The Middle East
and
North Africa
2024

The Middle East and North Africa 2024

70th Edition

LONDON AND NEW YORK

70th edition published 2023
by Routledge
4 Park Square, Milton Park, Abingdon, Oxon, OX14 4RN

and by Routledge
605 Third Avenue, New York, NY 10158

Routledge is an imprint of the Taylor & Francis Group, an informa business

© 2023 Routledge

All rights reserved. No part of this book may be reprinted or reproduced or utilised in any form or by any electronic, mechanical, or other means, now known or hereafter invented, including photocopying and recording, or in any information storage or retrieval system, without permission in writing from the publishers.

Trademark notice: Product or corporate names may be trademarks or registered trademarks, and are used only for identification and explanation without intent to infringe.

First published 1948

ISBN: 978-1-032-49274-2
ISSN: 0076-8502

Typeset in New Century Schoolbook
by Data Standards Limited, Frome, Somerset

Regional Editor: Jillian O'Brien

Regional Organizations Editor: Helen Canton

Senior Editor, Statistics: Philip McIntyre

Senior Editor, Directory: Iain Frame

Editorial Assistant: Avi Sharma

Editorial Research Manager: Surabhi Srivastava

Statistics Researchers: Mohd Khalid Ansari (Senior Team Leader), Ankita Nigam, Niti Rawat, Koustubh Saxena, Kumar Shaishav

Directory Editorial Researchers: Aditi Kapoor (Team Leader), Payal Singhal (Senior Editorial Researcher), Nini Benny, Waqar Momin

Contributing Editors: Catriona Holman (Regional Organizations), Gareth Vaughan (Major Commodities)

Publisher: Juliet Love

The Publishers make no representation, express or implied, with regard to the accuracy of the information contained in this book and cannot accept any legal responsibility for any errors or omissions that may take place.

Printed and bound by CPI Group (UK) Ltd, Croydon, CR0 4YY

FOREWORD

This edition of THE MIDDLE EAST AND NORTH AFRICA, the 70th in print, provides comprehensive coverage of political and economic life at the regional, subregional and national levels. The volume is divided into three separate, though complementary, sections. In Part One a collection of introductory essays discusses some of the most pertinent issues affecting the region. Topics covered include Saudi-Iranian relations, political Islam, China's growing presence in the region, US regional policy, the issue of Kurdish political autonomy and identity, the transition to sustainable energy in the Gulf states, and the religions of the region. In Part Two specialist authors, researchers and commentators examine in detail the main political and economic events in each of the countries and territories in the region. In addition, all statistical and directory material has been thoroughly updated. Extensive coverage of international organizations and research bodies active in the Middle East and North Africa is included in a section of Regional Information, together with a comprehensive archive of documents related to the history of Israel and the Palestinian territories, and bibliographies of essential publications for further study. A calendar of the key political events of 2022–23 enables rapid reference to the year's main developments.

While relatively quiet in terms of elections and changes of government, the year under review saw a number of potentially seismic shifts in intraregional relations. Most notable was the groundbreaking rapprochement and re-establishment of diplomatic relations in March 2023 between long-term adversaries Saudi Arabia and Iran—a development that could help to reduce tensions across the region and bring some stability to areas of conflict, particularly Yemen, where the ceasefire, although still holding, appeared very fragile. The fact that Saudi-Iranian 'normalization' was achieved largely through Chinese mediation is also perhaps indicative of a desire on the part of the People's Republic of China to play a greater diplomatic role in the Middle East at a time of perceived US disengagement from the region. A further sign of changes to the balance of power on the global stage that directly involved the Middle East and North Africa was the invitation in August by the BRICS (Brazil, Russia, India, China, South Africa) grouping to Egypt, Iran, Saudi Arabia and the United Arab Emirates (together with Argentina and Ethiopia) to join the bloc in January 2024.

Another significant development in the region in this period was the first step in the political rehabilitation of the long-ostracized Syrian Arab Republic in May 2023, when the League of Arab States (Arab League) initiated a process of normalization between Syria and other Arab countries by agreeing to reinstate Syria's membership (suspended in 2011 upon the outbreak of civil war in that country). Israel, conversely, appeared increasingly isolated in the region following the installation of a new Government headed by Benjamin Netanyahu that was dominated by right-wing nationalist parties. The Government's subsequent plans to introduce controversial legislation significantly reducing the powers of the Supreme Court provoked widespread domestic and international criticism and created serious divisions among the Israeli people.

President Recep Tayyip Erdoğan of Türkiye and President Kaïs Saïed of Tunisia both consolidated their hold on power: the former by securing a hard-fought victory in a general election in May 2023 and the latter by continuing to quash dissent through a variety of methods, including placing opposition activists on trial in military courts and dissolving local councils. Saïed's avowedly temporary intervention in running the country appeared ever-more likely to become effectively a long-term autocracy.

The stifling of opposition by those in power was a recurrent theme elsewhere in the region. The large-scale 'Women, Life, Freedom' protests that broke out across Iran in September 2022, following the death of a young Kurdish women in custody, appeared for a while to pose a significant challenge to the Islamist Government and attracted considerable support in the West. However, by early 2023 the protests had largely fizzled out as a result of a harsh crackdown by the authorities, and hopes of reform in Iran were, once again, dashed.

The entire content of the print edition of THE MIDDLE EAST AND NORTH AFRICA is available online at www.europaworld.com. This prestigious resource incorporates sophisticated search and browse functions as well as specially commissioned visual and statistical content. An ongoing programme of updates of key areas of information ensures currency of content, and enhances the richness of the coverage.

The Editors would like to express their thanks to all the contributors for their articles and advice, as well as to the numerous governments and organizations that provided statistical and other information.

September 2023

ACKNOWLEDGEMENTS

The Editors gratefully acknowledge the interest and co-operation of numerous national statistical and information offices, and government departments, as well as embassies in London and throughout the region, whose kind assistance in updating the material contained in THE MIDDLE EAST AND NORTH AFRICA is greatly appreciated.

We acknowledge particular indebtedness for permission to reproduce material from the following publications: the United Nations' statistical databases and *Demographic Yearbook, Statistical Yearbook and Monthly Bulletin of Statistics*; the United Nations Educational, Scientific and Cultural Organization's Institute for Statistics database; the *Human Development Report* of the United Nations Development Programme; the Food and Agriculture Organization of the United Nations' statistical database; the statistical databases of the World Health Organization; the statistical databases of the UNCTAD/WTO International Trade Centre; the International Labour Office's statistical database; the World Bank's statistical databases, especially the World Development Indicators database, and the *World Development Report*; the International Monetary Fund's statistical database, *International Financial Statistics* and *Government Finance Statistics Yearbook*; the World Tourism Organization's *World Tourism Barometer* and *Yearbook of Tourism Statistics, 2023 edition*, UNWTO, Madrid; the US Geological Survey; the International Telecommunication Union; the United Nations Economic and Social Commission for Western Asia's *National Accounts Studies of the ESCWA Region*; Lloyd's List; and *The Military Balance 2023*, a publication of the International Institute for Strategic Studies, Arundel House, 6 Temple Pl., London, WC2R 2PG, UK. We are also grateful to the Israeli embassy, London, for the use of two maps illustrating the disengagement agreements between Israel and Egypt, and Israel and Syria (both 1974).

HEALTH AND WELFARE STATISTICS: SOURCES AND DEFINITIONS

Total fertility rate Source: WHO Global Health Observatory. The number of children that would be born per woman, assuming no female mortality at child-bearing ages and the age-specific fertility rates of a specified country and reference period.

Under-5 mortality rate Source: WHO Global Health Observatory. Defined by WHO as the probability of a child born in a specific year or period dying before reaching the age of five, if subject to the age-specific mortality rates of the year or period.

HIV/AIDS Source: UNAIDS. Estimated percentage of adults aged 15 to 49 years living with HIV/AIDS. < indicates 'fewer than'.

COVID-19 Sources: Center for Systems Science and Engineering (CSSE) at Johns Hopkins University (JHU) via Our World In Data: Hannah Ritchie, Edouard Mathieu, Lucas Rodés-Guirao, Cameron Appel, Charlie Giattino, Esteban Ortiz-Ospina, Joe Hasell, Bobbie Macdonald, Diana Beltekian and Max Roser (2020)—'Coronavirus Pandemic (COVID-19)'. Published online at OurWorldInData.org. (Retrieved from https://ourworldindata.org/coronavirus); Our World in Data: Mathieu, E., Ritchie, H., Ortiz-Ospina, E. et al. 'A global database of COVID-19 vaccinations' (Nature Human Behaviour, 2021). For reasons of comparability, UN population estimates have been used for most calculations.
Cumulative confirmed deaths (per 100,000 persons)
Attribution of cause of death to COVID-19 is based on classifications from the World Health Organization's International Statistical Classification of Diseases and Related Health Problems (ICD) guidelines, supported by national advice to health practitioners. Data refer to confirmed deaths only, actual numbers are likely to be greater.
Fully vaccinated population (% of total population)
'Fully vaccinated' denotes receipt of all doses prescribed by specific vaccination regimes, this may vary depending on the vaccine. Alternative definitions of fully vaccinated, including receipt of only part of a dosing regime, or recovery from illness, have been disregarded. For the sake of best comparison, rates are based on the total rather than eligible population in each case.

Health expenditure Source: WHO Global Health Expenditure database. Covering the provision of health services (preventive and curative), family planning activities, and nutrition activities. Public sources include domestic revenue as internal transfers and grants, transfers, subsidies to voluntary health insurance beneficiaries, non-profit institutions serving households (NPISH) or enterprise financing schemes as well as compulsory prepayment and social health insurance contributions. External grants or loans for healthcare provided by international agencies and other national authorities are not included.
US $ per head (PPP)
International dollar estimates. Current domestic general government expenditures as a ratio of total population.
% of GDP
The share of domestic general government resources used to funs health expenditures, given as a percentage of the economy as measured by gross domestic product (GDP).
Public expenditure % of total health expenditure
Share of current health expenditures funded from general government sources, social health insurance and compulsory prepayment.

Access to water and sanitation Source: WHO/UNICEF Joint Monitoring Programme on Water Supply, Sanitation and Hygiene (JMP) (*Progress on Household Drinking Water, Sanitation and Hygiene, 2000–2020*). Defined in terms of the percentage of the population using improved facilities in terms of the type of technology and levels of service afforded. For water, this includes house connections, public standpipes, boreholes with handpumps, protected dug wells, protected spring and rainwater collection; allowance is also made for other locally defined technologies. Sanitation is defined to include connection to a sewer or septic tank system, pour-flush latrine, simple pit or ventilated improved pit latrine, again with allowance for acceptable local technologies. Access to water and sanitation does not imply that the level of service or quality of water is 'adequate' or 'safe'.

Carbon dioxide emissions Source: World Bank, World Development Indicators database, citing CAIT data. Climate Watch. 2020. GHG Emissions. Washington, DC: World Resources Institute. Available at: https://climatewatchdata.org/ghg-emissions. Emissions comprise those resulting from the burning of fossil fuels (including those produced during consumption of solid, liquid and gas fuels and from gas flaring) and from the manufacture of cement, but exclude emissions resulting from land-use transformation and forestry.

Human Development Index (HDI) Source: UNDP, *Human Development Report* (2021–22). A summary of human development measured by three basic dimensions: prospects for a long and healthy life, measured by life expectancy at birth; knowledge, measured by adult literacy rate (two-thirds' weight) and the combined gross enrolment ratio in primary, secondary and tertiary education (one-third weight); and standard of living, measured by GDP per head (PPP US $). The index value obtained lies between zero and one. A value above 0.800 indicates very high human development, between 0.700 and 0.799 high human development, between 0.550 and 0.699 medium human development, and below 0.550 low human development. A centralized data source for all three dimensions was not available for all countries. In some cases other data sources were used to calculate a substitute value; however, this was excluded from the ranking. Other countries, including non-UNDP members, were excluded from the HDI altogether. In total, 191 countries were ranked for 2021.

CONTENTS

The Contributors	page x
Abbreviations	xi
International Telephone Codes	xiv
Explanatory Note on the Directory Section	xiv
Transcription of Arabic Names	xv
Calendar of Political Events, September 2022–August 2023	xvi

PART ONE

General Survey

China's Growing Presence in the Middle East: From Economic Partnerships to Diplomatic Engagement?
JULIA GUROL 3

Political Islam
BARBARA ZOLLNER 9

Saudi Arabia and Iran: Islam, Security and Foreign Policy in the Middle East
SIMON MABON 18

US Middle East Policy
ROBERT E. LOONEY 28

The Kurdish Question in the Middle East
CENGIZ GUNES (Revised for this edition by LIAM ANDERSON) 39

Instituting a Sustainable Energy Transition in the Gulf: A Review of Saudi Arabia, the United Arab Emirates and Qatar
JUSTIN DARGIN 55

The Religions of the Middle East and North Africa
R. B. SERJEANT (Revised by the editorial staff) 77

PART TWO

Country Surveys

See page xiv for explanatory note on the Directory section of each country.

ALGERIA
Geography	87
History GIANNI DEL PANTA	87
Economy ROBERT E. LOONEY	97
Statistical Survey	106
Directory	111
Bibliography	122

BAHRAIN
Geography	125
History MARC JONES (Revised by KRISTIAN COATES ULRICHSEN)	125
Economy MARTIN HVIDT	133
Statistical Survey	138
Directory	142
Bibliography	150

CYPRUS
Geography	page 151
History ANDREAS STERGIOU	151
Economy Revised by ANDREAS STERGIOU	159
Statistical Survey	167
Directory	169
'Turkish Republic of Northern Cyprus'	178
History	178
Economy	181
Statistical Survey	182
Directory	183
Bibliography	187

EGYPT
Geography	189
History VAUGHN SHANNON	190
Economy CHAHIR ZAKI	199
Statistical Survey	205
Directory	211
Bibliography	225

IRAN
Geography	228
History EDWARD WASTNIDGE	229
Economy ROBERT E. LOONEY	241
Statistical Survey	251
Directory	257
Bibliography	269

IRAQ
Geography	273
History LIAM ANDERSON	274
Economy ROBERT E. LOONEY	308
Statistical Survey	316
Directory	320
Bibliography	331

ISRAEL
Geography	334
History VAUGHN SHANNON	335
Economy ROBERT E. LOONEY	346
Statistical Survey	354
Directory	359
Occupied Territories	373
East Jerusalem	373
The Golan Heights	374
Bibliography	375

JORDAN
Geography	page 379
History COURTNEY FREER	380
Economy ROBERT E. LOONEY	396
Statistical Survey	405
Directory	410
Bibliography	420

KUWAIT
Geography	422
History Revised by CLAIRE BEAUGRAND	422
Economy MÁTÉ SZALAI	438
Statistical Survey	447
Directory	452
Bibliography	460

LEBANON
Geography	462
History NATÁLIA CALFAT (Revised by the editorial staff)	463
Economy ALI NOUREDDEEN	477
Statistical Survey	483
Directory	488
Bibliography	499

LIBYA
Geography	502
History Revised by RONALD BRUCE ST JOHN	503
Economy AMIR MAGDY KAMEL	530
Statistical Survey	537
Directory	541
Bibliography	547

MOROCCO
Geography	549
History NEIL PARTRICK (Based on an original essay by RICHARD I. LAWLESS)	550
Economy NEIL PARTRICK (Based on an original essay by ALAN J. DAY)	581
Statistical Survey	593
Directory	598
Bibliography	609

OMAN
Geography	611
History Revised by MARC VALERI	611
Economy FRANCIS OWTRAM	619
Statistical Survey	626
Directory	631
Bibliography	638

PALESTINIAN TERRITORIES
Geography	640
Recent History Updated by NIGEL PARSONS (Revised for this edition by VAUGHN SHANNON)	640
Economy HABIB HINN, RAJA KHALIDI and ISLAM RABEE	682
Statistical Survey	695
Directory	699
Bibliography	704

QATAR
Geography	page 706
History DAVID ROBERTS	706
Economy FRANCIS OWTRAM	712
Statistical Survey	718
Directory	723
Bibliography	731

SAUDI ARABIA
Geography	732
History BRANDON FRIEDMAN	733
Economy NEIL PARTRICK (Based on an original essay by MOIN SIDDIQI)	745
Statistical Survey	767
Directory	772
Bibliography	784

SPANISH NORTH AFRICA
Ceuta	786
Melilla	792
Bibliography	798

SYRIAN ARAB REPUBLIC
Geography	799
History EYAL ZISSER	800
Economy OMAR S. DAHI and MOHAMMAD AL-ASADI	807
Statistical Survey	815
Directory	820
Bibliography	829

TUNISIA
Geography	831
History NEIL PARTRICK (Based on an original essay by RICHARD I. LAWLESS)	832
Economy NEIL PARTRICK (Based on an original essay by the editorial staff)	870
Statistical Survey	891
Directory	896
Bibliography	904

TÜRKIYE (TURKEY)
Geography	906
History Revised by GARETH JENKINS	907
Economy Revised by GARETH JENKINS	927
Statistical Survey	941
Directory	947
Bibliography	961

UNITED ARAB EMIRATES
Geography	965
History KRISTIAN COATES ULRICHSEN	965
Economy ROBERT E. LOONEY	971
Statistical Survey	981
Directory	986
Bibliography	998

YEMEN

Geography	page 1000
History VINCENT DURAC	1001
Economy CHARLES SCHMITZ	1011
Statistical Survey	1022
Directory	1026
Bibliography	1033

PART THREE
Regional Information

REGIONAL ORGANIZATIONS

The United Nations in the Middle East and North Africa	1037
Members, Contributions, Year of Admission	1037
Permanent Missions to the United Nations	1037
United Nations Information Centres/Services	1038
Economic Commission for Africa—ECA	1038
Economic and Social Commission for Western Asia—ESCWA	1041
United Nations Children's Fund—UNICEF	1044
United Nations Development Coordination Office	1047
United Nations Development Programme—UNDP	1048
United Nations Environment Programme—UNEP	1052
United Nations High Commissioner for Refugees—UNHCR	1060
United Nations Peacekeeping	1063
United Nations Political Missions and Peacebuilding	1068
United Nations Relief and Works Agency for Palestine Refugees in the Near East—UNRWA	1077
World Food Programme—WFP	1079
Food and Agriculture Organization of the United Nations—FAO	1081
International Atomic Energy Agency—IAEA	1087
International Bank for Reconstruction and Development—IBRD—World Bank	1091
International Development Association—IDA	1096
International Finance Corporation—IFC	1097
International Fund for Agricultural Development—IFAD	1098
International Monetary Fund—IMF	1100
World Health Organization—WHO	1103
Other UN Organizations active in the region	1109
African Development Bank—AfDB	1115
African Union—AU	1119
Arab Fund for Economic and Social Development—AFESD	1126
Arab League (*see* League of Arab States)	
Arab Monetary Fund	1127
Asian Infrastructure Investment Bank—AIIB	page 1129
Cooperation Council for the Arab States of the Gulf (Gulf Cooperation Council—GCC)	1131
European Bank for Reconstruction and Development—EBRD	1135
Economic Co-operation Organization—ECO	1138
European Union—EU	1140
Islamic Development Bank	1143
League of Arab States	1146
Organization of Arab Petroleum Exporting Countries—OAPEC	1154
Organization of Islamic Cooperation—OIC	1155
Organization of the Petroleum Exporting Countries—OPEC	1161
OPEC Fund for International Development	1164
Other Regional Organizations	1166

MAJOR COMMODITIES OF THE MIDDLE EAST AND NORTH AFRICA

Aluminium and Bauxite	1180
Chromium	1181
Cotton	1182
Gold	1183
Natural Gas	1185
Olives	1187
Petroleum	1189
Phosphate	1193
Sugar	1194
Tea	1196
Tobacco	1197
Wheat	1198

DOCUMENTS ON PALESTINE   1200

CALENDARS   1256

RESEARCH INSTITUTES   1257

SELECT BIBLIOGRAPHY (BOOKS)

THE MIDDLE EAST	1267
NORTH AFRICA	1275

SELECT BIBLIOGRAPHY (PERIODICALS)   1278

INDEX OF REGIONAL ORGANIZATIONS   1282

THE CONTRIBUTORS

Mohammad Al-Asadi. Research economist, Syrian Center for Policy Research, Vienna, Austria.

Liam Anderson. Professor of Political Science, School of Social Sciences and International Studies, Wright State University, Dayton, OH, USA.

Claire Beaugrand. Lecturer in Sociology of the Gulf and Arabian Peninsula, Institute of Arab and Islamic Studies, University of Exeter, UK; and CNRS Researcher at the Institut de Recherche Interdisciplinaire en Sciences Sociales (IRISSO), Université Paris Dauphine-PSL, France.

Natália Calfat. PhD Candidate, Department of Political Science, University of São Paulo, Brazil.

Kristian Coates Ulrichsen. Fellow for the Middle East, Baker Institute for Public Policy, Rice University, Houston, TX, USA.

Omar S. Dahi. Professor of Economics, Hampshire College, Amherst, Massachusetts, USA; and founding Director of 'Security in Context' research network.

Justin Dargin. Middle East Energy and Climate Scholar, Carnegie Endowment for International Peace, Washington, DC, USA; and former legal advisor to OPEC.

Alan J. Day. Former Editor of *The Annual Register*, London, United Kingdom; and former Joint Editor of the *Political Handbook of the World*, Binghamton University, New York, USA.

Gianni Del Panta. Junior Assistant Professor of Political Science, University of Pavia, Italy.

Vincent Durac. Associate Professor, School of Politics and International Relations, University College Dublin, Ireland.

Courtney Freer. Visiting Assistant Professor of Middle Eastern Studies, Emory University, Atlanta, GA, USA.

Brandon Friedman. Director of Research, Moshe Dayan Center for Middle Eastern and African Studies, Tel Aviv University, Israel.

Cengiz Gunes. Associate Lecturer in Politics and International Relations, Faculty of Social Sciences, Open University, Milton Keynes, UK.

Julia Gurol. Postdoctoral Researcher, Chair for International Relations, University of Freiburg and Arnold-Bergstraesser-Institute Freiburg, Germany.

Habib Hinn. Lecturer in Finance and Economics, Birzeit University, Ramallah, Palestinian Territories.

Martin Hvidt. Associate Professor and Head of Studies, Center for Modern Middle East and Muslim Studies, Department of Culture and Language, University of Southern Denmark, Odense, Denmark.

Gareth Jenkins. Non-resident Senior Fellow with the Silk Road Studies Program, based in Istanbul, Türkiye.

Marc Jones. Associate Professor in Middle East Studies, Hamad Bin Khalifa University, Doha, Qatar.

Amir Magdy Kamel. Senior Lecturer (Associate Professor), School of Security Studies and Fellow, Institute of Middle Eastern Studies, King's College London, UK; and Visiting Faculty, Abbasi Program, Stanford University, CA, USA, and Politics and International Studies, University of San Francisco, CA, USA.

Raja Khalidi. Director-General, Palestine Economic Policy Research Institute (MAS), Ramallah, Palestinian Territories.

Richard I. Lawless. Late Emeritus Reader in Middle Eastern Studies, Durham University, UK.

Robert E. Looney. Distinguished Professor Emeritus, Department of National Security Affairs, Naval Postgraduate School, Monterey, CA, USA.

Simon Mabon. Professor of International Politics, and Director of SEPAD, Lancaster University, UK.

Ali Noureddeen. Independent economic researcher and writer specializing in the Middle East and North Africa region.

Francis Owtram. Honorary Research Fellow, Institute of Arab and Islamic Studies, University of Exeter, UK.

Nigel Parsons. Senior Lecturer, Politics Programme, Massey University, Palmerston North, New Zealand.

Neil Partrick. Writer and analyst on the Arabian Peninsula and wider Middle East.

Islam Rabee. Assistant Researcher, Palestine Economic Policy Research Institute (MAS), Ramallah, Palestinian Territories.

David Roberts. Senior Lecturer, School of Security Studies, King's College London, UK; Adjunct Faculty, Paris School of International Affairs, Sciences Po, Paris, France; Non-resident Fellow at the Arab Gulf States Institute, Washington, DC, USA; and former Director of the Qatar office of the Royal United Services Institute for Defence and Security Studies.

Charles Schmitz. Professor and Chair, Department of Geography & Environmental Planning, Towson University, Towson, MD, USA.

R. B. Serjeant. Late Professor of Arabic and Director of the Middle East Centre, University of Cambridge, UK.

Vaughn Shannon. Professor of Political Science, School of Social Sciences and International Studies, Wright State University, Dayton, OH, USA.

Moin Siddiqi. Independent economist specializing in macroeconomic developments and the banking sector in the Middle East and Africa; also advises on trends in petroleum markets.

Andreas Stergiou. Professor, Department of Economics, University of Thessaly, Volos, Greece.

Ronald Bruce St John. Independent scholar specializing in the political economy of developing states.

Máté Szalai. Marie Skłodowska-Curie COFUND Fellow, Ca' Foscari University, Venice, Italy.

Marc Valeri. Associate Professor in Political Economy of the Middle East and Director of the Centre for Gulf Studies, University of Exeter, UK.

Edward Wastnidge. Senior Lecturer in Politics and International Studies, Faculty of Arts and Social Sciences, Open University, Milton Keynes, UK.

Onn Winckler. Professor, Department of Middle Eastern and Islamic Studies, University of Haifa, Haifa, Israel.

Chahir Zaki. Professor of Economics and World Trade Organization Chair Holder, Faculty of Economics and Political Science, Cairo University, Egypt.

Eyal Zisser. Vice Rector, and Yona and Dina Ettinger Chair in Contemporary History of the Middle East, Tel Aviv University, Israel.

Barbara Zollner. Independent scholar specializing in Middle East politics.

ABBREVIATIONS

AAHO	Afro-Asian Housing Organization
AAPSO	Afro-Asian People's Solidarity Organization
Acad.	Academy
AD	Algerian dinars
ADC	Aide-de-camp
Adm.	Admiral
AED	UAE dirhams
Admin.	Administrative, Administration, Administrator
Admin.-Gen	Administrator-General
AfDB	African Development Bank
Agric.	Agriculture
AH	anno Hegirae (year of the Hegira)
a.i.	ad interim
AIDS	acquired immunodeficiency syndrome
AIWO	Agudath Israel World Organization
ALF	Arab Liberation Front
AM	Amplitude Modulation
a.m.	ante meridiem (before noon)
Apdo	Apartado (Post Box)
API	American Petroleum Institute
approx.	approximately
apptd	appointed
ARE	Arab Republic of Egypt
AŞ	Anonim Şirketi (Joint-Stock Company)
Ass.	Assembly
asscn	association
Assoc.	Associate
Asst	Assistant
AU	African Union
auth.	authorized
Ave	Avenue
Avda	Avenida
BADEA	Banque Arabe pour le Développement Economique en Afrique (Arab Bank for Economic Development in Africa)
BCE	before common era
b/d	barrels per day
BD	Bahrain dinars
Bd	Board
Bde	Brigade
Bldg	Building
Blvd	Boulevard
BP	Boîte Postale (Post Box)
br.(s)	branch(es)
Brig.	Brigadier
BST	British Standard Time
Bul.	Bulvar (Boulevard)
C	Centigrade
c.	circa
Cad.	Caddesi (Street)
CAFRAD	Centre Africain de Formation et de Recherches Administratives pour le Développement
cap.	capital
Capt.	Captain
CARE	Co-operative for American Relief Everywhere
Cdre	Commodore
CE	common era
cen.	central
CEN-SAD	Community of Sahel-Saharan States
CEO	Chief Executive Officer
cf.	confer (compare)
Chair.	Chairman/person/woman
Cie	Compagnie (Company)
c.i.f.	cost, insurance and freight
C-in-C	Commander-in-Chief
circ.	circulation
cm	centimetre(s)
CMEA	Council for Mutual Economic Assistance
CNG	compressed natural gas
cnr	corner
c/o	care of
Co	Company
Col	Colonel
Comm.	Commission
Commdr	Commander
Commdt	Commandant
Commr	Commissioner
Conf.	Conference
Confed.	Confederation
Cons.-Gen.	Consul-General
COO	Chief Operating Officer
Corpn	Corporation
Cttee	Committee
cu	cubic
cwt	hundredweight
Del.	Delegate, Delegation
Dep.	Deputy
dep.	deposits
Dept	Department
Devt	Development
DFLP	Democratic Front for the Liberation of Palestine
Dir	Director
Div.	Division
Dr	Doctor
dcha	derecha (right)
DU	depleted uranium
dwt	dead weight tons
E	East, Eastern
ECOSOC	Economic and Social Council (UN)
ECU	European Currency Unit(s)
Ed.(s)	Editor(s)
edn	edition
EFTA	European Free Trade Association
e.g.	exempli gratia (for example)
ELA	emergency liquidity assistance
Eng.	Engineer
est.	established; estimate(d)
excl.	excluding
EU	European Union
Exec.	Executive
F	Fahrenheit
f.	founded
FAO	Food and Agriculture Organization of the UN
FAPS	Framework Agreement on Permanent Status
FDI	foreign direct investment
Fed.	Federal, Federation
Flt	Flight
FM	Frequency Modulation
fmr(ly)	former(ly)
f.o.b.	free on board
Fr.	Franc
ft	foot (feet)
g	gram(s)
GAFTA	Greater Arab Free Trade Agreement
GATT	General Agreements on Tariffs and Trade
GCC	Gulf Cooperation Council
GDP	gross domestic product
GEF	Global Environment Facility
Gen.	General
GHQ	General Headquarters
GMT	Greenwich Mean Time
GNP	gross national product
GONGO(s)	government-owned non-governmental organization(s)
Gov.	Governor
Govt	Government
GRE	government-related entity
grt	gross registered ton(s)
GSM	Global System for Mobile Communications
GW	gigawatt(s)
GWh	gigawatt hour(s)
ha	hectare(s)
HE	His (or Her) Excellency, His Eminence
HIV	human immunodeficiency virus
hl	hectolitre(s)
HLTF	High Level Task Force
HM	His (or Her) Majesty
Hon.	Honorary; Honourable
HQ	Headquarters
HRH	His (or Her) Royal Highness
IAEA	International Atomic Energy Agency
IATA	International Air Transport Association
ibid.	ibidem (from the same source)

ABBREVIATIONS

IBRD	International Bank for Reconstruction and Development (World Bank)	no.	number
ICAO	International Civil Aviation Organization	NPT	Non-Proliferation Treaty
ICATU	International Conference of Arab Trade Unions	nr	near
ICT	Information and Communication Technologies	nrt	net registered ton(s)
ID	new Iraqi dinars	NTC	National Transitional Council
IDA	International Development Association	NW	North-West
IDF	Israel(i) Defense Forces	OAPEC	Organization of Arab Petroleum Exporting Countries
i.e.	id est (that is to say)	OCHA	United Nations Office for the Co-ordination of Humanitarian Affairs
IFC	International Finance Corporation		
IISS	International Institute of Strategic Studies	OECD	Organisation for Economic Co-operation and Development
ILO	International Labour Office/Organization	OFF	Oil-for-Food
IMF	International Monetary Fund	OIC	Organization of Islamic Cooperation (previously Organization of the Islamic Conference)
in(s)	inch(es)		
Inc	Incorporated	OPEC	Organization of the Petroleum Exporting Countries
incl.	include, including	Org.(s)	Organization(s)
Ind.	Independent	oz	ounce(s)
Insp.	Inspector		
Inst.	Institute; Institution	p.	page
Int.	International	PA	Palestinian Authority
IPO	initial public offering	p.a.	per annum
IR	Iranian rials	Parl.	Parliament(ary)
IRF	International Road Federation	PCC	Palestinian Central Council
IRGC	Islamic Revolutionary Guard Corps	Perm.	Permanent
Is	Islands	Perm. Rep.	Permanent Representative
ISIC	International Standard Industrial Classification	PFLP	Popular Front for the Liberation of Palestine
IT	information technology	PhD	Doctor of Philosophy
ITU	International Telecommunication Union	PLC	Palestinian Legislative Council; Public Limited Company
ITUC	International Trade Union Confederation	PLO	Palestine Liberation Organization
IUU	illegal, unreported and unregulated	p.m.	post meridiem (after noon)
izqda	izquierda (left)	PNC	Palestine National Council
		POB	Post Office Box
JD	Jordanian dinars	PPP	purchasing-power parity
Jr	Junior	Pres.	President
Jt	Joint	Prof.	Professor
		Propr	Proprietor
KD	Kuwaiti dinars	Pty	Proprietary
kg	kilogram(s)	p.u.	paid up
KFAED	Kuwait Fund for Arab Economic Development	publ.(s)	publication(s), published, publishes
km	kilometre(s)	Publr	Publisher
kV	kilovolt(s)		
kW	kilowatt(s)	QE	Qatar Exchange
kWh	kilowatt hour(s)	QIA	Qatar Investment Authority
		QR	Qatari riyals
lb	pound(s)	q.v.	quod vide (to which refer)
LD	Libyan dinars		
Legis.	Legislative	RCC	Revolutionary Command Council (Iraq, Libya)
LNG	liquefied natural gas	RCD	Regional Co-operation for Development
Lot	Lotissement	Rd	Road
LPG	liquefied petroleum gas	RDA	Rassemblement Démocratique Africain
Lt	Lieutenant	REC	regional economic communities
Ltd	Limited	regd	registered
		Rep.	Representative
m	metre(s)	Repub.	Republic
m.	million	res	reserves
Mah.	Mahallesi (district)	retd	retired
Maj.	Major	Rev.	Reverend
Man.	Manager, Managing	RO	rial Omani
MB	Bachelor of Medicine	ro-ro	roll-on roll-off
MD	Doctor of Medicine		
mem.(s)	member(s)	S	South, Southern
Mfg	Manufacturing	SBA(s)	Sovereign Base Area(s)
Mgr	Monseigneur, Monsignor	SDR(s)	special drawing right(s)
Mil.	Military	SE	South-East
MINURSO	United Nations Mission for the Referendum in Western Sahara	Sec.	Secretary
		Secr.	Secretariat
mm	millimetre(s)	SITC	Standard International Trade Classification
MOC	memorandum of co-operation	Soc.	Society; Société
MOU	memorandum of understanding	Sok.	Sokak (Street)
MP	Member of Parliament	SpA	Società per Azioni (Limited Company)
MSS	Manuscripts	sq	square (in measurements)
Mt	Mount	Sq.	Square
MTBE	methyl tertiary butyl ether	SR	Saudi riyals
MW	megawatt(s); medium wave	Sr	Senior
MWh	megawatt hour(s)	St	Saint; Street
		STL	Special Tribunal for Lebanon
N	North, Northern	Stn	Station
n.a.	not available	subs.	subscribed
Nat.	National	Supt	Superintendent
NATO	North Atlantic Treaty Organization	SW	South-West
NE	North-East		
NEPAD	New Partnership for Africa's Development	Tapline	Trans-Arabian Pipeline Company
n.e.s.	not elsewhere specified	TAŞ	Türk Anonim Şirketi (Turkish Joint-Stock Company)
NGLs	natural gas liquids	TD	Tunisian dinars
NGO(s)	non-governmental organization(s)	tel.	telephone
n.i.e.	not included elsewhere	TEU	20-ft equivalent unit
NIS	new Israeli shekels	TL	Turkish lira

ABBREVIATIONS

toe	tons of oil equivalent	UNRWA	United Nations Relief and Works Agency for Palestine Refugees in the Near East
trans.	translated; translation		
Treas.	Treasurer	UNSCOM	United Nations Special Commission
TV	Television	UNTSO	United Nations Truce Supervision Organization
		UNUPR	United Nations Universal Periodic Review
UA	Unit(s) of Account	UNWTO	World Tourism Organization
UAE	United Arab Emirates	UPAF	Union Postale Africaine (African Postal Union)
UAR	United Arab Republic	UP	University Press
UBAF	Union des Banques Arabes et Françaises	USA (US)	United States of America (United States)
UHF	Ultra High Frequency	USAID	US Agency for International Development
UK	United Kingdom	USIS	United States Information Services
UN	United Nations	USSR	Union of Soviet Socialist Republics
UNAIDS	United Nations Joint Programme on HIV/AIDS	UTA	Union de Transports Aériens
UNCTAD	United Nations Conference on Trade and Development		
UNDOF	United Nations Disengagement Observer Force	VAT	value-added tax
UNDP	United Nations Development Programme	VHF	Very High Frequency
UNEF	United Nations Emergency Force	vol.(s)	volume(s)
UNEP	United Nations Environment Programme		
UNESCO	United Nations Educational, Scientific and Cultural Organization	W	West, Western
		WFTU	World Federation of Trade Unions
UNFICYP	United Nations Peace-keeping Force in Cyprus	WHO	World Health Organization
UNFPA	United Nations Population Fund	WSSD	World Summit on Sustainable Development
UNICEF	United Nations Children's Fund	WTI	West Texas Intermediate
UNIDO	United Nations Industrial Development Organization	WTO	World Tourism Organization; World Trade Organization
UNIFIL	United Nations Interim Force in Lebanon		
Univ.	University		
UNMEM	United Nations Middle East Mission	YR	Yemeni riyals
UNMOVIC	United Nations Monitoring, Verification and Inspection Commission	yr	year

INTERNATIONAL TELEPHONE CODES

To make international calls to telephone and fax numbers listed in THE MIDDLE EAST AND NORTH AFRICA, dial the international code of the country from which you are calling, followed by the appropriate country code for the organization you wish to call (listed below), followed by the area code (if applicable) and telephone or fax number listed in the entry.

	Country code		Country code
Algeria	213	Palestinian Territories	970 or 972
Bahrain	973	Qatar	974
Cyprus	357	Saudi Arabia	966
'Turkish Republic of Northern Cyprus'	90	Spain (for Spanish North Africa)	34
Egypt	20	Syria	963
Iran	98	Tunisia	216
Iraq	964	Türkiye	90
Israel	972	United Arab Emirates	971
Jordan	962	Yemen	967
Kuwait	965		
Lebanon	961		
Libya	218		
Morocco	212		
Oman	968		

Note: Telephone and fax numbers using the Inmarsat ocean region code 870 are listed in full. No country or area code is required, but it is necessary to precede the number with the international access code of the country from which the call is made.

EXPLANATORY NOTE ON THE DIRECTORY SECTION

The Directory section of each chapter is arranged under the following headings, where they apply:

THE CONSTITUTION
THE GOVERNMENT
   HEAD OF STATE
   CABINET/COUNCIL OF MINISTERS
   MINISTRIES
LEGISLATURE
ELECTION COMMISSION
POLITICAL ORGANIZATIONS
DIPLOMATIC REPRESENTATION
JUDICIAL SYSTEM
RELIGION
THE PRESS
PUBLISHERS
BROADCASTING AND COMMUNICATIONS
   TELECOMMUNICATIONS
   RADIO
   TELEVISION
FINANCE
   CENTRAL BANK
   STATE BANKS
   COMMERCIAL BANKS
   DEVELOPMENT BANKS
   INVESTMENT BANKS
   SAVINGS BANKS
   ISLAMIC BANKS
   FOREIGN BANKS
   SOVEREIGN WEALTH FUNDS
   STOCK EXCHANGE
   INSURANCE
TRADE AND INDUSTRY
   GOVERNMENT AGENCIES
   DEVELOPMENT ORGANIZATIONS
   CHAMBERS OF COMMERCE AND INDUSTRY
   INDUSTRIAL AND TRADE ASSOCIATIONS
   EMPLOYERS' ASSOCIATIONS
   HYDROCARBONS
   UTILITIES
   HOLDING COMPANIES
   MAJOR COMPANIES
   CO-OPERATIVES
   TRADE UNIONS
TRANSPORT
   RAILWAYS
   ROADS
   INLAND WATERWAYS
   SHIPPING
   CIVIL AVIATION
TOURISM
DEFENCE
EDUCATION

TRANSCRIPTION OF ARABIC NAMES

The Arabic language is used over a vast area. Though the written language and the script are standard throughout the Middle East, the spoken language and also the pronunciation of the written signs exhibit wide variation from place to place. This is reflected, and even exaggerated, in the different transcriptions in use in different countries. The same words, names and even letters will be pronounced differently by an Egyptian, a Lebanese or an Iraqi—they will be heard and transcribed differently by an English person, a French person or an Italian. There are several more or less scientific systems of transliteration in use, sponsored by learned societies and Middle Eastern governments, most of them requiring diacritical marks to indicate Arabic letters for which there are no Latin equivalents.

Arabic names occurring in the historical and geographical sections of this book have been rendered in the system most commonly used by British and American Orientalists, but with the omission of the diacritical signs. For the convenience of the reader, these are explained and annotated below. The system used is a transliteration—i.e. it is based on the writing, which is standard throughout the Arab world, and not on the pronunciation, which varies from place to place. In a few cases consistency has been sacrificed in order to avoid replacing a familiar and accepted form by another which, although more accurate, would be unrecognizable.

Consonants

- d   represents two Arabic letters. The second, or emphatic d, is transliterated $ḍ$. It may also be represented, for some dialects, by *dh* and by *z*, e.g. Qāḍī, qadhi, qazi.
- dh   in literary Arabic and some dialects, pronounced like English *th* in *this*. In many dialects pronounced *z* or *d*.
- gh   A strongly guttural *g*—sometimes written *g*, e.g. Baghdād, Bagdad.
- h   represents two Arabic letters. The second, more guttural *h*, is transliterated $ḥ$, e.g. Ḥusain, Husein.
- j   as English *j* in *John*, also represented by *dj* and *g*. In Egypt this letter is pronounced as a hard *g*, and may be thus transcribed (with *u* before *e* and *i*), e.g. Najib, Nadjib, Nagib, Naguib, Neguib.
- kh   as *ch* in Scottish *loch*, also sometimes represented by *ch* and *h*, e.g. Khalīl, Chalil, Halil.
- q   A guttural *k*, pronounced farther back in the throat. Also transcribed $k̇$, $ḳ$, and, for some dialects, *g*, e.g. Waqf, Wak̇f, Wakf, wagf.
- s   represents two Arabic letters. The second, emphatic *s*, is transliterated $ṣ$. It may also be represented by *ç*, e.g. Sāliḥ, Saleh, Çaleh.
- sh   as in English *ship*. The French transcription *ch* is found in Algeria, Lebanon, Morocco, the Syrian Arab Republic and Tunisia, e.g. Shaikh, Sheikh, Cheikh.
- t   represents two Arabic letters. The second, emphatic *t*, is transliterated $ṭ$.
- th   in literary Arabic and some dialects, pronounced as English *th* in *through*. In many dialects pronounced *t* or *s*, e.g. Thābit, Tabit, Sabit.
- w   as in English, but often represented by *ou* or *v*, e.g. Wādā, Vadi, Oued.
- z   represents two Arabic letters. The second, or emphatic z, is transliterated $ẓ$. It may also be represented, for some dialects, by *dh* or *d*, e.g. Ḥāfiẓ, Hafidh, Hafid.
- ʿ   A glottal stop, as in Cockney English *'li'l bo'ls'*.

Vowels

The Arabic script only indicates three short vowels, three long vowels, and two diphthongs, as follows:

- a   as in English *hat*, and often rendered *e*, e.g. balad, beled, emir, amir; with emphatics or gutturals usually pronounced as *u* in *but*, e.g. Khalīfa, Baghdād.
- i   as in English *bit*. Sometimes rendered *e*, e.g. jihād, jehād.
- u   as in English *good*. Often pronounced and written *o*, e.g. Muhammad, Mohammad.

In some Arabic dialects, particularly those of North Africa, unaccented short vowels are often omitted altogether, and long vowels shortened, e.g. Oued for Wādī, bled for balad, etc.

- ā   Long *a*, variously pronounced as in *sand, dart* and *hall*.
- ī   As *ee* in *feet*. In early books often rendered *ee*.
- ū   As *oo* in *boot*. The French transcription *ou* is often met in English books, e.g. Maḥmūd, Mahmood, Mahmoud.
- ai   Pronounced in classical Arabic as English *i* in *hide*, in colloquial Arabic as *a* in *take*. Variously transcribed as *ai, ay, ei, ey* and *â*, e.g. sheikh, shaikh, shaykh, etc.
- aw   Pronounced in classical Arabic as English *ow* in *town*, in colloquial Arabic as in *grow*. Variously rendered *aw, ew, au, ô, av, ev*, e.g. Tawfīq, Taufiq, Tevfik, etc.

Sun- and Moon-Letters

In Arabic pronunciation, when the word to which the definite article, *al*, is attached begins with one of certain letters called 'Sun-letters', the *l* of the article changes to the initial letter in question, e.g. *al-shams* (the sun) is pronounced *ash-shams*; *al-rajul* (the man) is pronounced *ar-rajul*.

There are 14 Sun-letters in the Arabic alphabet, which are transcribed as: d, dh, n, r, s, sh, t, th, z, zh (d, s, t and z, and their emphatic forms, ḍ, ṣ, ṭ and ẓ, are not differentiated in this book). The remaining 15 letters in the Arabic alphabet are known as 'Moon-letters'.

TURKISH ORTHOGRAPHY AND PRONUNCIATION

Turkish has been written in Roman characters since 1928. The following pronunciations are invariable:

- c   hard *j*, as in *majority, jam*.
- ç   *ch*, as in *church*.
- g   hard *g*, as in *go, big*.
- ğ   not voiced, or pronounced *y*; Ereğli is pronounced *erayly*.
- ı   short vowel, as the second vowel of *'centre'*, or French *'le'*.
- i   *i* sound of *India, bitter* (NOT as in *bite, might*).
- o   *o*, as in *hot, boss*.
- ö   *i* sound of *'birth'*, or French *'oeuvre'*.
- ş   *sh*, as in *cash*.
- u   as in *do, too*, German *'um'*.
- ü   as in *burette*, German *'Hütte'*.

CALENDAR OF POLITICAL EVENTS, SEPTEMBER 2022–AUGUST 2023

SEPTEMBER 2022

1 **Cyprus** Air Vice-Marshal Peter Squires was sworn in as Administrator of the Sovereign Base Areas and Commander of British Forces Cyprus, succeeding Maj.-Gen. Rob Thomson.

8 **Algeria** President Abdelmadjid Tebboune carried out a cabinet reorganization, including the appointment of Brahim Merad as Minister of the Interior, Local Authorities and Territorial Planning, replacing Kamel Beldjoud, who became Minister of Transport.

15 **Libya** Abdullah Abu Razizah replaced Mohammed al-Hafi as Chief Justice of the Supreme Court.

19 **Iran** Dr Rouhollah Dehghani Firouzabadi was appointed Vice-President for Science, Technology and Knowledge-based Economy, replacing Sorena Sattari.

26 **Iraq** Mohammed al-Halbousi submitted his resignation as Speaker of the Council of Representatives; on 28 September the legislature voted to reject al-Halbousi's resignation.

27 **Saudi Arabia** King Salman bin Abdulaziz Al Sa'ud issued a royal decree promoting Crown Prince Mohammed bin Salman bin Abdulaziz Al Sa'ud from his cabinet posts as Deputy Prime Minister and Minister of Defence to that of Prime Minister (a position hitherto held by the King himself). Responsibility for the defence portfolio was assigned to the Crown Prince's younger brother Prince Khalid bin Salman Abdulaziz Al Sa'ud. In addition, Yousef bin Abdullah bin Mohammed al-Benyan was appointed to replace Dr Hamad bin Mohammed al-Sheikh as Minister of Education.

29 **Kuwait** At elections to the National Assembly, opposition candidates made considerable gains, winning 28 of the chamber's 50 seats (compared with 24 seats at the elections in December 2020). The Muslim Brotherhood-affiliated Islamic Constitutional Movement secured five seats, while Shi'a Muslim candidates took nine seats. While there had been no female representation in the previous legislature, the new Assembly included two women. A total of 20 former legislators lost their seats, including three former cabinet ministers. According to official estimates, the electoral turnout was around 50% of eligible voters.

OCTOBER 2022

5 **Kuwait** Having been formally reappointed as Prime Minister by Crown Prince Sheikh Meshal al-Ahmad al-Jaber al-Sabah, Sheikh Ahmad Nawaf al-Ahmad al-Sabah named a new Council of Ministers, which was subsequently approved by the Crown Prince. While the majority of cabinet members had served in the former Government (including Minister of Foreign Affairs Dr Ahmad Nasser al-Mohammad al-Sabah), a number of new appointments were made, including that of Abdullah Ali Abdullah al-Salem al-Sabah as Minister of Defence. However, another new appointee, Minister of Public Works, and of Electricity, Water and Renewable Energy Ammar Mohammad al-Ajmi, announced his resignation only hours after taking office, citing a lack of public trust in a number of reappointed ministers. After the composition of the new administration was also rejected by several legislators, Prime Minister Sheikh Ahmad carried out an extensive ministerial reorganization on 16 October, including the replacement of Dr Ahmad Nasser as Minister of Foreign Affairs by Sheikh Salem Abdullah al-Jaber al-Sabah and the appointment of Bader Hamed al-Mullah as Deputy Prime Minister and Minister of Oil. The new ministers were sworn in on 17 October.

9 **Iraq** Following disagreements between the Patriotic Union of Kurdistan and the Kurdistan Democratic Party over various issues relating to the parliamentary elections that had been scheduled for 1 October 2022, the Iraqi Kurdistan Parliament voted to extend its current term by one year.

13 **Iraq** In an initial round of voting, the Council of Representatives failed to elect a new President; Abdul Latif Rashid secured 157 votes, while the incumbent, Barham Salih, won 99 votes. In a second round held later that day, Rashid was elected to the presidency, winning 162 votes against 99 for Salih. Having been sworn into office, President Rashid named Mohammed Shia al-Sudani (who was supported by the Co-ordination Framework coalition of Shi'a parties) as the Prime Minister-designate and tasked him with forming a new government within 30 days. On 15 October outgoing Prime Minister Mustafa al-Kadhimi appointed Hayam Nemat as acting Minister of Finance, after accepting the resignation of Ihsan Abdul Jabbar Ismail from that post.

18 **Kuwait** The National Assembly elected Ahmed Abdulaziz al-Saadoun (who was unopposed) as the new Speaker, succeeding Marzouq al-Ghanim.

19 **Iran** Seyed Solat Mortazavi was appointed Minister of Co-operatives, Labour and Social Affairs (replacing Mohammad Hadi Zahedivafa, who had held the position in an acting capacity since 14 June); Mortazavi's erstwhile post of Vice-President in charge of Executive Affairs was assumed by former Governor of Tehran, Mohsen Mansouri, on 1 November.

27 **Iraq** More than a year of political deadlock came to an end when the Council of Representatives approved the ministerial nominations of Prime Minister-designate Mohammed Shia al-Sudani; the new Council of Ministers took office on 28 October. Fuad Hussein retained responsibility for the foreign affairs portfolio (as well as being appointed as one of three Deputy Prime Ministers), while Hayan Abdul Ghani Abdul Zahra was appointed as Deputy Prime Minister and Minister of Oil and Taif Sami Muhammad as Minister of Finance. Two cabinet posts—the environment, and construction and housing—remained unfilled. On assuming office, Prime Minister al-Sudani promised to amend the electoral law within three months and to hold early legislative elections within a year.

27 **Israel/Lebanon** The Governments of Israel and Lebanon ratified an historic, US-brokered agreement regarding the demarcation of their maritime border, thereby opening the possibility for both countries of offshore hydrocarbons exploration within the formerly disputed area of the Mediterranean.

CALENDAR OF POLITICAL EVENTS, SEPTEMBER 2022–AUGUST 2023

27 **Jordan** King Abdullah bin al-Hussein issued a royal decree, approving a cabinet reorganization (involving 10 ministerial portfolios) effected by Prime Minister Bisher al-Khasawneh. The reshuffle included the appointment of Nasser Shraideh as a third Deputy Prime Minister and an increase in the number of female ministers from two to five. On 30 October the King appointed a new Senate; Faisal al-Fayez was retained as Speaker of the upper chamber.

28 **Palestinian Territories** President Mahmoud Abbas issued a presidential decree ordering the formation of a new Supreme Council of Judicial Bodies and Authorities, which was to have full supervisory power over the judicial system and of which he himself would be the head and appoint the other members.

30 **Kuwait** Mohammad bin Naji was sworn in as President of the Supreme Judicial Council, President of the Court of Cassation and President of the Constitutional Court, while Mohammad Abu Sulaib was sworn in as President of the Court of Appeal.

30 **Lebanon** Following four unsuccessful attempts (on 29 September and 13, 20 and 24 October) by the National Assembly to elect a new President to succeed Michel Aoun, the latter left office one day before his mandate officially expired, on 31 October, and without a designated successor. In accordance with the Constitution, in the event of the presidency falling vacant, presidential powers were to be assumed by the Cabinet, with the Prime Minister becoming acting head of state. However, since Prime Minister Najib Miqati and his Government held office in an acting capacity, their executive powers were limited.

31 **Ceuta** Rafael García Rodríguez was appointed to succeed Salvadora del Carmen Mateos Esdudillo as Government Delegate.

NOVEMBER 2022

1 **Israel** At the country's fifth legislative elections in less than four years, a right-wing electoral alliance led by former Prime Minister Benjamin Netanyahu's Likud won a parliamentary majority, largely at the expense of left-wing parties. The electoral turnout was 70.6% of the registered electorate. According to the official results, 10 parties obtained at least 3.25% of the valid votes, thereby securing representation in the Knesset. Likud won 32 of the 120 seats, the centrist Yesh Atid (headed by the incumbent Prime Minister, Yair Lapid) took 24 seats, the far-right party list comprising the Religious Zionist Party, Otzma Yehudit and Noam increased its representation from six to 14 seats, while National Unity (an alliance composed of Kahol Lavan/Chosen L'Yisrael and New Hope) obtained 12 seats and the ultra-Orthodox Shas 11 seats. The Arab-majority Ra'am (United Arab List) and Hadash-Ta'al (an electoral alliance comprising the Arab Movement for Renewal/Ta'al and the Hadash coalition) won five seats each. On 13 November President Isaac Herzog formally tasked Netanyahu with forming a new government.

10 **Lebanon** The National Assembly failed in a fifth attempt to elect a new President; six further attempts, on 17 and 24 November, on 1, 8 and 15 December and on 19 January 2023 also proved unsuccessful.

12 **Bahrain** In the first round of elections to the Council of Representatives only six of the 40 elective seats were won outright. The official turnout was 73% of registered voters. The remaining 34 deputies were elected at a run-off vote on 19 November. Many first-time deputies and a record total of eight women (two more than at the previous elections, in 2018) were elected to the Council. Individuals affiliated to opposition groups were not permitted to contest the elections. On 21 November King Hamad bin Isa Al Khalifa reappointed Crown Prince Sheikh Salman bin Hamad Al Khalifa as Prime Minister and requested that he form a new cabinet; this took place later that day, with only a small number of adjustments and no change in the key posts. Members of the new Consultative Council, the 40-member upper house of the bicameral legislature which holds a purely advisory role, were appointed by King Hamad on 27 November, under the renewed chairmanship of Ali bin Saleh al-Saleh.

13 **Jordan** Ahmad Safadi was elected as the new Speaker of the House of Representatives (in succession to Abdulkarim Dughmi), defeating his opponent, Firas Sawair, by 104 votes to 13.

22 **Iran** Rostam Ghasemi resigned as Minister of Roads and Urban Development on health grounds; Mehrdad Bazrpash was appointed as his successor in the post on 6 December.

DECEMBER 2022

3 **Iraq** The Council of Representatives approved the following two cabinet appointments, thereby completing the formation of Mohammed Shia al-Sudani's Government: Nizar Amedi as Minister of the Environment and Benkin Rikani as Minister of Construction and Housing.

12 **Bahrain** Sayyid Ahmed bin Salman al-Musallam was elected to succeed Fawzia bint Abdullah Yousef as Speaker of the Council of Representatives.

12 **Israel** Yariv Levin, a close ally of Prime Minister-designate Benjamin Netanyahu, was elected as acting Speaker of the Knesset, replacing Michael (Mickey) Levy. Levin was to oversee the passage of legislation aimed at facilitating Netanyahu's formation of a government.

15 **Kuwait** It was reported that Abdullah Ali Abdullah al-Salemal al-Sabah had resigned from his post as Minister of Defence; on 19 December First Deputy Prime Minister and Minister of the Interior Sheikh Talal Khaled al-Ahmad al-Sabah assumed responsibility for the defence portfolio in an acting capacity.

17 **Tunisia** At elections to the newly reconstituted Assembly of the Representatives of the People (ARP) (in which, according to new electoral legislation introduced in mid-September, candidates were elected directly rather than via party lists for a term of five years), only 21 candidates secured victory—including 10 unopposed. The official turnout was just 11.2% of the electorate, with the poll being boycotted by the majority of political parties, which denounced the vote as a sham and challenged the legitimacy of the new parliamentary lower chamber. Amid growing calls for the election process to be abandoned, a second round of voting took place on 29 January 2023 to fill a further 131 seats in the ARP; there were no candidates for the remaining nine seats. As in the first round, the turnout for the run-off poll was extremely low, again at around an estimated 11%.

22 **Jordan** Makram Queisi was appointed as Minister of Tourism and Antiquities, following the resignation from the post of Nayef al-Fayez.

29 **Iran** Mohammad Reza Farzin was appointed as Governor of the Central Bank, following the resignation from the post of Ali Salehabadi.

29 **Israel** Following intensive inter-party negotiations over the allocation of ministerial posts and the passage of new legislation allowing individuals who had been convicted of offences but not given custodial sentences to serve as ministers, a new coalition Government, headed by Benjamin Netanyahu, the Chairman of Likud, was sworn into office, having been endorsed by the Knesset by 63 votes to 54. The new administration, which was notable for its predominantly hardline, ultra-Orthodox composition, comprised representatives of Likud, Shas, the Religious Zionist Party, Otzma Yehudit, United Torah Judaism and Noam. The appointment of Itamar Ben Gvir, the leader of Otzma Yehudit, as Minister of National Security, provoked particular controversy, owing to his uncompromising, anti-Arab political stance. Also on 29 December Amir Ohana of Likud was elected as the new Speaker of the Knesset.

30 **Tunisia** President Kaïs Saïed decreed an extension of the state of emergency (in place since November 2015) until 30 January 2023 (subsequently further extended until the end of 2023).

JANUARY 2023

3 **United Arab Emirates** President Sheikh Mohammed bin Zayed Al Nahyan issued a federal decree appointing Lt-Gen. Eng. Issa Saif Mohammed al-Mazrouei as Chief of Staff of the Federal Armed Forces, in succession to Lt-Gen. Hamad Mohammed Thani al-Rumaithi.

6 **Tunisia** President Kaïs Saïed dismissed the Minister of Trade and Export Development, Fadhila al-Rabhi Ben Hamza, with no reason being specified; on 12 January the vacated post was allocated to Kalthoum Ben Rejeb.

16 **Israel** Maj.-Gen. Herzl 'Herzi' Halevi took office as Chief of Staff of the Israel Defense Forces, succeeding Lt-Gen. Aviv Kohavi.

18 **Israel** The Supreme Court ruled (by 10 votes to one) that the appointment of Aryeh Deri, the leader of the ultra-Orthodox Shas party and a key ally of Prime Minister Benjamin Netanyahu, to the posts of Vice Prime Minister and Minister of the Interior and of Health, should be revoked on the grounds of it being 'extremely unreasonable' in light of Deri's conviction in early 2022 for tax fraud and suspended prison sentence. The dramatic ruling was made amid controversial plans by the Government significantly to reform the judicial system, including a proposed severe curtailment of the Supreme Court's powers. On 22 January 2023 Netanyahu complied with the Supreme Court's ruling by dismissing Deri from his cabinet posts, with effect from 24 January. Deri was, however, to retain the title of Vice Prime Minister, which is largely honorific and carries no official authority or responsibility. On 24 January the Minister within the Ministry of Welfare, Yoav Ben-Tzur of Shas, also assumed the post of acting Minister of Health, while the Minister of Religious Services, Michael Malkieli (also of Shas), was given the additional responsibility of the interior portfolio on an interim basis.

23 **Iraq** Prime Minister Mohammed Shia al-Sudani removed Mustafa Ghaleb Mukheef from his post as Governor of the Central Bank of Iraq, replacing him with Ali Mohsen Ismail (who had held the governorship during 2014–20).

23 **Kuwait** Prime Minister Sheikh Ahmad Nawaf al-Ahmad al-Sabah tendered the resignation of the Council of Ministers, following disputes with the National Assembly over a proposed debt relief bill and plans by the legislature to question two ministers over alleged economic mismanagement. The resignation was accepted on 26 January by Amir Nawaf al-Ahmad al-Jaber al-Sabah, who asked that the cabinet remain in office in an acting capacity pending the formation of a new administration.

30 **Tunisia** President Kaïs Saïed carried out a minor cabinet reshuffle, replacing Fathi Slaouti as Minister of Education with Mohamed Ali Boughdiri and Mahmoud Elyes Hamza as Minister of Agriculture, Water Resources and Fisheries with Abdelmonem Belati.

FEBRUARY 2023

2 **Saudi Arabia** King Salman bin Abdulaziz Al Sa'ud issued a royal decree appointing Ayman al-Sayari as Governor of the Saudi Central Bank, in succession to Fahad al-Mubarak.

5 **Cyprus** At a presidential election, Nikos Christodoulides (an independent candidate, who had previously served as foreign affairs minister and who was supported by the Movement of Social Democrats—EDEK, the Democratic Party—DIKO, the Democratic Front—DEPA and the Solidarity Movement) and Andreas Mavroyiannis (an independent candidate supported by the Progressive Party of the Working People—AKEL and Generation Change) emerged as the leading candidates, winning 32.0% and 29.6% of the valid votes cast, respectively. Averof Neophytou of the Democratic Rally (DISY) was third-placed, with 26.1% of the vote. Christodoulides and Mavroyiannis subsequently contested a run-off election on 12 February, at which the former won a narrow victory, with just under 52.0% of the vote. Turnout was recorded at 72.1% of the electorate at the first round and 72.5% at the second round. Christodoulides took office as President on 28 February, succeeding Nikos Anastasiades, and a new Council of Ministers was sworn in on 1 March. The new Government mainly comprised independents, but also included a representative of DIKO and a representative of the Solidarity Movement.

7 **Tunisia** President Kaïs Saïed dismissed Othman Jerandi from his post as Minister of Foreign Affairs, Migration and Tunisians Abroad and replaced him with Nabil Ammar.

22 **Tunisia** President Kaïs Saïed dismissed the Minister of Employment and Vocational Training, Nasreddine Nsibi, with no reason being specified.

MARCH 2023

5 **Kuwait** Crown Prince Sheikh Meshal al-Ahmad al-Jaber al-Sabah issued a decree reappointing Sheikh Ahmad Nawaf al-Ahmad al-Sabah as Prime Minister and requesting that he form a new cabinet.

5 **Saudi Arabia** King Salman bin Abdulaziz Al Sa'ud appointed Salman al-Dosari as Minister of Media.

6 **United Arab Emirates** As part of a minor cabinet reorganization, Salem bin Khalid al-Qassimi replaced Noura bint Mohammed al-Kaabi as Minister of Culture and Youth, and Shamma al-Mazrui replaced

Hessa bint Essa Buhumaid as Minister of Community Development.

7 **Qatar** Having accepted the resignation of Sheikh Khalid bin Khalifa bin Abdulaziz Al Thani from his posts as Prime Minister and Minister of the Interior, Amir Sheikh Tamim bin Hamad Al Thani appointed erstwhile Deputy Prime Minister Sheikh Mohammed bin Abdulrahman bin Jassim Al Thani as the new Prime Minister (while also retaining the post of Minister of Foreign Affairs) and Sheikh Khalifa bin Hamad bin Khalifa Al Thani as the new interior minister.

10 **Iran/Saudi Arabia** In an unexpected development, following talks brokered by the People's Republic of China, Iran and Saudi Arabia formally agreed to restore diplomatic relations (severed in January 2016) and reopen their embassies in Riyadh and Tehran.

11 **Cyprus** Annita Demetrious was elected to replace Averof Neophytou as the leader of the Democratic Rally (DISY), following the latter's failed bid in the presidential poll in February.

13 **Tunisia** The new Assembly of the Representatives of the People, elected over two rounds, in December 2022 and January 2023, was officially inaugurated. By this date a total of 154 seats had been filled, with only 25 female representatives among them. Ibrahim Bouderbala, a staunch supporter of President Kaïs Saïed, was elected as the new Speaker of the Assembly.

15 **Algeria** Abderrezak Makri resigned as President of the opposition Mouvement de la Société pour la Paix.

16 **Algeria** President Abdelmadjid Tebboune carried out a ministerial reorganization, including the appointment of Ahmed Attaf as Minister of Foreign Affairs (replacing Ramtane Lamamra) and Laaziz Fayed as Minister of Finance (replacing Brahim Kassali).

17 **Tunisia** Tawfiq Sharafeddine resigned as Minister of the Interior for personal reasons; the following day the erstwhile Governor of Tunis, Kamal Feki, took office as the new interior minister.

19 **Kuwait** Amid renewed tension between the National Assembly and the Government, the Constitutional Court annulled the legislative elections of 29 September 2022, in which the opposition had secured a majority of seats, and ordered that the previous Assembly, in which the opposition had narrowly failed to achieve a majority, be reinstated with immediate effect. The reinstatement of the legislature included the return of Marzouq al-Ghanim, a long-term supporter of the executive, to the post of Speaker. The Court justified its action by citing appeals relating to the alleged invalidity of the electoral process owing to discrepancies in the decree issued by Crown Prince Sheikh Meshal al-Ahmad al-Jaber al-Sabah (acting on behalf of Amir Sheikh Nawaf al-Ahmad al-Jaber al-Sabah) on 22 June 2022 ordering the dissolution of the legislature.

26 **Israel** Prime Minister Benjamin Netanyahu dismissed Yoav Gallant from his post as Minister of Defense (although he did not send him a letter formally confirming his dismissal) in response to the minister's expressed support for the mass protests against the Government's proposed judicial reforms and his request that implementation of the proposed legislation be postponed. On 27 March the Government survived two no-confidence votes in the Knesset—rejected by 59 votes to 51 and by 60 votes to 51. Following the postponement of the judicial reforms, on 3 April Netanyahu announced that he had put Gallant's dismissal on hold and on 10 April he retracted it entirely.

28 **Bahrain** Rear Admiral Mohammed Ibrahim al-Binali was appointed to succeed Rear Admiral Mohammed Youssef al-Asam as Commander of the Royal Bahraini Navy; al-Binali was to hold the post in an acting capacity.

28 **Israel** The Knesset approved the appointment of David Amsalem of Likud as Minister of Regional Co-operation and Minister within the Ministry of Justice.

29 **Syrian Arab Republic** President Bashar al-Assad carried out a cabinet reorganization, including the appointment of a new Minister of Petroleum and Mineral Resources (Dr Firas Hassan Qaddour, replacing Bassam To'meh) and four other ministers.

29 **United Arab Emirates** President Sheikh Mohammed bin Zayed Al Nahyan issued a decree naming his eldest son, Sheikh Khalid bin Mohammed bin Zayed Al Nahyan, as Crown Prince of Abu Dhabi, making him the country's likely next head of state and consolidating the Al Nahyan family's hold on power. On the same day the President appointed his brother, Deputy Prime Minister and Minister of the Presidential Court Sheikh Mansour bin Zayed Al Nahyan, to hold the additional post of Vice-President, alongside Sheikh Mohammed bin Rashid Al Maktoum (the Ruler of Dubai).

APRIL 2023

2 **Israel** May Golan of Likud, was appointed to the newly created post of Minister for the Advancement of the Status of Women.

3 **Iran** Following the resignation of Yousef Nouri as Minister of Education amid widespread discontent at a delay in the payment of teachers' salaries, Reza Morad Sahraei was appointed to the post, in an acting capacity (confirmed in post on 30 May).

9 **Kuwait** An Amiri decree was issued forming a new Government, headed by Prime Minister Sheikh Ahmad Nawaf al-Ahmad al-Sabah.

9 **Morocco** Rear-Adm. Mohammed Tahin was appointed as Inspector General of the Royal Moroccan Navy, in succession to Rear-Adm. Mustapha el-Alami.

12 **Iran** Dr Seyed Massoud Mirkazemi was replaced as Vice-President and Head of the Planning and Budget Organization by Davoud Manzour, while Javad Sadatinezhad was replaced as Minister of Agriculture, on an acting basis, by Seyed Mohammad Aghamiri.

17 **Kuwait** Crown Prince Sheikh Meshal al-Ahmad al-Jaber al-Sabah (acting on behalf of Amir Sheikh Nawaf al-Ahmad al-Jaber al-Sabah) ordered the dissolution of the National Assembly that had been reinstated on 19 March and it was announced that fresh legislative elections would be held within two months.

19 **Iraq** Jalil Adnan Khalaf resigned as Chairman of the Independent High Electoral Commission (IHEC); on 17 May Omar Ahmed Mohammed was elected as the new Chairman of the IHEC.

19 **Israel** The Knesset approved the appointment of Moshe Arbel of Shas as Minister of the Interior and of Health.

22 **Morocco** King Mohammed VI appointed Lt-Gen. Mohammed Berrid to succeed Lt-Gen. Belkhir el-

CALENDAR OF POLITICAL EVENTS, SEPTEMBER 2022–AUGUST 2023

Farouk as Inspector General of the Royal Moroccan Forces.

26 **Iran** Ayatollah Abbasali Soleimani, a senior Shi'a Muslim cleric and member of the Assembly of Experts, was killed by a gunman in Babolsar in northern Iran.

26 **Tunisia** Opposition party Ennahdha appointed Mondher Lounissi to hold the post of party President in an caretaker capacity, in the absence of incumbent leader Rachid Ghannouchi, who had been arrested on 17 April on a number of charges (including terrorism).

30 **Iran** Seyed Reza Fatemi Amin was dismissed from his post as Minister of Industries, Mines and Trade; he was replaced, in an acting capacity, by Mehdi Niazi.

MAY 2023

1 **Kuwait** The National Assembly was formally dissolved and on 3 May it was announced that legislative elections would be held on 6 June.

7 **Syrian Arab Republic** At a meeting of the foreign affairs ministers of the Arab League held in Cairo, Egypt, the ministers voted to readmit Syria to the organization (from which it had been suspended in November 2011).

14 **Türkiye** According to the preliminary results of the first round of the presidential election, which attracted a turnout of 87.0% of the electorate, none of the three candidates secured an outright majority. The incumbent President, Recep Tayyip Erdoğan, representing the ruling Adalet ve Kalkınma Partisi (AKP, Justice and Development Party), won 49.5% of the vote, Kemal Kılıçdaroğlu of the opposition Cumhuriyet Halk Partisi (CHP, Republican People's Party) received 44.9% and Sinan Oğan, representing the right-wing ATA Alliance, garnered 5.2%. Despite Muharrem İnce, the leader of the recently formed Memleket Partisi (Homeland Party), having withdrawn from the contest on 11 May, his name appeared on the ballot papers and he received 0.4% of the vote. According to the final results of the run-off presidential poll held on 28 May (the first Turkish presidential election to go to a second round), Erdoğan was re-elected to the presidency, securing 52.2% of the vote against Kılıçdaroğlu's 47.8%; a turnout of 84.2% was reported. Meanwhile, in the legislative elections held concurrently on 14 May, the ruling AKP retained the largest (albeit reduced) representation in the Turkish Grand National Assembly, winning 268 of the 600 seats, while the CHP was second-placed, with 169 seats. A reported 87.0% of registered voters took part in the elections to the legislature.

22 **Iran** Rear Admiral Ali Shamkhani resigned from his post as Secretary of the Supreme National Security Council and was succeeded by Gen. Ali Akbar Ahmadian.

25 **Lebanon** Walid Joumblatt resigned as President of the Parti Socialiste Progressiste (a post which he had held since 1977).

28 **Ceuta** At elections to the 25-member local assembly, the Partido Popular remained the party with the largest representation, retaining nine seats. The Partido Socialista Obrero Español won six seats, VOX five, the Movimiento por la Dignidad y la Ciudadanía three and Ceuta Ya! two.

28 **Melilla** At elections to the local assembly, the Partido Popular increased its representation by four seats, winning an outright majority of 14 of the 25 seats. The Coalición por Melilla secured five seats, the Partido Socialista Obrero Español three, VOX two and Somos Melilla one.

30 **Iraq** The Federal Supreme Court ruled that the Iraqi Kurdistan Parliament's extension of its term by one year in October 2022 was unconstitutional, on the grounds that only 80 of the 111 legislators had taken part in the vote to approve the extension, and stated that all decisions issued by the Parliament from the end of its legal term, on 6 November 2022, were therefore considered null and void.

JUNE 2023

3 **Türkiye** Recep Tayyip Erdoğan was sworn in for a third term as President. He subsequently named his new Council of Ministers (with only two members of the previous administration being retained), including Hakan Fidan, the erstwhile head of the National Intelligence Organization, as Minister of Foreign Affairs and Mehmet Şimşek, a respected economist and former incumbent of the post, as Minister of Treasury and Finance. Also on 3 June, Erdoğan announced the appointment of Cevdet Yılmaz as his new Vice-President, in succession to Fuat Oktay; Yılmaz formally took office on 5 June. On the same day, in a third round of voting, the Grand National Assembly elected Numan Kurtulmuş of the ruling Adalet ve Kalkınma Partisi (AKP, Justice and Development Party) as the new Speaker; he was sworn in on 7 June.

6 **Kuwait** At elections to the National Assembly, opposition candidates won an outright majority of 29 of the chamber's 50 elective seats, representing a gain of one seat on the opposition's tally of 28 seats in the elections of 29 September 2022 (annulled by the Constitutional Court on 19 March 2023). Only one woman candidate (representing the opposition) won a seat in the National Assembly, while Shi'a candidates took seven seats and the Islamic Constitutional Movement three.

6 **Türkiye** Following the appointment of Gen. Yaşar Güler as Minister of National Defence, his previous position as Chief of the General Staff was allocated, on an interim basis, to the Commander of the Turkish Land Forces, Gen. Musa Avsever. On the same day Hafize Gaye Erkan was appointed to succeed Prof. Şahap Kavcıoğlu as Governor of the Central Bank, becoming the first woman to hold the post.

13 **Iran** The Majlis-e-Shura-e Islami approved the appointment of Dr Abbas Aliabadi as Minister of Industries, Mines and Trade.

13 **Kuwait** Crown Prince Sheikh Meshal al-Ahmad al-Jaber al-Sabah reappointed Sheikh Ahmad Nawaf al-Ahmad al-Sabah as Prime Minister. Sheikh Ahmad Nawaf announced his new cabinet on 18 June; six new ministers were named, including for the oil and defence portfolios, while Sheikh Talal al-Khaled al-Ahmad al-Sabah was reappointed as First Deputy Prime Minister and Minister of the Interior and Manaf Abdulaziz Hajri as Minister of Finance. The new Council of Ministers was sworn in on 19 June.

14 **Lebanon** A 12th attempt by the National Assembly to elect a new President proved unsuccessful; Jihad Azour secured 59 votes and Suleiman Frangieh 51.

20 **Algeria** President Abdelmadjid Tebboune dismissed Mohamed Bouslimani from his posts as Minister of Communication and Government Spokesman, following a number of Algerian media reports concerning the ambassador of the United Arab Emirates to Algeria that were denied by the foreign affairs ministry.

Mohamed Laagab was appointed as the new Minister of Communication on 3 September.

20 **Iran** The Majlis-e-Shura-e Islami approved the appointment of Mohammad Ali Nikbakht as Minister of Agriculture.

20 **Kuwait** At the inaugural session of the newly elected National Assembly, Ahmed al-Saadoun was elected as Speaker, in succession to Marzouq al-Ghanim.

24 **Ceuta** Mayor/President Juan Jesús Vivas Lara appointed a new Council of Government, comprising members of the Partido Popular.

JULY 2023

1 **Cyprus** Katerina Stamatiou took office as the President of the Supreme Court, succeeding Antonis Liatsos, who was to become the President of a new Supreme Constitutional Court.

3 **United Arab Emirates** Mohammed Hassan al-Suwaidi was appointed to hold the newly created post of Minister of Investment.

7 **Melilla** The Assembly elected Juan José Imbroda of the Partido Popular (PP) as the new Mayor/President, succeeding independent Eduardo de Castro González. A new Council of Government, comprising members of the PP, took office on 11 July.

11 **Kuwait** Manaf Abdulaziz al-Hajri resigned from his post as Minister of Finance; on the following day responsibility for the finance portfolio was allocated, on an interim basis, to Deputy Prime Minister, Minister of Oil and Minister of State for Economic Affairs Saad al-Barrak. Fahd al-Jarallah was appointed as the new Minister of Finance on 3 September.

23 **Spanish North Africa** In the Spanish general election, Javier Celaya Brey of the Partido Popular (PP) was elected as the Deputy to the Congress of Deputies in Madrid representing Ceuta, while Sofia Acedo Reyes, also of the PP, was elected to represent Melilla. The following members of the PP were elected to the Senate in Madrid: Cristina Diaz Moreno and Abdelhakim Abdeselam al-Lal, representing Ceuta; and Fernando Adolfo Gutiérrez Díaz de Otazu and Isabel María Moreno Mohamed, representing Melilla.

24 **Morocco** Maj.-Gen. Mohamed Galih was appointed as Inspector General of the Royal Moroccan Air Force, in succession to Maj.-Gen. Abed Alaoui Bouhamid.

27 **Libya** Prime Minister Abdul Dbeibah suspended Minister of Foreign Affairs and International Co-operation Najla el-Mangoush from her post after reports that she had held a covert meeting with her Israeli counterpart in Rome, Italy, sparked a political outcry and street protests in Libya. El-Mangoush was subsequently reported to have fled to Türkiye.

31 **Lebanon** As planned, Riad Salameh stood down as Governor of the central bank, the Banque du Liban, having held the post since 1993; following the Government's failure to name a permanent successor to Salameh, the erstwhile First Deputy Governor of the bank, Wassim Mansouri, was appointed as its new Governor, on an interim basis.

AUGUST 2023

1 **Iran** President Ebrahim Raisi accepted the resignation (on the grounds of ill health) of Minister of Sport and Youth Affairs Hamid Sajjadi and appointed Kioumars Hashemi to head the ministry on an acting basis.

1 **Tunisia** Amid a deepening economic and social crisis in the country, President Kaïs Saïed dismissed Prime Minister Najla Bouden and replaced her with Ahmed Hachani.

3 **Iraq** President Nechirvan Barzani issued a decree setting 25 February 2024 as the date for the next parliamentary elections in the Kurdish Autonomous Region.

3 **Türkiye** Gen. Metin Gürak was appointed as Chief of the General Staff, while Gen. Selçuk Bayraktaroğlu succeeded Gen. Musa Avsever as Commander of the Turkish Land Forces and Gen. Ziya Cemal Kadıoğlu succeeded Gen. Atilla Gülan as Commander of the Turkish Air Force.

6 **Iran** Mohammad Jafar Montazeri, the erstwhile Prosecutor-General, was appointed as Chief Justice of the Supreme Court, succeeding Ahmad Mortazavi Moghaddam.

6 **Libya** The High Council of State voted, by 67 votes to 62, in a run-off vote to appoint Mohammed Takala as its new President, replacing Khalid al-Mishri, who had held the post since April 2017.

9 **Syrian Arab Republic** Dr Muhammad Amer Mardini was sworn in as the new Minister of Education, following the dismissal of the previous incumbent, Dr Darem Taba'a.

11 **'Turkish Republic of Northern Cyprus'** Prime Minister Ünal Üstel carried out a cabinet reshuffle, including the replacement of Alişan Şan as Minister of Finance with Özdemir Berova, and the transfer of Dursun Oğuz from the post of Minister of Agriculture and Natural Resources to that of Minister of Interior Affairs.

24 **Egypt/Iran/Saudi Arabia/United Arab Emirates** At a summit meeting of the BRICS (Brazil, Russia, India, China and South Africa) grouping held in Johannesburg, South Africa, it was announced that Egypt, Iran, Saudi Arabia and the United Arab Emirates (together with Argentina and Ethiopia) had been invited to join the bloc, effective from 1 January 2024.

PART ONE
General Survey

CHINA'S GROWING PRESENCE IN THE MIDDLE EAST: FROM ECONOMIC PARTNERSHIPS TO DIPLOMATIC ENGAGEMENT?

JULIA GUROL

INTRODUCTION

Recent diplomatic advances by the People's Republic of China in the Middle East have made international headlines. China's facilitation of the Iran-Saudi rapprochement agreement in March 2023 sent geopolitical shock waves around the world, and the country's economic footprint in the region is continuing to grow. These developments have raised an essential question: what is China's future role in the Middle East going to look like? Moreover, maybe even more importantly, how is this going to affect the posture of the USA in the region? While the question of whether China is challenging the USA's role in the Middle East, or whether the declining US hegemony in the region is paving the way for deepening China-Middle East ties, is open to debate, it is certain that the Middle East is currently experiencing a major reconfiguration of power—both intra-regionally and with respect to external actors. This introduction therefore seeks to deconstruct the Chinese role in the Middle East, guided by the following questions: What is the extent and substance of China-Middle East relations? Why have both sides sought to deepen these relations? Will China replace the USA as the leading guarantor of security in the region? And what are the implications of China's growing presence for the regional (security) order?

As a relatively new, but increasingly influential, extra-regional power in the Middle East, China has become an important partner for most countries in the region, in terms of economic partnerships but also beyond. Given the changing role of the USA as a security guarantor and the disengagement of other Western actors in the region, more attention has been dedicated to the rationales, dynamics and implications of China's approach to the Middle East. While there is no single Chinese Middle East strategy, the importance of the broader Middle East region to China has undoubtedly increased over the past decades. Following the announcement of the Belt and Road Initiative (BRI) in 2013, China's economic, political, and, to a lesser extent, security footprint in the Middle East and its bilateral ties with individual countries in the region have deepened and the Middle East has become increasingly important to China.

According to China's *Arab Policy Paper* (Ministry of Foreign Affairs, 2016), released when Chinese President Xi Jinping visited the Middle East in 2016, China's approach to the region was described as a '1+2+3 co-operation pattern' in which energy security forms the core, followed by investment and trade, and finally the development of nuclear energy. Since then, China's partnerships in the Middle East and North Africa (MENA) have mainly taken two forms: multilateral and bilateral. The former refers to the collective co-operation between China and the League of Arab States (Arab League), the Gulf Cooperation Council (GCC), the China-Arab States Cooperation Forum (CASCF) and the Union of the Arab Maghreb, while the latter comprises a growing number of strategic partnerships with individual MENA countries. As of April 2023, China maintained comprehensive strategic partnerships with Algeria, Egypt, Saudi Arabia, the United Arab Emirates (UAE) and Iran, and strategic partnerships with Oman, Kuwait, Iraq, Morocco, Jordan and Qatar.

Traditionally, China's relationships with Middle Eastern countries have primarily revolved around two key issues, namely energy and the expansion of economic partnerships in the context of China's BRI. While economic co-operation and energy partnerships still remain firmly at the heart of China-Middle East relations, recent developments have shown a certain paradigm shift in China's Middle East policy, with the country transitioning from being a reactive bystander in terms of security and diplomacy towards being a more proactive diplomatic force. Fuelled by the decline of the long-standing dominance of the USA in the region, China's approach to the Middle East, as well as the role prescribed to it by countries within the region, is undergoing major changes. Against this backdrop, questions pertain regarding China's future role in the region in light of current power reconfigurations.

To answer these questions, we need to understand the key pillars of China's Middle East strategy and how countries within the region view China. Moreover, it is necessary to assess the changing US role in the region to predict how China's regional footprint might evolve in the future. To provide an overview of China's growing presence in the Middle East and the development from merely economic interactions to a more substantial Chinese political and diplomatic role, this essay discusses the evolution of China's approach to the Middle East. In addition, it considers the implications of China's rise for the regional order and the promise that an ascendant China holds for multipolarity in the Middle East. By means of providing a comprehensive overview of China-Middle East relations, it also examines the position of the Middle East in China's overall BRI strategy and considers the future of China-Middle East ties. As understanding this relationship is hardly possible without taking into account the role of the USA in the region and how countries in the Middle East view the waning US security guarantees, all sections of this essay will include the USA as a reference frame.

CHINA'S GROWING ECONOMIC FOOTPRINT IN THE MIDDLE EAST AND THE ROLE OF OIL AND NATURAL GAS

China's influence in the Middle East is growing steadily, particularly its economic influence. China's trade with Middle East countries far exceeds that of the USA. In 2021 China's imports from the region reached a total of US $130,000m., while the USA imported $34,000m. Similarly, China's exports to the region totalled $129,000m. in 2021, compared with $48,000m. of US exports. In addition, Chinese foreign direct investment (FDI) in the Middle East has grown steadily since 2003 (ChinaMED, 2023). Saudi Arabia and the UAE are China's main trading partners in the region. Chinese imports from Saudi Arabia reached $78,046m. in 2022, while imports from the UAE totalled $45,408m. (ChinaMED, 2023). Although the USA continues to maintain a significant economic presence in the region through FDI and the longevity of US company's interactions, China's economic footprint in the Middle East has increased rapidly, particularly since 2013.

In this overall context, energy has been a key driver. China is among the most important buyers of crude petroleum and liquefied natural gas (LNG) from Middle Eastern exporters. The majority of China's crude petroleum imports originate from countries in the Middle East, which has over time led to a certain degree of Chinese dependency on oil exporters in that region (Andrews-Speed and Yao, 2022). It is thus not surprising that since the beginning of the Russian Federation's invasion of Ukraine in February 2022 China has increased its imports of sharply discounted Russian crude petroleum to reduce this dependency and capitalize on the lower prices for Russian crude petroleum. However, China still imports around one-half of its oil from the Middle East as other efforts by China to diversify its energy sources and secure oil supplies from Africa and Canada have been unsuccessful. Saudi Arabia is the region's primary exporter to China. China has become by far the most important export market for Saudi crude petroleum. In 2020 Saudi Arabia exported US $24,700m. worth of crude petroleum to China. Oman (with $11,300m. worth of crude petroleum exports in 2020), Kuwait ($7,900m. in 2020) and the UAE ($8,600m. in 2018) are also major suppliers of oil to China (OEC, 2023a, 2023b, 2023c, 2023d), while Qatar exported approximately $7,800m. worth of natural gas to China in 2019. In November 2022 China and Qatar also signed a $60,000m. deal for the supply of LNG over a 27-year period (Dargin, 2022). The deal provided for the export of approximately 4m. metric tons of LNG to China per year and was considered the longest-term LNG supply contract signed to date. Competition with the USA was also evident in the context of Chinese oil imports from the Middle East: after the expiration of US waivers on Iranian oil imports in May 2019, China continued importing a small quantity of oil from Iran (Gurol and Scita, 2020), thereby supporting Iran financially in defiance of US oil sanctions. In December 2022 Chinese oil imports from Iran reached a record high, owing to concerns about international sanctions reducing Russian oil exports.

The importance of energy in China-Middle East relations is not only reflected in oil and gas purchases but also in the construction of critical infrastructure such as pipelines and terminals. For instance, the UAE has awarded a number of oil concessions and drilling licences to Chinese firms in recent years (Cahill, 2021). The Saudi Arabian Oil Company (Saudi Aramco) also entered into several joint ventures with the China Petroleum and Chemical Corporation (Sinopec) in 2022 to invest in refineries throughout the kingdom, and both parties signed a memorandum of understanding to expand their co-operation (Gulf Business, 2022).

The third element of China's '1+2+3' approach, namely the development of nuclear energy, has also increasingly come into prominence. In the past decade China has been eager to expand the market share of its nuclear power enterprises in the MENA region and to advance co-operation with countries such as Saudi Arabia, the UAE, Iran, Algeria, Türkiye (Turkey), Egypt and Jordan (Sun et al., 2022). For these countries, nuclear power is regarded as an important means to diversify their energy sources and to meet their increasing electricity needs. The examples of China-Middle East nuclear energy co-operation are manifold. For instance, after securing the support of the China National Nuclear Corporation (CNNC), in 2019 the Emirati authorities announced a platform for nuclear technology and finance (Andrews-Speed and Lixia, 2022), while Saudi Arabia, with the assistance of several Chinese companies, planned to construct up to 16 nuclear reactors, which were expected to enter into service by 2032 (Garlick and Havlová, 2019). Chinese nuclear companies have also offered to help locate and develop the kingdom's uranium resources. For instance, in 2017 the CNNC and the Saudi Geological Survey signed a memorandum of understanding on surveying uranium deposits, and in recent years China has helped Saudi Arabia to develop multiple uranium-prospecting sites (Wong et al., 2023).

THE MIDDLE EAST'S PARTICIPATION IN CHINA'S BELT AND ROAD INITIATIVE

China's BRI, launched in 2013 as a global infrastructure initiative and now a key component of China's foreign policy, comprised two complementary projects in its original form (National Development and Reform Commission, 2015; Ministry of Foreign Affairs, 2017). The first was the establishment of overland connectivity through the Silk Road Economic Belt (SREB), while the second was the Maritime Silk Road (MSR), connecting the maritime trade routes of Africa, Europe, Oceania, and South and South-East Asia. This was later followed by the Digital Silk Road (DSR) and, announced at the height of the first wave of the coronavirus disease (COVID-19) pandemic, the Health Silk Road (HSR). The HSR is intended to function in tandem with the DSR, bringing together digital and physical infrastructure with the goal of providing global health care. While the concept of the HSR is far from new—the first references to the development of an HSR date back to 2015—the political context of its official launch during the early stages of the COVID-19 pandemic in early 2020 was extremely advantageous for China and provided a unique opportunity for the country to position itself as a 'saviour' in the global crisis (Greene and Triolo, 2020; Gurol et al., 2023).

Virtually overnight, the digital and health elements became the main focus of the BRI (Rudolf, 2021).

For all four components (land, sea, digital and health) of the overarching BRI, the MENA region plays a central role (Ehteshami, 2018), accounting for 28.5% of total BRI investments in 2021 (Foreign Affairs Committee, 2022). As of 2022, China had signed BRI agreements with 21 states of the MENA region, including 18 Arab states. In line with the overall orientation of the BRI and China's own needs, investments and partnerships have focused primarily on the construction, transportation, logistics, energy, digital and security sectors. For example, Chinese companies and consortia are involved in the expansion of a high-speed rail line in Iran linking Mashhad to the capital, Tehran, are investing in the development of a new coal-fired power plant in Türkiye, and are seeking contracts to expand the Suez Canal in Egypt. Furthermore, the railway from Medina to Mecca in Saudi Arabia was built and financed by China Railway Construction Corporation.

From China's perspective, the Middle East's geographically strategic location and abundance of natural resources has made the region a major focus of the BRI. The Middle East is situated at the heart of the SREB routes and provides a gateway to Europe (Chaziza, 2020). In addition, the Middle East occupies a favourable geographic position for the MSR, owing to its proximity to the Red Sea, the Persian (Arabian) Gulf and the Gulf of Oman—and thus to some of the most significant maritime trade routes between Europe, the Middle East and Asia (Fulton, 2019; Chaziza, 2019). The Arabian Sea is a key focus of China's maritime strategy (Chan, 2022). In particular, the Strait of Hormuz, the Bab-el-Mandeb Strait and the Suez Canal are three of the most crucial trade routes in the global economy, which are of critical importance for the global energy transportation system and the BRI's connectivity framework, and thereby bestow the Middle East with great geostrategic weight (Gresh, 2017).

THE DIGITAL SILK ROAD AND CHINA-MIDDLE EAST TECHNOLOGY CO-OPERATION

A growing focus of many Middle Eastern countries' bilateral relations with China is digital infrastructure and technology (Mogielnicki, 2022). This is also a policy priority for China: the country's 13th Five-Year Plan for Economic and Social Development of March 2015 identified digital connectivity as a key goal (National Development and Reform Commission, 2016). In this context, China is investing internationally in fibre-optic links, data centres (which the Chinese Government describes as a 'fundamental strategic resource') and the gradual establishment of a digital ecosystem as part of the DSR. In this policy field, the changing role of the USA and the growing importance of China has become evident. While, historically, ties with the West have dictated the structure of the Middle East's digital environment (Soliman, 2023), China is now the preferred development partner for technology and digital infrastructure. China's role as a global technology exporter thus has both an economic and a security component that is of interest to regional actors (Gurol, Zumbrägel, and Demmelhuber, 2023; Gurol and Schütze, 2022). For China, promoting technological progress and boosting digital development is a key component of the DSR. Under the DSR, Chinese technology companies are building digital infrastructure to facilitate the collection, transmission, storage and processing of 'big data' from partner countries.

However, the importance of technology and digital infrastructure varies between different regions of the Middle East and North Africa. While the Levant (Iraq, Lebanon and the Syrian Arab Republic) is most affected by technology disparities and has fallen behind other countries in the region in terms of innovation and technology, the Greater Maghreb states are increasingly investing in technology and developing their digital infrastructure (Soliman, 2023), often with Chinese assistance. For instance, Chinese companies have played a key role in 'Morocco Digital 2025' and 'Digital Egypt', the respective Moroccan and Egyptian digital development plans. The Chinese technology firm Huawei has established a logistics centre at the Tanger Med port complex in Morocco, and is deeply integrated into Morocco's telecommunication systems

(Aluf, 2022). In Egypt, Huawei created an OpenLab in 2017, which focuses on public safety and the development of smart city, smart government and smart education technologies (ibid.).

However, it is the Gulf monarchies that have become the frontrunners regarding investments in Chinese digital technology, including e-commerce platforms, mobile payment systems, smart data centres, 5G networks, submarine cables, satellites, cloud storage, smart city technologies and artificial intelligence (AI). For example, various telecommunications companies in Bahrain, Kuwait, Qatar, Saudi Arabia and the UAE have signed 5G contracts with Huawei (Calabrese, 2019). Bahrain pioneered the rollout of 5G infrastructure, and Bahraini telecommunications operators have co-operated with Huawei to develop the country's AI and surveillance technologies (Demmelhuber et al., 2022). Similar developments can be seen in the relationship between China and the UAE. In 2017 the UAE became the first country in the Arab region to announce a strategy to expand AI governance in key areas such as transportation, health, space, renewable energy, water, technology, education and the environment. In 2019 the Emirati Government further adopted an updated initiative, the National AI Strategy 2031, which envisioned 'AI supremacy' by 2031. To achieve this goal, the UAE, along with Israel, is relying heavily on the Chinese technology industry and its AI capabilities (Araz, 2020). In a similar vein, the national police in Dubai, UAE, are using the facial recognition programme *Oyoon* ('Eyes') to record and analyze people's faces, behaviour and movements, in order to combat crime (Gurol and Schütze, 2022). The technology involved has been linked to the Chinese company Hikvision (Rajagopalan, 2019).

Particularly in the context of the COVID-19 pandemic, the DSR, and, with it, policy areas such as technological advancement, digitalization, innovation and AI, became a key element of Chinese diplomacy in the Middle East, especially in the Gulf region. For example, deepening co-operation occurred between the Emirati firm Group 42 Holding Ltd and Chinese technology companies such as Beijing YeeCall Interactive Network Technology regarding the development of tracking software during the pandemic. Another example of emerging co-operation during the pandemic was the collaboration between the Saudi Data and Artificial Intelligence Authority and the Chinese companies Alibaba and Huawei to create Saudi Arabia's National Artificial Intelligence Capability Development Program (Saudi Press Agency, 2020).

THE CHANGING ROLES OF CHINA AND THE USA IN THE MIDDLE EAST

With the USA's commitment to its longstanding role as the main security guarantor in the Middle East starting to weaken, China is becoming increasingly important to the region—not only economically, but also in terms of its security policy. China has adopted an extremely cautious and balanced approach to regional political and security challenges (Gurol and Scita, 2020; Ehteshami and Horesh, 2020) and has avoided direct involvement in regional conflicts. This has allowed China 'to expand its economic and military activities in a highly competitive environment without being bogged down in the turmoil of regional, political and security conflicts' (Gurol and Scita, 2020). At the same time, China's approach to relations with the Middle East largely accepted the USA's continuing dominance as a security guarantor in the region. The regional security architecture maintained by the USA offered China a cost-effective opportunity to expand its economic ties without having to take an active role as a security actor (Sun, 2022). Without attaching too much importance to the narrative that China could step into a 'vacuum' left by the USA, two trend reversals have become very apparent. First, it has become evident that China can no longer maintain its purely apolitical strategy focused on economic relations, but must become active itself in order to create a stable environment for Chinese projects and investments (Ghiselli, 2020; Ghiselli and Morgan, 2021). One vivid example of the security dimension attached to Chinese overseas investments became visible in 2014, when China evacuated hundreds of Chinese workers from Libya during an upsurge of violent unrest in the country (Zerba, 2014). Similarly, the attacks on oil tankers and Saudi oil facilities in 2019 demonstrated how increasing energy dependency and investments had exposed China to the risks of regional turmoil, necessitating a more proactive Chinese security approach to secure these investments.

Against this backdrop, China's Middle East security policies have slowly evolved. The first indication of this was an increase in Chinese arms exports. China has sold its latest weapons systems to countries that the USA is unwilling to supply with armaments. The UAE's purchase of Chinese unmanned aerial vehicles (UAVs—commonly known as drones) in 2018 was a case in point: after the USA had refused to sell its *MQ-9 Reaper* drones to the UAE, in deference to Israeli interests, the Emirati Government instead purchased Chinese *Wing-Loong II* drones (Gady, 2018). Moreover, China is involved in the construction of a production facility in Saudi Arabia for *CH-4* drones, similar to the USA's *MQ-1 Predator* drones (Defense News, 2022). Saudi Arabia also purchased the Chinese *Wing-Loong* model, and Chinese exhibitors dominated Saudi Arabia's World Defense Show in February 2022. Thus, with its *Wing-Loong*, *CH-3* and *CH-4* drone systems, China has become one of the largest suppliers of UAVs in the region, alongside Türkiye. Although Chinese arms sales to the region were not expected to exceed those of the USA in the near term, China role in the military sector supports the Gulf monarchies' overall diversification strategies and provides evidence of the country's growing importance in the military arena.

A second indicator of China's evolving security position in the region is the country's increasing military footprint, represented by its participation in multilateral operations in the Middle East. Albeit on a very small scale, China has provided security through these operations, such as in 2006 when it was one of the first countries to contribute to the United Nations (UN) peacekeeping force in Lebanon, and in 2008 when it sent deployed navy vessels to the Gulf of Aden to participate in UN-endorsed anti-piracy operations. According to Chaziza (2018), mediation diplomacy has also emerged as 'one of the central pillars of China's foreign policy objectives and practice', with China deliberately positioning itself as a peacemaker in the MENA region (Evron, 2017). In recent years China has become a more proactive security and diplomatic actor in the Middle East.

An example of this more proactive approach in the context of conflict mediation and diplomacy was the Chinese facilitation of the rapprochement agreement between Iran and Saudi Arabia in March 2023, which was a clear symbolic and diplomatic victory for China (Haghirian and Scita, 2023). In addition, the trilateral naval exercises held by China, Iran and Russia in the Gulf of Oman in the same month were interpreted by many experts as a sign of increasing military engagement by China in the Gulf region. In June 2023, moreover, China supported Iran's intention to form a naval alliance with Saudi Arabia, the UAE and other Gulf nations, as well as India and Pakistan (Reuters, 2023)—a potential sign of the USA's decreasing military role in the region.

Why and how has the formerly apolitical and merely economic-focused Chinese approach to the region transitioned to this more proactive and risky involvement in Middle Eastern affairs? Despite headlines describing this shift as a major surprise, this change in policy has been evident since 2019, when drone attacks on Saudi Aramco facilities made it clear that tensions between Iran and Saudi Arabia could affect China's core interest in the region—energy security. However, it was not just the need for a stable environment for China's oil and gas imports that encouraged this policy reversal. China's growing political, financial and economic engagement had reached a tipping point, beyond which its role as a marginal actor no longer fully guaranteed the protection of its interests. Consequently, China has adopted a more proactive stance in the Middle Eastern security sphere. The brokering of the Iran-Saudi Arabia deal supports China's broader strategy and interests in the Gulf (Ignatius, 2023). Moreover, it shows that countries in the Middle East no longer view China merely as an economic partner, but increasingly as a security actor and a diplomatic force. China's growing presence has thus led to a stronger determination to become more involved in regional security and politics, as reflected by the Chinese Global Security Initiative (Ministry of Foreign Affairs, 2023), which was announced in February 2023.

IMPLICATIONS FOR THE REGIONAL ORDER: TOWARDS GREATER MULTIPOLARITY?

The Middle East is characterized by intense competition between regional actors, as well as extra-regional actors, most notably China and the USA (Fardella and Friedman, 2023). The passive dependence of the Middle East on the USA as a security guarantor has been a topic of lively academic debate for many decades. The USA played a leading role in shaping the regional order in the Middle East, particularly in the post-Second World War era (Ehteshami and Horesh, 2020), and the country has long been regarded as the dominant security actor in the region. The USA's security role maintained a status quo that allowed other extra-regional actors to advance their interests without making a significant contribution to regional stability (Fulton, 2020; Gurol, 2020).

As the USA increasingly withdraws from the region, this status quo is shifting (Garver, 2016). During the Administration of US President Barack Obama (2009–17), the Middle East's longstanding reliance on the USA as a regional security guarantor began to wane, resulting in the diversification of extra-regional partnerships (Fulton, 2018; Ghiselli, 2023). This development was also driven by the perception that the partnership with the USA was highly asymmetrical, and that unilateral dependence could quickly become a security dilemma in the event of a possible US withdrawal. The lack of strategic continuity in US foreign policy in the region and recent geopolitical events have reinforced this trend. Finally, the poorly executed withdrawal of US troops from Afghanistan and Iraq brought to the fore the limits of US power and influence in the region, and increased Middle Eastern countries' distrust of the USA. In turn, China has slowly but steadily built credibility as a capable partner that has at times criticized the USA's disengagement from the region. In particular, through the brokering of the rapprochement agreement between Iran and Saudi Arabia, China has proven that it is able and willing to expand its role into areas hitherto dominated by the USA, namely security and diplomacy.

From a Chinese vantage point, in the context of growing tensions with the USA, the reliance on the US security umbrella increasingly involves an element of uncertainty and vulnerability. Therefore, the significance of a growing and more proactive role for China in the Middle East can only be understood against the backdrop of changing relations with the USA, as well as the general transition processes in the Middle East (Fulton, 2022; Ghiselli, 2023). This is because the USA, while still the most important security actor in the Middle East, still lacks what Martin Wight calls the 'justification of power' (1991), namely the legitimacy to set the rules of a hegemonic order. This has, ultimately, paved the way for greater Chinese engagement, not only in the economic sphere, but also in the diplomatic and—to a lesser extent—security realms. The number of relevant extra-regional actors has consequently grown. Although China is neither willing nor able to replace the USA as the main security actor in the region in the near term, China's expanding role suggests that multipolarity in the Middle East will steadily increase.

How might that unfold and what would it mean for the USA's future role in the region? Thus far, China's increasing involvement has not necessarily been perceived as a threat, as the USA remains the dominant military power in the Middle East. In fact, with China showing no willingness to challenge or replace the USA in that regard, its expanding geopolitical activities could lead to more co-operation with the USA, as China could leverage regional relationships that the USA lacks (with Iran, for example). US and Chinese interests converge more than they clash—both countries have an interest in securing trade flows (especially in energy), stabilizing the key maritime lines of communication and ensuring freedom of navigation. Co-operation in such areas could strengthen multipolar competition in the Middle East.

CONCLUSION AND OUTLOOK: WILL CHINA REPLACE THE USA IN THE MIDDLE EAST?

The Middle East is currently undergoing major power reconfigurations. The constellation of dominant extra-regional actors is changing, with the waning US security presence, a rising China and an altered geopolitical perception of Russia. In addition, the diversification of external actors in the region has facilitated the growth of regional agency and has enabled many countries in the Middle East to pursue a more strategic balance between these external actors. China is playing a significant role, regionally and internationally, with respect to these transitions.

As an emerging extra-regional actor in the Middle East, China's importance has grown significantly within a very short period of time. Since 2013 China's trans-regional ties, interactions and spheres of co-operation have steadily increased and now encompass numerous policy fields such as trade, energy, technology and security. The mutual dependency evident in the area of oil and gas exports is particularly significant. In conclusion, three main points should be noted. First, the importance of the relationship between China and the Middle East has increased sharply over time. Second, a certain trend reversal in the scope of these bilateral relations was evident during 2022 and 2023. For example, China is no longer seen merely as an economic partner and a market for regional raw materials, but is increasingly also regarded as a diplomatic player and a possible security actor. Third, the implications of the increased Chinese presence are already beginning to have an impact on the regional order. Not only are regional actors changing their perception of China, but the country itself is transitioning from an apolitical approach to the region, focused purely on economic co-operation, towards a more proactive strategy in areas such as mediation and diplomacy. Although these developments had started before the COVID-19 crisis, the pandemic served to advance the trans-regional partnerships between China and the Middle East and led to a significant expansion of bilateral relations. While in 2020 Tim Niblock had argued that Chinese strategists viewed the Middle East as a 'significant but limited place' (2020), the importance and commitment of China to the region has since increased significantly. Finally, it should be noted that China-Middle East relations are embedded within fluid power structures in the international system and are clearly influenced by global power shifts.

While it is too soon to make predictions regarding potential changes to China's regional stature following its adoption of a more proactive approach as a political and diplomatic actor in the Middle East, it is clear that China's importance to the region is growing, and that relations have advanced beyond economic partnerships. Moving forwards, China will have to decide what role it wishes to play in the Middle East: that of a diplomatic actor, a military sponsor and security guarantor, or a primarily economic force. Regardless of which direction developments may take, they will be strongly influenced by systemic tensions, competition between China and the USA on a broader global scale, as well as ongoing transitions in the Middle East and the region's growing agency.

SELECT BIBLIOGRAPHY

Aluf, Dale. 'China's digital footprint grows in the Middle East and North Africa'. *Map Global China*, 2022. mapglobalchina.com/research_briefs/chinas-digital-footprint-grows-in-the-middle-east-north-africa.

Andrews-Speed, Philip, and Lixia, Yao. 'China's evolving energy relations with the Middle East', in Fulton, Jonathan. *Routledge Handbook on China-Middle East Relations*. London and New York, Routledge, 2022.

Araz, Sevan. *The UAE eyes AI supremacy: A key strategy for the 21st century*. Middle East Institute, 2020. www.mei.edu/publications/United Arab Emirates-eyes-ai-supremacy-key-strategy-21st-century.

Cahill, Ben. *Everything at Once: Transformation of Abu Dhabi's Oil Policy*. Arab Gulf States Institute in Washington, 2021. agsiw.org/everything-at-once-transformation-of-abu-dhabis-oil-policy.

Calabrese, John. *The Huawei Wars and the 5G Revolution in the Gulf*. Middle East Institute, 2019. www.mei.edu/publications/huawei-wars-and-5g-revolution-gulf#_ftn1.

Chan, Edward Sing Yue. *China's Maritime Security Strategy: The Evolution of a Growing Sea Power*. London and New York, Routledge, 2022.

Chaziza, Mordechai. 'China's mediation efforts in the Middle East and North Africa: constructive conflict management'. *Strategic Analysis*, 42 (1), pp. 29–41, 2018.

China's Middle East Diplomacy: The Belt and Road Strategic Partnership. Sussex Academic Press, 2020.

ChinaMED. *ChinaMED INDEX for the Middle East*. 2023. www.chinamed.it/chinamed-data/middle-east.

Helou, Agnes. 'Chinese and Saudi firms create joint venture to make military drones in the kingdom'. *Defense News*, 2022. www.defensenews.com/unmanned/2022/03/09/chinese-and-saudi-firms-create-joint-venture-to-make-military-drones-in-the-kingdom.

Demmelhuber, Thomas, Gurol, Julia, and Zumbrägel, Tobias. 'The COVID-19 temptation? Sino–Gulf relations and autocratic linkages in times of a global pandemic', in Völkel, Jan, Möller, Lena-Maria, and Hobaika Khoury, Zeina (Eds). *The MENA Region and COVID-19: Impact, Implications and Future Prospects*. Routledge, pp. 19–35, 2022.

Ehteshami, Anoushiravan. 'Gold at the end of the Rainbow? The BRI and the Middle East'. *Global Policy*, 9 (3), pp. 387–397, 2018.

Ehteshami, Anoushiravan, and Horesh, Niv. *How China's Rise is Changing the Middle East*. London and New York, Routledge, 2020.

Evron, Yoram. 'China's diplomatic initiatives in the Middle East: The quest for a great-power role in the region'. *International Relations*, 31 (2), pp. 125–144, 2017.

Fardella, Enrico, and Friedman, Brandon. 'Dragon unbound? Regional influences on China's policies in the Middle East—Introduction'. *Global Policy*, 14 (1), pp. 4–6, 2023.

Foreign Affairs Committee, US House of Representatives. *China regional snapshot: Middle East and North Africa*. 2022. foreignaffairs.house.gov/china-regional-snapshot-middle-east-and-north-africa/.

Fulton, Jonathan. 'Domestic Politics as Fuel for China's Maritime Silk Road Initiative: The Case of the Gulf Monarchies'. *Journal of Contemporary China*, 29 (122), pp. 1–16, 2019.

Fulton, Jonathan. 'China in the Persian Gulf: Hedging under the US umbrella', in Kamrava, Mehran (Ed.). *Routledge Handbook of Persian Gulf Politics*. Routledge, pp. 492–505, 2020.

Gady, Franz-Stefan. 'Is the United Arab Emirates Secretly Buying Chinese Killer Drones?'. *The Diplomat*, 2018. thediplomat.com/2018/01/is-the-United Arab Emirates-secretly-buying-chinese-killer-drones/#:~:text=To%20date%2C%20neither%20the%20size,have%20publicly%20confirmed%20the%20purchase.

Garlick, Jeremy, and Havlová, Radka. 'China's "Belt and Road" Economic Diplomacy in the Persian Gulf: Strategic Hedging amidst Saudi-Iranian Regional Rivalry'. *Journal of Current Chinese Affairs*, 49 (1), pp. 82–105, 2020.

Garver, John W. *China's Quest: The History of the Foreign Relations of the People's Republic of China*. Oxford University Press, 2016.

Ghiselli, Andrea. *Protecting China's Interests Overseas: Securitization and Foreign Policy*. Oxford University Press, 2020.

China and the United States in the Middle East: Policy Continuity Amid Changing Competition. Middle East Institute, 2023. www.mei.edu/publications/china-and-united-states-middle-east-policy-continuity-amid-changing-competition.

Ghiselli, Andrea, and Morgan, Pippa. 'A Turbulent Silk Road: China's Vulnerable Foreign Policy in the Middle East and North Africa'. *The China Quarterly*, 247, pp. 641–661, 2021.

Greene, Robert, and Triolo, Paolo. *Will China Control the Global Internet via its Digital Silk Road?*. Carnegie Endowment, 2020. carnegieendowment.org/2020/05/08/will-china-control-global-internet-viaits-digital-silk-road-pub-81857.

Gresh, Geoffrey. 'A Vital Maritime Pinch Point: China, the Bab al-Mandeb, and the Middle East'. *Asian Journal of Middle Eastern and Islamic Studies*, 11 (1), pp. 37–46, 2017.

Gulf Business. 'Saudi Aramco, China's Sinopec sign MoU to boost strategic collaboration'. 2022. gulfbusiness.com/saudi-aramco-chinas-sinopec-sign-mou-to-boost-strategic-collaboration.

Gurol, Julia. 'The Role of the EU and China in the Security Architecture of the Middle East'. *Asian Journal of Middle Eastern and Islamic Studies*, 14 (1), pp. 18–34, 2020.

'The authoritarian narrator: China's power projection and its reception in the Gulf'. *International Affairs*, 99 (2), pp. 687–705, 2023.

Gurol, Julia, and Scita, Jacopo. 'China's Persian Gulf strategy: Keep Tehran and Riyadh content'. *MENA Source*, Atlantic Council, 2020. atlanticcouncil.org/blogs/Middle Eastsource/chinas-persian-gulf-strategy-keep-tehran-and-riyadh-content.

Gurol, Julia, and Schütze, Benjamin. 'Infrastructuring Authoritarian Power: Arab-Chinese Transregional Collaboration Beyond the State'. *International Quarterly for Asian Studies*, 53 (2), pp. 231–249, 2022.

Gurol, Julia, Zumbrägel, Tobias, and Demmelhuber, Thomas. 'Elite Networks and the Transregional Dimension of Authoritarianism: Sino-Emirati Relations in Times of a Global Pandemic'. *Journal of Contemporary China*, 32 (139), pp. 138–151, 2023.

Haghirian, Mehran, and Scita, Jacopo. 'The Broader Context Behind China's Mediation Between Iran and Saudi Arabia'. *The Diplomat*, 2023. thediplomat.com/2023/03/the-broader-context-behind-chinas-mediation-between-iran-and-saudi-arabia.

Ignatius, David. 'How China is heralding the beginnings of a multipolar Middle East'. *The Washington Post*, 2023. www.washingtonpost.com/opinions/2023/03/16/china-saudi-arabia-iran-middle-east-change.

Ministry of Foreign Affairs, People's Republic of China. *China's Arab Policy Paper*. 2016. english.www.gov.cn/archive/publications/2016/01/13/content_281475271412746.htm.

Vision for Maritime Co-operation under the Belt and Road Initiative. 2017. english.www.gov.cn/archive/publications/2017/06/20/content_281475691873460.htm.

The Global Security Initiative. 2023. www.fmprc.gov.cn/Ministry of Foreign Affairs_eng/wjbxw/202302/t20230221_11028348.html.

Mogielnicki, Robert. 'Technological dimensions of China-MENA economic relations', in Fulton, Jonathan (Ed.). *Routledge Handbook on China-Middle East Relations*. London and New York, Routledge, 2022.

National Development and Reform Commission, People's Republic of China. *Vision and Actions on Jointly Building Silk Road Economic Belt and 21st-Century Maritime Silk Road*. 2015. www.fmprc.gov.cn/eng/topics_665678/2015zt/xjpcxbayzlt2015nnh/201503/t20150328_705553.html.

The 13th Five-Year Plan for Economic and Social Development of the People's Republic of China (2016–2020). 2016. en.ndrc.gov.cn/policies/202105/P020210527785800103339.pdf.

Niblock, Tim. 'China and the Middle East: A Global Strategy Where the Middle East has a Significant but Limited Place'. *Asian Journal of Middle Eastern and Islamic Studies*, 14 (4), pp. 481–504, 2020.

OEC. *Crude Petroleum in Saudi Arabia*. 2023. oec.world/en/profile/bilateral-product/crude-petroleum/reporter/are (last accessed on 29 March 2023).

Crude Petroleum in United Arab Emirates. 2023. oec.world/en/profile/bilateral-product/crude-petroleum/reporter/are (last accessed on 29 March 2023).

Crude Petroleum in Oman. 2023. oec.world/en/profile/bilateral-product/crude-petroleum/reporter/omn (last accessed on 29 March 2023).

Crude Petroleum in Kuwait. 2023. oec.world/en/profile/bilateral-product/crude-petroleum/reporter/kwt (last accessed on 29 March 2023).

Rajagopalan, Megha. 'Facial Recognition Technology is Facing a Huge Backlash in the US. But Some of the World's Biggest Tech Companies Are Trying to Sell it in the Gulf'. *Buzzfeed News*, 2019. www.buzzfeednews.com/article/meghara/dubai-facial-recognition-technology-ibm-huawei-hikvision.

Reuters. 'Iran says to form naval alliance with Gulf states to ensure regional stability'. 2023. www.reuters.com/world/middle-east/iran-says-form-naval-alliance-with-gulf-states-ensure-regional-stability-2023-06-03.

Rudolf, Moritz. *China's Health Diplomacy during COVID-19*. German Institute for International and Security Affairs, 2021. www.swp-berlin.org/fileadmin/contents/products/comments/2021C09_ChinaHealthDiplomacy.pdf.

Saudi Press Agency. 'NCAI, HUAWEI Announce MoU to Develop AI Capabilities'. 2020. www.spa.gov.sa/viewfullstory.php?lang=en&newsid=2147393.

Soliman, Mohammed. *The Middle East in an era of great tech competition*. Middle East Institute, 2023. www.mei.edu/publications/middle-east-era-great-tech-competition.

Sun, Degang. 'China's "Zero-Enemy Policy" in the Gulf', in Fulton, Jonathan and Sim, Li-Chen (Eds). *Asian Perceptions of Gulf Security*. London and New York, Routledge, pp. 30–49, 2022.

Sun, Degang, and He, Shaoxin. 'From a By-stander to a Constructor: China and the Middle East Security Governance'. *Journal of Middle Eastern and Islamic Studies*, 9 (3), 2015.

Sun, Degang, Xu, Haiyan, and Tu, Yichao. 'In with the New: China's Nuclear Energy Diplomacy in the Middle East'. *Middle East Policy*, 29 (1), pp. 41–60, 2022.

Wong, Edward, Nereim, Vivian, and Kelly, Kate. 'Inside Saudi Arabia's global push for nuclear power'. *New York Times*, 2023. www.nytimes.com/2023/04/01/us/politics/saudi-arabia-nuclear-biden-administration.html.

Zerba, Shaio H. 'Libya Evacuation Operation: A new diplomatic imperative—overseas citizen protection'. *Journal of Contemporary China*, 23 (90), pp. 1093–1112, 2014.

Zoubir, Yahia H., and Tran, Emilie. 'China's Health Silk Road in the Middle East and North Africa amidst COVID-19 and a Contested World Order'. *Journal of Contemporary China*, 31 (135), pp. 335–350, 2022.

POLITICAL ISLAM

BARBARA ZOLLNER

DEBATING DEFINITIONS

Political Islam, Islamism or Islamist politics can be defined as religiously induced activities of actors, movements, groups and organizations that regard Islamic beliefs, practices, law, traditions, social interactions and early history as the parameters of their political agitation. It must be emphasized that not all Muslims regard politics as the core of their religious faith, even if they are politically active and their political views are influenced by their beliefs and practices. Key to understanding Islamism is that its proponents regard Islam as 'a complete divine system with a superior political model, cultural code, legal structure, and economic arrangement – in short, a system that responded to all problems'. Islamists thus regard politics and religion as intertwined and inseparable. As Islamists incite 'repertoires and frames of reference from Islamic traditions', they construct an ideologically motivated imagination of the past. Their retrospection fosters an inaccurate understanding of historical periods, particularly the early phase of the spread of Islam, and an erroneous view of Islamic theology and law that ignores the fact that neither the concept of state nor the theory of governance is part of Muslim revelation.

The recognition that Islamism is not merely the comeback of orthodox beliefs is also why academic work typically refrains from using the term 'Islamic fundamentalism'. This terminology was commonly used in US public debates and scholarship throughout the 1990s, where it was often juxtaposed with secularism. Yet, as all believing Muslims aim to take recourse to the fundamentals of Islam as a religion, the term 'Islamic fundamentalism' is neither meaningful to explain the political interpretation of religion nor helpful to describe the modern origin of this ideology.

Apart from the distorted perspective that political Islam can be traced back to the beginnings of Islam itself, definitions of Islamism are all too often tainted by the activities of extremist proponents and militant groups. Islamism is often outright equated to acts of political extremism and militancy as perpetuated by Muslim terrorists. While there is no doubt that various militant Islamist organizations represent a worrying trend that threatens the national and international security contexts, these groups have, compared with non-militant groups, relatively small numbers of followers. Moreover, the reduction of Islamism to terrorism ignores that there is a wide range of politico-Muslim actors, movements and non-movements. The exclusive focus on Islamist radicalism, extremism and militancy thus reduces the definition of Islamism to a limited, albeit admittedly very dangerous, minority phenomenon.

As the frames of reference from Islamic history and traditions resonate with Muslim listeners, Islamist ideologists construct a viewpoint that seems in accordance with Muslim dogma. Recurrent frames of reference include, among many others, *Shari'a* (Islamic law), *hukm Allah* (divine sovereignty), *kufr* (unbelief) and *takfir* (accusation of apostasy). These frames of reference are recognizable to most Muslims as they find occasional mention in sermons, yet their complex meaning is subject to continuous theological, juridical, societal and political debates. Hence, the call for the implementation of *Shari'a* and the claim that the application of law requires the existence of an Islamic state became an issue only upon the inception of modern forms of governance amid the decline of the Ottoman Empire, which resulted in the collapse of the caliphate. Yet, the debates surrounding the necessity of Islamic law and order seem to be a logical extension of classical religious precepts. This merger of what is assumed to be devotion to religious prescription on the one hand, and the dedication to strive for adaptation to a new political reality on the other hand, affirms Islamist ideologies.

The uncertainty about the meaning of these frames of reference in a modern context leaves much room for differences among proponents of various Islamist strains. There are, therefore, immense disparities between those with religiously reformist beliefs (e.g. the Strong Egypt Party, Al-Wasat Party and Al-Nahda) and those of a religiously neo-orthodox persuasion (e.g. the Wahhabi and Salafi movements), depending on differences in their understanding of *Shari'a*. Moreover, there is divergence on the issues surrounding the concept of an Islamic state—i.e. what an Islamic state is, whether the aim of instituting an Islamic state is central to political activism, and, above all, what means are legitimate for the struggle to establish such a state. While advocates of radical ideas consider it justified to vilify as apostates Muslims who do not actively engage in establishing an Islamic state, the issue of the legitimacy of using force marks the dividing line between militant and non-violent groups. Divergence on these issues is the source of much disagreement among Islamist actors and groups.

Benchmarks pinpointing differences in political and religious leanings are necessary for categorizing the plethora of Islamist actors, be they organized groups, movements or ideological figureheads, allowing us to compare them, and to point out commonalities or trace ideological developments. Such benchmarks also facilitate an assessment of whether a particular group or leader backs violence and militancy or champions non-violence, gradualism in activism and peaceful resolution of conflict. In latter cases, it needs to be further evaluated whether a group aspires to democratic ideals. Related to, but not necessarily congruent with, the stance on violence vs non-violence is the issue of whether a particular Islamist actor endorses revolutionary plans or holds state-supporting positions. As Islamic frames of reference are used to substantiate a specific political programme of Islamist groups, it needs to be assessed whether these views follow the interpretations of the orthodox schools of law or whether they question and challenge their methodology and juridical reasoning and are, therefore, reformist in nature.

Reviewing the span of Islamist actors is challenging indeed. It is difficult to capture adequately the commonalities and differences of the sheer multitude of groups that arose over the past century, each corresponding to diverse cultural settings, historical circumstances, national concerns and political campaigns. Moreover, it must be recognized that Islamist groups, particularly those with a longstanding operative record, do not remain ideologically and organizationally stagnant. Hence, any assessment of specific Islamist movements and organizations requires a subjective appraisal of the context to which they respond and an evaluation of their conceptual and organizational progression.

The problem becomes all too clear in debates about a group's strategic and behavioural moderation or any rejection of violence. In principle, it needs to be recognized that movements, groups and individuals have the potential for change over time. Islamism is no exception; as much as there is potential for radicalization, there are opportunities to de-escalate or perhaps deradicalize. However, the possibility of making overly optimistic evaluations based on recantations of violence can have severe consequences as there remains the concern that repudiation of violence might be merely a strategic decision rather than a more fundamental ideological retraction. Weighing heavily on sound assessments of Islamists is, furthermore, the issue of legitimate opposition to authoritarianism. What is regarded as an acceptable means of rightful opposition, or perhaps even armed resistance, often depends on the subjective political interests of prominent international actors in the network of international relations. Yet, there is undeniably a core of militant Islamist organizations that remain a substantive threat to peace and to the security of the international community.

REVIVALIST ISLAM AND THE IDEOLOGICAL GROUNDWORK OF POLITICAL ISLAM

The roots of political Islam lie in the Islamic revivalism (also known as the Islamic reformism) of the late 19th and early 20th centuries. During a drawn-out period when the Ottoman influence on the peripheries of its vast empire began to wane, calls for resistance to Turkish military and economic rule began to grow louder. At the same time, there was growing opposition to the increasing political influence of colonial powers. Considering religion and politics to be inseparable, proponents of the Islamic reform movement argued that the failure to adapt to modernity that accompanied religious interpretative stagnation was the main reason for the deterioration of political power. Identifying traditional Muslim learning as stagnant and ill-equipped to address modern problems, the Islamic revivalists also turned their back on religious orthodoxy. Thus, they called for sweeping reforms in religious institutions, the educational and administrative systems, the courts, the police, the military and the economic system. While the West was a source of inspiration for reform, Islamic revivalists regarded the growing influence of colonial powers as a cause of internal weakness.

Islamic revivalism was found with outstanding voices in Jamal al-Din al-Afghani, Muhammad 'Abduh and Rashid Rida, as well as Abul A'la Maududi on the Indian subcontinent. Al-Afghani epitomizes a restless political activism that leads him from Iran to India, Saudi Arabia, Turkey (now Türkiye), Egypt, France, the United Kingdom and the Russian Federation. His anti-British agitation still coalesced Pan-Islamism and nationalism as forces of resistance. Yet his understanding that Islam is congruent with rationality and natural law found resonance in various Islamic reformist movements and actors that called for internal reform. Among them are the *Tanzimat* (reordering) movement of Ottoman Turkey, the rising Arab nationalist movement in Egypt and the Levant, and the Iranian nationalist movement of the turn of the 19th century. He inspired a new generation of secular and religious activists and thinkers, including Sa'ad Zaghlul, Sati' al-Husri, Muhammad 'Abduh, Rashid Rida and Hassan al-Banna.

While al-Afghani set the tone, Muhammad 'Abduh developed Islamic reform into a consistent religious philosophy. 'Abduh, who was to become the Grand Mufti of Egypt and then rector of Al-Azhar University, despite his conflict with orthodox Islamic scholarship, was mainly concerned with the revival of theology and jurisprudence. In *The Theology of Unity* (published in 1898 and first translated into English in 1966), 'Abduh sets out to reconcile reason and revelation, arguing that Qur'anic revelation is the essence of divine reasoning. His emphasis on the congruity of Islam and human reason breaks with orthodox doctrine, calling for a fundamental revision of Islamic law. While 'Abduh's ideas remain a broad acceptance of reason as the core of Islam, he paved the way for a variety of more developed theories, among them religious utilitarian views held by Rashid Rida, 'Allal al-Fasi, and later Hassan al-Turabi, but also religious liberalism such as proposed by 'Ali 'Abd al-Raziq, Muhammad Sa'id al-'Ashmawi, Fazlur Rahman Malik and Muhammad Shahrur.

Rashid Rida, editor-in-chief of the magazine *Al-Manar* (The Lighthouse) and a close associate of 'Abduh, carried on the latter's vision of educational reform. Opening the Dar al-'Ulum teacher training college, Rida directly impacted the schooling of a new intellectual elite. As a direct challenge to Al-Azhar's traditional educational system, Rida favoured a more modern approach that included modern sciences on the curriculum, used modern pedagogical techniques, and taught religious education with an emphasis on a rational understanding of Islam. Although suspicious of Western colonialism, he introduced Western concepts of teaching that prepared pupils for the demands of the 20th century. Aside from his efforts in reforming education, Rida also directly impacted the political discourse of his time. His political treatise *The Caliphate of the Supreme Imamate* contributed to debates about the restoration of the caliphate. Blaming Turkish rule for the decline of the Muslim world, he called for the renewal of an *ummah* (worldwide community of Muslims) under Arab leadership. With its clear political tone, this work set the tone for future views of political renewal through the establishment of an Islamic state. Drawing extensively from classical works on the caliphate, Rida reimagined the first generation of Muslims as an ideal community that must be emulated. He argued that laws surrounding worship and rituals are *'ibadat* (laws of submission), which constitute an indissoluble covenant with God and hence must not be questioned. He regarded every legal consideration other than that as part of *mu'amalat* (literally: transactions). Guided by *maslaha* (public interest) as *ratio legis* (reason for the law), this legislative sphere leaves room for modern lawmaking.

Rida's view of the Islamic state and its utility for political unity, but also his attempts to reconcile traditional Islamic law with modern legislation, and his concerns with modern education were adopted by the so-called father of political Islam, Hassan al-Banna, and the first Islamist organization that was founded by him—the Muslim Brotherhood.

Muhammad bin Abdulwahhab must also be mentioned as a foundational thinker of political Islam. Although he pre-dates al-Afghani, 'Abduh and Rida, his ideas were to become a concern to the development of Islamism in the 20th century. It was not, as one might think, due to the impact of his ideas on the rise of the House of Sa'ud, which drew on the state-affirming viewpoints put forward in Abdulwahhab's seminal work *Kitab al-Tawhid* (The Book of Monotheism). Rather, it was Abdulwahhab's emphasis on interpretative literalism that highly influenced a neo-orthodox movement aiming to emulate the practices of the *salaf al-salih* (righteous ancestors). Drawing on Abdulwahhab, Salafis and Salafi *jihadists* regard all other concepts of state, politics, society and religion, including those of reformist Islamists, as heretical.

Abdulwahhab's lifetime pre-dates the beginnings of modernity, and his ideas were regressive even for his time. He did not propose that Islam needed reform but rather suggested the restoration of religious law by returning to a simplified version of the literalist Hanbali school of Islamic jurisprudence. Despite his immense influence on Salafism, Abdulwahhab is thus, strictly speaking, not a founding father of Islamist thought.

At the heart of Abdulwahhab's view lies the concept of *tawhid* (unity of God), thus emphasizing a strict form of monotheism. He cautioned against moral laxity in belief and practice that he saw as being present in Shi'ism, Sufism, saint worship and acts of remembrance of the dead, but also seemingly trivial practices such as intercessions and the use of charms and amulets. Crucially, he introduced a 'catechism' of morality that defined virtues and sinful behaviour. The three most damning sins are *shirk* (idolatry), disobedience to authority and false testimony. Based on the religious norm *amr bi 'l-ma'ruf wa 'n-nahy 'an al-munkar* (command to do good and avoid wrong), Abdulwahhab justified the exercise of *hisba* (literally: accountability) as an instrument of social and moral control. This opened the door for the construction of the authoritarian. As any view or practice that does not strictly follow neo-orthodox literal interpretations could be seen as a form of disobedience at best and *shirk* at worst, *hisba* becomes a religious and political tool for suppression. Although Abdulwahhab's ideas were a direct response to the decline of the Ottoman caliphate, for which he blamed immorality and social laxity, the legacy of his ideas in the 20th century is relevant for the development of Islamist ideology. For the Saudi state, which implements Wahhabism as state ideology, it is a means of controlling its citizens. At the same time, Salafi movements use it as an instrument with which to discredit beliefs and practices that they deem to be heretical.

Abdulwahhab thus lays the foundation for politico-religious trends that are, paradoxically, either used to affirm conservative state policies or, alternatively, to produce radical purist movements that oppose state authorities outside their group. This neo-orthodox Salafi trend encompasses a broad range of groups that span from pietist groups that adopt quietist social policies and thus disengage from the surrounding political order to those that aim to install a purist state by all possible means, including terrorism.

Hassan al-Banna initiated a new phase in the evolution of Islamism. Although he is often seen as the 'father' of Islamism, this does not stem from an extensive literary legacy or intricate theological explanations. Al-Banna cannot be described as an Islamist thinker per se. He was the founder of the Muslim Brotherhood and, as such, stood out as an organizer, activist and leader who managed to develop the organization into a political mass movement. His speeches and hagiographical stories about his life and political engagement during a turbulent period of Egypt's history remain the inspiration for many Islamists today. To the Muslim Brotherhood and its supporters, al-Banna's legacy remains the foremost point of reference. The corpus he leaves behind directly responds to the immediate political context of his time and contains inconsistencies. Al-Banna's legacy remains, therefore, subject to continuous debate among competing factions within the organization. For the same reason, critics of the Brotherhood regard the lack of definitive directives in al-Banna's works and deeds as a reason for suspecting hidden motives behind the organization's claimed strategy and aims.

Al-Banna established the Muslim Brotherhood in 1928, essentially adopting and putting into practice the ideas of reformist precursors, particularly al-Afghani, 'Abduh and Rida. Original to the ideological evolution of Islamism is that al-Banna relates being Muslim with the concept of *jihad* (literally: struggle). Unlike later radical Islamists, *jihad* carried for him the meaning of personal engagement with Islam. Although *jihad* already entails a political (i.e. politically activist) element, he did not regard the Brotherhood as a political party. In the age of universalist movements, and not dissimilar to nationalist, fascist, or communist mass organizations, al-Banna defined the Brotherhood broadly as a spiritual, social, religious and political 'home' that provides members and supporters with an identity in all walks of life. To al-Banna, the Brotherhood was 'a Salafi call, a Sunni way, a Sufi truth, a political organization, an athletic group, an intellectual and scientific association, an economic company and a social idea'. Likewise, while the stated aims of the organization are focused on taking power in a political system, al-Banna's vision is much broader as he aspires religious activism to be concerned with the private and personal as much as with societal, economic and political realms.

To put these aspirations into practice, al-Banna suggested a gradualist methodology, which should structure the personal growth of each brother and guide him toward the broader goal of living a genuinely Muslim life. Religious learning, physical activities, competency tests and selection, and gradual introduction to administrative and executive duties within the Muslim Brotherhood are part of this gradualist method. The incremental approach is also applied to the members' recruitment, selection and upward leadership mobility, thus making it possible to build a coherent and committed organizational hierarchy that benefits from a highly trained leadership core, a skilled and dedicated membership, and a supportive base. In addition, al-Banna asked members of the Brotherhood to commit to a code of practice that directly binds them to the organization's mission. It could also be said that the methodology and structure of the Brotherhood impose a degree of secrecy that enables the organization to guard against external subversion, and it lies right at the heart of debates about the Brotherhood's intentions and potential hidden agenda. However, al-Banna also saw the method as being applicable to society and politics, envisaging the rebuilding of strong family relations and the firm implementation of Islamic values in order to strengthen social ties and responsibilities, which would serve as an impetus for the revitalization of Muslim culture and education, economic recovery and the revival of a competent judicial and political system. Again, there is no doubt that al-Banna saw the Brotherhood as a mass movement that offered a universalist understanding of Islam.

Under al-Banna's leadership, the Muslim Brotherhood grew into an organization of immense size and political influence. The ups and downs of the organization over time largely coincide with the major political shifts and regime changes in Egypt. During the constitutional monarchy, particularly during the Second World War and the post-war period, the Brotherhood directly confronted the Egyptian state. The fact that al-Banna rejected the role of political parties yet also stood as a parliamentary candidate fuels discussions on the extent of the organization's commitment to democracy. Intra-organizational debates about the legitimate use of violence also go back to this time, not least because al-Banna sanctioned the formation of an armed unit. The Brotherhood committed acts of terrorism against the state, such as the assassination in 1948 of Prime Minister Mahmud Fahmi al-Nuqrashi, but was also the victim of state violence, including most notably when al-Banna was murdered by the Egyptian secret police in 1949.

Abul A'la Maududi is yet another early Sunni thinker who laid the foundation for a systematic political understanding of Islam. Like al-Banna, he was the founder and leader of an early Islamist organization, the Jamaat-e-Islami, which was formally established as a party in 1941 during the end phase of the British Raj. The organization continued to operate as a party and movement following the Partition of India and the establishment of Pakistan in 1947, under the new name Jamaat-e-Islami Pakistan. Although the organization has considerable influence and support among the lower middle class and educated circles, it remained politically relatively marginal. Maududi's substantial opus as a politico-religious author and thinker has impacted the ideological development of Islamism, and key authors, including most notably Sayyid Qutb (see *Ideological Developments: Radicalization or Moderation*), have borrowed from his renderings.

Like earlier reformists, Maududi held the suspicion that the clerical class was responsible for the stagnation in Islamic jurisprudence as it no longer addressed the concerns of Muslims. He thus wrote a Qur'anic commentary that was decidedly modern and intentionally comprehensible. Reform, to Maududi, entails a renewal of interpretative legal efforts that go hand in hand with the implementation of Islamic law as the law of the land, and the decline of Islam's social and political power had its roots in the seeping return of *jahiliyya* (literally: ignorance). Maududi reappropriated a classical concept that was previously used to describe the non-Islamic practices of pre-Islamic society with its state of religious ignorance, legal anarchy and political turmoil. Adapting the concept of *jahiliyya* to reject the 'un-Islamic' influences of Roman and Greek philosophical traditions, Maududi voiced his opposition to Western social and political thought as well as the British colonial legacy in India and Pakistan. To Maududi, Islamic revival can be accomplished only by the renunciation of modern *jahiliyya*. Imitating the manner in which pious ancestors adopted religion would lead Muslims to embrace fully God's sovereignty, which he surmises in the term *hakimiyyat Allah*. Maududi presents here a universalist understanding of divine authority, in which Islam finds expression in God's law (*Shari'a*), which requires implementation in a Muslim's private, social, economic and political affairs. Although this position brings Maududi close to religious neo-orthodox views, his interpretation of theo-democracy also, perhaps surprisingly, entrusts an area for political power-sharing that he links to the concept of *shura* (consultation). Through *shura*, elected representatives can debate and formulate manmade laws in areas upon which Islamic law is silent. While this is undoubtedly a modern idea, the actual limits of legislative power through democratic representation remain ill-defined.

IDEOLOGICAL DEVELOPMENTS: RADICALIZATION OR MODERATION

The name most connected to the ideological radicalization of Islamist movements is Sayyid Qutb. His work *Ma'alim fi al-Tariq* (Signposts Along the Road), published in 1964 and also known as *Milestones*, is perhaps the single most relevant manifesto that seeks to justify the use of violence, presenting a fundamental reinterpretation of ideas already existing in the repertoire of classical Muslim understandings of apostasy and rebellion. This brief manifesto initiated debates within the Muslim Brotherhood about whether armed resistance against a regime is justified if leaders have transgressed from Islam. Qutb argued that it was, and his unremitting rejection of *jahiliyya* also inspired *jihadi* groups as they deemed violence to be the only means of combatting *kufr*, which effectively includes all non-Muslim religions, societies and political systems.

Qutb was a mid-ranking member of the Muslim Brotherhood who joined the organization in the early 1950s. In July 1952 the constitutional monarchy was abolished following a coup carried out by the Free Officers Movement. The military leadership introduced a new political system that, at least initially, promised political freedom. The Muslim Brotherhood, now led by Hassan al-Hudaybi, demanded a stake in the politics of the newly established republic. During this period, Qutb authored books on social issues that he discussed from an Islamist perspective. As an activist, he believed that the Brotherhood should co-operate with the newly installed military regime. However, the period of collaboration did not last long. Accused of planning an assassination attempt against the Free Officers' rising star, Col Gamal Abdel Nasser, the Muslim Brotherhood was eventually banned in October 1954. Thousands of Brotherhood members and supporters were subsequently imprisoned, among them Qutb. *Milestones*, which was to become the most significant text for radical Islamist movements, was written as a manual to assist the revival of grassroots activities outside prison.

In *Milestones*, Qutb's radical ideas are based on three interlinked components: his interpretation of *jahiliyya*, his insistence on *hukm Allah* and his understanding of *jihad*. Qutb's views on *jahiliyya* and *hukm Allah* draw directly from those of al-Maududi, albeit Qutb presented them in much stricter dualistic, antithetical terms. Qutb argued that the concept of *tawhid* means that God possesses absolute authority that must not be regarded in abstract terms or merely as a philosophical or theological idea; it necessitates that laws set out in the Qur'an are obligatory and must be fully implemented as state law. To Qutb, it means that Muslims must enact their political existence from no other power than God, who is not just a transcendental overlord but the only legitimate sovereign in worldly matters. Muslims express their servitude to God through the *shahada* (profession of faith). Confessing to Islam, therefore, requires Muslims to fight for the installation of *hukm Allah*. With this mental loop, Qutb reduces Islam to a radical political concept. Although he primarily rejects any form of secular governance (in a nod to Nasser's Egypt), he also dismisses any form of non-political Muslim religiosity, political quietist movements or those adopting defensive political strategies.

Qutb's ideas on the preferred constitution of an Islamic state are rather vague. Although he insisted that God rules through the implementation of Islamic law, he regarded theorizing on this topic as treacherous. Nevertheless, his position is far removed from Maududi's idea of theo-democracy, which allows room for legislative and democratic institutions. Qutb proposes a robust executive leadership for an Islamic polity that oversees the implementation of *Shari'a*. As for the law, he rejected differentiating between *'ibadat* (religious duties) and *mu'amalat* (directives for social life); as such, any form of legislative representation would be unnecessary. In sum, Qutb advocated a totalitarian utopia in which all Muslims are educated within a compliant community that imposes a duty-bound version of Islamic law.

Like Maududi, Qutb argued that *jahiliyya* is in diametrical opposition to Islam. He also adopted Maududi's position that *jahiliyya* is a state of moral, philosophical, social, political and religious depravity rooted in rejecting God's absolute power. Yet, Qutb further implied that *jahiliyya* is synonymous with *kufr* (disbelief). Moreover, he also declared that *jahiliyya* poisoned all existing social orders, including communist, Western and, most astonishingly, Muslim societies. Although Qutb never mentions the word *takfir* (apostasy), this announcement amounts to accusing Muslim political leaders and systems, such as those in Egypt, with charges for which the classical legal repertoire would demand the death penalty. Qutb's dualistic worldview of Islam versus *kufr* is thus the foundation for a new radical Islamist ideology, which could be used to declare anyone who does not conform to Qutbian ideas of *hukm Allah*, or who does not regard belief as a commitment to radical activism, to be corrupted by *jahiliyya*. Consequently, they would be considered no longer Muslim, which makes them, if one follows this line of thought, traitors to the cause.

Jihad is, for Qutb, the logical solution that follows from his view that God's rule on earth must be installed. As much as the *shahada* is a call to political action, so too is *jihad*. The struggle for the divine cause needs to follow a methodology that copies the Prophet Muhammad's example for establishing his rule. Like the Prophet's exile in Yathrib (later Medina, Saudi Arabia), believers need to build a core community that epitomizes an ideal vanguard. The community is yet too small and therefore needs to shut itself off from any *jahiliyya* influence. This internal *hijra* (migration) is also a time to prepare for the ultimate fight against the *jahili* tyranny. However, Qutb does not directly issue a call to arms, even when referring to fighting *jahili* tyranny. The potency of the justification for violence does then not lie in any outspoken call to militancy but in the construction of a religious argument that interprets known precepts in a new and uncomplicated fashion setting 'true Muslims' apart from a 'deviant other'. Because the creation of an Islamic state is a divinely ordained duty, Qutb regards *jihad* as an obligation. It is this novel interpretation that is perhaps most impactful for the development of a militant Islamist movement that was to sanctify religious militancy as a command for the creation of an Islamic state.

While aware of Qutb's writing, the leadership of the Muslim Brotherhood did not react immediately to the radical turn of his ideas. One can only speculate that the organization, which was close to collapse due to the authorities' campaign of persecution and incarceration of its leadership and mid-ranking members, needed Qutb's influence in rebuilding cells outside prison. These units, branded Tanzim 1965 (Organization 1965) by the media after cell members stood trial in 1965, had chosen Qutb as their spiritual leader. Another reason might be that the Brotherhood leadership under al-Hudaybi did not give sufficient weight to Qutb's radical ideas and thus misjudged their gravity and influence. Only after Qutb's death by hanging in 1966—following his conviction in connection with the attempted assassination of Nasser—did al-Hudaybi react, and then only in the wake of the Six-Day War in June 1967, when internal debates threw up the issue of whether the Brotherhood should opt for violence as its strategic modus operandi or whether it should aim for political moderation and reconciliation with the state. Headed by al-Hudaybi, a circle of leaders began to work on a theological brief that would challenge the radical ideas of Qutbists, opting instead for non-violence, reconciliation and political pragmatism. Qutbists, on the other hand, influenced militant Islamist organizations that began to emerge during the late 1960s and 1970s (see below).

The Muslim Brotherhood's new emphasis on non-violence was expressed in *Du'at La Qudat* (Preachers not Judges), in which, like Qutb, al-Hudaybi starts his argument by defining the purpose of the *shahada*. His emphasis here is not on activism, let alone militant *jihad*. Instead, he reminds the reader that the *shahada* is a Muslim's declaration of faith. Based on this testimony of faith, a person must be regarded as Muslim, even if they commit sins. Al-Hudaybi thus cautions against the pronunciation of *takfir* and, at least implicitly, against the concept of a modern *jahiliyya*. Furthermore, he cites the *amr bi l-ma'ruf* not as a means of controlling the behaviour of fellow Muslims, as espoused by Abdulwahhab, but as a justification for resistance against injustice, particularly those committed by rulers. Holding on to the classical dictum that an illegitimate leader is better than *fitna* (civil strife), he warns against violence and calls for moderation in the strategies of opposition. Although he does not entirely repudiate the use of force as a final option, it leads him to appeal for restraint, endurance and gradualism, which he subsumes under the concept of *da'wa* (calling) towards religious, social and political change. The fact that Hasan al-Hudaybi speaks out against *takfir* and in favour of political moderation is important for the Muslim Brotherhood's political trajectory since the 1970s. Although al-Hudaybi talks in purely juridical terms that are seemingly detached from political implications or the urgency of strategic directives for Brotherhood members, the text represented an important ideological shift that called on the organization to retain al-Banna's gradualist approach. Responding to the radicalization within its ranks, the Muslim Brotherhood leadership under al-Hudaybi eventually reacted with its assurances of non-violence and gradualism.

Under 'Umar al-Tilmisani, who replaced al-Hudaybi as leader of the Muslim Brotherhood in 1972, this politically pragmatic policy bore fruit. While the presidency of Col Anwar Sadat facilitated a degree of political opening, it enabled the Brotherhood to rebuild its organizational strength. Despite rather precarious relations with the state during the presidencies of Sadat and his successor, Muhammad Hosni Mubarak, the Brotherhood made major inroads into Egyptian political circles. Throughout the 1980s and 1990s it established considerable support among the educated middle class, particularly via the organization's engagement in student movements, professional syndicates and independent parliamentary candidacies. By the time of the Arab Spring in the early 2010s, it was undoubtedly the largest informal opposition force. The Freedom and Justice Party, which has strong links to the Muslim Brotherhood, won the most seats in the parliamentary elections held between November 2011 and January 2012, and its candidate Muhammad Morsi was elected President in June 2012. Whether the Muslim Brotherhood stands for moderation or perhaps even democratic participation remains an issue of contentious debate, not least after the coup that removed Morsi from power in July 2013. The current discussion often veers back to the time of al-Banna and to the persecution of Brotherhood members during 1954–71 when looking for arguments either suggesting that the organization harbours militant objectives or maintaining that its members are non-violent actors that were wrongly targeted.

THE BEGINNINGS OF MILITANT ISLAMISM

While the Muslim Brotherhood held on to al-Banna's gradualism and to al-Hudaybi's moderate stance, violent Islamist groups, which later (most notably since the 1990s) were labelled *jihadist* or Salafi-*jihadist* organizations, started to appear from the 1970s onwards. In simple terms, Qutb posthumously became the spiritual father of militant groups, most notably including Tanzim al-Jihad (Islamic Jihad—later known as Egyptian Islamic Jihad), al-Qa'ida (Base) and Islamic State in Iraq (known during 2013–14 as Islamic State in Iraq and the Levant, and from 2014 as Islamic State) and its various subsidiaries.

The first Islamist group that adopted a militant stance was al-Jama'at al-Muslimun (Group of Muslims), widely known disparagingly as al-Takfir wa 'l-Hijra (Excommunication and Exile). The group was led by Mustafa Shukri, who was a member of Qutb's Organization 1965 and was imprisoned with several Qutbists. Picking up Qutb's methodology of establishing a vanguard, Shukri reduced all people outside his group as unbelievers. True Muslims, i.e. group members, must dissociate themselves from society and its institutions by forming a nuclear community. Shukri thus tried to put into practice Qutb's methodological suggestions for preparing an elite vanguard for the ensuing combat against the state. Living on the outskirts of the Egyptian capital, Cairo, in desert-like surroundings, the group embraced a form of physical and spiritual *hijra*. Internally, the group was organized in a strictly hierarchical and authoritarian fashion. Externally, Shukri's group dissociated itself from any social ties, thus stripping itself of popular support or the potential for growth. Because of the group's self-imposed isolation, it began to implode. Frequent clashes with the police and the military, which ensued from the mid-1970s, reduced the group further. Eventually, the group faltered in 1978.

A contrasting strategy for preparing to combat the state was adopted by Salah Siriyya's group, later known as al-Faniyya al-'Askariyya (the Military Academy Group). Motivated by the Muslim Brotherhood's organizational impasse during the Nasser years, and encouraged by the radical arguments of Qutbists who regarded violence as the only justified means to fight the state, Siriyya attracted a highly motivated circle of fighters who prepared for a coup. The recruitment efforts targeted members of the military, particularly those who showed neo-orthodox religious leanings. Without taking any significant precautions against the possibility of being infiltrated or exposed, Siriyya embraced a risky 'all-channel' recruitment strategy and an egalitarian organizational structure. As the stakes of exposure were high, Siriyya's group tried to seize the military barracks near Cairo. The attack and the attempted coup failed, Siriyya was executed and the group was disbanded. Although al-Faniyya al-'Askariyya could be regarded as a relatively inconsequential group, it became an example to subsequent organizations. In particular, the more egalitarian organizational cell structure that draws on the recruitment of already assenting individuals and its mixture of Qutbian and neo-orthodox Salafi leanings can be found in Egyptian Islamic Jihad.

Gama'ah al-Islamiyah (Islamic Group) is one of the largest Salafi-*jihadist* groups. Gama'ah al-Islamiyah was perhaps the earliest militant Islamist group that 'successfully' put Qutbian ideas into practice. At least until the beginning of its deradicalization process, it held on to an ideology of *jihad*, a strategy of militant resistance to the regime, and a method of building up an Islamic counter-society. It thus interspersed Qutbian ideas with a puritanical, Wahhabi-inspired Salafi creed that trickled into the religiously more conservative and more tribal social structures of southern Egypt.

Gama'ah al-Islamiyah shows a turbulent and notorious history that throws up questions on the causes of militancy but also offers discussions on reasons for deradicalization and ideological moderation. Gama'ah al-Islamiyah was established in 1970 as a countermovement to the Muslim Brotherhood, absorbing the Qutbian trend with its radical views on *jahiliyya*, *hukm Allah* and *jihad*. Having first enjoyed recruitment successes as a Salafi-leaning student movement in the early 1970s with its primary support on the university campuses at Asyout, Suhag and Menia, and lesser chapters in Alexandria and Cairo, Gama'ah al-Islamiyah then extended its stronghold in the religiously and socially more conservative environment of Egypt's southern regions, growing into a significant social network across the rural south and, by extension, its cities. By the mid-1970s Gama'ah al-Islamiyah had built a robust hierarchical organization under Nageh Ibrahim, Karam Zuhdi and Abd al-Salam Faraj as executive leaders and Sheikh Omar Abd al-Rahman as its spiritual guide.

Faraj was born in Egypt in 1952 into a family that continued supporting the Muslim Brotherhood during its persecution under Nasser. Faraj thus became familiar with Qutb's ideas during his youth and began to support the radicalization of Qutbists. Rejecting the Brotherhood mainstream under al-Hudaybi, Faraj regarded their reconciliation attempts with the Egyptian regime as a form of apostasy, and initially joined Gama'ah al-Islamiyah. In 1979 Faraj, along with Ayman al-Zawahiri, Sayyid Fadl and several others, formed a radical offshoot of Gama'ah al-Islamiyah that had its main base in the Cairo region. Merging both organizations under the umbrella of Egyptian Islamic Jihad in 1980, Faraj took charge of the preparations for the assassination of President Sadat in 1981. In around 1984 Gama'ah al-Islamiyah re-emerged as a separate group following the release from prison of several of its members. In the following years it rebuilt its clan-like networks in the south. In addition, it diversified its influence by gaining a foothold in poverty-stricken, predominantly Sa'idi quarters of Cairo, such as Imbaba and Bulaqa.

In this environment, Gama'ah al-Islamiyah was able to build a state within the state by applying a dual mobilization strategy. It thus borrowed the concept of *da'wa* from the Muslim Brotherhood to seek public support among the urban and rural poor. It offered, for example, neighbourhood support services, religious advice and education. Parallel to this, it applied the Salafi-Wahhabi concept of *hisba* to enforce a puritanical religious and social order. Gama'ah al-Islamiyah hoped to rebuild society from the bottom up based on this dual strategy. While believing that society would eventually rid itself of a *jahili* regime, Gama'ah al-Islamiyah held on to the Qutbian concept of *jihad* and the justification for armed resistance. It thus continued its militant strategy by attacking secular public figures and fighting a guerrilla war against the Egyptian military and police that particularly affected Egypt's southern regions. Gama'ah al-Islamiyah's militancy culminated in a terrorist attack in November 1997, which killed 58 tourists and four Egyptian nationals at a pharaonic temple in Luxor. The incident, which prompted widespread revulsion, was a turning point for the organization, which subsequently initiated a process of deradicalization and moderation. After several years of re-examining the group's ideological foundations, Gama'ah al-Islamiyah leader Karam Zuhdi edited a series of four books that contained articles written by the group's leading circle under the title *Silsila Tashih al-Mafahim* (Series for the Correction of Understanding), also known as (Muraja'at) (Revisions). In subsequent years the group continued to issue books that advocated non-violence and political engagement. Having remodelled itself, the organization established a Salafi-oriented political party during the Arab Spring. It then participated in the elections of 2011 and, after the coup of July 2013, supported the presidency of Gen. Abd al-Fatah al-Sisi.

Meanwhile, Faraj's book *Al-Farida Al-Ghaiba* (The Neglected Duty), which he issued in 1980, became the core text that guided the militant ideology of Egyptian Islamic Jihad, continuing to influence the group even after his execution in 1982. In fact, there is an ideological continuity as Ayman al-Zawahiri picked up on Faraj's ideas and incorporated these into his own work. As for Egyptian Islamic Jihad, it was to become the forerunner of al-Qa'ida. After a contingent of Egyptian Islamic Jihad fighters was released from Egyptian prisons, they continued their activities abroad, with Saudi Arabia and Afghanistan as major hubs. The group used Afghanistan as a safe haven and training camp during the 1980s, exploiting the political instability that was caused by the Union of Soviet Socialist Republics (USSR) occupation. By 1988 the *jihadi* training camp was to become the 'Base', otherwise known as al-Qa'ida. The ranks of Egyptian Islamic Jihad thus directly filtered into al-Qa'ida, which became the umbrella network under which local groups continued to operate.

In *Al-Farida Al-Gaiba*, Faraj repeated many of Qutb's arguments but he focused principally on the claim that the concept and practice of *jihad* had been disregarded by religious leaders and by the community of Muslims. In many ways, he took up Qutb's critique that *jihad* has only been understood in defensive terms. Faraj agreed but added that *jihad* must be regarded as the sixth pillar of Islam, thus making explicit what radical *jihadists* had previously only implied and elevating *jihad* (i.e. offensive *jihad*) to a fundamental religious duty on a par with the confession of faith, prayer, fasting, giving alms and pilgrimage. Faraj also followed Qutb's view that Muslims have an individual obligation to engage in *jihad*. In other words, every Muslim has to participate in *jihad* or might otherwise not be considered a Muslim. However, Faraj goes further than Qutb regarding militancy as a core aspect of *jihad*: believing Muslims become combatants who engage in revolutionary, militant activism. This is, of course, a very extreme position that has little in common with the peaceful practice of Islam. As for the priority target of militant *jihad*, Faraj remains feted to the 'near enemy' strategy that postulates that Muslim land must first be liberated from the claws of impious Muslim leaders before Jerusalem or global political masters can be targeted. Nevertheless, Faraj brings an international political aim into the picture and thus paves the way for global *jihadist* militancy.

SALAFI-*JIHADIS*, INTERNATIONAL POLITICS AND TERRORISM

When one thinks of militant Islamism, the names of organizations such as al-Qa'ida and Islamic State immediately come to mind. Both organizations are infamous for the impact that their terrorist activities have had on the global stage. While both draw from the same ideological pool and, although al-Qa'ida established a base and thus gave the impetus for transnational militant *jihad*, Islamic State went further in attempting to establish a state where it ruthlessly applied its version of an Islamist polity. As pointed out above, the foundations for a militant Islamist ideology were formulated by Sayyid Qutb and 'Abd al-Salam Faraj. The latter was also a leader of Egyptian Islamic Jihad, to which Ayman al-Zawahiri belonged. Through al-Zawahiri's input, Egyptian Islamic Jihad was incorporated into al-Qa'ida as the first truly global militant Islamist network. Still, an important link for the ideological transition from a 'near enemy' theory in Faraj's work to one that justified militancy against 'the far enemy' is Abdullah Yusuf Azzam, also poignantly called the Imam of Jihad.

Azzam was born in 1941 in Palestine (then administered under the British Mandate for Palestine). His radicalization was sparked by the Six-Day War in June 1967, as a result of which his family had to flee the West Bank. During his theological studies in Egypt, Azzam became close to Gama'ah al-Islamiyah circles and became friends with Sheikh Abd al-Rahman and al-Zawahiri. He later took on a post at the University of Jordan in Amman, but was dismissed due to his radical views, subsequently being appointed as a lecturer in Jeddah, Saudi Arabia, where he met Osama bin Laden. Following the Salafi-*jihadi* instigated occupation of the Grand Mosque in Mecca, Azzam was expelled from Saudi Arabia. He then moved to Afghanistan, where he established the Maktab al-Khidamat (Office of Services), which managed the arrival of Arab Jihadists. Azzam was killed by a roadside bomb in Peshawar, Pakistan, in November 1989, shortly after the withdrawal of Soviet forces from Afghanistan.

As well as being important for the organization of Arab *jihadists* and his close ties to al-Zawahiri and bin Laden, i.e. the highest tier of al-Qa'ida leaders, Azzam's ideas present the missing link that justified global *jihadi* combat. Azzam reasoned in his tract *Ilhaq bi 'l-Qawafila* (Join the Caravan) and the book *Al-Difa'a 'an Ardh al-Muslimin Ahamm Furud al-Ayan* (Defending Muslim Lands is Among the Most Important Collective Obligations, which included a key *fatwa* still used by al-Qa'ida, Islamic State and other Salafi-*jihadist* groups today) that *jihad* is the most important individual duty. Unlike Qutb or Faraj, Azzam's *jihad* theory is inspired by the classical law of war. The 'far enemy' position rests on the judicial position that Muslim lands must be defended against foreign invasion. The 'near enemy' theory, by contrast, rests on a far more complicated justification. To recall, Qutb argued that the leaders of Muslim societies were infected by *jahiliyya* and hence could no longer claim to be Muslims themselves. In other words, the 'near enemy' theory focuses on internal enemies as the primary target of its militancy. Declaring their rulers as apostates, they focus their operations on predominantly Muslim-populated states in the Middle East and North Africa. Thus, the theory is an extreme spin-off of apostasy law. The 'far enemy' theory derives its emphasis from orthodox instructions on war.

Azzam, therefore, reintroduced to Salafi-*jihadi* ideological thinking a more standard and much simpler explanation for armed combat. Afghanistan, which was first occupied by the USSR and later by allied Western forces, was thus seen by supporters of *jihadi* ideas as a legitimate case. In fact, as 'classical law for beginners' is often reiterated in basic training for preachers and Imams, the justification for armed engagement in Afghanistan resonated among many ordinary Muslims. It thus provided Salafi-*jihadists* with credence for external support, recruitment and building their militant base. Azzam's justification was first applied to combat against the USSR but, following his death, it became part of the Salafi-*jihadi* repository. It was used to justify terrorist attacks against US targets, including the events of September 2001. In this way, global militant *jihadists* insist that they act in defence.

However, there are novel aspects in Azzam's *jihad* theory that go beyond the influence of classical law of war or the recourse to Qutb and Faraj. Azzam lowered the threshold that the classical law set for participation in warfare. While classical judicial renderings on war instructed an individual Muslim to stay home if they needed to support their parents, spouse or children, Azzam saw no need for these conditionalities. Azzam regarded *jihad* to be singularly the most essential duty. To him, it is stronger than any responsibility towards family or friends. Implicitly, he makes a case for intensifying the recruitment to *jihad*, thus targeting particularly enthusiastic supporters who might otherwise feel obligated towards their families. Also new in Azzam's interpretation is his argument that wealthy Muslims must sponsor *jihad*, a logical stretch that was made by extending the concept of *zakat* (giving alms). To him, *zakat* was no longer an economic rule for the support of the needy and poor, but was now extended to include financing militancy.

Interestingly, Azzam also argued that *jihad* could be supported by infidels (non-believers) if this supported the purpose of the Salafi-*jihadi* cause. This might sound contradictory, but it effectively allows for temporary alliances with forces that militant Salafi-*jihadists* might otherwise regard as enemies. Examples here are manifold, such as the temporary alliance of al-Qa'ida and the USA during the Soviet occupation, the temporary collaboration of Islamic State with remnants of the Arab Renaissance (Baath) Socialist Party in Iraq, or its co-operation with the regime of Bashar al-Assad during the conflict in the Syrian Arab Republic.

Borrowing heavily from Qutb, Azzam reiterated the phases for successful *jihadi* activism, namely to close Salafi-*jihadi* ranks first by practising internal exile, and then to pursue training and preparations before engaging in combat. Interestingly, Azzam added a final stage, which he called the *Shari'a* phase and which suggested that he was contemplating the possibility of the establishment of an Islamic state in Afghanistan. However, Azzam also remarked that the four stages of *jihad* needed to be repeated by Salafi-*jihadists* in every conflict that they face. As such, his extended Qutbian method still remains part of the ideological core of Salafi-*jihadi* planning.

Osama bin Laden is perhaps the most instantly recognizable face of militant Salafi-*jihadism*. Bin Laden was born in Riyadh, Saudi Arabia, in 1957 into a rich Saudi family with a major stake in construction. The year 1979 was crucial: the Soviet invasion of Afghanistan was the trigger that turned bin Laden's attention to *jihad*. In the following years, he travelled repeatedly to Afghanistan. Initially a financial broker, he then supported Abdullah Azzam in establishing the Maktab al-Irshad for Arab fighters in Peshawar in the mid-1980s. Extending these activities into Afghanistan, bin Laden and al-Zawahiri established al-Qa'ida as a training camp and hub that allowed *jihadists* to prepare for combat.

Although bin Laden was typically seen as the frontman of al-Qa'ida, al-Zawahiri had perhaps more experience in organizing *jihadist* cells and had brought extensive links to Gama'ah al-Islamiyah and Egyptian Islamic Jihad into the formation of al-Qa'ida. Born into a prominent Egyptian family in Giza in June 1951, he studied medicine and became a surgeon in 1978. Al-Zawahiri joined Gama'ah al-Islamiyah as a teenager and then continued his *jihadi* career as a member of Egyptian Islamic Jihad. Following the assassination of President Sadat in 1981, al-Zawahiri was incarcerated for three years on minor charges. Upon his release, he resettled in Pakistan, where he met Abdullah Azzam and Osama bin Laden. As al-Qa'ida, at least initially, had the dual purpose of defending Afghanistan against Soviet invasion and establishing a base for a vanguard community, bin Laden and al-Zawahiri put into practice the militant ideology presented in the ideas of Qutb, Faraj and Azzam.

After the Soviet withdrawal from Afghanistan in 1989, bin Laden returned to Saudi Arabia while al-Zawahiri stayed in Afghanistan. The deployment of US troops on Saudi soil following the Iraqi invasion of Kuwait in August 1990 prompted bin Laden to condemn the Saudi monarchy in an open letter. In response, the Saudi authorities stripped bin Laden of his Saudi citizenship in 1992. He was expelled from Saudi Arabia and then from the Sudan. When he permanently settled in Afghanistan in 1996, the development of al-Qa'ida received fresh impetus. Bin Laden and al-Zawahiri began to solidify the organizational structure of al-Qa'ida. They extended the group's initial function of serving as a hub for the Salafi-*jihadists* by evolving into an umbrella organization that linked militant Islamist groups and individuals from various countries. In 1996 bin Laden issued a *fatwa* entitled *Declaration of War Against the Americans*, which criticized the USA for its actions in numerous countries. This was followed by a *fatwa* issued in February 1998 by bin Laden, al-Zawahiri and three other Islamist leaders, *World Islamic Front for Jihad against the Jews and Crusaders*, in which they accused the 'Zionist-Crusader alliance and their collaborators' of being responsible for atrocities in various Muslim-majority countries, and called on Muslims to 'kill the Americans and their allies—civilian and military'. In August of that year al-Zawahiri's published the tract *Al-Hasad al-Murr* (Bitter Harvest), in which he criticized the Muslim Brotherhood for its political pragmatism and, adopting the arguments of Faraj and Azzam, argued that militancy was the only way to achieve the success of *jihad*. These epistles were followed by bombings at the US embassies in Kenya and Tanzania in August 1998 and a suicide attack on the USS Cole in October 2000. Less than a year later, more than 2,600 people were killed and many more were injured in the September 2001 terror attacks in New York, Washington, DC, and Pennsylvania, USA. US President George W. Bush declared a 'War on Terror', and the USA began to attack Taliban forces and al-Qa'ida camps in Afghanistan from October.

Al-Zawahiri was unrepentant, issuing a series of essays under the title *Fursan Taht Rayah al-Nabi* (Knights under the Prophet's Banner) in which he preached in raging words to Salafi-*jihadis* about the inevitability of confrontation. Indeed, in the following years Afghanistan and, from 2003 onwards, Iraq became the targets of US-led military intervention. However, the focus of these wars was, by no means, only on eradicating militant Islamist organizations, and, even if combatting terrorism was one aspect of the intervention, its long-term success is indeed questionable. The trajectories of the Taliban, al-Qa'ida, and the Islamic State are examples of the failures of these drawn-out, costly and inhumane wars. The Taliban regime in Afghanistan, which stood accused of offering a safe haven to al-Qa'ida members, including its senior leadership, was dismantled rapidly. None the less, the movement was able to reorganize itself in the mountainous border region of Pakistan, from where it initiated a long-running campaign that eventually led to its return to power in 2022. Meanwhile, despite international efforts to capture members and curb its terror activities, al-Qa'ida managed to restructure its organization. The top-tier leaders went into hiding, but the group's scattered hierarchy continued to operate and establish affiliated sub-groups in the Middle East and North Africa, as well as in Europe and North America.

Al-Qa'ida initiated a new form of all-channel terrorism, based on the organizational input of al-Qa'ida's chief strategist, Abu Mus'ab al-Suri, who issued his recommendations for strategic change in the book *Da'wat l-muqawamah al-islamiyyah al-'alamiyyah* (Call to Global Islamic Resistance), which was published in 2005. Al-Suri presented a variety of operational changes, most crucially recommending that a future militant *jihad* could be successful only if it opened its recruitment and operational channels. Taking advantage of the internet age, this created the policy of an all-channel network through which al-Qa'ida evolved into an international network. Using the spread, limitlessness and undetectability of online communications, al-Qa'ida was able effectively to disseminate its ideology, distribute instructions to potential supporters and encourage individuals to form self-styled *jihadi* groups or commit acts of suicide terrorism. Al-Qa'ida and its affiliates were thus able to mobilize for terrorism that threatened public life throughout the 2000s. It was responsible for the loss of countless lives in acts of terror in numerous places, including Riyadh, Casablanca (Morocco), İstanbul (Türkiye), Barcelona and Madrid (Spain), London (UK), Paris (France) and Baghdad (Iraq).

Following the killing of bin Laden by US special operatives in Abbottabad, Pakistan, on 2 May 2011, al-Qa'ida continued under the auspices of al-Zawahiri. During his leadership, al-Qa'ida maintained ties to local affiliated Salafi-*jihadi* groups that tend to spread in countries weakened by intra-state conflicts and civil war. Even after al-Zawahiri too was killed, in a US drone attack on his hideout in Afghanistan in July 2022, al-Qa'ida has continued to operate, despite losing its hegemony as the dominant transnational Salafi-*jihadi* organization to Islamic State by the mid-2010s.

Al-Zawahiri's writings have had a lasting impact on Salafi-*jihadist* militant groups, even if they strategically veer away from al-Qa'ida. Apart from his 1998 *fatwa*, his essay *Bitter Harvest* and the book *Knights under the Banner*, al-Zawahiri wrote various texts that became the ideological drivers of Islamic State. Of particular importance is the debate with Sayyid Fadl, who was previously a close ally of al-Zawahiri and a known figurehead within Egyptian Islamic Jihad. Responding to Fadl's deradicalization attempts, al-Zawahiri repeated the approach of previous militant *jihadist* ideologues and, furthermore, introduced the concept of *maslaha* (public interest) into the debate. Reinterpreting the classical judicial concept, he argued that acts of terror are justified, even if they result in the killing of innocent civilians, which, to al-Zawahiri, constituted acceptable collateral damage. In his view, public interest also sanctions criminal acts such as theft, fraud and money laundering, as well as drug smuggling, kidnapping, human trafficking and slavery. Al-Zawahiri also extended Azzam's extreme views on lifting legal clauses for *jihad*, arguing that young people do not need the approval of their parents, even if for suicide missions. The influence of these views can be traced in the writings of numerous Salafi-*jihadist* authors. Among them are Jordanian-Palestinian theologian Abu Muhammad al-Maqdisi, who wrote a series of influential works, including *Millat Ibrahim* (The Creed of Abraham; published in 1985), and is perhaps best known for being the spiritual mentor of Abu Musab al-Zarqawi (see below); and Abu Bakr Naji, who, in *Management of Savagery* (published online in 2004), justified the use of violence, brutality and cruelty as a tolerable means of achieving the desired Islamic state. The ideology of al-Qa'ida thus finds continuity in a bulk of ideologues that form the foundations for the terrorist extremism that is ruthless in its pursuit of a totalitarian concept of an Islamist state system.

Islamic State originated from al-Qa'ida in Iraq, which was established in 1999 by al-Zarqawi. Born in Jordan in 1966, al-Zarqawi joined Arab *jihadi* fighters in 1989 in Afghanistan, shortly before the Soviet withdrawal. After a period in Pakistan, where he continued to be part of Salafi-*jihadi* cells, he returned to Jordan in 1992. There he was imprisoned after guns and explosives were found in his possession. In a general amnesty of 1999, al-Zarqawi was released from prison and, with the support of bin Laden and al-Zawahiri, established Jama'at al-Tawhid wa 'l-Jihad. Following the US-led invasion of Iraq in 2003, al-Zarqawi formally swore allegiance to al-Qa'ida in 2004 and was designated by bin Laden and al-Zawahiri as the Emir of Iraq. He renamed his group al-Qa'ida in Iraq, and offered a highly visible franchise that provided al-Qa'ida with the validation that the Salafi-*jihadi* organization continued in the defence of Muslim land. Al-Zarqawi became an increasingly ruthless and dangerous leader, who personally took part in beheadings that were streamed online. Furthermore, al-Qa'ida in Iraq was responsible for countless bombings in busy city centres and attacks on the Iraqi Shi'a-led Government, as well as against US and British forces. His campaign of violence became so brutal that al-Zawahiri issued a statement calling on him to restrain his extremism. The dispute with al-Zawahiri led al-Zarqawi to dissolve the alliance. Although al-Zarqawi was killed by a targeted action in June 2006, al-Qa'ida in Iraq continued its activities under Abu Omar al-Baghdadi and then Abu Bakr al-Baghdadi.

Ibrahim Awad Ibrahim al-Badri, commonly known as Abu Bakr al-Baqdadi, declared himself as Islamic State's first caliph in 2014. Born in July 1971 in the Iraqi city of Samarra, he studied Islamic theology at the University of Baghdad. Radicalized by the US-led invasion of Iraq, Abu Bakr al-Baghdadi joined al-Qa'ida in Iraq in 2003 and became an increasingly influential figure within the organization, which was reconstituted as Islamic State in Iraq in 2006, under al-Zarqawi's and Abu Omar al-Baqhdadi's leadership. Following the latter's death in May 2010, Abu Bakr al-Baghdadi became leader of Islamic State in Iraq.

With the descent of Iraq into political chaos, Abu Bakr al-Baqdadi managed gradually to extend the local pockets controlled by Islamic State in Iraq fighters. Through opportunistic temporary alliances with tribes and Sunni movements, some of which were previously close to Saddam Hussain's Baath Party, Islamic State in Iraq found support for its anti-Shi'a agitation and for its ambition in fighting US and British troops on Iraqi soil. The organization took further advantage of Syria's descent into civil war after Assad's hostile response to the Arab Spring protests of 2011, and by mid-2014, now known as Islamic State, it had seized control of large parts of Iraq, including the main cities in Al-Anbar (Anbar) and the Kurdish regions, as well as parts of eastern Syria, and in June 2014 al-Baghdadi declared the establishment of the Islamic State caliphate. Although the US-led international coalition made some efforts to combat Islamic State, substantial differences among global political players on the issue of how to respond to the civil conflict in Syria or a potential sectarian Shi'a crescent, and, above all, the confusion over shifting political and military alliances within Syria and Iraq played into Islamic State's hands. The organization imposed its view of an Islamic state onto the areas that it controlled through coercion, enslavement and terror, and atrocities committed by its members became daily news. A military breakthrough was not achieved until 2017, when Iraqi government forces regained control of Al-Raqqah (Raqqa), Syria, and then Al-Mawsil (Mosul), Iraq. Despite losing its territory and despite al-Baghdadi's death in October 2019, remnants of Islamic State still exist in Syria and Iraq, and many surviving fighters not captured by Iraqi, Kurdish or international forces moved on to join various groups in other countries. Despite being fragmented, militant Salafi-*jihadism* continues to threaten the international community, putting an immense strain on the stability of states in the Middle East and North Africa, and the Sahel region, but also in Central and East Asia.

SHI'A MOVEMENTS

Several notable Shi'a movements shape the political landscape of states with sizable Shi'a populations, such as Iran, Iraq, Lebanon, Saudi Arabia and Bahrain. Among the many Shi'a movements are, most notably, Hezbollah in Lebanon, the Second Khordad Movement, and later the Green Movement, in Iran, and the so-called Mahdi Army in Iraq.

It is impossible to recount here the rich history of Shi'a Islam, particularly the dominant branch of Twelver Shi'ism. However, Adoration of the *Ahl al-Bayt* (literally: People of the House, which designates the dynastic line from the Prophet Muhammad to his son-in-law, Ali), the martyrdom of Muhammad's grandson Hussain in Karbala in 680, and the *ghayba* (concealment) of the 12th Imam Mahdi in 941 are among the core frames that shape the identity of Shi'a Muslims. As such, they are central and recurrent references invoked by Shi'a movements to support their political aims. For example, the injustice attributed to the martyrdom of Hussain is used as a symbol for the enduring fight against oppression. At the same time, the story of Mahdi's *ghayba* carries messianic tenets that surface in support of the leaders of Shi'a movements. Thus, Ayatollah Ruhollah Khomeini, who became the inaugural Supreme Leader of the Islamic Republic of Iran in 1979, has been assigned an aura of infallibility comparable to that of the Imamate of the direct descendants of Ali, while other leaders such as Sheikh Hasan Nasrallah, Grand Ayatollah Ali al-Husaini al-Sistani and Muqtada al-Sadr have also invoked the narrative of the return of the righteous Imam and the battle at the end of times.

Yet, it must be pointed out that a politicized understanding of Shi'ism is, as it is with Sunni Islamism, a relatively modern phenomenon, having its roots in the 19th century, and reaching an ideological peak with Ayatollah Khomeini's success. The term *Wilayat al-Faqih* (Guardianship of the Islamic Jurist), which is commonly seen as the core idea of Khomeini, was actually coined by Mullah Ahmad Naraqi in the early 19th century, who argued that clerics needed to take charge of religious and some aspects of social life. Admittedly, Naraqi, who stood at the beginning of the *Usuli-Akhbari* debate, had spiritual leadership in mind, while Khomeini extended the concept to political leadership. Moreover, the basis for such a political leadership of a clerical cast was also the product of the 19th century. As a result of the *Usuli-Akhbari* debate during the late Qajar period, the clerical ranks of *ayatollah* and *hojatolislam* (commonly referred to as *mullahs*), as well as the concept of *marja'iyya* (clerical authority), were introduced. Proponents of an *Usuli* believe that the ordinary Muslim needs the religious guidance of a learned *mujtahid* (a person educated in spiritual interpretation). Around this time, Grand Ayatollah Murtaza Ansari Shushtari insisted on the need for clerical hierarchy, epitomized in the institution of *maraja'a at-taqlid* (authorities of interpretation), which is headed by *al-marja'a al-'azm* (the highest authority). In sum, the religious and clerical leadership that is today unquestioningly associated with Shi'a Islam is a product of modernity.

The political weakness and lack of modernization that caused the decline and eventual fall of the Qajar dynasty in 1925 was met with the increasing influence of Shi'a clerics, demonstrating its political power during the Persian Constitutional Revolution (1905–11). Although the reintroduction of monarchical rule under the Pahlavi dynasty from 1925 led to a temporary retreat of the clerical establishment from Iranian politics, it continued to control much of social and religious life. Clerics returned to instigate political protest in reaction to the US- and British-backed coup that brought down the nationalist Government of Prime Minister Mohammad Mussadeq in August 1953. The force of clerical-led political dissent became apparent with the so-called 15 Khordad Rebellion of 1963 against the reformist policies of Reza Shah Pahlavi's 'White Revolution'. Ayatollah Khomeini, who headed the protests, was imprisoned.

Following his discharge from prison, Khomeini was selected as *Marja'a al-Taqlid*, the highest clerical authority, holding this office until his death in June 1989. He was exiled from Iran in 1964, eventually settling in the Iraqi centre of Shi'a Islam, Al-Najaf (Najaf). In a series of lectures that were collated by his students and later published in an edited form under the title *Hukumat-e Islami* (Islamic Government), Khomeini revisited the concept of *Wilayat al-Faqih*, arguing that, in the absence of the occulted Imam Mahdi, the clerical hierarchy needed to take charge of religious, social and political affairs. Only then would governance be in accordance with *Shari'a*. He furthermore saw within the juristic dictum of *amr bi 'l-ma'ruf* (command to do good) a demand to oppose an unjust ruler and the introduction of a legalistic theocracy. After years of exile in Najaf and a short spell in Paris, Khomeini returned to Iran in the wake of the Iranian Revolution of 1979 that deposed Shah Muhammad Reza Pahlavi. Khomeini outplayed his political opponents using his clerical power and eventually turned the revolution to his advantage. In March 1979 the establishment Islamic Republic of Iran was confirmed via a referendum, and in December a new Constitution was adopted. Although Khomeini's views only partially fed into the legal framework of the newly established Islamic Republic, it gave him, as Supreme Leader, almost absolute power. The constitutional arrangements were the source of continuous political tensions, initially between the Supreme Leader and the Prime Minister and, even more so, after the constitutional amendment of 1989, between the Supreme Leader and the President. Hojatoleslam Seyed Ali Hosseini Khamenei, who relinquished the presidency to become Supreme Leader following the death of Khomeini in June 1989, managed to manipulate to his advantage by playing hardliners and reformists against each other.

Over the ensuing years there have been recurring reports of demonstrations and protest movements in Iran. Despite calls on the streets for the easing of social and political restrictions, there is, at least so far, little tangible evidence that such protests are demanding the end of the Islamic Republic, the return of the monarchy or the installation of a secular republic. On the contrary, it could be argued that the Iranian protest movements, such as the Second Khordad Movement, led by the cleric Mohammad Khatami, and later the Green Movement, led by Mir Hossein Mousavi, were Islamist protest movements. Moussavi and particularly Khatami stood for a different kind of Islam that emphasized a personal relationship with God. Still venerating Khomeini, both regarded Shi'a Islam as a reformist, liberal, pluralistic and democratic force. Yet, the idea of reform competes in Iran with the views of hardliners. This more conservative understanding of religious tenets—which is sometimes expressed on the streets but has its support base in rural areas, the military, the moral police and large parts of the clerical establishment—plays on concerns regarding the need to defend Shi'a and Iranian identity. Only time will tell whether other Shi'a Islamist or non-religious alternative movements appear, whether the Islamic Republic opens itself to reform or whether it remains a religiously conservative, oppressive regime.

The Iranian example of 1979 and Khomeini's views regarding clerical rule had a powerful influence on Shi'a movements outside Iran. Hezbollah, established in Lebanon in the early 1980s by a circle of clerics who received their clerical training in Najaf in the 1960s and 1970s, has particularly strong ties to the Islamic Republic. Having a strong clerical foundation, Khomeini's *Wilayat al-Faqih* became a core concept of Hezbollah. Yet, it is wrong to assume that the organization is merely an extension of Khomeini's and Khatami's Iran. Hezbollah has strong national Lebanese roots.

Other Shi'a organizations, such as Amal, Islamic Amal, the Lebanese Da'wa and the Association of Muslim Students, became incorporated into Hezbollah. Leaders of these organizations took seats in Hezbollah's *shura* council. Some of these Shi'a forerunner groups pursued armed strategies during the Lebanese civil war (1975–90) and the Israeli invasion of 1982. The paramilitary cells also found a new home in Hezbollah even after the Ta'if Accord of 1989 that provided for an eventual end to the civil war. Hezbollah continues to maintain a military wing (despite offering many assurances to the contrary), which regards defensive *jihad* and anti-Zionist rhetoric as a core frame of reference. Yet, the organization must not be reduced to a group that only pursues a militant Shi'a Islamist agenda. In fact, as a political organization, it has evolved into a significant player. As a social organization, it provides various services and facilities, from kindergartens, schools and libraries to hospitals and other health care. It has used these services to extend its influence beyond the Shi'a community. Nevertheless, reports on Hezbollah's involvement in the murder of Lebanese Prime Minister Rafiq Hariri in 2005 and, more recently, allegations of corruption and meddling among the political elite that surfaced in the wake of the devastating explosion in 2020 at the Port of Beirut have damaged the organization's credibility and prospects.

OUTLOOK

The issue of whether Islamist movements, and perhaps Islam more generally, is compatible with democracy has been subject to endless debates that are often tainted by partisan positions. At the outset, Muslims are neither more nor less adept than non-Muslims at accepting democratic values. Yet, the question of whether there are obstacles that inhibit Islamist movements from accepting democratic ideals is all too often related to religious arguments. In particular, the concept of God's sovereignty and the authority of *Shari'a* are often used to argue that Islam and Islamism are incompatible with democratic principles. This view is voiced by secularists who regard the severance of all religious frames from politics to be at the heart of modern democracy. Still, they are equally loudly articulated by Islamists with neo-orthodox Salafi leanings, who regard any attempts to disentangle religion from politics as an act of *kufr*. If one understands that Islamism, in all its shades and manifestations, is a product of modernity, one can appreciate that the question of its compatibility or non-compatibility is not so much shaped by religion itself but by the interpretations of those that intend to use Islam for a political purpose. Similarly, it helps to understand that there are immense variances among Islamist movements and actors. In fact, the ideological difference between neo-orthodox Salafi-*jihadists*, who believe in God's worldly authority, and liberal-minded reformists, who regard Islam as a source of democratic values, can hardly be starker. What complicates the analysis of Islamist organizations is the fact that the political context of most countries with majority Muslim populations is overshadowed by authoritarian and semi-authoritarian regimes. As long as democracy has not taken root in these contexts, it is hardly surprising that the ideological frames of Islamists do not veer more decidedly toward consensus-based formal politics.

BIBLIOGRAPHY

Akbarzadeh, Shahram. (Ed.). *Routledge Handbook of Political Islam*. New York and London, Routledge, 2011.

Ayubi, N. N. *Political Islam. Religion and Politics in the Arab World*. London and New York, Routledge, 1991.

Dalacoura, K. *Islamist Terrorism and Democracy in the Middle East*. Cambridge, Cambridge University Press, 2011.

Enayat, H. *Modern Islamic Political Thought: The Response of Shi'i and Sunni Muslims to the Twentieth Century*. London, Macmillan, 2005.

Gerges, F. *The Far Enemy: Why Jihad Went Global*. Cambridge, Cambridge University Press, 2005.

Ismail, S. *Rethinking Islamist Politics: Culture, the State and Islamism*. London, I. B. Tauris, 2006.

Mandaville, P. *Global Political Islam*. London, Routledge, 2007.

Meijer, R. (Ed.). *Global Salafism: Islam's New Religious Movement*. London, Hurst & Co, 2009.

Wiktorowicz, Q. (Ed.) *Islamic Activism: A Social Movement Theory Approach*. Bloomington, Indiana University Press, 2004.

SAUDI ARABIA AND IRAN: ISLAM, SECURITY AND FOREIGN POLICY IN THE MIDDLE EAST

SIMON MABON

In early January 2016 Saudi Arabia executed 47 people, most of whom had been accused of carrying out attacks on behalf of al-Qa'ida, a Sunni militant group. However, four of these people were Shi'a, including a prominent cleric and activist for Shi'a rights, Sheikh Nimr al-Nimr, who had been arrested for his involvement in protests in the restive Eastern Province of the Kingdom against repression of the Shi'a minority. The executions were condoned by the Council of Senior Ulama (a body of senior Islamic scholars with far-reaching influence over religious and legal affairs), whose head, Abdulaziz bin Abdallah Al al-Sheikh, emphasized that the sentences were in accordance with 'the *Shari'a* (Islamic law), and there is no doubt for these are the punishments set out in the *Koran* and they apply to everyone'. The executions were framed as essential for national security, amid allegations that al-Nimr was acting as an Iranian agent. There was widespread condemnation of the executions in Iran. The Iranian Supreme Leader, Ayatollah Ali Khamenei, stated that the measure was 'a political error on the part of the Saudi regime. God will not relinquish [avenging] the blood of the innocent. The blood spilled unjustly will rapidly deliver a blow to the politicians and officials of this [Saudi] regime'. Khamenei later predicted that Saudi Arabia would experience 'divine vengeance' as a consequence. Shortly after, the Saudi embassy in the Iranian capital, Tehran, was set on fire and the Saudi consulate in the Iranian city of Mashhad was looted. As a consequence, diplomatic relations between the two states were severed—a latest low point in an increasingly fractious relationship between the two regional powers.

The Islamic Revolution in Iran in 1979 added a religious dimension to strained ties between the two historical rivals, which became particularly acrimonious, given the existential importance of Islam to the Saudi and Iranian regimes. As a result, religion began to feature prominently in the political, security and foreign policies of both countries. The construction of the regional security environment provides opportunities for external involvement in the domestic affairs of regional actors, and with the increasing tensions between regime and society after the uprisings. Within this, political life became increasingly contested, as many struggled to meet their basic needs in the context of deteriorating and increasingly complex political and security situations. Such conditions provided scope for Riyadh and Tehran to increase their standing across the region by providing support for groups in contested spaces. To this end, this essay seeks to understand and engage with how the fragmentation of political life—and sovereignty broadly—has provided scope for the rivalry between Saudi Arabia and Iran to intensify and further escalate tensions across the region.

In recent years, the rivalry between Saudi Arabia and Iran has become increasingly important in shaping the nature of Middle Eastern politics. Building upon the spread of religious and ethnic identities and pre-existing schisms between regime and society that deepened with the 'Arab Spring' of revolutionary protests in Middle East and North African states in late 2010 and early 2011, Riyadh and Tehran capitalized upon a fragmenting region in an attempt to shape the Middle East in their image. To understand this—and indeed the importance of religion broadly—we must consider the importance of religion within the fabric of each state, which goes some way to explain the prominence of religion within foreign policy.

The nature of regional security calculations became determined by this rivalry, the consequences of which have spread out into the wider Middle East.

The USA had long been seen as a guarantor of regional security for Saudi Arabia—although the presence of external forces in the Persian (Arab) Gulf region was a source of concern for Iran—and as a result, condemnation by US President Barack Obama was met with a great deal of hostility in the Saudi Arabian capital, Riyadh. In response, Turki al-Faisal bin Abdulaziz, a prominent Saudi prince, sought to draw a comparison between '...the Kingdom's 80 years of constant friendship with America to an Iranian leadership that continues to describe America as the biggest enemy, that continues to arm, fund and support sectarian militias in the Arab and Muslim world, that continues to harbour and host Al-Qaeda leaders, that continues to prevent the election of a Lebanese president through Hezbollah, which is identified by your government as a terrorist organization, that continues to kill the Syrian Arab people in league with Bashar Assad?'

Of course, the sensitivity of Middle Eastern politics in the midst of the Arab Uprisings played a prominent role in such security concerns, with the struggle between the two states taking on increasing importance in the aftermath of the Arab Uprisings. Following the protests, the fragmentation of regime-society relations across a number of Middle Eastern states resulted in a wide range of socioeconomic and political challenges, all affecting human security and the ability to meet basic needs. In these cases, people turned elsewhere to ensure their survival. Such existential issues provided scope for the external penetration of a state, particularly with the existence of shared religious or ethnic bonds that create strong ties between different actors. The severity of the rivalry between Riyadh and Tehran meant that such penetration was seen in zero-sum terms through the prism of regional security. To the layperson, at the heart of this rivalry is a religious dimension that pits the most powerful Sunni state against the most powerful Shi'a state to shape the nature of regional politics. Despite the prominence of religion, it is important not to assume that religion is the sole driving force of the rivalry; indeed, sectarian differences need not necessarily be violent or result in animosity. They can do, however, when they become increasingly politicized and framed in such a way that the 'other' poses an existential threat to the survival of the state. We see that Islam plays a prominent role in the fabric of both countries and, as a consequence, also in their foreign policies. Yet in both cases, religion is used instrumentally as a means of securing legitimacy for domestic and external audiences. By the very nature of the *ummah*—the worldwide community of Muslims—states that have a prominent Islamic identity have the capacity to speak to people across state borders. Such capacity serves as a means of transcending state borders, or across the *Dawla*, and speaking to people of the same faith or doctrine in different communities, which is regularly used instrumentally. Of course, there also exists the perception that religion is used as a means of mobilizing particular communities, which is a prominent feature of regional politics. Perceptions are shaped not only by shared religious ties, but also by historical experience, which requires careful consideration.

Efforts to understand the rivalry between Riyadh and Tehran have produced a body of literature that can be separated into three camps. The first suggests that the rivalry is best understood through a balance of power in the Gulf. This position suggests that states compete for regional hegemony in a range of different arenas, and when state sovereignty fragments, the opportunity to increase power emerges. The second camp suggests that religion plays a prominent role in shaping the nature of the rivalry and that proxy conflicts have been drawn along sectarian lines. It boils the rivalry down to an existential struggle about religious difference, neglecting the complexity of identity construction—and change—or the political ramifications of identity politics. The third camp suggests that a more nuanced approach is needed, drawing upon concerns about regime power and legitimacy—externally and internally—with the instrumentalized use of religious difference.

This essay offers a genealogical approach to understanding the rivalry between Saudi Arabia and Iran, considering the importance of religion in the context of each state's foreign policy agenda. In doing this, the essay is broken down into five sections: the first considers the nature of relations between the two prior to the revolution; the second looks at the first decade of the Islamic republic; the third considers the scope for rapprochement after the death of Ayatollah Ruhollah Khomeini (the leader of the Islamic Revolution) in 1989; the fourth looks at the aftermath of the invasion of Iraq in 2003; and the fifth considers the Middle East after the Arab Spring protests. Within each of these sections is a reflection upon the nature of the rivalry, together with the exploration of the role of Islam in shaping policy and actions. Such a breakdown allows for the identification of different periods in the period of rivalry between Riyadh and Tehran, which allows us to acknowledge the importance of a range of different factors in shaping the nature of regional security.

DOMESTIC FACTORS

In search of an understanding of the nature of the rivalry between Saudi Arabia and Iran, the role of religion in both states must be considered. The preamble to the Iranian Constitution of 1979 notes that:

'The Constitution of the Islamic Republic of Iran advances the cultural, social, political, and economic institutions of Iranian society based on Islamic principles and norms, which represent an honest aspiration of the Islamic *Ummah*. This aspiration was exemplified by the nature of the great Islamic Revolution of Iran, and by the course of the Muslim people's struggle, from its beginning until victory, as reflected in the decisive and forceful calls raised by all segments of the populations. Now, at the threshold of this great victory, our nation, with all its beings, seeks its fulfilment.'

Similarly, Article 1 of the Saudi Constitution declares that:
'The Kingdom of Saudi Arabia is a sovereign Arab Islamic state with Islam as its religion; God's Book and the *Sunnah* of His Prophet, God's prayers and peace be upon him, are its constitution.'

It is hard to ignore the symbolic importance of Islam, reflected in the prominent use of green on both countries' flags, together with the *Shahada* on the flag of Saudi Arabia, which emphasizes the oneness of Allah and Muhammad's role as his messenger. It is clear that Islam is built into the fabric of both states, and such prominence positions religion as a prominent characteristic of regional politics. If one considers state-building processes in Saudi Arabia and Iran, the role of religion is paramount. For the Al Sa'ud dynasty in Saudi Arabia, the centuries-old alliance with the puritanical Wahhabi *ulama* provides an integral source of legitimacy, allowing a fringe tribe to claim rule over large swathes of the Arabian Peninsula. It is a state run in accordance with the *Shari'a*, which served as a source of the country's laws, and although a large number of people may not identify as Wahhabi, the importance of clerics should not be understated. Saudi Arabia is home to the two holiest sites in the Muslim world: the Grand Mosque in Mecca and the Prophet's Mosque in Medina. As a consequence, the Al Sa'ud dynasty has derived legitimacy as the custodian of the two holy places and in doing so, offers protection to all of those individuals who perform the annual *Hajj* pilgrimage.

In Iran, religion played a more private role prior to the Islamic Revolution, but in the months after the revolution, faith was positioned front and centre in the Islamic Republic. Khomeini's vision of *velayat-e faqih* (The Regency of the Jurist) suggested that in lieu of the return of the *Mahdi* (the revered twelfth imam of the Shi'a tradition who went into occultation in the 10th century CE, and whose return, so followers believe, will rid the world of evil in preparation for the Day of Judgement), only jurists of a certain status were qualified to rule. This position is a serious diversion from traditional Shi'a thought, which suggests that there should be a clear separation between religion and politics and, as a consequence, deep divisions emerged between clerics following Khomeini in Iran and clerics in the holy Shi'a city of Najaf, Iraq, under the tutelage of Grand Ayatollah Ali Sistani. In the Islamic Republic, a system of checks and balances was implemented to ensure that politics was run in accordance with the *Shari'a* and that Khomeini's political vision was maintained.

Shi'a history played a prominent role in Iran, particularly its construction of a foreign policy agenda. Of particular relevance was the Battle of Karbala, at which Hussein—the grandson of the Prophet Muhammad—was killed. Hussein spoke out against the impropriety of the caliphate at this time, which had accrued vast wealth and behaved in a way that was perceived to be un-Islamic. Over time, Hussein's martyrdom, which some theologians suggest was his desired outcome, located ideas of martyrdom, guilt and sacrifice in the Shi'a experience and Iranian foreign policy. It is with these domestic factors in mind that we turn to competition between Saudi Arabia and Iran and their respective foreign policies.

RIVALRY BEFORE REVOLUTION

To understand the characteristics of the contemporary rivalry, an examination of the rivalry prior to the Islamic Revolution must be considered. In 1929 the Saudi-Iranian Friendship Treaty was signed, following a dialogue that had included Iranian officials visiting Mecca to witness Wahhabi governance first hand. In the following decades, both states were predominantly concerned with the development of domestic infrastructure projects, paying scant attention to broader regional trends. Although there was a legacy of suspicion directed at the 'other' across the Gulf, stemming from a long history of Arab–Persian tensions, relations were largely positive. The first serious point of tension emerged from Iranian recognition of the state of Israel in 1950 (only the second Muslim country to do so at that time, after Turkey—now officially known as Türkiye). By doing so, Iran positioned itself in direct opposition to pan-Arab support for the Palestinian cause.

Despite this point of tension, in the late 1960s and early 1970s US President Richard Nixon attempted to resolve security concerns in the Persian (Arabian) Gulf by establishing a two-pillar approach, cultivating support from both Saudi Arabia and Iran, and encouraging co-operation between those two countries, to maintain stability in an increasingly important part of the world. Such security calculations were driven by a mutual suspicion—and indeed fear—of the military capabilities and intentions of the secular, socialist Baathist regime in Iraq, which had assumed power in 1968. Moreover, both Iran and Saudi Arabia were concerned by the influence of pan-Arab thought, which shaped regional politics during the 1950s and 1960s. Territorial tensions became a source of friction, particularly over the offshore boundaries in the Gulf. The two countries' respective coastlines vary between just 60 km (95 miles) away from each other at the northern end of the Persian Gulf to about 215 km (135 miles) at the southern end, and the two sides referred the demarcation of their maritime border to the International Court of Justice, which negotiated an accord in 1968. Such concerns were bound up in concerns about regional security mechanisms in light of the withdrawal of a significant proportion of British armed forces from the Persian Gulf after the Suez Crisis of 1956. During this period, Iranian influence across the Middle East had increased as a consequence of Iran's membership of a number of international institutions, together with maintaining a position of regional influence as an ally of the USA.

At this time, Gulf security was shaped by the presence of Western actors, particularly the British. With the decision to withdraw 'East of Suez' after 1956, a number of questions emerged, particularly with regard to the nature of regional security. The smaller Gulf states were also affected, with many gaining independence at around this time. In Bahrain, independence raised questions about identity, amid longstanding suggestions that Bahrain was the '14th province of Iran'. A survey organized by the United Nations in Bahrain in early 1970, asking the Bahraini population whether they preferred independence or Iranian rule, returned the result that Bahrainis wished to be independent (the country achieved independence from the United Kingdom in 1971), but Iranian claims to Bahrain continued.

THE IMPACT OF REVOLUTION

Unsurprisingly, revolutionary action in Iran dramatically altered regional security calculations across the Persian Gulf and Middle East. The events of 1978 and 1979, which forced Muhammad Reza Pahlavi to abdicate as Shah of Iran in February 1979, resulted in the establishment of *velayat-e faqih*, under Supreme Leader Ayatollah Khomeini. Khomeini's vision was anti-monarchical and anti-colonial, immediately pitting Iran against a number of states across the region. The revolution brought Islamic considerations to the forefront of the rivalry, raising fundamental questions about regime security and influence across both the Middle East and the wider *ummah*.

In the formative stages of the Islamic Republic, the importance of Islam was abundantly clear to the new regime in Tehran, yet also to Riyadh, where the Al Sa'ud dynasty was reliant upon its longstanding alliance with Wahhabi clerics to provide legitimacy. Given this, a spiral of rhetoric emerged that sought to demonstrate the Islamic credentials of each state. Things began positively, with King Khalid of Saudi Arabia welcoming the establishment of an Islamic Republic:

'It gives me great pleasure that the new republic is based on Islamic principles which are a powerful bulwark for Islam and Muslim peoples who aspire to prosperity, dignity, and well-being. I pray the Almighty to guide you to the forefront of those who strive for the upholding of Islam and Muslims, and I wish the Iranian people progress, prosperity, and stability.'

In turn, Khomeini also sought to emphasize cohesion across the Muslim world, transcending language and sectarian allegiance:

'There is no difference between Muslims who speak different languages, for instance the Arabs and the Persians. It is very probable that such problems have been created by those who do not wish the Muslim countries to be united [...] They create the issues of nationalism, of pan-Iranianism, pan-Turkism, and such isms, which are contrary to Islamic doctrines. Their plan is to destroy Islam and Islamic philosophy.'

Inevitably, when relations soured, this rhetoric became increasingly vitriolic and divisive. Khomeini's vision was explicitly stated:

'We will export our experiences to the whole world and present the outcome of our struggles against tyrants to those who are struggling along the path of God, without expecting the slightest reward. The result of this exportation will certainly result in the blooming of the buds of victory and independence and in the implementation of Islamic teachings among the enslaved Nations.'

Saudi Arabia was not immune to this criticism; after all, Khomeini's vision was explicitly anti-monarchical. Given this, coupled with Saudi Arabia's position of leadership in the Muslim world, it was hardly surprising for Khomeini to attack the Al Sa'ud dynasty.

'If we wanted to prove to the world that the Saudi Government, these vile and ungodly Saudis, are like daggers that have always pierced the heart of the Muslims from the back, we would not have been able to do it as well as has been demonstrated by these inept and spineless leaders of the Saudi Government.'

King Fahd, having succeeded King Khalid in 1982, referred to the new regime in Iran as 'hypocrites and pretenders who are using Islam to undermine and destabilize other countries'. While sovereign borders were transgressed, the argument put forward suggested that sovereignty was found in God and, as a result, both states were dealing with the *ummah*, rather than the Westphalian notion of a nation state. This point of tension would become a prominent feature across the international relations of Middle Eastern states, particularly among those that derived a large measure of legitimacy from Islam.

The Islamic Revolution brought a religious dimension to the rivalry that had previously been shaped by geopolitical considerations about the nature of regional security. Religious rituals would also take on a political dimension. The *Hajj* of 1987 was one such site of political contestation, when Shi'a Muslims on *Hajj* clashed with Saudi security forces, resulting in the deaths of at least 400 pilgrims, some 200 of whom were Iranian nationals. It was later argued that Iranian special agents were involved in creating discontent with political motivations. In protest at Saudi actions, Iran boycotted the *Hajj* in the following year.

In 1980 the onset of the Iran–Iraq war resulted in a large-scale loss of life, which also drew in regional and international actors, largely on the side of Iraq, who were concerned about the potential for Khomeini's Islamic revolutionary vision to spread. Although neither side was fully prepared for war, it was expected by many in Iran that the Shi'a of Iraq—long marginalized by the Baathist regime in that country—would join their sectarian kin from Iran. However, this view was misguided and underestimated the importance of Iraqi and Arab nationalism.

In 1981 the Cooperation Council for the Arab States of the Gulf (Gulf Cooperation Council—GCC) was established, predominantly in response to security concerns emanating from the Iranian revolution and the Iran–Iraq war. During the war, a number of incidents threatened to escalate tensions between Riyadh and Tehran, notably an Iranian attack on a Saudi oil tanker and a Saudi attack on an Iranian jet. Although the war threatened to escalate and draw in other Gulf states, the conflict remained between Iran and Iraq, ending in 1988 in a costly stalemate.

One of the main reasons for the onset of conflict was Khomeini's desire to spread his ideological vision across the Middle East, particularly to those with a significant Shi'a minority such as Saudi Arabia and Lebanon, and those with a disenfranchised Shi'a majority, such as Bahrain and Iraq. Of those states, two are of paramount importance to the discussion of the immediate aftermath of the Islamic Revolution, as a consequence of direct Iranian involvement in the domestic affairs of other states.

In Lebanon, members of the newly formed Iranian Revolutionary Guard Corps (IRGC)—the elite wing of the Iranian military, which answers only to the Supreme Leader—provided logistical and financial support to the Shi'a of Lebanon, working with them towards the establishment of Hezbollah, the Party of God. The establishment of Hezbollah provided Iran with a powerful actor in the eastern Mediterranean, which shared a border with Israel. The ideology of *velayat-e faqih* found traction among the downtrodden sections of the population in Lebanon, where Shi'a communities were marginalized politically, economically and socially. In the midst of a 15-year long civil war, Hezbollah provided support to the marginalized Shi'a communities and, over time, the group's ideology of resistance attracted a great deal of popular support. Alongside Hezbollah, Iran would eventually strengthen relations with the neighbouring Syrian Arab Republic, which also played a prominent role in Lebanon by supporting Hezbollah. The alliance between Iran, Syria and Hezbollah became known as the 'Axis of Resistance', challenging the regional order.

In Bahrain, which is viewed by many to be the epicentre of sectarian conflict as a consequence of its location in the Gulf between Saudi Arabia and Iran, the kingdom's demographic constitution has left it vulnerable to unrest. Several decades of marginalization of Shi'a communities have provided fertile ground for unrest, and once again, with the support of the IRGC, a Shi'a group—the Islamic Front for the Liberation of Bahrain (IFLB)—attempted to overthrow the ruling Al Khalifa monarchy. Although the coup was thwarted before it could begin, the legacy of Iranian involvement in Bahraini politics created the suspicion that Iran was the motivating force behind any regional unrest. Saudi fears were mitigated by the construction of the King Fahd causeway connecting Saudi Arabia to the island of Bahrain. Although it was ostensibly designed to improve economic links between the two Gulf kingdoms, the causeway served as a means to provide rapid military assistance to the Al Khalifa regime if required.

These two sets of events meant that whenever there was unrest among Shi'a groups in Bahrain, the belief that Iran was behind the unrest was widespread. Such claims, although understandable, were not always accurate. Indeed, the legacy of the Islamic Revolution can be felt in a number of different ways, serving to inspire Shi'a groups across the region, without necessarily having causal links, as has been the case in the unrest in the Eastern Province of Saudi Arabia since 2017. Irrespective of the circumstances, the perception that Iran was behind the unrest only served to fuel tensions between the Sunni Arab states and the Shi'a Islamic Republic of Iran.

ATTEMPTS AT RAPPROCHEMENT IN THE 1990s

At the end of the devastating Iran–Iraq war, a generation of Iranians had lost their lives, and the societal and economic consequences were severe, with both economies hit hard. Such consequences fed into Iranian strategic calculations at this time. Recognizing the need to develop more favourable relations with its neighbours and the international community, and with a lingering fear of Iraqi aspirations, Iran sided with Kuwait after it was invaded by Iraq in August 1990 and tacitly supported the international community's successful military campaign to liberate Kuwait in early 1991. The amelioration of relations across the Gulf became a key part of the Iranian presidencies of Ali Akbar Hashemi Rafsanjani and Mohammad Khatami over the next decade.

In 1990 a large earthquake hit Iran, killing some 30,000 people, and in response, Saudi Arabia sent aid to help. Diplomatic ties between the two were later restored, as a consequence of this episode. In December 1997 Saudi Crown Prince Abdullah attended a meeting of the Organization of the Islamic Conference (now Organisation of Islamic Cooperation—OIC) in Tehran, in doing so becoming the most senior Saudi official to visit since the Islamic Revolution. Two years later President Khatami visited Crown Prince Abdullah in Saudi Arabia, in the first visit by an Iranian leader since the Islamic Revolution.

Following Khomeini's death in 1989, space for rapprochement between the two states opened up. The presidency of Rafsanjani (1989–97) was one such opportunity, as the transition to Ali Khamenei as Supreme Leader—and Khamenei's legitimacy deficit compared with Khomeini—left space for Rafsanjani to take a greater role in the day-to-day politics of Iran. Under Rafsanjani, the two countries were able to restore diplomatic relations, and a frosty relationship gradually thawed, following visits of prominent state officials to each other's countries.

In 1999 President Khatami (1997–2005) visited Riyadh, becoming the first Iranian President to do so since the Islamic Revolution. A series of bilateral deals were signed between Riyadh and Tehran, while increasing security co-operation across the Persian Gulf aided the process of amelioration in bilateral ties. This led to a period of rapprochement in Saudi-Iranian relations, although the two states were still characterized by religious difference. One reason for this, apart from the trust that had been built in the aftermath of the earthquake of 1990, was the continued presence of Iraq as a prominent player in regional security calculations, where Tehran and Riyadh shared fear of a belligerent Iraqi foreign policy under President Saddam Hussain.

Despite this, a key historical dimension of the rivalry between Riyadh and Tehran has been over contrasting views of the role of external actors in maintaining regional security. Iran saw itself as uniquely qualified to ensure regional security, given its demographics and long history. In contrast, Saudi Arabia has been particularly reliant upon the USA for its security since the Gulf War of 1991. This issue would feature prominently in the years to come, particularly with an increased US presence in the Gulf in the first decade of the 21st century.

CONFLICT IN IRAQ AND THE OVERTHROW OF SADDAM HUSSAIN

At the beginning of the 21st century, relations between Riyadh and Tehran appeared to be cordial. The political rapprochement of the 1990s was supported by security co-operation, which resulted in the establishment of a security pact on terrorism and drug trafficking. However, the terrorist attacks on the USA on 11 September 2001 dramatically altered the construction of regional security across the Middle East. As previously noted, regional security in the Gulf had long been shaped by the interaction of three major powers: Iran, Iraq and Saudi Arabia. Any change to the ability of one state to shape regional security would have a serious effect on the ability of the other two states. Thus, in 2003, the toppling of Saddam Hussain would have a serious effect on regional Gulf security, creating a bipolar system that would have ramifications across the Middle East.

The invasion of Iraq in 2003 was a prominent part of President George W. Bush's 'war on terror'—the ideological response to the terrorist attacks of September 2001, which led to the invasion of Afghanistan in November and the toppling of the Baathist regime in Iraq in April 2003. In the early stages of the 'war on terror', there was a largely positive relationship between Washington and Tehran, with the latter permitting US air force planes to use Iranian airspace on missions to Afghanistan. President Bush's State of the Union speech in January 2002 ended any burgeoning rapprochement, however, as Iran was posited as being a member of an 'Axis of Evil', together with Iraq and the Democratic People's Republic of Korea (North Korea). From this point, as relations between Washington and Tehran became increasingly fraught, so did those between Riyadh and Tehran.

The US-led invasion of Iraq under the banner of 'Operation Iraqi Freedom' was hugely unpopular in the international community, but especially so in the Muslim world. Despite this, few observers were sad to see Saddam Hussain removed from power. This action created space within the Persian Gulf regional security complex for Iran and Saudi Arabia to compete for influence as a vacuum of power was created in Iraq.

The Iraqi rearguard action to the invasion of the country was short-lived, resulting in the establishment of the US-led Coalition Provisional Authority (CPA) in May 2003 and, ultimately, the transition to Iraq's first free elections. Under the CPA, the decision was taken to eviscerate the Baath party infrastructure in an attempt to prevent it from regaining control of Iraq, and all party members were dismissed from jobs in the police, army and state institutions. Little did the CPA realize the impact that such a move would have, however, as it resulted in several hundred thousand people being made redundant and struggling to provide for their families. Iranian involvement in Iraq's internal politics was multifarious, stemming in part from shared religious ties, the return of several Iraqi dissidents who had sought safe haven in Iran to frontline Iraqi politics and the presence of a number of powerful militias that received support from Tehran.

Rising sectarian violence, in part as a consequence of the presence and competing agendas of al-Qa'ida members, Shi'a militias and coalition forces, was rife, yet the CPA in Baghdad appeared to be either unable or unwilling to prevent it. Coupled with concerns about ensuring that basic needs were met, these became key factors in explaining why a number of Sunni tribes, particularly from Anbar province, would ultimately turn to groups like Islamic State in Iraq and the Levant (ISIL, renamed Islamic State). Such conditions, coupled with the presence of US forces in the region, notably in Iraq, Bahrain and Afghanistan, together with a number of other US military bases, would pose serious problems to a number of actors across the region, particularly those who believed that regional security should be ensured by states in the region, rather than external powers.

Although Iranian foreign policy became more progressive under the presidency of Khatami, particularly as he sought to reach out to global powers, this did not last. The election of Mahmoud Ahmadinejad, the bombastic former Mayor of Tehran, as President of Iran in 2005, was a further turning point in the construction of regional relations. Ahmadinejad fused a Shi'a outlook with a strong sense of Persian nationalism, which became an aggressive part of his foreign policy. Despite this bombastic outlook, Ahmadinejad travelled to Saudi Arabia in 2007, when GCC states were reaching out to Iran and attempting to build on increasingly positive relations between Saudi Arabia and Iran. Indeed, Ahmadinejad became the first Iranian President to attend a meeting of the GCC and also to perform the *Hajj* while serving as President.

Despite this growing rapprochement, a number of factors prevented a permanent thawing in relations, predominantly coalescing around security, albeit defined broadly. Such calculations revolve around national interests and maintaining territorial integrity, with a nod towards the Westphalian notion of non-interference in the domestic affairs of other states. However, it also involves an understanding of security that sees Islamic legitimacy—and its potential erosion—as an existential threat to regime survival.

Saudi efforts to address the Iranian threat by bolstering its own security date back to the Islamic Revolution in Iran, yet the invasion of Iraq in 2003 would cause consternation among many in Riyadh. On a number of occasions, Saudi officials spoke to their US counterparts, documenting the threat posed by Iran. In 2006 Prince Nayef bin Abdulaziz called for the USA not to 'leave Iraq until its sovereignty has been restored, otherwise it will be vulnerable to the Iranians'. Two years later, in a conversation between the US chargé d'affaires in Iraq, Patricia Buzenis, and Adel al-Jubeir, the Saudi ambassador to the USA, al-Jubeir expressed the seriousness with which senior Saudi officials were viewing the Iranian threat. Al-Jubeir recalled:

'...the King's frequent exhortations to the US to attack Iran and so put an end to its nuclear weapons program. "He told you to cut off the head of the snake," he recalled to the chargé d'affaires, adding that 'working with the US to roll back Iranian influence in Iraq is a strategic priority for the King and his government'.

In 2009 John Brennan, the US Homeland Security Advisor, met King Abdullah, who expressed his concerns about the Iraqi Prime Minister Nuri al-Maliki:

'The King said he had "no confidence whatsoever in (Iraqi PM) Maliki, and the Ambassador (Fraker) is well aware of my views". [...] For this reason, the King said, Maliki had no credibility. "I don't trust this man," the King stated, He's an Iranian agent." [...] Maliki has "opened the door for Iranian influence in Iraq" since taking power, the King said.'

Iranian involvement in the manipulation of domestic affairs can be seen across the region, which prompted increasing security co-operation between Saudi Arabia and the USA. Iranian influence could be seen in Lebanon, with the establishment of Hezbollah; in the Gaza Strip through Iranian support for Hamas; in Iraq with support for the Supreme Council of the Islamic Republic; in Bahrain with support for the IFLB; in Syria with support for the regime of President Bashar al-Assad; in Yemen with support for the Shi'a al-Houthi rebels; and in other states where there are serious tensions between Shi'a and Sunni communities. After the Islamic Revolution, rhetoric from Khomeini, coupled with Article 3.16 of the Iranian Constitution, set out an explicitly proselytizing agenda, grounded in Shi'a thought. In the following years, the fragmentation of regime-society relations across the Middle East and the marginalization of Shi'a communities across the region provided fertile ground for Iran to exploit, and also for perceptions of Iranian influence to develop.

In the years following the invasion of Iraq, the Axis of Resistance gained power and influence across the Middle East, stemming in part from the rising popularity of a number of key players, namely Ahmadinejad and Hassan Nasrallah (the leader of Hezbollah). The rising influence of Hezbollah in particular posed a serious problem for Saudi Arabia in light of the war between Israel and Hezbollah in mid-2006. Despite being an explicitly Sunni actor, the Al Sa'ud dynasty provided financial support for the rebuilding of Dahiya, the Shi'a-majority southern district of Beirut which had been largely destroyed by the Israeli armed assault. Iran provided financial assistance in the region of US $120m, while Saudi Arabia provided $1,200m. for the reconstruction efforts.

At this point, it becomes apparent that despite religious differences, the quest for legitimacy and the desire to be seen to do the right thing meant that Riyadh had to circumvent the concerns of Wahhabi clerics in Saudi Arabia to ensure that an external position of power and influence was maintained, much to the chagrin of the clerics.

THE ARAB UPRISINGS OF 2010-11 AND THE FRAGMENTATION OF REGIONAL ORDER

In late 2010 protests spread across the Middle East emanating from serious schisms between the regimes and large, disaffected parts of the population. These tensions resulted in the fragmentation of state sovereignty in a number of states, which provided new arenas for proxy competition between Riyadh and Tehran. Stemming from increased concerns about the nature of political organization and stagnating economies that prevented ordinary citizens from achieving a decent standard of living, growing popular dissatisfaction resulted in large numbers of people taking to the streets to express their frustration. The self-immolation of Muhammad Bouazizi—a youth in provincial Tunisia who killed himself in December 2010, in despair at the lack of economic prospects in his country, after being arrested for selling fruit and vegetables without a permit—was the catalyst for demonstrations across the region, leading to the toppling of political elites in Tunisia, Libya and Egypt in 2011 and Yemen in 2012, while the regimes in Bahrain and Syria were challenged to varying degrees. The failure of political structures, both formal and informal, left people feeling increasingly marginalized, which required large sections of the population to turn elsewhere to meet their basic needs.

In this context, both Riyadh and Tehran sought to exploit opportunities to strengthen themselves and weaken the other, amid a zero-sum game for ascendancy in the Middle East. Ultimately, the fracturing of political organization and the nature of state-society relations after the uprisings provided scope for the two to become involved in a number of proxy conflicts, increasingly along sectarian lines. In Syria, Bahrain, Iraq and Yemen, the two states supported opposing sides in the respective conflicts, exacerbating longstanding regional competition for influence in Lebanon. This behaviour—and the rivalry broadly—should not be viewed purely as a sectarian conflict; rather, as we have seen, sectarian dynamics have been used as a fig leaf for national interest.

Article 3.16 of the Iranian Constitution articulates 'the organization of the nation's foreign policy based on Islamic criteria, fraternal commitment to all Muslims, and unrestrained support for the impoverished people of the world'. In the context of the fragmentation of states and the failure of political elites to ensure the protection of people across the Middle East, the Iranian Constitution explicitly called on the state to protect marginalized members of society. Iranian foreign policy in the years following the Islamic Revolution created the perception that Tehran was behind unrest across the region, particularly in those states with Shi'a minorities. The narrative that Iran was the driving force behind the unrest in Bahrain and Yemen was compelling to many observers and, given the religious make-up of the Middle East, the spread of Shi'a groups would eventually leave a number of states open to (the perception of) external penetration.

For Ayatollah Khamenei, the uprisings of 2011-12 were framed as an extension of the Islamic Revolution of 1979, where, once again, Iran attempted to position itself at the vanguard of regional change. Although Middle Eastern and North African regimes sought to ensure their survival by emphasizing that the events were a consequence of sectarian schisms that were manipulated by external powers, this denied the agency of local protest groups and ignored the socioeconomic grievances that had led people to take their grievances to the streets.

The protests resulted in regimes referring to a range of strategies to ensure their survival, including the creation of sectarian master narratives as a mechanism of control. Such efforts largely distorted legitimate grievances and divided protest groups along sectarian grounds and by doing so, created a climate of fear and suspicion, which often turned to violence. Of course, sectarian differences need not necessarily be violent, but the existence of sectarian networks, albeit with different types of links between actors in the network, provided an easy opportunity through which messages could be spread and populations mobilized. The fear of the mobilization of a Shi'a network led to King Abdullah bin al-Hussain of Jordan referring to a 'Shi'a Crescent', mapping an arc of areas with Shi'a Muslims from Iran through Iraq and Syria to Lebanon. Despite failing to engage with differences within Shi'a thought, particularly over the role of clerics in politics, such concerns have shaped the perceptions of many Sunni states, particularly Saudi Arabia.

With the onset of the Arab uprisings, many regimes sought to frame the protest movements as a consequence of Iranian manipulation and interference, drawing on the Islamic Republic's history and foreign policy behaviour. This strategy involved framing unrest among Shi'a populations as a consequence of Tehran's 'propensity for mischief' and creating divisions within domestic populations, while securing regional support from powerful Sunni states. In the climate of uncertainty and instability, the securitization of protest movements solidified into a Saudi-led conservative bloc, the members of which were vehemently anti-Iranian and, as time went on, anti-Islamist.

This competition would spill over into a range of institutional arenas, including the OIC, which became the site for posturing and contesting legitimacy. The OIC took on an increasingly political dimension, when in 2016 the organization denounced 'Iran's interference in the internal affairs of the states of the region and other member states (including Bahrain, Yemen, Syria and Somalia) and its continued support for terrorism'. The need to maintain leadership over the Islamic world became of paramount importance in times of chaos.

Independent of the uprisings, negotiations were taking place that were designed to end Iran's nuclear programme and prevent the proliferation of nuclear weapons in the Middle East. Much to the chagrin of Israel and Saudi Arabia, the agreement that was concluded in July 2015 between Iran and the so-called E3/EU+3 group (comprising France, Germany and the UK, together with the People's Republic of China, the Russian Federation and the USA)—the Joint Comprehensive Plan of Action (JCPOA)—resulted in the lifting of economic sanctions that had decimated the Iranian economy. Over the course of 2015 the international price of a barrel of oil dropped from US $110 to $30, stemming in part from Saudi Arabia increasing supply in order to maintain a low price. Although the Saudi economy was also hit hard, the Saudi rationale was that its economy could withstand such pressures, whereas the Iranian economy could not. Driving this action was the concern that an empowered Iran would increase its sponsorship of its violent proxy groups, in particular Hezbollah in Lebanon and various Shi'a militia groups in Iraq. Such increased sponsorship would have the capacity to empower these groups and destabilize their local environments. Moreover, as regional security was increasingly seen in zero-sum terms, increasingly influential Iranian proxies would coincide with a reduction in Saudi influence.

Such sentiment—and indeed manifest suspicion—about Iranian aspirations was reflective of geopolitical shifts across the region. Within the context of what appeared to be an existential struggle for the Middle East, lines between a Saudi-led alliance of Sunni states (and Israel) and what was termed 'the Resistance Bloc', comprising Iran, Syria, Hezbollah and Hamas were drawn. Across a fragmenting region, such support for the 'marginalized' would be appealing.

As sectarian networks were mobilized, the importance of religion became increasingly apparent, and the failure to adhere to one's responsibilities to the Muslim world would be seriously damaging to claims to legitimacy. In 2015 the annual *Hajj* in Mecca was the site of thousands of deaths when a crane fell on pilgrims. The failure to prevent such events from happening was an opportunity to criticize the Al Sa'ud dynasty for failing in their duty to protect Muslims performing the *Hajj*, while attempting to erode the legitimacy of Saudi Arabia. In a meeting with the families of the victims, Ayatollah Khamenei stated how:

'The incompetence of the Saudis and the insecurity imposed by them against the *Hajj* pilgrims to the House of God indeed demonstrated that this government is not qualified to manage the Two Holy Mosques and this reality must be spread in the Muslim world and be understood.'

Although a number of Iranians died on *Hajj*, the event was used for political—and indeed geopolitical—ends, much like in 1987, to demonstrate Iran's position at the vanguard of the Islamic world once again.

Such concerns about hegemony and legitimacy within the Muslim world continue to play an important role in defining the nature of Saudi-Iranian relations. In attempting to facilitate this, both Saudi Arabia and Iran have provided financial support to clerics from across the world, hosting them for training and providing economic assistance in support of their vision of Islam.

Efforts to demonstrate vitality and legitimacy are coupled with desires to depict the weaknesses of the religious establishment in the other. For instance, the following remarks from Iranian officials speaking about the spread of Wahhabi ideology:

'Wahhabism is a tool for the enemies, and Muslims should stay away from the heretical Wahhabism (...) The disagreements and conflicts among Muslims have today risen to an unprecedented level. In Syria, Egypt, Iraq, Yemen, and Bahrain (...) the heretical Wahhabism is the chief cause of conflict. For hundreds of years, Shi'ites, Sunnis, Alawites, and Christians lived together in Syria, but when they [i.e. Wahhabi elements] entered [the arena]—look at the wars and bloodshed that began. Several Arab countries have become tools for the U.S. and Israel.'

In addition, others presented the view that 'The greatest danger threatening Islam today is the existence of takfiris, as with their fatwas they proclaim Shi'a to be inferior to [even] the Jews and Christians, and strive for Muslim infighting'. For their part, Saudi officials stated that:

'...the statements of the Iranian regime expose its true [character], as expressed by [its] support for terror, and continue the policy of undermining the security and stability of the region's countries... By defending the actions of terrorists and justifying them, the Iranian regime becomes a partner to their crimes, and it bears full responsibility for its policy of incitement and escalation'.

Such comments were also presented in Western news outlets, as al-Jubeir (who was appointed Minister of Foreign Affairs in 2015) presented Iran as responsible for widespread regional unrest, with Tehran attempting to 'obscure its dangerous sectarian and expansionist policies, as well as its support for terrorism, by levelling unsubstantiated charges against the Kingdom of Saudi Arabia'. Al-Jubeir also suggested that Iran was 'the single most belligerent actor in the region, and its actions display both a commitment to regional hegemony and a deeply held view that conciliatory gestures signal weakness either on Iran's part or on the part of its adversaries'. Once again, after the veneer of sectarianism is removed, we see how political and security considerations feature prominently in the calculations of both states.

THE TRUMP PRESIDENCY AND RAPID ESCALATION

The election of Donald Trump as the President of the USA in 2016 was met with much fanfare across the Gulf Arab states. Few had liked Trump's predecessor, Obama, and his overtures to Iran. Speaking with Jeffrey Goldberg in an interview published in *The Atlantic* in April 2016, Obama argued that:

'The competition between the Saudis and the Iranians—which has helped to feed proxy wars and chaos in Syria and Iraq and Yemen—requires us to say to our friends as well as to the Iranians that they need to find an effective way to share the neighborhood and institute some sort of cold peace.'

These comments were quickly rejected by many in Riyadh, as illustrated by the comments from Prince Turki, a former ambassador to the USA and the UK, cited above. Prince Turki's comments were supported by al-Jubeir, who later suggested that Iran was the 'number one state sponsor of terrorism'.

Central to Saudi concerns about Obama's policy towards the Middle East was the JCPOA, the nuclear deal agreed in 2015. The deal was quickly condemned as one that would allow Iran to develop 'break-out capacity' to obtain an atomic bomb and embolden its foreign policy activity, most notably through its support for Hezbollah in Lebanon and the al-Houthis in Yemen. In response, many actors across the Gulf, in Israel, and in the USA were critical of the deal.

Beyond the JCPOA, Trump had also cultivated positive relations with the new powerbroker in Riyadh, Crown Prince Mohammed bin Salman bin Abdulaziz Al Sa'ud. Trump's first official presidential visit abroad was to Saudi Arabia, in May 2017. After Mohammed bin Salman was appointed as Crown Prince, it was reported that Trump proclaimed 'We've put our man on top'. Trump later stated via social media, 'I have great confidence in King Salman and the Crown Prince of Saudi Arabia, they know exactly what they are doing...'. In addition to their burgeoning personal relationship, both men held strongly anti-Iranian views, which helped to reset relations between the USA and Saudi Arabia.

Over the course of his election campaign in 2016, Trump had articulated his foreign policy vision, which contained, at its core, a desire to withdraw from the JCPOA nuclear deal. Riyadh shared Washington's concerns about Iran, and the Trump Administration's decision to withdraw from the JCPOA in May 2018 was well received across the Kingdom. Explaining his decision, Trump argued that the deal 'was one of the worst and most one-sided transactions the USA has ever entered into'.

In the months following its withdrawal from the JCPOA, the USA imposed more sanctions on Iran, placing further pressure on the Islamic Republic. At the same time, Saudi Arabia continued its military campaign in Yemen, seeking to curtail al-Houthi activity and, ultimately, Iranian influence. However, international pressure grew on the Kingdom amid reports of humanitarian atrocities committed by the Saudi-led coalition and the murder of the Saudi dissident journalist Jamal Khashoggi in İstanbul, Türkiye, in October 2018.

As pressure increased on the Islamic Republic, officials in Tehran threatened to close the Strait of Hormuz, a narrow body of water through which around one-fifth of the world's oil supplies are transported daily. The Strait is also a key strategic point in global supply chains, meaning that its closure would have devastating consequences. In the months that followed, a series of incidents occurred that dramatically increased tensions between Iran and regional and international powers, notably Saudi Arabia and the USA.

On 13 June 2019 four commercial ships, including two Saudi oil tankers, were targeted in a 'sabotage attack' near the United Arab Emirates (UAE) port of Fujairah, close to the Strait of Hormuz. The USA and Saudi Arabia quickly blamed Iran for the incident, leading to a range of new sanctions being imposed on the Islamic Republic by the USA, including on the Supreme Leader. Designed to stop Iran from obtaining a nuclear weapon, the sanctions also sought to curtail Iranian activity across the region. While in Jerusalem, Israel, US National Security Advisor John Bolton said that Iran had not been granted a 'hunting licence' across the Middle East. After a US drone was shot down later in June—from international or Iranian airspace, depending on the account—Trump gave the order for air strikes on Iran. Although the order to strike was quickly withdrawn, he later authorized a cyber-attack on the Islamic Republic. British forces seized an Iranian oil tanker off the coast of Gibraltar in mid-July on suspicion that it was travelling to Syria, in breach of European Union sanctions against the Assad regime. In response, members of the elite IRGC sought to capture a British oil tanker in the following week.

While Iranian action following the US withdrawal from the JCPOA was directed principally at other states, Saudi Arabia continued to hold a firm line against the Islamic Republic. Speaking to the British Broadcasting Corporation in June 2019, al-Jubeir suggested that the Kingdom was consulting with allies about possible action and trying to 'send a message very clearly to the Iranians that this behaviour is not acceptable and must stop'. This message was firmly supported by the Trump Administration, together with Israel, under the leadership of Benjamin Netanyahu, whose anti-Iran stance created conditions to reshape regional politics, putting an end to longstanding tensions between Israel and some Arab states, amid shared concerns about the threat from Tehran. However, over the next few years, these dynamics began to shift.

ESCALATION AND MEDIATION

On 3 January 2020 a US drone strike on the outskirts of Baghdad killed Qasem Soleimani, the Commander of Iran's IRGC Quds Force, and Abu Mahdi al-Muhandis, the deputy leader of Iraq's pro-Iranian Popular Mobilization Forces militia. Soleimani had previously been considered a mysterious figure, heralded by many as the architect of Iran's vast networks of influence across the Middle East, and his death was commemorated by huge crowds on the streets of Tehran and other Iranian cities. In response, Iranian officials called for retribution, with Ayatollah Khamenei declaring that 'a harsh revenge awaits the criminal killers', and that 'the US regime will be responsible for all the consequences'. The Iranian response came five days later, on 8 January, when a barrage of missiles was launched at US bases in Iraq in what many viewed as a disproportionate attack in the face of Soleimani's assassination. Indeed, the same day Khamenei declared that the missile strikes were but a slap in the face to the USA, not sufficient retaliation.

The killing of Soleimani and ensuing revenge strikes against US targets in Iraq led to an increasingly precarious environment in the Gulf region and wider Middle East, with many fearing a dramatic escalation and all-out war. Yet key Saudi officials, notably al-Jubeir, called for de-escalation: 'the Kingdom of Saudi Arabia, in light of the rapid developments, calls for the importance of self-restraint to ward off all acts that may lead to aggravating the situation, with unbearable consequences'. When combined with the events of the tanker crisis a few months earlier, it was apparent that for all of the belligerent rhetoric of Crown Prince Mohammed bin Salman, the Kingdom was not willing to go to war with Iran, even if circumstances appeared to facilitate conflict.

While Soleimani had been responsible for cultivating Iranian influence in the region, it is suggested that he was in Iraq to pass on a message to Saudi Arabia about dialogue. Indeed, at this time, it was acknowledged by many that Iraq was acting as a mediator between Riyadh and Tehran. Shortly after the strike, Iraq's Prime Minister Adil Abd al-Mahdi articulated that Soleimani was in Iraq to deliver a message from Iran, in response to a message delivered to Iran from Saudi Arabia, raising a host of questions about US knowledge—and knowledge amongst various branches of the Trump Administration—about the ongoing dialogue facilitated by Iraq.

Later in the year, Pakistan, under the leadership of Prime Minister Imran Khan, made similar claims to mediation. Similarly well placed, with a society divided along sect-based lines and with cordial relations with both Riyadh and Tehran, the success of Khan's efforts remained to be seen.

THE PANDEMIC HITS

The emergence of the coronavirus disease (COVID–19) pandemic in the early months of 2020 had a dramatic impact on the Middle East, causing huge numbers of deaths in Iran and opening up schisms in societies across the region. Hosting large numbers of Shi'a pilgrims visiting religious shrines, Iran was quickly seen as the epicentre of the COVID-19 outbreak in the region. Citizens of neighbouring countries who had travelled to Iran, in many cases illegally, were told they would not face punishment as long as they came forward and helped with track and trace processes. Yet, in a political climate defined by hostility and suspicion, it was hardly surprising that anti-Shi'a and anti-Iranian sentiments rapidly spread.

In response to the devastation across Iran, a number of Gulf states sent medical and financial aid to the Islamic Republic, including the UAE, but notably excluding Saudi Arabia. While parallels can perhaps be drawn to the 1990s and the humanitarian crisis that followed the devastating earthquake, by 2020 Saudi Arabia was unwilling to provide aid, perhaps reflecting the nature of both domestic and regional politics, which prevented rapprochement.

DIALOGUE AND THE BIDEN ADMINISTRATION

The election of Joe Biden as the 46th President of the USA in late 2020 provoked concern among Arab Gulf states that feared a return to the accommodationist policies of the Barack Obama era. Fears of a possible Biden presidency had prompted a number of Arab states—notably the UAE and Bahrain—to normalize ties with Israel and strengthen the anti-Iranian front. Although Saudi Arabia did not formally normalize ties, it maintained a 'tacit security relationship' with Israel. Unlike other Arab states, the Kingdom was constrained by the need to (be seen to) support the Palestinian cause, owing to its position in the Muslim world and after having proposed a peace plan to resolve tensions between the Israelis and Palestinians in 2002.

Biden's inauguration in early 2021 brought about a period of instability in relations between the USA and the Kingdom of

Saudi Arabia, and prompted serious concerns for the latter about the organization of security across the Persian Gulf. The Biden Administration released documents declaring that Crown Prince Mohammed bin Salman had 'approved an operation' to capture or kill murdered journalist Khashoggi, sanctioning 76 lower-level Saudi officials as a consequence. Moreover, Washington sought to end the war in Yemen—albeit unsuccessfully—while also attempting to revive the moribund JCPOA, all contributing to Saudi Arabia's concern.

Behind the scenes, Saudi Arabia and Iran had been engaging in a range of diplomatic activities designed to improve relations and, ultimately, to reimagine regional security in a more positive light. Longstanding Track II initiatives evolved into more formal diplomatic initiatives across 2021, reflecting changes in global politics, perhaps most notably the Saudi realization that it could no longer rely on the USA to guarantee its security—opening new avenues of possibility.

Dialogue continued into 2022, albeit against a backdrop of conflict and increased tensions over the JCPOA. The Russian invasion of Ukraine on 24 February had a seismic impact on global politics, most obviously felt in the dramatic increase in oil prices and in countries that were reliant on wheat from Ukraine, but the conflict also had an impact on diplomatic relations, with Russia placing additional demands on diplomats involved in the nuclear negotiations. During an official visit to Saudi Arabia in July, amid the pressures arising from the war in Ukraine, President Biden walked back on previous comments that he had made about making the Kingdom a 'pariah state'. Biden's trip to the Middle East saw a recommitment to regional security through the Jerusalem Declaration, designed to deepen integration between states in the region and co-operation on security issues, notably to counter Iran. Such developments were felt in the nuclear negotiations, as all sides sought to assert dominance in the talks, with Iranian officials declaring that Iran was a 'nuclear threshold state', further escalating tensions.

Despite the achievement of a ceasefire in Yemen from 2 April 2022, conditions facing Yemenis deteriorated dramatically, while Saudi fears about al-Houthi attacks continued. In this climate, Crown Prince Mohammed bin Salman sought to make headway with his Saudi Vision 2030 development plan and its flagship NEOM project, hosting major sporting events in an effort to attract the necessary investment. The precarious nature of regional politics posed a challenge to both Saudi Arabia and Iran, with Tehran's influence in Iraq and Lebanon increasingly contested amid ongoing protests against elites, many of whom had links with the Islamic Republic.

RAPPROCHEMENT

By March 2023, backchannel dialogue between the Saudis and the Iranians made a breakthrough, culminating in the signing of a normalization agreement in China. While Beijing played a key role in getting the agreement across the line, work by a number of states and civil society organizations was essential in creating the broader conditions to allow for such an agreement. The normalization agreement set out a plan to re-establish diplomatic relations which had been severed after the execution in 2016 of Nimr al-Nimr, and to work towards the broader re-integration of Iran into the Gulf political fold. Underpinning the agreement was a range of security and economic concerns. For Saudi Arabia, the USA was increasingly unreliable as a security guarantor—particularly under a Democrat Administration—which prompted the reimagination of threat perceptions and strategic calculations. At a time when Mohammed bin Salman had put the Kingdom on a road of rapid socioeconomic transformation, it was deemed prudent to normalize relations with Iran and reduce the scope for conflict. For Saudi Arabia, Iran also opened up new economic opportunities. For Iran, years of crippling sanctions had provoked widespread unrest across the Islamic Republic. The country's isolation had taken a toll, meaning that normalization and re-integration into regional politics was invaluable.

Nevertheless, while significant, the agreement was not a panacea for the region's ills. It did little to address conflict in Yemen or Syria, although the broader transformation of regional relations could shift part of the context in which conflict played out. The agreement pointed to the broader realignment of regional security calculations, with the role of the USA, China and Russia increasingly uncertain.

CONCLUSIONS

The coming months will be key in making the normalization agreement work, requiring a host of other moves to build trust and transform perceptions of the other which reverberated across the security and political realms. The possible benefits of this transformation are huge, yet a number of issues remain unresolved.

The role of Islam as a means of deepening divisions between Saudi Arabia and Iran has become increasingly apparent in recent years. Prior to the Islamic Revolution, despite religious differences, the two states were able to work together on a range of issues affecting them. Even after the Revolution, it is possible to identify periods of rapprochement where relations between the two appeared far more favourable than at other times. Yet when sectarian differences become utilized for political ends and, perhaps more importantly, when this sectarian difference led to participants increasing their security and military capabilities for geopolitical ends, the divisions between the two become entrenched. When such positions emerge, it is important to look beyond what appears to be the driving force of violent differences, to consider structural factors, both domestically and externally, which provide scope for the possibility of action.

Such action occurs in a range of different guises, ranging from direct military action to support for proxy actors, to competition attempting to ensure legitimacy and primacy within the Islamic world. It is undeniable that religion has a role to play, but structural factors are equally important. The possibility for Saudi Arabia and Iran to improve their respective positions within the Persian Gulf or the wider Middle East, or an opportunity to solidify their legitimacy domestically, are perhaps more important factors, whatever the cost.

During the presidency of Donald Trump, Saudi Arabia became emboldened in its struggle to curtail Iranian influence across the Middle East, unlike under the Obama Administration, when the USA adopted a more conciliatory tone, seeking a diplomatic resolution of the rivalry. In contrast, following the USA's withdrawal from the JCPOA, Iran found itself on the periphery of international politics and faced increasing economic pressures. The new Administration in the USA has sought to address this, but it remains to be seen how successful President Biden will be in reintegrating Iran into the diplomatic fold and addressing the first and second order consequences of such developments. More important, however, is the ongoing diplomatic initiative designed to improve relations across the Gulf. Although it is subject to myriad spoilers and, as yet, has not provided a solution to key stumbling blocks such as the war in Yemen, there is hope that a significant breakthrough can be made. Although as of early September 2023 the ceasefire in Yemen was still holding, the situation remained precarious, with a range of structural issues—both domestic and regional—meaning that securing lasting peace posed a serious challenge.

What remains clear is that to understand the nature of the rivalry—and ultimately for there to be a de-escalation of tensions—we must recognize the complexity of the issues and their regional ramifications. By acknowledging the importance of myriad factors—local, regional and international—we are better placed to understand how such factors affect policy decisions and religious beliefs. By accepting this complexity, and with it the idea that Islam plays a significant yet not exclusive role in foreign policy behaviour, we are better placed to understand the rivalry between Saudi Arabia and Iran.

NOTE

This essay is an expanded and revised version of a chapter that first appeared in Akbarzadeh, Shahram (Ed.). *Routledge Handbook of the International Relations of the Middle East*. Abingdon, Routledge, 2011.

SELECT BIBLIOGRAPHY

Algar, Hamid. *Islam and Revolution I: Writings and Declarations of Imam Khomeini*. Berkeley, CA, Mizan Press, 1981.

— *Wahhabism: A Critical Essay*. New York City, NY, Islamic Publications International, 2002.

Alhasan, Hasan 'The Role of Iran in the Failed Coup of 1981: The IFLB in Bahrain'. *The Middle East Journal*, 65 (4), pp. 603–617, 2011.

Arab News. 'Saudi Arabia calls for restraint after Soleimani killing'. 3 January 2020. www.arabnews.com/node/1607896/saudi-arabia.

Alvandi, Roham. 'Muhammad Reza Pahlavi and the Bahrain Question, 1968-1970'. *British Journal of Middle East Studies*, 37 (2), 2010.

British Broadcasting Corporation. 'Saudi Arabia 'determined to push back against Iran'. 20 June 2019. www.bbc.co.uk/news/av/world-middle-east-48710384/saudi-arabia-determined-to-push-back-against-iran.

Commins, David D. *The Wahhabi Mission and Saudi Arabia*. London, I. B. Tauris, 2005.

Constitute Project. 'Iran (Islamic Republic of)'s Constitution of 1979 with Amendments through 1989'. www.constituteproject.org/constitution/Iran_1989.pdf?lang=en.

— 'Saudi Arabia's Constitution of 1992 with Amendments through 2013'. www.constituteproject.org/constitution/Saudi_Arabia_2013.pdf?lang=en.

Dawisha, Adeed. *Iraq: A Political History from Independence to Occupation*. Princeton, NJ, Princeton University Press, 2009.

Eiran, Ehud and Malin, Martin B. 'The Sum of all Fears: Israel's Perception of a Nuclear-Armed Iran'. *The Washington Quarterly*, Vol. 36, Issue 3, pp. 77–89.

Al-Faisal, Turki. 'Mr. Obama, We Are Not "Free Riders"'. *Arab News*, 14 March 2016. www.arabnews.com/columns/news/894826.

Fuccaro, Nelida. *Histories of City and State in the Persian Gulf: Manama since 1800*. Cambridge, Cambridge University Press, 2009.

Furtig, Henner. *Iran's Rivalry with Saudi Arabia Between the Gulf Wars*. Reading, Ithaca Press, 2006.

Goldberg, Jacob. 'The Saudi Arabian Kingdom', in Rabinovich, Itovar, and Shaked, Haim, (Eds). *Middle East Contemporary Survey Volume XI: 1987*. Boulder, CO, Westview Press, 1987.

Goldberg, Jeffery. 'The Obama Doctrine'. *The Atlantic*, April 2016. www.theatlantic.com/magazine/archive/2016/04/the-obama-doctrine/471525/#5.

Halliday, Fred. *Nation and Religion in the Middle East*. London, Saqi Books, 2000.

Hinnebusch, Raymond and Ehteshami, Anoushiravan (Eds). *The Foreign Policies of Middle East States*. London, Lynne Rienner Publishers, 2002.

El-Husseini, Rola. 'Hezbollah and the Axis of Refusal: Hamas, Iran and Syria'. *Third World Quarterly*, 31, Issue 5, 2010.

Al Jazeera. 'Khamenei Hails 'Islamic' Uprisings'. 4 February 2011. www.aljazeera.com/news/middleeast/2011/02/201124101233510493.html.

— 'Saudi FM: Iran 'Number One State Sponsor of Terrorism'. 10 Nov. 2017. www.aljazeera.com/news/2017/11/saudi-fm-seeks-pressure-iran-hezbollah-171109193012811.html.

— '"We Put Our Man on Top", Trump said on MBS, Book Claims. 5 Jan. 2018. www.aljazeera.com/news/2018/01/put-man-top-trump-mbs-book-claims-180105124054629.html.

Al-Jubeir, Adel bin Ahmed. 'Can Iran Change?' *The New York Times*, 19 January 2016. www.nytimes.com/2016/01/19/opinion/saudi-arabia-can-iran-change.html?_r=2.

Keynoush, Banafsheh. *Saudi Arabia and Iran: Friends or Foes?* London, Palgrave Macmillan, 2016.

Kostiner, Joseph. 'On Instruments and their Designers: The Ikhwan of Najd and the Emergence of the Saudi state'. *Middle East Studies*, 21, Issue 3, pp. 298–323, 1985.

— 'State, Islam and Opposition in Saudi Arabia, The Post-Desert Storm Phase'. *Middle East Review of International Affairs*, 1, Issue 2, 1997.

Lynch, Marc. *The New Arab Wars: Uprisings and Anarchy in the Middle East*. New York, NY, Public Affairs, 2016.

Mabon, Simon. 'The Battle for Bahrain'. *Middle East Policy*, 19, no. 2, pp. 84–97, 2012.

— *Saudi Arabia and Iran: Soft Power Rivalry in the Middle East*. London, I. B. Tauris, 2013.

Mabon, Simon, and Royle, Stephen. *The Origins of ISIS*. London, I. B. Tauris, 2017.

Marschall, Christian. *Iran's Persian Gulf Policy: From Khomeini to Khatami*. London, Routledge, 2003.

Mason, Robert. *Foreign Policy in Iran and Saudi Arabia: Economics and Diplomacy in the Middle East*. London, I. B. Tauris, 2014.

Merom, Gil. 'Israeli Perceptions of the Iranian Nuclear Threat'. *Political Science Quarterly*, 132 (1), 2017.

Middle East Media Research Institute. 'Iran Calls for Violent Shi'ite Reaction Against Saudi Arabia'. 12 February 2014. www.memri.org/reports/iran-calls-violent-shiite-reaction-against-saudi-arabia.

— 'Unprecedented Tension between Saudi Arabia, Iran following Execution of Shi'ite Cleric Nimr Al-Nimr'. 4 January 2016. www.memri.org/reports/unprecedented-tension-between-saudi-arabia-iran-following-execution-shiite-cleric-nimr-al.

— 'Iran Furious over Saudi Arabia's Execution of Shi'ite Sheikh Nimr Al-Nimr'. 4 Jan. 2016. www.memri.org/reports/iran-furious-over-saudi-arabias-execution-shiite-sheikh-nimr-al-nimr.

Nasr, Vali. *The Shia Revival: How Conflicts Within Islam Will Shape the Future*. New York, W. W. Norton, 2007.

The New York Times. 'Iran Debates Accepting Quake Relief Aid from Enemies'. 27 June 1990. www.nytimes.com/1990/06/27/world/iran-debates-accepting-quake-relief-from-enemies.html.

Norton, Augustus R. *Amal and the Shi'a: Struggle for the Soul of Lebanon*. Austin, TX, University of Texas Press, 1987.

— *Hezbollah*. Princeton, NJ, Princeton University Press, 2007.

Office of the Supreme Leader, Iran. *Saudis Not Competent to Run Islam's Holy Mosques*. 7 September 2016. www.leader.ir/en/content/16203/The-Leader's-meeting-with-families-of-Mina-and-Grand-Mosque-tragedies-in-Saudi-Arabia.

Organisation of Islamic Cooperation. *Final Communiqué of The Extraordinary Meeting of The Council of Foreign Ministers of The Organization of Islamic Cooperation on Aggressions on The Embassy of The Kingdom of Saudi Arabia in Tehran and its Consulate General in Mashhad*. 22 January 2016. www.oic-oci.org/iocv2/topic/?t_id=10837&t_ref=4262&lan=en.

Pandya, Sophia. 'Women's Shi'i Ma'atim in Bahrain'. *Journal of Middle East Women's Studies*. 6 (2), 2010.

Peterson, Scott. 'Imminent Iran Nuclear Threat? A Timeline of Warnings Since 1979'. *The Christian Science Monitor* 8, 2001.

Rubin, Lawrence. *Islam in the Balance: Ideational Threats in Arab Politics*. Stanford, CA, Stanford Security Studies, 52, 2014.

Samii, Abbas William. 'A Stable Structure on Shifting Sands: Assessing the Hizballah-Iran-Syria Relationship'. *The Middle East Journal*, 62 (1), pp. 32–53, 2008.

Shahram, Chubin and Tripp, Charles. *Iran-Saudi Arabia Relations and Regional Order*. London, Oxford University Press for International Institute for Security Studies, 1996.

Shai, Shaul. *The Axis of Evil: Iran, Hizballah, and the Palestinian Terror*. Piscataway, NJ, Transaction Books, 2005.

Szanto, Edith. 'Beyond the Karbala Paradigm: Rethinking Revolution and Redemption in Twelver Shi'a Mourning Rituals'. *Journal of Shi'a Islamic Studies*, 6 (1), 2013.

Tripp, Charles. *A History of Iraq*. Cambridge, Cambridge University Press, 2007.

Trump, Donald J. *Twitter*, 6 Nov. 2017.

The Washington Post. 'Netanyahu's Claim that Iran is "Six Months" from Having Nuclear Bomb Material', 16 Sept. 2012.

Wehrey, Frederic, et al. *Saudi-Iranian Relations Since the Fall of Saddam: Rivalry, Cooperation, and Implications for U.S. Policy*. Santa Monica, CA, RAND Corporation, 2009.

The White House. *President Donald J. Trump is Ending United States Participation in an Unacceptable Iran Deal*. 8 May 2018. www.whitehouse.gov/briefings-statements/president-donald-j-trump-ending-united-states-participation-unacceptable-iran-deal.

WikiLeaks. Saudi MOI Head Says If U.S. Leaves Iraq, Saudi Arabia Will Stand with Sunnis. 20 December 2006. wikileaks.org/plusd/cables/06RIYADH9175_a.html.

Saudi King Abdullah and Senior Princes On Saudi Policy Towards Iraq. 20 April 2008. wikileaks.org/plusd/cables/08RIYADH649_a.html.

Counterterrorism Adviser Brennan's Meeting with Saudi King Abdullah. 22 March 2009. wikileaks.org/plusd/cables/09RIYADH447_a.html.

Worrall, James, Mabon, Simon, et al. *Hezbollah: From Islamic Resistance to Government*. Santa Barbara, CA, Praeger, 2016.

Young, Richard. 'Equitable Solutions for Offshore Boundaries: The 1968 Saudi-Iran Agreement'. *The American Journal of International Law*, 64 (1), 1970.

US MIDDLE EAST POLICY

ROBERT E. LOONEY

INTRODUCTION

Until recently, to understand US policy in the Middle East, it was necessary only to have a passing knowledge of US interests in the region. Over the years, these have revolved around five primary goals. The first goal for many years was keeping oil and gas from the region flowing to global markets. A second objective, prominent in recent times, is neutralizing regional terrorist groups and eliminating the danger posed by these groups to US security. The third goal is preventing the proliferation of weapons of mass destruction. Some US Administrations have also emphasized a fourth objective, the importance of promotion of human rights and democracy, or at least the start of participatory government. All US Presidents have subscribed to a fifth goal of helping to ensure Israel's survival as a sovereign state. The first three goals reflect US strategic interests. The final two objectives can be considered more 'moral imperatives', which cut across Democratic and Republican party lines.

From time to time the relative priority of these goals has shifted, producing what appeared to be inconsistencies in the US stance. Added to these were trade-offs among the goals, the most obvious being the need to keep supplies of oil flowing, while encouraging the spread of human rights and democracy, leading to the USA's image of tolerating authoritarian regimes, particularly in many of the oil-exporting countries of the Persian (Arabian) Gulf, and countries of strategic value during the Cold War, such as Pakistan.

Long-run secular trends are also at play, the prime example being the weakening of the US commitment to the defence of Israel. In part, US concern for Israel's security has waned merely because the Jewish state has managed to become increasingly secure from external threats. However, Israeli actions, including its expansion of illegal settlements in the West Bank, and the suppression of Palestinian rights are also factors.

In recent years, the US shale oil boom has substantially reduced the reliance of the USA and its allies on Middle Eastern oil, thus lessening concern over the region's willingness and ability to supply world markets with their hydrocarbons.

The conduct of US policy towards the Middle East falls into two broad periods. The first covers the period from the end of the Second World War in 1945 up to 1990. During this time, the USA did not, as a rule, adopt military force (with the exception, most notably, of interventions in Lebanon to prop up a Christian-led government in 1958, and again in the Lebanese civil war in the early 1980s, which ended abruptly when the US embassy was attacked in one of the first significant instances of an Islamist-inspired suicide bombing against Western interests, in the Lebanese capital of Beirut in 1983, followed by an even bigger attack on a US barracks later that year), but rather a classic strategy of balance-of-power policy. The USA had some influence over outcomes through close security ties to several countries, allowing it to exert control without being directly involved. Under these circumstances, the US objective was to prevent any single country, first the Union of Soviet Socialist Republics (USSR), and more recently, Iran, from dominating the region. As long as that was the case, the USA was confident of ensuring the uninterrupted flow of oil from the Middle East to international markets.

An increased US military presence and the rising anti-US sentiment this situation generated among populations in the Middle East defines the second period, from 1990 to the present. Within each time frame, every US Administration has had its particular agenda for the region, or at least its style of policymaking, with some Administrations being much more engaged in Middle East issues than others. Finally, each period has seen several leading issues that have tended to define US policy.

Within this context, the US approach to the Middle East has been multi-layered and has employed a spectrum of policy instruments to achieve the USA's interests and implement its policies. These include various diplomatic, political and economic measures and strategic and military means. The provision of US economic and technical aid and military assistance has become an increasingly prominent instrument of the USA in the Middle East.

The overall role of the USA in the supply of arms to Middle Eastern regimes changed in the period following the October War (or Yom Kippur War) of 1967—a 19-day armed conflict fought between Israel and a coalition of Arab states led by Egypt and the Syrian Arab Republic. The USA became more extensively involved, not only through the provision of military equipment to Israel but also through the sale of increasingly sophisticated equipment to existing Arab clients as well as to new Arab customers, such as Egypt, which moved from the Soviet sphere to that of the USA. In the post-1990 period, the overall scale of US arms sales increased dramatically. Saudi Arabia has become the most significant military customer and has exerted its influence militarily, most notably in declaring war on the al-Houthi rebels in Yemen in March 2015 (see Saudi Arabia and Yemen).

Over time, with the rise of Islamist terrorist groups from the 1990s, the so-called Arab Spring revolutions in the early 2010s, deteriorating economic conditions and an increasingly militarized environment, US policymaking has shifted from the luxurious situation of being able to make clear-cut decisions for the better (at least as far as US interests are concerned), to that of often being forced to opt for the lesser of two evils.

US POLICY IN THE MIDDLE EAST UNTIL 1990

US leaders have traditionally had a good sense of knowing who their friends and enemies are in the Middle East. Furthermore, their goals in the region, if not always easily accomplished, were relatively straightforward. Unfortunately, this is no longer the case. Today there is considerable uncertainty about US interests and the willingness and ability of the country to pursue them, as in the past. Traditional US partners today are not as confident that they can count on US support. No consensus exists about how to deal with the complex mix of actors and forces now proliferating throughout the region. The situation has led many observers to conclude that the USA no longer has a Middle East strategy guiding its policy in the region. Although there is an element of truth in this assertion, the fact remains that the US strategy in place, especially since 1990, is not working. This development did not just begin with the US military presence, but has its roots in the USA's historic involvement in the region, which goes back many years.

US links with the Middle East did not develop significantly until the 20th century, and it was primarily in the period after the Second World War (1939–45) that the US role became substantial. In its earliest years, the USA had no official policy in the Middle East in the commonly accepted sense of the term. Throughout much of US history before the First World War (1914–18), and even later, US interests and involvement in the region were primarily private or commercial, involving non-political and non-strategic activities.

The Period Preceding the Second World War

US participation in the region expanded around the beginning of the 20th century, when the USA began to be concerned by international developments and altered its approach to several areas of the geopolitical arena, including the Middle East. The prime reason for the change was the outcome of the First World War, with the reconfiguration of centres of global political power and the creation and independence from colonial rule of many of the states of the area, amid the collapse of the Ottoman Empire in 1918. Although the USA was involved in some of the diplomatic discussions, the key arrangements were worked out by the British and the French.

In the inter-war period, the United Kingdom and France remained the predominant regional powers, although US activities increased somewhat. The USA did not have what might be called a formal Middle East policy during this period, however. Instead, US actions were undertaken more on an ad hoc basis, with their primary intent being to advance US private sector commercial activities in the region. In fact, the USA went to some lengths to avoid any entanglements that might necessitate longer-term commitments or obligations. The one exception in this regard was Palestine. President Woodrow Wilson expressed support for a Jewish homeland in Palestine as early as 1917, when the Balfour Declaration was made by the British Government, favouring the eventual creation of a Jewish state. However, that is about as far as it went. The USA made no concrete proposals either for financial assistance or direct involvement leading to the creation of a Jewish homeland in Palestine. Neither the US Congress nor the Executive was prepared to commit the USA to the Palestinian project, and indeed, as late as 1945 President Franklin D. Roosevelt had assured the Arabs that the USA would not intervene to decide the future of Palestine without consulting both the Jews and the Arabs in the region.

There were significant economic developments in the region in the inter-war period, with the USA's efforts being mainly confined to ensuring open access to the area so that US firms would not be at a commercial disadvantage to global competitors. Of the various commercial sectors available for US involvement, the oil industry became the most significant. In this arena, the US Government assisted companies and consortia in gaining access to the region. By the end of the Second World War, oil had become a primary US interest that loomed large in commercial and financial, if not political and strategic, calculations about the Middle East.

The Second World War forced the USA to take a more active role in the region. It precipitated a significant US physical presence, strategic involvement, and the formation of political and security policy. Although the role of the USA was secondary to the UK's, the USA did establish bases, supply depots, and transportation and communications links. Furthermore, during the war the USA stationed troops in the area (notably establishing an airbase in Dhahran, Saudi Arabia), concluded lend-lease agreements, and provided economic and technical assistance to allied countries, including Saudi Arabia, and, after it changed allegiance from the Axis powers to the Allied forces, to Iraq. Of US wartime concerns, among the most important was the supply of war material to the USSR through the Persian Gulf–Iran route. The Middle East provided a direct link to the USSR from territory under the control of the Allies. It was also during the Second World War that the focus of attention and activity of the Zionist movement, which was advocating for a Jewish state in Palestine, shifted from the British capital, London, to the US capital, Washington, DC.

Following the Second World War the economic potential of the Middle East region became apparent, and the increased US interest in the resources of the region, especially oil, added to the US assessment of the area's importance. The emergence of the USA as the dominant economic power after the war made it incumbent on the USA to assume a more significant role in the global economy, including the Middle East, with the dual objective of exploiting new markets and preventing the spread of Soviet communism.

Although initially after 1945 the USA had hoped to continue its reliance on the British and French proxies, the virtual withdrawal of the French from the Middle East (although not North Africa), and the diminution of British capability, worked to ensure the US assumption of responsibility in the region. At the start of the post-Second World War era, the USA did not have a precise or comprehensive plan for the area, although it did recognize the need to prevent local conflict that could escalate and involve extra-regional powers, potentially in a major international conflict.

The Truman Administration, 1945–53

Official US policy involvement in the Middle East began a few years after the end of the Second World War. Two significant developments at this time drew US attention to the region. The first centred on what later became known as 'the northern tier'. The USA sought to prevent hostile (mainly Soviet and communist) domination of Greece, Turkey (known as Türkiye from June 2022) and Iran. Waning British capability and political will brought the USA into Iran to shore up the shaky regime of the autocratic Shah, Muhammad Reza Pahlavi, through a series of bilateral arrangements, including the provision of economic and military assistance.

US involvement in Iran began with the stationing of US troops in that country during the Second World War. The US role at the time was to assist in the transfer of supplies to the USSR, as well as to protect Iranian oil assets. British and Soviet troops helped in this endeavour. After the war, the US presence continued as the US-Iranian alliance strengthened. It was at this point that the US tendency, for better or worse, to create 'special relationships' in the region began. Many of these relationships involved significant amounts of US foreign assistance. Over the years, these relationships have assisted the USA in maintaining regional stability. However, they have come at a high price financially and in limiting the ability of the USA to pursue a consistent regional strategy through standard diplomatic means. Also starting at that time was the US tendency to demonize individual countries whose actions appeared not to be in the USA's interests. This practice had the effect of making it impossible to co-operate with such regimes when at times their interests overlapped with those of the USA.

The second major post-war development was the end of the British Mandate in Palestine and the formation of the Israeli state. Immediately following the war, Palestine became a matter of concern for the USA and other powers interested in the Middle East, although no agreed position existed either in the USA or among US allies. It was only when the British indicated that they were no longer able to maintain their Mandate in Palestine and the obligations it entailed that the USA began to play a significant role in Palestine. Much of what transpired fell on the Administration of President Harry S. Truman, who first accepted the partition plan of the United Nations (UN) in November 1947 and then, in May 1948, recognized the establishment of Israel as a sovereign state, although in the subsequent war between Israel and its Arab neighbours the USA officially maintained an arms embargo against all belligerents; after an armistice was signed in 1949 between the two sides the USA was not involved in the ensuing negotiations.

The Eisenhower Administration, 1953–61

The Middle East policies of the Administration of Dwight D. Eisenhower were primarily responsive to individual events, rather than the implementation of a strategic vision for the region. The first such event occurred in 1953 with the overthrow of Mohammad Mussadeq as Prime Minister of Iran. Mussadeq, an ardent nationalist, had campaigned against US and British influence in Iranian domestic affairs, particularly as they concerned its economy, and, after becoming premier in 1951, oversaw the nationalization of the country's oil assets as a means to achieving economic independence. Although the details are controversial, President Eisenhower set in motion forces that eventually led to the ouster of the Mussadeq Government in August 1953, which, while staving off oil nationalization, cost popular Iranian goodwill towards the USA in the long term.

The second event occurred in 1956, with the British and French attack on Egypt following that country's nationalization of the Suez Canal (which had previously been under private, majority European ownership). Eisenhower did not come to the assistance of his European allies to help overturn the nationalization, as they had hoped, effectively ending the conflict in Egypt's favour.

Finally, in 1958 Eisenhower ordered the dispatch of US troops to Lebanon to prevent the overthrow of that country's Christian-led Government. The Eisenhower Administration reflected an increased willingness on the part of the USA to become involved in Middle Eastern affairs: to fill the void left by the declining presence of the UK and France, but more importantly to protect a broader set of US interests.

The Kennedy Administration, 1961–63

While President Eisenhower's Middle East policies were in line with those of his Republican Party at the time, those of his successor, John F. Kennedy, were consistent with the stance taken by the Democratic Party. In particular, President Kennedy was interested in strengthening the US relationship with Israel through increased financial and moral support, and he is considered to be the founder of the strategic military alliance with the Jewish state, ending the arms embargo that had been in place under the Eisenhower and Truman Administrations. Kennedy is also considered to have acquiesced in Israel's pursuit of building a nuclear arsenal with French technical assistance, apparently in contravention of the US policy of non-proliferation of atomic weapons. Furthermore, Kennedy attempted to move the USA away from viewing the region through a Cold War lens, as Eisenhower had done, where opposition to the USSR was the default position in policy making.

The Johnson Administration, 1963–69

As the Administration of Lyndon B. Johnson faced the ever-deepening US involvement in the war in Viet Nam, Middle East issues assumed a low priority until the Six-Day War of 1967. Fearing the involvement of the USSR in the Arab–Israeli conflict, President Johnson placed the US Mediterranean Sixth Fleet on alert to support Israel, instructing it to turn back from Gibraltar to the eastern Mediterranean, which prompted the deployment of the Soviet navy, raising the risk of a confrontation between the two major global powers. Johnson simultaneously pressurized the Jewish state to agree to a ceasefire and to consolidate its significant territorial gains.

The Nixon and Ford Administrations, 1969–77

The first direct involvement of the Administration of Richard Nixon (1969–74) in the Middle East came with the Yom Kippur war in 1973 when Egypt, Jordan and Syria attacked Israel to regain territories lost in the Six-Day War. On 19 October Nixon requested US $2,200m. from Congress to fund Israel's military response to the Arab threat. Israel fought back and was ready to launch a full-scale offensive when the USSR threatened to intervene and act 'unilaterally'. Nixon responded, first by putting US forces on alert, and second by convincing Israel to agree to a ceasefire. Nixon was not willing to risk a possible nuclear war with the USSR over a Middle East ally, however close US ties to Israel had now become. For their part, the Soviets, also not wanting to risk a nuclear exchange with the USA and unclear as to how far Nixon would be prepared to go in his defence of the Jewish state, withdrew their threat to intervene militarily on behalf of their Arab allies.

Following Nixon's positive support for Israel, the Organization of the Petroleum Exporting Countries (OPEC) imposed an oil embargo on the USA. Domestic oil prices in the USA consequently rose from about US $2.90 per barrel before the ban to more than $11 a barrel by January 1974. Disagreements among the OPEC countries on how long to impose the embargo eventually resulted in the lifting of the ban in March. However, high oil prices persisted in the USA and most of the important oil-consuming countries in the Western world, leading to temporary economic disruption.

Oil price increases, and the cost they imposed on the USA and other consumer countries, brought home the extent to which these states had become vulnerable to actions by Middle East countries, forcing them to view the region in a different light. However, in retrospect, the sharp increase in oil prices reflected fortuitous circumstances in the USA as much as OPEC market power. In mid-1973 the US economy was near full capacity, and many commodity prices other than oil were also rising rapidly. Furthermore, the US domestic oil industry at that time lacked excess capacity with which to replace imports. Under a more typical set of economic conditions in the USA, the embargo would have had much less of an effect.

The rapid escalation of oil prices triggered a recession in the USA and most of the advanced oil-importing countries. Although the USA considered forming a wheat cartel or even a food cartel, based on the model of OPEC, to break the oil producers' cartel, such considerations did not get past the planning stage. However, the USA and other major consumer countries did form a cartel of sorts in 1974: the International Energy Agency, located in Paris, France, which was charged with helping to ensure energy security for member nations.

The Carter Administration, 1977–81

The presidency of Jimmy Carter, coming after the Arab oil embargo, appeared more willing than previous Administrations to be involved in Middle East issues. The Administration's major accomplishment was the 1978 Camp David Peace Accord; the peace treaty consequently negotiated between Israel and its most powerful Arab neighbour, Egypt, in 1979 returned to Egypt the Sinai Peninsula, which had been occupied by Israel since 1967.

In addition to peace agreements, this was a period of increased US military assistance programmes for the region. The major programme at the time was the 1978 'package deal', under which F-5E fighter aircraft were delivered to Egypt and F-15 aircraft to Saudi Arabia; in addition, the number of F-15s previously pledged to Israel was increased. The agreements gave Egypt and Saudi Arabia greater access to sophisticated US weaponry. This increased access accelerated with the USA's decision in 1981 to allow Saudi Arabia to purchase a highly sophisticated airborne warning and control system aircraft (AWACS) and to enhance the capability of the previously delivered F-15s. These deals represented a significant turning point in the USA's role as arms provider in the Middle East and indicate a dramatic shift in US policy on sales to the Arab states in the region.

Despite unquestionable US largesse, it is debatable whether US foreign aid programmes for the region have been as effective as their advocates often argue. In an average year, the Middle East usually received at least one-third of US funds allocated to aid, even though poverty rates were much lower than in other parts of the developing world. Moreover, unforeseen social and political consequences of this US aid could have long-term effects on US security.

The most significant Middle East event during the Carter years was the Iranian Revolution and the establishment, on 1 April 1979, of the Islamic Republic in that country under Supreme Leader Ayatollah Ruhollah Khomeini. At the end of that year, 52 US diplomats and citizens were taken hostage for a period of 14 months.

Immediately after the hostage situation developed, the USA imposed economic sanctions on Iran for the first time in November 1979. These consisted mainly of freezing US $12,000m. of Iranian assets held in the USA and at US financial institutions overseas. Over time, additional sanctions would be imposed for a variety of reasons, including Iran's support of terrorism, notably terrorist acts perpetrated on behalf of Palestinians in Israel and the occupied territories, and the country's civil and military nuclear programmes. The Iran-Libya Sanctions Act enacted by the US Congress in 1995 would punish companies within US jurisdiction that invested more than $20m. in Iran's oil and gas sector. In the 1980s, during the period of Iranian attacks on merchant shipping, the Administration of Ronald Reagan would bar all imports from Iran, including oil, and prohibited arms exports to Iran. In 1995 the Administration of Bill Clinton would levy a total embargo on trade and investment with Iran.

The Reagan Administration, 1981–89

The Reagan presidency saw a general deterioration in US relations with the Middle East. Little or no progress was made in resolving the Israeli–Palestinian disputes. However, after initially condoning Israel's 1982 invasion of Lebanon, Reagan did eventually intervene to demand a ceasefire.

Violence in Lebanon, however, continued and a truck bomb nearly destroyed the US embassy in Beirut in April 1983, killing 63 people, including US diplomats and Lebanese civilians. Other bombings followed, eventually forcing Reagan to withdraw all US troops in early 1984 and much of the US diplomatic contingent from Lebanon, less than two years after the 1982 troop deployment.

The Reagan Administration suffered severe damage through its involvement in the Iran-Contra Affair in the mid-1980s. Hearings in Washington, DC, eventually documented the manner in which the Administration had, contrary to public statements and official government policy on negotiating with terrorists, made several deals with Iran. These transactions involved the selling of arms to the Iranian regime in exchange for the release of Western hostages in Iran and

Lebanon, and where Iranian payments assisted the Contra rebels fighting the pro-Soviet regime in Nicaragua.

The Reagan Administration also made several controversial decisions that profoundly affected the political dynamics of the Middle East and its relations with the West. First, it supported Israel's expanded settlement programme in the occupied Palestinian territories. Second, it actively supported Iraqi President Saddam Hussain in the 1980–88 Iran–Iraq war, giving the Iraqi leader the false impression that his actions in the region were without consequence. Saddam Hussain's stance against Iran was supported by both the USA and its allies, notably the UK and France.

Summing up US policy in the region from 1945 to 1990, the USA—except for limited military involvement in Iran (an attempted—and abortive—hostage rescue in April 1980) and Lebanon (in 1958 and again in the early 1980s)—used soft power to achieve its objectives in the region. In this regard, the USA's approach to the region stands in sharp contrast to the country's military deployment in Asia and Europe during that period. Instead of a military presence in the region, the USA relied on a series of local alliances with countries including the Gulf monarchies, Jordan, Morocco, Israel and, until 1979, with Iran. Israel enjoyed a string of victories over Soviet allies Egypt and Syria with US backing. The strategy was largely successful, eventually convincing Egyptian President Anwar Sadat to switch Egypt's allegiance during the mid-1970s from the USSR to the USA.

US POLICY IN THE MIDDLE EAST SINCE 1990

Towards the end of the 1980s, the USA began deviating from its Middle East strategy as Iraqi influence in the region rose. After supporting Iraq in the period after that country's invasion of Iran in 1980, the USA was forced to send troops to the region following Iraq's invasion of reliable US ally Kuwait in 1990 and the subsequent threat posed to the 'special relationship' with Saudi Arabia, which feared that Iraq had ambitions to seize oilfields within its own territory.

The George H. W. Bush Administration, 1989–93

In a move that is still not completely understood even today, Saddam Hussain invaded and took control of Kuwait on 2 August 1990. One theory holds that earlier in 1990, when Saddam Hussain had posited the idea of Iraq occupying Kuwait, the US ambassador to Iraq, April Glaspie, had responded by saying that the US Administration did not have an opinion on inter-Arab matters. Rightly or wrongly, Glaspie's message gave Iraq encouragement to believe that it could invade Kuwait without any US military response (against a backdrop of waning Soviet influence or threat of intervention, since the collapse of communism in Eastern Europe in the previous year, without any Soviet attempt to defend allied regimes). However, it was clear that the seizure of Kuwait presented two major concerns: the potential for damage to Saudi oilfields, and the possibility of Iraqi domination of a highly significant area of world oil production and reserves.

On 6 August 1990 King Fahd bin Abdulziz Al Sa'ud of Saudi Arabia formally requested US assistance and President Bush announced that the USA was committed to defending Saudi Arabia with its armed forces. Eventually, the USA formed a military coalition of some 30 countries, including most Arab states, with combined military forces swelling to more than half a million troops. A total of 18 additional countries provided humanitarian and economic aid. The liberation of Kuwait took only about six weeks, including a 38-day campaign of bombardment from the air that started in January 1991, followed by a ground war in February that lasted a matter of only four days, in which Saddam Hussain's forces were finally driven out of Kuwait and back towards Baghdad, the Iraqi capital.

The controversial decision by President Bush not actively to invade Iraq and overthrow Saddam Hussain has been the subject of fierce debate ever since 1991, with strong support both for and against his action. Given the firm conviction of US policymakers that the Iraqi people would rise up against the defeated Saddam Hussain and install a more stable regime, the decision appeared to make sense at the time. However, Bush's choice reflects another flaw in the USA's policymaking in the Middle East—a tendency to underestimate the tenacity and ruthlessness of its opponents in the region.

With President Bush's attention focused on the Iraq–Kuwait situation, Israel and the Palestinian territories received little official US attention, despite the start of the first Palestinian *intifada* (popular uprising) in 1987. Towards the end of his presidency, in late 1992, President Bush ordered a military intervention in Somalia, in support of a UN military and humanitarian operation intended to support an anti-famine programme arising from the ongoing civil war in that country. Some 25,000 US troops were involved. The action met with limited success and resulted in the deaths of 18 US soldiers in a battle in the Somali capital, Mogadishu, in October 1993. The incident prompted the withdrawal of the US contingent from the UN mission in March 1994 and led to a far more cautious approach to the deployment of US forces in the Middle East and other Muslim-majority countries by successor Administrations.

The Clinton Administration, 1993–2001

In sharp contrast to the assertiveness of the Bush Administration, most of the early involvement in the region of the successor Administration of President Bill Clinton focused on efforts to mediate a peace treaty between Jordan and Israel in 1994. Clinton also achieved diplomatic success, in the short term at least, through his efforts in concluding the 1993 Oslo Accords, which brought the first Palestinian *intifada* to an end and set Israel and the Palestinians on the so-called roadmap eventually to try to achieve a peaceful two-state solution to the impasse. The agreement also established the Palestinian (National) Authority (PA) and gave the Palestinians the right of limited self-determination in the occupied territories of the West Bank and Gaza Strip. The agreement additionally called on Israel to withdraw from the occupied territories. Unresolved issues included the right of Palestinian refugees to return to Israel, and the ongoing enlargement of Israeli settlements in the West Bank, which were considered illegal under international law. Also unresolved was the status of East Jerusalem, which was occupied by Israel but claimed by the Palestinians.

In a last-ditch effort to resolve these issues at the end of his presidency, Clinton organized a summit at Camp David, Maryland, USA in December 2000. Israeli Prime Minister Ehud Barak and Palestinian leader Yasser Arafat were in attendance, but the meeting failed and coincided with the second *intifada*, which had commenced in October of that year following a controversial visit by Barak's predecessor as premier, Ariel Sharon, to Temple Mount, the site of the revered al-Aqsa Mosque, in Jerusalem.

President Clinton also inherited a challenging situation in Iraq, where severe economic sanctions imposed by the UN Security Council in August 1993 were implemented to contain Saddam Hussain's regime and sustain a lengthy UN search for weapons of mass destruction (WMD). This policy of containment was continued throughout the Clinton Administration despite its evident failure, due to the lack of co-operation by Iraq's neighbours and the catastrophic toll of the sanctions on the Iraqi population, who lost the ability and will to rise up against the regime, preoccupied as they were with simply surviving, amid shortages of food, medicine and other essential items.

President Clinton signed the Iraq Liberation Act of 1998, making it 'the policy of the USA to seek to remove the Saddam Hussain regime from power in Iraq and to replace it with a democratic government.' This policy involved financial support for Iraqi opposition groups—US $97m. in military aid and several million dollars more in direct payments. Clinton also called on the UN to create an international criminal tribunal to indict and put on trial Saddam Hussain and his regime's senior officials for crimes against humanity.

This policy shift encouraged various Iraqi parties to visit Washington, DC, to present themselves as the legitimate spokespersons of the Iraqi people. Among these groups, a coalition of political operatives under the umbrella of the Iraqi National Congress, led by Ahmed Chalabi, rose to prominence. Chalabi and his associates welcomed the election of George W. Bush as President in November 2000 and the rise of a group of

US political appointees, notably in the Department of Defense, including Donald Rumsfeld, Paul Wolfowitz and Richard Perle, who had been advocating the ouster of Saddam Hussain's regime for several years.

The George W. Bush Administration, 2001–09

Following the terrorist attacks on New York and Washington, DC, in September 2001, which were attributed to the Islamist al-Qa'ida organization, recently elected President George W. Bush had almost unanimous worldwide support when he ordered an attack in October on Afghanistan against the Taliban regime, which he claimed had offered al-Qa'ida protection while the group was planning its attacks on the USA. George W. Bush's subsequent decision to invade Iraq in 2003, without seeking the assent of the UN Security Council, in order to topple Saddam Hussain as part of the so-called 'war on terror' mustered considerably less backing. According to George W. Bush's vision for the region, the removal of Saddam Hussain would initiate the start of a virtuous circle of reforms, leading to greater democracy in the Middle East. Bush also saw the creation of a strong democratic Iraq as the cornerstone against further instability in the Middle East, with Iraq as a vital ally, along with Saudi Arabia, in countering the threat posed by Shi'a Iran, an implacable enemy of Israel, and, as the 21st century progressed, also of the Sunni Gulf monarchies.

Despite the Iraqi regime falling within weeks of the US-led coalition's invasion in March 2003, and the capture of Saddam Hussain in December (he was put on trial in October 2005, and found guilty and executed in 2006), by the end of 2006 few of Bush's objectives had been fulfilled, and the chances of them ever being met were growing slim, as Iraq had descended into a vicious sectarian war, with the Sunni minority that had prospered under Saddam Hussain fighting the hitherto oppressed Shi'a majority, while an insurgency raged against the occupying US army and its allies. The US Administration had undertaken numerous shifts in strategy and policy since the invasion of 2003, but all proved ineffective in stimulating the economy and bringing peace and stability to Iraq.

In May 2003 the USA expanded its ambitions from quickly putting in place an appointed government in Iraq to imposing a longer-term military occupation. In November it reversed course and abruptly transferred authority to a provisional government. In 2004 it adjusted its military approach to focus more on building up the Iraqi Security Forces (ISF). In 2005 the US ambassador to Iraq, Zalmay Khalilzad, urged the application of 'focused stabilization'—namely co-ordinating military and civilian authorities to stabilize key Iraqi cities. In early 2006 the Administration's emphasis had shifted to the 'Battle for Baghdad', accompanied by a recognition that sectarian militias fighting each other posed as significant a danger to the future of Iraq as Sunni insurgents fighting the occupying forces. By that time US forces had adapted their training and tactics with little success.

From April 2003 to the end of 2006 US expectations about the ability and desire of Iraqi politicians to compromise and arrive at a peace deal were repeatedly disappointed, and Washington's timelines for the transition of local and provincial security to the ISF often experienced delays. The inescapable facts were that the security situation was deteriorating, the Iraqi provisional government was failing to improve its ability to deliver essential services, and Iraq's political factions had been unable to start a meaningful process of political reconciliation.

Several reasons explain the US failure to bring peace or stable governance to Iraq after the removal of Saddam Hussain. These range from an underfunded military effort, including the dispatch to the country of insufficient numbers of personnel immediately after the initial invasion, to the handling of the insurgency that gained ground soon after the overthrow of Saddam Hussain. There is an element of truth in these strategy-based explanations, but other factors, including the US approach to jump-starting the economy, also played a significant role.

While President George W. Bush hoped that Iraq would herald the start of a democratic revolution in the Arab world, others in Washington, DC, wanted to show how the right set of economic policies might have a more significant effect on the region's future. By introducing what had become known as the 'Washington Consensus' of neoliberal reforms, many in the George W. Bush Administration believed that the type of economic boom that had occurred in Chile in the mid-1970s (after the coup that removed a socialist regime and replaced it with a US-backed right-wing military junta) could quickly revitalize the economy and be a template for others in the region wishing to stimulate the most dysfunctional economies. In fact, even well before the invasion of Iraq, interest had been growing in Washington, DC, to find the means to achieve high, sustained rates of economic expansion in a region that for years had been lagging behind other parts of the developing world.

For many critical advisers in the George W. Bush Administration, Iraq represented a test case for whether the USA could create a system of US-style free market capitalism in the Middle East. In an address in February 2003 President George W. Bush spoke of 'a new Arab charter that champions internal reform, greater political participation, economic openness and free trade.' A new democratic government in Iraq, he added, 'would serve as a dramatic and inspiring example of freedom for other nations in the region.'

Unfortunately, although the neoliberal model to which Bush alluded might apply to a developed economy with stable governing, judicial and civic institutions, its introduction into post-Saddam Iraq was severely flawed. In their haste, US officials in the governing Coalition Provisional Authority pushed ahead with many free market reforms despite the absence of critical supporting institutions, such as a sound legal system for enforcing and respecting contracts. Also absent was a functioning financial authority to finance an expanding manufacturing sector. The neoliberal model relies on a surge in private investment to take advantage of the opportunities to make profits by allowing prices to be set by the market, and the laws of supply and demand. However, so soon after the US invasion there were very few Iraqis with capital to invest, or the skills needed to function in a modern capitalist economic system.

Towards the end of the George W. Bush presidency, anti-Americanism was on the increase. Middle Eastern and European governments and many other countries in Latin America, Asia and Africa formed an increasingly negative image of the USA in general and President George W. Bush in particular. The rise in anti-Americanism began at the start of the Bush Administration and worsened significantly after the US-led invasion of Iraq. By March 2007 a survey by the British Broadcasting Corporation of some 28,000 people in 27 countries found that only Israel, Iran and the Democratic People's Republic of Korea (North Korea) scored below the USA in terms of being considered to exert a negative influence on global affairs. President George W. Bush received an approval rating of only 8%–20% among the populations of the USA's Muslim allies Pakistan, Egypt and Indonesia. In the UK—a country that was a longstanding ally of the USA and an active supporter of the Iraqi invasion under Prime Minister Tony Blair—only 30% expressed confidence in President George W. Bush. In Germany and France (two other longstanding allies), this figure fell dramatically, to 25% and 15%, respectively. The most substantial decline occurred in fellow North Atlantic Treaty Organization (NATO) member state Turkey, where the share of those surveyed who expressed confidence in Bush dropped to a mere 3%.

In summary, the George W. Bush Administration largely failed to accomplish its objectives in the Middle East region. In addition to numerous policy errors, its credibility was also undermined by inconsistencies. This is exemplified by the case of Iraq in 2005–06. Even as the Administration pursued democratization in that country, it conspicuously avoided criticizing the Saudi regime on the same issue, or on the issue of ensuring fundamental human rights. Furthermore, the George W. Bush Administration encouraged Egypt to hold free and fair multi-party elections in 2005 but then failed to protest against the serious flaws and abuses that took place in the conduct of the polls, which gave an overwhelming majority to the party of President Hosni Mubarak. Such contradictions, as well as Bush's choosing not to make the Israeli–Palestinian conflict a priority until late into his Administration, and even then allowing the Israeli military to operate with near impunity in its assaults on southern Lebanon in mid-2006 and Gaza in late 2008–early 2009, undermined the US President's credibility and squandered his political capital.

The Obama Administration, 2009–17

Upon assuming office in January 2009, President Barack Obama put US Middle East policy on a distinctly different path from that of his predecessor. Some changes simply reflected a different vision for the region, which presupposed that regimes and societies should reform themselves, with Western support, rather than Western imposition, while others stemmed from the fact that Obama lacked the freedom to pursue the type of comprehensive transformational policy that George W. Bush had been free to adopt after the terrorist attacks of September 2001. Instead, his agenda consisted primarily of modest, near-term goals.

However, in order to demonstrate that the region was a high priority on his agenda, Obama announced a series of significant actions. First, he appointed former Senate majority leader George Mitchell as his special Middle East envoy. Second, Obama announced that the majority of US military personnel stationed in Iraq would be withdrawn by mid-2010. Third, he attempted to seek a rapprochement with Syria, and fourth, he toned down US rhetoric towards Iran. These actions suggested that Obama intended to reshape the US approach to the Middle East, amid high expectations, following a speech delivered in the Egyptian capital Cairo, in June 2009, titled 'A New Beginning', in which he called for improved understanding and relations between the West and the Islamic world. To the surprise of many, Obama appeared to side with the Palestinians by recognizing their desire for statehood. Obama's receipt of the Nobel Prize for Peace in late 2009 only added to the pressure on him to follow through with tangible achievements in the Middle East.

Statements early on in Obama's Administration suggested that he had selected four key goals to accomplish in the region. First and foremost among these was preserving gains in Iraq after several years of increasing instability. George W. Bush had succeeded in achieving significant security gains in Iraq, giving Obama the opportunity rapidly to reduce US troop numbers. The challenge facing Obama was one of winding down military operations and withdrawing US forces without jeopardizing Iraqi stability.

The second challenge facing Obama was Iran. In sharp contrast to the George W. Bush Administration, Obama accepted the fact that a policy advocating 'regime change' only provided ammunition for the right-wing elements in Iran to push harder for an expanded nuclear programme.

The third priority area involved restarting the Israeli-Palestinian peace process. Here Obama faced significant difficulties, given the Israeli assault on Gaza in late 2008–early 2009 and the increasing political sway of the Israeli right in that country's Government. By the time Obama took office, the Israeli–Palestinian conflict had reached a level of acrimony not witnessed for several decades. Even worse, the two sides appeared to believe that they had nothing to gain through further negotiation.

Finally, Obama wanted to restore US credibility in the region as much as possible. Obama and his advisers concluded that one reason for Bush's ineffectiveness in the region was his high level of unpopularity among most of the region's citizens. In this environment, co-operation with the USA was difficult, even though many agreed with the goals that Obama had set out upon coming to office and his likely courses of action.

Given Obama's goals and the extent and intensity of the region's problems, there was no way that he could avoid difficult choices and severe criticism for decisions made (or not made). None the less, at the start of his Administration, there were some promising signs that lessons had been learned from the George W. Bush years.

Compared with Bush's ideological perspective, Obama tended to approach policy issues with more of an analytical framework, preferring to see a variety of opinions rather than just those from a small group of advisers. Obama's early decisions also showed a more profound grasp of the interconnected nature of many of the region's problems, especially the influence of the Israeli–Palestinian conflict, as well as the problems between Sunni and Shi'a Islam. Finally, he was more inclined than Bush to use US soft power when needed, rather than seeking a military option as the default position.

These attributes were visible in the Administration's efforts to engage with Syria and tentative discussions with Iran concerning positive measures that it could take in Afghanistan and Iraq to improve security.

However, Obama's approach towards the region and his style of policymaking faced resistance from many Middle Eastern regimes, particularly the Gulf monarchies, such as the conservative ruling elite in Saudi Arabia. These regimes had supported George W. Bush's decision to overthrow Saddam Hussain and adopt a hard line against Iran. As a result, a number of them expressed concern over the Obama agenda, which sought to involve Iran and its regional allies, such as Syria and the Lebanese Shi'a group Hezbollah. Furthermore, several countries in the region perceived Obama as weak, due to his apparent preference for the use of diplomacy over military action.

In summary, at the start of the Obama Administration, it appeared that the US Government would not make the same mistakes that had resulted in George W. Bush's regional policy setbacks. It was unclear, however, whether Obama's approach would be so excessively cautious and risk-averse as to preclude any significant policy breakthroughs.

The Obama Administration faced one of its greatest challenges in January 2011 in the form of the beginning of a series of Middle East uprisings and regime changes commonly referred to as the Arab Spring, notably in Egypt, where long-time US ally President Mubarak was subsequently removed from office, creating enormous uncertainty over the future of that country and its relationship with Israel. For the recently installed Obama, the challenge was to find a consistent strategy that balanced the USA's national interests, democratic and humanitarian ideals, and the needs of its Middle East allies—a difficult task under any circumstances.

The Obama Administration's response contended that change in the Middle East 'would be determined by its people' and that such change 'is not something that we should fear'. Both statements generated intense criticism at home and abroad, pleasing few, particularly in Washington, DC. US liberals argued that the Administration had hesitated when it most mattered, being a latecomer to the democratic transitions in Tunisia and Egypt, an accomplice to repression in Bahrain, and embracing a 'no-fly zone' too late to avert chaos in Libya. Similarly, neoconservatives argued that Obama failed to lead, weakening US authority in a vital region. Some neoconservatives went so far as to claim that Iran or jihadist groups would fill the vacuum left by the USA and its allied regimes in the Middle East.

However, those subscribing to a realist approach to international relations, emphasizing the importance of policies that would preserve the existing balance of power, complained that the President's embrace of anti-regime protesters in countries where the Arab Spring was taking place sacrificed real US interests for fanciful goals. They suggested that the USA had little ability to change regional politics, and that the Administration's actions—taken to satisfy a domestic US audience—did little but alienate longstanding allies.

Friction with Israel was present throughout the term of the Obama Administration. The primary areas of the dispute were Israeli settlements in the occupied West Bank and the status of Jerusalem (where Israel occupied the whole of the city and considered it its undivided capital, while the Palestinians lived under Israeli occupation in East Jerusalem and also claimed the whole of the city as their capital).

No Middle East policy challenged the Obama Administration more than the USA's relationship with Iran and its potential to produce nuclear weapons. The USA's fear was that Iran's refusal to suspend its uranium enrichment programme, as required by UN Security Council resolutions, could spark increased tensions and open conflict at any time. Obama's stated and implied policy objectives suggested that achieving a lasting solution to the Iranian nuclear question was his highest priority during his second term.

The first Obama Administration (2009–13) was marked by an initial attempt to engage Iranian officials in dialogue, followed by three years of co-ordinating tighter economic sanctions against Iran. The leading champions of these sanctions were Secretary of State Hillary Clinton and Secretary of Defense Robert Gates. The goal of the sanctions was to change the internal calculus of Iranian officials and convince them that achieving an accommodation with the USA was better for Iran than enduring increasingly acute economic penalties.

Over the years, the more stringent sanctions inflicted considerable stress on Iran's economy but failed to induce a change in the Iranian regime's strategic calculus. None the less, Obama believed that tougher sanctions would strengthen its negotiating position vis-à-vis Iran. He announced his readiness to pursue aggressive diplomacy with Iran when the conditions were right, and this began to occur in the early years of his second term, from 2013.

At this time there were indications that Iran might be more willing to negotiate. The sanctions were working, and the broader strategic environment in the Middle East, including the slow-motion collapse of Iran's key regional ally in Syria, suggested that the regime would be increasingly inclined to reduce the risks to its survival—including through engagement with the USA.

The greatest obstacle continued to be Iran's long-held position that sanctions should be eased or eliminated before it took any significant action regarding its nuclear agenda. Iranian officials routinely stated that they could not be expected to negotiate under the threat of economic sanctions or military force.

The Obama Administration's position emphasized that sanctions relief would occur after Iran revealed the full extent of its past nuclear activities and complied with requirements to suspend its nuclear enrichment programme. The US position was determined, in part, by the reality that once removed, international sanctions would be hard—if not impossible—to re-impose.

In retrospect, Obama's assumptions and strategy proved the correct approach. In July 2015, after a marathon 18 months of negotiations, Iran and six major powers (three member states of the European Union (EU)—France, Germany and the UK—plus the three other permanent UN Security Council members—the People's Republic of China, the Russian Federation and the USA—collectively known as the E3/EU+3) agreed on the parameters of the Joint Comprehensive Plan of Action (JCPOA), a deal that limited Iran's nuclear programme to civilian and energy use, in exchange for sanctions relief.

In the final year of the Obama Administration, in 2016, Middle East priorities included reducing opposition within the region to the nuclear deal with Iran, securing greater commitments for the fight against the fundamentalist Islamic State group, and ending the Saudi-led campaign against the al-Houthi rebels in Yemen. At the same time, President Obama had to reassure friendly Gulf countries that earlier statements suggesting that the USA was about to make a 'pivot to Asia', together with closer engagement with Iran, did not signify an abandonment of their interests.

Obama's policies in the Middle East elicited a mixed response, with both strong advocates and detractors of his positions. Those who supported the Obama approach to the region noted that his Administration showed that the USA need not play as active a role in pursuit of longstanding regional interests as under his predecessors, such as guaranteeing Israel's security; countering the proliferation of WMDs; preventing the spread and entrenchment of jihadist groups; and maintaining steady shipments of hydrocarbons from the Gulf. However, Obama's critics claimed that his Administration's failure to intervene in the Middle East more stridently allowed the rise of Islamic State to threaten the wider region and export jihadist terrorism to the West, while allowing other actors to play a more significant role in the region, such as Russia with its military campaign to shore up the regime of Syrian President Bashar al-Assad; or Iran with its support for Shi'a allies and militia in Iraq, Lebanon, Syria, Bahrain and Yemen.

THE TRUMP ADMINISTRATION, 2017–21

Donald Trump's election as US President in late 2016 raised a series of questions concerning US policy in the Middle East. Would his Administration continue or break away from past policies? During the election campaign, Trump found fault with many aspects of US foreign policy. These included the USA's role as the provider of global security and the promotion of human rights and democracy around the world. These attitudes applied to the Middle East, as well. However, there is often little resemblance between what US politicians say in campaigns and what they do once elected.

What candidate Trump did say about the Middle East was often uninformed and inconsistent. He was highly critical of previous US Administrations, without elaboration on how previous US policies had fallen short of expectations. He described Iraq's invasion as 'a terrible thing', but then criticized President Obama as foolish for withdrawing troops from the country 'without finishing the job' or seizing the country's oil. Meanwhile, Trump characterized the Iran nuclear agreement as 'one of the worst deals in the history of our country'. As for Israel, Trump believed that the Obama Administration had treated the country 'very, very badly'. To members of the Washington foreign policy establishment, the Trump Administration's regional policies were ones of neglect and confusion. Others characterized the USA's strategy under Trump as childish, dangerous and corrupt. More cynical observers questioned whether the Trump Administration even had a Middle East policy.

Officially, the Administration's stated goals for the Middle East included containing Iran's influence, which Trump believed to be the most significant threat to US interests in the region. The Administration's second goal was the elimination of the militant Islamist group Islamic State in Syria and Iraq. The third was achieving a peace agreement between Israel and the Palestinians. However, it was unclear whether the Trump Administration's goal was the establishment of sustained peace in the region or merely to facilitate Israel's alliance with the USA, Saudi Arabia and the United Arab Emirates (UAE) in confronting Iran. As events played out, it became apparent that there were significant inconsistencies within the Administration's three paramount goals for the region.

The Administration's Iran policy started with the JCPOA signed in July 2015 by the E3/EU+3 countries and Iran regarding the latter's nuclear weapons capability development. As a candidate, Trump promised to 'rip up' the agreement. However, after taking office, Trump initially reversed this position, promising strict enforcement instead; in other words, a continuation of Obama-era policy. The JCPOA was meant to reintegrate Iran into the international community, whereby the country could play a constructive rather than belligerent role. Trump reversed his position again in May 2018 by pulling the USA out of the agreement, taking the USA back to looking at Iran from a containment perspective but not appearing to have a strategy for proceeding, other than tightening economic sanctions, and perhaps encouraging a regime change.

During the presidential campaign, Trump also criticized Obama for failing to defeat Islamic State, claiming that the Administration had been too involved in some areas of the Middle East and not enough in others that were more critical to the USA's direct interests. Here the Trump Administration intensified Obama-era strategies with greater resolve and direct involvement. However, following the defeats suffered by Islamic State at its headquarters in Raqqa (Syria) and Mosul (Iraq), the Trump Administration announced that it was formally suspending US military support for Kurdish-led Syrian rebels, the USA's main allies in the fight against Islamic State.

The third major Trump policy initiative involved the reaching of a peace agreement between the Palestinians and Israel. Since the signing of the Oslo Accords in 1993 and 1995, there has been a convergence of viewpoints among international actors toward a two-state solution. A two-state solution has been the USA's official position since the Administration of George H. W. Bush. However, over the subsequent years, the issue of illegal Israeli settlements in the West Bank has prevented the achievement of a final, definitive agreement between the Palestinians and the Israelis. As a candidate, Trump campaigned on reversing critical aspects of US policy in this regard. Furthermore, he promised to move the US embassy in Israel from Tel Aviv to Jerusalem, a longstanding goal of pro-Israel groups in Washington, DC. During his Administration's first year, Trump's position seemed open to whatever the two parties wanted.

In December 2017 the Administration's decision to act on Trump's promise to move the US embassy to Jerusalem provoked outrage throughout the region. To the Palestinians and most Arab governments, the decision provided clear evidence that the USA was no longer interested in a two-state solution and lasting peace between Israel and the Palestinians. The USA also lost any reputation that it might have had for being an honest broker in the region.

A final area of Middle East policy concerns efforts, starting with the George W. Bush Administration, to promote democracy in the region. However, in practice, this goal was always conditional. Although in theory the USA favoured improved democracy, it was under the condition that it did not undermine higher priorities such as the 'war on terror', the security of Israel or the flow of arms to allied regimes in the Gulf and the flow of oil out of them onto global markets.

As a candidate and as President, Trump failed to show any interest in promoting democracy or human rights in the Middle East. He praised Saudi Arabia and Egypt's authoritarian leaders, while refraining from expressing any criticism of alleged human rights violations. Although this approach may have been disappointing, compared with the Obama Administration's aspirations, it did not represent a significant deviation from past US policy over the long term.

Despite the announcement in March 2019 of the defeat of Islamic State, the group remained a severe threat to stability in Iraq and Syria, as well as in countries outside the region such as Afghanistan, Sri Lanka and Indonesia. The Trump Administration injected further uncertainty by breaking with international consensus, and law, in recognizing Israel's sovereignty over the Golan Heights.

The Trump Administration's policies toward Iran also produced little in the way of achieving its stated objectives of regime change or of that country renouncing its nuclear ambitions. After withdrawing the USA from the JCPOA in May 2018, Trump continued to ratchet up sanctions severely to restrict the Iranian economy and thus attempt to bring about regime change. Although the harsh economic sanctions dealt a blow to the Iranian economy, other nations continued to trade with Iran, including buying its oil. As in the past, sanctions were more of a uniting than dividing force among Iranians and strengthened the influence of Iranian hardliners.

During the negotiations that led to the JCPOA, Russia, China and Iran argued for the immediate lifting of a UN arms embargo that had been imposed on the Islamic Republic in 2005, but the USA insisted that it remain in place until 2020. The ban prohibited Iran from importing major military items such as fighter jets and naval vessels and from exporting any weaponry. In 2020 the Trump Administration pointed to Iran's violations of the JCPOA and its transfer of arms to non-state actors in Yemen and Iraq as justification for keeping the arms embargo in place. However, as most UN Security Council members were determined to save the JCPOA, the USA found little support when it circulated a draft resolution in June to extend the arms embargo on Iran indefinitely, even though Iran's regional transfers of weaponry were widely deplored.

The Trump Administration formally placed the draft resolution to extend the arms embargo on Iran on the agenda of the UN Security Council in late 2020. It was hoped that the timing of this action would help President Trump's re-election bid, as an extension of the embargo had bipartisan support in the US Congress. Even though the effort failed, Washington threatened to push for a full 'snapback' of all UN sanctions lifted under the JCPOA: if Trump's Democratic rival and the eventual victor in the presidential election held in November, former Vice-President Joe Biden, opposed this, he risked appearing 'soft' in terms of his policy towards Iran.

European states expressed their opposition to any US attempt to trigger the so-called snapback of UN sanctions that were lifted under the JCPOA. The legal basis for such an attempt was highly contentious because the USA was no longer a party to the 2015 accord. UN Security Council Resolution 2231 was carefully drafted to allow any JCPOA party to trigger renewed sanctions without a Security Council vote or option of imposing a veto. The US Administration argued that it still had the authority to invoke the clause, as the Resolution identified the eligible states (including the USA) by name, rather than merely as signatories. Iran vowed to end participation in the JCPOA if any country acted to reimpose UN sanctions, although it was not expected to react to a unilateral US declaration to do so.

By late 2019 the USA was no longer viewed as a credible interlocutor between Israelis and Palestinians, and as the possibility of a long-envisioned two-state solution receded, relations between the two sides continued to worsen. Questionable acts such as moving the US embassy from Tel Aviv to Jerusalem, cutting aid to the PA and closing its office in Washington, DC, led to despair and regular outbreaks of violence in Gaza and the West Bank.

The Trump Administration found that its foreign policy initiatives in the Middle East were often out of step with regional realities and that its insistence on 'America First' was not practical in today's globalized and transnational world, where the nation state is only one of many actors. Trump's inclination not to send troops to the Middle East and to reduce US involvement in the region found widespread support at home from a public weary of decades of engagement, expense and casualties. However, with a reduced footprint on the ground, the USA needed to find a way to work with Middle Eastern states and Europe, Russia and China—in addition to the UN and other international organizations—to achieve the policy results that it wanted. Unfortunately, most observers in the region saw no sign of meaningful movement in this direction. Whether this perception was correct or not was no longer the point.

Finally, a US-sponsored agreement between Israel and the UAE, along with Bahrain, to normalize diplomatic relations, was signed on 15 September 2020. In the agreement, Israel pledged to suspend its plans to annex parts of the West Bank in return for the full normalization of relations with the two Gulf Arab states. The agreement, officially titled the 'Abraham Accords', was hailed by some observers as a geopolitical game changer. In fact, it recognized and formalized political shifts that had been under way for more than a decade. In the 12 months preceding the signing of the agreement, US Secretary of State Mike Pompeo and Trump's Senior Advisor and son-in-law, Jared Kushner, visited a number of Arab countries, with the aim of pushing other regional governments towards recognizing Israel. Sudan and Oman were widely seen as the most likely candidates to do so; although neither country had publicly expressed interest in changing their stance towards Israel, they both congratulated Bahrain and the UAE on the Abraham Accords.

While the Accords called for an unspecified, 'just, comprehensive, realistic' Israeli-Palestinian solution, the President of the PA, Mahmoud Abbas, warned that they would not bring peace to the region while the USA and Israel failed to recognize Palestinian statehood rights. The Accords mentioned the Palestinian issue only in very general terms in their preamble, and the Israeli commitment to suspend potential West Bank annexations as a quid pro quo for Emirati diplomatic recognition was nowhere formally enshrined, although US pressure was reportedly aimed at blocking annexation until at least 2024.

THE BIDEN ADMINISTRATION, 2021–

Although the Administration of Joe Biden was slow to articulate a coherent Middle East policy, elements of his policies towards the region were coming into focus by early 2022. However, it isn't easy to assess the soundness of the Administration's approach. Should the basis of comparison be with the catholic Trump years? Or should it be with the more conventional approaches adopted by Democratic Administrations such as Obama's? Is Biden charting an alternative course for the USA or simply updating the standard set of decades-old policies? Does the Biden Administration aim to preserve the status quo or to move towards a 'post-American' era? Is Biden pursuing a long-term strategy of US disengagement from the

Middle East, or is his approach simply one of pragmatism in responding to threats to US interests in the region?

It is easier to say what the Biden approach is not than to articulate an explicit statement of its goals. The overriding theme that runs through the Biden approach toward the region is that for decades the USA has made too many commitments and promises that it has not delivered. Nor does the Biden Administration subscribe to the goals of transforming the Middle East through regime change or democratization. It is also not as willing as some past Administrations to strike bargains with authoritarian regimes. Regarding Iran, the Biden Administration has shifted from Trump's failed, heavy-handed approach to one of negotiation over the country's nuclear programme.

None the less, the Administration subscribes to the fundamental goals that have defined US policy in the region over the years. These include Israel's security, protecting vital waterways, especially those used to transport oil, and preventing outside powers (notably China and Russia) from gaining a strategic foothold. While traditional goals such as promoting democracy and human rights are still important, to the chagrin of liberals in the Democratic Party, they are not at the elevated levels often found in previous Administrations.

The conflict that erupted between Israel and Hamas, an Islamist armed group that controls Gaza, on 10 May 2021 was the first major foreign policy test of Biden's presidency. On 18 May he called for a ceasefire, but only after several days of intense fighting. The USA even blocked several UN Security Council resolutions calling for a truce. During this period, Biden attracted harsh criticism from some fellow Democrats for his slow response to the crisis. Several liberal Democrats urged Biden to pressure Israel towards a ceasefire, especially in light of the conflict's high civilian death toll.

Although President Biden himself has long been regarded as friendly to Israel, he has not tackled the Israeli–Palestinian conflict directly. However, some policy changes from the Trump era have been instigated. In April 2021 the Biden Administration announced that it was to resume sending aid to a UN programme directed at Palestinian refugees that had been ended by Trump. Earlier that year the Administration also suggested that it had no objection to reopening the Palestine Liberation Organization mission in Washington, DC, which Trump closed in 2018. However, any significant revision to US policy, such as reviewing recognition of Israel's sovereignty over the Golan Heights, remains unlikely. Biden's hesitancy to act against Israel stems from observing previous US Administrations consumed by the Israeli–Palestinian conflict. He has no wish to repeat that experience.

Under Biden, the USA has maintained Israel as a close strategic ally. Nevertheless, policy differences have made for a somewhat more fractious relationship, even though not all Trump-era actions have been reversed. The USA has continued to provide Israel with close strategic and military support, despite the fact that policy differences have caused more vocal criticism from both sides. In other areas, several signs suggest a shifting US policy toward long-term allies Saudi Arabia and Egypt. US relations with these countries are cooler, with the Biden Administration's foreign policy focusing more on promoting human rights and democracy.

On 4 February 2021, during his first foreign policy speech, President Biden announced the end of US support for Saudi Arabia's operations in Yemen, including 'relevant' arms sales. Later that month he also officially removed the designation of the Iranian-backed al-Houthi rebel movement as a foreign terrorist organization. Moreover, in comparison with the Trump presidency, which had worked closely with Saudi Crown Prince Mohammed bin Salman bin Abdulaziz Al Sa'ud, President Biden's first call to Saudi Arabia was somewhat delayed, and when it did take place, it was with King Salman, a signal that the Biden Administration intended to keep the Crown Prince at a distance. That said, the US response to the release of a classified intelligence report indicating that Crown Prince Mohammed bin Salman had approved the 2018 murder of US-based Saudi dissident journalist Jamal Khashoggi at the Saudi consulate in İstanbul, Türkiye, was, at its core, pragmatic. While imposing visa bans on 76 Saudi citizens under the new 'Khashoggi Policy', the USA did not take any action against the Crown Prince himself.

The USA stressed that it would focus on the 'future conduct' of Saudi Arabia to encourage Riyadh to improve its human rights record. Meanwhile, Saudi Arabia has taken several steps to appease Biden's Administration, ending its long-standing feud with Qatar (another US ally in the region) and releasing several prominent prisoners. Concerning Egypt, in the weeks leading up to the US presidential election in November 2020, Biden posted on social network Twitter that there would be 'no more blank checks for Trump's "favorite dictator"' (in reference to Egyptian President Abd al-Fatah al-Sisi). However, despite little progress made by Egypt in improving human rights, the Biden Administration still approved a US $200m. missile sale in February 2021, with the announcement coming just days after the Egyptian Government detained family members of US-based Egyptian-American human rights activist Mohamed Soltan. Thus, although US-Egyptian relations have, at times, been frosty, co-operation has remained robust.

Before Biden's inauguration, most observers held that the USA was likely to rejoin the Iran nuclear deal in 2021. Biden indicated that Iran must fully comply with the JCPOA before the resumption of talks and ruled out lifting sanctions to get Iran back to the negotiating table. Nevertheless, Iran stated that it remained up to the USA to compromise, as it was the USA that had pulled out of the agreement. Following a series of back-and-forth skirmishes between the two sides, by mid-2020 a draft agreement on a return to mutual compliance had virtually been completed, although one major issue remained outstanding. Iran demanded that the USA remove the Islamic Revolutionary Guard Corps (IRGC) from its list of foreign terrorist organizations. The Biden Administration has steadfastly refused to do so without a reciprocal gesture being made by Iran. Neither Iran nor the USA appears willing to back down, and the issue's binary nature makes compromise difficult. However, there is the threat of significant uncertainties and risks if the JCPOA collapses, and no party wants to be blamed for failure. As of mid-2023, therefore, it appeared likely that the fate of the agreement would remain in limbo, with no breakthroughs being made in negotiations in the short term, but no decisive collapse either.

Relations with Saudi Arabia remain a significant challenge for the Biden Administration. In an interview in March 2022, Crown Prince Mohammed bin Salman stated that he wished to maintain and strengthen ties with the USA. However, he went on to say that Saudi Arabia refused to respond to US pressure to increase its oil output in order to bring down elevated oil prices stemming from Russia's invasion of Ukraine in February. Furthermore, the Crown Prince obliquely threatened to reduce Saudi investment in the USA (currently totalling around US $800,000m.) and stated that he was seeking closer relations with Iran.

Two factors drove the tone of the interview. First, Crown Prince Salman wanted Biden to recognize that he was the kingdom's de facto ruler. Unlike his predecessor, Trump, Biden had, as of that date, refused to talk directly with the Crown Prince, instead dealing with the 86-year-old King Salman. Second, the Crown Prince wanted Biden to follow Trump's lead in supporting Saudi involvement in the civil war in Yemen. In the short term, relations between the USA and Saudi Arabia were expected to be dictated by whether Saudi boosted its oil production. In the longer term, the personal factor involved would likely continue to lead to periodic tensions.

By June 2022 high oil prices had become a key policy priority for the Biden Administration, with his domestic popularity declining ahead of crucial mid-term elections in November. This reality had prompted the USA to lobby for OPEC+ to raise oil production over and above the increments agreed in late 2021. OPEC+ (led by Saudi Arabia) had initially resisted US pleas and demands for higher-than-planned production, but acquiesced in early June 2022. At that time, the organization agreed to raise output by 648,000 barrels/day (b/d) in July and August. In addition, increased supplies could be made available in subsequent months to help ease international energy price pressures.

The agreement by OPEC+ to depart from its previous production schedule was viewed by some as the possible beginning of a breakthrough in relations leading to greater co-operation from Saudi Arabia and other countries such as the UAE as the sanctions imposed on Russia reduced oil output from that country. OPEC+'s decision to increase oil supplies risked breaking the organization's highly valued six-year pact with Russia. None the less, Saudi Arabia had shown willingness to do so before when its greater interests dictated such action (it launched an oil price war with Russia in March 2020), and whatever the current tensions, its relationship with the USA remained far more critical.

Also in June 2022, the Biden Administration announced that it was upgrading its diplomatic mission to the Palestinians, located within the US embassy to Israel in Jerusalem, in order to improve its line of communications with the PA. The Palestinian Affairs Unit (PAU) was redesignated as the US Office of Palestinian Affairs and was now able to deal directly with the US Department of State rather than via the US ambassador to Israel, as previously. However, the Administration failed to carry out the repeated promise of US Secretary of State Antony Blinken that it would reopen the US consulate for Palestinians in Jerusalem, which Trump had closed in 2018. The diplomatic upgrade of the PAU indicated that Biden aimed to establish closer relations with the PA despite the ongoing tensions between Israel and the Palestinians. Direct communications would allow the US Department of State to have separate channels of discourse with both sides. Nevertheless, the US Administration's failure to reopen the consulate disappointed Palestinians, who remained unconvinced that the USA was an 'honest broker' in the Israeli–Palestinian conflict.

The Biden Administration is under considerable pressure to conduct a comprehensive US Middle East policy evaluation. In light of disastrous outcomes in Iraq and Afghanistan, many in the USA feel the country to be overextended, particularly if more government resources are needed to counter China, support Ukraine's efforts against Russia, recover from the COVID-19 pandemic and repair the sorry state of US infrastructure. In this context, the US Middle East policy costs more than it is worth. Politically, events in Afghanistan (where the Taliban seized power in August 2021, following Biden's decision to withdraw the remaining US troops from the country) provide an opportunity to go back to basics and undertake a fresh analysis of US Middle East policy.

The established author and Middle Eastern analyst Gary Sick notes that in such a review, one objective worth considering is whether and how the USA might contribute to a self-regulating regional balance of power. In his words: 'Is there really a grave danger that one regional state will dominate all the others? Are regional states powerless to prevent such an outcome? Must we lie awake nights worrying that one or more regional states will refuse to sell their oil? Will one or more of them mount a sustained and effective attack against energy lines of communication? Is the extensive US military presence making things better or worse?'

The answers to these questions are already coming into focus. The US withdrawal from Afghanistan does not in itself indicate a change in direction for US foreign policy. Instead, the Afghanistan case suggests that US foreign policy is becoming more overtly pragmatic in its aims. The sense in Washington is that the USA cannot win a war in the Middle East, and that any control or influence that the USA wishes to retain there will have to be through non-military means.

The realities of the Biden Administration's Middle East policy were made evident during the President's first official visit to the region in July 2022. While he was in Israel, brief mention was made of issues that had consumed previous administrations. Differences between the USA and Israel over Iran and the Palestinians received scant attention. Rather than maintaining the semblance of being an honest broker between Israel and the Palestinians, Biden's focus was on obtaining Saudi permission for Israeli flights over Saudi Arabia's airspace.

On the Saudi leg of Biden's trip, there was little sign of his promise as both a candidate in 2020 and since taking office that he would treat Saudi Arabia as a 'pariah' because of the country's human rights record and its role in the murder of Khashoggi in October 2018. President Biden is not the first US President to formulate a Middle East policy centred on values and human rights. He is also not the first to backtrack on such a promise when it conflicts with US interests.

Biden's election pledge to ostracize Saudi Crown Prince Mohammed bin Salman, and his decision to release a Central Intelligence Agency (CIA) report implicating bin Salman in the murder of Khashoggi in 2018, only reinforced the perception that the White House would prefer another member of the Al Sa'ud family to lead the kingdom. As has historically been the case, primary among US interests in the region is maintaining stability in global energy markets. With soaring fuel prices in the USA as a result of the Western sanctions against Russia, Biden has come under growing pressure to persuade the Saudi authorities to increase oil production and ease global markets. Biden's reversal underscores the fact that condemning the Saudi Government involved costs—and that interests still trump values in the USA's engagement with the Middle East.

Biden visit to Saudi Arabia in July 2022 was undertaken in an attempt to improve US-Saudi relations. However, the President failed to achieve the oil- and security-related goals sought by his Administration. Instead, Saudi Arabia reaffirmed that it would abide by it OPEC+ commitments and would, thus, not immediately start pumping more oil. In addition, during Biden's visit to the Middle East, no agreement was reached on a regional security arrangement (involving Israel) to counter Iran. Furthermore, Saudi Arabia would not commit to seeking formal normalization with Israel. Finally, the Gulf states did not commit to reducing ties with Russia and China.

By September 2022 efforts to revive the Iran nuclear deal had shifted dramatically since March, when an agreement had appeared almost inevitable. Subsequent events, including the escalating war in Ukraine, had hampered co-operation. At the same time, the Biden Administration and some European signatories to the JCPOA were reluctant to accede to Iran's latest core demands, including binding a future US government to adhere to the agreement to stop it from reneging on the deal, as had happened under Trump, and the cancellation of the International Atomic Energy Agency's investigation into historical allegations about Iran's nuclear programme. In addition, President Biden was wary of the talks becoming a political liability in the November mid-term elections. Unless the situation changes dramatically, as of mid-2023 it appeared that a new deal would not be reached under the Biden Administration.

In March 2023 tensions between the USA and Israel flared up when President Biden criticized proposed Israeli judicial reforms in unusually frank terms and denied reported plans to invite Israeli Prime Minister Benjamin Netanyahu to the White House. Netanyahu, in turn, rebuffed Biden, sharply reasserting Israel's sovereignty and rejection of foreign pressure.

US engagement in Libya increased in early 2023, with the aim of countering Russian influence and removing mercenaries belonging to the Wagner Group (a Russian private paramilitary company) from the country. On 20–21 March US Assistant Secretary of State for Near Eastern Affairs, Barbara Leaf, held a meeting with representatives of the rival east- and west-based Libyan governments. Discussions with the commander of the east-based Libyan National Army (LNA), Khalifa Haftar, specifically focused on foreign fighters and the US Administration's decision to designate the Wagner Group as a transnational criminal organization.

However, the USA has few local allies in Libya to support its efforts to tackle Russia's presence there. Unlike in Ukraine, in Libya the USA is unable to rely on regional allies or NATO members to consolidate its position. Divisions exist among US allies regarding their support for the factions in Libya—Italy and France have backed different sides, as have, at various points, the UAE, Egypt, Türkiye and Qatar. The importance of keeping Libya's oil flowing has also meant that the military option is unviable, given potential damage to oil infrastructure. Moreover, the various Libyan factions are not capable of dealing with the Wagner Group militarily. Acknowledging that a military solution would be challenging, the Biden

Administration is therefore re-engaging in the Libyan political process in an attempt to limit Russia's political capital, including through unifying the international community's stance and rallying behind the UN plan to facilitate the holding of elections in Libya in 2023.

On 10 March 2023 China brokered a ground-breaking agreement between traditional adversaries Saudi Arabia and Iran to restore bilateral diplomatic relations, hosting a follow-up meeting of the two countries' foreign affairs ministers in the Chinese capital, Beijing, on 6 April, bypassing the USA. In the following month Saudi Arabia restored diplomatic ties with Syria and brokered its return to the Arab League, despite US opposition. After the Arab League agreed to readmit Syria as a member, the Biden Administration indicated that it did not support its allies normalizing ties with Syria. The latter's readmittance to the Arab bloc came amid a wave of rapprochements and a new regional emphasis on multipolarity. A number of the USA's allies, including the Gulf states, Israel and Egypt, have signalled that they do not share the USA's worldview of strategic rivalry with China and Russia.

Despite the long-awaited shift towards a 'post-American' order, the pace and goals of the Biden Administration in the Middle East remain unclear, and the approach taken is increasingly often reactionary and piecemeal. Correspondingly, there is growing uncertainty over US objectives in the region. After considerable delay, the Biden Administration released a new National Security Strategy (NSS) on 12 October 2022. The NSS states that the Administration is seeking to balance the strategic challenges of great power rivalry and the transnational threats that affect US security and prosperity. Russia's aggression in Ukraine has increased its perceived level of threat, compared with the level documented in the interim NSS published in March 2021, but China continues to pose the most significant challenges to US interests.

Because of the primary emphasis on China and secondary concerns about Russia, the Indo-Pacific and Europe are the key strategic areas for the USA. Other regions, including the Middle East, receive less attention, being broadly lumped together under an overarching theme of the need to 'revitalize' or 'renew' partnerships, promote economic resilience and support the spread of stable democracies—although without specific details being given on how these goals are going to be achieved.

For the remainder of the Biden Administration, the US policy engagement in the Middle East will likely take the form of low-key technocratic co-ordination across various security and defence issues. A muted approach will further reinforce perceptions of US disengagement, even if the reality is actually far less clear-cut. The muted US response to the flurry of meetings between China, Saudi Arabia and Iran and even to the reintegration of Syria into the Arab fold may partly reflect a sense that the USA is losing agency in the region and has far less ability to set the agenda.

Over the next 10 years or so, the USA will determine whether it can maintain a consistent foreign policy approach to the region across multiple Administrations. If the approach does not remain consistent, Washington's present-day correction will be one of many pendulum swings that will render it a powerful, if disruptive, pole in a multipolar regional landscape. However, looking at the current state of US policy in mid-2023, the approach appears to be one of pursuing solidly plausible, median outcomes. There are no dreams of transformation here, no pretence of spreading democracy or fostering greater human rights. Instead, in order to prevent being viewed as inattentive in the Middle East and as weak or incompetent in Washington owing to setbacks, the Biden Administration's policy will involve establishing modest goals for the region while simultaneously preparing for stumbling blocks.

SELECT BIBLIOGRAPHY

Barnes, Joe, and Barron, Robert, 'Trump Policy in the Middle East', *Baker Institute*, 29 January 2018. www.bakerinstitute.org/research/trump-policy-middle-east-iran.

Eriksson, Jacob. 'Master of None: Trump, Jerusalem and the Prospects of Israeli-Palestinian Peace', *Middle East Policy*, XXV 2, Summer 2018, pp. 51–63.

Feierstein, Gerald. 'Trump's Middle East Policy at One Year: Policy Lacks Strategic Coherence Despite Rhetoric', *Middle East Institute*, March 2018. www.mei.edu/content/trumps-middle-east-policy-one-year.

Gunter, Frank. *The Political Economy of Iraq: Restoring Balance in a Post-Conflict Society*. Cheltenham, Edward Elgar, 2013.

Indyk, Martin S. 'A Trump Doctrine for the Middle East', *Brookings Institution*, 16 April 2018. www.brookings.edu/blog/order-from-chaos/2018/04/16/a-trump-doctrine-for-the-middle-east.

Iran Sanctions. Washington Congressional Research Service, 22 February 2022.

Karlin, Mara and Cofman Wittes, Tamara. 'America's Middle East Purgatory: The Case for Doing Less', *Foreign Affairs*, January/February 2019. www.foreignaffairs.com/articles/middle-east/2018-12-11/americas-middle-east-purgatory?-cid=otr-authors-january_february_2019-121118.

Looney, Robert (Ed.). *Handbook of US-Middle East Relations*. London, Routledge, 2009.

Lynch, Marc. 'Belligerent Minimalism: The Trump Administration and the Middle East', *The Washington Quarterly*, Vol. 39, No. 4, pp. 127–144, 2016.

Oualaalou, David S. *The Ambiguous Foreign Policy of the United States toward the Muslim World*. New York, NY, Lexington Books, 2016.

Silverburg, Sanford, and Reich, Bernard. *United States Foreign Policy and the Middle East/North Africa*. Third edition, London, Routledge, 2016.

Snow, Donald. *The Middle East, Oil, and the U.S. National Security Policy: Intractable Conflicts, Impossible Solutions*. New York, NY, Rowman & Littlefield, 2016.

Thépaut, Charles. *A Vanishing West in the Middle East: The Recent History of US-Europe Cooperation in the Region*. Washington, DC, The Washington Institute for Near East Policy, Bloomsbury Publishing, 2022.

THE KURDISH QUESTION IN THE MIDDLE EAST

CENGIZ GUNES

Revised for this edition by LIAM ANDERSON

INTRODUCTION

The history of the Kurdish question in the Middle East is a long and complex one. Divided among the states of Iraq, Iran, the Syrian Arab Republic and Türkiye (as Turkey was redesignated in June 2022), the Kurds constitute one of the largest 'nations' in the world without their own state. The Kurds have a long presence in the region they populate, and their origin is often traced back to the ancient Medes who inhabited the mountainous area in north-western Iran and rose to prominence in the 7th century CE after they helped to overthrow the Assyrian Empire. The rise of the Ottoman Empire from the early 16th century onwards following the demise of the Abbasid Empire resulted in a military contest between the Ottoman and Persian Empires, and a large part of Kurdish-populated territory came under the rule of the Ottomans after the Battle of Chaldiran in August 1514. The Ottoman authorities adopted a policy of accommodation and a decentralized political system to win the support of Kurdish emirates and enlist them in dealing with the threat posed by the Persian Empire. Between the 16th and 18th centuries Kurdistan remained a borderland between the Ottoman and Persian Empires and the site of their long geopolitical competition, which prevented both the national unification of Kurdish-populated areas and consolidation of Kurdish political structures in the region.

The expansion of state authority into Kurdish territories during the early 19th century resulted in the elimination of the autonomy that the Kurdish emirates had held. The changes in the international relations of the region—particularly the end of hostility and establishment of a border between the Ottoman and Persian Empires after the signing of the Treaty of Erzurum in 1823 and the growing influence of Russia and the United Kingdom—ended the favourable conditions that had enabled the Kurdish emirates to flourish. The Kurdish emirates did not surrender their autonomy willingly and resisted the Ottoman forces in revolts during the 1840s, but ultimately they could not preserve their status. Once the political structures that could have evolved into a centre of Kurdish power were eliminated, the Kurdish regions remained deeply fragmented.

In the second half of the 19th century religious elites rose to prominence and began to act as the leaders of the Kurdish population. In particular, Sufi orders such as the *Naqshbandiyya* and *Qadiriyya* began to play a more important role in the social and political life of the Kurds. Furthermore, a number of Kurdish individuals rose to prominence in the Ottoman Empire's bureaucracy and attempts were made to establish organizations that campaigned for the development of Kurdish society and raised Kurdish national consciousness. However, efforts to organize a Kurdish movement and work towards the establishment of a Kurdish state were interrupted by the First World War. Small-scale Kurdish revolts took place in Iran, Iraq and Türkiye between 1918 and 1922, and Kurdish attempts to represent their interests and demands at the international conferences held by the dominant international powers to decide the future of the collapsing Ottoman Empire did not succeed. Initially a consensus on the establishment of Kurdish autonomy in Türkiye was reached under the Treaty of Sèvres, which was signed in August 1920 by the victorious Allied powers and had the aim of partitioning the remaining territory of the Ottoman Empire. The Treaty of Sèvres was never implemented, however, and in July 1923 it was replaced by the Treaty of Lausanne, which neither mentioned Kurdish autonomy nor offered a path towards the establishment of a Kurdish state, leaving the Kurds as a marginalized minority in the states of Iraq, Iran, Syria and Türkiye.

Accurate census data on the Kurdish population does not exist and the exact number of Kurds in the Middle East is unknown. Furthermore, estimating the Kurdish population is a contentious issue, with nation states tending to underestimate the size of their Kurdish population in order to downplay their demands, while Kurdish nationalists tend to overestimate their numbers. However, it is generally agreed that the Kurds constitute some 20% of the population of Iraq and Türkiye, and 10% of Iran and Syria, and the Kurdish population across the region is estimated to be around 35m. According to this estimate, nearly one-half of the Kurds in the region live in Türkiye, where the Kurdish population is estimated to be around 16m. The Kurdish population in Iraq is estimated at 7m. and those in Iran and Syria at 8m. and 2m., respectively. There is a large Kurdish diaspora in Europe, Lebanon and the southern states of the former Union of Soviet Socialist Republics (USSR), whose population is estimated at around 2m.

In Iraq the Kurds constitute the majority of the population in the governorates of Duhok, Irbil (Arbil/Erbil) and al-Sulaimaniya, and large Kurdish communities can also be found in the Iraqi capital city of Baghdad and in the governorates of al-Ta'meem (Kirkuk), Nineveh and Diyala. In Iran the Kurdish population is mainly concentrated in the north-western corner of the country in the provinces of Kurdistan, Ilam, Kerman and West Azerbaijan along the borders with Iraq and Türkiye. There are also pockets of Kurdish population in north-eastern Iran in the historic region of Khorasan. In Syria the Kurdish population is concentrated in the north-eastern and north-western regions, and large Kurdish communities existed before the Syrian civil war in Aleppo and the capital, Damascus. In Türkiye the Kurds' historic homeland is in the south-eastern and eastern regions of the country and currently around 80% or more of the population of the following provinces is Kurdish: Adıyaman, Ağrı, Batman, Bingöl, Bitlis, Diyarbakır, Hakkari, Mardin, Muş, Şanlıurfa, Siirt, Şırnak, Tunceli and Van. A significant number of Kurds populate the adjacent area of provinces including Elazığ, Erzurum, Gaziantep, Kahramanmaraş and Malatya. There are pockets of Kurdish population in central Anatolia and many Kurds have migrated to southern and western Türkiye since the 1950s for economic reasons. From the late 1980s until the early 2000s, with the intensification of conflict in the Kurdish-majority regions, many rural Kurds were forced by the army and security forces out of their villages and hamlets and settled in western and southern Türkiye.

The main Kurdish languages are Kurmanji and Sorani. Kurmanji is spoken mainly in Türkiye and Syria, but also in parts of Iraq and Iran. Sorani is spoken in Iraq and Iran and is the language of education in the semi-autonomous Kurdistan region of northern Iraq (the Kurdish Autonomous Region). In addition, a section of the Kurdish population in Türkiye, perhaps as many as 2m., speaks Zazaki or Dimili. The majority of Kurds follow the Sunni school of Islam, with a minority in Iraq and Iran being followers of the Shi'a school of Islam. A small number of adherents of minority religions, such as Alevis, Yazidis and Ahl-e Haqq, also exist.

THE KURDISH QUESTION IN IRAQ

Following the defeat of the Ottoman empire in the First World War, the Ottoman provinces of Baghdad, Basra and Mosul came under the control of British forces and in 1920 the state of Iraq was created under British mandate. As early as 1919 the region witnessed the first Kurdish revolt for greater recognition of Kurdish rights, under the leadership of Sheikh Mahmud, who was the Governor of Sulaimaniya. The British forces suppressed the revolt and exiled Sheikh Mahmud to India, but in order to end the subsequent unrest and re-establish order, Sheikh Mahmud was reinstated in 1922. Sheikh Mahmud subsequently continued his activities to establish a Kurdish kingdom until his headquarters were destroyed in 1924.

During the 1930s several Kurdish political and cultural publications appeared in Iraq and more determined attempts at political organization by the Kurds were made. In 1940 a new nationalist organization, called Hiwa (Hope), was established and in 1943 Mullah Mustafa Barzani organized a revolt against Iraqi rule, which was put down in 1945 with the help of the British air force. Barzani escaped to Iran, where he took part in the establishment of the Republic of Kurdistan in Mahabad in north-western Iran in December 1945. However, when Soviet troops were withdrawn from Iran in May 1946 and all external support for the Kurdish republic was severed, Barzani went into exile in the USSR and remained there until the overthrow of the Iraqi monarchy by Gen. Abd al-Karim Qasim in a *coup d'état* in July 1958. In Barzani's absence, Kurdish nationalist activities continued underground but there was an instant revival upon his return. Barzani subsequently established himself as a key figure in the Kurdish struggle in Iraq and became the leader of the Partiya Demokrat a Kurdistanê (KDP—Kurdistan Democratic Party).

The early years of Qasim's rule witnessed growing Kurdish cultural and political activism, but he soon began to target the political activities of the Kurdish movement. In March 1961 Barzani informed the Iraqi Government of the demand for greater Kurdish autonomy but this demand was flatly rejected by Qasim. In September 1961 the Iraqi army attacked the Kurdish regions; the Kurds organized a resistance movement and set up a government to administer the territories under their control. In February 1964 a ceasefire was agreed that lasted until 1965 when the second phase of armed conflict began. After the Baathist coup of 1968 Saddam Hussein was appointed as the Vice-President of Iraq and the conflict between the Kurdish forces and the Iraqi army continued until secret negotiations resulted in an autonomy agreement in March 1970.

The autonomy agreement recognized the Kurdish language as an official language of Iraq and the right to provide education in Kurdish in the majority Kurdish areas. It promised to provide state support for the development of Kurdish language and culture, to adopt policies to promote the development of Kurdish regions, to commit to the Kurds' full participation in the country's politics and administration and to lift the restrictions that blocked the development of Kurdish civil society organizations. Attempts were made to implement the agreement, but the Iraqi Government opposed the key Kurdish demand of the inclusion of the Kirkuk governorate within the Kurdish autonomous region, and the plan faltered.

In March 1974 an alternative 'take it or leave it' autonomy offer with significantly reduced terms was made by the Iraqi Government but refused by Barzani, leading to the resumption of armed conflict in 1974. The Iraqi army made territorial gains in the mountainous terrain of northern Iraq and Kurdish forces were unable to prevent the progress of Iraqi armed forces. The Kurdish position was further weakened by the signing of the Algiers Agreement between Iraq and Iran in March 1975, which resulted in Iran ending its military support for the Kurdish forces in exchange for Iraqi concessions in the territorial dispute in the Persian Gulf between the two states. Initially the KDP leadership took the decision to continue the insurgency but later in March it decided to end the insurgency and its forces withdrew to Iran.

A significant section of the KDP's leadership was in favour of continuing the resistance and it began to establish new political organizations. The most significant of these groups was the Yekîtiya Nîştimanî ya Kurdistanê (PUK—Patriotic Union of Kurdistan), which was established in June 1975 in Damascus under the leadership of Jalal Talabani and united the groups that had broken away from the KDP, such as the left-wing Komala Party of Iranian Kurdistan (commonly shortened to Komala), which was led by Nawshirwan Mustafa, and the Kurdistan Socialist Movement, led by Ali Askari. From May 1976 the KDP began to re-establish its presence in the Kurdish regions of Iraq. The initially tense relations that existed between the KDP and the PUK soon led to the outbreak of violence in mid-1976.

The Iran–Iraq War that broke out in 1980 offered Kurdish parties more room for manoeuvre and impetus in their attempts to re-establish their presence in Iraqi Kurdistan. With the reduced presence of the Iraqi army in the Kurdish regions, both the PUK and the KDP were able to increase their activities and exploit the war between Iran and Iraq to their advantage. The KDP leadership was based in Iran and began to receive military aid and logistical support from the Iranian state. During the 1980s the PUK managed to establish a strong support base in Sulaimaniya and Kirkuk governorates and developed a left-wing political discourse. The KDP continued to receive military support and money from Iran during 1979 and the early 1980s. The PUK was initially allied with Syria then signed a ceasefire agreement with the Iraqi Government in October 1983. From October 1986 the PUK began to form an alliance with Iran and to develop closer ties with the KDP.

During the mid-1980s the Iraqi state intensified its campaign to bring Kurdish-controlled areas under its control, adopted a policy of 'Arabization' and initiated the Anfal Campaign, which involved destruction of the traditional Kurdish rural economy and infrastructure, the forced displacement of rural Kurdish communities, the summary executions of Kurdish nationalist activists and forced disappearances of others. In total some 4,000 villages were destroyed and around 182,000 people were killed, according to Kurdish sources. According to the estimates of the US non-governmental organization Human Rights Watch, as many as 100,000 people, many of them women and children, lost their life during the Anfal Campaign. The chemical attack on the town of Halabja on 16 March 1988 alone killed an estimated 5,000 Kurds.

Iraq's unexpected invasion of Kuwait in August 1990 and the ensuing international condemnation and US-led invasion of Iraq in January 1991 brought further instability to the region. After US forces succeeded in expelling the Iraqi army from Kuwait in February, Kurdish Iraqis in the north of the country and Shi'a Iraqis in the south were encouraged by the US victors to rise up against Saddam's rule. An uprising on 1 March in Iraq's south soon spread to central and northern Iraq. On 5 March a popular uprising (known locally as *Raparin* in Sorani Kurdish) took place in the town of Ranya in Sulaimaniya governorate and culminated in Kurdish *peshmerga* fighters taking control of the town. On the following day the popular uprising spread to the main cities of the region, Irbil and Sulaimaniya. However, shortly afterwards the Iraqi military regrouped and began to suppress the uprising, which resulted in a massive exodus of Kurds in March–April. Türkiye refused to take in the Kurdish civilians and in order to prevent a humanitarian disaster, on 5 April the United Nations (UN) Security Council adopted resolution 688 and began implementing a 'no-fly zone' in northern and southern Iraq. This UN action proved to be a significant development in the history of the Kurds and enabled them to establish their de facto autonomy in 1991.

The consolidation of Kurdish autonomy was not straightforward, however, and in the mid-1990s the region witnessed a violent conflict between militias allied to the KDP and the PUK, with the KDP driven out of the regional capital, Irbil. The KDP forces sought the support of the Iraqi army and took back Irbil in August 1996, and subsequently two separate Kurdish administrations came into being, with the KDP controlling Duhok and Irbil governorates and the PUK controlling Sulaimaniya governorate. The invasion of Iraq in March 2003 by US and British forces, the subsequent ouster of President Saddam Hussein and the chain of events triggered by those developments had a major effect on the fortunes of the Kurds in Iraq. In 2005 Kurdish autonomy came to be recognized as part of Iraq's new governmental structure and Kurds managed to secure some of the key political positions in the Iraqi state, including the presidency and foreign ministry.

The new Iraq that came into being was conceived of as a federal state. The areas under the Kurdish administration came to be recognized as the 'region of Kurdistan' (article 117 of the new Iraqi Constitution, which came in effect in December 2005) and the Kurdish language was constitutionally recognized as one of the two official languages of Iraq (article 4). As citizens of Iraq, Kurds are represented in federal-level institutions including the Council of Representatives, Iraq's legislative body. The Kurdish Autonomous Region has control over and responsibility for its own internal security and the organization of its police and security forces, and its own military forces, the *peshmerga*, are outside the command of the Iraqi military forces. However, some of the Kurdish-majority areas, including the oil-rich city of Kirkuk, remained outside of the Kurdish Autonomous Region and the final status of these 'disputed' territories was to be decided at a referendum. Article 140 of the Constitution makes provisions for such a referendum to be held, but for various reasons the referendum has not yet been held. Following an offensive in August 2014 (see below) in northern Iraq by the Salafi fundamentalist militant group Islamic State (which had been known until June of that year as Islamic State in Iraq and the Levant), the disputed territories fell under the control of Kurdish *peshmerga* forces.

A number of developments during the 2010s exposed the weaknesses of the Kurdish autonomy model in Iraq. The issue of the exploitation and management of natural resources of the Kurdish Autonomous Region became a major source of disagreement between the Kurdistan Regional Government (KRG) and the Iraqi federal Government. In October 2011 the KRG reached an agreement with the US petroleum company ExxonMobil to produce and sell oil independent of the Iraqi federal Government. Similar agreements were reached in July 2012 with US oil company Chevron and French oil company Total. The steps the KRG took to increase its economic autonomy have been interpreted as unilateral and unconstitutional by the federal Government in Baghdad, which in turn suspended federal budget payments to the KRG in 2014. More recently, in 2017 the Russian state-owned oil company Rosneft began operating in the Kurdish Autonomous Region in the areas of oil exploration and the development of infrastructure for the eventual export of oil.

The Kurdish Autonomous Region's inability to consolidate its military forces under one central command structure has proved a major weakness, which became apparent at the beginning of 2014, when Islamic State attacked Nineveh and Kirkuk governorates and increasingly targeted the Kurdish controlled or populated territories. On 1 August Islamic State began to take control of the territory formerly controlled by the Kurdish forces, including the towns of Zumar and Sinjar. Islamic State came as far as the towns of Gwer and Makhmour in Nineveh governorate and came within 40 km of reaching the Kurdish Autonomous Region's capital city, Irbil, causing widespread panic among its population. Islamic State attacks in Sinjar and surrounding areas against the Yazidi Kurds in early August resulted in a humanitarian crisis.

The KRG and the Iraqi federal Government's inability to reach an agreement on the final status of the disputed territories led to the Kurdish Autonomous Region holding a referendum on its independence on 25 September 2017, at which, according to the Independent High Elections and Referendum Commission, 92.7% of those who took part cast a vote in favour of independence; the reported turnout was 72.2%.

However, due to the opposition of the Iraqi federal Government and regional and international powers, the KRG reversed its decision of pursuing independence. In mid-October 2017 the Iraqi army and allied Shi'a militias attacked and took back control of the disputed territories that were held by the Kurds, including the oil-rich city of Kirkuk.

On 29 October 2017, before the full impact of losing Kirkuk and other disputed territories could be absorbed, Masoud Barzani announced that he would stand down from the Kurdish presidency on 1 November; he none the less retained the presidency of the KDP and, consequently, remained influential within that party. The KDP won a narrow victory in parliamentary elections in the Kurdish Autonomous Region in September 2018, gaining 45 seats in the 111-seat chamber. In December the party nominated Masrour Barzani, the son of Masoud Barzani, as the new Prime Minister of the KRG. In June 2019, as widely expected, but following months of negotiations between the KDP and the other parties represented in the legislature, the outgoing Prime Minister of the KRG (and nephew of Masoud Barzani) Nechirvan Barzani was elected by the regional legislature as the new Kurdish President. Masrour Barzani was sworn in as Prime Minister in July.

Meanwhile, the KDP performed well in the Iraqi parliamentary elections held on 12 May 2018, obtaining 25 seats in the enlarged, 329-seat Council of Representatives. The PUK secured 18 seats. A former Prime Minister of the Kurdish Autonomous Region, Barham Salih, was elected as the President of Iraq on 2 October 2018. Following the elections of 2018 and the formation of its new Government in July 2019, relations between the Kurdish Autonomous Region and the Iraqi federal Government appeared to be in the process of normalization. However, mass protests by mainly young people began in Iraq from October 2019, leading to the resignation of Prime Minister Adil Abd al-Mahdi and the fall of his Government in November 2019 (see Iraq). The continued protests, compounded by the social and economic effects of the coronavirus disease (COVID-19) pandemic, hampered the ability of politicians to govern the country. Although the protests did not spread into the Kurdish Autonomous Region, the instability of Iraqi governance adversely affected the Region. A new Baghdad Government, under the leadership of former head of the intelligence services, Mustafa al-Kadhimi, eventually emerged with the support of the Kurdish political parties in May 2020. However, whether this new administration would be able effectively to address the myriad issues complicating relations between the Kurdish Autonomous Region and the Iraqi federal Government remained to be seen.

Frequent rocket attacks targeted the Kurdish Autonomous Region's critical infrastructure, such as Irbil International Airport, during 2020–21. These attacks were attributed to a predominantly Shi'a group of militias known as the Popular Mobilization Units (PMU—or Hashd al-Shaabi). The KRG's failure to pay civil servants' salaries precipitated protests in December 2020, with the police taking harsh measures to disperse the demonstrators. In several towns, angry protesters set fire to KDP and PUK offices and government buildings, and in total 150 attacks took place across the Sulaimaniya governorate.

Several rounds of negotiations between the federal Government and the KRG took place during March 2021, and a deal was eventually reached on 28 March. Media reports suggested that the KRG's share of the federal budget was set at 12.7%. As part of the agreement, the KRG was to transfer the revenue from the sale of at least 250,000 barrels of oil per day. Around 50% of non-oil income received by the KRG would also be handed over to the federal Government, and the KRG would start to repay a loan of ID 5,000,000m. (US $3,400m.) from the Trade Bank of Iraq.

The issue of media freedom in the Kurdish Autonomous Region attracted international attention in 2021. On 16 February a court in Irbil sentenced journalists Sherwan Sherwani, Guhdar Zebari, Hariwan Issa, Ayaz Karam and Shvan Saeed to six years in prison. The KRG claimed the journalists were convicted because they had gathered declassified information and passed it to foreign agents in exchange for payments. However, lawyers defending the journalists reported many irregularities during the trial and described the evidence used to secure the conviction as 'insufficient and baseless'. The journalists had been detained due to their critical coverage of the protests, the KRG's management of its budget and the failure to pay civil servants' salaries. On 28 April the Kurdish Autonomous Region's Court of Cassation upheld the six-year prison sentences, rejecting the defendants' claims of ill-treatment during detention, and irregularities during the trial. The human rights organization Amnesty International issued an 'Urgent Action' urging the Kurdish Autonomous Region authorities to release all the defendants immediately. In June the Court of Cassation again confirmed the prison sentences imposed on the five journalists.

Tensions between forces of the Partiya Karkerên Kurdistanê (PKK—Kurdistan Workers' Party—see below) and the KDP also dominated the politics of the Kurdish Autonomous Region from mid-2020 onwards, with several incidents bringing the two groups to the verge of a full-scale military conflict. In October the Kurdish Autonomous Region's Internal Security Forces, known as the Asayish, accused the PKK of responsibility for the killing of Ghazi Salih, the head of security of a border crossing in Duhok governorate, but the PKK denied any involvement. In November an armed clash between PKK militants and the KDP *peshmerga* fighters took place. According to KRG sources, one *peshmerga* was killed and nine were injured in the attack. Several high-ranking KRG officials released statements condemning the attack and claiming that the PKK was undermining the authority of the KRG by occupying villages in the Kurdish Autonomous Region. In a further escalation in tensions, in December a skirmish took place between the KDP *peshmerga* and PKK guerrillas at a checkpoint near Amedi town in Duhok governorate. A vehicle used by the PKK was halted at a checkpoint, and then came under attack. Initially, sources stated that one PKK member had died, but according to subsequent reports three had been injured. The KDP, however, reported that the PKK had attacked the checkpoint and one *peshmerga* had been killed. In June 2021 another incident between the two parties took place in Mount Matina in Duhok governorate, an area under the control of the PKK and the site of conflict between PKK militants and the Turkish armed forces. A convoy of *peshmerga* was on its way to be deployed near the Turkish border when a vehicle came under attack, killing five *peshmerga* fighters and injuring seven. The KRG blamed the PKK for the attack, but the PKK's commander in the region denied that his forces were responsible.

The elections held on 10 October 2021 to the Council of Representatives of Iraq was marked by a low turnout, which apparently dented the performance of the 'Kurdistani Coalition' formed by the PUK and the Gorran (Change) Movement, which won 17 seats. The KDP secured 31 seats, while the New Generation Movement increased its tally of seats from four in 2018 to nine. Discussions begun in December to form a coalition government had made little noticeable progress by early 2022, although the KDP had indicated that it would work with the Shi'a Sadrist Movement and the Sovereignty Alliance (a Sunni bloc) to form Iraq's next administration. However, by July the Iraqi political parties had failed to agree on a new President or to form a broad-based coalition government. The presidential post, which is constitutionally held by a Kurd and had been occupied since 2004 by individuals affiliated with the PUK, proved challenging to fill, after the KDP insisted on securing election for its candidate, Rebar Ahmed. The PUK supported the Co-ordination Framework alliance forged by former Prime Minister (2006–14) Nuri Kamal al-Maliki and the Shi'a, pro-Iranian Fatah Alliance. Following the 2021 elections, the Co-ordination Framework did not have a sufficient number of legislators to lead the formation of a new coalition government or secure election for its preferred presidential candidate, although it had enough support to frustrate the process.

In an unexpected turn of events, efforts by the political parties to form a new government gathered new momentum when the 73 legislators from the Sadrist Movement political bloc, loyal to Shi'a cleric Muqtada al-Sadr, resigned in June 2022, in an effort to break the impasse in Iraq's government formation process. According to Iraqi law, if any seat in the legislature becomes vacant, the candidate who obtained the second-highest number of votes in the electoral constituency replaces the candidate who resigned. Following the resignation of legislators loyal to al-Sadr, therefore, the Co-ordination Framework alliance, supported by the PUK, had enough seats in the Council of Representatives potentially to form the next government.

Meanwhile, in February 2022 Iraq's Federal Supreme Court issued a ruling on the Kurdish Autonomous Region's Oil and Gas Law No. 22, which was enacted in 2007 and had been used by the KRG as the legal framework for its agreements with international oil companies to explore for and produce hydrocarbons in the Kurdish Autonomous Region. The ruling prevented the KRG from exporting oil and gas independently and deprived it of the right to explore for and extract oil and gas in the Kurdish Autonomous Region. Kurdish institutions and KRG representatives have since attempted to engage Iraqi political actors to reverse the Supreme Court's decision and prevent it from further undermining intergovernmental relations.

The long-rumoured internal power struggle between the co-Presidents of the PUK became public in mid-2021, with co-President Lahur Talabani being forced to resign from his position on 20 July. His fellow co-President, Bafel Talabani, had nominated a candidate to head the Zanyari Agency (the PUK's intelligence agency), but the party had refused to endorse it, which exacerbated the rivalry between the two leaders and led to Lahur's resignation. These developments shook Iraqi Kurdish politics and were likely to add to the political polarization in the Kurdish Autonomous Region. Lahur Talabani and Bafel Talabani had reached a power-sharing agreement in 2019 following the death in 2017 of the PUK's long-term leader Jalal Talabani, which resulted in their election as co-Presidents of the party in 2020.

In recent years there has been a marked increase in attacks by the Turkish armed forces using unmanned aerial vehicles (or 'drones') targeting various Kurdish groups in Syria and Iraq, including the Yezidis in Sinjar. The Kurdish Autonomous Region and the regions populated by Kurds that remain part of the disputed territories have been targeted by Türkiye. Clashes between PKK fighters and Turkish soldiers in the Metinah and Avashin districts of Duhok governorate near the Turkish–Iraqi border took place in September–October 2021. The Turkish army carried out several air strikes in early 2022, targeting the Makhmour refugee camp (which is under the control of the Iraqi federal Government) and Sinjar in February. The strike on Makhmour killed eight people and injured 17 others.

In April 2022 the Turkish armed forces launched 'Operation Claw-Lock' in the mountainous districts of Zap, Metinah and Avashin against PKK guerrillas. Prior to the commencement of the operation, these areas were heavily bombed by air and artillery, and Turkish troops were airdropped in specific locations. Clashes between PKK guerrillas and Turkish troops soon broke out, around 10 km–15 km from the Turkish–Iraqi border, but Turkish media reported that Turkish soldiers were expected to penetrate about 50 km–60 km into the Kurdish Autonomous Region as part of the operation. Turkish media subsequently published occasional updates on the progress made in the operation, and Türkiye's Ministry of National Defence claimed that the operation was 'a key link' in the counter-terrorism operations that the Turkish army had carried out in past years. The Turkish media broadcast footage of airborne actions against PKK positions and claimed that the PKK had suffered heavy losses. For its part, the PKK asserted that the Turkish ground operation had not progressed as initially planned. In addition, the PKK circulated footage of its attacks against Turkish army positions and alleged that the number of Turkish casualties was far higher than the figures provided by the Turkish Ministry of National Defence. Türkiye also carried out a number of drone attacks against PKK guerrillas in the Kurdish Autonomous Region that resulted in the deaths of several civilians. One such attack took place in May in the Chamchamal district of Sulaimaniya governorate, killing three guerrillas and two civilians. In June Farhad Shibli, the deputy co-chair of the Executive Council of the Autonomous Administration of North and Eastern Syria (AANES), who was on an official visit to the Kurdish Autonomous Region, was killed in a Turkish drone attack in the Kalar district of Sulaimaniya governorate, which left three other people dead.

During 2020 the Kurdish Autonomous Region's security forces are believed to have detained about 100 journalists and activists in the Bahdinan region. Legal proceedings against some of the detainees have been concluded, resulting in convictions. In the case of the remaining detainees, in mid-2023 the proceedings of some were under way, while others still awaited trial. In April 2021 the Court of Cassation in the Kurdish Autonomous Region approved the imprisonment of five journalists and activists in Bahdinan, who were charged with various crimes, including spying for the USA, the UK and Germany, sending sensitive information to foreign entities and co-operating with the PKK; the ruling provoked widespread condemnation among the international community. Reports of the detainees' poor health and mistreatment have circulated in the media; in September 2021 reports emerged that some of the so-called 'Bahdinan detainees' had begun a hunger strike.

The glacial process of forming a new government inched forward in late September 2022 with the announced formation of the State Administration Coalition, which consisted of the various Co-ordination Framework parties, the PUK, the KDP, both major Sunni alliances and the Babylon Movement (a small Chaldean Christian party). The onus was now on the two Kurdish parties to reach a consensus on a nominee for president, and with the PUK continuing to insist on Barham

Saleh as the nominee, the KDP opted to withdraw the candidacy of Rebar Ahmed and instead nominate Abdul Latif Rashid. Although technically an independent, Rashid was the brother-in-law of the late PUK leader Jalal Talabani and had strong historical links to the PUK. This should have made him more acceptable to the PUK, but the PUK's insistence on backing Saleh meant a contested election for president involving two Kurdish candidates. As neither candidate received the necessary two-thirds' parliamentary majority in the first round of voting, the election went to a second round, where a simple majority of the vote is sufficient. Rashid emerged as the clear winner, obtaining 162 votes to Salih's 99, and on the same day the newly elected President named Mohammed Shia al-Sudani as Prime Minister designate. Twenty-one of the 23 members of al-Sudani's new cabinet were approved by parliament on 27 October, including two Kurds: the KDP's Fuad Hussein was retained as foreign affairs minister, while the PUK's Khaled Shwani was appointed as Minister of Justice. The failure to approve appointees for the remaining two portfolios—of the environment and of construction and housing—was the result of yet more intra-Kurdish fighting. Nominees for these two posts were eventually approved at the end of November, with the former being allocated to Nizar Amedi of the PUK and the latter to Benkin Rikani of the KDP.

Relations between the PUK and the KDP were no better at the regional level. In the absence of agreement on issues relating to the parliamentary elections in the Kurdish Autonomous Region scheduled for 1 October 2022, such as the drawing up of electoral districts and the allocation of reserved seats for minority groups, the Iraqi Kurdistan Parliament was forced to convene and on 9 October voted to extend its current term by one year. This extension vote was a rare moment of KDP-PUK consensus, but several other parties, including the Kurdistan Islamic Union and the New Generation Movement, opted to boycott the parliamentary session, meaning that only 80 of the 111 legislators were present to approve the extension. Members of the New Generation Movement then filed a lawsuit with the Federal Supreme Court, arguing that the extension violated the Iraqi Constitution.

Meanwhile, the situation for Iraqi Kurds deteriorated in late 2022 and into 2023. In October 2022 the assassination of Hawkar Abdullah Rasoul, known as Hawkar Jaff, in Irbil in a car bombing provoked a major crisis in relations between the PUK and the KDP. Jaff was a former colonel in the PUK's counter-terrorism service who had been ousted from his post in 2021 during the power struggle between Lahur and Bafel Talabani. Reports suggested that Jaff had been targeted by PUK operatives because he was in the process of defecting to the KDP. Video evidence released by the KDP-dominated regional security council, together with confessions from suspects, appeared to substantiate this claim. In response to this accusation, the PUK opted to boycott weekly meetings of the KRG. A meeting held in January 2023 between delegations from the two parties in an effort to resolve outstanding issues proved fruitless, and the PUK's boycott continued until May. From a Kurdish perspective, this was unfortunate, as the intervening period was a critical time for Kurdish unity, given the evolution of relations between Irbil and Baghdad. Of central concern for Kurdish leaders was securing a stable income from the federal Government that was sufficient, at a minimum, to cover the costs of the salaries of KRG employees; receiving these payments on a regular basis had been a central Kurdish demand in return for supporting al-Sudani's Government. Accordingly, the federal Government authorized the disbursement of approximately US $140m. to the KRG in December. However, this ad hoc arrangement was challenged in the Federal Supreme Court, which duly decreed that the payments violated the 2021 budget law as well as the Constitution. The ruling greatly complicated negotiations about a new budget for Iraq (the first since 2021).

The budget deal that was eventually concluded in March 2023 allocated 12.7% of the budget to the Kurdish Autonomous Region, in return for which the Kurds were required to produce 400,000 barrels of oil per day from the Region's oilfields. The deal gave Iraq's State Oil Marketing Organization control over the pricing, export and marketing of oil produced in the Kurdish Autonomous Region, with the proceeds to be deposited in a bank account controlled by the KRG but supervised by the federal Government. In most respects, all this did was to formalize the terms of the oil-for-revenue arrangement that was supposed to have already been in place for several years. At the same time, it effectively officially codified what the Federal Supreme Court had already determined—that the Kurdish Autonomous Region's natural resources were controlled by the federal Government and not by the KRG.

Another setback to the autonomy of the KRG came in the form of a provision in Article 14 of the budget law, which allowed individual governorates within the Kurdish Autonomous Region to petition the federal Government directly for a separate share of the Region's budget allocation in the event that the KRG was held to have dispersed revenue unfairly across the Region. The inclusion of this provision, which was advocated by the PUK, reflected the PUK's long-held belief that the KDP-dominated KRG had deprived PUK-dominated governorates (Sulaimaniya and Halabja) of revenue in favour of those governorates in which the KDP was dominant (Irbil and Duhok). There may be some truth in this contention, but the broader significance of the provision was that it potentially allowed the federal Government to determine how the KRG allocated its resources across the Kurdish Autonomous Region.

Another controversial decision by the Federal Supreme Court, handed down on 30 May 2023, declared that the October 2022 vote to extend the term of the Iraqi Kurdistan Parliament was 'unconstitutional' and that it 'undermined democracy'. Accordingly, the Court ruled that all decisions made by the Parliament subsequent to the end of its legal term (6 November 2022) were also unconstitutional and therefore null and void. Although many Kurds had opposed the extension of the parliamentary term and welcomed the Court's decision, the deeper constitutional implications of the ruling were troubling. Iraq's Constitution places no limitations on regions in terms of their conduct of elections or their power to determine the terms of office of elected regional institutions, and the federal Government has no constitutional powers to dictate these to regions. Therefore, it appeared that a supreme court that itself had no constitutional standing, and on which Kurdish judges were heavily outnumbered, had now awarded itself the power to dictate these issues to Iraq's only region.

It is easy to pin the blame for the erosion of Kurdish autonomy on the decisions of an unelected court, but Kurdish leaders themselves bear some of the responsibility. The extension of the parliamentary term would not have been necessary, had the PUK and the KDP been able to reach a consensus on how to conduct an election. Indeed, about a week before the Federal Supreme Court's ruling in May 2023, members of the two parties engaged in what was described as a brawl in parliament caused by disagreements about the composition of the Kurdish electoral commission. The Court may be no friend of the Kurds, but Kurdish leaders also seem entirely capable of being their own worst enemies. In the end, it took intensive pressure from the USA and the UN Assistance Mission for Iraq to force the issue, and on 3 August President Barzani issued a decree setting 25 February 2024 as the date for the next parliamentary elections in the Kurdish Autonomous Region.

THE KURDISH QUESTION IN TÜRKIYE

The majority of Kurds found themselves within the borders of Türkiye after the collapse of the Ottoman Empire following the First World War, and Türkiye adopted wide-ranging policies to suppress Kurdish culture and language. The Kurds resisted Turkish nationalism during the 1920s and 1930s, with a considerable number taking part in a series of revolts in that period. While the early Kurdish rebellions mobilized a significant proportion of Kurdish society, they did not manage to mobilize the entire rural population, and Kurds living in towns and cities played no part in the revolts. The 1940s and 1950s were notable for a distinct lack of organized activity by Kurdish opposition groups, and they have been described colloquially as the 'quiet years' or era of 'silence'. The transition to multi-party democracy in Türkiye in 1946, the rise of the Kurdish national movement in Iraq and the emergence of a new generation of politically active Kurdish activists influenced the politicization of the Kurds in Türkiye during the

1960s. The limited freedoms provided by the 1961 Constitution made room for the political opposition to mobilize its struggle, and the Kurds were able to express some of their demands and concerns.

During the 1950s a new generation of Kurdish activists emerged, including Edip Karahan, Musa Anter, Yusuf Azizoğlu, Ziya Şerefhanoğlu, Faik Bucak, Mehmet Emin Bozarslan, Sait Kırmızıtoprak and Sait Elçi. The latter two men helped to found the Türkiye Kürdistan Demokrat Partisi (TKDP—Kurdistan Democrat Party of Türkiye) in 1965. Anter and Karahan published the Kurdish political magazines *Dicle-Fırat* (1962–63) and *Deng* (1963), and in 1968 Bozarslan transliterated the Kurdish epic *Mem-û-Zîn* into Kurdish-Latin script and also published a Turkish translation of the work. A number of other cultural publications were founded during that time and enjoyed wide readerships, including *İleri Yurt* (1959), *Reya Rast*, *Roja Newe* (1963) *and Yeni Akış* (1966). Furthermore, a book on Kurdish grammar was published in 1965. Kurdish culture was revived through such activities and the publication of titles in Kurdish provided a forum where Kurdish national rights could be debated. A significant number of Kurds were active within the Türkiye İşçi Partisi (TİP—Workers' Party of Türkiye) and subsequently played a leading role in the establishment of the Kurdish movement in the late 1960s.

During the late 1950s and early 1960s a series of episodes in Türkiye brought the Kurdish question under the political spotlight and highlighted the oppression that the Kurdish population endured. Public attention was drawn in particular to an incident that became known as 'the 49'ers incident' (*49'lar Olayı*) and involved some 50 Kurdish political activists and students who were arrested in December 1959 (one of whom died in police custody); their trials lasted until 1967. The authorities justified the arrests by citing a public statement that had been signed by 102 Kurdish students, in which they condemned a number of anti-Kurdish remarks made by Asım Eren, a Turkish nationalist politician, in 1959. Political repression of Kurds continued after the coup in May 1960 with the arbitrary arrest, detention and exile of Kurds.

In the second half of the 1960s Kurdish activism was marked by a development towards a more rigorous structure. The evolution of the Kurdish self-determination movement was re-invigorated directly by the Kurdish national movement in Iraq, an example of which was the establishment of the TKDP in Türkiye, which proposed a similar programme as the KDP in Iraq. The TKDP was the first secret Kurdish political party to be founded in Türkiye, in the early 1960s, and it united disparate strands of Kurdish society, including intellectuals and professionals, artisans and students. However, soon after the TKDP was founded, the party suffered internal divisions, and many of its most senior members were arrested in January 1968.

The TİP and the socialist movement in Türkiye in general provided another arena for Kurdish activism in the 1960s. The TİP offered Kurds a forum within which to debate and formulate their political, economic and social demands. In fact, the pressure exerted by Kurdish members participating in the fourth party congress in 1970 resulted in the open acknowledgement of the Kurds in eastern Türkiye and their plight and Kurdish activists in the TİP played an important part in advancing the debate on the Kurdish question. Kurds who were active in left-wing groups began to develop and make public an alternative interpretation of their social reality, which challenged the official ideology and narrative of the Turkish state. Initially, the Kurdish question in Türkiye was formulated in the context of the economic and social underdevelopment of the Kurdish region, but from the 1970s it assumed a new and more profound character and was considered as a national problem, and indeed as an example of colonialism.

The emerging Kurdish movement began to attract widespread popular support, notably articulated at the so-called 'meetings of the East' (*Doğu Mitingleri*) during which Kurdish nationalists publicly voiced their demands. Such activities culminated in the emergence and increasing influence of Devrimci Doğu Kültür Ocakları (DDKO—Revolutionary Cultural Eastern Hearths) in 1969, an association which formulated its programme on popular grievances, such as a lack of Kurdish economic and social development, and a dearth of government investment in most Kurdish regions. The military coup in 1971 intensified political oppression, leading to the closing down of the DDKO and the prosecution of its leaders and members.

Several Kurdish left-wing groups and political parties emerged in the 1970s, including the Türkiye Kürdistan Sosyalist Partisi (TKSP—Socialist Party of Turkish Kurdistan) in 1974, which was renamed the Partiya Sosyalîst a Kurdistan (Socialist Party of Kurdistan) following its third party congress in 1992. The Partiya Karkeren Kurdistan (PKK—Kurdistan Workers' Party) was founded in 1978 (see below), but it had existed as a small political cell since 1973. Other groups formed in this period included Rizgarî (Liberation, 1976), Kürdistan Ulusal Kurtuluşçuları (KUK—Kurdistan National Liberationists 1978), Kawa (1978), Ala Rizgarî (Flag of Liberation, 1979) and Tekoşin (Struggle, 1979). In varying degrees, all of these groups were committed to the Kurdish struggle and embraced socialism. The PKK and the KUK advocated Kurdish autonomy and armed resistance against the Turkish state, while smaller groups such as Ala Rizgarî, Kawa, Rizgarî and Tekoşin disseminated political pamphlets and periodicals. Others, such as the TKSP, had to adapt to changing circumstances. Following the military coup in Türkiye in September 1980 most TKSP activities took place in Europe, where the party had established a wide political network, particularly in Germany and Sweden.

The PKK was formally established in November 1978 as a secret organization that advocated the liberation of Kurdistan from Türkiye, and which found inspiration from national liberation and anti-imperialist movements around the world. The party sought to unify the 'people of Kurdistan' in an independent, united and socialist republic. It propounded a philosophy of national liberation based on the need to challenge Türkiye by force of arms, in the form of a protracted popular struggle. In August 1984 the PKK embarked on a guerrilla war and during the late 1980s and early 1990s, as its insurgency intensified, the PKK attracted popular support from the Kurds and greatly increased its influence in Kurdish communities. At its zenith in the early 1990s its guerrilla army comprised some 15,000 fighters, and it was supported by several million members and sympathizers in all parts of Kurdish-majority regions, as well as among the Kurdish diaspora in Europe.

In the spring of 1991 and of 1992 large numbers of Kurds took part in popular uprisings, known as *Serhildan*, across Kurdish towns and cities in the south-east of Türkiye, in a popular demonstration of support for the PKK and its political objectives. The PKK-led Kurdish rebellion is the most radical to date of any revolt in the history of the Kurds in Türkiye and has lasted for the longest time. The conflict has cost the lives of more than 45,000 people (mainly soldiers, guerrillas, village guards and Kurdish civilians), and resulted in the forced evacuation of some 3,500 villages and hamlets. Through the expulsion of rural Kurds, the Turkish authorities severed the support that the PKK had been giving to rural Kurdish communities. As a consequence of these developments, the PKK's military capability diminished from the mid-1990s.

In October 1998 the PKK's leader, Abdullah Öcalan, was forced to leave Syria, where he had been based since the early 1980s. In February 1999 he was captured in the Kenyan capital, Nairobi. He subsequently received a death sentence, although this was commuted to life imprisonment, following international diplomatic pressure and fears on the part of the Turkish authorities that making a martyr of Öcalan risked provoking a conflict that could descend into civil war. Since Öcalan's imprisonment, the PKK has undergone a number of organizational and ideological transformations. In August 1999 the party withdrew its combatants from Türkiye to the Kurdish region in northern Iraq and declared a permanent ceasefire, which transformed the nature of the conflict. In 2005 the PKK issued a new manifesto, which notably proposed a 'democratic solution' to the Kurdish question. The central plank of the programme proposed a 'democratic transformation' of the current state system in the Middle East into two entities: federal and confederal. It proposed reconstituting the Kurds as a nation without establishing a nation-state or defining particular Kurdish territory. The proposed confederal Kurdish entity would neither undermine established and internationally recognized boundaries nor resort to ethnic nationalism or founding a nation-state. Its priority was the development of a bureaucratic framework for Kurdish self-government.

The pro-Kurdish democratic movement has expressed its political demands in Türkiye through legal means, and it is represented in parliament in the Turkish capital, Ankara, by the Halkların Demokratik Partisi (HDP—Peoples' Democratic Party). The pro-Kurdish democratic movement emerged in 1990 and despite the numerous instances of repression it has suffered since then, it has none the less survived. In 1991, through co-operation with the Sosyaldemokrat Halkçı Parti (Social Democratic Populist Party) the then pro-Kurdish party Halkın Emek Partisi (HEP—People's Labour Party) won 22 seats in the parliament. Owing to the nature of the political demands they raised, such as the constitutional recognition of Kurdish national identity, these parties were viewed as political 'outsiders'. As a result of their demands for the promotion of Kurdish separatism, they attracted repression from the Turkish authorities. The authorities eventually outlawed pro-Kurdish groups, including the HEP in 1993, the Demokrasi Partisi (Democracy Party, the successor to HEP) in 1994, the Halkın Demokrasi Partisi (People's Democracy Party) in 2003 and the Demokratik Toplum Partisi (DTP—Democratic Society Party) in 2009. Hence, since its formation the pro-Kurdish democratic movement has been represented by a series of political parties.

After the general election of July 2007 the pro-Kurdish parliamentary opposition returned with the election of 21 DTP legislators who stood as independent candidates in order to avoid the 10% threshold for political party representation in the Turkish parliament. In the municipal elections held in March 2009 the DTP consolidated its position as a leading political force in the Kurdish-majority regions. The successor to the DTP, the Barış ve Demokrasi Partisi (BDP—Peace and Democracy Party), contested the general election of June 2011 as part of the pro-democracy 'Labour, Peace and Democracy Block' and it too supported independent candidates, resulting in the election of 35 such candidates. At the local elections held in March 2014 the BDP won some 100 councils, including the municipalities of Ağrı, Batman, Bitlis, Diyarbakır, Hakkari, Iğdır, Mardin, Şırnak, Siirt, Tunceli and Van; as a result of persecution by the authorities, however, the BDP decided effectively to dissolve itself and most of its members joined the HDP. The HDP took part in the general election in June 2015; the party won the electoral support of some 6m. voters and secured 80 seats in parliament.

However, violence broke out between the security forces and the PKK in mid-2015 and the Turkish Government began to pursue repressive policies and aggravated the conflict further. In May 2016 the Turkish parliament passed legislation to lift the immunity from prosecution of legislators—a measure designed to end, or at least significantly weaken, the HDP representation in parliament. Legal proceedings began against a number of HDP legislators, of whom 11 were detained on 4 November. At mid-2023 the majority of them were still in custody, including the former co-Chairs of the party, Selahattin Demirtaş and Figen Yüksekdağ. Despite the repression, the HDP appears to be maintaining its electoral base: in the elections of November 2015 and June 2018 the party won 10.8% and 11.7% of the national vote and 59 and 67 seats in parliament, respectively. At local elections held in March 2019 the HDP concentrated its efforts in the Kurdish majority provinces. Its main objective was to take back control over the municipal and district councils won by the BDP in 2014, the elected officials having been effectively replaced by government-appointed 'trustees' in 2016. Despite a decline in the HDP's overall share of the vote compared with that of the BDP in 2014, it managed to win in the municipalities of Batman, Diyarbakır, Hakkari, Iğdır, Kars, Mardin, Siirt and Van. In addition, it won 50 district councils. The HDP chose not to field candidates in most of western Türkiye and encouraged its supporters to back opposition candidates, in an attempt to weaken the power base of the governing Adalet ve Kalkınma Partisi (AKP—Justice and Development Party). This support proved crucial, enabling the opposition Cumhuriyet Halk Partisi (CHP—Republican People's Party) to gain control of councils in a number of major municipalities formerly governed by the AKP or by its ally, the Milliyetçi Hareket Partisi (MHP—Nationalist Movement Party), notably including the Turkish capital, İstanbul. There are also smaller Kurdish political parties such as the left-wing Hak ve Özgürlükler Partisi (Rights and Freedoms Party) and the Islamist Hür Dava Partisi (Free Cause Party) but they have not managed to win sufficient votes in either parliamentary or local elections to gain representation.

Prior to the local elections in March 2019, Turkish President Recep Tayyip Erdoğan hinted that the government policy of removing the elected mayors and replacing them with district and provincial governors would continue, and in late August the HDP co-mayors of Diyarbakır, Mardin and Van municipal councils were removed from their positions and replaced by the provincial governors who were appointed as 'trustees'. By mid-November the co-mayors of 24 councils, including of Diyarbakır, Hakkari, Mardin and Van provinces, had been removed from their positions, and it was expected that more HDP-run councils would be taken over by government-appointed 'trustees'. Nevertheless, in the short term, winning back the municipalities in the Kurdish region boosted the morale of the HDP's support base and strengthened the party's efforts to counter the Government's depiction of it as an illegitimate political movement. It has also increased the relevance of the HDP in the national efforts to reverse the authoritarian turn in Turkish politics, particularly as its supporters helped the opposition defeat AKP candidates in the country's main urban centres.

Throughout 2019 and during the first six months of 2020, Türkiye continued to target and kill high-level PKK commanders using drones. These attacks also resulted in civilian casualties and prompted increasingly tense relations between the KRG and Türkiye. In June 2020 Türkiye launched a ground and air cross-border operation in KRG territory, targeting suspected PKK bases and hideouts. Turkish air strikes, meanwhile, targeted a larger area, including the Sinjar and the Qandil mountains, and the Makhmour refugee camp. The ground operation continued into late 2020, focusing on the border regions such as Haftanin, which was an area known to have a strong PKK presence.

The current situation of the Kurds in Türkiye is rather precarious and the positive developments that took place in the conflict during the 2000s and the first half of the 2010s have all been reversed in a short space of time. In the past decade, despite significant opportunities to resolve the conflict, Türkiye has failed to develop a new policy framework to transform and eventually end the fighting. The recognition of Kurdish identity, and the associated rights, requires major changes in Türkiye's identity as a state, but the public debate so far has revealed the ideological rigidity of Turkish nationalism and its hesitation in accepting the legitimacy of Kurdish political demands and rights, which continue to be rejected by the state and Government in Türkiye on the grounds that they promote separatism.

Suppression of the HDP was a dominant feature in Türkiye during 2020 and 2021, with the arrest of large numbers of party officials and the initiation of a court case aimed at closing down the party permanently. In September 2020 many former HDP legislators were arrested as part of a reopened case. In total, some 20 former or currently active officials of the HDP were detained. Their trial began in Ankara on 26 April 2021.

On 22 December 2020 the European Court of Human Rights (ECHR) delivered its verdict in the case of former HDP co-Chair Selahattin Demirtaş, who had been imprisoned since 4 November 2016. The Court concluded that Türkiye had violated four articles of the European Convention on Human Rights. It ordered Demirtaş's immediate release and awarded him €28,500 in damages. Demirtaş's lawyers applied for his release, but the Ministry of Justice rejected the application. On 26 April 2021 Türkiye's Court of Cassation upheld a prison sentence of four years and eight months that Demirtaş had received in 2018 for a speech he had delivered in İstanbul in March 2013, on the occasion of the Nowruz festival (Kurdish New Year). On 22 March 2021 Demirtaş received a further three-and-a-half-year prison sentence for insulting President Erdoğan. The charge related to a statement made by Demirtaş at Istanbul Airport on 24 December 2015, following his return from a visit to the Russian Federation, which criticized the President and Prime Minister for a deterioration in Türkiye's relations with Russia.

On 2 March 2021 the Office of the General Prosecutor of the Supreme Court of Appeals announced that it was launching an investigation into the HDP and accused the party of having ties with the PKK. The investigation was initiated after several demands by the MHP leader, Devlet Bahçeli, in February for the permanent closure of the HDP. On 17 March the Office of the General Prosecutor completed the indictment for the closure of the HDP. The indictment claimed that the HDP had 'become the focus of actions against the indivisible unity of the state with its territory and nation', and demanded that 687 former and current members of the party be banned from politics for five years. The indictment also included requests that the HDP be wholly deprived of the financial aid paid by the Treasury to political parties, its bank accounts blocked, and the financial aid paid to it in the past reclaimed. The voluntary dissolution of the HDP and establishment of a new political party with a similar mission was discussed by its members as a possible strategy to circumvent the closure, but was rejected. The HDP decided to defend itself in court and to build national and international support and solidarity around the case. However, on 31 March the Constitutional Court's rapporteurs found numerous inadequacies in the file during their initial assessment, and the Court returned the indictment to the General Prosecutor's Office of the Supreme Court of Appeals.

On 7 June 2021 a second indictment for the HDP's closure was submitted to the Constitutional Court. The indictment, prepared by the General Prosecutor of the Supreme Court of Appeals, Bekir Şahin, contained accusations that 'the HDP is the focus of terrorist acts, aimed at disrupting and eliminating the indivisible unity of the state'. The Constitutional Court announced that it would conduct its initial review of the second indictment by 21 June. On 18 June the Court's rapporteurs stated that their initial evaluation had established that the previously identified shortcomings had been addressed in the second indictment. The next stage in the case was to involve the HDP's submission of its preliminary defence. Following this, Şahin would present his opinion on the merits of the HDP's defence. The Constitutional Court's rapporteurs would then prepare a report on the merits of the General Prosecutor's opinion. A two-thirds' majority, or 10 votes, would be required for the Constitutional Court to close the party.

In the early morning of 24 April 2021 the Turkish armed forces launched cross-border ground and air operations against PKK positions in the mountainous Metina and Zap regions of Iraq's Kurdish Autonomous Region. The area was hit with artillery fire, and air strikes targeted hideouts believed to be used by PKK militants. Troops were airdropped to the region, and engaged with the PKK forces in a ground battle. By the end of April the Turkish armed forces announced that six soldiers had been killed in the operation. The PKK reported a much higher number of Turkish casualties and claimed that the Turkish army had not succeeded in capturing its bases and positions in the ongoing operations in the region. On 2 May Türkiye's Minister of National Defence, Hulusi Akar, visited Turkish bases inside the Kurdish Autonomous Region, drawing criticism from the Iraqi Ministry of Foreign Affairs. Türkiye's state news agency, Anadolu Ajansı, reported that on 15 and 16 June alone air strikes targeting 500 PKK targets had been carried out by the Turkish military. On 17 May President Erdoğan announced that the Turkish security forces had killed a high-ranking commander of the PKK, known as Sofi Nurettin, in an air strike. On the following day, however, the PKK issued a statement denying that Sofi had been killed.

Seven members of a Kurdish family were killed in July 2021 in an apparently racially motivated attack in the Meram district of Konya province in central Türkiye, after which their house was burned down. In August parts of Türkiye were engulfed by wildfires, and the Government's inability swiftly to manage the extinguishing of the blazes resulted in a public outcry against the authorities. In an apparent effort to shift responsibility, government representatives and the Turkish nationalist groups affiliated to the Government popularized the claim that the wildfires had been started by arsonists within the PKK.

On 11 October 2021 President Erdoğan renewed his threat of an attack against Kurdish-led forces in northern Syria. Later that month the Turkish Government appealed to the legislature to authorize the use of military force in Iraq and Syria for two more years; this was approved by the votes of the governing coalition and the opposition İyi Partisi (Good Party). However, the CHP opposed the Government's decision, on the grounds that it did not address the critical aspects of the Syrian conflict and raised concerns about Türkiye's role in the Syrian governorate of Idlib (see Syrian Arab Republic).

Meanwhile, on 2 September 2021 Türkiye's Constitutional Court considered the HDP's request for extra time to submit its defence to the Court regarding the threatened closure of the party. The Court extended by 60 days the deadline of 7 September set for the HDP to submit its initial defence and the defence of its members who faced political bans. In early November the HDP submitted its preliminary legal defence in the closure case to the Constitutional Court. The following week the Court forwarded the HDP's preliminary defence to the Chief Public Prosecutor of the Court of Cassation for him to respond to the Constitutional Court within a month. The HDP's defence lawyers highlighted procedural issues in the casework file and asked the Constitutional Court to reject the closure case. The HDP stated that its final defence would respond fully to all allegations against the party. In April 2022 the HDP submitted its 220-page written defence in the closure case to the Constitutional Court.

The 11th hearing of the so-called Kobani trial took place on 8 April 2022, in which 108 people were charged with involvement in the deaths of 37 individuals during violent protests in Türkiye in October 2014 against the Government's refusal to launch a military operation in defence of the Kurdish city of Kobani in northern Syria which was under siege by the Islamic State. Among the defendants were the former HDP co-Chairs Demirtaş and Yüksekdag and former HDP legislators. The HDP's lawyers argued that the prosecutors in the trial had repeatedly interfered with the case from the outset and that the Government had unlawfully influenced the court's position in order to persecute the HDP on political grounds. On 9 April 2022 the Public Prosecutor's Office in Ankara issued arrest warrants for 91 HDP members as part of the Kobani investigation. A few days later 46 people were detained in raids on residential properties in 13 Turkish cities. By that time the Turkish authorities had frozen the assets of 90 people, mainly HDP politicians, as part of the ongoing case and investigation. In February the ECHR had ruled that Türkiye had violated the freedom of expression of 40 HDP legislators, including Demirtaş, when parliament removed their immunity in 2016 to pave the way for their trial and subsequent pre-trial detention. Senior HDP officials and lawyers of the legislators in question demanded their immediate release.

The ongoing persecution of the HDP and its members for alleged ties to the PKK was especially salient during 2022 and the first half of 2023, given that presidential and parliamentary elections in Türkiye were scheduled for May 2023, and an unfavourable ruling in the closure case would mean that the HDP would not be able to field candidates. The HDP's strategy for the elections was complicated not just by the impending closure case, but also because the only chance to prevent yet another victory for President Erdoğan and his party was for all parties of the opposition to forge a common front. However, when an opposition alliance of six parties, running under the National Alliance banner, but colloquially referred to as the 'Table of Six', did emerge in mid-2022 to challenge Erdoğan, it pointedly excluded the HDP. Although the major opposition party—the CHP—appeared willing to countenance a strategic alliance with the HDP, other opposition parties were adamantly hostile to the idea. In September, for example, CHP legislator Gürsel Tekin suggested that the HDP's participation in a successful opposition alliance could be rewarded with a ministerial portfolio; almost immediately, a spokesman for the staunchly nationalist İyi Partisi (Good Party) stated that 'We will not be at the table where the HDP is'. The problem for the leaders of the opposition was that the major point of agreement among the Table of Six parties was a shared desire to unseat Erdoğan, and while the inclusion of the HDP would certainly have increased the probability of this occurring, it would equally certainly have led to the Table of Six fragmenting beyond repair, owing to stark differences of opinion within the alliance on the Kurdish question. With only limited options available, the HDP chose to forge its own opposition bloc, and in October it officially announced the formation of the 'Labour and Freedom Alliance', an electoral alliance comprising the HDP and a number of small left-wing parties.

Alongside the Turkish Government's efforts to target the HDP politically, its military targeting of PKK bases inside the Kurdistan Autonomous Region in Iraq continued unabated. The attacks involved a combination of air strikes, artillery launched from the Turkish army's increasing number of quasi-permanent military outposts inside Iraq and, increasingly, drone strikes. Most of these attacks generated little in the way of attention or controversy. An exception to this was an artillery strike on the Zakho district of Duhok in July 2022, which killed nine tourists and injured another 23. Iraq's Minister of Foreign Affairs, Fuad Hussein, condemned the attack and accused Türkiye of 'occupying Iraq'. At a subsequent emergency session of the UN Security Council that was convened to discuss the attack, Hussein demanded the 'full withdrawal' of all Turkish forces from Iraq; however, the harsh reality of the situation was that Iraq lacked the military power to force the issue, and Türkiye had powerful Western allies, most of which considered the PKK to be a terrorist organization, so there was almost no international pressure on Türkiye to withdraw its military presence in Iraq. The ability to target the PKK with impunity inside Iraq also served a useful political purpose for Erdoğan, in that being seen as tough on terrorism helped to safeguard the AKP's ongoing alliance with the ultra-nationalist MHP. This was especially important in an election year, because, in many respects, the prospect of Erdoğan being defeated at the ballot box had probably never been more likely. A stubbornly high unemployment rate, coupled with an inflation rate of about 80% and a currency that continued to lose value against the US dollar, made Erdoğan vulnerable on economic issues. There was also no indication that the Turkish Government had a coherent endgame in mind for Türkiye's involvement in the Syrian conflict. While government officials made repeated statements during 2022 and the first half of 2023 about Türkiye's intentions to 'normalize' relations with Syria, the latter's progressive reintegration into the Arab fold (see below) and the continued support for Syria of important allies in Iran and Russia meant that Syria had no real incentive to make concessions to Türkiye.

Potentially adding to President Erdoğan's electoral vulnerability was the perceived inadequacy of the Government's response to two catastrophic earthquakes that struck the south of Türkiye on the border with Syria in early February 2023. The two earthquakes, measuring 7.8 and 7.5 in magnitude on the Richter scale, killed nearly 50,000 people and caused massive property damage over an extensive area of southern Türkiye and northern Syria. The Turkish Government's initial response to the disaster was lethargic, and as the scale of destruction became evident, important questions began to emerge about the sheer number of collapsed buildings, many of which had been built during a construction boom under Erdoğan, and all of which were supposed to have been built according to strict legal guidelines to make them resistant to earthquakes. The obvious failure of many of the buildings in the affected area to withstand the two earthquakes raised troubling questions about the Government's enforcement (or lack thereof) of the guidelines, and the extent to which corruption had driven the process.

In the run-up to the general election of May 2023, therefore, there were certainly vulnerabilities for the opposition to exploit. Changes to the electoral law regarding representation in parliament that were approved in April 2022 meant that individual parties, or electoral alliances, now only needed to surpass a threshold of 7% of the vote (down from 10%) to achieve representation in parliament. This diminished the importance of having a unified opposition to challenge the ruling parties for purposes of parliamentary elections. At the same time, a divided opposition would be fatal to efforts to unseat Erdoğan in the presidential election. Hence, the main dilemma for the HDP was whether to field its own presidential candidate, thereby dividing the opposition vote, or to support the National Alliance's proposed candidate, Kemal Kılıçdaroğlu. The other main problem for the HDP was the uncertainty regarding the outcome of the closure case. Given that an adverse ruling delivered prior to the elections would result in a ban on the HDP presenting candidates for parliament, in March 2023 the party announced that its candidates would run under the banner of the Yeşil Sol Parti (YSP—Green Left Party) as part of the broader Labour and Freedom Alliance. About a month later, the HDP reached agreement with the CHP to support Kılıçdaroğlu's bid for the presidency. In return for Kurdish support, Kılıçdaroğlu made a number of pledges, including the release of the HDP's leader, Selahattin Demirtaş, from prison and an end to Erdoğan's practice of replacing elected Kurdish mayors with state-appointed 'administrators'.

Elections for the 600-seat Grand National Assembly took place on 14 May 2023 and delivered a disappointing result for those seeking to end President Erdoğan's dominance. While the AKP's share of the vote share fell, compared with the 2018 elections, and it lost 27 seats in parliament, the parties of the People's Alliance (of which the AKP was a member) collectively garnered a comfortable governing majority of 323 seats. Meanwhile, the main party of the National Alliance, the CHP, improved on its 2018 performance, adding 23 seats to its previous total of 146. From a Kurdish perspective, the results were disappointing, not just because the ruling parties maintained their majority, but also because the share of the vote secured by the main pro-Kurdish party (the YSP) declined by nearly three percentage points compared with 2018. However, the key prize in Turkish politics subsequent to the constitutional reforms of 2017 is the office of the presidency, and most of the polls leading up to the presidential election had suggested that with Kurdish support, Kılıçdaroğlu had a good chance of defeating Erdoğan.

The three main candidates running for the presidency were Erdoğan, representing the People's Alliance, the National Alliance's Kılıçdaroğlu and Sinan Oğan, the nominee of a new formation—the Ata İttifakı (ATA—Ancestral Alliance). The ATA consisted of several parties that had collectively won less than 3% of the votes in the parliamentary elections, and so Oğan's candidacy was not expected to make a difference to the outcome. However, his ultra-nationalist campaign, which focused on the immediate expulsion of Syrian refugees and a categorical refusal to negotiate with terrorists (namely the PKK) and their associated entities (the HDP), appeared to resonate beyond this limited base of voters, and in the first round of the election, Oğan's 5.2% of the vote was sufficient to deprive either of the two other candidates of an outright majority. Under Türkiye's two-round electoral system, if no candidate secures a majority in the first round of voting, the top two candidates take part in a run-off poll to determine the winner. For Kurds, this was arguably the worst possible outcome, as it made Oğan's endorsement potentially decisive to a second-round victory for either of the two remaining candidates, leading both to spend the time between the two ballots trying to outdo each other in terms of anti-immigrant and anti-Kurdish rhetoric. Oğan's eventual endorsement of Erdoğan led to the disintegration of the ATA, but it was also pivotal to Erdoğan's ultimate victory in the second round. The manner of Erdoğan's victory and his growing reliance on ultra-nationalist support makes any softening of Türkiye's approach toward the Kurdish question extremely implausible for the foreseeable future.

THE KURDISH QUESTION IN SYRIA

Syria emerged as a state in 1920 after the collapse of the Ottoman Empire and was under a French mandate until 1946. Syria and Lebanon became the centres of pan-Kurdish political and cultural activities during the 1920s and 1930s, which were spearheaded by the Kurdish intellectuals and nationalist leadership exiled from Türkiye, including Celaded Bedir Khan, Nureddin Zaza, Ekrem Cemilpaşa and Memduh Selim. The political and cultural activities of the exiled Kurdish intellectuals were important contributions to the development of Kurdish nationalism in the region and they were involved in the establishment of the Xoybûn (Being Oneself) nationalist organization. Important work on the grammatical development and standardization of the Kurmanji Kurdish language was produced by the exiled intellectuals during the 1930s and 1940s.

The Kurdish-majority areas in Syria do not constitute a continuous enclave, and areas populated by Arabs and other ethnic groups divide the Kurds' population centres. The first Kurdish political party in Syria, the Partiya Demokrat a Kurdistanê li Sûriyê (KDPS—Kurdistan Democratic Party of Syria), was established in 1957 under the leadership of Nureddin Zaza. The party advocated a similar political programme to the KDP in Iraqi Kurdistan and the origins of most of the current Kurdish political parties in Syria can be traced to the KDPS. However, soon after its establishment, the party was engulfed in a leadership struggle, with the modernist and traditional sections vying for control. In 1964 an internal struggle between the party's left and right wings took place, leading to the party splitting in 1965. The issue of whether Kurdish demands in Syria should be framed as a minority issue or a national one—that is, whether the Kurds of Syria were represented as part of the Kurdish nation or only an ethnic minority within Syria—constituted another source of conflict and disagreement and caused further divisions among the Kurdish political parties in the subsequent decades. The personal conflicts and disagreements among the leadership of these parties also contributed to the divisions the political parties experienced. From the 1970s onwards numerous other divisions emerged, with several groups breaking away to form new parties, which led to the further fragmentation of the Kurdish national movement in Syria.

Several incidents that took place in Kurdish regions of Syria in the 1960s symbolized the vulnerability and repression of Syria's Kurds. A fire in a cinema in the town of Amuda in 1960 that killed some 200 children left a huge mark on the Kurds' collective memory. Furthermore, as part of the Arabization policy of the Syrian state, following the population census of 1962 Syrian citizenship of around 120,000 Kurds was revoked, on the grounds that they were not native to Syria. This meant that nearly 20% of the Kurdish population in Syria was left stateless and described as either *ajanib* (foreigners) or *maktumiin* (unregistered people). Other Arabization policies pursued by successive Syrian governments during the 1960s and 1970s included taking away agricultural land from Kurds and redistributing it to ethnic Arabs in the Jazira region of northeastern Syria. The Government's aim was to create an 'Arab belt' along the Syrian–Turkish border as a protection against future Kurdish unrest in neighbouring Türkiye. Syria began implementing the policy from 1973 when it first settled ethnic Arabs who had been displaced by the construction of the Tabqa Dam on lands owned by Kurds. The policy was abandoned in 1976, but the Arabs who had settled on Kurdish land were not removed from the region.

The Kurdish political parties in Syria were illegal and conducted their activities clandestinely. As political parties had to conduct their activities in an environment of authoritarian rule, high risks associated with engaging in political mobilization dissuaded most people from engaging in politics, and Kurdish political parties from confronting the Syrian state. Consequently, the Kurdish political parties could not develop a popular base or initiate the types of struggles that have developed in Iraq or Türkiye. The unsuitability of the local geography was another factor behind the low levels of mass political mobilization in Syria. The Kurdish political parties framed their demands around ending the discrimination that the Kurds faced, around political and cultural rights for the Kurds, and democracy in Syria. While Kurdish grievances in Syria were not given a voice, the periodic bursts of Kurdish demands, particularly in 2004 and 2005 in the northeastern town of al-Qamishli, close to the border with Türkiye, demonstrated their potential effect.

Although the Syrian state kept a close eye on the activities of its native Kurdish political parties, it tolerated the activities of the Kurdish movements from Iraq and Türkiye on its territory. This created a paradoxical situation during the 1980s and 1990s in which Kurds were politicized and radicalized through Kurdish political organizations, most notably the PKK, but the oppression of the Kurds in Syria was not at the centre of Kurdish political activism in Syria. The view that Kurdish rights in Syria would be achieved only if the Kurdish movements in Iraq or Türkiye were successful was accepted widely among the Kurdish political parties in Syria. Even though the Syrian Kurdish political parties were not able to generate notable political mobilization in Syria, the support that the Kurdish political parties from Iraq and Türkiye drew from Syria's Kurds during the 1980s and 1990s was instrumental in their success, and meant that in that period the Kurds of Syria were, once again, making significant contributions to pan-Kurdish political developments. Furthermore, since the 1980s cultural output by Kurdish individuals in Syria, such as the poetry of Cigerxwîn (Sheikhmous Hasan) and the music of Ciwan Haco, has made a significant contribution to the wider Kurdish cultural renewal.

At the onset of the civil conflict in Syria in 2011 there were around 20 Kurdish political parties in Syria. Many of these political parties were brought together under the umbrella of the Encûmena Niştimanî ya Kurdî li Sûriyê (KNC—Kurdish National Council) later that year, although a number of them left in subsequent years. Since 2011 the Partiya Yekîtiya Demokrat (PYD—Democratic Union Party) has been the dominant political force in the Kurdish-majority regions of Syria and has spearheaded political developments there. The PYD was established by former Syrian Kurdish members of the PKK in 2003. The PKK leader Abdullah Öcalan was based in Syria or Syrian-controlled territories of Lebanon from 1979 to 1998. From the early 1980s the PKK began to organize among the Kurdish population in Syria, and in subsequent years managed to win their popular support. A number of other Kurdish representative organizations have been established in Syria since 2011, including the Tevgera Civaka Demokratîk (Movement for a Democratic Society) and the Meclîsa Gel a Rojavayê Kurdistanê (People's Council of Western Kurdistan). These organizations act as umbrella bodies for the local and district councils and have been involved in the development of Kurdish-led autonomy in Syria.

One of the main factors behind the PYD's success is the effectiveness of its military forces—the Yekîneyên Parastina Gel (YPG—People's Protection Units) and the Yekîneyên Parastina Jin (YPJ—Women's Protection Units)—in defending the communities of northern Syria against the attacks of Islamic State, particularly since 2013. The jihadist threat has continued, but has been repelled due to the discipline, dedication and military acumen of the YPG fighters, combined with the support received from 2014 from the international military coalition fighting Islamic State. There has not been a significant confrontation between the Syrian army and Kurdish forces. From October 2015 the YPG, along with a number of other opposition groups, established the Hêzên Sûriya Demokratîk (SDF—Syrian Democratic Forces), which strengthened the Kurds' commitment to a democratic united Syria. The Arab and Syriac groups within the SDF include the Syriac Military Council and the Jaysh al-Thuwar (Army of Revolutionaries), plus smaller groups previously affiliated to the Free Syrian Army (FSA) and Arab tribal militias. Current estimates of the number of fighters in the SDF range between 80,000 and 100,000; Mazloum Kobani Abdi has been the Commander-in-Chief of the SDF since its formation. The size of the Arab component of the SDF has been steadily increasing since 2015, with new fighters recruited and trained as part of the Raqqa and Deir el-Zor campaigns against Islamic State; currently Arab fighters comprise the majority of the total. As the Kurdish–Islamic State conflict accelerated, many Kurds from Türkiye and some Turkish left-wing activists also joined the YPG and YPJ, while in recent years Western fighters (mainly leftist revolutionaries, internationalists and former soldiers) began to join the Kurdish forces in small numbers. There are a number of other armed organizations at local level: these include the Syrian Civil Defence Forces, the local military councils and the Asayish.

Although intra-Kurdish relations since 2011 in Syria have not always been cordial, the tensions have not resulted in an armed conflict. The PYD has been accused of suppressing the activities of the political parties linked to the KNC and of generally being intolerant to dissent. Such political disagreements have continued despite attempts to secure an agreement among the Syrian Kurdish political parties. In July 2012 the KRG brokered an agreement that led to the creation of the Desteya Bilind a Kurd (Kurdish Supreme Committee)—an umbrella organization bringing together the PYD and the KNC—and the establishment of a form of power sharing in the administration of Kurdish-controlled areas, including the co-ordination of the activities of the YPG. However, the agreement was not implemented: the resultant continuation of tensions led to a new round of talks being held in Duhok, in the Kurdish Autonomous Region, in October 2014, which in turn produced a fresh power-sharing agreement.

Kurdish political parties in Syria do not advocate the creation of their own independent Kurdish state. Rather, their goals consist of: extensive autonomy for Kurds; a pluralist democratic system; and recognition of the rights of all the ethnic and religious minorities in Syria. The Kurds have been managing their own affairs in the areas they control since the withdrawal of Syrian state forces in July 2012. The Kurds' autonomous administration took a more organized form in January 2014 when the cantons of Rojava were established. The term 'Rojava', meaning 'west' in the Kurdish language, refers to the Kurdish areas in Syria that are popularly referred to as Rojavayê Kurdistanê (Western Kurdistan). Initially three cantons were established, in Jazira, Kobani and Afrin in the north-east, north and north-west of the country, respectively. In March 2016 the cantons of Rojava were brought together under the umbrella federal administration of the Democratic Federal System of Rojava–Northern Syria. However, at an organizing council meeting held in December, the term 'Rojava' was removed from the federal administration's name and it became known formally as the Democratic Federation of Northern Syria (DFNS). The Kurdish leadership argued that such a step had become necessary, especially after the capture of territories historically populated by Arabs, such as Tell Abyad, Manbij and Raqqa. In September 2018 the autonomous entity changed its name once more, to the Autonomous Administration of North and East Syria (AANES). Although the Kurds are the main force behind the AANES, it is not organized along ethnic lines and aspires to be a multi-ethnic entity with decentralized administration and representative bodies to accommodate all of the ethno-cultural groups in northern Syria. From its establishment in 2016 until September 2018, the DFNS's most senior officials were its co-Presidents Hediya Yousef, a Kurd, and Mansur Selum, an Arab from Tell Abyad. Following the formation of the AANES, a Syriac Christian politician, Siham Qairou, and Farid Ati, a Kurd from Kobani, were elected as the organization's co-Chairs.

The AANES is designated as a decentralized self-governing entity, which brings together several autonomous entities and seeks to remain part of a decentralized and federal Syria. The internal territorial decentralization of the federation is considered necessary to provide representation to the region's diverse ethnic groups and to promote co-existence among them. The AANES is the highest-level representative body, and its objective is to strengthen the position of the Democratic Autonomous Administrations at the Syrian, regional and international levels. It embodies the principle of decentralization and grassroots democracy organized at the level of local councils. This structure is considered essential for the involvement of the local population in the decision-making process, and it enables the population to elect delegates to represent the local councils in higher representative bodies, including at district, provincial and regional levels.

There are a number of other representative organizations, including the Meclîsa Sûriya Demokratîk (Syrian Democratic Council), which was established in December 2015 and comprises representatives of different ethnic and political groups. One of the main features of the Kurdish military and political mobilization in Syria has been the central role women have played as part of the militias and the Asayish, which is estimated to number around 15,000. Women are part of the political representative institutions at the local and regional level, with all of the significant political offices being shared by women and men through the co-chairing system. The system has been developed to promote gender equality in terms of political representation. Since its establishment, the Kurdish-led AANES has made significant strides, but the uncertainty about its long-term future continues. Its prospects are connected to and conditional upon finding a durable long-term political solution to the ongoing conflict in Syria. To date, Kurdish representatives have not been included in the international attempts to find a solution to the conflict, such as the UN-sponsored talks in Geneva, Switzerland, due to the opposition from Türkiye and Syrian opposition groups. The AANES has strengthened its position by cultivating stronger political and military relations with the international powers involved in the region, including the USA and France. The AANES administration has maintained a willingness to enter into dialogue and negotiations with the Syrian state, but it remains to be seen whether the level of autonomy demanded by the Kurds will be recognized.

Assessing Kurdish prospects in Syria is a difficult task because of the fluidity of the situation in that country. Since the beginning of 2015 the Kurdish-led SDF has increased the territory it controls by capturing areas under the control of Islamic State. However, since August 2016 Türkiye has increased its military presence in northern and north-western Syria. Turkish military intervention has increasingly targeted the Kurdish-controlled regions and is primarily based on empowering its Turkmen and Arab allies. In April 2016 the Turkish Air Force carried out attacks against several YPG positions, and in November, supported by FSA and Islamist militias, it launched an operation in al-Bab in northern Aleppo to prevent the SDF from capturing more territory and establishing a land connection to the Kurdish canton of Afrin. In January 2018 Turkish troops and FSA units loyal to Türkiye began a ground offensive with the stated aim of clearing the YPG presence from Afrin, which was completed in mid-March. As a result of the Turkish and FSA offensive, according to the UN, an estimated 183,500 Kurds were displaced from Afrin and sought refuge in Tal Refaat. Türkiye continued its threats to invade the territory under the control of the AANES. Such threats resulted in an agreement between the USA and Turkey in August 2019 to set up a security zone along the Turkish–Syrian border to be jointly monitored by both countries.

However, despite the establishment of the security zone along the Turkish–Syrian border, Türkiye pursued its objective to invade the majority-Arab populated towns of Tell Abyad (Girê Spî) and Ras al-Ayn (Serê Kaniye) in northern Syria in October 2019. The Turkish invasion resulted in widespread displacement of the Kurdish population from these cities and the settlement of ethnic Arabs close to the Turkish-backed Syrian military groups. In order to prevent a full Turkish invasion, the AANES accepted the stationing of Russian and Syrian military forces along the Turkish–Syrian border.

Another significant consequence of the Turkish invasion of northern Syria was the US Administration's decision to withdraw from Syria its forces supporting the SDF in the fight against Islamic State. The desire to withdraw all US military personnel stationed in Syria was first mentioned by US President Donald Trump in December 2018, and this was expected to be a phased withdrawal. However, in February the Administration had decided to keep a small number of US troops in Syria indefinitely. Following the Turkish invasion, US forces began withdrawing from the border areas and relocated in the north-eastern and eastern regions of Syria, mainly tasked with preventing the Government of Syrian President Bashar al-Assad from accessing those regions' oil and gas resources. In early August 2020 the SDF signed an agreement with an unnamed US oil company, covering rights to explore for oil deposits in the region under SDF control and to build a US $150m. refinery.

Nevertheless, no significant armed clashes between the YPG/SDF and the Syrian army have taken place, and since 2018 representatives of the AANES and the Assad Government have engaged in dialogue. Syrian state officials have frequently reiterated their desire to bring under its control the areas held by the Kurdish-led forces and have rejected Kurdish demands for extensive autonomy. After the Turkish invasion in October 2019, dialogue with the Syrian Government to find a political agreement for the reintegration of the AANES into

Syria intensified. However, while the dialogue continued, the Assad Government and the AANES remained far apart on the issue of autonomy.

There were efforts to broker a further power-sharing agreement between the different Kurdish political factions during 2020 and 2021. However, the dialogue process between the KNC and the political bloc headed by the PYD reached an impasse in October 2020. The USA and France had supported the talks, which began in March, with a second phase commencing in August. Some progress was made on the establishment of a joint Kurdish administration ('Kurdish High Council'), with each main bloc being allocated 16 seats, and four seats being reserved for independent political figures, but the talks broke down without a final agreement.

The territories under the control of the AANES experienced a relatively calm period during 2020 and 2021. Some instances of tension and armed conflict between the Asayish and the regime's National Defence Forces (NDF) militia in the city of al-Qamishli, in the al-Hasakah governorate, took place in early 2021. In late April clashes between the NDF and the Asayish took place in the al-Tay neighbourhood of al-Qamishli. On 23 April the NDF forces withdrew from the al-Tay neighbourhood to villages under their control in the surrounding region, following an agreement mediated by Russia, leaving the Asayish in control.

On 28 March 2021 a large-scale anti-terrorist operation was launched by the Asayish, with the support of the SDF, in the al-Hol camp against Islamic State members and underground cells operating in the camp. The operation was carried out following an increase in the number of murders carried out in the camp, and more than 30 people linked to Islamic State were detained on the first day. Several high-ranking Islamic State leaders and members were captured, and in total, the operation resulted in the arrest of 125 people linked with Islamic State. The operations continued throughout May and June, and resulted in the capture of several Islamic State cells, particularly in the Deir el-Zor governorate.

Reports of human right violations against Kurds in Afrin continued to emerge during 2020 and 2021. In many instances, Kurds were arbitrarily detained by Turkish-backed Syrian groups and their properties appropriated. Some of the confiscated properties were sold by the Turkish-backed groups to Arabs who had settled there after the Turkish invasion. Similar human rights violations frequently occured in other areas under the control of these groups. In some cases, people were detained for long periods, and in others they were detained randomly following an event or attack. Media reports detailed many cases of the kidnapping of girls and young women, some of whom were killed and denounced as terrorists. They were often subjected to sexual violence and threatened with rape if their families failed to pay a demanded ransom to these armed groups.

A potentially significant development affecting the AANES since 2021 has been severe water shortages in the region, resulting from damage to the Alouk water pumping station and a substantial reduction in the amount of water flowing into the region from the Euphrates River. The Alouk water station is based in the countryside of Ras al-Ayn, in the northern part of the al-Hasakah governorate, and distributes water to nearly 1m. people in al-Hasakah city and the surrounding towns and villages. The AANES authorities have tried to transport water to al-Hasakah city in tankers but have not been able to meet the residents' needs.

Attacks by Turkish-backed Syrian groups on the rural areas controlled by the AANES have increased in recent years, as have the human rights violations committed against the Kurds in the areas under the control of Turkish-backed Syrian groups. Türkiye increased its drone attacks on these targets in August 2021, primarily targeting SDF commanders. A drone attack in mid-August targeted a building used as a communication centre by the SDF in Til Temir district, killing two SDF commanders and two fighters. In November a Turkish drone attack targeted the city of al-Qamishli, hitting a military vehicle and killing three people, and in the following month Türkiye carried out a drone attack in Kobani that targeted a youth centre. Six members of the Revolutionary Youth Movement died in the attack, and three were injured.

In February 2022 Türkiye carried out six drone attacks targeting vehicles associated with the SDF and officials linked with the AANES or the PYD, killing eight individuals, including five SDF fighters and two children, and injuring 13 others. Shelling of AANES territories by the Turkish-backed Syrian National Army (SNA, a coalition of armed Syrian opposition groups) continued in early 2022, resulting in several civilians suffering injuries. Arrests of Kurdish civilians in areas under the control of the SNA also continued. According to Kurdish sources, 88 civilians were arrested in Afrin alone in the first two months of the year. In May the Turkish Ministry of National Defence claimed that the SDF had shelled the border gendarmerie station in Karkamish, but the SDF denied any involvement in the incident. Turkish soldiers attacked several positions of the SDF in northern Syria in the same month, and Turkish drone attacks targeting individuals associated with the SDF and the AANES authorities have continued since May.

On 23 May 2022 President Erdoğan announced that Türkiye was taking steps to complete the remaining sections of a 30 km-wide security zone along its southern border. On 1 June Erdoğan again threatened to launch a military operation in northern Syria and specified the targets as the cities of Manbij and Tel Rifaat in the north of the governorate of Aleppo, which hosted many internally displaced persons (IDPs) from the Afrin area. The Turkish Government subsequently intensified its diplomatic efforts to obtain a green light for the operation from Russia, Iran and the USA. In mid-June Turkish officials met Iranian and Russian officials under the aegis of the Syrian peace negotiations known as the Astana Process. However, the meetings did not conclusively indicate that either Iran or Russia supported a new Turkish military operation. In response to the Turkish threats of launching a fresh offensive in northern Syria, Russia and Iran reinforced their bases in and around Manbij and Tel Rifaat.

The decision to withdraw US troops from Afghanistan, and the chaotic scenes that the world witnessed as the 31 August 2021 deadline for their evacuation approached, heightened Kurdish fears that US troops would also withdraw from Syria and abandon the Kurdish-led forces in that country. The Administration of US President Joe Biden reassured the Kurds in Syria that the USA had no immediate plans to withdraw from the region. The US embassy in Syria announced via social media that a meeting had taken place on 29 August between Acting Assistant Secretary of State for Near Eastern Affairs Joey Hood and the SDF, during which the USA had emphasized its 'commitment to the campaign against Islamic State and stability in the region'. Hood also stated that he expected 'stronger political and military support' from the Biden Administration. The Commander of the SDF, Mazloum Abdi, reported in September that the US delegation had reassured him that there would not be any changes on the ground in terms of the US military presence in Syria.

An Islamic State attack on Sina'a prison, in the Ghuwayran district of al-Hasakah city, in January 2022 was the most significant attack carried out by the militant group since March 2019, when it lost territorial control over much of Syria. Sina'a prison, the largest prison in the AANES, held about 4,000 Islamic State prisoners, including some 700 minors known as the 'Cubs of the Caliphate'. According to the SDF, about 200 Islamic State militants were involved in the attack, which began with the explosion of a car bomb at the main prison gate, which destroyed a prison wall. The Islamic State militants were thought to have crossed into AANES territory from areas under the control of the SNA and attacked the prison from multiple directions using heavy artillery. The attack was followed by prisoners starting a riot; after seizing weapons, they killed many of the prison guards and ancillary staff and took some staff hostage. A small number of prisoners escaped from the prison and were at large for nine days before being recaptured. Clashes between the Islamic State and Kurdish-led forces outside the prison continued for several days before the SDF declared the prison and the surrounding areas secure on 30 January 2022. According to figures released by SDF, 374 Islamic State militants and prisoners died in the attack, as well as 77 prison guards and other staff, 40 SDF fighters and seven civilians.

In March 2022 the SNA began a blockade of the shipment of medicines and other products to the Kurdish-majority neighbourhoods of Sheikh Maksud and Ashrafiye in Aleppo; the group had previously blocked the entry of fuel, flour and other basic foodstuffs into the area. In response to the blockade, on 9 April the SDF blocked the entrances and exits of areas controlled by the Syrian regime forces in the eastern cities of al-Hasakah and al-Qamishli. Local sources reported that SNA forces and AANES officials held a meeting in al-Qamishli, mediated by Russian officials, to discuss the lifting of the blockade on the Kurdish neighbourhoods in Aleppo in exchange for an end to the SDF's counter-blockade on regime forces in al-Qamishli and al-Hasakah. From mid-April the Russian mediation efforts intensified, and at the end of the month the two sides agreed to lift their respective blockades.

The situation for Syria's Kurds remained precarious during the rest of 2022 and the first half of 2023. As Türkiye was apparently unable to reach agreement with the Syrian Government on a mutually acceptable way to end the conflict, Türkiye's fallback strategy continued to consist of using artillery and drone and air strikes to attack SDF targets inside Syria. These attacks escalated significantly in November 2022, when the Turkish armed forces launched Operation Claw-Sword. The operation was prompted by a bombing on 13 November in a busy street in İstanbul that killed six people and injured more than 80 others. According to the Turkish authorities, the perpetrator was a Syrian Kurdish woman who had entered Türkiye from Afrin, which naturally led the Turkish Government to accuse the PKK and the YPG of orchestrating the attack. Operation Claw-Sword marked a significant escalation in Türkiye's military involvement in northern Syria and risked destabilizing an already delicate geopolitical environment. On 19 November, for example, Turkish air strikes in northern Syria resulted in the deaths of 11 civilians and dozens of SDF fighters, but also killed 18 members of the Syrian army. Other strikes targeted SDF personnel in close proximity to bases occupied by US troops. In response to the air strikes and a threatened ground invasion by the Turkish armed forces, SDF officials announced a suspension of anti-Islamic State operations in order to prepare for an all-out Turkish military assault that could 'occur at any time', according to the Turkish Government. What seems to have prevented the threatened invasion was the strong opposition of Russia and, more importantly, the USA. In a telephone call on 30 November with his Turkish counterpart, US Secretary of State for Defense Lloyd Austin warned that Turkish air strikes were threatening the lives of US troops in Syria and undermining efforts to combat Islamic State. Austin called for de-escalation and expressed the USA's 'strong opposition to a new Turkish military operation in Syria'.

It is, unfortunately, not easy to envisage a positive outcome for any of the participants in the ongoing Syrian conflict. As made clear in the Turkish elections in May 2023, the continued presence of more than 3.5m. Syrian refugees in Türkiye has become an explosive issue in Turkish politics. However, a minimum requirement for any resettlement plan, given the large number of people involved, is a degree of stability in Syria that simply does not currently exist, coupled with some sort of agreement between Türkiye and the Assad regime that the latter seems unwilling to countenance. Ongoing efforts by Türkiye to 'normalize' relations have been consistently rebuffed by the Assad regime and, in any case, are adamantly opposed by Turkish-backed opposition forces inside Syria. Furthermore, an unknown, but probably large, number of the refugees are in that situation because they actively opposed the Syrian regime and do not want to return to Syria for obvious reasons. This makes 'voluntary' resettlement on any scale implausible. In the absence of an agreement, large swathes of territory in northern Syria, including most of Idlib governorate, will remain outside the control of the Syrian Government and occupied by armed opponents of the regime. In the midst of this, the position of the Kurds and the future status of the AANES remain tenuous, at best. The one point of consensus between the Governments of Türkiye and Syria is implacable hostility to any sort of formal autonomy for the AANES, so whatever the eventual outcome of the conflict, the Kurds will face a fight to preserve what they have. The lifeline for the Kurds is the presence of US troops in Syria, and the critical role played by the SDF in Operation Inherent Resolve (the ongoing multinational military intervention against Islamic State). Hence, the survival of the AANES is contingent on decisions made in Washington, DC, and, quite possibly, the outcome of the US presidential election in November 2024.

THE KURDISH QUESTION IN IRAN

The origins of the contemporary Kurdish movement in Iran dates back to the early 1940s. The Hizbi Demokirati Kurdistani Eran (Democratic Party of Iranian Kurdistan—PDKI) has historically been the main Kurdish political party in Iran. The origin of the PDKI dates back to the Komalay Jiyanaway Kurdistan (Komalay J. K.—Society for the Revival of Kurdistan), which was established as a clandestine organization in September 1942 in Mahabad. It was organized in small cells and one of its main activities was the publication of its newspaper *Nishtiman* (Fatherland). Komalay J. K. was abolished and integrated into the PDKI when the party was formally established in August 1945. The PDKI's main demand was the establishment of an autonomous Kurdish region within Iran.

One of the main developments that the PDKI initiated was the formation of the Kurdish republic in Mahabad, which came about as a result of the Soviet occupation of northern Iran during the Second World War. The Kurdish Republic was formally established on 22 January 1946 and existed for almost a year. In May, when the Soviet forces withdrew from Iran, the existence of the Republic came under threat, and, in the significantly changed domestic context in Iran, numerous Kurdish tribes soon began to withdraw their support from the PDKI and its leader Qazi Muhammad. In December Iranian troops entered Mahabad and recaptured the city from Kurdish forces, and in March 1947 Qazi Muhammad, his brother and cousin were executed by hanging in Mahabad.

During the mid-1960s, under its new leader Abd-Allah Ishaqi, the PDKI began moving towards the right ideologically, and closer to Mullah Mustafa Barzani's line within the KDP. As part of the conditions of military aid that the KDP was receiving from Iran, Mullah Mustafa Barzani demanded that the PDKI end its activities against Iran. The demand was not met by some of the leaders and supporters of the PDKI, who formed a Revolutionary Committee and, in March 1967, launched an armed campaign against Iran. The insurgency lasted for 18 months, but ultimately the Kurdish forces were not able to withstand the counterattack by the Iranian army, whose task was facilitated by help provided by the KDP. During this period many of the PDKI members, including one of its leaders, Suleiman Moini, were killed by the KDP *peshmerga*. Moini's body was handed over to the Iranian authorities. In 1973, during the third conference of the PDKI, Abdul Rahman Ghassemlou was elected as the party's leader, replacing Ahmed Tawfiq, who supported the conservative faction of the party and was a close associate of the KDP leader Barzani. The party's third congress also adopted the slogan 'Democracy for Iran, Autonomy for Kurdistan' and committed itself to armed struggle.

Komala (or, to use its full name, the Komala Party of Iranian Kurdistan) was the other main Kurdish political party in Iran. It has been claimed that the party was formed in 1969 in Tabriz by a group of students, but its existence was declared publicly only in 1979. It was not openly a Kurdish nationalist group and advocated a more social liberationist programme; its main objectives were administrative decentralization and co-operation with other communities in Iran to defeat the central Government. Komala was particularly strong in the Sanandaj and Mariwan regions and its formulation of Kurdish autonomy demands was similar to that of the PDKI; the main difference was Komala's greater emphasis on 'workers' rights and agrarian policies' in its political programme. Together with a number of other Iranian left-wing political groups, Komala formed the Communist Party of Iran (CPI) in 1982. However, its members gradually drifted away from the CPI and Komala reappeared under its own name in 1991. Komala's existence challenged the PDKI's claim to be the sole leader of the Kurdish people in Iran.

As the protests and upheaval in Iran intensified in late 1978 against the increasingly despotic rule of Reza (Shah) Pahlavi, Kurds seized large quantities of weapons and became the main force on the ground in the majority Kurdish regions. Large numbers of Kurds took part in the Islamic Revolution of January–February 1979 and in April the PDKI established control in Kurdish areas and the main towns of the region, including Sanandaj, Mariwan, Naqadeh and Saqiz. However, instead of the recognition of their autonomy that the Kurds demanded, their rule came under military attack once the hardliners consolidated their rule following the resignation of the interim Prime Minister, Mehdi Bazargan, in November. Kurds had taken part in the parliamentary elections held in mid-1979 and elected candidates from the Kurdish political parties, although the elected Kurdish representatives were never allowed to attend the parliament.

The PDKI's demands for extensive autonomy and the creation of a Kurdish administrative region in Iran were not met by the newly established Islamist Government. Until 1983 fighting took place between the Kurdish militias and the regime's armed forces, with Kurdish rural areas being largely under Kurdish control and Kurdish towns under regime control. In mid-1982 the Iranian army began a large-scale assault on Kurdish-held territories, and by the end of 1983 almost all Kurdish-held territory had been captured. In total an estimated 10,000 Kurds died in the conflict during the late 1970s and early 1980s as a result of fighting between Kurdish forces and the Iranian army, including the summary executions of Kurdish civilians and political activists by the Iranian army.

Since 1982 the PDKI has operated inside Iraq and has received assistance from the PUK. Between 1981 and 1982 the PDKI and Komala co-operated militarily and managed to re-launch an armed struggle against Iran. The Iran–Iraq war (1980–88) opened up opportunities for the Kurdish political parties, and the military aid that the Kurdish parties in Iran received from the Iraqi Government led to the decision to restart the armed struggle against Iran. However, in November 1984 they faced each other in an internal conflict that lasted until 1988. In the late 1980s both the PDKI and Komala were beset by multiple internal divisions and they remained fragmented, with a number of opposing factions in existence, into the 21st century.

Due to the severe restrictions placed on Kurdish political activism, the leadership of Kurdish nationalist parties was based outside of Iran, mainly in Iraqi Kurdistan and in Europe. The PDKI split into two factions in 1988 and its leader, Ghassemlou, was assassinated in the Austrian capital, Vienna, in July 1989. A senior Komala leader was assassinated in Larnaca, Cyprus in 1989, and in September 1992 two of the PDKI's senior leaders and its Secretary-General, Sadegh Sharafkandi, were assassinated in the German capital, Berlin. There were many other victims of Iran's campaign against politically active Kurds, and according to some estimates Iranian agents murdered more than 200 Kurds in Iraqi Kurdistan during the early 1990s. These assassinations significantly weakened Iran's Kurdish movement. As a reaction against the assassination of its leaders, the PDKI intensified its armed campaign against Iran in 1991, and its forces remained active until 1996, when the party agreed to pull its fighters out of the country. Since then, the PDKI has mainly been based in the Kurdish Autonomous Region of Iraq.

The years since 2004 have witnessed the emergence of the Partiya Jiyana Azad a Kurdistanê (PJAK—Party of Free Life in Kurdistan) and its sporadic attacks against Iranian soldiers in Kurdish-majority regions of north-western Iran. Headquartered in the remote Qandil Mountains, the PJAK has demonstrated a significant degree of resilience. It is considered as an offshoot of the PKK in Türkiye and has been involved in an insurgency and occasional clashes with the Iranian forces since its establishment. It advocates decentralization of political power in Iran, an end to restrictions on Kurdish freedom of association and culture, recognition of the Kurds as a nation and their linguistic rights in education and broadcasting, and the political representation of the Kurds in Iran. There have been occasional clashes between PJAK guerrillas and the Iranian Revolutionary Guard Corps (IRGC) which have often resulted in casualties. One of the largest operations carried out by Iran against PJAK guerrillas was in mid-2011, which, according to the commander of the IRGC, resulted in the deaths of over 180 PJAK fighters. Since then, the level of violence in the conflict has declined substantially. However, it has not been completely eliminated, as occasional clashes between the PJAK guerrillas and the IRGC continue to take place.

In addition to the occasional military clashes between PJAK guerrillas and the IRGC, during mid-2016 PDKI fighters carried out attacks against the IRGC. These attacks were perpetrated by the dominant faction of the PDKI led by Mustafa Hijri, who has been the leading figure in the party since the assassination of Sharafkandi in 1992. A minority wing of the PDKI had been led by Abdullah Hasanzadeh as a separate organization since 2006, and its members deserted the PDKI in late 2006 and regrouped themselves as the KDP-Iran. Komala suffered similar fragmentation in 2007, and there are currently two distinct branches that are active. The Komala-CPI is led by Ebrahim Alizadeh and retains a stronger affinity to the CPI, while the Komala-PIK (Party of Iranian Kurdistan) is led by Abdullah Mohtadi and has a stronger focus on Kurdish rights.

The tensions in 2016 continued for several weeks but they did not lead to an escalation in the conflict. The different factions of the PDKI and Komala have made a stronger attempt to revive the Kurdish struggle in Iran. The desire to re-establish themselves and preserve their status as important actors in Kurdish politics in Iran can be seen as a reaction against the PJAK's resurgence and subsequent dominance. At the same time, they have been framing a solution to the Iran's Kurdish question in new terms; for example, since 2004 the PDKI has been calling for a solution to the Kurdish question in Iran on the basis of a 'federalist framework' that involves the establishment of a federal Kurdish region 'within a democratic federalist Iran'.

Mass protests and civil unrest by Kurds have taken place frequently in Iran in recent years. These events have had many different causes, but by and large they reflect the growing discontent among Kurds. One of the last major incidents of protest occurred in May 2015 in Mahabad, triggered by the death of a young Kurdish woman, Farinaz Khosrawani, who fell from the fourth floor of the hotel at which she was working as she tried to escape from a security guard accused of attempting to sexually assault her. The protests spread to the city of Sardasht, where clashes between the police and Kurdish protesters also took place. In 2005 Kurds in Iran had taken part in widespread demonstrations that lasted for three weeks and were triggered by the shooting of a Kurdish rights activist by the Iranian security forces. Kurds also participated in nationwide protests after President Mahmoud Ahmadinejad was elected to a second term in office in May 2009. The continuation of discriminatory practices against the Kurdish minority and the failure by successive governments to address Kurdish grievances have resulted in growing widespread anti-establishment feelings among the Kurds. This was reflected in the large numbers of Kurds participating in the anti-Government protests that took place in Iran in December 2017 and January 2018.

The anti-regime protests that broke out in September 2022 were the most serious since the Green Revolution of 2009–10 and arguably represented the most significant challenge to the legitimacy of the Islamic regime since its inception. As is often the case, Iranian Kurds were at the forefront of the protests, which were sparked by the death of a 22-year-old Kurdish woman from Saqqez, named Mahsa Amini. Amini had been arrested by the Guidance Patrol (colloquially known as the 'morality police') in the Iranian capital, Tehran, for allegedly wearing her *hijab* (Islamic headscarf) improperly and subsequently died in police custody. The focus of Western media attention was overwhelmingly on the victim's gender identity and the regime's repressive policies towards women, but Amini's Kurdish ethnicity was also a relevant factor that helps to explain why the Kurdish-inhabited regions of Iran became both the epicentre of resistance and also bore the brunt (along with Sistan and Baluchestan province) of the Government's harsh response.

During the week following Amini's death, as demonstrations spread across Iran, the government crackdown led to the deaths of over 50 protesters and nearly 900 others being injured in Kurdish-majority areas alone. In an effort to curb the growing tide of anger, the regime shut down access to the internet across Iran and imposed curfews on Kurdish cities. The IRGC also launched artillery strikes against Iranian Kurdish opposition groups based in the Kurdish Autonomous Region of Iraq, accusing them of orchestrating the protests. In response, the umbrella Cooperation Center of Iranian Kurdistan's Political Parties issued a statement supporting the goals of the protests, but rejecting any attempt to militarize the protest movement. While the initial armed strikes did not result in casualties, this changed in late September 2022, when the IRGC attacked the Kurdish Autonomous Region with 'suicide drones' and ballistic missiles, killing 18 people and injuring more than 50 others. Although widely condemned by Western powers, the IRGC vowed to continue targeting parties inside Iraq, unless the KRG expelled all Iranian Kurdish opposition groups from its territory.

In the end, the 'Mahsa Revolution' followed a similar trajectory to most mass protests that had taken place in Iran since 1979. The harshly repressive approach adopted by the authorities to initial displays of dissent provoked widespread international outrage and served to fuel popular anger inside Iran in the short term, leading many Western analysts to predict the imminent demise of the Islamic regime. In December 2022 the Iranian leadership appeared sufficiently concerned about the course of events to make concessions to protesters' demands, and it was widely reported in the Western media that the 'morality police' was to be disbanded and that parliament would be reviewing the law governing the wearing of the *hijab* in public. Over time, however, the relentlessness of the regime's crackdown took its toll. Although exact numbers are impossible to determine, by the end of 2022 the number of protesters killed by the Basij (a division of the IRGC) probably exceeded 500, with thousands more injured and tens of thousands arrested. Contrary to Western media reports, the 'morality police' was not disbanded; its patrols were temporarily suspended and renewed in July 2023. Meanwhile, proposed new legislation was announced in August, which, if approved, would not end the requirement for women to wear the *hijab* in public, but would merely change the punishments for infractions and place the onus on businesses to enforce the law.

The ability of the protest movement to attract support that transcended social class, region, age and ethnic identity was viewed as an important source of strength, but in terms of achieving tangible concessions from the regime, it was also a source of weakness. Any movement as diverse as this inevitably lacks a coherent leadership capable of articulating clear-cut demands, and while the focus of attention was obviously centred on women's rights and the enforcement of restrictive dress codes by the 'morality police', many participants were animated by other concerns, such as the regime's treatment of ethnic minorities or the perpetually dire state of the Iranian economy. All of the protesters may have shared a desire to displace the current regime, but there was no shared vision concerning the nature of what should replace it.

Much the same problem afflicts organized opposition to the regime. The two main exiled movements that seek Western support for replacing the Islamic regime are the Mujahidin-e-Khalq (People's Mojahedin Organization of Iran) and the Alliance for Democracy and Freedom in Iran, led by the former Crown Prince of Iran, Reza Pahlavi. In an effort to capitalize on the protest movement, the latter brought together several key opposition figures to draft a 'Charter of Solidarity and Alliance for Freedom'. Dubbed the 'Mahsa Charter', the four-page document was published in March 2023 and was strongly supported by one of the Iranian Kurdish parties (Komala), but equally strongly opposed by the other major Iranian Kurdish parties. From a Kurdish perspective, the sharpness of this division was unfortunate because during 2022 and into 2023 there had been growing unity among Iranian Kurdish parties. In August 2022, for example, it emerged that the PDKI and the KDP-Iran were in the final stages of a two-year process to reunite following the schism of 2006. The reunification of the two parties was officially announced at a ceremony held in August 2022. This was followed in November by an announcement that the two main factions of Komala were also reuniting as a single entity. By June 2023, however, the reunification deal had apparently broken down irreparably, and the two factions of Komala were openly engaging in military confrontations in the Iraqi Kurdish Autonomous Region.

The Islamic regime in Iran apparently continues to command the loyalty of powerful coercive institutions—most importantly the Basij and the IRGC; but even if the regime were somehow to be overthrown, the seeming inability of Iranian Kurdish political leaders to transcend their differences, whether these be personal, ideological or over tactics and strategy, would remain a major impediment to the achievement of full Kurdish rights in Iran.

KURDISH PROSPECTS

In Iraq since 1991 and Syria since 2011 the sovereign control of the states over the Kurdish populated territories has significantly weakened, but the existing state of order in the region remains intact and attempts at a new configuration that reflects the ethnopolitical divisions face strong regional and international opposition. The Kurdish Autonomous Region's independence bid in Iraq in September 2017 demonstrated that there are significant barriers to the establishment of a Kurdish state, particularly regarding the attainment of the necessary recognition from neighbouring states and the international community. Therefore, forms of autonomy and self-governance within the existing states to address the popular Kurdish demands remain a more realizable objective for the Kurds.

Kurdish demands can be accommodated within existing state boundaries if the current centralized structure of the existing states in the region is decentralized and a new political culture that recognizes diversity and political pluralism takes root. For this to be realized, a new regional-level framework for the accommodation of Kurdish rights is needed. More broadly, the transformation and peaceful resolution of Kurdish conflicts in the region need to be incorporated into the international community's efforts to build peace and stability in the wider region. A new regional consensus on the accommodation of Kurdish demands for autonomy within existing state boundaries needs to be built.

Historically, the policies of the states with Kurdish populations have been shaped around repression and denial of Kurdish rights, and such a framework still dominates the thinking of national policymakers. For Iran and Türkiye—the two regional powers that have significant Kurdish populations—the Kurdish question in the Middle East is seen as a domestic and regional-level security threat as well as a barrier to the countries' ambitions to extend their political influence in the region. The positions of Kurdish actors and entities have been strengthened by the stronger ties that they have managed to build with the international powers involved in the anti-Islamic State campaign in Iraq and Syria. In these two countries, Kurdish resurgence has been aided by US protection and support, and the Kurds' future success is strongly tied to their continuation. However, the USA does not have a long-term Kurdish strategy. Despite the absence of an overall grand strategy, the view that the Kurds have played an important role in combating Islamic State has gained widespread acceptance within international security circles. Whether the Kurds' involvement in the international campaign against Islamic State and the support that they have received from international powers will prompt a reassessment of the Kurdish question in the region remains to be seen.

SELECT BIBLIOGRAPHY

Allsopp, Harriet. *The Kurds of Syria: Political Parties and Identity in the Middle East*. London, I. B. Tauris, 2014.

Gunes, Cengiz. *The Kurdish National Movement in Turkey: From Protest to Resistance*. Abingdon, Routledge, 2012.

Gunes, Cengiz and Welat Zeydanlıoğlu (Eds). *The Kurdish Question In Turkey: New Perspectives on Conflict, Representation and Reconciliation*. Abingdon, Routledge, 2014.

Koohi-Kamali, Farideh. *The Political Development of the Kurds in Iran: Pastoral Nationalism*. New York, Palgrave Macmillan, 2003.

Romano, David and Gurses, Mehmet (Eds). *Conflict Democratization, and the Kurds in the Middle East: Turkey, Iran, Iraq, and Syria*. Basingstoke, Palgrave Macmillan, 2014.

Stansfield, Gareth. *Iraqi Kurdistan: Political Developments and Emergent Democracy*. London, Routledge, 2003.

Tejel, Jordi. *Syria's Kurds: History, Politics and Society*. Abingdon, Routledge, 2009.

Tudgar, Elif. E. and Serhun, Al (Eds). *Comparative Kurdish Politics in the Middle East: Actors, Ideas, and Interests*. New York, Palgrave Macmillan, 2018.

Vali, Abbas. *Kurds and the State in Iran: The Making of Kurdish Identity*. London, I. B. Tauris, 2011.

Voller, Yaniv. *The Kurdish Liberation Movement in Iraq: From Insurgency to Statehood*. Abingdon, Routledge, 2014.

INSTITUTING A SUSTAINABLE ENERGY TRANSITION IN THE GULF: A REVIEW OF SAUDI ARABIA, THE UNITED ARAB EMIRATES AND QATAR

JUSTIN DARGIN

INTRODUCTION: BACKGROUND OF THE ARAB SOCIAL CONTRACT AND THE DEVELOPMENT OF REGIONAL ENERGY PRICING

Sustainable development, and the prudent utilization and consumption of natural resources, has emerged as one of the most critical issues in the 21st century. (Sustainable development is defined within this text as development that meets the needs of the present without compromising the ability of future generations to meet their own needs.) Indeed, it is likely going to be the principal issue that global leaders must contend with in the medium to long term. However, the Persian (Arabian) Gulf countries, until recently, granted scant regard to sustainable development as they sought to pursue economic growth regardless of the environmental cost. Industrialization and urbanization were the twin pillars of their macroeconomic programmes. Similarly, policymakers in the Gulf region, particularly those in Saudi Arabia, Qatar and the United Arab Emirates (UAE), mirroring their counterparts in other rapidly developing nations, viewed the negative impacts associated with the extraction of natural resources and ensuing pollution as unavoidable consequences of their economic expansion. Prior to this rapid evolution, the foundational norms rooted in their tribal and religious traditions prescribed a duty towards responsible environmental custodianship.

Prophetic doctrines, constituting a significant part of these traditions, imparted wide-ranging lessons concerning various environmental dimensions, including prudent use of natural resources, restoration of barren lands and the maintenance of environmental cleanliness. In the countryside, the nomadic Bedouin communities enforced an eco-conscious principle known as *Hima*. This concept, centred on the rotation of grazing fields, served to moderate overgrazing, thus ensuring the longevity of their pastures. Conversely, in the urbanized regions, dwellers embraced recycling as a habitual practice, contributing significantly to pollution abatement.

This scenario, however, began to alter with the emergence of state centralization in the Gulf nations. This structural change ushered in a novel cultural paradigm of modernization, which gradually eclipsed the time-honoured practices of environmental management, generating new challenges for these rapidly modernizing societies. When the governing authorities transferred ecological regulation from the local and tribal leaders to central government, the authorities declared that land was state property, thereby abolishing the ancient *Hima* system. Therefore, we can trace the first significant shift that privileged economic development over environmental stewardship to the beginning of petroleum production in the mid-20th century. The advent of hydrocarbon production in the region precipitated a whole host of ecological modifying events, such as increased urbanization and housing, industrial development, expanded agricultural production, and expansive water desalination. Alongside the relatively low environmental awareness of the populace, which engaged in ecologically unfriendly behaviour, were the institutional attitudes that sponsored massive industrialization drives favouring large-scale construction and industrial 'megaprojects' at the expense of the environment.

From the perspective of Gulf policymakers, Western nations had achieved their industrial prowess with scant regard for the associated environmental degradation. Consequently, they perceived environmental issues as 'luxuries' that only affluent societies could afford to prioritize. Accordingly, much like their counterparts in other developing regions globally, the leadership in the Gulf subscribed to the notion that rapid industrialization was an expedient path towards increasing their geopolitical clout and elevating their citizens to a standard of living comparable to that seen in the West.

Therefore, the governments in the Gulf region asserted that the advancement of industrialization should proceed unhindered. This perspective emanated from the belief that economic growth and environmental conservation were fundamentally antithetical to each other, a belief formed by observing the Western trajectory of development.

This commitment to vigorous industrialization remains firmly in place today. However, it has taken on an added layer of complexity and urgency as these governments grapple with the imperative to construct resilient, diversified economies capable of thriving in the imminent 'post-oil' era. This era is characterized by dwindling oil reserves, an increasing global push towards sustainable energy, and a transformational shift in the global energy landscape, making the need for economic diversification not just a strategic goal, but a matter of existential significance.

However, the industrialize-at-all-costs notions are evolving as Gulf governments realize that long-term economic development cannot succeed at the expense of environmental degradation. To a certain degree, it may be said that the Gulf's Overton Window (i.e. the range of policies politically acceptable to the mainstream population at a given time) rapidly expanded in the 2010s, when climate change and decarbonization issues were becoming much better understood among political leaders as they sought to transform their role in global environmental stewardship. As such, while continuing to champion industrialization, these nations are simultaneously confronted with the challenge of integrating environmental considerations into their development agenda, a nuance that calls for a delicate and strategic balance. This balance would then align them with the evolving global norms of sustainable development, ensuring their continued progress without compromising the environmental legacy for future generations.

While the Gulf states depend on hydrocarbon production and exports, they are caught between a rock and a hard place, as the region is one of the most susceptible to the dire impact of climate change. What fuels the Gulf economies also provides the impetus for potentially making the area literally uninhabitable for humans. Recent studies have predicted that deadly heatwaves could ripple throughout the region by the late 21st century, resulting in temperatures too high for basic human survival. For example, in June 2021 the temperature in Kuwait reached 53.2°C (127.8°F), with Oman, the UAE and Saudi Arabia all registering temperatures in excess of 50°C (122°F). A month later Iraq was subjected to a heat spike of 51.5°C (124.7°F), while Iran endured a high of 51°C (123.8°F).

Alarmingly, this pattern of extreme heat is not an isolated incident, but rather the inception of an escalating trend. The rate of warming in the Middle East is double the global average. Projections indicate that by 2050, the region's temperature will be 4°C higher, in contrast to the 1.5° increase deemed the threshold for environmental safety by the scientific community. The World Bank has asserted that such extreme climatic conditions will become the norm, forecasting that the region could be subjected to a relentless, scorching sun for as much as four months each year.

This essay argues that the focus of pricing reform in the region, primarily in the power and water sectors, can be understood as an indirect approach to natural gas pricing reform. This connection arises from the significant amount of gas utilized in these sectors. Additionally, while Saudi Arabia, Qatar and the UAE have made substantial investments in alternative energy production and have assumed leading roles in international climate negotiations, they have, at the same time, rapidly expanded their hydrocarbon production and export capacity. The aim of this strategic move is to preserve their revenue inflows for as long as possible.

The reduction in domestic hydrocarbon demand, driven by decarbonization and energy efficiency policies, enables these three countries effectively to increase their hydrocarbon exports. It also helps to reduce the opportunity cost of supplying hydrocarbons to the domestic market at below-market rates. Therefore, their climate change mitigation policies need to be viewed not only as a sudden embrace of environmental advocacy but also as part of a broader strategy. These policies reflect self-interest and align with economic and geopolitical goals, blending environmental concerns with the practical need to safeguard revenue streams and leverage natural resources most efficiently.

The essay addresses the interrelationship between energy and electricity pricing reform in the region related to climate change and greenhouse gas emissions mitigation, alternative energy development, energy demand reduction policies and domestic political stability. It also reviews the motivations behind the Gulf countries' policy decisions, such as energy efficiency measures, fuel switchovers from more carbon-intensive oil to natural gas, and alternative energy deployment.

The essay is organized into several sections, each addressing a specific aspect of the Gulf region's industrialization and energy landscape. The following section reviews the historical industrialization of the Gulf area, highlighting the utilization of natural gas as the primary fuel for development. The third section assesses how administrative gas prices have led to a range of unintended and adverse economic outcomes throughout the region.

The fourth section explores energy pricing reform efforts undertaken by Saudi Arabia, the UAE and Qatar to reduce their domestic energy consumption. In the fifth section the focus shifts to the various strategies that these three selected Gulf countries have adopted for the deployment of alternative energy. Finally, the conclusion provides an overview of the commonalities and differences between Saudi Arabia, the UAE, and Qatar in terms of their energy and power pricing reform initiatives. This section also emphasizes how these reforms are poised to shape and influence their renewable energy investments in the future.

ENERGY SECTOR-BASED INDUSTRIALIZATION IN THE GULF REGION

When the Gulf countries began to develop economically in the 1970s, policymakers viewed natural gas as perhaps the most effective means of creating a domestic industrial base. Since the 1970s, in the wake of the 'first oil price revolution' emanating from the Organization of Arab Petroleum Exporting Countries (OAPEC) oil embargo, the Gulf countries have directed numerous investment streams into industrial megaprojects to reduce their dependence on hydrocarbon exports and the inherent volatility of the global oil market. However, since the beginning of the 2000s, several significant economic forces have morphed the contours of the worldwide energy sector, consequently affecting Gulf economic growth. The 'second oil price revolution', a period of increased oil prices from 2000 to 2008, reflected a slow but steady rise in prices to more than US $100 per barrel that enriched the economies of the Gulf countries. (The first oil price revolution—or 'oil super cycle'—was the several-fold price increase that occurred in the wake of the Organization of the Petroleum Exporting Countries—OPEC—oil embargo of 1973.) For instance, during 2000–08 the economies of the Cooperation Council for the Arab States of the Gulf (more generally known as the Gulf Cooperation Council—GCC) collectively tripled in size to $1,100,000m.

However, the 2007–08 global financial crisis undercut what had seemed like an inevitable upward trend in Gulf economic growth. When alarm about the global financial crisis reached a peak in December 2008, oil prices dropped precipitously to approximately US $30 per barrel. Combined with capital flight and constrained capital markets, the GCC countries were significantly affected by the economic turmoil. Nevertheless, relief was in sight as international oil prices began steadily to increase until they reached over $100 per barrel during 2010–14. Much of the surge in international oil prices that occurred in 2014 was driven by the political crisis in Iraq during the middle months of that year, as well as by various geopolitical issues relating to the 'Arab Spring' protests and the expansion of the militant Islamic State organization. (There are various forms of oil sold on the international market, termed as 'benchmark oils'. The pricing differentials depend upon the production location and the relative quality. Therefore, when the term 'global oil prices' is used, typically it comprises Brent, West Texas Intermediate and Dubai/Oman, although other crudes can also form a benchmark crude.)

Despite the economic setbacks of the global financial crisis, the second oil price revolution heralded a period of unparalleled industrial expansion in the Gulf region. The Gulf countries initiated enormous value-added (petrochemicals, fertilizers), energy-intensive (cement manufacturing, aluminium smelting), and power expansion projects in the region. Additionally, during the same period of 2000–08 the regional population increased from 28m. to 39m. (Population growth in the Gulf is approximately 2.5% per year, at which rate the population in the Gulf is expected to double within 30 years.) Most of the demographic bulge was composed of youths (aged under 25 years), which spurred the Gulf countries to focus on job creation as a tool to alleviate potential socioeconomic discontent, particularly in the wake of the 'Arab Spring' protests in the early 2010s. This rapid population growth also caused the Gulf governments to focus on infrastructure development and housing construction, which led directly to a rise in energy/power consumption across all sectors.

Regional gas consumption has evolved. The industrial sector became a critical driver of gas demand, accounting for an increasing proportion of gas demand over the years. If the demand rates continue this trend, then industrial gas usage will expand even as power demand is projected to plateau over the next decade.

Gas has been at the centre of most Gulf countries' industrial expansion and economic diversification plans. This development model did not pose any risks for the Gulf countries until the expansionary pressure became too great by the mid- to late 2000s, and the region's associated natural gas could not match the demand growth. For Saudi Arabia, the UAE and Qatar, as well as the other Gulf countries, until recently their energy balances were composed of oil and gas, and virtually nothing else. By 2007 the widening supply-demand imbalance fissures had become starkly apparent as blackouts and allocation disruptions metastasized throughout the region.

Gulf countries also faced growing economic pressures due to the massive expansion of government expenditures in the wake of the 'Arab Spring'. The combined social spending by Gulf countries to stave off social discontent reached approximately US $150,000m. during the first year alone of the protests. The significant rise in government spending programmes increased the 'breakeven oil price'—the price of oil per barrel required for an oil-producing country to remain fiscally solvent. (There are two kinds of breakeven price frameworks in energy-related literature. One refers to the price that a barrel of oil needs to garner on the market for a production project to remain fiscally viable. The other, and the definition used in this essay, is the price a government needs to obtain for a barrel of oil to maintain its budgetary outlays.) For example, on the eve of the US invasion of Iraq in 2003, the breakeven price for a barrel of oil in much of the region was approximately $30 (in nominal prices). The regional breakeven oil price increased to $90–$100 per barrel nearly a decade later. (The variability is because different methodologies are utilized by different organizations. However, within the region, there is significant variability, at the low and high ends of the spectrum.) None the less, in 2017 the average breakeven oil price for government solvency in the Gulf declined for the first time since 2003 to almost $80 per barrel in the wake of improved government budgets and subsidy reforms. In 2018–19, prior to the coronavirus disease (COVID-19) pandemic, Saudi Arabia's breakeven oil price was approximately $78, while the UAE's breakeven price was $90. Qatar's breakeven oil price defied its neighbours' trends and rose from $24 in 2008 to $47 in 2018. Prices declined to around $30 per barrel in 2020, creating significant problems for the oil- and gas-producing countries. Although the price had rebounded to more than $10 per barrel by the end of 2022, the global oil market's overall volatility and cyclical nature have left regional governments facing alternating periods of feast and famine.

In the aftermath of the global pandemic, countries in the Gulf region have had varying responses and outcomes in terms of their fiscal breakeven oil prices. The UAE has been remarkably resilient, managing to lower its fiscal breakeven price to below US $65 per barrel in 2023. This significant achievement can largely be attributed to the introduction of a new corporate tax in that year, which was designed to bolster non-hydrocarbon revenue in 2024–25. This strategic fiscal policy aligns with the UAE's broader goals of diversification away from sole reliance on oil.

Qatar, meanwhile, has succeeded in reducing its breakeven oil price to approximately US $40–$43 per barrel in 2023. This decrease has been driven by a combination of efficient energy management, strategic investments in non-oil sectors and a continued emphasis on natural gas exports, which has further solidified Qatar's position in the global energy market.

Conversely, Saudi Arabia has seen its breakeven oil price increase to more than US $81 per barrel in 2023. This rise is tied to the nation's ambitious industrialization projects that form part of a grand strategy aimed at macroeconomic diversification. By investing heavily in various industries, Saudi Arabia is seeking to reduce its economic dependence on oil, but this approach has resulted in a short-term increase in its fiscal breakeven price. These projects align with Saudi Arabia's 'Vision 2030', a comprehensive plan that aims to reshape the kingdom's economy, society and global standing.

A dual-pronged development approach appears to be gaining ground in several Gulf nations, with Saudi Arabia being a notable example. As these countries strive to capitalize on their competitive edge and broaden their industrial foundation via economic diversification and the creation of backward and forward linkages within their domestic economies, the goal is to reduce their exclusive dependency on oil exports.

The countries' burgeoning industries necessitate access to affordably priced—or, at the very least, consistently priced—natural gas and oil. This requirement is crucial to maintain the global competitiveness of their offerings, particularly with regard to petrochemicals and other downstream products. In effect, low and steady energy costs underpin their efforts to stand their ground in the international market. However, simultaneously, as their economies expand and government expenditures increase through infrastructure development and subsidization of various economic sectors, there is a greater incentive to develop the downstream oil sector and defend higher oil prices to capture the lost opportunity cost.

The primary challenge for governments in the Gulf region is the fact that their legacy gas pricing policies actively discourage the development of their non-associated and unconventional gas reserves, which have a production cost several-fold higher than their conventional associated gas production. The crux of the problem for the Gulf countries is that their gas deficits are not related to the scarcity of natural gas; instead, they are a result of the failure to create effective policies that would promote upstream exploration and production and demand reduction.

Additionally, the petrochemical sector, which is the basis of Gulf economic diversification, is also threatened by the lack of comprehensive energy price reform as the gas shortages impact allocation to these national industries as the Gulf countries attempt to transition away from hydrocarbon dependence and develop diversified and sustainable modern economies. However, as the next section will discuss, the low-cost pricing structure of natural gas hinders the ability of regional policymakers to realize these strategic goals.

THE BIRTH OF GULF ENERGY PRICING

Rapidly increasing natural gas demand in the Gulf region has historically been driven mainly by administrative pricing. These prices tended to be much lower than international natural gas prices. For example, until the pricing reform that took place in the mid-2010s, the legacy average natural gas price in the Gulf hovered around US $1.50 per metric million British thermal unit (MMBTU). Since then, Gulf governments have been undertaking incremental energy price restructuring. As a result, the average regional legacy price of natural gas supplied to the various economic sectors has increased, and as of mid-2023 it was around $3.00 per MMBTU. This represents a doubling of the price over the past decade, reflecting the region's efforts to align more closely with global energy market dynamics, while balancing domestic economic considerations. None the less, despite the increases, these prices are below the global average for natural gas prices.

These administrative natural gas prices are not, strictly speaking, 'subsidies', as is often reported in the international media. However, there are a wide range of actual subsidies in other segments of the energy and power sector. For example, there are subsidies in the power sector, for both consumption and generation, as well as subsidies for petrol.

Finding a universally accepted definition of 'subsidies' has proven to be an exceptionally challenging task, as various countries and multilateral organizations have each formulated their own unique definitions. This complexity is further highlighted when considering the most prevalent interpretations of the term 'subsidy', such as those that define it as measures keeping prices below market levels for consumers, or above market levels for producers, or those that define it as measures reducing costs for both consumers and producers. The intricate nature of this concept was starkly illustrated during the 2020 G20 (Group of 20) meeting hosted by Saudi Arabia. In a strategic move reflecting its perspective, the kingdom chose to remove the phrase 'fossil fuel subsidies' from expert briefings, replacing it with the more nuanced term 'fossil fuel incentives'. This subtle shift in language underscores the multifaceted and often politically charged nature of defining subsidies, reflecting deeper economic and ideological considerations that vary from one context to another.

The Agreement on Subsidies and Countervailing Measures (ACMS) of the World Trade Organization (WTO) provides a definition for subsidies that all WTO members have accepted. Article 1 of the ACMS states that a 'subsidy' exists when there is a 'financial contribution' by a government or public body that confers a 'benefit'. A 'financial contribution' arises where: (i) a government practice involves a direct transfer of funds (e.g. grants, loans or equity infusion), potential direct transfers of funds or liabilities (e.g. loan guarantees); (ii) government revenue that is otherwise due is foregone or not collected (e.g. fiscal incentives such as tax credits); (iii) a government provides goods or services other than general infrastructure, or purchases goods; or (iv) a government entrusts or directs a private body to carry out one or more of the above functions. A 'benefit' is conferred when the 'financial contribution' is provided to the recipient on terms that are more favourable than those that the recipient could have obtained from the market.

In contrast, the International Energy Agency (IEA) utilizes the 'price-gap' approach, comparing domestic energy prices with the international market prices. This approach tends only to consider consumer subsidies. The price-gap method tends to be attractive due to the overall complexity of the myriad of energy policy interventions; however, it can also be criticized because it neglects to assess many different forms of subsidies. The price-gap limitations centre upon two primary factors: the challenges in accurately estimating the data inputs required to calculate the price-gap and the types of policy interventions that this analytic tool cannot capture. In terms of the data inputs, it is challenging to track patterns across various countries and fuels. In addition, there are difficulties in establishing pricing benchmarks with commodities that are not traded easily, such as natural gas, which has regional pricing variations.

Price-gap assessment utilizes long-run marginal cost (LRMC) estimates as a stand-in that incorporates the notion that the alternative supply would arrive by new production instead of imports. (The LRMC is the change in long-run total cost of production of a certain good or service resulting from a change in the quantity produced. This is often utilized in price-gap calculations whereby alternative supply sources cannot be imported.) However, applying the new capacity cost in advance is difficult for extensive and complicated capital projects as volatility in the commodity markets and credit market dysfunction make determining accurate prices somewhat challenging. Furthermore, even global price benchmarks for commodities may be distorted. They may contain some level of embedded subsidies, and back-calculating the extent of the subsidies may be nearly impossible in many jurisdictions.

Finally, another limitation of the IEA's price-gap approach is that it does not explain how governments may ultimately compensate producers for providing the product for sale at a lower price. The IEA merely calculates the price difference and labels it as a subsidy, even though the difference could have been through a direct budgetary transfer (a subsidy) or from a tax concession (which is not often considered a subsidy). In any case, the IEA's price-gap method does not report this. The gas markets in the three countries discussed in this essay have undergone some modest reform, although the forward momentum has slightly stalled. As a result, by the early 2020s the regional gas markets were nowhere near to being even modestly liberalized.

When these commonly utilized definitions are compared with the negligible marginal production cost of each additional unit of associated natural gas in the region, Gulf gas prices are not set below the cost of production or domestic 'market' levels, and thus terming the gas sectors in the three selected countries as being subsidized may be inaccurate. This is the case because the gas market is not liberalized in the region, so there is no effective 'market' price as the price is not a function of supply and demand. Furthermore, there is effectively no unified global price for natural gas (the market is still segmented regionally). Therefore, it is difficult to judge the domestic prices against a worldwide gas price (which does not yet exist). However, the Gulf states' domestic natural gas pricing policies are causing gas allocation disruptions and exacerbating budgetary pressures to keep their industrialization and diversification strategies on schedule by providing low-priced natural gas feedstock to their national industries. This is occurring as all the Gulf countries, with the notable exception of Qatar, experienced gas shortages during the 2010s as demand consistently outpaced production from around 2008. As a result, while the situation has since stabilized, from 2008 until the mid-2010s there were power outages in many countries, with many of their energy-intensive industries and petrochemical companies unable to acquire the gas that they needed to maintain operations.

In the past, and as is the current situation, when most of the natural gas produced was associated natural gas, i.e. low production cost and easily accessible, having such a low-cost framework was economically feasible (i.e. there was an abundance of gas, and it could be freely allocated to the various nascent industries). Although natural gas and power consumption has substantially increased, along with rising upstream production costs in non-associated and unconventional natural gasfields (ultra-sour, tight and shale), the current natural gas pricing framework (approximately US $3.00 per MMBTU) has remained affordable in Saudi Arabia and the UAE as long as the governments of those countries underwrite the gap between production costs and delivery costs. This is unsustainable chiefly because the gas price is too low to stimulate production at unconventional gasfields that have much higher production costs, and because the low price encourages overuse of the resource, resulting in crippling gas deficits. (In Qatar, the cost of gas production is roughly equal to the long-run marginal cost, and therefore does not imply a subsidy by the definitions specified above.) Furthermore, being affordable does not necessarily mean that it is sustainable when considering the regional governments' ever-expanding budgetary commitments and rising production costs. In addition, the cost of producing from non-associated complex (or unconventional) gas reservoirs is significantly greater (at approximately $4–$7 per MMBTU) than the production cost of conventional associated natural gas.

Consequently, if the same administrative gas pricing framework for associated natural gas is utilized for non-associated and unconventional natural gas (or imports of liquefied natural gas—LNG), it would allocate natural gas at below the new cost of production (or import), which would then, by most commonly used definitions, result in a subsidy. However, the extremely low-cost pricing framework, rapid population growth and the expansion of downstream gas industries caused regional gas demand to increase at an average annual rate of approximately 6%–8% from the beginning of the 21st century. As a result of this demand pressure, the investment logic that caused foreign energy-intensive industries to relocate to the region has concomitantly evolved, with many downstream and energy-intensive companies migrating to the USA to take advantage of low-cost shale gas inputs. Many Gulf countries are starting to consider utilizing US Henry Hub pricing as a benchmark so that their downstream gas industries may more effectively compete with their US rivals in terms of cost.

Using the IEA definition, subsidies declined substantially in 2019–20 because of the sharp reduction in regional spot prices, which in early 2020 hovered around US $1.50–$2.00 per MMBTU. However, they increased significantly in 2021, to approximately $10 per MMBTU; the price of internationally traded LNG, which is the incremental source of domestic supply for the UAE, is considerably higher than the Emirati domestic gas price. Therefore, considering all factors, the IEA's definition tends to be problematic when applied in a period of extreme price volatility. For all their problems, the LRMC and delivery cost versus domestic price are better definitions.

As previously articulated, the international oil market is much more fungible, and also more volatile, owing to relatively low storage and transportation expenditures, and the presence of a cohesive market structure that facilitates trade. Conversely, the establishment of an integrated global gas market with a standardized price is still in its nascent stages. Consequently, natural gas is predominantly traded within continental markets, including North America, Europe and Asia-Pacific. Distinct benchmark fuels are utilized in these regional markets to determine the pricing of natural gas, which serves as a standardized price index for gauging the value of natural gas in specific markets.

In the North American market, prices primarily hinge on the Henry Hub benchmark. This market is characterized by liberalization and fierce competition, and operates based on structural supply and demand equilibriums, with active spot and futures markets.

In the United Kingdom, another competitive and deregulated market, the UK National Balancing Point benchmark fosters gas-to-gas competition. Conversely, the continental European market retains a high degree of regulation, with long-term bilateral contracts dominating. The principal European benchmark fuel, known as the Dutch Transfer Title Facility (TTF) benchmark, applies to both LNG and pipeline gas. However, in the wake of the natural gas crisis precipitated by the Russian invasion of Ukraine in February 2022, the European Union (EU) is contemplating instituting a new benchmark for the region's wholesale gas prices. Owing to significant geopolitical strain and structural supply-demand dynamics, many EU policymakers consider the TTF price as no longer reflective of the true value of LNG imports into Europe, particularly considering the marked increase in LNG imports in 2022.

In Asia, the Japan Korea Marker (JKM) functions as the benchmark. This system bears a similarity to Europe's in terms of its rigid structure and heavy reliance on external imports. Asian purchasers typically engage in long-term negotiated bilateral LNG contracts, with oil indexation serving as the base. This methodology causes their contractual natural gas import prices to correlate closely with international oil prices. Due to the scarcity of Asian trade by pipeline, LNG is the primary form of traded natural gas.

Global buyers of LNG usually price their acquisitions according to benchmarks such as Henry Hub or the JKM, along with a modest spread that incorporates regasification and grid transfer costs. Nevertheless, as previously mentioned, the burgeoning spot market and expanding LNG trade are steering the industry towards the potential development of a unified global LNG benchmark price in the foreseeable future.

The potential for a regional Gulf natural gas price benchmark to materialize in the future is plausible. As indicated in 2020 by the then Bahraini oil minister, Sheikh Mohammed Al Khalifa, covert discussions within the GCC were in progress regarding the possible establishment of a cross-Gulf gas pipeline infrastructure that would interconnect all GCC nations. However, realizing such an ambitious project would require the Gulf countries to confront numerous challenges, including geopolitical discord, gas price adjustments, technical hurdles and deficits in economic co-ordination.

Historical endeavours provide a cautious outlook: in the 1980s, the Gulf countries considered the development of a regional gas pipeline to distribute natural gas from Qatar's substantial North Field to other gas-needy Gulf nations. GCC policymakers anticipated that such a regional pipeline would instigate enhanced integration within the Gulf, extending to security, economic and political domains. Yet, at a summit held in December 1990, consensus was reached on all pivotal points except for the establishment of a regional gas price. Ultimately, diplomatic conflicts, territorial disputes and political tensions led to the abandonment of the proposed initiative.

Despite this, it could reasonably be contended that the Dolphin natural gas pipeline, which exports Qatari gas to the gas networks of the UAE and Oman, represents a scaled-down iteration of a Gulf regional natural gasfield. This suggests that, notwithstanding the persistent political friction between Qatar and its neighbours, the possibility for such co-operative ventures exists.

Until either a global gas price convergence or a regional Gulf gas benchmark is established, using current international market rates (which are predicated on regional benchmarks) to assess Gulf domestic prices remains a complex and challenging task. The domestic natural gas pricing structures employed by the Gulf states have historically created what is known in economic terms as 'perverse incentives'.

These incentives have been manifested in heightened gas demand pressure, leading to several negative consequences. For instance, in the late 2000s and early 2010s these pricing structures contributed to gas distribution disruptions and power blackouts. The demand for low-cost natural gas exceeded supply, causing interruptions that affected both consumers and industries. Furthermore, these 'perverse incentives' place strain on government budgets. Gulf states have pursued ambitious industrialization and diversification strategies, which often rely on supplying low-cost natural gas feedstock to national industries. The desire to fuel these initiatives with affordable energy has sometimes conflicted with the need for sustainable pricing and energy management.

None the less, the significant challenges are not just limited to the natural gas sector; regional oil demand is also high. This is due to two interrelated factors. First, as natural gas shortfalls spread through the regional economies, Gulf states such as Saudi Arabia and Kuwait, as well as the northern emirates, utilized more fuel oil for power generation. When hydrocarbons are consumed domestically at below-market prices instead of being exported at international market rates, this results in a significant opportunity cost and less foreign revenue inflows for the government. (In well-functioning markets, cost equals opportunity cost. However, in imperfectly functioning markets, opportunity cost equals the best available alternative.)

In Saudi Arabia, for example, oil demand is partly due to the country's expansive petrochemical sector. However, the principal source of demand is from the kingdom's large power generation sector, which is supported by low-priced heavy fuel oil and crude petroleum. (Saudi Arabia has been attempting to compensate for the decline in oil exports by prioritizing the export of more expensive oil grades. However, this is merely a short-term response to a deep-seated structural problem. Annual power demand has been growing at a rate of 8% over the past several years and seems likely to continue increasing at this rate until renewable energy projects come online later in the 2020s.) The average transfer prices from the state-owned Saudi Arabian Oil Company (Saudi Aramco) to the power utilities is US $2.20 per barrel for heavy fuel oil and $4.24 per barrel for crude petroleum. These low oil prices encourage exceptionally high consumption rates and do not incentivize power utilities to make capital investments in energy-efficient equipment. However, since 2018 Saudi Arabia's oil consumption has been declining, despite its increasing population and electricity consumption, while natural gas consumption has been plateauing since the late 2010s due in large part to the pricing reconfiguration implemented during the mid-2010s.

ENERGY AND POWER PRICING REFORM IN SAUDI ARABIA, THE UAE AND QATAR

The Basis of the Gulf Social Contract

Reform of domestic energy pricing is a regional trend that most countries in the Middle East and North Africa have been grappling with to varying degrees. The challenge, particularly in the three selected countries, but also across the region as a whole, is that detailed data on pricing is often poor or entirely unavailable. Much of the information about gas prices is hidden from public view, adding a layer of complexity to the true economic burden.

Policymakers throughout the region have come to recognize that energy pricing reform is necessary to strike a balanced relationship between hydrocarbon consumption and supply. Prior to the oil price collapse of 2014, oil-exporting countries were reaping substantial profits from sales on the global market. However, at the same time, they were encountering the opportunity cost of providing hydrocarbons and power to the domestic market at artificially low energy prices.

This situation changed dramatically when oil prices plummeted in 2014. The Gulf countries, on average, experienced a staggering revenue decline of nearly 10% of their gross domestic product (GDP) within just one year. This financial shock further underscored the importance of a carefully calibrated approach to domestic energy pricing. The post-2014 era has seen a renewed purpose in addressing these pricing challenges, driven by the recognition that long-term fiscal stability and economic diversification require a more sustainable and transparent pricing model.

The Gulf countries faced a pressing need to increase domestic energy prices in order to balance their government budgets, a move that significantly restructured their 'rent' distribution frameworks, which encompassed the allocation of fuel, gas, water and electricity at below-market prices. The urgency of energy price reforms was exacerbated by the global oil price decline in 2014, especially as every energy-rich country in the Middle East and North Africa had begun to experience natural gas allocation shortfalls during 2008–14.

To fully grasp the emergence of energy price reform in the region, it is essential to consider the broader context of the Arab social contract, which serves as the centrepiece of this complex puzzle. The Gulf countries operate within a political system that is predicated on state-led distribution of welfare through various subsidies, including energy, water and food, along with a substantial public sector to employ university graduates.

At the core of this social contract is a unique exchange: the ruling families maintain relatively unrestricted political autonomy, while the citizenry accepts the state's authority and responsibility for security matters, as well as the distribution of rent, primarily in the form of hydrocarbon income. This arrangement financed a socio-political framework that has been foundational to the region, embodying the fundamental tenet of rentier state theory.

The production and exportation of natural resources supported this intricate structure, creating a delicate equilibrium between state control, economic benefits and social stability. However, the shifting dynamics of global energy markets and the acute pressures of the 2014 oil price collapse drove home the reality that this model was in need of serious re-evaluation and reform, sparking a new era of change and adaptation in the Gulf's approach to domestic energy pricing.

However, it should be noted that this Gulf social contract only applies to citizens. Unlike many other countries in the world, obtaining citizenship is nearly impossible for the vast numbers of expatriate workers, even though they comprise about 33% of the Saudi population, almost 85% of the Emirati population and approximately 95% of the Qatari workforce. Overall, in the Gulf region, expatriate workers are thought to account for nearly 70% of the total regional population. There was a colossal influx of foreign workers in the wake of the OAPEC oil embargo of 1973, with the Gulf states using their new oil revenues to hire foreign workers to industrialize their countries.

Gulf citizenship was particularly difficult to acquire due to several overlapping factors. The Gulf states, being recently formed, were concerned about 'culture dilution'. Given the large numbers of foreign workers, concerns arose that the local populations could easily be displaced, both demographically and culturally. Additionally, as the Gulf countries have generous and extensive welfare frameworks, incorporating large numbers of individuals into these frameworks would place burdens on government finances. Finally, there is a security dimension to these issues in that the Gulf governments are also concerned that bestowing citizenship on large numbers of people with varied religious backgrounds would disrupt the delicate sectarian balance in their countries and could potentially lead to unrest and sectarian violence, as regularly occurs in other countries in the Middle East and North Africa. High on the list of concerns of Gulf policymakers is that the flow of foreign workers represents a form of 'colonization' that could undermine the indigenous populations. An example of such concerns is illustrated by a development that took place in the UAE in 2011. In that year, mindful of potential socio-political discord, the Emirati leadership surreptitiously hired Erik Prince, the founder of the US private security services company Blackwater, to construct, at a cost of nearly US $500m., a desert military base in Abu Dhabi, which would be used to quell internal conflict if an Arab Spring-style protest movement arose or if foreign workers rebelled. An interesting point is that most of the mercenaries recruited were veterans of violent conflicts in South America and Africa. In general, Muslim operatives were not preferred, as the guiding notion was that South American mercenaries would be more likely to follow mission directives without having to take religious identity into account if it were necessary to conduct large-scale pacification campaigns against Muslim workers.

Even though many expatriate workers have lived in the Gulf countries for decades and have raised families there, they are not able to acquire citizenship. The Gulf states have a highly specific form of labour regime based on rigid market division between foreigners and nationals. However, even though the Gulf countries have been engaging with varying degrees of success in labour indigenization, the need to participate and compete in the global market obligates them to modify their existing social constructs. Saudi Arabia and the UAE are tentatively experimenting with granting citizenship to select groups of talented individuals. The Gulf states have also been under external pressure from international human rights organizations and the home governments of expatriate workers in relation to alleged human rights violations against foreign workers. These international recriminations have caused the Gulf states to seek to remedy publicly some of the most prevalent excesses associated with their treatment of foreign workers, who are not accorded the same legal and social rights as the local citizenry.

While it appears exceedingly unlikely that a radical wholesale restructuring of the social contract and the extension of the franchise will be undertaken during the 2020s, it is undeniable that, as many Western countries are attempting to restrict immigration, the Gulf countries will move in the other direction in tandem with the reimagining of their welfare and subsidization regimes.

Social contract theory is nearly as old as the study of philosophy itself, yet it was not fully developed until the 17th century by English philosopher Thomas Hobbes in his 'second law of nature'. (After Hobbes, both John Locke and Jean-Jacques Rousseau developed the theory even further and with additional elements.) In essence, Hobbes explained that the bedrock of the social contract is that citizens surrender their individual liberties in exchange for some form of common security, whether physical or otherwise. The contract, according to Hobbes, is the 'mutual transferring of rights'. The social contract is central to most rentier states, the Gulf states being no exception. In countries with robust democracies, the social contract encompasses the unspoken 'bargain' between the representatives of the state, labour and capital. However, in Middle Eastern rentier states, the social contract incorporates the position of state institutions rather than formalized citizen input as in more democratic countries.

While Saudi Arabia, the UAE and Qatar are actively engaging in sweeping macroeconomic reform, and in Saudi Arabia's case, social reform as well, they are met with substantial barriers in the path of energy pricing reform. The underlying concern that resonates among Gulf policymakers, as emphasized by regional scholars, lies in the potential public reaction to alterations being made to the social contract, of which energy pricing is a crucial element.

Historically, drastic changes in commodity prices have ignited social unrest, riots and uprisings in various countries. This historical precedence has guided the three selected Gulf countries to approach energy price revisions with a certain level of caution. Pricing is not just a matter of economics, but is deeply intertwined with the societal fabric and public sentiment in these nations. Moreover, it is essential to recognize that the gas prices discussed are presented in nominal terms. In real terms, the situation appears different as prices have been declining due to inflation. This could potentially negate the pricing and efficiency gains achieved since the mid- to late 2010s, thereby complicating the reform process and its intended outcomes.

With the exception of Qatar and the UAE, all of the Gulf countries experienced increasing poverty rates and domestic energy demand when global oil prices declined in 2014. They only succeeded in managing the situation by using high budgetary revenues from previous years to expand the current outflows. Saudi Arabia, Oman and Bahrain began to run fiscal deficits and were obligated to reform their respective domestic energy prices. Even countries that had smaller populations and large hydrocarbon reserves were running deficits by 2016. Among the three selected countries of this study, Saudi Arabia, the UAE and Qatar, the pace of energy pricing reforms reflects the relative importance that each respective Government places on the need to transition from an allocative state to a productive state that would be able to create a more significant role for its private sector in the broader macroeconomy.

Despite the evident necessity of increasing domestic energy prices, the road to pricing reform is still fraught with hazards. Additionally, gas pricing reform, for the most part, lagged behind after its initial progress in the mid-2010s. However, reform of power sector prices can be used as a substitute for direct gas pricing reform to a large degree due to the substantial amount of natural gas consumed by regional power generation.

The following sections will discuss each of the three selected countries' efforts to reform their domestic energy pricing frameworks and the challenges that they have yet to overcome.

Saudi Arabia Launches Energy Price Reform

Low-priced natural gas allocation to the domestic economy has long been a defining feature of Saudi Arabia's social contract and a crucial element in its industrialization strategy. This policy was formalized in 1984, when the Saudi Government set the domestic natural gas price at US $0.50 per MMBTU, a rate maintained until 1998 when it was modestly increased to $0.75 per MMBTU. Even as global natural gas prices surged over the following decades, Saudi policymakers resisted the urge to adjust domestic prices to reflect these trends, maintaining a stable pricing structure until the mid-2010s.

This approach was not accidental but rather part of a broader domestic energy-pricing framework designed to serve various interconnected objectives. By keeping energy prices low, the Government facilitated wealth transfers to low-income citizens, making essential services more accessible. This, in turn, fostered the competitive advantage of the country's energy-intensive industries, enabling a wave of industrialization and making the kingdom attractive to foreign investors. These policies were intertwined with the underlying principles of the Arab social contract, as described above, which allowed political elites to wield considerable power without direct popular representation or enfranchisement, a system underpinned by the provision of economic benefits.

However, the collapse of oil prices in 2014 presented the Saudi Government with a new and pressing fiscal challenge. With substantial commitments to welfare programmes, the decrease in oil revenue forced the Government to reconsider its budget priorities and seek ways to reduce deficits. The

Table 1: Saudi Arabia Price Reform

	2015	2016	Increase (%)	2018	Increase (%)
Natural gas (US $ per MMBTU)	0.75	1.25	67	unchanged	–
Ethane (US $ per MMBTU)	0.75	1.75	133	unchanged	–
Low-grade petrol (US $ per litre)	0.12	0.20	67	0.37	83
High-grade petrol (US $ per litre)	0.16	0.24	50	0.54	127
Diesel—transport (US $ per litre)	0.07	0.12	79	unchanged	–
Diesel—industry (US $ per barrel)	9.11	14.10	55	16.15	15
Arab light crude (US $ per barrel)	4.24	6.35	50	unchanged	–
Arab heavy crude (US $ per barrel)	2.67	4.40	65	unchanged	–
Kerosene (US $ per barrel)	23.00	25.70	12	unchanged	–

Source: Arab Petroleum Investments Corporation.

diversification of the economy away from oil also became an urgent imperative. These challenges prompted serious discussions at the highest levels of government, culminating in the difficult decision to undertake comprehensive price reforms.

The first phase of these reforms was launched in late 2015, targeting an increase in the prices of natural gas, diesel, power, water and petrol. While the increases were modest compared to international standards and still significantly below global levels, they marked a notable policy shift. The Government signalled its readiness to make tough decisions to rectify its fiscal situation and catalyze macroeconomic transformation.

Despite the potentially disruptive nature of these changes, the first phase of price reforms was met with relatively little resistance. Saudi domestic prices remained low compared to those of most other countries, mitigating the immediate impact on consumers. Moreover, the gradual and considered approach adopted by the authorities, and their careful communication of the underlying reasons for the reforms, likely contributed to the relatively smooth transition. (see Table 1).

As the Saudi populace generally accepted the first phase of price reform, the Government did not feel the need to publicize the reforms nor to introduce compensatory programmes. While the Government deemed the first phase to have attained its goals, it decided to implement subsequent price increases more incrementally and delayed its initial plan to reach the level of international prices by 2020 by five years, until 2025. On 1 January 2018 the Government proceeded with the second phase of pricing reform, which increased power tariffs for residential and commercial consumers and raised petrol prices to a predetermined reference price. This could be considered a part of gas pricing reform, as a large share of power generation uses natural gas; therefore, the increase in government revenues from power pricing reform could help to bridge the natural gas allocation cost/price gap.

The second phase of the energy price reform involved a cash transfer programme, valued at approximately US $6,700m., under a 'Citizen's Account' scheme for low- and middle-income families in predefined income brackets. As the IMF argues, a compensation scheme is perhaps one of the most essential pillars of any significant energy price reform policy as it is needed to manage any potential adverse impact upon the more impoverished demographics of a country. Cash transfers also tend to encourage public acceptance of reform measures. With the programme's initial inception on 21 December 2017, more than 3.7m. households applied, representing over one-half of the country's 5.5m. households. Saudi policymakers chose a gradual phase-in of the energy pricing reform to allow the economy to acclimatize to the increased prices and to enable the country to diversify away from oil so that the private sector would have a more significant role in the macroeconomy.

Overall, the Saudi Government successfully implemented the initial two phases of energy price reform; none the less, there are still multiple challenges that lie ahead. First, higher energy and power prices tend to apply upward pricing pressure on other products and services that require power and fuel for transportation, even though it remains difficult for many of the state-owned enterprises to pass these costs directly on to customers. Higher power and energy prices influence wage expectations as citizens begin demanding higher future wages as a corollary. Second, the Saudi Government experienced data complications in identifying eligible recipients. Third, the Government must ensure that its databases are robust and coherent to enable the reforms to progress successfully. Finally, the Government failed to increase natural gas and diesel prices for the industrial sector during the second phase. In 2017, when the Saudi economy contracted due to output reductions, the Government extended the timetable for full implementation of the subsidy reform programme until 2025. The COVID-19 pandemic, which began in early 2020, further delayed subsidy reform.

Natural gas pricing reform in Saudi Arabia experienced a noticeable stall after 2016, highlighting a complex interplay of economic and political factors within the country. This slowdown can be seen as an illustration of the influential power still wielded by energy-intensive industries and downstream gas sectors. These industries are vital to the Saudi economy, and any change in energy pricing has a direct impact on their operating costs, profit margins and overall competitiveness.

For example, SABIC, a global leader in diversified chemicals headquartered in Riyadh, announced that its annual costs had risen by more than 5% due to fuel and electricity price increases. Simultaneously, Saudi Arabia Fertilizers Co (SAFCO) indicated an 8% increase in production costs, while Yanbu National Petrochemical Co (Yansab) expected a 6.5% rise in costs. Even the Saudi Cement Co, a prominent player in the construction industry, announced an anticipated increase in production costs by SR 68m. (US $18.1m.).

These figures are not just numbers on a balance sheet; they translate into real challenges for the industries. Higher energy costs increase input costs across a broad spectrum of sectors, but the impact is particularly acute for energy-intensive industries such as petrochemicals and cement. These sectors often operate on thin margins and are heavily reliant on energy as a primary input.

In the petrochemical industry, competition is fierce, and the ability to pass on increased costs to end buyers is limited. Companies must remain price-competitive on the global market, where they are contending with producers benefiting from lower energy costs, such as with North American petrochemical companies that benefited from the shale gas boom. In the case of the cement industry, government price controls further restrict the ability to adjust prices in response to increased production costs.

The stalling of natural gas pricing reform, therefore, must be viewed in the broader context of the Saudi Government's need to balance economic reform with maintaining the competitiveness of key domestic industries. The influential role of these sectors may have acted as a barrier to more rapid reform.

It appears that the Saudi Government delayed the reform timeline and other parts of its austerity programme because of concerns about the potential impact on private sector growth, economic competitiveness and the politics of the social contract. As illustrated elsewhere in this essay, there is always some disquiet among policymakers about potentially upsetting the delicate sociopolitical balance by reforming too rapidly. Many other countries in the Middle East and beyond that abruptly modified their energy-pricing regimes embedded in the social contract experienced severe unrest. Unless the Saudi Government is willing to restart and accelerate energy sector reform, full liberalization of the country's natural gas market seems likely to be a long-term prospect. This situation demonstrates the inherent tension in transitioning towards a market-based energy pricing mechanism while preserving the health of industries critical to the national economy and social stability.

Nevertheless, in the Government's fiscal plan announced in December 2017 it was revealed that residential, commercial and industrial power consumption would be fully linked to international benchmark prices by 2025. However, the Saudi Government did not indicate to which international benchmark they would form the link. To date, while prices have increased, there has been no firm progress in terms of an international linkage.

To bolster its pricing reform policies, the Saudi Government has incorporated a comprehensive energy efficiency strategy through the Saudi Energy Efficiency Program (SEEP), established in 2012. Through the efforts of SEEP, the Government hopes to manage the impact of inflationary pressures on the competitiveness of its energy-intensive and downstream gas industries. Despite Saudi goals of stimulating the growth of the non-oil sector, downstream and energy-intensive industries, such as petrochemicals and aluminium smelting, will likely remain significant drivers of future economic growth.

Before the Saudi pricing reforms were implemented, the prevailing opinion was that the deeply entrenched social contract within Saudi Arabia was too rigid to permit significant alterations to energy pricing. This perspective was rooted in a longstanding tradition of government subsidies for fuel, which had become symbolic of the social compact between rulers and citizens. Any attempt to disrupt this balance was seen as potentially destabilizing.

However, the onset of pricing reforms revealed a more complex reality. While the historical essence of the Saudi social contract may never fully vanish, it is becoming clear that the model is more adaptable and resilient than previously thought. It is being reshaped to meet the demands of a changing world and to align with Saudi Arabia's broader economic transformation goals.

Despite the stalled progress and uneven implementation, Saudi Arabia's incremental pricing reform might still be considered a philosophical 'success'. The reason for this success lies in the Government's acknowledgment that macroeconomic reform is not just desirable but necessary. The rulers recognized the need to transition from a petrostate dependent on oil revenues to a modern economy with a diversified industrial and financial base. This understanding has come in conjunction with the Saudi Government's growing realization that climate change is both a threat and an opportunity.

Climate change poses existential risks to the nation's long-term survival due to its reliance on fossil fuels. However, it also presents opportunities for Saudi Arabia to reinvent itself, embarking on diversification schemes that are predicated upon comprehensive decarbonization and macroeconomic reformation and liberalization. This approach aligns with global trends towards sustainability and positions the nation to take advantage of emerging economic opportunities in renewable energy and other green industries.

The somewhat peaceful public response to the pricing reforms further illustrates that the Saudi social contract has not lost its historical articulation involving fuel subsidies. Instead, the contract is evolving, reflecting a new understanding between the state and its citizens. This transformation is not just a reaction to economic pressures but part of a broader vision for Saudi Arabia's future, embracing both the challenges and opportunities presented by a rapidly changing global landscape.

The History of Emirati Energy Price Reform

Like its neighbours, the UAE considered its prevalent energy pricing framework almost inviolable. As previously discussed, low energy and power prices were an essential pillar of the general Arab social contract. However, as stated above, Gulf governments began to amend their energy prices in some form in the early 2010s; by 2018 all Gulf countries had implemented energy pricing reform in one way or another. The UAE was the first Gulf country to institute electricity price reforms, as Dubai began implementing tariff reforms in 2008, with additional pricing reforms in 2011. In January 2015 Abu Dhabi introduced another round of reforms, while electricity prices in the northern emirates of Fujairah, Ras al-Khaimah, Umm al-Qaiwain and Ajman were also modified in 2015, although the focus of their policy shift was on expatriates. In Sharjah, the local Government announced a new commercial and industrial electricity tariff framework in 2014. More broadly, throughout the UAE, petrol and diesel prices were liberalized to meet global pricing benchmarks set each month. However, there has not yet been any substantive gas price reconfiguration in Dubai.

Dubai was one of the first emirates to take pricing reform seriously due to its dependence on energy imports and the austerity measures that it had undertaken in the wake of the global financial crisis. However, in the 2000s energy demand rose precipitously and rapidly outpaced available supply. Consequently, Dubai imported pipeline gas (via the Dolphin pipeline, which transports gas from Qatar's North Field to the UAE and Oman) and LNG to manage the shortfall. However, while the gas import bill was higher than locally produced associated gas, domestic gas tariffs did not rise in tandem; as a result, the Dubai leadership recognized that in order to curb the demand growth it would have to reform energy and power prices.

In 2008 the Dubai Electricity and Water Authority (DEWA) introduced a slab framework of tariff increases based on projected electricity consumption in 2011, initially only applying to expatriates. (Slab tariff pricing is when the designated price of a unit of energy increases progressively with increases in the amount of energy consumed.) Additionally, a fuel surcharge was added to cover the additional cost of LNG importation. Subsidy reform was critical for Dubai and the other emirates due to their power companies' inability to absorb significant financial losses over the long term.

The Dubai Government subsequently commenced an extensive public relations campaign to explain the necessity of the energy and power price reforms and to encourage lower consumption. DEWA designed this system to reward more efficient energy consumption, with higher prices charged for higher consumption levels. In 2011 the Dubai Government implemented a 15%–20% increase in the slab unit cost of power for residential expatriates, government and industry. The authorities also implemented incremental electricity and water price increases for Emirati nationals. (Generally, Emirati nationals had paid three to four times less than expatriates for electricity and water, which had resulted in expatriates effectively cross-subsidizing citizens.) Unlike Saudi Arabia, the Dubai Government did not initially offer a compensation programme to offset the rise in prices. However, following a public outcry, the authorities rescinded the power tariff increases for citizens in a lower income bracket. None the less, the Government retained the power tariff increases for most citizens. As a result, by 2012 power demand had declined by an average of 3%.

Abu Dhabi began to consider energy and power tariff reform after Dubai implemented its changes; however, Abu Dhabi did not institute its reforms until August 2015. Abu Dhabi differed from Dubai in that it did not have a large LNG import bill and it did not suffer economically to the same extent as Dubai during the global financial crisis. Nevertheless, Abu Dhabi faced an increased cost burden for its non-associated gas production as it typically has a higher hydrogen sulphide ratio. The authorities in Abu Dhabi felt that the time was opportune to increase tariffs as costs were rising while the global oil price was declining. Furthermore, anecdotally, the youth population was more amenable to accepting economic reform than previous generations, owing to the growth in environmental sustainability awareness.

In late 2014 the Abu Dhabi Government made a significant announcement regarding adjustments to tariffs, particularly affecting expatriates. The changes, implemented in January 2015, included an increase in tariffs for expatriates, while Emirati nationals faced only a minor rise in power rates and incremental increases for water consumption. This move was seen as a strategic decision to balance the fiscal demands of the state with the welfare considerations for its citizens.

Like Dubai, Abu Dhabi launched a public relations campaign in anticipation of these changes. The campaign emphasized sustainability and conservation as the main reasons behind the need for price adjustments. The message was clear: these changes were necessary to promote responsible consumption and to ensure the long-term viability of the energy and water sectors.

In Sharjah and the northern emirates, similar changes were implemented, but with a focus on electricity prices. These were raised for expatriates as well as commercial and industrial users. The move aligned with broader efforts across the UAE to rationalize energy prices and reduce subsidies, reflecting a shift in economic thinking.

At the federal level, the Emirati Government took an even more decisive step by removing price controls on transportation fuels. This allowed prices to move in tandem with global benchmarks, a move that both signalled a more market-oriented approach and aligned the UAE's domestic pricing with international market dynamics.

With regard to natural gas pricing, changes were even more noticeable. The legacy wholesale gas price in the UAE stood at approximately US $1.25 per MMBTU in 2016. This was then raised to nearly $1.60 per MMBTU in 2017, followed by another increase, to $2.20 per MMBTU, by 2018, where it remained as of the end of 2020.

These incremental adjustments in natural gas prices reflect the UAE's broader strategy to bring domestic energy prices closer to global levels. This not only helps in reducing the fiscal burden of subsidies but also encourages energy efficiency and rationalizes consumption across various sectors.

The Government's systematic and well-communicated approach to these pricing reforms has been crucial. By carefully planning these changes and communicating the underlying rationale to the public, the UAE has been able to implement significant pricing reforms without provoking widespread resistance or misunderstanding. The focus on sustainability and alignment with global practices demonstrated a nuanced understanding of both domestic needs and international economic dynamics. These changes are indicative of the UAE's ongoing commitment to modernize its economy and align its domestic policies with broader global trends and best practices.

Qatar's Incremental Energy Subsidy Reform
Unlike Saudi Arabia and the UAE, Qatar has not experienced pressing fiscal difficulties nor natural gas allocation challenges due to its energy pricing framework. Therefore, it adopted an ad hoc approach to energy pricing reform. However, it did incur budget deficits of 9% of GDP in 2015–16 due to the 2014 global oil price decline. The Qatari Government also directed state-owned institutions to reduce operations and dismiss redundant expatriate staff to limit financial outlays.

Due to the aforementioned, Qatar's domestic energy pricing strategy is still relatively inchoate. The Government increased transportation fuel prices in 2011 by approximately 25% and announced that it would eventually index them to global prices. In 2014 diesel prices increased from US $1.04 per gallon to $1.58 per gallon, while petrol prices rose by 30%, from $1.04 per gallon to $1.38 per gallon. In terms of the power sector, Qatar is an outlier among its GCC peers as electricity is free to citizens, although power prices were increased for expatriates based on monthly consumption rates. Moreover, since June 2016 the Government has begun to adjust fuel prices monthly. From June 2016 until March 2017 fuel transportation prices increased by nearly 30% and diesel prices by about 10%.

The Government announced that it would set future prices based on a formula that includes global prices, and production and distribution costs within Qatar and the Gulf region. However, Qatar will likely continue to allocate free power to its citizens and provide low-cost natural gas to its industries. Natural gas used for power generation represents just 7% of Qatar's gas production, with nearly 80% of it being exported. The cost of producing natural gas is extremely low, with condensates and liquefied petroleum gas (LPG) covering any differences between the production cost and the domestic gas price.

According to the 2022 International Gas Union Wholesale Price Survey, Qatar's wholesale gas price saw significant fluctuations over the years immediately prior, standing at approximately US $1.50 per MMBTU in 2021. This marked an increase from around $0.90 per MMBTU in 2019 and $0.75 in 2017. Despite these changes, Qatar's pricing was still lower than most other countries, with only Kazakhstan, Algeria, Venezuela, Libya and Turkmenistan reporting lower prices.

Unlike some of its neighbouring countries, Qatar does not incur financial losses by allocating gas at comparatively low prices. This distinct economic position is illustrated by examining the Barzan Gas Project, a crucial US $10,300m. undertaking that is expected to sustain and fuel Qatar's ongoing and future major infrastructure initiatives.

The Barzan Gas Project, encompassing both offshore and onshore developments, is being implemented by RasGas, a joint venture between Qatargas and ExxonMobil. This project serves as a window onto the unique dynamics of Qatari gas production and pricing strategy.

By using the costs of the Barzan gas project as a reference point and setting aside any potential cost overruns, a comprehensive analysis of Qatar's domestic gas pricing model can be formulated. Assuming an upstream market return of 12%, and considering the potential yields of condensates and LPG in line with the North Field LNG supply developments from the 1990s and 2000s, the efficiency and innovation of Qatar's gas production system come into sharp focus.

This analysis reveals a production system that has been meticulously optimized to serve the country's strategic goals. Through careful planning, the utilization of cutting-edge technology, and leveraging the vast experience gained from previous projects, Qatar has positioned itself to offer natural gas to domestic industries at a competitive rate without any significant fiscal burden. Qatar's ability to provide domestic industries with natural gas at near-free rates is not solely a reflection of abundant natural resources. It also stems from strategic planning, targeted technological investments and the country's geologically favourable conditions.

This capability to provide domestic industries with low-cost natural gas without substantial economic burdens sets Qatar apart from many other gas-producing nations. It underscores the success of the country's long-term energy strategy, supporting local industrial development and solidifying Qatar's standing as one of the world's foremost LNG exporters.

The absence of fiscal losses in allocating gas at these prices, compared with neighbouring countries, is attributed to Qatar's lower production costs. Unlike other Gulf nations where the majority of incremental natural gas production costs can be significantly higher due to the characteristics (e.g. tight, sour or shale) of non-associated and unconventional gasfields, Qatar's North Field enjoys several advantages. Large economies of scale, extensive field homogeneity and a favourable physical location enable Qatar to maintain a lower cost structure. High yields of valuable by-products such as condensate, ethane and LPG further boost the profitability of the field compared to its nearest competitors.

Qatar's strategic approach allows it to allocate natural gas to domestic industries at an exceptionally low price without significant financial drawbacks. The combination of geological advantages, economies of scale, efficient utilization of technology and strategic planning contributes to this favourable position, reflecting a nuanced understanding of the global energy landscape and a commitment to both domestic growth and international competitiveness.

THE ALTERNATIVE GULF: RENEWABLE AND NUCLEAR ENERGY

Prospects and Challenges
The governments of the Gulf region are taking significant strides towards embracing alternative energy sources, such as renewables and nuclear energy, in their efforts to lessen reliance on domestic hydrocarbon consumption. This concerted move is not only a step towards reducing carbon emissions but also a fundamental part of transitioning the region's economies from being primarily allocative to being more productive and diverse.

The region's historical dependence on oil and gas has not deterred these nations from aligning with global sustainability initiatives. In fact, all the Gulf nations have either announced new targets or reaffirmed their commitments to the Paris Agreement (an international treaty adopted in 2015 covering climate change mitigation, adaptation and finance) within the past two years. This reflects a growing recognition of the role they must play in global efforts to mitigate climate change.

The power sector, as one of the largest sources of emissions in the region, has become a focal point in these national decarbonization plans. Consequently, substantial investments in renewable energy are expected throughout the current decade. The increased emphasis on solar power, in particular, positions the Gulf as a global leader in photovoltaic deployment and pricing.

As of 2023, however, regional power generation in the Gulf is still primarily dependent on oil and gas. This reliance not only consumes a substantial portion of domestically produced oil and gas, incurring significant opportunity costs, but also drives the growth in power demand, consequently increasing regional carbon emissions. The sector responsible for heat and power generation is the single most significant contributor to carbon emissions in the region.

This situation is both caused and exacerbated by the historically low administrative pricing of electricity and hydrocarbons, which promotes higher consumption rates. The high level of power consumption has long-term environmental consequences, making the transition to alternative energy sources even more urgent.

Fortunately, the Gulf states are uniquely positioned to exploit renewable energy, particularly solar energy. Boasting some of the highest solar irradiance levels in the world, these nations have access to a virtually untapped reservoir of solar power. Wind resources, although less abundant, also present opportunities for diversification of energy sources.

Several Gulf countries have begun to invest in solar and wind projects, recognizing the potential for both environmental stewardship and economic diversification. By harnessing these natural resources, they can reduce reliance on traditional fossil fuels, curb carbon emissions and create a more sustainable energy future.

The shift towards renewable energy in the Gulf region represents not just an environmental imperative but also a strategic economic opportunity. By transitioning from a hydrocarbon-based economy, these nations can create new industries, drive technological innovation and foster economic growth in sectors beyond oil and gas.

Historically, the low administrative pricing regime of hydrocarbons was one of the most significant barriers to the broad deployment of renewable energy regionally. However, renewables, particularly solar, have proven to be a low-cost method of power generation in the region. Nevertheless, slowing power demand, global economic uncertainty and increased investments in non-associated natural gas in the late 2010s could still potentially curb solar investment.

While energy efficiency policies have indeed lowered per capita power demand in the Gulf region, potentially reducing the immediate need for solar investment, both Saudi Arabia and the UAE have reaffirmed their stated commitments to renewable energy production, with a particular emphasis on solar power.

Saudi Arabia and the UAE, the two largest economies in the GCC, are leading the way in climate-related initiatives within the region. By the end of 2021, these nations were responsible for roughly 90% of the GCC's renewable energy capacity, with the UAE alone contributing an impressive 77%. These figures underline their substantial commitments to renewable energy, further emphasized by their ambitious pledges to achieve net zero emissions—the UAE by 2050 and Saudi Arabia by 2060.

These commitments align with the obligations under the Paris Agreement, which mandates that all signatories establish and adhere to goals known as nationally determined contributions (NDCs). Across the Gulf region, governments have publicly declared net zero targets and are actively pursuing renewable energy deployment to fulfill their NDC climate commitments. Given that the power sector is a primary source of emissions, these efforts are crucial.

The UAE and Saudi Arabia, the largest greenhouse gas emitters in the GCC, have made significant investments in renewables. In 2022 the UAE even increased its target for reducing GHG emissions to 31% by 2030, compared with its previous commitment of 23.5%. The new NDC limits the UAE's emissions in 2030 to 208m. metric tons of carbon dioxide equivalent (CO_2e), compared with 301.2m. tons of CO_2e under its business-as-usual (BAU) scenario.

Furthermore, the UAE's Renewable Energy Strategy 2050 emphasizes the decarbonization of the power sector as a key priority. Unlike organizations such as the International Renewable Energy Agency (IRENA), which exclude nuclear power from renewable energy statistics, the UAE considers both nuclear and renewables as 'clean energy'. Its goal is to achieve 30% of its energy mix from clean sources by 2030, rising to 50% by 2050.

While renewable energy investment was principally intended to reduce domestic hydrocarbon demand, the Gulf governments view it as a bedrock of their economic diversification efforts, with many benefits that accrue beyond the electricity-generating potential.

Regional energy pricing reform was a focus of regional governments in the mid- to late 2010s. However, much of the initial momentum has stalled, with further reforms proceeding extremely slowly. There is still much work to be completed and many obstacles to be overcome. Nevertheless, as previous sections have illustrated, alternative energy is becoming much more attractive to the regional governments because it is potentially less expensive than the incremental gas from complex and non-associated fields, would require less domestic price adjustment and would reduce hydrocarbon demand and carbon emissions (see Table 1). 'Less domestic price adjustment' refers to the fact that as complex, higher-cost natural gasfields come online, in order for electricity tariffs to meet the cost of production from incremental fields, they would have to be increased. Solar power generation costs are typically on a downward trajectory. Solar-powered generation prices of under US $0.03 per kWh, which have been consistently realized in the Gulf since 2016, are considered the first 'tipping point' for solar to become more economically viable than coal and the higher-cost unconventional natural gas production.

Since 2016 the Gulf region has emerged as a significant player on the global stage in terms of photovoltaic (solar) energy deployment and pricing. In the five-year span from 2015 to 2020, nearly 7 GW of solar power capacity was ordered in the region under long-term power purchase agreement frameworks. This development continually set new pricing records, positioning the Gulf as a model for solar power generation investment and deployment worldwide.

The region is not only thriving in current solar market dynamics but is also seen at the forefront of potential future developments in the solar power market. This transformation has been rapid, marking the Gulf as a global template for renewable energy expansion.

Despite Kuwait's early adoption of solar power in the 1970s and 1980s, the UAE has become the regional frontrunner in installed renewable energy capacity. As a mature market, the pace of renewable projects in the UAE is expected to grow more slowly compared to Saudi Arabia. According to an estimate by the Arab Petroleum Investments Corporation, renewables will comprise 22% of the value of all power projects in Saudi Arabia between 2021 and 2025, in contrast to just 8% in the UAE.

These dynamics indicate that by 2030 Saudi Arabia is projected to overtake the UAE in installed renewable capacity, potentially reaching nearly twice that of its neighbour. This ambitious goal aligns with Saudi Arabia's declared national targets and reflects the country's commitment to decarbonization at the domestic level.

Solar power generation in the region has a lower cost structure than domestic associated and complex non-associated natural gas (when considering the total cost, including capital investment and operating costs) or LNG imports. (In 2019 the Saudi Arabian company ACWA Power submitted a tariff of US $0.0169 per kWh for the 900-MW fifth phase of Dubai's Mohammed bin Rashid al-Maktoum Solar Park.) These prices do not include the significant opportunity cost that these countries accrue from supplying their domestic markets at the production cost of oil and natural gas instead of supplying the international market at several-fold higher prices. Therefore, it is vital not just to consider the cost differential between hydrocarbon power generation and renewable energy generation; it is also essential to broaden the analysis to understand the impact of supplying oil and natural gas to the domestic market for power generation as opposed to exporting them, which makes solar an even more attractive option.

Initially, there was widespread scepticism about the viability of solar investment in the Gulf region, with the common belief that many of the low prices were only achieved due to substantial embedded subsidies hidden from public view that could not be emulated in other jurisdictions. However, that is not the case, as it is structural factors, such as steadily declining solar technology prices, local business environments and the provision of generous but financially viable terms, that have led to the record low solar prices. That this phenomenon is not limited to the Gulf is evident by the observation that average global prices for utility-scale capital expenditures in the solar market have declined precipitously to the levels present in the Gulf region at the beginning of the 2020s.

If artificial barriers were removed, then the adoption of alternative energy would occur rapidly as the region has significant solar capital available year-round. Solar power investment is likely to be the most effective option for Gulf countries to reduce domestic or imported natural gas dependence. Saudi Arabia, the UAE and Qatar are each engaging in large-scale alternative energy development strategies.

Overall, a new solar pricing regime has been realized in the Gulf, with power purchase agreements (PPAs) consistently awarded for prices significantly below US $0.02 per kWh. This pricing point is crucial because it represents the second 'tipping point' at which solar power is rapidly becoming more economically favourable than existing fossil fuel capacity.

Saudi Arabia: Moving Ahead with Solar and Wind Investments

Saudi Arabia has attempted sporadically to craft an alternative energy policy over the past few decades. Historically, this was never taken seriously until Crown Prince Mohammed bin Salman bin Abdulaziz Al Sa'ud announced a comprehensive renewable energy policy in late 2021 to transform the country's position from simply being a crude petroleum producer/exporter to an international force in the clean energy marketplace. However, many hurdles must be overcome as Saudi Arabia is still the largest oil-consuming country in the Middle East and North Africa. The country's domestic hydrocarbon consumption incurs a significant opportunity cost for oil that could be exported at international prices.

For example, domestic oil consumption in the kingdom has increased significantly over the past four decades, growing by an average of 5.7% per year and reaching nearly 3m. barrels per day (b/d)—about one-quarter of production. As a corollary, Saudi Arabia obtains almost three-fifths of its power generation from oil, and crude petroleum consumption has increased markedly over the decades due to rapid industrial development, rising population levels, and subsidized energy and power prices.

Saudi Arabia's escalating domestic oil consumption, driven by both transport needs and oil-fuelled power generation, presents a complex challenge. If the current trends persist, internal energy consumption may eventually surpass national energy production capacity, leading to a situation where the country might need to import oil within the next decade. Such a scenario is particularly concerning for a nation that has long been a leading global oil exporter.

Confronted with the rising trend of domestic oil consumption, Saudi Arabia is turning its attention towards solar power, identifying it as a promising and potentially revolutionary avenue for its energy needs. The stakes are high and the allure is profound: by tapping into its solar potential, the country could theoretically meet one-third of its domestic power demand. This shift could allow Saudi Arabia to boost its oil exports by an additional 300,000 b/d, translating into a windfall of tens of billions of US dollars in additional export revenue.

Yet, this promising scenario currently resides in the realm of theory rather than practice. Saudi Arabia's continued alignment with the OPEC+ quota framework, as of the early 2020s, places substantial constraints on such an ambitious shift in its energy policy. The commitment to these quotas limits the extent to which the country can reduce its reliance on oil and pivot towards renewable energy.

The numbers further illustrate the complexity of the situation. Despite boasting the seventh largest average annual solar power potential of any country, according to World Bank data, Saudi Arabia ranks only 45th globally in terms of actual solar capacity. As of 2023 the nation's 1 GW of installed solar power pales in comparison to the 75 GW installed in Germany, 173 GW in the USA and massive 482 GW in the People's Republic of China.

The discrepancy between potential and reality underscores a significant gap in Saudi Arabia's renewable energy ambitions. While the opportunities presented by solar energy are indeed enticing, bridging this gap will require more than mere recognition of the potential. It demands dedicated efforts, innovative policies, substantial investments and perhaps a re-evaluation of existing international commitments. Without these elements, Saudi Arabia's solar dreams may continue to remain a distant vision, overshadowed by the dominant role of hydrocarbons in its energy landscape. Even if Saudi Arabia manages to avoid becoming a net oil importer through the expansion of solar energy or other means, the country will still need to pursue diversification in its power generation. At the very least, this might involve switching to more natural gas-fired power generation to prevent its spare capacity from being consumed by large domestic demand. Yet such a transition would not be without consequences.

Switching to natural gas or another alternative to oil could potentially diminish Saudi Arabia's geopolitical power and influence. The country's role as a leading global oil supplier has long been a source of strength in international relations. Any significant deviation from this position would require careful consideration and strategic planning, weighing the economic benefits against the potential loss of global standing.

None the less, the pursuit of solar energy is not solely about economics. Saudi Arabia's current domestic energy policies have led to high carbon emissions, a matter of growing global concern. The leadership in Riyadh recognizes that transitioning to alternative energy sources is not only a strategic economic decision but also a necessary step toward creating a sustainable future. Embracing renewable energy supports private sector growth, aligns with global efforts to combat climate change and positions the nation as a responsible player on the international stage.

The integration of solar power into Saudi Arabia's energy mix represents more than just a short-term solution to an immediate problem. It is part of a broader vision that seeks to diversify the economy, reduce reliance on fossil fuels and align with international efforts to mitigate the effects of climate change. It is a critical pillar in the Saudi leadership's long-term strategy to foster sustainable economic growth and environmental stewardship. Given Saudi Arabia's significant solar potential, the investment in this renewable resource appears to be a logical move.

Significant steps were taken in 2012, when the Saudi Government announced somewhat ambitious plans for US $109,000m. worth of investment in renewable energy, which would create a solar industry that could potentially supply nearly one-third of domestic power by 2032. (This would comprise 41 GW of solar power and another 21 GW of geothermal and wind power. In 2018 less than 1% of Saudi Arabia's energy supply was derived from renewables.) By 2020 Saudi Aramco was operating the country's largest solar farm (a 10-MW photovoltaic project), located in the car park of the company's headquarters in Dhahran and generating just enough power for a nearby office block.

Saudi Arabia's journey towards adopting renewable energy has been marked by several key shifts and milestones. In 2015 the Government announced a delay in its renewable energy target date, postponing it to 2040 to allow for further studies into the technology. A year later, in 2016, the renewable power generation targets were dramatically reduced from 50% of the total to just 10%, and the role of natural gas in the energy mix was simultaneously increased.

However, despite these initial setbacks, the Government renewed its commitment to the deployment of renewable energy when it introduced the Saudi Vision 2030 framework in April 2016. This strategic framework highlighted the importance of economic diversification and reducing the country's reliance on oil.

Subsequently, in 2018 Saudi Arabia unveiled a plan to seek investment of up to US $7,000m. to supply about 10% of its power requirements (9,500 MW) from renewable sources by 2023. The Government did not stop there and later announced an ambitious plan to achieve a 50% share of renewables in its power capacity mix by 2030. The targets were set at 58.7 GW of renewable energy capacity by 2030, with solar energy contributing 40 GW and wind energy contributing 16 GW.

Simultaneously, the Government implemented strategic reforms and initiatives. In 2016 the Government restructured itself by merging several resource-related ministries to form the Ministry of Energy, Industry and Mineral Resources. This was a strategic move designed to streamline decision-making processes. In January 2017 Saudi Arabia officially announced its first global solar power tender, signalling its earnest intentions.

Moreover, in the first quarter of 2019 the Saudi company Ajlan & Bros and Hanergy Thin Film Power Group of China signed a memorandum of understanding (MOU) to construct the first thin-film solar industrial park in the Middle East and North Africa. The project, with a projected cost of over US $1,000m., demonstrated Saudi Arabia's commitment to bolster its renewable energy manufacturing capability.

Saudi Arabia's pursuit of renewable energy has seen remarkable progress, particularly in the solar and wind power sectors, when compared to its lack of interest and political will to see projects through in the 2000s and the first half of the 2010s. In March 2022 the kingdom underscored its commitment to diversifying its energy mix by awarding contracts for two major solar projects with a combined capacity of 1 GW. The first of these projects, the Ar Rass solar photovoltaic (PV) project, was awarded to ACWA Power, a leading company in Saudi Arabia's solar power development. Located in the central region of the country, the project will boast a capacity of 700 MW, making it the largest PV project tendered as of 2023. ACWA Power will operate the project under a 25-year power purchase agreement (PPA). The second project, involving the construction of the 300-MW Saad solar PV park, was awarded to the Chinese company Jinko Power Technology. Located about 80 km from Riyadh, this project illustrates the ongoing international collaboration in Saudi Arabia's renewable energy transformation.

Simultaneously, wind energy is gaining traction in the kingdom. Marking a significant milestone, the Dumat Al Jandal project, the largest wind farm in the Middle East, was fully connected to the national power grid at the end of 2021 and began generating electricity. This 400-MW utility-scale wind power project, developed by a consortium led by EDF Renewables and the Emirati company Masdar, highlights the growing role of pan-Gulf investment, with Masdar expanding its influence across the wider Middle East and North Africa region.

The Dumat Al Jandal wind farm is expected to provide enough clean energy to power up to 70,000 Saudi households, offsetting nearly 1m. metric tons of carbon emissions annually. Additionally, the project is expected to create more than 600 local jobs during construction, aligning with Saudi Arabia's goal to diversify its economy and boost employment outside the government and oil sectors.

Saudi Arabia's wind energy potential is vast, with average wind speeds ranging from 6.0 to 8.0 metres per second across most of the country. The Government has set an ambitious target of achieving 10 GW of wind energy capacity by 2025. According to the Global Wind Energy Council, the technical potential for onshore wind in the kingdom is in excess of 200 GW in seven regions, with mean wind speeds at 100 metres altitude ranging from 6.7 to 7.9 metres per second. Moreover, Saudi Arabia's offshore wind potential adds further prospects, offering up to 28 GW of conventional fixed-bottom installations and 78 GW of floating offshore wind capacity.

However, renewable energy deployment has had a somewhat difficult inception as various high-profile projects have been delayed or cancelled. For instance, in October 2018 the Saudi Government cancelled a US $200,000m. 200-GW solar plant that had been announced in March by the Saudi Public Investment Fund and SoftBank Corpn of Japan. The two parties had developed the erstwhile deal in a rather haphazard manner. Many senior Saudi officials had been excluded from the negotiations, and there were also concerns about integrating the project into the national grid. Additionally, the MOU did not detail how export tariffs would be estimated, nor how the expansion of logistics and manufacturing capacity would be resolved in a country with just 50 MW of installed power capacity—less than Kyrgyzstan or the US state of Louisiana. A further complication is that Saudi Arabia is seeking to become a regional hub of renewable energy manufacturing and, perhaps, a global exporter of renewable energy technology, with 60%–80% of solar power components to be manufactured domestically as part of the country's National Renewable Energy Program. The Government has imposed local manufacturing rules (local content stipulations) for domestic projects to develop this aim further. However, even Saudi officials have recognized the trade-off between the somewhat strict local content rules and their desire to achieve local job growth, low project bidding costs and the expansion of Saudi technical capacity.

Photovoltaic solar generation costs have been declining in Saudi Arabia, with levelized costs (lifetime costs divided by energy production) expected to reach around US $0.07 per kWh by 2025. As previously noted, it is essential to remember that solar energy generation costs are significantly lower than the current administered domestic power tariffs of between $0.18 and $0.32 per kWh. When considering that fuel oil provides nearly 39% of Saudi Arabia's power generation, there are also significant opportunity costs associated with this domestic allocation as opposed to its export at international market rates.

While Saudi Arabia's ambitious renewable energy investments are certainly commendable, a nuanced view reveals a more complex picture. The country still produces about 99% of its power from hydrocarbons, and the shift towards renewables has been gradual and fraught with challenges. Indeed, although Saudi Arabia's renewable energy goals mark a departure from its previous reluctance to engage fully in the renewable energy sector, the road to realization is lined with significant barriers. These include a strong carbon lock-in, where existing investments and infrastructure tied to fossil fuels create resistance to change. The situation is further complicated by a lack of environmental awareness among the general population and leadership, perpetuating a reliance on traditional energy sources, although there are signs that awareness is growing.

Additionally, the country's power and energy subsidization policies have historically favoured fossil fuels, making the transition to renewables more financially challenging. This economic situation is exacerbated by limited technical knowledge of renewable energy among both Saudi leadership and the population at large. Without a well-informed populace and decision-makers, the drive towards renewable energy can become mired in misconceptions and inertia.

Furthermore, the lack of supporting institutions and frameworks for innovation, such as intellectual property rights, hampers the development and deployment of new technologies. This institutional void can stifle creativity and hinder collaboration between researchers, industries and policymakers.

The combination of these factors leads to a situation where progress, although significant in terms of investments, has been incremental in actual implementation. Without strong, dedicated leadership to address these barriers and develop enabling factors, Saudi Arabia's achievement of its stated renewable energy targets within the planned time frame appears a challenging indertaking.

It is essential to recognize that the transition to renewable energy is not merely a matter of investment or technological capability; it requires a multifaceted approach that considers economic policies, educational initiatives, legal frameworks and cultural shifts. The Saudi Government's commitment to renewable energy is clear, but achieving the transformation will require concerted efforts across multiple domains, from policy reforms and financial incentives to education and public engagement. Without a holistic and robust strategy, the transition to a sustainable energy future in Saudi Arabia may continue to be a slow and complex process.

Investing in the Atom: Saudi Nuclear Energy Development

In December 2006 the GCC made a notable announcement: it would commission research into the development of nuclear energy for peaceful purposes. Both France, with its advanced nuclear technology, and Iran, with its vested interests in nuclear development, pledged their support and co-operation. The announcement came in a year that was already fraught with significant developments in the nuclear domain. In April Iran made a groundbreaking proclamation that it had successfully enriched uranium for the first time. This marked a critical milestone for the country, aligning with its stated goal of pursuing nuclear energy. Then, in October, the Democratic People's Republic of Korea (North Korea) alarmed the international community with the announcement of its successful detonation of a nuclear device.

These events, with repercussions beyond their immediate geographical confines, created ripples in the already complex landscape of global nuclear politics. Some observers and analysts were quick to connect the dots, suggesting that the GCC's newfound interest in nuclear energy might have been a direct response to these occurrences.

The issue of nuclear energy introduces another complex dimension to the already labyrinthine geopolitical intricacies of the Middle East. Iran's unyielding advancement of its domestic nuclear power industry has not only been a subject of international attention but has also induced growing apprehension among its regional neighbours, especially Saudi Arabia. This concern is not merely tied to Iran's potential energy self-sufficiency but also extends to the possibility of the weaponization of its nuclear capabilities.

This concern, often cloaked in the diplomatic subtleties of international relations, has fuelled extensive speculation that Saudi Arabia may be quietly cultivating the ambition to develop its own nuclear capabilities. Such ambitions, however, extend beyond mere energy requirements and encapsulate a broader strategic vision. Should Iran achieve a nuclear breakthrough, Saudi Arabia's pursuit of nuclear technology could serve as a critical counterbalance in maintaining regional equilibrium.

Such speculation is far from baseless. In 2009 the late Saudi King Abdullah bin Abdulaziz delivered a stern warning to the Administration of US President Barack Obama. He stated explicitly that if Iran were to obtain nuclear weapons, Saudi Arabia would respond in kind, pursuing nuclear capabilities of its own. The concern was echoed nearly a decade later by the Crown Prince and de facto ruler of Saudi Arabia, Prince Mohammed bin Salman. In 2018 he somewhat stridently acknowledged these anxieties, affirming that Saudi Arabia would indeed seek to develop nuclear weapons if Iran were to achieve this capability. This revelation, while disconcerting to some, offered a transparent view into the strategic thinking of the Saudi leadership.

It is essential to recognize that any civilian nuclear program inherently contains dual-use elements. These components, while primarily intended for peaceful purposes, could feasibly be redirected to aid in the production of weapons-grade material. The nexus between civilian and potential military applications of nuclear technology renders the entire subject highly sensitive and fraught with risk.

The strategic considerations surrounding nuclear energy within the Gulf region reveal the multifaceted and intricate dynamics at play. The GCC's announcement in 2006 of research into the peaceful utilization of nuclear energy indicated recognition of its broader potential. However, this was not merely a pursuit of an alternative energy source; it was deeply interwoven with regional security concerns, strategic rivalries and geopolitical manoeuvring. The balance that needed to be struck between the aspiration for energy diversification and the imperatives of regional stability was delicate.

This interplay between energy, politics and security was further highlighted in subsequent developments. In February 2007 the six GCC member states, in collaboration with the International Atomic Energy Agency (IAEA), agreed on a framework that saw Saudi Arabia leading a feasibility study for a regional nuclear power and desalination programme. This regional approach appeared to align with the co-operative spirit of the GCC. However, in August 2009 Saudi Arabia diverged from this path, announcing an independent inquiry into domestic nuclear energy development. The Government unambiguously stated that nuclear power was not just an option but a necessity for achieving its future energy sustainability goals. The Saudi Government further underlined its commitment in April 2010 when it issued a royal decree that articulated the essential role of atomic energy in the kingdom's future. It stated: 'The development of atomic energy is essential to meet the kingdom's growing requirements for energy to generate electricity, produce desalinated water and reduce reliance on depleting hydrocarbon resources.'

In a landscape where nuclear energy remained contentious and laden with risks, Saudi Arabia's determination stood out even more starkly in the aftermath of the 2011 disaster at the Fukushima Daiichi nuclear power plant in Japan. While the catastrophe led several countries to rethink or even scale back their preliminary nuclear power developments, Saudi Arabia steadfastly maintained its course.

Saudi Arabia has the second most developed nuclear energy programme in the Arab world, after the UAE. To facilitate its nuclear energy goals, in April 2010 the Saudi Government established the King Abdullah City for Atomic and Renewable Energy (K.A.CARE) in Riyadh. K.A.CARE was tasked with formulating a strategy to reduce hydrocarbon consumption, and was also given responsibility for managing nuclear energy treaties signed by the kingdom and for supervising nuclear energy and radioactive waste projects. According to Saudi nuclear energy assessments announced in April 2013, nuclear power plant construction was scheduled to commence in 2016, with K.A.CARE projecting 17 GW of nuclear capacity by 2032 out of a planned total of 123 GW. Of this total, 16 GW would be solar photovoltaic, 25 GW concentrated solar power (CSP) and 4 GW geothermal, as well as waste. The plans stated that the Government would construct 16 nuclear power reactors over the following 20 years at a cost of more than US $80,000m., which would generate nearly 20% of Saudi Arabia's electricity needs.

The timeline for the completion of nuclear power plants in Saudi Arabia has experienced a series of delays, pushing the completion date back to 2040. In July 2017 Saudi Arabia made strides in its atomic energy pursuits by approving a National Atomic Energy Project. This project encompassed plans to build both large and small nuclear reactors for electricity production and water desalination. By November 2017 the Saudi authorities were actively soliciting technical bids to construct the first two 1.4-GW reactors, initiating discussions with China, France, the Republic of Korea (South Korea), the Russian Federation and the USA. Although progress was slowed by the global pandemic, it resumed in 2023 with the receipt of numerous bids to build the country's first reactors.

Parallel to these developments, the Saudi authorities have been diligent in establishing the necessary legal and regulatory frameworks with the assistance of the IAEA. This collaboration included a nuclear infrastructure review conducted in 2018 and a final report issued in January 2019. Saudi Arabia further consolidated its commitment by establishing the Nuclear and Radiological Regulatory Commission in March 2018 and the Saudi Nuclear Energy Holding Company (SNEHC) in March 2022, which was to develop and operate the planned nuclear facilities.

While Saudi Arabia has expressed an openness to collaborate with any nation that could aid its nuclear endeavours, it has notably favoured US nuclear technology. Saudi leaders are eager to establish a joint US-Saudi partnership in the nuclear energy sector, mirroring the existing co-operation between the USA and Saudi Aramco.

However, these ambitions have been hindered by a significant disagreement between the two countries, centring on Saudi Arabia's insistence that uranium enrichment should occur within its borders. In support of this stance, Saudi energy minister Prince Abdulaziz bin Salman Al Sa'ud declared in 2019 that Saudi Arabia aimed to control the entire nuclear cycle, including the production and enrichment of uranium.

This was reiterated in January 2023 with an emphasis on utilizing domestic uranium resources for producing low enriched uranium (LEU).

In contrast, the USA's position aligns with the precedent set in a 2009 agreement with the UAE, referred to as the 'gold standard'. This agreement permits US collaboration but requires a commitment from the partner country to abstain from enrichment and fuel reprocessing within its territory. The fundamental difference in perspectives presents a complex challenge to achieving a mutually beneficial nuclear collaboration between Saudi Arabia and the USA, casting uncertainty on the future of the nuclear energy partnership.

The disagreements have led to frustration within Saudi Arabia, prompting officials to explore alternative partnerships with other nations, including China, Russia or US allies. Saudi Arabia's aspirations for uranium enrichment and nuclear fuel production, including potential exportation, are viewed as even more vital than the proposed reactors within the country.

In February 2022 Saudi Arabia further signalled its international co-operation by signing an MOU with France, covering nuclear energy, hydrogen and electrical interconnection. In December the IAEA conducted a workshop with Saudi officials in Riyadh, the purpose of which was to 'support the implementation of its nuclear energy programme in a safe, secure and transparent manner', according to an official press release. The Saudi energy ministry emphasized that the kingdom's 'peaceful nuclear power programme' would adhere to 'transparency and international best practices'. It pledged to collaborate closely with the IAEA and nations that had signed general agreements with Saudi Arabia, including China, Russia, South Korea and France.

Simultaneously, Saudi Arabia continues to engage with the USA, its preferred partner, and has offered to 'normalize' relations with Israel in return for US collaboration on building nuclear reactors and other assurances.

Although Saudi Arabia's geographical and climatic advantages position it as a prime candidate for low-cost solar power production, its pursuit of nuclear energy has raised eyebrows and prompted further doubts regarding the underlying motives of its nuclear ambitions. The choice of nuclear energy, often viewed as a more expensive and complex path, leads to questions about the true dimensions and purposes behind this strategic decision. None the less, despite the scepticism and concerns expressed by some external observers, Saudi Arabia appears resolute in progressing with its nuclear energy plans, an initiative reflecting a multifaceted energy strategy within the broader context of regional dynamics.

Ahead of the Pack: The UAE's Renewable Energy Deployment

The UAE has made the most progress among its Gulf peers in renewable energy implementation and deployment. The country has also taken on the unofficial role of global sustainability advocate for the Middle East and North Africa to showcase its renewable energy investments. The UAE's path towards renewable energy is not just predicated on environmental issues. The structural problems of declining low-cost conventional gas supply and rising power demand spurred the Emirati leadership to develop renewable energy. In 2022 the UAE announced that it was proceeding with plans to invest approximately US $163,000m. to diversify its energy mix throughout the decade to better its chances of meeting its goal of becoming net zero by 2050.

In January 2017 Sheikh Mohammed bin Rashid Al Maktoum, the Emirati Vice-President and Prime Minister, and the Ruler of Dubai, unveiled the UAE Energy Plan 2050. This ambitious strategy aims to transform the country's energy landscape by increasing the utilization of alternative energy sources, including renewables and nuclear, by 50% and enhancing energy efficiency by 40%. The plan lays out a vision for the UAE's energy mix by 2050, projecting that 44% will be sourced from renewable energy, 38% from natural gas, 12% from coal (though this percentage may have been revised, as discussed in subsequent sections) and 6% from nuclear energy.

These targets are part of a broader commitment by the UAE to sustainable energy and environmental stewardship. Alongside its 2050 renewables target, the country has set ambitious goals to reduce greenhouse gas emissions by 31.5% by 2030 and to achieve carbon neutrality by 2050. Yet, despite these clear targets, uncertainty looms regarding the UAE's commitment to oil production and export.

Renewable energy, particularly solar energy, has emerged as a compelling option for the UAE, thanks to a confluence of favourable circumstances. First, the country's geographical location offers a distinct advantage for harnessing solar energy. With an average of nearly 10 hours of sunlight daily and approximately 350 days of sunshine per year, the potential for solar power generation is immense.

Second, the UAE's leadership has demonstrated a robust commitment to addressing climate change. Between 2010 and 2020 the country increased its renewable energy portfolio by 400%, signalling a profound shift towards sustainable energy solutions. This commitment is not merely symbolic; the Emirati Government has concrete targets to reduce greenhouse gas emissions by 2030, aligned with its obligations under the Paris Agreement.

Third, renewable energy costs declined significantly during the mid-2010s, with solar photovoltaic costs reaching record lows through foreign direct investment (FDI) and technology transfer. Finally, renewable energy is a vital pillar of the UAE's diversification goals, with the country aiming to reduce the domestic consumption of natural gas to allow more exports to the international market and a greater allocation to the downstream sector, and to develop an expansive renewable energy technology manufacturing base through FDI and technology transfer.

Since the beginning of the 2010s, the UAE has become a leading force in renewable energy in the Middle East and North Africa region, inaugurating numerous renewable energy projects. Among these initiatives, solar energy has emerged as a prominent component of the UAE's energy strategy, reflecting a broader global shift toward sustainable power sources.

In Dubai alone, the commitment to renewable energy is evident. Power demand in Dubai grew by 9.8% in 2021, reaching 50,202 gigawatt hours (GWh), up from 45,712 GWh the previous year. Remarkably, renewable energy, primarily from solar sources, has kept pace with this growth. In 2021 renewables accounted for 11.4% of Dubai's total energy production, an increase from 9.0% in 2020. By the end of 2022, this figure had risen further, with renewables meeting approximately 14% of Dubai's energy needs. The Emirate's ambitious plan to meet 100% of its energy requirements through renewable energy by 2050 underscores the central role that renewables, and particularly solar energy, are expected to play in its future energy landscape.

The UAE's projections for the country as a whole are equally ambitious. It anticipates a fourfold increase in solar energy production by 2025 and aims to achieve 50 GW of combined PV and concentrated solar power (CSP) capacity by 2035. Several factors are driving this robust growth, including a steady decline in the levelized cost of solar PV energy. This cost reduction is making solar power an increasingly attractive and economical option compared with traditional energy generation methods.

However, despite these advancements in renewable energy, the UAE's total energy capacity is still heavily dominated by natural gas and oil. As of 2022 the UAE's total solar capacity stood at 18.13 terrawatt hours (TWh), a significant improvement from 1.98 TWh five years previously, but dwarfed by the natural gas and oil capacities, at 698.48 TWh and 607.25 TWh, respectively. This disparity highlights the ongoing challenges on the path ahead for the UAE in shifting its energy mix.

In a bid to progress even further, as part of the revised UAE National Energy Strategy 2050, the UAE has committed to an extensive investment plan, involving as much as an additional US $54,400m. being invested in the energy sector as a whole. This initiative, announced by Prime Minister Sheikh Al Maktoum in July 2023, is formulated potentially to triple the nation's renewable energy output by 2030. The strategy also includes a targeted focus on developing infrastructure for electric vehicles and low-emissions hydrogen fuel.

Over the past decade the UAE has made remarkable progress in augmenting its renewable energy capacity, leading the world in this area. The country's ambitious plans envisage investment of US $40,000m.–$54,000m. to increase this capacity threefold by 2030, reaching a total of 14.2 GW.

Abu Dhabi's current solar infrastructure demonstrates a significant investment in renewable energy, with an installed capacity of 1.3 GW. This figure is the cumulative result of several key projects. The Noor Abu Dhabi (Sweihan) project provides the majority of the solar capacity (1.17 GW). Emirati solar capacity is further enhanced by the Abu Dhabi virtual battery, which contributes 108 MW. The immense size of this virtual battery system is particularly noteworthy, as it can provide up to six hours of backup power in the event of a failure in Abu Dhabi's electricity grid.

In line with its sustainability objectives, Abu Dhabi commissioned the Shams 1 CSP plant, which became operational in 2014. This 100-MW facility was financed with a US $600m. investment from a consortium of international banks. Shams 1 has earned recognition as the largest CSP plant outside of Spain and the USA, and is the first such facility in the Middle East and North Africa. Since its inauguration, Shams 1 has been instrumental in shaping Abu Dhabi's energy profile. Over the past 10 years, the plant has provided power to more than 200,000 homes and offset the production of 1.75m. metric tons of carbon emissions. On a yearly basis, these emissions savings are equivalent to planting 1.5m. trees or taking 15,000 cars off Abu Dhabi's roads.

Initially, the Abu Dhabi Government planned the Noor Abu Dhabi project in collaboration with Marubeni of Japan and JinkoSolar of China for a plant capacity of 350 MW. The landscape dramatically changed when the consortium submitted a groundbreaking bid of just US $0.024 per kWh in September 2016. Recognizing the opportunity, the Abu Dhabi Water and Electricity Authority (ADWEA) quickly revised the plan. The authorities expanded the project's capacity to 1.17 GW, almost quadrupling the original design. The completed project features 3.2m. solar panels and has the capacity to power the daily lives of 90,000 family units.

Furthering its commitment to expanding solar power generation, Abu Dhabi is currently developing the Al Dhafra Solar PV Independent Power Producer project, situated about 35km from Abu Dhabi city. Set for completion before the UN Climate Change Conference (COP 28) conference in Dubai in November 2023, the 2-GW project will be the world's largest single-site solar power plant. The plant, which will utilize nearly 3.5m. solar panels, is to supply power to the Emirates Water and Electricity Company (EWEC—which assumed responsibility for major infrastructure from ADWEA in 2018) and is expected to generate enough electricity to power approximately 160,000 homes across the UAE. It has been calculated that the project will help significantly to reduce carbon emissions in the country, with the potential to mitigate 2.4m. metric tons of carbon dioxide on an annual basis.

The Al Dhafra solar project is a collaborative venture between the Abu Dhabi National Energy Company (TAQA) and Masdar, which together control a 60% stake, while partners EDF (of France) and JinkoPower control the remaining 40%. In April 2023 Masdar confirmed the completion of the solar PV module installation at Al Dhafra. This marked a key milestone in the project's progress, laying the groundwork for its full commissioning, anticipated by November of that year.

EWEC also took another step towards enhancing Abu Dhabi's renewable energy portfolio with the announcement in 2023 of the 1.5-GW Al Ajban solar project, scheduled to be operational by 2026. The plant will boost Abu Dhabi's solar capacity to approximately 4 GW, supplementing existing facilities such as Noor Abu Dhabi and Al Dhafra. EWEC planned to select the winning bid for the development, financing, construction, operation, maintenance and ownership of the plant and related infrastructure by the end of 2023. The successful bidder will own up to 40% of the project, with the remaining equity indirectly held by the Abu Dhabi Government. In addition, the developer will enter into a long-term power purchase agreement (PPA) with EWEC. The PPA will be structured as an energy purchase agreement, meaning that EWEC will pay solely for the net electrical energy supplied by the plant.

The Al Ajban solar project is aligned with EWEC's earlier call in March 2023 for the UAE to increase its solar PV capacity sixfold by 2030, aiming for a total capacity of 7.3 GW. This proposed expansion is seen as a response to the growing power demand, which is expected to rise by 30% by 2029, and as part of the UAE's broader sustainability goals.

Abu Dhabi's renewable energy landscape is further shaped by the strategic presence of IRENA, the international organization that supports countries in their transition to a sustainable energy future. The location of IRENA's headquarters in Abu Dhabi reinforces the Emirate's narrative that it is committed to global collaboration on renewable energy policy, technology and best practices.

The completion of key projects represents tangible progress towards these objectives. These initiatives contribute significantly to Abu Dhabi's targeted solar PV capacity of 5.6 GW, set to be achieved by the end of 2026. The combination of governmental support, international collaboration, strategic investment and a thriving ecosystem of renewable energy companies is propelling Abu Dhabi towards becoming a global leader in this sector.

Meanwhile in Dubai, DEWA launched the Mohammed bin Rashid Al Maktoum Solar Park development in October 2013. By 2030, when it is expected to be fully commissioned, it is planned that the plant will have a capacity of 5 GW, produce enough power for 270,000 single-family residential units, and displace more than 6.5m. metric tons of carbon emissions per year. By 2022 the plant was already meeting 15% of Dubai's power requirements. When completed, the project will supplant Al Dhafra as the largest single-site solar power plant in the world, created under the build-own-operate model. The project was registered under the Clean Development Mechanism of the UN Framework Convention on Climate Change in November 2016, with an initial crediting period of seven years. The Mohammed bin Rashid Al Maktoum Solar Park will be central in helping Dubai to achieve its goal of generating 25% of its power through renewable energy by 2030, and 75% by 2050.

The project was initially structured in three distinct phases, but was subsequently expanded to comprise five, each contributing to a landmark initiative in solar energy. The first phase, consisting of a 13-MW solar farm, was constructed by the US company First Solar and was inaugurated in October 2013. Phase two, which came online in March 2017, was a 200-MW PV plant built by a consortium led by ACWA Power International of Saudi Arabia and TSK Electrónica y Electricidad of Spain, at a cost of US $320m. DEWA awarded the contract for the 800-MW third phase to a consortium led by Masdar in June 2016; the third phase was implemented in three stages, in 2018, 2019 and 2020. The 950-MW fourth phase was a collaboration between China's Silk Road Fund, Shanghai Electric (also of China) and ACWA Power International, built with an investment of US $4,290m. It includes CSP thermal and PV technologies, generating 700 MW from CSP (600 MW from a parabolic basin complex and 100 MW from a solar tower) and 250 MW from PV, with a thermal system that can store energy for up to 15 hours. The 900-MW fifth phase was inaugurated in Dubai in June 2023. Developed with an investment of $544m., DEWA holds a 60% stake in this phase, with the remaining 40% held by a consortium of ACWA Power and the Gulf Investment Corporation. This sequential and collaborative development represents a significant step in large-scale renewable energy project development in the UAE.

The observed decline in solar generation costs in the UAE and surrounding Gulf region indicates a potential shift in the economic dynamics of renewable energy compared with fossil fuel-based generation. This trend, combined with significant investments in projects such as Al Dhafra and other renewable initiatives, aligns with the UAE's stated renewable energy targets and its goal of net-zero emissions. By pursuing these objectives, the UAE is positioning itself in a broader context of renewable energy development and sustainability goals, a process that continues to evolve in response to technological advancements, economic factors and policy decisions.

THE EMIRATI NUCLEAR SECTOR AND THE FUTURE OF COAL DEVELOPMENT

In contrast to the misgivings surrounding the Saudi nuclear programme, the Emirati nuclear sector has fully complied with the IAEA from its inception. The Emirati decision to engage in nuclear power development began in 2006 and followed an in-depth assessment of the UAE's predicted future energy requirements in 2007. The 2007 study projected that annual domestic peak power demand would likely increase to more than 40,000 MW by 2020, representing an average annual growth rate of approximately 9% from the initial assessment. The projected power demand alarmed Emirati officials as it was well beyond their capacity at that time.

Upon reviewing the projected power demand, the Emirati Government promulgated an additional study to determine the best available technologies for power generation to meet the increasing demand. The results indicated that readily available natural gas resources would be insufficient to meet future power demand; utilizing liquid fuels (crude petroleum and/or diesel) could be viable, but would be expensive and ecologically damaging; coal-fired power generation would likely be less expensive, but would be environmentally unviable and potentially vulnerable from a supply security vantage point; and, finally, while renewable energy would be desirable, it would probably only meet 6%–7% of projected energy demand by 2020.

Therefore, due to the above assessment, it was concluded that nuclear power 'emerged as a proven, environmentally promising and commercially competitive option which could make a significant base-load contribution to the UAE's economy and future energy security'.

In a region where the development of nuclear power by a Middle Eastern Arab nation could be met with scepticism and concern, often coloured by potential prejudice, the UAE has taken decisive and transparent steps to alleviate any apprehensions about its nuclear energy programme.

In April 2008 the Emirati Government explicitly outlined its peaceful objectives in a policy document entitled 'Policy of the United Arab Emirates on the Evaluation and Potential Development of Peaceful Nuclear Energy'. This document served as a clear and official statement of the UAE's commitment to harnessing nuclear energy solely for peaceful purposes. To reinforce this commitment, the UAE promulgated domestic legislation permanently to forego the ability to enrich uranium and reprocess plutonium. This move, uncommon among nations pursuing nuclear energy, further underscored the UAE's commitment to non-proliferation. In addition, the Emirati Government signed the 2009 nuclear co-operation and non-proliferation '123 Agreement' with the USA. This agreement established a legal framework for civil nuclear co-operation between the two countries and emphasized adherence to international non-proliferation norms.

The UAE's commitment to peaceful nuclear energy development extends to its engagement with international non-proliferation treaties, regimes and organizations. It joined the UN Treaty on the Non-Proliferation of Nuclear Weapons in 1995, signed a safeguards agreement with the IAEA in 2003 and acceded to the IAEA Additional Protocol in 2010.

These concerted efforts have led to the UAE being widely recognized as having set the 'gold standard' precedent for nuclear energy newcomers. The nation's comprehensive approach, characterized by transparency, international co-operation and strict adherence to global norms, serves as a model for other countries exploring nuclear energy. It also demonstrates how, even in a region where nuclear development might be viewed with suspicion, a country can successfully pursue nuclear energy while maintaining trust and co-operation with the international community.

However, despite its efforts in implementing non-proliferation confidence-building measures, the UAE faces challenges that may require time and significant foreign assistance to overcome. The emergence of a 'commitment-compliance gap', whereby the Emirati Government may find itself without the necessary institutional capacity fully to meet its pledges, is a concern.

Historical context adds complexity to this issue. For example, the UAE has been a central transit area for illicit transactions with Iran and other countries. Dubai, in particular, was a known trafficking hub for Pakistan's so-called A. Q. Khan network, which was involved in smuggling nuclear weapons technology to Libya, the Syrian Arab Republic, Iran and North Korea. These past associations raise questions about the UAE's ability to ensure the security and transparency needed to meet international expectations.

Given this backdrop, the UAE's ambitions to achieve its renewable energy targets and net-zero emissions goal could face scrutiny and reservations. Success in these areas will likely depend on the country's ability to build strong regulatory frameworks, foster international collaborations, invest in capacity-building, and demonstrate a clear and unwavering commitment to global non-proliferation standards and regional co-operation.

While international concerns regarding Saudi nuclear activities were primarily focused on non-proliferation, a separate issue emerged during the diplomatic rift between Qatar and other Middle Eastern states, which lasted from June 2017 to January 2021. At the height of this schism, in March 2019, the Qatari Ministry of Foreign Affairs expressed concerns to the IAEA about the Emirati nuclear plants. Specifically, Qatar claimed that these nuclear facilities could pose a threat to regional stability and the environment, and it requested that the IAEA establish a framework to ensure the safe operation of nuclear energy in the Gulf region. Central to Qatar's concerns was the fear that any accidental discharge from the Emirati nuclear plants might send radioactive material to Doha (the Qatari capital) within hours. The UAE firmly rejected these concerns, maintaining that its nuclear facilities were operated under strict safety protocols and in accordance with international standards.

Moreover, concerns have arisen regarding the vulnerability of Emirati nuclear facilities to potential threats. These concerns include the risk of attack from regional entities, such as Iran or its al-Houthi allies, or even from terrorist groups such as al-Qa'ida or Islamic State, both of which have previously targeted critical energy infrastructure in the region. For instance, in 2017 the al-Houthis in Yemen claimed to have fired a cruise missile towards the Barakah nuclear power plant, a report that the UAE officially denied. The al-Houthis have also issued repeated threats to target critical infrastructure in the UAE.

In response to these concerns, the Emirati Federal Authority for Nuclear Regulation (FANR) issued a statement to reassure the public and international community. The regulator affirmed that the UAE's nuclear power plant was well protected against both physical and cyber threats, emphasizing the comprehensive security measures in place to defend against any potential attacks. The announcement by FANR was seen as a critical step in alleviating fears and maintaining confidence in the UAE's commitment to the safe and secure operation of its nuclear energy programme.

In the face of reservations from certain international quarters, the UAE's progress in its nuclear energy programme has been marked by a steadfast commitment to adhere to international nuclear regulations and standards. In a significant move, the Emirates Nuclear Energy Corporation (ENEC) awarded a contract in December 2009 to a consortium led by the Korea Electric Power Corporation (KEPCO) for the construction of four APR-1400 reactors at the Barakah nuclear power plant. The construction process began in 2012 with an ambitious target completion date of 2022. However, the project faced delays, not due to mismanagement or lack of effort, but stemming from an intense focus on safety and quality assurance. Concerns over specific components and systems were addressed meticulously, reflecting the UAE's serious and responsible approach to nuclear energy development. These delays, rather than undermining confidence, served rather to emphasize the UAE's commitment to maintaining the highest standards in the pursuit of its nuclear energy goals, recognizing that the project was under the international spotlight.

The progress of the UAE's nuclear energy programme has been consistent and methodical. The first reactor at the Barakah plant began start-up operations and was connected to the grid in August 2020, before commencing commercial operations in April 2021. Reactor 2 followed a similar trajectory, becoming grid-connected in September 2021 and initiating commercial operations in March 2022. Reactor 3 added to this momentum, coming online in February 2023. Additionally, ENEC has announced the successful completion of hot functional testing for the fourth and final reactor at the Barakah plant, setting the stage for the reactor to start operating in 2024.

As of December 2022 the three reactors already operational provided over 80% of the Abu Dhabi's clean electricity consumption. Once all four reactors are online, the Barakah complex is expected to meet up to 25% of the UAE's electricity requirements and prevent 22.4m. metric tons of carbon emissions annually. In contrast to the perennial cost overruns and the (often multi-year) delays common in the global nuclear industry, the Barakah operations teams were able to leverage their experiences from constructing the first two reactors to reduce the time taken to reach commercial operations after fuel loading in the third reactor. According to ENEC, this process took four months less than it did for Reactor 2, and more than five months less than it did for Reactor 1. This efficiency demonstrates a learning curve within the UAE's nuclear programme and reflects a growing expertise in the nuclear energy sector. The total value of the contract for the construction, commissioning and fuel loads of the four reactors was US $20,400m., with most of the contract being offered under a fixed-price arrangement.

Despite some international criticism, Dubai commenced the construction of the 3.6-GW ultra-supercritical Hassyan clean coal power station in Saih Shuaib in November 2016. This US $3,400m. plant was initially set to become fully operational by 2023 and to increase Dubai's power generation capacity by 25%. The plant, designed with advanced carbon capture equipment to minimize emissions, would be the region's first coal-fired facility.

At the time of the Hassyan plant's commissioning, coal was perceived as a more cost-effective option than renewables. However, Dubai's regulatory authorities implemented stringent carbon emission standards, in line with the recommendations by the International Finance Corporation and exceeding EU standards for coal plants. The emissions factors from the Hassyan plant were expected to vary depending on the specific type and origin of the coal used, so the exact figures could not be determined until the coal was purchased.

The UAE's national energy strategy of 2017 included plans for about 11.5 GW of ultra-supercritical coal plants, compatible with carbon capture and storage technology, and employing highly efficient technologies to curb carbon emissions. This was in line with the UAE's broader power generation and emission reduction targets for 2050.

However, in a significant development, in February 2022 Dubai announced that the Hassyan plant would be converted to use natural gas. This shift aligned with the UAE's pledge to achieve net-zero carbon emissions by 2050, although details regarding the conversion's cost and its impact on the plant's timeline were not disclosed. The plant's design also includes a desalination facility to support the region's water needs.

China has been heavily involved in the construction of the Hassyan power plant, describing it as a 'major engineering project of the Belt and Road Initiative'. With the General Electric Co of the USA also participating in the construction, China anticipated that the plant would meet 20% of Dubai's electrical demand. The conversion of the plant from coal to natural gas reflects a strategic shift in Dubai's energy planning, responding to both economic and environmental considerations in line with regional and global sustainability goals.

For its part, Ras al-Khaimah announced in 2016 that it would construct its own 1,800-MW clean coal plant at a cost of nearly US $3,000m. However, while initially due to come online in 2021, the project was delayed and placed on hold as it required a construction transmission line. A bureaucratic reorganization contributed to the delay as the Federal Electricity and Water Authority was absorbed into the Abu Dhabi Water and Electricity successor agency, the Emirates Water and Electricity Company. In addition, the Emirati authorities were concerned about Asian coal export prices, which had increased significantly. It appeared that the Hassyan facility would likely be the first and last coal-fired plant constructed in the region, as when the agreement between the Ras al-Khaimah authorities and ACWA Power International was signed in 2016, the electricity prices agreed upon were less than $0.05 per kWh; however, by 2020 solar power costs had declined substantially, to less than $0.02 per kWh.

At mid-2023 the future of the Hassyan plant remained somewhat uncertain, and the information available was limited. However, the UAE's initial pursuit of coal-fired plants appears contradictory to its image as a leader in clean energy. This seeming contradiction can be understood in the context of the nation's desire for a form of energy independence akin to the US model. Specifically, the UAE aims to diversify its energy mix to reduce dependency on neighbouring countries such as Iran and Qatar for natural gas imports.

This goal aligns with the Government's 2011 Integrated Energy Strategy and 2015 Clean Energy Strategy, which set the path for Dubai to transition from almost complete reliance on gas to a more balanced mix of 61% gas, 7% clean coal, 7% nuclear and 25% solar by 2030. This energy diversification strategy is designed to enhance Dubai's resilience and ability to withstand 'black swan' events (i.e. unforeseen and unpredictable occurrences with potentially severe consequences, ranging from environmental to geopolitical challenges).

In the aggregate, the plan does raise concerns, especially considering the higher emissions typically associated with coal. Clean coal technology has often fallen short of delivering consistent emissions reductions, and there are widespread doubts regarding the long-term efficacy of carbon capture and storage technology in coal-fired plants. However, the UAE's broader energy strategy also incorporates nuclear power and renewables, coupled with efforts to improve energy efficiency. As such, despite the potential risks associated with coal, the overall approach is expected to lead to a structural decline in carbon emissions from the Emirati power sector throughout the 2020s. This illustrates the UAE's complex and nuanced approach to energy independence and sustainability, striving to balance economic, environmental and geopolitical considerations.

The UAE has already reduced its carbon dioxide emissions through an emphasis on renewable energy generation, greater power plant operational efficiency and more fuel switching to natural gas in its power plants. For example, in 1990 the UAE produced 32.6 metric tons of per capita carbon dioxide emissions per year, but this had declined to 21.9 tons by 2010. Moreover, in Dubai emissions declined by 33% in 2020, more than double the target set in the official *Dubai Carbon Abatement Strategy 2021*. As more renewable and nuclear energy comes online, carbon emissions are projected to decline even further.

Qatar's Renewable Energy Goals

Qatar's rapid economic transformation has been primarily driven by the North Field, home to extensive recoverable reserves of offshore gas. Revenues from gas exports reached US $132,000m. in 2022, making Qatar one of the world's wealthiest countries, with GDP per head in excess of $84,000. This wealth has fuelled the growth of the sovereign wealth fund (SWF), estimated at $450,000m., supported the expansion of the private sector and enhanced Qatar's foreign policy reach.

The construction boom ahead of Qatar's hosting of the Fédération Internationale de Football Association (FIFA) 2022 World Cup powered the Qatari economy in recent years. Additionally, the expansion of the country's LNG production and export capacity is likely to drive the economy for many years to come. This is true despite, and partly because of, the market turmoil caused by Russia's invasion of Ukraine in February 2022.

Unlike some of its GCC peers, Qatar has not faced challenges with natural gas production shortfalls. As a result, it has not shown the same level of interest in developing renewable energy as some of its neighbours. However, several enabling factors could support a shift toward renewable energy in Qatar. With an average of 9.5 hours of sunshine per day, low cloud cover and expansive land areas, the nation has significant potential for solar energy development.

Qatar has positioned itself as a leader in global climate change discussions, aiming to decrease its reliance on hydrocarbons for domestic energy needs. Since 2005, the country has been exploring the potential role of renewables in its national energy mix. While Qatar has shown a *stated* interest in renewable energy and certainly possesses the natural resources to harness it, the nation's approach to this sector has been more cautious and ambiguous. Although the country has established a few solar projects and is working towards some measure of decarbonization of its LNG sector, a lack of definitive goals and specific action plans has created a degree of uncertainty. Qatar's abundant natural gas reserves may have lessened the urgency to diversify into renewable energy. However, the global push towards sustainability and the potential economic and environmental benefits of renewables might prompt more decisive action in the future.

The country's acknowledgment of the significance of renewable energy has been articulated in a number of ways. Initially, in 2008 Qatar's National Vision 2030 identified environmental protection and sustainable consumption of hydrocarbons as guiding principles for future development. Within this framework, the Qatari Government crafted an environmentally conscious strategy, emphasizing ecological protection. However, this strategy was somewhat ambiguous and lacked clear, defined targets for renewable energy adoption. The absence of concrete goals led to questions about the Government's seriousness with regard to the development of renewable energy sources.

In 2010 the Ministry of Development, Planning and Statistics further clarified Qatar's stance by announcing its first National Development Strategy, covering the period 2011–16. This strategy expanded upon the role of renewable energy in fostering economic development in the country. However, an underlying assumption of the document was that it would be necessary for renewable energy technology to become more cost efficient. Consequently, the Qatari Government created a National Renewable Energy Committee to forge a renewable energy policy as part of this strategy. In March 2018 the Ministry of Development, Planning and Statistics launched a second National Development Strategy, for the period 2018–22, in which it directly addressed the importance of renewable energy. The document recognized that Qatar had made relatively limited gains in renewable energy production despite possessing significant renewable energy potential.

As a result, in 2017 the Ministry of Energy and Industry, the state-owned Qatar General Electricity and Water Corporation (Kahramaa), and various other stakeholders began to develop the country's first large-scale renewable energy project, the Al Kharsaah Solar PV Independent Power Producer Project, also known as Siraj 1. Siraj 1 is being constructed in the village of Al Kharsaah, located 80 km west of Doha. Once fully operational, the facility will have a capacity of 800 MWp (mega watt peak, a unit of measurement representing the maximum potential output of power from a renewable energy source, such as solar or wind, which may vary due to weather conditions).

In October 2018 Kahramaa announced the prequalification of 16 international power firms for the construction of Siraj 1, and by 2019 it had received five bids from international developers for the project's first phase. Utilizing a public-private partnership framework, Siraj 1 was to be operated by Siraj SPV, a consortium composed of TotalEnergies of France and Marubeni (together holding 40% of the shares) and Siraj Energy (60%), the latter being a joint venture between state-owned QatarEnergy (formerly Qatar Petroleum) and the Qatar Electricity and Water Company (QEWC).

Although the start-up of the first 400-MW phase was delayed from its initial 2021 schedule, TotalEnergies confirmed in late July 2022 that the phase had been completed and the Siraj 1 plant had come online. The plant was inaugurated in October, in time to supply power for the FIFA World Cup tournament held in November and December.

In a significant move, QatarEnergy agreed in October 2022 to acquire QEWC's remaining 49% stake in Siraj Energy. Details of the sums involved in the deal remain confidential, but it marked an essential step in QatarEnergy's sustainability strategy, which aimed to generate 5 GW of solar power by 2035. According to Saad bin Sherida al-Kaabi, Qatar's Minister of State for Energy Affairs and CEO of QatarEnergy, the acquisition was pivotal for QatarEnergy's efforts in the renewables sector. Upon the deal's closure, Siraj Energy was expected to be integrated within QatarEnergy Renewable Solutions, the company's investment arm specializing in renewable and sustainable energy projects. Al-Kaabi further emphasized that the acquisition signified Siraj Energy's transition to becoming a wholly-owned affiliate of QatarEnergy, consolidating QatarEnergy's position in the renewable energy business. The move increased the total solar power capacity under QatarEnergy's direct control to 1,675 MW and unified all utility-scale solar power generation projects in Qatar under its supervision.

Siraj 1 represents a significant milestone for Qatar as it embarks on its journey towards promoting renewable energy and mitigating carbon emissions. This pioneering project holds great importance for Qatar's commitments under the Paris Agreement, as it aims to reduce its greenhouse gas emissions by 25%, relative to its BAU baseline, by 2030. However, it is essential to note that in the short term the Siraj 1 plant will not immediately contribute additional LNG volumes for export. This limitation arises from Qatar's current production capacity, as of the third quarter of 2023, which stands at the maximum amount (77m. metric tons per year) at its LNG export facilities.

Looking ahead, the North Field expansion project is set to unfold in two phases. During phase one (North Field East), annual production capacity is forecast to increase by an impressive 43%, from 77m. metric tons of LNG to 110m. tons by 2025. Building on this progress, phase two (North Field South) is predicted further to increase production capacity to 126m. tons per year, achieving a total overall increase of 64% by 2027.

Qatar has also been making progress with other solar energy projects. In August 2022 QatarEnergy awarded a contract to South Korean firm Samsung C&T for the construction of the country's second utility-scale solar project, the Industrial Cities Solar Power Project (IC Solar), costing approximately US $630m. The project involves the construction of two solar PV plants with a combined clean power generation capacity of 875 MW. Samsung C&T will be responsible for the engineering, procurement and construction (EPC) of the plants, which are expected to be commissioned by the end of 2024. The two plants to be constructed are a 417-MW solar PV plant in Mesaieed Industrial City and a 458-MW solar PV facility in Ras Laffan Industrial City. Through the construction of the IC Solar project and the Siraj 1 plant, Qatar's renewable energy generation capacity is projected to reach 1.68 GW by 2024. This aligns with Qatar's goal to enhance its green energy capacity and supports QatarEnergy's aim of achieving 5 GW of solar-generated power by 2035.

Qatar, a nation that has long been dependent on LNG and natural gas as a transitional 'green' fuel, has worked to position itself as a premier supplier of this in-demand commodity and a supporter of global decarbonization efforts. However, it is worth noting that its proactive stances have often been accompanied by clear economic benefits, as evidenced by its actions since 2012. Through initiatives such as reducing routine gas flaring, QatarEnergy has shown an early interest in environmental stewardship, but economic considerations have also constituted an integral part of this process.

In 2021 the announcement of the Qatar National Environment and Climate Change Strategy marked a significant step in the country's environmental policy. The strategy's goal of reducing carbon intensity in LNG plants and upstream operations by 25% by 2030 is commendable, although some might argue it remains to be seen how these targets will be met in practice.

The scaling-up of Qatar's energy transition investments seems to demonstrate a willingness to engage with the commercial risks associated with meeting demand in a world focused on net-zero emissions. Yet, it is worth recognizing that these moves align with Qatar's broader economic and sustainability goals. The North Field expansion projects, including the planned largest carbon capture and storage (CCS) facility in the LNG industry in Ras Laffan, are designed to showcase Qatar's leadership in environmental innovation.

A substantial aspect of Qatar's strategic planning involves integrating renewable energy development with its prominent LNG sector. The CCS facility at Ras Laffan aims to capture up to 11m. metric tons per year of carbon dioxide through sequestration. This is not a new area for Qatar, however, with existing capture/sequestration efforts averaging 2.5m. tons annually since 2015/16. Through these concerted efforts, Qatar is attempting to position itself as a leader in environmental responsibility within the LNG industry, although the full impact of these initiatives will only be revealed with time and implementation.

Qatar's renewable energy ambitions reflect a measured and strategic approach to balancing economic interests with environmental responsibility. While the country has made significant strides in aligning with worldwide sustainability trends, the implementation of these plans will ultimately determine the success of Qatar's transition to a more environmentally responsible energy sector. Its efforts in renewable energy and carbon reduction offer promise, but the tangible impacts of these initiatives are yet to be fully realized. The global push towards sustainability, coupled with the potential economic and environmental benefits of renewables, may prompt further action in the future, but Qatar's path toward these goals remains an unfolding story.

CONCLUSION

The Gulf countries, historically known for their resistance to climate change initiatives, made a significant shift in 2012 with their support for the promulgation of the UN's Durban Platform and subsequent acceptance of the Paris Agreement in 2015. This transformation marked a new era of embracing decarbonization through the reform of energy pricing and the deployment of alternative energy sources.

However, progress across the region has been uneven. While some countries, such as Bahrain and Kuwait, have made little headway in alternative energy, others such as Saudi Arabia and the UAE have taken more substantial strides. The levelized cost of solar power generation has notably declined in these latter two countries, reaching rates as low as US $0.11 per kWh and $0.02 per kWh, respectively. This has enabled solar power to compete with conventional natural gas-powered generation across the Gulf.

In contrast, natural gas pricing reform has been more of a challenge to implement. Although countries such as Saudi Arabia, the UAE and Qatar made some initial progress in this area during the mid-2010s, efforts have since stalled. Directly reforming energy pricing, such as by eliminating energy subsidies and implementing market pricing for natural gas inputs, has been hindered by complex social, political and economic factors.

One significant obstacle to reform is the so-called Arab social contract, an implicit agreement between rulers and citizens that has endured since independence. According to this understanding, governments provide low-priced energy and generous subsidies under a comprehensive welfare system, and, in return, citizens grant the government unquestioned loyalty. The lingering effects of the Arab Spring and the deeply entrenched beliefs associated with this social contract continue to influence the region's approach to energy reform.

None the less, some countries have made greater progress in power price liberalization, which could be seen as an indirect form of natural gas pricing reform. This, coupled with the falling cost of solar power, indicates a positive trend towards more sustainable energy practices.

The energy landscape in the Gulf region is marked by a dynamic and sometimes paradoxical set of strategies. The situation is not merely an economic or environmental challenge; it carries significant national security implications as well. Failure to achieve sustainable economic growth and intergenerational equity through well-designed energy policy reform could lead to severe economic and sociopolitical repercussions, threatening the stability, security and prosperity of future generations in the region.

The energy strategies of Saudi Arabia, the UAE and Qatar can be understood through the lens of the Green Paradox, a concept that highlights the potential for counterproductive outcomes in response to environmental policies. Facing the prospect of tightening regulations and the impending transition to a 'post-oil world', the three countries have aggressively expanded their investment in hydrocarbon production and export capacity. This strategy is driven by a desire to capitalize on fossil fuel assets that might depreciate rapidly or become stranded assets in the near future.

By focusing on domestic decarbonization and energy efficiency policies, Saudi Arabia, the UAE and Qatar are positioning themselves to increase hydrocarbon exports, thus leveraging higher global prices compared to the still-regulated and typically lower domestic prices. Despite ongoing reforms to align with the global norm, the domestic prices remain substantially lower.

However, this approach has not been without criticism. The simultaneous expansion in hydrocarbon production alongside commitments to climate change mitigation has led to scepticism regarding the countries' true intentions. Doubts have emerged, overshadowing the significant investments that the three countries have made in alternative energy and casting a complex light on their roles in the global effort to combat climate change. The situation underscores the multifaceted and often conflicting demands faced by nations rich in fossil fuel resources as they navigate the transition to a more sustainable energy future.

Saudi Arabia has witnessed decades of surging demand for natural gas, driven by rapid industrialization and urban/demographic growth. As a result, in recent year Saudi leadership has recognized the need for a more sustainable and forward-thinking approach to energy management. This awareness has culminated in efforts to implement demand-side reduction policies, specifically targeting sectors such as transportation and housing. These policies aim to make energy consumption more efficient and environmentally responsible, aligning with global initiatives to combat climate change. Additionally, the country has initiated reforms in power and natural gas pricing, potentially leading to more market-driven energy dynamics and diversification away from heavy reliance on hydrocarbons.

This strategic shift is projected to lower overall domestic energy demand, marking a notable departure from previous growth trends. However, it is essential to understand this transformation in its broader context. One of the key drivers behind Saudi Arabia's motivation is not merely sustainability but, as discussed previously, also a practical economic strategy to reduce domestic hydrocarbon consumption. By doing so, the country aims to increase oil exports and downstream expansion, thereby maintaining its budgetary inflows for as long as possible.

Capitalizing on the global decline in renewable energy costs, the Saudi leadership has embarked on an ambitious journey to transform its energy landscape. It has set targets and secured investments to foster the growth of renewable energy sources such as wind and solar power. Although the early stages of this transformation were met with scepticism, as some of the goals seemed unlikely to be achieved within the original timelines, there has been a concerted effort to turn vision into reality. The efforts have begun to bear fruit, with renewable energy capacity expected to reduce the share of natural gas and oil in the Saudi power sector by the mid-to-late 2020s.

The UAE, recognized for its investment in renewable energy and domestic decarbonization policies, has recently come under scrutiny for a different aspect of its energy strategy. In November 2022 the UAE revealed ambitious plans for oil and gas expansion, positioning itself as the third largest player in the world in terms of such expansion, surpassed only by Saudi Arabia and Qatar.

The Abu Dhabi National Oil Company (ADNOC, the world's 11th largest oil and gas producer), is playing a significant role in these plans. Delivering more than 1,000m. barrels of oil equivalent (BOE) in 2021, ADNOC announced a massive US $150,000m. investment over five years to enable an accelerated growth strategy for oil and gas production. The strategy included significant short-term expansion, with plans to add 7,600m. BOE to the company's production portfolio in the coming years. These ambitious expansion plans have led to sharp criticism from various quarters. The contrast between the UAE's promotion of renewable energy on the one hand, and its plans for significant fossil fuel expansion on the other has drawn attention and concern, particularly as the country is hosting the UN climate summit (COP 28) in November 2023.

Critics include environmental campaigners who have targeted the CEO of ADNOC, Sultan al-Jaber, calling for his resignation as President of COP 28, a tenure that some have likened to 'putting the head of a tobacco company in charge of negotiating an anti-smoking treaty'. This pointed comparison underscores the perceived conflict of interest between the UAE's stated commitment to renewable energy and its simultaneous expansion in oil and gas production. Others involved in UN climate talks have been more circumspect in their criticisms, likely recognizing the need to work with ADNOC and other UAE officials in the future. However, the tension between the country's public commitment to renewable energy and its private investment in fossil fuels is clear.

Building on the multifaceted energy strategy outlined earlier, ADNOC's gas policy is noteworthy, encompassing a series of strategic goals such as achieving self-sufficiency in gas production, significantly expanding its LNG exports and exploring gas-to-chemicals opportunities, all while maintaining its current LNG output levels. These goals are indicative of a broader commitment to diversify and expand the UAE's energy profile.

In tandem with these policies, solar power has emerged as a key element of the UAE's energy landscape, particularly in Dubai and Abu Dhabi, where record low prices have been achieved. This represents not only a financial advantage but also aligns with the country's efforts to incorporate renewable energy into its portfolio.

Beyond solar power, the discovery of promising gas and condensate reservoirs in Sharjah in 2020 adds another layer to the UAE's energy picture. Interestingly, Emirati gas demand appears to have peaked during 2020–21, and there are indications that it may have begun to plateau. This trend is likely influenced by the country's nuclear power coming online and the introduction of new solar projects, which have undoubtedly reduced the reliance on traditional gas sources.

While projections indicate that LNG imports to the UAE will persist until at least 2025, there is an evolving understanding of the nation's future relationship with gas imports, particularly those from Qatar. Abu Dhabi, specifically, appears to be progressing toward independence from Qatari gas by 2025–26. Despite moving towards self-sufficiency in energy, Abu Dhabi is anticipated to continue pipeline gas imports from Qatar until 2032. This protracted timeline might represent a measured strategy, acknowledging the benefits of sustaining diversified energy sources and capitalizing on existing agreements and infrastructure. Furthermore, it may illustrate a strategic synchronization with long-term energy requirements and geopolitical factors. The broader region's political and economic conditions have significantly shaped Emirati energy policy. Notably, plans to develop a potential pipeline from Iran have met with various obstacles, while the 2017–21 blockade against Qatar did not, unexpectedly, impact imports from the Dolphin Gas Project.

In summary, the UAE's energy landscape is characterized by complexity and ambition. Building on the country's considerable investments in both fossil fuels and renewable energy, the policies, discoveries and market trends of the 2020s are shaping a future in which the UAE may moderate and even reduce its domestic gas demand, while becoming a leader in renewable energy production and also significantly expanding its hydrocarbon exports to the global market. These developments reflect a concerted effort to balance energy security, economic growth and environmental sustainability, while navigating the political and economic challenges unique to the region.

Qatar's situation differs from that of Saudi Arabia and the UAE as it is the world's largest LNG producer. Although much of Qatar's initial LNG strategy in the 2000s was predicated on expected exports to the USA, it successfully transitioned its exports to the lucrative Asia-Pacific market. Even though competition in the international LNG market has increased, Qatar still has several core advantages, such as its physical location and the high yield of liquids produced alongside its gas, which indicates that it will still have the world's lowest cost base, and the most competitive break-even price for gas in most markets. In spite of the increased competition in the LNG market and co-ordination between Asian buyers, which places sustained downward pressure on prices, Qatar will still benefit from Asia's long-term demand growth potential. Additionally, due to the ongoing conflict in Ukraine, Qatar is benefiting from Europe's transition from Russian energy exports and has adeptly positioned itself as a stable business partner not influenced by geopolitical shifts. This stance, differing markedly from Russia's approach, was highlighted when Qatar chose not to let the fluctuations of the 2017–21 blockade affect its natural gas exports to the countries imposing the blockade, including the UAE. Furthermore, the blockade did not hinder Qatar's participation in the GCC Interconnection Project (a regional power grid) or the management of the Al-Bunduq joint oilfield shared with Abu Dhabi. Although Qatar's withdrawal from OPEC in 2019 was influenced by geopolitical factors, there were also strong economic reasons that supported the country's decision to leave the organization.

Qatar has also embarked on efforts to reform energy and power pricing and is beginning to invest in renewable energy, as seen with the Siraj 1 solar project. Unlike its neighbours, Qatar's small geographical and demographic size, as well as its substantial natural gas reserves, mean that it does not face the same balance of demand and production pressures commonly found in the region. None the less, Qatar continues to signal its desire to be at the forefront of global climate discussions, an aspiration that is primarily motivating its gradual reformation of the domestic energy sector.

In conclusion, the three selected countries—Saudi Arabia, the UAE and Qatar—face a complex interplay of ambition and scepticism in their pursuit of climate change mitigation. On the one hand, they have made significant strides in the development of alternative energy, investing vast sums in decarbonization projects and expressing strong intentions to shift away from traditional hydrocarbon reliance. On the other hand, their concurrent expansion in and advocacy of oil and gas production have given rise to doubts about their true commitment to environmental stewardship.

Institutional challenges further complicate the landscape, as the lack of indigenous technical expertise represents a major obstacle to the successful implementation of alternative energy projects. This gap in know-how not only slows down the pace of progress but also raises questions about the long-term viability and impact of the countries' renewable energy endeavours.

Despite these concerns, the transformative investments in alternative energy and the reforms in domestic energy pricing cannot be ignored. They mark a substantial change in the approach of these nations, reflecting not merely a policy shift but a potential psychological transformation. This altered mindset, aligning with global trends and emphasizing a future beyond fossil fuels, is a signal of a new direction in both regional and global economic development.

This highlights the complexity and nuance of the energy transition in these countries, acknowledging both their concrete achievements and the substantial challenges that remain. It recognizes that their energy strategies are intertwined with broader economic and geopolitical considerations and underscores the importance of ongoing vigilance, collaboration and innovation to ensure that their investments in renewable energy translate into meaningful and sustainable change.

SELECT BIBLIOGRAPHY

Aboueldahab, Noha. *Social Protection, Not Just Legal Protection: Migrant Workers in the Gulf,* Brookings Institution. 23 August 2021.

Alnaser, W. E., and Alnaser, N. W. 'The Impact of the Rise of Using Solar Power in GCC Countries'. *Renewable Energy and Environmental Sustainability,* Vol. 4, 31 August 2019.

Altomonte, Carlo, and Ferrara, Massimiliano (Eds). *The Economic and Political Aftermath of the Arab Spring: Perspectives from Middle East and North African Countries.* Edward Elgar Publishing, 2014.

Anchondo, Carlos. 'CCS 'Red Flag?' World's Sole Coal Project Hits Snag'. *Energy Wire,* 10 January 2022.

Anwer, Murad, and Matar, Walid. *Reforming Industrial Fuel and Residential Electricity Prices in Saudi Arabia.* KAPSARC, July 2017, p. 9.

APICORP Energy Research. 'Energy Price Reform in the GCC: Long Road Ahead'. Vol. 1, No. 4, January 2016, p. 2.

APICORP Energy Research. 'Renewables in the Arab World: Maintaining Momentum'. Vol. 3, No. 8, May 2018.

Al-Badi, Abdullah, and Al-Mubarak, Imtenan. 'Growing Energy Demand in the GCC Countries'. *Arab Journal of Basic and Applied Sciences*, Vol. 26, Issue 1, 2019.

Baffes, John, et al. 'Understanding the Plunge in Oil Prices: Sources and Implications', in *Global Economic Prospects*. World Bank Group, 5 October 2013.

Belbagi, Zaid. *Renegotiating the Social Contract in the GCC: Lessons from the Rousseau Playbook*. The Oxford Gulf and Arabian Studies Forum.

Bellini, Emiliano. 'Dubai: Tariff for Large-Scale PV Hits New Low at $0.024/kWh'. *PV Magazine*, 5 November 2018.

Boersma, Tim, and Griffiths, Steve. 'Reforming Electricity, Water and Fuel Subsidies in the United Arab Emirates'. *The Oxford Energy Forum*, No. 108, March 2017.

> *Reforming Energy Subsidies: Initial Lessons from the United Arab Emirates*. The Brookings Institution, January 2016, p. 11.

Bohra, Moiz, and Shah, Nilay. 'Optimizing Qatar's Energy System for a Post-Carbon Future'. *Energy Transition*, Vol. 4, 2019, p. 7.

Bolinger, M., et al. *Utility-Scale Solar: Empirical Trends in Project Technology, Cost, Performance, and PPA Pricing in the United States–2019 Edition*. Electricity Markets & Policy, Berkeley Lab, 2019.

Brockway, P. E., et al. 'Estimation of global final-stage energy-return-on-investment for fossil fuels with comparison to renewable energy sources'. *Nature Energy*, Vol. 4, No. 7, 2019, pp. 612–621.

Byrne, Megan. 'Qatar Joins Solar Revolution with Al Kharsaah Start Up'. *MEES*, Issue 65/30, 29 July 2022.

Cafiero, Giorgio. *Qatar Cuts Spending to Cope with Low Oil Prices*. Middle East Institute, 1 March, 2016.

Chevron. *Chevron to Establish Sustainable Energy Efficiency Center in Qatar*.

Chiesa, Matteo, et al. 'What is Going On with Middle Eastern Solar Prices, and What Does it Mean for the Rest of Us?'. *Progress in Photovoltaics*, Vol. 29, No. 6, June 2021, pp. 638–639.

Collins, Catherine, and Frantz, Douglas. 'The Long Shadow of A.Q. Khan'. *Foreign Affairs*, 31 January 2018.

Crystal, Jill. *Oil and Politics in the Gulf: Rulers and Merchants in Kuwait and Qatar*. Cambridge, Cambridge University Press, 1990.

Dargin, Justin. *'The Dolphin Natural Gas Project', The Development of a Gulf Gas Initiative*. The Oxford Institute of Energy Studies, 2008.

> *Desert Dreams: The Quest for Arab Integration from the Arab Revolt to the Gulf Cooperation Council*. Republic of Letters, 2012.

Darwish, Mohamed, and Mohtar, Rabi. 'Prime Energy Challenges for Operating Power Plants in the GCC'. *Energy and Power Engineering*, Vol. 5, 2013, pp. 109–128.

Davidson, Christopher. *After the Sheikhs: The Coming Collapse of the Gulf Monarchies*. London, Hurst, 2012.

> *The United Arab Emirates: A Study in Survival*. Boulder, Lynne Rienner, 2005.

Devlin, Julia. *Challenges of Economic Development in the Middle East and North Africa Region*. World Scientific, 2010, pp. 3–10.

De Clercq, Geert. 'Qatar Asks IAEA to Intervene Over "Threat" Posed by UAE Nuclear Plant'. *Reuters*, 20 March 2019.

DiPaola, Anthony. 'Saudi Arabia Delays $109 Billion Solar Program Eight Years'. *Bloomberg*, 21 January 2015.

Early, Bryan. *Export Control Development in the United Arab Emirates: From Commitments to Compliance*. Belfer Center for Science and International Affairs at the Harvard Kennedy School, 6 July 2009.

Al-Garni, Hassan Z., et al. 'Design and economic assessment of alternative renewable energy systems using capital cost projections: A case study for Saudi Arabia'. *Sustainable Energy Technologies and Assessments*, Vol. 48, 2021.

Al-Ghanim, Kaltham, 'Contradictory Forces in the Gulf Environment: Old and New Cultural Values and Knowledge'. in Sillitoe, Paul (Ed.). *Sustainable Development: An Appraisal from the Gulf Region*. Berghahn, 2014.

Growth Through Diversification and Energy Efficiency: Energy Productivity in Saudi Arabia. KAPSARC, November 2017.

International Gas Union. *Wholesale Gas Price Survey 2016 Edition*. 2016.

> *Wholesale Gas Price Survey 2018 Edition*. 2018.
> *Wholesale Gas Price Survey 2022 Edition*. 2022.

International Monetary Fund. *Regional Economic Outlook Middle East and Central Asia*. May 2018.

Kamel, Deena. 'Sharjah Reveals First New Onshore Natural Gas Discovery in Three Decades'. *The National*, 28 January 2020.

Kamrava, Mehran. *Beyond the Arab Spring: The Evolving Ruling Bargain in the Middle East*. Oxford University Press, 2014.

El-Katiri, Laura. 'The GCC and the Nuclear Question'. *Oxford Energy Comment*, December 2012.

Koplow, Doug. *Measuring Energy Subsidies Using the Price Gap Approach: What Does it Leave Out?*. International Institute of Sustainable Development, August 2009.

Krane, Jim, and Hung, Shih Yu. 'Energy Subsidy Reform in the Persian Gulf: The End of the Big Oil Giveaway'. *Issue Brief*, Baker Institute for Public Policy, 28 April 2016, p. 4.

Krane, Jim and Monaldi, Francisco. *Oil Prices, Political Instability, and Energy Subsidy Reform in MENA Oil Exporters*. Baker Institute for Public Policy, June 2017.

Krane, Jim. 'Dubai's Coal Push Upends Abu Dhabi's Clean Energy Strategy'. *MEES*, Issue 63/35, 28 August 2020.

> *Energy Governance in Saudi Arabia: An Assessment of the Kingdom's Resources, Policy and Climate Approach*. Baker Institute for Public Policy, January 2019.

> *The Political Economy of Subsidy Reform in the Persian Gulf Monarchies*. Baker Institute for Public Policy, 8 August 2016, p. 5.

Larbi, Hedi. *Rewriting the Arab Social Contract*. Belfer Center, 16 May 2016.

Mahdi, Wael, and Nereim, Vivian. 'Saudi Arabia Scales Back Renewable Energy Goal to Favor Gas'. *Bloomberg*, 7 June 2016.

Mahmood, Haider, et al. 'Industrialization, Urbanization and CO2 Emissions in Saudi Arabia: Asymmetry Analysis', *Energy Reports*, Vol. 6, 2020, pp. 1553–1560.

Mills, Robin. *Under a Cloud: The Future of Middle East Gas Demand*. Center on Global Energy Policy, April 2020, p. 36.

Moerenhout, Tom. *Energy Pricing Reforms in the Gulf: A Trend, Not (Yet) a Norm*. International Institute for Sustainable Development, January 2018, p. 2.

Moerenhout, Tom, and Hamaizia, Adel. *Five Takeaways from a Decade of Energy Subsidy Reform in MENA*. Chatham House, 16 February 2022.

Myers Jaffe, Amy. et al. *The Geopolitics of Natural Gas: The Gulf Cooperation Council Natural Gas Conundrum: Geopolitics Drive Shortages Amid Plenty*. Harvard Belfer Center, October 2013.

National Renewable Energy Program. KSA Climate website. www.ksa-climate.com/making-a-difference/nrep/.

O'Keefe, Phillip, et al. *The Future of Energy Use*. Earthscan, 2010.

Pal, Jeremy, et al. 'Future Temperature in Southwest Asia Projected to Exceed a Threshold for Human Adaptability'. *Nature Climate Change*, Vol. 6, February 2016.

Qatar National Vision 2030. www.gco.gov.qa/en/about-qatar/national-vision2030.

Raffoul, Alexandre and Al-Zahra Hewaidi, Fatima. *How Industrialization Could Future-Proof MENA's Gulf Economies*. World Economic Forum, 28 June 2021.

S&P Global Platts. *Dubai's Energy Demand Climbs 9.8% as Renewables Gain Bigger Share*. 24 January 2022.

Al-Saleh, Yasser M. 'An Empirical Insight into the Functionality of Emerging Sustainable Innovation Systems: The Case of Renewable Energy in Oil-Rich Saudi Arabia'. *International Journal of Transitions and Innovation Systems*, Vol. 1, No. 3, 2011.

Sarrakh, Redouane, et al. 'Impact of Subsidy Reform on the Kingdom of Saudi Arabia's Economy and Carbon Emissions'. *Energy Strategy Reviews*, Vol. 28, March 2020.

Scott, Mike. 'Saudi Arabia Plans to Source 10% of its Power from Renewable Energy Within Five Years'. *Forbes*, 18 January 2018.

Scully, Jules. 'UAE Solar Capacity to Increase Fourfold by End of 2025 Thanks to 'Robust' Development Pipeline'. *PV-Tech*, 10 Febraury 2022.

Seznec, Jean-François, and Kirk, Mimi. *Industrialization in the Gulf: A Socioeconomic Revolution*. Routledge, 2010.

Al-Soliman, Tarik M. 'Environmental Impacts and the Need for a National Environmental Policy in Saudi Arabia'. *Journal of Architectural and Planning Research*, Vol. 10, No. 3, 1993, p. 221.

Stern, Jonathan (Ed.). *The Future of Gas in the Gulf: Continuity and Change*. OIES Press, 2019.

Sweidan, Osama. 'The Environmental and Energy Policies to Enable Sustainable Consumption and Production in the Gulf Cooperation Council Countries'. *Clean Technologies and Environmental Policy Journal*, Vol. 23, 2021, pp. 2639–2654.

The UAE's Response to Climate Change. The United Arab Emirates Government Portal. u.ae/en/information-and-services/environment-and-energy/climate-change/theuaesresponsetoclimatechange

Williamson, Nick, and Garcia, Mhari Main. 'Gas Shortages in the Middle East: An Unlikely Paradox'. in *The International Comparative Legal Guide to Gas Regulation*. Global Legal Group, 2011.

World Bank. *Solar Photovoltaic Power Potential by Country*. July 2020.

World Nuclear Association. *Nuclear Power in Saudi Arabia*. April 2019.

World Trade Organization. *Agreement on Subsidies and Countervailing Measures*. www.wto.org/english/docs_e/legal_e/24-scm.pdf.

THE RELIGIONS OF THE MIDDLE EAST AND NORTH AFRICA

R. B. SERJEANT

Revised by the editorial staff

ISLAM

Islam is a major world religion and the faith predominating throughout the Middle East (with the exception of Israel) and North Africa. There are substantial Christian minorities in some countries (e.g. Lebanon and Egypt) and communities of oriental Jews and other faiths, for centuries integrated with the Muslim majority. Islam is not only a highly developed religious system, but also an established and distinctive culture embracing every aspect of human activity from theology, philosophy and literature to the visual arts and even the individual's routine daily conduct. Its characteristic intellectual manifestation, therefore, is in the field of Islamic law, the *Shari'a*. Though in origin a Semitic Arabian faith, Islam was also the inheritor of the legacy of classical Greek and Roman civilization and, in its major phase of intellectual, social and cultural development after its emergence from Arabia, it was affected by Christian, Jewish and Persian civilization. In turn, Greek scientific and philosophical writings—in the form of direct translations into Arabic or as a principal element in the books of Arab scholars—began to enter medieval Europe in Latin renderings about the early 12th century CE from the brilliant intellectual circles of Islamic Spain, and formed a potent factor in the little Renaissance of Western Europe.

Islamic civilization had, by about the 18th century, clearly lost its initiative to the ascendant West and has not since regained it. Today, however, certain oil-rich Arab states of the Persian (Arabian) Gulf, notably Saudi Arabia and Kuwait, have made significant progress in the world of international finance and mercantilism, engaging in activities such as the provision of Islamic banking services—for which there has been a significant increase in demand since the latter part of the 20th century. The tiny kingdom of Bahrain has also become a leading centre of Islamic banking and finance in recent years, while other countries in the region are promoting considerable growth in this area.

History

The founder of the religion of Islam was the Prophet Muhammad b. 'Abdullah, born about 570 CE, a member of the noble house of Hashim, belonging to the 'Abd Manaf clan, itself a part of the Quraish tribal confederation of Mecca. 'Abd Manaf may be described as semi-priestly, since they had the privilege of certain functions during the annual pilgrimage to the Meccan Ka'ba—a cube-shaped temple set in the sacred enclave (*haram*). Quraish controlled this enclave, which was maintained inviolate from war or killing, and they had established a pre-eminence and even loose hegemony over many Arabian tribes which they had induced to enter a trading alliance extending over the main Arabian land routes, north and south, east and west. Muhammad clashed with the powerful Quraish leaders in Mecca (temple guardians, chiefs and merchant adventurers), when, aged about 40, he began to proclaim the worship of one God, Allah, as against their multiplicity of gods. The Quraish leaders were contemptuous of his mission.

While his uncle Abu Talib, head of the house of Hashim, lived, he protected Muhammad from physical harm, but after Abu Talib's death Muhammad sought protection from tribes outside Mecca. However, even after he had asked to remain quietly without preaching, they would not accept him and Thaqif of Taif (al-Ta'if, south of Mecca) drove him away. Ultimately, pilgrims of the Aws and Khazraj tribes of Yathrib (Medina), some 200 miles north of Mecca, agreed to protect him there, undertaking to associate no other god with Allah and accepting certain moral stipulations. Muhammad left Mecca with his Companion, Abu Bakr, in 622 CE—this is the year of the *Hijra* or Hegira ('flight' or migration).

Arriving in Yathrib, Muhammad formed a federation or community (*umma*) of Aws and Khazraj known as the 'Supporters' (*Ansar*), followed by their Jewish client tribes, and the 'Emigrants' (*Muhajirun*—his refugee Quraish adherents), with himself as the ultimate arbiter of the *umma* as a whole. However, there remained a local opposition covertly antagonistic to him, the *Munafiqun*, rendered as 'Hypocrites'. Two internal issues had now to be fought by Muhammad—the enforcement of his position as theocratic head of the federation, and the acquisition of revenue to maintain his position; externally, he adopted an aggressive attitude towards the Meccan Quraish.

In Yathrib Muhammad's disposal of the Jewish tribes who made common cause with the 'Hypocrites' improved his financial position. Muhammad overcame the Meccan Quraish more as a result of skilful political manoeuvring than of occasional armed clashes, and in year 8 he entered Mecca peacefully. He had previously declared Yathrib a *haram*, renaming it *Madinat al-Nabi* (Medina, the City of the Prophet)—the two cities, known as al-Haraman, have become the holy land of Islam. Muhammad was conciliatory towards his defeated Quraish kinsmen, and, after his success in al-Ta'if, deputations came from the Arabian tribes to make terms with the Prophet—the heritor of the influence of the Meccan Quraish.

Early Islam

The two main tenets of Islam are embodied in the formula of the creed, 'There is no god but Allah and Muhammad is the Apostle of God'. Unitarianism (*tawhid*), as opposed to polytheism (*shirk*) or making partners with God, is Islam's basic principle, coupled with the authority conferred on Muhammad by God. Muhammad made little change to the ancient Arabian religion—he abolished idolatry but confirmed the pilgrimage to the Ka'ba; the Koran, the sacred Book in Arabic revealed to Muhammad for his people, lays down certain social and moral rules. Among these are the condemnation of usury or interest (*riba*) on loans and the prohibition of wine (*khamr*)—both ordinances have always been difficult to enforce. In many respects, the similarities between the old and new faiths enabled Arabia to embrace Islam with relative ease. While there is incontrovertible evidence of Muhammad's contact with Judaism, and even with Christianity, and the Koran contains versions of narrative known to the sacred books of these faiths, these are used to point to purely Arabian morals. The limited social law laid down by the Koran is supplemented by a body of law and precept derived from the *Hadith* or Tradition of Muhammad's practice (*Sunna*) at Medina, and welded into the Islamic system, mainly in its second and third centuries.

Subsequent History

Immediately after Muhammad's death in 632 CE, Abu Bakr, delegated by the Prophet to lead the prayer during his last indisposition, became his successor or Caliph. Some Medinan 'Supporters' had attempted a breakaway from Quraish overlordship, but Abu Bakr adroitly persuaded them to accept his succession. Office in Arabia, generally speaking, is hereditary within a family group, though elective within that group, and Abu Bakr's action had taken no account of the claims of 'Ali, the Prophet's cousin and son-in-law. The house of Hashim, to which Muhammad and 'Ali belonged, was plainly aggrieved that a member of a minor Quraish clan, not of the 'house' (*bayt*) of their ancestor, Qusaiy, the holder of religious offices in Mecca which he bequeathed to his descendants, should have snatched supreme power. Muhammad's Arabian coalition also weakened, the tribes particularly objecting to paying taxes to Medina, but Abu Bakr's uncompromising leadership reasserted cohesion. Expansionist campaigns beyond Arabia undertaken during his Caliphate were continued under his successors 'Umar and 'Uthman, diverting tribal energies to profitable warfare in Mesopotamia, Palestine-Syria, Egypt and Persia. Muslim armies were eventually to conquer North Africa, much of Spain, parts of France, and even to besiege Rome, while in the east they later penetrated as far as Central Asia and India.

During 'Uthman's tenure the pace of conquest temporarily slackened and the turbulent tribes, now settled in southern Iraq and Egypt, began to dispute the Caliph's disposal of plunder and revenue, maintaining that he favoured members of his own house unduly. A delegation of tribal malcontents from Egypt murdered 'Uthman in the holy city of Medina, and in the resultant confusion 'Ali, Muhammad's cousin, was elected Caliph with the support of the tribesmen responsible for the murder. This raised grave constitutional problems for the young Muslim state, and is regarded as the origin of the first and greatest schism in Islam.

If legitimist arguments were the sole consideration, 'Ali's claims to succession would appear to be superior, but his claim had already been superseded by 'Uthman—whose father belonged to the Umaiya clan which had opposed Muhammad, but whose mother was of Hashim ancestry. 'Uthman naturally appointed Umaiya men loyal to him to commands in the Empire, notably Mu'awiya—the son of Abu Sufyan who had led Quraish opposition to Muhammad at Mecca, but was later reconciled with him—as governor of Syria. Mu'awiya demanded that 'Uthman's murderers be brought to justice in accordance with the law, but 'Ali, unable to deliver the murderers from among his supporters, was driven by events to take up arms against Mu'awiya. When they clashed at Siffin, Syria, 'Ali was forced, against his better judgement, to submit to the arbitration of the Koran and *Sunna*, thus automatically losing the position of supreme arbiter, inherited by the Caliphs from Muhammad. Although history is silent as to what the arbiters actually judged upon, it was most likely as to whether 'Ali had broken the law established by Muhammad, and that he was held to have sheltered unprovoked murderers. The arbiters deposed him from the Caliphial office, though historians allege that trickery entered into their action.

'Ali was murdered shortly afterwards by one of a group of his former supporters which had come out against the arbitration it had first urged upon him. This group, the Khawarij, is commonly held to be the forerunner of the Ibadis of Oman and elsewhere. Mu'awiya became Caliph and founder of the Umaiyad dynasty, with its capital in Damascus. The ambitions of the Hashim house were not allayed, however, and when Umaiyad troops slew 'Ali's son, Husain, at Karbala in southern Iraq, they created the greatest Shi'a martyr (see *Religious Groupings*).

The house of Hashim also included the descendants of 'Abbas, the Prophet's uncle, but 'Abbas had opposed Muhammad until late in his life. The 'Abbasids made common cause with the 'Ali-id Shi'a against the Umaiyads, but were evidently more able in the political field. In the Umaiyad empire the Arabian tribes formed a kind of military elite, but were constantly at factious war with one another. The Hashemites rode to power on the back of a rebellion against the Umaiyads which broke out in Khorasan in eastern Persia; however, it was the 'Abbasid branch of Hashim which assumed the Caliphate and ruled from the capital they founded at Baghdad.

The 'Abbasid Caliphate endured up to the destruction of Baghdad in 1258 by the devastating Mongol invaders of the eastern empire, but the Caliphs had long been mere instruments in the hands of Turkish and other mercenaries, and the unwieldy empire had fragmented into independent states which rose and fell, though they mostly conceded nominal allegiance to the 'Abbasid Caliphs.

The Mongol Ilkhanid sovereigns, now converted to Islam, were in turn displaced by the conquests of Tamerlane at the end of the 14th century. In fact the Islamic empire had largely been taken over by Turkic soldiery. The Mameluke or Slave rulers of medieval Egypt, who followed the Aiyubid (Kurdish) dynasty of Salah ul-Din (Saladin), were mainly Turks or Circassians. It was they who checked the Mongol advance at 'Ain Jalut in Palestine (1260). The Ottoman Turks captured Constantinople in 1453, and seized Egypt from the Mamelukes in 1516, subsequently occupying the Hedjaz where the Ashraf, descendants of the Prophet, ruled in Mecca and Medina, under first Mameluke then Turkish suzerainty. In 1533 the Turks took Baghdad, and Iraq became part of the Ottoman Empire. The Ottoman Sultans assumed the title of Caliph—though in Islamic constitutional theory it is not easy to justify this. The Ottoman Caliphs endured until the Caliphate was abolished by Mustafa Kemal (later called Atatürk, or 'Father of the Turks') in 1924. The Turks have always been characterized by their adherence to Sunni orthodoxy.

Throughout history the 'Ali-ids have constantly asserted their right to be the Imams or leaders of the Muslim community—this in the religious and political senses, since Islam is fundamentally theocratic. The Shi'a, or followers of 'Ali and his descendants, were in constant rebellion against the 'Abbasids and came to form a distinct schismatic group of legitimist sects—at one time the Fatimid Shi'a rulers of Egypt were close to conquering the main part of the Islamic world. The principal Shi'a sects today are the Ithna'asharis, the Isma'ilis and the near-orthodox Zaidis of Yemen. The Safavids who conquered Persia at the beginning of the 16th century brought it finally into the Shi'a fold. Sunni Hashemite dynasties flourish today in Jordan and Morocco, as they did until fairly recently in Iraq and Libya, and the Shi'a Zaidi ruler of Yemen was only displaced in 1962. The main difference between Sunnis and Shi'a concerns the Imamate, i.e. the temporal and spiritual leadership of Islam: for Sunnis, while they respect the Prophet's house, do not consider that the Imam must be a member of it; the Shi'a, on the other hand, insist on an Imam of the descendants of 'Ali and his wife Fatima, daughter of the Prophet.

It has been too readily assumed that, during the later Middle Ages and long Turkish domination, the Islamic Middle East was completely stagnant. The shift in economic patterns after the discovery of the New World and the Cape route to India, coupled with widening Western intellectual horizons and the development of science and technology, did push European culture far ahead of the Muslim Middle East. It was confronted by a vigorous and hostile Christianity intent on proselytizing in its very homelands. Muslim thinkers like Muhammad Abduh (1849–1905) of Egypt and his school asserted that Islam had become heavily overlaid with false notions—hence its decline; like earlier reformers, they were convinced that the present difficulties could be resolved by reversion to an (idealized) pure, primitive Islam. Sometimes, in effect, this meant reinterpreting religious literature to suit attitudes and ideas of modern times—as for instance when the virtual prohibition of polygamy was identified in the restrictions which define the practice. Since the earlier modern days political leaders such as Atatürk have often taken drastic measures, secularizing the state itself even in the sensitive field of education, and accusing the more conservative forms of Islam of blocking progress. In recent years the Islamic Middle East has witnessed regimes ranging from the firm supporters of traditional Islam—for example Saudi Arabia and Libya—to the anti-religious Marxist group which controlled Aden (the People's Democratic Republic of Yemen) until 1990. In Libya, nevertheless, Muammar al-Qaddafi in the 1970s published *The Green Book*, embodying his personal, socialist solution of problems of democracy and economics. Theocratic Shi'a Iran has a distinctive character of its own.

Islamic Law

Orthodox Sunni Islam finds its main expression in *Shari'a* law, which it regards with great veneration. The Sunnis have crystallized into four schools or rites (*madhhab*), all of which are recognized as valid. Although in practice the adherents of one school can sometimes have profound disagreement with another, in modern times it is claimed that the law of any one of these rites can be applied to a case. The schools, named after their founders, are the Hanbali, regarded as the strictest, with adherents mainly in Saudi Arabia; the Shafi'is, the widest in extent, with adherents in Egypt, Palestine-Syria, South Arabia and the Far East; the moderate Hanafi school, which was the official rite of the Ottoman Turkish empire and to which most Muslims in the Indian sub-continent belong; and the Malikis of the North African states, as well as Nigeria and Sudan. The Shi'a sects have developed their own law and give prominence to *ijtihad*, the forming of independent judgement, whereas the Sunnis are more bound by *taqlid* or following ancient models. However, since the law of Sunnis, the moderate Shi'a and the Ibadis is basically derived from the same sources, the differences are generally more of emphasis than of principle.

The completely Islamic state as the theorists envisage it, organized in total conformity with the rules of the *Shari'a*, has probably never been achieved, and people's practice is often at variance with some or other requirements of *Shari'a*. Nevertheless, the imprint of Islam is unmistakably evident, in one way or another, on virtually every country in the region.

Civil Courts

In modern states of the Islamic world there exists, side by side with the *Shari'a* court (judging cases on personal status, marriage, divorce, etc.), the secular court which has a wide jurisdiction (based on Western codes of law) in civil and criminal matters. This court is competent to give judgment irrespective of the creed or race of the defendant.

Islamic Law as Applying to Minorities

In cases of minorities (Christian or Jewish) residing as a community in Muslim countries, spiritual councils are established where judgment is passed according to the law of the community, in matters concerning personal status, under the jurisdiction of the recognized head of that community.

Tribal Courts

In steppe and mountain areas of some countries a proportion of the population maintain tribal courts which administer law and justice in accordance with ancient custom and tribal procedure. Among tribes these courts are often more popular than *Shari'a* courts, because justice is swifter. Conciliation (*sulh*) is generally their objective. There is, none the less, constant pressure to eliminate customary practices where these are unequivocally seen to be contrary to Islamic principles.

Awqaf

In Muslim countries the law governing *awqaf* (singular, *waqf*), called in North Africa *habous* (*hubus*), is the law applied to religious and charitable endowments, trust and settlements. This important Islamic institution is administered in most Muslim countries by a special ministry of *awqaf*. *Awqaf*, or endowments, are pious bequests made by Muslims for the upkeep of religious institutions, public benefits, etc. Family *awqaf* provide an income partly for religious purposes and partly for the original donor's family.

Belief and Practice

'Islam' means the act of submitting or resigning oneself to God, and a Muslim is one who resigns or submits himself to God. Muslims disapprove of the term 'Muhammadan' for the faith of Islam, since they worship Allah, and Muhammad is only the Apostle of Allah whose duty it was to convey revelation, though he is regarded as the 'Best of Mankind'. He is the Seal (*Khatam*) of the prophets, i.e. the ultimate Prophet in a long series in which both Moses and Jesus figure. They are revered, but, like Muhammad the Prophet, they are not worshipped.

Nearly all Muslims agree on acceptance of six articles of the faith of Islam: Belief (i) in God; (ii) in His angels; (iii) in His revealed books; (iv) in His Apostles; (v) in the Resurrection and Day of Judgement; and (vi) in His predestination of good and evil.

Faith includes works, and certain practices are obligatory for the Muslim believer. These are five in number.

1. The recital of the creed (*Shahada*)—'There is no god but God (Allah) and Muhammad is the Apostle of God.' This formula is embodied in the call to prayer made by the *muezzin* (announcer) from the minaret of the mosque before each of the five daily prayers.
2. The performance of the Prayer (*Salat*) at the five appointed canonical times—in the early dawn before the sun has risen above the horizon, in the early afternoon when the sun has begun to decline, later when the sun is about midway in its course towards setting, immediately after sunset, and in the evening between the disappearance of the red glow in the west and bedtime. In prayer Muslims face towards the Ka'ba in Mecca. They unroll prayer mats and pray in a mosque (place of prostration), at home or wherever they may be, bowing and prostrating themselves before God and reciting set verses in Arabic from the Koran. On Fridays it is obligatory for men to attend congregational Prayer in the central mosque of the quarter in which they live; women do not normally attend. On this occasion formal prayers are preceded by a sermon.
3. The payment of the legal alms (*Zakat*). In early times this contribution was collected by officials of the Islamic state, and devoted to the relief of the poor, debtors, travellers and to other charitable and state purposes, and it often became, in effect, a purely secular tax on crops. Nowadays the fulfilment of this religious obligation is left to the conscience of the individual believer. The *zakat* given at the breaking of the fast at the end of Ramadan, for example, is a voluntary gift of provisions.
4. The 30 days of the fast in the month of Ramadan, the ninth month in the lunar year. As the lunar calendar is shorter by 11 days than the solar calendar, Ramadan moves from the hottest to the coldest seasons of the solar year. It is observed as a fast from dawn to sunset each day by all adults in normal health, during which time no food or drink may be taken. The sick, pregnant women, travellers and children are exempt; some states exempt students, soldiers and factory workers. The fast ends with one of the two major Muslim festivals, 'Id al-Fitr.
5. The pilgrimage (*Hajj*) to Mecca. Every Muslim is obliged, circumstances permitting, to perform this at least once in his lifetime, and when accomplished he may assume the title, *Hajji*. More than 2m. pilgrims go each year to Mecca (including some 1.5m. non-Saudi Muslims), but the holy cities of Mecca and Medina are prohibited to non-Muslims.

Before entering the sacred area around Mecca by the seventh day of Dhu'l-Hijja, the 12th month of the Muslim year, pilgrims must don the *ihram*, consisting of two unseamed lengths of white cloth, indicating that they are entering a state of consecration and casting off what is ritually impure. The pilgrims circumambulate the Ka'ba seven times, endeavouring to kiss the sacred Black Stone. Later they run seven times between the nearby twin hills of Safa and Marwah (now covered in by an immense hall), thus recalling Hagar's desperate search for water for her child Ishmael (from whom the Arabs claim descent). On the eighth day of the month the pilgrims leave the city for Mina, a small town six miles to the east. Then, before sunrise of the next day, all make for the plain below Mount 'Arafat, some 12 miles east of Mecca, where they pass the day in prayers and recitation until sunset. This point is the climax of the pilgrimage when the whole gathering returns, first to Muzdalifah where it spends the night, then to Mina where pilgrims stone the devil represented by three heaps of stones (*jamra*). The devil is said to have appeared to Abraham here and to have been driven away by Abraham throwing stones at him. This day, the 10th of Dhu'l-Hijja, is 'Id al-Adha, the Feast of the Sacrifice, and the pilgrims sacrifice an animal, usually a sheep, and have their heads shaved by one of the barbers at Mina. They return to Mecca that evening. In recent years the increasing number of pilgrims arriving (especially by air) has presented the Saudi authorities, guardians of the Holy Places, with major problems of organization, supply, health and public order. In 1988, following the tragic events of July 1987, when 402 people (including 275 Iranian pilgrims) lost their lives in clashes between the Iranians and Saudi security forces, and in order to reduce overcrowding, the Saudi Government imposed national quotas for the numbers of pilgrims performing the *Hajj*. However, overcrowding has continued to present serious problems, and tragic incidents similar to that of 1987 have not been infrequent in recent years. In January 2006 at least 345 pilgrims died in a stampede near the Jamarat Bridge in Mina. As a result of such accidents, restructuring of the bridge area and procession routes was undertaken; the final stage of this work was completed in November 2009. Despite the structural improvements, in September 2015 more than 2,000 pilgrims were reportedly killed in a stampede in the streets leading up to the bridge; the Saudi Government put the death toll at 769.

The Holy War (*Jihad*) against the infidel was the means whereby Arab Muslim rule made its immense expansion in the first centuries of Islam, but despite pressures to do so, it has never been elevated to form a sixth Pillar of Islam. Today some

GENERAL SURVEY

theologians interpret *jihad* in a less literal sense as the combating of evil, but it is significant that the Afghan guerrillas who resisted the Soviet presence in their country called themselves *mujahidin*, i.e. those who wage the *jihad* against the enemies of Islam.

The Koran (*Quran*—'recital' or 'reading') is for Muslims the very Word of God. The Koran consists of 114 chapters (*surah*) of uneven length, the longest coming first after the brief opening chapter called *al-Fatiha*. (The Koran is about as long as the Christian New Testament.) *Al-Fatiha* (The Opener) commences (as does every chapter) with the words, '*Bismillahi 'l-Rahmani 'l-Rahim*', 'In the name of God, the Compassionate, the Merciful', and forms part of the ritual five prayers (*Salat*). Other special verses and chapters are also used on a variety of occasions, and Muslim children are taught to recite by heart a portion of the Koran or, preferably, the whole of it. The Koran has been the subject of vast written commentaries, but translation into other languages is not much approved by Muslims, although interlinear translations (a line of Koran underneath which is a line of translation) are used, and a number of modern translations into English and most other languages exist. The earlier (Meccan) chapters of the Koran speak of the unity of God and his wonders, of the Day of Judgement and Paradise, while the Medinan chapters tend to be occupied more with social legislation for marriage, divorce, personal and communal behaviour. The definitive redaction of the Koran was ordered by the Caliph 'Uthman (644–56).

Sufis

In common with other religions where simple observance of a code of law and morals proves spiritually unsatisfying, some Muslims have turned to mysticism. From early times Islamic mystics existed, known as Sufis, allegedly owing to their wearing a woollen garment. They seek complete identification with the Supreme Being, and annihilation of the self—the existence of which they term polytheism (*shirk*). The learned doctors of Islam often think ill of the Sufis, and indeed rogues and wandering mendicants found Sufism a convenient means of livelihood. Certain Sufi groups allowed themselves dispensations and, as stimulants, even used hashish and opium, which are not sanctioned by the Islamic moral code. The Sufis became organized in what are loosely called brotherhoods (*turuq*; singular, *tariqa*), and have to a large extent been incorporated into the structure of orthodox Islamic society. Some *turuq* induce ecstatic states by their performance of the *dhikr*, meaning, literally, the mentioning (of Allah). Today there is much disapproval of the more extravagant manifestations of the Sufis, and in some places these have been banned entirely.

Holy Places

Mecca (Makkah): Hedjaz province of Saudi Arabia. Mecca is centred around the Ka'ba, the most venerated building in Islam, traditionally held to have been founded by Abraham, recognized by Islam also as a prophet. It stands in the centre of the vast courtyard of the Great Mosque and has the form of a cube; its construction is of local grey stone and its walls are draped with a black curtain embroidered with a strip of writing containing verses from the Koran. In the eastern corner is set the famous Black Stone. The enlarging of the Great Mosque commenced under the second Caliph 'Umar. Both the Ka'ba and Great Mosque have undergone many renovations, notably since 1952. Mecca is the centre of the annual pilgrimage (*Hajj*) from all Muslim countries.

Medina (Al-Madinah—The City, i.e. of the Prophet): Hedjaz province of Saudi Arabia. Medina, formerly called Yathrib, was created as a sacred enclave (*haram*) by Muhammad, who died there in the year 11 of the *Hijra* ('flight' or migration) and was buried in the Mosque of the Prophet. Close to his tomb are those of his companions and successors, Abu Bakr and 'Umar, and a little further away, that of his daughter Fatima. Frequently damaged, restored and enlarged, the mosque building was extensively renovated by the Saudi Government in 1955.

Jerusalem (Arabic *al-Quds* or *Beit al-Maqdis*, The Hallowed/Consecrated): West Bank (annexed by Israel). Jerusalem is Islam's next most holy city after al-Haraman (Mecca and Medina), not only because it is associated with so many pre-Islamic prophets, but because Muhammad himself is popularly held to have made the 'Night Journey' there. Jerusalem contains the magnificent Islamic shrine, the Dome of the Rock (688–91), built by the Caliph 'Abd al-Malik, and the famous al-Masjid al-Aqsa (al-Aqsa Mosque).

Hebron (Al-Khalil): West Bank. The Mosque of Abraham, called al-Khalil, the 'Friend of God', is built over the tomb of Abraham, the Cave of Machpelah; it also contains the tombs of Sarah, Isaac, Rebecca, Jacob and Leah. The shrine is revered by Muslims and Jews, and is also important to Christians.

Qairawan (Kairouan): Tunisia. The city is regarded as a holy place for Muslims, seven pilgrimages to the Great Mosque of Sidi 'Uqbah b. Nafi' (an early Muslim general who founded Qairawan as a base for the Muslim invaders of North Africa) being considered the equivalent of one pilgrimage to Mecca.

Muley Idris: Morocco. The shrine at the burial place of the founder of the Idrisid dynasty in the year 687, at Walili, near Fez.

Every Middle Eastern country has a multitude of shrines and saints' tombs held in veneration, except Wahhabi states which consider saint cults to be polytheism (*shirk*). In Turkey (officially known as Türkiye from June 2022), however, the policy of secularization led to Aya Sofya Mosque (St Sophia) being turned into a museum.

The following shrines are associated with the Shi'a or Legitimist sects of Islam.

Meshed (Mashad): Iran. The city is famous for the shrine of Imam 'Ali al-Rida/Riza, the eighth Imam of the Ithna'ashari group, which attracts many thousands of pilgrims each year. The shrine is surrounded by buildings with religious or historical associations.

Qom: Iran. A Shi'a centre, it is venerated as having the tomb of Fatima, the sister of Imam al-Rida/Riza, and those of hundreds of saints and kings including Imams 'Ali b. Ja'far and Ibrahim, Shah Safi and Shah 'Abbas II. Following the Iranian Revolution of 1979 it became the centre favoured by Ayatollah Khomeini.

Najaf (Al-Najaf): Iraq. Mashhad 'Ali, reputed to be constructed over the place where 'Ali b. Abi Talib, fourth Caliph, the cousin and son-in-law of Muhammad, is buried, is a most venerated Shi'a shrine, drawing many pilgrims.

Kerbala (Karbala): Iraq. The shrine of Husain b. 'Ali where, at Mashhad Husain, he was slain with most of his family, is today more venerated by the Shi'a than the Mashhad 'Ali. 'Ashoura Day (10th Muharram), when Husain was killed, is commemorated by passion plays (*ta'ziya*) and religious processions during which the drama of his death is re-enacted with extravagant expressions of emotion.

Baghdad: Iraq. The Kazimain/Kadhimain Mosque is a celebrated Shi'a shrine containing the tomb of Musa al-Kazim/Kadhim, the seventh Imam of the Ithna'asharis.

RELIGIOUS GROUPINGS

Sunnis

The great majority, probably over 80% of Muslims, are Sunni, followers of the *Sunna*, i.e. the way, course, rule or manner of conduct of the Prophet Muhammad; they are generally called 'orthodox'. The Sunnis recognize the first four Caliphs (Abu Bakr, 'Umar, 'Uthman and 'Ali) as Rashidun, i.e. following the right course. They base their *Sunna* upon the Koran and 'Six Books' of Traditions, and are organized in four orthodox schools or rites (*madhhab*), all of equal standing within the orthodox fold. Many Muslims today prefer to avoid identification with any single school and simply call themselves Muslim or Sunni.

Wahhabis

The adherents of 'Wahhabism' strongly disapprove of this title by which they are known outside their own group, for they call themselves Muwahhidun or Unitarians. In fact they belong to the strict Hanbali school, following its noted exponent, the 13th/14th century Syrian reformer Ibn Taimiyah. The founder of 'Wahhabism', Muhammad bin Abdulwahhab of Arabian Najd (1703–87), sought to return to the pristine purity of early Islam, freed from all accretions and from what he regarded as innovations contrary to its true spirit, such as saint worship, lax sexual practices and superstition. His doctrine was accepted by the chief Muhammad bin Sa'ud of Dar'iya (near Riyadh). Ibn Sa'ud and his son Abdulaziz—who proved a capable general—conquered much of Arabia. Medina fell in 1804 and Mecca in 1806 to Sa'ud, son of Abdulaziz, but after his death in 1814 the Wahhabis were gradually broken by the armies of the Pasha of Egypt, Muhammad 'Ali, acting nominally on behalf of the Ottoman Sultan of Turkey. After varying fortunes in the 19th century, the Wahhabis emerged as an Arabian power in the opening years of the 20th century. By the close of 1925 they held the Holy Cities and Jeddah, and are today the strongest power in the Arabian Peninsula. Although Wahhabism remains the strictest of the orthodox groups, Saudi Arabia has made some accommodation to modern times.

The Turuq or Religious Orders

In many Middle Eastern countries the religious orders (*turuq*) have important political-cum-religious roles in society. There are the widely spread Qadiriya who, with Tijaniya, are found in North Africa, the Khatmiya in Sudan, and the Rifa'iya in Egypt and the Syrian Arab Republic, to name a few. The West has no organizations exactly equivalent to these Sufi orders into which an individual has to be initiated, and in which, by dint of ascetic exercises and study, he may attain degrees of mystical enlightenment—this can also bring moral influence over his fellow men. The Orders may be Sunni or Shi'a; some few Orders are even so unconventional as to be hardly Islamic at all. Although Sufism is essentially uninterested in worldly politics, the *turuq* have, at times, been drawn into the political arena. It was the orthodox reformist Sanusi Order that played the most significant role in our time. The Grand Sanusi, Muhammad ibn Ali, born at Mustaghanem in Algeria of a Sharif family, founded the first *zawiya* or lodge of the Sanusis in 1837. The Sanusi *tariqa* is distinguished for its exacting standards of personal morality. The Sanusis established a network of lodges in Cyrenaica (Libya) and put up strong resistance to Italian colonization. The Grand Sanusi was recognized as King Idris of Libya in 1951, but lost his throne in the military revolt led by Qaddafi in 1969.

Shi'a

The Legitimist Shi'a pay allegiance to 'Ali, as mentioned above. 'Ali's posterity, which must number at least hundreds of thousands scattered all over the Muslim world, are customarily called Sharifs if they trace descent to his son al-Hasan, and Sayyids if descended from his second son al-Husain, but while the Sharifs and Sayyids, the religious aristocracy of Islam, are traditionally accorded certain privileges in Islamic society, not all are Shi'a, many being Sunnis. By the ninth century many strange sects, and even pagan beliefs, had become associated with the original Shi'a or Party of 'Ali; however, these extremist sects, called *ghulat*, have vanished except for a few, often practising a sort of quietism or dissimulation (*taqiyya*) for fear of persecution. All Shi'a accord 'Ali an exalted position, the extreme (and heretical) Shi'a at one time even according him a sort of divinity. Shi'a Islam does not in the main differ on fundamental issues from the Sunni orthodox since they draw from the same ultimate sources, but Shi'a *mujtahids* have, certainly in theory, greater freedom to alter the application of law since they are regarded as spokesmen of the Hidden Imam.

The Ithna'asharis (Twelvers)

The largest Shi'a school or rite is the Ithna'ashariya or Twelvers, acknowledging a succession of 12 Imams. From 1502 Shi'ism became the established school in Iran under the Safavid ruler Sultan Shah Isma'il, who claimed descent from Musa al-Kazim. There are also Ithna'ashariya in southern Iraq, al-Hasa (Saudi Arabia), Bahrain and the Indian subcontinent.

The last Shi'a Imam, Muhammad al-Mahdi, disappeared in 878, but the Ithna'asharis believe that he is still alive and will reappear in the last days before the Day of Judgement as the Mahdi (Guided One)—a sort of Messiah—who will rule personally by divine right.

The 12 Imams recognized by the Twelver, Ithna'ashari Shi'a are:

(1) 'Ali b. Abi Talib, cousin and son-in-law of the Prophet Muhammad.
(2) Al-Hasan, son of 'Ali.
(3) Al-Husain, second son of 'Ali.
(4) 'Ali Zain al-'Abidin, son of Husain.
(5) Muhammad al-Baqir, son of 'Ali Zain al-'Abidin.
(6) Ja'far al-Sadiq, son of Muhammad al-Baqir.
(7) Musa al-Kazim, son of Ja'far al-Sadiq.
(8) 'Ali al-Rida, son of Musa al-Kazim.
(9) Muhammad al-Taqi, son of 'Ali al-Rida.
(10) 'Ali al-Naqi, son of Muhammad al-Taqi.
(11) Al-Hasan al-Zaki, son of 'Ali al-Naqi, al-'Askari.
(12) Muhammad al-Mahdi, son of al-Hasan b. 'Ali, al-'Askari, known as al-Hujja, the Proof.

Isma'ilis

This group of Shi'a does not recognize Musa al-Kazim as the seventh Imam, but holds that the last Imam visible on earth was Isma'il, the other son of Ja'far al-Sadiq. For this reason they are also called the Sab'iya or Seveners. There is, however, much disagreement among the Seveners as to whether they recognized Isma'il himself as the seventh Imam, or one of his several sons, and the Fatimids of Egypt (10th–12th centuries) in fact recognized a son of Isma'il's son Muhammad. Schismatic offshoots from the Fatimid-Isma'ili group are the Druzes, the Musta'lians, first settled in Yemen but now with their main centre in Mumbai, India—where the Daudi section, under the chief 'missionary' (Da'i al-Du'a), is known as Bohoras, but who are properly called the Fatimi Taiyibi Da'wa—and the Nizari Isma'ilis, of whom the Agha Khan is the spiritual head. These sects have a secret literature embodying their esoteric philosophies. Both groups are very active and a large Isma'ili Institute, sponsored by the Agha Khan, was opened in London, United Kingdom, in 1985. Small groups of Isma'ilis are to be found in north-west Syria, Iran, Afghanistan, East Africa and Zanzibar, and larger numbers in India and Pakistan.

'Alawis (Nusairis)

The 'Alawis (or Alawites) believe that Muhammad was a mere forerunner of 'Ali and that the latter was an incarnation of Allah. This extremist Shi'a sect, established in the ninth century, has also adopted practices of both Christian and pagan origin. Most of its members today live in north-west Syria; the President of that country, Bashar al-Assad, is Alawi.

Druze

The Druze are heretics, an offshoot of the Fatimid-Isma'ilis, established in Lebanon and Syria. Their name (Duruz) derives from al-Darazi, a missionary of Persian origin who brought about the conversion of these Syrian mountaineers to the belief of the divine origin of the Fatimid Caliph al-Hakim. The origins of this sect and its subsequent expansion are still obscure. Hamza b. 'Ali, a Persian contemporary of al-Darazi, is the author of several of the religious treatises of the Druze. This community acknowledges one God and believes that he has on many occasions become incarnate in man. His last appearance was in the person of the Fatimid Caliph al-Hakim (disappeared 1020). The Druze have played a distinctive role in the political and social life of their country and are renowned for their independence of character. They engaged ardently in *jihad* against the Israeli invaders of Lebanon and their Christian allies. Druze morale is reinforced by the inspiration of the Islamic Revolution in Shi'a Iran.

Zaidis

The Zaidis are a liberal and moderate sect of the Shi'a, close enough to the Sunnis to call themselves the 'Fifth School' (*al-madhhab al-khamis*). Their name is derived from a grandson of al-Husain b. 'Ali called Zaid b. 'Ali, whom they recognize as the fifth Imam. They reject religious dissimulation (*taqiyya*) and are extremely warlike. Zaidism is the dominant school of Islam in Yemen, its main centres being San'a and Dhamar, but Shafi'is form roughly one-half of the population.

Ibadis

The Ibadis are commonly held to have their origins in the Khawarij, who disassociated themselves from 'Ali b. Abi Talib when he accepted arbitration in his quarrel with Mu'awiya; however, this is open to question. They broke off early from the mainstream of Islam and are usually regarded as heretics, though with little justification. Groups of the sect, which has often suffered persecution, are found in Oman (where Ibadism is the majority religion), Zanzibar, Libya and Algeria, mainly in the Mzab.

CHRISTIANITY

Development in the Middle East

Christianity was adopted as the official religion of the Roman empire in 313 CE, and the Christian Church came to be based on the four leading cities, Rome, Constantinople (capital from 330 CE), Alexandria and Antioch. From the divergent development of the four ecclesiastical provinces there soon emerged four separate churches: the Roman Catholic or Latin Church (from Rome), the Greek Orthodox Church (from Constantinople), the Syrian or Jacobite Church (from Antioch) and the Coptic Church (from Alexandria).

Later divisions resulted in the emergence of the Armenian (Gregorian) Church, which was founded in the fourth century, and the Nestorian Church, which grew up in the fifth century in Syria, Mesopotamia and Iran, following the teaching of Nestorius of Cilicia (d. 431). From the seventh century onwards followers of St Maron began to establish themselves in northern Lebanon, laying the foundations of the Maronite Church.

Subsequently, the Uniate Churches were brought into existence by the renunciation by formerly independent churches of doctrines regarded as heretical by the Roman Church and by the acknowledgement of Papal supremacy. These churches—the Armenian Catholic, Chaldean (Nestorian) Catholic, Greek Catholic, Coptic Catholic, Syrian Catholic and Maronite Church—did, however, retain their Oriental customs and rites. The independent churches continued to exist alongside the Uniate Churches, with the exception of the Maronites who reverted to Rome.

Holy Places

Bethlehem (Beit Lahm): West Bank. The traditional birthplace of Jesus is enclosed in the Basilica of the Nativity, revered also by Muslims. Christmas is celebrated here by the Roman and Eastern Rite Churches on 25 December, by the Greek Orthodox, Coptic and Syrian Orthodox Churches on 6 and 7 January, by the Ethiopian Church on 8 January, and by the Armenian Church on 19 January. The tomb of Rachel, important to the three faiths, is just outside the town.

Jerusalem: West Bank (annexed by Israel). The most holy city of Christianity has been a centre for pilgrims since the Middle Ages. It is the seat of the patriarchates of the Roman, Greek Orthodox and Armenian Churches, who share the custodianship of the Church of the Holy Sepulchre and who each own land and buildings in the neighbouring area.

The Church of the Holy Sepulchre stands on the hill of Golgotha in the higher, north-western part of the Old City. In the central chamber of the church is the Byzantine Rotunda built by 12th-century crusaders, which shelters the small shrine of the traditional site of the tomb. Here the different patriarchates exercise their rights in turn. Close by is the Rock of Calvary, revered as the site of Jesus's Crucifixion.

Most pilgrims devoutly follow the Way of the Cross, leading from the Roman Praetorium through several streets of the Old City to the Holy Sepulchre. Franciscan monks, commemorating the journey to the Crucifixion, follow the course of this traditional route each Friday; on Good Friday this procession marks a climax of the Easter celebrations of the Roman Church.

Outside the Old City stands the Mount of Olives, the scene of Jesus's Ascension. At the foot of its hill is the Garden of Gethsemane, which is associated with the vigil on the eve of the Crucifixion. The Cenaculum, or traditional room of the Last Supper, is situated on Mount Zion in Israel.

Nazareth: Israel. This town, closely associated with the childhood of Jesus, has been a Christian centre since the fourth century CE. The huge, domed Church of the Annunciation has recently been built on the site of numerous earlier churches to protect the underground Grotto of the Annunciation. Nearby the Church of St Joseph marks the traditional site of Joseph's workshop.

Galilee: Israel. Many of the places by this lake (the Sea of Galilee, or Lake Tiberias) are associated with the life of Jesus: Cana, scene of the miracle of water and wine, which is celebrated by an annual pilgrimage on the second Sunday after Epiphany; the Mount of Beatitudes; Tabgha, scene of the multiplication of the loaves and fish; and Capernaum, scene of the healing of the Centurion's servant.

Mount Tabor: Israel. The traditional site of the Transfiguration, which has drawn pilgrims since the fourth century, is commemorated by a Franciscan Monastery and a Greek Basilica, where the annual Festival of the Transfiguration is held.

Jericho (Ariha): West Bank. The scene of the baptism of Jesus; nearby is the Greek Monastery of St John the Baptist.

Nablus (Nabulus): West Bank. This old town contains Jacob's Well, associated with Jesus, and the Tomb of Joseph.

Qubaibah (Emmaus): Jordan. It was near this town that two of the Disciples encountered Jesus after the Resurrection.

'Azariyyah (Bethany): Jordan. A town frequented by Jesus, the home of Mary and Martha, and the scene of the Raising of Lazarus.

Mount Carmel: Haifa, Israel. The Cave of Elijah draws many pilgrims, including Muslims and Druzes, who celebrate the Feast of Mar Elias on 20 July.

Ein Kerem: Israel. Traditional birthplace of John the Baptist, to whom a Franciscan church is dedicated; nearby is the church of the Visitation.

Ephesus: Türkiye. The city was formerly a great centre of pagan worship, where Paul founded the first of the seven Asian Churches. The Basilica, built by Justinian, is dedicated to John the Evangelist, who, according to legend, died here; a fourth-century church on Aladag Mountain commemorating Mary's last years spent here now draws an annual pilgrimage in August.

JUDAISM

There are two main Jewish communities, the Ashkenazim and the Sephardim. The former originate from central, northern and eastern Europe (Ashkenaz being the old Hebrew word for Germany), while the latter come from the historic Spanish community and their descendants (Sepharad being the old Hebrew word for Spain). In popular use, however, the term Sephardim is often expanded to include all Jews of non-European origin and thus those communities from the Balkans, the Middle East and North Africa. The term Mizrahim (meaning 'easterners') has also emerged in Israel to describe Jews descended from communities in Asia and Africa. The majority of immigrants into Israel were from the Ashkenazim, and their influence predominates there, although the Hebrew language follows Sephardim usage. There is no doctrinal difference between the two communities, but they observe distinct rituals.

Holy Places

Wailing Wall: Jerusalem. This last remnant of the western part of the wall surrounding the courtyard of Herod's Temple, finally destroyed by the Romans in 70 CE, is visited by devout Jews, particularly on the Fast Day of the ninth of Av, to grieve at the destruction of the First and Second Temples which had once stood on the same site.

Mount Zion: Israel. A hill to the south-west of the Old City of Jerusalem, venerated particularly for the tomb of David, acknowledged by Muslims as Abi Dawud (the Jebuzite hill on which David founded his Holy City is now known as Mount Ophel, and is in Jordan, just to the east of the modern Mount Zion). Not far from the foot of the hill are the rock-cut tombs of the family of King Herod.

Cave of Machpelah: West Bank. The grotto, over which was built a mosque, contains the tombs of Abraham and Sarah, Isaac and Rebecca, Jacob and Leah.

Bethlehem: West Bank. The traditional tomb of Rachel is in a small shrine outside the town, venerated also by Muslims and Christians.

Mount Carmel: Israel. The mountain is associated with Elijah, whose Cave in Haifa draws many pilgrims. (See *Christianity*.)

Safad: Israel. Centre of the medieval Cabbalist movement, this city contains several synagogues from the 16th century associated with these scholars, and many important tombs, notably that of Rabbi Isaac Louria.

Meiron: Israel. The town contains the tombs of Shimon bar Yohai, reputed founder in the second century of the medieval Cabbalist movement, and his son Eleazer. A yearly Hassidic pilgrimage is held to the tomb to celebrate Lag Ba'Omer with a night of traditional singing and dancing in which Muslims also participate.

Tiberias: Israel. An ancient city containing the tombs of Moses Maimonides and Rabbi Meir Baal Harness. Famous as a historical centre of Cabbalist scholarship, it is—with Jerusalem, Safad and Hebron—one of the four sacred cities of Judaism, and once accommodated a university and the Sanhedrin.

OTHER COMMUNITIES

Zoroastrians

Zoroastrianism developed from the teaching of Zoroaster, or Zarathustra, who lived in Iran some time between 700 and 550 BCE. Later adopted as the official religion of the Persian empire, Zoroastrianism remained predominant in Iran until the rise of Islam. Many adherents were forced by persecution to emigrate, and the main centre of the faith is now Mumbai, where followers are known as Parsis. Technically a monotheistic faith, Zoroastrianism retained some elements of polytheism. It later became associated with fire-worship.

Yazd: Iran. This city was the ancient centre of the Zoroastrian religion, and was later used as a retreat during the Arab conquest. It contains five fire temples and still remains a centre for this faith, of which an estimated 30,000–60,000 adherents live in Iran.

Bahá'ís

Bahá'ísm developed in the mid-19th century CE from Babism. The Bab, or Gateway (to Truth), Saiyid Ali Muhammad of Shiraz (1821–50), was opposed to the corrupt Shi'a clergy in the Iran of his day and was executed in 1850. His remains were later taken to Haifa and buried in a mausoleum on the slopes of Mount Carmel. Mirza Husain Ali Bahá'ullah ('Splendour of Allah', 1817–92), a follower of Babism, experienced a spiritual revelation while in prison and in 1863 declared himself to be 'he whom Allah shall manifest' as predicted by the Bab. A member of the Persian nobility, he devoted his life to preaching against the corruption endemic in Persian society and as a result spent many years in exile. He died at Acre in Palestine in 1892 and is buried in a shrine adjacent to the mansion in which the Bab died, at Bahji, some miles north of Acre on the road to Beirut.

It was in the will and testament of Abdul Bahá, the eldest son and successor of Bahá'ullah, that after his death (in 1921) the head of the Bahá'í faith would be Shoghi Effendi, known as the Guardian of the Bahá'í faith ('Guardian of Allah's Command'), and that he would be the 'President' of the Universal House of Justice which would be elected in due course. In fact Shoghi Effendi died in London in 1957 after 36 years as Guardian, but the Universal House of Justice was not elected from the Bahá'í world until 1963. The presidency was never assumed and there is no possibility of a second Guardian being appointed.

In 1846 the Babis declared their secession from Islam, and the Bahá'ís claim independence from all other faiths. They believe that the basic principles of the great religions of the world are in complete harmony and that their aims and functions are complementary. Other tenets include belief in the brotherhood of man, opposition to racial and colour discrimination, equality of the sexes, progress towards world peace, monogamy, chastity and the encouragement of family life. Bahá'ísm has no priesthood and discourages asceticism, monasticism and mystic pantheism. The number of Bahá'ís worldwide is variously reported as being between 5m. and 8m, some 1.8m.–2.2m. of whom live in India. Most of Bahá'ísm's Middle Eastern adherents live in Iran and, on a temporary basis, Israel, but since the 1979 Islamic Revolution those in Iran have suffered from severe official persecution.

Haifa: Israel. Shrine and gardens of the Bab on Mount Carmel, the world centre of the Bahá'í faith. Pilgrims visit the Bahá'í holy places in Haifa and in and around Acre. The Pilgrimage lasts for nine days and the pilgrimage period extends over the whole year, with the exception of August and September.

PART TWO
Country Surveys

ALGERIA

Geography

Algeria is the largest of the three countries in north-western Africa that comprise the Maghreb, as the region of mountains, valleys and plateaux lying between the sea and the Sahara desert is known. It is situated between Morocco and Tunisia, with a Mediterranean coastline of nearly 1,000 km and a total area of some 2,381,741 sq km (919,595 sq miles), over four-fifths of which lies south of the Maghreb proper and within the western Sahara. Its extent, both from north to south and west to east, exceeds 2,000 km. The Arabic name for the country, el-Djezaïr (the Islands), is said to derive from the rocky islands along the coastline.

The climate of northernmost Algeria, including the narrow coastal plain and the Tell Atlas southwards to the margin of the High Plateaux, is of 'Mediterranean' type with warm, wet winters and hot, dry summers. Rainfall varies from over 1,000 mm annually on some coastal mountains to less than 130 mm in sheltered situations, and occurs mostly during the winter. Complete drought lasts for three to four months during the summer, when the notorious sirocco (Chehili) also occurs. This is a scorching, dry and dusty southerly wind blowing from the Sahara, prevailing for some 40 days a year over the High Plateaux, although nearer the coast its duration is closer to 20 days. With the arrival of the sirocco, shade temperatures often rise rapidly to more than 40°C (104°F). The climate of Saharan Algeria is characterized by extremes of temperature, wind and aridity. Daily temperature ranges reach 32°C, and maximum shade temperatures of over 55°C have been recorded. Sometimes very high temperatures are associated with violent dust storms. Average annual rainfall, although extremely irregular, is less than 130 mm everywhere, and in some central parts of the desert it is less than 10 mm.

Along the northern margin of the High Plateaux 'Mediterranean' conditions give way to a semi-arid or steppe climate, in which summer drought lasts from five to six months and winters are colder and drier. Rainfall is limited to 200 mm–400 mm annually and tends to occur in spring and autumn rather than in winter. It is, moreover, variable from year to year. South of the Saharan Atlas annual rainfall decreases to below 200 mm and any regular cultivation without irrigation becomes impossible.

The total population of Algeria increased from 23,038,942 in April 1987 to 29,100,867 (excluding 171,476 Sahrawi refugees in camps) at the census of June 1998. At a new census conducted in April 2008, the total population was recorded at 34,080,030. At mid-2023, according to United Nations (UN) estimates, the population was 45,606,481. The great majority of the inhabitants reside in the northern part of the country, particularly along the Mediterranean coast where both the capital, Algiers or el-Djezaïr (including suburbs, estimated by the UN at 2,901,810 at mid-2023), and the second largest town, Oran (935,947), are located. Many settlements reverted to their Arabic names in 1981. The population is almost wholly Muslim. A majority speak Arabic and the remainder Tamazight, the principal language of the Berber minority who were the original inhabitants of the Maghreb. Many Algerians also speak French.

History

GIANNI DEL PANTA

INTRODUCTION

The invasion of Ukraine by the Russian Federation in February 2022 resulted in two positive developments for the Algerian ruling elite. The first was a rapid and unprecedented rise in hydrocarbon prices. Between February 2022 and July 2023 the oil price remained above US $65 per barrel, reaching a high of $123.70 per barrel in March 2022. Although the conflict in Ukraine did not initiate this upward trend, as hydrocarbon prices had been increasing steadily throughout 2021, it strengthened the already ongoing dynamic, pumping extra revenue into the Algerian state's coffers. Algeria's macroeconomic indicators consequently improved significantly during 2022 and the first half of 2023, with the budget deficit and public debt both declining markedly, and a fiscal surplus expected in 2023. Second, in an effort to reduce their strong dependence on Russian natural gas, Western European countries sought to purchase natural gas from other producers. Owing to its geographical location, Algeria benefited the most from this increase in European demand, and the country rapidly established itself as the second largest gas supplier to Europe (after Norway), supplanting Russia. More than 85% of Algeria's gas exports are now purchased by European countries, primarily Italy. Unsurprisingly, it was the economic and diplomatic relationship between Algeria and Italy that most noticeably improved. During 2022 and the first half of 2023 Italian Prime Ministers Mario Draghi and Giorgia Meloni made three official visits to Algeria, while the Algerian Minister of Foreign Affairs, Ahmed Attaf, who had been appointed in March 2023, chose Italy for his first official visit abroad. In mid-2023 the two countries were also considering the feasibility of constructing a new gas pipeline between Algeria and the Italian island of Sardinia.

In addition, two other elements contributed to the strengthening of the relationship between Algeria and Italy. The first was a disagreement between Algeria and Spain after the latter reversed its neutral stance in the Western Sahara dispute (see below) by announcing its support for the position of Algeria's main geopolitical rival, Morocco. In response, Algeria unilaterally suspended its two decade-long friendship treaty with Spain in June 2022, fostering a diplomatic crisis that drew the involvement of European institutions. As expected, economic relations were also affected. By May 2023 Spanish exports to Algeria had declined by more than 80%, while Algerian gas exports to Spain (which was the second largest importer after Italy in 2021) decreased by more than 35% in 2022. The second factor that led to the strengthening of the Algerian-Italian relationship was the strained ties between Algeria and France (the third most important international market for Algerian gas). In August 2022 French President Emmanuel Macron visited Algeria in an attempt to improve relations between the two countries, followed by French Prime Minister Elisabeth Borne and more than a dozen government ministers a few weeks later. These efforts by France to improve bilateral ties were prompted by a controversy in October 2021, when President Macron had questioned whether Algeria had existed as a nation before French colonization, causing outrage in Algeria. This demonstrates how the anti-colonial revolution that began in 1954 continues to affect Algerian politics and the country's international relations after almost 70 years, providing a set of values that still pertain today. The main reason for this is the exceptionally long armed struggle that ended France's century-long occupation of Algeria, which dated back to 1830.

COLONIZATION AND FRENCH RULE

On 25 May 1830 a fleet of 635 ships sailed from Toulon and Marseille, heading for Algiers. A few weeks later the North African city had been conquered by French troops. This event marked the end of more than 300 years of Ottoman rule of Algiers and its environs, leading to France's colonization of today's Algeria. Owing to its intensity and brutality, the colonial control of Algeria for 132 years represents an exception even for the highly colonialized region of the Middle East and North Africa. There are at least three main aspects of French rule in Algeria that should be considered. First is the fact that the country became a settlement colony. Mainly in response to the rapidly growing population in southern Europe, large numbers of Spanish, French and Italians, often from very poor backgrounds, were encouraged to move to Algeria. In the 1840s alone, for instance, the European population of Algeria more than quadrupled from 26,987 to 125,963. By the turn of the century, also as a result of a dramatic decrease in the native population, with the disappearance of some 600,000 people between 1861 and 1872, the more than half a million Europeans represented about one-sixth of the entire population. At the outbreak of the War of Independence in 1954 the European population had grown to 984,000. Secondly, rural properties, often owned collectively by native Algerians, were systematically expropriated, which had a great impact on Algerian society, hitherto overwhelmingly peasant and nomadic. By the mid-1900s the European population had acquired a total monopoly of land, as shown by its ownership of some 2,700,000 ha of the most cultivable part of the country, almost entirely located in the north. Finally, Algerian territory was divided into four parts—that is, the departments of Algiers, Constantine and Oran, and the territories of the south—and became part of France. Despite this, French citizenship was not automatically granted to all those living in Algeria. To obtain it, non-European people had to renounce their Muslim civil status: a very hard step, taken by only 1,557 individuals between 1865 and 1913. In this way, the political and legal inequality of the two peoples was fully institutionalized.

Considering the intrusiveness of French colonial rule in Algeria it is not surprising that a strong and violent resistance developed, especially in the early years. From 1830 to 1848, for instance, the anti-colonial movement led by figures such as Abd al-Qadir and Ahmed Bey limited significantly the capacity of French troops to impose their domination, before being decisively defeated. Important layers of Algerian traditional elites were forced into exile, and those resisting French domination left the major cities of the coast for the mountains and oases, where the roughness of the terrain made it difficult for Europeans to fight. The last great revolt took place in 1871 and was concentrated in Kabylia, the main Amazigh (Berber) region of the country. From that moment on French rule appeared fully institutionalized in Algeria and the native population defeated, fragmented and passive. In many cases the mere existence of the notion of Algerian nationalism became contested. Paradoxically, it was on French soil that the anti-colonial movement truly developed a few decades later.

The arrival of the French, as already mentioned, profoundly disrupted Algeria's pre-capitalist society, forcing Algerians who had lost access to land to work as wage labourers on European-owned farms. However, owing to land concentration, population growth and technological advancements, about one-half of the rural population of working age was unemployed and inhabiting shanty towns on the outskirts of the main cities. Finding a job in these urban settings, considering the very limited industrial development of the country, was not easy. In such a context, emigration to Europe was one of the very few alternatives. By the mid-1920s the North African worker community in France, almost entirely Algerian, had already grown to about 100,000. It was in a situation of harsh exploitation, cultural isolation and strong ideological polarization of French society that a small group of Algerians joined the French Communist Party and its affiliated trade union. The French extreme left sponsored the holding of a congress of Maghrebi workers in 1924, paving the way for a series of meetings that led to the foundation, under the leadership of Messali Hadj, of the Etoile Nord-Africaine (North African Star) in 1926. The group openly campaigned for Algerian independence and adopted an anti-capitalist rhetoric. Alongside the Etoile Nord-Africaine, renamed the Parti du Peuple Algérien (PPA—Algerian's People Party) after Messali began the process of transferring the movement to his native soil in 1936–37, other strands of Algerian nationalism included the moderate Islamic reform movement led by Abd al-Hamid Ben Badis; a liberal-orientated group of newly educated Algerian elite whose most prominent figure was Ferhat Abbas; and the tiny Parti Communiste Algérien (PCA—Algerian Communist Party).

The worsening of economic conditions in the wake of the Second World War and the weakening of France's political position strengthened the Algerian nationalist movement, which appealed for demonstrations in May 1945. Violent clashes between nationalists and Europeans followed, leading to a failed insurrection that cost the lives of thousands of Algerians, especially in Sétif, Guelma and Kherrata. The bloodshed polarized further the two communities and contributed to fostering the idea, especially among younger Algerians, that independence could only be won by force. By 1947 the outlawed PPA had renamed itself the Mouvement pour le Triomphe des Libertés Démocratiques (MTDL—Movement for the Triumph of Democratic Liberties) and created a secret paramilitary structure, known as the Organisation Spéciale (OS—Special Organization), which attracted some of the leaders of the coming revolution, such as Hocine Aït Ahmed and Ahmed Ben Bella, who later became President of independent Algeria. Wihin a few years, however, the OS had been disbanded by the colonial police, strengthening Messali's view that revolutionary methods could not work. Accordingly, the MTDL rejected all requests to reconstitute the OS. The decision frustrated some of the most militant elements in Algerian society, who started deserting the movement. This happened at a time when a severe conflict erupted between Messali and his followers, on the one hand, and the central committee of the party, on the other, paralysing the organization. In reaction to this, a group of young nationalists created a third force, the Comité Révolutionnaire d'Unité et d'Action (CRUA—Revolutionary Committee of Unity and Action), with the initial aim of mediating between the two factions. Once it became clear, in mid-1954, that the reunification of the MTDL was impossible, the 22 young men of the CRUA began to plan the revolution, which was officially launched on 1 November 1954.

Right from the start, the confrontation between the CRUA, which soon became the Front de Libération Nationale (FLN—National Liberation Front), and the French army was evidently uneven. By mid-1957, when it was clear that an attempt by the FLN to move the battle from the countryside to the capital had failed, the revolution reached its nadir. Profound conflicts, moreover, broke out within the ranks of the FLN. On the one hand, these concerned the different ideological positions taken by the less and more radical wings of the liberation movement. On the other hand, and more importantly, tensions developed between the Gouvernement Provisoire de la République Algérienne (GPRA—Provisional Government of the Algerian Republic), officially formed in Cairo, Egypt, in September 1958, but de facto created during the FLN's clandestine congress of Soummam held two years earlier, and the military. The latter was also split between the Armée de Libération Nationale (National Liberation Army), which operated on the borders of Algeria, especially in Morocco, and the guerrillas of the interior, who bore the brunt of the actual fighting and suffered extensive losses. These divisions led Algeria to the brink of civil war after independence. For the moment, however, the necessity to fight a common and much stronger enemy bonded the different layers of the liberation movement, which increasingly attracted substantial international support and indirectly unleashed severe contradictions in the French camp. The engagement of nearly half a million French troops on Algerian soil, most of whom were conscripts, brought war home to France in a direct way, raising questions about the necessity to defend colonial domination in Algeria. Under pressure from public opinion, the French Government turned towards the idea of a negotiated settlement for Algeria. As expected, this outraged French citizens in Algeria, who started an insurrection that came close to spreading to the mainland and threatening the republic. To deal with the crisis, Gen. Charles de Gaulle, who had fought against Nazi Germany in the Second World War and chaired France's Provisional Government between 1944 and 1946, received exceptional and unprecedented political powers. De Gaulle moved gradually from generic positions on the future of Algeria, to self-determination without the involvement of the FLN, right up to consideration of an Algerian republic. As shown by the referendum on self-determination for Algeria held in France in January 1961, this latter option was by far the prevalent feeling in French society. Despite a long series of terrorist attacks by the Organisation Armée Secrète (Secret Army Organization)—the final and most lethal paramilitary organization set up to defend French's colonial possession—the Evian Accords were signed on 18 March 1962. After more than seven years and an unspecified number of casualties, possibly amounting to around 300,000 people in total, the war ended with full independence for Algeria. A referendum ratified the decision on 1 July 1962.

THE POLITICAL SYSTEM AFTER INDEPENDENCE

At the end of the revolutionary war Algeria was a broken country: more than 2m. Algerians had been forced into internment camps, some 300,000 had found refuge in Tunisia and Morocco, and about 400,000 had been arrested. By 1962 more than 3m. rural Algerians—that is, almost one in two of those living in the countryside—had been displaced, resulting in a rapid increase in the country's urban population. In the months that followed the signing of the Evian Accords there was the precipitous departure of about 90% of Europeans, many of whom had occupied prominent positions in the administrative and economic sectors. Before leaving Algeria, as typical in military retreats, they blew up buildings, torched libraries and destroyed the vast communication network that they had built over many decades. Capital fled as well as the Europeans. Algeria's gross domestic product (GDP) contracted by about 35% between 1960 and 1963 alone, and up to 70% of the active male labour force was unemployed or underemployed. As many as 1,400 out of some 2,000 construction enterprises disappeared, while textile factories were operating at about 60% of their capacity. The number of industrial workers shrank from about 110,000 to 80,000 between 1962 and 1963. Moreover, manufacturing largely remained a subordinate branch of agriculture, with food-processing factories accounting for some 40% of industrial output and providing employment for about 25% of the workforce as late as 1966. In the mean time, the hitherto covert struggle among the various factions of the national liberation movement became open and public.

In June 1962, after a meeting in Tripoli, Libya, had geared Algeria towards 'socialism', prioritizing agricultural development over industrialization, the GPRA tried to assert its supremacy over the military wing by dismissing three top officers of the General Staff, among them Col Houari Boumedienne. In reaction to this, the General Staff, backed by Ben Bella, entered Algiers, and the GPRA, supported by the former guerrillas, based itself in Tizi Ouzou, in Kabylia. The showdown between the two sides, which came close to escalating into a full-scale civil war, cost the lives of hundreds, possibly thousands, of Algerians and was eventually won by Ben Bella and Boumedienne's forces. In September voters were asked to ratify a list of 196 candidates who would comprise the National Constituent Assembly, whose first president was Abbas. About a year later the Assembly ratified the Constitution, which declared the FLN the sole legal party of Algeria and established a presidential republic in which power was hugely concentrated in the executive branch. In September 1963 almost 97% of those voting in a national referendum approved the Constitution, and Ben Bella was elected President in an election in which he was the only candidate. Holding the positions of head of government, head of state and Secretary-General of the FLN, Ben Bella had clearly won the post-independence struggle for political power in Algeria by late 1963. Despite this, he still faced internal threats. The most serious of these was the guerrilla movement organized and led by Aït Ahmed.

Aït Ahmed resigned from the GPRA in mid-1962 and organized resistance to Ben Bella's rise to power in Kabylia. In September 1963, he founded the Front des Forces Socialistes (FFS—Socialist Front Forces) and urged Algerians to fight for supposedly authentic socialist values and against the institutionalization of what he described as a 'fascist regime'. The FFS carried out a series of sabotages and attacks against government forces, but largely failed to create a national organization. Rather, it remained limited to Kabylia, where a long-lasting anti-Arab feeling contributed to the insurrection. The outbreak of a border war between Morocco and Algeria in October 1963, which created a patriotic fervour in the country and weakened internal opposition to Ben Bella's rule, as well as the deployment of significant military forces in Kabylia, curbed the development of the FFS guerrilla movement. Following Aït Ahmed's arrest in October 1964 the insurrection came to a decisive end. After being sentenced to death—a verdict that Ben Bella himself commuted to life imprisonment—Aït Ahmed escaped and fled to Europe in 1966. He would return to Algeria only in 1989.

Meanwhile, Ben Bella summoned the long-awaited congress of the FLN, which took place in April 1964. The congress provided an opportunity to legitimize Ben Bella's position and institutionalize the sharing of power among the three leading groups: Ben Bella's inner circle, Boumedienne's followers and the leaders of the *wilayat* (departments). An attempt to transform the FLN into an avant-garde party, however, proved a fiasco. The class-based rhetoric that pervaded the document approved by the congress, known as the Algiers Charter, was at odds with what the party had already become, i.e., a mass-based party with 150,000 full and 600,000 aspirant members, coming from different social classes and representing a broad spectrum of ideological positions. The FLN was, therefore, a secondary apparatus, performing public and diplomatic functions on behalf of a state machine that it never controlled. In a similar way, students' organizations and the so-called revolutionary family (the generation of mujahidin and subsequently their children) were brought under the strict control of the regime, whereas the Union Générale des Travailleurs Algériens (UGTA—General Union of Algerian Workers) became the sole legal and compulsory channel of workers' representation. At the helm of the state machine stood the bureaucracy and, above all, the military, which was significantly empowered by the bloodless *coup d'état* against Ben Bella on 19 June 1965.

In the short term, the military takeover, led by Minister of Defence Houari Boumedienne and carried out by a small clique of military officers who subsequently named themselves the Council of the Revolution, was a reaction to Ben Bella's planned dismissal of Minister of Foreign Affairs Abdelaziz Bouteflika, who was Boumedienne's ally and later served as President of Algeria from 1999 until 2019. From a larger perspective, the coup represented a firm rejection of Ben Bella's economic policies. In the wake of independence and the abrupt departure of the Europeans, abandoned colonial properties, generally known as *bien vacants*, were occupied by Algerians. Out of necessity, peasants and workers resumed production. The so-called self-management movement (*autogestion*) attracted international support on the left and was officially backed by Algeria's Government in March 1963. However, owing to the fact that subsidiaries of French metropolitan firms were left untouched in order not to jeopardize Algeria's vital economic aid from France, self-management in the industrial sector remained limited. By 1964 only between 345 and 413 industrial units were being managed by self-management committees, accounting for no more than 15% of the total industrial workforce. The situation was different, however, in agriculture. Former agricultural properties were reorganized into larger self-managed units that included some of the most fertile lands and produced more than one-half of gross agricultural product. Ben Bella's Government tried gradually to expand the magnitude of the self-management experiment, nationalizing all landholdings belonging to Europeans and incorporating them into the self-managed sectors. In October 1964 about 200,000 ha that were considered to have been wrongly acquired by the Algerian propertied classes were also added to the self-management system. Such a move impacted some of the families (and threatened many more) of the new rural middle and upper classes that had benefitted enormously from the departure of the colonial Europeans, either buying their properties at excessively low prices or simply occupying them. In a context characterized by a strong socialist rhetoric, these classes did not find any clear political expression. Their resentment added, however, to the strong opposition to the self-management movement among the bureaucracy and the army, who opposed the top priority given to the agricultural sector (which received about 50% of the total government budget in 1963) and supported a more central role for state apparatuses.

Apart from a series of demonstrations staged by youth and student organizations, Ben Bella's removal was not seriously contested. In the aftermath of the coup, the 1963 Constitution was suspended and the National Assembly abolished, while Ben Bella was arrested, remaining in prison until 1979 when he was transferred to house arrest and finally liberated the following year. Power was fully concentrated in the Council of the Revolution, composed of 26 men and led by Boumedienne. At local level, the first communal assemblies were elected in 1967 by direct universal suffrage from lists of candidates drawn up by the FLN. Two years later the same mechanism was used to elect *wilayat* assemblies. It was only in 1975, to celebrate the 10th anniversary of what had become known as the 'revolutionary readjustment', that Boumedienne announced plans for the drafting of a new national constitution; the charter was approved by more than 99% of those who took part in a popular referendum in November 1976. The Constitution confirmed Islam as the state religion and socialism as the country's economic system. Presidentialism became the form of government and enormous authority was concentrated in the executive branch. The President of the republic was nominated by a congress of the FLN, which remained the sole legal party, and then elected by a popular vote for five years without any term limit. The President named the cabinet directly and, optionally, a Prime Minister; the ministers were not responsible to the parliament. The latter was a unicameral legislature, whose 261 members were elected for five-year terms from larger lists of candidates drawn up by the FLN. In December Boumedienne officially became President, running as the sole candidate nominated by the ruling party, and at legislative elections held in February 1977 (the first since 1964) the FLN won all 261 seats in the National People's Assembly, as the only party to contest the polls.

THE POLITICAL ECONOMY OF INDEPENDENT ALGERIA

France's colonial domination had transformed Algeria into a commodity-extracting hinterland for the metropole and an importer of manufactured consumer goods, determining an inconsistent process of industrialization. By the time of the 1965 coup, Ben Bella's self-management experiment had already proved incapable of breaking the chain of dependence on core capitalist states and transforming Algeria into an autonomous and independent centre of capital accumulation. Under Boumedienne the new implicit alliance between the military and the bureaucracy, under the leadership of the former, switched towards state-led economic development in which top priority was given to state-owned and vertical-integrated industries, favouring capital intensive sectors such as steel, heavy machinery, iron metallurgy, organic and inorganic chemistry and electricity. The whole strategy was built around three basic priorities: capital accumulation over consumption; industrialization over agriculture; and capital equipment over consumer goods. After nationalizing all the natural gas reserves of the country in February 1971, hydrocarbon rents paid in hard currencies were used to finance state investments, which skyrocketed in the following years. In scarcely more than a decade, state-led development transformed Algeria. Between 1967 and 1978 the average annual growth of the economy was an impressive 7.2%, industrial production doubled and the output of basic industries nearly quadrupled.

These impressive economic data were not, however, the effect of an accelerated capital accumulation. Rather, the two real driving forces behind this process were the astonishing amount of resources invested and the two global oil shocks that caused unprecedented high hydrocarbons prices. The industrialization strategy was little more than a gigantic spending programme, under which workers were hired liberally—receiving social and economic benefits in exchange for their political quiescence—and plants were managed in a way that ignored cost-benefit calculations. As unequivocally demonstrated by the fact that hydrocarbons accounted for 98% of export earnings in the mid-1970s, Algerian industrialization was never a success story. During 1969–82, for example, all state enterprises, excluding Sonatrach, the national oil and gas company, registered negative operating incomes every year except 1978. When Boumedienne died suddenly in December 1978 a profound reshaping of the model of development was already on its way to being launched. This happened under the presidency of Col Ben Djedid Chadli, who was nominated by the FLN, on the army's recommendation, to succeed Boumedienne.

The shortcomings in Boumedienne's economic policies and the emergence of a private bourgeoisie, concentrated in commercial and trade activities as well as in small-scale manufacturing enterprises, increasingly exacerbated pressure on market openings, eventually determining the end of the military-technocracy alliance and its replacement with a military-private bourgeoisie nexus in the course of the 1980s. The whole process started in 1980 when, during an extraordinary congress of the FLN, the first five-year plan of Chadli's presidency was announced. It aimed to concentrate resources away from capital-intensive industries and towards social infrastructure, light industry and agriculture. For the first time since independence, private sector initiative was encouraged, while state-owned enterprises were restructured and decentralized. Despite the modest results of the first five-year plan, the pace of economic reforms sped up quickly after Chadli's re-election for a second five-year presidential term in January 1984, by about 95% of the votes cast. Investments in industry were further curtailed, while the attempt to revitalize agriculture through privatization of land and irrigation schemes became an absolute priority for a country that by 1986 was importing no less than three-quarters of its food requirements. Likewise, investments in social infrastructure increased to more than 27% of the total, focusing particularly on housing. Hydrocarbons revenue supported the entire system, making Algeria particularly vulnerable to fluctuations in oil prices; a situation that first emerged in 1985 when hydrocarbons prices on the global markets started decreasing.

By 1986 the price of oil per barrel had fallen below US $10, leading to a sharp decline in hydrocarbons export earnings. Unable to borrow again on the international market, Chadli was forced to impose austerity measures. GDP growth slowed from 5.2% in 1984 to 2.7% in 1985 and 0.6% in 1986. It turned negative in 1987 and plummeted in 1988. Unemployment increased from 11% to 25% between 1984 and 1988. Those who did not lose their jobs suffered diminishing purchasing power as a result of stagnant salaries combined with rising inflation. Moreover, the Government's sharp cuts to food subsidies led to a huge price increase in many basic foodstuffs in a society that reached an astonishingly high level of social inequality: the richest 5% of the population earned 45% of the national income, while the poorest 50% earned less than 22%. It was in this context that huge anti-regime protests broke out.

FROM THE EVENTS OF OCTOBER 1988 TO THE FIS VICTORIES

The political temperature had been rising in Algeria since the late 1970s. In March 1980, in response to a government ban on a conference at the university of Tizi Ouzou on the use of the Amazigh language, teachers and students occupied the university, starting a long series of protests concentrated in Kabylia and known as the 'Berber Spring', in recollection of the 1968 events in Prague, Czechoslovakia (now the Czech Republic). Although the uprising was violently suppressed by the security forces, it raised the issues caused by the diversity of the Algerian population for the first time and indirectly indicated the limits of Boumedienne's push for Arabization of the administrative sphere and education. Despite this push by the regime, francophone students in fact enjoyed significantly better career opportunities than Arabized students. In protest, the latter undertook a two-month strike at the University of Algiers in 1979–80. Fearing that Islamist fundamentalists would take control of the movement, Chadli's Government strengthened the process of Arabization of Algerian society. However, the move enjoyed little success, creating the context for the outbreak of the above mentioned 'Berber Spring' and failing to appease the Islamists, who were growing at an accelerated pace and clashing with left-wing students on university campuses. In the course of one of these violent confrontations, a left-wing student was killed in November 1982 at the university house complex of Ben Aknoun, in the hills of Algiers. In response, the regime cracked down on the fundamentalists, arresting about 400 of them, among them Sheikh Abdellatif Soltani and former FLN loyalist Abbassi Madani, who later became one of the leaders of the Front Islamique du Salut (FIS—Islamic Salvation Front). When Soltani died shortly after being released from prison in March 1984, tens of thousands of people attended the funeral, which rapidly degenerated into clashes between Islamists and the security forces. A small number of militants joined a guerrilla movement led by Mustapha Bouyali, the Mouvement Islamique Armé (MIA—Armed Islamic Movement), which mainly operated in the mountains south of Algiers and defied police efforts to track it down for about five years.

In this atmosphere, the collapse of oil and gas revenues in 1985–86 proved catastrophic for the regime. Riots erupted in poor neighbourhoods of Algiers, particularly in the Casbah, as early as 1985. In November 1986 student demonstrations took place in Algiers, Oran, Skikda, Sétif and Constantine. Thousands of people occupied the buildings of the communal authorities in Aïn Abid in September 1987, inspiring inhabitants of other peripheral centres to do the same in the following months. Subsequently, the organized labour movement made its appearance on the scene and unrest spread quickly from one economic branch to another. By September 1988 the entire northern industrial zone had been affected by the strike movement. On 5 October riots targeting public buildings, symbols of state power and luxury shops proliferated. In the following days the movement spread rapidly throughout Algeria, affecting all the main cities. The regime quickly declared a state of emergency, but demonstrations continued. For the first time the Islamists took to the streets en masse on 7 October, leading to violent clashes with the police. In response, the military was deployed onto the streets and ultimately resorted to open repression. On 8 October the army opened fire near a mosque in Algiers, causing about 50 deaths. Two days later a rally of 20,000 Islamists led by the imam from the Sunna mosque in Bab el-Oued, Ali Belhadj, who was later one of the founders and leaders of the FIS, was fired on by the army and broken up. By then hundreds of Algerians had been killed and thousands arrested, but calm was eventually restored across the country.

The events of October 1988 were a critical turning point in Algeria's recent history, seriously affecting the reputation of the army, which had long been seen as the guardian of the popular will. Moreover, in what was a surprising move given that the uprising had been crushed, President Chadli decided to open up the political system. Arguably, the decision was an attempt both to counteract the discontent caused by the phase of painful economic reforms and to sideline the old guard of the FLN by depriving it of its political monopoly. After having been re-elected for a third term as President in the December 1988 election where he ran unopposed, winning 81% of the vote, Chadli proposed a new Constitution in early 1989. The charter, which was overwhelmingly approved in a plebiscite, was a sharp departure from the 1976 Constitution. It no longer referred to socialism as the founding ideology of the country and it described the armed forces as a strictly military institution. Even more significantly, the FLN was not mentioned and freedom of expression, association and meeting were guaranteed. The one-party system was eventually abandoned and already established illegal opposition groups, as well as newly founded political forces, started being recognized after a new law on the establishment of political parties was approved on 5 July 1989. By early 1991 as many as 33 parties had obtained official recognition. Among these were parties led by prominent political figures who had spent years, if not decades, in exile, such as Ben Bella's Mouvement pour la Démocratie en Algérie (MDA—Movement for Democracy in Algeria) and Aït Ahmed's FFS, which organized a 100,000-strong demonstration in Algiers in May 1990. As with the FFS, the Rassemblement pour la Culture et la Démocratie (RCD—Rally for Culture and Democracy), led by one of the leaders of the 1980 'Berber Spring', Saïd Sadi, mainly derived its support from Kabylia. Neither of the two parties was, however, a regionalist force in the full sense of the word, in that they promoted cultural pluralism and supported a non-religious state. The more socialist-orientated appeal of the FFS and the RCD's greater emphasis on individual rights and liberal values differentiated the two parties. On the left, the main force was the Parti de l'Avant-Garde Socialiste (PAGS—Socialist Vanguard Party), which was formed in 1966 in the wake of the dissolution of the PCA and operated just beyond the fringe of legality, providing critical support to the regime and penetrating the most radical sections of the UGTA. From June 1990 the PAGS was joined by the Parti des Travailleurs (PT—Workers' Party), which grew out of the clandestine and Trotskyist-orientated Organisation Socialiste des Travailleurs (Socialist Workers' Organization). In the centre of the political spectrum, was the Parti Social-Démocrate (PSD—Social Democratic Party), which supported liberal-orientated values and pro-market policies and was mainly composed of entrepreneurs, academics and members of the professions.

The most important political force was, however, in the Islamist camp. The FIS was a broad and particularly heterogeneous coalition of informal and organized Islamist groups that officially came together in March 1989. Only a few Islamist groups, among them Mahfoud Nahnah's Hamas and Abdallah Djaballah's Mouvement de la Renaissance Islamique (MRI—Islamic Renaissance Movement), did not join the new coalition. The FIS was mainly composed of two wings, perfectly personified by its most prominent leaders. On the one hand, university professor, PhD graduate and honorific attendee of the liberation war Madani, who appealed to middle-class professionals and small tradesmen fed up with socialist claims and the state's strict control over economic activities. On the other, the young imam Belhadj, who drew support from disgruntled and frustrated youth.

The first actual test for all political forces were the local and provincial elections in June 1990. Ben Bella's MDA and, especially, Aït Ahmed's FFS appealed for a boycott, arguing that the elections were rigged against them. The absence of the two most prominent non-Islamist forces limited electoral participation to only 65% of voters and determined a huge concentration of votes for the two main parties. The relative balance of support for them was, however, completely unexpected. In the municipal elections the FIS obtained 4.3m. votes (54.2%), while the FLN obtained 2.3m. (28.1%). In addition, as an effect of a majoritarian electoral law, the Islamists assumed control of 856 out of 1,541 communal councils and 31 out of 48 *wilayat* assemblies. In the wake of these results, political attention switched towards the parliamentary elections, initially planned for early 1991 but subsequently postponed owing to the outbreak of the Gulf crisis. In the mean time, the parliament approved a new electoral law in April 1991 which adopted majoritarian criteria, raised the number of seats in the legislature from 295 to 542, and assigned a greater weight to those rural districts in which the FLN had performed well in the 1990 local and provincial elections. Moreover, the law also banned campaigning in mosques—the focus of Islamist organization—and forbade men to cast votes for their wives, a practice that had been allowed in 1990 and that had been particularly used by the Islamists. In response to what was seen as a frontal attack by the regime, the FIS appealed for a general strike of indefinite duration from 25 May 1991. The Islamists achieved little success in mobilizing workers, but the urban unemployed took the upper hand in the protests, which remained largely peaceful. As the protests entered their second week, the military pressured President Chadli to declare a state of emergency. Once this happened, clashes between the security forces and Islamists ensued. In a replay, albeit on a smaller scale, of the events of October 1988, 50 protesters were killed and hundreds arrested. A few weeks later, as a consequence of the greater role that the armed forces had acquired after a government reorganization, hundreds of Islamists were arrested, including Madani and Belhadj. Following minor amendments to the electoral law, which reduced the number of parliamentary seats to 430 but maintained the majoritarian principle, the first round of the parliamentary elections was scheduled to be held on 26 December 1991. The success of the Islamists was unquestionable. The FIS secured 188 seats, against only 15 won by the FLN. The FFS was dominant in Kabylia, taking 25 seats. The FIS was expected easily to obtain an absolute majority following the second round of the elections for the remaining 199 seats, which was scheduled to take place on 16 January 1992. To prevent this from happening, the military intervened on 11 January, forcing Chadli out of power and halting the electoral process.

THE OUTBREAK OF CIVIL WAR AND THE REMAKING OF THE SYSTEM

On 13 January 1992 the coup leaders announced the creation of a Haut Comité d'Etat (HCE—High Committee of State), composed of five men, among them defence minister and strongman of the regime Gen. Khaled Nezzar. The HCE, led by war independence hero Mohamed Boudiaf, who had lived in exile since 1964, was expected to rule the country for about two years. While the military coup left many Algerian citizens deeply troubled, it also received the backing of some important constituencies that feared the establishment of an Islamist theocracy more than anything else, such as the French-speaking community, intellectuals, feminist organizations and segments of the Amazigh community in Kabylia. Among political parties, the PAGS and, above all, Sadi's RCD emerged as the most vociferous supporters of the military intervention. However, other forces opposed the idea of a binary choice between an Islamic state or a military dictatorship. Amid growing rumours of an imminent military coup, under the slogan 'neither with the Islamic republic nor with the police state', the FFS organized what became, on 2 January 1992, the largest demonstration in Algerian history at that time, attracting some 400,000 people to gather in the capital. The PT, the MDA and the FLN expressed similar positions.

From the outset, the top priority of the HCE was the repression of the FIS and its supporters. The crackdown on the Islamists escalated rapidly: hundreds were arrested and violent clashes erupted in many parts of the country. On 9 February 1992 a state of emergency was declared and the FIS was outlawed in early March. In June the already imprisoned Madani and Belhadj were each given a 12-year sentence, which they served until 2003. The harsh repression of the Islamists by the state created the ideal conditions for the outbreak of an insurrection. Small armed groups had proliferated within a few months, mainly composed of the marginalized youth of the suburbs. In 1993 most of these groups agreed on the importance of converging under the same organizational structure, leading to the formation of the Groupe Islamique Armé (GIA—Armed Islamic Group), which became the most violent wing of the Islamist movement and mainly operated in the Algiers region. In May 1994, as a result of the coming together of other armed groups in the eastern part of the country, the Armée Islamique du Salut (AIS—Islamic Salvation Army) was created. In contrast to the position of the GIA, which condemned the FIS for its supposedly conciliatory stance towards the regime, the AIS proclaimed itself the armed wing of the FIS. Between February 1992 and December 1994 some 30,000 people lost their lives either in attacks by Islamist groups or in actions of reprisal by the Algerian security forces. By late 1993 the violence was also aimed at opposition groups, foreigners, journalists, intellectuals and teachers, almost tearing the country apart and polarizing Algerian society even more between supporters and opponents of the re-legalization of the FIS.

The Government, whose inner circle was strongly dominated by the army, was equally divided between hardliners, known as 'eradicators', and moderates or 'conciliators'. After Boudiaf's assassination in June 1992, another veteran of the war of independence against France, Ali Kafi, took his place at the helm of the HCE. Kafi headed the Committee until its dissolution in January 1994, when defence minister Gen. Liamine Zéroual was appointed President of the country for an anticipated three-year transitional period. In a context in which secret negotiations between Zéroual's Government and the FIS were taking place with very little progress being made, several Algerian parties tried to break the impasse, meeting with exiled FIS leaders in Rome, Italy, under the auspices of the Sant'Egidio Catholic lay community in January 1995. While the RCD, Hamas, UGTA and Ettahadi—the main offshoot of the PAGS after its split in late 1992—refused to take part in the dialogue, the FIS, the FLN, Aït Ahmed's FFS, Ben Bella's MDA, Louisa Hanoune's PT and Djaballah's MRI signed a pact that formalized the request for a return to free and multi-party parliamentary elections. Considering that the Sant'Egidio Platform accused the military of acts of extreme violence and demanded its return to the barracks, it was not a surprise that Zéroual's Government rejected the pact. At the same time, mainly in an attempt to re-establish the fading authority of the regime and legitimize his leadership, Zéroual called a presidential election. The major parties that had negotiated in Rome refused to participate in the poll, whereas Saïd Sadi for the RCD, Mahfoud Nahnah for Hamas and Noureddine Boukrouh for the small Parti du Renouveau Algérien (Party of Algerian Renewal) joined the contest.

On 16 November 1995 Algerians voted for the first time in a multi-candidate presidential election. Despite threats against those going to the polls by the AIS and, above all, the GIA, as well as the appeal to boycott the election by the three most popular parties in the first round of the 1991 parliamentary elections—the FIS, the FLN and the FFS—the turnout was considerably high, at nearly 75% of registered voters. In what has been hitherto the most free and fair presidential election in Algerian history, Zéroual obtained 61.0% of the valid votes, Nahnah 25.6%, Sadi 9.8% and Boukrouh 3.8%. In the aftermath of the presidential election came the drafting of a new Constitution. Algeria's fourth national charter strengthened the role of the executive branch and transformed the unicameral legislature into a parliament with two chambers. The lower house, the National People's Assembly, was to be directly elected by voters for a five-year term, while two-thirds of the members of the upper house, the Council of the Nation, were to be selected by communal and provincial assemblies and one-third appointed by the President. As a result of the fact that the Constitution forbade political parties founded on a religious basis, Nahnah's Hamas became the Mouvement de la Société pour la Paix (MSP—Movement of Society for Peace) and Djaballah's MRI was renamed Ennahda. The presidential election and the new Constitution did not halt the violent confrontations between the security forces and armed Islamist groups, which peaked in 1996–97. None the less, after five years of war the Islamists had not succeeded in demolishing the Algerian state and taking power. In the face of an endless spiral of violence and meaningless atrocities committed by both sides, the population increasingly favoured a political solution to the conflict. In an attempt to capitalize on the situation, the regime took the initiative, launching major military operations against the Islamist strongholds and announcing the holding of parliamentary elections in 1997. In contrast to what had happened in the 1995 presidential election, none of the major parties boycotted the polls, marking the definitive ending of the 1995 Sant'Egidio Platform. The newly created Rassemblement Nationale Démocratique (RND—National Democratic Rally), led by Ahmed Ouyahia, who had been appointed Prime Minister at the end of December 1995, was the most popular party, obtaining about one-third of the votes cast and 156 of the 380 seats in the National People's Assembly. The MSP came second, receiving 14.8% of the votes and 69 seats, while the FLN took 62 seats, Ennahda 34, the FFS 20, the RCD 19 and the PT 4. Ouyahia subsequently formed a coalition Government, which not only included the RND and the FLN, but also the moderate Islamist MSP.

BOUTEFLIKA'S ALGERIA IN THE 2000s

In September 1998, in a surprising move, Zéroual announced that a fresh presidential election would be held in a few months and that he would not take part in the contest. The regime candidate was Abdelaziz Bouteflika, who had served as Minister of Foreign Affairs from 1963 to 1979 and had been close to winning the FLN's nomination to succeed Boumedienne. Several other candidates tried to join the presidential campaign, but ultimately only six collected the 75,000 signatures required: former Prime Ministers who ran as independents Mouloud Hamrouche and Mokdad Sifi, former education and foreign minister Ahmed Taleb Ibrahimi, Hocine Aït Ahmed for the FFS, and Abdallah Djaballah for the Mouvement pour la Réforme Nationale (MRN—Movement for National Reform), a party created as a breakaway faction from Ennahda, after most of the leadership of the latter had started collaborating with the Government. However, just 24 hours before the scheduled presidential election on 14 April 1999 all the opposition candidates withdrew, claiming evident irregularities in the voting procedure and appealing for a public boycott of the poll. Despite this, the official turnout was relatively high (60.3% of registered voters) and more than one-quarter of those who participated in the polling still voted for withdrawn candidates. Bouteflika obtained 73.4% of the votes and a few weeks later was sworn into the presidency, which would prove the longest to date in Algerian history.

From the start Bouteflika faced two main challenges: finding a solution to the internal conflict and restarting economic growth. In June 1999 he issued the Law of Civil Concord, through which an amnesty was granted to Islamist fighters, excluding those involved in mass killings, sexual crimes and bombing of public places. Bouteflika's policy of reconciliation was strongly opposed by various forces: some sectors of the military considered it outrageous to pardon many of those they had been fighting for several years; while most of the GIA militants refused to surrender and joined the Groupe Salafiste pour la Prédication et le Combat (Salafist Group for Preaching and Combat), which later pledged support for the Islamist group al-Qa'ida and became Al-Qaïda au Maghreb Islamique (al-Qa'ida in the Islamic Maghreb) in 2007. Meanwhile, some FIS leaders such as Abbassi Madani condemned the Law of Civil Concord for holding only Islamists responsible for the long-lasting internal conflict. In September 1999, however, when Algerians were asked to vote on the law in a national referendum, 98.6% of those who voted (on a turnout of 85% of the electorate) approved it. After eight years of war that had caused some 200,000 deaths, the conflict gradually abated. As a consequence, economic policies then became the single most important issue.

Algeria entered the period 1988–92 suffering a profound economic crisis, which was further exacerbated by the Islamist uprising. During 1990–95 GDP grew by an average of only 0.1% per year. In 1994 Algeria signed a stand-by agreement with the International Monetary Fund, committing itself to a comprehensive package of neoliberal reforms. Among these was the reduction of the budget deficit, unrestricted access for foreign investors, and privatization of state-owned enterprises, excluding, however, the extremely sensitive hydrocarbons sector. The social costs of these reforms were high. Real public wages dropped by more than 30% between 1993 and 1996, nearly 500,000 public sector workers were laid off, and 12m. out of a population of some 30m. people were living below the poverty line. In the second half of the 1990s, however, the Algerian economy started recovering and macroeconomic indicators stabilized. This was mainly the effect of an increase in hydrocarbons exports, with the price of oil per barrel increasing from US $13 in 1998 to $28.50 in 2000.

However, the vast resources coming from the boom in oil prices (which reached a record of more than US $140 per barrel in 2008) were used to finance largely unnecessary public works. These projects were carried out by private companies owned by well-connected businessmen and senior officials, especially in the armed forces, strengthening the existing alliance between the security apparatuses—embodied by the Département du Renseignement et de la Sécurité, led by the enigmatic figure of Gen. Mohamed 'Toufik' Mediène between 1990 and 2015—and a rapacious and unproductive capitalist class. The latter was grouped around Bouteflika's brother Saïd, benefitting from state licensing, operating in import-export and trade activities, and acting as the agent of Western countries and multinationals on Algerian soil. The balance of power among the leading groups and clans in Algerian society changed constantly in relative terms in Bouteflika's years, but never swung far enough to affect fundamentally the structure of an environment in which multiple, competing power centres struggled to control the massive hydrocarbon revenues and broaden their influence and clientelistic networks at the expense of the others.

In political terms, post-civil war Algeria was a partly liberalized autocracy, in which political parties were allowed to operate and multi-party elections regularly held, although they were neither free nor fair. To campaign and provide parliamentary support the regime relied, in a rather peculiar way, on two ruling parties—the FLN and the RND. As already seen, Ouyahia's RND secured a majority of seats in the 1997 parliamentary elections, but the tally fell from 156 to 47 seats in the legislative elections of 2002, when the FLN obtained 34.3% of the votes cast and won a majority of 199 seats out of 389. Djaballah's recently created MRN made substantial gains and took 43 seats, emerging as the third largest parliamentary force, while the other moderate Islamist party, the MSN, lost more than one-half of its votes and won 38 seats. The parliamentary representation of Hanoune's PT jumped from four to 21 seats, benefiting from the electoral boycott of the FFS and RCD, in a context in which overall participation fell to 46% of registered voters. The decision of the two main Kabylia-based parties not to participate in the poll was a reaction to the powerful anti-regime movement that had developed in the region in 2001, when a violent revolt, known as the 'Black Spring' developed. Although limited to Kabylia and lasting only around seven weeks, the movement was a serious threat to the regime. Huge demonstrations took place in Tizi Ouzou (attracting some 500,000 participants on 21 May) and Algiers (about 200,000 demonstrators on 31 May and probably even more on 14 June). The response of the security forces was brutal, resulting in the deaths of more than 100 protesters.

The anti-regime stance of the RCD, was, however, short-lived, and its leader, Saïd Sadi, ran in the 2004 presidential election, when Bouteflika was comfortably re-elected for a second five-year term with 85% of the votes. Ali Benflis, the Secretary-General of the FLN and Prime Minister from 2000 to 2003, obtained 6.4%, Djaballah of the MRN 5.0%, Sadi of the RCD 1.9%, Hanoune of the PT 1.1% and Ali Fawzi Rebaine of the small nationalist party Ahd 54 just 0.6%. The FFS boycotted the election once again and official turnout was 58% of registered voters. Opposition leaders alleged electoral fraud at all levels and Benflis resigned from his post in protest. Following the election, Bouteflika appointed Ouyahia as Prime Minister for the second time, a position that he was to hold, excluding the period between May 2006 and June 2008, until September 2012. During his second presidential term Bouteflika speeded up the process of demilitarizing Algerian politics and concentrating power in the executive branch. In August 2004 Lt-Gen. Mohamed Lamari, Chief of Staff of the Algerian army since 1993 and regarded as the most powerful military figure in the country, was forced to resign, and Larbi Belkheir, the director of the President's office and a highly influential retired general, was dismissed from his post and a year later was sent to Morocco to serve as the Algerian ambassador there. Bouteflika's attempt to oust the entire 'old guard' from the security apparatuses was, however, unsuccessful, as three of the senior military officers who had played a critical role in the 1992 military coup—Abdelmalek Guenaizia, Smain Lamari (unrelated to Mohamed Lamari) and 'Toufik' Mediène—were not dismissed. Moreover, Bouteflika underwent complex surgery in Paris, France, in November 2005, taking several months to recover and undermining his political position.

After the 2007 legislative elections, at which turnout was just 35.7% of registered voters and the two main parties of the presidential coalition—the FLN, whose representation fell from 199 to 136 seats, and the RND, whose seats increased from 47 to 61—were again the most successful, Bouteflika won an important political battle in November 2008 in gaining the approval of the parliament for a partial reform of the 1996

Constitution that abolished the two-term presidential limit; only RCD deputies voted against the reform. Consequently, Bouteflika was able to present his candidacy for a third mandate in the 2009 presidential election. Many credible candidates—from former President Zéroual to MRN leader Djaballah and Sadi for the RCD—as well as political forces such as the FFS and former Ettahadi, which had been renamed the Mouvement Démocratique et Social (MDS—Democratic and Social Movement) in 1998, abstained from running. As expected, Bouteflika achieved a landslide victory in the 2009 poll, obtaining 90.2% of the votes, while Hanoune for the PT took 4.5%, Moussa Touati for the right-wing Front National Algérien (FNA—Algerian National Front) 2.0%, former MRN leader Djahid Younsi 1.5%, independent Mohamed Said 0.9% and Rebaine for Ahd 54 just 0.8%.

FROM BOUTEFLIKA FOR LIFE TO GROWING SOCIAL MOBILIZATION

After scarcely more than a year, Bouteflika's third presidential term faced the serious threat of the 2010–11 uprisings, commonly known as the 'Arab Spring', which engulfed almost the entire Middle East and North Africa region. However, owing to a low level of social mobilization and an extremely fragmented political environment in which opposition forces distrusted one another as much as they distrusted the regime, Algeria's protest movement remained weak. The regime exploited this situation and reacted quickly to prevent the spread of social discontent by deploying the security forces en masse onto the streets, announcing a reversal of the recent high price increases on food items and lifting the state of emergency that had been in place for 19 years on 22 February 2011. Finally, a US $25,000m. plan, promising more social housing, higher public sector salaries and larger subsidies for basic goods, was announced in April. In this way, Bouteflika and his regime weathered the storm; however, the political context became increasingly challenging for them. Mass uprisings in neighbouring countries had shown that apparently undefeatable autocrats could be brought down in a few weeks. The established Algerian opposition forces tried to exploit this situation in the 2012 legislative elections.

After about a decade during which the FFS had boycotted all electoral contests, Aït Ahmed's party announced that it would participate in the May 2012 parliamentary elections, and the main Islamist parties launched the Alliance de l'Algérie Verte (AAV—Green Alliance of Algeria). Both the FLN and the RND lost votes, but, owing to the use of proportional representation and a very high level of party fragmentation, the two parties actually increased their number of seats (to 221 and 70 seats, respectively), achieving an overall majority in the enlarged 462-seat National People's Assembly. The AAV did not perform particularly well, obtaining 47 seats, while the FFS won 21, the PT 17 and Abdallah Djaballah's newly founded Front de la Justice et du Développement (FJD—Justice and Development Front) just seven. A few months after the elections Abdelmalek Sellal, who had held several cabinet posts between 1995 and 2012, replaced Ahmed Ouyahia as Prime Minister, remaining in office until 2017. In April 2013 Bouteflika suffered from a debilitating stroke that made him reliant on a wheelchair and raised rumours about his capacity to rule. For several months speculation about the President being on the verge of complete incapacitation through ill health, but no such downturn actually took place. Rather, the various apparatuses of the regime, incapable of reaching agreement on a new candidate for the presidency, decided to support Bouteflika's bid for a fourth mandate in the 2014 presidential election, hoping that an ill and weak President would increase their room for manoeuvre. To contest this decision, a new movement Barakat (Enough) was formed in early March 2014. In the 45 days or so between its foundation and the holding of the election, Barakat tried to mobilize in the streets on no less than six occasions, but attracted few participants. On 17 April there were no surprises when the results were announced: 81.5% of those who took part in the poll (on a turnout of 51.7% of the electorate) voted for Bouteflika; 12.2% for Ali Benflis, Bouteflika's former Prime Minister (who had become mildly critical of the regime since standing down); 3.3% for former FLN deputy Abdelaziz Belaïd, who had founded the pro-regime Front El-Moustakbal (Future Front) in 2012; 1.4% for Hanoune (PT); 1.0% for Ali Fawzi Rebaine (Ahd 54); and 0.6% for Touati (FNA). All the main opposition parties, such as the Kabylia-based FFS and RCD, as well as the moderate Islamist MSP, Ennahda and FJD, boycotted the presidential election. Bouteflika's fourth and final term as Algerian President was marked by three main issues: the 2016 constitutional reform, the outbreak of a severe economic and fiscal crisis, and the development of a long series of social and labour protests.

In February 2016 important amendments to the 1996 Constitution, already partly revised in 2008, were approved by the National People's Assembly. For the first time Tamazight was recognized as one of the country's official languages and the two-term presidential limit, which had been previously abolished to allow Bouteflika to run for a third mandate in 2009, was reintroduced. Under development since 2011 to meet the popular expectations raised by the Arab uprisings, the partial reform of the Constitution was also an attempt to show the supposedly reformist character of a regime that was suffering from a deep economic crisis. During Bouteflika's presidency Algeria's economy remained heavily dependent on the oil and gas sectors, which accounted for about 97% of Algeria's exports, two-thirds of government spending and one-third of the country's GDP. When oil prices declined in the mid-2010s, macroeconomic indicators deteriorated rapidly. This situation forced the Government to approve a package of austerity measures, ranging from the freezing of public wage increases during 2011–16 to the introduction of a pension reform in November 2016 that raised the retirement age from 55 to 60 years. In reaction to these measures, social mobilization increased dramatically during Bouteflika's fourth mandate, involving four main actors: public sector workers in education, health and transport who mobilized through independent trade unions; industrial workers in some of the remaining huge state-owned factories created during Boumedienne's state-led development; the lower classes of the south who protested against fracking activities; and workers operating in the strategic oil and gas sectors.

The May 2017 legislative elections, however, did not really reflect the growing ferment within Algerian society. Although the FLN lost 60 seats, it remained the largest parliamentary party with 161 seats, and the RND's representation increased from 70 to 100 seats. Moreover, the regime enjoyed the support of two other parties—the Rassemblement de l'Espoir pour l'Algérie (Rally for Hope for Algeria), founded by former MSP member Amar Ghoul in 2012, and the Mouvement Populaire Algérien (Algerian Popular Movement) led by Amara Benyounès. Both Ghoul and Benyounès had served as ministers in the previous cabinet, and their parties won 20 and 13 seats, respectively. The opposition performed poorly. In the Islamist camp, the MSP obtained 34 seats and Ennahda 15, while among 'secular' forces the FFS took 14 seats, the PT 11, and the RCD nine. The official turnout was just 35.4% of registered voters, the lowest in Algeria's history. In the aftermath of the elections Bouteflika dismissed Sellal and nominated FLN loyalist and former minister Abdelmadjid Tebboune as the new Prime Minister—a position that he held for only three months. Tebboune's attempt to implement anti-corruption measures was reportedly unpopular among the upper echelons of the regime, leading to his replacement by RND leader Ahmed Ouyahia, who became Prime Minister for the fourth time.

THE HIRAK, BOUTEFLIKA'S REMOVAL AND THE CONTINUATION OF AUTHORITARIANISM

As the presidential election approached, through a message conveyed to the nation on 10 February 2019 Bouteflika formally announced his intention to run for another presidential term. Although the announcement had largely been expected, the subsequent attempt by leading social and political groups to rally support for a President who had completely disappeared from the public scene since 2013 sparked a strong and autonomous reaction from below. A wave of minor protests took place in various parts of the country between 11 and 19 February 2019. In an effort to capitalize on this growing political ferment, the Mouwatana (Citizenship) movement, which had been established in June 2018 to contest the possibility of Bouteflika seeking a fifth term in the presidency, announced a demonstration on 24 February 2019. Hundreds of thousands of Algerians, however, independently took to the streets two days before, starting the popular protest movement known as the Hirak, which led to Bouteflika's fall in scarcely over a month. The Hirak staged million-strong protests in all of Algeria's main cities on Fridays, and the student movement protested every Tuesday. A five-day general strike from 10 March tilted the balance of power in favour of the opposition, and on 11 March Bouteflika was compelled to announce the indefinite postponement of the presidential election and his intention not to run. Realizing that the protest movement was not ebbing, recognizing that the political system was not able to solve the crisis, and fearing that the support that the Seventh Armoured Brigade had publicly given to the uprising could affect other units, the military took the initiative, declaring Bouteflika 'unfit to rule' and removing him from office on 2 April. He died in political isolation in September 2021.

After Bouteflika's removal from office, the President of the Council of the Nation, Abdelkader Bensalah, became Algeria's acting President, while Ahmed Gaïd Salah, deputy defence minister and Chief of Staff of the Algerian army since 2004, briefly emerged as Algeria's strongman, until his sudden death in December 2019. Despite the arrest of high-ranking politicians, tycoons and Bouteflika's relatives, as well as an attempt by the authorities to co-opt more moderate parts of the protest movement, the Hirak continued to mobilize every Friday, demanding the demilitarization of the country, social justice and genuine democracy. It was in this context that the military was forced to postpone the presidential election from 4 July to 12 December. Despite an active boycott by all opposition forces, with protests staged outside polling stations, the election was eventually held. The official turnout was 39.9% of registered voters, and the five candidates who took part in the poll were all part of the political establishment. A former Prime Minister and the army's preferred choice, Abdelmadjid Tebboune, was elected President with 58.2% of the votes cast, defeating former tourism minister and one of the founders in 2013 of the Mouvement El-Bina (or National Construction Movement), Abdelkader Bengrina (17.4%), former Prime Minister and leader of Talaie El-Houriat, Ali Benflis (10.6%), former culture minister and RND's acting Secretary-General, Azzedine Mihoubi (7.3%), and leader of the Front El-Moustakbal, Abdelaziz Belaïd (6.7%). In late December 2019 Tebboune appointed university professor Abdelaziz Djerad as Prime Minister, and a new cabinet was inaugurated in early January 2020. Despite this, the Hirak and the student movement continued to stage weekly protests (on Fridays and Tuesdays, respectively). It was only the outbreak of the coronavirus disease (COVID-19) pandemic that forced the protest movement to suspend street demonstrations in March.

The regime took full advantage of the unprecedented situation. In early 2020 President Tebboune had already established a commission comprising 17 experts tasked with proposing revisions to the Constitution. The authorities now even more pushed the project as representing the first step in Tebboune's attempt to build a supposedly new Algeria. In May the commission, led by Ahmed Laraba, a member of the International Law Commission at the United Nations, published a pre-draft document of the revised Constitution. The proposed amendments reinforced the role of Islam as the religion of the state and promised to strengthen the separation of powers between the executive and the legislature, to enhance the independence of the judiciary and to combat corruption. The reforms proposed modifying the existing presidential system to transform it into a semi-presidential model and to give parliament the power to dismiss the Prime Minister or head of government by means of a vote of no confidence. However, the powers of the President remained extensive. Two significant aspects of the proposed amendments are worth mentioning in this regard: first is the fact that the President would be empowered to veto legislation by demanding that draft laws be read once again. This would then require approval by either a two-thirds' majority in the National People's Assembly or by a three-quarters' majority in the Council of the Nation; this latter threshold would be difficult for the Council of the Nation to achieve, as one-third of its members are directly appointed by the President and would therefore be unlikely to vote for any measure that contravened his wishes. Second, under the amended Constitution, the President's role as head of the Conseil Supérieur de la Magistrature (CSM—Superior Council of the Judiciary) was constitutionalized, and he would maintain firm control over the courts, with the power to appoint and dismiss judges without seeking the approval of parliament. Among the most notable other reforms that the commission proposed were: expanding the two-term limit on the presidency to encompass both consecutive terms (as reintroduced in 2016) and non-consecutive terms; restricting members of the National People's Assembly to a maximum of two terms; and reversing a founding principle of post-independence Algeria by permitting, for the first time, Algerian armed forces to be deployed outside national territory in order to support international peacekeeping missions.

Various groups, such as the Hirak and the recently formed Forces du Pacte de l'Alternative Démocratique (FPAD—Forces of the Pact of the Democratic Alternative—a broad coalition of associations, civil society groups, intellectuals and secular parties including the RCD, the FFS, the MDS, the PT, the Union pour le Changement et le Progrès (UCP—Union for Change and Development) and the Parti Socialiste des Travailleurs (PST—Socialist Workers' Party), strongly criticized the draft Constitution, both in terms of the contents of the proposed amendments and the way in which they had been presented. They contended that by selecting a small group of experts, President Tebboune had chosen to revise the Constitution in a clearly undemocratic way. Moreover, the draft had been published at a time when the Algerian authorities were taking advantage of the COVID-19 pandemic to increase repression against political activists, trade unionists and journalists, including certain online independent media, such as *Maghreb Emergent* and Radio M. The Council of Ministers and both houses of parliament none the less approved the constitutional reforms in September 2020, and they were submitted to a popular referendum, scheduled for 1 November—a date that symbolically marks the outbreak of Algeria's war of liberation against France. In a clear attempt to present himself and his Government as heirs of the anti-colonial war, Tebboune used the slogan 'November 1954: liberation. November 2020: change'. The Hirak, the FPAD, civil rights groups and Islamist parties called for a boycott of the referendum. The opposition was no less eager to frame their struggle as a new liberation movement, drawing a parallel between the pro-independence mobilization against France's domination and their attempt to liberate Algeria from a coterie of rapacious capitalists, foreign multinational companies, corrupt politicians and powerful generals. In total, 66.8% of those who took part in the referendum approved the proposed reforms. In the event, the official turnout was just 23.1%, but as no minimum rate of participation was required for the proposals to be enacted, the Constitution was duly amended.

In early 2021 the pro-democracy movement took to the streets again after a hiatus of about a year. The chosen date for the first mass demonstration was 22 February, the second anniversary of the first public protests by the Hirak. However, following the resumption of anti-regime protests, the Hirak was unable seriously to threaten authoritarian institutions, owing to a lower rate of participation in demonstrations and harsh repression by the regime. Between February and July more than 6,000 anti-Government activists and protesters were detained, and from May a large police presence in the streets, especially in Algiers, prevented the Hirak from staging protests in many cities. The regime's repression of protests escalated at a time when a deep economic crisis, owing to the COVID-19 pandemic and a global fall in oil prices, prompted demonstrations by ordinary working Algerians, but made social or economic concessions from the Government impossible.

In February 2021, as part of a strategy aimed at consolidating his power, President Tebboune dissolved the National People's Assembly and scheduled early legislative elections for June; groups that actively campaigned to boycott the vote were repressed. On 14 May, in a repeat of the fate that the PT's leader Hanoune had suffered in 2019, several dozen journalists and political activists were arrested, including the leaders of the RCD, the MDS and the FFS. A few days later, the Mouvement pour l'Autodétermination de la Kabylie (Movement for the Self-determination of Kabylia) was declared a terrorist organization. The Algerian authorities also sought the dissolution of the PST, the UCP and the civil society organization Rassemblement Actions Jeunesse (Youth Action Rally). In such a context, legislative elections took place on 12 June 2021. For the first time since the outbreak of the Hirak protests, the major Islamist parties, including the MSP and the FJD, broke with other anti-regime parties, which had implicitly coalesced around the issue of rejecting regime-orchestrated initiatives, by taking part in the elections. This was not enough, however, to activate popular participation. The official turnout was the lowest in Algeria's history and failed to reach the threshold of 23% of registered voters. In Kabylia, less than 1% of the adult population went to the polls. The fact that about four-fifths of the votes cast were for independent candidates provided further evidence of the popular rejection of the regime-led political transition. One of the effects of this was that parties that received very limited electoral support gained significant parliamentary representation. The FLN received the largest number of votes of any party (although it secured just 6.2% of the total), yet it won 98 seats (almost one-quarter of the total of 407). The MSP took 65 seats, followed by the RND with 58, the Front El-Moustakbal with 48 and the Mouvement El-Bina with 39, while independent candidates won a record 84 seats. In the wake of the elections, Prime Minister Djerad announced his resignation. Tebboune appointed the Minister of Finance Aïmen Benabderrahmane as the new premier (while retaining the finance portfolio). In July Benabderrahmane formed a cabinet comprising 33 ministers, about two-thirds of whom were technocrats without party affiliation.

As part of the process of institutionalizing his regime, Tebboune's third and final step—after the constitutional referendum in November 2020 and the parliamentary elections in June 2021—was to hold local and regional elections in November 2021. According to official data, turnout at the polls was higher than in the recent legislative elections, recorded at 36.5% and 34.8% of eligible voters, respectively. The FLN finished in first place in the local elections, obtaining 5,978 seats and an overall majority in 124 communes, and the RND came second, with 4,584 seats. The lists of independents came third, with 4,430 seats, followed by the Front El-Moustakbal with 3,262 seats, the Mouvement El-Bina with 1,848 and the MSP with 1,820. At the regional level, the results were similar. The FLN finished in first place (471 seats), followed by the RND (366 seats), the Front El-Moustakbal (304 seats), the MSP (239 seats), the Mouvement El-Bina (230 seats) and independents (100 seats). After the participation of Islamist parties in the legislative elections in June 2021, the anti-regime front lost two additional parties from its boycott, upon the decision of the FFS and the PT to participate in the local and regional elections. However, both parties performed poorly: notably, the FFS lost seats in its traditional strongholds in Kabylia, despite the fact that the party's main rival, the RCD, boycotted the vote.

The formation of a new Government did not result in any moderation of regime repression against critical voices. A notable example of this was the arrest in July 2021 of opposition leader and head of the left-wing MDS Fethi Ghares. As of October 2022, according to the US-based non-governmental organization Human Rights Watch, the Algerian authorities continued to hold at least 250 political activists, most of them associated with the Hirak. In a clear sign of the regime's growing authoritarianism, in April 2022 the liberal-orientated, French-language newspaper *Liberté* was forced to close after 30 years, as a result of the ownership's independent editorial line. The owner of the newspaper, Issad Rebrab, had been sentenced to 18 months in prison in January 2020, having already spent eight months in pre-trial detention. It is likely that judicial proceedings against Rebrab were carried out first and foremost as retaliation against his participation in the Hirak protests in March 2019. In December 2022 the Algerian authorities also forced Radio M, one of the very few remaining independent media outlets in the country, to close. In April 2023 Radio M's director, Ihsane El Kadi, was found guilty of receiving undeclared funds from abroad and sentenced to five years in prison (increased to seven years following an appeal in June). This growing authoritarianism also targeted workers and trade unions. In late 2022 the Government announced its intention to introduce a new labour law, which was subsequently ratified by parliament in March 2023. This increased the legal requirements for the establishment of a public sector trade union and made it more difficult for unions to initiate strike action, especially in sectors regarded as strategic. In reaction to the Government's crackdown, independent trade unions called for a national strike, while the traditionally pro-regime UGTA also took a critical stance towards the new law. In apparent retaliation, several UGTA officials were subsequently charged by the authorities with embezzling public funds. Meanwhile, the detention of Amira Bouraoui, one of the most prominent figures in the Hirak, by the Tunisian authorities in February 2023 prompted an international crisis that was only resolved when the French authorities intervened and helped her to avoid extradition to Algeria by granting her safe passage to France, despite protests by the Algerian Government.

Another sign of the growing confidence of the regime was a general tendency to reduce the sentences of leading political figures from the Bouteflika era, as illustrated by the cases of Bouteflika's brother Saïd, former Prime Ministers Ouyahia and Sellal, and UGTA's leader, Abdelmadjid Sidi Saïd. One of the reasons that helps to explain this new course is the rapid improvement in Algeria's economic situation. Hydrocarbons prices started to recover in 2021, and they rose dramatically after the Russian invasion of Ukraine in February 2022. Algeria benefited twice over, enjoying higher revenues from hydrocarbons exports as well as urgent requests for oil and gas from Western European countries seeking to reduce their dependence on Russian hydrocarbons.

In March 2023 Tebboune announced a major cabinet reorganization, affecting 11 portfolios. Most notably, after months of reciprocal distrust, the President replaced the Minister of Foreign Affairs, Ramtane Lamamra, with Ahmed Attaf, who had previously served in this position during the 1990s.

At mid-2023 the legitimacy of the new regime in the eyes of the general populace remained weak and superficial. The opportunity of a genuine movement towards democracy that the emergence of the Hirak presented in 2019 had dissipated, and Algeria's authoritarian institutions and actors—first and foremost, the very powerful armed forces—remained the kingmakers of the system. This does not mean, however, that there are no monumental challenges looming on the horizon for Tebboune and his allies. The country remains overdependent on hydrocarbons revenue, the rate of unemployment is very high, especially among the young, corruption is rampant, and the political system appears unable to respond to popular demands for social and economic change. In addition, Algeria's international position is challenging. On the one hand, its financial stability remains deeply dependent on selling oil and gas to European countries. In so doing, however, Algeria has essentially adopted a position of subordination towards more economically developed countries by exporting raw materials and importing high value-added finished products. On the other hand, in a gradual attempt to delink its economic development from Europe, Algeria has sought to increase economic engagement with Russia and the People's Republic of China. Nevertheless, the Government will have to move cautiously in this direction, since it risks crossing red lines and jeopardizing its relationship with the West. In November 2022 Algeria and China signed a five-year strategic co-operation plan, which was shortly followed by an executive plan for joint development under China's Belt and Road Initiative. While the Algerian-Chinese relationship is mostly economic, the ties between Algeria and Russia are predominantly focused on political and military co-operation. Like many other countries in the 'Global South', Algeria took an independent position on the war in Ukraine, expressing neither support for the Russian invasion nor condemnation. Algeria adopted this posture because of its concerns over two vital national interests. The first was related to Algeria's desire to join the BRICS (Brazil, Russia,

India, China and South Africa) grouping of rapidly developing countries. Tebboune visited Russia in June 2023 and appealed for an acceleration of Algeria's accession process. Secondly, Algeria's armed forces are heavily dependent on military equipment supplied by Russia. In 2023 Algeria was the third largest importer of Russian weapons in the world. Bilateral military co-operation had been further strengthened in November 2022 after Algeria signed a contract with Russia to purchase arms supplies worth between US $12,000m. and $17,000m.

This significant military investment has to be considered in the context of the rising diplomatic tensions between Algeria and Morocco over the past few years. The long-lasting Western Sahara conflict between Morocco and the Polisario Front, whose armed campaign for independence is supported by Algeria, arguably remains the single most important issue. Recently, however, other areas of dispute between the two countries have arisen. In July 2021, for instance, Algeria recalled its ambassador from Rabat, the Moroccan capital, to protest against the declaration in favour of Kabylia's independence made by Moroccan diplomats during a meeting of the Non-Aligned Movement in New York, USA, a few days earlier. Furthermore, recently established military co-operation, as well as formal diplomatic ties, between Israel and Morocco is threatening Algeria's leading military position in the region. In November the Israeli Minister of Defense, Benny Gantz, and his Moroccan counterpart, Abdellatif Loudiyi, signed the first ever memorandum of understanding on defence and security between the two countries. As a result of this development, Morocco could eventually overtake Algeria's military capacity in sectors such as electronic warfare and unmanned combat aerial vehicles (drones), which are proving to be of strategic importance in the Ukraine war. Mounting tensions between the two North African countries reached a new high in January 2022, when Morocco established an additional military zone bordering Algeria, which, in response, began increasingly to target Morocco's strong dependence on energy imports. In April Algeria threatened to terminate its natural gas export agreement with Spain if any Algerian gas were routed to Morocco. Moreover, the announcement in June of the Spanish Government's decision to support Morocco's position in the Western Sahara dispute provoked a major diplomatic and economic crisis between Algeria and Spain, which at mid-2023 was still unresolved. At that time, however, the outbreak of hostilities between Algeria and Morocco remained unlikely, and there were tentative signs of a rapprochement between the two countries, such as Algeria inviting King Mohammed VI of Morocco to attend the League of Arab States (Arab League) summit that it hosted in November 2022. Nevertheless, ongoing competition in the military sphere was expected to continue, especially since Algeria and Morocco were on opposite sides of the international schism between the West on the one hand and Russia and China on the other. These international tensions could escalate, potentially forcing Algeria and Morocco to spend additional resources on bolstering their armed forces and thereby undermining their overall economic development and social welfare.

Economy

ROBERT E. LOONEY

INTRODUCTION

Algeria is the sixth largest economy in the Middle East and North Africa, slightly larger than Qatar, but smaller than Iraq. With a population of 44.9m. in 2022, Algeria is the third most populous country in the Arab world, behind Sudan (46.9m.), but ahead of Iraq (42.2m.). As with many hydrocarbon-based economies, economic growth has been volatile. The economy expanded at an average annual rate of 2.1% during 1980–89, declining to 1.9% during 1991–2001 as a result of civil war and unrest. With the end of the civil war and the advent of a commodity supercycle, the average annual rate of growth increased to 3.7% during 2002–14. A reduction in oil prices in 2014, and a further decline in 2020, combined with the coronavirus disease (COVID-19) pandemic, resulted in growth slowing to an average of 1.5% per year during 2015–22.

On a purchasing power parity (PPP) basis, per capita income (in 2017 international dollars) was US $9,013 in 1980. However, by 2001 per capita income had declined to $8,848. Partly owing to a commodity boom, per capita income reached $11,263 in 2014, declining to $10,897 by 2022. Per capita income contracted by an average of 0.1% annually during 1980–90, remained constant during 1991–2001, increased by an average of 1.9% per year during 2002–14 and contracted at an average annual rate of 0.4% during 2015–22. Over the entire period of 1980–2022 per capita income averaged growth of only 0.5% per year.

Despite many attempts at diversification, Algeria's dependence on hydrocarbons is increasing. Oil rent alone (revenue minus production costs) accounted for 14.8% of gross domestic product (GDP) during 1980–2001, rising to 19.6% in 2002–22. Hydrocarbons also dominate exports, with the country's top three exports being hydrocarbon-based. In 2021 Algeria's exports of liquefied petroleum gas (LPG) totalled US $14,300m., of crude petroleum $10,700m. and of refined petroleum $6,230m.

In contrast to most emerging economies, agriculture has increased its share of GDP, rising from 6.2% in 1980 to 9.0% in 2000 and 11.9% in 2022. Industry (including construction, oil and manufacturing) contributed 42.2% of GDP in 1980, increasing to 58.1% in 2000 before declining to 44.1% in 2022. The contribution of the services sector to overall output in Algeria also deviated from the norm seen in most developing countries by not following a steadily upward trajectory. Services accounted for 51.6% of GDP in 1980, 32.9% in 2000 and 44.0% in 2022. Although agriculture has increased its share of GDP in recent years, employment in the sector declined from 22.3% of the labour force in 2000 to 11.9% in 2010 and to 10.3% in 2021. The corresponding figures for industry were 24.9%, 30.2% and 31.0%, respectively, while the services sector expanded its share of the labour force from 52.8% in 2000 to 57.9% in 2010 and to 58.6% in 2021.

The industrial sector has experienced a series of difficulties, characterized by the obsolescence of the production base, underutilized production capacities, poor productivity rates, and low competitiveness compared with imported products.

The composition of GDP expenditures has also experienced significant shifts in recent years. Most significantly, exports averaged 34.2% of GDP in 2002–14, but this figure declined to 21.2% in 2015–22. Also significant was an increase in investment from an average of 33.0% of GDP in 2002–14 to 42.5% in 2015–22, while over the same period the share of private consumption increasing from 36.4% to 42.2%. Lesser shifts were registered in government consumption, which increased from an average of 20.3% of GDP in 2002–14 to 21.9% in 2015–22, and in the share of imports, which rose from 27.5% to 28.6%.

The COVID-19 pandemic caused significant disruption in Algeria in 2020, with GDP contracting by 5.1% in that year, as public health restrictions weakened industrial and household demand. In addition, a sharp decline in global oil prices adversely affected government finances. However, the recovery of oil prices following the easing of strict COVID-19 restrictions in 2021–22, and the boycotts of oil exports from the Russian Federation by Western nations during 2022 enabled the Government to reverse several negative trends that followed the 2014 oil price decline and the COVID-19 pandemic.

None the less, popular discontent lingers. In response to recent demonstrations against the Government, the authorities will probably increase spending on social programmes and welfare benefits, especially given current inflationary pressures and food shortages owing to global supply chain disruptions. However, the underlying causes of the anti-Government protests remain unresolved, creating an ongoing risk of further social unrest.

THE DEMOGRAPHIC SITUATION

As in many other countries in the Middle East and North Africa, Algeria has experienced rapid population growth over the last several decades. As a result, the country's population is relatively young, with large numbers entering the workforce. Job creation will be critical for maintaining social stability. During the 1960s Algeria's population grew at an average annual rate of 2.7%, increasing to 2.9% in the 1970s and 3.0% in the 1980s. However, during the 1990s, civil war and high rates of emigration caused population growth to decrease to a yearly average of 2.0%. During 2002–14 average annual growth declined further, to 1.7%, before increasing to 1.9% in 2015–21.

Changes in the population growth rate followed the same trend as the birth rate: a decrease from 30.5 live births per 1,000 people in 1970 to 19.7 live births per 1,000 people in 2002, increasing to an average of 24.9 live births per 1,000 people during 2015–21. The crude death rate per 1,000 people averaged 4.6 in 2015–21, while the infant mortality rate (per 1,000 live births) averaged 20.5% over the same period.

The decline in the fertility rate stems primarily from improvements in women's socioeconomic status, particularly their education level, their place in the family and in society, and their access to contraceptive methods. The authorities' desire to control the birth rate has also played a significant role. Among the factors relating to the status of women, educational levels are fundamental. Indeed, as Algerian women have become better educated, the better they have become informed about the means of managing their fertility.

By 2021 30.7% of the population were aged 0–14 years, up from 28.7% in 2015. A total of 63.1% were in the working-age group, aged 15–64 years, down from 65.9% in 2015. Those aged 65 years and older comprised 6.2% of the population, compared with 5.4% in 2015. With its birth rates and age structure, the country is expected to experience a 'demographic dividend', with a larger share of the population in the working-age group. The percentage of those aged 15–64 years is forecast to reach 66.2% of the population by 2040. However, by 2050, the working-age population is predicted to decline to 62.7% of the total population.

These forecasts are always subject to change, however, with one crucial factor being migration. Migration between Algeria and France has historically had a special status in terms of its scale and specific migratory regime. France is the primary destination for Algerian migrants, although, in the last 30 years, there has been some diversification towards the United Kingdom, Germany, Spain, Belgium and Canada.

Algeria had a unique status in the French Empire. Before independence in 1962, Algerians were—in theory—French citizens benefiting from freedom of movement across the Mediterranean. Since 1962 Algerians have held a special status of ambiguous benefit to those seeking to move temporarily or permanently to France. This status has included bilateral agreements which mean that Algerians are not subject to some immigration controls and they have access to specific migratory routes not available to other foreigners. Many Algerians, however, have not benefited from these exceptions and have been subject to arbitrary administrative decisions because they do not come under the standard rules.

Since the late 1960s France has increasingly limited Algerian immigration (as part of a broader reduction in immigration), and since the late 1980s has brought the migratory regime applied to Algerians more in line with that of other foreigners.

Mass labour migration (beyond limited seasonal work and highly qualified professionals) ended in the 1970s. Today, family reunification and higher education are the principal routes to permanent migration. In 2020, of a total of 30,579 first residence permits issued to Algerians in the European Union (EU), 59% were for family reasons and 23% for educational reasons. Remnants of the French patchwork of previous rules and practices, however, do still apply and take on heightened importance in a context in which the usual routes to migration involve increasing conditions and costs, as well as the likelihood of refusal.

An announcement in September 2021 that France planned to reduce by 50% the number of visas given to Algerians (as well as Tunisians and Moroccans) was issued in response to the Algerian Government's reluctance to participate in forcible repatriations of its citizens. The action was also aimed at appealing to domestic audiences in the run-up to the April 2022 French presidential election.

In November 2021 French interior minister Gérald Darmanin announced that 31% of Algerian visa requests had been rejected in January–August (10,828 of 34,169), and that approximately 50% had been denied (11,867 of 24,474) since the announcement in September that visas would be reduced. These statistics likely represent only a fraction of the Algerians who want a visa but cannot obtain one.

For the most desperate, there are illegal border crossings, which increased across the Mediterranean in 2021 following an initial decline driven by COVID-19 travel restrictions. Algerian nationals comprised 11% of detected illegal border crossings into the EU in 2020, the third largest nationality after Syrians and Moroccans, and a growing percentage of the total. Undocumented Algerians living in Europe are also increasing, in contrast to the more stable figures for undocumented Moroccans and Tunisians. Algerians were the main nationality issued deportation orders from the EU in 2020 (8.6% of the total). The sociological profile of undocumented migrants attempting illegal border crossings is also shifting. Previously dominated by poorer young men with only primary or secondary education, it is now more likely to include university students, women and children.

THE LABOUR MARKET

The growth of the Algerian labour force has failed to keep pace with that of the total population, with average annual rates of expansion of 3.3% in 1991–2002, 1.6% in 2003–14 and 1.5% in 2015–22. This slowdown did not stem from a decline in the labour participation rate, which has been relatively stable at 46.5% of the total population aged 15–64 years in 1980–2001 and 44.7% in 2002–21. However, the participation rates of females and males have changed. The male participation rate averaged 79.3% in 1980–2001, falling to 72.2% in 2002–21. For females, the corresponding rates were 12.4% and 16.0%.

Structural Shifts

Several notable shifts in the labour force occurred between 2003 and 2019. First, there was an increase in the share of female permanent (by 4.0 percentage points) and non-permanent (by 8.4 percentage points) employees. The share of women in the employer/self-employed sector and the unpaid family worker sector decreased by 7.8 percentage points and 4.6 percentage points, respectively. The share of men in the employer/self-employed sector increased by 5.5 percentage points, although the share in permanent employment decreased by 4.9 percentage points.

Second, between 2003 and 2019 the share of the employed population who had completed higher education increased by 3.8 percentage points for men and by 19.3 percentage points for women. Meanwhile, the share of uneducated workers and those with only a primary school education decreased for both men and women.

Third, during this period net annual job creation did not always rise. International factors strongly influence the local labour market. Indeed, during 2007–09 (the global financial crisis), 2011 (the beginning of the 'Arab Spring' protests) and 2014 (a decline in demand from European markets and a sharp reduction in oil prices) the Algerian economy shed jobs. In 2019 the agricultural, industrial and construction sectors recorded job losses of 63,000, 40,000 and 11,000, respectively. In contrast, the commerce/services and administration sectors created 101,000 and 243,000 jobs, respectively, in that year.

Significant shifts in the structure of Algeria's labour force occurred between 1991 and 2021. During this time, the agricultural sector's share of employment decreased from 23.8% of the employed population to just 10.3%. Over the same period, industry's share increased from 25.6% to 31.0%, while the services sector's share increased from 50.6% to 58.6%.

Patterns of Unemployment

Unemployment in Algeria has gone through three distinct phases since the mid-1960s. The first lasted from 1966 to 1985—the 'pre-crisis' period, during which the unemployment rate decreased considerably from 34% to less than 10%. During this period there was massive recruitment by public companies. Algeria established co-operation agreements for labour migration with several countries, most notably France, managed by the Office National Algérien de la Main-d'Oeuvre (ONAMO—National Manpower Office), which was created by decree in November 1962. Its primary function was to manage the migration of Algerian workers to France and the German Democratic Republic (East Germany). In 1990 ONAMO was succeeded by the Agence National de l'Emploi (National Employment Agency).

The second distinct phase lasted from 1986 until 1996: this was a period of crisis prompted by the decline in hydrocarbons prices in 1986, which led to a slowdown of the Algerian economy; production capacity fell to 30%, and companies reduced their operations and stopped recruiting, which resulted in an increase in unemployment. The onset of the civil war from 1991 only exacerbated this trend.

The third distinct phase began in 1997: this was the post-crisis period, during which the unemployment rate decreased considerably because of a period of global expansion, especially in Algeria's principal export markets. Domestically, the economic climate benefited from a ceasefire in the civil war (which eventually ended in 2002). The overall unemployment rate declined considerably during 2003–22, from 23.7% to 11.6%. The unemployment rate among people aged 15–24 years, which was significantly higher than for adults (25 years and older), decreased from 43.8% in 2003 to 29.0% in 2022. However, the unemployment rate of females aged 15–24 increased from 39.8% in 2003 to 47.8% in 2022, while the corresponding rate for males in this age group decreased from 44.5% to 24.9%.

In 2022 unemployment rates were likely substantially higher than official figures suggested. Many young people had given up looking for formal employment and were thus labelled inactive in the official employment statistics. Frustration with the lack of employment opportunities, particularly in the south and other more geographically isolated areas, will continue to generate social unrest. Even among the employed, poor wage growth and a lack of career opportunities have led to rising labour unrest, especially as emigration has become increasingly complex, with more restrictive policies in the EU towards migrants.

Education and Gender Factors

Historically, graduates have found jobs quickly. However, in recent years the situation has changed, with graduate unemployment rates increasing. This situation stems partly from a significant rise in higher education enrolment and weak employment opportunities, especially for university graduates. For higher education graduates, the unemployment rate was 18.0% in 2017; however, the rate was 23.9% for women, compared with only 11.0% for men.

For women, the unemployment rate systematically increases in line with level of education. However, for men, the rate decreases for those educated to secondary and higher levels. Nevertheless, the overall unemployment rate of individuals who have completed higher education remains higher than that of individuals who have completed their education only to primary level or who have little education.

Although the unemployment rate had declined overall by 2019, the level of unemployment among members of the labour force with higher education remained high, at 17.4%, compared with 10.6% for those who had studied up to secondary education level, 11.8% for up to middle education level, 6.8% for up to primary education level and just 3.0% for those who had undertaken no education. The situation was more pronounced for females, with the number of unemployed women with higher education qualifications having risen substantially. Women who have completed higher education are more likely to be unemployed than those who have not. For men, those with an 'average' level of education appear most likely to be unemployed.

In 2019 women were more likely to be employed in jobs in line with their level of education (54.4%) than men (48.4%). More than 22.0% of men were overqualified (23.5% of women), and 29.3% were underqualified (22.1% of women). By age, young people (15–24 years old) were more likely to be employed in jobs that aligned with their education level (61.5%) than older people. This alignment decreased with age: 56.0% of those aged 25–35 were in jobs in line with their level of education, compared with 44.1% of those aged 35–59 and 21.3% of those aged 60–64. Older people were more likely to be underqualified (72.1% of those between 60 and 64 years of age). However, workers aged 15–24 and 25–34 were most likely to be employed in jobs for which they were overqualified.

This mismatch between the level of qualification and the supply of jobs may result from two factors. First, there is pressure on the labour market, as growing numbers of young people have been entering the workforce, many of whom are better educated (there were about 300,000 graduates in 2017/18) than in the past. Second, the economy needs to create more skilled jobs to absorb the cohorts of graduates entering the labour market.

SOCIOECONOMIC PROGRESS

The 2021/22 United Nations Development Programme (UNDP) Human Development Index (HDI) ranked Algeria 91st out of the 191 countries and territories surveyed, placing it in the 'High Human Development' group. According to the HDI, life expectancy at birth in Algeria was 76.4 years in 2021, with mean years of schooling totalling an estimated 8.1 years. The country ranked 13 places higher in human development than in gross national income (GNI) per capita, suggesting that oil revenues positively contributed to the population's well-being. While there was no change in Algeria's ranking as a member of the 'High Human Development' group during 2014–21, improvements in human development appeared to be slowing, with average annual rates of progress declining from 1.1% in 2000–10 to 0.3% in 2010–21.

Algeria has one of the more equitable income distributions in the Middle East and North Africa, with a Gini coefficient (a measure of income inequality, whereby 0 signifies perfect equality and 1 maximal inequality) of 0.276 in 2010–21. During 2010–21 the poorest 40% of the population accounted for 23.1% of the nation's income, with the wealthiest 10% having 22.9% and the richest 1% controlling 9.9%. There are considerable gender differences in Algeria, with GNI per capita (2017 PPP) in 2021 being US $3,550 for females and $17,787 for males. World Bank data for 2011 placed only 0.4% of the population in poverty at the $1.90 per day rate and 3.7% at the $3.20 per day rate.

Women's average educational levels have risen sharply in recent years, and the gap in years of schooling has narrowed between women and men, with mean years of education in 2021 reaching 7.7 years for females and 8.4 years for males. The narrowing of the educational attainment gap between the sexes is even more apparent among the younger age groups. The proportion of women with higher secondary education among the younger generations (starting with the 1980 cohort) has already exceeded the ratio of men at this level of education.

Algeria was ranked 109th out of 167 countries in the Legatum Institute's 2023 Prosperity Index. Algeria's six highest rankings in the Index, which is a composite of 12 dimensions reflecting various aspects of prosperity, were in safety and security (60th), living conditions (70th), health (70th), education (92nd), infrastructure and market access (99th), and governance (107th). Areas of deficiency, mainly relating to the economy, included social capital (155th), natural environment (144th), enterprise conditions (138th), economic quality (132nd), investment environment (131st) and personal freedom (128th).

THE INFORMAL ECONOMY

Algeria's informal economy has thrived for years, and formalizing it has been a long-term aim of the country's politicians, who present this as a solution to Algeria's economic problems.

They intend to increase domestic revenue and reduce reliance on hydrocarbon exports by formalizing activities. However, this approach fails to recognize that the informal economy is more a symptom than a cause of the economy's structural weaknesses. Therefore, the authorities can only safely eliminate the informal sector once they have provided alternatives in the formal economy. The informal economy is simply too important a lifeline for Algerians unable to support themselves in the formal economy. In 2020 the informal economy accounted for 30% of economic activity and 20% of employment among non-graduate youths.

While much of the underground economy provides jobs for Algeria's unemployed youths, it also creates smuggling opportunities for many, including politicians. As a result, politicians have blocked many economic reforms because they would eliminate their lucrative underground activities.

Take the case of subsidies. Algeria's enormous subsidy programme amounts to nearly 20% of GDP. Reducing subsidies would dramatically ease budgetary pressures. To that end, the Government's 2022 budget included a provision for removing subsidies on essential food items and replacing them with individual tax breaks and means-tested benefits. The reforms were intended to address the deterioration in state finances following the slump in oil prices in 2014. The Government must enact these reforms to ensure the long-term sustainability of the country's finances. However, if implemented, the reforms would cause a significant incursion into the informal economy.

The situation presents a dilemma for the Government. In 2022 shortages of foodstuffs often stemmed from speculators buying large volumes of low-priced, subsidized goods in the informal markets to smuggle out of the country, thus perpetuating the scarcity. However, as queues for basic foodstuffs grew and more Algerians struggled to afford them, the public were likely to hold the Government accountable for the decision to end subsidies. With oil prices rising to near-record levels and the 2022 budget on course for a US $22,000m. surplus by the end of the year, the authorities were expected to postpone the removal of subsidies to limit the prices that Algerians paid.

AGRICULTURE

Algeria's agricultural sector grew at an average annual rate of 3.2% in 1980–90, rising to 5.0% in 1991–2001 and 6.8% in 2002–14, before decelerating to 2.3% in 2015–22. In 2000 the sector accounted for 9.0% of GDP, increasing to 12.6% in 2015 and 15.0% in 2020 (primarily because of the COVID-19-related decline in GDP that year). As GDP recovered, agriculture's share declined, to 13.1% in 2021 and 11.9% in 2022. In 1997 the agricultural sector employed 23.1% of the country's workforce. By 2010 agricultural employment had declined to 11.0%, decreasing further to 10.3% by 2021.

The sector faces several challenges. Poor topographical conditions and an arid climate make the cultivation of most types of agricultural goods nearly impossible. A lack of adequate irrigation infrastructure has weakened the sector's potential. Previous government-led plans to increase domestic production and reduce reliance on imports have had mixed success.

During the colonial era Algeria exported significant volumes of agricultural goods to Europe. However, after independence, the country soon became a major food importer. This shift partly stemmed from the Government's focus on industrialization and on policies that encouraged mass migration from rural areas to urban locations. The agricultural sector became neglected as a succession of administrations focused on developing the far more valuable hydrocarbons sector.

Over time, the Government took greater interest in agriculture, providing technical and economic assistance to improve grain yields. Support included interest-free loans for seeds, irrigation, equipment and other inputs, although, initially, these programmes proved ineffective. However, growth in grain production accelerated in the 1990s as new seed varieties and greater access to fertilizers and pesticides resulted in average yields increasing sharply. Despite the improvement, current Algerian wheat yields lag significantly behind other regional producers, such as Egypt. However, output per agricultural worker has improved substantially, growing at an average annual rate of 7.1% between 2000 and 2019.

Currently, the main constraints on agricultural production involve irrigation. Only around 2% of grain production receives irrigation, leaving farmers dependent on increasingly volatile weather patterns caused by climate change. While the Government has acknowledged the problem, solutions are expensive. Another obstacle to increasing grain output is farmers' poor access to credit. The state owns and leases to farmers almost 40% of Algeria's agricultural land. Smallholders own, often without official titles, most of the remaining land. Without titles, farmers are unable to access the market to invest in output-boosting resources.

Algeria is a significant cereal consumer, with wheat being the primary staple. Consumers use wheat mainly for bread and couscous. Consumption continues to expand due to increased urbanization and population growth. Wheat production in Algeria fluctuates considerably depending on the weather, and the sector has experienced several periods of growth and decline. In 1961 production was 685,723 metric tons, increasing to 1.8m. tons in 1972, before declining to 750,080 tons in 1990. Production, with large yearly fluctuations, gradually rose to reach 3.0m. tons in 2003, 3.4m. tons in 2012 and 4.0m. tons in 2018, before decreasing to 3.1m. tons in 2020. In percentage terms, wheat production increased by 9.1% in 2015, and contracted by 8.2% in 2016 and by 0.2% in 2017, before expanding by 63.4% in 2018. Owing to adverse weather conditions, production declined by 2.6% in 2019, by 19.9% in 2020 and by 30.2% in 2021, in which year production totalled 2.1m. tons.

Since 1977 wheat yields have gradually increased, albeit with wide fluctuations. In 1977 wheat yields were 4,337 hectograms per hectare (hg/ha), rising to 13,090 hg/ha in 1996 and to 19,100 hg/ha in 2013. After declining to 11,501 hg/ha in 2017, yields increased to 20,433 hg/ha in 2018. However, by 2020 yields had decreased to 16,811 hg/ha.

Maize production in Algeria also fluctuates widely. In 1961 maize production reached 5,689 metric tons, rising to 6,718 tons in 1975. Production declined rapidly thereafter to reach 231 tons in 1990, rising to 2,456 tons in 2006, before decreasing to 359 tons in 2010. Production rose to 6,369 tons in 2019, but contracted by 49.4% in 2020 to 3,223 tons. Year-to-year fluctuations in maize output are more extreme than wheat production, with a growth rate of 32.0% in 2016, followed by a contraction of 28.6% in 2017. Production increased by 109.3% in 2018 and by 15.5% in 2019. With maize consumption averaging around 4.5m. tons per year during 2018–20 and annual output totalling approximately 5,000 tons, the country depended on imports for more than 99% of its consumption requirements.

Barley production also exhibits wide fluctuations around a gradually increasing trend. In 1961 Algeria produced 211,919 metric tons of barley, increasing to 1.8m. tons in 1991. However, production decreased to 163,287 tons in 2000, before rising to a high of 2.2m. tons in 2009. Output declined to 919,907 tons in 2016, with subsequent growth rates of 5.4% in 2017 and 101.9% in 2018, followed by decreases of 15.8% in 2019 and 26.4% in 2020.

For major grain importers such as Algeria, Russia's invasion of Ukraine in February 2022 and the subsequent significant increase in grain prices on the global market added to inflationary pressures and raised concerns about food shortages. In response, on 13 March President Abdelmadjid Tebboune announced a ban on exports of essential staples, including cooking oils, sugar, semolina, pasta and wheat-based products.

The imposition of agribusiness export restrictions throughout 2022 further raised import costs. The United Nations' FAO Food Price Index (FFPI—a measure of the monthly change in international prices of a basket of food commodities) averaged 143.7 during the year as a whole, the highest annual average level on record; during May to December the monthly average reached 158.1. The spike in food prices raised concerns about the impact that it would have on Algeria's economic growth prospects and political and social stability. However, in December the headline FFPI had fallen to 131.8, while the price of edible oils was 42.7% lower and that of cereals 13.4% lower than in March. In year-on-year terms, food prices in December were 1.0% lower than in the same month in 2021, edible oil prices were down by 19.1%, but cereal prices were up by 4.8%.

Algeria is far from self-sufficient in a number of essential commodities. In 2022 the country was 31.7% self-sufficient in wheat, 0.0% self-sufficient in maize, 82.1% self-sufficient in barley, 21.5% self-sufficient in butter and 5.4% self-sufficient in cheese. The Government aims to reduce its annual food and grain import bill, which has been approaching the US $20,000m. mark according to the latest estimates. Multiple incentives are under way to bolster domestic self-sufficiency. The Government has been striving to increase domestic agricultural production and reduce imports. The goal of the current agriculture plan (2020–24) is to reduce imports, including those of grains, sugar, vegetable oils and milk powder, by $2,500m. To date, the Government's attempts to increase domestic production have had mixed results. For example, in its previous five-year plan (2015–19), the Government had aimed to double wheat production from 3.3m. metric tons in 2014 to almost 7.0m. tons in 2019, but output only reached 3.9m. tons in that year.

HYDROCARBONS

Algeria is a significant and established hydrocarbons producer with a mature, but substantial, oil and natural gas reserves base. However, the bulk of production lies in maturing fields, which face heavy rates of decline. Despite the recent implementation of reforms, foreign investors remain broadly unattracted to the country's licensing and fiscal regime. A high level of state intervention and enduring security concerns make the operational environment challenging. The heavily subsidized gas prices act as a deterrent to foreign investment in the upstream sector. The Government's aspirations to develop Algeria's unconventional resources remain distant, with enduring concerns over cost, water scarcity and a lack of domestic technical expertise.

The hydrocarbons sector contracted by 2.4% in 2017, 6.4% in 2018, 4.9% in 2019 and 10.2% in 2020, before recovering to grow by 10.5% in 2021 and 1.7% in 2022. During this period the non-hydrocarbons sector took a much different path, expanding by 2.3% in 2017, 2.9% in 2018 and 2.2% in 2019, contracting by 4.1% in 2020 (as a result of the COVID-19 pandemic), and returning to positive growth of 2.1% in 2021 and 3.2% in 2022.

If oil prices remain high, the hydrocarbons sector can further expand and continue to play a critical role in the economy. The country's territory remains relatively underexplored, with potential in known and frontier basins and offshore. Algeria also has extensive technically recoverable shale gas resources. In early 2022 the state-owned hydrocarbons company, Société Nationale pour la Recherche, la Production, le Transport, la Transformation et la Commercialisation des Hydrocarbures (SONATRACH), confirmed the existence of commercially viable oil and natural gas reserves at its Touggourt Est I exploration area in el-Bayadh. However, these discoveries are unlikely substantially to increase Algeria's hydrocarbons production capacity in the near term. In Touggourt, the confirmation of holdings in SONATRACH's WOEN-2 delineation well increased the total of estimated reserves in the area from 546m. barrels of oil to 961m. barrels. In el-Bayadh, west of the well-established production area of Hassi R'Mel, SONATRACH discovered new reserves with a potential output of 925 barrels per day (b/d) of oil and 6,456 cu m per day of gas.

However, these discoveries alone will not significantly affect forecasts of Algeria's hydrocarbons output, underlining the need for the country's energy authorities to increase exploration and development efforts to counter many years of under-investment in the energy sector. Investment in Algeria's gas sector will be increased because of the Russian invasion of Ukraine, which has prompted EU countries to diversify away from Russian gas supplies and seek alternative energy sources. Algeria is in a prime position to help Europe to end its dependence on Russian energy and is also actively pursuing new US interest in developing the country's hydrocarbons reserves.

Algeria possesses the world's 10th largest natural gas reserves. Before the outbreak of the war in Ukraine in February 2022, Algeria met just over 10% of the EU's gas needs. Since then, European countries have courted Algeria competitively as an existing supplier with infrastructure and corporate links across the Mediterranean. France and Italy, in particular, have engaged in intensive political outreach. French President Emmanuel Macron's visit to Algeria in August 2022 was partly prompted by France's looming energy shortages. European Council President Charles Michel visited in September, with the Algeria-EU energy dialogue being revived the following month. In January 2023 Algeria was the first overseas official visit for Italy's new Prime Minister, Giorgia Meloni; her predecessor, Mario Draghi, had visited twice in 2022.

The surge in European interest has brought Algeria new diplomatic leverage, allowing it to act from a position of economic and geopolitical confidence. This development was evident in Algeria's relations with Spain, which suffered a rift in June 2022 after Spain expressed support for Morocco's claim to the disputed territory of Western Sahara. The Algerian Government exacted a price for this shift in Spain's policy: a decrease in the volume of gas exports and a substantial increase in the contract price for the gas. Algeria's use of gas against Spain may deter other European states from adopting a similar stance vis-à-vis Western Sahara; as of mid-2023 no other state had followed Spain's lead.

The global shortage of gas and the consequent price surge has positively affected Algeria's fiscal and external balances. The 2022 budget registered a surplus of 2.1% of GDP, compared with a deficit of 7.2% in 2021, although the International Monetary Fund (IMF) predicted that the budget would return to deficits of 6%–7% of GDP over the next several years. Having recorded deficits equivalent to 12.8% of GDP in 2020 and 2.8% in 2021, the current account recorded a surplus of 7.6% of GDP in 2022 and was expected to remain in surplus in 2023.

SONATRACH's sales revenue totalled more than US $50,000m. in 2022, representing a year-on-year increase of more than 40%. Algeria used the European gas crunch to negotiate favourable new supply contracts, for example, with the French energy company ENGIE. SONATRACH also signed a contract with Italy's Eni for increased gas volumes. The agreement allowed for greater supply flexibility and a gradual rise in supply to 9,000m. cu m annually in 2023–24.

Algeria's three gas pipelines, Trans-Mediterranean (with an annual capacity of 34,000m. cu m), Trans-Saharan Gas (30,000m. cu m) and Medgaz (10,500m. cu m), have a combined total capacity of carrying 74,500m. cu m per year, and the country's liquefied natural gas (LNG) export terminals have an operational annual capacity of about 30,000m. cu m. However, as a result of decades of under-investment is that, upstream production growth has yet to keep pace with rapidly rising domestic and international demand. Consequently, there is now a push to increase oil and gas production.

Algeria now aims to attract further European investment. Even before the Russian invasion of Ukraine, new reforms (see *New Hydrocarbons Legislation*) were sufficient to persuade Eni to enter a new exploration and production sharing agreement (PSA) in December 2021. In July 2022 TotalEnergies of France and Eni, together with Occidental Petroleum Corporation of the USA, signed a PSA with SONATRACH to invest US $4,000m. in developing oil reserves in the Berkine Basin. Because of the lengthy period of time involved in progressing from discovery to production, the Algerian authorities encourage existing producers to develop 'near-field' opportunities—close to existing production infrastructure—to deliver swifter output increases. In early 2023 US oil giant Chevron became the latest hydrocarbons firm to enter talks on exploration in Algeria.

Algeria is further exploiting the allure of its gas supplies to mobilize European support in moving towards the adoption of cleaner forms of fuel—including embryonic efforts to create a hydrogen industry. In December 2022 SONATRACH signed a memorandum of understanding with German gas company VNG to co-operate in developing 'green' (renewables-based) hydrogen production in Algeria for export to Germany.

New Hydrocarbons Legislation

One of President Tebboune's first acts upon taking office in December 2019 was to approve a new hydrocarbons law. This legislation reintroduced PSAs and streamlined the fiscal framework. Algeria had struggled to attract foreign investment since the adoption of a law in 2005 that was regarded as unfavourable to the interests of international oil companies. Four previous amendments to the legislation (in 2006, 2013, 2014 and 2015) attempted to introduce more attractive provisions for foreign investors. However, these proved inadequate because they failed to improve upon the country's vague licensing terms and unfavourable tax schemes.

The new hydrocarbons legislation, which entered force in January 2020, stipulated that the state owned Algeria's oil and gas resources. It also retained the two state agencies created in 2005 to oversee domestic oil and gas activities. The Agence Nationale pour la Valorisation des Ressources en Hydrocarbures is in charge of promoting the development of hydrocarbon resources in Algeria, while the Autorité de Régulation des Hydrocarbures (ARH) oversees regulations concerning technical issues, safety and environmental standards.

Under the new legislation, every oil and gas development in Algeria would need to be preceded by an environmental impact assessment study, which would then have to be verified and approved by the ARH and the Ministry of Environment and Renewable Energy. The Ministry of Environment and Renewable Energy and the Ministry of Energy were also to be in charge of matters related to carbon credits.

The new legislation also defined the various taxes on oil and gas activities in Algeria. Most notably, it reduced the taxes and duties imposed on exploration and production activities, often blamed for deterring foreign investment in Algeria over the previous decade; these included the production levy, the petroleum income tax and the complementary income tax. The new law also removed duties and levies on most equipment imports, while providing tax exemptions for eligible professional activities in the sector.

Finally, the new legislation sought to simplify the licensing regime for upstream contractors, which had often been criticized as being too complex and ambiguous. The three types of contract now available in Algeria are: (a) Participation Agreements, in which SONATRACH holds at least a 51% interest; (b) Production Sharing Agreements, whereby international companies acquire a share of the produced oil and gas proportionate to their investment; and (c) Risk Service Agreements, whereby international companies receive fees per barrel of oil produced above a predetermined minimum level of production.

SONATRACH is continuing to work towards attracting increased investment in upstream activities. In addition, the company planned to invest US $39,000m. between 2022 and 2026, focusing on oil and gas exploration and output maintenance efforts across existing assets.

Gas Production

Algerian proven natural gas reserves increased slightly from 4,523,000m. cu m in 2000 to 4,545,000m. cu m in 2003, before declining to 4,505,000m. cu m in 2005, at around which level they remained until 2021. Output continues to be heavily dependent on the giant Hassi R'Mel field. The field is maturing, with annual production having decreased over the last few years. Underinvestment in maintaining the field and infrastructure is partly to blame. The Hassi R'Mel field was also severely overproduced in the early 2000s, which caused lasting damage to the reservoir. Work is due to be carried out to increase the reservoir pressure.

Algeria's gas production totalled 2,998m. cu m in 1970. Production increased gradually to reach 11,650m. cu m in 1980, after which output expanded rapidly, reaching 35,590m. cu m in 1983, 54,760m. cu m in 1991 and 93,860m. cu m by 2003. However, from 2003 production levelled off, decreasing to 76,600m. cu m in 2009, before reaching 93,800m. cu m in 2018. Output declined by 7.3% in 2019 and by 6.3% in 2020, but rose by 23.7% in 2021 to reach 100,770m. cu m. The sector's strong performance in 2021 was a result of gas supply shortages in Algeria's key European export markets due to low stocks, disrupted pipeline flows from Russia and a post-pandemic rebound in demand. As European nations needed to detach themselves from reliance on Russian gas, strong demand for alternative gas sources provided sufficient incentive for Algeria to maintain elevated production throughout 2022, although the annual total dipped slightly to 99,200m. cu m.

Algeria has demonstrated that it will allocate its spare production and export capacities to meet additional demand from Europe. However, the country's fields are producing at or near peak rates; thus, further output increases would need to come from new exploration. In April 2022 SONATRACH indicated that it only had a 'few billion additional cubic meters' of gas available, although it expressed optimism that further exploration could unlock more production in about four years.

However, foreign involvement will remain limited because of Algeria's constrictive regulatory and licensing environment. Algeria is planning several small and medium-sized project developments, but these will offer only a temporary boost to output. Most significant is the South West Gas Field project, which comprises several distinct developments, including Reggane North (with estimated reserves of 2,900m. cu m), Timimoun (1,600m. cu m), Touat (4,500m. cu m) and Ahnet (4,000m. cu m). The project will involve the construction of gas-gathering facilities, a gas treatment plant and connecting pipeline infrastructure.

According to the US Energy Information Administration, Algeria possesses vast recoverable shale gas resources of around 19,800,000m. cu m. (an estimated 5,700m. barrels). Prospective resources are located in the Ghadames and Illizi basins in east Algeria, the Timimoun, Ahnet and Mouydir basins in central Algeria, and the Reggane and Tindouf basins in south-west Algeria. However, there has been little movement towards the development of these resources. In a licensing round held in 2014, the Timissit licence awarded to Norway's Statoil and the British-Dutch hydrocarbons firm Shell was the only shale licence to receive a bid.

The exploration programme has been relatively unambitious, involving just two exploration wells by 2017. Furthermore, local protests erupted in January 2015 after SONATRACH started a pilot shale well in the Ahnet Basin, suggesting that there would be domestic opposition to shale development.

Despite the enormous below-ground potential, critical barriers to investment in unconventional exploration remain, and it is unlikely that there will be any significant momentum towards exploiting these resources in the short term.

Oil Production

In 1963 oil production in Algeria totalled 569,940 b/d. Production reached 1.3m. b/d in 1979, before declining to 1.0m. b/d in 1983. Production then rose again, reaching 2.0m. b/d in 2007. From 2007, however, production declined almost every year for more than a decade. After contracting by 2.3% in 2017, 1.9% in 2018, 1.6% in 2019 and 10.4% in 2020, production amounted to 1.3m. b/d in 2020. However, in 2021, production increased by 1.7%, bringing output to 1.4m. b/d.

Algeria's oil output further increased to 1.6m. b/d in 2022, following the implementation of production target increases by the Organization of the Petroleum Exporting Countries Plus (OPEC+, of which Algeria is a member), which led the country to produce oil at levels close to pre-COVID levels. Output was expected to stagnate or fall slightly in 2023. The near-term outlook remains favourable, with global supply tightness set to incentivize high production levels. However, the longer-term outlook for the sector is more sombre, amid a dearth of significant new projects under development and high above-ground risks. None the less, as earlier noted, there has been some interest shown by international oil companies in the Algerian oil sector following the enactment of the new hydrocarbons legislation in January 2020.

MANUFACTURING

Algeria's manufacturing sector is underdeveloped, as in most hydrocarbon-producing emerging economies. The sector contracted by an average of 0.3% per year during 2002–14 and by 0.2% during 2015–21. As a result, manufacturing as a share of GDP declined from 38.8% in 2002 to 30.0% in 2021.

With the decline in oil prices in 2014, it became apparent that the economy was overdependent on hydrocarbons and that vigorous efforts should be made by the Government to diversify. To this end, the Government made manufacturing the focus of a five-year investment plan for 2015–19. The strategy centred on three main areas: developing other industries and mines, improving competitiveness, and strengthening the business climate. The Government implemented a classic import substitution strategy, banning the import of 851 products in 2018 in an attempt to make local production more profitable. However, following the implementation of the plan, manufacturing contracted by 4.6% in 2018, 3.5% in 2019 and 9.0% in in the pandemic year of 2020, before recovering to grow by 9.0% in 2021. Moreover, during this period the Government made little progress in improving competitiveness or the business climate.

Petrochemicals were one area that received attention. However, in 2020 the Government was forced to suspend plans for the construction of an international-scale petrochemicals complex owing to the COVID-19 crisis. Decreasing oil revenues from 2014 significantly reduced the funds available for investment, while the decline in oil prices reduced the cost of naphtha feedstock and, therefore, the competitiveness of ethane feedstock. However, the situation may change with the rise in oil prices from 2021 and the extra funds that the Government will consequently have for projects in this sector.

The automotive sector reflects many of the shortcomings of the Government's import substitution strategy, with production having all but collapsed. Algeria still has to import most parts used in the assembly of automotives, while vehicle production has effectively halted following the failure of the Government's previous 'semi-knock-down' (SKD)/'complete knock-down (CKD)' automotive production model. Local vehicle production declined from 70,597 units in 2018 to 60,012 units in 2019, before collapsing to just 754 units in 2020. In November 2021 it was reported that Renault Algérie (a joint venture between French vehicle manufacturer Renault and the Algerian Government) had completed the assembly of 4,650 SKD kits that had been released by customs in May, with local media reporting that the Oran plant would soon enter a one-month 'technical shutdown'. With the assembly of these cars completed, the future of the Algerian automotive sector remained unclear in 2022. By mid-2023 it was readily apparent that automotive production had effectively stopped in Algeria.

However, with Algeria's new-found importance as a gas exporter to Europe cementing an improvement in relations with some EU members, it was forecast that this would result in greater foreign investment in the country and would probably lead to a return of European automotive manufacturers to the local market.

In part, the manufacturing sector's problems stem from very low competitiveness in areas that the 2015–19 plan did not address. Algeria was ranked 89th out of 141 countries in the World Economic Forum's 2019 Competitiveness Index. Of the 12 components of the Index, Algeria scored the lowest in terms of its labour market (131st), product market (125th), financial system (111th), institutions (111th) and macroeconomic stability (102nd). The country scored highest in terms of its market size (38th), health (56th), and information and communications technology adoption (77th).

Specific areas of concern include corporate governance, for which Algeria ranked 133rd. Algeria was also placed 123rd for auditing and accounting standards and 133rd for conflict-of-interest regulation. Regarding trade openness, the country was ranked 127th for the prevalence of non-tariff barriers and 139th for trade tariffs. In terms of its labour market, Algeria was ranked 125th for the ease of hiring foreign labour and 113th for workers' rights. With respect to finance, Algeria was ranked 112th for domestic credit to the private sector as a share of GDP and 123rd for market capitalization as a percentage of GDP.

Algeria belongs on the long list of countries for which import substitution failed to produce a dynamic manufacturing industry capable of sustaining growth and entering export markets. As with many other developing oil producers, Algeria did not implement the governance and economic reforms required to support the economy and its manufacturing component.

Governance is a concern because of its importance in establishing a firm foundation for economic growth and because it has been deteriorating in Algeria in recent years. The World Bank's Governance Indicators comprise six dimensions: voice and accountability; political stability/absence of violence; government efficiency; regulatory quality; the rule of law; and control of corruption. Using an average of the six dimensions, Algeria ranked in the 16th percentile in 1996, improving to the 33rd percentile by 2005. However, governance standards have declined gradually since then, reaching the 21st percentile in 2020. In that year Algeria ranked the lowest in regulatory quality (an approximate measure of the business environment). In 2005 the country ranked in the 43rd percentile, but by 2020 it had declined to the ninth percentile. Control of corruption decreased from the 40th percentile in 2005 to the 28th by 2020, while the rule of law declined from the 31st percentile in 2013 to the 22nd by 2020. The erosion of government efficiency was less extreme, with the country dropping from the 39th percentile in 2005 to the 34th in 2020. Voice and accountability (a rough measure of democracy) decreased from the 25th percentile in 2005 to the 18th percentile in 2020, while over the same period political stability/absence of violence declined from the 20th percentile to the 17th.

The Heritage Foundation's 2023 Index of Economic Freedom ranked Algeria as the 168th freest nation out of the 184 countries included in the survey. The country ranked 15th among the 17 countries in the Middle East and North Africa and its overall score (which was 2.6 points lower than in 2022) remained lower than the regional and world averages. After initially being placed in the Index's 'mostly unfree' grouping, Algeria joined the 'moderately free' group for one year in 2002. However, the country's economic freedom levels subsequently regressed, with Algeria being placed in the 'repressed' group in 2017, where it has since remained. The picture is similar for the Index's subcomponents, with Algeria placed in the 'repressed' group in 2023 for property rights, judicial effectiveness, government integrity, investment freedom, financial freedom and fiscal health. The recent decline in business freedom is striking. In 2015, at the start of the Government's five-year plan, Algeria was ranked in the middle of the 'moderately free' group for this category. By 2022, however, the country had been placed in the 'repressed' group, although there was a slight improvement in its ranking in 2023 to that of 'mostly unfree'.

The manufacturing sector has also been undermined by Algeria's high minimum wage (by African/Middle Eastern and North African standards). The monthly minimum wage on 1 January 2022 was US $144. By comparison, the minimum wage was $140 in Tunisia and just $76 in Egypt. Finally, Algeria is also one of the most challenging places in the world in which to do business, ranking 157th in the World Bank's 2020 Ease of Doing Business index.

ELECTRICITY

Electricity production has increased steadily in recent years, rising from 12.3 terawatt hours (TWh) in 1985 to 25.4 TWh in 2000 and 45.7 TWh in 2010. Production reached 81.5 TWh in 2019, before declining by 3.4% to 78.8 TWh in 2020. The impact of the COVID-19 pandemic resulted in a downturn in household and industrial consumption, leading to a 5.7% decrease in thermal generation. Production totalled 77.6 TWh in 2021 and 83.5 TWh in 2022. Algeria's current level of electricity generation is more than sufficient to meet domestic consumption demands, although grid losses remain high, which can put pressure on supply during peak periods.

By 2020 99.8% of Algerians had access to electricity, up from 99.0% in 2000. Almost 99% of electricity generation in Algeria comes from gas-fired thermal power. However, the levelling-off of gas production and the Government's desire to increase gas exports suggest that renewables will begin to supply a significant amount of the country's electricity needs.

In May 2015 the Government adopted an ambitious target for renewable energy development, aiming to install 22 gigawatts (GW) of renewable electricity capacity by 2030, representing around 35% of Algeria's total power capacity. Solar energy would account for 13.5 GW of this capacity. It was estimated that total investment of between US $60,000m. and $120,000m. would be required to reach this target.

In early 2020 Prime Minister Abdelaziz Djerad reported that Algeria was targeting 16 GW of renewable capacity by 2035, including 4 GW by 2024, a more attainable target than 22 GW by 2030. In June 2021 the target was adjusted slightly to 15 GW by 2035.

The Government has highlighted solar power as the technology with the most potential in the country, owing to the high insolation levels in the Sahara desert. In 2015 the Government introduced a feed-in tariff for wind and solar energy to encourage development in the sector.

In March 2023 Algeria's state-owned utility Sonelgaz issued a tender for developing and constructing 15 solar power plants with a total combined capacity of 2,000 MW. The individual capacities of the plants would range from 80 MW to 220 MW.

CONSTRUCTION

In 2022 the construction sector accounted for around 11% of GDP. The COVID-19 pandemic caused significant damage to the sector in 2020 as lockdowns resulted in the suspension of construction projects and the disruption of supply chains of materials and equipment. The Government introduced lockdown measures in March, which remained in place until mid-July, when some of the stricter conditions were lifted. With limited activity, the sector contracted by 3% in 2020. Construction work resumed in 2021 following the lifting of restrictions and increased government spending stemming from recovering oil prices. The construction sector expanded by 5.9% in 2021 and by 4.5% in 2022.

The construction sector has several strengths. Large multinational contractors such as France's Alstom and Orascom Construction of Egypt have significant established presences in Algeria. In addition, revenue from gas exports helps to fund the Government's infrastructure programmes. In this regard, the Government's Public Investment Programme has successfully driven growth in the sector.

However, the construction industry also suffers from several weaknesses. The sector faces a shortage of suitable-sized firms with the requisite expertise. Road and rail infrastructure in some parts of the country is underdeveloped, and there is limited access to the electricity grid in rural areas. The availability of domestic skilled labour is limited, and attracting qualified foreign workers can be challenging. Potential investors have security concerns over political unrest, the country's proximity to instability in Libya, and the kidnapping of foreign workers in Algeria by members of the militant Islamic State group.

Despite these problems, the sector's future looks promising. Algeria is enhancing its relationship with the People's Republic of China, which could drive further investment. The Government approved a national policy for renewable energy in 2015, which could result in US $60,000m.–$120,000m. of infrastructural investment over the medium term (see Electricity). Algeria continues to suffer from a severe housing shortage; the country would need to build around 175,000 new housing units every year over the next 10 years to absorb the housing deficit.

Several major construction projects are under way or about to commence, including the new cities of Sidi Abdellah and Boughezoul, the latter of which was to incorporate a new railway station and airport. The construction of Algeria's first 'green' mosque has commenced in Sidi Abdellah. The innovatory development, due to be completed in 2024, includes solar panels which will provide 50% of the energy consumed by the site and wastewater recycling for irrigation facilities. Meanwhile, in June 2022 it was announced that cement manufacturer LafargeHolcim Algeria was to receive a €9.4m. loan from the Algerian subsidiary of the French bank Société Générale to fund efforts to make the manufacture of building materials (cement, concrete and aggregate production) at the company's sites in Algeria carbon neutral. In November the Minister of Housing, Urban Planning and Towns, Mohamed Tarek Belaribi, reported that 800,000 new housing units had been completed during the previous three years.

TOURISM

Algeria's tourism industry is relatively small compared with those of Morocco and Egypt, but the country has been gaining in popularity with tourists in recent years. The major visitor attractions include the Kasbah of Algiers, the Hamma Test Garden in Algiers, the Basilica of Our Lady of Africa, Santa Cruz Fort, the Emir Abdelkader Mosque and the El Mechouar Palace. In 1995 there were 520,000 tourist arrivals. By 2008 arrivals had increased to 1.8m., and by 2013 arrivals had reached a record 2.7m. However, the tourism sector contracted by 15.8% in 2014 and by a further 25.7% in 2015, partly owing to Algeria's lack of competitiveness. In 2015 the World Travel and Tourism Council ranked Algeria 132nd out of 140 countries in terms of travel and tourism competitiveness. Nevertheless, arrivals increased to just under 2.7m. in 2018, before declining by 10.8% to 2.4m. in 2019. The COVID-19 pandemic, and the associated lockdowns and flight cancellations, caused tourist arrivals to decrease by 75.1% in 2020 to just 591,000 and to a mere 125,000 in 2021. Although there was a partial recovery in tourist arrivals, to 1.4m., in 2022, given Algeria's political and social instability and the lack of competitiveness of the country's tourism sector, it may take years for tourist numbers to return to their pre-COVID levels.

In 2019 tourism provided 5.6% of Algeria's GDP, declining to 3.6% in 2020. In 2019 tourism accounted for 5.8% of jobs in Algeria, decreasing to 4.4% in 2020. Tourism provided 0.4% of the country's exports in 2019, declining to just 0.1% in 2020.

In 2022 66% of tourists arriving in Algeria (excluding arrivals of Algerian nationals resident abroad) were from Tunisia, 9% were from France, 3% from Morocco and 2% from Türkiye (Turkey).

FOREIGN TRADE AND BALANCE OF PAYMENTS

Algeria is less open to international trade than Morocco and Tunisia, with imports and exports equivalent to a combined 45.2% of GDP in 2020. Comparable figures for Morocco and Tunisia were 78.6% and 107.9%, respectively. In 2021 Algeria's principal exports were LPG (US $14,300m.), crude petroleum ($10,700m.), refined petroleum ($6,230m.), nitrogenous fertilizers ($1,210m.) and ammonia ($714m.). The country's primary export market in that year was Italy ($7,320m.), followed by Spain ($5,060m.), France ($4,600m.), the Republic of Korea ($1,680m.) and the USA ($1,680m.). Algeria's principal imports in 2021 included wheat ($2,200m.), followed by concentrated milk ($1,270m.), cars ($800m.), soybean oil ($798m.) and maize ($795m.). China ($6,340m.) was the main exporter to Algeria in that year, followed by France ($4,350m.), Spain ($2,190m.), Germany ($2,160m.) and Italy ($2,070m.).

As with most hydrocarbon-exporting developing countries, imports and exports follow a somewhat distinct pattern, with little correlation between the two. For Algeria, exports of goods and services grew at an average annual rate of 2.2% in 1980–90, increasing to 2.9% in 1991–2001. However, during 2002–14 exports of goods and services declined by an average of 1.1% per year, before recovering to expand at an average annual rate of 1.2% during 2015–22. Imports of goods and services contracted at an average rate of 0.8% per year during 1980–90, before expanding at an average yearly rate of 0.4% during 1991–2002 and 11.1% during 2002–14. However, the period 2015–22 saw an average annual contraction in imports of goods and services of 5.7%.

These trade patterns translated into an average current account deficit of 0.8% of GDP in 1980–90 and an average surplus of 3.4% of GDP in 1991–2001, increasing to 10.9% in 2002–15. However, during 2016–22, a period that witnessed falling oil prices and the onset of the COVID-19 pandemic, an average current account deficit of 9.3% of GDP was recorded.

Foreign direct investment (FDI) had a limited impact on the current account balance, averaging just 1.3% of GDP in 2002–14 and only 0.6% of GDP in 2015–21. By comparison, during 2018–20 FDI as a percentage of GDP averaged 7.7% in Egypt, 2.3% in Morocco and 1.7% in Iran.

Instead, the Government financed much of the deficit by depleting the country's foreign exchange reserves. Algeria's foreign exchange reserves increased from US $4,343m. in 1999 to $146,129m. in 2009, reaching a maximum of $193,273m. in February 2014. However, owing first to the decline in oil prices and later to the COVID-19 pandemic, reserves progressively decreased to $97,300m. in 2017, $79,900m. in 2018, $62,800m. in 2019, $48,200m. in 2020 and $46,700m. in 2021. In that year the Government even drew down its extra allocation of

$2,670m. of Special Drawing Rights (SDRs) from the IMF. Following a rebound in oil prices from 2021, Algeria's reserve position began to reverse its recent downward trend, with reserves increasing to $62,000m. in 2022.

MONETARY POLICY

Algeria's central bank, the Banque d'Algérie (established in 1962), issues the nation's currency, the Algerian dinar (AD). Officially, the bank became independent of political and economic pressure groups in 1990, but in 1999 President Abdelaziz Bouteflika assumed de facto control of the bank's policymaking.

Following the oil price crash of 2014, the Government adopted a loose monetary policy in 2015 to weaken the dinar, thus increasing the local currency value of oil exports. In 2014 the exchange rate was US $1 = AD 80.58. However, the rate had declined to $1 = AD 116.59 by 2018 and to $1 = AD 139.9 by the end of 2021.

The Banque d'Algérie's loss of independence became apparent in 2016, when Bouteflika ordered the bank to print money to cover the treasury's deficit. When the Governor of the central bank refused to do so, he was dismissed. The practice of monetizing the Government's budget deficit became formalized with a law approved in September 2017 that allows the Government to borrow from the central bank. With its control over the money supply thereby lost, the central bank's primary policy instrument now is its ability to control the reserve requirements of the nation's banks.

Since late 2017 it has been difficult to separate Algeria's monetary policy from its fiscal actions. The monetary authorities began expanding the central bank's balance sheet to purchase sovereign bonds. This approach essentially finances government debt. The IMF estimated that by the end of 2018 monetary financing amounted to 23% of GDP, and in March 2019 issued a sharply critical assessment of the Government's practice of borrowing from the central bank to cover the fiscal deficit. The Fund also noted a series of restrictions announced by the Algerian Government in January 2018 banning the importation of almost 1,000 items. The IMF warned that these short-term measures carried the risk of inflation and the further erosion of foreign reserves, which had declined sharply since 2014.

The IMF recommended that the Government consider alternatives, particularly raising external loans to fund investment projects and financing the fiscal deficit through domestic borrowing at market rates. However, the Government rejected these recommendations. Despite concerns that the central bank's actions would lead to hyperinflation, the inflation rate decreased to 5.6% in 2017 (down from 6.4% in 2016). Inflation declined further to 4.3% in 2018 and to 2.0% in 2019.

The COVID-19 pandemic began to disrupt the Algerian economy in mid-March 2020, prompting the central bank to lower reserve requirements from 10% to 8%. As the severity of the economic crisis grew, the monetary authorities opted for another reduction in April 2020, to 6%. A third reduction was implemented in September, with the minimum reserve requirement set at 3%. However, by 2021 a weakening currency and loose monetary policy began to have an impact on prices, with inflation rising to 7.2% in that year and further to 9.3% in 2022.

FISCAL POLICY

As with most hydrocarbons exporters, Algeria's public finances remain primarily driven by developments in the international oil market. From 1991 to 2001 government revenue averaged 31.2% of GDP, increasing to 38.6% in 2002–14, before declining to 31.4% during 2015–22. As a result of the accommodative monetary policy adopted in 2016/17, government expenditure has become more independent of oil price movements. After averaging 31.3% of GDP during 1991–2001, government expenditure increased to 36.3% of GDP in 2002–14 and to 40.3% of GDP in 2015–22.

Government revenue and expenditure patterns resulted in slight budgetary deficits averaging 0.1% of GDP during 1991–2001, transforming into budgetary surpluses averaging 2.3% of GDP in 2002–14, before returning to deficits averaging 8.9% of GDP during 2015–22. Government debt rose from 7.7% of GDP in 2014 to 46.2% in 2019 and to 62.8% in 2021, before declining to 53.4% in 2022. However, the IMF predicts that Algeria will register persistent budgetary deficits of around 8% of GDP until 2028 and that government debt will reach 66.4% of GDP in 2026 and 70.2% in 2028.

PROSPECTS

Algeria will follow a pattern familiar in the Middle East and North Africa: propose reforms to improve economic performance during periods of low energy prices and then postpone them (often indefinitely) when energy prices recover. In December 2021 the World Bank noted that the Algerian economy was 'enjoying temporary breathing space'. Algeria's successive governments have posed complex challenges for the multilateral lenders, whose advice has traditionally been taken selectively. The World Bank warned starkly that 'absent decisive implementation of the reform agenda, the economic outlook points to a fragile recovery, and to deteriorating fiscal and external balances in the medium term'.

Government policy in the near term will focus on addressing the cost-of-living crisis, especially high food inflation, through subsidies and social spending. Over the next few years, the Algerian Government will most likely focus on maintaining social stability and reducing the risk of civil unrest through higher welfare spending. A probable scenario will see the basic state pension increasing by 50% and unemployment benefit by 15% in 2023. Government policy will therefore remain statist and financed by a hydrocarbons-based rentier economy, which will continue to undermine investor confidence given the Government's persistent fiscal mismanagement and inconsistency.

The large number of young people entering the job market in the next five years will exert additional pressure on the Government to provide both sufficient jobs and housing. This will potentially become largest source of social unrest in the country. Although in mid-2021 the Government imposed a ban on unauthorized demonstrations, as part of a heightened crackdown on protests by the authorities, there will likely be a resurgence in popular discontent if living conditions continue to deteriorate.

Over the longer term, Algeria will face the effects of climate change, for which the country is ill-prepared. Extreme weather events, including wildfires and droughts, will increase in frequency as global temperatures rise. Algeria will be vulnerable to the effects of climate change but is likely to be slow to adapt amid political constraints that reduce the space for mitigating its impact. The Government's inability to respond to more frequent natural disasters will exacerbate political unrest and may lead to increasingly violent protests.

ALGERIA

Statistical Survey

Source (unless otherwise stated): Office National des Statistiques, 8 rue des Moussebilines, BP 202, Ferhat Boussad, Algiers; tel. (21) 63-99-74; fax (21) 63-79-55; e-mail ons@ons.dz; internet www.ons.dz.

Area and Population

AREA, POPULATION AND DENSITY

Area (sq km)	2,381,741*
Population (census results)	
25 June 1998	29,100,867
16 April 2008	
Males	17,232,747
Females	16,847,283
Total	34,080,030
Population (UN estimates at mid-year)†	
2021	44,177,969
2022‡	44,903,225
2023‡	45,606,481
Density (per sq km) at mid-2023‡	19.1

* 919,595 sq miles.
† Source: UN, *World Population Prospects: The 2022 Revision*.
‡ Projection.

POPULATION BY AGE AND SEX
('000, UN projections at mid-2023)

	Males	Females	Total
0–14 years	7,090.1	6,796.7	13,886.7
15–64 years	14,678.4	14,027.4	28,705.8
65 years and over	1,448.7	1,565.2	3,013.9
Total	23,217.2	22,389.3	45,606.5

Note: Totals may not be equal to the sum of components owing to rounding.
Source: UN, *World Population Prospects: The 2022 Revision*.

POPULATION BY WILAYA (ADMINISTRATIVE DISTRICT)
(2008 census)

	Area (sq km)	Population	Density (per sq km)
Adrar*	439,700	399,714	0.9
Aïn Defla	4,897	766,013	156.4
Aïn Témouchent	2,379	371,239	156.0
Algiers (el-Djezaïr)	273	2,988,145	10,945.6
Annaba	1,439	609,499	423.6
Batna	12,192	1,119,791	91.8
el-Bayadh	78,870	228,624	2.9
Béchar*	162,200	270,061	1.7
Béjaïa	3,268	912,577	279.2
Biskra (Beskra)*	20,986	721,356	34.4
Blida (el-Boulaïda)	1,696	1,002,937	591.4
Borj Bou Arreridj	4,115	628,475	152.7
Bouira	4,439	695,583	156.7
Boumerdès	1,591	802,083	504.1
Chlef (el-Cheliff)	4,795	1,002,088	209.0
Constantine (Qacentina)	2,187	938,475	429.1
Djelfa	66,415	1,092,184	16.4
Ghardaïa*	86,105	363,598	4.2
Guelma	4,101	482,430	117.6
Illizi*	285,000	52,333	0.2
Jijel	2,577	636,948	247.2
Khenchela	9,811	386,683	39.4
Laghouat	25,057	455,602	18.2
Mascara (Mouaskar)	5,941	784,073	132.0
Médéa (Lemdiyya)	8,866	819,932	92.5
Mila	9,375	766,886	81.8
Mostaganem	2,175	737,118	338.9
M'sila	18,718	990,591	52.9
Naâma	29,950	192,891	6.4
Oran (Ouahran)	2,121	1,454,078	685.6
Ouargla*	211,980	558,558	2.6
el-Oued*	54,573	647,548	11.9
Oum el-Bouaghi	6,768	621,612	91.8
Relizane (Ghilizane)	4,870	726,180	149.1
Saïda	6,764	330,641	48.9
Sétif (Stif)	6,504	1,489,979	229.1
Sidi-bel-Abbès	9,096	604,744	66.5
Skikda	4,026	898,680	223.2
Souk Ahras	4,541	438,127	96.5
Tamanrasset (Tamanghest)*	556,200	176,637	0.3
el-Tarf	3,339	408,414	122.3
Tébessa (Tbessa)	14,227	648,703	45.6
Tiaret (Tihert)	20,673	846,823	41.0
Tindouf	159,000	49,149	0.3
Tipaza	2,166	591,010	272.9
Tissemsilt	3,152	294,476	93.4
Tizi Ouzou	3,568	1,127,607	316.0
Tlemcen	9,061	949,135	104.7
Total	**2,381,741**	**34,080,030**	**14.3**

* In December 2019 10 new wilayas were created: Béni Abbès (162,200 sq km, from territory formerly part of Béchar); Bordj Badji Mokhtar (439,700 sq km, from territory formerly part of Adrar); Djanet (285,000 sq km, from territory formerly part of Illizi); In Guezzam (556,200 sq km, from territory formerly part of Tamanrasset); el-Meghaier (54,573 sq km, from territory formerly part of el-Oued); el-Meniaa (86,105 sq km, from territory formerly part of Ghardaïa); Ouled Djellal (20,986 sq km, from territory formerly part of Biskra); In Salah (556,200 sq km, from territory formerly part of Tamanrasset); Timimoun (439,700 sq km, from territory formerly part of Adrar); Touggourt (211,980 sq km, from territory formerly part of Ouargla).

PRINCIPAL TOWNS
(population at 1998 census)

Algiers (el-Djezaïr, capital)	1,519,570	Tébessa (Tbessa)	153,246
Oran (Ouahran)	655,852	Blida (el-Boulaïda)	153,083
Constantine (Qacentina)	462,187	Skikda	152,335
Batna	242,514	Béjaïa	147,076
Annaba	215,083	Tiaret (Tihert)	145,332
Sétif (Stif)	211,859	Chlef (el-Cheliff)	133,874
Sidi-bel-Abbès	180,260	el-Buni	133,471
Biskra (Beskra)	170,956	Béchar	131,010
Djelfa	154,265		

Mid-2023 (incl. suburbs, UN projections): Algiers 2,901,810; Oran 935,947; Djelfa 570,543; Blida 511,672; Qacentina 417,768; Annaba 368,782; Batna 346,016; Sétif 331,801 (Source: UN, *World Urbanization Prospects: The 2018 Revision*).

BIRTHS, MARRIAGES AND DEATHS*

	Registered live births†		Registered marriages		Registered deaths†	
	Number	Rate (per 1,000)	Number	Rate (per 1,000)	Number	Rate (per 1,000)
2016	1,066,559	26.1	356,600	8.7	165,648	4.4
2017	1,060,000	25.4	340,000	8.1	190,000	4.6
2018	1,038,000	24.4	332,000	7.8	193,000	4.5
2019	1,034,000	23.8	315,000	7.3	198,000	4.6
2020	992,000	n.a.	283,000	n.a.	236,000	n.a.

* Figures refer to the Algerian population only; including adjustment for underenumeration.
† Rounded estimates, excluding live-born infants dying before registration of birth.

Life expectancy (years at birth, estimates): 76.4 (males 74.9; females 78.0) in 2021 (Source: World Bank, World Development Indicators database).

ALGERIA

ECONOMICALLY ACTIVE POPULATION
('000 persons aged 15 years and over at May 2019)

	Males	Females	Total
Agriculture	1,006	77	1,083
Mining and quarrying	141	13	153
Manufacturing	908	389	1,297
Construction	1,862	28	1,890
Trade	1,684	91	1,775
Transport and communication	690	39	729
Public administration	1,525	287	1,812
Health and social work	746	931	1,676
Other services	658	207	865
Total employed	**9,219**	**2,062**	**11,281**
Unemployed	920	529	1,449
Total labour force	**10,140**	**2,591**	**12,730**

Note: Totals may not be equal to the sum of components owing to rounding.

Health and Welfare

KEY INDICATORS

Total fertility rate (children per woman, 2021)	2.9
Under-5 mortality rate (per 1,000 live births, 2021)	22.3
HIV/AIDS (% of persons aged 15–49, 2021)	<0.1
COVID-19: Cumulative confirmed deaths (per 100,000 persons at 30 June 2023)	15.3
COVID-19: Fully vaccinated population (% of total population at 4 September 2022)	14.4
Physicians (per 1,000 head, 2018)	1.7
Hospital beds (per 1,000 head, 2015)	1.9
Domestic health expenditure (2020): US $ per head (PPP)	460.5
Domestic health expenditure (2020): % of GDP	4.0
Domestic health expenditure (2020): public (% of total current health expenditure)	62.6
Access to improved water resources (% of persons, 2020)	94
Access to improved sanitation facilities (% of persons, 2020)	86
Total carbon dioxide emissions ('000 metric tons, 2019)	171,250
Carbon dioxide emissions per head (metric tons, 2019)	4.0
Human Development Index (2021): ranking	91
Human Development Index (2021): value	0.745

Note: For data on COVID-19 vaccinations, 'fully vaccinated' denotes receipt of all doses specified by approved vaccination regime (Sources: Johns Hopkins University and Our World in Data). Data on health expenditure refer to current general government expenditure in each case. For more information on sources and further definitions for all indicators, see Health and Welfare Statistics: Sources and Definitions section (europaworld.com/credits).

Agriculture

PRINCIPAL CROPS
('000 metric tons)

	2019	2020	2021
Almonds	72	61	55
Apples	559	567	522
Apricots	209	187	190
Artichokes	120	127	121
Aubergines (Eggplants)	184	178	193
Barley	1,648	1,213	555
Beans, green	95	100	88
Broad beans, dry	55	50	40
Cabbages and other brassicas	116	124	158
Carrots and turnips	420	448	414
Cauliflowers and broccoli	205	243	239
Chick peas	40	40	39
Chillies and peppers, green	675	718	352
Cucumbers and gherkins	166	184	183
Dates	1,136	1,152	1,189
Figs	114	116	107
Garlic	223	171	196
Grapes	550	554	630
Lemons and limes	87	85	84
Oats	101	69	40
Olives	869	1,080	705
Onions, dry	1,614	1,666	1,710
Oranges	1,200	1,175	1,137
Peaches and nectarines	202	186	186
—continued	2019	2020	2021
Pears	223	155	150
Peas, green	200	209	204
Plums and sloes	113	99	97
Potatoes	5,020	4,659	4,361
Pumpkins, squash and gourds	420	435	405
Rapeseed*	23	23	23
Tangerines, mandarins, etc.	295	302	290
Tobacco, unmanufactured	15	11	9
Tomatoes	1,478	1,636	1,642
Watermelons	2,207	2,287	2,076
Wheat	3,877	3,107	2,168

* FAO estimates.

Aggregate production ('000 metric tons, may include official, semi-official or estimated data): Total cereals 5,634 in 2019, 4,393 in 2020, 2,784 in 2021; Total fruit (primary) 7,070 in 2019, 7,055 in 2020, 6,838 in 2021; Total roots and tubers 5,020 in 2019, 4,659 in 2020, 4,361 in 2021; Total vegetables (primary) 7,295 in 2019, 7,986 in 2020, 7,652 in 2021.

Source: FAO.

LIVESTOCK
('000 head, year ending September unless otherwise indicated)

	2019	2020	2021
Asses	86	84	80
Camels	417	435	448
Cattle	1,786	1,740	1,734
Chickens (million)*	136	137	137
Goats	4,929	4,908	5,029
Horses	50	48	50
Sheep	29,379	30,906	31,126

* FAO estimates.
Source: FAO.

LIVESTOCK PRODUCTS
('000 metric tons)

	2019	2020	2021
Camels' milk*	15	15	15
Cattle meat*	152	144	146
Cattle offals, edible*	23	22	22
Cows' milk	2,478	2,415	2,409
Chicken meat*	258	258	258
Goat meat*	19	18	19
Goats' milk	326	333	314
Sheep meat	329	335	342
Sheep offals, edible*	42	42	43
Sheep's (Ewes') milk	524	592	525
Sheepskins, fresh*	52	53	54
Turkey meat*	24	24	n.a.
Hen eggs*	322	308	305
Honey (natural)	6	5	5
Wool, greasy	35	38	33

* FAO estimates.
Source: FAO.

Forestry

ROUNDWOOD REMOVALS
('000 cubic metres, excl. bark, FAO estimates)

	2019	2020	2021
Sawlogs, veneer logs and logs for sleepers	28	28	28
Pulpwood	59	59	59
Other industrial wood	52	52	52
Fuel wood	8,738	8,791	8,843
Total	**8,877**	**8,930**	**8,982**

Sawnwood production ('000 cubic metres, incl. railway sleepers, FAO estimates): 13 per year in 1975–2021.

Source: FAO.

ALGERIA

Fishing

('000 metric tons, live weight)

	2019	2020	2021
Capture	100.6	71.5*	79.2*
Bogue	3.2	3.4	0.3
Jack and horse mackerels	12.0	5.8	2.5*
Sardinellas	24.7	26.4	23.3
European pilchard (sardine)	24.9	18.4	29.9
Other marines fishes	32.8	15.2	20.1
Aquaculture	4.8	5.4	4.8
Total catch	105.4	76.9*	84.0*

* FAO estimate.

Source: FAO.

Mining

('000 metric tons unless otherwise indicated)

	2016	2017	2018
Crude petroleum*	68,417	66,648	65,332
Natural gas (dry basis, million cu m)*	91,392	92,977	93,844
Iron ore (gross weight)	826	497	497
Phosphate rock†	1,275	1,100‡	1,200‡
Barite (Barytes)	52	40‡	40‡
Salt (unrefined)	158	160‡	160‡
Gypsum (crude)	2,200	2,500‡	2,500‡

* Source: Energy Institute, *Statistical Review of World Energy*.
† Figures refer to gross weight. The estimated phosphoric acid content in '000 metric tons, estimated) was 375 in 2016; 330 in 2017; 340 in 2018.
‡ Estimated production.

2019: Crude petroleum ('000 metric tons) 64,330; Natural gas 86,952m. cu m (Source: Energy Institute, *Statistical Review of World Energy*).
2020: Crude petroleum ('000 metric tons) 57,625; Natural gas 81,425m. cu m (Source: Energy Institute, *Statistical Review of World Energy*).
2021: Crude petroleum ('000 metric tons) 58,200; Natural gas 101,098m. cu m (Source: Energy Institute, *Statistical Review of World Energy*).
2022: Crude petroleum ('000 metric tons) 63,649; Natural gas 98,175m. cu m (Source: Energy Institute, *Statistical Review of World Energy*).

Source (unless otherwise indicated): US Geological Survey.

Industry

SELECTED PRODUCTS
('000 metric tons unless otherwise indicated)

	2018	2019	2020
Olive oil (metric tons)*	87	106	114
Naphthas	7,715	7,375	7,437
Motor spirit (petrol)	3,749	3,253	3,105
Jet fuel	1,497	1,221	992
Gas-diesel (distillate fuel) oils	10,189	9,590	9,503
Residual fuel oils	5,822	5,915	5,920
Lubricating oils	98†	110	n.a.
Petroleum bitumen (asphalt)	115	110	177
Liquefied petroleum gas	8,972	8,917	8,413
Pig iron for steel†	300	n.a.	n.a.
Crude steel (ingots)	2,000†	n.a.	n.a.
Electrical energy (million kWh)	76,662	81,533	79,155

* Unofficial figures.
† Estimated production.

Sources: FAO; UN Energy Statistics Database; US Geological Survey.

Finance

CURRENCY AND EXCHANGE RATES

Monetary Units
100 centimes = 1 Algerian dinar (AD).

Sterling, Dollar and Euro Equivalents (31 May 2023)
£1 sterling = 169.308 dinars;
US $1 = 136.936 dinars;
€1 = 146.289 dinars;
1,000 Algerian dinars = £5.91 = $7.30 = €6.84.

Average Exchange Rate (dinars per US $)
2020   126.777
2021   135.064
2022   141.995

GOVERNMENT FINANCE
(central government operations, '000 million AD)

Revenue

Revenue*	2021	2022†	2023†
Hydrocarbon revenue	2,609	5,400	4,950
Other revenue	3,971	3,863	4,501
Tax revenue	2,762	2,982	3,577
Non-tax revenue	1,209	881	923
Bank of Algeria dividends and interests	900	500	500
Total	6,581	9,262	9,451

Expenditure

Expenditure by economic type‡	2021	2022†	2023†
Current expenditure	5,444	5,919	8,113
Personnel expenditure	2,363	2,414	3,241
War veterans' pensions	206	260	281
Material and supplies	171	131	228
Current transfers	2,560	2,844	3,940
Interest payments	144	270	422
Capital expenditure	1,985	1,889	2,412
Total	7,429	7,808	10,525

* Excluding grants received ('000 million AD): 6 in 2021; 0 in 2022–23 (projection).
† Projections.
‡ Excluding lending minus repayments ('000 million AD): 748 in 2021; 857 in 2022 (projection); 920 in 2023 (projection).

Source: IMF, *Algeria: 2022 Article IV Consultation—Press Release; and Staff Report* (February 2022).

INTERNATIONAL RESERVES
(excl. gold, US $ million at 31 December)

	2020	2021	2022
IMF special drawing rights	1,295	3,914	4,238
Reserve position in IMF	717	758	749
Foreign exchange	46,870	41,382	56,752
Total	48,882	46,055	61,739

Source: IMF, *International Financial Statistics*.

MONEY SUPPLY
('000 million AD at 31 December)

	2020	2021	2022
Currency outside depository corporations	6,140.68	6,712.16	7,392.81
Transferable deposits	4,401.60	5,493.86	6,478.31
Other deposits	5,565.00	6,247.56	7,380.54
Broad money	16,107.28	18,453.58	21,251.65

Source: IMF, *International Financial Statistics*.

ALGERIA

COST OF LIVING
(Consumer Price Index for Algiers; base: 2001 = 100)

	2019	2020	2021
Food and beverages	212.2	212.6	240.4
Clothing and footwear	205.9	218.0	234.9
Housing	162.1	164.4	167.8
All items (incl. others)	206.2	211.2	234.2

All items (Consumer Price Index; base 2010 = 100): 155.0 in 2020; 166.2 in 2021; 181.6 in 2022 (Source: IMF, *International Financial Statistics*).

NATIONAL ACCOUNTS
('000 million AD at current prices)
Expenditure on the Gross Domestic Product

	2020	2021	2022
Government final consumption expenditure	3,472.1	3,846.5	4,287.2
Private final consumption expenditure	8,828.4	9,798.2	10,954.9
Gross fixed capital formation	7,101.9	7,696.5	8,251.8
Changes in inventories	994.5	677.7	1,081.8
Total domestic expenditure	20,396.8	22,018.9	24,575.7
Exports of goods and services	3,227.9	5,902.8	9,834.0
Less Imports of goods and services	5,147.8	5,842.4	6,720.8
GDP at purchasers' values	18,476.9	22,079.3	27,688.8

Gross Domestic Product by Economic Activity

	2020	2021	2022
Agriculture	2,546.9	2,688.3	3,207.8
Mining (including associated industries)	2,657.3	5,034.9	8,776.2
Construction	2,285.1	2,455.4	2,737.6
Other industry	1,148.4	1,230.8	1,354.2
Transport and communications	2,045.3	2,125.7	2,241.1
Trade	2,317.2	2,620.9	2,846.8
Financial institutions and real estate	3,985.4	4,179.3	4,535.7
Other services	796.5	921.1	1,054.8
Sub-total	17,782.1	21,256.5	26,754.2
Taxes on products (net)	1,480.6	1,604.0	1,774.6
Less Imputed bank service charges	785.8	781.1	839.7
GDP at purchasers' values	18,476.9	22,079.3	27,688.8

BALANCE OF PAYMENTS
(US $ million)

	2020	2021	2022
Exports of goods f.o.b.	21,915.0	38,628.4	65,079.9
Imports of goods f.o.b.	−34,907.2	−37,395.0	−38,692.9
Balance on goods	−12,992.3	1,233.3	26,387.0
Exports of services	2,986.9	3,222.2	3,584.5
Imports of services	−7,439.8	−6,939.2	−8,290.5
Balance on goods and services	−17,445.1	−2,483.6	21,681.0
Primary income received	845.8	688.8	798.9
Primary income paid	−3,841.1	−4,702.0	−6,230.5
Balance on goods, services and primary income	−20,440.4	−6,496.9	16,249.5
Secondary income received	2,599.8	2,311.6	2,489.1
Secondary income paid	−346.4	−361.3	−459.4
Current balance	−18,187.1	−4,546.5	18,279.2
Capital account (net)	−41.3	−53.5	−17.7
Direct investment assets	−14.6	51.8	−70.6
Direct investment liabilities	1,143.9	869.2	75.2
Other investment assets	1,597.1	−261.2	−769.4
Other investment liabilities	−327.7	2,498.7	852.3
Net errors and omissions	−674.0	−73.8	475.8
Reserves and related items	−16,503.6	−1,515.5	18,824.8

Source: IMF, *International Financial Statistics*.

External Trade

Note: Data exclude military goods. Exports include stores and bunkers for foreign ships and aircraft.

PRINCIPAL COMMODITIES
(distribution by SITC, million AD)

Imports c.i.f.	2018	2019	2020
Food products and live animals	933,127.0	892,149.0	953,781.1
Inedible raw materials, except fuels	133,672.1	153,073.7	204,433.0
Mineral fuels, lubricants and related products	88,265.5	162,299.6	107,030.2
Chemicals and related products	827,789.3	784,121.5	769,980.3
Manufactured items	1,011,487.1	966,086.2	762,091.2
Machinery and transport equipment	1,998,487.6	1,632,547.4	1,190,682.4
Miscellaneous manufactured items	266,101.2	275,659.3	223,897.6
Total (incl. others)	5,403,233.0	5,016,837.0	4,363,653.1

Exports f.o.b.	2018*	2019*	2020
Food products and live animals	41,706.6	46,208.5	50,832.6
Mineral fuels, lubricants and products	4,547,206.2	3,963,719.1	2,578,800.2
Chemicals and related products	253,413.3	204,791.1	166,217.7
Total (incl. others)	4,889,278.6	4,271,648.8	2,846,371.4

*Preliminary.

2018 ('000 million AD): Total exports (revised) 4,812.5.
2019 ('000 million AD): Total exports (revised) 4,206.2.
Total imports ('000 million AD): 5,097.5 in 2021; 5,705.3 in 2022.
Total exports ('000 million AD): 5,391.9 in 2021; 9,157.4 in 2022.

PRINCIPAL TRADING PARTNERS
(million AD)

Imports c.i.f.	2018	2019	2020
Argentina	220,619.6	216,352.9	175,474.9
Brazil	140,185.4	135,627.6	169,429.8
China, People's Republic	916,522.9	913,686.1	733,366.8
France (incl. Monaco)	559,246.8	510,888.6	462,988.8
Germany	371,126.6	343,141.3	284,431.8
Italy	428,452.6	407,264.0	307,744.9
Korea, Republic	144,566.2	100,602.1	54,807.7
Spain	412,699.3	349,552.6	271,203.2
Türkiye	269,699.0	256,310.9	187,461.3
USA	191,868.0	169,431.2	177,583.7
Total (incl. others)	5,403,233.0	5,016,837.0	4,363,653.1

Exports f.o.b.	2018*	2019*	2020
Australia	29,003.8	55,057.8	16,845.6
Belgium	145,453.2	100,897.3	80,716.7
Brazil	263,204.7	151,631.2	86,233.8
Canada	35,655.1	7,772.8	19,912.1
China, People's Republic	149,422.7	201,519.8	138,170.4
Egypt	44,284.8	25,151.3	22,305.9
France (incl. Monaco)	588,101.4	587,280.7	390,197.9
Greece	30,937.4	45,847.0	97,427.7
India	178,607.4	188,593.7	77,863.2
Italy	705,995.5	547,802.5	409,613.5
Korea, Republic	144,102.3	167,301.4	68,011.2
Malta	8,695.4	69,027.9	74,378.2
Morocco	76,744.4	50,641.0	57,407.7
Netherlands	249,195.5	192,216.2	121,696.2
Portugal	140,120.0	110,855.2	55,368.5
Singapore	22,081.7	68,579.6	46,251.8
Spain	593,112.1	485,182.8	289,682.4
Tunisia	111,162.0	164,099.2	122,500.8
Türkiye	276,868.1	249,959.0	251,644.9
United Kingdom	319,424.4	270,121.8	n.a.
USA	472,994.4	259,124.9	50,064.4
Total (incl. others)	4,889,278.6	4,271,648.8	2,846,371.4

*Preliminary.

2018 ('000 million AD): Total exports (revised) 4,812.5.
2019 ('000 million AD): Total exports (revised) 4,206.2.
Total imports ('000 million AD): 5,097.5 in 2021; 5,705.3 in 2022.
Total exports ('000 million AD): 5,391.9 in 2021; 9,157.4 in 2022.

ALGERIA

Transport

RAILWAYS
(traffic)

	2016	2017	2018
Passengers carried ('000)	37,686	42,974	39,536
Freight carried ('000 metric tons)	3,486	4,005	4,422
Passenger-km (million)	1,337	1,550	1,602
Freight ton-km (million)	885	1,009	1,025

ROAD TRAFFIC
(motor vehicles in use at 31 December)

	2017	2018	2019
Passenger cars	3,984,250	4,151,041	4,245,307
Lorries and vans	1,693,431	1,626,241	1,644,298
Buses and coaches	86,741	87,968	88,707
Motorcycles and mopeds	77,568	139,780	181,458

SHIPPING

Flag Registered Fleet
(at 31 December)

	2020	2021	2022
Number of vessels	204	208	215
Total displacement ('000 grt)	728.8	720.6	727.1

Source: Lloyd's List Intelligence (www.bit.ly/LLintelligence).

CIVIL AVIATION
(traffic on scheduled services)

	2013	2014	2015
Kilometres flown (million)	60	67	73
Passengers carried ('000)	4,492	5,021	5,911
Passenger-km (million)	5,452	6,246	7,249
Total ton-km (million)	18	22	25

Source: UN, *Statistical Yearbook*.

2021 (domestic and international): Departures 27,650; Passengers carried 1.9m.; Freight carried 13m. ton-km (Source: World Bank, World Development Indicators database).

Tourism

FOREIGN TOURIST ARRIVALS BY COUNTRY OF ORIGIN*

	2019	2021†	2022
China, People's Republic	39,437	5,192	5,848
France	164,907	11,964	66,979
Italy	24,430	2,615	9,706
Morocco	79,505	1,492	21,654
Spain	35,828	3,961	14,882
Tunisia	1,323,709	7,648	496,278
Türkiye	32,593	7,152	14,890
Total (incl. others)	1,933,778	66,995	757,380

* Excluding arrivals of Algerian nationals resident abroad: 437,278 in 2019; 58,243 in 2021; 640,668 in 2022.
† Figures for 2020 were not available.

Source: Ministère du Tourisme et de l'Artisanat, Algiers.

Tourism receipts (US $ million, excl. passenger transport): 112 in 2019; 43 in 2020; 73 in 2021 (provisional) (Source: World Tourism Organization).

Communications Media

	2019	2020	2021
Telephones ('000 main lines in use)	4,635.7	4,785.8	5,097.1
Mobile telephone subscriptions ('000)	45,425.5	45,555.7	47,015.7
Broadband subscriptions, fixed ('000)	3,582.7	3,790.5	4,177.0
Broadband subscriptions, mobile ('000)	38,670.2	39,740.7	42,913.4
Internet users (% of population)	59.0	63.9	70.8

Source: International Telecommunication Union.

Education

(2019/20 unless otherwise indicated)

	Institutions	Teachers	Pupils
Primary*	19,308	205,848	5,175,274
Middle education*	5,630	162,733	3,123,435
Secondary	2,488	104,585	1,262,641
Higher†	50‡	58,647	1,523,985

* Primary education covers the first and second cycles of basic education, while middle education comprises the third cycle of basic education.
† 2017/18 figures.
‡ Universities only.

2019/20 (pre-primary only): 17,927 teachers; 505,857 pupils.

Pupil-teacher ratio (qualified teaching staff, primary education, UNESCO estimate): 24.2 in 2019/20 (Source: UNESCO Institute for Statistics).

Adult literacy rate (UNESCO estimates): 81.4% (males 87.4%; females 75.3%) in 2018 (Source: UNESCO Institute for Statistics).

Directory

The Constitution

A new Constitution for the People's Democratic Republic of Algeria was promulgated on 22 November 1976, with subsequent amendments approved on 30 June 1979, 3 November 1988, 23 February 1989, 28 November 1996, 8 April 2002 and 7 February 2016. Further amendments were approved at a national referendum on 1 November 2020. The principal changes on this occasion were the expansion of the two-term limit on the presidency to encompass both consecutive terms (as reintroduced in 2016) and non-consecutive terms; the imposition of a two-term limit on members of the National People's Assembly; the establishment of rules regarding the appointment of the Prime Minister; and the constitutionalization of the national independent election authority. The main provisions of the Constitution (as amended) are summarized below:

The Preamble recalls that Algeria owes its independence to a war of liberation which led to the creation of a modern sovereign state, guaranteeing social justice, equality and liberty for all. It emphasizes Algeria's Islamic, Arab and Amazigh (Berber) heritage, and stresses that, as an Arab Mediterranean and African country, it forms an integral part of the Great Arab Maghreb. The text refers specifically to the Hirak protest movement, which began in early 2019, citing its desire to build a 'new Algeria' via 'profound' social and political reforms. It states the purpose of the Constitution to guarantee individual and collective rights and freedoms, to protect the principle of free choice by the people and to enshrine the principle of the peaceful transfer of power via means of regular, free elections. The Preamble also reaffirms the separation and balance of powers among state institutions, judicial independence and oversight of state actions. It also emphasizes Algeria's commitment to upholding human rights, as defined by the 1948 Universal Declaration of Human Rights and subsequent international treaties to which Algeria is a party.

FUNDAMENTAL PRINCIPLES OF THE ORGANIZATION OF ALGERIAN SOCIETY

The Republic

Algeria is a popular, democratic state. Islam is the state religion, and Arabic and Tamazight are considered national and official languages of the state. Algiers is its capital city.

The People

National sovereignty resides in the people and is exercised through its elected representatives. The institutions of the state consolidate national unity and protect the fundamental rights of its citizens. The exploitation of one individual by another is forbidden.

The State

The state is exclusively at the service of the people and is founded on the principles of democratic representation, separation of powers, guaranteed rights and freedoms, and social justice. Those holding positions of responsibility must live solely on their salaries and may not, directly or by the agency of others, engage in any remunerative activity.

Fundamental Freedoms and the Rights of Man and the Citizen

Fundamental rights and freedoms are guaranteed. All discrimination on grounds of sex, race or belief is forbidden. Law cannot operate retrospectively, and a person is presumed innocent until proved guilty. Victims of judicial error shall receive compensation from the state.

The state guarantees the inviolability of the home, of private life and of the person. The state also guarantees the secrecy of correspondence, the freedom of conscience and opinion, freedom of intellectual, artistic and scientific creation, and freedom of expression and assembly.

The state guarantees the right to form political associations (on condition that they are not based on differences in religion, language, race, gender or region), the right to join a trade union, the right to strike, the right to work, to protection, to security, to health, to leisure, to education, etc. It also guarantees the right to leave the national territory, within the limits set by law.

Duties of Citizens

Every citizen must respect the Constitution, and must protect public property and safeguard national independence. The law sanctions the duty of parents to educate and protect their children, as well as the duty of children to help and support their parents. Every citizen must contribute towards public expenditure through the payment of taxes.

The People's National Army

The army safeguards national independence and sovereignty.

Principles of Foreign Policy

Algeria subscribes to the principles and objectives of the United Nations. It advocates international co-operation, the development of friendly relations between states, on the basis of equality and mutual interest, and non-interference in the internal affairs of states.

POWER AND ITS ORGANIZATION

The Executive

The President of the Republic is head of state, head of the armed forces and responsible for national defence. He or she must be of Algerian origin, a Muslim and more than 40 years old. He or she is elected by universal, secret, direct suffrage. The presidential mandate is for five years, and no individual may serve as President for more than two terms, consecutive or non-consecutive. The President embodies the unity of the nation. The President presides over meetings of the Council of Ministers. He or she decides and conducts foreign policy and appoints the Prime Minister, who must be supported by a majority of the members of the legislature. The Prime Minister, who is responsible to the National People's Assembly, must appoint a Council of Ministers within 30 days of being appointed. He or she drafts, co-ordinates and implements his or her Government's programme, which he or she must present to the Assembly for ratification. Should the Assembly reject the programme, the Prime Minister and the Council of Ministers resign, and the President appoints a new Prime Minister. Should the newly appointed Prime Minister's programme be rejected by the Assembly, the President dissolves the Assembly, and a general election is held. Should the President of the Republic be unable to perform his or her functions, owing to a long and serious illness, the President of the Council of the Nation assumes the office for a maximum period of 45 days (subject to the approval of a two-thirds' majority in the National People's Assembly and the Council of the Nation). If the President of the Republic is still unable to perform his or her functions after 45 days, the presidency is declared vacant by the Constitutional Court. Should the presidency fall vacant, the President of the Council of the Nation temporarily assumes the office and organizes presidential elections within 60 days. He or she may not himself or herself be a candidate in the election. The President of the Republic presides over a High Security Council, which advises on all matters affecting national security.

The Legislature

The legislature consists of the National People's Assembly and the Council of the Nation (which was established by constitutional amendments approved by national referendum in November 1996). The members of the lower chamber, the National People's Assembly, are elected by universal, direct, secret suffrage for a five-year term. Two-thirds of the members of the upper chamber, the Council of the Nation, are elected by indirect, secret suffrage from regional and municipal authorities; the remainder are appointed by the President of the Republic. The Council's term of office is six years; one-half of its members are replaced every three years. The deputies enjoy parliamentary immunity. The legislature sits for two ordinary sessions per year, each of not less than four months' duration. The commissions of the legislature are in permanent session. The two parliamentary chambers may be summoned to meet for an extraordinary session on the request of the President of the Republic, or of the Prime Minister, or of two-thirds of the members of the National People's Assembly. Both the Prime Minister and the parliamentary chambers may initiate legislation, which must be deliberated upon respectively by the National People's Assembly and the Council of the Nation before promulgation. Any text passed by the Assembly must be approved by three-quarters of the members of the Council in order to become legislation.

The Judiciary

Judges obey only the law. They defend society and fundamental freedoms. The right of the accused to a defence is guaranteed. The Supreme Court is the highest judicial instance, while the Council of State has jurisdiction over administrative cases. The High Council of Magistracy, the regulatory body of the judiciary, is presided over by the President of the Republic. Appointments to various judicial posts (including judges of the Supreme Court) are made by presidential decree, based on the proposals of the High Council of Magistracy. All magistrates are answerable to the High Council for the manner in which they fulfil their functions. The High Court of State is empowered to judge the President of the Republic in cases of high treason, and the Prime Minister for crimes and offences.

The Constitutional Court

The Constitutional Court is responsible for ensuring that the Constitution is respected, and that referendums, the election of the President of the Republic and legislative elections are conducted in accordance with the law. The Constitutional Court comprises 12 members, of whom four are appointed by the President of the Republic (including the President and Vice-President of the Court), and two each by the National People's Assembly, the Council of the Nation, the Supreme Court and the Council of State. The Constitutional Court's term of office is six years; one-half of the membership of the Court is replaced every three years.

The High Islamic Council

The High Islamic Council is an advisory body on matters relating to Islam. The Council comprises 15 members and its President is appointed by the President of the Republic.

Constitutional Revision

The Constitution can be revised on the initiative of the President of the Republic (subject to approval by the National People's Assembly and by three-quarters of the members of the Council of the Nation), and must be approved by national referendum. Should the Constitutional Court decide that a draft constitutional amendment does not in any way affect the general principles governing Algerian society, it may permit the President of the Republic to promulgate the amendment directly (without submitting it to referendum) if it has been approved by three-quarters of the members of both parliamentary chambers. Three-quarters of the members of both parliamentary chambers, in a joint sitting, may propose a constitutional amendment to the President of the Republic, who may submit it to referendum. The basic principles of the Constitution may not be revised.

The Government

HEAD OF STATE

President: ABDELMADJID TEBBOUNE (took office 19 Dec. 2019).

COUNCIL OF MINISTERS
(September 2023)

Prime Minister: AÏMEN BENABDERRAHMANE.
Minister of Foreign Affairs: AHMED ATTAF.
Minister of the Interior, Local Authorities and Territorial Planning: BRAHIM MERAD.
Minister of Finance: ABDELAZIZ FAYED.
Minister of Justice and Attorney-General: ABDERRACHID TEBBI.
Minister of Energy and Mining: MOHAMED ARKAB.
Minister of War Veterans and Related Persons: LAÏD REBIGUA.
Minister of Religious Affairs and Awqaf (Religious Endowments): YOUCEF BELMEHDI.
Minister of National Education: ABDELHAKIM BELABED.
Minister of Higher Education and Scientific Research: KAMEL BIDARI.
Minister of Vocational Training and Professional Education: YACINE MERABI.
Minister of Transport: YOUCEF CHORFA.
Minister of Culture and the Arts: SORAYA MOULOUDJI.
Minister of Youth and Sports: ABDERRAHMANE HAMMAD.
Minister of Digitization and Statistics: MERIEM BENMILOUD.
Minister of Postal Services and Telecommunications: KARIM BIBI TRIKI.
Minister of National Solidarity, the Family and Women: KAOUTAR KRIKOU.
Minister of Industry and Pharmaceutical Production: ALI AOUN.
Minister of Agriculture and Rural Development: MOHAMED ABDELHAFID HENNI.
Minister of Housing, Urban Planning and Towns: MOHAMED TAREK BELARIBI.
Minister of Trade and Export Promotion: TAYEB ZITOUNI.
Minister of Communication: MOHAMED LAAGAB.
Minister of Public Works and Basic Infrastructure: LAKHDAR RAKHROUKH.
Minister of Water Resources and Water Safety: TAHA DERBAL.
Minister of Tourism and Handicrafts: MOKHTAR DIDOUCHE.
Minister of Health, Population and Hospital Reform: ABDELHAK SAIHI.
Minister of Labour, Employment and Social Security: FAISAL BENTALEB.
Minister of Relations with Parliament: BASMA AZOUAR.
Minister of Environment and Renewable Energy: FAZIA DAHLEB.
Minister of Fisheries and Fish Production: AHMED BIDANI.
Minister of Knowledge Economy, Startups and Micro-enterprises: YACINE EL-MAHDI.
Secretary-General to the Government: YAHIA BOUKHARI.

MINISTRIES

Office of the President: Présidence de la République, el-Mouradia, Algiers; tel. (21) 69-15-15; fax (21) 69-15-95; internet www.elmouradia.dz.
Office of the Prime Minister: rue Docteur Saâdane, Palais du Gouvernement, Algiers; tel. (21) 73-12-00; fax (21) 71-07-83; internet www.cg.gov.dz.
Ministry of Agriculture and Rural Development: 12 ave Col Amirouche, Algiers; tel. (23) 50-32-38; fax (23) 50-31-17; internet madrp.gov.dz.
Ministry of Communication: Algiers; tel. (21) 54-10-15; fax (21) 56-39-99; internet www.ministerecommunication.gov.dz.
Ministry of Culture and Arts: BP 100, Palais de la Culture 'Moufdi Zakaria', Plateau des Annassers, Kouba, Algiers; tel. (23) 70-11-11; e-mail sg@m-culture.gov.dz; internet www.m-culture.gov.dz.
Ministry of Digitization and Statistics: Algiers.
Ministry of Energy and Mining: BP 229, Tower A, Val d'Hydra, Ben Aknoun, Algiers; tel. (21) 48-85-26; fax (21) 48-85-57; e-mail info@memalgeria.org; internet www.mem-algeria.org.
Ministry of Environment and Renewable Energy: 4 rue des Quatre Canons, Algiers; tel. (23) 49-59-50; fax (23) 49-57-64; e-mail contact@me.gov.dz; internet www.me.gov.dz.
Ministry of Finance: Immeuble Ahmed Francis, Ben Aknoun, Algiers; tel. (21) 59-51-51; e-mail mfmail@mf.gov.dz; internet www.mf.gov.dz.
Ministry of Fisheries and Fish Production: route des Quatre Canons, Algiers; tel. (21) 43-39-47; fax (21) 43-31-68; e-mail ministre@mpeche.gov.dz; internet www.mpeche.gov.dz.
Ministry of Foreign Affairs: place Mohamed Seddik Benyahia, el-Mouradia, Algiers; tel. (21) 29-12-12; fax (21) 50-43-63; internet www.mae.gov.dz.
Ministry of Health, Population and Hospital Reform: 125 rue Abderrahmane Laâla, el-Madania, Algiers; tel. (21) 27-92-11; fax (21) 27-99-50; e-mail secretariatgeneral@sante.gov.dz; internet www.sante.gov.dz.
Ministry of Higher Education and Scientific Research: 11 chemin Doudou Mokhtar, Ben Aknoun, Algiers; tel. (23) 23-80-66; fax (23) 23-80-14; e-mail webmaster@mesrs.dz; internet www.mesrs.dz.
Ministry of Housing, Urban Planning and Towns: 135 rue Mourad Didouche, Algiers; tel. (21) 74-07-22; e-mail ministere_mhuv@mhuv.gov.dz; internet www.mhuv.gov.dz.
Ministry of Industry and Pharmaceutical Production: Immeuble de la Colisée, 2 rue Ahmed Bey, el-Biar, Algiers; tel. (21) 74-75-48; e-mail contact@industrie.gov.dz; internet www.industrie.gov.dz.
Ministry of the Interior, Local Authorities and Territorial Planning: 1 rue Docteur Saâdane, Algiers; tel. (21) 73-23-40; e-mail webmaster@interieur.gov.dz; internet www.interieur.gov.dz.
Ministry of Justice: 8 place Bir Hakem, el-Biar, Algiers; tel. (21) 92-41-83; fax (21) 92-29-56; e-mail contact@mjustice.dz; internet www.mjustice.dz.
Ministry of Knowledge Economy, Startups and Micro-enterprises: Algiers.
Ministry of Labour, Employment and Social Security: 44 rue Muhammad Belouizdad, 16600 Algiers; tel. (21) 65-99-99; fax (21) 66-12-92; internet www.mtess.gov.dz.
Ministry of Mining: Algiers.
Ministry of National Defence: Les Tagarins, el-Biar, Algiers; tel. (21) 71-15-15; fax (21) 72-51-73; internet www.mdn.dz.
Ministry of National Education: 8 rue de Pékin, el-Mouradia, Algiers; tel. (21) 60-55-60; fax (21) 60-67-02; e-mail education@men.dz.
Ministry of National Solidarity, the Family and Women: BP 31, route nationale no. 1, Les Vergers, Bir Khadem, Algiers; tel. (21) 44-99-46; fax (21) 44-97-26; e-mail contact@msnfcf.gov.dz; internet www.msnfcf.gov.dz.
Ministry of Postal Services and Telecommunications: 4 blvd Krim Belkacem, 16027 Algiers; tel. (21) 71-12-20; fax (21) 73-00-47; e-mail contact@mpttn.gov.dz; internet www.mpttn.gov.dz.

ALGERIA

Ministry of Public Works and Basic Infrastructure: 6 rue Moustafa Khalef, Ben Aknoun, Algiers; tel. (21) 37-56-17; fax (21) 37-56-53; internet www.mtp.gov.dz.

Ministry of Religious Affairs and Awqaf (Religious Endowments): 4 rue de Timgad, Hydra, Algiers; tel. (23) 48-44-20; fax (21) 69-15-69; e-mail info@marw.dz; internet www.marw.dz.

Ministry of Tourism and Handicrafts: 119 rue Didouche Mourad, Algiers; tel. and fax (21) 71-45-45; e-mail contact@mta.gov.dz; internet www.mta.gov.dz.

Ministry of Trade and Export Promotion: Cité Zerhouni Mokhtar les El Mohamadia, Algiers; tel. (21) 89-00-74; fax (21) 89-00-34; internet www.commerce.gov.dz.

Ministry of Transport: 1 chemin ibn Badis el-Mouiz (ex Poirson), el-Biar, 16300 Algiers; tel. (21) 92-98-85; fax (21) 92-98-94.

Ministry of Vocational Training and Professional Education: rue des Frères Aîssou, Ben Aknoun, Algiers; tel. (23) 25-52-66; fax (23) 25-52-97; e-mail contacts@mfep.gov.dz; internet www.mfep.gov.dz.

Ministry of War Veterans: 2 ave du Lt Muhammad Benarfa, el-Biar, Algiers; tel. (21) 92-23-55; fax (21) 92-35-16; internet www.m-moudjahidine.dz.

Ministry of Water Resources: 3 rue du Caire, Kouba, Algiers; tel. (23) 33-69-78; internet www.mree.gov.dz.

Ministry of Youth and Sports: 3 rue Muhammad Belouizdad, Algiers; tel. (21) 51-24-24; fax (21) 65-71-74; e-mail mjs@mail.com; internet www.mjs.gov.dz.

President

Presidential Election, 12 December 2019

Candidate	Votes	%
Abdelmadjid Tebboune	4,945,116	58.15
Abdelkader Bengrina	1,477,735	17.38
Ali Benflis	896,934	10.55
Azzedine Mihoubi	617,753	7.26
Abdelaziz Belaid	566,808	6.66
Total	**8,504,346***	**100.00**

* Excluding 1,255,046 invalid votes.

Legislature

NATIONAL PEOPLE'S ASSEMBLY

National People's Assembly: ave Zighout Youcef, 16000 Algiers; tel. (21) 73-86-00; e-mail contact@apn.gov.dz; internet www.apn.dz.
President: IBRAHIM BOUGHALI.

General Election, 12 June 2021

	Seats
Front de Libération Nationale (FLN)	98
Mouvement de la Société pour la Paix (MSP)	65
Rassemblement National Démocratique (RND)	58
Front El-Moustakbal (FM)	48
Mouvement El-Bina	39
Parti Voix du Peuple (PVP)	3
Parti de la Justice et le Développement	2
Parti de la Liberté et de la Justice (PLJ)	2
Parti el-Fedjr el-Jadid (PFJ)	2
Front de la Bonne Gouvernance (FBG)	2
Front de l'Algérie Nouvelle (FAN)	1
Parti El-Karama (PK)	1
Parti de Jil Jadid	1
Front National Algérien (FNA)	1
Independents	84
Total	**407**

COUNCIL OF THE NATION

Council of the Nation: 7 blvd Zighout Youcef, 16000 Algiers; tel. (21) 74-60-85; fax (21) 74-60-79; e-mail sg@majliselouma.dz; internet www.majliselouma.dz.
President: SALAH GOUDJIL.

Elections, 29 December 2018 and 5 February 2022*

	Seats
Front de Libération Nationale (FLN)	54
Rassemblement National Démocratique (RND)	22
Front El-Moustakbal (FM)	7
Mouvement El-Bina	5
Front des Forces Socialistes (FFS)	4
Parti Voix du Peuple (PVP)	2
Parti el-Fedjr el-Jadid (PFJ)	2
Mouvement de la Société pour la Paix (MSP)	1
Tajamoua Amel El-Djazaïr (TAJ)	1
Independents	18
Appointed by the President	58
Total	**174**

* Deputies of the 174-member Council of the Nation serve a six-year term; one-half of its members are replaced every three years. Elected representatives are selected by indirect, secret suffrage from regional and municipal authorities. Following the creation of 10 new departments (*wilayat*) in December 2019, for the elections in February 2022 the number of elected deputies was increased from 96 to 116 and the number of presidential appointees from 48 to 58.

Election Commission

L'Autorité Nationale Indépendante des Élections (ANIE): Palais des Nations, Algiers; fax (21) 37-68-74; internet ina-elections.dz; f. 2019; Pres. MOHAMED CHARFI.

Political Organizations

Until 1989 the FLN was the only legal party in Algeria. Amendments to the Constitution in February of that year permitted the formation of other political associations, with some restrictions. The right to establish political parties was guaranteed by constitutional amendments in November 1996; however, political associations based on differences in religion, language, race, gender or region were proscribed. The most prominent political organizations currently active are listed below.

Ahd 54 (Oath 54): 53 rue Larbi Ben M'Hedi, Algiers; f. 1991; small nationalist party; Pres. ALI FAWZI REBAÏNE.

Alliance El-Itihad: Algiers; f. 2017; electoral alliance formed by 3 Islamist parties—Mouvement de la Renaissance Islamique (Al-Nahda), Front pour la Justice et le Développement (FJD—El-Addala) and Mouvement El-Binaa—to contest the 2017 legislative elections.

Alliance Nationale Républicaine (ANR): 1 lot Bouchaoui, Algiers; f. 1995; anti-Islamist; Sec.-Gen. Dr BELKACEM SAHLI.

Front de l'Algérie Nouvelle (FAN): Algiers; Pres. DJAMEL BENABDESLAM.

Front de la Bonne Gouvernance: Algiers; internet fb.com/front-de-la-bonne-gouvernance-720638968002388; Sec.-Gen. AISSA BELHAD.

Front des Forces Socialistes (FFS): 56 ave Souidani Boudjemaâ, el-Mouradia, 16000 Algiers; tel. (23) 47-15-06; fax (23) 47-15-08; e-mail communication@ffs.dz; internet www.ffs.dz; f. 1963; revived 1989; seeks greater autonomy for Berber-dominated regions and official recognition of the Berber language; First Sec. YOUCEF AOUCHICHE.

Front pour la Justice et le Développement (FJD): Baba Hassen, Algiers; tel. and fax (21) 41-55-79; f. 2011; moderate Islamist party; Leader ABDELLAH DJABALLAH.

Front de Libération Nationale (FLN): rue Mohammed Baq, Hydra, Algiers; tel. (23) 48-04-49; internet www.pfln.dz; f. 1954; sole legal party until 1989; socialist in outlook, the party is organized into a Secretariat, a National Council, an Executive Committee, Federations, Kasmas and cells; under the aegis of the FLN are various mass political orgs, incl. the Union Nationale de la Jeunesse Algérienne and the Union Nationale des Femmes Algériennes; Sec.-Gen. ABOU EL-FADL BAADJI.

Front El-Moustakbal (FM): Algiers; tel. (23) 72-70-35; e-mail parti.fm.info@gmail.com; internet fb.com/parti.fm; f. 2012; Pres. ABDELAZIZ BELAÏD.

Front du Militantisme National (FMN): Algiers; f. 2012; Pres. ABDALLAH HADDAD.

Front National Algérien (FNA): 18 rue Chaib Ahmed, 16100 Algiers; e-mail touatimoussa@yahoo.fr; f. 1999; advocates eradication of poverty and supports the Govt's peace initiative; Pres. MOUSSA TOUATI.

ALGERIA

Front National pour la Justice Sociale (FNJS): Algiers; f. 2012; Pres. REDOUANE KHELIF.

Mouvement pour l'Autodétermination de la Kabylie (MAK): Tizi Ouzou; internet makabylie.org; f. 2001; founded as the Mouvement pour l'Autonomie de la Kabylie; present name adopted 2013; advocates autonomy for the north-eastern region of Kabylia within a federal Algerian state; outlawed by the Govt in 2021; Pres. FERHAT MEHENNI.

Mouvement El-Bina: Algiers; Pres. ABDELKADER BENGRINA.

Mouvement des Citoyens Libres (MCL): Algiers; f. 2012; Pres. MUSTAPHA BOUDINA.

Mouvement Démocratique et Social (MDS): 67 blvd Krim Belkacem, 16200 Algiers; tel. (21) 63-86-05; fax (21) 63-89-12; e-mail mdsalgerie.dz@gmail.com; f. 1998 by fmr mems of Ettahadi; left-wing party; Sec.-Gen. FETHI GHARES.

Mouvement de l'Entente Nationale (MEN): Algiers; e-mail men.national@yahoo.com; Sec.-Gen. ALI BOUKHEZNA.

Mouvement El-Infitah (ME): Algiers; f. 1997; present name adopted 2007; Pres. OMAR BOUACHA.

Mouvement El Islah (MRN) (Mouvement de la Réforme Nationale): Algiers; tel. (23) 54-22-79; internet fb.com/elislah.algeria; f. 1998; radical Islamist party; contested May 2012 legislative elections as part of Alliance de l'Algérie Verte; Pres. FAYÇAL BOUSSEDARIA.

Mouvement Populaire Algérien (MPA): 53 Coopérative des Médecins, Ben Aknoun, Algiers; tel. (21) 94-67-07; fax (21) 94-67-27; Sec.-Gen. AMARA BENYOUNES.

Mouvement de la Renaissance Islamique (Al-Nahda) (Harakat al-Nahda al-Islamiyya): blvd des Martyrs, 16100 Algiers; tel. (21) 74-85-14; e-mail medias.nahda@gmail.com; internet fb.com/nahdadz01; fundamentalist Islamist group; contested 2017 legislative elections as part of Alliance El-Itihad; Sec.-Gen. MOHAMED ZWAIBI.

Mouvement de la Société pour la Paix (MSP) (Harakat Mujtamaa al-Silm): 63 rue Ali Haddad, el-Mouradia, Algiers; tel. (21) 27-35-02; fmrly known as Hamas; adopted current name in 1997; moderate Islamist party; favours the gradual introduction of an Islamic state; Pres. ABDELAALI HASSANI-CHERIF.

Parti Algérien Vert pour le Développement (PAVD) (Algerian Green Party for Development): Algiers; internet pavd-dz.com; f. 2012; Pres. ALI AMARA.

Parti el-Fedjr el-Jadid (PFJ): Algiers; Pres. TAHAR BENBAÏBECHE.

Parti de Jil Jadid: Zeralda, Algiers; tel. (23) 32-20-34; e-mail contact@jiljadid.org; internet jiljadid.org; Pres. SOUFIANE DJILALI.

Parti El-Karama (PK): Algiers; f. 2012; Sec.-Gen. MOHAMED DAOUI.

Parti de la Liberté et de la Justice (PLJ): 12 rue Ali Boumendjel, Algiers; tel. (21) 73 94 72; e-mail plj.national@yahoo.com; internet www.plj.dz; Pres. DJAMEL BENZIADI.

Parti du Renouveau Algérien (PRA): 8 ave de Pékin, 16209 el-Mouradia, Algiers; tel. (21) 59-43-00; Pres. KAMEL BENSALEM.

Parti des Travailleurs (PT): 2 rue Belkheir Hassan Badi, el-Harrach, 16000 Algiers; tel. (23) 82-71-56; fax (23) 82-71-58; e-mail contact@pt.dz; internet www.pt.dz; workers' party; Leader LOUISA HANOUNE.

Parti des Jeunes (PJ): Algiers; f. 2012; Gen. Co-ordinator HAMANA BOUCHERMA.

Parti National pour la Solidarité et le Développement (PNSD): BP 110, Staouéli, Algiers; tel. and fax (21) 39-40-42; e-mail cherif_taleb@yahoo.fr; f. 1989 as Parti Social Démocrate; Leader MUHAMMAD CHÉRIF TALEB.

Parti Voix du Peuple (PVP): 29 rue el-Kadous, Birkhadem, Algiers; tel. (23) 59-75-53; e-mail pvpparti@gmail.com; internet parti-pvp.org; f. 2019; Pres. LAMINE OSMANI.

Rassemblement Algérien (RA): Cité Ahcène Mahiouz, BP 158, Ben Aknoun, 16000 Algiers; f. 2008; Pres. Dr ALI ZEGHDOUD.

Rassemblement pour la Culture et la Démocratie (RCD): 40 rue Muhammad Chabane, el-Biar, Algiers; f. 1989; social democratic and secular party; advocates inclusion of Berber traditions into the Algerian identity; Pres. ATMANE MAZOUZ.

Rassemblement National Démocratique (RND): BP 10, Cité des Asphodèles, Ben Aknoun, Algiers; tel. (21) 91-64-10; fax (21) 91-47-40; e-mail contact@rnd-dz.com; f. 1997; centrist party; Sec.-Gen. TAYEB ZITOUNI.

Rassemblement Patriotique Républicain (RPR): Algiers; Pres. ABDELKADER MERBAH.

Tajamoua Amel El-Djazaïr (TAJ) (Rassemblement de l'Espoir de l'Algérie): Algiers; tel. (796) 03-61-63; e-mail tajcomme@gmail.com; internet fb.com/tajwatani; f. 2012; Pres. FATIMA-ZOHRA ZEROUATI.

Union des Forces Démocratiques et Sociales (UFDS—El-Ittihad): 3 ave Frères Bouadou, F05, Bir Mourad Rais, Algiers; tel. (21) 54-06-15.

The following groups are in armed conflict with the Government:

Al-Qa'ida Organization in the Land of the Islamic Maghreb (AQIM): f. 1998 as the Groupe Salafiste pour la Prédication et le Combat (GSPC), a breakaway faction from the Groupe Islamique Armé; adopted current name in Jan. 2007, when it aligned itself with the militant Islamist al-Qa'ida network; particularly to the east of Algiers and in Kabylia; as the GSPC, traditionally responded to preaching by Ali Belhadj, the second most prominent member of the proscribed Front Islamique du Salut; Leader Sheikh MUJAHID YAZID MUBARAK (also known as Abu Ubaida Yusuf al-Annabi).

Groupe Islamique Armé (GIA): f. 1992; was the most prominent and radical Islamist militant group in the mid-1990s, but has reportedly split into several factions that do not all adhere to one leader.

Diplomatic Representation

EMBASSIES IN ALGERIA

Angola: rue 90 Domine Ben Haddadi Said-Dar Diaf Chéraga, Algiers; tel. (23) 27-94-17; fax (23) 27-94-15; e-mail embaixada.argelia@mirex.gov.ao; Ambassador TOKO DIAKENDA.

Argentina: 5 chemin Mackley, Ben Aknoun, 16028 Algiers; tel. (23) 18-74-40; fax (23) 18-74-39; e-mail earge@cancilleria.gov.ar; internet earge.cancilleria.gob.ar; Ambassador MARIANO SIMÓN PADRÓS.

Austria: 17 chemin Abdelkader Gadouche, Hydra, 16035 Algiers; tel. (23) 47-28-15; fax (23) 47-28-22; e-mail algier-ob@bmeia.gv.at; internet www.bmeia.gv.at/oeb-algier; Ambassador CHRISTINE MOSER.

Azerbaijan: 29 rue Abu Nuwas, Hydra, Algiers; tel. (23) 47-41-99; fax (23) 47-42-24; Ambassador TURAL RZAYEV.

Bahrain: 17 rue Yahia Belhayat, Hydra, Algiers; tel. (23) 45-92-13; fax (23) 45-92-12; e-mail algiers.mission@mofa.gov.bh; internet www.mofa.gov.bh/algiers; Ambassador FUAD SADIQ AL-BAHARNA.

Bangladesh: 24 Cheikh Bachir Ibrahimi, el-Biar, Algiers; tel. (23) 05-30-01; fax (21) 79-74-01; e-mail mission.algiers@mofa.gov.bd; internet algiers.mofa.gov.bd; Ambassador MUHAMMAD ZULQAR NAIN.

Belgium: BP 341, 22 rue Mohammed Benadache, chemin Youssef Tayebi, 16030 el-Biar, Algiers; tel. (23) 05-24-11; fax (23) 05-24-06; e-mail algiers@diplobel.fed.be; internet algeria.diplomatie.belgium.be; Ambassador ALAIN LEROY.

Brazil: 55 bis, chemin Cheikh Bachir el-Ibrahimi, el-Biar, 16030 Algiers; tel. (23) 05-28-19; fax (23) 05-28-16; e-mail brasemb.argel@itamaraty.gov.br; internet argel.itamaraty.gov.br; Ambassador FLÁVIO MAREGA.

Bulgaria: 13 blvd Col Bougara, el-Biar, Algiers; tel. (21) 23-00-14; fax (21) 23-05-33; e-mail embassy.algiers@mfa.bg; internet www.mfa.bg/embassies/algeria; Ambassador MARIANA BOYADZHIEVA.

Burkina Faso: BP 212, 23 Lot el-Feth, chemin ibn Badis el-Mouiz (ex Poirson), el-Biar, Didouche Mourad, Algiers; tel. (21) 30-67-61; e-mail abfalger@yahoo.fr; internet www.fb.com/abfalger; Ambassador OUMAROU SADOU.

Cameroon: 5 rue J. Aprement, Air de France, Algiers; tel. (21) 78-81-95; fax (21) 92-11-25; e-mail ambacam.alger@diplocam.cm; Ambassador KOMIDOR HAMIDOU NJIMOLUH.

Canada: BP 464, 18 rue Mustapha Khalef, Ben Aknoun, 16306 Algiers; tel. (770) 08-30-00; fax (770) 08-30-40; e-mail alger@international.gc.ca; internet www.canadainternational.gc.ca/algeria-algerie; Ambassador MICHAEL CALLAN.

Chad: Villa 18, Cité DNC, chemin Ahmed Kara, Hydra, Algiers; tel. (23) 48-92-08; fax (23) 48-92-09; Ambassador MOUKHTAR WAWA DAHAB.

Chile: 5 impasse chemin du Resérvoire, Hydra, Algiers; tel. (21) 48-47-61; fax (21) 60-34-27; e-mail echiledz@minrel.gob.cl; internet chile.gob.cl/argelia; Ambassador FRANCISCO JAVIER BERGUNO HURTADO.

China, People's Republic: 34 blvd des Martyrs, Algiers; tel. (23) 46-90-20; fax (21) 69-30-56; e-mail chinaemb_dz@mfa.gov.cn; internet dz.chineseembassy.org; Ambassador LI JIAN.

Colombia: 5 impasse chemin du Réservoir, Hydra, Algiers; tel. (21) 60-22-97; e-mail eargelia@cancilleria.gov.co; internet argelia.embajada.gov.co; Ambassador JOSÉ ANTONIO SOLARTE GÓMEZ.

Congo, Republic: 86 ave des Frères Abdeslami, Vieux Kouba, Algiers; tel. (21) 44-85-93; fax (21) 28-39-70; Ambassador JEAN-PIERRE LOUYEBO.

Côte d'Ivoire: BP 260, Immeuble 'Le Bosquet', Parc Paradou, Hydra, Algiers; tel. (21) 69-28-28; fax (21) 69-30-32; e-mail acialg@yahoo.fr; Ambassador ALPHONSE VOHO SAHI.

Croatia: 26 bis, rue Hadj Ahmed Mohamed, Hydra, 16405 Algiers; tel. (23) 48-01-34; fax (23) 48-01-32; e-mail croemb.algeria@mvep.hr; Ambassador ILIJA ŽELALIĆ.

ALGERIA

Cuba: 22 rue Larbi Allik, Hydra, Algiers; tel. (21) 69-21-48; fax (21) 69-32-81; e-mail embajada@dz.embacuba.cu; internet misiones.minrex.gob.cu/fr/algerie; Ambassador ARMANDO VERGARA BUENO.

Czech Republic: BP 358, Villa Koudia, 3 chemin Ziryab, Algiers; tel. (21) 23-00-56; fax (21) 23-01-33; e-mail algiers@embassy.mzv.cz; internet www.mzv.cz/algiers; Ambassador JAN CERNY.

Denmark: 7 chemin Doudou Mokhtar, Ben Aknoun, Algiers; tel. (770) 08-23-10; fax (770) 23-86-05; e-mail algamb@um.dk; internet algeriet.um.dk; Ambassador KATRINE F. HOYER.

Egypt: BP 297, 8 chemin Abdelkader Gadouche, 16300 Hydra, Algiers; tel. (21) 69-16-73; fax (21) 69-29-52; e-mail embassy.algeria@mfa.gov.eg; Ambassador MOKHTAR GAMIL TAWFIK WARIDA.

Finland: 10 rue des Cèdres, el-Mouradia, Algiers; tel. (23) 52-75-80; fax (23) 52-75-84; e-mail sanomat.alg@formin.fi; internet www.finlandalgeria.org; Ambassador MARJA JOENUSVA.

France: 25 chemin Abdelkader Gadouche, 16035 Hydra, Algiers; tel. (21) 98-17-17; internet dz.ambafrance.org; Ambassador STÉPHANE ROMATET.

Germany: BP 664, 165 chemin Sfindja, Alger-Gare, 16000 Algiers; tel. (21) 74-19-56; fax (21) 74-05-21; e-mail info@algier.diplo.de; internet www.algier.diplo.de; Ambassador ELISABETH WOLBERS.

Ghana: 62 rue des Frères Benali Abdellah, Hydra, Algiers; tel. (23) 47-40-65; fax (21) 69-28-56; e-mail algeria@mfa.gov.gh; internet algiers.mfa.gov.gh; Ambassador YAW BIMPONG.

Greece: 60 blvd Col Bougara, 16030 el-Biar, Algiers; tel. (23) 37-80-91; fax (23) 37-79-81; e-mail gremb.alg@mfa.gr; internet www.mfa.gr/algiers; Ambassador GEORGIOS ZACHARIOUDAKIS.

Guinea: 47 blvd Central Saïd Hamdine, Hydra, Algiers; tel. (21) 69-36-11; fax (21) 69-34-68; e-mail ambaga49@yahoo.fr; Ambassador (vacant).

Guinea-Bissau: BP 32, Villa 17, rue Ahmad Kara, Colonne Volrol, Hydra, Algiers; tel. and fax (21) 60-84-00; e-mail mbagbalg@yahoo.com.br; Ambassador MAMADOU ALIOU JALLOW.

Holy See: 1 rue Noureddine Mekiri, 16021 Bologhine, Algiers (Apostolic Nunciature); tel. (23) 15-40-65; fax (23) 15-40-60; Apostolic Nuncio KURIAN MATHEW VAYALUNKAL (Titular Archbishop of Ratiaria).

Hungary: BP 68, 18 ave des Frères Oughlis, el-Mouradia, Algiers; tel. (23) 52-69-57; fax (23) 52-69-78; e-mail mission.alg@mfa.gov.hu; internet algir.mfa.gov.hu; Ambassador GYÖRGY PÁNTOS.

India: 26 rue Belkacem Amani, Paradou, Hydra, Algiers; tel. (23) 47-25-21; fax (23) 47-29-04; e-mail hoc.algiers@mea.gov.in; internet www.indianembassyalgiers.gov.in; Ambassador GAURAV AHLUWALIA.

Indonesia: BP 62, 61 ave Souidani Boudjemaa, el-Mouradia, Algiers; tel. (23) 47-15-61; fax (23) 47-15-38; e-mail alger.kbri@kemlu.go.id; internet www.kemlu.go.id/algiers; Ambassador CHALIEF AKBAR.

Iran: Jardin Olof Palme, chemin Sidi Yahia, Hydra, Algiers; tel. (23) 47-81-79; fax (23) 47-81-93; internet algeria.mfa.gov.ir; Ambassador MOHAMMAD REZA BABAEI.

Iraq: BP 249, 4 rue Abri Arezki, Hydra, Algiers; tel. (21) 69-31-25; fax (21) 69-10-97; internet www.mofa.gov.iq/algeria; Chargé d'affaires MEKDAD ABDUL HAMID.

Italy: 18 rue Muhammad Ouidir Amellal, 16030 el-Biar, Algiers; tel. (23) 05-14-34; fax (23) 05-14-20; e-mail segreteria.algeri@esteri.it; internet www.ambalgeri.esteri.it; Ambassador GIOVANNI PUGLIESE.

Japan: BP 80, 1 chemin el-Bakri, Ben Aknoun, el-Biar, Algiers; tel. (23) 37-55-11; fax (23) 37-54-97; internet www.dz.emb-japan.go.jp; Ambassador KONO AKIRA.

Jordan: 44 blvd Said Hamdine, Hydra, Algiers; tel. (21) 69-20-31; fax (21) 69-15-54; e-mail jordan@ambassade-jordanie.dz; Ambassador SHAKER AL-AMOUSH.

Kenya: 6 lot Borsas, Haute Site, Hydra, 16035 Algiers; tel. (23) 23-08-54; fax (23) 23-08-75; e-mail algiers@mfa.go.ke; internet algiers.mfa.go.ke; Ambassador PETER KATANA ANGORE.

Korea, Democratic People's Republic: 48 rue Madeline Bourssas, Hydra, Algiers; tel. (21) 23-04-19; fax (21) 23-04-32; e-mail agkoem@gmail.com; Ambassador SONG CHANG-SIK.

Korea, Republic: 5 chemin el-Bakri, Ben Aknoun, Algiers; tel. (23) 18-77-17; fax (23) 47-28-51; e-mail koemal@mofa.go.kr; internet overseas.mofa.go.kr/dz-fr/index.do; Ambassador YOU KI-JUN.

Kuwait: BP 340, 2 chemin al-Bakri, Hydra, Algiers; tel. (21) 59-20-20; fax (21) 59-22-33; e-mail q8alg@hotmail.com; Ambassador MOHAMMAD AL-SHABO.

Lebanon: 14 rue du Hoggar, Hydra, Algiers; tel. (21) 69-39-70; fax (21) 69-23-97; e-mail libalg@wissal.dz; Ambassador MUHAMMAD MAHMOUD HASSAN.

Libya: 15 chemin Cheikh Bachir el-Ibrahimi, Algiers; tel. (21) 92-52-93; fax (21) 92-46-87; e-mail ambassadedelibyaenalgerie@gmail.com; Ambassador SALEH MOHAMED HIMMA BAKDA.

Madagascar: BP 65, 22 rue Abd al-Kader Aouis, 16090 Bologhine, Algiers; Chargé d'affaires JENIN PERTHIN.

Malaysia: Villa 9, chemin Said Hamdine, 16406 Hydra, Algiers; tel. (21) 60-68-12; fax (21) 60-68-18; e-mail mwalgiers@kln.gov.my; internet www.kln.gov.my/web/dza_algiers; Ambassador MOHAMMAD FAIZAL RAZALI.

Mali: Quartier Diplomatique, Ain Allah, Dély Ibrahim, Algiers; tel. (23) 21-15-17; e-mail ambamalialger@gmail.com; Ambassador MAHAMANE AMADOU MAIGA.

Mauritania: rue 32, Les Caroubiers, Dély Ibrahim, Algiers; tel. (21) 91-71-72; fax (21) 91-08-15; e-mail ambrimalger@yahoo.fr; Ambassador WEDADY SIDI HAIBA.

Mexico: BP 329, 25 chemin El-Bakri, Ben Aknoun, 16306 Algiers; tel. (21) 91-46-00; fax (21) 91-46-01; e-mail embamexargelia@gmail.com; internet embamex.sre.gob.mx/argelia; Ambassador GABRIEL ROSENZWEIG PICHARDO.

Mozambique: Coopérative el-Bina, Lot 3, rue Hai el-Bina, Dély Ibrahim, Algiers; tel. (23) 30-43-97; fax (23) 30-47-67; e-mail ambassademozambiquealger@yahoo.fr; Ambassador CARVALHO MUÁRIA.

Netherlands: BP 72, 23/27 chemin Cheikh Bachir el-Ibrahimi, el-Biar, Algiers; tel. (23) 05-28-47; e-mail alg@minbuza.nl; internet www.paysbasmondial.nl/pays/algerie; Ambassador JANNA VAN DER VELDE.

Niger: 54 rue Vercors Rostamia, Bouzaréah, Algiers; tel. (21) 93-71-90; fax (21) 93-99-49; e-mail ambassadenigeralger@hotmail.fr; Ambassador AMINOU ELH MALAM MANZON.

Nigeria: 6 rue Paradou, Hydra, Algiers; tel. (21) 69-10-83; fax (21) 69-13-29; e-mail nigerianalgiers@hotmail.com; Ambassador AISHA MOHAMMED GARBA.

Norway: 7 chemin Doudou Mokhtar, Ben Aknoun, 16035 Algiers; tel. (23) 23-85-12; fax (23) 23-85-11; e-mail emb.alger@mfa.no; internet www.norway.no/fr/algeria; Ambassador THERESE LOKEN-GISELLE.

Oman: BP 456, Villa 5, rue Doudou Mokhtar, Ben Aknoun, Algiers; tel. (21) 91-28-35; fax (21) 91-47-37; e-mail algeria@fm.gov.om; Ambassador SAIF BIN NASSER BIN RASHID AL-BADAEI.

Pakistan: BP 395, Villa 18, rue des Idrissides, el-Biar, Algiers; tel. (21) 79-37-56; fax (21) 79-37-58; e-mail parepalgiers@mofa.gov.pk; internet www.mofa.gov.pk/algeria; Ambassador MUHAMMED TARIQ.

Peru: 14 rue 3, Parc Paradou, Hydra, 16016 Algiers; tel. (21) 47-81-98; e-mail ambaperou@hotmail.com; Ambassador JORGE EDUARDO WURST CALLE.

Poland: rue Olof Palme, Nouveau-Paradou, Hydra, Algiers; tel. (21) 60-99-50; fax (21) 60-99-59; e-mail algier.amb.sekretariat@msz.gov.pl; internet www.msz.gov.pl; Chargé d'affaires a.i. JAN LINKOWSKI.

Portugal: 3 blvd du 11 Décembre 1960, Val d'Hydra, Algiers; tel. (21) 92-55-82; fax (21) 92-53-13; e-mail secretariado.argel@mne.pt; internet www.argel.embaixadaportugal.mne.pt; Ambassador LUÍS DE ALBUQUERQUE VELOSO.

Qatar: BP 35, Quartier Diplomatique, Dély Ibrahim, Algiers; tel. (23) 31-28-12; fax (23) 31-25-59; e-mail algiers@mofa.gov.qa; internet algeria.embassy.qa; Ambassador ABDULAZIZ NAAMA AL-NAAMA.

Romania: 24 rue Abri Arezki, Hydra, 16035 Algiers; tel. (23) 48-55-87; fax (23) 48-55-86; e-mail alger@mae.ro; internet alger.mae.ro; Ambassador GRUYA OTILIO JACOTA.

Russian Federation: 7 chemin du Prince d'Annam, el-Biar, Algiers; tel. (23) 37-68-65; fax (23) 37-68-67; e-mail ambrussie@yandex.ru; internet www.algerie.mid.ru; Ambassador VALERIAN SHUVAEV.

Saudi Arabia: BP 256, 5 chemin Doudou Mokhtar, Ben Aknoun, el-Biar, Algiers; tel. (23) 23-84-29; fax (23) 23-84-43; e-mail dzemb@mofa.gov.sa; internet embassies.mofa.gov.sa/sites/algeria; Ambassador ABDULLAH BIN NASSIR ABDULLAH AL-BASSIRI.

Senegal: 11 chemin Doudou Mokhtar, Ben Aknoun, Algiers; tel. (21) 23-07-63; fax (21) 23-07-65; e-mail secretariat@ambassadesenegal.dz; internet www.ambassadesenegal.dz; Ambassador SERIGNE DIEYE.

Serbia: 42 rue des Frères Benali Abdellah, 16035 Hydra, Algiers; tel. (23) 47-41-50; fax (23) 47-41-47; e-mail ambasada@ambserbie-alger.com; internet alger.mfa.gov.rs; Chargé d'affaires a.i. MILOS JASTREBIĆ.

South Africa: 21 rue du Stade, Hydra, 16035 Algiers; tel. (21) 48-44-18; fax (21) 48-44-19; e-mail algiers.embassy@dirco.gov.za; internet www.dirco.gov.za/algiers; Chargé d'affaires a.i. Dr S. P. RANKHUMISE.

Spain: BP 185, 3 chemin Youcef Ziryab, Algiers; tel. (21) 23-97-86; fax (21) 23-99-28; e-mail emb.argel@mae.es; internet www

.exteriores.gob.es/embajadas/argel; Ambassador FERNANDO MORAN CALVO-SOTELO.

Sudan: 27 rue des Frères Benhafid, Hydra, Algiers; tel. (44) 19-10-64; fax (44) 19-12-72; e-mail ambassadesdn5@gmail.com; Ambassador NADIA MOHAMED KHAIR OTHMAN.

Sweden: BP 263, rue Olof Palme, Nouveau Paradou, Hydra, Algiers; tel. (21) 54-83-33; fax (21) 54-83-34; e-mail ambassaden.alger@gov.se; internet www.swedenabroad.se/sv/utlandsmyndigheter/algeriet-alger/; Ambassador BJÖRN HÄGGMARK.

Switzerland: 9–11 rue Slimane Amirat, el-Mouradia, Algiers; tel. (21) 98-10-00; fax (21) 98-10-29; e-mail alger@eda.admin.ch; internet www.eda.admin.ch/alger; Ambassador PIERRE-YVES FUCHS.

Syrian Arab Republic: 11 chemin Abdelkader Gadouche, Ben Aknoun, Algiers; tel. (23) 38-12-86; fax (23) 38-12-82; Ambassador (vacant).

Tanzania: Villa 13, rue Carthage, Hydra, Algiers; tel. (23) 48-44-11; fax (23) 48-44-22; e-mail algiers@nje.go.tz; internet www.dz.tzembassy.go.tz; Ambassador IMANI SALUM NJALIKAI (designate).

Tunisia: 11 rue du Bois de Bologne, el-Mouradia, Algiers; tel. (21) 69-15-67; e-mail at.alger@diplomatie.gov.tn; internet www.diplomatie.gov.tn/mission/etranger/ambassade-de-tunisie-a-alger-algerie/; Ambassador ROMDHANE EL-FAYEDH.

Türkiye (Turkey): 19 Villa Dar el-Oued, chemin de la Rochelle, blvd Col Bougara, el-Biar, 16000 Algiers; tel. (21) 23-00-04; fax (21) 23-01-12; e-mail ambassade.alger@mfa.gov.tr; internet www.algiers.emb.mfa.gov.tr; Ambassador MUHAMMET MÜCAHIT KÜÇÜKYILMAZ.

Uganda: Villa 90, Domaine Ben Haddadi Said, Dar Diaf Cherega, 16014 Algiers; tel. (23) 27-80-83; fax (23) 27-80-91; e-mail algiers@mofa.go.ug; internet algiers.mofa.go.ug; Ambassador ALINTUMA NSAMBU.

Ukraine: 28 rue de Carthage, Hydra, 16016 Algiers; tel. (23) 48-48-32; fax (23) 48-49-13; e-mail emb_dz@mfa.gov.ua; internet algeria.mfa.gov.ua; Chargé d'affaires a.i. OLEKSANDR SERHIYOVYCH.

United Arab Emirates: BP 165, Alger-Gare, 14 rue Muhammad Drarini, Hydra, Algiers; tel. (23) 47-39-24; e-mail algeriaemb@mofa.gov.ae; internet www.mofaic.gov.ae/en/missions/algeria; Ambassador YOUSEF SAIF KHAMIS SUBAA AL-ALI.

United Kingdom: 3 chemin Capitaine Hocine Slimane, Hydra, Algiers; tel. (770) 08-50-00; fax (21) 68-10-58; e-mail britishembassy.algiers@fco.gov.uk; internet www.gov.uk/world/organisations/british-embassy-algiers; Ambassador SHARON WARDLE.

USA: BP 549, 5 chemin Cheikh Bachir el-Ibrahimi, el-Biar, 16030 Algiers; tel. (770) 08-20-00; e-mail algiers_webmaster@state.gov; internet dz.usembassy.gov; Chargé d'affaires a.i. KATHRYN (KATIE) KISER.

Venezuela: 21–22 lotissement el-Fath, rue Sables Rouge, el-Biar, Algiers; tel. (21) 48-39-22; fax (21) 79-31-15; Ambassador JUAN BAUTISTA ARIAS PALACIOS.

Viet Nam: 30 rue de Chénoua, Hydra, Algiers; tel. (23) 48-54-70; e-mail sqvnalgerie@yahoo.com.vn; internet fb.com/vietnamembassyinalgeria; Ambassador TRAN QUOC KHANH.

Yemen: 10 cité la Madeleine, Hydra, Algiers; tel. (23) 23-04-87; fax (23) 23-02-07; Ambassador ALI AL-YAZIDI.

Zimbabwe: 43 rue 1er Novembre, Château Neuf, el-Biar, Algiers; tel. (21) 79-13-89; fax (21) 79-14-22; e-mail zimalgiers@zimfa.gov.zw; Ambassador VUSUMUZI NTONGA.

Judicial System

Justice is exercised through 183 courts (Tribunaux) and 31 appeal courts (Cours d'Appel), grouped on a regional basis. The highest court of justice is the Supreme Court (Cour Suprême). Legislation promulgated in March 1997 provided for the eventual establishment of 214 courts and 48 appeal courts. The Court of Accounts (Cour des Comptes) was established in 1979. Algeria adopted a penal code in 1966, retaining the death penalty. In February 1993 three special courts were established to try suspects accused of terrorist offences; however, the courts were abolished in February 1995. Constitutional amendments introduced in November 1996 provided for the establishment of a High Court of State (empowered to judge the President of the Republic in cases of high treason, and the head of government for crimes and offences), and a Council of State to have jurisdiction over administrative cases. In addition, a Conflicts Tribunal was established to adjudicate in disputes between the Supreme Court and the Council of State. In February 1989 a constitutional amendment enabled the creation of a Constitutional Council, which was responsible for ensuring 'respect for the Constitution', and that plebiscites were conducted in accordance with the law. A further amendment in March 2016 empowered the Council to adjudicate on challenges to the constitutional propriety of legislation. In accordance with further constitutional amendments which entered into effect on 1 January 2021 (having been approved at a national referendum in November 2020), the Constitutional Council was replaced by a Constitutional Court.

Constitutional Court: Algiers; f. 2021 to replace the Constitutional Council (f. 1989); 12 mems; Pres. OMAR BELHADJ.

Supreme Court: rue du 11 Décembre 1960, Ben Aknoun, Algiers; tel. (23) 24-07-23; e-mail coursupreme@coursupreme.dz; internet www.coursupreme.dz; f. 1963; comprises 150 judges; Pres. TAHER MAMOUNI.

Minister of Justice and Attorney-General: ABDERRACHID TEBBI.

Religion

ISLAM

Islam is the official religion, and the vast majority of Algerians are Muslims.

High Islamic Council: 6 rue du 11 Décembre 1960, Ben Aknoun, 16030 Algiers; tel. (21) 91-54-10; fax (21) 91-54-09; e-mail hci@hci.dz; internet www.hci.dz; Pres. BOUABDELLAH GHLAMALLAH.

CHRISTIANITY

The majority of the European inhabitants, and a small number of Arabs, are Christians.

The Roman Catholic Church

Algeria comprises one archdiocese and three dioceses (including one directly responsible to the Holy See).

Archbishop of Algiers: Most Rev. PAUL JACQUES MARIE DESFARGES, 13 rue Khalifa Boukhalfa, 16000 Alger-Gare, Algiers; tel. (21) 63-37-18; fax (21) 63-38-42; e-mail redac_chef@eglise-catholique-algerie.org; internet www.eglise-catholique-algerie.org.

Protestant Church

Eglise Réformée d'Alger: 31 rue Reda Houhou, 16110 Alger-HBB, Algiers; tel. and fax (21) 71-62-38; e-mail protestants_alger@yahoo.com; 38 parishes; Pres. SALAHEDDINE CHALAH.

The Press

DAILY NEWSPAPERS (PRINT AND ONLINE)

El Acil: 24 blvd Belouizdad, Constantine; tel. and fax (31) 92-46-13; e-mail elacilquotidien@yahoo.fr; internet www.elacil.com; f. 1993; French; Dir-Gen. NACEUR-DINE KHENFAR.

Akher Saâ: Intersection Bougandoura Miloud et Sakhri Abdelhamid, Annaba; tel. (38) 43-17-90; e-mail akhersaapub@yahoo.fr; internet www.akhersaa-dz.com; Arabic; Dir SAÏD BELHADJOUDJA.

Le Courrier d'Algérie: Maison de la Presse, Kouba, Algiers; tel. (23) 70-94-30; fax (21) 70-94-26; e-mail redaction_courrier@yahoo.fr; internet www.lecourrier-dalgerie.com; f. 2003; French; Dir AHMED TOUMIAT.

La Dépêche de Kabylie: 60 rue Abane Ramdane, Cité des 60 Logements, Batiment OPGI, Tizi-Ouzou; tel. (26) 12-26-48; e-mail ladepechedekabylie@gmail.com; internet www.depechedekabylie.com; f. 2001; Dir IDIR BENYOUNÈS.

Ech-Cha'ab (The People): POB 95, El Shohada St, 16000 Algiers; tel. (21) 60-69-55; fax (21) 60-70-35; internet www.ech-chaab.com; f. 1962; Arabic; journal of the Front de Libération Nationale; Dir-Gen. DJAMEL LAÂLAMI.

Echorouk El-Youmi: Maison de la Presse, Kouba, Algiers; tel. and fax (21) 29-89-41; internet www.echoroukonline.com; f. 2000; Arabic; Dir ALI FOUDIL.

L'Expression: Maison de la Presse, Kouba, Algiers; tel. (23) 70-94-01; fax (21) 70-93-98; e-mail laredaction@lexpressiondz.com; internet www.lexpressiondz.com; f. 2000; French; Dir AHMED FATTANI.

Al-Fedjr: Maison de la Presse Tahar Djaout, 1 rue Bachir Attar, place du 1er Mai, 16016 Algiers; tel. and fax (21) 65-76-60; internet www.al-fadjr.com; f. 2000; Arabic; Dir ABDA HADDA HAZEM.

Horizons: 20 rue de la Liberté, Algiers; tel. (23) 50-21-13; fax (23) 50-21-17; internet www.sudhorizons.dz; f. 1985; evening; French; Pres. and Dir-Gen. NOURIA BOURIHANE; Editorial Dir LIESSE DJERAOUD.

Le Jeune Indépendant: Maison de la Presse Tahar Djaout, 1 rue Bachir Attar, place du 1er Mai, 16016 Algiers; tel. (21) 67-07-48; fax (21) 67-07-46; e-mail redaction@jeune-independant.net; internet www.jeune-independant.net; f. 1990; French; Man. Dir TAYEB MECHERI; Dir KAMEL MANSARI.

ALGERIA

Directory

El-Joumhouria (The Republic): 6 rue Bensenouci Hamida, Oran; tel. (41) 89-66-29; fax (41) 40-21-29; e-mail djoumhouria@yahoo.fr; internet www.eldjoumhouria.dz; f. 1963; Arabic; Dir BOUZIANE BEN ACHOUR.

Le Jour d'Algérie: 2 blvd Mohamed V, Algiers; tel. (21) 78-14-16; fax (21) 78-14-15; e-mail lejourdalgerie@hotmail.fr; internet lejourdalgerie.com; French.

El Khabar: 32 rue El Feth bin Khlakane, Hydra, Algiers; tel. (23) 47-71-79; fax (21) 47-71-43; e-mail redaction@elkhabar.com; internet www.elkhabar.com; f. 1990; Arabic; Dir-Gen. ZAHR EL-DIN SAMATI.

El-Massa: Maison de la Presse, Kouba, 16000 Algiers; tel. (23) 70-96-31; fax (21) 70-90-49; e-mail info@el-massa.com; internet www.el-massa.com; f. 1977; evening; Arabic; Dir-Gen. SAMIRA BELAMRI.

Le Matin: Maison de la Presse Tahar Djaout, 1 rue Bachir Attar, place du 1er mai, 16016 Algiers; tel. (21) 28-83-86; fax (21) 66-20-97; e-mail redactionlematindz@gmail.com; internet www.lematindalgerie.com; French; Dir HAMID ARAB.

El-Moudjahid (The Fighter): 20 rue de la Liberté, Algiers; tel. (21) 73-70-81; fax (21) 73-90-43; e-mail info@elmoudjahid.com; internet www.elmoudjahid.com; f. 1965; govt journal in French and Arabic; Pres. and Dir-Gen. LARBI TIMIZAR.

An-Nasr (The Victory): BP 388, Zone Industrielle, La Palma, Constantine; tel. (31) 60-70-78; fax (31) 60-70-77; e-mail annasr@annasronline.com; internet www.annasronline.com; f. 1963; Arabic; Dir ABD AL-KADIR TAWABI.

La Nouvelle République: Maison de la Presse Tahar Djaout, 1 rue Bachir Attar, place du 1er Mai, 16016 Algiers; tel. (21) 67-10-44; fax (21) 67-10-75; e-mail lnr98redaction@yahoo.fr; internet www.lnr-dz.com; French; Dir ABDELWAHAB DJAKOUNE.

Ouest Tribune: 13 Cité Djamel, 31007 Oran; tel. (41) 85-80-48; fax (41) 85-82-54; e-mail redaction@ouestribune-dz.com; internet www.ouestribune-dz.com; French; Dir ABDELMADJID BLIDI.

Le Quotidien d'Oran: BP 110, 63 ave de l'ANP, 1 rue Laid Ould Tayeb, Oran; tel. (41) 23-25-22; fax (41) 23-25-20; e-mail infos@lequotidien-oran.com; internet www.lequotidien-oran.com; French; Dir-Gen. MUHAMMAD ABDOU BENABBOU.

Le Soir d'Algérie: Maison de la Presse Tahar Djaout, 1 rue Bachir Attar, place du 1er Mai, 16016 Algiers; tel. (21) 67-06-58; fax (21) 67-06-76; e-mail info@lesoirdalgerie.com; internet www.lesoirdalgerie.com; f. 1990; evening; ind. information journal in French; Dir NACER BELHADJOUDJA.

El Watan: Maison de la Presse, 1 rue Bachir Attar, place du 1er mai, 16016 Algiers; tel. (21) 68-21-83; fax (21) 68-21-87; e-mail admin@elwatan.com; internet www.elwatan.com; f. 1990; French; Dir MOHAMED TAHAR MESSAOUDI.

PERIODICALS

L'Auto Marché: 139 blvd Krim Belkacem; tel. (21) 74-44-59; fax (21) 74-14-63; e-mail contact@lautomarche.com; internet lautomarche.com; f. 1998; fortnightly; French; motoring.

Bibliographie de l'Algérie: Bibliothèque Nationale d'Algérie, BP 127, Hamma el-Annasser, 16000 Algiers; tel. (21) 67-57-81; fax (21) 67-23-00; internet www.biblionat.dz; f. 1963; 2 a year; lists books, theses, pamphlets and periodicals publ. in Algeria; Arabic and French; Dir-Gen. MUHAMMAD AÏSSA OUMOUSSA.

Le Buteur: Maison de la Presse Tahar Djaout, 1 rue Bachir Attar, place du 1er Mai, 16016 Algiers; fax 73-14-17; e-mail info@lebuteur.com; internet www.lebuteur.com; Mon., Thur. and Sat.; French; sports; Dir BOUSAÂD KAHEL.

Al-Cha'ab al-Thakafi (Cultural People): Algiers; f. 1972; cultural monthly; Arabic.

Al-Chabab (Youth): Algiers; 24 a year; journal of the Union Nationale de la Jeunesse Algérienne; Arabic and French.

Al-Djeich (The Army): Office de l'Armée Nationale Populaire, Algiers; f. 1963; monthly; Arabic and French; Algerian army review.

IT Mag: 5è groupe, Bat J, 1er Mai, Algiers; tel. (21) 71-47-76; fax (21) 65-03-28; e-mail info@itmag-dz.com; internet www.itmag-dz.com; f. 2002; French; telecommunications and IT in North Africa; Dir ABDERRAFIQ KHENIFSA.

Journal Officiel de la République Algérienne Démocratique et Populaire: pl. Seddik Ben Yahia, el-Mouradia, Algiers; tel. (21) 68-65-50; internet www.joradp.dz; f. 1962; Arabic and French.

Révolution et Travail: Maison du Peuple, 1 rue Abdelkader Benbarek, place du 1er mai, Algiers; tel. (21) 66-73-53; monthly; journal of the Union Générale des Travailleurs Algériens (central trade union) with Arabic and French edns; Editor-in-Chief RACHID AÏT ALI.

Revue Algérienne du Travail: BP 5, rue de Sidi Lakhel, Draria, Algiers; tel. (21) 31-07-66; e-mail derp@int.dz; f. 1964; quarterly; labour publ; French.

Al-Thakafa (Culture): 2 place Cheikh Ben Badis, Algiers; tel. (21) 62-20-73; f. 1971; 6 a year; cultural review; Editor-in-Chief CHEBOUB OTHMANE.

NEWS AGENCY

Algérie Presse Service (APS): BP 444, ave des Frères Bouadou, Bir Mourad Raïs, 16300 Algiers; tel. (23) 56-96-90; fax (23) 56-96-47; e-mail contact@aps.dz; internet www.aps.dz; f. 1961; provides news reports in Arabic, English and French; Dir-Gen. SAMIR GAID.

Publishers

BERTI Editions: Lot Ennadjah No. 24, 16320 Dély Ibrahim, Algiers; tel. (23) 36-24-19; fax (23) 36-24-20; e-mail berti@berti-editions.com; internet www.berti-editions.com; f. 1995; publishes books on medicine, law, finance and IT; Dir MUHAMMAD GACI.

Casbah Editions: 6 chemin Saïd Hamdine, Hydra, 16012 Algiers; tel. (21) 54-79-10; fax (21) 54-72-77; e-mail contact@casbah-editions.com; internet casbah-editions.com; f. 1995; literature, essays, memoirs, textbooks and children's literature; Dir-Gen. SMAÏN AMZIANE.

Editions Dahlab: 28 rue des Pins, Hydra, Algiers; tel. and fax (21) 51-66-69; e-mail editionsdahlab@yahoo.fr; internet editions-dahlab.com; history, social sciences, economics; Dir ABDELLAH CHEGHNANE.

Editions du Tell: 3 rue des Frères Yacoub Torki, 09000 Blida; tel. (25) 31-10-35; fax (25) 31-10-36; e-mail contact@editions-du-tell.com; internet fr-fr.facebook.com/editions.tell.blida; f. 2002; publishes books on literature, history, economics and social sciences.

Entreprise Nationale des Arts Graphiques (ENAG): BP 75, Zone industriel de Réghaia, Algiers; tel. (23) 96-56-10; fax (21) 96-56-18; e-mail edition@enag.dz; internet www.enag.dz; f. 1983; art, literature, social sciences, economics, science, religion, lifestyle and textbooks; Dir-Gen. HAMIDOU MESSAOUDI.

Office des Publications Universitaires (OPU): 1 place Centrale de Ben Aknoun, 16306 Algiers; tel. (23) 38-46-25; fax (23) 38-46-24; e-mail info@opu-dz.com; internet www.opu-dz.com; publishes university textbooks; Dir-Gen. NOUREDDINE LACHEB.

Sedia: Cité les Mandariniers, Lot 293, al-Mohammadia, 16211 Algiers; tel. 770973861; fax (23) 75-01-41; e-mail sedia@sedia-dz.com; internet www.sedia.dz; f. 2000; literature and educational textbooks; Pres. and Dir-Gen. BRAHIM DJELMAMI-HANI.

Broadcasting and Communications

TELECOMMUNICATIONS

Algérie Télécom: route Nationale 5, Cinq Maisons, Mohammadia, 16130 Algiers; tel. (21) 82-38-38; fax (21) 82-38-39; e-mail contact@algerietelecom.dz; internet www.algerietelecom.dz; f. 2001 to manage and develop telecommunications infrastructure; Pres. and Dir-Gen. ADEL BEN TOUMI.

Mobilis: Quartier des Affaires, Bab Ezzouar, Algiers; tel. (23) 92-13-13; fax (23) 92-12-80; internet www.mobilis.dz; f. 2003; subsidiary of Algérie Télécom; Pres. and Dir-Gen. CHAOUKI BOUKHEZANI.

Djezzy GSM: Orascom Télécom Algérie, rue Mouloud Feraoun, Lot No. 8A, el-Beida, Algiers; e-mail service-clientele@djezzy.dz; internet www.djezzy.dz; f. 2001; 96.6% owned by Fonds National d'Investissement; Pres. and Dir-Gen. MAHIEDDINE ALLOUCHE (acting).

Ooredoo Algérie: 66 route d'Ouled Fayet, Chéraga, 16001 Algiers; tel. 50000333; e-mail mtouati@wta.dz; internet www.ooredoo.dz; f. 2004 as Wataniya Telecom Algérie (Nedjma); acquired by Ooredoo QSC (Qatar) in 2013; Dir-Gen. RONI TOHME.

Regulatory Authority

Autorité de Régulation de la Poste et des Communications Electroniques (ARPCE): 1 rue Kaddour Rahim, Hussein Dey, 16005 Algiers; tel. (23) 77-16-64; fax (23) 77-25-73; e-mail info@arpce.dz; internet www.arpce.dz; f. 2001; Pres. ZINEDDINE BELATTAR; Dir-Gen. MOHAMED KHEMIS.

BROADCASTING

Radio

Radio Algérienne (ENRS): 21 blvd des Martyrs, Algiers; tel. (23) 50-03-01; fax (21) 23-08-23; e-mail contact@radioalgerie.dz; internet www.radioalgerie.dz; govt-controlled; operates 48 local radio stations; Dir-Gen. MOHAMED BAGHALI.

Arabic Network: transmitters at Adrar, Aïn Beïda, Algiers, Béchar, Béni Abbès, Djanet, El Goléa, Ghardaïa, Hassi Messaoud,

ALGERIA

In Amenas, In Salah, Laghouat, Les Trembles, Ouargla, Reggane, Tamanrasset, Timimoun, Tindouf.

French Network: transmitters at Algiers, Constantine, Oran and Tipaza.

Kabyle Network: transmitter at Algiers.

Television

The principal transmitters are at Algiers, Batna, Sidi-Bel-Abbès, Constantine, Souk-Ahras and Tlemcen. Television plays a major role in the national education programme.

Etablissement Public de Télévision (EPTV): BP 16070, 21 blvd des Martyrs, el-Mouradia, Algiers; tel. (23) 53-10-10; fax (23) 53-10-93; internet www.entv.dz; f. 1986; govt-controlled; Dir-Gen. CHABANE LOUNAKEL.

Télédiffusion d'Algérie (TDA): BP 50, Algiers; tel. (23) 18-10-01; fax (23) 18-10-41; e-mail contact@tda.dz; internet www.tda.dz; f. 1991; govt-controlled; Dir-Gen. RACHID BESTAM.

Finance

BANKING

Central Bank

Banque d'Algérie: Immeuble Joly, 38 ave Franklin Roosevelt, 16000 Algiers; fax (23) 48-71-38; e-mail contact@bank-of-algeria.dz; internet www.bank-of-algeria.dz; f. 1962 as Banque Centrale d'Algérie; present name adopted in 1990; bank of issue; Gov. SALAH EDDINE TALEB.

Nationalized Banks

Banque Al-Baraka d'Algérie: Haï Bouteldja Houidef, Villa 1, Ben Aknoun, Algiers; tel. (21) 38-12-73; fax (21) 38-12-77; e-mail fil-istimaa@albaraka-bank.com; internet www.albaraka-bank.com; f. 1991; Algeria's first Islamic financial institution; owned by the Saudi Arabia-based Al-Baraka Investment and Devt Co (56%) and the local Banque de l'Agriculture et du Développement Rural (44%); Chair. HOUSSEM BEN HAJ AMOR; Gen. Man. HAFID MUHAMMAD SEDDIK.

Banque Extérieure d'Algérie (BEA): 11 blvd Col Amirouche, Algiers; tel. (21) 56-92-95; fax (21) 56-92-99; e-mail dtm-direction@bea.dz; internet www.bea.dz; f. 1967; chiefly concerned with energy and maritime transport sectors; Pres. and Dir-Gen. LAZHAR LATRECHE.

Banque du Maghreb Arabe pour l'Investissement et le Commerce (BAMIC): 7 rue Dubois, Hydra, Algiers; tel. (23) 48-45-44; fax (23) 48-45-40; e-mail bamic@bamic-dz.com; internet www.bamic-dz.com; f. 1988; owned by Libyan Arab Foreign Bank (50%) and by Banque Extérieure d'Algérie, Banque Nationale d'Algérie, Banque de l'Agriculture et du Développement Rural and Crédit Populaire d'Algérie (12.5% each); Pres. LAZHAR LATRECHE; Dir-Gen. ALI BENHAMZA.

Banque Nationale d'Algérie (BNA): 8 blvd Ernesto Ché Guévara, 16000 Algiers; tel. (23) 48-80-43; fax (23) 49-80-80; e-mail sec.dg@bna.dz; internet www.bna.dz; f. 1966; specializes in industry, transport and trade sectors; Chair. MUHAMMAD BELKACEM; Pres. and Dir-Gen. MOHAMED LAMINE LEBBOU.

Crédit Populaire d'Algérie (CPA): BP 411, 2 blvd Col Amirouche, 16000 Algiers; tel. (23) 50-32-62; fax (23) 50-32-64; e-mail info@cpa-bank.com; internet www.cpa-bank.dz; f. 1966; specializes in light industry, construction and tourism; Chair. MOHAMMED RACHID LARBI; Dir-Gen. ALI KADRI.

Development Banks

Banque de l'Agriculture et du Développement Rural (BADR): BP 484, 17 blvd Col Amirouche, 16000 Algiers; tel. (21) 68-92-23; e-mail contact@badr-bank.dz; internet badrbanque.dz; f. 1982; wholly state-owned; finance for the agricultural sector; Pres. and Dir-Gen. MOHAND BOURAI.

Banque de Développement Local (BDL): 5 rue Gaci Amar, Staouéli, 16000 Algiers; tel. (21) 99-48-00; e-mail clientele@bdl.dz; internet www.bdl.dz; f. 1985; regional devt bank; Chair. SAID DIB; Dir-Gen. YOUCEF LALMAS.

Caisse Nationale d'Epargne et de Prévoyance (CNEP-Banque): 61 blvd Souidani Boujemaa, Chéraga, Algiers; tel. (23) 36-60-07; e-mail communication@cnepbanque.dz; internet www.cnepbanque.dz; f. 1964; savings and housing bank; Chair. MUSTAPHA CHAABANE; Dir-Gen. SAMIR TAMRABET.

Fonds National d'Investissement (FNI): 170 rue Hassiba Ben-bouali, Algiers; tel. (23) 82-43-10; fax (23) 82-41-79; internet www.fni.dz; f. 1963; fmrly Banque Algérienne de Développement, name changed as above in 2009; a public establishment with fiscal sovereignty; aims to contribute to Algerian economic devt through long-term investment programmes; Dir-Gen. KAMEL MANSOURI.

Private Banks

Arab Leasing Corpn: Cité Bois des Cars III, Dély Ibrahim, 16320 Algiers; tel. (23) 31-89-89; fax (23) 31-86-28; e-mail contact@arableasing-dz.com; internet www.arableasing-dz.com; f. 2001; owned by Arab Banking Corpn (41%), the Arab Investment Co (25%), CNEP (27%) and other small shareholders; Dir-Gen. ABDELHAKIM DJEBARNI.

Bank ABC Algérie: BP 367, 38 ave des Trois Frères Bouadou, Algiers; tel. (23) 56-95-23; fax (23) 56-92-08; e-mail information@bank-abc.com; internet bit.ly/3hZSNS9; f. 1998; 87.62% stake owned by Arab Banking Corpn BSC (Bahrain); Chair. HISHAM A. MOUZUGHI; CEO JAWAD SACRE.

BNP Paribas El-Djazair: Bab Ezzouar, 16024 Algiers; tel. (23) 98-13-31; fax (23) 92-40-68; internet www.bnpparibas.dz; f. 2001; Dir-Gen. PIERRE BEREGOVOY; Sec.-Gen. ALI RAFRAFI.

Gulf Bank Algeria: 190 ave Ali Khodja, Commune d'el Biar, Algiers; tel. (21) 98-49-04; e-mail crc@agb.dz; internet www.agb.dz; f. 2004; owned by United Gulf Bank, Bahrain (60%), Tunis Int. Bank (30%) and Jordan Kuwait Bank (10%); Chair. ABDELKRIM AL-KABARITI; Dir-Gen. RABIH SOUKARIEH.

Trust Bank Algeria: 70 chemin Larbi Allik, Hydra, Algiers; tel. (21) 54-97-55; fax (21) 54-97-50; e-mail direction@trustbank.dz; internet www.trustbank.dz; f. 2002; Pres. GHAZI KAMEL ABU NAHL; Dir-Gen. GHALIB BENHAMOUDA.

Banking Association

Association des Banques et des Etablissements Financiers (ABEF): 3 chemin Romain, Val d'Hydra, Algiers; tel. (21) 91-55-77; fax (21) 91-56-08; e-mail contact@abef-dz.org; internet www.abef-dz.org; f. 1995; serves and promotes the interests of banks and financial institutions in Algeria; Pres. ACHOUR ABBOUD.

STOCK EXCHANGE

Bourse d'Alger (Algiers Stock Exchange): 27 blvd Col Amirouche, 16000 Algiers; tel. (23) 49-22-23; fax (23) 49-22-16; internet www.sgbv.dz; f. 1999; Pres. YACINE BOUGUERRI; Dir-Gen. YAZID BENMOUHOUB.

Commission d'Organisation et de Surveillance des Opérations de Bourse (COSOB): 17 Campagne Chkiken, 16045 Hydra, Algiers; tel. and fax (23) 47-27-93; internet www.cosob.org; f. 1993; Pres. (vacant).

INSURANCE

L'Algérienne des Assurances (GIG): 1 rue de Tripoli, 16040 Hussein-Dey, Algiers; tel. (23) 77-21-12; fax (23) 77-21-73; e-mail contact@gig.dz; internet www.gig.dz; f. 1999; general; Pres. and Dir-Gen. MOURAD KAOULA.

Caisse Nationale de Mutualité Agricole (CNMA): 24 blvd Victor Hugo, 16100 Algiers; tel. (21) 74-33-28; fax (21) 74-50-21; e-mail cnma@cnma.dz; internet www.cnma.dz; f. 1972; Dir-Gen. CHERIF BENHABILES.

Cie Algérienne d'Assurance et de Réassurance (CAAR): 48 rue Didouche Mourad, 16000 Algiers; tel. (21) 63-20-72; e-mail contact@caar.dz; internet www.caar.dz; f. 1963 as a public corpn; Pres. and Dir-Gen. HADJ MOHAMED SEBA.

Cie Algérienne d'Assurances (CAAT): 52 rue des Frères Bouadou, Bir Mourad Raïs, Algiers; tel. (23) 56-93-24; fax (23) 59-93-78; e-mail info@caat.dz; internet www.caat.dz; f. 1985; general; majority state ownership; Pres. and Dir-Gen. NACER SAIS.

Cie Centrale de Réassurance (CCR): Lot 133, Cité Administrative Plateau, Ouled Fayet, Algiers; tel. (23) 31-40-75; fax (23) 31-40-69; e-mail contact@ccr.dz; internet ccr.dz; f. 1973; general; Pres. and Dir-Gen. ABDELLAH BENSEIDI.

Société Nationale d'Assurances (SAA): Immeuble SAA, lot 234, Bab Ezzouar, Algiers; tel. (21) 22-50-00; internet www.saa.dz; f. 1963; state-sponsored co; Pres. and Dir-Gen. YOUCEF BENMICIA.

Trust Algeria Assurances-Réassurance: BP 187, 70 chemin Larbi Allik, 16405 Hydra, Algiers; tel. (23) 40-05-96; fax (23) 48-92-46; e-mail www.trustalgeriains.com; internet trust-dz.com; f. 1987; 77.5% owned by Trust International (Bahrain), 22.5% owned by Qatar General Insurance; Dir-Gen. ABDELHAKIM HADJOU.

ALGERIA

Trade and Industry

GOVERNMENT AGENCIES AND DEVELOPMENT ORGANIZATIONS

Agence Algérienne de Promotion du Commerce Extérieur (ALGEX): 5 route Nationale, Cinq Maisons, el-Mohamadia, Algiers; tel. (23) 83-87-89; fax (23) 83-87-18; e-mail info@algex.dz; internet www.algex.dz; f. 2004; Man. ABDELATIF EL-HOUARI.

Agence Nationale de l'Aménagement du Territoire (ANAT): 30 ave Muhammad Fellah, Kouba, Algiers; tel. (21) 68-78-16; fax (21) 68-85-03; f. 1980.

Agence Nationale de Développement de l'Investissement (ANDI): 1 rue Kaddour Rahim, Hussein Dey, Algiers; tel. (23) 73-85-80; fax (23) 73-85-75; e-mail secretariat_dg@andi.dz; internet www.andi.dz; f. 1994; Dir-Gen. MUSTAPHA ZIKARA.

Agence Spatiale Algérienne (ASAL): 14 rue Omar Aissaoui, el-Hammadia, Bouzareah, Algiers; tel. (23) 27-05-31; fax (23) 27-05-24; e-mail info@asal.dz; internet asal.dz; f. 2002; Dir-Gen. AZZEDINE OUSSEDIK.

Institut National de la Productivité et du Développement Industriel (INPED): 35000 Boumerdès; tel. (24) 79-47-52; e-mail dg@inped.edu.dz; internet www.inped.edu.dz; f. 1967; Dir-Gen. FOUZIA OSMANI.

Office Algérien Interprofessionnel des Céréales (OAIC): 5 rue Ferhat-Boussaad, Algiers; tel. (21) 23-73-04; fax (21) 23-73-13; internet oaic-office.com; f. 1962; responsible for the regulation, distribution and control of the national market and the importation of cereals and vegetables; Dir-Gen. NASREDDINE MESSAOUDI.

Office National de Recherche Géologique et Minière (ORGM): 8 rue des Aures, El Harrach, Algiers; tel. (24) 79-10-46; fax (24) 79-10-52; f. 1992; mining, cartography, geophysical exploration; Dir-Gen. DJAMEL KHELOUF.

CHAMBERS OF COMMERCE

Chambre Algérienne de Commerce et d'Industrie (CACI): BP 100, Palais Consulaire, 6 blvd Amilcar Cabral, place des Martyrs, 16003 Algiers; tel. (23) 16-04-74; fax (23) 16-14-89; e-mail infos@caci.dz; internet www.caci.dz; f. 1980; Dir-Gen. NADIRA FATHI.

Chambre de Commerce et d'Industrie Algéro-Française (CCIAF): Villa Malglaive, 1 rue du Professeur Vincent Telemly, Algiers; tel. (23) 50-70-19; fax (21) 60-95-09; e-mail cciaf@cciaf.org; internet www.cciaf.org; f. 1975; c. 24,500 mems; Pres. MICHAL BISAC; Dir-Gen. RIDA EL-BAKI.

INDUSTRIAL ASSOCIATIONS

Centre d'Etudes et de Services Technologiques de l'Industrie des Matériaux de Construction (CETIM): BP 93, Cité Ibn Khaldoun, 35000 Boumerdès; tel. (24) 79-10-20; fax (24) 79-10-18; e-mail contact@cetim-dz.com; internet www.cetim-dz.com; f. 1982; CEO LYES MADI.

Institut National Algérien de la Propriété Industrielle (INAPI): 42 rue Larbi Ben M'hidi, 16000 Algiers; tel. (44) 19-6866; e-mail info-dpitt@inapi.dz; internet www.inapi.org; f. 1973; Dir-Gen. ABDELHAFID BELMEHDI.

EMPLOYERS' ORGANIZATIONS

Confédération Algérienne du Patronat Citoyen (CAPC): 23 rue Hadj Ahmed, Hydra, Algiers; tel. (770) 88-90-80; e-mail info@capc.dz; internet capc.dz; f. 2000 as Forum des Chefs d'Entreprises; present name adopted in 2020; Pres. RAHMOUN ZERGOUNE.

Confédération Générale des Entreprises Algériennes (CGEA): C1 N11, Cité des abattoirs, Staouali, Algiers; tel. (23) 39-24-20; e-mail contact@cgea.dz; internet www.cgea.dz; f. 1989; Pres. SAÏDA NEGHZA.

Confédération de Industriels et Producteurs Algériens (CIPA): Algiers; tel. (23) 93-94-92; fax (23) 93-94-98; Pres. ABDELWAHAB ZIANI.

L'Union Nationale des Investisseurs (UNI): Pins Maritimes el Mohammadia, 16211 Algiers; tel. (21) 89-15-16; fax (21) 89-15-17; e-mail contact@uni.dz; internet www.uni.dz.

UTILITIES

Regulatory Authority

Commission de Régulation de l'Electricité et du Gaz (CREG): Immeuble du Ministère de l'Energie et des Mines, Tour B, Val d'Hydra, Algiers; tel. (21) 48-81-48; fax (21) 48-84-00; e-mail contact@creg.energy.gov.dz; internet www.creg.gov.dz; f. 2002; Pres. WASSILA ATIMENE.

Directory

Electricity and Gas

Algerian Energy Co SPA: 168 rue Hassiba Ben Bouali, Hamma, Algiers; tel. (23) 82-43-98; fax (23) 82-43-89; internet aec.dz; f. 2001 as a jt venture between Sonatrach and Sonelgaz; 100% owned by Sonatrach since 2018; Pres. and Dir-Gen. ABDENNOUR KIMOUCHE.

Linde Gas Algérie SpA (GI): BP 247, 23 ave de l'ALN, Hussein-Dey, Kouba, Algiers; tel. (21) 49-73-91; fax (21) 49-71-94; internet www.linde.dz; f. 1972 as Entreprise Nationale des Gaz Industriels; production, distribution and commercialization of industrial and medical gas.

New Energy Algeria (NEAL): 15 Haouche Kaouche, Dély Ibrahim, 16302 Algiers; tel. (21) 37-28-83; fax (21) 37-29-23; internet www.neal-dz.com; a jt venture between Sonatrach and Sonelgaz; promotion and devt of new and renewable energy sources, and the completion of related projects.

Société Algérienne de l'Electricité et du Gaz (Sonelgaz SpA): 2 blvd Col Krim Belkacem, Algiers; tel. (21) 72-31-00; fax (21) 71-26-90; e-mail communication@sonelgaz.dz; internet www.sonelgaz.dz; f. 1969; production, distribution and transportation of electricity, and transportation and distribution of natural gas; subsidiaries include l'Opérateur du Système Electrique (OSE), La Société de Gestion du Réseau de Transport de l'Electricité (GRTE), La Société de Gestion du Réseau de Transport Gaz (GRTG), La Compagnie de l'Engineering de l'Electricité et du Gaz (CEEG), La Société de Distribution de l'Electricité et du Gaz d'Alger (SDA); Chair. and CEO MOURAD ADJAL.

La Compagnie de l'Engineering de l'Electricité et du Gaz (CEEG): rue Nacional, N 38, Gué de Constantin, Algiers; tel. (23) 61-24-69; fax (23) 61-24-32; internet www.ceeg.dz; f. 2009; Pres. and Dir-Gen. OUIDAD HAMROUR.

La Société Algérienne de Production de l'Electricité et du Gaz (SPE): Immeuble des 600 Bureau, route nationale N38, Gué de Constantine, Algiers; tel. (23) 61-27-31; fax (23) 61-27-30; e-mail boiteaidees@spe.dz; internet www.spe.dz; f. 2004; production and marketing of electricity and natural gas; Pres. and Dir-Gen. KHALED NOUASRI.

Water

L'Algérienne des Eaux (ADE): Zone Industrielle de Oued Smar, Algiers; tel. (23) 93-00-37; internet www.ade.dz; f. 2001; state-owned co responsible for management of water production, treatment and distribution network; directly manages water supply in 14 zones; jt-venture Société de l'Eau et de l'Assainissement d'Alger manages water supply in the capital; Dir-Gen. MUSTAPHA REQIQ.

STATE HYDROCARBONS AGENCIES AND COMPANIES

Agence Nationale pour la Valorisation des Ressources en Hydrocarbures (Alnaft): Sis chemin Kaddous, Lot G8, Hydra, Algiers; tel. (23) 23-09-87; e-mail contact-alnaft@alnaft.dz; internet www.alnaft.dz; f. 2005; Pres. NOURREDINE DAOUDI.

Autorité de Régulation des Hydrocarbures (ARH): Ministère de l'Energie et des Mines, Tour B, Val d'Hydra, Algiers; tel. (21) 48-81-83; fax (21) 48-83-15; internet www.arh.gov.dz; f. 2005; Dir-Gen. RACHID NADEL.

Société Nationale pour la Recherche, la Production, le Transport, la Transformation et la Commercialisation des Hydrocarbures (SONATRACH): Djenane el-Malik, Hydra, Algiers; e-mail sonatrach@sonatrach.dz; internet sonatrach.com; f. 1963; exploration, exploitation, transport and marketing of petroleum, natural gas and their products; Pres. and Dir-Gen. TOUFIK HAKKAR.

The following companies are wholly owned subsidiaries of Sonatrach:

Entreprise Nationale de Canalisation (ENAC): 32 rue Tripoli, Algiers; tel. (21) 77-01-53; e-mail contact@enac-dz.com; internet www.enac-dz.com; piping; Pres. and Dir-Gen. ABDELHAKIM CHEHILI.

Entreprise Nationale de Forage (enafor): BP 211, Zone Industrielle, Bir Messaoud, Hassi Messaoud, 30500 Ouargla; tel. (29) 73-71-35; fax (29) 73-21-70; e-mail enafor@enafor.dz; internet www.enafor.dz; f. 1981; drilling; Chair. and CEO MOHAMMED BENNEZZAR.

Entreprise Nationale de Géophysique (ENAGEO) (National Company of Geophysics): 140 Zone Industrielle Hassi Messaoud, 30500 Ouargla; tel. (29) 73-77-00; fax (29) 73-72-12; e-mail communication@enageo.com; internet www.enageo.com; f. 1981; seismic acquisition, geophysics; CEO ABDELKADER CHERFAOUI.

Entreprise Nationale des Grands Travaux Pétroliers (GTP): BP 09, Zone Industrielle, Reghaïa, Algiers; tel. (23) 96-51-00; fax (21) 96-50-32; internet www.engtp.com; f. 1980; major industrial projects; Dir-Gen. BENYOUCEF MAMMERI.

Entreprise Nationale des Services aux Puits (ENSP): BP 83, 30500 Hassi Messaoud, Ouargla; tel. (29) 79-79-73; fax (29) 79-82-

01; internet www.enspgroup.com; f. 1981; oil well services; Pres. and Dir-Gen. ABDALLAH KHELLOUT.

Entreprise Nationale des Travaux aux Puits (ENTP): BP 206–207, Base du 20 Août 1955, 30500 Hassi Messaoud, Ouargla; tel. (29) 79-88-50; fax (29) 73-84-06; internet entp.dz; f. 1981; oil well construction; Pres. MOSTEFA CHEIKH; Dir-Gen. ABDUL GHAFOOR GHALLAB.

Société Nationale de Commercialisation et de Distribution des Produits Pétroliers (NAFTAL, SpA): BP 73, route des Dûnes, Chéraga, Algiers; tel. (21) 38-13-13; fax (21) 38-19-19; e-mail webmaster@naftal.dz; internet www.naftal.dz; f. 1987; international marketing and distribution of petroleum products; Pres. and Dir-Gen. ABDELKADER CHAFI.

Société Nationale de Génie Civil et Bâtiment (GCB, SpA): BP 110, blvd de l'ALN, 35000 Boumerdès-Ville; tel. (24) 79-76-88; fax (24) 79-76-75; e-mail contact@gcb.dz; internet www.gcb.dz; civil engineering; Pres. and Dir-Gen. ABDELGHANI BENDJEBBA.

MAJOR COMPANIES

A large part of Algerian industry is nationalized. Following the implementation of an economic reform programme in the 1980s, however, privatizations were undertaken during the 1990s and 2000s. In 2006 a new privatization programme was launched to attract investment in over 1,000 companies (although some were unprofitable and in need of restructuring and those in strategic sectors remained exempt from sale).

Biopharm SPA: Zone Industrielle, Oued Smar, 16000 Algiers; tel. (21) 50-63-10; fax (21) 50-63-96; internet www.biopharmdz.com; f. 1990; production, distribution, promotion and logistics services of pharmaceuticals; Pres. SOFIANE LAHMAR.

Cevital: Bejaia; tel. (34) 20-20-00; e-mail conso@cevital.com; internet www.cevital-agro-industrie.com; operations in food processing and distribution, automotive, and real estate industries; CEO MALIK REBRAB.

Direction Générale des Forêts: BP 232, chemin Doudou Mokhtar, Ben Aknoun, 16306 Algiers; tel. (23) 23-82-63; fax (23) 23-82-86; internet www.dgf.org.dz; f. 1971; production of timber, management of forests; Dir-Gen. DJAMEL TOUAHRIA.

Entreprise Nationale d'Approvisionnement en Bois et Dérivés (ENAB): 2 blvd Muhammad V, 16026 Algiers; tel. (21) 78-13-97; fax (21) 78-13-98; internet www.enab-dz.com; f. 1970; import and distribution of wood and wood products; Pres. EL HADJ REKHROUKH.

Entreprise Nationale d'Ascenseurs (ENASC): 86 rue Hassiba Ben Bouali, 16000 Algiers; tel. (21) 66-75-23; e-mail secretariat.dg@enasc.dz; internet www.enasc.org; f. 1983; manufacture of elevators and escalators; Pres. SAÏD BRAHIMI.

Entreprise Nationale de Charpentes et de Chaudronnerie (ENCC): BP 435, 8 rue Capitaine Azzoug, Hussein-Dey, Algiers; tel. (23) 75-62-67; fax (23) 75-62-66; e-mail dg@encc-dz.com; internet encc-dz.com; f. 1983; 6 subsidiary cos, manufacturing, supplying and maintaining industrial equipment.

Entreprise Nationale de Construction de Matériaux et d'Equipements Ferroviaires (Ferrovial): BP 63, route d'El Hadjar, Annaba; tel. (38) 52-17-32; fax (38) 52-20-96; e-mail dgferrovial@yahoo.fr; internet www.ferrovial.dz; f. 1983; production, import and export of railway equipment; Dir-Gen. LAMRI BOUYOUCEF.

Entreprise Nationale de Produits Miniers Non-Ferreux et des Substances Utiles (ENOF): 31 rue Muhammad Hattab, el-Harrach, Algiers; tel. (23) 82-71-73; fax (21) 82-71-69; e-mail sec_dg@enof.dz; internet enof.dz/v; f. 1983; production and distribution of minerals; CEO FATEH DRIFI.

Entreprise Nationale des Appareils de Mesure et de Contrôle (AMC): BP 248, route de Djemila, el-Eulma, Sétif; tel. (36) 76-10-56; e-mail direction.commerciale@enamc.dz; internet www.en-amc.dz; f. 1984; production of measuring, checking and regulation equipment; ownership transferred to Sonelgaz in 2010.

Entreprise Nationale des Industries de l'Electroménager (ENIEM): BP 71A, blvd Stiti Ali, Chikhi, Tizi Ouzou; tel. (26) 20-02-15; fax (26) 20-04-24; e-mail commerciale@eniem.dz; internet www.eniem.com.dz; consortium of mfrs of household equipment; Pres. and Dir-Gen. MUSTAPHA CHAOUI.

Entreprise Nationale des Matériels de Travaux Publics (ENMTP): BP 67, Aïn Smara, Constantine; tel. (31) 97-36-81; fax (31) 97-36-48; e-mail somatel@enmtp.com; internet www.enmtp.com; f. 1983; Dir SLIMANE BOULEBD.

Entreprise Publique Economique Asmidal, SpA (ASMIDAL): BP 326, 2 rue Mohamed Sidi Brahim Hamza, 23000 Annaba; tel. (38) 43-53-53; fax (38) 43-58-58; e-mail info@asmidal-dz.com; internet www.asmidal-dz.com; f. 1985; production of ammonia, fertilizers, pesticides and sodium tripolyphosphate; Pres. and Dir-Gen. MOHAMED TAHAR HEOUAINE.

Groupe Boissons d'Algérie (GBA): BP 417, 21 rue Belhouchat Mouloud, Hussein-Dey, 16008 Algiers; tel. (21) 23-18-17; fax (21) 23-18-15; e-mail gba@cojub.com; internet www.cojub.com/gba/gba.htm; f. 1983; mineral water, carbonated beverages and beer.

Groupe Industriel du Papier et de la Cellulose (GIPEC): route de la Gare, Baba Ali, Algiers; tel. (23) 58-97-92; e-mail infogipec@gipec.dz; internet www.gipec.dz; pulp and paper; CEO KOUADRI LILA.

Groupe des Industries Métallurgiques et Sidérurgiques (IMETAL): 7 rue Belkacem Amani, Site Sider, Hydra, Algiers; tel. (23) 53-41-37; fax (23) 53-41-18; e-mail dg@imetal.dz; internet www.imetal.dz; f. 2015; comprises 16 subsidiaries; Chair. LATRECH LAZHAR.

Entreprise Publique Economique Bâtiments Industrialisés SPA (EPE BATIMETAL): BP 88, route de Dar el Beida, Oued-Smar, 16270 Algiers; tel. (23) 92-30-64; fax (21) 51-64-60; e-mail dg@epebatimetal.dz; internet www.epebatimetal.dz; f. 1983; owned by Groupe des Industries Métallurgiques et Sidérurgiques (IMETAL); study and commercialization of buildings, metalic structures and boilermaking; Dir-Gen. HASSEN YAHI.

Entreprise de Transformation des Produits Longs (ENTPL): BP 1005, 19 rue Mekki Khelifa, el-Manouar, Oran; tel. (41) 24-66-48; fax (41) 24-66-39; e-mail marketing@entpl.dz; internet www.entpl.dz; f. 1983; production and distribution of steel girders.

Groupe SIDER: BP 342, Chaiba Sidi Amar, Annaba; tel. (38) 57-42-19; e-mail contact@groupesider.com; internet www.groupesider.com; f. 1964 as Société Nationale de Sidérurgie; restructured in 1983, then again in 1995 as Groupe SIDER; holds shares in Emarat Dzayer Steel and Algerian Qatari Steel (AQS); steel, cast iron, zinc and products.

Groupe Valorisation des Produits Agricoles (GVAPRO): BP 116, 28 rue des Fusillés, El Anassers, Algiers; tel. (21) 68-54-17; fax (21) 67-44-53; e-mail contact@gvapro-dz.com; internet gvapro-dz.com; agricultural production and marketing; operates 6 subsidiary cos; Man. Dir MUSTAPHA BELHANINI.

NCA-Rouiba SPA: Zone Industrielle de Rouiba, route Nationale 5, Algiers; tel. (23) 87-37-86; internet www.rouiba.com.dz; f. 1966 as Nouvelle Conserverie Algérienne (NCA); present name adopted in 2008; production and distribution of beverages.

SAIDAL Production Pharmaceutique: BP 141, 11 route de Wilaya, A16100 Dar el-Beida, Algiers; tel. (23) 92-01-76; fax (23) 92-01-78; internet www.saidalgroup.dz; f. 1982 as Entreprise Nationale de Production Pharmaceutique; name changed as above in 1985; production of pharmaceuticals; partially privatized; Pres. and Dir-Gen. WASSIM KOUIDRI.

Société des Emballages et Arts Graphiques (EMBAG): BP 60, route d'Alger, 34000 Bordj Arréridj; tel. (35) 87-31-38; fax (35) 87-31-36; e-mail embag@gipec.dz; f. 1985; packaging; subsidiary of GIPEC.

Société des Mines de Phosphates (SOMIPHOS): BP 122, Tébessa; tel. (38) 58-52-83; e-mail contact@somiphos.com; internet somiphos.com; f. 1983 as Entreprise Nationale du Fer et du Phosphate (FERPHOS); wholly owned by MANAL Gropu; reorganized as present in 2005; production, import and export of phosphate products; Pres. and Dir-Gen. MOKHTAR LEKHAL.

TRADE UNIONS

Association Générale des Entrepreneurs Algériens (AGEA): Villa 28, Quartier Aïn Soltane, les Oliviers, Birkhadem, Algiers; tel. (21) 83-83-31; fax (23) 83-83-33; f. 1989; Pres. MOULOUD KHELOUFI.

Syndicat National des Journalistes (Algerian Journalists' Union): Maison de la Presse Tahar Djaout, 1 rue Bachir Attar, place du 1er Mai, 16016 Algiers; tel. and fax (21) 67-36-61; e-mail snjalgerie2006@yahoo.fr; f. 2001; Sec.-Gen. KAMEL AMARNI.

Union Générale des Travailleurs Algériens (UGTA): Maison du Peuple, place du 1er Mai, Algiers; tel. (21) 65-07-36; e-mail sgeneral@ugta.dz; internet www.ugta.dz; f. 1956; there are 10 national 'professional sectors' affiliated to the UGTA; Sec.-Gen. AMAR TAKDJOUT.

Union Nationale des Paysans Algériens (UNPA): f. 1973; Sec.-Gen. ABDELLATIF DILMI.

Transport

RAILWAYS

A metro system was in operation in Algiers, as part of a plan to construct 54 km of lines in the capital and the surrounding areas by 2025. Construction of a 19.7-km metro network for the city of Oran was under way in 2023. Tramways are in operation in Algiers, Constantine, Oran, Ouargla, Sétif and Sidi Bel Abbès. A tramway network in the port city of Mostaganem entered commercial service in February 2023.

ALGERIA — Directory

Entreprise du Métro d'Alger (EMA): 170 rue Hassiba Ben Bouali, Algiers; tel. (23) 51-20-06; fax (21) 51-20-40; internet metroalger-dz.com; initial 9-km section of Algiers Metro Line 1 (10 stations) commenced operations in 2011; further extensions of Line 1 inaugurated in 2015 and 2018; operates the tramway system in Algiers and in six other cities, plus the metro system in Oran (under construction as of 2023); Pres. and Dir-Gen. ALI AREZKI.

Infrafer (Entreprise Publique Economique de Réalisation des Infrastructures Ferroviaires): BP 208, 15 rue Col Amirouche, 35300 Rouiba; tel. (23) 89-41-04; e-mail info@infrafer.com; internet www.infrafer.com; f. 1986; responsible for construction and maintenance of track; Dir-Gen. ABDERAHMANE AKTOUF.

Société Nationale des Transports Ferroviaires (SNTF): 21–23 blvd Muhammad V, Algiers; tel. (21) 73-00-00; fax (21) 63-32-98; e-mail contact@sntf.dz; internet www.sntf.dz; f. 1976 to replace Société Nationale des Chemins de Fer Algériens; daily passenger services from Algiers to the principal provincial cities and services to Tunisia and Morocco; Dir-Gen. KARIM AYACHE.

ROADS

The French administration built a good road system (partly for military purposes), which, since independence, has been allowed to deteriorate in places. New roads have been built linking the Sahara oilfields with the coast, and the Trans-Sahara highway is a major project. Construction of the 1,216-km East–West highway, linking el-Tarf with Tlemcen, was completed in August 2023, at an estimated cost of more than US $11,000m. Construction of a 773-km highway connecting Tindouf in Algeria to Zoerate in Mauritania was under way in 2023.

L'Algérienne des Autoroutes (ADA): BP 72, Les Bananiers, Mohammadia; tel. (23) 79-61-24; fax (23) 79-61-00; internet www.ada.dz; f. 2016 by merger of Agence Nationale des Autoroutes (ANA) and Algérienne de Gestion des Autoroutes (AGA); Dir-Gen. ALI KHELIFAOUI.

Groupe Logitrans: 24 rue des Trois Frères Bouadou, Bir Mourad Raïs, Algiers; tel. (21) 54-05-04; fax (21) 54-05-35; internet www.groupe-logitrans.dz; f. 1967 as Société Nationale des Transports Routiers (SNTR); present name adopted 2016; goods transport by road; maintenance of industrial vehicles; Pres. and Dir-Gen. BOUALEM KINI.

Société Nationale des Transports des Voyageurs (SNTV): Algiers; tel. (21) 66-00-52; f. 1967; long-distance passenger transport by road; Man. Dir MUHAMMAD DIB.

SHIPPING

Algiers is the main port, with anchorage averaging 20 m in the Bay of Algiers. Anchorage for the largest vessels in Agha Bay reaches up to 36 m. The port has a total quay length of 8,352 m. In 2008 United Arab Emirates-based DP World signed a 30-year contract with the Algerian Government to manage and redevelop the ports at Algiers and Djen-Djen. The proposed redevelopment at Algiers port included an expansion of capacity from 500,000 20-ft equivalent units (TEUs) to 800,000 TEUs. DP World formally commenced operations at both ports in 2009. Construction of a deep-water port in the industrial zone of el-Hamdania, at an estimated cost of US $3,300m., began in May 2021. There are also important ports at Annaba, Arzew, Béjaïa, Djidjelli, Ghazaouet, Mostaganem, Oran, Skikda and Ténès. Petroleum and liquefied gas are exported through Arzew, Béjaïa and Skikda. Algerian crude petroleum is also exported through the Tunisian port of La Skhirra.

Port Authorities

Entreprise Portuaire d'Alger (EPAL): BP 259, 2 rue d'Angkor, Alger-Gare, Algiers; tel. (21) 42-36-14; fax (21) 42-36-03; e-mail epal@portalger.com.dz; internet www.portalger.com.dz; f. 1982; responsible for management and growth of port facilities and sea pilotage; Dir-Gen. MOHAMMED LARBI.

Entreprise Portuaire d'Annaba (EPAN): BP 1232, Môle Cigogne, quai Nord, 23000 Annaba; tel. (38) 45-47-37; fax (38) 45-47-49; e-mail epan@annaba-port.com; internet www.annaba-port.com; Pres. and Dir-Gen. MOHAMED KHIR EDDINE BOUMENDJEL.

Entreprise Portuaire d'Arzew (EPA): BP 46, 7 rue Larbi Tebessi, 31200 Arzew; tel. (41) 79-12-03; e-mail direction.generale@arzewports; internet www.arzewports.dz; Pres. and Dir-Gen. BENSALEM KAIDARI.

Entreprise Portuaire de Béjaïa (EPB): BP 94, 13 ave des Frères Amrani, 06000 Béjaïa; tel. (34) 16-76-31; fax (34) 16-75-71; e-mail portbj@portdebejaia.dz; internet www.portdebejaia.dz; Dir-Gen. KASMI HALIM.

Entreprise Portuaire de Djen-Djen (EPJ): BP 87, El Achouat Taher-Wilaya de JIJEL, 18000 Jijel; tel. (34) 54-21-88; fax (34) 54-21-60; e-mail officiers@djendjen-port.com; internet www.djendjen-port.com; f. 1984; Pres. Dir-Gen. ABDESLEM BOUAB.

Entreprise Portuaire de Ghazaouet (EPG): BP 217, Wilaya de Tlemcen, 13400 Ghazaouet; tel. (43) 46-97-25; e-mail contact@portdeghazaouet.com; internet www.portdeghazaouet.com; f. 1982; Pres. and Dir-Gen. MOHAMMED KARIM MERAD.

Entreprise Portuaire de Mostaganem (EPM): BP 131, quai du Maghreb, 27000 Mostaganem; tel. (45) 35-13-22; fax (45) 35-11-15; e-mail dg@port-mostaganem.dz; internet www.port-mostaganem.com; Pres. and Dir-Gen. SEBANE NASREDDINE.

Entreprise Portuaire d'Oran (EPO): 1 rue du 20 août, 31000 Oran; tel. (41) 33-24-41; fax (41) 33-24-98; e-mail pdg@port-oran.dz; internet www.port-oran.dz; construction of extension to container port began in 2014; Dir-Gen. MOKHTAR KORBA.

Entreprise Portuaire de Skikda (EPS): BP 65, 46 ave Rezki Rahal, 21000 Skikda; tel. (38) 75-23-70; fax (38) 75-20-15; e-mail infos@skikda-port.com; internet www.skikda-port.com; Pres. and Dir-Gen. IMAD TANFOUR.

Entreprise Portuaire de Ténès (EPT): BP 18, Wilaya de Chlef, 02200 Ténès; tel. (27) 76-72-76; fax (27) 76-61-77; e-mail dgport@portdetenes.dz; internet www.portdetenes.dz; f. 1985; Man. Dir ALI ASSENOUNI.

CIVIL AVIATION

Algeria's principal international airport, Houari Boumedienne, is situated 20 km from Algiers. A new terminal building was inaugurated in 2019, and the construction of another terminal was expected to begin in 2028. A new runway became operational in July 2023, increasing the airport's passenger handling capacity. A new terminal at Ahmed Ben Bella international airport, which serves Oran, was officially opened in June 2022. Other international airports are situated at Annaba, Constantine and Tlemcen.

Société de Gestion des Services et Infrastructures Aéroportuaires d'Alger (SGSIA): BP 295, Aeroport d'Alger, Algiers; internet www.aeroportalger.dz; f. 2006; CEO OMAR HALIS.

Air Algérie (Entreprise Nationale d'Exploitation des Services Aériens): BP 858, 1 place Maurice Audin, Algiers; tel. (21) 98-63-63; e-mail helpdesk@airalgerie.dz; internet www.airalgerie.dz; f. 1953 by merger; state-owned from 1972; internal services and extensive services to Europe, North and West Africa, and the Middle East; flies to more than 70 destinations; CEO AMINE DEBAGHINE MESROUA (acting).

Air Express Algeria: 02 Ilôt 08, lotissement Krim Belkacem, Dar el-Beida, Algiers; tel. (21) 50-88-94; internet airexpressdz.com; f. 2002; specializes in transportation of passengers and light cargo, medical evacuation for the petroleum and gas sector; total fleet of 15 aircraft; Pres. and Dir-Gen. CHAKIB BELAILI.

Tassili Airlines: 168 rue Hassiba Ben Bouali, Algiers; tel. (21) 73-78-00; e-mail delegationhme@tassiliairlines.com; internet www.tassiliairlines.dz; f. 1997; wholly owned by Sonatrach; domestic passenger services; Pres. and Man. Dir ABDESSAMAD OURIHAN (acting).

Tourism

Agence Nationale de Développement Touristique (ANDT): BP 78, Complexe Touristique de Sidi Fredj, Staoueli, Algiers; tel. (21) 37-60-43; fax (21) 37-67-16; e-mail contact@andt-dz.org; tourism promotion; Dir-Gen. NOUREDDINE NEDRI.

Office de l'Entreprise Nationale Algérienne de Tourisme (ONAT): 126 bis A, rue Didouche Mourad, 16000 Algiers; tel. (21) 64-09-00; e-mail contact@onat.dz; internet www.onat.dz; f. 1983; Dir-Gen. AREZKI TAHAR.

Office National du Tourisme (ONT): 2 rue Ismail Kerrar, 16000 Algiers; tel. (21) 43-80-60; fax (21) 43-80-59; internet ont.dz; f. 1988; state institution; oversees tourism promotion policy; Dir-Gen. SALIHA NECER BEY.

Touring Club d'Algérie (TCA): 30 rue Hassène Benaâmane, Les Vergers, Bir Mourad Raïs, Algiers; tel. (21) 54-13-13; fax (21) 22-24-86; e-mail sg_touring@algeriatouring.net; internet www.algeriatouring.net; f. 1963; Pres. ABDERRAHMANE ABDEDAÏM.

Touring Voyages Algérie: 30 rue Hassen Benaamane, Les Vergers, Bir Mourad Raïs, Algiers; tel. (21) 54-13-13; fax (21) 54-15-11; e-mail contact@touring-algerie.com; internet www.touring-algeria.com; f. 1995 to manage the commercial activities of Touring Club d'Algérie; 89% owned by Touring Club d'Algérie; Pres. and Dir-Gen. TAHAR SAHRI.

Defence

As assessed at November 2022, the People's National Armed Forces had an estimated total strength of 139,000: army 110,000 (incl. 75,000 conscripts); navy 15,000; air force 14,000. In addition, there was a reserve force of some 150,000 and a paramilitary force estimated at 187,200 (National Security Forces 16,000; Republican Guards 1,200; 150,000 legitimate defence groups; and a gendarmerie of 20,000).

Defence Budget: AD 1,300,000m. in 2022.

Chief of Staff of the People's National Army: Gen. SAÏD CHENGRIHA.

Commander of the Land Force: Maj.-Gen. AMMAR ATAMNIA.

Commander of the Air Force: Maj.-Gen. MAHMOUD LARABA.

Commander of the Naval Forces: Maj.-Gen. MAHFOUD BENMEDDAH.

Commander of the Territory Air Defence Forces: Maj.-Gen. ABDELAZIZ HOUAM.

Commander of the National Gendarmerie: Gen. YAHIA ALI OUELHADJ.

Commander of the Republican Guard: Maj.-Gen. BENALI BENALI.

Education

Education is officially compulsory for a period of nine years, for children between six and 15 years of age. Primary education begins at the age of six and lasts for six years. Middle education begins at 11 years of age and comprises one cycle of three years. Secondary education lasts for up to three years. Most education at primary level is in Arabic, but at higher levels French is still widely used. In 2003 the Government agreed to permit the use of the Berber language, Tamazight, as a language of instruction in Algerian schools. According to UNESCO, enrolment at primary schools in 2019/20 included 99.8% of children in the relevant age-group. According to UNESCO, spending on education constituted 15.4% of total government expenditure in 2022.

Bibliography

Achy, Lahcen. *The Price of Stability in Algeria*. Beirut, Carnegie Middle East Center, 2013. carnegieendowment.org/files/price_stability_algeria.pdf.

Ageron, Charles-Robert. *Modern Algeria: A History from 1830 to the Present*. London, Hurst, 1992.

Aghrout, Ahmed, with Bougherira, Redha (Eds). *Algeria in Transition: Reforms and Development Prospects*. London, Routledge, 2004.

Aïssaoui, Ali. *Algeria: The Political Economy of Oil and Gas*. New York and Oxford, Oxford University Press, 2001.

Aissaoui, Rabah, and Eldridge, Claire (Eds). *Algeria Revisited: History, Culture and Identity*. London, Bloomsbury Academic, 2017.

Aït-Aoudia, Myriam. *L'expérience Démocratique en Algérie, 1988–1992*. Paris, Les Presses de Sciences Po, 2015.

Aït-Chaalal, Amine. *Algérie–Etats-Unis; des relations denses et complexes*. Louvain-la-Neuve, CERMAC, 1998.

Akre, Philip J. 'Algeria and the Politics of Energy-Based Industrialization', in Entelis, John, and Naylor, Philip (Eds). *State and Society in Algeria*. Boulder, CO, Westview Press, 1992, pp. 73–95.

Alexander, Christopher. 'Opportunities, Organizations, and Ideas: Islamists and Workers in Tunisia and Algeria', *International Journal of Middle East Studies*. Vol. 32, Issue 4, 2000, pp. 465–490.

'The Architecture of Militancy: Workers and the State in Algeria, 1970-1990', *Comparative Politics*. Vol. 34, Issue 3, 2002, pp. 315–335.

Allais, M. *Les Accords d'Evian, le référendum et la résistance algérienne*. Paris, 1962.

Assaad, Ragui, Hendy, Rana, Lassassi, Moundir, and Yassin, Shaimaa. 'Explaining the MENA Paradox: Rising Educational Attainment Yet Falling Female Labour Force Participation', *Demographic Research*. Vol. 43, Issue 28, 2020, pp. 817–850.

Amir-Aslani, Ardavan. *L'Age d'Or de la Diplomatie Algérienne*. Paris, Du Moment, 2015.

Aussaresses, Gen. Paul. *Services spéciaux Algérie 1955–1957: Mon témoignage sur la torture*. Paris, Perrin, 2001.

The Battle of the Casbah: Terrorism and Counter-Terrorism in Algeria 1955–1957. Silver Spring, MD, Enigma Books, 2004.

Balta, Paul, and Rulleau, Claudine. *L'Algérie des algériens*. Paris, Editions Ouvrières, 1982.

Bedjaoui, Youcef, et al. (Eds). *An Inquiry into the Algerian Massacres*. Geneva, Hoggar, 1999.

Belakhdar, Naoual. 'When Unemployment Meets Environment. The Case of the Anti-Fracking Coalition in Ouargla', *Mediterranean Politics*. Vol. 24, Issue 4, 2019, pp. 420–442.

Belalloufi, Hocine. *La Démocratie en Algérie: reforme ou révolution?* Algiers, Les Editions Apic, 2012.

Belarbi, Ahcene. *Demain, la mémoire: Chroniques de l'Algérie massacrée*. Paris, Editions des Ecrivains, 2000.

Benabdallah, Youcef. 'Rente et désindustrialisation', *Confluences Méditerranée*. Vol. 4, Issue 71, 2009, pp. 85–100.

Benamou, Georges-Marc. *Un mensonge français: Enquête sur la guerre d'Algérie*. Paris, Laffont, 2003.

Bennoune, M. *The Making of Contemporary Algeria (1830–1987): Colonial Upheavals and Post-Independence Development*. Cambridge, Cambridge University Press, 1988.

Binoche, Jacques. *L'Algérie et sa représentation parlementaire, 1848–1962*. Paris, L'Harmattan, 2018.

Bonner, Michael, Reif, Megan, and Tessler, Mark (Eds). *Islam, Democracy and the State in Algeria: Lessons for the Western Mediterranean and Beyond*. Abingdon, Routledge, 2005.

Bonora, C. *France and the Algerian Conflict*. Aldershot, Ashgate Publishing Ltd, 2000.

Boudiaf, Muhammad. *Où va l'Algérie?* Algeria, Rahma, 1992.

Bougherira, Redha M., and Agrout, Ahmed (Eds). *Algeria in Transition: Reforms and Development Prospects*. London, Routledge, 2004.

Boukhobza, M'Hammed. *Ruptures et transformations sociales en Algérie*. Algiers, OPU, 1989.

Boukra, Liess. *Algérie: La terreur sacrée*. Paris, Favre, 2002.

Bourdieu, Pierre. *The Algerians*. Boston, 1962.

Bouyacoub, Ahmed. 'Quel développement économique depuis 50 ans?', *Confluences Méditerranée*. Vol. 2, Issue 81, 2012, pp. 83–102.

Brand, Laurie A. *Official Stories: Politics and National Narratives in Egypt and Algeria*. Rosewood City, CA, Stanford University Press, 2014.

Brun, Catherine. *Algérie: D'Une Guerre à l'Autre*. Paris, Presses Sorbonne Nouvelle, 2014.

Butcher, Charity. 'Can Oil-Reliant Countries Democratize? An Assessment of the Role of Civil Society in Algeria', *Democratization*. Vol. 21, Issue 4, 2014, pp. 722–742.

Byrne, Jeffrey James. *Mecca of Revolution: Algeria, Decolonization, and the Third World Order*. New York, Oxford University Press, 2016.

Cavatorta, Francesco. *The International Dimension of the Failed Algerian Transition: Democracy Betrayed?* Manchester, Manchester University Press, 2009.

Chikhi, Said. 'Algeria: From Mass Rebellion in October 1988 to Workers' Social Protest', *Current African Issues*. Vol. 13, 1991, pp. 1–23.

Christelow, Allan. *Algerians Without Borders: The Making of a Global Frontier Society*. Gainesville, FL, University Press of Florida, 2012.

Cook, Steven A. *Ruling But Not Governing: The Military and Political Development in Egypt, Algeria, and Turkey*. Baltimore, MD, The Johns Hopkins University Press, 2007.

Crowley, Patrick. *Algeria: Nation, Culture and Transnationalism, 1988-2015*. Liverpool, Liverpool University Press, 2017.

D'Amato, Silvia. and Del Panta, Gianni. 'Does Rentierism Have a Conditional Effect on Violence? Regime Oil Dependency and Civil War in Algeria', *The Extractive Industries and Society*. Vol. 4, Issue 2, 2017, pp. 361–370.

De Gaulle, Charles. *Mémoires d'espoir: Le Renouveau 1958–1962*. Paris, Plon, 1970.

Del Panta, Gianni. 'Weathering the Storm: Why Was There No Arab Uprising in Algeria?' *Democratization*. Vol. 24, Issue 6, 2017, pp. 1085–1102.

Derradji, A. *The Algerian Guerrilla Campaign: Strategy and Tactics*. Edwin Mellen Press, 1997.

Dillman, Bradford, L. *State and Private Sector in Algeria: The Politics of Rent-Seeking and Failed Development*. Boulder, CO, Westview Press, 2000.

Driessen, Michael D. 'Public Religion, Democracy, and Islam: Examining the Moderation Thesis in Algeria', *Comparative Politics*. Vol. 44, Issue 1, 2012, pp. 171–189.

Encyclopaedia of Islam. *Algeria*. New edn, Vol. I. London and Leiden, 1960.

Emery, Meaghan. *The Algerian War Retold: Of Camus's Revolt and Postwar Reconciliation*. Abingdon, Routledge, 2021.

Entelis, John. 'SONATRACH: The Political Economy of an Algerian State Institution', *Middle East Journal*. Vol. 53, Issue 1, 1999, pp. 9–27.

'Algeria: Democracy Denied, and Revived?' *The Journal of North African Studies*. Vol. 16, Issue 4, 2011, pp. 653–678.

Evans, Martin. *Algeria: France's Undeclared War*. Oxford, Oxford University Press, 2011.

Evans, Martin, and Phillips, John. *Algeria: Anger of the Dispossessed*. New Haven, CT, Yale University Press, 2007.

Faivre, Maurice. *Les archives inédites de la politique algérienne 1958–1962*. Paris, L'Harmattan, 2000.

Favrod, Ch.-H. *Le FLN et l'Algérie*. Paris, 1962.

Forestier, Patrick, with Salam, Ahmed. *Confession d'un émir du GIA*. Grasset et Fasquelle, Paris, 1999.

Francos, Avia, and Séréri, J.-P. *Un Algérien nommé Boumedienne*. Paris, 1976.

Fuller, Graham E. *Algeria: The Next Fundamentalist State*. Rand Corporation, 1996.

Garon, Lise. *L'obsession unitaire et la Nation trompée: La fin de l'Algérie socialiste*. Montreal, University of Laval Press, 1993.

Ghanem, Dalia. *Understanding the Persistence of Competitive Authoritarianism in Algeria*. Cham, Palgrave Macmillan, 2022.

Ghettas, Mohammed Lakhdar. *Algeria and the Cold War: International Relations and the Struggle for Autonomy*. London, I. B. Tauris, 2018.

Gordon, David. *The Passing of French Algeria*. Oxford, 1966.

Goytisolo, Juan. *Argelia en el vendaval*. Madrid, El País-Aguilar, 1994.

Guignard, Didier, and Grangaud, Isabelle. *Propriété et Société en Algérie Contemporaine: Quelles Approches?* Aix-en-Provence, Institut de Recherches et d'Etudes sur le Monde Arabe et Musulman, 2017.

Hachemaoui, Mohammed. *Clientélisme et patronage dans l'Algérie contemporaine*. Paris, Karthala, 2013.

Harbi, Muhammad. *L'Algérie et son destin*. Paris, Arcantère, 1992.

Hafez, Mohammed M. 'Armed Islamist Movements and Political Violence in Algeria', *The Middle East Journal*. Vol. 54, Issue 4, 2000, pp. 572–591.

Hamouchene, H. and Rouabah, B. 'The Political Economy of Regime Survival: Algeria in the Context of the African and Arab Uprisings', *Review of African Political Economy*. Vol. 43, Issue 150, 2016, pp. 668–680.

Hill, J. N. C. *Identity in Algerian Politics: The Legacy of Colonial Rule*. Boulder, CO, Lynne Rienner Publishers, 2009.

Hill, Jonathan. *Democratization in the Maghreb*. Edinburgh, Edinburgh University Press, 2016.

'The Evolution of Authoritarian Rule in Algeria: Linkage versus Organizational Power', *Democratization*. Vol. 26, Issue 8, 2019, pp. 1382–1398.

Horne, Alistair. *A Savage War of Peace: Algeria 1954–1962*. London, Macmillan, 1977.

House, Jim, and McMaster, Neil. *Paris 1961: Algerians, State Terror, and Memory*. New York, NY, Oxford University Press, 2009.

Ibrahimi, A. Taleb. *De la décolonisation à la révolution culturelle (1962–72)*. Algiers, SNED, 1973.

Joesten, Joachim. *The New Algeria*. New York, 1964.

Joffé, George. *Algeria: The Failed Revolution*. Abingdon, Routledge, 2009.

Johnson, Jennifer. *The Battle for Algeria: Sovereignty, Health Care, and Humanitarianism*. Philadelphia, PA, Pennsylvania University Press, 2016.

Julien, Charles-André. *Histoire de l'Algérie contemporaine, conquête et colonisation, 1827–1871*. Paris, Presses Universitaires de France, 1964.

Kadri, Aïssa, and Bouaziz, Moula. *La Guerre d'Algérie Revisitée: Nouvelles Générations, Nouveaux Regards*. Paris, Karthala, 2015.

Kalman, Samuel. *French Colonial Fascism: The Extreme Right in Algeria, 1919–1939*. Basingstoke, Palgrave Macmillan, 2013.

Keenan, Jeremy. *The Lesser Gods of the Sahara*. London, Frank Cass, 2004.

Kettle, Michael. *De Gaulle and Algeria*. London, Quartet, 1993.

Khalil, Andrea. *Crowds and Politics in North Africa Tunisia, Algeria and Libya*. Abingdon, Routledge, 2014.

Khelladi, A. *Les islamistes algériens face au pouvoir*. Algiers, Alfa, 1992.

Klose, Fabian. *Human Rights in the Shadow of Colonial Violence: The Wars of Independence in Kenya and Algeria*. Philadelphia, PA, University of Pennsylvania Press, 2013.

Laffont, Pierre. *L'Expiation: De l'Algérie de papa à l'Algérie de Ben Bella*. Paris, Plon, 1968.

Lakehal, M. *Algérie: De l'indépendance à l'Etat d'urgence*. Paris, L'Harmattan, 1992.

Lambotte, R. *Algérie, naissance d'une société nouvelle*. Paris, Editions Sociales, 1976.

Laremont, Ricardo René. *Islam and the Politics of Resistance in Algeria 1783–1992*. Trenton, NJ, Africa World Press, 2000.

Lassassi, Assassi. *Non-Alignment and Algerian Foreign Policy*. Aldershot, Dartmouth, 1988.

Lassassi, Moundir, and Tansel, Aysit. 'The Dynamics of Female Labour Force Participation in Selected MENA Countries', *Economic Research Forum Working Paper*, 2019.

Lawless, Richard I. 'Algeria: The Contradictions of Rapid Industrialization', in Lawless, Richard and Findlay, Allan (Eds). *North Africa: Contemporary Politics and Economic Development*. London, Croom Helms, 1984, pp. 153–190.

Algeria. World Bibliographical Series Vol. 19. Denver, CO, Clio Press, 1995.

Layachi, Azzedine. 'The Private Sector in the Algerian Economy: Obstacles and Potentials for a Productive Role', *Mediterranean Politics*. Vol. 6, Issue 2, 2001, pp. 29–50.

Lazreg, Marnia. *The Emergence of Social Classes in Algeria. A Study of Colonialism and Socio-Political Change*. Boulder, CO, Westview Press, 1976.

The Eloquence of Silence: Algerian Women in Question. London, Routledge, 1994.

Le Sueur, James D. *Uncivil War: Intellectuals and Identity Politics during the Decolonization of Algeria*. Philadelphia, PA, University of Pennsylvania Press, 2001.

Between Terror and Democracy: Algeria since 1989. London, Zed Books, 2010.

Lebjaoui, Mohamed. *Vérités sur la Révolution Algérienne*. Paris, Gallimard, 1970.

Leca, Jean, and Vatin, Jean-Claude. *L'Algérie politique, institutions et régime*. Paris, Fondation nationale des sciences politiques, 1974.

Liverani, Andrea. *Civil Society in Algeria: The Political Functions of Associational Life*. Abingdon, Routledge, 2008.

Lowi, Miriam R. *Oil Wealth and the Poverty of Politics: Algeria Compared*. Cambridge, Cambridge University Press, 2009.

McDougall, James. *A History of Algeria*. Cambridge, Cambridge University Press, 2017.

Maamri, Malika Rebai. *The State of Algeria: the Politics of a Postcolonial Legacy*. London, I. B. Tauris, 2016.

Majumdar, Margaret A., and Saad, Mohammed. *Transition and Development in Algeria: Economic, Social and Cultural Challenges*. Bristol, Intellect Books, 3rd edn, 2005.

Malley, Robert. *The Call from Algeria: Third Worldism, Revolution and the Turn to Islam*. Berkeley, CA, University of California Press, 1996.

Mandouze, André. *La révolution algérienne par les textes*. Paris, 1961.

Martens, Jean-Claude. *Le modèle algérien de développement (1962–1972)*. Algiers, SNED, 1973.

Martin, Claude. *Histoire de l'Algérie française 1830–1962*. Paris, 1962.

Martinez, Luis. *The Algerian Civil War, 1990–1998*. London, C. Hurst and Co, 2000.

Martínez, Luis, and Boserup, Rasmus Alenius. *Algeria Modern: From Opacity to Complexity*. New York, Oxford University Press, 2016.

Meynier, Gilbert. *L'Algérie Révélée: la Guerre de 1914–1918 et le Premier Quart du XXe Siècle*. Saint-Denis, Bouchène Editions, 2015.

Mohand-Amer, Amar, and Benzenine, Belkacem (Eds). *Le Maghreb et l'indépendance de l'Algérie*. Paris, Karthala, 2012.

Mortimer, Robert. 'Islamists, Soldiers, and Democrats: The Second Algerian War', *The Middle East Journal*. Vol. 50, Issue 1, 1996, pp. 18–39.

Murphy, Emma. 'The Initiation of Economic Liberalization in Algeria, 1979-1989', in Nonneman, Gerd (Ed.). *Political and Economic Liberalization: Dynamics and Linkages in Comparative Perspectives* London, Lynne Rienner Publishers, 1996, pp. 181–197.

Nabi, Muhammad. *L'Algérie aujhourd'hui ou l'absence d'alternatives à l'Islam politique.* Paris, L'Harmattan, 2000.

Northey, Jessica Ayesha. *Civil Society in Algeria: Activism, Identity and the Democratic Process.* London, I. B. Tauris, 2018.

Ottaway, David and Marina. *Algeria. The Politics of a Socialist Revolution.* Berkeley, CA, University of California Press, 1970.

Ouzegane, Amar. *Le Meilleur Combat.* Paris, Julliard, 1962.

Parks, Robert P. 'Algeria and the Arab Uprisings', in Henry, Clement. and Ji-Hyang, Jang (Eds.) *The Arab Spring: Will It Lead to Democratic Transitions?* New York, Palgrave MacMillan, 2012, pp. 101–126.

Pfeifer, Karen. 'Economic Liberalization in the 1980s: Algeria in Comparative Perspective', in Entelis, John and Naylor, Philip (Eds). *State and Society in Algeria.* Boulder, CO, Westview Press, 1992, pp. 97–116.

Porch, Douglas. *The Conquest of the Sahara.* New York, Farrar, Straus and Giroux, 2005.

Quandt, William B. *Revolution and Political Leadership: Algeria, 1954-1968.* MIT Press, 1970.

Between Ballots and Bullets: Algeria's Transition from Authoritarianism. Brookings Institution Press, 1998.

Algeria, 1830–2000: A Short History. New York, Cornell University Press, 2004.

Redjala, R. *L'opposition en Algérie depuis 1962.* Paris, L'Harmattan, 1988.

Rey-Goldzeiguer, Annie. *Aux origines de la guerre d'Algérie 1940–1945. De Mers el-Kébir aux massacres du Nord-Constantinois.* Paris, La Découverte, 2002

Rivet, Daniel. *Le Maghreb à l'épreuve de la colonisation.* Paris, Hachette Littératures, 2002.

Roberts, Hugh. *The Battlefield: Algeria, 1988–2002. Studies in a Broken Polity.* London, Verso, 2003.

'Demilitarizing Algeria', *Carnegie Paper.* Washington, DC, Carnegie Endowment for International Peace. No. 86, May 2007. carnegieendowment.org/files/cp_86_final1.pdf.

Ruedy, John D. *Modern Algeria: The Origins and Development of a Nation.* Bloomington, IN, Indiana University Press, 2nd edn, 2005.

Samraoui, Muhammad. *Chronique des années de sang.* Paris, Denoël, 2003.

Sifaoui, Mohamed. *Histoire de l'Algérie Indépendante.* Paris, Nouveau Monde Éditions, 2014.

Simon, Jacques. *Le Nationalisme Algérien selon Benjamin Stora.* Paris, L'Harmattan, 2014.

Sivan, Emmanuel. *Communisme et Nationalisme en Algérie (1920–1962).* Paris, 1976.

Smith, Tony. *The French Stake in Algeria 1945–1962.* New York, Cornell University Press, 1978.

Stora, Benhamin. *Algeria, 1830–2000: A Short History.* Ithaca, NY, and London, Cornell University Press, 2001.

Historie de l'Algérie coloniale. 4th edn, Paris, Editions La Découverte, 2004.

Sulzberger, C. L. *The Test, de Gaulle and Algeria.* London and New York, 1962.

Temlali, Yassine. *La Genèse de la Kabylie: Aux origines de l'affirmation berbère en Algérie (1830–1962).* Algiers, Editions Barsakh, 2015.

Vatin, Jean-Claude. *L'Algérie politique, histoire et société.* Paris, Fondation nationale des sciences politiques, 1974.

Vidal-Naquet, Pierre. *L'Affaire Audin.* Paris, Les éditions de Minuit, 1989.

Face à la raison d'Etat: Un historien dans la guerre d'Algérie. Paris, La Découverte, 1989.

Vince, Natalya. *Our Fighting Sisters: Nation, Memory and Gender in Algeria, 1954–2012.* Manchester, Manchester University Press, 2015.

Volpi, Frédéric. *Islam and Democracy: The Failure of Dialogue in Algeria.* London, Pluto Press, 2002.

'Algeria Versus the Arab Spring', *Journal of Democracy.* Vol. 24, Issue 3, 2013, pp. 104–115.

'Algeria: When Elections Hurt Democracy', *Journal of Democracy.* Vol. 31, Issue 2, 2020, pp. 152–65.

Wall, Irwin M. *France, the United States and the Algerian War.* Berkeley, CA, University of California Press, 2001.

Werenfels, Isabelle. 'Obstacles to Privatization of State-Owned Industries in Algeria: The Political Economy of a Distributive Conflict', *The Journal of North African Studies.* Vol. 7, Issue 1, 2002, pp. 1–28.

Managing Instability in Algeria: Elites and Political Change since 1995. Abingdon, Routledge, 2009.

Willis, Michael. *The Islamist Challenge in Algeria: A Political History.* New York, NY, New York University Press, 1996.

Politics and Power in the Maghreb: Algeria, Tunisia and Morocco from Independence to the Arab Spring. London, Hurst & Co, 2014.

Algeria: Politics and Society from the Dark Decade to the Hirak. Oxford, Oxford University Press, 2023.

Zoubir, Yahia H. (Ed.). *The Politics of Algeria: Domestic Issues and International Relations.* Abingdon, Routledge, 2019.

Yous, Nesroulah. *Qui a tué à Bentalha?* Paris, La Découverte, 2000.

Zahraoui, Saïd. *Entre l'horreur et l'espoir 1990-1999: Chronique de la nouvelle guerre d'Algérie.* Paris, Laffont, 2000.

Zeraoui, Zidane. 'Algeria: Revolution, Army, and the Political Power', *Language and Intercultural Communication.* Vol. 12, Issue 2, 2012, pp. 133–145.

Zhang, Chuchu. 'From Peak to Trough: Decline of the Algerian 'Islamist Vote', *Chinese Political Science Review.* Vol. 1, Issue 4, 2016, pp. 717–735.

BAHRAIN

Geography

The Kingdom of Bahrain consists of some 33 natural islands and a number of man-made islands, situated midway along the Persian (Arabian) Gulf, about 24 km from the east coast of Saudi Arabia and 28 km from the west coast of Qatar.

The total area of the Bahrain archipelago is 770.9 sq km (297.7 sq miles). Bahrain itself, the principal island, is about 50 km long and between 13 km and 25 km wide. To the north-east of Bahrain, and linked to it by causeway and road, lies Muharraq island, which is approximately 6 km long. A causeway also links Bahrain island to Sitra island. Other islands in the state include Nabih Salih, Jeddah, Hawar, Umm Nassan and Umm Suban. The King Fahd Causeway, linking Bahrain and Saudi Arabia, opened in 1986, and plans were under way in 2023 to construct a second—to be named the King Hamad Causeway. The construction of a 40-km road/rail causeway linking eastern Bahrain to Qatar was approved in 2004 and was scheduled to commence by the end of 2009. However, as a result of various issues including financial problems and diplomatic disputes between the two countries (see History), the project suffered serious delays and as of mid-2023 construction work had not yet commenced.

Between April 1971 and the census of 27 April 2010 the total population of Bahrain increased from 216,078 to 1,234,571, of whom 568,399 were Bahraini citizens. According to the results of the most recent census, of 17 March 2020, the population had increased further, to 1,501,635 (males 942,895, females 558,740). Of the total, 712,362 were Bahrainis and 789,273 non-Bahraini nationals. According to official estimates, at mid-2023 the total population stood at some 1,609,000. In 2001 the port of Manama (on Bahrain island)—the capital and seat of government—had a population of 153,395; the United Nations estimated that the capital and its suburbs were home to 688,558 people by mid-2022. Bahrain's Muslim population (74% of the total—Bahraini and non-Bahraini—in 2020) is estimated to consist of almost 60% Shi'a and just over 40% Sunnis. According to the 2020 census, 99.7% of Bahraini citizens were Muslims. The ruling family are Sunnis. The Bahraini labour force was estimated to have doubled between 1989 and the end of the 20th century. However, the economy continues to rely heavily upon expatriate labour: 79.1% of the employed population were estimated to be of non-Bahraini origin at the end of June 2023.

History

MARC JONES

Revised by KRISTIAN COATES ULRICHSEN

THE AL KHALIFA AND THE BRITISH

Bahrain's history since the 16th century CE has been characterized by colonial intervention by a number of rival regional and European powers, from the Portuguese, to the Persians, to the Omanis. However, the country's most recent era of rule began in 1783, when members of the Al Khalifa family, from the Bani Utub tribe (part of the larger Aniza tribal confederation), conquered the island of Bahrain from their base in Zubara (in modern-day Qatar), driving out the Persians. Since this time, despite a brief interlude during 1800–02, the Al Khalifa have dominated the governance of Bahrain, creating a dynasty based on the insular nature of the ruling family, whose feudal conquest of the indigenous *bahārna* has created a lasting chasm between society and state.

What emerged from the Al Khalifa conquests of 1783 was a feudal society in which various tribal chiefs allied to the Al Khalifa were allocated fiefdoms over which they could extract tax and levies. These small territories were often date gardens or agricultural land, themselves administered by *bahārna* tenants. Despite a relative precariousness to the rule of the tribal leaders, who were often warring with others in the region, engaged in piracy or embroiled in internecine conflict, the period of *Pax Britannica* brought not only stability to the region, but the crystallization of Al Khalifa rule. The ruling family's ascendency to a number of treaties with the United Kingdom established their legitimacy as the rulers of Bahrain. The first of these was the General Maritime Treaty of 1820. A subsequent agreement was signed in 1861, and in 1880 the British concluded a treaty with the Chief of Bahrain in which they forbade the Al Khalifa from engaging in negotiations or treaties with foreign powers without prior consent; this was updated in 1892. However, in exchange for control over Bahrain's foreign policy, the UK was now bound to protect the Bahraini Government from external aggression.

Another of the most significant reforms was that the British agreed to a system of primogeniture, acknowledging that the first born of Sheikh Isa bin Ali Al Khalifa, Hamad, would be the Amir. However, while Isa was growing increasingly frail, a wing of the family, led by his wife and Hamad's brother, Abdullah bin Isa Al Khalifa, was opposing British reforms and undermining British encroachment. For these reasons, it was the British who, essentially, deposed Sheikh Isa in 1923, installing Hamad in his place. Through the malleable Hamad, the British were able to exercise influence via 'indirect and pacific' means, even though Isa, technically, remained Amir until his death in 1932. None the less, rivalry within the ruling family continued to cause significant instability, itself aggravated by the fact that Europeans, whom the UK was treaty-bound to protect, were beginning to bear the brunt of these tensions.

Following an attack on a representative of a German trader in 1904 by the retainers of Sheikh Ali bin Ahmed Al Khalifa, when he intervened to protect another employee from Ali bin Ahmed's men, the British took disciplinary measures against the Khalifa family that represented a significant encroachment in Bahrain's internal affairs. The measures included banning the long-held practice of *sukhra* (forced labour) and taking the heir apparent Hamad as hostage on a British ship until Sheikh Ali bin Ahmed came out of hiding to face punishment for his orchestration of the assault. The attack also provoked the ire of Persia, as Persian subjects were affected. Increasingly under pressure from regional and European powers, the British trade project was untenable, unless it could provide security for traders, and thus the British had to take strong measures in order to reassure investors.

The British role, initially designed to secure trade routes with India from piracy and to suppress the slave trade, soon extended into moderating internal conflict. This became more concrete upon the application of the Order in Council of 1913, which brought Bahrain into the informal empire as an overseas imperial territory. The British-led Government of India, wanting to retain a light touch in intervention, often came into conflict with the opinions of many political agents on the ground, who sometimes felt a moral compunction to intervene. This moral desire frequently resulted from the treatment of the indigenous *bahārna* population, who were mistreated by their feudal sheikhs, often suffering attacks on their persons and property or extortion by the sheikh's armed retainers. In one instance, up to 2,000 *bahārna* camped at the British residency in Bahrain to protest against Al Khalifa oppression. Indeed, the British officials' disdain for many members of the ruling family, especially in the 1920s and 1930s, indicated how British policy and protection of the Al Khalifa was a pragmatic affair, born of a need to protect British geostrategic and trade interests.

Soon, British intervention took the form of administrative reform. The British Political Agent, Maj. H. R. P. 'Harold' Dickson, created the Manama municipality in 1919—a form of quasi-democratic government, the main purpose of which was to generate taxes in Manama, the capital, as well as providing a form of security independent of the previous system of what was arbitrary tax collection by members of the Al Khalifa and their *al-fidawiyya* (armed retainers). However, the creation of the Manama municipality represented a focus on the urban, at the expense of the rural. As British trade interests were considered paramount, stability in Manama—a perceived result of establishing the municipality—took precedence over the country. Thus, British encroachment began not only reluctantly, but also asymmetrically and in a localized fashion. This divide reflects an enduring contract between the ruling elite and its external protectors that has generated a chasm between rulers and ruled, urban and rural, and merchants and the poor.

The might of British gunboat diplomacy sometimes concealed a willingness to compromise, which was itself born out of a desire to intervene only to the minimum extent necessary, yet enough to counter any potential objections to British rule by competing forces, such as Turkey (known as Türkiye from June 2022), the Al Saud family and Persia. For example, the British sought to improve the lot of the *bahārna* population to appease the Persians, yet not to the extent that it would threaten the neighbouring Al Saud. Although the need for stability in Bahrain—driven by the imperative of maintaining British ascendancy in trade through the Persian (Arabian) Gulf—was paramount, some reforms, however well-intentioned, contributed to a growing class divide. For example, the British reformed the pearling industry in the 1920s, which had hitherto relied on indebted labour relations between a wealthy merchant class and poorer divers. Even attempts to reform land in the 1920s and 1930s were designed to mitigate conflict between the Al Khalifa feudal chiefs and their mostly indigenous *bahārna* tenants. However, while the pearl industry reforms resulted in short-term demonstrations, the creation of a cadastral survey and a court system had longer-term consequences, consolidating land ownership in a manner that benefited the existent landowners, such as wealthy merchants and members of the Al Khalifa family. British officials themselves acknowledged that the Al Khalifa had appropriated most of the land from the indigenous inhabitants, but this was regarded as a *fait accompli*, the effects of which could now only be mitigated.

Aside from the Manama municipality and other municipalities that were steadily being built, such as in the towns of Muharraq and Hidd, the British created a police force to ensure order around the country. Although Bahrain's Shi'a population welcomed, to a certain extent, the protection that the British provided to them, growing political opportunity and increasing awareness of progress in countries like India prompted a desire for political change. During 1934–35 a group of Shi'a led by notable merchants pressed the Amir for changes to the legal system and for more access to trade; however, little became of this, other than promises to codify the legal system.

The nascent political movement in 1935 emerged shortly after the discovery of oil, in 1932, which created opportunities for Bahrain's increasingly educated residents. However, many of the job opportunities created by the developing oil industry caused discontent among Bahrainis, as much of the labour was imported, owing to the shortage of a skilled workforce in the country. In addition, political progress in neighbouring countries, such as the creation of a (short-lived) legislative council in Kuwait in 1938, forced a re-examination of local policies. Questions were also being raised about the allocation of the new oil revenues. British officials, concerned about winning oil concessions for British entities while keeping the Al Khalifa united, agreed that one-third of all oil revenues would go to the ruling family. This resulted in the ruling family effectively securing up to 25% of the country's gross domestic product between 1926 and 1975. Thus, the price of stability, at least in this form of incentivizing unity within the ruling family, came at a huge cost to the economy, fuelling accusations of ruling family corruption and expropriation, not least because of the increased expectations that oil wealth would be distributed to develop new political and economic institutions. Yet this redistribution did occur, and emergent political movements seized the relative opportunity provided by political reforms to make their demands felt.

In 1938, for the first time in modern history, Shi'a and Sunni groups submitted a joint petition to the ruler demanding various reforms, including for more democratic governing institutions. However, the British administration in India, which had broad oversight over political arrangements in the Gulf, did not wish to encourage democracy at this time, and along with the ruling Al Khalifa, sought to divide the Sunni and Shi'a by offering differential reforms for both. Yet the momentum did not abate immediately; following strikes and protests, the administration was forced into some concessions, including improvements in the codification of law that had been promised in 1935, and the formation of various committees, including one that sought to represent the Shi'a in matters of education. Nevertheless, the implementation of reforms was not aided by the death of the Amir, Sheikh Hamad bin Isa Al Khalifa, in 1942, who was succeeded by the more conservative Sheikh Salman bin Hamad Al Khalifa.

Despite the expansion of education and new job opportunities in the oil sector, sectarianism and the slow pace of reform still prevailed. This came to a head on 1 June 1954, when a group of Shi'a civilians, angry at the sentencing of a co-religionist, protested at the police fort. The police opened fire and killed three civilians. In 1956 police opened fire in a market, killing five people and injuring 17, after a minor altercation over a vegetable stand. Despite the anger directed at the institutions of government, the injustice of the shootings contributed to the popularity of the National Union Committee (NUC)—a broad political grouping that viewed sectarianism as a divisive ruling tactic used by British colonial forces. In addition to the anger prompted by the police shootings, the influence of Arab nationalism, and its tenets of anti-colonialism, coupled with growing local discontent with slow reform and ruling family corruption, contributed to the movement's popularity. The perception of autocratic British influence in governance through Charles Belgrave, the Commandant of the police and Financial Advisor to the Amir, also fuelled suspicions of colonial misrule. Chants of 'Down, down, Advisor!', were scrawled on walls in Manama, echoing the chants of 'Down, down, Hamad' that are more commonplace today.

The British employed a pragmatic approach in their dealings with the NUC, using delaying tactics to allow for the possibility of the group fragmenting while they decided on future strategy. Co-operation with the NUC was not out of the question, especially given the political burden and recalcitrance of the Al Khalifa family, but geostrategic concerns were paramount. Reflecting on their eventual decision to side with the Al Khalifa in 1956, the British decided that the Cold War and the importance of protecting Kuwait in the Gulf were sufficient justification for not disturbing the status quo that they had facilitated. Assured support from the Al Khalifa, who permitted a British military presence, might not be so forthcoming if the British were to agree to support an elected assembly in Bahrain. For these reasons, the NUC was eventually dismantled following the arrest of several of its members and the deportation of its main leaders. Following a highly politicized trial in 1956, in which a British police officer acted as government prosecutor, three leaders of the High Executive Committee of the NUC were illegally deported to the British island of Saint Helena.

The removal of the NUC destroyed elements of organized political activity, yet the reforms initiated by the regime in response, including the creation of an Administrative Council, were criticized for incorporating too many appointed members of the ruling family. Other key demands by the NUC were introduced, including a penal code; this was also criticized for being used as a legal vehicle for cracking down on political expression, along with an emergency law which severely curtailed any public gatherings. These unfulfilled expectations carried through into the 1960s and culminated in the March *intifada* (uprising) in 1965, which was instigated by the National Liberation Front (NLF) and the Arab Nationalist Movement, which positioned themselves against the British and in favour of a new social order. After the state oil firm, the Bahrain Petroleum Company, dismissed a number of workers, protests resulted in the deaths of six Bahrainis. The Government responded to the riots with further limited reforms, including the creation of partial labour committees at the oil company. However, these committees were considered merely a superficial arena for the expression of dissent, and were organized deliberately to avoid effecting meaningful social and political reforms. The Government took other measures to control dissent, such as the creation of a security ordinance, which gave the state almost unlimited powers of detention and arrest over anyone deemed to threaten national security.

BAHRAIN POST-INDEPENDENCE

Foreign interdiction on internal matters had shaped the nature of the regime and the institutions of state. British influence had not only created emergent state structures, but shaped the growth of law, land ownership, urban development and the security apparatus. Indeed, the colonial legacy and the accompanying industrialization had rapidly changed a feudal society into one in which the tribal class monopolized the instruments of state, while tenants who had recently been feudal subjects now largely worked in industries in which they had few legal rights to organize collectively. Without a vote, the indigenous class had now become workers, whose livelihoods were contingent on the policies enacted by government and foreign multinationals. Thus, Bahrain's eventual transition into a sovereign state in 1971 (with Britain's withdrawal from the Gulf) coincided with industrial unrest, while the country's reliance on foreign powers for protection appeared to continue, when the US Navy opened its Fifth Fleet base in Bahrain.

The continuation of neo-colonialism and the rise of US hegemony, coupled with multiple labour grievances, meant the leftist influence from those going to study in the Union of Soviet Socialist Republics (USSR) or the Soviet satellite states resonated strongly with many Bahraini workers, and presented a challenge to the nascent feudal-industrial capitalism forming in Bahrain. As the more overt oppression under the British was still in recent memory, the ruling classes' ownership of not simply the means of production but also the resources of the state—mainly in the form of oil revenues—fuelled anger. This was aggravated by the influx of workers from South Asia, who were being sold to companies in Bahrain as cheap and compliant labour. It was believed that trade unions could be subverted by employing foreign nationals whose services could be terminated if economic hardship prevailed. This was compounded by what was seen as the reluctance of the indigenous workers to take on menial jobs. Expectations, heightened by signs of modernization in neighbouring states, as well as by local, but often asymmetric, demonstrations of progress, compounded Bahrainis' political and economic grievances.

While the British administration had been hostile to the idea of democracy in the 1930s, it increasingly recognized its benefits as a tool to relieve growing pressures within Bahrain and to guard against revolution. Yet the ruling classes, which included the Al Khalifa and, according to one British ambassador, important merchant families, were hesitant about instituting democracy. In particular, the conservative Prime Minister, Sheikh Khalifa bin Salman Al Khalifa, opposed such policies. None the less, the Amir, against the wishes of more conservative elements of the regime, as well as King Faisal of Saudi Arabia, introduced democratic reforms, perhaps more so at the behest of the British and more progressive members of the regime. The Amir issued a decree in 1972 ordering the formation of a constituent assembly to draft a constitution for the newly independent state. The Constitution, which was enacted by Amiri decree in 1973, allowed for men to elect 30 members of a 44-seat unicameral National Assembly. The remaining 14 seats were held by government ministers appointed by Amiri decree.

The parliament proved more obstructive than the Government had imagined, regularly thwarting its proposals, especially those concerning security. The pressure to abandon democracy was highlighted by the fact that the National Assembly was dissolved in 1975, ostensibly because it had refused to approve a State Security Law that granted substantial powers of detention and arrest to the security forces. The law, which would remain in place until 2001, replaced the security ordinance of 1965. Given the importance of security to the regime, the economic privileges enjoyed by the elite and Saudi fears that democracy might create a domino effect in the region, it is hardly surprising that the National Assembly lasted only two years. Following its dissolution, Saudi Arabia sought to influence members of the Bahraini ruling family with gifts, conditional on the basis that they abandon any demands for democratic experimentation. Saudi Arabia also provided 300 of its citizens to bolster the Bahraini armed forces, and regulated Bahraini purchases of military equipment. By the time of the Iranian Revolution in 1979, any possibility of a reinstatement of democracy in Bahrain had evaporated.

Bahrain's short parliamentary experiment had seen brief, but surprising, co-operation between the left and religious elements in the National Assembly. Following the dissolution of parliament, the Government was reluctant to see further co-operation between these two groupings, on the principle that a united, cross-sect and diverse ideological opposition would be a more formidable force. The regime increasingly targeted and stigmatized the country's Shi'a population. Although this paranoia was partly augmented by the Iranian Revolution in 1979, and the fear that Ayatollah Ruhollah Khomeini of Iran wished to export the revolution across the Gulf, the Bahraini authorities had always exhibited antipathy towards the Shi'a, especially now that British influence, which had hitherto offered some protection, was diminished. This was demonstrated in 1981, when the Prime Minister ordered the arrest of up to 850 Shi'a, even though they had shown no visible support for Khomeini. Even Ian Henderson, the British head of the State Security Investigation Directorate, expressed his concerns about ruling family conservatism in 1982, reporting that the Prime Minister and the Crown Prince, Hamad bin Isa Al Khalifa, were deporting hundreds of Shi'a without any legal basis.

Although leftist opposition did exist, much of it, including the NLF, had been infiltrated by the security forces, using tactics previously employed by Henderson during his time in the colonial police force in Kenya. This left a vacuum that was filled to some extent by Shi'a Islamism, the ranks of which were swollen by the Government's ongoing persecution. Encroaching Saudi influence was formalized with a security pact in 1982, itself prompted by an attempted coup by the Islamic Front for the Liberation of Bahrain (IFLB). With Saudi protection formalized over Bahrain, the country was politically, economically and socially evermore reliant on Saudi support. Despite the continued, but diminishing influence of the UK in the security forces, and the presence of a US naval base, the Al Khalifa and, in particular, the Prime Minister—influenced to a large extent by Saudi conservatism—seemed to be paving their own way in defining Bahrain's future. The rising authoritarianism was marked by an increasing number of deaths in custody: six Bahrainis were believed to have been tortured to death in custody between 1975 and 1986.

THE 1990S *INTIFADA*

The ongoing oppression of Bahrain's political opposition, particularly the Shi'a community at large throughout the 1980s, combined with growing economic challenges, laid the foundations for the unrest of the 1990s, often referred to as the 1990s *intifada*. Between 1992 and 1994 influential public figures wrote a series of petitions to the Amir, Sheikh Isa bin Salman Al Khalifa, who had governed the country since 1961. The majority of these petitions called for the reinstatement of the National Assembly which had been dissolved in 1975. One such petition, known as the Elite petition, was signed by a Shi'a religious scholar and former member of the National Assembly, Sheikh Abd al-Amir al-Jamri; a Sunni university professor, Dr Abd al-Latif al-Mahmud; a Sunni religious scholar, Sheikh Isa al-Jawdar; and a former leftist and member of the National Assembly, Muhammad Jabir al-Sabah. It was also signed by 300 of Bahrain's notables. Although the petition was accepted for consideration by the Amir, stalling by the regime led to further petitions and a statement by the Bahrain Freedom Movement, the IFLB, the NLF and the Popular Front for the Liberation of Bahrain, which reiterated the demands of the Elite petition. The Amir refused them and, after an initial meeting with the Elite petitioners, insisted on meeting Sunni and Shi'a groups individually—a move that reflected the regime's tactic of deliberately exacerbating communal tensions in order to dilute and weaken any unified opposition.

The spark for further tensions came on 25 November 1994, when marathon runners clad in shorts and T-shirts attempted to run through a crowd of protesters in a Shi'a village. The residents of the village, who did not object to the presence of foreigners, did, however, object to the perceived immodesty of the runners' apparel. As the runners tried to push through the blockade, scuffles broke out with the inhabitants of the village. Following the arrests of about 20 villagers and Ali Salman, a Shi'a notable, and the latter's subsequent deportation, massive demonstrations broke out in Bahrain, sparking almost a decade of unrest. Indeed, although 1992 and 1994 had been marked by petitions and lobbying, the period between December 1994 and August 1995 was characterized by street protests, rallies and sit-ins. This was due in part to continued repression by the Government, which involved the deportation and arrest of key movement leaders, such as Ali Salman and Sheikh al-Jamri.

Considerable unrest continued between 1995 and 1997. Stonewalling by the Government and police brutality—itself facilitated by the broad mandate of the State Security Law—encouraged more militant groups to counter the authorities with more extreme means, including arson attacks and the throwing of Molotov cocktails. Two percussion bombs exploded at the Yatim Centre in Manama on 31 December 1995. In January 1996 bombs went off at the Royal Le Méridien Hotel, and in February a bomb exploded at the Diplomat Hotel in Manama. Other bombings occurred throughout 1996, most of which targeted hotels throughout the country. While many of these explosions did not cause casualties, a later attack on a restaurant frequented by South Asian migrant labourers resulted in a number of deaths.

This violence amid Bahrain's central infrastructure and the killing of two police officers prompted an even harsher reaction from the authorities. Two Shi'a mosques in Sanabis, a suburb of Manama, were destroyed—a move that would be a precursor to larger mosque demolitions in 2011. Although the violence abated in 1997, in 1998–99 there was constant unrest, as new, innovative forms of protest began to occur. However, the regime began the collective punishment of the almost exclusively poor Shi'a neighbourhoods that were perceived as giving succour to the opposition movement, by switching off their water and electricity periodically. The Government's heavy-handed initial response fanned the flames of discontent and reflected the authoritarian instincts of the Prime Minister, who was attempting to undermine the comparatively conciliatory approach of his nephew, Crown Prince Hamad.

Despite the repression, the Government showed a willingness to offer some concessions, although none substantial enough to halt demands for a reinstatement of the Constitution. In a 'carrot and stick' fashion, the Government first responded in 1992 by creating an appointed Consultative Council (Majlis al-Shura), yet this did little to curb the demands for a return to an elected parliament, even after the number of members was expanded. The growth of the Gulf Cooperation Council (GCC, established in 1981) and the collective fears among traditional monarchies about unrest in Bahrain resulted in Gulf regimes attempting to salvage the policy of *makramāt* (gifts bestowed by the Amir) and paternalism in order to undermine any efforts towards genuinely inclusive politics. Reflecting its continued influence in the region, Saudi Arabia raised Bahrain's allotment from the Abu Saafa oilfield from 70,000 barrels a day (b/d) to 100,000 b/d. A subsequent increase in the intensity of the unrest simply resulted in Saudi Arabia giving Bahrain the full allocation of 140,000 b/d, while the United Arab Emirates (UAE) reportedly resumed annual subsidies of US $50m. to Bahrain. Although ownership of Abu Saafa had once been contested between Saudi Arabia and Bahrain, negotiations meant that the oilfield went to Saudi Arabia, but the revenues from it were directed to Bahrain, giving Saudi Arabia considerable economic leverage.

As had become common, the Government, through the state media, framed the uprising as an externally motivated plot by Shi'a Islamists based in Iran and Lebanon. In 1996 the Government claimed that it had uncovered an Iranian-backed plot by the military wing of Hezbollah Bahrain. The confessions of the alleged plotters were broadcast on television and implicated local notables, who were perceived to be influential in the unrest. Yet with continued accusations of torture, the allegations appeared to be attempts to delegitimize the opposition and brand them as sectarian Islamists. In fact, the reasons for the *intifada* were better explained by several factors, including rising unemployment; a growing but acute gap between the upper middle-class and the lower middle-class and rural poor; the spread of exclusive housing around the capital at the expense of affordable, urgently required housing for Bahraini citizens; and the continued discrimination against and exclusion of the Shi'a majority in certain jobs, particularly in security institutions such as the army.

BAHRAIN UNDER KING HAMAD

In accordance with the tradition of following unrest with an ostensible top-down act of benevolence, Bahrain's most recent democratic turn began upon the death of the former Amir, Sheikh Isa bin Salman Al Khalifa, in 1999. His successor and son, Sheikh Hamad bin Isa Al Khalifa, drove forward a number of political reforms designed to introduce elements of democratic rule to Bahrain. In his first address, Sheikh Hamad pledged that he would not tolerate discrimination against the Shi'a community, or favouritism towards the country's Sunni population. He ordered the release of 350 political detainees, and after Sheikh al-Jamri wrote a letter expressing his regret for organizing protests in the 1990s, he was pardoned. Hamad even visited a number of Shi'a villages to extend an olive branch to these disenfranchised communities. In addition, political prisoners were given permission to return, and those charged with crimes against the state were absolved.

The conciliatory mood was accompanied by the publication of the National Action Charter (NAC) of 2001—a document listing numerous political reforms that was approved by 98% of those who voted when it was put to a national referendum in February of that year. Yet those voting on the NAC were to be disappointed by the implementation of the proposed changes. The promised new constitution, proposed by royal decree in 2002, essentially clarified and amended key expectations laid out in the NAC. Although many had believed that a unicameral, elected parliament would be established (as in 1973), or a bicameral parliament with one elected house and another comprising technocrats, what was actually created was a bicameral parliament in which the upper house was not only appointed by royal decree, but also had the power of veto over the lower house. Thus, the upper house (Consultative Council) effectively had ultimate power over the elected lower house (Council of Representatives). Constitutional amendments required a two-thirds' majority of the combined houses, making amendments entirely unlikely and change virtually impossible. Only the Cabinet was allowed to initiate laws, and the parliament had power only to vote on them. Rather than being a democratic regime with some authoritarian tendencies, the constitutional changes had shown that the Bahraini Government was an authoritarian regime with democratic accoutrements. In addition, Hamad, who in February 2002 had declared Bahrain a kingdom and thereby assumed the title of King, retained the right to rule by decree, ensuring that power remained firmly in the palace.

Further political sleight of hand undermined confidence in the reform processes. Through the Decree 56 law of 2002, those accused of crimes committed before 2001 were exempt from prosecution. However, although the law granted amnesty to those accused of crimes against the state, it also extended immunity to those accused of torture. Thus, the price for what turned out to be limited democratic institutions was a denial of redress to victims of state crime and their inability to absolve themselves of the deprivations that they had suffered. Other legislation hastily passed before the first session of parliament in 2002 included a strict press law and other laws regulating political expression. None of these could now be amended without parliament's consent.

Despite what King Hamad had said at his inaugural address about rejecting discrimination against Bahrain's Shi'a majority, Shi'a enfranchisement was undermined by a number of procedures that aggravated grievances within the country's opposition. In addition to removing citizenship from Shi'a dissidents, the Government embarked on an extensive programme of naturalizing Sunni foreigners in exchange for their service in the military or the police. Estimates suggest that since the reforms of 2001, some 50,000 people may have been naturalized each year. The Sunni vote was also strengthened by the partial reintegration into Bahrain society of the descendants of the Sunni Dawasir—a tribe expelled by the British to Saudi Arabia in 1926 for their refusal to accept the reforms of the 1920s. Up to 20,000 of them, most of whom lived in Dammam in Saudi Arabia, were permitted to hold dual Bahraini-Saudi citizenship under a decree of 2002. A report by the Bahrain Centre for Human Rights (BCHR), an outlawed non-governmental organization (NGO), revealed in 2002 that the Dawasir were receiving housing and state benefits from Bahrain while also voting in the Bahrain elections in polling stations set up on the King Fahd Causeway joining Bahrain and Saudi Arabia. This sectarian social engineering became evident in other forms. It was revealed that Bahrain's electoral boundaries were also drawn in such a way as to reduce the power of the Shi'a vote, while some Sunni constituencies numbering only a few hundred were given the same voting power to elect one deputy as Shi'a areas numbering several thousand. In the most extreme case, one Sunni vote equalled 21 Shi'a votes.

Despite these developments, between 2002 and 2010 Bahrain's rating on the index produced by the independent watchdog Freedom House went from a rating of 'not free' to 'partly free', reflecting some quantifiable improvements. Moderate progress was evident in the creation of political societies, journalists' associations and labour unions. Bahrain briefly became the most progressive Gulf nation for migrant rights in 2009, when it approved legislation amending the *kafala* (sponsorship) system, henceforth allowing migrants to change jobs once in Bahrain if their expected contractual conditions were not met (see *Reasserting Authoritarianism*). Progress for women was partly evident in the Government's desire to introduce a universal personal status law, although it backed down on this after members of the Shi'a clergy, and thousands of other Bahrainis, protested against government encroachment on religious matters. The proposed universal law had been driven forward by the newly appointed Supreme Council for Women (SCW). Its cancellation is often used to criticize the human rights record of current Shi'a activists. However, in 2007 the Women's Petition Committee (an independent group of female activists), criticized the SCW for being too closely linked to the Government and the Royal Court, providing an illusion of women's empowerment rather than substantive change.

Some of the other new political societies created in the 2000s included Islamist groupings such as al-Menbar, the Salafist al-Asala, and secular movements such as the Jamiyat al-Amal al-Watani al-Dimoqrati (al-Wa'ad—National Democratic Action Society). However, in the 2002 elections a number of societies, including the newly established Jamiyat al-Wefaq al-Watani al-Islamiyya (al-Wefaq) and al-Wa'ad, boycotted the vote on the principle that the reforms of 2001 gave little authority to the elected house. It is perhaps unsurprising that this weakening of the Shi'a vote had the corollary effect of creating sect-based societies like al-Wefaq, which capitalized on addressing Shi'a grievances, an issue that struggled to gain purchase among secular or Sunni members of society. Yet even then, the Shi'a community in Bahrain was not a monolithic block, a fact that became self-evident when Hassan Mushaima, a founding member of al-Wefaq, left the group and created the al-Haq movement following disagreement about al-Wefaq's decision to contest the 2006 elections. The fragmentation arguably weakened the Shi'a as a collective movement, but also reflected frustration among members of the community who felt al-Wefaq's more conciliatory approach to political engagement would yield little benefit.

The fractious politics of Bahrain, built on the diluted promises of the 2001 reforms, meant that demands for change did not deviate significantly from historic precedent. However, even before the 'Arab Spring' uprising of 2011, there appeared to be a resurgent conservative mood in the ruling elite that found its way into the ranks of the security apparatus. As early as 2007 the international NGO Human Rights Watch reported that the use of torture was creeping back into Bahraini police stations. The country was also shaken by allegations made by Salah al-Bandar, a British former adviser to the Royal Court, about a plan by high-level members of the Al Khalifa family to reduce the power of the Shi'a vote. Al-Bandar's 216-page report documented US $2.65m. in payments to a network of people that included an electronic propaganda cell, a bogus human rights organization and a newspaper. The alleged head of the cabal was Sheikh Ahmed bin Attiyatallah Al Khalifa, the Minister of Cabinet Affairs. While 'Bandargate' implied a high-level cabal operating within the Royal Court, it was suspected that the group enjoyed broad support within the ruling family. Powerful hardliners, exemplified by the Prime Minister and the Minister of the Royal Court, Khalid bin Ahmad Al Khalifa, were wary about empowering the Shi'a and disagreed with King Hamad's more overtly conciliatory approach.

THE BAHRAIN UPRISING OF 2011

With growing evidence of corruption, sectarian naturalization and a continued lack of faith in the political process, the Egyptian uprising that began on 25 January 2011 (see Egypt) provided moral courage to many of Bahrain's disenfranchised. A 'Day of Rage' was called for on 14 February, three days after Egypt's President was ousted from power and the 10th anniversary of the 2001 vote to approve the National Action Charter of reform, and activists, initially anonymous, expressed their anger at corruption, oppression and lack of accountability. When people took to the streets, government forces responded with tear gas, bird-shot and rubber bullets, which resulted in the death of 21-year-old protester Ali Mushaima. On the following day, at Mushaima's funeral, the authorities opened fire, killing another young Bahraini. The sequence of events prompted thousands of people to set up camp at Bahrain's Pearl Roundabout, an ageing monument to GCC unity located near the business district of Manama, the capital of Bahrain. On 17 February security forces cleared the roundabout, killing four protesters and injuring hundreds. The Pearl Roundabout became a symbolic site of resistance, similar to the role of Tahrir Square in the Egyptian uprising, and the next day thousands returned there to participate in the funerals of those killed. The military, which had subsequently been stationed at the roundabout, opened fire, killing another protester. In a move designed to assuage rapidly growing anger, the troops withdrew, and the Crown Prince, Sheikh Salman bin Hamad Al Khalifa, assured civilians that they could remain at the roundabout. Meanwhile, a generally loyalist and mostly Sunni grouping gathered at the Al-Fateh Mosque, itself a symbol of the conquest of Bahrain by the Al Khalifa family in 1783, and expressed their support for the ruling family. Led by Sheikh Abd al-Latif al-Mahmud, this gathering was the foundation for the creation of the National Unity Gathering. The movement subsequently lost momentum, however, and failed to win a seat in Bahrain's 2014 elections.

Despite the initial brutality and hostility towards the presence of thousands of activists at the Pearl Roundabout, the symbolic home of the uprising, late February–early March 2011 was characterized by some degree of hope. The more conciliatory Crown Prince, in dialogue with several opposition leaders, including Ali Salman, announced on 13 March his 'Seven Principles' reform plan, which included initiatives to increase the powers of the elected house, fair voting districts and a government that would accommodate the will of the people. Although these proposals fell short of demands for a constitutional monarchy, the Government appeared to seize on an escalation in protests, which spilled over from the Pearl Roundabout into the nearby Financial Harbour, a property owned by the Prime Minister. Government forces once again cleared the roundabout, resulting in more deaths, including a number of police officers. Any real hope of concessions being made in 2011 was ended abruptly in mid-March by the intervention of the GCC Peninsula Shield Force, a military alliance comprising troops from Saudi Arabia, the UAE and Qatar. At this point, and with the Bahrain Defence Force and National Guard on the streets, the Government did not concede to the demands of the opposition. While the Government's response might have been planned all along, with the Crown Prince's dialogue with the opposition appearing to have been a delaying tactic, divisions among the ruling members of the Al Khalifa family and Saudi influence also partly explain the change in approach to the protests. The apparently more placatory attitude of Crown Prince Salman, who led discussions with the opposition, clashed with the more draconian attitudes of palace hardliners, including Royal Court ministers and the Prime Minister. As in the 1970s, it is probable that Saudi Arabia objected to the Crown Prince's reform plan, which risked empowering Bahrain's Shi'a to what the Saudis perceived to be an unacceptable level. After 2011 the Crown Prince, who became First Deputy Prime Minister in 2013, lost influence, while the leverage of hardliners grew amid a more reactionary approach to opposition protests and demands.

Meanwhile, in February 2011, when government forces shot and killed protesters, certain radical flanks of the movement split from the main opposition, escalating their demands by calling for a republic. Among these were Hassan Mushaima, the leader of al-Haq, Abd al-Wahab Hussain, head of Tiyar al-Wafa al-Islami (al-Wafa) and Saeed al-Shehabi, head of the British-based Harakat Ahrar al-Bahrain al-Islami (Bahrain Freedom Movement). Jamiyat al-Wefaq al-Watani al-Islamiyya (al-Wefaq), in the mean time, had formed an alliance with a number of other societies, including the Jamiyat al-Amal al-Watani al-Dimoqrati (al-Wa'ad), a society whose roots lay in Bahrain's leftist Arab nationalist and socialist movements. This split in the opposition was capitalized upon by the Government, which emphasized that those wanting a republic were engaged in potentially treasonous demands.

As during the 1990s *intifada*, the government-controlled media portrayed the uprising to the national and international community as an Iranian-backed move designed to install theocratic rule. Consultative Council member (and later Minister of Information Affairs) Samira Rajab appeared on the Al Jazeera Arabic News channel and propagated an erroneous story about protesters waving Bahraini flags containing 12 points—supposedly to reflect their loyalty to Ithna'ashara ('Twelver') Shi'a Islam, the dominant theology in Iran. A string of stories in other Gulf media outlets, later denounced as false, contained tales of ships from Iran carrying arms being intercepted en route to Bahrain. An independent commission of international legal experts subsequently found that there had been no Iranian involvement. However, in 2013 the Government continued with its rhetoric, and blamed exiled cleric Hadi al-Modarresi for being the leader behind the 14 February Youth Coalition, Bahrain's anonymous youth movement. The fearmongering was not without impact, and contributed to the splitting of some secular and Sunni support for the movement. It also heightened the climate of fear, increasing demands for protection and security.

Since 2011, dozens of leading human rights activists, religious notables and political figures, including a group known as the 'Bahrain 13', have been arrested. Among them was Ibrahim Sharif, the former Secretary-General of al-Wa'ad, who was sentenced to five years in gaol in 2011 for allegedly inciting hatred against the regime. Sharif's arrest was notable owing to the fact that he was a Sunni Muslim, amid accusations that the Government sought to maintain the appearance that the uprising was exclusively Shi'a in nature and sectarian in composition. Similarly, displays of cross-sect co-operation were undermined. The leader of an online social media campaign called #UniteBH (Unite Bahrain) was arrested and questioned about his motives, and a 'human chain' stretching from the Pearl Roundabout to the Al-Fateh mosque was broken up. Other members of the 'Bahrain 13' include Abd al-Hadi al-Khawaja, the co-founder of the BCHR and a long-time political activist, who went on a 110-day hunger strike in 2012 to protest against his incarceration. In addition to these high-profile figures, thousands of citizens have been incarcerated, dozens killed and many tortured by the state's security apparatus. The BCHR recorded approximately 100 deaths between 2011 and 2015 as a result of the excessive use of force by the Government.

Most significant in the early days of the Bahrain uprising was the failure of traditional ruling strategies to placate the opposition. A promised US $20,000m. aid package from other GCC states failed to make any short-term impact on people's demands. As a result, the Government increased sanctions against dissidents, including the removal of scholarships from government-funded students studying overseas and the expulsion of up to 500 students from Bahrain universities for alleged involvement in the protests. Approximately 2,500 people were dismissed from their jobs, many for absenteeism during the unrest. However, many of those were engaged in what an independent international commission found to be legal strikes. The repressive measures introduced in March 2011 included the 'state of national safety', which was a constitutionally enshrined form of quasi-martial law. The state of national safety created a two-tier military court system that severely curtailed civil and political rights. When asked about the harsh nature of the penalties passed down by the mostly Sunni judges, the legal officials argued that the provisions of the state of national safety overruled constitutionally protected civil rights.

REASSERTING AUTHORITARIANISM

Reforms designed to appease the opposition were not substantial, and included a constitutional amendment that permitted the Council of Representatives to pass a vote of no confidence in the Prime Minister. The amendment requires a two-thirds' majority of the elected chamber to agree, although the King still has the power to overrule the parliament's decision. In addition to this, the Government sponsored a National Dialogue that attempted to include all facets of Bahraini society. However, the dialogue, which was launched in July 2011, subverted the representation afforded by the elected house: Al-Wefaq, which secured 45% of the seats in the 40-seat Council of Representatives at the October 2010 legislative elections, was granted only five of the 300 seats in the dialogue, while the entire opposition was allocated just 35 seats in total. This, once again, convinced al-Wefaq that the Government was not serious about representing the will of the people, prompting it to withdraw from the dialogue. A second dialogue launched by King Hamad in 2013 fared little better. An emerging Sunni coalition comprising Tajammu al-Wahda al-Watani (al-Tajammu), al-Menbar and al-Asala used it as an opportunity to pursue their own demands for socioeconomic changes, including improvements to housing and health care. The growing sectarianism in the country did not help matters, and the Sunni Islamist groupings, with their focus on moral issues, failed to agree with demands for fundamental political reform by what they viewed as a largely Shi'a opposition. The opposition again withdrew from the dialogue after al-Wefaq's deputy was charged under new anti-terrorism laws.

Both dialogues indicated that the Government was either buying time while attempting to consolidate the security situation, or rejecting full-scale authoritarianism by implementing token gestures. While the dialogues had been criticized by organizations such as al-Wefaq, they represented the Government's need to create some form of popular forum for discussion, following al-Wefaq's decision in February 2011 to withdraw from the legislature. Although the National Dialogues were regarded by many observers as a way to distract attention from government stalling, the announcement by the King of the appointment of an international committee to investigate the events of 2011 was widely praised. The committee, comprising international legal experts such as Cherif Bassiouni of Egypt, was given significant access to government departments. Its report, published in November 2011, was highly critical of the Government, but also criticized the opposition. Crucially, it revealed that the security forces had engaged in the systematic torture of Bahraini detainees. It made a number of recommendations, which included asking the Government to investigate all officials thought to have engaged in human rights abuses. The King, in a public address, accepted the findings of the report and commissioned a committee to follow through with the implementation of the recommendations. However, this process was criticized by members of the international community, including Bassiouni himself, who noted that of the 26 recommendations, only 10 were carried out. Crucially, the two most important recommendations singled out by Bassiouni were the need to release political prisoners, and the undertaking of investigations into those believed to be responsible for torture that led to deaths. The failure to implement these recommendations followed what has become a familiar pattern in Bahraini politics: a sense of immunity for agents of the state accused of human rights violations. Despite the prosecution of low-level officers for their role in the mistreatment of detainees and protesters, no high-level officials were implicated. Fears of impunity were compounded in July 2013 when a recording was leaked of the Prime Minister visiting a *majlis* (assembly), where he assured loyalists, and an officer recently acquitted of torture, that they were above the law.

Following the killing of protesters by the security forces in February 2011, al-Wefaq withdrew from the Council of Representatives, vacating 18 out of 40 seats. The ensuing by-elections resulted in the election of pro-Government independent loyalists. While the elected chamber provided some semblance of public legitimacy to new anti-terrorism legislation passed from 2013 onwards, opposition activists bore the brunt of their implementation. Protests were almost entirely banned in Manama, and the penalties were made stricter for those who harmed or even insulted the security forces. The parents of those under the age of 16 years were also targeted, facing the possibility of prosecution if their children attended illegal protests. The 2006 anti-terrorism law was also amended to allow detainees to be held for up to 28 days without charge. Since 2014 it has been illegal to insult the Bahraini flag, while those who criticize the King can face up to seven years in prison. In dealing with the protest movement, the Government has taken the opportunity to consolidate its position through both legal and military means. Even though the legal forms of recourse that the regime has at its disposal have been amended to make detention and arrest easier, the authorities still resort to illegal means, when necessary. In June 2016, for example, the President of the BCHR, Nabeel Rajab, was arrested and charged with 'spreading false news and rumours about the internal situation in a bid to discredit Bahrain', in relation to a series of social media posts discussing the conflict in Yemen and the alleged use of torture in Bahraini prisons. At the conclusion of his trial, in February 2018, Rajab was found guilty of the charges and given a five-year prison sentence; however, in early June 2020 his punishment was converted to a non-custodial term.

Achievements earned by workers from the 1960s onwards were undone following the 2011 uprising, when the Government began to dismantle the General Federation of Bahrain Trade Unions (GFBTU), the umbrella trade union organization that had been created following the reforms of 2001. GFBTU leaders were arrested, while those who had agreed to engage in strikes were targeted. Those leaders who were seen to be involved in the strikes of 2011 were also prohibited from running for a similar position for five years. The trade union law was also amended to strengthen government control over union bargaining, so that only unions chosen by the Ministry of Labour could represent Bahraini workers in national and international discussions. The Government also allowed the creation of a rival union in 2012. Originally named the Bahrain Labour Union Free Federation (BLUFF), it was not long before the group changed its name to the Bahrain Free Labour Unions Federation. The move, widely seen as an attempt to split the movement and create unions based on sect, was condemned by activists and opposition members alike. As well as the crackdown on the GFBTU, the Government undid changes to the *kafala* system which had been progressively reformed in 2009. Henceforth, migrant workers had to remain with their employers for one year before changing jobs without consent.

Civil society organizations also faced stricter conditions regarding their operations. Legislation was introduced to ensure that political societies and NGOs were less able to draw international criticism to Bahrain. The Minister of Justice and Islamic Affairs issued an order in 2013 stipulating that political societies wishing to meet any foreign official or representatives must first seek permission from the Ministry of Foreign Affairs, so that the ministry could send a representative to the meeting. The Government dissolved the Islamic Scholars Council in 2014, after it was accused of supporting political activities under the cover of religious sectarianism. The Islamic Action Society (Amal), another political society, was dissolved in 2012 after the Government asserted that it had violated both the Constitution and the society's own standing orders. A total of 23 of the society's high-ranking members were tried on charges ranging from 'inciting hatred against the regime' to 'broadcasting false and tendentious news and rumours'.

While these more stringent measures were implemented, the Government, concerned about its standing in the international community, established multiple government-owned NGOs (GONGOS) to create an impression of civil society in the country and to convince people that issues were being dealt with. Among these GONGOS were the Bahrain Human Rights Watch Society, Bahrain Monitor and the Manama Human Rights Centre. In addition to providing evidence that the Bahraini Government is fulfilling its commitments to human rights, these GONGOS represent Bahrain in international arenas such as the United Nations Universal Periodic Review (UNUPR). Conversely, Bahrainis attempting to raise issues of torture and mistreatment at UNUPR reportedly faced harassment from the Bahraini authorities.

Although street protests in small villages still take place, and male youths engage in violent clashes with the police, the legal opposition has been gradually dismantled. Al-Wefaq, which had generally showed a willingness to engage with the regime, was officially dissolved in June 2016. Its spiritual leader, Sheikh Isa Qassim, also had his Bahraini citizenship removed in that month, after the regime accused him of serving foreign interests and promoting sectarianism. The action against Qassim provoked mass sit-ins around his home in the village of Diraz. In May 2017 Qassim was fined and given a suspended sentence of one year, on charges of money laundering, and Ali Salman, the Deputy Secretary of al-Wefaq, formerly exiled during the 1990s *intifada*, was given a nine-year prison sentence on charges related to the promotion of violence and attempting to change the regime by force. Despite the release of al-Wa'ad's Sharif in July 2016, that year was characterized by the continued harassment of other human rights activists, including Nabeel Rajab (see above).

The first half of 2016 witnessed a renewed hard-line approach to dissent in Bahrain, exacerbated by Saudi Arabia's increasing fears of Iranian-led subversion throughout the Gulf region. The hard-line approach was abetted by developments on the international political scene. The election of Donald Trump as US President in November, and his visit to the Saudi capital, Riyadh, in May 2017 cemented an alliance that his predecessor, Barack Obama, had been accused of damaging. With the apparently unequivocal support for Trump's Administration from the Sunni Gulf monarchies, the Bahraini Government adopted an even more draconian stance towards any domestic opposition in 2017, especially anything that the regime deemed to be supported or fomented by Iran. This tough stance was characterized by the deaths of multiple civilians: in January the Government executed three Shi'a men accused of killing three policemen in an attack in Manama in March 2014. Despite accusations that the trials had been flawed and the convictions unsafe, the executions went ahead—the first such since 2010. The executions prompted demonstrations in Shi'a villages near the capital. Three men were reportedly shot at sea in February 2017 after they escaped from prison in Jau and attempted to flee to Iran; and in May five men were killed when security forces raided houses in Diraz, ending a siege that had been in place since 2016.

The events of 2017 reflected not only a growing authoritarianism in Bahrain, but also a departure from the recommendations laid out in the Bahrain Independent Commission of Inquiry (which had been established in June 2011 to investigate the incidents that led to the unrest earlier that year, and the consequences) and from Bahrain's stated commitments to democratic principles. The closure in June 2017 of *Al-Wasat*, the country's only daily newspaper that was considered to be independent, on charges of 'sowing division', further illustrated the increasing prominence of an authoritarian stance. While the newspaper had been suspended temporarily since 2011, *Al-Wasat* dismissed its entire staff in June 2017. In the same month the Ministry of the Interior announced that anyone expressing criticism of a policy recently introduced by the Government (along with two other GCC member states) of isolating Qatar could face up to five years in prison. Commentators remarked that increasing Saudi political influence on its Gulf neighbours was undoubtedly part of the reason for the growing conservativism in Bahrain, besides the apparent failure of the US Administration to comment on or criticize repressive measures introduced by Gulf leaders.

In April 2018 a base for British naval personnel was opened by the Duke of York and Crown Prince Salman bin Hamad. The Naval Support Facility, which was located at Khalifa bin Salman port, was the UK's first permanent military base in the Middle East since 1971.

King Hamad published a decree in early September 2018, declaring that parliamentary elections would take place on 24 November. Run-off polls were scheduled for 1 December. In October al-Wefaq, which was barred from standing in the elections, called for a boycott of the polls. In the first round of the parliamentary elections, only nine of the 40 seats were won outright. The official turnout was reported to be 67%, although the opposition disputed this figure. The remaining 31 deputies were elected at the run-off vote. Independent candidates won 34 seats in total. Pro-Government Sunni groups took just four seats: Al-Asala Islamic Society won three, while the National Unity Assembly, a movement established following the civil unrest in 2011, won one. A former partner of al-Wefaq, the socialist Progressive Tribune Society, secured two seats. Of the 24 outgoing deputies who stood for re-election, only three retained their seats, in an indication of the electorate's frustration with the ongoing policy of economic austerity. However, the polls took place without any reported violent incidents. The Prime Minister, Sheikh Khalifa, effected a minor cabinet reorganization in December 2018. Notably, Sheikh Salman bin Khalifa Al Khalifa was appointed as Minister of Finance and National Economy, replacing Sheikh Ahmed bin Muhammad Al Khalifa.

Meanwhile, in November 2018 a court sentenced Sheikh Ali Salman to life imprisonment on charges of spying for Qatar in 2011; he continued to serve sentences previously handed down in 2014 and 2017. Salman's appeal against the latest verdict was rejected in January 2019 and he remained in gaol in mid-2021, despite calls by human rights organizations for opposition activists such as Salman to be released owing to the threat posed to prisoners by the coronavirus disease (COVID-19) pandemic. (Near the start of the pandemic, in mid-March 2020, the Bahraini authorities had allowed 1,486 prisoners to be freed: of these, 901 were pardoned for humanitarian reasons, while the remainder were permitted to serve non-custodial terms.) The Ministry of Health had announced Bahrain's first case of COVID-19 in February 2020, and the authorities introduced measures to curb the spread of the virus (see Economy). Restrictions were relaxed from July as the rate of infection fell. Bahrain launched a national vaccination programme in December. By late August 2021 almost two-thirds of Bahrain's population had been fully vaccinated against the virus—one of the highest rates in the world.

In February 2020 Abdullatif bin Rashid al-Zayani, who at that time had served as the Secretary-General of the GCC since 2011, succeeded Sheikh Khalid bin Ahmed al-Khalifa as Bahrain's Minister of Foreign Affairs.

Bahrain was at the heart of a significant regional development in September 2020. At a ceremony presided over by President Trump in Washington, DC, USA, al-Zayani and the UAE's Minister of Foreign Affairs and International Co-operation, Sheikh Abdullah bin Zayed Al Nahyan, signed the so-called Abraham Accords with the Israeli Prime Minister, Binyamin Netanyahu. This US-brokered agreement provided for the establishment of diplomatic relations with Israel by Bahrain and the UAE, which became the third and fourth Arab countries to do so, after Egypt and Jordan. In return, the Israeli Government agreed to suspend plans to annex parts of occupied Palestinian territory in the West Bank. Following the signing of the Abraham Accords, Bahrain's Crown Prince expressed his view that the agreement with Israel would 'strengthen regional security, stability and prosperity', amid the prospect of future bilateral trade and co-operation. However, many Bahraini opposition groups were opposed to the normalization of relations with Israel, and several—including the February 14 Youth Coalition—urged their supporters to participate in a 'Day of Rage' on the day that the Abraham Accords were signed. The Iranian and Palestinian leaderships also denounced the normalization of ties between the two Gulf states and Israel.

An Israeli ministerial delegation visited Manama in October 2020, when full diplomatic relations were formally re-established; seven memoranda of understanding, covering finance and the economy, civil aviation, communications and agriculture, were also signed. During the visit, al-Zayani expressed to Israel the Bahraini Government's support for direct negotiations towards a two-state solution to the Israeli–Palestinian conflict. There was considerable opposition to the normalization of relations among the Bahraini population, and hundreds of protesters gathered in Manama and other cities across Bahrain from September. In November the first official Bahraini government delegation to the Israeli capital, Tel Aviv, led by al-Zayani, coincided with a visit to that city by US Secretary of State Mike Pompeo; the two ministers held joint meetings with senior Israeli officials, including Prime Minister Netanyahu and Minister of Foreign Affairs Gabi Ashkenazi. At the inaugural US-Bahrain Strategic Dialogue, which was conducted remotely in December, discussions focused on defence co-operation, regional security and prosperity, economic development and trade, and human rights. Bahrain welcomed the US Department of State's recognition in December of Saraya al-Mukhtar, a Bahraini-based militant group founded during the unrest of 2011, as a terrorist organization and a proxy of Iran's Islamic Revolutionary Guard Corps. The group, which was reported to have carried out a number of attacks, predominantly against Bahraini security personnel, during 2011–17, was alleged to have been plotting further attacks against Bahraini officials as well as against US personnel in Bahrain.

An event of great domestic significance for Bahrain was the death, in November 2020, of Prince Khalifa, who had served as Prime Minister since independence in 1971. Crown Prince Salman was appointed as premier in his place. It was hoped that the change in leadership might prove beneficial to social cohesion and democratic reform efforts, as Crown Prince Salman had sought in his previous roles to display willingness to introduce democratic initiatives and to seek dialogue with the opposition. Also in November 2020, however, the High Representative of the European Union for Foreign Affairs and Security Policy, Josep Borrell Fontelles, condemned the 'dire condition' of human rights in Bahrain, drawing particular attention to the situation concerning pro-democracy activists Mohamed Ramadan and Hussain Ali Moosa, who had been tortured in detention, and whose death sentences on terrorism charges following a bomb attack in 2014 had been upheld by Bahrain's Court of Cassation in July 2020.

On 4 January 2021 Saudi Arabia reopened its border with Qatar, following discussions on the sidelines of the annual GCC summit meeting, convened in Al-Ula, Saudi Arabia, which brought to an end the three-year dispute with Qatar.

The following day the leaders of Bahrain and the other GCC member states, together with Egypt, signed the Al-Ula Declaration, pledging their commitment to the stability and security of the group. Bahrain reopened its airspace to Qatar on 11 January and invited the Qatari Ministry of Foreign Affairs to send a delegation to Bahrain for bilateral discussions. However, poor pre-existing relations between Qatar and Bahrain meant that bilateral ties post-2021 were the slowest to improve relative to the other 'blockading states', and were only in fact restored in April 2023, more than two years after the Al-Ula Declaration.

By contrast, Bahrain's relations with Israel continued to expand and evolve. The two countries exchanged ambassadors in 2021, conducted joint military exercises in the Red Sea (together with Emirati and US forces), and in February 2022 Naftali Bennett became the first Israeli Prime Minister to carry out an official visit to Bahrain. Also in February, at a public ceremony in Manama, the Israeli Deputy Prime Minister and Minister of Defence, Benjamin (Benny) Gantz, and King Hamad signed a memorandum of understanding regarding security co-operation, the first such agreement between Israel and a Gulf state. The following month saw the foreign affairs ministers of Bahrain, the UAE and Morocco—the three countries which had normalized relations with Israel in 2020—meet their Israeli, Egyptian and US counterparts in Israel. Held amid the economic fallout arising from the Russian–Ukrainian war, the Negev Summit aimed to co-ordinate joint efforts in areas such as food and water security, clean energy, health care and tourism.

The rise in oil prices that began in 2021 as geopolitical tensions heightened in Europe in the run-up to the Russian invasion of Ukraine in February 2022 provided some respite to Bahrain's economy after a decade of ever-widening budget deficits. The lessening of fiscal pressures contributed to a sense of growing confidence among the Bahraini elite that was illustrated by a government reorganization in June 2022 that saw 17 of the 25 cabinet members being replaced—albeit none of the key office holders (Prime Minister, foreign affairs minister, interior minister or defence minister). The reshuffle was noteworthy for two reasons, the first being the replacement of allies of the late Prime Minister, Prince Khalifa, including his son, Prince Ali bin Khalifa (who had been a Deputy Prime Minister), and the second being the allocation of a record nine cabinet positions to Shi'a. Eleven years after the uprising, it appeared that key stakeholders across the communal spectrum were preparing to move beyond the shadow of 2011 and the events that followed. The elections to the Council of Representatives, which took place on 12 and 19 November 2022, reinforced the sense of moving forward, as opposition candidates remained largely banned, candidates who ran on individual slates rather than as part of political societies performed strongly, and turnout was the highest since the events of 2011. A record eight women were elected, up from six in 2018, and the sense that political stability was returning to Bahrain, albeit in a highly authoritarian context, led Standard & Poor's to revise its outlook on Bahrain's B+ credit rating from 'stable' to 'positive' after the budget returned to surplus and economic growth was at its strongest level since 2011.

Economy

MARTIN HVIDT

INTRODUCTION

From an economic perspective, Bahrain exhibits the same characteristics as the surrounding oil-rich Gulf states, namely that plentiful incomes from petroleum and natural gas have created a so-called 'rentier economy', in which the state has no need to tax its citizens or businesses to finance its budgets, and where the personal wealth of citizens is secured by the state through well-paid jobs in the public sector, cheap housing and abundant welfare services. In such economies, there is generally less incentive for citizens to become entrepreneurs, pursue education and work long hours.

Bahrain's modern development started in 1934 when the first shipment of oil left the island heading to Japan. Prior to that, income was generated by trade, fishing, agriculture and, not least, pearl fishing. The modern state of Bahrain was built with oil, meaning that state institutions and procedures were established on the basis of a steady flow of revenue, produced by a relatively small group of Bahrainis and international engineers. The key challenge in the early days of the oil discoveries was for the Government to distribute the oil income, which led to the establishment of a range of benefits for citizens, such as public sector jobs, subsidies on water, electricity and fuel, and welfare, education and health services.

However, the 'oil era' is slowly grinding to a halt. Bahrain has experienced declining oil output, and over the last decade has only produced around 190,000 barrels per day (b/d): 150,000 b/d from the oilfield shared with Saudi Arabia and 40,000 b/d from its onshore fields. Earlier, with high oil prices and a small population the rentier model was successful, but it has become vulnerable. The oil price collapse in 2014, when oil prices fell from above US $100 per barrel to about $40, was a stark reminder of exactly how dependent Bahrain is on income from oil. The combined effects of relatively low hydrocarbon production, the oil price collapse in 2014, the lost income from tourism during the coronavirus disease (COVID-19) pandemic in 2020–21 and the substantial economic support packages extended by the Government to sustain the economy during the pandemic resulted in the accumulation of significant debt.

In its *Regional Economic Outlook* of April 2022, the International Monetary Fund (IMF) noted that Bahrain's public debt had risen to the equivalent of 125% of its gross domestic product (GDP). However, on the positive side, the global surge in demand for oil due to the economic recovery in the wake of the COVID-19 pandemic, and particularly following the Russian invasion of Ukraine in February 2022, has brought oil prices back to their pre-2014 level, securing Bahrain greater economic flexibility. In May 2023 the IMF noted that Bahrain had experienced strong growth in 2022 as a result of the improvement in oil prices, ongoing fiscal reforms and growth in non-oil sectors. Consequently, a large fiscal surplus had been recorded and government debt had been reduced to 117% of GDP by the end of 2022.

Income from hydrocarbons remains of utmost importance for the Bahraini economy. The price of oil largely determines the ability of the state to finance its activities. The World Bank estimated that the so-called 'break-even' oil price for 2023 (the price that Bahrain, with its current level of oil production, needed in order to generate sufficient income to finance its state budget) was US $124 per barrel. Hence, if the price fell below this level, Bahrain would need to reduce its spending or contract additional debt. Bahrain had the highest 'break-even' price of the six Gulf Cooperation Council (GCC) members (Bahrain, Kuwait, Oman, Qatar, Saudi Arabia and the United Arab Emirates—UAE).

From the outset, Bahrain's oil resources were estimated to be quite limited. Accordingly, the Bahraini authorities from an early date were aware that the revenue from oil could not be the sole source of income. As part of a first major drive to diversify its economy away from petroleum and natural gas, Bahrain in 1971 inaugurated the Aluminium Bahrain (ALBA) aluminium smelter, which, following several expansions, is now one of the world largest smelters (see *Industry and Manufacturing*). While most of the produce is exported as raw aluminium, Bahrain has succeeded in establishing both public and private firms that process a substantial part of the aluminium for domestic or regional use, but also into high-value car wheel hubs for European and US vehicle manufacturers and various parts for the aerospace industries.

Another noteworthy element in the diversification policy has been the growth of the banking and financial sector. Due to an open market economy, stability and a credible regulatory framework, Bahrain became the country of choice in the mid-1970s when international banks and financial institutions chose to leave Lebanon due to civil war. There were 370 financial institutions in Bahrain at the end of December 2020, including 91 banking institutions, 34 insurance companies, 53 investment business firms and 86 specialized licensees. The financial sector is the largest single employer in Bahrain, employing nearly 14,000 people and contributing 17.2% of GDP in 2020. In close competition with Dubai and Saudi Arabia, Bahrain aims to become the centre for Islamic finance in the Gulf region.

Due to the initiatives taken over the years, Bahrain has become one of the most mature and diverse economies in the GCC. The World Bank's *Doing Business 2020* index (since discontinued) ranked Bahrain as the 43rd easiest country out of the 190 ranked in which to open, operate and close a business. This ranking compared favourably with the surrounding Gulf states (apart from the UAE, in 16th place): Saudi Arabia was ranked 63rd, Oman 68th, Qatar 77th and Kuwait 83rd. Moreover, Bahrain aims to continue the process of creating a more business friendly environment, according to its New Economic Growth and Fiscal Balance Plan announced in October 2021.

Bahrain has a tiny population, numbering 1,501,635 at the census of 2020, of whom 712,362, or 47%, were Bahraini nationals. Approximately one-half of the total population are below the age of 25 years and thus are not likely to be a part of the labour force, together with the small group of only 3% aged over 65 years of age. In addition, in Bahrain as in the surrounding Arab Gulf countries, a significant proportion of the adult female population choose not to enter the labour market. Overall, the number of Bahrainis available for the labour market is small, likely between 200,000 and 300,000 persons. This fact has necessitated a vast influx of migrant workers who are employed not only in construction and industry, or as domestic helpers and chauffeurs, but also in high-skilled and high-paid jobs, such as doctors, engineers, bankers, IT experts and university professors.

On the Human Development Index (HDI), which evaluates the health status of a population, its educational level and its wealth (gross national income), in 2021 Bahrain ranked 35th out of 191 countries, about the same level as countries such as Greece, Poland and Portugal. Among the Arab Gulf countries, Bahrain ranked the same as Saudi Arabia, seven places higher than Qatar and about 15 places higher than Oman and Kuwait, while the UAE was the highest ranked of the Gulf states (26th). Bahrain scored well on expected years of schooling, but comparatively low on life expectancy at birth (indicating the health standards of the country), and on the present average educational level of the population. These factors, in combination with the relative wealth of the country, resulted in Bahrain's relatively low overall value on the HDI index. It could also be concluded that Bahrain has not yet succeeded in transforming its economic wealth into social benefits for its population such as a long and healthy life and good educational standards.

Bahrain has a significant lack of qualified people among its citizens, among whom there are high rates of unemployment. The Bahrain Economic Vision 2030, launched in 2008, bluntly stated that 'even for those medium- to high-wage jobs created, Bahrainis are not the preferred choice for employers in the private sector, since the education system does not yet provide young people with the skills and knowledge needed to succeed in our labour market'. The Vision 2030 plan aimed to create more high value-added and better paid jobs for Bahraini citizens in private sector businesses. The plan focused on moving the rentier economy established over the past many decades to a modern productive economy where a large percentage of citizens participate in the creation of the wealth of the society. The plan stated 'We aspire to shift from an economy built on oil wealth to a productive, globally competitive economy, shaped by the government and driven by a pioneering private sector—an economy that raises a broad middle class of Bahrainis who enjoy good living standards through increased productivity and high-wage jobs.' Current reform efforts to enhance labour market mobility, contain public sector wages and reduce skill mismatches in the labour market through coordinated training programmes are aimed at enhancing employment opportunities for Bahrainis in the public sector.

The COVID-19 pandemic had significant economic and human implications in most countries worldwide, and Bahrain was no exception. One of the most visible effects of the pandemic was the 14-month closure of the King Fahd Causeway, which in normal years brings around 9m. Saudi visitors into the country. As part of the public health measures taken in response to the pandemic, the Government imposed significant restrictions on economic activity, including partial lockdowns at various points, resulting in GDP contractions of 8.9% and 6.9%, respectively, during the second and third quarters of 2020. The IMF, in an Article IV consultation with Bahrain concluded in June 2022, noted that GDP for 2020 overall had contracted by 5.4%, while the overall fiscal deficit that year increased to 18.2% of GDP and public debt reached 133% of GDP.

However, the IMF noted that a gradual post-pandemic recovery of the economy was under way, supported by high oil prices. Growth of 4.9% was achieved in 2022. In response to a sharp increase in Bahrain's public debt, in October 2021 the Government announced the New Economic Growth and Fiscal Balance Plan, which aimed to support the post-pandemic recovery and postponed a zero-deficit fiscal target from 2022 to 2024. Furthermore, it raised value-added tax (VAT) from 5% to 10%.

The Plan included some significant reforms: a National Labour Market Plan, aiming for the creation of 20,000 jobs; a Regulatory Reform Package designed to ease the inflow of foreign direct investment (FDI); a Strategic Projects Plan, which allocated more than US $30,000m. of investments to various projects; a new Priority Sectors Plan for oil and natural gas, tourism, etc.; and revision of the Fiscal Balance Program, including a target to balance the budget by 2024. In May 2023 the IMF expressed satisfaction with the aims and implementation of the measures in the Plan, and noted that the 'authorities remain strongly committed to their reform agenda' and 'the 2023/24 budget is guided by the Fiscal Balance Program targets, which focus on reducing the fiscal deficit and public debt'.

AGRICULTURE

From its earliest days, the northern part of Bahrain was comparatively well endowed with fresh water from underground aquifers, which made it possible to grow various crops and keep livestock. Date palms dominated Bahrain's agriculture and enough dates were produced for both domestic consumption and export. Between the 1950s and the 1970s date farming was reduced, due to changing food consumption habits and increasing lack of freshwater, after aquifers were overused and became saline. In the 1980s large parts of the palm groves were transformed into vegetable gardens, nurseries for trees and flowers, and poultry and dairy farms.

The cultivated area of land shrunk from approximately 6,000 ha in 1971 to 1,600 ha in 2018, and agricultural farmland is now concentrated in the hands of around 800 owners. Of these, the ruling Al Khalifa family own the greatest number of plots, including the most productive ones. Absentee landlordism is pervasive, resulting in a high percentage of farmers who do not own the land that they work on, and thus tend to under-invest in land and machinery. As such, food items are a permanent part of Bahrain's imports.

According to the World Bank, in 2020 approximately 2.0% of land in Bahrain was arable. The agricultural sector accounted for only 0.3% of GDP in 2022 and employed just 0.4% of the total labour force at mid-2015, according to the United Nations Food and Agriculture Organization.

PETROLEUM AND GAS

The hydrocarbon sector remains central to the Bahraini economy. However, the sector's share of GDP has fallen significantly over time. In 1980 nearly 70% of GDP was generated by oil, but due to declining production and the significant expansion of other sources of income, notably aluminium and financial services, the exploitation of crude petroleum and natural gas accounted for only 18.0% of GDP in 2022—the lowest level in any Arab Gulf country.

Bahrain currently produces oil and natural gas from the onshore Awali field and the offshore Abu Saafa oilfield, which it shares with Saudi Arabia. The Awali field was the site of the first oil discovery on the Arab peninsula in 1932. The field peaked in 1970, with production of 79,000 b/d, but by 2009 this had fallen to 32,000 b/d as reserves became depleted. Tatweer Petroleum (see below) has increased efforts to revitalize this mature field, which produced 43,000 b/d in 2020. The Abu Saafa field produces approximately 300,000 b/d, of which Bahrain's share is one-half. According to the US Census Bureau's World Population Review, domestic consumption accounted for 58,000 b/d in 2020.

Total crude petroleum production in Bahrain, according to official figures, was 69.1m. barrels in 2022, including 54.7m. barrels from the Abu Saafa oilfield. Bahrain's exports of crude petroleum were reported at 151,917 b/d in December 2021. In addition, Bahrain exports around 219,000 b/d of refined petroleum products annually, mostly using crude petroleum imported from Saudi Arabia, but refined in Bahrain.

Bahrain's proven onshore oil reserves are relatively small, estimated at 124.6m. barrels, all located in the Awali field. However, in April 2018 the Bahraini Government announced a major oil discovery in the Khalij al-Bahrain basin off the west coast, believed to total oil reserves of 80,000m. barrels, which would represent the second largest deposit of shale oil in the world. Furthermore, Bahraini shale oil is relatively cheap to extract, at around an estimated US $35 per barrel. Due in part to the COVID-19 situation, the tendering process through which Bahrain aims to attract international oil companies was delayed, and surveys to determine the field's commercial viability were still ongoing in mid-2023.

Gas

Bahrain's proven natural gas reserves were estimated at 228,950m. cu m at the end of 2020, sufficient to maintain production (at 2020 levels) for around only four years. However, at the same time as the huge oil discovery in 2018, it was announced that onshore Pre-Unayzah gas reserves of some 10,000,000m.–20,000,000m. cu ft had been discovered beneath the Awali field. Total gas production in 2022 amounted to 906,700m. cu ft.

Prior to the recent gas discovery, various initiatives were taken in order to secure a plentiful and steady inflow of gas for electricity generation, and not least to support further industrial development. One of these initiatives involved the construction of a floating liquefied natural gas (LNG) import/export facility at the Hidd industrial area, on Muharraq Island, with capacity to handle 800,000 cu ft per day. The LNG terminal began operations in May 2019 and allows Bahrain to import LNG from suppliers worldwide.

Refining

In 1936 Bahrain established its own petroleum refinery, located on the island of Sitra, south of Manama. From an initial capacity of 10,000 b/d, the refinery has been expanded several times. It was expected that the latest expansion would be completed in late 2023 and would raise the capacity of the refinery from 267,000 b/d to 400,000 b/d.

The refinery imports about 85% of the crude petroleum that it processes from Saudi Arabia via a 54-km underwater pipeline. The Bahrain Petroleum Company (BAPCO) sells 8% of output from the refinery to the domestic market in Bahrain in the form of products such as petrol, jet fuel and diesel, and exports the remaining 92%.

Organization

In 2005 Bahrain centralized the regulatory and policymaking capabilities within the hydrocarbon sector in the National Oil and Gas Authority (NOGA), which replaced the Supreme Oil Council. NOGA operated a holding company, the Oil and Gas Holding Company (Nogaholding), which fully owned a number of production companies and administered the Government's share in various international companies. Among those companies were BAPCO, the Bahrain National Gas Company (Banagas), the Gulf Petrochemical Industries Company (GPIC), the Bahrain Aviation Fuelling Company (BAFCO), the Bahrain National Gas Expansion Company (BNGEC), Tatweer Petroleum, the Bahrain Lube Base Oil Company, the Bahrain Liquefied Natural Gas Company (Bahrain LNG) and the Arab Shipbuilding and Repair Yard (ASRY). NOGA was abolished in September 2021, with its regulatory functions and obligations being transferred to the Ministry of Oil and Environment, while Nogaholding continued to operate as a semi-independent agency within the ministry.

INDUSTRY AND MANUFACTURING

In recognizing that Bahrain only possessed relatively meagre oil and gas resources (prior to the vast discoveries in 2018), it has been imperative for the country to establish other sources of income, i.e. to diversify its economy away from the dependence on oil and gas incomes. The process of diversification commenced in the 1970s and has been intensified since the 1990s. The initial emphasis has been to promote export-oriented industries related to aluminium and petrochemical products, but the Economic Development Board (EDB), which sets policies in the economic domain, plans to diversify further into the fields of pharmaceuticals, industrial services, logistics, packaging and fast-moving consumer goods.

ALBA, which started production in 1971, is now the world's largest single-site aluminium smelter outside the People's Republic of China. In 1971 the ALBA smelter had an annual production capacity of 120,000 metric tons, but this has been progressively expanded over the years. A sixth potline was inaugurated in November 2019, bringing annual capacity to more than 1.6m. tons in 2022. The Bahraini state, represented by the Bahrain Mumtalakat holding company, owns a 69.4% stake in ALBA, with the Saudi Basic Industries Corporation (SABIC) owning 20.6% and the general public 10.0%. ALBA has a workforce of around 3,100 employees, of whom 84% are Bahrainis, and sells around 35%–40% of its products within Bahrain.

The Bahraini authorities have made efforts to create an enabling environment for both public and private businesses manufacturing raw aluminium into articles such as. building materials, doors, window frames and cladding, but also into high-value products such as car wheel hubs for European and US vehicle manufacturers, and various parts for the aerospace industries. As part of continued efforts to expand capacity, the possibility of adding a seventh potline to the ALBA smelter is currently under discussion. Aluminium exports comprised 23.2% of Bahrain's total export revenue in 2021; the sector contributed 11.1% of GDP in 2020.

In 1980 the Bahraini Government established GPIC to produce ammonia and methanol from supplies of natural gas. By 1988 GPIC produced 1,700 metric tons of petrochemicals daily, leading to the creation of new downstream industries in Bahrain. Within the petrochemical sector, five sub-sectors have grown rapidly in recent years: construction chemicals, water treatment chemicals, polymer and plastic additives, paints and coating additives, and oilfield chemicals.

In a further effort to diversify the economy, ASRY was established in 1977 as a multi-service yard. Its activities are focused in four main areas: ship repair and conversion, rig repairs and conversions, naval repair and conversions, and fabrication and engineering. The shipyard is located at the Hidd industrial area and has a workforce of more than 3,000 employees. In April 2022 ASRY signed a memorandum of understanding with the ONEX business group of Greecein order to place itself in a better position in the highly competitive ship repair industry in the Gulf, where Saudi Arabia, Dubai (UAE) and Oman aim to become the region's largest shipbuilding and repair sites.

The construction sector is highly dependent on the income from oil. Consequently, activities in this sector were modest following the sharp fall in oil prices in 2014. In 2020 activities were further reduced due to the COVID-19 pandemic. However, the government budget for 2021–22 increased the allocation for construction spending. Expenditure over the two years included US $1,600m. for a variety of construction projects related to sectors including infrastructure, housing, health, education, sports, culture, electricity and water.

To overcome a significant shortage of affordable housing units, the Bahraini Ministry of Housing and Urban Planning has launched several large housing development projects, including Salman Town (to comprise more than 15,000 housing units and 10 reclaimed islands), Khalifa Town (around 6,000 housing units) and other smaller housing programmes. More than 3,000 housing units had been completed in Salman Town by early 2022. The residential development at Khalifa Town was expected to be completed in 2026.

POWER AND WATER

In 2020 around 99.9% of electricity production in Bahrain was generated from natural gas and 0.1% from oil. Per capita annual electricity generation was 18,477 kWh in 2020. In line with rising demand, electricity consumption increased by 326% between 1990 and 2019. The main factors behind this development were rapid population growth, national housing programmes and growing demand from the industrial sector, especially desalination plants and aluminium smelters. An additional factor was the fact that electricity in Bahrain has been heavily subsidized. By 2013 the cost of these subsidies amounted to about US $935m. annually.

In 2009 53% of electricity in Bahrain was consumed by the residential sector, 34% by the commercial and public services sector and 12% by industry. This has made it politically challenging to reform prices. Consequently, Bahraini nationals continue to pay only a minimal fee for water and electricity, while the expatriate community now pay considerably more. Following the 2014 oil price collapse, austerity measures were adopted throughout the economy. As a part of these measures, fees for water and electricity were raised for the expatriate community through a four-year phased plan. In 2021 expatriates paid BD 0.029 per unit of electricity while Bahrainis paid BD 0.003 for the same amount.

Under the GCC's grid interconnection programme, Bahrain is connected to Saudi Arabia, Qatar and Kuwait, and is able to receive as much as 600 MW of additional power capacity.

Renewable Energy

The Sustainable Energy Unit was established in 2014 as a joint initiative between the Ministry of Electricity and Water Affairs and the United Nations Development Programme (UNDP). The key objectives of the Unit are to develop a cohesive and sustainable energy policy and to promote renewable energy and energy efficiency in Bahrain. The Unit also works towards bridging the legal, institutional and capacity gaps to ensure that the Bahrain energy sector is capable of meeting future challenges.

In 2017 the Sustainable Energy Authority published the National Energy Efficiency Action Plan (NEEAP), which set a national renewable energy target of 5% by 2025, rising to 10% by 2035. The plan also contained 22 specific initiatives to improve efficiency in both energy supply and demand in all sectors of the economy.

So far only modest initiatives have been taken to meet the goals related to implementation of renewable energy. Two small solar parks have been established. A 5-MW solar park owned by BAPCO was commissioned in 2014, and a 3-MW solar plant established by Tatweer Petroleum at the Awali site was commissioned in 2019. A 100-MW solar park is, however, under construction at the Askar landfill site, in the Southern Governorate, by a consortium comprising Saudi-based ACWA Power, Mitsui & Co of Japan and Bahrain's Almoayyed Contracting Group. ACWA Power has the majority stake in the consortium (60%), followed by Mitsui (30%) and the Almoayyed Contracting Group (10%).

Bahrain obtains its water supplies through the desalination of sea water. The current annual capacity is approximately 277.9m. cu m, which is expected to rise to 515m. by 2030. In order to meet the increase in demand four main initiatives are planned. The construction of a new private sector power and water production plant with a capacity of 80m. cu m per year is planned in the al-Dur water and electricity complex. A new desalination plant with a capacity of 84m. cu m per year is to be built south of the existing Ras Abu Jarjur reverse osmosis plant by 2023–24. A new desalination plant with a capacity of 50m. cu m per year is to be built to supply the new Northern City housing project by 2028. Finally, a new desalination plant with a capacity of 40m. cu m per year is to be constructed by 2029 to replace the Sitra multistage flash desalination plant. In addition to these proposed projects, the Bahraini authorities plan to increase wastewater reuse.

TRANSPORT AND COMMUNICATIONS

Bahrain's transport sector is seen as an important and enabling factor of the country's drive toward further economic diversification. This is first because good connectivity is essential for an efficient and diversified economy, second because a well-developed infrastructure is essential to attract FDI by international firms, and lastly because Bahrain is located in a region where several states (not least the UAE and Qatar) have established superior infrastructure.

In addition to an extensive road system, Bahrain possesses Bahrain International Airport (BIA), its own air carrier (Gulf Air), a major seaport, Khalifa bin Salman Port (KBSP), and operates the 25-km low-bridge King Fahd Causeway, connecting Bahrain to Saudi Arabia. However, much of this infrastructure is outdated and congestion occurs on a daily basis. Therefore, Bahrain, supported by a recent US $10,000m. financing agreement with its GCC neighbours, plans significantly to upgrade its transport infrastructure in the coming years. Bahrain's Ministry of Transportation and Telecommunications is the primary government entity responsible for the development of the sector in the kingdom.

The King Fahd Causeway was inaugurated in 1986 and the higher traffic load on the roads that ensued led to a subsequent upgrade of the road network within Bahrain, including the construction of a 2.5-km causeway connecting Manama to Muharraq in 1997 and a causeway linking Hidd with Manama in 2003. The daily average number of travellers crossing the King Fahd Causeway is 75,000, and it brings more than 9m. Saudi tourists to Bahrain each year. In other words, the Causeway is a huge asset to Bahrain. Saudis from the east of the country use Bahrain as a weekend destination, due to its less stringent enforcement of Islamic law and entertainment facilities. The Causeway was closed for some 14 months during the COVID-19 pandemic, but was reopened in May 2021.

Due to increased traffic volume, the King Fahd Causeway is subject to significant congestion during weekends and the traffic is expected to double by 2030. In response, there are plans to construct a new causeway. The King Hamad Causeway is to run parallel to the existing causeway and will consist of a four-lane road and two-line railway, with a 70-km rail link connecting the rail terminal in Saudi Arabia's eastern city of Dammam with KBSP in Bahrain. It is forecast that by 2050 the rail link will be used annually by not only 8m. passengers but also 600,000 container vehicles carrying 13m. tons of bulk freight, and it is envisaged that KBSP will act as a logistic hub for most of eastern Saudi Arabia. It is planned that the new King Hamad Causeway will connect Bahrain to the proposed 2,177-km GCC railway network, which, it is envisaged, will eventually span the region from north to south and east to west. The causeway and the rail link are to connect with the kingdom's planned metro system, which is scheduled to become operational by 2030.

Another planned project is the construction of a 40-km causeway, the Qatar Bahrain Causeway, linking northern Qatar with the east coast of Bahrain. This project has been under consideration since 2001, when a preliminary engineering and environmental investigation was conducted. In May 2008 the formal contract to start construction work was signed with an international consortium. However, the process was subsequently delayed, due to a decision by the two Governments to add a railway line to the design.

BIA was inaugurated on Muharraq Island in 1971 and had a maximum annual capacity of 4m. passengers by the 1980s. An upgrade to the airport was completed in 1994. Passenger numbers increased steadily thereafter, reaching a record high of 9.1m. in 2018. The airport has recently undergone a significant expansion, which was completed in January 2021, bringing the airport's capacity to 14m. passengers and 130,000 aircraft movements annually. An upgrade of the airport's existing terminal is also planned, with an emphasis on increasing cargo handling capacity. The expansion is part of Bahrain's strategy to develop BIA as a stopover destination for long-haul flights between Asia and Europe.

The airport is the headquarters of Gulf Air, the national carrier of Bahrain. Gulf Air commenced operations in 1950, and was at that time jointly owned by the Governments of Abu Dhabi (UAE), Oman and Qatar until they withdrew their stakes in 2005, 2007 and 2002, respectively. Due to its strategic importance to Bahrain, the Government has on several occasions provided the airline with substantial financial support, notably in 2014 when Gulf Air introduced a new strategic plan.

KBSP was established on 110 ha of reclaimed land in Hidd's industrial zone next to ASRY. The port was inaugurated in 2009 and has facilities to handle containers, general cargo, roll-on/roll-off ships and cruise ships. Its container section has an annual handling capacity of 1m. 20-ft equivalent units. The port is managed and operated by APM Terminals Bahrain, a subsidiary of A. P. Møller—Mærsk of Denmark, under a 25-year concession agreement, which was signed in 2006 and entered into effect in April 2009. KBSP has four times the capacity of Mina Salman port, in Manama, and the two ports are connected by a 5-km causeway. The Government of Bahrain aims to make the port the key transshipment centre in the northern part of the Gulf region, in competition with both Saudi Arabia and Kuwait. The planned rail link in conjunction with the King Hamad Causeway, however, creates the possibility that containers from a large part of Saudi Arabia could be shipped through KBSP.

Bahrain has a well-developed telecommunications sector, overseen by the Telecommunications Regulatory Authority (TRA). The number of mobile telephone subscribers totalled 2.1m. in the first quarter of 2023, which represented a market penetration of 137%. Similarly, the number of broadband subscriptions totalled 2.48m., representing a penetration rate of 158%. Three companies hold licences to provide mobile and other telecommunications services (including 5G technology). These are the Bahrain Telecommunications Co BSC (BATELCO), Zain Bahrain and the Saudi Telecom Company (STC—through its subsidiary, stc Bahrain), which currently share the Bahraini market equally among them.

FINANCE AND THE BUDGET

Since a large proportion of Bahrain's state budget is derived directly from oil and natural gas revenue (which accounted for 62.3% of total government revenue in 2022), the economy reflects the overall international trends in the oil market. In recent years there have been four distinct periods reflecting fluctuations in oil prices. The period between 2000 and 2014 was marked by rising oil prices, apart from a setback associated with the financial crisis in 2008–09. Prices rose from about US $30 to $115 per barrel, leading to positive fiscal balances. This was followed by a second period starting with the oil price collapse of 2014, after which prices dropped from $115 per barrel to around $40–$60 during the second half of the 2010s. The Bahraini Government responded to this crisis with various initiatives, such as suspending development projects, introducing austerity measures, cutting subsidies on meat and fuel, doubling excise duties on alcohol and cigarettes, and raising electricity and water tariffs for industrial and commercial users and expatriates. Furthermore, in an attempt to stabilize state revenues, the Government introduced VAT of 5% on goods and services from 1 January 2019, which was later raised to 10%. However, despite all these measures, Bahrain accumulated significant amounts of debt.

The COVID-19 crisis from March 2020 until early 2022 marked a third period. As in other countries worldwide, the Bahraini Government closed down significant parts of the country's business life, together with leisure facilities, and paid out large amounts of compensation in support of the sectors that had been affected. The King Fahd Causeway (see *Transport and Communications*) was closed for 14 months (between 8 March 2020 and 17 May 2021), resulting in significant losses of income from Saudi tourists.

A fourth period began with the end of the COVID-19 pandemic in early 2022 and the Russian invasion of Ukraine in February of that year, which caused a sharp increase in oil and prices, surpassing US $110 per barrel. This resulted in a significant windfall gain for Bahrain, leaving the country in a favourable position to carry out fiscal and other reforms, and to reduce public debt and restore macroeconomic sustainability. However, the Bahraini population has, like populations around the world, been negatively affected by the rising costs of food and other staple items throughout this period.

FOREIGN TRADE AND TOURISM

In the five-year period from 2014 to 2019 10m.–12m. tourists visited Bahrain annually. Around 90% of them were weekend tourists from Saudi Arabia, attracted by Bahrain's relaxed interpretation of Islamic law allowing for cinemas, non-gender separated shopping malls, sports events, restaurants and a liberal alcohol policy. As a result of the pandemic and the widespread travel restrictions, tourist numbers fell from 11.1m. in 2019 to 1.9m. in 2020, before rebounding to 3.6m., in 2021 and 9.9m. in 2022. The tourism sector contributed an estimated US $1,813m. of revenue in 2021, compared with $3,681m. in 2019.

The Bahrain Tourism and Exhibitions Authority (BTEA) organizes and oversees festivals, conferences and exhibitions in the fields of art, music, entertainment and sports to attract tourists. Bahrain hosts a number of major tourism and entertainment events, including the Bahrain Formula One Grand Prix motor race, the Bahrain Food Festival and the Manama Gold Festival.

Under the Bahrain Tourism Strategy 2022–26, the aim is to position Bahrain as an international tourism hub and increase the sector's share of GDP. The plan is to be achieve this by increasing the number of annual tourist arrivals, making tourist visits longer and encouraging visitors to spend more money while they are in Bahrain. More tourist attractions are to be established and more exhibitions held, in addition to the development of beaches, waterfronts and resorts.

Bahrain's economy is closely linked to the price of oil (see *Finance and the Budget*). In 2020, at the height of the COVID-19 pandemic, Bahrain recorded a visible merchandise trade deficit of BD 47.8m. and there was a deficit of BD 1,220.0m. on the current account of the balance of payments. However, a current account surplus of BD 978.5m. was achieved in 2021, which increased to BD 2,571m. in 2022, the highest level for 25 years.

Exports of mineral fuels and oils accounted for 32% of total exports in 2022, while exports of aluminium accounted for 31%. Other exports included chemical products, transport equipment, electrical equipment and textiles. In 2022 the principal source of imports was Saudi Arabia (accounting for 15.0% of the total). Other major suppliers were Brazil, Australia, the UAE and the USA. Saudi Arabia was the principal customer for Bahrain's exports in that year (taking 21% of the total), followed by the USA and the UAE.

Bahrain was a signatory of a GCC agreement in 1999 that provided for the creation of a full customs union by 2005. From January 2003 restrictions were removed on all goods and services traded within the GCC. The six GCC member states later announced plans for the creation of a single market and currency by January 2010. The UAE withdrew from the initiative in May 2009 (as Oman had done in 2006). None the less, an accord on Gulf Monetary Union was signed in 2009 by Bahrain, Kuwait, Qatar and Saudi Arabia.

In 2004 Bahrain signed a Free Trade Agreement (FTA) with the USA that abolished customs duties (with a few exceptions) on consumer and industrial products. Most agricultural products were to be duty free, and the remainder of Bahraini tariffs were to be phased out over 10 years. Market access was also to be liberalized in the service sectors, particularly in financial services, telecommunications, health care and construction. In September 2016 Bahrain opened Investment Gateway Bahrain, its first freehold trade zone. The zone permits the freehold purchase of land on Muharraq Island for commercial and light industrial use, and 100% foreign ownership.

Statistical Survey

Sources (unless otherwise stated): Information and eGovernment Authority, POB 33305, Manama; tel. 17878130; e-mail Statistics@iga.gov.bh; internet www.data.gov.bh/en/ResourceCenter; Central Bank of Bahrain, POB 27, Bldg 96, Block 317, Rd 1702, Manama; tel. 17547777; fax 17530399; e-mail info@cbb.gov.bh; internet www.cbb.gov.bh.

Area and Population

AREA, POPULATION AND DENSITY

Area (sq km)	770.9*
Population (census results)	
27 April 2010	1,234,571
17 March 2020	
Males	942,895
Females	558,740
Total	1,501,635
Bahrainis	712,362
Non-Bahrainis	789,273
Population (official estimates at mid-year)	
2021	1,504,365
2022†	1,565,000
2023†	1,609,000
Density (per sq km) at mid 2023†	2,087.2

* 297.7 sq miles.
† Projection; rounded figure.

POPULATION BY AGE AND SEX
(official estimates at mid-2021)

	Males	Females	Total
0–14 years	148,782	143,045	291,827
15–64 years	747,928	410,774	1,158,702
65 years and over	29,037	24,799	53,836
Total	925,747	578,618	1,504,365

GOVERNORATES
(population estimates at mid-2021)

	Area (sq km)	Population	Density (per sq km)
Capital	75.4	538,965	7,148.1
Muharraq	64.8	263,430	4,065.3
Northern	145.5	396,779	2,727.0
Southern	485.0	305,191	629.3
Total	770.9	1,504,365	1,951.4

Note: Area total may not be equal the sum of components, owing to rounding.

PRINCIPAL TOWNS
(at 2001 census)

Manama (capital)	153,395	Hamad Town	52,718
Muharraq	91,939	Jidd Hafs	52,450
Rifa'a	79,985		

Mid-2022 (incl. suburbs, UN projection): Manama 688,558 (Source: UN, *World Urbanization Prospects: The 2018 Revision*).

BIRTHS, MARRIAGES AND DEATHS

	Registered live births		Registered marriages		Registered deaths	
	Number	Rate (per 1,000)	Number	Rate (per 1,000)	Number	Rate (per 1,000)
2016	20,714	14.6	7,019	4.9	2,858	2.0
2017	20,581	13.7	6,691	4.5	2,902	1.9
2018	19,740	13.1	6,039	4.0	3,052	2.0
2019	18,611	12.5	5,524	3.7	3,010	2.0
2020	18,042	12.3	6,026	4.1	3,488	2.4

2021: Registered marriages 6,369 (per 1,000 persons 4.2).

Life expectancy (years at birth, estimates): 78.8 (males 77.8; females 80.0) in 2021 (Source: World Bank, World Development Indicators database).

ECONOMICALLY ACTIVE POPULATION
(persons aged 15 years and over, at 2010 census)

	Males	Females	Total
Agriculture, fishing and animal husbandry	7,479	72	7,551
Mining and quarrying	1,678	58	1,736
Manufacturing	77,137	7,237	84,374
Electricity, gas and water	1,109	60	1,169
Construction	155,042	5,666	160,708
Trade and repairs	95,771	13,723	109,494
Restaurants and hotels	29,318	6,194	35,512
Transport, storage and communications	19,961	4,080	24,041
Banks, insurance and finance	12,330	5,023	17,353
Real estate and business	34,624	6,733	41,357
Government, defence, social affairs and security	67,824	15,233	83,057
Education	10,710	13,563	24,273
Health	1,427	1,989	3,416
Community, social and personal services	11,723	4,098	15,821
Households with employed persons	24,666	59,737	84,403
Sub-total	550,799	143,466	694,265
Activities not adequately defined	7,145	1,797	8,942
Total employed	557,944	145,263	703,207
Unemployed	2,466	5,557	8,023
Total labour force	560,410	150,820	711,230

2013: Total employed 716,473 (males 566,350, females 150,123).

2020 census (persons aged 15 years and over): Total employed 863,088; Total employed 12,470; Total labour force 875,558.

Health and Welfare

KEY INDICATORS

Total fertility rate (children per woman, 2021)	1.8
Under-5 mortality rate (per 1,000 live births, 2021)	6.9
HIV/AIDS (% of persons aged 15–49, 2021)	0.1
COVID-19: Cumulative confirmed deaths (per 100,000 persons at 30 June 2023)	104.3
COVID-19: Fully vaccinated population (% of total population at 21 December 2022)	83.3
Physicians (per 1,000 head, 2016)	0.8
Hospital beds (per 1,000 head, 2017)	1.7
Domestic health expenditure (2020): US $ per head (PPP)	1,492.0
Domestic health expenditure (2020): % of GDP	3.0
Domestic health expenditure (2020): public (% of total current health expenditure)	62.7
Total carbon dioxide emissions ('000 metric tons, 2019)	33,257
Carbon dioxide emissions per head (metric tons, 2019)	22.3
Human Development Index (2021): ranking	35
Human Development Index (2021): value	0.875

Note: For data on COVID-19 vaccinations, 'fully vaccinated' denotes receipt of all doses specified by approved vaccination regime (Sources: Johns Hopkins University and Our World in Data). Data on health expenditure refer to current general government expenditure in each case. For more information on sources and further definitions for all indicators, see Health and Welfare Statistics: Sources and Definitions section (europaworld.com/credits).

Agriculture

PRINCIPAL CROPS
('000 metric tons)

	2019	2020	2021
Aubergines (Eggplants)	1.4	1.5	1.6
Bananas*	1.0	1.0	n.a.
Cauliflowers and broccoli	1.2	1.2	1.2
Chillies and peppers, green	1.0	1.0	1.0
Cucumbers and gherkins	2.8	2.9	3.3
Dates	13.5	13.8	14.1
Lemons and limes*	1.1	1.1	1.1
Lettuce and chicory	0.9	1.0	1.1
Onions, dry	0.2	0.2	0.2
Pumpkins, squash and gourds	3.0	3.3	3.4
Tomatoes	6.8	7.0	7.8

* FAO estimates.

Aggregate production ('000 metric tons, may include official, semi-official or estimated data): Total fruit (primary) 21.4 in 2019, 21.7 in 2020; 22.3 in 2021; Total vegetables (primary) 18.3 in 2019, 19.3 in 2020; 20.9 in 2021.

Source: FAO.

LIVESTOCK
('000 head, year ending September)

	2019	2020	2021
Cattle	8	7	8
Chickens*	1,600	1,500	1,534
Goats	26	21	25
Sheep	63	60	60

* FAO estimates.

Source: FAO.

LIVESTOCK PRODUCTS
('000 metric tons)

	2019	2020	2021
Cattle meat*	0.8	0.8	0.8
Cows' milk	11.6	10.0	10.0
Chicken meat	8.9	7.3	8.3
Goat meat*	0.3	0.2	0.2
Sheep fat*	1.5	1.4	1.4
Sheep meat*	26.1	25.0	25.0
Sheep offals, edible*	4.3	4.2	4.2
Sheepskins, fresh*	4.1	3.9	3.9
Hen eggs	4.4†	3.9	n.a.

* FAO estimates.
† Unofficial figure.
Source: FAO.

Fishing

('000 metric tons, live weight, FAO estimates)

	2019	2020	2021
Capture	14.9	14.4	15.7
Spangled emperor	1.0	1.0	1.1
Spinefeet (Rabbitfishes)	2.3	2.2	2.4
Blue swimming crab	4.5	4.4	4.8
Green tiger prawn	2.8	2.6	2.8
Aquaculture	0.0	0.0	0.0
Total catch	14.9	14.4	15.7

Source: FAO.

Mining

	2020	2021	2022
Crude petroleum ('000 barrels)*	71,073	70,442	69,100
Natural gas ('000 million cu ft)	886.9	921.3	906.7

* Including a share of production from the Abu Saafa offshore oilfield, shared with Saudi Arabia: 55,220,000 barrels in 2020; 54,897,140 barrels in 2021; 54,700,000 in 2022.

Industry

SELECTED PRODUCTS
('000 barrels unless otherwise indicated)

	2019	2020	2021
Liquefied petroleum gas	1,584	1,442	n.a.
Butane	432	376	297
Propane	299	251	176
Naphtha	14,909	13,649	14,294
Motor spirit (petrol)	6,416	4,561	4,012
Kerosene and jet fuel	24,065	18,073	15,010
Distillate fuel oil	30,438	28,534	32,099
Residual fuel oil	17,620	12,893	14,892
Electrical energy (million kWh)	17,854	17,934	n.a.

Aluminium (unwrought, metric tons): 981,016 in 2017; 1,011,101 in 2018; 1,365,005 in 2019 (Source: US Geological Survey).

Finance

CURRENCY AND EXCHANGE RATES

Monetary Units
1,000 fils = 1 Bahraini dinar (BD).

Sterling, Dollar and Euro Equivalents (31 May 2023)
£1 sterling = 465 fils;
US $1 = 376 fils;
€1 = 402 fils;
10 Bahraini dinars = £21.51 = $26.60 = €24.90.

Average Exchange Rate
Note: This has been fixed at US $1 = 376 fils (BD 1 = $2.6596) since November 1980.

BUDGET
(BD million, budget figures)

Revenue	2020	2021	2022
Net petroleum and gas	2,096.3	1,517.5	1,531.3
Non-petroleum	850.2	548.3	565.8
National bureau for revenue	—	340.0	360.0
Total	2,946.5	2,405.8	2,457.1

Expenditure	2020	2021	2022
Recurrent expenditure	1,966.4	1,959.8	1,965.2
Government subsidies	586.4	497.0	451.3
Reserve budget	97.5	96.5	95.2
Government debt interest	697.0	708.0	757.0
Other expenditures	200.0	52.5	—
Total	3,547.2	3,313.8	3,268.7

Source: partly Ministry of Finance and National Economy, Manama.

BAHRAIN

INTERNATIONAL RESERVES
(US $ million at 31 December)

	2020	2021	2022
Gold (national valuation)	0.2	0.2	0.2
IMF special drawing rights	96.4	623.7	593.8
Reserve position in IMF	196.2	190.6	181.3
Foreign exchange (central bank)*	1,946.8	3,905.9	3,728.0
Total*	2,239.6	4,720.4	4,503.3

* Excluding foreign exchange reserves held by government.

Source: IMF, *International Financial Statistics*.

MONEY SUPPLY
(BD million at 31 December)

	2020	2021	2022
Currency outside banks	593.0	558.0	506.5
Demand deposits at commercial banks	3,288.0	3,952.1	3,398.6
Foreign currency	959.9	1,285.3	841.8
Time and savings	8,959.0	8,955.4	10,079.7
Broad money	12,840.0	13,465.5	13,984.8

Source: Central Bank of Bahrain, Manama.

COST OF LIVING
(Consumer Price Index; base: April 2019 = 100)

	2020	2021	2022
Food and non-alcoholic beverages	105.4	105.4	116.3
Clothing and footwear	91.7	89.5	85.1
House-related expenses, water, electricity, gas and other fuels	95.8	94.6	93.7
All items (incl. others)	97.6	97.0	100.5

NATIONAL ACCOUNTS
(BD million at current prices)

Expenditure on the Gross Domestic Product

	2019	2020	2021
Government final consumption expenditure	2,280.3	2,230.9	2,335.4
Private final consumption expenditure	5,871.9	5,484.4	5,784.0
Gross fixed capital formation	4,039.3	3,761.5	3,635.9
Change in stocks	703.9	807.0	143.7
Total domestic expenditure	12,895.4	12,283.8	11,899.0
Exports of goods and services	11,116.2	9,493.7	13,248.2
Less Imports of goods and services	9,478.1	8,759.6	10,369.1
GDP in purchasers' values	14,533.8	13,017.8	14,778.1
GDP at constant 2010 prices	12,991.3	12,387.9	12,718.6

GDP at constant 2010 prices (provisional): 13,336.8 in 2022.

Gross Domestic Product by Economic Activity

	2020	2021	2022
Agriculture and fishing	40.8	41.2	43.0
Mining	1,520.9	2,316.7	3,051.0
Petroleum and gas	1,367.9	2,154.4	2,880.0
Manufacturing	2,381.5	3,035.0	3,578.2
Electricity and water	205.4	209.0	229.2
Construction	1,082.6	1,082.3	1,134.4
Transport and communications	894.9	946.1	958.8
Trade	589.1	587.9	600.7
Hotels and restaurants	195.7	211.7	252.0
Real estate and business activities	704.5	715.2	746.5

—continued	2020	2021	2022
Finance and insurance	2,340.9	2,496.8	2,616.8
Government services	1,785.6	1,817.2	1,913.6
Education	295.9	301.7	322.0
Health	281.8	298.0	285.2
Other social and personal services	791.3	805.4	794.6
Private non-profit institutions serving households	4.6	4.4	4.6
Households with employed persons	106.1	103.7	113.2
Sub-total	12,644.0	14,372.6	16,036.6
Import duties	373.8	405.5	654.3
GDP in purchasers' values	13,017.8	14,778.1	16,690.9

* Provisional.

BALANCE OF PAYMENTS
(BD million)

	2020	2021	2022*
Exports of goods	5,288.7	8,410.9	11,352.9
Imports of goods	−5,336.5	−6,566.6	−8,252.9
Balance on goods	−47.8	1,844.3	3,100.0
Exports of services	4,205.0	4,837.3	5,409.9
Imports of services	−3,423.1	−3,802.5	−4,181.0
Balance on goods and services	734.1	2,879.1	4,328.9
Primary income received	946.4	970.0	1,558.4
Primary income paid	−1,871.0	−1,920.5	−2,296.4
Balance on goods, services and primary income	−190.5	1,928.60	3,590.9
Secondary income (net)	−1,029.5	−950.1	−1,019.6
Current balance	−1,220.0	978.5	2,571.3
Capital account (net)	293.1	212.1	177.8
Direct investment (net)	461.1	644.8	1.3
Portfolio investment assets	−472.2	−1,316.4	−341.9
Portfolio investment liabilities	1,289.5	891.4	530.3
Other investment assets	−420.9	−397.3	−1,912.3
Other investment liabilities	42.9	494.5	−139.9
Net errors and omissions	−521.3	−561.3	−973.2
Overall balance	−547.8	946.3	−86.6

* Provisional.

External Trade

PRINCIPAL COMMODITIES
(distribution by HS, US $ million)

Imports f.o.b	2019	2020	2021
Live animals and animal products	595.1	602.2	574.6
Vegetables and vegetable products	469.2	505.6	469.7
Prepared foodstuffs; beverages, spirits, vinegar; tobacco and articles thereof	713.3	651.4	642.1
Mineral products	6,804.5	3,969.3	7,286.5
Ores, slag and ash	1,016.7	788.9	2,272.9
Iron ores and concentrates	1,010.1	783.8	2,267.5
Mineral fuels, oils and products of their distillation	5,632.5	3,031.1	4,866.9
Crude petroleum	5,333.7	2,776.5	4,482.8
Chemicals and related products	1,897.2	1,826.0	2,059.1
Inorganic chemicals	999.9	972.3	1,139.0

BAHRAIN

Statistical Survey

Imports f.o.b—*continued*	2019	2020	2021
Plastics, rubber, and articles thereof	430.8	466.3	545.1
Iron and steel, other base metals and articles of base metal	1,124.7	1,022.2	1,044.0
Articles of iron or steel	395.9	552.3	439.5
Machinery and mechanical appliances; electrical equipment; parts thereof	2,961.3	3,476.6	2,800.1
Machinery, boilers, etc.	1,680.8	2,170.2	1,732.2
Electrical and electronic equipment	1,280.5	1,306.4	1,067.8
Vehicles, aircraft, vessels and associated transport equipment	1,544.8	1,073.8	1,021.2
Vehicles other than railway and tramway	1,199.5	1,017.5	994.0
Cars and station wagons	895.1	750.0	715.6
Total (incl. others)	18,589.1	15,459.4	18,675.9

Exports (incl. re-exports) f.o.b.	2019	2020	2021
Mineral products	7,328.9	4,257.8	9,277.2
Ores, slag and ash	1,355.6	807.9	2,361.0
Iron ores and concentrates	1,354.0	806.3	2,358.7
Mineral fuels, mineral oils	5,971.8	3,446.9	6,915.2
Petroleum oils and oils obtained from bituminous minerals, crude	5,962.5	3,442.8	6,915.0
Chemicals and related products	699.5	608.3	827.6
Pearls, precious or semi-precious stones, precious metals, and articles thereof	532.9	264.0	355.4
Iron and steel, other base metals and articles of base metal	2,971.3	3,798.1	5,927.0
Iron and steel	468.7	615.8	975.1
Aluminium and articles thereof	2,048.5	2,792.7	4,488.7
Unwrought aluminium	918.5	1,979.0	3,225.8
Aluminium wire	628.7	467.3	580.0
Plates, sheets and strip, of aluminium	318.0	170.1	425.8
Machinery and mechanical appliances; electrical equipment; parts thereof	540.1	674.2	717.9
Machinery, appliances, boilers	395.8	507.1	520.5
Vehicles, aircraft, vessels and associated transport equipment	560.3	601.5	602.2
Vehicles other than railway and tramway	497.3	447.4	418.2
Total (incl. others)	14,167.3	11,559.7	19,331.7

Source: Trade Map-Trade Competitiveness Map, International Trade Centre, marketanalysis.intracen.org.

PRINCIPAL TRADING PARTNERS
(US $ million)

Imports	2019	2020	2021
Australia	936.9	878.1	1,026.8
Brazil	854.1	788.0	2,006.8
China, People's Republic	2,065.5	1,751.0	1,847.5
France	305.1	202.1	233.0
Germany	576.1	528.0	478.5
India	685.4	565.7	736.6
Italy	362.4	525.3	507.8
Japan	705.6	700.6	550.1
Korea, Republic	256.4	472.5	231.0
Saudi Arabia	6,260.2	3,712.3	5,452.8
Spain	149.1	181.7	194.8
Switzerland	315.3	529.7	259.4
Thailand	169.4	178.9	155.9
Türkiye	281.7	218.8	201.5
United Arab Emirates	927.7	827.2	1,050.8
United Kingdom	491.2	353.8	463.5
USA	843.3	812.2	741.5
Total (incl. others)	18,589.1	15,459.4	18,675.9

Exports	2019	2020	2021
China, People's Republic	317.2	131.8	341.1
Egypt	378.6	343.4	729.9
India	214.7	308.9	395.4
Italy	101.3	144.4	226.1
Korea, Republic	150.0	173.6	418.3
Kuwait	292.2	224.4	284.0
Malaysia	16.4	400.1	167.3
Netherlands	272.7	411.9	415.1
Oman	439.3	479.4	569.7
Saudi Arabia	2,027.4	1,943.1	2,460.7
Spain	51.8	125.7	273.2
Taiwan	88.5	128.3	162.4
Thailand	148.8	138.8	154.8
Türkiye	190.9	194.9	275.2
United Arab Emirates	1,435.6	1,019.2	1,623.4
USA	792.3	697.3	1,335.7
Total (incl. others)	14,167.3	11,559.7	19,331.7

Source: Trade Map-Trade Competitiveness Map, International Trade Centre, marketanalysis.intracen.org.

Transport

ROAD TRAFFIC
(motor vehicles in use at 31 December, estimates)

	2018	2019	2020
Passenger cars	562,723	569,390	573,687
Buses and coaches	13,873	13,789	14,028
Lorries and vans	71,979	73,701	75,315
Motorcycles and mopeds	18,429	20,172	21,818

SHIPPING

Flag Registered Fleet
(at 31 December)

	2020	2021	2022
Number of vessels	334	315	297
Total displacement ('000 grt)	573.0	548.1	501.3

Source: Lloyd's List Intelligence (www.bit.ly/LLintelligence).

BAHRAIN

CIVIL AVIATION
(traffic on scheduled services)

	2013	2014	2015
Kilometres flown (million)	73	76	80
Passengers carried ('000)	4,672	5,171	5,314
Passenger-km (million)	8,052	8,692	8,908
Total ton-km (million)	266	258	240

Source: UN, *Statistical Yearbook*.

2021 (domestic and international): Departures 29,475; Passengers carried 1.8m.; Freight carried 523m. ton-km (Source: World Bank, World Development Indicators database).

Tourism

FOREIGN VISITOR ARRIVALS BY NATIONALITY
('000)

	2019	2021*	2022
Egypt	9,095	73.5	236.8
Germany	101.0	9.1	30.0
India	1,266.0	210.0	736.5
Kuwait	294.6	74.7	300.3
Pakistan	5,156	81.2	257.6
Russian Federation	39.0	3.4	20.3
Saudi Arabia	7,961.3	2,699.5	6,973.0
United Kingdom	263.5	56.4	140.0
Total (incl. others)	11,061.2	3,612.1	9,948.6

* Full data for 2020 were not available.

2020: Total arrivals 1,909,004.

Receipts from tourism (US $ million, excl. passenger transport): 3,681 in 2019; 673 in 2020; 1,813 in 2021 (provisional).

Source: partly World Tourism Organization.

Communications Media

	2019	2020	2021
Telephones ('000 main lines in use)	273.1	274.1	262.2
Mobile telephone subscriptions ('000)	1,900.4	1,748.7	1,923.4
Broadband subscriptions, fixed ('000)	141.0	151.0	167.1
Broadband subscriptions, mobile ('000)	2,011.7	1,861.2	1,978.4
Internet users (% of population)	99.7	99.7	100.0

Source: International Telecommunication Union.

Education

(state schools only, 2018/19 unless otherwise indicated)

	Institutions	Teachers	Students
Primary	111	5,511	72,074
Primary/Intermediate	22	1,470	72,074
Intermediate	37	2,695	37,048
Intermediate/Secondary	1	42	979*
Secondary	35	4,138	34,511
Religious institutes	3	186	2,005†
University level	16‡	1,915§	38,260§

* 2012/13 figure.
† 2013/14 figure.
‡ 2011/12 figure.
§ 2014/15 figure.

Private education (2018/19 unless otherwise indicated): *Students* Pre-primary 38,914; Primary 43,051; Intermediate 15,263; Secondary 11,378; Higher secondary 157 (2012/13).

Pupil-teacher ratio (qualified teaching staff, primary education, UNESCO estimate): 12.2 in 2018/19 (Source: UNESCO Institute for Statistics).

Adult literacy rate (UNESCO estimates): 97.5% (males 98.8%; females 94.9%) in 2018 (Source: UNESCO Institute for Statistics).

Directory

The Constitution

The 108-article Constitution that came into force on 6 December 1973 stated that 'all citizens shall be equal before the law' and guaranteed freedom of speech, of the press, of conscience and of religious beliefs. Other provisions included compulsory free primary education and free medical care. The Constitution also provided for a National Assembly, composed of 14 members of the Cabinet and 30 members elected by popular vote, although this was dissolved in August 1975. A National Action Charter was approved in a nationwide referendum held on 14–15 February 2001. (The Charter had been prepared by a Supreme National Committee, created by Amiri decree in late 2000 with the task of outlining the future evolution of Bahrain's political system.) Principal among the Committee's recommendations were that there should be a transition from an emirate to a constitutional monarchy (the Amir proclaimed himself King on 14 February 2002), with a bicameral parliament (comprising a directly elected legislature and an appointed consultative chamber) and an independent judiciary. Bahraini women were to be permitted for the first time to hold public office and to vote in elections. The amended Constitution, promulgated on 14 February 2002, guaranteed the provisions of the National Action Charter. The kingdom's first direct elections to the 40-member Majlis al-Nuwab (Council of Representatives) took place on 24 October, and the new Majlis al-Shura (Consultative Council), also comprising 40 members, was appointed by the King on 17 November. Members of both chambers are appointed for terms of four years. Members of the lower house are required to be Bahraini nationals of at least 30 years of age, while those of the Consultative Council—who must also be Bahraini citizens—are to be aged at least 35.

The Government

HEAD OF STATE

King and Supreme Commander of the Bahrain Defence Force: HM Sheikh HAMAD BIN ISA AL KHALIFA (acceded as Amir 6 March 1999; proclaimed King 14 February 2002).

CABINET
(September 2023)

Prime Minister: Crown Prince Sheikh SALMAN BIN HAMAD AL KHALIFA.
Deputy Prime Minister: Sheikh KHALID BIN ABDULLAH AL KHALIFA.
Minister of Cabinet Affairs: HAMAD BIN FAISAL AL-MALKI.
Minister of the Interior: Gen. Sheikh RASHID BIN ABDULLAH AL KHALIFA.
Minister of Foreign Affairs: ABDULLATIF BIN RASHID AL-ZAYANI.
Minister of Finance and National Economy: Sheikh SALMAN BIN KHALIFA AL KHALIFA.
Minister of Education: MOHAMMED MUBARAK JUMA.
Minister of Legal Affairs: YOUSSEF BIN ABDULHUSSEIN KHALAF.
Minister of Social Development: OSAMA BIN AHMED KHALAF AL-ASFOOR.
Minister of Electricity and Water Affairs: YASSER BIN IBRAHIM HUMAIDAN.
Minister of Justice, Islamic Affairs and Endowments: NAWAF BIN MOHAMMED AL-MAAWDA.
Minister of Works: IBRAHIM BIN HASSAN AL-HAWAJ.

BAHRAIN

Minister of Municipal Affairs and Agriculture: WAEL BIN NASSER AL-MUBARAK.

Minister of Labour: JAMEEL BIN MOHAMMED ALI HUMAIDAN.

Minister of Transportation and Telecommunications: MOHAMMED BIN THAMER AL-KAABI.

Minister of Housing and Urban Planning: AMNA BINT AHMED AL-ROMAIHI.

Minister of Shura Council and Parliament Affairs: GHANEM BIN FADHIL AL-BUAINAIN.

Minister of Health: JALILA BINT AL-SAYYED JAWAD HASSAN.

Minister of Youth and Sports Affairs: RAWAN BINT NAJEEB TAWFIQI.

Minister of Defence Affairs: Lt-Gen. ABDULLA BIN HASSAN AL-NUAIMI.

Minister of Sustainable Development: NOOR BINT ALI AL-KHULAIF.

Minister of Industry and Commerce: ABDULLA BIN ADEL FAKHRO.

Minister of Tourism: FATIMA BINT JAFFER AL-SAIRAFI.

Minister of Information Affairs: RAMZAN BIN ABDULLA AL-NUAIMI.

Minister of Oil and Environment: Dr MOHAMMED BIN MUBARAK BIN DAINA.

MINISTRIES

Royal Court: POB 555, Riffa Palace, Manama; tel. 17666666; fax 17663070.

Prime Minister's Court: POB 1000, Government House, Government Rd, Manama; tel. 17200000; fax 17533033.

Ministry of Cabinet Affairs: POB 26613, Manama; tel. 17223366; fax 17225202.

Ministry of Defence: POB 245, West Rifa'a.

Ministry of Education: POB 43, Manama; tel. 17278999; fax 17273656; e-mail moe@moe.gov.bh; internet www.moe.gov.bh.

Ministry of Electricity and Water Affairs: POB 2, Manama; tel. 17996333; fax 17541182.

Ministry of Finance and National Economy: POB 333, Diplomatic Area, Manama; tel. 17575000; fax 17532853; internet www.mofne.gov.bh.

Ministry of Foreign Affairs: POB 547, Government House, Government Rd, Manama; tel. 17227555; fax 17212603; e-mail contactus@mofa.gov.bh; internet www.mofa.gov.bh.

Ministry of Health: POB 12, Bldg 1228, Rd 4025, Juffair 340, Manama; tel. 17288888; fax 17286691; e-mail pir@health.gov.bh; internet www.moh.gov.bh.

Ministry of Housing and Urban Planning: POB 5802, Manama; tel. 17533000; fax 17531182; e-mail pr.media@housing.gov.bh; internet www.housing.gov.bh.

Ministry of Industry and Commerce: POB 5479, Diplomatic Area, Manama; tel. 17574777; fax 17581403; e-mail info@moic.gov.bh; internet www.moic.gov.bh.

Ministry of Information Affairs: al-Istighlal Hwy, Isa Town, Manama; tel. 17871111; internet www.mia.gov.bh.

Ministry of the Interior: POB 13, Police Fort Compound, Manama; tel. 17390900; e-mail info@interior.gov.bh; internet www.interior.gov.bh.

Ministry of Justice and Islamic Affairs: POB 450, Diplomatic Area, Manama; tel. 17513000; fax 17536343; internet www.moj.gov.bh.

Ministry of Labour: POB 32868, Isa Town; tel. 17873666; fax 17686999; e-mail minister.office@mlsd.gov.bh; internet www.mlsd.gov.bh.

Ministry of Legal Affairs: Manama.

Ministry of Oil and Environment: Manama.

Ministry of Municipal Affairs and Agriculture: Manama.

Ministry of Shura Council and Parliament Affairs: Manama; internet www.msrc.gov.bh.

Ministry of Social Development: Manama.

Ministry of Sustainable Development: Manama.

Ministry of Tourism: Manama.

Ministry of Transportation and Telecommunications: POB 10325, Diplomatic Area, Manama; tel. 17337878; fax 17534041; e-mail pr@mtt.gov.bh; internet www.mtt.gov.bh.

Ministry of Works: POB 53, Manama; tel. 17981000; fax 17211767; e-mail prinfo@mun.gov.bh; internet www.mun.gov.bh.

Ministry of Youth and Sports Affairs: POB 5498, al-Seef, Manama; tel. 17114000; fax 17114422; e-mail info@mys.gov.bh; internet www.mys.gov.bh.

Legislature

COUNCIL OF REPRESENTATIVES

The most recent elections to the Council of Representatives (Majlis al-Nuwab), the directly elected lower house of the bicameral legislature, took place in November 2022. In the first round of the elections, held on 12 November, only six of the 40 elective seats were won outright. The official turnout was 73% of registered voters. The remaining 34 deputies were elected at a run-off vote on 19 November. A total of 33 first-time deputies and a record eight women (two more than at the previous elections, in 2018) were elected to the Council. Individuals affiliated to opposition groups were not permitted to contest the elections.

Council of Representatives: POB 54040, Manama; tel. 17748444; fax 17748445; e-mail info@nuwab.bh; internet www.nuwab.bh.

Speaker: Sayyid AHMED BIN SALMAN AL-MUSALLAM.

CONSULTATIVE COUNCIL

Members of the new Consultative Council (Majlis al-Shura), the 40-member upper house of the bicameral legislature which holds a purely advisory role, were appointed by King Hamad on 27 November 2022.

Consultative Council: POB 2991, Manama; tel. 17748888; fax 17715715; e-mail info@shura.bh; internet www.shura.bh.

Chairman: ALI BIN SALEH AL-SALEH.

Political Organizations

Political parties are still prohibited in Bahrain. However, several political and civic societies (many of which were previously in exile) are now active in the country, and a number of new groups have been established since 2001. Restrictions on campaigning by political groups were revoked prior to the first elections to the new Council of Representatives, held in October 2002. By mid-2013 it was reported that there were 20 political alliances or blocs functioning in Bahrain.

In a controversial move, the Government of Bahrain dissolved the Al-Wefaq National Islamic Society, the country's largest political opposition group, in 2016. The decision was upheld by the Court of Cassation in 2018.

Al-Asala Islamic Society: Muharraq; tel. 17331255; fax 17331266; internet www.alasalah-bh.org; f. 2002; Sunni Islamist; promotes the implementation of strict Salafi principles in society and law.

Al-Menbar Islamic Society (Islamic National Tribune Society): Bldg 30, Sheikh Salman St, Muharraq; tel. 17324997; fax 17324996; internet www.almenber.bh; Sunni Islamist; political wing of the Al-Islah Soc., affiliated with the Muslim Brotherhood; Sec.-Gen. Eng. MUHAMMAD AL-EMADI.

Other prominent groups include al-Adala (National Justice Movement—a secular, liberal society established in 2006), Al-Haq (Movement for Liberty and Democracy—a radical breakaway faction of Al-Wefaq, opposed to participation in parliamentary politics), the Islamic Action Society (Shi'a Islamist) and Al-Meethaq (liberal, pro-democracy).

Diplomatic Representation

EMBASSIES IN BAHRAIN

Algeria: Villa 1220, Rd 3324, Blk 333, Umm al-Hassam, Manama; tel. 17740659; fax 17740652; e-mail algerian.embassy@gmail.com; Ambassador MAHMOUD BRAHEM.

Bangladesh: POB 26718, Villa 71, Rd 56, Blk 356, al-Qufool, Manama; tel. 17233925; fax 17233683; e-mail bangla@batelco.com.bh; internet manama.mofa.gov.bd; Ambassador Dr MOHAMMAD NAZRUL ISLAM.

Brunei Darussalam: POB 15700, Villa 892, Rd 3218, Blk 332, al-Mahooz, Manama; tel. 17720222; fax 17741757; e-mail manama.bahrain@mfa.gov.bn; internet www.mfa.gov.bn/bahrain-manama; Chargé d'affaires a.i. NAZIRAH BINTI Haji ZAINI.

China, People's Republic: POB 3150, Bldg 158, Rd 4156, Blk 341, Juffair Ave, Manama; tel. 17723093; fax 17727304; e-mail chinaemb_bh@mfa.gov.cn; internet bh.china-embassy.gov.cn; Ambassador NI RUOXI.

Egypt: POB 818, Villa 18, Rd 33, Blk 332, al-Mahooz, Manama; tel. 17720005; fax 17721518; Ambassador YASSER MOHAMED AHMED SHA'BAN.

France: POB 11134, Villa 51A, Rd 1901, Blk 319, Diplomatic Area, Manama; tel. 17298660; fax 17298607; e-mail chancellerie

.manama-amba@diplomatie.gouv.fr; internet www.ambafrance-bh.org; Ambassador ERIC GIRAUD-TELME.
Germany: POB 10306, Bldg 39, Rd 322, Blk 327, Salmaniya Ave, Manama; tel. 17745277; fax 17714314; e-mail info@manama.diplo.de; internet www.manama.diplo.de; Ambassador CLEMENS HACH.
India: Bldg 1090, Rd 2819, Blk 428, al-Seef, Manama; tel. 17712785; fax 17715527; e-mail hoc.bahrain@mea.gov.in; internet eoi.gov.in/bahrain; Ambassador VINOD K. JACOB.
Indonesia: Villa 2113, Rd 2432, Blk 324, Juffair, Manama; tel. 17400164; fax 17400267; e-mail indonesia.manama@batelco.com.bh; internet www.kemlu.go.id/manama; Ambassador ARDI HERMAWAN.
Iraq: POB 26477, Bldg 396, Rd 3207, Blk 332, al-Mahooz, Manama; tel. 17741472; fax 17720756; internet www.mofa.gov.iq/manama; Chargé d'affaires a.i. MUAYYAD OMAR ABDULRAHMAN.
Israel: Manama; Ambassador EITAN NA'EH.
Italy: POB 347, Villa 1554, Rd 5647, Blk 356, Manama; tel. 17252424; fax 17277020; e-mail ambasciata.manama@esteri.it; internet www.ambmanama.esteri.it; Ambassador PAOLA AMADEI.
Japan: POB 23720, Villa 55, Blk 327, Salmaniya Ave, Manama; tel. 17716565; fax 17715059; e-mail nippon@bh.mofa.go.jp; internet www.bh.emb-japan.go.jp; Ambassador MASAYUKI MIYAMOTO.
Jordan: POB 5242, Bldg 43, Rd 1901, Blk 319, Manama; tel. 17291109; fax 17291980; e-mail bahrain@fm.gov.jo; Ambassador RAMI SALEH ABDUL KARIM WREIKAT AL-ADWAN.
Korea, Republic: POB 20554, Villa 401, Rd 915, Blk 309, Salmaniya, Manama; tel. 17531120; fax 17530577; e-mail korembbah@mofa.go.kr; internet overseas.mofa.go.kr/bh-en/index.do; Ambassador KOO HEON SANG.
Kuwait: POB 786, Villa 76, Rd 1702, Blk 317, Manama; tel. 17534040; fax 17536475; Ambassador Sheikh THAMER AL-JABER AL-AHMAD AL-SABAH.
Lebanon: Villa 1556, Rd 5647, Salihiya 356, Manama; tel. 17579001; fax 17232535; e-mail lebembassy@gmail.com; Ambassador MILAD NAMMOUR.
Libya: POB 26015, Villa 787, Rd 3315, Blk 333, Umm al-Hassam, Manama; tel. 17722252; fax 17722911; e-mail libyan.bbb@batelco.com.bh; Ambassador FAWZI TAHER ABDULA'ALI.
Malaysia: POB 18292, Bldg 1617, Rd 3437, Blk 334, al-Mahooz, Manama; tel. 17564551; fax 17564552; e-mail mwmanama.kln@1govuc.gov.my; internet www.kln.gov.my/web/bhr_manama/; Ambassador SHAZRIEL BIN ZAHIRAN.
Morocco: POB 26229, Villa 2743, Rd 2771, Blk 327, Manama; tel. 17180444; fax 17180555; e-mail sifamana@batelco.com.bh; Ambassador MUSTAPHA BENKHIYI.
Nepal: POB 75933, Villa 2397, Rd 2437, Blk 324, Juffair, Manama; tel. 17725583; fax 17720787; e-mail eonmanama@mofa.gov.np; internet bh.nepalembassy.gov.np; Ambassador TIRTHA RAJ WAGLE.
Oman: POB 26414, Bldg 37, Rd 1901, Blk 319, Diplomatic Area, Manama; tel. 17293663; fax 17293540; e-mail oman@batelco.com.bh; Ambassador FAISAL BIN HAREB BIN HAMAD AL-BUSAIDI.
Pakistan: POB 563, Bldg 35, Rd 1901, Blk 319, Manama; tel. 17244113; fax 17255960; e-mail parepbahrain@mofa.gov.pk; internet mofa.gov.pk/manama-bahrain; Ambassador MUHAMMAD AYUB.
Philippines: Bldg 2186, Rd 2755, Blk 327, Adliya, Manama; tel. 17721234; fax 17720827; e-mail manama.pe@dfa.gov.ph; internet manamape.dfa.gov.ph; Ambassador ANNE GALLANDON LEWIS.
Russian Federation: POB 26612, Villa 877, Rd 3119, Blk 331, Zinj, Manama; tel. 17231914; fax 17725921; e-mail bahrain@mid.ru; internet bahrain.mid.ru; Ambassador ALEXEY SKOSYREV.
Saudi Arabia: POB 1085, Bldg 82, Rd 1702, Blk 317, Diplomatic Area, Manama; tel. 17537722; fax 17533261; e-mail bhemb@mofa.gov.sa; internet embassies.mofa.gov.sa/sites/bahrain; Ambassador Prince SULTAN BIN AHMED BIN ABDUL AZIZ AL SA'UD.
Senegal: Villa 25, Rd 33, Blk 333, al-Mahooz, Manama; tel. 17821060; fax 17721650; e-mail sengemb@batelco.com.bh; Ambassador ABDOU LAHAT SOURANG.
Sri Lanka: Villa 25, Umm-Shoom Ave, Blk 333, al-Mahooz, Manama; tel. 17008410; e-mail slemb.bahrain@mfa.gov.lk; internet fb.com/slembbahrain; Ambassador HERATH MUNDIYANSELAGE.
Sudan: POB 5438, Villa 423, Rd 3614, Blk 336, al-Adliya, Manama; tel. 17717959; fax 17710113; e-mail sudanimanama@hotmail.com; internet www.sudanimanama.com; Ambassador EBRAHIM MUHAMMAD AL-HASSAN.
Syrian Arab Republic: POB 11585, Villa 867, Rd 3315, Blk 333, al-Mahooz, Manama; tel. 17722484; fax 17740380; e-mail syremb@batelco.com.bh; Ambassador MOHAMMED ALI IBRAHIM.
Thailand: POB 26475, Villa 132, Rd 66, Blk 360, Zinj, Manama; tel. 17274142; fax 17272714; e-mail thaimnm@mfa.go.th; internet manama.thaiembassy.org; Ambassador PIYAPAK SRICHAROEN.
Tunisia: POB 26911, Villa 54, Rd 3601, Blk 336, Adliya, Manama; tel. 17714149; fax 17715702; e-mail atmanama@batelco.com.bh; Chargé d'affaires a.i. MUNA AL-MALOUL.
Türkiye (Turkey): POB 10821, Villa 924, Rd 3219, Blk 332, Manama; tel. 17533448; fax 17536557; e-mail embassy.manama@mfa.gov.tr; internet www.manama.emb.mfa.gov.tr; Ambassador ESIN ÇAKIL.
United Arab Emirates: POB 26505, Villa 270, Rd 2510, Blk 325, Manama; tel. 17748333; fax 17717724; e-mail ManamaEMB@mofa.gov.ae; internet www.mofaic.gov.ae/en/missions/manama; Ambassador Sheikh SULTAN BIN HAMDAN BIN ZAYED AL NAHYAN.
United Kingdom: POB 114, Blk 306, 21 Govt Ave, Manama; tel. 17574100; internet www.gov.uk/government/world/organisations/british-embassy-manama; Ambassador ALASTAIR LONE.
USA: POB 26431, Bldg 979, Rd 3119, Blk 331, Zinj, Manama; tel. 17242700; fax 17272594; e-mail manamaconsular@state.gov; internet bh.usembassy.gov; Ambassador STEPHEN C. BUNDY.
Yemen: POB 26193, Villa 195, Rd 3305, Blk 333, Umm al-Hassam, Manama; tel. 17822110; fax 17822078; Ambassador Dr ALI HASSAN AL-AHMEDI.

Judicial System

Since the termination of British legal jurisdiction in 1971, intensive work has been undertaken on the legislative requirements of Bahrain. All nationalities are subject to the jurisdiction of the Bahraini courts, which guarantee equality before the law irrespective of nationality or creed. The 1974 Decree Law on State Security Measures and the State Security Court were both abolished in February 2001. The adoption of the amended Constitution in 2002 provided for the establishment of an independent judiciary; however, all judges are appointed by royal decree. The Criminal Law is at present contained in various Codes, Ordinances and Regulations; a new Code of Criminal Procedure was introduced in 2002.

Constitutional Court: POB 18380, Manama; tel. 17578181; fax 17224475; e-mail info@ccb.bh; internet www.ccb.bh; f. 2002 to undertake review of, and to settle disputes concerning the constitutionality of, laws and regulations; consists of 7 members appointed by the King; Pres. ABDULLAH BIN HASSAN AHMED AL-BUAINAIN.

Court of Cassation: f. 1990; serves as the final court of appeal for all civil and criminal cases; Pres. Sheikh KHALID BIN ALI BIN ABDULLA AL KHALIFA.

Civil Law Courts: All civil and commercial cases, including disputes relating to the personal affairs of non-Muslims, are settled in the Civil Law Courts, which comprise the Higher Civil Appeals Court, Higher Civil Court and Lesser Civil Courts.

Criminal Law Courts: Higher Criminal Court, presided over by three judges, rules on felonies; Lower Criminal Courts, presided over by one judge, rule on misdemeanours.

Religious Courts: Shari'a Judiciary Courts operate according to Islamic principles of jurisprudence and have jurisdiction in all disputes relating to the personal affairs of Muslims, including marriage contracts and inheritances. They are structured according to the following hierarchy: Higher *Shari'a* Appeals Court, Greater *Shari'a* Court, Lesser *Shari'a* Court; each court has separate Sunni and Shi'a departments.

Supreme Judicial Council: Founded in 2000, and further regulated by law decree in 2002, the Supreme Judicial Council, headed by the King, is made up of the most senior figures from each branch of the judiciary. The Council supervises the performance of the courts and recommends candidates for judicial appointments and promotions.

Attorney-General: ALI BIN FADHEL AL-BUAINAIN.

Religion

At the 2010 census the total population was recorded at 1,234,571, of whom 866,888 were Muslims. According to the census data, Bahraini citizens totalled some 568,399, of whom some 99.8% were Muslims. Of the 666,172 non-Bahrainis resident in the country, 55.0% were classified as adhering to religions other than Islam.

ISLAM

Muslims are divided between the Sunni and Shi'a sects. The ruling family is Sunni, although the majority of the Bahraini Muslim population are Shi'a.

CHRISTIANITY

The Anglican Communion

Within the Episcopal Church in Jerusalem and the Middle East, Bahrain forms part of the diocese of Cyprus and the Gulf. There are two Anglican churches in Bahrain: St Christopher's Cathedral in Manama and the Community Church in Awali. The congregations are entirely expatriate. The Bishop in Cyprus and the Gulf is resident in Cyprus.

Dean: Very Rev. Dr BILL SCHWARTZ, St Christopher's Cathedral, POB 36, al-Mutanabi Ave, Manama; tel. 17253866; fax 17246436; e-mail cathedra@batelco.com.bh; internet www.stchcathedral.org.

Roman Catholic Church

A small number of adherents, mainly expatriates, form part of the Apostolic Vicariate of Northern Arabia.

Vicar Apostolic: PAUL HINDER (Titular Bishop of Macon), Bishop's House, POB 25362, Rd 4603, House 137/125, Blk 946, Awali; tel. and fax 17490929; e-mail mail@camilloballin.com; internet www.avona.org.

The Press

DAILY NEWSPAPERS (PRINT AND ONLINE)

Akhbar al-Khaleej (Gulf News): POB 5300, Manama; tel. 17620111; fax 17621566; e-mail local@aaknews.net; internet www.akhbar-alkhaleej.com; f. 1976; Arabic; Chair. and Editor-in-Chief ANWAR ABD AL-RAHMAN.

Al-Ayam (The Days): POB 3232, Manama; tel. 17617777; fax 17617111; e-mail jm1111@alayam.com; internet www.alayam.com; f. 1989; Arabic; publ. by Al-Ayam Establishment for Press and Publications; Editor-in-Chief ISA AL-SHAIJI.

The Daily Tribune: Strategic Publicity and Advertising Co WLL, Bldg 1351, Blk 333, Umal Hassam, nr Tropicana Hotel, POB 11148, Manama; tel. 36453899; e-mail mail@newsofbahrain.com; internet www.newsofbahrain.com; f. 1997; English; Editor-in-Chief Capt. MAHMOOD AL-MAHMOOD.

Gulf Daily News: POB 5300, Manama; tel. 17620222; fax 17622141; e-mail gdnnews@gdn.com.bh; internet www.gdnonline.com; f. 1978; English; publ. by Al-Hilal Publishing and Marketing Group; Chair. ANWAR ABD AL-RAHMAN; Editor-in-Chief (vacant).

Al-Watan: POB 38801, Rifa'a; tel. 17496666; fax 17496678; e-mail mbusaibea@alwatannews.net; internet www.alwatannews.net; f. 2005; Arabic; Man. Editor IHAB AHMED.

WEEKLY NEWSPAPERS (PRINT AND ONLINE)

The Gulf: POB 1100, Manama; tel. 17293131; fax 17293400; e-mail info@thegulfonline.com; internet www.thegulfonline.com; f. 2008; English; business and current affairs; publ. by Al-Hilal Publishing and Marketing Group; Editor DIGBY LIDSTONE.

Gulf Weekly: POB 1100, Manama; tel. 17299187; fax 17293400; e-mail mail.alkhatib@gulfweekly.com; internet www.gulfweekly.com; f. 2002; English; publ. by Al-Hilal Publishing and Marketing Group; Editor MAI AL-KHATIB.

Huna al-Bahrain (Here is Bahrain): POB 26005, Isa Town; tel. 17870166; fax 17686600; e-mail bahrainmag@info.gov.bh; f. 1957; Arabic; publ. by the Ministry of Information Affairs; Editor ABD AL-QADER AQIL.

Oil and Gas News: POB 1100, Manama; tel. 17299135; fax 17293400; e-mail editor@ognnews.com; internet www.ognnews.com; f. 1983; English; publ. by Al-Hilal Publishing and Marketing Group; Editor ABDULAZIZ KHATTAK.

PERIODICALS

Arab Agriculture: POB 10131, Bahrain Tower, 8th Floor, Manama; tel. 17213900; e-mail fanar@batelco.com.bh; internet www.fanarpublishing.net/arabagriculture; f. 1984; annually; English and Arabic; publ. by Fanar Publishing WLL; Editor-in-Chief ABDUL WAHED ALWANI.

Arab World Agribusiness: POB 10131, Bahrain Tower, 8th Floor, Manama; tel. 17213900; e-mail fanar@batelco.com.bh; internet www.fanarpublishing.net/arabworldagribusiness; f. 1985; 9 per year; English and Arabic; publ. by Fanar Publishing WLL; Editor-in-Chief ABDUL WAHED ALWANI.

Al-Bahrain ath-Thaqafia: POB 2199, Manama; tel. 17290210; fax 17292678; internet www.mia.gov.bh; quarterly; Arabic; publ. by the Ministry of Information Affairs; Editor ABD AL-QADER AQIL.

Bahrain This Month: POB 20461, Manama; tel. 17813777; fax 17813700; e-mail contact@redhousemarketing.com; internet www.bahrainthismonth.com; f. 1997; monthly; English; publ. by Red House Marketing; Publr and Chair. GEORGE F. MIDDLETON.

Gulf Construction: POB 1100, Manama; tel. 17293131; fax 17293400; e-mail editor@gulfconstructiononline.com; internet www.gulfconstructiononline.com; f. 1980; monthly; English; publ. by Al-Hilal Publishing and Marketing Group; Editor BINA PRABHU GOVEAS.

Gulf Industry: POB 1100, Manama; tel. 17299104; fax 17293400; e-mail editor@gulfindustryonline.com; internet www.gulfindustryonline.com; English; industry and transport; publ. by Al-Hilal Publishing and Marketing Group; Editorial Dir SREE BHAT.

Al-Mohandis (The Engineer): POB 835, Manama; tel. 17727100; fax 17729819; e-mail mohandis@batelco.com.bh; internet www.mohandis.org; f. 1972; quarterly; Arabic and English; publ. by Bahrain Society of Engineers; Editor MAHMOUD MOHAMMED YAQOOB.

Al-Musafir al-Arabi (Arab Traveller): POB 10131, Bahrain Tower, 8th Floor, Manama; tel. 17213900; e-mail fanar@batelco.com.bh; internet www.fanarpublishing.net; f. 1985; 6 per year; Arabic; publ. by Fanar Publishing WLL; Editor-in-Chief ABDUL WAHED ALWANI.

Al-Quwwa (The Force): POB 245, Manama; tel. 17291331; fax 17659596; internet www.bdf.gov.bh; f. 1977; monthly; Arabic; publ. by Bahrain Defence Force; Editor-in-Chief Maj. AHMAD MAHMOUD AL-SUWAIDI.

Travel and Tourism News Middle East: POB 1100, Manama; tel. 17293131; fax 17293400; e-mail kim.thomson@tradearabia.ae; internet www.ttnworldwide.com; f. 1983; monthly; English; travel trade; publ. by Al-Hilal Publishing and Marketing Group; Publishing Dir KIMBERLY THOMPSON.

Woman This Month: POB 20461, Manama; tel. 17813777; fax 17813700; e-mail contact@womanthismonth.com; internet www.womanthismonth.com; f. 2003; English; monthly; publ. by Red House Marketing; Editor FARAH BAIG; Publr and Man. Dir GEORGE F. MIDDLETON.

NEWS AGENCY

Bahrain News Agency (BNA): Information Affairs Authority, POB 253, Manama; tel. 17372000; e-mail info@bna.bh; internet www.bna.bh; f. 2001 to cover local and foreign news; replaced Gulf News Agency as national news agency; Dir-Gen. ABDULLAH KHALIL BUHEJJI.

PRESS ASSOCIATION

Bahrain Journalists' Association (BJA): Villa 2057, Rd 4156, Block 341, Juffair, Manama 341; tel. 17003311; fax 17003322; internet www.bahrainijournalists.org; f. 2000; Chair. ISA AL-SHAIJI.

Publishers

Arabian Magazines Group: 6th Floor, Bldg 741, Rd 3616, Blk 436, al-Seef District, Manama; tel. 17822388; fax 17721722; e-mail info@arabianmagazines.com; internet www.arabianmagazines.com; f. 2001; publs include *Bahrain Confidential*, *Areej*, *Gulf Insider*, *Bahrain 101*; Man. Dir NICHOLAS COOKSEY.

Fanar Publishing WLL: POB 10131, Bahrain Tower, 8th Floor, Manama; tel. 17213900; fax 17211765; e-mail fanar@batelco.com.bh; internet www.fanarpublishing.net; publs incl.: *Arab Oil and Gas*, *Arab World Agribusiness*, *The Arab Agriculture Year Book* and *The Arab Traveller*; f. 1985; Editor-in-Chief ABDUL WAHED ALWANI.

Al-Hilal Publishing and Marketing Group: POB 1100, Manama; tel. 17293131; fax 17293400; e-mail hilalpmg@tradearabia.net; internet www.alhilalgroup.com; f. 1978; specialist magazines, newspapers and websites of commercial interest, incl. *Gulf Daily News*, *Gulf Weekly*, *Gulf Construction*, *Gulf Industry*, *Travel & Tourism News*, etc.; Man. Dir RONNIE MIDDLETON.

Al-Maseerah Printing & Publishing House Co WLL: POB 5981, Manama; tel. 17258882; fax 17276178; f. 1981.

Primedia International BSC: POB 2738, Manama; tel. 17490000; fax 17490001; internet www.primediaintl.com; f. 1977; fmrly Tele-Gulf Directory Publications WLL; publrs of, inter alia, annual *Gulf Directory* and *Arab Banking and Finance*, as well as *Bahrain Telephone Directory with Yellow Pages*, *Qatar Telephone Directory with Yellow Pages* and *Banks in Bahrain*; CEO ALDRIN S. MENEZES.

Red House Marketing: POB 20461, Rd 2426, Blk 324, Juffair, Manama; tel. 17813777; fax 17813700; e-mail contact@redhousemarketing.com; internet www.redhousemarketing.com; British-owned; publs include *Bahrain This Month*, *Woman This Month*, *Bahrain Hotel & Restaurant Guide*, maps, tourist guides and various specialist trade publs; Man. Dir and Publr GEORGE F. MIDDLETON.

GOVERNMENT PUBLISHING HOUSE

Directorate of Press and Publications: POB 253, Manama; tel. 17711010; fax 17717515; e-mail jamaldawood@hotmail.com; publs include *Official Gazette* and *Huna Al-Bahrain Magazine*; Dir JAMAL DAWOOD AL-JLAHMA.

Broadcasting and Communications

TELECOMMUNICATIONS

The telecommunications sector in Bahrain was fully opened to private sector competition in 2002. Since liberalization of the sector Bahrain has been at the forefront of the development of new infrastructure and technologies in the region. Several companies provide fixed-line services and international telecommunications services. Three providers have been awarded mobile telecommunications licences; the third mobile licence was awarded to Saudi Telecom (STC) in 2009.

Bahrain Telecommunications Co BSC (BATELCO): POB 14, Manama; tel. 17881881; fax 17611898; e-mail public.relations@batelcogroup.com; internet www.batelco.com; f. 1981; 100% owned by Govt of Bahrain, financial institutions and public of Bahrain; launched mobile telecommunications service, Sim Sim, 1999; provides fixed-line and mobile telephone services, broadband internet and data services; Chair. Sheikh ABDULLAH BIN KHALIFA AL KHALIFA; CEO MIKKEL VINTER.

Infonas WLL: 12th Floor, NBB Tower, Government Ave, Manama; tel. 16500110; fax 16500109; e-mail info@infonas.com; internet www.infonas.com; f. 2004 as 2Connect Bahrain; present name adopted in 2016; provides fixed-line telephone, broadband internet and data-hosting services; Man. Dir HAMAD AL-AMER.

Nuetel Communications: NOC Bldg 2420, Rd 5718, Blk 257, Amwaj Islands; tel. 16033000; fax 16033001; e-mail info@nue-tel.com; internet www.nue-tel.com; f. 2006; provides fixed-line telephone, broadband internet, internet telephony and data services; Chair. SAUD KANOO.

stc Bahrain: Bldg 15, Blk 428, Seef, Manama; internet www.stc.com.bh; f. 2010 as VIVA Bahrain; present name adopted 2019; subsidiary of Saudi Telecommunications Co—Saudi Telecom; mobile telephone and broadband internet services; Chair. MOHAMED AL-HAKBANI; CEO Eng. NEZAR BANABEELA.

Zain Bahrain: POB 266, Rd 2806, Bldg 401, Blk 428, Manama; tel. 36107107; e-mail customercare@bh.zain.com; internet www.bh.zain.com; f. 2003 under the name MTC Vodafone Bahrain; present name adopted in 2007; acquired Celtel International (Netherlands) 2005; 60% owned by Mobile Telecommunications Co (Kuwait), 40% by Bahraini Govt; provides mobile telephone services; Chair. Sheikh AHMED BIN ALI AL KHALIFA; Man. Dir MOHAMMED ZAIN AL-ABEDIN; CEO DUNCAN HOWARD.

Regulatory Authority

Telecommunications Regulatory Authority (TRA): 5th Floor, Bldg 852, Rd 3618, Seef 436; POB 10353, Manama; tel. 17520000; fax 17532125; e-mail contact@tra.org.bh; internet www.tra.org.bh; f. 2002; Chair. Eng. MARYAM AHMED JAMAAN; Gen. Dir PHILIP MARNICK.

BROADCASTING

Radio

Bahrain Radio and Television Corpn: POB 702, Manama; tel. 17871405; fax 17681622; f. 1955; state-owned; two 10-kW transmitters; programmes are in Arabic and English, and include news, drama and discussions; Asst Undersecretary ABDULLAH KHALED AL-DOSARI.

Radio Bahrain: POB 702, Manama; tel. 17871585; fax 17780911; internet www.radiobahrain.fm; f. 1977; English-language commercial radio station; Dir YOUNIS SALMAN.

Television

Bahrain Radio and Television Corpn: POB 1075, Manama; tel. 17686000; fax 17681544; internet www.bahraintv.com; commenced colour broadcasting in 1973; broadcasts on 5 channels, of which the main Arabic and the main English channel accept advertising; offers a 24-hour Arabic news and documentary channel; covers Bahrain, eastern Saudi Arabia, Qatar and the United Arab Emirates; an Amiri decree in early 1993 established the independence of the Corpn, which was to be controlled by a committee; Asst Undersecretary ABDULLAH KHALED AL-DOSARI.

Finance

BANKING

In 2022 there were 86 banks operating in Bahrain, including 72 conventional banks and 14 Islamic banks.

Central Bank

Central Bank of Bahrain (CBB): POB 27, Bldg 96, Blk 317, Rd 1702, Diplomatic Area, Manama; tel. 17547777; fax 17530399; e-mail info@cbb.gov.bh; internet www.cbb.gov.bh; f. 1973 as Bahrain Monetary Agency; in operation from Jan. 1975; present name adopted 2006; controls issue of currency, regulates exchange control and credit policy, organization and control of banking and insurance systems, bank credit and stock exchange; Chair. HASSAN KHALIFA AL-JALAHMA; Gov. RASHEED MOHAMMED AL-MARAJ.

Locally Incorporated Commercial Banks

Ahli United Bank BSC (AUB): POB 2424, Bldg 2495, Rd 2832, al-Seef District 428, Manama; tel. 17585858; fax 17580569; e-mail info@ahliunited.com; internet www.ahliunited.com; f. 2001 by merger of Al-Ahli Commercial Bank and Commercial Bank of Bahrain; acquired by Kuwait Finance House in 2022; Chair. MESHAL ABDUL AZIZ AL-OTHMAN; Group CEO and Man. Dir ADEL EL-LABBAN.

Bahrain Islamic Bank BSC: POB 5240, al-Salam Tower, Diplomatic Area, Manama; tel. 17515151; fax 17535808; e-mail contactcentregroup@bisb.com; internet www.bisb.com; f. 1979; Chair. Dr ESSAM ABDULLAH FAKHRO; CEO YASER ABDULJALIL AL-SHARIFI.

BBK BSC: POB 597, 43 Government Ave, Area 305, Manama; tel. 17223388; fax 17229822; e-mail feedback@bbkonline.com; internet www.bbkonline.com; f. 1971 as Bank of Bahrain and Kuwait BSC; name changed as above 2005; Chair. MURAD ALI MURAD; Chief Exec. ABDULRAHMAN ALI SAIF.

Ithmaar Bank BSC: POB 2820, Ground Floor, Seef Tower, al Seef, Manama; tel. 17585000; fax 17585151; e-mail info@ithmaarbank.com; internet www.ithmaarbank.com; f. 1984 as Faisal Investment Bank of Bahrain EC, a wholly owned subsidiary of Shamil Bank of Bahrain BSC; acquired by Dar al-Maal al-Islami and assumed name as above 2003; merged with Shamil Bank of Bahrain 2010; Chair. Prince AMR MUHAMMAD AL-FAISAL; CEO ABDULLA ABDULAZIZ TALIB.

National Bank of Bahrain BSC (NBB): POB 106, Government Ave, Manama; tel. 17214433; fax 17228998; e-mail nbb@nbbonline.com; internet www.nbbonline.com; f. 1957; 55% govt-owned; Chair. FAROUK YOUSUF AL-MOAYYED; CEO and Dir JEAN-CHRISTOPHE DURAND.

Al-Salam Bank Bahrain BSC: POB 18282, 13th Floor, East Tower, Bahrain World Trade Center, Manama; tel. 17005500; fax 17560003; internet www.alsalambahrain.com; f. 2006; acquired Bahraini Saudi Bank 2014; Islamic bank; Chair. Sheikh KHALID BIN MUSTAHAIL AL-MASHANI; CEO RAFIK NAYED.

Specialized Financial Institutions

Bahrain Development Bank (BDB): POB 20501, Manama; tel. 17511111; fax 17530116; internet www.bdb-bh.com; f. 1992; invests in manufacturing, agribusiness and services; Chair. KHALID OMAR AL-RUMAIHI; Group CEO DALAL AL-QAIS.

First Energy Bank BSC: POB 209, 20th floor, West Tower, Bahrain Financial Harbour, Manama; tel. 17100000; fax 17170170; f. 2008; owned by Gulf Finance House BSC and other Gulf shareholders; Islamic wholesale bank providing investment and advice for energy projects; Chair. ZAYED A. R. AL-AMIN; CEO MUHAMMAD SHUKRI GHANEM.

Offshore Banking Units

Bahrain has been encouraging the establishment of offshore banking units (OBUs) since 1975. An OBU is not permitted to provide local banking services, but is allowed to accept deposits from governments and large financial organizations in the area and make medium-term loans for local and regional capital projects.

Bank ABC Islamic: POB 2808, ABC Tower, Diplomatic Area, Manama; tel. 17543000; e-mail webmaster@bank-abc.com; internet www.bank-abc.com/world/IslamicBank; f. 1987 as ABC Investment and Services Co (EC); name changed as above 1998 when converted into Islamic bank; 100% owned by Arab Banking Corpn BSC; Chair. AMR EL-NOKALY; Man. Dir HAMMAD HASSAN.

Alubaf Arab International Bank BSC: POB 11529, Alubaf Tower, al-Seef, Manama; tel. 17517722; fax 17540094; e-mail info@alubafbank.com; internet www.alubafbank.com; f. 1982; 99.5% owned by Libyan Foreign Bank; Chair. MORAJA GAITH SULAYMAN; CEO HASAN K. ABULHASAN.

Arab Bank PLC (Jordan): Bldg 540/542, Rd 1706, Blk 317, Diplomatic Area, Manama; tel. 17549000; internet www.arabbank.bh; f. 1930; Chair. SABIH AL-MASRI.

Arab Banking Corpn BSC: POB 5698, ABC Tower, Diplomatic Area, Manama; tel. 17543000; fax 17533163; e-mail webmaster@bank-abc.com; internet www.bank-abc.com; f. 1980; Chair. SADDEK AL-KABER; Pres. and Chief Exec. SAEL AL-WARRY.

Arab Investment Co SAA (Saudi Arabia): POB 5559, Manama; tel. 17588945; fax 17588983; e-mail jamri@taicobu.com; internet www.taic.com; f. 1974; Chair. ABDULAZIZ SALIH O. AL-FURAIH; CEO IBRAHIM H. AL-MAZYAD.

BNP Paribas (France): POB 5241, Bahrain Financial Harbour, West Tower, Manama; tel. 17866202; fax 17866601; e-mail csd.bahrain@bnpparibas.com; internet mea.bnpparibas.com; f. 1975; Gen. Man. RAMI FALAH.

Gulf International Bank BSC (GIB): POB 1017, Al-Duwali Bldg, 3 Palace Ave, Area 317, Manama; tel. 17534000; fax 17522530; e-mail info@gibbah.com; internet www.gib.com; f. 1975; Chair. Eng. ABDULLA BIN MOHAMMED AL-ZAMIL; Group CEO ABDULAZIZ A. AL-HELAISSI; CEO, GIB BSC JAMAL AL-KISHI.

First Abu Dhabi Bank (UAE): Bldg 1565, Rd 1722, Blk 317, Diplomatic Area, Manama; tel. 17560870; fax 17583281; e-mail customersupport.bahrain@nbad.com; internet www.bankfab.com; f. 1977 as National Bank of Abu Dhabipresent name adopted 2017 after merger with First Gulf Bank (FGB); Group CEO HANA AL-ROSTAMANI.

KEB Hana Bank (Repub. of Korea): POB 5767, Yateem Centre Bldg, 5th Floor, al-Khalifa Rd, Manama; tel. 17229333; fax 17225327; e-mail bahrain@hanafn.com; internet www.kebhana.com; f. 1977; Pres. and CEO PAR SUNG-HO.

MCB Bank Ltd (MCB) (Pakistan): Of. 132, 13th Floor, NBB Tower, Bldg 113, Rd 383, Blk 316, Govt Ave, Manama; tel. 17533306; e-mail complaint@mcb.com.bh; internet www.mcb.com.pk; f. 1947 as Muslim Commercial Bank Ltd, name changed as above 2005; Chair. MUHAMMAD MANSHA.

National Bank of Kuwait KSC (NBK): POB 5290, Bldg 1411, Rd 4626, Blk 346, Manama; tel. 17155555; fax 17104860; internet www.nbk.com/bahrain; f. 1987; Group CEO ISAM J. AL-SAGER; Group Chair. HAMAD MOHAMED AL-BAHAR; Gen. Man. ALI FARDAN.

Standard Chartered Bank (United Kingdom): POB 29, Manama; tel. 17223636; fax 17225001; internet www.sc.com/bh; f. 1976; CEO ABDULLA ABDULRAZAQ BUKHOWA.

State Bank of India: POB 5466, GBCorp Tower, Bahrain Financial Harbour, Manama; tel. 17505175; fax 17224692; e-mail wbbbah@statebank.com; internet bh.statebank; f. 1977; CEO MUNNA PRASAD THAKUR.

Yapi ve Kredi Bankasi AS (Türkiye): POB 10615, Wind Tower, 10th Floor, Bldg 404, Rd 1705, Blk 317, Diplomatic Area, Manama; tel. 17530313; fax 17530311; internet www.yapikredi.com; f. 1982; Group CEO GÖKHAN ERÜN.

Investment Banks

Bahrain Middle East Bank BSC (BMB Investment Bank): POB 797, BMB Centre, Diplomatic Area, Manama; tel. 17532345; fax 17530526; e-mail info@bmb.com.bh; internet www.bmb.com.bh; f. 1982; fmrly Bahrain Middle East Bank EC; Chair. Sheikh KHALIFA BIN DUAIJ AL KHALIFA; CEO ABDULLA MOHAMMED DAWOOD (acting).

Al-Baraka Islamic Bank BSC (EC): POB 1882, Bldg 370, Rd 4611, Block 346, Manama; tel. 13300400; e-mail complaints@albaraka.bh; internet www.albaraka.bh; f. 1984 as Al-Baraka Islamic Investment Bank BSC (EC); current name adopted 1998; owned by Al-Baraka Banking Group BSC; Chair. SALEH SALMAN AL-KAWARI; CEO HAMAD ABDULLA AL-OQAB.

Global Banking Corpn (GBCORP): POB 1486, GBCORP Tower, Bahrain Financial Harbour, Manama; tel. 17200200; fax 17200300; e-mail info@gbcorponline.com; internet www.gbcorponline.com; f. 2007; Islamic investment bank; 50.4% stake owned by Gulf Finance House BSC; Chair. HISHAM AL-RAYES; CEO MOHAMED AHMED BUHAJEEH (acting).

Gulf Finance House BSC: POB 10006, Bahrain Financial Harbour, Manama; tel. 17538538; fax 17540006; e-mail info@gfh.com; internet gfh.com; f. 1999 as Gulf Finance House EC, name changed as present 2004; Chair. Sheikh GHAZI AL-HAJERI; CEO HISHAM AHMAD AL-RAYES.

Ibdar Capital BSC: POB 1001, 6th floor, Al Zaml Bldg, Al Khalifa Ave, Manama; tel. 17510000; fax 17510051; e-mail info@ibdar.com; internet ibdarcapital.com; f. 2013 by merger of Capital Management House, Capinvest and Elaf Bank; Islamic investment bank; 30.1% stake owned by Kuwait Finance House; Chair. MOHAMMAD AL-HAJERI; CEO AHMED MOSTAFA.

INVESTCORP Bank BSC: POB 5340, Investcorp House, Manama; tel. 17532000; fax 17530816; e-mail investcorp.bahrain@investcorp.com; internet www.investcorp.com; f. 1982 as Arabian Investment Banking Corpn (Investcorp) EC, present name adopted 1990; Chair. MUHAMMAD ALARDHI; Co-CEOs RISHI KAPOOR, HAZEM BEN-GACEM.

Nomura International PLC: POB 26893, BMB Centre, 7th Floor, Diplomatic Area, Manama; tel. 17530531; fax 17530365; internet www.nomuraholdings.com; f. 1982; Regional CEO, EMEA JONATHAN LEWIS.

United Gulf Bank BSC: POB 5964, UGB Tower, Diplomatic Area, Manama; tel. 17533233; fax 17533137; e-mail info@ugbbah.com; internet www.ugbbah.com; f. 1980; Chair. MASAUD M. J. HAYAT; CEO HUSSAIN A. LALANI.

Venture Capital Bank BSC: POB 11755, Bldg 247, Rd 1704, Blk 317, Diplomatic Area, Manama; tel. 17518888; e-mail info@vc-bank.com; internet www.vc-bank.com; f. 2005; Islamic investment bank; Chair. ABDULFATAH MUHAMMAD RAFIE MARAFIE; CEO ROBERT C. WAGES.

Other investment banks operating in Bahrain include Al-Amin Bank, Amex (Middle East) EC, Capital Union EC, Daiwa Securities SMBC Europe Ltd (Middle East), Global Banking Corpn BSC, Investors Bank EC, Al-Khaleej Islamic Investment Bank (BSC) EC and Merrill Lynch Int. Bank Ltd.

STOCK EXCHANGE

Bahrain Bourse: POB 3203, Manama; tel. 17261260; fax 17256362; e-mail info@bahrainbourse.com.bh; internet www.bahrainbourse.com; f. 1989; scheduled for privatization; 41 listed cos at Dec. 2022; Chair. ABDULKARIM AHMED BUCHEERY; CEO Sheikh KHALIFA BIN EBRAHIM AL KHALIFA.

INSURANCE

In 2020 there were 22 locally incorporated insurance firms and 11 foreign-owned companies operating in Bahrain. The principal local firms include:

Arab Insurance Group BSC (ARIG): POB 26992, Arig House, Bldg 131, Rd 1702, Diplomatic Area 317, Manama; tel. 17544444; fax 17531155; e-mail info@arig.com.bh; internet www.arig.net; f. 1980; owned by Govts of Kuwait, Libya and the UAE (49.5%), and other shareholders; reinsurance and insurance; Chair. SAEED MOHAMMED AL-BAHHAR; CEO SAMUEL VERGHESE (acting).

Bahrain Kuwait Insurance Co BSC (gigBahrain): BKIC Tower 2775, Rd 2835, Blk 428, al-Seef District; tel. 80008777; fax 17921111; e-mail info@gig.com.bh; internet www.gigbh.com; f. 1975; 56.1% owned by Gulf Insurance Group (Kuwait); CEO Dr ABDULLA SULTAN.

Bahrain National Holding Co BSC (BNH): POB 843, BNH Tower, 9th Floor, al-Seef District, Manama; tel. 17587300; fax 17583099; e-mail bnh@bnhgroup.com; internet www.bnhgroup.com; f. 1999 by merger of Bahrain Insurance Co and Nat. Insurance Co; all classes incl. life insurance; Chair. FAROUK YOUSIF AL-MOAYYED; Chief Exec. SAMEER AL-WAZZAN.

Gulf Union Insurance and Reinsurance Co: POB 10949, Bldg 331, Rd 5616, Blk 356, Sheikh Salman Hwy, Manama; tel. 17255292; fax 17255090; e-mail info@gulfunion.com.bh; internet www.gulfunion.com.bh; Chair. ABDULAZIZ AL-TURKI; CEO WALEED MAHMOOD.

Solidarity General Takaful BSC: POB 5282, Seef Tower, al-Seef District, Manama; tel. 17130000; fax 17585200; e-mail mail@solidarity.com.bh; internet www.solidarity.com.bh; f. 2004 by Qatar Islamic Bank; Chair. TAWFEEQ SHEHAB; Gen. Man. JAWAD MOHAMMED.

Takaful International Co: POB 3230, Bldg 680 Rd 2811, al-Seef District 428, Manama; tel. 17565656; e-mail takaful@gigtakaful.bh; internet www.gigtakaful.bh; f. 1989 as Bahrain Islamic Insurance Co; restructured and renamed as above 1998; subsidiary of Gulf Insurance Group (Kuwait); Chair. EBRAHIM MOHAMED AL-RAYES; CEO ESSAM M. AL-ANSARI.

Insurance Association

Bahrain Insurance Association (BIA): POB 2851, Office 901, Amani Tower, 6th Floor, Blk 436, Rd 3620, Bldg 964, al-Seef District, Manama; tel. 17532555; fax 17536006; e-mail info@bia-bh.com; internet www.bia-bh.com; f. 1993; 50 mems; Chair. JAWAD MOHAMMED.

Trade and Industry

GOVERNMENT AGENCIES

Economic Development Board (EDB): POB 11299, Manama; tel. 17589999; fax 17589900; e-mail investorenquiries@bahrainedb.com; internet www.bahrainedb.com; f. 2000; assumed duties of Bahrain Promotions and Marketing Board (f. 1993) and Supreme Council for Economic Devt (f. 2000) 2001; provides national focus for Bahraini marketing initiatives; attracts inward investment; encourages devt and expansion of Bahraini exports; Chair. Crown Prince Sheikh SALMAN BIN HAMAD AL KHALIFA (Prime Minister); CEO KHALID IBRAHIM HUMAIDAN.

National Space Science Agency (NSSA): POB 5115, Bldg 702, 2nd Floor, Rd 1510, Blk 115, Hidd; tel. 17558811; fax 17337976; e-mail nssa@nssa.gov.bh; internet www.nssa.gov.bh; f. 2019; Chair. MOHAMMED BIN THAMER AL-KAABI; CEO Dr MOHAMED E. AL-ASEERI.

Sustainable Energy Authority (SEA): POB 60005, Bahrain Financial Harbour, W Tower, 38th Floor, Manama; tel. 17799950; fax 17799960; e-mail inquiry@sea.gov.bh; internet sea.gov.bh; f. 2014; aims to promote renewable energy technologies and energy efficiency practices in Bahrain; Pres. Dr ABDUL HUSSAIN BIN ALI MIRZA.

DEVELOPMENT ORGANIZATION

Bahrain Mumtalakat Holding Co (Mumtalakat): Arcapita Bldg, 4th Floor, Bldg No. 551, Rd 4612, Sea Front 346, Bahrain Bay, Manama; POB 820, Manama; tel. 17561111; fax 17561109; e-mail contactus@mumtalakat.bh; internet www.mumtalakat.bh; f. 2006; investment holding co; manages state non-hydrocarbons assets; Chair. Sheikh SALMAN BIN KHALIFA AL KHALIFA (Minister of Finance and National Economy); CEO Sheikh ABDULLA BIN KHALIFA AL KHALIFA.

CHAMBER OF COMMERCE

Bahrain Chamber of Commerce and Industry (BCCI): Manama; internet www.bahrainchamber.bh; f. 1939; Chair. SAMEER ABDULLA AHMED NASS; CEO Dr ABDULLAH BADER AL-SADA (acting).

STATE HYDROCARBONS COMPANIES

Bahrain National Gas Co BSC (BANAGAS): POB 29099, Rifa'a; tel. 17756222; fax 17756991; e-mail bng@banagas.com.bh; internet www.banagas.com.bh; f. 1979; responsible for extraction, processing and sale of hydrocarbon liquids from associated gas derived from onshore Bahraini fields; 75% owned by Govt of Bahrain, 12.5% by Chevron and 12.5% by Boubyan Petrochemical Co; produces approx. 6,300 barrels per day (b/d) of propane, 5,800 b/d of butane and 8,600 b/d of naphtha (2022); Chair. MARK THOMAS; Chief Exec. Dr Sheikh MOHAMED BIN KHALIFA AL KHALIFA.

Bahrain Petroleum Co BSC (BAPCO): POB 25555, Awali; tel. 17704040; fax 17704070; e-mail enquiries@bapcobmp.com; internet www.bapco.net; f. 1999 by merger of Bahrain Nat. Oil Co (f. 1976) and Bahrain Petroleum Co (f. 1980); 100% govt-owned; fully integrated co responsible for exploration, drilling and production of oil and gas; supply of gas to power-generating plants and industries; refining crude petroleum; international marketing of crude petroleum and refined petroleum products; supply and sale of aviation fuel at Bahrain International Airport; and local distribution and marketing of petroleum products; Chair. ABDULLA JEHAD AL-ZAIN; CEO ABDULRAHMAN JAWAHERY.

Gulf Petrochemical Industries Co BSC (GPIC): POB 26730, Manama; tel. 17731777; fax 17731047; e-mail gpic@gpic.com; internet www.gpic.com; f. 1979 as jt venture between the Govts of Bahrain, Kuwait and Saudi Arabia, each with one-third equity participation; a petrochemical complex at Sitra, inaugurated 1981; produces 1,200 metric tons of both methanol and ammonia per day; Chair. Eng. KAMAL BIN AHMED MOHAMMED; Pres. YASSER A. RAHIM AL-ABBASI.

UTILITIES

Electricity and Water Authority: POB 2, Manama; tel. 17999111; e-mail customercare-ewa@ewa.bh; internet www.ewa.bh; f. 2007; privatization of electricity production was approved December 2003; Pres. Sheikh KAMAL BIN AHMED MOHAMMED.

MAJOR COMPANIES

Aluminium Bahrain BSC (Alba): POB 570, Manama; tel. 17830000; fax 17830083; e-mail info@alba.com.bh; internet www.albasmelter.com; f. 1971; operates a smelter owned by the Bahrain Mumtalakat Holding Co (69.38%), Saudi Public Investment Fund (20.38%); production 1.56m. metric tons (2021); Chair. Sheikh DAIJ BIN SALMAN AL KHALIFA; CEO ALI AL-BAQALI; 3,100 employees (2021).

Awal Dairy Co WLL: POB 601, Rd 55, Blk 463, al-Hajar; tel. 17598598; fax 17591150; e-mail business@awaldairy.com; internet www.awaldairy.com; f. 1963 as Bahrain Danish Dairy Co WLL; current name adopted in 2006; 51% owned by Gen. Trading and Food Processing Co BSC; processing, packaging and distribution of milk, ice cream and fruit juice.

Bahrain Aluminium Extrusion Co BSC (BALEXCO): POB 1053, Manama; tel. 17730073; fax 17736924; e-mail blxsales@balexco.com.bh; internet www.balexco.com.bh; f. 1977; supplies aluminium profiles in mill finish, powder coated and anodized; capacity 32,000 metric tons per year; Chair. JASSIM MOHAMED SEYADI.

General Trading and Food Processing Co BSC (TRAFCO): POB 20202, Manama; tel. 17729000; fax 17727380; e-mail info@trafco.com; internet www.trafco.com; f. 1977; importation and distribution of food products; subsidiaries include Awal Dairy Co WLL, Kuwait Bahrain Dairy Co WLL, Trafco Logistics Co WLL, Bahrain Fresh Fruits Co WLL, Bahrain Water Bottling and Beverages Co WLL; Chair. IBRAHIM MOHAMED ALI ZAINAL; Group CEO AZZAM MOUTRAGI.

Gulf Aluminium Rolling Mill Co BSC (GARMCO): POB 20725, North Sitra Industrial Area, Manama; tel. 17731000; internet www.garmco.com; f. 1981 as a jt venture between the Govts of Bahrain, Saudi Arabia, Kuwait, Iraq, Oman and Qatar; annual production capacity of 165,000 metric tons; Chair. ARIF RAHIMI; CEO MOHAMED RAFEA; 597 employees (2022).

Al-Khajah Establishment and Factories: POB 5042, Manama; tel. 17730811; e-mail alkhajah@alkhajahfactory.com; internet www.alkhajahfactory.com; f. 1972; contracting, trading and manufacture of switchgear and light fittings; numerous subsidiaries within the Gulf; Gen. Man. ESAM AL-KHAJAH.

Maskati Bros and Co BSC: POB 24, 321 Delmon House, Rd 1506, Bahrain International Investment Park, Hidd 115, Manama; tel. 17464646; fax 17464600; e-mail info@maskatibros.com; internet www.maskatibros.com; f. 1956; paper converters, polyethylene manufacture, injection moulders.

Midal Cables Ltd: POB 5939, Bldg 744, Rd 5128, Blk 951, Askar; tel. 17832832; fax 17832932; e-mail midalcbl@midalcable.com; internet www.midalcable.com; f. 1977; manufacture of aluminium and aluminium alloy electrical and mechanical rods and conductors for overhead transmission and distribution lines; Chair. KHALID RASHID AL-ZAYANI; Man. Dir HAMID AL-ZAYANI; CEO KERSI MASTER.

Nass Group: POB 669, Manama; tel. 17725522; e-mail nassbah@batelco.com.bh; internet www.nassgroup.com; f. 1963; construction and associated industries, incl. manufacturing, marine transport, offshore engineering and ship repair; 58 subsidiary cos, incl. Nass Corpn BSC, Nass Int. Trading and Gulf Devt Corpn; 32 associated cos; affiliated offices in Kuwait, Qatar, Saudi Arabia and the United Arab Emirates; Chair. SAMEER ABDULLA NASS; Man. Dir SAMI ABDULLA NASS.

Shaheen Group: Bldg 285, Rd 4306, 343 Manama; tel. 17814646; e-mail info@shaheengroup.com; internet www.shaheengroup.com; f. 1958 as AWALCO Group; 4 subsidiary cos: Awal Products (heating and ventilation), Gulf Services (security and safety), Gypsum Products (manufacture and installation of gypsum products), Shaheen Electromechanical (after-sales services); Chair. and CEO SAGER SHAHEEN.

TRADE UNIONS

In November 2002 legislation was ratified to permit the establishment of independent trade unions. The law established the General Federation of Bahrain Trade Unions (GBFTU) and allowed the formation of one trade union per company. In July 2012 the Bahrain Labour Union Free Federation (now Bahrain Free Labour Unions Federation) was founded, following an amendment to the Workers Trade Union Law to permit the formation of more than one federation. According to the Bahrain Center for Human Rights, there were more than 70 trade unions operating in Bahrain in 2021.

Bahrain Free Labour Unions Federation: POB 32806, Villa 3776, Rd 915, Blk 809, Isa, Manama; tel. 17226522; fax 17226422; e-mail bflufbh@bflufbh.com; internet www.bflufbh.com; f. 2012; established as Bahrain Labour Union Free Federation; Chair. YAQOOB MUHAMMAD YOUSIF.

General Federation of Bahrain Trade Unions (GFBTU): POB 26805, Manama; tel. 17727333; fax 17729599; e-mail gcbw@batelco.com.bh; internet www.gfbtu.org; f. 2002 under the Workers Trade Union Law; Sec.-Gen. ABDULQADER AL-SHEHABI.

Transport

RAILWAYS

There are currently no railways in Bahrain. In 2011 a detailed feasibility study was initiated into plans for a 184-km domestic rail network, to be constructed in three phases by 2030. The Bahraini project was to form part of a planned regional rail network, connecting Bahrain with the other member countries of the Cooperation Council for the Arab States of the Gulf (or Gulf Cooperation Council—GCC).

In October 2021 the Government approved the commencement of work on phase one of a planned, US $2,000m. four-line 109-km light rail network. The contract for the construction of the first phase (comprising two lines with a total track length of nearly 29 km and 20 stations) was awarded to the Delhi Metro Rail Corpn in February 2023.

ROADS

The King Fahd Causeway, a 25-km causeway link with Saudi Arabia, was opened in 1986. A three-lane dual carriageway links the causeway to Manama. Other causeways link Bahrain with Muharraq island and with Sitra island. In October 2019 a consultancy contract was awarded for the construction of a second, 25-km causeway, which was to carry both motor vehicles and trains and which was to be named after King Hamad. It was estimated that the new causeway, which would form part of the planned GCC rail network, would cost some US $3,500m.

The Strategic Roads Masterplan 2021, launched by the Ministry of Works in 2005, outlined plans for the modernization of Bahrain's road network in anticipation of significant increases in road traffic volume. The planned construction of a 40-km road/rail causeway linking Askar in eastern Bahrain with Ras Ishairij in Qatar (the Qatar Bahrain Friendship Bridge) was approved in 2004; when completed, the causeway would be the longest fixed causeway in the world. The project was to be supervised and funded by a joint committee established in 2005 by the Governments of the two countries. However, as a result of various issues including financial problems and diplomatic disputes between Bahrain and Qatar, the project suffered serious delays and as of August 2023 construction work had not yet commenced.

SHIPPING

In 1999 work began on the construction of a new port and industrial zone at Hidd, on Muharraq island. Incorporating the Bahrain Gateway Terminal, the new port, Khalifa bin Salman, which became operational in 2009, has an annual handling capacity of 1.1m. 20-foot equivalent units (TEUs). The port is managed and operated by APM Terminals Bahrain, under the terms of a 25-year contract effective from 2009.

Port and Regulatory Authorities

APM Terminals Bahrain BSC: PO Box 50490, Khalifa bin Salman Port, Hidd; tel. 17365500; fax 17365505; e-mail combah@apmterminals.com; internet www.apmterminals.com/en/operations/africa-middle-east/bahrain; f. 2006; 64% owned by APM Terminals BV, 16% by Yusuf bin Ahmad Kanoo Holdings; management and operation of Bahrain's commercial port; Man. Dir MAUREEN BANNERMAN.

General Organization of Sea Ports: POB 75315, Manama; tel. 17359595; fax 17359558; e-mail info@gop.gov.bh; responsible for regulation, devt and promotion of maritime and logistics zones; Chair. Sheikh DAIJ BIN SALMAN BIN DAIJ AL KHALIFA; Dir-Gen. HASSAN ALI AL-MAJID.

Principal Shipping Companies

Alsharif Group WLL: Bldg 1315A, Rd 114, Block 101, Hidd; tel. 17911321; fax 17515051; e-mail alsharif@batelco.com.bh; internet www.alsharifbahrain.com; f. 1957; shipping agency; Pres. and CEO KHALID AL-SHARIF.

Arab Shipbuilding and Repair Yard Co (ASRY): POB 50110, Hidd; tel. 17671111; fax 17670236; e-mail info@asry.net; internet www.asry.net; f. 1974 by OAPEC mems; 500,000-metric-ton dry dock opened 1977; 2 floating docks in operation since 1992; new twin slipway completed 2008; Chair. YOUSSEF ISSA BUBASHIT; Man. Dir MAZEN MATAR.

Al-Jazeera Shipping Co WLL: POB 302, Mina Salman Industrial Area, Manama; tel. 17728837; fax 17728217; e-mail almelaha@ajsco.com; internet ajsco.com; operates a fleet of tugboats and barges; Man. Dir ALI HASSAN MAHMOUD.

UCO Marine Contracting WLL: POB 1074, Bldg 840, Rd 115, Block 601, Manama; tel. 17730816; fax 17732131; e-mail admin@ucomarine.biz; internet ucomarine.co; owns and operates a fleet of bulk carriers, tugboats, barges and dredgers; Man. Dir ALI AL-MUSALAM.

CIVIL AVIATION

Following the completion in January 2021 of the expansion of the terminal building at Bahrain International Airport (BIA), the airport's total capacity was increased to 14m. passengers per year. A terminal for private jet passengers was inaugurated at BIA in October.

Bahrain Airport Co (BAC): Bldg 212, al-Muharraq; internet www.bahrainairport.com; f. 2008; manages operations and devt of Bahrain International Airport; Chair. MOHAMMED BIN THAMER AL-KAABI (Minister of Transportation and Telecommunications); CEO MOHAMED YOUSIF AL-BINFALAH.

Civil Aviation Affairs (CAA): POB 586, Manama; tel. 17337878; e-mail andinfo@caa.gov.bh; internet mtt.gov.bh/directorates/civil-aviation; part of the Ministry of Transportation and Telecommunications.

Gulf Air: POB 138, Manama; tel. 17373737; internet www.gulfair.com; f. 1950 as Gulf Aviation Co; name changed 1974; wholly owned by the Govt of Bahrain; services to the Middle East, South-East Asia, the Far East, Australia, Africa and Europe; Chair. ZAYED BIN RASHID AL-ZAYANI; CEO Capt. WALEED ABDULHAMEED AL-ALAWI.

Tourism

Bahrain Tourism Co (BTC): POB 5831, Manama; tel. 17530530; fax 17530867; e-mail btc@alseyaha.com; internet www.alseyaha.com; f. 1974; Chair. HAMED MOHAMMED AL-AWADHI; Gen. Man. ABDULLA AL-AWADHI.

Bahrain Tourism and Exhibitions Authority (BTEA): Bldg 158, Ave 28, Sanabis, Block 410, POB 11644, Manama; tel. 17558800; e-mail info@btea.bh; internet www.btea.bh; f. 2015; Chair. FATIMA BINT JAFFER AL-SAIRAFI (Minister of Tourism); CEO Dr NASSER ALI QAEDI.

Defence

As assessed at November 2022, the Bahrain Defence Force had an estimated total strength of 8,200: army 6,000; navy 700; air force 1,500. There were also an estimated 11,260 paramilitary forces (police 9,000; national guard est. 2,000; coastguard est. 260). Military service is voluntary. The United Kingdom maintained a naval base in Bahrain and had 1,000 navy personnel in the country. A total of 4,700 US navy personnel were also stationed in Bahrain.

Defence Budget: BD 526m. in 2022.

Supreme Commander of the Bahrain Defence Force: HM Sheikh HAMAD BIN ISA AL KHALIFA.

Commander-in-Chief of the Bahrain Defence Force: Field Marshal Sheikh KHALIFA BIN AHMAD AL KHALIFA.

Chief of Staff of the Bahrain Defence Force: Lt-Gen. DHIAB BIN SAQR AL-NUAIMI.

Commander of the Royal Bahraini Navy: Rear-Adm. MOHAMMED IBRAHIM AL-BINALI.

Commander of the Royal Bahraini Air Force: Vice-Marshal Sheikh HAMAD BIN ABDULLAH AL KHALIFA.

Education

Basic education (between the ages of six and 14 years) is compulsory and is provided free of charge in government schools, although private establishments are also available. Basic education is divided into two levels: children attend primary school from six to 11 years of age and intermediate school from 12 to 14. Secondary education, beginning at the age of 15, lasts for three years; students choose to follow a general (science or literary), commercial, technical or vocational curriculum. According to UNESCO, enrolment at pre-primary schools in 2019/20 was equivalent to 52.6% of children (boys 49.9%; girls 55.7%) in the relevant age-group, while enrolment at primary schools in 2018/19 was 97.7% of children (boys 98.1%; girls 97.2%) in the relevant age-group. In 2018/19 enrolment at lower secondary schools included 96.3% of children (boys 93.0%; girls 99.9%) in the relevant age-group, while the comparable figure for upper secondary schools was 87.3% of children (boys 81.9%; girls 93.7%) in the relevant age-group. In 2022 recurrent expenditure by the Ministry of Education was equivalent to 9.3% of total government recurrent expenditure.

The University of Bahrain, established by Amiri decree in 1986, comprises nine Colleges: of Engineering, Arts, Science, Information Technology, Law, Applied Studies, Business Administration, Health and Sports Sciences, and Bahrain Teachers College. Higher education is also provided by the Arabian Gulf University (AGU), funded by seven Arab governments. The AGU comprises the College of Medicine and Medical Science, and the College of Graduate Studies. The Medical University of Bahrain, a constituent university of the Royal College of Surgeons in Ireland, was founded in 2004.

Bibliography

Abd Allah Abd al-Rahman, Yatim. *Bahrain, Society and Culture, Anthropological Studies*. Beirut, Arab Institute for Research and Publishing, 2016.

Abu-Hakima, Ahmad Mustafa. *History of Eastern Arabia 1750–1800: The Rise and Development of Bahrain, Kuwait and Wahhabi Saudi Arabia*. London, Probsthain, 1965.

Adamiyat, Fereydoun. *Bahrain Islands: A Legal and Diplomatic Study of the British-Iranian Controversy*. New York, Praeger, 1955.

Al-Arayed, Jawad Salim. *A Line in the Sea: The Qatar Versus Bahrain Border Dispute in the World Court*. Berkeley, CA, North Atlantic Books, 2003.

Al-Hassan, Omar, and Sincock, Peter. *Iranian Interference in Bahrain's Internal Affairs: Official and Semi-official Declarations from February 14, 2011 until December 31, 2015*. 2nd edn, London, Gulf Centre for Strategic Studies, 2016.

Alkooheji, Lamya, and Sinha, Chitra. *Discourse and Identity Formation: Parliamentary Debates in Bahrain*. Amsterdam, John Benjamins Publishing Co, 2017.

AlShehabi, Omar H. *Contested Modernity: Sectarianism, Nationalism, and Colonialism in Bahrain*. London, Oneworld, 2019.

Al-Tajir, M. A. *Bahrain 1920-1945: Britain, The Shaikh and the Administration*. Abingdon, Routledge, 2023.

Andersen, Lars Erslev. *Bahrain and the Global Balance of Power After the Arab Spring*. Copenhagen, Danish Institute for International Studies, 2012.

Brown, Rajeswary Ampalavanar. *Islam and Capitalism in the Making of Modern Bahrain*. Oxford, Oxford University Press, 2023.

Burton, Paul, and Hassan, Omar. *Bahrain and its Development Philosophy*. London, Gulf Centre for Strategic Studies, 1998.

Clarke, Angela. *Bahrain: Oil and Development, 1929–1989*. London, Immel, 1998.

Coates Ulrichsen, Kristian. *Bahrain's Aborted Revolution*, May 2012, www.lse.ac.uk/IDEAS/publications/reports/pdf/SR011/FINAL_LSE_IDEAS__BahrainsAbortedRevolution_Ulrichsen.pdf.

Dabrowska, Karen. *Bahrain Briefing: The Struggle for Democracy*. London, Colourmast, 1997.

Farah, Talal T. *Protection and Politics in Bahrain, 1869–1915*. Beirut, American University of Beirut, 1985.

Gengler, Justin. *Group Conflict and Political Mobilization in Bahrain and the Arab Gulf: Rethinking the Rentier State*. Bloomington, IN, Indiana University Press, 2015.

Al-Ghatam, Dr Mohammed, and Galal, Dr Mohammed Nomal. *A Strategic Outlook on Bahrain and the Arab Region in an International Context (No. 3)*. Manama, Bahrain Centre for Studies and Research, 2006.

Hamad bin Isa Al Khalifa, Sheikh. *First Light: Modern Bahrain and its Heritage*. London, Kegan Paul International, 1995.

Hassan, Omar. *Border Dispute Between Bahrain and Qatar and the Challenges of Gulf Co-operation*. London, Gulf Centre for Strategic Studies, 1997.

Insoll, Timothy R. *The Land of Enki in the Islamic Era: Pearls, Palms, and Religious Identity in Bahrain*. New York, Columbia University Press, 2004.

Jones, Marc Owen. *Political Repression in Bahrain*. Cambridge, Cambridge University Press, 2020.

Joyce, Miriam. *Bahrain from the Twentieth Century to the Arab Spring*. New York, Palgrave Macmillan, 2012.

Kinninmont, Jane. *Bahrain: Beyond the Impasse*. London, Royal Institute of International Affairs (Chatham House), 2012.

Lahn, Glada. *Democratic Transition in Bahrain: A Model for the Arab World*. London, Gulf Centre for Strategic Studies, 2004.

Lawson, Fred H. *The Modernization of Autocracy*. Abingdon, Routledge, 2022.

Matthiesen, Toby. *Sectarian Gulf: Bahrain, Saudi Arabia, and the Arab Spring that Wasn't*. Stanford, CA, Stanford Briefs, 2013.

Mohammed, Nadeya Sayed Ali. *Population and Development of the Arab Gulf States: The Case of Bahrain, Oman and Kuwait*. Aldershot, Ashgate Publishing, 2003.

Mojtahedzadeh, Pirouz. *Security and Territoriality in the Persian Gulf: A Maritime Political Geography*. Richmond, Curzon Press, 1999.

Nakhleh, Emile A. *Bahrain: Political Development in a Modernizing Society* (2nd edn). Lexington, MA, Lexington Books, 2011.

Routine Abuse, Routine Denial: Civil Rights and the Political Crisis in Bahrain. New York, Human Rights Watch, 1997.

Niethammer, Katja. *Political Reform in Bahrain: Institutional Transformation, Identity Conflict and Democracy*. Abingdon, Routledge, 2014.

Payne, Anna, and Steele, Katie (Eds). *Foreign Policy in Bahrain*. London, Gulf Centre for Strategic Studies, 2004.

al-Rumaihi, Mohammed. *Bahrain: Social and Political Change since the First World War*. Durham Univ., Bowker, in association with the Centre for Middle Eastern and Islamic Studies, 1977.

Shehabi, Ala'a, and Jones, Marc Owen (Eds). *Bahrain's Uprising: Resistance and Repression in the Gulf*. London, Zed Books, 2015.

Terterov, Marat, and Shoult, Anthony (Eds). *Doing Business with Bahrain*. London, GMB Publishing, revised edn, 2005.

Wehrey, Frederic. *The Precarious Ally: Bahrain's Impasse and U.S. Policy*, Carnegie Endowment for International Peace, February 2013, carnegieendowment.org/files/bahrain_impasse.pdf.

Wheatcroft, Andrew. *The Life and Times of Sheikh Salman bin Hamad Al Khalifa: Ruler of Bahrain 1942–61*. London, Kegan Paul International, 1995.

Winkler, David F. *Amirs, Admirals and Desert Sailors: Bahrain, the U.S. Navy and the Arabian Gulf*. Annapolis, MD, Naval Institute Press, 2007.

Worthington, Joe. *British Diplomacy in Oman and Bahrain: 50 Years of Change*. Abingdon, Routledge, 2022.

Yanai, Shaul. *The Political Transformation of Gulf Tribal States: Elitism and the Social Contract in Kuwait, Bahrain and Dubai, 1918–1970s*. Eastbourne, Sussex Academic Press, 2015.

CYPRUS

Geography

The island of Cyprus, with an area of 9,251 sq km (3,572 sq miles), is situated in the north-eastern corner of the Mediterranean Sea, closest to Türkiye (which was known as Turkey prior to June 2022, and which is easily visible from Cyprus's northern coast), but also less than 160 km (100 miles) from the Syrian coast. Its greatest length (including the long, narrow peninsula of Cape Andreas) is 225 km. The island has been divided since 1974 into separately Greek Cypriot- and Turkish Cypriot-administered areas by a demilitarized zone monitored by the United Nations (UN), which extends for more than 180 km across the island. The two-thirds of the island to the south of the UN zone constitute the Republic of Cyprus, which is recognized internationally as the legitimate authority for the whole island. The Turkish-occupied areas to the north of the UN zone form the de facto 'Turkish Republic of Northern Cyprus' ('TRNC'), which is recognized only by Türkiye.

PHYSICAL FEATURES

Cyprus owes its peculiar shape to the occurrence of two ridges that were once part of two much greater arcs running from the mainland of Asia westwards towards Crete. The greater part of these arcs has disappeared, but remnants are found in Cyprus and on the eastern mainland, where they form the Amanus range of Türkiye. In Cyprus the arcs are visible as two mountain systems—the Kyrenia range of the north, and the much larger and imposing Troödos massif in the centre. Between the two mountain systems lies a flat lowland, open to the sea in the east and west and spoken of as the Mesaoria. Here also lies the chief town, Nicosia (Lefkoşa in Turkish).

The mountain ranges are actually very different in structure and appearance. The Kyrenia range is a single narrow fold of limestone, with occasional deposits of marble, and its maximum height is 900 m. As it is mainly porous rock, rainfall soon seeps below ground, and so its appearance is rather arid, but picturesque, with white crags and isolated pinnacles. The soil cover is thin. The Troödos, on the other hand, has been affected by folding in two separate directions, so that the whole area has been fragmented, and large quantities of molten igneous rock have forced their way to the surface from the interior of the earth, giving rise to a great dome that reaches 1,800 m above sea level. As it is impervious to water, there are some surface streams, rounder outlines, a thicker soil, especially on the lower slopes, and a covering of pine forest.

CLIMATE

The climate in Cyprus is strongly Mediterranean in character, with the usual hot dry summers and warm, wet winters. As an island with high mountains, Cyprus receives a fair amount of moisture, and up to 1,000 mm of rain falls in the mountains, with a minimum of 300 mm–380 mm in the Mesaoria. Frost does not occur on the coast, but may be sharp in the higher districts, and snow can fall fairly heavily in regions over 900 m in altitude. In summer, despite the proximity of the sea, temperatures are surprisingly high, and the Mesaoria, in particular, can experience over 38°C (100°F). There is a tendency for small depressions to form over the island in winter, giving a slightly greater degree of changeability in weather than is experienced elsewhere in the Middle East.

In 2020, according to the World Bank, 11.1% of the total land area of Cyprus was under cultivation—a figure higher than that for quite a number of Middle Eastern countries. This can partly be explained by the relatively abundant rainfall, the expanses of impervious rock that retain water near the surface, and the presence of rich soils derived from volcanic rocks which occur around the Troödos massif. The export markets in wine and early vegetables add to the incentives to development.

POPULATION

The census of 1 October 1982, which was held only in Greek Cypriot areas, but included an estimate for the Turkish-occupied region, recorded a total population of 642,731. At the census of October 2011, the population of the Republic of Cyprus was recorded at 840,407 (excluding the Turkish-occupied region). This figure had risen to 918,100, according to preliminary figures, by the time of the census of October 2021, giving a population density of 155.7 people per sq km in the government-controlled area. The 'TRNC' had a population of 390,745 at 31 December 2021, according to official projections. Nicosia (Lefkoşa) is the capital of both the Republic of Cyprus and the 'TRNC'. The Greek Cypriot-administered part of the city had a population of 256,400 at December 2019, according to official estimates. The section of the city in the 'TRNC' had a population of 61,378, according to that territory's 2011 census.

History

ANDREAS STERGIOU

HISTORICAL BACKGROUND UNTIL 1974

Owing to its pivotal position at the crossroads of three continents—a 'staging post' for the Middle East, according to Henry Kissinger (US Secretary of State in 1973–77)—and its importance for the control of the Eastern Mediterranean, Cyprus came under the rule of many external powers throughout its long history: the Romans, the French dynasty of the Lusignans, the Venetians, the Ottomans and lastly the British. In 1925 Cyprus was proclaimed a British Crown Colony.

The arrival of the British gave a new impetus to the desire for self-determination, namely, in that period the unification of Cyprus with the Greek motherland, (*Enosis*). Later, after the proclamation of independence in 1960, the notion of 'self-determination' referred rather to a desire for sovereignty. Throughout the period of British rule, each time that Greek Cypriots petitioned or agitated for *Enosis*, the British encouraged Turkish Cypriot opposition to counter pro-Greek agitation. Omnipresent guard of the national ideology and main agitator for *Enosis* was the Greek Orthodox Church. Headed in Cyprus by Archbishop Makarios III, the Church started a relentless campaign to internationalize the Cyprus question and force the United Kingdom to accept *Enosis*. The UK's categorical refusal to consider an independent Cyprus or to cede the island to Greece created an unbridgeable rift between the Greek Cypriots and the UK, which developed into a full-scale armed revolt against colonial rule from 1955 until 1959.

As the UK came under increasing international pressure over Cyprus, it tried in various ways to draw international attention, and above all that of Turkey (officially known as Türkiye since June 2022, but, for the sake of clarity, referred to as Turkey throughout this essay), to the 'threatened rights of the Turkish minority'. The UK followed the same divisive course on the internal front. Between 1955 and 1959 the Greek Cypriot armed revolt took place, led by the underground movement, the Ethniki Organosis Kyprion Agoniston (EOKA—National Organization of Cypriot Combatants), under the command of Cypriot-born, former Colonel of the Greek Army Georgios Grivas, and Makarios as its clandestine political leader. EOKA's chief aim was to harass British military personnel and undermine the UK's hold on the island. In order to confront these armed fighters, the British recruited almost exclusively Turkish Cypriots into the police force, while encouraging the formation of their own paramilitary movement, which became known as the Türk Mukavemet Teşkilatı (Turkish Resistance Organization). Turkish staff officers took over military command of this organization and Turkish Cypriot Rauf Denktaş assumed its political leadership. In 1958 communal violence erupted when the Turkish Cypriot and Greek Cypriot paramilitary organizations began to clash with each other and terrorize minorities in mixed villages.

It was amid this upheaval, in February 1959 in Zürich, Switzerland, that the motherlands, Greece and Turkey, agreed to establish an independent Cyprus. A few days later, the Zürich Agreements were endorsed by the UK during the London Conference, at which representatives of the two Cypriot communities were invited to sign the Agreements, although neither had been offered the opportunity to participate in the negotiations that produced them. The Agreements provided for the establishment of a Cypriot state, whose independence, constitutional order and territorial integrity were guaranteed by the UK, Greece and Turkey. The arduous independence process formally came to an end on 16 August 1960, when the Treaty of Establishment and the Treaty of Guarantee were signed by Cyprus, Greece, Turkey and the UK, and the Treaty of Alliance was signed by Cyprus, Greece and Turkey, in the Cypriot capital, Nicosia, formally creating the Republic of Cyprus. Makarios took office as the first President of the Republic, having been elected to the post in December 1959. The Treaty of Establishment included a clause on Sovereign Base Areas (SBAs—Akrotiri and Dhekelia), which provided for a territory remaining under British sovereign control and granting the UK a variety of rights and facilities such as the use of Cyprus's roads, ports and overflight in Cyprus's airspace. This privileged and *sui generis* status of the SBAs is comparable to the USA's rights in the Panama Canal and the Guantánamo Bay base in Cuba. Unlike Greece and Turkey, Cyprus chose not to join the North Atlantic Treaty Organization (NATO) and to become instead one of the 25 founding members of the Non-Aligned Movement upon its creation at the Belgrade Conference in 1961.

The Constitution of the Republic of Cyprus had a complex and dysfunctional structure. It was tailored to balance power between the Greek and Turkish Cypriot communities in a way that would prevent the numerically much smaller Turkish Cypriot population from being marginalized by the Greek Cypriots. To prevent majority rule, the Turkish Cypriot community was granted veto rights in several domains, including fiscal, defence and foreign policy. Separate majorities in both communities were required for the enactment of certain legislation. Hence, rather than encouraging co-operation between the ethnic communities, it boosted separatist tendencies via the provision of separate municipalities, separate communal chambers and separate electoral rolls. Executive power was divided between the President, who was elected by the Greek Cypriot community, and the Vice-President, who was elected by the Turkish Cypriot community. The criterion of membership to the civil service, security forces and army was also ethnicity (Greek Cypriots 78%, Turkish Cypriots 18%, and Latins, Maronites and Armenians a combined 4%). A House of Representatives of 50 members, also with a seven-to-three ratio, was to be elected separately by communal balloting on a universal suffrage basis. In addition, separate Greek Cypriot and Turkish Cypriot communal chambers were set up to exercise control in matters of religion, culture and education. The legislative veto system caused deadlocks in communal and state politics on many occasions. This complex ethnic system of checks and balances broke down after just three years.

In December 1963 inter-communal violence erupted in Nicosia, soon spilling over to the rest of the island. Hardliners in both communities, bitterly opposed to the Zürich and London Treaties, found a unique opportunity to undermine the Republic. Many Turkish Cypriots withdrew from their posts in order to form their own administration, while others were hindered by radical Greek Cypriots from carrying out their duties. Following the inter-communal violence, the representatives of the Turkish Cypriot community in the House of Representatives resigned, prompting constitutional gridlock. The crisis nearly led to the collapse of the state and resulted in the incapacity of key state organs to operate properly. To ensure the continuous functioning of the state institutions, the Supreme Court of Cyprus ruled that the provisions of a law that would otherwise be unconstitutional could be justified on the 'doctrine of necessity'. Ever since then, and given the fact that the seats allocated to the Turkish Cypriot community in the House of Representatives remain empty, the 'doctrine of necessity' has been recognized by the Supreme Court as a source of law in the constitutional order of Cyprus.

To stop the civil strife and prevent the risk of a Greek–Turkish war, the US Government decided to get involved in Cypriot affairs. In a letter dated June 1964 that was published a short time later in the Turkish press, US President Lyndon Johnson warned Turkish President İsmet İnönü that if Turkey interfered, the USA would no longer support Turkey in the event of an attack by the Union of Soviet Socialist Republics (USSR). Unfortunately, this coincided with Archbishop Makarios's approach to the USSR and his domestic co-operation with the very popular Cypriot communist party, the Anorthotiko Komma Ergazomenou Laou (AKEL—Progressive Party of the Working People), resisting efforts to impose a purely NATO solution. The Cyprus conflict had thus become entangled in the Cold War confrontation.

On 21 April 1967 a coup in Greece brought to power a military junta which was deeply mistrustful of Archbishop Makarios. In November, apparently with the encouragement of the Greek junta, former EOKA leader Grivas and other Greek Cypriot nationalists attacked the Turkish enclave of Kofinou in the Larnaca district of Cyprus, provoking widespread condemnation and an immediate international intervention. The junta was forced to capitulate, recalling Grivas and removing most of its troops from the island. However, in September 1971 Grivas returned secretly to the island, and formed EOKA B, an extremist pro-union paramilitary organization with an overriding objective to organize the resistance against Makarios. Capitalizing on the weakness of the Greek Cypriots, the Turkish Cypriots proclaimed their own provisional administration, and worked systematically towards a final dichotomization of the island. The EOKA of the 1960s and early 1970s, led by Grivas and some Greek junta officers, was not an authentic popular movement as in the 1950s, but, with a pretext of *Enosis*, waged a terrorist campaign against the Makarios Government, and sometimes also the Turkish Cypriot citizens. In March 1970 an assassination attempt was made on Archbishop Makarios, and two years later the so-called 'Bishop's revolt' took place, when senior members of the Orthodox Church sought to remove him from the presidency. In late 1973 Brig.-Gen. Demetrios Ioannides, who was determined to force a Union of Cyprus with Greece as soon as possible, became head of a new military junta in the Greek capital, Athens. In mid-July 1974 he ordered the overthrow of Archbishop President Makarios and his replacement by a puppet regime in Nicosia. Makarios succeeded in fleeing to Paphos, a stronghold of his supporters in the south-west of Cyprus, and subsequently, with the assistance of the British Government, to the UK capital, London. Meanwhile, the new regime in Nicosia proclaimed the establishment of the 'Hellenic Republic of Cyprus'. The installation of Nikos Sampson as President of Cyprus, a fierce critic of the Turkish Cypriot community, was a blatant provocation to the Turkish Government and the Turkish Cypriot community. On 20 July Turkey invaded northern Cyprus in order to resist the puppet regime, and soon occupied the whole of the northern part of the island. On 23 July, finding themselves under enormous pressure, both the military junta in Athens and the regime in Nicosia collapsed, and two days later formal peace talks began in Geneva, Switzerland, between Greece, Turkey and the UK.

In mid-August 1974, and while another round of discussions was being held in Geneva, Turkey surprisingly resumed its offensive in Cyprus, this time extending its occupation over about 37% of the island. Two days later, the UN Security Council recorded 'its formal disapproval of the unilateral military actions undertaken against the Republic of Cyprus'.

The Turkish invasion was accompanied by mass executions of hundreds of civilians and war prisoners, rapes and ill-treatment of captives, and most of the Greek Cypriot inhabitants of the seized territory (approximately 180,000) were forced to flee towards the south. In the southern part of the island, Turkish Cypriots were also exposed to violent reprisals and approximately 50,000 were also forced to flee, either towards the north or to the British military bases. The fear generated by the war facilitated the separation of the communities. For the Turkish Cypriot hardliners who had long pursued a separate Turkish Cypriot territory and government, this state of affairs offered the ideal opportunity to attain what had been hitherto unimaginable. The result was large-scale ethnic cleansing and, when the ceasefire was eventually declared, the island had been partitioned along ethnic lines and 1,600 Greek Cypriots had gone missing. Within a period of 10 years, a 400-year-long peaceful co-existence between the two ethnic Cypriot communities had been destroyed.

To the present day, Türkiye refers to the Turkish invasion as a peace operation stemming from the state's guarantor power obligations, and carried out solely with a view to restoring the *status quo ante* in the Republic of Cyprus. According to the 1959 and 1960 Agreements, however, the commitment of the guarantor powers was limited only to the restoration of constitutional order. The continued occupation of the north of the island has been declared illegal by all international organizations.

1974–2004: THE CONSOLIDATION OF DIVISION

The effects of the division were devastating on both sides of the island. The gross domestic product of the country dropped by 70%. Important farming areas such as Morphou, the home of the island's citrus industry, and most of the once renowned tourism accommodation came under Turkish Cypriot control. The port of Famagusta remained out of service and the main international airport in Nicosia was turned into a United Nations (UN)-controlled buffer zone (known as the Green Line). Nevertheless, within a short time the southern part, unlike the occupied part, began to prosper economically, owing to the rapid development of trade, tourism and shipping, as well as to its transformation into a robust and reliable offshore centre. With the onset of prosperity, the *Enosis* ideology faded away.

In December 1974 Makarios returned to Cyprus and resumed the presidency. In February 1975 the Turkish Cypriots announced the formation of the 'Turkish Federated State of Northern Cyprus', thereby signalling the de facto division of the island. Despite this, UN-sponsored intercommunal talks began. After repeated rounds of discussions between Makarios and the Turkish Cypriot leader, Denktaş, a major breakthrough was achieved in January 1977, when the two sides reached an agreement (the 'High-Level Agreement') designed to remodel Cyprus into a bi-zonal and bi-communal federal state. The term 'bi-zonal' identified two areas, with a Greek Cypriot and a Turkish Cypriot administration, respectively. The term 'bi-communal' indicated that the two communities would participate effectively in the organs and decisions of the central federal government, although the precise meaning of the word 'effectively' had yet to be defined. The new state would have a single sovereignty, a single citizenship and a single international personality. For a transitional period, freedom of movement and settlement would be restricted. In August Makarios died. He was replaced by Spyros Kyprianou, the former foreign affairs minister, who was President of the House of Representatives at the time of Makarios's death. Kyprianou also took over as the main representative of the Greek-Cypriot side in the ongoing negotiations. In 1979 the two sides reached a new agreement, which re-affirmed the 1977 High-Level Agreement, but also included provisions for the demilitarization of the island and a commitment to refrain from destabilizing actions. Nevertheless, shortly after, Denktaş demanded that the Turkish Cypriot federal state be exclusively Turkish Cypriot and the Greek Cypriot state exclusively Greek Cypriot. This represented a revival of the 'two-state solution' and a torpedoing of the agreement.

From 1979, multiple negotiations and high-level meetings aimed at the re-unification of the island took place, revolving around the same set of interrelated issues: the establishment of a federal state, security guarantees, the right of intervention of the guarantor powers, the maintenance or withdrawal of the Turkish military forces, the return of refugees and institutional power-sharing. The profound mistrust on both sides, combined with Denktaş's personal intransigence, as well as his authoritarian governing style, impeded meaningful progress over the following decades.

On 15 November 1983 the Turkish Cypriots took advantage of post-election political instability in Turkey and unilaterally declared independence. Although the 'Turkish Republic of Northern Cyprus' ('TRNC') was soon recognized by Turkey, the rest of the international community condemned the move. The UN Security Council shortly afterwards passed a resolution (by a 14–1 vote; only Pakistan opposed the proposal) stating that the act was 'legally invalid' and calling for the withdrawal of the unilateral declaration of independence. With this and a further resolution adopted in May 1984, the UN Security Council condemned the proclamation as a secessionist action and reaffirmed that the sole legitimate government on the island was that of the Republic of Cyprus. Furthermore, the European Court of Human Rights resolved that the 'TRNC' was a 'puppet state' under the 'effective control' of Turkey.

The Turkish side argued that the 'TRNC' was established through the exercise of the right of self-determination that justified the proclamation of statehood. However, according to the criteria for statehood laid down in article 1 of the 1933 Montevideo Convention on the Rights and Duties of States, formal recognition for an entity is subsequent and consequential to achieving international legal personality as a nation-state. Since 1983 the international community has acted on the assumption that the Republic of Cyprus that was established in 1960 continues to exist, and as a result it has withheld formal recognition of the 'TRNC'.

At the same time, Turkey authorized the settlement of many thousands of settlers from Anatolia in the occupied areas of Cyprus, dramatically changing the existing economic, social and demographic situation in the northern part of the island. Entire families from mainland Anatolian Turkey were transferred to settle in occupied Cyprus, and were offered houses and land on generous subsidized terms. Moreover, a massive process of Turkification, entailing the changing of 3,000 Greek-language place names, the building of mosques and the conversion of churches into mosques, took place. Turkish forces consolidated their position on the island and a military airfield was developed. In 1976, 1983 and 2001, to mention only a few dates, the European Court of Human Rights found Turkey guilty of repeated violations of the European Convention on Human Rights with regard to the 'TRNC'.

From 1983, whenever a fresh round of negotiations was embarked upon, Denktaş, with the support or the acquiescence of whichever government was then in power in Turkey, repeatedly declared that he considered the *status quo ante* the solution to the Cypriot problem. Furthermore, he insisted on recognition of the 'TRNC' as part of any settlement, a demand completely unacceptable not only to the Greek side but, more importantly, also to the international community. Gradually, both sides hardened their stance, so that any concession or deviation from the official policy ran the risk of being equated with defeatism, a lack of patriotism and willingness to serve foreign interests.

In July 1990 the Republic of Cyprus officially submitted an application for full membership of the European Union (EU). This came as a result of an Association Agreement signed in 1972 with the European Economic Community. Many European states objected to it, arguing that it would import a serious problem right into its bosom and complicate its relationship with Turkey. The subsuming of a divided Cyprus into the European family would actually mean that Turkey, a powerful eastern neighbour and EU member state candidate, would occupy the territory of a member state. In April 2003, however, the European Parliament consented to Cyprus's accession to the EU and in May 2004 the Mediterranean island joined the bloc on the basis of a *sui generis* legal formula: the whole island became officially part of the EU, but EU legislation was suspended in the northern part of the island where the Cypriot Government did not exercise any control.

In the EU's 2003 Progress Report on Turkey's EU membership bid, Turkey was reminded that the Cyprus problem could become an obstacle to achieving this goal. Under considerable international pressure, the two communities' leaders, Tassos Papadopoulos of the Greek Cypriot community and Denktaş of the Turkish Cypriot community, reluctantly agreed in February 2004 to resume negotiations with the intention of reaching a deal before the island's accession to the EU. A set of proposals, presented by the UN Secretary-General, Kofi Annan, known as the Annan Plan, served as a basis for the resumed talks. Consequently, both communities were scheduled to vote on the proposals in a simultaneous referendum held on 24 April, just one week before Cyprus officially became an EU member on 1 May.

Under the Annan Plan, the Republic of Cyprus would cease to exist in its current form and would be transformed into a new state, the United Cyprus Republic—a loose federation composed of two constituent states with some consociational power-sharing features. Ostensibly, the plan strove to accommodate different perceptions and aspirations, but what eventually came out of it was a nebulous and dysfunctional arrangement with very little, if any, chance of success. It borrowed features from various models of federalism—mainly the Swiss and Belgian ones—and was encapsulated in a document comprising more than 130 laws and other agreements in a number of fields running to approximately 9,000 pages.

As in most cases of federalism, under the Annan Plan the constituent states would exercise all powers not vested in the Constitution of the federal Government and there would be no hierarchy between federal and constituent state laws. The northern Turkish Cypriot constituent state would encompass about 28.5% of the island and the southern Greek Cypriot constituent state the remaining 71.5%. Even though the state would have a single international personality, every person would have two citizenships—that of the common state and that of the constituent state in which he or she resided. The plan allowed for a rotating presidency on the basis of two terms for Greek Cypriots followed by one term for Turkish Cypriots. Within all institutions, proportionality norms would have to prevail. Minority veto provisions regarding legislation would also be prevalent throughout the institutions. A bicameral parliament would be established: composed of a Chamber of Deputies, in which Turkish Cypriots would hold 25% of the seats, and a Senate, consisting of equal numbers from each ethnic group. As in Switzerland, executive power would be vested in a six-member presidential council, whose members would be elected by both houses of parliament and from a single list.

Many parts of the plan sparked controversy; for example, the property provisions for displaced persons and the number of Turkish settlers allowed to remain on the island. However, what really determined the Greek Cypriots' electoral behaviour in the ensuing referendum was the issue of security guarantees. Although the plan proposed a gradual reduction in the number of Greek and Turkish troops stationed on the island, which after six years would be limited to 6,000, falling further to 600 after 19 years, it failed to remove the Treaty of Guarantee which had granted the UK, Greece and Turkey the right to intervene militarily in the new state.

Another contentious point was the legalization of residency of a large number of Turkish settlers, in addition to those who had acquired the right by marrying a Turkish Cypriot citizen. For the Greek Cypriot community, the presence of those settlers was not only regarded as an illegal modification of the demographic structure of the island, but also as a source of tension and discontent among the indigenous population as well as a threat to the security of the new state.

Aside from these considerations, there were also geopolitical obstacles to the reunification of the island, which would have major consequences reaching far beyond the inter-communal sphere and affect the strategic equilibrium in the Eastern Mediterranean region. Against this background, the plan was supported by the EU and the USA, but opposed by the Russian Federation, which held that its strategic interests in the region were threatened.

Since AKEL, Russia's old ally on the island, was the most influential political and social actor in the Greek Cypriot community, the outcome of the referendum depended mainly on the party's position towards the Annan Plan. Despite strong scepticism about the settlement's future viability, broad segments of the party supported it. AKEL called upon the UN and the international community to postpone the plebiscite for several months so that the plan's security deficiencies could be corrected and a broader consensus among the Cypriot population be secured. To address these concerns, UN Secretary-General Annan prepared a draft UN resolution that incorporated sufficient security guarantees for the plan's implementation. Russia, however, torpedoed the UN resolution at the Security Council and, as a result, the AKEL leadership officially rejected the plan, thereby prejudicing the outcome of the referendum. Consequently, just as the Turkish Cypriots overwhelmingly endorsed the plan, so too did the Greek Cypriots overwhelmingly reject it.

Papadopoulos, a former prominent member of EOKA and President of Cyprus since February 2003, also urged the Greek Cypriot electorate to reject the Annan Plan, claiming that the negative consequences resulting from a 'yes' vote far outweighed those from a 'no' vote.

There was a significant difference in the attitude of the two communities towards the plan's envisaged security arrangements. While the Turkish Cypriots considered the arrangements to be at least sufficient, the Greek Cypriots felt that their security needs were not adequately addressed.

2004–22: ENTANGLEMENT IN EASTERN MEDITERRANEAN POWER POLITICS AND THE DISPUTE OVER MARITIME ZONES

The collapse of the Annan Plan, which was rejected by 66.7% of those who voted in a referendum held on 24 April 2004 (75.8% of Greek Cypriot participants voted against it, as did 35.1% of Turkish Cypriot participants) was followed by a diplomatic hiatus in the efforts to find a solution to the Cyprus question. However, the hiatus was filled by one of the most intractable issues within the EU and NATO: specifically, the outstanding question of Turkey's accession to the EU. Turkey, an EU applicant state, is a leading member of NATO that does not recognize Cyprus, which, for its part is a member of the EU but not of NATO. Furthermore, Turkey has denied the use of its sea and airports to Greek Cypriot ships and aircraft, and has frequently prevented the holding of high-level formal meetings between NATO and the EU's Political and Security Committee and obstructed discussions over military operations and intelligence issues whenever Cyprus has wished to participate, on the grounds that Cyprus does not possess any security clearance from NATO.

Beyond this, from 2007 onwards, the geopolitical architecture of the region shifted as the Republic of Cyprus initiated hydrocarbon exploration efforts, by licensing the US company Noble Energy to explore for natural gas in Cypriot territorial waters. Four years later Noble Energy announced a breakthrough: the discovery of the Aphrodite gasfield in Cyprus's southern exclusive economic zone (EEZ), containing estimated gas reserves of 127,425m. cu m. This discovery off the southern shores of Cyprus was seen by many as a unique opportunity to bring the Greek Cypriots and the Turkish Cypriots to the negotiating table and find a solution to the political conflict. Many analysts expressed hope that the prospect of huge revenue from gas exploitation would cause both sides to seek a resolution to their long-term conflict, despite their disagreements and the unsettled issues from the past. Unfortunately, resource endowment did not become a peace incentive but rather another cause of contention.

The prospect of discovering new hydrocarbons reserves pushed Cyprus and its neighbouring countries to define their EEZs. The delimitation of maritime zones is often an extremely difficult and contentious political issue, since it addresses sovereignty rights and economic interests at the same time. Israel signed an EEZ delimitation agreement with Cyprus in 2010 without having declared such a zone prior to the conclusion of the agreement, and having only partially acceded to the 1982 United Nations Convention on the Law of the Sea (UNCLOS). Cyprus delineated its EEZ with Egypt in 2003 and with Lebanon in 2007. The Lebanese parliament, however, did not ratify this agreement, probably due to political pressure from Turkey. (In July 2010 the Lebanese Government sent a new list of geographical co-ordinates to the UN that contradicted the 2007 agreement.)

The leadership of the breakaway 'TRNC' regime, backed by Turkey, immediately raised objections to actions taken by the Republic of Cyprus pertaining to the delimitation of the maritime borders and the joint development of cross-boundary resources. The 'TRNC' asserted that, according to the 1960 Constitution, two equal constituent communities exist, and therefore any unilateral action represents a *fait accompli* and runs counter to their own legitimate rights and interests. Furthermore, Turkey has argued that the Greek Cypriot Government lacks any legal authority over affairs concerning the entire island, including the right to claim a continental shelf and an EEZ. Consequently, according to Turkey, all agreements reached by Greek Cypriot authorities with international oil companies for the purpose of offshore oil and gas exploration are invalid. This has led the Turkish military to engage in direct confrontational action against foreign companies conducting exploration activities in Cyprus's EEZ, seriously disrupting the development of its offshore fields.

In 2014 Turkey submitted a diplomatic note to the UN Secretary-General mapping out the geographical co-ordinates of its continental shelf in the Eastern Mediterranean, as established by a delimitation agreement with the internationally non-recognized 'TRNC', which had been signed in September 2011 and ratified by Turkey in June 2012. The delimitation agreement, which apparently failed to meet basic international legal standards, as one of the signatories was not recognized by the international community, outlined some of Turkey's longstanding positions on the law of the sea. The agreement only concerned the continental shelf and did not provide for the delineation of an EEZ. In this manner, Turkey endeavoured to avoid the impression that it accepted the right of islands to create such zones. Its official position that islands in certain regions (implying the Aegean Sea) should not be entitled to claim maritime zones of their own other than territorial sea is associated with the dispute between Turkey and Greece over the sovereignty of some islands and the delimitation of the maritime space in the Aegean Sea that dates back to the 1970s.

To counterbalance 'the Turkish menace' Cyprus forged an alliance with Israel, which was driven by a shared concern over regional (in)stability during the Arab Spring in the early 2010s, a mutual desire to profit from discovery of large offshore gas reserves in the Mediterranean, and a severe deterioration in Israeli-Turkish relations following a military incident in 2010.

The state of Israel had long considered Cyprus highly important, both because of its geographical proximity (the distance from Israel's northern port of Haifa to Cyprus is only 225 km) and because it viewed Cyprus as an integral part of its 'peripheral policy' aimed at breaking its isolation from the Arab states. In this context, Benjamin Netanyahu made a historic visit to Cyprus in February 2012, the first ever undertaken by an Israeli Prime Minister to the island. During Netanyahu's visit, the two countries signed a military agreement, to the dismay of Turkey and the Turkish Cypriots, allowing the Israeli air force to use the airspace and territorial waters around Cyprus to protect vital energy resources. One year later, Israeli energy companies Delek Drilling and Avner Oil & Gas signed an agreement to acquire a 30% stake in exploration rights in Cyprus's offshore field. In June 2013 the two companies signed a statement of intent for the development of an onshore liquefied natural gas (LNG) plant in the area of Vasilikos. The economic benefits expected from the substantial natural gas and oil resources discovered in the Israeli and Cypriot adjacent EEZs have also contributed to the materialization of an unprecedented political, military and energy relationship between the two countries and, by extension, Greece, with the backing of the EU.

The EU-Cyprus-Greece-Israel co-operation, however, clashed with Turkey's geopolitical aspirations in the region. Turkish economic and political elites perceived a possible export route to European markets through the Mediterranean, connecting Israel, Cyprus and Greece, as a threat to their own ambition to transform Turkey into the major non-Russian transit route for gas sales and a regional energy hub. Turkey has contested the fact that the areas that contain gas reserves in the eastern basin of the Mediterranean, stretching from the Levant coast to southern Crete and potentially beyond, are situated in clearly divided national waters. Moreover, the geopolitical and geo-economic shift of power triggered renewed antagonism among the regional players. Turkey and Russia fostered energy co-operation in the field of nuclear power, in order to counterbalance the US- and EU-backed hydrocarbons activities, fuelling yet another form of US-Russian rivalry in the region.

Despite these rivalries, the two communities of Cyprus resumed talks in 2015 aimed at the reunification of the island. This development was prompted by the election in April of Mustafa Akıncı to the position of President of the breakaway Turkish Cypriot regime. Akıncı, a moderate leftist, was known for his co-operation with the Greek Cypriots during his term as Mayor of North Nicosia from 1976 to 1990. The gestures of goodwill between the 'TRNC' and the Republic of Cyprus that followed his election to the presidency, and the expectation of sharing the revenues from the impending exploitation of the island's energy resources created a positive climate around the time of the negotiations.

Between November 2015 and July 2017, during perhaps the most promising talks held since the collapse of the Annan Plan, the two communities failed again to make a breakthrough, although for the first time hitherto taboo subjects were discussed and maps exchanged with a view to defining future boundaries. Disagreements about territorial and security issues, including the withdrawal of all troops, and about the Treaty of Guarantee, proved insurmountable obstacles. More precisely, the Turkish Cypriot leadership demanded that Turkey remain a guarantor power and a continued presence of Turkish troops on the island. This cast doubts on the true willingness of the negotiating sides to establish a federation. It is also noteworthy that the return of the Morphou area (under the control of the 'TRNC') to the Greek Cypriots, which was also an important issue in these talks, had been included in the Annan Plan that was eventually rejected in the April 2004 referendum.

The deterioration of the wider political climate and renewed tensions in neighbouring states, appeared also to have played an important role in the failure of the talks. In February 2018 Turkish warships obstructed gas exploration in Block 3 of Cyprus's EEZ by blocking a drilling vessel operated by Italian energy company ENI. Therefore, when US hydrocarbons firm ExxonMobil sent a drilling vessel to the area (Block 10) in March, the US Sixth Fleet operating in the area accompanied and monitored the vessel. In early October, on the occasion of the Republic of Cyprus's invitation to international companies to bid for offshore hydrocarbons exploration licences in Block 7, Turkey's foreign affairs ministry stated that: 'any exploration activity regarding natural resources on Turkey's continental shelf, the outer limits of which were conveyed to the UN via our Notes dated 2 March 2004 and 12 March 2013, can only be carried out by obtaining Turkey's permission... Turkey has never allowed and will never allow any foreign country, company or ship to conduct unauthorized research activities regarding natural resources within its maritime jurisdiction areas.' The Greek Cypriot authorities denounced Turkey's naval action as an illegal use of force and a violation of Cyprus's sovereign rights.

Since then, Turkish researchers accompanied by military vessels have repeatedly collected seismic and geological data, in preparation for Turkey's own exploration in areas where drilling activities are already taking place, thus increasing the risk of a direct military confrontation. In May 2019 Turkey went a step further by sending Turkish ships to drill for hydrocarbons within the Cypriot EEZ, an action that has been repeated many times since. Turkey's aggressive stance has deepened its isolation. EU leaders have repeatedly condemned the country's actions in the Eastern Mediterranean and the Aegean as illegal, and deplored its failure to respond to the EU's repeated demands that it cease such activities and respect the sovereignty of Cyprus, in accordance with international law. In November the EU adopted a framework for the imposition of targeted restrictive measures, including asset freezes and travel bans, on persons or entities involved in unauthorized drilling activities for hydrocarbons in the Eastern Mediterranean.

Meanwhile, Egypt strongly defended not only the Cypriot offshore gas exploration projects but also its 2003 EEZ delineation agreement with Cyprus. Moreover, Egypt joined the informal alliance between Israel, Cyprus and Greece, in a move that was perceived to increase the threat to Turkish strategic interests in the Eastern Mediterranean. Turkey was left further isolated when by the end of 2018 the US Congress had lifted an arms embargo on Cyprus and increased foreign aid to the island, in a show of support for its gas exploration and against Turkish aggression.

In January 2019 Greece, Cyprus, Israel and Egypt proceeded to deepen their co-operation with the so-called Cairo Declaration establishing the Eastern Mediterranean Gas Forum (EMGF), with its headquarters in Egypt. The forum institutionalized co-operation regarding the development of natural gas reserves in the Eastern Mediterranean Sea among seven countries: Egypt, Israel, Cyprus, Jordan, the Palestinian territories, Greece and Italy. The EMGF's member states agreed to expand their co-operation to develop a common energy policy towards the establishment of a competitive regional gas market and infrastructure while respecting each other's rights over natural resources, protecting the environment and adhering to international law. Even though the establishment of the EMGF can be regarded as one of the most important steps toward a regional order based on optimal exploitation of natural gas in the Eastern Mediterranean, its exclusive nature hinders the forum's economic rationale. Although it was announced that membership of the EMGF would be open to additional countries willing to accept its governing rules (France was admitted as a member in March 2021), the membership structure of the forum does not currently include certain littoral states in the Eastern Mediterranean such as Turkey, Lebanon, the Syrian Arab Republic and Libya. In other words, almost one-half of the countries of the Eastern Mediterranean are not members of this regional institution.

Yet, Turkey is less interested in gas exploration than in challenging Greek and Cypriot sovereignty, as well as adhering to its position that the two countries have contiguous continental shelves. Therefore, it deliberately chose a location 62 km within the Cypriot EEZ to undertake drilling activities.

Turkey's claims in the Aegean and the Eastern Mediterranean are more or less encapsulated in the country's strategy of a 'Blue Homeland' (Mavi Vatan), referring to a vast area of Turkish interests expanding across half of the Eastern Mediterranean, including the continental shelves of Cyprus and those of the Greek islands of Rhodes, Kastellorizo, Karpathos, Kassos and the eastern section of Crete. In this area of the Mediterranean in May 2019 Turkey conducted its largest ever naval military exercise, named 'Operation Sea Wolf', involving 131 warships, 57 warplanes and 33 helicopters.

In November 2019 Turkey submitted to the UN a series of claims to EEZs in the Eastern Mediterranean that are also claimed by Greece. These included an area extending west of the south-eastern Aegean island of Rhodes and an area south of Crete. In the same month Turkey signed a bilateral agreement with Libya on maritime boundaries, in exchange for a security pact involving military training and equipment.

Meanwhile, the initial enthusiasm about the energy reserves south of Cyprus has moderated. Despite the widespread euphoria over the natural endowments of the region, and its perceived potential to transform the EU's energy security in the short to medium term, the East Mediterranean natural gas 'bonanza' is rather overestimated. The gas deposits remain, apart from the Tamar and Zohr fields, so far largely undeveloped and exploration is proceeding slowly, since there is no available export route for the large volumes of gas that could potentially be produced.

Given that natural gas exports from the area, in the best-case scenario and probably after many years, would reach an annual volume of 20,000m. cu m, and that the EU market consumes more than 400,000m. cu m per year, the perception of their significance appears rather misguided. In July 2020 ratification by the Cypriot parliament of an agreement signed between Greece, Cyprus and Israel in January regarding construction of the so-called EastMed pipeline, designed to transport Israeli and Cypriot gas to Greece and on to Western Europe, coincided with US energy corporation Chevron's announcement of its US $5,000m. acquisition of Noble Energy, one of the region's leading operators. However, the proposed pipeline, which would transport 10,000m. cu m of gas per year and be among the longest undersea gas links in the world, with 1,300 km of its total length of 1,900 km being offshore, has, to date, been for economic and technical reasons more of a pipedream than a realistic project. In the economic environment in the wake of the coronavirus disease (COVID-19) pandemic there will be tough competition with other existing and potential gas suppliers to Europe, and, in the case of LNG imports, with exporters across the globe. Furthermore, the prospects for the development of the discovered reserves are not only affected by Turkish aggression but inevitably also by the challenging global situation and the current crisis engulfing the oil and gas industry. In January 2022 the USA announced the withdrawal of its support for the EastMed project, which excluded Turkey, citing environmental reasons, and the project's perceived lack of economic and commercial viability.

The surge in global energy prices, which began in 2021 and was compounded by the Russian invasion of Ukraine on 24 February 2022 and the ensuing conflict, revived interest in the Cypriot natural gas reserves, and created impetus for the stakeholders to seek alternative options for their exploitation.

In August 2022 ENI announced the discovery of a gasfield in the Cronos-1 well in Block 6 of Cyprus's EEZ; the Italian company is the operator of Block 6, in which it holds a 50% stake, as does France's TotalEnergies. Preliminary estimates indicated reserves of about 2,500,000m. cu ft of gas, a rather modest quantity that was not expected to have much of an impact on regional or global markets. However, the discovery was significant insofar as it increased Cyprus's known gas reserves to around 13,000,000m. cu ft and confirmed that the area incorporating Blocks 5, 6, 7, 10 and 11 was prolific in gas. In December ENI announced the discovery of a further gasfield, which was estimated to contain 2,000,000m.–3,000,000m. cu ft of gas, in the Zeus-1 well (also within Block 6).

Meanwhile, the EU has come up with an ingenious idea which also serves to address the daunting environmental challenges that the region faces (the Eastern Mediterranean being regarded as a prominent hotspot of climate change). The President of the EU Commission, Ursula von der Leyen, announced in August 2022 that the EU was advancing the idea of establishing a bicommunal solar park in Cyprus's buffer zone which would contribute to the energy needs of both Cypriot communities. It was hoped that the construction of the park would act as a confidence-building measure and as an incentive for wider discussions between the two sides.

Nevertheless, in November 2022 the EU condemned Türkiye's endorsement of the acceptance of the 'TRNC' as an observer state at the Organization of Turkic States, branding the decision as a violation of the UN Security Council Resolutions that recognize only the Republic of Cyprus as a subject of international law.

THE RUSSIA FACTOR

Another important factor in the Eastern Mediterranean security environment has been Russia. Traditionally, Russia has been a major geopolitical player in the region. The Mediterranean is a significant component of Russia's military strategy:

the basin provides an access point to southern Europe, the Middle East and North Africa. Moreover, Russia has been viewing the Mediterranean as an arena of competition with the USA and NATO. Like the USSR, post-communist Russia has followed, for geopolitical but also purely economic reasons, a policy of 'fishing in muddy waters'—that is a slow but steady penetration in the region. Historically, this penetration was achieved mainly through indirect methods. Rather than sending in its armed forces to annex territories, the USSR, as well as its allies, wilfully extended its support to various political groups and governments in order to erode Western ties in these countries and thereby spread their influence southward.

Official Cypriot-Russian relations date back to the 1960s when the USSR established diplomatic relations with the newly independent Republic of Cyprus. In 1982 the two states signed a waiver agreement of double taxation that was extremely positive for taxpayers, providing for zero withholding taxes on dividends, interest and royalties. As a result, at the beginning of the 1990s Cyprus was one of the few capitalist countries with an institutional framework for Russian capital outflows and inflows already in place. The 1982 double taxation agreement was also adopted by most of the former republics of the USSR after they gained independence. Western investors were familiar with Cyprus's legal and commercial infrastructure, based on the common law legacy left by the UK, the former colonial power, and had far more confidence in it than in the evolving and initially unreliable legal systems of the newly capitalist countries. As a result, over the next two decades Cyprus not only became one of the favoured destinations for Russian capital, but also the preferred jurisdiction for channelling wealth and investment from the West into Russia and Eastern Europe, providing stability, predictability, transparency and substantial tax savings. Moreover, from the early 1990s onwards, Russians were among the most active non-resident portfolio investors on the Cyprus Stock Exchange, with the overwhelming majority of the invested funds deriving from Russian capital.

Cyprus's accession into the EU in 2004 prompted a series of legislative changes, but did not halt the inflow of Russian funds. In October 2010 the two countries signed a new bilateral agreement (the Convention for the Avoidance of Double Taxation of Income and Property) that further increased the flow of investment. Cyprus does not impose withholding tax on payments of dividends, interest and royalties paid by international business companies. Therefore, a Cypriot company with international operations is more likely to receive dividend interest, royalties and capital gains from another treaty country, in order for the withholding tax to be reduced. The interest and royalty payments are in most cases a deductible expense in a high tax jurisdiction, whereas the capital gains are tax exempt. Cypriot private capital was also a major source of investment in the Russian securities market. These investments were often considered inflows of Russian capital, acting as safety nets for Russian companies to protect themselves from political uncertainties in the domestic environment. However, the prominent position of Cyprus in Russian economic affairs may also indicate that many foreign companies wishing to trade with Russia used Cypriot subsidiaries in order to take advantage of the favourable taxation in Cyprus. The increased capital circulation captured the attention of various observers, who estimated that money laundering and tax evasion were the main driving forces behind capital movements.

After Cyprus recognized Russia as the successor to the USSR in 1992, defence co-operation between the two countries flourished. As the Republic of Cyprus has not been constrained by any alliance restrictions (it is not a member of NATO, for example) and given the US arms embargo on Cyprus (which was not lifted until 2020), there were only two obstacles to the acquisition of Russian arms: the reaction of Turkey and British objections. The latter derived from the presence of the two British SBAs on the island under the terms of the 1960 Treaty of Independence. The first Russian-Cypriot agreement on military technical co-operation was signed in March 1996. During 1991–2011 Russia and the Republic of Cyprus concluded €430.5m. worth of deals regarding the purchase of Russian military hardware. Following the 1996 agreement the Cypriot defence ministry began to purchase significant quantities of Russian weapons, including 43 BMP-3 and 41 T-80U tanks, as well as six Tor-M1 surface-to-air missiles systems. During the 2000s Cyprus bought four BM-21 'Grad' self-propelled multiple rocket launchers, 12 Mi-24P combat helicopters, three Mi-8MT helicopters and an additional fleet of 41 T-80U tanks in 2010.

Cyprus's acquisition of the Russian-made S-300 anti-aircraft missile system in January 1997 provoked strong opposition from the USA and Turkey. The US Administration was concerned that the deployment of S-300 missiles in Cyprus would bring the Eastern Mediterranean under Russian control, and it exerted pressure on the Greek and Cypriot Governments to cancel the acquisition. According to declassified presidential records, which former US President Bill Clinton subsequently made public, Clinton was very troubled by the deal because of the Russian connection and hence asked the then British Prime Minister, Tony Blair, to exert pressure on Cypriot President Glafkos Klerides to stop the delivery of the missiles. After more than two years of diplomatic tug-of-war, in September 1999 the Greek and Cypriot Governments finally bowed to US pressure, agreeing to install the weapons on the island of Crete rather than in Cyprus. The weapons system, having been installed on Crete, was not tested until 2013.

The harmonious defence co-operation between Cyprus and Russia was also reflected on a political level. Cyprus was frequently an ardent supporter of Russian interests within the EU and was considered as one of Russia's most reliable allies in the bloc. During the Russian–Georgian conflict of August 2008, President Demetris Christofias was among the few international leaders and the only leader of an EU member state to support Russia. He also backed Russian demands to limit the installation of US missile defence systems in Eastern Europe. In July 2016 the Cypriot parliament voted for a resolution to lift EU sanctions against Russia, following its annexation of the Crimean region of Ukraine in 2014.

Gradually, Cyprus's reputation evolved towards being the money-laundering hub of the Mediterranean, a haven for Russians and Serbians escaping political turmoil and a magnet for capital flows, which are then channelled to the Russian economy. Therefore, some observers deemed Cyprus as a 'weak link' in Europe's banking system because of its lax approach to questionable Russian money that could pose a threat to other countries' banks in the single market and create hazards for European democracy. Against this background, the imposition by the Central Bank of Cyprus of severe restrictions on shell companies in November 2017 was a turning point because it caused a mass exodus of Russian money from Cyprus.

Following extensive negotiations, in September 2020 the Cypriot Minister of Finance, Constantinos Petrides, and the Russian Deputy Minister of Finance, Alexey Sazanov, signed a protocol amending the double taxation treaty. The Cypriot side ensured, among other things, exemption from a 15% withholding tax on dividends for regulated entities, such as pension funds and insurance companies, as well as listed companies, and on interest payments from corporate and government bonds, as well as Eurobonds.

Despite pressure on Russian companies to repatriate assets, there are still numerous Russian companies based in Cyprus. Most of them are located in Limassol, where a sizeable Russian-speaking community lives and Russian schools, Orthodox churches, Russian-language television and radio services have been established.

The sanctions that the EU imposed on Russian businesses, as part of wide-ranging measures against Russia in response to its invasion of Ukraine on 24 February 2022, have, as of mid-2023, had only a limited impact on the Cypriot economy. Under pressure from the EU, in May Cyprus, together with Malta, revoked the so-called golden passports of dozens of wealthy Russian and Belarusian nationals who were subject to EU sanctions. Cyprus's Golden Passport scheme, in place between 2007 and 2020, offered Cypriot citizenship in exchange for a financial investment of at least €2.5m.

RECENT POLITICAL DEVELOPMENTS

In October 2020 Ersin Tatar, a politician regarded as a hardliner, was elected as the President of the 'TRNC'. Immediately after his election, Tatar drew attention to the 53-year-long stagnation in negotiations between the Turkish Cypriots and the Greek Cypriots and stated that official discussions could only be initiated by two states with sovereign equality. Since the Greek Cypriot side demanded adherence to a federal settlement with political equality, as formally agreed in 1977 and 1979 and stipulated in UN resolutions, any new effort to resume negotiations appeared pointless. Nevertheless, in late April 2021 an informal five-plus-one summit on the Cyprus problem attended by the leaders of the island's two communities and the foreign affairs ministers of the guarantor countries of Greece, the UK and Turkey, took place in Geneva. The purpose of the summit, co-ordinated and led by the UN, was to attempt to find common ground that would allow substantive negotiations on the Cyprus issue to resume. Unsurprisingly, UN Secretary-General António Guterres announced at the end of the summit that this had not been achieved. Tatar repeated his demand that the 'TRNC' be recognized as an independent state, while Greek Cypriot President Nikos Anastasiades suggested examining a model of a decentralized federation, in which the constituent states would have increased responsibilities. According to the United Nations Peacekeeping Force in Cyprus (UNFICYP), at the same time Turkey continued to embark on a series of illegal and provocative activities in the territorial sea, the continental shelf and the EEZ of Cyprus, and violations of the military status quo along the Turkish forces' ceasefire line as well as in the border town of Strovilia and the fenced area of Varosha (Maraş—the abandoned southern quarter of Famagusta), in outright defiance of UN Security Council resolutions.

Nevertheless, Greek Cypriot aid to the 'TRNC' continued, increasing by €1.4m. year on year to reach €40.4m. in 2021, according to the Greek Cypriot Ministry of Finance. Total aid to the 'TRNC' during the five years to 2021 totalled €199.4m.

Legislative elections in the Republic of Cyprus in May 2021 unfolded in the shadow of various corruption scandals, which allegedly implicated both the Government and much of the opposition. An independent investigation into Cyprus's now defunct investment-for-citizenship programme found that the Government had unlawfully granted passports to thousands of relatives of wealthy investors, some of whom were believed to have links with criminal organizations. For the first time ever, the electoral campaign was not preoccupied by the Cyprus issue but by other topics such as corruption, the Government's management of the COVID-19 pandemic and migration.

The far-right Ethniko Laiko Metopo (ELAM—National People's Front), with its strident anti-migration platform, and a centrist splinter group called Dimokratiki Parataxi (Democratic Front) made large gains in the legislative elections of 30 May 2021 (attaining 6.8% and 6.1% of the votes, respectively), as a significant proportion of the electorate appeared to have turned their backs on the traditionally dominant three parties, amid widespread voter disenchantment with the political status quo. The conservative Dimokratikos Synagermos (DISY—Democratic Rally) secured the most votes with 27.8% of the total, while communist party AKEL was second-placed with 22.3%. The centre-right Dimokratiko Komma (DIKO—Democratic Party) was placed third with 11.3% of the votes, and the socialist Kinima Sosialdimokraton EDEK (Movement of Social Democrats EDEK), a traditional power in the Cypriot political landscape, in alliance with Symmaxia Politon (Citizens' Alliance), was placed fifth (just behind the far-right ELAM) with 6.7%.

In July 2021 tensions between the Greek Cypriot and 'TRNC' administrations ran high. During a visit to northern Cyprus in that month, Turkish President Recep Tayyip Erdoğan announced the partial opening of Varosha (Maraş), the abandoned southern quarter of Famagusta, for settlement under 'TRNC' control. Varosha is perhaps the quintessential embodiment of the Cyprus problem: the town was, prior to 1974, one of the most popular tourist destinations in the world, but since then has remained a ghostly collection of derelict high-rise hotels and residences in a military zone that nobody has been allowed to enter. The 1979 reaffirmation of the 1977 High-Level Agreement stipulated that the resettlement of Varosha was to be a unified Cypriot priority, that both sides were open to such acts of goodwill, and that the UN should play a role in the resolution to the Cyprus problem. As multiple UN resolutions had appealed for Varosha to be handed over to UN administration, and for former residents to be allowed to return to their homes, the USA, the EU and the UN Security Council all condemned Erdoğan's announcement of unilateral action.

In a report submitted to the UN Security Council in January 2023, UN Secretary-General António Guterres stated that public confidence regarding the prospects for reaching a negotiated settlement in Cyprus remained low, with both camps remaining firmly entrenched in their opposing views as to the best way forward. Guterres noted a deterioration in relations between the two sides, as well as with the UN, during the reporting period (June–December 2022), with mutual mistrust exacerbated and the political landscape further complicated by disputes over areas in and around the buffer zone and in Varosha, including over civilian activities. However, some progress was achieved by the technical committees in reducing existing barriers to intercommunal contact and trade, as had been called for by the Security Council, including the easing by the Greek Cypriot Government of certain restrictions on the trade of processed food items of non-animal origin under the EU's Green Line Regulation, which led to an increase in the volume of bilateral trade.

The devastating earthquake that struck southern Türkiye and Syria in early February 2023 affected the Turkish Cypriot community as well, with 39 students, parents and teachers from Famagusta killed in the disaster. Many Greek Cypriots expressed a strong desire to transcend the political divide, but co-operation through the bicommunal Technical Committees on Crisis Management and on the Environment (in line with the EU's disaster resilience goals) unfortunately fell prey to the Cyprus problem. While the general population mostly welcomed the Greek Cypriot assistance, some Turkish Cypriot politicians accused the Greek Cypriots of seeking politically to manipulate the humanitarian crisis.

During the first half of 2023 political attention was firmly focused on domestic priorities, with elections being held in the Republic of Cyprus in February 2023 and in both Greece and Türkiye in May. Consequently, there was limited opportunity and incentive for the principal parties to invest political capital on the resolution of the Cyprus question.

The presidential election held in the Republic of Cyprus in February 2023 was contested by a record-high 14 candidates. Of these, the three main candidates were DISY President Averof Neophytou, whose candidacy was endorsed by the incumbent President Anastasiades; the independent Nikos Christodoulides, who held the post of Minister of Foreign Affairs during 2018–22 and who was supported by EDEK, the centrist parties Dimokratiki Parataxi (DEPA—Democratic Front) and Dimokratiko Komma (DIKO—Democratic Party), and the Kinima Allileggii (Solidarity Movement); and AKEL-backed independent Andreas Mavroyiannis, the longstanding chief negotiator in reunification talks.

Regarding the Cyprus question, Christodoulides and Mavroyiannis seemed to support a bizonal, bicommunal federal solution. Christodoulides, however, appeared less committed to that model as a result of his backing by EDEK, DIKO and the Solidarity Movement, all of which are considered to be 'rejectionist' parties (i.e. they reject the federal model as a basis for a solution to the Cyprus problem). Furthermore, Christodoulides pledged to seek greater EU involvement and to establish a team of experts within the Office of the President to support the Greek Cypriot negotiator and to renegotiate the Guterres framework, which was designed to resolve the outstanding points of disagreement between the sides during the UN-mediated international Conference on Cyprus talks held over three rounds in Switzerland in 2017. Neophytou, on the contrary, was well disposed to retaining the Guterres framework, and instead placed emphasis on NATO candidacy, a longstanding issue in Cypriot politics, and energy as the two keys with which to unlock the current stalemate and ultimately lead to a solution of the Cyprus problem. Mavroyiannis, an experienced diplomat, attached importance to the role of the international community and the Turkish Cypriot community as key components of unlocking the process of bilateral negotiations, as well as the incorporation of Varosha within the buffer zone.

Aside from the Cyprus problem, two other key issues in the pre-electoral agenda were inflation and immigration. In recent years Cyprus has recorded the highest number of asylum seekers per capita among the EU member states, and one consequence of this has been growing support for far-right politicians, several of whom stood as candidates in the presidential election. Most prominent among these was the President of ELAM, Christos Christou.

Against this backdrop, in the first round of the presidential election, held on 5 February 2023, no candidate secured a majority of votes, necessitating a run-off poll between the top two candidates—Christodoulides (who garnered 32.0% of the vote in the first round) and Mavroyiannis (29.6%). To the surprise of many observers, Neophytou came third in the first round, with 26.1% of the vote—the first time in Cypriot electoral history that a DISY candidate had failed to advance to a second round of a presidential election; this was doubtlessly due to the fact that Christodoulides attracted a significant number of DISY voters, at the expense of Neophytou. Christou came fourth with 6.0%, which appeared to indicate a consolidation of support for ELAM, and for far-right ideology more generally, within the Cypriot political party system.

At the second round of the presidential election, held on 12 February 2023, Christodoulides secured a narrow victory, winning the 52.0% of the ballot against Mavroyiannis's 48.0%. Christodoulides thus became the eighth president of the Republic of Cyprus, and, notably, the first to be elected without the official support of any of the major Cypriot political parties.

Tensions between the Greek Cypriots and Turkish Cypriots were heightened on 18 August 2023 when three UN peacekeepers were injured in scuffles with Turkish Cypriot security forces over unauthorized construction work being carried out by Turkish Cypriot workers inside the UN buffer zone near Pyla (Pile). The UN Security Council condemned the violence and expressed serious concerns over the construction work, stressing that it contravened UN Security Council resolutions and constituted a violation of the status quo in the buffer zone.

Economy

Revised by ANDREAS STERGIOU

Note: The Cyprus pound (C£) was in use until the Republic of Cyprus's adoption of the euro (€) on 1 January 2008. Some historical data in this essay continues to be presented in terms of Cyprus pounds, with the euro equivalent at the prevailing conversion rate indicated in brackets.

Since July 1974 Cyprus has been divided into two areas, one to the north and one to the south of the 'Attila Line', or 'Green Line' (a buffer zone monitored by the United Nations—UN). The northern two-fifths of the country, under Turkish Cypriot control and not formally recognized by the international community, is closely linked to the economy of Turkey (officially designated Türkiye from June 2022), and has had little economic contact with the south of the island since partition, despite recent attempts to stimulate intra-island trade. The unilateral declaration of independence from the (Greek Cypriot) Republic of Cyprus (in the south) by the 'Turkish Republic of Northern Cyprus' ('TRNC') in November 1983, which was condemned by the UN Security Council, and subsequent international court judgments reinforced the economic separation of the northern sector. Both areas suffered severe disruption as a result of the events of 1974.

ECONOMIC PERFORMANCE SINCE PARTITION

The economy of the south made a remarkable recovery following partition in 1974, despite having lost 38% of the island's territory, 70% of its productive resources, 30% of its factories, 60% of the tourist installations, the main port (Famagusta), 66% of the grain-producing land and 80% of the citrus fruit groves, all of which were on the northern side of the line.

Since 1974 the economy has undergone huge structural changes, with the commercial and service sectors having gradually gained in importance, while small-scale industry (mainly textiles) and agriculture have declined. Two-year economic plans were devised and implemented with great efficiency. International aid was used effectively, producing significant added value for the economy. In addition, bilateral agreements were signed with Czechoslovakia, Bulgaria and Greece, providing job opportunities for Cypriot workers and refugees in those countries. Within the framework of reconstruction measures, a major reform was initiated that was radically to change the economic and social development of the island—the transformation of Cyprus into a centre for offshore companies. Foreign companies wishing to establish themselves in Cyprus had to pay income tax at a rate of only 4.25% and were permitted to import cars and office equipment duty-free. The companies' foreign employees living in Cyprus paid only half the national rate of income tax, and clients of foreign banks enjoyed a similar level of protection of confidentiality as those of Swiss banks. All of these measures had an extremely positive impact on the Cypriot economy, which experienced a rehabilitation in the following years that can only be compared with that recorded in Germany during the 1950s after the Second World War.

Unemployment was reduced from almost 30% of the labour force in late 1974 to just 1.7% in 1979, partly by the emigration of workers but largely through the promotion of labour-intensive industry and massive expansion of the construction sector, both for private housing and for development projects. By 1980, however, it became clear that the post-1976 boom had concealed a deeper instability in the economy. Rising wages and the growing cost of imported petroleum contributed to an increase in inflation to 13.5% in 1980. The Greek Cypriot Government was also confronted with widening balance-of-payments and budgetary deficits. It consequently adopted a stabilization programme, which had successfully reduced the inflation rate to 5.0% by 1985.

The Government's Five-Year Economic Plan for 1989–93 achieved average annual gross domestic product (GDP) growth of 5.2%. However, during that period annual growth rates were extremely volatile. The average annual growth rate then decreased to 3.8% in 1996–2000, largely owing to the negative impact on the tourism sector of controversy in 1996–97 over a Russian missile system that the Government planned to deploy on the island (see History). The average annual growth rate decreased again during 2001–05, following the September 2001 suicide attacks in the USA, the consequences in 2002 of the crash that came after a poorly regulated stock market boom and the US-led military campaign in Iraq in 2003. A revival in the tourism industry, as well as an upsurge in construction fuelled by rising credit, contributed to a recovery over the next few years, with GDP growth averaging 4.3% per year in 2004–08.

An important feature of economic policy from 1992 was the gradual adaptation of economic practices and procedures to prepare for full membership of the European Community (EC, now European Union—EU), followed by the adoption of the euro in January 2008. The Cyprus Government had applied for membership in July 1990 (having achieved customs union with the EC from 1 January 1988) and joined the EU on 1 May 2004. In addition to the introduction of value-added tax (VAT), in June 1992 the Government linked the Cyprus pound initially to the European Currency Unit and then to the euro at a rate of C£1 = €1.708601. This proved to be a remarkably successful policy for currency stability as the Cyprus pound traded very closely to this rate for well over a decade and joined the Exchange Rate Mechanism (ERM) at the same rate (inverted, therefore, at C£0.585274 per euro) in May 2005. It was also the rate at which the Cyprus pound was converted to the euro.

Cyprus's formal accession to the EU on 1 May 2004 was overshadowed by the failure to reach a political settlement, with the result that only the (de facto) Greek Cypriot area came under the EU's *acquis communautaire* (at mid-2023 this remained suspended in the northern part of the island due to the continuing Turkish occupation), and that the potential economic benefits of a reunified island being in the EU—in particular, building commercial relations with the island's largest neighbouring market—were deferred. Nevertheless, the Cyprus Government was not obliged to meet the cost of reunification, estimates of which varied wildly (for political reasons), from a low of about C£4,000m. (€6,834m.) to a high of some C£16,000m. (€27,337m.), at a time when its finances were in substantial deficit. In an early warning to Cyprus, the European Commission announced in May 2004 that the Government's fiscal consolidation plans had significantly diverged from targets, resulting in levels of budget deficit and public debt well above the Maastricht convergence criteria. The high budget deficit prompted the European Commission to launch a formal 'excessive deficit procedure', which effectively delayed Cyprus's entry into the ERM, and thus adoption of the euro, by a year. The Government responded to the Commission in June by announcing new measures for the progressive reduction of the deficit, which had the effect of reducing it from 6.3% of GDP in 2003 to 2.3% in 2005. On 2 May 2005 the Cyprus pound was admitted to the ERM, beginning the obligatory minimum two-year transitional stage towards adoption of the euro (see *Budget, Investment and Finance*). On 16 May 2007 the European Commission stated that the Maastricht convergence criteria had been met and recommended that Cyprus adopt the euro on 1 January 2008, which it duly did.

Foreign capital, supported by a well-functioning public administration, lack of bureaucratic 'red tape' and a favourable legal framework, continued to flow into the tourism and real estate sectors, boosting the construction industry and generating jobs that could not be satisfied by the local labour force. Since the transitional arrangements introduced by the EU suspending the free movement of citizens from the new accession countries for seven years did not apply to Cyprus, there were, subsequently, waves of legal and illegal immigration, including from low-wage EU member states (including Bulgaria and Romania) but also from further afield (including from the Philippines and Sri Lanka). Owing to the mass immigration of cheap labour, initially with the consent of the trade unions, violations of the migrants' labour and human rights were widespread. As a general rule, third-country nationals work under less favourable conditions than EU citizens, especially as the employment and residence permits of the former are tied to a specific employer, thereby restricting the opportunity to change jobs. Officially, the employment contracts of third-country nationals are controlled by the Government and trade unions. However, in practice, employers have been able to draw up their own contracts, often involving worse working conditions, and leading to 'wage dumping' and unfair competition with local workers.

By the end of 2008 the economy had started to decelerate as a result of the global economic downturn, with the bursting of the real estate 'bubble' and declining consumer demand contributing to a slowdown. According to the World Bank, the economy contracted during 2009, by 2.0%, but returned to growth in 2010, expanding by 2.0% in that year and by 0.4% in 2011, buoyed by increased activity in real estate services, and the hotels and restaurants sector. Although the banking sector continued to show relatively healthy profits into 2010, by the end of 2011 a substantial write-down of high exposure to Greek sovereign and commercial debt by the island's two largest banks had resulted in serious capitalization issues (see *Industry, Manufacturing and Services*). This, together with continuing international concerns over the Government's fiscal policy, which had resulted in a rapid downgrading of Cyprus's credit rating and consequently prevented access to international financial markets, obliged the Government to apply on 25 June 2012 for aid from the European Financial Stability Facility (EFSF—see *Budget, Investment and Finance*). According to the World Bank, GDP contracted by 3.4% in 2012 and by 6.6% in 2013, before the rate of contraction slowed to 1.8% in 2014. Following successful measures to stabilize and reform the banking sector, GDP growth resumed in 2015, at a rate of 3.4%. The recovery accelerated in 2016, with growth of 6.6%. GDP grew by 5.7% in 2017, and remained buoyant in 2018 and 2019, at 5.6% and 5.5%, respectively.

With the onset of the global coronavirus disease (COVID-19) pandemic in early 2020, Cyprus was in a strong fiscal position, having recorded a series of fiscal surpluses which had allowed some reduction of government debt. However, the impact of the global health emergency on the country was substantial, particularly owing to its strong dependence on the tourism sector. GDP contracted by 4.4% in 2020, but a return to positive growth was achieved in 2021, with GDP expanding by 6.6% in that year.

In the Heritage Foundation's 2023 Index of Economic Freedom, Cyprus's overall score was 72.3, making its economy the 18th most free among the 176 ranked countries and the 12th most free among the 44 European countries, with its overall score above the regional and world averages. Public debt reached an unprecedented high of 102.5% of GDP in 2018, but subsequently declined to 95.7% in 2019, 89.1% in 2020 and 83.0% in 2021.

Economic activity remained strong in 2022, despite the adverse external environment. According to the World Bank, GDP grew by 5.6% in 2022, largely due to a better than expected performance by the tourism sector and the continued expansion of exports in other service sectors. In terms of domestic demand, consumption in the first nine months of 2022 increased by 10.8%, compared with the corresponding period of 2021; public consumption increased by 1.6% and private consumption by 7.4% over the same period. Gross fixed capital formation increased by 6.6% in 2022 as a whole. In terms of external demand, exports increased by 23.7% in 2022, while imports increased by 29.4%. From a sectoral perspective, growth in 2022 was recorded in nearly all sectors, with a contraction being recorded only in the construction sector.

The Cypriots are among the most prosperous people in the Mediterranean region—Cyprus being the only country in the region that can compete with Israel in this respect—with GDP per capita in 2023 of an estimated US $33,807 in nominal terms and $54,611 on a purchasing-power-parity basis, according to the International Monetary Fund (IMF). According to the 2021–22 Human Development Index published by the United Nations Development Programme (UNDP), Cyprus was ranked 29th out of 191 countries and territories, comfortably within the 'very high human development' category.

AGRICULTURE

Until only a few decades ago agriculture was the single most important economic activity in Cyprus, but—following the economic dislocation caused by the 1974 invasion—it has since been superseded by tourism, manufacturing and financial services. In the Greek Cypriot area, only 2.4% of the employed population was engaged in agriculture (including forestry and fishing) in 2022. Agriculture accounted for a preliminary 1.9% of GDP in that year. According to the World Bank, the GDP of the agricultural sector declined by an average of 0.7% per year in 2012–21; it decreased by 1.4% in 2020, but decreased by 0.1% in 2021. The main crops in both parts of the island are citrus fruits, potatoes, olives, carobs, wheat and barley.

Periodic drought conditions have made agricultural production volatile, and have led environmentalists to question the logic of producing crops that need large amounts of water, such as citrus fruits. Production of cereals reached 164,280 metric tons in 2003, but declined to 70,195 tons by 2011, rising slightly to 89,848 tons by 2015. Output of cereals fell to only 10,424 tons in 2016, before rising again to 59,033 tons by 2019. The potato crop peaked at 234,000 tons in 1995. Since then, annual production has fluctuated, rising to 122,803 tons in 2016, before declining progressively over the next four years to 80,300 tons in 2020, but increasing to 88,500 tons in 2021. The production of grapes and bananas has declined markedly since 2003, in part owing to the trend for sizeable tracts of agricultural land in certain areas to be sold for property development, and stood at 22,600 tons and 5,600 tons, respectively, in 2021. The production of olives experienced a resurgence in recent years, reaching 25,520 tons in 2019, although output decreased to 22,100 tons in 2020 and further to 17,000 tons in 2021. The production of oranges, the main citrus fruit, declined from 63,000 tons in 1990 to 18,100 tons in 2021. The main livestock products are pork and poultry meat, with production of 43,700 tons and 26,600 tons, respectively, in 2021. Exports of products of agricultural origin, such as halloumi cheese, are becoming more important to the agricultural sector. Dairy and other edible animal products accounted for 6.4% of total export revenue in 2022.

INDUSTRY AND SERVICES

After continued weak performance in the overall industrial sector during the 1990s, the sector demonstrated a strong recovery in 2000–05, mainly as a result of growth in mining and quarrying and electricity, gas and water, but only a modest recovery for the sub-sector of manufacturing. The 2000–05 period was characterized by a sharp decline in output from the traditional manufacturing sectors, such as clothing, textiles and leather products, as these sectors failed to compete with lower-cost manufacturers abroad, together with a strong increase in certain higher value-added sectors such as pharmaceuticals and machinery and equipment. However, output of petroleum refining declined by 35.3% in 2001–05, owing to the closure of the oil refinery in Larnaca in April 2004. This overall trend continued in 2006–08. A decline in output of textiles and pulp and paper products offset a healthy increase in output of chemicals (including pharmaceuticals), electrical and optical equipment, and transport equipment. According to the World Bank, industrial GDP increased by an average of 3.1% per year in 2012–21; it decreased by 6.4% in 2020, but increased by 7.1% in 2021. The contribution of manufacturing to GDP at current market prices declined steadily from 14.4% in 1995 to 10.4% in 2000, 7.6% in 2005 and a preliminary 6.5% in 2022. The industrial sector overall (comprising mining, manufacturing, power and construction) provided a preliminary 15.4% of GDP and engaged 17.1% of the employed labour force in 2022.

In contrast to the relative decline in the contribution of the manufacturing sector, the services sector has increased its share of GDP over recent years, based on constant annual growth in total gross value added. It rose from 64.7% of GDP in 1995 to 69.6% in 2000, then declined gradually to 66.4% of GDP in 2008 as construction boomed. When the construction sector declined sharply in 2009, the contribution of the services sector rose accordingly to 69.9% of GDP. Services contributed 71.6% of GDP in 2010, rising to a preliminary 81.9% in 2022, when it engaged 76.6% of the employed labour force. According to the World Bank, the GDP of the services sector increased at an average annual rate of 2.0% in 2012–21; it decreased by 4.4% in 2020, but decreased by 5.3% in 2021.

The virtual standstill in both the construction and real estate sectors from 2009 raised concerns over the commercial banks' exposure to property developers, evidenced by a significant rise in the rescheduling of loans and provision for non-performing loans. Given the crucial role of the banking sector in the economy, a far greater worry emerged in 2010 and deepened in 2011 regarding the Cypriot commercial banks' substantial exposure to the crisis-ridden economy of Greece. In April 2011 credit ratings agency Standard & Poor's (S&P) estimated this exposure at some €6,400m. in Greek sovereign and bank debt, in addition to significant amounts lent to Greek companies and households through the Cypriot banks' substantial networks in Greece. Most Greek-related exposure was held by the three largest Cypriot banks: Bank of Cyprus (BoC), Marfin Popular Bank (MPB) and Hellenic Bank. Despite the banks' apparent compliance with the Central Bank of Cyprus's instruction to improve capital adequacy ratios to levels that would accommodate 50% write-offs as the loans fell due and were rolled over, BoC and MPB proved unable to cope with the impact of the 76.4% 'haircut' on their sovereign Greek assets as part of a bailout plan agreed by Greece with the so-called troika, comprising the European Commission, the IMF and the European Central Bank (ECB) in October 2011.

MPB had bought heavily into Greek sovereign debt between 2007 and 2009, adding to a large commercial and consumer debt portfolio—amounting to the most substantial Greek exposure of all the Cypriot banks. The non-executive Chairman of MPB, Andreas Vgenopoulos, was forced to resign in November 2011, just before MPB posted a record net loss for that year of €2,830m., which included a 65% write-down (€1,969m.) of its €3,052m. Greek sovereign debt holding. In April 2012 the bank, which had recently reverted to its original name of Cyprus Popular Bank (CPB), revised its final 2011 losses upwards to €3,650.4m., incorporating a write-down of the full 76.4% (€2,331m.) of the nominal value of its Greek government bond holdings. By May 2012 it was evident that CPB would not be able to raise from a strategic investor the €1,800m. that it needed for recapitalization and it appealed for assistance from the Government, which agreed to underwrite the €1,800m. capital issue. The state bought €1,797m. of the share issue in June, gaining an interest in the bank of 84%, and named new board members in July.

However, CPB's difficulties worsened, as concerned depositors began to withdraw their funds, leaving it increasingly dependent on the emergency liquidity assistance (ELA) provided by the central bank. The terms of the bailout agreed by the Government with the troika in March 2013 specified the winding down of CPB. This involved the sale of CPB's business in Cyprus (excluding its subsidiaries and branches abroad) to BoC, and the division of CPB into a 'good' bank with performing loans (to be absorbed by BoC) and a 'bad' bank with non-performing loans (to be run down over time). Although BoC received around €4,000m. from CPB in insured deposits (i.e. less than €100,000), it was also required to assume some of CPB's obligations, including the €9,200m. that the latter had accumulated in ELA debt, adding to BoC's own ELA liability of around €2,000m. At the Government's insistence, 2,390 CPB employees in Cyprus were also transferred to BoC's payroll, prior to an eventual reduction of the total workforce and branch network. Meanwhile, following the Greek bailout agreement in October 2011 with its attached 'haircut', BoC posted post-tax losses of €1,380m. in its 2011 full-year results, incorporating a €1,682m. write-down of the €2,083m. nominal value of its Greek sovereign debt holdings. Group CEO Andreas Eliades resigned in July 2012, after the BoC announced that it needed funding of €500m., which it could only secure through temporary state assistance.

Under the initial terms of the March 2013 bailout agreement, uninsured depositors with BoC were subjected to a 'bail-in', involving the automatic conversion of 37.5% of net funds into Class A shares in BoC, with voting rights and dividends. A further 22.5% of uninsured depositors' net funds were temporarily frozen against eventual conversion into Class A shares when the final 'bail-in' figure was agreed; this was set at 47.5% in July. Under the new structure, former CPB depositors owned some 18% of BoC—but were only able to sell those shares after the 'bad' part of CPB had been finally wound down. The bank employees' union became BoC's second-largest shareholder after the 'bail-in' of its provident fund deposits. As part of the CPB resolution process, in March both banks' boards were dismissed by the central bank in its capacity as the resolution authority to facilitate the restructuring of the banking sector. On 30 July BoC formally exited administration by the resolution authority and it regained access to cheaper liquidity via the Eurosystem the following day. In mid-September a new board of directors was elected, including six Russians.

The operations abroad of the three largest Cypriot banks began to be curtailed in the second quarter of 2013, with BoC taking steps to sell its units in Romania, the Russian Federation and Ukraine. Under the terms set by the Eurogroup for the bailout agreement, Piraeus Bank was chosen by the Greek Government to assume the Greek units of BoC, CPB and Hellenic, with the total price set at €524m. The deal was approved, despite opposition from the boards of both BoC and CPB. However, the enforced sale of the Cypriot banks' Greek units resulted in CPB selling to Piraeus Bank assets that were pledged against its ELA liability, without Piraeus Bank assuming the corresponding ELA liability. CPB was therefore left with an 'unsecured' ELA liability amounting to some €3,800m., which was then imposed on BoC as a result of the Eurogroup decision. As part of the rescue programme agreed by the troika with the Government, which provided €1,500m. for co-operative banks to correct a capital shortfall, their number was to be reduced from 96 to 18, mainly through mergers. Some 150 branches of the co-operative banks were also to be closed, leaving 250. Under an approved arrangement designed to recapitalize and restructure the co-operative credit sector before the end of 2013 without a depositor 'bail-in', the state was to use the bailout funds to buy 99% of shares, effectively becoming the exclusive owner of the sector, and thus liable for any losses, but also eligible for dividends. The Government agreed to receive 10% annual interest on the capital, allowing the co-operative banks to use any surplus to buy back shares.

Deposits in the banking system increased in 2016, for the first time since the 2013 'bail-in', amid strengthening confidence and relatively high interest rates. A Single Supervisory Mechanism review in 2016 assessed the capital positions of the three largest Cypriot banks as adequate; however, the non-performing loan (NPL) ratio in the three banks remained extremely high. The Cyprus Co-operative Bank (CCB—formerly the Co-operative Central Bank), which had become state-owned following a capital injection of €1,800m. by the Government in 2012, and had received further capital injections (see *Budget, Investment and Finance*) in 2014 and 2015, suffered another setback in March 2017 when the financial Ombudsman ordered the return of €111m. to overcharged borrowers, resulting in a €75m. decrease in the bank's capital. The CCB's 60% NPL ratio continued to hamper plans for it to secure a CSE listing that would enable the reduction of the state holding to 25%. Meanwhile, in January 2017, after the creation of an Ireland-based holding company, BoC was admitted to listing and trading on the London Stock Exchange; BoC also repaid the remaining balance on its ELA.

Amid increasing uncertainties regarding a worsening of the CCB's funding situation, a run on deposits in early 2018 prompted the Government in April to deposit around €2,520m. in the bank, principally financed by government bonds at a total value of €2,350m., with maturities of 15–20 years, purchased by the CCB. Meanwhile, in March the Government issued an invitation for expressions of interest in acquisition of the 'good' part of the CCB. In June an agreement was finalized under which Hellenic Bank was to acquire the operations of the bank, in exchange for increasing its capital by €150m. The CCB's banking licence was formally withdrawn by the central bank at the end of August, and it was decidedthat the bank would be transformed into the Co-operative Asset Management Company (SEDIPES), with a subsidiary Cyprus Asset Management Company (KEDIPES), which would manage former assets of the CCB amounting to €8,300m., including NPLs of €7,000m. that would be removed from the banking system. In September it was announced that Hellenic Bank had completed the acquisition of certain assets and liabilities of the CCB.

The effects of the COVID-19 pandemic on the domestic financial sector were largely contained in 2021, mainly owing to the better-than-anticipated performance of the economy. Domestic private sector deposits increased significantly to reach the equivalent of 5.8% of GDP in December 2021, compared with 2.5% in December 2020. According to the Central Bank of Cyprus, this upward trend in deposits reflected fiscal support measures introduced by the Government for businesses and households (see *Budget, Investment and Finance*), increased forced/precautionary savings, and the general recovery in economic activity. The level of non-performing facilities in the banking system decreased by €2,100m. in 2021 to stand at €3,000m. (11.1% of total loans) by the end of December. Overall lending and deposit interest rates in Cyprus remained low at mid-2022, creating an environment conducive to growth.

In March 2022 RCB Bank (formerly Russian Commercial Bank—an international bank founded in 1995 and headquartered in Limassol) announced that it was to cease operating as a bank and was to become an asset management company. In the previous month the principal shareholder, the VTB Bank, had sold its shares in RCB Bank to Cypriot interests amid the economic fallout from Russia's invasion of Ukraine, which had begun on 24 February, thus making the bank entirely Cypriot-owned for the first time in its history. Regulators at the ECB had long been concerned about RCB Bank's alleged links to the Russian Government. Furthermore, many of the bank's executives appeared to have acquired Cypriot passports under dubious circumstances, most likely via the country's notorious (and now defunct) so-called 'golden passport' scheme, which allowed 6,700 foreign nationals (including around 2,900 Russians) effectively to purchase passports by investing or depositing large sums of money in Cyprus.

The construction sector grew rapidly after the 1974 Turkish invasion, partly owing to the need to house refugees from the north. The manufacturing and construction sectors were hampered, in the early 1980s, by the adverse effects of the Government's deflationary measures and by the accumulated results of wage inflation over several years. Rapid expansion in the second half of the decade led to oversupply, however, and during 1990–94 growth in the construction sector decelerated overall. During 1995–99 value added in construction rose only in 1995. One of the reasons for the poor performance of construction in 1999–2000 was the stock market 'bubble', which diverted money temporarily into investment in (overvalued) stocks. The spectacular crash of the stock market, combined with restrictions on taking money out of Cyprus that were only fully lifted in 2004, led Cypriots to return to the more traditional practice of investing in land. Thus, a long recovery in the construction sector began from 2001 onwards, assisted initially by a decrease in interest rates and later by increased foreign demand for holiday homes. The number of authorized building permits rose from 6,096 (valued at €1,055.1m.) in 2000 to 9,794 (€2,473.4m.) in 2006.

The significant devaluation of the pound sterling against the euro, combined with heightened concern over delays in the issuing of title deeds for properties already purchased, greatly reduced demand from British buyers for new holiday homes in 2009. Despite the sharp economic downturn, offer prices for real estate during that year remained high in a stagnant market, resulting in a 44% decrease in sales, according to Land Registry data, with purchase prices only beginning to decline in 2010. In the ensuing years the construction sector expanded further, contributing a preliminary 6.0% of GDP in 2022 and engaging 9.1% of the employed labour force in that year (there were, in addition, large numbers of foreign workers employed in the sector). During 2022 a total of 7,604 building permits were issued, compared with 8,164 in the previous year, representing a 7% decline. The total value of these permits remained virtually unchanged, at €2,496.6m., while the total area declined by 6% and the number of dwelling units also fell by 6%. Despite the effects of the termination, in October 2020, of the Cyprus Investment Programme (CIP), which were significant since real estate investments through the CIP comprised about 60% of total programme investments, growth prospects in the construction sector were expected to remain positive. Although the GDP of the construction sector declined at an average annual rate of an estimated 0.4% during 2021–23 (representing a cumulative decrease of around 1.3%), the negative impact of the termination of the CIP was expected to be negligible from 2024.

According to data released by the Ministry of Finance, the GDP of the retail sector grew by 2.0% in 2014 and by 3.5% in 2015, and the upward trend continued in 2016 and 2017, with respective increases of 5.3% and 6.0%. The retail sector expanded by 5.4% in 2018 and by 3.5% in 2019. Due to the COVID-19 pandemic, sectoral GDP declined by 1.5% in 2020. However, the sector recovered strongly in 2021, increasing by 6.9%, and expanded further in 2022, by 2.2%.

ENERGY

In January 2001 the Greek Cypriot Government approved plans for the concentration of all refining and energy production facilities at Vassiliko on the southern coast. The Vassiliko Energy Centre was ultimately to host all existing and new electricity generation and oil-refining installations. The Government subsequently confirmed that, owing to cost and environmental grounds, and to meet the requirements of EU membership, Cyprus would eventually switch to the use of natural gas rather than petroleum for generating electricity. To that end, the Government entered into talks with Syria and

Egypt on the supply of Egyptian natural gas to Cyprus via Syria and an underwater pipeline. However, in the light of cost and supply uncertainties, the Government announced in December 2002 that it had chosen the option of importing liquefied natural gas (LNG) by tanker. International tenders would be invited for contracts to bring LNG to Cyprus and also for the construction of a terminal at Vassiliko on a build-operate-transfer basis.

The possibility that Cyprus might be able to exploit recently discovered gas reserves in its exclusive economic zone (EEZ—see below) was one of the reasons for an extended pause in the LNG terminal project. Following the completion of a feasibility study in 2016, the Government in October 2018 issued a tender for the construction of the LNG terminal in Vassiliko Bay, near Limassol, and associated infrastructure. The EU Connecting Europe Facility financing instrument was to provide a grant of €116m. towards the project's estimated total cost of €500m. In August 2019 it was announced that the Natural Gas Public Company (DEFA/CYGAS) had selected a consortium led by the China Petroleum Pipeline Engineering Company (from three bidding consortiums, the other two comprising Japanese and European companies, respectively). The European Investment Bank reportedly finalized €150m. of funding for the project in June 2020, and construction officially commenced in July. The terminal was originally scheduled to be operational by the end of 2022. However, owing to various delays, the completion date was pushed back, initially until July 2023 and subsequently until October.

Against a background of austerity measures and severe economic recession which persisted into 2015, hopes for future economic growth were vested in the confirmed existence of major gas deposits to the south of Cyprus, within its 200-mile EEZ. Having had its EEZ mapped out in detail and signed EEZ delimitation agreements with Egypt, Israel and Lebanon, the Greek Cypriot Government intended to exploit at least an estimated gross mean 7,000,000m. cu ft (198,240,000m. cu m) of natural gas. The presence of these first reserves had been confirmed in December 2011 by US company Noble Energy, which held the concession to a 2,000-sq-km area known as Block 12 following the first licensing round in 2007. This block is located some 60 km from Israel's Leviathan gasfield, which contains some 19,000,000m. cu ft of natural gas. The proximity of Israeli gasfields and the collaboration between Noble Energy and Israeli company Delek Drilling (renamed NewMed Energy in 2022) in the Israeli gas finds naturally led to high-level contact between Cyprus and Israel over the possibility of co-operating on the exploitation of their respective gas resources. In February 2013 the Greek Cypriot Government signed an agreement transferring 30% of Noble Energy's gas exploitation rights in offshore Block 12 to Avner Oil & Gas and Delek Drilling, the US firm's Israeli partners. In March Noble Energy confirmed that it would explore a second prospect within Block 12, believed to hold up to 8,000,000m. cu ft of natural gas, and began an appraisal well in June. It was reported in early 2014 that the results of Noble's test confirmed that reserves in Block 12 (the Aphrodite gasfield) were smaller than initially estimated, although still 'substantial', at 3,600,000m.–6,000,000m. cu ft.

Despite threats from Turkey, which disputes the Republic of Cyprus's right to exploit the EEZ for hydrocarbons, in May 2012 the Greek Cypriot Government concluded a second licensing round for the remaining 12 blocks in its EEZ. In October the Government announced the award of four licences for contiguous blocks to the north and north-east of Block 12: for Blocks 2 and 3, licences were awarded to a consortium of Italy's ENI and Korea Gas Corpn (KOGAS); the licence for Block 9 went to a consortium comprising Total E&P Activités Pétrolières, Russia's NOVATEK Overseas Exploration & Production GMBH and GPB Global Resources BV; and the licence for Block 11 went to Total E&P Activités Pétrolières. In February 2013 the Government signed an exploration agreement with Total for oil and gas in Blocks 10 and 11.

Following a third licensing round, in early 2016, a consortium of the USA's ExxonMobil and Qatar Petroleum (renamed Qatar Energy in 2021) announced in April 2017 that an exploration and production sharing contract for Block 10 had been signed with the Greek Cypriot Government. In July the *West Capella* drilling vessel contracted by Total and ENI began exploration operations in Block 11 (resulting in increased tensions with Turkey, which staged naval exercises in the region). After the exploratory drilling was completed in September the initial results released indicated that the reserves were too small for commercial development. However, in February 2018 it was reported that ENI and Total had made what was believed to be a large gas discovery at the Calypso prospect in Block 6. Tensions with Turkey again escalated shortly afterwards, when Turkish vessels conducting military exercises prevented a drill ship operated by ENI from moving a drilling rig to Block 3 from Block 6.

In September 2018 the energy ministers of Cyprus and Egypt signed an agreement providing for the construction of a sub-sea pipeline, at a cost of US $800m.–$1,000m., to transport gas from Cyprus' Aphrodite offshore field, located approximately 170 km south of Limassol, to Egypt, where it would be liquefied for export to Europe. The agreement was ratified by the Cypriot House of Representatives in April 2019.

In January 2020 the energy ministers of Greece, Cyprus and Israel signed a framework agreement providing for the construction of the 1,900-km sub-sea EastMed pipeline, with a capacity to transport 10,000m. cu m of natural gas annually, which would connect Israel's Leviathan and Cyprus's Aphrodite gasfields in the Eastern Mediterranean to Cyprus, the Greek island of Crete, and thence to mainland Greece and Italy. However, in January 2022 the US Department of State withdrew its diplomatic support for the pipeline owing to environmental concerns, the pipeline's purported lack of economic and commercial viability, and regional tensions arising from the project, which, if undertaken, would effectively thwart Turkey's aspirations of becoming a regional energy hub.

Aside from the Aphrodite gasfield, in 2015 ENI discovered sizeable deposits of gas in Block 6 of the Cypriot EEZ, close to the maritime border with Egypt, while exploratory activities carried out by ExxonMobil and Qatar Petroleum in Block 10 in 2019 revealed a gasfield (dubbed Glaucus) containing an estimated 5,000,000m.–8,000,000m. cu ft of gas. In December 2022 the Ministry of Energy announced that the consortium of ENI and France's TotalEnergies had found gas reserves of 2,000,000m.–3,000,000m. cu ft at the Zeus-1 well in Block 6 of the Cypriot EEZ. A similar discovery, at the Cronos-1 well, had been announced in August and was expected to yield around 2,500,000m. cu ft of gas, according to preliminary estimates. Cyprus hopes to begin exporting gas from the Aphrodite gasfield by 2026, most probably via the proposed pipeline connecting the field to terminals in Egypt.

In July 2012 the Electricity Authority of Cyprus (EAC) signed a memorandum of co-operation (MOC) with the Israel Electric Corporation regarding the use of their countries' respective hydrocarbons discoveries in the eastern Mediterranean. The MOC included provisions for connecting the two organizations' electricity grids via submarine cable and jointly developing electricity production stations using natural gas, for export to third countries. The MOC was motivated partly by progress in feasibility studies for the EuroAsia Interconnector project, which aimed to construct a submarine power cable connecting the power grids of Israel, Cyprus and Greece. The initial feasibility studies were completed in late 2012 and a revised proposal was presented to the Governments of the three countries in May 2013. In July the project was recognized by the EU as a cross-border project of common interest, qualifying it for EU funding. The first tripartite meeting between government leaders took place in Nicosia in January 2016, and in February 2017 the European Commission approved €14.5m. in financial support towards the planned EuroAsia Interconnector, which, it was envisaged, would end the energy isolation of Cyprus. An agreement on the cross-border cost allocation of the EuroAsia Interconnector was signed by the Cyprus Energy Regulatory Authority (CERA) and Greece's Regulatory Authority for Energy in October. In March 2021 Cyprus, Greece and Israel signed an initial agreement to build the EuroAsia Interconnector traversing the Mediterranean seabed, at a projected cost of about US $900m. It was announced that the Interconnector would have a capacity of 1,000 MW–2,000 MW and, at a length of about 1,500 km, would be the longest and deepest sub-sea electricity cable ever constructed. Construction of the Interconnector formally commenced in October 2022 and was expected to be completed by the end of 2025.

Electricity production capacity rose gradually after the first phase of the Vasilikos power station was commissioned in 2000. At the beginning of July 2011 the EAC owned and operated three power stations with a total nominal capacity of 1,568 MW: Vasilikos (878 MW), Dhekelia (360 MW) and Moni (330 MW). The EAC also distributed electricity generated by three operational privately owned wind farms: Orites (82 MW), Ayia Anna (20 MW) and Alexigros (31.5 MW). The total installed capacity of the three EAC power stations in 2022 was 1,478 MW: Vasilikos (868 MW), Dhekelia (460 MW) and Moni (150 MW).

Although more than 80% of the Greek Cypriot sector's energy still comes directly from oil, in recent years the Government has promoted renewable energy sources subsidy schemes, involving primarily the exploitation of solar and wind energy, as part of its European obligation to increase renewable energy production. By 2014 six wind farms were operational, producing a total of around 150 MW. In May 2012 the Government announced new subsidy schemes for renewable energy, focusing on photovoltaic (PV) units for household and commercial purposes. By the end of July 2020 the number of households with PV systems totalled 16,546. In 2018 electricity production from combustible fuels totalled an estimated 4,626.7m. kWh, while electricity production from renewable energy sources amounted to an estimated 514.8m. kWh (of which wind energy provided 238.6m. kWh and solar photovoltaic output contributed 218.3m. kWh). Total electricity consumption in that year was 4,615.4m. kWh, and imports of petroleum products accounted for 18.4% of the value of total imports.

TRANSPORT AND COMMUNICATIONS

As part of a programme of economic diversification, the Greek Cypriot sector has become a major maritime trading centre. By the end of 1996 Cyprus had climbed to fifth position in the world in terms of displacement, with a displacement totalling more than 26m. grt. However, since then the ship registry has been in decline. Under a new policy introduced in January 2000 to improve the safety record of Cyprus-registered ships, the age limit for registration was reduced from 17 to 15 years. These and other quality improvements, as well as a ban imposed by Turkey on Cyprus-flagged ships docking in Turkish ports, resulted in the Cyprus registry slipping to 11th position in the world (third in the EU, after Malta and Greece) by 2018, in which position it remained in 2020. According to Lloyds' List Intelligence, the registered fleet had declined to 1,245 vessels and 21.9m. grt by the end of 2022.

Famagusta formerly handled around 83% of Cyprus's freight traffic, but since becoming Turkish-controlled the port was declared closed by the Cypriot Government and has been superseded by Larnaca and Limassol for shipments from the Republic of Cyprus-controlled area. Gross tonnage of goods loaded increased from 3.1m. metric tons in 2014 to 4.3m. tons in 2018, while over the same period tonnage of goods unloaded rose from 5.3m. tons to 8.1m. tons. As a result of the COVID-19 pandemic, goods loaded and unloaded declined to 3.7m. tons and 7.4m. tons, respectively, in 2020. Port development schemes have been instituted at Larnaca and Limassol, and new marina projects are under way or have recently been completed in Paphos, Larnaca, Limassol and Ayia Napa.

In 2001 the Government secured parliamentary approval for plans to privatize the operation and development of the two international airports, at Larnaca and Paphos. A contract was eventually awarded in 2005 to an international consortium, Hermes Airports Ltd, which secured a 25-year concession from the Cypriot Government for the development and management of the two airports. The new terminal building at Paphos airport opened in November 2008, while the new terminal at Larnaca airport was inaugurated in November 2009.

Consecutive Greek Cypriot governments have given priority to establishing Cyprus as a centre for regional telecommunications and as a staging post for satellite communications between Europe, the Middle East and Asia. In a major step towards achieving this objective, in May 2003 Cyprus and Greece jointly launched the Hellas Sat satellite from Cape Canaveral, Florida, USA, using a US rocket to provide voice, digital television, internet and broadband services to as many as 25 countries. The telecommunications sector was traditionally dominated by the state-owned Cyprus Telecommunications Authority (CYTA), but in March 2003 CYTA's monopoly effectively ended, with the granting of licences to four Cyprus-registered information technology (IT) companies for the provision of various fixed-line services. In August the Telecommunications and Post Office Commission awarded a 20-year special licence to the EAC for the provision of fixed-line telephone services and in October the Lebanese-funded Scancom (Cyprus) group won an auction for a 20-year mobile telephone licence, operating first under the name Areeba, then as MTN and then as Epic, for which it paid the Government C£12.75m. (€21.8m.). In April 2004 another licence for the provision of telephone services was awarded to the private enterprise Callsat. Complying with EU requirements, in June 2013 the Government announced a tender for a third mobile network operator licence, despite protests from CYTA and MTN that the island's market was too small to accommodate it. In 2006 there were 385,538 fixed-line telephone subscribers and 867,785 mobile telephone subscriptions. By 2021 the former had declined to 304,581 and the latter stood at 1,320,800. In that year there were around 340,100 fixed-line broadband internet subscriptions and 1,233,000 mobile broadband internet subscriptions.

TOURISM

Tourism was one of the areas of the Greek Cypriot economy that was most adversely affected by the 1974 war, as 90% of the island's hotels came under Turkish Cypriot control. However, the sector expanded rapidly in the 1980s and 1990s, becoming the Republic of Cyprus's largest source of income. Tourist arrivals and revenue continued to rise in 1998–2001, reaching a peak of 2,696,732 arrivals and €2,173.3m. in revenue in 2001. Tourism then entered a difficult period, with either declining arrivals or dwindling revenue in many years. Occasional indirect factors included the onset of the Iraq crisis in 2003, but industry experts more often cite an ageing product and a comparative lack of infrastructure.

The global economic crisis, the full effects of which did not manifest in Cyprus until 2009, hit the tourism sector especially hard; total arrivals declined to 2,141,193 (down by 10.9% from 2008), and receipts from tourism decreased by 16.7% to €1,493.2m. However, total arrivals in 2011 rose to 2,392,228, marking a return to 2008 levels, and receipts from tourism increased to €1,749.3m. Total arrivals in 2012 rose to 2,464,908, the highest level since 2001, and receipts from tourism to €1,927.7m. A record level in tourist arrivals of 3,186,500 was recorded in 2016 (representing a year-on-year rise of 19.8%), with increases in visitors from all the major markets. Tourism receipts rose by 11.9% to €2,363.4m. in that year. Tourist arrivals again increased, by 14.6%, in 2017, to 3,652,100, while revenue from tourism rose to €2,639.1m. In 2018 tourist arrivals rose by 7.8% to 3,938,625 and receipts by 2.7% to €2,710.6m. A slight rise, to 3,976,777 arrivals, was recorded in 2019, when receipts amounted to €2,683.0m. However, the tourism sector was one of the most severely affected by the COVID-19 pandemic in 2020: despite a limited resumption of tourist activity in the second half of the year, tourist arrivals totalled only 631,609 overall, representing a year-on-year drop of 84.1%. Revenue from tourism likewise fell by 85.4% in 2020, to €392.0m. Amid an easing of international travel restrictions in many parts of the world for much of 2021, tourist arrivals in Cyprus recovered to 1,936,931 in that year, representing an increase of 206.7% on 2020's total, but still 51.3% down on that recorded in 2019. Tourist arrivals recovered strongly in 2022 to reach 3,201,080, while revenue from tourism was estimated at €2,439.2m., up from €1,513.6m. in 2021.

The Government's efforts to upgrade the quality of tourism on offer have been beset by delays. For example, in May 2000 approval was given for the construction of six new marinas by the end of 2002, as part of the Government's strategy of promoting 'high-value' tourism; however, construction of the first marina in Limassol did not begin until late 2010, and the marina facilities and linked commercial area became fully operational only in mid-2014. Securing finance for the other marina projects, notably the €700m. project in Larnaca, became increasingly difficult in 2013, and in July 2015 the Government revoked the contract awarded to an international consortium. Meanwhile, the Government of President Nikos Anastasiades indicated that it would include casinos in its strategy to encourage foreign investment. The Cyprus Tourism Organisation commissioned a study by private consultants into the potential impact of casinos on tourism, and in July 2013 it announced a plan to grant a licence for an integrated casino resort (ICR) that would have a large bed capacity and offer a number of auxiliary services, including theme parks, restaurants and retail space. In July 2015 the House of Representatives approved a bill facilitating the development of the resort and four 'satellite' gambling establishments. In June 2017 a 30-year contract to build and operate the casino resort was signed between the National Gaming Authority and the Melco Hard Rock consortium (comprising Macao's Melco International Development Ltd and Hard Rock International of the USA); it was announced that the complex, based in Limassol, and to include four satellite casinos in Nicosia, Larnaca, Ayia Napa and Paphos, would be the only ICR in Europe, and would attract an additional 300,000 tourists a year to Cyprus, provide 4,000 jobs and generate €100m. annually in taxes. In June 2019 Melco Resorts and Entertainment acquired a 75% stake in the ICR venture, having purchased the shares of Hard Rock international. The City of Dreams Mediterranean ICR in Limassol was officially inaugurated in July 2023. Meanwhile, plans for the expansion and privatization of Larnaca port and marina were finalized in February 2020, with a Cypriot-Israeli consortium taking on the project.

As part of its National Tourism Strategy 2030, in January 2022 the Greek Cypriot Government announced 12 grant schemes that were to come into effect over the course of the year. The main objectives of the plans for the tourism sector included the improvement of Cyprus's tourism product, the extension of the tourist season and the improvement or creation of the necessary infrastructure to facilitate certain forms of specialized tourism. The plans also aimed to promote and showcase Cypriot handicrafts and winemaking.

BUDGET, INVESTMENT AND FINANCE

Budget policy in recent years has been largely defined by EU and eurozone membership requirements, Cyprus having joined the EU on 1 May 2004 and the eurozone on 1 January 2008. In May 2000 the Government secured approval for a programme of tax cuts and other measures designed to compensate the lower paid for an increase in VAT from 8% to 10%, which came into effect on 1 July, as the first step towards the minimum 15% rate required by EU accession. Legislation adopted in December 1999 provided for the existing 9% statutory ceiling on interest rates to be removed with effect from 1 January 2001.

Declining share prices in early 2000 culminated in a major correction to the Cyprus Stock Exchange (CSE) index in March. Market capitalization of quoted companies decreased to less than C£8,000m. (€13,669m.), while the CSE index declined by more than one-half. Further significant decreases in the following months inflicted heavy losses on new investors, some of whom staged angry demonstrations in protest against what they alleged were fraudulent activities by brokers with the connivance of the CSE authorities. The Government responded in August by announcing various measures to restore investor confidence, including a strengthening of the CSE's legal framework and the introduction of greater transparency in its operations. In March 2005 the CSE and the Athens Stock Exchange agreed to create a common trading platform, which became operational in October 2006 and resulted in a transfer from trading in Cyprus pounds to trading in euros. Meanwhile, under constitutional amendments enacted in June 2002, the Central Bank of Cyprus became fully independent from the Government on 1 July, in accordance with the norm in EU member states.

In June 2004 the Government, under pressure from the European Commission, announced new austerity measures intended to contain the fiscal deficit to 5.2% of GDP in that year and then to reduce it to less than 3% in 2005 and to under 2% by 2007, to allow Cyprus to qualify for entry into the eurozone. These measures helped to restrain the 2004 deficit to 3.7% of GDP. Supported by receipts of €119.6m. from an income tax amnesty that expired on 31 March, the actual out-turn for 2005 was a budget deficit of 2.2% of GDP. The fiscal performance in 2006 would be one of the main criteria used for assessing whether Cyprus had fulfilled all of the preconditions for adopting the euro on 1 January 2008 as planned. In the event, the budget deficit out-turn was only 1.0% of GDP, well below the 3% ceiling. The 2007 budget projected a deficit of 1.6% of GDP, but, as it turned out, a large surplus of €563.5m., or 3.2% of GDP, was recorded. On 16 May the European Commission declared that Cyprus had met all of the (Maastricht) criteria for adoption of the euro, and Cyprus duly adopted the euro on 1 January 2008.

In 2008 there was a fiscal surplus of €164.6m., equivalent to 0.9% of GDP, and public debt was reduced to 45.5% of GDP. The surplus was soon applied to raising state pensions closer in line with EU norms and to increasing other welfare allowances to mitigate the initial effects of the economic downturn. The Government expressed public optimism that the economy could ride out the economic crisis in 2009 without serious difficulties. However, in the event, Cyprus's economy contracted by 2.0% in 2009, while the budget deficit amounted to €1,014.7m., equivalent to 5.4% of GDP. In June 2010 the European Commission recommended opening an Excessive Deficit Procedure for Cyprus, owing to the sizeable 2009 budget deficit and a forecast increase in public debt. The out-turn for 2010 was a narrowing of the budget deficit to €911.6m., equivalent to 4.7% of GDP (lower than the anticipated 6.0%–7.0%, owing to the unforeseen profit made on an interest-swap agreement and the transfer of higher-than-usual central bank profits). However, in 2011 the budget deficit rose to €1,122.1m. (equivalent to 5.7% of GDP), while general government gross debt increased to €13,057.9m. (65.9% of GDP).

As of 30 June 2012 Cyprus had only €3,829m. of debt under its euro-denominated note programme, reflecting the unavailability of the international capital markets since June 2011 due to its poor credit rating. However, the budget deficit and public debt rose sharply, despite the adoption of two austerity packages, in September and December 2011, which comprised a 10% cut in salary for senior government officials, a two-year freeze in basic civil service salaries, a freeze on new recruitment in the civil service and a staggered increase in income tax rates. The decision by Fitch Ratings in June 2012 to lower Cyprus's sovereign rating to 'junk' status meant that the country lost its investment grade status with all three of the largest credit rating agencies, obliging the ECB to stop accepting Cypriot government bonds as collateral for commercial bank borrowing. Having already had to rely heavily on short-term borrowing for its own refinancing needs by turning to the domestic bank markets and semi-governmental organizations like CYTA and the EAC (short-term borrowing represented just 19% of the state's overall loans in 2010, but increased to 46% in 2011), and with yields on its 10-year benchmark bond of around 16%, the Government had little option but to apply on 25 June 2012 for aid from the EFSF for both the state and the banks.

The projected size of the European bailout grew very rapidly from the minimum €2,300m. needed for the recapitalization of CPB and BoC to include some €4,500m. for state (re-)financing needs into 2013. When S&P announced in August 2012 its further downgrading of Cyprus to 'BB', the credit rating agency referred to a base case scenario involving a €11,000m. financial support package. By the time the Government and the troika resumed negotiations in November on the specifics of the memorandum of understanding relating to the financial support package, the European Commission had downwardly revised its forecast for the Cypriot economy, citing record unemployment (especially in the construction sector) and a high degree of economic uncertainty leading to reduced private consumption. The out-turn for 2012 was a budget deficit of €1,120.3m., equivalent to 5.8% of GDP, and general government gross debt reached €15,618.5m. (80.3% of GDP).

By January 2013, six months after Cyprus made its formal request for a bailout and still without a final agreement, it had become clear that the rescue programme would need to be delayed by at least two more months, amid mounting disagreement over how to reduce the cost to a manageable level for the debt-laden Government. Within the troika, the IMF was insisting on significant amounts of debt relief before it agreed to participate, and the option of a 'bail-in' of creditors began to be promoted strongly. At the beginning of March EU finance ministers pledged to agree a bailout for Cyprus by the end of the month. At the newly elected President Anastasiades's first European Council meeting in mid-March, he was presented with the ultimatum of an unprecedented levy on all deposits held by all Cypriot banks as a precondition for a rescue programme. These bailout terms were rejected by the House of Representatives. Under a revised bailout plan, which was approved by the House of Representatives later in March, a levy of up to 40% was to be imposed on deposits of more than €100,000 held in BoC and CPB. Additionally, CPB was to be closed and some of its assets transferred to BoC (see *Industry, Manufacturing and Services*). To allay fears of mass deposit withdrawals, the Government temporarily closed the country's banks, and subsequently imposed strict controls on financial transactions. The European Stability Mechanism (ESM) was to provide €9,000m. and the IMF €1,000m. to finance the Cypriot authorities' three-year economic adjustment programme. In addition to the recapitalization of the banking sector, the programme required austerity reforms to reduce the budget deficit and a privatization programme.

The terms of Cyprus's bailout agreement were adopted by the House of Representatives on 30 April 2013, following its approval by EU member states, and the first instalment (of some €3,000m.) was received by the Government in two stages, in May and June. In August the Russian Government agreed to extend the terms of the €2,500m. loan it had provided to the Republic of Cyprus over a five-year period in late 2011, to allow repayment of the debt in eight six-monthly instalments from 2016; the interest rate was also to be reduced to ease Cyprus's financial burden. In mid-2014 the Cypriot Government returned to the international markets with the issuance of a five-year bond at an average yield of 4.85%, raising €750m. The sale of a seven-year bond with an average 4.0% yield, generating €1,000m., took place in April 2015, followed by that of a €1,000m., 10-year bond, at an average yield of 4.25%, in October. Following the third issuance, and after Fitch Ratings upgraded Cyprus's sovereign credit rating to 'B+' from 'B-' in October, Minister of Finance Harris Georgiades declared the country to be 'creditworthy', also announcing that funds raised would strengthen state reserves and assist in the management of public debt. In 2013 the budget deficit declined to €1,007.7m. (5.6% of GDP), although general government gross debt increased substantially to €18,706.5m. (104.0% of GDP). However, in 2014, due to a €1,500m. recapitalization of the CCB in March of that year, the budget deficit rose to a high of €1,538.6m. (8.8% of GDP) and general government gross debt to €19,013.8m. (109.1% of GDP).

By 2015 the budget deficit, including a further capital injection of €175.0m. for the CCB, had been substantially reduced to €163.5m. (0.9% of GDP), but general government gross debt rose slightly to €19,164.1m. (107.2% of GDP). In early March 2016 the Government announced the early completion of its economic adjustment programme, by which time it had borrowed only €7,300m. of the €10,000m. available under the terms of the bailout (following a further seven disbursements during 2013–15). The troika commended the Cypriot authorities for having stabilized and reformed the banking sector, exceeded their fiscal targets, reduced public debt, and completed a successful return to international capital markets. However, in the banking sector, the NPL ratio remained very high at 60%, equivalent to 150% of GDP. In addition, owing to strong parliamentary and public opposition, including strike action, the Government had failed to implement plans to privatize the state-owned CYTA and restructure the EAC. Later in March 2016 the Government succeeded in securing parliament's adoption of legislation finalizing the privatization of commercial operations at the primary port of Limassol. The Government's budget and reform policies were to remain subject to post-programme monitoring by the European Commission until at least 75% of the financial assistance received had been repaid, expected to be until 2029.

In 2016 the overall budget balance moved to a small surplus of €48.6m. (equivalent to 0.3% of GDP), although general government gross debt increased slightly to €19,509.3m. (103.1% of GDP). At the end of 2016 the level of NPLs in the banking system had fallen by €5,000m. since their 2014 peak, to €24,200m. (though remaining extremely high, at 46% of total loans and 135% of GDP), following repayments, write-downs and loan-to-real estate exchanges. In March 2017 S&P raised its long-term sovereign credit ratings on Cyprus to 'BB+', from 'BB' with a stable outlook, based on stronger-than-expected economic growth and fiscal progress. In 2017 the overall budget surplus increased to €384.5m. (1.9% of GDP), while general government gross debt fell significantly to €18,814.1m. (92.9% of GDP).

The budget balance moved to a deficit of €784.9m. (3.6% of GDP) in 2018, due to a one-off expenditure of around €1,720m., resulting from the restructuring of the CCB and its sale to Hellenic Bank (see *Industry and Services*). General government gross debt rose to €21,256.3m. (98.4% of GDP). The removal of the CCB's large NPL portfolio from the banking system (together with legislation adopted in July 2018 that significantly strengthened the framework for addressing NPLs) resulted in a significant reduction in NPLs, to 30.5% of loans, or 50% of GDP, at the end of 2018 (from 43% of loans, or 106% of GDP, at the end of 2017). Largely in response to that reform, S&P in September 2018 (followed by Fitch Ratings in October) raised Cyprus's sovereign credit rating to BBB–, i.e. to investment grade, thereby allowing Cypriot government bonds again to be accepted by the ECB as collateral. Shortly afterwards, the Cypriot authorities announced the issue of a €1,500m., 10-year sovereign bond with a yield of 2.4%, which was to be used to refinance existing debt.

A fiscal surplus of €293.8m. was recorded in 2019, amounting to 1.3% of GDP. General government gross debt decreased marginally to €20,958.0m., or 91.1% of GDP. However, in order to mitigate the impact of the COVID-19 pandemic, the Government implemented an economic support package amounting to around €800m. (3.9% of GDP) in 2020 for the health sector, households and businesses. The measures, some of which were extended, included support of €40m. for the health sector to combat the pandemic, income support for households, a wage subsidy scheme for affected businesses to maintain jobs, grants for small businesses and the self-employed, assistance for the tourism sector, a two-month deferral of VAT payments, and a temporary VAT cut to stimulate the tourism and hospitality sector. The cost of support measures for 2021 was estimated to be around 3.6% of GDP, including a loan guarantee scheme (amounting to €1,000m.) and other special support plans for businesses and employees severely affected by the pandemic. The budget deficit narrowed from €1,275.0m. (5.8% of GDP) in 2020 to €482.0m. (2.0% of GDP) in 2021, while general government gross debt declined from €24,924.0m. in 2020 (113.8% of GDP) to €24,310.7m. (101.2% of GDP) in 2021. A budget surplus of €570.2m. (2.1% of GDP) was recorded in 2022, facilitated by the rescindment of the vast majority of COVID-19 restrictions, as well as by continued improvements in the economic environment.

Total employment increased by 3.4% during 2021 and by 4.4% in 2022, to reach 450,541 persons in the latter year. In 2022 the unemployment rate stood at 6.7%, youth unemployment at 18.4% and long-term unemployment at 2.3%. In 2022 12,650 companies were registered, compared with 12,532 companies in 2021, representing an increase of 0.9%, while new sale contracts increased by 29.6% year on year.

FOREIGN TRADE AND BALANCE OF PAYMENTS

Cyprus has registered a persistent trade deficit for many years (with imports regularly being three or four times as great as exports in terms of value), only partly offset by an 'invisibles' balance, arising mainly from earnings from tourism and, more recently, income from accounting and legal services. This has led to a growing current account deficit, which is primarily funded by inflows of bank deposits from non-residents (the traditional offshore sector) and partly by foreign direct investment. Cyprus has been acting as a transshipment centre, meaning that total exports and total imports exceed goods produced or consumed domestically.

According to official figures, the merchandise trade deficit decreased by 3.3% year on year to €4,895.5m. in 2020, before widening to €5,278.3m. in 2021 and €7,100.9m. in 2022. Particularly owing to the decline in travel-related services as a result of COVID-19, the current account deficit widened significantly to the equivalent of 10.1% of GDP in 2020 (up from 5.7% in 2019). The current account balance recorded an improvement in 2021, with the deficit narrowing to 6.8% of GDP, predominantly owing to a larger services surplus and a smaller secondary income deficit. However, high energy prices helped to increase the current account deficit to 9.1% of GDP in 2022.

From the late 1980s EC countries began to replace Arab countries (chiefly Lebanon, Egypt, the states of the Arabian peninsula and Libya) as Cyprus's principal trading partners. In 1995 the UK was Cyprus's largest individual trading partner, but by 2007 it had fallen as a supplier to third place behind Greece and Italy. In 2020 EU countries received 31.4% of Greek Cypriot exports and supplied 58.0% of imports. The principal individual source of imports in 2022 was Greece (23.4%), followed by Italy (10.5%), the People's Republic of China (8.0%) and Israel (7.4%). Hong Kong was the leading export destination in that year, accounting for 10.7% of the total, followed by Lebanon (7.5%), Greece (7.1%), Liberia (5.8%) and the UK (5.6%).

ECONOMIC OUTLOOK

According to the baseline macroeconomic scenario laid out by the Greek Cypriot Ministry of Finance, growth in the medium term is expected to continue on a positive path, albeit at a decelerated pace, with real annual growth in 2023 expected at a rate of 3%. This slowdown in growth is predicated on a deterioration in the external economic environment and the continued impact of high energy prices, coupled with increases in interest rates, which will put pressure on both domestic and external demand. The main risk to the outlook is the ongoing war between Russia and Ukraine and the ensuing sanctions, as well as consolidation of the banking sector and the sale of NPLs. In addition, the devaluation of the Russian rouble and the ban on the use of EU airspace by Russia, and vice versa, are expected to have a significant impact on the number of Russian tourists visiting Cyprus, although the magnitude of the impact will depend on the duration and extent of the war and the sanctions imposed. Moreover, the increase in energy prices will in turn affect the cost of electricity production in Cyprus, given that Cyprus is a highly oil-dependent country. This additional cost, or part of it, could be transmitted to the consumer energy prices, thus affecting consumption and temporarily increasing the rate of inflation. Professional legal, accounting, consulting and other services to companies of Russian origin and/or interests may also be significantly affected, through a reduction in their turnover and profits, with a subsequent impact on government revenues.

From a macroeconomic perspective, debt portfolio risk metrics have improved significantly despite the challenges of 2022, while weighted average cost has remained at low levels. Cyprus maintains its successful presence in international markets. The downward trajectory of public debt in 2022 is expected to continue. Cyprus enjoys a very strong cash position (equivalent to around 9.7% of GDP as of the end of 2022), which would enable the state to offset any further negative effects from either the Russia–Ukraine crisis or additional interest rate increases by the ECB, or indeed in the event of a resurgence in COVID-19 infections.

In the medium term, further improvement in the fiscal balance is expected, with a fiscal surplus of 1.7% of GDP forecast in 2023 and 2.3% in 2024. The primary balance (the fiscal balance excluding net interest payments on public debt) is forecast to reach 3.0% of GDP in 2023 and 3.6% in 2024. Productivity is predicted to grow by 2.2% in 2023, primarily owing to the recovery of the economy and an increase in full-time and part-time employment. Productivity growth is forecast to decelerate to 1.9% and 1.0% in 2024 and 2025, respectively, signalling a return to more steady levels.

Statistical Survey

Source (unless otherwise indicated): Statistical Service of Cyprus, Michael Karaoli St, CY-1444 Nicosia; tel. (22) 22602129; fax (22) 22661313; e-mail enquiries@cystat.mof.gov.cy; internet www.cystat.gov.cy.

Note: Since July 1974 the northern part of Cyprus has been under Turkish occupation. As a result, the majority of statistics relating to subsequent periods do not cover the whole island. See section on the 'Turkish Republic of Northern Cyprus' for detailed data on the Turkish-occupied region.

AREA AND POPULATION

Area: 9,251 sq km (3,572 sq miles), incl. Turkish-occupied region; 5,896 sq km (2,276 sq miles), government-controlled area only.

Population: 840,407 (males 408,780, females 431,627), excl. Turkish-occupied region, at census of 1 October 2011; 918,100, excl. Turkish-occupied region, at census of 1 October 2021 (preliminary).

Density (excl. Turkish-occupied region, at 2021 census): 155.7 per sq km.

Population by Age and Sex ('000, excl. Turkish-occupied region, official estimates at 31 December 2019): *0–14 years:* 142.4 (males 72.7, females 69.7); *15–64 years:* 600.8 (males 295.0, females 305.8); *65 years and over:* 144.8 (males 66.8, females 78.0); *Total* 888.0 (males 434.5, females 453.5). Note: Estimates not adjusted to take account of 2021 census.

Population by Ethnic Group (estimates at 31 December 2001): Greeks 639,400 (80.6%), Turks 87,600 (11.1%), Others 66,100 (8.3%); Total 793,100.

Districts ('000, excl. Turkish-controlled region, at 2021 census, preliminary): Ammochostos 51.5; Larnaka (Larnaca) 154.2; Lefkosia 351.6; Lemesos (Limassol) 258.9; Pafos (Paphos) 101.9; *Total* 918.1.

Principal Towns (official population estimates at 31 December 2019): Nicosia (capital) 256,400 (excl. Turkish-occupied portion); Limassol 189,600; Larnaca 88,200; Paphos 67,800. Note: Estimates not adjusted to take account of results of 2021 census.

Births, Marriages and Deaths (government-controlled area, 2019): Registered live births 9,548 (birth rate 10.8 per 1,000); Registered marriages 14,854 (incl. 7,846 residents of Cyprus); Registered deaths 6,239 (death rate 7.1 per 1,000).

Life Expectancy (years at birth, estimates): 81.2 (males 79.2; females 83.2) in 2021. Source: World Bank, World Development Indicators database.

Immigration and Emigration (2019): Immigrants 26,170; Emigrants 17,373.

Economically Active Population (government-controlled area, '000 persons aged 15 years and over, excl. armed forces, labour force survey, 2022): Agriculture, forestry and fishing 10.7; Mining and quarrying 0.5; Manufacturing 29.5; Electricity, gas and water 6.0; Construction 41.2; Wholesale and retail trade; repair of motor vehicles, motor cycles and personal and household goods 76.6; Restaurants and hotels 35.8; Transport, storage and communications 34.4; Financial intermediation 26.9; Real estate, renting and business activities 54.6; Public administration and defence 39.8; Education 30.4; Health and social work 25.0; Other community, social and personal service activities 21.8; Private households with employed persons 15.9; Extraterritorial organizations 1.3; *Total* 450.5; Unemployed 32.8; *Total labour force* 483.3.

HEALTH AND WELFARE

Total Fertility Rate (children per woman, 2021): 1.3.

CYPRUS

Under-5 Mortality Rate (per 1,000 live births, 2021): 2.8.

HIV/AIDS (% of persons aged 15–49, 2021): 0.1.

COVID-19: Cumulative Confirmed Deaths (per 100,000 persons at 30 June 2023): 152.2.

COVID-19: Fully Vaccinated Population (% of total population at 22 February 2023): 72.1.

Physicians (per 1,000 head, 2021): 5.4.

Hospital beds (per 1,000 head, 2017): 3.4.

Domestic Health Expenditure (2020): US $ per head (PPP): 2,519.3.

Domestic Health Expenditure (2020): % of GDP: 6.3.

Domestic Health Expenditure (2020): public (% of total current health expenditure): 78.3.

Total Carbon Dioxide Emissions ('000 metric tons, 2019): 7,190.

Carbon Dioxide Emissions Per Head (metric tons, 2019): 6.0.

Human Development Index (2021): ranking: 29.

Human Development Index (2021): index: 0.896.

Note: For data on COVID-19 vaccinations, 'fully vaccinated' denotes receipt of all doses specified by approved vaccination regime (Sources: Johns Hopkins University and Our World in Data). Data on health expenditure refer to current general government expenditure in each case. For more information on sources and further definitions for all indicators, see Health and Welfare Statistics: Sources and Definitions section (europaworld.com/credits).

AGRICULTURE

Principal Crops (government-controlled area, '000 metric tons, 2021 unless otherwise indicated): Apples 2.7; Barley 25.6; Bananas 5.6; Cabbages and other brassicas 3.5; Cantaloupes and other melons 7.3; Carobs 7.5 (2017); Cucumbers and gherkins 7.7; Grapes 22.6; Grapefruit and pomelos 16.6; Lemons and limes 6.8; Olives 17.0; Onions, dry 5.0; Oranges 18.1; Potatoes 88.5; Tangerines, mandarins, etc. 18.6; Tomatoes 15.1; Watermelons 14.4; Wheat 25.6.

Livestock (government-controlled area, '000 head, 2021 unless otherwise indicated): Cattle 84.6; Chickens 2,786.0 (2020); Goats 261.1 (2020); Sheep 326.3 (2020); Pigs 360.7.

Livestock Products (government-controlled area, '000 metric tons, 2021): Chicken meat 26.6; Cows' milk 298.1; Goat meat 2.5; Pig meat 43.7; Sheep meat 2.6.

Forestry (government-controlled area, '000 cubic metres, 2021): Roundwood removals (excl. bark) 10.0; Sawnwood production (incl. railway sleepers) 1.7.

Fishing (government-controlled area, metric tons, live weight, 2021): Capture 1,401 (Albacore 513; Bogue 96); Aquaculture 7,862 (European seabass 2,680; Gilthead seabream 5,097); *Total catch* 9,264 (FAO estimate).

Source: FAO.

MINING

Selected Products (government-controlled area, '000 metric tons, 2019): Sand and gravel 6,148; Gypsum 531.9; Bentonite 83.1; Umber 12.5.

INDUSTRY

Selected Products (government-controlled area, 2019 unless otherwise indicated): Wine 10.2m. litres; Beer 40.4m. litres; Soft drinks 13,2m. litres; Cigarettes 3,803m. (2001); Footwear 89,974 pairs (2011); Bricks 25.2m.; Floor and wall tiles 39,000 sq m; Cement 1,018,537 metric tons (2016); Electrical energy 5,060.6m. kWh (2018).

FINANCE

Currency and Exchange Rates: 100 cent = 1 euro (€). *Sterling and Dollar Equivalents* (31 May 2023): £1 sterling = €1.157; US $1 = €0.936; €10 = £8.64= US $10.68. *Average Exchange Rate* (euros per US dollar): 0.8755 in 2020; 0.8455 in 2021; 0.9496 in 2022. Note: The Cyprus pound (C£) was formerly in use. On 1 January 2008 the government-controlled area of Cyprus adopted the euro, which became the sole legal tender in that area from the end of the same month.

Budget (government-controlled area, € million, 2022): *Revenue:* Taxation 8,863.5 (Direct taxes 3,014.7, Indirect taxes 3,542.6, Social security contributions 2,306.2); Other current revenue 991.3; Total 9,854.9 (excl. grants from abroad 420.7). *Expenditure:* Current expenditure 9,423.2 (Wages and salaries 2,223.6, Other goods and services 754.9, Social security payments 2,949.6, Subsidies 139.7, Interest payments 432.0, Pensions and gratuities 695.4, Social pension 81.2, Other current transfers 1,966.4, Unallocated 180.5); Capital expenditure (investments) 411.2; Total 9,834.4. Source: Budgets and Fiscal Control Directorate, Ministry of Finance, Nicosia.

International Reserves (government-controlled area, US $ million at 31 December 2022): Gold (Eurosystem valuation) 813.4; IMF special drawing rights 567.7; Reserve position in IMF 113.2; Foreign exchange 232.0; *Total* 1,726.3. Source: IMF, *International Financial Statistics*.

Money Supply (government-controlled area, € million at 31 December 2021): Transferable deposits 27,383; Other deposits 13,619; *Total (incl. others)* 45,912. Source: IMF, *International Financial Statistics*.

Cost of Living (government-controlled area, Consumer Price Index; base: 2015 = 100): 100.1 in 2020; 102.6 in 2021; 111.2 in 2022.

Gross Domestic Product (government-controlled area, € million at current prices): 21,896.5 in 2020; 24,019.0 in 2021 (preliminary); 27,006.4 in 2022 (preliminary).

Expenditure on the Gross Domestic Product (government-controlled area, € million at current prices, 2022, preliminary): Government final consumption expenditure 5,078.4; Private final consumption expenditure 16,565.1; Change in inventories 54.6; Gross fixed capital formation 5,409.6; *Total domestic expenditure* 27,107.7; Exports of goods and services 24,716.6; *Less* Imports of goods and services 24,817.9; *GDP in market prices* 27,006.4.

Gross Domestic Product by Economic Activity (government-controlled area, € million at current prices, 2022, preliminary): Agriculture, forestry and fishing 445.8; Mining and quarrying 34.2; Manufacturing 1,545.4; Electricity, gas and water supply 639.5; Construction 1,418.5; Wholesale and retail trade 2,684.2; Restaurants and hotels 1,036.1; Transport, storage and communications 3,582.8; Financial intermediation 2,407.0; Real estate, renting and business activities 4,661.9; Public administration and defence 2,034.7; Education 1,360.5; Health and social work 980.7; Other community, social and personal services 629.2; Private households with employed persons 187.1; *Sub-total* 23,647.4; Net taxes on products 3,359.0; *GDP in market prices* 27,006.4.

Balance of Payments (government-controlled area, US $ million, 2022): Exports of goods 4,789; Imports of goods −10,993; *Balance on goods* −6,203; Exports of services 21,162; Imports of services −15,103; *Balance on goods and services* −144; Primary income received 16,004; Primary income paid −18,253; *Balance on goods, services and primary income* −2,393; Secondary income received 762; Secondary income paid −995; *Current balance* −2,625; Capital account (net) 48; Direct investment assets −2,620; Direct investment liabilities 11,132; Portfolio investment assets −1,383; Portfolio investment liabilities −313; Financial derivatives and employee stock options (net) 179; Other investment assets 1,764; Other investment liabilities −6,857; Net errors and omissions 825; *Reserves and related items* 150. Source: IMF, *International Financial Statistics*.

EXTERNAL TRADE

Principal Commodities (distribution by HS, government-controlled area, € million, 2022): *Imports c.i.f.:* Vegetables and vegetable products 392.4; Prepared foodstuffs; beverages, spirits, vinegar; tobacco and articles thereof 952.8; Mineral products 2,653.8 (Mineral fuels, oils, distillation products, etc. 1,571.7); Chemicals and related products 1,031.0 (Pharmaceutical products 335.1); Plastics, rubber, and articles thereof 374.2; Textiles and textile articles 383.9; Iron and steel, other base metals and articles of base metal 583.8; Machinery and mechanical appliances; electrical equipment; parts thereof 1,211.4 (Machinery, boilers, etc. 497.6; Electrical and electronic equipment 517.1); Vehicles, aircraft, vessels and associated transport equipment 2,052.2 (Vehicles other than railway, tramway 528.3; Ships, boats and floating structures 898.9); Total (incl. others) 11,290.0. *Exports f.o.b.:* Live animals and animal products 347.3 (Dairy products, eggs, honey and edible animal products 268.4); Prepared foodstuffs; beverages, spirits, vinegar; tobacco and articles thereof 123.0; Mineral products 1,024.7 (Mineral fuels, oils, distillation products, etc. 641.5); Chemicals and related products 559.0 (Medicinal and pharmaceutical products 352.4); Machinery and mechanical appliances; electrical equipment; parts thereof 266.0 (Electrical and electronic equipment 143.9); Vehicles, aircraft, vessels and associated transport equipment 1,416.3 (Ships, boats and floating structures 1,091.7); Total (incl. others) 4,189.0.

Principal Trading Partners (government-controlled area, € million, 2022): *Imports c.i.f.:* Belgium 245.7; Bulgaria 162.2; China, People's Republic 898.2; France (incl. Monaco) 192.9; Germany 600.5; Greece 2,640.9; Ireland 172.3; Israel 835.9; Italy 1,183.9; Japan 115.9; Korea, Republic 196.4; Netherlands 467.3; Romania 141.9; Russian Federation 208.3; Singapore 248.1; Spain 389.6; Türkiye 184.5; United Kingdom 353.8; Total (incl. others) 11,290.0. *Exports f.o.b.* (incl. re-exports): France (incl. Monaco) 64.2; Germany 100.4; Greece 296.8; Hong Kong 448.3; India 57.1; Israel 102.8; Italy

46.2; Lebanon 314.7; Liberia 242.3; Libya 126.3; Marshall Islands 164.3; Singapore 77.4; United Arab Emirates 162.2; United Kingdom 232.5; USA 97.3; Total (incl. others) 4,189.0.

TRANSPORT

Road Traffic (government-controlled area, licensed motor vehicles, 31 December 2021): Private passenger cars 564,526; Taxis and self-drive cars 22,567; Buses and coaches 2,774; Lorries and vans 117,926; Motorcycles 41,141; Total (incl. others) 776,149.

Shipping (government-controlled area, freight traffic, '000 metric tons, 2020): Goods loaded 3,662; Goods unloaded 7,420. *Flag Registered Fleet:* At 31 December 2022 a total of 1,245 merchant vessels (combined displacement 21,888,822 grt) were registered in Cyprus (Source: Lloyd's List Intelligence, www.bit.ly/LLintelligence).

Civil Aviation (government-controlled area, 2019): Overall passenger traffic 11,255,762; Total freight transported 32,600 metric tons.

TOURISM

Foreign Tourist Arrivals (government-controlled area, '000): 631.6 in 2020; 1,936.9 in 2021; 3,201.1 in 2022.

Arrivals by Country of Residence (government-controlled area, '000, 2022): United Kingdom 1,212.6; Israel 277.4; Germany 198.4; Poland 186.8; Greece 169.8; Sweden 118.9; Austria 70.1; Denmark 67.6; France 61.3; Switzerland 60.8; Russian Federation 51.8; Hungary 50.7; Total (incl. others) 3,201.1.

Tourism Receipts (government-controlled area, € million): 392.0 in 2020; 1,513.6 in 2021; 2,439.2 in 2022.

COMMUNICATIONS MEDIA

Telephones (main lines in use, 2021): 304,581.
Mobile Telephone Subscriptions ('000, 2021): 1,320.8.
Internet Subscribers (% of population, 2021): 90.8.
Broadband Subscriptions, Fixed ('000, 2021): 340.1.
Broadband Subscriptions, Mobile ('000, 2021): 1,233.0.

Source: International Telecommunication Union.

EDUCATION

Government-controlled Area (2020/21): *Pre-primary:* 734 institutions, 2,705 teachers, 32,958 pupils. *Primary:* 360 institutions, 4,676 teachers, 58,093 pupils. *Secondary (Gymnasiums and Lyceums):* 168 institutions, 6,500 teachers, 56,714 pupils. *Tertiary (incl. University of Cyprus):* 55 institutions, 1,928 teachers, 53,508 students. Note: 19,199 Cypriot students were studying abroad in 2010/11.

Pupil-teacher Ratio (primary education): 12.4 in 2020/21.

Adult Literacy Rate (2011 census): 98.7% (males 99.3%; females 98.1%).

Directory

The Constitution

The Constitution, summarized below, entered into force on 16 August 1960, when Cyprus became an independent republic.

THE STATE OF CYPRUS

The State of Cyprus is an independent and sovereign Republic with a presidential regime.

The Greek Community comprises all citizens of the Republic who are of Greek origin and whose mother tongue is Greek or who share the Greek cultural traditions or who are members of the Greek Orthodox Church.

The Turkish Community comprises all citizens of the Republic who are of Turkish origin and whose mother tongue is Turkish or who share the Turkish cultural traditions or who are Muslims.

The official languages of the Republic are Greek and Turkish.

The Republic shall have its own flag of neutral design and colour, chosen jointly by the President and the Vice-President of the Republic.

The Greek and the Turkish Communities shall have the right to celebrate respectively the Greek and the Turkish national holidays.

THE PRESIDENT AND VICE-PRESIDENT*

Executive power is vested in the President and the Vice-President, who are members of the Greek and Turkish Communities respectively, and are elected by their respective communities to hold office for five years.

The President of the Republic as Head of the State represents the Republic in all its official functions; signs the credentials of diplomatic envoys and receives the credentials of foreign diplomatic envoys; signs the credentials of delegates for the negotiation of international treaties, conventions or other agreements; signs the letter relating to the transmission of the instruments of ratification of any international treaties, conventions or agreements; confers the honours of the Republic.

The Vice-President of the Republic, as Vice-Head of the State, has the right to be present at all official functions; at the presentation of the credentials of foreign diplomatic envoys; to recommend to the President the conferment of honours on members of the Turkish Community, which recommendation the President shall accept unless there are grave reasons to the contrary.

The election of the President and the Vice-President of the Republic shall be direct, by universal suffrage and secret ballot, and shall, except in the case of a by-election, take place on the same day but separately.

The office of the President and of the Vice-President shall be incompatible with that of a Minister or of a Representative or of a member of a Communal Chamber or of a member of any municipal council including a Mayor or of a member of the armed or security forces of the Republic or with a public or municipal office.

The President and Vice-President of the Republic are invested by the House of Representatives.

The President and the Vice-President of the Republic in order to ensure the executive power shall have a Council of Ministers composed of seven Greek Ministers and three Turkish Ministers. The Ministers shall be designated respectively by the President and the Vice-President of the Republic who shall appoint them by an instrument signed by them both. The President convenes and presides over the meetings of the Council of Ministers, while the Vice-President may ask the President to convene the Council and may take part in the discussions.

The decisions of the Council of Ministers shall be taken by an absolute majority and shall, unless the right of final veto or return is exercised by the President or the Vice-President of the Republic or both, be promulgated immediately by them.

The executive power exercised by the President and the Vice-President of the Republic conjointly consists of:

Determining the design and colour of the flag.

Creation or establishment of honours.

Appointment of the members of the Council of Ministers.

Promulgation by publication of the decisions of the Council of Ministers.

Promulgation by publication of any law or decision passed by the House of Representatives.

Appointments and termination of appointments as in Articles provided.

Institution of compulsory military service.

Reduction or increase of the security forces.

Exercise of the prerogative of mercy in capital cases.

Remission, suspension and commutation of sentences.

Right of references to the Supreme Constitutional Court and publication of Court decisions.

Address of messages to the House of Representatives.

The executive powers which may be exercised separately by the President and Vice-President include: designation and termination of appointment of Greek and Turkish Ministers respectively; the right of final veto on Council decisions and on laws concerning foreign affairs, defence or security; the publication of the communal laws and decisions of the Greek and Turkish Communal Chambers respectively; the right of recourse to the Supreme Constitutional Court; the prerogative of mercy in capital cases; and addressing messages to the House of Representatives.

* A constitutional amendment approved in December 2019 restricted the number of consecutive terms in office that a President or Vice-President could serve to a maximum of two.

THE COUNCIL OF MINISTERS

The Council of Ministers shall exercise executive power in all matters, other than those which are within the competence of a Communal Chamber, including the following:

General direction and control of the government of the Republic and the direction of general policy.

Foreign affairs, defence and security.

Co-ordination and supervision of all public services.

Supervision and disposition of property belonging to the Republic.

Consideration of Bills to be introduced to the House of Representatives by a Minister.

Making of any order or regulation for the carrying into effect of any law as provided by such law.

Consideration of the Budget of the Republic to be introduced to the House of Representatives.

THE HOUSE OF REPRESENTATIVES†

The legislative power of the Republic shall be exercised by the House of Representatives in all matters except those expressly reserved to the Communal Chambers.

The number of Representatives shall be 50, subject to alteration by a resolution of the House of Representatives carried by a majority comprising two-thirds of the Representatives elected by the Greek Community and two-thirds of the Representatives elected by the Turkish Community.

Out of the number of Representatives 70% shall be elected by the Greek Community and 30% by the Turkish Community separately from among their members respectively, and, in the case of a contested election, by universal suffrage and by direct and secret ballot held on the same day.

The term of office of the House of Representatives shall be for a period of five years.

The President of the House of Representatives shall be a Greek, and shall be elected by the Representatives elected by the Greek Community, and the Vice-President shall be a Turk and shall be elected by the Representatives elected by the Turkish Community.

† Following a constitutional amendment in 1985, the number of seats in the House of Representatives was increased to 80 (of which 56 were allocated to Greek Cypriot deputies and 24 reserved for Turkish Cypriots).

THE COMMUNAL CHAMBERS

The Greek and the Turkish Communities respectively shall elect from among their own members a Communal Chamber.

The Communal Chambers shall, in relation to their respective Community, have competence to exercise legislative power solely with regard to the following:

All religious, educational, cultural and teaching matters.

Personal status; composition and instances of courts dealing with civil disputes relating to personal status and to religious matters.

Imposition of personal taxes and fees on members of their respective Community in order to provide for their respective needs.

THE PUBLIC SERVICE AND THE ARMED FORCES

The public service shall be composed as to 70% of Greeks and as to 30% of Turks.

The Republic shall have an army of 2,000 men, of whom 60% shall be Greeks and 40% shall be Turks.

The security forces of the Republic shall consist of the police and gendarmerie and shall have a contingent of 2,000 men. The forces shall be composed as to 70% of Greeks and as to 30% of Turks.

OTHER PROVISIONS‡

The following measures have been passed by the House of Representatives since January 1964, when the Turkish members withdrew:

The amalgamation of the Supreme Court and the Supreme Constitutional Court into a unified Supreme Court.

The abolition of the Greek Communal Chamber and the creation of a Ministry of Education.

The unification of the municipalities.

The unification of the police and the gendarmerie.

The creation of a military force by providing that persons between the ages of 18 and 50 years can be called upon to serve in the National Guard.

The extension of the term of office of the President and the House of Representatives by one year intervals from July 1965 until elections in February 1968 and July 1970 respectively.

New electoral provisions; abolition of separate Greek and Turkish rolls; abolition of post of Vice-President, which was re-established in 1973.

‡ Following the enactment of legislative amendments in July 2022, the Supreme Court was divided back into two separate courts—the Supreme Constitutional Court and the Supreme Court—as had been the situation during 1960–64.

The Government

HEAD OF STATE

President: NIKOS CHRISTODOULIDES (took office 28 February 2023).

COUNCIL OF MINISTERS
(September 2023)

The Government is formed by independents (Ind.), the Democratic Party (DIKO) and the Solidarity Movement.

Minister of Foreign Affairs: CONSTANTINOS KOMBOS (Ind.).

Minister of Finance: MAKIS KERAVNOS (DIKO).

Minister of the Interior: CONSTANTINOS IOANNOU (Ind.).

Minister of Defence: MICHALIS GIORGALLAS (Solidarity Movement).

Minister of Education, Sport and Youth: ATHINA MICHAELIDOU (Ind.).

Minister of Transport, Communications and Works: ALEXIS VAFEADES (Ind.).

Minister of Energy, Commerce and Industry: GIORGOS PAPANASTASIOU (Ind.).

Minister of Agriculture, Rural Development and the Environment: PETROS XENOFONTOS (Ind.).

Minister of Labour and Social Insurance: YIANNIS PANAYIOTOU (Ind.).

Minister of Justice and Public Order: ANNA PROKOPIOU (Ind.).

Minister of Health: POPI KANARI (Ind.).

Government Spokesman: CONSTANDINOS LETYMPIOTIS (Ind.).

MINISTRIES

Office of the President: Presidential Palace, 1400 Nicosia; tel. 22867400; fax 22663799; e-mail info@presidency.gov.cy; internet presidency.gov.cy.

Ministry of Agriculture, Rural Development and the Environment: 6 Amfipoleos St, 2025 Strovolos, Nicosia; tel. 22408300; fax 22770397; e-mail registry@moa.gov.cy; internet www.moa.gov.cy.

Ministry of Defence: 172–174 Strovolou Ave, 2048 Strovolos, Nicosia; tel. 22807500; fax 22676182; e-mail defence@mod.gov.cy; internet www.mod.gov.cy.

Ministry of Education, Culture, Sport and Youth: Kimonos and Thoukididis, 1434 Nicosia; tel. 22800600; e-mail registry@moec.gov.cy; internet www.moec.gov.cy.

Ministry of Energy, Commerce, Industry and Tourism: 6 Andreas Araouzos St, 1421 Nicosia; tel. 22867100; fax 22375120; e-mail perm.sec@mcit.gov.cy; internet www.mcit.gov.cy.

Ministry of Finance: Cnr Michalakis Karaolis St and Gregoriou Afxentiou St, 1439 Nicosia; tel. 22602723; e-mail registry@mof.gov.cy; internet www.mof.gov.cy.

Ministry of Foreign Affairs: Presidential Palace Ave, 1447 Nicosia; tel. 22651000; fax 22661881; e-mail info@mfa.gov.cy; internet www.mfa.gov.cy.

Ministry of Health: 1 Prodomou and 17 Chilonos, 1448 Nicosia; tel. 22605300; e-mail perm.sec@moh.gov.cy; internet www.moh.gov.cy.

Ministry of the Interior: Demosthenis Severis Ave, Ex Secretariat Compound, 1453 Nicosia; tel. 22867800; fax 22671465; e-mail info@moi.gov.cy; internet www.moi.gov.cy.

Ministry of Justice and Public Order: 125 Athalassa Ave, 1461 Strovolos, Nicosia; tel. 22805950; fax 22518356; e-mail registry@mjpo.gov.cy; internet www.mjpo.gov.cy.

Ministry of Labour and Social Insurance: 7 Byron Ave, 1463 Nicosia; tel. 22401600; fax 22670993; e-mail administration@mlsi.gov.cy; internet www.mlsi.gov.cy.

Ministry of Transport, Communications and Works: 28 Achaeon St, 1424 Nicosia; tel. 22800100; e-mail permsec@mcw.gov.cy; internet www.mcw.gov.cy.

President

Presidential Election, First Ballot, 5 February 2023

Candidate	Votes	%
Nikos Christodoulides (Ind., with support from EDEK, DIKO, DEPA and the Solidarity Movement)	127,309	32.04
Andreas Mavroyiannis (Ind., with support from AKEL and Generation Change)	117,551	29.59
Averof Neophytou (DISY)	103,748	26.11
Christos Christou (ELAM)	23,988	6.04
Achilleas Demetriades (Ind.)	8,137	2.05
Constantinos Christofides (Neo Kyma)	6,326	1.59
Giorgos Kolokasides (Ind.)	5,287	1.33
Alexios Savvides (Ind.)	2,395	0.60
Others	2,576	0.60
Total*	397,317	100.00

* Excluding 7,004 abstentions and blank or invalid votes (1.73% of the total votes cast).

Presidential Election, Second Ballot, 12 February 2023

Candidate	Votes	%
Nikos Christodoulides (Ind., with support from EDEK, DIKO, DEPA and the Solidarity Movement)	204,867	51.97
Andreas Mavroyiannis (Ind., with support from AKEL and Generation Change)	189,335	48.03
Total*	394,202	100.00

* Excluding 12,404 and blank and invalid votes (3.05% of the total votes cast).

Legislature

The House of Representatives originally consisted of 50 members, 35 from the Greek community and 15 from the Turkish community, elected for a term of five years. In January 1964 the Turkish members withdrew and set up the 'Turkish Legislative Assembly of the Turkish Cypriot Administration'. At the 1985 elections the membership of the House was expanded to 80 members, of whom 56 were to be from the Greek community and 24 from the Turkish community (according to the ratio of representation specified in the Constitution).

House of Representatives: 1402 Nicosia; tel. 22407300; fax 22668611; e-mail vouli@parliament.cy; internet www.parliament.cy.
President: ANNITA DEMETRIOU.

Elections for the Greek Representatives, 30 May 2021

Party	Votes	%	Seats
Democratic Rally (DISY)	99,328	27.77	17
Progressive Party of the Working People (AKEL)	79,915	22.34	15
Democratic Party (DIKO)	40,395	11.30	9
National People's Front (ELAM)	24,255	6.78	4
Movement of Social Democrats (EDEK)	24,022	6.72	4
Democratic Front (DEPA)	21,832	6.10	4
Cyprus Greens (KOSP)	15,762	4.41	3
Total (incl. others)*	357,712	100.00	56

* Excluding 6,826 invalid votes and 2,070 blank votes.

Political Organizations

Afoa: Nicosia; internet www.fb.com/afoa.cy; f. 2023; feminist, environmentalist and anti-capitalist.

Allagi Genias (Generation Change): Nicosia; e-mail info@anex.com.cy; internet anex.com.cy; f. 2019; Founding Leader ANNA THEOLOGOU.

Anorthotiko Komma Ergazomenou Laou (AKEL) (Progressive Party of the Working People): POB 21827, 4 E. Papaioannou St, 1075 Nicosia; tel. 22761121; fax 22761574; e-mail info@akel.org.cy; internet www.akel.org.cy; f. 1941; successor to the Communist Party of Cyprus (f. 1926); Marxist-Leninist; supports united, sovereign, independent, federal and demilitarized Cyprus; Sec.-Gen. STEPHANOS STEPHANOU.

Dimokratiki Parataxi (DEPA) (Democratic Front): 58 Digeni Akrita, Ghinis Bldg, 1061 Nicosia; tel. 22270007; fax 22270008; e-mail info@depa.cy; internet depa.cy; f. 2018 by fmr mems of DIKO; centrist; Pres. MARIOS GAROYIAN.

Dimokratiko Komma (DIKO) (Democratic Party): Grivas Dhigenis Ave, 1096 Nicosia; tel. 22873800; e-mail contact@diko.org.cy; internet www.democraticparty.org.cy; f. 1976; absorbed Enosi Kentrou (Centre Union, f. 1981) in 1989; supports settlement of the Cyprus problem based on UN resolutions; Pres. NICOLAS PAPADOPOULOS; Gen. Sec. GEORGE SOLOMOU.

Dimokratikos Synagermos (DISY) (Democratic Rally): POB 25305, 25 Pindarou St, 1308 Nicosia; tel. 22883000; e-mail epikinonia@disy.org.cy; internet www.disy.org.cy; f. 1976; absorbed Democratic National Party (DEK) 1977, New Democratic Front (NEDIPA) 1988 and Liberal Party 1998; advocates the reunification of Cyprus on the basis of a bizonal federation; also advocates market economy with restricted state intervention and increased state social role; Pres. ANNITA DEMETRIOU.

Enomeni Dimokrates (EDI) (United Democrats): POB 23494, 1683 Nicosia; tel. 22663030; fax 22664747; e-mail edicy@spidernet.com.cy; internet www.edi.org.cy; f. by merger of Ananeotiko Dimokratiko Socialistiko Kinima (ADISOK—Democratic Socialist Reform Movement) and Kinima ton Eleftheron Dimokraton (KED—Movement of Free Democrats); Pres. PRAXOULA ANTONIADOU KYRIAKOU; Gen. Sec. Dr GEORGE D. CHRISTODOULIDES.

Ethniko Laiko Metopo (ELAM) (National People's Front): POB 1070, Nicosia; tel. 22318051; fax 22318049; e-mail kd@elamcy.com; internet www.elamcy.com; right-wing, nationalist; Pres. CHRISTOS CHRISTOU.

Kinima Allileggii (Solidarity Movement): 60 Athalassis St, Strovolos, 2023 Nicosia; tel. 22007048; e-mail info@allileggii.com; internet fb.com/allileggii2015; f. 2016 by fmr mem. of DISY; absorbed Evropaiko Komma (Evro.Ko—European Party); Chair. (vacant).

Kinima Oikologon–Synergasia Politon (KOSP) (Cyprus Greens—Citizens' Co-operation): POB 29682, 1722 Nicosia; tel. 22518787; fax 22512710; e-mail info@cyprusgreens.org; internet cyprusgreens.org; f. 1996 as the Kinima Oikologon Perivallontiston (Movement of Ecologists and Environmentalists); present name adopted 2016; promotes the principles of sustainable devt; Pres. CHARALAMPOS THEOPEMPTOU.

Kinima Sosialdimokraton EDEK (Movement of Social Democrats EDEK—EDEK): Lordou Vyronos 40, 1096 Nicosia; tel. 22476000; fax 22678894; e-mail info@edek.org.cy; internet www.edek.org.cy; f. 1969 as Eniaia Dimokratiki Enosi Kentrou (United Democratic Centre of the Union—EDEK; name changed to Socialistiko Komma Kyprou EDEK (Socialist Party of Cyprus EDEK) in 1973 and as above in 2000; Pres. MARINOS SIZOPOULOS.

Neo Kyma (New Wave–Volt Cyprus): POB 24944, 1305 Nicosia; tel. 70001019; e-mail info@neokyma.org.cy; internet neokyma.org.cy; f. 2019; Gen. Sec. CONSTANTINOS CHRISTOFIDES.

Diplomatic Representation

EMBASSIES AND HIGH COMMISSIONS IN CYPRUS

Australia: 27 Pindarou St, Blk A, Alpha Business Centre, 7th Floor, 1060 Nicosia; tel. 22697555; fax 22766486; e-mail nicosia.ahc@dfat.gov.au; internet www.cyprus.embassy.gov.au; High Commr FIONA MCKERGOW.

Austria: 34 Demosthenis Severis Ave, 1080 Nicosia; tel. 22410151; fax 22680099; internet www.bmeia.gv.at/botschaft/nikosia; Ambassador Dr DOROTHEA AUER.

Brazil: 14 Acheon St, Ayios Andreas, 1101 Nicosia; tel. 22592300; fax 22354538; e-mail brasemb.nicosia@itamaraty.gov.br; internet nicosia.itamaraty.gov.br; Ambassador EDUARDO AUGUSTO IBIAPINA DE SEIXAS.

Bulgaria: POB 24029, 13 Constantinou Paleologos St, 2406 Engomi, Nicosia; tel. 22672486; fax 22676598; e-mail embassy.nicosia@mfa.bg; internet www.mfa.bg/embassies/cyprus; Ambassador NEDIALTCHO D. DANTCHEV.

China, People's Republic: POB 24531, 30 Archimedes St, 2411 Engomi, Nicosia; tel. 22352184; fax 22353530; e-mail chinaemb_cy@mfa.gov.cn; internet cy.china-embassy.org; Ambassador LIU YANTAO.

Cuba: Pentelis 26, 2013 Strovolos, Nicosia; tel. 22769743; fax 22753820; e-mail embajada@cy.embacuba.cu; internet misiones.minrex.gob.cu/en/cyprus; Ambassador ANGEL GUSTAVO SUAREZ CORDERO.

CYPRUS
Directory

Czech Republic: Office 202, 2nd Floor, 18 Kyriakou Matsi Ave, Ayioi Omoloyites, 1082 Nicosia; tel. 22421118; fax 22421059; internet www.mzv.cz/nicosia; Ambassador VLADIMÍR NĚMEC.

Egypt: POB 21752, 14 Ayios Prokopios St, Engomi, 1512 Nicosia; tel. 22449083; fax 22449081; e-mail embassy.nicosia@mfa.gov.eg; Ambassador AMR MOHSEN HAMZA.

Finland: POB 21438, 9 Arch. Makarios III Ave, 1508 Nicosia; tel. 22458020; fax 22447880; e-mail sanomat.nic@formin.fi; internet finlandabroad.fi/web/cyp; Ambassador HARRI MÄKI-REINIKKA.

France: 34 Demostheni Severi Ave, 2nd Floor, Agioi Omologitai, 1080 Nicosia; tel. 22585300; fax 22585335; e-mail contact .nicosie-amba@diplomatie.gouv.fr; internet cy.ambafrance.org; Ambassador SALINA GRENET-CATALANO.

Georgia: 3 Vasilissis Amalias St, 1101 Ayios Andreas, Nicosia; tel. 22357327; fax 22357307; e-mail cyprus.emb@mfa.gov.ge; internet cyprus.mfa.gov.ge; Ambassador TEIMURAZ KEKELIDZE.

Germany: 10 Nikitaras St, Ayioi Omoloyites, 1080 Nicosia; POB 25705, 1311 Nicosia; tel. 22790000; fax 22790079; e-mail info@nikosia.diplo.de; internet www.nikosia.diplo.de; Ambassador ANKE SCHLIMM.

Greece: POB 21799, 8–10 Byron Ave, 1096 Nicosia; tel. 22445111; fax 22680649; e-mail gremb.nic@mfa.gr; internet www.mfa.gr/cyprus; Ambassador IOANNIS PAPAMELETIOU.

Holy See: POB 22099, 1517 Nicosia (Apostolic Nunciature); tel. 22522231; fax 22522271; Apostolic Nuncio Most Rev. GIOVANNI PIETRO DAL TOSO (Titular Archbishop of Foratiana—also Apostolic Nuncio to Jordan, resident in Amman).

India: POB 25544, 3 Indira Gandhi St, Engomi, 2413 Nicosia; tel. 22351741; fax 22352062; e-mail hoc.nicosia@mea.gov.in; internet hci .gov.in/nicosia; High Commr Shri MANISH (designate).

Iran: 8 Elias Papakyriako St, Acropolis, Nicosia; tel. 22314459; internet cyprus.mfa.ir; Ambassador Seyed ALIREZA SALARIAN.

Ireland: 7 Aiantas St, Ayioi Omoloyites, 1082 Nicosia; POB 23848, 1686 Nicosia; tel. 22818183; fax 22660050; e-mail nicosiaembassy@dfa.ie; internet www.dfa.ie/irish-embassy/cyprus; Ambassador CONOR LONG.

Israel: POB 25159, 4 Ioanni Grypari St, 1090 Nicosia; tel. 22369500; fax 22369555; e-mail info@nicosia.mfa.gov.il; internet embassies.gov .il/nicosia; Ambassador OREN ANOLIK.

Italy: POB 27695, 11 25th March St, Engomi, 2408 Nicosia; tel. 22357635; fax 22357616; e-mail ambnico.mail@esteri.it; internet www.ambnicosia.esteri.it; Ambassador FEDERICA FERRARI BRAVO.

Japan: 5 Esperidon St, Acropolis, 1087 Nicosia; tel. 22394800; fax 22319077; e-mail embjapan@cy.mofa.go.jp; internet www.cy .emb-japan.go.jp; Ambassador YOSHIO YAMAWAKI.

Jordan: 29 Eleonon St, Strovolos, 2057 Nicosia; tel. 22041555; fax 22041551; e-mail nicosia@fm.gov.jo; internet jordanembassynicosia .com; Ambassador MUHAMMAD SHARARI AL-BAKHIT AL-FAYEZ.

Kuwait: 38 Armenias St, Strovolos, 2003 Nicosia; tel. 22465566; fax 22454424; e-mail kuwait.emb@cytanet.com.cy; Ambassador ABDULLAH M. AL-KHORAFI.

Lebanon: POB 21924, 6 Chiou St, Ayios Dhometios 2373, 1515 Nicosia; tel. 22878282; fax 22878293; e-mail lebanon.emb@cytanet .com.cy; internet www.nicosia.mfa.gov.lb; Ambassador CLAUDE EL-HAJAL.

Libya: POB 22487, 7 Stassinos Ave, 1060 Nicosia; tel. 22460055; fax 22452711; e-mail info@libyanembassy.com.cy; Ambassador QUWAYDIR ABRAHIM QUWAYDIR.

Netherlands: POB 23835, 34 Demosthenis Severis Ave, 1080 Nicosia; tel. 22873666; fax 22872399; e-mail nic@minbuza.nl; internet www.netherlandsandyou.nl/your-country-and-the -netherlands/cyprus; Ambassador ELKE MERKS-SCHAAPVELD.

Oman: 135 Eleonon St, Strovolos, 2060 Nicosia; tel. 22376064; fax 22374436; e-mail embassyofoman@cytanet.com.cy; Ambassador MUHAMMAD BIN ABDULLAH BIN AWAD AL-NAHDI.

Poland: POB 22743, Office 601, 12–14 Kennedy Ave, 1087 Nicosia; tel. 22753517; fax 22751981; e-mail nikozja.amb.sekretariat@msz .gov.pl; internet nikozja.msz.gov.pl; Ambassador IRENA LICHNEROWICZ-AUGUSTYN.

Portugal: POB 21404, Severis Bldg 1065, 9 Arch. Makarios III Ave, 1508 Nicosia; tel. 22375131; e-mail nicosia@mne.pt; internet fb.com/embportcyp; Ambassador VANDA MARIA DIAS STELZER SEQUEIRA.

Qatar: 21–23 Agias Annas St, 2054 Nicosia; tel. 22466864; fax 22466893; e-mail nicosia@mofa.gov.qa; internet nicosia.embassy .qa; Ambassador ALI YOUSEF ABDULRAHMAN AL-MULLA.

Romania: POB 22210, 27 Pireos St, Strovolos, 2023 Nicosia; tel. 22495535; fax 22517383; e-mail nicosia@mae.ro; internet nicosia .mae.ro; Ambassador DAN MIHALACHE.

Russian Federation: POB 21845, Ayios Prokopias St and Archbishop Makarios III Ave, Engomi, 2406 Nicosia; tel. 22774622; fax 22774854; e-mail russia1@cytanet.com.cy; internet www.cyprus.mid .ru; Ambassador MURAT ZYAZIKOV.

Saudi Arabia: Ionos 4, Engomi, 2406 Nicosia; tel. 22667300; e-mail cyemb@mofa.gov.sa; internet fb.com/ksaembassycy; Ambassador KHALED BIN MOHAMMED AL-SHARIF.

Serbia: 2 Vasilissis Olgas St, Engomi, 1101 Nicosia; tel. 22777511; fax 22775910; e-mail nicosia@serbia.org.cy; internet www.nicosia .mfa.gov.rs; Ambassador MARKO BLAGOJEVIĆ.

Slovakia: POB 21165, 4 Kalamatas St, 2002 Strovolos, Nicosia; tel. 22879681; fax 22311715; e-mail emb.nicosia@mzv.sk; internet www .mzv.sk/nicosia; Ambassador MARTIN BEZAK.

Spain: POB 28349, 5 Nikolaou Katalanou St, Ayios Andreas, 1100 Nicosia; tel. 22450410; fax 22491291; e-mail emb.nicosia@maec.es; internet www.exteriores.gob.es/embajadas/nicosia; Ambassador GABRIEL FERRÁN CARRIÓN.

Sweden: POB 21621, 9 Archbishop Makarios III Ave, Severis Bldg, 2nd Floor, 1065 Nicosia; tel. 22458088; e-mail ambassaden.nicosia@gov.se; internet www.swedenabroad.se/sv/utlandsmyndigheter/cypern-nicosia; Ambassador MARTIN HAGSTRÖM.

Switzerland: Prodromou/2 Dimitrakopoulou St, 2nd Floor, 1090 Nicosia; POB 20729, 1663 Nicosia; tel. 22466800; fax 22766008; e-mail nicosia@eda.admin.ch; internet www.eda.admin.ch/nicosia; Ambassador CHRISTOPH BURGENER.

Syrian Arab Republic: POB 21892, 24 Nikodimos Mylona St, Ayios Antonios, 1071 Nicosia; tel. 22817333; fax 22756963; e-mail syrianembassy@cytanet.com.cy; Chargé d'affaires a.i. HAYDAR ALI AHMAD.

Ukraine: 10 Andrea Miaouli St, Makedonitissa, Engomi, 2415 Nicosia; tel. 22464380; fax 22464381; e-mail emb_cy@mfa.gov.ua; internet cyprus.mfa.gov.ua; Ambassador RUSLAN NIMCHYNSKYI.

United Arab Emirates: 39–41 Evagorou Ave, 1066 Nicosia; tel. 22375777; fax 22375778; e-mail nicosiaemb.amo@mofaic.gov.ae; internet www.mofaic.gov.ae/en/missions/nicosia; Ambassador MOHAMMED SAIF AL-SHEHHI.

United Kingdom: POB 21978, Alexander Pallis St, 1587 Nicosia; tel. 22861100; fax 22861125; e-mail ukincyprus@fcdo.gov.uk; internet www.gov.uk/world/cyprus; High Commr IRFAN SIDDIQ.

USA: Metochiou and Ploutarchou St, 2407 Engomi, Nicosia; tel. 22393939; fax 22780944; e-mail consularnicosia@state.gov; internet cy.usembassy.gov; Ambassador JULIE D. FISHER.

Judicial System

As required by the Constitution, a law was adopted in 1960 providing for the establishment, jurisdiction and powers of courts of civil and criminal jurisdiction, i.e. of six District Courts and six Assize Courts. In accordance with the provisions of new legislation, approved in 1991, a permanent Assize Court, with powers of jurisdiction in all districts, was established.

In addition to a single Military Court, there are specialized courts concerned with cases relating to industrial disputes, rent control and family law.

After many years of discussion, legislative amendments were approved in July 2022 to reform Cyprus's judicial system. The reforms included the division of the Supreme Court into two separate courts: the Supreme Constitutional Court and the Supreme Court, as provided for in the 1960 Constitution before the enactment of legislation in 1964 (following the withdrawal of the Turkish Cypriot judges) under which one unified Supreme Court (with 13 judges) had been established to exercise the jurisdiction of both courts. The two 'new' courts were established in July 2023, together with a Court of Appeal. Two additional courts, an Admiralty Court and a Commercial Court, were to commence operations in September.

Supreme Constitutional Court: Nicosia; f. 2023; comprises nine judges appointed by the President of the Republic; final appellate court and adjudicator in matters of constitutional and administrative law; Pres. ANTONIS R. LIATSOU.

Supreme Court: Charalambos Mouskos St, 1404 Nicosia; tel. 22865741; fax 22304500; e-mail chief.reg@sc.judicial.gov.cy; internet www.supremecourt.gov.cy; f. 2023; comprises seven judges appointed by the President of the Republic; court of final appeal for criminal and civil matters; Pres. KATERINA STAMATIOU.

Court of Appeal: Nicosia; f. 2023; comprises 16 judges; exercises appellate jurisdiction over the first instance courts, in civil and criminal cases, as well as cases involving judicial review of administrative decisions, and other decisions of courts of special jurisdiction.

Attorney-General: GIORGOS SAVVIDES.

Religion

The majority of the Greek Cypriot community are adherents of the Orthodox Church, although there are also adherents of the Armenian Apostolic Church, the Anglican Communion and the Roman Catholic Church (including Maronites).

CHRISTIANITY

The Orthodox Church of Cyprus

The Autocephalous Orthodox Church of Cyprus, founded in 45 CE, is part of the Eastern Orthodox Church; the Church is independent, and the Archbishop, who is also the Ethnarch (national leader of the Greek community), is elected by representatives of the towns and villages of Cyprus. The church comprises 16 dioceses.

Archbishop of Nova Justiniana and all Cyprus: Archbishop GEORGIOS III, Holy Archdiocese of Cyprus, Archbishop Kyprianou Sq., 1016 Nicosia; tel. 22554600; fax 22431796; e-mail office@churchofcyprus.org.cy; internet www.churchofcyprus.org.cy.

Metropolitan of Kitium: Bishop NEKTARIOS.

Metropolitan of Kyrenia: Bishop CHRYSOSTOMOS.

Metropolitan of Limassol: Bishop ATHANASIOS.

Metropolitan of Morphou: Bishop NEOPHYTOS.

Metropolitan of Paphos: Bishop GEORGIOS.

The Roman Catholic Church

Latin Rite

The Patriarchate of Jerusalem covers Israel, Jordan and Cyprus. The Patriarch is resident in Jerusalem (see Israel).

Vicar Patriarchal for Cyprus: Fr JERZY KRAJ, Holy Cross Catholic Church, Paphos Gate, POB 21964, 1010 Nicosia; tel. 22662132; fax 22660767; e-mail holcross@logos.cy.net; internet www.cypruscatholicchurch.org.

Maronite Rite

Most of the Roman Catholics in Cyprus are adherents of the Maronite rite. Prior to June 1988 the Archdiocese of Cyprus included part of Lebanon.

Archbishop of Cyprus: Most Rev. SELIM JEAN SFEIR, 10 Karaiskaki St, 2012 Strovolos, 1519 Nicosia; tel. 22427966; fax 22314919; e-mail betmorounincyprus@cytanet.com.cy; internet www.maronitearcheparchy.org.cy.

The Anglican Communion

Anglicans in Cyprus are adherents of the Episcopal Church in Jerusalem and the Middle East, officially inaugurated in January 1976. The Church has four dioceses. The diocese of Cyprus and the Gulf includes Cyprus, Iraq and the countries of the Arabian peninsula.

Bishop in Cyprus and the Gulf, President Bishop of the Episcopal Church in Jerusalem and the Middle East: Right Rev. MICHAEL LEWIS, POB 22017, 1517 Nicosia; tel. 22671220; e-mail info@cypgulf.org; internet www.cypgulf.org; Archdeacon in Cyprus Very Rev. CHRISTOPHER FUTCHER.

Other Christian Churches

Among other denominations active in Cyprus are the Armenian Apostolic Church and the Greek Evangelical Church.

The Press

DAILY NEWSPAPERS (PRINT AND ONLINE)

Alithia (Truth): 5 Archbishop Kyprianos St, 2235 Latsia, 1502 Nicosia; POB 21695, 1512 Nicosia; tel. 22471300; fax 22763945; e-mail news@alfamedia.press.cy; internet www.alithia.com.cy; f. 1952 as a weekly, 1982 as a daily; morning; Greek; right-wing; Man. Dir FRIXOS N. KOULERMOS.

Cyprus Mail: 5 Limassol Ave, 2112 Nicosia; POB 21144, 1502 Nicosia; tel. 22818585; fax 22676385; e-mail mail@cyprus-mail.com; internet www.cyprus-mail.com; f. 1945; morning; English; independent; Chair. IOANNIS KASOULIDES; Man. Editor KYRIACOS IACOVIDES.

Haravgi (Dawn): POB 20255, 7 Larnakos Ave, Doriforos Bldg, Blk B, Offices 301–401, 2101 Aglantzia, Nicosia; tel. 22864500; fax 22765154; e-mail info@dialogos.com.cy; internet dialogos.com.cy/haravgi; f. 1956; morning; Greek; owned by Dialogos Media Group; Group Dir ELENI MAVROU.

MAXH (Combat): POB 27628, 1st Floor, Block D, 109 office, 2113 Engomi, Nicosia; tel. 22356676; fax 22356701; internet www.maxhnews.com; f. 1960; weekly; Greek; right-wing; Gen. Man. MINA SAMPSON; Chief Editor FROSSO GEORGIOU.

O Phileleftheros (Liberal): POB 21094, 1501 Nicosia; tel. 22744000; fax 22744050; e-mail mailbox@phileleftheros.com; internet www.philenews.com; f. 1955; morning; Greek; independent; moderate; Exec. Dir MYRTO MARKIDOU-SELIPA; Editor-in-Chief ARISTOS MICHAELIDES.

Politis (Citizen): 8 Vassilios Voulgaroktonos St, 1010 Nicosia; POB 22894, 1524 Nicosia; tel. 22861861; fax 22861871; e-mail info@politis-news.com; internet www.politis.com.cy; f. 1999; morning; Greek; independent; Publr YIANNIS PAPADOPOULOS.

WEEKLY NEWSPAPERS (PRINT AND ONLINE)

Athlitiki tis Kyriakis (Sunday Sports News): 53 Demosthenis Severis Ave, 9th Floor, 1080 Nicosia; tel. 22664344; fax 22664543; e-mail fellouka@cytanet.com.cy; f. 1996; Greek; athletics; Dir PANAYIOTIS FELLOUKAS; Chief Editor NICOS NICOLAOU.

The Blue Beret: POB 21642, HQ UNFICYP, 1590 Nicosia; tel. 22614634; fax 22614461; e-mail unficyp-hq-mil-pio@un.org; internet www.unficyp.org; f. 1965; bi-monthly journal of the UN Peacekeeping Force in Cyprus (UNFICYP); English; Editor ALEEM SIDDIQUE.

The Cyprus Lion: 55 AEC Episkopi, BFPO 53; tel. 25962052; fax 25963181; distributed to British Sovereign Base Areas, UN Forces and principal Cypriot towns; includes British Forces Broadcasting Services programme guide; Editor LOUISE CARRIGAN.

Cyprus Weekly: POB 21094, 1 Diogenous St, Engomi, 2404 Nicosia; tel. 22744000; fax 22744440; e-mail incyprus@phileleftheros.com; internet in-cyprus.com; f. 1979; English; independent; became online only in 2017; Editors BOULI CHATZIOANOU, STELIOS MARATHOVOUNIOTIS.

Dimosios Ypallilos (Civil Servant): 3 Demosthenis Severis Ave, 1066 Nicosia; tel. 22844445; fax 22668639; e-mail pasydy@pasydy.org; internet www.pasydy.org; f. 1927; Greek; publ. by the Cyprus Civil Servants' Trade Union (PASYDY).

Ergatiki Phoni (Workers' Voice): POB 25018, SEK Bldg, 11 Strovolos Ave, Strovolos, 2018 Nicosia; tel. 22849849; fax 22849858; e-mail ergatikifsek@cytanet.com.cy; f. 1947; Greek; organ of SEK trade union; Dir NICOS MOYSEOS.

Ergatiko Vima (Workers' Tribune): 29 Arhermos St, 1045 Nicosia; POB 21185, 1514 Nicosia; tel. 22866400; fax 22346828; e-mail portal@ergatikovima.com; internet www.ergatikovima.com; f. 1956; Greek; organ of PEO trade union; Chief Editor LEFTERIS GEORGIADIS.

Financial Mirror: POB 16077, 2085 Nicosia; tel. 22678666; fax 22776799; e-mail info@financialmirror.com; internet www.financialmirror.com; f. 1993; English (with Greek-language supplement); independent; Publr and Dir MASIS DER PARTHOGH.

I Kathimerini: 7E Nicou Kranidioti St, Engomi 2411, Nicosia; tel. 22472500; fax 22472550; e-mail info@kathimerini.com.cy; internet www.kathimerini.com.cy; f. 2008; Greek and English; Dir ANDREAS PARASCHOS.

Middle East Economic Survey (MEES): POB 24940, 23 Alkeos St, Politica Business Centre, 1355 Nicosia; tel. 22665434; fax 22671988; e-mail info@mees.com; internet www.mees.com; f. 1957 (in Beirut, Lebanon); review and analysis of petroleum, finance and banking, and political devts; Publr Dr SALEH S. JALLAD; Man. Editor JAMES COCKAYNE.

Official Gazette: Printing Office of the Republic of Cyprus, 1445 Nicosia; tel. 22405824; fax 22303175; e-mail pspanos@gpo.mof.gov.cy; internet www.mof.gov.cy/gpo; f. 1960; Greek; publ. by the Govt of the Republic of Cyprus.

Reporter: POB 21185, 5 Egaleo St, Strovolos 2057, Nicosia; tel. 22505555; fax 22679820; e-mail reporter@imhbusiness.com; internet www.reporter.com.cy; f. 1991; Greek; Gen. Dir GIORGOS MICHAEL; Chief Editor YIANNIS ANTONIOU.

Simerini (Today): POB 21836, 31 Archangelos Ave, Strovolos, 2054 Nicosia; tel. 22580580; fax 22580570; e-mail mail@simerini.com; internet www.sigmalive.com/simerini; f. 1976; morning; Greek; right-wing; supports DISY; Publr KOSTAS HADJIKOSTIS; Exec. Dir CHRYSANTHOS TSOUROULLIS; Editor-in-Chief SKÉVI STÁVROU.

Vestnik Kipra: POB 58236, Park Tower 1, 14 Byron St, Limassol; tel. 22580530; fax 25584920; e-mail official@vkcyprus.com; internet vkcyprus.com; f. 1995; Russian; news, general interest; Fri.

PERIODICALS

Agrotis: 6 Amphipoleos St, Strovolos, 2025 Nicosia; tel. 22408599; fax 22771385; 4 a year; Greek; publ. by Ministry of Agriculture, Rural Development and the Environment.

Cypria (Cypriot Woman): POB 28506, 56 Kennedy Ave, 11th Floor, Strovolos, 2080 Nicosia; tel. 22494907; fax 22427051; e-mail pogo@spidernet.com.cy; f. 1983; every 2 months; Greek; Owner MARO KARAYIANNI.

CYPRUS

The Cyprus Review: POB 24005, 46 Makedonitissas Ave, 1700 Nicosia; tel. 22842306; fax 22842222; e-mail cy_review@unic.ac.cy; internet www.unic.ac.cy/publications/the-cyprus-review; f. 1989; 2 a year; English; publ. by University of Nicasia; Editor-in-Chief Assc. Prof. CHRISTINA IOANNOU.

Cyprus Time Out: POB 3697, 4 Pygmalionos St, 1010 Nicosia; tel. 22472949; fax 22360668; f. 1978; monthly; English; Dir ELLADA SOPHOCLEOUS; Chief Editor LYN HAVILAND.

Cyprus Today: c/o Ministry of Education, Culture, Sport and Youth, Cultural Services, 27 Ifigenias St, Strovolos 2007, Nicosia; tel. 22809841; fax 22663730; e-mail aanastassiades@culture.moec.gov.cy; f. 1963; quarterly; English; cultural and information review; publ. and distributed by Press and Information Office; Chair. PAVLOS PARASKEVAS.

Cyprus Tourism: POB 51697, Limassol; tel. 25337377; fax 25337374; f. 1989; bi-monthly; Greek and English; tourism and travel; Man. Dir G. EROTOKRITOU.

Enosis (Union): 71 Piraeus & Tombazis, Nicosia; tel. 22756862; fax 22757268; f. 1996; monthly; Greek; satirical; Chief Editor VASOS FTOCHOPOLILOS.

Eva: 6 Psichikou St, Strovolos, Nicosia; tel. 22322959; fax 22322940; f. 1996; Greek; Dir DINOS MICHAEL; Chief Editors CHARIS PONTIKIS, KATIA SAVVIDOU.

Hermes International: POB 24512, Nicosia; tel. 22570570; fax 22581617; f. 1992; quarterly; English; lifestyle, business, finance, management; Chief Editor JOHN VICKERS.

I Kypros Simera (Present Day Cyprus): 1 Apellis St, 1456 Nicosia; tel. 22801186; fax 22666123; e-mail kvrahimis@pio.moi.gov.cy; f. 1983; fortnightly; Greek; publ. by the Press and Information Office of the Ministry of the Interior; Principal Officers MILTOS MILTIADOU, MICHALAKIS CHRISTODOULIDES.

Nicosia This Month: POB 20365, 2 Agathokleous St, Strovolos, Nicosia; tel. 22441922; fax 22519743; e-mail info@gnora.com; internet www.gnora.com; f. 1984; monthly; English; Publr MARINOS MOUSHIOTTAS; Man. Dir ANDREAS HADJKYRIACOS.

Omicron: 1 Diogenous St, 2404 Engomi; POB 21094, 1501 Nicosia; tel. 22744000; fax 22590516; e-mail omikron@phileleftheros.com; f. 1996; Greek; Dir NIKOS CHR. PATTICHIS; Chief Editor THANASIS PHOTIOU.

Paediki Chara (Children's Joy): 184 Kyrenia St, 2112 Nicosia; tel. 22817585; fax 22817599; e-mail paidikichara@mail.com; internet www.paidikichara.com; f. 1962; monthly; for pupils; publ. by the Pancyprian Union of Greek Teachers; Dir DIMITRIS SAVVIDIS.

Synergatiko Vima (The Co-operative Tribune): Kosti Palama 5, 1096 Nicosia; tel. 22680757; fax 22660833; e-mail coop.confeder@cytanet.com.cy; f. 1983; quarterly; Greek; official organ of Pancyprian Co-operative Confed. Ltd; Pres. ANDREAS MOUSKALLIS.

Synthesis (Composition): 6 Psichikou St, Strovolos, Nicosia; tel. 22322959; fax 22322940; f. 1988; every 2 months; Greek; interior decorating; Dir DINOS MICHAEL.

Tele Ores: POB 28205, 4 Acropoleos St, 1st Floor, 2091 Nicosia; tel. 22513300; fax 22513363; f. 1993; fortnightly; Greek; television guide; Chief Editor PROMETHEAS CHRISTOPHIDES.

TV Kanali (TV Channel): POB 25603, 5 Aegaleo St, Strovolos, Nicosia; tel. 22353603; fax 22353223; f. 1993; Greek; Dirs A. STAVRIDES, E. HADJIEFTHYMIOU; Chief Editor CHARIS TOMAZOS.

NEWS AGENCY

Cyprus News Agency: 21 Glafkos Clerides Ave, Aglantzia 2107, Nicosia; tel. 22556009; fax 22556103; e-mail director@cna.org.cy; internet www.cna.org.cy; f. 1976; Greek, Turkish, Arabic and English; Dir GEORGE PENINTAEX; Chair. of Bd IOSIF IOSIF.

Publishers

Andreou Chr. Publishers: POB 22298, 67A Regenis St, 1010 Nicosia; tel. 22666595; fax 22666878; e-mail andreou2@cytanet.com.cy; f. 1979; biography, literature, history, regional interest.

Cyprus Research Centre (CRC): POB 21952, 1515 Nicosia; tel. 22456319; fax 22456309; e-mail archeiokee@moec.gov.cy; internet www.moec.gov.cy/kee; Dir ANNA LOIZIDOU-POURADIER DUTEIL.

Anastasios G. Leventis Foundation: 40 Gladstonos St, POB 22543, 1095 Nicosia; tel. 22667706; fax 22675002; e-mail info@leventis.org.cy; internet www.leventisfoundation.org; f. 1980; Dir CHARALAMBOS BAKIRTZIS.

MAM Ltd (The House of Cyprus and Cyprological Publications): POB 21722, 19 Constantinou Paleologou St, 1512 Nicosia; tel. 22753536; fax 22375802; e-mail mam@mam.com.cy; internet mam.com.cy; f. 1965; Man. MICHAEL MICHAELIDES.

Nikoklis Publishing House: POB 20300, 2150 Nicosia; tel. 22334918; fax 22330218; history, geography, culture, travel; Man. Dr ANDREAS SOPHOCLEOUS.

Pierides Foundation: POB 40025, 6300 Larnaca; tel. 24814555; fax 24817868; internet www.pieridesfoundation.com.cy; f. 1974.

Broadcasting and Communications

TELECOMMUNICATIONS

Cyprus Telecommunications Authority (CYTA): POB 24929, Telecommunications St, Strovolos, 1396 Nicosia; tel. 22701000; fax 22494940; e-mail enquiries@cyta.com.cy; internet www.cyta.com.cy; f. 1961; provides fixed-line telecommunications services and broadband internet access; signed partnership agreement with Vodafone PLC (UK) in 2004 to offer mobile telecommunications services under brand name Cytamobile-Vodafone; Chair. MICHAEL IOANNIDES; CEO ANDREAS NEOCLEOUS.

Epic Ltd: 87 Kennedy Ave, 1077 Nicosia; tel. 96222222; fax 96969375; e-mail contactus@epic.com.cy; internet www.epic.com.cy; f. 2004 as Areeba and later rebranded as MTN Cyprus; acquired by Monaco Telecom in 2018; present name adopted in 2019; provides mobile telecommunications services; CEO, MTN Cyprus THANOS CHRONOPOULOS.

PrimeTel PLC: POB 51490, The Maritime Center, 141 Omonia Ave, 3045 Limassol; tel. 22102210; internet primetel.com.cy; f. 2003; provides fixed-line telecommunications services, broadband internet access and cable television to domestic customers under brand name PrimeHome; Man. Dir HERMES N. STEPHANOU.

BROADCASTING

Regulatory Authority

Cyprus Radio Television Authority: POB 23377, 42 Athalassas Ave, 1682 Nicosia; tel. 22512468; fax 22512473; e-mail crtauthority@crta.org.cy; internet www.crta.org.cy; f. 1998; Pres. RONA KASAPI; Dir NEOPHYTOS EPAMINONDAS.

Radio

British Forces Broadcasting Services, Cyprus: Akrotiri, BFPO 57; tel. 25275161; e-mail cyprus@bfbs.com; internet radio.bfbs.com/stations/bfbs-cyprus; f. 1948; broadcasts daily radio and television services in English.

Cyprus Broadcasting Corpn (CyBC): 2120 Nicosia; tel. 22862000; fax 22314050; e-mail info@cybc.com.cy; internet cybc.com.cy; f. 1952; four 24-hour radio channels, two of which are mainly Greek; channel 2 broadcasts programmes in Turkish, English and Armenian; Pres. MICHALIS P. MICHAEL; Dir-Gen. THANASIS TSOKOS.

Kanali Exi: POB 54845, 69 Irinis St, 3041 Limassol; tel. 25820500; internet www.kanali6.com.cy; Dir MICHALIS PAPAEVAGOROU.

Logos: 2054 Strovolos, Nicosia; tel. 22355701; e-mail alithinoslogos@cy.net; internet www.logosradio.com.cy.

Radio Astra: 7 Larnaca Ave, Block B, Office 301–401, 2101 Nicosia; tel. 22864500; e-mail info@dialogos.com.cy; internet dialogos.com.cy/astra; Chair. ELENI MAVROU; Dir ORIANA PAPANTONIOU.

Radio Proto: 31 Andy Hadjikostis and Archangelou cnr, 1513 Nicosia; tel. 22580400; e-mail onairstudio@radioproto.com.cy; internet www.radioproto.com.cy; f. 1990; Man. PETROS ATHANASIOU.

Super FM: POB 22795, 4 Annis Komninis St, Solea Court, 6th Floor, 1060 Nicosia; tel. 22460150; e-mail info@superfmradio.com; internet www.superfmradio.com; Dir ZENON ZINTILIS.

Super Sport FM: POB 12669, 5 Archibishop Kyprianou, Latsia, 2235 Nicosia; tel. 22471444; fax 22571000; e-mail info@sport-fm.com.cy; internet www.sport-fm.com.cy; Gen. Man. YIOTA KOURI.

Television

Greek Cypriot viewers have access to Greek television channels via satellite.

Antenna TV Cyprus (ANT1 Cyprus): 5 Megaron, Strovolos, 2032 Nicosia; tel. 22200200; e-mail info@antenna.com.cy; internet www.ant1.com.cy; f. 1983.

British Forces Broadcasting Services, Cyprus: BFPO 57, Akrotiri; tel. 7504567; e-mail servicedelivery@bfbs.com; internet www.bfbs.com/region/cyprus; f. 1948; broadcasts a daily TV service; Station Man. ANTHONY BALLARD.

Cyprus Broadcasting Corpn (CyBC): POB 24824, CyBC St, 1397 Nicosia; tel. 22862020; fax 22312720; e-mail riknews@cybc.com.cy; internet www.riknews.com.cy; f. 1957; Pik 1 (CyBC 1) one Band III 100/10-kW transmitter on Mount Olympus; Pik 2 (CyBC 2) one Band IV 100/10-kW ERP transmitter on Mount Olympus; ET1 one Band IV 100/10-kW ERP transmitter on Mount Olympus for transmission of the ETI Programme received, via satellite, from Greece; the above three TV channels are also transmitted from 80 transposer stations; Dir-Gen. THANASIS TSOKOS.

Music TV: 49 Archbishop Makarios III Ave, Office 101, Latsia, 2222 Nicosia; tel. 22210001; fax 22210002; e-mail info@musictv.com; Man. MARIOS AHAS.

Omega Channel: 15 Patriarchi Petrou, 7 St, 2054 Strovolos, Nicosia; tel. 22477777; fax 22477737; e-mail info@omegatv.com.cy; internet www.omegatv.com.cy; CEO IOANNIS CHASIKOS.

Sigma Radio TV Ltd: 31 Andy Hadjicostis & Archangelos Ave, 2057 Nicosia; tel. 22580100; fax 22580308; e-mail info@sigmatv.com; internet www.sigmatv.com; f. 1995; island-wide coverage.

Finance

BANKING

Central Bank

Central Bank of Cyprus: POB 25529, 80 Kennedy Ave, 1076 Nicosia; tel. 22714100; e-mail cbcinfo@centralbank.cy; internet www.centralbank.cy; f. 1963; became fully independent from govt control 2002; Gov. CONSTANTINOS HERODOTOU.

Principal Commercial Banks

Alpha Bank Cyprus Ltd: POB 21661, 3 Lemesos Ave, 2112 Nicosia; tel. 22888888; fax 22668234; e-mail riskmanagement@alphabank.com.cy; internet www.alphabank.com.cy; f. 1960 as Lombard Banking (Cyprus) Ltd; name changed to Lombard NatWest Banking Ltd 1989 and as above 1998; locally incorporated although foreign-controlled; 100% owned by Alpha Bank (Greece); Chair. MICHAEL COLAKIDES; Man. Dir KONSTANTINOS D. KOUTENTAKIS.

AstroBank: 1 Spyrou Kyprianou Ave, 1065 Nicosia; tel. 22575655; fax 22767741; e-mail info@astrobank.com; internet www.astrobank.com; f. 2008; Chair. MICHALIS SARRIS; CEO ARISTIDES VOURAKIS.

Bank of Cyprus Public Company Ltd: POB 21472, 51 Stassinos St, Ayia Paraskevi, Strovolos, 1599 Nicosia; tel. 22128000; e-mail info@bankofcyprus.com; internet www.bankofcyprus.com; f. 1899; reconstituted 1943 by the amalgamation of Bank of Cyprus, Larnaca Bank Ltd and Famagusta Bank Ltd; Chair. EFSTRATIOS-GEORGIOS (TAKIS) ARAPOGLOU; CEO PANICOS NICOLAOU.

Hellenic Bank Public Co Ltd: 200 cnr Limassol and Athalassa Ave, 2025 Nicosia; tel. 22500000; fax 22500050; e-mail contact@hellenicbank.com; internet www.hellenicbank.com; f. 1974; financial services group; 15.8% owned by Eurobank Gp; Chair. Dr EVRIPIDES A. POLYKARPOU; CEO OLIVER GATZKE.

National Bank of Greece (Cyprus) Ltd: 15 Arch. Makarios III Ave, 1597 Nicosia; tel. 22040000; fax 22840010; e-mail cloizou@nbg.com.cy; internet www.nbg.com.cy; f. 1994 by incorporating all local business of the National Bank of Greece SA; full commercial banking; Chair. (vacant); Man. Dir MARINIS STRATOPOULOS.

Investment Organization

The Cyprus Investment and Securities Corpn Ltd: 1 Agiou Prokopiou and Posidonos, 1st Floor, Engomi, 2406 Nicosia; tel. 22121700; fax 22123740; e-mail ciscoinfo@bankofcyprus.com; internet www.cisco-online.com.cy; f. 1982 to promote the devt of capital market; brokerage services, fund management, investment banking; mem. of Bank of Cyprus Group; Gen. Man. CHRISTOS KALOGERIS.

Development Bank

The Cyprus Development Bank Public Co Ltd: POB 21415, Alpha House, 50 Archbishop Makarios III Ave, 1065 Nicosia; tel. 22846500; fax 22846600; e-mail info@cdb.com.cy; internet www.cdb.com.cy; f. 1963; aims to accelerate the economic devt of Cyprus by providing medium- and long-term loans for productive projects, developing the capital market, encouraging jt ventures, and providing technical and managerial advice to productive private enterprises; Chair. CHRISTODOULOS PATSALIDES; CEO LOUCAS MARANGOS.

STOCK EXCHANGE

Cyprus Stock Exchange: POB 25427, 71–73 Lordou Vyronos Ave, 1309 Nicosia; tel. 22712300; fax 22570308; e-mail info@cse.com.cy; internet www.cse.com.cy; f. 1996; official trading commenced March 1996; 65 cos listed in Dec. 2020; Chair. MARINOS CHRISTODOULIDES; Gen. Man. NIKOS TRIPATSAS (acting).

INSURANCE

Insurance Companies Control Service: Ministry of Finance, POB 23364, 1682 Nicosia; tel. 22602990; fax 22302938; e-mail insurance@mof.gov.cy; internet bit.ly/3FtdbVk; f. 1969 to control insurance cos, insurance agents, brokers and agents for brokers in Cyprus; Superintendent TONIA TSANGARIS (acting).

Insurance Companies

Atlantic Insurance Co Public Ltd: POB 24579, 15 Espiridon St, 2001 Strovolos, 1301 Nicosia; tel. 22886000; fax 22886111; e-mail atlantic@atlantic.com.cy; internet www.atlantic.com.cy; f. 1983; general, non-life; Chair. and Man. Dir EMILIOS PYRISHIS.

CNP Asfalistiki Ltd: POB 20819, 17 Acropoleos St, 2006 Strovolos, Nicosia; tel. 22887600; fax 22887651; internet www.cnpasfalistiki.com; f. 1981; owned by CNP Assurances SA (France); general; Chair. SONIA BARRIÈRE; CEO TAKIS PHIDIA.

CNP Cyprialife Ltd: POB 20819, 17, Akropoleos Ave, 2006 Strovolos, 1664 Nicosia; tel. 22111213; fax 22363407; e-mail cyprialife@cnpcyprus.com; internet www.cnpcyprialife.com; f. 1995; life, accident and health; Chair. SONIA BARRIÈRE; CEO TAKIS PHIDIA.

Cosmos Insurance Co Public Ltd: POB 21770, Cosmos Tower, 46 Griva Digeni St, 1080 Nicosia; POB 21770, 1513 Nicosia; tel. 22796000; fax 22022000; e-mail info@cosmosinsurance.com.cy; internet www.cosmosinsurance.com.cy; f. 1981; present name adopted 2004; general; Pres. MARIOS LOUCAIDES; Man. Dir KYRIAKOS TYLLIS.

Eurolife Ltd: Eurolife House, 4 Evrou, Strovolos 2003 Nicosia; tel. 22124000; fax 22341090; e-mail info@eurolife.bankofcyprus.com; internet www.eurolife.com.cy; wholly owned subsidiary of Bank of Cyprus; life, accident and health; CEO AVRAAM PEKRIS.

General Insurance of Cyprus Ltd: POB 21668, 2–4 Themistoklis Dervis St, 1066 Nicosia; tel. 80008787; e-mail complaints@gic.bankofcyprus.com; internet www.gic.com.cy; f. 1951; wholly owned subsidiary of Bank of Cyprus; general, non-life; CEO STELIOS CHRISTODOULOU.

Hellenic Life: 66 Griva Digeni, 1095 Nicosia; tel. 80005433; e-mail infoheli@hellenicbank.com; internet www.helleniclife.com; f. by merger of Hellenic Bank PCL and Alico AIG Life; 100% owned by Hellenic Bank PCL; Chair. Dr EVRIPIDES A. POLYKARPOU.

Minerva Insurance Co Public Ltd: POB 23544, 165 Athalassas Ave, 2024 Strovolos, 1684 Nicosia; tel. 77771414; fax 22551717; e-mail info@minervacy.com; internet minervacy.com; f. 1970; general and life; Chair. and CEO MARIOS KOUTSOKOUMNIS.

Pancyprian Insurance Ltd: POB 21352, Pancyprian Tower, 66 Grivas Dhigenis Ave, 1095 Nicosia; tel. 77772171; e-mail pancyprian@pancyprianinsurance.com; internet www.pancyprianinsurance.com; f. 1992; wholly owned subsidiary of Hellenic Bank PCL; general, non-life; Chair. Dr EVRIPIDES A. POLYKARPOU; CEO CHRISTOS PATSALIDES.

Prime Insurance Co Ltd: POB 22475, 1070 Nicosia; tel. 22896000; fax 22896001; e-mail info@primeinsurance.eu; internet www.primeinsurance.eu; fmrly Interlife Insurance Co; acquired by Demco Insurance Ltd (Greece) and present name adopted in 2011; life and general; Chair. MARIA KONTOMINA; CEO PANAYIOTIS PANAYIOTOU.

Universal Life Insurance Public Co Ltd: POB 21270, Universal Tower, 85 Dhigenis Akritas Ave, 1505 Nicosia; tel. 22882222; fax 22882200; e-mail info@unilife.com.cy; internet www.universallife.com.cy; f. 1970; life, accident, health and general; Chair. PHOTIADES PAVLOS; CEO and Man. Dir GAVAS EVAN.

Insurance Association

Insurance Association of Cyprus: POB 22030, Insurance Centre, 23 Zenon Sozos St, 1st Floor, 1075 Nicosia; tel. 22452990; fax 22374288; e-mail info@iac.org.cy; internet www.iac.org.cy; 29 mem. cos; Chair. EVANGELOS ANASTASIADES; Dir-Gen. ANDREAS ATHANASIADES.

Trade and Industry

CHAMBERS OF COMMERCE AND INDUSTRY

Cyprus Chamber of Commerce and Industry: POB 21455, 38 Grivas Dhigenis Ave, 1509 Nicosia; tel. 22889800; fax 22669048; e-mail chamber@ccci.org.cy; internet www.ccci.org.cy; f. 1927; Pres. CHRISTODOULOS ANGASTINIOTIS; Sec.-Gen. MARIOS TSIAKKIS; 8,000 mems, 140 affiliated trade asscns (2020).

Famagusta Chamber of Commerce and Industry: 152 Georgiou Gourounia, Ruidoso Shopping Centre, 1st Floor, 5281 Paralimni; tel. 23829264; fax 23829267; e-mail info@famagustachamber.org.cy; internet www.famagustachamber.org.cy; f. 1952; Pres. AVGOUSTINOS PAPATHOMAS.

Larnaca Chamber of Commerce and Industry: POB 40287, 12 Gregoriou Afxentiou Ave, Skouros Bldg, 4th Floor, 6302 Larnaca; tel.

24823855; fax 24628281; e-mail info@larnakachamber.com.cy; internet larnacachamber.cy; f. 1954; Pres. STAVROS STAVROU; Sec. GEORGE PSARAS.

Limassol Chamber of Commerce and Industry: 170 Franklin Roosevelt Ave, 3045 Limassol; POB 55699, 3781 Limassol; tel. 25855000; fax 25661655; e-mail info@limassolchamber.eu; internet www.limassolchamber.eu; f. 1962; Pres. ANDREAS TSOULOFTAS; Sec. and Dir CHRISTOS ANASTASSIADES.

Nicosia Chamber of Commerce and Industry: POB 21455, 38 Grivas Dhigenis Ave, 3 Deligiorgi St, 1509 Nicosia; tel. 22889600; fax 22667433; e-mail reception@ncci.org.cy; internet www.ncci.org.cy; f. 1952; Pres. MICHALIS MOUSIOUTTAS; Dir SOCRATES HERACLEOUS; 1,520 mems.

Paphos Chamber of Commerce and Industry: POB 82, Tolmi Court, 1st Floor, cnr Athinon Ave and Alexandrou Papayou Ave, 8100 Paphos; tel. 26818173; fax 26944602; e-mail info@pcci.org.cy; internet www.pcci.org.cy; Pres. GEORGE MAIS; Sec. MARINOS STYLIANOU; 550 mems.

EMPLOYERS' ORGANIZATION

Cyprus Employers' & Industrialists' Federation: POB 21657, 2 Acropoleos Ave, 1511 Nicosia; tel. 22643000; fax 22669459; e-mail info@oeb.org.cy; internet www.oeb.org.cy; f. 1960; over 100 mem. trade asscns, and over 10,000 direct and indirect mems; the largest of the trade asscn mems are: Cyprus Building Contractors' Asscn; Land and Building Developers' Asscn; Asscn of Cyprus Tourist Enterprises; Cyprus Shipping Asscn; Cyprus Footwear Mfrs' Asscn; Cyprus Metal Industries Asscn; Cyprus Bankers Employers' Asscn; Cyprus Asscn of Business Consultants; Mechanical Contractors Asscn of Cyprus; Union of Solar Energy Industries of Cyprus; Chair. ANTONIOS ANTONIOU; Dir-Gen. ANTONIOU MICHALIS.

UTILITIES
Regulatory Authority

Cyprus Energy Regulatory Authority (CERA): POB 24936, 1305 Nicosia; 20 Agias Paraskevis, 2002 Strovolos, Nicosia; tel. 22666363; fax 22667763; e-mail regulator.cy@cera.org.cy; internet www.cera.org.cy; f. 2003; regulates the electricity and gas market in Cyprus; Chair. Dr ANDREAS POULLIKKAS; Dir PANAGIOTIS KELIRIS.

Electricity

Electricity Authority of Cyprus (EAC): POB 21413, 1508 Nicosia; tel. 22202243; fax 22202388; e-mail eac@eac.com.cy; internet www.eac.com.cy; f. 1952; generation, transmission and distribution of electric energy in govt-controlled area; also licensed to install and commercially exploit wired telecommunication network; total installed capacity 1,478 MW in 2018; Chair. DESPINA PANAYIOTOU THEODOSIOU; Gen. Man. ADONIS JASEMIDIS.

Water

Water Development Department: 100–110 Kennedy Ave, 1047 Pallouriotissa, Nicosia; tel. 22609000; fax 22675019; e-mail director@wdd.moa.gov.cy; internet www.moa.gov.cy/wdd; f. 1939; owned by Ministry of Agriculture, Rural Development and the Environment; Dir PANAGIOTA HATZIGEORGIOU.

MAJOR COMPANIES

Cyprus Canning Co Ltd: POB 50209, 1 Franklin Roosevelt Ave, 3602 Limassol; tel. 25853100; fax 25573429; f. 1954.

Cyprus Forest Industries Public Ltd: Ayias Sofias 1, Palaiometocho, 2682 Nicosia; tel. 22872700; fax 22833564; e-mail cfi@cfi.com.cy; internet www.cfi.com.cy; f. 1970; Chair. EFTHYMIA AGATHOCLEOUS; CEO CHARIS CHARALAMBOUS.

Cyprus Hydrocarbons Co (CHC): 53 Strovolou Ave, Victory Bldg, 2018 Strovolos; tel. 22203880; e-mail info@chc.com.cy; internet chc.com.cy; f. 2012; established as Cyprus National Hydrocarbons Co (KRETYK); present name adopted 2014; responsible for exploration, production and monetization of offshore oil and gas reserves; state-owned; Pres. TOULA ONOUFRIOU; Gen. Man. DEMETRIS FESSAS (acting).

Cyprus Phassouri Plantations Co Ltd: POB 50180, 3601 Limassol; tel. 25876000; fax 25952225; e-mail info@redseal-quality.com; internet www.redseal-quality.com.

Cyprus Trading Corpn Public Ltd: POB 21744, Shacolas House, 200 Lemesos Ave, 2025 Strovolos, 1589 Nicosia; tel. 22740300; fax 22485385; e-mail ctc@ctcgroup.com; internet www.ctcgroup.com; Chair. DEMETRIS DEMETRIOU.

Keo PLC: POB 50209, 1 Franklin Roosevelt Ave, 3602 Limassol; tel. 25020000; fax 25020001; e-mail keo@keogroup.com; internet www.keogroup.com; f. 1927 as Keo Ltd; present name adopted 2006; mfrs of wine, beer and spirits, fruit juices, canned vegetables and mineral water; Chair. COSTAS KOUTSOS.

Natural Gas Public Co (DEFA/CYGAS): 13 Limassol Ave, Demetra Tower, 4th Floor, 2112 Nicosia; tel. 22761761; e-mail info@defa.com.cy; internet defa.com.cy; f. 2007; has sole responsible for the import, storage, distribution, transmission, supply and trading of natural gas in Cyprus; Chair. NIKOS KASTELLANIS.

Vassiliko Cement Works Ltd: POB 22281, 1A Kyriakos Matsis Ave, 1519 Nicosia; tel. 22458100; fax 22762741; e-mail info@vassiliko.com; internet www.vassiliko.com; f. 1963; cement mfrs; Exec. Chair. ANTONIOS ANTONIOU.

TRADE UNIONS

Cyprus Civil Servants' Trade Union (PASYDY): 3 Demosthenis Severis Ave, 1066 Nicosia; tel. 22844445; fax 22668639; e-mail e.stratios@pasydy.org; internet www.pasydy.org; f. 1927; regd 1966; restricted to persons in the civil employment of the Govt and public authorities; 6 brs with a total membership of 15,383; Pres. ANTONIS KOUTSOULIS; Gen. Sec. STRATIS MATTHEOU.

Dimokratiki Ergatiki Omospondia Kyprou (DEOK) (Democratic Labour Federation of Cyprus): POB 21625, 40 Byron Ave, Nicosia 1511; tel. 77772070; e-mail contact@deok.org.cy; internet www.deok.org.cy; f. 1962; 6 workers' unions; Chair. JOSEPH ANASTASIOU.

Pankypria Ergatiki Omospondia (PEO) (Pancyprian Federation of Labour): POB 21885, 29 Archermos St, 1045 Nicosia; tel. 22886400; e-mail peo@peo.org.cy; internet www.peo.org.cy; f. 1946; regd 1947; previously the Pancyprian Trade Union Cttee (f. 1941, dissolved 1946); 8 unions and 176 brs with a total membership of 75,000; affiliated to WFTU; Gen. Sec. SOTIROULA CHARALAMBOUS.

Pankypria Omospondia Anexartition Syntechnion Organoseon (POASO) (Pancyprian Federation of Independent Trade Unions): 168 Athalassa Ave, Office 401, Minos Court, 2025 Nicosia; tel. 22516600; fax 22516717; e-mail info@poaso.org.cy; internet www.poaso.org.cy; f. 1957; regd 1957; has no political orientation; Chair. KOSTAS IOANNOU; Sec.-Gen. PANAGIOTIS GEORGIOU.

Synomospondia Ergazomenon Kyprou (SEK) (Cyprus Workers' Confederation): POB 25018, 11 Strovolos Ave, 2018 Strovolos, 1306 Nicosia; tel. 22849849; fax 22849850; e-mail sek@sek.org.cy; internet www.sek.org.cy; f. 1944; regd 1950; 7 federations, 5 labour centres, 47 unions, 12 brs with a total membership of 65,000; affiliated to ITUC and the European Trade Union Confed; Gen. Sec. ANDREAS MATSAS.

Union of Cyprus Journalists: POB 23495, Rik Ave 12, 2152 Nicosia; tel. 22446090; fax 22446095; e-mail cyjourun@logosnet.cy.net; internet www.esk.org.cy; f. 1960; Pres. GEORGE FRANGOS; Gen. Sec. RALLI PAPAGEORGIOU.

Transport

RAILWAYS

There are no railways in Cyprus.

ROADS

The Nicosia–Limassol four-lane dual carriageway, which was completed in 1985, was extended with the completion of the Limassol and Larnaca bypasses. Highways also connect Nicosia and Larnaca, Nicosia and Anthoupolis-Kokkinotrimithia, Larnaca and Kophinou, Aradippo and Dhekelia, Limassol and Paphos, and Dhekelia and Ammochostos (Famagusta). The north and south are now served by separate transport systems, and there are no services linking the two sectors.

Cyprus Public Transport: Thali 4, 2200 Geri, Nicosia; tel. 1416; e-mail contactus@publictransport.com.cy; internet www.publictransport.com.cy; Chair. FELIPE COSMEN.

SHIPPING

Until 1974 Famagusta, a natural port, was the island's most important harbour, handling about 83% of the country's cargo. Since its capture by the Turkish army in August of that year the port has been officially declared closed to international traffic. However, it continues to serve the Turkish-occupied region.

The main ports that serve the island's maritime trade at present are Larnaca and Limassol. There is also an industrial port at Vassiliko, and there are three specialized petroleum terminals, at Larnaca, Dhekelia and Moni. Work on a project to redevelop Larnaca port and marina commenced in April 2022 and was to be carried out in four phases over 15 years at an estimated total cost of €1,200m.

In addition to serving local traffic, Limassol and Larnaca ports act as transshipment load centres and as regional warehouse and assembly bases.

CYPRUS — Directory

Port and Regulatory Authorities

Deputy Ministry of Shipping: POB 56193, Kylinis St, Mesa Geitonia, 4007 Limassol; tel. 25848100; fax 25848200; e-mail maritimeadmin@dms.gov.cy; internet www.shipping.gov.cy; f. 2018; established as an autonomous body dedicated solely to the maritime industry of Cyprus; Dep. Minister of Shipping VASSILIOS DEMETRIADES.

Cyprus Ports Authority: POB 22007, 5 Limassol Ave, 1516 Nicosia; tel. 22817200; fax 22765420; e-mail cpa@cpa.gov.cy; internet www.cpa.gov.cy; f. 1973; Chair. ANTONIS ST. STYLIANOU.

Shipping Companies

Amer Shipping Ltd: POB 27363, 701 Ghinis Bldg, 58–60 Dhigenis Akritas Ave, 1644 Nicosia; tel. 22875188; fax 22756556; e-mail ateam@amershipping.com; internet www.amershipping.com; f. 1989; Man. Dir ANIL DESHPANDE.

Cyprus Shipping Chamber: POB 56607, City Chambers, 1st Floor, 6 Regas Fereos St, 3309 Limassol; tel. 25360717; e-mail csc@csc-cy.org; internet www.csc-cy.org; f. 1989; Pres. THEMIS PAPADOPOULOS.

CIVIL AVIATION

There is an international airport at Nicosia, which has been closed since 1974, following the Turkish invasion. A new international airport was constructed at Larnaca, and commenced operating in 1975. Another international airport, at Paphos, began operations in 1983. Two new terminals were opened, one at Paphos airport in 2008 and the other at Larnaca airport in 2009. The national carrier, Cyprus Airways, entered into liquidation in 2015. In July 2016 Charlie Airlines acquired the rights to use the trademarks and branding of Cyprus Airways; the airline was acquired by the SJC Group of Malta in June 2021 and was to continue operating under the name of Cyprus Airways.

Cyprus Airways: Larnaka Int. Airport, POB 43027, 6650 Larnaka; tel. 24000053; e-mail callcenter@cyprusairways.com; internet www.cyprusairways.com; acquired by the SJC Group (Malta) in 2021; services throughout Europe and the Middle East; CEO and COO PAUL SIES.

Tourism

Deputy Ministry of Tourism: POB 24535, 19 Leoforos Lemesou, Aglantzia, 1390 Nicosia; tel. 22691100; fax 22334696; e-mail cytour@visitcyprus.com; internet www.visitcyprus.com; fmrly Cyprus Tourism Organisation; under Ministry of Energy, Commerce, Industry and Tourism; Dep. Minister SAVVAS PERDIOS.

Defence

The House of Representatives authorized the formation of the National Guard in 1964, after the withdrawal of the Turkish members. Men aged between 18 and 50 years are liable to 14 months' conscription. As assessed at November 2022, the National Guard comprised an army of 12,000 regulars and 50,000 reserves. A total of 950 Greek army personnel were stationed in Cyprus at that time. There was also a Greek Cypriot paramilitary police force of some 250. A United Nations peacekeeping force is also based in Cyprus, and there are UK military bases at Akrotiri and Dhekelia. Cyprus was one of 25 European Union (EU) member states to commit to the joint Permanent Structured Co-operation (PESCO) on security and defence, a framework for co-operation in various aspects of military organization, initiated in 2017 as part of the EU's Common Security and Defence Policy.

Defence Budget: €470m. in 2022.

Commander of the National Guard: Lt-Gen. DIMOKRITOS ZERVAKIS.

UNITED NATIONS PEACEKEEPING FORCE IN CYPRUS (UNFICYP)

POB 21642, 1590 Nicosia; tel. 22464000; e-mail unficyp-public-information-office@un.org; internet unficyp.unmissions.org.

UNFICYP was established for a three-month period in March 1964 by a UN Security Council resolution (subsequently extended at intervals of three or six months by successive resolutions) to keep the peace between the Greek and Turkish communities and help to resolve outstanding issues between them. In mid-1993, following an announcement by troop-providing countries that they were to withdraw a substantial number of troops, the Security Council introduced a system of financing UNFICYP by voluntary and assessed contributions. As prescribed by a UN Security Council resolution adopted in October 2004, there was a significant reduction in the size of UNFICYP. The contingent numbered 1,013 uniformed personnel (746 troops, 64 police, 52 staff officers and 151 civilians) at June 2022.

Commander: Maj.-Gen. INGRID GJERDE (Norway).

Special Representative of the UN Secretary-General and Head of Mission: COLIN WILLIAM STEWART (Canada).

See also the section on UN Peacekeeping Operations in the Regional Organizations section of Part Three.

BRITISH SOVEREIGN BASE AREAS

Akrotiri and Dhekelia

Headquarters British Forces Cyprus, Episkopi 3370, BFPO 53; tel. 25967295; fax 25963521; e-mail cosba@cytanet.com.cy; internet www.sbaadministration.org.

Under the Cyprus Act 1960, the UK retained sovereignty in two base areas and this was recognized in the Treaty of Establishment signed between the UK, Greece, Turkey (now known as Türkiye) and the Republic of Cyprus in August 1960. The base areas cover 98 sq miles. The Treaty also conferred on the UK certain rights within the Republic, including rights of movement and the use of specified training areas. As assessed at November 2022, military personnel in the sovereign base areas numbered 2,260.

Administrator of the Sovereign Base Areas and Commander of British Forces Cyprus: Air Vice-Marshal PETER SQUIRES.

Education

Until 1965 each community in Cyprus managed its own schooling through a Communal Chamber. In March, however, the Greek Communal Chamber was dissolved and a Ministry of Education was established to take its place. Intercommunal education has been placed under this Ministry (now entitled the Ministry of Education, Culture, Sport and Youth). According to UNESCO, spending on education in the Greek Cypriot area constituted 12.4% of total government expenditure in 2022.

Primary education is compulsory and is provided free in six grades to children between five-and-a-half and 12 years of age. Secondary education is also free for all years of study and lasts for six years, with three compulsory years at a general secondary school (gymnasium) being followed by three non-compulsory years at a technical school or lyceum. In 2019/20, according to estimates by UNESCO, enrolment at pre-primary level was equivalent to 86.7% of children (boys 87.7%; girls 85.5%) in the relevant age-group, while primary enrolment included 99.6% of children in the relevant age-group. In the same academic year, enrolment at lower secondary schools and upper secondary schools included 99.2% and 92.5% of children in the appropriate age-groups, respectively.

The University of Cyprus was established in 1992. The Higher Technical Institute offers sub-degree courses, leading to a diploma, in civil, electrical, mechanical and marine engineering and in computer studies. Other specialized training is provided at the Cyprus Forestry College, the Higher Hotel Institute, the Mediterranean Institute of Management and the School of Nursing. In 2023 the Cyprus International Institute of Management (founded in 1990) was upgraded to university status and renamed the University of Limassol.

CYPRIOT SECESSIONIST TERRITORY

'TURKISH REPUBLIC OF NORTHERN CYPRUS'

The northern one-third of the island of Cyprus has been administered as a separate territory since the invasion of Cyprus by Turkey (officially known as Türkiye from June 2022) on 20 July 1974. On 15 November 1983 the 'Turkish Federated State of Cyprus' (as the de facto governing authority had hitherto referred to itself) issued a unilateral declaration of independence as the 'Turkish Republic of Northern Cyprus' ('TRNC'). While the 'TRNC' has enjoyed de facto political and military support from, and full diplomatic relations with, Türkiye, the territory is not formally recognized by any other state.

Contemporary Political History

Cyprus achieved independence from British rule on 16 August 1960. There was serious fighting between the Greek and Turkish Cypriot communities following a constitutional dispute, which resulted in the withdrawal of the Turks from the central Government in December 1963. Consequently, separate political and judicial institutions were established for the Turkish community. Meanwhile, in March 1964 a United Nations Peace-keeping Force in Cyprus (UNFICYP, see p. 1067) was formed in an effort to stem the intercommunal violence.

Following a Greek-led military coup, which had led to the replacement of Cyprus's President Makarios by a Greek Cypriot politician who sought a union with Greece, on 20 July 1974 Turkish armed forces invaded Cyprus to protect the Turkish community and prevent Greece from taking over the island. Cyprus thus became divided along the so-called Green Line (or Attila Line), extending from Morphou through Nicosia to Famagusta. The Turkish Cypriots subsequently established a de facto Government in the northern third of the island, and in February 1975 declared a 'Turkish Federated State of Cyprus' ('TFSC'), with Rauf Denktaş as President.

In the 'TFSC' a new Council of Ministers was formed in December 1978, under Mustafa Çağatay of the Ulusal Bırlık Partisi (UBP—National Unity Party). UN-sponsored peace negotiations were relaunched in September 1980 between the Greek and Turkish Cypriots, with the latter demanding equal status for the two communities and equal representation in government (despite constituting less than 20% of the island's population). At elections held in June 1981 President Denktaş was returned to office. In March 1982 Çağatay formed a coalition Government, comprising the UBP, the Demokratik Halk Partisi (Democratic People's Party) and the Türkiye Bırlık Partisi (Turkish Unity Party). In May 1983 the UN General Assembly adopted a resolution demanding the removal of Turkish forces from Cyprus. Denktaş responded, on 15 November, by making a unilateral declaration of independence for the 'TFSC' (which had already adopted the Turkish lira as its currency); it was designated the 'Turkish Republic of Northern Cyprus' ('TRNC'). Like the 'TFSC', the 'TRNC' was recognized only by Turkey (officially known as Türkiye from June 2022), and the declaration of independence was condemned by the UN Security Council.

Events following the Establishment of the 'TRNC'

After Denktaş's announcement, Çağatay resigned as premier and UBP leader; an interim Government was formed in December 1983 under Nejat Konuk. The 'TRNC' and Turkey established diplomatic relations in April 1984, and the 'TRNC' rejected UN proposals for a suspension of its declaration prior to further talks.

During 1984 a 'TRNC' Constituent Assembly drafted a new Constitution, which was approved by 70% of those who voted at a referendum in May 1985. At a presidential election held in June, Denktaş was returned to office. A general election followed later in June, at which the UBP, led by Derviş Eroğlu, won 24 of the 50 seats in the legislature, the Assembly of the Republic. In July Eroğlu became Prime Minister, leading a coalition Government comprising the UBP and the Toplumcu Kurtuluş Partisi (TKP—Communal Liberation Party).

UN-sponsored direct negotiations between Denktaş and the new Greek Cypriot President, Georghios Vassiliou, began in September 1988. However, the intermittent talks were abandoned in March 1990, reportedly after the Turkish Cypriot President insisted on self-determination for Turkish Cypriots.

In April 1988 Eroğlu resigned as premier, following a disagreement between the UBP and its coalition partner since September 1986, the Yeni Doğuş Partisi (New Dawn Party). In May 1988 Eroğlu formed a new, UBP-dominated Council of Ministers, which also included independents. In April 1990 Denktaş secured re-election at an early presidential poll. Eroğlu remained Prime Minister, after the UBP won 34 of the 50 seats in the Assembly at elections in May. (Following by-elections for 12 seats in October 1991, the party held a total of 45 seats.)

Settlement Proposals following Cyprus's Application to Join the European Community

In July 1990 Denktaş condemned the Government of Cyprus' application for membership of the European Community (EC, now European Union—EU), since the 'TRNC' leadership had not been consulted. Direct discussions between Vassiliou and Denktaş, brokered by the new UN Secretary-General, Boutros Boutros-Ghali, resumed in 1992. However, Denktaş rejected a draft settlement based on Boutros-Ghali's proposals for a federal political structure with separate Greek and Turkish Cypriot areas of administration, which proposed a Turkish administrative area that was around 25% smaller than the 'TRNC'.

At an early general election in December 1993, the UBP lost its majority in the Assembly, securing only 17 of the 50 seats. A coalition Government was subsequently formed by the Demokrat Parti (DP—Democrat Party), which had been supported by President Denktaş, and the left-wing Cumhuriyetçi Türk Partisi (CTP—Republican Turkish Party). DP leader Hakkı Atun took office as Prime Minister. In response to the adoption in July 1994 by the UN Security Council of Resolution 939 (see the Republic of Cyprus), the 'TRNC' legislature approved measures seeking to co-ordinate foreign and defence policies with those of Turkey.

At a presidential election held in mid-April 1995, Denktaş received a mere 40.4% of votes cast in the first poll, only securing victory against Eroğlu, with 62.5%, at a second round in late April. A new coalition of the DP and the CTP, under Atun, took office in June. However, Atun and his Government resigned in November, after Denktaş rejected a new list of CTP ministers. A new DP-CTP coalition, led by Atun and with the CTP's Mehmet Ali Talat as deputy premier, took office in December.

The Government resigned in July 1996 following persistent internal disputes over policy, and in August Eroğlu regained the premiership after a new coalition agreement between the DP and UBP. In December the European Court of Human Rights ruled that Turkey was in breach of the European Convention on Human Rights by denying a woman access to her property in the north, thus implicating Turkey as fully responsible for activities in the 'TRNC' and for the consequences of the 1974 invasion.

Direct negotiations between Denktaş and the Greek Cypriot President, Glavkos Klerides, in the presence of the UN's new Secretary-General, Kofi Annan, collapsed in August 1997 after Denktaş demanded that Cyprus suspend its application to join the EU. Cyprus's EU accession talks began in March 1998. In August Denktaş rejected a UN plan for reunification, instead proposing a confederation of equal status; however, Klerides dismissed this proposal since it would legitimize the status of the 'TRNC'.

At the December 1998 legislative elections, the UBP increased its representation in the Assembly to 24 seats, while the DP won only 13 seats. The TKP took seven seats and the CTP the remaining six. At the end of the month the President approved a new UBP-TKP Council of Ministers, with Eroğlu as Prime Minister and TKP leader Mustafa Akıncı as his deputy. At the first round of the presidential poll on 15 April 2000, Denktaş won 43.7% of the votes cast, thus again failing to secure the majority necessary for outright victory. However, on 19 April his closest contender, Eroğlu, withdrew from the process and Denktaş was consequently proclaimed President.

Resolution 1303, which was adopted by the UN Security Council in mid-June 2000 and included the customary six-month extension to UNFICYP's mandate, notably excluded any reference to the authority of the 'TRNC'. At the end of the month the 'TRNC' retaliated, restricting the movement of UNFICYP forces and imposing new tariffs for UN vehicles and for the use of utilities supplied by the north. 'TRNC' and Turkish forces also crossed into the buffer zone and established a checkpoint at a village inhabited by Greek Cypriots. UN-sponsored proximity talks held by Klerides and

Denktaş from July 2000 achieved little, and in November Denktaş, with the apparent support of Turkey, withdrew from the talks and demanded that the 'TRNC' be afforded international recognition.

The governing coalition collapsed in May 2001, following disagreement between the UBP and the TKP over the reconciliation talks. In June a new UBP-DP coalition assumed office, with Eroğlu continuing as Prime Minister.

The 'Annan Plan'

On 11 November 2002 the UN presented the Turkish and Greek Cypriot leaders with a comprehensive new peace plan (the 'Annan Plan'). This included proposals for the creation of a common federal state with two equal components, but with a single international legal identity. It required the 'TRNC' to reduce its share of the island from 36% to 28.5%, and pledged to compensate dispossessed property owners. However, Denktaş rejected a revised version of the Annan Plan in December.

At the EU summit held in Copenhagen, Denmark, in December 2002, Cyprus was formally invited to join the Union in 2004. However, upon taking office in February 2003 the newly elected Greek Cypriot President, Tassos Papadopoulos, demanded that the Annan Plan be amended to allow all Greek Cypriot refugees to return to the north. Despite a concerted effort by Annan to persuade Denktaş and Papadopoulos to agree a settlement that would allow a unified Cyprus to accede to the EU, the Turkish Cypriot President denounced the Annan Plan as unacceptable, and refused to continue discussions. Following confirmation that Cyprus would join the EU on 1 May 2004, on 23 April the 'TRNC' Government declared that it would open its border to the Greek part of the island for the first time in 30 years. Henceforth Turkish Cypriots would be permitted to visit the south for one-day trips, while Greek Cypriots could visit the north for up to three nights.

Legislative elections held in December 2003 resulted in the pro-EU CTP narrowly defeating the ruling UBP; however, parliamentary seats were distributed equally between pro-EU parties and parties that opposed the terms of the Annan Plan. Talat was appointed as Prime Minister, and in January 2004 formed a new CTP-DP Government. The President's son, Serdar Denktaş, became Deputy Prime Minister and Minister of Foreign Affairs.

Efforts to finalize the details of a settlement intensified from February 2004. Discussions in Switzerland in March also involved the Turkish and Greek premiers; Talat replaced President Denktaş as head of the Turkish Cypriot delegation. At the end of March Annan presented a final version of his peace plan, which was accepted by the 'TRNC', Turkish and Greek Governments; however, Papadopoulos signalled his opposition. At concurrent referendums held in both parts of the island on 24 April, 64.9% of Turkish Cypriot participants approved the Annan Plan, while 75.8% of Greek Cypriot participants rejected the plan. Consequently, only the Greek Cypriot-administered part of the island joined the EU on 1 May.

Domestic Developments after Cyprus's EU Accession

In April 2004 the coalition Government lost its parliamentary majority, after two DP deputies withdrew their support and resigned from the Assembly. At early legislative elections held in February 2005, Talat's CTP secured 24 of the 50 seats, while the UBP took 19 and the DP six. The CTP could therefore only command a parliamentary majority in a renewed alliance with the anti-reunification DP. In March President Denktaş approved a new, largely unchanged coalition Government, under Talat.

Shortly after the referendums of April 2004, Rauf Denktaş announced that he would retire from public office following the 2005 presidential election. At that poll, held on 17 April, Talat was elected as President outright, with 55.6% of votes cast. Eroğlu secured 22.7% of the vote. Talat, who pledged his commitment to achieving reunification, was inaugurated on 24 April. The CTP Secretary-General, Ferdi Sabit Soyer, replaced him as Prime Minister at the head of a new CTP-DP coalition Government later that month.

Eroğlu resigned as UBP leader in November 2005, and was replaced in February 2006 by Hüseyın Özgürgün. A new political party, the Özgürlük ve Reform Partisi (ORP—Freedom and Reform Party), was formed in September by three parliamentary deputies from the UBP and one from the DP. Soyer subsequently dissolved the Government and formed a new coalition administration with the ORP, which included that party's leader, Turgay Avcı, as Deputy Prime Minister and Minister of Foreign Affairs. The new Government secured a motion of confidence in the legislature in October, despite opposition from the DP and the UBP.

In December 2006 EU foreign ministers partially suspended Turkey's accession negotiations, owing to Turkey's refusal to open its ports and airports to all EU member states, including the Republic of Cyprus, by the end of 2006. In March 2007 the demolition by the Greek Cypriot authorities of a wall at Ledra Street in Nicosia was hailed as a significant step towards ending the division of the city.

The Resumption of Reunification Talks and Elections during 2009–10

During talks between Talat and the new President of the Republic of Cyprus, Demetris Christofias, in Nicosia in March 2008, the two leaders agreed to open the Ledra Street crossing point in central Nicosia (this was achieved in early April); formulate an agenda for future negotiations; and establish working groups and technical committees to support further talks (this occurred in mid-April).

At a UN-sponsored meeting held in May 2008, the two leaders again emphasized their 'commitment to a bizonal, bicommunal federation with political equality, as defined by relevant Security Council resolutions'. Long-awaited, fully fledged negotiations finally commenced in September, but issues of contention such as power sharing prevented any immediate breakthrough.

The 'TRNC' held early parliamentary elections in April 2009. The UBP secured an overall majority, winning 26 seats. President Talat's CTP garnered only 15 seats, while the DP won five, and the ORP and the Toplumcu Demokrasi Partisi (TDP—Communal Democracy Party) two each. (The TDP had been established in 2007 following a merger between the TKP and the Barış ve Demokrasi Hareketi—Peace and Democracy Movement.) Eroğlu, who had regained the UBP leadership in November 2008, formed a new Government in May

In June 2009 discussions on economic matters were concluded and talks on territorial issues commenced. Later that month an agreement was reached on the opening of an additional crossing point at the north-eastern village of Limnitis (Yeşilırmak); this took place in October 2010. In August 2009, following the 40th meeting between Talat and Christofias since the resumption of fully fledged negotiations, the first round of reunification negotiations was concluded. A second round of talks ended in January 2010, after the two leaders agreed to conduct twice-weekly meetings from October 2009.

At a presidential election, held in mid-April 2010, Eroğlu won 50.4% of the valid votes cast, while Talat received 42.9%. A minority Government—under the premiership of the new UBP leader, İrsen Küçük—took office in May, with the support of DP and ORP deputies.

Protests against Austerity Measures and the Stalling of Reunification Negotiations

In January 2011 tens of thousands of Turkish Cypriot public sector workers began industrial action and protested in Nicosia against economic austerity measures imposed by the Government. General strikes and protests continued into April, when Küçük effected an extensive cabinet reorganization.

The UN-sponsored reunification talks restarted in October 2011, but stalled in February 2012, shortly before the Republic of Cyprus was set to assume the rotating EU presidency. In April the UN restricted its role as a mediator to negotiations on technical issues and confidence-building measures. Following Cyprus's assumption of the EU presidency for a six-month period starting on 1 July, Turkey suspended all high-level contacts with EU member states.

The Collapse of the Küçük Government and Early Legislative Elections

After eight deputies from Küçük's UBP defected to the DP, in June 2013 the Assembly approved a motion of no confidence in the Prime Minister, prompting his resignation. President Eroğlu subsequently appointed Sibel Siber of the CTP to lead an interim Council of Ministers.

The July 2013 legislative elections resulted in a victory for the CTP, which secured 21 seats. The UBP won only 14 seats, the DP 12 and the TDP three. A new CTP-DP coalition Government took office in September. CTP leader Özkan Yorgancıoğlu became Prime Minister and the DP leader, Serdar Denktaş, was appointed Deputy Prime Minister and Minister of Economy, Tourism, Culture and Sport. In November the EU agreed to restart negotiations with Turkey on one of the chapters relating to the country's application to join the Union, despite ongoing concerns about Turkey's democratic and human rights credentials.

Hopes for progress in the reunification talks were raised in February 2014 following the signing of a joint declaration by Eroğlu and the Greek Cypriot President, Nikos Anastasiades (who had been elected in February 2013). In September 2014 the newly elected Turkish President, Recep Tayyip Erdoğan, emphasized Turkey's commitment to the 'TRNC' by making it the location of his first official visit. However, in October Anastasiades suspended Greek Cypriot participation in the reunification talks, following Turkey's commencement of drilling activity in Cyprus's exclusive economic zone (EEZ) off the south coast of the island.

The 2015 Presidential Election and Intensified Talks

At the presidential election held on 19 April 2015, Eroğlu (standing as an independent) emerged as the leading candidate, securing 28.2% of the valid votes cast. His closest rival, Mustafa Akıncı (the former Deputy Prime Minister and mayor of the Turkish Cypriot area of Nicosia), won 26.9%. Siber, now Speaker of the Assembly, was placed third, with 22.5% of the vote, while Kudret Özersay, who had served as the 'TRNC' chief negotiator in the reunification talks until October 2014, took 21.3%. Eroğlu and Akıncı contested a run-off election on 26 April 2015, at which Akıncı was elected with 60.5% of the vote; he was sworn into office as President on 30 April.

The new 'TRNC' President's more ambivalent stance over relations with Turkey, and stated determination to reinvigorate the reunification talks, was welcomed by Anastasiades. The two leaders held their first direct meeting, under UN auspices, on 15 May 2015, and agreed to meet on a twice-monthly basis thereafter.

Former President Talat was re-elected as CTP leader in June 2015, prompting the resignation of Yorgancıoğlu as Prime Minister in July 2015; President Akıncı appointed Ömer Kalyoncu, also of the CTP, to replace him in the post and a new CTP-UBP coalition Government was formed.

Prime Minister Kalyoncu submitted the resignation of his Council of Ministers to President Akıncı in April 2016, following the Government's loss of its parliamentary majority as a result of the UBP's withdrawal from the governing coalition. The UBP and DP subsequently reached a coalition agreement, with UBP leader Hüseyın Özgürgün becoming Prime Minister. Serdar Denktaş was appointed as Deputy Prime Minister and Minister of Finance, while the UBP's Tahsin Ertuğruloğlu became Minister of Foreign Affairs.

Akıncı attended the World Economic Forum in Davos, Switzerland, in January 2016—the first time that a 'TRNC' President had been allowed to participate in the annual international summit. Following two rounds of UN-brokered discussions in Mont Pélerin, Switzerland, during November, Anastasiades and Akıncı attended a summit meeting in Geneva, Switzerland, on 9–11 January 2017; for the first time, both the Greek and Turkish Cypriot delegations presented the UN with maps showing their proposals for a future internal boundary of a reunified, federal Cyprus. The new UN Secretary-General, António Guterres, chaired an international Conference on Cyprus on 12 January.

Peace Talks Fail; 2018 Assembly Elections

The optimism generated by the acceleration of peace talks dissipated as 2017 progressed. A further round of UN-mediated talks between Anastasiades and Akıncı in Switzerland in June concluded with the two sides having failed to agree on a number of issues. In August Prime Minister Özgürgün announced that there would be no further negotiations based on UN parameters of bizonality and bicommunality, and that talks would not restart until the Greek Cypriot side recognized the unconditional equality of the Turkish Cypriot people.

At elections to the Assembly held in January 2018, the UBP secured 21 seats. The CTP won 12 seats, the newly formed People's Party (Halkın Partisi—HP) obtained nine, while the TDP and the DP took three apiece. Another new party, the Rebirth Party (Yeniden Doğuş Partisi—YDP), won the remaining two seats. A new CTP-led coalition administration took office in February, under Tufan Erhürman as Prime Minister. The HP, the TDP and the DP joined the Government, with HP leader Özersay becoming Deputy Prime Minister and Minister of Foreign Affairs.

During a visit to the 'TRNC' in July 2018, Turkish President Erdoğan expressed his determination to achieve a 'just and lasting' solution to the Cyprus issue. In September Erdoğan denied rumours that Turkey intended to establish a new military base in the 'TRNC', but suggested that it would increase the number of military personnel stationed there. Meanwhile, in November an additional two crossing points were opened between the north and south of the island (see the Republic of Cyprus).

The 'TRNC' authorities condemned the signing, in September 2018, of an agreement between the Republic of Cyprus and Egypt providing for the construction of an undersea pipeline which would export natural gas from Cyprus's EEZ to Egypt from 2022; however, this was subsequently deferred until 2025.

On 9 May 2019 Erhürman submitted the resignation of his Government, following the HP's withdrawal from the coalition on the previous day, citing a lack of trust among the four parties. On 22 May a new UBP-HP coalition Government took office. UBP leader Ersin Tatar became Prime Minister, while Özersay regained the posts of Deputy Prime Minister and Minister of Foreign Affairs. Olgun Amcaoğlu of the UBP was appointed as Minister of Finance, following the resignation of Denktaş earlier in May.

Presidents Akıncı and Anastasiades continued to hold informal discussions, under UN auspices, during 2019, agreeing a number of confidence-building measures. In November Guterres hosted a meeting between the two leaders in Berlin, Germany, at which both reportedly expressed their preparedness to restart the reunification negotiations. However, in February 2020 Akıncı warned that Cyprus's partition could become permanent if the two sides failed to reach an 'equitable' solution soon concerning the creation of a bicommunal federation, as he believed that their differences were increasing.

During 2019 the 'TRNC' authorities frequently protested against 'unilateral' actions by their Greek Cypriot counterparts with regard to drilling for potential hydrocarbon reserves in disputed waters. The 'TRNC' Government also condemned as 'hostile and provocative' the signing of the so-called EastMed pipeline agreement in January 2020 between the Republic of Cyprus, Greece and Israel (see the Republic of Cyprus).

Following the 'TRNC's first confirmed case of the coronavirus disease (COVID-19) on 10 March 2020, strict measures were brought in to control the virus, including border closures, a ban on public gatherings and a curfew. Certain restrictions were eased from mid-May, although some were reintroduced in mid-January 2021 following a sharp rise in the number of cases.

Meanwhile, the presidential election due to have been held on 26 April 2020 was postponed for six months. In September an official list of six presidential candidates was announced by the Supreme Board of Elections, comprising Akıncı; Tatar (who had stated in an interview in March that he favoured the permanent partition of Cyprus and would seek closer ties with Turkey if elected as President); CTP leader Erhürman; YDP leader Erhan Arıklı; Deputy Prime Minister Özersay, who resigned as HP leader to contest the election as an independent; and Serdar Denktaş, who similarly stood down as leader of the DP to stand as an independent.

On 6 October 2020 the HP withdrew its support for the UBP-led coalition, citing its disagreement with Tatar's decision to pursue the reopening of the abandoned city of Varosha (Maraş). However, the HP ministers remained in post pending the appointment of a new administration. The Republic of Cyprus Government denounced the reopening of Varosha as being contrary to international law, while many Turkish Cypriots also opposed this decision as well as a high-profile visit by Erdoğan to the city on 15 November.

Recent Developments: The 2020 Presidential Election and 2022 Legislative Elections

At the rescheduled presidential election, held on 11 October 2020, Prime Minister Tatar was placed first, with 32.3% of the vote, and the incumbent, Akıncı, second with 29.8%. Erhürman won 21.7% of the vote, while Özersay received 5.7%, Arıklı 5.4% and Denktaş 4.2%. At a run-off election between Tatar and Akıncı on 18 October, Tatar secured an unexpected victory, with 51.7% of the vote; his inauguration took place on 23 October. The start of Tatar's presidency was warmly welcomed by Erdoğan, who had backed his campaign. Akıncı, meanwhile, complained about Turkey's political interference in the election.

President Tatar named the UBP's Ersan Saner as acting Prime Minister on 6 November 2020. However, he failed to secure a coalition agreement within the required two-week period, and on 21 November President Tatar appointed Erhürman to lead further talks. These also concluded without agreement, and on 3 December Saner regained the mandate to form an administration. Saner finally formed a coalition Government—comprising the UBP, the DP and the YDP—on 9 December. Arıklı was appointed Deputy Prime Minister and Minister of Economy and Energy.

In April 2021 a UN-led informal summit on the Cyprus issue took place in Geneva between the island's two communities and the Greek, Turkish and British foreign affairs ministers, but ended without an agreement to resume formal talks. Shortly prior to the talks, Tatar had reiterated his preference for a two-state solution to the conflict (for which Turkish President Erdoğan had recently expressed support), which, he contended, would bring 'new vision' to the proceedings, despite the Greek Cypriot side having repeatedly rejected this scenario. Following informal discussions between Tatar and Anastasiades in New York, USA, in September, Tatar asserted that the 'TRNC' would not agree to the formal resumption of talks unless its 'sovereign equality' and 'equal international status' were recognized.

Amid ongoing divisions within the coalition 'TRNC' Government, on 11 October 2021 the Speaker of the Assembly, Önder Sennaroğlu, announced that the Government and opposition parties had agreed to stage early legislative elections on 6 February 2022. On 13 October 2021 Saner tendered his Government's resignation, citing repeated failures to convene the Assembly owing to quorum issues, disagreements between the coalition parties and a lack of co-operation from the opposition parties. Saner was to remain as premier in an interim capacity pending the election of a new administration.

However, on 20 October 2021 Saner was forced to resign as Prime Minister, as well as UBP Chairman, after compromising video footage involving Saner and a young woman was widely circulated on social media; Saner denied any wrongdoing, alleging that the video had been edited as part of a politically motivated campaign to discredit him. Faiz Sucuoğlu was elected as the new leader of the UBP at the end of October, and on 1 November he was charged by President Tatar with forming a new government. On 8 November Sucuoğlu's new cabinet, comprising representatives of the UBP and the DP, and backed by independent deputies, received the President's approval. While the majority of the ministers from Saner's outgoing administration retained their posts, there were a number of new appointments. Later that day the six political parties with parliamentary representation agreed to hold fresh elections on 23 January 2022.

At the elections, the UBP increased its representation in the Assembly to 24 seats (two seats short of an outright majority), defeating the CTP, which secured 18 seats. The DP and the HP each won three seats, while the YDP won the remaining two. Turnout was estimated at 57.6% of the registered electorate. With the CTP, in contrast to Tatar's UBP, favouring a bicommunal and bizonal federal solution to the Cyprus problem, the relatively close contest between the two leading parties appeared to indicate significant divisions among the Turkish Cypriot population over the issue of reunification. On 21 February 2022 Prime Minister Sucuoğlu formed a new coalition Government, comprising members of the UBP, the DP and the YDP. However, following President Tatar's refusal on 19 April to endorse Sucuoğlu's proposed dismissal of Minister of Finance Sunat Atun (the Prime Minister and Atun were in disagreement over recent increases in electricity prices), on 20 April the Prime Minister submitted the resignation of the entire Council of Ministers, which was accepted by the President. At the President's request, Sucuoğlu formed a new Government on 25 April, including the appointment of Olgun Amcaoğlu as Minister of Finance. However, on 30 April Sucuoğlu submitted the resignation of this new administration, which was accepted by the President. On 9 May President Tatar mandated the Minister of Interior Affairs, Ünal Üstel of the UBP, to form a new administration. A new coalition Government, headed by Üstel as Prime Minister and comprising members of the UBP, the DP and the YDP, took office on 12 May; notably, Atun was retained as Minister of Finance. However, on 26 July Atun stood down as finance minister, citing disagreements with Prime Minister Üstel, and was replaced by Alişan Şan.

In a statement issued in August 2022, Minister of Foreign Affairs Ertuğruloğlu categorically rejected the federation model as a basis for negotiations between the 'TRNC' and the Greek Cypriot administration, arguing that a solution based on two equal sovereign states was the only path to cordial relations. Ertuğruloğlu's statement was scathing in its assessment of the role played by the EU in the Cyprus problem, accusing the bloc of seeking merely to preserve the status quo, which, he argued, better served the Greek Cypriot administration. Addressing the UN General Assembly in September, Turkish President Erdoğan criticized the decision to invite Anastasiades (but not Tatar) to address the Assembly, and pledged Türkiye's support for the 'new vision' proposed by the 'TRNC', in an apparent veiled reference to Turkish Cypriot calls for a two-state solution. At an Organization of Islamic Cooperation (OIC) foreign affairs ministers' meeting held a few days later in New York, Ertuğruloğlu urged OIC member states to grant official recognition to, and establish formal relations with, the 'TRNC', and to reaffirm its sovereign equality and equal international status.

The USA's decision, announced in September 2022, to lift defence trade restrictions on the Greek Cypriot Government for the 2023 fiscal year was denounced as 'unacceptable' by Tatar, who argued that it would increase intercommunal tensions. Tatar also called for the lifting of longstanding 'inhumane' restrictions imposed on the 'TRNC' by the international community, while Erdoğan announced that Türkiye was to reinforce its military presence in the 'TRNC'.

Also in September 2022, construction of a new presidential complex—projected to cost some 2,500m. Turkish liras and to be funded by the Turkish Government—commenced in the Turkish Cypriot area of Nicosia. There was widespread criticism over the project, which was to include a mosque and palace as well as a new parliamentary building, with critics arguing that it was disrespectful to the many people within the 'TRNC' and Türkiye struggling to afford basic essentials. A legal objection to the construction was dismissed in November.

In October 2022 the 'TRNC' administration issued an ultimatum to UNFICYP, giving it one month to conclude a separate agreement with the 'TRNC' regarding its continued presence on the island or the mission's personnel would no longer be welcome in northern Cyprus; the deadline passed without incident. In November UNFICYP announced that it was to increase its patrols inside the buffer zone in the wake of a series of close encounters between Greek Cypriot farmers and Turkish troops. Following the adoption in January 2023 of a UN Security Council resolution extending UNFICYP's mandate for a further year, a statement released by the 'TRNC' Ministry of Foreign Affairs noted that once again the consent of the 'TRNC' had not been sought for the extension, and accused the Council of being 'unable to free itself from Greek Cypriot influence'.

In a setback for the coalition administration, the CTP, which continued to advocate a bicommunal, bizonal federal solution to the Cyprus problem, secured control of the largest number of municipalities at local elections held in December 2022, taking seven against the UBP's six, again serving to highlight the stark polarization of the political landscape. The DP and the TDP took one municipality apiece, while independent candidates won three.

Despite the local elections confirming strong public support for a bicommunal solution, ahead of the Greek Cypriot presidential poll in February 2023 Tatar reiterated that, while the Turkish side wished for a settlement and co-operation with the Greek Cypriots, no negotiations would take place until formal recognition of the 'equal sovereignty' of the 'TRNC' had been granted. Following the victory of Nikos Christodoulides at the Greek Cypriot presidential poll, the President-elect pledged to secure a resumption of talks with the 'TRNC', with a view to finally solving the Cyprus question; however, it remained to be seen whether Christodoulides' election would have any significant bearing on relations between the island's two communities.

Tensions between the Greek Cypriots and Turkish Cypriots were heightened on 18 August 2023 when three UN peacekeepers were injured in scuffles with Turkish Cypriot security forces over unauthorized construction work being carried out by Turkish Cypriot workers inside the UN buffer zone near Pyla (Pile). The UN Security Council condemned the violence and expressed serious concerns over the construction work, stressing that it contravened UN Security Council resolutions and constituted a violation of the status quo in the buffer zone.

Meanwhile, following a steep increase in the number of COVID-19 cases in northern Cyprus, and amid concerns over the emergence of the more contagious Omicron variant of the coronavirus, new restrictions on travel and assembly were introduced from November 2021. Further entry restrictions were imposed on international arrivals in January 2022, and vaccination of children aged between five and 11 years commenced later that month. Many domestic COVID-related restrictions were eased or lifted in early 2022, and in April all border restrictions were removed for vaccinated travellers. According to Johns Hopkins University and Our World in Data, by 6 December 2022 81.8% of the total population of the 'TRNC' had been fully vaccinated.

Economic Affairs

Gross national product (GNP) in the 'TRNC' was officially estimated at 30,188.9m. Turkish liras, or US $11,129 per head, in 2021. Real gross domestic product (GDP) decreased at an average annual rate of 0.5% in 2015–21. GDP decreased by 16.2% in 2020, but increased by 3.9% in 2021, according to the State Planning Organization.

The agricultural sector (including forestry and fishing) contributed 9.1% of GDP in 2021, and engaged 4.2% of the employed labour force in October 2022. The principal crops are citrus fruit, vegetables, potatoes, barley and wheat. The 'TRNC' imports water from Türkiye in order to address the problem of drought. The GDP of the agricultural sector increased at an average annual rate of 0.5% in 2015–21. Agricultural GDP increased by 1.8% in 2020, but decreased by 1.5% in 2021.

The industrial sector (comprising mining, manufacturing, utilities and construction) contributed 16.3% of GDP in 2021, and engaged 18.3% of the employed labour force in October 2022. Industrial GDP remained constant in 2015–21. The GDP of the industrial sector decreased by 21.1% in 2020, but increased by 20.1% in 2021.

Mining and quarrying contributed 2.4% of GDP in 2021, and engaged 0.3% of the employed labour force in October 2020. The GDP of the mining sector increased at an average annual rate of 0.3% in 2015–21; mining GDP decreased by 21.1% in 2020, but increased by 20.2% in 2021.

The manufacturing sector provided 2.5% of GDP in 2021, and engaged 7.3% of the employed labour force in October 2020. Manufacturing GDP declined at an average annual rate of 4.9% in 2015–21; it decreased by 16.6% in 2020, but increased by 18.4% in 2021. In September 2022 it was announced that production of electric cars was to commence in the 'TRNC' during 2023.

The construction sector provided 8.1% of GDP in 2021, and engaged 9.9% of the employed labour force in October 2022. The GDP of the construction sector increased at an average annual rate of 3.0% in 2015–21; sectoral GDP decreased by 25.6% in 2020, but increased by 23.0% in 2021.

Mineral fuels and lubricants comprised 21.9% of total imports in 2021. In October 2016 the 'TRNC' signed an energy protocol with Turkey which envisaged the construction of an underwater electricity cable between the two territories by the end of 2017, as well as further co-operation in hydrocarbons exploration and the development of renewable energy. In October 2017 the route of the 800-MW electricity connection was announced and a further agreement between the two sides was concluded in July 2023 which stated that the project would be completed in 2028 at a cost of US $400m. to Türkiye. Meanwhile, discussions were under way concerning the construction of an 80-km pipeline to transport natural gas from Türkiye to the 'TRNC' by 2025. The Greek Cypriot Government agreed to supply around 4,000 MWh of electricity to the 'TRNC' in August 2021 at the latter's request, owing to ongoing power supply issues; electricity was also supplied from the Greek side to the Turkish side in December–January 2022, with the 'TRNC' agreeing to reciprocate at a later date, and the 'TRNC' submitted a further request for electricity from the Greek side in July.

The services sector contributed 74.6% of GDP in 2021, and engaged 77.5% of the employed labour force in October 2022. In 2021 a total of 552,307 tourists (438,696 of whom were from Turkey) visited the 'TRNC'. Tourism receipts in that year were estimated at US $340.3m. Services GDP decreased at an average annual rate of 0.9% in 2015–21; sectoral GDP decreased by 17.1% in 2020, but increased by 0.7% in 2021.

The 'TRNC' recorded a visible merchandise trade deficit in 2021 of US $1,578.1m. and there was a deficit of $47.5m. on the current account of the balance of payments (excluding foreign aid and loans from Turkey). In 2021 the principal imports were machinery and transport equipment, mineral fuels and lubricants, food and live animals, basic manufactures, and miscellaneous manufactured products, chemicals, and beverages and tobacco; the principal exports were food and live animals, basic manufactures, and miscellaneous manufactured products. Türkiye is by far the territory's most significant trading partner, supplying 62.9% of imports and taking 47.0% of exports in 2021.

The 'TRNC' registered a budgetary deficit of 1,446.3m. Turkish liras in 2021. Consumer prices increased by an average of 30.3% per year in 2015–22; the annual average rate of inflation was 21.4% in 2021 and 99.7% in 2022. The unemployment rate was recorded at 6.3% in October 2022.

The Turkish Cypriot economy continues to suffer from its international isolation, and remains heavily dependent on financial aid from Türkiye. Despite the objections of the Greek Cypriot Government, in May 2019 the Turkish Petroleum Corporation commenced drilling for hydrocarbons in Cyprus's exclusive economic zone (EEZ), in an area 75 km off the west coast of Cyprus. Further drilling began off the east coast in July, and in October Turkey prepared to drill for hydrocarbons in waters in which the Republic of Cyprus had already granted exploration rights to French, Italian, US and Qatari companies. Turkish offshore hydrocarbon exploration was halted in December 2020, but resumed in August 2022. Proposals to end international trade restrictions against the 'TRNC' have been prevented by continued Greek Cypriot opposition, while goods produced in the north must also be re-exported via Türkiye, making them more costly and therefore less competitive in global markets. Since 2011 economic conditions and pressure from the Turkish Government have led successive 'TRNC' administrations to persist with unpopular austerity measures. The high rate of inflation that has prevailed since 2013 has been exacerbated by a series of steep declines in the value of the Turkish lira, including in 2018, mid-2020 and late 2021. Meanwhile, GDP growth declined from 5.5% in 2017 to 1.3% in 2018, and to just 0.2% in 2019, before contracting by 16.2% in 2020 owing to the impact of the COVID-19 pandemic, which led to a large decrease in tourist arrivals and receipts in that year. Total arrivals increased to 552,307 in 2021 (from 388,842 in 2020), but this still fell far short of the 1.75m. recorded in 2019. Nevertheless, the partial recovery in the lucrative tourism industry contributed to a return to positive overall GDP growth in 2021 of 3.8%; growth in that year was also supported by rebounds in the construction and manufacturing sectors. In April 2022 the 'TRNC' and Turkey signed a new financial co-operation protocol, according to which Turkey pledged to allocate the 'TRNC' a total of 4,250m. Turkish liras in that year, mainly in the form of grants. However, the 'TRNC' noted that of the 3,250m. Turkish liras promised by Turkey under the 2021 protocol, only 1,833m. Turkish liras had actually been received. The economy of the 'TRNC' remained weak throughout 2022 and into 2023, suffering from the combined effects of the currency crisis in Türkiye, soaring global food and fuel prices (arising from the invasion of Ukraine by the Russian Federation in February 2022), ongoing disruptions to the power supply (attributed principally to chronic under-investment) and a persistently high rate of unemployment. However, it was hoped that the easing of COVID-19 restrictions would facilitate a continued recovery in the valuable tourism sector. Plans for a new national airline were under consideration, and a new terminal at Ercan airport was opened, after protracted delays, in July 2023. With the high rate of inflation depleting the real-term value of employees' wages, in July 2022 the 'TRNC' administration announced an increase in the minimum net monthly wage, from 6,900 Turkish liras to 8,600 Turkish liras, in a bid to limit the number of lower-income households falling into poverty; the minimum wage was further increased to 11,800 Turkish liras in January 2023 and to 15,750 Turkish liras in July. Meanwhile, in July 2022 Prime Minister Ünal Üstel announced that a planned 20% reduction in public sector wages (for those whose monthly wage was more than 15,000 Turkish liras) had been revoked; the decision came after the Public Servants Union had filed a legal challenge to the pay cuts at the Constitutional Court.

Statistical Survey

Sources: Statistics and Research Dept, State Planning Organization, Prime Ministry, Lefkoşa (Nicosia), Mersin 10, Türkiye; tel. 6011200; fax 2285988; e-mail info.dpo@gov.ct.tr; internet www.devplan.org; 'TRNC' Statistical Institute, Selçuklu Cad. 3, Kızılay, Lefkoşa (Nicosia), Mersin 10, Türkiye; tel. 6013000; fax 2270913; e-mail info@stat.gov.ct.tr; internet www.stat.gov.ct.tr.

AREA AND POPULATION

Area: 3,242 sq km (1,251 sq miles).

Population: 256,644 at census of 30 April 2006; 286,257 (males 150,483, females 135,774) at census of 4 December 2011. *2021* (official projection at 31 December): 390,745.

Density (at 31 December 2021): 120.5 per sq km.

Population by Age and Sex (official projections at 31 December 2021): *0–14 years:* 53,733 (males 27,992, females 25,741); *15–64 years:* 298,801 (males 166,737, females 132,064); *65 years and over:* 38,211 (males 17,806, females 20,405); *Total* 390,745 (males 212,535, females 178,210).

Population by Country of Nationality (self-declaration at census of 4 December 2011): 'TRNC' 136,362; Türkiye 80,550; Joint 'TRNC' and other 54,132 (with Türkiye 38,085, with Other 16,047); United Kingdom 3,691; Turkmenistan 1,760; Nigeria 1,279; Iran 1,152; Pakistan 1,075; Bulgaria 920; Azerbaijan 835; Other 4,501; *Total* 286,257. Note: Classification of nationality reflects local methodology.

Districts (population at census of 4 December 2011): Lefkoşa 94,824; Mağusa 69,741; Girne 69,163; Güzelyurt 30,037; İskele 22,492; *Total* 286,257.

Principal Towns (population within the municipal boundary at census of 4 December 2011): Lefkoşa (Nicosia) 61,378 (Turkish-occupied area only); Gazi Mağusa (Famagusta) 40,920; Girne (Kyrenia) 33,207; Güzelyurt 18,946.

Births, Marriages and Deaths (registered, 2021): Live births 3,614 (birth rate 9.3 per 1,000); Marriages 1,234 (marriage rate 3.0 per 1,000); Deaths 1,693 (death rate 4.4 per 1,000).

Life Expectancy (years at birth, 2021): 81.0 (males 79.0; females 83.1).

Economically Active Population (labour force survey, October 2020): Agriculture, forestry and fishing 4,066; Mining and quarrying 333; Manufacturing 9,752; Construction 10,104; Electricity, gas and water 3,517; Wholesale and retail trade 25,101; Hotels and restaurants 8,709; Transport, storage and communications 8,043; Financial institutions 5,295; Real estate and renting 9,220; Public administration 17,955; Education 14,981; Health 6,256; Other community services 9,551; *Total employed* 132,883; Unemployed 14,950; *Total labour force* 147,833. 2022 (labour force survey, October 2022): Agriculture, forestry and fishing 5,797; Industry (excl. construction) 11,704; Construction 13,668; Services 107,439; Total employed 138,609; Unemployed 9,340; Total labour force 147,949.

HEALTH AND WELFARE

Total Fertility Rate (children per woman, 2020): 1.8.

Under-5 Mortality Rate (per 1,000 live births, 2006): 13.9.

COVID-19: Fully Vaccinated Population (% of total population at 30 December 2022): 81.8.

Physicians (per 1,000 head, 2010): 2.7.

Hospital Beds (per 1,000 head, 2018): 4.1.

Note: For data on COVID-19 vaccinations, 'fully vaccinated' denotes receipt of all doses specified by approved vaccination regime (Sources: Johns Hopkins University and Our World in Data). For more information on sources and further definitions for all indicators, see Health and Welfare Statistics: Sources and Definitions section (europaworld.com/credits).

AGRICULTURE

Principal Crops ('000 metric tons, 2021): Artichokes 8.2; Barley 54.6; Cantaloupes and other melons 2.6; Carobs 2.5; Cucumbers 2.4; Grapefruits 2.1; Legumes 3.9; Lemons 6.1; Olives 5.0; Onions 5.4; Oranges 59.3; Potatoes 15.4; Tangerines, etc. 40.6 Tomatoes 5.6; Watermelons 3.2; Wheat 16.4.

Livestock ('000 head, 2021): Cattle 69.2; Goats 88.8; Poultry 9,896; Sheep 528.1.

Livestock Products ('000 metric tons unless otherwise indicated, 2021): Cattle meat 4.9; Cows' milk 159.9; Chicken meat 15.0; Goat meat 1.1; Goats' and sheep's milk 24.2; Sheep meat 4.0; Poultry eggs (dozens) 8.1m.; Wool 0.3.

Fishing (metric tons, 2001): Total catch 400.

FINANCE

Currency and Exchange Rates: Turkish currency: 100 kuruş = 1 Turkish lira. *Sterling, Dollar and Euro Equivalents* (28 April 2023): £1 sterling = 24.234 liras; US $1 = 19.444 liras; €1 = 21.352 liras; 100 Turkish liras = £4.13 = $5.14 = €4.68. Note: A new currency, the new Turkish lira, equivalent to 1m. of the former units, was introduced on 1 January 2005. Some figures in this survey have been converted retrospectively to reflect this development. (The name of the currency reverted to Turkish lira on 1 January 2009, although new Turkish lira banknotes and coins were to remain in circulation for a further year.) *Average Exchange Rate* (liras per US $): 7.009 in 2020; 8.850 in 2021; 16.549 in 2022.

Budget (million Turkish liras, 2021): *Revenue:* Local revenue 7,591.9 (Direct and indirect taxes 5,897.3, Other income 792.9, Fund revenues 901.7); Foreign aid 1,348.0; Total 8,939.8. *Expenditure:* Personnel 3,300.1; Other goods and services 928.5; Transfers 4,128.0; Investments 1,352.5; Defence 677.1; Total 10,386.1.

Cost of Living (Consumer Price Index; base: 2015 = 100): 201.9 in 2020; 245.1 in 2021; 489.5 in 2022.

Gross Domestic Product (million Turkish liras at constant 1977 prices): 18,557.0 in 2019; 15,548.6 in 2020; 16,154.4 in 2021.

Expenditure on the Gross Domestic Product ('000 Turkish liras at current prices, 2003, provisional figures): Government final consumption expenditure 482,674; Private final consumption expenditure 1,071,916; Increase in stocks 30,900; Gross fixed capital formation 300,218; *Total domestic expenditure* 1,885,707; Net exports of goods and services −56,763; *GDP in purchasers' values* 1,828,944.

Gross Domestic Product by Economic Activity ('000 Turkish liras, 2021): Agriculture, forestry and fishing 2,525,767.7; Mining and quarrying 658,236.2; Manufacturing 689,836.3; Electricity and water 925,922.4; Construction 2,247,766.8; Wholesale and retail trade 3,142,668.5; Restaurants and hotels 1,011,090.9; Transport and communications 2,764,184.8; Finance 2,678,856.6; Ownership of dwellings 2,206,501.8; Business and personal services 4,272,004.7; Government services 4,670,800.5; *Sub-total* 27,793,637.2; Import duties 2,350,093.3; *GDP in purchasers' values* 30,143,730.5.

Balance of Payments (US $ million, 2021): Merchandise exports f.o.b. 150.1; Merchandise imports c.i.f. −1,578.1; *Trade balance* −1,428.0; Services and unrequited transfers (net) 1,380.5; *Current balance* −47.5; Capital movements 83.2; *Overall balance* −35.8.

EXTERNAL TRADE

Principal Commodities (US $ million, 2021): *Imports c.i.f.:* Food and live animals 248.7; Beverages and tobacco 78.8; Mineral fuels, lubricants, etc. 344.6; Chemical and related products 126.1; Basic manufactures 245.2; Machinery and transport equipment 361.2; Miscellaneous manufactured articles 147.6; Total (incl. others) 1,572.1. *Exports f.o.b.:* Food and live animals 89.6; Beverages and tobacco 2.8; Chemicals and related products 1.6; Basic manufactures 19.9; Miscellaneous manufactured articles 18.6 Total (incl. others) 134.8.

Principal Trading Partners (US $ million, 2021): *Imports c.i.f.:* Argentina 12.1; Belgium 13.7; China, People's Republic 85.4; Germany 59.6; Israel 81.8; Italy 21.6; Japan 35.7; Netherlands 10.9; Romania 10.8; Russian Federation 13.6; Türkiye 988.2; United Arab Emirates 14.3; United Kingdom 51.5; USA 16.9; Total (incl. others) 1,572.1. *Exports f.o.b.:* Cyprus (govt-controlled) 6.3; Iraq 5.8; Kuwait 10.3; Russian Federation 5.7; Saudi Arabia 5.3; Türkiye 63.4; United Arab Emirates 4.8; USA 15.7; Total (incl. others) 134.8.

TRANSPORT

Road Traffic (registered motor vehicles, 2021): Saloon cars 208,655; Estate cars 11,743; Pick-ups 184; Vans 43; Buses 4,719; Trucks 34,866; Lorries 13,524; Motorcycles 34,432; Agricultural tractors 11,154; Total (incl. others) 352,332.

Shipping (2021): *Freight Traffic* ('000 metric tons): Goods loaded 245.8; Goods unloaded 1,632.4; Vessels entered 1,563.

Civil Aviation (2001): Passenger arrivals and departures 691,431; Freight landed and cleared (metric tons) 4,297.

TOURISM

Visitors (2021): 552,307 (incl. 438,696 Turkish visitors).

Tourism Receipts (US $ million, 2021): 340.3.

COMMUNICATIONS MEDIA

Radio Receivers (2001, provisional): 82,364 in use.

Television Receivers (2001, provisional): 70,960 in use.

Telephones (2019): 237 per 1,000 population.

Mobile Telephone Subscriptions (2018): 2,357 per 1,000 population.

EDUCATION

2021/22 (unless otherwise indicated): *Pre-primary schools:* 113 institutions, 768 teachers, 7,556 pupils; *Primary schools:* 95 institutions, 1,799 teachers, 20,434 pupils; *Secondary Schools:* 40 institutions, 2,397 teachers, 11,925 students; *General High Schools:* 32 institutions, 2,397 teachers, 11,327 students; *Vocational Schools:* 12 institutions, 596 teachers, 3,814 students; *Special Education (2019/20):* 13 institutions, 61 teachers, 390 students; *Universities (2018/19):* 18 institutions, 102,953 students (of which 12,507 Turkish Cypriots, 54,966 from Türkiye, 35,480 from other countries). Note: 3,828 'TRNC' students were studying abroad in 2018/19.

Pupil-teacher Ratio (primary education): 11.0 in 2021/22.

Adult Literacy Rate (at census of 15 December 1996): 93.5%.

Directory

Constitution

The Turkish intervention in Cyprus in July 1974 resulted in the establishment of a separate area in northern Cyprus under the control of the Autonomous Turkish Cypriot Administration, with a Council of Ministers and separate judicial, financial, police, military and educational machinery serving the Turkish community.

On 13 February 1975 the Turkish-occupied zone of Cyprus was declared the 'Turkish Federated State of Cyprus', and Rauf Denktaş declared President. At the second joint meeting held by the Executive Council and Legislative Assembly of the Autonomous Turkish Cypriot Administration, it was decided to set up a Constituent Assembly, which would prepare a constitution for the 'Turkish Federated State of Cyprus' within 45 days. This Constitution, which was approved by the Turkish Cypriot population in a referendum held on 8 June 1975, was regarded by the Turkish Cypriots as a first step towards a federal republic of Cyprus. The main provisions of the Constitution are summarized below:

The 'Turkish Federated State of Cyprus' is a democratic, secular republic based on the principles of social justice and the rule of law. It shall exercise only those functions that fall outside the powers and functions expressly given to the (proposed) Federal Republic of Cyprus. Necessary amendments shall be made to the Constitution of the 'Turkish Federated State of Cyprus' when the Constitution of the Federal Republic comes into force. The official language is Turkish.

Legislative power is vested in the Assembly of the Republic, composed of 50 deputies, elected by universal suffrage for a period of five years. The President is head of state and is elected by universal suffrage for a period of five years. No person may be elected President for more than two consecutive terms. The Council of Ministers shall be composed of a Prime Minister and 10 Ministers. Judicial power is exercised through independent courts.

Other provisions cover such matters as the rehabilitation of refugees, property rights outside the 'Turkish Federated State', protection of coasts, social insurance, the rights and duties of citizens, etc.

On 15 November 1983 a unilateral declaration of independence brought into being the 'Turkish Republic of Northern Cyprus', which, like the 'Turkish Federated State of Cyprus', was not granted international recognition.

The Constituent Assembly, established after the declaration of independence, prepared a new Constitution, which was approved by the Turkish Cypriot electorate on 5 May 1985. The new Constitution was similar to the previous one, but the number of deputies in the legislature was increased to 50.

The Government of the 'Turkish Republic of Northern Cyprus'

HEAD OF STATE

President of the 'Turkish Republic of Northern Cyprus': ERSIN TATAR (inaugurated 23 October 2020).

COUNCIL OF MINISTERS
(September 2023)

A coalition Government formed by the National Unity Party (UBP), the Democrat Party (DP) and the Rebirth Party (YDP).

CYPRIOT SECESSIONIST TERRITORY — 'Turkish Republic of Northern Cyprus'

Prime Minister: ÜNAL ÜSTEL (UBP).
Deputy Prime Minister and Minister of Tourism, Culture, Youth and Environment: FIKRI ATAOĞLU (DP).
Minister of Public Works and Transportation: Prof. Dr ERHAN ARIKLI (YDP).
Minister of Economy and Energy: OLGUN AMCAOĞLU (UBP).
Minister of Finance: ALIŞAN ŞAN (UBP).
Minister of Interior Affairs: ZIYA ÖZTÜRKLER (UBP).
Minister of Foreign Affairs: TAHSIN ERTUĞRULOĞLU (UBP).
Minister of National Education: NAZIM ÇAVUŞOĞLU (UBP).
Minister of Agriculture and Natural Resources: DURSUN OĞUZ (UBP).
Minister of Health: İZLEM GÜRÇAĞ (UBP).
Minister of Labour and Social Security: HASAN TAÇOY (UBP).

MINISTRIES

Office of the President: Şht Selahattin Sonat Sok., Lefkoşa (Nicosia), Mersin 10, Türkiye; tel. 2283444; fax 2272252; e-mail info@kktcb.org; internet www.kktcb.org.

Prime Minister's Office: 3 Selçuklu Cad., Lefkoşa (Nicosia), Mersin 10, Türkiye; tel. 2283141; fax 2275281; e-mail info.basbakanlik@gov.ct.tr; internet kktcbasbakanlik.org.

Ministry of Agriculture and Natural Resources: 11 Mehmet Vural Ahmet Sok., Yenişehir, Lefkoşa (Nicosia), Mersin 10, Türkiye; tel. 2283735; fax 2286945; e-mail info.tarim@gov.ct.tr; internet tarim.gov.ct.tr.

Ministry of Economy and Energy: Lefkoşa (Nicosia), Mersin 10, Türkiye; tel. 2289629; fax 2273976.

Ministry of Finance: Lefkoşa (Nicosia), Mersin 10, Türkiye; tel. 2283116; fax 2278230; e-mail kktcmaliyebasin@gmail.com; internet www.maliye.gov.ct.tr.

Ministry of Foreign Affairs: Selçuklu Cad., Lefkoşa (Nicosia), Mersin 10, Türkiye; tel. 2283241; fax 2284290; e-mail info@mfa.gov.ct.tr; internet mfa.gov.ct.tr.

Ministry of Health: 142 Bedreddin Demirel Cad., Lefkoşa (Nicosia), Mersin 10, Türkiye; tel. 2283173; fax 2283893; e-mail info.saglik@gov.ct.tr; internet saglik.gov.ct.tr.

Ministry of Interior Affairs: Lefkoşa (Nicosia), Mersin 10, Türkiye; tel. 6111100; fax 6111170; e-mail info.icisleri@gov.ct.tr; internet icisleri.gov.ct.tr.

Ministry of Labour and Social Security: 82 Atatürk Cad., Yenişehir, Lefkoşa (Nicosia), Mersin 10, Türkiye; tel. 2279781; fax 2288234; internet csgb.gov.ct.tr.

Ministry of National Education: Lefkoşa (Nicosia), Mersin 10, Türkiye; tel. 2287376; fax 2283136; internet www.mebnet.net.

Ministry of Public Works and Transportation: 4 Selçuklu Cad., Lefkoşa (Nicosia), Mersin 10, Türkiye; tel. 2283666; fax 2281891; e-mail info.ulastirma@gov.ct.tr; internet bub.gov.ct.tr.

Ministry of Tourism, Culture, Youth and Environment: Lefkoşa (Nicosia), Mersin 10, Türkiye; tel. 2289629; fax 2279675; e-mail kktcturizmbakanligi@gmail.com; internet turizm.gov.ct.tr.

President

Presidential Election, First Ballot, 11 October 2020

Candidate	Votes	%
Ersin Tatar (UBP)	35,872	32.3
Mustafa Akıncı (Ind.)	33,058	29.8
Tufan Erhürman (CTP)	24,075	21.7
Kudret Özersay (Ind.)	6,365	5.7
Erhan Arıklı (YDP)	5,999	5.4
Serdar Denktaş (Ind.)	4,627	4.2
Others	919	0.8
Total*	**110,915**	**100.0**

* Excluding 5,051 invalid votes.

Presidential Election, Second Ballot, 18 October 2020

Candidate	Votes	%
Ersin Tatar (UBP)	67,322	51.7
Mustafa Akıncı (Ind.)	62,910	48.3
Total*	**130,232**	**100.0**

* Excluding 3,699 invalid votes.

Legislature

Assembly of the Republic: Bedrettin Demirel Cad., Köşklüçiftlik, Lefkoşa (Nicosia), Mersin 10, Türkiye; tel. 2283281; e-mail info@cm.gov.nc.tr; internet www.cm.gov.nc.tr.
Speaker: ZORLU TÖRE.

General Election, 23 January 2022

Party	Votes	%	Seats
National Unity Party (UBP)	2,025,768	39.6	24
Republican Turkish Party (CTP)	1,631,758	31.9	18
Democrat Party (DP)	379,658	7.4	3
People's Party (HP)	342,263	6.7	3
Rebirth Party (YDP)	329,497	6.4	2
Total (incl. others)*	**5,113,684**	**100.0**	**50**

* Under the Elections and Referendums Law of 2016, the entire territory of the 'Turkish Republic of Northern Cyprus' comprises a single electoral district and each party presents a list of candidates to voters across the territory. Each voter is permitted to express preferences for up to 50 candidates.

Election Commission

Yüksek Seçim Kurulu (YSK) (Supreme Board of Elections): Lefkoşa (Nicosia), Mersin 10, Türkiye; tel. 6122000; e-mail ymgenelsekreter@hotmail.com; internet ysk.mahkemeler.net; Pres. NARIN FERDI ŞEFIK.

Political Organizations

Communal Democracy Party (Toplumcu Demokrasi Partisi—TDP): Osman Paşa Cad., 10 Köşklüçiftlik, Lefkoşa (Nicosia), Mersin 10, Türkiye; tel. 2272555; e-mail info@tdpkibris.org; internet tdpkibris.org; f. 2007, by merger between the Barış ve Demokrasi Hareketi (Peace and Democracy Movement) and the Toplumcu Kurtuluş Partisi (Communal Liberation Party); Pres. MINE ATLI; Sec.-Gen. Dr HALIL HIZAL.

Cyprus Justice Party (Kıbrıs Adalet Partisi—KAP): 1 Osman Paşa Ave., Köşklüçiftlik, Lefkoşa (Nicosia), Mersin 10, Türkiye; tel. 2270274; fax 2289938; Leader OĞUZ KALEIOĞLU.

Cyprus Socialist Party (Kıbrıs Sosyalist Partisi—KSP): Yüzbaşı Tekin, Lefkoşa (Nicosia), Mersin 10, Türkiye; tel. 8614144; e-mail kibrissosyalistpartisi@gmail.com; internet www.kibrissosyalistpartisi.org; Gen. Sec. MEHMET BIRINCI.

Democrat Party (Demokrat Parti—DP): Servet Somuncuoğlu Sok., Lefkoşa (Nicosia), Mersin 10, Türkiye; tel. 2271240; e-mail merkez@kktcdemokratparti.com; internet www.kktcdemokratparti.com; f. 1992 by disaffected representatives of the Ulusal Birlik Partisi; merged with the Yeni Doğuş Partisi (New Dawn Party; f. 1984) and Sosyal Demokrat Partisi (Social Democrat Party) in May 1993; Leader FIKRI ATAOĞLU; Gen. Sec. SERHAT AKPINAR.

National Unity Party (Ulusal Birlik Partisi—UBP): Mehmet Akif Cad. 40/42, Lefkoşa (Nicosia), Mersin 10, Türkiye; tel. 2284151; fax 2285801; internet ulusalbirlikpartisi.com; f. 1975; right of centre; opposes reunification of Cyprus; Pres. ÜNAL ÜSTEL; Sec.-Gen. OĞUZHAN HASIPOĞLU.

New Cyprus Party (Yeni Kıbrıs Partisi—YKP): 64/1 Tanzimat Sok., Arabahmet Mah., Lefkoşa (Nicosia), Mersin 10, Türkiye; tel. 2274917; fax 2288931; e-mail ykp@ykp.org.cy; internet www.ykp.org.cy; f. 1989; operated as Patriotic Unity Movement (Yurtsever Birlik Hareketi) during 1998–2004; publishes weekly newsletter Yeniçag; Gen. Sec. MURAT KANATLI.

The People's Party (Halkın Partisi—HP): Mehmet Akif Cad., Okay Apt. 7, Daire 2, Kumsal, Lefkoşa (Nicosia), Mersin 10, Türkiye; tel. 4440047; e-mail info@halkinpartisi.biz; internet www.halkinpartisi.biz; f. 2016; Pres. KUDRET ÖZERSAY; Sec.-Gen. AHMET TOKATLIOĞLU.

Rebirth Party (Yeniden Doğuş Partisi—YDP): Burhan Nalbantoğlu Cad., Tevfik Mut İşhanı Kat 3, Daire 3, Lefkoşa (Nicosia), Mersin 10, Türkiye; tel. 8625509; e-mail ydpkuzeykibris@gmail.com; internet www.ydp.com.tr; f. 2016; Pres. Prof. Dr ERHAN ARIKLI; Sec.-Gen. TALIP ATALAY.

Republican Turkish Party (Cumhuriyetçi Türk Partisi—CTP): 99 Şehit Salahi, Şevket Sok., Lefkoşa (Nicosia), Mersin 10, Türkiye; tel. 26001970; fax 26001980; e-mail info@ctpkibris.org; internet www.cumhuriyetciturkpartisi.org; f. 1970 by mems of the Turkish community in Cyprus; district orgs at Gazi Mağusa (Famagusta), Girne (Kyrenia), Güzelyurt (Morphou) and Lefkoşa (Nicosia); Pres. TUFAN ERHÜRMAN; Gen. Sec. ASIM AKANSOY.

United Cyprus Party (Birleşik Kıbrıs Partisi—BKP): Kaymaklı Yolu Sok. 28, Çağlayan, Lefkoşa (Nicosia), Mersin 10, Türkiye; tel. 2281845; fax 2281617; e-mail bkp@birlesikkibris.com; internet www.birlesikkibris.com; f. 2002; Marxist-Leninist; Pres. İZZET İZCAN; Sec.-Gen. SALIH SONÜSTÜN.

Diplomatic Representation

Türkiye (formerly Turkey) is the only country officially to have recognized the 'Turkish Republic of Northern Cyprus'.

Türkiye (Turkey): Bedrettin Demirel Cad., T. C. Lefkoşa Büyükelçisi, Lefkoşa (Nicosia), Mersin 10, Türkiye; tel. 6003100; fax 2282209; e-mail lefkosa.konsolosluk@mfa.gov.tr; internet nicosia.emb.mfa.gov.tr; Ambassador METIN FEYZIOĞLU.

Judicial System

Supreme Court: Lefkoşa (Nicosia), Mersin 10, Türkiye; tel. 6122000; e-mail arsiv.mahkemeler@gov.ct.tr; internet www.mahkemeler.net; The Supreme Court is the highest court in the 'TRNC', and functions as the Constitutional Court, the Court of Appeal and the High Administrative Court. The Supreme Court, sitting as the Constitutional Court, has exclusive jurisdiction to adjudicate finally on all matters prescribed by the Constitution. The Supreme Court, sitting as the Court of Appeal, is the highest appellate court in the 'TRNC' in both civil and criminal cases. It also has original jurisdiction in certain matters of judicial review. The Supreme Court, sitting as the High Administrative Court, has exclusive jurisdiction on matters relating to administrative law. The Supreme Court is composed of a President and 7 judges; Pres. NARIN FERDI ŞEFIK.

Subordinate Courts: Judicial power other than that exercised by the Supreme Court is exercised by the Assize Courts, District Courts and Family Courts.

Supreme Council of Judicature: The Supreme Council of Judicature, composed of the president and judges of the Supreme Court, a member appointed by the President of the 'TRNC', a member appointed by the Assembly of the Republic, the Attorney-General and a member elected by the Bar Association, is responsible for the appointment, promotion, transfer and matters relating to the discipline of all judges. The appointments of the president and judges of the Supreme Court are subject to the approval of the President of the 'TRNC'.

The Attorney-General's Office: The office of the Attorney-General is not attached to any Ministry. The Deputy Attorney-General acts for the Attorney-General in case of his absence; Attorney-General SARPER ALTINCIK.

Religion

Most adherents of Islam in the 'TRNC' are Sunni Muslims of the Hanafi sect. The religious head of the Muslim community in the 'TRNC' is the Grand Mufti.

Grand Mufti of the 'TRNC': Dr AHMET ÜNSAL, PK 142, Lefkoşa (Nicosia), Mersin 10, Türkiye.

The Press

DAILIES

Afrika: Lefkoşa (Nicosia), Mersin 10, Türkiye; tel. 2271338; fax 2274585; e-mail avrupa@kktc.net; internet www.afrikagazetesi.net; fmrly *Avrupa*; Turkish; independent; Editor ŞENER LEVENT.

Halkın Sesi (Voice of the People): 172 Girne Cad., Lefkoşa (Nicosia), Mersin 10, Türkiye; tel. 2273141; fax 2272612; e-mail haber@halkinsesikibris.com; internet www.halkinsesikibris.com; f. 1942; morning; Turkish; independent Turkish nationalist; Chair. MEHMET KÜÇÜK.

Kıbrıs (Cyprus): Dr Fazıl Küçük Bul., Yeni Sanayi Bölgesi, Lefkoşa (Nicosia), Mersin 10, Türkiye; tel. 2252555; fax 2255176; e-mail kibris@kibrisgazetesi.com; internet www.kibrisgazetesi.com; Turkish; Chair. ASIL NADIR; Editor-in-Chief ALI BATURAY.

Ortam (Political Conditions): 7 Cengiz Han Sok., Kösklüciflik, Lefkoşa (Nicosia), Mersin 10, Türkiye; tel. 2280852; fax 2283784; e-mail info@ortamgazetesi.com; internet www.ortamgazetesi.com; f. 1981; Turkish; Editor-in-Chief HALDUN CAMBAZ.

Vatan (Homeland): 21. Sok., 66 Organize Sanayi Bölgesi, Lefkoşa (Nicosia), Mersin 10, Türkiye; tel. 2258341; fax 2258342; internet www.arti392.com; f. 1991; Turkish; Editor MEHMET KASIMOĞLU.

Yeni Düzen (New System): Organize Sanayi Bölgesi, Lefkoşa (Nicosia), Mersin 10, Türkiye; tel. 2256658; fax 2253240; e-mail web@yeniduzen.com; internet www.yeniduzengazetesi.com; f. 1975; Turkish; organ of the CTP; Chief Editor CENK MUTLUYAKALI.

WEEKLIES

Cyprus Observer: 18 Aytekin Zekai Sok., Kyrenia (Girne), Mersin 10, Türkiye; POB 29085, Nicosia; tel. 8155387; fax 8155585; internet www.observercyprus.com; f. 2005; English; Exec. Editor HASAN ERCAKICA; Editor UMUT URAS.

Cyprus Today: Dr Fazıl Küçük Bul., PK 831, Lefkoşa (Nicosia), Mersin 10, Türkiye; tel. 2252555; e-mail cyprustoday@yahoo.com; internet www.cyprustodayonline.com; f. 1991; English; political, social, cultural and economic; Man. Co-ordinator MARIA DJEMAL.

Ekonomi (The Economy): 90 Bedrettin Demirel Cad., Lefkoşa (Nicosia), Mersin 10, Türkiye; tel. 2283760; fax 2270782; e-mail ktto@ktto.net; f. 1958; Turkish; publ. by the Turkish Cypriot Chamber of Commerce; Editor-in-Chief DENIZ GÜRGÖZE.

Yeniçağ: 64/1 Tanzimat Sok., Arabahmet Mah., Lefkoşa (Nicosia), Mersin 10, Türkiye; tel. 2274917; fax 2288931; e-mail ykp@ykp.org.cy; internet www.ykp.org.cy/category/yenicag/; f. 1990; Turkish; organ of the YKP; Editor MURAT KANATLI.

PERIODICALS

Güvenlik Kuvvetleri Magazine: Lefkoşa (Nicosia), Mersin 10, Türkiye; tel. 2275680; publ. by the Security Forces of the 'TRNC'.

Halkbilimi (Folklore): POB 199, Küçük Kaymaklı Spor Kulübü Karşısı, Lefkoşa (Nicosia), Mersin 10, Türkiye; tel. 2272427; e-mail hasder@hasder.org; internet www.hasder.org; f. 1986; annual; publ. by Hasder Folk Arts Foundation; academic, folkloric; Turkish, with a short summary in English; Chief Editor KANI KANOL.

Kıbrıs—Northern Cyprus Monthly: c/o Ministry of Foreign Affairs, Lefkoşa (Nicosia), Mersin 10, Türkiye; tel. 2283365; fax 2287641; f. 1963; Editor GÖNÜL ATANER.

Kıbrıslı Türkün Sesi: 44 Mecidiye St, Lefkoşa (Nicosia), Mersin 10, Türkiye; tel. 2278520; fax 2287966; monthly; political; Exec. Dir DOGAN HARMAN; Gen. Co-ordinator CEVDET ALPARSLAN.

Kuzey Kıbrıs Kültür Dergisi (North Cyprus Cultural Journal): PK 157, Lefkoşa (Nicosia), Mersin 10, Türkiye; tel. 2231298; f. 1987; monthly; Turkish; Chief Editor GÜNSEL DOĞASAL.

NEWS AGENCY

TürkAjansı-Kıbrıs (TAK) (Turkish News Agency of Cyprus): PK 355, 30 Mehmet Akif Cad., Lefkoşa (Nicosia), Mersin 10, Türkiye; tel. 4441881; fax 2271213; e-mail turkajansikibris@gmail.com; internet www.tak.gov.ct.tr; f. 1973; Pres. and CEO FEHMI GURDALLI.

Publishers

Action Global Communications: 6 Kondilaki St, 1090 Lefkoşa (Nicosia), Mersin 10, Türkiye; tel. 22818884; fax 22873632; e-mail action@actionprgroup.com; internet www.actionprgroup.com; f. 1971; affiliate of Weber Shandwick; has 44 offices in the emerging markets; travel, aviation and hospitality; CEO CHRIS CHRISTODOULOU.

Halkın Sesi Ltd: 172 Girne Cad., Lefkoşa (Nicosia), Mersin 10, Türkiye; tel. 2285645; fax 2272612; internet www.halkinsesi.org.

Kıbrıs Araştırma ve Yayın Merkezi (North Cyprus Research and Publishing Centre—CYREP): PK 327, Lefkoşa (Nicosia), Mersin 10, Türkiye; tel. 8555179; fax 2272592; Dir AHMET C. GAZIOĞLU.

Broadcasting and Communications

TELECOMMUNICATIONS

Kıbrıs Mobile Telekomünikasyon Ltd (Kuzey Kıbrıs Turkcell): Arif Salih Sok. 12, Yenişehir, Lefkoşa (Nicosia), Mersin 10, Türkiye; tel. 8780533; e-mail info@kktcell.com; internet www.kktcell.com; f. 1999; subsidiary of Turkcell; provides mobile telecommunications services; Gen. Man. MURAT KÜÇÜKÖZDEMIR.

KKTC Telekomünikasyon Dairesi (KKTC Telekom): Şehit Arif Salih Sok. 1, Küçük Kaymaklı, Lefkoşa (Nicosia), Mersin 10, Türkiye; tel. 2283111; fax 2281030; e-mail info.telekom@gov.ct.tr; internet telekom.gov.ct.tr; f. 1963; state-owned; fixed-line telephone and internet services; Gen. Man. ENIZ ELAGÖZ.

KKTC Telsim: Ali Rıza Efendi Cad. 33/A, Lefkoşa (Nicosia), Mersin 10, Türkiye; tel. 8880542; fax 2270584; e-mail vmol.info@vodafone.com; internet www.kktctelsim.com; f. 1995; provides mobile telecommunications services; subsidiary of Vodafone Türkiye; Gen. Man. SEFER TÜZ.

BROADCASTING

Radio

Bayrak Radio and TV Corpn (BRTK): BRTK Sitesi, Dr Fazıl Küçük Bul., Lefkoşa (Nicosia), Mersin 10, Türkiye; tel. 2255555; e-mail info@brtk.net; internet www.brtk.net; f. 1963 as Bayrak Radio; became independent Turkish Cypriot corpn, partly financed by the 'TRNC' Govt, in July 1983; now has 5 radio stations on air: Radio Bayrak, Bayrak International (international music, 24-hour, and news in English, Greek, Russian, Arabic and German), Bayrak FM (popular music, 24-hour), Bayrak Classic (classical music, 24-hour) and Bayrak Turkish Music (Turkish classical and folk music, 18-hour); Dir MERYEM ÖZKURT.

First FM and Interfirst FM: Dr Fazıl Küçük Bul., Meral Birinci Sok 1, Lefkoşa (Nicosia), Mersin 10, Türkiye; tel. 4447396; fax 2254219; f. 1996.

Kıbrıs FM/Kıbrıs TV: Dr Fazıl Küçük Bul., Yeni Sanayi Bolgesi, Lefkoşa (Nicosia), Mersin 10, Türkiye; tel. 2252555; fax 2253707.

Radio Emu: Eastern Mediterranean University, Gazi Mağusa (Famagusta), Mersin 10, Türkiye; tel. 6302352; fax 6302317; e-mail fcms@emu.edu.tr; internet fcms.emu.edu.tr.

Television

In addition to those listed below, several Turkish channels are also transmitted to the 'TRNC'.

Bayrak Radio and TV Corpn (BRTK): BRTK Sitesi, Dr Fazıl Küçük Bul., Lefkoşa (Nicosia), Mersin 10, Türkiye; tel. 2255555; e-mail info@brtk.net; internet www.brtk.net; f. 1976; in July 1983 it became an independent Turkish Cypriot corpn, partly financed by the 'TRNC' Govt; Bayrak TV; transmits programmes in Turkish, Greek and English; Dir MERYEM ÖZKURT.

Kanal T: Şehit Üsteğmen Mustafa Orhan Sok. 10, Lefkoşa (Nicosia), Mersin 10, Türkiye; tel. 4444424; e-mail haberkanalt@gmail.com; internet www.kanalt.com; Chair. SIBEL TATAR.

Kıbrıs Genç TV: Dr Fazıl Küçük Bul., Meral Birinci Sok. 1, Lefkoşa (Nicosia), Mersin 10, Türkiye; tel. 4444255; e-mail info@kibrisgenctv.com; internet www.kibrisgenctv.com; Chair. TEKIN E. BIRINCI; Gen. Man. YAVUZ APAYDIN.

Finance

BANKING

Central Bank

Central Bank of the 'Turkish Republic of Northern Cyprus': POB 857, 63 Bedreddin Demirel Cad., Lefkoşa (Nicosia), Mersin 10, Türkiye; tel. 6115000; fax 2288607; internet www.kktcmerkezbankasi.org; f. 1984; Pres. RIFAT GÜNAY.

Principal Commercial Banks

Asbank Ltd: 8 Mecidiye Sok., PK 448, Lefkoşa (Nicosia), Mersin 10, Türkiye; tel. 4443678; fax 2287790; e-mail bilgi@asbank.com.tr; internet www.asbank.com.tr; f. 1986; Chair. TAŞTAN ALTUNER; Gen. Man. ÇAĞATAY KARIP.

CreditWest Bank Ltd: 1 Ozanköy Yolu Mülk Pl., Çatalköy, Lefkoşa (Nicosia), Mersin 10, Türkiye; tel. 4449378; fax 8245624; e-mail catalkoy@creditwestbank.com; internet www.creditwestbank.com; f. 1993 as Kıbrıs Altinbaş Bank Ltd; name changed as above 2006; Gen. Man. MAZHER ZAHEER.

Kıbrıs Iktisat Bankasi Ltd (Cyprus Economy Bank Ltd): 151 Bedreddin Demiral Cad., Lefkoşa (Nicosia), Mersin 10, Türkiye; tel. 6004000; fax 2281311; e-mail info@iktisatbank.com; internet www.iktisatbank.com; f. 1990; Chair. METE OZMERTER; Gen. Man. OLGUN ÖNAL.

Kıbrıs Türk Kooperatif Merkez Bankası Ltd (Cyprus Turkish Co-operative Central Bank): PK 823, 49–55 Mahmut Paşa Sok., Lefkoşa (Nicosia), Mersin 10, Türkiye; tel. 6221000; fax 2276787; e-mail info@koopbank.com; internet www.koopbank.com; f. 1959; banking and credit facilities to mem. societies and individuals; Chair. ŞERIFE KANAN; Gen. Man. KEMAL ATAMAN.

Kıbrıs Vakiflar Bankası Ltd (Cyprus Vakiflar Bank Ltd): PK 212, Atatürk Cad. 66, Yenişehir, Lefkoşa (Nicosia), Mersin 10, Türkiye; tel. 6006000; e-mail info@vakiflarbankasi.com; internet www.vakiflarbankasi.com; f. 1982; Chair. ERCAN IBRAHIMOĞLU; Gen. Man. MUSTAFA CENGIZ ERCAĞ.

Limasol Türk Kooperatif Bankası Ltd (LKTB) (Limassol Turkish Co-operative Bank Ltd): Atatürk Cad. 38, Yenişehir, Lefkoşa (Nicosia), Mersin 10, Türkiye; tel. 2280333; fax 2281350; e-mail info@limasolbank.com.tr; internet www.limasolbank.com.tr; f. 1939; Chair. GÜLHAN ALP; Gen. Man. İLKIN YOĞURTCUOĞLU.

Türk Bankası Ltd (Turkish Bank Ltd): 92 Girne Cad., PK 242, Lefkoşa (Nicosia), Mersin 10, Türkiye; tel. 6003333; fax 2279447; e-mail tmmk@turkishbank.net; internet www.turkishbank.com; f. 1901; Chair. IBRAHIM HAKAN BÖRTEÇENE; CEO MITHAT ARIKAN.

Viyabank Ltd: Atatürk Cad., 16 Muhtar Yusuf Galleria, Lefkoşa (Nicosia), Mersin 10, Türkiye; tel. 2285286; fax 2285878; e-mail gm@viyabank.com; internet www.viyabank.com; f. 1998; Pres. ŞÜKRÜ ATAMEN; Gen. Man. RAIF ERKIVANÇ.

Yakin Doğu Bank Ltd (Near East Bank Ltd): POB 47, 1 Girne Cad., Lefkoşa (Nicosia), Mersin 10, Türkiye; tel. 4440632; e-mail iletisim@neareastbank.com; internet www.neareastbank.com; Chair. ENVER HASKASAP; Gen. Man. SELAMI KAÇAMAK.

INSURANCE

Akfinans Sigorta Insurance Ltd: 130 Girne Cad., Lefkoşa (Nicosia), POB 451, Mersin 10, Türkiye; tel. 2287020; fax 2287077; internet www.akfinansbank.com.tr/subelerimiz; f. 1996; Chair. ADEM KADER.

Anadolu Anonim: Memduh Asaf Sok. 8, Köşklüçiftlik, Lefkoşa (Nicosia), Mersin 10, Türkiye; tel. 2279595; fax 2279596; e-mail kibrissube@anadolusigorta.com.tr; internet www.anadolusigorta.com.tr; Chair. FÜSUN TÜMSAVAŞ; Gen. Man. MEHMET SENÇAN.

Gold Insurance Ltd: Salih Ilhan Guven Sok. 19, Lefkoşa (Nicosia), Mersin 10, Türkiye; tel. 2286500; e-mail info@gold-insurance.com; internet www.gold-insurance.com; f. 1996; Man. Dir ULKER FAHRI.

Groupama Sigorta: Şehit Tuncer Hasan Sok. 21, Lefkoşa (Nicosia), Mersin 10, Türkiye; tel. 2280208; fax 2286160; e-mail kibris-gs@groupama.com.tr; internet www.groupama.com.tr; Man. PHILIPPE-HENRI BURLISSON.

Kıbrıs Sigorta STI Ltd (Cyprus Insurance Co Ltd): Abdi İpekçi Cad., Eti Binaları, Lefkoşa (Nicosia), Mersin 10, Türkiye; tel. 4445757; e-mail info@kibrissigorta.com; internet www.kibrissigorta.com; Chair. OZGUR ARIKAN; Gen. Man. HASAN BASRI BEYCANLI.

Şeker Sigorta (Kıbrıs) Ltd: İlhan Savut Sok. 7, PK 664, Köşklüçiftlik, Lefkoşa (Nicosia), Mersin 10, Türkiye; tel. 4440404; fax 2274074; e-mail contact@sekersigorta-kibris.com; internet www.sekerinsurance.com; f. 1996; Chair. TÜRKER YÜKSEL; Man. Dir MEHMET BETMEZOĞLU.

Insurance Association

Kuzey Kıbrıs Sigorta ve Reasürans Şirketleri Birliği (Insurance and Reinsurance Association of Northern Cyprus): Selim Cad. 49, Arca Apartment No. 3, Köşklüçiftlik, Lefkoşa (Nicosia), Mersin 10, Türkiye; tel. 2280937; e-mail info@kksrsb.org; internet www.kksrsb.org; 32 mem. cos; Chair. RAIF ÇUKUROVALI.

Trade and Industry

CHAMBERS OF COMMERCE AND INDUSTRY

Turkish Cypriot Chamber of Commerce: 90 Bedrettin Demirel Cad., PK 718, Lefkoşa (Nicosia), Mersin 10, Türkiye; tel. 2283645; fax 2270782; e-mail ktto@ktto.net; internet www.ktto.net; f. 1958; Pres. TURGAY DENIZ; Sec.-Gen. AYSUN ÖNET ILERI; more than 9,000 mems.

Turkish Cypriot Chamber of Industry: 2 Organize Sanayi Bölgesi, 19 Cad., Lefkoşa (Nicosia), Mersin 10, Türkiye; tel. 2258131; fax 2258130; e-mail info@kibso.org; internet www.kibso.org; f. 1977; Pres. CANDAN AVUNDUK; Sec.-Gen. DOĞA DÖNMEZER.

EMPLOYERS' ORGANIZATION

Kıbrıs Türk İşverenler Sendikası (Turkish Cypriot Employers' Association): PK 674, Lefkoşa (Nicosia), Mersin 10, Türkiye; tel. 2273673; fax 2277479; internet fb.com/kibristurkisverenlersendikasi; Chair. HASAN SUNGUR.

UTILITIES

Cyprus Turkish Electricity Corpn (Kib-Tek): 140 Bedreddin Demirel Cad., Lefkoşa (Nicosia), Mersin 10, Türkiye; tel. 6000900; fax 2283851; e-mail info@kibtek.com; internet www.kibtek.com; Chair. HÜSEYIN PAŞA; Gen. Man. GÜRCAN ERDOĞAN.

MAJOR COMPANIES

Cypfruvex Ltd: Güzelyurt, PK 433, Lefkoşa (Nicosia), Mersin 10, Türkiye; e-mail info@cypfruvex.com; internet www.cypfruvex.com; f. 1974; state-owned; fruit exporters.

Cypri-Cola Co Ltd: Güzelyurt Karayolu, Kanlıköy Kavşağı, Alayköy, Lefkoşa (Nicosia), Mersin 10, Türkiye; tel. 2233420; fax 2233429; e-mail info@cypricola.com; internet www.cypricola.com; f. 1993; bottled water supplier.

Kıbrıs Türk Petrolleri Ltd, Şti (Turkish Cypriot Petroleum Co Ltd): Gazi Mağusa (Famagusta), Kalecik Tesisleri, PK 117, Mersin 10, Türkiye; tel. 3832646; fax 3832666; e-mail info@ktpetrolleri.com; internet www.ktpetrolleri.com; import, storage and distribution of petroleum and petroleum derivatives; 52% owned by OMV Petrol Ofisi AŞ (Türkiye); Gen. Man. CEM ARAT.

Kıbrıs Türk Tütün Endüstrisi Ltd (Turkish Cypriot Tobacco Industry Ltd): 27 Atatürk Cad., Lefkoşa (Nicosia), Mersin 10, Türkiye; tel. 2273403; fax 2273394; e-mail ktt@kibristutun.com; internet kibristutun.com; state-owned; cigarette mfrs; Chair. and Gen. Man. RAGIP BINGÖL.

TAŞEL (Turkish Spirits and Wine Enterprises Ltd): PK 48, Gazi Mağusa (Famagusta), Mersin 10, Türkiye; fax 2366330; e-mail sales@taselltd.com; internet www.taselltd.com; f. 1961; state-owned; mfrs of alcoholic beverages.

Toprak Ürünleri Kurumu (Agricultural Products Board): 12 Şht. Hüseyin Ali Arabacı Sok., Lefkoşa (Nicosia), Türkiye; tel. 2283211; fax 2284167; e-mail toprakkurum@hotmail.com; internet tuk.gov.ct.tr; state-owned; potato exporters; Chair. GÜRSEL UZUN.

TRADE UNIONS

Devrimci İşçi Sendikaları Federasyonu (Dev-İş) (Federation Of Revolutionary Workers' Trade Unions): 6 Serabioğlu Sok., 748 Lefkoşa (Nicosia), Mersin 10, Türkiye; tel. 2272640; fax 2286463; e-mail dev-is@dev-is.org; internet www.dev-is.org; f. 1976; affiliated to WFTU; Pres. KORAL AŞAM; Gen. Sec. ÖMER NAŞIT.

Kıbrıs Türk İşçi Sendikaları Federasyonu (TÜRK-SEN) (Turkish Cypriot Trade Union Federation): POB 829, 7–7A Şehit Mehmet R. Hüseyin Sok., Lefkoşa (Nicosia), Mersin 10, Türkiye; tel. 2272444; fax 2287831; internet www.turk-sen.org; f. 1954; regd 1955; affiliated to ITUC, the European Trade Union Confed., the Commonwealth Trade Union Council and the Confed. of Trade Unions of Türkiye (Türk-İş); Pres. ARSLAN BIÇAKLI; Gen. Sec. TAMAY SOYSAN.

Transport

SHIPPING

Until 1974 Gazi Mağusa (Famagusta), a natural port, was the island's most important harbour, handling about 83% of the country's cargo. Since its capture by the Turkish army in August of that year the port has been officially declared closed to international traffic. However, it continues to serve the Turkish-occupied region. Girne (Kyrenia) has also been declared closed to international traffic. A hydrofoil service operates between Girne (Kyrenia) and Mersin on the Turkish mainland. A ferry service between the Turkish provinceof Hatay and Gazi Mağusa (Famagusta) commenced operating in May 2022.

Ak-Günler Co Ltd: Girne (Kyrenia), Mersin 10, Türkiye; tel. 6508888; fax 8158647; e-mail info@akgunlerdenizcilik.com; internet akgunlerdenizcilik.com; f. 1978; operates a fleet of 5 passenger and cargo vessels; Man. Dir İÇIM KAVUKLU; Gen. Man. İBRAHIM BAŞTUĞ.

Fergün Shipping Co: Girne Yeni Liman Yolu, Fergün Apt 1, Girne (Kyrenia), Mersin 10, Türkiye; tel. 8151770; fax 8151989; e-mail info@fergun.net; internet www.fergun.net; ferries to Turkish ports; Owner FEHIM KÜÇÜK.

CIVIL AVIATION

In 1975 the Turkish authorities opened Ercan (formerly Tymbou) airport, and a second airport was opened at Geçitkale (Lefkoniko) in 1986. However, only Türkiye and Azerbaijan recognize the airports as legitimate points of entry; flights from all other countries involve a preliminary stopover at one of Türkiye's airports.

Fly Kıbrıs Havayolları (Fly KHY): Dr Burhan Nalbantoğlu Cad., Ortaköy 14A/14B, Lefkoşa (Nicosia), Mersin 10, Türkiye; tel. 8000549; e-mail yolcu@flykhy.com; internet www.flykhy.com; f. 2023; operated by Freebird Airlines (Türkiye); flights to Ankara, İzmir and Istanbul.

Tourism

North Cyprus Tourism Centre: Ministry of Tourism, Culture, Youth and Environment, Lefkoşa (Nicosia), Mersin 10, Türkiye; tel. 2289629; fax 2279675; e-mail info@northcyprus.cc; internet www.northcyprus.cc; headquarters based in London, UK.

Turkish Cypriot Tourism and Travel Agencies Association (Kıbrıs Türk Turizm ve Seyahat Acenteleri Birliği—KITSAB): Lefkoşa (Nicosia), Mersin 10, Türkiye; tel. 2285238; e-mail info@kitsab.org; internet kitsab.org; Pres. ORHAN TOLUN.

Defence

As assessed at November 2022, the 'TRNC' had an army of an estimated 3,000 regulars and 15,000 reserves. There was also a paramilitary armed police force of about 150. Men between 18 and 50 years of age are liable to 15 months' conscription. The 'TRNC' forces were being supported by an estimated 33,800 Turkish troops.

Defence Budget: TL 305.2m. in 2017.

Commander of 'TRNC' Security Forces: Maj.-Gen. ZORLU TOPALOĞLU.

Education

With the exception of private kindergartens, a vocational school of agriculture attached to the Ministry of Agriculture and Natural Resources, a training school for nursing and midwifery attached to the Ministry of Health, and a school for hotel catering attached to the Ministry of Tourism, Culture, Youth and Environment, all schools and educational institutes are administered by the Ministry of National Education.

Formal education covers pre-primary, primary, secondary and higher education. Pre-primary education is provided by kindergartens for children between the ages of 5 and 6. Primary education lasts for five years and caters for children aged 7–11. Secondary education is provided in two stages. The first stage (junior), lasting three years, is intended for pupils aged 12–14. The second stage consists of a three-year programme of instruction for pupils aged 15–17. Pupils elect either to prepare for higher education, to prepare for higher education with vocational training, or to prepare for vocational training only. This stage of education is free, but not compulsory.

The Eastern Mediterranean University, which is located near Gazi Mağusa (Famagusta), was opened in 1986. Other institutions providing higher education in the Turkish Cypriot zone are the Near East University in Lefkoşa (Nicosia); the Girne (Kyrenia) American University; the Anadolu University; the European University of Lefke (Levka); the International American University; the Cyprus International University; and the Teachers' Training College in Lefkoşa (Nicosia), which trains teachers for the elementary school stage. In 1982 an International Institute of Islamic Banking and Economics was opened to provide postgraduate training.

Bibliography

Aktar, Ayhan, Kızılyürek, Niyazi, and Özkırımlı, Umut (Eds). *Nationalism in the Troubled Triangle: Cyprus, Greece and Turkey.* Basingstoke, Palgrave Macmillan, 2010.

Alastos, D. *Cyprus in History.* London, Zeno Publishers, 1955.

Anastasiou, Harry. *The Broken Olive Branch: Nationalism, Ethnic Conflict and the Quest for Peace in Cyprus.* Two vols, Syracuse, NY, Syracuse University Press, 2006.

Asmussen, Jan. *Cyprus at War: Diplomacy and Conflict during the 1974 Crisis.* London, I. B. Tauris, 2008.

Bozkurt, Umut, and Trimikliniotis, Nicos (Eds). *Beyond a Divided Cyprus: A State and Society in Transformation.* New York, Palgrave Macmillan, 2012.

Burke, John. *Britain and the Cyprus Crisis of 1974: Conflict, Colonialism and the Politics of Remembrance in Greek Cypriot Society.* Abingdon, Routledge, 2017.

Briguglio, Lino. (Ed.) *Small States and the European Union: Economic Perspectives* (Europa Economic Perspectives series). Abingdon, Routledge, 2016.

Bryant, Rebecca. *Imagining the Modern: The Cultures of Nationalism in Cyprus.* New York, I. B. Tauris, 2004.

Calotychos, Vangelis (Ed.). *Cyprus and its People: Nation, Identity and Experience in an Unimaginable Community, 1955–97.* Abingdon, Routledge, 2021.

Charalambous, Giorgos, and Christophorou, Christophoros (Eds). *Party-Society Relations in the Republic of Cyprus: Political and Societal Strategies.* Abingdon, Routledge, 2015.

Cyprus: Treaty of Guarantee. Nicosia, 16 August 1960.

Crawshaw, Nancy. *The Cyprus Revolt: An Account of the Struggle for Union with Greece.* Abingdon, Routledge, 2022.

Diez, Thomas, and Tocci, Nathalie. (Eds). *Cyprus: A Conflict at the Crossroads.* Manchester, Manchester University Press, 2009.

Dodd, Clement H. (Ed.). *The Political, Social and Economic Development of Northern Cyprus*. Huntingdon, Eothen Press, 1993.

The History and Politics of the Cyprus Conflict. Basingstoke, Palgrave Macmillan, 2010.

Faustmann, Hubert, and Ker-Lindsay, James (Eds). *The Government and Politics of Cyprus*. Bern, Peter Lang, 2008.

Faustmann, Hubert, and Varnava, Andrekos (Eds). *Reunifying Cyprus: The Annan Plan and Beyond*. London, I. B. Tauris, 2009.

French, David. *Fighting EOKA: The British Counter-Insurgency Campaign on Cyprus, 1955-1959*. Oxford, Oxford University Press, 2015.

Foot, Sir Hugh. *A Start in Freedom*. London, Hodder & Stoughton Ltd, 1964.

Grivas (Dhigenis), George. *Guerrilla Warfare and EOKA's Struggle*. London, Longman, 1964.

Hakkı, Murat Metin. *The Cyprus Issue: A Documentary History, 1878–2006*. London, I. B. Tauris, 2007.

Hannay, David. *Cyprus: The Search for a Solution*. London, I. B. Tauris, 2005.

Hatzivassiliou, Evanthis. *Britain and the International Status of Cyprus, 1955–59* (Minnesota Mediterranean and East European Monographs). Minneapolis, MA, University of Minnesota, 1997.

The Cyprus Question, 1878-1960: the Constitutional Aspect (Minnesota Mediterranean and East European Monographs). Minneapolis, MA, University of Minnesota, 2002.

Henn, Francis. *A Business of Some Heat: The United Nations Force in Cyprus before and during the 1974 Turkish Invasion*. Barnsley, Pen and Sword Books, 2004.

Hill, Sir George. *A History of Cyprus*. 4 vols, London, 1940–1952.

Hitchens, Christopher. *Hostage to History: Cyprus from the Ottomans to Kissinger*. London, Verso Books, 1997.

Holland, Robert. *Britain and the Revolt in Cyprus, 1954–59*. Oxford, Clarendon Press, 1998.

Ker-Lindsay, James. *The Cyprus Problem: What Everyone Needs to Know*. Oxford, Oxford University Press, 2011.

Resolving Cyprus: New Approaches to Conflict Resolution. London, I. B. Tauris, 2014.

Ker-Lindsay, James, Faustmann, Hubert, and Mullen, Fiona. (Eds). *An Island in Europe: The EU and the Transformation of Cyprus*. London, I. B. Tauris, 2011.

Kızılyürek, Niyazi. *Bir hınç ve şiddet tarihi: Kıbrıs'ta statü kavgası ve etnik çatışma (A History of Resentment and Violence: The Fight for Status and Ethnic Conflict in Cyprus)*. İstanbul, İstanbul Bilgi University Press, 2016.

Koumoulides, John A. *Cyprus: The Legacy*. Bethesda, MD, University Press of Maryland, 1999.

Kyriakides, S. *Cyprus—Constitutionalism and Crisis Government*. Philadelphia, PA, University of Pennsylvania Press, 1968.

Kyris, George. *The Europeanisation of Contested Statehood: The EU in Northern Cyprus*. Farnham, Ashgate, 2015.

Leventis, Yiorghos. *The Struggle for Self-Determination in the 1940s: Prelude to Deeper Crisis*. New York, Peter Lang Publishing, 2002.

Loizides, Neophytos. *Designing Peace: Cyprus and Institutional Innovations in Divided Societies*. Philadelphia, PA, University of Pennsylvania Press, 2016.

Luke, Sir Harry C. *Cyprus under the Turks 1571–1878*. Oxford, Hurst & Co, 1921.

Mallinson, William. *Cyprus: A Modern History*. Revised edn, London, I. B. Tauris, 2008.

Partition through Foreign Aggression: The Case of Turkey in Cyprus (Minnesota Mediterranean and East European Monographs). Minneapolis, MN, Modern Greek Studies, University of Minnesota, 2010.

Kissinger and the Invasion of Cyprus: Diplomacy in the Eastern Mediterranean. Newcastle-upon-Tyne, Cambridge Scholars Publishing, 2016.

Markides, Diana Weston. *Cyprus 1957–1963: From Colonial Conflict to Constitutional Crisis: The Key Role of the Municipal Issue* (Minnesota Mediterranean and East European monographs). Minneapolis, MN, Modern Greek Studies, University of Minnesota, 2001.

Mehmet, Ozay. *Sustainability of Micro-States: The Case of North Cyprus*. Salt Lake City, UT, University of Utah Press, 2009.

Michael, Michális S., and Vural, Yücel (Eds). *Cyprus and the Roadmap for Peace: A Critical Interrogation of the Conflict*. Cheltenham, Edward Elgar Publishing, 2018.

Mirbagheri, Farid. *Cyprus and International Peacemaking, 1964–86*. London, Routledge, 1998.

Moran, Michael (Ed.). *Rauf Denktash at the United Nations: Speeches on Cyprus*. Huntingdon, Eothen Press, 1997.

Sovereignty Divided: Essays on the International Dimensions of the Cyprus Problem. Nicosia, CYREP, 1999.

Morgan, Tabitha. *Sweet and Bitter Island: A History of the British in Cyprus*. London, I. B. Tauris, 2010.

Panteli, Dr Stavros. *Historical Dictionary of Cyprus*. Lanham, MD, Scarecrow Press, 1995.

The History of Modern Cyprus. London, Interworld Publications, 2005.

Papadakis, Yiannis, Peristianis, N., and Welz, Gisela. (Eds). *Divided Cyprus: Modernity, History and an Island in Conflict*. Bloomington, IN, Indiana University Press, 2006.

Pericleous, Chrysostomos. *The Cyprus Referendum: A Divided Island and the Challenge of the Annan Plan*. London, I. B. Tauris, 2009.

Purcell, H. D. *Cyprus*. London, Benn, 1969.

Rappas, Alexis. *Cyprus in the 1930s: British Colonial Rule and the Roots of the Cyprus Conflict*. London, I. B. Tauris, 2014.

Richmond, Oliver P. *Mediating in Cyprus: The Cypriot Communities and the United Nations*. London, Frank Cass, 1998.

Richter, Heinz A. *A Concise History of Modern Cyprus: 1878–2009*. Ruhpolding, Verlag Frantz Philipp Rutzen, 2010.

Richter, Heinz A., and Fouskas, Vassilis K. (Eds). *Cyprus and Europe: The Long Way Back*. Möhnesee, Bibliopolis, 2003.

Sevcenko, Nancy P., and Moss, Christopher F. *Medieval Cyprus*. Princeton, NJ, Princeton University Press, 1999.

Sonyel, Salahi R. *Cyprus: The Destruction of a Republic. British Documents 1960–65*. Huntingdon, Eothen Press, 1997.

Soulioti, Soula. *Fettered Independence: Cyprus, 1878–1964* (Minnesota Mediterranean and East European Monographs). Minneapolis, MN, University of Minnesota, 2006.

Stefanidis, Ioannis D. *Isle of Discord: Nationalism, Imperialism and the Making of the Cyprus Problem*. New York, New York University Press, 1999.

Stefanou, Constantin. *Cyprus and the EU: The Road to Accession*. London, Ashgate, 2005.

Stergiou, Andreas. 'Turkey's Neo-Ottoman policy and the Greece-Israel-Cyprus Axis: Historical and Geopolitical Parameters', *Thetis*, Vol. 20, 2013, pp. 487–499.

'The exceptional case of the British Military Bases on Cyprus', *Middle Eastern Studies*, Vol. 51, No. 2, 2015, pp. 285–300.

'The Communist Party of Cyprus and Soviet policy in the Eastern Mediterranean', *Modern Greek Studies Yearbook*, Vol. 30/31, 2014/15, pp. 199–221.

'Euroscepticism in Cyprus' in Moreau, Patrick, and Wassenberg, Birte (Eds). *European Integration and New Anti-Europeanism Volume 2: the 2014 European Election and New Anti-European Forces in Southern, Northern and Eastern Europe*. Stuttgart, Franz Steiner, 2016, pp. 55–66.

Stergiou, Andreas, Kivanç, Ulusoy, and Blondheim, Menahem (Eds). *Conflict & Prosperity: Geopolitics and Energy in the Eastern Mediterranean*. Mamaroneck, NY, Israel Academic Press, 2017.

Theodore, John. *Cyprus and the Financial Crisis: The Controversial Bailout and what it Means for the Eurozone*. Basingstoke, Palgrave Macmillan, 2015.

Xypolia, Ilia. *British Imperialism and Turkish Nationalism in Cyprus, 1923-1939: Divide, Define and Rule*. Routledge, Abingdon, 2017.

Yennaris, Costas. *From the East: Conflict and Partition in Cyprus*. Sarasota, FL, Elliot & Thompson, 2004.

Yiangou, Anastasia, and Heraclidou, Antigone. *Cyprus from Colonialism to the Present: Visions and Realities: Essays in Honour of Robert Holland*. Routledge, Abingdon, 2017.

EGYPT

Geography

The Arab Republic of Egypt occupies the north-eastern corner of the African continent, with an extension across the Gulf of Suez into the Sinai region, which is usually regarded as lying in Asia. The area of Egypt is 1,009,450 sq km (389,751 sq miles). Egypt lies between latitudes 22°N and 32°N; the greatest distance from north to south is about 1,024 km (674 miles), and that from east to west is 1,240 km (770 miles), giving the country a roughly square shape, with the Mediterranean and Red Seas forming, respectively, the northern and eastern boundaries. Egypt has political frontiers on the east with Israel, on the south with Sudan and on the west with Libya. The actual frontiers run, in general, as straight lines drawn directly between defined points, and do not normally conform to geographical features. Between June 1967 and October 1973 the de facto frontier with Israel was the Suez Canal. As a result of the 1979 Peace Treaty, the frontier reverted to a line much further to the east (Documents on Palestine, see p. 1215). In June 2017 the Government prompted controversy within Egypt after President Abd al-Fatah al-Sisi ratified an agreement over the country's maritime border with Saudi Arabia, which included the concession of the Red Sea islands of Tiran and Sanafir to the latter (see History for further details).

PHYSICAL FEATURES

The remarkable persistence of cultural cohesion among the Egyptian people may largely be explained by the geography of the country. Egypt consists essentially of a narrow, trough-like valley, some 3 km–15 km wide, cut by the Nile river in the plateau of north-east Africa. At an earlier geological period a gulf of the Mediterranean Sea probably extended as far south as Cairo, but deposition of silt by the Nile has entirely filled this gulf, producing the fan-shaped Delta region (22,000 sq km in area), through which flow two main distributary branches of the Nile—the eastern, or Damietta, branch (240 km long) and the western, or Rosetta, branch (235 km), together with many other minor channels. As deposition of silt takes place, large stretches of water are gradually impounded to form shallow lakes, which later become firm ground. At present there are four such stretches of water in the north of the Delta: from east to west, and in order of size, lakes Menzaleh, Brullos, Idku and Mariut.

Upstream from Cairo the Nile Valley is at first 10 km–15 km in width, and, as the river tends to lie close to the eastern side, much of the cultivated land, and also most of the major towns and cities, lie on the western bank. Towards the south the river valley gradually narrows until, at about 400 km from the border with Sudan, it is no more than 3 km wide. Near Aswan there is an outcrop of resistant rock, chiefly granite, which the river has not been able to erode as quickly as the rest of the valley. This gives rise to a region of cascades and rapids that is known as the First Cataract. Four other similar regions occur on the Nile, but only the First Cataract lies within Egypt. The cataracts form a barrier to human movement upstream and serve to isolate the Egyptian Nile from territories further south. In Ancient Egypt, when river communications were of paramount importance, there was a traditional division of the Nile Valley into Lower Egypt (the Delta), Middle Egypt (the broader valley above the Delta) and Upper Egypt (the narrower valley as far as the cataracts). Nowadays, however, it is usual to speak merely of Upper and Lower Egypt, with the division occurring at Cairo.

The fertile strip of the Nile Valley is separated to the south by the cataracts and by the deserts and swamps of Sudan; to the north by the Mediterranean Sea; and to the east and west by desert plateaux. The land immediately to the east of the Nile Valley, known as the Eastern Highlands, is a complex region with peaks that rise 1,800 m to 2,100 m, but also deep valleys, which make travel difficult. Owing to aridity the whole region is sparsely populated, with a few partly nomadic shepherds, one or two monasteries and a number of small towns associated chiefly with the exploitation of minerals—petroleum, iron, manganese and granite—that occur in this region. Difficult landward communications mean that contact is mostly by sea, except in the case of the iron-fields. The Sinai, separated from the Eastern Highlands by the Gulf of Suez, is structurally very similar, but the general plateau level is tilted, giving the highest land (again nearly 2,100 m in elevation) in the extreme south, where it rises in bold scarps from sea level. Towards the north the land gradually slopes down, ultimately forming the low-lying sandy plain of the Sinai desert, which fringes the Mediterranean Sea. Owing to its low altitude and accessibility, the Sinai, in spite of its desert nature, has been for many centuries an important corridor linking Egypt with Asia.

West of the Nile occur the vast expanses known as the Western Desert. Though by no means uniform in height, the land surface is much lower than that to the east of the Nile, and within Egypt rarely exceeds 300 m above sea level. Parts are covered by extensive masses of light, shifting sand, which often form dunes, but in addition there are a number of large depressions, some of which actually reach to below sea level. These depressions seem to have been hollowed out by wind action, breaking up rock strata that were weakened by the presence of underground water, and most hollows still contain supplies of artesian water. In some instances (as, for example, the Qattara depression and the Wadi Natrun, respectively south-west and south-east of Alexandria) the subterranean water is highly saline and consequently useless for agriculture; however, in others—notably the oases of the Fayum, Siwa, Dakhlia, Behariya and Farafra—the water is suitable for irrigation purposes, and settlements have grown up within the desert.

CLIMATE

The main feature of the Egyptian climate is the almost uniform aridity. Alexandria, the wettest part, receives only 200 mm of rain annually, and most of the south has 80 mm or less. In many districts rain may fall in quantity only once every two or three years; consequently, throughout most of Egypt, including Cairo itself, the majority of the people live in houses made of unbaked, sun-dried brick. During the summer temperatures are extremely high, sometimes reaching 38°C–43°C and even 49°C in the southern and western deserts. The Mediterranean coast has cooler conditions, with a maximum of 32°C; as a result, the wealthier classes tend to move to Alexandria for the three months of summer. Winters are generally warm, with very occasional rain, but cold spells occur from time to time and light snow is not unknown. Owing to the large expanse of desert, hot dry sand-winds (called *khamsin*) are fairly frequent, particularly in spring, and much damage can be caused to crops; it has been known for the temperature to rise by 20°C in two hours, and the wind to reach 150 km per hour. Another unusual condition is the occurrence of early morning fog in Lower Egypt during spring and early summer. This has a beneficial effect on plant growth as it supplies moisture and is a partial substitute for rainfall.

IRRIGATION

With insufficient rainfall over the entire country, human existence in Egypt is heavily dependent on irrigation from the Nile. The river rises in the highlands of East Africa, with its main stream issuing from Lakes Victoria and Albert. In southern Sudan it flows sluggishly across a flat, open plain, where the fall in level is only 1:100,000. Here the shallow waters become a vast swamp, full of dense masses of papyrus vegetation, and this section of the Nile is called the Sudd ('blockage'). Finally, in the north of Sudan, the Nile flows in a well-defined channel and enters Egypt. In Upper Egypt the river is in the process of cutting its bed deeper into the rock floor, but in the lower part of its course silt is deposited, and the level of the land is rising—in some places by as much as 10 cm per century.

The salient feature of the Nile is its annual flood, which is caused by the onset of summer rains in East Africa and Ethiopia. The flood waters travel northward, reaching Egypt during August, and within Egypt the normal rise in river level was at first 6.4 m, declining to 4.6 m as irrigation works developed. This cycle of flooding had been maintained for many thousands of years until the construction of the Aswan High Dam made it a feature of the past so far as Egypt is concerned.

Originally, the flood waters were simply retained in specially prepared basins with earthen banks, and the water could then be used for three to four months after the flood. Within the last century, the building of large barrages, holding water all the year round, has allowed cultivation in any season. The old (basin) system allowed one or two crops per holding per year; the newer (perennial) system allows three or even four. In the past, barley and wheat were the main crops; under perennial irrigation maize and cotton, which can tolerate the great summer heat, provided they are watered, have assumed equal importance.

With most Egyptians entirely dependent upon Nile water, almost all the water entering Egypt is fully utilized. However, there are enormous losses by evaporation, which at present amount to some 70% of the total flow. Difficulties and opportunities over the use of Nile water were exemplified by the High Dam scheme at Aswan, which created a lake 500 km in length and 10 km wide that extends southwards across the Sudanese border. The High Dam is 3,600 m across, with a girth of 980 m at the river bed and 40 m at the top. It holds back one of the largest artificial lakes in the world (Lake Nasser), and enables large-scale storage of water from year to year, and the regular planned use of all Nile water independently of the precise amount of annual flood. Furthermore, 12 generator units incorporated into the dam give considerable quantities of low-cost electric power. The dam was completed in July 1970 and officially inaugurated in January 1971.

However, adverse effects were soon noticed: scouring of the Nile bed below the dam; increased salinity in the lower stretches; reduced sedimentation below the dam and heavy deposition within the basin, resulting in the need for greater use of artificial fertilizers, which must be imported; and, perhaps more seriously, the disappearance of fish (particularly sardines) off the Mediterranean coast of Egypt. Possibly the most disturbing effect of all was a notable rise in the water table in some areas, owing to hydrostatic pressures, and the year-round presence of water. Besides disturbing irrigation systems (which are adapted to pre-existing conditions), salinity and gleying of a more permanent nature began to appear; reports of bilharzia and other parasitic diseases increased; and the appearance of the plant water hyacinth threatened to choke irrigation systems.

POPULATION

According to the census of 2006, the population of Egypt stood at 72,798,031. By the next census, held in April 2017, this figure had risen to 94,798,827. Official estimates put the population at 102,878,749 at 1 January 2022, giving a population density of 101.9 people per sq km. However, this figure obscured the fact that the overwhelming majority of the population lives within the Nile Valley (just 4% of the country's total area) and, therefore, population density in its major settlements is much higher. According to projections by the United Nations, the capital, Cairo (and its suburbs), had a population of 22,183,201 at mid-2023. Other major cities included Alexandria (5,588,477) and Port Said (778,280). Work on the construction of a new administrative capital city, situated 45 km to the east of Cairo, began in 2018. The country's key state institutions (including government ministries, parliament and the presidential headquarters) began to be transferred to the new city in late 2021. When fully constructed, the new city was expected to accommodate 6.5m. people.

Arabic, the official language, is the language of almost all Egyptians, although there are very small numbers of Berber language-speaking villages in the western oases. Newspapers in English and French have an important circulation in Cairo and Alexandria. Small groups of Greeks and Armenians are also a feature of the larger Egyptian towns. The Arabic name for Egypt, Misr, is always used within the country itself.

History

VAUGHN SHANNON

Egypt has a long, storied past as a place of civilization, an empire, a protectorate and a modern state. Successive Egyptian rulers conquered and were conquered, and the country has played a major role in antiquity as well as contemporary regional and international politics. This essay traces Egypt's history through the ages, with an emphasis on the defining domestic and international trends of the country today.

DYNASTIES AND EMPIRES THROUGH THE AGES

Early inhabitant settlements of the Nile Valley can be traced as far back as 7,000 BCE, bringing one of the earliest human civilizations and, with it, techniques of agriculture and irrigation, as well as the development of the hieroglyphic writing system. The 'pre-dynastic era' gave way to Egyptian dynastic empires, often divided into Old Kingdom, Middle Kingdom and New Kingdom periods. Each period had several dynasties and rulers within those dynasties, some of great historical consequence. The Old Kingdom (between c. 2575 BCE and 2130 BCE) included the construction and use of the Great Pyramids of Giza as burial temples. The Middle Kingdom (c. 1938 BCE–1630 BCE) was characterized by less powerful and centralized rule, as well as the flourishing of art and literature. Fortresses constructed in this period indicated the need to defend against rising outside powers; external threats included recurrent episodes of conflict with the Nubian kingdoms, leading to a brief period of Nubian rule, which ended the Middle Period.

A blend of Assyrian and Persian influences characterized the later dynastic cultural and political regimes of the New Kingdom (c. 1539 BCE–1075 BCE). Notable during this period was the reign of the first female ruler, Hatshepsut (born c. 1507 BCE), who ruled between c. 1473 BCE and 1458 BCE; Akhenaten's controversial flirtation with monotheism (1379 BCE–1336 BCE); and the reign of Akhenaten's son, Tutankhamun (Tut Ankh Amon), although the latter is renowned in the West more for the spectacle of his archaeological discovery than for any accomplishments achieved during his lifetime, given his premature demise at the age of around 19 years, in 1325 BCE. In the fourth century BCE, Alexander the Great of the ancient Greek kingdom of Macedon and his successor Ptolemaic kingdoms ruled the Mediterranean, developing the port city of Alexandria into a centre of power and learning. Cleopatra, the last vestige of the dynastic era, was of Ptolemaic lineage and ruled with her brother Ptolemy XIV in 51 BCE–30 BCE before Egypt succumbed to the Roman Empire. Her affair with the Roman statesman Julius Caesar and, following the latter's assassination, her subsequent marriage to the Roman politician and general Mark Antony intertwined the fates of all involved, with the forces of Caesar's successor, Octavian (also known as Caesar Augustus), defeating the allied forces of Antony and Cleopatra in 31 BCE.

The Byzantine Empire, the successor to the Roman Empire, held sway over most of modern Egypt until the arrival of the Islamic armies from Arabia. The Rashid Caliphate, which ruled the Islamic community following the death of the Prophet Muhammad in 632 CE, spread the religion far and wide, including to Egypt in 640. The Umayyad Caliphate came to power in 661 and quickly adopted dynastic characteristics of its own, ruling Egypt and elsewhere out of Damascus, Syria, until being overthrown by the Sunni Muslim Abbasid dynasty in 750, which governed from Baghdad, Iraq, with a less firm hand on the further reaches of the Islamic world. Umayyads in Spain and Idrisids in Morocco broke away from a united Islamic caliphate, and Egypt would see local challenges as well, with the Shi'a Muslim Fatimids coming to power in the 10th century.

Roman and Byzantine crusades to 'take back' the holy lands in Palestine and fight for safe pilgrimage for Christians against Seljuk Turk raiders led to the formation of a Crusader state in neighbouring Jerusalem and the eastern shores of the Mediterranean. Saladin, a Kurdish Sunni Muslim who abolished the weakening Fatimid Caliphate in 1171 and formally reinstituted Sunni Islam in Egypt, became the first Sultan of Egypt in 1171, subsequently proving his mettle on the battlefield, and in politics and diplomacy, from Syria. Subsequent Crusader invasions were repelled with the help of the Mamluk, who then overthrew the Ayyubid dynasty to rule Egypt from the 13th century until the advent of the Ottoman Empire in the 16th century. This vast Turkish empire, based in the Anatolian Plateau, ruled over a large area stretching from North Africa to Arabia and Eastern Europe.

ENTER EUROPE

Although the Ottoman Empire would last until the First World War (1914–18), its hold on Egypt was challenged by rising European powers France and the United Kingdom. Napoleon's forces landed in 1798 as part of his ambitions of conquest and cultural exploration. The British joined the Ottomans in repelling the French from Egypt, and Muhammad Ali assumed control in 1805. Ali and his sons ruled an increasingly modern and expansive territory in Egypt, which enjoyed growing autonomy from a weakening Ottoman Empire.

One modernizing project implemented in conjunction with the French was the construction of the Suez Canal between 1859 and 1869, which deepened involvement from European commercial and colonial interests within Egypt and the broader Middle East region. Falling on economic hard times and struggling under the burden of accumulating debts, the Egyptian Government reached out to the British Government for financial assistance, giving the UK a stake in the Suez Canal and the country, both of which the latter regarded as of key importance in the defence of British India. Opposition to the British military presence and Tawfiq Pasha, who was appointed *khedive* (viceroy) of Egypt in 1879, precipitated a nationalist uprising. The British quashed the Urabi Revolt in September 1882 and occupied Egypt, establishing firm control over the country in a period of rule dubbed the Veiled Protectorate, although Egypt remained, nominally, an Ottoman province. British conquest extended to form Anglo-Egyptian Sudan, provoking uprisings and independence movements in both countries of the condominium. Formal protectorate status was conferred on Egypt in 1914.

Among the forces pushing for change within Egypt was the Wafd Party, a nationalist liberal political party that was founded in 1919. In 1866 the first ever Arab parliament had been formed, although it lacked effective power under Ottoman and subsequently British rule. A Wafd delegation headed by Saad Zaghlul pressed for liberal reforms, and for a presence at the Paris Peace Conference following the end of the First World War. Nominal independence was granted to Egypt in 1922, with a constitutional monarchy under King Fuad and, from 1936, his successor King Farouk. Although the 1936 Anglo-Egyptian Treaty led to a withdrawal of British forces, functionally, the British remained the power behind the throne. Some British troops were permitted to remain in the Suez Canal Zone to ensure the waterway's security.

Opposition to British rule came in many forms, and nominal independence did not buy legitimacy for the British-backed monarchs. A major force in Egyptian and regional politics for decades to come was the Muslim Brotherhood. Founded by Islamic scholar Hassan al-Banna, this Sunni Muslim organization promoted charity, religious piety and an anti-colonial political agenda against the Western-backed regime. It sought the creation of an Islamic state in Egypt, if not the broader Islamic world, thus putting it at odds with not only Western powers but also local monarchical or secular nationalist rulers.

The Second World War (1939–45) led the UK to reassert itself in Egypt, given the strategic value of the Suez Canal amid the conflict in North Africa against Nazi Germany. In 1942 Britain forced King Farouk to allow the formation of a pro-British Wafdist Government under the premiership of Nahas Pasha. The pan-Arab Nahas left office in October 1944, but returned to power in January 1950, abrogating the Anglo-Egyptian Treaty and calling for the withdrawal of British forces from the Suez Canal Zone. An increasingly activist Muslim Brotherhood protested against Wafd rule and embarked upon a campaign of bombings and assassinations, as a result of which the movement was banned. The battle between the state and the Muslim Brotherhood continued, however, with the assassination of Prime Minister Mahmud Fahmi al-Nuqrashi in 1948, and the apparent reprisal killing of al-Banna in 1949.

Despite domestic political disgruntlement and efforts to force the British out of the Suez Canal Zone, the British clung on to power in Egypt. However, as in other post-war colonial holdings, British control was strained by anti-colonial fervour and British military decline in an increasingly bipolar world shaped by US and Soviet influence.

THE INDEPENDENT EGYPTIAN REPUBLIC

In July 1952 the Free Officers Movement, a group of Egyptian nationalist officers serving in the Egyptian and Sudanese armed forces, seized power in the Egyptian capital, Cairo, forcing the abdication of the Western-backed King Farouk but allowing his (infant) son Ahmad Fuad II to ascend to the throne, alongside a government of amenable politicians. Political wrangling ensued, leading power increasingly to devolve to the Free Officers' nine-member Revolutionary Command Council (RCC). The RCC abrogated the Constitution in December and dissolved all political parties in January 1953. In June the monarchy was formally abolished and Egypt was proclaimed a republic, which was to be governed by the RCC for a three-year transition period.

A truly independent Egypt took the world stage on the backs of military power and revolutionary nationalism that would reverberate throughout the region and in Egypt's political future. Military officers assumed political positions: Gen. Muhammad Nagib (Neguib) as President and Prime Minister, and Col Gamal Abdel Nasser as Deputy Prime Minister and Minister of the Interior. Internal struggles led eventually to Neguib's removal in 1954 and Nasser's accession to the presidency, in an interim capacity, in November of that year. In June 1956 a new Constitution was approved by public referendum, and Nasser was elected President, with 99.9% of the vote.

The resulting Arab Republic was a unitary presidential system of limited democratic participation. A one-party state, the Arab Socialist Party dominated the People's Assembly (Majlis al-Sha'ab). Wary of monarchical dynastic regimes, as well as of other Arabist movements such as the Baathists of Syria and Iraq, Nasser peddled instead 'Nasserism', a combination of pan-Arabism, anti-colonialism and Arab socialism (an agenda remarkably similar to the Baathist platform). The recovery of wealth and resources from the former colonial masters and their redistribution among the people became a popular theme in the Arab world, Iran and other post-colonial countries in the 1950s.

Pan-Arabism was a phenomenon, and Nasser was the charismatic face of the regional movement, but he was not without international detractors, regional competitors and domestic opponents. The Muslim Brotherhood, seeing Nasser's message rooted in Arabism rather than Islam, and seeing ego rather than humility to God, opposed his regime despite its anti-Western stance. The attempted assassination of Nasser by members of the Muslim Brotherhood on 26 October 1954 led to a cycle of arrests and violence between the military and state on the one hand and conservative Islamist elements of society on the other that echoed through the decades. Among the leaders imprisoned was Sayyid Qutb, whose writings from prison connected external rulers and apostate rulers who strayed from the path of true Islam, advocating and justifying violent jihad on religious and historical grounds in his book *Ma'alim fi al-Tariq* (Signposts Along the Road), published in 1964. In 1966 Qutb was convicted of plotting the attempt to assassinate Nasser and was executed. However, his writings became widely shared following his death and helped to spawn violent radicalized groups, including Islamic Jihad (later reconstituted as Egyptian Islamic Jihad) in 1979.

REGIONAL AND INTERNATIONAL DETRACTORS

A key foreign policy concern for Egypt was the fate of the British mandate of Palestine on Egypt's eastern border. Having been controlled by the Ottoman Empire until the First World War, Palestine and Transjordan came under British control from 1920, as a result of the League of Nations' Mandate for Palestine. After the British relinquished control in 1948, an international proposal to partition Palestine into separate Jewish and Arab sovereign states (UN Security Council Resolution 181 of November 1947) was accepted by the Jewish leadership but opposed by Egypt and other Arab states. The World Zionist Organization and the Jewish Agency for Palestine (subsequently renamed the Jewish Agency for Israel) declared an independent State of Israel on 14 May 1948, triggering the 1948 Arab-Israeli War, in which multiple countries jockeyed for position in Palestine, with Egyptian forces fighting as much to gain territory as to oppose Israel's creation per se. By the end of the war in July 1949, Egypt had gained control of the Gaza Strip along the Mediterranean, abutting Egypt's Sinai Peninsula.

From the start, the League of Arab States (Arab League) refused to acknowledge the State of Israel, which was seen as a European colonial occupier of Arab lands forced upon the region by outside great powers. Egypt notably ramped up its rhetoric against Israel after Nasser became President in the wake of the Free Officers' coup. Egypt blockaded Israel's Straits of Tiran in the Red Sea, despite UN resolutions calling for Israel's right to transit international waters. Skirmishes increased around demilitarized zones established in the 1949 armistice, and raids into Israel from Egyptian-controlled Gaza began, using what came to be known as Palestinian fedayeen (militants). Israel engaged in raids of its own into Gaza, including in February 1955 against an Egyptian base, escalating bilateral tensions.

The USA was initially wary of openly extending economic and military support to Israel, partly out of concern for Arab world opposition in an emerging Cold War climate in which diplomatic battles for allies were constant against the superpower foe, the Union of Soviet Socialist Republics (USSR). Israel tried to sow discord between the USA and Arab states, at one point staging a bombing of a US installation in Egypt and blaming Egypt for the violence, in the so-called Lavon Affair in 1954.

Egypt's concerns and politics led it to seek assistance of its own in the East. The publicity surrounding a Czech arms deal in 1955, which revealed the possibility of Egypt becoming a client of the USSR, raised alarm in Israel and the West. At first, the USA and the UK tried to court Egypt, collectively promising US $70m. in aid to help finance the construction of the Aswan High Dam on the River Nile in December 1955. However, owing to the escalation of Nasser's anti-Western rhetoric and flirtations with the USSR, the USA and the UK both withdrew their offers of support in mid-July 1956. This pushed Nasser firmly into the camp of the Soviets, who had offered to help fund and build the High Dam.

THE SUEZ CRISIS, 1956

On 26 July 1956 President Nasser announced the nationalization of the Suez Canal, stating that revenue earned from the canal would help to finance construction of the High Dam. Both the British and French were concerned by this development, as was the young state of Israel, which still lived in the shadow of Egypt and other Arab states that refused to recognize its existence. Israel conspired with the UK and France to stage an operation during which Israel would invade the Sinai Peninsula, and French and British forces would then seize the Suez Canal in the name of peacekeeping between the warring parties. By intervening militarily, the British would regain control of the Canal and with it the vital waterway connecting the Mediterranean with the Indian Ocean.

The plan unfolded on the eve of the 1956 US presidential election, with Israeli forces crossing into Sinai on 29 October and advancing towards the Suez Canal. Incumbent US President Dwight Eisenhower, coasting to re-election, was playing golf when informed about the development. Security briefings indicated Israel's collusion with the USA's erstwhile allies France and the UK, prompting anger from Washington owing to the implications for the West's standing in the so-called Third World (countries that were not aligned either with communism or democratic capitalism). The USA and the USSR, Cold War nemeses, were united in their condemnation of Israel's actions as well as the French and British charade of conducting a peacekeeping operation. The USA reasserted its leadership in the West, chided Israel and made efforts to clarify that the USA and the 'Free World' were not in the business of imperialism.

At the same time, the USA negotiated a withdrawal of warring parties that granted Israel some security guarantees related to safe passage in the Straits of Tiran and the stationing of UN peacekeepers in Sinai. During 1956–66 a fairly stable, albeit fragile, peace was maintained, punctuated by skirmishes and reprisals conducted by Israeli forces and Palestinian fedayeen and nationalists operating across the borders from Syria, Gaza and the Jordanian-controlled West Bank.

Pan-Arabism set the region alight in revolutionary anti-colonial fervour well beyond Egypt, including Syria. In February 1958 Egypt and Syria combined to form the United Arab Republic (UAR), based on mutual defence agreements forged during the Suez crisis. Both were hostile to Israel and the West, and increasingly clients of the USSR. They invited Yemen to join a looser confederation of United Arab States in 1958, in a show of Arab unity that appeared to confirm the concerns of Western powers.

However, the UAR of Egypt and Syria proved short-lived. The first National Assembly of the UAR opened in Cairo in July 1960, and by December 1961 the experiment was over. Syrian elements were unhappy as junior partners, and after the Syrian military seized control in Damascus in September 1961, Nasser acquiesced to the insurgents' demands to end the union. Attempts at Arab unity under the UAR banner took place sporadically thereafter, and a new National Congress of Popular Forces', with broader representation across both Egypt and Syria, met in Cairo in May 1962. The Arab Socialist Union was founded as Egypt's sole political organization, chaired by Nasser, and a new system of government was introduced, based on quasi-democratic elections and patronage. However, coups in Iraq and Syria in February and March 1963, respectively, brought Baathists to power, who were aligned with one another and in opposition to Nasser's visions and power. More changes disrupted Syrian-Iraqi collaboration and from early 1965 Egypt worked with Iraq under a Unified Political Command, although progress was limited. The remnants of the UAR faced economic hurdles and loan default, as well as political splintering in the Arab world, especially against the Gulf monarchies with whom Egypt fought a proxy war over the fate of Yemen in the Arabian Peninsula. Meanwhile, Nasser was re-elected as President at a referendum held in March 1965, securing more than 99% of the votes cast.

THE SIX-DAY WAR, 1967

Emboldened by the signing of a mutual defence pact between Egypt and Syria in November 1966, a newly assertive Syria both increased both support to the Palestinians and intensified air raids on Israel's north-eastern frontier. In early 1967 Syria and Israel exchanged artillery fire in the disputed Golan

Heights area. Nasser warned Israel of Egypt's commitments to Syria under the joint defence pact. Following further clashes with Israel in April, Syria reached out to Egypt for assistance, which Nasser gave in the form of more vague threats as well as the mobilization of Egyptian forces. In the ensuing crisis, other Arab states also mobilized their armies. By the end of May Egypt had ordered UN peacekeepers to leave Egypt and had blockaded the Straits of Tiran. Nasser asserted that the armies of Egypt, Jordan, Syria and Lebanon were 'poised on the borders ... to face the challenge', noting that 'the critical hour has arrived', in which their actions would 'astound the world'.

Most accounts suggest that the Arab side was full of bluff and bluster, rather than genuinely preparing to initiate an invasion intent on annihilation. The USA, mindful of handing a propaganda victory to the USSR, adopted the middle ground, trying to constrain Israeli action while reassuring them of US support on the matter of security and the blockade. Perhaps sensing more an opportunity than a threat, Israel chose pre-emptively to wage war and thus end the stalemate, hoping to capitalize on the element of surprise to seize territory and shore up its defences. Thus, on 5 June 1967 the so-called 'Six-Day War' began, with Israel launching attacks on Egyptian forces, followed by attacks against Syria and Jordan. A UN call for a ceasefire was issued, and Israeli incursions into Syria on 9 June led the USSR to threaten to stop Israel by any necessary means, 'including military', risking a global escalation of the situation. However, Syria agreed to a truce on 10 June and all fighting had ceased by the following day.

The consequences of the Six-Day War for Egypt were twofold. First, Israel delivered a humiliating defeat to Nasser and his array of pan-Arab allies, already bogged down in Yemen's civil war. In the immediate aftermath of the defeat, Nasser announced his resignation as President, accepting responsibility for Egypt's humiliation. Following widespread public protests against his decision, he retracted his resignation, remaining in office until his death in 1970. However, Nasser was forced to withdraw from Yemen, reducing his clout as a regional player and leader. Second, Israel seized control of areas of land that became known as the Occupied Territories, including the Gaza Strip and the Sinai Peninsula from Egypt. This development had significant security and economic consequences for Egypt, leading to austerity policies that fuelled anti-Government protests into 1968.

No state recognized Israel's right to retain the Occupied Territories as its own, and the question of who should control them became the focus of intense diplomacy and, at times, conflict. The pre-1967 borders of Israel, which were themselves intended as demarcation lines rather than permanent borders and were effectively frozen in armistice pending future settlement, are conventionally known as the Green Line (related to the colour of the line drawn in the 1949 armistice map). The post-war Occupied Territories were clearly located outside the Green Line. In November 1967 UN Security Council Resolution 242 set out the international position on the war and the territories—a position that has guided most negotiations ever since. In short, the resolution is a 'land for peace' formulation based on two expectations: first, the withdrawal of Israeli forces from territories occupied in the Six-Day War; and second, the termination of all claims of belligerency, as well as respect for and acknowledgement of the sovereignty, territorial integrity and political independence of every state in the area and their right to live in peace within secure and recognized boundaries.

While seemingly clear at first sight—Israel returns the Occupied Territories, while the Arab states recognize Israel and make peace with it—the ambiguities upon closer scrutiny of the wording of Resolution 242 included a lack of clarity about whether withdrawal or recognition should come first and whether Israel needed to withdraw from all, or just some, of the territories occupied during the Six-Day War (the word 'the' not appearing before 'territories' in the English-language version of the resolution). Arab states argued that Israel should withdraw from all of the Occupied Territories before any discussion regarding formal recognition took place, while Israel maintained that withdrawal could be a matter of discretion and, in any case, would be effected only after recognition and assurances of peace from its neighbours. Despite exhortations and diplomatic efforts by multilateral forums and bilateral allies, there was no immediate change in the new status quo.

The Arab League summit meeting held in Khartoum, Sudan, in August–September 1967 had affirmed the 'Three Noes of Khartoum'—no peace with, no negotiations with and no recognition of Israel. Resolution 242 would not change this. Instead, the emboldened Israelis ploughed ahead with settlement building in the Occupied Territories, while Arab states, smarting from the humiliation of the war, continued to harass and seek to isolate Israel, in what came to be known as the 'War of Attrition', while simultaneously promoting the Palestinian cause on the world stage. Among these states, Egypt and Syria would seek to avenge themselves and to recover their lost lands.

FROM PAN-ARABISM TO EGYPTIAN NATIONALISM

Following Nasser's sudden death on 28 September 1970, the Vice-President, Col Anwar Sadat, was appointed interim President; he was subsequently confirmed in the role at a national referendum. A pragmatic Egyptian nationalist, President Sadat abandoned the pan-Arab populist agenda in favour of focusing on reclaiming the Sinai Peninsula. A reformed Constitution introduced in 1971 permitted opposition parties, interest groups and limited press freedom in a system that some observers described as 'authoritarian but with a greater tolerance of political pluralism'. Even the Muslim Brotherhood was permitted a degree of freedom. The Arab Socialist Union was dissolved in October 1978 and was succeeded by the National Democratic Party (NDP), although many of the same establishment interests were represented in the new party.

Sadat's pragmatic nationalism made Egypt less radical internationally. A US-initiated ceasefire plan in June 1970, which called for a 90-day ceasefire in the still unsettled Sinai Peninsula and the Suez Canal Zone, had been agreed to by Nasser shortly before his death. Sadat reaffirmed Egypt's commitment to the ceasefire, and extended it indefinitely. Jordan and Israel followed suit. However, ceasefires do not equate to peace, and Sadat remained determined to restore pride and territory, by force if necessary. He publicly sought a partial Israeli withdrawal from the Sinai Peninsula by the end of 1971, which was advocated by the USA; however, this did not happen, increasing the possibility of renewed conflict.

On 6 October 1973—the Jewish holiday of Yom Kippur—Egypt and Syria attacked Israeli positions in Sinai and the Golan Heights. Initial attacks penetrated deep into Israeli-held territory, as Israeli forces were unprepared. Through the lens of the Cold War, the USA became concerned about the fate of Israel against its Soviet-sponsored Arab neighbours, and began to supply the country with arms and aid, while at the same time pressurizing it to accept a ceasefire proposal. When Egypt rejected the ceasefire proposal, the Administration of US President Richard Nixon ordered a full-scale airlift to Israel and raised the US military state of alert to defense readiness condition (DefCon) 3, largely to send a message to the USSR that, in the words of US Secretary of State Henry Kissinger, the USA would not 'allow a Soviet-supported operation to succeed against an American-supported operation'. At the same time, the USA was under the new pressure of an oil embargo imposed by Arab members of the Organization of Petroleum Exporting Countries (OPEC), creating an economic toll for US support for Israel. Seeking to defuse the crisis, the USA and the USSR jointly brokered UN Security Council Resolution 338, adopted on 22 October 1973, which called for a ceasefire, the implementation of Resolution 242 and negotiations for a 'just and durable peace in the Middle East'. Although both Egypt and Israel accepted the terms of Resolution 338, the fighting continued, necessitating the adoption of a follow-up resolution, adopted on 23 October, which reasserted the conditions of Resolution 338 and requested that the UN Secretary-General dispatch UN observers to monitor the observance of the ceasefire by both sides. After 18 days of fighting, the war (subsequently dubbed the Yom Kippur War or October War) was over.

The 1973 conflict proved a costly awakening for all sides: Egypt found that it could not win back land by force of arms, Israel found that it was not invincible, and the USA found that there was a price for its complicated relationship with Israel, vis-à-vis the Arab world as well as within the broader Cold War context. The USA worked enthusiastically after the war to be a leader in promoting Middle East peace, with Kissinger, during the Administrations of Presidents Nixon and Gerald Ford, engaging in 'shuttle diplomacy' to secure agreements for disengagement between a chastened Israel and Egypt, as well Syria. Sadat's openness to peace coincided with the election in Israel in 1977 of the Likud (Consolidation) Government, led by Prime Minister Menachem Begin. Sadat stunned the region with a call to address the Israeli parliament, the Knesset, which Israel accepted. Sadat's public call for peace in the seat of Israeli government signalled historic opportunities for the two states, even as it signalled the end of pan-Arabism and of Sadat's clout in the Arab world. Nevertheless, US President Jimmy Carter, who had taken office in January 1977, nurtured talks between the two countries, inviting both heads of state to the Camp David presidential retreat. The main document of the resultant Camp David Accords of 1978 concerned a pledge for a phased Israeli withdrawal from the occupied Sinai Peninsula in exchange for normalization of relations. US pledges of aid and assistance helped to solidify the deal, so Egypt had gone from Soviet client to US ally within the decade. (While Egypt made a good show of promoting Palestinian rights, concerns about Palestinians were put in a separate document, with vague pledges for future conferences and discussions.) A formal Egypt-Israel peace treaty was signed in March 1979. Begin thus won peace on Israel's western front, which persists to the present day, while Sadat, who had been awarded the Nobel Peace Prize in 1978, secured the return to Egypt of Sinai. However, Sadat's peace with Israel and secular nationalist rule inflamed extremist members into action against him. In October 1981, during a parade to commemorate the October 1973 war, military officers connected with the Egyptian Islamic Jihad opened fire on Sadat, killing the President and six diplomats.

STATE OF EMERGENCY: MUBARAK YEARS

With Sadat's assassination came a new leader and a new sense of crisis. Hosni Mubarak assumed the presidency in October 1981, and imposed martial law under a state of emergency that would remain in place for the next three decades.

Radical Islamist groups were a cause of concern for the regime and its allies, but eventual distinctions and relaxations were made within the context of emergency rule. In 1992 extremist Islamist groups such as Gama'ah al-Islamiyah and Egyptian Islamic Jihad carried out attacks on government targets and tourists, threatening lives as well as an important economic lifeline in Egypt. Attacks on tourists continued through the 1990s, as did attacks on indigenous Coptic Christians and even attempts on the life of Mubarak himself. In November 1997 six members of Gama'ah al-Islamiyah killed 58 foreign tourists and four Egyptian nationals at Deir el-Bahri (the Temple of Hatshepsut) in Luxor, one of Egypt's most popular tourist attractions. Revulsion over the Luxor massacre—which was orchestrated by prominent cleric Ayman al-Zawahiri, the leader of Egyptian Islamic Jihad—had a devastating impact on the Egyptian tourism industry in the short term, and turned public opinion in Egypt firmly against radical Islamism.

The Government responded with crackdowns on militant groups and increased security at tourist sites. At the same time, it reached out to groups that were willing to renounce violence. Legislation implemented in 1998 eased restrictions on some apolitical non-governmental organizations (NGOs) while cracking down more firmly on oppositional advocacy groups. Muslim Brotherhood was banned under the law, while Gama'ah al-Islamiyah disavowed violence and its members were eventually granted prison releases in exchange for the cessation of armed acts of violence.

EGYPT'S INTERNATIONAL RELATIONS AFTER THE COLD WAR

The end of the Cold War allowed Egypt to rebuild its regional and international relations. Egypt's participation in a coalition against Iraq's invasion of Kuwait in August 1990 repaired some political ties with the Gulf states and Syria. Egypt became a leader in promoting nuclear non-proliferation, hosting the signing of the African Nuclear-Weapon-Free Zone Treaty in Cairo in April 1996. Following the signing by Israel and the Palestine Liberation Organization of the Oslo Accords—the Declaration of Principles on Interim Self-Government Arrangements, signed in Washington, DC, USA, in September 1993; and the Interim Agreement on the West Bank and the Gaza Strip, signed in Taba, Egypt, in September 1995, which led to the creation of the Palestinian National Authority, Egypt offered its hand as intermediary in negotiations between the two sides. However, this role was suspended after Israel's Likud Government refused to implement the Wye River Memorandum, which was signed between Israel and the Palestinians in Maryland, USA, in October 1998, and which was intended to resume implementation of the 1995 Interim Agreement.

Meanwhile, Omar Abd al-Rahman, an Egyptian cleric and leader of Gama'ah al-Islamiyah, plotted a bomb attack on the World Trade Center in New York, USA, which killed six people in February 1993 but failed in its goal of bringing down the North and South 'Twin' Towers. Prominent Egyptian cleric Ayman al-Zawahiri, together with Osama bin Laden, the Saudi-born leader of the militant Islamist group al-Qa'ida, and three others jointly issued a World Islamic Front Statement in February 1998, calling on Muslims to 'kill the Americans and their allies—civilian and military' as 'an individual duty ... in order for their armies to move out of all the lands of Islam'. Later that year the US embassies in Kenya and Tanzania were attacked, prompting a US retaliatory strike against suspected al-Qa'ida targets in Sudan and Afghanistan. Egypt criticized the US strikes, as well as subsequent attacks against Iraq in December 1998, straining tensions with the USA for a time.

After the 11 September 2001 terrorist attacks in the USA, the Administration of US President George W. Bush ramped up its Global War on Terrorism and a Freedom Agenda that sought to promote democracy in the Middle East and elsewhere. Egypt would factor into both aspects of US foreign policy. Both the US Government and the Egyptian Government had an interest in combating Islamist terror networks, increasing security for US citizens and other nationals and pushing ahead with the prosecution of suspected terrorists. The USA deported a member of Egyptian Islamic Jihad to Egypt for trial in 2002 in connection with the assassination of President Sadat, while Egypt assisted with the investigation into a fatal shooting at Los Angeles International Airport perpetrated by an Egyptian immigrant (although this was ultimately deemed not to have been terrorism-related).

The push from Washington for democratic reforms in the Middle East pressurized authoritarian allies to soften their touch and implement reforms. In May 2005 the People's Assembly in Egypt approved a constitutional amendment providing for multi-candidate presidential elections, although opposition parties, including for the New Wafd Party (New Delegation Party), the Arab Democratic Nasserist Party and the National Progressive Unionist Party (NPUP, or Tagammu), criticized the strict conditions placed on the eligibility of prospective candidates. Independent candidates seeking to run for the presidency were henceforth required to obtain 250 signatures in support of their nomination, including 65 from parliamentarians, 25 from members of the upper house—the Majlis al-Shura or Advisory Council—and 10 from local councillors in each of Egypt's 14 provinces. Parties wishing to nominate candidates were required to hold at least 5% of the seats in both the People's Assembly and the Advisory Council. The constitutional amendment also mandated that parties seeking to contest any future presidential elections would need to have been in existence for at least five years at the time of the poll and would have to nominate candidates who had held a senior leadership position within the party for at least one year.

Given that none of the existing opposition parties at that time held 5% of the seats in both chambers of parliament, a clause was added to the constitutional amendment, which allowed all legalized political parties to nominate candidates for the 2005 election. At the election, held on 7 September, Mubarak secured re-election, but with a reduced share of the vote—89%, compared with 98.5% in 1981, 97% in 1987, 96% in 1993 and 94% in 1999. Ayman al-Nour of the liberal al-Ghad (Tomorrow) Party, Mubarak's main challenger for the presidency, was arrested following the election in connection with allegations that he had forged many of the signatures required to register his party in 2004; in December 2005 he was sentenced to five years' imprisonment, but his conviction was widely denounced as being politically motivated. The Press Secretary of the US Government released a statement asserting that the USA was 'deeply troubled' by al-Nour's conviction and called on the Egyptian Government to release him from detention. Meanwhile, in November–December Egypt held the freest multi-party parliamentary elections to date, at which the NDP's representation declined to 324 seats, from 417 at the previous election in 2000. New Wafd won six seats, al-Ghad, the NPUP and the left-leaning Nasserist party Hizb al-Karama (Dignity Party) each secured two seats, while independents affiliated to the Muslim Brotherhood won 88 (a gain of 71 seats from 2000) and other independents took eight. However, the NDP still dominated the legislature, with 324 of the 454 seats.

The limited easing measures implemented by the Government did encourage greater organization in civil society, which was facilitated by the rise of social media including Facebook and Twitter, which allowed disparate individuals to congregate online in relative anonymity. Meanwhile, a state-affiliated National Council for Women was created in 2000 to increase female participation and representation within society and its constitutional institutions and empower them socially, culturally, economically and politically. In 1976 just 2% of parliamentarians were female; by 2010 this had increased to 12%.

Following through on his 2005 election pledge, in late 2006 Mubarak initiated an overhaul of the 1971 Constitution. Based on his own recommendations, the President instructed the NDP's Policy Secretariat to draw up a detailed proposal of constitutional amendments. Following two months of parliamentary debate, the proposed constitutional changes were approved by the Advisory Council, and in March 2007 they were ratified by the People's Assembly, although more than 110 deputies voted against the proposals, including all members of the parliamentary opposition.

The final draft of the proposed amendments contained 34 changes to the 1971 Constitution. Of these, the most far-reaching amendments focused on the economy; the organization of elections and party political activities; and the incorporation of stringent new anti-terrorism provisions. With regard to the economy, the proposed amendments withdrew all reference to the 'socialist character of the state' stipulated in the 1971 Constitution, and the revised Constitution now stated that Egypt's economy rested on 'market principles'. On the political front, important changes were made to four articles of the Constitution. Article 5, which defines Egypt as a multi-party system, was amended explicitly to prohibit the formation of political parties (and the pursuit of political activities) on the basis of religion. Also changed was Article 76, which stipulates the candidacy requirements for presidential elections. According to the new provisions, political parties seeking to participate would need to hold at least 3% of all seats in either the People's Assembly or the Advisory Council, compared with a previous requirement of 5% in both upper and lower chambers. No changes were made, however, to any of the stringent requirements for independent candidates. Changes to Article 88 involved the establishment of a government-appointed Higher Election Commission, which was to replace full judicial supervision of elections. To prepare for new anti-terrorism legislation, which was to replace the existing emergency law, the regime amended Article 179 of the Constitution. Introducing new anti-terrorism measures, the revised article confirmed the President's right to refer civilians to military courts and broadened the police's powers of surveillance, interrogation and arrest. Some human rights advocates criticized the measures for entrenching the emergency regime. Other notable amendments to the Constitution concerned the President's right unilaterally to dissolve parliament without calling for a national referendum; the rebalancing of executive legislative powers; and the introduction of quotas for female representation in local councils.

Shortly after being ratified by the People's Assembly on 19 March 2007, the Government announced that the 34 constitutional amendments would be put to a national referendum on 26 March. The referendum was boycotted by a broad coalition of opposition parties, civil society organizations and prominent individuals. According to the official results, 27.1% of all registered voters took part in the referendum, of whom 75.9% voted in favour of the constitutional amendments. However, independent observers and opposition representatives suggested that actual turnout had been only 5%–7%, and there were numerous reports that the referendum process had been marred by widespread voter intimidation and vote-tampering.

Following the formation in early 2008 of the April 6 Youth Movement, which was established to support workers who were planning to strike on 6 April, subsequent rallies were met with state violence, creating a sustained spiral of protest and repression amid economic hardships and food price inflation that frayed the edges of Egyptian society. The rise in food prices was partly linked to the economic instability that followed the implementation of austerity measures to appease the International Monetary Fund, including the privatization of state-owned businesses and the reduction of costly subsidies to an increasingly struggling society. Public discontent was further exacerbated by numerous allegations of police brutality, including the fatal beating in June 2010 by police officers in Alexandria of Khaled Said, a young man who had recently posted online a video purporting to show police officers handling illegal drugs. Said's killing sparked a popular movement on Facebook called 'We are All Khaled Said', which campaigned against police brutality. The movement encouraged thousands of its followers to participate in anti-Government rallies in a 'day of rage' on 25 January 2011, to coincide with Egypt's National Police Day. This was to become a much bigger spark in the so-called Arab Spring, culminating in the downfall of Mubarak.

THE ARAB SPRING

From its emergence in December 2010 in Tunisia, the Arab Spring was a series of anti-Government demonstrations throughout the Middle East and North Africa, protesting against economic and political policies and undemocratic regimes. The ousting of Tunisia's long-time pro-USA autocratic leader Zine al-Abidine Ben Ali on 14 January 2011, inspired similar protesters and movements in Egypt and elsewhere. National Police Day on 25 January was already a focal point of Egyptian protests. The Government briefly cut off all mobile telephone lines, as well as internet services, on 26 January. The services were restored a few days later, but their suspension seemed to encourage more people (from all sections of society) to join the protests. Buoyed by events in Tunisia, the crowds in Cairo's Tahrir (Liberation) Square burgeoned to an estimated 1m. people at one point, and for 18 days protests took place involving thousands of people on the streets of the capital, Alexandria, Ismailia and in many cities and villages in the Nile Delta and Nile Valley, calling for Mubarak's immediate resignation. Although the protests themselves were mostly peaceful, the interaction between supporters of the regime (especially the undercover police) and those seeking the removal of the President were not. During the principal days of protests (on 25 January–11 February), more than 800 people were killed (according to a subsequent government inquiry) and many others injured in Tahrir Square and elsewhere throughout Egypt, increasing calls for an end to the regime.

Mubarak pivoted to offering concessions, pledging not to seek re-election and replacing Prime Minister Ahmad Nazif and his Government in late January 2011 with a new administration headed by Gen. Ahmad Muhammad Shafiq, releasing a number of political prisoners, and increasing state salaries and pensions. After a defiant televised speech on 10 February, in which he insisted that he would remain in power, on the very next day—at the urging of the military—Mubarak, President since 1981, announced his resignation.

What followed was a story of attempted, managed reform. The military, which had not used its full force against the people but which was also not ready to let the country fall into revolution, earned the trust of Egyptians initially with promises of a military-controlled transition to democracy. In a communiqué issued on 13 February 2011, the Supreme Council of the Armed Forces (SCAF) declared itself in charge of this transition—under the leadership of the Commander-in-Chief of the Armed Forces, Deputy Prime Minister and Minister of Defence, Field Marshal Muhammad Hussain Tantawi—and successfully persuaded protesters to return to their homes and trust the process of reform. The SCAF's communiqué announced the dissolution of parliament and the suspension of the Constitution, and declared that the SCAF would 'run the affairs of the country on a temporary basis for six months or until the end of parliamentary and presidential elections'. A judicial committee was instructed to formulate amendments to the Constitution in preparation for a national referendum in March. The communiqué also confirmed that Tantawi, as Chairman of the SCAF, was to act as de facto head of state. On 3 March Prime Minister Shafiq's resignation was announced; former Minister of Transport Dr Essam Sharaf was subsequently appointed to replace him. Sharaf named his new Council of Ministers on 7 March. These arrangements, however, were unacceptable to many political activists, and protests continued in Cairo.

The draft amendments to the Constitution included provisions for the judicial supervision of elections, the limiting of a four-year presidency to two terms and the mandated appointment of a Vice-President. Other amended articles stipulated the removal of a controversial counter-terrorism provision and the narrowing of the criteria under which a President could institute a state of emergency.

On 19 March 2011, despite opposition from the anti-Mubarak protest movement, the constitutional amendments were approved by 77.3% of voters; voter turnout was recorded at 41.2% (a remarkable showing, given Egypt's historically low voter participation). Accordingly, on 23 March the SCAF issued a Constitutional Declaration—including the amendments approved at the referendum—which was temporarily to replace the former Constitution until a new charter could be formulated. Legislative elections were scheduled for later in the year.

After Mubarak's ousting the masses stopped gathering on a daily basis in Tahrir Square, although significant protests continued. Increasingly, the new military rulers were criticized for not delivering change in an expeditious manner—promising reform, but undertaking repressive measures against their opponents, many of whom were sentenced to death. During the SCAF's first eight months, more than 12,000 people were reportedly subjected to military trials on charges including curfew violations to insulting the military. Substantiated allegations also involved the military beating unarmed protesters, firing live ammunition at protesters, assaulting medics attempting to render aid to the injured, and physically attacking journalists reporting its actions. Domestic and international NGOs also came under attack from the SCAF. By late 2011 a total of 17 groups had been raided on the order of the Prosecutor's Office, and numerous foreign staff were prohibited from leaving the country or faced criminal proceedings. The SCAF was reportedly concerned that the NGOs were fomenting unrest. On 25 November Kamal al-Ganzouri (Prime Minister in 1996–99) formed a new 'national unity' government and was given the SCAF's presidential powers, excluding those relating to military and judicial matters. A new cabinet was sworn in on 7 December.

Genuine multi-party parliamentary elections, held between November 2011 and January 2012, reshaped the political landscape, with the Freedom and Justice Party (FJP—formed in April 2011, with strong links to the Muslim Brotherhood) winning 235 of the 498 elective seats, followed by the conservative Islamist Al-Nour Party with 123 seats and the New Wafd Party with 38 seats. Pro-state nationalist parties, tied as they were to the apparatus of Mubarak, fared less well. The young, liberal forces behind the social media mobilizations and protests were less organized and numerous when it came to party politics and election turnout. The secular liberal al-Ghad had joined other disparate groups in a coalition with the FJP. This left the so-called Egyptian Bloc, comprising the Free Egyptians Party, the Social Democratic Party and Tagammu, as the representatives of the liberal wing of the revolution; they collectively garnered 34 seats in the new legislature. At elections to the Advisory Council, which were held in January–February 2012, the FJP won 105 of the 180 contested seats, while Al-Nour won 45 and New Wafd took 14.

Attention then turned to the presidential election. The first round of voting, held on 23–24 May 2012, yielded no outright winner, necessitating a run-off between the two highest-polling candidates—former Prime Minister Ahmed Shafiq (who had won 23.7% of the vote in the first round) and Mohamed Mursi of the FJP (24.8%). In the second round of voting, held on 16–17 June, Mursi narrowly prevailed with 51.7% of the 25.6m. valid votes cast. Meanwhile, on 31 May the state of emergency, which had been imposed following President Sadat's assassination in 1981, fully expired, as earlier authorized by the SCAF.

On 14 June 2012 the Supreme Constitutional Court proclaimed the law governing the recent parliamentary elections, at which the FJP had been so successful, to be unconstitutional. The Court maintained that one-third of the chamber's elective seats had been contested by representatives of political parties rather than being reserved for independent candidates. Consequently, the SCAF dissolved the Islamist-dominated People's Assembly on 15 June, on the eve of the presidential run-off poll, assuming interim legislative powers pending the drafting of a new constitution and fresh elections, and setting up a contentious period over the legitimacy of the different branches of government. Al-Ganzouri announced his Government's resignation on 25 June. Mursi, who resigned from the Muslim Brotherhood and as FJP Chairman shortly after his victory, was sworn in as President on 30 June. Meanwhile, in early June former President Mubarak was sentenced to life imprisonment for failing to protect the 846 protesters who had died during the uprising against his regime, although he was not held responsible for their deaths. Habib al-Adli, Minister of the Interior at the time of Mubarak's ousting, was also imprisoned for life. (Following a retrial, in March 2017 Mubarak was acquitted of the charges and released from gaol, while al-Adli was acquitted of all charges against him and released in May 2019.)

On 8 July 2012 President Mursi contravened the June ruling of the Supreme Constitutional Court and subsequent SCAF decree by ordering the reconstitution of the People's Assembly. However, the Supreme Constitutional Court countered that its decision was final and not subject to appeal. Ultimately, Mursi conceded the dissolution of the People's Assembly until new elections could be held. On 24 July Mursi named Hisham Qandil, an independent, as Prime Minister. A largely non-affiliated cabinet was inaugurated on 2 August, including four Muslim Brotherhood ministers. On 12 August Mursi announced that SCAF Chairman Tantawi was to retire from public life; he was replaced as Minister of Defence and Commander-in-Chief of the Armed Forces by Gen. Abd al-Fatah al-Sisi. Mursi concurrently revoked the amendments to the interim Constitutional Declaration approved by the SCAF in June, under which the SCAF had assumed legislative powers.

Democratic elections had brought conservative Islamists to power, raising concerns both inside Egypt and abroad about what sort of future this Egypt would chart. However, this situation was not altogether surprising: despite the youthful and liberal face of the Arab Spring protests, polling by the Pew Research Center indicated that 62% of Egyptians wanted the country strictly to adhere to the teachings of the Qur'an, and 75% held favourable views of the Muslim Brotherhood, while 70% held favourable views of the April 6 Movement.

The legitimacy of the new Government was challenged from the start. A 100-member Constituent Assembly (comprising 50 parliamentarians and 50 trade union and civil group representatives charged with drawing up a new Constitution) was formed in March and then reconstituted in July. It was influenced by military authorities and a cross-section of the establishment. Given the Islamist successes in the recent elections, a battle over the evolving document centred on the powers outlined in it as well as control of the document itself. The Constituent Assembly engaged in constitutional discussions and hearings, but its efforts to expedite completion of the drafting of the new charter and stage a referendum were met with opposition.

The SCAF still wielded constitutional powers, and immediately set about attempting to expand its authority under the new system by proposing constitutional amendments that would consolidate its control over the military, its immunity from civilian control or oversight, and its power to object to or replace the Constituent Assembly if its final product was considered unacceptable. Mursi's actions indicated that the power struggle with the SCAF would go both ways. Releasing hundreds of SCAF-detained political prisoners, Mursi then dismissed the establishment chief of the General Intelligence Service and the Minister of Defence, and used his presidential powers to reject the SCAF's constitutional amendment proposals, setting up a legal challenge.

However, Mursi moved to consolidate his authority in ways that undermined his legitimacy. In November 2012 he purged state prosecutors and reduced the powers of the judiciary by removing its rights to dissolve either the Constituent Assembly or Advisory Council, and to challenge presidential decisions. Furthermore, he began a campaign to prosecute all those behind the suppression of the Arab Spring protests of 2011, which riled establishment political and police figures. Mursi's decrees left open the possibility that nobody could check or overrule the President's decisions, drawing concern from all quarters about the future of government and society. By the end of 2012 many Egyptians had begun to believe that the country had exchanged one authoritarian leader for another.

The draft Constitution, which was to be put to a national referendum over two rounds, on 15 and 22 December 2012, limited the President to two four-year terms, abolished the post of Vice-President and required that candidates nominated by the President for the role of Prime Minister be approved via a parliamentary vote of confidence. The President was to be designated Supreme Commander of the Military and Head of the National Defence Council, wherein military budgets and declarations of war could be made. The opposition, given voice in the secular National Salvation Front alliance, demanded that the referendum be postponed to allow for consensus-building talks. Mursi made overtures, calling for national dialogue talks and on 8 December he annulled the decree announced the previous month that had removed his judicial accountability.

In the referendum, which was held as scheduled, the draft charter was approved by 63.8% of the votes cast, although many of its opponents boycotted the polls (a turnout of 32.9% was recorded). The new Constitution was signed into law by Mursi on 26 December 2012. Sustained protests against Mursi's power moves began to destabilize Egypt in early 2013. The security forces were reluctant to crack down on the protests on behalf of an Islamist Government of which they were sceptical and by which they felt threatened. A Republican Guard force protected the presidential palace, outside of which supporters and opponents of the President confronted each other, with some incidents escalating into violence.

BACK TO THE FUTURE?

On 3 July 2013, on the pretext of restoring order after months of uncertainty and instability, the Commander-in-Chief of the Armed Forces and Minister of Defence and Defence Production, Gen. Abd al-Fatah al-Sisi, led a military operation that ousted Mursi from power, arresting him and again placing Egypt under the control of the military. Al-Sisi appointed Adli Mahmoud Mansour, hitherto President of the Supreme Constitutional Court, as interim President, while Hazem al-Biblawi, who had served in the transitional Government of 2011, was appointed as Prime Minister, pending new presidential and parliamentary elections. The 2012 Constitution was suspended and a new charter was to be drafted.

In the aftermath of the coup, supporters and opponents of Mursi and the Muslim Brotherhood inevitably clashed with one another, leading to the deaths of more than 1,000 people. Accusing the Muslim Brotherhood of terrorism, the military leadership began a campaign to round up the group's members and supporters. Charges, including incitement to murder, were levied against Muslim Brotherhood leaders, including Mursi, and a judicial panel called for the organization to be disbanded.

Al-Sisi promised to restore order, while stoking fears regarding Islamic extremism by connecting the supporters of Mursi and the Muslim Brotherhood with the rising agitation and violence being perpetrated in various parts of the world by the militant Islamist group Islamic State. Unlike in 2011, the military was not prepared to indulge sustained street protests, and began forcibly to clear Tahrir Square. Interim President Mansour reimposed the state of emergency, which had been lifted by the SCAF in 2012. Violent repression of crowds by the security forces on 8 and 27 July 2013 was overshadowed by a definitive crackdown operation on 13–14 August at Raba'a al-Adawiya Square, during which, according to some estimates, 800–1,000 protesters were killed. Thousands more were detained then or thereafter. The Muslim Brotherhood was formally designated as a terrorist organization and outlawed by the authorities in December, although many observers deemed this to be a politically motivated act. Upwards of 1,200 Islamists and Muslim Brotherhood members were sentenced to death in trials during 2014.

All of these actions were taken in the name of righting the ship of a new democratic Egypt, but it became clear that the procedural electoral democracy was tilting back in favour of establishment military and business interests. With conservative Islamist forces banned and on the run, and liberals still under-represented in society, those who longed for a return to the relative law and order of the old regime threw their support behind al-Sisi.

At the presidential election, held on 26–28 May 2014, al-Sisi, who had resigned from the military in March, secured a resounding victory. According to official results, he won 96.9% of the 24.5m. valid votes cast, defeating liberal candidate and former journalist and activist Hamdeen Sabbahi of the Popular Current Party

Following its endorsement at a national referendum (by 98.1% of those who voted, on a turnout of 38.1%) on 14–15 January 2014, a new Constitution was promulgated later that month. The new charter, known as the Deep State Constitution, had been drafted by a 50-member constitutional committee that excluded members of the Muslim Brotherhood. It removed religious elements of the 2012 Constitution, related to blasphemy and granting constitutional authority to Cairo's Al-Azhar University in matters of Islamic law (*Shari'a*), banned political parties based on religion and retained considerable powers for the Egyptian military. The President was granted the power to appoint 5% of the legislature—which was to be reconstituted as a unicameral body, the House of Representatives, comprising no less than 450 members, with the Advisory Council being abolished—as well as the power to make appointments to cabinet posts (formerly the responsibility of the Prime Minister).

After protracted delays, elections to the House of Representatives were finally held in October–December 2015. Of the 596 seats, 448 were to be elected by single-member district elections and 120 by party-list seats in four constituencies, with the remaining 28 legislators to be selected by the President. The ban on Muslim Brotherhood defanged Islamist parties and led many to boycott the elections, as they had done with the presidential poll. Turnout was recorded at just 28.3% of the registered electorate. Independents secured 351 of the 596 seats, giving al-Sisi the support needed to rule and reform the system in a manner reminiscent of pre-Arab Spring Egypt. Coptic Christians were elected to 36 single-member district seats, and to 24 of the 120 party-list seats. Women were elected to 75 seats, with a further 14 being appointed by al-Sisi; female representation in the legislature thus increased from just 1.8% in the conservative Islamist parliament of 2012 to 14.6% in the new House of Representatives.

Egypt's Coptic Christians, who account for around 10% of the population, were largely happy with al-Sisi's promises of protection and support. Islamist attacks on Coptic sites and neighbourhoods had increased under Mursi's rule, and Islamic State attacks in 2015 and 2016 in Cairo and the Sinai Peninsula fuelled support for a crackdown on the sources of terror. On 11 December 2016, for example, 25 people were killed and 49 injured in Islamic State attacks on St Mark's Coptic Orthodox Cathedral in Cairo. On 9 April 2017 attacks at St Mark's Cathedral and at Mar Gorges Church collectively claimed the lives of 44 people and injured more than 110 others. Dozens were killed and injured in an attack on 26 May at St Samuel Monastery, targeting both Christian worshippers and foreign tourists. Against this backdrop of violence, the Coptic Church officially endorsed the post-coup al-Sisi Government. Manal Awad Mikhail was appointed governor of Damietta in August 2018, thereby becoming the first Coptic Christian woman (and only the second woman ever) to be appointed as a governor in Egypt.

However, in the name of fighting terror, al-Sisi's Egypt reverted to a state of emergency in April 2017, which facilitated a general crackdown on dissent of any kind. After a brief window in which it was rated as 'partly free' in the *Freedom in the World* annual study of political rights and civil liberties worldwide, compiled by US-based non-profit organization Freedom House, Egypt returned to being listed in the 'not free' category in 2018 (remaining there as of 2023). The Freedom House report claimed that 'women, Christians, Shiite Muslims, people of color, and LGBT people face indirect forms of discrimination that limit their political participation to varying degrees'.

Legislation introduced in 2017 provided for the closure and prosecution of NGOs that did not comply with newly implemented regulations. Office raids became routine as a new regulatory body was charged with determining which groups and individuals were harmful to 'national security, public order, public morality, or public health'.

After the ouster of Mursi, a rise in assaults, arrests and imprisonments of journalists was evident. Internet freedom was inhibited in terms of both access and content, with over 500 websites being blocked in the first few years of al-Sisi's presidency alone, likely reflecting the regime's concerns regarding online activism and mobilization, such as seen in the run-up to the Arab Spring.

In 2018 al-Sisi ran for re-election, as was his constitutional right. On this occasion, presidential opponents faced obstacles and intimidation. Former premier Ahmed Shafiq was forcibly detained in November 2017 shortly after declaring his candidacy, and subsequently announced his withdrawal from the race. Col Ahmad Konsowa was sentenced to six years' imprisonment in December, a month after announcing that he intended to contest the election. Three other candidates withdrew their respective candidacies in January 2018—human rights lawyer Khaled Ali, who pulled out amid an ongoing court case against him; Sami Anan, a retired general and former member of the SCAF, who withdrew from the race after being arrested for incitement and other charges just days after announcing his candidacy; and Muhammad Anwar Sadat, a nephew of former President Sadat, who dropped out citing an 'environment of fear' surrounding the vote.

The presidential election was held on 26–28 March 2018. Al-Sisi overwhelmingly defeated his only remaining challenger, al-Ghad leader Moussa Moustafa Moussa, taking 97.1% of the valid votes. Turnout was reported at 41%. Al-Sisi was inaugurated for a second presidential term on 2 June, and a new cabinet, led by Mustafa Madbouly, was sworn in later that month.

At a constitutional referendum held on 20–22 April 2019, a series of proposals to amend the Constitution was approved by 88.8% of those who voted, on a turnout of 44.3%. Under the amendments, the maximum number of consecutive presidential terms was increased from two to three and the term was extended from four to six years, while a 'transitional article' included the retrospective extension of the presidential term of office to six years (thus allowing al-Sisi, whose second four-year term was due to expire in 2022, to remain in post until 2024 at least and potentially until 2030). The amendments also gave the President the authority to make senior judicial appointments, such as the Chief Justice of the Supreme Constitutional Court; granted the military increased political and judicial powers; reserved 25% of seats in the House of Representatives for women; and provided for the re-establishment of a second parliamentary chamber.

On 2 July 2020 President al-Sisi approved legislation providing for the establishment of an upper parliamentary chamber, the 300-member Senate, with one-third of its members to be elected directly via a list system, one-third via an individual system and one-third to be appointed by the President. On 9–12 August elections were held for the new Senate. Run-off polls took place on 6–9 September. The electoral campaign was low-key and mostly one-sided. Voter turnout in the first round was only 14.2%. According to results announced following the second round, the pro-Government National Unified List, led by Mostaqbal Watan (Nation's Future Party—formed in 2014), had won all 100 of the seats reserved for party-list candidates, including 50 seats for Mostaqbal Watan, which also took 68 of the 100 individual seats. Al-Sisi appointed the remaining 100 members of the Senate on 17 October, and its inaugural session was held on the following day.

The first stage of elections to the House of Representatives was held on 24–25 October 2020 (with turnout reported at 29.5%) and the second stage on 7–8 November (with turnout of 28.1%). In both the upper and lower chamber elections, it was unclear whether the exceptionally low turnout rates were principally owing to COVID-related concerns or to general disillusionment with Egypt's political system. Run-off contests took place on 23–24 November and 7–8 December. According to final results, Mostaqbal Watan secured 316 of the 568 elective seats, while the Republican People's Party and the New Wafd Party—also members of the National Unified List—won 50 and 25 seats, respectively. The new House of Representatives was dominated by al-Sisi supporters, but included representatives from 13 political parties.

Al-Sisi's coup and subsequent re-election to the presidency has returned Egypt to the politics of soft—and, at times, not so soft—authoritarianism that characterized the final years of the Mubarak regime. Elections are still constitutionally provided for, but the societal rights of free speech, free assembly and a free press have once again become severely restricted.

BACK TO THE FUTURE IN INTERNATIONAL POLITICS

Al-Sisi has successfully forced the world to deal with the reality of his regime, after some brief hesitation in the West over the nature of his return to power and Egypt's human rights record since his assumption of the presidency. The USA struggled under the Administration of President Barack Obama to determine how best to respond to democracy movements that ousted an ally in Mubarak and replaced it with a Muslim Brotherhood Government, then struggled again when that Government was ousted by al-Sisi and a return to authoritarianism. To call the events of 2013 a coup would put the USA in an awkward position, since US law, under the Arms Export Control Act of 1976, prohibits the selling of arms to military regimes that foster coups against democratically elected governments. While the USA waivered, Egypt flirted with the idea of procuring Russian arms and support. Ultimately, however, the USA resumed politics as usual with the important Arab state. US President Donald Trump embraced al-Sisi's regime unreservedly in the name of countering Iranian regional power, consolidating continued peace with Israel and battling the threat posed by Islamic State.

The Democratic Administration of Trump's successor as President, Joe Biden, has adopted a firmer stance on Egypt's human rights record, withholding US $130m. in military aid (around 10% of annual US military aid to Egypt) in September 2022 in response to concerns raised by the US Congress regarding alleged human rights abuses. However, another $170m. was approved, in response to progress reportedly made by Egypt in releasing political prisoners and under statutory rules about counterterrorism and security assistance.

Egypt hosted the 27th United Nations Climate Change Conference (COP27) in November 2022 in Sharm el-Sheikh, during which Presidents Biden and al-Sisi and others in attendance shored up their commitment to tackling the climate change crisis. Biden also expressed his Administration's 'solidarity with Egypt in the face of the global economic and food security challenges'. Economic struggles in Egypt have resulted in an increase in the number of migrants seeking to reach Europe, including via illegal smuggling operations. This has led to co-operation between Egypt and the European Union on migration and people smuggling issues, which were already problems for Europe from other parts of North Africa. Egyptian nationals were among those on board a fishing boat carrying hundreds of migrants that sank off the coast of Pylos, Greece, on 14 June 2023, resulting in the confirmed deaths of 82 people, with around 500 others missing, presumed dead, including around 100 children. By 16 June nine men, all of Egyptian descent, had been arrested on suspicion of organizing the people smuggling operation.

Regionally, if the Arab Spring challenged old authoritarian governance from Egypt to Syria, the rise of al-Sisi and the survival of the regime of Syrian President Bashar al-Assad after a decade of civil war signal a return to business as usual in the Arab world. Assad's Syria was readmitted to the Arab League in May 2023, after a 12-year suspension of its membership amid staunch opposition to Assad's violent suppression of anti-Government protests, his ties to Iran and previous marginalization of Syria's Sunni Arab majority. In June Syria's newly appointed representative at the Arab League, Houssam al-Din Ala, was allocated the additional post of Syrian ambassador to Egypt. Following the ousting of the Muslim Brotherhood regime, Egypt and Saudi Arabia had worked to improve bilateral relations. In April 2016 al-Sisi had signed an accord providing for the transfer to Saudi sovereignty of two uninhabited islands in the Red Sea, Tiran and Sanafir (which had been controlled by Egypt since 1950). Despite a public backlash and legal challenges, the accord was finally ratified in June 2017. Egypt subsequently dragged its heels on the finalization of the transfer, partly to exact more economic concessions from Syria amid Egypt's financial woes, which pre-dated but were worsened by the coronavirus disease (COVID-19) pandemic from early 2020 and resulting global economic downturn. Following US mediation, Egypt and Saudi Arabia agreed to implement the transfer agreement by 31 December 2022. However, as of August 2023 the transfer remained pending, with Egypt reported to be stalling implementation owing to ongoing tensions with the USA.

Economy

CHAHIR ZAKI

INTRODUCTION

In the Middle East and North Africa (MENA) region, Egypt is considered one of the most diversified and booming economies. It is characterized by a large market (with a population of more than 100m.), a relatively diversified economy (with mineral products—predominantly petroleum oils and gases—accounting for 39.3% of export revenue in 2022, according to the International Trade Centre) and a large services sector (which contributed 54.1% of gross domestic product—GDP—in 2021/22). Nevertheless, Egypt has faced a number of political and economic challenges since 2011, with political turmoil in January 2011 followed by a significant currency devaluation in 2016, the health crisis of the coronavirus disease (COVID-19) pandemic in 2020 and the onset of the war in Ukraine in 2022. While the economy has been relatively resilient at the macroeconomic level, the country's overall economic and social performance has been modest, especially compared with other emerging countries (Ikram, 2007 and Zaki, 2017). In fact, social outcomes have not improved and a number of structural challenges have not been addressed, despite different reform programmes, leaving the economy in 2023 under serious pressure, as will be discussed later.

From a historical perspective, Adly (2021) shows that Egypt's development model and performance were related to the country's political position in the world order. Indeed, during the period of British occupation (1882–1956) much of the trajectory of domestic growth, state-economic relations and economic nationalism was affected by the struggle for independence. In 1920, Egyptian entrepreneur Talaat Harb established Banque Misr, which played a key role in developing the industrial and services sectors in Egypt, as well as several companies in the textiles, aviation and film-making sectors. After 1952, and following full independence in 1956 (with the decolonization and non-alignment movement under Gamal Abdel Nasser), a state-led development model was adopted, including nationalist domestic policies, heavy industrialization, economic planning and an import substitution strategy. With President Anwar Sadat (who held power from 1970 to 1981) and the signing of the peace treaty with Israel in 1979, an *infitah* or open-door policy was adopted, with Egypt realigning with the West. During Hosni Mubarak's regime (1981–2011), the role of the public sector was re-emphasized without changing earlier liberalization measures. After the political turmoil of the Arab Spring in 2011 and the political instability that lasted until 2014, while growth was primarily driven by infrastructure mega-projects, the role of military-run firms increased in the economy (Ikram and Nassar, 2022).

Against this background, the objective of this essay is twofold. First, it analyzes the main economic policies and characteristics of the Egyptian economy. Second, it examines why several reforms and different programmes agreed with the International Monetary Fund (IMF) failed to improve the competitiveness and the dynamism of the economy. In fact, while stabilization reforms were necessary to address the main cyclical challenges faced by the Egyptian economy, they did not prove sufficient and failed to diversify the economy further, boost the private sector, increase exports or create more jobs.

The rest of the chapter is structured as follows: *Structural Characteristics* presents the main characteristics of the Egyptian economy, *Overview of Economic Policies* analyzes the different economic policies that have recently been implemented, *Implications for Development* focuses on the main reasons behind the stagnation of the private sector, and *Conclusion and the Way Forward* sums up the situation and discusses policy implications.

STRUCTURAL CHARACTERISTICS

In order to analyze the structural characteristics of the Egyptian economy, it is important to look at the composition of GDP by economic activity, factors of production and by expenditure. First, the GDP disaggregation shows that the Egyptian economy depends heavily on services, with sector's contribution to GDP increasing from 46.5% in 2000 to 51.5% in 2022. Meanwhile, the contribution of agriculture to GDP fell steadily over the same period, from 15.5% to 10.9%, despite the sector continuing to be a large employer in Egypt. The manufacturing sector's share of GDP has remained relatively stable, increasing slightly from 30.7% in 2000 to reach 32.7% in 2022. The increase in the services sector's contribution was primarily due to growth in the information and communications technology (ICT) and tourism sub-sectors, while the manufacturing sector was dominated by capital-intensive sub-sectors.

In terms of factors of production, different social accounting matrices show that the share of labour in GDP declined from 42.8% in 1977 to 32.0% in 2019. This is in line with the findings of Kheir-El-Din and Moursi (2007), who argue that capital accumulation was the main driving force behind economic growth between 1960 and 1998. Amer et al. (2021) also show that one of the reasons behind this trend is the substantial supply of unqualified labour and prevailing employment laws that foster the adoption of capital-intensive production techniques. In the same vein, Herrera et al. (2010) show that energy-intensive sectors that are also capital intensive (such as cement, iron and steel) have dominated the economy over several decades, due to subsidized oil.

In terms of expenditure, private consumption has the highest share (82.5% of GDP in 2022, up from 75.8% in 2000), followed by investment, whose share of GDP decreased from 19.0% to 15.2% over the same period, and government consumption, whose share decreased from 11.2% to 7.2%. The share of exports and imports (by value) remained relatively stable, standing at 16.2% and 22.8% of GDP, respectively, in 2000 and 15.1% and 22.0% in 2022. A closer look at investment shows that the contribution of public investment to GDP increased from 0.2% in 2014 to 2.5% in 2018, while that of private investment increased from 0.1% to 0.3% over the same period. Domestic private investment decreased from 9.0% of GDP in 2016/17 to 2.2% in 2021/22, while foreign direct investment (FDI) decreased from 2.4% of GDP to 1.2% over the same period, reflecting the shrinking role of the private sector in the Egyptian economy. The situation was different, however, in the mid-2000s; during 2004–08 the contribution of private investment to GDP was three times higher (Herrera et al. 2010), with the majority of investment being concentrated in the construction sector.

At the social level, poverty increased from 27.8% of the population in 2015 to 32.5% in 2018, before falling back to 29.7% in 2019. In addition, the living standards of the middle class has deteriorated (Othman et al., 2021). El-Baba and Khawaja (2023) show that, among different Arab countries, the largest decline in middle class was observed in Egypt; between 2006 and 2018 the number of people defined as members of the middle class decreased by 12%, indicating the failure of economic and social reforms to support and sustain an educated middle class.

The structural characteristics of the Egyptian economy did not change over time despite different policies and waves of reform. The next section focuses on the various economic policies that have been implemented, and attempts to illustrate how the latter failed to address the structural challenges that both face and characterize the Egyptian economy.

OVERVIEW OF ECONOMIC POLICIES

The literature on the subject distinguishes between two types of economic policies: stabilization and structural. While stabilization policies focus on the short-term, structural ones focus on the longer term. The second difference between the two types of policy pertains to their implications. While stabilization policies help to maintain balance within the economy by reducing the output gap (the difference between growth and its potential level), structural policies attempt to increase the level of potential GDP through a more efficient allocation of resources (Gersbach, 2004). This latter approach increases factors' productivity and stimulates economic growth. Stabilization policies include fiscal, monetary and exchange rate policies, whereas structural policies include, among others, trade, competition, sectoral and social policies.

The Egyptian Government has focused on macroeconomic stabilization, especially since 2016. In 2011, as mentioned above, Egypt suffered from political unrest, which led to several internal and external macroeconomic imbalances— increased budget and current account deficits, larger domestic and external debts and a widening gap between official exchange rates and the black market rate. These economic imbalances resulted in reductions in FDI and international reserves to a critical level, which in turn hindered economic growth. A few years later, Egypt experienced two external shocks, namely the COVID-19 pandemic and the war in Ukraine, which also had negative effects at the macroeconomic level. This is why, having suffered these internal and external shocks, the Government attempted to stabilize the economy through different macroeconomic policies and with the support of the IMF. At the same time, there was less focus on structural policies.

Stabilization Policies

The goal of macroeconomic policies is to provide a stable economic environment conducive to growth and development. The following three sections focus on macroeconomic policies covering the fiscal, monetary and exchange rate areas, and show how such policies succeeded in stabilizing the economy without, however, fostering long-term growth and development. The fourth section looks at the issue of recurrent loans from the IMF and their positive and adverse effects on the economy.

Fiscal Policy

At the fiscal level, one can distinguish between current (or non-productive) and productive spending. While productive government spending facilitates higher yields within the economy (with higher investment in physical and human capital) and hence has a direct impact on long-term growth, non-productive expenditure affects citizens' welfare (through subsidies, wages and compensation of employees and government purchases) and might have no rea impact on economic growth since the money involved is spent and consumed in the short term (Kneller et al. 1999 and Chu et al. 2020). In Egypt, whereas productive spending (including spending on education, health and infrastructure) represents, on average, 16% of the Government's total expenditure, current expenditure (compensation of employees, interest payments, purchases of goods and services, and subsidies and social benefits) represents 84%. This distribution shows how public spending is skewed towards the short term and does not invest sufficiently in long-term human capital (Othman et al., 2021). It is worth noting that the Government has adopted an expansionary fiscal policy by increasing public investment in funding various mega-projects.

While government expenditure was equivalent to 23.1% of GDP in 2022 (down from 29.3% in 2011), revenue had remained fairly stable over the years and amounted to 17% of GDP, with 75% of government revenue coming from taxes (income, value-added, property and custom duties). The remainder of the revenue came from the Suez Canal Authority, the Egyptian General Petroleum Corporation, economic authorities and state-owned companies. As a result, the fiscal deficit reached 6.1% of GDP in 2022, down from 12.5% in 2016 (before Egypt received an IMF loan). It is also worth noting that, after 2016, the Government started to generate a primary surplus (revenue minus expenditure before interest payments on debt), indicating that the Government has larger levels of income relative to current spending, which might help make the domestic debt more sustainable.

Since 2016 Egypt's debt has increased, especially external debt. Until 2015/16 domestic debt had been increasing, while external debt had remained relatively stable. However, in 2016 this trend changed as domestic debt decreased (from 95% of GDP in 2015/16 to 68% in 2021/22) and external debt increased to reach a record level of around 37% of GDP in 2021/22. This tendency has also been associated with a deterioration in several external variables such as the ratio of total reserves to external debt service and the ratio of debt service to exports and primary income. Notably, the interest payments on external debt place greater strain on the balance of payments and have been increasing, along with the principal reimbursement.

Monetary Policy

The Central Bank of Egypt (CBE) is responsible for Egypt's monetary policy. When the Banking Law No. 88 was issued in 2003, monetary policy became formally geared towards achieving price stability. According to its website, the CBE was entrusted with the 'formulation and implementation of monetary policy, with price stability being the primary and overriding objective'. The goal was, over the medium term, to ensure low rates of inflation, maintain confidence and sustain high rates of investment and economic growth.

The main policy tools utilized by the CBE are the minimum reserve requirement for commercial banks, standing facilities, deposit auctions and the exchange rate. First, the required reserve ration was increased to 18% in 2022, up from 14% in

2017, to tighten financial conditions and support the currency. Second, regarding the standing facilities, the CBE provides two standing facilities, namely the overnight deposit and overnight lending facilities, by setting the rates of these facilities that are used as the lower and upper bounds of the CBE's corridor system around the main policy rate in order to manage liquidity imbalances of commercial banks. Third, the CBE conducts deposit auction operations to manage liquidity during surplus periods in order to absorb commercial banks' excess liquidity. Finally, and as will be shown later, the exchange rate is one of the most important policy tools used to control inflation and price stability in Egypt. This is why the CBE, despite a *de jure* floating exchange rate regime, adopted an administered exchange rate policy to curb price increases and reduce the pass-through

Inflation has recently soared as a result of a lax monetary policy and a series of currency devaluations. Indeed, both headline (overall) and core (without administered prices and fruit and vegetables) inflation increased to reach around 32% and 40%, respectively, in February 2023. The prices of fruit and vegetables were more volatile, with inflation for these products reaching a peak of 48% in April 2022, shortly after the Russian invasion of Ukraine.

In terms of policy implementation, and although the CBE instigated the pronouncement of a preannounced target (with a leeway of several percentage points either way) in 2019, the bank needs to have stronger operational transparency (by publishing regular reports including projected inflation rates) and a greater level of de facto independence in order to have a more credible monetary policy.

Exchange Rate Policy

The CBE maintained, globally, a fixed adjustable peg of the Egyptian pound to the US dollar to keep inflation low. Until 2003, the exchange rate was kept within an implicit band at around US $1 = £E 3.33. This policy was accompanied by foreign exchange controls and multiple exchange rates. In order to have a more active monetary policy, the Government announced the abandonment of the exchange rate peg in January 2003 and in December 2004 a foreign exchange interbank market was established that eliminated the parallel foreign exchange market and stabilized the nominal exchange rate from December 2005 (at around US $1 = £E 5.7). In the wake of the political turmoil in 2011 international reserves declined rapidly, falling from US $36,000m. in December 2010 to $26,400m. in June 2011, $15,500m. in June 2012 and $15,400m. in January 2015 (equivalent to just 2.8 months of imports). This trajectory reflects the CBE's efforts to protect the Egyptian pound, which lost only around 4% of its value against the US dollar between January 2011 and December 2012.

In December 2012 the CBE introduced a new system for buying and selling foreign currency. The system featured regular currency auctions to allow the Egyptian pound to float more freely, leading to a low value of US $1 = £E6.70 in March 2013. The Egyptian pound experienced a further depreciation in early 2015, when the CBE announced that the value of the dollar was US $1 = £E7.61. The new system for buying and selling foreign currency resulted in a rise in black market rates; the dollar reached an official rate of US $1 = £E8.88 in March 2016, while on the black market it was US $1 = £E18.00.

In November 2016, amid negotiations with the IMF, the CBE announced its decision to adopt a liberalized exchange rate regime and the Egyptian pound was floated against the US dollar at US $1 = £E13.00. By early 2017 the exchange rate stood at US $1 = £E18.00. Thereafter, there was a slight appreciation in the Egyptian pound and in February 2022 the exchange rate was US $1 = £E15.70. However, in response to the effects of the pandemic and the war in Ukraine and the consequent pressure on Egypt's foreign reserves, the CBE commenced a series of currency devaluations in early 2022 and by May 2023 the official exchange rate was US $1 = £E31.00.

Therefore, despite the floating announcements that were made on several occasions, the CBE adopted an administered exchange rate regime. While such policy was not sustainable with the surge in external debt and the scarcity of foreign currencies in the economy, the currency devaluation was inevitable. In addition, while such a devaluation was supposed to increase Egypt's competitiveness, Zaki et al. (2019) show that a depreciation of the real exchange rate increases the value of exports without affecting the quantity of exports. One of the reasons behind this can be attributed to the fact that Egypt is a net importer of capital goods and raw materials used in exportable goods (they represent around 70% of Egypt's imports). Thus, the devaluation of the currency increases the import costs of these goods. As they are used as inputs in the production of other goods, the cost of production increases and thus brings about cost-push inflation, especially if the demand for imports is rigid. The benefits of depreciation are thereby eroded.

Stabilization through IMF Recurrent Loans

Egypt embarked on several stabilization programmes with the IMF and the World Bank aimed at steadying the economy, correcting chronic imbalances and stimulating sustained economic growth. The first IMF programme was supposed to be signed under Sadat in 1976. However, large food riots in Egypt in 1977 compelled Sadat to reverse his earlier decision, leading to a halt of the IMF programme (Adly, 2021). Following the resultant surge in external debt and decrease in different rents, Egypt signed a stand-by agreement with the IMF and accepted the long-term involvement of the World Bank through a structural adjustment programme introduced in 1990. This Economic Reform and Structural Adjustment Program (ERSAP), included liberalization of the economy, the privatization of many state-owned companies and the rectification of various macroeconomic imbalances (Seddon, 1990).

Following the accumulation of economic problems between 2011 and 2016, a second programme was developed, including the signing of a three-year Extended Fund Facility agreement with the IMF in November 2016 for US $12,000m. The main components of the reform programme included: floating the currency, replacing the sales tax with a value-added tax (VAT), removing subsidies and freezing public hiring. This led in 2019 to an acceleration in the rate of economic growth to 5.6% (compared with 4.3% in 2016), a decrease in the average annual inflation rate to 13.8% (down from 23.3% in 2016), a fall in the unemployment rate to 7.9% (compared with 12.7% in 2016), a narrowing of the overall budget deficit to 8.0% of GDP (compared with 12.5% in 2016) and an increase in international reserves to $44,000m. (compared with $15,000m. in 2016). However, social outcomes deteriorated, as levels of informal employment, poverty and inequality increased. Moreover, the bottlenecks that confronted the private sector and impeded its expansion were not addressed, as will be discussed in the following sections.

The COVID-19 health crisis in 2020 led to a decline in FDI, domestic investment and tourism, as well as a decrease in exports, owing to a fall in demand from Egypt's main trading partners (mainly European countries and Arab states). Accordingly, Egypt obtained another stand-by loan from the IMF, amounting to US $5,200m.

The outbreak of war in Ukraine in February 2022 placed additional pressure on Egypt's expansionary fiscal policies and led to a rise in external debt (to 40% of GDP, compared with 16.5% in 2010) and a decrease in foreign exchange reserves (already affected by declining tourism, exports and FDI). This resulted in Egypt concluding another loan with the IMF, of US $3,000m.

These recurrent IMF loans corroborate the literature on IMF and recidivism (Bird et al., 2004 and Conway, 2007). Indeed, while most of its conditionality is focused on macroeconomic stabilization (Dreher, 2009), frequent users of IMF credit have recurring balance of payments problems and weak access to capital markets, therefore leading to their frequent resort to the Fund and illustrating the 'recidivism' in the use of Fund resources. Bird et al. (2004) find that recidivist borrowers have lower international reserves, larger current account deficits and capital outflows, larger debt service and external debt ratios, lower investment rates and per capita income, and weak checks and balances. Obviously, most of these characteristics apply to Egypt, which explains why these loans had limited impact on the economy. While the recurrent loans from the

IMF have enabled short-term macroeconomic stabilization, they have not solved Egypt's long-term structural problems, in particular the revitalization of the private sector, the improvement of the competitiveness of exports and job creation.

Structural Policies

Trade Policy

Trade policy can be a powerful tool to promote exports and increase the competitiveness of the economy. However, this cannot take place unless trade policy is backed up by a clear and strong industrial policy. Juhász et al. (2023) argue that contemporary industrial policies target outward orientation and export promotion, and should not be perceived as inward-looking or associated to protectionist trade policies. This essay argues that, while Egypt liberalized its trade policy, industrial policy was unclear or, indeed, almost absent. Thus, despite the currency devaluation and trade liberalization, Egyptian exports did not increase (Zaki, 2021).

A more detailed look at Egypt's trade policy shows that, since the country's accession to membership of the World Trade Organization (WTO), nearly 99% of Egypt's tariff lines are bound to the WTO. Most-favoured-nation (MFN) tariffs applying to non-agricultural products are generally lower than those for agricultural goods, with an average of 12.8% and 66.4%, respectively. Yet, while tariffs declined, fewer efforts have been made to address non-tariff measures (NTMs), including technical barriers to trade, and sanitary and phyto-sanitary measures. Such NTMs are implemented to meet legitimate non-trade objectives such as the protection of human health. However, they have been increasingly used as a protectionist tool with lower tariffs. Consequently, they prevent the Egyptian economy from being more integrated in the world economy. It is also worth noting that NTMs can be politically motivated. Indeed, during Mubarak's term, Eibl and Malik (2016) argue, political incumbents relied on trade policy-induced rents to protect their businesses. This is why sectors with prior exposure to cronyism benefitted significantly more from the new NTMs compared with non-crony sectors.

In addition to NTMs, behind-the-border constraints are among the most serious impediments to trade. Indeed, according to the World Bank Enterprise Survey of 2020, 20% of the surveyed exporting firms identified customs and trade regulations as a major constraint, compared with 9% in 2013. This is mainly due to the period of time needed to clear exports and imports, with the time required for the clearance of imports increasing from 9.2 to 12.3 days, while that for exports remained relatively stable, but high, at 7.5 days.

Finally, despite the conclusion of various trade agreements, most of them focused on tariff liberalization without addressing other issues such as non-tariff measures, mobility of persons, capital mobility and trade in services. This is the reason why such trade agreements had a limited effect on Egypt's exports (Adly, 2018).

Competition Policy

While from a *de jure* perspective, competition policy has improved in Egypt, from a *de facto* perspective, it still suffers from several drawbacks. First, despite the introduction in 1990 of ERSAP, which implied an orientation towards a market economy structure, the Government did not adopt an explicit competition law at that time. With the Government's implementation of the second wave of business environment reforms in 2004, the road was made ready for the adoption of the competition law in 2005 (Law No. 3 of 2005).

Under this legislation, the Egyptian Competition Authority (ECA) was created and assigned the role of overseeing and enforcing competition policy. Yet, it faced a number of challenges. For instance, despite the fact that the law stipulated a variety of fines, it did not grant the ECA the power to impose fines directly (this was held by the economic courts). In terms of its independence, the ECA has at times been affiliated to the Prime Minister and at other times to the Minister of Trade, whereas it should really be more independent and not part of the executive. Second, in addition to the ECA, Article 215 of the 2014 Constitution provided for different independent bodies and regulatory agencies that have legal personality, and technical, financial and administrative independence, and are consulted about draft legislation. These bodies and agencies include the CBE, the Financial Supervisory Authority, the Central Auditing Organization, and the Administrative Control Authority. At the sectoral level, the roles of some regulators overlap to some extent with those of the ECA. These regulators include the National Telecommunications Regulatory Authority (NTRA) and regulatory bodies that oversee water, electricity, gas, insurance, and bids and auctions by the Ministry of Supply and Internal Trade. While the mandates of these different institutions are not strictly related to competition policy, their existence is indispensable in the bid to reduce corruption, make the market function more smoothly and hence become more competitive.

Despite these developments, Youssef and Zaki (2022) argue that the adoption of legislation is not sufficient on its own and that what really matters is the implementation and enforcement of the legislation. For instance, during 2000–10 the Egyptian private sector suffered from monopolization by firms controlled by politically-connected businessmen (Diwan et al., 2020). In addition, military-owned companies have recently flourished in different sectors as they are privileged compared to other market players. For example, in 2016 the military and other security institutions were given exemptions with regard to the VAT law that was introduced as part of the IMF programme. They were exempted from paying VAT on goods, equipment, machinery, services and raw materials needed for the purposes of defence and national security, and the Ministry of Defence was given the power to determine which goods and services were eligible (Reuters, 2018). This indeed raises questions on the effectiveness of the competition policy in place and highlights the importance of strengthening the competition framework and ensuring a competitive level playing field. Finally, in some sectors there is no separation between the regulator and state actors, which can negatively affect actors in the private sector. For instance, the CBE acts as the regulator and supervisory body of the banking sector, while at the same time controlling the fully state-owned banks.

In order to increase the contestability of the markets, particularly following the introduction of the IMF programme in 2022, in early 2023 the Government announced that more than 10 military-affiliated companies would be listed as part of its initial public offering (IPO) programme (Salah, 2023). While this was a positive move, deeper reforms are needed in order to make the market more competitive and, thus, attract both domestic and foreign investors.

Social Policy

Social policies can be perceived as both structural and stabilization policies. They can be considered as stabilization policies as they aim to help vulnerable sections of the population during economic recessions. Yet, they need to play a more proactive role in helping people to move out of poverty and become more resilient during crisis times, and in protecting the middle-income class.

At the macroeconomic level, with current or non-productive spending in decline, the increase in productive spending was mainly driven by a surge in public investments (concentrated in infrastructure and construction), which did not improve the human capital of the population. Government expenditure on health and education in 2022 was equivalent to 1.4% (the same level as 2014) and 2.1% (down from 4.0% in 2014) of GDP, respectively. These figures are significantly lower than those stipulated in the Constitution (3% for health and 4% for basic education). Hence, such relatively low levels of expenditure do not result in an efficient or socially desired outcome, bearing in mind that human capital is the most important determinant of long-term economic growth (Lucas, 2015).

In addition to this macroeconomic overview, several programmes and initiatives have recently been implemented. In 2014 the Government launched two targeted cash transfer schemes, Takaful ('solidarity') and Karama ('dignity'). While Takaful is a family income-support scheme that provides a monthly cash transfer, with an increment per child in school for up to three children (conditional on the child attending school and visiting the health clinic), Karama is a programme for individuals who are unable to work due to age (above 65 years) or disability. Although Takaful was initially perceived as a conditional cash transfer programme, these conditions have not been enforced to date. In 2017 the Government launched the national Forsa ('opportunity') programme, offering diverse economic inclusion interventions (such as job placements, asset transfers, training and skills development). The programme is targeted at working-age individuals who benefit from any form of social assistance or who have applied for social benefits but did not meet the conditions. In 2022 the Forsa programme was piloted in eight governorates, covering 50,000 households. Meanwhile, in 2019 the Government launched the first phase of a universal health insurance project in some governorates. The objective of this programme was to reform the entire health care system and provide health care services for all individuals. Also in 2019, the Government launched Hayah Karima ('decent life'), a programme aimed at raising the standard of living of the poorest rural households. This programme is of particular importance given that poverty is concentrated in rural areas with limited access to social and physical infrastructure. Finally, the Government implemented additional measures in response to exogenous shocks. Amid the COVID-19 pandemic, the Ministry of Social Solidarity allocated extra funds to the Takaful and Karama programmes in order to accommodate an additional 411,000 families in 2020, reaching a total number of 4m. families (15m. individuals). Furthermore, an exceptional monthly allowance of £E500 for a period of six months was provided to informal and irregular workers who were at increased risk of falling into poverty. Following the outbreak of the war in Ukraine in early 2022 and the subsequent escalation in food and fuel prices, an emergency support fund for irregular workers was announced in May 2023 and a subsidy of £E1,000 (US $32.5) per month was to be disbursed to irregular workers who were not covered by other social protection programmes.

To conclude, while there are several social protection programmes and initiatives in operation in Egypt, social protection policies remain largely reactive, rather than proactive. In addition, Othman et al. (2021) argue that social protection allocations are generally perceived as a drain on the budget rather than a gain for the country. This is why a change in paradigm is needed in order to make social protection policies better conceived and implemented.

IMPLICATIONS FOR DEVELOPMENT

Despite the macroeconomic stabilization and because of the policies dicussed above, the Egyptian model did not experience any real development given that economic growth was jobless (i.e. failed to create employment), the private sector remained relatively constrained and export levels were rather stagnant.

A Jobless Growth Model

As mentioned before, the share of labour in GDP declined owing to the fact that capital-intensive production techniques and capital accumulation were the main driving forces behind economic growth. In addition, FDI, although coming from developed regions (the European Union and the USA), was chiefly concentrated in the oil sector which has very low value-added and is capital intensive. This is why economic growth was jobless. The concept of jobless growth (Caballero and Hammour, 1998) refers to a scenario where an economy expands due to stabilization policies, with employment outcomes not matching such growth.

Because of the policies and the developments presented above, and despite a high (but volatile) rate of economic growth, employment outcomes in Egypt were rather modest. Indeed, Amer et al. (2021) and Said and Zaki (2022) show that, despite a generally declining trend in the unemployment rate, other indicators of the Egyptian labour market did not improve. While the unemployment rate declined until 2019 (before the pandemic), employment rates were also in decline, indicating an increase in the extent of discouraged workers. (The concept of discouraged job seekers was introduced during the 19th International Conference of Labour Statisticians in 2013 and refers to persons of legal employment age who are not actively seeking employment or who have not found employment after long-term unemployment, but who would prefer to be working. This is usually because such individuals have given up looking, hence the term 'discouraged'.)

In addition, informal employment has increased, especially among women and school leavers and university graduates, and real wages and access to health insurance and holiday provisions have been decreasing. Thus, while economic growth was jobless during the period under analysis because of the dominance of capital-intensive sectors, the quality of the jobs that were created deteriorated.

A Shrinking Private Sector

The private sector has faced several problems that have affected its competitiveness. First, the quality of institutions does not help firms to expand. Indeed, Egypt, when compared with other comparable economies such as Morocco, Jordan, Brazil, Poland and Türkiye (formerly Turkey), is suffering from a lack of rule of law, low levels of protection of property rights and a lack of market competition. Second, with the surge in public debt, the banking sector has been primarily lending to the Government, at the expense of the private sector. Credit to the private sector, as a share of total domestic credit, declined from 46% in 2004 to 18% in 2018, while the share of credit to the Government increased from 26% to 50% over the same period. Third, several investment climate variables have deteriorated, according to data from the World Bank Enterprise Survey of 2020. The percentage of Egyptian businesses that identified informal sector practices, corruption, tax administration, tax rates, and customs and trade regulations as major constraints to their operations increased between 2013 and 2020. This indicates that there is an urgent need to reform economic institutions (in terms of, for example, when to set up a business, exports and imports, or enforcing a contract) in order to increase private sector participation. Fourth, as mentioned before, competitiveness in the market remains weak. Indices compiled by the Economist Intelligence Unit (EIU) show that the freedom to compete index has deteriorated in Egypt since 2015 and remains below the MENA average. Consequently, domestic private investment decreased from 9% of GDP in 2016/17 to 2.2% in 2021/22 and FDI decreased from 2.4% of GDP to 1.2% over the same period.

Lack of Export Promotion

The Egyptian model has not followed that of Asian countries that have succeeded in diversifying and increasing their exports. Indeed, export revenue decreased from 12.0% of GDP in 2010 to 7.1% of GDP in 2021. This share is lower than that of middle-income countries and for the MENA region as a whole (being a large exporter of petroleum and petroleum products). In terms of the structure of exports, Egypt is moderately diversified given that the share of manufacturing exports amounts to 45.2% of total merchandise exports, compared with 22.5% in the MENA region as a whole and 66.0% in middle-income countries. The share of Egypt's fuel exports averages around 34% of total merchandise exports. Finally, Egypt is rather specialized in traditional sectors that are not intensive in complex know-how. According to the Economic Complexity Index, despite a slight improvement, Egypt ranks below economies such as Jordan, Tunisia and Türkiye. In terms of destinations, Egypt's exports remain relatively concentrated, as the main trading partner for both exports and imports is Europe (with 43% of exports and 35% of imports).

To sum up, Egypt's relatively poor export performance can be attributed to: a declining private sector, weak institutions that do not help in the upgrading of exports (Karam and Zaki, 2019), and the absence of a clear industrial policy.

CONCLUSION AND THE WAY FORWARD

In order to create a more inclusive and sustainable development model, several points have to be taken into account:

Stabilization—Necessary but Not Sufficient

At the fiscal level, growth has mainly been driven by an increase in public spending that led to a surge in Egypt's debt. This is why, in the short term, two reforms are necessary. First, in order to reduce the pressure on foreign currency and pay off the external debt, the option of restricting imports that are mainly inelastic goods and intermediate inputs may not be a plausible option. Instead, a more comprehensive approach of debt restructuring (renegotiation of terms of servicing existing debt, co-ordination among creditors, etc.) may be required.

Second, fiscal consolidation is needed to reduce the domestic debt, which will require limiting spending on infrastructure projects.

The exchange rate policy needs to be more credible and more sustainable to avoid managing an overvaluation of the Egyptian pound and to reduce the burden on foreign exchanges to keep the currency stable. While this is necessary to improve the competitiveness of exports, some structural reforms are also needed to foster and diversify domestic production and to remove administrative and unjustified non-tariff measures that affect exports and therefore production.

Towards Deeper and More Structural Reforms

More structural and deeper reforms are needed to improve the investment climate, generate externalities and help companies to improve their productivity. This applies to competition policy, the simplification of business procedures, and the application of the one-stop-shop approach (whereby investors can finalize all procedures to reduce the cost of starting a business, delays in processing and the reproduction of documents). To improve competition, it is necessary not only to develop a transparent public ownership policy and governance framework but also to limit the cases where state actors are excluded from laws or granted exemptions. Furthermore, it is important that the institutional mandate of the ECA be strengthened. This would help the private sector to increase its productivity. It is also important to attract more FDI in the manufacturing sector (not just the oil sector), in order to increase the transfer of technology, particularly in the high value-added sectors, which absorb labour.

Finally, a clearer industrial policy must be developed and better linked to trade policy. To determine the most important products for Egypt to focus on, both supply (measured by the country's capabilities) and demand (measured by global demand) must be considered to ensure that Egypt specializes in products that are in high demand. More manufacturing exports would lead to greater demand, higher production and therefore more jobs. Importantly, this would require a specific industrial strategy that focuses on specific labour-intensive sectors.

Bibliography and Sources

Adly, A. 'A Brief History of Nation, State and Market', in Springborg, R., Saad, A. I., Adly, A. I. A., Gorman, A. P., Moustafa, T., Sakr, N., and Smierciak, S. (Eds). *Routledge Handbook of Contemporary Egypt*. London, Routledge, 2021.

Adly, A. 'Liberalization without Integration. Egypt and PTAs (1990–2010)', in Looney, R. E. (Ed.). *Handbook of International Trade Agreements: Country, Regional and Global Approaches*. London, Routledge, 2018.

Amer, M., Selwaness, I., and Zaki, C. 'Patterns of economic growth and labor market vulnerability in Egypt', in Assaad, R., and Marouani, M. A. (Eds). *Regional Report on Jobs and Growth in North Africa 2020*. International Labor Office and Economic Research Forum, 2021.

Bird, G., Hussain, M., and Joyce, J. P. 'Many happy returns? Recidivism and the IMF'. *Journal of International Money and Finance*, 23 (2), pp. 231–251, 2004.

Caballero, R. J., and Hammour, M. L. 'Jobless Growth: Appropriability, Factor Substitution, and Unemployment'. *Carnegie-Rochester Conference Series on Public Policy*, 48, 1998.

Chu, T. T., Hölscher, J., and McCarthy, D. 'The impact of productive and non-productive government expenditure on economic growth: an empirical analysis in high-income versus low-to middle-income economies'. *Empirical Economics*, 58, pp. 2403–2430, 2020.

Conway, P. 'The revolving door: Duration and recidivism in IMF programs'. *The Review of Economics and Statistics*, 89 (2), pp. 205–220, 2007.

Diwan, I., Keefer, P., and Schiffbauer, M. 'Pyramid capitalism: Cronyism, regulation, and firm productivity in Egypt'. *The Review of International Organizations*, 15, pp. 211–246, 2020.

Dreher, A. 'IMF conditionality: theory and evidence'. *Public Choice*, 141, pp. 233–267, 2009.

Eibl, F., and Malik, A. *The Politics of Partial Liberalization: Cronyism and Non-Tariff Protection in Mubarak's Egypt*. Centre for the Study of African Economies, 2016.

El-Baba, W. and Khawaja, M. 'Middle class in Arab countries'. *Working Paper Series on the Middle Class*. Beirut, Economic and Social Commission for Western Asia, 2023.

Gersbach, H. 'Structural reforms and the macroeconomy: The role of general equilibrium effects', in Solow, R. M. (Ed.). *Structural Reform and Economic Policy*. Palgrave Macmillan, pp. 9–22, 2004.

Herrera, S., Selim, H., Youssef, H., and Zaki, C. *Egypt Beyond the Crisis—Medium Term Challenges for Sustained Growth*. The World Bank Policy Research Working Paper No. 5451, 2010.

Ikram, K. *The Egyptian Economy, 1952–2000: Performance Policies and Issues*. London, Routledge, 2007.

Ikram, K., and Nassar, H. (Eds). *The Egyptian Economy in the Twenty-first Century: The Hard Road to Inclusive Prosperity*. American University in Cairo Press, 2022.

Juhász, R., Lane, N. J., and Rodrik, D. *The New Economics of Industrial Policy*. National Bureau of Economic Research, Working Paper No. W31538, 2023.

Karam, F., and Zaki, C. 'Why Can't MENA Countries Trade More? The Curse of Bad Institutions'. *Quarterly Review of Economics and Finance*, 73, pp. 56–77, 2019.

Kheir-el-Din, H., and Moursi, T. 'Sources of Economic Growth and Technical Progress in Egypt: An Aggregate Perspective', in Nugent, J., and Pesaran, H. (Eds). *Explaining Growth in the Middle East, Contributions to Economic Analysis*. Elsevier, 2007.

Kneller, R., Bleaney, M. F., and Gemmell, N. 'Fiscal policy and growth: evidence from OECD countries'. *Journal of Public Economics*, 74 (2), pp. 171–190, 1999.

Othman, A., Sholkamy, H., and Zaki, C. 'On mainstreaming social thinking in macroeconomic policies'. *Social Protection in Egypt: Mitigating the Socio-Economic Effects of the COVID-19 Pandemic on Vulnerable Employment*, 2021. fount.aucegypt.edu/faculty_journal_articles/501.

Reuters Staff 'From war room to boardroom. Military firms flourish in Sisi's Egypt.' *Reuters*, 2018. www.reuters.com/investigates/special-report/egypt-economy-military.

Said, M., and Zaki, C. 'Growth and employment through the COVID-19 pandemic: The case of Egypt', in Assaad, R., and Marouani, M. A. (Eds). *Second Report on Jobs and Growth in North Africa and Sudan (2021–2022)*. International Labor Office and Economic Research Forum, 2022.

Salah, A. 'Egypt to list over 10 military-affiliated companies soon: PM'. *Al-Ahram*, 2023. english.ahram.org.eg/NewsContent/3/12/498693/Business/Economy/Egypt-to-list-over-militaryaffiliated-companies-s.aspx.

Seddon, D. 'The politics of adjustment: Egypt and the IMF, 1987–1990'. *Review of African Political Economy*, 17 (47), pp. 95–104, 1990.

Youssef, J., and Zaki, C. 'A. Decade of Competition Policy in Arab Countries: A De jure and De facto Assessment'. *International Journal of Economic Policy in Emerging Economies*, 2022.

Zaki, C. 'An Overview of Structural Imbalances in Egypt'. *Egypte Monde Arabe*, 'L'État égyptien en quête de stabilité', 16 (3), pp. 99–124, 2017.

Zaki, C. 'Why Egypt's Trade Policy Failed to Improve its External's Competitiveness?', in Springborg, R., Saad, A.I., Adly, A. I. A., Gorman, A. P., Moustafa, T, Sakr, N., and Smierciak, S. (Eds). *Routledge Handbook of Contemporary Egypt*. London, Routledge, 2021.

Zaki, C., Ehab, M., and Abdallah, A. 'How Do Trade Margins Respond to Exchange Rate? The Case of Egypt'. *Journal of African Trade*, 1–2, pp. 60–80, 2019.

EGYPT

Statistical Survey

Sources (unless otherwise stated): Central Agency for Public Mobilization and Statistics, POB 2086, Cairo (Nasr City); tel. (2) 4020574; fax (2) 4024099; e-mail nic@capmas.gov.eg; internet www.capmas.gov.eg; Central Bank of Egypt, 31 Sharia Qasr el-Nil, Cairo; tel. (2) 27702770; fax (2) 25976081; e-mail info@cbe.org.eg; internet www.cbe.org.eg.

Area and Population

AREA, POPULATION AND DENSITY

Area (sq km)	1,009,450*
Population (census results)†	
21 November 2006	72,798,031
18 April 2017	
Males	48,892,493
Females	45,906,334
Total	94,798,827
Population (official estimates at 1 January)	
2020	99,845,720
2021	101,478,581
2022	102,878,749
Density (per sq km) at 1 January 2022	101.9

* 389,751 sq miles.
† Excluding Egyptian nationals abroad, totalling an estimated 3,901,396 in 2006 and an estimated 9,470,674 in 2017.

POPULATION BY AGE AND SEX
(official estimates at 1 January 2022)

	Males	Females	Total
0–14 years	18,170,239	17,072,690	35,242,929
15–64 years	32,655,637	31,009,882	63,665,519
65 years and over	2,109,760	1,860,541	3,970,301
Total	52,935,636	49,943,113	102,878,749

GOVERNORATES
(official population estimates at 1 January 2022)

	Area (sq km)	Population	Density (per sq km)	Capital
Alexandria	2,679.36	5,469,480	2,041.3	Alexandria
Aswan	678.45	1,614,967	2,380.4	Aswan
Asyout	1,553.00	4,903,763	3,157.6	Asyout
Behera	10,129.48	6,723,269	663.7	Damanhour
Beni-Suef	1,321.50	3,492,903	2,643.1	Beni-Suef
Cairo	214.20	10,100,166	47,153.0	Cairo
Dakahlia	3,470.90	6,930,797	1,996.8	El-Mansoura
Damietta	589.17	1,593,610	2,704.8	Damietta
El-Wadi el-Gidid	376,505.00	261,167	0.7	El-Kharga
Fayoum	1,827.10	3,970,083	2,172.9	El-Fayoum
Gharbia	1,942.21	5,343,756	2,751.4	Tanta
Giza	85,153.56	9,323,196	109.5	Giza
Ismailia	1,441.59	1,419,631	984.8	Ismailia
Kafr el-Sheikh	3,437.12	3,645,111	1,060.5	Kafr el-Sheikh
Kalyoubia	1,001.09	6,024,438	6,017.9	Banha
Luxor	55.00	1,364,640	24,811.6	Luxor
Matruh	212,112.00	520,459	2.5	Matruh
Menia	2,261.70	6,148,074	2,718.3	El-Menia
Menoufia	1,532.13	4,640,003	3,028.5	Shebien el-Kom
North Sinai	27,574.00	496,386	18.0	El-Areesh
Port Said	72.07	783,433	10,870.4	Port Said
Qena	1,795.60	3,531,018	1,966.5	Qena
Red Sea	203,685.00	393,551	1.9	Hurghada
Sharkia	4,179.55	7,744,815	1,853.0	Zagazig
South Sinai	33,140.00	113,795	3.4	El-Tour
Suez	17,840.42	778,970	43.7	Suez
Suhag	1,547.20	5,547,268	3,585.4	Suhag
Total	997,738.40*	102,878,749	103.1*	—

* The official, rounded national total is 1,009,450 sq km, producing an overall density figure of 101.9 per sq km.

PRINCIPAL TOWNS
(incl. suburbs, UN projections at mid-2023)

Cairo (Al-Qahirah, the capital)	22,183,201	Asyout (Asyut)	480,732
Alexandria (Al-Iskandariyah)	5,588,477	El-Fayoum (Al-Fayyum)	432,726
Port Said (Bur Sa'id)	778,280	Zagazig (Al-Zaqaziq)	373,685
Suez (Al-Suways)	672,826	Ismailia (Al-Ismailiyah)	370,146
El-Mansoura (Al-Mansurah)	584,952	Aswan	364,528
El-Mahalla el-Koubra (Al-Mahallah al-Kubra)	538,658	Kafr el-Dawar (Kafr al-Dawwar)	361,301
Tanta	522,994		

Source: UN, *World Urbanization Prospects: The 2018 Revision.*

BIRTHS, MARRIAGES AND DEATHS

	Registered live births		Registered marriages		Registered deaths	
	Number ('000)	Rate (per 1,000)	Number	Rate (per 1,000)	Number ('000)	Rate (per 1,000)
2017	2,557	26.8	912,606	9.6	547	5.7
2018	2,382	24.5	887,315	9.1	560	5.8
2019	2,305	23.3	927,840	9.4	571	5.8
2020	2,235	22.2	902,502	9.0	665	6.6
2021	2,147	21.0	947,493	9.3	732	7.2

Life expectancy (estimates, years at birth): 70.2 (males 67.9; females 72.6) in 2021 (Source: World Bank, World Development Indicators database).

ECONOMICALLY ACTIVE POPULATION
('000 persons aged 15 years and over, 2021)

	Males	Females	Total
Agriculture, hunting, forestry and fishing	4,432	800	5,232
Mining and quarrying	39	1	40
Manufacturing	3,142	272	3,414
Electricity, gas and water supply (incl. water support, drainage and recycling)	457	42	499
Construction	3,715	24	3,738
Wholesale and retail trade; repair of motor vehicles, motorcycles, and personal and household goods	3,450	627	4,077
Hotels and restaurants	781	39	820
Transport, storage and communications	2,572	70	2,642
Financial intermediation	146	54	201
Real estate, renting and business activities	716	126	842
Public administration and defence; compulsory social security	1,131	330	1,461

EGYPT

—continued	Males	Females	Total
Education	1,044	1,081	2,126
Health and social work	373	630	1,003
Other community, social and personal service activities	736	61	797
Private households with employed persons	145	86	230
Extraterritorial organizations and bodies	2	1	3
Sub-total	**22,881**	**4,244**	**27,125**
Activities not classified	57	6	63
Total employed	**22,937**	**4,251**	**27,188**
Unemployed	1,359	811	2,170
Total labour force	**24,296**	**5,063**	**29,359**

Note: Totals may not be equal to the sum of components, owing to rounding.

Health and Welfare

KEY INDICATORS

Total fertility rate (children per woman, 2021)	2.9
Under-5 mortality rate (per 1,000 live births, 2021)	19.0
HIV/AIDS (% of persons aged 15–49, 2021)	<0.1
COVID-19: Cumulative confirmed deaths (per 100,000 persons at 30 June 2023)	22.4
COVID-19: Fully vaccinated population (% of total population at 21 May 2023)	38.2
Physicians (per 1,000 head, 2019)	0.7
Hospital beds (per 1,000 head, 2017)	1.4
Domestic health expenditure (2020): US $ per head (PPP)	167.3
Domestic health expenditure (2020): % of GDP	1.4
Domestic health expenditure (2020): public (% of total current health expenditure)	31.9
Access to improved sanitation facilities (% of persons, 2020)	97
Total carbon dioxide emissions ('000 metric tons, 2019)	249,370
Carbon dioxide emissions per head (metric tons, 2019)	2.5
Human Development Index (2021): ranking	97
Human Development Index (2021): value	0.731

Note: For data on COVID-19 vaccinations, 'fully vaccinated' denotes receipt of all doses specified by approved vaccination regime (Sources: Johns Hopkins University and Our World in Data). Data on health expenditure refer to current general government expenditure in each case. For more information on sources and further definitions for all indicators, see Health and Welfare Statistics: Sources and Definitions section (europaworld.com/credits).

Agriculture

PRINCIPAL CROPS
('000 metric tons)

	2019	2020	2021
Apples	701.4	751.2	793.3*
Apricots	76.7	66.3	71.0*
Artichokes	307.1	311.0	315.4*
Aubergines (Eggplants)	1,347.2	1,278.4	1,286.5*
Bananas	1,330.3	1,347.0	1,285.1*
Barley	107.0	109.0	102.8*
Beans, green*	264.2	265.0	265.4
Broad beans, dry	100.4	125.1	105.1*
Cabbages and other brassicas	534.3	473.3	487.6*
Cantaloupes and other melons	120.4	135.2	179.1*
Carrots and turnips	189.6	195.6	221.3*
Cauliflowers and broccoli	105.7	115.0	120.5*
Chillies and peppers, green	956.3	867.0	862.1*
Cucumbers and gherkins	566.2	443.5	433.4*
Dates	1,644.2	1,711.2	1,747.7*
Figs	215.5	299.5	298.5*
Garlic	363.5	377.1	348.2*
Grapes	1,595.4	1,184.0	1,435.0†
Groundnuts, with shell	198.8	219.5	104.0*
Lemons and limes	313.5	376.2	361.0*
Lettuce and chicory	79.0	78.0	78.9*
Maize	7,593.1	7,593.2	7,500.0†
Mangoes, mangosteens and guavas	1,396.5	1,544.4	1,327.9*
Okra	61.0	87.4	82.4*
Olives	981.0	968.4	976.1*
Onions, dry	3,077.3	3,199.3	3,312.5*
Oranges	3,067.6	3,966.2	3,000.0†
Peaches and nectarines	349.6	273.5	244.2*
Peas, green	151.5	152.0	156.2*
Potatoes	5,200.6	6,786.3	6,902.8*
Pumpkins, squash and gourds	389.4	415.2	417.1*
Rice, paddy	4,804.3	4,804.0	4,841.3*
Sorghum	758.4	758.2	764.9*
Strawberries	545.3	438.7	470.9*
Sugar beet	12,247.2	15,336.0	14,826.9*
Sugar cane	15,336.0	10,284.4	12,360.6*
Sweet potatoes	447.0	531.3	511.7*
Tangerines, mandarins, etc.*	985.3	993.8	988.1
Taro (Coco yam)	122.0	133.5	129.9*
Tomatoes	6,814.5	6,494.0	6,245.8*
Watermelons	1,401.3	1,129.0	1,311.3*
Wheat	8,558.8	9,101.8†	9,000.0†

* FAO estimate(s).
† Unofficial figure.

Aggregate production ('000 metric tons, may include official, semi-official or estimated data): Total cereals 21,913.8 in 2019, 22,458.4 in 2020, 22,301.2 in 2021; Total fruit (primary) 14,350.8 in 2019, 14,835.5 in 2020, 14,127.4 in 2021; Total oilcrops 1,573.4 in 2019, 1,485.1 in 2020, 1,380.1 in 2021; Total roots and tubers 5,774.6 in 2019, 7,456.2 in 2020, 7,549.5 in 2021; Total vegetables (primary) 16,118.6 in 2019, 15,667.2 in 2020, 15,570.9 in 2021.

Source: FAO.

LIVESTOCK
('000 head, year ending September)

	2019	2020	2021*
Asses*	908	1,069	967
Buffaloes	1,427	1,348	1,263
Camels	91	79	100
Cattle	2,809	2,745	2,819
Chickens*	166,593	171,578	176,564
Ducks*	5,595	4,682	3,999
Geese and guinea fowls*	7,028	7,019	7,011
Goats	977	925	862
Horses*	83	84	84
Rabbits and hares*	7,000	6,485	6,800
Sheep	2,082	1,936	2,239
Turkeys*	1,800	1,793	2,314

* FAO estimates.
Source: FAO.

LIVESTOCK PRODUCTS
('000 metric tons)

	2019	2020	2021
Buffalo meat	217.0	183.0	166.7*
Buffalo offals, edible*	34.6	29.2	26.6
Buffaloes' milk	1,226.0	1,265.0	1,567.5*
Camel meat*	11.5	9.3	10.2
Cattle hides, fresh*	44.6	42.2	37.0
Cattle meat	425.0	402.0	352.4*
Cattle offals, edible*	57.4	54.2	47.6
Cows' milk	3,967.0	4,281.0	3,709.9*
Chicken meat	1,542.0	2,034.0	2,232.2*
Duck meat	55.0	49.0	41.8*
Goat meat	12.0	16.0	13.9*
Goats' milk	34.0	32.0	28.7*
Goose and guinea fowl meat	14.0	13.0	14.4*
Rabbit meat	75.0	69.1	72.0*
Sheep meat	42.0	54.0	55.8*
Sheep's (Ewes') milk*	72.3	65.1	65.8
Turkey meat	19.0	25.0	20.9*
Hen eggs*	540.2	450.0	413.0
Honey (natural)	4.5	4.6	4.4*
Wool, greasy*	11.6	11.8	11.9

* FAO estimate(s).
Source: FAO.

Forestry

ROUNDWOOD REMOVALS
('000 cubic metres, excluding bark, FAO estimates)

	2019	2020	2021
Sawlogs, veneer logs and logs for sleepers	134	134	134
Other industrial roundwood	134	134	134
Fuel wood	17,861	17,893	17,926
Total	18,129	18,161	18,194

Source: FAO.

SAWNWOOD PRODUCTION
('000 cubic metres, incl. railway sleepers)

	2019	2020	2021
Total (all broadleaved)	12	12	12

Note: Output assumed to be unchanged from 2005 (unofficial figures).
Source: FAO.

Fishing

('000 metric tons, live weight)

	2019	2020	2021
Capture	397.0	418.7	425.8
Nile tilapia	140.7	160.1	169.9
Aquaculture*	1,641.9	1,591.9	1,576.2
Cyprinids	216.7	199.5	145.5
Nile tilapia	1,081.2	954.2	963.8
Flathead grey mullet*	244.0	317.8	351.2
Total catch*	2,039.0	2,010.6	2,002.0

* FAO estimates.

Note: Figures exclude capture data for sponges (metric tons, FAO estimates): 1 in 2019–21.
Source: FAO.

Mining

('000 metric tons unless otherwise indicated, fiscal year)

	2016/17	2017/18	2018/19
Crude petroleum	32,178	32,844	31,812
Natural gas (million cu m)	48,813	58,558	64,939
Aluminium	314	300*	300*
Iron ore†	565	500	500
Salt (unrefined)*	1,750	1,700	1,700
Phosphate rock	4,800	5,000*	5,000*
Gypsum (crude)*	1,000	1,000	1,000
Kaolin*	232	230	230
Granite (cu m)*	5,000	5,000	5,000

* Estimated production.
† Figures refer to gross weight. The estimated iron content is 50%.

2014/15: Marble 40,000 cu m.

2020: Crude petroleum ('000 metric tons) 31,066; Natural gas (million cu m) 58,465.

2021: Crude petroleum ('000 metric tons) 29,601; Natural gas (million cu m) 67,799.

2022: Crude petroleum ('000 metric tons) 29,921; Natural gas (million cu m) 64,488.

Sources: mostly US Geological Survey; Energy Institute, *Statistical Review of World Energy*.

Industry

SELECTED PRODUCTS
('000 metric tons unless otherwise indicated)

	2018	2019	2020
Cement	52,000	48,700	n.a.
Jet fuels	2,162	2,744	2,261
Kerosene	33	41	43
Distillate fuel oils	7,640	8,046	9,901
Motor spirit (gasoline)	4,827	5,258	5,314
Residual fuel oil (mazout)	7,444	9,009	7,869
Petroleum bitumen (asphalt)	633	691	762
Electrical energy (million kWh)	202,838	194,279	197,201

2016: Cigarettes (million) 53,423; Caustic soda ('000 metric tons) 133.

Electrical energy (million kWh): 177,144 in 2019/20; 183,246 in 2020/21; 194,009 in 2021/22.

Sources: mostly UN Energy Statistics Database; US Geological Survey.

Finance

CURRENCY, EXCHANGE RATES AND FISCAL YEAR

Monetary Units
1,000 millièmes = 100 piastres = 5 tallaris = 1 Egyptian pound (£E).

Sterling, Dollar and Euro Equivalents (28 April 2023)
£1 sterling = £E38.435;
US $1 = £E30.838;
€1 = £E33.863;
£E100 = £2.60 sterling = $3.24 = €2.95.

Average Exchange Rate (Egyptian pound per US $)
2020   15.759
2021   15.645
2022   19.160

Note: From February 1991 foreign exchange transactions were conducted through only two markets, the primary market and the free market. With effect from 8 October 1991, the primary market was eliminated, and all foreign exchange transactions are effected through the free market. In January 2001 a new exchange rate mechanism was introduced, whereby the value of the Egyptian pound would be allowed to fluctuate within narrow limits: initially, as much as 1% above or below a rate that was set by the Central Bank of Egypt, but would be adjusted periodically in response to market conditions. The trading band was widened to 3% in August, and in January 2003 the Government adopted a floating exchange rate.

Fiscal Year
The fiscal year ends on 30 June.

EGYPT

Statistical Survey

GOVERNMENT FINANCE
(budgetary central government operations, £E million, fiscal year)

Revenue

	2020/21	2021/22	2022/23*
Tax revenue	833,993	990,138	1,168,795
Income tax	321,246	385,499	428,789
Property tax	72,404	89,777	114,459
Taxes on goods and services	384,913	453,944	540,983
Taxes on international trade and transactions	36,130	43,297	46,014
Other taxes	19,300	17,621	38,550
Non tax revenue	274,633	335,433	349,059
Grants	2,955	2,889	912
Other revenue	271,678	332,544	348,147
Total	**1,108,625**	**1,325,571**	**1,517,854**

Expense

Expense by economic type	2020/21	2021/22	2022/23*
Compensation of employees	318,806	358,184	400,000
Use of goods and services	81,462	95,578	125,600
Interest payments	565,497	584,819	690,149
Subsidies, grants and social benefits	263,886	341,854	355,994
Other payments	99,751	113,417	122,700
Purchases of non-financial assets	249,372	318,223	376,429
Total	**1,578,774**	**1,812,074**	**2,070,872**

* Budget figures.

Source: Ministry of Finance, Cairo.

INTERNATIONAL RESERVES
(US $ million at 31 December)

	2020	2021	2022
Gold (national valuation)	4,390	4,228	7,326
IMF special drawing rights	279	2,657	13
Reserve position in the IMF	394	383	364
Foreign exchange	33,423	32,050	24,447
Total	**38,485**	**39,318**	**32,150**

Source: IMF, *International Financial Statistics*.

MONEY SUPPLY
(£E million at 31 December)

	2020	2021	2022
Currency outside depository corporations	611,203	701,882	831,227
Transferable deposits	668,259	837,629	1,218,258
Other deposits	3,641,063	4,283,138	5,353,255
Broad money	**4,920,525**	**5,822,649**	**7,402,740**

Source: IMF, *International Financial Statistics*.

COST OF LIVING
(Consumer Price Index; base: 2018/19 = 100)

	2020	2021	2022
Food and non-alcoholic beverages	99.4	104.6	130.9
Clothing and footwear	105.8	107.8	118.3
Housing and utilities	109.2	114.2	121.5
All items (incl. others)	107.8	114.0	131.0

NATIONAL ACCOUNTS
(£E million at current prices, fiscal year)

Expenditure on the Gross Domestic Product

	2019/20	2020/21	2021/22
Government final consumption expenditure	463,900	503,600	570,000
Private final consumption expenditure	5,146,400	5,730,600	6,471,800
Gross capital formation	984,100	1,010,900	1,334,700
Total domestic expenditure	**6,594,400**	**7,245,100**	**8,376,500**
Exports of goods and services	767,400	703,700	1,183,200
Less Imports of goods and services	1,209,200	1,285,700	1,717,200
GDP in purchasers' values	**6,152,600**	**6,663,100**	**7,842,500**
GDP at constant 2016/17 prices	**5,855,000**	**4,347,400**	**4,633,800**

Note: Figures are rounded to the nearest £E hundred million.

Gross Domestic Product by Economic Activity

	2019/20	2020/21	2021/22
Agriculture, hunting, forestry and fishing	687,050	762,054	858,421
Mining and quarrying	422,072	411,261	565,562
Manufacturing	1,007,824	1,031,800	1,252,489
Electricity, gas and water	141,574	153,805	178,445
Construction	420,092	481,197	568,898
Wholesale and retail trade, restaurants and hotels	961,881	1,027,152	1,216,475
Transport, storage and communications	516,218	575,272	678,341
Suez Canal	91,969	92,773	114,626
Finance, insurance, real estate and business services	912,050	998,594	1,119,046
Public administration and defence	403,510	437,417	488,465
Other services	407,360	458,180	530,981
GDP at factor cost	**5,879,631**	**6,336,732**	**7,457,123**
Indirect taxes, *less* subsidies	272,969	326,368	385,377
GDP in purchasers' values	**6,152,600**	**6,663,100**	**7,842,500**

Source: Ministry of Finance, Cairo.

BALANCE OF PAYMENTS
(US $ million)

	2019	2020	2021
Exports of goods	28,472.1	25,049.0	36,442.2
Imports of goods	−57,757.6	−54,282.9	−70,912.8
Balance on goods	**−29,285.5**	**−29,233.9**	**−34,470.6**
Exports of services	25,050.5	15,052.7	21,897.1
Imports of services	−21,193.2	−18,199.5	−23,126.0
Balance on goods and services	**−25,428.2**	**−32,380.7**	**−35,699.5**
Primary income received	1,047.8	544.6	944.3
Primary income paid	−12,640.9	−11,560.0	−15,012.8
Balance on goods, services and primary income	**−37,021.3**	**−43,396.2**	**−49,768.1**
Secondary income received	27,384.0	30,039.6	31,990.1
Secondary income paid	−584.6	−879.4	−832.8
Current balance	**−10,221.9**	**−14,236.0**	**−18,610.8**
Capital account (net)	−169.5	−232.6	−154.9
Direct investment assets	−405.0	−326.5	−367.0
Direct investment from liabilities	9,010.1	5,851.8	5,122.3
Portfolio investment assets	60.6	−1,572.5	−106.3
Portfolio investment liabilities	10,393.8	2,587.7	6,078.7
Other investment assets	−12,595.2	−2,539.3	5,479.7
Other investment liabilities	6,535.0	5,466.0	12,271.5
Net errors and omissions	−4,642.9	−9,059.0	−10,611.1
Reserves and related items	**−2,035.0**	**−14,060.3**	**−897.8**

Source: IMF, *International Financial Statistics*.

External Trade

Note: Figures exclude trade in military goods.

PRINCIPAL COMMODITIES
(distribution by HS, US $ million)

Imports c.i.f.	2020	2021	2022
Live animals and animal products	3,215.9	2,802.9	3,246.4
Vegetables and vegetable products	8,118.6	9,115.9	10,772.4
Cereals	4,627.7	4,938.5	6,408.0
Wheat and meslin	2,693.9	2,465.1	3,803.0
Maize or corn	1,880.9	2,411.1	2,500.9
Oil seeds and oleaginous fruits	1,949.1	2,447.1	2,456.1
Mineral products	7,964.0	11,825.4	16,570.0
Mineral fuels, oils, distillation products, etc.	7,072.1	10,409.4	15,071.7
Crude petroleum oils	3,806.6	3,728.8	4,389.8
Non-crude petroleum oils	1,643.6	3,806.0	6,202.8
Petroleum gases	1,227.0	2,297.4	3,230.3
Chemicals and related products	6,475.4	8,281.5	8,895.3
Pharmaceutical products	2,264.3	3,565.7	3,434.2
Medicaments consisting of mixed or unmixed products for therapeutic or prophylactic uses	1,968.1	2,750.4	2,981.5
Plastics, rubber, and articles thereof	3,720.0	4,903.3	5,342.0
Plastics and articles thereof	2,978.6	4,093.2	4,618.5
Textiles and textile articles	3,165.4	3,486.8	3,352.7
Iron and steel, other base metals and articles of base metal	6,142.3	7,045.5	8,573.3
Iron and steel	2,636.8	3,514.2	4,277.4
Articles of iron or steel	1,909.8	1,312.0	1,652.4
Machinery and mechanical appliances; electrical equipment; parts thereof	9,235.8	11,063.1	9,891.3
Machinery, boilers, etc.	5,255.9	6,181.4	5,843.3
Electrical, electronic equipment	3,979.9	4,881.7	4,048.0
Vehicles, aircraft, vessels and associated transport equipment	5,007.4	6,389.3	4,077.8
Vehicles other than railway, tramway	4,619.3	4,976.7	2,906.5
Motor cars and other motor vehicles	2,751.8	3,432.8	1,610.4
Total (incl. others)	60,279.6	73,781.2	79,712.1

Exports f.o.b.	2020	2021	2022
Vegetables and vegetable products	3,062.2	3,407.3	3,960.5
Vegetables, roots and tubers	1,033.9	1,067.2	1,441.1
Fruit, nuts, peel of citrus fruit and melons	1,454.1	1,660.9	1,806.3
Prepared foodstuffs; beverages, spirits, vinegar; tobacco and articles thereof	1,429.1	1,875.8	2,090.3
Mineral products	5,210.8	13,908.9	18,908.8
Mineral fuels, oils, distillation products, etc.	4,724.2	13,164.2	17,972.7
Crude petroleum oils	1,197.8	2,916.2	2,963.1
Non-crude petroleum oils	2,900.8	6,030.9	4,525.3
Petroleum gases	497.5	4,037.0	10,316.1
Chemicals and related products	3,178.8	3,903.4	5,588.6
Fertilizers	1,163.7	1,471.3	2,344.8
Nitrogenous fertilizers	939.2	1,152.1	1,876.6
Plastics, rubber, and articles thereof	1,849.7	2,804.9	2,775.2
Plastics and articles thereof	1,731.6	2,666.8	2,610.9
Textiles and textile articles	2,810.0	3,833.7	4,331.1
Non-knitted articles of apparel and accessories	891.8	1,264.5	1,658.2
Articles of stone, plaster, cement, asbestos; ceramic and glass products	909.3	1,290.1	1,311.1
Pearls, precious stones, metals, coins, etc.	2,956.4	1,154.0	1,616.5
Gold, unwrought or semi-manufactured	2,924.5	1,103.3	1,608.2
Iron and steel, other base metals and articles of base metal	1,860.2	3,470.8	2,856.9
Iron and steel	696.2	1,723.3	1,256.4
Machinery and mechanical appliances; electrical equipment; parts thereof	1,761.7	2,767.9	2,857.0
Electrical and electronic equipment	1,563.9	2,380.4	2,562.6
Total (incl. others)	26,815.1	40,701.7	48,148.7

Source: Trade Map-Trade Competitiveness Map, International Trade Centre, marketanalysis.intracen.org.

PRINCIPAL TRADING PARTNERS
(US $ million)*

Imports c.i.f.	2020	2021	2022
Argentina	911.4	1,305.4	775.0
Belgium	960.6	1,549.3	1,061.8
Brazil	1,931.2	1,612.4	2,794.0
Bulgaria	233.8	251.3	920.1
China, People's Republic	9,051.9	10,009.6	11,371.3
France (incl. Monaco)	1,427.9	1,438.3	1,892.2
Germany	3,486.0	3,297.1	3,290.8
India	2,284.2	2,470.4	3,427.6
Indonesia	1,043.8	1,179.6	1,272.1
Israel	53.8	44.0	1,260.1
Italy	2,606.5	2,381.4	2,936.1
Japan	1,017.4	745.9	709.4
Korea, Republic	1,033.3	1,387.3	1,521.5
Kuwait	1,988.8	1,216.0	3,329.2
Netherlands	951.3	1,025.1	1,159.5
Romania	452.8	623.1	901.7
Russian Federation	2,522.1	2,481.8	3,355.2
Saudi Arabia	3,817.9	6,251.3	7,082.4
Spain	1,428.2	1,400.3	1,354.2
Sweden	692.7	718.6	1,009.3
Switzerland	746.8	913.3	854.8
Thailand	785.5	768.1	993.5
Türkiye	2,957.2	3,131.2	3,137.6
Ukraine	1,582.7	1,397.6	901.2
United Arab Emirates	1,359.6	1,934.8	2,649.6
United Kingdom	1,217.0	1,195.2	1,562.8
USA	4,026.3	5,105.4	5,706.4
Total (incl. others)	60,279.6	73,781.2	79,712.1

EGYPT

Exports f.o.b.	2020	2021	2022
Algeria	490.1	507.2	699.7
Belgium	253.6	406.0	603.5
Canada	704.4	785.4	925.0
China, People's Republic	603.1	1,288.0	1,735.6
France (incl. Monaco)	537.3	928.5	1,591.7
Germany	576.2	821.7	926.7
Greece	682.0	1,407.1	1,700.8
India	1,224.3	2,327.3	1,761.4
Iraq	421.8	460.8	490.0
Japan	153.0	545.2	238.0
Italy	1,396.0	2,579.5	3,333.2
Jordan	568.0	631.8	680.9
Kenya	350.7	339.4	335.9
Korea, Republic	361.9	587.5	1,963.8
Lebanon	299.1	331.3	408.4
Libya	572.8	796.2	977.5
Malta	489.1	1,632.2	144.7
Morocco	446.1	683.9	803.6
Netherlands	459.8	629.9	1,673.1
Russian Federation	406.0	402.3	560.0
Saudi Arabia	1,703.8	1,999.1	2,386.6
Singapore	132.1	505.4	303.0
Spain	764.1	1,693.8	3,530.5
Sudan	474.5	716.0	793.8
Syrian Arab Republic	288.7	301.1	350.8
Türkiye	1,671.6	2,647.3	3,783.9
United Arab Emirates	2,863.6	1,196.5	1,888.4
United Kingdom	763.7	1,057.0	1,577.7
USA	1,472.4	2,159.2	2,145.6
Yemen	312.9	311.1	311.7
Total (incl. others)†	26,815.1	40,701.7	48,148.7

*Imports by country of consignment, exports by country of destination. Totals include trade in free zones, not classifiable by country.
† Including bunkers and ships' stores (US $ million): 184.4 in 2020; 488.6 in 2021; 1,146.5 in 2022.

Source: Trade Map-Trade Competitiveness Map, International Trade Centre, marketanalysis.intracen.org.

Transport

RAILWAYS
(traffic, year ending 30 June)

	2018/19	2019/20	2021/22
Passengers carried ('000, paying passengers only)	269,977	263,106	253,759
Freight carried ('000 metric tons)	4,628	4,596	n.a.
Passenger-km (million)	38,773	38,374	38,579
Freight ton-km (million)	1,316	1,200	n.a.

ROAD TRAFFIC
(licensed motor vehicles in use at 31 December)

	2019	2020	2021
Passenger cars	5,238,260	4,817,176	5,021,762
Buses and coaches	159,576	183,245	180,008
Lorries and vans	1,460,428	1,286,653	1,255,785
Motorcycles and mopeds	3,689,678	3,605,884	3,559,632
Total (incl. others)	11,495,730	10,801,239	10,909,456

SHIPPING
Flag Registered Fleet
(at 31 December)

	2020	2021	2022
Number of vessels	500	511	535
Displacement ('000 grt)	1,382.0	1,356.3	1,381.0

Source: Lloyd's List Intelligence (www.bit.ly/LLintelligence).

Suez Canal Traffic

	2019	2020	2021
Transits (number)	18,880	18,829	20,694
Displacement ('000 net tons)	1,207,087	1,168,999	1,274,900
Total cargo volume ('000 metric tons)	1,031,192	n.a.	n.a.

Source: Suez Canal Port Authority.

CIVIL AVIATION
(traffic on scheduled services)

	2013	2014	2015
Kilometres flown (million)	175	164	165
Passengers carried ('000)	10,594	9,525	10,159
Passenger-km (million)	22,125	20,008	20,507
Total ton-km (million)	387	419	398

Source: UN, *Statistical Yearbook*.

2021 (domestic and international): Departures 57,871; Passengers carried 5.6m.; Freight carried 589m. ton-km (Source: World Bank, World Development Indicators database).

Tourism

ARRIVALS BY NATIONALITY
('000)

	2018	2019	2020
Belarus	274.0	327.2	135.2
China, People's Republic	234.7	214.2	44.2
France	217.5	298.8	89.2
Germany	1,707.4	1,729.1	352.8
Israel	405.4	530.2	37.9
Italy	422.0	619.4	95.8
Jordan	208.3	203.6	42.5
Kazakhstan	133.0	156.6	58.1
Kuwait	164.5	164.9	39.9
Libya	410.7	440.3	135.6
Netherlands	189.7	218.5	65.0
Palestinian Territories	136.0	163.6	48.0
Poland	303.7	413.9	111.3
Russian Federation	145.6	264.1	80.6
Saudi Arabia	909.1	891.6	150.9
Sudan	459.6	575.6	239.8
Ukraine	1,174.2	1,551.7	741.9
United Kingdom	435.8	455.6	114.7
USA	287.8	349.6	118.1
Yemen	164.6	175.8	93.4
Total (incl. others)	11,346.4	13,026.4	3,676.9

Tourism receipts (US $ million, excl. passenger transport): 13,030 in 2019; 4,398 in 2020 (provisional); 8,895 in 2021 (provisional).

Source: World Tourism Organization.

Communications Media

	2019	2020	2021
Telephones ('000 main lines in use)	8,760.4	9,858.3	11,030.9
Mobile telephone subscriptions ('000)	95,340.3	95,357.4	103,449.7
Broadband subscriptions, fixed ('000)	7,598.9	9,361.6	10,861.2
Broadband subscriptions, mobile ('000)	59,572.8	66,272.9	84,164.8
Internet users (% of population)	57.3	71.9	n.a.

* Persons aged 6 years and over.

Source: International Telecommunication Union.

Education

(2022/23 unless otherwise indicated)

	Schools	Teachers	Students
Pre-primary	13,063	59,186	1,237,331
Primary	19,877	417,886	13,680,455
Preparatory	13,693	237,747	6,013,856
Secondary:			
general	4,482	96,007	2,124,450
technical	3,114	127,914	2,250,281
Special education	1,164	9,520	46,393
University*	52	n.a.	2,678,184

* 2020/21 figures.

Source: Ministry of Education, Cairo.

Al-Azhar University (2020/21 unless otherwise indicated): *Primary:* 3,635 schools; 75,934 teachers (2018/19); 1,022,492 students. *Preparatory:* 3,508 schools; 45,264 teachers (2018/19); 401,835 students. *Secondary:* 2,314 schools; 42,726 teachers (2018/19); 336,448 students.

Pupil-teacher ratio (qualified teaching staff, primary education, UNESCO estimate): 25.0 in 2018/19 (Source: UNESCO Institute for Statistics).

Adult literacy rate (UNESCO estimates): 73.1% (males 78.8%; females 67.4%) in 2021 (Source: UNESCO Institute for Statistics).

Directory

The Constitution

Following the ouster of former President Muhammad Hosni Mubarak and his Government in early February 2011, the 1971 Constitution was suspended pending the approval of amendments at a national referendum held on 19 March 2011. At the referendum, the proposed amendments were approved by 77.3% of participating voters and a temporary Constitutional Declaration was subsequently published by the Supreme Council of the Armed Forces. A draft for a new, permanent Constitution was presented to President Mohamed Mursi by the outgoing Constituent Assembly on 1 December 2012. At a referendum, held in two rounds on 15 and 22 December, the document was approved by 63.8% of participating voters, according to official results. The new Constitution entered into effect on 26 December.

However, the 2012 Constitution was suspended on 3 July 2013, following Mursi's removal from office, and on 8 July a 33-article Constitutional Declaration was announced by Interim President Adli Mahmoud Mansour. Under the provisions of the Declaration, Mansour appointed a committee of judges to study amendments to the 2012 Constitution within 25 days of his assumption of office; the recommendations of this committee were then to be submitted to a second committee, comprising representatives of the armed forces and religious institutions, for approval in September 2013. The second committee adopted the final draft of a new Constitution on 3 December. A national referendum was subsequently scheduled for 14–15 January 2014, at which the new Constitution was approved by some 98.1% of participating voters, according to the Higher Election Commission. Voter turnout was recorded at 38.1%. The document entered into effect on 18 January. Under the new Constitution, the unicameral legislature, the House of Representatives, comprised 596 members, 568 of whom were directly elected and the remaining 28 were appointed by the President.

In February 2019 the House of Representatives overwhelmingly approved proposed amendments to the 2014 Constitution, including the extension of the presidential term of office (renewable only once) from four to six years; the reservation of 25% of seats in the House of Representatives for women; and the re-establishment of a second parliamentary chamber, the Senate (with 200 senators being directly elected and 100 senators being appointed by the President). The term of both legislative chambers would be five years. The constitutional changes were endorsed by almost 89% of participants at a nationwide referendum held in April 2019.

The Government

HEAD OF STATE

President: Abd al-Fatah al-Sisi (took office 8 June 2014; re-elected 26–28 March 2018).

COUNCIL OF MINISTERS
(September 2023)

Prime Minister: Dr Mostafa Madbouly.
Minister of Defence and Military Production: Gen. Mohamed Ahmed Zaki.
Minister of the Interior: Gen. Mahmoud Tawfik Kandil.
Minister of Education and Technical Education: Reda Hegazy.
Minister of Health and Population: Dr Khaled Atef Abdel Ghaffar.
Minister of Higher Education and Scientific Research: Prof. Ayman Ashour.
Minister of Planning and Economic Development: Dr Hala Helmy al-Saeed.
Minister of Agriculture and Land Cultivation: El-Sayed el-Quseir.
Minister of Awqaf (Islamic Endowments): Muhammad Mokhtar Gomaa.
Minister of Foreign Affairs: Sameh Hassan Shoukry.
Minister of Manpower: Hassan Mohamed Hassan Shehata.
Minister of Supply and Internal Trade: Dr Ali al-Said el-Moselhy.
Minister of Electricity and Renewable Energy: Dr Mohamed Hamed Shaker.
Minister of Finance: Dr Mohamed Ahmed Maait.
Minister of Social Solidarity: Niveen el-Qabbag.
Minister of Civil Aviation: Lt-Gen. Mohamed Abbas Helmy.
Minister of Trade and Industry: Ahmed Samir.
Minister of Culture: Nevine al-Kilani.
Minister of Communications and Information Technology: Dr Amr Ahmed Talaat.
Minister of Petroleum and Mineral Resources: Eng. Tarek Ahmed el-Molla.
Minister of Transport: Eng. Kamel Abd el-Hady al-Wazir.

Minister of Housing, Utilities and Urban Communities: Dr ASEM ABD EL-HAMID AL-GAZZAR.
Minister of State for Sports and Youth Affairs: Dr ASHRAF SOBHY AMER.
Minister of Local Development: HISHAM AMNA.
Minister of Environment: Dr YASSMIN FOUAD.
Minister of International Co-operation: Dr RANIA ABD EL-MONEIM AL-MASHAT.
Minister of Parliamentary Affairs: ALAA EL-DIN FOUAD.
Minister of Water Resources and Irrigation: HANY SEWILAM.
Minister of State for Military Production: MOHAMED SALAH EL-DIN.
Minister of Immigration and Egyptian Expatriates Affairs: SOHA AL-GENDY.
Minister of Justice: OMAR MARWAN.
Minister of Antiquities and Tourism: AHMED ISSA TAHA.
Minister of Public Enterprise Sector: MAHMOUD ESMA.

MINISTRIES

Ministries began relocating their operations to the New Administrative Capital in late 2021.

Office of the Prime Minister: 2 Sharia Majlis al-Sha'ab, Cairo 11582; tel. (2) 55508688; e-mail questions@cabinet.gov.eg; internet www.cabinet.gov.eg.

Ministry of Agriculture and Land Cultivation: 1 Sharia Nadi el-Seid, Cairo (Dokki); tel. (2) 33372677; fax (2) 37498128; e-mail info.malr@agr-egypt.gov.eg; internet www.agr-egypt.gov.eg.

Ministry of Antiquities and Tourism: 3 Sharia el-Adel Abu Bakr, Cairo (Zamalek); tel. 19654; fax (2) 27354532; e-mail egymonuments@moantiq.gov.eg; internet egymonuments.gov.eg.

Ministry of Awqaf (Islamic Endowments): Sharia Sabri Abu Alam, Bab el-Louk, Cairo; tel. (2) 23931216; fax (2) 23929828.

Ministry of Civil Aviation: Sharia Cairo Airport, Cairo; tel. (2) 22677610; fax (2) 22679470; e-mail info@civilaviation.gov.eg; internet www.civilaviation.gov.eg.

Ministry of Communications and Information Technology: Smart Village, km 28, Sharia Cairo–Alexandria, Cairo; tel. (2) 35341300; fax (2) 35371111; e-mail webmaster@mcit.gov.eg; internet www.mcit.gov.eg.

Ministry of Culture: 2 Sharia Shagaret el-Dor, Cairo (Zamalek); tel. (2) 27485065; fax (2) 27353947; e-mail media@moc.gov.eg; internet www.moc.gov.eg.

Ministry of Defence: Sharia 23 July, Kobri el-Kobba, Cairo; tel. (2) 22602566; fax (2) 22906004; e-mail mmc@afmic.gov.eg; internet www.mod.gov.eg.

Ministry of Education: 12 Sharia el-Falaky, Cairo; tel. (2) 27963273; fax (2) 27921351; internet moe.gov.eg.

Ministry of Electricity and Renewable Energy: POB 11517, 8 Sharia Ramses, Abbassia Sq., Cairo (Nasr City); tel. (2) 26855549; fax (2) 22616234; e-mail info@moere.gov.eg; internet www.moee.gov.eg.

Ministry of Finance: Ministry of Finance Towers, Cairo (Nasr City); tel. (2) 23428830; fax (2) 26861561; internet www.mof.gov.eg.

Ministry of Foreign Affairs: Corniche el-Nil, Cairo (Maspiro); tel. (2) 25749820; fax (2) 25767967; e-mail contact.us@mfa.gov.eg; internet www.mfa.gov.eg.

Ministry of Health and Population: 3 Sharia Majlis al-Sha'ab, Lazoughli Sq., Cairo; tel. (2) 27943462; fax (2) 27953966; e-mail webmaster@mohp.gov.eg; internet www.mohp.gov.eg.

Ministry of Higher Education and Scientific Research: 101 Sharia Qasr el-Eini, Cairo; tel. (2) 27950682; fax (2) 27941005; e-mail info@mohesr.gov.eg; internet mohesr.gov.eg.

Ministry of Housing, Utilities and Urban Communities: 1 Sharia Ismail Abaza, 3rd Floor, Qasr el-Eini, Cairo; tel. (2) 27921365; fax (2) 27957836; e-mail egypt@ad.gov.eg; internet www.mhuc.gov.eg.

Ministry of Immigration and Egyptian Expatriates Affairs: Cairo; tel. (2) 33036433; fax (2) 33035332; e-mail egyptiansabroad@emigration.gov.eg; internet www.emigration.gov.eg.

Ministry of the Interior: 25 Sharia Sheikh Rihan, Bab el-Louk, Cairo; tel. (2) 24060785; fax (2) 24060579; e-mail center@moi.gov.eg.

Ministry of Investment and International Co-operation: 8 Sharia Adli, Cairo; tel. (2) 23908819; fax (2) 23908159; internet www.miic.gov.eg.

Ministry of Justice: Cairo; tel. (2) 27922263; fax (2) 27958103; internet www.jp.gov.eg.

Ministry of Local Development: 4 Sharia Nadi el-Seid, Cairo (Dokki); tel. (2) 33356708; e-mail info@mld.gov.eg; internet www.mld.gov.eg.

Ministry of Manpower: 3 Sharia Yousuf Abbas, Cairo (Nasr City); tel. (2) 22609359; fax (2) 23035332; internet www.manpower.gov.eg.

Ministry of Military Production: 5 Sharia Ismail Abaza, Qasr el-Eini, Cairo; tel. 19827; e-mail momp@momp.gov.eg; internet www.momp.gov.eg.

Ministry of Parliamentary Affairs: Cairo; tel. (2) 27926599; fax (2) 27942721.

Ministry of Petroleum and Mineral Resources: 1 Sharia Ahmad el-Zomor, Cairo (Nasr City); tel. (2) 26706401; e-mail contact@petroleum.gov.eg; internet www.petroleum.gov.eg.

Ministry of Planning and Economic Development: POB 11765, Sharia Salah Salem, Cairo (Nasr City); tel. (2) 24000100; fax (2) 24014619; e-mail contact@mop.gov.eg; internet www.mpmar.gov.eg.

Ministry of Public Enterprise Sector: Cairo.

Ministry of Social Solidarity: 13 Sharia al-Alfy, al-Fahra, Cairo; tel. (2) 25912453; internet www.moss.gov.eg.

Ministry of Supply and Internal Trade: 99 Sharia Qasr el-Eini, Cairo; tel. (2) 27958481; fax (2) 27956835; e-mail info@msit.gov.eg; internet www.msit.gov.eg.

Ministry of Tourism: 1 Abbasya Sq, Cairo; e-mail promotion@mota.gov.eg; internet www.egypt.travel.

Ministry of Trade and Industry: 2 Sharia Latin America, Cairo (Garden City); tel. (2) 27921224; fax (2) 27957487; internet www.mti.gov.eg.

Ministry of Transport: 105 Sharia Qasr el-Eini, Cairo; tel. (2) 2604884; fax (2) 2610510; internet www.mot.gov.eg.

Ministry of Water Resources and Irrigation: 1 Sharia Gamal Abd al-Nasser, Corniche el-Nil, Imbaba, Cairo; tel. (2) 35449420; fax (2) 35449410; e-mail minister_office@mwri.gov.eg; internet www.mwri.gov.eg.

President

Presidential Election, 26–28 March 2018

Candidate	Votes	%
Abd al-Fatah al-Sisi	21,835,378	97.08
Moussa Moustafa Moussa	656,534	2.92
Total*	22,491,912	100.00

* Excluding 1,762,240 invalid votes (7.26% of total votes cast).

Legislature

HOUSE OF REPRESENTATIVES

House of Representatives: 1 Sharia Majlis Sha'ab, Cairo; tel. (2) 227931211; fax (2) 227948977; e-mail publicopinion@parliament.gov.eg; internet www.parliament.gov.eg.

Speaker: HANAFY ALI EL-GEBALY.

Elections, 24 October–24 November 2020 (first round); 7 November–8 December 2020 (second round)

Party	Seats
Mostaqbal Watan	316
Republican People's Party	50
New Wafd Party	25
Homeland Defenders Party	23
Modern Egypt Party	11
Others*	46
Independents	97
Nominees	28
Total†	596

* Other parties represented in the chamber included Al-Nour and the National Progressive Unionist Party (Tagammu); none of these secured more than nine seats.

† Of the 568 elective seats, 284 seats were allocated to party lists under a system of proportional representation, while the remaining 284 seats were allocated to individual candidates who may or may not be affiliated to political organizations. A further 28 seats are allocated to persons nominated by the President.

SENATE

On 2 July 2020 President Abd al-Fatah al-Sisi approved legislation which provided for the formation of a second legislative chamber, the Senate. The chamber comprises 300 members, 100 of whom are elected via closed lists, 100 on an individual basis and a further 100 appointed by the President. Some 10% of the total seats are reserved for female candidates. The first phase of elections to the new chamber took place on 9–12 August, with run-off polls on 6–9 September. The pro-Government National Unified List, led by the Mostaqbal Watan party, secured all of the 100 seats reserved for party lists, with 50 of those won by Mostaqbal Watan. That party also secured 68 of the seats allocated to individual candidates, taking its total to 118 seats. On 17 October the President appointed the remaining 100 members and the opening session of the Senate took place on the following day.

Senate: Cairo.
Speaker: ABDEL WAHAB ABDEL RAZEQ.

Election Commission

National Election Authority (NEA): Cairo; internet www.elections.eg; f. 2017 to replace the Higher Election Commission; 10-mem. board of dirs and 4-mem. exec; Chair. WALID HASSAN HAMZA.

Political Organizations

Arab Democratic Nasserist Party (ADNP): 8 Sharia Talaat Harb, Cairo; tel. (2) 25781004; internet fb.com/profile.php?id=100064551857969; f. 1992; advocates maintaining the principles of the 1952 Revolution, achieving a strong national economy and protecting human rights; split into two factions in 2021 following the death of its leader, Sayed Abdel-Ghani; Chair. MOHAMED EL-NIMER.

The Constitution Party: Cairo; f. 2012; Leader JAMILA ISMAIL.

Democratic Generation Party (Hizb al-Geel al-Dimuqrati): Bldg 26, Sharia Ismail Abaza, Saad Zaghloul Metro Station, Cairo; tel. and fax 3103010; internet info@hzpelgeel.com; internet dgparty.org; f. 2002; advocates improvements in education and youth-based policies; Chair. NAGUI EL-SHEHABY.

Democratic Peace Party: Cairo; f. 2005; Chair. AHMAD MUHAMMAD BAYOUMI AL-FADALI.

Egyptian Arab Socialist Party (Hizb Misr al-Arabi al-Ishtiraki): f. 1976; seeks to maintain principles of the 1952 Revolution and to preserve Egypt's Islamic identity; f. 1985; Leader AHMED BAHAA EL-DIN SHAABAN.

Egyptian Communist Party: Cairo; tel. (2) 75469934; e-mail cpegypt@gmail.com; internet fb.com/c.pegypting; f. 1922; Marxist-Leninist; Leader SALAH ADLY.

Egyptian Progressive Green Party (Hizb al-Khudr al-Misri): 9 Sharia al-Tahrir, Cairo (Dokki); tel. and fax (2) 33364748; e-mail awad@egyptiangreens.com; internet www.egyptiangreens.com; f. 1990; Pres. MUHAMMAD AWAD.

Egyptian Islamic Labour Party: 12 Sharia Awali el-Ahd, Cairo; e-mail magdyahmedhussein@gmail.com; internet www.el3amal.net; f. 1978; official opposition party; pro-Islamist; seeks establishment of economic system based on *Shari'a* (Islamic) law, unity between Egypt, Sudan and Libya, and the liberation of occupied Palestinian territory; Sec.-Gen. MUHAMMAD MAGDI AHMAD HUSSEIN.

Free Egyptians Party (Hizb al-Masryin al-Ahrar): 15 Sharia al-Amal, Cairo; e-mail press.almasreyeenelahrar@gmail.com; internet fb.com/almasreyeenalahrrar; f. 2011; merged with Democratic Front Party (f. 2007) in Jan. 2014; seeks to promote liberal democracy, the rule of law and a civil society; mem. of the Egyptian Bloc; Pres. ESSAM KHALIL.

Al-Ghad (Tomorrow) Party: Cairo; internet www.elghad.com; f. 2004; aims to combat poverty and to improve the living conditions of Egypt's citizens; Chair. Eng. MOUSSA MUSTAFA MOUSSA.

Homeland Defenders Party: Cairo; left-wing party; Sec.-Gen. TAREK NOSSEIR.

Misr el-Fatah (Young Egypt Party): f. 1990; pursues a socialist, nationalist and reformist agenda; Chair. OSAMA KAMEL.

Modern Egypt Party: Cairo; f. 2011; liberal democratic; Leader Dr WALID DEIBIS.

Mostaqbal Watan (Nation's Future Party): 16 Hussein Hegazy, el-Sayeda Zainab, Cairo; e-mail info@mostaqbal-watan.org; f. 2014; Leader ABDEL WAHAB ABDEL RAZEK.

Muslim Brotherhood (Al-Ikhwan al-Muslimun): internet www.ikhwanonline.com; f. 1928, with the aim of establishing an Islamic society; banned in 1954; transnational org.; advocates the adoption of *Shari'a* (Islamic) law as the sole basis of the Egyptian legal system; founded Freedom and Justice Party to contest at least one-half of the seats at 2011–12 legislative elections; proscribed by the interim Govt in Dec. 2013; Supreme Guide Dr SALAH ABDEL-HAQ (acting).

National Accord Party (Hizb al-Wifaq al-Qawmi): f. 2000; Arab nationalist; Chair. MOHAMED REFAAT.

National Progressive Unionist Party (NPUP) (Hizb al-Tagammu' al-Watani al-Taqadomi al-Wahdawi—Tagammu): 1 Sharia Karim el-Dawlah, Cairo; e-mail altagamoa@altagamoa.com; internet fb.com/tagamoa.party; f. 1976; left-wing; seeks to defend the principles of the 1952 Revolution; was part of the Coalition for Egypt for the 2020 legislative elections; Chair. SAYID ABD AL-AAL.

New Wafd Party (New Delegation Party): POB 357, 1 Boulos Hanna St, Cairo (Dokki); tel. (2) 33383111; fax (2) 37603060; internet www.alwafd.org; f. 1919 as Wafd Party; banned 1952; re-formed as New Wafd Party Feb. 1978; disbanded June 1978; re-formed 1983; seeks further political, economic and social reforms, greater democracy, the abolition of emergency legislation, and improvements to the health and education sectors; Chair. ABDEL-SANAD YAMAMA.

Al-Nour Party: 6–7, Mohamed Rushdy, Cairo; tel. (1) 5491742; e-mail info@alnourpartyeg.com; internet alnourpartyeg.com/ar; f. 2011; Salafist; Chair Dr MOHAMED IBRAHIM MANSOUR.

The Reform and Development Party (al-Islah wa al-Tanmiya): 28 Samir Mokhtar St, Ard El Golf, Cairo; tel. 1001506771; e-mail rdp.egypt@gmail.com; internet www.rdpegypt.org; f. 2009; was denied licence 2010; formed by merger of the Reformation and Development Party with the Masrena Party; Chair. MOHAMED ANWAR ESMAT EL-SADAT.

Republican People's Party: Cairo; f. 1992; Chair. HAZEM OMAR.

Al-Wasat Party: 8 Pearl St, Mokattam, Cairo; tel. (2) 23646016; internet fb.com/alwasatparty; f. 2011; originally formed 1996 but denied licence under rule of former President Hosni Mubarak; Pres. ABUL ELA MADI.

Diplomatic Representation

EMBASSIES IN EGYPT

Afghanistan: 59 Sharia el-Orouba, Cairo 11341 (Heliopolis); tel. (2) 24177236; e-mail cairo@mfa.af; internet fb.com/afghanistanineg; Ambassador (vacant).

Albania: Ground Floor, 27 Sharia Gezira al-Wissta, Cairo (Zamalek); tel. (2) 27361815; fax (2) 27356966; e-mail embassy.cairo@mfa.gov.al; internet www.ambasadat.gov.al/egypt; Ambassador EDUARD SULO.

Algeria: 14 Sharia Bresil, Cairo (Zamalek); tel. (2) 7368527; fax (2) 7364158; Ambassador ABDELAZIZ BEN ALI ECHERIF (designate).

Angola: 256 Sharia, Bldg 6, New Maadi, Cairo; tel. (2) 25173572; fax (2) 25173564; e-mail angoembcai@angolaeg.net; internet www.angolaeg.net; Ambassador NELSON MANUEL COSME.

Argentina: 1st Floor, 8 Sharia el-Saleh Ayoub, Cairo (Zamalek); tel. (2) 27351501; fax (2) 27364355; e-mail eegip@cancilleria.gob.ar; internet eegip.cancilleria.gov.ar; Ambassador GONZALO URRIOLABEITIA.

Armenia: 20 Sharia Muhammad Mazhar, Cairo (Zamalek); tel. (2) 27374157; fax (2) 27374158; e-mail armegyptembassy@mfa.am; internet egypt.mfa.am; Ambassador HRACHYA POLADIYAN.

Australia: 11th Floor, World Trade Centre, Corniche el-Nil, Cairo 11111 (Boulac); tel. (2) 27706600; fax (2) 27706650; e-mail cairo.austremb@dfat.gov.au; internet www.egypt.embassy.gov.au; Ambassador AXEL WABENHORST.

Austria: 3 Sharia Abu el-Feda, 15th Floor, Zamalek, Cairo 11211 (Giza); tel. (2) 35702975; fax (2) 35702979; internet www.bmeia.gv.at/kairo; Ambassador Dr GEORG PÖSTINGER.

Azerbaijan: Villa 16/24, 10 Sharia, Maadi Sarayat, Cairo; tel. (2) 23583761; fax (2) 23583725; e-mail embassy.azerbaijan.cairo@gmail.com; internet cairo.mfa.gov.az; Ambassador ELKHAN POLUKHOV.

Bahrain: POB 1111, 15 Sharia Bresil, Cairo (Zamalek); tel. (2) 27357996; fax (2) 27366609; e-mail cairo.mission@mofa.gov.bh; internet www.mofa.gov.bh/cairo; Ambassador FAWZIA BINT ABDULLAH ZAINAL.

Bangladesh: 259 Sharia, Bldg 3, New Maadi, Cairo; tel. (2) 25162808; fax (2) 25162819; e-mail mission.cairo@mofa.gov.bd; internet cairo.mofa.gov.bd; Ambassador SAMINA NAZ (designate).

Belarus: 26 Sharia Gaber bin Hayan, Cairo (Dokki); tel. (2) 37499171; fax (2) 33389545; e-mail egypt@mfa.gov.by; internet egypt.mfa.gov.by; Ambassador SERGEI TERENTIEV.

Belgium: POB 37, 20 Sharia Kamal el-Shennawi, Cairo 11511 (Garden City); tel. (2) 27949163; e-mail cairo@diplobel.fed.be; internet egypt.diplomatie.belgium.be; Ambassador FRANÇOIS CORNET D'ELZIUS.

Bolivia: 21 New Ramses Centre, Sharia B. Oman, Cairo 11794 (Dokki); tel. (2) 37624361; fax (2) 37624360; e-mail info@emboliviaeg.com; internet fb.com/emboliviaegypt; Ambassador RUBEN DOMINGO VIDAURRE ANDRADE.

Bosnia and Herzegovina: 42 Sharia al-Sawra, Cairo (Dokki); tel. (2) 37499191; fax (2) 37499190; e-mail ambbihcairo@gmail.com; Ambassador SABIT SUBAŠIĆ.

Brazil: Nile City Towers, North Tower, 2005C, Corniche el-Nil, Cairo; tel. (2) 24619837; fax (2) 24619838; e-mail consular.cairo@itamaraty.gov.br; internet cairo.itamaraty.gov.br; Ambassador ANTONIO PATRIOTA.

Brunei Darussalam: Villa 191, M6, 1st District, 5th Settlement, Cairo; tel. (2) 25652463; fax (2) 25652465; e-mail embassy@mfa.gov.bn; Ambassador Haji MOHD. SALIMIN BIN Haji MOHD. DAUD.

Bulgaria: 6 Sharia el-Malek el-Afdal, Cairo (Zamalek); tel. (2) 27366077; fax (2) 27363826; e-mail embassy.cairo@mfa.bg; internet www.mfa.bg/en/embassies/egypt; Ambassador DEYAN KATRATCHEV.

Burkina Faso: 22 Sharia Wadi el-Nil, Mohandessin, Cairo 11794; tel. (2) 23808956; internet fb.com/ambassade-du-burkina-faso-au-caire-177479782932824; Ambassador ALASSANE MONE.

Burundi: 27 Sharia el-Ryad, Mohandessin, Cairo; tel. (2) 33024301; fax (2) 33441997; Chargé d'affaires a.i. JULES ARISTIDE NDATIMANA.

Cambodia: Villa 2E, Sharia Gamal Hemdan, Cairo (Dokki); tel. (2) 37629973; e-mail camemb.egy@mfaic.gov.kh; Ambassador UK SARUN.

Cameroon: POB 2061, 15 Sharia Muhammad Sedki Soliman, Mohandessin, Cairo; tel. (2) 33441101; fax (2) 33459208; e-mail ambacam@ambacamcaire.com; internet ambacamcaire.com; Ambassador Dr MOHAMADOU LABARANG.

Canada: Nile City Towers, South Tower, 18th Floor, 2005A Sharia Corniche el-Nil, Cairo 11221; tel. (2) 24612200; fax (2) 24612201; e-mail cairo@international.gc.ca; internet www.international.gc.ca/world-monde/egypt-egypte/cairo-caire.aspx; Ambassador LOUIS DUMAS.

Chad: POB 1869, 12 Midan al-Refaï, Cairo 11511 (Dokki); tel. (2) 37493403; fax (2) 37492733; Ambassador TCHONAI ELIMI HASSAN.

Chile: 1 Saleh Ayoub, Suite 31, Cairo (Zamalek); tel. (2) 27358711; fax (2) 27353716; e-mail echile.egipto@minrel.gov.cl; internet chile.gob.cl/egipto; Ambassador ROBERTO GERARDO EBERT GROB.

China, People's Republic: 14 Sharia Bahgat Ali, Cairo (Zamalek); tel. (2) 27363556; fax (2) 27359459; e-mail webmaster_eg@mfa.gov.cn; internet eg.china-embassy.org; Ambassador LIAO LIQIANG.

Colombia: 6 Sharia Guezira, Cairo (Zamalek); tel. (2) 27364203; fax (2) 27357429; e-mail eegipto@cancilleria.gov.co; internet egipto.embajada.gov.co; Ambassador ANA MILENA MUÑOZ DE GAVIRIA.

Congo, Democratic Republic: 5 Sharia Mansour Muhammad, Cairo (Zamalek); tel. (2) 23403662; fax (2) 23404342; Ambassador KASINGO MUSINGA.

Côte d'Ivoire: Villa 2, 212 Maadi Degla Medan, Victoria, Cairo; tel. (2) 25214012; fax (2) 25214107; e-mail ambacicaire@yahoo.fr; internet www.egypte.diplomatie.gouv.ci; Ambassador TIMOTHÉE EZOUAN.

Croatia: 3 Sharia Abou el-Feda, Cairo (Zamalek); tel. (2) 27383155; fax (2) 27355812; e-mail croemb.caire@mvep.hr; internet mvep.gov.hr/eg/en; Ambassador TOMISLAV BOŠNJAK.

Cuba: Villa 14, 202 Sharia, Degla Maadi, Cairo; tel. (2) 25195762; fax (2) 25213324; e-mail embajada@eg.embacuba.cu; internet misiones.minrex.gob.cu/es/egipto; Ambassador TANIA AGUIAR FERNÁNDEZ.

Cyprus: Apt 301, 3rd Floor, 23 Sharia Muhammad Mazhar, Cairo (Zamalek); tel. (2) 27377012; fax (2) 27377016; e-mail cairoembassy@mfa.gov.cy; Ambassador POLLY IOANNOU.

Czech Republic: 1st Floor, 4 Sharia Dokki, Cairo 12511 (Giza); tel. (2) 33339700; fax (2) 37485892; e-mail cairo@embassy.mzv.cz; internet www.mfa.cz/cairo; Ambassador IVAN JUKL.

Denmark: Nile City Tower, North Tower, 7th Floor, Corniche el-Nil, Ramlet Boulaq, Cairo 11221; tel. (2) 24616630; fax (2) 24619330; e-mail caiamb@um.dk; internet www.egypten.um.dk; Ambassador ANNE DORTE RIGGELSEN.

Djibouti: 11 Sharia Muhammad Abdou el-Said, Cairo (Dokki); tel. (2) 33366436; fax (2) 33366437; Ambassador AHMED ALI BARREH.

Ecuador: 5 Sharia Ibn el-Nabih, Cairo (Zamalek); tel. (2) 27361839; e-mail eecuegipto@cancilleria.gob.ec; internet www.cancilleria.gob.ec/map_maps/egipto/; Ambassador DENYS TOSCANO AMORES.

Equatorial Guinea: 56 Sharia Abdel Moneim Riad, Mohandessin, Cairo (Giza); tel. (2) 33450495; fax (2) 33450497; e-mail embajadadeguineaecuatorial.eg@gmail.com; Ambassador GERMAN EKUA SIMA ABAGA.

Eritrea: 6 Sharia el-Fallah, Mohandessin, Cairo; tel. (2) 33033503; fax (2) 33030516; e-mail eritembe@yahoo.com; Ambassador FASIL GEBRESELASIE.

Estonia: 8th Floor, Abou el-Feda Bldg, 3 Sharia Abou el-Feda, Cairo 11211 (Zamalek); tel. (20) 1844753; fax (2) 27384189; e-mail embassy.cairo@mfa.ee; internet cairo.mfa.ee; Ambassador INGRID AMER.

Ethiopia: 21 Sharia Sheikh Muhammad el-Gehzali, Cairo (Dokki); tel. (2) 33355958; fax (2) 33353699; Ambassador HASSAN IBRAHIM.

Finland: 13th Floor, 3 Sharia Abou el-Feda, Cairo 11211 (Zamalek); tel. (2) 25869000; fax (2) 27371376; e-mail sanomat.kai@formin.fi; internet finlandabroad.fi/web/egy; Ambassador PEKKA KOSONEN.

France: POB 1777, 29 Sharia Charles de Gaulle, Cairo (Giza); tel. (2) 35673200; internet eg.ambafrance.org; Ambassador MARC BARETY.

Gabon: 17 Sharia Mecca el-Moukarama, Cairo (Dokki); tel. (2) 33379699; Ambassador NAZIH GUY ROGER.

Georgia: 11 Sharia Tanta, Aswan Sq., Mohandessin, Cairo; tel. (2) 33044798; fax (2) 33044778; e-mail cairo.emb@mfa.gov.ge; internet www.egypt.mfa.gov.ge; Chargé d'affaires a.i. MIKHEIL TIGISHVILI.

Germany: 2 Sharia Berlin (off Sharia Hassan Sabri), Cairo (Zamalek); tel. (2) 27282000; fax (2) 27282159; e-mail info@kairo.diplo.de; internet www.kairo.diplo.de; Ambassador FRANK HARTMANN.

Ghana: 6 Sharia Tanta, Agouza, off Aswan Sq., Cairo; tel. (2) 33032290; e-mail cairo@mfa.gov.gh; internet ghanaembassy-egypt.com; Ambassador OBED BOAMAH AKWA.

Greece: 18 Sharia Aicha al-Taimouria, Cairo 11451 (Garden City); tel. (2) 27950443; fax (2) 27963903; e-mail gremb.cai@mfa.gr; internet www.mfa.gr/egypt; Ambassador NIKOLAOS PAPAGEORGIOU.

Guinea: 46 Sharia Muhammad Mazhar, Cairo (Zamalek); tel. (2) 27358109; fax (2) 27361446; Ambassador SORIBA CAMARA.

Holy See: Apostolic Nunciature, Safarat al-Vatican, 5 Sharia Muhammad Mazhar, Cairo (Zamalek); tel. (2) 27353350; Apostolic Nuncio Most Rev. NICOLAS HENRY MARIE DENIS THEVENIN (Titular Archbishop of Aeclanum).

Honduras: 8th Floor, 5 Sharia el-Israa, Mohandessin, Cairo; tel. (2) 33441337; fax (2) 33441338; e-mail hondemb@idsc.net.eg; Ambassador NELSON VALENCIA.

Hungary: 29 Sharia Muhammad Mazhar, Cairo 11211 (Zamalek); tel. (2) 27358634; fax (2) 27358648; e-mail mission.cai@kum.hu; internet kairo.mfa.gov.hu; Ambassador ANDRÁS KOVÁCS.

India: 5 Sharia Aziz Abaza, Cairo (Zamalek); tel. (2) 27363051; fax (2) 27364038; e-mail info.cairo@mea.gov.in; internet www.eoicairo.gov.in; Ambassador AJIT VINAYAK GUPTE.

Indonesia: POB 1661, 13 Sharia Aicha al-Taimouria, Cairo (Garden City); tel. (2) 24715561; fax (2) 24726772; e-mail info@kbri-cairo.org; internet kemlu.go.id/cairo; Ambassador LOTFI RAOUF.

Iraq: 9 Sharia Mohamed Mazhar, Cairo (Zamalek); tel. (2) 37622731; fax (2) 37622517; e-mail caiemb@mofa.gov.iq; internet www.mofa.gov.iq/cairo; Ambassador AHMED NAYEF AL-DULAIMI.

Ireland: 18 Sharia Hassan Sabri, Cairo 11211 (Zamalek); tel. (2) 27287100; fax (2) 27362863; e-mail cairoembassy@dfa.ie; internet www.dfa.ie/irish-embassy/egypt; Ambassador NUALA O'BRIEN.

Israel: 25 Sharia Moustafa Kamel, Maadi, Cairo; tel. (2) 33321500; fax (2) 33321555; e-mail info@cairo.mfa.gov.il; Ambassador AMIRA ORON.

Italy: 15 Sharia Abd al-Rahman Fahmi, Cairo (Garden City); tel. (2) 27943194; fax (2) 27940657; e-mail ambasciata.cairo@esteri.it; internet www.ambilcairo.esteri.it; Ambassador MICHELE QUARONI.

Japan: POB 500, 81 Sharia Corniche el-Nil, Maadi, Cairo; tel. (2) 25285910; fax (2) 25285905; e-mail culture@ca.mofa.go.jp; internet www.eg.emb-japan.go.jp; Ambassador HIROSHI OKA.

Jordan: 6 Sharia Basem al-Kateb, Cairo (Dokki); tel. (2) 37485566; fax (2) 37601027; e-mail cairo@fm.gov.jo; Ambassador AMJAD ODEH AL-ADAYLEH.

Kazakhstan: Villa 371, South Academy, Area A, Sharia Ammar bin Yasser, 5th Settlement, New Cairo, Cairo; tel. (2) 5378079; e-mail cairo@mfa.kz; internet www.gov.kz/memleket/entities/mfa-cairo; Ambassador KAIRAT LAMA SHARIF.

Kenya: 60 Sharia al-Kanal, Maadi, Cairo; tel. (2) 23581260; fax (2) 23580713; e-mail info@kenemb-cairo.com; internet kenemb-cairo.com; Ambassador Maj.-Gen. AYUB G. MATIIRI.

Korea, Democratic People's Republic: 6 Sharia al-Saleh Ayoub, Cairo (Zamalek); tel. (2) 3408219; fax (2) 3414615; Ambassador MA TONG HUI.

Korea, Republic: 3 Sharia Boulos Hanna, Cairo (Dokki); tel. (2) 33611234; fax (2) 33611238; e-mail egypt@mofa.go.kr; internet overseas.mofa.go.kr/eg-ar/index.do; Ambassador HONG JIN-WOOK.

Kuwait: 6 Sharia Dr Mohamed Sobhy, Cairo; tel. (2) 27372120; fax (2) 27371199; e-mail kwcairo@hotmail.com; Ambassador GHANEM SAQER AL-GHANEM.

Latvia: 8th Floor, Abou el-Feda Bldg, 3 Sharia Abou el-Feda, Cairo (Zamalek); tel. (2) 27384188; fax (2) 27384189; e-mail embassy.egypt@mfa.gov.lv; internet www.mfa.gov.lv/egypt; Ambassador ANDRIS RAZĀNS (designate).

Lebanon: 22 Sharia Mansour Muhammad, Cairo (Zamalek); tel. (2) 27382823; fax (2) 27382818; internet www.cairo.mfa.gov.lb; Ambassador ALI HASSAN AL-HALABI.

Lesotho: 5 Sharia Ahmed el-Meleby, Cairo (Dokki); tel. (2) 33369161; fax (2) 25211437; Ambassador BOMO FRANK SOPHONIA.

Liberia: 23 Sharia Qadi Ben Hamadi Senhaji, Souissi, Cairo; e-mail liberianembassycairo@yahoo.com; Ambassador (vacant).

Libya: 4 Sharia Patrice Lumumba, Cairo; tel. (2) 24940286; fax 23934643; Ambassador MOHAMED ABDEL-ALI MESBAH.

Lithuania: 23 Sharia Muhammad Mazhar, Cairo (Zamalek); tel. (2) 27366461; fax (2) 27365130; e-mail amb.eg@mfa.lt; internet eg.mfa.lt; Ambassador ARTŪRAS GAILIŪNAS.

Malaysia: 21 Sharia el-Aanab, Mohandessin, Cairo (Giza); tel. (2) 37610013; fax (2) 37610216; e-mail mwcairo@kln.gov.my; internet www.kln.gov.my/web/egy_cairo; Ambassador ZAMANI ISMAIL.

Mali: POB 844, 3 Sharia al-Kawsar, Giza (Mohandessine); tel. (2) 33371641; fax (2) 33371841; e-mail ambmalicaire@yahoo.fr; Ambassador BOUBACAR DIALLO.

Malta: 9th Floor, N Tower, Nile City Towers, Cairo (Ramlet Boulak); tel. (2) 24619961; fax (2) 27362371; e-mail maltaembassy.cairo@gov.mt; internet fb.com/maltainegypt; Ambassador ROBERTO PATCH.

Mauritania: 114 Mohi el-Din, Abou-el Ezz, Mohandessin, Cairo; tel. (2) 37490671; fax (2) 37491048; Ambassador SIDI MOHAMED MOHAMED ABDALLAHI.

Mauritius: 1st Floor, 33 Sharia Ismail Muhammad, Cairo (Zamalek); tel. (2) 27365208; fax (2) 27365206; e-mail cairoemb@govmu.org; internet mauritius-cairo.govmu.org; Ambassador DATAKARRAN GOBURDHUN.

Mexico: 25 Sharia al-Hadayek, Maadi, 11431 Cairo; tel. (2) 23580256; fax (2) 23780059; e-mail oficial@embamexcairo.com; internet embamex.sre.gob.mx/egipto; Ambassador LEONORA ROSAURA RUEDA GUTIERREZ.

Mongolia: 14 Sharia 152, Maadi, Cairo; tel. (2) 23586012; e-mail cairo@mfa.gov.mn; internet www.fb.com/embassy-of-mongolia-cairo-1618980501695605; Ambassador BULGAN ENKTOVSHIN.

Morocco: 10 Sharia Salah el-Din, Cairo (Zamalek); tel. (2) 27359849; fax (2) 27361937; e-mail ambmorocco-egypt@maec.gov.ma; Ambassador AHMAD TAZI.

Mozambique: 24 Sharia Babel, off Mosaddek, Cairo (Dokki); tel. (2) 37605505; fax (2) 37486378; e-mail embamoc.egipto@minec.gov.mz; Ambassador FILIPE CHIDUMO.

Myanmar: 24 Sharia Muhammad Mazhar, Cairo (Zamalek); tel. (2) 27362644; fax (2) 27357712; e-mail me.cairo@gmail.com; internet mecairo.org; Ambassador MYINT LWIN.

Nepal: 23B Sharia Muhammad Mazhar, Cairo (Zamalek); tel. (2) 27369482; fax (2) 27369481; e-mail eoncairo@mofa.gov.np; internet eg.nepalembassy.gov.np; Ambassador SHUSIL KUMAR LAMSAL.

Netherlands: 18 Sharia Hassan Sabri, Cairo 11211 (Zamalek); tel. (2) 27395500; fax (2) 27363821; e-mail kai@minbuza.nl; internet www.netherlandsworldwide.nl/countries/egypt; Ambassador HENRICUS MAURITIUS SCHAAPVELD.

New Zealand: N Tower, 8th Floor, Nile City Bldg, Sharia Corniche el-Nil, Cairo (Boulac); tel. (2) 24616000; fax (2) 24616099; e-mail enquiries@nzembassy.org.eg; Ambassador AMY LAURENSON.

Niger: 101 Sharia Pyramids, Cairo (Giza); tel. (2) 33865607; fax (2) 33865690; e-mail ambanigercaire@yahoo.fr; Ambassador SANI NANA AÏCHA ANDIA.

Nigeria: 13 Sharia Gabalaya, Cairo (Zamalek); tel. (2) 27356042; fax (2) 27357359; Ambassador NURA ABBA RIMI.

Norway: 8 Sharia el-Gezirah, Cairo (Zamalek); tel. (2) 27283900; fax (2) 27283901; e-mail emb.cairo@mfa.no; internet www.norway.no/egypt; Ambassador HILDE KLEMETSDAL.

Oman: 29 Sharia Taha Hussein, Zamalek, Cairo; tel. (2) 27373182; fax (2) 27373188; e-mail cairo@mofa.gov.om; Ambassador ABDULLAH BIN NASSER AL-RAHBI.

Pakistan: 8 Sharia el-Salouli, Cairo (Dokki); tel. (2) 37487806; fax (2) 37480310; e-mail parepcairo@hotmail.com; internet pakistanembassycairo.org; Ambassador SAJID BILAL.

Panama: POB 62, 4A Sharia Ibn Zanki, Cairo 11211 (Zamalek); tel. (2) 27361093; fax (2) 27361092; e-mail embpanamaegipto@mire.gob.pa; internet www.fb.com/embajadadepanama.egipto; Ambassador ALEJANDRO IVÁN MENDOZA GANTES.

Peru: 41 Sharia el-Nahda, Maadi, Cairo; tel. (2) 23590306; e-mail emperucairo@yahoo.es; Ambassador JOSÉ JESÚS GUILLERMO.

Philippines: Villa 28, 200 Sharia, Cairo (Degla Maadi); tel. (2) 25213064; fax (2) 25213048; e-mail cairo.pe@dfa.gov.ph; internet cairope.dfa.gov.ph; Ambassador EZZEDIN H. TAGO.

Poland: 5 Sharia el-Aziz Osman, Cairo (Zamalek); tel. (2) 27367456; fax (2) 27355427; e-mail cairo.secretariat@msz.gov.pl; internet kair.msz.gov.pl; Ambassador MICHAŁ RAFAŁ ŁABENDA.

Portugal: 25 Ahmad Heshmat, Cairo (Zamalek); tel. (2) 27350779; fax (2) 27350799; e-mail cairo@mne.pt; internet www.cairo.embaixadaportugal.mne.pt; Ambassador RUI TERENO.

Qatar: 10 Sharia al-Thamar, Midan al-Nasr, Madinet al-Mohandessin, Cairo; tel. (2) 37604693; e-mail cairo@mofa.gov.qa; internet cairo.embassy.qa; Ambassador SALEM BIN MUBARAK BIN SHAFI AL-SHAFI.

Romania: 6 Sharia el-Kamel Muhammad, Cairo (Zamalek); tel. (2) 27359546; fax (2) 27360851; e-mail cairo@mae.ro; internet cairo.mae.ro; Ambassador Dr MIHAI ŞTEFAN STUPARU.

Russian Federation: 95 Sharia Giza, Cairo (Dokki); tel. (2) 37489353; fax (2) 37609074; e-mail rus.egypt@mail.ru; internet www.egypt.mid.ru; Ambassador GEORGY BORISENKO.

Rwanda: Cairo; internet fb.com/rwandaembassyegypt; Ambassador DAN MUNYUZA (designate).

Saudi Arabia: Sharia al-Yemen, Cairo (Giza); tel. (2) 37625000; fax (2); e-mail egemb@mofa.gov.sa; internet embassies.mofa.gov.sa/sites/Egypt; Ambassador OSAMA NUGALI.

Senegal: 46 Sharia Abd al-Moneim Riad, Mohandessin, Cairo (Dokki); tel. (2) 33460946; fax (2) 33461039; e-mail mamadousow@hotmail.com; Ambassador KÉMOKO DIAKITE (designate).

Serbia: 33 Sharia Mansour Muhammad, Cairo (Zamalek); tel. (2) 27365494; fax (2) 27353913; e-mail serbia@serbiaeg.com; internet www.cairo.mfa.gov.rs; Ambassador MIROSLAV ŠESTOVIĆ.

Sierra Leone: Villa No. 18, St 18, Sarayat, Maadi, Cairo; tel. (2) 23801398; e-mail info@eg.slembassy.gov.sl; Ambassador SADIQ SILLAH.

Singapore: 40 Sharia Adnan Omar Sedki, Cairo 11511 (Dokki); tel. (2) 37490468; fax (2) 37480562; e-mail singemb_cai@mfa.sg; internet www.mfa.gov.sg/cairo; Ambassador DOMINIC GOH.

Slovakia: POB 450, 3 Sharia Adel Hussein Rostom, Dokki, Cairo (Giza); tel. (2) 33358240; fax (2) 33355810; e-mail emb.cairo@mzv.sk; internet www.mzv.sk/web/kahira; Ambassador LENKA MIHALIKOVA.

Slovenia: 21 Sharia Soliman Abaza, Mohandessin, Cairo 12311; tel. (2) 37498171; fax (2) 37497141; e-mail sloembassy.cairo@gov.si; internet cairo.embassy.si; Ambassador SAŠO PODLESNIK.

Somalia: 27 Sharia el-Somal, Cairo (Dokki), Giza; tel. (2) 33374038; fax (2) 33374577; e-mail cairoembassy@mfa.gov.so; Ambassador ILYAS SHEIKH OMAR.

South Africa: Bldg 11, 200–203 Sharia Degla, Maadi, Cairo; tel. (2) 25353000; fax (2) 25213261; e-mail essaemb@idsc.net.eg; internet www.dirco.gov.za/cairo; Ambassador NTSIKI MASHIMBYE.

Spain: 41 Sharia Ismail Muhammad, Cairo (Zamalek); tel. (2) 27356437; fax (2) 27352132; e-mail emb.elcairo@maec.es; internet www.exteriores.gob.es/embajadas/elcairo; Ambassador ÁLVARO IRANZO GUTIÉRREZ.

Sri Lanka: POB 1157, 8 Sharia Sri Lanka, Cairo (Zamalek); tel. (2) 27351406; e-mail slemb.cairo@mfa.gov.lk; internet fb.com/slembcairo; Ambassador M. K. PATHMANAATHAN.

Sudan: 3 Sharia el-Ibrahimi, Cairo (Garden City); tel. (2) 27949661; fax (2) 27942693; Ambassador AL-SADIQ OMAR ABDULLAH.

Sweden: POB 131, 13 Sharia Muhammad Mazhar, Cairo (Zamalek); tel. (2) 27289200; fax (2) 27289260; e-mail ambassaden.kairo@gov.se; internet www.swedenabroad.com/cairo; Ambassador HÅKAN EMSGÅRD.

Switzerland: POB 633, 10 Sharia Abd al-Khalek Sarwat, 11511 Cairo; tel. (2) 25758284; fax (2) 25745236; e-mail cairo@eda.admin.ch; internet www.eda.admin.ch/cairo; Ambassador YVONNE BAUMANN.

Syrian Arab Republic: 24 Sharia Kamel el-Shenawi, Cairo (Garden City); tel. (2) 27924325; fax (2) 27924326; Ambassador HOUSSAM AL-DIN ALA.

Tajikistan: POB 11431, Villa 15, Sharia 2251, Cairo (Degla Maadi); tel. 23783210; fax 23803955; e-mail tajembcairo@mfa.tj; internet www.mfa.tj/en/cairo; Ambassador ZAROBIDDIN QOSIMI.

Tanzania: 10 Sharia Anas Ibn Malek, Mohandessin, Cairo; tel. (2) 33374155; fax (2) 33374286; e-mail cairo@nje.go.tz; internet eg.tzembassy.go.tz; Ambassador Maj.-Gen. RICHARD MUTAYOBA MAKANZO (designate).

Thailand: Villa 19, Sharia Abdallah al-Ketab, Cairo (Dokki), Giza; tel. (2) 37603553; fax (2) 37605076; e-mail thaiemb.cairo@gmail.com; internet cairo.thaiembassy.org; Ambassador PUTTAPORN EWTOKSAN.

Tunisia: 26 Sharia el-Jazirah, Cairo (Zamalek); tel. (2) 27368962; e-mail at.caire@diplomatie.gov.tn; internet www.diplomatie.gov.tn/en/nc/mission/etranger/ambassade-de-tunisie-a-le-caire-egypte; Ambassador MOHAMED BEN YOUSSEF.

Türkiye (Turkey): 25 Sharia Felaki, Cairo (Bab el-Louk); tel. (2) 27978400; fax (2) 27978477; e-mail embassy.cairo@mfa.gov.tr; internet cairo.emb.mfa.gov.tr; Ambassador SALIH MUTLU ŞEN.

EGYPT

Uganda: 66 Rd 10, Maadi, Cairo; tel. (2) 23802514; fax (2) 23802504; e-mail ugembco@link.net; internet cairo.mofa.go.ug; Ambassador SAM MALE SEBULIBA.

Ukraine: 50 Sharia 83, Maadi, Cairo; tel. (2) 23786871; fax (2) 23786873; e-mail emb_eg@mfa.gov.ua; internet egypt.mfa.gov.ua; Ambassador NAGORNY MYKOLA.

United Arab Emirates: 4 Sharia Ibn Sina, Cairo (Giza); tel. (2) 37766101; fax (2) 35700844; e-mail cairoemb@mofaic.gov.ae; internet www.mofaic.gov.ae/en/missions/cairo; Ambassador MARYAM KHALIFA JUMA AL-KAABI.

United Kingdom: 7 Sharia Ahmad Ragheb, Cairo (Garden City); tel. (2) 27916000; fax (2) 27916131; e-mail cairo.press@fco.gov.uk; internet www.gov.uk/world/organisations/british-embassy-cairo; Ambassador GARETH BAYLEY.

USA: 5 Sharia Tawfik Diab, Cairo (Garden City); tel. (2) 27973300; fax (2) 27973200; e-mail pressinfoegypt@state.gov; internet eg.usembassy.gov; Chargé d'affaires JOHN DESROCHER.

Uruguay: 6 Sharia Lotfallah, Cairo (Zamalek); tel. (2) 27353589; fax (2) 27368123; e-mail uruegipto@mrree.gub.uy; Ambassador FERNANDO ARDIANA LISSIDINI.

Uzbekistan: 18 Sharia Sad el-Aali, Cairo (Dokki); tel. (2) 33361723; fax (2) 33361722; e-mail uzembegypt@gmail.com; internet www.uzembegypt.com; Ambassador MANSURBEK KILICHEV.

Venezuela: POB 11543, Villa 25, Sharia 79, el-Nahda Sq., Maadi, Cairo; tel. (2) 23594871; fax (2) 23581639; e-mail embve.egcro@mppre.gob.ve; internet egipto.embajada.gob.ve; Ambassador WILMER OMAR BARRIENTOS FERNÁNDEZ.

Viet Nam: Villa 47, Sharia Ahmed Heshmat, Cairo (Zamalek); tel. (2) 27364327; fax (2) 27366091; e-mail vnemb.eg@mofa.gov.vn; internet vnembassy-cairo.mofa.gov.vn; Ambassador NGUYEN HUI ZONG.

Yemen: 28 Sharia Amean al-Rafai, Cairo (Dokki); tel. (2) 37614224; fax (2) 37604815; internet www.yemenembassy-cairo.com; Ambassador Dr MOHAMED MAREM.

Zimbabwe: 40 Sharia Ghaza, Mohandessin, Cairo; tel. (2) 33059743; fax (2) 33059741; e-mail zimcairo@thewayout.net; Ambassador SHEBBA SHUMBAYAONDA.

Judicial System

The Courts of Law are principally divided into two juridical court systems: Courts of General Jurisdiction and Administrative Courts. Since 1969 the Supreme Constitutional Court has been at the top of the judicial structure.

Supreme Constitutional Court: Corniche el-Nil, Maadi, Cairo; tel. (2) 25246323; fax (2) 27958048; e-mail info@sccourt.gov.eg; internet sccourt.gov.eg; has specific jurisdiction over: (i) judicial review of the constitutionality of laws and regulations; (ii) resolution of positive and negative jurisdictional conflicts and determination of the competent court between the different juridical court systems, e.g. Courts of General Jurisdiction and Administrative Courts, as well as other bodies exercising judicial competence; (iii) determination of disputes over the enforcement of two final but contradictory judgments rendered by two courts each belonging to a different juridical court system; (iv) rendering binding interpretation of laws or decree laws in the event of a dispute in the application of said laws or decree laws, always provided that such a dispute is of a gravity requiring conformity of interpretation under the Constitution; Pres. BOULOS FAHMY ISKANDAR.

Court of Cassation: f. 1931; highest court of general jurisdiction. Its sessions are held in Cairo. Final judgments rendered by Courts of Appeal in criminal and civil litigation may be petitioned to the Court of Cassation by the Defendant or the Public Prosecutor in criminal litigation and by any of the parties in interest in civil litigation on grounds of defective application or interpretation of the law as stated in the challenged judgment, on grounds of irregularity of form or procedure, or violation of due process, and on grounds of defective reasoning of judgment rendered. The Court of Cassation is composed of the President, 41 Vice-Presidents and 92 Justices; Pres. HOSNI HASSAN ABDEL LATIF ABU ZEID.

Courts of Appeal: Cairo; each Court of Appeal has geographical jurisdiction over one or more of the governorates of Egypt, and is divided into Criminal and Civil Chambers. The Criminal Chambers try felonies, and the Civil Chambers hear appeals filed against such judgment rendered by the Tribunals of First Instance where the law so stipulates. Each Chamber is composed of three Superior Judges. Each Court of Appeal is composed of the President, and sufficient numbers of Vice-Presidents and Superior Judges.

Tribunals of First Instance: In each governorate there are one or more Tribunals of First Instance, each of which is divided into several Chambers for criminal and civil litigations. Each Chamber is composed of: (a) a presiding judge, and (b) two sitting judges. A Tribunal of First Instance hears, as an Appellate Court, certain litigations as provided under the law.

District Tribunals: Each District Tribunal is a one-judge ancillary Chamber of a Tribunal of First Instance, having jurisdiction over minor civil and criminal litigations in smaller districts within the jurisdiction of such a Tribunal of First Instance.

Public Prosecution: Cairo; represented at all levels of the Courts of General Jurisdiction in all criminal litigations and also in certain civil litigations as required by the law. It also controls and supervises enforcement of criminal law judgments; Prosecutor-General HAMADA EL-SAWY.

Administrative Courts System: Has jurisdiction over litigations involving the state or any of its governmental agencies. It is divided into two courts: the Administrative Courts and the Judicial Administrative Courts, at the top of which is the Supreme Administrative Court.

The State Council (Conseil d'Etat): An independent judicial body, which has the authority to make decisions in administrative disputes and disciplinary cases within the judicial system; Chair. ADEL FAHIM AZAB.

The Supreme Judicial Council: Reinstituted in 1984, having been abolished in 1969. It exists to guarantee the independence of the judicial system from outside interference and is consulted with regard to draft laws organizing the affairs of the judicial bodies; Pres. and Chair. HOSNI HASSAN ABDEL LATIF ABU ZEID.

Religion

ISLAM

A Supreme Council for Islamic Affairs functions under the auspices of the Ministry of Awqaf (Islamic Endowments). The Minister acts as Chairman, while other members include the Grand Sheikh of the al-Azhar Mosque; the President and Vice-President of Al-Azhar University; the Grand Mufti of Egypt; and the Council's Secretary-General.

Grand Sheikh of Al-Azhar: Sheikh AHMED MUHAMMAD EL-TAYEB.

Grand Mufti of Egypt: Sheikh SHAWQI IBRAHIM ABD AL-KARIM ALLAM.

CHRISTIANITY

Orthodox Churches

Armenian Apostolic Orthodox Church: POB 48, 179 Sharia Ramses, Faggalah, Cairo; tel. (2) 25901385; fax (2) 25906671; e-mail armpatrcai@yahoo.com; Prelate Bishop ASHOT MNATSAKANIAN; 7,000 mems.

Coptic Orthodox Church: St Mark's Cathedral, POB 9035, Anba Ruess, 222 Sharia Ramses, Abbassia, Cairo; tel. (2) 22857889; fax (2) 22825683; internet www.copticpope.org; f. 61 CE; Patriarch Pope TAWADROS II; c. 13m. followers in Egypt, Sudan, other African countries, the USA, Canada, Australia, Europe and the Middle East.

Greek Orthodox Patriarchate: POB 2006, Alexandria; tel. (3) 4868595; fax (3) 4875684; e-mail patriarxeio.alexandreias@gmail.com; internet www.patriarchateofalexandria.com; f. 43 CE; Pope and Patriarch of Alexandria and All Africa THEODOROS II; 3m. mems.

The Roman Catholic Church

Armenian Rite

The Armenian Catholic diocese of Alexandria is suffragan to the Patriarchate of Cilicia. The Patriarch is resident in Beirut, Lebanon.

Bishop of Alexandria: Rt Rev. KRIKOR-OKOSDINOS COUSSA, Patriarcat Arménien Catholique, 36 Sharia Muhammad Sabri Abou Alam, 11121 Cairo; tel. (2) 23938429; fax (2) 23932025; e-mail pacal@tedata.net.eg.

Chaldean Rite

Bishop of Cairo: (vacant), Evêché Chaldéen, Basilique-Sanctuaire Notre Dame de Fatima, 141 Sharia Nouzha, 11316 Cairo (Heliopolis); tel. and fax (2) 26355718; e-mail fatimasarraf@yahoo.com. Patriarchal Administrator FR PAULUS SATI.

Coptic Rite

Egypt comprises the Coptic Catholic Patriarchate of Alexandria and five dioceses.

Patriarch of Alexandria: Archbishop IBRAHIM ISAAC SIDRAK, Patriarcat Copte Catholique, POB 69, 34 Sharia Ibn Sandar, Koubbeh Bridge, 11712 Cairo; tel. (2) 22571740; e-mail p_coptcattolico@yahoo.it; internet coptcatholic.net.

Latin Rite

Egypt comprises the Apostolic Vicariate of Alexandria (incorporating Heliopolis and Port Said).

Vicar Apostolic: Rt Rev. Bishop CLAUDIO LURATI, 10 Sharia Sidi el-Metwalli, Alexandria; tel. (3) 4876065; fax (3) 4878169.

Maronite Rite

Bishop of Cairo: Rt Rev. GEORGES CHIHANE, Evêché Maronite, 15 Sharia Hamdi, Daher, 11271 Cairo; tel. (2) 25939610; e-mail maronite.egypt@gmail.com; internet www.maronite-egypt.com.

Melkite Rite

His Beatitude Joseph Absi (resident in Damascus, Syria) is the Greek-Melkite Patriarch of Antioch and all the East, of Alexandria, and of Jerusalem.

Patriarchal Exarchate of Egypt and Sudan: Greek Melkite Catholic Patriarchate, 16 Sharia Daher, 11271 Cairo; tel. (2) 25905790; fax (2) 25935398; 6,200 adherents (2018); General Patriarchal Vicar for Egypt and Sudan Rt Rev. Bishop JEAN-MARIE CHAMI (Titular Bishop of Tarsus dei Greco-Melkiti).

Syrian Rite

Bishop of Cairo: Rt Rev. ÉLIE JOSEPH WARDE, Evêché Syrien Catholique, 46 Sharia Daher, 11271 Cairo; tel. (2) 25901234; fax (2) 25923932.

The Anglican Communion

In June 2020 the Anglican diocese of Egypt was separated from the Episcopal Province of Jerusalem and the Middle East, and formally inaugurated as the Episcopal/Anglican Province of Alexandria, with the Archbishop of Alexandria as its primate. The Province of Alexandria has four dioceses: Egypt, North Africa, the Horn of Africa and Gambella. These dioceses cover 10 countries in total, including Algeria, Chad, Djibouti, Egypt, Eritrea, Ethiopia, Libya, Mauritania, Somalia and Tunisia.

Archbishop of Alexandria and Bishop of Egypt: Most Rev. SAMI FAWZI, Diocesan Office, POB 87, 5 Sharia Michel Lutfalla, 11211 Cairo (Zamalek); tel. (2) 27380829; fax (2) 27358941; e-mail info@dioceseofegypt.org; internet www.dioceseofegypt.org.

Other Christian Churches

Coptic Evangelical Organization for Social Services: POB 162, 11811 El Panorama, Cairo; tel. (2) 26221425; fax (2) 26221434; internet ceoss-eg.org; Chair. Dr MERVAT AKHNOUKH ABASKHARON; Pres. Rt Rev. Dr ANDREA ZAKI.

Other denominations active in Egypt include the Coptic Evangelical Church (Synod of the Nile) and the Union of the Armenian Evangelical Churches in the Near East.

JUDAISM

The 1986 census recorded 794 Jews in Egypt, and there were reported to be around 16 remaining by 2020.

Jewish Community: Main Synagogue, Shaar Hashamayim 17, Adly St, Cairo; tel. (2) 24824613; fax (2) 27369639; e-mail bassatine@yahoo.com; f. 19th century; Pres. MAGDA HAROUN.

The Press

All newspapers and magazines are supervised, according to law, by the National Press Authority. The four major state-owned publishing houses of Al-Ahram Establishment, Dar al-Hilal, Dar Akhbar el-Yom and El-Tahrir Printing and Publishing House operate as separate entities and compete with each other commercially.

National Press Council: Cairo; f. 2017 to replace the Supreme Press Council; Chair. ABDEL-SADEQ EL-SHORBAGY.

DAILY NEWSPAPERS (PRINT AND ONLINE)

Al-Ahaly (The People): Sharia Kareem al-Dawli, Tala'at Harb Sq., Cairo; tel. (2) 25791628; fax (2) 23900412; internet www.al-ahaly.com; f. 1978; publ. by Nat. Progressive Unionist Party; Editor-in-Chief NAJIB ALAWANI.

Al-Ahram (The Pyramids): Sharia al-Galaa, Cairo 11511; tel. (2) 25801600; fax (2) 25786023; e-mail ahramdaily@ahram.org.eg; internet www.ahram.org.eg; f. 1875; morning, incl. Sun.; Arabic; international edn publ. in London, UK; North American edn publ. in New York, USA; Chair. ABDUL MOHSEN SALAMA; Chief Editor MAJID MOUNIR.

Al-Akhbar (The News): Dar Akhbar el-Yom, 6 Sharia al-Sahafa, Cairo; tel. (2) 25782600; fax (2) 25782530; internet akhbarelyom.com; f. 1952; Arabic; Chair. AHMED GALAL; Editor-in-Chief KHALED MERY.

Arev: 10 Sharia Menouf, Cairo; tel. (2) 24170204; fax (2) 24170203; e-mail arev@link.net; f. 1915; evening; Armenian; official organ of the Armenian Liberal Democratic Party; Editor SEVAN SEMERDJIAN.

Al-Dustour (The Constitution): nr Kobri al-Gamaa, Cairo (Giza); tel. (2) 33379008; fax (2) 33379766; internet www.dostor.org; f. 1995; banned by the authorities 1998; relaunched 2005; daily and weekly edns; independent; Chair. MOHAMMED EL-BAZ.

The Egyptian Gazette: 111–115 Sharia Ramses, Cairo; tel. (2) 25781010; e-mail info@egyptian-gazette.com; internet egyptian-gazette.com; f. 1880; morning; English; Chair. EYAD ABUL-HAGGAG; Editor-in-Chief MOHAMED FAHMY.

Al-Gomhouriya (The Republic): 24 Sharia Zakaria Ahmad, Cairo; tel. (2) 25781515; fax (2) 25781717; e-mail eltahrir@eltahrir.net; internet www.algomhuria.net.eg; f. 1953; morning; Arabic; mainly economic affairs; Chair. MOHAMED ABOULHAGAG; Editor-in-Chief ABDEL-RAZEK TAWFIQ ABU ZEID.

Al-Masry al-Youm: 49 Sharia Qasr al-Aini, Cairo; tel. (2) 27980100; fax (2) 27926331; e-mail admin@almasry-alyoum.com; internet www.almasryalyoum.com; f. 2003; Arabic; independent, privately owned; Editor-in-Chief HAMDI RIZK.

Al-Misaa' (The Evening): 24 Sharia Zakaria Ahmad, Cairo; tel. (2) 25783333; fax (2) 25781555; internet almessa.gomhuriaonline.com; f. 1956; evening; Arabic; political, social and sport; Chair. EYAD ABUL-HAGGAG; Editor-in-Chief ABDUL NABI AL-SHAHAT.

Le Progrès Egyptien: 24 Sharia Zakaria Ahmad, Cairo; tel. (2) 25783333; fax (2) 25781110; internet www.progres.net.eg; f. 1893; morning incl. Sun.; French; Chair. EYAD ABUL-HAGGAG; Editor-in-Chief CHAÏMAA ABD EL-ILLAH.

Al-Wafd: 1 Sharia Boulos Hanna, Cairo (Dokki); tel. (2) 33383111; fax (2) 37603060; e-mail contact@alwafd.org; internet alwafd.news; f. 1984; organ of the New Wafd Party; Editor-in-Chief WAJDI ZAINUDDIN.

Al-Youm Al-Sab'ei (Youm7): Cairo; tel. (2) 33355776; fax (2) 33355920; e-mail article@youm7.com; internet www.youm7.com; f. 2008; online only; Editor-in-Chief OLA AL-SHAFEI.

PERIODICALS

Al-Ahram al-Arabi: Sharia al-Galaa, Cairo 11511; tel. (2) 25786100; e-mail arabi@ahram.org.eg; internet arabi.ahram.org.eg; f. 1997; weekly (Sat.); Arabic; political, social and economic affairs; Editor-in-Chief JAMAL AL-KASHKI.

Al-Ahram al-Dimouqratiyah (Democracy Review): Sharia al-Galaa, Cairo 11511; tel. (2) 25786960; fax (2) 27705238; e-mail democracy@ahram.org.eg; internet democracy.ahram.org.eg; f. 2001; quarterly; politics; Arabic and English; publ. by Al-Ahram Establishment; Editor-in-Chief HINA OBAID.

Al-Ahram Hebdo: POB 1057, Sharia al-Galaa, Cairo 11511; tel. (2) 27703314; fax (2) 27703314; e-mail hebdo@ahram.org.eg; internet hebdo.ahram.org.eg; f. 1993; weekly (Wed.); French; publ. by Al-Ahram Establishment; Editor-in-Chief NEVINE MOHAMED KAMEL OMAR.

Al-Ahram al-Iqtisadi (The Economic Al-Ahram): Sharia al-Galaa, Cairo 11511; tel. (2) 25786100; fax (2) 25786833; e-mail ik@ahram.org.eg; internet ik.ahram.org.eg; Arabic; weekly (Mon.); economic and political affairs; publ. by Al-Ahram Establishment; Chief Editor KHALIFA ADHAM.

Al-Ahram Weekly (The Pyramids): Al-Ahram Bldg, Sharia al-Galaa, Cairo 11511; tel. (2) 25786100; fax (2) 25786833; e-mail weekly-web@ahram.org.eg; internet weekly.ahram.org.eg; f. 1989; English; weekly; publ. by Al-Ahram Establishment; Man. Editor SHADEN SHEHAB; Editor-in-Chief EZZAT IBRAHIM.

Akhbar al-Adab: 6 Sharia al-Sahafa, Cairo; tel. (2) 25795620; fax (2) 25782706; internet www.dar.akhbarelyom.com/issuse/?mag=a; f. 1993; literature and arts for young people; Editor-in-Chief ALA AL-DIN ALI AHMED ABDEL HADI.

Akhbar al-Hawadith: 6 Sharia al-Sahafa, Cairo; tel. (2) 25782600; fax (2) 25782510; e-mail diwan_elmazalem@yahoo.com; internet hawadeth.akhbarelyom.com; f. 1993; weekly; crime reports; Editor-in-Chief IHAB FATHY IMBABI DARWISH.

Akhbar al-Nogoom: 6 Sharia al-Sahafa, Cairo; tel. (2) 25807000; fax (2) 25782510; e-mail nogoomsite21@yahoo.com; internet nogoom.akhbarelyom.com; f. 1991; weekly; theatre and film news; Editor-in-Chief ISLAM AFIFI.

Akhbar al-Riadah: 6 Sharia al-Sahafa, Cairo; tel. (2) 25782600; fax (2) 25782510; e-mail akhbarriadasports@gmail.com; internet reyada.akhbarelyom.com; f. 1990; weekly; sport; Editor-in-Chief AYMAN BADRA.

Akhbar al-Sayarat: 6 Sharia al-Sahafa, Cairo; tel. 25806063; fax 25782530; e-mail sayarat@akhbarelyom.com; internet sayarat

.akhbarelyom.com; f. 1998; car magazine; Editor-in-Chief SHARIF KHAFAJI.

Akhbar el-Yom (News of the Day): 6 Sharia al-Sahafa, Cairo; tel. (2) 25807113; fax (2) 25782520; internet akhbarelyom.com; f. 1944; weekly (Sat.); Arabic; Chair. AHMED GALAL; Editor-in-Chief AMR EL-KHAIAT.

Akher Sa'a (Last Hour): Dar Akhbar el-Yom, Sharia al-Sahafa, Cairo; tel. (2) 25782600; fax (2) 25782530; internet www.dar.akhbarelyom.com/issue/?mag=akh; f. 1934; weekly (Sun.); Arabic; independent; consumer and news magazine; Editor-in-Chief ESSAM MUHAMMAD AL-SIBAI.

Business Monthly: 33 Soliman Abaza St, Cairo (Giza); tel. (2) 33336900; fax (2) 33381060; e-mail info@amcham.org.eg; internet www.amcham.org.eg/publications/business-monthly; f. 1985; monthly; business; English; publ. by the American Chamber of Commerce in Egypt; Man. Editor TAMER HAFEZ.

Business Today Egypt: 3A Sharia 199, IBA Media Bldg, Degla, Maadi, Cairo; tel. (2) 27555000; fax (2) 27555050; e-mail editor@businesstodayegypt.com; internet www.businesstodayegypt.com; f. 1994; English; monthly; business, economics and politics; publ. by IBA Media Group; Editor-in-Chief MOHAMED ABD EL-BAKY.

Egypt Today: 3A Sharia 199, IBA Media Bldg, Degla, Maadi, Cairo; tel. (2) 33355776; fax (2) 33355920; e-mail editor@egypttoday.com; internet www.egypttoday.com; f. 1979; monthly; English; current affairs; publ. by IBA Media Group; Editor-in-Chief MOHAMED ABD EL-BAKY.

Egyptian Cotton Gazette: POB 1772, 12 Sharia Muhammad Talaat Nooman, Ramel Station, Alexandria; tel. (3) 4806971; fax (3) 4873002; e-mail info@alcotexa.org; internet www.alcotexa.org; f. 1947; 2 a year; English; organ of the Alexandria Cotton Exporters' Asscn.

The Employer: Villa 126, 5th Settlement First Zone, First District, New Cairo; tel. and fax (2) 26162255; e-mail info@the-employer.com; internet www.the-employer.net; English; bi-monthly; employment; Man. Dir DINA MAKKAWI.

El-Fagr (The Dawn): 8 Sharia al-Sadd al-Aali, Dokki, Giza; tel. (2) 33366164; e-mail elfagr@elfagr.org; internet www.elfagr.org; f. 2005; weekly; independent; Arabic; Editor-in-Chief MANAL LASHIN.

Hawa'a (Eve): Dar al-Hilal, 16 Sharia Muhammad Ezz el-Arab, Cairo 11511; tel. (2) 23625450; fax (2) 23625469; internet hawaamagazine.com; f. 1955; weekly (Sat.); Arabic; women's magazine; Chief Editor SAMAR IBRAHIM MOHAMED DESSOUKI.

Al-Hilal: Dar al-Hilal, 16 Sharia Muhammad Ezz el-Arab, Cairo 11511; tel. (2) 23625450; fax (2) 23625469; f. 1895; monthly; Arabic; literary; Editor KHALED NAJEH MAHMOUD IBRAHIM.

Horreyati: 24 Sharia Ramses, Cairo; tel. (2) 25785666; fax (2) 25784747; e-mail horreyati@yahoo.com; internet www.horreyati.net.eg; f. 1990; weekly; social, cultural and sport; Editor-in-Chief ESSAM OMRAN.

Al-Kawakeb (The Stars): Dar al-Hilal, 16 Sharia Muhammad Ezz el-Arab, Cairo 11511; tel. (2) 23625450; fax (2) 23625469; f. 1952; weekly; Arabic; film magazine; Editor-in-Chief SAMAR IBRAHIM MOHAMED DESSOUKI.

Al-Kora wal-Malaeb (Football and Playgrounds): 24 Sharia Zakaria Ahmad, Cairo; tel. (2) 5783333; fax (2) 5784747; internet koura.net.eg; f. 1976; Editor-in-Chief MOHAMED SALAH DEMERDASH; weekly; Arabic; sport.

Magallat al-Mohandessin (The Engineer's Magazine): 30 Sharia Ramses, Cairo; tel. (2) 25747479; fax (2) 25748634; e-mail info@eea.org.eg; internet www.eea.org.eg; f. 1945; publ. by The Engineers' Syndicate; 10 a year; Arabic and English.

Medical Journal of Cairo University: POB 11252, 20 Sharia el-Manial, Faculty of Medicine, Cairo University, Cairo; tel. and fax (2) 23655768; e-mail info@medicaljournalofcairouniversity.net; internet www.medicaljournalofcairouniversity.net; f. 1933; Qasr el-Eini Clinical Society; quarterly; English; Assoc. Editors NADER A. ABULATA, MOHAMED HANY HAFEZ.

Al-Mussawar: Dar al-Hilal, 16 Sharia Muhammad Ezz el-Arab, Cairo 11511; tel. (2) 23625450; fax (2) 23625469; f. 1924; weekly; Arabic; news; Editor-in-Chief AHMED AHMED ABDEL BAQI AYOUB.

Nesf al-Donia: Sharia al-Galaa, Cairo 11511; tel. (2) 25786100; e-mail nisfelduniaweb@ahram.org.eg; internet nisfeldunia.ahram.org.eg; f. 1990; weekly; Arabic; women's magazine; publ. by Al-Ahram Establishment; Editor-in-Chief MARWA MAMDOUH ANIS AL-TOBJI.

October: Dar al-Maaref, 1119 Sharia Corniche el-Nil, Cairo; tel. (2) 25777077; fax (2) 25744999; internet www.octobermag.com; f. 1976; weekly; Arabic; Chair. and Editor-in-Chief MUHAMMAD AMIN ALI.

Rose al-Yousuf: 89A Sharia Qasr el-Eini, Cairo; tel. (2) 27920536; fax (2) 27956413; e-mail portal@rosaelyoussef.com; internet www.rosaelyoussef.com; f. 1925; weekly; Arabic; political; circulates throughout all Arab world; Editor-in-Chief AYMAN FATIH TAWFIK.

Sabah al-Kheir (Good Morning): 89A Sharia Qasr el-Eini, Cairo; tel. (2) 27950367; fax (2) 27923509; internet www.rosaonline.net/Sabah; f. 1956; weekly (Tue.); Arabic; light entertainment; Chief Editor MUHAMMAD ABD AL-NOUR.

Al-Siyassa al-Dawliya: Al-Ahram Bldg, 12th Floor, Sharia al-Galaa, Cairo 11511; tel. (2) 25786071; fax (2) 25792899; e-mail siyassa@ahram.org.eg; internet www.siyassa.org.eg; f. 1965; quarterly; politics and foreign affairs; publ. by Al-Ahram Establishment; Editor-in-Chief AHMED NAJI QAMHA.

Watani (My Country): 27 Sharia Abd al-Khalek Sarwat, Cairo; tel. (2) 23927201; fax (2) 23935946; e-mail info@wataninet.com; internet www.wataninet.com; f. 1958; weekly (Sun.); Arabic and English, with French supplement; independent newspaper addressing Egypt's Christian Copts; Editor-in-Chief YOUSSEF SIDHOM.

NEWS AGENCY

Middle East News Agency (MENA): POB 1165, 17 Sharia Hoda Sharawi, Cairo; tel. (2) 23933000; fax (2) 23935055; e-mail newsroom@mena.org.eg; internet www.mena.org.eg; f. 1955; regular service in Arabic, English and French; Chair. and Editor-in-Chief ALI HASSAN.

PRESS ASSOCIATIONS

Egyptian Syndicate of Journalists: 4 Sharia Abd al-Khalek Sarwat, Cairo; tel. 25741555; e-mail elsahfyeen@gmail.com; internet www.ejs.org.eg; Chair. DIAA RASHWAN.

Foreign Press Association: 2 Sharia Ahmad Ragheb, Cairo (Garden City); tel. (2) 27943727; fax (2) 27943747; internet www.fpaegypt.net; f. 1972; Chair. VOLKHARD WINDFUHR.

Publishers

The General Egyptian Book Organization: POB 235, Sharia Corniche el-Nil, Cairo (Boulac) 1194; tel. (2) 25775367; fax (2) 25789316; e-mail walaakotb@gebo.gov.eg; internet www.gebo.gov.eg; f. 1961; affiliated to the Ministry of Culture; editing, publishing and distribution; organizer of Cairo International Book Fair; Chair. HAITHAM AL-HAJ; Gen. Dir AHMAD SALAH ZAKI.

Al-Ahram Establishment: Al-Ahram Bldg, 6 Sharia al-Galaa, Cairo 11511; tel. (2) 25786100; fax (2) 25786023; e-mail english@ahram.org.eg; internet www.ahram.org.eg; f. 1875; state-owned; publishes newspapers, magazines and books, incl. Al-Ahram; Chair. ABDELMOHSEN SALAMA; Dep. Chair. and Gen. Man. ALI GHONEIM.

Dar Akhbar el-Yom: 6 Sharia al-Sahafa, Cairo; tel. (2) 25948223; fax (2) 25784444; e-mail kitabelyom@gmail.com; internet ketabelyom.akhbarelyom.com; f. 1944; state-owned; publs include Al-Akhbar (daily), Akhbar el-Yom (weekly) and Akher Sa'a (weekly); Chair. ALAA ABD AL-WAHAB.

American University in Cairo Press: 113 Sharia Qasr el-Eini, POB 2511, Cairo 11511; tel. (2) 27976926; fax (2) 27941440; e-mail aucpress@aucegypt.edu; internet aucpress.com; f. 1960; political history, economics, Egyptology, and Arabic literature in English translation; Dir Dr NIGEL FLETCHER-JONES.

Boustany's Publishing House: 4 Sharia Aly Tawfik Shousha, Cairo (Nasr City) 11371; tel. (2) 24035455; fax (2) 22623085; e-mail boustany@boustanys.com; internet www.boustanys.com; f. 1900; fiction, poetry, history, biography, philosophy, language, literature, politics, religion, archaeology and Egyptology; Chief Exec. FADWA BOUSTANY.

Elias Modern Publishing House: 1 Sharia Kenisset al-Rum El-Kathulik, Daher, Cairo 11271; tel. (2) 25903756; fax (2) 25880091; e-mail info@eliaspublishing.com; internet www.eliaspublishing.com; f. 1913; publishing, printing and distribution; publ. dictionaries, children's books, and books on linguistics, poetry and arts; Chair. NADIM ELIAS; Man. Dir LAURA KFOURY.

Dar al-Farouk: 3 Sharia Mansour, Cairo (Giza); tel. (2) 27953032; fax (2) 27943643; e-mail support@darelfarouk.com.eg; internet www.darelfarouk.com.eg; wide range of books incl. educational, history, science and business; Chair. FAROUK MUHAMMAD AL-AMARY; Gen. Man. Dr KHALED FAROUK AL-AMARY.

Dar al-Gomhouriya: 24 Sharia Zakaria Ahmad, Cairo; tel. (2) 25781010; fax (2) 25784747; e-mail eltahrir@eltahrir.net; internet www.algomhuria.net.eg; state-owned; affiliate of El-Tahrir Printing and Publishing House; publs include the dailies Al-Gomhouriya, Al-Misaa', The Egyptian Gazette and Le Progrès Egyptien; Pres. MUHAMMAD ABOUL HADID.

Dar al-Hilal: 16 Sharia Muhammad Ezz el-Arab, Cairo 11511; tel. (2) 23625450; fax (2) 23625469; f. 1892; state-owned; publs include Al-Hilal, Kitab al-Hilal, Tabibak al-Khass (monthlies); Al-Mussawar, Al-Kawakeb, Hawa'a (weeklies); Chair. ABD AL-KADER SHUHAYIB.

Dar al-Kitab al-Masri: POB 156, 33 Sharia Qasr el-Nil, Cairo 11511; tel. (2) 23922168; fax (2) 23924657; e-mail info@daralkitabalmasri.com; internet www.daralkitabalmasri.com; f. 1929; publishing, printing and distribution; publrs of books on Islam and history, as well as dictionaries, encyclopaedias, textbooks, children's and general interest books; Pres. and Dir-Gen. Dr HASSAN EL-ZEIN.

Dar al-Maaref: 1119 Sharia Corniche el-Nil, Cairo; tel. (2) 25777077; fax (2) 25744999; e-mail dmf17@yahoo.com; internet daralmaref.com; f. 1890; publishing, printing and distribution of wide variety of books in Arabic and other languages; publrs of *October* magazine; Editor ATEF ABDEL GHANI.

Maktabet Misr: POB 16, 3 Sharia Kamal Sidki, Cairo; tel. (2) 25898553; fax (2) 27870051; f. 1932; fiction, biographies and textbooks for schools and universities; Man. AMIR SAID GOUDA EL-SAHHAR.

Dar al-Masri al-Lubnani: 16 Sharia Abd al-Khalek Sarwat, Cairo; tel. (2) 23910250; fax (2) 23909618; e-mail info@almasriah.com; internet www.almasriah.com; Arabic literature, history, sciences, textbooks and children's books; Chair. MUHAMMAD RASHED.

Nahdet Misr Group: al-Nahda Tower, 21 Sharia Ahmad Orabi, Sphinx Sq., Mohandessin, Cairo (Giza); tel. (2) 33464903; fax (2) 33462576; e-mail marketing@nahdetmisr.com; internet www.nahdetmisr.com; f. 1938; fiction, children's literature and educational books; also publishes magazines, incl. *Mickey* (weekly); Chair. MUHAMMAD AHMAD IBRAHIM.

Dar al-Nashr (fmrly Les Editions Universitaires d'Egypte): POB 1347, 41 Sharia Sherif, Cairo 11511; tel. (2) 23934606; fax (2) 23921997; f. 1947; university textbooks, academic works and encyclopaedias.

National Centre for Educational Research and Development: 12 Sharia Waked, el-Borg el-Faddy, POB 836, Cairo; tel. (2) 23930981; f. 1956; fmrly Documentation and Research Centre for Education (Ministry of Education); bibliographies, directories, information and education bulletins; Dir Prof. ABD EL-FATTAH GALAL.

National Library Press (Dar al-Kutub): POB 11638, 8 Sharia al-Sabtteya, Cairo; tel. (2) 25750886; fax (2) 25765634; internet www.darelkotob.org; bibliographic works; Chair. Dr MUHAMMAD SABER ARAB.

Safeer Publishing: Saraya Mall, 4th Floor, Sheikh Zayed City, Giza; tel. (11) 44455199; fax (2) 37608650; e-mail info@safeer.com.eg; internet safeerpublishing.com; f. 1982; children's books; Pres. MUHAMMAD ABD EL-LATIF.

Dar al-Shorouk: 8 Sibaweh al-Masri, Cairo (Nasr City) 11371; tel. (2) 24023399; fax (2) 24037567; e-mail dar@shorouk.com; internet www.shorouk.com; f. 1968; publishing, printing and distribution; publrs of books on current affairs, history, Islamic studies, literature, art and children's books; Chair. IBRAHIM EL-MOALLEM.

El-Tahrir Printing and Publishing House: 24 Sharia Zakaria Ahmad, Cairo; tel. (2) 25781222; fax (2) 22784747; e-mail eltahrir@eltahrir.net; internet www.eltahrir.net; f. 1953; state-owned; Pres. and Chair. ALI HASHIM.

Dar el-Thaqafa: Coptic Evangelical Organization for Social Services, Sharia Dr Ahmed Zaki, Cairo; tel. (2) 26221425; internet www.darelthaqafa.com; publishing dept of the Coptic Evangelical Org. for Social Services; publishes books on social issues, as well as on spiritual and theological topics; Dir Rev. Dr ANDREA ZAKI STEPHANOUS.

PUBLISHERS' ASSOCIATION

Arab Publishers' Association (APA): Saridar Tower, 2nd Floor, 92 Sharia el-Tahrir, Dokki, Cairo (Giza); tel. (2) 37622058; fax (2) 37622058; e-mail info@arab-pa.org; internet www.arab-pa.org; f. 1995; Pres. MOHAMED RASHAD; 1,039 mems (2021).

Broadcasting and Communications

TELECOMMUNICATIONS

Etisalat Misr: POB 11, S4 Down Town, Sharia 90, 5th Compound, New Cairo; tel. (2) 35346333; internet www.etisalat.eg; f. 2007 as Egypt's third mobile telephone service provider; subsidiary of Etisalat (United Arab Emirates); Chair. GAMAL EL-SADAT; CEO HAZEM METWALLY.

Global Telecom Holding: Nile City Towers, North Tower, 2005 Corniche el-Nil, Ramlet Boulaq, Cairo 11221; tel. (2) 24618559; internet www.gtelecom.com; fmrly Orascom Telecom, present name adopted following merger with VimpleCom Ltd (Russian Federation); owns and operates mobile telecommunications providers in North Africa, sub-Saharan Africa, North America and South Asia; approx. 88m. subscribers worldwide; Chair. MICHAEL SCHULZ; Man. Dir GERBRAND NIJMAN.

Orange Egypt for Telecommunications SAE (Orange Egypt): Nile City Bldg, 2005C, Corniche el-Nil, Ramlet Boulaq, Cairo 11221; tel. (2) 23202020; e-mail info@orange.com; internet www.orange.eg; f. 1998 as Egyptian Company for Mobile Services; present name adopted 2016; owned by M.T. Telecom SCRL (98.9%); 33.5m. subscribers (2017); Chair. ELON NDIAYE; CEO YASSER SHAKER.

Telecom Egypt: POB 2271, Sharia Ramses, Cairo 11511; tel. 5000111; e-mail customer.care@te.eg; internet www.te.eg; f. 1957; provider of fixed-line telephone services; Chair. MAGED OSMAN; CEO and Man. Dir MOHAMED NASR EL-DIN.

Vodafone Egypt: Smart Village, Bldg C2, KM 28, 1st Cairo–Alexandria Desert Rd, 12573 Giza; tel. (2) 25292000; fax (2) 25292100; e-mail public.relations@vodafone.com; internet www.vodafone.com.eg; f. 1998 by the MisrFone consortium; mobile telephone service provider; 55% owned by Vodacom Group (South Africa) since 2021; CEO MOHAMED ABDALLAH.

Regulatory Authority

National Telecommunications Regulatory Authority (NTRA): Smart Village, Bldg No. 4, Km 28, Sharia Cairo–Alexandria, Cairo (Giza); tel. (2) 35344000; fax (2) 35344155; e-mail info@tra.gov.eg; internet www.tra.gov.eg; f. 2000; Chair. Dr AMR AHMED TALAAT (Minister of Communications and Information Technology); CEO HOSSAM EL-GAMAL.

BROADCASTING

Radio and Television

Supreme Council for Media Regulation: Cairo; f. 2017; Chair. KARAM KAMIL JABR.

Dream TV Network: 23 Polis Hana St, Cairo (Giza); tel. (2) 38582302; e-mail info@dreamonline.tv; internet www.dreamonline.tv; f. 2001; privately owned satellite television station; broadcasts on Dream 1 and Dream 2 networks, providing sports, music and entertainment programmes; Chair. Dr AHMAD BAHGAT.

El-Mehwar TV: Cairo; tel. (2) 32652145; e-mail info@elmehwartv.com; internet www.elmehwartv.com; f. 2001; privately owned; entertainment and current affairs programmes; Founder Dr HASSAN RATEB.

Nagham FM: Cairo; tel. (2) 38555316; e-mail info@naghamfm1053.com; internet www.naghamfm1053.com.

National Media Authority (NMA): Radio and TV Bldg, Sharia Maspero, Corniche el-Nil, Cairo; e-mail info@maspero.eg; internet www.maspero.eg; f. 1945 as Egyptian Radio and Television Union; state-owned; reorg. as NMA in 2019; operates radio and television stations; Pres. HUSSEIN ZEIN.

Nile Radio Productions (NRP): Media City Free Zone, 6th of October City; tel. (2) 38555055; e-mail socialmedia@nileradioproductions.net; internet www.nilefm.com; f. 2003; owned by Nile Radio Productions Holdings; operates radio stations in English (Nile FM) and Arabic (Nogoum FM); Group CEO AYMAN SALEM; Man. Dir and Group COO HALA HEGAZI.

Finance

BANKING

Central Bank

Central Bank of Egypt (CBE): 54 Sharia El Gomhoureya, 11511 Cairo; tel. 16777; e-mail info@cbe.org.eg; internet www.cbe.org.eg; f. 1961; controls Egypt's monetary policy and supervises the banking sector; Gov. and Chair. HASSAN ABDALLA.

Commercial and Specialized Banks

Abu Dhabi Commercial Bank (Egypt) (ADCB Egypt): POB 3865, 16 Sharia Gameat al-Dowal al-Arabia, Mohandesin, Cairo (Giza); tel. (2) 33011300; e-mail adc-helpdesk@adcb.com.eg; internet www.adcb.com.eg; f. 2020 by merger of Union National Bank, Al Hilal Bank and the Abu Dhabi Commercial Bank; Chair. MOHAMED AL-HAMLY; Man. Dir and CEO IHAB EL-SEWERKY.

Abu Dhabi Islamic Bank (Egypt) (ADIB Egypt): 9A Sharia Rostom, Cairo (Garden City); tel. (2) 38289300; fax (2) 27984053; e-mail adibegypt@adib.eg; internet www.adib.eg; f. 1980; fmrly National Development Bank; 49.62% share owned by Abu Dhabi Islamic Bank; offers *Shari'a*-compliant banking services; Exec. Dir KHALIFA MATAR AL-MHEIRI; CEO MOHAMED ALY.

Agricultural Bank of Egypt (ABE): 1 Nadi al-Said Sq., Dokki, Cairo (Giza); tel. (2) 33327259; internet www.abe.com.eg; f. 1976 to succeed former credit orgs; state-owned; Chair. ALAA FAROUK.

Bank of Alexandria (ALEXBANK): 49 Sharia Qasr el-Nil, Cairo; tel. (2) 23992000; e-mail csr@alexbank.com; internet www.alexbank

.com; f. 1957; 80% stake owned by Intesa Sanpaolo SpA (Italy); Chair. Dr ZIAD AHMED BAHAA EL-DIN; CEO and Man. Dir DANTE CAMPIONI.

Banque du Caire, SAE: Banque du Caire Tower, 6 Sharia Dr Moustafa Abu Zahra, Nasr City, Cairo 11371; tel. (2) 22646401; fax (2) 24037751; e-mail intl.division@bdc.com.eg; internet www.bdc.com.eg; f. 1952; state-owned; privatization pending; Chair. and CEO TARIQ FAYED.

Banque Misr, SAE: 151 Sharia Muhammad Farid, Cairo; tel. (2) 23912172; fax (2) 23908464; e-mail bm19888@banquemisr.com; internet www.banquemisr.com; f. 1920; merger with Misr Exterior Bank 2004; privatization pending; Chair. MUHAMMAD MAHMOUD ELETREBY.

Beltone Financial Holding: Nile City Tower, North Tower, 33rd Floor, Corniche el-Nil 2005 A, Cairo 11221; tel. (2) 24616300; fax (2) 24619850; e-mail marketing@beltonefinancial.com; internet www.beltonefinancial.com; f. 2002; services include investment banking, asset management and securities brokerage; 55.9% owned by Chimera Investment LLC; Exec. Chair. ONSI SAWIRIS; CEO DALIA KHORSHID.

CI Capital: West Tower, 3rd Floor, Galleria 40, 26th of July Corridor, Sheikh Zayed City; tel. (2) 21292511; e-mail media@cicapital.com.eg; internet www.cicapital.com; f. 2005; services include microfinance, asset management, leasing, securities brokerage and investment banking; Chair. and Man. Dir MAHMOUD ATTALLA; Man. Dir and Group CEO AMR HELAL.

Commercial International Bank (Egypt), SAE: POB 2430, Nile Tower Bldg, 21–23 Sharia Charles de Gaulle, Cairo (Giza); tel. (2) 37472000; fax (2) 35703172; e-mail info@cibeg.com; internet www.cibeg.com; f. 1975 as Chase Nat. Bank (Egypt), SAE; adopted present name 1987; Chair. SHERIF SAMY; CEO HUSSEIN ABAZA.

Egyptian Arab Land Bank: 78 Sharia Gameat al-Dowal al-Arabia, Mohandessin, Cairo 12311; tel. (2) 33383579; fax (2) 33383569; e-mail info@eal-bank.com; internet www.eal-bank.com; f. 1880; state-owned; Chair. MEDHAT AHMED AHMED KAMAR.

Export Development Bank of Egypt (EBE): 108 Mohi el-Din Abou al-Ezz, Cairo 12311 (Dokki); tel. (2) 37619006; fax (2) 33385938; e-mail info@edbebank.com; internet ebank.com.eg; f. 1983 to replace Nat. Import-Export Bank; Chair. MERVAT ZOHDY AL-SAYED SOLTAN.

HSBC Bank Egypt, SAE: POB 126, Abou el-Feda Bldg, 3 Sharia Abou el-Feda, Cairo (Zamalek); tel. (2) 35359800; fax (2) 27364010; internet www.egypt.hsbc.com; f. 1982 as Hong Kong Egyptian Bank; name changed to Egyptian British Bank 1994, and as above 2001; 94.5% owned by Hongkong and Shanghai Banking Corpn; Chair. NASSER AL-SHAALI; CEO RODNEY TODD WILCOX.

National Bank of Egypt (NBE): POB 11611, National Bank of Egypt Tower, 1187 Corniche el-Nil, Cairo; tel. (2) 20219623; fax (2) 25945137; internet www.nbe.com.eg; f. 1898; merged with Mohandes Bank and Bank of Commerce and Devt 2005; privatization pending; handles all commercial banking operations; Chair. HISHAM AHMAD OKASHA.

Société Arabe Internationale de Banque (SAIB): POB 54, 56 Sharia Gamet el-Dowal al-Arabia, Mohandessin, Cairo (Giza); tel. (2) 16668; e-mail customer.care@saib.com.eg; internet www.saib.com.eg; f. 1976; 46% owned by Arab Int. Bank; Chair. and Man. Dir TAREK MOHAMMED BADAWI AL-KHOLY.

The United Bank (UBE): POB 85, Cairo Center, 106 Sharia Qasr el-Eini, Cairo; tel. (2) 33326000; e-mail info@theubeg.com; internet www.theubeg.com; f. 1981 as Dakahlia Nat. Bank for Devt; renamed United Bank of Egypt 1997; current name adopted 2006, when merged with Nile Bank and Islamic Int. Bank for Investment and Devt; purchased by Kuwait Investment Authority in 2023; CEO ASHARF AL-KADY.

Social Bank

Nasser Social Bank: POB 2552, 35 Sharia Qasr el-Nil, Cairo; tel. (2) 23932126; fax (2) 23924484; internet nsb.gov.eg; f. 1971; state-owned; interest-free savings and investment bank for social and economic activities, participating in social insurance, specializing in financing co-operatives, craftsmen and social institutions; Chair. NIVEEN EL-QABBAG (Minister of Social Solidarity).

Multinational Banks

Arab African International Bank: 5 Midan al-Saray al-Koubra, POB 60, Majlis al-Sha'ab, Cairo 11516 (Garden City); tel. (2) 24886679; fax (2) 27925599; e-mail inquiry@aaib.com; internet www.aaib.com; f. 1964 as Arab African Bank; renamed in 1978; acquired Misr-America Int. Bank in 2005; commercial investments and retail banking; shareholders are Central Bank of Egypt, Kuwait Investment Authority (49.37% each), and individuals and Arab institutions; Chair. AMR KAMEL; Man. Dir SHERIF ELWY.

Arab International Bank: POB 1563, 35 Sharia Abd al-Khalek Sarwat, Cairo; tel. (2) 23918794; fax (2) 23938743; e-mail cairobranch@aib.com.eg; internet www.aib.com.eg; f. 1971 as Egyptian Int. Bank for Foreign Trade and Investment; renamed 1974; owned by Egypt, Libya, Oman, Qatar, the United Arab Emirates and private Arab shareholders; offshore bank; aims to promote trade and investment in shareholders' countries and other Arab countries; Chair. AMR MOHAMED KAMEL; CEO and Man. Dir HISHAM RAMEZ ABDELHAFEZ.

Commercial Foreign Venture Banks

Ahli United Bank (Egypt): 81 Sharia El-Tesseen, Sector A, Fifth Settlement; tel. (2) 26149500; fax (2) 26135160; e-mail egypt.callcenter@ahliunited.com; internet www.ahliunited.com; f. 1978 as Delta Int. Bank; name changed as above 2007; 89.3% stake owned by Ahli United Bank BSC (Bahrain) and other Gulf-based financial institutions; Chair. MOHAMMAD FOUAD AL-GHANIM; CEO HALA HATEM SADEK.

Al-Ahli Bank of Kuwait-Egypt (ABK): Km 28, Bldg B227–B228, Sharia Cairo–Alexandria Desert, 6th of October, Cairo 12577; tel. (2) 35352790; internet www.abkegypt.com; f. 2006, following acquisition of Egyptian Commercial Bank by Piraeus Bank Group (Greece); 98.5% stake owned by Al-Ahli Bank (Kuwait); Chair. ALI EBRAHIM HAJJI HUSSAIN MARAFI; CEO and Man. Dir KHALID NABIL AL-SALAWY.

Attijariwafa Bank, SAE: POB 110, 12 Midan el-Sheikh Yousuf, Cairo (Garden City); tel. (2) 25296100; fax (2) 23662810; internet www.attijariwafabank.com.eg; f. 1975 as Cairo Barclays Int. Bank; renamed Banque du Caire Barclays Int. 1983, Cairo Barclays Bank 1999 and Barclays Bank Egypt 2004; present name adopted 2017 after acquisition by Attijariwafa Bank (Morocco); Chair. HALLA SAKR; Man. Dir MOUAWIA ESSEKELLI.

alBaraka Bank Egypt, SAE: New Admin. Bldg, Blk 75, 5th Settlement, New Cairo; tel. 19373; e-mail central@albaraka-bank.com.eg; internet www.albaraka-bank.com.eg; f. 1980 as Pyramids Bank; renamed Egyptian-Saudi Finance Bank 1988; present name adopted 2010; 73.7% owned by Al-Baraka Banking Group (Bahrain); Chair. ABDEL AZIZ MOHAMED ABDO YAMANI; Vice-Chair. and CEO HAZEM HEGAZY.

Blom Bank Egypt: POB 410, el-Tagamoaa el-Khames, Cairo; tel. (2) 33322778; fax (2) 37494508; e-mail blomcallcenter@blombankegypt.com; internet www.blombankegypt.com; f. 1977 as Misr Romanian Bank, name changed as above in 2006; 99.5% stake acquired by Bank ABC (Bahrain) in 2021; Chair. SAEL AL-WAARY; Man. Dir MOHAMED OZALP.

Crédit Agricole Egypt, SAE: POB 364, Downtown Mall, Sharia 90, 5th Settlement, New Cairo 11835; tel. (2) 23146010; e-mail webmaster.egypt@ca-egypt.com; internet www.ca-egypt.com; f. 2006 by merger of Calyon Bank Egypt (Egyptian affiliate of Crédit Agricole Group—France) and Egyptian American Bank; owned by Crédit Agricole Groupe, Mansour and Maghrabi Investment and Devt, and Egyptian investors; Chair. OSAMA SALEH; Man. Dir JEAN-PIERRE TRINELLE.

Egyptian Gulf Bank: POB 56, El-Orman Plaza Bldg, 8–10 Sharia Ahmad Nessim, Cairo (Giza); tel. (2) 26733118; internet eg-bank.com; f. 1981; Misr Insurance Co has 19.3% interest; Chair. RAED JAWAD AHMED BUKHAMSEEN; CEO and Man. Dir NIDAL EL-KASSEM MOHAMED ASSAR.

Emirates NBD Egypt: Plot 85, Sharia el-Tesseen, New Cairo; tel. (2) 23661000; e-mail egyptcsr@emiratesnbd.com; internet www.emiratesnbd.com.eg; f. 2013; subsidiary of Emirates NBD (UAE); fmrly BNP Paribas SAE; Chair. HESHAM ABDULLAH AL-QASSIM; Man. Dir MOHAMED BERRO.

Faisal Islamic Bank of Egypt, SAE: POB 2446, 3 Sharia 26 July, Galaa Sq., Cairo (Dokki); tel. (2) 27868723; fax (2) 27866744; e-mail publicrelat@faisalbank.com.eg; internet www.faisalbank.com.eg; f. 1979; all banking operations conducted according to Islamic principles; Chair. Prince AMR AL-FAISAL AL SA'UD; Gov. ABD AL-HAMID ABU MOUSSA.

National Bank of Kuwait: POB 63, 13 Sharia Semar, Dr Fouad Mohi el-Din Sq., Gameat el-Dewal al-Arabia, Mohandessin, Cairo 12655; tel. (2) 26149400; internet nbk.com/egypt; f. 1980 as Al-Watany Bank of Egypt; Chair. SHAIKHA K. AL-BAHAR; CEO and Man. Dir YASSER ABD EL-KODDOUS EL-TAYEB.

Suez Canal Bank, SAE: POB 76, 7–9 Sharia Abd el-Kader Hamza, Cairo (Garden City); tel. 19093; e-mail info@scbank.com.eg; internet www.scbank.com.eg; f. 1978; Chair. and Man. Dir HUSSEIN AHMAD ISMAIL REFAEI.

Non-commercial Banks

Arab Banking Corpn—Egypt: 39B Sharia N Teseen, 5th Settlement, New Cairo; e-mail abcegypt@bank-abc.com; internet www.bank-abc.com/world/egypt/en/pages/default.aspx; f. 1982 as Egypt Arab African Bank; acquired by Arab Banking Corpn (Bahrain) 1999; Arab Banking Corpn has 93% interest, other interests 7%; commercial and investment bank; Chair. Dr YOUSEF AL-AWADI; Man. Dir and CEO AMR THARWAT.

Arab Investment Bank (Federal Arab Bank for Development and Investment): POB 826, Cairo Sky Center Bldg, 8 Sharia Abd al-Khalek Sarwat, Cairo; tel. (2) 25760031; fax (2) 25770329; e-mail arinbank@mst1.mist.com.eg; internet www.aibegypt.com; f. 1978 as Union Arab Bank for Devt and Investment; acquired by EFG Hermes Holding in 2021; Chair. TARIQ KABIL ABDULAZIZ KABIL; CEO and Man. Dir TAMER SEIF EL-DIN.

EFG-Hermes: Bldg B129, Phase 3, Smart Village, Km 28, Sharia Cairo–Alexandria Desert, 6th of October, Cairo 12577; tel. (2) 35356584; fax (2) 35357111; e-mail corporate@efg-hermes.com; internet www.efghermes.com; f. 1984; offices in Cairo, Alexandria and Mansoura; Chair. MONA ZULFICAR; CEO KARIM AWAD.

Housing and Development Bank, SAE: 26 Sharia el-Kroum, Mohandessin, Cairo (Giza); tel. (2) 21270600; e-mail customer.rights@hdb-egy.com; internet www.hdb-egy.com; f. 1979; Chair. and Man. Dir HASSAN ESMAIEL GHANEM.

Industrial Development and Workers Bank of Egypt (IDWBE): 110 Sharia al-Galaa, Cairo 11511; tel. (2) 25772468; fax (2) 25751227; internet www.idbe-egypt.com; f. 1947 as Industrial Bank; re-established as above 1976; Chair. and Man. Dir MAGED FAHMY ATTIYA.

Misr Iran Development Bank: POB 219, Nile Tower Bldg, 21 Charles de Gaulle Ave, Cairo 12612 (Giza); tel. (2) 35727311; fax (2) 35701185; e-mail midb@mst1.mist.com.eg; internet www.midb.com.eg; f. 1975; Iran Foreign Investment Co 40.14% interest, National Investment Bank 29.93%, Misr Insurance Co 16.06%; Misr For Life Insurance Co 13.87%; Chair. HISHAM ARAFAT MAHDI AHMED; CEO and Man. Dir AMR ALGARHY.

QNB Al Ahli: POB 2664, 5 Sharia Champollion, 11111 Cairo; tel. (2) 20219700; e-mail info.qnbaa@qnbalahli.com; internet www.qnbalahli.com; f. 1978; 97.12% stake held by QNB Group (Qatar), other investors 2.88%; Chair. ALI RASHID AL-MOHANNADI; CEO MOHAMED MAHMOUD BEDEIR.

REGULATORY AUTHORITY

Financial Regulatory Authority (FRA): Bldg 136B, Alexandria Desert Rd, km 28, Cairo 12577; tel. (2) 35345350; fax (2) 35370037; e-mail info@fra.gov.eg; internet fra.gov.eg; f. 2009, following the merger of the Capital Market Authority, the Egyptian Insurance Supervisory Authority and the Mortgage Finance Authority; also assumed the regulatory functions of the General Authority for Investment and Free Zones, and the Egyptian Exchange; supervision of all non-banking financial markets and institutions, incl. the stock exchange, the capital market, and the insurance and mortgage sectors; Chair. Dr MOHAMED FARID SALEH.

SOVEREIGN WEALTH FUND

The Sovereign Fund of Egypt (THARAA): 3 Sharia Abul Feda, 12th Floor, Cairo (Zamalek); fax (2) 27375048; e-mail info@sovfundegypt.com; internet tsfe.com; f. 2018; focused on sustainable economic development; CEO AYMAN SOLIMAN.

STOCK EXCHANGE

The Egyptian Exchange (EGX): 4A Sharia el-Sherifein, Cairo 11513; tel. (2) 23941900; e-mail info@egx.com.eg; internet www.egx.com.eg; f. 1883 as the Cairo and Alexandria Stock Exchanges; present name adopted 2008; Exec. Chair. Dr AHMED EL-SHEIKH.

INSURANCE

Allianz Egypt: Business Park A, Bldg A1, Cairo Festival City, New Cairo; tel. (2) 23223000; fax (2) 23223001; e-mail info@allianz.com.eg; internet www.allianz.com.eg; f. 1976 as Arab Int. Insurance Co; Allianz AG (Germany) purchased 80% stake 2000; name changed as above 2004; general and life insurance; Chair. and CEO AYMAN HEGAZY.

MetLife Egypt: 75, Sharia 90, New Cairo; tel. (2) 24616500; e-mail service-egypt@metlife.com; internet www.metlife.eg; f. 1997; first multinational insurance co to be granted licence to offer life insurance service in Egypt; Man. Dir HAITHAM TAHER.

Misr Insurance Co: 44 Sharia Dokki, Cairo (Dokki); tel. (2) 33355350; e-mail info@misrins.com.eg; internet www.misrins.com.eg; f. 1934; merged with Al-Chark Insurance Co and Egyptian Reinsurance Co in 2007; scheduled for privatization; all classes of insurance and reinsurance; Chair. MUHAMMAD JAMAL AL-DIN HAMZAH; Man. Dir OMAR JUDEH.

Mohandes Insurance Co: POB 62, 3 el-Mesaha Sq., Cairo (Dokki); tel. (2) 33368101; fax (2) 33361365; e-mail info@mohins.com; internet www.mohins.com; f. 1980; privately owned; insurance and reinsurance; Chair. ATEF AL-MAHMOUDI; Man. Dir KHALED ABDEL SADEK.

National Insurance Co of Egypt, SAE: POB 592, 41 Sharia Qasr el-Nil, Cairo; tel. (2) 23910731; fax (2) 23933051; internet www.ahlya.com; f. 1900; scheduled for privatization; Chair. SADEK HASSAN SADEK.

Trade and Industry

GOVERNMENT AGENCIES

Egyptian Mineral Resource Authority (EMRA): 3 Sharia Salah Salem, Abbassia, 11517 Cairo; tel. (2) 26828013; fax (2) 24820128; e-mail info@emra.gov.eg; internet www.emra.gov.eg; f. 1896 as the Egyptian Geological Survey and Mining Authority; state supervisory authority concerned with geological mapping, mineral exploration and other mining activities; Chair. KHALED EL-SHESHTAWY.

General Authority for Investment and Free Zones (GAFI): 3 Sharia Salah Salem, 11562 Cairo (Nasr City); tel. 16035; e-mail investinegypt@gafi.gov.eg; internet www.investinegypt.gov.eg; Exec. Dir MOHAMED ABDEL WAHAB.

Information Technology Industry Development Agency (ITIDA): Bldg B121, Sharia Cairo-Alex Desert, Smart Village, Cairo (Giza) 12577; tel. (2) 35345022; internet www.itida.gov.eg; f. 2004; aims to develop the information and communication technology industry in the country; CEO Eng. AMR MAHFOUZ.

CHAMBERS OF COMMERCE

Federation of Egyptian Chambers of Commerce (FEDCOC): 73 Sharia South Taseen, 5th Settlement, New Cairo; tel. (2) 28105002; fax (2) 28105006; e-mail fedcoc@hotmail.com; internet www.fedcoc.org.eg; f. 1955; Chair. IBRAHIM AL-ARABI; Sec.-Gen. ADEL ABDEL-FATTAH NASSER.

Alexandria Chamber of Commerce: 31 Sharia el-Ghorfa Altogariya, Alexandria; tel. (3) 4837804; fax (3) 4837806; e-mail acc@alexcham.org; internet www.alexcham.org; f. 1922; Chair. AHMAD EL-WAKIL.

American Chamber of Commerce in Egypt: 33 Sharia Sulayman Abaza, Cairo (Dokki) 12311; tel. (2) 33336900; fax (2) 33381060; e-mail info@amcham.org.eg; internet www.amcham.org.eg; f. 1981; Pres. TAREK TAWFIK; CEO SYLVIA MENASSA.

Cairo Chamber of Commerce: 4 el-Falaki Sq., Cairo; tel. (2) 27962091; fax (2) 27963603; e-mail info@cairochamber.org.eg; internet cairochamber.org.eg; f. 1913; Pres. IBRAHIM MAHMOUD EL-ARABY; Sec.-Gen. ASHRAF AL-SHIMIY.

In addition, there are 24 other local chambers of commerce.

EMPLOYERS' ORGANIZATION

Federation of Egyptian Industries: 1195 Corniche el-Nil, Ramlet Boulaq, Cairo; and 65 Gamal Abdel Nasser Ave, Alexandria; tel. (2) 25796590; fax (2) 25796953 (Cairo); tel. and fax (3) 34916121 (Alexandria); e-mail info@fei.org.eg; internet www.fei.org.eg; f. 1922; Chair. MUHAMMAD ZAKI EL-SEWEDY.

STATE HYDROCARBONS COMPANIES

Egyptian General Petroleum Corpn (EGPC): POB 2130, 4th Sector, Sharia Palestine, New Maadi, 11742 Cairo; tel. (2) 27066900; fax (2) 27028813; e-mail egpc@egpc.com.eg; internet egpc.com.eg; state supervisory authority generally concerned with the planning of policies relating to petroleum activities in Egypt with the object of securing the devt of the petroleum industry and ensuring its effective administration; Chair. Eng. ALAA EL-BATAL.

Arab Petroleum Pipelines Co (SUMED): POB 158, el-Saray, 431 el-Geish Ave, Louran, Alexandria; tel. (3) 5824138; fax (3) 5831295; internet www.sumed.org; f. 1974; EGPC has 50% interest, Saudi Arabian Oil Co 15%, Int. Petroleum Investment Co (UAE) 15%, Kuwait Real Estate Investment Consortium 14.22%, Qatar Petroleum 5%, other Kuwaiti cos 0.78%; Suez–Mediterranean crude oil transportation pipeline (capacity: 117m. metric tons per year) and petroleum terminal operators; Chair. and Man. Dir Eng. MUHAMMAD ABDELHAFEZ.

Belayim Petroleum Co (PETROBEL): POB 7074, Sharia el-Mokhayam, Cairo (Nasr City); tel. (2) 22621738; fax (2) 22609792; f. 1977; capital equally shared between EGPC and Int. Egyptian Oil Co, which is a subsidiary of Eni of Italy; petroleum and gas exploration, drilling and production; Chair. and Man. Dir KHALED MOWAFI.

Egyptian Natural Gas Co (GASCO): Ring Rd, Exit 12, Sharia el-Tesien, 5th Settlement, Cairo; tel. (2) 25384500; fax (2) 26171514; e-mail int.relations@gasco.com.eg; internet www.gasco.com.eg; f. 1997; 70% owned by EGPC, 15% by Petroleum Projects and Technical Consultations Co (PETROJET), 15% by Egypt Gas; transmission and processing of natural gas; operation of the national gas distribution network; Chair. and Man. Dir Eng. YASSER SALAH EL-DIN.

EGYPT

General Petroleum Co (GPC): POB 743, 8 Sharia Dr Moustafa Abou Zahra, Cairo (Nasr City); tel. (2) 24030975; fax (2) 24037602; internet www.gpc.com.eg; f. 1957; wholly owned subsidiary of EGPC; operates mainly in Eastern Desert; Chair. Eng. NABIL ABDELSADEK.

Gulf of Suez Petroleum Co (GUPCO): POB 2400, 4th Sector, Sharia Palestine, New Maadi, Cairo 11511; tel. (2) 23520985; fax (2) 23531286; f. 1965; jt venture between EGPC and BP Egypt (UK/USA); developed the el-Morgan oilfield in the Gulf of Suez, also holds other exploration concessions in the Gulf of Suez and the Western Desert; Chair. and Man. Dir Eng. MOHAMED EL-MELIGY.

Middle East Oil Refinery (MIDOR): Sharia el-Teseen, Plot 209, City Center, Sector 2, 5th Settlement, New Cairo; tel. (2) 26733500; fax (2) 26733600; e-mail info@midor.com.eg; internet www.midor.com.eg; f. 1994; 79% owned by EGPC, 10% by Engineering for the Petroleum and Process Industries (Enppi), 10% by Petroleum Projects and Technical Consultations Co (PETROJET), 1% by Suez Canal Bank; operation of oil-refining facilities at Ameriya, Alexandria; capacity 115,000 b/d; Chair. and CEO GAMAL KAREISH.

Western Desert Petroleum Co (WEPCO): POB 412, Borg el-Thagr Bldg, Sharia Safia Zagloul, Alexandria; tel. (3) 3928710; fax (3) 3934969; internet wepco-eg.com; f. 1967 as partnership between EGPC (50% interest) and Phillips Petroleum (35%) and later Hispanoil (15%); developed Alamein, Yidma and Umbarka fields in the Western Desert and later Abu Qir offshore gas field 1978, followed by NAF gas field 1987; Chair. Eng. IBRAHIM MASSOUD.

Egyptian Natural Gas Holding Co (EGAS): POB 8064, 85c Sharia Nasr, 11371 Cairo (Nasr City); tel. (2) 24055830; fax (2) 24055876; e-mail egas@egas.com.eg; internet www.egas.com.eg; f. 2001 as part of a restructuring of the natural gas sector; strategic planning and promotion of investment in the natural gas industry; Chair. Eng. MAGDY GALA.

UTILITIES

Electricity

Egyptian Electricity Holding Co: Sharia Ramses, Cairo (Nasr City); tel. (2) 24030681; fax (2) 24031871; e-mail isats_eehc@yahoo.com; internet www.eehc.gov.eg; fmrly Egyptian Electricity Authority; renamed as above 2000; Chair. GABER DESOUKY.

Gas

Egypt Gas: 30 el-Mofatechine St, Cairo; tel. (2) 22901942; fax (2) 24178607; e-mail egyptgas@egyptgas.com.eg; internet www.egyptgas.com.eg; f. 1983; Chair. WA'EL GOWAIED.

Egyptian Natural Gas Holding Co (EGAS): see State Hydrocarbons Companies.

Water

Holding Co for Water and Wastewater: Corniche el-Nil, Cairo; tel. (2) 24583591; fax (2) 24583884; e-mail hcww@hcww.com.eg; internet www.hcww.com.eg; f. 2004; operation, maintenance and devt of water and wastewater facilities; oversees the operations of 20 affiliated regional water cos; Chair. MAMDOUH ISMAIL AHMAD RASLAN.

National Organization for Potable Water and Sanitary Drainage (NOPWASD): Sharia Ahmed Orabi, Mohandessin, Cairo; tel. (2) 33023055; fax (2) 33023052; f. 1981; water and sewerage authority; Chair. Eng. EHAB AHMED KHADER.

STATE HOLDING COMPANIES

The following holding companies, under the supervision of the Ministry of Investment and International Co-operation, are responsible for the management of the public sector companies and state investments in the relevant sectors. In addition, the holding companies promote and implement the Government's privatization programme.

Holding Co for Chemical Industries: POB 38, 5 Sharia Tolombat, 11516 Cairo (Garden City); tel. (2) 27954006; fax (2) 27964597; e-mail info@cihc-eg.com; internet www.cihc-eg.com; 22 affiliated cos incl. Egyptian Chemical Industries Co (KIMA), Misr Chemical Industries Co, National Cement Co, Rakata Paper Co, Eastern Tobacco Co; mfrs of industrial chemicals; fertilizers; tyres, rubber and leather; cement; paper and packaging; cigarettes; vehicle components; Chair. MOHAMED ZAKARIA MOHIELDIN.

Holding Co for Construction and Development: 17 Sharia Republic, Cairo (Heliopolis); tel. (2) 23953155; fax (2) 23908673; e-mail info@hccd-construction.com; internet www.hccd-construction.com; affiliated to the Ministry of Public Enterprise Sector; 11 subsidiary cos; Chair. FATHALLAH FAWZI MUHAMMAD FATHALLAH.

Holding Co for Food Industries (FIHC): 1 el-Sawah Sq., Cairo; tel. (2) 22845573; e-mail info@hcfi-egy.com; internet hcfi-egy.com; 31 affiliated cos; manufacture, processing and distribution of foodstuffs and agricultural commodities; Man. Dir Prof. AHMED HASSANEIN.

Holding Co for Metallurgical Industries: 5 Sharia al-Tolomabat, Cairo (Garden City); tel. (2) 27954844; fax (2) 27962079; e-mail info@mih.eg; internet mih.eg; affiliated cos incl. Egypt Aluminium Co, Egyptian Iron and Steel Co, El-Nasr Mining Co, Egyptian Ferro Alloys Co; Chair. Eng. MOHAMED EL-SAADAWI.

Holding Co for Pharmaceuticals, Chemicals and Medical Appliances (HoldiPharma): 12 Sharia Waked, 2078 Cairo; tel. (2) 25912825; fax (2) 25916866; e-mail chairman@holdipharma.com; internet www.holdipharma.com; 12 affiliated cos incl. Nile Co for Pharmaceuticals, Kahira Co for Pharmaceuticals and Chemical Industries, Alexandria Co for Pharmaceuticals and Chemical Industries.

Holding Co for Tourism and Hotels (HOTAC): 4 Sharia Latin America, Cairo (Garden City); tel. (2) 27940036; fax (2) 27952056; e-mail info@hotac.com.eg; internet www.hotac.com.eg; 9 affiliated cos incl. Egyptian General Co for Tourism and Hotels (EGOTH), Misr Travel Co, Misr Hotels Co; Chair. and CEO MERVAT ALI HATABA; Man. Dir ADEL AMIN WALI.

MAJOR COMPANIES

Abu Qir Fertilizers and Chemical Industries Co: Sharia al-Tabia-Rashid, Alexandria 21911; tel. (3) 5603053; internet abuqir.net; f. 1976; production of nitrogen-based fertilizers; Chair. ABD EZZ RIJAL ABDELAAL.

AJWA Group Egypt: 95c Sharia Merghany, Cairo (Heliopolis); tel. (2) 24178182; fax (2) 24146721; e-mail oroubamail@orouba.ajwa.com; internet www.ajwagroup.com; f. 1985; processing, distribution and marketing of edible oils and food products.

Alexandria Mineral Oils Co (AMOC): POB 5, Sharia el-Sad el-Ali, Wadi el-Qamar, el-Max, Alexandria; tel. (3) 2205646; fax (3) 2205651; e-mail info@amoceg.com; internet amoceg.com; manufacture and distribution of refined petroleum products incl. paraffin wax, transmission fluid, lubricants, LPG and base oils; Chair. and CEO AMR LOTFY.

Alexandria Spinning and Weaving Co (SPINALEX): al-Bar al-Kebli, al-Mahmoudaya, al-Nozha, Alexandria 21511; tel. (3) 3818046; fax (3) 3810485; e-mail spinalexco@yahoo.com; internet www.spinalex.com; f. 1959; production of cotton yarns; operates four mills; Chair. and Man. Dir RIFAAT HELAL.

Amiral Group: 29 Sharia Farid, Cairo (Heliopolis) 11341; tel. (2) 4149944; fax (2) 4148877; e-mail info@amiral.com; internet www.amiral.com; active in maritime, livestock, engineering and technology, and bio-fuels industries; most of group's operations based at Sokhna Port; subsidiaries incl. Royal Logistics, International Shipping and Transport Co, Amiral Management Corpn, Bulk Liquids Terminal and Bunkering (Sonker); Pres. and CEO OSAMA AL-SHARIF.

Cairo Poultry Co: POB 42, 32H Sharia Mourad, Cairo (Giza); tel. (2) 35714124; fax (2) 5726485; e-mail info@cpg.com.eg; internet www.cpg.com.eg; f. 1977; breeding and distribution of poultry and poultry products; controls 14 subsidiary cos; Chair. Eng. TAREK TAWFIK; Man. Dir ADEL AL-ALFI.

Eastern Co SAE: 6th Industrial Zone, Sharia al-Wahat, 6th of October City, Cairo (Giza); tel. (2) 38164310; fax (2) 38164444; e-mail eastern@easternegypt.com; internet www.easternegypt.com; f. 1920; partial privatization began in 1995; currently 55% state-owned; manufacture and distribution of tobacco and associated products; Chair. Eng. TAMER GAD ALLAH; CEO HANI AMAN.

Egypt Aluminium Co (Egyptalum): Nag Hammadi, Qena; tel. (2) 25744295; fax (2) 23906793; e-mail info@egyptalum.com.eg; internet www.egyptalum.com.eg; f. 1972; operates a smelting plant at Nag Hammady; Chair. SYED AHMED KASIB MOHAMED; Man. Dir MAHMOUD ALI AHMED SALEM.

Egyptian Financial and Industrial Co: Kafr el-Zayat, Gharbia; tel. (2) 2548881; fax (2) 2542773; e-mail efic@efic-eg.com; internet efic-eg.com; f. 1929; fmrly 100% state-owned; initial public offering of 65% of shares issued in 1996; production of phosphate fertilizers and sulphuric acid; Chair. ABDUL AZIM MUHAMMAD AL-ABSI.

Egyptian International Pharmaceutical Industries Co (EIPICO): POB 149, Industrial Zone B1, 10 Ramadan City, Cairo (Giza); tel. (15) 499199; fax (15) 499306; e-mail tenth@eipico.net; internet www.eipico.com.eg; f. 1985; production and distribution of pharmaceutical products; Chair. and Gen. Man. Dr AHMED KILANI.

Egyptian Iron and Steel Co (HADISOLB): Helwan, el-Tebeen, Cairo; tel. (2) 27155491; e-mail adv@hadisolb.com; internet www.hadisolb.com; f. 1954; state-owned; affiliate of the Holding Co for Metallurgical Industries; Chair. FAROUK KHAMIS BADAWY.

Elsewedy Electric: POB 311, Plot 27, District 1, Settlement 5, New Cairo 11835; tel. (2) 27599700; fax (2) 27599731; e-mail info@elsewedy.com; internet www.elsewedyelectric.com; f. 1984; privately owned; mfrs of cables and electrical products for the telecommunications and energy industries; Chair. and Man. Dir SADEK AHMED SADEK EL-SEWEDY.

Ezzsteel: Four Seasons Nile Plaza, Corporate Bldg, 1089 Corniche el-Nil, Garden City, Cairo; tel. (2) 27989800; fax (2) 27931953; e-mail info@ezzsteel.com; internet www.ezzsteel.com; f. 1994; mfrs of long and flat steel products; subsidiaries include Al-Ezz Dekheila Steel Co; Chair. MAMDOUH EL-RUBY; Man. Dir HASSAN NOUH.

Ghabbour Auto Group (GB Auto): POB 60 Giza, Abu Rawash Industrial Zone, km 28, Cairo–Alexandria Desert Rd, Cairo; tel. (2) 35391047; fax (2) 35390139; e-mail info@ghabbour.com; internet www.ghabbourauto.com; f. 1956 as Ghabbour Brothers; automotive assembly and distribution; CEO NADER GHABBOUR; 21,593 employees (2020).

Juhayna Food Industries: Bldg 2, Beverly Hills, Sheikh Zayed, Cairo (Giza); tel. 38508393; fax 38200655; e-mail contactus@juhayna.com; internet www.juhayna.com; f. 1983; producer of dairy, juice and cooking products; Chair. AHMED EL-WAKIL; over 4,000 employees (2023).

Lafarge Egypt: Summit 15, Sharia el-Teseen, City Center, Sector 1, 5th Settlement, New Cairo; tel. (2) 27689200; fax (2) 27681131; internet www.lafarge.com.eg; f. 2008; producers of cement, concrete and aggregates; CEO JIMMY KHAN.

Orascom Construction Industries: Nile City Towers, Corniche el-Nil, 11221 Cairo; tel. (2) 24611000; e-mail contactus@orascom.com; internet www.orascom.com; f. 1976; international construction contractor with operations in the Middle East, Africa, Europe and Cen. Asia; three construction divisions: Orascom Construction, BESIX Group(50% ownership), Contrack Int; also active in the manufacture of fertilizer products through subsidiaries incl. Egyptian Fertilizers Co; Chair. JÉRÔME GUIRAUD; CEO OSAMA BISHAI.

Oriental Weavers Carpet Co: Sharia Ismailia, 10 Ramadan City, Industrial Area A1, Cairo; tel. (5) 4411137; fax (5) 4411136; e-mail owc@orientalweavers.com; internet www.orientalweavers.com; f. 1980; mfrs of rugs, carpets and associated products; Chair. YASMINE MOHAMED FARID KHAMIS; CEO and Man. Dir SALAH ABD EL-AZIZ.

Pharco Corpn: Sharia Alexandria-Cairo Desert, Km 31, Ameriya, Alexandria; tel. (3) 4480130; fax (3) 4480730; e-mail pharco@pharco.com.eg; internet www.pharco.org; f. 1987; devt, manufacturing, marketing, distribution and exporting of pharmaceutical products; subsidiaries include Pharco Pharmaceuticals, Amriya Pharmaceutical Industries, European Egyptian Pharmaceutical Industries, Safe Pharma, Technopharma Egypt, Pharco B International; CEO Dr SHERINE HASSAN ABBAS HELMY.

Sidi Krier Petrochemicals (Sidpec): Sharia Cairo-Alexandria Desert, Km 36, el-Ameriya, Alexandria; tel. (3) 4770131; fax (3) 4770129; e-mail info@sidpec.com; internet www.sidpec.com; f. 1997; 20% owned by Egyptian Petrochemicals Holding Co; mfrs of polyethylene products; Chair. and CEO Eng. MOHAMED IBRAHIM.

Suez Cement: Km 30, Sharia Maadi-Ain Sokhna, Cairo (Helwan); tel. (2) 25222000; fax (2) 25222077; e-mail scc-communication@suezcem.com; internet www.suezcement.com.eg; f. 1977; 55% owned by HeidelbergCement Group (Germany); four production facilities; Chair. YASSER EL-NAGGAR; Man. Dir MOHAMED ABDEL RAHEM EL-SAYED HEGAZY.

Talaat Moustafa Group Holding (TMG): 34–36 Sharia Mussadak, Cairo; tel. (2) 33016701; fax (2) 33362198; e-mail tmgh@tmg.com.eg; internet www.talaatmoustafa.com; f. 1975; community real estate devt, and devt of hotels and resorts; 21 subsidiary cos, in the real estate, construction and agriculture sectors; Chair. TAREK TALAAT MOSTAFA; CEO and Man. Dir HISHAM TALAAT MOSTAFA.

TRADE UNIONS

Egyptian Democratic Labour Congress (EDLC): 88 Sharia Qasr el-Eini, 1st Floor, Apt no. 7, Downtown, Cairo; tel. (2) 27962564; e-mail edlc.labourcongress@gmail.com; f. 2012; mem. of Arab Trade Union Confed; Leader SAAD SHAABAN; 271 affiliated unions and more than 1m. mems.

Egyptian Federation of Independent Trade Unions (EFITU): Cairo; f. 2011; Pres. KAMAL ABU EITA; 261 affiliated unions and 2.4m. mems.

Egyptian Trade Union Federation (ETUF): 90 Sharia al-Galaa, Cairo; tel. (2) 25740362; fax (2) 25753427; e-mail office@etufegypt.com; internet www.etufegypt.com; f. 1957; govt-controlled; affiliated to Int. Confed. of Arab Trade Unions and to the Org. of African Trade Union Unity; 27 affiliated unions; Pres. MOHAMED GOBRAN.

Transport

RAILWAYS

The area of the Nile Delta is well served by railways. Lines also run from Cairo southward along the Nile to Aswan, and westward along the coast to Salloum. In April 2021 Egypt and Sudan agreed plans to build a 363.5-km railway line connecting their two rail networks. The first stage of the project would connect Aswan to Toshka and Abu Simbel in southern Egypt, with the second stage extending the line to Halfa in northern Sudan. The railway project would include the construction of a 6-km suspension bridge over Lake Nasser. In July 2022 the first phase (incorporating 70 km of track and 12 stations) of an electrified light rail transit (LRT) system was inaugurated, connecting Cairo with the New Administrative Capital and 10th of Ramadan City. When completed, the LRT project was expected to extend over 103 km with 19 stations. The first phase of a two-line monorail rapid transit system in Greater Cairo, incorporating 56.5 km of track and 22 stations, was expected to begin operating 2023.

Egyptian National Railways: Station Bldg, Midan Ramses, Cairo 11794; tel. (2) 25753555; fax (2) 25774295; e-mail support@enr.gov.eg; internet enr.gov.eg; f. 1852; length 9,570 km (2020); a 346-km line to carry phosphate and iron ore from the Bahariya mines, in the Western Desert, to the Helwan iron and steel works in south Cairo, was opened in 1973, and the Qena–Safaga line (length 223 km) commenced operating in 1989; restructured in 2012; Chair. MUSTAFA ABDEL LATIF ABU AL-MAKAREM.

Alexandria Passenger Transport Authority: POB 466, Aflaton, el-Shatby, Alexandria 21111; tel. (3) 5975223; fax (3) 5971187; internet www.alexapta.org; f. 1860; controls City Tramways (100.5 km), Ramleh Electric Railway, suburban buses and minibuses; Chair. and Tech. Dir MOHAMED ZAKARIA.

Cairo Transport Authority: Sharia Ramses, el-Gabal el-Ahmar, Cairo (Nasr City); tel. (2) 26845712; fax (2) 28654858; owned by the Governorate of Cairo; provider of public transport services in Greater Cairo, incl. tram, surface metro, bus and ferry services; rail system length 78 km (electrified); gauge 1,000 mm; operates 16 tram routes and 24 km of light railway; 720 cars; Chair. SALAH FARAG.

Egyptian Co for Metro Management and Operations (Cairo Metro): POB 466, Ramses Bldg, Midan Ramses, Cairo 11794; tel. (2) 25748353; e-mail contact.us@cairometro.gov.eg; internet www.cairometro.gov.eg; f. 2003; construction of the first electrified, 1,435-mm gauge underground transport system in Africa and the Middle East began in Cairo in 1982; Line 1, which opened to the public in 1987, has a total of 35 stations (5 underground), connects el-Marg el-Gedida with Helwan and is 44 km long with a 4.7-km tunnel beneath central Cairo; Line 2 links Shoubra el-Kheima with Giza, at el-Monib station, totalling 21.6 km (13 km in tunnel), and with 20 stations (12 underground), two of which interconnect with Line 1; Line 3 currently links Attaba and al-Ahram in Heliopolis, following the inauguration of the second phase of construction in 2014; two further phases will eventually connect Attaba with Mohandessin and Imbaba, and al-Ahram with Cairo International Airport; it was planned that, upon completion, Line 3 would have 39 stations (26 underground); Chair. and Man. Dir ALY FADALY.

ROADS

There are good metalled main roads as follows: Cairo–Alexandria (desert road); Cairo–Banha–Tanta–Damanhour–Alexandria; Cairo–Suez (desert road); Cairo–Ismailia–Port Said or Suez; and Cairo–Fayoum (desert road). The Ahmad Hamdi road tunnel (1.64 km) beneath the Suez Canal was opened in 1980. A second bridge over the Suez Canal was completed in 2001. In 2019 a new 342-km road from the Ahmed Hamdi tunnel to Sharm el-Sheikh was inaugurated.

General Authority for Roads, Bridges and Land Transport—Ministry of Transport (GARBLT): 105 Sharia Qasr el-Eini, Cairo; tel. (2) 27952344; fax (2) 23892176; e-mail garblt@idsc.gov.eg; Chair. Eng. SA'AD AL-GOYOUSHI.

SHIPPING

Egypt's principal ports are Alexandria, Port Said and Suez. A port designed to handle up to 16m. metric tons of cargo per year in its first stage of development, was opened at Damietta in 1986. By 2021 handling capacity at Damietta had increased to 21.8m. tons. Egypt's first privately operated port was opened in 2002 at Ain Sokhna on the Red Sea coast, near the southern entrance of the Suez Canal. Sokhna's cargo handling capacity increased from 6m. tons in 2005 to 23.5m. tons in 2021. Following the completion in 2015 of a major expansion project at the Suez Canal Container Terminal at Port Said, total annual throughput capacity was increased to 5.4m. 20-foot equivalent units (TEUs). In August 2023 the Government awarded a 30-year contract to the General Authority for Land and Dry Ports to develop and operate the 10th of Ramadan Dry Port and Logistics Centre.

Port and Regulatory Authorities

Maritime Transport Sector: Ministry of Transport, 4 Sharia Ptolemy, Bab Sharqi, 21514 Alexandria; tel. (3) 4842119; fax (3) 4842041; e-mail contact@mts.gov.eg; internet www.mts.gov.eg; supervision of the maritime sector; Dir-Gen. Rear-Adm. REDA AHMED ISMAIL.

Alexandria Port Authority: 106 Sharia el-Hourriya, Alexandria 26514; tel. (3) 4800627; fax (3) 4800866; e-mail info@apa.gov.eg; internet www.apa.gov.eg; f. 1966; management of Alexandria and Dakahlia ports; Chair. Rear-Adm. TARIQ SHAHIN ALI SHAHIN.

Damietta Port Authority: POB 13, Damietta; tel. (57) 2290007; e-mail chairman@dpa.gov.eg; internet www.dpa.gov.eg; Chair. WALID MOSTAFA AWAD.

Port Said Port Authority: Intersection Sharia Moustafa Kamel and Sharia Azmy, Port Said; tel. (66) 3348210; fax (66) 3348262; Gov. ADEL EL-GHADBAN.

Red Sea Ports Authority: POB 1, Port Tawfik, Suez; tel. (62) 3191124; fax (62) 3191117; e-mail info@rspa.gov.eg; internet www.rspa.gov.eg; responsible for ports incl. Suez, Sokhna and Hurghada; Chair. Adm. MOHAMED ABDEL RAHIM HAMID.

Principal Shipping Companies

Arab Maritime Petroleum Transport Co (AMPTC): POB 143, 9th Floor, Nile Tower Bldg, 21 Sharia Giza, 12211 Giza; tel. (2) 35701311; fax (2) 33378080; e-mail amptc.cairo@amptc.net; internet www.amptc.net; f. 1973; affiliated to the Org. of Arab Petroleum Exporting Countries; 10 vessels; Gen. Man. AHMED EL-DEMERDASH.

Egyptian Navigation Co (ENC): 2 el-Nasr St, el-Gomrok, Alexandria; tel. (3) 4877805; fax (3) 4871345; e-mail enc@dataxprs.com.eg; internet www.enc.com.eg; f. 1961; owners and operators of Egypt's mercantile marine; international trade transportation; 12 vessels; Chair. and Man. Dir AMR GAMAL EL-DIN ROUSHDY.

Holding Co for Maritime and Land Transport: 19 Sharia el-Maahad el-Eshteraky, Cairo (Heliopolis); tel. (3) 22586139; fax (3) 22586140; e-mail itc_cairo@hcmlt.com; internet www.hcmlt.com; govt-owned; 17 affiliated cos, incl. General Co for River Nile Transportation, Port Said Container and Cargo Handling Co, General Egyptian Warehouses Co; Chair. and Man. Dir SALAH EL-DIN HELMY ABD EL-KADER.

National Navigation Co: 4 Sharia El-Hegaz, Cairo (Heliopolis); tel. (2) 24525575; fax (2) 24526171; e-mail nnc@nnc.com.eg; internet www.nnc.com.eg; f. 1981; specializes in bulk cargoes; operates passenger services between Egypt and Saudi Arabia; 18 vessels; Chair. Eng. HANY SAYED DAHI; Man. Dir and CEO ABDEL KADER GABALLAH.

Red Sea Navigation Co: 10 Gowhar el-Khaled St, Port Tawfik, Suez; tel. (62) 3196971; fax (62) 9136915; e-mail suez@rdnav.com; internet www.rdnav.com; f. 1986; operates a fleet of eight cargo vessels; shipping agency, Suez Canal transit and stevedoring; Chair. ABD EL-MAJID MATAR.

THE SUEZ CANAL

Length of canal: 193.3 km; maximum permissible draught: 20.12 m (66 ft); breadth of canal at water level and breadth between buoys defining the navigable channel at −11 m: 313 m and 225 m, respectively.

A second parallel channel (dubbed the New Suez Canal), totalling 35 km in length, was inaugurated in 2015. This channel was designed to increase the total daily capacity of the Canal from 49 vessels to 97 and augment total revenue to more than US $13,000m. per year by 2023.

Suez Canal Authority (Hay'at Canal al-Suways): Irshad Bldg, Ismailia; Cairo Office: 6 Sharia Lazoughli, Cairo (Garden City); tel. (64) 3396222; fax (64) 3392515; e-mail info@suezcanal.gov.eg; internet www.suezcanal.gov.eg; f. 1956; govt-owned; Chair. and CEO Lt-Gen. OSAMA RABIE.

Suez Canal Container Terminal: POB 247, Port Said; tel. (66) 3258970; fax (66) 3258960; e-mail scct@scctportsaid.com; internet scct.com.eg; f. 2000, with 30-year concession to operate the East Port Said container terminal; Man. Dir STEVEN YOOGALINGAM.

CIVIL AVIATION

The main international airports are at Cairo (located at Heliopolis, 23 km from the centre of the city), Sharm el-Sheikh and Hurghada. A new international airport at Borg el-Arab (40 km south-west of Alexandria) was inaugurated in 2010. Borg el-Arab became the main airport serving Alexandria in December 2011, owing to the closure of the city's main international airport, el-Nouzha, which was to undergo expansion. However, it was subsequently announced that el-Nouzha was to close permanently. A new international airport, Sphinx International Airport, serving the city of Giza to the west of Cairo, commenced operations in 2019.

EgyptAir: Administration Complex, Cairo International Airport, Cairo (Heliopolis); tel. (2) 22657226; fax (2) 22663773; e-mail callcenter@egyptair.com; internet www.egyptair.com; f. 1932 as Misr Airwork; known as United Arab Airlines 1960–71; restructured as a holding co with 9 subsidiaries 2002; operates internal services in Egypt and external services throughout the Middle East, Far East, Africa, Europe and the USA; Chair. and CEO AMR ABO EL-ENEIN.

Egyptian Civil Aviation Authority: ECAA Complex, Sharia Airport, Cairo 11776; tel. (2) 22677610; fax (2) 22679470; e-mail contact_us@civilaviation.gov.eg; internet www.civilaviation.gov.eg; f. 2000; Chair. SAMEH AHMED HEFNI.

Egyptian Holding Co for Airports and Air Navigation (EHCAAN): EHCAAN Bldg, Airport Rd, Cairo; tel. (2) 24175388; fax (2) 22666013; e-mail info@ehcaan.com; internet www.ehcaan.com; f. 2001; responsible for management and devt of all Egyptian airports; Chair. MOHAMED SAIED MAHROUS.

Cairo Airport Co: Cairo International Airport, 11776 Cairo (Heliopolis); tel. (2) 26966300; fax (2) 22653214; e-mail cac@cairo-airport.com; internet www.cairo-airport.com; under management of Egyptian Holding Co since 2003; Chair. AHMED FAWZY ABDUL AZIM.

Egyptian Airports Co: Cairo; tel. (2) 22739417; fax (2) 22739416; e-mail info@eac-airports.com; internet www.eac-airports.com; f. 2001; management and devt of 19 regional airports; Chair. AHMED MANSOUR.

Tourism

Egyptian Tourist Authority: 11 Abassya Sq., Cairo; tel. (2) 22854509; fax (2) 22854363; e-mail info@egypt.travel; internet www.egypt.travel; f. 1965; brs in Alexandria, Port Said, Suez, Luxor and Aswan; Chair. AMR EL-EZABI.

Egyptian General Co for Tourism and Hotels (EGOTH): 4 Sharia Latin America, 11519 Cairo (Garden City); tel. (2) 27942914; e-mail headoffice@egoth.com.eg; internet www.egoth.com.eg; f. 1961; affiliated to the Holding Co for Tourism, Hotels and Cinema; Chair. and Man. Dir SHERIF MOHAMED SALAH BENDARY.

Defence

As assessed at November 2022, the total strength of the armed forces was 438,500: army 310,000; air defence command 80,000; navy 18,500 (including 10,000 conscripts); air force 30,000 (10,000 conscripts). There were also 479,000 reserves. Paramilitary forces were estimated at 397,000: Central Security Forces 325,000; National Guard 60,000; and Border Guard 12,000. Military service is selective and lasts for 1–3 years.

Defence Budget: £E86,000m. in 2022.

Commander-in-Chief of the Armed Forces: Gen. MOHAMED AHMED ZAKI.

Chief of Staff of the Armed Forces: Lt-Gen. OSAMA ASKAR.

Commander of the Air Force: Maj.-Gen. MAHMOUD FOUAD ABDEL-GAWAD.

Commander of the Air Defence Forces: Maj.-Gen. MOHAMED HEGAZY ABDEL-MAWGOUD.

Commander of the Navy: Rear Adm. ASHRAF IBRAHIM ATWA MUJAHID.

Education

Education is compulsory for eight years between six and 14 years of age. Primary education, beginning at six years of age, lasts for five years. Secondary education, beginning at 11 years of age, lasts for a further six years, comprising two cycles of three years each. In 2018/19, according to estimates by UNESCO, enrolment at pre-primary schools was equivalent to 29.3% of children (boys 29.3%; girls 29.3%) in the relevant age-group, while primary enrolment included 99.3% of children in the relevant age-group, lower secondary enrolment 97.6% (boys 96.9%; girls 98.4%) and upper secondary enrolment 76.6% (boys 77.3%; girls 75.9%). The Al-Azhar University and its various preparatory and associated institutes provide instruction and training in several disciplines, with emphasis on adherence to Islamic principles and teachings. Education is free at all levels. According to UNESCO, spending on education constituted 12.3% of total government expenditure in 2020.

Bibliography

General and Historical Context

Abdel-Malek, Anwar. *Egypte, société militaire*. Paris, 1962.

Idéologie et renaissance nationale / L'Egypte moderne. Paris, 1969.

Adly, Amr. *State Reform and Development in the Middle East: Turkey and Egypt in the Post-Liberalization Era*. Abingdon, Routledge, 2013.

Aishima, Hatsuki. *Public Culture and Islam in Modern Egypt: Media, Intellectuals and Society*. London, I. B. Tauris, 2016.

Aldridge, James. *Cairo: Biography of a City*. London, Macmillan, 1970.

Avram, Benno. *The Evolution of the Suez Canal State 1869–1956. A Historico-Juridical Study*. Geneva, Librairie E. Droz, and Paris, Libraire Minard, 1958.

Baer, Gabriel. *Studies in the Social History of Modern Egypt*. Chicago, IL, and London, University of Chicago Press, 1969.

Berque, Jacques. *Egypt: Imperialism and Revolution*. London, Faber, 1972.

Blunt, Wilfred Scawen. *Secret History of the English Occupation of Egypt*. London, Martin Secker, 1907.

Cannuyer, Christian. *Les Coptes*. Turnhout, Editions Brepols, 1991.

Chevillat, Alain and Evelyne. *Moines du désert d'Egypte*. Lyons, Editions Terres du Ciel, 1991.

Chih, Rachida. *Le Soufisme au quotidien: confréries d'Egypte au XXe siècle*. Arles, Sinbad: Actes Sud, 2000.

Collins, Robert O. *The Nile*. New Haven, CT, Yale University Press, 2003.

Cook, Steven A. *The Struggle for Egypt: From Nasser to Tahrir Square*. Oxford, Oxford University Press, 2013.

Cromer, Earl of. *Modern Egypt*. 2 vols, London, 1908.

Dawisha, A. I. *Egypt in the Arab World*. London, Macmillan, 1976.

Dodwell, H. *The Founder of Modern Egypt*. Cambridge, 1931, reprinted 1967.

Efendi, Husein. *Ottoman Egypt in the Age of the French Revolution* (trans. and with introduction by Stanford J. Shaw). Cambridge, MA, Harvard University Press, 1964.

Empereur, Jean-Yves. *Alexandria. Past, Present and Future*. London, Thames & Hudson, 2002.

Gerges, Fawaz. *Making the Arab World: Nasser, Qutb, and the Clash that Shaped the Middle East*. Princeton, NJ, Princeton University Press, 2018.

Haeri, Niloofar. *Sacred Language, Ordinary People. Dilemmas of Culture and Politics in Egypt*. Basingstoke, Palgrave Macmillan, 2004.

Harris, C. P. *Nationalism and Revolution in Egypt: The Role of the Muslim Brotherhood*. The Hague, Mouton and Co, 1964.

Harris, J. R. (Ed.). *The Legacy of Egypt*. Oxford, Oxford University Press, 2nd edn, 1972.

Hopkins, Harry. *Egypt, The Crucible*. London, Secker and Warburg, 1969.

Hurst, H. E. *The Nile*. London, 1952.

The Major Nile Projects. Cairo, 1966.

Iskandar, Adel. *Egypt in Flux: Essays on an Unfinished Revolution*. Cairo, American University of Cairo Press, 2013.

Kepel, Gilles. (trans. Jon Rothschild). *The Prophet and Pharaoh: Muslim Extremism in Egypt*. London, Saqi Books, 1985.

King, Joan Wucher (Ed.). *An Historical Dictionary of Egypt*. Metuchen, NJ, Scarecrow Press, 1984.

Kinross, Lord. *Between Two Seas: The Creation of the Suez Canal*. London, John Murray, 1968.

Lacouture, Jean and Simonne. *Egypt in Transition*. London, Methuen, 1958.

Lauterpacht, E. (Ed.). *The Suez Canal Settlement*. London, Stevens and Sons, under the auspices of the British Institute of International and Comparative Law, 1960.

Lengye, Emil. *Egypt's Role in World Affairs*. Washington, DC, Public Affairs Press, 1957.

Lia, Brynjar. *The Society of the Muslim Brothers in Egypt: The Rise of an Islamic Mass Movement 1928–1942*. Reading, Ithaca Press, 2006.

Little, Tom. *Modern Egypt*. London, Ernest Benn, and New York, Praeger, 1967.

Lloyd, Lord. *Egypt since Cromer*. 2 vols, London, 1933–34.

Makari, Peter E. *Conflict and Cooperation: Christian-Muslim Relations in Contemporary Egypt*. Syracuse, NY, Syracuse University Press, 2007.

Marsot, Afaf Lutfi al-Sayyid. *Egypt and Cromer: A Study in Anglo-Egyptian Relations*. London, John Murray, and New York, Praeger, 1968.

Mehrez, Samia. *Egypt's Culture Wars: Politics and Practice*. Abingdon, Routledge, 2008.

Morkot, Robert. *Egyptians: An Introduction*. Abingdon, Routledge, 2005.

Osman, Ahmed. *Christianity: An Ancient Egyptian Religion*. Rochester, VT, Inner Traditions International Ltd, 2005.

Owen, Robert, and Blunsum, Terence. *Egypt, United Arab Republic. The Country and its People*. London, Queen Anne Press, 1966.

Pollard, Lisa. *Nurturing the Nation: The Family Politics of Modernizing, Colonizing, and Liberating Egypt, 1805–1923*. Berkeley, CA, University of California Press, 2005.

Richmond, J. C. B. *Egypt, 1798–1952: Her Advance towards a Modern Identity*. London, Methuen, 1977.

Safran, Nadav. *Egypt in Search of Political Community: An Analysis of the Intellectual and Political Evolution of Egypt, 1804–1952*. Cambridge, MA, Harvard University Press, and London, Oxford University Press, 1961.

Sharnoff, Michael. *Nasser's Peace: Egypt's Response to the 1967 War with Israel*. Abingdon, Routledge, 2017.

Smith, Simon C. *Reassessing Suez 1956: New Perspectives on the Crisis and its Aftermath*. Abingdon, Routledge, 2016.

Waterfield, Gordon. *Egypt*. London, Thames and Hudson, 1966.

Weaver, Mary Ann. *A Portrait of Egypt: A Journey Through the World of Militant Islam*. New York, Farrar, Straus and Giroux, 1998.

Wilson, John A. *The Burden of Egypt*. Chicago, IL, 1951.

Zaki, Abdel Rahman. *Histoire Militaire de l'Epoque de Mohammed Ali El-Kebir*. Cairo, 1950.

Contemporary Political History

Abdelrahman, Maha M. *Egypt's Long Revolution: Protest Movements and Uprisings*. Abingdon, Routledge, 2014.

Abouelnaga, Shereen. *Women in Revolutionary Egypt: Gender and the New Geographies of Identity*. Cairo, American University in Cairo Press, 2016.

Aboul Gheit, Ahmed. *Witness to War and Peace: Egypt, the October War, and Beyond*. Cairo, American University in Cairo Press, 2018.

Achrainer, C. *Egyptian Foreign Relations Under al-Sisi: External Alignments Since 2013*. London, Routledge, 2022.

Alexander, Anne. *Nasser*. London, Haus Publishing, 2005.

Arafat, Alaa al-Din. *Hosni Mubarak and The Future of Democracy in Egypt*. New York, NY, Palgrave Macmillan, revised edn, 2011.

Al-Awadi, Hisham. *The Muslim Brothers in Pursuit of Legitimacy: Power and Political Islam in Egypt Under Mubarak*. London, I. B. Tauris, 2014.

Amin, Galal. *Whatever Happened to the Egyptian Revolution?* (trans. by Jonathan Wright). Cairo, American University of Cairo Press, 2013.

Anani, Khalil. *Inside the Muslim Brotherhood: Religion, Identity, and Politics*. New York, Oxford University Press, 2016.

Ayata, B., and Harders, C. (Eds). *The Affective Dynamics of Mass Protests: Midān Moments and Political Transformation in Egypt and Turkey*. London, Routledge, 2023.

Baker, Raymond William. *Egypt's Uncertain Revolution under Nasser and Sadat*. Cambridge, MA, Harvard University Press, 1979.

Baker, Raymond William. *Sadat and After: Struggles for Egypt's Political Soul*. London, I. B. Tauris, 1990.

Bassiouni, M. Cherif. *Chronicles of the Egyptian Revolution and its Aftermath: 2011–2016*. Cambridge, Cambridge University Press, 2016.

Beinin, Joel. *Workers and Thieves: Labor Movements and Popular Uprisings in Tunisia and Egypt*. Stanford, CA, Stanford Briefs, 2015.

Brand, Laurie A. *Official Stories: Politics and National Narratives in Egypt and Algeria*. Redwood City, CA, Stanford University Press, 2014.

Brehony, Noel, and el-Desouky, Ayman Ahmed (Eds). *British-Egyptian Relations from Suez to the Present Day*. London, Saqi Books, 2007.

Brownlee, Jason. *Democracy Prevention: The Politics of the U.S.-Egyptian Alliance*. Cambridge, Cambridge University Press, 2012.

Cohen, Raymond. *Culture and Conflict in Egyptian-Israeli Relations: A Dialogue of the Deaf*. Bloomington, IN, Indiana University Press, 1994.

Connell, John. *The Most Important Country. The Story of the Suez Crisis and the Events leading up to it.* London, Cassell, 1957.

Cook, Steven A. *The Struggle for Egypt: From Nasser to Tahrir Square.* New York, Oxford University Press, 2012.

Cooper, Mark N. *The Transformation of Egypt.* London, Croom Helm, 1982.

Elsässer, Sebastian. *The Coptic Question in the Mubarak Era.* Oxford, Oxford University Press, 2014.

Fahmy, Ninette S. *The Politics of Egypt: State-Society Relationship.* London, Routledge, 2002.

Farnie, D. A. *East and West of Suez. The Suez Canal in History, 1854–1956.* Oxford, Clarendon Press, 1969.

Finklestone, Joseph. *Anwar Sadat: Visionary Who Dared.* London, Frank Cass, 1998.

Frampton, Martin. *The Muslim Brotherhood and the West: A History of Enmity and Engagement.* Cambridge, MA, Harvard University Press, 2018.

Heikal, Muhammad. *Sphinx and Commissar: The Rise and Fall of Soviet Influence in the Arab World.* London, Collins, 1978.

Autumn of Fury: The Assassination of Sadat. London, André Deutsch, 1983.

Cutting the Lion's Tail: Suez through Egyptian Eyes. London, André Deutsch, 1986.

Herrera, Linda. *Revolution in the Age of Social Media: The Egyptian Popular Insurrection and the Internet.* London, Verso, 2014.

Herrold, Catherine. *Delta Democracy: Pathways to Incremental Civic Revolution in Egypt and Beyond.* New York, Oxford University Press, 2020.

Hoyakem, Emile, and Taha, Hebatalla. *Egypt after the Spring: Revolt and Reaction.* London, International Institute for Strategic Studies, 2016.

Iskander, Elizabeth. *Sectarian Conflict in Egypt: Coptic Media, Identity and Representation.* Abingdon, Routledge, 2012.

Ismael, Tareq Y., and El-Said, Rifa'at. *The Communist Movement in Egypt 1920–1988.* Syracuse, NY, Syracuse University Press, 1990.

Issawi, Charles. *Egypt in Revolution.* Oxford, 1963.

Joesten, Joachim. *Nasser: The Rise to Power.* London, Odhams, 1960.

Joya, Angela. *The Roots of Revolt: a Political Economy of Egypt from Nasser to Mubarak.* Cambridge, Cambridge University Press, 2020.

Jumet, Kira D. *Contesting the Repressive State: Why Ordinary Egyptians Protested During the Arab Spring.* New York, Oxford University Press, 2018.

Kamel, Muhammad Ibrahim. *The Camp David Accords: A Testimony by Sadat's Foreign Minister.* London, Routledge and Kegan Paul, 1986.

Kassem, Maye. *In the Guise of Democracy: Governance in Contemporary Egypt.* Reading, Ithaca Press, 1999.

Egyptian Politics: The Dynamics of Authoritarian Rule. Boulder, CO, Lynne Rienner, 2004.

Kassem, Maye, and Kraetzschmar, Hendrik J. *Egypt.* Abingdon, Routledge, 2006.

Kienle, Eberhard. *A Grand Delusion: Democracy and Economic Reform in Egypt.* London, I. B. Tauris, 2001.

Krause, Wanda. *Civil Society and Women Activists in the Middle East: Islamic and Secular Organizations in Egypt.* London, I. B. Tauris, 2012.

Kyle, Keith. *Suez: Britain's End of Empire in the Middle East.* London, I. B. Tauris, 2002.

Loewe, Markus. *Industrial Policy in Egypt 2004-2011.* Bonn, Deutsches Institut für Entwicklungspolitik, 2013.

Mansfield, Peter. *Nasser's Egypt.* London, Penguin, 1965.

The British in Egypt. London, Weidenfeld and Nicolson, 1971.

Marsot, Afaf Lutfi al-Sayyid. *A History of Egypt: From the Arab Conquest to the Present.* Cambridge, Cambridge University Press, 2nd edn, 2007.

Masoud, Tarek E. *Counting Islam: Religion, Class, and Elections in Egypt.* New York, Cambridge University Press, 2014.

McMahon, Sean F. *Crisis and Class War in Egypt: Class Warfare, the State and Global Political Economy.* London, Zed Books, 2016.

Meital, Yoram. *Revolutionary Justice: Special Courts and the Formation of Republican Egypt.* New York, Oxford University Press, 2016.

Mellor, Noha. *The Egyptian Dream: Egyptian National Identity and Uprisings.* Edinburgh, Edinburgh University Press, 2015.

Moustafa, Tim. *The Struggle for Constitutional Power: Law, Politics and Economic Development in Egypt.* Cambridge, Cambridge University Press, 2007.

Nasser, Gamal Abdel. *Egypt's Liberation: The Philosophy of the Revolution.* Washington, DC, 1955.

Neguib, Mohammed. *Egypt's Destiny: A Personal Statement.* New York, 1955.

Nutting, Anthony. *No End of a Lesson: The Story of Suez.* London, Constable, 1967.

Nasser. London, Constable, 1972.

O'Ballance, E. *The Sinai Campaign 1956.* London, Faber, 1959.

Osman, Tarek. *Egypt on the Brink: From Nasser to Mubarak.* New Haven, CT, Yale University Press, 2010.

Quandt, William B. *Camp David: Peacemaking and Politics.* Washington, DC, Brookings Institution, 1986.

Resta, V. *Tunisia and Egypt after the Arab Spring: Party Politics in Transitions from Authoritarian Rule.* London, Routledge, 2023.

Riad, Hassan. *L'Egypte Nassérienne.* Paris, Editions de Minuit, 1964.

Roccu, Roberto. *The Political Economy of the Egyptian Revolution: Mubarak, Economic Reforms and Failed Hegemony.* Basingstoke, Palgrave Macmillan, 2013.

Rubin, Barry. *Islamic Fundamentalism in Egyptian Politics.* London, Macmillan, 1990.

Rutherford, Bruce K. *Egypt after Mubarak: Liberalism, Islam, and Democracy in the Arab World* (2nd edn). Princeton, NJ, Princeton University Press, 2013.

Schielke, Samuli. *Egypt in the Future Tense: Hope, Frustration, and Ambivalence before and After 2011.* Bloomington, IN, Indiana University Press, 2015.

Schonfield, Hugh A. *The Suez Canal in Peace and War, 1869–1969.* London, Vallentine Mitchell, 2nd edn, 1969.

Scott, Rachel M. *The Challenge of Political Islam: Non-Muslims and the Egyptian State.* Stanford, CA, Stanford University Press, 2010.

El-Shazli, Heba F. *Trade Unions and Arab Revolutions: Challenging the Regime in Egypt.* New York, Routledge, 2019.

El-Shazly, Gen. Saad. *The Crossing of Suez: The October War (1973).* London, Third World Centre for Research and Publishing, 1980.

Shama, Nael. *Egyptian Foreign Policy from Mubarak to Morsi: Against the National Interest.* Abingdon, Routledge, 2014.

Shehata, Dina. *Islamists and Secularists in Egypt: Opposition, Conflict and Co-operation.* Abingdon, Routledge, 2009.

Sirrs, Owen L. *A History of the Egyptian Intelligence Service: A History of the Mukhabarat, 1910–2009.* Abingdon, Routledge, 2010.

Springborg, Robert. *Egypt.* Cambridge, Polity, 2018.

Stachursky, Benjamin. *The Promise and Perils of Transnationalization: NGO Activism and the Socialization of Women's Human Rights in Egypt and Iran.* Abingdon, Routledge, 2013.

Tadros, Mariz. *The Muslim Brotherhood in Contemporary Egypt: Democracy Redefined or Confined?* Abingdon, Routledge, 2012.

Resistance, Revolt, & Gender Justice in Egypt: Gender, Culture, and Politics in the Middle East. New York, NY, Syracuse University Press, 2016.

Takeyh, Ray. *The Origins of the Eisenhower Doctrine: The US, Britain and Nasser's Egypt, 1953–57.* London, Macmillan, 2000.

Tal, Nachman. *Radical Islam in Egypt and Jordan.* Eastbourne, Sussex Academic Press, 2005.

Tohamy, Ahmed. *Youth Activism in Egypt: Islamism, Political Protest and Revolution.* London, I. B. Tauris, 2016.

Tsourapas, Gerasimos. *The Politics of Migration in Modern Egypt: Strategies for Regime Survival in Autocracies.* Cambridge, Cambridge University Press, 2018.

Vatikiotis, P. J. *A Modern History of Egypt.* New York, Praeger, 1966; London, Weidenfeld and Nicolson, 1969, revised edn, 1980.

The Egyptian Army in Politics. Bloomington, IN, Indiana University Press, 1961.

Wahba, D. *Counter Revolutionary Egypt: From the Midan to the Neighbourhood.* London, Routledge, 2023.

Waterbury, John. *The Egypt of Nasser and Sadat: The Political Economy of Two Regimes.* Princeton, NJ, Princeton University Press, 1983.

Wilbur, D. N. *The United Arab Republic.* New York, 1969.

Wynn, Wilton. *Nasser of Egypt: The Search for Dignity.* Cambridge, MA, 1959.

Zahid, Mohammed. *The Muslim Brotherhood and Egypt's Succession Crisis: The Politics of Liberalisation and Reform in the Middle East.* London, I. B. Tauris, 2010.

Economy

Abdel-Khalek, Gouda. *Stabilization and Adjustment in Egypt: Reform or Deindustrialization?* Cheltenham, Edward Elgar, 2001.

AlAzzawi, Shireen. 'Do Endowments Matter? Exploring The Gender Dimensions Of Poverty In Egypt'. *Review of Income and Wealth*, Vol. 64, Issue 1, 2018. DOI:10.1111/roiw.12390.

'Regional and income disparities in cost of living changes: evidence from Egypt', *Middle East Development Journal*, 2020. DOI: 10.1080/17938120.2020.1770476.

Arab Republic of Egypt. 'National Anti-Corruption Strategy (2019–22)'. www.aca.gov.eg/arabic/AntiCorruption/PublishingImages/Pages/nationalstrategy/English.pdf.

Assaad, Ragui (Ed.). *The Egyptian Labor Market Revisited*. Cairo, American University in Cairo Press, 2009.

Assaad, Ragui, and Krafft, Caroline. *The Egyptian Labor Market in an Era of Revolution*. Oxford, Oxford University Press, 2015.

Assaad, Ragui, Krafft, Caroline, Roemer, John, & Salehi-Isfahani, Djavad. 'Inequality of Opportunity in Wages and Consumption in Egypt'. *The Review of Income and Wealth*, Vol. 64, Issue 1, 2018. doi.org/10.1111/roiw.12289.

Bush, Ray. *Economic Crisis and the Politics of Reform in Egypt*. New York, Routledge, 2019.

Commander, Simon. *The State & Agricultural Development in Egypt Since 1973*. London, Ithaca Press (for the Overseas Development Institute), 1987.

Farah, Nadia Ramsis. *Egypt's Political Economy: Power Relations in Development*. Cairo, American University of Cairo Press, 2009.

El Ghonemy, M. Riad. *Economic and Industrial Organization of Egyptian Agriculture since 1952, Egypt since the Revolution*. London, Allen and Unwin, 1968.

Egypt in the Twenty-First Century: Challenges for Development. London, Routledge, 2003.

El-Haddad, Amirah. *The Egyptian Economy: Structural Transformation and Growth in the Middle East*. Abingdon, Routledge, 2021.

Hlasny, Vladmir, and Alazzawi, Shireen. 'Informality, Market Fragmentation and Low Productivity in Egypt', *The Forum: ERF Policy Portal*. 15 Aug. 2020. theforum.erf.org.eg/2020/08/08/informality-market-fragmentation-low-productivity-egypt.

Hvidt, Martin. *Water, Technology and Development: Upgrading Egypt's Irrigation System*. London, Tauris Academic Studies, 1997.

Ikram, Khalid. *The Egyptian Economy 1952–2000: Performance, Policies and Issues*. Abingdon, Routledge, 2005.

The Political Economy of Reforms in Egypt: Issues and Policymaking Since 1952. Cairo, American University in Cairo Press, 2018.

Jadallah, Dina. *US Economic Aid in Egypt: Strategies for Democratisation and Reform in the Middle East*. London, I. B. Tauris, 2016.

Kardouche, G. S. *The UAR in Development*. New York, Praeger, 1967.

Korayem, Karima. *Structural Adjustment, Stabilization Policies, and the Poor in Egypt*. Cairo, American University Press, 1996.

Mabro, Robert. *The Egyptian Economy 1952–1972*. London, Oxford University Press, 1974.

Mead, Donald C. *Growth and Structural Change in the Egyptian Economy*. Homwood, IL, Irwin, 1967.

Ministry of Finance and United Nations Children's Fund (UNICEF). *Co-Published Brief on State Budget for FY 20/21: Including Public Spending on Covid-19*, Transparency Brief No. 4, 2020. www.mof.gov.eg/MOFGallerySource/English/PDF/Budget_2020-2021/Preliminary_document_Co-published.pdf.

O'Brien, Patrick. *The Revolution in Egypt's Economic System 1952–65*. Oxford, 1966.

Posusney, Marsha Pripstein. *Labour and the State in Egypt: Workers, Unions and Economic Restructuring*. New York, Columbia University Press, 1998.

Saab, Gabriel S. *The Egyptian Agrarian Reform 1952–1962*. London and New York, Oxford University Press, 1967.

Utvik, Bjørn Olav. *Islamist Economics in Egypt: The Pious Road to Development*. Boulder, CO, Lynne Rienner Publishers, 2006.

Warriner, Doreen. *Land Reform and Economic Development*. Cairo, 1955.

Land Reform and Development in the Middle East—A Study of Egypt, Syria and Iraq. London, Oxford University Press, 2nd edn, 1962.

IRAN

Geography

The Islamic Republic of Iran is bounded on the north by the Caspian Sea, Armenia, Azerbaijan and Turkmenistan, on the east by Afghanistan and Pakistan, on the south by the Persian (Arabian) Gulf and the Gulf of Oman, and on the west by Iraq and Türkiye (formerly Turkey).

PHYSICAL FEATURES

Structurally, Iran is an extremely complex area and, owing partly to political difficulties and partly to the difficult nature of the terrain itself, complete exploration and investigation have not so far been achieved. In general, Iran consists of an interior plateau, 1,000 m to 1,500 m above sea level, ringed on almost all sides by mountain zones of varying height and extent. The largest mountain massif is that of the Zagros, which runs from the north-west, first south-westwards to the eastern shores of the Persian (Arabian) Gulf, and then eastwards, fronting the Arabian Sea, and continuing into Balochistan (Pakistan). Joining the Zagros in the north-west, and running along the southern edge of the Caspian Sea, is the narrower but equally high Alborz range; along the eastern frontier of Iran are several scattered mountain chains, less continuous and imposing than either the Zagros or the Alborz, but sufficiently high to act as a barrier.

The Zagros range begins in north-western Iran as an alternation of high tablelands and lowland basins, the latter containing lakes, the largest of which is Lake Urmia. This lake, having no outlet, is saline. Further to the south-east the Zagros becomes much more imposing, consisting of a series of parallel hog's-back ridges, some of which reach over 4,000 m in height. In its southern and eastern portions the Zagros becomes distinctly narrower, and its peaks much lower, though a few exceed 3,000 m. The Alborz range is very much narrower than the Zagros, but equally, if not more, abrupt, and one of its peaks, the volcanic cone of Mt Damavand, at 5,604 m, is the highest in the country. There is a sudden drop on the northern side to the flat plain occupied by the Caspian Sea, which lies about 27 m below sea level. The eastern highlands of Iran consist of isolated massifs separated by lowland zones, some of which contain lakes from which there is no outlet, the largest being the Hirmand Basin, on the border with Afghanistan.

The interior plateau of Iran is partly covered by a salt swamp (termed *kavir*) and partly by loose sand or stones (*dasht*), with stretches of better land mostly round the perimeter, near the foothills of the surrounding mountains. In these latter areas much of the cultivation of the country is practised, but the lower-lying desert and swamp areas, towards the centre of the plateau, are largely uninhabited. The Kavir is an extremely forbidding region, consisting of a surface formed by thick plates of crystallized salt, which have sharp, upstanding edges. Below the salt lie patches of mud, with, here and there, deep drainage channels—all of which are very dangerous to travellers and are hence unexplored. Owing to the presence of an unusually intractable 'dead heart', it has proved difficult to find a good central site for the capital of Iran—many towns, all peripheral to a greater or lesser degree, have in turn fulfilled this function, but none has proved completely satisfactory. The choice of the present capital, Tehran, dates only from the end of the 18th century.

Iran suffers from occasional earthquakes, which can cause severe loss of life, damage to property and disruption of communications. A particularly bad earthquake occurred around Tabas in the north-eastern Khurasan province in September 1978, when an estimated 20,000 lives were lost; severe damage was inflicted, extending over 2,000 sq km. Even more devastating was the major earthquake that struck north-western Iran (principally the provinces of Gilan and Zanjan) in June 1990. Estimates put the total number of those killed during the quake and a series of severe tremors and aftershocks at some 40,000. In December 2003 more than 26,000 people were killed by an earthquake in the region of the ancient city of Bam, in south-eastern Iran.

CLIMATE

The climate of Iran is one of great extremes. Owing to its southerly position, adjacent to Arabia and near the Thar Desert, the summer is extremely hot, with temperatures in the interior rising possibly higher than anywhere else in the world—certainly a temperature exceeding 55°C has been recorded. In winter, however, the great altitude of much of the country and its continental situation result in far lower temperatures than one would expect to find in such low latitudes. Temperatures of −30°C have been recorded in the north-western Zagros, and −20°C is common in many places.

Another unfortunate feature is the prevalence of strong winds, which intensify the temperature contrasts. Eastern Iran is subject to the so-called 'Wind of 120 Days', which blows regularly throughout the summer, occasionally reaching a velocity of more than 160 km per hour and raising sand to such an extent that the stone walls of buildings are sometimes scoured away and turn to ruins.

Most of Iran is arid; but in contrast, parts of the north-west and north receive considerable rainfall—up to 2,000 mm along parts of the Caspian coast, producing very special climatic conditions in this small region, recalling conditions in the lower Himalayas. The Caspian coast has a hot, humid climate and this region is by far the most densely populated of the whole country. Next in order of population density comes the north-western Zagros area—the region of Azerbaijan, with its capital, Tabriz, the sixth largest city in Iran. Then, reflecting the diminished rainfall, next in order come the central Zagros area, and adjacent parts of the interior plateau, around Esfahan, Hamadan, Shiraz and Bakhtaran (Kermanshah), with an extension as far as Tehran. The extreme east and south, where rainfall is very scarce, were historically extremely lightly populated, except, in the few parts where water is available, by nomadic groups.

POPULATION

At the census of 2011, the population was recorded at 75,149,669. By the time of the next census—September 2016—that figure had increased to 79,926,270. The United Nations (UN) estimated that the population had reached 89,172,767 by mid-2023. The capital, Tehran, is Iran's largest city, with a population of 8,693,706 at the 2016 census. Other major cities include Mashhad (Meshed—3,012,090) and Esfahan (Isfahan—2,112,767).

Several languages are current in Iran. Farsi (Persian), an Indo-Aryan language related to the languages of Western Europe, is spoken in the north and centre of the country, and is the only official language of the state. As the north is by far the most densely populated region of Iran, Farsi has an importance somewhat greater than its territorial extent would suggest. Various dialects of Kurdish are current in the north and central Zagros mountains, and alongside these are found several Turkic-speaking tribes. Baluchi is spoken in the extreme south-east.

History

EDWARD WASTNIDGE

REVOLUTION

During the 1970s Iran's coffers began to swell from record high international oil prices, which had approximately doubled following the 1973 Arab–Israeli War and the resultant oil embargo that targeted Western supporters of Israel. By 1974 Iranian oil revenues were some seven times higher than they had been just two years previously, expanding from US $2,400m. to $17,400m. As a consequence, the Shah (Emperor) of Iran, Muhammad Reza Pahlavi, vastly increased government spending, injecting enormous sums into the Iranian economy without considering the possible knock-on effects of inflation and severe shortages as the country struggled to keep up with the rapid pace of development that he had envisaged on the march to achieving his proposed 'Great Civilization' of Iranian society. The Shah also ramped up Iranian spending in the military sphere, with US President Richard Nixon allowing him to buy whatever non-nuclear weapons he wanted from the USA, as Iran sought to consolidate its position as a regional military heavyweight and 'policeman' of the Persian (Arabian) Gulf. The promises offered by the oil boom resulted in a rapid increase of Iran's urban population as millions of Iranians moved to the cities in search of work, and also sharpened the increasing inequalities between rich and poor in the country. The masses experienced little improvement, however, while inflation became rampant and political repression escalated at the hands of the SAVAK, the Shah's feared and ruthless government security agency. Any attempts at organization by opposition forces were brutally suppressed, with illegal detention and torture of the Shah's political opponents commonplace.

Iranian political opposition to the Shah had historically centred around nationalist and leftist coalitions such as the National Front and the communist Tudeh Party. These opposition groups had suffered under the Shah, but they too shared Reza Pahlavi's misgivings about the potential power of the religiously informed political opposition to the Shah, consisting of the religious scholars (*ulema*) and lay intellectuals such as Ali Shariati, who harnessed religious populism as a means of channelling the discontent of the masses who had failed to reap the benefits of the Shah's rapid modernization plans. Ayatollah Ruhollah Khomeini had been exiled by the Shah in 1964, having spoken out against the modernization plans laid out in the monarch's so-called White Revolution. Following his exile to Najaf in Iraq, via Turkey (officially designated as Türkiye from June 2022), Khomeini began to formulate his ideas on a revolutionary form of Islamic government which would become enshrined in the constitution of the future Islamic Republic of Iran following the Islamic Revolution in 1979. Khomeini's text, the *Hukumat-e Islami* (Islamic Government), which was published in 1971, introduced the idea of *velayat-e faqih* (Guardianship of the Jurist), which envisioned the establishment of clerical rule in Iran in place of the monarchy. Clerical authority in Shi'a Islam is centred around the principal of *marja'iyat* whereby a number of high-ranking clerics act as spiritual guides or 'sources of emulation' (*marja-e taqlid*) to the Shi'a community worldwide. Khomeini, as one such *marja*, argued that the highest-ranking *faqih* (Islamic jurist), who is also a source of emulation, should therefore be the ruler, and that accepting the rule of their religious guardians, in the form of the *ulema*, was a religious duty.

The Shah had sought to reduce the power and influence of the *ulema* in Iranian society, realizing his modernization plans through an attempted Westernization and secularization of Iranian society. Religious leaders were imprisoned or exiled, and it was from exile that Khomeini tapped into growing discontent with the Shah's regime. Recordings of his sermons began to be smuggled into Iran from his place of exile in Najaf, Iraq, aided by improving relations between Iran and Iraq at that time and the subsequent increase in Iranian pilgrims visiting one of Shi'a Islam's holiest sites there. Prayer leaders in mosques throughout Iran became increasingly hostile to the Shah, echoing the increasing discontent of the urban poor left behind by the Shah's vision—and ultimately his mismanagement—of Iran's rapid economic development.

In January 1978 the Iranian daily newspaper *Ettela'at* published a hostile article slandering Khomeini, which acted as a lightning rod for anger directed at the Shah. The resultant protests by religious students in the holy city of Qom were brutally suppressed, with scores killed. A subsequent rally based on the Shi'a practice of holding mourning ceremonies on the 40th day, was held in Tabriz and was again violently suppressed. Protests spread to Iran's other major cities, and the Shah's forces reacted with increasing harshness, creating more martyrs and beginning the mourning cycle again, each time with increasing numbers and mounting public fury against the Shah, as dissatisfaction against his rule surged into the open. The prominence of Shi'a ritual and increasing identification of the opposition with religious symbolism gave the rapidly growing protest movement a religious hue which began to coalesce around Khomeini's leadership.

Huge nationwide strikes that took place throughout 1978 placed further pressure on the Shah, and despite attempts by the ailing monarch, who was suffering from terminal cancer, to institute some reforms to appease the protests, it was too little, too late. Khomeini's popularity was growing, and his move to Paris, France in October 1978, after being forced to leave Iraq (most likely owing to pressure on the Iraqi leadership from Iran) proved decisive, giving him the tools of the world's media to broadcast his demands that the Shah abdicate. The Shah left Iran on 16 January 1979, ostensibly a 'temporary' move ordered by the Shah's recently appointed Prime Minister, Shapour Bakhtiar, who subsequently ordered the release of political prisoners and the disbanding of the SAVAK. This was not enough, however, and Khomeini returned triumphantly to Iran on 1 February to a rapturous welcome.

ESTABLISHING THE ISLAMIC REPUBLIC

Once Khomeini had returned to Iran, he established a provisional government, appointing the leader of the Freedom Movement of Iran, Mehdi Bazargan, as his Prime Minister. During this time Khomeini's closest clerical supporters established themselves within the parallel Islamic Revolutionary Council, which had oversight of the revolutionary movement, guiding its direction. During the Iranian Revolution a wide range of groups of varying political persuasions joined forces to oust the Shah. The immediate post-revolutionary political landscape witnessed fierce competition and debate for influence over the future direction of the country. The main power broker was the Islamic Republican Party, formed by Khomeini's supporters immediately after his return to Iran. Other key groups included the more secular-minded opposition groups that had participated in the Islamic Revolution, such as the liberal religious Freedom Movement of Iran, the liberal nationalist National Front, the Tudeh Party, and Marxist-Islamist groups such as the Mujahidin-e-Khalq and Fedayin-e-Khalq. The clerics set about consolidating their power at the expense of liberals, nationalists and leftist forces which had supported Khomeini as a figurehead of the Islamic Revolution. In a referendum held at the end of March 1979, Iranian voters were given a choice to vote in support of, or against the establishment of an Islamic Republic. The vote in support of the proposal was approved by 99.3% of voters, and the Islamic Republic of Iran was declared on 1 April.

Following the declaration of Iran as an Islamic Republic, an assembly of experts dominated by the Islamic Republican Party was elected and tasked with creating a new constitution. This was approved in a nationwide vote in December 1979 by 99.5% of voters. The Constitution enshrined the concept of *velayat-e faqih* in law, making Khomeini the undisputed leader of the Islamic Republic and conferring upon him the title of Supreme Leader. It created key political organs, combining Islamic and republican elements in a unique form of theocratic government. The three main popularly elected bodies were the Majlis-e-Shura (Consultative Assembly), which acts as the parliament; the presidency; and the Assembly of Experts (not to be confused with the assembly tasked with drafting the constitution in 1979), made up of Islamic jurists and whose main task is to supervise, dismiss and elect the Supreme Leader. Unelected bodies that are appointed through these three arms of government are the cabinet (appointed by the President and approved by the Majlis) and the Supreme Leader (appointed by the Assembly of Experts). The Supreme Leader also appoints the head of the armed forces and the head of the judiciary. Perhaps the most important government body after the Supreme Leader and established by the new constitution was the Council of Guardians. It comprises six jurists, appointed by the Majlis, and six theologians, appointed by the Supreme Leader. It has vast oversight powers, with three main constitutionally mandated functions, namely: jurisdiction/veto power over all legislative decisions; interpretation of the constitution; and supervision of elections, thus having final approval of candidates in parliamentary, presidential and Assembly of Experts elections.

In addition to the governmental organs that were set up in the new Constitution, several key foundations or welfare organizations (bonyads) were established following the Islamic Revolution. These were tasked with redistributing the country's wealth, which helped in consolidating the power of Khomeini and his supporters in the post-Islamic Revolution political landscape. The assets of the Shah, most notably the riches of the Pahlavi Foundation, were given over to the newly founded Foundation for the Dispossessed who went on to acquire properties and possessions of the former elite, and became not only the most powerful bonyads, but one of the largest commercial enterprises in the country and wider region. Other notable bonyads included the Martyrs Foundation and Imam Khomeini Relief Committee. To this day the bonyads exercise huge economic power and as independent bodies remain largely free from government interference and scrutiny, answering only to the Supreme Leader.

As Khomeini's supporters consolidated their political power in Iran, the country also underwent a cultural revolution with an increasing Islamization of public life. From 1980 to 1983 more uncompromising members of the new government sought to drive out all secular, leftist and moderate groups, focusing primarily on academics, overseeing the closing of universities until 1983. Khomeini had been fiercely critical of the Shah's Westernizing tendencies and on coming to power he sought to counter this by imposing Islamic principles not only in law and government, but also in wider society. Thus, mandatory wearing of the veil was enforced for women, the expression of Western fashion, art and culture was censured, and Shari'a-compliant laws were enacted, resulting in religiously sanctioned punishments for offences such as the consumption of alcohol and adultery.

IRAN'S FOREIGN RELATIONS, 1979–88

After the Islamic Revolution Khomeini had sought to steer the country on a self-sufficient course, with an independent foreign policy reflecting the view of his famous maxim of 'neither east nor west, only Islamic Republic'. A feature of this approach was the strident anti-Americanism that typified Khomeini's political thought, as he represented the very antithesis of the Shah's close alliance with the USA. Chants of 'down with America' and references to the USA as the 'Great Satan' were common refrains during the Islamic Revolution. In the early days of the provisional government, Bazargan and other moderate figures sought to maintain relations with the USA, but with power increasingly being centred around Khomeini and his closest allies within the Islamic Revolutionary Council, such moves were ultimately undone by the hostage crisis, which started in November 1979. With the Shah's health rapidly declining, and by that time an itinerant exile, Iran's former leader had travelled for medical treatment to the USA in late October. The US offer of medical sanctuary to the ailing Shah stoked fears in Iran that the USA was plotting a counter-revolution. This, together with Bazargan's meeting with US National Security Advisor Zbigniew Brzezinski in the Algerian capital, Algiers, a few days later, prompted a scathing response from Khomeini's supporters culminating in the takeover on 4 November of the US embassy in Tehran by a group of radical students calling themselves the Muslim Student Followers of the Imam's Line. A total of 53 US embassy staff were held hostage for 444 days, and the events drew a firm line under any pretence of normalized relations between the USA and post-revolutionary Iran. Domestically, it prompted the resignation of the entire provisional government of Iran, thus further consolidating the Khomeinists' grip on power. The USA responded by freezing several billion dollars' worth of Iranian assets, severing all diplomatic relations with Iran and placing it under a trade embargo.

Of primary importance to the early Islamic Republic was solidarity with oppressed groups and support for Muslim communities worldwide. This manifested itself through a rhetorical and material export of the Islamic Revolution, particularly to countries with large Shi'a populations, which had the effect of antagonizing many of the governments of the region. This was especially important with regards to Lebanon. Throughout the early 1980s Iran lent support via its Islamic Revolutionary Guard Corps (IRGC) to disenfranchised Shi'a groups resisting the Israeli occupation of southern Lebanon, which eventually coalesced leading to the establishment of the militant group (and later political party) Hezbollah. The founding manifesto of Hezbollah, issued in 1985, pledged allegiance to Khomeini and his vision of Islamic government, and called for the expulsion of all Western and Israeli forces from Lebanon. The Islamic Republic's support for anti-US and anti-Israeli movements was an important feature of its foreign policy in its formative years. However, Iran's foreign relations in the decade following the Islamic Revolution were primarily dominated by the eight-year war with Iraq (see below).

Iran's relations with Iraq had been problematic during the 1970s, with disputes over the shared Shatt al-Arab waterway that formed part of the southern section of the border between the two nations. Iraqi designs on Iran's Khuzestan province—historically an ethnically Arab area—and the Shah's patronage of Kurdish rebels in Iraq further strained ties. The 1975 Algiers Agreement normalized relations in exchange for Iraqi territorial concessions, and ties between the two states improved as a result. However, the Islamic Revolution caused a further rupture, with the Iraqi regime becoming increasingly fearful of the appeal of the Islamic Republic's revolutionary model among its own, largely disenfranchised Shi'a majority. Khomeini had called for the overthrow of Iraqi President Saddam Hussain's Ba'athist regime, but Saddam was quick to crush anti-regime protests, and further exacerbated already tense relations by expelling thousands of Iraqi Shi'a who were suspected of having Iranian antecedents, to Iran. Following border skirmishes, Iraq invaded Iran along three separate fronts in September 1980, seizing several hundred square kilometres of territory, including the strategic port city of Khorramshahr in Khuzestan. The resulting war lasted nearly eight years, claiming up to 1m. lives by some estimates, and was characterized by trench warfare, the use of chemical weapons by Saddam's forces, and so-called 'human wave' attacks by Iranian soldiers and volunteer forces.

Iraqi forces were largely expelled from Iranian territory by mid-1982, and as the Islamic Republic went on the offensive, Iran's regional neighbours, fearful of the appeal of the Islamic Revolution, increased their financial support for Saddam's regime. Iraq also benefitted from huge military support from both the USA and the Union of Soviet Socialist Republics (USSR), while Iran relied on arms from the Democratic People's Republic of Korea (North Korea) and the People's Republic of China, as well as support from the Syrian Arab Republic and Libya. The war was a source of contention between Iran and the USSR, owing mainly to the latter's role as one of Iraq's chief suppliers of arms. However, Iran was able to separate political and economic relations, and economic co-operation with the USSR—referred to by Khomeini as the 'Lesser Satan'—continued throughout the war. Iran was also able to use its patronage of Hezbollah to help secure some US armaments and spare parts for some of its US-made hardware. In what was to become known as the Iran-Contra Affair, US weapons were secretly channelled to Iran in exchange for the release of US hostages held by Hezbollah in Lebanon. Part of the resultant payment made to Israel for supplying the weapons was diverted to fund anti-communist Contra rebels fighting the pro-Soviet Government in Nicaragua. The eight-year war ended in stalemate, with the passing of United Nations (UN) Security Council resolution no. 598 in August 1988; Khomeini famously likened the acceptance of the ceasefire to 'drinking from a poisoned chalice'.

POLITICS IN THE ISLAMIC REPUBLIC, 1980–89

Khomeini's followers continued to consolidate power in the domestic political arena in the 1980s, while other groups that had taken part in the Islamic Revolution were increasingly marginalized. The largely secular provisional government had disbanded following the hostage crisis, and Khomeini's decree in January 1980 barring those who had opposed voting on the establishment of an Islamic Republic from contesting the forthcoming presidential election meant that the Mujahidin-e-Khalq's leader, Massoud Rajavi, was prevented from running. In the following year Rajavi went into hiding and his organization began a violent campaign against the Iranian Government, which included targeted assassinations and bomb attacks. Rajavi fled to Paris in July 1981, with the Mujahidin-e-Khalq, by that time operating as the National Council of Resistance of Iran coalition, where they continue to be based and from where they oppose the Islamic Republic to this day. The group also sided with Saddam Hussain during the Iran–Iraq war, and launched an unsuccessful invasion of Iran following the 1989 ceasefire. It remains a vocal opposition group to the Islamic Republic, centred around the personality cult of Rajavi (who disappeared in Iraq in 2003 and has not been heard from since) and his wife Maryam Rajavi, his successor as leader. It regularly courts hawkish US politicians who support regime change in Iran, but its reach and popularity inside Iran is severely limited.

Post-revolutionary Iran's first head of state, Abolhassan Bani Sadr, was elected as President of the Islamic Republic on 25 January 1980, having received some 75% of the votes. A representative of the Marxist-inspired Islamic intellectuals based in the West who had opposed the Shah and returned to Iran with Khomeini, Bani Sadr struggled to contain clerical influence in politics upon becoming President. His nominations for the post of Prime Minister and cabinet were rejected by the Islamic Republican Party-dominated Majlis and he had to work with a cabinet largely imposed by the Islamic Revolutionary Council, which set the tone for his presidency. Bani Sadr also disagreed with the hard-line stance taken in relation to the US embassy hostage crisis and the use of irregular forces and 'human wave' attacks in the war with Iraq, as he became increasingly vocal in his opposition to being marginalized by Khomeini's allies. By June 1981 he had been stripped of his role as Commander-in-Chief of the armed forces and compelled to go into hiding while calling for an uprising; he eventually escaped to France, together with Masud Rajavi. The Majlis voted to impeach Bani Sadr and he was officially dismissed by Khomeini on 22 June. Following a period of interim administrations and assassinations of key political figures during mid-1981, including Bani Sadr's successor Muhammad Ali Rajai, future Supreme Leader Ali Khamenei was elected President in October, with Mir Hossein Mousavi taking up the post of Prime Minister and thus cementing Islamist control of the principal organs of power. Further opposition purges led to the Tudeh party being outlawed in 1983, and its leadership and notable members were imprisoned, making the Islamic Republican Party's dominance in Iranian politics complete. The party was disbanded in 1987 by the Speaker of the Majlis, Ali Akbar Hashemi Rafsanjani, and President Khamenei, owing to internal differences between conservatives aligned with Khamenei and Rafsanjani, and more leftist figures, notably Prime Minister Mousavi. These groups reconfigured broadly along 'Islamic left' and 'traditionalist right' lines, with the former represented by the Association of Combatant Clergy and Organization of the Mujahidin, and the latter through the Society of Combatant Clergy and Coalition of Islamic Associations.

One of the principal aims of the Islamic Revolution was to improve economic performance, particularly with regard to the *mostazafin* (the 'oppressed' or 'disinherited'). Khomeini espoused goals of social justice and egalitarianism which gave an often leftist flavour to the provisional government's economic policy. This was exemplified in the widespread nationalization of major industry that took place after the Islamic Revolution. Despite the Islamic Revolution's aims of improving the country's economic condition, the 1979–87 period witnessed economic decline, with real per head income falling during this time. Also problematic was Iran's dependence on oil export revenue; its economic difficulties were compounded by a fall in international oil prices during the mid-to-late 1980s, and a drop in production during the war with Iraq. Iran's economic situation was hampered by the war and a lack of clear direction economically, with disputes over the extent to which Iran should engage with the West, and crippling power struggles between the different arms of government—most notably the Majlis and the Council of Guardians. A further obstacle to re-engaging with the West came with the Salman Rushdie affair in 1989, when the British author was subject to a *fatwa* from Khomeini that called for his death for committing blasphemy, which led to a severing of diplomatic relations between Iran and the United Kingdom. (Rushdie's novel *The Satanic Verses* included an irreverent depiction of the Prophet Muhammad.) In the same year, as Khomeini's health began to deteriorate, attention turned to planning for his succession. Ayatollah Hossein Ali Montazeri had been designated as Khomeini's successor by the Assembly of Experts in 1985. However, by 1986 he had begun to criticize certain aspects of Khomeini's rule, including the mass executions of Mujahidin-e-Khalq members and that of other political prisoners, the export of the Islamic Revolution abroad, and the negative effects of the Rushdie *fatwa*. Montazeri was ultimately stripped of his title and position as Supreme Leader-designate and went on to become an outspoken critic of uncompromising elements within the Islamic Republic until his death in 2009.

Cognizant of the damaging effect that intra-governmental power struggles were having on political life in the Islamic Republic in the late 1980s, and aware of the need to secure an orderly transition of power to his successor, Khomeini sanctioned two key changes to the Iranian political system before his death on 3 June 1989. First, in February 1988 he ordered the establishment of the Expediency Council, which was tasked with mediating the disputes between the Majlis and the Council of Guardians. Second, he convened a Council for the Reappraisal of the Constitution in April 1989, less than two months before his death. The council was made up of 20 members picked by Khomeini, with a further five selected by the Majlis. Perhaps the most significant revision concerned the position of the Supreme Leader, removing the stipulation that the leader needed to be religiously qualified to the level of being a 'source of emulation' (*marja-e taqlid*). The role of Prime Minister was also abolished, giving greater executive power to the role of President. The Expediency Council was made into a permanent constitutional body, and the Supreme National Security Council was created to take charge of the Islamic Republic's foreign policy. Khomeini had previously not tolerated division within the regime, and often acted as a mediator in any conflicts between the various branches of government. Thus, it was only after Khomeini's death, and in the absence of his charismatic rule, that the development of independent political institutions in effect began to take place in Iran. On 28 July the Speaker of the Majlis, Rafsanjani, was elected to the newly empowered role of President in an election that also put the constitutional revisions to a national plebiscite. The constitutional changes were also approved, by an overwhelming 97% of those who voted.

Following Khomeini's death, the Assembly of Experts chose then President Ali Khamenei as his successor. Prior to assuming the post of supreme leader, Khamenei had held only the position of *hojat-ul Islam*—a clerical ranking below that of an Ayatollah. His promotion to this post can be seen as a politicization of the role of the Supreme Leader. The amendment to Article 107 of the Constitution, enacted in 1989, made it no longer necessary for the *faqih* to be a leading cleric. It was more important for the guide to be 'aware of the times', and therefore be more politically minded rather than have certain religious qualifications. In effect this led to the idea of *velayat-e-faqih* becoming politicized, as ultimate leadership no longer rested with the highest religious authority. It should be noted, however, that Khamenei is today seen as a *marja* among significant sections of the global Shi'a community, and indeed now takes the title of Ayatollah. The amendments helped to secure an orderly transition of rule, and also acted as a means of challenging the authority of the now defrocked Ayatollah Montazeri, the previous Supreme Leader-designate.

RAFSANJANI AND POST-WAR RECONSTRUCTION, 1989–97

Having secured 94% of the vote in the 1989 elections, Rafsanjani had the political mandate and newly enshrined presidential powers to oversee important developments in Iran's political trajectory, as it faced the challenges of post-war reconstruction. The economic crisis that prevailed in Iran by the end of the 1980s led to recognition of the need for a change in economic policy. One aspect of such change was to allow greater economic liberalism and the implementation of pragmatic reforms—for example increasing the scope of privatization of state-owned assets, and the re-opening of the Tehran stock exchange in 1990. Khomeini's death in 1989 accelerated the advance of a more pragmatist outlook in Iranian politics and economic planning. Rafsanjani was a principal figure in promoting economic reform, including efforts for greater integration into the global economy to stimulate economic development at home, through increased foreign investment. Rafsanjani sought to implement an era of reconstruction following the war with Iraq, and grand infrastructure projects were proposed to show that the economy was improving. Plans to reduce both rising unemployment and the dependency on oil revenue were also given prominence. His strategy was to closely ally himself with the bazaar and thus cultivate a more mercantilist outlook for the economy of the Islamic Republic. Although he aimed to liberalize the economy and reduce state control, many of Rafsanjani's ideas never extended beyond rhetoric and he also had his own vested interests (being a major actor in the pistachio trade), which became a running theme in measures taken against him during the Mahmoud Ahmadinejad era in the early 21st century. Rafsanjani was seen at the time as a moderate and an enlightened reformer who could solve Iran's economic ills, but his ideas created a society and economy not so much based on reform, but rather on the servicing of the commercial community. The concentration of economic power in such a community, and his patrimonial style of leadership, were seen by some as a return to a similar situation that had existed under the Shah—one that the Islamic Revolution had aimed to correct.

There were, none the less, some positive economic achievements, and a genuine social and cultural opening took place during the Rafsanjani era. The economy grew by an annual average of 8% during the early 1990s, while borrowing for state expenditure decreased, as did the rate of unemployment during 1989–94. However, this period also witnessed an increase in loans from the World Bank, higher foreign debt, rising inflation and a currency devaluation. Iran also remained susceptible to fluctuations in the oil market—for example, the drop in oil prices in the late 1990s intensified the economic difficulties faced by the Mohammad Khatami administration that followed Rafsanjani. Consequently, there was less money to invest, forcing the Government to cut public capital outlays by some 30%. The Rafsanjani period was also characterized by openings in the social and cultural sphere, with less rigid adherence to the perceived 'correct' Islamic cultural norms in society. Rafsanjani appointed his eventual presidential successor Khatami as Minister of Culture and Islamic Guidance in his first cabinet, who liberalized the arts and publishing in an attempt to foster greater civil society in Iran. During his tenure, art galleries reopened and there was a substantial increase in both film-making and publishing.

Politically, Rafsanjani worked in tandem with Khamenei, and while Rafsanjani's supporters began to coalesce under a modern, pragmatic right-wing grouping (distinct from the traditionalist right of Khamenei), the first half of the Rafsanjani era can be seen as something of a period of dual leadership in Iran, albeit with Rafsanjani arguably steering the country's direction. Rafsanjani began to promote technocrats into positions of influence at the expense of more traditional conservatives, and the beginnings of a backlash against his liberalizing tendencies were seen in increasing conservative press criticism of Khatami's reforms, leading to his eventual forced resignation in July 1992. Rafsanjani secured a second term of office, winning 63% of the vote in the 1993 presidential election, but the traditionalist right still held sway in the Majlis and would block or dilute much of his liberalization efforts and also acted as a check on attempts to open up to the West. Furthermore, Khamenei began to emerge as the key power in the Iranian polity, using his allies in the traditionalist right-wing camp to constrain Rafsanjani. By the time of the 1996 Majlis elections, Rafsanjani's allies had formed their own party, the Servants of Construction, thus formalizing the split between the traditionalist right and the technocratic modern right. Rafsanjani's supporters would go on to ally themselves with leftist groups including the Association of Combatant Clergy, paving the way for the victory of reformist candidate Khatami in the 1997 presidential election.

KHATAMI AND THE REFORMIST MOVEMENT, 1997–2005

The election of Mohammad Khatami as President in 1997 signified one of the first discernible signs of popular dissatisfaction with the political regime expressed through the ballot box. Khatami secured the presidency in the first round with 69% of the vote. His opponent, the parliamentary speaker Ali Akbar Nateq Nouri, was the officially endorsed candidate and was seen by voters as representing the revolutionary 'old guard'. Khatami represented a more tolerant voice, and was considered as something of a moderate intellectual who helped to engender a more tolerant and open society, which gave him the support of students and much of the press. He also appealed to female voters, following his well-received interview with women's magazine *Zanan* during the campaign. He was, none the less, viewed by his opponents as a political lightweight, despite having served as Minister of Culture and Islamic Guidance, and this engendered a kind of complacency among the Nateq Nouri camp. As a scholar well versed in Western as well as Islamic philosophy, Khatami sought to appeal to the cultural heart of Iranian society, and through his calls for a 'dialogue among civilizations' in foreign policy, and promotion of greater press freedoms, he was considered to represent an advancement for civil society in Iran.

Khatami's accession to the presidency can be seen as heralding the beginning of the reformist movement's active involvement in Iranian politics. He was able to draw on support from the traditional leftist and also moderate conservative camps in what became known as the Second of Khordad Movement—named after the date in the Persian calendar on which he was elected. Having previously been responsible for initiating the openings in the cultural and social sphere under Rafsanjani, Khatami spent time as head of the National Library, where he published his own works on Islamic and Western philosophy, paying particular attention to modern Shi'a thinkers who sought to reconcile Islam with modernity. Khatami's main strategist in his election campaign was Saeed Hajjarian, a reformist, lay intellectual who sought to assert political legitimacy over religious rule through Islamic democracy, and this harnessing of reform-minded discourse, together with the backing of Rafsanjani's Servants of Construction faction, helped Khatami to secure a large victory that shook the conservative establishment. Khatami's promotion of civil society in Iran through the encouragement of a more dynamic and freer press enabled the rapid growth of publications that brought discussion of previously taboo subjects into the public arena.

A conservative backlash subsequently took place against the reformist movement that Khatami represented, with uncompromising elements utilizing their institutional power to purge those close to him. The popular mayor of Tehran and Khatami supporter Gholamhossein Karbaschi was imprisoned in 1998 on charges of corruption and embezzlement, and interior minister Abdollah Nouri was removed from office and eventually imprisoned in 1999, owing in part to his support of Montazeri. Moreover, Minister of Culture and Islamic Guidance Ayatollah Mohajerani was also forced out of government in 2000, having been perceived as excessively liberal with regard to social and cultural issues. Meanwhile, student protests against the closure of reformist newspaper Salam in 1999 turned violent after their dormitories were attacked by right-wing vigilantes from the Ansar-e Hezbollah, as well as Basij paramilitaries. The assassination of a number of secular intellectuals in late 1998 and the attempted assassination of Hajjarian in 2000 were further signs of increasing fear among hard-line elements that the revolution was under threat. Disagreement also became evident in foreign policy, with Khamenei and conservatives resisting attempts at rapprochement with the USA. Khatami's economic programme, although more populist and arguably more left-leaning than Rafsanjani's, also aimed to increase foreign investment. Key to this was his more conciliatory approach towards relations with the West, and a continuation of Iran's course of cultivating an improved image on the international scene, which will be explored further in the foreign policy section below.

Reformists secured victory in the 2000 Majlis elections and this was followed by a clear victory by Khatami in the 2001 presidential election, where he gained 77% of the vote. However, despite his popular mandate, a political impasse developed as result of the polarization in Iranian politics between those seeking to empower its democratic and civil society institutions and those wishing to emphasize the religious aspect and adherence to its core revolutionary ideals. Turnout in the 2001 presidential election was down by over 13 percentage points from the 77.9% who had participated in the 1997 vote, as apathy among the educated and middle classes began to take hold. The widespread closure of publications linked to the reformist movement had silenced much of Khatami's support, and reformist legislative proposals were regularly vetoed by the Council of Guardians. Khatami thus became somewhat ineffectual as President during his second term of office (2001–05). Despite significant electoral victories for the reformists, conservative factions in Iran were able to exert considerable power in stymieing the reformist front, as occurred when the Council of Guardians banned over 2,500 reformist candidates, including 85 deputies who were already in post, from standing for the 2004 Majlis elections, which resulted in a conservative-dominated parliament.

MAHMOUD AHMADINEJAD, POPULIST PRESIDENT, 2005–13

In the run-up to the June 2005 presidential election, most attention had centred around the candidacies of Rafsanjani (looking to secure the presidency again), the reformist Mostafa Moin, and Mohammed Bagher Ghalibaf, the conservative head of Iran's police and former mayor of Tehran. The first round produced a significant shock, with the populist mayor of Tehran, Mahmoud Ahmadinejad coming a close second behind Rafsanjani, with former Majlis speaker Mahdi Karrubi finishing closely behind him in third place. As no single candidate was able to secure the requisite majority to win outright, Iran witnessed its first presidential run-off, between Rafsanjani and Ahmadinejad. It had been expected that the main contest in the election would be between Rafsanjani and Moin, both offering different visions of how to build on Khatami's legacy. Instead, the run-off pitted an establishment figure—albeit one who could potentially offer a significant challenge to the traditional conservatives and potentially the authority of Khamenei—against a relatively unknown candidate. Ahmadinejad had campaigned on a populist platform, emphasizing his 'man of the people' credentials through his frugal lifestyle and championing of the poor, in marked contrast to the more polished campaign operations of his election rivals. He had little outward support from conservative power brokers in Iran until the second round, after which key state institutions offered their backing as a means of checking Rafsanjani's ascent to the presidency for a third time. Support from the IRGC and Basij paramilitaries helped to mobilize their constituencies behind Ahmadinejad, and he won the run-off round comfortably, with 61.7% of the valid votes cast.

In keeping with his populist rhetoric, Ahmadinejad's presidency was characterized by policies that sought to fight poverty and corruption, promote justice and to protect and promote the aims of the Islamic Revolution. He sought to redistribute Iran's oil wealth to the poor, and his presidency coincided with high international oil prices, allowing him to initiate assistance programmes to benefit his core constituency. He revised the privatization programmes instigated under Rafsanjani, distributing 40% of shares from privatized firms to low-income households at a discounted price, as so-called 'justice shares'. Ahmadinejad also oversaw an attempt to reform Iran's long-standing subsidy programme, under which the prices of fuel and other basic goods had been kept low. This resulted in a gradual removal of the subsidies by the administration, the effects of which were intended to be cushioned by a further monthly subsidy paid out in the form of cash payments by the government. The payments were initially intended for low-income households only, but were eventually offered to all, thus negating any positive reduction in the financial burden placed on the Government by the subsidy programme.

Another feature of Ahmadinejad's tenure as President, drawn in part from his populist leanings, was the strong current of Messianism that characterized his political thinking. His emphasis on social justice was couched in terms of providing the foundations for the return of the Mahdi—the revered 12th imam of the Shi'a tradition who went into occultation in the 10th century CE and whose return, so followers believe, will rid the world of evil in preparation for the Day of Judgment. Ahmadinejad's justice-oriented outlook led him to rally against perceived corruption among members of the Iranian political elite, most notably against Rafsanjani and his significant business interests. In foreign relations, Ahmadinejad's presidency was marked by a return to confrontation with the West, particularly over the resumption of the Iranian nuclear programme and repeated denials of the Holocaust.

Ahmadinejad stood for a second term in the 2009 presidential election. The campaign was noted for its openness, with live debates between the candidates taking place on television for the first time. Reformist support swung decisively behind former Prime Minister Mousavi, who was seen as the main challenger to Ahmadinejad. The incumbent was pronounced the victor on 12 June with 63.1% of the vote, to Mousavi's 34.2%. The result was hotly disputed by Mousavi and fellow candidates Karrubi and Mohsen Rezaei, who cited widespread fraud, although Rezaei's complaints were later withdrawn, and the resultant protests escalated to become the most serious threat to the Islamic Republic since the Iranian Revolution. In the subsequent crackdown over 1,000 people were arrested, including prominent reformist political figures and activists, and more than 30 people were killed in post-election violence. Mousavi and Karrubi continued their protest, forming the Green Movement to co-ordinate their continued opposition to the election results, and Khamenei's position hardened in the face of a perceived 'velvet revolution' being promoted by the opposition leaders. After calling for their supporters to demonstrate in solidarity with the uprisings that were sweeping Arab states in early 2011, Mousavi and Karrubi were placed under house arrest, where they remained in late 2021.

Although Ahmadinejad secured a victory with the support of conservative power brokers such as the IRGC, his second term was marked by problems as the economy began to feel the effect of sanctions imposed by Western powers over Iran's disputed nuclear programme (see Breakthrough and the JCPOA). Questions over Ahmadinejad's economic mismanagement led to him being called to answer questions from the Majlis, and disputes over his cabinet nominations caused relations between Ahmadinejad and the Supreme Leader to fray. Of particular concern was Ahmadinejad's elevation of cabinet member and close aide Esfandiar Rahim-Mashaei to the position of First Vice-President in 2009. Mashaei was a controversial figure on account of alleged comments regarding relations with Israel, perceived hostility towards clerical rule, and Persian nationalist tendencies. Khamenei vetoed the appointment, although

Ahmadinejad responded by making him his chief of staff. In 2011 Ahmadinejad in effect went on strike, refusing to attend cabinet meetings for 11 days after Khamenei had again intervened in his cabinet choices by reinstating the intelligence minister Heydar Moslehi, following the President's request for him to resign from his post. Ahmadinejad announced his intention to run in the 2017 presidential election, and despite a public rebuke from Khamenei he registered as a candidate in open defiance of the Supreme Leader. However, his candidature was subsequently rejected by the Council of Guardians.

HASSAN ROUHANI, THE MODERATE PRAGMATIST, 2013–21

Rouhani entered the race for the 2013 presidential election having previously been very much a political insider, holding a number of important positions, particularly in relation to the internal machinations of Iranian foreign and defence policy. He served as Khamenei's representative on the Supreme National Security Council and acted as its chair from its inception in 1989 until 2005. He had also served in the Majlis and held important roles co-ordinating the war effort against Iraq in the 1980s. In terms of Iranian political factions, Rouhani was very much a moderate centrist, or pragmatic conservative. His moderate tendencies thus made him palatable to a broad spectrum of not only the Iranian political elite, but also the population as a whole. He campaigned under a slogan of moderation, seeking to roll back perceived extremist forces that had harmed Iran's economy and international standing. His campaign utilized the symbol of a key to emphasize his aim of 'unlocking' Iran's problems, and he placed great emphasis on improving Iran's relations with the rest of the world after the combative Ahmadinejad years. Central to this was the resumption of talks over Iran's disputed nuclear programme, something he had been involved in himself during negotiations with the so-called EU3 countries (France, Germany and the UK) between 2003 and 2005, where he earned the nickname the 'Diplomat Sheikh'. The Ahmadinejad administration's stance on the issue (see *Breakthrough and the JCPOA*) had led to successive waves of punitive sanctions that damaged the Iranian economy. Rouhani thus saw a chance to rectify the damage by recommencing negotiations with Western powers and reintegrating Iran into the global economy, making this a principal part of his campaign. He won the June 2013 election in the first round, with 50.7% of the total votes cast; turnout was recorded at 72%.

Rouhani was able to count on the support of reformist figures such as Khatami, and moderate conservatives and sometime reformists such as Rafsanjani, who had initially sought to stand in the election but was barred from doing so by the Council of Guardians. Rouhani was able to court reformists through his support of an easing of social restrictions and allowing greater press freedom. In the economic sphere, the Rouhani administration oversaw modest improvements in economic growth and inflation as a more optimistic outlook prevailed on account of the resumption of the nuclear discussions.

Public support for his administration's handling of the country's nuclear negotiations, economic policies and message of moderation in Iran's international affairs was evident in the concurrently held 2016 Majlis and Assembly of Expert elections. In the Majlis the Rouhani-affiliated 'List of Hope'—a coalition of reformists and moderate conservatives—secured a majority over the 'Principlist' coalition of traditional and so-called hard-line conservatives. Rouhani stood for re-election as President in 2017, winning a second term, in a victory seen as a further endorsement of his policy of reducing Iran's international isolation through the Joint Comprehensive Plan of Action (JCPOA) nuclear deal that had been secured with international powers in his first term of office. In his campaign he again pitched his message as one of moderation, reiterating his support for civil liberties, but he was bolder in his rallying against forces of extremism in Iranian politics and society. Conservatives countered that Rouhani and his allies' liberalism and overtures to the West were a threat to core revolutionary values. In the election Rouhani secured 57.1% of the votes in the first round, ahead of the conservative-backed candidate Ebrahim Raisi, the head of the powerful Astan-e Qods Razavi charitable foundation that manages the shrine of Imam Reza in Mashhad.

Having served as Ayatollah Khamenei's representative on the Supreme National Security Council, Rouhani was entrusted with arguably greater power than previous presidents in the foreign policy domain. This was evidenced by the role played by his foreign minister Mohammad Javad Zarif in the nuclear negotiations, entrusted as he was with one the most critical issues in the foreign relations of the Islamic Republic. Following a pattern seen with previous Presidents, Ayatollah Khamenei's criticisms increased during Rouhani's second term of office. His objections to elements of Rouhani's programme were laid bare shortly after the election victory where he publicly cautioned against the President sowing division in society in the same way that Bani-Sadr had done during his tenure as head of state. Rouhani also had to contend with sporadic small-scale protests against rising prices and widening economic inequities across Iran from December 2017. Economic pressures were compounded by the US decision to abrogate the JCPOA in May 2018 (see *Foreign Relations under Rouhani*).

With foreign investors withdrawing from Iran, owing to the threat of US sanctions, Khamenei publicly criticized Rouhani and Zarif for their roles in securing the agreement, claiming that they had made too many concessions.

The Majlis was the scene of heated debates throughout 2018 and early 2019 as Iranian legislators discussed proposals for Iran to sign up to the recommendations of an international inter-governmental organization, the Financial Action Task Force (FATF). Iran's failure to comply with FATF-imposed deadlines led to its 'blacklisting' by the organization in February 2020.

Iran has been the victim of several terrorist attacks in recent years. In September 2018 a total of 30 people died, including members of the IRGC and civilians, when gunmen attacked a military parade in the city of Ahvaz, in Khuzestan province, close to the border with Iraq. Following initial claims of responsibility for the attack by local Arab separatists that were subsequently refuted, Islamic State claimed responsibility. Iran responded by claiming that Saudi Arabia and the United Arab Emirates (UAE) had funded the attacks and carried out missile strikes on Islamic State targets in Syria in response. In December Baluchi separatists operating under the banner of a Sunni militant group, Ansar al-Furqan, claimed responsibility for a suicide bombing in Chabahar, in Sistan and Baluchestan province, which killed two police officers. In February 2019 at least 27 members of the IRGC were killed in a suicide bomb attack in Sistan and Baluchestan province, which was claimed by the Sunni militant group Jaish al-Adl, based in Pakistan. Throughout 2020 a number of suspicious explosions and fires targeting critical infrastructure, including at sensitive nuclear sites, were reported in Iran. No state or credible opposition group has claimed responsibility, but Iranian commentators and figures within the Government have accused the US and Israeli authorities of involvement. Israel has begun to adopt a less ambiguous policy stance, acknowledging that it carried out covert operations in Iran during 2021–22.

In November 2019 an unexpected reduction in the government subsidy of petroleum led to a price hike of some 50%. This provoked large protests across Iran, especially by poorer sections of the population most seriously affected by the increase. Several international organizations condemned the response of the authorities, which had resulted in the deaths of some protesters, while the Iranian Government decried such reports as part of a Western-backed conspiracy against the Islamic Republic. The efforts at containing the protests were accompanied by a week-long, near total internet blackout in Iran. As the protests subsided, Iran was rocked by the assassination on 3 January 2020 of the commander of the IRGC's elite Quds Force, Qassem Soleimani, in Baghdad, the Iraqi capital, by a US drone (unmanned aerial vehicle) strike (see *Foreign Relations under Rouhani*). Having fought in the Iran–Iraq war and risen through the ranks of the IRGC during the 1990s, Soleimani had played a major role in advancing Iran's interests in the Middle East over the previous two decades. He was a revered figure within the country and feared by many of Iran's regional and international rivals. The commemorations of his death included the largest popular gatherings seen in the Islamic Republic since the death of its founder Khomeini in 1989.

A turbulent period was further compounded by the accidental shooting down of a Ukrainian passenger aircraft shortly after take-off from Imam Khomeini International Airport in January 2020, resulting in the deaths of all 176 passengers and crew on board. As Iran reeled from the triple shock of domestic protests, Soleimani's killing and the airliner tragedy, attention turned towards the Majlis elections in February. The outcome of these was a major victory for conservative factions, with a large number of the formerly dominant, reformist-aligned legislators being barred from standing. In May three-time presidential candidate and former Mayor of Tehran Mohammed Bagher Ghalibaf was elected as Speaker of the Majlis, ensuring conservative dominance of Iran's legislature for the foreseeable future.

In early 2020 Iran became one of the first countries outside China to be seriously affected by the coronavirus disease (COVID-19) global pandemic. Efforts at securing a loan worth some US $5,000m. from the International Monetary Fund to help combat the virus were blocked by the US Administration as it continued to tighten its own sanctions against Iran.

EBRAHIM RAISI AND THE CONSERVATIVE ASCENDANCY

Prior to his victory in the 2021 presidential election, Ebrahim Raisi was already a well-known figure on the Iranian political stage. He had previously worked in a number of high-ranking roles, including Deputy Prosecutor of Tehran, and in later years had been the director of Astan-e Qods Razavi. His role as Tehran's Deputy Prosecutor caused a degree of controversy among Western media outlets, owing to his association with a large number of executions of Iranian dissidents that took place in the capital in the late 1980s. Having stood unsuccessfully against Rouhani in the 2017 presidential election, Raisi became the Head of the Judiciary in 2019, a position that he held until his victory in the presidential poll in June 2021. He won the vote in the first round, with 72.4% of the valid votes cast. His nearest challenger was a perennial presidential candidate, the conservative Rezaei, who took just 13.8% of the votes. In an election in which there were no serious challengers from either the reformist or pragmatic conservative camps, Raisi was the establishment's anointed candidate and frontrunner. Well-known figures whose candidacies were rejected by the Guardian Council in the course of its vetting process included former President Ahmadinejad and former Speaker of the Majlis, Ali Larijani. The election produced a record-low turnout of just 49%. While a number of Raisi's appointments to the cabinet had traditionally been outspoken in their opposition to the JCPOA, during his electoral campaign Raisi vowed to continue negotiations on Iran's nuclear programme.

For the first time in over a decade, the main centres of power in Iranian politics were largely aligned, arguably even more closely than during the early Ahmadinejad years, given the continued squeeze on both the reformists and the more pragmatic conservative camps that had maintained a foothold in Iranian politics during that period. The Majlis continued to be dominated by conservatives following the 2020 elections, while Raisi's replacement as Head of the Judiciary, Gholamhossein Mohseni Ejehi, was a former Minister of Intelligence who served under the first Ahmadinejad Government. During the first years of his tenure, Raisi had to contend with a number of challenges, including the continuing impact of the COVID-19 pandemic, high inflation rates, protests and strikes over resources, working conditions and economic hardships, as well as ongoing sabotage operations by Israel (see *New Presidents, Same Old Mistrust*). Iran's economy continued to cause the new administration unease throughout its early years in office. The broader impact of the Russian Federation's invasion of Ukraine in February 2022 on global commodity prices has been a mixed blessing for Iran economically, on the one hand driving up the country's oil revenues but also impacting on its stubbornly high inflation figures. Inflation surged to more than 50% in 2022, although it began to fall from this peak during the first half of 2023. Iranian oil exports, by volume, also reached a five-year high in mid-2023, on account of increasing sales to China and in defiance of US sanctions.

The latter half of 2022 saw the Islamic Republic facing a significant domestic challenge in the shape of the 'Women, Life, Freedom' protests that broke out in September. The spark for these protests, the largest seen in Iran since the 2009 Green Movement, was the death in police custody of 22-year-old Iranian Kurd, Mahsa Jina Amini. Amini had been arrested by members of the Guidance Patrol (or 'religious morality police') for allegedly wearing her compulsory *hijab* (Islamic headscarf) incorrectly. Both Amini's relatives and local news sources claimed that she had died as a result of being severely beaten; the police denied the allegations, citing natural causes. The subsequent protests drew widespread global attention, with hopes among many Iranian diaspora and exiled groups that the unrest could represent a serious challenge to the Islamic Republic. However, by early 2023 the protests had largely fizzled out, with Iranian security forces able to stymie further dissent. In response to the protests, whose varied aims included protesting against the rigid enforcement of Iran's mandatory *hijab* laws, conservative legislators sought to introduce a new 'chastity' bill through the Majlis in mid-2023. Prominent voices within Iran's long-suppressed reform movement, including former President Khatami, have voiced their opposition to the current government crackdown on dissent, and have questioned the value of enforcing mandatory *hijab* laws.

IRANIAN FOREIGN POLICY, 1988–2013

During the 1980s Iran's foreign relations were shaped by the war with Iraq and the export of the Islamic Revolution. The first revolutionary decade thus witnessed radical idealism in the ascendancy as the Islamic Republic sought to find its footing domestically and on the world stage. By the end of the decade a confluence of key events, including the end of the war with Iraq, the death of Khomeini and the end of the Cold War all helped set the scene for a shift away from the more ideological and revolutionary concerns that had shaped Iranian foreign policy. During the Rafsanjani era, as with domestic economic policies, an increasingly pragmatic trend shaped the foreign policy front—one that tended to put national over ideological interests. Central to this dynamic were relations with the Persian Gulf monarchies, including Saudi Arabia, and the wider Arab world, which—with the exception of those with Syria—had remained poor since the Islamic Revolution. In these countries the fear of the appeal of the Islamic Revolution, and potential 'fifth columns' emerging from their own Shi'a minority populations, as well as their support for Iraq in its war against Iran, had clouded relations between Iran and its Arab neighbours throughout the 1980s. Iraq's defeat in the 1991 Gulf War with the USA and its allies—a conflict in which Iran had remained neutral—meant that Iran was in a position to reassert itself as a power in the Persian Gulf once again. However, cognizant of the need to improve relations with states in the region as a means of aiding its post-war reconstruction, and of a still-hostile USA, Iran sought, and gained, improved ties with its Arab neighbours. Diplomatic ties with Saudi Arabia were resumed in 1991, having been suspended since 1988 following the deaths of Iranian pilgrims in clashes with security forces during the Hajj pilgrimage in Makkah (Mecca), Saudi Arabia. Iranian-Qatari ties were also strengthened following a 1990 joint agreement on developing the shared South Pars/North Dome gas deposit in the Persian Gulf—the world's largest natural gasfield. Diplomatic ties with the UAE remained strained on account of a territorial dispute over the Abu Musa and Greater and Lesser Tunb islands in the Persian Gulf, but this was offset by growing commercial ties as the UAE underwent major economic development.

A NEW INTERNATIONAL ENVIRONMENT

Another major event that had important ramifications for Iran's foreign relations in this period was the break-up of the USSR in 1991, which led to the emergence of eight independent republics in Central Asia and the Caucasus. This gave Iran a chance to expand its influence in regions with which it had longstanding historical and cultural links. Persian had historically served as the cultural and literary language in parts of Central Asia, and remains the main language spoken in Tajikistan. Areas of Central Asia and the Caucasus had also come under nominal Iranian control until expansion there by Tsarist Russia. Iran had to be cautious not to antagonize its northern neighbour by engaging too readily in a region that the newly independent Russian Federation considered its own 'near abroad'. Russia has since become a close ally of Iran, providing Iran with technological assistance relating to its nuclear programme, arms sales and common positions on key regional issues, most notably the Syrian conflict (see *Foreign Relations under Rouhani*). During the 1990s Iran therefore chose to pursue a pragmatic foreign policy towards its newly independent neighbours to the north. The Islamic Republic was fully cognizant of the opportunities that this opening provided, allowing it the chance to build new relationships and demonstrate its commitment to international norms. Iran's leaders knew that there was little appetite for its brand of revolutionary Islam in the newly independent Muslim states of Central Asia and Azerbaijan. Hence, rather than seeking to export its ideology to the former Soviet republics, Iran emphasized its common historical and cultural links, and the desire for regional co-operation. Tehran was a keen proponent of reinvigorating the previously moribund Regional Cooperation for Development grouping of Iran, Pakistan and Turkey, sponsoring its enlargement and subsequent transformation into the Economic Cooperation Organization incorporating newly independent Azerbaijan, Kazakhstan, Kyrgyzstan, Tajikistan, Turkmenistan and Uzbekistan, together with Afghanistan. Iran also played a mediating role in regional conflicts, helping bring an end to Tajikistan's civil war (1992–97), and the Armenian–Azerbaijani conflict over the disputed territory of Nagornyi Karabakh. The moves made by Iran in assuming a more constructive regional role helped its international image, showing the Islamic Republic as a willing and co-operative partner which adhered to international norms.

Relations with the USA remained strained during the 1990s, with the USA accusing Iran of supporting terrorism and seeking to acquire weapons of mass destruction. US President Bill Clinton ordered a trade embargo against the Islamic Republic in 1995, and the USA also made unsubstantiated accusations against Iran in relation to the 1996 Khobar Towers bombing in Khobar, Saudi Arabia, in which 19 US servicemen were killed. Further sanctions were imposed in 1996 under the aegis of the Iran-Libya Sanctions act, which targeted both states' oil and natural gas industries. In terms of other Western powers, a cautious rapprochement between Iran and the European Union (EU) had started to take place during the Rafsanjani era, under the EU's policy of 'critical dialogue'. However, relations were hampered by alleged Iranian government complicity in the assassination of Kurdish dissidents at the Mykonos restaurant in the German capital, Berlin, in 1992. Following a 1997 German indictment citing Iranian involvement, a number of EU member states withdrew their ambassadors from Iran in protest.

KHATAMI, DETENTE AND DIALOGUE

The election of Khatami as President in 1997 represented a landmark change not only in Iran's domestic politics, but also in its foreign relations, as Khatami introduced a foreign policy based on detente and the principle of 'dialogue among civilizations'. The detente was based on three main areas, which built on the gains made during the Rafsanjani presidency: continuing to prohibit the active export of the Islamic Revolution; promoting rapprochement with Arab states, particularly those neighbouring Iran; and normalization of relations with EU states. Khatami wooed Western audiences with a well-publicized interview with the US news channel CNN in 1998, in which he expressed his respect for US civilization, and the need for greater cultural exchange between the two countries as a means of advancing mutual understanding. Some tentative steps at cultural exchange were explored, such as reciprocal visits by sports teams, particularly in the field of wrestling. European nations noted Khatami's willingness to improve ties with the West: EU member state ambassadors returned to Tehran in November 1997, and Khatami made successful official visits to France, Germany and Italy during his first term. Anglo-Iranian relations also improved, with Khatami telling the UN in 1998 that the *fatwa* calling for the death of Rushdie would no longer be carried out.

Further foreign policy success came with Iran's chairmanship of the Organisation of Islamic Conference (OIC, now Organisation of Islamic Cooperation, see p. 1155) and hosting of its summit in Tehran in 1997. Leaders of Iran's neighbours were in attendance, including Crown Prince Abdullah, who became the first senior Saudi leader to visit Iran since the Islamic Revolution. Relations with Saudi Arabia witnessed a marked improvement as a result, with Khatami making a reciprocal visit in 1999 and co-operation between the two states on oil quotas and security concerns soon followed. Khatami's message at the summit was a conciliatory one, introducing as it did, his principle of 'dialogue among civilizations'. Perhaps the centrepiece of Iran's foreign relations during the Khatami era, the 'dialogue among civilizations' was an attempt by Khatami to provide an answer to the US historian Samuel Huntington's 'clash of civilizations' thesis. Drawing on his intellectual background in Western and modern Islamic philosophy, Khatami's call for dialogue was based on advancing mutual understanding between the world's great civilizations as a first step in securing world peace. For Khatami, Iran, as the inheritor of a great civilization, should be in dialogue with other nations of similar historical and cultural depth. This involved enhancing cultural exchanges and co-operation between such nations, and was arguably a significant public relations coup for the Islamic Republic, with the UN proclaiming 2001 as the 'Year of Dialogue among Civilizations'. Iran sought to use the initiative to enhance its relations with countries including Greece, Italy, India and Egypt, as well as institutionalizing the project through international bodies such as the UN Educational, Scientific and Cultural Organisation (UNESCO) and the OIC.

Despite the more positive sentiment toward Iran's international role, the Islamic Republic still faced challenges during this period. One significant issue was the rise of the Sunni fundamentalist Islamic Government led by the Taliban in Afghanistan. Iran was strongly opposed to the regime, giving material and logistical support to the opposition Northern Alliance, which in turn complicated relations with neighbouring Pakistan, which was one of the main supporters of the Taliban. In August 1998 Iran and the Taliban came close to direct conflict following the murder of Iranian diplomats and journalists from the Iranian consulate in the Afghan city of Mazar-i-Sharif, and Iran subsequently massed troops on the border with Afghanistan. The aftermath of the terrorist attacks on the USA in September 2001 also presented Iran with challenges. The subsequent launching of the so-called 'War on Terror' by US President George W. Bush, starting with the US invasion of Afghanistan in October, and its extension to incorporate the ouster of Saddam Hussain from power in Iraq in 2003, left Iran surrounded by US forces in two of its neighbouring states, in addition to an increased US presence in the Persian Gulf. However, the War on Terror rid Iran of two hostile governments on its borders. Iran provided covert assistance to the USA in its efforts to overthrow the Taliban, but despite conciliatory messages from Khatami, the USA chose instead to confront Iran, with President George W. Bush infamously referred to Iran as forming part of an 'Axis of Evil' (together with Iraq and North Korea) during his State of the Union address in January 2002. The USA subsequently cited alleged Iranian obfuscation over its nuclear programme, claiming later that year that Iran was clandestinely developing a nuclear weapons programme. In 2003 a so-called 'grand bargain' with the USA was offered by Iran. In a fax delivered to the US Administration via the Swiss ambassador in the US capital, Washington, DC, Iran allegedly offered direct talks on the nuclear issue, a reining in of its support for Hezbollah and the Palestinian organization Hamas, and co-operation over Iraq, in return for an ending of sanctions and the provision of security guarantees. The USA, viewing itself at that time in a position of strength before becoming lodged in its Afghan and

Iraqi quagmires, rebuffed the offer. From this point, the nuclear issue began to assume a central role in Western states' policy towards Iran.

THE REVOLUTION STRIKES BACK

During the Ahmadinejad era, the rhetoric from the Islamic Republic was marked by something of a return to the combativeness witnessed in the early years of the Revolution, which in turn reversed some of the gains made in rapprochement with the West under Khatami. This was a period during which the sanctions regime against Iran was tightened as a result of its nuclear programme, isolating the country economically and diplomatically, while Ahmadinejad sought to elevate the nuclear programme to an issue of national pride. Iran's foreign relations were increasingly shaped by the ongoing impasse over the nuclear issue, forcing it to seek alternative partners as Western economic investors began to withdraw from the country. Iran sought to build on the economic ties fostered with China and Russia to counter-balance Western efforts at using economic pressure to halt its nuclear development. The Ahmadinejad presidency witnessed renewed emphasis on the constitutionally defined priorities of the Islamic Republic's foreign policy that had been less prominent under Khatami. This meant promoting an independent, justice-seeking foreign policy that challenged US hegemony and offered a more stringent opposition to Israel, together with a renewed emphasis on solidarity with the developing world and non-alignment with the major global power. Iran also adopted a 'look east' policy, under which China became an increasingly important partner, with trade between the two nations increasing from US $4,000m. in 2003 to $53,000m. by 2013. As part of this policy, Iran gained observer status in the Shanghai Cooperation Organisation (SCO) in 2005.

Ahmadinejad also cultivated pragmatic alliances with fellow 'anti-Imperialist' leaders in Latin America, such as the Venezuelan President Hugo Chávez and Bolivian head of state Evo Morales. He also enhanced relations with a number of African countries, and sought accommodation with rising powers such as Turkey and Brazil, in order to circumvent US-led efforts at containment. In terms of regional relations, Iran sought to improve ties with Pakistan through a joint natural gas pipeline, but the project was delayed and in 2020 its completion date was estimated at 2024. Relations were also tested by cross-border raids from Baluchi separatists operating from inside Pakistan. However, Iran's relations with Turkey remained cordial and both sides co-operated against Kurdish separatists. Ahmadinejad also sought good relations with Saudi Arabia and the other Arab Gulf states, making several visits across the region, but there was a more cautious approach from their side, with concerns voiced over Iran's increasing assertiveness and the advance of its nuclear programme. In addition to its efforts at securing SCO membership, Iran also attempted to strengthen ties with the fellow Persian-speaking nations of Afghanistan and Tajikistan. Ahmadinejad called for the establishment of a 'Union of Persian Speaking Nations' in an effort to make use of its soft power potential in reaffirming common cultural bonds. Despite attempts to establish initiatives, such as a joint television station, the grouping ultimately struggled to move past a rhetorical commitment to greater co-operation.

Despite his very public condemnation of US foreign policy, Ahmadinejad did attempt his own form of outreach in letters to Presidents George W. Bush and Barack Obama, as well as an open letter to the American people, but these were dismissed by the US Government as insincere. The continued US presence in Iraq, although perceived negatively by Iran, did pave the way for the first direct high-level talks between the two sides in 2007, when the Iranian and US ambassadors to Iraq met in the Iraqi capital, Baghdad, to discuss the deteriorating security situation in that country, with both seeking the same outcome of a united, democratic Iraq rid of extremist forces. The US ouster of Saddam Hussain had given Iran unprecedented influence in Iraq, with many in the newly formed Government coming from Shi'a political groups that had operated in exile from Iran during Saddam's period of rule. Iran also cemented its position in Lebanon by helping with the reconstruction of the predominantly Shi'a areas that had suffered following Israel's campaign against Hezbollah in 2006. Iran and Syria considered Hezbollah's claim of victory in the conflict as a triumph for their mutual resistance to Israel (which also claimed victory, and to have defeated Hezbollah), and from this point began to refer to the alliance of the three, at times, together with Hamas in the Gaza Strip, as the 'Axis of Resistance'.

The series of uprisings in the Arab world that began in 2011 were initially welcomed by Iran. Khamenei characterized the protests that challenged authoritarian regimes in the region as part of an 'Islamic Awakening' that cast illegitimate rulers aside, and citing Iran's own revolution in 1979 as a model to be emulated. The brief, year-long interregnum of democratic rule in Egypt, during which the Muslim Brotherhood's Muhammad Mursi took power as head of state following his victory in a democratic election in 2012, facilitated the first presidential visits between the two countries since the Islamic Revolution. However, the uprisings also posed challenges for Iran, as seen in accusations of complicity in the uprising of the Shi'a majority in Bahrain against the monarchy. Iran subsequently opposed the Saudi-led intervention there which quelled the uprising and secured the rule of the Sunni Al Khalifa monarchy. Iran's relations with Arab states, Iraq and Syria notwithstanding, were also tested by Tehran's continued support for Syrian President Bashar al-Assad as his country descended into civil war. Syria remains Iran's longest-standing ally in the Middle East, and the challenge to Assad's rule there was characterized as a terrorist threat by Iran, with the Islamic Republic seeking to maintain its strategic interests in the region and a conduit to Hezbollah in Lebanon. This led to a rupture between Iran and Hamas, as the Palestinian group was a supporter of the Syrian opposition fighting Assad. Iran's involvement in the conflict was initially limited to military advice and logistical support, although this subsequently grew to open acknowledgement of a direct military role in conjunction with Hezbollah. Iran also supported Syria through providing help in allowing its oil exports to evade embargoes against the country, and offered over US $4,000m. in loans to help shore up the Syrian economy in 2013.

THE NUCLEAR ISSUE

Although Iran's nuclear programme has been the focus of much international attention since the early 2000s, its beginnings date back to the Shah's regime when the USA provided Iran with a nuclear reactor for research purposes in 1967. Work on the Bushehr nuclear power plant began in 1975 but following the Islamic Revolution, Iran's nuclear plans were suspended. Iran's interest in resuming its nuclear programme began under Rafsanjani, who signed an agreement with Russia to develop the Bushehr plant in 1995. It was during this period that Khamenei issued a *fatwa* (which was not publicly reported at the time) prohibiting the development of nuclear weapons, which built on Khomeini's stated opposition to developing weapons of mass destruction in response to Iraqi chemical attacks on Iran towards the end of the war. Although cited as a potential cause for concern among Western states, and as one of the reasons for US sanctions as enshrined in the Iran-Libya Sanctions Act in 1996, the nuclear programme received comparatively little attention until 2002, when members of the Mujahidin-e-Khalq released documents revealing the development of undeclared nuclear facilities. The discovery of a uranium enrichment facility in Natanz and a heavy water plant in Arak came just as Russian technical staff were beginning the long-delayed construction of Iran's nuclear reactor at Bushehr. This prompted demands for access to the sites by the International Atomic Energy Association (IAEA). With negotiations with the USA off the table, and the rejection of Khatami's 'grand bargain' offer earlier that year, Iran commenced negotiations with the E3/EU countries (France, Germany and the UK) in October 2003 as a means of avoiding punitive action. Iran's negotiating team were led by the then secretary of the Supreme National Security Council, and future president, Rouhani. In the resultant Tehran Declaration, Iran agreed to suspend elements of its programme, and signed up to the IAEA's 'Additional Protocol' which allowed for increased inspections, which took place in the same month.

The IAEA concluded in November that although Iran had previously failed in some of its obligations regarding the declaration of its activities, there was no evidence of a nuclear weapons programme in the country. In 2004 Iran was rebuked by the IAEA for a lack of co-operation and announced a temporary suspension of activities, pending further negotiations.

THE SANCTIONS REGIME

Ahmadinejad's assumption of the presidency in 2005 marked a new phase in Iran's nuclear development. The President cited Iran's programme as an 'inalienable right' and project of national pride, and its enforced curtailment was seen as indicative of the bullying and hegemonic aspirations of Western powers. Iran subsequently resumed its uranium enrichment activities at its research centre in Esfahan. The Islamic Republic continued to maintain that its nuclear activities were directed only towards nuclear energy and research. IAEA seals were broken at the Natanz plant in January 2006, with enrichment resuming in the following month. The IAEA reported Iran to UN Security Council, which in turn demanded that Iran suspend all enrichment activities or face sanctions. Sanctions were imposed by the E3/EU+3 (referring to the nations that led the negotiations over Iran's nuclear programme—the E3, plus China, Russia and the USA) in December 2006, targeting nuclear and ballistic missile technologies. In April 2007 Ahmadinejad announced that Iran had attained the level of industrial-scale enrichment and would continue to expand its activities with a greater number of centrifuges. Iran agreed to IAEA inspections at Arak in July 2007, but new US sanctions were implemented in October, and further UN Security Council-mandated sanctions came into force in March 2008. A proposal mandated by the E3/EU+3 to ship Iran's low-enriched uranium abroad for further enrichment was initially rejected by Iran in November 2009, although the plan was revived by Turkey and Brazil in May 2010. Iran agreed to ship half of its low-enriched uranium stock to Turkey as a confidence-building measure, but the proposal was rejected by the E3/EU+3. With negotiations stalling, a new raft of sanctions targeting Iran's shipping sector and the economic activities of the IRGC came into force in June 2010. These sanctions also included a complete arms embargo against Iran. The year 2010 also witnessed the first of four assassinations of scientists linked to Iran's nuclear programme. The attacks all took place in Tehran between January 2010 and January 2012, and were widely attributed to the Israeli external security services agency, Mossad, although the Israeli Government has refused to deny or admit responsibility for the killings. The announcement of further US and British sanctions in 2011 led to the ransacking of the British embassy in November 2011 by hardline students protesting the move. The UK withdrew its ambassador and full diplomatic relations were not restored until 2014, with the British embassy fully re-opening in the following year. The EU imposed sanctions of its own on Iran in February 2012 which led to an oil embargo starting in November. Although increasingly suffering economically, the Iranian Government announced a further expansion of its nuclear programme in February, with Ahmadinejad unveiling Iran's first consignment of domestically produced nuclear fuel. This led to the offer of more talks from the E3/EU+3, but negotiations in Baghdad in May failed to reach an agreement and as a result, the sanctions regime continued to tighten.

BREAKTHROUGH AND THE JCPOA

Rouhani's presidential election campaign promises to restart negotiations and ease the sanctions burden were realized when the representatives of the E3/EU+3 convened and met with Rouhani's foreign minister Zarif in Geneva, Switzerland, in October 2013. Zarif was allowed to take charge of the negotiations, as opposed to the head of the Supreme National Security Council who had historically acted as Iran's chief nuclear negotiator. This move, which was backed by the Supreme Leader Khamenei, who had mandated the talks under pragmatic aegis of 'heroic flexibility', meant that the negotiations were brought under Rouhani and Zarif's control. As a result, Zarif was more empowered than any previous Iranian foreign minister, although both were ultimately still required to defer to the wishes of the Supreme Leader and his personal 'red lines' for the negotiations. The red lines included a continuation of nuclear research during negotiations, a refusal to permit the inspection of military sites, and the demand that sanctions be lifted upon the signing of any agreement on nuclear matters. The first set of negotiations between Iran and the E3/EU+3 under Rouhani and Zarif led to an interim deal in November 2013 known as the Joint Plan of Action, which would act as the starting point for a comprehensive final plan. This involved Iran acquiescing to a partial curb of its enrichment activities and greater inspection access for the IAEA, in return for partial sanctions relief, totalling some US $7,000m. The IAEA confirmed in April 2014 that Iran had reduced its stockpile of highly enriched uranium by one-half, thus showing its commitment to the interim deal reached in Geneva. Six rounds of negotiations took place in 2014 but the parties failed to reach a self-imposed deadline for a final settlement, so all sides agreed to extend the talks into 2015.

On 14 July 2015 Iran and the E3/EU+3 signed the historic Joint Comprehensive Plan of Action (JCPOA), in which the Islamic Republic accepted limitations on its nuclear programme in return for a lifting of sanctions. The JCPOA was subsequently enshrined in a UN Security Council resolution that endorsed the plan and laid the ground for removal of UN sanctions that had been previously imposed on Iran. The talks that led to the final deal were cited as the longest continuous international negotiations since the Camp David Accords were signed between Israel and Egypt in 1979, representing a triumph of multilateral diplomacy. The JCPOA ensured the exclusively peaceful nature of Iran's nuclear programme, reaffirming Iran's commitment not to pursue the development of nuclear weapons. Among its stipulations, Iran agreed drastically to curtail the scale and depth of its uranium enrichment programme until 2025; to ratify the IAEA Additional Protocol, thus submitting its nuclear facilities to rigorous inspection; to accept a 97% reduction in its stockpile of enriched uranium; and to convert its Fordow enrichment plant to a research and development facility. The IAEA inspections—some of the most stringent ever carried out—resulted in quarterly reports on Iran's upholding of its commitments, which it consistently met. The UN sanctions were officially lifted in January 2016 following IAEA verification of Iran's implementation of JCPOA conditions, and EU and US sanctions that had previously been imposed independently of the UN were also withdrawn. In addition to the removal of restrictions that had been placed on Iranian state entities and Iran's integration with the global economy, a huge tranche of funds relating to frozen assets were also released as part of the deal. This included a US $1,700m. cash settlement from the USA that related to an unfulfilled order for military equipment owed to Iran from before the Islamic Revolution. It also allowed Iran once again to access a reported $30,000m. worth of state assets held in Asian banks that had been frozen as the UN sanctions regime against it was tightened.

FOREIGN RELATIONS UNDER ROUHANI

President Rouhani staked his political capital on reducing Iran's international isolation and securing increased foreign direct investment in Iran's economy following the nuclear deal. Initially, this proved to be successful with restored international trade resulting in improved economic indicators and Iranian oil production increasing to reach pre-2012 levels. Much of the foreign investment came from large European companies and governments that were particularly keen to capitalize on the re-opening of the Iranian market. Such investments, although showing the potential and desire for international business engagement with the Iranian economy, were still contingent on full US adherence to the JCPOA, something that began to appear increasingly unlikely after Donald Trump won the US presidential election in November 2016: during his election campaign, Trump had referred to the JCPOA as 'the worst deal ever'.

Away from the nuclear deal, Iran's leaders had other pressing foreign policy concerns, and it undertook its most significant military engagements since the war with Iraq. US and

Israeli threats against it notwithstanding, the Islamic Republic faced perhaps one of its most serious threats to its national security following the lightning gains made by the Salafi militant group Islamic State in Iraq and Syria in 2014. Syria is the Islamic Republic's longest-standing ally in the region, and Iran offered support to President Assad early on in the Syrian civil conflict (which began in 2011), keen to retain Syria as a key component of the 'Axis of Resistance'. Iran applied something of a defensive lens to the conflict, taking the threat to Assad as a threat to its own security, and once Islamic State began making inroads into Syria in 2014, it dispatched members of the IRGC's elite Quds Force to the country. Its desire to maintain a friendly government in Syria was borne of its desire to consolidate its strategic role in the region, acting as a counterweight to Israeli and US interests. In doing so, Iran cemented close diplomatic and military co-operation with Russia as the principal diplomatic and military supporter of Assad's regime in Syria.

Although Rouhani and his Government offered their support to Assad, the key player in Iran's engagements with both Syria and Iraq has been the IRGC. The Quds Force leader, Gen. Soleimani, became a ubiquitous presence in the Syrian conflict, often being seen directing operations on the battlefield, and gained increased popularity in Iran as a result. In addition to Iranian support for Hezbollah, which has actively supported Assad since the early days of the conflict, Iran also facilitated the participation of Shi'a volunteer forces from Afghanistan, Pakistan and Iraq to fight in Syria. Iranian and Russian military support for Assad has been responsible for the war turning back in the Syrian leader's favour, with Islamic State largely defeated by late 2019, and the foreign-backed opposition forces fighting the Syrian Government largely contained in Idlib province in northern Syria. The Iranian presence in Syria has also caused an escalation in tensions with Israel, with several Israeli attacks against Iranian positions launched inside Syria as Israel sought to roll back Iranian influence in the region.

Iran's military involvement in Iraq also stems from a defensive posture and the desire to protect its borders from external threats. As with its gains in Syria, the expanding presence of Islamic State on Iran's borders was seen as an existential threat to the Islamic Republic and Iran was one of the first countries to provide support to Iraq, sending weapons to both the Iraqi and Kurdish Regional Governments. As the Iraqi army melted away in the face of Islamic State gains in 2014, Ayatollah Ali Sistani issued a *fatwa* calling for Iraqi Shi'a to help defend Iraqi cities. This led to the formation of the predominantly Shi'a 'Popular Mobilization Units' (PMUs), important contingents of which were armed and trained by Iran.

Iran's involvement in Iraq and Syria has allowed it to maintain and arguably increase its strategic depth in the region. Iran's narrative for justifying its military engagement in both Syria and Iraq has been to pitch it in terms of Iran fighting its own 'war on terror' against Wahabi-inspired Sunni extremists. For Iran's leaders this was indicative of a war being waged by extremist Sunni groups against Iran and Shi'a communities across the region, something that was aided by support from the Saudis and wealthy Persian Gulf states. Although the aim of much of this involvement was to preserve Iran's own national security in keeping Islamic State from its borders, Iran was subject to an attack by the group in June 2017. Islamic State operatives from Iran launched simultaneous attacks in Tehran, on the Majlis and the shrine of Ayatollah Khomeini, killing 17 people and injuring 43 others. As noted above, the group also claimed responsibility for an attack on a military parade in Ahvaz in September 2018. In addition to Islamic State's admitted culpability, Iranian officials also pointed to US, Israeli and Saudi Arabian intelligence agencies as co-conspirators in the attacks—charges that all three denied.

Although Rouhani came to power promising to reopen Iran to the world, and improve ties with its neighbours, the signing of the JCPOA was not welcomed by all members of the international community. Saudi Arabia, in particular, joined Israel in opposing the deal, which was seen as further strengthening an Iran that was already increasing its military strength and reach in the region, counter to both states' interests. Iranian-Saudi relations had already been strained following the Arab uprisings of early 2011, and allegations of Iranian support for the largely Shi'a pro-democracy movement in Bahrain that was crushed following a Saudi-led intervention later that year. The Saudis also alleged Iranian complicity in anti-Government protests that took place in Saudi Arabia's predominantly Shi'a eastern provinces in 2012. In Syria, Iran and Saudi Arabia supported opposing sides—with the Saudis providing support to Islamist opposition groups, and Iran backed the Syrian Government. Iran's relationship with Saudi Arabia also deteriorated in line with the increasing power assumed by Crown Prince (and de facto head of state) Mohammed bin Salman Al Sa'ud who has adopted a stringently anti-Iranian agenda. As defence minister, Mohammed bin Salman was responsible for initiating the ongoing, Saudi-led military campaign against Shi'a al-Houthi rebels in Yemen, in March 2015. Alleged Iranian backing of the Houthis has been cited by the Saudi Government as evidence of malign intent by the Islamic Republic, although Iran denied offering material support and insisted that its support did not go beyond rhetorical backing and solidarity with the Houthis. Ties were further strained by the Saudi regime's execution of Shi'a cleric and opposition figure Sheikh Nimr al-Nimr in January 2016, prompting demonstrations and the ransacking of the Saudi embassy in Tehran, which resulted in the severing of diplomatic relations.

DONALD TRUMP AND A RETURN TO CONFRONTATION

The election of Donald Trump as the President of the USA in November 2016 represented a major setback for Iran's ambitions to reap the economic benefits of the JCPOA. Having railed against the nuclear deal during his election campaign, Trump set about undermining it once in office, despite this stance placing him at odds with all other signatories to the internationally recognized agreement. Although Trump signed sanctions waivers during his first year in office, in October 2017 he announced that he would not be recertifying the JCPOA deal, despite continued confirmations from IAEA inspectors that Iran was meeting all of its obligations. Attempts by Israeli and US politicians to highlight alleged transgressions of the spirit of the deal by Iran were met with strong European support for maintaining the JCPOA, including a joint statement by the leaders of France, Germany and the UK declaring their continued commitment to the agreement.

In May 2018 President Trump formally withdrew the USA from the JCPOA and signalled his intention to impose sweeping economic sanctions on Iran. In violating the terms of the deal, the USA was immediately placed at odds with its European partners, all of which continued to endorse it and pledged to work with Iran on upholding their commitments. The USA aimed to impose what the then Secretary of State, Mike Pompeo, described as 'the strongest sanctions in history', seeking to restrict virtually all trade with Iran and cripple its economy as a means of bringing it to the negotiating table on purely US terms, which Tehran refused to do. Despite efforts by European governments to keep the deal afloat and their offer of economic assistance as a means of helping Iran to combat the sanctions, the already struggling Iranian economy had suffered considerably following Trump's decision (see Economy).

The USA continued to increase pressure on the Islamic Republic, cancelling all waivers that it had granted to nations that had been purchasing Iranian oil since the initial lifting of US sanctions following the signing of the JCPOA in 2015. Trump's increasingly hawkish foreign policy team sought to impose a policy of 'maximum pressure' on Tehran, simultaneously seeking to ruin the Iranian economy by driving down its oil exports to zero while expressing its openness to negotiations with the Islamic Republic. The USA sought to exert further pressure on Iran by designating the IRGC as a 'foreign terrorist organization' in April 2019, thus sanctioning its leaders and subsidiary enterprises; however, in reality these sanctions had little effect on the group's ability to function in Iran and the wider region.

Despite regular pillorying by Iranian leaders of US efforts against the Islamic Republic, Iran was initially guarded in its response to the US withdrawal from the JCPOA and its increasing efforts to pressurize Iran to comply with its demands. However, in May 2019, on the anniversary of the US withdrawal from the agreement, President Rouhani announced that Iran would begin gradually to scale back its compliance with certain aspects of the accord, in areas including the resale of its stockpile of low-enriched uranium and the limits set on its uranium enrichment activities. In July Iran announced that it would exceed the 3.67% limit that had been placed on its uranium enrichment activities as part of the JCPOA. There was also a significant escalation in tensions in the Persian Gulf in mid-2019 as a number of commercial vessels in that body of water came under attack from unidentified assailants. The USA subsequently announced that it would increase its military presence in the Persian Gulf as a means of protecting its commercial interests and those of its allies.

The continued ratcheting up of unilateral US sanctions against Iran by the Trump Administration contributed to increased tension between the two nations during 2020. The spectre of all-out military conflict intensified following the extra-judicial killing by the US military of Gen. Soleimani in Iraq in January. Widely seen as the architect of Iran's military and broader strategic policy in the region since the 2000s, Soleimani had been in Iraq to meet senior Iraqi figures. These included the deputy chief of Iraq's Popular Mobilization Forces and key Iranian ally in the country, Abu Mahdi al-Muhandis, who was killed in the same drone strike. Iran vowed to respond in punishing fashion, declaring that US troops stationed in the region were now legitimate targets. Five days later Iran launched successive rounds of ballistic missiles at US bases in Iraq.

In terms of wider diplomacy, Iran continued to play a prominent role in the tripartite Astana peace process, along with Russia and Turkey, as talks continued in an effort to resolve the Syrian conflict. Iran also sought to circumvent continued US sanctions by enhancing its relations with the Russian-led Eurasian Economic Union, entering a free trade agreement with the bloc in November 2019. Similarly, Iran spent much of 2020 and early 2021 finalizing details of a major 25-year strategic agreement with China, which was signed in March 2021 and aimed to secure Iran's position as a key node within Beijing's massive Belt and Road Initiative.

Regional tensions were exacerbated in 2021, owing to incidents involving Israeli and Iranian-linked shipping operations in the Mediterranean Sea and the Gulf of Oman. The increasing sense of a 'shadow war' between the two states was compounded by probable Israeli involvement in several operations against critical and nuclear infrastructure on Iranian territory, including a sabotage attack on the Natanz nuclear facility in April. Israel also continued its bombing campaigns against suspected Iranian targets (and those of its local allies) in Syria and was widely believed to have carried out the assassination in November 2020 of Mohsen Fakhrizadeh, a senior Iranian nuclear scientist, in Damavand, near Tehran.

NEW PRESIDENTS, SAME OLD MISTRUST

In terms of Iranian-US relations, Trump's defeat in the US presidential election of November 2020 initially led to hopes in Iran that the USA might take a less confrontational approach. This was based on US President-Elect Joe Biden's campaign promises to resume negotiations and rejoin the JCPOA. Successive rounds of talks in Vienna, Austria, between the remaining signatories of the JCPOA during 2021 and into 2022 were aimed at securing a US return to the agreement, in return for Iran scaling back recent advancements in its uranium enrichment capacity, which had resumed following the USA's withdrawal from the deal in May 2018. At his inauguration in August 2021, President Raisi sought to emphasize a new direction in Iranian foreign policy. He claimed that Iran would prioritize relations with neighbouring countries while adhering to the terms of the JCPOA (on condition of the USA's return to the agreement). Raisi's appointee as Minister of Foreign Affairs, Hossein Amir Abdollahian, had previously served as Deputy Minister for Arab and African Affairs and as ambassador to Bahrain.

Iran and the remaining signatories to the JCPOA resumed the JCPOA talks in Vienna in November 2021, with further rounds of discussions being held in the following month and in February 2022. The talks were initially based on the drafts that had been agreed by the previous administration, but were suspended in March owing to differences between the USA (which was excluded from direct participation in the talks) and Iran, with both accusing the other of shifting position. The impasse was further entrenched by the Biden Administration's imposition of new sanctions against Iran in December 2021 and throughout 2022, primarily in response to non-nuclear related issues, including human rights issues, and, ironically, Iranian efforts to evade existing sanctions. Moreover, Iran's willingness to increase its uranium enrichment levels in response to actions that it perceived as being hostile to Iranian interests was of concern to the USA and other Western powers.

Despite the February 2022 round of JCPOA negotiations yielding some positive sound bites from all sides, including broad agreement on a final text, the talks were ultimately stymied by Russia's invasion of Ukraine later that month. With world attention firmly focused on Ukraine, and with oil and gas prices soaring as a result of the conflict, Iran found itself in a stronger bargaining position as European states dependent on Russian fuel scrambled desperately to source alternative supplies. A further round of negotiations in Vienna in August was seen by many observers as the last real chance to salvage the JCPOA. During the first half of 2023 the USA and Iran continued back channel talks, facilitated by Oman, seeking to find agreement on prisoner exchanges and the release of frozen Iranian assets; in August some US $6,000m. of Iranian frozen funds in the Republic of Korea (South Korea) were released to be used for humanitarian purposes.

Meanwhile, Iran's 'shadow war' with Israel showed no signs of abating in 2022 and the first half of 2023, with continued Israeli attacks on critical infrastructure in Iran as well as air strikes against Iranian and allied targets in Syria, and repeated efforts by the Israeli Government to dissuade Western powers from reviving the JCPOA. Cyberattacks attributed to both sides also continued. In addition, Israel admitted to the assassination of a former IRGC military officer, Hassan Sayyad Khodaei, in Tehran in May 2022.

Following protracted negotiations, Iran and the UK finally reached agreement in early 2022 on the status of two British-Iranian dual nationals, Nazanin Zaghari-Ratcliffe and Anoosheh Ashoori, who had been detained by the Iranian Government since their respective arrests in 2016 and 2017; both were released and returned to the UK in March 2022. Despite official deflection around the subject, the high-profile release of Zaghari-Ratcliffe was widely linked to an agreement on the UK's repayment of a longstanding £400m. debt owed to Iran for the non-delivery of tanks ordered by the latter prior to the Iranian Revolution.

Signs of a tentative rapprochement with Saudi Arabia were evident in 2021–22, and the Iraqi Government hosted a number of confidential and public rounds of talks between Iranian and Saudi representatives. Iran's desire for improved ties with its neighbours was given a further boost by a visit to Tehran in December 2021 by the UAE's National Security Advisor, Sheikh Tahnoun bin Zayed Al Nahyan. In mid-August 2022 Iran and Kuwait upgraded their bilateral relations and Kuwait dispatched its first ambassador to Tehran since 2016, followed by the appointment of the UAE's first ambassador to Tehran, also since 2016, in April 2023. The sense of a broader regional rapprochement was given a major boost with the China-brokered Iran-Saudi talks that took place in early 2023. In March China publicly announced that its mediation had produced a successful agreement between the two sides to restore full diplomatic relations. Iranian and Saudi diplomats resumed their positions in mid-2023, followed by the full reopening of embassies in Riyadh and Tehran. Reciprocal visits by the Iranian and Saudi foreign affairs ministers were also hosted by Tehran and Riyadh in June and August, respectively, as a prelude to meetings between the heads of both countries later in the year.

As well as prioritizing relations with neighbouring countries in the Middle East, the Raisi administration has been keen to extend existing relations with its partners in Central and East Asia. After 15 years as an observer, Iran's bid to become a full member of the SCO was finally approved in September 2021, a decision that was due to be ratified by the organization's member states in September 2022, with full accession taking place in July 2023. Iran also continued to express its readiness to join the BRICS (Brazil, Russia, India, China and South Africa) grouping of countries, following its official application in June 2022; in late August 2023, at a BRICS summit meeting held in Johannesburg, South Africa, it was announced that Iran (together with five other applicant countries) had been invited to join the bloc, effective from 1 January 2024. Russia's invasion of Ukraine, and the subsequent imposition of Western sanctions on Russia have helped to further co-operation between Russia and Iran, particularly in light of the latter's longstanding experience of living under similar economic sanctions. The alleged provision of Iranian drones and other military equipment to Russia, which have been cited by Ukrainian officials as contributing to Russia's war effort, has been denied by Iran.

Economy

ROBERT E. LOONEY

INTRODUCTION

Like so many other oil-rich countries lacking the legal and political institutions of a modern market-based economy, pre-revolutionary Iran suffered from what is known as the resource curse—a dependence on natural wealth that undermined balanced economic development and sustained inefficiency, and a culture of corruption. Indeed, discontent over the inequities stemming from how oil revenues flowed through the economy was one of the factors that led to mass mobilizations and the eventual overthrow of the Shah, Muhammad Reza Pahlavi, in 1979.

After the consolidation of power as an Islamic republic under Ayatollah Ruhollah Khomeini, the Government proposed adopting an economic development model capable of reversing the damage wrought by oil by using oil revenues to secure social and economic justice. This model has worked better than predicted by many sceptics in the early 1980s. Now, 44 years after the revolution, income per person has increased by about one-half (in terms of purchasing power) since 1980 and is more equitably distributed. The health of the population has improved significantly, as measured by factors such as infant mortality and life expectancy. Average years of education have increased dramatically for both men and women.

However, the formula has hardly proved a panacea for solving the country's many economic ills. Since the revolution, Iran has struggled almost continuously with high inflation rates and unemployment (especially youth unemployment). The country also suffers from a massive 'brain drain' that has created a diaspora of well-educated emigrants. In the past 15 years, most of the growth (and job creation) has occurred in urban areas, leading to extensive internal migration from the countryside. Subsidies and price controls have severely distorted market prices—a problem that is impeding growth but stubbornly resisting a solution.

Iran currently faces highly restrictive sanctions, significantly reducing oil revenues and thus limiting the Government's ability to provide essential resources to support the economy's expansion and provide safety nets for the disadvantaged. The politically controlled banking system constrains credit to the private sector. The military retains a significant presence in the economy, making it difficult for the private sector to acquire inputs and establish competitive firms. The regulatory environment remains highly challenging, deterring both domestic and foreign investment. Lower oil exports brought on by the renewal of US sanctions in 2018 pushed the economy into a recession, worsened by the devastating spread of the coronavirus disease (COVID-19) pandemic and crippling water shortages. In addition, anti-Government demonstrations were staged during 2022–23 in protest against corruption, increasing authoritarianism, low salaries and rising consumer prices (with Iran's depreciating currency, the rial, driving high inflation). In view of the low likelihood of a nuclear deal being agreed in the near future (see History), most observers expected the economic situation to remain strained as Western sanctions stayed in place.

EVOLUTION OF THE ECONOMY

Iran's economic growth has fluctuated widely over the years, reflecting developments in oil markets, the revolution, wars, sanctions and the policy effectiveness of various governments. Within the general policy context of attempting to diversify the economy away from its over-dependence on oil, developments in that sector have been critically important in accounting for movements in gross domestic product (GDP). During the Shah's reign (1941–79), annual GDP growth averaged 7.8%. With the coming to power of the Islamic regime, average annual growth declined to 1.6% in the 1980s and 1990s, before increasing to 3.1% during 2000–22. During these periods, oil rents as a share of GDP followed the same pattern, averaging 28.5% in the 1960s and 1970s, falling to 15.7% in the 1980s and 1990s, and increasing to an average of 22.9% during 2000–22. Despite the Government's efforts, the economy has undergone little structural change since the revolution. Agriculture accounted for 11.3% of GDP in 1980, 9.1% in 2000 and 12.5% in 2020, while the corresponding shares for industry—35.9% (1980), 40.6% (2000) and 37.0% (2020)—and the services sector—52.8% (1980), 50.3% (2000) and 47.1% (2020)—also remained relatively static.

The struggles of Iran's post-revolutionary administrations stem from the values attributed to the Islamic Republic's founding father, Ayatollah Khomeini (1902–89). Khomeini believed that economic growth was an unworthy pursuit—a sentiment incorporated into the 1979 Constitution. From this starting point, the Islamic Republic's economy has gone through several phases. The one constant affecting policy-making during these phases has been the tension between the two dominant factions within the regime: the conservative 'Islamists' and the more pragmatic 'modernists'. With the conservatives in charge, wholesale nationalization, together with the exodus of middle-class Iranians, the decline in international oil prices and the destruction caused by the war of attrition with Iraq, had devastating economic consequences. GDP declined at an average annual rate of 2.1% during 1980–88, and capital formation decreased by about one-third.

Following the death of Ayatollah Khomeini in 1989, the authoritarian (but also pragmatic) Ali Akbar Hashemi Rafsanjani became Iran's President and began an economic liberalization phase. He prioritized rebuilding after the devastating war with Iraq (1980–88). Rafsanjani implemented his initiatives in a structural adjustment programme—the so-called 'Rafsanjani perestroika'. One of its key elements was the proposed privatization of many of the increasingly inefficient state enterprises. This proposal met with vigorous opposition from state employees and other beneficiaries and led to heated clashes between liberal and conservative factions, with the conservatives winning. Unable to make significant gains through privatization, Rafsanjani tried a different tack, stimulating competition among state entities—especially in the reconstruction of facilities damaged in the war. Annual growth picked up, averaging 4.7% during 1989–97.

In 1997 the ascension of Mohammad Khatami to the presidency ushered in a period of social reform that was vigorously opposed by the conservatives. Although Khatami's policies maintained an Islamic framework, they attempted to strengthen the rule of law while transitioning the economy towards modernization and globalization. Annual growth averaged a respectable 4.2% during the Khatami years of 1997–2005.

The administration of Mahmoud Ahmadinejad (2005–13) represented a pronounced shift towards a populist economic agenda designed to confront the country's longstanding economic malaise. Ahmadinejad's 'petro populism' condemned the size of the state and its bureaucracy, the budget's undue reliance on income from oil exports, and the country's vast wealth and income differentials, low wages, high unemployment, corruption, nepotism and monopolies. However, his policies to address these issues suffered from poor implementation and mismanagement. Despite record-high oil prices in the first several years of Ahmadinejad's administration, average annual growth rates declined to 2.0% during his presidency.

Hassan Rouhani, who took office as President in August 2013, thought that the lifting of economic sanctions would revitalize the country's economy—only to discover that the initial benefits fell short of expectations. Growth averaged 1.3% per annum during 2014–20. With the reimposition of sanctions on Iran that had been lifted or waived by the USA in 2015 under the Joint Comprehensive Plan of Action (JCPOA) nuclear agreement (see History), GDP contracted by 1.8% in 2018 and by 3.1% in 2019. These declines reflected the most stringent US sanctions imposed on Iran, notably on its energy, shipping, shipbuilding and financial sectors. However, despite the sanctions and the COVID-19 pandemic, there was a return to positive growth, of 3.3%, in 2020.

Ebrahim Raisi, a hardline cleric, won Iran's presidential election on 18 June 2021. The poll produced a record-low turnout for a presidential election. Such extensive voter abstention indicated increasingly widespread disillusionment with the political system, particularly among younger moderate and reformist voters.

Although growth increased to 4.7% in 2021, it slowed to 2.5% in 2022, as the fading prospect of a nuclear deal and ongoing US sanctions caused the Iranian economy to weaken. At mid-2023 President Raisi's Government had few policy options to improve economic and social conditions, leaving many citizens frustrated and angry. Although there had been a fall in the number of street demonstrations during that year, the protest movement was unlikely to fade away completely, particularly as the regime had launched a fresh crackdown on women who refused to wear the mandatory *hijab* (Islamic head covering).

SOCIOECONOMIC PROGRESS

By 2022 average per capita income in Iran stood at US $15,782 on a purchasing-power parity (PPP) basis, up from $10,773 in 1980 and $15,347 in 2010. Over time, the country's economic growth had supported significant gains in human development, with Iran ranking 76th out of 189 countries in the 2021/22 United Nations Development Programme (UNDP) Human Development Index (HDI). Iran's HDI ranking was 15 places higher than the one based on gross national income (GNI) per capita, suggesting a concerted effort to address basic needs, and elevating the country into the UNDP's High Human Development group, albeit somewhat below other oil-rich countries in the Middle East. By comparison, the United Arab Emirates (UAE) ranked 26th, Saudi Arabia and Bahrain joint 35th, Qatar 42nd, and Kuwait 50th. There has been a slowdown in HDI improvement over time, with Iran's HDI score growing at an average annual rate of 1.3% in 1990–2000, before decelerating to 0.8% in 2000–10 and further to 0.4% in 2010–21.

The Legatum Institute's 2023 Prosperity Index painted a more pessimistic picture, with Iran ranked 126th out of 167 countries (down from 120th in 2020). The country ranked low in personal freedom (165th), enterprise conditions (162nd), natural environment (158th), governance (146th), economic quality (138th), safety and security (130th), investment environment (129th), and social capital (122nd). Iran scored best in health (58th), education (78th), living conditions (81st) and social capital (89th).

Until recently, it appeared that the Government had almost eradicated poverty, with World Bank data showing only 1.0% of the population in 2019 living below US $1.90 a day (on a 2017 PPP basis). The corresponding rates for $3.20 and $5.50 per day were 6.0% and 21.0%. However, by early 2023 deteriorating economic conditions, high inflation, a collapsing currency and increasing unemployment may have resulted in over 60% of the population living below the poverty line. The legislature approved an expansionary budget for 2023/24, which increased social welfare spending significantly above the inflation rate, highlighting the Government's concern that worsening economic conditions could precipitate further protests.

Iran has one of the region's more unequal distributions of incomes, and in recent years it has worsened. The country's Gini index (a broad measure of inequality) rose from 37.4 in 2013 to 40.0 in 2016 and 42.0 in 2018, before declining to 40.9 in 2019. In 2010–21 the income share of the poorest 40% of the population was 16.3%. In sharp contrast, the wealthiest 10% and 1% income shares were 31.7% and 18.2%, respectively.

Although Iranian education has progressed since the revolution, it still ranks relatively low by international standards. In 2019 the Trends in International Mathematics and Science Study, published by the Institute of Education Sciences, found that Iranian students slightly underperformed in terms of global averages on mathematics and science aptitude metrics. Grade 8 pupils in Iran received an average score of 446 for mathematics achievement and 449 for science achievement, both of which were below the international benchmark averages. While Iranian students performed better than their peers in other countries in the region, including Saudi Arabia, Oman, Egypt and Kuwait, they ranked below pupils in countries such as Singapore, Canada and the Russia Federation. Given the Ministry of Education's intense focus on STEM subjects (science, technology, engineering and mathematics), it was expected that there would be a concerted effort for improvement. These results also reflected stagnation in education quality, which could constrain the competitiveness of Iran's labour market over the medium-to-long term.

While Iran has made some progress in governance, improvements have been difficult to sustain, with gains in one administration often eroded by its successor. The World Bank's Worldwide Governance Indicators show a gradual deterioration of voice and accountability (a proxy for the extent of democratic institutions), declining from the 23rd percentile in 1998 to the fifth by 2013. The highest erosion of democracy occurred during the Ahmadinejad administration (2005–13). However, under President Rouhani (2013–21), this dimension improved to the 12th percentile by 2016, before declining to the ninth percentile in 2021. Political stability and absence of violence also deteriorated under Ahmadinejad, falling from the 24th percentile in 2005 to the 10th in 2012. Subsequently, this measure improved under Rouhani to the 18th percentile in 2015 and 2016, before declining to the 15th in 2017, the 10th in 2018 and the seventh in 2021. This pattern of sharp improvements in the first few years of Rouhani's administration, followed by their erosion in the next few years, occured in several other areas of governance (see Manufacturing).

Iran's ranking in the World Bank's government effectiveness measure also declined during Ahmadinejad's presidency, decreasing from the 33rd percentile in 2005 to the 29th by 2013. Under Rouhani, it improved dramatically, increasing to the 45th percentile by 2017. However, a decline set in at that point, with Iran's ranking falling to the 18th percentile by 2021. Regulatory quality (a proxy for the business climate) has been very depressed since 1996, with little in the way of a pattern of change according to which administration is in power. Under Ahmadinejad, regulatory quality declined from the 12th percentile in 2005 to the sixth by 2013. Subsequently, under Rouhani, it rose to the 10th percentile in 2017, but had regressed to the fifth by 2021.

The rule of law deteriorated under Ahmadinejad, falling from the 23rd percentile in 2005 to the 16th at the end of his administration. Under Rouhani, improvements brought the country to the 27th percentile in 2016. However, as with other governance dimensions, a decline set in, with the rule of law falling to the 18th percentile in 2021. Control of corruption also followed this pattern of improvement, then erosion. In 2005 Iran ranked in the 40th percentile for control over corruption, only to decline to the 28th in 2013. Under Rouhani, Iran's ranking reached the 32nd percentile in 2015 before decreasing to the 13th percentile in 2021. The poor state of governance in Iran was expected to hinder growth for the foreseeable future. There was little prospect of reforms being implemented following the accession to power of the hard-line Raisi administration in 2021. Iran ranked last among Middle Eastern and North African countries—at 169th overall—on the US-based Heritage Organization's 2023 Economic Freedom Index. Its economy was ranked in the bottom group of countries and was classified as 'repressed'.

DEMOGRAPHICS AND LABOUR MARKETS

Iran's population reached an estimated 89.2m. in mid-2023, up from 21.9m. in 1960, 39.3m. in 1980 and 63.5m. in 2000. Population growth has slowed in recent years. After averaging increases of 3.4% in the 1980s, growth declined to an average annual rate of 1.6% in the 1990s and 2000s and 1.2% during 2010–22. The country's labour force numbered 28.8m. in 2022, with Iran having the third largest working-age population in the Middle East and North Africa, after Turkey (officially designated as Türkiye from June 2022) and Egypt. The 'baby boom' of the 1980s resulted in a large youth population and the creation of a so-called 'demographic dividend', with the working-age population (those aged 15–64 years) increasing as an average share of the total population from 53.2% in the 1980s to 56.0% in the 1990s, 68.5% in the 2000s and 70.7% in 2010–21.

The migrant population is insignificant and consists mainly of unskilled refugees from Afghanistan and Iraq. Female participation in the labour force is meagre, and the labour force is predominantly urban based, with the country's urbanization rate at 76.3% in 2021, up from 64.0% in 2000 and 70.6% in 2010. The other main characteristic of the labour force is its tendency to exceed the demand for workers, especially for younger workers. The unemployment rate has remained in double digits since 1990, with 11.0% of the labour force unemployed in 2022. Youth unemployment is considerably higher, reaching 29.1% in 2016, before declining to 26.0% in 2022. However, while the youth unemployment rate for males was 22.8% in 2022, down from 25.3% in 2016, the female youth unemployment rate was 38.8% in 2022, down from 43.5% in 2016.

Unemployment in Iran stems from a variety of factors. The demand for workers has slowed, owing to a decline in domestic manufacturing industries, which have lost their competitive advantage. Moreover, the implementation of international sanctions has further limited Iran's economic growth and significantly restricted the number of jobs and employment opportunities. The country's labour code is also a significant factor restricting job creation in the formal sector as it provides considerable rights and generous benefits for workers and stipulates a national minimum wage, resulting in additional business costs. The large public sector protects older workers by virtually guaranteeing them a job for life. In addition, the average redundancy package is 23.1 weeks of salary—representing one of the most generous payments in the world. The mandatory redundancy pay for workers with at least 10 years of tenure is even higher, at 43.3 weeks. The country's labour code thus makes firms overly cautious in hiring new workers. The resulting large pool of young unemployed workers has depressed wages and helped to fuel a 'brain drain' that has seen Iran lose some of its most talented workers.

AGRICULTURE

Iran's agricultural sector has seen a long-term sectoral decline, with an average annual expansion rate of 4.6% in the 1960s and 1970s, falling to 4.2% in the 1980s and 1990s, and to 3.4% during 2000–22. As a result, the sector's share in GDP decreased from an average of 13.9% in the 1960s and 1970s to 12.4% in the 1980s and 1990s, and to 8.6% during 2000–22. A similar drop occurred in employment, with the sector employing 16.3% of the labour force in 2021, down from 24.6% in 1991 and 18.0% in 2010.

Despite its relative decline, Iranian agriculture possesses several advantages, including a diverse landscape and climate that enable the country to grow various crops. Also, the Government maintains generous agricultural support policies and aims for self-sufficiency. However, the climate poses a challenge, as many parts of Iran suffer severe water deficits, with 70% of the country's water concentrated in just 25% of its area.

Landholding patterns in Iran have not changed significantly since the early 1960s. The first agriculture census in 1960, before the White Revolution's land reforms of 1962, found that 50% of the landholding farmers owned just 15% of the total area under cultivation, with an average holding of less than 3 ha. The next census, in 1973, found an increase in concentration, with 43% owning 4.3% of the area under cultivation and an average of less than 3 ha. The first census after the 1979 revolution showed a rise in the number of landholders and a decrease in agricultural land. By the 1992 agricultural census, 33.4% of farmers owned 3.8% of the cultivated land and an average of less than 3 ha.

Iran's principal crops are wheat, barley, rice, oilseeds, sugar cane, sugar beet and cotton. Fresh and dried fruits and nuts are exported on a large scale. Grains are cultivated throughout Iran and are a vital part of the local farming sector. Wheat is the primary grain, accounting for almost 70% of aggregate cereal production, followed by barley and corn. These crops, mainly wheat and barley, are grown extensively on farmland in mountainous areas of the country.

Wheat production was 14.5m. metric tons in 2019, before decreasing to 10.4m. tons in 2020 and 10.1m. tons in 2021. A severe drought during 2021–22 had a highly detrimental impact on domestic agriculture. Iran's self-sufficiency level in wheat declined from meeting 86.2% of total domestic demand in 2021 to 65.9% in 2022. Compounding factors during times of below-average rainfall include the inefficiency of the country's water system and the Government's somewhat contradictory aims of managing declining groundwater levels while attempting to achieve agricultural self-sufficiency. In 2022 Iran was just 57.4% self-sufficient in barley, 14.0% in corn, 61.3% in rice, 64.9% in sugar, and 50.1% in beef and veal. However, the country was 107.6% self-sufficient in poultry.

The Government regulates grain production, with producers receiving subsidized inputs and guaranteed prices for their crops. In 2022, however, there was widespread discontent among farmers over low crop prices. Government support programmes have also enabled the survival of inefficient farmers and inhibited the development of larger, more efficient farms. However, US-led sanctions have stifled the modernization of the agricultural sector and deterred investment.

Declining groundwater levels represent a further challenge for the agricultural industry, while the unsustainable use of irrigation has increased the likelihood of salination reducing soil fertility. In addition, climate change is expected to increase the frequency, and severity, of droughts in the country, presenting a long-term threat to the agricultural sector. Although agriculture remains the largest source of water usage in Iran, demand from other end users, such as urban centres with growing populations and hydroelectric power facilities, is projected to rise, placing further pressure on groundwater resources.

MINING

Iran possesses around 68 minerals, including coal, iron ore, copper, lead, zinc, chromium, uranium and gold. Overall, Iran possesses about 7.0% of global mineral reserves and accounts for approximately 75% of total mineral production in the Middle East. The sector's growth has been steady, with rates averaging 11.3% per annum in the 1960s and 1970s, 6.1% in the 1980s and 1990s, and 9.2% during 2000–19. However, with the reimposition of US sanctions, contractions of 13.3% in 2019 and 32.8% in 2020 were recorded, although positive growth of 5.2% was achieved in 2021.

Economic sanctions have resulted in reduced investment in the mining industry and outdated capital stock. A lack of modern equipment and machinery means that most mining firms operate at only 50%–60% capacity. The industry is dominated by domestic and state-owned mining companies, discouraging new firms from entering the market. However, the sector has benefited from relatively low labour costs and government-subsidized power. The Government has also implemented a 20-year plan aimed at attracting US $20,000m. into the mining sector. As part of this programme, the Government requires banks to prioritize lending for mining activities.

The state-owned National Iranian Copper Industries Company (NICICO) is the largest copper-mining firm in the country and has a near monopoly over copper production. NICICO is one of the largest companies listed on the Tehran Stock Exchange and is among Iran's largest non-oil exporters. There are currently 19 active copper mines in the country. The largest copper mines are the Sarcheshmeh (Kerman province), Meidouk (Kerman province) and Songoon (Azarbayejan-e-Sharqi—East Azerbaijan—province). In 2022 Iran had the 17th largest copper reserves globally, containing about 4% of total worldwide reserves. In 2004 the country produced 153,000 metric tons of copper (metal content), increasing to 316,000 tons by 2021. The copper industry has the potential for accelerated growth in the long term. However, with the reinstatement of US sanctions, underdeveloped infrastructure, corruption and inefficient bureaucracy, the sector was expected to register, at best, only muted growth. Nevertheless, in January 2023 the Government announced its intention to invest US $15,000m. to expand copper production over the following five years. The proposed investment was projected to increase the value of Iran's annual copper exports from $1,700m. to more than $10,000m.

Iran has extensive zinc reserves. There are two significant mines: the Mehdiabad mine, with 154m. metric tons of zinc ore reserves, and the Angouran mine, with 9m. tons of reserves. At mid-2019 domestic smelters were operating at only 30% of capacity because of a shortage of concentrates for ingot production. Shortages had arisen mainly as a result of supply chain problems associated with the transport system.

Iran is the largest iron ore producer in the Middle East and North Africa region and has more than 200 iron ore deposits, containing an estimated 2,700m. metric tons of reserves—the world's ninth largest in 2021. Iron production increased rapidly, from 12.2m. tons in 2000 to 33.6m. tons in 2007. Production reached 93.4m. tons in 2018 and 104.9m. tons in 2021. Several state-owned mining companies dominate the iron ore sector: National Iranian Steel Company, Mobarakeh Steel Company, Esfahan Steel Company and Khouzestan Steel Company. The Government has prioritized the iron ore and steel industry and is inviting foreign companies to invest in the sector, although progress is likely to be minimal as long as the current sanctions regime is in effect.

PETROLEUM AND GAS

Like most member states of the Organization of the Petroleum Exporting Countries, Iran has experienced several periods of boom followed by bust, owing to rapid fluctuations in international oil prices. In Iran's case, several other factors have significantly affected production levels. The country's oil output increased from 1.9m. barrels per day (b/d) in 1965 to 6.1m. b/d in 1974. However, production declined to 1.4m. b/d in 1981, following the Islamic Revolution in 1979. Production gradually increased to reach 4.1m. b/d in 2005, but fell to 3.1m. b/d by 2013 as Western-imposed sanctions were tightened. As sanctions were loosened, production rose to 4.4m. b/d by 2017. However, another round of sanctions led to production falling by 5.4% in 2018, 30.4% in 2019 and 9.9% in 2020, bringing output to 2.6m. b/d in that year. Production expanded by 17.6% in 2021, to 3.1m. b/d, rising further to 3.6m. b/d in 2022. The outlook for exploration activity in Iran has improved in line with higher oil prices and rising export levels, increasing the funds available for investment.

The petroleum and gas sector contributes significantly to Iran's foreign exchange earnings and government revenues. In non-sanction years, oil revenues have accounted for around 40% of government revenues. Currently, Iran possesses the world's fourth largest oil reserves, according to the US Energy Information Administration. Onshore fields account for around 70% of total reserves, with 80% of onshore fields situated in Khuzestan. Iran's onshore reserves are mainly located in five fields. The Marun field is the largest, with estimated reserves of 22,000m. barrels, with the Ahwaz-Asmari field (18,000m. barrels) and the Aghajari field (17,000m. barrels) close behind.

Despite their enormous oil reserves, producing Iranian oilfields are very mature. Years of international sanctions and the country's resulting inability to develop more challenging fields have prevented the modernization and further development of the sector. Around 60% of Iran's current production comes from oilfields discovered before the nationalization of the industry in 1951.

The sanctions have not received 100% compliance. The People's Republic of China opposed them in November 2018 and has continued to question their applicability. Also, Iran has several options to move its oil out to market, including non-US dollar and barter transactions, ship-to-ship transfers, blending into other regional grades and trucking barrels across its borders. Although such trading involves considerable risk, the combination of limited exposure to the US banking system, a tight oil market and high prices encourages companies to do so. Notably, the amount of cargo exported to 'unknown' destinations has been higher under the latest round of sanctions.

In early 2019 Iran's Government accused the European Union (EU) of breaching the JCPOA by neglecting to support the Iranian economy sufficiently against the impact of the US sanctions, warning that it would enrich uranium beyond the stipulated 3.67% limit if its co-signatories did not step in to preserve EU-Iranian trade. In July Iran confirmed that it had breached the JCPOA by amassing enriched uranium and threatened further action if trade with the deal's remaining signatories were not increased. During most of 2020 the country remained determined in its efforts to secure economic and trade support from the JCPOA's signatories and it continued to enrich uranium beyond the agreement's limits (reportedly to 4.5%, still well below the approximately 90% enrichment point for weapons-grade status).

In order to circumvent US sanctions, France, Germany and the United Kingdom created a special-purpose vehicle (SPV) under the EU called the Instrument in Support of Trade Exchanges (Instex). The SPV conducted trade with Iran through a system of bartering, thereby avoiding a direct violation of US sanctions and supporting Iran's economy by sustaining trade. However, the absence of oil trade through Instex created further tension with Iran, which announced in July 2019 that the use of its oil in bartering was a non-negotiable prerequisite to its adherence to the JCPOA. Despite this, Instex members stated that they would refrain from purchasing (or bartering with) oil from Iran if the state did not abide by the terms of the JCPOA.

The electoral victories of President Joe Biden in the USA in November 2020 and of ultra-conservative cleric Raisi in Iran's presidential election on 18 June 2021 enabled negotiations between the USA and Iran over a return to the 2015 nuclear deal to proceed, since—in both countries—in a government controlled primarily by hardliners there would be less political benefit in criticizing or attempting to derail the agreement.

The governance and operations of Iran's hydrocarbons sector are complex. The Supreme Energy Council, which was founded in 2001 and is chaired by the President, supervises the sector. All upstream oil projects come under the purview of the National Iranian Oil Company (NIOC). A subsidiary of NIOC, the National Iranian South Oil Company, accounts for some 80% of Iran's oil production. NIOC is also responsible for refining and local distribution networks through another subsidiary, the National Iranian Oil Refining and Distribution Company. Seventeen production companies operate under NIOC and oversee various activities, including drilling services, fuel conservation, oil terminal management, investment and financing in the country's international oil trade, oil refining, distribution, shipment, engineering and development projects.

Iran has an estimated 32,100,000m. cu m of natural gas reserves—the second largest after Russia and accounting for 17.1% of global reserves. However, Iran produced only

250,800m. cu m (just 6.5% of global output) of gas in 2020, increasing to 257,100m. cu m in 2021 and 268,800m. cu m in 2022, but still well behind the outputs of the USA and Russia. Reserves are predominantly located in offshore non-associated fields. The South Pars/North Dome field is the largest, accounting for about two-thirds of Iran's proven reserves. Other sizeable natural gas fields include the Kish, North Pars, Tabnak, Forouz, Kangan and Ferdowsi fields. As with oil, international sanctions have limited Iran's ability to develop these fields and the associated infrastructure needed to get the gas to significant export markets.

In early 2022 the international gas market changed dramatically following Russia's invasion of Ukraine. On 10 March the EU set a deadline of 2027 to 'achieve independence' from Russian gas. Given the size of its gas reserves, Iran has the potential to become a major supplier to European countries. Indeed, on 23 February 2022 (the day before the Russian invasion) President Raisi had expressed readiness to supply gas to Europe. However, Iran will struggle to become a significant gas supplier to EU member states by 2027.

Iran has limited export capability and no direct means of exporting gas to the bloc. Its principal pipeline connections are with Türkiye, Azerbaijan and Iraq on the export side and with Turkmenistan on the import/transit side. In 2020 Iran's exports of gas totalled some 16,000m. cu m, of which about two-thirds went to Iraq; most of the rest went to Türkiye. Iran has no liquefied natural gas (LNG) export facilities, nor does it have a pipeline connection to a country that does.

With its current export infrastructure, the only means by which Iranian gas could reach EU countries in the short term is through gas swaps with Türkiye and Azerbaijan. In order to achieve this, Iran would first have to obtain commercial agreements with end customers in Europe. After then reaching agreements with Türkiye or Azerbaijan, Iran would supply the requested volumes of gas to these two countries, which would then deliver equivalent volumes to the end customers. Such complex commercial arrangements would also face challenges from sanctions and existing gas suppliers. Owing to US and EU sanctions, European customers cannot conclude such Iranian gas supply agreements. These sanctions have also resulted in Russian and Chinese companies leaving Iran. Furthermore, Türkiye and Azerbaijan would want to prioritize the latter's gas over Iranian exports to capture market share in Europe.

For Iran to become a long-term significant gas supplier to Europe would require the construction of new facilities, such as a dedicated pipeline or LNG export facilities. There are currently no concrete proposals for either type of project, although Iran harbours ambitions to develop an LNG industry. It is likely to take many years before such infrastructure becomes a reality. Both types of projects would require tens of billions of US dollars of investment. A pipeline would require an agreement with neighbouring countries—probably Türkiye—in order to be workable. An LNG plant would also require Iran to have access to technology that is not currently available to the country because of sanctions. Even if Iran were to construct an LNG facility, it would be a late entrant in the field and would face competition from established and lower-cost suppliers such as Qatar.

As long as the sanctions regime remains in place, Iran cannot fill the gas supply gap in Europe. Uncertainties persist over the resumption of the JCPOA or the conclusion of a new nuclear deal. Even if a new nuclear deal were signed and sanctions lifted, it would take several years before major international companies had the confidence to invest significant funds in Iran's gas sector, despite high global prices. The principal concerns of potential investors include fears that a new deal could be terminated because of political change in Washington, DC, or Tehran; the challenging legal and regulatory environment in Iran; and unfair competition from state-linked companies in Iran. The latter two issues would require significant political will and time to address.

MANUFACTURING

Iran's major manufacturing industries include petrochemicals, steel, vehicle manufacturing, aviation and defence. The sector has seen strong but declining growth rates over the years, expanding at an average annual rate of 10.7% in 1960–70, 6.6% in 1980–99 and 5.0% during 2000–21. With the sector's growth being faster than that of the economy as a whole, manufacturing's average share of GDP increased from 10.4% in the 1960s and 1970s to 12.9% in the 1980s and 1990s, and to 15.3% in 2000–21. Growth has fluctuated in recent years: an expansion of 7.0% in 2014, a contraction of 8.2% in 2015, increases of 8.0% in 2016 and 5.1% in 2017, another contraction, of 6.6%, in 2018, and a recovery to growth of 4.0% in 2019, 7.2% in 2020 and 3.3% in 2021.

Iran's petrochemicals industry began with the establishment of a fertilizer factory in 1958 and further developed in 1964 with the foundation of the National Iranian Petrochemical Co (NIPC). The industry provides raw materials for many of Iran's other industrial activities, such as textiles and paper. The sector has several advantages, including the country's oil and gas industry, which provides petrochemicals producers with easy and inexpensive access to feedstocks. Import and export incentives are provided in special economic zones, and the industry has a large domestic market.

The petrochemical industry plays a crucial role in Iran's non-oil economy, with petrochemical exports constituting Iran's second largest hard currency earner after crude petroleum. Exports of petrochemicals account for nearly one-third of the country's non-oil exports by value. However, US sanctions have forced the industry to become heavily integrated with the Chinese petrochemicals market. Iran signed an agreement with China in 2022 to support exports to the Chinese market.

The NIPC's strategy is to complete the value chain and diversify production to add value to basic chemicals. Petrochemical hubs in Parsian, Makran, Qeshm Island and Jask will be instrumental in ending the export of raw materials, transforming Iran into a fully integrated producer of polymers and manufactured products. Developing the massive South Pars gasfield and higher associated oil and gas utilization in other fields will increase the available raw feedstock. As with the oil and gas sectors, international sanctions have adversely affected the petrochemicals sector's exports and caused a decline in capacity utilization, with joint ventures and technology transfers with foreign firms being delayed or abandoned. The industry is also at a disadvantage in being a late developer, placing its progress at least a decade behind regional rivals such as Qatar and Saudi Arabia. In addition, a historical lack of expertise at the state-owned NIPC makes it challenging to design and successfully commission new petrochemical plants. Finally, the prices of petrochemical products in Iran are about 50%–70% lower than international market prices.

The US Department of the Treasury's Office of Foreign Assets Control placed Iran's petrochemicals industry on its anti-terrorism sanctions list in June 2019. The USA had previously imposed sanctions on several Iranian petrochemical companies, but this was the first time that the industry as a whole had been targeted. Among the companies targeted was the Persian Gulf Petrochemical Industry Commercial Company (PGPICC), Iran's most important petrochemical company and one of the largest of its kind in the world. The US Treasury announced that the sanctions were being imposed because of PGPICC support for the Islamic Revolutionary Guard Corps (IRGC), a group on the USA's list of foreign terrorist organizations.

Iran's steel industry started with the establishment of the privately owned National Iranian Steel Group in 1963, followed by the state-owned National Iranian Steel Company in 1972. The two companies merged after the revolution; the new entity was the country's sole steel manufacturer until 2002. Iran has an estimated 3,400m. metric tons of iron ore reserves. In 2022 the country was the world's eighth largest iron ore producer, with 75m. tons extracted. By 2021 Iran's annual production of steel totalled 28.5m. tons, behind Turkey's output of 40.4m. tons, but well ahead of Egypt's 10.3m. tons.

The automotive industry has operated for more than 45 years in Iran. In 1967 the Paykan was the first motor car produced in Iran, under licence from a British manufacturer. Currently, over 20 producers are manufacturing more than 100 different auto models in Iran. In 1976 there were only five vehicles per 1,000 persons in Iran, but this figure had increased to 200 vehicles per 1,000 persons by 2012. The country's three leading vehicle producers are Iran Khodro, Saipa and Pars Khodro, which together account for more than 98% of all motor cars produced in Iran. Annual output increased from 35,000 vehicles in 1970 to more than 1.6m. in 2011, and during the period 2000–07 alone, the share of automotive production in total industrial output increased from 10% to 20%. However, the impact of sanctions reduced output by more than one-half, to 743,680 vehicles, in 2013, although output recovered to reach 1.1m. vehicles in 2014. By 2017 production had increased to 1.5m. vehicles.

After the resumption of US sanctions in August 2018, German car manufacturer Daimler announced the suspension of its business activities in Iran (following previous joint venture plans in the country). Meanwhile, in 2017 the French automotive group Renault signed a US $150m. deal to manufacture up to 150,000 cars in Iran. Even though this was the largest foreign auto deal in Iranian history, it never came to fruition, with Renault withdrawing from the agreement owing to the US sanctions. Another French automotive company, the PSA Group (formerly known as PSA Peugeot Citroën), the largest automobile manufacturer in Iran, also announced in 2018 that it was to leave the Iranian automotive market. Annual production fell to 1.1m. vehicles in 2018 and further to 821,060 in 2019. However, there was a modest recovery in output during the next two years, to 880,997 in 2020 and 894,298 in 2021.

In 2022 Russian automotive firms began requesting exports of Iranian vehicles. Russian manufacturers required additional car parts and components because of the restrictions imposed by ongoing sanctions. By August over 50 Iranian automotive component suppliers and local car manufacturers had signed agreements with Russian automotive companies to develop regional supply chains and to start selling Iranian-made vehicles in Russia.

The Iranian defence industry started production in 1925. Its first product was the Brno rifle, named after its city of origin, Brno. Since the revolution, domestic specialists have supplied munitions, weapons and armour. In recent years the industry has made significant progress in missile, electronic, optical, marine and aerospace technologies.

If the Iranian manufacturing sector is to survive the harsh conditions in which it finds itself, it will have to find ways of overcoming its lack of competitiveness. Several country compilations suggest the magnitude of what this would entail. The World Bank's *Doing Business 2020* report ranked Iran 127th out of 190 countries, identifying it as one of the most challenging countries in which to do business in the region, although it was ranked higher than Yemen, Libya, the Syrian Arab Republic, Iraq, Algeria and Lebanon. The World Economic Forum's *Global Competitiveness Report 2019* ranked Iran 99th out of 141 countries, a decline of 10 places from the previous year. It ranked 12th among the 14 participating Middle East and North African economies. In terms of specific competitiveness pillars, Iran ranked 120th in supporting institutions, 134th for macroeconomic stability, 133rd for product market competition, 140th for its labour market, 132nd for business dynamism and 123rd for its financial system. In specific areas, Iran ranked 133rd for the burden of government regulation, 122nd for efficiency of the legal framework in settling disputes, 126th for long-term government vision, 125th for fibre internet subscriptions per 100 people, 136th for the skill set of graduates, 139th for trade openness and 132nd for co-operation in labour-employer relations.

Even if the political will existed, the Iranian regime would find it challenging to liberalize the economy and allow greater foreign involvement, given the threat that such changes would pose to the IRGC's extensive business interests. There have been reports of the IRGC arbitrarily arresting foreign business people connected to firms with activities that overlapped with its own. This type of intervention is likely to continue, damaging the business environment by reducing policy predictability and transparency.

POWER AND WATER

Electricity coverage is widespread throughout Iran, with access in both urban and rural areas approaching 100% of the population. Although tariffs may increase as a result of subsidy cuts, electricity costs remain among the lowest in the region. The plentiful domestic oil and gas supply means that the country is self-sufficient in energy generation, reducing the risk of disruption to fuel supply chains. The primary threat to business activities regarding the electricity network is the difficulty that the country has faced in meeting demand in recent years (despite being a net exporter of energy), which has led to managed power outages.

In 2022 Iran's sources of electricity were natural gas (82.8%), oil (11.4%), hydropower (4.1%), nuclear (1.0%), non-hydropower renewables (0.6%) and coal (0.2%). The procedure for connecting to the grid has become more efficient since 2015, with the abolition of the requirement to obtain an excavation permit for electricity connection works.

Electricity generation has increased at a relatively regular pace, averaging 3%–4% per annum, with production rising from 57,660m. kilowatt-hours (KWh) in 1990 to 235,680m. KWh in 2010 and 280,240m. KWh in 2015. Production increased by 2.1% in 2016, 6.7% in 2017, 2.4% in 2018, 2.1% in 2019, 5.8% in 2020 and 6.1% in 2021, in which year it reached 357,840m. KWh. Although Iran enjoys high levels of general energy security, the country's power supply has historically struggled to meet demand. Sanctions on the oil and gas sector severely restricted foreign involvement, with many multinationals having pulled out of the country since 2010. This exodus has hindered production and prevented investment in power generation and distribution networks, which require updates to boost supply and improve reliability. Consequently, Iran's electricity sector has suffered from a severe lack of investment and has been unable to keep pace with rising domestic demand.

Iran's Government has ambitious plans to increase electricity generation from nuclear power plants. The Islamic Republic has one operating nuclear power plant, the 1-GW Bushehr power station. The plant, built under an agreement between the Governments of Iran and Russia, entered into operation in 2011. In September 2014 Iran announced its intention to build two new reactors at the Bushehr nuclear power plant, with an estimated capacity of 2.1 GW, and that it had signed an agreement with the Russian state nuclear agency, Rosatom, to undertake the work. Construction of this second phase—Bushehr-2—began in 2017 and was due for completion in 2026. The Atomic Energy Organization of Iran (AEOI) estimated that, upon completion, the Bushehr plant would account for 8%–10% of Iran's total electricity supply. However, a representative of the AEOI announced in March 2021 that the Bushehr plant was at risk of closure, citing challenges caused by the US sanctions in making payments outside Iran to procure components essential to the plant's maintenance.

The AEOI announced in February 2022 that Iran planned to invest US $50,000m. in developing new nuclear power plants over the coming years. Without specifying project names, locations or individual capacities, the plan envisaged the construction of an overall 10 GW of new nuclear power capacity. While it is safe to assume that this figure includes the 2.1-GW second phase of the Bushehr plant, the AEOI released no information about the projects that would account for the remaining capacity.

The Government's plans for non-hydropower renewables are very ambitious. According to the Renewable Energy and Energy Efficiency Organization, in 2014 the Government set itself a target of creating 4 GW of new renewable capacity by 2020, although it ultimately failed to achieve this goal by a significant margin. The Government has also adopted a German-style feed-in tariff to offer a fixed rate for renewable projects.

The Ministry of Energy aimed to increase the country's renewable power capacity by 10,000 MW before the end of the current Government's term in August 2025. This would represent a 13-fold increase, as capacity was only around 800 MW when the Government came to office in August 2021.

Iran possesses the most abundant renewable internal freshwater resources per capita in the Middle East and North Africa, giving it a significant advantage over its peers. While this means that there is, theoretically, higher water availability for industrial use, the country also has the second-highest water withdrawal rate in the region, placing pressure on the supply. The share of agriculture in freshwater withdrawals is larger in Iran than in any other country in the region. Annual freshwater withdrawals in agriculture (as a percentage of total freshwater withdrawals) in 2020 amounted to 92%, compared with a global average of 71%.

In 2019 96.2% of the population had access to safe drinking water. However, Iran is facing severe problems with its water supply, owing to the increasing prevalence of drought and inefficient water usage resulting from subsidies, which hinder freshwater replenishment rates and extraction capacity. The supply of freshwater to the industrial sector remains severely constrained, as priority is given to household consumption. As a result, businesses in water-intensive industries have to source their own supplies or run the risk of shortages.

From late May 2021 Iran experienced rolling blackouts and dramatic water shortages related to severe drought and the long-term environmental crisis. On 5 July the Government issued a critical water shortage warning, affecting some 300 Iranian towns. Two weeks later, protests began in Iran's oil-rich Khuzestan province. The demonstrations prompted an intensive security crackdown in which at least eight people died. Further demonstrations were staged, expressing solidarity, in larger cities such as Tehran and Tabriz. The crisis partly reflected the impact of the USA's 'maximum pressure' sanctions, which had constrained government spending and investment, including investment in water infrastructure. The protests also formed part of a continuing series, from large-scale nationwide demonstrations against petrol price rises in early 2019 to more recent labour strikes.

The Government had previously announced plans to alleviate pressure on the water supply in drier regions, including a proposal to transfer desalinated water from the Persian (Arabian) Gulf and the Gulf of Oman to Iran's arid central provinces, which suffer from severe water shortages. However, environmental campaigners have heavily criticized the proposed water transfer projects as short-term solutions that could damage existing ecosystems and water supplies.

TRANSPORT

Iran's transport network provides excellent coverage throughout the country, with substantial road and rail connections to urban areas and ports, and airports to neighbouring states. It connects the railways of Central Asia to those of Europe. Many of the world's major oil producers lie in the Persian Gulf to the south, and the Caspian Sea in the north connects Iran with Russia, Kazakhstan, Turkmenistan and Azerbaijan. Iran has essential transit roads and communication routes, including about 1,000 km of strategic border routes. Routes to the east bring Iran close to the countries of Central Asia, and those to the north-west allow access to European markets.

By the time of the Islamic Revolution in 1979, Iran had 56,000 km of urban roads and 11,000 km of rural roads. The road network extended over 190,000 km in 2000, of which over 90,000 km were asphalt roads. By 2010 there were more than 200,000 km of major, minor and rural roadways, and by 2019 the total length of the country's highways was 198,866 km, 19.4% of which were unpaved. Iran's longest highway, at 600 km, is from Tehran to Tabriz, connecting the capital with the north-west; its longest road is the 978-km Ilam–Julfa road, which connects the west to the north-west. Roads remain the dominant transport mode for freighted goods and provide vital supply chain links for businesses. Roads account for 79% of internal freight tonnage.

Traffic congestion in urban areas has become a severe problem, causing delays to supply chains heavily reliant on the road network. A more severe issue is the high frequency of road accidents. According to figures from the World Health Organization, in 2020 Iran had one of the highest rates of road deaths in the region (22.2 per 100,000 people) and the 65th highest rate globally. Most accidents are the result of poor driving standards, inadequate road maintenance and unsafe vehicles.

The railway network accounts for a significant proportion of total freight tonnage in Iran. It provides an attractive diversification option for supply chains because of its excellent coverage and secure international connections. Rail freight caters primarily for containerized goods such as manufacturing and agricultural products, fuel and cotton.

Iran's rail network is the longest in the region, extending 13,437 km in 2016/17, with 94 km of broad gauge and the rest standard gauge. The network connects Tehran to most other major cities, including Tabriz in the north, Shiraz in the south, Mashhad and Zahedan in the east, and the country's main seaports at Bandar Abbas and Bandar Imam Khomeini. In 2018/19 rail freight amounted to 50.5m. metric tons, decreasing to 47.0m. tons in 2019/20.

There are rail connections to five of Iran's seven direct neighbours, but there is a break of gauge with these countries apart from Türkiye and Iraq. These connections help to integrate Iran with the more extensive Middle Eastern and Asian railway networks, but the break of gauge adds time delays and costs on trains travelling north or east out of Iran.

International sanctions have had a particularly severe impact on Iran's port sector and have been explicitly targeted at the country's port operators and the state-owned Islamic Republic of Iran Shipping Lines, hindering its operational abilities. In addition, international shipping companies ceased calling at Iran's ports, leading to a decline in container throughput and more limited maritime trade connections. The lifting of sanctions in early 2016 began to strengthen links to global shipping routes and boosted international investment in port infrastructure, but the reintroduction of US secondary sanctions in 2018 limited further gains, and significant obstacles to development remain.

Bandar Abbas (the premier container terminal), Bandar Imam Khomeini, and Chabahar are all located on the Persian Gulf, while Bandar Anzali (formerly Bandar Pahlavi) and Amirabad are on the Caspian Sea. These terminals mainly cater for containerized imports. The Caspian seaports play an essential role in importing cereals from Russia and Kazakhstan to Iran and other Persian Gulf countries. Iran's principal export, oil, is transported to dedicated oil terminals on the Persian Gulf at Kharg Island, Sirri Island, Lavan Island and Bandar Abbas. Although Iran has 5,279 km of navigable inland waterways, ranking it highest in this respect in the region, the Karun River is the only waterway suitable for freight transport, running from the Persian Gulf to Khorramshahr. Inland waterways for supply chains are minimal and do not offer a viable alternative to roads and rail for inland freight transport.

Iran has many international airports located throughout the country, with the busiest terminals in Tehran. Mehrabad Airport is the central domestic air transport hub, while Imam Khomeini International Airport (IKIA) caters for international services. Air travel facilitates domestic passenger and freight transport. The national airline is IranAir, which operates frequent direct flights to many destinations in Europe, the Middle East and Asia, including London, Paris, Frankfurt, İstanbul, Dubai, Mumbai, Beijing and Kuala Lumpur. International airlines, including AirAsia, Emirates and Etihad, also operate out of IKIA. In 2016 British Airways, KLM and Lufthansa resumed passenger flights from Iran to the UK, the Netherlands and Germany, respectively, but the former two airlines suspended flight connections once again in September 2018.

The sanctions regime has seriously affected Iran's air transport sector, preventing national airlines from upgrading their ageing fleets. This situation has contributed to poor safety standards, which has hindered international connectivity and the development of the air freight sector. Numerous deals to replace planes and rehabilitate airport infrastructure following the initial lifting of sanctions are now unlikely to materialize, which will restrict improvements to freight and passenger air travel over the coming years.

BANKING AND FINANCIAL SERVICES

Iran's financial services sector has seen explosive growth. During the boom years of the 1960s and 1970s, the sector expanded at an average annual rate of 17.0%. With the revolution and its aftermath, the sector contracted at an average annual rate of 2.6% in the 1980s and 1990s. The sector recovered to record an average annual growth rate of 11.9%

during 2000–09, but expanded at a more modest rate, averaging 2.7% per year, during 2010–19. The sector's share of GDP declined from 2.5% in 2011 to 1.9% in 2019.

Iran's banking and financial services industry has several strengths: key public sector banks continue to receive government support; the banking system and the Government's limited reliance on external funding reduces the risk of severe financial instability; and limited options outside the domestic banking system mean that sudden, large-scale withdrawals are unlikely. However, weaknesses currently dominate the industry's outlook. In particular, the insurance and asset management sectors remain small owing to a lack of access to foreign markets and investors. Despite some steps towards privatization, the industry remains under tight government control, while banks continue to suffer from significant liquidity and solvency issues. Sanctions-related restrictions on using the US dollar in financial transactions and Iran's exclusion from the SWIFT international transfer system continue to affect growth. The sector also faces the likelihood of increased loan defaults as the economy struggles with incomes remaining depressed due to low growth, high rates of inflation and a rapidly depreciating currency.

The Iranian banking sector is dominated by domestic companies, with state-owned firms holding most banking assets. Ongoing US sanctions have limited the presence of foreign firms in Iran's banking sector and have also affected domestic banks' ability to operate their overseas subsidiaries successfully. Iran also has a large shadow banking sector, which is gradually transitioning into the regulatory framework. The Government maintains a significant presence in the banking sector, and the dominance of large state-owned banks limits competition.

The three major state-owned banks are Bank Melli Iran (BMI), Bank Saderat Iran (BSI) and Bank Sepah. BMI is the country's largest commercial bank, founded in 1928. It has around 3,277 active branches in Iran and 13 outside (mainly in the UAE and Oman) and four foreign subsidiaries in London, Kabul, Bahrain and Moscow. The bank also has two affiliated companies: the Tehran-based BMI Investment Company, founded in 1992, which operates through its subsidiaries in the cement, agrochemical, trading and textiles industries; and Bank Melli Brokerage, also based in Tehran. BSI is a market leader in Iran's banking sector, as the second largest entity on the Tehran Stock Exchange and with the most robust international presence out of all Iranian banks.

Bank Sepah was the first Iranian bank, being established in 1925, and is Iran's third largest bank. It has over 1,750 domestic branches, three foreign branches (in Frankfurt, Paris and Rome), and a wholly-owned subsidiary, Bank Sepah International, based in the UK. All three of Iran's major state-owned banks have seen their domestic and international activities affected by sanctions. In June 2008 the EU froze BMI's assets located within the bloc under sanctions designed to discourage the Iranian Government's nuclear weapons programme. This action came after the EU and the British Government accused the bank of being a secret financial channel for the programme.

Meanwhile, the operating environment of Bank Sepah's London subsidiary came under pressure in 2007, after it was added to the UN Security Council's blacklist for allegedly providing financial support to the Iran Aerospace Industries Organization, reportedly involved in the production and distribution of weapons of mass destruction. Moreover, all three banks were implicated in a US $2,600m. embezzlement scandal in 2011, accused of forging illegal credit documents to buy out public companies, with executives fleeing the country to avoid prosecution, causing severe reputational damage.

Major private banks in Iran include Eghtesad Novin Bank (EN Bank), Bank Pasargad (BPI) and Bank Tejarat. EN Bank was established in 2001 by a consortium of industrial, construction and business entities seeking to provide financial services to Iran's private sector and to small and medium-sized enterprises (SMEs). The lender offers complementary financial services, including securities trading, insurance and foreign exchange. BPI, founded in 2005, provides various retail and wholesale banking and investment banking services. The bank is the second largest in Iran in terms of deposits and loans, with a network of 325 branches. It is part of the Pasargad Financial Group, which has insurance, leasing and money exchange operations.

President Raisi and Ehsan Khandouzi, the Minister of Economic Affairs and Finance, announced, in an address to the Islamic Consultative Assembly (Majlis-e-Shura-e Islami) in August 2021, that the Government would prioritize banking sector reform. This policy represented a sharp break from previous administrations. The political establishment had delayed banking reforms for many years, leaving the sector with numerous seemingly intractable problems and exacerbating the unintended consequences of any future reforms. The critical issue undermining implementation of reform is the complexity of the links between Iranian banks and public or parastatal institutions.

Severe deficiencies in the local banking sector include undercapitalization, high levels of non-performing loans, and weak risk management and credit allocation policies. These deficiencies have significantly hindered the development of the local private sector and non-oil growth. The previous moderate administration also attempted some reform, such as introducing new capital-adequacy requirements in 2017, but without substantive impact. As in other policy areas, the new Government may benefit from having all the levers of state power held by those of a similar ideological persuasion, but their vested interest in the status quo militates against meaningful change.

During the confirmation hearings, Raisi claimed to have comprehensive reform plans in place. Similarly, Khandouzi emphasized the need for loans to be redirected towards productive sectors, especially manufacturing, rather than towards the 'speculative activities' that drove high credit growth in the previous 2020/21 Iranian year (21 March–20 March), during which lending roughly doubled, to IR 19,000,000,000m. (around US $450,000m.). However, despite being consistent with the conservatives' commitment to a 'resistance economy' based on domestic production, better credit allocation was also a declared aim of the previous Government and Bank Markazi Jomhouri Islami Iran (Central Bank of Iran—CBI). The Majlis approved an outline for a three-part banking sector reform package in December 2019, but local bankers strongly criticized it as being poorly drafted by non-specialists. Persistent fiscal pressures are likely to be resolved partly by continued monetization of the deficit, further crowding out lending to the private sector.

One driver behind the banking sector's problems has been the Government's interpretation of the *Shari'a* (Islamic law) principle that prohibits the charging of interest. Iranian religious scholars have allowed banks to 'cleanse' such forbidden payments on savers' deposits by lending money (often to government-sponsored projects) at a lower rate, against all banking norms. Chronic high inflation means that by the time loans mature, the combined value of repayments and interest is almost always below the initial value of the loan. Thus, the credit system is habitually loss-making. To compensate for such losses, the Government has repeatedly injected cash into the banking system, expanding the monetary base and driving inflation. This practice began when hydrocarbons exports were booming, but continued when money was printed by fiat when revenues declined.

The banking sector's total debt to the CBI expanded from 16% to 50% of the monetary base under President Ahmadinejad. The Governor of the central bank reported in 2020 that the sum had reached IR 800,000,000m. (around US $3,000m.). Banks pay a flat 34% fee annually to the CBI, generally rolling their debts over to the following year, when they also typically increase their borrowing.

In a bid to boost the banks' balance sheets, in 2016 President Rouhani reduced the permitted interest rates on savings deposits. The new rates were so far below inflation that most banks, especially those in the private sector, ignored the rules and created complex contracts that re-labelled higher interest rates as, for example, 'time-adjusted bonuses', in order to attract customers.

Over the long term, the Government's constant cash injections into the Iranian banks have created unrealistic expectations about their ability to invest in development and infrastructure projects. The practice has created an imbalance between supply and demand in the credit market and a growing shortage of financing for the public and private sectors alike.

A related problem stems from the banking system's opaque operations. The lack of transparency in offering low-interest loans has encouraged rent-seeking behaviour and exacerbated corruption: the number of embezzlement cases has risen sharply since the 2000s. The authorities have cracked down by imposing heavy sentences on offenders, but many observers consider enforcement to be selectively politicized. For example, the conservative Raisi Government has targeted centrist Rouhani associates. A court even sentenced the former Governor of the central bank to 10 years in prison in October 2021. In the same month, the CBI published a list of 1,432 holders of bank debts (many of whom were allies of Rouhani), each exceeding IR 10,000m. and including 900 of more than IR 100,000m., as a 'naming and shaming' exercise. The top 13 debtors were all government-owned or partially government-owned companies.

There are growing concerns that if the Iranian banking system continues along its current path, it will eventually collapse. Some smaller, supposedly 'private' financial institutions have already gone bust without state intervention, causing many customers to lose their savings. At mid-2023 several larger banks were also on the verge of collapse and were only surviving by being propped up by the Government.

The Iranian banking sector currently suffers from poor regulatory oversight, excessive government involvement, unreliable financial reports and the expansion of unlicensed credit institutions. In recent years the Government has taken steps to reduce the state's role in the banking sector via bank privatizations and the reform of internal management structures. Moves are also under way by the Government to sell its stakes in several banks via exchange-traded funds and by divesting banks' non-financial assets. Progress towards more significant reform will be slow, however, as the Government continues to face resistance from key stakeholders, as well as criticism from supporters of reform, who contend that the proposed measures need to go further.

As with banking, domestic firms in both the life and non-life sectors dominate the insurance industry in Iran. The insurance market remains small, and the impact of sanctions are visible through the absence of international companies and their subsidiaries, which are needed to grow the industry. However, if the sanctions were removed, the insurance industry's competitive landscape has great potential to grow over the medium-to-long term. Iran's reinsurance market is expanding as demand has grown while sanctions remain in place.

TOURISM

Iran boasts many archaeological and historical attractions, including Persepolis (dating back to 515 BCE) in Shiraz. The country also hosts some important religious sites—principally the Imam Reza shrine and Goharshad mosque in Mashhad, the Hazrat-e Masumeh shrine in Qom, the Shah Abdul Azim shrine in Tehran, the Shah Cheragh mausoleum in Shiraz, and the tomb of the Prophet Daniel in Shush—which attract significant numbers of foreign visitors, particularly Shi'a Muslims from other Middle East countries such as Kuwait, Bahrain, Lebanon and Saudi Arabia.

During 1967–77 Iran had the most prominent tourism industry among Middle East countries, mainly as a result of the development of tourist accommodation and infrastructure and the widening of Iran's international relations. By 1980, however, the number of arrivals had fallen to about 150,000, owing to the revolution and the onset of war with Iraq. The number of foreign tourists had declined to about 70,000 by 1988. With the renewed development of the sector after the war, the number of tourists began increasing. In 1995 452,000 tourists visited Iran. Tourist numbers grew steadily, reaching 2.0m. in 2008. At that point, after the global financial crisis, tourism accelerated notably, with arrivals increasing to 5.2m. in 2015. After contracting by 5.6% in 2016 and by 1.5% in 2017, arrivals increased by 49.9% in 2018 and by 24.8% in 2019, when they reached 9.1m. The World Travel & Tourism Council (WTTC) placed Iran 20th among 185 countries in its 2017 ranking, which evaluated travel and tourism growth during 2011–17.

As expected, the lockdowns and suspension of travel during most of 2020 stemming from the COVID-19 pandemic had a devastating effect on Iran's tourism sector, with arrivals declining by 83% to about 1.6m. Although tourists began to return, the number of arrivals in 2021 was still considerably smaller than in 2019. The WTTC estimated that the contribution of tourism to Iran's GDP in 2019 was 5.8%. Owing to the impact of the pandemic on tourism, the sector's GDP contribution fell to 3.1% in 2020, before partially recovering to 4.1% in 2021. The number of jobs created by tourism rose by 7.2% in 2019, 4.8% in 2020 and 5.1% in 2021. In 2021 34% of Iran's tourists came from Iraq, followed by Turkey (15%), Pakistan (10%), Azerbaijan (9%) and Kuwait (2%).

FOREIGN TRADE AND BALANCE OF PAYMENTS

Due to economic sanctions over the years, Iran's economy has relied on international trade less than other countries in the Middle East. Total trade (imports plus exports) accounted for 52.5% of GDP in 1980, declining to 41.3% in 2000 and 37.6% by 2022. In contrast, the corresponding 2022 numbers were 160.9% for the UAE, 142.4% for Bahrain, 98.2% for Kuwait, 90.0% for Oman and 50.6% for Saudi Arabia. Egypt was the only major economy in the region with a lower share of trade in 2022, with 34.0%.

Exports have fluctuated considerably in recent years, owing to the reimposition of sanctions and the COVID-19 pandemic. Exports of goods and services grew by 0.1% in 2017, before decreasing by 15.0% in 2018, 19.6% in 2019 and 4.4% in 2020. However, they recovered to record growth of 14.5% in 2021, due largely to higher oil prices, before declining by 6.2% in 2022. Imports of goods and services followed a similar pattern, with growth of 10.0% in 2017, followed by contractions of 16.4% in 2018, 5.3% in 2019 and 27.4% in 2020. Imports increased by 22.0% in 2021, before declining by 4.4% in 2022. During 1980–99 Iran ran a current account deficit averaging 1.0% of GDP. This deficit turned into an average surplus of 4.1% of GDP during 2000–22.

In part, Iran's current account surpluses reflect the country's limited ability to borrow internationally. External public debt as a percentage of GDP averaged 0.5% during 2010–19, decreasing to 0.1% in 2020, rising to 0.2% in 2021, before declining again to 0.1% in 2022.

Foreign direct investment has been stagnant for decades, with annual inward flows averaging only 1.0% of GDP during 2000–09 and 0.6% during 2010–22. Iran is essentially closed to foreign investment and trade, particularly with Western firms, despite holding huge business potential in its hydrocarbons, infrastructure and consumer-facing industries. This situation and troubled relations with some regional neighbours, such as Saudi Arabia and Israel, leave Iran with limited trading partners.

PUBLIC FINANCE

Iran's public finances have deteriorated over time. After averaging 19.5% of GDP in the 1990s, revenues declined to an average of 16.4% in the 2000s and 12.5% during 2010–22. Government expenditures have also steadily declined, falling from 22.4% of GDP in the 1990s to 18.3% in the 2000s and 14.7% during 2010–22. As a result of these patterns, Iran ran an average fiscal deficit of 2.9% of GDP in the 1990s, 2.4% in the 2000s and 2.2% during 2010–22. This deficit has increased in the past few years, from 1.6% of GDP in 2018 to 4.5% in 2019, 5.8% in 2020, 4.2% in 2021 and 4.0% in 2022. The International Monetary Fund (IMF) forecast that the fiscal deficit would expand to 5.8% of GDP in 2023, 6.2% in 2024 and 6.4% in 2025, eventually widening to 7.4% in 2028.

The Government will likely continue to cover the widening fiscal deficits via domestic debt issuance. The central Government's debt has increased considerably in recent years, from 12.6% of GDP in 2014 (the year of the oil price collapse) to 34.0% in 2022. The Government is also liable for the enormous debt and payment arrears accumulated by state-owned enterprises. The process of migrating some of this debt onto the sovereign balance sheet is ongoing. Moreover, state-owned enterprises are still able to spend without oversight and obtain financing directly from local banks. This situation raises the risk of Iran potentially experiencing severe fiscal instability further down the line, particularly if US sanctions restrict trade for a prolonged period.

In the longer term, the Government will probably face a significant fiscal crisis. There is growing public acknowledgment that the pension system is in urgent need of reform. The current situation is fiscally unsustainable. Based on the current rate of retirement and existing trajectories, the Government would need to use its entire budget to cover pension payments within 10 years. Possible reforms include a higher retirement age (the current retirement age in Iran is 60 years for men and 55 years for women, whereas 65 years would be more in line with international norms), an end to government-sponsored early retirement schemes, reforms to labour market regulation and reduced public sector involvement in vital economic activities. However, significant progress is unlikely. Such measures would carry high economic, social and political costs for the Government, especially considering the sanctions, the economic downturn and probable increases in unemployment. This situation implies that there is a significant risk of a collapse of the pension system in the longer term if rising fiscal pressures mean that the Government can no longer afford to make direct payments to all the ailing funds. In such a scenario, many households would lose their primary source of income, causing widespread social unrest. The collapse of the Iran Social Security Organization alone, which is the largest fund in the country and relies heavily on government support, would affect an estimated 42m. employees, pensioners and dependants.

The Government is addressing its budgetary challenges by reducing subsidies. In a televised interview in May 2022, President Raisi announced plans for further subsidy cuts. Subsidies on essential goods and services account for about 12% of government spending. However, while the subsidy system creates fiscal stress, it does so without necessarily reaching the poorer segments of the population. The removal of subsidies is taking place at a time when relations between state and society are already fraught. Their removal will add further upward pressure to already rising food prices in Iran, which by mid-2022 had increased by around 50% year on year. The fading prospect of a nuclear deal and ongoing US sanctions will ensure that the economy continues to weaken. Raisi's Government has few policy options to improve conditions, leaving citizens frustrated and angry. This combination of factors could lead to worse social unrest and raise the spectre of regime change in the long term.

MONETARY POLICY

The CBI, established in 1960, is the principal banking regulator. Its responsibilities include supervising the banks, issuing notes and coins, and managing foreign exchange, gold transactions and the flow of currency. It also acts as a banker to the Government.

The CBI lists 32 financial institutions under its supervision: commercial government-owned banks (three); private banks (20); specialized government banks (five); Gharzolhasaneh banks (two); a bi-national bank (one); and a non-bank credit institution (one). The Money and Credit Council is the highest decision-making body of the CBI, comprising representatives from the CBI and the Ministry of Economic Affairs and Finance, and other legislators. Its duties involve co-operating with the CBI Governor in the general management of the bank; directing and supervising all banking affairs, as provided in the Banking and Monetary Act; defining what constitutes banking operations, and approving the granting of banking licences on a case-by-case basis.

All banks operating in Iran—domestic and foreign—are required to implement the Council's directions and may not engage in any banking activities or ancillary services (such as marketing and cross-border marketing activities) without its approval. Foreign banks (classified as such if non-Iranian individuals or entities hold over 40% of the capital) must formally include the proposed activities of their entity in Iran in their application. Foreign firms with 51% Iranian ownership are considered Iranian companies, and only the Iranian Government has the authority to form joint banks with foreign entities. Banks operating in Iran must also adhere to Islamic jurisprudence and interest-free lending, regardless of the currency of the loan, under the 1983 Law for Usury (Interest)-Free Banking.

The CBI has been actively bailing out banks by providing massive liquidity injections. As a result, inflation has risen rapidly in Iran amid the reimposition and further tightening of US sanctions on the Islamic Republic. Annual price growth averaged 9.6% in 2017, increasing to 30.2% in 2018, 34.6% in 2019, 36.4% in 2020, 40.1% in 2021 and 49.0% in 2022. US sanctions have drastically reduced Iranian exports and investment inflows while also constraining cross-border financial transactions. This has restricted foreign currency availability and undermined Iranians' confidence in the rial, thus fuelling depreciation of the unit in the 'free market' (where most transactions take place) and making imports more costly.

Further contributing to price growth is the continued expansion of Iran's monetary base. Money supply growth has historically been high in the Islamic Republic, mainly because of the monetization of public debt. Currently, much of the expansion is to provide enough liquidity to prevent the insolvency of the banking system. With the increase in government budget deficits, liquidity expansion will continue rising, and with it, the rate of inflation.

Owing partly to rising inflation, the rial has depreciated sharply, falling from around IR 22,000 = US $1 in May 2021 to IR 42,300 = US $1 in July 2022 and to IR 601,500 = US $1 in March 2023. The CBI is attempting to bring US dollars into the market and halt the rial's slide. The depreciating currency increases the costs of imported goods and services, thereby raising consumer prices. By mid-2023 the country appeared to be in an inflation-devaluation spiral.

PROSPECTS

Iran's economy was negatively affected by the reimposition of US sanctions in 2018, the COVID-19 crisis and anti-Government protests. US sanctions, which will probably remain in place for the foreseeable future, and deep-rooted structural problems will continue to constrain economic growth. The weakness of the economy could have enormous consequences for the longevity of the Iranian regime. Previously, most of the population tolerated political repression since life could be relatively stable and prosperous if they ignored politics. Now, even the most loyal elements of Iranian society, who previously never complained about the regime, are struggling to make ends meet. This is causing people to question the competence of the entire system and, therefore, demand change. However, the Government may secure some reprieve through increased access to assistance after Iran was one of six countries invited, in August 2023, to join the BRICS (Brazil, Russia, India, China and South Africa) grouping, with effect from 1 January 2024.

Statistical Survey

The Iranian year runs from approximately 21 March to 20 March

Sources (except where otherwise stated): Statistical Centre of Iran, POB 14155-6133, Dr Fatemi Ave, Tehran 14144; tel. (21) 88965061; fax (21) 88963451; e-mail sci@sci.org.ir; internet www.amar.org.ir; Bank Markazi Jomhouri Islami Iran (Central Bank), POB 15875-7177, 144 Mirdamad Blvd, Tehran; tel. (21) 29954855; fax (21) 29954780; e-mail g.secdept@cbi.ir; internet www.cbi.ir.

Area and Population

AREA, POPULATION AND DENSITY

Area (sq km)	1,648,195*
Population (census results)	
24 October 2011	75,149,669
24 September 2016	
Males	40,498,442
Females	39,427,828
Total	79,926,270
Population (UN estimates at mid-year)†	
2021	87,923,433
2022‡	88,550,570
2023‡	89,172,767
Density (per sq km) at mid-2023‡	54.1

* 636,372 sq miles.
† Source: UN, *World Population Prospects: The 2022 Revision*.
‡ Projection.

POPULATION BY AGE AND SEX
('000, UN projections at mid-2023)

	Males	Females	Total
0–14 years	10,631.0	10,105.0	20,736.1
15–64 years	31,056.9	30,304.8	61,361.7
65 years and over	3,314.5	3,760.5	7,075.0
Total	45,002.4	44,170.4	89,172.8

Source: UN, *World Population Prospects: The 2022 Revision*.

PROVINCES
(population at 2016 census)

Province (Ostan)	Area (sq km)*	Population	Density (per sq km)	Provincial capital
Alborz†	5,122	2,712,400	529.6	Karaj
Ardebil	17,800	1,270,420	71.4	Ardebil
Azarbayejan-e-Gharbi (West Azerbaijan)	37,411	3,265,219	87.3	Orumiyeh
Azarbayejan-e-Sharqi (East Azerbaijan)	45,651	3,909,652	85.6	Tabriz
Bakhtaran (Kermanshah)	25,009	1,952,434	78.1	Bakhtaran
Bushehr	22,743	1,163,400	51.2	Bushehr
Chaharmahal and Bakhtiyari	16,328	947,763	58.0	Shahr-e-Kord
Esfahan	107,018	5,120,850	47.9	Esfahan
Fars	122,608	4,851,274	39.6	Shiraz
Gilan	14,042	2,530,696	180.2	Rasht
Golestan	20,367	1,868,819	91.8	Gorgan
Hamadan	19,368	1,738,234	89.7	Hamadan
Hormozgan	70,697	1,776,415	25.1	Bandar Abbas
Ilam	20,133	580,158	28.8	Ilam
Kerman	180,726	3,164,718	17.5	Kerman
Khuzestan	64,055	4,710,509	73.5	Ahvaz
Kohgiluyeh and Boyerahmad	15,504	713,052	46.0	Yasuj
Kordestan (Kurdistan)	29,137	1,603,011	55.0	Sanandaj
Lorestan	28,294	1,760,649	62.2	Khorramabad
Markazi (Central)	29,127	1,429,475	49.1	Arak
Mazandaran	23,842	3,283,582	137.7	Sari
North Khorasan	28,434	863,092	30.4	Bojnurd
Qazvin	15,567	1,273,761	81.8	Qazvin
Qom	11,526	1,292,283	112.1	Qom
Razavi Khorasan	118,851	6,434,501	54.1	Mashhad
Semnan	97,491	702,360	7.2	Semnan
Sistan and Baluchestan	181,785	2,775,014	15.3	Zahedan
South Khorasan	95,385	768,898	8.1	Birjand
Tehran (Teheran)†	13,692	13,267,637	969.0	Tehran (Teheran)
Yazd	129,285	1,138,533	8.8	Yazd
Zanjan	21,773	1,057,461	48.6	Zanjan
Total	1,628,771	79,926,270	49.1	—

* Excluding inland water; densities are calculated on basis of land area only.
† In June 2010 the legislature enacted a law dividing the existing province of Tehran to create a new province, Alborz, with the city of Karaj as its capital.

PRINCIPAL TOWNS
(population at 2016 census)

Tehran (Teheran, the capital)	8,693,706	Yazd	611,466
Mashhad (Meshed)	3,012,090	Zahedan	592,968
Esfahan (Isfahan)	2,112,767	Hamadan	577,458
Karaj	1,940,554	Bandar Abbas	543,218
Shiraz	1,712,745	Arak	531,523
Tabriz	1,623,096	Ardabil (Ardebil)	531,454
Qom	1,229,964	Eslamshahr (Islam Shahr)	512,156
Ahvaz	1,192,439	Qazvin	485,488
Bakhtaran (Kermanshah)	952,285	Zanjan	433,475
Orumiyeh	750,805	Sanandaj	414,069
Rasht	748,711	Khorramabad	380,829
Kerman	632,162		

BIRTHS, MARRIAGES AND DEATHS

	Registered births	Registered marriages	Registered deaths
2016/17	1,528,053	704,716	369,751
2017/18	1,487,913	611,399	376,731
2018/19	1,366,519	555,301	376,929
2019/20	1,196,132	535,254	395,231
2020/21	1,114,115	561,395	511,830
2021/22	1,116,212	570,618	544,517

Crude birth rates (UN estimates, rates per 1,000): 15.1 in 2019; 14.2 in 2020; 13.7 in 2021 (Source: UN, *World Population Prospects: The 2022 Revision*).

Crude death rates (UN estimates, rates per 1,000): 4.9 in 2019; 5.6 in 2020; 6.4 in 2021 (Source: UN, *World Population Prospects: The 2022 Revision*).

Life expectancy (years at birth, estimates): 73.9 (males 71.2; females 76.8) in 2021 (Source: World Bank, World Development Indicators database).

IRAN

Statistical Survey

ECONOMICALLY ACTIVE POPULATION
(labour force survey year ending 20 March 2019, '000 persons aged 10 years and over, incl. armed forces and unpaid family workers)

	Males	Females	Total
Agriculture, hunting, forestry and fishing	3,357.1	856.1	4,213.2
Mining and quarrying	186.0	9.5	195.5
Manufacturing	3,018.8	1,108.8	4,127.6
Electricity, gas and water supply	290.0	14.3	304.3
Construction	2,964.1	36.1	3,000.2
Wholesale and retail trade; repair of motor vehicles, motorcycles and personal and household goods	3,389.3	345.2	3,734.5
Hotels and restaurants	319.2	51.6	370.8
Transport, storage and communications	2,359.9	94.9	2,454.8
Financial intermediation	259.7	67.8	327.5
Real estate, renting and business activities	626.5	176.5	803.0
Public administration and defence; compulsory social security	1,201.2	153.2	1,354.4
Education	643.8	778.3	1,422.1
Health and social work	346.5	393.1	739.6
Other community, social and personal service activities	486.2	234.3	720.4
Private households with employed persons	15.8	24.4	40.1
Extraterritorial organizations and bodies	0.4	0.8	1.2
Sub-total	19,464.5	4,344.9	23,809.2
Activities not adequately defined	3.4	0.5	3.9
Total employed	19,467.8	4,345.3	23,813.0
Unemployed	2,250.3	1,010.5	3,260.8
Total labour force	21,718.0	5,355.8	27,073.8

2020 (labour force survey year ending 20 March, '000 persons aged 15 years and over, incl. armed forces and unpaid family workers): Agriculture 4,296.4; Manufacturing 7,767.5; Services 12,209.6; *Total employed* 24,273.5; Unemployed 2,893.6; *Total labour force* 27,167.1.

Note: Totals may not equal sum of components, owing to rounding.

Health and Welfare

KEY INDICATORS

Total fertility rate (children per woman, 2021)	1.7
Under-5 mortality rate (per 1,000 live births, 2021)	12.6
HIV/AIDS (% of persons aged 15–49, 2021)	<0.1
COVID-19: Cumulative confirmed deaths (per 100,000 persons at 30 June 2023)	165.2
COVID-19: Fully vaccinated population (% of total population at 20 June 2023)	66.2
Physicians (per 1,000 head, 2018)	1.6
Hospital beds (per 1,000 head, 2017)	1.6
Domestic health expenditure (2020): US $ per head (PPP)	414.5
Domestic health expenditure (2020): % of GDP	2.9
Domestic health expenditure (2020): public (% of total current health expenditure)	53.9
Access to improved water resources (% of persons, 2020)	97
Access to improved sanitation facilities (% of persons, 2020)	90
Total carbon dioxide emissions ('000 metric tons, 2019)	630,010
Carbon dioxide emissions per head (metric tons, 2019)	7.6
Human Development Index (2021): ranking	76
Human Development Index (2021): value	0.774

Note: For data on COVID-19 vaccinations, 'fully vaccinated' denotes receipt of all doses specified by approved vaccination regime (Sources: Johns Hopkins University and Our World in Data). Data on health expenditure refer to current general government expenditure in each case. For more information on sources and further definitions for all indicators, see Health and Welfare Statistics: Sources and Definitions section (europaworld.com/credits).

Agriculture

PRINCIPAL CROPS
('000 metric tons)

	2019	2020	2021
Almonds, with shell	177.0	161.9*	163.6*
Apples	2,241.1	2,241.1*	2,241.1†
Apricots	329.6	332.0*	323.0*
Aubergines (Eggplants)*	594.1	595.3	598.3
Barley	3,600.0†	2,940.6	2,814.3
Beans, dry	158.8*	167.5	138.2
Cabbages and other brassicas*	293.5	293.2	294.0*
Cantaloupes and other melons	887.6*	752.9	676.3
Cherries, sweet	128.4	161.9*	156.1*
Cherries, sour	124.8	121.8*	122.7*
Chick peas	191.6*	172.9	168.1
Chillies and peppers, green*	93.6	94.1	93.5
Cucumbers and gherkins	663.8*	571.4	483.1
Dates	1,307.9	1,282.0*	1,303.7*
Figs	130.3	112.5*	83.9*
Garlic*	59.2	59.5	59.9
Grapes	1,945.9	1,982.6*	1,888.8*
Lemons and limes*	476.6	477.8	479.0
Lentils*	80.2	79.4	79.7
Lettuce and chicory*	424.2	438.5	436.0
Maize	1,400.0†	437.9	320.2
Olives	101.4	109.1*	115.0*
Onions, dry	2,308.7	2,214.2*	2,139.9*
Oranges	2,308.7	2,214.2*	2,139.9*
Peaches and nectarines	591.4	650.0*	687.2*
Pears	106.8	127.6*	124.0*
Pistachios	337.8	190.0†	135.0†
Plums and sloes	359.2	374.4*	388.2*
Potatoes	3,465.7*	3,215.0	2,599.1
Pumpkins, squash and gourds*	193.4	196.9	193.3
Rice, paddy	2,486.4†	1,820.4	1,595.3
Soybeans (Soya beans)†	180.0	190.0	200.0
Sugar beet	5,550.2*	5,435.2	5,146.9
Sugar cane	7,550.0*	7,840.0	8,258.2
Tangerines, mandarins, etc.	586.6	572.2*	527.0*
Tea	90.8	85.0*	83.5*
Tomatoes	4,367.4*	3,615.9	3,392.2
Walnuts, with shell	321.1	356.9*	387.0*
Watermelons	1,672.9*	1,410.5	1,251.4
Wheat	14,500†	10,416.2	10,093.6

* FAO estimate(s).
† Unofficial figure(s).

Aggregate production ('000 metric tons, may include official, semi-official or estimated data): Total cereals 21,998.9 in 2019, 15,627.8 in 2020, 14,836.1 in 2021; Total fruit (primary) 17,450.6 in 2019, 17,119.4 in 2020, 16,649.4 in 2021; Total oilcrops 1,632.6 in 2019, 1,429.3 in 2020, 1,383.8 in 2021; Total roots and tubers 3,465.7 in 2019, 3,215.0 in 2020, 2,599.1 in 2021; Total sugar crops 13,100.2 in 2019, 13,275.2 in 2020, 13,405.1 in 2021; Total vegetables (primary) 10,554.2 in 2019, 10,055.4 in 2020, 9,331.1 in 2021.

Source: FAO.

LIVESTOCK
('000 head, FAO estimates unless otherwise indicated)

	2019	2020	2021
Asses	1,557	1,556	1,556
Buffaloes	148	171*	162
Camels	147	152*	152
Cattle	5,241	5,324*	5,344
Chickens	973,721	1,017,615	1,030,666
Ducks	1,535	1,533	1,532
Geese and guinea fowl	994	994	994
Goats	15,034*	16,664*	16,955
Horses	133	132	131
Mules	180	180	181
Sheep	41,304*	46,587*	45,270
Turkeys	1,912	1,843	1,760

* Official figure.
Source: FAO.

LIVESTOCK PRODUCTS
('000 metric tons, FAO estimates unless otherwise indicated)

	2019	2020	2021
Buffaloes' milk	128	128	128
Cattle hides, fresh	22	32	43
Cattle meat	173	250	336
Cattle offals, edible	38	55	74
Cows' milk	6,800	7,509*	7,036
Chicken meat	2,332	2,430*	1,982
Goat meat	24	31	38
Goat offals, edible	4	5	7
Goats' milk	277	351*	302
Sheep meat	116	152	238
Sheep offals, edible	23	29	46
Sheep's (Ewes') milk	328	376*	386
Sheepskins, fresh	19	25	39
Hen eggs	869	756	783
Honey (natural)	73	74	77
Silk-worm cocoons, reelable	1	2	2
Wool, greasy	56	54	52

* Official data.
Source: FAO.

Forestry

ROUNDWOOD REMOVALS
('000 cubic metres, excl. bark)

	2014*	2015	2016
Sawlogs, veneer logs and logs for sleepers	286	201	162
Pulpwood	196	99	116
Other industrial wood	248	165	138
Fuel wood	52	34	30
Total	782	499	446

* FAO estimates.

2017–21: Annual production assumed to be unchanged from 2016.
Source: FAO.

SAWNWOOD PRODUCTION
('000 cubic metres, incl. railway sleepers)

	2014	2015	2016
Total (all broadleaved)	33	25	21

2017–21: Annual production assumed to be unchanged from 2016.
Source: FAO.

Fishing

('000 metric tons, live weight)

	2019	2020	2021
Capture	824.6	790.9	779.5
Caspian sprat	24.6	20.1	20.1
Indian oil sardine	90.2	80.2	93.8
Kawakawa	33.3	35.6*	39.6
Skipjack tuna	40.0	44.5	68.1
Longtail tuna	49.0	56.6	51.7
Yellowfin tuna	58.0	48.3	44.3
Aquaculture*	458.1	480.5	478.7
Silver carp	117.0	122.9	119.3
Rainbow trout	187.9	197.4	193.8
Total catch*	1,282.7	1,271.4	1,258.2

* FAO estimate(s).
Source: FAO.

Production of caviar (metric tons, fiscal year): 2 in 2017/18; 1 in 2018/19; 1 in 2019/20.

Mining

('000 metric tons unless otherwise indicated, fiscal year)

	2016/17	2017/18	2018/19
Iron ore: gross weight	33,967	36,435	33,093
Iron ore: metal content	22,200	23,900	21,700
Copper concentrates*	296	316	315†
Bauxite	1,047	805	780†
Lead concentrates*	48	48	50
Zinc concentrates*†	140	140	140
Manganese ore‡	101	129	134
Chromium concentrates§	292	119	122
Molybdenum concentrates (metric tons)*	3,300	1,700	700
Gold (kilograms)*†	7,000	7,600	7,600
Bentonite	518	424	425
Kaolin	860	1,160	1,160
Other clays†	600	600	n.a.
Magnesite	156	130†	25†
Fluorspar (Fluorite)	55	55†	55†
Feldspar	1,340	2,060	2,100
Barite (Barytes)	239	202	202†
Salt (unrefined)†	2,800	2,500	2,500
Gypsum (crude)†	16,000	16,000	16,000
Mica (metric tons)†	1,500	1,500	1,500
Talc†	82	85	85
Turquoise (kilograms)†	21,000	21,000	21,000
Coal†	1,518	1,644	2,000

* Figures refer to the metal content of ores and concentrates.
† Estimate(s).
‡ Figures refer to gross weight. The estimated metal content ('000 metric tons) was: 39 in 2016/17, 45 in 2017/18; 45 in 2018/19.
§ Figures refer to gross weight. The estimated chromic oxide content ('000 metric tons) was: 129 in 2016/17, 53 in 2017/18, 54 in 2018/19.
Source: US Geological Survey.

Crude petroleum ('000 metric tons, estimates): 144,368 in 2020; 168,793 in 2021; 176,541 in 2022 (Source: Energy Institute, *Statistical Review of World Energy*).

Natural gas (excl. flared or recycled, '000 million cu m): 249,530 in 2020; 256,650 in 2021; 259,399 in 2022 (Source: Energy Institute, *Statistical Review of World Energy*).

Industry

PETROLEUM PRODUCTS
(average cu m per day, fiscal year)

	2016/17	2017/18	2018/19
Liquefied petroleum gas	9,068	10,774	9,467
Motor spirit (petrol)	62,177	81,911	64,888
Kerosene	20,710	17,035	21,640
Gas-diesel (distillate fuel) oil	80,339	84,795	83,857
Residual fuel oils	69,942	56,853	73,045

2009/10: Burning oil (for electricity) 18,519; Jet fuel 4,188; Petroleum bitumen (asphalt) 698.

IRAN

OTHER PRODUCTS
(fiscal year)

	2013/14	2014/15	2015/16
Refined sugar ('000 metric tons)	2,324	2,331	2,324
Soft drinks (million bottles)	1,714	1,921	1,714
Malt liquor (million bottles)	320	335	320
Cigarettes (million)	25,532	13,110	25,532
Threads ('000 metric tons)	363	358	363
Finished fabrics (million metres)	282	244	282
Machine-made carpets ('000 sq m)	30,697	33,256	30,697
Hand-woven carpets (moquette—'000 sq m)	66,779	62,947	66,779
Paper ('000 metric tons)	549	673	549
Detergent powder ('000 metric tons)	549	580	549
Soap (metric tons)	80,797	81,660	80,797
Cement ('000 metric tons)	77,465	66,519	77,465
Washing machines ('000)	245	272	245
Radio receivers ('000)	190	477	190
Television receivers ('000)	1,196	1,214	1,196
Water meters ('000)	606	571	606
Electricity meters ('000)	1,461	1,511	1,461
Passenger cars and jeeps ('000)	652	995	652
Electrical energy (million kWh)	262,434	274,438	280,689

Electrical energy ('000 million kWh): 308.0 in 2017/18; 310.9 in 2018/19; 326.4 in 2019/20; 343.1 in 2020/21.

Finance

CURRENCY, EXCHANGE RATES AND FISCAL YEAR

Monetary Units
100 dinars = 1 Iranian rial (IR).

Sterling, Dollar and Euro Equivalents (31 August 2022)
£1 sterling = 48,787.2;
US $1 = 42,000.0 rials;
€1 = 42,000.0 rials;
100,000 Iranian rials = £2.05 = $2.38 = €2.38.

Average Exchange Rate (rials per US $)
2019   42,000.0
2020   42,000.0
2021   42,000.0.

Note: A new unified exchange rate, based on the market rate (regulated by the central bank), took effect from 21 March 2002. The foregoing information on average exchange rates refers to this official rate (used for most inter-governmental transactions); however, the unofficial prevailing free market rate was reported to have reached more than 330,000 per US dollar in early October 2022. In 2020 the authorities initiated legislation to replace the rial with the toman as the official currency.

Fiscal Year
The fiscal year ends on 20 March.

BUDGET
(consolidated accounts of central government and Oil Stabilization Fund—OSF, '000 million rials, fiscal year)

Revenue	2007/08	2008/09*	2009/10†
Oil and gas revenue	578,708	569,951	436,159
Budget revenue	444,278	559,589	498,071
Transfers from OSF	209,098	184,235	223,099
Revenues transferred to OSF	134,430	10,362	−61,912
Non-oil budgetary revenue	237,893	283,918	354,315
Tax revenue	162,579	203,042	240,454
Taxes on income, profits and capital gains	97,097	130,453	153,994
Domestic taxes on goods and services	16,663	15,900	29,771
Taxes on international trade and transactions	48,819	56,689	56,689
Non-tax revenue	75,314	80,876	113,861
Non-oil OSF revenues	4,551	6,038	6,223
Total	821,152	859,906	796,697

Expenditure	2007/08	2008/09*	2009/10†
Central government expenditures	710,022	841,093	884,798
Current expenditure	562,306	595,254	676,682
Wages and salaries	151,583	211,000	229,000
Interest payments	7,371	5,982	5,982
Subsidies	62,862	61,000	68,000
Goods and services	39,119	55,000	71,600
Grants	13,823	50,800	28,700
Social benefits	64,492	139,605	181,000
Gasoline imports	33,820	60,867	34,300
Other expenses	189,236	11,000	58,100
Capital expenditure	147,716	245,839	208,116
OSF expenditures	40,289	19,148	—
Total	750,311	860,240	884,798

* Estimates.
† Projections.

Source: IMF, *Islamic Republic of Iran: 2009 Article IV Consultation-Staff Report; Staff Supplement; Public Information Notice on the Executive Board Discussion; and Statement by the Executive Director for Iran* (March 2010).

2015/16 ('000 million rials): *Revenue:* Tax revenue 791,890 (Taxes on income, profits and capital gains 405,448; Taxes on property 24,153; Domestic taxes on goods and services 246,747; Taxes on international trade and transactions 115,542); Other revenue 1,002,210 (Property income 817,743); Total 1,794,100. *Expenditure:* Current expenditure 1,716,637; Net acquisition of non-financial assets 273,766; Total 1,990,403 (Source: IMF—see below).

2016/17 ('000 million rials): *Revenue:* Tax revenue 1,014,600 (Taxes on income, profits and capital gains 467,100, Taxes on property 26,700, Domestic taxes on goods and services 337,900, Taxes on international trade and transactions 182,900); Other revenue 1,184,000 (Property income 936,529); Total 2,198,600. *Expenditure:* Current expenditure 2,070,200; Net acquisition of non-financial assets 417,000; Total 2,487,200 (Source: IMF—see below).

2017/18 ('000 million rials, projections): *Revenue:* Tax revenue 1,085,118 (Taxes on income, profits and capital gains 482,547; Taxes on property 29,815; Domestic taxes on goods and services 345,621; Taxes on international trade and transactions 227,135); Other revenue 1,226,845 (Property income 950,501); Total 2,311,962. *Expenditure:* Current expenditure 2,320,632; Net acquisition of non-financial assets 335,799; Total 2,656,431 (Source: *Islamic Republic of Iran: 2018 Article IV Consultation—Press Release; Staff Report; and Statement by the Executive Director for the Islamic Republic of Iran*, March 2018).

INTERNATIONAL RESERVES
(US $ million at 31 December)*

	2020	2021	2022
IMF special drawing rights	2,236	6,958	6,622

* IMF estimates of gross usable official reserves were estimated at $13,800m. in 2020, $17,700m. in 2021 and $25,400m. in 2022.

Source: IMF, *International Financial Statistics* and *May 2023 Regional Economic Outlook: Middle East and Central Asia*.

MONEY SUPPLY
('000 million rials, rounded figures, fiscal year)

	2019/20	2020/21	2021/22
Currency outside banks	611,400	735,000	864,300
Sight deposits	3,661,600	6,174,600	9,001,500
Non-sight deposits (quasi-money)	20,448,500	27,852,100	38,458,600
Total money	24,721,500	34,761,700	48,324,400

COST OF LIVING
(Consumer Price Index, fiscal year; base: 2021/22 = 100)

	2019/20	2020/21	2022/23
Food and non-alcoholic beverages	47.3	65.8	171.2
Clothing and footwear	47.6	66.1	147.5
Housing, water, electricity, gas, and other fuels	62.9	78.8	132.3
All items (incl. others)	52.3	71.3	145.8

IRAN

NATIONAL ACCOUNTS
('000 billion rials at current prices, fiscal year)

Expenditure on the Gross Domestic Product

	2019/20	2020/21	2021/22
Final consumption expenditure	17,155	23,219	35,860
Private	14,237	19,197	29,362
Public	2,918	4,023	6,498
Changes in inventories*	11,656	17,711	27,667
Gross fixed capital formation	6,582	11,123	18,657
Total domestic expenditure	35,393	52,054	82,184
Exports of goods and services	6,364	8,675	16,865
Less Imports of goods and services	6,309	8,400	11,724
GDP at market prices	35,448	52,329	87,325
GDP at constant 2011/12 prices	7,184	7,254	7,570

* Changes in inventories includes statistical discrepancy.

Gross Domestic Product by Economic Activity

	2019/20	2020/21	2021/22
Hydrocarbon GDP	4,946	6,505	14,197
Non-hydrocarbon GDP	30,338	45,642	72,905
Agriculture	3,285	4,654	7,548
Industry	10,164	16,499	27,368
Mining	466	851	1,606
Manufacturing	5,774	9,968	15,934
Construction	1,255	2,223	3,626
Electricity, gas and water	2,669	3,456	6,203
Services	16,889	24,489	37,989
Transport, storage and communication	2,848	4,133	6,553
Banking and insurance	866	2,056	2,315
Trade, restaurants and hotels	5,169	7,903	12,817
Real estate and professional services	4,342	5,906	8,893
Public services	3,424	4,312	7,089
Other services	240	180	321
GDP at factor prices	35,284	52,146	87,102
Net indirect taxes	165	183	223
GDP at market prices	35,448	52,329	87,325

Note: Totals may not be equal to the sum of components, owing to rounding.

BALANCE OF PAYMENTS
(US $ million, fiscal year)

	2019/20	2020/21	2021/22
Exports of goods f.o.b.	59,975	49,848	79,470
Petroleum and gas	26,049	21,043	38,723
Non-petroleum and gas exports	33,926	28,805	40,748
Imports of goods f.o.b.	−58,090	−46,612	−63,626
Petroleum and gas	111	—	—
Trade balance	1,885	3,236	15,844
Exports of services	11,509	4,214	6,518
Imports of services	−16,013	−8,212	−11,877
Balance on goods and services	−2,619	−762	10,485
Income received	2,123	1,148	1,276
Income paid	−2,108	−1,747	−1,771
Balance on goods, services and income	−2,604	−1,361	9,990
Transfers (net)	953	655	1,153
Current balance	−1,652	−708	11,144
Capital account (net) / Financial account (net)	−249	−6,318	−9,333
Errors and omissions	2,572	4,385	−916
Overall balance	671	−2,641	895

External Trade

PRINCIPAL COMMODITIES
(US $ million, fiscal year)

Imports c.i.f. (distribution by SITC)	2016/17	2017/18	2018/19
Food and live animals	6,345	7,638	7,971
Cereals and cereal preparations	2,806	3,430	4,466
Crude materials (inedible) except fuels	2,579	3,129	3,024
Mineral products	1,018	2,865	1,712
Animal and vegetable oils and fats	877	1,203	1,053
Vegetable oils and fats	873	1,198	1,049
Chemicals and related products	6,016	7,234	6,386
Chemical elements and compounds	1,246	1,586	1,506
Medical and pharmaceutical products	1,667	1,854	1,868
Plastic, cellulose and artificial resins	1,459	1,666	1,208
Basic manufactures	6,922	7,767	4,801
Paper, cardboard and articles thereof	959	1,086	899
Iron and steel	2,509	2,677	1,561
Machinery and transport equipment	17,704	21,916	16,151
Non-electrical machinery	7,321	8,818	7,754
Electrical machinery, apparatus, etc.	5,034	5,429	3,957
Transport equipment	5,350	7,668	4,440
Miscellaneous manufactured articles	1,738	2,300	1,677
Total (incl. others)	43,684	54,459	43,169

Exports f.o.b.*	2016/17	2017/18	2018/19
Agricultural and traditional goods	5,523	5,702	5,186
Carpets	360	426	239
Fruits (fresh and dried)	2,257	2,273	1,731
Metallic mineral ores	1,103	1,868	1,139
Industrial manufactures	30,004	32,194	33,233
Oil and gas products	9,686	9,017	9,184
Iron and steel	2,999	4,007	4,636
Organic chemicals	3,688	3,897	4,037
Plastic materials and products	4,940	6,076	5,639
Articles of stone, plaster, cement and ceramic products	1,376	1,510	1,405
Total (incl. others)	36,723	39,920	39,580

* Excluding exports of crude petroleum and associated gas (US $ million): 53,362 in 2016/17; 62,768 in 2017/18; 60,735 in 2018/19.

Total imports: 44,058 in 2019/20; 38,893 in 2020/21.

Total exports: 40,996 in 2019/20; 34,998 in 2020/21.

Note: Imports include registration fee, but exclude defence-related imports and imports of refined petroleum products.

IRAN

PRINCIPAL TRADING PARTNERS
(US $ million, fiscal year)

Imports c.i.f.	2017/18	2018/19	2020/21*
Austria	337	556	326
Belgium	688	398	n.a.
Brazil	675	492	334
China, People's Republic	13,236	10,414	9,843
France	1,771	1,074	284
Germany	3,094	2,489	1,851
India	2,258	2,761	2,140
Italy	1,437	1,154	687
Japan	668	437	102
Korea, Republic	3,719	2,065	586
Netherlands	1,440	1,173	889
Russian Federation	728	1,354	1,070
Singapore	951	915	591
Sweden	706	343	64
Switzerland	2,160	2,116	933
Türkiye	3,222	2,636	4,400
United Arab Emirates	10,059	6,618	976
United Kingdom	1,105	1,036	n.a.
Total (incl. others)	54,459	43,169	38,893

Exports f.o.b.	2017/18	2018/19	2020/21*
Afghanistan	2,785	2,948	2,308
Azerbaijan	326	417	511
China, People's Republic	8,762	8,828	9,077
India	2,563	2,045	1,281
Indonesia	649	755	674
Iraq	6,555	8,991	7,448
Italy	423	257	n.a.
Korea, Republic	454	n.a.	n.a.
Oman	552	n.a.	n.a.
Pakistan	919	1,267	1,002
Russian Federation	292	284	505
Taiwan	577	332	81
Thailand	734	n.a.	n.a.
Türkiye	3,963	2,381	2,537
Turkmenistan	418	406	137
United Arab Emirates	4,438	4,316	4,662
Total (incl. others)	39,920	39,580	34,998

* Full data were not available for 2019/20, although total imports were reported as 44,058, and total exports 40,996.

Note: Exports exclude crude petroleum and associated gas.

Transport

RAILWAYS
(traffic, fiscal year)

	2017/18	2018/19	2019/20
Passengers carried ('000)	24,480	28,094	28,599
Passenger-km (million)	13,272	15,239	14,890
Freight carried ('000 metric tons)	46,766	50,478	46,976
Freight ton-km (million)	30,299	34,859	33,646

ROAD TRAFFIC
(registered motor vehicles, fiscal year)

	2017/18	2018/19	2019/20
Passenger cars*	1,463,956	847,205	823,798
Pick-ups and light trucks	75,766	52,924	68,908
Motorcycles	153,119	164525	116974
Total (incl. others)	1,752,206	1,117,301	1,108,811

* Including ambulances.

SHIPPING
Flag Registered Fleet
(at 31 December)

	2020	2021	2022
Number of vessels	983	1,155	1,612
Total displacement ('000 grt)	12,068.1	12,149.2	12,043.6

Source: Lloyd's List Intelligence (www.bit.ly/LLintelligence).

International Seaborne Freight Traffic
(fiscal year, '000 metric tons)

	2017/18	2018/19	2019/20
Goods loaded	90,958	80,783	85,234
Crude petroleum and petroleum products	26,853	25,351	27,655
Goods unloaded	59,612	51,101	58,844
Petroleum products	20,912	19,614	19,142

CIVIL AVIATION
(fiscal year)

	2017/18	2018/19	2019/20
Passengers ('000):			
domestic flights	23,702	19,913	18,539
international arrivals	5,997	4,836	4,217
international departures	6,046	4,898	4,246
Freight (excl. mail, metric tons):			
domestic flights	12,322	12,576	12,952
international arrivals	65,990	58,724	45,836
international departures	31,769	34,535	22,846
Mail (metric tons):			
domestic flights	2,412	1,262	1,173
international arrivals	1,512	1,114	1,028
international departures	906	1,612	1,094

Tourism

FOREIGN TOURIST ARRIVALS
(fiscal year)

Country of nationality	2016/17	2017/18	2018/19
Afghanistan	683,241	860,079	1,034,275
Azerbaijan	981,200	959,653	829,434
Iraq	1,398,201	1,356,185	2,598,230
Pakistan	242,087	273,273	304,677
Türkiye	444,200	573,849	947,033
Turkmenistan	104,859	149,949	170,984
Total (incl. others)	4,901,084	5,113,524	7,804,113

2019/20: Total tourist arrivals 8,832,050.

Source: Iran Cultural Heritage and Tourism Organization, Tehran.

Tourism receipts (US $ million, excl. passenger transport): 3,868 in 2015; 3,713 in 2016; 4,402 in 2017 (Source: World Tourism Organization).

Communications Media

	2019	2020	2021
Telephones ('000 main lines in use)*	28,954.9	29,093.6	29,306.8
Mobile telephone subscriptions ('000)*	118,061.4	127,625.0	135,889.4
Broadband subscriptions, fixed ('000)	8,626.2	9,564.2	10,674.9
Broadband subscriptions, mobile ('000)	66,533.7	77,706.9	91,844.3
Internet users (% of population)	72.5	75.6	78.6
Book production*:			
titles	105,486	n.a.	n.a.
copies ('000)	148,638	n.a.	n.a.
Newspapers and periodicals: titles*			
daily	356	n.a.	n.a.
others	6,924	n.a.	n.a.

* Twelve months beginning 21 March of year stated.

Source: partly International Telecommunication Union.

Education

(2019/20 unless otherwise indicated)

	Institutions	Teachers	Students ('000) Males	Females	Total
Special	1,701	14,399	49.8	30.5	80.3
Pre-primary	31,350	1,898*	519.7	505.1	1,024.8
Primary	66,484	229,226	4,266.4	4,027.3	8,293.6
Lower secondary:					
mainstream	26,020	} 129,671	1,769.2	1,652.4	3,421.6
adult	968		11.7	8.0	19.7
Upper secondary:					
mainstream	18,988	} 151,144	1,372.0	1,311.8	2,683.8
adult	5,235		149.2	101.0	250.2
Pre-university:					
mainstream*	8,593	} n.a.	177.3	263.3	440.6
adult*	1,068		24.1	19.3	43.4
Teacher training*	98	n.a.	16.6	18.9	35.5
Islamic Azad University†	n.a.	93,186	1,008.4	628.4	1,636.8
Other higher†	n.a.	192,879	1,541.8	1,625.4	3,167.2

* 2011/12.
† 2013/14.

Pupil-teacher ratio (qualified teaching staff, primary education, UNESCO estimate): 28.5 in 2016/17 (Source: UNESCO Institute for Statistics).

Adult literacy rate (UNESCO estimates): 88.7% (males 92.4%; females 85.0%) in 2021 (Source: UNESCO Institute for Statistics).

Directory

The Constitution

A draft constitution for the Islamic Republic of Iran was published on 18 June 1979. It was submitted to an Assembly of Experts, elected by popular vote on 3 August, to debate the various clauses and to propose amendments. The amended Constitution was approved by a national referendum on 2–3 December 1979. A further 45 amendments to the Constitution were approved by a referendum on 28 July 1989.

The Constitution states that the form of government of Iran is that of an Islamic Republic, and that the spirituality and ethics of Islam are to be the basis for political, social and economic relations. Persians, Turks, Kurds, Arabs, Balochis, Turkomans and others will enjoy completely equal rights.

The Constitution provides for a President to act as Chief Executive. The President is elected by universal adult suffrage for a term of four years. The President may not serve more than two terms consecutively. Legislative power is held by the Majlis-e-Shura-e Islami (Islamic Consultative Assembly), with 290 members (effective from the 2000 election) who are similarly elected for a four-year term. Provision is made for the representation of Zoroastrians, Jews and Christians.

All legislation passed by the Islamic Consultative Assembly must be sent to the Council for the Protection of the Constitution (Article 94), which will ensure that it is in accordance with the Constitution and Islamic legislation. The Council for the Protection of the Constitution consists of six religious lawyers appointed by the Wali Faqih (Guardian Jurist) and six lawyers appointed by the High Council of the Judiciary and approved by the Islamic Consultative Assembly. Articles 19–42 deal with the basic rights of individuals, and provide for equality of men and women before the law and for equal human, political, economic, social and cultural rights for both sexes.

The press is free, except in matters that are contrary to public morality or insult religious belief. The formation of religious, political and professional parties, associations and societies is free, provided they do not negate the principles of independence, freedom, sovereignty and national unity, or the basis of Islam.

Under the Constitution, the Wali Faqih acts as the Supreme Leader of the country, in the absence of the Imam Mehdi (the hidden Twelfth Imam). The amendments to the Constitution that were approved in July 1989 increased the powers of the presidency by abolishing the post of Prime Minister, formerly the Chief Executive of the Government.

The Government

SUPREME LEADER

Wali Faqih (Guardian Jurist): Ayatollah Seyed ALI HOSSEINI KHAMENEI.

HEAD OF STATE

President: Dr Seyed EBRAHIM RAISI (assumed office 5 August 2021).
First Vice-President: MOHAMMAD MOKHBER.
Head of the Presidential Office and Chief of Staff: GHOLAM HOSSEIN ESMAEILI.
Vice-President in charge of Executive Affairs: MOHSEN MANSOURI.
Vice-President and Head of the Administrative and Recruitment Affairs Organization: Dr MEYSAM LATIFI.
Vice-President and Head of the Planning and Budget Organization: Dr DAVOUD MANZOUR.
Vice-President and Head of the Foundation of Martyrs' and Veterans' Affairs: Dr Seyed AMIR HOSSEIN GHAZIZADEH HASHEMI.
Vice-President in charge of Legal Affairs: Dr MOHAMMAD DEHGHAN.
Vice-President for Parliamentary Affairs: Dr Seyed MOHAMMAD HOSSEINI.
Vice-President for Women and Family Affairs: Dr ENSIEH KHAZALI.
Vice-President and Head of the Atomic Energy Organization: MOHAMMAD ESLAMI.
Vice-President and Head of the Department of the Environment: Dr ALI SALAJEGHEH.
Vice-President for Science, Technology and Knowledge-based Economy: Dr ROUHOLLAH DEHGHANI FIROUZABADI.
President of the State Information Council: Dr SEPEHR KHALAJI.

CABINET
(September 2023)

Minister of Education: Dr REZA MORAD SAHRAEI.
Minister of the Interior: AHMAD VAHIDI.
Minister of Foreign Affairs: HOSSEIN AMIR ABDOLLAHIAN.
Minister of Intelligence: Seyed ESMAEIL KHATIB.

Minister of Energy: ALI AKBAR MEHRABIAN.
Minister of Economic Affairs and Finance: EHSAN KHANDOUZI.
Minister of Communications and Information Technology: EISA ZAREPOR.
Minister of Cultural Heritage, Tourism and Handicrafts: EZZATOLLAH ZARGHAMI.
Minister of Co-operatives, Labour and Social Affairs: Seyed SOLAT MORTAZAVI.
Minister of Science, Research and Technology: Dr MOHAMMAD ALI ZOLFIGOL.
Minister of Defence: MOHAMMAD REZA GHARAEI ASHTIANI.
Minister of Agriculture: Seyed MOHAMMAD ALI NIKBAKHT.
Minister of Health and Medical Education: BAHRAM EINOLLAHI.
Minister of Culture and Islamic Guidance: MOHAMMAD MEHDI ESMAEILI.
Minister of Industries, Mines and Trade: Dr ABBAS ALIABADI.
Minister of Petroleum: JAVAD OJI.
Minister of Justice: AMIR HOSSEIN RAHIMI.
Minister of Roads and Urban Development: MEHRDAD BAZRPASH.
Minister of Sport and Youth Affairs: KIOUMARS HASHEMI (acting).

MINISTRIES

Office of the President: POB 1423-13185, Pasteur Ave, Tehran 13168-43311; tel. (21) 64451; internet www.president.ir.

Ministry of Agriculture: Ayatollah Taleghani Ave, Vali-e-Asr Sq., Tehran; tel. (21) 64582040; fax (21) 64582042; e-mail pmaj@agri-jahad.ir; internet www.maj.ir.

Ministry of Communications and Information Technology: POB 15875-4415, Shariati St, Tehran 16314; tel. (21) 88431513; fax (21) 88464949; e-mail khajeh@ict.gov.ir; internet www.ict.gov.ir.

Ministry of Co-operatives, Labour and Social Affairs: Azadi St, Tehran; tel. (21) 64492425; fax (21) 66580102; e-mail infopack@mcls.gov.ir; internet www.mcls.gov.ir.

Ministry of Cultural Heritage, Tourism and Handicrafts: Tehran.

Ministry of Culture and Islamic Guidance: POB 11365-1515, Baharestan Sq., Tehran 11365; tel. (21) 33966050; fax (21) 33966059; e-mail info@farhang.gov.ir; internet www.farhang.gov.ir.

Ministry of Defence and Armed Forces Logistics: Shahid Yousuf Kaboli St, Sayed Khandan Area, Tehran; tel. (21) 26126988; e-mail info@mod.ir; internet www.mod.ir.

Ministry of Economic Affairs and Finance: Bab Homayoon St, Imam Khomeini Sq., Tehran 1114-943661; tel. (21) 33967208; fax (21) 33967615; e-mail info@mefa.ir; internet mefa.ir.

Ministry of Education: Si-e-Tir St, Imam Khomeini Sq., Tehran; tel. (21) 82281111; fax (21) 88805431; e-mail prm@medu.ir; internet www.medu.ir.

Ministry of Energy: POB 19968-33913, Niayesh Highway, Vali-e-Asr Ave, Tehran; tel. (21) 81606000; fax (21) 81606132; e-mail info@moe.gov.ir; internet www.moe.gov.ir.

Ministry of Foreign Affairs: Imam Khomeini Sq., Tehran; tel. (21) 66739191; fax (21) 61154275; e-mail info@mfa.gov.ir; internet www.mfa.gov.ir.

Ministry of Health and Medical Education: POB 310, Jomhouri Islami Ave, Hafez Crossing, Tehran 11344; tel. (21) 88363560; fax (21) 88364111; e-mail pr@behdasht.gov.ir; internet www.behdasht.gov.ir.

Ministry of Industries, Mines and Trade: POB 15996-91379, Somayyeh St, Ostad Negatollahi St, Karimkhan Ave, Tehran; tel. (21) 88907030; fax (21) 88907819; e-mail info@mimt.gov.ir; internet www.mimt.gov.ir.

Ministry of Intelligence: POB 16765-1947, Second Negarestan St, Pasdaran Ave, Tehran; tel. (21) 233031; fax (21) 23305.

Ministry of the Interior: Fatemi St, Tehran; tel. (21) 84861; fax (21) 88964678; internet www.moi.ir.

Ministry of Justice: Vali Asr Ave, Tehran 14167-83619; tel. (21) 82210000; fax (21) 82210000; e-mail info@justice.ir; internet www.justice.ir.

Ministry of Petroleum: Hafez Crossing, Taleghani Ave, Tehran 15936-57919; tel. (21) 61651; fax (21) 88939304; internet www.mop.ir.

Ministry of Roads and Urban Development: Dadman Tower, Africa Blvd, Tehran; tel. (21) 88878031; fax (21) 88888127; e-mail pr.mrud@mrud.ir; internet www.mrud.ir.

Ministry of Science, Research and Technology: Sanat Sq., Khovardin St, Tehran 14666–64891; tel. (21) 82231000; fax (21) 88575751; e-mail info@msrt.ir; internet www.msrt.ir.

Ministry of Sport and Youth Affairs: Building A, Seoul St, Enqelab Sport Complex, Tehran 19956-14118; tel. (21) 22662295; fax (21) 22660921; e-mail info@msy.gov.ir; internet msy.gov.ir.

President

Presidential Election, 18 June 2021

Candidate	Votes	%
Ebrahim Raisi	17,926,345	72.38
Mohsen Rezaei	3,412,712	13.77
Abdolnaser Hemmati	2,427,201	9.80
Amir-Hossein Ghazizadeh Hashemi	999,718	4.03
Total	**24,765,976***	**100.00**

* Excluding 4,167,028 invalid votes (14.40% of total votes cast).

Legislature

MAJLIS-E-SHURA-E ISLAMI—ISLAMIC CONSULTATIVE ASSEMBLY

Elections to the 11th Majlis took place on 21 February 2020. According to the Ministry of the Interior, overall voter turnout was 42.6%. Around 221 of the 290 seats were secured by conservatives and principlists (including those affiliated to the main principlist list, Unity of the Revolutionary Forces Coalition), while independents won some 38 seats and reformists 20; many reformist and centrist candidates had been disqualified by the Council of Guardians in advance of the elections. Five seats were reserved for candidates representing religious minorities. Run-off polls for 10 seats where no single candidate had secured more than 25% of the votes cast eventually took place on 11 September (having originally been scheduled for April, they were delayed owing to the COVID-19 pandemic).

Islamic Consultative Assembly: POB 11575-177, Baharestan Sq., Tehran 11576-12811; tel. (21) 39931; fax (21) 33440309; e-mail en@parliran.ir; internet www.parliran.ir.

Speaker: MOHAMMAD BAGHER GHALIBAF.

SHURA-YE ALI-YE AMNIYYAT-E MELLI—SUPREME NATIONAL SECURITY COUNCIL

Formed in July 1989 (in place of the Supreme Defence Council) to co-ordinate defence and national security policies, the political programme and intelligence reports, and social, cultural and economic activities related to defence and security. The Council is chaired by the President and includes a representative of the Wali Faqih, the Minister of the Interior, the Speaker of the Majlis, the Head of the Judiciary, the Chief of the Supreme Command Council of the Armed Forces, the Minister of Foreign Affairs, the Head of the Management and Planning Organization, and the Minister of Intelligence.

Secretary: Rear Adm. ALI AKBAR AHMADIAN.

MAJLIS-E KHOBREGAN—ASSEMBLY OF EXPERTS

Elections were held on 10 December 1982 to appoint an Assembly of Experts which was to choose an eventual successor to the Wali Faqih (then Ayatollah Khomeini) after his death. The Constitution provides for a three- or five-man body to assume the leadership of the country if there is no recognized successor on the death of the Wali Faqih. The Assembly comprises 88 clerics, who are elected by direct suffrage for an eight-year term. In accordance with electoral legislation approved in 2009, elections to a fifth term of the Assembly were delayed in order that they be held concurrently with elections to the Majlis on 26 February 2016. President Hassan Rouhani was among those elected on that date. Partial elections to the Assembly took place on 21 February 2020.

Assembly of Experts: Tehran; e-mail info@majleskhobregan.com; internet www.majlesekhobregan.ir.

Chairman: Ayatollah AHMAD JANNATI.

SHURA-E-NIGAHBAN—COUNCIL OF GUARDIANS

The Council of Guardians, composed of six qualified Muslim jurists appointed by Ayatollah Khomeini and six lay Muslim lawyers, appointed by the Majlis from among candidates nominated by the Head of the Judiciary, was established in 1980 to supervise elections and to examine legislation adopted by the Majlis, ensuring that it accords with the Constitution and with Islamic precepts.

Secretary: Ayatollah AHMAD JANNATI.

IRAN

SHURA-YE TASHKHIS-E MASLAHAT-E NEZAM—COUNCIL TO DETERMINE THE EXPEDIENCY OF THE ISLAMIC ORDER

Formed in February 1988, by order of Ayatollah Khomeini, to arbitrate on legal and theological questions in legislation approved by the Majlis, in the event of a dispute between the latter and the supervisory Council of Guardians. Its permanent members, defined in March 1997, are Heads of the Legislative, Judiciary and Executive Powers, the jurist members of the Council of Guardians, and the Minister or head of organization concerned with the pertinent arbitration. In October 2005 the powers of the Expediency Council were extended, allowing it to supervise all branches of government. The members of the Council are appointed for a term of five years.

Chairman: Ayatollah SADEQ AMOLI LARIJANI.

Political Organizations

Numerous political organizations were registered in the late 1990s, following the election of President Mohammad Khatami in 1997, and have tended to be regarded as either 'conservative' or 'reformist', the principal factions in the legislature. There are also a small number of centrist political parties. Under the Iranian electoral system, parties do not field candidates *per se* at elections, but instead back lists of candidates, who are allowed to be members of more than one party. In the mid-2000s there were estimated to be more than 100 registered political organizations, some of which are listed below:

Democratic Coalition of Reformists: Tehran; f. 2010; Sec.-Gen. MASSOUMEH EBTEKAR.

Eslahteleban-e Motedel (Moderate Reformists): Tehran; Leader ALI MOTAHARI.

Jebhe-ye Besiret ve Bidari-ye Eslami (Insight and Islamic Awakening Front): Tehran; Leader SHAHABEDDIN SADRI.

Jebhe-ye Istadegi (Resistance Front): Tehran.

Jebhe-ye Mottehed-e Osulgeraian (United Front of Principlists): Tehran; officially formed in 2008; reformed in 2012.

Jebhe-ye Paydari-ye Enghelab-e Eslami (Front of Islamic Revolution Stability): Tehran; internet www.jebhepaydari.ir; f. 2011; Sec.-Gen. SADEGH MAHSOULI.

Jebhe-ye Seda-ye Mellet (People's Voice Front): Tehran; f. 2011; Leader MOHSEN REZAI; Sec.-Gen. ALI MOTAHARI.

Jebhe-ye Touhid ve Edalet (Monotheism and Justice Front): Tehran; f. 2012; Leader MANOUCHEHR MOTTAKI; Sec.-Gen. ESFANDIAR RAHIM-MASHAE.

Labour Coalition (LC): Tehran; f. 2000; Leader HOSSEIN KAMALI; Sec.-Gen. SOHEILA JOLODARZADEH.

Most of the following are either registered political parties that have boycotted elections to the Majlis-e-Shura-e Islami (Islamic Consultative Assembly), or are unregistered organizations or guerrilla groups:

Alliance for Democracy and Freedom in Iran (ADFI): e-mail contact@adfiran.com; internet adfiran.com; f. 2023; seeks the establishment of a secular democracy in Iran; Leader REZA PAHLAVI.

Ansar-e Hezbollah (Helpers of the Party of God): f. 1995; militant, ultra-conservative youth movement; pledges allegiance to the Wali Faqih (supreme religious leader).

Daftar-e Tahkim-e Vahdat (Office for Strengthening Unity): Tehran; f. 1979; org. of Islamist university students who supported Mohammad Khatami in the presidential election of 1997 and reformist candidates in the Majlis elections of 2000; Sec.-Gen AMIRREZA BAKSHIPOUR.

Democratic Party of Iranian Kurdistan (PDKI) (Hizbi Demokirati Kurdistani Eran): 17 ave d'Italie, Paris 75013, France; tel. 1-45-85-64-31; fax 1-45-85-20-93; e-mail info@pdki.org; internet www.pdki.org; f. 1945; seeks a federal system of govt in Iran, in order to secure the national rights of the Kurdish people; faction led by Abdullah Hasanzadeh broke away in 2006 to form the Kurdistan Democratic Party-Iran (KDP-Iran), but reunited with the PDKI in Aug. 2023; consultative mem. of the Socialist International; Sec.-Gen. MUSTAFA HIJRI.

Fedayin-e-Khalq (Organization of the Iranian People's Fedayeen—Majority): Postfach 260268, 50515 Köln, Germany; e-mail kar@kar-online.com; internet kar-online.com; f. 1971; Marxist; Leader BEHROUZ KHALIQ.

Fraksion-e Hezbollah: f. 1996 by deputies in the Majlis who had contested the 1996 legislative elections as a loose coalition known as the Society of Combatant Clergy; Leader ALI AKBAR HOSSAINI.

Free Life Party of Kurdistan (Parti Jiyani Azadi Kurdistan—PJAK): f. 2004; militant org. that operates in mountainous areas of Iran and northern Iraq; apparently has close links with the Kurdistan Workers' Party (PKK—Partiya Karkeren Kurdistan) of Türkiye (Turkey); seeks a federal, secular system of govt in Iran, in order to secure the national rights of the Kurdish people; Leader ZILAN VEJIN.

Hezb-e Etemad-e Melli (National Confidence Party—NCP): Tehran; tel. (21) 88373305; fax (21) 88373306; f. 2005 by Mahdi Karrubi, fmrly of the Militant Clergy Association, shortly after his defeat in the presidential election of June; reformist, centrist; Sec.-Gen. MAHDI KARRUBI.

Hezb-e Hambastegi-ye Iran-e Islami (Islamic Iran Solidarity Party): f. 1998; reformist; Sec.-Gen. EBRAHIM ASGHARZADEH.

Hezb-e-Komunist Iran (Communist Party of Iran): POB 70445, 107 25 Stockholm, Sweden; e-mail dabirxane.cpi@gmail.com; internet cpiran.org; f. 1979 by dissident mems of Tudeh Party; Sec.-Gen. 'AZARYUN'.

Iran National Front (Jebhe Melli Iran): US Section, POB 136, Audubon Station, New York, NY 10032, USA; internet jebhemeliiran.org; f. late 1940s by the late Dr Muhammad Mussadeq; secular, pro-democracy opposition group, which also seeks to further religious freedom within Iran; Sec.-Gen. Seyyed HOSSEIN MOUSAVIAN.

Jame'e-ye Eslaami-e Mohandesin (Islamic Society of Engineers): f. 1988; conservative; mems incl. fmr President Mahmoud Ahmadinejad; Sec.-Gen. MUHAMMAD REZA BAHONAR.

Jebbeh-ye Mosharekat-e Iran-e Islami (Islamic Iran Participation Front): e-mail mail.emrooz@gmail.com; f. 1998; reformist, leftist; reportedly proscribed by the Iranian authorities in March 2010; Sec.-Gen. MOHSEN MIRDAMADI.

Komala Party of Iranian Kurdistan (Komala): e-mail secretariat@komala.org; internet www.komala.org; f. 1969; founded as Kurdish wing of the Communist Party of Iran (CPI); Marxist-Leninist; a breakaway faction led by Ebrahim Alizadeh retains a stronger affinity to the CPI; Sec.-Gen. ABDULLAH MOHTADI.

Marze Por Gohar (Glorious Frontiers Party): 1351 Westwood Blvd, Suite 111, Los Angeles, CA 90024, USA; tel. (310) 473-4763; fax (310) 477-8484; e-mail info@marzeporgohar.org; internet www.marzeporgohar.org; f. 1998 in Tehran; nationalist party advocating a secular republic in Iran; Chair. ROOZBEH FARAHANIPOUR.

Mujahidin-e-Khalq (Holy Warriors of the People): e-mail mojahed@mojahedin.org; internet www.mojahedin.org; Marxist-Islamist guerrilla group opposed to clerical regime; 10,000–15,000-strong military wing, the National Liberation Army, established 1987; mem. of the National Council of Resistance of Iran; based in Paris, France 1981–86 and in Baghdad, Iraq, 1986–2003; Leaders MARYAM RAJAVI, MASSOUD RAJAVI.

National Movement of the Iranian Resistance (NAMIR): Paris, France; internet www.namir.info; f. 1980; founded by Shapour Bakhtiar; centre-left.

Nehzat-e Azadi-ye Iran (Liberation Movement of Iran): e-mail nehzateazadi1340@gmail.com; f. 1961; emphasis on basic human rights as defined by Islam; Sec.-Gen. MOHAMMAD TAVASOLI.

Pan-Iranist Party: POB 31535-1679, Karaj; e-mail iran@paniranism.info; internet www.paniranist.org; calls for a Greater Persia.

Sazeman-e Mujahidin-e Enqelab-e Islami (Organization of the Mujahidin of the Islamic Revolution): reformist; Sec.-Gen. MUHAMMAD SALAMATI.

Sazeman e-Peykar dar Rahe Azadieh Tabaqe Kargar (Organization Struggling for the Freedom of the Working Class): Marxist-Leninist.

Tudeh Party of Iran (Party of the Masses): POB 100644, 10566 Berlin, Germany; tel. and fax (30) 3241627; e-mail dabirkhaneh_hti@yahoo.de; internet www.tudehpartyiran.org; f. 1941; declared illegal 1949; resumed legal activities 1979; banned April 1983.

Diplomatic Representation

EMBASSIES IN IRAN

Afghanistan: Dr Beheshti Ave, cnr of 4th St, Pakistan St, Tehran; tel. (21) 88737050; fax (21) 88372346; e-mail admin@afghanembassy.ir; internet www.afghanembassy.ir; Ambassador ABDUL QAYYUM SULAIMANI (acting).

Algeria: No. 20, 11th Alley, Sharia Mahestan, Shahrak-e-Ghods, Tehran 146575-3111; tel. (21) 88561882; fax (21) 88377031; e-mail embalg_teheran@yahoo.com; internet www.algeriaemb.ir; Ambassador ALI OROUJ.

Argentina: 6 Ghoo Alley, Yar Mohammadi Ave, Darrous, Tehran 15875-4335; tel. (21) 22577433; fax (21) 22577432; e-mail eiran@mrecic.gob.ar; internet eiran.cancilleria.gob.ar; Chargé d'affaires a.i. JORGE MARIANO JORDAN.

Armenia: 32 Ostad Shahriar St, Razi St, Jomhouri Islami Ave, Tehran 11337; tel. (21) 66704833; fax (21) 66700657; e-mail armiranembassy@mfa.am; internet iran.mfa.am; Ambassador Arsen Avakian.

Australia: 11 Yekta St, Valie Asr Ave, Tehran 19736-33651; tel. (21) 72068666; fax (21) 72068777; e-mail dfat-tehran@dfat.gov.au; internet www.iran.embassy.gov.au; Ambassador Lyndall Sachs.

Austria: 6–8 Bahonar St, Moghaddasi St, Ahmadi Zamani St, Tehran 19796-33755; tel. (21) 22750040; fax (21) 22705262; e-mail teheran-ob@bmeia.gv.at; internet www.bmeia.gv.at/oeb-teheran; Ambassador Wolf Dietrich Heim.

Azerbaijan: 16 Ratovan St, 3rd Neyestan St, Pasdaran, Tehran 19449-65114; tel. (21) 22554255; fax (21) 22558183; e-mail az.embassy.tehran@gmail.com; internet tehran.mfa.gov.az; Ambassador Ali Alizade.

Bangladesh: House No. 7, 64th St, 1st Alley, north of Yousef Abad, Tehran 14368-12345; tel. (21) 88601781; fax (21) 88605445; e-mail info@bangladoot.ir; internet tehran.mofa.gov.bd; Ambassador Manjurul Karim Khan Chowdhury.

Belarus: House 1, Azar Alley, Shahid Taheri St, Fallahi St, Zafaraniyeh Ave, Tehran 19887-93483; tel. (21) 22752229; fax (21) 22751382; e-mail iran@mfa.gov.by; internet iran.mfa.gov.by; Ambassador Dmitry Koltsov.

Belgium: POB 11365-115, 4 Agha Bozorghi St, Elahieh, Tehran 19646-16451; tel. (21) 22391909; fax (21) 22247313; e-mail teheran@diplobel.fed.be; internet iran.diplomatie.belgium.be; Ambassador Gianmarco Rizzo.

Benin: Abadan St, 3rd E Alley, Tehran; tel. (21) 22474820; fax (21) 22474821; Ambassador Azizo Imorou.

Bolivia: 79 Qareh Tapehei St, 2nd Floor, Kosar Sq., Saadat Abad Ave, Tehran; tel. (21) 88686807; fax (21) 88686808; Ambassador Romina Pérez.

Bosnia and Herzegovina: POB 19858, No. 4, 7th St, Iranzamin Ave, Shahrak Qods, Tehran; tel. (21) 88086929; fax (21) 88086930; e-mail bhembassyir@gmail.com; Ambassador Samir Veladžić.

Brazil: 2 Yekta St, Vali-e-Asr Ave, Zafaraniyeh, Tehran 19886-33854; tel. (21) 22753108; fax (21) 22752009; e-mail brasemb.teera@itamaraty.gov.br; internet teera.itamaraty.gov.br; Ambassador Laudemar Gonçalves de Aguiar Neto.

Brunei Darussalam: No. 7 Mina Blvd, Africa Ave, Tehran; tel. (21) 88797946; fax (21) 88770162; e-mail tehran.iran@mfa.gov.bn; Ambassador Avanj Ismail Abdul Manap.

Bulgaria: POB 11365-7451, Vali-e-Asr Ave, Tavanir Ave, 40 Nezami-e-Ganjavi St, Tehran; tel. (21) 88775662; fax (21) 88779680; e-mail embassy.tehran@mfa.bg; internet www.mfa.bg/embassies/iran; Ambassador Nikolina Kuneva.

Burkina Faso: Tehran; Ambassador (vacant).

Chile: 4 Hormouz St, Khazar Shomali Ave, Tehran; tel. (21) 26643700; fax (21) 26643826; e-mail echile.iran@minrel.gob.cl; internet chile.gob.cl/iran; Chargé d'affaires a.i. Sergio Toro Mendoza.

China, People's Republic: No. 73, Movahed Danesh Ave, Aghdassiyeh, Tehran; tel. (21) 22291240; fax (21) 22290690; e-mail chinaemb_ir@mfa.gov.cn; internet ir.chineseembassy.org; Ambassador Chang Hua.

Croatia: No. 213, W Lavasani St, Tehran; tel. (21) 22705090; fax (21) 22724222; e-mail iran@mvep.hr; Ambassador Dr Drago Štambuk.

Cuba: Bldg 54, 17th West, Khodaverdi St, Niavaran Sq., Tehran; tel. and fax (21) 22282749; e-mail embajada@ir.embacuba.cu; internet misiones.minrex.gob.cu/en/iran; Ambassador Alberto Gonzalez Casals.

Cyprus: No. 9, Mahmoud Razi St, Reza Ali Hosseini St, Zaferanieh, Tehran 19889-34611; tel. (21) 22219842; fax (21) 22219843; e-mail tehranembassy@mfa.gov.cy; internet www.mfa.gov.cy/embassytehran; Ambassador Andrias P. Kosopis.

Czech Republic: POB 11365-4457, No. 36, Nastaran Alley, Bostan St, North Pasdaran Ave, Upper Farmaniyeh Crossroads, Tehran; tel. (21) 26118851; fax (21) 22802079; e-mail teheran@embassy.mzv.cz; internet www.mzv.cz/tehran; Ambassador Josef Rychtar.

Denmark: POB 19395-5358, 10 Dashti St, Dr Shariati Ave, Hedayat St, Tehran 19148-61144; tel. (21) 28155000; fax (21) 22640007; e-mail thramb@um.dk; internet iran.um.dk; Ambassador Jesper Vahr.

Finland: POB 19395-1733, No. 2, Haddadian Alley, Mirzapour St, Dr Shariati Ave, Tehran 19336; tel. (21) 23512000; fax (21) 23512225; e-mail sanomat.teh@formin.fi; internet www.finland.org.ir; Ambassador Kari Kahiluoto.

France: 64–66 Neauphle-le-Château Ave, Tehran; tel. (21) 64094000; fax (21) 64094092; e-mail contact@ambafrance-ir.org; internet www.ambafrance-ir.org; Ambassador Nicolas Roche.

The Gambia: No. 10, Malek St, Shariati Ave, Tehran; tel. (21) 77500074; fax (21) 77529515; e-mail gambiaembassy_tehran@yahoo.co.uk; Ambassador Saeed Zare.

Georgia: 92, 2nd Golestan St, Pasdaran Ave, Tehran; tel. (21) 22782386; fax (21) 22542692; e-mail tehran.emb@mfa.gov.ge; internet www.iran.mfa.gov.ge; Ambassador Ioseb Chakhvashvili.

Germany: POB 11365-179, 324 Ferdowsi Ave, Tehran 11446-43416; tel. (21) 39990000; fax (21) 39991960; e-mail info@tehe.diplo.de; internet teheran.diplo.de; Ambassador Hans-Udo Mutzel.

Ghana: House No. 5, Amirie Sourie St, Zafarenieh, Tehran; tel. (21) 26230773; e-mail tehran@mfa.gov.gh; internet www.ghanaembassy-iran.com; Ambassador Eric Owusu-Boateng.

Greece: POB 11155-1151, 43 Esfandiar Ave, Vali-e-Asr Ave, Tehran 19679-15681; tel. (21) 22050533; fax (21) 22057431; e-mail gremb.teh@mfa.gr; internet www.mfa.gr/missionsabroad/en/iran.html; Ambassador Stylianos Gavril.

Holy See: Apostolic Nunciature, POB 11155-178, 84 Razi Ave, Crossroad Neauphle-le-Château Ave, Tehran; tel. (21) 66403574; fax (21) 66419442; e-mail nuntius_fars@fastmail.fm; Apostolic Nuncio Andrzej Józwowicz.

Hungary: POB 6363-19395, No. 10, Shadloo St, Hedayat Sq., Darrous, Tehran; tel. (21) 22596020; fax (21) 22596022; e-mail mission.thr@mfa.gov.hu; internet teheran.mfa.gov.hu; Ambassador Zoltan Varga.

India: POB 15875-4118, 22 Mir-Emad St, cnr of 9th St, Dr Beheshti Ave, Tehran; tel. (21) 88755103; fax (21) 88755973; e-mail hoc.tehran@mea.gov.in; internet www.indianembassytehran.gov.in; Ambassador Rudra Gaurav Shresth.

Indonesia: POB 11365-4564, Ghaem Magham Farahani Ave, No. 180, Tehran; tel. (21) 88716865; fax (21) 88718822; e-mail tehran.kbri@kemlu.go.id; internet kemlu.go.id/tehran; Ambassador Ronny Prasetyo Yuliantoro.

Iraq: 1640 Vali-e-Asr Ave, Damascus St, Tehran; tel. (21) 88938865; fax (21) 88938877; e-mail tehemb@mofa.gov.iq; internet mofamission.gov.iq/en/IranTeh; Ambassador Nasir Abdul Mohsen Abdullah Taki.

Italy: POB 4813-4863, 66–68 Neauphle-le-Château Ave, Tehran 11348-34814; tel. (21) 66726958; fax (21) 66726961; e-mail segreteria.teheran@esteri.it; internet www.ambteheran.esteri.it; Ambassador Giuseppe Perrone.

Japan: No. 162, Moghaddas Ardebili St, Tehran 19856-93653; tel. (21) 22660710; fax (21) 22660747; e-mail infoeoj@th.mofa.go.jp; internet www.ir.emb-japan.go.jp; Ambassador Ikawa Kazutoshi.

Jordan: No. 1553, 2nd Alley, North Zarafshan, Phase 4, Shahrak-e-Ghods, Tehran; tel. (21) 88088356; fax (21) 88080496; e-mail tehran@fm.gov.jo; Chargé d'affaires a.i. Nizar Nathir Mustafa al-Qaisi.

Kazakhstan: 83 North Hedayet St, cnr of Masjed Alley, Darrous, Tehran; tel. (21) 22565933; e-mail tehran@mfa.kz; internet www.mfa.gov.kz/tehran; Ambassador Askhat Orazbay.

Kenya: POB 19395-4566, 12 M. Ravanpour St, Africa Ave, Tehran; tel. (21) 22651080; fax (21) 22651083; e-mail tehran@mfa.go.ke; internet kenyaembassytehran.ir; Ambassador Joshua Gatimu.

Korea, Democratic People's Republic: 349 Shahid Dastjerdi Ave, Africa Ave, Tehran; tel. (21) 44828066; fax (21) 44815292; Ambassador Han Sung-Joo.

Korea, Republic: POB 11155-3581, No. 2, West Daneshvar St, Shaikhbahai Ave, Vanak Sq., Tehran; tel. (21) 88054900; fax (21) 88064899; e-mail emb-ir@mofa.go.kr; internet irn.mofa.go.kr; Ambassador Yun Kang-Hyeon.

Kuwait: Africa Ave, Mahiyar St, No. 15, Tehran; tel. (21) 88785997; fax (21) 88788257; Ambassador Bader Abdullah al-Munaikh.

Kyrgyzstan: POB 19579-35611, Bldg 12, 5th Naranjestan Alley, Pasdaran St, Tehran; tel. (21) 22854303; fax (21) 22281720; e-mail kgembassy.ir@mfa.gov.kg; internet mfa.gov.kg/en/dm/Embassy-of-the-Kyrgyz-Republic-in-the-Islamic-Republic-of-Iran; Ambassador Turdaqun Sediqov.

Lebanon: POB 11365-3753, No. 31, Shahid Kalantari St, Gharani Ave, Tehran; tel. (21) 88908451; fax (21) 88907345; Ambassador Hassan Abbas.

Libya: No. 72, Jasmine St, N Dibaji, Fermaneh, Tehran; tel. (21) 22418322; fax (21) 26418322; Ambassador Ali Juma Hassan Fudhail.

Malaysia: POB 868, North Zarafshan St, Eyvanak Blvd, Phase 4, Shahrak Qods, Tehran; tel. (21) 88072444; fax (21) 88078716; e-mail mwtehran@kln.gov.my; internet www.kln.gov.my/web/irn_tehran; Ambassador Khairi Omar.

Mali: No. 16, Aroos Alley, Istanbul St, Shariati Ave, Tehran; tel. (21) 22207278; fax (21) 22234631; e-mail malimissiontehran@yahoo.com; Ambassador Mohammed Maïga.

Mexico: POB 19156, No. 12, Golfam St, Nelson Mandela Ave, Tehran; tel. (21) 22057586; fax (21) 22057589; e-mail embiran@sre.gob.mx; internet embamex.sre.gob.mx/iran; Ambassador Guillermo Alejandro Puente Ordorica.

IRAN

Netherlands: POB 11155-138, No. 60 West Arghavan, Farmaniyeh, Tehran; tel. (21) 23660000; fax (21) 23660190; e-mail teh@minbuza.nl; internet www.netherlandsworldwide.nl/countries/iran; Ambassador FRANCISCOS JOHANS MARIA MOLLEN.

New Zealand: No. 1, 2nd Park Alley, 34 Sousan St, North Golestan Complex, Aghdassiyeh Ave, Niavaran, Tehran; tel. (21) 26122175; fax (21) 26121973; e-mail nzembassytehran@hotmail.co.nz; Ambassador MIKE WALSH.

Nicaragua: No. 79, 4th Floor, Ghare Tapei (25) St, Saadat Abad Ave, Tehran; tel. (21) 88685070; fax (21) 88685073; Ambassador ISAAC LENIN BRAVO JAEN.

Nigeria: 11 Sarvestan St, Elahieh, Tehran; tel. (21) 22636317; fax (21) 22636315; e-mail ngrembtehran@yahoo.com; internet nigeriaembassyiran.com; Ambassador SULEIMAN YAKUBU.

Norway: No. 72, Yasaman St. North Dibaji, Dr Lavasani Ave (Ex-Farmanieh), Tehran 19536-83513; tel. (21) 22291333; fax (21) 22292776; e-mail emb.tehran@mfa.no; internet www.norway.no/iran; Ambassador SIGVALD TOMIN HAUGE.

Oman: No. 12, Tandis Alley, Africa Ave, Tehran; tel. (21) 22128352; fax (21) 22044672; e-mail tehran@mofa.gov.om; Ambassador IBRAHIM BIN AHMAD AL-MOEINI.

Pakistan: Block No. 1, Ahmed Eitmadzadeh St, West Dr Hussain Fatemi Jamshedabad Shomali, Tehran 14118; tel. (21) 66944898; fax (21) 66944887; e-mail eoptehran@gmail.com; internet www.mofa.gov.pk/tehran; Ambassador MUHAMMAD MUDASSIR TIPU (designate).

Philippines: POB 19395-4797, 9 Khayyam St, Vali-e-Asr Ave, Tehran 19656-35113; tel. (21) 22668774; fax (21) 22668990; e-mail tehran.pe@dfa.gov.ph; internet tehranpe.dfa.gov.ph; Ambassador ROBERTO G. MANALO.

Poland: POB 11155-3489, No. 2, Pirouz St, Africa Expressway, Tehran 19176-63113; tel. (21) 88787262; fax (21) 87015222; e-mail teheran.amb.sekretariat@msz.gov.pl; internet teheran.msz.gov.pl; Ambassador MACIEJ FAŁKOWSKI.

Portugal: No. 16, Rouzbeh Alley, Hedayat Ave, Darrous, Tehran; tel. (21) 22582760; fax (21) 22552668; e-mail teerao@mne.pt; internet teerao.embaixadaportugal.mne.pt; Ambassador CARLOS RICO ANTONIO DA COSTA NEVES.

Qatar: No. 4, Nelson Mandela St, Tehran; tel. (21) 22029336; e-mail tehran@mofa.gov.qa; internet tehran.embassy.qa; Ambassador MOHAMMED BIN HAMAD AL-HAJRI.

Romania: 22 Shahid Meshki, Baharestan Ave, Tehran; tel. (21) 77647570; fax (21) 4569985; e-mail teheran@mae.ro; internet teheran.mae.ro; Ambassador MIRELA-CARMEN GRECU.

Russian Federation: 39 Neauphle-le-Château Ave, Tehran 11317-13811; tel. (21) 66701161; fax (21) 66701652; e-mail rusembiran@mid.ru; internet iran.mid.ru; Ambassador ALEXEY DEDOV.

Senegal: 39 Fereshteh St, Elahiyeh, Tehran; tel. (21) 22619569; fax (21) 22619579; e-mail senegal.embassy.ir@gmail.com; internet www.embassentehran.com; Ambassador SALIO DIENG.

Serbia: POB 11365-118, 4th St, N Falamak Ave, Shahrak-e-Quds, Tehran 19858; tel. (21) 88091529; fax (21) 88578291; e-mail serbembteh@neda.net; internet www.mfa.gov.rs; Ambassador DRAGAN TODOROVIĆ.

Sierra Leone: POB 11365-1689, No. 4, Bukan St, Sadeghi Ghomi St, Bahonar Ave, Niavaran, Tehran; tel. (21) 22721474; fax (21) 22721485; e-mail slembsy_tehran@yahoo.com; Ambassador ALIMAMY A. KAMARA.

Slovakia: POB 19395-6341, 72 Moghadassi St, Bahonar St, Niavaran, Tehran 19718-36199; tel. (21) 22740466; fax (21) 22758528; e-mail emb.tehran@mzv.sk; internet www.mzv.sk/web/teheran; Ambassador LADISLAV BALLEK.

Slovenia: N Kamranieh, Sheybani St, 24 Homayoun Farokh Alley, Tehran; tel. (21) 26152692; e-mail sloembassy.tehran@gov.si; internet tehran.embassy.si; Ambassador IGOR YUKICH (designate).

South Africa: POB 11365-7476, No. 5, Yekta St, Bagh-e-Ferdows, Vali-e-Asr Ave, Tehran; tel. (21) 22702866; fax (21) 2719516; e-mail tehran.admin@foreign.gov.za; internet www.southafricanembassy.ir/embassy; Ambassador VIKA MAZWI KHUMALO.

Spain: No. 10 Shadi St, Abbas Asadi St, Sharzad Blvd, Darrous, Tehran; tel. (21) 22568681; fax (21) 22568018; e-mail emb.teheran@maec.es; internet www.exteriores.gob.es/embajadas/teheran/es/paginas/inicio.aspx; Ambassador ÁNGEL LOSADA FERNÁNDEZ.

Sri Lanka: No. 66, Kafiabadi Alley, Shahid Fallahi St, Zafaranieh, Tehran; tel. (21) 22425297; fax (21) 22175471; e-mail slembiran@yahoo.com; Ambassador G. M. V. WISHWANATH APONSU.

Sweden: POB 19575-458, 27 Nastaran St, Boostan Ave, Tehran; tel. (21) 23712200; fax (21) 22296451; e-mail ambassaden.teheran@gov.se; internet www.swedenabroad.com/tehran; Ambassador MATTIAS LENTZ.

Switzerland: POB 19395-4683, No. 2 Yasaman St, Sharifimanesh Ave, Elahieh, Tehran 19649; tel. (21) 22008333; fax (21) 22006002; e-mail tehran@eda.admin.ch; internet www.eda.admin.ch/tehran; Ambassador NADIN OLIVIERI LOZANO; also represents interests of the USA in Iran.

Syrian Arab Republic: 19 Iraj St, Africa Ave, Tehran; tel. (21) 22052780; fax (21) 22059409; Ambassador SHAFIQ DAYOUB.

Tajikistan: No. 10, 3rd Alley, Shahid Zeynali St, Niavaran, Tehran; tel. (21) 22299584; fax (21) 22809299; e-mail tajemb.iran@gmail.com; internet mfa.tj/tg/main/country/ir; Ambassador NIZOMIDDIN ZOHIDI.

Thailand: No.7, Nahid Alley, N Kamranieh Rd, Tehran; tel. (21) 22808198; fax (21) 77532022; e-mail thaiembassy.thr@mfa.mail.go.th; internet tehran.thaiembassy.org; Ambassador PICHIT BOONSUD.

Tunisia: No. 7, 2nd Alley, North Zarafshan St, Sharak-e Ghods, Tehran; tel. (21) 88591639; fax (21) 88591647; e-mail at.teheran@diplomatie.gov.tn; Ambassador IMED RAHMOUNI (designate).

Türkiye (Turkey): POB 11446-43463, No. 337 Ferdowsi Ave, Tehran; tel. (21) 35951100; fax (21) 33117928; e-mail embassy.tehran@mfa.gov.tr; internet tehran.emb.mfa.gov.tr; Ambassador HICABI KIRLANGIÇ.

Turkmenistan: 34 Barati St, Vatanpour St, Tehran; tel. (21) 22206731; fax (21) 22206732; e-mail iran_mfa@online.tm; internet iran.tmembassy.gov.tm; Ambassador AKHMED GURBANOV.

Uganda: 59 Taheri St, Africa Blvd, Tehran; tel. (21) 22658506; fax (21) 22658516; e-mail tehran@mofa.go.ug; internet tehran.mofa.go.ug; Ambassador (vacant).

Ukraine: 10 Ghaderi Lane, Shahid Bahonar St, Tehran 19797-63417; tel. (21) 22397195; fax (21) 22397292; e-mail emb_ir@mfa.gov.ua; internet iran.mfa.gov.ua; Chargé d'affaires a.i. EVGENY KRAVCHENKO.

United Arab Emirates: POB 19395-4616, No. 337, Vahid Dastjerdi Ave, Vali-e-Asr Ave, Tehran; tel. (21) 42792000; fax (21) 88094293; e-mail tehranemb@mofa.gov.ae; Chargé d'affaires ALI EISSA AL-ZAABI.

United Kingdom: 172 Ferdowsi Ave, Tehran 11316-99813; tel. (21) 64052000; internet ukiniran.fco.gov.uk; Ambassador SIMON SHERCLIFF.

Uruguay: POB 19395-4718, No. 6, Mina Blvd, Africa Expressway, Tehran; tel. (21) 88679690; fax (21) 88782321; e-mail uruiran@mrree.gub.uy; Ambassador BERALDO NICOLA.

Uzbekistan: No. 6, Nastaran Alley, Boustan St, Pasdaran Ave, Tehran; tel. (21) 22299780; fax (21) 22299158; e-mail uzembiri@mail.ru; internet www.uzbekembassy.ir; Ambassador ABDULLAEV B. BAROTOVICH.

Venezuela: No. 17, Tajiki St, Kamranieh St North, Tehran; tel. (21) 22284450; fax (21) 26124886; internet emveniran.net; Ambassador JOSÉ RAFAEL SILVA APONTE.

Viet Nam: No. 54, Borzou St, Zaferanieh, Tehran; tel. (21) 22411670; fax (21) 22416045; e-mail vnemb.ir@mofa.gov.vn; internet vnembassy-tehran.mofa.gov.vn; Ambassador LUONG QUOC HUY.

Yemen: No. 8, 5 St, Velenjak Ave, Tehran; tel. (21) 22419945; fax (21) 22419934; e-mail emb.yemntehran@gmail.com; Ambassador IBRAHIM AL-DAILAMI (appointed by the al-Houthi government).

Zimbabwe: 6 Shad Avar St, Mogghadas Ardabili, Tehran; tel. (21) 88075479; e-mail zimtehran@zimfa.gov.zw; internet zimembassytehran.com; Ambassador BRIGHT KUPEMBA.

Judicial System

In August 1982 the Supreme Court revoked all laws dating from the previous regime that did not conform with Islam; in October all courts set up prior to the Islamic Revolution of 1979 were abolished. In June 1987 Ayatollah Khomeini ordered the creation of clerical courts to try members of the clergy opposed to government policy. A new system of *qisas* (retribution) was established, placing the emphasis on swift justice. Islamic codes of correction were introduced in 1983, including the amputation of a hand for theft, flogging for fornication and violations of the strict code of dress for women, and stoning for adultery. The Islamic revolutionary courts try those accused of crimes endangering national security, corruption, drug trafficking, and moral and religious offences. The Supreme Court has 33 branches, each of which is presided over by two judges.

Head of the Judiciary: GHOLAMHOSSEIN MOHSENI EJEHI.

Supreme Court: Chief Justice MOHAMMAD JAFAR MONTAZERI.

Prosecutor-General: MOHAMMAD MOVAHEDI AZAD.

IRAN

Religion

According to the 1979 Constitution, the official religion is Islam of the Ja'fari sect (Shi'a), but other Islamic sects, including Zeydi, Hanafi, Maleki, Shafe'i and Hanbali, are valid and will be respected. Zoroastrians, Jews and Christians will be recognized as official religious minorities. According to the 2016 census, there were 79,598,054 Muslims, 130,158 Christians (mainly Armenian), 23,109 Zoroastrians and 9,826 Jews in Iran.

ISLAM

The great majority of the Iranian people are Shi'a Muslims, but there is a minority of Sunni Muslims. Persians and Azerbaijanis are mainly Shi'a, while the other ethnic groups are mainly Sunni.

CHRISTIANITY

The Roman Catholic Church

Armenian Rite

Bishop of Esfahan: SARKIS DAVIDIAN, Armenian Catholic Bishopric, POB 11318, Hafez Ghazzali 29, Tehran; tel. (21) 66707204; fax (21) 66727533; e-mail arcaveso@yahoo.com.

Chaldean Rite

Archbishop of Ahvaz: (vacant), Archbishop's House, 334 Suleiman Farsi St, Ahvaz; tel. (61) 2224980ADMINISTRATOR RAMZI GARMOU (ARCHBISHOP OF TEHRAN).

Archbishop of Tehran: THOMAS MERAM, Archevêché, Enghelab St, Sayed Abbas Moussavi Ave 91, Tehran 15819; tel. (21) 88823549; fax (21) 88308714.

Archbishop of Urmia (Rezayeh) and Bishop of Salmas (Shahpour): THOMAS MERAM, Khalifagari Kaldani Katholiq, POB 338, 7 Mirzaian St, Orumiyeh 57135; tel. (441) 2222739; fax (441) 2236031; e-mail thmeram@yahoo.com.

Latin Rite

Archbishop of Esfahan: DOMINIQUE MATHIEU, Consolata Church, POB 11155-445, 73 Neauphle-le-Château Ave, Tehran; tel. (21) 66703210; fax (21) 66724749; e-mail latin.diocese@gmail.com.

The Anglican Communion

Anglicans in Iran are adherents of the Episcopal Church in Jerusalem and the Middle East, formally inaugurated in January 1976. The Bishop in Cyprus and the Gulf is resident in Cyprus.

Bishop in Iran: (vacant), POB 135, 81465 Esfahan; tel. (21) 5420452; fax (21) 88906908; internet dioceseofiran.org; diocese founded 1912.

Presbyterian Church

Synod of the Evangelical (Presbyterian) Church in Iran: POB 14395-569, Assyrian Evangelical Church, Khiaban-i Hanifnejad, Khiaban-i Aramanch, Tehran; tel. (21) 88006135; Moderator Rev. ADEL NAKHOSTEEN.

OTHER COMMUNITIES

Communities of Armenians, and somewhat smaller numbers of Zoroastrians, Jews, Assyrians, Greek Orthodox Christians, Uniates and Latin Christians are also found as officially recognized faiths. The Bahá'í faith, which originated in Iran, has about 350,000 Iranian adherents as of 2019, although at least 10,000 are believed to have fled since 1979 in order to escape persecution. The Government banned all Bahá'í institutions in August 1983.

The Press

Tehran dominates the media, as many of the daily papers are published there, and the bi-weekly, weekly and less frequent publications in the provinces generally depend on the major metropolitan dailies as a source of news. A press law announced in August 1979 required all newspapers and magazines to be licensed, and imposed penalties of imprisonment for insulting senior religious figures. Offences against the Act will be tried in the criminal courts. Under the Constitution, the press is free, except in matters that are contrary to public morality, insult religious belief, or slander the honour and reputation of individuals.

DAILY NEWSPAPERS (PRINT AND ONLINE)

Aftab-e-Yazd (Sun of Yazd): POB 13145-1134, Tehran; tel. (21) 66495833; fax (21) 66495835; e-mail aftab.yz@gmail.com; internet www.aftabeyazd.ir; f. 2000; Farsi; pro-reform.

Alik: POB 11365-953, 16 Mohebi St, North Sohrevardi Ave, Tehran 155588; tel. (21) 88768567; fax (21) 88760994; e-mail info@alikonline.ir; internet www.alikonline.ir; f. 1931; afternoon; Armenian; political, literary, cultural, social, sport; Editor DERENIK MELIKIAN.

Donya-e-Eqtesad (Economic World): POB 14157-44344, Tehran; tel. (21) 42710202; fax (21) 42710509; e-mail infotc@den.ir; internet www.donya-e-eqtesad.com; Farsi; Editor ALI MIRZAKHANI.

Entekhab (Choice): 16 Bayati St, Ibn Sina Sq., Tehran; tel. (91) 92673685; fax (21) 89773382; e-mail entekhab.news.agency@gmail.com; internet www.entekhab.ir; online only; Farsi; centrist; Man. Dir ALI MORADI.

Etemad (Confidence): e-mail info@etemaad.com; internet www.etemaad.ir; Farsi; pro-reform; Man. Dir ELIAS HAZRATI; Editor BEHROUZ BEHZADI.

Ettela'at (Information): Ettela'at Bldg, Mirdamad Ave, South Naft St, Tehran 15499; tel. (21) 29999; fax (21) 22258019; e-mail ettelaat@ettelaat.com; internet www.ettelaat.com; f. 1925; evening; Farsi; political and literary; operates under the direct supervision of velayat-e-faqih (religious jurisprudence); Man. Dir IRAJ JAVID.

Hambastegi (Solidarity): Tehran; internet www.hambastegidaily.com; Farsi; pro-reform; Editor SALEH ABADI.

Hamshahri (Citizen): POB 19395-5446, Tehran; tel. (21) 23023000; fax (21) 22046067; e-mail sales@agahihamshahri.com; internet www.hamshahrionline.ir; f. 1993; Farsi; conservative; economics, society and culture; owned by the Municipality of Tehran; Editor-in-Chief HOSSEIN GORBANZADEH.

Iran: POB 15875-5388, Tehran; tel. (21) 88761720; fax (21) 88761254; internet www.iran-newspaper.com; Farsi; conservative; connected to the Islamic Republic News Agency; Man. Dir MOHAMMAD FAZELI; Editor-in-Chief JAWAD DALIRI.

Iran News: POB 15875-8551, No. 13, Pajouhesh Lane, Golestan St, Marzdaran Blvd, Tehran; tel. (21) 44253448; fax (21) 44253395; e-mail info@irannewsdaily.com; internet www.irannewsdaily.com; f. 1994; English; Man. Dir FEREYDOON TAHERPOUR ASL.

Jam-e Jam: 129 Mirdamad Ave, Tehran; tel. (21) 23004000; fax (21) 22226252; e-mail info@jamejamonline.ir; internet www.jamejamonline.ir; online only; Farsi, English and French; conservative; linked to Islamic Republic of Iran Broadcasting; Man. Editor GHOLAM REZA NOURI.

Jomhouri-e-Eslami (Islamic Republic): Baharestan Sq., 115491-7711 Tehran; tel. (21) 77644420; fax (21) 77644418; e-mail info@jomhourieslami.net; internet www.jomhourieslami.net; f. 1980; Farsi; conservative; Man. Dir MASIH MOHAJERI.

Kayhan (Universe): Institute Kayhan, POB 11365-3631, Shahid Shahcheraghi Alley, Ferdowsi Ave, Tehran 11444; tel. (21) 33110251; fax (21) 33111120; e-mail kayhan@kayhan.ir; internet www.kayhannews.ir; f. 1941; evening; Farsi; political; also publishes Kayhan International (f. 1959; daily; English; Editor HAMID NAJAFI), Kayhan Arabic (f. 1980; daily; Arabic), Kayhan Persian (f. 1942; daily; Farsi), Zan-e Rooz (Today's Woman; f. 1964; weekly; Farsi), Kayhan Varzeshi (World of Sport; f. 1955; daily and weekly; Farsi), Kayhan Bacheha (Children's World; f. 1956; weekly; Farsi), Kayhan Farhangi (World of Culture; f. 1984; monthly; Farsi); owned and managed by Mostazafin Foundation from October 1979 until January 1987, when it was placed under the direct supervision of velayat-e-faqih (religious jurisprudence); Man. Dir HUSSEIN SHARIATMADARI.

Khorasan: Mashhad; Head Office: Khorasan Daily Newspapers, 14 Zohre St, Mobarezan Ave, Tehran; tel. (51) 37634000; fax (51) 37624395; e-mail info@khorasannews.com; internet www.khorasannews.com; f. 1948; Farsi; Editor SAEED ALI ALVI.

Quds Online: POB 91735-577, Khayyam Sq., Sajjad Blvd, Mashhad; tel. (51) 7685011; fax (511) 7684004; e-mail info@qudsonline.ir; internet www.qudsonline.ir; f. 1987; Farsi; owned by Astan Quds Razavi, the org. that oversees the shrine of Imam Reza at Mashhad; also publ. in Tehran.

Resalat (The Message): POB 11365-777, 53 Ostad Nejatollahi Ave, Tehran; tel. (21) 88902642; fax (21) 88900587; internet www.resalat-news.com; f. 1985; organ of right-wing group of the same name; Farsi; conservative; political, economic and social; Propr Resalat Foundation; Man. Dir SAYED MORTEZA NABAVI.

Shargh (East): 6 Alvand St, Arjantin Sq., Tehran; tel. (21) 88654392; internet www.sharghdaily.ir; f. 2003; Farsi; reformist; publ. suspended in August 2009, allowed to resume in March 2010; Man. Dir MEHDI RAHMANIAN; Editor AHMAD GHOLAMI.

Tehran Times: POB 14155-4843, 18 Bimeh Alley, Ostad Nejatollahi Ave, Tehran; tel. (21) 43051601; fax (21) 88808214; e-mail info@tehrantimes.com; internet www.tehrantimes.com; f. 1979; English; independent; Man. Dir MOHAMMAD SHOJAEIAN; Editor-in-Chief MOHAMMAD GHADERI.

PRINCIPAL PERIODICALS

Acta Medica Iranica: Shafa Bldg, Faculty of Medicine, Tehran University of Medical Sciences, 49 Italia St, Tehran 14174; tel. (21) 42910700; e-mail acta@tums.ac.ir; internet acta.tums.ac.ir; f. 1956; monthly; English; Editor-in-Chief AHMAD REZA DEHPOUR; circ. 2,000.

Bukhara: POB 15655-166, Tehran; tel. 9121300147; fax (21) 88958697; e-mail info@bukharamag.com; internet www.bukharamag.com; bi-monthly; Farsi; arts, culture and humanities; Editor ALI DEHBASHI.

Bulletin of the National Film Archive of Iran: POB 11155, Baharestan Sq., Tehran 11499-43381; tel. (21) 38512583; fax (21) 38512710; e-mail khoshnevis_nfai@yahoo.com; f. 1989; English; Editor M. H. KHOSHNEVIS.

Daneshmand (Scientist): POB 15875-3649, Tehran; tel. and fax (21) 86087211; e-mail info@daneshmandonline.ir; internet daneshmandonline.ir; f. 1963; monthly; Farsi; owned by Mostazafari Foundation; science and technology in Iran and abroad; Editor-in-Chief HAMED AZIMZADEGAN.

Donyaye Varzesh (World of Sports): Tehran; tel. (21) 3281; fax (21) 33115530; internet www.donyayevarzesh.com; weekly; sport; Editor G. H. SHABANI.

The Echo of Iran: 7104 Dudrow Ct., Springfield, VA 22150, USA; e-mail info@iranalmanac.com; internet www.iranalmanac.com; f. 1952; monthly; English; news, politics and economics; Editor FARJAM BEHNAM.

Echo of Islam: POB 14155-3899, Tehran; tel. (21) 88897663; fax (21) 88902725; internet www.echoofislam.com; quarterly; English; publ. by the Islamic Thought Foundation; Man. Dir Dr MAHDI GOLJAN; Editor-in-Chief S. MOUSAVI.

Iran Almanac: POB 14155-1168, 4 Hourtab Alley, Hafez Ave, Tehran; tel. and fax (932) 9139201; e-mail info@iranalmanac.com; internet www.iranalmanac.com; f. 2000; English; reference; history, politics, trade and industry, tourism, art, culture and society; Researcher and Editor FARJAM BEHNAM.

Iran Tribune: POB 111244, Tehran; e-mail matlab@iran-tribune.com; internet www.iran-tribune.com; monthly; English and Farsi; socio-political and cultural; Editor SALAH IRANDOOST.

Iran Who's Who: POB 14155-1168, 4 Hourtab Alley, Hafez Ave, Tehran; e-mail info@iranalmanac.com; internet www.iranalmanac.com; annual; English; Editor FARJAM BEHNAM.

Kayhan Bacheha (Children's World): Institute Kayhan, POB 11365-3631, Shahid Shahcheraghi Alley, Ferdowsi Ave, Tehran 11444; tel. (21) 33110251; fax (21) 333900025; e-mail keyhanbacheha@gmail.com; internet www.kayhanbacheha.ir; f. 1956; weekly; illustrated magazine for children; Editor ALI DANESHVAR.

Kayhan Varzeshi (World of Sport): Institute Kayhan, POB 11365-3631, Shahid Shahcheraghi Alley, Ferdowsi Ave, Tehran 11444; tel. (21) 33110246; fax (21) 33114228; internet www.kayhanvarzeshi.ir; f. 1955; weekly; Farsi; Man. Dir SEYYED MOHAMMAD SAEED MADANI.

Mahjubah: POB 14155-3899, Tehran; tel. (21) 88899663; fax (21) 88902725; internet www.mahjubah.com; Islamic family magazine; publ. by the Islamic Thought Foundation; Editor-in-Chief MINA SALIMI.

Soroush: Shahid Mostafa Motahari Ave, Tehran; tel. and fax (21) 88847602; internet www.soroushpub.com; f. 1972; one weekly magazine; four monthly magazines, one for women, two for adolescents and one for children; one quarterly review of philosophy; all in Farsi; Editor-in-Chief ALI AKBAR ASHARI.

Tavoos: POB 19395-6434, 6 Asgarian St, East Farmanieh Ave, Tehran 19546-44755; tel. (21) 22370597; fax (21) 22825447; e-mail info@tavoosonline.com; internet www.tavoosonline.com; quarterly; Farsi and English; arts; Man. Dir MANIJEH MIREMADI.

Tchissta: POB 13145-593, Tehran; tel. (21) 678581; e-mail daneshvamardom@tchissta.com; internet tchissta.com; Farsi; politics, society, science and literature; Editor-in-Chief PARVIZ SHAHRIARI.

ZamZam: POB 14155-3899, Tehran; tel. (21) 88934301; fax (21) 88902725; internet www.zamzam-mag.com; children's magazine; English; publ. by the Islamic Thought Foundation; Man. Dir MUHAMMAD HUSSEIN AHMEDI; Editor-in-Chief SHIVA MIRHASSANI.

NEWS AGENCIES

Fars News Agency: Ferdawsi Sq., 36717-15999 Tehran; tel. (21) 42082000; e-mail info@farsnews.ir; internet www.farsnews.ir; f. 2003; independent; news in Farsi and English; Man. Dir Dr PAYAM TIRANDAZ.

Iranian Quran News Agency (IQNA): 97 Bozorgmehr St, Qods Ave, Tehran; tel. (21) 66470212; fax (21) 66970769; e-mail info@iqna.ir; internet www.iqna.ir; f. 2003; general news and news on Koranic activities.

Islamic Republic News Agency (IRNA): POB 764, 873 Vali-e-Asr Ave, Tehran; tel. (21) 88902050; fax (21) 88800171; e-mail irna@irna.ir; internet www.irna.ir; f. 1934; state-controlled; Man. Dir ALI NADERI.

Mehr News Agency: 32 Bimeh Alley, Nejatollahi St, Tehran; tel. (21) 43051000; fax (21) 88805801; e-mail info@mehrnews.com; internet www.mehrnews.com; f. 2003; news in Farsi, English and Arabic; Man. Dir MOHAMMAD MAHDI RAHMATI.

PRESS ASSOCIATION

Association of Iranian Journalists: No. 87, 7th Alley, Shahid Kabkanian St, Keshavarz Blvd, Tehran; tel. (21) 88956365; fax (21) 88963539; e-mail generalsecretary@aoij.org; Pres. RAJABALI MAZROOEI; Sec. BADRALSADAT MOFIDI.

Publishers

Amir Kabir Book Publishing and Distribution Co: POB 11365-4191, Jomhouri Islami Ave, Esteghlal Sq., Tehran; tel. (21) 33900751; fax (21) 33903747; e-mail info@amirkabir.net; internet www.amirkabir.net; f. 1948; historical, philosophical, social, literary and children's books; Dir AHMAD NESARI.

Avayenoor Publications: 99 Shahid Nazari St, Farvardin St, Inqelab Sq., Tehran; tel. (21) 66967355; fax (21) 66488058; e-mail info@avayenoor.com; internet www.avayenoor.com; f. 1988; sociology, politics and economics; Editor-in-Chief SAYED MOHAMMAD MIRHOSSEINI.

Caravan Books Publishing House: POB 186-14145, 18 Salehi St, Sartip Fakouri Ave, Northern Karegar Ave, Tehran 14136; tel. (21) 88007421; fax (21) 88029486; e-mail info@caravan.ir; internet caravan.ir; f. 1997; fiction and non-fiction; Chief Editor ARASH HEJAZI.

Echo Publishers & Printers: POB 14155-1168, 4 Hourtab Alley, Hafez Ave, Tehran; tel. and fax (21) 22930477; e-mail info@iranalmanac.com; internet www.iranalmanac.com; f. 2000; politics, economics and current affairs; Man. FARJAM BEHNAM.

Eghbal Publishing Organization: 273 Dr Ali Shariati Ave, Tehran 16139; tel. (21) 77500973; fax (21) 7768113; f. 1903; Man. Dir SAEED EGHBAL.

Farhang Moaser: 28 Fariman St, Taleghani Ave, Tehran 13147; tel. (21) 66952632; fax (21) 66417018; e-mail info@farhangmoaser.com; internet www.farhangmoaser.com; dictionaries.

Gooya Publications: 91 Karim Khan St, Tehran; tel. (21) 88313431; fax (21) 46293860; e-mail gooya.publishing@gmail.com; internet www.gooyabooks.com; f. 1981; art; Dir NASER MIR BAGHERI.

Iran Chap Co: Ettela'at Bldg, Mirdamad Ave, South Naft St, Tehran; tel. (21) 29999; fax (21) 22258022; e-mail ettelaat@ettelaat.com; internet www.ettelaat.com; f. 1966; newspapers, books, magazines, book-binding and colour printing; Man. Dir IRAJ JAVID.

Iran Exports Publication Co Ltd: POB 16315-1773, 41 First Mehr Alley, Mirzapour St, Shariati Ave, Tehran; tel. (21) 22200646; fax (21) 22888505; internet www.iranexportsmagazine.com; f. 1987; business and trade pubs in English; Editor-in-Chief and Dir of Int. Affairs AHMAD NIKFARJAM.

Ketab Sara Co: POB 15117-38951, Tehran; tel. (21) 88717636; fax (21) 88717819; e-mail info@ketabsara.ir; internet www.ketabsara.ir; f. 1980; CEO SADEGH SAMII.

Kowkab Publishers: POB 14455-168, Tehran; tel. (21) 36454585; fax (21) 36454585; e-mail fatemi.bahman@gmail.com; internet www.kowkabpublishers.com; engineering, science, medicine, humanities, reference; Man. Dir Dr AHMAD GHANDI.

The Library, Museum and Documentation Center of the Islamic Consultative Assembly (Ketab-Khane, Muze va Markaz-e Asnad-e Majlis-e-Shura-e Islami): POB 11365-866, Ketab-Khane Majlis-e-Shura-e Islami No. 1, Baharestan Sq., Tehran; tel. (21) 33137810; fax (21) 33137813; f. 1912 as Majlis Library; renamed as above in 1996; arts, humanities, social sciences, politics, Iranian and Islamic studies; Dir SAYED MOHAMMAD ALI AHMADI ABHARI.

Ofoq Publishers: 181 Nazari St, 12th Farvardin St, Tehran 13145-1135; tel. (21) 66413367; fax (21) 66414285; e-mail info@ofoqco.com; internet www.ofoqco.com; f. 1990; illustrated books for children and teenagers, adult fiction and non-fiction; Dir REZA HASHEMINEJAD.

Qoqnoos Publishing Group: 111 Shohadaye Jandarmeri St, Enqelab Ave, Tehran; tel. (21) 66408640; fax (21) 66413933; e-mail pub@qoqnoos.ir; internet www.qoqnoos.ir; f. 1977; fiction, history, philosophy, law, sociology, psychology, and children's books; privately owned; Owner and Gen. Man. AMIR HOSSEINZADEGAN.

Sahab Geographic and Drafting Institute: POB 11365-617, 30 Somayeh St, Hoquqi Crossroads, Dr Ali Shariati Ave, Tehran 16517; tel. (21) 77535706; fax (21) 77535876; e-mail info@sahabmap.com;

internet www.sahabmap.com; f. 1936; maps, atlases, and books on geography, science, history and Islamic art; Man. Dir MUHAMMAD REZA SAHAB.

Soroush Press: POB 15875-1163, Soroush Bldg, Motahari Ave, Mofatteh Crossroads, Tehran; tel. (21) 88300760; fax (21) 88345488; internet www.soroushpub.com; part of Soroush Publication Group, the publs dept of Islamic Republic of Iran Broadcasting; publishes books, magazines and multimedia products on a wide range of subjects; Man. Dir ALI AKBAR ASHARI.

Tehran University Press: 16th St, North Karegar St, Tehran; tel. (21) 88012080; fax (21) 88012077; e-mail press@ut.ac.ir; internet press.ut.ac.ir; f. 1944; univ. textbooks; Man. Dir Dr MUHAMMAD SHEKARCIZADEH.

Broadcasting and Communications

TELECOMMUNICATIONS

Telecommunications Co of Iran (TCI): 60 Lotfi St, Haft Tir Sq., Tehran 15898-53811; tel. (21) 87870000; e-mail pr@tci1.ir; internet tci1.ir; fmrly 100% state-owned; 51% stake acquired by Etemad-e-Mobin consortium 2009; Chair. MOHAMMAD SHAHSAWARI.

Mobile Communications Co of Iran (MCI): 88 Hamrah Tower, Vanak St, Vanak Sq., Tehran, 19919-54651; tel. (21) 81711; fax (21) 29999900; e-mail info@mci.ir; internet www.mci.ir; f. 2004; wholly owned subsidiary of TCI; CEO MEHDI AKHAVAN BEHABADI.

MTN Irancell: 5 Alidoust Alley, Qaderi St, Heravi Sq., Tehran; tel. 9377000000; e-mail cs@mtnirancell.ir; internet irancell.ir; f. 2004 as Irancell, name changed as above 2005; mobile telecommunications; consortium of Iran Electronic Devt Co (51%) and MTN (South Africa—49%); 50.4m. subscribers (Dec. 2021); Chair. and CEO BIJAN ABBASI.

RighTel Telecommunications Services Co: 8 Mehrdad St, West Armaghan St, Past Niyayesh Crossroad, Vali-e-Asr St, Tehran 19678-63311; tel. (21) 22047085; fax (21) 26214696; e-mail pr@rightel.ir; internet www.rightel.ir; f. 2007 as Tamin Telecom; owned by the Social Security Investment Org; launched 3G mobile telephone services in 2013; Chair. MOHAMMAD REZA SHAHRIARI; Man. Dir YASER REZAKHAH.

Regulatory Authority

Communications Regulatory Authority (CRA): CRA Tower, Shariati St, Sayyad Khandan Bridge, Tehran 16317-13761; tel. (21) 89661204; e-mail public_relation@cra.ir; internet www.cra.ir; f. 2003; affiliated to the Ministry of Communications and Information Technology; Pres. HOSSEIN FALLAH JOUSHAGHANI.

BROADCASTING

Article 175 of Iran's Constitution prohibits the establishment of private television channels and radio stations that are deemed to be 'un-Islamic'. However, in addition to the channels operated by the state-controlled Islamic Republic of Iran Broadcasting, many Iranians have access to foreign television programmes transmitted via satellite dishes (although ownership of these is officially banned).

Islamic Republic of Iran Broadcasting (IRIB): Jam-e Jam St, Vali-e-Asr Ave, Tehran 19395-3333; tel. (21) 22652880; e-mail pr.media@irib.ir; internet www.irib.ir; semi-autonomous authority, affiliated with the Ministry of Culture and Islamic Guidance; non-commercial; operates seven national and 30 provincial television stations, and nine national radio networks; broadcasts worldwide in 27 languages; launched Al-Alam (international Arabic-language news channel) in 2002 and Press TV (English-language satellite channel) in 2007; Pres. PEYMAN JEBELI.

Radio

Radio Network 1 (Voice of the Islamic Republic of Iran): Covers the whole of Iran and also reaches Europe, Asia, Africa and part of the USA via short-wave and the internet; medium-wave regional broadcasts in local languages: Arabic, Armenian, Assyrian, Azerbaijani, Balochi, Bandari, Dari, Farsi, Kurdish, Mazandarani, Pashtu, Turkish, Turkoman and Urdu; external broadcasts in English, French, German, Spanish, Italian, Turkish, Bosnian, Albanian, Russian, Georgian, Armenian, Azeri, Tajik, Kazakh, Arabic, Kurdish, Urdu, Pashtu, Dari, Hausa, Bengali, Hindi, Japanese, Mandarin, Kiswahili, Indonesian and Hebrew.

Television

Television Network 1 (Vision of the Islamic Republic of Iran): 625-line, System B; Secam colour; two production centres in Tehran producing for national networks and 30 local television stations.

Finance

BANKING

Central Bank

Bank Markazi Jomhouri Islami Iran (Central Bank of Iran—CBI): POB 15875-7177, 198 Mirdamad Blvd, Tehran; tel. (21) 29954855; fax (21) 29954780; e-mail g.secdept@cbi.ir; internet www.cbi.ir; f. 1960; Bank Markazi Iran until 1983; issuing bank, govt banking; Gov. MOHAMMAD REZA FARZIN.

State-owned Commercial Banks

Bank Keshavarzi Iran (Agriculture Bank of Iran): POB 14155-6395, 247 Patrice Lumumba Ave, Jalal al-Ahmad Expressway, Tehran 14459–94316; tel. (21) 88287070; fax (21) 88253625; e-mail info@bki.ir; internet www.bki.ir; f. 1980 by merger of Agricultural Co-operative Bank of Iran and Agricultural Devt Bank of Iran; Chair. and Man. Dir FARSHID FARROKHNEJAD.

Bank Mellat (Nation's Bank): Head Office Bldg, 327 Taleghani Ave, Tehran 15817; tel. (21) 82962440; fax (21) 88515919; e-mail info@bankmellat.ir; internet www.bankmellat.ir; f. 1980 by merger of 10 fmr private banks; Chair. and Man. Dir REZA DOLATABADI.

Bank Melli Iran (National Bank of Iran): POB 11365-171, Ferdowsi Ave, Tehran; tel. (21) 66731382; fax (21) 66738606; e-mail pr@bmi.ir; internet bmi.ir; f. 1928; present name since 1943; Chair. ABOLFAZL NAJJARZADEH (acting).

Bank Refah Kargaran: 2584 before Vanak Sq., Vali Asr Ave, Tehran 19917-56783; tel. (21) 88653991; fax (21) 42504292; e-mail farad@bankrefah.ir; internet www.refah-bank.ir; f. 1960; CEO Dr ISMAIL ALLAHGANI.

Bank Saderat Iran: POB 15745-631, Bank Saderat Tower, 43 Somayeh Ave, Tehran; tel. (21) 8829469; fax (21) 88839539; e-mail hbsi@bsi.ir; internet www.bsi.ir; f. 1952; Man. Dir SIDZIA IMANI.

Bank Sepah: Negin Sepah Bldg, Nowrouz St, Africa Hwy, Argentina Sq., Tehran 15196-62840; tel. (21) 88647001; fax (21) 88647028; e-mail info@banksepah.ir; internet www.banksepah.ir; f. 1925; nationalized in June 1979; CEO Dr AYATOLLAH EBRAHIMI.

Post Bank of Iran (PBI): 237 Motahari Ave, Tehran 15876-18118; tel. (21) 88505885; fax (21) 88502027; e-mail info@postbank.ir; internet www.postbank.ir; f. 2006; Man. Dir BEHZAD SHIRI.

Private Commercial Banks

Bank Pasargad (BPI): POB 19697-74511, 430 Mirdamad Ave, Tehran; tel. (21) 88649502; fax 88649501; e-mail info@bpi.ir; internet bpi.ir; f. 2005; CEO Dr MAJID GHASEMI.

Eghtesad Novin Bank (EN Bank): POB 19395-3796, 24 Esfandiar Blvd, Vali-e-Asr Ave, Tehran 196865-5944; tel. (21) 82330000; fax (21) 88880166; e-mail info@enbank.ir; internet enbank.ir; f. 2001; granted operating licence in 2001; CEO ALIREZA BOLGOURI.

Karafarin Bank: POB 196691-6461, No. 97, West Nahid St, Vali-e-Asr Ave, Tehran; tel. (21) 26215000; fax (21) 26214999; e-mail info@karafarinbank.net; internet www.karafarinbank.ir; f. 1999 as Karafarin Credit Institute; converted into private bank in 2001; CEO Dr AHMED BAHARUNDI.

Parsian Bank: 4 Zarafshan St, Farahzadi Blvd, Shahrak Ghods, Tehran 14677-93811; tel. (21) 81151000; fax (21) 88362744; e-mail info@parsian-bank.ir; internet parsian-bank.ir; f. 2002; Man. Dir Dr KOUROSH PARVIZIAN.

Saman Bank Corpn: 2 Tarkeshdooz St, Vali-e-Asr Ave, Tehran; tel. (21) 23095100; fax (21) 26211043; e-mail info@sb24.com; internet www.sb24.com; f. 2001; CEO ALIREZA MARAFET.

Sarmayeh Bank: POB 19395-6415, 24 Arak St, Gharani Ave, Tehran; tel. (21) 84245245; fax (21) 84245138; e-mail info@sbank.ir; internet www.sbank.ir; f. 2005; Chair. MORTEZA POURMARASHI; Man. Dir FARAJOLLAH QADAMI.

Tejarat Bank: POB 11365-5416, 130 Taleghani Ave, Nejatoullahie, Tehran 15986–17818; tel. (21) 88826690; fax (21) 88893641; e-mail info@tejaratbank.ir; internet www.tejaratbank.ir; f. 1979 by merger of 12 banks; partially privatized in 2009, with the Govt retaining a 20% minority share; Chair. A. M. RAZAZAN; Man. Dir HADI AKHLIK FAIZ ATAR.

Development Banks

Bank of Industry and Mine (BIM): POB 15875-4456, Firouzeh Tower, 2917 Vali-e-Asr Ave (above Park Way Junction), Tehran; tel. (21) 22029811; fax (21) 22029854; e-mail info@bim.ir; internet www.bim.ir; f. 1979 by merger of Industrial Credit Bank, Industrial and Mining Devt Bank of Iran, Devt and Investment Bank of Iran, and Iranian Bankers Investment Co; state-owned; CEO ALI KHORSANDIAN.

Export Development Bank of Iran (EDBI): POB 151674-7913, Tose'e Tower, 15th St, Ahmad Ghasir Ave, Argentina Sq., Tehran

151383–5711; tel. (21) 88709022; fax (21) 88702848; e-mail info@edbi.ir; internet www.edbi.ir; f. 1991; state-owned; Chair. and Man. Dir Dr Seyed ALI HOSSEINI.

Housing Bank

Bank Maskan (Housing Bank): POB 19947-63811, 14 Attar St, Vali-e-Asr Ave, Vanak Sq., Tehran; tel. (21) 82932339; fax (21) 82932735; e-mail intl_div@bank-maskan.ir; internet bank-maskan.ir; f. 1979; state-owned; provides mortgage and housing finance; Chair. NADER GHASEMI; Man. Dir ALI ASGARI.

SOVEREIGN WEALTH FUND

National Development Fund of Iran: 25 National Development Fund Bldg, Gandhi St, Argentina Sq, Tehran; tel. (21) 42855000; fax (21) 88640440; internet www.ndf.ir; f. 2011; Chair. Dr MEHDI GHAZANFARI.

STOCK EXCHANGE

Tehran Stock Exchange: 192 Hafez Ave, Tehran 11355; tel. (21) 66719535; fax (21) 66710111; e-mail int@tse.ir; internet www.tse.ir; f. 1967; 334 listed cos (31 March 2020); Dir-Gen. Dr MAHMOUD GOUDARZI.

INSURANCE

The nationalization of insurance companies was announced in June 1979. However, as part of the reforms to the financial sector undertaken by the former Khatami administration, four new private insurance companies were licensed to commence operations in May 2003.

Bimeh Alborz (Alborz Insurance Co): POB 4489-15875, Alborz Bldg, 234 Sepahboad Garani Ave, Tehran 19137-7151; tel. (21) 88803821; fax (21) 88908088; e-mail info@bimehalborz.ir; internet www.alborzinsurance.ir; f. 1959; all types of insurance; Chair. MAJID ALIPANAHI; Man. Dir MOHSEN POURKIANI.

Bimeh Asia (Asia Insurance Co): POB 15815-1885, Taleghani Ave, Tehran; tel. (21) 88800950; e-mail info@asiainsurance.ir; internet www.bimehasia.com; f. 1959; all types of insurance; Chair. FAZLULLAH MOAZZAMI; Man. Dir M. BADIN.

Bimeh Dana (Dana Insurance Co): 2 15th St, Ghandi Ave, Tehran 151789-1197; tel. (21) 88770971; fax (21) 88792997; e-mail info@dana-insurance.com; internet www.dana-insurance.com; f. 1988; 56% govt-owned; life, personal accident and health insurance; CEO REZA JAFARI.

Bimeh Day (Day Insurance Co): 239 Mirdamad Blvd, Tehran 191895-5311; tel. and fax (21) 22900516; e-mail info@dayins.com; internet www.dayins.com; f. 2004; privately owned; all types of insurance; Chair. SEYYED MAJID BAKHTIARI.

Bimeh Iran (Iran Insurance Co): 107 Western Brazil Ave, Vanak, Tehran 14155-6363; tel. (21) 86092238; fax (21) 88954698; e-mail iad@iraninsurance.ir; internet www.iraninsurance.ir; f. 1935; state-owned; all types of insurance; Chair. and CEO HASAN SHARIFI.

Bimeh Karafarin (Karafarin Insurance Co): No. 5, 17th St, Qasir St, Tehran 151384-6911; tel. (21) 42563000; fax (21) 88713988; e-mail info@karafarin-insurance.ir; internet www.karafarin-insurance.ir; f. 2003; privately owned; all types of insurance; Man. Dir MOHAMMAD HEYDARI.

Bimeh Novin (Novin Insurance Co): POB 5888-15875, 11 Behrouz St, Madar (Mohseni) Sq., Mirdamad Blvd, Tehran 191193-3183; tel. (21) 22277775; fax (21) 22923846; e-mail info@novininsurance.com; internet www.novininsurance.com; f. 2006; privately owned; all types of insurance; CEO HUSSEIN KARIM KHAN ZAND.

Bimeh Saman (Saman Insurance Co): 433 Seyed Jamaluddin Asadabadi St, Tehran 143493-3574; tel. (21) 8943; e-mail mailroom@samaninsurance.ir; internet www.si24.ir; f. 2005; privately owned; Chair. KHOSROW FAKHIM HASHEMI; Man. Dir AHMAD REZA ZARABIEH.

Bimeh Sina (Sina Insurance Co): 225 Mir Damad Blvd, Tehran; tel. (21) 88342966; fax (21) 28371030; e-mail info@sinainsurance.com; internet www.sinainsurance.com; f. 2003; privately owned; Man. Dir ABDULLAH SOLTANI THANI.

Mellat Insurance Co: 48 Shahid Haghani Expressway, Vanak Sq., Tehran; tel. and fax (21) 88878814; e-mail info@melat.ir; internet www.mellatinsurance.com; privately owned; property, life, engineering, aviation and marine insurance; Chair. BEHRANG ESADI; Man. Dir Dr ALIREZA YAZDANDOOST.

Regulatory Authority

Bimeh Markazi Iran (Central Insurance of Iran): POB 19395-5588, 2 Maryam St, Africa Ave, Tehran 196786-4111; tel. (21) 24551000; fax (21) 22054099; e-mail secretariat@centinsur.ir; internet www.centinsur.ir; f. 1971; regulates and supervises the insurance market and tariffs for new types of insurance cover; the sole state reinsurer for domestic insurance cos, which are obliged to reinsure 50% of their direct business in life insurance and 25% of business in non-life insurance with Bimeh Markazi Iran; CEO MAJID BEHZADPOUR.

Trade and Industry

GOVERNMENT AGENCIES

Atomic Energy Organization of Iran (AEOI): Tehran; tel. (21) 82060; fax (21) 88221042; e-mail web_publicr@aeoi.org.ir; internet aeoi.org.ir; f. 1974; Pres. MOHAMMAD ESLAMI.

Iranian Space Agency (ISA): 34 Shahid Soltani St, Vali Asr Ave, Tehran; tel. (21) 233440; fax (21) 22029000; e-mail info@isa.ir; internet isa.ir; f. 2003; Pres. HASSAN SALARIEH.

CHAMBERS OF COMMERCE

Iran Chamber of Commerce, Industries and Mines: 175 Taleghani Ave, Tehran 15836-48499; tel. (21) 85730000; e-mail info@iccima.ir; internet en.iccima.ir; supervises the affiliated 32 local chambers; Pres. GHOLAM HOSSEIN SHAFEI; Sec.-Gen. MOHAMMAD REZA MOLLA RAMEZANI.

Esfahan Chamber of Commerce, Industries, Mines and Agriculture: POB 81656-336, Feyz Sq., Esfahan; tel. (3) 6560000; fax (3) 6613636; e-mail info@eccim.com; internet www.eccim.com; Pres. MASOUD GOLSHIRAZI; Sec.-Gen. BEHNAM EBRAHIMI.

Shiraz Chamber of Commerce, Industries and Mines: POB 71867-89565, Qasr Dasht St, Shiraz; tel. (71) 36294901; fax (71) 36294910; e-mail info@Sccim.ir; internet fccima.ir; Chair. JAMAL RAZEGHI.

Tabriz Chamber of Commerce, Industries and Mines: 65 North Artesh Ave, Tabriz; tel. (41) 35264111; fax (41) 35264115; e-mail info@tzccim.ir; internet www.tzccim.ir; f. 1906; privately owned; Chair. YOUNES ZHAELEH.

Tehran Chamber of Commerce, Industries and Mines: 82 Khalid Islamboli Ave, Tehran; tel. (21) 88107732; fax (21) 88715828; e-mail info@tccim.ir; internet www.tccim.ir; Chair. Eng. MASOUD KHANSARI; Sec.-Gen. BAHMAN ESHGHI.

INDUSTRIAL AND TRADE ASSOCIATIONS

National Iranian Industries Organization (NIIO): POB 15875-1331, No. 11, 13th Alley, Miremad St, Tehran; tel. (21) 88744198; fax (21) 88757126; f. 1979; owns 400 factories in Iran; Man. Dir ALI TOOSI.

National Iranian Industries Organization Export Co (NECO): No. 8, 2nd Alley, Bucharest Ave, Tehran; tel. (21) 44162384; fax (21) 212429.

STATE HYDROCARBONS COMPANIES

The following are subsidiary companies of the Ministry of Petroleum:

National Iranian Gas Co (NIGC): POB 6394-4533, 7th Floor, No. 401, Saghitaman, Taleghani Ave, Tehran; tel. (21) 84877250; fax (21) 88912656; e-mail boujarzadeh@nigc.ir; internet www.iraniangas.ir; f. 1965; Man. Dir MAJID CHEGENI.

National Iranian Oil Co (NIOC): 214 Khorramshahr Ave, Tehran 15337-43911; tel. (21) 88518601; e-mail publicrelations@nioc.ir; internet www.nioc.ir; f. 1948; controls all upstream activities in the petroleum and natural gas industries; incorporated April 1951 on nationalization of petroleum industry to engage in all phases of petroleum operations; in Feb. 1979 it was announced that in future Iran would sell petroleum directly to the petroleum companies, and in Sept. 1979 the Ministry of Petroleum assumed control of the NIOC; Chair. JAVAD OJI (Minister of Petroleum); Man. Dir MOHSEN KHOJASTEH MEH; subsidiary cos include the following:

Iranian Offshore Oil Co (IOOC): POB 5591, 12 Tooraj St, Vali-e-Asr Ave, Tehran 19395; tel. (21) 22664470; fax (21) 22664401; e-mail info@iooc.co.ir; internet www.iooc.co.ir; f. 1980; devt, exploitation and production of crude petroleum, natural gas and other hydrocarbons in all offshore areas of Iran in the Persian (Arabian) Gulf and the Caspian Sea; Chair. and CEO ALIREZA MEHDIZADEH.

Pars Oil and Gas Co (POGC): POB 14141-73111, 1 Parvin Etesami Alley, Dr Fatemi Ave, Tehran; tel. (21) 88966031; fax (21) 88989273; e-mail info@pogc.ir; internet www.pogc.ir; f. 1999; Man. Dir MUHAMMAD MESHKIN FAM.

National Iranian Oil Refining and Distribution Co (NIORDC): POB 15815-3499, NIORDC Bldg, 140 Ostad Nejatollahi Ave, Tehran 15989; tel. (21) 88928220; fax (21) 88498950; e-mail info@niordc.ir; internet www.niordc.ir; f. 1992 to assume responsibility for refining, pipeline distribution, engineering, construction and research in the petroleum industry from NIOC; Chair. JAVAD OJI (Minister of Petroleum); Man. Dir JALIL SALARI.

National Iranian Petrochemical Co (NIPC): POB 19395-6896, North Sheikh Bahaei St, Tehran; tel. 84991; e-mail info@nipc.ir; internet www.nipc.ir; f. 1964; oversees the devt and operation of Iran's petrochemical sector; directs activities of over 50 subsidiaries; Chair. JAVAD OJI (Minister of Petroleum); Man. Dir MORTEZA SHAHMIRZAEI.

CO-OPERATIVES

Central Union of Rural and Agricultural Co-operatives of Iran: Bldg 514, North Palestine St, Tehran; tel. (21) 84082200; fax (21) 88964166; e-mail info@trocairan.com; internet www.trocairan.com; f. 1963; educational, technical, commercial and credit assistance to rural co-operative societies and unions; Man. Dir ALI AKBARKHANI.

UTILITIES

Electricity

Iran Power Generation, Transmission and Distribution Co (Tavanir): POB 19988-36111, Tavanir Blvd, Rashid Yasami St, Vali-e-Asr Ave, Tehran; tel. (21) 27938000; fax (21) 88779543; e-mail info@tavanir.org.ir; internet www.tavanir.org.ir; f. 1979; state-owned; operates a network of 16 regional electricity cos, 27 generating cos and 42 distribution cos; also responsible for electricity transmission; Chair. and Man. Dir MOHAMMAD HASSAN MOTAVILIZADEH.

Water

Iran Water Resources Management Co: 517 Felestin Ave, Tehran; tel. (21) 43680000; fax (21) 88916600; e-mail info@wrm.ir; internet www.wrm.ir; f. 2003; govt agency reporting to the Ministry of Energy; in charge of Iran's Regional Water Authorities; Man. Dir MUHAMMAD HAJRASOULIHA.

MAJOR COMPANIES

Aabsal Public Co: No. 3, Hengam St, Daneshgah Ave, Tehran; tel. (21) 77451002; fax (21) 77203355; e-mail info@aabsalco.com; internet www.aabsalco.com; f. 1956; mfrs of domestic appliances.

Alborz Darou Pharmaceutical Co: 3–5 Floor, Africa Ave, Tehran 15186–46177; tel. (21) 88658764; fax (21) 88192770; e-mail info@alborzdarouco.com; internet www.alborzdarouco.com; f. 1976 as International Products Co; present name adopted in 1989; engaged in formulation, development, manufacturing and marketing of pharmaceutical products; CEO ELIAS KOHZADI.

Alborz Tire Manufacturing Co: 6 Chahardangeh Chamran St, Tehran; tel. (21) 55249500; e-mail info@kiantireco.com; internet www.kiantireco.com; f. 1958 as Kian Tire Manufacturing Co; present name adopted in 2001; mfrs of vehicle tyres; Exec. Dir MEHRDAD SHAFIEI.

Ama Industrial Co: POB 37515-355, Km 17, Jaddeh Makhsoos Karaj, Tehran; tel. (21) 44983935; fax (21) 44987769; e-mail fpd@ama-co.com; internet www.ama-co.com; f. 1959; mfrs of arc welding consumables; Chair. ALIZADEH RAD.

Bahman Group (Sherkat-e Iran Vanet): Km 13, Shahid Lashkari Highway, Tehran; tel. (21) 48027; e-mail info@bahman.ir; internet bahman.ir; f. 1952 as Iran Khalidj Co, renamed Iran Vanet Co in 1984; in 1998 became a holding co under the name Bahman Group; mfrs of pick-up trucks and other motor vehicles, automotive spare parts; 18 subsidiaries; Chair. JAMSHED IMANI; Man. Dir B. ALIMIRADOLU.

Behnoush Iran Co: POB 13185-571, 5 Shahid Poori St, Km 9, Shahid Lashkari Rd, Tehran; tel. (21) 44556003; e-mail info@behnoushiran.com; internet www.behnoushiran.com; f. 1966; mfrs of non-alcoholic beverages; Chair. NABIULLAH MAJD; CEO YASSER DAVARI.

Behpak Industrial Co: 22 Ghaem Moqam Farahani St, Tehran; tel. (21) 88322414; fax (21) 88341945; e-mail info@behpak.com; internet www.behpak.com; mfrs of soya protein and vegetable oils; Chair. Seyyed ABULFAZL ALI MORAD; Man. Dir ALI DANA.

Behran Oil Co: 2 Sharifi Alley, Dastgerdi St, Shariati Ave, Tehran; tel. (21) 22264124; fax (21) 22264131; internet www.behranoil.co; f. 1963; mfrs of engine and industrial lubricants, anti-freeze and paraffin wax; Chair. Seyed NURUDDIN TAHERI; Man. Dir ASAD AZIZI.

Borujerd Textile Co: 22 Banisi St, Nelson Mandela Blvd, Tehran; tel. (21) 43907000; e-mail info@borujerdtextile.com; internet www.borujerdtextile.com; f. 1983; textile mfrs; Man. Dir OMID ALAEE.

Chadormalu Mining and Industrial Co: 56 Esfandiar Blvd, Vali-e Asr, Tehran 19686-53647; tel. (21) 88882858; fax (21) 88775935; e-mail info@chadormalu.com; internet www.chadormalu.com; f. 1992; owned by Iranian Mines and Mining Industries Development and Renovation Org. (IMIDRO); producer of iron ore concentrate and crushed iron ore; Man. Dir AMIR ALI TAHERZADEH.

Chemi Darou Industrial Co: POB 16575-361, Abali Rd, Km 3, Tehran 17467-73611; tel. (21) 77330872; fax (21) 77336458; e-mail office@chemidarou.com; internet www.chemidarou.com; f. 1965; publicly owned; mfrs of pharmaceuticals and chemicals; Man. Dir Dr Seyyed AHMAD REZA MAHDIAN.

Damafin Thermal Technology Co: Zamyad St, Iran Khodro Blvd, Km 14, Karaj Special Rd, Tehran; tel. (21) 44922312; fax (21) 44922494; e-mail info@damafin.com; internet www.damafin.com; f. 1992; mfrs of air coolers and finned tubes; Chair. Seyed MOHAMMAD HOSSEIN WAZIRI; Man. Dir MOHSEN MELAI.

Darou Pakhsh Pharmaceutical Chemical Co: POB 13185-877, 1 Talaghani Ave, Darou Pakhsh Ave, Km 18, Karaj Freeway, Tehran; tel. (21) 44981191; fax (21) 44985053; e-mail info@dppcco.com; internet www.dppcco.com; f. 1992; mfrs of human and veterinary pharmaceuticals; Chair. and Man. Dir ALI MOGHADASI RAD.

Defence Industries Organization (DIO): POB 19585-777, Pasdaran St, Permanent Expo of Defence Industries Organization, Tehran; tel. (21) 22562883; fax (21) 22551961; e-mail marketing@dio1.org; internet www.diomil.ir; f. 1981; subsidiary of the Ministry of Defence and Armed Forces Logistics; supplies the Iranian armed forces; exports weapons, engineering and technical services.

Esfahan Petrochemical Co: POB 81395-313, Petrochemical Blvd, Tehran Rd, Esfahan; tel. (311) 33922000; fax (311) 33922681; e-mail info@epciran.com; internet www.epciran.com; f. 1992; mfrs of aromatics; Chair. MOHSEN GHADIRI; Man. Dir Seyed MOSTAFA ELAHI.

Exir Pharmaceutical Co: No. 2, Darupakhsh St, Karaj Rd, Tehran; tel. (66) 44992677; fax (66) 42606022; e-mail info@exir.co.ir; internet exir.co.ir; f. 1984; mfrs over 180 pharmaceutical products; Chair. Dr ISSA MALMIR; Man. Dir Eng. MOHSEN KURD.

Fars & Khuzestan Cement Co: POB 15875-3343, 4th Alley, Pakistan St, Dr Beheshti Ave, Tehran 153163-5113; tel. (21) 41002000; fax (21) 88736323; e-mail info@fkcco.com; internet www.fkcco.com; f. 1950; mfrs of cement; Chair. MAJID VAFAPOUR; CEO MOSTAFA SHAHRIARI.

Fars Chemical Industries Co (FCIC): 45 Rahimi St, Vali Asr Ave, Tehran; tel. (21) 22053247; fax (21) 22053247; e-mail info@farschemical.com; internet www.farschemical.com; f. 1980; mfrs of melamine, formalin and glue; CEO BABAK HENDIZADEH.

Firouza Engineering Co: Sahel Sq., Nima Yoshij St, Tehran; tel. (21) 48092000; e-mail info@firouzacranes.com; internet www.firouzacranes.com; f. 1967; cranes and load-handling machines.

Ghazvin Glass Co: POB 15875-1665, 13 Shahid Sarafraz St, Shahid Beheshti St, Tehran; tel. (21) 88731515; e-mail info@ghazvinglass.com; internet en.ghazvinglass.com; f. 1965; mfrs of sheet glass.

Glass Wool Co of Iran: 221 Motahari Ave, Tehran 158763-9111; tel. (71) 38224527; fax (21) 88735815; e-mail sale@iranglasswool.com; internet www.iranglasswool.com; f. 1964; mfrs of glass fibre insulation; Chair. ARJMAND SOLTANIZADEH; Man. Dir JAHANGIR BAGHERI.

Golgohar Mining & Industrial Co: No. 273, Opp. Laleh Hotel, Dr Fatemi Ave, Tehran; tel. (21) 88977261; fax (21) 88977260; e-mail info@geg.ir; internet geg.ir; f. 1969; mfrs of different types and forms of iron ore.

Hakim Pharmaceutical Co: POB 11365-5465, 1370 Dr Shariati Ave, Gholhak, 191377-4951 Tehran; tel. (21) 22263051; fax (21) 22267978; e-mail info@hakimpharm.com; internet www.hakimpharm.com; f. 1962; mfrs of pharmaceutical products.

Hamadan Glass Co: 2 Ghazali St, Hafez St, Tehran 113184-7113; tel. (21) 66704528; fax (21) 66713016; e-mail info@hamadanglass.com; internet www.hamadanglass.com; f. 1975; mfrs of glass bottles and jars; Man. Dir KHOSROW FAKHIM HASHEMI.

Iran Cable Manufacturing Co: Tehran; tel. (21) 66939278; fax (21) 66939404; e-mail sales@irancable.com; internet www.irancable.com; f. 1965; mfrs of power cables and earthing wires; Chair. MOHAMMED HOSSEIN ALADI.

Iran Diesel Engine Manufacturing Co (IDEM): 4 Sanat St, W Industrial Rd, Tabriz, Azarbayejan-e-Sharqi; tel. (41) 34450011; fax (41) 34451885; e-mail info@idem.ir; internet www.idem.ir; f. 1969; 47.5% owned by Iran Khodro Diesel Co, 30% owned by Daimler Chrysler and 22.5% owned by Iran Khodro Co; mfrs of diesel engines and spare parts.

Iran Electronics Industries Co (SAIRAN): POB 19575-365, Tehran; tel. (21) 22988006; fax (21) 22549664; e-mail info@ieicorp.ir; f. 1973; mfrs of electronic products, incl. audio-visual, communications, IT, optics, security systems, training aids and electro-medical; six subsidiaries: Shiraz Electronics Industries, Iran Communications Industries, Information Systems of Iran, Electronic Components Industries, Isfahan Optics Industries and Iran Electronics Research Center; Man. Dir AMIR ADMIR RASTEGARI.

Iran Insulator Co: 4 Niloofar Alley, South Bahar St, Enghelab Ave, Tehran; tel. (21) 77528642; fax (21) 77523311; e-mail iic@iraninsulator.com; internet www.iraninsulator.com; mfrs and exporters of ceramic insulators; Man. Dir REZA KIANI.

Iran International Engineering Co (IRITEC): 19 Khodami St, Wali Asr Ave, Tehran 19946-45411; tel. (21) 812801; fax (21)

IRAN

88678750; e-mail info@iritec.com; internet www.iritec.com; f. 1975; engineering consultancy and contracting; CEO Eng. AZIZ MOHAMMADI.

Iran Khodro Industrial Group: POB 13895-111, Gate 1, Km 14, Karaj Rd, Tehran; tel. (21) 48901; fax (21) 44934000; e-mail info@ikco.ir; internet www.ikco.ir; f. 1962; publicly owned; mfrs of cars, pickups, ambulance minibuses and buses; Chair. MOHAMMAD REZA FAIZBAKHSH; CEO MEHDI KHATIBI.

Iran Tire Manufacturing Co: Opposite Ghods Air Industries, Km 5, Karaj Makhsoos Rd, 139883–4711 Tehran; tel. (21) 44503460; fax (21) 44503500; e-mail info@irantireco.com; internet www.irantireco.com; f. 1964; mfrs of vehicle tyres; Chair. SEYYED AMIR HOSSEIN SHAMS DOLATABADI; CEO HAMID REZA ABDOLMALAKI.

Iran Tractor Manufacturing Co (Sherkat-e Teraktor Sazi-e Iran): Iran Tractor Complex, Sardroud Rd, Tabriz, Azarbayejan-e-Sharqi; tel. (41) 34255800; fax (41) 34245857; e-mail info@itmco.ir; internet itmco.ir; f. 1967; publicly owned; mfrs of tractors; Chair. YUSUF ELHI SHAKIB; CEO MUSTAFA VAHIZADEH.

Iran Zinc Mines Development Co: Haft Tir Sq., Shahid Motahari St, Qaem Magam Farahani St, 8th Alley, Tehran; tel. (21) 88540094; fax (21) 88540093; e-mail info@izmdc.com; internet www.izmdc.com; f. 1997; zinc mining; 16 subsidiary cos (2022); Chair. MEHDI MOHAMMAD KHANI; CEO MAHMOUD ALIPOUR JEDI.

Iranian Aluminum Co: 49 Mullah Sadra St, Tehran; tel. (21) 88049760; fax (21) 88049028; e-mail info@iralco.ir; internet www.iralco.ir; mfrs of aluminium ingots and alloys; CEO Seyed MOHAMMAD REZA MIRI LAVASANI.

Iranian Offshore Engineering and Construction Co (IOEC): POB 19395-5999, 27 Ostad Nejatollahi Ave, Arak St, 15989-66911 Tehran; tel. (21) 82840; fax (21) 88806607; e-mail info@ioec.com; internet www.ioec.com; f. 1993; owned by Nat. Iranian Oil Co and Industrial Devt and Renovation Org. of Iran; designs, procures, builds, installs and services offshore infrastructure for the offshore petroleum and gas industry; Chair. ALIREZA ZEIGHAMI; Man. Dir MOHAMMAD REZA ZAHIRI.

Khorasan Steel Complex Co: Km 15, Neyshabur; tel. (251) 41520000; fax (21) 2453231; e-mail info@kscco.ir; internet kscco.ir; operates steel making and rolling mill plants; also maintains several auxiliary plants; Man. Dir KASRA GHAFOURI.

Loabiran Co: 25 km Shiraz-Esfahan Rd, Kargar St, Tehran; tel. (21) 2622424; e-mail factory@loabiran.com; internet www.loabiran.com; f. 1987; mfrs of glazes and coatings for the ceramics and tile industries; Chair. BEHROUZ FARHANGIAN; Man. Dir NADER REZAEI MANESH.

Maadiran Industries: Maadiran Bldg, Aftab Interchange, Khodami St, Vanak Sq., Tehran; tel. (21) 82266; fax (21) 88623730; e-mail contactus@maadiran.com; internet www.maadiran.com; f. 1964 as Iran Office Machines Industries; present name adopted in 2001; 100% privately owned; subsidiaries include Iran Office Machines Co, Maadiran Home Appliances Co, Maadiran Electronic Industries Co, Sasha Development Co; Chair. MASOUD AMIRI; CEO ALI KARAMI.

Mapna Group: 231 Mirdamad Blvd, Tehran 191895-3651; tel. (21) 81981001; e-mail info@mapnagroup.com; internet www.mapnagroup.com; f. 1993; public jt-stock co; activities include construction, operation of power plants, petroleum and gas, and rail transport; CEO MOHAMMAD OWLIA.

Margarine MFG Co: Km 3, Varamin Rd, Tehran; tel. (21) 35811; fax (21) 33400430; e-mail info@margarineco.com; internet www.mmc.ir; f. 1953; mfrs of margarine, edible vegetable oils and fats; Man. Dir KHASHAYAR QAJAR.

Melli Agrochemical Co (MAC): 501 Pasdaran St, Narenjestan II cnr, Tehran 195791-6435; tel. (21) 26104583; fax (21) 26104731; e-mail info@mac-ir.com; internet mac-ir.com; f. 1984; mfrs of agrochemicals.

Minoo Industrial Group: POB 13885-118, Km 10, Tehran–Karaj Rd, Tehran 139973-6311; tel. (21) 48831040; fax (21) 44543004; e-mail info@minoogroup.com; internet www.minoogroup.com; f. 1959; foodstuffs, pharmaceuticals, cosmetics and hygiene products; consists of 12 separate cos; Chair. HOSSEIN ALI AKBARZADEH; CEO ALIREZA EYASIANFAR.

Mobarakeh Steel Co: No. 2, Gol Azin St, Koushestan St, Ketab Sq., Sa'adat Abad, Tehran; tel. (311) 52732200; fax (311) 33324324; e-mail info@msc.ir; internet msc.ir; f. 1993; iron and steel milling; CEO MOHAMMAD YASER TAYEBNIA.

Motogen MFG Co: W Industrial Zone, Tabriz, Azarbayejan-e-Sharqi; tel. (41) 34453001; e-mail info@motogen.com; internet www.motogen.com; f. 1973; mfrs of industrial and household electrical motors; Chair. TAHER RAHIMI; Man. Dir HADI EBADI.

National Iranian Copper Industries Co (NICICO): POB 15115-416, No. 1091, Vali-e-Asr Ave, Tehran 15115; tel. (21) 88721723; fax (21) 88721737; e-mail info@nicico.com; internet www.nicico.com; f. 1972 as Sarcheshmeh Copper Mine Co of Kerman; copper extraction and mfrs of copper products; Man. Dir ALI ROSTAMI.

Directory

Navard Aluminum Manufacturing Group: 28 Homa St, Sindokht St, Dr Fatemi St, 141865–4381 Tehran; tel. (21) 54709000; fax (21) 54709100; e-mail info@navardaluminum.com; internet www.navardaluminum.com; f. 1972; mfrs and exporters of rolled aluminium; Chair. REZA HAMIDI; CEO MEHRDAD MOHAMMADI.

Niroumokarekeh Machine Tools Co (NMT): 103 Passage Vanak, Vanak Ave, Vanak Sq., Tehran 19919; tel. (21) 88797216; fax (21) 88775402; e-mail info@nmt-co.com; internet www.nmt-co.com; f. 1990; mfrs of machine tools; Chair. ABD AL-RAHMAN HADDAD.

Osvah Pharmaceutical Co: 17 Shahrivar St, Shad Abad, Karaj Old Rd, Tehran; tel. (21) 66801075; e-mail info@osvahpharma.com; internet www.osvahpharma.com; f. 1966 as Iran Merck; adopted present name 1981; Man. Dir Dr MEHDI BAKHSHAYESH.

Pak Dairy Co: 26 Rudsar St, Hafez St, Tehran; tel. (21) 37886897; e-mail info@pakdairy.com; internet www.pakdairy.com; f. 1959; producers of dairy products and ice cream; Chair. AMIR ALI AWSAT; CEO ALI ABDI.

Pars Appliance MFG Co (Lavazem Khanegi Pars): 181 Taleghani Ave, Tehran; tel. (21) 88845045; fax (21) 88304077; e-mail info@parsappliance.com; internet www.parsappliance.com; f. 1975; domestic appliances; Man. Dir FARIBARZ ZAROUFI.

Pars Darou Co: POB 11365-4688, No. 13, East 144 Ave, 1st Tehranpars Sq., Tehran 165471–3691; tel. (21) 77704061; fax (21) 77877700; e-mail info@parsdarou.ir; internet www.parsdarou.ir; f. 1960; mfrs of pharmaceuticals; CEO Dr SOHEIL SOHEILI.

Pars Shahab Lamp Co (PSLC): 49 Sepahbod Gharani Ave, Tehran 533151–5816; tel. (21) 88823142; fax (21) 88841910; e-mail parslamp@parsshahab.com; internet www.parsshahab.com; f. 1969; jt venture with Toshiba (Japan); mfrs and exporters of light bulbs; Chair. HOUSHANG DADASH; Man. Dir BAHMAN DZHAKAM.

Paxan PLC: POB 13774, Km 8, Fath Highway, Tehran; tel. (21) 64562361; fax (21) 66250563; e-mail crm@paxanco.com; internet www.paxanco.com; f. 1963; household and personal hygiene products; Chair. SEYED SADR AL-DIN HASINI; Man. Dir MOHAMMADI RAD.

Persian Gulf Petrochemical Industry Commercial Co (PGPICC): Ryan Vanak Bldg, Tehran; tel. (21) 86092477; e-mail info@pgpdig.com; internet en.pgpdig.ir; CEO RASHID QANEI.

Petrochemical Industries Investment Co: No. 14, Third St, Seyed Jamaledin Asadabadi St, Tehran 143361–3433; tel. (21) 88551371; e-mail ece@piicgroup.com; internet www.piicgroup.com; f. 1991; finance/investment; subsidiary of state-owned Nat. Petrochemical Co; Chair. HAMID MASEEN ASL; CEO HOJATOLLAH BARAMAKI YAZDI.

Pumpiran Co: Vali-e-Asr Ave, Mirdamad Junction, Eskan Tower 2, Tehran 1969613313; tel. (21) 88654811; fax (21) 88654814; e-mail info@pumpiran.com; internet www.pumpiran.co; f. 1963; mfrs of household pumps, industrial pumps and industrial electric motors; Chair. AHMAD CHERAGH; Man. Dir MOHAMMAD HOSSEIN HIHAT.

Radiator Iran Co: POB 13445-159, Km 15, Old Karaj Rd, Tehran 138618-3731; tel. (21) 44922710; e-mail info@irradiator.com; internet www.irradiator.com; mfrs of radiators and heat exchangers; Chair. MOHAMMADREZA ATAEE; Man. Dir MAHDI HOSSEINNEJAD.

Razak Laboratories Co: POB 13185-1671, Km 10 Karaj Rd, Tehran; tel. (21) 44537027; e-mail info@razakpharma.com; internet www.razakpharma.com; f. 1964; mfrs of human and veterinary drugs; Chair. Dr QAIS BADRI.

Rehabilitation and Maintenance of Petrochemical Co (RAMPCO): 50 Bahrami St, Valiasr Ave, Tehran; tel. (21) 88209878; fax (21) 88193878; internet rampcogroup.com; f. 1992; repair, rehabilitation and installation of machinery and equipment in petrochemical plants and other industries; over 5,000 employees; Chair. ABBAS SHARI MOGHADAM; Man. Dir IRAJ MASROORI.

Sadra (Iran Marine Industrial Co): POB 14665-495, 2 Toheed Bldg, Shafagh Ave, Dadman Blvd, Phase 7, Shahrak Ghods, Tehran 146695–6491; tel. (21) 83362000; fax (21) 88576186; e-mail info@sadra.ir; internet www.sadra.ir; f. 1968; shipbuilding and repairs; Man. Dir ASADOLLAH ABVISANI.

Saipa Diesel Co: POB 13895-141, Km 14, Karaj Makhsoos Rd, Tehran 139618–8783; tel. (21) 44196513; fax (21) 44196518; e-mail info@saipadiesel.ir; internet saipadiesel.ir; f. 1963; mfrs of motor vehicles; Man. Dir MOHAMMAD HASSAN MOHAMMADZADEH.

Sepahan Cement Co: 211 Vahid Dastgardi E St, Tehran; tel. (21) 52454471; fax (21) 52457383; e-mail info@sepahancement.com; internet www.sepahancement.com; f. 1970; mfrs and exporters of cement; Chair. Eng. MOHAMMAD REZA SOLEIMIAN; Man. Dir Eng. ABBAS ALI MOEINIAN.

Sepahan Industrial Group Co: POB 15857-6617, 1 Ahmad Ghassir Ave, Tehran 151461-3146; tel. (21) 88739010; internet www.sepahan.com; f. 1973; mfrs of industrial pipes and scaffolding tubes.

Shahdiran Inc: POB 91775-1174, Km 5 Mashhad-Ghouchan Rd, 91971–75199 Mashhad; tel. (51) 36514300; fax (51) 336514299;

e-mail info@shahdiran.ir; internet www.shahdiran.ir; f. 1982; fruit juice mfrs.

Shahid Bahonar Copper Industries Co (CSP): No. 19, Gandhi St, 7th Alley (Palizvani), Tehran; tel. (34) 31227999; e-mail info@csp.ir; internet www.csp.ir; f. 1983; Chair. ABBAS HASSANI; CEO MAJID ZIAEI.

Shargh Cement Co: No. 47, 1/2 Asrar St, 21 University St, Mashhad; tel. (51) 38424212; e-mail info@sharghcement.ir; internet www.sharghcement.ir; f. 1953; mfrs of Portland cement; Chair. HASSAN KHOSHPOUR; Man. Dir MOHAMMAD MEHDI EBRAHIMI.

Shazand Petrochemical Co (Arak): POB 14155-6589, 68 W Taban St, Vali-e-Asr Ave, Tehran 196891-3751; tel. (21) 82120; fax (21) 82121; e-mail infoarpc@arpc.ir; internet www.arpc.ir; mfrs of plastics, rubber and chemicals; CEO ALIREZA KHALILINIA.

Sina Chemical Industrial Co: POB 15875-8537, No. 12, 6th St, Bucharest Ave, Tehran 15146-45711; tel. (21) 88501038; e-mail sci@sinachem.com; internet www.sinachem.com; f. 1989; mfrs of formalin, hexamine and paraformaldehyde.

Sina Darou Laboratories Co: POB 11155-3851, Km 15, Makhsoos Karaj Rd, 52 Blvd, Tehran 33561; tel. (21) 44194521; fax (21) 44196603; e-mail info@sinadarou.com; internet www.sinadarou.com; f. 1962; mfrs of pharmaceuticals; Man. Dir Dr HASSAN BAYRAMI.

Social Security Investment Co (Shasta): 11 South Gandhi St, Tehran; tel. (21) 82109000; fax (21) 88779412; internet ssic.ir; Man. Dir EBRAHIM BAZIAN.

Soufian Cement Co: No. 4 Amdi St, Mirdamad St, Africa Ave, Tehran,; tel. (21) 42147000; fax (21) 42147000; e-mail info@soufiancement.com; internet www.soufiancement.com; f. 1966; mfrs of Portland cement; Chair. KOUROSH JAMEI; Man. Dir SAEED DELFKAR.

Varziran Co: Africa Blvd, Amadi Alley, Tehran 15189-54714; tel. (21) 88773124; fax (21) 88780963; e-mail sales@varziran.com; internet www.varziran.com; f. 1982; mfrs of pipe coating, waterproofing membranes and bitumen for use in pipelines, building and road construction.

Zahravi Pharmaceutical Co: Km 19, Tabriz; tel. (41) 36309401; fax (41) 36309400; e-mail info@zahravipharma.com; internet www.zahravi.com; f. 1986; Chair. FARHAD GHAFOURIAN; Man. Dir Dr FARHAD KIAFAR.

Zamyad Co: POB 13185-943, Km 15, Old Karaj Rd, Tehran; tel. (21) 44922911; fax (21) 44922012; e-mail info@zamyad.co.ir; internet www.zamyad.co.ir; f. 1963; part of the Saipa Group; mfrs of vans, trucks and minibuses; Man. Dir Seyed MOHSEN MORTAZAVI.

Transport

RAILWAYS

Government plans to expand the rail network to 28,000 km by 2020 were severely impeded by a shortage of foreign investment resulting from the imposition of US-led sanctions. None the less, construction of a 506-km rail link between Esfahan and Shiraz was completed in June 2009. In the same month a 250-km Zahedan–Kerman line was inaugurated, linking the rail networks of Iran and Pakistan and facilitating the launch of a direct Islamabad (Pakistan)–Tehran–İstanbul (Türkiye) freight service in August. Construction of a 1,350-km railway along Iran's eastern border, linking Mashhad, in the north-east, with Chabahar on the Persian (Arabian) Gulf, commenced in 2010. The final link in a 930-km north–south railway corridor (for freight alone) connecting Iran, Turkmenistan and Kazakhstan was officially inaugurated in December 2014. In early 2015 a Chinese consortium headed by China Railway Engineering Corporation commenced construction of a 410-km high-speed line connecting Tehran and Esfahan via Qom. In December 2020 a 225-km railway was inaugurated, connecting the city of Khaf in Iran with Herat in Afghanistan. The railway was part of the planned Five Nations Railway Corridor linking Iran and the People's Republic of China via Afghanistan, Tajikistan and Kyrgyzstan. In July 2021 a 271-km railway line connecting the cities of Yazd and Eqlid was inaugurated.

Islamic Republic of Iran Railways: Railways Central Bldg, Argentina Sq., Africa Blvd, Tehran; tel. (21) 55651415; fax (21) 88646570; e-mail iranrailways@rai.ir; internet www.rai.ir; f. 1934; affiliated to Ministry of Roads and Urban Development; CEO SEYED MIAD SALEHI.

Raja Passenger Trains Co: POB 15875-1363, 1 Sanaie St, Karimkhan Zand Ave, Tehran; tel. (21) 88310880; e-mail info@raja.ir; internet www.raja.ir; f. 1996; state-owned; affiliated to Islamic Republic of Iran Railways; Man. Dir MOHAMMAD RAJABI.

Tehran Metro

Construction of the Tehran metro system commenced in 1977. As of March 2023 the system consisted of seven active lines, with 257 km of track and 148 stations.

Tehran Urban and Suburban Railway Co (Tehranmetro) (TUSRC): 956 Hafez St, Enghelab St, Tehran; tel. (21) 66747500; fax (21) 66747900; e-mail info.metro@tehran.ir; internet metro.tehran.ir; f. 1976; CEO SHAYESTEH ASL.

ROADS

There is a paved highway (A1, 2,089 km) from Bazargan on the Turkish border to the Afghanistan border. The A2 highway runs 2,473 km from the Iraq border to Mir Javeh on the Pakistan border. A 122–km highway linking the eastern city of Dogharun to Herat in Afghanistan was opened in 2005. The 121–km Tehran-Shomal Freeway linking the capital with the cities of western Mazandaran province is currently under construction; by early 2020 some 52 km of the freeway had been completed and were in use.

INLAND WATERWAYS

Lake Urmia (formerly Lake Rezaiyeh): 80 km west of Tabriz in north-western Iran; from Sharafkhaneh to Golmankhaneh there is a regular service of tugs and barges for the transport of passengers and goods.

Karun River: Flowing south through the oilfields into the Shatt al-Arab waterway, and thence to the head of the Persian (Arabian) Gulf near Abadan; there is a regular cargo service, as well as daily motor-boat services for passengers and goods.

SHIPPING

The main oil terminal on the Persian (Arabian) Gulf is at Kharg Island. The principal commercial non-oil ports are Bandar Shahid Rajai (which was officially inaugurated in 1983 and handles a significant proportion of the cargo passing annually through Iran's Gulf ports), Bandar Imam Khomeini, Bushehr, Bandar Abbas and Chabahar. The Bandar Abbas port complex, which predates the 1979 Islamic Revolution, comprises two separate ports, Shahid Rajai and Shahid Bahonar. A major expansion project at the Shahid Beheshti port of the Chabahar port complex (which also includes the Shahid Kalantari port), was agreed between Iran, India and Afghanistan in May 2016. The first phase of the project, which increased Chabahar's annual handling capacity from 2.5m. metric tons to 8.0m. tons, was inaugurated in December 2017. Iran's principal ports on the Caspian Sea include Bandar Anzali (formerly Bandar Pahlavi) and Bandar Nowshahr.

Port Authority

Ports and Maritime Organization (PMO): POB 15875-6377, 1 Shahidi St, Shahid Haghani Highway, Vanak Sq., Tehran; tel. (21) 88809280; fax (21) 88651191; e-mail info@pmo.ir; internet www.pmo.ir; f. 1960 as Ports and Shipping Org.; affiliated to Ministry of Roads and Urban Development; Man. Dir ALI-AKBAR SAFAEI.

Principal Shipping Companies

Islamic Republic of Iran Shipping Lines (IRISL): POB 19395-1311, 37 Asseman Tower, Sayyad Shirazee Sq., Pasdaran Ave, Tehran; tel. (21) 20100369; fax (21) 20100367; e-mail e-pr@irisl.net; internet www.irisl.net; f. 1967; 18 vessels; Man. Dir MOHAMMAD REZA MODARRES KHIYABANI.

National Iranian Tanker Co (NITC): POB 19395-4833, 67–68 Atefis St, Africa Ave, Tehran; tel. (21) 66153220; fax (21) 22224537; internet nitcshipping.com/index.jsp?siteid=2; Man. Dir HOSSEIN SHIVA.

CIVIL AVIATION

The principal international airport is Imam Khomeini International Airport (IKIA), to the south of Tehran. IKIA opened fully in May 2005, and, by mid-2006, had taken over all international flights from Mehrabad Airport (west of Tehran). There are several other international airports, including those at Esfahan, Mashhad, Shiraz and Tabriz.

Civil Aviation Organization (CAO): POB 13445-1798, Taleghani Ave, Tehran; tel. (21) 66078700; fax (21) 66025405; e-mail pr@cao.ir; internet www.cao.ir; affiliated to Ministry of Roads and Urban Development; Pres. MOHAMMAD MOHAMMADI BAKHSH.

Caspian Airlines: 5 Sabonchi St, Shahid Beheshti Ave, Tehran; tel. (21) 44535052; fax (21) 44561112; internet caspian.aero; f. 1992; operates more than 50 flights per week from Tehran to other cities in Iran, as well as scheduled flights to the United Arab Emirates, Lebanon, the Syrian Arab Republic, Türkiye (formerly Turkey) and several European destinations; rep. offices abroad; Gen. Dir Capt. ASGAR RAZZAGHI.

IranAir (Airline of the Islamic Republic of Iran): POB 13185-775, IranAir HQ, Mehrabad Airport, Tehran; tel. (21) 46625949; fax (21) 46628224; e-mail pr@iranair.com; internet www.iranair.com; f. 1962; serves the Middle East and Persian (Arabian) Gulf area, Europe, Asia and the Far East; CEO Brig.-Gen. SHAMSEDDIN FARZAZADIPOUR (acting).

Iran Airtour: 520 Taleghani St, Sarparast Ave, Cross Rd, Tehran; tel. (21) 89317000; e-mail info@iranairtour.ir; internet iranairtour.ir; f. 1973; low-cost subsidiary of IranAir, offering flights from Tehran, Tabriz and Mashhad; serves domestic routes and destinations in Türkiye (formerly Turkey); Chair. MAJID SHEKARI; Man. Dir REZA MOUSAVI.

Iran Aseman Airlines: POB 141748, Mehrabad Airport, Tehran 13145-1476; tel. (21) 61106663; fax (21) 66002810; e-mail info@iaa.ir; internet www.iaa.ir; f. 1980 as result of merger of Air Taxi Co (f. 1958), Pars Air (f. 1969), Air Service Co (f. 1962) and Hoor Asseman; domestic routes and charter services to destinations in Central Asia and the Middle East; Man. Dir MEHDI QADERI.

Kish Air: POB 19395-4639, 215 Africa Ave, Tehran 19697; tel. (21) 48680000; fax (21) 48681030; internet www.kishairline.com; f. 1989, under the auspices of the Kish Devt Org.; domestic routes and flights to Türkiye (formerly Turkey) and the United Arab Emirates; Chair. MAJID MELANOROZI; Man. Dir Dr FARZANEH SHARFAFAFI.

Mahan Air: POB 14515-411, Mahan Air Tower, 21 Azadegan St, Karaj Highway, Tehran 14816-55761; tel. (21) 48380; fax (21) 48381450; internet www.mahan.aero; f. 1992; domestic routes and charter services to other Middle Eastern, Asian and European destinations; Man. Dir HAMID ARABNEJAD.

Qeshm Air: 12 Riahi St, Karaj Makhsoos Rd, 13919-46611 Tehran; tel. (21) 47999; e-mail crm@qeshm-air.com; internet qeshm-air.com; operates regular flights from Qeshm Island to the Iranian mainland and the United Arab Emirates.

Saha Airlines: Ayat-e-Said Ave, Tehran; tel. (21) 66630101; fax (21) 66698016; e-mail info@sahaair.com; internet sahaair.com; f. 1990; owned by the Iranian Air Force; operates passenger and cargo charter domestic flights and services to Europe, Asia and Africa; Man. Dir Capt. MANSOUR NIKUKAR.

Tourism

Iran Tourism and Touring Organization (ITTO): 154 Keshavarz Blvd, Tehran; tel. (21) 88737065; fax (21) 88736800; internet www.itto.org; f. 1985; administered by Govt.

Defence

As assessed at November 2022, Iran's regular armed forces totalled an estimated 610,000 personnel: army 350,000; navy 18,000; air force 37,000; air defence 15,000. There was also a 350,000-strong reserve force. The Islamic Revolutionary Guard Corps (*Pasdaran Inqilab*), which has its own land, navy and marine units, comprised some 190,000 personnel. The Basij War Volunteers Corps was estimated to include up to 12.6m. members, of which around 600,000 were thought to be combat capable. There were also some 40,000–60,000 paramilitary forces under the command of the Ministry of the Interior.

Defence Budget: IR 2,225,000,000m. in 2022.

Secretary of the Supreme National Security Council: Gen. ALI AKBAR AHMADIAN.

Chief of Staff of the Armed Forces: Maj.-Gen. MOHAMMAD HOSSEIN BAGHERI.

Commander of the Army: Maj.-Gen. ABDOLRAHIM MOUSAVI.

Commander of the Air Force: Brig.-Gen. HAMID VAHEDI.

Commander of the Navy: Adm. SHAHRAM IRANI.

Chief of Staff of the Islamic Revolutionary Guard Corps (Pasdaran Inqilab): Maj.-Gen. HOSSEIN SALAMI.

Commander of the Islamic Revolutionary Guard Corps Ground Forces: Brig.-Gen. MOHAMMAD PAKPOUR.

Commander of the Islamic Revolutionary Guard Corps Air Force: Brig.-Gen. AMIR ALI HEJIZADEH.

Commander of the Islamic Revolutionary Guard Corps Navy: Rear-Adm. ALIREZA TANGSIRI.

Commander of the Islamic Revolutionary Guard Corps Quds Force: Brig.-Gen. ESMAIL QA'ANI.

Commander of Basij (Mobilization) War Volunteers Corps: Brig.-Gen. GHOLAMREZA SOLEIMANI.

Education

Primary education, beginning at the age of six and lasting for five years, is compulsory for all children and provided free of charge. Secondary education, from the age of 11, lasts for up to seven years, comprising a first cycle of three years and a second of four years. In 2019/20, according to UNESCO estimates, enrolment at pre-primary schools was equivalent to 72.5% of children (boys 71.3%; girls 73.7%) in the relevant age-group, while primary enrolment included 99.9% of children in the relevant age-group. Enrolment at lower secondary schools in 2019/20 included 98.3% of children (boys 99.2%; girls 97.2%) in the relevant age-group, while the comparable figure for upper secondary schools was 82.7% of children (boys 83.0%; girls 82.5%).

Apart from Tehran, there are universities in Bakhtaran, Esfahan, Hamadan, Tabriz, Ahwaz, Babolsar, Meshed, Kermanshah, Rasht, Shiraz, Zahedan, Kerman, Shahrekord, Urmia and Yazd. There are colleges of higher education, technological institutes, teacher-training colleges, colleges of advanced technology, and colleges of agriculture in Hamadan, Zanjan, Sari and Abadan. Vocational training schools also exist in Tehran, Ahwaz, Meshed, Shiraz and other cities. According to UNESCO, expenditure on education by the central Government in 2020 was equivalent to 23.1% of total spending.

Bibliography

General and Historical Context

Akram, A. I. *The Muslim Conquest of Persia*. Karachi, Oxford University Press Pakistan, 2004.

Alaedini, Pooya. *Social Policy in Iran: Main Components and Institutions*. Abingdon and New York, Routledge, 2022.

Alikarami, Leila. *Women and Equality in Iran: Law, Society and Activism*. London, I. B. Tauris, 2019.

Amanat, Abbas. *Apocalyptic Islam and Iranian Shi'ism*. London and New York, I. B. Tauris, 2009.

Iran: a Modern History. New Haven, CT, Yale University Press, 2017.

Amanat, Abbas, and Ashraf, Assef (Eds). *The Persianate World: Rethinking a Shared Sphere*, Boston, MA, Brill. 2019.

Amirahmadi, Hooshang, and Entessar, Nader. *Iran and the Arab World*. Basingstoke, Macmillan, 1993.

Amirsadeghi, Hossein. *Twentieth Century Iran*. London, Heinemann, 1977.

Ansari, Ali M. *Modern Iran since 1921: The Pahlavis and After*. Harlow, Longman, 2nd edn, 2007.

Perceptions of Iran: History, Myths and Nationalism from Medieval Persia to the Islamic Republic. London, I. B. Tauris and Iran Heritage Foundation, 2014.

Iran's Constitutional Revolution of 1906: Narratives of the Enlightenment. London, Gingko Library, 2016.

Modern Iran Since 1797: Reform and Revolution. Abingdon, Routledge, 2019.

Ansari, Sarah, and Martin, Vanessa. *Women, Religion and Culture in Iran*. Abingdon, Routledge, 2014.

Arberry, A. J. (Ed.). *The Cambridge History of Iran*. Cambridge, Cambridge University Press, 1969.

Axworthy, Michael. *Iran, Empire of the Mind: A History from Zoroaster to the Present Day*. London, Penguin Books, 2008.

Revolutionary Iran: A History of the Islamic Republic. London, Allen Lane, 2013.

Iran: What Everyone Needs to Know. New York, Oxford University Press, 2017.

Azimi, Fakhreddin. *Iran: The Crisis of Democracy 1941–1953*. London, I. B. Tauris, 1990.

Bahramitash, Roksana, and Hooglund, Eric (Eds). *Gender in Contemporary Iran: Pushing the Boundaries*. Abingdon, Routledge, 2014.

Brosius, Maria. *The Persians*. Abingdon, Routledge, 2006.

Bunya, Ali Akbar. *A Political and Diplomatic History of Persia*. Tehran, 1955.

Byrne, Malcolm, and Gasiorowski, Mark J. (Eds). *Mohammad Mossadeq and the 1953 Coup in Iran*. Syracuse, NY, Syracuse University Press, 2004.

Cambridge History of Iran (8 vols). Cambridge University Press, reissued edn, 1993.

Chehabi, H. E., Jafari, Peyman, and Jefroudi, Maral. *Iran in the Middle East: Transnational Encounters and Social History*. London, I. B. Tauris, 2015.

Colledge, M. A. R. *The Parthians*. London, Thames and Hudson, 1968.

Cronin, Stephanie. *The Army and the Creation of the Pahlavi State in Iran 1910–1926*. London and New York, I. B. Tauris, 1997.

The Making of Modern Iran: State and Society under Riza Shah, 1921–1941. London, Routledge, 2003.

Tribal Politics in Iran: Rural Conflict and the New State, 1921–1941. Abingdon, Routledge, 2006.

Culican, William. *The Medes and the Persians*. 1965.

Daryaee, Touraj. *The Oxford Handbook of Iranian History*. New York, Oxford University Press, 2014.

De Groot, Joanna. *Religion, Culture and Politics in Iran: From the Qajars to Khomeini*. London, I. B. Tauris, 2007.

Delannoy, Christian. *Savak*. Paris, Editions Stock, 1991.

Ebadi, Shirin. *Iran Awakening: A Memoir of Revolution and Hope*. London, Rider, 2006.

Farzaneh, Mateo Mohammad. *The Iranian Constitutional Revolution and the Clerical Leadership of Khurasani*. Syracuse, NY, Syracuse University Press, 2015.

Foltz, Richard C. *Iran in World History*. Oxford, Oxford University Press, 2016.

Forbes Manz, Beatrice. *Power, Politics and Religion in Timurid Iran*. Cambridge University Press, 2007.

Frye, Richard N. *Persia*. London, Allen and Unwin, 3rd edn, 1969.

Houshisadat, Seyed Mohammad. *Iran's Regional Relations: A History from Antiquity to the Islamic Republic*. London, Routledge, 2020.

Hovannisian, Richard, and Sabagh, Georges. *The Persian Presence in the Islamic World*. Cambridge, Cambridge University Press, 1999.

Huot, Jean Louis. *Persia* Vol. I. London, Muller, 1966.

Katouzian, Homa. *State and Society in Iran: the Eclipse of the Qajars and the Emergence of the Pahlavis*. London and New York, I. B. Tauris, 2000.

Kashani-Sabet, Firoozeh. *Frontier Fictions: Shaping the Iranian Nation, 1804–1946*. Princeton, NJ, Princeton University Press, 1999.

Keddie, Nikki R., and Gasiorowski, Mark (Eds). *Neither East nor West: Iran, the Soviet Union and the United States*. New Haven, CT, Yale University Press, 1990.

Khaniki, Hadi. 'Dialogue of Civilisations: Objective Grounds and Theoretical Guidelines', in Dallmayr, Fred, and Manoochehri, Abbas (Eds). *Civilisational Dialogue and Political Thought: Tehran Papers*. Lanham, MD, Lexington Books, 2007, pp. 83–100.

Khazeni, Arash. *Tribes and Empire on the Margins of Nineteenth-century Iran*. Seattle, WA, University of Washington Press, 2010.

Khomeini, Ayatollah Ruhollah. *A Clarification of Questions*. Boulder, CT, Westview Press, 1985.

Kondo, Nobuaki. *Islamic Law and Society in Iran: a Social History of Tehran*. Abingdon, Routledge, 2017.

Lockhart, L. *The Fall of the Safavi Dynasty and the Afghan Occupation of Persia*. Cambridge, Cambridge University Press, 1958.

Mackey, Sandra. *The Iranians: Persia, Islam and the Soul of a Nation*. New York, NY, Plume Penguin, 1998.

Martin, Vanessa (Ed.). *Anglo-Iranian Relations since 1800*. Abingdon, Routledge, 2009.

Mishal, Shaul. *Understanding Shiite Leadership: The Art of the Middle Ground in Iran and Lebanon*. Cambridge, Cambridge University Press, 2014.

Melville, Charles (Ed.). *Safavid Persia*. 1996.

Millspaugh, A. C. *Americans in Persia*. Washington, DC, 1946.

Minoui, Delphine (Ed.). *Jeunesse d'Iran: Les voix du changement*. Paris, Autrement, 2001.

Monshipouri, Mahmood. *Inside the Islamic Republic: Social Change in post-Khomeini Iran*. London, Hurst & Co Publishers, 2016.

Moore, Eric D. *Russia-Iran Relations since the End of the Cold War*. Abingdon, Routledge, 2014.

Nabavi, Negin. *Modern Iran: a History in Documents*. Princeton, NJ, Markus Wiener, 2016.

Nashat, Guity. *Women and Revolution in Iran*. Abingdon, Routledge, 2022.

Offiler, Ben. *US Foreign Policy and the Modernization of Iran: Kennedy, Johnson, Nixon and the Shah*. Basingstoke, Palgrave Macmillan, 2015.

Olmstead, A. T. *History of the Persian Empire, Achaemenid Period*. Chicago, IL, 1948.

Ramazani, Rouhollah K. *The Foreign Policy of Iran 1500–1941*. Charlottesville, VA, University Press of Virginia, 1966.

The Persian Gulf: Iran's Role. Charlottesville, VA, University Press of Virginia, 1972.

Rice, Cyprian. *The Persian Sufis*. London, Allen and Unwin, 1964.

Sabahi, Hushang. *British Policy in Persia 1918–1925*. London, Frank Cass, 1990.

Sanghvi, Ramesh. *Aryamehr: The Shah of Iran*. London, Macmillan, 1968.

Sansarian, Eliz. *Religious Minorities in Iran*. Cambridge, Cambridge University Press, 2000.

Sarshar, Houman. *The Jews of Iran: The History, Religion and Culture of a Community in the Islamic World*. London, I. B. Tauris, 2014.

Shah of Iran. *Mission for My Country*. London, Hutchinson, 1961.

Shakibi, Zhand. *Pahlavi Iran and the Politics of Occidentalism: the Shah and the Rastakhiz Party*. London, I. B. Tauris, 2020.

Shearman, I. *Land and People of Iran*. London, 1962.

Siavoshi, Sussan. *Montazeri: the Life and Thought of Iran's Revolutionary Ayatollah*. Cambridge, Cambridge University Press, 2017.

Sirdar, Ikbal Ali Shah. *Persia of the Persians*. London, 1929.

al-Suwaidi, Jamal S. (Ed.). *Iran and the Gulf: A Search for Stability*. Abu Dhabi, Emirates Centre for Strategic Studies and Research, 1996. (Distrib. I. B. Tauris, London).

Sternfeld, Lior. *Between Iran and Zion: Jewish Histories of Twentieth-Century Iran*. Stanford, CA, Stanford University Press, 2018.

Sykes, Sir Percy. *Persia*. Oxford, 1922.

A History of Persia (2 vols; 3rd edn, with supplementary essays). London, 1930.

Vali, Abbas. *Kurds and the State in Iran: The Making of Kurdish Identity*. London, I. B. Tauris, 2014.

Wiesehofer, Josef. *Ancient Persia*. London, I. B. Tauris, 2001.

Wilber, Donald N. *Iran: Past and Present: From Monarchy to Islamic Republic*. Princeton University Press, 9th edn, 1982.

Wright, Robin B. *The Last Great Revolution: Turmoil and Transformation in Iran*. New York, Alfred A. Knopf, 2000.

Yaghoubian, David N. *Ethnicity, Identity, and the Development of Nationalism in Iran*. Syracuse, NY, Syracuse University Press, 2014.

Yıldız, Kerim, and Taysi, Tanyel B. *The Kurds in Iran: The Past, Present and Future*. London, Pluto Press, 2007.

Zabih, Sepehr. *The Communist Movement in Iran*. Berkeley, CA, University of California Press, 1967.

Contemporary Political History

Abdolmohammadi, Pejman, and Cama, Giampiero. *Contemporary Domestic and Foreign Policies of Iran*. London, Palgrave Macmillan, 2020.

Abrahamian, Ervand. *Iran between Two Revolutions*. Princeton, NJ, Princeton University Press, 1982.

A History of Modern Iran. Cambridge, Cambridge University Press, 2008.

Adebahr, Cornelius. *Explaining and Shaping European-Iranian Relations Beyond the Nuclear File*. Abingdon, Routledge, 2017.

Adib-Moghaddam, Arshin. *Iran in World Politics: The Question of the Islamic Republic*. New York, Columbia University Press, 2008.

Akbarzadeh, Shaharam, and Conduit, Dara (Eds). *Iran in the World: President Rouhani's Foreign Policy*. London, Palgrave Macmillan, 2017.

Alikhani, Hossein. *Sanctioning Iran: Anatomy of a Failed Policy*. London, I. B. Tauris, 2000.

Ansari, Ali M. *Iran, Islam and Democracy: The Politics of Managing Change*. London, Royal Institute for International Affairs (Chatham House), 2nd edn, 2006.

Iran under Ahmadinejad: The Politics of Confrontation. Abingdon, Routledge, 2007.

The Politics of Nationalism in Modern Iran. Cambridge, Cambridge University Press, 2012.

Arjomand, Saïd Amir. *The Turban for the Crown: The Islamic Revolution in Iran.* New York, Oxford University Press, 1989.

After Khomeini: Iran Under His Successors. New York, Oxford University Press, 2009.

Ashton, Nigel, and Gibson, Bryan (Eds). *The Iran-Iraq War: New International Perspectives.* Abingdon, Routledge, 2012.

Assadollah, Alam. *The Shah and I: The Confidential Diaries of Iran's Royal Court, 1969–77.* London, I. B. Tauris, 1991.

Bajoghli, Narges. *Iran Reframed: Anxieties of Power in the Islamic Republic.* Stanford, CA, Stanford University Press, 2019.

Beck, Lois. *Nomads in Postrevolutionary Iran: The Qashqa'i in an Era of Change.* Abingdon, Routledge, 2015.

Bani-Sadr, Abol-Hassan. *My Turn to Speak: Iran, the Revolution and Secret Deals with the US.* New York, Brassey's, 1991.

Behrouz, Maziar. *Rebels with a Cause: the Failure of the Left in Iran.* London and New York, I. B. Tauris, 2000.

Blight, James G. *Becoming Enemies: U.S.-Iran Relations and the Iran-Iraq War, 1979-1988.* Lanham, MD, Rowman & Littlefield, 2014.

Boroujerdi, Mehrzad, and Rahimkhani, Kourosh. *Postrevolutionary Iran: A Political Handbook.* Syracuse, NY, Syracuse University Press, 2018.

Brumberg, Daniel. *Reinventing Khomeini: The Struggle for Reform in Iran.* Chicago, IL, University of Chicago Press, 2001.

Calabrese, John. *Revolutionary Horizons: Regional Foreign Policy in Post-Khomeini Iran.* Basingstoke, Macmillan, 1994.

Cheema, Sujata Ashwarya. *India-Iran Relations: Progress, Problems and Prospects.* Abingdon, Routledge, 2017.

Chubin, Shahram. *Iran's Nuclear Ambitions.* Carnegie Endowment for International Peace, 2006.

Chubin, Shahram, and Tripp, Charles. *Iran and Iraq at War.* London, I. B. Tauris, 1988.

Chubin, Shahram, and Zabih, Sepehr. *The Foreign Relations of Iran: A Developing State in the Zone of a Great-Power Conflict.* Berkeley, CA, University of California Press, 1975.

Cohen, Ronen A. *The Rise and Fall of the Mojahedin Khalq, 1987–1997: Their Survival After the Islamic Revolution and Resistance to the Islamic Republic of Iran.* Brighton, Sussex Academic Press, 2008.

Cordesman, Anthony H. *The Iran–Iraq War and Western Security 1984–87.* London, Jane's Publishing Company, 1987.

Iran's Developing Military Capabilities (Significant Issues Series). Washington, DC, Center for Strategic and International Studies, 2005.

Cottam, Richard W. *Iran and the United States: A Cold War Case Study.* Pittsburgh, PA, University of Pittsburgh Press, 1988.

Cronberg, Tarja. *Nuclear Multilateralism and Iran: Inside EU Negotiations.* Abingdon, Routledge, 2017.

Delpech, Thérèse. *Iran and the Bomb: The Abdication of International Responsibility.* London, C. Hurst & Co, 2006.

Donovan, Jerome. *The Iran-Iraq War: Antecedents and Conflict Escalation.* Abingdon, Routledge, 2014.

Ehteshami, Anoushiravan. *After Khomeini: The Iranian Second Republic.* London and New York, Routledge, 1995.

Iran: Politics, Economy and International Relations. Abingdon, Routledge, 2017.

Ehteshami, Anoushiravan, and Molavi, Reza. (Eds). *Iran and the International System.* Abingdon, Routledge, 2011.

Ehteshami, Anoushiravan, and Zweiri, Mahjoob. *Iran and the Rise of its Neoconservatives: The Politics of Tehran's Silent Revolution.* London, I. B. Tauris, 2007.

Ehteshami, Anoushivaran, and Zweiri, Mahjoob. (Eds). *Iran's Foreign Policy: From Khatami to Ahmadinejad.* Reading, Ithaca Press, 2012.

Elling, Rasmus Christian. *Minorities in Iran: Nationalism and Ethnicity after Khomeini.* New York, Palgrave Macmillan, 2013.

Esfandiary, Dina, and Tabatabai, Arianne. 'Iran's ISIS policy', *International Affairs.* Volume 91, Issue 1, 2015, pp. 1–15.

Triple Axis: Iran's Relations with Russia and China. London, I. B. Tauris, 2018.

European External Action Service. *Joint Comprehensive Plan of Action,* 14 July 2015. eeas.europa.eu/statements-eeas/docs/iran_agreement/iran_joint-comprehensive-plan-of-action_en.pdf.

Fathollah-Nejad, Ali. *Iran in an Emerging New World Order: From Ahmadinejad to Rouhani.* London Palgrave Macmillan, 2021.

Fayazmanesh, Sasan. *The United States and Iran: Sanctions, Wars and the Policy of Dual Containment.* Abingdon, Routledge, 2008.

Fischer, M. J. *Iran: From Religious Dispute to Revolution.* Cambridge, MA, Harvard University Press, 1980.

Fitzpatrick, Mark. *The Iranian Nuclear Crisis: Avoiding Worst-case Outcomes.* Abingdon, Routledge, 2008.

Fitzpatrick, Mark, Elleman, Michael, and Izewicz, Paulina. *Uncertain Future: the JCPOA and Iran's Nuclear and Missile Programmes.* Abingdon, Routledge, 2019.

Forozan, Hesam. *The Military in Post-Revolutionary Iran: the Evolution and Roles of the Revolutionary Guards.* Abingdon, Routledge, 2018.

Furtig, Henner, and Ehteshami, Anoushiravan. *Iran's Rivalry with Saudi Arabia between the Gulf Wars.* Reading, Ithaca Press, 2001.

Gärtner, Heinz and Shahmoradi, Mitra. *Iran in the International System: Between Great Powers and Great Ideas.* London, Routledge, 2019.

Gheissari, Ali (Ed.). *Contemporary Iran: Economy, Society, Politics.* Oxford, Oxford University Press, 2009.

Gheissari, Ali, and Nasr, Vali. *Democracy in Iran: History and the Quest for Liberty.* New York, Oxford University Press, 2006.

Gohardani, Farhad, and Tizro, Fahra. *The Political Economy of Iran: Development, Revolution and Political Violence.* Cham, Palgrave Macmillan, 2019.

Goodarzi, Jubin M. *Syria and Iran: Diplomatic Alliance and Power Politics in the Middle East.* London, I. B. Tauris, 2009.

Goode, James F. *The United States and Iran, 1946–51: The Diplomacy of Neglect.* New York, St Martin's Press, 1989.

Halliday, Fred. *Iran: Dictatorship and Development.* London, 1978.

Harris, Kevan. *A Social Revolution: Politics and the Welfare State in Iran.* Oakland, CA, University of California Press, 2017.

Herzig, Edmund. *Iran and the Former Soviet South.* London, Royal Institute of International Affairs (Chatham House), 1996.

Heydemann, Steven, and Leenders, Reinoud (Eds). *Middle East Authoritarianisms: Governance, Contestation, and Regime Resilience in Syria and Iran.* Redwood City, CA, Stanford University Press, 2013.

Hiro, Dilip. *Iran under the Ayatollahs.* London, Routledge and Kegan Paul, 1984.

Neighbours, Not Friends: Iraq and Iran after the Gulf Wars. London, Routledge, 2001.

Holliday, Shabnam. *Defining Iran: Politics of Resistance.* Farnham, Ashgate Publishers, 2011.

Hooglund, Eric, and Stenberg, Leif. (Eds). *Navigating Contemporary Iran: Challenging Economic, Social and Political Perceptions.* Abingdon, Routledge, 2012.

Hoveyda, Ferydoun. *The Fall of the Shah.* London, Weidenfeld and Nicolson, 1979.

Jafarzadeh, Alireza. *The Iran Threat: President Ahmadinejad and the Coming Nuclear Crisis.* London, Palgrave Macmillan, 2008.

Jervis, Robert, and Wirtz, James J. (Eds). *The 2007 Iran Nuclear Estimate Revisited: Anatomy of a Controversy.* Abingdon, Routledge, 2022.

Joshi, Shashank. *The Permanent Crisis: Iran's Nuclear Trajectory.* Abingdon, Routledge, 2012.

Karsh, Efraim. *The Iran–Iraq War: 1980–1988 (Essential Histories).* Oxford, Osprey, 2002.

Katouzian, Homa, and Shahidi, Hossein. *Iran in the 21st Century: Politics, Economics and Conflict.* Abingdon, Routledge, 2007.

Kaussler, Bernd. *Iran's Nuclear Diplomacy: Power Politics and Conflict Resolution.* Abingdon, Routledge, 2013.

Kazemzadeh, Masoud. *Iran's Foreign Policy: Elite Factionalism, Ideology, the Nuclear Weapons Program, and the United States.* London, Routledge, 2020.

Keddie, Nikki R. *Modern Iran: Roots and Results of Revolution.* New Haven, CT, Yale University Press, revised edn, 2006.

Khatami, Mohammad. *Islam, Dialogue and Civil Society.* Canberra, Centre for Arab and Islamic Studies, Australian National University, 2000.

Khomeini, Ayatollah Ruhollah. *Islam and Revolution: Writings and Declarations of Imam Khomeini* (trans. and ed. by Hamid Algar). Berkeley, CA, Mizan Press, 1982.

Kinzer, Stephen. *All the Shah's Men: An American Coup and the Roots of Middle Eastern Terror.* John Wiley & Sons, Inc, 2004.

Kozanov, Nikolai. *Iran's Strategic Thinking: The Evolution of Iran's Foreign Policy, 1979-2018.* Berlin, Gerlach Press, 2018.

Krause, Joachim (Ed.). *Iran's Nuclear Programme: Strategic Implications.* Abingdon, Routledge, 2011.

Kurzman, Charles. *The Unthinkable Revolution in Iran.* Cambridge, MA, Harvard University Press, 2004.

Lenczowski, George. (Ed.). *Iran under the Pahlavis*. Stanford, CA, Hoover Institution Press, 1978.

Leslie, Jonathan G. *Fear and Insecurity: Israel and the Iran Threat Narrative*. Oxford, Oxford University Press, 2023.

Litvak, Meir. *Constructing Nationalism in Iran: from the Qajars to the Islamic Republic*. Abingdon, Routledge, 2017.

Mabon, Simon. *The Struggle for Supremacy in the Middle East: Saudi Arabia and Iran*. Cambridge, Cambridge University Press, 2023.

Malek-Ahmadi, Farshad. *Trapped by History: 100 Years of Struggle for Constitutionalism and Democracy in Iran*. Abingdon, Routledge, 2006.

McEachern, Patrick, and O'Brien McEachern, Jaclyn. *North Korea, Iran and the Challenge to International Order: A Comparative Perspective*. Abingdon, Routledge, 2017.

Mir-Hosseini, Ziba, and Tapper, Richard. *Islam and Democracy in Iran: Eshkevari and the Quest for Reform*. London, I. B. Tauris, 2006.

Mirsepassi, Ali. *Democracy in Modern Iran: Islam, Culture and Political Change*. New York, New York University, 2010.

Mohammadi, Ali (Ed.). *Iran Encountering Globalization: Problems and Prospects*. Abingdon, Routledge, 2006.

Moin, Baqer. *Khomeini: Life of the Ayatollah*. London and New York, I. B. Tauris, 1999.

Moshirzadeh, Homeira. 'Discursive Foundations of Iran's Nuclear Policy', *Security Dialogue*. Volume 38, Issue 4, 2007, pp. 521–543.

Moslem, Mehdi. *Factional Politics in Post-Khomeini Iran*. Syracuse, NY, Syracuse University Press, 2002.

Mousavian, Seyed Hossein. *Iran-Europe Relations: Challenges and Opportunities*. Abingdon, Routledge, 2010.

Mousavian, Seyed Hossein, and Shahidsaless, Shahir. *Iran and the United States: An Insider's View on the Failed Past and the Road to Peace*. New York, Bloomsbury Academic, 2014.

Murray, Donette. *US Foreign Policy and Iran: American-Iranian Relations since the Islamic Revolution*. Abingdon, Routledge, 2010.

Nick Pay, Vahid. *Republican Islam: Power and Authority in Iran*. London, I. B. Tauris, 2016.

Ostovar, Afshon. *Vanguard of the Imam: Religion, Politics, and Iran's Revolutionary Guards*. New York, Oxford University Press, 2016.

Pargoo, Mahmoud. *Secularization of Islam in Post-Revolutionary Iran*. London, Routledge, 2021.

Parsa, Misagh. *Democracy in Iran: Why it Failed and How it Might Succeed*. Cambridge, MA, Harvard University Press, 2016.

Parsons, Sir Anthony. *The Pride and the Fall: Iran 1974–79*. London, Jonathan Cape, 1984.

Patrikarakos, David. *Nuclear Iran: The Birth of an Atomic State*. London, I. B. Tauris, 2012.

Pedram, Ali M. *Parliament and the Process of Democratization in the Islamic Republic of Iran*. Reading, Ithaca Press, 2009.

Perkes, Volker. *Iran—Eine politische Herausforderung: die Prekäre Balance von Vertrauen und Sicherheit*. Berlin, Suhrkamp Verlag, 2008.

Potter, Lawrence G., and Sick, Gary G. (Eds). *Iran, Iraq and the Legacies of War*. London, Palgrave Macmillan, 2006.

Rahnema, Ali. *Superstition as Ideology in Iranian Politics: From Majlesi to Ahmadinejad*. Cambridge, Cambridge University Press, 2011.

Rakel, Eva Patricia. *Power, Islam, and Political Elite in Iran: A Study on the Iranian Political Elite from Khomeini to Ahmadinejad*. Boston, MA, Brill, 2009.

Ramazani, Rouhollah K. 'Iran's Foreign Policy: Both North and South', *Middle East Journal*, Volume 46, Issue 3, 1992, pp. 393-412.

Rezun, Miron (Ed.). *Iran at the Crossroads: Global Relations in a Turbulent Decade*. Oxford, Westview Press, 1990.

Sadeghi-Boroujerdi, Eskandar. 'Strategic Depth, Counter-insurgency & the Logic of Sectarianization: The Islamic Republic of Iran's Security Doctrine and Its Regional Implications', in Hashemi, Nader, and Postel, Danny (Eds). *Sectarianization: Mapping the New Politics of the Middle East*. London, C. Hurst & Co, 2016.

Samore, Gary (Ed.). *Iran's Strategic Weapons Programmes: A Net Assessment*. Abingdon, Routledge, 2005.

Schirazi, Asghar. *The Constitution of Iran: Politics and the State in the Islamic Republic*. London, I. B. Tauris, 1998.

Schwerin, Ulrich von. *The Dissident Mullah: Ayatollah Montazeri and the Struggle for Reform in Revolutionary Iran*. London, I. B. Tauris, 2015.

Sedghi, Hamideh. *Women and Politics in Iran: Veiling, Unveiling, and Reveiling*. Cambridge, Cambridge University Press, 2007.

Takeyh, Ray. *Guardians of the Revolution: Iran and the World in the Age of the Ayatollahs*. New York, Oxford University Press, 2009.

Tazmini, Ghoncheh. *Khatami's Iran: the Islamic Republic and the Turbulent Path to Reform*. London, I. B. Tauris, 2009.

Vahman, Fereydun. *175 Years of Persecution: A History of the Babis and Baha'is of Iran*. Oxford, Oneworld, 2019.

Vatanka, Alex. *The Battle of the Ayatollahs in Iran: The United States, Foreign Policy, and Political Rivalry Since 1979*. London, I. B. Tauris, 2021.

Wastnidge, Edward. 'The Modalities of Iranian Soft Power: From Cultural Diplomacy to Soft War', *Politics*, Vol. 35 (3-4), 2015, pp. 364–377.

Diplomacy and Reform in Iran: Foreign Policy under Khatami. London, I. B. Tauris, 2016.

Zaccara, Luciano (Ed.). *The Foreign Policy of Iran under President Hassan Rouhani*. London, Palgrave Macmillan, 2018.

Zarif, Mohammad Javad. 'What Iran Really Wants: Iranian Foreign Policy in the Rouhani Era', *Foreign Affairs*, Vol. 93, Issue 3, 2014, pp. 49–59.

Zonis, Marrin. *Majestic Failure: The Fall of the Shah*. Chicago, IL, University of Chicago Press, 1991.

Economy

Alizadeh, Parvin (Ed.). *The Economy of Iran: The Dilemmas of an Islamic State*. London, I. B. Tauris, 2001.

Alizadeh, Parvin, and Hakimian, Hassan (Eds). *Iran and the Global Economy: Petro Populism, Islam and Economic Sanctions*. Abingdon, Routledge, 2013.

Amid, Mohammad Javad. *Poverty, Agriculture and Reform in Iran*. London, Routledge, 1990.

Amuzegar, Jahangir. *Iran's Economy Under the Islamic Republic*. London, I. B. Tauris, 1997.

The Islamic Republic of Iran: Reflections on an Emerging Economy. Abingdon, Routledge, 2014.

Bharier, Julian. *Economic Development in Iran 1900–1970*. London, Oxford University Press, 1971.

Congressional Research Service. *Iran Sanctions*. Washington, DC, 11 Sept. 2019. crsreports.congress.gov/product/pdf/RS/RS20871/299.

Elm, Mostafa. *Oil, Power and Principle: Iran's Oil Nationalization and its Aftermath*. Syracuse, NY, Syracuse University Press, 1992.

Heiss, Mary Ann. *Empire and Nationhood: The United States, Great Britain and Iranian Oil, 1950–1954*. New York, Columbia University Press, 1998.

Issawi, Charles. *The Economic History of Iran, 1800–1919*. University of Chicago Press, 1972.

Looney, Robert E. *Economic Origins of the Iranian Revolution*. New York, NY, Pergamon Press, 1982.

'Iran's Beleaguered Economy', *Milken Institute Review*, 20 September 2017. www.milkenreview.org/articles/irans-beleaguered-economy.

Mazarei, Adnan. *Iran Has a Slow Motion Banking Crisis*. Washington, DC, Peterson Institute for International Economics, June 2019. www.piie.com/publications/policy-briefs/iran-has-slow-motion-banking-crisis.

Mofid, Kamran. *The Economic Consequences of the Gulf War*. London, Routledge, 1990.

Pesaran, Evaleila. *Iran's Struggle for Economic Independence: Reform and Counter-Reform in the Post-Revolutionary Era*. Abingdon, Routledge, 2011.

Shakoori, Ali. *The State and Rural Development in Post-Revolutionary Iran*. New York, St Martin's Press, 2001.

IRAQ

Geography

Iraq is bounded to the north by Türkiye (as Turkey was officially known from June 2022), to the east by Iran, to the south by Kuwait and the Persian (Arabian) Gulf, to the south-west by Saudi Arabia and Jordan, and to the north-west by the Syrian Arab Republic. The actual frontier lines present one or two unusual features. First, there exists between Iraq, Kuwait and Saudi Arabia a Neutral Zone, which was devised to facilitate the migrations of pastoral nomads, who cover great distances each year in search of pasture for their animals and who move regularly between several countries. Second, the frontier with Iran in its extreme southern portion, below Basra, follows the course of the Shatt al-Arab waterway (the confluence of the Tigris and Euphrates), which flows into the Gulf. Under the Algiers Agreement of March 1975, accepted by Iraq in 1988, the border follows the Thalweg Line in the middle of the deepest shipping channel in the Shatt al-Arab estuary. Third, the inclusion of the northern province of Mosul within Iraq was agreed only in 1926. Owing to its petroleum deposits, this territory was in dispute between Türkiye, Syria and Iraq. Again, the presence of large numbers of migratory nomads, journeying each season between Iran, Türkiye, Syria and Iraq, was a complicating factor. In March 1984 a treaty was signed by Jordan and Iraq that finally demarcated the border between the two countries and under which Iraq ceded some 50 sq km to Jordan.

PHYSICAL FEATURES

The old name of Iraq (Mesopotamia = land between the rivers) indicates the main physical aspect of the country—the presence of the two river valleys of the Tigris and Euphrates, which merge in their lower courses. On the eastern side of this double valley the Zagros Mountains appear as an abrupt wall, overhanging the riverine lowlands, particularly in the south, below the capital, Baghdad. North of the latitude of Baghdad the rise to the mountains is more gradual, with several intervening hill ranges, such as the Jebel Hamrin. These ranges are fairly low and narrow at first, with separating lowlands, but towards the main Zagros topography becomes more imposing, and summits over 3,000 m in height occur. This region, lying north and east of Baghdad, is the ancient land of Assyria; nowadays the higher hill ranges lying in the extreme east are known as Iraqi Kurdistan, since many Kurdish tribes inhabit them.

On the western side of the river valley the land rises gradually to form the plateau that continues into Syria, Jordan and Saudi Arabia, and its maximum height in Iraq is about 1,000 m. In places it is possible to trace a cliff formation, where a more resistant bed of rock stands out prominently, and from this the name of the country is said to be derived (Iraq = cliff). There is no sharp geographical break between Iraq and its western neighbours comparable with that between Iraq and Iran; the frontier lines are artificial.

The Tigris, 1,850 km (1,150 miles) in length, rises in Türkiye, and is joined by numerous and often large tributaries both in Türkiye and Iraq. The Euphrates, 2,350 km in length, also rises in Türkiye and flows first through Syria and then Iraq, joining the Tigris in its lower course at Qurnah, to form the stream known as the Shatt al-Arab (or Arvand river, as it is called by the Iranians), which is 185 km in length. Unlike the Tigris, the Euphrates receives no tributaries during its passage through Iraq. Above the region of Baghdad both rivers flow in well-defined channels, with retaining valley walls. Below Baghdad, however, the vestiges of a retaining valley disappear, and the rivers meander over a vast open plain with only a slight drop in level—in places merely 1.5 m or 2.0 m in 100 km. Here the rivers are raised on great levees, or banks of silt and mud (which they have laid down), and now lie several feet above the level of the surrounding plain. One remarkable feature is the change in the relative level of the two river beds—water can be led from one to the other according to the district, and this possibility, utilized by irrigation engineers for centuries, still remains the basic principle of present-day development. Old river channels, fully or partially abandoned by the river, are also a feature of the Mesopotamian lowland, associated with wide areas of swamp, lakes and sandbars. The Tigris, though narrower than the Euphrates, is swifter, and carries far more water.

As the sources of both rivers lie in the mountains of Türkiye, the current is fast, and upstream navigation is difficult in the middle and upper reaches. In spring, following the melting of snows in Asia Minor, both rivers begin to rise, reaching a maximum in April (Tigris) and May (Euphrates). Floods of 3.6 m to 6.0 m occur, and 10.0 m is known—this in a region where the land may fall only 4 m or less in level over 100 km. Immense areas are regularly inundated, levees often collapse, and villages and roads, where these exist, must be built on high embankments. The Tigris is particularly liable to sudden flooding. In lower Iraq wide expanses are inundated every year. Construction of the Wadi Tharthar control scheme, however, greatly reduced the incidence of severe flooding, particularly along the Tigris.

Roads were formerly difficult to maintain because of floods, and the rail system was of different gauges. Standard-gauge rail links were constructed: north–south from Mosul to Basra via Baghdad; various cross-country lines; and an extension along the Euphrates valley towards north-eastern Syria.

As a result of the former difficulties in communication, many communities of differing cultures and ways of life have persisted. Minority groups have thus been a feature of Iraq.

CLIMATE

The summers are overwhelmingly hot, with shade temperatures of over 43°C. Winters may be surprisingly cold: frost, though very rare in the south, can be severe in the north. Sudden hot spells during winter are another feature in the centre and south of Iraq. Rainfall is scanty over all of the country, except for the north-east (Assyria), where annual precipitation of 400 mm–600 mm occurs—enough to grow crops without irrigation. Elsewhere farming is entirely dependent upon irrigation from river water. The great extent of standing water in many parts of Iraq leads to an unduly high air humidity, which explains the notorious reputation of the Mesopotamian summer.

POPULATION

According to the Constitution ratified in 2005, Arabic and Kurdish are the official languages of Iraq. Arabic is the most widely used and the first language in the Arab governorates, while Kurdish is the primary language in the Kurdish Autonomous Region. Dialects of Turkish are current in the north, while variants of Persian are spoken by tribes in the east. The total population of the country was estimated by the United Nations (UN) at 45,504,560 at mid-2023, giving a density of 104.8 people per sq km. According to UN estimates, Baghdad is Iraq's largest city, with a population of 7,711,305 (incl. suburbs) at mid-2023. Other major cities included Mosul (1,792,020), Basra (1,448,124) and Kirkuk (1,074,884).

Important minorities live in, or close to, the hill country of the north: the Kurds; the Yazidis of the Jebel Sinjar; the Assyrian Christians (the name refers to their geographical location, and has no historical connection); and various communities of Uniate and Orthodox Christians. In addition, there were important groups of Jews—more than in most other Muslim countries—although, since the establishment of the State of Israel, much emigration has taken place. Nowadays only a tiny, and rapidly dwindling, Jewish community remains in Baghdad. The majority of the Muslims follow Shi'a rites, although there is a significant minority of Sunni Muslims, particularly in the western governorates.

History

LIAM ANDERSON

OTTOMAN IRAQ

The leader of the Sunni Ottoman Turks, Sultan Suleyman I (Suleyman the Magnificent), conquered Baghdad in 1534–35 during his campaign against Safavid Ismail, the Shah of Persia. Although Persian control was restored between 1623 and 1638, Iraq was to remain, at least nominally, under Ottoman control until the First World War. A series of Mamluk pashas in the 18th century engaged in wars with Persia, and towards the end of the century had to contend with Kurdish insurrection in the north and raids by Wahhabi tribesmen from the south. In the early 19th century the Ottoman Sultan decided to regain direct possession of Iraq and end the Mamluk system. Sultan Mahmoud II sent Ali Ridha Pasha to perform this task in 1831. A severe outbreak of plague hampered the Mamluks, the Mamluk ruler Da'ud Pasha was deposed, and the Mamluk regiments were exterminated.

WESTERN INFLUENCE

Although some of the European nations had long been in contact with Iraq through their commercial interests in the Persian (Arabian) Gulf, Western influences were slow to penetrate the province. By 1800 there was a British Resident at Basra and two years later a British Consulate in Baghdad. France also maintained agents in these cities, and French and Italian religious orders had settlements in the land. During the tanzimat reform period of the mid-19th century, the Ottoman Government did much to impose direct control over Kurdistan and the mountainous areas close to the Persian border, but serious reform did not begin until 1869, when Midhat Pasha arrived in Baghdad. After his departure in 1872, reform and European influence continued to advance, albeit slowly.

In November 1914 the United Kingdom and the Ottoman Empire were at war. British troops occupied the Shatt al-Arab region and, through the necessity of war, transformed Basra into an efficient and well-equipped port. A premature advance on Baghdad in 1915 ended in the retreat of the British forces to Kut and their eventual capitulation to the Ottomans in April 1916. A new offensive launched from Basra in late 1916 brought about the capture of Baghdad in March 1917. Kirkuk was taken in 1918, but before the Allies could seize Mosul, the Ottoman Government sought and obtained an armistice in October. For two years, until late 1920, the Commander-in-Chief of the British forces, acting through a civil commissioner, continued to be responsible for the administration of Iraq from Basra to Mosul, all the apparatus of a modern system of rule being created in Baghdad.

The last phase of Ottoman domination in Iraq, especially after the Young Turk Revolution in 1908, had witnessed a marked growth of Arab nationalist sentiment. The prospect of independence, which the Allies held out to the Arabs during the war, strengthened and extended the nationalist movement. In April 1920 the UK received a mandate for Iraq from the conference at San Remo, Italy. This news was soon followed by a serious insurrection among the tribesmen of the south. The revolt, caused partly by instinctive dislike of foreign rule but also by vigorous nationalist propaganda, was not wholly suppressed until early in the next year. However, in October military rule in Iraq was formally terminated. An Arab Council of State, advised by British officials and responsible for the administration, now came into being, and in March 1921 the Amir Faisal bin Hussain agreed to rule as King in Baghdad. His ceremonial accession took place in August.

The Najdi (Saudi Arabian) frontier with Iraq was defined in the Treaty of Mohammara in May 1922. Saudi concern over loss of traditional grazing rights resulted in further talks between Ibn Sa'ud and the British Civil Commissioner in Iraq, and a Neutral Zone of 7,000 sq km was established adjacent to the western tip of the Kuwait frontier. A further agreement concerning the administration of this zone was signed between Iraq and Saudi Arabia in May 1938.

MODERN IRAQ

Despite the opposition of the more extreme nationalists, an Anglo-Iraqi Treaty was signed on 10 October 1922. It embodied the provisions of the mandate, safeguarded the judicial rights of foreigners and guaranteed the special interests of the UK in Iraq. An electoral law facilitated the choice of a constituent assembly, which met in March 1924 and ratified the treaty with the UK. It accepted, too, an organic law declaring Iraq to be a sovereign state with a constitutional hereditary monarchy and a representative system of government. In 1925 the League of Nations recommended that the wilaya (administrative district) of Mosul, to which the Turks had laid claim, be incorporated into the new kingdom, a decision finally implemented in the treaty of July 1926 between the interested parties: the UK, Turkey (officially designated as Türkiye from June 2022) and Iraq. By 1926 a fully constituted parliament was in session in Baghdad, and all the ministries, as well as most of the larger departments of the administration, were in effective control. In 1930 a new treaty was signed with the UK, establishing a close alliance between the two countries for 25 years and granting the UK the use of airbases at Shuaiba and Habbaniya. On 3 October 1932 Iraq entered the League of Nations as an independent power, the mandate now being terminated.

Numerous difficulties confronted the kingdom after 1932: for example, the animosities between the Sunni Muslims and the powerful Shi'a tribes on the Euphrates, which tended to divide and embitter political life; the problem of relations with the Kurds, some of whom wanted a separate Kurdish state, and with other minorities such as the Assyrians; and the complicated task of reform in land tenure and of improvement in agriculture, irrigation, flood control, public services and communications. During these years the Government was little more than a facade of democratic forms concealing faction and intrigue. It is not surprising, therefore, that the first years of full independence made rather halting progress towards efficient rule. The dangerous nature of domestic tensions was demonstrated by the Assyrian massacre of 1933, perpetrated by Iraqi armed forces. Political intrigue from Baghdad was partly responsible for the outbreak of tribal revolt along the Euphrates in 1935–36. The army crushed the insurrection without much difficulty and then, under the leadership of Gen. Bakr Sidqi, and in alliance with disappointed politicians and reformist elements, brought about a coup in October 1936. The new regime failed to fulfil its assurances of reform; its policies alienated the tribal chieftains and gave rise to serious tensions even within the armed forces, which led to the assassination of Bakr Sidqi in August 1937.

In 1937 Iraq joined Turkey, Iran (as Persia had been renamed in 1935) and Afghanistan in the Sa'dabad Pact, which arranged for consultation in all disputes that might affect the common interests of the four states. A treaty signed with Iran in July 1937 and ratified in the following year provided for the specific acceptance of the boundary between the two countries as it had been defined in 1914. Relations with the UK deteriorated after 1937, mainly because of the growth of anti-Zionist feeling and of resentment at British policy in Palestine. German influence in Iraq increased greatly at this time, especially among those political and military circles associated with the army group later to be known as the Golden Square. Iraq severed its diplomatic connections with Germany at the beginning of the Second World War, but in 1941 the army commanders carried out a new coup, establishing, under the nominal leadership of Rashid Ali al-Gaylani, a regime that announced its non-belligerent intentions. A disagreement over the passage of British troops through Iraq left no doubt of the pro-German sympathies of the Gaylani Government and led to hostilities that ended with the Allied occupation of Basra and Baghdad in May 1941. Thereafter, Iraq co-operated with the Allies and declared war on the Axis powers in 1943.

Iraq, during the years after the Second World War, was to experience much internal tension and unrest. In January 1948 a new Anglo-Iraqi agreement was signed, replacing that of 1930 and incorporating substantial concessions, among them the British evacuation of the airbases at Shuaiba and Habbaniya and the creation of a joint board for the co-ordination of all matters relating to mutual defence. The animosities arising from the situation in Palestine provoked riots in Baghdad, directed against the new agreement with the UK; the unrest was sufficiently disturbing to oblige the Iraqi Government to repudiate the settlement.

FOREIGN RELATIONS, 1955–58: THE BAGHDAD PACT AND THE SUEZ CRISIS

Iraq during these years found itself caught between the growing presence of the Union of Soviet Socialist Republics (USSR) in Middle Eastern (specifically Arab) affairs and the efforts of the Western Powers to counter that presence. In February 1955 Iraq made an alliance with Turkey for mutual co-operation and defence, a pact to which the UK acceded in April, agreeing also to end the Anglo–Iraqi agreement of 1930 and surrender its airbases at Shuaiba and Habbaniya. When Pakistan and Iran followed suit in late 1955, the so-called Baghdad Pact was completed. A defensive cordon now existed along the southern fringe of the USSR.

The outbreak of hostilities between Israel and Egypt on 29 October 1956 and the armed intervention of British and French forces against Egypt (31 October–6 November) emboldened opposition in Iraq to all connections with the Western Powers. Indeed, Iraq broke off diplomatic relations with France and announced that it could give no assurance of taking part in further sessions of the Council of the Baghdad Pact if delegates from the UK were present. However, the equivocal attitude of the Baghdad Government during the Suez crisis provoked unrest in Iraq, with fatal disturbances in Najaf and Mosul. Martial law was imposed on 31 October and was not lifted until 27 May 1957. In February 1958 King Faisal of Iraq and King Hussein of Jordan joined together in an abortive Arab Federation (see Jordan).

OVERTHROW OF THE MONARCHY AND INTERNAL UPHEAVAL, 1958–68

King Faisal II, the Crown Prince of Iraq and Gen. Nuri al-Said were all killed during a coup, initiated on 14 July 1958 by units of the Iraqi army. Iraq became a republic and power was placed in the hands of a Council of Sovereignty exercising presidential authority, and of a Cabinet led by Brig. Abd al-Karim Kassem, with the rank of Prime Minister. However, a power struggle soon developed between the two main architects of the coup—Brig. (later Gen.) Kassem, the Prime Minister, and Col. (later Field Marshal) Abd al-Salam Muhammad Aref, the Deputy Prime Minister and Minister of the Interior. Aref was associated with the influential Baath Party and had shown himself to be a supporter of union between Iraq and the United Arab Republic (UAR—the union of Egypt and Syria). In September he was dismissed and, in November, was tried on a charge of plotting against the interests of Iraq. Upon its reconstitution in February 1959, the new regime proved to be hostile to the UAR and favoured a form of independent nationalism with left-wing tendencies. One of the new regime's earliest acts, in March, was to withdraw from the Baghdad Pact. Shortly afterwards, the British Royal Air Force contingent at Habbaniya was recalled.

In early 1959 the Iraqi communists, operating mainly under the aegis of the so-called People's Resistance Force (PRF), were refused representation in the Government, but had otherwise already infiltrated the armed forces and the civil service. Kassem began to introduce measures to limit communist influence inside the Government and the administration of the country. In July fighting occurred at Kirkuk between the Kurds (supported by the PRF) and the Turkomans, with the result that Kassem disbanded the PRF. More important for the Government was the fact that, in March 1961, much of the Kurdish population in northern Iraq rose in rebellion under Mustafa Barzani, the President of the Kurdistan Democratic Party (KDP)—a party established in 1958 after Barzani's return from an exile occasioned by an earlier unsuccessful revolt in 1946—owing to the Government's refusal to accede to repeated demands for Kurdish autonomy; Barzani proclaimed an independent Kurdish state. By September 1961 the rebels controlled the mountainous territory for some 400 km along the Iraq–Turkey and Iraq–Iran frontiers, from Zakho in the west to Sulaimaniya in the east. The Kurds were able to consolidate their hold over much of northern Iraq during 1962, and by December 1963 Kurdish forces had advanced south towards the Khanaqin area and the main road linking Iraq with Iran. Negotiations for peace began near Sulaimaniya in January 1964 and led to a ceasefire on 10 February. The national claims of the Kurds were to be recognized in a new provisional Constitution for Iraq, but the Kurdish tribes refused to lay down their arms until their political demands had been granted. Despite the negotiation of this settlement, no definitive solution to the Kurdish problem had emerged.

Kassem was killed on 8 February 1963 in a military coup against his regime that had been planned by nationalist army officers and the Baath Party. Aref was now promoted to the office of President and a new Cabinet was created under Brig. (later Gen.) Ahmad Hassan al-Bakr. The Baath Party, founded in 1941 (in Syria) and dedicated to the ideas of Arab unity, socialism and freedom, drew its main support from military elements, intellectuals and the middle classes, but in Iraq it was divided into a pro-Egyptian wing advocating union with the UAR and a more independent wing disinclined to accept authoritarian control from Egypt. The coup triggered the arrest of pro-Kassem and communist elements, mass trials, several executions, confiscations of property and a purge of the officer corps and civil service.

The schism between the extremist and the more moderate Baath elements soon widened. At the end of September 1963 the extremists dominated the Baath Regional Council in Iraq, and their position was strengthened by an international Baath conference held in Damascus, the Syrian capital, in October, which supported a federal union between Syria and Iraq and put forward more radical social and economic policies. None the less, a further Baathist conference in Baghdad in November enabled the moderates to elect a new Baath Regional Council in Iraq with their own adherents in control. At this juncture the extremists attempted a coup, during which elements of the air force attacked the presidential palace and the Ministry of Defence. On 18 November President Aref assumed full powers in Iraq, with the support of the armed forces, and a new Revolutionary Command was established in Baghdad.

In July 1965 several pro-Egyptian ministers resigned, and at the beginning of September a new administration was installed, with Brig. Aref Abd al-Razzaq as Prime Minister. Abd al-Razzaq, reputed to be pro-Egyptian, tried to seize full power in Iraq, but his attempted coup failed, and on 16 September he, together with some of his supporters, found refuge in Cairo, Egypt. On 13 April 1966 President Aref was killed in a helicopter crash. His brother, Maj.-Gen. Abd al-Rahman Aref, succeeded him as President with the approval of the Cabinet and of the National Defence Council. In late June Abd al-Razzaq led a second abortive coup. Meanwhile, the war against the Kurds continued during 1964–66, and fighting in December 1965 close to the Iraq–Iran border led to several frontier violations, which exacerbated tensions between the two states.

THE 1968 COUP AND ITS AFTERMATH

Popular perceptions of the regime were that it was corrupt and inefficient, and consequently the sudden bloodless coup of 17 July 1968 did not surprise many observers. Former Prime Minister al-Bakr became President; the deposed President Abd al-Rahman Aref went into exile and his Prime Minister, Taher Yahya, was imprisoned on corruption charges. A new Government was soon dismissed by President Bakr, who accused it of 'reactionary tendencies'. He then appointed himself Prime Minister and Commander-in-Chief of the Armed Forces. However, by November there were frequent reports of a purge being directed against opponents of the new regime, and freedom of political expression seemed to have disappeared. A former Minister of Foreign Affairs, Dr Nasser al-Hani, was murdered, and former Prime Minister Dr Abd al-Rahman al-Bazzaz was arrested as a 'counter-revolutionary leader'. Open hostilities with the Kurds erupted in October 1968 for the first time since the June 1966 ceasefire. The Baghdad Government had little success in gaining military control, claiming that the rebels were receiving aid from Iran and Israel. Fighting continued unabated throughout 1969, the Kurds demanding autonomy within the state and asking for United Nations (UN) mediation.

In June 1972 Iraq nationalized the interests of the Iraq Petroleum Co, and agreement on outstanding points of dispute was finally reached in February 1973. The company agreed to settle Iraqi claims for retrospective royalties by paying £141m., and to waive its objections to Law No. 80, under which the North Rumaila fields had been seized in 1961.

An abortive coup took place in July 1973, led by the security chief, Nazim Kazzar. The Minister of Defence, Gen. Hammad Shehab, was killed, but the coup was ultimately unsuccessful. There was some speculation that the coup had been attempted by a civilian faction within the Baath Party to eliminate President Bakr and the military faction. Consequences of the attempted coup included an amendment to the Constitution giving more power to the President and the formation of a National Front between the Baath Party and the Iraqi Communist Party (ICP).

SETTLEMENT WITH THE KURDS

In March 1970 a 15-article peace plan was announced by the Revolutionary Command Council (RCC) and the Kurdish leaders. The plan conceded that the Kurds should participate fully in government; that Kurdish officials should be appointed in areas inhabited by a Kurdish majority; that Kurdish should be the official language, together with Arabic, in Kurdish areas; that development of Kurdish areas should be implemented; and that the Provisional Constitution should be amended to incorporate the rights of the Kurds. The agreement was widely accepted by the Kurdish community and fighting ceased, thus ending a costly war, which had delayed the national development programme.

According to the agreement, the deadline for its implementation was 11 March 1974. On expiry of the deadline, Saddam Hussain al-Tikriti, the Vice-President of the RCC, announced the granting of autonomy to the Kurds. The KDP claimed that the Iraqi offer did not fulfil its demands for full government representation, which included membership of the RCC, but a minority of Kurds welcomed the proposals. Barzani and his *peshmerga* ('those who confront death') militia commenced an armed insurgency in northern Iraq. By August the Kurdish war had reached a new level of intensity; the Government in Baghdad was directing large military resources against the *peshmerga*, deploying tanks, field guns and bombers. About 130,000 Kurds, largely civilians, took refuge in Iran, which was also supplying arms to the *peshmerga*. However, the Kurdish rebellion collapsed after Iraq and Iran signed an accord at the meeting of the Organization of the Petroleum Exporting Countries (OPEC, see p. 1161) in Algiers, Algeria, in March 1975, ending their border dispute and agreeing to end 'infiltrations of a subversive character'; Barzani decided that he could not continue his struggle without Iran's aid and fled to the Iranian capital, Tehran. (He died in the USA in 1979, and was succeeded as leader of the KDP by his son, Masoud.)

On 16 July 1979 Saddam Hussain replaced Bakr as President of Iraq and Chairman of the RCC. A few days later an attempted coup was reported, and several members of the RCC were sentenced to death for their alleged part in the plot.

WAR WITH IRAN

Iraq was dissatisfied with the 1975 peace agreement with Iran (although from a domestic aspect it had virtually ended the Kurdish rebellion) and wanted to re-establish the Shatt al-Arab boundary, whereby it controlled the whole waterway. The Iranian Revolution of 1979 increased tensions, as the new regime in Tehran accused Iraq of fomenting demands for Arab autonomy in the Iranian province of Khuzestan. In addition, Iraq's Sunni leadership feared that the Islamic Revolution in Iran could inspire Iraq's Shi'a majority. Fighting on the border between Iran and Iraq occurred frequently as 1980 progressed, and open warfare began on 22 September when Iraqi forces advanced into Iran along a 480-km front. Iran had ignored Iraqi demands for the withdrawal of Iranian forces from Zain ul-Qos on the border, Iraq maintaining that this territory should have been returned by Iran under the 1975 agreement. Iraq had therefore abrogated the Shatt al-Arab agreement on 16 September 1980.

Most commentators agree that Saddam Hussain's real intention when he invaded Iran was to topple the Islamic revolutionary regime. However, resistance was fiercer than he expected, and a stalemate was soon reached along the invasion front, while various international peace missions sought in vain for a solution. In early 1982 Iranian forces launched successful counter-offensives, one in the region of Dezful in March and another in April that resulted in the recapture of Khorramshahr by the Iranians in May. By late June Saddam Hussain had to acknowledge that the invasion of Iran had been a failure, and he arranged for the complete withdrawal of Iraqi troops from Iranian territory. In July the Iranian army crossed into Iraq, giving rise to the heaviest fighting of the war thus far.

From October 1983 Iran launched a series of attacks across its northern border with Iraq. About 700 sq km of Iraqi territory were gained, threatening the last outlet for Iraqi exports of petroleum through the Kirkuk pipeline. Iraq intensified its missile attacks and bombing raids against Iranian towns and petroleum installations.

In February 1984 Iran launched an offensive in the marshlands around Majnoon Island, the site of rich oilfields in southern Iraq, near the confluence of the Tigris and Euphrates rivers. Iraq failed to regain control of this territory and was condemned for using mustard gas in the fighting. Iraq subsequently established extensive and formidable defences, including a system of dams and embankments, along the southern front, near Basra, in anticipation of a possibly decisive offensive by Iran, which massed some 500,000 men there.

The anticipated offensive occurred in March 1985, when Iran committed an estimated 50,000 troops to an attack on the southern front in the region of the Hawizah marshes, east of the Tigris. Iranian forces succeeded in crossing the Tigris and for a time closed the main road connecting Baghdad and Basra before being repulsed. Iraq was again accused of using chemical weapons during this engagement.

In August 1985 Iraq made the first of a concentrated series of raids on the main Iranian petroleum export terminal on Kharg Island. This caused a reduction in Iranian oil exports from 1.2m. barrels per day (b/d)–1.5m. b/d, in the months leading up to the raids, to less than 1m. b/d in September. By the end of 1985 exports from Kharg had reportedly been reduced to a trickle compared with its capacity of 6.5m. b/d.

From mid-1986 Iran launched offensives along the length of the Iraqi border and, in the south, the Karbala-5 offensive brought Iranian troops to within 10 km of Iraq's second most populous city, Basra. Iraq, meanwhile, continued to attack tankers shuttling Iranian oil from Kharg Island to the floating terminals at Sirri and Larak islands during the first half of the year. However, an apparently accidental attack in the Gulf by an Iraqi Mirage F-1 fighter plane on the frigate USS *Stark*, part of the US naval force which had been deployed in the Gulf to protect shipping, created a crisis in Iraqi–US relations. The plane fired two Exocet missiles at the *Stark*, one of which exploded, killing 37 US sailors. Iraq apologized for the 'error' and desisted from attacks on tankers for the next five weeks.

Tension in the Gulf escalated in May 1987 after the USA's decision to accede to a request from Kuwait for 11 Kuwaiti tankers to be re-registered under the US flag, entitling them to US naval protection. Apart from the financial aid that it gave to Iraq, Kuwait was a transit point for goods (including military equipment) destined for Iraq and for exports of oil sold on Iraq's behalf. Iran warned Kuwait on several occasions of dire consequences if it continued to support Iraq, and between October 1986 and April 1987 some 15 ships bound to or from Kuwait were attacked in the Gulf by Iran, and several Kuwaiti cargoes were seized. After the USA made its navy available to escort re-registered Kuwaiti tankers through the Gulf, Iran announced that it would not hesitate to sink US warships if provoked. Contrary to advice from Western governments, in August 1987

Iraq resumed attacks on Iranian oil installations and industrial targets and on tankers in the Gulf transporting Iranian oil.

CEASEFIRE IN THE IRAN–IRAQ WAR

During 1987–88, for the first time in six years, owing to poor mobilization, disorganization and a shortage of volunteers, Iran was unable to launch a major winter offensive and began to lose ground to Iraqi advances on the war front. However, this was not before Kurdish guerrillas, in February 1988, had advanced into government-controlled territory in Iraqi Kurdistan, where Iranian forces, with Kurdish assistance, had established bridgeheads, particularly in the Mawat region, along the Iranian border. The Kurdish part in these operations represented the largest Kurdish offensive since 1974–75, uniting forces from the KDP and the Patriotic Union of Kurdistan (PUK), which, in November 1986, had agreed to co-ordinate their military and political activities and were in the process of forming a coalition of Kurdish nationalist groups. In March 1988, in a retaliatory attack against the captured town of Halabja, Iraq used chemical weapons to kill up to 5,000 Kurdish civilians. In April Iraqi forces regained control of the Faw peninsula, where the Iranians, who had been unable to make further territorial gains since capturing the area in 1986, had scaled back their presence. In May 1988 Iraq recaptured the Shalamcheh area, south-east of Basra, driving the Iranians back across the Shatt al-Arab.

Following a series of military defeats in 1988, Iran accepted the terms of a ceasefire, which came into force on 20 August, monitored by a specially created UN observer force of 350 officers—the UN Iran-Iraq Military Observer Group. On 16 August 1990, shortly after Iraq's invasion of Kuwait (q.v.), Saddam Hussain abruptly sought an immediate, formal peace with Iran by accepting almost all of the claims that Iran had pursued since the declaration of a ceasefire. On 10 September Iran and Iraq formally agreed to resume diplomatic relations.

IRAQI SUPPRESSION OF THE KURDS

The introduction of a ceasefire in the Iran–Iraq War in August 1988 allowed Iraq to divert more troops and equipment to Kurdistan, apparently to effect a final military solution to the problem of the Kurdish separatist movement. At the end of August an estimated 60,000–70,000 Iraqi troops launched a new offensive to conquer guerrilla bases near the borders with Iran and Turkey, bombarding villages, allegedly using chemical weapons, and forcing thousands of Kurdish civilians and *peshmerga* to escape into Iran and Turkey. By mid-September more than 100,000 Kurdish refugees were estimated to have fled across the border into Turkey, while Iraqi Kurds seeking refuge in Iran joined an estimated 100,000 others from their country, some 40,000 of whom had escaped from Halabja after the chemical attack on the city in March. The death toll from the new offensive was estimated at 15,000 in early September.

In September 1988 the Government began to evacuate inhabitants of the Kurdish Autonomous Region to the interior of Iraq as the first step towards the creation of a 30 km-wide uninhabited 'security zone' along the whole of Iraq's border with Iran and Turkey.

IRAQ'S INVASION OF KUWAIT

Prior to a meeting of the OPEC ministerial council in Geneva, Switzerland, on 25 July 1990, Iraq had implied that it might take military action against countries that continued to flout their oil production quotas. It had also accused Kuwait of violating the Iraqi border in order to steal Iraqi oil resources worth US $2,400m. and suggested that Iraq's debt to Kuwait, accumulated largely during the Iran–Iraq War, should be waived.

Direct negotiations between Iraq and Kuwait commenced in Saudi Arabia at the end of July 1990, with the aim of resolving disputes over territory, oil pricing and Iraqi debt. Kuwait was expected to accede to Iraqi demands for early negotiations to draft a border demarcation treaty, while Iraq was expected to focus on its claim to the strategic islands of Bubiyan and Warbah, situated at the mouth of the Shatt al-Arab. However, on 1 August the talks collapsed, and on 2 August Iraq invaded Kuwait, taking control of the country and establishing a (short-lived) Provisional Free Government.

The immediate response, on 2 August 1990, of the UN Security Council to the invasion of Kuwait was to convene and unanimously to adopt a resolution (No. 660) which: condemned the Iraqi invasion of Kuwait; demanded the immediate and unconditional withdrawal of Iraqi forces from Kuwait; and appealed for a negotiated settlement of the conflict. On 6 August the UN Security Council adopted resolution No. 661, which imposed mandatory economic sanctions on Iraq and occupied Kuwait, affecting all commodities with the exception of medical supplies and foodstuffs 'in humanitarian circumstances'.

On 7 August 1990, at the request of King Fahd of Saudi Arabia, the USA dispatched combat troops and aircraft to Saudi Arabia to secure the country's border with Kuwait against a possible attack by Iraq. US troops began to occupy positions in Saudi Arabia on 9 August, one day after Iraq announced its formal annexation of Kuwait. On the same day the UN Security Council unanimously adopted a further resolution (No. 662), which declared the annexation of Kuwait to be null and void and urged all states and institutions not to recognize it.

The dispatch of US troops signified the beginning of Operation Desert Shield for the defence of Saudi Arabia, in accordance with Article 51 of the UN Charter. By the end of January 1991 some 30 countries had contributed ground troops, aircraft and warships to the multinational force in Saudi Arabia and the Gulf region. By far the biggest contributor was the USA, which, it was estimated, had deployed some 500,000 military personnel. Arab countries participating in the multinational force were Egypt, the Syrian Arab Republic, Morocco and the members of the Cooperation Council for the Arab States of the Gulf (Gulf Cooperation Council). It was estimated that by the end of January Iraq had deployed some 555,000 troops in Kuwait and southern Iraq.

On 29 November 1990 the UN Security Council adopted a US-drafted resolution (No. 678), which, with reference to the UN's previous resolutions regarding Iraq's occupation of Kuwait, authorized all necessary means to enforce the removal of Iraqi forces from Kuwait. As part of the initial phase of Operation Desert Storm, hostilities commenced on 16–17 January 1991 with air raids on Baghdad. On 30 January the multinational force claimed air supremacy over Iraq and Kuwait, and air attacks were refocused on the fortified positions of Iraqi ground troops in Kuwait, in preparation for a ground offensive.

During the night of 23–24 February 1991 the multinational force launched a ground offensive for the liberation of Kuwait. Iraqi troops defending Kuwait's border with Saudi Arabia offered little resistance and were quickly defeated. On 28 February US President George Bush announced that the war to liberate Kuwait had been won, and he declared a ceasefire. Iraq had agreed to renounce its claim to Kuwait and release all prisoners of war. It also indicated that it would comply with the remaining relevant UN Security Council resolutions. On 3 March Iraq accepted the ceasefire terms that had been dictated by the commander of the multinational force, US Gen. Norman Schwarzkopf, at a meeting with Iraqi military commanders.

On 3 April 1991 the UN Security Council adopted a resolution (No. 687) that stipulated the terms for a full ceasefire in the Gulf. Among these was the requirement that Iraq dismantle its weapons of mass destruction stockpiles and production facilities. A UN Special Commission (UNSCOM) was created by the UN to monitor Iraq's compliance. These terms were accepted on 5 April by Iraq's RCC and on the following day by the National Assembly.

INTERNAL REVOLT

Following the rout of the Iraqi army by the UN-sponsored multinational force in February 1991, armed rebellion broke out among the largely Shi'a population of southern Iraq and the Iraqi Kurds in the Kurdish northern governorates (provinces).

In the south, Basra was the centre of the rebellion. On 4 March it was reported that supporters of the Tehran-based Supreme Council for the Islamic Revolution in Iraq (SCIRI) had gained control of the towns of Basra, Amarah, Samawah and al-Nasiriyah (Nasiriya). Already, on 5 March, the assessment of US intelligence sources that the southern rebellion lacked sufficient organization to succeed appeared to be corroborated: armed forces loyal to the Government were reported to be regaining control of the rebel-held areas. Crucially, there was no military intervention by the multinational force in support of the rebellion. By mid-March pro-Government forces had effectively crushed the rebellion in the south, but their deployment there had allowed a simultaneous revolt by Kurdish guerrilla groups in the Kurdish northern governorates of Iraq to gather momentum. In late March it was reported that Kurdish rebels had gained control of Kirkuk and of important oil installations to the west of the city, and in early April Kurdish leaders claimed that as many as 100,000 guerrillas were involved in hostilities against government forces. By early April government forces had recaptured Kirkuk, Irbil (Arbil/Erbil), Duhok and Zakho. Some 50,000 Kurds were reported to have been killed in the hostilities, and, fearing genocide, an estimated 1m.–2m. Kurds fled across the northern mountains into Turkey and Iran.

As the 'Kurdish crisis' had developed, France, the UK and the USA had all committed troops to maintain a 'safe haven' for the Kurds in northern Iraq. On 8 April 1991 a proposal by the British Prime Minister, John Major, that a UN-supervised enclave be created in northern Iraq for the protection of the Kurdish population was approved by the leaders of the member states of the European Community (now European Union—EU). The US Government withheld its formal approval of the proposal, but on 10 April it warned Iraq that any interference in relief operations north of latitude 36°N would prompt military retaliation. On 17 April the UN Secretary-General, Javier Pérez de Cuéllar, cautioned that the Iraqi Government's permission would have to be obtained before foreign troops were deployed in northern Iraq, and that the UN Security Council would need to approve the policing of the Kurdish enclave by a UN-backed force. However, in late April UN relief agencies reported that Kurdish refugees were returning to Iraq in large numbers.

As international diplomacy sought to create secure conditions for Iraqi Kurds within Iraq, negotiations between the leaders of Kurdish groups and the Iraqi Government soon collapsed and, in the absence of a negotiated autonomy agreement with the Iraqi Government, the Kurds organized elections to a 105-member Iraqi Kurdistan National Assembly and for a paramount Kurdish leader.

CONCLUSION OF AGREEMENT ON PETROLEUM SALES

After rejecting the UN's initial plan to allow Iraq to export oil in return for supplies of essential civilian goods, in May 1996 Iraq finally accepted the conditions of Resolution 986, allowing for UN monitoring of the distribution of humanitarian supplies and the supply of specified amounts of food and medicine to the Kurdish-controlled enclave in the north. The memorandum of agreement, which had to be renewed every six months, detailed stringent conditions for the sale of up to US $4,000m. of Iraqi oil per year in order to fund the purchase of food and medicine and finance UN operations in Iraq. Petroleum began to flow through the pipeline to Turkey in December. Part of Iraq's oil revenue was to be allocated to the UN Compensation Commission, which had been unable to settle the majority of Gulf War compensation claims owing to inadequate funds. The first shipments of food and humanitarian supplies purchased under the new agreement reached Iraq in March 1997.

In June 1998 the UN Security Council unanimously adopted Resolution 1115, condemning the Iraqi authorities for repeatedly refusing to allow inspection teams access to sites and indicating that failure to co-operate could prompt the imposition of further sanctions. Relations between UNSCOM and the Iraqi Government deteriorated rapidly, provoked mainly by an ongoing dispute over the inspection of Iraq's presidential palaces. More broadly, Iraq continued to insist that it had destroyed all its weapons of mass destruction, but was unable to verify this to the satisfaction of UNSCOM.

ECONOMIC CRISIS, MILITARY INSTABILITY AND CONFLICTS WITHIN THE REGIME

By October 1994 the living standards of large sections of the Iraqi population had reportedly been reduced to subsistence level. The Iraqi Government appeared increasingly desperate to maintain order in the face of this economic crisis. Dissatisfaction within the armed forces was a particular source of concern for the regime. An unsuccessful coup attempt in January 1995 prompted a comprehensive reorganization of military ranks. In March another coup attempt, organized by the former head of Iraqi military intelligence during the 1990–91 hostilities in the Gulf, and supported by Kurdish insurgents in the north and Shi'a rebels in the south, was also thwarted.

A new Minister of Defence and a new Chief of the General Staff of the Armed Forces were appointed in July 1995 in an attempt to consolidate support for the President. However, in August further significant divisions within Saddam Hussain's power base became apparent following the defection to Jordan of two of the President's sons-in-law, Lt-Gen. Hussain Kamel al-Majid and his brother Col Saddam Kamel, together with their wives. Hussain Kamel had been Minister of Industry and Military Production, responsible for Iraq's weapons development programme, and Saddam Kamel the head of the Presidential Guard. It was rumoured that they had become alarmed at the increasing concentration of power in the hands of Saddam Hussain's two sons, Uday and Qusay, and that they feared for their lives. The two men were immediately granted political asylum by King Hussein of Jordan. Iraq condemned both men as traitors, and a wave of arrests and executions followed their defection as Saddam Hussain ordered a purge of senior army officers and government officials who had been close to the two brothers.

In February 1996 the two defectors, Hussain and Saddam Kamel, returned to Baghdad, having been granted a pardon by Saddam Hussain. Immediately after their return to Iraq the two men were assassinated, allegedly by men under the command of Saddam Hussain's son Uday. In June reports emerged of a new coup plot involving senior officers of the Republican Guard and close associates of Saddam Hussain from Tikrit. More than 100 officers, including two army commanders, were arrested and subsequently executed. Mounting opposition to the President from within the armed forces was widely considered to have prompted his decision to transfer responsibility for the national military intelligence department from the Ministry of Defence, and to create new paramilitary units entrusted with the protection of his own family.

Tensions in southern Iraq were greatly exacerbated in February 1999 when Ayatollah Mohammad Baqir al-Sadr was assassinated in the holy city of Najaf, becoming the third senior Shi'a cleric to be murdered in less than a year. In his final sermon, a week before his death, al-Sadr had called on the authorities to release an estimated 100 Shi'a clerics who had been arbitrarily arrested. The Iraqi Government again denied any involvement in the murder and swiftly suppressed widespread riots throughout the southern governorates and a major suburb of Baghdad, which erupted following al-Sadr's murder.

OPERATION DESERT FOX

In December 1998 UNSCOM submitted a new report to the UN Security Council that was critical of Iraq's attitude towards UNSCOM. On 16 December, as the Security Council considered UNSCOM's report, the USA and the UK launched an intensive bombing campaign against Iraq over four consecutive nights. The stated aim of the campaign—termed Operation Desert Fox—was to diminish and degrade Saddam Hussain's ability to deploy weapons of mass destruction.

Operation Desert Fox signalled the end of any effort by Iraq to co-operate with UNSCOM. It was also the last significant attempt by the Administration of US President Bill Clinton to precipitate the downfall of Hussain's regime through military force. Instead, the emphasis shifted to containment, specifically through the vigorous enforcement of the two 'no-fly' zones.

US and British forces continued to attack military targets in both zones, extending the range from surface-to-air missile batteries to their command and control infrastructure, and began attacking some oil-related installations. Iraq insisted that these attacks had resulted in civilian casualties.

IRAQ IN THE AFTERMATH OF 11 SEPTEMBER 2001

Following the swift victory of US-led forces against the Taliban regime in Afghanistan in late 2001 (after the major terrorist attacks against targets on the US mainland on 11 September), demands within the US political establishment for a similar campaign in Iraq increased. Statements made by senior US officials appeared to suggest that, if Iraq did not agree to the prompt return of UN weapons inspectors, the Administration of US President George W. Bush was prepared to resort to military action.

In November 2002, following months of tension between the USA and Iraq regarding the re-admittance of weapons inspectors, the UN Security Council unanimously adopted Resolution 1441, which demanded that Iraq must declare all details of its weapons programmes and provide immediate and unconditional access to weapons inspectors, or else face serious consequences. The resolution did not authorize the automatic use of force against Iraq. Hans Blix, in charge of weapons inspections, presented his first report to the UN Security Council in January 2003, amid a tense political atmosphere. The report, which highlighted Iraqi co-operation, but also indicated areas in need of improvement, only served to heighten the already fraught divisions within the Security Council. Blix's second report, in mid-February, offered similarly ambiguous conclusions, stating that, although no Iraqi weapons of mass destruction had been found, inspectors doubted Saddam Hussain's intentions to disarm. With the British Prime Minister, Tony Blair, particularly insistent upon at least attempting to secure a UN resolution authorizing the use of military force against Iraq, the USA, the UK and Spain submitted a draft resolution in late February emphasizing the serious consequences faced by Iraq as a result of its 'continued violation of its obligations'. After the French threatened to veto any resolution authorizing the use of force, it became clear that any attack on Iraq would proceed without UN backing.

OPERATION IRAQI FREEDOM

The military undertaking to remove Saddam Hussain started from a weakened position, owing to the refusal of the Turkish Grand National Assembly to permit the use of Turkish territory as a base for an attack on the Iraqi regime. This left Kuwait as the US-led coalition's only base of operations for land forces. Operation Iraqi Freedom commenced on 20 March 2003 with an air strike on central Baghdad in an attempt to assassinate the Iraqi President. The attack failed, but was followed by a precise but overwhelming onslaught of aerial firepower in a strategy that came to be labelled as 'shock and awe'. The land assault began almost simultaneously. The coalition forces remained convinced that Saddam Hussain enjoyed little popular support among the Iraqi people and expected little opposition on the ground. British forces tentatively occupied Basra on 6 April, but failed for several days adequately to secure the city. The US conquest of Baghdad commenced on 3 April, with US forces consolidating their hold on the capital by 9 April. Coalition forces were left exposed to guerrilla attacks, with daily losses being announced. The removal of Saddam Hussain from power was symbolized by the toppling of his statue in the centre of Baghdad. However, it soon became apparent that the lightning speed with which the coalition forces had entered and occupied Iraq had bypassed significant pockets of pro-Saddam Hussain groups.

POST-WAR TURBULENCE

The ousting of Saddam Hussain's Government was followed by a period of civil unrest. The USA moved quickly to place an administrator for Iraq in Baghdad in order to bring order to the city and country. A retired general, Jay Garner, and the Office of Reconstruction and Humanitarian Assistance (ORHA) were given the task of restoring basic services and law and order to Iraq. Arriving in the country on 21 April 2003, Garner proved unable to resolve the immediate problems facing Iraqi society and was subsequently replaced by the Department of State's appointee, Paul Bremer, in May. Bremer was to head the Coalition Provisional Authority (CPA), the replacement for the ORHA. He made clear his intention to remove the last vestiges of Saddam Hussain's authority by outlawing the Baath Party and demobilizing the Iraqi army and institutions of state deemed to be corrupted by the Baathists, including the Ministries of Defence and of Information, and the security apparatus. However, attacks attributed by the US-led coalition to remnants of Saddam Hussain's regime, including the Fedayeen Saddam, grew in number and intensity: 31 US troops were killed in guerrilla attacks between 1 May (when President Bush announced the end of major combat operations in Iraq) and 21 July. Towards the end of April the Sunni-dominated town of Fallujah, 55 km west of Baghdad, became the focal point for anti-US attacks. The subsequent response by US forces, which resulted in 13 Iraqis being killed on 28 April alone, only served to heighten the tension. The British army faced a less intense, but no less damaging, response in Basra.

On 13 July 2003 a 25-member Governing Council was established in Baghdad; unelected, and with no executive power, its remit was to draw up a new constitution, appoint ministers and diplomatic representatives and set a date for free elections. It was a situation that satisfied none of the political parties, but one they had little choice but to accept. However, it put the occupying powers in the unenviable position of committing themselves to an extended period of administrative involvement in an Iraqi state galvanized more by an anti-occupation sentiment than by acceptance of US hegemony.

In the first of three major attacks against non-coalition targets in August 2003, 19 people were killed when the Jordanian embassy was severely damaged by a car bomb on 7 August. More worrying, from an international viewpoint, was the destruction of the UN building in Baghdad on 19 August. The UN Special Representative for Iraq, Sergio Vieira de Mello, and more than 20 others were killed when a truck laden with explosives was driven into the UN compound and detonated. On 29 August a car bomb exploded in the city of Najaf, killing the Shi'a cleric and leader of SCIRI, Muhammad Bakir al-Hakim, and up to 125 of his followers. Abd al-Aziz al-Hakim, a member of the Governing Council and brother of the murdered cleric, assumed the leadership of SCIRI. By early September a total of 139 US troops had reportedly been killed in Iraq since 1 May—this exceeded the number of soldiers who had died during the conflict itself. In late September Aquila al-Hashimi, one of only three female members of the Governing Council, was assassinated by unidentified gunmen in Baghdad.

THE RETURN OF SOVEREIGNTY TO IRAQ

The upsurge in attacks committed by Iraqi insurgent forces against the CPA, the Governing Council and US-led coalition military targets continued unabated in mid-2003. Amid sporadic bombings and shootings, structures of local governance rapidly broke down, and political life within Iraq became localized and communalized. In southern Iraq, clerics loyal to Muqtada al-Sadr (the son of Mohammad Baqir al-Sadr) gained prominence in the town councils of Basra and Kut al-Amara. In the Sunni-dominated areas of Tikrit, Mosul and Baquba, religious groups continued to consolidate their support base, and Baghdad itself became increasingly divided according to sectarian identity. The predominantly Shi'a slums in north-eastern Baghdad, formerly known as Saddam City, were renamed Sadr City, clearly reflecting the allegiances of its inhabitants. In northern Iraq, the Kurds were increasingly concerned about how to maintain their relative autonomy. The Governing Council failed to gain support from the majority of Iraqis, who viewed it as a US creation, staffed solely by returning exiles. Even when it did make decisions, these still had to be accepted by the CPA before they were made law.

Apparently unable to improve the security situation within Iraq, and still facing criticism from the international community regarding the occupation of the country, the USA moved towards the handover of sovereignty to Iraqis at the earliest opportunity. In this atmosphere of heightened violence (US casualties alone reached 500 by January 2004), the CPA revealed that the creation of a Transitional National Assembly (TNA) would not take place as planned. Instead, the CPA extended the remit of the Governing Council and gave it the task of drafting a Transitional Administrative Law (TAL) to serve as an interim constitution. The Kurds succeeded in including a reference to the autonomous region governed by the Kurdistan Regional Government (KRG), while the Shi'a compromised by having Islam cited as 'a' source of legislation rather than 'the' source. The TAL also contained a provision by which a two-thirds' majority vote in any three governorates could block the adoption of a new constitution, referred to by Arab Iraqis as 'the Kurdish veto'. The TAL, which was to serve as Iraq's constitution until a permanent replacement could be approved by the Iraqi people, was signed on 8 March 2004.

A new phase of anti-coalition attacks commenced at the end of March 2004, and this time included Shi'a groups in addition to the Sunni groups already identified. On the Shi'a side, al-Sadr remained a dangerous focal point for many Shi'a Iraqis opposed to coalition forces, and he had steadily consolidated his hold on Sadr City and Kufa, while becoming increasingly influential in Basra, Najaf and Karbala. What became known as the 'Sadr Insurgency' steadily gained momentum, and Sadr's 'Mahdi Army' fought openly with coalition forces across Iraq.

The Sunni-associated insurgency gained increased notoriety on 31 March 2004 when four civilian contractors from the CPA were captured and killed in Fallujah, and their corpses put on public display. The killings by Sunni insurgents caused outrage in the USA, forcing the CPA to take an increasingly aggressive line towards them. Insurgents quickly gained control of many areas outside Baghdad, and in Fallujah widespread fighting left approximately 450 Iraqis (including many civilians) and 40 US soldiers dead, and several foreign workers were kidnapped. The scale of the Shi'a insurgency and the failure of the US Marine Corps to pacify Fallujah forced the USA to back down on several of its threats. Instead of capturing al-Sadr, as threatened, the USA proved unwilling to venture into the Shi'a strongholds of Najaf and Kufa for fear of consolidating Shi'a support behind al-Sadr. Instead, US forces struck a deal with the cleric in June, bringing his insurgency to an end but leaving his forces intact. In Fallujah, the US Marine Corps were replaced with Iraqis under the command of one of Saddam Hussein's former generals. In addition, the CPA announced in April that it would be reinstating members of the former Baathist security forces.

Dr Ayad Allawi, leader of the opposition Iraqi National Accord, was appointed Prime Minister of the new Interim Government (IG) on 28 May 2004. The position of President was awarded to the Sunni tribal figure Sheikh Ghazi Mashal Ajil al-Yawar on 1 June. The positions of Vice-President went to Ibrahim al-Ja'fari, spokesman of the Shi'a Islamic Dawa Party, and to Dr Rozh Nuri Shawais of the KDP.

As the handover date of 30 June 2004 approached, there was a significant increase in the number of attacks launched by insurgency forces and in the kidnapping and killing of foreigners in Iraq. In an attempt to forestall a probable large-scale assault by the insurgency forces, the handover of sovereignty to the IG was brought forward in secret to 28 June.

Security remained the most pressing concern of the new Government. Most of the indigenous security forces that had been trained in the year preceding the IG's selection had proved unwilling to fight against fellow Iraqis during the siege of Fallujah in April 2004. Most units had either deserted or defected to join the insurgents. The only Iraqi troops that actually fought during the siege were reported to be elements of the Kurdish *peshmerga*. In the absence of capable Iraqi security forces, US troops were forced to confront a stubbornly persistent threat from al-Sadr's Mahdi Army and an increasingly violent 'Sunni Triangle'. The Mahdi Army continued its sporadic attacks on coalition forces in mid-2004. Notably, Sadr City became virtually inaccessible, and there was a major Mahdi Army uprising in August in the holy cities of Karbala and Najaf. Al-Sadr's supporters succeeded in occupying the Imam Ali mosque (Shi'ism's most sacred shrine) and fought running battles with US troops for control of Najaf. Ultimately, it required the direct intervention of Grand Ayatollah Sistani to broker a truce between the two sides, and once again al-Sadr escaped punishment with his Mahdi Army depleted, but intact. In November Fallujah was once more the scene of an intense battle between US troops and insurgents, with the US military amassing almost 15,000 troops to attack the city. After a fierce encounter that resulted in the deaths of over 50 US troops and perhaps 1,000 insurgents, Fallujah was eventually 'pacified'.

THE JANUARY 2005 ELECTIONS

With attacks on coalition forces running at more than 70 per day by January 2005, there seemed little likelihood that the elections to the TNA scheduled for 30 January could safely be conducted, still less that they would constitute a crucial turning point in Iraq's democratic development. Prominent Sunni groups—most notably, the Association of Muslim Scholars—denounced the electoral process as illegitimate and urged Sunnis to boycott the elections. Meanwhile, Grand Ayatollah Sistani issued a *fatwa* declaring it to be the religious obligation of every Shi'a to vote, while Kurds in the relative security of the north prepared to participate in massive numbers. Abu Musab al-Zarqawi, a Jordanian national with suspected links to the Islamist group al-Qa'ida who was thought to be the leader of an insurgent network responsible for numerous kidnappings, executions and bomb attacks, reportedly declared a 'war on this evil principle of democracy' and threatened to 'wash the streets with blood' on election day.

Within the Shi'a community, the dominant political force was the United Iraqi Alliance (UIA), an uneasy coalition of primarily religious groupings that included SCIRI and its armed faction, the Badr Organization (previously named the Badr Brigades), the Islamic Dawa Party and several individuals with ties to al-Sadr. Also included was Ahmad Chalabi and the remnants of the INC, as well as representatives of other ethnicities and sects.

The main secular Shi'a alternative was Allawi's Iraqi List, a coalition that included Sunnis and former Baathists. The two main Kurdish parties—the PUK and the KDP—pooled resources to form the Democratic Patriotic Alliance of Kurdistan (DPAK). From the Sunni Arab community, only interim President al-Yawar's Iraqis party chose to participate seriously in the elections.

The results represented a clear triumph for the religious Shi'a bloc, which obtained an overall majority of seats (140 out of a total 275) in the TNA, with just under 48% of the valid votes cast. Overall, overtly religious parties and coalitions of various parties obtained almost 54% of the Assembly's seats. The Kurdish list also performed disproportionately well, relative to the numerical presence of Kurds in the population as a whole, winning 75 of the Assembly's seats with just under 26% of the valid votes cast. Conversely, Allawi's Iraqi List and other moderate, secular parties performed poorly. The Iraqi List obtained only 40 seats in the Assembly and less than 14% of the valid votes cast. The only Sunni Arab party represented in the Assembly was al-Yawar's Iraqis, which gained five seats with less than 2% of the vote.

Iraqis voted concurrently to elect 18 governorate councils, and in the Kurdish Autonomous Region to elect a Kurdistan National Assembly (KNA). The outcome followed much the same pattern as the results at the national level, with the Kurds and religious Shi'a parties emerging as dominant. Kurdish parties won majorities in all five of the northernmost governorates, including Kirkuk and Nineveh, while all governorates south of Baghdad fell to religious parties. The remaining four governorates produced highly fragmented councils, with the exception of Anbar governorate, where voter turnout was so low (less than 0.5% of the electorate) that the results were meaningless. Voting for the KNA was dominated by a joint PUK-KDP list.

Much of the upsurge in post-electoral violence can be attributed to a vacuum in legitimacy that arose following a three-month delay in the formation of the new government. This delay was due largely to the rules on forming the new administration that were written into the TAL requiring (in effect) a two-thirds' majority of votes in the National Assembly to endorse a new government. This meant that the UIA controlled too few votes to form a government on its own, despite controlling a majority in the Assembly, and was forced to rely on a tactical alliance with the Kurdish list. As kingmakers in this process, the Kurds managed to secure the presidency in the person of PUK leader Jalal Talabani, who assumed office in April 2005. Including Sunnis in a government of national unity was deemed essential to the country's future stability, but there were only 17 potential candidates to choose from, and it was not clear that any spoke credibly for the broader Sunni population. Under the eventual compromise deal, the UIA's Ibrahim al-Ja'fari emerged as the Prime Minister, with Dr Adil Abd al-Mahdi (Shi'a Arab) and al-Yawar (Sunni Arab) as the two Vice-Presidents. Sunnis were awarded seven of the 37 ministerial portfolios, including the Ministry of Defence, while the remaining portfolios were allocated (broadly) on the basis of seat percentage in the Assembly.

In addition to combating the insurgency and trying to rebuild Iraq's still dilapidated infrastructure, the major task of the elected Transitional Government was to organize the drafting of Iraq's permanent Constitution. A referendum on the new Constitution was scheduled for 15 October 2005, with elections by 15 December. The initial decision of al-Ja'fari's Government to allocate places on the constitutional council in proportion to each party's share of seats in the Assembly meant that 28 seats on the council went to the UIA, 15 to the Kurds, eight to Allawi's faction and one seat each to a communist, a Turkmen, a Christian and a Sunni Arab. The almost total absence of Sunni Arabs from the body charged with drafting Iraq's permanent Constitution was an obvious source of concern; to alleviate this problem, the Government asked groups believed to represent at least some proportion of the broader Sunni community, such as the IIP and the National Dialogue Council, to propose a list of 15 Sunnis to sit on a panel to operate alongside the main council.

Following a series of extensions beyond the original deadline of 15 August 2005, due to persistent difficulties in reaching consensus among all groups, the parliamentary committee charged with drafting the Constitution presented a finalized text to the TNA for consideration on 28 August. Much of the text of the draft Constitution was imported unchanged from the TAL, and the institutional structure of government remained much as before. The Constitution outlined a parliamentary system in which primary executive authority was vested in the Prime Minister and the Council of Ministers. Ambiguities remained regarding the division of powers between the federal and regional governments. However, arguably the most controversial feature was Article 119, which stated that 'one or more governorates shall have the right to establish a region', a provision from which only Baghdad was excluded. This seemingly minor change in wording meant that there was now no longer an upper limit on the number of governorates that could amalgamate into regions, thereby opening up the possibility of sectarian or ethnically-based 'super-regions'. Another controversial item, Article 140, envisaged a three-stage process for the resolution of the status of Kirkuk and the other disputed territories in northern Iraq. The third stage—a referendum to determine the will of the people—was to be held no later than 31 December 2007.

Although the final draft of the Constitution satisfied most of the aspirations of Shi'a and Kurdish leaders, it offered almost nothing to Sunni Arabs. Hence, the referendum on the draft Constitution on 15 October 2005 yielded predictable results. The Constitution was endorsed in Shi'a- and Kurdish-dominated governorates by large margins. In the multi-communal governorates, the vote in favour of the Constitution prevailed by narrower margins, and in two Sunni-dominated governorates (Anbar and Salah al-Din) the vote went overwhelmingly against it. Voters in Nineveh governorate (ethnically mixed, but with a Sunni Arab majority) rejected the Constitution, but the vote failed to reach the necessary two-thirds' threshold. Overall, the Constitution was approved by 79% of those who voted.

Having boycotted the January 2005 elections and paid a heavy price in terms of loss of influence over the drafting of the Constitution, Sunni Arab leaders this time contested the legislative elections held in December. Once again, parties standing for election were dominated by ethno-sectarian identity. The UIA, the major Shi'a religious grouping, suffered the defection of Chalabi's Iraqi National Congress (INC) faction, which chose to run as an independent party, but was joined by the Sadrists. The major secular Shi'a alternative, Allawi's Iraqi National List (INL), was strengthened by the inclusion of two factions that had run independently in January—al-Yawar's Iraqis and the communist People's Union. With the exception of the Kurdistan Islamic Union (KIU), most major Kurdish parties ran on the same ticket as before, namely the DPAK. Two significant coalitions represented the interests of the Sunni Arab community. The Iraqi Accord Front (IAF) comprised an amalgam of Sunni religious groupings including, most notably, Adnan al-Dulaimi's General Council for the People of Iraq and Tariq al-Hashimi's IIP. The Iraqi Front for National Dialogue (IFND) purported to offer a 'non-sectarian' alternative, but was generally thought to represent the interests of secular Sunnis and former Baathists.

When the Independent High Electoral Commission (IHEC) of Iraq finally certified the results of the elections, nearly two months after the polls, the composition of the new parliament was remarkably similar to that of its predecessor. With just over 41% of the vote, the UIA emerged as the largest single party, claiming 128 of the 275 available seats, while the Kurdish alliance secured 53 seats with 22% of the vote. The participation of the two Sunni Arab parties meant that both the UIA and the Kurdish alliance experienced declines in their share of the popular vote, and, as a consequence, their share of seats. The IAF polled over 15% of the vote and obtained 44 seats, while the IFND's 4% of the vote yielded 11 seats. The Iraqi Turkmen Front, the National Rafidain List (Assyrians) and the Al-Ezediah Movement for Progress and Reform (a Yazidi grouping) obtained one seat each. The performance of Allawi's INL (25 seats from an 8% share of the vote) was a major disappointment for those who had hoped to see a strengthening of the moderate, secular vote. Likewise, Chalabi's INC achieved no representation in parliament. Overall, this pattern of results accurately reflected the prevailing reality of Iraq's political climate. By December 2005 the politics of communal identity had, if anything, become even more deeply entrenched than in January.

As inter-communal violence intensified in early 2006, political leaders in Baghdad struggled to forge a government of national unity to avert all-out civil war. The deadlock persisted for over six weeks until, finally, Ayatollah Sistani was able to broker a deal between various factions within the UIA to coalesce behind the nomination of a compromise candidate, Nuri Kamal (Jawad) al-Maliki. Like former Prime Minister al-Ja'fari, al-Maliki came to prominence as a leading member of the Islamic Dawa Party, and ideologically the two were almost indistinguishable. The national unity Government officially came into being on 20 May, when the National Assembly finally approved al-Maliki's 37-member cabinet, comprising principally the UIA, the Kurdish alliance, the IAF and the INL. Together with three smaller parties, the Government controlled 240 of the 275 seats in the Council of Representatives.

FROM INSURGENCY TO CIVIL WAR

As politicians in Baghdad struggled to form a consensus on the direction of policy, the violence in Iraq began to shift in an ominous direction. The problem of sectarian violence was not unknown before 2005. Al-Zarqawi had made attacks on Iraq's Shi'a population central to his campaign to destabilize the country. The ultimate goal, many observers concluded, was to provoke all-out civil war between Sunni and Shi'a communities. Under strict instructions from Ayatollah Sistani and other Shi'a clerics, the Shi'a community mostly refrained from exacting revenge. However, following the formation of the UIA-dominated Government in April 2005, this restraint eroded rapidly. Prime Minister al-Ja'fari's appointment of prominent SCIRI hardliner Bayan Jabr as Minister of the Interior led to a dramatic reorganization of the ministry's security forces. Significant elements of the Badr Organization were incorporated into effective counter-insurgency commando units, which swiftly acquired a reputation for brutality and violent excesses against Iraq's Sunni population. Viewed by the Sunni community as little more than state-sponsored death squads, these commando units were heavily criticized by human rights organizations for indiscriminate violence and the use of torture. The low-level civil war escalated in February 2006 when insurgents, believed to be associated with al-Zarqawi's group, destroyed the golden dome of the Al-Askari Mosque in Samarra. Over the next few days mobs of Shi'a militia forces, led by al-Sadr's Mahdi Army, exacted revenge on the Sunni community, torching dozens of Sunni mosques and assassinating Sunni clerics. During the first five days after the attacks the official death toll was 1,300, although unofficially the total was believed to be much higher, and a period of shadowy, but intense, sectarian warfare followed. By the end of June a UN report estimated that over 150,000 Iraqis had been displaced by the violence since February.

During an address to the nation in January 2007, President Bush announced an increase in US troop levels of between 20,000 and 30,000. The majority of these troops were to be deployed to Baghdad, with a smaller number (approximately 4,000) of marines assigned to Anbar governorate. By October evidence from multiple sources indicated that violence of all types was in decline. During this month 38 US troop deaths were recorded, compared with more than 100 each month from April to June. Iraqi civilian deaths, meanwhile, declined from nearly 2,000 during January to fewer than 900 in October. By mid-2008 almost every available indicator showed that violence in Iraq had declined to its lowest level since the declared end of combat operations in May 2003.

One reason for the significant decline in sectarian killings in Baghdad was that by the end of 2007 the city was almost completely segregated into sectarian neighbourhoods. Many of the remaining Sunni Arab neighbourhoods had been sealed off from surrounding Shi'a districts by the construction of vast walls that enabled security forces to control points of entry and exit. Another plausible reason for the decline in violence was the USA's strategy of empowering Sunni Arab militias through the so-called 'Awakening' (*sahwa*) movement, which clearly had a dramatic effect on violence levels in Sunni Arab areas. From its beginnings in 2005 in Anbar governorate, the movement spread throughout north-central Iraq and into Baghdad, and by mid-2008 had nearly 100,000 members. The short-term benefit of the *sahwa* movement was the virtual elimination of attacks on coalition forces and the defeat of radical Islamist insurgent groups in places like Anbar.

LEGISLATIVE AND CONSTITUTIONAL IMPASSE

Despite the reduction in violence, politics in Baghdad remained gridlocked. The fundamental problem confronting Iraq's political leaders was a deepening divide between those—mainly the Kurds and the Islamic Supreme Council of Iraq (ISCI)—who perceived Iraq's permanent Constitution to be a largely finished document, and those who sought major amendments to its provisions. This division reflected the broader 'federalist versus nationalist' confrontation, and was viewed by many Western observers as a positive development for the Iraqi political system, as it suggested that Iraqis were moving beyond the politics of ethnicity and sect towards a more ideologically driven brand of politics. However, the depths of this division made it almost impossible for Iraq's political leaders to compromise on constitutional amendments.

The Constitutional Review Committee (CRC), which had laboured since November 2006 to arrive at a set of mutually acceptable amendments, issued its 'final report' in July 2008. No agreement could be reached on several issues, including the powers of the President, which Sunni members of the CRC had sought to strengthen by granting the President power over Iraq's armed forces. The CRC was also divided over those articles of the Constitution that dealt with the management of the hydrocarbons sector and the powers of regions and governorates relative to the federal Government. Finally, the CRC was utterly divided about how to proceed with Article 140. The inability of the CRC to reach consensus on these core issues had at least three important implications for Iraqi politics. First, a CRC at impasse demonstrated that Iraq's major political factions were still bitterly divided over the very structure of governance, including the nature of executive power, the federal system and the future status of territories disputed by the Iraqi Kurdish Autonomous Region and the federal Government. Second, in the absence of a finished founding document that enjoyed popular legitimacy, it had been almost impossible to make progress in areas such as hydrocarbons legislation. Third, the absence of consensus on the CRC left Iraq without an upper house of parliament (the Federation Council) and, critically, without a constitutional court (the Federal Supreme Court), which both remained hostage to the stalled constitutional revision process. With no constitutional court, Iraq's political system lacked a vital check on the power of its political leaders, particularly the Prime Minister, and the integrity of the Constitution itself was progressively eroding.

THE ASCENT OF NURI AL-MALIKI

One of the more remarkable political developments during 2008–09 was the emergence of Prime Minister Nuri al-Maliki as the single most powerful political leader in Iraq. Once regarded as a weak and ineffectual politician, al-Maliki had originally been a compromise candidate for Prime Minister and was generally assumed to be a pliable puppet of the Shi'a religious establishment. However, from early 2008 al-Maliki began to use the powers of his office to assert his authority. In February the Prime Minister announced his intention to mount a major military operation in Basra 'to take on criminals and gang leaders' in the city. The operation involved over 40,000 Iraqi troops who were intended to operate without the assistance of coalition forces. The assault on Basra was accompanied by serious clashes between the Mahdi Army and Iraqi troops in several major southern cities, including Amarah, Kut and Nasiriya. Subsequently, US forces sealed off the Sadrist stronghold of Sadr City in Baghdad, and joint US-Iraqi attacks commenced in April and continued for seven weeks. In mid-May al-Sadr announced a ceasefire and agreed to allow Iraqi government troops, but not US forces, to enter Sadr City. The attacks on al-Sadr's militia forces were indecisive from a military perspective, but they demonstrated al-Maliki's willingness to confront militias within the Shi'a community and thereby enhanced his claims to be a champion of the Iraqi nationalist cause.

In the wake of his military campaigns against rival militias in the south, al-Maliki established a network of so-called tribal support councils (*isnad*) throughout the region. Modelled on the *sahwa* movement in the predominantly Sunni parts of the country, these *isnad* operated outside any legal or constitutional framework and received their funding directly from the office of the Prime Minister. As they proliferated throughout the south, al-Maliki acquired what he and his Islamic Dawa Party had previously lacked—a support base and an organizational means through which to challenge the ISCI's power in southern Iraq. In July 2008 al-Maliki turned his attention northwards, launching a large-scale military offensive in the troubled governorate of Diyala on 29 July. The offensive involved up to 30,000 Iraqi troops and police supported by US forces and initially focused on the governorate's capital, Baquba. The stated target of the operation was al-Qa'ida in Iraq, but the operation soon developed into a confrontation between Iraqi government forces and local Sunni insurgent (Sons of Iraq—SOI) groups, and more dangerously, with the forces of the Kurdish *peshmerga* stationed in the disputed northern districts of the governorate. What started as a counter-insurgency operation soon assumed the appearance of an attempt by the Prime Minister to eliminate rivals and impose his will on the governorate, including the arrests of five key SOI leaders and hundreds of fighters, together with members of the Sunni IAF. Matters came to a head in mid-August when Iraqi forces reached the northern district of Khanaqin, a predominantly Kurdish district, and threatened a confrontation with the 4,000-strong *peshmerga* brigade stationed there. The stand-off was resolved only when the President of the Kurdish Autonomous Region, Masoud Barzani, visited Baghdad to negotiate a deal directly with al-Maliki. The result was an agreement whereby security in the city of Khanaqin would be provided by local police, *peshmerga* forces would withdraw to positions some 25 km north and south of the city, and control over Arab sub-districts in the south of the city would be transferred to Iraqi forces.

The effectiveness of this strategy was evident in the January 2009 governorate elections, when al-Maliki's State of Law Coalition won sweeping victories from Baghdad southwards, where the ISCI was reduced to a minor political force. Of the 14 governorates in which elections were held, the State of Law Coalition won in nine, including Basra and Baghdad, either by capturing more seats than any other coalition, or by winning an outright majority. Consequently, the State of Law Coalition secured control (either alone or in a coalition) of eight governorates. The ISCI fared badly in almost every southern governorate and emerged from the election in control of only one council—Muthanna. These results represented a personal triumph for al-Maliki and his brand of Iraqi nationalism and suggested that he was emerging as exactly the sort of powerful, centralizing leader that most Arab Iraqis (but few Kurds) appeared to favour.

In Baghdad al-Maliki consolidated his hold on power by establishing a network of security institutions, such as the Baghdad Brigade and the National Counterterrorism Force, which were directly funded by, and answerable to, the office of the Prime Minister. Moreover, the constitutional and legal constraints that required the approval of the Iraqi parliament for the appointment of senior army officers had been routinely ignored; in practice this meant that the upper ranks of the armed forces were personally beholden to the Prime Minister for their career progression (or regression). In a classic example of his emerging strategy, al-Maliki ordered a new military offensive in Diyala in May 2009. Much like the operation in July 2008, the sequel was portrayed as an attempt to root out remaining al-Qa'ida forces in the governorate, but evolved swiftly into an attack on Diyala's Sunni political leaders, who had excluded al-Maliki's State of Law Coalition from participating in the provincial government. On 18 May 2009 the regional head of the IAF in Diyala, Abd al-Jabbar al-Khazraji and SOI leader Sheikh Riyad al-Mujami, were arrested following accusations of attacks on civilians.

THE DEMISE OF ARTICLE 140

The major political victims of the emerging nationalist bloc were the Kurds. Already facing harsh criticism from all sides in Baghdad for circumventing the federal Government in the signing of oil contracts, the Kurdish negotiators only barely managed to retain the Kurds' 17% share of revenues during budget negotiations and failed to receive financial compensation to help cover the costs of *peshmerga* deployments in support of Iraqi government troops. However, the major casualty of the upsurge in anti-Kurdish sentiment was the Kurds' effort to secure a favourable resolution to the issue of Kirkuk and other 'disputed territories'. Article 140 of the Constitution had envisaged a three-stage process leading to a resolution of Kirkuk's final status. Stage one—normalization—involved the return of those Kurds deliberately displaced by Saddam Hussain as part of his campaign to change the demography of Kirkuk, and the return to their governorates of origin of Arabs brought into the region as part of the same campaign. Stage two involved a census and stage three a referendum on the future status of the territories, to be conducted by 31 December 2007.

Of the various territories generally considered to be 'disputed', Kirkuk was by far the most controversial, both because of its large oil resources and because the city (and governorate) contained sizeable populations of Kurds, Arabs and Turkmen. The Kurdish effort to incorporate Kirkuk into the territory of the Kurdish Autonomous Region was bitterly opposed by almost every non-Kurdish group in Iraq and by most states in the region (especially Turkey), and the Kurds faced determined opposition at all levels of government to their drive to complete the necessary stages in time for a December 2007 vote. Although the political decision to reverse the effects of Arabization was approved by Prime Minister al-Maliki in March, it was not until September that the necessary finances were made available to compensate those Kurds and Arabs affected. Consequently, the normalization stage of Article 140 had barely begun by the time that the referendum deadline came around. In addition, only about 5% of the tens of thousands of Kirkuk property disputes had been resolved, and no agreement had been reached on the restoration of Kirkuk governorate to its pre-Baathist boundaries.

When the deadline expired without the completion of even stage one of the process, the future of Article 140 was thrown into political limbo. In the absence of a favourable resolution to the Kirkuk issue, the Kurds refused to approve the package of constitutional amendments recommended by the CRC. As a result, the single most important dimension of the political reconciliation process, namely, amending the Constitution to assuage Sunni Arab concerns, could not be completed without a resolution of the Kirkuk issue.

US WITHDRAWAL

With the UN mandate authorizing the presence of coalition forces in Iraq set to expire on 31 December 2008, the latter half of that year saw an intensifying effort on the part of the outgoing Bush Administration and the Iraqi Government to craft a mutually acceptable status of forces agreement (SOFA) to provide a legal basis for a continued US military presence beyond that date. The process was fraught with complexity and controversy. The agreement that eventually emerged offered several important concessions to Iraq. The most significant articles were Article 27, which prohibited Iraqi 'land, sea, and air' from being used as a 'launching or transit point for attacks against other countries' (i.e. Iran), and Article 24, which appeared to establish an unambiguous timetable for the withdrawal of US forces: Section 3 required all US 'combat' forces to withdraw from Iraqi cities no later than 30 June 2009 and the withdrawal of all 'United States Forces' from Iraqi territory by 31 December 2011. In August 2010 US President Barack Obama officially declared an end to combat operations in Iraq, and the military-led Operation Iraqi Freedom was transformed into the civilian-led Operation New Dawn. The new mission of the 50,000 remaining US troops in Iraq was to train, equip and advise Iraqi military forces and protect the remaining US civilian presence in the country. Meanwhile, the US Administration worked diligently behind the scenes to convince Iraqi politicians of the need to retain some form of US military presence beyond the deadline. The politics of this remained complicated, however. Ending the war in Iraq was a key pledge of Obama's presidential electoral campaign, while Prime Minister al-Maliki used the signing of the SOFA, complete with its requirement for a withdrawal of all US troops, to strengthen his credentials as an Iraqi nationalist. Hence, both sides sought an agreement that would allow for the longer-term presence of US forces while retaining public support.

This idea of a long-term deployment appeared to gain momentum in October 2011, when a meeting of Iraq's key leaders in Baghdad authorized the Government to allow an unspecified number of US trainers to remain in Iraq beyond December. Although the USA insisted on immunity from Iraqi law for any remaining trainers, there appeared to be a consensus among Iraqi leaders that this should not be granted. Despite lengthy talks between the USA and Iraq, a proposal to maintain a US military presence in the country under the auspices of the North Atlantic Treaty Organization (NATO) was rejected in December for the same reason. Hence, all remaining US military units departed Iraq ahead of schedule on 19 December.

ELECTIONS IN THE KURDISH AUTONOMOUS REGION

In July 2009 Kurds went to the polls in northern Iraq to elect the Kurdish Autonomous Region's President and legislature, the Iraqi Kurdistan Parliament. Once again, the PUK and the KDP formed an electoral alliance (the Kurdistan List); however, many of the lesser parties that had previously participated in the DPAK ran in direct opposition to the PUK-KDP alliance.

Leading the assault on the status quo was the Movement for Change (Gorran), founded by a former Deputy Secretary-General of the PUK, Nawshirwan Mustafa, following his defection from that party in protest against its failure to address internal corruption. Gorran campaigned on an anti-establishment platform that was overtly critical of the PUK and the KDP for their alleged corruption and failure to establish a clear distinction between their own institutions and those of government. Gorran tapped into popular discontent that had been festering in the Kurdish Autonomous Region since the 2005 elections.

Turnout at the polls on 25 July 2009 was nearly 80% of the registered electorate. As expected, the Kurdistan List garnered the most votes (57% of the total), to secure 59 of the 111 seats; however, this was over 20% fewer votes, and 45 fewer seats, than the DPAK had obtained in 2005. Gorran polled 24%, securing 25 seats, including the PUK's home base of Sulaimaniya. The Service and Reform List (led by the KIU) secured 13% of the vote to win 13 seats. The Islamic Movement in Iraqi Kurdistan took two seats and the Freedom and Social Justice List one seat, while the remaining 11 seats were reserved for representatives of various minority groups. In the concurrent presidential election, the KDP's Masoud Barzani was re-elected by a comfortable margin, securing 69.6% of the vote.

THE MARCH 2010 LEGISLATIVE ELECTIONS

Unlike the 2005 elections, in which most of the Shi'a parties had joined forces to form the UIA, the 2010 elections saw an important split in Shi'a ranks. In August 2009 the remnants of the UIA, most notably the ISCI and the Sadrists, combined under the Iraqi National Alliance banner, together with an assortment of religious and secular Shi'a independents, including former premier al-Ja'fari's small National Reform Movement, Chalabi's INC, a breakaway faction of the Islamic Dawa Party, Fadillah, and even a Sunni Arab leader of the Anbar Awakening, Hamed al-Hayes. The ISCI-Sadrist alliance was undeniably a marriage of convenience. The two movements represented starkly different Shi'a constituencies, with the ISCI attracting support mainly from the middle classes and the Sadrists from the poor. Moreover, the respective positions of the two parties on several key ideological issues—federalism, for example—bordered on the mutually incompatible. However, they were united in a shared hostility towards al-Maliki and a mutual determination to prevent him from securing another term as Prime Minister. The State of Law Coalition was reconstituted around al-Maliki's own Islamic Dawa Party, to which were added two other Dawa factions, an independent bloc led by Minister of Oil Dr Hussain al-Shahristani and various other individuals with localized appeal.

Pitted against the two Shi'a-dominated lists were two secular, nationalist alliances, Iraqiya and the Iraqi Unity Coalition (IUC). Forged by Minister of the Interior Jawad al-Bulani in October 2009, the IUC had genuine trans-sectarian appeal; as well as al-Bulani (a secular Shi'a), it included several prominent Sunni tribal leaders, including Ahmad Abu Risha, who had helped to initiate the Anbar Awakening. Meanwhile, Allawi's Iraqiya, formed in January 2010, attempted to secure a broader appeal than the now defunct INL, particularly in the Sunni-dominated governorates in northern Iraq, by the addition of several prominent Sunni Arab movements and individuals, including Salih al-Mutlaq and his IFND, Vice-President al-Hashimi and the influential al-Hadbaa list from Nineveh.

The most prominent Kurdish contender—the Kurdistan Alliance—was contesting the 2010 elections as a two-party alliance of the KDP and PUK. Also competing for Kurdish votes were Gorran and the two Islamic parties (the KIU and the Islamic Group of Kurdistan—IGK), which all ran on separate slates.

According to the final results (including compensatory seats) announced by the IHEC in late March 2010, Iraqiya had secured 91 seats with 24.7% of the vote, narrowly defeating the State of Law Coalition, which won 89 seats, having garnered 24.2% of the vote. The Iraqi National Alliance won 70 seats (18.0% of the vote), while the Kurdistan Alliance obtained 43 seats (14.6%). The Kurdistan Alliance's loss of 10 seats from the 2005 elections was due mainly to the performance of the three other Kurdish parties—Gorran (which won eight seats), the KIU (four seats) and the IGK (two seats). Other than the eight seats reserved for minorities, only two other parties achieved representation in parliament—the IAF (which secured six seats) and the Iraqi Unity Coalition (four). The pattern of results nationally served to reinforce the impression that Iraqi voters had yet to transcend the politics of ethno-sectarianism. The Shi'a Arab-dominated parties (the State of Law Coalition and the Iraqi National Alliance) won all but 17 of the 119 seats available in the nine predominantly Shi'a governorates south of Baghdad, but only one seat in the governorates north of Baghdad. The Sunni Arab-dominated parties (Iraqiya and the IAF) won convincing victories in all the Sunni Arab majority governorates in the north, and the Kurdish parties swept the board in the Kurdish Autonomous Region.

In the absence of a clear legislative majority, the Constitution required the President to assign the responsibility for government formation to 'the biggest bloc in parliament in numerical terms', which appeared to be Allawi's Iraqiya. However, the Constitution failed to define the term 'bloc' and, crucially, whether or not one could be formed after an election. In an attempt to capitalize on this constitutional loophole, the State of Law Coalition and the Iraqi National Alliance announced that they had agreed to form a unified parliamentary bloc—the National Alliance (NA)—in early May 2010. With a combined total of 159 seats, the NA would have the right to form a new government as the largest parliamentary bloc.

Although nominally a unified force, the NA's major problem concerned the nomination of the new premier. In late October 2010 a series of meetings between the leaders of the major blocs as part of the so-called Barzani initiative resulted in the Irbil Agreement. The broad principles of the accord were believed to involve the retention of al-Maliki as Prime Minister, the establishment of a new National Council for Strategic Policy, to be headed by Allawi and the maintenance of 'balance' in terms of government appointments among Iraq's various communities. The Irbil Agreement succeeded in preparing for a broad consensus on government formation. Accordingly, in November the Council of Representatives re-elected Talabani as President; Talabani invited al-Maliki to form a new governing coalition. In accordance with the Agreement, Iraqiya's Osama al-Nujaifi was elected parliamentary Speaker.

Three days before the expiration of a 25 December 2010 deadline for government formation, Prime Minister al-Maliki presented an incomplete list of ministers to the Council of Representatives for approval. Controversially, al-Maliki nominated himself as temporary head of all three crucial security ministries—defence, national security affairs and the interior. The major winners in the division of government positions were the State of Law alliance, with 11 ministries, and the Sadrists, with six. In stark contrast, the once all-powerful ISCI emerged from the process in control of just one ministry (transportation). On 22 December al-Maliki's new (partial) Government was approved by the necessary majority.

In January 2011 the Federal Supreme Court placed certain critical institutions, including the IHEC and the Central Bank, under the control of the executive branch. This measure, constituting a massive extension of the powers of the Prime Minister, appeared to contravene the Constitution, which stated that these bodies were 'considered independent commissions subject to monitoring by the Council of Representatives'. In conjunction with al-Maliki's tendency to create new security and intelligence offices that were responsible solely to the Office of the Prime Minister, and his demonstrated willingness to utilize these against political opponents, there was an understandable concern among opponents of al-Maliki that his intentions were not benign.

A second dynamic that shaped the post-election political landscape was the sharp deterioration in the relationship between al-Maliki and Allawi. Since the conclusion of the coalition agreement, al-Maliki had done nothing to indicate that he was serious about sharing power with Allawi. He rejected all of Allawi's nominations for Minister of Defence and claimed that creating a National Strategic Policy Council with meaningful powers (i.e. the capacity to check the Prime Minister) would violate the Constitution. By mid-2011 communications between the two had ended. Simultaneously, the US departure from Iraq in 2011 left Prime Minister al-Maliki virtually unchecked in his exercise of power. Within hours of the exit of the last US troops and just days after al-Maliki's visit to Washington, DC, USA to meet President Obama, Iraq's Supreme Judicial Council issued an arrest warrant for Vice-President al-Hashimi on terrorism charges. In response to the charges, al-Hashimi fled to the Kurdish Autonomous Region, where he enjoyed the protection of Kurdish leaders until he departed for Qatar in April 2012 and thereafter travelled to Turkey. Al-Hashimi's trial on 150 separate terrorism-related charges began, in absentia, in May. In September al-Hashimi was found guilty of planning and facilitating the murder of two men and sentenced to death. Al-Hashimi rejected the verdict as 'unjust', and Iraqiya issued a statement claiming that the court's decision had been politically motivated.

OPPOSITION TO AL-MALIKI

Prime Minister al-Maliki's capacity to confront and outmanoeuvre his opponents became a defining feature of politics in Baghdad. The most serious threat to al-Maliki gathered pace in April 2012 when the leaders of the major opposition blocs—the Kurds, Iraqiya and the Sadrists—met in Irbil to plan a strategy for confrontation. The result was a nine-point letter, delivered in the form of an ultimatum, which demanded that the premiership be limited to two terms and that al-Maliki adhere to the Irbil Agreement. The Prime Minister was given a deadline of 15 days to deliver a satisfactory response, in the absence of which a vote of no confidence would be organized in the Council of Representatives. Following the expiry of the deadline, a concerted effort began to mobilize enough votes to remove al-Maliki from office. In June it was revealed that a petition had been submitted to President Talabani requesting that he authorize a vote of no confidence in the Prime Minister, but the number of signatories to the petition fell three short of the absolute majority of 163 votes required to remove the Prime Minister and his Government.

Iraq's other nominally independent commissions proved less resilient in the wake of the Supreme Court's decision of January 2011. In that year the Chairman of the Trade Bank of Iraq, Hussein al-Azri, was forced to flee to Lebanon, after al-Maliki launched a corruption investigation against him and the bank. Al-Azri was later sentenced to 15 years' imprisonment and replaced by al-Maliki's nominee, Hamdiyah al-Jaff. Iraq's Integrity Commission, the body charged with investigating government corruption, was targeted next. After facing the familiar corruption charges levelled by the Prime Minister, Judge Rahim al-Ogaili resigned, to be replaced by an al-Maliki ally, Izzat Tawfiq. Finally, accusations of money laundering and the irregular conduct of foreign exchange auctions against the Governor of Iraq's Central Bank, Sinan al-Shabibi, led to his formal removal in October 2012, together with the resignation of many of his staff. Within two years al-Maliki had succeeded in replacing the heads of nearly all of Iraq's nominally independent institutions with his own allies.

While the political opposition in Baghdad struggled to rise against the increasingly authoritarian tendencies of the Prime Minister, a more serious threat to al-Maliki's authority began to emerge in mid-2010 in the form of widespread popular demonstrations against the Government. Initially, popular discontent was directed at government officials for their failure to provide basic services, which was exacerbated by widespread government corruption. From February 2011 the demonstrations became larger and more organized. In keeping with the wave of popular uprisings throughout the Middle East, protest organizers in Iraq designated 25 February as a 'day of rage' and urged 1m. Iraqis to participate. Al-Maliki's response to the impending protests was to claim they were being manipulated by Baathists and al-Qa'ida and to ban all traffic in Baghdad on the day of the protests, on security grounds. In the end, protests took place in 18 cities across Iraq, although attendance fell far short of 1m. Al-Maliki's main approach to addressing the protest movement was repression. By March it had become almost impossible to obtain permission to demonstrate, and journalists reporting on the demonstrations were routinely beaten and arrested by security forces.

From December 2012 the protests assumed a more dangerous form. In that month arrest warrants were issued for several bodyguards of the Minister of Finance, Fallujah-born Rafie al-Issawi. This action prompted large-scale protests in Fallujah and Ramadi, which spread to cities throughout the Sunni-populated areas of the country. The initial demands of the protesters were predictable—a reversal of de-Baathification, the release of prisoners and the resignation of al-Maliki. In January 2013, however, events escalated when the Iraqi army opened fire on protesters in Fallujah, killing nine and injuring more than 50. In April an attack on a police checkpoint outside Hawija (in Kirkuk governorate) prompted Iraqi security forces to attack a protest site in Hawija. In the resulting confrontation, approximately 40 protesters were killed and over 150 injured. Over the following days violence escalated throughout central Iraq as insurgent groups, such as al-Qa'ida and the Baathist Naqshibandi group, capitalized on the Hawija incident to launch attacks against government forces and Shi'a civilians. As a result, April and May were the most violent months in Iraq since 2008, in terms of the number of deaths. The main threat presented by the 2013 protest movement was that, unlike in 2010–11, when demonstrations were staged throughout Iraq, the 2013 protests were conducted exclusively in Sunni areas and were overtly sectarian in nature. Hence, the sectarian attacks that followed raised fears of a return to the large-scale violence of the civil war years (2005–08). What prevented the protests from coalescing into something more threatening to al-Maliki's Government were the internal divisions among the protesters, in terms of their ultimate aims and the means that they were prepared to use to achieve them. By late 2013 the Sunni protest movement appeared to have lost momentum.

RELATIONS WITH THE KURDISH AUTONOMOUS REGION

Together with the future status of the disputed territories, the other key concern that has dominated relations between the central Government and the Kurdish authorities is the management of Iraq's oil and gas sector, particularly whether the KRG has the constitutional right to sign contracts with international oil companies (IOCs) without the approval of the Ministry of Oil in Baghdad. Efforts to adopt a comprehensive package of legislation relating to the hydrocarbons sector in Iraq began during mid-2006. Almost immediately there was controversy over issues such as the terms of private sector involvement in Iraq's petroleum industry, whether oil revenues should be controlled by the central or regional governments, and the mechanism by which revenues would ultimately be distributed across the country as a whole. The failure of Iraq's political leaders to pass a national oil and gas law prompted the KRG to pass its own regional oil and gas law in 2007. This offered more favourable terms to IOCs than those being offered by Baghdad. Subsequently, the KRG signed contracts with more than 40 IOCs to develop the hydrocarbons sector in the Kurdish Autonomous Region. In response, the Ministry of Oil declared the contracts to be illegal and threatened to blacklist any company that signed an agreement with the KRG.

Initially, most of the IOCs that signed contracts were small-scale operations, but in November 2011 several petroleum exploration agreements were signed by US oil giant Exxon-Mobil and the KRG to develop several fields in the Kurdish Autonomous Region. At least three of these fields were wholly or partly situated in disputed areas of Nineveh and Kirkuk outside the recognized Kurdish Autonomous Region. Predictably, the central Government condemned the agreements as illegal and in violation of the Constitution and threatened ExxonMobil with several negative consequences, including the termination of its existing participation in the exploitation of the large-scale West Qurna field in Basra. Moreover, the company was banned from a hydrocarbons bidding round in May 2012. In June al-Maliki reportedly urged President Obama to intervene to halt ExxonMobil's dealings with the KRG, claiming that they were undermining Iraq's stability. However, the company's success in concluding agreements with the Kurds while retaining its West Qurna contract inspired other major hydrocarbons firms to pursue the significantly better deals offered by the KRG. French oil company Total, US oil giant Chevron and the oil arm of the Russian

Federation's Gazprom also acquired exploration blocs in the Kurdish Autonomous Region. The major problem facing the KRG and IOCs operating in the Kurdish Autonomous Region was how to transport oil to market without relying on Iraq's existing infrastructure. A potential solution to this problem emerged in May, when it was announced that the KRG and Turkey had agreed to export Kurdish crude petroleum via a new pipeline to the Turkish border from 2013.

Despite these promising developments for the Kurds, the Iraqi authorities retain de facto control over the oil industry in the Kurdish Autonomous Region, not just via their control of the pipeline network, but also because the Government dictates the distribution of all hydrocarbons revenues. The KRG relies on Baghdad for over 90% of its income, including the revenue necessary to compensate IOCs for the costs of hydrocarbons development in the region.

GOVERNORATE ELECTIONS IN 2013

With the three Kurdish-dominated governorates still avoiding elections, and the status of Kirkuk too controversial for the authorities to risk organizing a vote, balloting actually took place in only 12 of Iraq's 19 governorates on 20 April 2013. The elections did very little to upset the existing balance of power. Al-Maliki's State of Law, which was joined by the Badr Organization, the Islamic Virtue Party and several Shi'a members of Iraqiya, was placed first in seven governorates, including Baghdad and Basra, and took joint first place with the ISCI in Wasit. In Najaf and Salah al-Din, local independent lists (the Alliance of Iraqi People and Loyalty to Najaf, respectively) prevailed, while the Sadrists were successful in Maysan. In Diyala, a pan-Shi'a list that included the ISCI, the Sadrists and the State of Law was placed first. Although it secured the highest number of governorate council seats across Iraq as a whole, the State of Law actually lost representation compared with its performance in 2009, and in no governorate was the party's margin of victory sufficient to govern without coalition partners. Allawi's Iraqiya performed worst: despite being the only list to present candidates in all 12 governorates, Iraqiya's best result was fourth place in Diyala and Salah al-Din. The main beneficiary appeared to be a new Sunni coalition assembled by parliamentary Speaker al-Nujaifi, Mutahhidun ('the Uniters'), which was placed second in Baghdad, Salah al-Din and Diyala (in alliance with al-Mutlaq's Iraqi Front for National Dialogue).

Despite emerging from the April 2013 elections as the preeminent Sunni political movement, however, Mutahhidun suffered a sharp reversal in fortunes in its home base of Nineveh when the delayed voting was held in June. Mutahhidun's share of council seats declined from 22 to just eight. A joint KDP/PUK coalition—the Brotherhood and Coexistence Alliance—unexpectedly emerged victorious, securing 11 of the council's seats. Mutahhidun performed better in June's rescheduled election in Anbar, taking eight of the council's 30 seats. In Nineveh the party reached an agreement with the KDP/PUK list to form a coalition government and preserve the Governor's position. Likewise, in Anbar and Diyala Mutahhidun was able to assemble coalition governments of various Sunni factions, while in Baghdad a surprising governing coalition was formed with the Sadrists that excluded al-Maliki's party from power. In total, al-Maliki's State of Law emerged from the elections as the dominant force in only six of the 14 councils.

The September 2013 elections to choose the 111 members of the Iraqi Kurdistan Parliament marked a sea change in the region's politics, as this was the first time since 2003 that the KDP and the PUK had competed separately. The final results delivered a stunning blow to the PUK. As expected, the KDP emerged with the largest share of the vote (38%) and the most seats (38); however, with 18% of the vote and 18 seats, the PUK was beaten by Gorran's 24% (and 24 seats). The KIU also performed well, securing 10 seats with 9% of the vote, as did the IGK, with 6% and six seats. There were several contributory factors to the PUK's poor performance, including the untainted appeal of the anti-establishment Gorran and the continued association of the PUK with corruption and nepotism, but the most important factor was that the party had been effectively leaderless since December 2012, when Talabani left Iraq for medical treatment in Germany. The party leadership was nominally in the hands of Talabani's wife, Hero Ibrahim Ahmed, but it was clear that the party was highly factionalized and directionless. The diminution of the PUK's political influence in the Kurdish Autonomous Region risked disturbing the delicate power-sharing balance that had prevailed in the region since the 1990s.

THE APRIL 2014 LEGISLATIVE ELECTIONS

In early November 2013 the Iraqi parliament finally approved a measure to amend the electoral law in line with a June 2010 Supreme Court ruling that had declared the existing legislation unconstitutional. The purpose of the amendment was to change the formula for seat allocation across parties to make the overall system more proportional and in keeping with the 'principles of democracy' as required by the Constitution. This change to the electoral system, which was (erroneously) believed by Iraqi politicians to benefit small parties at the expense of large parties, together with the Supreme Court's 2010 ruling that electoral blocs could be formed after an election as well as before, resulted in fragmentation of the party system. In October 2013 the former constituent parties of Iraqiya—most importantly Allawi's INL, al-Nujaifi's Mutahhidun and al-Mutlaq's al-Arabiya Coalition—announced that each would run separately in the April 2014 elections. In November 2013 the two main constituent elements of the National Alliance—the ISCI and the Sadrists—also announced their intention to participate in the elections as independent entities, the former to run as the Citizens' Alliance (Muwatin) and the latter as the Liberal Coalition (Ahrar). Later that month the two main Kurdish parties—the KDP and the PUK—also stated their intention to run on separate tickets, leaving al-Maliki's State of Law as the only electoral alliance to survive largely intact from the 2010 elections. As with previous elections, there was little in the way of serious campaigning on substantive issues. Moreover, campaigning was all but impossible in much of Anbar governorate, owing to ongoing violence, particularly in Ramadi and Fallujah. Another problem for Anbar was the displacement of up to one-third of the governorate's population by ongoing violence associated with government security operations.

Despite the ongoing violence in northern and western Iraq, the elections went ahead as scheduled on 30 April 2014, with turnout reportedly only marginally lower than in 2010, at about 60% of eligible voters. When the official results were released by the IHEC three weeks later, they confirmed that al-Maliki's State of Law had emerged with the largest share of parliamentary seats. Factoring in lists affiliated with the State of Law, the incumbent Prime Minister increased his group's representation from 89 seats out of 325 to 94 out of 328. Elsewhere among the main Shi'a lists, the Sadrists gained 31 seats and Fadillah six seats, while the ISCI's (Citizens' Alliance) seat allocation increased from 21 to 30. Among the main Sunni lists, Mutahhidun confirmed its status as the dominant political force within the Sunni community, with a total of 28 seats. Notably, the party appeared to have regained lost ground in its Nineveh stronghold, more than doubling its share of the vote compared with the 2013 provincial elections. Elsewhere, the INL/Wataniya list obtained 21 seats, 10 of which were in Baghdad, while al-Arabiya secured 11 seats. Among the various Kurdish parties, the KDP predictably emerged with the largest share of seats (25), but the PUK, with 19 seats, staged something of a comeback after its dismal performance in the 2013 elections to the Kurdish parliament. The elections were held in the PUK's traditional stronghold of Kirkuk for the first time since 2005, where the PUK secured one-half of the 12 seats. The other Kurdish parties obtaining parliamentary seats were Gorran (nine), the KIU (four) and the IGK (three), bringing the total Kurdish representation to 62 seats.

Overall, this pattern of results represented a small but important victory for the Prime Minister. His party won more seats than any other, and he remained the single most popular political figure in the country. Moreover, the disintegration of large coalitions such as Iraqiya and the National

Alliance meant that potential opposition to a continuation of al-Maliki's tenure at the helm was now more divided than ever. The general picture was one of continuity: the main Kurdish parties scored overwhelming victories in Kurdish-populated areas, the Shi'a lists won almost all the seats on offer south of Baghdad and only a handful of seats to the north, and the Sunni parties won almost all the seats in Sunni regions, indicating that Iraqi politics was still ordered primarily around ethnicity and sect.

Unlike after previous elections, in 2014 the three top positions—Speaker, Prime Minister and President—were elected sequentially, rather than as part of a single agreement. First, in mid-July parliament elected the moderate Sunni Arab politician Salim al-Jaburi, an outspoken critic of al-Maliki, as its Speaker. Just over a week later, the Kurdish politician Fouad Masoum was overwhelmingly endorsed to succeed the ailing Talabani as President, thus activating the constitutionally mandated 15-day deadline for the nomination and approval of a Prime Minister. As leader of the largest parliamentary bloc, al-Maliki was ideally placed to mount a bid for a third successive term, but faced strong opposition from Sunnis, Kurds and even many within his own Shi'a community. On 25 July Ayatollah Sistani issued a statement urging Iraq's leaders not to 'cling to power'—a thinly veiled reference to al-Maliki's efforts to retain his post and a stance that was subsequently endorsed by Iran's Supreme Religious Leader, Sayed Ali Khamenei. The effect of this statement was to divide the State of Law Coalition. Ultimately, in early August the group nominated Haidar al-Abadi in preference to al-Maliki by a vote of 50 to 45. Al-Abadi's nomination as premier was confirmed by President Masoum on 11 August. A new Council of Ministers under al-Abadi's leadership was approved by the legislature and took office in September. Significantly, al-Maliki, Allawi and al-Nujaifi were all appointed as Vice-Presidents. Although the removal of al-Maliki from power was widely regarded as a positive development for Iraqi politics, it remained to be seen whether al-Abadi would be any more successful in satisfying the conflicting demands of Iraq's various ethnic and sectarian factions, or whether the new Government would be capable of dealing with the myriad problems confronting it in late 2014. Arguably, the most serious of these problems was the dramatic ascent of the insurgent group ISIL (known as Islamic State in Iraq and the Levant until its expansion into Syria in 2013) in the north and west of the country from June.

ISIL ASCENDANCY

In early June 2014 a series of notable victories by ISIL, which was headed by Abu Bakr al-Baghdadi, resulted in Iraq's security forces losing control of large parts of north-western Iraq. Although ISIL was often referred to in the media as an al-Qa'ida-related group, the leadership of al-Qa'ida officially disowned the group in February 2014, following military confrontations between ISIL and the official al-Qa'ida affiliate in Syria, Jabhat al-Nusra (al-Nusra Front; renamed Jabhat Fatah al-Sham—Levant Conquest Front—in July 2016). Isil's financial resources were reported to derive from control of Syrian and Iraqi oilfields and illicit trading in oil, the sale of raw materials and stolen antiquities, kidnapping, protection rackets and bank heists. ISIL was able to capitalize on the discontent manifest in the Sunni protest movement in Iraq to sell itself as a champion of the Sunni community against the 'Persian' occupation of Baghdad. In some areas, notably Ramadi, ISIL faced the hostility of local tribes and other insurgent groups, but in Fallujah ISIL co-operated with local forces to present a unified front against the Iraqi Government.

During 2013 and the first half of 2014 ISIL demonstrated its capacity to conduct operations throughout Iraq, including waves of simultaneous attacks with vehicle-borne improvised explosive devices targeting Shi'a civilians in Baghdad and in cities further south. By June 2014 it was estimated that ISIL was responsible for some 75%–95% of all insurgent attacks in Iraq. It was also in June that ISIL began to implement its stated strategy of seizing control of territory in the region. On 5 June the group took control of five out of seven districts of the city of Samarra in Salah al-Din governorate before being driven out by the security forces. On the following day ISIL launched a more successful attack against Iraq's second largest city, Mosul. Within three days the security forces and the local police had collapsed, and ISIL had taken control of the city, seizing military equipment, including helicopters, and freeing hundreds of prisoners from the city's main prison. On 10 June ISIL also took control of Tikrit and by mid-June controlled large parts of Anbar, Nineveh, Kirkuk, Salah al-Din and Diyala governorates. At the end of the month the group announced a name change from ISIL to Islamic State, following its proclamation of the establishment of a new caliphate stretching 'from Aleppo to Diyala', with al-Baghdadi as the caliph.

At this time it was considered highly unlikely in the long term that Islamic State could retain the territory that it had seized and even less plausible that the group could fulfil its strategic goal of taking Baghdad. The real danger presented by Islamic State in June–July 2014 appeared to be that it risked further inflaming ethno-sectarian tensions within Iraq. In this context, the active participation in the conflict of the Quds Force of the Iranian Islamic Revolutionary Guard Corps (IRGC), the re-mobilization of Shi'a militia groups to confront the threat posed by Islamic State and the *fatwa* issued by Grand Ayatollah Sistani that was interpreted as calling for a Shi'a defensive jihad against Sunni insurgents were all ominous developments. Meanwhile, the Kurdish leadership moved quickly to capitalize on the weakening of central government authority to reoccupy disputed territory, including Kirkuk. In early July, moreover, Kurdish President Masoud Barzani described Iraq as 'effectively partitioned', and charged members of the Iraqi Kurdistan Parliament with forming an electoral commission to prepare for a referendum on Kurdish independence before the end of 2014.

In August 2014, however, Kurdish forces suffered a significant blow when Islamic State launched a large-scale assault on the Kurdish-controlled district of Sinjar in Nineveh governorate. Although theoretically in place to protect the district's minority Yazidi population, up to 10,000 Kurdish *peshmerga* withdrew from their positions, leaving the civilian population to their fate. Confronting the possibility of a massacre at the hands of Islamic State, significant numbers of Yazidi civilians fled for the safety of Sinjar mountain, creating a potential humanitarian disaster. From a positive perspective, the plight of the Yazidis prompted meaningful action from the USA. On 7 August President Obama announced that the USA would commence air strikes against Islamic State targets in northern Iraq, with the aims of defending US military and civilian personnel in Iraq, blocking an advance on Irbil by the group and preventing a 'potential act of genocide' against the Yazidis in Sinjar. The first air strikes were confirmed by the US Department of Defense on 8 August. US military aircraft had undertaken the delivery of humanitarian aid to Yazidi refugees earlier that week. In mid-August US air support helped Kurdish forces to regain control of the strategic Mosul dam from Islamic State. By the end of that month it was reported that the USA had around 1,000 combat forces stationed in Iraq and had conducted nearly 120 air strikes against Islamic State targets. In early September Obama announced that the scope of the USA's intervention against the militant group would be widened to encompass neighbouring Syria, and several other countries, including a group of Arab states led by Saudi Arabia, indicated their willingness to contribute to the military effort against Islamic State.

In a speech to the UN General Assembly in September 2014, President Obama claimed that more than 40 countries had pledged to assist the US-led coalition. In addition to NATO allies, members of the coalition included four Arab countries (Bahrain, Jordan, Saudi Arabia and the United Arab Emirates—UAE) which carried out air strikes against Islamic State targets in Syria. Although the military campaign against Islamic State could claim some early successes, it was hampered by the absence of reliable ground forces capable of capitalizing on the opportunities created by coalition air strikes. This problem was brought into stark relief during September and October when first the town of Hit in Anbar governorate, then a nearby military training base at Saqlawiya, fell to Islamic State forces. Up to 500 Iraqi security forces were executed in the aftermath of the battle for Saqlawiya, and a further 200 were taken prisoner. Hopes of mobilizing a tribal uprising in Anbar against Islamic State were dealt a severe blow in October when a prominent tribe opposed to the militant group, the Albu Nasir, suffered a series of losses and were then pursued and executed by Islamic State fighters. In all, some 500 tribe members had been executed by the end of October, all but eliminating the tribe as a serious fighting force. By the end of November Islamic State's offensive in Anbar had left the group in control of approximately 90% of the governorate. Of Anbar's important towns and cities, only Ramadi and Haditha remained outside the control of Islamic State fighters.

Elsewhere in Iraq, the news was more positive. In Salah al-Din governorate, for example, Iraqi government forces were able first to block Islamic State's expansion and then win some morale-boosting victories. The most important of these was the successful lifting of the Islamic State's siege of Amerli at the end of August 2014 by a joint force of Kurdish *peshmerga*, Shi'a militia groups and the Iraqi army, assisted by coalition air strikes. However, the propaganda value of the victory was seriously undermined by the behaviour of Shi'a militias in the aftermath of the battle. According to a March 2015 report by the US-based non-governmental organization (NGO) Human Rights Watch, members of the so-called Popular Mobilization Units (or Hashd al-Shaabi) proceeded to loot Sunni villages around Amerli, set fire to a large number of residents' houses and Sunni mosques and mete out 'vicious reprisals' against suspected Islamic State sympathizers. Similar incidents were reported in Diyala as Shi'a militias stepped up efforts to drive Islamic State out of the governorate. By the end of January 2015, following a series of military operations in Diyala, Hashd commander Hadi Ameri claimed, somewhat implausibly, that Islamic State had been defeated in Diyala and that the entire governorate was now liberated.

THE PREMIERSHIP OF AL-ABADI: A DIFFICULT FIRST YEAR

The challenges confronting al-Abadi as he assumed office in September 2014 were daunting. Most obviously, in Islamic State, he faced a motivated, well-trained and resourced insurgent army that occupied up to one-third of Iraq's territory. The Iraqi army, meanwhile, had essentially disintegrated in the face of Islamic State's onslaught of mid-2014, which meant that al-Abadi would have to rely heavily on Shi'a militia forces (the Hashd) and Kurdish *peshmerga* to stem the militant group's advance and retake captured territory. Islamic State's success at seizing and governing territory in Iraq's Sunni-inhabited regions indicated that the group enjoyed some measure of support within the beleaguered Sunni community. From a political perspective, therefore, the key to defeating Islamic State lay in convincing the Sunni population to reject the group in favour of an Iraqi Government that had comprehensively marginalized the community under al-Maliki's leadership. Efforts to move in the direction of sectarian reconciliation began promisingly. In October al-Abadi successfully steered his nominees for the Ministries of the Interior and of Defence through parliament to complete his first Government. The defence portfolio went to a Sunni, Mutahhidun's Khalid al-Obeidi, a former air force officer from Mosul. Despite opposition from the Kurds, who accused al-Obeidi of having participated in repression of the Kurds under Saddam Hussain, and the protestations of the Accountability and Justice Commission (AJC—the successor body to the de-Baathification Commission), which claimed that his Baathist past precluded his appointment to office, al-Obeidi's appointment was approved by parliament. More controversial was the appointment of Muhammad al-Ghabban as Minister of the Interior. As a member of the Badr Organization, al-Ghabban's appointment revived memories of the 2005–08 period, when Badr's infiltration of the Ministry of the Interior's counter-terrorism units had led to widespread atrocities against the Sunni community and ultimately led to civil war.

Like all Iraqi governments since 2005, al-Abadi's was a Government of national unity that allocated portfolios on the basis on ethnicity and sect in almost exactly the same proportion as al-Maliki's second Government. The Shi'a parties received 51% of the ministries, the Sunnis secured 27% and the Kurds 17%. However, al-Abadi's first Government was a significant improvement over its predecessors. First, it was notably smaller than al-Maliki's second Government, comprising 29 ministers—a reversal of al-Maliki's practice of creating meaningless government posts to satisfy the demands of various factions for access to power and patronage. Second, unlike al-Maliki, who had either appointed loyal allies to key security posts or kept these posts for himself, al-Abadi's appointment of al-Obeidi as Minister of Defence and al-Ghabban as Minister of the Interior suggested that the Prime Minister was fully cognizant of the urgent need to overhaul Iraq's corrupt and incompetent security apparatus. The process began in September 2014 with the elimination of up to 50,000 'ghost' soldiers from the Ministry of Defence's payroll. Subsequently, hundreds of officers, including numerous senior officers, were dismissed in a more far-reaching purge of the military. In addition, al-Abadi began the long process of dismantling al-Maliki's personalized security architecture by eliminating the Office of Commander-in-Chief—a post that al-Maliki had created.

Al-Abadi won support for his national unity Government from Sunni political leaders by pledging to address the key demands of the Sunni community. The most important of these were an end to the indiscriminate shelling of Sunni towns and cities, which estimates suggested were killing more Sunnis than Islamic State; a general amnesty that would include the release of large numbers of Sunnis detained without trial; an end to the Accountability and Justice (de-Baathification) process; and the creation of a system of provincially based National Guard (NG) units that would be funded and equipped by the Iraqi Government but would remain under provincial command. The Prime Minister even expressed his openness to the idea of the creating one or more Sunni federal regions. This was in stark contrast to al-Maliki, who had simply ignored requests from Salah al-Din and Diyala governorates in 2011 to initiate the referendum process in order to transform both governorates into federal regions. The creation of an NG system had been strongly encouraged by the USA, and was viewed as a critical first step towards integrating the Sunni community into the fight against Islamic State. By mid-2015, however, parliament had taken no action on either the revised draft of the NG bill (which was released in February and, unlike the original version, placed the NG under the command of the Prime Minister rather than the provincial governors and excluded the *peshmerga* from the arrangement) or the amended version of the Accountability and Justice Law, providing a powerful indication of the magnitude of problems faced by al-Abadi.

AL-ABADI'S REFORM PROGRAMME

By mid-2015 the popular demonstrations that had occurred sporadically since 2011 began to escalate. In early August 2015 a wave of protests swept the southern cities of Basra, Najaf, Karbala and Nasiriya, culminating in the tens of thousands of mostly young, secular demonstrators in Baghdad's Tahrir Square on consecutive Fridays in that month to protest, initially, against the Government's failure reliably to provide essential services such as electricity and potable water. The protests soon developed into calls for more fundamental and radical political reforms to address the country's chronic political corruption problem and the system of allocating ministerial portfolios on the basis of ethnic and sectarian quotas, which led to biased and incompetent performance. Demands for reform were endorsed by the Shi'a clerical establishment. A key focus of the protesters' demands was reform of the judicial system, including the removal of the controversial Chief Justice and head of the Supreme Judicial Council, Medhat al-Mahmoud (on account of his extensive record of judicial service under al-Bakr and Saddam Hussain). On 8 August al-Abadi duly announced a sweeping package of reforms aimed at tackling corruption, reducing the size of government and ending the system of ethnic and sectarian quotas. Notably absent, however, was any effort to initiate serious judicial reforms; instead, the judiciary was simply instructed to devise a plan to reform itself. The package was approved unanimously by the Council of Representatives on 11 August, but little progress was made in terms of its implementation. However, al-Abadi did enjoy some success in reducing the size of a bloated Council of Ministers that had reached as many as 40 members during al-Maliki's second term. By eliminating some ministries and merging others, al-Abadi reduced the size of his cabinet from 29 members to 22, but left unchanged the more important issue of ethnic and sectarian quotas; in fact, the ethnic and sectarian composition of the new, slimmed-down cabinet was almost identical to that of the preceding administration.

On the vital question of tackling high-level corruption, al-Abadi's reform programme achieved predictably little in terms of the functioning of government, and while examples were made of certain individuals, the basic system of patronage that lies at the heart of Iraq's political system remained undisturbed.

The complexity of the political calculations involved in reforming a fundamentally dysfunctional political system were brought into sharp relief in February 2016 when al-Sadr announced his own reform package that involved replacing the existing cabinet with a cabinet of non-partisan technocrats. Al-Sadr gave al-Abadi a 45-day deadline to enact meaningful political reforms and pledged to organize protest demonstrations in the mean time. In response, al-Abadi announced in late February that he was replacing his cabinet with a slate of non-partisan technocrats and presented the list of names to the Council of Representatives for approval on 31 March. Almost immediately, two of al-Abadi's nominees—for the oil and finance ministries—withdrew their names from consideration, owing to the strength of opposition from the major political groupings in parliament (with the exception of the Sadrist bloc). The major parties accused al-Abadi of failing to consult them on the list of nominees and demanded the right to nominate their own candidates. This led al-Abadi to present a second list of nominees who, he hoped, were more acceptable to the major blocs, but, in response, dozens of deputies staged a sit-in in the chamber of the Council of Representatives to protest against al-Abadi's perceived capitulation to vested interests. Amid scenes of chaos in parliament, during which water bottles and punches were thrown, there were calls for al-Abadi and Kurdish President Masoum to resign and claims that the Sunni Speaker, al-Jaburi, had been voted out of office. Al-Abadi eventually succeeded in securing parliamentary approval for five of his proposed 16 nominees in late April, but was unable to make any progress on the other cabinet posts. Al-Abadi's efforts to reform the political system placed him in a difficult position; to stay in power and enact a reform package required the support of at least some of the parties that had shared power since 2005, yet it was precisely these parties that had the most to lose in terms of access to state resources and patronage opportunities if al-Abadi's reforms were eventually to succeed.

In mid-July 2016, amid the ongoing stalemate over the appointment of a technocratic cabinet, al-Abadi accepted the resignations of the Ministers of Oil, Transportation, Construction and Housing, Industry and Minerals, Water Resources, and the Interior. (The latter, al-Ghabban, had submitted his resignation in early July, following a bomb attack in a predominantly Shi'a district of Baghdad, in which more than 300 civilians were killed.) Nominees for five vacant posts were approved by parliament in mid-August. Most notably, Jabar Ali al-Luaibi became Minister of Oil. However, the Government was further destabilized by votes of no confidence by parliament in the Minister of Defence, al-Obeidi, in late August and the Minister of Finance, Hoshyar al-Zebari, in September.

Meanwhile, al-Sadr succeeded in co-opting an increasingly strident protest movement to demand the very reforms that al-Abadi lacked the political support to deliver. Following a brief lull in protests during April 2016, al-Sadr's supporters stormed the so-called 'Green Zone' in Baghdad on two occasions in May, and on the second of these, when they entered the parliament building and briefly even the prime ministerial office, security forces responded with tear gas and live ammunition, killing four protesters.

A DEAL WITH THE KURDS UNRAVELS

Initial relations between the new Prime Minister and Kurdish leaders were tense, owing to al-Abadi's refusal to approve Kurdish demands in return for obtaining Kurdish support for his new administration. In fact, Kurdish MPs were not even present in Baghdad when al-Abadi presented the names of his cabinet members for parliamentary approval in early September 2014, nor had Kurdish leaders officially confirmed their willingness to participate in the new Government. A threatened Kurdish boycott of parliament and the Government was avoided only after the USA and the UN brought intense diplomatic pressure to bear on the Kurds to join the national unity Government. Together with longstanding Kurdish demands, such as the implementation of Article 140 and passage of a national hydrocarbons law, the Kurds sought assurances from the new Prime Minister that the freeze on central government funding for the Kurdish Autonomous Region imposed by al-Maliki in January 2014 would end, and that the *peshmerga* would receive equipment and funding to carry on the fight against Islamic State. In return for their participation in government, the Kurds reportedly came to an agreement with al-Abadi that established deadlines of one year for resolving the problem of the disputed territories, six months for the passage of a hydrocarbons law and one month for the release of frozen budget funds. Despite the implausibility of any progress on a hydrocarbons law and the fact that large swathes of the area in question were occupied by Islamic State, an important breakthrough in relations between Irbil and Baghdad took place in December through the conclusion of a formal agreement for the Kurds to provide 550,000 b/d to the Iraqi state oil marketing organization—SOMO (300,000 b/d of which were to come from the Kirkuk oilfields, and 250,000 b/d from oilfields in the recognized Kurdish Autonomous Region) in return for a 17% share of the budget and a $1,000m. payment for the *peshmerga*. The agreement was widely considered to represent a 'win-win' situation, as it increased oil production for Iraq as a whole at a time when the low global price of oil was causing chronic budget shortfalls in Baghdad, and it finally allowed the KRG to resume paying the salaries of government workers and security forces. Almost immediately, however, the deal came under strain, owing to the inability of the Kurds to produce oil in the quantities required and the Iraqi Government's failure to provide funding at the agreed levels. The KRG was therefore unable to pay the salaries of government employees or to make repayments on the more than $3,000m. in debt that the region had accrued in 2014–15. Further exacerbating the Kurdish Autonomous Region's financial crisis was the steep decline in the international price of oil from late 2014 and the unreliability of the one pipeline—from Kirkuk, through Turkey to the port of Ceyhan on Turkey's Mediterranean coast—that allowed the Kurds to export oil independently. The pipeline was repeatedly out of use during early 2016, owing to sabotage and sporadic attacks by the Partiya Karkeren Kurdistan (PKK) in Turkey.

The KRG's dire financial state was compounded by a political crisis that erupted in August 2015, precipitated by the expiry of Barzani's term as President following a previous deal in 2013 to extend his tenure by two years. By law, Barzani's term expired on 19 August, and the vacant position should then have been occupied temporarily by the parliamentary Speaker, Gorran's Yousuf Muhammad Sadiq, until elections could be held. However, Barzani refused to step down, citing the threats posed by the economic crisis and Islamic State, and with key external players, such as Turkey and the USA, seemingly unconcerned by Barzani's extended tenure as President, there was limited pressure on him to compromise. Barzani also retained the capacity to play the nationalist card, as he did in February 2016 when announcing that a (non-binding) referendum on Kurdish independence would be held in either October or November. Even if the referendum were to go ahead as planned and resulted in a vote for Kurdish independence from Iraq, Barzani would not be able to act on the result without the assent of Turkey and the USA; however, the move sent a clear warning to Baghdad about the potential consequences of continued intransigence over the KRG's budget, while reinforcing the perception among Kurds throughout their communities in the

Middle East that Barzani was the true champion of the Kurdish nationalist movement.

THE FIGHT AGAINST ISLAMIC STATE: TURNING THE TIDE

In March 2015 the Iraqi Government launched a series of offensives aimed at liberating the city of Tikrit in Salah al-Din from the control of Islamic State forces. Roughly two-thirds of the government forces advancing on Tikrit were estimated to be Hashd members, but they were backed by a small number of Sunni tribal fighters, up to 1,000 members of the Iranian IRGC, Iranian air power and, reportedly, 150 members of the Lebanese Hezbollah. In support of the operation, Kurdish *peshmerga* launched an offensive against the Islamic State stronghold of Hawija in Kirkuk in an effort to disrupt the militant group's supply lines into Salah al-Din. Notably absent from the proceedings, at least initially, was the USA, partly due to the prominent and very public role played by Iran in the operation, but also driven by the stated determination of Hashd commander Ameri to retake Tikrit without US assistance. After initial successes in the surrounding areas, the advance stalled in the face of poor co-ordination, a lack of training in urban warfare and a fierce rearguard action by the remaining Islamic State fighters. After two weeks the death toll among government forces had risen to over 1,000. At this point, al-Abadi opted to overrule Ameri and request US air strikes. In return, the US Administration asked that Hashd forces be held back and regular Iraqi security forces be used for the final push to take Tikrit. The town finally fell to government forces on 31 March, after a month of fighting. Although this was an important victory for the Iraqi Government and Islamic State's most significant defeat to date, the battle for Tikrit revealed the limitations of Iraqi ground forces. Despite government forces vastly outnumbering those of Islamic State, and the significant assistance provided by the Iranians, it is questionable whether Tikrit would have been retaken without US air power.

Hopes that the fall of Tikrit would mark the beginning of the end for Islamic State in Iraq were short-lived. In April–May 2015 Islamic State launched offensives in Anbar governorate that overran several army bases and captured the Tharthar dam just north of Fallujah. In mid-May the group launched a massive assault on Ramadi, the capital of Anbar. Using armoured bulldozers and multiple suicide car bombs, Islamic State fighters overran the government centre on 14–15 May. An attack on the Anbar Operations Command on 17 May routed remaining government forces, and the entire city was in the hands of Islamic State by the end of the day.

More broadly, Islamic State's success in Anbar provided a graphic illustration of the magnitude of the problems facing Prime Minister al-Abadi in his efforts to combat the militant organization. On the one hand, Iraqi government forces were for the most part unmotivated and ill-equipped to defeat an army as capable as Islamic State; on the other, the one force that was motivated and had demonstrated a willingness to stand and fight, the Hashd, had a history of committing grievous human rights violations against the civilian populations of retaken territory. Unleashing the Hashd to spearhead offensive operations in the Sunni heartland of Anbar, as was announced by the Iraqi Government in July 2015, therefore risked transforming a counter-insurgency campaign against a common enemy into a full-blown sectarian civil war. A second problem was a lack of clarity in terms of command and control. In theory, the Hashd was overseen by the Hashd Commission under the control of al-Abadi as Commander-in-Chief, but in practice, key military decisions were made by Hashd Deputy Commander Abu Mahdi al-Muhandis and Assistant Commander Hadi al-Ameri (of the Badr Organization). The absence of a unified and coherent chain of command created unnecessary problems during the early stages of the campaign to retake Anbar, as al-Abadi ordered Iraqi forces to focus on liberating Ramadi from Islamic State, and al-Ameri unilaterally decided to launch an assault on Fallujah. Given that the total number of Iraqi troops available for the Anbar campaign was less than half the number that had been needed to retake Tikrit, al-Abadi's compromise decision to attack both cities left neither force with sufficient troop strength to hold captured territory, and by the end of August the Anbar offensive appeared to have ground to a halt.

There was better news from Salah al-Din, where a combined Iraqi force (Hashd and government troops) of some 13,000, reportedly under the command of al-Ameri, finally prevailed in the year-long struggle for the city of Baiji in October 2015. Baiji's huge oil-refining complex had historically given the city a vital strategic significance, but the refinery was largely destroyed during the fighting. However, Baiji retained a strategic location on the main highway from Baghdad to Mosul. Following the devastating loss of Ramadi to Islamic State forces in May 2014, this was a critical victory for the morale of Iraqi forces and freed up troops to join the Anbar offensive. In Anbar a critical breakthrough occurred in December 2015 when Iraqi government forces, together with Sunni tribal militia and supported by coalition air strikes, advanced into Ramadi and recaptured the government complex. Although it would take many months to clear the city of remaining pockets of resistance and dismantle the huge number of booby traps and improvised explosive devices left in place by retreating Islamic State forces, the victory in Ramadi was highly important.

Following the victory in Ramadi, Iraqi forces advanced rapidly through western Anbar, capturing Hit in April 2016 and Haditha and Rutba in May. By the middle of that month Iraqi forces were in place to begin the final assault on Fallujah. Despite predictions of a costly battle of attrition, the campaign to liberate Fallujah took just five weeks. As in Ramadi, the lead was taken by Iraqi armed forces and Sunni tribal fighters, backed by Iraqi air force and US air strikes, with Shi'a militias confined to a largely supporting role. However, disturbing reports soon surfaced of Shi'a militia groups perpetrating atrocities. In particular, the UN High Commissioner for Human Rights, Prince Zeid Ra'ad Zeid al-Hussein, accused the Iranian-backed Hezbollah Brigades of killing up to 50 Sunni civilians and abducting nearly 900 others in the aftermath of the fight for Fallujah. The genuine danger that Islamic State still posed to Iraq's political stability no longer derived from its occupation of large swathes of Iraqi territory, but from its capacity to inflame sectarian tensions, either through targeted attacks against the Shi'a civilian population, such as the massive truck bomb detonated in the Shi'a-majority Karrada district of Baghdad in early July, killing over 300 civilians, or through retaliatory actions by the various Iranian-backed Shi'a militia formations that comprised the Hashd, and without which Islamic State could not be defeated militarily.

THE BATTLE FOR MOSUL

The latter months of 2016 and the first half of 2017 were dominated by the planning and execution of the military campaign to retake Mosul, Islamic State's prize possession in Iraq, and site of the al-Nuri Mosque from which the group's leader, al-Baghdadi, had proclaimed the establishment of the caliphate. Although this was primarily a military operation, political considerations were never far from the surface. Among the various armed formations vying for a lead role in the fight were the Iraqi Government's security forces: specifically, the Golden Division of the counter-terrorism forces; the federal police; the Rapid Reaction Division of the interior ministry; and various elements of Iraq's army, each answering to a different chain of command. The various components of the Iranian-backed Hashd were also pushing for an active role, as were the Kurdish *peshmerga*, the PKK from its base in Sinjar, and a Sunni militia force, the Hashd al-Watani, which was headed by a former governor of Nineveh, Atheel al-Nujaifi. External players with a vested interest in the outcome included, obviously, Iran, the special forces of several Western powers (notably, the USA, the UK, Canada and France) and Turkey, which had established a base in northern Nineveh in December 2015 (just outside the disputed territory of Bashiqa) with the stated goal of fighting Islamic State, and was largely responsible for training and equipping al-Nujaifi's militia.

Prime Minister al-Abadi's challenge of transforming this diverse array of forces, each under a separate chain of command and with its own conflicting agenda, into a coherent fighting force was not helped by the loss of his Minister of Defence, al-Obeidi, in August 2016. The parliamentary vote of no confidence in al-Obeidi was orchestrated by al-Maliki and was considered as a thinly veiled attempt to undermine the authority of al-Abadi. (Minister of the Interior al-Ghabban had resigned in July over the Karrada bombing, and Minister of Finance Hoshyar al-Zebari was dismissed in September.) With his Government in chaos, in October al-Abadi officially announced the beginning of the military campaign to retake Mosul. Although the Hashd and the *peshmerga* were both to be involved in the campaign, neither force would be permitted to enter the city itself, according to al-Abadi. Given the disparity in size between the two sides, with some 100,000 pro-Government forces versus fewer than 5,000 Islamic State fighters, al-Abadi felt able to predict with confidence that the fight to reclaim Mosul would be over by the end of 2016.

The original plan was for the various pro-Government forces to advance on Mosul and surround the city on three sides, leaving a channel to the west through which members of Islamic State could withdraw from the city, thereby creating a 'kill box' in the open ground between Mosul and the Syrian border and avoiding a fight to the death in Iraq's second most populous city. This channel would also provide a way out for the 1m.–1.5m. inhabitants still believed to be present in the city and thus allow government forces to bring their superior firepower (air strikes and artillery) to bear on the enemy without excessive civilian casualties.

At some point between the official start of the campaign and the end of October 2016, however, the plan changed, apparently at the instigation of Iran, which feared that large numbers of Islamic State fighters might take advantage of the escape channel to cross the border back into Syria and re-join the fight against the regime of President Bashar al-Assad. Accordingly, on 28 October it was announced that Hashd forces had been dispatched and tasked with re-taking the city of Tal Afar, to the west of Mosul, and sealing off the Syrian border to prevent the escape of Islamic State fighters.

Elsewhere in the campaign, Kurdish *peshmerga* and the Golden Division initially made rapid advances in the towns and villages to the east of Mosul. The *peshmerga*'s role was to spearhead an advance to the east, paving the way for the Golden Division, and, by some accounts, the Hashd al-Watani, to launch an assault on eastern Mosul. By the end of October 2016 Kurdish forces had recaptured the town of Bashiqa, at which point they halted their advance and began digging defensive trenches. After overwhelming a fierce defence of the town of Bartella—viewed as the 'eastern gate to Mosul'—the Golden Division was ordered to continue its advance into the city. The campaign plan had called for elements of the Iraqi army and the federal police to advance simultaneously into the city from the north and south, with the goal of spreading out defensive forces as thinly as possible. However, as the advances along northern and southern fronts ground to a halt several kilometres from the city during November, the Golden Division was caught badly exposed and facing the full force of Islamic State resistance. In the first five weeks of the campaign alone Islamic State launched over 600 suicide car bomb attacks against pro-Government forces, leading to an estimated attrition rate among the Golden Division of 40%–50%.

In early December 2016 an order was given that federal police forces and Iraqi army units be diverted from the southern front to support the Golden Division's advance on Mosul. By the end of January 2017 Islamic State's lines of defence in the eastern part of the city had effectively collapsed; on 24 January east Mosul was declared 'liberated'. The operation to reclaim west Mosul was launched in February with an attack from the south by the Iraqi army, federal police and the Rapid Reaction Division, later supported by the Golden Division. The combined forces made good progress along three axes of advance, capturing Mosul airport and university quickly, but ground to a standstill on the outskirts of the Old City district, where the bulk of Islamic State fighters were holed up. A new front from the north, led by the army's Ninth Division, helped to disperse defenders, and the decision to skirt the Old City enabled most of the areas west of the Tigris to be captured by early June. On 29 June Iraqi forces captured the al-Nuri Mosque, and on 10 July the last areas occupied by Islamic State fighters were cleared, allowing Prime Minister al-Abadi finally to declare victory in the battle for Mosul.

The eviction of Islamic State from its Mosul stronghold left the group in possession of Tal Afar in the west, Hawija south of Kirkuk and some isolated pockets of territory along the Syrian border, but it also left Iraq with any number of unresolved issues. Foremost among these were the post-Islamic State political status of the Hashd and the issue of the disputed territories formerly occupied by Islamic State.

POST-ISLAMIC STATE PROBLEMS

The term Hashd al-Shaabi refers to a diverse array of militia factions of varying sizes, capabilities and loyalties. Although the vast majority of the fighters who comprise the various units are Shi'a, the Hashd is not a coherent organization. Some units were formed in response to Sistani's *fatwa* and remain loyal to the Grand Ayatollah; others, such as al-Sadr's Peace Brigades, owe loyalty to powerful political individuals; others to Iran; and still others are the armed wings of established political parties. Some of these units were thought likely to demobilize in the wake of an Islamic State defeat, but the more powerful—the Badr Organization, the Asa'ib Ahl al-Haq, and the Peace Brigades—were likely to seek to translate their successes on the battlefield into political power. Efforts to finalize the legal and political status of the Hashd continued to generate controversy, given that the 2015 Law on Political Parties prohibits militias from forming parties and forbids parties from being affiliated with any armed force.

The initial approach to dealing with the Hashd was to codify its legal status as a separate branch of the armed forces under civilian control (at least theoretically). This was the thinking behind the law passed by the Iraqi parliament in November 2016 which established a new force from the Hashd, independent of the armed forces, but under the Prime Minister's direct control. The law limited the number of troops in the new force to 50,000 (a proposed reduction of 100,000) and required a quota of 15,000 of the 50,000 fighters to be Sunnis. The legal recognition of the Hashd as a national institution was an attempt formally to separate armed militias from political parties by creating a non-partisan security force. It remained to be seen, however, whether fighters would place loyalty to the new institution over loyalty to a specific individual or party. Moreover, the chances of forging a coherent fighting force from the hugely diverse factions of the Hashd seemed slim. The problem of coherence was compounded in December when the Prime Minister issued an order to integrate al-Nujaifi's Hashd al-Watani into the new force, reportedly at the behest of Turkey. By this point a warrant had already been issued for Nujaifi's arrest, based on the accusation that he had conspired with a foreign country by inviting Turkey to establish a base in Nineveh. Thus al-Nujaifi's militia was legalized at a time when its leader remained criminalized.

Like most laws passed by the Iraqi parliament, the law on the Hashd was not immediately implemented and, meanwhile, the power of Shi'a militia groups outside state control continued to grow. Various Hashd factions established political bureaus in liberated Sunni cities, such as Fallujah and Ramadi, others undertook serious recruitment programmes in Iraqi universities, and in March 2017 the head of Asa'ib Ahl al-Haq, Sheikh Qais al-Khazali, announced his intention to establish a Hashd University. The unenviable conundrum facing al-Abadi was that the implementation of the Hashd law was bitterly opposed by Sunni and (most) Kurdish political leaders; to forge ahead, therefore, would greatly complicate the task of post-Islamic State ethno-sectarian reconciliation, essential for future stability in Iraq. Failure to implement the law, however, would alienate powerful Hashd factions as well as Iran.

Besides the formidable challenges of dealing with militias and rebuilding large swathes of northern Iraq, at an estimated cost of US $100,000m., amid chronic fiscal problems with deficits and debt, the other major post-Islamic State political issue that urgently needed to be addressed concerned the disputed territories, almost all of which were now under de facto Kurdish control. However, it was obviously unrealistic to assume that there would be no discussions about the status of the disputed territories. In particular, a complex and volatile situation had emerged in the disputed territory of Sinjar. Although a combination of Kurdish forces, including the PKK and the Syrian Kurdish Yekîneyên Parastina Gel, had re-taken Sinjar from Islamic State in November 2015, the Hashd's advance into the region west of Mosul after October 2016 dramatically changed the dynamic. After surrounding Tal Afar and taking up positions along the Syrian–Iraqi border, in May 2017 Hashd forces moved into Sinjar and began liberating Yazidi villages and recruiting heavily from the local population. The Hashd move was a direct challenge to the Kurds, most notably the KDP, and could be understood on two different levels. The Hashd's presence in Sinjar meant that the district's incorporation into the Kurdish Autonomous Region would inevitably be contested; more importantly, if the Iranian-backed Hashd could control the region west of Mosul that abuts the Syrian border, it would help to advance the realization of the long-held Iranian goal of creating a land corridor, protected by allies, from Tehran to the Mediterranean.

The situation in Kirkuk was also complex. By mid-2017 control of Kirkuk governorate was divided, with Kurdish forces (mainly *peshmerga* affiliated to the PUK) controlling just over one-half of the territory, including the city itself and the oil infrastructure, and Islamic State dominating most of the southern half of the governorate. A diverse range of Hashd forces were also present, including Shi'a Turkmen formations affiliated with the Badr Brigades in the sub-district of Taza and in neighbouring Tuz Khurmatu, together with Sunni and Shi'a Arab Hashd forces gathering along the Hamreen mountains in preparation for the forthcoming assault on the Islamic State stronghold of Hawija. An agreement concluded between Kurdish *peshmerga* and the various Hashd formations in February 2015 on the provision of security in Kirkuk appeared to have held firm, and the *peshmerga* and Hashd even conducted joint military operations against Islamic State. However, the final defeat of Islamic State in its remaining stronghold of Hawija in early October 2017 changed the situation significantly, by removing the shared enemy from Kirkuk. The situation had also changed dramatically as a consequence of the Kurdish independence referendum on 25 September.

THE KURDISH GAMBLE

The announcement via social media in June 2017 that a date had been set for a Kurdish independence referendum brought the issues of the Kurds' future status in Iraq and the disputed territories into sharp relief. President Barzani had originally authorized the vote via an executive order, which led some Kurds to question the legal status of the entire process. In an effort to legitimize the referendum, Barzani convened the Kurdish parliament, which had been suspended for some two years, for a single session on 15 September. The intention was to secure legislative approval for the vote, but the effect was to reveal the extent of intra-Kurdish divisions. Only 68 deputies in the 111-member body attended the session, 65 of whom voted in favour of the referendum. Notably, members from Gorran and the right-wing, Islamist Kurdistan Islamic Group (KIG) boycotted the vote, as did several members of the PUK. The wording of the question—'Do you want the Kurdistan Region and the Kurdistani areas outside the administration of the Region to become an independent state?'—seemed designed to produce an overwhelmingly positive response, but the referendum was non-binding. The intention was that a strongly positive vote would provide Barzani with the authority to engage in negotiations with Baghdad over the terms of the Kurds' eventual separation from Iraq. Controversially, the referendum was scheduled to be held throughout the disputed territories—or at least those territories controlled by Kurdish forces—including Kurdish-controlled parts of Kirkuk. A strongly positive result in these areas would enable Barzani to argue that the 'will of the people' (as per Article 140) to join the Kurdish Autonomous Region had duly been expressed.

Unlike the Kurdish political parties, which were divided between and within themselves over the wisdom of staging the referendum, the international community was almost entirely united in its opposition. Alongside the predictably strident opposition of the Iraqi Government, Turkey and Iran, almost all of the most important global players, including the UN, the EU, Russia, the UK, France and Germany, opposed the vote. Critically, the USA made its strong opposition clear in the weeks leading up to the vote. Two days before the vote, US Secretary of State Rex Tillerson delivered a letter to Barzani urging a delay in the referendum and proposing a 'new and accelerated framework for negotiation' on all issues between the Kurds and the Iraqi Government that would last 'no longer than a year'. In the event, Tillerson's plea came too late to derail the vote, which took place as scheduled on 25 September 2017 and delivered the result that had been widely predicted. More than 92% of those who voted supported independence for the Kurdish Autonomous Region and, significantly, the 'Kurdistani areas outside the administration of the Region'. However, the strength of this endorsement was undermined by the surprisingly low turnout. Data from the Kurdistan Independent High Elections and Referendum Commission indicated that about 70% of eligible voters participated in the referendum, but unofficial reports suggested that turnout was significantly lower in areas not controlled by the KDP. In Sulaimaniya and Halabja, for example, turnout was unofficially estimated at about 55%, suggesting a distinct lack of enthusiasm for the process in regions not dominated by the KDP.

The Iraqi Government's response to the vote was swift. In the weeks following the referendum a series of measures was enacted to isolate and punish the Kurds, including a ban on flights into and out of the Kurdish Autonomous Region, the exclusion of the Region's banks from the Iraqi banking system, the issuing of arrest warrants for the organizers of the referendum, joint military exercises between Iraqi government forces and those of Turkey and Iran along the Region's external borders, and a vote by the Iraqi parliament to authorize the use of force to reclaim disputed territories, if necessary. An opportunity for Prime Minister al-Abadi to act on this authorization came in mid-October 2017, when Iraqi government forces, supported by Hashd forces, finally defeated Islamic State in Hawija. On 16 October the combined anti-Islamic State forces marched into Kirkuk and by the end of that day they had seized control of the city and key strategic sites, including the K1 military base and the two oilfields of Avana and Bai Hassan, which had provided the Kurds with almost one-half of their oil revenues since 2014. The lack of Kurdish resistance surprised many observers, but it soon became clear that the PUK's *peshmerga*, which comprised the bulk of the Kurdish forces present in Kirkuk, had staged a planned withdrawal in line with the terms of a deal struck with the Iraqi Government during the preceding days. The PUK's retreat left the KDP's much smaller contingent with no option but to withdraw. The PUK also withdrew from parts of disputed territories that it had occupied in other governorates, and by the end of October 2017 the Kurds had ceded almost all of the disputed territories, including territory, such as Khanaqin, which had been under de facto Kurdish control since 2003. At the end of October 2017 Iraqi government forces also took control of the key strategic town of Fishkhabur in Dohuk, thereby gaining control of the location at which the Kurds' independent oil pipeline crossed into Turkey. On 30 October Barzani announced that he was to stand down as President. In his statement Barzani stated that he was not retiring from politics, but that he would not seek another term as President and that his powers would be distributed among the KRG Prime Minister, parliament and judiciary.

The events of October 2017 were a disaster for the Kurds. In losing control over almost all of the disputed territories, they also lost vital oilfields and the pipeline that allowed the Kurds to export oil independently of Baghdad. This deprived the Kurdish Autonomous Region of its independent revenue stream and returned the Region to a position of, in effect, total dependence on Baghdad for its income. The loss of Kirkuk—the Kurds' 'Jerusalem' as it was characterized by Kurdish leaders—also laid bare the extent and depth of intra-Kurdish divisions. The agreement for the KRG to yield disputed territories to the Iraqi Government had been agreed by the PUK without the knowledge of the KDP. Within the PUK itself, significant divisions had emerged even before the death of its leader Talabani in early October. In September the party lost one of its dominant figures when Barham Salih, former Prime Minister of the KRG and former vice-premier of Iraq, left the party to form his own political movement. His intention was to unite the various political factions that opposed the duopoly of the two main parties and favoured wholesale reform of the Kurdish Autonomous Region's political system under a new umbrella organization named the Coalition for Democracy and Justice. The PUK was also starkly divided over the wisdom of proceeding with the referendum. On the one hand, prominent PUK political figures, including acting head of the party, Kosrat Rasul, and the Governor of Kirkuk, Najmaldin Karim, were strong supporters of the referendum and staunch opponents of the deal to cede Kirkuk without a fight; on the other, it was a powerful PUK faction clustered around Talabani's immediate family that had actually concluded the agreement with Baghdad.

The Kurds' loss of territory and vital resources translated into a sharply diminished political bargaining position vis-à-vis the federal Government. Flush with political capital from the defeat of Islamic State and the largely bloodless recapture of disputed territory from the Kurds, Prime Minister al-Abadi was in no rush to reach accommodation with the Kurds. Although the Kurds offered to 'freeze' the results of the referendum, al-Abadi refused even to hold talks unless and until Kurdish leaders issued a statement to annul the results. In November 2017 Iraq's Supreme Court issued a ruling that the referendum had been 'unconstitutional' and that the result was annulled. The KRG's Prime Minister, Nechirvan Barzani (nephew of former President Masoud Barzani), described the ruling as unilateral, but notably declined to challenge its basic premise. Henceforth, negotiations between Baghdad and Irbil led to the former's slow release of the economic chokehold that it had maintained on the latter since the referendum. For their part, the Kurds had no option but to try to reach an accommodation with Baghdad. With no major independent source of income and reportedly in debt of some US $17,000m. (borrowed in order to finance huge budget deficits) in the midst of an acute economic crisis, the KRG was forced to impose economic austerity measures and was unable to pay salaries to public sector employees. By December the dire economic situation in the KRG and the ruling parties' inability or unwillingness to address it effectively had provoked large-scale popular protests, mainly in Sulaimaniya governorate. A sharp reminder of the Kurds' lack of political leverage had come in November when the draft budget included a cut in the Kurds' share of government disbursements from 17.0% to 12.7%. When the budget was finally approved in March 2018, it included no specific allocation for Kurdistan as an entity in its own right, but instead pledged a share to each of the three Kurdish-dominated governorates proportionate to their share of Iraq's total population. Given the strength of anti-Kurdish and anti-Barzani sentiment among Arab Iraqis since the September referendum, al-Abadi's decision to confront the Kurds over the budget was a logical tactic in the run-up to the legislative elections in May 2018.

THE 2018 LEGISLATIVE ELECTIONS

Since the December 2005 elections, when the various factions representing the Shi'a community competed as an umbrella coalition (the United Iraqi Alliance), a key trend in Iraqi politics had been the increasing fragmentation of the political landscape, and the 2018 parliamentary elections promised to be the most fragmented to date. However, although prospective Iraqi voters had a greater range of choice than ever, and most of the major blocs made some attempt to appeal beyond a single ethno-sectarian base, the political space remained dominated by a familiar cast of characters, suggesting that a radical change to the system was not on the cards. Frontrunners within the Shi'a community included the party that had won the most seats in the 2014 election—Nuri al-Maliki's State of Law Coalition. Al-Maliki largely ignored Kurdish and Sunni parts of the country and focused the campaign on the part of the Shi'a base—rural and lower-class Shi'a in central and southern Iraq—that had delivered victory, if not the premiership, in 2014. Undermining the State of Law's prospects for a repeat of its 2014 success were the perceived culpability of al-Maliki in creating Islamic State in the first place, the shocking performance of Iraq's security forces under his leadership, and several important defections. Most notably, Prime Minister al-Abadi split from the State of Law Coalition ranks to form his own coalition—the Victory Alliance (Nasr Coalition). Al-Abadi's defection split both the State of Law Coalition and the Islamic Dawa Party, but was accepted by Dawa leaders on the grounds that it would maximize the chances of the party retaining control of the premiership. Another important defection came with the formation of a political coalition to harness the popular appeal of the Hashd. The al-Fatah (Conquest) Alliance, spearheaded by the Badr Organization and fronted by Badr's leader, al-Ameri, comprised the bulk of the various pro-Iranian Shi'a militias that had helped to defeat Islamic State, but also included a small number of Sunni and Turkmen Hashd formations and was expected to have an electoral appeal that transcended its main support base in the Shi'a heartland. These three coalitions were viewed as the most likely contenders to secure the most seats in parliament, but the Shi'a community was further divided by two alliances: the National Wisdom Movement (al-Hikmah), formed from an offshoot of ISCI and led by its former head Ammar al-Hakim; and an unlikely union between followers of al-Sadr and the Iraqi Communist Party (ICP). The Saairun (Forward) Alliance—referred to hereafter as simply Saairun—was intended to build on the momentum of the protest movement that began in 2015 and campaigned on a platform of anti-corruption and an end to the *muhassasa* system by which positions of power are allocated on the basis of ethno-sectarian quotas rather than merit. These same issues, together with an improvement in public services and job creation, were, to some extent, championed by all the major Shi'a coalitions during the campaign.

The two main coalitions vying (primarily) for the votes of the Sunni community were the National Accord (Wataniya) led by Allawi, and the Mutahhidun led by al-Nujaifi. While the former had, as in previous elections, a demonstrable appeal among secularists which transcended ethno-sectarian identity, the latter ran candidates only in Sunni-dominated governorates and focused its platform on Sunni concerns, such as post-Islamic State reconstruction and the establishment of an autonomous Sunni federal region. Kurdish interests were represented by the two main parties—the KDP and the PUK—running on separate tickets; by the two most prominent religious parties in the KRG, the KIG and the KIU; by Gorran; and by two new creations: Salih's Coalition for Democracy and Justice; and the New Generation Movement (NGM), created and led by media mogul Shaswar Abdulwahid. The NGM was formed in the aftermath of the independence referendum, which Abdulwahid had strongly opposed, and ran a dynamic campaign against the perceived corruption of the KDP and the PUK.

The legislative elections took place on 12 May 2018 as scheduled; the electorate's apathy towards the Iraqi political process was indicated in a low turnout of just 44%. Perhaps the most surprising aspect of the results was the poor showing of Prime Minister al-Abadi's party. Prior to the vote, it was assumed that defeating Islamic State and adopting a tough approach towards the Kurds would translate into a comfortable electoral victory. However, Nasr obtained only 42 seats out of the 329 seats, placing the party third behind the election's winner, Saairun, with 54 seats, and the al-Fatah Alliance, with 47. The strong showing by Saairun was the elections' other main surprise. Overall, Saairun was placed first in terms of seats in six governorates, including Baghdad, and finished second in a further four. As opinion polls predicted, al-Maliki's State of Law Coalition performed poorly, winning only 26 seats. This represented a loss of 66 seats from its 2014 seat total. The various Kurdish parties performed in line with expectations, winning a combined total of 58 seats. The only surprise, given the events of 16 October 2017, was the strong showing by the PUK, which secured 18 seats. The Kurdish reform parties—the NGM, Gorran and Salih's Coalition for Democracy and Justice—collectively obtained 11 seats, while the two main Islamic parties garnered two seats each. Elsewhere, the major Sunni parties fared less well. Allawi's Wataniya, which included prominent Sunni politicians Salim Jabouri and al-Mutlaq, came joint first in terms of seats in

Diyala governorate, but otherwise performed below expectations, winning just 21 seats overall. Al-Nujaifi's Mutahhidun took just 14 seats overall and was placed fifth in Nineveh governorate with only 7% of the vote.

DELAYS IN FORMING A NEW GOVERNMENT

Delays in ratification of the election results scheduled for the end of July 2018 were the result of several factors, including accusations of fraud across multiple governorates, alleged problems with the electronic voting machines, manual recounts and concerns about the independence and credibility of the IHEC. After all members of the IHEC were summarily dismissed by the Prime Minister and replaced with a panel of judges to supervise the partial recount, the process finally began in early July in 13 of the 18 governorates. When the Supreme Court officially certified the results on 19 August, the only change was a gain of one seat for the al-Fatah Alliance. However, the recount process had raised serious doubts about the overall credibility of Iraq's election and served further to undermine public trust in the country's political institutions.

The ratification of the vote paved the way for the official process of government formation to commence. Accordingly, on the same day representatives of four political groups—Saairun, al-Hikmah, Nasr and Wataniya—announced the formation of a 'nucleus for an alliance' that could constitute the basis of a new government. By the end of August 2018 the contest to form the largest bloc in parliament had distilled down to a stand-off between two sides: a 'reformist' bloc termed Reform and Construction (al-Islah), centred on al-Sadr's Saairun and controlling approximately 130 seats, and a 'conservative' bloc—Construction (al-Binaa)—crystallized around the al-Fatah Alliance and al-Maliki's State of Law Coalition and controlling 74 seats. The standard practice after all preceding elections had been for all Shi'a parties to coalesce to form the largest bloc, but this split in the Shi'a ranks left neither bloc close to a majority in parliament. Confusing matters further was a dispute over whether the term 'bloc' referred to an alliance of parties or a collection of individual legislators. The question arose from several prominent defections from al-Abadi's Nasr, including the Chair of the National Security Council, Faleh al-Fayadh, who was promised the interior ministry portfolio in return for deserting al-Islah and joining al-Binaa. The question was never definitively resolved, but the net effect was that each bloc could claim to be the largest and nominate rival candidates for the position of Speaker. As a result, the first parliamentary session convened to elect the Speaker, on 4 September 2018, was unable to reach a decision, and parliament was forced to adjourn until 15 September.

Although intra-Shi'a contestation dominated the post-election strategic environment, the Sunni and Kurdish parties were also divided. Within the Sunni community, the two major election winners, Allawi's Wataniya and al-Nujaifi's Mutahhidun, were challenged almost immediately by a prominent Sunni businessman, Khamis al-Khanjar, who joined forces with Jamal al-Karbouli's National Movement for Development and Reform (al-Hal) to forge the National Axis Alliance. The Alliance picked off members of the two main Sunni parties with such success that it soon emerged as the largest Sunni group in parliament, with some 50 members. Despite a track record of hostility between al-Khanjar and al-Maliki, the Alliance opted to side with al-Binaa, leaving the remnants of Wataniya and Mutahhidun to align with al-Islah. Officially, both main Kurdish parties pledged to stay out of negotiations until the largest bloc had been formed. Informally, however, the Kurdish parties were also divided between the two main blocs, with the KDP favouring al-Binaa and the PUK and others gravitating toward al-Islah. For the first time since post-war elections had begun, therefore, all three of Iraq's main ethno-sectarian communities were divided into two rival blocs challenging for executive power. On the positive side, this could have indicated that Iraq was moving toward a political system that was no longer starkly defined by ethnicity and sect; on the negative side, it made the government formation process even more tortuous than usual, leaving the country with no effective government to address the increasingly violent demands of the population during mid-2018.

PROTESTS ESCALATE VIOLENTLY IN MID-2018

Iraqi civilians taking to the streets during the summer months to protest against the repeated failings of successive Iraqi governments has become something of a tradition, and 2018 was no exception. What differed from previous years were the scale and intensity of the protests and the violence of the Government's response. When the protest season began in early July, the grievances expressed by protesters were familiar: unemployment, especially among the youth, endemic political corruption and the inability of the Government to provide reliable essential services, such as electricity and potable water. In terms of electricity, Iraq's infrastructure was capable only of generating 15,700 MW of electricity, but needed more than 23,000 MW to ensure a continuous supply during the summer months. Some of the shortfall was met by electricity imports from Iran, but on 7 July Iran ceased exporting electricity to Iraq, citing unpaid bills and the needs of its own population.

The problems with respect to water supply were, if anything, even more ominous than those relating to electricity. In terms of quantity, water shortages owing to extremely high temperatures and a drought were exacerbated by a significant reduction in the quantity of water flowing down the Tigris river. In terms of quality, this reduction, combined with an increase in the salinity of water moving up the Shatt al-Arab waterway, created an environmental and public health crisis in Basra that came to a head in July and August 2018. By the end of August several tens of thousands of people in Basra had fallen ill after consuming contaminated water, and there were fears of a large-scale cholera outbreak in the city. Against this background, the protest movement began in May but escalated rapidly from the beginning of July. On 8 July a large protest near the West Qurna 1 oilfield in Basra led to clashes with police and resulted in the deaths of two protesters. Over the following week, protests intensified and spread across southern Iraq. The main targets of the protesters were government buildings, airports, ports and infrastructure relating to the oil industry, which is run by international oil companies, which tend to employ foreign workers rather than Iraqis. Increasingly, protesters also vented their anger on the various political parties that seemed incapable of even forming a government, let alone addressing the demands of an angry population. On 13 July, for example, protesters in Maysan governorate stormed the provincial council building and set fire to the headquarters of the Islamic Dawa Party and al-Hikmah. On the following day Badr's headquarters in Basra was set on fire, and the day after, Saairun's office in Hillah, Babil, was attacked. The targeting of Saairun, a movement that had emerged ostensibly to champion the cause of the protesters, was a telling indication of the level of anger behind the protests.

Prime Minister al-Abadi's response to the escalating protests was a mix of repression and empty promises. In an effort to stem the tide, the Government shut off access to the internet and launched a concerted media campaign to discredit the protesters as 'Baathists' and 'terrorists'. Simultaneously, security forces adopted a harder line, using tear gas and live ammunition on demonstrations throughout southern Iraq. There were also reports of a campaign to arrest and even assassinate activists and journalists, although it is not clear that this was government-sponsored. In an effort to buy off the protesters, al-Abadi promised emergency funding for Basra, to increase supplies of electricity and potable water and to create 10,000 new government jobs. Temporarily at least, this combination of carrot and stick appeared to take the steam out of the protest movement. However, Basra's ongoing water crisis, which had caused illness among some 22,000 people by the end of August 2018, prompted a revival of protests; seven protesters died on 4 September, the single most violent day of protests.

The core problem facing any Iraqi government is that the demands of protesters cannot easily be addressed in a meaningful way. Corruption is so deeply embedded in Iraq's political system that it is probably impossible to root out. The country's electricity infrastructure is in dire need of an overhaul, but this would require an estimated US $30,000m., and even then, demand would still far outstrip supply. Problems with the water supply are predictable, but largely beyond the control of the Iraqi authorities. Finally, Iraq's economy remains heavily dependent on oil, which is not a labour-intensive industry; creating government jobs to reduce unemployment might alleviate anger in the short term, but further bloating the public sector would only undermine the future health of the Iraqi economy. Hence, Iraq is caught in a negative spiral whereby political parties repeatedly campaign on promises to address the demands of protesters but are unable to deliver when they get into government, which leads to increased cynicism on the part of the Iraqi population and more protests against the political establishment.

AGREEMENT OF THE AL-MAHDI GOVERNMENT

The most high-profile casualty of the summer protests was probably al-Abadi in his bid to retain the premiership. By early September 2018 he was being criticized on all sides for his inability to address the demands of protesters and for the harshness of his crackdown. Once al-Abadi's political toxicity had become clear, Saairun's al-Sadr and al-Ameri of the al-Fatah Alliance met to discuss a viable alternative on 6 September. On the following day, the al-Fatah Alliance, Saairun and al-Hikmah all called for al-Abadi's resignation, while Ayatollah al-Sistani's office issued a statement saying that the next premier should be someone new (i.e. neither al-Abadi nor al-Maliki). At this stage, the deal between al-Sadr and al-Ameri appeared to have stopped short of an intention to forge the largest bloc, because when parliament reconvened on 15 September, both al-Islah and al-Binaa nominated candidates for the post of Speaker. In the event, al-Binaa's Mohammed al-Halbousi comfortably defeated al-Islah's al-Obeidi, and Saairun's Hassan Karim al-Kaabi and the KDP's Bashir al-Haddad were subsequently elected as Deputy Speakers.

Failed efforts by the two main Kurdish parties to reach an agreement on a consensus nominee for the largely ceremonial post of President meant that for the first time, MPs had to choose between two Kurdish candidates—the PUK-nominee, Salih, and the KDP's Fuad Hussein. Salih defeated Hussein by 219 votes to 22 in the second round of voting. The newly elected Salih then announced Abd al-Mahdi as Prime Minister-designate, triggering a 30-day period for the approval of al-Mahdi's incoming cabinet.

The choice of al-Mahdi was as much a process of elimination as anything else. Al-Abadi was unacceptable to al-Ameri, al-Maliki was rejected by al-Sadr, and both preferred an independent who was not backed by an established political party. Beyond this, al-Mahdi could bring considerable political experience to the table, having served as Vice-President, as well as Minister of Finance and of Oil under various post-war administrations. He could also offer some Islamist credentials (he was a former member of the ISCI), as well as a background in the ICP. Finally, he had enjoyed historically good relations with Kurdish leaders as well as with Iran, but was also acceptable to the USA. He was, in short, the ultimate compromise. With no established power base, however, the success of the new administration would depend heavily on al-Mahdi's political skills to broker deals between two blocs that agreed on little. In his efforts to form a cabinet that transcended the problem of ethno-sectarian quotas, al-Mahdi was aided by al-Sadr's willingness to allow al-Mahdi himself to select the posts claimed by al-Islah as part of the al-Islah/al-Binaa deal, but only if the selections were independent technocrats. Al-Mahdi's first attempt to balance a multitude of competing political interests resulted in the approval of 14 of the 22 cabinet positions at a parliamentary session on 24 October 2018. Notable appointees included the KDP's Fuad Hussein as finance minister and Thamer al-Ghadhban as oil minister. While posts were shared proportionally among Shi'a, Sunni and Kurd in a familiar pattern, most of the appointees could plausibly claim to be independent of a political party, and many had relevant prior experience, making this a genuine, albeit incomplete, cabinet of independent technocrats. The problem for al-Mahdi came in filling the other eight posts, especially the key ministries of justice, the interior and defence. The remaining five posts—culture, education, higher education, planning and migration—should have been less controversial, but remained unfilled until they were finally approved in December. The new female Minister of Education, Shaila al-Hayali, was forced to resign following accusations that her brother was an Islamic State collaborator. This meant that four posts remained unfilled more than 100 days into the new al-Mahdi administration.

A long, drawn-out process of government formation is the rule rather than the exception in Iraq, but in other ways, the al-Mahdi administration marked a break with the past. Notably, for the first time a Government was appointed without the prior formation of a 'largest bloc' in parliament. Instead, executive appointees were determined on the basis of an understanding between two large blocs, al-Islah and al-Binaa, and included many political independents. Although some observers argued that this provided a less stable foundation for al-Mahdi's Government, it was also a more flexible arrangement. There was no prior consensus on a platform for al-Mahdi's Government, which meant that the Prime Minister would have to piece together majority coalitions on an issue-by-issue basis. In the short term, al-Mahdi's political mettle would be tested to the full by a sharp increase in tension between two of Iraq's most important external partners, Iran and the USA.

TREADING A FINE LINE

The US Administration's 'maximum pressure' campaign against Iran was launched in the aftermath of the US withdrawal from the nuclear agreement that the two countries had signed, together with other major powers, in 2015 (the Joint Comprehensive Plan of Action—see Iran). Following its withdrawal, the USA imposed targeted sanctions against senior Iranian leaders and designated the IRGC as a terrorist organization, but above all it sought to inflict maximum damage on Iran's economy. To this end, the Administration of President Donald Trump reimposed economic sanctions unilaterally, but also imposed secondary sanctions that threatened to punish private companies and third countries trading with Iran. Caught squarely in the middle as tensions escalated was Iraq. The growing resentment among Iraqis over external interference in Iraqi politics had become increasingly evident in 2018. For example, the anger violently expressed by protesters at the Shi'a political establishment in mid-2018 involved setting fire to the offices of Iranian-linked political parties, but also targeted symbols of Iranian influence directly, such as billboards depicting Iran's Supreme Leader, Ayatollah Khamenei. The most dramatic manifestation of anti-Iranian sentiment came on 7 September when protesters set fire to the Iranian consulate in Basra. Likewise, during the extended government formation period, all the major factions (except the Kurds) issued statements condemning efforts by the USA and Iran to influence the process. The task for Iraqi political leaders was to maintain a delicate balance between two strategically necessary partners to preserve the benefits of both relationships, and this meant not picking a side.

The problem posed by Trump's 'maximum pressure' campaign was that it required Iraq to side with the USA by imposing economic sanctions on Iran. The dangers of following this course became evident in August 2018 when al-Abadi announced that Iraq would adhere to the US sanctions regime and began turning back Iranian goods at several border crossings. The announcement was highly unpopular in Iraq and contributed in no small measure to the failure of al-Abadi to retain the premiership. There were also more practical considerations to take into account. As Iraq's second largest trading partner after Türkiye, Iran is an indispensable source of critical commodities, such as electricity and natural gas for Iraq's power stations, as well as being an important importer of Iraqi oil from the Kirkuk oilfield. Confusing the issue were the conflicting messages emanating from the Trump Administration, which combined ultimatums to the Iraqi Government to cut off power imports from Iran completely within a specified period with a succession of sanctions waivers that enabled this trade to continue.

Meanwhile, a key factor in every summer of protests is the inadequacy of Iraq's electricity supply, making it a very dangerous proposition for any government to reduce this still further by cutting off Iranian imports. For the most part, Prime Minister al-Mahdi succeeded in preventing Iraq from getting sucked deeper into the US–Iranian confrontation by engaging with both sides. Although stating publicly that he disagreed with the US sanctions regime, his Government took steps to appease the Trump Administration, such as prohibiting Iran from participating in US dollar auctions on the foreign exchange market and reaching a deal with the Kurds to reactivate the pipeline from Kirkuk to Turkey, thereby ending exports to Iran. Likewise, in June 2019, when Shi'a militia forces launched a series of rocket attacks at bases housing US troops, possibly at the instigation of Iran, al-Mahdi responded by issuing an executive order requiring all Hashd units to integrate fully into the Iraqi security forces, reportedly after pressure from Washington. Meanwhile, in December 2018 Iran's Minister of Petroleum, Bijan Zangeneh, visited Baghdad to sign a memorandum of understanding (MOU) on long-term energy co-operation with his Iraqi counterpart, and in March 2019 Iranian President Hassan Rouhani visited Iraq to sign several MOUs designed to increase bilateral trade from US $12,000m. per year to $20,000m.

THE KURDS GO TO THE POLLS

The Kurdish regional elections, scheduled for 30 September 2018, offered a potential way out of the political crisis that had gripped the region since 2015. Notably, if the Kurdish people chose to punish the KDP for the referendum debacle and the loss of Kirkuk by voting for opposition parties, some equilibrium could be restored to the regional power balance. For the PUK, the vote would provide an indication of whether the party's role in the events of October 2017 (seen by many as a betrayal) and the subsequent intensification of factional infighting would accelerate the party's decline by enhancing the appeal of rival challengers like Gorran and the NGM. The elections took place against a background of increasing tension between the PUK and the KDP over the nomination of Iraq's President (a Kurd) in Baghdad.

In the event, the fragmentation of the opposition to the two main parties helped to preserve the status quo: when the official results were released on 23 October 2018, both parties had performed above expectations. The KDP was the clear winner, obtaining 45 of the 111 seats available—an increase of seven seats from 2013. The PUK, meanwhile, secured 21 seats, three more than in 2013. Of the main opposition parties, Gorran saw its seat count halved from 24 in 2013 to 12, to the benefit of the NGM, which emerged in fourth place with eight seats. The other main story of the 2018 election was the dismal level of voter turnout. In most of the region, turnout was below 60%, which although far higher than the turnout across Iraq for the May 2018 national election, was still low by Kurdish standards. Like voters throughout Iraq, it seemed that Kurdish voters were becoming increasingly sceptical of a democratic process that yielded minimal change in the overall distribution of power.

KURDISH GOVERNMENT AGREED

Despite a relatively clear victory for the KDP, the process of government formation in the Kurdish Autonomous Region ended up being almost as tortuous as its national counterpart. With 45 seats, the KDP lacked the majority necessary to govern alone. With several opposition parties refusing to participate in government, the KDP realistically needed to draw the PUK and/or Gorran into the government formation process, but efforts to reach a deal with the PUK initially foundered over the latter's reluctance to accept a role as junior partner, as well as the KDP's insistence on claiming both the presidency and the premiership. For its part, Gorran reiterated its longstanding demand for legislation to limit the powers of the presidency and demanded the posts of vice-president and deputy prime minister as the price for its participation in government. Further complicating the process was the PUK's requirement that negotiations must include all outstanding issues, including the election of a PUK-approved Governor of Kirkuk and the party's claim to the still-vacant justice ministry in Baghdad.

It took until March 2019 to secure a working KDP-PUK agreement and a further month to secure the consent of Gorran. The eventual deal was for the KDP to take the two chief executive positions—President and Prime Minister—and for the remainder of cabinet posts to be distributed proportionally between the other two parties. An amendment to the law on the presidency, meanwhile, gave the Iraqi Kurdistan Parliament, rather than the Kurdish people, the power to select the President. This equated to a diminution of the President's de facto power relative to the Prime Minister, as the President could no longer claim a popular mandate. For the time being, this was largely academic, as in June 2018 the Kurdish parliament selected the outgoing Prime Minister, Nechirvan Barzani, to be President. At the same time, Masrour Barzani, Masoud's son, was elected premier. Gorran was awarded four posts in the Cabinet, including the Minister of Finance, together with the newly created post of Vice-President. The PUK secured six posts, including the powerful portfolio of *peshmerga* affairs and the position of parliamentary Speaker. Jalal Talabani's son, Qubad, was appointed Deputy Prime Minister, and the PUK was also allocated the post of 'second vice-president'.

As part of the agreement, the KDP also approved a PUK figure as Governor of Kirkuk and agreed to support the PUK's candidate for the justice ministry in Baghdad. The PUK's Farouq Amin Shwani was subsequently confirmed in this post by the Iraqi parliament on 24 June 2019. This was also the day that the Iraqi Government acquired new Ministers of the Interior and of Defence. The appointment of the interior minister, typically the preserve of the Shi'a parties, had proven especially contentious. Al-Binaa had insisted on al-Fayadh, the former head of the Hashd and al-Abadi's national security adviser, for the post. However, his nomination was repeatedly rejected by al-Islah, owing partly to his close ties to Iran, but also because he had defected from al-Abadi's Nasr during the government formation process and was therefore seen as unreliable. The eventual appointee, Yassin Tara al-Yassri, was a compromise candidate proposed by al-Hikmah. The new Sunni Arab defence minister, Najah al-Shammari, was a former military officer and special forces commander who enjoyed the support of al-Alawi's Wataniya.

PROTESTS ESCALATE AGAIN

In a break from the tradition of a protest season during the summer months, in 2019 the most dramatic period of protests in Iraq so far began on 1 October with major demonstrations in 10 governorates. In response, the Government shut down the internet, and the Iraqi security forces adopted repressive measures to break up the protests, using tear gas, water cannons, rubber bullets and, eventually, live ammunition. The result was that within about a week, over 100 demonstrators had been killed, and more than 6,000 injured. Prime Minister al-Mahdi's decision in late September to remove the publicly revered Gen. Abdul-Wahab al-Saadi from his position as commander of the Counter-Terrorism Service and transfer him to a non-combat role in the Ministry of Defence explains some of the anger. Al-Mahdi gave no reason for the decision, but unnamed 'Iraqi officials' claimed that the Prime Minister had caved in to pressure from Hashd leaders, who perceived al-Saadi and counter-terrorism forces as a threat to their political ambitions. The removal from office of a national hero who had led the liberation of Mosul at the behest of leaders widely seen as puppets of Iran may have galvanized the protests, but the root causes remained much as before: unemployment, a corrupt political system, the excessive influence of foreign powers in the political affairs of Iraq and the lack of adequate basic services. Likewise, the new Government's inability, or unwillingness, to do much about any of these problems remained much the same. What differed this time around, other than the scale of the movement, was the harshness of the Government's response, and the increasing involvement of shadowy militia groups in the repression. Although Iraqi government forces were undeniably responsible for many of the deaths, as demonstrated in numerous video recordings, some of the actions taken against protesters, such as kidnappings, the use of snipers, and the violent intimidation of journalists attached to media outlets deemed sympathetic to the protesters, were attributed to 'extrajudicial' forces with assumed connections to pro-Iranian militia groups.

As Iran became more deeply embedded in the crisis, Iraq's most revered religious figure, Ayatollah Sistani, threw his considerable political weight behind the protesters. On 4 October 2019 Sistani called for an end to government-instigated violence against protesters and blamed the crisis on Iraq's political leaders for failing to deliver promised political and economic reforms. Ever the opportunist, al-Sadr capitalized on the moment to call for the resignation of al-Mahdi's Government and the staging of early elections, and reactivated his dormant militia, the Peace Brigades. Equipped with blue baseball caps, al-Sadr's 'blue hats' were then deployed to protest sites to act as a protection force. Al-Abadi soon followed with demands for early elections. The initial response of the al-Mahdi administration was defiance. For example, national security adviser Faleh al-Fayyad threatened to deploy the Hashd against protesters who were engaged in a plot to 'bring down the Iraqi state'. Al-Mahdi himself delivered a televised address on 3 October in which he denied any involvement of security forces in the violence, blamed protesters for their own deaths and refused to make any concessions to the protest movement. Subsequently, Speaker al-Halbousi came out in support of the protests. With political support eroding and the protests escalating in response to the violence of the crackdown, al-Mahdi was forced to change strategy. On 6 October he announced a 17-point proposal, which included an increase in government jobs, an expansion of welfare programmes and the forgiveness of debt on agricultural land. On 8 October further 'reforms' were announced, including the payment of stipends to students and vocational training for the unemployed, and the following day al-Mahdi promised a transparent investigation into those responsible for the use of live ammunition against protesters, the payment of compensation to the families of those killed and the immediate release of those detained during the protests. In a further effort to appease the demands of protesters, the Iraqi parliament passed a resolution to suspend all activities of governorate and municipal councils until new elections scheduled for April 2020 could be held. By this point, however, nothing less than the resignation of the Government and the dismantling of the entire political edifice would have sufficed to quell the anger driving the protests. Moreover, this anger only increased as reports from reliable news outlets, such as Reuters, began to uncover the extent of Iran's involvement in the violent suppression of demonstrations, and leaked Iraqi government estimates put the death toll as high as 400, with a further 250 'disappeared'. The report of the government committee tasked with investigating the violence against demonstrators that was published on 22 October absolved senior political figures of all responsibility, and mostly blamed low-ranking security officers for losing control of their forces.

Al-Mahdi made a further effort at appeasement on 25 October 2019, promising gradual reforms, a cabinet reshuffle and, implausibly, constitutional amendments to meet the demands of protesters. However, on the same day protests recommenced and more than 40 protesters were killed. A pivotal event occurred on 28 October when an unidentified group attacked a protest camp in Karbala, killing 30–40 people and wounding up to 800. The Government denied all knowledge of the attack and many officials denied the attack had even taken place, but from this point onwards, al-Mahdi's Government was plainly living on borrowed time. By mid-November most of the major political factions in parliament had withdrawn their support for al-Mahdi, and on 29 November Ayatollah Sistani delivered a sermon in which he called upon the Government to 'reconsider its options'. The Prime Minister announced his intention to submit his resignation to parliament on the same day, and on 1 December this decision was duly accepted. The brevity of the Government's lifespan—fewer than six months between the completion of al-Mahdi's Government and its collapse—brought into sharp relief the immense complexities involved in translating election results into functioning governments under current circumstances. Prior to al-Mahdi, government appointees had to be simultaneously acceptable to the multiple political factions in parliament, the USA and Iran, at a minimum. Al-Mahdi's fall indicated that the voice of the Iraqi people, expressed through sometimes violent protests and demonstrations, could no longer be ignored. For the Iraqi people, the logical lesson to be learned from these events was that voting changed nothing, and that the only way to effect meaningful change was to take to the streets. This was potentially dangerous for the future health of Iraq's fragile democracy. Meanwhile, the response to the protests revealed in stark terms that the Iraqi state was incapable of exercising the most basic requirement of sovereignty—namely a monopoly over the legitimate use of force within a given territory. The involvement of various pro-Iranian Hashd formations in the violent suppression of protests occurred outside the formal command and control structure of the Iraqi state, and most analysts concluded that their orders were coming from Tehran rather than Baghdad. Powerful Iranian-affiliated groups like Kataeb Hezbollah and Asa'ib Ahl al-Haq continued to operate with impunity as instruments of Iranian policy, which put Iraq in a precarious position as tensions between Iran and the USA continued to escalate.

REINING IN MILITIAS

Prime Minister al-Mahdi's attempt to control the Hashd yielded an executive order issued on 19 June 2019 which came in the wake of several rocket attacks launched by pro-Iranian militia forces against US-linked facilities. The order stated, among other things, the 'actions of any Iraqi or non-Iraqi armed forces outside the framework of the Iraqi armed forces or outside the command and supervision of the commander-in-chief... shall be prohibited'. In July further reforms were promised that aimed at the full integration of Hashd units into the Iraqi armed forces. A critical test of the Prime Minister's willingness to enforce his own orders came in August, when he ordered the Hashd's 30th brigade, an outfit staffed mainly by ethnic Shabaks, to withdraw from the Nineveh plains and Mosul and hand over control to regular armed forces. The commander of the brigade refused to comply with the order, organized protests that blocked the Mosul–Irbil road, and even clashed with Iraqi troops who were sent there to enforce the order. Faced with this challenge to his authority, al-Mahdi backed down and allowed the brigade to remain. Simultaneously, a series of Israeli air strikes on Hashd rocket storage facilities inside Iraq prompted threats of retaliation from Hashd leaders and threatened to drag Iraq into an international conflict. However, the greatest threat to Iraq's stability posed by the Hashd was its targeting of US facilities in the country. This placed Iraq at the heart of escalating tensions between Iran and the USA and with very little control over the outcome. This became clear in late December when the USA launched missile strikes against three Kataeb Hezbollah bases in Iraq and a further two in Syria, in response to the group's rocket and mortar attacks on US-linked infrastructure. The breaking point came with a Kataeb Hezbollah rocket strike against the K1 air base outside Kirkuk, which killed a US contractor and wounded four US troops. In response, a US air strike on Baghdad Airport on 3 January 2020 killed, among others, Gen. Qassem Soleimani, head of the Quds Force of the IRGC, and the vice-chair of the Hashd Committee and leader of Kataeb Hezbollah, Abu Mahdi al-Muhandis. Iran's retaliation came on 7 January when 15 missiles were launched at bases in Anbar and Irbil that hosted US forces. The attacks seemed deliberately calibrated to avoid casualties, which implied that Iran was in no mood for an escalation of the conflict.

Meanwhile, on 5 January 2020 an emergency session of the Iraqi parliament was convened by caretaker Prime Minister al-Mahdi, which passed a resolution demanding the full withdrawal of all US troops from Iraq. While the Prime Minister was fully supportive of the resolution, observers noted that most Sunni and Kurdish legislators boycotted the session, suggesting that the issue of US troop withdrawal was one that divided Iraqis along ethno-sectarian lines, at least at the level of political elites. In response to the resolution, US President Trump threatened to impose sanctions on Iraq that would 'make Iranian sanctions look somewhat tame', and further pledged to make Iraq pay for the military installations constructed by the USA since 2003 if Iraq forced US troops to pull out. The difficult reality for any Iraqi government was that any attempt to enforce the withdrawal resolution would potentially create a very dangerous enemy in the form of the USA, while simultaneously dividing the Iraqi population along ethno-sectarian lines, and leaving the field clear for a further extension of Iranian influence.

REPLACING AL-MAHDI

Al-Mahdi's resignation in late November 2019 demoted his Government to caretaker status and left Iraq's political factions with the task of appointing another government. Constitutionally, the job of nominating a replacement should have fallen to the 'largest bloc' in parliament, but, as previously, identifying this largest bloc was easier said than done. President Salih began the tortuous process of negotiation on 1 December by meeting with all the leaders of major factions in parliament, and over the following days, he also canvassed the opinions of academics, activists and protesters. The epicentre of the protest movement in Baghdad, the so-called 'Turkish Restaurant' near Tahrir Square, announced a list of seven qualities required of any incoming prime minister. Among these were that the candidate must have no party attachments, no prior political experience in elected office, no 'foreign loyalties', and that they must commit to leaving office after early elections; this narrowed the field of acceptable candidates considerably. The decisive role played by the protests in bringing down the previous Government meant that protesters now had a de facto veto over any prospective nominee. This they exercised when an apparent frontrunner emerged in the shape of the State of Law Coalition's Mohammed Shi'a al-Sudani. In a desperate attempt to make himself eligible in the eyes of protesters, al-Sudani resigned from the State of Law Coalition and declared himself an 'independent', but he was immediately rejected by protesters as a continuation of the status quo. Over the next month or so, some 75 candidates were proposed by various parliamentary factions, but none was deemed capable of commanding majority support in parliament and meeting the requirements of protesters. By the end of January 2020, and with no end to the impasse in sight, President Salih gave parliament until 1 February to nominate a candidate acceptable to the public and threatened to appoint his own candidate if no name was forthcoming. On 1 February political support appeared to coalesce around the nomination of Mohammed Tawfiq Allawi. On the positive side, Allawi was an independent who had resigned from his position as Minister of Communications in two al-Maliki Governments in protest against the Prime Minister's sectarian agenda. As a minister, he had also spearheaded a well-publicized anti-corruption drive. Most importantly, he was at least minimally acceptable to the two main power brokers in parliament—Saairun and the al-Fatah Alliance (and Iran)—because of his stated support for the removal of US troops from Iraq. On the negative side, he was a dual (British/Iraqi) citizen who was the cousin of Ayad Allawi and who had participated in the exiled opposition movement during the 1990s that was blamed by many for creating the *muhassasa* system in the first place. The President's official nomination of Mohammed Tawfiq Allawi on 1 February 2020 triggered the 30-day period for the nominee to complete his government and earn a vote of confidence in parliament. It also triggered a popular backlash, as large numbers of protesters took to the streets of Baghdad and throughout the south brandishing posters depicting Allawi with a large red cross over his face and the slogan 'rejected by orders of the people'. Undaunted, Allawi delivered a speech in which he pledged to form a government staffed by non-partisan technocrats that would organize early elections, combat corruption and hold accountable those accused of killing and wounding protesters. Despite the evident lack of public support for an Allawi administration, the Prime Minister-designate persevered and by early March had managed to assemble a cabinet to put before a parliamentary vote. He was aided in his quest by the support of Saairun and the al-Fatah Alliance and by an agreement between these two that Allawi would be left to choose his own candidates. The problem for Allawi was that a government of independents that did not include representative quotas of Kurds and Sunnis would be unacceptable to most of the Kurdish and Sunni factions. Divisions over the demands for a withdrawal of US troops also fell mainly along ethno-sectarian lines. Most Shi'a factions refused to approve any government that would not explicitly commit to removing US troops from Iraqi soil; most Kurdish and Sunni factions demanded they stay, in part to continue the fight against what remained of Islamic State, but also because the US presence provided a counterweight to Iranian influence. Allawi was also opposed by some Shi'a factions, notably al-Maliki's State of Law Coalition. The upshot was that Allawi's political opponents were sufficiently numerous that their absence from parliament denied the body a quorum. On four separate occasions, the vote to approve Allawi's cabinet was postponed owing to the lack of a quorum, and eventually Allawi bowed to the inevitable and withdrew his candidacy.

Efforts to agree on a new candidate commenced almost immediately. On 10 March 2020 the major Shi'a factions announced they had formed a committee to determine a consensus candidate, but within a week, al-Sadr announced that negotiations had collapsed and called upon the President to exercise his constitutional prerogative to appoint a new prime minister-designate. On 16 March, in response to a query from President Salih, Iraq's Supreme Court issued a ruling that the president has the 'exclusive choice' to designate a new prime minister in line with Article 76 of the Constitution. Accordingly, on 17 March Salih charged former Najaf Governor Adnan al-Zurfi with the task of forming a new government.

Unlike Allawi, who at least had the support of the two largest parties in parliament, al-Zurfi's nomination was immediately rejected by both Ameri's al-Fatah Alliance and al-Maliki's State of Law Coalition. As a dual Iraqi-US citizen, al-Zurfi was also opposed by powerful pro-Iranian militias. As the parliamentary leader of the Nasr coalition, he was very clearly not a political independent, which made him automatically unacceptable to the protesters. On 17 March 2020 protesters in Baghdad and throughout the south began displaying portraits of al-Zurfi with large red crosses drawn through them to indicate his rejection.

PROBLEMS ESCALATE

As Iraq's political leaders struggled to produce a government that could satisfy the often incompatible demands of all major political players, a number of developments compounded the problems that any new administration would have to confront. Along with the persistence of rocket attacks by pro-Iranian militia groups against US targets in Iraq, which risked retaliation and escalation, and the ongoing protests that had now become a permanent presence on the political scene, an oil war between Russia and Saudi Arabia coupled with a collapse in demand due to the coronavirus disease (COVID-19) pandemic drove down the price of oil from US $50 a barrel in February 2020 to around $30 a barrel by mid-March. The Iraqi Government needed some $3,500m. a month just to pay its employees, and by March oil revenues stood at around $2,000m. per month. Another problem related to the nature of oil contracts signed with foreign companies: these 'technical service contracts' required the Government to pay a flat fee per month to oil companies regardless of the price of oil, which equated to an additional $1,000m. a month of expenditure. In an effort to control the spread of COVID-19, the Kurdish Autonomous Region imposed a two-day curfew on 13 March, which evolved into a complete 'lockdown' in early April, accompanied by a ban on travel between the region's three governorates. Many other governorates followed suit, but the relentless spread of the virus meant that by the end of June, the Ministry of Health was reporting the number of cases in Iraq at nearly 40,000, with a record 14,000 new cases per week. In early July a report on the economic impact of the virus by the International Rescue Committee indicated that nearly 90% of 1,500 respondents had lost their jobs, and 73% were forced to eat less food in order to save money. Without adequate resources to fund an already stretched health care system, Iraq witnessed a steady growth in COVID-19 cases throughout mid-2020 and by the beginning of August the number of cases had surpassed 140,000.

IRAQ GETS A NEW PRIME MINISTER

Once it became obvious that al-Zurfi's chances of winning a confidence vote in parliament were slim to none in the face of strong popular opposition and the al-Fatah Alliance's (and Iran's) hostility to his candidacy, it fell to the major Shi'a factions to come up with an alternative. On 31 March 2020 Iran's new Quds Force commander, Brig.-Gen. Ismael Ghaani, arrived in Baghdad to meet the leaders of all major Shi'a factions in an effort to reach consensus on a new nominee. The following day, al-Zurfi announced that he was close to completing the formation of his cabinet, but on 6 April the leaders of three parties—al-Hikmah, the al-Fatah Alliance and the State of Law Coalition—sent a letter to President Salih rejecting al-Zurfi's nomination and announcing Mustafa al-Kadhimi, the chief of the Iraqi National Intelligence Service (INIS), as their chosen candidate. The same day, al-Sadr stated that he was open to accepting any candidate who was prepared to appoint a cabinet based on merit rather than ethno-sectarian quotas. Over the following days, declarations of support for al-Kadhimi from Speaker al-Halbousi and KRG President Nechirvan Barzani effectively sealed al-Zurfi's fate, and on 9 April President Salih formally announced al-Kadhimi as the new Prime Minister-designate. As head of Iraq's intelligence agency, al-Kadhimi had worked closely with the USA and Iran during the campaign to eliminate Islamic State and was on good terms with both. Protesters were less enthusiastic, but seemed by this point willing to tolerate anyone in preference to the status quo. Al-Kadhimi also enjoyed the backing of almost all the major factions in parliament. The strongest opposition to the new nominee came from militia groups Asa'ib Ahl al-Haq and Kataeb Hezbollah, which accused al-Kadhimi of complicity in the assassinations of Soleimani and Muhandis; however, with the al-Fatah Alliance on board, the political implications of this opposition were negated.

Initially, al-Kadhimi's efforts to piece together a cabinet appeared to be heading in a familiar direction. Local media sources surfaced in mid-April 2020 suggesting that al-Kadhimi was attempting to form a cabinet of 22 members, with 11 posts allocated to Shi'a parties, six to Sunni parties, four to the Kurds and the final post reserved for a minority group: in other words, a continuation of the *muhassasa* system. However, when the final list of candidates was presented to parliament for a confidence vote on 6 May, all of those approved were independent technocrats. Of the 20 nominees presented, 15 were approved and five rejected, with the ministers of oil and foreign affairs to be determined at a later date. Finally, on 6 June the remaining seven cabinet members received parliamentary approval. The two key 'sovereign' ministries up for grabs—oil and foreign affairs—went to Ihsan Ismael, the former head of the Basra Oil Company, and Fuad Hussein, the former Minister of Finance, respectively. Assembling a cabinet that satisfied the demands of parties for the share of posts to which they considered themselves 'entitled', while simultaneously securing approval for 22 candidates who were almost entirely free of partisan affiliation, was a considerable achievement. However, the main task of the new Government was to stage early elections to find its own replacement. Beyond this, a daunting array of challenges faced the incoming administration, from combating the spread of COVID-19, to dealing with an economic crisis of monumental proportions, to navigating a safe path through the simmering tensions between the USA and Iran. Regarding the last of these, there was less pressure on al-Kadhimi to force a US troop withdrawal than there had been on previous nominees: as 2020 progressed, a slow but steady increase in the number and scale of attacks launched by the remnants of Islamic State provided a reminder of the importance of continued US military support. In an effort to mend frayed relations with the USA, the two sides conducted a virtual 'strategic dialogue' in June, in which the USA apparently pledged a reduction in troop numbers and to enter into discussions on the status of the remaining troops. In return, al-Kadhimi promised to crack down on rocket and mortar attacks by pro-Iranian militias on US assets and to expand the role of US companies in Iraq's energy sector.

Al-Kadhimi also made some progress with respect to staging early elections—a key demand of protesters. At the end of July 2020 he announced that the elections would take place on 6 June 2021. The Council of Representatives had already approved a new election law in December 2019, but had yet to finalize the details. The new electoral system marked a significant change from the existing system of proportional representation based on governorate-wide electoral districts, envisaging the restructuring of the governorates into districts, each of which would elect multiple legislators. Instead of choosing from party lists, voters would be able to cast their votes for individual candidates, with the winners in each district being decided on a first-past-the-post basis. Thus, in a district allocated to elect five legislators, the five candidates receiving the highest number of votes would secure election. This single non-transferable vote (SNTV) electoral system has been used in other countries of the Middle East, such as Jordan and Libya, to elect their parliaments. It is designed to provide more proportional outcomes than the standard single-member district, first-past-the-post system, which tends to penalize small parties and artificially inflate the seat total of the largest parties.

The failure of the Government to secure passage of a complete electoral law in December 2019 was due to the inability of the major parties to agree on the number of districts, and their size and form. The Council of Representatives was unable to agree on a formula until October 2020, but eventually settled on a plan under which the number of districts for each governorate would be based on its 25% quota of seats allocated to women by the Constitution. Thus, each governorate's existing seat allocation in parliament would be divided by four, to establish a total of 83 districts country-wide, each of which would elect multiple members. For example, Baghdad's 69 seats in parliament yielded 17 districts, while Salah al-Din's 12 seats resulted in three districts. The number of candidates elected from each district would vary according to the population of the district, although in the absence of an accurate census, which data would be used to determine each district's population was unclear. The Council of Representatives approved this formula on 10 October, and two weeks later voted on the delineation of district boundaries for 16 of the country's 18 governorates. District maps for the two most contentious governorates—Nineveh and Kirkuk—were finally approved in late October.

The successful passage of an election law was a significant achievement for the al-Kadhimi Government, and, equipped with a newly designed electoral system, it could now focus attention on addressing the remaining obstacles to staging early elections—namely, approving funding for the IHEC to commence preparations, and, more dauntingly, ensuring that a duly constituted and fully staffed Federal Supreme Court would be in place to certify early election results.

BUDGET PROBLEMS AND STRUGGLES WITH COVID-19

Despite talk of reform and a radical restructuring of Iraq's economy, the 2021 draft budget presented to the Council of Representatives in December 2020 set record levels of government spending and a record budget deficit. The subsequent delay in approving the budget (which was not endorsed until March 2021) was almost entirely caused by disputes over funding for the Kurdish Autonomous Region. Eventually, an agreement was reached under which the KRG would send 250,000 b/d of oil to the federal Government in exchange for the settlement of outstanding funds owed to it from the 2014–19 period and the payment of public sector salaries in the Region. The net effect was that the Region as a whole was allocated more than three times the sum allocated to Iraq's most populous governorate (Baghdad). Elsewhere, any effort to adhere to the constitutional requirement that revenues be distributed on the basis of population size appeared to have been abandoned. For example, Nineveh is the second most populous governorate in Iraq, but received a budget allocation 10 times smaller than that of Thi-Qar. Notably, the three Sunni-dominated governorates—Nineveh, Salah al-Din and Anbar—received the smallest allocations of all 18 governorates. Once again, the budget process illustrated the difficulties involved in implementing major economic reforms; Iraq's economic problems were easy to identify, as revealed by the contents of the Government's white paper, and the solutions were equally self-evident, but political realities precluded meaningful action being taken to implement these solutions.

Iraq's acute financial and economic crisis could not have come at a worse time, given the relentless spread of the COVID-19 pandemic worldwide. In August 2020 the World Health Organization issued a report on the escalation of COVID-19 in Iraq, warning that cases were 'exponentially rising to an alarming and worrying level, suggesting a major health crisis soon'. By that time, Iraq had recorded some 175,000 confirmed cases and nearly 6,000 deaths, almost all of which had occurred during the preceding three months. By November that year confirmed cases had risen to nearly 530,000, and were increasing at a rate of about 20,000 per week. The number of cases rose to more than 1m. in April 2021, at which point the number of new cases was rising at a rate of more than 50,000 a week. Like many other countries, Iraq's response to the COVID-19 outbreak was haphazard and sporadic. At times, parts of the country were placed under complete curfew, a national requirement for the compulsory wearing of face coverings was announced and public gatherings prohibited, but these measures were never pursued consistently. The Kurdish Autonomous Region simply ignored any orders emanating from the federal Government, and adopted its own inconsistent policies to stem the spread, including, at various times, bans on travel between the Region and the rest of the country. A major problem was the excessively slow pace of the national vaccination programme. The first vaccines only arrived in Iraq from the People's Republic of China in March, and even then, the total available for distribution was just 50,000. By the end of the first week of July the number of vaccinated people in Iraq had reached roughly 1m., equating to a vaccination rate of approximately 4% of the adult population. Another problem was the inability of Iraq's crumbling health care infrastructure to cope with a pandemic of this magnitude and severity. Symptomatic of the dire conditions of many Iraqi hospitals were two fires that occurred in 2021. The first of these broke out in April at the Ibn al-Khatib hospital, a COVID-19 isolation centre in Baghdad, and resulted in the deaths of over 80 people. The immediate cause of the blaze was an exploding oxygen tank, but a parliamentary report on the incident cited hospital administration negligence, corruption, the absence of a functioning fire-suppression system and the slow response of emergency services as contributory factors. A second massive fire, in which more than 90 people died, occurred in June in the COVID-19 intensive care ward of the al-Hussein Teaching Hospital in Nasiriya, Thi-Qar. Outraged demonstrators took to the streets of Nasiriya when details of the fire emerged; for example, the roof of the three-month-old ward had collapsed, making rescue impossible, because the walls were constructed with cheap, but highly flammable, material. In addition, the ward lacked any form of fire-alarm or sprinkler system, and the fire services ran out of water soon after arriving at the blaze. The standard approach of Iraqi governments is to respond to such disasters by dismissing the officials deemed responsible in order to appease the public, but the problem runs far deeper than this. In his resignation letter some 10 days after the Baghdad fire, the Minister of Health and Environment, Hassan al-Tamimi, highlighted the lack of government support for health care and 'haphazard' policies, and also stated that the blaze at the Ibn al-Khatib hospital 'could happen again' in any medical facility in Iraq.

PROTESTS DIMINISH

The brutal crackdown against demonstrators launched by the previous administration had provoked international condemnation and outrage among ordinary Iraqis. The ultimate result was the demise of the al-Mahdi Government. Cognizant of al-Mahdi's fate, al-Kadhimi adopted a different approach. In August 2020 his Government officially recognized all those killed during the October 2019 protests as 'martyrs', thus entitling them to specific rights under the Martyrs Foundation Law of 2009, such as government payments to remaining family members. When large-scale protests resumed on 1 October 2020 to commemorate the anniversary of the protest movement, al-Kadhimi issued a statement reaffirming his Government's loyalty to the demonstrators and their demands, and calling on protesters to continue to defend the country's independence against 'foreign interference'. Then, upon the anniversary of the previous year's largest day of protest (25 October), al-Kadhimi ordered security forces to show restraint, and to 'protect demonstrations' and public and private property against efforts by armed groups to provoke violence. In the event, large-scale demonstrations that took place across 10 governorates from Baghdad to the south were mostly peaceful. The exception was in Baghdad, were demonstrators launched rocks and petrol bombs at security forces and were met with tear gas and water cannon. None the less, the al-Kadhimi Government's generally less confrontational approach to the protest movement and the Prime Minister's rhetorical commitment to addressing their concerns may have helped to defuse the protest movement. Another factor that undoubtedly took a toll on the movement was a campaign of intimidation, kidnapping and assassinations by shadowy militia forces (generally assumed to be pro-Iranian militia groups) that targeted prominent activists. Facing persistent intimidation and harassment, riven by internal splits, and devoid of cohesive leadership and organization, the protest movement seemed in terminal decline by mid-2021.

A NEW FEDERAL SUPREME COURT

The most daunting impediment to early elections was neither the passage of an election law, nor securing funding for the IHEC, but a problem relating to the status of Iraq's Federal Supreme Court. The Court, which is constitutionally required to certify election results, was established as part of the TAL interim Constitution, as codified by a 2005 law. Like all other provisions of the interim Constitution, the Court should have been dissolved upon the passage of the permanent Constitution in October 2005. However, the drafters of the Constitution were unable to agree on a number of issues, such as the number of justices, and their method of selection, so Article 92 charged parliament with the responsibility of enacting a law, to be adopted by a two-thirds' majority, to resolve these outstanding issues. Obtaining a two-thirds' vote for anything had been virtually impossible in Iraq since 2005, and in the absence of agreement, the task of interpreting the Constitution was claimed by the interim Supreme Court. However, this ad hoc arrangement collapsed in 2019 when Justice Farouq al-Sami announced his retirement from the Court. The 2005 law did not contain provisions for replacing judges on the Court, and the Government's effort to appoint a replacement was overturned by the Iraqi judiciary. Then in October 2020 Justice Aboud al-Tamimi died, leaving the Court two short of a full quorum, and therefore unable to certify election results. Hence, for elections to take place, Iraq's political leaders were required to face the task of reaching a deal on all aspects of the Court's design, and then securing a two-thirds' majority for parliamentary approval. Initial efforts to pass the law began on 4 March 2021, and 18 of the law's 24 articles were approved on that day. Three further articles were approved two days later, but no agreement was reached on the remaining articles, which dealt with the most contentious issues, such as the Court's composition and decision-making rules of the Court (majority vs unanimity). At this point, in an astute political manoeuvre, President Saleh proposed amending the 2005 law, which could be done by a simple majority, rather than attempting to pass an entirely new law by a two-thirds' majority. This proved to be a workable compromise, and on 18 March 2021 the Council of Representatives voted to create the new Federal Supreme Court via the First Amendment of Order No. 30 of 2005. Within a week, nine new justices had been appointed, and while critics complained, with justification, that the Court's composition followed the familiar *muhassasa* system (the President of the court was Shi'a, the Vice-President was Sunni, and the Kurds had two guaranteed seats), the creation of the new Supreme Court was an important step forward in Iraq's political evolution.

FOREIGN RELATIONS UNDER AL-KADHIMI: A STEP IN THE RIGHT DIRECTION

The most pressing problem facing al-Kadhimi when he assumed office was the brewing confrontation between Iraq's two most important international partners, Iran and the USA. The basic problem remained straightforward. The Iraqi Government needed a US military presence to prevent the resurgence of Islamic State, and to help train and equip its security forces. This presence was unacceptable to Iran, several pro-Iranian political parties, and most of the numerous militia groups that comprised the Hashd. The result had been an escalating cycle of reprisal attacks in which militias targeted US assets and the USA retaliated with air strikes against militias in either Syria or Iraq. Since these militias operated beyond the control of the Prime Minister, there was a limit to which any Iraqi government could affect this basic dynamic. The intensification of militia rocket attacks on US military and diplomatic targets prompted US Secretary of State Mike Pompeo to threaten to close the US embassy and withdraw completely from Iraq. According to an informed source, Pompeo also threatened military and economic retaliation, and promised that US forces 'would kill every Kataeb Hezbollah member' in the event of a withdrawal. The threats did little to curtail militia attacks—there were 27 such attacks on US targets in September 2020—but it did lead Iran to condemn the targeting of diplomatic facilities and divided opinion among Shi'a political leaders. In October a spokesperson for Kataeb Hezbollah announced that the group was offering a 'conditional ceasefire' in return for a 'retreat' by US forces, but in the same month the head of US Central Command, Gen. Kenneth McKenzie, stated that the USA had no intention of withdrawing from Iraq, and that its presence there would be 'long term'. Negotiations over the fate of US troops in Iraq continued sporadically in the form of the ongoing 'strategic dialogue' between the two countries. The second stage of this process commenced in Washington, DC, in August, and included various agreements in areas such as energy co-operation, and cultural and educational exchanges. A reduction in US troop numbers was also apparently agreed at the time (although not announced) because in September Gen. McKenzie confirmed a reduction in US troops from 5,200 to 3,000 by the end of that month. Then, in November, the Trump Administration instructed the Pentagon to begin the withdrawal of a further 500 troops. These troop reductions were widely viewed in the USA as a pre-election ploy to convince voters that Trump had successfully ended the war in Iraq, but these moves changed very little on the ground in Iraq. Rocket attacks against bases housing US troops continued much as before, as did bomb attacks on the convoys supplying these troops. From the perspective of Iran and associated militia groups, the presence of any US troops on Iraqi territory was the problem, and their exact number was largely irrelevant. Trump himself had stated his intention to leave some troops in Iraq in the long term to 'keep an eye on Iran', so the prospects of a complete withdrawal appeared minimal, at least in the short term. This was confirmed indirectly following 'strategic talks' between Iraq's Minister of Foreign Affairs and the new US Secretary of State of the Joe Biden Administration, Antony Blinken, in April 2021. The rhetorical formula that took shape after the April meeting was to reiterate that US troops were present in Iraq 'at the request of the Iraqi government', that there were no US military bases in Iraq (all US forces being hosted in Iraqi bases), and to make a distinction between 'combat' troops and those fulfilling advisory or training functions. Significantly, the talks yielded only a vague pledge to hold future talks on a timetable to redeploy 'combat' troops outside of Iraq. Following the US air strike of 3 January 2020, the best that the al-Kadhimi Government could hope for was to avoid further escalations in tensions between the USA and Iran. In this context, preserving the status quo probably counted as a success, but the status quo remained unacceptable to Iran and many powerful players in Iraq, so whatever the outcome the Government would have to resolve this issue at some point.

In other aspects of foreign relations, the al-Kadhimi Administration achieved some notable victories. In particular, relations between Iraq and the Gulf monarchies improved significantly under al-Kadhimi. In September 2020, for example, Iraq's Ministry of Transportation announced plans to reopen Anbar's Arar border crossing that linked Iraq and Saudi Arabia. The Arar border post had been shut down by the Saudis 30 years previously, in response to Iraq's invasion of Kuwait. A follow-up teleconference between al-Kadhimi and Saudi Crown Prince Mohammed bin Salman bin Abdulaziz Al Sa'ud in November confirmed this decision, along with plans to open a Saudi business attaché office in Baghdad and a shared commitment to abide by the decisions of OPEC. Then in March 2021, a visit by al-Kadhimi to the Saudi capital, Riyadh, yielded promises of a US $3,000m. Saudi investment in the Iraqi economy to help fund reconstruction, a figure matched by a similar commitment from the UAE the following month. Given the nature of relations between Saudi Arabia (and the UAE) and Iran, Iraq's capacity to tread a fine line that avoided choosing sides was notable. In fact, there was potential for Iraq to serve as a broker between the two sides. In April al-Kadhimi was reported to have successfully mediated direct talks in Baghdad between the Governments of Saudi Arabia and Iran over their involvement in regional conflicts. Both Saudi Arabia and Iran declined to acknowledge that the meeting had taken place, but credible sources, such as the Associated Press news agency, provided confirmation of what constituted a significant diplomatic coup for the al-Kadhimi Government.

THE 2021 LEGISLATIVE ELECTIONS

The build-up to the early elections demanded by the protest movement and scheduled for 10 October 2021 was shrouded in uncertainty. In July al-Sadr announced that the Sadrist Movement would join swathes of the protest movement and the ICP in boycotting the polls. However, in a characteristic volte-face, al-Sadr announced in late August that he was reversing his earlier decision. With al-Sadr back in the race, the line-up of Shi'a parties for the October 2021 elections did not differ greatly from the 2018 polls. Alongside the Sadrist Movement (albeit without its former ally, the ICP), the al-Fatah Alliance and al-Maliki's State of Law Coalition were the major contenders, while al-Abadi's Nasr joined forces with al-Hakim's Hikma to form the Alliance of Nation State Forces, presumably in an attempt to reverse the electoral declines that both had experienced in 2018.

The two main groups vying for the vote in Sunni areas were the Taqaddum (Progress) Alliance, headed by the parliamentary Speaker and former Governor of Anbar governorate, Mohammed al-Halbousi, and Khamis al-Khanjar's al-Azm (Determination) Alliance. Notably absent from the contest was Iyad Allawi, who chose to boycott the polls rather than face probable electoral annihilation. Both leaders of the two main Sunni parties were prominent (and wealthy) businessmen who had proven willing to co-operate strategically with parties and regional actors, regardless of their nominal sectarian or ethnic affiliation; for example, both were on good terms with Hashd leaders and Iran, although al-Khanjar was also the target of ongoing US sanctions, on the grounds of corruption.

Among the Kurdish parties, the clear front runner was the KDP. The PUK's political decline was expected to continue, owing both to the party's bitter internecine fight over the choice of successor to Jalal Talabani as party leader and the anticipated strength of the challenge posed by the protest-inspired NGM, which was expected to perform well in traditional PUK strongholds such as Sulaimaniya. To counter this threat, the PUK teamed up with Gorran to form the Kurdistan Coalition—an ironic development, given that the Gorran originated as a breakaway, reformist faction of the PUK.

Together with the NGM, which sought to capitalize on the growing strength of the protest movement in the Kurdish Autonomous Region, were several parties formed explicitly to represent the interests of protesters. The two most prominent of these were the Imtidad Movement (led by Dr Alaa al-Rikabi, a prominent leader of the 'October Revolution') and Ishraqat Kanoon. There was also a large number of candidates running as independents, although it was impossible to discern how many of these were genuinely independent of the established parties.

The other significant uncertainty surrounding the October 2021 elections related to the mechanics of the new electoral system and how successfully each party would navigate these to maximize representation in parliament. First and foremost, SNTV is an electoral system that rewards parties that have accurate data on the distribution of the party's support base across districts and can communicate effectively with the party's support base to provide direction on strategic voting. This all costs money, so the system typically favours larger, established parties with access to greater resources. In the case of Iraq, this advantage was magnified by a decision of the IHEC in July 2021 to impose no official limits on the funds that candidates could spend in the elections.

Despite the usual spate of pre-election reports about parties buying votes, voter intimidation and even 6m. missing voter cards, the elections that took place on 10 October 2021 were not marked by a significant level of fraud. The UN pronounced the elections 'technically sound', while the EU's observer mission described them as 'peaceful, orderly, and well-organized'. However, the pattern of early results, which indicated that the al-Fatah Alliance's seat total was set to decline from 48 to 17, prompted the party's leaders to reject the results outright. On 12 October Hadi al-Ameri claimed that the initial results were 'fabricated' and pledged to reject them 'no matter the cost'.

The disastrous performance of the al-Fatah Alliance and the seemingly clear-cut victory for the Sadrist Movement, which emerged from the elections with 73 seats, dominated the immediate post-elections narrative, but these results were deceptive. The Sadrist Movement actually received about 400,000 fewer votes than Saairun had received in 2018, but al-Sadr had clearly understood the mechanics of the new electoral system better than his rivals and was able to translate a 10% share of the vote into a 22% share of seats in parliament. Meanwhile, with about one-half of the votes going to the Sadrist Movement, the al-Fatah Alliance earned fewer than one-quarter the number of seats secured by the Sadrist Movement. Part of the problem for the al-Fatah Alliance was that it made almost no attempt to 'game' the new system, and in many districts it ended up competing against other Hashd-associated parties, such as Kataeb Hezbollah's political vehicle, Haqooq, for the same pool of voters. Elsewhere among Shi'a parties, al-Maliki's State of Law Coalition performed well, increasing its tally of parliamentary seats from 25 in 2018 to 33 in 2021, but the Hakim-Abadi alliance performed dismally, obtaining only four seats in total. Between the two main Sunni parties, al-Halbousi's Taqaddum Alliance was the clear winner, with 37 seats against the al-Azm Alliance's 14. Votes for Kurdish parties followed a predictable pattern. With a tally of 31 seats, the KDP secured nearly twice as many seats as its former rival, the PUK. Of the Kurdistan Coalition's 16 seats, all went to PUK candidates, marking the demise of Gorran as a viable political movement.

Another major story to emerge from the 2021 elections was the relative success of parties linked to the protest movement. In the Kurdish Autonomous Region, the NGM took nine seats—five in Sulaimaniya, three in Irbil and one in Kirkuk, while the Imtidad Movement also won nine seats and Ishraqat Kanoon secured six. These totals would undoubtedly have been higher, had a significant portion of the protest movement not boycotted the elections. More impressive still was the performance of independent candidates. Collectively, with nearly 1.7m. votes, independents won almost twice as many votes as the nominal 'winner', the Sadrist Movement. Importantly, independents won at least one seat in each governorate in the country, except Karbala, receiving a total of 43. Less clear was how many of these were authentically independent of the established parties, and how many would remain so during the process of government formation.

A final notable feature of the 2021 elections was the extremely low turnout, officially reported at about 44%, although this figure represented turnout as a percentage of registered voters; as a percentage of eligible voters, the figure was about 38%—the lowest turnout of any election since the fall of Saddam Hussain. This reflected the pervasive disenchantment of Iraqis, particularly among the young, with the established parties and, more generally, with the existing political system, and represented a serious challenge to the credibility of the country's fledgling democracy.

PROTESTS AND GOVERNMENT FORMATION

On the day after the initial results were announced, al-Sadr pledged to join forces with the KDP and al-Halbousi's Taqaddum Alliance to form a majority government that would exclude rival Shi'a parties such as the al-Fatah Alliance and the State of Law Coalition. Furthermore, al-Sadr made clear his intention to form a government that would lean 'neither east nor west'—referring to Iran and the USA—and said that all weapons 'must be exclusively in the hands of the state', in pointed reference to Shi'a militias. In response, the losing Shi'a parties—the al-Fatah Alliance, the State of Law Coalition and the Hakim-Abadi Alliance—formed the Co-ordination Framework (CF) and embarked on a two-track approach to thwarting al-Sadr's ambitions. The first track involved the use of 'people power' in an attempt to pressurize election officials either to annul the results completely or at least to conduct a time-consuming manual recount of all the ballots. This was the line pursued by Hashd-affiliated parties, and sporadic protests began to break out across the country to contest the results. More ominously, a Kataeb Hezbollah spokesman issued a statement likening the elections to the rigged polls staged by Saddam Hussain and accusing the IHEC of involvement in a foreign conspiracy to defraud the Hashd. When the IHEC's full list of preliminary results, issued on 19 October 2021, proved broadly similar to the initial results, large crowds of Hashd supporters began to assemble near the Green Zone in Baghdad. Following two weeks of mostly peaceful demonstrations, matters threatened to spiral out of control in early November when clashes between demonstrators and security forces outside the Green Zone led to exchanges of live fire, causing at least two deaths and injuries to hundreds of others. This was followed on 7 November by an attack on the Baghdad residence of Prime Minister al-Kadhimi using unmanned aerial vehicles (drones) armed with explosives. No group claimed responsibility for this apparent assassination attempt, which injured several members of the Prime Minister's security detail, but left the Prime Minister unharmed. The incident prompted widespread international outrage; many Western observers simply assumed that Iran had orchestrated it via one of its militia proxies, but the Iranian Ministry of Foreign Affairs immediately condemned the attack and called for calm and restraint. The al-Fatah Alliance leader, al-Ameri, also denounced the attack, while suggesting the involvement of an unidentified 'third party', and a spokesman for Kataeb Hezbollah accused al-Khadimi of 'playing victim' in an effort to distract attention from the violent actions of security forces against protesters on the previous day.

If nothing else, the seriousness of the attack on Prime Minister al-Kadhimi appeared to defuse a tense stand-off between the Hashd protesters and security forces and, as the option of achieving its objectives through coercion was seemingly off the table, the CF focused on pursuing a second track, which involved bombarding the Federal Supreme Court with law suits in an effort to annul the election results or at least delay their ratification. None of these was successful. On 30 November 2021 the IHEC released the final election results, which did not differ significantly from earlier iterations, and on 27 December the Supreme Court rejected a last-ditch law suit presented by the al-Fatah Alliance, officially ratified the results and called on President Salih to convene parliament to begin the process of forming a new government. To the surprise of many observers, key Hashd leaders issued statements accepting the Court's decision. Al-Ameri, for example, stated that 'out of concern for Iraq's security and political stability', he was prepared to accept the decision—a sentiment echoed by the leader of Asa'ib Ahl al-Haq, Qais al-Khazali, who pledged to pursue 'peaceful' measures to rectify the flaws in the political process. On the following day the CF called on all of its supporters to cease demonstrations and to withdraw from the streets.

On 30 December 2021 President Salih issued a decree calling for parliament to convene on 9 January 2022 to initiate the process of government formation. Unlike previous polls that had invariably yielded some variant of power-sharing government of national unity, the 2021 election results raised the prospect of a new dynamic. Al-Sadr's clear victory and determination to push ahead with forming a majority government threatened important Shi'a parties with being excluded from the new administration, which would deprive them of access to the spoils of office. For parties like the al-Fatah Alliance, moreover, al-Sadr's periodic pledges to disarm—or even dismantle—the Hashd represented an existential threat. The Sadrist Movement's alliance with the KDP and the Taqaddum Alliance potentially gave the Sadrist Movement control over 141 seats in parliament, which was enough comfortably to make it the largest parliamentary bloc but was still 24 seats short of the necessary majority actually to form a government. Ranged against the Sadrist Movement were the parties that constituted the CF, which could collectively muster between 60 and 70 seats. Clearly the balance of forces favoured the Sadrist Movement, but much depended on the choices made by the other parties threatened with exclusion from government, such as the PUK and the al-Azm Alliance, and on the actions of the 40 or so independents, whose ultimate loyalties were difficult to predict.

By mid-December 2021 media reports suggested that a number of independent legislators had effectively renounced their status as independents, with six opting to align with the Taqaddum Alliance, another six with the al-Azm Alliance, six with the State of Law Coalition and seven with the al-Fatah Alliance. At about the same time, the two main Sunni parties—the Taqaddum Alliance and the al-Azm Alliance—issued a joint statement announcing their formation of a unified bloc for the purpose of negotiating with other parties in the process of government formation. On 21 December the two main Kurdish parties, the KDP and PUK, also declared their intention to put aside their differences and engage in negotiations jointly. Spokesmen for the two parties further claimed that any decision about nominations for the post of President would be reached on the basis of consensus. However, this agreement on the need for a consensus nominee appears to have lasted less than three weeks, as on 10 January 2022 the PUK announced that it was backing the re-election of incumbent President Salih—a decision made apparently without the knowledge or consent of the KDP. In response, the KDP stated that it would support its own nominee, Hoshyar al-Zerbari, for the post.

When parliament reconvened on 9 January 2022, the first order of business was to elect a Speaker and two Deputy Speakers. As predicted, al-Halbousi stood again as Speaker and was comfortably re-elected with 200 votes, against 14 for his sole opponent. Also elected in the session were the Sadrist Movement's Hakim al-Zamili and the KDP's Shakhwan Abdullah as Deputy Speakers. Al-Halbousi then announced the beginning of the 15-day period within which a President had to be elected and adjourned the session. This first session was, however, controversial, with both al-Sadr and the CF producing documents that claimed to prove that each was the largest bloc in parliament. In the ensuing chaos, the eldest legislator, Mahmoud al-Mashhadani, who was constitutionally required to preside over the first session, collapsed and had to be hospitalized. The CF boycotted the rest of the session and claimed that the process of government formation was unconstitutional, owing to the absence of the eldest legislator. A subsequent request to the Supreme Court to adjudicate on the issue resulted in the Court temporarily 'suspending' the election of the Speaker and his two deputies, before finally ruling on 25 January that the session and its outcome were indeed constitutional; by this point, however, it was unclear whether the 15-day period for the election of the President had yet to begin or whether it was almost over. In the end, the question proved largely academic, as the two Kurdish parties were unable to agree on a consensus nominee for the post, and by 31 January a total of 25 candidates had confirmed their intention to contest the presidency, including Salih and al-Zebari. Asked to arbitrate on the identity of the largest bloc in parliament, the Supreme Court stated that this could be determined only after the election of the President. The Court was again required to step into the fray, on 6 February, when the eligibility of the KDP's candidate, al-Zebari, was called into question because of a parliamentary no-confidence vote against him for corruption in 2016. The Court temporarily barred al-Zebari from standing for the post, but on 7 February 2022, an effort by parliament to vote for a different candidate failed, owing to the lack of a quorum. When the Court ruled on 13 February that al-Zebari's candidacy was constitutionally invalid, the KDP put forward a new candidate, Reber Ahmed Barzani, for the post.

It was not until 26 March 2022 that parliament convened again to elect a new President, but at this point a new complication emerged. Under the Constitution, if parliament fails to elect a President by at least a two-thirds' majority, the two candidates who won the most votes in the first round then proceed to contest a second round in which the winner is determined by a simple majority vote. The Supreme Court had issued a ruling in February, however, that even to stage the first vote would require a quorum of at least two-thirds of the legislators. In practice, this meant that the vote could not proceed if more than one-third of members chose to boycott the session, which gave opponents of al-Sadr's plans a way to block the entire process of government formation. Accordingly, the parliamentary session on 26 March was boycotted by the CF and its allies, thus denying al-Sadr the numbers necessary to elect a President and initiate the government formation process. A further two attempts to elect a President were thwarted using the same tactics. On 31 March al-Sadr abandoned the process and gave his rivals in the CF 40 days to negotiate with other factions to form a government. However, although al-Sadr's opponents could muster the numbers to block the formation of a new government, they very clearly lacked the two-thirds' majority required to form an administration without the involvement of the Sadrist Movement and its allies. Al-Sadr's empty gesture summed up the exercise in futility that the government formation process had become, and on 12 June al-Sadr instructed all 73 legislators from his party to resign from parliament, in a move that he described cryptically as 'a sacrifice for the homeland and the people to save them from the unknown'.

Under Iraqi electoral law, a resigning legislator is replaced by the candidate who obtained the second-largest number of votes at the most recent election in the same constituency, which meant in effect that the seats vacated by al-Sadr's men would be redistributed among (mostly) rival Shi'a parties. When an extraordinary session of parliament was convened on 23 June 2022 to fill 64 of the 73 seats (nine of the designated replacement legislators having declined their seats), the major beneficiaries were the al-Fatah Alliance, which picked up 11 seats, the Hakim-Abadi alliance, which gained nine, and the Imtidad Movement and al-Maliki's State of Law Coalition, which both secured seven additional seats. Eleven of the vacated seats were filled by independents.

In theory, this new seat distribution should have made it easier to form a new government, but, in practice, al-Sadr's action exposed fault lines within the CF. In a surprise move, the political wing of Kataeb Hezbollah, Haqooq, announced that it would withdraw from parliament rather than take over the five former Sadrist Movement seats to which it was entitled. Others in the CF, such as al-Ameri of the al-Fatah Alliance, argued that forming a new government without the consent of the Sadrist Movement would be unsustainable. For its part, the State of Law Coalition vowed to push ahead with the process, and by the end of June 2022 appeared set to nominate al-Maliki as a candidate for Prime Minister. Given the bitter historical rivalry between al-Sadr and al-Maliki, it is inconceivable that the former would ever give his blessing to the latter's return to the premiership.

The already slim prospect of a return to power for al-Maliki appeared to suffer a terminal setback in mid-July 2022 when a series of recordings emerged via Twitter purporting to be of a meeting between al-Maliki and representatives of an obscure militia group named the Kataib A'immat al-Baqi' (Imams of al-Baqi' Battalions). Over the course of the five recordings, a voice that sounded like that of al-Maliki is heard to describe al-Sadr as a murderer, thief and a coward, while leaders of the paramilitary Popular Mobilization Forces are dismissed as cowards and crooks. The recordings also referred to an alleged British-led plot to restore Arab Sunni rule to Iraq, and spoke of the need to prepare the armed forces for an imminent civil war. Not surprisingly, al-Maliki claimed that the recordings were fabrications and a conspiracy by 'secret agencies at home and abroad that seek to turn Iraq into a battlefield'. Regardless of the authenticity or otherwise of the recordings, their release effectively put paid to al-Maliki's prospective candidacy for the post of Prime Minister. This was officially acknowledged on 25 July when the CF announced the nomination of Mohammed Shi'a al-Sudani for the premiership. Al-Sudani had been briefly considered for the post as a replacement for former Prime Minister al-Mahdi back in 2019, but had been comprehensively rejected by the protest movement. As a close associate of al-Maliki—he had served as human rights minister during al-Maliki's second term in office and was a member of the State of Law Coalition until 2019—al-Sudani was predictably unacceptable to al-Sadr. In response to the nomination, al-Sadr mobilized his supporters to march on the Green Zone in Baghdad on 27 July 2022. Protesters entered the parliament building chanting anti-Iranian slogans, stayed for the day, then withdrew in the evening on al-Sadr's command. Simultaneously, supporters of al-Sadr staged demonstrations in multiple southern cities. On 29 July, a speech by al-Hikmah's Ammar al-Hakim in which he pledged support for the nomination of al-Sudani resulted in al-Sadr's supporters ransacking al-Hikmah's offices in Baghdad and Basra. The following day, al-Sadr's supporters stormed the parliament building for a second time, and declared an open-ended occupation until their demands, specifically, for early elections and amendments to the Constitution, were met. An escalation into serious violence appeared imminent on 1 August when rival demonstrators organized by the CF began marching toward the Green Zone. However, CF leaders issued strict instructions to their supporters to stop short of the Green Zone and the tense stand-off ended without incident. While violence was thereby avoided, the immediate impact of the Sadrist occupation of parliament was to lead Speaker al-Halbousi to suspend the parliamentary session indefinitely. This meant that no new government could be formed, which was presumably al-Sadr's primary intent. In early August al-Sadr issued instructions to his followers to withdraw from parliament but to continue their sit-in in the Green Zone until certain demands were met. Foremost among these were the dissolution of parliament and the staging of snap elections. A possible compromise seemed to be emerging over the following days as CF leaders announced that they were not opposed to fresh elections. However, the CF also demanded that parliament reconvene and a new government be appointed prior to staging early elections. Constitutionally, parliament cannot be dissolved without a parliamentary vote, which obviously requires it to be in session. In turn, if parliament were in session without the attendance of the Sadrist deputies, there would be nothing to prevent it from approving a new government that might prove inimical to al-Sadr's interests.

The process of government formation in Iraq is routinely tortuous and frustrating, but the events following the polls in October 2021 were particularly so. The pivotal moment in the process was the Supreme Court's seemingly inexplicable ruling in February 2022 that a two-thirds' quorum in parliament was necessary to even begin the process. The Court's decision guaranteed that incoming governments effectively needed the support of two-thirds of parliament; this locked in *muhassasa*-style governments in perpetuity. The only way to change this would be via a constitutional amendment, but this too would require the consent of two-thirds of parliament.

Hopes that the new electoral system would transform the basic dynamics of Iraqi politics were short-lived. Although the new system facilitated the election of new protest parties and a large list of independent candidates, the envisaged formation of a loyal opposition did not come to fruition. The 40 or so independent legislators were unable to agree on anything much and were sharply divided about whether to join the Sadrist Movement, the CF or not to participate at all in the process of government formation. Even more disappointing was the performance of the protest parties. After helping to form the 'For the People' bloc in parliament, the Imtidad Movement suffered a series of defections and eventually ended up removing its founder and Secretary-General, al-Rikabi, from his post, owing to management problems. As the head of the UN Assistance Mission to Iraq, Jeanine Hennis-Plasschaert, aptly put it in May 2022, Iraq remained trapped in an 'incessant loop of zero-sum politics', with no obvious escape route.

With Baghdad consumed by the process of government formation, the outgoing administration of Prime Minister al-Kadhimi assumed caretaker status in late 2021, which meant that it was unable to initiate significant legislation to address Iraq's many problems, or even to draft and pass a budget. In view of these circumstances, as of mid-2022 the only significant political development since the election of 2021 occurred as a result of a Supreme Court decision, which fundamentally affected the relationship between the federal Government in Baghdad and the Kurdish Autonomous Region in a way that was extremely detrimental to the latter. Prior to this point, relations between the two sides had been relatively stable, owing to an ad hoc deal agreed in July 2021 by which the federal Government allocated about US $140m. a month to the Region without demanding anything in return. This changed dramatically in February 2022 when the Court handed down its ruling in a case brought by the federal Ministry of Oil challenging the constitutionality of the Region's Oil and Gas Law of 2007. In its decision, the Court asserted that the regional law violated articles 110, 112, 115, 121 and 130 of the Iraqi Constitution. Consequently, the Court required the KRG to hand over control of all oil facilities and all of the hydrocarbons produced in the Kurdish Autonomous Region to the federal Government. Furthermore, the Court authorized the Government to pursue the nullification of all existing contracts signed between the KRG and foreign states and oil companies since 2007. The validity and integrity of this decision was indubitably questionable, and it immediately provoked a furious reaction from Kurdish leaders. In early June 2022 the Kurdish Autonomous Region's own judicial council issued a ruling invalidating the decision of the Federal Supreme Court, which prompted the Iraqi Ministry of Oil to initiate legal proceedings against many of the foreign oil companies operating in the Region. On 15 June the Ministry of Oil issued instructions to the Iraqi National Oil Company to begin the process of taking control of all oil operations in the Kurdish Autonomous Region and threatened to blacklist all oil companies that did not terminate operations in the Region within a three-month period.

AL-SADR ESCALATES THE SITUATION

While the 73 members of the Sadrist Movement could have blocked the formation of a new government indefinitely, their resignations from parliament left al-Sadr with limited options for moving forward. As of early August 2022 the only things preventing the formation of a new government were a preference on the part of some parties for the inclusion of al-Sadr in the process, and the inability of the Kurdish parties to agree on a consensus candidate for president. Futile efforts to draw al-Sadr back into the political process continued during August. On 17 August, for example, al-Sadr was invited to a meeting convened by Prime Minister Kadhimi of the leaders of all major political parties to find a way out of the political impasse. The meeting yielded five vaguely worded commitments, including agreements to negotiate in good faith to resolve the crisis and preserve the constitutional system of government and to avoid 'all forms of escalation'. The only notable outcome of the meeting was a statement suggesting that participants were not opposed to staging early elections—one of al-Sadr's key demands. Not surprisingly, al-Sadr boycotted the meeting and issued a statement the following day describing it as useless and 'of no concern to the people'. A week later, crowds of al-Sadr's supporters raised the stakes by surrounding the Supreme Judicial Council complex in the Green Zone, and demanding, among other things, the resignation of the Council's President, Faiq Zidan, and that the Council issue a ruling to dissolve parliament. In response, the Council issued a statement reiterating that it had no constitutional power to dissolve parliament and announcing its suspension of all operations in protest at al-Sadr's actions. This prompted al-Sadr to order the withdrawal of his supporters. Then, on 29 August, al-Sadr announced his 'final retirement' from all forms of political activity, and ordered all institutions associated with the Sadrist Movement to cease operations. The announcement appeared to have been triggered by the retirement of Iran-based cleric Ayatollah Kadhim al-Haeri. As the anointed successor of Muqtada al-Sadr's father, Muhammad Sadiq al-Sadr, al-Haeri is often viewed as Muqtada's spiritual mentor. However, in a statement accompanying his resignation, al-Haeri instructed his followers to pledge allegiance to Iran's Supreme Leader, and pointedly accused al-Sadr of dividing the Shi'a community and of lacking both the authority and credentials to lead the Sadrist Movement. On the same day, al-Sadr's followers staged protests in many southern cities and marched on the Green Zone to confront security forces and supporters of the CF. The result was a night-long battle in Baghdad that resulted in the deaths of at least 30 people. With the country on the brink of an intra-Shi'a civil war, al-Sadr backed down the following day and issued an apology to the people of Iraq for the involvement of his followers in the violence. Al-Sadr's voluntary political exile left the stage free for the CF and its allies to push ahead with the formation of a new government. The only remaining barrier was the apparent inability of the two main Kurdish parties to agree on a nominee for president. Since 2006, all presidents had been Kurds, and all had been representatives of the PUK, but by 2022 the differential in political power between the two parties was such that the KDP was no longer willing to allow the PUK to 'own' the office of president. Accordingly, the KDP refused to back the PUK's preferred candidate, incumbent Barham Salih, and continued to advocate the nomination of Reber Ahmed. For its part, the PUK claimed to be willing to compromise on the identity of the presidential nominee, but only on the understanding that it would then be allowed to appoint the next governor of Kirkuk.

A NEW GOVERNMENT IS FORMED

The incremental process of government formation advanced a step with the announcement on 25 September 2022 of the establishment of the State Administration Coalition (SAC). The SAC consisted of the various CF components, the two main Kurdish parties, both major Sunni alliances and the small Chaldean Christian party, the Babylon Movement. Collectively, the SAC claimed to enjoy the support of 180 legislators, which very clearly made it the largest bloc in parliament, but which was also some way short of the two-thirds' majority necessary to establish a quorum and elect a new president. When parliament reconvened on 13 October, however, 277 deputies were in attendance, comfortably surpassing the two-thirds' quorum threshold required to proceed with the election. In a last-ditch effort at compromise, the KDP dropped its support for Reber Ahmed and instead nominated Abdul Latif Rashid for the presidency. As the former spokesperson for the PUK in the UK, and a Minister of Water Resources in several post-war governments, Rashid was an experienced political actor with strong links to the PUK. Despite this, the PUK opted to back Barham Salih, resulting in a head-to-head contest between the two Kurdish politicians. In the first round of voting, Rashid obtained 157 votes to Salih's 99. With neither candidate achieving the two-thirds' threshold, the voting proceeded to a second round, in which a simple majority would be sufficient to ensure election. Rashid emerged as the clear winner, securing 162 votes to Salih's 99. On the same day, the newly elected President identified al-Sudani as Prime Minister designate, thereby initiating the 30-day period for an al-Sudani government to be approved by parliament.

On 27 October 2022 parliament duly approved al-Sudani's nominees for 21 of 23 cabinet posts, leaving two posts unfilled—Environment, and Construction and Housing. Appointees to these two posts were subsequently approved at the end of November, with the former going to Nizar Amedi of the PUK and the latter to Benkin Rikani of the KDP. In most respects, the hallmark of al-Sudani's incoming Government was continuity rather than change. The various posts were allocated on the basis of a points-based quota system in line with *muhassasa* principles, and while seven of the ministers, including al-Sudani himself, were technically 'independent', most of these had deep-rooted histories with one or other of the established parties. Much like his two immediate predecessors, al-Sudani lacked an established power base. Although often labelled as a (former) member of the Islamic Dawa Party, al-Sudani is actually affiliated with the much smaller al-Dawa offshoot, the Islamic Dawa Party–Iraq Organization, a party that possesses no militia and controls just three seats in parliament. Consequently, as with former administrations, the success of al-Sudani's Government was entirely contingent on the consent and co-operation of the leaders of more powerful political forces, most of whom, at least in the eyes of many Western analysts, were beholden to Iran.

Reinforcing the image of the al-Sudani Government as a Hashd-dominated puppet of Iran was the appointment of a former spokesman for Asa'ib Ahl al-Haq, Naim al-Aboudi, as Minister of Higher Education and Scientific Research, which meant that the USA would now have to do business with a government that contained a representative of an officially designated terrorist organization. Also controversial was the appointment of Rabee Nader, a previous media operative for both Kataeb Hezbollah and Asa'ib Ahl al-Haq, as head of communications in the Prime Minister's Office. However, while the four cabinet posts allocated to representatives of the al-Fatah Alliance—Communications, Higher Education and Scientific Research, Labour and Social Affairs, and Transportation—offered opportunities for financial gain and patronage, all were second-tier ministries and none security-related. Indeed, none of the appointees to the key security-related posts was controversial. The defence portfolio was assigned to Thabet al-Abassi of the al-Azm Alliance, while the critical post of interior minister was awarded to Abdul Amir al-Shammari, a career military officer who is no friend of the Hashd and who is perhaps best known for ordering the storming of Kataeb Hezbollah's headquarters in 2015. Elsewhere, al-Sudani retained the incumbent head of the Counter-Terrorism Service, and opted to install himself, temporarily, as head of the powerful INIS. Thus, Western analysts who rushed to label the incoming Government as the 'Hashd Government' were wide of the mark, as were predictions that the new Government would act expeditiously to expel all US troops from Iraqi soil. As al-Sudani made clear in an interview with the *Wall Street Journal* in January 2023, his administration had no intention of picking sides in the US–Iranian standoff. As al-Sudani stated, 'I don't see this as an impossible matter, to see Iraq have a good relationship with Iran and the U.S.'. In the same interview, the Prime Minister argued that the presence of US troops was still necessary in the ongoing fight against Islamic State, and refused to set a timetable for their withdrawal. Notably, al-Sudani's remarks provoked almost no backlash from the CF. Predictably, Kataeb Hezbollah immediately issued a statement demanding that the Government implement the (non-binding) 2020 parliamentary vote to remove all US troops, but a spokesman for Asa'ib Ahl al-Haq expressed support for the Government's position, arguing that 'The U.S. forces are in Iraq today to train Iraqi security forces…We are trying to make the relationship with the United States based on partnership and interests'.

As with all previous Iraqi administrations, the appointees to al-Sudani's Government were intended to balance the demands of participating parties for access to the spoils of office, while simultaneously enabling Iraq to preserve productive, or at least non-adversarial, relations with both Iran and the USA. Unfortunately for Iraq, this delicate balancing act also tends to produce dysfunctional governments that are incapable of effectively addressing the country's most serious problems, and there was no initial indication that al-Sudani's Government would be any different in this respect.

AL-SUDANI'S AGENDA UNFOLDS

The incoming Government's programme was approved by parliament on 27 October 2022 and included the usual mix of vague promises—to improve public services, fight corruption, etc.—and more concrete, but highly implausible pledges, such as enacting legislation to create a Federation Council and a new Supreme Court, and to resolve the problem of internally displaced persons within six months. Among the elements that were both specific and potentially achievable, the most important were a commitment to hold new legislative elections within a year, and another to stage the first governorate elections since 2013. The former pledge was obviously intended to appease followers of al-Sadr and what remained of the protest movement, but its authenticity was questionable. Less than a week after the investiture of the new Government, President Rashid suggested that there was no agreement on staging early elections because 'the political crisis is over'. In late November a report written by representatives of all the major parties in government recommended that governorate elections be held by October 2023, but argued against early elections due to the 'sensitive' situation in the country. Thereafter, the idea of early national elections was quietly shelved, and attention focused on amending the elections law to regulate the conduct of governorate elections. In December 2022 deputies from Kataeb Hezbollah's political wing, Haqooq, mooted a proposal to draft a revised elections law to change the electoral system used at both national and provincial levels. In place of the STV system used in the previous national election, Haqooq argued for a reversion to the Sainte Lague system of proportional representation for both levels, based on the division of each governorate into two large districts in place of the 83 districts used in October 2022. The proposal soon gained traction among the parties that had performed poorly in 2022 (i.e. components of the CF), and on 13 February 2023, a revised elections law was introduced into parliament that proposed the use of proportional representation, treating each governorate as a single electoral district at both levels. Understandably, these proposals were met with hostility by independents and small parties in parliament, but on 20 March parliament approved the revised law, which included a provision that governorate elections must be held by 20 December. Accordingly, in June 2023 the Government determined 18 December as the date for staging the first governorate elections in more than a decade.

Assessments of al-Sudani's efforts to crack down on corruption have been mixed. While al-Sudani himself is widely seen as a 'clean' politician—an anomaly in Iraqi politics—corruption is so pervasive among the establishment parties and within the bureaucracy that rooting it out is all but impossible. Moreover, the removal and punishment of political and administrative actors is routinely justified under the banner of 'fighting corruption' but is often a tactic used to damage or eliminate political rivals. Hence, it is difficult to evaluate the motives behind al-Sudani's efforts to 'clean house' during his first year in office. These efforts included the removal from office of most al-Kadhimi-era appointees and more than half a dozen governors, and a purge of up to 150 permanent administrators at the director-general level from the bureaucracy in May 2023. The stated justification for these removals was either corruption or inadequate performance, but the suspicion was that many were motivated by a desire to eliminate enemies of the CF parties. In this context, the Government's response to news of the so-called 'heist of the century' in October 2022 is instructive. The theft in question involved hundreds of unauthorized withdrawals from the account of the General Commission for Taxes at the state-owned Rafidain Bank between September 2020 and August 2021; the scale of the theft—approximately US $2,500m.—was staggering, even by Iraq's standards. While al-Sudani immediately pledged to track down all of the stolen money, the greater part of the governing parties' attention over the next six months appeared to focus on exacting revenge on high-level officials in al-Kadhimi's former administration. In late October 2022, for example, a representative of Asa'ib Ahl al-Haq's political wing sent an official letter to the Speaker of parliament demanding that he instruct the Integrity Commission to freeze the assets of members of al-Kadhimi's former cabinet, and impose a travel ban on them. The following week Kataeb Hezbollah issued a statement demanding the doubling of efforts to prosecute 'Kadhimi and his spy team'. The standard way for an incoming prime minister to demonstrate seriousness of intent at tackling corruption is to dismiss some people and create a new anti-corruption institution. Accordingly, al-Sudani dismissed the head of the Integrity Commission in November and announced the creation of a new High Commission for Combating Corruption (HCCC) to deal with major corruption cases. Among the HCCC's first actions was to impose a travel ban on Raed Johi, al-Kadhimi's former chief of staff, and subsequent director of INIS. This was followed by a purge of the INIS's senior ranks, prompting INIS to issue a statement describing the attacks on its officials as a politically-motivated witch hunt on the part of unnamed political forces 'who are threatened by the service's effective role in protecting Iraq's national security'. In March 2023 the parliamentary committee that had been established to investigate the thefts from the Rafidain Bank issued its final report, which essentially placed all blame for the crime on al-Kadhimi and his closest associates. Subsequently, judicial authorities issued arrest warrants for three of al-Kadhimi's most senior advisors and former finance minister Ali Allawi, and in June reports indicated that a Baghdad court had issued instructions to seize al-Kadhimi's 'moveable and immovable' assets. It is impossible to determine with certainty whether targeting the former administration constituted the legitimate pursuit of the guilty parties or, as al-Kadhimi himself claimed, 'indicates an open political approach in targeting and terminating everyone associated with working with the previous government'. That Allawi was involved to any significant degree seems implausible given that there had been no prior accusations of corruption levelled at him, and that Allawi himself had identified nefarious activities at the Rafidain Bank as early as November 2021. That none of the established parties was involved in any way seems equally implausible. Perhaps the more relevant point is that al-Sudani's stated determination to recover all of the stolen money seems optimistic, as by mid-2023, less than 10% of the looted funds had actually been tracked down.

THE SLOW DEATH OF FEDERALISM IN IRAQ

On the face of it, the Government's decision to set a date for new governorate elections was a positive development for Iraq's system of federalism, but the reality is different. Governorate councils are powerless entities, provincial governors can be appointed and dismissed at the whim of the federal Government, and provinces are entirely dependent on Baghdad for funding. The Kurdish Autonomous Region, with its self-determined election cycle and independent oil and gas revenues, was the exception to this pattern, at least until the Supreme Judicial Council's 2022 decision invalidating the KRG's oil and gas law. This left the region entirely dependent on the federal Government for its income in the form of a monthly payment of approximately US $140m. During negotiations on government formation, the Kurdish parties had made a continuation of these payments a prerequisite for supporting an al-Sudani government, and in December 2022 al-Sudani's cabinet duly signed off the latest transfer. Controversy arose almost immediately in the form of a lawsuit filed at the Supreme Judicial Council by a member of parliament contesting the constitutionality of the payment, and in late January 2023 the Council declared that such payments violated the 2021 budget law and the Constitution. As negotiations between Irbil and Baghdad over the 2023 budget dragged on into March, al-Sudani attempted to circumvent the Council's decision by making March's payment to the KRG a 'loan' paid through the Trade Bank of Iraq, and repayable once the Kurds' share of the budget had been finalized. When the Council of Ministers eventually reached agreement and presented its budget for ratification to parliament in mid-March, it earmarked 12.7% of the total for the Kurdish Autonomous Region, and also contained the terms of a new oil agreement between Irbil and Baghdad. The deal required the Kurds to produce 400,000 b/d and gave SOMO control over the pricing, export and marketing of oil produced in the region, with the proceeds to be deposited in a bank account controlled by the KRG, but supervised by the federal Government. The deal was intended to be a temporary arrangement until a national oil and gas law was approved, and while it imparted clarity to the oil and gas sector in Kurdistan, it also effectively signified the end of Kurdish efforts to create an oil industry that was capable of generating revenue independent of Baghdad.

The political autonomy of the Kurdish Autonomous Region was also compromised in May 2023 by another Supreme

Judicial Council ruling. In the absence of agreement among Kurdish parties over the terms on which to hold the next regional election, in October 2022 the Iraqi Kurdistan Parliament had voted to extend its term by a year. This extension was opposed by several Kurdish parties, including the New Generation Movement, which had filed a suit at the Supreme Judicial Council. In its ruling, the Council declared that the vote in October had violated the Constitution and that the Kurdish parliament's term had officially ended in that month, and that all decisions taken thereafter were thereby null and void. While the merits of the decision were debatable, the end result was that the Kurdish Autonomous Region no longer controlled the timing of its own elections.

A final blow to Kurdish autonomy was a largely self-inflicted wound that came in the form of little-noted provision (Article 14) of the budget law that was finally approved by Iraq's parliament in June 2023. The budget itself was for a three-year period and notable for being the largest in Iraq's history, due mainly to a massive expansion in the size of the government payroll. In total, the budget allocated revenue for about half a million new public sector jobs, including more than 300,000 in the education sector alone. This was an obvious attempt to appease the protest movement, which is disproportionately drawn from Iraq's youth, many of whom are university graduates, and most of whom have no prospect of gainful employment in Iraq's anaemic private sector. For the numbers to add up would require Iraq to export 3.5m. barrels of oil per day, with 400,000 b/d of this total being supplied by the Kurdish Autonomous Region, and for the price of oil to stay at or above the US $70 per barrel mark over the three-year period. Leaving aside the problem of inherently unpredictable oil prices, the ability of the KRG to meet its quota over a three-year period is questionable. A Reuters report in August 2022, based on the KRG's own analysis, predicted that in the absence of massive investment in the Kurdish Autonomous Region's oil and gas industry, production would decline to about 250,000 b/d by 2027. A more immediate problem arose as a result of a decision handed down by the Paris-based International Court of Arbitration in March 2023. The case dated back to 2014 and involved claims by the Iraqi Government that Türkiye was in violation of a bilateral agreement on the use of the Iraq-Türkiye export pipeline that connects Kirkuk to the Turkish port of Ceyhan by allowing it to be used to transport Kurdish oil without the consent of Baghdad. The Court agreed, and ordered Türkiye to pay US $1,500m. in compensation to Iraq. In response, the Turkish Government effectively shut down the pipeline, thereby blocking the export of most of the oil produced in the Kurdish Autonomous Region. This meant that for the first six months of 2023 oil exports from Iraq averaged 3.2m. b/d, considerably short of the 3.5m. b/d needed to balance the budget.

Article 14 of the budget law appeared to have been included at the insistence of the PUK and in the face of opposition from the KDP. It allowed individual governorates in the Kurdish Autonomous Region to petition the federal Government directly for a separate budgetary allocation in the event that the KRG dispersed revenues 'unfairly' across the region. The PUK had long maintained that the KDP-dominated KRG had systematically favoured the two KDP-controlled governorates in the distribution of revenues and had starved the PUK's stronghold (Sulaimaniya) of resources. Regardless of the merits of this argument, the effect was to cede power to the federal Government over the distribution of the Kurds' share of the budget, thereby diminishing the power of the KRG and affording the federal Government an ongoing mechanism through which to divide and conquer the two main Kurdish parties. Exploiting intra-Kurdish divisions is a tried and tested approach for Baghdad to 'manage' Iraq's Kurdish problem, and the KDP and PUK have rendered this task all the easier through their chronic inability to sustain a united front in their interactions with the Iraqi Government.

Relations between the two parties had been on a downward spiral since the aftermath of the independence referendum in 2017 and deteriorated still further during 2022 and the first half of 2023. The PUK boycotted KRG cabinet meetings for much of this period in protest at what the PUK viewed as the KDP's 'unilateralism and monopoly of power' in the Kurdish Autonomous Region, and there were the usual squabbles over the dispersal of payments from Baghdad across the region, and over the selection of the Kurdish nominee for the Iraqi presidency. However, a more disturbing indication of the state of relations between the two parties came in October 2022, when Hawkar Abdullah Rasoul, a colonel in the counter-terrorism force of the PUK, was assassinated in Irbil. Reports later surfaced that Abdullah Rasoul had been in the process of defecting from the PUK to the KDP, leading the KDP to accuse the head of PUK's counter-terrorism force, Wahab Halabjay, of orchestrating the killing. Subsequently, when Halabjay and five of his colleagues were found guilty of the assassination and sentenced to death by an Irbil court, the PUK refused to turn over Halabjay and the KDP reportedly responded by refusing to pay the salaries of all members of the PUK's counter-terrorism service.

On a more positive note, in July 2023 the two parties finally agreed on the necessary conditions for staging new legislative elections and jointly sent an official request to the IHEC to oversee the polls. None the less, it is difficult to see how the holding of elections will change the situation to any significant degree. The crux of the problem is that the KDP is by far the dominant political force in the region, due, in part at least, to the chronic weakness of the PUK since the death of Jalal Talabani in October 2017; the Kurds' loss of Kirkuk, a PUK stronghold, in the same month further tipped the balance of power in favour of the KDP. At the same time, there is no prospect of an alternative party emerging to challenge the KDP's dominance because the PUK still controls patronage networks in important parts of the region and has powerful coercive forces at its disposal. Hence the PUK is too weak to challenge the KDP, but simultaneously too powerful to be replaced by a more viable challenger.

The broader pattern is the continued erosion of what remains of Iraq's system of federalism. Iraq still has no second legislative chamber to represent regional interests and is still subject to the decisions of a Supreme Judicial Council that panders to the interests of the powerful. There has been no pretence for a decade or so that what the Constitution terms 'governates not organized into a region' enjoy any degree of independence from federal government control, and the last meaningful vestige of federalism—the autonomy enjoyed by the Kurdish Autonomous Region—has now been stripped back to the bare minimum.

Economy

ROBERT E. LOONEY

INTRODUCTION

Although at mid-2023 the Iraqi economy possessed a number of strengths, it was at the same time faced with an array of challenges. While containing the world's fifth largest proven crude oil reserves, with low extraction costs by international standards, Iraq faced considerable impediments to its growth and development. The onset of a series of conflicts from the early 1980s led to the destruction of a significant amount of the country's resources. Despite having access to various international financial and security aid sources, successive governments have largely been unable to mitigate the damage caused by the various conflicts. The economy remains undiversified and heavily dependent on the oil sector. Severe tensions exist between the Shi'a majority and the rest of the country, including Kurdistan, a significant oil source. Across the country, severe deficiencies exist in education, health and the welfare system. A poor security environment and an unfavourable business climate continue to hamper investment and productive activity. Moreover, US–Iranian tensions periodically spill over into Iraq, threatening economic activity further and delaying the country's ongoing reconstruction. Higher oil prices since late 2021 have provided relief from some of these factors but not a cure for their underlying determinants.

THE POST-2003 ERA

In March 2003 the USA led an international military coalition that invaded Iraq and brought down the regime of Saddam Hussain in what became known as the second Gulf War. This war followed non-compliance by the Iraqi Government with United Nations (UN) inspections of its alleged programme to pursue the production of weapons of mass destruction. The war led to the occupation of Iraq from March 2003 to June 2004.

Shortly after the ousting of Saddam Hussain, in April 2003, the US-led Coalition Provisional Authority (CPA) assumed office as Iraq's transitional government. During its 13-month tenure, the CPA issued sweeping orders and regulations covering vast areas of public life that sought to re-establish Iraqi political and economic institutions in forms appropriate to an open market democracy.

Economically, the CPA's policies mirrored the 'shock therapy' structural adjustment programmes introduced in many former Soviet and Eastern European states in the mid-1990s, when applied neoliberal economic theories had limited sensitivity to the general nature of the local society. Iraq's state-owned companies, except those in the hydrocarbons sector, were to be privatized. While the US Government hoped that the CPA's programmes would bolster the Iraqi economy, the occupying power's inability to build institutional strength and efficiency and the slow reconstruction and upgrading of the national infrastructure presented long-term obstacles to economic growth and sustainability.

Oil production in Iraq between the invasion in March 2003 and 2004 was below the levels recorded during the period of the UN Oil-for-Food programme. While in 2000 Iraq produced 2.6m. barrels per day (b/d), in 2003 it produced only 1.3m. b/d and in 2004 only 2.0m. b/d. Despite the lower production levels, Iraq benefited from increasing oil prices—the price of a barrel of Brent crude oil averaged US $25.02 in 2002 and climbed to $38.27 by 2004. During the US occupation period, economic indicators primarily benefited from the increased international oil prices and the aid money that poured into the country. These two factors helped gross domestic product (GDP) per capita to return to a similar level to that seen pre-2003. In 2002 GDP per capita was $3,880 (at constant 2010 US dollar prices); it declined to $2,526 in 2003 due to the much decreased productivity of the oil sector, but recovered to $3,792 in 2004.

The primary source of foreign financial assistance was the USA, which between 2003 and 2012 provided US $60,000m.–$63,000m. to fund humanitarian aid and the reconstruction of Iraq. The primary beneficiaries of this aid were large infrastructure and defence corporations such as Bechtel, Fluor, Raytheon and Halliburton, which pledged to rebuild Iraq's infrastructure or supplied armaments used to defeat the insurgency. Furthermore, these funds enabled Iraq to eradicate most of its external debt, thus freeing the economy from one of the main burdens accumulated during the 1980s and 1990s. Iraq's total debt amounted to $140,000m. in 2003. Following negotiations with the International Monetary Fund (IMF) and the 'Paris Club' of international creditors, 80% of this debt was cancelled (except for the debt incurred from the Gulf countries, estimated at some $45,000m.).

Priority in reconstruction went to the repair and upgrade of the electricity sector—which, besides domestic usage, was essential for medical services, industry and the powering of the oil sector. However, soon after the March 2003 invasion, a violent insurgency erupted in Iraq and quickly spread. It targeted infrastructure, foreign contract workers and, above all, military occupation forces. Also during this period, there was a proliferation of violent, organized criminal activities. Shortly after the USA transferred sovereignty from the CPA to an interim Iraqi Government in June 2004, a new phase of violence erupted. Between 2006 and 2007 Iraq witnessed an inter-communal civil war for the first time since the state's foundation in 1920. Finally, in June 2014 the fundamentalist Sunni Islamic State militant group captured and occupied northern and western Iraqi territory. The Iraqi forces subsequently achieved a considerable degree of success in reversing Islamic State's territorial gains—in particular, taking back control of the group's stronghold of Raqqa, in the north of the Syrian Arab Republic, in October 2017, three months after recapturing the principal north-eastern Iraqi city of Mosul—although the negative economic and social consequences of the insurgency continue to linger.

These episodes delayed reconstruction efforts due to the direct and indirect targeting of crucial infrastructure, and the shifting of resources from development and reconstruction to security enhancement measures. By 2017 the Islamic State insurgency had caused significant losses in economic production in the territories under its control, the concomitant loss of tax revenues for the federal Government in Baghdad, the destruction of infrastructure and the disruption of major trading routes. It had also led to the internal displacement of some 4m. Iraqis and an influx of Syrian refugees from the war in that country (where Islamic State had also captured territory) into the north and east, thus putting Iraqi economic resources under greater pressure and creating further unemployment.

Since 2003 the Iraqi political system has undergone significant changes, leading to the creation of a federal system. Under the federal system, the Kurdish region has its own government, the Kurdish Regional Government (KRG). After the imposition of sanctions in the 1990s, the Kurdish region enjoyed relative economic autonomy, as it was protected from the Saddam Hussain regime by the establishment of a so-called no-fly zone enforced by the US and British air forces following the first Gulf War (August 1990–February 1991). However, the KRG has been in near-constant dispute with the federal Government in Baghdad over the management of oil resources and revenues.

At the centre of these mechanisms is the Iraq Hydrocarbon Law, first submitted for debate in the Iraqi Council of Representatives in 2007, but the subject of many objections and controversies since. The law would allow foreign oil companies to hold long-term contracts in Iraq and would give different regions the right to award contracts to those companies. The Iraq National Oil Company (INOC) would be restructured as an independent holding company and a federal council would be created to oversee national oil policy. The law would also allocate oil revenues among the 18 governorates of Iraq, based on their respective population levels.

The terms of the law, however, remain a point of dispute between the KRG and Baghdad. In November 2014 the KRG and the federal Government reached an agreement on the law's mechanisms pertaining to the Kurdish Autonomous Region. However, this agreement was suspended in mid-2015 when the KRG increased its independent oil sales beyond the level that had been agreed upon and Baghdad's transfer of oil revenue funds to the KRG was lower than agreed. Following a referendum on independence held by the KRG in September 2017 (see History), Iraqi federal forces regained control of the major oilfields that had provided significant oil revenues to the KRG and of the pipeline that allowed for direct exports of the oil, thus rendering the KRG once again financially dependent upon the central Government.

While the various episodes of violence and disorder since 2003 have had a significant impact on the reconstruction and recovery of Iraq's economy and infrastructure, allegations of corruption and management inefficiencies have also been notable factors in causing delays. The spread of institutional corruption and inefficiencies has been unprecedented in recent decades. Since the transfer of sovereignty to an Iraqi government in 2004, there have been many accusations of widespread institutional corruption by local and international observers, such as the International Crisis Group study in 2011. The study criticized an almost total absence of oversight of government operations. It singled out the administration of Prime Minister Nuri al-Maliki for exacerbating the problem by interfering in anti-corruption cases and intimidating critics to prevent replication of the type of popular movements that arose during the so-called Arab Spring of early 2011 against authoritarian regimes perceived as being economically corrupt.

Despite these many obstacles, Iraq experienced relatively rapid economic growth rates following the overthrow of Saddam Hussain, averaging 5.8% per year during 2005–13. However, growth decelerated to an average annual rate of 3.1% during 2014–22, owing to falling oil prices in 2014, the invasion and occupation by Islamic State in 2014–15, and the coronavirus (COVID-19) pandemic in 2020–22. Over the same period similar declines occurred in the rate of growth of fixed investment, from 45.5% to a contraction of 0.8%; of government consumption, from 4.7% to 2.1%; and of private consumption, from 9.0% to a contraction of 1.3%.

As of 2022 Iraq was the fifth largest economy in the Middle East and North Africa, with annual GDP at US $270,400m., after Saudi Arabia, Iran, the United Arab Emirates (UAE) and Egypt. With 44.5m. people, the country was the third most populous, after Egypt and Iran. Iraq's GDP per capita in 2021 was $10,436 (on a purchasing-power parity basis at 2017 constant prices), down from a high of $11,603 in 2016, but up from $7,624 in 2005.

In mid-2023, five-and-a-half years after the apparent defeat of Islamic State, the Iraqi economy presented a mixed picture. Thousands of Iraqis remained displaced and dependent on aid. The health care system, crippled by the conflict and the sudden collapse of oil prices in early 2020, had been unable to cope effectively with the onset of the COVID-19 pandemic. None the less, after contracting by 15.7% in 2020, the economy expanded by 7.7% in 2021 and by 8.1% in 2022. However, there are concerns that these rates are not sustainable in the current environment. Iraq's rent-seeking economy relies heavily on government expenditure, which crowds out the private sector and limits productivity. Heavy reliance on government spending to shore up popular support fuels chronic inflation. Moreover, high operational and political risk levels deter much-needed investment and prevent local businesses from leaving the informal economy. Finally, the economy still lacks diversity, with oil accounting for 57.3% of GDP in 2022, while manufacturing accounted for only 1.8%, electricity and water 1.2%, construction 2.3%, and banking and finance 0.6%.

SOCIOECONOMIC DEVELOPMENT

According to the UN Development Programme's Human Development Index (HDI) for 2022 (with data for 2021), Iraq was ranked 121st out of 189 countries, placing it in the medium human development category. While Iraq's ranking had risen by six places since 2014, this position was still 12 places below the country's ranking in terms of gross national income (GNI) per capita, suggesting that, as is the case in many oil-dependent countries, a significant disparity exists between the country's wealth and the population's standard of living. Improvement in Iraq's HDI score has declined over time, from an average of 0.83% in 2000–10 to 0.63% in 2010–21. With a Gini coefficient (a measure of inequality) of 0.295 (2010–21), the country's has a high rate of income equality. In 2021 the poorest 40% of the population had 21.9% of the income, while between 2010 and 2021 the top 10% had 23.7% and the top 1% had 22.0%. However, according to Ministry of Planning data, poverty rates are very high, averaging 20% at the end of 2018 and over 50% in some governorates. Ordinary Iraqis have few economic buffers to see them through hard times.

Iraq scores low on the World Bank's Human Capital Index for 2020. The data suggests that a child born in Iraq today will be only 41% as productive when they grow up as they could be if they enjoyed a complete education and full health. This outcome is lower than the average both for the Middle East and North Africa region and for upper middle-income countries.

The Legatum Prosperity Index for 2023 illustrates the gap between the country's wealth and its citizens' prosperity. The Index attempts to overcome the limitations of inferring well-being from simple per capita measures. Instead, it looks at prosperity as stemming from various dimensions associated with 'quality of life'. In 2023 Iraq ranked 140th out of 167 countries (down from 137th in 2020), scoring exceptionally low in the areas of natural environment (167th), safety and security (163rd), enterprise conditions (144th), social capital (138th), governance (135th), personal freedom (133rd), economic quality (132nd) and investment environment (127th). The country's highest rankings were in living conditions (87th), infrastructure and market access (107th) and health (115th).

The country's ranking in many areas probably stems from the underdevelopment of institutions and the lack of progress in improved governance. The World Bank's Governance Indices show that the country's percentile ranking in all the significant governance dimensions is low and in most cases falling. In the critical area of controlling corruption, Iraq ranked in the ninth percentile in 2021. Although this was an improvement on its ranking in 2015, when it was ranked in the fifth percentile, in 2011 the country had been ranked in the 11th percentile. In another essential governance dimension, government effectiveness, the country's 2021 ranking was in the 10th percentile, down from the 14th in 2014. Similarly, regulatory quality (the business environment) declined from the 17th percentile in 2009 to the 13th in 2021. For rule of law, the decline was from the seventh percentile in 2014 to the third by 2021. For political stability and absence of violence/terrorism, the decline was from the fifth percentile in 2012 to the second in 2021. The one relatively bright spot was voice and accountability, where Iraq appeared to have stabilized at around the 22nd percentile in 2021, up from the 10th in 2006.

The Government's difficulties in combating the COVID-19 crisis illustrate the many problems associated with deficiencies in the country's institutional development and governance structures. The Government has long prioritized short-term stability through investment in the security forces and political allies, while neglecting institutions that support health care, education and prosperity (see *Fiscal Policy*). Only around 2.5% of the federal budget is allocated to health care. The Government's response to the pandemic relied largely on the federal police collaborating with the Ministry of Health and Environment to impose curfews.

The Government's strict lockdown (with the imposition of restrictions on businesses, public services and freedom of movement) initially appeared to have successfully curbed the spread of COVID-19. However, recorded cases soon mounted sharply, with no sign of the curve flattening after the authorities lifted the national lockdown on 1 June 2020. According to the World Health Organization (WHO), the cumulative number of confirmed cases by that date stood at 18,950, but by 1 August this had risen to 124,609. Although COVID-19 increased pressure for a change of approach in the Government's health care policies, this was difficult to implement, given the rapidly growing youth population, lack of resources, weak infrastructure and poor governance structures—low levels of government efficiency, combined with high levels of corruption.

After levelling off, having reached 627,416 confirmed cases by 1 February 2021, cases again began to accelerate, prompting the Iraqi authorities to reintroduce restrictions. The Government permanently relaxed these restrictions in late March, even though cases had reached 844,260 by the end of that month. The relaxation of restrictions was driven by their harmful impact on a population already suffering severe economic hardship and by the fiscal strains that precluded substantial financial assistance from the Government.

Despite the rolling out of a national vaccination programme from March 2021, by late July 2022 the cumulative number of confirmed cases had risen to some 2.33m. and more than 25,000 COVID-related deaths had been recorded. Furthermore, by December only around 17.9% of the population had been fully vaccinated. Nevertheless, the rate of new infections flattened off during the latter half of 2022 and first half of 2023, and by July of that year the total number of confirmed cases amounted to just over 2.46m.

DEMOGRAPHICS AND LABOUR MARKETS

Iraq's population reached 45,504,560 in mid-2023, according to UN estimates. It has one of the world's more rapidly growing populations, with average annual population growth rates of 3.2% in the 1970s, falling to 2.5% during the 1980s. Growth increased to 2.9% in 1990–2002, only to decline to 2.1% in 2003–09 as Iraq was invaded and descended into civil war. However, growth rebounded to an average annual rate of 2.6% in 2010–21. The labour force grew at an average annual rate of 3.4% in 1990–2002, 2.2% in 2003–09 and 3.7% in 2010–21. In 2021 the labour force stood at some 10.7m., up from about 7.1m. in 2010. High rates of population growth have produced a relatively young population, with those aged 0–14 years accounting for an estimated 37.0% of the total population in 2022 and those aged 65 years and over just 3.5%.

Thus, Iraq is experiencing and will continue to experience the so-called demographic dividend, with a high proportion of the population in the labour force. This age group (15–64 years) increased from 49.9% of the population in the 1970s to 52.4% in 1990–2002 and an estimated 59.5% by 2022. However, before this can be turned into a valuable asset, considerable attention will have to be given to improving the country's education system, which is in a poor state, the infrastructure, teachers and resources having suffered underfunding for decades owing to war and sanctions.

The ongoing conflict in Iraq since the early 2000s has contributed to severe damage to national infrastructure and a loss of people of working age and has significantly reduced the human capital stock by lowering levels of educational attainment and creating shortages of skilled workers. An offsetting factor to a certain extent is the large number of Iraqi workers who possess basic skills. The minimum wage is also comparatively low, given productivity levels.

Iraq has experienced substantial outward migration since the US-led invasion in 2003, mainly of highly qualified academics, doctors and other technical workers and professionals. These workers have fled the chronic instability in the country to seek safer and more lucrative working conditions elsewhere. In 2019 7.6% of Iraqi emigrants left for the USA, 7.5% went to Turkey (officially known as Türkiye from June 2022), 7.0% to Jordan, 6.6% to Syria and 4.6% to Sweden. As the number of Iraqis opting to leave the country exceeds the number of inward migrants, Iraq faces a long-term shortage of skilled labour. Unfortunately, the country's educational system is not currently capable of offsetting this decline in human capital.

The Ministry of Education oversees the Iraqi education system. It once boasted widespread literacy, strong enrolment rates and a flourishing tertiary education sector. However, standards began to decline with the Iran–Iraq war in the 1980s, during which government spending was diverted away from education towards the military. This trend continued after the first Gulf War and the imposition of sanctions on Saddam Hussain's regime. The 2003 US-led invasion then caused the almost total collapse of Iraqi society, with widespread damage to school infrastructure and the deaths and displacement of hundreds of teachers and academics. Until its apparent defeat in 2017, the rise of Islamic State from 2014 compounded the perilous situation.

Compulsory schooling in Iraq begins at six and lasts for six years until 11, when children complete primary school. This first stage is intended to give students a grounding in necessary skills such as literacy and numeracy; however, compulsory years of schooling are far too short to ensure that children develop skill sets that will enable them to seek formal employment. The mean years of schooling in Iraq stands at just 7.3, around the regional average, suggesting that most children who attend school only remain there for the compulsory primary cycle. For those who stay on in school, the primary level is followed by three years of intermediate secondary education from ages 12 to 15, and three years of preparatory secondary education. At this level, students are equipped with the skills necessary to undertake vocational training or further academic study or to enter the workforce. At the higher education level, Bachelor's degrees are usually completed in four years.

In early 2019 the Government announced a five-year plan to support and develop graduates in agriculture and industry. The plan seeks to integrate training and programmes aimed at poverty alleviation in rural and more impoverished communities.

There are approximately 27,000 educational institutions (including pre-primary schools) across Iraq, and the UN Educational, Scientific and Cultural Organization (UNESCO) has instituted several Community Learning Centres in the country. In recent years, the country's private education sector has flourished. The growth of private education presents two notable advantages for potential employers over the long term. First, private institutes compete to produce the best students to attract further enrolment, boding well for skills development and learning among future generations of workers. Second, comparisons with the performance of public institutions place pressure on the Government to reform and invest in state education. On a more short- to medium-term basis, private education is perhaps more convenient for relocating foreign workers, especially higher-income workers who would be reluctant to enrol their children in state-operated schools.

In February 2020 the UN announced that more than 2.5m. children in Iraq had struggled to find adequate learning opportunities since the defeat of Islamic State in December 2017. Lack of documentation has been a critical constraint on children's access to education, particularly refugee children, whose lack of identification documents has restricted their movement, preventing them from moving freely in and out of the camps and therefore from attending school. In the long term, the lack of access to schools for Iraq's youth will result in a relatively large labour force without the requisite skills.

In another setback, as of May 2020, due to the COVID-19 pandemic, some 9m. students in Iraq were without physical access to education. Several innovative attempts were under way to rectify the situation. The Kurdish Autonomous Region's Ministry of Education, with support from the UN Children's Fund (UNICEF), launched a television channel dedicated to supporting children's education during school closures. The channel provided an opportunity for those without access to online facilities—primarily children from impoverished backgrounds—to keep up with their academic curriculum. Although this may not have been the best form of education, in the short term it supported progression in the academic year until all students were able to return to school.

CRIME AND SECURITY

Nationally, the Iraqi economy continues to be adversely affected by petty and violent crime. The country has never fully recovered from the breakdown in law and order after the 2003 war and its accompanying widespread poverty, proliferation of arms and absence of effective state security services. Furthermore, following the emergence of Islamic State in 2014, the rule of law became practically non-existent, with criminal activities flourishing in many areas. Despite the apparent ending of the conflict with Islamic State in December 2017, the group appears not to have been completely eradicated from the landscape as a security threat. Since 2020 there have been reports that the militant organization is employing guerrilla tactics in an effort to regain some of its lost ground. The risk of kidnapping by Islamic State operatives remains high, with state security forces incapable of providing sufficient security for civilians and businesses in many parts of the country, particularly in the Kirkuk area and in Anbar governorate.

The lack of policing in the southern region has enabled a flourishing drug trade, exposing businesses to risks of being co-opted into the trafficking of illicit substances. Without significant improvements to state capacity, businesses will be constrained by poor security over the long term. The state's inability to provide and enforce cybersecurity regulations and measures will also continue to place businesses at an increased risk of cybercrime. Poor corporate governance heightens the risks of reputational damage, criminal charges and increased operating costs to businesses. Money laundering and financial crime also remain salient concerns. However, the country is improving its capacity to investigate and prosecute offences, providing businesses with scope for an improved operating environment over the long term. In July 2019 the Financial Action Task Force removed Iraq from its monitoring list. Nevertheless, risks from cybercrime and cybersecurity breaches, as well as organized criminal activities, remain high.

AGRICULTURE

Iraqi agriculture is rain-fed, mainly in the north, and irrigated along the country's major rivers and in the south. The country was once self-sufficient in food, but the agricultural sector has been in decline for years. Much of the irrigation system is crumbling, soil salinity is a significant problem, and there has been a severe lowering of the water table owing to increasingly frequent droughts. Wheat is the principal crop, with sheep, cattle and goats being the most important livestock. Iraq's agricultural sector accounted for an average of 11.8% of annual GDP during 1992–2002, before the overthrow of Saddam Hussain in 2003. Since then, the sector has been unable to sustain this level, with its share averaging 5.0% in 2005–13 and 3.9% in 2014–22. The sector grew at an average annual rate of 5.5% during 1994–2002, decelerating to 4.9% in 2005–13 and 2.5% in 2014–22.

The occupation by Islamic State, particularly in the Nineveh, Kirkuk and Salah al-Din governorates, resulted in significant damage to agricultural infrastructure and crop losses. This region typically contributes almost one-half of Iraq's national production of cereals, and the losses there were a considerable blow to the country's food security. The invasion by Islamic State in 2014 occurred just after the harvest, causing many farmers to lose their crops and disrupting the subsequent (2015) cropping cycle. All three governorates reported reduced yields in the land area cultivated with cereals. Moreover, much of the existing irrigation infrastructure was destroyed. Storage facilities and greenhouses also suffered significant damage. Even after the cessation of hostilities, ongoing arson attacks in the rural areas continued to cause considerable loss of facilities, crops and livestock. As a result of the disruptions and weather conditions, the agricultural sector contracted by 36.9% in 2015, 0.3% in 2016 and 16.0% in 2017. There was a return to positive growth of 36.7% in 2018, 46.2% in 2019 and 22.5% in 2020, before the sector contracted by 17.5% in 2021, owing to the disruptive effects of the COVID-19 pandemic, and by a further 11.2% in 2022, as a result of a poor harvest season. Despite the extremely high volatility of output, the number of workers in agriculture remains relatively high, accounting on average for 30.1% of the total in 1991–2002, 24.7% in 2005–13 and 20.8% in 2014–21.

Cereals production, which had increased from 2.2m. metric tons in 2008 to 7.0m. tons in 2014, fell to 3.5m. tons in 2015. Production growth has been volatile in recent years, with contractions of 6.8% in 2017 and 30.0% in 2018, followed by an expansion of 164.4% in 2019 and 28.5% in 2020, in which year output totalled 8.9m. tons. However, production fell by 40.3% in 2021, to 5.3m. tons. Maize production was particularly hard hit, falling from 831,345 tons in 2013 to 182,340 tons in 2015. However, production rose to 473,064 tons in 2019, before decreasing to 419,345 in 2020 and 374,400 tons in 2021. Wheat production has followed a unique pattern, increasing from 1.3m. tons in 2008 to 5.1m. tons in 2015. After falling to 2.2m. tons in 2018, production almost doubled in 2019 to 4.3m. tons, before rising by a further 44% to reach 6.2m. tons in 2020. However, production declined by 32.1% in 2021, to 4.2m. tons.

PETROLEUM AND GAS

In 2022 Iraq had the world's fifth largest proven oil reserves (after Venezuela, Saudi Arabia, Canada and Iran) and the 11th largest proven natural gas reserves. Over the years the hydrocarbons sector has faced many challenges ranging from wars and sanctions to mismanagement, underinvestment, theft, lack of maintenance, and sabotage by various warring groups. Despite the lifting of sanctions, Iraq was unable to exceed its pre-2003 oil production levels until 2012, when it produced an average of 3.0m. b/d; production increased to 4.5m. b/d in 2016 and 2017 and to 4.6m. b/d in 2018. It rose again in 2019, to 4.8m. b/d, before falling to just over 4.1m. b/d in 2020 due to the decline in international prices and demand associated with the COVID-19 pandemic. Despite a rebound in prices from late 2021, production declined in that year to just under 4.1m. b/d, before increasing to 4.6m. b/d in 2022.

Meanwhile, annual average Brent spot crude oil prices began to climb from their 2009 global recession low of US $61.50 per barrel, reaching $111.63 in 2012. However, prices decreased to an average of $108.56 in 2013 and $98.97 in 2014 (crashing in the later months of that year). In 2015 Brent prices averaged $52.32, falling to $43.67 in 2016. Prices then began firming, rising to $54.25 in 2017 and $74.34 in 2018. They subsequently slipped to $64.30 in 2019, before plummeting to $41.96 in 2020 with the onset of the pandemic and its disruptive effects on economic activity and transport. With a steady global economic recovery under way and an agreement in place (involving substantial production quotas) between members of the Organization of the Petroleum Exporting Countries (OPEC) and other major oil-producing countries (known collectively as OPEC+), Brent prices increased to an average of $70.86 per barrel in 2021. Following the invasion of Ukraine by the Russian Federation in February 2022 and the subsequent imposition of international sanctions on exports of Russian oil, prices over that year as a whole rose to an average of $100.93 per barrel.

Oil reserves are located mainly in the southern part of the country near Basra, and in Kirkuk and Kurdistan. The western governorates and Kurdistan offer the best potential for new exploration, although they have a higher security risk, containing, as they do, remnants of Islamic State. Most of southern Iraq's oil is contained in the giant oilfields of Rumaila, West Qurna (I and II), Majnoon, Zubair, Halfaya and Nahr Umr. Future production growth will probably come from development projects carried out in these fields.

In April 2018 the Ministry of Oil held a bidding round for 11 new blocks. All of the blocks offered lie in cross-border areas, including five shared with Iran, three with Kuwait and one in the Persian (Arabian) Gulf. Six blocks were awarded, with only Crescent Petroleum (three blocks), Geo-Jade Petroleum (two) and United Energy Group (one) taking new acreage. There were no bids on the remaining five blocks, despite 13 international oil companies participating in the auction. The Italian oil and gas company Eni made two unsuccessful bids. There is a significant oilfield in East Baghdad in Central Iraq, but other smaller fields also exist.

Like southern Iraq, the central region is relatively well explored. In 2017 the Russian oil major Lukoil made an oil discovery at its Eridu-1 well in Block 10, and in 2019 it conducted 3D seismic work to support the appraisal of discoveries made in the previous year. Western Iraq fares worse because the region is vastly under-explored and has been more substantially affected by Islamic State incursions. Experts hold that the western region is more gas-prone than oil-prone and could hold considerable resources to boost Iraq's economy.

Iraq's proclaimed victory over Islamic State in 2017 changed the Kurdish Autonomous Region's exploration outlook and led to Chevron recommencing operations in the Sarta block. Given the production-sharing agreement in place in the Kurdistan region, steady payments from the federal Government will be essential to support reinvestment in exploration. In 2018 the federal Government finalized an agreement with BP to investigate the Kirkuk field's production potential.

The Khurmala dome in the Kurdish Autonomous Region currently has a production capacity of around 115,000 b/d, while the Avana and Baba domes in central Iraq can produce approximately 95,000 b/d and 100,000 b/d, respectively. There is considerable export capacity through the Port of Basra and pipelines via Türkiye, and by late March 2019 Iraq had completed 'technical preparations' to enable a new double pipeline to transport 1m. b/d of Iraqi oil to Jordan.

At the same time, the country presents a challenging operating environment. Although the situation has improved in recent years, the hydrocarbons sector still incurs additional costs for protecting personnel and infrastructure. Flaring of associated gas continues on a large scale, limiting gas availability for use in the domestic power market. Furthermore, Iraq has limited refining capacity to add value to crude oil. The sector also exists in a state of uncertainty, unsure if future OPEC quotas will curb production or whether another conflict will threaten output or market access. A worrying trend for Kurdistan has been the relinquishment of licences by major international oil companies in recent years, indicating that the region's geology is less promising than initially expected.

In 2017 Iraq raised its official reserve estimates from 143,000m. barrels of oil to 153,100m. barrels. Improved recovery techniques, such as seawater injection, could increase recovery further. In mid-2018 the Minister of Energy Affairs suggested that the country's actual reserves might be double the current official level.

In 2018 the Ministry of Oil relinquished its role as operator of the country's four regional oil companies; this responsibility was handed over to the re-established INOC. Henceforth, the ministry was to concentrate on downstream operations, strategic planning and creating the conditions for increased investment in the sector. However, in early 2019 Iraq's Federal Supreme Court ruled that several articles of INOC law were unconstitutional, thus casting doubt on the re-established company's status.

The OPEC-led output cuts in 2017–18 were the first round that Iraq had participated in for several decades, having left the quota system in 1998 due to its degraded production capacity. However, for much of the 2017–18 round of cuts, Iraq missed its compliance targets for various reasons, including the lack of federal control over production in the Kurdistan Autonomous Region. In the next round of cuts, which began in January 2019, Iraq complied with its quota of 4.65m. b/d agreed with OPEC. Iraq's re-engagement with OPEC is crucial for the organization's efforts to influence global oil prices, given that in 2019 Iraq was the second largest oil producer among its members. In addition, Iraq has the most scope among OPEC members to increase its production capacity further.

In 2021 Iraq continued to meet its OPEC+ production targets/quotas, registering compliance of 106%. In mid-2022 the overall level of compliance by OPEC+ members remained strong, with output steadily increasing in line with an easing of production cuts. However, Iraq continued to over-comply with targets (i.e. fall short of production quotas); in May OPEC data recorded 130% compliance, with Iraq's output averaging 4.405m. b/d (57,000 b/d lower than the target). The June meeting of OPEC+ set an accelerated schedule for the tapering off of production cuts, with an end to the cuts expected by August—one month earlier than originally planned. The OPEC+ member countries committed to increase output by 0.648m. b/d in both July and August—up from the 0.432m. b/d increases in May and June. The raised output target would potentially lead to Iraq's quota increasing by 71,000 b/d in July and August. However, at the time of the meeting in June, Iraq was consistently falling short of its production targets. In early 2023 OPEC+ announced a new set of crude production cuts, amounting to an overall reduction in output of 1.16m. b/d from May. The cuts were made across a handful of producers, including Iraq, which received the second largest proportion of the cuts, 18%, after Saudi Arabia's 43%. From May to December Iraq was to reduce its production of crude petroleum by an average of 211,000 b/d.

In its 2019 assessment of Iraq's prospects, the International Energy Agency (IEA) expressed its opinion that Iraq was likely to become the world's third largest oil producer by 2030. In early 2021 Iraq's Ministry of Oil announced a new, more ambitious target of 8m. b/d of production capacity by 2027, an increase of nearly 3m. b/d over the existing output of just below 5m. b/d. Both of these assessments are unlikely, however, given Iraq's current underinvestment and lack of momentum in enacting fiscal and licensing reforms. In addition, multiple high-profile international oil companies (including BP and ExxonMobil) have sought to divest stakes in several of Iraq's giant southern fields, suggesting that the sector remains unattractive given the current fiscal and regulatory terms of the technical services contracts. Most current licence holders cite frustration with production caps and governmental approval of capital expenditures, both of which have reduced profitability potential, as the main reasons for divestment.

However, one company, TotalEnergies of France, is planning a major expansion in Iraq. In July 2023 the company and the Iraqi Government signed a long-delayed agreement for a four-part energy project costing a combined total of US $27,000m. Although only partly focused on the upstream oil sector, the project could have lasting positive effects. The largest impact could come from the plan to construct a $4,000m. seawater treatment plant, which would enable the use of seawater (rather than limited freshwater from rivers and marshes) in the water-intensive production processes at the giant southern oilfields in drought-stricken Iraq. Two other proposals involved an increase in production capacity at the Ratawi oilfield to 210,000 b/d within four years and the construction of gas-processing facilities to allow the capture of flared gas from operations in the West Qurna II, Majnoon, Ratawi, Tuba and Luhais oilfields. The final element of the four-part deal was the proposed development of a 1-GW solar power plant to supply electricity to the Basra regional grid. It was agreed that shares in the project would be divided thus: TotalEnergies would hold the largest stake of 45%, the Iraqi state 30% and QatarEnergy 25%. The agreement awaited formal ratification by the Iraqi Government.

However, the Iraqi hydrocarbons sector remains a high-risk arena for investors. Iraqi crude petroleum exports might be limited by the new OPEC+ production cuts imposed in May 2023, owing to falling international oil prices and a slowdown in the global economy. Furthermore, the Iraqi Government must address the revocation and rewriting of oil licences in the restive Kurdistan region.

INFRASTRUCTURE

Many years of war and conflict have left the Iraqi transport network of roads, railways and air links severely damaged. However, the reconstruction of Iraqi infrastructure has experienced significant volatility in recent years. The rise of Islamic State and subsequent military intervention by Western powers led to further extensive damage to the country's energy, transport and urban networks. Volatile oil prices have also constrained funding and made long-term plans difficult for the federal Government to implement.

Since the defeat of Islamic State in 2017, with the support of various regional and global backers, the Iraqi Government has focused on reconstruction, but progress has been slow. An opaque bureaucratic environment marred by corruption continues to hinder the development of new projects. In addition, a lack of access to financing, supply-chain issues and limitations in terms of skilled labour are also constraints on growth. The COVID-19 pandemic compounded these issues. At the same time, reduced oil revenue during much of 2020 restricted the ability of the authorities to fund the capital budget.

Roads provide the dominant mode of freight transport in Iraq. The country's 59,623-km road network has been developed to cater for the onward transport of containerized imports arriving at the main ports in the south and entering from Jordan and Syria in the west. Consequently, the main highway runs from the port of Umm Qasr in the south, via Basra, north to Baghdad, where it turns west to provide the primary connection with Jordan and Syria. Two major highways run north from Baghdad to Mosul: one via Kirkuk and the other via Tikrit.

The Iraq Transport Corridors Project, for which funding of US $355m. was approved by the World Bank in December 2013, aims not only to develop transport projects to boost trade within Iraq and with neighbouring countries, but also to remedy the institutional weaknesses that have dogged the implementation of such projects in the past. The project was to be implemented by the World Bank in partnership with the Iraqi Government and the Islamic Development Bank, which would contribute US $384m. and $217m., respectively, to the first phase.

Iraq has 2,272 km of standard gauge railway. The main railway line links the ports of Umm Qasr and Basra in the south to Baghdad, Mosul and the Syrian border, while branches run south from Kirkuk and east from Al-Qa'im to link up with the main line. The entire network is standard gauge, which enables faster transportation of heavy freight goods. Plans have been discussed for several years to expand Iraq's railway network. Some progress has been made, but many of the ambitious plans have stalled, reflecting the lack of capacity to carry out significant projects in the sector and limited funds to undertake new construction. Iraq's National Investment Commission has listed several major rail projects, including the Baghdad-Kut-Amara-Basra line and the Baghdad-Baqubah-Kirkuk-Irbil-Mosul line, with estimated costs of US $13,700m. and $8,700m., respectively. However, as of mid-2023, with little information available, the status of these projects was unclear.

Efforts have also been made to revive projects delayed by internal politics and constrained public spending power. In October 2020 a consortium led by Alstom of France and Hyundai Engineering & Construction of the Republic of Korea (South Korea) signed a letter of intent with the Iraqi Ministry of Transport regarding the construction of a 31-km elevated light-rail system in Baghdad with 14 stations. In 2013 Alstom had signed a US $40m. deal for phase one of the project, involving feasibility and engineering studies. The new metro should ease traffic congestion in the Iraqi capital, but delays have occurred, owing to disputes among stakeholders in the project and a shortage of funding. The project was expected to cost around $2,500m. and was to be financed either through private investment or as a public-private partnership. There are also plans to extend Iraq's railway network to connect with Türkiye, including the construction of a 120-km railway line between Mosul and the Iraqi-Turkish border.

Iraq and Iran are also increasing co-operation in terms of their railway networks and in 2021 signed an initial agreement to start work on a 32-km connecting railway line. The line, which is projected to cost around US $230m., will link Basra in Iraq with the Iranian border city of Shalamjah and, when completed, will be the first cross-border rail connection between the two countries. Funds from the Iranian-based Mostazafan Foundation will support the project.

By mid-2022 Iraq's ports were experiencing an increase in throughput volumes which they were struggling to handle, and the resultant congestion threatened to disrupt the supply chain as the economy continued to expand. The reconstruction of the country's ports is essential and would help further to stabilize the economy as post-war rebuilding progresses.

Iraq has several international airports which provide connections to regional and international air transport and economic hubs. Although there is great potential for expanding the air transport sector in Iraq, this remains restricted, owing to the unstable security situation and the lack of demand for high-end consumer goods commonly transported by air. In addition, the COVID-19 crisis significantly impaired air travel in Iraq. Nevertheless, there are plans to expand the country's major existing airports in Baghdad, Basra and Najaf (among others). These plans include the construction of new terminals, the expansion of operations and new air traffic management contracts. The national carrier, Iraqi Airways, is optimistic about the potential for future growth and in recent years has ordered 55 new aircraft (at a cost of US $2,600m.) from Bombardier and Boeing.

Iraq's utilities network has suffered a similar fate to that of its transport sector. Even though the country has abundant natural gas and crude oil resources, it remains reliant primarily on imports of natural gas and electricity for its power supply and refined fuel, thus raising the cost and the risk of shortages in these areas. Electricity production increased from 26,660m. KWh in 2003 to 50,840m. KWh in 2011. After falling to 43,480m. KWh in 2012, production once again expanded, reaching 97,260m. KWh in 2021. However, production has not kept pace with demand, resulting in a series of blackouts in the summer of 2018 that devastated economic activity and precipitated widespread demonstrations. Similar protests in October 2019 and in July and August 2020 resulted in some 560 fatalities. These protests focused on inferior services, notably a lack of electricity in record-breaking temperatures above 50°C. This unrest is seen as a critical corruption indicator, as massive past investment in the oil-exporting country has failed to upgrade the power network or end dependence on energy imports from Iran.

Iran has a contract to supply 1.2 GW of electricity and 50m. cu m of gas daily to Iraq via pipelines to Basra, in the south, and the Baghdad area. The gas is sufficient to generate about 8 GW of power, meaning that Iran accounts for 40%–50% of Iraq's total available electricity.

Iraq's domestic gas supply has improved since 2015 because of the increased capture of previously flared gas, but this increase is less significant than the addition of Iranian supplies. Iraq flares approximately one-half of its associated gas (a by-product of oil production), equating to 17,000m. cu m per year—roughly the same as the 18,000m. cu m contracted from Iran. Iraqi power plants are fuelled mainly by fuel oil, crude oil and diesel, reducing the stocks available for export. The situation is exacerbated by persistent shortages in gas supply from Iran, which at 6,100m. cu m in 2019 was only about one-third of the contracted amount.

Investments are being made to relieve the power shortages. The majority (about 80%) of new power plant projects are gas-fired, offering investment opportunities for companies such as General Electric (GE) and Siemens, which specialize in providing gas-fired power equipment. Much investment is also focused on transmission and distribution infrastructure, which requires upgrading and expanding to reduce capacity losses. In recent years Saudi Arabia and Kuwait have both stepped in to help stabilize the situation, with the former offering to build a solar power plant in Iraq and sell electricity at one-quarter of the price charged by Iran. Kuwait has sent fuel to restart operations at power stations that had gone out of service and has supplied several generators. It is noteworthy that as of August 2018 Iran resumed exporting electricity to Iraq.

Although Iraq was water-rich in the 1970s, its water table has since declined dramatically, especially in the south. Water scarcity is rising, principally because of the construction of upstream dams in Türkiye and Iran. However, climate change issues and domestic mismanagement also play a significant role. The UN deems Iraq to be one of the five countries most exposed to the effects of climate change. The potential consequences for the country include displacement of the population, disruption to the agriculture sector and the risk of yet further conflict.

The Tigris and Euphrates rivers provide 98% of Iraq's surface water. However, their levels have declined sharply since the 1960s. For example, the quantity of water in the Tigris entering Iraq has dropped to just 35% of its average over the past century. The water intake from both rivers is decreasing at an unprecedented rate. Over the past five decades Türkiye has built dams on the Tigris and Euphrates to develop its south-eastern provinces, significantly reducing Iraq's water supply. From its superior position in terms of regional power and political stability, Türkiye has refused to negotiate an agreement with downstream users Iraq and Syria regarding water allocation.

Iran has built dams that have reduced the water flowing into eastern governorates of Iraq. All but three of the 45 tributaries shared by Iran and Iraq have been blocked or diverted by the construction of dams. The Sirwan river, one of the two main tributaries of the Tigris originating in Iran, has seen its water flow reduced by over 60% because of Iran's Daryan dam. More dams have also been built in Iraq itself, addressing water shortages locally but further disadvantaging downstream users. For example, the authorities in the Kurdistan region have proposed the construction of 245 dams, of which, to date, 14 have been completed.

There have been ongoing violent protests in Iraq's second largest city, Basra, since June 2018 over water shortages in the city; some 20 people were killed in one such protest in September 2018. In August of that year approximately 1,000 people were hospitalized daily in Basra due to intestinal infections. This situation stemmed from salinity levels in the city's drinking water, which reduced the ability of chlorine to kill bacteria in the water supply.

In 2015 the Ministry of Water Resources presented a plan to invest several billions of dollars in repairing damaged water infrastructure, including pipes, irrigation channels and pumping stations. However, it faced significant funding challenges because of the sharp fall in global oil prices in 2014–15 and the rise of Islamic State. There have been no serious efforts made since that time to revamp the plan.

In March 2023 Iraq pressurized Türkiye to release more water from upstream dams (as it had done in October 2018), gaining a temporary concession, but future flows remain subject to broader political disputes. There are also plans to increase water storage and to centralized control under the water resources ministry. However, the long track record of poor state management does not bode well for such an approach. It will be many more years before Iraq's water infrastructure reaches international standards.

TELECOMMUNICATIONS

There is little reliable data available on the fixed-line sector in Iraq. The latest information from the International Telecommunications Union indicates that there were about 3m. fixed lines in the country in 2021.

In the broadband sector, several satellite broadband players cater to enterprise and government customers in Iraq. However, these services remain too expensive to drive broadband take-up in the consumer market. By contrast, the Kurdistan Autonomous Region's government has awarded several wireline broadband licences, which has fostered stiff competition between key players, including Newroz, Fastlink and O3 Telecom. These providers, and companies such as the independent infrastructure provider IQ Networks, are also the principal source of international bandwidth for Iraq, linking to terrestrial networks through Türkiye and offering the only alternative landing station to the Iraqi Telecommunications and Post Company's (ITPC) Al-Faw facility in the Persian Gulf. The Ministry of Communications is trying to address the capacity problem and hopes to exploit Iraq's geographic position by routing data moving between South-East Asia and Europe via its new backbone network.

Businesses requiring high-speed internet services will continue to face significant problems in Iraq, as the country has one of the lowest broadband penetration rates in the region. This situation has been exacerbated by the fact that the ITPC maintains a monopoly over fixed wireline services in Iraq, and it has confronted a myriad of challenges over the past decade or so, including war and insecurity, underinvestment in network development and, more recently, intense competition for voice and data subscribers from mobile voice and wireless data service providers. As a result, fibre optic fixed broadband coverage is minimal, and prices are far beyond the reach of most Iraqi consumers. However, the situation should improve somewhat in the near term. Since 2017 Iraq's Ministry of Communications has been installing 90,000 fibre optic access lines in partnership with fibre network operator ScopeSky, a 100% Iraqi-owned firm licensed to build, operate and maintain Iraq's fibre infrastructure.

The mobile telephone market reached a total of just under 39m. subscriptions in 2022. Although the security and economic situations remain volatile, current forecasts anticipate that by 2025 subscriptions will reach 40.3m., equal to a penetration rate of 89.2%. A steady expansion of third-generation (3G) mobile data services took place following the commercial 3G launches of Zain and Asiacell at the start of 2015. Operators have reported substantial growth in mobile data usage since 2019, building on momentum during 2017–18. As long as state-owned ITPC retains a monopoly over wireline services in southern Iraq, access to fixed broadband services will remain limited and far too expensive for most consumers. Therefore, 3G offers the first opportunity for the vast majority of people outside the Kurdistan region.

The advent of fifth-generation (5G) services remains a distant prospect, given the current market conditions. The launch of fourth-generation (4G) services will inevitably replace 3G offerings. However, given the abysmal level of regulatory effort, there is high uncertainty regarding a potential 4G long-term evolution (LTE) launch.

FOREIGN TRADE AND BALANCE OF PAYMENTS

Iraq's leading exports in 2021 were crude petroleum (US $72,000m.), refined oil ($5,490m.), gold ($2,080m.), petroleum coke ($542m.) and petroleum gas ($157m.). The principal destinations for the country's exports in that year were India ($23,500m.), the People's Republic of China ($23,300m.), Greece ($8,700m.), South Korea ($4,670m.) and Italy ($3,970m.).

Iraq's leading imports in 2021 were refined petroleum (US $5,540m.), broadcasting equipment ($3,110m.), cars ($2,220m.), jewellery ($2,210m.) and packaged medicaments ($1,090m.). The main sources of imports in that year were the UAE ($14,300m.), Türkiye ($11,100m.), China ($10,700m.), India ($2,030m.) and Germany ($1,060m.). Iraq was the world's largest importer of wheat flour in 2021, with imports of the commodity totalling $488m.

Exports and imports have fluctuated considerably since the 1970s, with the share of exports in the country's GDP averaging 51.0% in the 1970s before falling to 27.8% in the war-torn 1980s. Exports increased to 33.8% of GDP in 1990–2002, despite sanctions, and to 51.3% during 2005–13, only to decrease to an average of 38.9% in 2014–22, reflecting the fall in international oil prices at the start of that period. By contrast, imports increased from an average of 30.3% of GDP in the 1970s to 35.1% in the 1980s. Sanctions during 1990–2002 caused imports to fall to an average of 25.3% of GDP over that period. Annual imports averaged 39.4% of GDP in 2005–13, rising slightly to 38.9% in 2015–22.

Iraq's oil exports account for over 90% of total exports. They are facilitated by minimal bureaucratic barriers and direct pipelines to ports on the Persian Gulf. However, trade in non-oil goods is much more complicated. Iraq's non-membership of the World Trade Organization is a significant issue for businesses engaged in international trade, resulting in opaque tariff schedules and customs procedures, arbitrary regulatory enforcement, and limited recourse for trade dispute resolution. A convoluted import tariff system creates difficulties for firms reliant on intermediate inputs and results in misreporting, undervaluation, smuggling and corruption, further complicating business trade. In this unfavourable environment, Iraq recorded current account surpluses averaging 3.2% of GDP per year in 2005–13, while in 2014–22 the country registered deficits averaging 0.1% of GDP per year. The deficits were driven mainly by oil price declines. In 2015 the current account deficit rose to 6.4% of GDP from a surplus of 2.6% in 2014. Similarly, the deficit of 10.8% of GDP in 2020 followed surpluses of 4.3% in 2018 and 0.5% in 2019. With rebounding oil prices, the current account returned to record surpluses of 7.7% of GDP in 2021 and 11.2% in 2022. Although the IMF projected that the current account would register a further surplus, of 4.4% of GDP in 2023, it forecast deficits averaging some 3%–4% during 2024–28.

In January 2019 Iraq and Iran announced their intention to sign a zero-tariff trade agreement. Meanwhile, following the USA's reimposition of sanctions on Iran in August 2018, the US Administration granted Iraq a 45-day sanctions waiver in November. Extensions to the waiver were repeatedly issued during 2019–23, to allow the Iraqi Government to continue importing Iranian gas and electricity supplies, on which it remained dependent.

In terms of new international investment flows, despite the apparent defeat of Islamic State in 2017, FDI remains low by international standards, with rates of 1.6% of GDP in 2019, 1.7% in 2020 and 1.3% in both 2021 and 2022. Iraq offers an unattractive and extremely high-risk environment for trade and investment. The country's undiversified and oil-reliant economy provides few opportunities for investors, and security remains a concern, despite the suppression of Islamic State. The investment climate is undermined by rampant corruption, high levels of bureaucracy and an opaque regulatory environment, while the banking sector is underdeveloped and unable to offer attractive financing options. Given the slow pace of reform, there is little hope of significant improvements in the medium term. Consequently, Iraq will continue to struggle to attract substantial foreign direct investment in the non-oil sectors of its economy.

However, inflows of Chinese investment are expected to increase significantly following the 'oil for (re)construction' deal that Iraq concluded with China in 2019. This arrangement involves China receiving about 20% of Iraq's daily oil production, earning Iraq more than US $1,500m. in 2020, with much of this capital being diverted to the import of goods from Chinese companies for infrastructure development in Iraq.

MONETARY POLICY

The primary monetary policy goal of the Central Bank of Iraq (CBI) is to maintain the value of the Iraqi dinar, and its principal instrument for achieving this goal is fixing the exchange rate of the dinar for US dollars through dollar auctions to Iraqi banks. The market exchange rate—the rate at which Iraqis can exchange dinars against US dollars at the banks—can differ widely from this auction exchange rate, particularly when the economy's external position deteriorates, as happened with the massive drop in global oil prices from June 2014. The CBI also holds a mandate to control inflation. Nevertheless, given the underdeveloped nature of the Iraqi financial markets, the monetary policy's transmission mechanism is minimal.

After averaging annual inflation rates of 15.3% in 2005–13, price increases averaged only 1.8% in 2014–22, with average consumer prices increasing at a rate of just 0.5% in 2016, 0.1% in 2017 and 0.4% in 2018, before contracting by 0.2% in 2019. In 2020 inflation was only 0.6%, but it increased to 6.0% in 2021 and remained relatively high in 2022, at 5.0%.

Russia's invasion of Ukraine in February 2022 led to a surge in commodity prices, keeping inflation high in the first half of 2022 after its increase in 2021 owing to the devaluation of the dinar in December 2020. As government revenues plummeted, the Iraqi authorities devalued the currency by nearly 23% in that month, causing a public outcry. In a country that depends heavily on imports of food and medicines, the devaluation soon led to a sharp increase in consumer prices, eroding purchasing power.

Even though Iraq has recently enjoyed high oil revenues, the CBI can only access them through the Federal Reserve (the US central bank), which has held Iraq's foreign exchange reserves since the invasion of 2003. Under the agreement, the CBI requests its US dollars from the Federal Reserve and sells them to commercial lenders and exchange houses for dinars. The process is known as the 'daily dollar auction'. However, US and Iraqi officials have long complained about suspicious transactions that have allowed sizeable sums to be taken out of the country, with some dollars ending up in the hands of armed groups such as Iran's Islamic Revolutionary Guard Corps. Worsening relations with Iran resulted in a decision by the USA in November 2022 to crack down on the flow of dollars through CBI auctions. The result was a severe shortage of dollars in Iraq and a sharp depreciation of the dinar. In a positive development, in February 2023 Minister of Foreign Affairs Fuad Hussein announced that the USA and Iraq had established a joint mechanism to track the outflow of dollars from Iraq.

FISCAL POLICY

The Government's fiscal position has shifted in recent years. After averaging 51.9% of GDP annually in 2005–13, government revenue decreased to an average annual of 35.7% of GDP in 2014–22. Similarly, over the same two periods government expenditure dropped from 51.1% of GDP to 39.7%. Due to these movements in revenue and expenditure, the Government's fiscal position declined from an average budgetary surplus of 0.8% of GDP in the first period to an annual average budgetary deficit of 4.0% of GDP in the latter period. The 2014–22 period saw several massive deficits associated with oil price declines. In 2015 the Government ran a deficit of 12.8% of GDP, increasing to 14.5% in 2016. In the pandemic year of 2020 a deficit of 12.6% of GDP was recorded. However, following a significant rebound in oil prices from late 2021, a budgetary surplus of 1.9% of GDP was registered in that year. Iraq has no fiscal rule or sovereign wealth fund to help manage expenditure derived from oil revenues. As a result, the budget tends to be pro-cyclical, increasing during periods of high oil prices and falling during periods of declining prices, thus reinforcing the business cycle.

In June 2023 Iraq's parliament approved an expansionary three-year budget (covering fiscal years 2023–25). The 2023–25 budget envisaged a 36.5% rise in total expenditure compared with 2022: annual spending was projected to reach US $152,000m. (about ID200,000,000m.) in 2025, driving a deficit of about $50,000m. (approximately 10% of GDP). However, the sharp deterioration in Iraq's fiscal outlook (the country having recorded a surplus of an estimated 6.4% of GDP in 2022) made the country vulnerable to several risks. Oil exports were likely to account for over 90% of government revenue in 2023–27, exposing the country to future fluctuations in global oil prices and demand. Iraq's fiscal vulnerability to future oil market shocks stemmed from a sharp rise in recurrent spending envisaged in the 2023–25 budget; recurrent spending accounted for about 75% of all government expenditure in 2022. Spending on civil servants' salaries, pensions and additional welfare payments to low-income families were projected to increase by 21% in 2023, expanding Iraq's already unsustainable levels of expenditure, which would be difficult to reduce if oil revenue deteriorated more sharply than expected in 2023–25. The growing fiscal deficit was likely to receive funding through the accumulation of both external and domestic debt, which would lead to an increase in Iraq's overall debt from an already high level of 43.3% of GDP in 2022, presenting another potential source of volatility as repayment obligations mounted and interest rates remained high globally.

The budget for 2023–25 also included a 26% increase in funding for the Popular Mobilization Units (PMUs, a group of primarily Shi'a-dominated, Iranian-backed militias), bringing total annual funding for the PMUs over the three-year period to US $2,600m. The budget also envisaged a 20% expansion of PMU personnel, with numbers being increased from 170,000 in 2021 to 204,000 in 2023–25. Most observers believed that the higher level of funding would bolster the strength and efficacy of the PMUs. In this sense, the budget verged on state capture, further eroding the Government's political authority over Iraq's collection of state-aligned militias.

PROSPECTS

Eventually, the Government will have to reduce its footprint on the economy by cutting back on public wages and its subsidy programme. This shift is likely to come gradually, given the elevated political cost associated with dismantling the Iraqi social framework, which is no longer sustainable. Moreover, efforts to reduce politically sensitive current spending (including the onerous public sector wage bill) will proceed only slowly as high global oil prices reduce the requirement for immediate action. The need for parliamentary approval will be the chief obstacle to more controversial reforms, as supporters of the status quo in parliament will attempt to obstruct such measures.

Statistical Survey

Sources (unless otherwise indicated): Central Organization for Statistics and Information Technology (COSIT), Ministry of Planning, 929/29/6 Arrasat al-Hindiya, Baghdad; tel. and fax (1) 885-3653; e-mail info@cosit.gov.iq; internet cosit.gov.iq; Central Bank of Iraq, POB 64, al-Rashid St, Baghdad; tel. (1) 816-5170; fax (1) 816-6802; e-mail cbi@cbi.iq; internet www.cbi.iq.

Area and Population

AREA, POPULATION AND DENSITY

Area (sq km)	434,128*
Population (census results)	
17 October 1987	16,335,199
17 October 1997	
Males	10,987,252
Females	11,058,992
Total	22,046,244
Population (UN estimates at mid-year)†	
2021	43,533,593
2022‡	44,496,122
2023‡	45,504,560
Density (per sq km) at mid-2023‡	104.8

* 167,618 sq miles. This figure excludes 924 sq km (357 sq miles) of territorial waters and also the Neutral Zone, of which Iraq's share is 3,522 sq km (1,360 sq miles). The Zone lies between Iraq and Saudi Arabia, and is administered jointly by the two countries. Nomads move freely through it, but there are no permanent inhabitants.
† Source: UN, *World Population Prospects: The 2022 Revision*.
‡ Projection.

POPULATION BY AGE AND SEX
('000, UN projections at mid-2023)

	Males	Females	Total
0–14 years	8,706.3	8,280.4	16,986.7
15–64 years	13,473.7	13,502.0	26,975.7
65 years and over	626.5	915.7	1,542.2
Total	22,806.5	22,698.1	45,504.6

Source: UN, *World Population Prospects: The 2022 Revision*.

GOVERNORATES
(official population estimates at 2021)

	Area (sq km)*	Population	Density (per sq km)
Nineveh	37,323	4,030,006	108.0
Salah al-Din	24,363	1,723,546	70.7
Al-Ta'meem (Kirkuk)	9,679	1,726,409	178.4
Diyala	17,685	1,768,920	100.0
Baghdad	4,555	8,780,422	1,927.6
Al-Anbar (Anbar)	137,808	1,914,165	13.9
Babylon	5,119	2,231,136	435.9
Karbala	5,034	1,316,750	261.6
Al-Najaf (Najaf)	28,824	1,589,961	55.2
Al-Qadisiya	8,153	1,394,885	171.1
Al-Muthanna	51,740	879,874	17.0
Thi-Qar	12,900	2,263,695	175.5
Wasit	17,153	1,489,631	86.8
Maysan	16,072	1,202,175	74.8
Al-Basrah (Basra)	19,070	3,142,449	164.8
Kurdish Autonomous Region			
Duhok	6,553	1,396,480	213.1
Irbil (Arbil)	15,074	2,003,963	132.9
Al-Sulaimaniya (Sulaimaniya)†	17,023	2,336,191	137.2
Total	434,128	41,190,658	94.9

* Excluding territorial waters (924 sq km).
† A fourth governorate, Halabja, was created in the Kurdish Autonomous Region in 2014 from territory previously part of al-Sulaimaniya, but was only formally recognized by the Iraqi authorities in March 2023.

PRINCIPAL TOWNS
(incl. suburbs, UN projections at mid-2023)

Baghdad (capital)	7,711,305	Al-Hillah (Hilla)	641,301
Al-Mawsil (Mosul)	1,792,020	Karbala	589,207
Al-Basrah (Basra)	1,448,124	Diwaniyah	572,122
Kirkuk	1,074,884	Al-Kut (Kut)	500,215
Al-Najaf (Najaf)	958,487	Ramadi	480,036
Irbil (Arbil)	896,716	Al-Fallujah (Faloojah)	367,830
Al-Sulaimaniya (Sulaimaniya)	800,793	Baqubah (Baaqoobah)	355,457
Al-Amarah (Amara)	729,276	Samarra	330,994
Al-Nasiriyah (Nasiriya)	671,412		

Source: UN, *World Urbanization Prospects: The 2018 Revision*.

BIRTHS AND DEATHS
(UN estimates)

	2019	2020	2021
Birth rate (per 1,000)	28.1	27.7	27.4
Death rate (per 1,000)	4.3	5.2	4.8

Source: UN, *World Population Prospects: The 2022 Revision*.

Births: 1,205,236 in 2018; 1,231,697 in 2019; 1,258,028 in 2020.

Deaths: 213,168 in 2018; 218,668 in 2019; 224,279 in 2020.

Registered marriages: 317,221 in 2018; 297,401 in 2019; 273,076 in 2020.

Life expectancy (years at birth, WHO estimates): 70.4 (males 68.2; females 72.4) in 2021 (Source: World Bank, World Development Indicators database).

ECONOMICALLY ACTIVE POPULATION
('000 persons 15 years and over, labour force survey, 2021)

	Males	Females	Total
Agriculture, hunting and forestry	582.6	142.8	725.4
Mining and utilities	266.2	28.6	294.7
Manufacturing	454.8	80.6	535.5
Construction	1,397.1	6.4	1,403.4
Trade; transportation; accommodation and food; business and administrative services	2,658.8	98.1	2,756.9
Public administration, community, social and other services	2,074.0	626.2	2,700.2
Sub-total	7,433.5	982.7	8,416.2
Activities not adequately defined	239.9	18.8	258.7
Total employed	7,673.4	1,001.5	8,674.9
Unemployed	1,278.2	395.4	1,673.7
Total labour force	8,951.6	1,396.9	10,348.6

Source: ILO.

Health and Welfare

KEY INDICATORS

Total fertility rate (children per woman, 2021)	3.5
Under-5 mortality rate (per 1,000 live births, 2021)	24.5
HIV/AIDS (% of persons aged 15–49, 2003)	<0.1
COVID-19: Cumulative confirmed deaths (per 100,000 persons at 30 June 2023)	57.0
COVID-19: Fully vaccinated population (% of total population at 2 January 2023)	17.9
Physicians (per 1,000 head, 2020)	1.0
Hospital beds (per 1,000 head, 2017)	1.3
Domestic health expenditure (2020): US $ per head (PPP)	254.4
Domestic health expenditure (2020): % of GDP	2.8
Domestic health expenditure (2020): public (% of total current health expenditure)	54.8
Access to improved water resources (% of persons, 2020)	98
Total carbon dioxide emissions ('000 metric tons, 2019)	174,560
Carbon dioxide emissions per head (metric tons, 2019)	4.4
Human Development Index (2021): ranking	121
Human Development Index (2021): value	0.686

Note: For data on COVID-19 vaccinations, 'fully vaccinated' denotes receipt of all doses specified by approved vaccination regime (Sources: Johns Hopkins University and Our World in Data). Data on health expenditure refer to current general government expenditure in each case. For more information on sources and further definitions for all indicators, see Health and Welfare Statistics: Sources and Definitions section (europaworld.com/credits).

Agriculture

(excluding data for Kurdish-controlled areas)

PRINCIPAL CROPS
('000 metric tons)

	2019	2020	2021
Apples	76	79	79
Apricots	35	35	34
Aubergines (Eggplants)	137	207	216
Barley	1,518	1,756	267
Canteloupes and other melons	158	201	205
Cauliflowers and broccoli	7	12	15
Chillies and peppers, green	23	46	59
Cucumbers and gherkins	149	243	185
Dates	639	735	750
Grapes	420	422	427
Lettuce and chicory	31	31	38
Maize	473	419	374
Okra	59	94	93
Olives	35	34	33
Onions, dry	29	66	74
Onions and shallots, green	50	41	60
Oranges	134	143	158
Peaches and nectarines	3	4	4
Pears	16	16	16
Plums	15	17	15
Potatoes	392	675	466
Pumpkins, squash and gourds	22	39	36
Rice, paddy	575	464	422
Sugar beet	32	32	32
Tangerines, mandarins, etc.	4	4	4
Tomatoes	620	755	744
Watermelons	338	420	378
Wheat	4,343	6,238	4,234

Aggregate production ('000 metric tons, may include official, semi-official or estimated data): Total cereals 6,914 in 2019, 8,885 in 2020, 5,302 in 2021; Total fruit (primary) 1,923 in 2019, 2,161 in 2020, 2,156 in 2021; Total roots and tubers 392 in 2019, 675 in 2020, 466 in 2021; Total vegetables (primary) 1,240 in 2019, 1,683 in 2020, 1,608 in 2021.

Source: FAO.

LIVESTOCK
('000 head, year ending September)

	2019	2020	2021
Asses*	379	379	379
Buffaloes	225	233	242
Camels	91	98	106
Cattle	1,979	2,020	2,061
Chickens	74,302	78,534	62,862*
Goats	1,329	1,352	1,376
Horses*	52	52	51
Sheep	6,694	6,724	6,754

* FAO estimate(s).

Source: FAO.

LIVESTOCK PRODUCTS
('000 metric tons)

	2019	2020	2021
Buffalo meat*	5.7	6.0	6.2
Buffaloes' milk	36.0	37.7	39.4
Cattle meat*	33.4	34.1	34.8
Cattle offals, edible*	6.1	6.2	6.3
Cows' milk	218.7	223.1	218.7*
Chicken meat	148.2	156.5	122.4*
Goat meat*	9.5	9.6	11.6
Goats' milk	21.6	22.0	22.4
Sheep meat	46.5	46.7	46.9
Sheep offals, edible*	7.8	7.8	7.9
Sheep's milk	57.8	58.1	58.3
Sheepskins, fresh*	8.7	8.7	8.8
Hen eggs*	48.5	55.9	49.0
Wool, greasy*	15.1	14.5	13.7

* FAO estimate(s).

Source: FAO.

Forestry

ROUNDWOOD REMOVALS
('000 cubic metres, excl. bark, FAO estimates)

	2019	2020	2021
Sawlogs, veneer logs and logs for sleepers	25	25	25
Other industrial wood	34	34	34
Fuel wood	118	118	118
Total	177	177	177

Note: Annual production assumed to be unchanged from 1998.
Source: FAO.

SAWNWOOD PRODUCTION
('000 cubic metres, incl. railway sleepers, FAO estimates)

	2019	2020	2021
Total (all broadleaved)	12	12	12

Note: Annual production assumed to be unchanged from 1998.
Source: FAO.

IRAQ

Fishing

('000 metric tons, live weight)

	2019	2020	2021
Capture	40.1	34.8	43.7*
Cyprinids (incl. Common carp)	19.7	12.8	16.3*
Freshwater siluroids	1.3	1.4	4.7
Other freshwater fishes	2.9	4.0	3.5*
Hilsa shad	1.7	0.7	0.3
Abu mullet	3.9	4.4	6.9
Aquaculture	22.3	22.7	22.7
Common carp	18.8	19.2	19.2
Total catch	62.4	57.5	66.4*

* FAO estimate.
Source: FAO.

Mining

('000 metric tons unless otherwise indicated)

	2017	2018	2019
Crude petroleum	222,382	227,012	234,220
Natural gas (million cu m)*	10,118	10,574	10,967
Ammonia (nitrogen content)†	100	90	90
Sulphur†	40	40	40
Salt (unrefined)†	240	270	270

* Figures refer to gross production.
† Estimated production.
Crude petroleum: 202,038 in 2020; 200,829 in 2021; 221,310 in 2022.
Natural gas (million cu m): 7,005 in 2020; 9,107 in 2021; 9,429 in 2022.

Sources: Energy Institute, *Statistical Review of World Energy*; US Geological Survey.

Industry

SELECTED PRODUCTS
('000 metric tons unless otherwise indicated)

	2018	2019	2020
Naphtha	1,522	1,890	2,063
Motor spirit (petrol)	2,832	2,553	2,063
Kerosene	1,447	1,526	1,329
Jet fuel	212	235	106
Gas-diesel (distillate fuel) oil	5,291	5,825	5,239
Residual fuel oils	16,182	16,880	14,169
Paraffin wax	3	3	4
Petroleum bitumen (asphalt)	153	190	208
Liquefied petroleum gas	1,792	1,780	1,776
Cement*†	14,000	15,000	n.a.
Electrical energy (million kWh)	82,507	88,867	91,423

* Source: US Geological Survey.
† Estimated production.
Source (unless otherwise indicated): UN Energy Statistics Database.

2020 ('000 metric tons unless otherwise indicated): White sugar 853; Vegetable fats 59; Beverages (million units) 758; Bricks (million units) 3,479; Cement 2,288.

Finance

CURRENCY AND EXCHANGE RATES
Monetary Units
1,000 fils = 20 dirhams = 1 new Iraqi dinar (ID).

Sterling, Dollar and Euro Equivalents (28 April 2023)
£1 sterling = 1,620.3 Iraqi dinars;
US $1 = 1,300.0 Iraqi dinars;
€1 = 1,427.5 Iraqi dinars;
10,000 Iraqi dinars = £6.17 = $7.69 = €7.01.

Average Exchange Rate (Iraqi dinars per US $)
2020 1,192.00
2021 1,450.00
2022 1,450.00

Note: Following the overthrow of the regime of Saddam Hussain in 2003, the new Coalition Provisional Authority established an exchange rate of US $1 = 1,400 dinars. A new dinar currency, the new Iraqi dinar (ID), was introduced on 15 October to replace both the 'Swiss' dinar (at ID 1 = 150 'Swiss' dinars), the currency in use in the Kurdish autonomous regions of northern Iraq since 1991, and the 'Saddam' dinar (at par), the official currency of the rest of Iraq. The new currency was to be fully convertible.

BUDGET
(ID '000 million)

Revenue	2021	2022*	2023†
Petroleum revenues	96,700	154,000	167,200
Non-petroleum revenues	13,100	8,400	10,300
Tax revenue	3,700	3,800	4,200
Non-tax revenue	8,700	3,400	5,100
Total	109,900	162,400	177,500

Expenditure	2021	2022*	2023†
Current expenditure	90,300	100,100	119,000
Salaries and pensions	57,600	58,000	69,500
Goods and services	13,400	18,000	26,200
Transfers	14,900	20,600	20,700
Interest payments	1,500	3,500	2,600
War reparations	3,000	—	—
Capital expenditure	20,700	37,200	34,800
Total	111,000	137,300	153,800

* Estimates.
† Projections.
Source: IMF, *Iraq: 2022 Article IV Consultation—Press Release; and Staff Report* (February 2023).

INTERNATIONAL RESERVES
(US $ million at 31 December)

	2020	2021	2022
Gold (national valuation)	5,853.4	5,633.6	7,598.5
IMF special drawing rights	1.9	5.8	17.3
Reserve position in IMF	417.6	405.8	385.9
Foreign exchange	48,142.6	58,177.1	89,012.3
Total	54,415.5	64,222.3	97,014.0

Source: IMF, *International Financial Statistics*.

MONEY SUPPLY
(ID '000 million at 31 December)

	2019	2020	2021
Currency outside depository corporations	47,638.6	59,987.1	71,526.1
Transferable deposits	39,132.4	43,366.5	48,418.0
Other deposits	16,520.2	16,421.3	19,793.1
Broad money	103,291.2	119,774.9	139,737.1

Source: IMF, *International Financial Statistics*.

IRAQ

COST OF LIVING
(Consumer Price Index; base: 2012 = 100)

	2020	2021	2022
Food and non-alcoholic beverages	97.0	101.7	108.6
Clothing and footwear	101.9	104.9	109.4
Housing, water, electricity, gas and other fuels	113.8	116.0	121.3
All items (incl. others)	105.1	111.5	117.0

NATIONAL ACCOUNTS
(ID '000 million at current prices)

Expenditure on the Gross Domestic Product

	2019	2020	2021
Government final consumption expenditure	57,893.0	50,141.0	61,916.9
Private final consumption expenditure	128,783.4	127,044.8	153,981.4
Changes in inventories	8,921.8	26,816.4	—
Gross fixed capital formation	59,237.8	16,679.0	20,887.9
Total domestic expenditure	254,836.0	220,681.2	236,786.2
Exports of goods and services	114,050.9	61,794.3	131,016.3
Less Imports of goods and services	92,729.1	66,814.0	85,724.5
Statistical discrepancy	—	—	13,727.9
GDP in market prices	276,157.9	215,661.5	295,805.9
GDP at constant 2015 prices	237,648.3	207,177.8	212,944.2

Gross Domestic Product by Economic Activity

	2019	2020	2021
Agriculture, hunting, forestry and fishing	10,411.2	13,130.9	11,912.8
Mining and utilities	122,186.6	68,886.0	129,912.5
Manufacturing	5,903.0	5,582.2	5,809.5
Construction	18,576.3	11,303.2	17,808.6
Wholesale, retail trade, restaurants and hotels	23,035.0	19,635.7	24,233.8
Transport, storage and communication	23,906.2	22,723.5	26,022.7
Other activities	75,739.5	75,865.7	79,560.2
GDP at factor cost	279,757.6	217,127.3	295,260.2
Indirect taxes (net)*	−3,599.8	−1,465.8	545.7
GDP in market prices	276,157.9	215,661.5	295,805.9

*Figures obtained as a residual.

Source: UN National Accounts Main Aggregates Database.

2022 (ID '000 million at current prices): Agriculture, hunting, forestry and fishing 10,922.8; Mining 219,563.8 (Crude petroleum 219,353.6); Manufacturing 6,852.6; Electricity, gas and water 5,190.9; Construction 8,761.8; Wholesale, retail trade, restaurants and hotels 23,275.9; Transport, storage and communications 33,402.2; Finance, insurance, real estate and other business services 18,588.3; Social and personal services 57,996.9; GDP at factor cost 384,555.2; Indirect taxes (net) −1,491.1; GDP in market prices 383,064.2.

BALANCE OF PAYMENTS
(US $ million)

	2019	2020	2021
Exports of goods	81,585.2	46,829.0	73,083.8
Imports of goods	−49,417.6	−40,927.3	−34,721.1
Balance on goods	32,167.6	5,901.7	38,362.7
Exports of services	7,317.7	3,802.7	5,176.7
Imports of services	−22,864.9	−13,794.6	15,985.8
Balance on goods and services	16,620.4	−4,090.2	27,553.6
Primary income received	1,712.0	873.4	501.6
Primary income paid	−2,878.0	−2,680.3	2,565.8
Balance on goods, services and primary income	15,454.4	−5,897.1	25,489.4
Secondary income received	2,021.6	1,436.8	1,618.0
Secondary income paid	−1,713.4	−1,737.3	2,544.0
Current balance	15,762.6	−6,197.6	24,563.4

—continued	2019	2020	2021
Capital account (net)	−11.1	−8.1	−17.5
Direct investment assets	−194.2	−147.2	−134.6
Direct investment liabilities	−3,075.6	−2,859.1	−2,637.3
Portfolio investment assets	6,159.4	−2,519.4	270.1
Portfolio investment liabilities	−2.9	8.2	0.0
Other investment assets	−5,812.3	8,086.5	−7,866.8
Other investment liabilities	392.9	−3,538.1	−1,565.6
Net errors and omissions	−3,800.8	100.2	−822.2
Reserves and related items	9,417.9	−7,074.6	11,789.5

Source: IMF, *International Financial Statistics*.

External Trade

PRINCIPAL COMMODITIES
(US $ million)

Imports c.i.f.	2019	2020	2021
Food and live animals	3,139	2,600	2,199
Animal and vegetable oils and fats	3,721	3,082	2,607
Beverages and tobacco	756	626	530
Crude materials (inedible) except fuels	1,046	867	733
Mineral fuels, lubricants, etc.	5,698	4,718	3,992
Chemicals and related products	3,895	3,226	2,729
Basic manufactures	6,628	5,489	4,644
Machinery and transport equipment	22,383	18,538	15,684
Miscellaneous manufactured articles	9,186	7,608	6,437
Total (incl. others)	58,138	48,150	40,736

Exports c.i.f.	2019	2020	2021
Food and live animals	16	12	22
Crude materials (inedible) except fuels	29	33	51
Mineral fuels, lubricants, etc.	81,412	46,692	72,603
Basic manufactures	128	92	146
Total (incl. others)	81,585	46,829	72,822

PRINCIPAL TRADING REGIONS
(US $ million)

Imports	2019	2020	2021
Arab nations	3,601	3,664	3,100
Asia	41,212	34,148	28,890
European Union	7,910	6,577	5,565
Other Europe	1,441	1,006	851
North and South America	3,767	2,552	2,159
Total (incl. others)	58,138	48,150	40,736

Exports f.o.b.	2019	2020	2021
Arab nations	2,398	1,616	2,512
Asia	55,218	36,550	56,838
European Union	17,113	5,999	9,328
North and South America	6,442	2,252	3,503
Total (incl. others)	81,585	46,829	72,822

Transport

RAILWAYS
(traffic)

	2019	2020	2021
Passengers carried ('000)	435	77	127
Freight carried ('000 tons)	372	1,293	593
Passenger-km (million)	164	31	45
Freight ton-km (million)	190	559	335

SHIPPING

Flag Registered Fleet
(at 31 December)

	2020	2021	2022
Number of vessels	84	89	89
Total displacement ('000 grt)	118.9	123.2	123.2

Source: Lloyd's List Intelligence (www.bit.ly/LLintelligence).

CIVIL AVIATION

	2019	2020	2021
International:			
Aircraft movements	34,742	5,398	10,269
Passengers carried ('000)	3,087	456	819
Domestic:			
Aircraft movements	17,046	5,752	10,107
Passengers carried ('000)	1,091	330	617
Total cargo transported (metric tons)	52,906	35,407	8,701

Tourism

ARRIVALS AT FRONTIERS OF VISITORS FROM ABROAD*

Country of nationality	2011	2012	2013
India	17,949	27,530	25,726
Iran	1,430,908	989,787	787,195
Pakistan	23,594	38,259	38,081
Total (incl. others)	1,510,174	1,111,492	891,836

* Including same-day visitors.

Tourism receipts (US $ million, excl. passenger transport): 3,593 in 2019; 955 in 2020; 1,963 in 2021 (provisional).

Source: World Tourism Organization.

Communications Media

	2019	2020	2021
Telephones ('000 main lines in use)	2,859.1	2,699.8	3,048.7
Mobile telephone subscriptions ('000)	37,224.8	37,475.3	37,649.1
Broadband subscriptions, fixed ('000)	4,559.1	6,254.1	6,588.4
Broadband subscriptions, mobile ('000)	16,532.7	18,459.8	20,678.8
Internet users (% of population)	44.3*	n.a.	n.a.

* Excluding Kurdish-controlled regions, where an additional 15.7% of the total Iraqi population were estimated to be internet users.

Source: International Telecommunication Union.

Education

(2019/20)

	Institutions	Teachers	Students
Pre-primary	1,244	8,465	209,935
Primary	17,945	291,904	6,637,127
Secondary:			
academic	8,612	173,805	3,258,718
vocational	316	10,741	52,131
Fine arts	24	1,239	8,819
Higher	586*	50,791	247,555†

* Including 30 institutes and 556 colleges.
† Students admitted to undergraduate programmes at universities, technical education commissions and private colleges.

Postgraduate: 19,156 students in 2019/20.

Pupil-teacher ratio (primary education, UNESCO estimate): 17.0 in 2006/07 (Source: UNESCO Institute for Statistics).

Adult literacy rate (UNESCO estimates): 85.6% (males 91.2%; females 79.9%) in 2017 (Source: UNESCO Institute for Statistics).

Directory

The Constitution

On 15 November 2003 the US-led Coalition Provisional Authority (CPA), established following the overthrow of the regime of Saddam Hussain in April, and the Governing Council, inaugurated in July, agreed on a timetable for the restoration of full Iraqi sovereignty, the drafting of a permanent constitution and the holding of free national elections. However, this plan was superseded by the Transitional Administrative Law signed by the Governing Council in March 2004, which outlined a new timetable for the establishment of sovereign, elected organs of government.

Accordingly, an Iraqi Interim Government and interim President assumed power in June, and the CPA and Governing Council were dissolved. Following elections in January 2005 to a 275-member Transitional National Assembly (TNA), the Interim Government was replaced in April by an Iraqi Transitional Government, consisting of a state Presidency Council (comprising a President and two Vice-Presidents appointed by the TNA) and a Prime Minister and Council of Ministers (appointed by the Presidency Council). The TNA presented a draft Constitution, drawn up by a constitutional committee, to the United Nations in September. The draft Constitution was ratified following its endorsement by 78.6% of the votes cast in a national referendum in October. National elections for a permanent legislature, the 325-seat Council of Representatives, took place in December. The size of the legislature was expanded to 328 seats at elections held in April 2014, and to 329 at elections in May 2018. The President is elected by the Council of Representatives by at least a two-thirds' majority and is limited to two four-year terms. The term in office of the Council of Representatives is also four years.

The Government

HEAD OF STATE

President: ABDUL LATIF RASHID (assumed office 13 October 2022).

IRAQ

COUNCIL OF MINISTERS
(September 2023)

Prime Minister: MOHAMMED SHIA AL-SUDANI.
Deputy Prime Minister and Minister of Foreign Affairs: FUAD HUSSEIN.
Deputy Prime Minister and Minister of Planning: MUHAMMAD ALI TAMIM.
Deputy Prime Minister and Minister of Oil: HAYAN ABDUL GHANI ABDUL ZAHRA.
Minister of Finance: TAIF SAMI MOHAMMED.
Minister of Defence: THABET MUHAMMAD SAEED REDA AL-ABBASI.
Minister of the Interior: ABDUL AMIR AL-SHAMMARI.
Minister of Health: SALEH MAHDI AL-HASNAWI.
Minister of Displacement and Migration: IVAN FAEQ.
Minister of Transportation: RAZZAK MUHAIBES AL-SAADAWI.
Minister of Water Resources: AOUN DIAB.
Minister of Labour and Social Affairs: AHMED AL-ASADI.
Minister of Youth and Sports: AHMED MOHAMED AL-MUBARQA.
Minister of Education: IBRAHIM AL-JUBOURI.
Minister of Culture, Tourism and Antiquities: AHMED FAKKAK.
Minister of Justice: KHALED SHWANI.
Minister of Electricity: ZIAD ALI FADEL.
Minister of Communications: HIAM ABBOUD AL-YASIRI.
Minister of Agriculture: ABBAS JABR AL-ALAWI.
Minister of Higher Education and Scientific Research: NAIM AL-ABOUDI.
Minister of Industry and Minerals: KHALED BATTAL.
Minister of Trade: ATHEER DAOUD AL-GHURAIRI.
Minister of the Environment: NIZAR MOHAMMED SAEED AMEDI.
Minister of Construction and Housing: BENKIN ABDALLAH RIKANI.

MINISTRIES

Ministry of Agriculture: Khulafa St, Khullani Sq., Baghdad; tel. (1) 719-5381; e-mail minis_of_agr@moagr.org; internet www.zeraa.gov.iq.
Ministry of Communications: Baghdad; tel. (1) 718-4555; e-mail info@moc.gov.iq; internet www.moc.gov.iq.
Ministry of Construction and Housing: Museum Sq., Baghdad; tel. (1) 537-2381; e-mail moch@moch.gov.iq; internet www.moch.gov.iq.
Ministry of Culture, Tourism and Antiquities: POB 624, Qaba bin Nafi Sq., Sadoun St, Baghdad; tel. (1) 538-3171; internet www.mocul.gov.iq.
Ministry of Defence: Baghdad; tel. (1) 548-5852; e-mail shakawa@mod.mil.iq; internet www.mod.mil.iq.
Ministry of Displacement and Migration: Baghdad; tel. 5370049; e-mail webmaster@momd.gov.iq; internet momd.gov.iq.
Ministry of Education: Saad State Enterprises Bldg, nr the Convention Centre, Baghdad; tel. (1) 883-2571; internet www.moedu.gov.iq.
Ministry of Electricity and Alternative Energy: Baghdad; e-mail infocen@moelc.gov.iq; internet www.moelc.gov.iq.
Ministry of Energy Affairs: Baghdad.
Ministry of the Environment: POB 10026, Baghdad; tel. 7809166641; e-mail moen.iraq@moen.gov.iq; internet www.moen.gov.iq.
Ministry of Finance: Khulafa St, nr al-Russafi Sq., Baghdad; tel. (1) 887-4871; e-mail emof@mof.gov.iq; internet www.mof.gov.iq.
Ministry of Foreign Affairs: opp. State Organization for Roads and Bridges, Karradat Mariam, Baghdad; tel. (1) 537-0091; e-mail press@iraqmfamail.com; internet www.mofa.gov.iq.
Ministry of Health: Baghdad; e-mail minister-office@moh.gov.iq; internet www.moh.gov.iq.
Ministry of Higher Education and Scientific Research: POB 55509, 52 Rusafa St, Baghdad; tel. and fax (1) 717-0709; e-mail info@mohesr.gov.iq; internet mohesr.gov.iq.
Ministry of Industry and Minerals: POB 5815, Baghdad; tel. (1) 816-2006; e-mail minister@industry.gov.iq; internet www.industry.gov.iq.
Ministry of the Interior: Baghdad; e-mail media@moi.gov.iq; internet www.moi.gov.iq.
Ministry of Justice: Baghdad; fax (1) 537-2269; e-mail minister_moj@moj.gov.iq; internet www.moj.gov.iq.
Ministry of Labour and Social Affairs: Baghdad; e-mail info@molsa.gov.iq; internet www.molsa.gov.iq.
Ministry of Oil: Oil Complex Bldg, Port Said St, Baghdad; tel. (1) 817-7000; fax (1) 747-0341; e-mail ministryofoil@oil.gov.iq; internet www.oil.gov.iq.
Ministry of Planning: Yafa St, Baghdad; tel. (1) 778-3899; internet www.mop.gov.iq.
Ministry of Trade: POB 5833, Khullani Sq., Baghdad; tel. (1) 887-2681; fax (1) 790-1907; e-mail motcenter@motiraq.org; internet www.mot.gov.iq.
Ministry of Transportation: nr Martyr's Monument, Karradat Dakhil, Baghdad; tel. (1) 776-6041; e-mail mt_office@motrans.gov.iq; internet www.motrans.gov.iq.
Ministry of Water Resources: Palestine St, Baghdad; tel. (1) 772-0240; fax (1) 774-0672; e-mail waterresmin@mowr.gov.iq; internet www.mowr.gov.iq.
Ministry of Youth and Sports: Baghdad; e-mail iraq_sport1010@yahoo.com; internet www.moys.gov.iq.

Legislature

COUNCIL OF REPRESENTATIVES

Council of Representatives: Baghdad International Zone Convention Center, Baghdad e-mail press@parliament.iq; internet www.parliament.iq.
Speaker: MOHAMMED AL-HALBOUSI.

Election, 10 October 2021

	Seats
Sadrist Movement*	73
Taqaddum (Progress) Alliance	37
State of Law Coalition	33
Kurdistan Democratic Party (KDP)	31
Al-Fatah Alliance	17
Patriotic Union of Kurdistan (PUK)	17
Al-Azm (Determination) Alliance	14
New Generation Movement	9
Imtidad Movement	9
Ishraqat Kanoon	6
Tasmeem Alliance	5
National Contract Alliance	4
Nation State Forces Alliance	4
Babylon Movement	4
Our People's Identity Alliance	3
Hasm Reform Movement	3
Independents	43
Others	17
Total	**329**

* The 73 Sadrist legislators resigned from the Council of Representatives on 12 June 2022. In accordance with electoral legislation, the vacated seats were offered to the candidates who had obtained the second-largest number of votes in each of the 73 constituencies in the election of 10 October 2021. On 23 June 2022 64 new legislators were sworn in (nine of the designated replacement legislators declined their seats).

Kurdish Autonomous Region

A 15-article accord signed by the Iraqi Government and Kurdish leaders in 1970 provided for: the creation of a unified autonomous area for the Kurdish population, comprising the administrative departments of Sulaimaniya, Duhok and Irbil (Arbil/Erbil), and the Kurdish sector of the city of Kirkuk; and the establishment of a 50-member Kurdish Legislative Council. Following the recapture of Kuwait from Iraqi forces by a multinational military coalition in early 1991, renewed negotiations between the Iraqi Government (under Saddam Hussain) and Kurdish groups stalled over the status of Kirkuk, and in October 1991 the Government effectively severed all economic and administrative support to the region. In May 1992 the Kurdish Iraqi Front (KIF), an alliance of several Kurdish factions—including the two largest, the Patriotic Union of Kurdistan (PUK) and the Kurdistan Democratic Party (KDP)—established in 1988, organized elections to a new 105-member Iraqi Kurdistan National Assembly. However, by September 1996 bitter factional disputes had led to the effective disintegration of the KIF, and prompted the Government to reassert full Iraqi sovereignty over the Kurdish areas. At a meeting in Washington, DC, USA, in September 1998, representatives of the PUK and the KDP reached a formal peace agreement, which provided for a unified regional administration, the sharing of local revenues and co-operation in implementing the United Nations-sponsored 'oil-for-food' programme. In December 1999 the KDP announced the composition of a new 25-member coalition administration (comprising the KDP, the Iraqi Communist Party, the Assyrian Movement, the Independent Workers' Party of Kurdistan, the Islamic Union and independents) for the areas under its control, principally the departments of Irbil and Duhok. Municipal elections (to select 571 officials) were conducted in the KDP-administered region in May 2001; according to official KDP sources, KDP candidates received 81% of votes cast. Negotiations between representatives of the KDP and the PUK for the full implementation of the Washington accord were held during 2002, and resulted in the resumption of a transitional joint session of the Iraqi Kurdistan National Assembly in October. The autonomous regions retained their status following the removal of the regime of Saddam Hussain in early 2003, but the status of Kirkuk remained highly controversial. On 12 June 2005 the Iraqi Kurdistan National Assembly appointed Masoud Barzani, the leader of the KDP, as President of the Kurdish Autonomous Region.

On 25 September 2017 an advisory referendum on independence was conducted throughout the Kurdish Autonomous Region, despite criticism from the Iraqi federal Government, Turkey and governments around the world. According to preliminary results, 92.7% of those who participated approved the creation of an independent Kurdish state. Following the vote, President Barzani celebrated the result as an expression of popular will. However, the Iraqi federal Government, which refused to recognize the poll's legitimacy, reacted by urging the closure of external consulates in the Kurdish Autonomous Region and of airports in the region. It also appealed for those areas of northern Iraq that had fallen into the control of Kurdish *peshmerga* fighters after the defeat of Islamic State to be transferred to the Iraqi army. The Iraqi armed forces began a military campaign to regain territory from the Kurdish *peshmerga*, taking Kirkuk and its surrounding oilfields on 16 October. Following this major defeat, Masoud Barzani announced that he would not seek to continue as President after the expiry of his current term on 1 November. The powers of the presidency were exercised by the Cabinet until 10 June 2019 when the outgoing Prime Minister of the Kurdish Regional Government, Nechirvan Barzani of the KDP, was sworn in as President. Nechirvan Barzani, the nephew of Masoud Barzani, had been elected to the post by the Iraqi Kurdistan Parliament on 28 May. A new Government took office on 10 July, with the KDP's Masrour Barzani, the son of Masoud Barzani, as Prime Minister.

THE PRESIDENCY OF THE KURDISH AUTONOMOUS REGION

President: NECHIRVAN IDRIS BARZANI (assumed office 10 June 2019).

THE CABINET
(September 2023)

A coalition comprising the Kurdistan Democratic Party (KDP), the Patriotic Union of Kurdistan (PUK), the Kurdistan Islamic Union (Yakgrtui Islami Kurdistan), the Islamic Group (Komaleh Islami) and independents.

Prime Minister: MASROUR BARZANI.
Deputy Prime Minister: QUBAD TALABANI.
Minister of Justice: FARSAT AHMAD ABDULLAH.
Minister of Peshmerga Affairs: SHORESH ISMAIL ABDULLA.
Minister of the Interior: REBER AHMAD KHALID.
Minister of Finance and Economy: AWAT JANAB NOORI.
Minister of Health: SAMAN HUSSEIN MUHAMMAD.
Minister of Education: ALAN HAMA SAEED SALIH.
Minister of Housing and Construction: DANA ABDULKAREEM HAMASALIH.
Minister of Municipalities and Tourism: SASAN OTHMAN AWNI HABIB.
Minister of Higher Education and Scientific Research: ARAM MOHAMMAD QADIR.
Minister of Planning: DARA RASHID MAHMUD.
Minister of Labour and Social Affairs: KWESTAN MOHAMAD ABDULLA MAAROUF.
Minister of Youth and Culture: MOHAMMAD SAID ALI.
Minister of Martyrs and Anfal Affairs: ABDULLAH MAHMOOD MOHAMMAD.
Minister of Agriculture and Water Resources: BEGARD DLSHAD SHUKRALLA.
Minister of Trade and Industry: KAMAL MUSLIM SAEED.
Minister of Transport and Communications: ANO JAWHAR ABDULMASEEH ABDOKA.
Minister of Endowment and Religious Affairs: PSHTIWAN SADIQ ABDULLAH.
Minister of Electricity: KAMAL MOHAMMAD SALIH KHALIL.
Ministers of State: AYDIN MARUF SELIM, VALA FAREED IBRAHIM.

The President of the Divan of the Council of Ministers, the Secretary of the Cabinet, the Chief of Staff of the Presidency, the Head of the Department of Foreign Relations and the Chairman of the Investment Board also have full ministerial status.

LEGISLATURE

In May 1992 negotiations with the Iraqi Government over the full implementation of the 1970 accord on Kurdish regional autonomy having stalled, the KIF unilaterally organized elections to a 105-member Iraqi Kurdistan National Assembly, in which almost the entire electorate of 1.1m. participated. The KDP and the PUK were the only parties to achieve representation in the new Assembly, and subsequently agreed to share seats equally (50 seats each—five having been reserved for two Assyrian Christian parties). However, the subsequent disintegration of the KIF and prolonged armed conflict between elements of the KDP and the PUK prevented the Assembly from becoming properly instituted. Relations between the KDP and the PUK improved following the Washington, DC, agreement of September 1998, and on 8 September 2002 representatives of the two parties signed an agreement providing for the inauguration of a transitional joint parliamentary session (with representation based on the results of the May 1992 elections) before the end of the year. On 4 October 2002 a joint session of the Iraqi Kurdistan National Assembly was convened for the first time since 1996.

Following the removal of the regime of Saddam Hussain by US-led forces in early 2003, elections to a new Iraqi Kurdistan National Assembly took place on 30 January 2005, concurrently with elections to the Transitional National Assembly in Baghdad. The Kurdistan Democratic List won 104 of the 111 seats. In February 2009 the Iraqi Kurdistan National Assembly was renamed the Iraqi Kurdistan Parliament. A draft Constitution for the Kurdish Autonomous Region, which included territorial claims to Kirkuk and other disputed regions, was approved by the Iraqi Kurdistan Parliament on 24 June 2009. However, a planned referendum on the draft Constitution was subsequently postponed, owing to opposition from the Independent High Electoral Commission and the Iraqi parliament. At elections to the Iraqi Kurdistan Parliament held on 25 July, the Kurdistani List, which comprised the PUK and the KDP, secured 59 of the 111 seats in the legislature. The significant reduction in the two main parties' majority was largely due to the success of the Movement for Change (Gorran), which received 25 seats; the group had been established in 2006 by former members of the PUK, and campaigned on a pro-reform and anti-corruption platform. At legislative elections held on 21 September 2013, the KDP emerged as the leading party, winning 38 seats, while Gorran became the second largest party, with 24 seats, surpassing the PUK, which took just 18 seats.

Final results of the most recent elections to the Iraqi Kurdistan Parliament, held on 30 September 2018, are detailed below. Following disagreements between the PUK and the KDP over various issues relating to the parliamentary elections that had been scheduled for 1 October 2022, on 9 October the Iraqi Kurdistan Parliament voted to extend its current term by one year. On 30 May 2023 the Federal Supreme Court ruled that the extension was unconstitutional, on the grounds that only 80 of the 111 legislators had taken part in the vote to approve the extension, and stated that all decisions issued by the Iraqi Kurdistan Parliament from the end of its legal term, on 6 November 2022, were therefore considered null and void. On 3 August 2023 President Nechirvan Barzani issued a decree setting 25 February 2024 as the date for the next parliamentary elections in the Kurdish Autonomous Region.

Iraqi Kurdistan Parliament: Irbil (Hewlêr), Kurdistan, Iraq; e-mail parliamentsite@perleman.org; internet www.perleman.org.

Speaker: Dr REWAZ FAEQ HUSSAIN.

Election, 30 September 2018

	Seats
Kurdistan Democratic Party (KDP)	45
Patriotic Union of Kurdistan (PUK)	21
Movement for Change (Gorran)	12
New Generation Movement	8
Islamic Group of Kurdistan	7
Towards Reform*	5
Kurdistan Communist Party†	1
Sardam List	1
Seats reserved for minority groups	11
Total	**111**

* An alliance of the Kurdistan Islamic Union and the Kurdistan Islamic Movement.
† Contested election as part of the Azadi List.
‡ Includes five seats reserved for parties representing the Assyrian, Chaldean and Syriac communities, five seats for representatives of the Turkoman community and one seat for the Armenian community.

Election Commission

Independent High Electoral Commission (IHEC): 14 Ramadan Bridge, Baghdad; internet www.ihec.iq; f. 2004 as Independent Electoral Comm. of Iraq by fmr Coalition Provisional Authority; renamed as above 2007; Chair. OMAR AHMED MOHAMMED.

Political Organizations

Following the removal from power of the Baathist regime, restrictions were effectively lifted on opposition political organizations that were either previously declared illegal, forced to operate clandestinely within Iraq or were based abroad.

Arab Baath Socialist Party: revolutionary Arab socialist movement founded in Damascus, Syria, in 1947; governed Iraq during 1968–2003 as principal constituent of ruling coalition, the Nat. Progressive Front (NPF); the NPF was removed from power by US-led forces in May 2003, whereupon membership of the Baath Party was declared illegal and former party mems were barred from govt and military posts; subsequently thought to be involved in insurgent activities in Iraq; in Feb. 2008 new legislation was ratified permitting certain former Baathists to be reinstated to official posts; in Jan. 2007, following the execution of former Iraqi President Saddam Hussain, former Vice-President Izzat Ibrahim al-Douri was named as the party's new leader. After al-Douri died in Oct. 2020, it was reported that former diplomat SALAH AL-MUKHTAR became the leader of the party.

Assyrian Democratic Movement (Zowaa Dimuqrataya Aturaya—Zowaa): e-mail info@zowaa.org; internet www.zowaa.org; f. 1979; seeks recognition of Assyrian rights within framework of democratic national govt; Sec.-Gen. YOUNADAM YOUSUF KANNA.

Al-Azm Alliance: Baghdad; f. 2021; Sunni party formed to contest Oct. 2021 elections; Leader MUTHANA AL-SAMARAI.

Babylon Movement: f. 2014; political wing of the Babylon Brigade, a pro-Iran Christian militia; Leader RAYAN AL-KILDANI.

Constitutional Party: Baghdad; f. 2004; Shi'a; Founder and Leader JAWAD AL-BULANI.

Al-Fateh Alliance: Baghdad; internet alfateh.iq; comprises Iran-aligned Shi'a parties, including several militia groups; Pres. HADI AL-AMIRI.

Imtidad Movement: Dhi Qar; formed during the anti-Govt protests of Oct. 2019; Leader ALAA AL-RIKABI.

Iraqi Accord (Jabhat al-Tawafuq al-Iraqiya): e-mail info@altawafoq.com; f. 2005 as the Iraqi Accord Front; reformed to contest the March 2010 legislative elections; mainly Sunni; secular; coalition of the Iraqi Islamic Party and the Nat. Gathering of the People of Iraq; Leader ADNAN AL-DULAIMI.

Iraqi Communist Party (ICP): al-Andalus Sq., Baghdad; e-mail iraqicp@hotmail.com; internet www.iraqicp.com; f. 1934; legally recognized in July 1973 on formation of NPF; left NPF March 1979; Sec.-Gen. RAED FAHMI.

Iraqi Constitutional Movement: Baghdad; f. 1993; fmrly Constitutional Monarchy Movement.

Iraqi Front for National Dialogue (Hewar National Iraqi Front): f. 2005 as breakaway party from Iraqi Nat. Dialogue Council; coalition of minor Sunni parties; Founder and Leader SALEH AL-MUTLAQ.

Iraqi Islamic Party (IIP) (al-Hizb al-Islami al-Iraqi): e-mail iraqiparty@iraqiparty.com; internet www.iraqiparty.org; f. 1960; Sunni; branch of the Muslim Brotherhood; contested March 2010 legislative elections as part of the Iraqi Accord list; Sec.-Gen. RASHID AL-AZZAWI.

Iraqi National Accord (INA): Baghdad; f. 1990; contested March 2010 legislative elections as mem. of Iraqi Nat. Movement; Founder and Sec.-Gen. Dr AYAD ALLAWI.

Iraqi National Alliance: list of mainly Shi'a parties, incl. the ISCI, the Sadr II Movement, the Iraqi Nat. Congress, the Nat. Reform Movement and the Islamic Virtue Party, which contested the March 2010 legislative elections as a single coalition; Leader AMMAR AL-HAKIM.

Iraqi National Congress (INC): f. 1992 in London, United Kingdom, as a multi-party coalition supported by the US Govt; following the removal of the regime of Saddam Hussain, the INC moved to Baghdad and was transformed into a distinct political party; formed Nat. Congress Coalition before 2005 legislative elections, at which it failed to win any seats; contested March 2010 elections as part of the Iraqi Nat. Alliance; Sec.-Gen. ARAS HABIB KARIM.

Iraqi National Movement (Iraqiya): secular electoral list formed to contest the March 2010 legislative elections, comprising a no. of political orgs, incl. the INA, the Iraqi Front for Nat. Dialogue, the Renewal List and Iraqis; Leader Dr AYAD ALLAWI.

Iraqi Turkmen Front (Irak Türkmen Cephesi): Kirkuk; f. 1995; coalition of Turkmen groups; seeks autonomy for Turkmen areas in Iraq and recognition of Turkmen as one of main ethnic groups in Iraq, and supports establishment of multi-party democratic system in Iraq; contests status of Kirkuk with Kurds; Leader HASAN TURAN.

Iraqis (Iraqiyun): f. 2004; moderate; includes both Sunnis and Shi'a; Leader AMMAR AL-HAKIM.

Islamic Dawa Party (Hizb al-Da'wa al-Islamiya): Baghdad; f. 1957 in Najaf; banned 1980; fmrly based in Tehran, Iran, and London, UK; re-established in Baghdad 2003; part of State of Law coalition; predominantly Shi'a, but with Sunni mems; advocates govt centred on the principles of Islam; Gen. Sec. NURI KAMAL (JAWAD) AL-MALIKI.

Islamic Movement of Kurdistan (IMK): Halabja; e-mail bzotnawa@yahoo.com; f. 1987; Islamist movement seeking to obtain greater legal rights for Iraqi Kurds; Founder and Leader IRFAN ABDULAZIZ.

Islamic Supreme Council of Iraq (ISCI): Najaf; f. 1982 as the Supreme Council for the Islamic Revolution in Iraq; name changed as above in 2007; Shi'a; seeks govt based on principle of *wilayat-e-faqih* (guardianship of the jurisprudent); armed faction, the Badr Organization (fmrly Badr Brigade), assisted coalition forces in Iraq after the removal of Saddam Hussain's regime; Leader AMMAR AL-HAKIM.

Islamic Virtue Party (Hizb al-Fadhila al-Islamiya—IVP): Basra; Shi'a; an offshoot of the Sadrist Movement; follows the spiritual leadership of Ayatollah al-Sayyid Muhammad al-Ya'qubi; Sec.-Gen. Dr ABDUL HUSSEIN AL-MUSSAWI.

Kurdistan Democratic Party (KDP): European Office (Germany), 10749 Berlin, POB 301516; tel. (70) 7904097; fax (73) 5094097; e-mail party@kdp.se; internet www.kdp.se; f. 1946; seeks to protect Kurdish rights and promote Kurdish culture and interests through regional political and legislative autonomy, as part of a federative republic; Pres. MASOUD BARZANI, Vice-Pres. NECHIRVAN BARZANI.

Kurdistan Islamic Union (Yakgrtui Islami Kurdistan): e-mail info@kurdiu.org; internet kurdiu.org; f. 1991; seeks establishment of an Islamic state in Iraq that recognizes the rights of Kurds; branch of the Muslim Brotherhood; Sec.-Gen. SALAHADDIN MUHAMMAD BAHADDIN.

Kurdistan Justice Group (Komal): Khurmal; f. 2001 as Islamic Group of Kurdistan; splinter group of IMIK; present name adopted in 2021; moderate Islamist, aligned with the PUK; Founder and Leader Mullah ALI BAPIR.

Kurdistan Socialist Democratic Party (KSDP): Sulaimaniya; e-mail info@psdkurdistan.org; f. 1994; splinter group of the KDP, aligned with the PUK; Sec.-Gen. MUHAMMAD HAJI MAHMOUD.

Kurdistan Toilers Party (Hizbi Zahmatkeshani Kurdistan): f. 1985; advocates a federal Iraq; closely associated with the KSDP; Sec.-Gen. BALEN ABDULLAH.

Movement for Change (Gorran): tel. 7708106636; e-mail info@gorran.net; internet gorran.net; f. 2006; established by fmr members of the PUK; advocates political and economic reform, anti-corruption measures and the independence of the judiciary; advocates a federal Iraq; Leader OMAR SAYID ALI.

National Contract Alliance: Baghdad; Leader ABDULAMIR AL-MAYAHI.

National Reform Movement: f. 2008 by fmr mems of Islamic Dawa Party; Shi'a; Leader IBRAHIM AL-JA'FARI.

National State Forces Alliance: Baghdad; Shi'a; Leader AMMAR AL-HAKIM.

National Wisdom Movement (al-Hikmah): f. 2017; Leader AMMAR AL-HAKIM.

New Generation Movement (NGM): Baghdad; f. 2017; Kurdish; Pres. SHASWAR ABDULWAHID QADIR.

Patriotic Union of Kurdistan (PUK): European Office (Germany), 10502 Berlin, POB 210213; tel. (30) 34097850; fax (30) 34097849; e-mail puk@puk.org; internet www.puk.org; f. 1975; seeks to protect and promote Kurdish rights and interests through self-determination; Pres. BAFEL TALABANI.

Sadrist Movement (al-Tayyar al-Sadri): Najaf; f. 2003; contested the 2018 legislative elections as a member of the Saairun (Forward) Alliance, together with the Iraqi Communist Party and four smaller parties; opposes presence of US-led coalition in Iraq; Leader Hojatoleslam MUQTADA AL-SADR.

State of Law Coalition (Dawlat al-Kanoon): f. prior to 2009 provincial elections; predominantly Shi'a alliance of parties and independent candidates, incl. the Islamic Dawa Party, the Independent Arab Movement and the Anbar Salvation Nat. Front; Leader NURI KAMAL (JAWAD) AL-MALIKI.

Taqaddum (Progress) Alliance: Baghdad; internet takadum.org; Sunni; Leader MOHAMMED AL-HALBOUSI.

Tasmeem Alliance: Baghdad; f. 2021; formed to contest Oct. 2021 elections; Leader ASAAD AL-EDANI.

Major militant groups that have launched attacks against Iraqis and the US-led coalition include: **Fedayeen Saddam** (Saddam's Martyrs; f. 1995 by mems of the former Baathist regime; paramilitary group); **Ansar al-Islam** (f. 1998; splinter group of IMIK; Islamist; suspected of having links with al-Qa'ida); **Hezbollah** (Shi'a Marsh Arab; Leader ABD AL-KARIM MAHOUD MOHAMMEDAWI—'ABU HATEM'); **Ansar al-Sunnah** (f. 2003 by mems of Ansar al-Islam; Islamist); **Imam al-Mahdi Army** (armed wing of the Sadrist Movement—al-Tayyar al-Sadri); **Base of Holy War in Mesopotamia** (Tanzim Qa'idat al-Jihad fi Bilad al-Rafidain; Sunni insurgent network, also known as al-Qa'ida in Iraq; Leader AL-NASSER LIDEEN ALLAH ABU SULEIMAN, who was reported to have been killed in Feb. 2011); **Islamic State** (al-Dawlat al-Islamiyya; network of Sunni insurgent groups; seized control of territory in Anbar, Kirkuk, Nineveh and Salah al-Din governorates—including the city of Mosul—from June 2014, as well as territory in northern Syria; proclaimed an independent Islamic state—or 'caliphate'—in those areas under its control in June, changing its name from Islamic State in Iraq and the Levant; however, by early 2018 much of this territory had been returned to govt control; Leader ABU HAFS AL-HASHIMI AL-QURAISHI).

Diplomatic Representation

EMBASSIES IN IRAQ

Algeria: Hay al-Mansour, Baghdad; tel. (1) 543-4137; fax (1) 542-5829; e-mail ambalgabaghdad@yahoo.com; Ambassador DJIHAD EDDINE BELKAS.

Australia: International Zone, Baghdad; tel. 780-9237565; e-mail info.baghdad@dfat.gov.au; internet www.iraq.embassy.gov.au; Ambassador Dr PAULA GANLY.

Bahrain: al-Rashid Hotel, Baghdad; tel. 781-4256980; e-mail baghdad.mission@mofa.gove.bh; internet www.mofa.gov.bh/baghdad; Chargé d'affaires a.i. KHALID AHMED AL-MANSOUR.

Bangladesh: 24/18/601 al-Mansour, Baghdad; tel. 782-7883680; e-mail bangladoot.baghdad.dip@gmail.com; internet baghdad.mofa.gov.bd; Ambassador MD FAZLUL BARI.

Bulgaria: 12/25/624 al-Ameriya, Baghdad; tel. (1) 400-9612; e-mail embassy.baghdad@mfa.bg; internet www.mfa.bg/embassies/iraq; Chargé d'affaires a.i. NIKOLA DRAGANOV.

Canada: International Zone, Baghdad; tel. 783-3035357; e-mail bghdd.consular@international.gc.ca; internet www.international.gc.ca/world-monde/iraq-irak/baghdad-bagdad.aspx; Ambassador KATHY BUNKA (designate).

China, People's Republic: POB 2386, al-Jadryaa Post Office, Baghdad; tel. 790-1912315; e-mail chinaemb_iq@mfa.gov.cn; internet iq.chineseembassy.org; Ambassador CUI WEI.

Czech Republic: POB 27124, 37/11/601 Hay al-Mansour, Baghdad; tel. 790-1912411; e-mail baghdad@embassy.mzv.cz; internet www.mzv.cz/baghdad; Ambassador PETR STĚPÁNEK.

Denmark: Baghdad; tel. (3) 3921112; internet irak.um.dk; Ambassador CHRISTIAN THORNING.

Egypt: International Zone, Hay al-Mansour, Baghdad; tel. (1) 543-0572; fax (1) 556-6346; e-mail egyemb.bgd@gmail.com; Ambassador WALID MOHAMED ISMAIL.

Finland: 22 St, Karadat Mariam, District 220, Baghdad; tel. (3) 573-7481; e-mail sanomat.bag@formin.fi; internet www.finlandabroad.fi/web/irq; Ambassador MATTI LASSILA.

France: POB 118, 7/55/102 Abu Nawas, Baghdad; tel. 790-1912365; e-mail cad.bagdad-amba@diplomatie.gouv.fr; internet www.ambafrance-iq.org; Ambassador ERIC CHEVALLIER.

Germany: POB 2036, Hay al-Mansour, Baghdad; tel. 790-1922526; e-mail info@bagdad.diplo.de; internet irak.diplo.de; Ambassador MARTIN JÄGER.

Greece: 2/4/609, Hay al-Mansour, Baghdad; tel. 783-1372165; fax (210) 3681717; e-mail gremb.bag@mfa.gr; internet www.mfa.gr/missionsabroad/iraq; Ambassador GEORGIOS ALMANOS.

Holy See: Apostolic Nunciature, POB 2090, 904/2/46 Saadoun St, Baghdad; tel. 781-1204663; e-mail nuntiusiraq@yahoo.com; Apostolic Nuncio Most Rev. MITJA LESKOVAR (Titular Archbishop of Beneventum).

India: 18/16/609, al-Mansour, Baghdad; tel. 772-6739642; e-mail hoc.baghdad@mea.gov.in; internet www.eoibaghdad.gov.in; Ambassador L. PRASHANT PISE.

Iran: POB 39095, al-Salhiya, Karadeh Maryam, Baghdad; tel. (1) 884-3033; fax (1) 537-5636; internet iraq.mfa.ir; Ambassador MOHAMMAD KAZEM AL-SADEQ.

Italy: International Zone, Baghdad; e-mail ambasciata.baghdad@esteri.it; internet www.ambbaghdad.esteri.it/ambasciata_baghdad; Ambassador MAURIZIO GREGANTI.

Japan: International Zone, Baghdad; tel. 770-4942032; e-mail embjp.info.iraq@bd.mofa.go.jp; internet www.iraq.emb-japan.go.jp; Ambassador MATSUMOTO FUTOSHI.

Jordan: Diplomatic Area, Dijlah Complex 2, Villa No. 3, Baghdad; tel. 781-2777667; fax (1) 541-2009; e-mail Baghdad@fm.gov.jo; Ambassador MONTASER AL-ZOUBI.

Korea, Republic: Villa W5, Green Zone Diplomatic Complex, Baghdad; tel. 770-0405883; e-mail kembiraq@mofa.go.kr; internet overseas.mofa.go.kr/iq-ko/index.do; Ambassador JOY TONG-SU.

Kuwait: International Zone, Baghdad; tel. 783-1111333; e-mail iraq@mofa.gov.kw; Ambassador TARIQ AL-FARAJ.

Lebanon: Bldg 51, al-Askari St, 116 al-Sarafiya Area, Baghdad; tel. (1) 414-2711; fax (1) 885-6731; e-mail lebembbaghadad@yahoo.com; internet www.baghdad.mfa.gov.lb; Ambassador ALI ADIB AL-HABHAB.

Mauritania: al-Mansour, Area 609, St 10, House 20, Baghdad; tel. 770-4625186; fax (1) 541-5786; e-mail embassymauritania.baghdad2013@gmail.com; internet www.ambarimbaghdad.com; Ambassador EL-HACEN MOHAMED ELEYATT.

Morocco: Baghdad; Chargé d'affaires ABDEL KARIM BIN SALAM.

Netherlands: POB 2064, 7/15/215 International Zone, Baghdad; tel. (1) 778-2571; fax (1) 776-3513; e-mail bag@minbuza.nl; internet www.netherlandsandyou.nl/your-country-and-the-netherlands/iraq; Ambassador JOHANNES LINDERT SANDE.

Oman: Baghdad; tel. 783-3886007; e-mail baghdad@fm.gov.om; Ambassador HAMID BIN AHMED AIDROOS.

Pakistan: al-Mansour Hotel, al-Salhiya, Baghdad; tel. 770-4843092; fax 781-2369544; e-mail parepbaghdad@gmail.com; internet www.mofa.gov.pk/baghdad-iraq; Ambassador AHMED AMJAD ALI.

Philippines: Hay al-Jamiyah, House 5, 915 St, Zukak 22, al-Jadriya, Baghdad; tel. 781-6066822; e-mail baghdad.pe@dfa.gov.ph; internet dfa.gov.ph/iraq; Chargé d'affaires a.i. CHRISTOPHER P. CASTILLO.

Poland: International Zone, Baghdad; tel. 780-9051068; e-mail bagdad.amb.sekretariat@msz.gov.pl; internet www.gov.pl/web/iraq; Ambassador MARCIN KUBIAK.

Qatar: POB 6027, House No. 114, District 611, Sector 15, Baghdad; tel. 773-5707000; e-mail baghdad@mofa.gov.qa; Ambassador SULTAN MUBARAK KHALIFA AL-KUBAISI (designate).

Romania: al-Mansur St, Baghdad; tel. 780-4462039; e-mail bagdad@mae.ro; Ambassador RADU OCTAVIAN DOBRE.

Russian Federation: 4/5/605 Hay al-Mutanabi, Baghdad; tel. and fax 790-1909674; e-mail rusembassyiraq@mid.ru; internet www.iraq.mid.ru; Ambassador ELBRUS KUTRASHEV.

Saudi Arabia: al-Rashid Hotel, International Zone, Baghdad; tel. 772-9905904; Ambassador ABD AL-AZIZ BIN KHALID AL-SHAMMARI.

Serbia: POB 2061, 16/35/923 Hay Babel, Baghdad; tel. 790-1912334; e-mail embsrbag@yahoo.com; internet www.baghdad.mfa.rs; Ambassador UROŠ BALOV.

Somalia: al-Salhiya, Baghdad; tel. 781-3753506; e-mail baghdadembassy@mfa.gov.so; Ambassador LIBAN SHEIKH MOHAMUD.

Spain: POB 2072, 55/3/609 al-Mansour, Baghdad; e-mail emb.bagdad@maec.es; internet www.exteriores.gob.es/embajadas/bagdad; Ambassador PEDRO MARTÍNEZ-AVIAL MARTÍN.

Sudan: al-Salhiya, Al Sikak, Sector 220, St 12, House 13/1, Baghdad; tel. 771-3955550; e-mail sudanbaghdad@gmail.com; Ambassador ABDUL RAHIM SAR AL-KHATIM.

Sweden: POB 55550, al-Salhiya, Baghdad; tel. 780-1987450; e-mail ambassaden.bagdad@gov.se; internet www.swedenabroad.com/baghdad; Ambassador (vacant).

Syrian Arab Republic: Hay al-Mansour, Princesses St, District 609, Alley 3, House 34, Baghdad; tel. 780-0700516; e-mail syrembagh@gmail.com; internet syrianembassybagh.com; Ambassador SATTAM JAD'AN AL-DANDAH.

Tunisia: 1/49/617 Hay al-Andalus, Baghdad; tel. (1) 542-4569; e-mail at.baghdad@diplomatie.gov.tn; Ambassador CHOKRI LETAÏEF (designate).

Türkiye (Turkey): POB 14001, 406/4213 Kerradet Meryem, International Zone, Baghdad; tel. (312) 218-6010; fax (312) 218-6110; e-mail embassy.baghdad@mfa.gov.tr; internet www.baghdad.emb.mfa.gov.tr; Ambassador ALI RIZA GUNEY.

Ukraine: POB 15192, 50/1/609 al-Mansour, al-Yarmouk, Baghdad; tel. 790-5577791; e-mail emb_iq@mfa.gov.ua; internet iraq.mfa.gov.ua; Chargé d'affaires a.i. OLEKSANDER BURAVCHENKOV.

United Arab Emirates: 81/34/611 Hay al-Andalus (al-Daoudi), Baghdad; tel. 780-7144444; fax 2494652; e-mail baghdademb@

mofaic.gov.ae; internet www.mofaic.gov.ae/en/missions/baghdad; Ambassador SALEM ISSA AL-QATTAM AL-ZAABI.

United Kingdom: International Zone, Baghdad; e-mail britishconsulbaghdad@fcdo.gov.uk; tel. 70085000; internet www.gov.uk/government/world/iraq; Ambassador STEPHEN HITCHEN.

USA: al-Kindi St, International Zone, Baghdad; tel. 760-0303000; e-mail baghdadirc@state.gov; internet iq.usembassy.gov; Ambassador ALINA L. ROMANOWSKI.

Venezuela: 34 St, al-Mansour, al-Dawoody, Baghdad; tel. 772-1096612; e-mail embve.irak@mppre.gob.ve; Ambassador ARTURO ANÍBAL RAMIREZ.

Yemen: 4/36/904 Hay al-Wahada, Baghdad; tel. (1) 718-6682; fax (1) 717-2318; Ambassador AL-KHADER MARMASH.

Judicial System

Supreme Judicial Council: Baghdad; e-mail iraqinfocenter@yahoo.com; internet www.hjc.iq; supervises and manages the affairs of the federal Judiciary, nominates candidates for judicial appointments and proposes annual budget draft of the Federal Judicial Authority to the Council of Representatives; Pres. FAIQ ZIDAN.

Federal Supreme Court: comprises a number of judges and experts in Islamic jurisprudence; reviews the constitutionality of laws and regulations; settles disputes concerning application of the federal laws, regulations and instructions issued by the federal authorities; settles disputes between the Federal Government, the Kurdish Regional Government and the governments of governorates; ratifies the results of elections to the Council of Representatives; Pres. JASSIM MOHAMMED ABBOUD.

Supreme Iraqi Criminal Tribunal: following the ousting of the Baath regime, the judicial system was subject to a process of review and de-Baathification. In June 2003 the former Coalition Provisional Authority (CPA) established a **Judicial Review Committee**, the task of which was to review and repair the material status of the courts and to assess personnel. In December the Governing Council created the **Iraqi Special Tribune**, in order to bring to trial those senior members of the former regime accused of war crimes, crimes against humanity and genocide. The statute of the Tribune was amended by the Transitional National Assembly in October 2005, when it was renamed the **Supreme Iraqi Criminal Tribunal**.

Central Criminal Court of Iraq: consists of an **Investigative Court** and a **Trial Court**. It was created by the CPA in July 2003 as the senior court in Iraq, with jurisdiction over all crimes committed in the country since 19 March 2003. With a few exceptions, the application of justice was to be based upon the 1969 Penal Code of Iraq and the 1971 Criminal Proceedings Code of Iraq.

Religion

ISLAM

About 95% of the population are Muslims, some 60% of whom are of the Shi'a sect. The Arabs of northern Iraq, the Bedouins, the Kurds, the Turkomans and some of the inhabitants of Baghdad and Basra are mainly of the Sunni sect, while the remaining Arabs south of the Diyali are Shi'a.

Grand Mufti of Iraq: Shekih ABDUL-MAHDI AL-SUMAIDAIE.

CHRISTIANITY

There are Christian communities in all the principal towns of Iraq, but their main villages lie mostly in the Mosul district. The Christians of Iraq comprise three groups: the free Churches, including the Nestorian, Gregorian and Syrian Orthodox; the churches known as Uniate, since they are in union with the Roman Catholic Church, including the Armenian Uniates, Syrian Uniates and Chaldeans; and mixed bodies of Protestant converts, New Chaldeans and Orthodox Armenians. There were estimated to be fewer than 250,000 Christians of various denominations in Iraq in 2021.

The Assyrian Church

Assyrian Christians, an ancient sect having sympathies with Nestorian beliefs, were forced to leave their mountainous homeland in northern Kurdistan in the early part of the 20th century. The estimated 550,000 members of the Apostolic Catholic Assyrian Church of the East are now exiles, mainly in Iraq (about 50,000 adherents), the Syrian Arab Republic, Lebanon and the USA. Their leader is the Catholicos Patriarch, His Holiness MAR DINKHA IV.

The Orthodox Churches

Armenian Apostolic Church: Diocese of the Armenian Church of Iraq, POB 2280, al-Jadriya, Tayaran Sq., Baghdad; tel. (1) 815-1856; fax (1) 815-1857; e-mail centralcom@iraqiarmenian.church; internet iraqiarmenian.church; f. 1639; Primate Archbishop OSHAGAN GULGULIAN; 12 churches (four in Baghdad).

Syrian Orthodox Church: Syrian Orthodox Archbishopric, POB 843, al-Seenah St, Baghdad; tel. (1) 719-6320; fax (1) 719-7583; Archbishop of Baghdad and Basra SEVERIUS JAMIL HAWA; 12,000 adherents in Iraq.

The Greek Orthodox Church is also represented in Iraq.

The Roman Catholic Church

Armenian Rite

Archbishop of Baghdad: Most Rev. NERSÈS (JOSEPH) ZABBARA, 27/903 Archevêché Arménien Catholique, POB 2344, Karrada Sharkiya, Baghdad; tel. (1) 719-2461; e-mail dabbaghianemm@hotmail.com.

Chaldean Rite

Iraq comprises the patriarchate of Baghdad, five archdioceses (including the patriarchal see of Baghdad) and five dioceses (all of which are suffragan to the patriarchate). Altogether, the Patriarch has jurisdiction over 21 archdioceses and dioceses in Iraq, Egypt, Iran, Lebanon, the Syrian Arab Republic, Türkiye (formerly Turkey) and the USA, and the Patriarchal Vicariate of Jerusalem.

Chaldean Patriarch of Baghdad: Cardinal LOUIS RAPHAËL I SAKO, POB 6112, Patriarcat Chaldéen Catholique, al-Mansour, Baghdad; tel. (1) 537-9164; e-mail info@st-addayyahoo.com; internet saint-adday.com.

Archbishop of Arbil: Most Rev. BASHAR MATTI WARDA, Archevêché Catholique Chaldéen, Ainkawa, Arbil; tel. (750) 410-6267.

Archbishop of Baghdad: the Chaldean Patriarch of Baghdad (q.v.).

Archbishop of Basra: Most Rev. HABIB HORMUZ AL-NAUFALI, Archevêché Chaldéen, POB 217, Ashar-Basra; tel. (772) 180-5115.

Archbishop of Kirkuk: Most Rev. YOUSIF THOMAS MIRKIS, Archevêché Chaldéen, POB 490, Kirkuk; tel. (790) 191-4702.

Archbishop of Mosul: Most Rev. NAJEEB MIKHAEL MOUSSA, Archevêché Chaldéen, POB 757, Mayassa, Mosul; tel. (60) 815831; fax (60) 816742; e-mail archdioceseofmossul@yahoo.com.

Latin Rite

The archdiocese of Baghdad is directly responsible to the Holy See.

Archbishop of Baghdad: Most Rev. JEAN BENJAMIN SLEIMAN, Archevêché Latin, POB 35130, Hay al-Wahda—Mahallat 904, rue 8, Immeuble 44, 12906 Baghdad; tel. (780) 607-4001.

Melkite Rite

The Greek-Melkite Patriarch of Antioch (GRÉGOIRE III LAHAM) is resident in Damascus, Syria.

Patriarchal Exarchate of Iraq: Exarchat Patriarchal Grec-Melkite, Karradat IN 903/10/50, Baghdad; tel. (770) 723-9025; Administrator YOUSSEF ABSI.

Syrian Rite

Iraq comprises two archdioceses and the Patriarchal Exarchate of Basra.

Archbishop of Baghdad: Most Rev. EPHREM YOUSIF ABBA MANSOOR, Archevêché Syrien Catholique, 903/2/1 Baghdad; tel. (770) 414-9010; fax (1) 719-0166.

Archbishop of Mosul: (vacant), Archevêché Syrien Catholique, Hosh al-Khan, Mosul; tel. (770) 517-5000.

The Anglican Communion

Within the Episcopal Church in Jerusalem and the Middle East, Iraq forms part of the diocese of Cyprus and the Gulf. Expatriate congregations in Iraq meet at St George's Church, Baghdad. The Bishop in Cyprus and the Gulf is resident in Cyprus.

JUDAISM

A tiny Jewish community, numbering only four people, remained in Baghdad as of early 2021.

OTHERS

Sabian Community: al-Nasiriyah (Nasiriya); est. to be less than 5,000 adherents in 2017; Mandeans, mostly in Nasiriya; Head Sheikh SATTAR JABBAR HILU.

Yazidis: Ainsifni; Religious Leader ALI ALYAS.

The Press

Since the overthrow of the regime of Saddam Hussain by US-led coalition forces in early 2003, the number of publications has proliferated. Security issues have resulted in severe distribution problems, and some newspaper offices have either relocated or chosen to publish online-only editions following threats being issued against journalists by militant groups, militias and security forces.

DAILIES (PRINT AND ONLINE)

Al-Adala (Justice): Baghdad; e-mail aliisadik@yahoo.com; internet www.aladalanews.net; f. 2003; twice weekly; Arabic; organ of the Islamic Supreme Council of Iraq; publ. by the Al-Adala Group for Press, Printing and Publishing; Owner Dr ADIL ABD AL-MAHDI.

Al-Bayan (The Manifesto): Baghdad; f. 2003; Arabic; organ of Islamic Dawa Party; Man. Editor SADIQ AL-RIKABI.

Dar al-Salam (House of Peace): Baghdad; Arabic; organ of Iraqi Islamic Party.

Al-Dustur (The Constitution): Baghdad; f. 2003; Arabic; politics; independent; publ. by Al-Dustur Press, Publishing and Distribution House; Editor BASIM AL-SHEIKH.

Al-Jarida (The Newspaper): Baghdad; f. 2003; Arabic; organ of the Iraqi Arab Socialist Movement; Editor Prof. QAYS AL-AZZAWI.

Kul al-Iraq (All Iraq): Baghdad; e-mail info@kululiraq.com; internet www.kululiraq.com; f. 2003; Arabic; independent; Editor-in-Chief Dr ABBAS AL-SIRAF.

Al-Mada: 41/1 Abu Nuwas St, Baghdad; tel. 780-8080800; fax (1) 881-3256; e-mail info@almadapaper.net; internet www.almadapaper.com; f. 2004; Arabic; independent; publ. by Al-Mada Foundation for Media, Culture and Arts; Editor-in-Chief FAKHRI KARIM.

Al-Mannarah (Minarets): Basra; tel. (40) 315758; e-mail almannarah@almannarah.com; Arabic; publ. by South Press, Printing and Publishing Corpn; Editor-in-Chief Dr KHALAF AL-MANSHADI.

Al-Mashriq: Baghdad; internet www.almashriqnews.com; f. 2004; Arabic; independent; publ. by Al-Mashriq Institution for Media and Cultural Investments.

Al-Mutamar (Congress): Baghdad; e-mail almutamer@yahoo.com; internet www.almutmar.com; f. 1993; Arabic; publ. by Iraqi Nat. Congress; Editor-in-Chief LUAY BALDAWI.

Al-Sabah: Baghdad; e-mail sabah@alsabaah.iq; internet www.alsabaah.iq; f. 2003; Arabic and English; state-controlled; publ. by the Iraqi Media Network; Deputy Editor-in-Chief ADNAN SHERKHAN.

Al-Sabah al-Jadid (New Morning): Baghdad; e-mail assabahaljaded@yahoo.com; internet www.newsabah.com; f. 2004; Arabic; independent; Editor-in-Chief ISMAIL ZAYER.

Sawt al-Iraq (Voice of Iraq): Baghdad; tel. 44839373; e-mail sotaliraq-com@hotmail.com; internet www.sotaliraq.com; online only; Arabic; independent.

Al-Taakhi (Brotherhood): tel. 770-3941395; e-mail taakhipress@gmail.com; internet www.altaakhipress.com; f. 1967; Kurdish and Arabic; organ of the Kurdistan Democratic Party (KDP); publ. by Al-Taakhi Publishing and Printing House; Editor-in-Chief AHMED NASSER AL-FAILY; circ. 20,000 (Baghdad).

Tariq al-Sha'ab (People's Path): Saadoun St, Baghdad; e-mail altareeq_1934@yahoo.com; f. 1974; Arabic and English; organ of the Iraqi Communist Party; Editor ABD AL-RAZZAK AL-SAFI.

Xebat: Irbil; tel. 2969696; e-mail info@xebat.net; internet www.xebat.net; f. 1959; Arabic and Kurdish; organ of the KDP; Editor-in-Chief SALAM ABDULLAH.

Al-Zaman (Time): Baghdad; tel. (1) 717-7587; e-mail postmaster@azzaman.com; internet www.azzaman.com; f. 1997 in the United Kingdom, f. 2003 in Baghdad; Arabic, with some news translated into English; Editor-in-Chief SAAD AL-BAZZAZ.

WEEKLIES

Al-Ahali (The People): Baghdad; tel. 770-1641069; e-mail hevalzaxoyi@yahoo.com; internet www.ahali-iraq.net; Arabic; politics; Editor HAVAL ZAKHOUBI.

Alif Baa al-Iraq: Baghdad; Arabic and English; general, social and political affairs.

Habazbuz fi Zaman al-Awlamah (Habazbuz in the Age of Globalization): Baghdad; f. 2003; Arabic; satirical; Editor ISHTAR AL-YASIRI.

Iraq Today: Baghdad; f. 2003; English; current affairs; Founder and Editor-in-Chief HUSSAIN SINJARI.

Al-Iraq al-Yawm (Iraq Today): Baghdad; internet www.iraqalyoum.net; Arabic and English; Editor ISRA SHAKIR.

Al-Ittihad (Union): Baghdad and Sulaimaniya; tel. (1) 543-8954; e-mail alitthad@alitthad.com; internet www.alitthad.com; Arabic and Kurdish; publ. by the Patriotic Union of Kurdistan; Editor ABD AL-HADI; circ. 30,000 (Baghdad).

Al-Ittijah al-Akhar (The Other Direction): Baghdad; tel. (1) 776-3334; fax (1) 776-3332; e-mail alitijahalakhar@yahoo.com; Arabic; organ of Reconciliation and Liberation Bloc; Chair. and Editor MISHAAN AL-JUBURI.

Kurdish Globe: Salah al-Din Highway, Pirzeen, Irbil; tel. 750-7747784; e-mail info@kurdishglobe.net; internet www.kurdishglobe.net; f. 2005; English; Kurdish news and issues; Exec. Editor (vacant); circ. 40,000.

Majallati: POB 8041, Children's Culture House, Baghdad; Arabic; children's newspaper; Editor-in-Chief Dr SHAFIQ AL-MAHDI.

Al-Muajaha (The Witness): 6/41/901, Karrada Dakhil, Baghdad; f. 2003; Arabic and English; current affairs; independent; Editor RAMZI MAJID JARRAR.

Al-Nahda (Renaissance): Basra; f. 2003; Arabic; organ of the Independent Democratic Gathering; Publr ADNAN PACHACHI.

Regay Kurdistan: Irbil; tel. 750-4635797; e-mail salammr@yahoo.com; internet www.regaykurdistan.com; Arabic and Kurdish; organ of the Iraqi and Kurdistan Communist Parties; Editor-in-Chief HANDREN AHMAD.

Al-Sina'i (The Industrialist): Baghdad; Arabic; general; publ. by the Nat. Industrialist Coalition; Editor-in-Chief Dr ZAYD ABD AL-MAJID BILAL.

Al-Waqai al-Iraqiya (Official Gazette of the Republic of Iraq): Ministry of Justice, Baghdad; tel. (1) 537-2023; e-mail Hashim_Jaffar_alsaieg@yahoo.com; f. 1922; Arabic and English; Dir HASHIM N. JAFFAR; circ. 5,000.

PERIODICALS

Hawlati: tel. 770-1570625; e-mail Hawlati2000@gmail.com; internet hawlati.co; f. 2001; fortnightly; Kurdish, Arabic and English; independent, privately owned; mainly Kurdish politics; Publr TARIQ FATIH; Editor KAMAL RAOUF.

Majallat al-Majma' al-'Ilmi al-Iraqi (Journal of the Academy of Sciences): POB 4023, Waziriya, Baghdad; tel. (1) 422-4202; fax (1) 422-2066; e-mail iraqacademy@yahoo.com; internet www.iraqacademy.iq; f. 1950; quarterly; Arabic; scholarly magazine on Arabic Islamic culture; Editor-in-Chief Prof. Dr MOHAMMED HUSSEIN AL-YASEEN.

Al-Sa'ah (The Hour): Baghdad; twice weekly; Arabic; organ of the Iraqi Unified Nat. Movement; Publr AHMAD AL-KUBAYSI; Editor NI'MA ABD AL-RAZZAQ.

Sawt al-Talaba (Voice of the Students): Baghdad; fortnightly; Arabic; publ. by New Iraq Youth and Students' Org; Editor MUSTAFA AL-HAYIM.

NEWS AGENCIES

National Iraqi News Agency: Baghdad; tel. 770-5352514; e-mail subscription@ninanews.com; internet www.ninanews.com; f. 2005; Arabic and English; independent; Chair. Dr FARID AYAR; Man. Dir ABD AL-MUHSEN HUSSAIN JAWAD.

PRESS ORGANIZATION

National Union of Iraqi Journalists: Bldg 12, Alley 20, al-Saadoun, Baghdad; tel. 770-4300067; e-mail info@nuijiraq.org; internet nuijiraq.org; Chair. ABD AL-MENEIM AL-ASAM.

Publishers

Afaq Arabiya Publishing House: POB 4032, Adamiya, Baghdad; tel. (1) 443-6044; fax (1) 444-8760; publr of literary monthlies, periodicals and cultural books; Chair. Dr MOHSIN AL-MUSAWI.

Dar al-Ma'mun for Translation and Publishing: POB 24015, Karradat Mariam, Baghdad; tel. (1) 538-3171; publr of newspapers and magazines.

Al-Hurriyah Printing Establishment: Karantina, Sarrafiya, Baghdad; f. 1970.

Al-Jamaheer Press House: POB 491, Sarrafiya, Baghdad; tel. (1) 416-9341; fax (1) 416-1875; f. 1963; publr of a number of newspapers and magazines; Pres. SAAD QASSEM HAMMOUDI.

Kurdish Culture and Publishing House: Baghdad; f. 1976.

Al-Ma'arif Ltd: Mutanabi St, Baghdad; f. 1929; publishes periodicals and books in Arabic, Kurdish, Turkish, French and English.

Al-Mada Foundation for Media, Culture and Arts: 141 Abu Nuwas St, Baghdad; tel. 770-2799999; e-mail info@almadapaper.net; internet www.almadapaper.net; f. 1994; Dir FAKHRI KARIM.

Al-Muthanna Library: POB 14019, Mutanabi St, Baghdad; tel. 770-3649664; e-mail mail@almuthannabooks.com; internet www

IRAQ

.almuthannabooks.com; f. 1936; booksellers and publrs of books and monographs in Arabic and oriental languages; Propr ANAS AL-RAJAB; Dir IBRAHIM AL-RAJAB.

Al-Nahdah: Mutanabi St, Baghdad; tel. (1) 416-2689; e-mail yehya_azawy@yahoo.com; politics, Arab affairs.

National House for Publishing, Distribution and Advertising: POB 624, al-Jumhuriya St, Baghdad; tel. (1) 425-1846; f. 1972; publishes books on politics, economics, education, agriculture, sociology, commerce and science in Arabic and other Middle Eastern languages; Dir-Gen. M. A. ASKAR.

Al-Thawra Printing and Publishing House: POB 2009, Aqaba bin Nafi's Sq., Baghdad; tel. (1) 719-6161; f. 1970; Chair. (vacant).

PUBLISHERS' ASSOCIATION

Iraqi Publishers' Association: Baghdad; tel. (1) 416-9279; fax (1) 416-7584; e-mail al_nasheren@yahoo.com; Chair. Dr ABD AL-WAHAB AL-RADI.

Broadcasting and Communications

REGULATORY AUTHORITY

Communications and Media Commission (CMC): POB 2044, Hay Babel, al-Masbah, Baghdad; tel. (1) 919-3144; e-mail enquiries@cmc.iq; internet www.cmc.iq; f. 2004 by fmr Coalition Provisional Authority; independent telecoms and media regulator; responsibilities include the award and management of telecommunications licences, broadcasting, media and information services, as well as spectrum allocation and management; Chair. BASSAM SALEM HUSSEIN; CEO ALI AL-MOAYYED.

TELECOMMUNICATIONS

Asiacell: Headquarters Bldg, Sulaimaniya; e-mail customercare@asiacell.com; tel. 770-1197649; internet www.asiacell.com; f. 1999; 49% owned by Al-Rowad Co for General Services and 15% by Barzan Holding Co SPC; 14m. subscribers (2021); Chair. of Bd FAROUK MUSTAFA RASOUL.

Iraqi Telecommunications and Posts Co (ITPC): POB 2450, Abu Nuwas St, Baghdad; tel. (2) 222-7725; e-mail infomedia@itpc.gov.iq; internet www.itpc.gov.iq; state-owned; Dir-Gen. OSAMA JIHAD QASSEM AL-HAMASHI.

Korek Telecom: Bldg 2, Media City, Shaqlawa Rd, Irbil; tel. 445-0022; e-mail info@korektel.com; internet korektel.com; f. 2001; 44% owned by jt-venture of Agility Logistics (Kuwait) and France Telecom—Orange; Chair. SIRWAN SABER MUSTAFA; CEO NAWZAD JUNDE.

Zain: Bldg 27, St 14, Hay al-Mutanabi, al-Mansoor, Baghdad; tel. 780-2999107; e-mail info@iq.zain.com; internet www.iq.zain.com; f. 2003 as MTC Atheer, a subsidiary of Mobile Telecommunications Co (Kuwait); acquired Iraqna Co for Mobile Phone Services Ltd (operated by Orascom Telecom Holding—Egypt) in 2007; name changed to above in 2008; 14m. subscribers (April 2019); CEO ALI AL-ZAHID.

BROADCASTING

Iraqi Media Network (IMN): Baghdad; e-mail info@imn.iq; internet imn.iq; f. 2003.; Chair. Dr NABIL JASSIM.

Al-Iraqiya Television: Baghdad; internet www.imn.iq/pages/iraqia-tv; terrestrial and satellite television.

Iraq Media Network—Southern Region: internet www.imnsr.com.

Republic of Iraq Radio: Baghdad; internet www.imn.iq.

Radio

Hawler Radio: Shorsh St, next to Shangri-La Hotel, Arbil; tel. 750-7361177; e-mail hawlerradio@yahoo.com; internet www.hawlerradio.com; f. 2009; Kurdish-language; covers Arbil, D'hok, Kirkuk and Sulaimaniya.

Radio Dijla: House 3, Hay al-Jamia Zone 635/52, Baghdad; tel. 771-5661010; internet radiodijla.net; f. 2004; privately owned; first talk radio station to be established in post-invasion Iraq; also broadcasts music programmes; Founder Dr AHMAD AL-RIKABI.

Voice of Iraq: Baghdad; internet voiraq.com; f. 2003; privately owned AM radio station; broadcasts music, news and current affairs programmes in Arabic, Turkmen and English.

Other independent radio stations include Radio Al Bilad, Radio Nawa, Radio Shafak and Sumer FM.

Television

Al Sharqiya: 10/13/52 Karrada Kharj, Baghdad; tel. 751-8320424; e-mail info@alsharqiya.co.uk; internet www.alsharqiya.com; f. 2004; privately owned; independent; broadcasts news and entertainment programming 24 hours a day terrestrially and via satellite; Founder and CEO SAAD AL-BAZZAZ.

Alsumaria Iraqi TV: Baghdad; tel. (1) 717-0843; e-mail contactus@alsumaria.tv; internet www.alsumaria.tv; f. 2004; privately owned, independent satellite network; broadcasts news, entertainment and educational programming 24 hours a day.

Finance

BANKING

Central Bank

Central Bank of Iraq (CBI): POB 64, al-Rashid St, Baghdad; tel. (1) 816-5171; e-mail cbi@cbi.iq; internet www.cbi.iq; f. 1947 as Nat. Bank of Iraq; name changed as above 1956; has the sole right of note issue; Gov. ALI MOHSEN ISMAIL.

State-owned Commercial Banks

Rafidain Bank: POB 11360, al-Rasheed St, Baghdad; e-mail info@rafidain-bank.gov.iq; internet www.rafidain-bank.gov.iq; f. 1941; Dir-Gen. Dr ALI KARIM HUSSEIN.

Rasheed Bank: POB 53926, al-Rashid St, Baghdad; tel. (1) 885-3478; e-mail fatca_rash@rasheedbank.gov.iq; internet www.rasheedbank.gov.iq; f. 1988; Chair. and Gen. Man. BASSEM ABD ALI YOUSSEF.

Private Commercial Banks

Babylon Bank: Babylon Bank Bldg, al-Karada, Baghdad; tel. 790-1911374; fax (1) 719-1014; e-mail info@bbk.iq; internet www.bbk.iq; f. 1999; Chair. MUHAMMAD QASSIM AL-NADOSI; Gen. Dir ZIENA AL-BANAA.

Bank of Baghdad: POB 3192, Karada Kharj, Alwiya, Baghdad; tel. 782-8893173; e-mail info@bankofbaghdad.com.iq; internet www.bankofbaghdad.com; f. 1992; 50.6% stake owned by Burgan Bank (Kuwait); Chair. USAM ISMAIL SHARIF; Man. Dir BASIL AL-DHAHI.

Commercial Bank of Iraq PSC (CBIQ): al-Saadoun St, Alwiya, Baghdad; tel. 783-3955530; e-mail cbiq.info@cbiq.com.iq; internet cbiq.com.iq; f. 1992; Ahli United Bank BSC (Bahrain) acquired 49% stake in 2005; Chair. MOHAMMED HAMID DARAG ALDRAGH; CEO and Man. Dir FAISAL AL-HAIMOUS.

Credit Bank of Iraq: POB 3420, Saadoun St, Alwiya, Baghdad; tel. 790-1907114; fax (1) 717-0156; e-mail creditbkiq@yahoo.com; internet creditbankofiraq.com.iq; f. 1998; 84.3% owned by Nat. Bank of Kuwait SAK, 10% by World Bank's Int. Finance Corpn and 15% by private investors; Chair. MOHAMMED ALI RADHI AL-JARJAFJI; Man. Dir ATHEER TALIB ABDULJABAR.

Gulf Commercial Bank: al-Saadoun St, Alwiya, Baghdad; tel. (1) 719-8534; fax (1) 778-8251; e-mail info@gcb.iq; internet gcb.iq; f. 2000; Chair. MOHAMED SALEH FARAJ; Man. Dir ADEL NOORI AL-ALAM.

National Bank of Iraq (al-Ahli al-Iraqi Bank): Head Quarter Bldg, Saadoun St, nr al-Firdous Sq., Baghdad 11194; tel. 780-9270683; e-mail main.branch@nbi.iq; internet www.nbi.com; f. 1995; 61.9% owned by Capital Bank of Jordan; Chair. BASSEM KHALIL AL-SALEM; CEO AYMAN OMRAN ABU DHAIM.

Sumer Commercial Bank: Uqba Bin Nafi Sq., Baghdad; tel. 772-7636399; e-mail care@sumerbank.iq; internet sumerbank.iq; Chair. ALI IBRAHIM. KATIE; Man. Dir FOUAD HAMZA AL-SAEED.

Specialized Banks

Agricultural Co-operative Bank of Iraq: POB 2421, al-Rashid St, Baghdad; tel. 5222071; internet www.agbank.gov.iq; f. 1936; state-owned; Chair. and Acting Gen. Man. RASHAD KHUDAIR WAHEED.

Dar el-Salaam Investment Bank: POB 3067, al-Saadoun Park 103/41/3, Alwiya, Baghdad; tel. (1) 719-6488; e-mail info@desiraq.com; f. 1999; 70.1% share owned by HSBC (UK); Chair. SARBEST BAYEZ ABAS; Man. Dir ZEYAD HASHIM ABAS.

Economy Bank for Investment and Finance (EBIF): 14 Ramadan St, al-Mansour Sq., Baghdad; tel. 770-4621125; fax (1) 298-7713; e-mail info@ebi-iq.com; internet www.ebi-iq.com; f. 1997; Chair. HAFEZ ABDUL ABBAS WALI AL-TAI.

Industrial Bank of Iraq: al-Sinak, al-Khalani Sq., Baghdad; tel. 783-0403040; e-mail info@indbk.gov.iq; internet www.indbk.gov.iq; f. 1940; state-owned; Chair. and Gen. Man. BILAL SABAH HUSSEIN.

Investment Bank of Iraq: POB 3724, 902/2/27 Hay al-Wahda, Alwiya, Baghdad; tel. (1) 719-9042; e-mail info@ibi-bankiraq.com;

internet www.ibi-bankiraq.com; f. 1993; Chair. HUSSEIN SALIH SHARIF; Gen. Man. MOHAMMED YAS.

Iraqi Islamic Bank for Investment and Development: POB 6003, 14 Ramadan St, al-Mansour, Baghdad; tel. (1) 542-9008; fax (1) 542-4042; e-mail webmaster@iraqiislamicb.iq; internet www.iraqiislamicb.iq; f. 1992; Chair. AHMAD W. AHMAD; Man. Dir HAMMAM THAMER KAZEM.

Iraqi Middle East Investment Bank: POB 10379, Bldg 65, Hay Babel, 929 Arasat al-Hindiya, Baghdad; tel. (1) 717-5545; internet imeib.iq; f. 1993; Chair. SAIF YOUSEF GHULAM; Man. Dir MAHASIN KHAIRY AHMED.

Kurdistan International Bank for Investment and Development: Gulan St, Irbil; tel. (66) 211-2000; e-mail admin@kib.iq; internet www.kib.iq; f. 2005; private bank; Man. Dir HAMAD SAAD HAMADNEH.

Mosul Bank for Development and Investment: POB 1292, Nidhal St, Mosul; tel. (80) 188-2200; e-mail customers_care@almosulbank.iq; internet www.almosulbank.iq; Man. Dir TAMKEEN ABDUL SARHAN AL-HANSNAWEI.

Real Estate Bank of Iraq: POB 8118, Jaffa St, al-Karada, Baghdad; tel. (773) 620-1530; e-mail estatebank194@yahoo.com; internet www.reb-iraq.com; f. 1949; state-owned; gives loans to assist the building industry; acquired the Co-operative Bank 1970; Dir-Gen. ABDUL MOHSEN ALWAN.

United Bank for Investment: 906/14/69, al-Wathiq Sq., Hay al-Wehda, Baghdad; tel. 781-1888944; e-mail hq2019@unitedbank.iq; internet unitedbank.iq; f. 1995; Chair. FADHEL JASSIM MUHAMMAD AL-DABBAS; Man. Dir MOHANAD QASIM ZGHAIR.

Trade Bank

Trade Bank of Iraq (TBI): POB 8186, 609/16/22 al-Mansour District, Baghdad; tel. (1) 543-3561; fax (1) 543-3560; e-mail info@tbiraq.com; internet tbi.com.iq; f. 2003 by fmr Coalition Provisional Authority to facilitate Iraq's exports of goods and services and the country's reconstruction; independent of Central Bank of Iraq; Chair. BILAL AL-HAMDANI (acting).

INSURANCE

Iraqi Insurance Diwan: Ministry of Finance, 147/6/47 Hay al-Eloom, Baghdad; tel. (1) 416-8030; internet insurancediwan.gov.iq; f. 2005 as independent regulator for the insurance sector.

Ahlia Insurance Co: Bldg 10/1, 52 St, Alley 80, District 904, Baghdad; tel. 7836351411; e-mail info@aic-iraq.com; internet aic-iraq.com; f. 2001; privately owned; general, marine, engineering, motor, health and life insurance; Chair. MUHAMMAD AHMED AL-HASSAN.

Al-Hamra'a Insurance Co: Bldg 27, Arasat al-Hindya, Baghdad; tel. (1) 717-7573; internet www.alhamraains.com; f. 2001; private co; general and life insurance; CEO Dr YASIR RAOOF.

Iraq Insurance Co: POB 989, Khaled bin al-Walid St, Aqaba bin Nafi Sq., Baghdad; tel. (1) 719-2185; fax (1) 719-2606; state-owned; life, fire, accident and marine insurance; proceedings for a merger with National Insurance Co were initiated in 2016.

Iraq Reinsurance Co: POB 297, Aqaba bin Nafi Sq., Khalid bin al-Waleed St, Baghdad; tel. (1) 719-5131; fax (1) 719-1497; e-mail iraqre@yahoo.com; f. 1960; state-owned; transacts reinsurance business on the international market; Chair. and Gen. Man. SAID ABBAS M. A. MIRZA.

National Insurance Co: POB 248, National Insurance Co Bldg, al-Khullani St, Baghdad; tel. (1) 885-3026; fax (1) 886-1486; f. 1950; state-owned; all types of general and life insurance, reinsurance and investment; proceedings for a merger with Iraq Insurance Co were initiated in 2016; Chair. and Gen. Man. MUHAMMAD HUSSAIN JAAFAR ABBAS.

STOCK EXCHANGE

Iraq Stock Exchange (ISX): POB 3607, Baghdad; tel. 783-4000034; e-mail info-isx@isx-iq.net; internet www.isx-iq.net; f. 2004, following the closure of the fmr Baghdad Stock Exchange by the Coalition Provisional Authority in March 2003; 103 cos listed in Jan. 2023; CEO TAHA AHMAD AL-RUBAYE.

Trade and Industry

DEVELOPMENT ORGANIZATION

National Investment Commission (NIC): Baghdad; e-mail info@investpromo.gov.iq; internet investpromo.gov.iq; seeks to attract inward private sector investment into Iraq and to stimulate domestic capital resources for growth and innovation, as well as promote Iraqi businesses; Chair. SUHA AL-NAJJAR.

CHAMBERS OF COMMERCE

Federation of Iraqi Chambers of Commerce: POB 3388, Saadoun St, Alwiya, Baghdad; tel. (1) 717-1798; fax (1) 719-2479; e-mail info@ficc.org.iq; internet www.ficc.org.iq; f. 1969; all 18 Iraqi chambers of commerce are affiliated to the Federation; Chair. ABD AL-RAZZAQ AL-ZUHAIRI.

Baghdad Chamber of Commerce: POB 5015, al-Sanal, Baghdad; tel. 771-8810607; e-mail info@bcc-iq.com; internet bcc-iq.net; f. 1926; Chair. FIRAS AL-HAMDANI.

Basra Chamber of Commerce: Manawi Pasha, Ashar, Basra; tel. (40) 614630; e-mail info@basrachamber.org; internet www.basrachamber.org; f. 1926; Chair. FALAH HAMEED SHABEB AL-BAIDHANI.

Erbil Chamber of Commerce and Industry: Chamber of Commerce and Industry Bldg, Gulan St, Irbil (Erbil); tel. (66) 2640103; e-mail erbilchamberofcommerce@yahoo.com; internet www.erbilchamber.org; f. 1966; Chair. DARA JALIL KHAYAT.

Kirkuk Chamber of Commerce: Kirkuk; tel. 780-0435899; e-mail kirkukofchamber@yahoo.com; internet kirkukchamber.org; f. 1957; Chair. SABAHUDDIN AL-SALIHI.

Mosul Chamber of Commerce: POB 35, Mosul; tel. 772-4140394; e-mail mcc19262017@yahoo.com; internet mcc1926.org; Chair. MUKBIL SIDIQ AL-DABAGH.

Sulaimaniya Chamber of Commerce and Industry: Salim St, Sulaimaniya; tel. 533-203293; e-mail info@sulcci.com; internet www.sulcci.com; Chair. SIRWAN MOHAMMED MAHMOUD.

EMPLOYERS' ORGANIZATION

Iraqi Federation of Industries: 191/22/915 al-Zaweya, Karada, Baghdad; tel. 790-191486; fax (1) 776-3041; e-mail fed_ind@yahoo.com; internet www.iraqifi.org; f. 1956; Chair. ADEL AKAB HUSSEIN.

PETROLEUM AND GAS

Ministry of Oil: Baghdad; tel. 728-477353; e-mail oilmc@oilgov.iq; internet www.oil.gov.iq; merged with INOC in 1987; affiliated cos: Oil Marketing Co, Oil Projects Co, Oil Exploration Co, Oil Products Distribution Co, Iraqi Oil Tankers Co, Gas Filling Co, Oil Pipelines Co, Iraqi Drilling Co, North Oil Co, South Oil Co, Missan Oil Co, North Refineries Co, Midland Refineries Co, South Refineries Co, North Gas Co, South Gas Co.

Basrah Gas Co: POB 2705, al-Ashar Post, Khor al-Zubair, Basrah; e-mail communications@basrahgas.com; internet www.basrahgas.com; jt venture of South Gas Co (51%), Royal Dutch Shell (44%) and Mitsubishi Co (5%); Man. Dir MALCOLM MAYES.

UTILITIES

Electricity

Electricity production in Iraq was greatly diminished as a result of the US-led military campaign in 2003, subsequent looting and sabotage by Baathist loyalists, and disruptions in fuel supplies to power stations. Power outages were common, especially in Baghdad and the surrounding area, and the Government resorted to power-rationing. With ongoing reconstruction of the means of generation, transmission and distribution, the Ministry of Electricity was achieving peak production levels of 6,750 MW by early 2009, supplying intermittent power for only 14 hours per day. According to a report by the Middle East Economic Survey (MEES), Iraq's peak electricity generation capacity stood at an estimated 18,500 MW at the end of 2019.

Water

The Ministry of Water Resources manages the supply of water throughout Iraq. Water resources are diminishing, and a large-scale investment programme is currently under way, which includes funding for new dam and irrigation projects, repairs to damaged facilities, and improvements in technology. Following years of neglect during the period of UN sanctions, infrastructure has also been damaged since the US-led military campaign in 2003, largely as a result of vandalism and looting. The Baghdad Water Authority is responsible for the management of water resources in the capital.

MAJOR COMPANIES

Agmest Group: POB 2489, Karrada Kharij, Hay Babil, Jodriah, Baghdad; tel. (1) 719-8822; fax (1) 717-3136; e-mail office2@agmest.com; internet www.agmest.com; f. 1989; nine cos; telecommunications, general trading, construction, engineering, pharmaceutical supplies.

Alousi Associates Technical Studies Bureau: Hasib Saleh Bldg, Nidhal St, Baghdad; tel. (1) 719-2833; e-mail faisal@alousi-associates.com; internet www.alousi-associates.com; f. 1974; architectural design and planning; offices in Cyprus and Singapore.

American-Iraqi Solutions Group: Sector 317, Rd 4, House 21, Al Baradiah, Basra; e-mail info@aisginc.com; internet www.aisginc.com; 11 cos involved in reconstruction projects, incl. real estate, construction, security, travel, recruitment and investment; Chair. CARTER ANDRESS; CEO CHRISTOPHER (KIFFER) ANDRESS.

Baghdad Factory for Furniture: TAJI Rd, near TAJI Electricity Stn, Baghdad; f. 1996; under supervision of Ministry of Industry and Minerals.

Al-Baqier Co: Saadon St, Naser Sq., Baghdad; tel. 7702586606; e-mail albakierco@gmail.com; internet albaqier.net; f. 2005; construction, electrical and mechanical contracting, general trading; Man. Dir MOHAMMED AL-TURKI.

Basrah East Co Ltd: POB 2141, Basra; tel. (40) 640-691; fax (40) 623-919; e-mail info@basraheast.com; internet www.basraheast.com; civil, electrical and mechanical engineering, construction of oil and gas pipelines, water treatment, industrial equipment trading.

Al-Burhan Group: al-Burhan St, Baghdad; tel. 77252280; e-mail enquiries@alburhangroup.com; internet www.alburhangroup.com; offices in London (UK), Amman (Jordan) and Dubai (UAE); construction, flour milling, railways, automobile manufacturing; Chair. and Man. Dir IMAD AL-BURHAN.

Danube Group: Bldg 13, St 2, Karrada 929, Baghdad; tel. 7901920484; fax (6) 5686520; e-mail info@danubegroup.com; internet www.danubegroup.com; f. 1989; engineering, contracting, mine clearance, general trading.

Darin Group: Darin Bldg Brayati, 40m St, Arbil; tel. (750) 7654321; e-mail info@daringroup.com; internet www.daringroup.com; f. 1998; construction, manufacture of building materials, telecommunications; Chair. MALASHENE BASHIR; over 8,000 employees (2022).

Diala State Co for Electrical Industries: Baquba, Diala; tel. (770) 7520059; e-mail info@dialacompany.com; internet www.dialacompany.com; f. 1974; mfrs of electrical transformers, ceiling fans, optical fibre cables and steam irons; produces oxygen and argon gases; Dir-Gen. ABDUL SATTAR MIKHLIF.

Diamond Group: Bldg 16, Baghdad University Main St, al-Jadriya, Baghdad; tel. 7901309294; e-mail service.desk@diamond-grp.com; internet www.diamond-grp.com; 11 cos in a range of fields, incl. construction, port equipment, security, flight catering, oil and gas equipment supplies, medical and pharmaceutical supplies; offices in Jordan and the UAE.

Dijla Group: Dijla Group Complex, Tunis St, Nasser Sq., Baghdad; tel. 7700434491; fax (1) 719-9380; e-mail dijlaco@nol.com.jo; internet www.dijlagroup.com; offices in Jordan, Lebanon and Dubai (UAE); f. 1978; 14 cos; construction, real estate, import and export; Branch Man. MUEED ABD AL-WAHED.

Dnana Group: Salam Faik St, Baghdad; tel. (1) 719-8993; e-mail info@dnana-co.com; internet www.dnana-co.com; oil services, construction, tourism, general trading, transport, food manufacturing; Man. Dir KARIM HASSAN DNANA.

Eng. Sabah al-Shammery and Partners Group (SAPCO): POB 50300, 69/1/21, al-Mansour al-Maneerat St, Baghdad; tel. (1) 541-2787; fax (1) 541-8155; internet www.shammery.com; 16 cos; engineering, construction, general trading, transport, computer and oil services; Chair. SABAH AL-SHAMMARI.

Al-Fadha'a Co Ltd: Bldg 18/1, St 43, 627, Hay al-Jamea, Baghdad; tel. (1) 556-4394; f. 2000; general trading, construction, water and waste water services.

General Co for Food Products: POB 2379, Baghdad; tel. (1) 718-2076; fax (1) 718-2356; internet www.vegoil-iraq.com; f. 2016 by the merger of General Cos for Vegetable Oils, Dairy Industries, Sugar Industry, and Tobacco and Cigarettes; state-owned.

Al-Ghalib Co Ltd: Bldg 21, St 12, Sector 601, al-Ameerat St, al-Mansour, Baghdad; tel. (1) 542-3163; fax (1) 541-0890; e-mail info@alghalib.org; internet www.alghalib.com; contractors and manufacturers.

Al-Ghodwa Group: Bldg 81, St 19, District 929, Arasat al-Hindiya, Karrad, Baghdad; tel. 7901918356; e-mail info@alghodwagroup.com; internet www.alghodwagroup.com; f. 1997; general trading and contracting, importer of construction, oil and gas equipment; CEO SABAH I. GHAIDAN; Man. Dir KHALID S. ISSA.

Al-Haitham Group: Al Jazair St, Basra; tel. 7801390025; e-mail info@alhaithamgroup.com; internet www.alhaithamgroup.com; f. 1985; oil and gas pipelines, general construction, water pipelines.

Hakkak Investment Group: al-Warqaa Trading Compound, Bldg 94, St 18, 929, al-Sharqiya, al-Karrada, Baghdad; tel. (1) 719-3220; fax (1) 718-6539; e-mail info@hakkak.com; internet www.hakkakgroup.com; general trading, construction, telecommunications, transport; Chair. MAHDI KAREEM SALIH AL-HAKKAK.

Ibn Majid State Co for Heavy Engineering and Marine Industries: Basra; e-mail info@ibnmajid.gov.iq; internet www.ibnmajid.gov.iq; f. 1990.

Iraq Projects Co Ltd (IPCO): Istiqlal St, Khora Bridge, Asharr, Basra; tel. 7901906889; internet www.ipco.net; construction and engineering services within the fields of communications, infrastructure, oil and gas and transport.

Iraqi Cement State Co: POB 2050, Jadriya, Baghdad; tel. (1) 773-6071; fax (1) 773-3625; e-mail iraqicement@icsc.gov.iq; internet icsc.gov.iq; f. 1936; Gen. Man. Eng. HUSSEIN MOHSEN AL-KHAFAJI.

Al-Mahara Co Ltd: Muhammad Asker Bldg, Quarter 123, St 53, Sheikh Omar, Bab al-Sheikh, Baghdad; e-mail info@almaharaco.com; internet almaharaco.com; f. 1971 as The Productive Industrial Factory; reorg. and renamed as above 1984; mfrs of metal equipment, incl. automobile parts, knives, moulds and machinery.

Al-Maysoon Trading Agencies Ltd: Bldg 16, St 90, Mahala 615, al-Mansour, Baghdad; tel. 7825396068; e-mail info@al-maysoon.com; internet www.al-maysoon.com; medical equipment suppliers.

Al-Merjal General Contracting Co (MERGCC): al-Rasikh Bldg, al-Mansour, Baghdad; tel. 7703967662; e-mail r.abbo@almerjal.com; internet www.almerjal.com; f. 1991; power plant construction.

Muhandis Inbehar Group (MIG): Nidhal St, al-Saadoun Park, 103/34/11, Baghdad; tel. (1) 717-7776; fax (1) 719-3313; internet www.migcompanies.com; f. 2003; construction; consortium of 15 cos; Owners KHALID ALI AHMAD, WATHIQ ABD AL-JABBAR; 368 employees.

Nabeel Contracting Bureau: 2nd Floor, al-Saher Bldg, 14 Ramadan St, al-Mansour, Baghdad; tel. and fax (1) 543-8522; internet www.nabeelcb.com; engineering and construction of power plants, water treatment systems and gas turbine units; Technical Man. NABEEL KHALAF.

Naseem Al-Aftan Group: al-Wathiq Sq., Baghdad; tel. 7827437510; e-mail trade@naseemaftan.com; internet www.naseemaftan.com; 12 cos; engineering, construction, medical supplies, transport, general trading.

Al-Noaman Co: internet www.alnoamanco-iraq.com; f. 1985; state-owned; mfrs of plastics, especially for irrigation systems.

Northern Cement State Co: POB 13, Mosul; tel. (60) 780280; fax (60) 65440; e-mail cement_planning@yahoo.com; internet www.ncsc-iraq.com.

Pioneer Engineering Contracting Co (PCC): Wahda District, Baghdad; tel. 7901914620; fax (1) 555-3488; e-mail pcc@pcciraq.org; internet www.pcciraq.org/index.php; general construction, power stations, water treatment.

Pioneers Pharma: Shoresh Rd, Qirga, Sulaimaniya; tel. (53) 33265881; e-mail info@pioneerpharma.org; internet www.pioneerpharma.org; medical and pharmaceutical supplies.

Al-Qabas Group: Bldg No. 26, M. 609, 14 Ramadan St, al-Mansour, Baghdad; tel. 7901906291; fax (1) 541-2779; e-mail info@alqabasgroup.com; internet www.alqabasgroup.com; f. 1961; five cos; contracting, engineering, power and electricity services, general trading.

Al-Qarya Group: al-Mansour, Dawodi, Baghdad; tel. (1) 542-3886; e-mail imad@alqaryagroup.com; internet www.alqaryagroup.com; f. 2001; construction, trading, information technology and telecommunications; Chair. IMAD MAKKI.

Al-Qudrah Alfania Co: Bldg 17, St 57, Bab al-Sheikh, Baghdad; tel. (1) 817-4827; internet www.alqudraco.com; mechanical and civil engineering, construction, water treatment.

Al-Rahmani Group: Harthiya, Hay al-Kindy, Baghdad; tel. 7901907253; e-mail baghdad@alrahmanigroup.com; internet www.alrahmanigroup.com; f. 1921; offices in Jordan and Dubai (UAE); transport, construction, import and export, oil and gas services, logistics.

Rowad Baghdad Construction Ltd: Zayouna, Baghdad; tel. 7901343190; e-mail info@rowadbaghdad.com; internet www.rowadbaghdad.com; f. 1985; civil and construction works.

Al-Sadda Group: tel. (780) 100-2279; fax (780) 100-2872; internet www.alsaddaco.com; construction, electrical and communications projects, general trading; seven cos.

Saham Babil Co: 1st Floor, al-Fateh Bldg, al-Andalous Sq., al-Nidhal St, Baghdad; tel. (1) 717-5309; fax (1) 719-4173; internet www.sahambabil.com; f. 1996; construction, general trading.

Salihi Group International (SGI): Villa 301/19, Alwazyria St, Alwazyria, Baghdad; tel. 7481107600; e-mail info@salihi.net; internet www.salihi.biz; f. 2003; construction; Chair. and CEO ABD AL-RAHMAN AUBEED.

Al-Salman Group: Baghdad; tel. 763665014; e-mail info@aalsalman-group.com; internet www.aalsalman-group.com; f. 1925; general trading, construction, real estate, marine, petroleum, media and security services; Chair. FARIS AL-SALMAN.

Al-Sameem Co: Baghdad; tel. (1) 817-7547; fax (1) 816-6216; internet www.alsameem.com; f. 1990; construction, import and export; office in Jordan.

Al-Sawari State Co for Chemical Industries: POB 337, Baghdad; tel. 7901281699; e-mail alsawwar1@yahoo.com; internet www.alsawwary-iraq.com; f. 1994; Dir-Gen. RAISAN SADDAM HASSAN; 961 employees.

Southern Cement State Co: POB 9, Kufa; tel. 7801036003; e-mail info@southern-cement.com; internet www.southern-cement.com; f. 1996; Dir-Gen. SINAN AL-SAIDI.

State Battery Manufacturing Co: POB 190, al-Waziriya, Baghdad; e-mail sbmc@sbmc.industry.gov.iq; internet www.sbmc.industry.gov.iq; f. 1987; Dir-Gen. Eng. SALAM SAEED AHMED; 1,929 employees.

State Co for Automotive Industry (SCAI): POB 138, Iskandariya-Babylon; internet www.scai.industry.gov.iq; f. 1976; specializes in assembling buses, trucks and semi-trailers; Man. Dir Eng. MAZHAR SADIQ SABA AL-TAMIMI.

State Co for Construction Industries: 931/27/2 Hay Babel, Baghdad; tel. 7901374431; f. 1987 by merger of state orgs for gypsum, asbestos, and the plastic and concrete industries; Dir ALI SALIM OMAR; 3,123 employees.

State Co for Cotton Industries: Khadimiya, Baghdad; internet www.cottonindiraq.com; f. 1964; 6,720 employees.

State Co for Dairy Industries: POB 21072, Abu Ghraib, Baghdad; tel. (1) 511-0923; fax (1) 511-0154; f. 1956; 1,251 employees.

State Co for Drinks and Mineral Water: POB 5689, Sara Khatoon Camp, Baghdad; POB 2108, al-Za'afaraniya, Baghdad; f. 1987 by merger of enterprises responsible for soft and alcoholic drinks.

State Co for Import and Export: POB 5642-5670, al-Nidal St, Baghdad; tel. (1) 719-0397; fax (1) 719-8732; f. 1987 to replace the five state orgs responsible to the Ministry of Trade for productive commodities, consumer commodities, grain and food products, exports and imports; Gen. Dir FOUZI H. AL-DHAHIR.

State Co for Leather Industries: Karrada Kharij, Baghdad; tel. (1) 778-5081; fax (1) 778-3828; f. 1976 by merger of State Co for Leather and Bata Co.

State Co for Petrochemical Industries (SCPI): POB 933, Khor al-Zubair, Basra; tel. 7727048765; e-mail scpipc1khor@yahoo.com; internet pchemiq.com; f. 1977; Dir-Gen. AQEEL A. ABD ALI.

State Co for Steel Industries: Baghdad; tel. 7809161812; e-mail info@scosi-mim.com; internet scosi-mim.com; f. 2016 by merger of Nasser State Co for Mechanical Industries and Al-Sumood Co for Steel Industries; Man. Dir Eng. MOHAMMED FAEQ JUMAA.

State Co for the Sugar Industry: POB 42, Gizlani St, Mosul; internet www.statesugarcompany.com; f. 1987 by merger of sugar enterprises in Mosul and Sulaimaniya; Dir-Gen. AKEEL MUHAMMAD NOORI.

State Co for Textile Industries: POB 2, Hilla, nr Najaf; tel. (30) 243-200; fax (30) 242-627; internet www.nasseg-hilla.com; f. 1967.

State Co for Tire Industry: Najaf; tel. and fax (30) 333-239; e-mail scrit.iq@gmail.com; internet www.scti-iraq.com; f. 1997.

State Co for Tobacco and Cigarettes: POB 10026, al-Habibiya, Baghdad; 2,246 employees.

State Co for Woollen Industries: POB 9114, Khadhumiya, Baghdad.

State Cos for Fertilizer (Northern and Southern Regions): POB 74, Khor al-Zubair Factories, Basra; e-mail scf@scf.gov.iq; internet www.scf.gov.iq; f. 1975; Dir-Gen. FAWZI ABBAS ALI.

Sweer Co Contracting: Jumhuriya St, Baghdad; tel. 7822752574; e-mail info@sweerco.com; internet www.sweerco.com; mechanical and electrical contracting.

T. al-Shayei and Partner Co: 203/22, al-Rashid St, al-Sanak, Baghdad; tel. 7507395811; fax (1) 886-4550; e-mail info@al-shayei.com; internet www.al-shayei.com; f. 1989; oil and chemical industry supplies, construction; Man. Dir TARIQ AL-SHAYEI.

Taha and Partners Group: Taha Group Bldg, Jaderiyah, Baghdad; tel. 907-500; e-mail info@taha-partners.com; internet www.taha-partners.com; five cos; construction and printing; Chair. WALID K. ISSA TAHA.

Technical United Oilfields Services and Supplies Co Ltd (TUOSSCO): al-Mansour, Baghdad; tel. (1) 541-1424; fax (1) 541-5498; internet tuoss-co.com; f. 1992; suppliers of oil equipment and machinery; offices in Jordan and the UAE.

That Al-Sawary State Co for Chemical Industries: POB 337, Baghdad; tel. (1) 543-3701; e-mail alsawwary1@yahoo.com; internet www.alsawwary-iraq.com; f. 1994.

Uruk Group: POB 828, 4 St, Mahalla 228, Karradat Maryam, Baghdad; tel. (1) 190-9202; e-mail info@urukgroup.com; internet www.urukgroup.com; f. 2003; construction, engineering and management; CEO and Gen. Man. JAFAR D. JAFAR.

Al-Wakeel International Co: al-Jeesr St, al-Samawah; tel. 7801013252; internet www.alwakeelint.com; f. 2004; fmrly Al-Hadi Engineering Co; construction, contracting, civil and mechanical engineering, power supply; Dir AMAD AZIZ.

Al-Yaqut Group: Bldg 36, St 16, al-Yarmouk, 612, Baghdad; tel. 7901909737; e-mail info@alyaqutgroup.com; internet alyaqutgroup.com; f. 1988; import and export, construction consultancy, engineering.

ZamZam Group: POB 19184, Zayounah Post Office, Baghdad; tel. 7901908175; e-mail info@zamzam-group.com; internet www.zamzam-group.com; f. 1972; construction, engineering, hotels, general trading.

Zurafa Co: POB 6086, 39/6/605, al-Mansour, Baghdad; tel. 5430196; e-mail info@zurafacompany.com; internet www.zurafacompany.com; f. 2009; construction, general trading, consultancy; Man. Dir Dr RAID K. AL-SAIDI.

TRADE UNIONS

General Federation of Trade Unions in Iraq: Baghdad; e-mail tradeunions.iq@gmail.com; Pres. SATAR DANBOUS BARAK.

Iraqi Teachers' Union (ITU): al-Mansour, Baghdad; e-mail nakaba.center.2018@gmail.com; internet fb.com/iraqi.teachers.union; f. 2003; Pres. ABBAS AL-SUDANI.

There are also unions of doctors, pharmacologists, jurists, writers, journalists, artists, engineers, electricity and railway workers.

Transport

RAILWAYS

The main railway line covers the length of the country, from Rabia, on the Syrian border, via Mosul, to Baghdad (534 km), and from Baghdad to Basra and Umm Qasr (608 km), on the Persian (Arabian) Gulf. There are also a number of branch lines, including one that runs westwards from Baghdad, connecting the capital with the cities of Al-Qa'im and Husayba, and another that runs east–west, connecting Haqlaniya with Kirkuk via Bayji. In December 2021 the Government announced plans for the construction of a 1,220-km, double-track railway line connecting the Grand Port of Al-Faw (the first stage of which had recently been completed) in southern Iraq with the port of Mersin in Türkiye (Turkey). Construction of a 31-km elevated light-rail system in Baghdad was expected to commence in 2023. In September of that year construction work began of a 32-km railway line to link Basra with the Iranian border city of Shalamjah; when completed, this line will be the first cross-border rail connection between the two countries.

General Co for Railways: Ministry of Transportation, nr Martyr's Monument, Karradat Dakhil, Baghdad; e-mail iraqitransport@yahoo.com; internet www.scr.gov.iq; Dir JAWAD AL-HUSSEINI.

Iraqi Republic Railways Co (IRRC): West Station, Baghdad; tel. (1) 537-0011; internet www.iraqrailways.com; f. 1914; Dir-Gen. RAFIL YUSSEF ABBAS.

ROADS

Iraqi Land Transport Co: Baghdad; e-mail info@sclt.gov.iq; internet sclt.gov.iq; f. 1988 to replace State Org. for Land Transport; fleet of more than 1,000 large trucks; Dir-Gen. ABBAS OMRAN MUSA.

State Organization for Roads and Bridges: POB 917, Karradat Mariam, Karkh, Baghdad; tel. (1) 32141; responsible for road and bridge construction projects under the Ministry of Construction and Housing.

SHIPPING

In December 2020 it was reported that the Government had agreed the terms of a contract with a South Korean company to build a new deep-water port at Al-Faw in Basra governorate. It was anticipated that the new facility would, upon completion (at an estimated cost of $7,000m.), replace Umm Qasr as Iraq's main commercial port and—with the planned building of nearly 100 berths by 2032—be the largest port in the Middle East. The Grand Port of Al-Faw project included the planned construction of a 2.5-km underwater road tunnel (passing under the Khor al-Zubair navigational channel), linking the new port with Iraq's highway network. The first phase of the project was completed in September 2021 and the tunnel was expected to be finished by 2025.

General Co of Iraqi Ports (GCPA): Malik bin Dinar St, Basra; tel. 781-0535742; e-mail info@scp.gov.iq; internet scp.gov.iq; f. 1919; owned by the Ministry of Transportation; Dir-Gen. Dr Eng. FARHAN MUHESEN AL-FARTOSI.

General Co for Maritime Transport: POB 13038, al-Jadriya al-Hurriya Ave, Baghdad; Basra office: POB 766, 14 July St, Basra; tel. (1) 776-3201; internet scmt.gov.iq; f. 1952 as State Enterprise for Maritime Transport; renamed as above 2009; Dir-Gen. ABDUL KARIM KANHAL AL-JABRI.

State Enterprise for Iraqi Water Transport: POB 23016, Airport St, al-Furat Quarter, Baghdad; f. 1987, when State Org. for Iraqi Water Transport was abolished; responsible for the planning, supervision and control of six nat. water transportation enterprises, incl. General Co for Maritime Transport.

CIVIL AVIATION

There are international airports at Irbil, Baghdad, Basra, Mosul, Najaf and Sulaimaniya.

Iraq Civil Aviation Authority (ICAA): Baghdad; tel. 790-5319779; fax (1) 543-0689; e-mail info@iraqcaa.com; internet www.iraqcaa.com; f. 1987; Dir-Gen. NAEL SAAD ABDUL HADI.

Iraqi Airways Co: Baghdad International Airport, Baghdad; tel. 781-1000036; e-mail contactus@ia.com.iq; internet www.iraqiairways.com.iq; f. 1945; operates flights to other Arab countries, Iran, Türkiye (Turkey), Greece and Sweden; Dir-Gen. ABBAS MUSA.

Tourism

Iraq Tourism Board: POB 7783, Haifa St, Baghdad; tel. (1) 543-3912; Chair. HAMOUD MOHSEN AL-YACOUBI.

Defence

As assessed at November 2022, Iraq's armed forces totalled an estimated 193,000: army 180,000; navy 3,000; air force 5,000; air defence 5,000. There were also paramilitary forces numbering c. 266,000, including 36,000 members of the Iraqi Federal police, 50,000 members of the Border Enforcement forces and 180,000 members of various militia or 'popular mobilization forces'.

Defence and Security Budget: ID 12,600,000m. in 2022.

Chief of the General Staff of the Armed Forces: Lt-Gen. ABDUL AMIR YARALLAH.

Commander of the Ground Forces: Maj.-Gen. QASSIM AL-MUHAMMADI.

Commander of the Air Force: Maj.-Gen. SHIHAB JAHID ALI SHAKARCHI.

Commander of the Navy: Rear Adm. MAZEN ABDUL WAHED GHABIAN.

Education

During the mid-1970s free education was established at all stages from pre-primary to higher. Primary education, beginning at six years of age, is compulsory and lasts for six years. According to UNESCO estimates, in 2006/07 enrolment at primary schools included 88% of pupils in the relevant age-group. Secondary education, from 12 years of age and lasting for up to six years, is divided into two cycles of three years each. Enrolment at secondary schools in 2006/07 included some 43% of children in the appropriate age-group, according to UNESCO. Following the change of regime in Iraq in April 2003, a comprehensive reform of the country's education system was implemented. According to UNESCO, spending on education constituted 14.0% of total government expenditure in 2016.

Bibliography

General and Historical Context

Abdul-Jabar, Faleh. (Ed.). *Ayatollahs, Sufis and Ideologues: State, Religion and Social Movements in Iraq*. London, Saqi Books, 2006.

The Shi'ite Movement in Iraq. London, Saqi Books, 2006.

Allawi, Ali A. *Faisal I of Iraq*. New Haven, CT, Yale University Press, 2014.

Bashkin, Orit. *New Babylonians: A History of Jews in Modern Iraq*. Rosewood City, CA, Stanford University Press, 2012.

Bengio, Ofra. *The Kurds of Iraq: Building a State Within a State*. Boulder, CO, Lynne Rienner Publishers, 2012.

Çetinsaya, Gökhan. *Ottoman Administration of Iraq, 1890–1908*. Abingdon, Routledge, 2006.

Danilovich, Alex. *Iraqi Federalism and the Kurds: Learning to Live Together*. Farnham, Ashgate, 2014.

Franzén, Johan. *Red Star over Iraq: Iraqi Communism Before Saddam*. New York, Columbia University Press, 2012.

Helfont, Samuel. *Compulsion in Religion: Saddam Hussein, Islam, and the Roots of Insurgencies in Iraq*. Oxford, Oxford University Press, 2021.

Ihsan, Muhammad. *Nation Building in Kurdistan: Memory, Genocide and Human Rights*. Abingdon, Routledge, 2017.

Khoury, Dina Rizk. *Iraq in Wartime: Soldiering, Martyrdom, and Remembrance*. New York, Cambridge University Press, 2013.

Korn, David A. *Human Rights in Iraq*. New Haven, CT, Yale University Press, 1990.

Lloyd, Seton. *Iraq*. Oxford Pamphlet in Indian Affairs, No. 13. Bombay, 1943.

Twin Rivers: A Brief History of Iraq from the Earliest Times to the Present Day. Oxford, 1943.

Foundations in the Dust. Oxford, 1949.

Longrigg, S. H. *Four Centuries of Modern Iraq*. Oxford, 1925.

Lukitz, Liora. *A Quest in the Middle East: Gertrude Bell and the Making of Modern Iraq*. London, I. B. Tauris, 2013.

Mahdi, Kamil. A. *Oil and Oil Policy in Iraq: Past and Present*. Ann Arbor, MI, University of Michigan Press, 2007.

Al-Marashi, Ibrahim, and Salama, Sammy. *Iraq's Armed Forces: An Analytical History*. Abingdon, Routledge, 2009.

McNabb, David E. *Oil and the Creation of Iraq: Policy Failures and the 1914-1918 War in Mesopotamia*. Abingdon, Routledge, 2016.

Al-Musawi, Muhsin J. *Reading Iraq: Culture and Power in Conflict*. London, I. B. Tauris, 2006.

Niblock, Tim. *Iraq: The Contemporary State*. Abingdon, Routledge, 2022.

Polk, William R. *Understanding Iraq: The Whole Sweep of Iraqi History from Genghis Khan's Mongols to the Ottoman Turks to the British Mandate to the American Occupation*. New York, HarperCollins, 2005.

Rutledge, Ian. *Enemy on the Euphrates: The British Occupation of Iraq and the Great Arab Revolt, 1914-1921*. London, Saqi Books, 2014.

Seierstad, Åsne. *A Hundred and One Days: A Baghdad Journal*. London, Virago, 2004.

Spät, Eszter. *The Yezidis*. London, Saqi Books, 2006.

Stansfield, Gareth. *Iraqi Kurdistan: Political Development and Emergent Democracy*. London, Routledge, 2003.

Stevenson, Wendell. *The Weight of a Mustard Seed*. London, Atlantic Books, 2009.

Stewart, Desmond, and Haylock, John. *New Babylon: A Portrait of Iraq*. London, Collins, 1956.

Voller, Yaniv. *The Kurdish Liberation Movement in Iraq: From Insurgency to Statehood*. Abingdon, Routledge, 2014.

Wien, Peter. *Iraqi Arab Nationalism: Authoritarian, Totalitarian and Pro-Fascist Inclinations, 1932–1941*. Abingdon, Routledge, 2006.

Contemporary Political History

Ali, Hawraman. *The Iraqi Kurds and the Cold War: Regional Politics, 1958–1975*. London, Routledge, 2020.

Alkifaey, Hamid. *The Failure of Democracy in Iraq: Religion, Ideology and Sectarianism*. London, Routledge, 2019.

Allawi, Ali A. *The Occupation of Iraq: Winning the War, Losing the Peace*. New Haven, CT, Yale University Press, 2007.

Anderson, Liam, and Stansfield, Gareth. *The Future of Iraq: Dictatorship, Democracy or Division?* New York, Palgrave Macmillan, 2004.

Crisis in Kirkuk: The Ethnopolitics of Conflict and Compromise. Philadelphia, PA, University of Pennsylvania Press, 2009.

Arburish, Said. *Saddam Hussein: The Politics of Revenge*. London, Bloomsbury, 2000.

Arnove, Anthony (Ed.). *Iraq Under Siege: The Deadly Impact of Sanctions and War*. London, Pluto Press, 2000.

Ashton, Nigel, and Gibson, Bryan (Eds). *The Iran-Iraq War: New International Perspectives*. Abingdon, Routledge, 2012.

Axelgard, Frederick W. *Iraq in Transition: A Political, Economic, and Strategic Perspective*. New York. Routledge, 2019.

Barakat, Sultan. *Reconstructing Post-Saddam Iraq*. Abingdon, Routledge, 2006.

Baram, Amatzia. *Culture, History and Ideology in the Formation of Baathist Iraq, 1968–89*. Basingstoke, Macmillan, 1991.

Saddam Husayn and Islam, 1968–2003: Ba'thi Iraq from Secularism to Faith. Washington, DC, Woodrow Wilson Center Press, 2014.

Baram, Amatzia, Rohde, Achim, and Zeidel, Ronen. *Iraq between Occupations: Perspectives from 1920 to the Present*. Basingstoke, Palgrave Macmillan, 2010.

Batatu, Hanna. *The Old Social Classes and the Revolutionary Movements of Iraq*. Princeton, NJ, Princeton University Press, 1978.

Bengio, Ofra. *Saddam's World: Political Discourse in Iraq*. Oxford, Oxford University Press, 1998.

Bennis, Phyllis, and Moushabeck, Michael (Eds). *Beyond the Storm: A Gulf Crisis Reader*. Edinburgh, Canongate Press, 1992.

Brigham, Robert K. *The United States and Iraq since 1990: A Brief History with Documents*. Oxford, Wiley-Blackwell, 2014.

Butler, Richard. *Saddam Defiant: The Threat of Weapons of Mass Destruction, and the Growing Crisis of Global Security*. London, Weidenfeld & Nicolson, 2000.

Chandrasekaran, Rajiv. *Imperial Life in the Emerald City: Inside Baghdad's Green Zone*. London, Bloomsbury, 2007.

Chubin, Shahram, and Tripp, Charles. *Iran and Iraq at War*. London, I. B. Tauris, 1988.

Cockburn, Patrick. *The Occupation: War and Resistance in Iraq*. London, Verso, 2006.

Muqtada: Muqtada Al-Sadr, the Shia Revival, and the Struggle for Iraq. New York, Scribner Book Company, 2008.

The Rise of Islamic State: ISIS and the New Sunni Revolution. London, Verso, 2015.

Danchev, Alex, and Macmillan, John (Eds). *The Iraq War and Democratic Politics*. London, Routledge, 2004.

Danilovich, Alex. *Iraqi Kurdistan in Middle Eastern Politics*. Abingdon, Routledge, 2016.

Federalism, Secession and International Recognition Regime: Iraqi Kurdistan. Abingdon, Routledge, 2019.

Dann, Uriel. *Iraq under Qassem: A Political History 1958–63*. New York, Praeger, 1969.

Dawisha, A. I. *Iraq: A Political History*. Princeton, NJ, Princeton University Press, 2013.

DeFronzo, James. *The Iraq War: Origins and Consequences*. Boulder, CO, Westview Press, 2009.

Denselow, James. *Iraq and Syria: Diplomacy and Geopolitics since the Fall of Saddam*. London, I. B. Tauris, 2012.

Dodge, Toby. *Inventing Iraq: The Failure of Nation Building and a History Denied*. London, C. Hurst & Co, 2003.

Iraq's Future: The Aftermath of Regime Change. Abingdon, Routledge, 2006.

Iraq: From War to a New Authoritarianism. London, International Institute for Strategic Studies, 2012.

Donovan, Jerome. *The Iran-Iraq War: Antecedents and Conflict Escalation*. Abingdon, Routledge, 2014.

Dougherty, Beth. *Historical Dictionary of Iraq*. Lanham, MD, The Scarecrow Press, 2nd edn, 2013.

Farouk-Sluglett, Marion, and Sluglett, Peter. *Iraq since 1958: From Revolution to Dictatorship*. London, I. B. Tauris, revised edn, 2001.

Fawn, Rick, and Hinnebusch, Raymond. *The Iraq War: Causes and Consequences*. Boulder, CO, Lynne Rienner Publishers, 2006.

Franzén, Johan. *Pride and Power: A History of Modern Iraq*. London, Hurst & Co, 2020.

Greenstock, Jeremy. *Iraq: the Cost of War*. London, William Heinemann, 2016.

Gunter, Frank R. *The Political Economy of Iraq: Restoring Balance in a Post-Conflict Society*. Cheltenham, Edward Elgar, 2014.

Gunter, Michael. *The Kurds Ascending: The Evolving Solution to the Kurdish Problem in Iraq and Turkey*. Basingstoke, Palgrave Macmillan, 2nd edn, 2011.

Haddad, Fanar. *Sectarianism in Iraq: Antagonistic Visions of Unity*. London, C. Hurst & Co, 2011.

Hahn, Peter L. *Missions Accomplished? The United States and Iraq since World War I*. Oxford, Oxford University Press, 2012.

Hallenberg, Jan, and Karlsson, Håkan (Eds). *The Iraq War: European Perspectives on Politics, Strategy and Operations*. Abingdon, Routledge, 2006.

Hamoudi, Haider Ala. *Negotiating in Civil Conflict: Constitutional Construction and Imperfect Bargaining in Iraq*. Chicago, IL, The University of Chicago Press, 2014.

Harrer, Gudrun. *Dismantling the Iraqi Nuclear Programme: The Inspections of the International Atomic Energy Agency, 1991–1998*. Abingdon, Routledge, 2014.

Hashim, Ahmed S. *Iraq's Sunni Insurgency*. Abingdon, Routledge, 2009.

Heikal, Mohammed. *Illusions of Triumph: An Arab View of the Gulf War*. London, HarperCollins, 1992.

Helfont, Samuel. *Iraq against the World: Saddam, America, and the Post-Cold War Order*. New York, Oxford University Press, 2023.

Hiro, Dilip. *The Longest War: The Iran–Iraq Military Conflict*. London, Grafton, 1989.

Desert Shield to Desert Storm: The Second Gulf War. London, Routledge, 1992.

Secrets and Lies: Operation Iraqi Freedom and the Collapse of American Power in the Middle East. New York, Nation Books, 2005.

Secrets and Lies: The Planning, Conduct and Aftermath of Blair and Bush's War. London, Politico's Publishing, 2005.

Hussein, Saddam. *Social and Foreign Affairs in Iraq (Routledge Revivals)*. Abingdon, Routledge, 2009. (First published 1979.)

Isakhan, Benjamin. *The Legacy of Iraq: From the 2003 War to the 'Islamic State'*. Edinburgh, Edinburgh University Press, 2015.

Democracy in Iraq: History, Politics, Discourse. Farnham, Ashgate, 2012.

Israeli, Raphael. *Global Institutions: The Internationalization of ISIS: The Muslim State in Iraq and Syria*. Abingdon, Routledge, 2016.

Karsh, Efraim. *The Iran–Iraq War: 1980–1988 (Essential Histories)*. Oxford, Osprey, 2002.

Karsh, Efraim, and Ravtsi, Inari. *Saddam Hussein: A Political Biography*. London, Brasseys, 1992.

Khadduri, Majid. *Independent Iraq 1932–58, A Study of Iraqi Politics*. Oxford, Oxford University Press, 2nd edn, 1960.

Republican Iraq: A Study in Iraqi Politics since the Revolution of 1958. Oxford, Oxford University Press, 1970.

Socialist Iraq: A Study in Iraqi Politics since 1968. Washington, DC, The Middle East Institute, 1978.

Kiely, Patrick, and Ryan, David. *America and Iraq: Policy-making, Intervention and Regional Politics*. Abingdon, Routledge, 2008.

Kienle, Eberhard. *Ba'th versus Ba'th: The Conflict between Iraq and Syria*. London, I. B. Tauris, 1990.

Kinsey, Christopher. *Private Contractors and the Reconstruction of Iraq: Transforming Military Logistics*. Abingdon, Routledge, 2009.

Iraq 1900–1950: A Political, Social and Economic History. London, 1953.

MacArthur, Brian (Ed.). *Despatches from the Gulf War*. London, Bloomsbury, 1991.

Mahnken, Thomas G., and Keaney, Thomas A. (Eds). *War in Iraq: Planning and Execution*. Abingdon, Routledge, 2007.

Makiya, Kanan. *Republic of Fear: The Politics of Modern Iraq*. Berkeley, CA, University of California Press, 2nd edn, 1998.

Malkasian, Carter. *Illusions of Victory: the Anbar Awakening and the Rise of the Islamic State*. New York, Oxford University Press, 2017.

Malone, David M. *International Struggle over Iraq: Politics in the UN Security Council 1980–2005*. Oxford, Oxford University Press, 2006.

Marr, Phebe. *The Modern History of Iraq*. Boulder, CO, Westview Press, 3rd edn, 2012.

Mosallam, Mosallam Ali. *The Iraqi Invasion of Kuwait: Saddam Hussein, his State and International Politics*. London, I. B. Tauris, 1996.

Nixon, John. *Debriefing the President: the Interrogation of Saddam Hussein*. London, Corgi Books, 2017.

Nouri, Bamo. *Elite Theory and the 2003 Iraq Occupation by the United States: How US Corporate Elites Created Iraq's Political System*. Abingdon, Routledge, 2021.

Osman, Khalil. *Sectarianism in Iraq: The Making of State and Nation since 1920*. Abingdon, Routledge, 2014.

Patel, David Siddhartha. *Order out of Chaos: Islam, Information, and the Rise and Fall of Social Orders in Iraq*. Ithaca, Cornell University Press, 2022.

Rafaat, Aram. *Kurdistan in Iraq: The Evolution of a Quasi-State*. London, Routledge, 2018.

Rahman, H. *The Making of the Gulf War: Origins of Kuwait's Longstanding Territorial Dispute with Iraq*. Reading, Ithaca Press, 1997.

Rasheed, A. *Power and Paranoia in Syria-Iraq Relations: The Impact of Hafez Assad and Saddam Hussain*. London, Routledge, 2023.

Rear, Michael. *Intervention, Ethnic Conflict and State-Building in Iraq: A Paradigm for the Post-Colonial State*. Abingdon, Routledge, 2012.

Ritchie, Nick, and Rogers, Paul. *The Political Road to War with Iraq: Bush, 9/11 and the Drive to Overthrow Saddam*. Abingdon, Routledge, 2006.

Rohde, Achim. *State-Society Relations in Baathist Iraq: Facing Dictatorship*. Abingdon, Routledge, 2010.

Sakai, Keiko, and Marfleet, Philip (Eds). *Iraq Since the Invasion: People and Politics in a State of Conflict*. Abingdon, Routledge, 2020.

Salih, Khalid. *State-Making, Nation-Building and the Military: Iraq 1941–1958*. Gothenburg, Göteborg University Press, 1996.

Sayej, Caroleen Marji. *Patriotic Ayatollahs: Nationalism in Post-Saddam Iraq*. Ithaca, NY, Cornell University Press, 2018.

Schofield, R. *Kuwait and Iraq: Historical Claims and Territorial Disputes*. London, Royal Institute of International Affairs, 2nd edn, 1993.

Shakir, Farah. *The Iraqi Federation: Origin, Operation and Significance*. Abingdon, Routledge, 2017.

Springborg, Robert (Ed.). *Oil and Democracy in Iraq*. London, Saqi Books, 2007.

Talmon, Stefan. *The Occupation of Iraq. Volume II: The Official Documents of the Coalition Provisional Authority and the Iraqi Governing Council*. Oxford, Hart Publishing, 2013.

Al-Tamimi, Huda. *Women and Democracy in Iraq: Gender, Politics and Nation-Building*. London, I. B. Tauris, 2019.

Tejel, Jordi. *Writing the Modern History of Iraq: Historiographical and Political Challenges*. Hackensack, NJ, World Scientific, 2012.

Tripp, Charles. *A History of Iraq*. Cambridge, Cambridge University Press, 2000.

Visser, Reidar, and Stansfield, Gareth. *An Iraq of its Regions: Cornerstones of a Federal Democracy?* New York, Columbia University Press, 2007.

Economy

Alnasrawi, Abbas. *Iraq's Burdens: Oil Sanctions and Underdevelopment*. Westport, CT, Greenwood Press, 2002.

Al-Asady, Janan. *Iraq's Oil and Gas Industry: The Legal and Contractual Framework*. Abingdon, Routledge, 2021.

Gunter, Frank R. *The Political Economy of Iraq: Restoring Balance in a Post-Conflict Society*. Cheltenham, Edgar Elgar, 2013.

Rebuilding Iraq's Public Works Infrastructure Following the Defeat of ISIS. Foreign Policy Research Institute, 21 Nov. 2018. www.fpri.org/article/2018/11/rebuilding-iraqs-public-works-infrastructure-following-the-defeat-of-isis.

International Energy Agency. 'Iraq's Energy Sector: A Roadmap to a Brighter Future'. 25 April 2019.

'Iraq: Country Brief'. *Food and Agriculture Organization of the United Nations*, 11 April 2019. www.fao.org/giews/countrybrief/country.jsp?code=IRQ.

Looney, Robert. 'The Business of Insurgency: The Expansion of Iraq's Shadow Economy', in *The National Interest* 81, Fall 2005, pp. 67–72.

'After ISIS Can Iraq Get Reconstruction Right this Time?'. *World Politics Review*, 18 July 2017, www.worldpoliticsreview.com/articles/22730/after-isis-can-iraq-get-reconstruction-right-this-time.

Iraq's Informal Economy: Reflections of War, Sanctions and Policy Failure. Abu Dhabi, Emirates Center for Strategic Studies and Research, 2007.

'New Developments on the Iraqi Economic Front'. *The Journal of South Asian and Middle Eastern Studies*, 32(1), Fall 2008, pp. 1–29.

Tollast, Robert, Water, Nick, and Krebs, Lutz. *Harsh Summer, Wet Winter? A Long Term View of Iraq's Water Resources*. Baghdad, Iraq Energy Institute, 15 May 2019.

ISRAEL

Geography

The State of Israel is bounded on the north by Lebanon, on the north-east by the Syrian Arab Republic, on the east by Jordan and the Palestinian territory in the West Bank, and on the south and south-west by the Gulf of Aqaba and the Sinai Desert, occupied in 1967 and returned in April 1982 to Egyptian sovereignty. The so-called 'Gaza Strip', a small piece of territory some 40 km long, formed part of Palestine but was, under the Armistice Agreement of February 1949, then left under Egyptian control. Since May 1994 the Gaza Strip has been under the limited jurisdiction of the Palestinian (National) Authority (PA); however, Israel completed its disengagement from the territory in August–September 2005 (see History). The territories that were occupied after the war of June 1967 are not recognized internationally as forming part of the State of Israel. (Geographical descriptions of these territories are given in a supplementary section on the Occupied Territories at the end of this chapter.)

PHYSICAL FEATURES

The physical geography of Israel is surprisingly complex and, though the area of the state is small, a considerable number of regions are easily distinguished. In the extreme north the hills of the Lebanon range continue without break, though of lower altitude, to form the uplands of Galilee, where the maximum height is just over 1,200 m. The Galilee hills fall away steeply on three sides: on the east to the well-defined Jordan Valley (see Jordan), on the west to a narrow coastal plain, and to the south at the Vale of Esdraelon or 'Emek Yezreel'. This latter is a rather irregular trough formed by subsidence along faults, with a flat floor and steep sides, and it runs inland from the Mediterranean south-eastwards to reach the Jordan Valley. At its western end the vale opens into the wide Bay of Acre, 25 km–30 km in breadth, but it narrows inland to only a few km before opening out once again where it joins the Jordan Valley. This lowland area has a very fertile soil and an annual rainfall of 400 mm, which is sufficient, with limited irrigation, for agriculture. Formerly highly malarial and largely uncultivated, the vale is now very productive. For centuries it has been a corridor of major importance linking the Mediterranean coast and Egypt with the interior of south-west Asia, and has thus been a passageway for ethnic, cultural and military invasions.

South of Esdraelon there is an upland plateau extending for about 150 km. This is a broad upfold of rock, consisting mainly of limestone and reaching 900 m in altitude. In the north, where there is a moderate rainfall, the plateau has been eroded into valleys, some of which are fertile, though less so than those of Esdraelon or Galilee. This district, centred on Jenin and Nablus, is the ancient country of Samaria, until 1967 part of Jordan. Further south rainfall is reduced and erosion is far less prominent; hence this second region, Judea proper, stands out as a more strongly defined ridge, with far fewer streams and a barer open landscape of a more arid and dusty character. Jerusalem, Bethlehem and Hebron are the main towns. Towards the south-east rainfall becomes scarce and the Wilderness of Judea, an area of semi-desert, unfolds. In the extreme south the height of the plateau begins to decline, passing finally into a second plateau only 300 m–450 m above sea level, but broader, and broken by occasional ranges of hills that reach 900 m in height. This is the Negev, a territory comprising nearly one-half of the total area of Israel, and bounded on the east by the lower Jordan Valley and on the west by the Sinai Desert. Agriculture, entirely dependent on irrigation, is carried on in a few places in the north, but for the most part the Negev consists of steppe or semi-desert. Irrigation schemes have been developed in those areas where soils are productive.

Between the uplands of Samaria-Judea and the Mediterranean Sea there occurs a low-lying coastal plain that stretches southwards from Haifa as far as the Egyptian frontier at Gaza. In the north the plain is closely hemmed in by the spur of Mount Carmel (550 m), which almost reaches the sea; but the plain soon opens out to form a fertile lowland—the Plain of Sharon. Still further south the plain becomes broader again, but with a more arid climate and a sandier soil—this is the ancient Philistia. Ultimately the plain becomes quite arid, with loose sand dunes, and it merges into the Sinai Desert.

CLIMATE

Israel has the typical 'Mediterranean' cycle of hot, dry summers, when the temperature reaches 32°C–38°C, and mild, rainy winters. Altitude has a considerable effect, in that although snow may fall on the hills, it is not frequent on the lowlands. Several inches of snow may fall in Jerusalem in winter, whereas Upper Galilee may receive several feet. The valleys, especially Esdraelon and adjacent parts of the upper Jordan, lying below sea level, can become extremely hot (more than 40°C) and very humid.

Rainfall varies greatly from one part of Israel to another. Parts of Galilee receive over 1,000 mm annually, but the amount decreases rapidly southwards, until in the Negev and Plain of Gaza it is 250 mm or less. This is because the prevailing south-westerly winds blow off the sea to reach the north of Israel, but further south they come from Egypt, with only a short sea track, and therefore lack moisture.

POPULATION

At a census held in December 2008, the total population was recorded at 7,412,180 (males 3,663,910, females 3,748,270). By 31 December 2022, according to official estimates, this had increased to 9,656,000. Jerusalem is the country's largest city, with the population of its municipal area recorded at a preliminary 979,079 in December 2022. Other major cities included Tel Aviv—Jaffa (population 473,841) and Haifa (289,535). The Israeli Government designates Jerusalem as the country's capital, although this designation is not recognized by the United Nations and most foreign governments have their embassies in Tel Aviv. At mid-2023 only the USA, Guatemala, Kosovo and Honduras had embassies in Jerusalem.

Hebrew is the official language of the State of Israel. Following the passage of controversial new legislation in July 2018, Arabic was effectively downgraded from being an official language to having a 'special status in the state'. Although English no longer has official status, it retains a prominent place in the functions of the state. All laws and regulations must be published in Hebrew and Arabic, and, in practice, are also translated into English.

Hebrew was largely eclipsed as a spoken language after the dispersal of Jewish people by the Romans, and until relatively recently its use was largely restricted to scholarship, serious literature and religious observance. Immigrants to Palestine since 1890, however, were encouraged to use Hebrew in normal everyday speech and its revival has been a potent agent in the unification of the Israeli Jewish people, since most Jewish immigrants spoke yet another language according to their country of origin. (The census of 1931 recorded more than 60 such languages in common usage within Palestine.) Hebrew is now dominant among Israeli-born citizens, while Arabic has declined following the flight of Arab refugees. English is also less important, though it remains the first foreign language of many Israelis. Owing to large-scale immigration from the countries of the former Union of Soviet Socialist Republics (USSR) following the disintegration of that state in the early 1990s, Russian has also become prevalent in Israel. It has been reported that 15%–20% of the population speak Russian as their first language, and a significant minority of those do not speak any Hebrew. Many state services are, therefore, also provided in Russian, alongside Hebrew and Arabic.

History

VAUGHN SHANNON

INTRODUCTION

The modern state of Israel is located at the eastern edge of the Mediterranean Sea, south of Lebanon, west of the Syrian Arab Republic and Jordan, and east of Egypt. Founded in 1948, its borders, politics and sheer existence have invited controversy and debate. Israel is a recent incarnation of previous efforts at establishing a 'Jewish state'. The space that modern Israel occupies has also been home—past and present—to other, non-Jewish peoples and governments, including Turks, British and Arabs. Palestinian Arabs lay claim to some or all of what constitutes Israel today, leading to much of the dynamics of insecurity that define its contemporary domestic and international politics. The following essay reviews the history of Israel and its predecessors, focusing on the 75 years of Israel's modern statehood.

CIVILIZATIONS OF THE EASTERN MEDITERRANEAN

The cradle of civilizations spanned the Nile Valley through the Fertile Crescent of Mesopotamia, and modern Israel stands today at the crossroads of those civilizations of antiquity. Semitic peoples settled the area circa 3500 BCE, with nascent settlements of Aramites, Edomites and Canaanites located along the edge of the eastern Mediterranean region by 2500 BCE. By the time of biblical stories of Abraham's journey from Ur to this area, Hittite and Egyptian empires bestrode the Mediterranean rim surrounding the so-called Promised Land of Jewish and Christian texts. Estimates of the dates for the settlement of Abraham's descendants, including Moses's exodus from Egypt and invasion of Canaan, range between the 15th–14th centuries BCE and the 11th–10th centuries BCE.

The 'United Kingdom of Israel' flourished under King David and King Saul, amid rival civilizations of Phoenicians, Philistines, Ammonites, Moabites, Edomites and Arameans. The Jewish dominion eventually split into the Kingdom of Judah in the south and the Kingdom of Israel in the north, with Jerusalem occupying a central spiritual space, with a holy Temple for Judaism. These two kingdoms were not to last: the rising Assyrian Empire swept through, destroying the Kingdom of Israel in 721 BCE. The Kingdom of Judah, and Jerusalem with it, fell to the Babylonians in the sixth century BCE. The resulting diaspora after these two conquests spread Jewish people, faith and ideas further abroad to places such as Persia. The Persians, who pushed west and enveloped the lands of the eastern Mediterranean, allowed interested Jews to migrate back to Jerusalem and its environs. Alexander the Great's Macedonian armies vanquished the Persians in the fourth century BCE and his successors ruled next, imposing Greek culture and desecrating the remains of the Jewish First Temple. A local Jewish group, the Maccabees, staged a revolt, eventually leading to the establishment of the Hasmonean Empire in the 160s BCE. During this Empire, a second temple was built in Jerusalem. Living under the Roman Empire at the time of Jesus of Nazareth (the beginning of the 'common era', according to the Christian Gregorian calendar), Jewish zealots agitated against Roman rule and repression. The final stand of one revolt against the Romans, at Masada in 73 CE, ended in mass suicide rather than surrender. The suppression of the Bar Kokhba revolt in 135 CE brought an end to the Jewish revolts, as the Romans destroyed the Jewish Second Temple. The Jews were once more in diaspora. While the Jewish population scattered again, the area of the eastern Mediterranean saw successive rule by the Byzantines to the Islamic caliphate, from crusader state in the 11th century to the Ayyubid and Mamluk dynasties into the 1500s. From the 1500s through to the First World War (1914–18), the Turkish-led multicultural Ottoman Empire ruled the area containing Jerusalem, including the Jewish Wailing Wall (the last remnant of the destroyed Second Temple) as well as the Temple Mount/Haram al-Sharif ('Noble Sanctuary') compound (the site of the Dome of the Rock and the al-Aqsa Mosque, built in the era of Muslim rule).

ZIONISM

In the 1880s a transnational political movement emerged around the idea of Jewish nationalism and statehood. Responding to the poor treatment of Jewish minorities in European countries, including the pogroms of Russia in which populations were expelled from their homes and land, the world Jewry experienced both surges in immigration as well as intellectual and political pressure to find a home for the dispossessed and downtrodden people. A Russian group, Hovevei Zion (Lovers of Zion), helped to lead some Jewish immigrants to Palestine in the first wave of 'aliya' ('ascent'). The group's founder, Leon Pinsker published *Auto-Emancipation* in 1881, which, together with Theodor Herzl's *The Jewish State* (published in 1896), brought powerful and popular voices to the movement, the latter lamenting 'the futility of combating anti-semitism'. The 1897 Basel Congress inaugurated an organized movement around the World Zionist Organization (WZO), which was to seek funding and lobby for both safe passage immigration and a homeland for the Jews.

WORLD WAR AND THE BRITISH MANDATE

The First World War is fundamental to the understanding of the modern state of Israel. The Ottomans sided with Germany and the Austro-Hungarian Empire (the Central Powers) against the British, French and Russians, and the eventual defeat of the Central Powers would leave the fate of the Levant in the hands of the Allied Powers. Zionists such as Chaim Weizmann lobbied the British for the creation of a Jewish homeland in Palestine (as the area had been called since Roman times). The 1917 Balfour Declaration publicly stated the support of the British Foreign Secretary, Arthur Balfour, for such an entity, although, importantly, the declaration did not specify an independent state but only a homeland, and added the caveat that 'nothing shall be done which may prejudice the existing civil and religious rights of existing non-Jewish communities in Palestine'.

The British had also made other vague wartime promises. In the McMahon-Hussein Correspondence of 1915–16, the British courted Arab support for a revolt against the Ottoman Turk forces, in exchange for promises of Arab self-rule to be determined in the future. Sharif Hussein of Mecca pushed for control and independence over much of the Arab world, including Palestine, whereas the British hedged their bets regarding details, having plans for themselves—especially in Palestinian territories such as the port of Haifa. These British aspirations were revealed in publicized secret promises made in the Sykes-Picot Agreement with wartime ally France, which involved plans to carve much of the Arab Middle East into spheres of influence between the two European powers, with Palestine reserved for possible other plans.

The basic outlines of the Sykes-Picot agreement were incorporated in the formal peace plans endorsed by the League of Nations after the war. So-called 'mandates' under British and French rule included Palestine as a creation to come under British tutelage. Both Zionists and Palestinian and other Arabs would lobby the British for eventual control of this area of land. The British administration recognized the Jewish Agency for Palestine (now the Jewish Agency for Israel), which had been founded by Weizmann in 1929 'as a public body for the purpose of advising' on the administration of Palestine, feeding Zionist aspirations for eventual statehood. Jewish immigration into Palestine increased from 5,500 in 1920 to over 33,000 by 1925. The Zionist leadership settled in Palestine at this time and created the proto-state institutions for a future government. A democratic Assembly of Representatives operated on behalf of the Jewish community (Yishuv), as did the General Federation of Labour in Israel (known as Histadrut), headed by

David Ben-Gurion. A Zionist militia, the Haganah, served as a regular armed force from the 1920s.

The Arab and Palestinian constituents lacked the same level of formalized legitimacy as well as internal unity, with the British favouring the Grand Mufti Hajj Amin al-Husseini as head of an Arab Higher Committee and Supreme Muslim Council, at the expense of marginalized rivals such as the Palestinian Arab Congress and members of the Nashashibi clan and of the Hizb al-Istiqlal (Independence Party). Arabs were placated by an early decision to divide the Palestine mandate, separating the area between the Jordan River and the Mediterranean (Palestine) from an all-Arab Transjordan which would not indulge Jewish settlement and favour. None the less a series of Arab revolts, protesting against British rule and increasing Zionist immigration, favouritism and land sales, occurred in 1920, 1921 and 1929, culminating in the Great Revolt of 1936–39. Izz ad-Din al-Qassam headed local militias in more violent aspects of these multifaceted strikes and protests, until he was killed in the 1935 uprising. Hajj Amin al-Husseini ended up being removed and exiled, turning, infamously, towards Nazi Germany in attempts to gain influence over the future of Palestine.

The British, facing ongoing governance struggles amid the ongoing Great Revolt, proposed successive plans to divide Palestine into Jewish and Arab entities. The 1937 Peel Commission and 1938 Woodhead Commission heard from all sides, and published findings and recommendations that included maps for two states, each with a continued British presence. By 1939 a British White Paper had abandoned proposals both from the Commissions and from the Balfour Declaration, and had curbed Jewish land sales and immigration with the goal of withdrawing from Palestine in about a decade. Despite objections by local Palestinians such as al-Husseini and the Hizb al-Istiqlal, in 1944 Musa al-Alami was appointed to head the Arab Higher Committee, representing not only Palestinian but also broader Arab interests.

The White Paper, aimed at placating the Arab majority of Palestine, was viewed as a betrayal by the Zionist movement. Coming at the start of the Second World War and the Nazi 'Final Solution' programme, the immigration curbs seemed especially insensitive, with Jewish immigration to Palestine decreasing from 16,000 in 1939 to 4,500 in 1940. By 1942 the Zionist movement had turned to the USA for patron support, affirming in the New York-based Zionist Conference's Biltmore Declaration the desire for an independent Jewish state in Palestine.

The costs of occupation and the Second World War led the British to seek a way out, or to share the burden with superpower ally the USA, in a future plan for Palestine. The Anglo-American Committee of Inquiry, established in January 1946, was sceptical about allowing the formation of a Jewish state—seemingly legitimizing continued British rule—even as it proposed a resumption of Jewish immigration to post-war Palestine. Problems persisted, as radical Zionist groups, including Irgun and Lehi (known as the Stern Gang), militarized not only against Arab rivals in the territory but against British targets as well. The King David Hotel in Jerusalem, which served as the headquarters of the British mandatory government, was bombed by Irgun activists in July 1946, and the British added this group and Lehi (and their leaders) to their terrorist watch lists.

One further federal plan, based on the earlier Morrison-Grady Plan for partition, was proposed by British Foreign Secretary Ernest Bevin, but was rejected by Arab and Jewish Agency representatives. Turning to the newly created United Nations (UN) for a multilateral solution, the British and Americans endorsed the majority proposal of the UN Special Committee on Palestine (UNSCOP) for a two-state solution—one Jewish, one Arab—with Jerusalem being proposed as an international trusteeship, owing to its religious and political importance to Jews, Muslims and Christians. In a final vote held on 29 November 1947, UN General Assembly Resolution 181 was passed by 33 votes to 13 (with 10 abstentions), with the USA supporting it and the United Kingdom abstaining. Notably, no affirmative votes came from the Arab and Muslim world, signalling their opposition to the proposal to cede Palestinian land to a Jewish state. Zionists too were reluctant about Resolution 181, for opposite reasons: it did not give Jerusalem (and the Temple grounds) to a Jewish state, and involved the allocation of far less territory than they had aspired to. None the less, the official position of the Jewish Agency was to accept Resolution 181, and the affirmative vote represented a formal legalized endorsement for the long-desired goal of a Jewish state. Given Arab and Palestinian opposition, however, violence and war became inevitable in the lead-up to the British administration's declared intent to withdraw by May 1948.

WAR AND THE FOUNDING OF ISRAEL

Locally, in the first half of 1948 a Palestinian Arab irregular force, headed by Abd al-Qadir al-Husseini and known as the Army of the Holy War, mobilized against Zionist forces and aimed to create an independent state in Palestine. Zionist militias successfully worked together to oppose the various jihadist fronts, scattering the Arab fighters and consolidating around a new State of Israel, which was declared upon the termination of the British mandate for Palestine on 14 May 1948. The League of Arab States (Arab League) responded the following day by ordering the dispatch to Palestine of a multi-national Arab Liberation Army, which was, at least on paper, a Joint Command of national forces from Egypt, Syria, Jordan, Iraq and Lebanon. Rather than acting as a unified Arab world, however, each country acted for its own benefit. An example of this was the Zionist-Hashemite Non-Aggression Pact, by which Israel and Jordan agreed, as early as November 1947, not to fight each other but rather to focus on territorial acquisition. Both before and after independence, Israeli forces pressed on against the various Arab armies, while driving into Palestinian territories to purge coveted areas for the fledgling state.

The UN offered and urged truces and proposals in mid-1948, but there was little interest. In September UN mediator Count Folke Bernadotte proposed a two-state partition plan, with Palestinian Arabs joining Transjordan, but he was assassinated by a member of Lehi.

Israeli forces gained control of 73% of the erstwhile Palestinian mandate—more than the 55% allocated under UN Security Council Resolution 181. Israel agreed an armistice with Arab states in early 1949, leaving unsettled issues of statehood, borders, Jerusalem (now divided between Jordanian-controlled East Jerusalem and Israeli-controlled West Jerusalem) and a new Palestinian refugee problem in the surrounding countries and territories. Some 750,000 Palestinian Arabs in total were displaced through a combination of war and intentional 'ethnic cleansing' operations by Israeli forces in places such as Deir Yassin. UN General Assembly Resolution 194 affirmed the 'right of return' for those displaced in the war who wished to return, but in practice the warring parties avoided peace solutions in favour of consolidating gains in Palestine, including not just Israel's gains but Egypt's control of the Gaza Strip and Jordan's control of the West Bank and East Jerusalem. All of these issues would return in future iterations of the so-called Arab–Israeli conflict.

The New State of Israel

What was this new state of Israel, which came into being with a Declaration of Independence on 14 May 1948? Who was involved and what vision did they have for a state? The Declaration itself was made by David Ben-Gurion, the founder of the Histadrut trade union federation and previously leader of both the WZO and the Jewish Agency, who is widely considered to be the founding father of Israel. Ben-Gurion was appointed Prime Minister of a provisional government based on the members of the Jewish Agency Executive. Amid a war for independence, these founders would build institutions for the Zionist-declared goal of a 'Jewish State'. This would prove challenging, not least because many in the country would be non-Jewish and the founders were committed to notions of Western representative democracy

The provisional government, in the form of the Provisional State Council, was tasked with governing, winning a war and planning an enduring state; its 37 members were drawn from a broader National Council of the Yishuv and the Jewish Agency Executive Committee and it was chaired by Chaim Weizmann of the WZO. After independence, the Provisional State Council acted as the temporary legislature, while the executive comprised a cabinet of 13 ministers (all members of the Provisional State Council), headed by Prime Minister Ben-Gurion.

Early government decisions included lifting Jewish immigration restrictions into Israel and the merger of irregular forces and Haganah regular forces into a new body, the Israel Defense Forces (IDF). Taxes were raised, public services provided and a census taken: providing basic functionality for the duration of the war and pending the first elections for a permanent government to replace the provisional one.

Elections were held in January 1949 for a Constituent Assembly, which at its inaugural meeting in February declared itself the first Knesset ('assembly'). The new body was (and still is) a unicameral parliament of 120 seats which was elected on a nationwide basis in a multiparty poll according to the rules of proportional representation. Of the tallied 712,000 Jews and 69,000 Arabs from a census, there was a turnout of about 87% of the 506,000 eligible voters. Ben-Gurion's party, Mapai (Workers' Party of the Land of Israel), won the largest share, 46 of the 120 seats, leading to the formation of a coalition Government under the continuing premiership of Ben-Gurion.

With a democratically elected Government and the war coming to an end, in 1949 Israel turned its attention to the drawing up of a constitution and laws. On the issue of a constitution, differences quickly emerged over not just the contents but on the question of whether the country should have one at all. While the Knesset agreed eventually to draw up a written constitution, it consciously chose, in the 1950 Harari Resolution, to draft the charter piecemeal and gradually through a series of 'Basic Laws' rather than immediately drafting a single, formal constitution. Another significant piece of legislation that was passed in 1950 was the Law of Return, which stated that 'every Jew has the right to come to this country' and offered Israeli citizenship to all people 'born of a Jewish mother' or who 'has become converted to Judaism and who is not a member of another religion'. This law spurred massive immigration to the new state in fairly rapid order, adding to an already large influx of post-war European refugees; the population doubled from 120,000 in 1948 to 240,000 in 1949. As the law took effect and the bureaucracy to manage immigration was consolidated, Jewish immigration rose dramatically, including 50,000 from Yemen, 113,000 from Iraq and thousands more from other neighbouring Arab majority states. By 1956 the population of Israel exceeded 1.6m.

Meanwhile, characteristic of the self-defined 'Jewish state' was a dual track for handling non-Jews, citizens or otherwise. While the Law of Return generated a massive influx of Jews to Israel, the 1952 Citizenship Law restricted non-Jews from immigrating to Israel or obtaining citizenship. The 2008 Amendment 9 to Article 11 empowers the courts to revoke citizenship for any so-called 'breach of allegiance', which could include becoming a citizen or permanent resident of certain Arab and Muslim states; and the 2011 Amendment 10 permits revocation of citizenship as a form of punishment for those convicted in criminal proceedings of treason, espionage or terrorist acts.

The 1950 Absentees' Property Law removed refugee Palestinians from their land and entitlements, transferring property to an Israeli Custodian of Absentee Property. Combined with the 1960 Basic Law, which created the Israeli Land Administrations, property owned by the State of Israel, the Development Authority or the Jewish National Fund (totalling 93% of Israel) cannot be sold or transferred. These laws, taken together, prevent Arab settlement or return, helping to explain how the Arab majority of mandatory Palestine, already depleted from the war and *nakba* (as Palestinians called the depopulation of homes and homeland in 1948), fell to 160,000 within Israel's borders. Palestinians who were already resident in Israel were allowed to remain and become Israeli citizens, but the door was effectively shut on Arabs, Palestinian or otherwise, who wished to move to or return to Israel.

Domestic Politics of Early Israel
In the early years of Israel, politics was dominated by Mapai and secular socialist influences from the largely European Ashkenazim—the founding Yyishuv. As Sephardim and other Oriental Jewish (Mizrahi) émigrés arrived in Israel, and more religiously orientated Jews joined the ranks of the citizenry, political dynamics shifted, culminating in a political 'earthquake' in the 1970s. Until then, however, Ben-Gurion and his successors enjoyed an extended honeymoon period of relative unity and hegemony.

Ben-Gurion himself retired from political life in January 1954, ceding the office of Prime Minister to Moshe Sharett for a time. However, Ben-Gurion returned to government in 1955, and was reappointed as Prime Minister in November, in which post he remained until June 1963. The office of President, created as a largely symbolic post and elected by the Knesset, was first was held by Chaim Weizmann, the former head of the WZO. Weizmann was elected as the Israeli head of state in February 1949 and remained in the presidency until his death in late 1952, when he was succeeded by Yitzhak Ben-Zvi.

One major area of debate in the founding of an explicitly Jewish state was the relationship between religion and state. Some demanded that Israel be constituted religiously a Jewish state, while many of the secular European Jews in Israel expected separation of religion and state. The ruling Mapai—which merged with two other Labor groups in 1968 to form the Israeli Labor Party—adopted a compromise position by cementing a long partnership with the National Religious Party (NRP) in coalition Government. Carrying over from the Yishuv's pre-state policies, the compromise was effectively a continuation of the status quo on matters of the Sabbath (allowing Jewish law or *halacha* to extend to public operations on Saturdays); on marriage and divorce rites (which were to be handled by religious law and authority, Jewish and otherwise); and on permitting the exemption from military service of ultra-orthodox Jews attending *Yeshivot* (religious schools).

International Politics of Early Israel
An early goal of Israel internationally was to secure its survival by building legitimacy. On the day that Israel declared its independence, the USA and the Union of Soviet Socialist Republics (USSR) recognized the new state, and in 1949 the UN voted to admit Israel to its ranks, by a vote of 37 votes to 12. Israel would eventually gain recognition from a total of more than 160 countries. Those refusing to recognized Israel were largely from the Arab and Muslim world, together with others from the post-colonial non-Western world. From the outset, the Arab League states refused to acknowledge what was viewed as a European colonial occupier of Arab lands, forced upon the region by external Great Powers. In line with the anti-colonial ideologies of the 1950s, Arab nationalism adopted hard-line positions against both the West and Israel. Egypt blockaded Israel's Straits of Tiran in 1967, despite UN Security Council resolutions calling for Israel's right to transit international waters.

Neighbouring Egypt ramped up its rhetoric against Israel, especially after the rise of Gamal Abd al-Nasir (Nasser) in the wake of the Free Officers' coup that brought down the pro-British King Farouk in 1952. Beyond rhetoric, skirmishes increased around demilitarized zones established after the 1949 armistice, and raids were launched into Israel from Egyptian-controlled Gaza by Palestinian fedayeen forces. Israel carried out retaliatory raids into Gaza, including 'Operation Black Arrow' in February 1955 against an Egyptian base, escalating tensions with its Arab neighbour.

Israel found regional allies where it could through Ben-Gurion's strategy of the 'periphery doctrine', starting with non-Arab centres of power in Iran, Turkey (now known as Türkiye) and Ethiopia, as a means of navigating a hostile Arab world intent on embargoing and isolating Israel. However, more important for the Jewish state was to secure Great Power patronage. Despite the early recognition by the USA, US presidents were initially wary of giving economic and military support to Israel, partly out of concern for Arab world opposition in an emerging Cold War climate in which diplomatic battles for allies were constant against the USA's superpower adversary, the USSR. Israel would continue to court the USA in the years to come, but meanwhile it attempted to sow discord between the USA and Arab states, at one point in 1954 conducting a covert operation involving the bombing of US civilian targets in Egypt and blaming Egypt for the violence (the Lavon Affair). The well-publicized arms deal between Egypt and Czechoslovakia in 1955 indicated that the former was becoming a client of the USSR, raising alarm in Israel and the West.

A case where the Cold War framed Israeli relations with world powers was the Suez crisis of 1956. Egypt's President Nasser nationalized the Suez Canal in that year—a strategically vital waterway for the UK, which had purchased substantial shares in the Suez Canal Company in 1875. Alarmed by these actions, Israel and the UK, together with France, conspired to stage an operation in which Israel would invade Egypt's Sinai Peninsula, followed by French and British forces seizing the Suez Canal, citing the need to act as peacekeepers between the warring parties. By intervening militarily, the British hoped to regain control of the Canal and with it the waterway connecting the Mediterranean with the Indian Ocean

The operation took place on the eve of the 1956 US presidential election. Incumbent US President Dwight D. Eisenhower, coasting to re-election, was playing golf when he was informed of the Israelis' actions. After briefings indicated collusion with erstwhile US allies France and the UK, the USA responded with anger at having been kept in the dark about such a dramatic operation, which had implications for the West's standing in the so-called Third World (countries that were not aligned either with communism or democratic capitalism). Eisenhower joined his country's Cold War nemesis, the USSR, in condemning Israel's actions as well as the charade of a peacekeeping operation staged by France and the UK. The USA reasserted its leadership in the West, chided Israel and made efforts to clarify that the USA and the 'Free World' were not in the business of imperialism.

At the same time, the USA negotiated a withdrawal of the warring parties that granted Israel some security guarantees related to safe passage through the Straits of Tiran in the Red Sea, and the stationing of UN peacekeepers in the Sinai Peninsula (UN Emergency Force—UNEF I). During 1956–66, a fairly stable, albeit fragile, peace was maintained, where incidents reverted to skirmishes and reprisals between Israeli forces and Palestinian fedayeen and nationalists operating across the borders from the Syrian Arab Republic, Gaza and the Jordanian-controlled West Bank.

By the time of the next crisis, in 1967, the USA and Israel had developed what President John F. Kennedy called a 'special relationship'. It involved the beginning of arms sales to Israel, and Kennedy's successor, Lyndon B. Johnson, strengthened relations by upgrading arms sales to tank sales and by using rhetoric such as saying that the USA was 'one of the best friends Israel ever had'. Given the gravitation of Arab nationalist regimes such as Egypt and Syria to the orbit of the USSR in the 1950s and 1960s, Israel was increasingly viewed as a necessary regional check on perceived Soviet expansionism.

Six Days in 1967

A newly assertive Syria, after a decade of coups and instability, increased both its support for the Palestinians and air raids across Israel's north-east border. Emboldened by Nasser's promises of pan-Arab defence, Syria's actions in 1966–67 provoked an escalation with Israel that led to a crisis. In early 1967, with Syria and Israel exchanging artillery fire in the disputed Golan Heights area, Nasser warned Israel of Egypt's commitments to Syria under its mutual defence pact. After an air battle on 7 April with Israel, Syria reached out to its Egyptian patron for assistance. Nasser responded by issuing more vague threats and mobilizing troops. In the ensuing crisis, multiple Arab state armies were mobilized. By the end of May the Egyptian Government had ordered UNEF peacekeepers to leave Egypt and had closed the Straits of Tiran to Israeli shipping, effectively (as in 1956) blockading the Israeli port of Eilat. Nasser asserted that 'the armies of Egypt, Jordan, Syria and Lebanon are poised on the borders of Israel [...] to face the challenge', noting that 'This act will astound the world', and that 'the critical hour has arrived. We have reached the stage of serious action.'

Most accounts—including Israeli analyses at that time—claim that the Arab stance was more bluster and bluff than a pending invasion of annihilation. The USA, mindful of handing the USSR 'a propaganda victory', sought a middle ground, attempting to restrain Israeli action while reassuring the country of US support on the matter of security and the blockade. Sensing an opportunity perhaps more than a threat, the Israeli Cabinet chose pre-emptive war to end the stalemate and use the advantage of surprise to shore up defences and the seizure of territory. On 5 June 1967 the so-called Six-Day War began with Israeli forces first attacking Egypt, followed by Jordan and Syria, and making substantial territorial gains. In response to a demand by the UN, Israel issued a ceasefire, which Jordan and Egypt agreed to on 8 June. Israeli incursions into Syria on 9 June prompted the USSR to threaten to stop Israel by any 'necessary actions, including military', risking a global escalation. However, Syria also promptly agreed to a truce and all fighting had ceased by 11 June.

The consequences of the Six-Day War were seismic for Israel in terms of both domestic and international politics: Israel had not only achieved a rather impressive victory against a number of its Arab neighbours but had also seized five areas of land that became known as the Occupied Territories—from Egypt, the Sinai Peninsula and Gaza Strip; from Syria, the Golan Heights; and from Jordan, the West Bank and—within it—a united Jerusalem. Israel's victory and occupation altered the Arab–Israeli conflict fundamentally from one of existential Israeli survival to one of Arab land for peace. Domestically, control of more than double the area contained within Israel's pre-war borders, including Judaism's holiest site of Old Jerusalem and the Temple Mount, caused both euphoria and debate about what to do with the acquired land.

From War to War

The effects of the 1967 war on Israel's general (Jewish) population were very different from the effects on Arab Israelis and the people in the Occupied Territories themselves. For most of Israel's Jewish population, the war was a triumph. Amid the crisis of May 1967, Israel had formed a national unity Government that included representatives of opposition parties Gahal and Rafi. The aftermath of the war, from victory to gaining control of a united Jerusalem, strengthened the sense of unity and nationalism in the country. Israel, from the start, asserted that Jerusalem would never be divided again, and Zionists began to contemplate the retention and settlement of historic Jewish lands now under their possession. What was called the West Bank by Jordanians and in international circles, was the Judea and Samaria of old to Zionist Jews. Labor retained its popularity in Israeli politics, which was not surprising amid the fanfare of celebrations. Prime Minister Levi Eshkol (who had succeeded Ben-Gurion in 1963) died in 1969 and the premiership was assumed by Golda Meir, who had served as Minister of Foreign Affairs from 1956 to 1966. Meir would steer Israel through the crisis of another war in 1973, which would damage her standing for leaving the country vulnerable and unprepared.

Whatever hopes and dreams Israelis had for 'Judea and Samaria', Jerusalem, Golan and Gaza, there was the small matter of international and regional expectations to deal with. Nowhere did anyone recognize Israel's right to keep the Occupied Territories as its own. The issue of who would control them was the arena of diplomacy and, sometimes, war. The pre-1967 borders of Israel, which were themselves intended as demarcation lines rather than permanent borders and were effectively frozen in armistice pending future settlement, are conventionally known as the Green Line (related to the colour of the line drawn in the 1949 armistice map). The post-war Occupied Territories were clearly located outside the Green Line. In November 1967 UN Security Council Resolution 242 laid out the international position on the war and the territories that has guided most negotiations ever since. In short, the resolution was a 'land for peace' formulation based on two expectations: first, the withdrawal of Israeli forces from territories occupied in the recent conflict; and second, the termination of all claims of belligerency, and respect for and acknowledgement of the sovereignty, territorial integrity and political independence of every state in the area and their right to live in peace within secure and recognized boundaries.

While seemingly clear at first sight—Israel returns the Occupied Territories and Arab states recognize Israel and make peace with it—the complications surrounding Resolution 242 included the lack of clarity about which should come first (withdrawal or recognition) and whether Israel needed to withdraw from all of territories (the word 'the' not appearing before 'territories' in the English-language version of the resolution). Arab states argued yes to the 'all' question and that Israel should withdraw before any discussion; Israel held that withdrawal could be a matter of discretion and, in any case, only after peace had been achieved with its hostile neighbours. Despite exhortations and diplomacy from multilateral forums and bilateral allies, the outcome of the UN Security Council resolution was no immediate change in the new status quo.

The Arab League summit of August–September 1967, held in Khartoum, Sudan, affirmed what became known as the 'Three Noes': no peace with Israel, no negotiations with Israel and no recognition of Israel. Resolution 242 would not change this. Instead, the emboldened Israelis would plough ahead with settlement building, while Arab governments, smarting from the humiliation of the war, would continue on the path of harassing and isolating Israel in a low-level 'war of attrition', combined with promoting the Palestinian cause on the world stage. Furthermore, in some cases, such as Egypt and Syria, they would plan to avenge themselves by recovering their lost lands.

In Egypt, following Israel's victory in the Six-Day War, a humiliated Nasser had immediately offered to resign from the presidency, but, in response to a public outpouring of support for him, withdrew his resignation the following day and remained as President until his death in 1970. His successor, Col Anwar Sadat, gave up pan-Arabism for Egyptian nationalism and pride. This change of policy made Egypt less radical internationally. The 1970 initiative of US Secretary of State William Rogers, calling for a 90-day ceasefire in the still unstable Sinai and Suez Canal area, was agreed to by Nasser and Sadat, with the latter extending the ceasefire indefinitely. Jordan and Israel followed suit.

However, ceasefires do not equate to peace. President Sadat remained bent on restoring Egyptian pride and territory—by force if necessary. He publicly sought an Israeli partial withdrawal from the Sinai Peninsula by the end of 1971, which the USA advocated for but which did not happen, raising prospects of war at the start of 1972. On 6 October 1973, the Jewish holiday of Yom Kippur (the Day of Atonement), Egyptian and Syrian troops attacked Israeli positions in the Sinai and Golan Heights. Prime Minister Golda Meir had been warned by Israeli intelligence of a possible attack; she failed, however, to alert the country and go onto a war footing, which effectively spelled the end of her political career.

Initial attacks penetrated deep into Israeli-held territory, as Israeli forces were unprepared, even though their leaders had not been entirely uninformed. Egyptian forces crossed the Suez Canal and reoccupied part of Sinai, while Syrian troops tried to reclaim the Golan Heights. Viewed through the lens of Cold War, the USA became concerned about the fate of Israel against these Soviet-sponsored Arab enemies, and so began the flow of arms and aid to Israel, even as it pressured Israel to offer a ceasefire. When Egypt rejected the ceasefire proposed by Israel, the Administration of US President Richard Nixon (1969–74) ordered a full-scale airlift to Israel and raised the US military state of alert to defense readiness condition (DefCon) 3, largely to attract the attention of the USSR. US Secretary of State Henry Kissinger declared that 'the US would not allow a Soviet-supported operation to succeed against an American-supported operation'. At the same time, the USA was under the added pressure of an oil embargo imposed by Arab members of the Organization of the Petroleum Exporting Countries (OPEC), creating an economic toll for US support for Israel against the Arab belligerents. Seeking to defuse the crisis, the superpowers attempted to end the conflict through UN Security Council Resolution 338, adopted on 22 October 1973, which called for a ceasefire, the implementation of Resolution 242, and negotiations for a 'just and durable peace in the Middle East'. Having successfully repelled the advances of the Egyptian and Syrian troops, Israel agreed ceasefires with Egypt and Syria on 24 October.

Legislative elections held in Israel on 31 December 1973 reflected the changed mood in the country from the 1967 war to that of 1973. Although the Labor Alignment (an alliance comprising the Labor Party and Mapam/the United Workers' Party) secured the most votes to form a Government, the new centre-right Likud (Consolidation) bloc (an alliance of several parties, including Gahal—comprising the Herut (Freedom) Party and the Liberal Party) was second-placed, with 39 seats. Meir ended up resigning over the Yom Kippur War (alternatively known as the October War) in June 1974, as the interim report of the Agranat Commission, published in April, publicized the Government's knowledge of and lack of preparedness for the attacks leading up to the conflict.

Meir's replacement as Prime Minister, Itzhak Rabin, began a push for Arab-Israeli peace, offering territorial concessions to Jordan from the gains of the 1967 war. Jordan had sought to claim the West Bank for itself, but had met resistance from the Palestinians there, leading to civil war in 1970 and the forcible expulsion of the Palestinian Liberation Organization (PLO) from Jordan. The rest of the Arab world was not interested in territorial concessions and peace at that moment, instead throwing its weight behind the PLO as the 'sole legitimate representative of the Palestinian people'. Nor did Rabin's proposals win great support in Israel itself. Likud's popularity increased on the platform of not granting territorial concessions, but settling the lands for Israel on the grounds of security, and religious and historical ties. The Gush Emunim ultranationalist Orthodox Jewish movement gained prominence in the 1970s on this basis, providing a bedrock of religious and nationalist support for the more religious and right-wing Israeli parties.

The so-called 'political earthquake' came in 1977 as the culmination of not only frustrations over war but also demographic changes, the increased religiosity of immigrants, and the socioeconomic marginalization of more recent immigrants from Asia and North Africa. Almost 30 years after Israel's foundation, Labor's long run of party hegemony came to an end with the legislative elections in May, which saw the Labor Alignment's representation in the Knesset reduced to 32 seats, while the Likud bloc, led by Menachem Begin of the Herut Party, secured the largest number of seats, with 43. Begin was appointed Prime Minister and formed a coalition with a number of ultra-Orthodox parties as well as the NRP (a former Labor ally despite its religious bent).

Among the major consequences of Likud's rise to power was the exponential growth of Israeli settlements in the Occupied Territories. Although not implemented, thee Allon Plan for partitioning the West Bank after the 1967 war, had authorized settlements along the Jordanian border for the purpose of 'secure frontiers', but Likud increased the proposed number of settlements in the name of Eretz Yisrael (Land of Israel). On 29 July 1980 the Begin Government passed a Basic Law that declared 'Jerusalem, whole and united, is the capital of Israel'. In December 1981 the Government approved the Golan Heights Law—effectively representing the formal annexation of the territory—despite the objections of international actors and law.

As for the Israeli Arab population, the 1967 war had quite different effects. Israeli Arab politics prior to the war have been described as a time of 'political quietude', partly owing to deliberate Israeli policies of de-Palestinianization to undermine the Palestinians' ability to organize, identify and mobilize. Aside from belonging to something literally called the Jewish State, Israeli Arabs lived under military rule up to 1966, and were denied land ownership and allocated unequal shares of economic and political resources. Until the 1967 war, Arabism seemed the dominant force through which to vent Israeli Arab frustrations. The war, by all accounts, discredited pan-Arab ideology and dashed hopes that Nasser or another international guardian would assist. Palestinian Arab nationalism, while nascent in some quarters for decades previously, was primarily fuelled by the creation of the PLO in 1964 and its constituent radical entities, and secondly by the 1967 Six-Day

War. Almost overnight, it became clear that Palestinians would have to fend for themselves.

For Israeli Arabs, Palestinian national consciousness seeped back into the mainstream. Israel was now dominating and militarily controlling fellow Palestinians and their lands. While militant exile groups, from Fatah (the Palestine National Liberation Movement), whose founding leader was Yasser Arafat, to the Popular Front for the Liberation of Palestine (PFLP) promoted Palestinian rights at the point of the gun, Israeli Arabs became more active on their own behalf as well as for the plight of their fellow Palestinians under occupation. Pre-1967 Arab activity in Israel was limited, partly due to restrictions such as the laws banning parties and candidates that undermine the 'fundamental constitutional premise' of Israel as a Jewish State. Among the active Israeli Arab bodies was Al-Ard, a political movement established in 1958 to promote Palestinian identity and pan-Arabism. The 1965 Yeredor case saw Al-Ard's political wing, the Arab Socialist Party, disqualified from Knesset elections on the basis of the challenge that it represented to the concept of the Jewish state. The Communist Party of Israel (Maki), an Arab-Jewish party, remained the only party allowed to contest elections and register a platform of Arab rights and frustrations. After the end of military government and the occupation of the lands beyond the Green Line, other parties and organizations came to prominence in Israel. Hadash, a breakaway group from Maki, became an Arab-Jewish party that advocated the end of occupation and the creation of a Palestinian state. The Progressive List for Peace (PLP, founded in 1984) was another Arab-Jewish party that promoted Palestinian national identity and rights until its dissolution in the 1990s. The Arab Democratic Party, established in 1988, was all Arab. The Abnaa el-Balad (Sons of the Land) boycotted elections in Israel, but otherwise promoted Arab and Palestinian rights. In terms of organized social movements, there was the National Committee of the Heads of Arab Local Authorities (established in 1974), the National Committee for the Defense of Arab Lands (NCDAL) and the High Follow-Up Committee for Arab Citizens of Israel (established in 1982). A benchmark day for Israeli Arabs occurred on 30 March 1976. On that day, which came to be known as Land Day, the NCDAL called a general strike and staged demonstrations to protest against the 'judaization of Galilee'—which is, it should be noted, in Israel, and not in the West Bank. This protest led to arrests and violent skirmishes with Israeli police, in which six Palestinians were killed and dozens of people injured. The protest subsequently became an annual event. When Gaza and West Bank Palestinians organized strikes and protests during the 1987 *intifada* (uprising or, literally, shaking off—see *The Palestine Question*), Israeli Arabs protested in solidarity, adding to Israel's troubles over occupation.

The Road to Peace
The October/Yom Kippur War of 1973 proved a costly awakening for all sides: Egypt found that it could not win and recover land by force of arms; Israel found that it was not invincible; and the USA found that there was a price for its complicated relationship with Israel, vis-à-vis the Arab world as well as within the broader Cold War context. Additionally, amid US efforts to promote nuclear non-proliferation, Israel admitted to the Nixon Administration that it had covertly developed nuclear weapons. Both sides agreed to neither confirm nor deny the weapons' existence, but the addition of an Israeli nuclear arsenal raised the stakes of war, even as it may have served to deter future aggression by Israel's Arab neighbours.

The USA worked enthusiastically after the war to be a leader in promoting Middle East peace, with Secretary of State Kissinger engaging in shuttle diplomacy to secure agreements for disengagement between a chastened Israel and Egypt as well Syria. As Kissinger's efforts under President Nixon and his successor, Gerald Ford, gave way to the new Administration of Jimmy Carter (1977–81), Sadat's openness to peace coincided with the Likud Government of Prime Minister Begin, which took office in June 1977. Sadat stunned the region with a request to address the Knesset, which Israel accepted. His public call for peace in the seat of Israeli government signalled historic opportunities for the two states, even as it signalled the end of pan-Arabism and of Sadat's prestige in the Arab world. President Carter nurtured talks between the two countries, inviting both heads of state to the US presidential retreat at Camp David, Maryland. While Egypt made a good show of promoting Palestinian rights, concerns about Palestinians were placed in a separate document, with vague pledges for future conferences and discussions. The main document of the Camp David Accords, signed in September 1978, concerned a pledge for an Israeli phased withdrawal from the occupied Sinai Peninsula, in exchange for normalization of relations. US promises of aid and assistance helped to solidify the deal. Egypt had therefore gone from being a Soviet client to a US ally within a decade. In a formal peace treaty signed in March 1979 in Washington, DC, USA, in 1979, Begin won peace on Israel's western front that still persists to this day, while Sadat recovered Sinai for Egypt (the Israeli withdrawal being completed in April 1982).

The Palestine Question
Meanwhile, the Palestinian cause was taking centre stage internationally, partly due to high-profile hijackings and the kidnapping of Israeli athletes by Palestinian militants at the 1972 Olympics in Munich, West Germany. Diplomatically, the Arab League endorsed the PLO, whose charismatic leader, Yasser Arafat, was making inroads in the post-colonial world, garnering sympathy in the face of Israel's continued occupation and Palestinian statelessness. In November 1975 the Soviet-supported UN Security Council Resolution 3379 went so far as to call Zionism 'a form of racism and racial discrimination', and was passed by a vote of 72 to 35 (the resolution would be repealed in another UN vote, in 1991).

The Camp David Accords did not end Israel's border problems. Despite a pledge in the Accords to address the Palestinian question, little was done internationally while the PLO and others were continuing to conduct guerrilla warfare across Israel's many frontiers. After its expulsion from Jordan in 1970, the PLO found a haven amid the civil war in Lebanon, on Israel's northern border. So, in the same year that it signed the Accords with Egypt, Begin's Government ordered the invasion of southern Lebanon in Operation Litani, which sought to drive out PLO forces from the border region. The incursion was of limited duration and effect, but in 1982 Israeli forces returned to Lebanon to 'once and for all be rid of the menace of Palestinian terror'. This time Israel would occupy southern Lebanon until 2000.

One result of Israel's involvement in Lebanon was the eventual negotiated withdrawal of the PLO from the country to faraway Tunisia. The USA sent peacekeepers to help to ensure an orderly withdrawal, at the request of the Lebanese Government. However, one of the consequences of the PLO's withdrawal was the formation of Lebanese Hezbollah, an Iranian-supported Shi'a fundamentalist group, political party and militia rolled into one. Hezbollah forces would use suicide truck bomb tactics against the US embassy and the US Marine Corps peacekeepers' barracks, both in Beirut, the Lebanese capital, in 1983.

Another significant event linked to Israel's operation in Lebanon was the raid mounted on Palestinian refugee camps at Sabra and Chatila in west Beirut in September 1982. In conjunction with Lebanese Government and Maronite Christian Phalangist militias, and in the wake of the assassination earlier that month of Lebanese President Bachir Gemayel, Israel cordoned off the refugee camps on the grounds of suspected militant activity. With the apparent complicity of the occupying Israeli forces, Lebanese forces entered the camps and massacred some 2,000 people, including women and children. Israel's investigatory Kahan Commission found Israeli Minister of Defense Ariel Sharon indirectly responsible for the atrocities, a finding that forced him eventually to resign from his cabinet post. Israeli forces remained in southern Lebanon, as did the UN Interim Force in Lebanon (UNIFIL), a peacekeeping mission dating back to the 1978 crisis.

With the PLO in Tunisia and UNIFIL peacekeepers in southern Lebanon, with Israeli forces acting as a buffer, the Palestinian question could arguably be seen as less pressing for Israel. However, that view emphasizes the formal role of international groups and militias, when in fact millions of

Palestinians had been living in the Occupied Territories under Israeli military rule since the 1967 Six-Day War. The Likud Governments under Begin and—upon his resignation—his successor Itzhak Shamir continued overseeing the establishment of Israeli settlements in the occupied Gaza Strip and West Bank; by 1987 there were 19 settlements with 2,500 settlers in Gaza, and 130 settlements with 175,000 settlers in the West Bank. Since neither the Labor Alignment nor Likud could form a viable coalition after the election in 1984, the Labor leader, Shimon Peres, had to form a national unity Government with Likud, pulling Israel in different directions on matters of international peace initiatives. In 1985 Israel rejected a Jordanian proposal to hold a conference to attempt to resolve outstanding issues, on the grounds that representatives of the PLO would be invited to take part. In turn, Jordan rejected Israeli calls for direct talks without the PLO's involvement. Peres supported an initiative by US Secretary of State George Shultz to organize an international peace conference to seek to find a final settlement on the Occupied Territories, only for Shamir to scuttle the plans when he resumed the premiership in 1986. At the November 1988 elections to the Knesset, the Likud-Labor national unity Government retained control, and the paralysis in policy advancements continued.

Escalating street protests by Palestinians in the Occupied Territories and Israeli violence culminated in the first *intifada*, a sustained territory-wide movement uprising. Triggered by the deaths of four Palestinians in Gaza in December 1987, in a collision with an Israeli military vehicle, the *intifada* drew international attention to the Occupied Territories and upended the West's widely held view of Israel as the innocent victim. News coverage of children throwing rocks at Israeli armoured tanks and of the Israeli forces employing US-supplied ammunition raised concerns in Israel and the West. UN Security Council resolutions condemned Israeli violence and deportations, with only the USA and Israel voting against them, strengthening the impression that the USA both enabled and protected Israel's behaviour.

The *intifada* generated co-operation among disparate Palestinian actors from Fatah to the PFLP, under a coalition entitled the Unified National Leadership of the Uprising, giving Arafat inroads to influence in the territories again. In November 1988, at a meeting in the Algerian capital, Algiers, the Palestinian National Council (PNC) of the PLO declared an independent Palestinian state (notionally comprising the West Bank and Gaza) and, surprisingly, endorsed UN Security Council Resolutions 242 and 338, thereby implicitly recognizing Israel and indicating that Palestinian aspirations were now defined by Green Line 1967 borders rather than by the 1948 mandate. Numerous countries recognized the new Palestinian 'state', and Jordan relinquished all claims to the West Bank and Jerusalem. The declaration also provoked more violence and the creation of radicalized groups, such as the Islamic Resistance Movement (Hamas—Harakat al-Muqawama al-Islamiyya), which rejected recognition of Israel and spoke in terms of liberating all of Palestine.

Following Iraq's invasion of Kuwait in August 1990, the *intifada* attracted greater international attention, as Iraqi President Saddam Hussain pointed out the hypocrisy of Western moralizing against the occupation of Kuwait while Israel maintained its hold on Gaza, the West Bank and the Golan Heights. Iraq tried to provoke Israel into joining the Gulf War in 1991, firing Scud missiles at the state, which refrained from retaliating at the request of the USA in the name of coalition unity. In order to maintain the support of Arab states against Iraq, the Administration of US President George H. W. Bush (1989–93) also called for an international conference to address the Palestinian question. The ensuing 1991 Madrid Conference was ambitious, but ultimately resulted in little of substance. With a Likud Government back in sole control in Israel since June 1990, Israeli opposition to peace initiatives irked the US President, who delayed a US $10,000m. loan guarantee to Israel by demanding that the latter first freeze its settlement building in the Occupied Territories as part of a jump-start to a possible peace deal with the Palestinians.

Out of the new hopes arising from the Madrid Conference and the end of the Cold War came a new path to peace. The use of back channels and track-two diplomacy, under the mediation of Norway, was begun between the PLO and Israel's Labor party leadership. The resulting Declaration of Principles on Palestinian Self-Rule in the Occupied Territories, or Oslo Accords, were revealed in September 1993, after Labor had been returned to power at the head of a new coalition Government, under the premiership of Itzhak Rabin, following the elections of June 1992. The Declaration of Principles was announced at a White House ceremony hosted by the new US President, Bill Clinton (1993–2001). Under the terms of the Oslo Accords, the PLO would recognize Israel and renounce terrorism, while Israel would recognize the PLO as the sole representative of the Palestinian people for the purposes of negotiation. Furthermore, the Oslo Accord established a detailed timetable for Israel's disengagement from the Occupied Territories, stipulating that a permanent settlement of all outstanding issues pertaining to the Palestinian question be in place by early May 1999.

A transitional period of Palestinian self-rule in the Gaza Strip and Jericho began on 13 December 1993. On 4 May 1994 Israel and the PLO signed the Gaza–Jericho Agreement (commonly known as the 1994 Cairo Agreement), which provided for Israel's military withdrawal from the Gaza Strip and Jericho, and the deployment of a 9,000-strong Palestinian police force. A nominated Palestinian (National) Authority (PA) was to assume control of these areas, with the exception of external security and foreign affairs. The withdrawal was completed on 13 May, and on 17 May the PLO assumed control of the Israeli Civil Administration's departments in Gaza and Jericho. On 26–28 May the PA held its first meeting in the Tunisian capital, Tunis. Arafat made a symbolic return to Gaza City in July, and the PA was formally inaugurated in Jericho.

The Oslo process continued into the second half of the 1990s. The Oslo II Accord, formally known as the Interim Agreement on the West Bank and the Gaza Strip, which was signed in September 1995, stipulated the creation of Areas A, B and C in the West Bank. In areas designated Area A the Palestinians would have 'full control', while Israeli security would be maintained in those designated Area B and those designated Area C would remain under Israeli control pending later agreements.

The Oslo Accords were welcomed by the West and by moderates in Israeli and Palestinian circles. However, hardliners on both sides were suspicious of the terms. Israeli opponents of the agreement recoiled at their head of state legitimizing PLO Chairman Yasser Arafat, who for a generation had been a terrorist in the eyes of many. Palestinian hardliners saw Arafat as naive at best or treasonous at worst for negotiating with the 'Zionist entity' and, in their opinion, receiving so little in return at the outset. Yet Arafat did get something from the outset: a seat at the table and international legitimacy, and a chance to return to his homeland in Ramallah, West Bank. Opposition from Hamas was partly a result of the group having been shut out of the negotiation process and marginalized, and it appeared to embrace playing the role of spoiler to the peace process by carrying out terrorist bombings in 1995–96 in Israel and elsewhere.

In the mean time, Jordan made some conciliatory moves towards Israel in 1994; the two countries commenced trade and sharing water resources. These moves by Jordan, a Western-supported 'moderate' regime, provoked controversy in the Arab world. At various points the prospect of successful negotiations with Syria over Golan appeared hopeful, but ultimately came to little.

Extremist and rejectionist forces also stirred amid the optimism of the ongoing peace process. In February 1994 Israeli-American Baruch Goldstein killed 29 Palestinian Muslims and wounded more than 100 others who were at prayer at a mosque in Hebron in the West Bank. In November 1995 Israeli Prime Minister Itzhak Rabin was assassinated by Israeli nationalist Yigal Amir, at a peace rally in Tel Aviv in support of the Oslo Accords. This act horrified the nation and highlighted the strength of hostility among the radical Israeli right towards Rabin's actions of perceived appeasement towards their long-standing foe, and of ceding territory considered either ancestral or important for national security. Rabin's successor, Shimon Peres, continued implementing the Oslo process and governing Israel ahead of a general election to be held in May 1996. Hamas attacks continued throughout 1994–96 and throughout the Peres Government, provoking Israeli reprisals that undermined the trust being built on both sides to proceed with the land transfers. In March 1996 Hezbollah attacks on settlements in northern Israel prompted the election-wary Peres to order a sustained campaign of air and artillery attacks (code-named Operation Grapes of Wrath) on alleged Hezbollah positions in Lebanon against targets in Lebanon the following month. Some 400,000 Lebanese were displaced northwards, while the Israeli shelling of a UNIFIL base at Qana killed more than 100 Lebanese civilians who were sheltering there and four UN peacekeepers.

A NEW PRIME MINISTER AND A NEW SYSTEM OF ELECTING A PRIME MINISTER

If Peres thought that his militaristic response to Hezbollah's aggression would help in his re-election, he was wrong. In May 1996 Benjamin Netanyahu, the leader of Likud, achieved a marginal victory over Peres in Israel's first direct prime ministerial election (separate from the legislative poll). For three election cycles, 1996, 1999 and 2001, Israel experimented with a system of direct elections for the office of Prime Minister—akin to the US presidential election, which is conducted separately from elections to Congress. Based on legislation approved in 1992, Israeli voters received two ballots on election day, one for the Knesset party list and one for the candidates for the post of Prime Minister. The reasons for this change to the election system were that the existing system made it almost impossible for one party to win a majority and a sense that too much power rested with party leaderships; further electoral reforms decentralized party power to allow other party members to initiate policy and activities. By 2003, however, Israeli elections had reverted to using party ballots alone, with the Prime Minister again being chosen from within the ranks of a governing coalition.

Netanyahu, who has since become a defining figure in Israeli politics, entered the scene in 1996 as a young, brash nationalist who channelled the scepticism of Israel's right-wing about the peace process and land concessions, considering Arafat either 'unable or unwilling' to curb the violence in the Palestinian territories. Troop withdrawals promised in Oslo II were delayed by Netanyahu, who blamed the inaction on continuing violence. None the less, the Hebron Protocol, which was signed by Netanyahu and Arafat in January 1997, stipulated that Israeli forces withdraw from 80% of Hebron within 10 days, with redeployment of the IDF in the remaining 20% of the territory to be completed by mid-1998.

President Clinton himself took part in intensive negotiations with Arafat and Netanyahu in Maryland, USA in October 1998, resulting in the Wye River Memorandum, which aimed to progress the Israeli land concessions and redeployments in exchange for undertakings by the Palestinians to intensify measures to prevent terrorism and finally officially alter the wording of the Palestinian National Charter to recognize the state of Israel. The Memorandum outlined a three-month timetable for the implementation of the 1995 Interim Agreement and signalled the commencement of 'final status' talks—originally scheduled for May 1996 In November 1998 the Israeli Government implemented the first stage of renewed redeployment from the West Bank, also releasing 250 Palestinian prisoners and authorizing the opening of an international airport at Gaza. In December US President Clinton attended a session of the PNC, where delegates reaffirmed the removal from the Palestinian National Charter of all clauses seeking Israel's destruction. Netanyahu announced that the second phase of Israeli troop deployment envisaged by the Wye River Memorandum, scheduled for mid-December, would not be undertaken, citing the Palestinians' failure to address their security commitments. The Knesset subsequently voted to suspend implementation of the Wye River Memorandum, effectively suspending the peace process. Divisions within Netanyahu's coalition over the Memorandum led to the collapse of the Government, and the Knesset voted to hold elections in early 1999. In the second direct polls to elect Israel's Prime Minister, held on 17 May 1999, Netanyahu, with 44% of the vote, lost to Labor's Ehud Barak, who secured 56% and went on to from a broad-based coalition Government.

With a Labor Prime Minister back in charge shortly after the expiry, on 4 May 1999, of the interim stage as defined in the Oslo Accords, there was hope of a final settlement at last, after a decade of setbacks and half measures. Yet so much remained unresolved: notably, full Palestinian sovereignty, the delineation of the borders of a future Palestinian entity, the status of refugees and the future status of Jerusalem. In September Barak and Arafat signed the Sharm el-Sheikh Memorandum (or Wye Two accords) in Egypt. This outlined a revised timetable for implementation of the outstanding provisions of the Wye River Memorandum in order to facilitate the resumption of 'final status' talks: a new deadline—13 September 2000—was set to conclude a comprehensive settlement. In November 1999 Israel and the PA commenced talks on 'final status' issues in Ramallah.

US President Clinton opened the Camp David talks, aimed at reaching a framework agreement for a final peace settlement, on 11 July 2000. However, the summit ended on 25 July without agreement, and optimism in the peace process faded. There were differing views as to why the talks failed. The US and Israeli side claimed that a Palestinian state was proposed which incorporated the whole of Gaza and 91% of the West Bank, with an Israeli security presence along 15% of the Jordanian border, and a land swap of 1% of Israeli territory as compensation for the Israeli settlements that were retained. Arafat stated that he rejected the proposals because the Palestinians would not get Jerusalem, and asserted that Israel was willing to give up only 83% of the West Bank. No formal written offer was committed to paper to confirm what was actually discussed at Camp David, which may itself have been part of the problem.

The peace process effectively collapsed with the end of the Clinton Administration and the start of a second Palestinian *intifada* against Israeli occupation. Clinton's attempt at a final summit, held in Taba, Egypt, in January 2001, yielded nothing. Between the summits at Camp David and Taba, violence had been re-ignited in the Occupied Territories. In September 2000 Likud Chairman Ariel Sharon made a highly controversial visit to the Temple Mount/Haram al-Sharif compound in Jerusalem, asserting his right to do so with an entourage. In view of Sharon's role in the Sabra and Chatila massacres of 1982, this visit was an affront to Palestinians and sparked rioting and violence, which spread rapidly throughout the Palestinian territories. Deaths on both sides quickly indicated that this was not like the first *intifada*, but was a more weaponized and militarized affair, reflecting heightened frustrations on both sides. Of especial note, for the first time, Israeli Arabs clashed with security forces in Israel. In February 2001 Ariel Sharon defeated Barak in an early prime ministerial election and declared the peace process dead. Barak had notably lost the Israeli Arab vote, and his defeat was interpreted as a decisive rejection of the Oslo peace process by most Israelis.

After Oslo

In the spiralling violence in the early 21st century, pessimism about peace seemed to increase in Israeli and Palestinian quarters, but the notion of a two-state solution became the object of optimistic attention internationally. From the 2001 Mitchell and Tenet Plans put forward by the US Administration of George W. Bush (2001–09), to the 2002 Arab Peace Initiative and the 2003 Quartet Roadmap for Peace, external actors were willing to suggest solutions for an eventual return to negotiations. The Arab Peace Initiative, proposed by Saudi Arabia was finally approved by the Arab League at a summit in March 2007. It proposed normalization of relations between Israel and the Arab world, in exchange for a two-state solution with an Israeli withdrawal to the Green Line, giving Gaza, the West Bank and East Jerusalem to an independent Palestinian state. The Quartet, which involved representatives from the USA, the European Union, the Russian Federation and the UN, offered a more process-based phased plan with a goal of 'two states side by side in peace and security'. Phase I of this 'Performance-based Roadmap to a Permanent Two-State Solution to the Israeli–Palestinian Conflict' called for Palestinians to end all violence and Israeli affirmation of support for an independent, viable, sovereign Palestinian state. Phase II would be the creation of a provisional Palestinian state 'as a way station to a permanent status settlement'. This would include establishing a democratic Palestinian constitution to be aided by an international conference and monitoring. Phase III would be a formal international conference to determine a permanent final settlement of all outstanding issues, including 'just, fair and realistic' solutions on matters such as refugees and the status of Jerusalem.

None of these plans succeeded in ending the Israel–Palestine conflict. Talks aimed at relaunching the Middle East peace process were held over the ensuing years—at Annapolis, Maryland, in 2007 under the George W. Bush Administration, and with US Secretary of State John Kerry in 2013–14, during the presidency of Barack Obama (2009–17) administration—but it was not clear whether either the Israelis or the Palestinians were interested in the bilateral solutions proposed by these outside actors. Israel's position has hardened in line with its politics, adopting a centre-right posture that is sceptical about ceding territory or allowing a sovereign Palestinian state. Israeli proposals refer to demilitarized states with Israeli forces on the Jordanian border. The most useful concept, perhaps, for Israel's post-Oslo stance on Palestinian affairs is disengagement, a policy created under the watch of Prime Minister Ariel Sharon (2001–06). In November 2005 Sharon left Likud to establish a new centrist party, Kadima (Forward), which favoured a new, 'third way' regarding the revival of the peace process. Kadima suggested that the peace and concessions of Labor were foolish, yet Likud's desire to retain all of the land would lead to perpetual occupation and the absorption of Arab populations that would jeopardize the Jewish nature of the state of Israel. Disengagement, as proposed by Sharon, offered a managed withdrawal to defensible borders surrounding a Jewish majority. In 2004–05 the Sharon Government uprooted—by force at times—Jewish settlements in the Gaza Strip, abandoning control of the territory behind a newly constructed 'separation barrier'. While maintaining Israeli settlements in the West Bank and East Jerusalem, Sharon ordered the construction of a separation barrier (comprising a wall and fence) around the West Bank as well, which would physically divide Israel and its settlements from the Palestinian lands and peoples. This West Bank barrier did not conform to the 1949 Green Line, which was one of the objections of the International Court of Justice in its advisory ruling of July 2004 against the barrier's legality. Israel, however, claimed to have 'no partner in peace' and that the barrier protected Israel from rampant violence and bombings from the Occupied Territories. While there was a steep decline in suicide bombings—from 28 attacks and 173 fatalities in 2002 to two attacks and 15 fatalities in 2006—Palestinian militants responded with an increase in rocket and mortar attacks over the barrier. Israel countered these attacks with its 'Iron Dome' missile defence system, coupled with occasional incursions into Gaza or the West Bank to dismantle points of attack. These operations, included Operation Cast Lead, beginning in December 2008, Operation Pillar of Defense in November 2012 and Operation Protective Edge, beginning in July 2014. These, and lesser skirmishes in 2018 and beyond, have resulted in a disproportionate number of Palestinian deaths and recurring accusations of Israeli war crimes for the use of white phosphorus, excessive force and live ammunition on unarmed civilians. At times the UN has issued resolutions condemning the violence on both sides, often subject to a US veto.

After Sharon lapsed into an extended coma in January 2006, acting Prime Minister, Ehud Olmert, was named as Kadima's interim leader. Following elections in March 2006, Olmert became Prime Minister at the head of a new, Kadima-led coalition Government. In July 2008, facing a police inquiry into alleged corruption, Olmert declared his intention to resign the premiership in September, following the election of a new Kadima leader. In September Tzipi Livni won the Kadima leadership. Olmert duly resigned as Prime Minister, in order to contest the various corruption charges against him. However, when Livni proved unable to form a new government, a general election was scheduled for February 2009. In an election that illustrates well the quirks of the Israeli political system, Kadima secured 28 seats in the Knesset, while Likud (on a joint list with the right-wing, nationalist Ahi party) won 27. As a case study of the Israeli electoral system, the 2009 election showed that, despite custom or habit, the keys to forming a government do not automatically go to the highest vote winner. In fact, there resides with the office of the President the power to 'entrust to one of the members of the Knesset the duty of forming a government'. Until 2009 that duty was entrusted to the leader of the party with the largest share of the vote. In 2009, however, Israeli President Shimon Peres gave the task of forming a government not to Kadima leader Livni but to Likud's Benjamin Netanyahu. It was a controversial decision that led to charges of the 'old boys network' operating against the young, female Livni, although a more pedestrian explanation for Peres' decision is that a candidate must demonstrate the ability to control 61 seats in a coalition. It could be that Livni did not have the clout to convince Peres of her ability to control 61 seats, whereas Netanyahu could. It should be noted that the President was a member of the Labor Party, which was one of the constituent parties in the Likud-led coalition Government.

Whatever the circumstances, Netanyahu's ascension to the office of Prime Minister would initiate an era of unparalleled power and leadership, with the dominance of Likud and Netanyahu rivalling the hegemony of Labor during the early years of the Israeli state. Netanyahu remained as Prime Minister through several coalition changes from 2009 until 2022. In 2009 Likud formed a coalition with the secular, centre-left Labor Party but also with the religious Shas party, with the right-wing, nationalist Jewish Home (HaBayit HaYehudi) and the ultranationalist Israel Beytenu. In January 2011 the Deputy Prime Minister and Minister of Defense, Ehud Barak, resigned as Labor Chairman to form a new party, Ha'atzmaut (Independence). His fellow Labor ministers also subsequently resigned from the party. A renewed coalition agreement, facilitating the appointment of Ha'atzmaut representatives, was approved by the Knesset two days later. The revised Cabinet included four members of Ha'atzmaut, among them Barak, who retained the defence portfolio. Shelly Yachimovich succeeded Barak as Labor leader in September. In May 2012 the possibility of early elections was thwarted by another coalition change that brought Kadima into a unity coalition Government that controlled 94 seats. Kadima withdrew from the Government in July, however, following a dispute over the Tal Law, which allowed principally ultra-Orthodox students to defer military conscription. At a general election held in January 2013, an alliance of Likud and Israel Beytenu won the highest number of seats (31) in the Knesset and Netanyahu formed a new coalition Government in March. Following early elections in March 2015, Likud secured victory, with 30 seats, and formed another coalition which included a new centre-right party, Kulanu, while excluding the polarizing Israel Beytenu. As indicated in the above brief summary, Israeli politics has been increasingly turbulent, even though the centre-right holds a stable plurality in post-Oslo Israel. The peacemakers and secularists fare less well now.

Constituting 21% of the Israeli population as of the 2019 census, many Israeli Arabs in the post-Oslo era have become jaded and despondent. Amid the second *intifada*, voter turnout among Arabs dropped from 75%–79% in the first decades of the country's democracy to 18% in 2001, with calls for boycotts. Turnout rebounded to 62% in 2003, 56% in 2006 and 54% in 2009, but the debate over how to participate in the Jewish state has continued. More Arabs are calling for a 'state for all its citizens', against a background of laws demanding loyalty to the 'Jewish state' as a prerequisite for running for office. Even during the Oslo process, Israeli Arabs voiced their concerns through the Association for the Defense of the Rights of the Internally Displaced Persons in Israel, demanding the right to return to their homes lost in the War of Independence. Israeli Arabs held a *Nakba* ('catastrophe') Day on 15 May 1997. The so-called 'watershed vision documents' put together by prominent Israeli Arab in December 2006 spelled out the hopes and demands for a Future Vision of the Palestinian Arabs in Israel, an 'Equal Constitution for All' for the 'Collective Rights of Arab Citizens'. The right-wing shift in Israeli politics after Oslo included the implementation of more legislation that undermined Arab power and rights. The so-called governability bill, which was approved in March 2014, increased the minimum share of the national vote required for representation in parliament from 2% to 3.25%; critics claimed that the changes would prevent small and minority parties (particularly Israeli Arab parties) from gaining seats. A controversial new Basic Law, on Israel as the Nation-State of the Jewish People, which was approved in July 2018, defined Israel as 'the national home of the Jewish people' and stated that the right to exercise national self-determination in that country was 'unique to the Jewish people'. The legislation also defined Hebrew as the 'state's language', thereby effectively demoting Arabic—which had hitherto had been an official language, equal with Hebrew—to 'special status'. Opponents claimed that the legislation enshrined discrimination against Israeli Arabs in constitutional law, although Netanyahu insisted that the Israeli Government would continue to respect 'the rights of all its citizens'. In July 2022 the Israeli Supreme Court upheld a 2008 Citizenship Law which allowed the Government to revoke citizenship for those who committed a 'breach of loyalty'.

The Palestinian side of the Israel–Palestine conflict equation is even more complicated and is effectively a tale of two Palestines. When Yasser Arafat died in November 2004 Mahmoud Abbas was elected as the new Executive President of the PA. However, the Quartet—especially the USA—pushed for democratic elections in the Palestinian territories to give the PA greater legistimacy, which led to elections being held to the Palestinian Legislative Council (PLC) in January 2006. Hamas—which contested the polls as the Change and Reform list—secured a decisive majority in the PLC, and Abbas asked it to form a new administration. This result was unacceptable not only to Fatah but also to the USA, Israel and numerous conservative Arab governments, including Saudi Arabia. The resulting dispute over authority led to a civil war in Gaza in which Hamas prevailed and PLO forces were ejected. Since 2007 Hamas has held power in Gaza and claimed the mantle of legitimacy in the form of legislative elections. Abbas and the PLO claim the mantle of legitimacy in Ramallah as the holders of the Palestinian presidency recognized by outside powers and receiving outside aid. Hamas's rejectionist posture towards Israel leads to skirmishes and conflicts, as discussed above. As for the PA in the West Bank, its attempts at maintaining legitimacy among Palestinians has proven difficult, given the suspension of future elections and operating under emergency law while taking Israeli and Western aid. The Abbas approach has been to try to circumvent Israel and to gain recognition from the international community while attempting to isolate Israel. A 2012 Palestinian push for UN statehood was blocked by the USA in the Security Council, but in November the UN General Assembly voted, by 138 votes to nine (with 41 abstentions), to accord 'Palestine' the status of non-member observer state—giving the PA a voice but not a vote. International efforts to isolate or shame Israel through the actions of the Palestinian-led BDS (Boycott, Divestment, Sanctions) Movement have borne little fruit, although there is evidence that the political left in many parts of the world, including the USA, has become more sympathetic to the Palestinians and more critical of Israel, framing the occupation as akin to South Africa's former apartheid regime. A Gallup poll in March 2023 showed that, for the first time, Democratic Party sympathies in the USA were more with the Palestinians than with the Israelis, by a margin of 49% to 38%. The USA began giving aid to the PA under the Oslo process, as Abbas is viewed as a moderate potential partner for peace—a preferable alternative to Hamas and to what chaos would ensue if the West Bank lacked basic amenities.

International relations remained turbulent under Netanyahu's premiership. The 2011 'Arab Spring', hailed by many liberals and the West as a chance for democracy to bloom in the Middle East and North Africa, posed a potential threat to Israel's stability. Egypt's President Hosni Mubarak having been ousted in February, the country experienced rapid democratization that put the anti-Israel Muslim Brotherhood leaders in power, both in the presidency and parliament. However, the new President, Mohamed Mursi, promised to honour previous agreements, and thus the Egypt-Israel peace treaty of 1979. Mursi was himself toppled in July 2013 and replaced by Gen. Abd al-Fatah al-Sisi, restoring some stability to Israel's western frontier, even if democracy in Egypt was undermined as a result. In Syria, the anti-Israel regime of Bashar al-Assad faced civil war that apparently delighted Israel even as it created challenges of regional instability. Porous borders with Lebanon meant that Hezbollah and Iranian support for Assad could also threaten Israel, which took to liberally striking pro-Assad convoys deemed to be threatening Israel's national interests.

In terms of US relations, the Administration of Donald Trump (2017–21) tilted heavily towards Israel in its four years in office. In a highly controversial move, the Administration announced in December 2017 that it formally recognized the city of Jerusalem as Israel's capital, moving the US embassy there from Tel Aviv in March 2018, despite vehement Palestinian and Arab opposition and protests, in which dozens were killed and hundreds injured by Israeli forces. Under Trump, the USA cut aid to both the PA as well as the UN Relief and Works Agency (UNRWA), citing concerns about aid funding terrorist activity but also in attempt to pressurize the Palestinians into accepting a peace plan, entitled 'Peace to Prosperity', proposed by the President's son-in-law and senior adviser, Jared Kushner. The plan, like many before, was for a two-state solution and included a map delineating the proposed borders; however, it was not seriously considered by either side. Instead, the Trump Administration pivoted to circumventing the Palestinians altogether with the 2020 Abraham Accords. Focusing on Arab-Israeli reconciliation and normalization rather than on Palestinian issues, the USA brokered a deal for mutual recognition between Israel and the Arab states of Bahrain and the United Arab Emirates, in exchange for US supply of financial, military and surveillance technology, and on the premise that Iran posed a common threat to them all. In the words of the US Administration, 'the dispute between Israelis and Palestinians [...] need not hold up Israel's relations with the broader Arab world'. Morocco and Sudan subsequently joined the Abraham Accords by normalizing relations with Israel in December and January 2021, respectively.

While Netanyahu showed impressive political strength by continuing in power, that power was under continuous challenge, revealing a declining mandate to lead the country. In the legislative elections of April 2019 a serious challenge came from a new, centrist electoral alliance, Kahol Lavan ('Blue and White'—the colours of the Israeli flag), led by former Chief of General Staff Benjamin (Benny) Gantz. Although the 35 seats in the Knesset secured by Kahol Lavan were not enough to build a coalition, they were enough to block Likud (which had also won 35 seats) from forming a coalition of its own. This led to an election re-run in September, when Kahol Lavan became the largest group in the Knesset, winning 33 of the 120 seats, against Likud's 32 seats. Once again, neither party was able to form a coalition, with Israel Beytenu thwarting the formation of a Likud government in protest over draft legislation to repeal an exemption from military conscription granted to ultra-Orthodox religious students. A caretaker Government under Netanyahu continued in office as the country faced an unprecedented third poll to elect a new administration. Meanwhile, Netanyahu was faced with corruption allegations. In November he was formally charged with breach of trust, accepting bribes and fraud, legally requiring him to stand down from his various ministerial posts other than his role as acting Prime Minister.

Netanyahu could have been upended in the legislative elections held on 2 March 2020, as although neither of the leading parties appeared to have enough parliamentary support to form a majority government (Likud won 36 seats and Kahol Lavan 33), President Reuven Rivlin instructed Gantz to lead discussions over the formation of a new administration. However, Gantz chose to align with Likud and to share power with Netanyahu rather than forging a complicated coalition of many small parties that could have included the United Arab List (Ra'am). On 20 April Netanyahu and Gantz formally agreed to establish a unity Government, with Gantz serving as Deputy Prime Minister before replacing Netanyahu as Prime Minister after 18 months (and retaining the premiership for the same length of time). Part of the reasoning behind the decision to form a national unity Government was the outbreak in early

2020 of the coronavirus disease (COVID-19) pandemic, coinciding with the election season.

One week after being sworn in again as Prime Minister, on 24 May 2020 Netanyahu appeared at the Jerusalem District Court for the start of his corruption trial. It was the first time that a serving Israeli premier had faced trial proceedings. However, Netanyahu dismissed the charges against him as an attempt by police and prosecutors to remove him from power. During his second appearance in court, on 8 February 2021, just six weeks prior to another general election (see below), Netanyahu pleaded not guilty to all of the charges.

US-Israeli relations have been more unstable in recent years, given the dynamic of a centre-left US administration with the Likud-led Israeli Government. Since taking office in January 2021, the Administration of US President Joe Biden has not altered the Abraham Accords, although it has resumed aid to UNRWA and the PA. It abstained from, rather than vetoed, an UNRWA resolution reaffirming the Palestinian right of return stipulated in UN Security Council Resolution 194. In June 2023 the USA supported a UN Security Council resolution opposing Israel's continued construction and expansion of settlements in the West Bank. Although involving relatively mild and toothless measures, it appeared that the US tradition of vetoing UN resolutions and shielding Israel could no longer be taken for granted.

The Netanyahu era appeared finally to have come to an end following the legislative elections of 23 March 2021. Although Likud again secured the largest representation, winning 30 seats, once again, neither the Likud-led right-wing bloc, nor the anti-Netanyahu bloc appeared to have enough support to guarantee a majority in the Knesset. Netanyahu's attempts to form a coalition government failed, largely owing to the fact that parties centred around Jewish identity—whether religious or secular—were reluctant to enter into any pact with Ra'am, an avowedly Islamist party. President Rivlin then passed the prime ministerial mandate to Yair Atid, a former well-known media personality and founding leader of the secular centrist party Yesh Atid (There is a Future). On 2 June Lapid succeeded in reaching a coalition agreement with a disparate alliance of opposition parties, including Yemina, an ultra right-wing alliance established by Naftali Bennett in 2018. This broad-based 'government of change' was to be led by Bennett, thereby marking the end of Netanyahu's 12-year premiership. The main factor bonding the constituent members of the new administration, comprising parties from across the political spectrum, was their shared opposition to Netanyahu.

Bennett took office as Prime Minister on 13 June 2021, having narrowly (by 60 votes to 59) secured parliamentary approval for his coalition Government. The Cabinet included the right-wing parties Yemina and New Home, left-wing Labor and Meretz, and centrist Yesh Atid, Kahol Lavan and Israel Beytenu. The new Government also enjoyed the parliamentary support of Ra'am (an historic achievement by an Israeli Arab party), although the party was not allocated any ministerial posts. This first-ever involvement of an Israeli Arab party in government illustrated the breadth and unity of opposition to Netanyahu, but also the division within Arab political circles, as Ra'am left the Joint List alliance of parties representing Israeli Arab citizens in its willingness to join with conservative Israeli political forces. According to the terms of the coalition agreement, Bennett was to serve as Prime Minister until 27 August 2023, when Lapid would assume the premiership. Meanwhile, Lapid was appointed Alternate Prime Minister and Minister of Foreign Affairs.

Despite surviving two votes of no confidence in the Knesset, on 20 June 2022 Bennett's Government announced plans to dissolve the legislature and appoint Yair Lapid as Prime Minister pending fresh elections later that year. On 30 June the Knesset unanimously voted to dissolve itself and it was announced that a general election would be held on 1 November. Lapid took office as Prime Minister on 1 July (while retaining responsibility for foreign affairs), and Bennett assumed the post of Alternate Prime Minister.

At Israel's fifth general election in less than four years, held as scheduled on 1 November 2022, Netanyahu's showed his political resilience when a right-wing electoral alliance led by Likud won a parliamentary majority, largely at the expense of left-wing parties. A new coalition Government, headed by Netanyahu as Prime Minister, was sworn into office on 29 December. The new administration was notable for its predominantly hardline, ultra-Orthodox composition, comprising representatives of Likud, Shas, the Religious Zionist Party, Otzma Yehudit, United Torah Judaism and Noam. The appointment of Itamar Ben Gvir, the leader of Otzma Yehudit, as Minister of National Security, provoked considerable controversy, owing to his uncompromising, anti-Arab stance.

Once again, Netanyahu proved to be a political lightning rod, announcing controversial plans significantly to reform the judicial system by severely curtailing the Supreme Court's powers. The proposals included granting the Government control over judicial appointments and limiting the Court's mandate to exercise judicial review by giving the Knesset the authority to override rulings by the Court that deemed legislation approved by the Knesset as unconstitutional. A separate law was also proposed which Netanyahu's critics believed was intended to protect him in light of his ongoing corruption trial, since it would effectively limit the power to declare an incumbent Prime Minister unfit for office to the premier himself or to a two-thirds' cabinet majority; this legislation was adopted by the Knesset in March. The proposed judicial reforms provoked widespread opposition and large street protests among Israelis that escalated during the first half of 2023. In early March these protests coincided with violent incidents between Israeli settlers and Palestinians in the West Bank. The protests reached an unprecedented scale in late March, as the date approached for the Knesset to vote on the legislation. On 25 March Minister of Defense Yoav Gallant expressed his support for the mass protests and urged Netanyahu to postpone the implementation of the proposed legislation to allow for negotiations between the Government and the opposition. He argued that the proposals posed a serious threat to Israel's security, not least as many military reservists planned to protest against the judicial reforms by withdrawing from training. On 26 March Netanyahu responded to Gallant's remarks by dismissing him from the Cabinet. Within hours of Gallant's dismissal, spontaneous protests took place across Israel, with tens of thousands of demonstrators holding a mass rally in Tel Aviv and chanting that Israeli democracy was under threat. The unrest intensified on 27 March, when Israel's largest trade union, the Histradrut, called for a general strike until the Government withdrew the proposals. With security officials warning of the risk of serious violence and despite certain right-wing cabinet members continuing to pressurize Netanyahu not to reverse his plans, later that day the Prime Minister issued a statement that his Government would postpone the reforms until the next session of the Knesset, to allow sufficient time for dialogue with the opposition. However, following the collapse in June of negotiations aimed at reaching a compromise and the Government's decision in mid-July to proceed with introducing the judicial reform bill in the Knesset, on 18 July tens of thousands of protesters across the country took part in a 'National Day of Resistance'. The security forces responded forcefully, using stun grenades and other coercive measures against the protesters.

Given the level of unrest and schisms within society and politics caused by the sustained and intense protests against judicial reform, and the, at times, violent state response, some of the more histrionic analyses speculated about the prospect of civil war breaking out in Israel in 2023. Israeli President Isaac Herzog himself warned of Israel standing at the 'edge of an abyss'. On 24 July the Knesset passed a bill to limit the power of the Supreme Court to veto government decisions on the grounds of them being 'unreasonable'. Notably, the vote was passed by 64 votes to 0, owing to the absence of the opposition legislators, who had staged a boycott in protest at the bill. The implications of the bill's passage on the continuing deterioration of Israeli national unity were expected to be the focus of Israeli domestic politics for the remainder of 2023.

Economy

ROBERT E. LOONEY

INTRODUCTION

Israel has a strong and varied economy that encourages entrepreneurship and innovation. The services sector is the primary driver of economic activity largely owing to high levels of private consumption and tourism income. Additionally, Israel has developed manufacturing industries in high-value sectors such as electronics and pharmaceuticals, which are important exports. The largest sectors in terms of value added are the tertiary and secondary sectors, which are much larger than the primary sector.

The economy has recorded high, albeit declining, average annual rates of growth since the 1960s, averaging 6.6% in 1966–79, 4.6% in 1980–99 and 3.9% in 2000–22. With this sustained expansion, Israel attained one of the highest per capita incomes in the Middle East, with per capita incomes (on a purchasing-power parity—PPP—basis, in 2017 international dollar terms) increasing from US $19,251 in 1980 to $30,545 in 2000 and further to $44,335 in 2022, placing Israel roughly on a par with Spain and Italy.

The success of the economy stems from several critical factors. Israel's strong institutions and business environment stand out in the region, giving the country a diversified economy with many start-ups. Israel has invested heavily in education and spends a higher proportion of its gross domestic product (GDP) on civilian research and development than any other country. More than 50% of the population has enrolled in tertiary education. The highly skilled workforce enables the country to attract large volumes of foreign direct investment (FDI) into growth sectors such as information technology and pharmaceuticals, making Israel the region's technology hub.

Israel's high spending on military research has had positive knock-on effects for the civilian technology sector. The country's close ties with the USA provide it with substantial military support and a level of security not found elsewhere in the region. Israel has historically had few natural resources, but sizeable natural gas finds in the past decade have changed this. The country has mitigated the effects of low rainfall through desalination and water recycling projects and is a significant exporter of water technologies.

None the less, the economy is facing major challenges. Opposition to Israeli policy in the West Bank is growing, and this could lead to foreign (mostly European) firms pulling out of investments or to foreign governments imposing sanctions. The Israeli economy remains highly exposed to the USA and Europe in terms of trade and investment. It is also experiencing low productivity growth. This is mainly because of productivity and wage gains being limited to a few high-technology manufacturing and services industries, while the other sectors of the economy lag behind. Another issue is the quality of the education system and the integration of specific segments of the population into it. Policymakers need to address these deficiencies in order to improve productivity growth in Israel.

ECONOMIC GROWTH

Israel's economic progress in the 1980s and 1990s stemmed partly from the progressive fall in defence expenditure from more than 40% of GDP in 1973 to 18.9% in 1989 and 6.5% by 1999. The positive effects of the reduction of defence spending were reinforced by continuing substantial levels of official US military assistance and other aid, as well as by large financial donations from the USA and other Jewish communities abroad. These funds were used in particular to assist the absorption of Jewish migrants into Israel. Also beneficial was the introduction in 1980 of the shekel as the official currency unit, in succession to the previous Israeli pound (or lira), after a period of rapid currency depreciation and rampant inflation. The successful reform of many socialist structures and institutions, enabling the economy to compete in critical export markets, has also been significant.

Israel's annual economic growth averaged 5.6% in the 1990s, 3.5% in the 2000s and 4.2% in 2010–22. These long-term figures, however, mask numerous short-term fluctuations. One such period of volatility, and one that is at the root of many of today's issues with the economy, is the international financial crisis of 2008–09.

After five years of high growth, Israel's economy suffered a reversal in the second half of 2008, as the international credit crisis provoked a global economic downturn. Although GDP increased by 3.2% in 2008 as a whole, it contracted in the fourth quarter (and again, by an annual rate of 3.6%, in the first quarter of 2009), reflecting steep declines in exports, tax revenues and private consumption. The fall in fiscal revenue led to an increase in the budget deficit to 3.4% of GDP for 2008. Meanwhile, the inflation rate, which peaked at 5.5% in September 2008, declined sharply, and the Bank of Israel reduced the interest rate several times to reach a record low of 0.5% by April 2009.

Although the credit crisis led to upheaval in Israel's financial sector, its effects were moderate compared with those in other small open economies. The sector's relative strength reflected Israel's conservative banking practices, with comprehensive regulation and transparency, and an implicit government guarantee to support the banks. Furthermore, the period of negative growth was short-lived, and the economy started to recover in the second quarter of 2009, although GDP grew by only 0.9% in 2009 as a whole. Annual inflation in that year averaged 3.3%, and the Bank of Israel raised the interest rate on three separate occasions between August 2009 and March 2010, the rate reaching 1.25% in the latter month. Meanwhile, in December 2009 the International Monetary Fund (IMF) issued an upbeat assessment of Israel's economy but expressed concern about the size of the fiscal deficit, which widened to 6.6% of GDP in 2009, and the overall level of public debt, which was averaging 70%–80% of GDP.

GDP grew by 5.7% in 2010, underlining Israel's recovery from the global economic downturn and reflecting, according to the IMF, 'the fruit of decisive policies and strengthened macrofinancial policy frameworks'. There were rapid increases in fixed investment, exports and private consumption, a rise in employment and a marked decline in the budget deficit to 3.7% of GDP in 2010. The debt-to-GDP ratio also fell, from 74.5% to 70.6%. However, inflationary pressures from domestic factors, particularly rising housing prices and rents, and global price increases for energy and commodities, prompted the Bank of Israel to raise the interest rate to 2% by December 2010 and to 3.25% by June 2011.

Economic momentum continued in 2011, with growth of 4.7%, led by robust private consumption and buoyant business investment. However, the global slowdown meant that there was a deceleration in the second half of the year. The unemployment rate declined to an annual average of 5.6% (from 6.7% at the end of 2010), its lowest level since 1983, while the budget deficit decreased to 3.0% of GDP, and the debt-to-GDP ratio again contracted, to 68.9% of GDP. With the global and domestic economy slowing, the Bank of Israel began monetary easing in September 2011, incrementally reducing the interest rate from 3.25% to 2.5% by February 2012. The Government's fiscal policy and the rising cost of housing and essential consumer goods and services prompted nationwide social protests in mid-2011. In response, the Government changed its tax policy and increased support for working families. Continuing political turmoil across much of the Arab world heightened concerns about Israel's existing economic and trading links and their longer-term viability.

GDP growth in 2012 slowed to 2.8%, but this still compared favourably with the performance of other developed economies. Exports, which accounted for about 40% of GDP, struggled in the context of the sluggishness in Israel's main overseas markets, particularly in Europe. However, FDI inflows remained high, at 3.5% of GDP in 2012; industrial production grew by 3.7%, led by a surge in high-technology output, and annual inflation remained subdued, at 1.7%. The Bank of Israel further cut the benchmark interest rate in 2012 to 1.75%. In May 2013 an additional cut, to 1.5%, was made to protect the export sector in the context of the continued appreciation of the shekel; another cut, to 1.25%, swiftly followed. Meanwhile, in April of that year the new coalition Government under Benjamin Netanyahu approved draft legislation to establish a sovereign wealth fund (the Israeli Citizens Fund) to invest state revenue from Israel's new natural gas output.

An IMF report in early 2014 praised the strengths of the Israeli economy, notably welcoming the progress made in reducing public debt (although this remained high) and the Government's commitment to fiscal discipline. However, rapidly rising house prices were among the risks faced domestically. GDP growth was robust in 2013, at 4.8%, while unemployment was relatively low and the budget deficit declined to 4.1% of GDP (from 4.4% in 2012). The central bank made further benchmark interest rate reductions in 2014, reflecting the international economic environment, the appreciation of the shekel, and fears that the security situation could cause an economic slowdown.

In 2014 GDP grew by 4.1%, and the budget deficit declined to 2.4% of GDP. However, the fiscal outlook deteriorated, and overall economic activity slowed, owing to renewed Israeli–Palestinian confrontations in Gaza in July and August. Moreover, Israeli exports lagged owing to continued weakness in European demand. The unemployment rate averaged 5.9% for the year, down from 6.3% in 2013, while inflation fell to 0.5%, from 1.6% in 2013.

The economy expanded by 2.3% in 2015, and the fiscal deficit, at 1.1% of GDP, was below the government target of 2.9%. Although investment and export earnings declined, private consumption remained buoyant during the year, aided by lower unemployment, which fell to 5.3%, and a cut in the value-added tax rate, to 17%, in October. Meanwhile, the public debt-to-GDP ratio declined to 64% in 2015, and in March the Bank of Israel reduced the benchmark interest rate from 0.25% to a record low of 0.1%.

GDP grew by 4.5% in 2016, driven primarily by a double-digit increase in net investment, although exports suffered from weak growth in global trade, and the merchandise trade deficit rose sharply to US $13,100m. Inflation remained below the Bank of Israel's 1%–3% target range, and unemployment continued to fall, averaging 4.8% over the year. The Bank maintained the benchmark interest rate at 0.1% until November 2018, when it was increased to 0.25%. Meanwhile, significant real increases in revenue contained the fiscal deficit to 1.4% of GDP in 2016, and the public debt ratio declined further, to 62.1% of GDP. The IMF commended Israel's sound macro-economic performance and noted that the short-term outlook remained favourable. However, it cautioned that the country faced significant structural challenges from the inflated housing market, high levels of poverty and inequality, poor labour productivity and low labour force participation among some elements of the population.

The economy grew by 4.4% in 2017 and by 4.1% in 2018, with exports showing a slightly more robust performance than other components of GDP. In 2018 there was an overall surplus on the current account of the balance of payments equivalent to 3.0% of GDP. In that year unemployment fell to an average of 4.0%, declining further to 3.8% in 2019. The budget deficit increased to 2.9% of GDP in 2018 (up from 1.9% in 2017) and 3.6% in 2019 (the highest level since 2013). In June 2019 the Government agreed on a package of wide-ranging budget cuts, with some NIS 800m. to be diverted from other ministries' budgets to fund classified projects run by the Ministry of Defense. Further measures taken during 2019 to reduce the burgeoning deficit included petroleum tax increases and a levy on purchases of luxury electric cars.

Tourism continued to be a significant driver of GDP growth in 2019, with international visitor arrivals increasing from 3.6m. in 2017 to 4.1m. in 2018 and 4.6m. in 2019. GDP grew by 4.2% in 2019. However, foreign investment and capital spending fell, including that on significant infrastructure projects, partly owing to ongoing political instability in that year, following elections in April and September that failed to deliver a decisive majority or agreement to form a workable coalition (see History).

Following yet another election, in March 2020, Netanyahu and his main political rival, Benny Gantz, agreed in May to form a coalition under which Netanyahu would serve as Prime Minister until November 2021, when he would be succeeded by Gantz. However, any prospect of a more stable economic climate ended with the spread of the coronavirus disease (COVID-19) pandemic to Israel in March 2020, prompting a lockdown of non-essential parts of the economy and a suspension of international travel. In April the Knesset (parliament) approved a significant increase to the state budget, totalling some NIS 80,000m., to enable the Government to meet the economic and social costs of tackling the outbreak of COVID-19. In early April the Bank of Israel cut its key policy interest rate from 0.25% to 0.1%—its first rate cut since 2015. Some of the lockdown restrictions were eased during May 2020, but the number of cases of infection and fatalities rose significantly from June, prompting the Government to impose a second lockdown in mid-September, which once again severely curtailed economic activity. By August the unemployment rate had increased to 5.4% (although observers remarked that many members of the workforce were not economically active by that point and were receiving government support for their income).

Besides the enormous economic disruption caused by the pandemic and lockdown measures, large public protests against Netanyahu's administration took place from July 2020, directed at the Prime Minister's perceived mishandling of the pandemic response and his refusal to stand down as premier despite criminal proceedings against him for corruption (see History). Meanwhile, the launch of the Israeli Citizens Fund, which had been due to commence operations in 2020, was postponed until 2021. GDP contracted by 1.9% in 2020, but this was much less than the 6.3% contraction projected by the IMF as well as those recorded by many other advanced economies. However, Israel's fiscal deficit soared to 11.3% of GDP, from 3.6% in 2019. General government debt levels rose from 58.8% of GDP in 2019 to 70.6% in 2020.

The economy contracted during the first quarter of 2021, compared with the previous quarter, owing to a national lockdown imposed before the roll-out of Israel's mass rapid COVID-19 vaccination programme, which allowed the lifting of restrictions to begin in February 2021. However, business sector GDP expanded by almost 20% in the second quarter of the year, after a slight drop in the previous quarter. Although overall GDP growth was slower during the first half of 2021 than in the second half of 2020, when Israel was first emerging from its initial national lockdown, it was still a significant rebound from the slump recorded in the first half of 2020. Annualized seasonally adjusted real GDP growth in the second quarter of 2021 was 15.4%.

In October–December 2021 real GDP surged by a record 16.6%, compared with the previous quarter. Israel's economy built on this momentum to grow by 8.6% over 2021 as a whole, the fastest pace since 2000. This growth rate was well above the Government's optimistic expectations for Israel's recovery from the effects of the pandemic. The surge in growth reflected the importance of the country's technology sector, which boomed amid strong global demand. The high growth rate also reflected two key government achievements since mid-2021—first, the rapid vaccination programme and targeted public health measures that averted the need for further lockdown measures during subsequent surges in the COVID-19 infection rate, and second, the successful passage of the 2021 and 2022 budgets in November 2021, which unlocked a significant increase in government spending in the fourth quarter.

In 2021 services exports overtook goods exports for the first time, with expectations that their share would continue to increase in the economy and external accounts. However, there were several areas of concern. The number of hours worked rebounded in 2021 but did not fully regain 2018–19 levels, reflecting the fact that growth had been in high value-added sectors, such as technology services, which were only modest employers. The labour share in GDP was at its lowest level since 2015. Bank of Israel calculations suggested that even after the rebound in 2021, GDP per head was less than if it had continued on its pre-pandemic trajectory.

Following another surge in COVID-19, with cases exceeding 3.9m. by 31 March 2022, the economy contracted by 0.4% in the first quarter of that year. Inflation reached 4.0% year on year in April, the highest level in more than a decade, prompting the central bank to tighten its monetary policy. In that month it raised the benchmark interest rate to 0.35%, having held the rate at 0.1% since April 2020. The rate was raised further in May to 0.75%, and again in July to 1.75%, the most significant single rise since 2011. Another increase, to 2.0%, followed in late August.

In early 2023 inflation reached nearly 5%, prompting the Government to introduce temporary relief measures. Although the Bank of Israel had raised its base rate 10 times since April 2022, to 4.75%, this failed to reverse inflationary pressures or the shekel's depreciation against other currencies, raising imported inflation. However, data for the first quarter of 2023 showed that wages had more than kept pace with inflation, although this was because of a one-off bonus given to civil servants and other specific developments. Consumers have seen income erode in real terms and have been cutting back on spending. Credit card purchases fell by 1.3% year on year in February–April 2023. Although the Israeli political agenda continues to be dominated by judicial reform and security (see History), the cost of living is emerging as a primary concern among the electorate.

SOCIOECONOMIC DEVELOPMENT

Israel's strong growth rates since the 1960s have supported the transition to a high standard of living, as reflected by a ranking of 22nd out of 191 countries and territories in the 2022 United Nations' Human Development Index (HDI), with data for 2021. This ranking, although three places lower than in 2020, placed Israel in the HDI's 'very high human development' group, just behind the USA and the Republic of Korea (South Korea). According to the Index, life expectancy at birth in Israel was 82.3 years, while expected years of schooling were 16.1. Israel's HDI ranking was 10 places higher than its gross national income (GNI) per capita ranking, suggesting that Israel's quality of life is considerably higher than its resource base. However, improvements in the country's HDI have been slowing over time, with average annual growth of HDI of 0.7% in 1990–2000, falling to 0.6% in 2000–10 and further to 0.3% in 2010–21.

Income distribution is more unequal in Israel than in most of Europe. In 2018 the country's Gini coefficient of 0.386 reflected an income distribution more equal than the USA (0.414), but less equal than Germany (0.318), France (0.324), Greece (0.329), the United Kingdom (0.337) or Spain (0.347). The income share of the poorest 40% of the population in 2010–21 was 16.1%, while that of the wealthiest 10% was 27.6%. In 2021 the wealthiest 1% had slightly more than the poorest 40%, at 16.6%.

The Legatum Institute's Prosperity Index for 2023 reflects Israel's broad-based prosperity. This index views prosperity more broadly than the HDI, incorporating 12 elements commonly associated with quality of life. In 2023 Israel ranked 33rd out of 167 countries and territories, immediately behind Lithuania, Latvia and Italy. Israel's highest rankings were in health (6th), living conditions (12th), investment environment (15th), economic quality (19th) and governance (the extent to which there are checks and restraints on power and whether governments operate effectively and without corruption—22nd). Israel's lowest ranking was in safety and security (124th), followed by the natural environment category (96th) and social capital (56th).

The World Bank's Worldwide Governance Indicators (WGI), which provide a detailed examination of the institutional foundations of over 200 countries and territories, corroborate the Legatum Institute's findings on Israel. Israel's overall WGI ranking (the aggregate of six individual governance indicators) was ranked in the 70th percentile in both 1996 and 2021, with only modest fluctuations being registered over the intervening years. The country's best-performing individual governance indicators have been government effectiveness, for which Israel's ranking was in the 76th percentile in 1996, improving to the 87th in 2021, and regulatory quality (an approximate measure of the business climate), for which Israel improved from the 83rd percentile in 1996 to the 85th in 2021. While Israel generally ranks highly in terms of rule of law and control of corruption, the country's ranking for the former declined from the 88th percentile in 1996 to the 82nd in 2021, while there was a corresponding decline over the same period for control of corruption, from the 88th percentile to the 81st. Israel ranks somewhat lower in the voice and accountability category (a rough proxy for strength of democracy), scoring in the 69th percentile in 1996 and the 68th in 2021, with minimal fluctuation in between. The one governance area in which Israel lags is political stability and the absence of violence. Even here, however, there was a slight improvement from the 13th percentile in 1996 to the 14th in 2021.

DEMOGRAPHY

Israel's population reached 9,661,600 in 2022, of whom 21.1% were Arabs, a slight increase from 20.4% in 2010. Population growth has been rapid, with average annual rates of 3.4% in 1960–69, 2.7% in 1970–79, 2.2% in 1980–89, 3.0% in 1990–99, 2.0% in 2000–10 and 1.9% in 2010–22. The demographic structure is favourable for long-term growth, with those of working age (15–64 years) projected to increase from 59.8% in 2020 to a peak of around 61.1% in 2035.

Immigration trends have shaped Israel's demographic structure, with immigrants accounting for more than 40% of the country's population growth since Israel gained statehood in 1948, when the population totalled just 790,000. Just under 1m. people came to Israel from the former Union of Soviet Socialist Republics (USSR) between 1989 and 2004, following the relaxation of restrictions on emigration after the fall of communism. Immigration inflows fell as the decade drew to a close, before settling at 15,000–20,000 a year until an upturn in 2014–15, when an average of nearly 26,000 immigrants a year was recorded. Inflows fell back again in 2016, reflecting improved economic conditions in Europe. A total of 26,916 immigrants were recorded in 2018, rising to 31,484 in 2019. In 2020 the number fell to 18,665, largely as a result of COVID-related travel restrictions. There was a steep increase in the number of immigrants in 2022, to 74,203, with 66.7% of the total in the working-age bracket.

The most significant increase in immigration to Israel has been from Europe, where poor economic performance, fears of heightened violence against Jews in Western Europe and conflict in Ukraine have encouraged emigration. France and Ukraine, which both have large Jewish populations, will continue to be important sources of immigration. Government policy aims to encourage immigration by people with sufficient Jewish ancestry to meet the requirements of the Law of Return (that at least one grandparent be Jewish). Ethnic-nationalist and religious factors appear to play a more significant role than economic considerations in emigration to Israel. However, the convergence of salaries, particularly for high-skilled private sector workers, with Western levels has helped support immigration from North America and the European Union (EU).

There are around 90,000 registered foreign workers (excluding Palestinians) in Israel, while estimates of the number of unauthorized foreigners working vary between 200,000 and 300,000. The number of Palestinian workers in Israel peaked in 1993 and then fell during the second *intifada* (uprising) in 2000–04. However, the number of legally and illegally employed Palestinian workers subsequently rebounded, reaching around 87,000 by mid-2021. The Israeli military has argued for more work permits to be issued to Palestinians, contending that it would help to lower the number of illegal workers and stave off violent attacks. In August 2021 the Israeli Cabinet approved a proposal to increase by 15,000 the number of work permits granted to Palestinians employed in the Israeli construction sector in the West Bank.

Following a decline in the fertility rate during the 1990s and early 2000s, the rate subsequently recovered from 2.84 births per woman in 2005 to 3.09 in 2015, led by a substantial increase in Jewish births, particularly among the moderate Orthodox population. Fertility rates vary across different communities, with higher (but falling) average rates among Israeli Muslim Arabs (3.32 births per woman in 2015, down from 4.67 in 2000) and the Jewish Haredi (ultra-Orthodox) community. Consequently, the proportion of Israeli Arabs and Haredi Jews in the population is rising, exacerbating social and economic tensions, since these two groups tend to have low labour force participation rates (a pattern that the Government has been trying to change), greater dependence on welfare and relatively low levels of education. Welfare reforms in 2002–04 and subsequent efforts by the 2013–14 Government and later administrations have sought to integrate the ultra-Orthodox community within the workforce and the mainstream education system and end their exemption from military service. Other reforms have focused on greater labour force participation and education initiatives for Arab women, who have also traditionally had low participation rates. With solid employment growth for much of the past decade, there has been a significant increase in the participation rate.

The proportion of those over 65 years of age had exceeded 10% of the total population by 2001 and reached 12.3% in 2021. Although the growing number of older adults will place greater demands on social security and health services, the dependency ratio is more favourable than in Western Europe. Moreover, the impact on pensions will be limited, as reforms in 2005 raised the retirement age for men to 67 and for women to 62, moved the pension system onto a defined contribution basis, and prevented the 'old' (pre-reform) pension funds from having an actuarial deficit. Nevertheless, the Government will continue to broaden private pension provision and maintain the pension burden's fiscal sustainability. Older immigrants from the former USSR with little or no pension savings or pension rights from Israeli employment present a specific problem for the future. In any event, Israel's population will remain relatively young, and the labour force will continue to expand.

GROWTH DYNAMICS

Israel's economic growth reflects the development of solid institutions, high levels of governance and progress in economic reforms. High levels of attainment of each are often associated with improved competitiveness, and in Israel's case this generalization holds. Israel ranked 20th out of 141 countries in the World Economic Forum (WEF)'s 2019 Global Competitiveness Report. The WEF looks at a country's competitiveness from the perspective of 12 fundamental building blocks contributing to improved productivity. In 2019 Israel ranked highest in macroeconomic stability (1st), business dynamism (4th), health (9th), skills (14th), innovation capability (15th), the labour market (18th), infrastructure and the financial system (both 23rd) and institutions (27th). The country's lowest rankings were for market size (56th) and information and communications technology adoption (45th).

Economic reforms have also contributed to high levels of economic freedom, as measured by Heritage House. In its latest rankings (for 2022), Israel ranked 34th, down from 26th in 2020. Improvements in economic freedom began in 2004 when the country was on the cusp of being downgraded from the 'moderately free' group to that of 'mostly unfree'. With relatively constant improvements, Israel moved into the 'mostly free' grouping in 2015. However, with a sharp decline in freedom in 2021, the country fell back to 'moderately free', where it remained in 2022. While government integrity improved from 'repressed' in 2016 to 'mostly free' in 2019, it subsequently fell to nearly 'mostly unfree' by 2022. There was also a dramatic decline in fiscal health, with the country slipping from 'free' in 2019 to 'repressed' in 2022. Currently, Israel's strengths lie in monetary, trade and investment freedom. Areas of weakness are labour freedom and government spending.

With solid levels of governance and a moderately free economy, the Israeli economy has the requirements for converging with the advanced economies. Is the level of Israel's per capita income catching up with those of the advanced countries? Are the standards of living converging? There is some evidence that this is the case. As noted in the Introduction, per capita income in Israel in 1980 in international dollar terms was US $19,251, equivalent to 72.2% of the average per capita income among the advanced countries, which was $26,650. By 2022 Israel's per capita income had increased to $44,335, 82.2% of per capita income among the advanced countries, which averaged $53,292. Thus, standards of living have been slowly converging.

In another positive sign, productivity in Israel, as measured by GDP per hour worked, compares favourably with many member countries of the Organisation for Economic Co-operation and Development (OECD), equalling US $47.60 (in constant 2010 prices on a PPP basis) in 2022. This rate placed Israel ahead of Japan ($47.3), New Zealand ($43.3) and South Korea ($42.9), but below the OECD average of $53.6. Israel's GDP per head increased at an average annual rate of 1.4% in 2000–09 and 2.1% in 2010–22, while, over the same two periods, the average annual growth rate of the OECD average GDP per head decreased from 1.2% to 1.0%. Manufacturing output per head in Israel increased by an average of 1.3% per year in 2000–09 and by 3.1% in 2010–22. The corresponding growth rate figures for the euro area were 1.5% and 2.6%.

Overall productivity gains in Israel will be critical if convergence with the advanced economies is to continue. Unfortunately, this variable has been in decline, with average annual growth rates of 3.9% for 1955–70, 1.5% in the 1970s, 1.3% in the 1980s, 0.6% in the 1990s, 0.7% in the 2000s and 0.3% in 2010–19, according to the USA's Federal Reserve Bank of St. Louis.

Given the country's already high levels of governance and economic freedom, it may be challenging to turn stagnant or declining productivity rates in traditional sectors such as agriculture, manufacturing, construction and finance into high rates of positive gain. If Israel hopes to continue to converge towards standards of living enjoyed by the advanced economies, it will have to be through diverting resources away from the more traditional sectors of the economy and towards new high-technology industries.

AGRICULTURE

Agriculture is a declining industry in Israel. Between 1996 and 2009 the sector expanded at an average annual rate of 4.2%; however, between 2010 and 2022 the sector contracted at an average annual rate of 0.5%. The sector is relatively small, contributing 1.3% of GDP in 2022, down from 2.3% in 1995. It employed only 0.8% of the country's workforce in 2012, down from 3.5% in 1991. Agricultural productivity has fallen dramatically, from an average of 8.7% annually during 1996–2009 to 0.4% in 2010–19.

Israeli agriculture has attracted much international attention and, more than any other sector of the economy, has been the focus of ideological pressure. For centuries, Jews in the diaspora were prohibited from owning land. The Zionist movement, therefore, saw land settlement as one of its chief objectives.

Since the establishment of the State of Israel, government agricultural policy has centred chiefly on attaining self-sufficiency in foodstuffs, given military considerations and Israel's possible isolation from its principal foreign food supplies. Other motives for government support of agriculture have included saving foreign exchange through import substitution, promoting agricultural exports and absorbing large numbers of immigrants into the agricultural sector. In line with these objectives, promoting mixed farming and co-operative farming settlements has also been an essential element of government policy.

Cultivation has undergone a profound transformation into modern intensive irrigated husbandry. A distinct feature of Israel's agriculture is its communal settlements that are designed to meet the particular needs and challenges encountered by a farming community in its surroundings and its profession. While there are several different forms of collective settlements, all resemble two basic types: the *moshav* and the *kibbutz*. The *moshav* is a co-operative smallholders' village, where individual farms are of equal size. Each farmer manages his or her farm, but economic and social security is guaranteed by the co-operative structure of the village, which oversees the marketing of produce, purchases farm and household equipment, and provides credit and many other services. At the end of December 2021 351,500 people inhabited 447 *moshavim* and collective *moshavim*. The *kibbutz*, meanwhile, is a unique form of collective settlement developed in Israel. Each member is expected to work to the best of their ability; they receive no wages, but are supplied by the *kibbutz* with all necessary goods and services. The *kibbutz* is based on voluntary action, mutual liability and equal rights for all members, and it assumes for its members full material responsibility. At the end of December 2021 188,800 people inhabited 266 *kibbutzim*.

During the years following the establishment of the State of Israel, there was a large-scale expansion of the area under cultivation. By 2020 the cultivated area included 1,152,000 dunums (1 dunum = 1,000 sq m) of field crops, about 702,470 dunums of vegetables, potatoes and melons, and 1,014,500 dunums of citrus and other fruit plantations.

The crucial factor limiting agricultural development is not the availability of land, but rather that of water. Further development of the sector would involve intensifying the yield of existing land and reusing treated wastewater to preserve fresh water essential for household consumption. According to a report published in early 2018 by the Knesset Research and Information Center, water consumption totalled 2,346m. cu m in 2016, of which about 55% was attributable to agriculture, 34% to domestic households and public use, and 5% to industry. The state-owned Mekorot (Israel National Water Co) supplies about 60% of Israel's freshwater. In 2004 the Government announced a restructuring of Mekorot to divide it into a cluster of companies separating the supply operations (a natural monopoly) and all the other operations in competitive sectors. Under a Water Commissioner, the Government also established a unique Water Administration with statutory powers to control and regulate both supply and consumption of water.

The Water Administration's responsibilities include the conveyance of water from the north to southern Judaea and the Negev; the storage of excess supplies of water from winter to summer, and from periods of heavy rainfall to periods of drought; and the regulation of the various regional water supply systems.

In 2005 Israel, Jordan and the Palestinian (National) Authority (PA) announced that they had agreed terms regarding a feasibility study for a proposed 180-km Dead Sea–Red Sea pipeline canal to arrest the alarming water losses from the Dead Sea and increase fresh water supplies to the three territories. The study investigated the technical aspects and the social and environmental impact of the scheme in a process overseen by the World Bank. In January 2013 the Bank released a draft report declaring that the project was viable from engineering, environmental and economic perspectives. In December of that year representatives from Israel, Jordan and the PA signed a memorandum of understanding (MOU) covering three water-sharing initiatives. In February 2015 Israel and Jordan signed a US $900m. contract to start construction of the canal and in November they issued a joint tender for the first phase of the project. By mid-2021 construction of the canal had yet to commence and in June of that year Jordan was reported to have withdrawn from the project, citing a lack of interest on the part of Israel.

Israel exports a variety of agricultural products. In 2021 avocados were the leading agricultural export, at US $198.9m., followed by dates ($182.8m.), potatoes ($82.9m.), peppers ($77.8m) and carrots ($38.0m.). Citrus fruit production, one of the oldest and most important agricultural activities, increased rapidly, from 515,700 metric tons in 1961 to 1,800,350 tons in 1982. However, production declined thereafter, to 510,490 tons in 2004. After reaching 666,030 tons in 2005, production gradually fell to 421,979 tons in 2021. Citrus fruit export levels have generally been declining over the last two decades. A total of 461,900 tons of citrus were exported in 1990, but by 2003 the figure had decreased to 120,100 tons. Higher levels have been recorded more recently, with 162,000 tons being exported in 2019 and 159,000 tons in 2020. Exports of citrus were valued at NIS 1,457.5m. in 2020. The Plants Production and Marketing Board supervises all aspects of growing and marketing agricultural products.

PETROLEUM, GAS AND OTHER MINERALS

Israel's energy security changed dramatically with the discovery in 2000 of vast offshore reserves of natural gas in the Eastern Mediterranean. Dry natural gas production increased from 1,550m. cu m in 2010 to 7,000m. cu m in 2014, 10,290m. cu m in 2019 and 23,800m. cu m in 2022, with forecasts of 26,800m. cu m in 2023 and 27,800m. cu m in 2024. However, production was expected to decline to 26,200m. cu m in 2027. With domestic consumption totalling 11,700m. cu m in 2021, 12,100m. cu m in 2022 and a projected 14,200m. cu m in 2027, substantial amounts of gas are available for export markets at a time of high global demand and prices.

The country's innovative and competitive economy has facilitated the rapid switch to gas, increasing the domestic market size and improving energy security. Israel also has a large and modern refining sector, allowing the country to export motor petrol and diesel. With these assets, Israel has the potential to be at the centre of an East Mediterranean hub with Cyprus and Egypt.

In May 2016 the Government approved a revised offshore gas plan. The plan's framework foresaw the sale of the Tanin and Karish gasfields to a new investor (Greece's Energean Oil & Gas), supporting further exploration and development. Energean's entry into the Israeli oil and gas sector was the first manifestation of the anti-monopoly regulation and the first introduction of competition into the Israeli gas market. A final investment decision on the project was made in March 2018. The new gas outline agreement also allowed Israel's Exclusive Economic Zone (EEZ) to reopen for oil and gas exploration.

Following a successful licensing round in Cyprus, which attracted major hydrocarbons companies such as ExxonMobil and Total, Israel auctioned 24 new deep offshore blocks in 2017. The region's potential is substantial, with untested geological structures identified and licence areas on offer surrounding the giant Leviathan and Tamar gasfields. In July 2017 Delek Drilling reported that Tamar held 13% more gas than previously estimated after analysis of wells and production data, highlighting the field's solid geological potential.

A successful second offshore bidding round followed in July 2019. At August 2023 no official announcement had yet been made on the results of the third licensing round, which was launched in June 2020.

The question of how to transport Israel's gas to international markets has been a major issue ever since the first discoveries. Besides an existing short pipeline to Egypt, connections via immediate neighbours are unlikely. With most of the population living on the coast, a proposal to construct a liquefied natural gas (LNG) plant proved politically unpopular. Plans have been put forward to construct a new pipeline to Europe via Cyprus and Greece, known as EastMed. After protracted discussion, the EU continues to support the pipeline, which it has deemed a 'project of common interest', and has contributed €34.5m. (US $39m.) in funding. The EastMed pipeline would provide access to an alternative gas source for the EU, which could help reduce its dependence on Russian gas. It would also connect the energy markets of Greece and Cyprus to the rest of the EU. However, despite the EU's political and financial support, questions remain about the technical and commercial viability of the EastMed pipeline. The construction and transport costs could render the gas uneconomic. Also, the EU's commitment to decarbonize its economy by 2050 places in doubt the pipeline's lifespan and, thus, its viability. Pipelines typically require at least three decades fully to recover their construction and operating costs.

Finally, in June 2022 Israel, the EU and Egypt signed an agreement regarding the export of Israeli gas to Europe via LNG terminals in Egypt. The EU-Israel-Egypt agreement was advantageous to each signatory. The EU could reduce its dependency on Russian gas, while Egypt had under-used capacity in its LNG terminals and increased exports would help to contain its current account deficit. For Israel, the project would ease concerns that it was not able fully to exploit its substantial gas reserves; a 2021 government report expressed fears that 50% of Israeli natural gas would never be used.

In October 2022 Israel and Lebanon resolved the outstanding differences over their maritime boundaries in the eastern Mediterranean. Under the final maritime agreement, Israel retained full rights over the Karish gasfield, while Lebanon received the Qana gasfield, but would be obliged to give 17% of the profits from it to Israel.

In February 2023 the Israeli Government launched its fourth offshore bidding round for natural gas exploration. The round encompassed 20 new exploration blocks within four zones totalling an area of 5,888 sq km. Israel had accelerated its plans to launch the bidding round in response to Europe's urgent need for alternative gas sources following its ban on imports of gas from the Russian Federation in response to the latter's invasion of Ukraine in February 2022. However, Israel's options for greater exports of gas to Europe are limited, given that the EastMed pipeline project stalled in January 2022 due to the USA withdrawing its support and Egypt already exporting LNG at maximum capacity.

Israel's energy sector continues to face difficulties from another front. Security risks remain high for any high-profile energy project in Israel and oil and gas infrastructure has been a target of the Palestinian Islamic Resistance Movement (Hamas) in the past.

Israel has potentially huge recoverable oil shale reserves, mainly located in the northern Negev desert near the Dead Sea. Some estimates have suggested that the country could possess the world's third largest oil shale deposit after the USA and the People's Republic of China.

INDUSTRY AND MANUFACTURING

Industry (comprising mining, manufacturing, utilities and construction) grew at an average annual rate of 1.8% during 1996–2009, increasing to 4.0% in 2010–22. In 1996 industry accounted for 24.2% of GDP, falling to 19.6% in 2022. Value-added per worker increased at an average annual rate of 2.1% between 1996 and 2009, but the rate of growth declined to 1.2% in 2010–19. The industrial sector employed 14.9% of the labour force in 2022, down from 28.8% in 1991 and 19.7% in 2010. The manufacturing (and mining) sub-sector expanded at an average annual rate of 2.5% during 1996–2009, increasing to 3.6% in 2010–22. Manufacturing (and mining) accounted for 16.9% of GDP in 1995, falling to 12.0% in 2022.

Israel's manufacturing industry was initially developed to supply essential commodities such as soap, vegetable oil, margarine, bread, ice, farm implements, printing and electricity for the domestic market. The industry used raw materials available locally to produce citrus juices and other citrus by-products, canned fruit and vegetables, cement, glass and bricks. The Government curtailed imports of manufactured goods in order to save foreign exchange, thus giving local industry the opportunity to add local labour value to semi-manufactures imported from abroad. Although most of Israel's manufacturing production is still primarily for domestic consumption, the share of manufacturing products in the country's merchandise exports increased from 60.5% in 1963 to 93.1% in 1999. After dropping to 75.7% in 2007, manufacturing exports rose to 94.0% of total merchandise exports in 2009. They fluctuated around that level in subsequent years, dipping to 90.0% in 2022.

The composition of manufacturing exports is also changing, with medium- and high-technology exports increasing their share of the total from 36.7% in 2007 to 59.7% in 2009. After declining to 53.4% in 2011, the contribution of medium- and high-technology exports to total manufacturing exports rose to 64.3% in 2020.

Israel's principal industrial export is cut and polished diamonds, and in 2021 the country was the eighth largest exporter of these products. In 2018 Israel exported polished diamonds to the value of US $4,559m. However, the value of such exports decreased to $3,404m. in 2019 and $2,242m. in 2020, before partially rebounding to $3,529m. in 2021.

Mining accounts for a tiny proportion of the manufacturing and mining sector. The Dead Sea, which contains potash, bromides, magnesium and other salts in high concentration, is the country's chief source of mineral wealth. Dead Sea Works Ltd owns the potash works on the southern shore of the Dead Sea. Phosphates are mined at Oron in the Negev and in the Arava. According to the United States Geological Survey, in 2019 the mining operations produced 2.8m. metric tons of beneficiated phosphate rock.

As in many countries, Israel's construction sector has experienced significant volatility in recent years, averaging annual growth of 0.1% during 1996–2009, increasing to 5.2% in 2010–22. The sector's share of GDP declined from 7.2% in 1995 to 6.2% in 2022.

The Israeli construction sector has several strengths. Opportunities for growth are present in transport, energy and residential/non-residential domains. The major construction companies have a sound record and considerable expertise in implementing large infrastructure projects. Furthermore, the existing energy infrastructure is well-developed, ensuring access to the national grid for new projects. The country's close ties with the USA provide Israel with substantial financial assistance for economic and military projects. However, the construction sector faces the challenge of Israel's protracted conflict with the Palestinians, resulting in persistent security risks, which could threaten infrastructure assets. Moreover, the industry is comparatively slow to adopt new technology, reducing the efficiency of project implementation. The industry is highly dependent on Palestinian and foreign workers for its low-skilled labour force.

The construction sector's prospects are, nevertheless, good, given the potential opportunities. Owing to severe water shortages, Israel is looking to develop a desalination capacity of 350m. cu m a year, while the country's very high solar irradiance levels mean that there is strong potential for solar power projects of various sizes. Expanding the nascent natural gas sector will create opportunities in Israel's energy infrastructure, particularly if regional gas exports are successful.

TRANSPORT

Israel's transport sector has expanded steadily, with average annual growth of 3.9% in 1996–2009 and 5.3% in 2010–22. However, the last few years have witnessed wide fluctuations, with the sector growing by 0.6% in 2019, before contracting by 20.3% in the pandemic year of 2020. The sector subsequently recovered, expanding by 19.6% in 2021 and by 15.0% in 2022. In 1995 the sector contributed 4.6% of GDP, declining to 3.8% in 2022.

Israel has an extensive transport network incorporating roads, airports and ports with strong international connectivity. The transport network meets the country's supply chain needs, although it offers negligible diversification, with road being the dominant freight mode. There are some risks of supply chain disruption, mainly from road congestion, underdeveloped ports, and a high possibility of strike action by port and airport workers.

Israel has a well-developed road system of more than 18,000 km in length. The system includes several multi-lane highways, allowing faster traffic speeds and reducing freight transportation times. Two of these highways run north–south, one from Be'er Sheva to just south of Haifa, the other from Tel Aviv to Haifa. Another primary route links Tel Aviv to Jerusalem. The rest of the country is well served by major roads, although the lack of a significant highway south of Be'er Sheva limits the speed of freight transport to and from the Red Sea port of Eilat. Although Israel's connections with its neighbours are minimal, there is, in any case, little trade with these countries or hope for more. Israel has the second highest road density in the Middle East and North Africa, after Bahrain.

Israel's railways do not offer an attractive alternative to road-based supply chains. Their capacity for freight transport is limited and, at present, primarily geared towards transporting chemicals and minerals to ports for export. In addition, the limited passenger rail and metro services increase the pressure on the road network, adding to congestion and supply chain delays. The rail sub-sector will be a significant beneficiary of infrastructure investment in the coming years, improving passenger and freight services that will boost supply chains over the medium term. Israel's railway network centres on Tel Aviv, with four standard gauge main lines: one going north to

Haifa and Nahariya, one to Ben Gurion International Airport, one east to Jerusalem and one south to Be'er Sheva.

Ports are essential to Israel's economy, with 98% of the country's trade being seaborne. However, the port sector in Israel has suffered from a lack of investment that threatens to hinder the currently good connectivity to international shipping routes, as the country's terminals do not have the capacity to cater for the largest container ships in service on the Asian-European routes that link Israel to its Asian trading partners. Privatizing port management will improve the quality and efficiency of ports, although the risk remains of trade union action causing disruption.

Israel has three container ports, two on the Mediterranean coast, at Ashdod and Haifa, and a smaller one on the Red Sea at Eilat. Container throughput at Eilat has declined to negligible amounts in recent years, and the terminal is now used primarily for automobile imports.

The air transport sector offers good connections to a variety of destinations around the world for both passenger and freight traffic. Given the country's regional isolation, the importance of air transport is likely to continue; nevertheless, the sector faces several risks, including the unstable security situation in Gaza and frequent labour disputes.

Israel has 33 airports with paved runways, but only three are long enough to cater to the largest aircraft in service. The main airport, with a strong network of international connections, is Ben Gurion International in Tel Aviv, home to national carrier El Al Israel Airlines. Air travel has historically been a necessary means of international transport in Israel because of the lack of overland connections and the massive demand for global links from the large Jewish diaspora.

COMMUNICATIONS AND INFORMATION TECHNOLOGY

Israel's communications and information technology (IT) sectors have seen vigorous growth, with combined expansion rates averaging 12.4% per year during 1996–2009 and 8.4% during 2010–22. These high growth rates propelled the sector's contribution to GDP from 4.1% in 1995 to 13.2% in 2022. Israel's high-technology sector, heavily geared towards start-up companies, has been a critical economic driver for the past two decades. Although it employs only about 10% of the labour force, it accounts for more than one-half of goods and services exports and the bulk of FDI inflows.

The privatization of Bezeq Israel Telecom, the state-owned telecommunications company, which previously had a monopoly over the domestic market, was completed in 2005, when the state's remaining shares were sold to the private Apax-Saban-Arkin group for NIS 4,237m. In November 2015 Cellcom Israel, the largest mobile telephone operator in the country, agreed to a merger with Golan Telecom, one of four other rivals in the mobile market. However, Israel's Antitrust Authority subsequently blocked the deal, and in January 2017 Golan Telecom agreed to a US $91m. takeover by an Israeli electronics company, Electra Consumer Products. Electra also signed a 10-year network-sharing agreement with Cellcom Israel. In December 2016 the Knesset had adopted legislation requiring Bezeq to give competitors access to its nationwide network with its dominant landline and internet position.

Israel has an extensive IT ecosystem and a highly educated, linguistically skilled and entrepreneurial workforce. The industry is a leader in innovative hardware and solutions, and has the potential to be a leader in critical trends around the internet, such as advanced driver assistance in cars, advanced industrial automation and artificial intelligence (AI). The sector has received considerable political support from the Government through its policies and initiatives to expand IT and other high-technology industries.

The high-technology electronics industry specializes in equipment for military and communications purposes and computer and internet software in Israel's so-called Silicon Wadi. The rapid development of the country's IT sector attracted substantial investment from US corporations. In response to an impending shortage of skilled labour in the high-technology sector, the Israeli Government approved a six-year training programme in January 2017 to increase the supply of qualified staff. In December 2019 Intel announced the acquisition of Habana Labs, an Israeli start-up company specializing in AI processors and chips, for US $2,000m.

The 'cloud' computing market developed rapidly after migration momentum accelerated during the COVID-19 pandemic in 2020, when firms began to place greater value on scalability, flexibility and resilience. Amid the Fourth Industrial Revolution (4IR), there is momentum towards adopting advanced automation technologies built on cloud and edge computing, robotics, 5G technology, sensors and machine learning in fields such as automotives, manufacturing and logistics. Trends within 4IR and the Internet of Things are an opportunity for Israel's chip industry to diversify beyond personal computer (PC) and server products.

Israel is a major production centre in the Middle East for integrated circuits, mainly owing to the role of Intel Israel. The US chip giant reported that its operations continued in Israel during the pandemic, with its production facilities considered an essential industry and non-production roles able to be carried out remotely (with 80% of its staff in Israel working from home for much of 2020).

However, the sector does face challenges. Israel represents a relatively small market, and the already high penetration of computer devices limits volume growth potential. There is also a severe digital divide, with only a minority of the lowest income decile having home internet access. Regional political and security issues continue to pose a downside risk to Israel's economy and population. For instance, cyber attacks in the region could disrupt the operation of and demand for networked solutions. Labour shortages and wage rises could squeeze the competitiveness of Israel as a research and development hub over the longer term.

Israel's high-technology sector is currently experiencing a sudden drop in investment. The decline in start-up fundraising began in 2022, after a record year of nearly US $26,000m. in investment in 2021, with the rate of decrease accelerating from mid-2022. In addition, the number and value of start-up exits in the first quarter of 2023 were low, with the latter at $1,090m., compared with $20,600m. for the whole of 2022. The decline in Israeli capital raising mirrors a global downward trend prompted by rising policy interest rates and plunging technology share prices, as investors have become more risk-averse. Many observers believe that these external factors have been compounded since early 2023 by the Israeli Government's plans to curb the power of the courts. eBusiness, particularly the high-technology sector, is vociferously opposed to the proposed legislation, claiming that it would damage Israel's previously strong business environment. Several technology companies and investment funds have announced that they are moving their money out of the country. However, it is unclear whether the judicial controversy is playing that significant a role in the downturn in high-technology investment, with other global fundraising hubs, such as the UK, experiencing even sharper drops than Israel.

The fall in total funds raised is not the only concern, however; it is also alarming that of the total funds raised in the first quarter of 2023, almost 40% was provided by only three companies. The number of new start-ups in the first quarter of 2023 was about 50% lower than in 2015, a worrying development in an industry fuelled by the formation of new companies. If compounded by the passage of the controversial judicial reforms (see History), a prolonged funding drought could see more start-ups domicile abroad and eventually move their operations there.

TOURISM

In 1995 2.2m. tourists visited Israel. Arrivals gradually increased to reach 2.4m. in 2000. However, the Palestinian uprising in 2000, followed by the 11 September suicide attacks on the USA in 2001, contributed to a marked decline in arrivals, to just 0.9m., in 2002. Arrivals gradually increased thereafter, reaching 2.6m. in 2008, before falling back to 2.3m. in 2009. Arrivals slowly recovered to 2.9m. in 2016 before jumping to 4.6m. in 2019. However, amid the suspension of international travel and the imposition by many countries of national lockdowns to combat the COVID-19 pandemic, arrivals fell to just 887,100 in 2020.

As a result of the pandemic, the total contribution of tourism to Israel's GDP in 2020 fell to just 2.6%, from 5.7% in 2019, while tourism's share of total employment declined to 5.5%, from 5.9%. In addition, international tourism expenditure decreased from 7.2% of total exports in 2019 to just 2.3% of total exports in 2020. The number of tourist arrivals fell to 402,300 in 2021, before recovering to 2.9m. in 2021 as COVID-related restrictions were eased or lifted.

The USA dominates tourism to Israel, with arrivals from that country totalling 969,400 in 2019, before dropping to 205,800 in 2020 and 150,600 in 2021. However, in 2022 tourist arrivals from the USA numbered 858,500, not much less than the total in 2019. The other largest inward markets are France, Russia, the UK and Germany.

FOREIGN TRADE

Unlike most countries in Europe, which trade heavily among themselves, more of Israel's trade is with the major economies of the world, especially the USA. In 2022 the USA was the destination for 25.7% of Israeli exports, followed by China (with 6.4%), India (4.6%) and the UK (4.3%). In that year Israel received 12.2% of its imports from China, followed by the USA (8.9%), Germany (6.6%) and Switzerland (5.7%). In 2021 Israel's major exports were machinery, electrical equipment and parts (27.2%), chemicals and chemical products, excluding refining (18.8%), optical, photographic and medical instruments (13.2%), and polished diamonds (9.4%). Its leading imports in that year were machinery, electrical equipment and parts (24.3%), chemicals and chemical products, excluding refining (10.2%), fuel (9.9%) and diamonds (5.6%).

Dramatic shifts occurred in Israel's import and export growth patterns following the global financial crisis of 2007–08. During 1990–2007 exports of goods and services increased at an average annual rate of 7.6%. However, during 2008–22 average annual growth dropped to 3.8%. Similarly, imports of goods and services grew at an average annual rate of 7.4% in 1990–2007, before falling to 4.6% in 2008–22. The current account also showed a dramatic shift, averaging a small deficit equivalent to 0.9% of GDP during 1990–2007, but an average surplus equivalent to 3.3% of GDP during 2008–22. The improvement in Israel's current account stemmed from changes in the country's savings and investment pattern, with investment falling from 25.7% of GDP in the earlier period to 23.0% in the latter, and savings increasing from 23.4% of GDP to 26.3%. With the increase in savings over investment, domestic demand did not outrun supply, which would have required added imports.

Meanwhile, in 1995 Israel concluded a free trade agreement (FTA) with the EU covering financial services, government procurement, co-operation in research and development, additional agricultural products and improved Israeli access to European markets in the high-technology sector. An association agreement between the EU and Israel entered into force on 1 June 2000. In November 2015 the EU issued guidelines requiring Israeli agricultural products originating from settlements in the Occupied Territories to be labelled as such.

Several recent trade agreements are noteworthy. In May 2021 South Korea became the first East Asian country to sign an FTA with Israel. A more significant breakthrough in political terms, if not financially, was the signing of an FTA with the United Arab Emirates in April 2022.

BANKING AND FINANCIAL SERVICES

Israel's financial sector expanded at an average annual rate of 4.4% during 1996–2009 and 3.5% during 2010–22. However, growth in the sector was particularly robust in the last few years (with the exception of 2021): 8.1% in 2019, 10.5% in 2020, 0.3% in 2021 and 12.5% in 2022. The financial sector's share of GDP increased from 4.8% in 1995 to 5.7% in 2022. The Israeli banking sector has several significant strengths. While only a few large banks dominate the industry, these have strong capital buffers providing stability to the system. The three largest commercial banks with worldwide subsidiaries are Bank Leumi le-Israel, Bank Hapoalim and the Israel Discount Bank. The country's high per capita income ensures an ample market for a full range of banking and insurance-related services.

The sector is also experiencing change. Israeli banks and insurance companies are increasingly moving towards digital solutions for their customers, including digital branches and online-only products. Regulators promote greater competition across the financial services sector, including the adoption of fintech/insurtech solutions.

However, the system faces some challenges. Accounting for around 5% of GDP, the sector remains relatively small on an international scale, limiting room for new entrants or for banks to grow domestically. The adoption of a dovish monetary policy by the Bank of Israel and a corresponding ultra-low policy rate restricted Israeli banks' margins for much of the 2010s. Moreover, limited competition in the market raises the cost for customers and limits borrowing growth. The banks' traditional focus on real estate investment has made it harder to boost trading volumes and liquidity on the stock exchange.

Rising inflation will be the primary driver of tighter monetary policy. Inflation in February 2022, averaging 3.8% year on year, was above the Bank of Israel's target range of 1.0%–3.0%. This upward trend continued throughout 2022 and into 2023, mainly owing to cost-push factors, such as higher energy and food prices, caused by supply disruptions following Russia's invasion of Ukraine in February 2022. However, on 10 July 2023 the Bank of Israel's monetary policy committee held the benchmark interest rate at 4.75%, as inflation concerns began to ease. Figures released in mid-July showed that prices in June had stayed flat month on month, pushing year-on-year inflation down to 4.2%.

Among other areas of concern in the financial sector is the fact that the US Government has investigated several of Israel's largest banks over allegations of tax evasion. In addition, the Israeli Government's objective of reducing concentration could break up major banks and cause instability in the medium term.

FISCAL POLICY

The global financial crisis of 2007–08 profoundly affected Israel's public finances. During 1990–2007 general government revenue averaged 40.8% of GDP per year. However, average annual revenue dropped to 35.9% of GDP in 2008–22. Similarly, annual government expenditure experienced a significant shift, averaging 44.1% of GDP in 1997–2007 and only 35.9% in 2008–22. Despite these sharp shifts in revenue and expenditure, the Government's fiscal deficit remained broadly stable, averaging 3.2% of GDP annually during 1990–2007 and 3.6% in 2008–22. However, while the deficit averages over each period were similar, there were significant year-to-year fluctuations. Notably, the fiscal deficit of 11.3% of GDP in the pandemic year of 2020 was up from a deficit of 3.6% in the previous year. The deficit decreased to 4.4% of GDP in 2021 and a small surplus, of 0.6%, was recorded in 2022; the IMF forecast a deficit of 0.9% in 2023. Government debt increased from 58.8% of GDP in 2019 to 70.6% in 2020, subsequently falling to 68.0% in 2021 and 61.0% in 2022; the IMF predicted a gradual further decline to 55.0% by 2025.

Although there is some disagreement between the Bank of Israel and the Ministry of Finance over the exact fiscal policy direction that should be taken in the medium to longer term, both institutions agree that numerous structural reforms are urgently required without any further delay to address the long-term problems facing Israel's economy and society. There is also considerable consensus among bureaucrats as to the nature of these problems, and considerable common ground for solving them. The Bank of Israel defines 'four axes' on which to advance: investment in physical, technological and infrastructure capital; development of the financial system; improved regulation; and applying technology to streamline public sector functionality. All of these also appear in the Ministry of Finance's proposals, albeit with different weightings.

Both sets of plans implicitly agree that the most significant challenge facing the economy is within the labour market; although parts of Israel's economy operate at high levels of efficiency and productivity, there are a number of fundamental structural issues within the labour market. Both the Bank of Israel and the Ministry of Finance identify a two-fold challenge: first, to increase the level of labour force participation, requiring policies designed to integrate the two significant marginalized population groups (Israeli Arabs and ultra-orthodox Jews); and second, to enhance the human capital of these new employees as well as of existing workers, by improving the quality of education at all levels and by upgrading and expanding training and retraining programmes.

The disagreement between the two institutions centres on the question of how to finance so many necessary reforms. Whereas the Bank of Israel maintains its longstanding view that higher taxes are required and justified to pay for additional and better services, the Ministry of Finance is less specific about the cost details, sometimes indicating that it expects the reforms to pay for themselves (by boosting growth and thus tax revenue).

PROSPECTS

Israel's financial metrics remain strong, with budget and current account surpluses, and a decreasing debt-to-GDP ratio in 2022. The IMF forecast that GDP growth of 2.5% would be achieved in 2023, accelerating to 3.4% in both 2024 and 2025. None the less, the international credit rating agencies have expressed concern that the Government's judicial reforms will further undermine Israel's relatively weak institutional rating and create deep political divisions. However, only Moody's has acted, lowering Israel's outlook from 'positive' to 'stable' in April 2023. By August of that year Israel still enjoyed relatively high ratings—Moody's A1, Standard &Poor's AA– and Fitch Ratings A+. A downgrade at the agencies' next review, in November, would raise borrowing costs, but this looked unlikely. None the less, despite initially seeming improbable, it was feared that the widespread and persistent resistance to the judicial reforms proposed by the right-wing governing coalition might have significant economic consequences. There were concerns that the controversial reforms could lead to numerous high-technology companies and their educated employees relocating from Israel. Furthermore, foreign investors were growing anxious about the nation's prospects and delaying their investments.

Statistical Survey

Source (unless otherwise indicated): Central Bureau of Statistics, POB 13015, Hakirya, Romema, Jerusalem 91130; tel. 2-6592037; fax 2-6521340; e-mail yael@cbs.gov.il; internet www.cbs.gov.il.

Area and Population

AREA, POPULATION AND DENSITY

Area (sq km)	
Land	21,643
Inland water	429
Total	22,072*
Population (*de jure*; census results)†	
4 November 1995	5,548,523
27 December 2008	
Males	3,663,910
Females	3,748,270
Total	7,412,180
Population (*de jure*; official estimates at 31 December)†	
2020	9,289,800
2021	9,453,000
2022	9,656,000
Density (per sq km) at 31 December 2022	446.1‡

* 8,522 sq miles. Area includes East Jerusalem, annexed by Israel in June 1967, and the Golan sub-district (1,154 sq km), annexed by Israel in December 1981.
† Including the population of East Jerusalem and Israeli residents in certain other areas under Israeli military occupation since June 1967. Figures also include non-Jews in the Golan sub-district, an Israeli-occupied area of Syrian territory. Census results exclude adjustment for underenumeration.
‡ Land area only.

POPULATION BY AGE AND SEX
('000, at 31 December 2021)

	Males	Females	Total
0–14 years	1,355.1	1,285.1	2,640.1
15–64 years	2,822.2	2,828.2	5,650.5
65 years and over	518.6	643.9	1,162.5
Total	4,695.9	4,757.1	9,453.0

Note: Totals may not be equal to the sum of components, owing to rounding.

POPULATION BY RELIGION
('000, at 31 December 2021)

	Number	%
Jews	6,982.6	73.9
Muslims	1,708.9	18.1
Christians*	183.2	1.9
Druze	148.6	1.6
Unclassified†	429.7	4.5
Total	9,453.0	100.0

* Including Arab Christians.
† Including Lebanese not classified by religion.

DISTRICTS
(31 December 2021)

	Area (sq km)*	Population ('000)†	Density (per sq km)
Central	1,294	2,304.3	1,780.8
Haifa	866	1,092.7	1,261.8
Jerusalem‡	653	1,209.7	1,852.5
Northern§	4,473	1,513.6	338.4
Southern	14,185	1,386.0	97.7
Tel Aviv	172	1,481.4	8,612.8
Total	21,643	9,453.0†	436.8

* Excluding lakes, with a total area of 429 sq km.
† Components exclude, but total includes, Israelis residing in Jewish localities in the West Bank totalling some 465,300 at 31 December 2021.
‡ Including East Jerusalem, annexed by Israel in June 1967.
§ Including the Golan sub-district (area 1,154 sq km, population an estimated 53,700 at 31 December 2021), annexed by Israel in December 1981.

PRINCIPAL TOWNS
(population estimates at 31 December 2022, preliminary)

Jerusalem (capital)*	979,079	Netanya	232,762
Tel Aviv—Jaffa	473,841	Ashdod	226,866
Haifa	289,535	Bene Beraq	217,137
Rishon LeZiyyon	260,272	Beersheba	213,972
Petach Tikva	254,880	Holon	197,935

* The Israeli Government has designated the city of Jerusalem (including East Jerusalem, annexed by Israel in June 1967) as the country's capital, although this is not recognized by the United Nations.

ISRAEL

BIRTHS, MARRIAGES AND DEATHS*

	Registered live births		Registered marriages		Registered deaths†	
	Number	Rate (per 1,000)	Number	Rate (per 1,000)	Number	Rate (per 1,000)
2017	183,648	21.1	50,029	5.7	44,923	5.2
2018	184,370	20.8	49,410	5.6	44,850	5.0
2019	182,016	20.1	48,056	5.3	46,326	5.1
2020	177,307	19.2	39,984	4.3	49,006	5.3
2021	185,040	19.7	n.a.	n.a.	50,912	5.4

* Including East Jerusalem.
† Including deaths abroad of Israelis residing outside of Israel less than one year.

Note: Data include marriages involving a spouse not resident in Israel and those in which spouses may be of different religions.

Life expectancy (years at birth, estimates): 82.5 (males 80.5; females 84.6) in 2021 (Source: World Bank, World Development Indicators database).

IMMIGRATION*

	2019	2020	2021
Immigrants on immigrant visas	27,293	14,362	19,864
Immigrants on tourist visas†	4,191	4,303	4,409
Total	31,484	18,665	24,273

* Excluding immigrating citizens (4,251 in 2019; 1,373 in 2020; 1,820 in 2021) and Israeli residents returning from abroad.
† Figures refer to tourists who changed their status to immigrants or potential immigrants.

ECONOMICALLY ACTIVE POPULATION
(sample surveys, annual averages, '000 persons aged 15 years and over, excluding armed forces)*

	2020	2021	2022
Agriculture, hunting, forestry and fishing	37.0	32.1	33.8
Industry†	379.8	395.3	403.1
Electricity, gas and water supply	32.9	33.6	33.6
Construction	198.1	195.4	211.8
Wholesale and retail trade; repair of motor vehicles, motorcycles and personal and household goods	414.0	407.5	426.9
Hotels and restaurants	139.9	136.5	166.1
Transport, storage and communications	399.0	402.8	463.3
Financial intermediation	126.2	130.8	135.8
Real estate, renting and business activities	496.0	496.8	525.1
Public administration and defence; compulsory social security	408.3	424.0	420.0
Education	487.7	498.5	512.7
Health and social work	459.5	456.6	487.5
Other community, social and personal service activities	184.6	174.2	186.2
Private households with employed persons	62.9	73.7	70.2
Extraterritorial organizations and bodies	3.0	2.8	1.6
Sub-total	3,828.9	3,860.6	4,077.7
Not classifiable by economic activity	84.5	96.5	109.3
Total employed	3,913.4	3,957.0	4,187.0
Unemployed	177.0	206.3	163.4
Total labour force	4,090.4	4,163.3	4,350.4
Males	2,125.7	2,150.4	2,241.4
Females	1,964.7	2,012.9	2,109.0

* Totals may not be equal to the sum of components, owing to independent estimation methodologies.
† Comprising mining and quarrying, and manufacturing.

Health and Welfare

KEY INDICATORS

Total fertility rate (children per woman, 2021)	3.0
Under-5 mortality rate (per 1,000 live births, 2021)	3.4
HIV/AIDS (% of persons aged 15–49, 2018)	0.2
COVID-19: Cumulative confirmed deaths (per 100,000 persons at 30 June 2023)	133.0
COVID-19: Fully vaccinated population (% of total population at 4 May 2023)	65.2
Physicians (per 1,000 head, 2021)	3.7
Hospital beds (per 1,000 head, 2019)	1.8
Domestic health expenditure (2020): US $ per head (PPP)	2,448.6
Domestic health expenditure (2020): % of GDP	5.9
Domestic health expenditure (2020): public (% of total current health expenditure)	70.8
Total carbon dioxide emissions ('000 metric tons, 2019)	62,650
Carbon dioxide emissions per head (metric tons, 2019)	6.9
Human Development Index (2021): ranking	22
Human Development Index (2021): value	0.919

Note: For data on COVID-19 vaccinations, 'fully vaccinated' denotes receipt of all doses specified by approved vaccination regime (Sources: Johns Hopkins University and Our World in Data). Data on health expenditure refer to current general government expenditure in each case. For more information on sources and further definitions for all indicators, see Health and Welfare Statistics: Sources and Definitions section (europaworld.com/credits).

Agriculture

PRINCIPAL CROPS
('000 metric tons)

	2019	2020	2021
Apples	104.0	104.0	101.0
Aubergines (Eggplants)	49.2	47.4	51.0
Avocados	138.8	147.0	165.0
Bananas	144.0	153.0	147.0
Cabbages and other brassicas	52.0	49.2	51.6
Cantaloupes and other melons	32.9	33.1	33.2
Carrots and turnips	252.8	192.0	186.3
Cauliflowers and broccoli	28.6	22.4	24.0
Chillies and peppers, green	171.3	146.9	145.2
Cucumbers and gherkins	94.6	91.9	92.5
Dates	43.4	49.0	55.4
Grapefruit and pomelos	148.8	145.7	129.0
Grapes	57.1	46.2	60.5
Lemons and limes	75.6	71.3	74.8
Lettuce and chicory	22.4	25.0	16.6
Maize	77.8	74.5	68.2
Mangoes, mangosteens and guavas	53.2	35.4	58.4
Olives	108.0	83.0	70.0
Onions, dry	73.9	84.9	81.3
Oranges	74.9	75.8	46.6
Peaches and nectarines	56.2	58.1	39.1
Pears	23.5	24.0	24.7
Persimmons	27.0	21.9	30.0
Plums and sloes	25.0	21.0	17.0
Potatoes	524.4	528.0	509.4
Seed cotton	21.8	14.9	10.2
Sweet potatoes	35.0	34.3	40.0
Tangerines, mandarins, etc.	211.1	192.0	161.4
Tomatoes	299.1	343.4	374.1
Watermelons	100.1	105.1	119.1
Wheat	84.8	116.7	150.0

Aggregate production ('000 metric tons, may include official, semi-official or estimated data): Total cereals 184.1 in 2019, 246.8 in 2020, 268.3 in 2021; Total fruit (primary) 1,454.7 in 2019, 1,429.6 in 2020, 1,410.9 in 2021; Total oilcrops 202.7 in 2019, 163.3 in 2020, 137.7 in 2021; Total roots and tubers 559.4 in 2019, 562.2 in 2020, 549.4 in 2021; Total vegetables (primary) 1,307.8 in 2019, 1,266.6 in 2020, 1,281.8 in 2021.

Source: FAO.

ISRAEL

LIVESTOCK
('000 head, year ending September)

	2019	2020	2021
Cattle	553	526	530
Chickens	49,038	51,140	47,093
Ducks*	179	178	178
Geese and guinea fowls*	918	915	912
Goats	107	116	116
Pigs	166	184	164
Sheep	519	500	520
Turkeys	2,852	3,074	3,228

* FAO estimates.
Source: FAO.

LIVESTOCK PRODUCTS
('000 metric tons unless otherwise stated)

	2019	2020	2021
Cattle hides, fresh*	14.4	14.1	14.2
Cattle meat	141.1	138.7	139.7
Cattle offals, edible*	22.9	22.5	22.7
Cows' milk	1,542.1	1,563.1	1,528.3
Chicken meat	517.1	578.2	541.3
Goats' milk	24.4	24.5	25.0
Goose and guinea fowl meat*	3.1	3.1	3.1
Pig meat	13.6	15.1	13.4
Sheep meat	38.6	39.8	38.4
Sheep's (Ewes') milk	17.5	18.0	18.9
Turkey meat	94.4	81.4	85.7
Hen eggs	148.2	148.6	166.0
Honey (natural)	3.8	4.0	4.0

* FAO estimates.
Source: FAO.

Forestry

ROUNDWOOD REMOVALS
('000 cubic metres, excl. bark, FAO estimates)

	2019	2020	2021
Sawlogs, veneer logs and logs for sleepers	11	11	11
Pulpwood	7	7	7
Other industrial wood	7	7	7
Fuel wood	2	2	2
Total	27	27	27

Note: Figures assumed to be unchanged from 2001.
Source: FAO.

Fishing

(metric tons, live weight, FAO estimates)

	2019	2020	2021
Capture	2,046	2,016	2,035
Aquaculture	16,940	15,280	14,875
Common carp	3,060	3,100	3,000
Tilapias	6,500	5,300	5,300
Gilthead seabream	2,950	2,750	2,650
Flathead grey mullet	1,900	2,100	2,000
Total catch	18,996	17,296	16,910

Source: FAO.

Mining
('000 metric tons unless otherwise indicated)

	2017	2018	2019
Crude petroleum ('000 barrels)	480	552	627
Natural gas (million cu m)	9,570	10,480	10,500
Phosphate rock*	3,332	3,550	2,807
Potash salts†	1,900	2,200‡	2,040
Salt (unrefined, marketed)	514	377	301
Gypsum	116.0	75.8	72.0
Bromine (elemental)	180	175	180

* Figures refer to beneficiated production; the phosphoric acid content (in '000 metric tons) was: 1,030 in 2017; 1,100 in 2018; 870 in 2019.
† Figures refer to K_2O content.
‡ Estimate.
Source: US Geological Survey.

Industry

SELECTED PRODUCTS
('000 metric tons unless otherwise indicated)

	2017	2018	2019
Wine*	3.1	2.8	2.1
Sulphuric acid†	700	680	700
Cement	6,361	5,858	5,000†
Electrical energy (million kWh)	67,712	69,280	72,377

* FAO estimates.
† Estimate(s).

Electrical energy (million kWh): 72,760 in 2020; 73,796 in 2021.
Wine ('000 metric tons): 1.7 in 2020 (estimate).
Sources: FAO; US Geological Survey.

Finance

CURRENCY AND EXCHANGE RATES

Monetary Units
100 agorot (singular: agora) = 1 new sheqel (plural: sheqalim) or shekel (NIS).

Sterling, Dollar and Euro Equivalents (31 May 2023)
£1 sterling = NIS 4.593;
US $1 = NIS 3.715;
€1 = NIS 3.969;
NIS 100 = £21.77 = $26.92 = €25.20.

Average Exchange Rate (NIS per US $)
2020   3.4424
2021   3.2302
2022   3.3596

BUDGET
(NIS '000 million)

Revenue*	2021	2022	2023†
Taxes	428.4	488.4	491.3
Taxes on income, profits, and capital gains	191.1	227.3	209.3
Taxes on goods and services	188.5	210.1	226.9
Taxes on international trade and transactions	3.7	3.0	3.2
Other taxes	45.2	48.0	51.9
Social contributions	88.4	97.4	105.0
Other revenue	49.2	55.8	60.1
Interest income	2.5	3.0	3.0
Total	566.0	641.6	656.4

ISRAEL

Statistical Survey

Expenditure‡	2021	2022	2023†
Expense	636.1	653.4	695.0
Compensation of employees	148.9	157.3	170.7
Purchases/use of goods and services	101.8	105.8	113.2
Interest expense	44.3	58.8	55.6
Social benefits	200.8	210.0	227.9
Other expenses	140.3	121.4	127.6
Net acquisition of non-financial assets	–1.0	–8.0	–2.0
Total	635.1	645.4	693.0

* Excluding grants received NIS '000 million): 11.1 in 2021; 14.6 in 2022; 15.8 in 2023 (projection).
† Projections.
‡ Excluding net lending (NIS '000 million): –58.0 in 2021; –10.9 in 2022; –20.8 in 2023 (projection).

Source: IMF, *Israel: 2023 Article IV Consultation—Press Release; Staff Report; and Statement by the Executive Director for Israel* (June 2023).

INTERNATIONAL RESERVES
(excluding gold, US $ million at 31 December)

	2020	2021	2022
IMF special drawing rights	1,286.2	3,883.2	3,732.2
Reserve position in IMF	763.9	730.5	757.2
Foreign exchange	171,242.0	208,320.0	189,742.0
Total	173,292.1	212,933.7	194,231.4

Source: IMF, *International Financial Statistics*.

MONEY SUPPLY
(NIS million at 31 December)

	2020	2021	2022
Currency outside depository corporations	97,093.0	104,649.9	110,403.0
Transferable deposits	737,724.7	898,961.3	769,926.5
Other deposits	573,102.5	648,419.3	836,067.1
Securities other than shares	63,985.8	60,225.4	111,640.1
Broad money	1,471,906.0	1,712,255.9	1,828,036.7

Source: IMF, *International Financial Statistics*.

COST OF LIVING
(Consumer Price Index; base: 2020 = 100)

	2021	2022
Food (excl. vegetables and fruit)	101.5	106.7
Clothing and footwear	95.1	90.5
Housing	101.4	106.1
All items (incl. others)	101.5	105.9

NATIONAL ACCOUNTS
(NIS million at current prices)

National Income and Product

	2020	2021	2022
Gross domestic product in market prices	1,422,635	1,578,038	1,755,965
Net income paid abroad	–12,564	–23,782	–22,635
Gross national income (GNI)	1,410,071	1,554,256	1,733,330
Less Consumption of fixed capital	218,566	233,752	257,510
Net national income	1,191,505	1,320,504	1,475,820

Expenditure on the Gross Domestic Product

	2020	2021	2022
Final consumption expenditure	1,020,298	1,124,523	1,235,413
Private	688,863	775,783	869,402
General government	331,436	348,740	366,011
Gross capital formation	338,774	391,103	461,815
Total domestic expenditure	1,359,072	1,515,626	1,697,228
Exports of goods and services	393,724	464,874	560,619
Less Imports of goods and services	330,161	402,462	501,881
GDP in market prices	1,422,635	1,578,038	1,755,965

Gross Domestic Product by Economic Activity

	2020	2021	2022
Agriculture, hunting, forestry and fishing	18,728	19,899	20,525
Manufacturing, mining and quarrying	158,875	160,404	190,897
Electricity, gas and water supply	27,069	27,035	23,604
Construction	72,128	83,543	98,248
Wholesale, retail trade, repair of motor vehicles, motorcycles and personal and household goods; hotels and restaurants	144,978	169,176	184,667
Transport, storage and communications	192,515	234,400	271,100
Financial intermediation; real estate, renting and business activities	232,529	265,049	290,353
Housing services	156,314	156,494	162,898
Education	83,281	89,200	98,003
Public administration and defence	95,419	98,222	256,108
Human health and social work	83,154	91,109	
Arts, entertainment and recreation; households as employers; other service activities	33,487	39,616	
Sub-total	1,298,477	1,434,147	1,596,403
Net taxes on products	124,158	143,891	159,563
GDP in market prices	1,422,635	1,578,038	1,755,965

BALANCE OF PAYMENTS
(US $ million)

	2020	2021	2022
Exports of goods	59,321.8	70,132.4	80,032.3
Imports of goods	–70,997.0	–91,618.4	–105,889.5
Balance on goods	–11,675.2	–21,486.0	–25,857.2
Exports of services	55,099.8	73,751.2	86,065.8
Imports of services	–24,980.3	–32,959.8	–43,299.4
Balance on goods and services	18,444.3	19,305.4	16,909.2
Primary income received	12,038.9	18,033.7	19,316.9
Primary income paid	–15,849.3	–25,566.7	–26,629.3
Balance on goods, services and primary income	14,633.9	11,772.4	9,596.8
Secondary income received	12,833.5	14,789.9	14,973.2
Secondary income paid	–4,981.3	–5,472.3	–5,358.5
Current balance	22,486.1	21,090.0	19,211.5
Capital account (net)	435.4	470.8	498.1
Direct investment assets	–4,424.6	–9,455.5	–9,241.3
Direct investment liabilities	23,109.2	21,486.3	27,760.1
Portfolio investment assets	–15,202.3	–15,636.4	1,884.4
Portfolio investment liabilities	19,327.1	31,124.2	4,932.0
Financial derivatives and employee stock options (net)	–1,264.0	–281.5	–8,827.5
Other investment assets	–9,040.0	–13,501.4	–9,151.3
Other investment liabilities	1,048.7	10,037.1	–4,380.7
Net errors and omissions	1,467.5	–5,556.3	–20,045.9
Reserves and related items	37,943.1	39,777.3	2,639.4

Source: IMF, *International Financial Statistics*.

ISRAEL

External Trade

PRINCIPAL COMMODITIES
(US $ million)

Imports c.i.f.	2020	2021	2022
Food and live animals	5,705.5	7,098.1	8,290.4
Mineral fuels, lubricants, etc.	5,120.0	9,131.2	14,670.9
Petroleum, petroleum products, etc.	4,887.8	8,133.8	12,401.8
Chemicals and related products	9,577.9	11,524.5	12,915.6
Medical and pharmaceutical products	3,384.3	3,730.7	3,696.2
Basic manufactures	12,573.3	17,486.1	19,371.8
Non-metallic mineral manufactures	5,316.7	8,072.9	8,549.9
Iron and steel	1,874.6	2,938.8	3,546.8
Machinery and transport equipment	24,945.7	30,976.6	35,465.9
General industrial machinery, equipment and parts	3,260.8	3,732.2	4,046.1
Office machines and automatic data processing machines	2,311.0	2,738.4	3,104.0
Telecommunications and sound equipment	3,426.2	4,237.6	4,235.3
Other electrical machinery, apparatus, etc.	5,300.1	7,213.0	8,412.0
Road vehicles and parts	5,812.2	7,560.8	9,158.1
Miscellaneous manufactured articles	8,725.1	11,557.7	12,159.8
Total (incl. others)	70,326.2	92,158.8	107,755.6

Exports f.o.b.	2020	2021	2022
Food and live animals	1,719.5	1,925.7	1,923.3
Mineral fuels, lubricants and related products	2,370.5	4,283.6	7,021.7
Chemicals and related products	12,188.8	10,623.7	14,462.3
Organic chemicals	4,136.6	1,425.1	1,946.7
Medical and pharmaceutical products	1,705.4	2,167.8	3,240.7
Basic manufactures	8,464.1	12,339.3	14,614.3
Non-metallic mineral manufactures	5,795.9	9,277.4	11,496.9
Machinery and transport equipment	16,005.6	18,850.7	21,241.1
General industrial machinery, equipment and parts	1,758.0	2,008.5	2,063.7
Telecommunications and sound equipment	3,193.7	3,609.3	4,010.1
Other electrical machinery, apparatus, etc.	5,864.5	7,560.0	8,608.4
Road vehicles and other transport equipment and parts	2,269.6	2,392.2	3,062.2
Miscellaneous manufactured articles	8,423.3	10,837.2	12,066.1
Professional, scientific and controlling instruments, etc.	4,258.4	5,801.9	6,601.7
Total (incl. others)	50,154.1	60,158.4	72,565.1

PRINCIPAL TRADING PARTNERS
(US $ million)*

Imports (excl. military goods) c.i.f.	2020	2021	2022
Belgium-Luxembourg	3,616.3	4,787.7	4,730.4
China, People's Republic	7,669.9	10,728.1	13,150.7
France	2,137.6	2,368.3	3,551.0
Germany	5,230.2	6,560.4	7,075.7
Hong Kong	2,162.3	2,920.1	3,206.2
India	1,723.8	2,629.9	2,702.6
Ireland	1,216.1	1,975.7	1,920.0
Italy	2,686.6	3,366.3	3,470.3
Japan	1,239.4	1,439.5	1,401.2
Korea, Republic	1,692.7	2,251.7	2,796.6
Netherlands	2,902.1	3,712.3	4,278.2
Singapore	1,074.1	1,735.6	2,166.5
Spain	1,526.3	2,032.6	2,110.8
Sweden	706.5	782.3	1,126.5
Switzerland-Liechtenstein	5,254.3	6,618.0	6,089.2
Taiwan	938.1	1,106.0	1,319.2
Türkiye	3,497.1	4,764.3	5,700.3
United Arab Emirates	115.8	836.9	1,890.9
United Kingdom	2,973.8	2,990.2	3,186.8
USA	8,327.1	8,630.8	9,639.0
Total (incl. others)	70,326.2	92,158.8	107,755.6

Exports f.o.b.	2020	2021	2022
Belgium-Luxembourg	1,480.0	1,994.6	2,039.8
Brazil	1,006.7	1,259.7	1,942.0
Canada	567.0	612.1	1,042.4
China, People's Republic	4,240.5	4,398.3	4,631.3
Cyprus	316.7	575.0	1,054.1
France	1,153.8	1,412.9	2,081.4
Germany	1,681.1	1,792.5	1,880.6
Hong Kong	1,239.5	1,384.9	1,622.1
India	1,599.0	2,735.0	3,354.4
Ireland	198.0	1,435.4	2,576.1
Italy	786.7	1,378.1	1,524.4
Japan	948.2	989.0	906.0
Korea, Republic	787.7	1,153.7	1,304.2
Netherlands	2,462.8	2,234.1	2,439.3
Russian Federation	671.9	794.2	653.3
Singapore	513.9	693.7	1,143.0
Spain	874.7	1,120.8	1,198.4
Switzerland-Liechtenstein	445.1	742.9	1,530.3
Taiwan	733.1	1,062.9	1,395.6
Türkiye	1,430.7	1,919.0	2,338.9
United Kingdom	3,712.6	2,057.5	3,121.2
USA	13,132.3	16,318.9	18,616.8
Total (incl. others)	50,154.1	60,158.4	72,565.1

* Imports by country of purchase; exports by country of destination.

Transport

RAILWAYS
(traffic)

	2020	2021	2022
Passengers carried ('000 journeys)	24,155	35,021	54,718
Passenger-km (million)	1,253	1,956	3,019
Freight carried ('000 metric tons)	8,029	7,355	6,168
Freight ton-km (million)	1,250	1,085	992

ROAD TRAFFIC
(motor vehicles in use at 31 December)

	2020	2021	2022
Private passenger cars	3,173,595	3,312,626	3,433,446
Taxis	20,616	21,488	22,413
Minibuses	14,745	14,969	15,296
Buses and coaches	22,292	22,968	24,016
Lorries, vans and road tractors	303,660	305,724	308,202
Special service vehicles	5,970	6,379	6,742
Motorcycles and mopeds	148,895	156,475	163,807

SHIPPING

Flag Registered Fleet
(at 31 December)

	2020	2021	2022
Number of vessels	45	49	47
Displacement ('000 grt)	345.5	349.6	267.3

Source: Lloyd's List Intelligence (www.bit.ly/LLintelligence).

International Seaborne Freight Traffic
('000 metric tons)

	2020	2021	2022
Goods loaded	19,124	19,141	19,247
Goods unloaded*	38,329	40,624	41,467

* Including traffic between Israeli ports.

CIVIL AVIATION
(traffic on scheduled services)

	2013	2014	2015
Kilometres flown (million)	107	112	116
Passengers carried ('000)	5,566	5,887	6,064
Passenger-km (million)	18,828	19,677	20,290
Total ton-km (million)	802	651	759

Source: UN, *Statistical Yearbook*.

2021 (domestic and international): Departures 23,090; Passengers carried 2.4m.; Freight carried 716m. ton-km (Source: World Bank, World Development Indicators database).

Tourism

TOURIST ARRIVALS
('000)*

Country of residence	2020	2021	2022
Brazil	14.2	2.3	68.0
Canada	16.4	10.1	68.2
France	58.6	41.8	242.3
Germany	52.1	16.7	169.6
Italy	26.8	7.1	91.3
Korea, Republic	17.3	0.8	13.1
Poland	50.1	2.4	45.0
Romania	25.9	2.1	51.9
Russian Federation	59.8	14.5	174.5
Spain	17.0	5.4	60.1
Ukraine	33.7	14.5	73.5
United Kingdom	47.1	32.7	191.1
USA	205.8	150.6	858.5
Total (incl. others)	887.1	402.3	2,851.3

* Excluding arrivals of Israeli nationals residing abroad.

Tourism receipts (US $ million, excl. passenger transport): 2,500 in 2020; 2,217 in 2021 (provisional); 5,474 in 2022 (provisional) (Source: World Tourism Organization).

Communications Media

	2019	2020	2021
Telephones ('000 main lines in use)	3,140	3,370	3,500
Mobile telephone subscriptions ('000)	11,700	12,270	12,500
Broadband subscriptions, fixed ('000)	2,481	2,602	2,657
Broadband subscriptions, mobile ('000)	9,800	10,500	11,000
Internet users (% of population)	86.8	90.1	90.3

Source: International Telecommunication Union.

Education

(2021/22 unless otherwise indicated)

	Schools	Pupils	Teachers*
Hebrew			
Kindergarten	n.a.	705,638†	16,216
Primary schools	2,673	865,958	69,583
Special needs	278	14,197	n.a.
Intermediate schools	694	235,924	31,087
Secondary schools	1,707	367,168	44,220
Vocational schools	112‡	131,737	n.a.
Teacher training colleges	56‡	33,893‡	5,359§
Arab			
Kindergarten	n.a.	124,700†	3,175
Primary schools	667	252,453	21,866
Special needs	83	3,502	n.a.
Intermediate schools	225	82,524	8,591
Secondary schools	402	110,692	11,312
Vocational schools	24‡	46,705	n.a.
Teacher training colleges	4‡	2,827‡	491§

* 2020/21.
† 2016/17.
‡ 2008/09, provisional.
§ 2006/07.

Pupil-teacher ratio (primary education, UNESCO estimate): 12.1 in 2015/16 (Source: UNESCO Institute for Statistics).

Adult literacy rate (UNESCO estimates): 97.8% (males 98.7%; females 96.8%) in 2011 (Source: UNESCO Institute for Statistics).

Directory

The Constitution

There is no written constitution. In June 1950 the Knesset (parliament) voted to adopt a state constitution by evolution over an unspecified period. A number of laws, including the Law of Return (1950), the Nationality Law (1952), the State President (Tenure) Law (1952), the Education Law (1953) and the 'Yad-va-Shem' Memorial Law (1953), are considered as incorporated into the state Constitution. Other constitutional laws are: the Law and Administration Ordinance (1948), the Knesset Election Law (1951), the Law of Equal Rights for Women (1951), the Judges Act (1953), the National Service and National Insurance Acts (1953), and the Basic Law: the Knesset (1958). A further constitutional law, the Nation State of the Jewish People, received Knesset approval in 2018. The provisions of constitutional legislation that affect the main organs of state and government are summarized below:

THE STATE

The Land of Israel is the historical homeland of the Jewish people, in which the State of Israel was established. The State of Israel is the nation state of the Jewish People, in which it realizes its natural, cultural, religious and historical right to self-determination. The exercise of the right to national self-determination in the State of Israel is unique to the Jewish People.

ISREAL — Directory

The name of the State is 'Israel'. The State flag is white, with two light blue stripes close to the edge, and a light blue Star of David at the centre.

Jerusalem, complete and united, is the capital of Israel. Hebrew is the State language. The Arabic language has a special status in the State; arrangements regarding the use of Arabic in state institutions or vis-à-vis them will be set by law.

The State shall be open for Jewish immigration, and for the Ingathering of the Exiles. The State shall strive to ensure the safety of members of the Jewish People and of its citizens, who are in trouble and in captivity, due to their Jewishness or due to their citizenship. The State shall act, in the Diaspora, to preserve the ties between the State and members of the Jewish People. The State shall act to preserve the cultural, historical and religious heritage of the Jewish People among Jews in the Diaspora.

The State views the development of Jewish settlement as a national value, and shall act to encourage and promote its establishment and strengthening.

THE PRESIDENT

The President is elected by the Knesset for a maximum of one seven-year term.

Ten or more Knesset members may propose a candidate for the Presidency.

Voting will be by secret ballot.

The President may not leave the country without the consent of the Government.

The President may resign by submitting a letter of resignation in writing to the Speaker of the Knesset.

The President may be relieved of his duties by the Knesset for misdemeanour.

The Knesset is entitled to decide by a two-thirds' majority that the President is too incapacitated owing to ill health to fulfil his duties permanently.

The Speaker of the Knesset will act for the President when the President leaves the country, or cannot perform the duties of the office owing to ill health.

THE KNESSET

The Knesset is the parliament of the state. There are 120 members.

It is elected by general, national, direct, equal, secret and proportional elections.

Every Israeli national of 18 years or over shall have the right to vote in elections to the Knesset unless a court has deprived him of that right by virtue of any law.

Every Israeli national of 21 and over shall have the right to be elected to the Knesset unless a court has deprived him of that right by virtue of any law.

The following shall not be candidates: the President of the State; the two Chief Rabbis; a judge (*shofet*) in office; a judge (*dayan*) of a religious court; the State Comptroller; the Chief of the General Staff of the Defence Army of Israel; rabbis and ministers of other religions in office; senior state employees and senior army officers of such ranks and in such functions as shall be determined by law.

The term of office of the Knesset shall be four years.

The elections to the Knesset shall take place on the third Tuesday of the month of Marcheshvan in the year in which the tenure of the outgoing Knesset ends.

Election day shall be a day of rest, but transport and other public services shall function normally.

Results of the elections shall be published within 14 days.

The Knesset shall elect from among its members a Chairman (Speaker) and Vice-Chairman.

The Knesset shall elect from among its members permanent committees, and may elect committees for specific matters.

The Knesset may appoint commissions of inquiry to investigate matters designated by the Knesset.

The Knesset shall hold two sessions a year; one of them shall open within four weeks after the Feast of the Tabernacles, the other within four weeks after Independence Day; the aggregate duration of the two sessions shall not be less than eight months.

The outgoing Knesset shall continue to hold office until the convening of the incoming Knesset.

The members of the Knesset shall receive a remuneration as provided by law.

THE GOVERNMENT

The Government shall tender its resignation to the President immediately after his election, but shall continue with its duties until the formation of a new government. After consultation with representatives of the parties in the Knesset, the President shall charge one of the members with the formation of a government. The Government shall be composed of a Prime Minister (elected on a party basis from 2003) and a number of ministers from among the Knesset members or from outside the Knesset. After it has been chosen, the Government shall appear before the Knesset and shall be considered as formed after having received a vote of confidence. Within seven days of receiving a vote of confidence, the Prime Minister and the other ministers shall swear allegiance to the State of Israel and its Laws and undertake to carry out the decisions of the Knesset.

The Government

HEAD OF STATE

President: ISAAC HERZOG (took office 7 July 2021).

THE CABINET
(September 2023)

A coalition of Likud, Shas, the Religious Zionist Party, Otzma Yehudit, United Torah Judaism and Noam (whose sole representative in the Knesset was appointed as a deputy minister).

Prime Minister: BENJAMIN NETANYAHU (Likud).
Deputy Prime Minister and Minister of Justice: YARIV LEVIN (Likud).
Minister of Foreign Affairs: ELI COHEN (Likud).
Minister of Defense: YOAV GALLANT (Likud).
Minister of National Security: ITAMAR BEN GVIR (Otzma Yehudit).
Minister of Finance and Minister within the Ministry of Defense: BEZALEL YOEL SMOTRICH (Religious Zionist Party).
Minister of the Interior and of Health: MOSHE ARBEL (Shas).
Minister of Agriculture and Rural Development: AVI DICHTER (Likud).
Minister of Communications: SHLOMO KARHI (Likud).
Minister in the Prime Minister's Office and Minister of Construction and Housing: YITZHAK GOLDKNOPF (United Torah Judaism).
Minister of Culture and Sport: MAKHLUF MIKI ZOHAR (Likud).
Minister of Diaspora Affairs and of Social Equality and Pensioners: AMICHAI CHIKLI (Likud).
Minister of Labor: YOAV BEN TZUR (Shas).
Minister of the Economy and Industry: NIR BARKAT (Likud).
Minister of Education: YOAV KISCH (Likud).
Minister of Energy: ISRAEL KATZ (Likud).
Minister of Environmental Protection: IDIT SILMAN (Likud).
Minister of Immigration and Absorption: OFIR SOFER (Religious Zionist Party).
Minister for the Advancement of the Status of Women: MAY GOLAN (Likud).
Minister of Intelligence: GILA GAMLIEL (Likud).
Minister of Public Diplomacy: GALIT DISTEL ATBARYAN (Likud).
Minister of Jerusalem Affairs and Heritage: AMICHAY ELIYAHU (Otzma Yehudit).
Minister of Welfare and Social Affairs: YAKOV MARGI (Shas).
Minister of National Missions: ORIT MALKA STROCK (Religious Zionist Party).
Minister of Regional Co-operation, Minister within the Prime Minister's Office and the Ministry of Justice, and Liaison Minister between the Knesset and Government: DAVID AMSALEM (Likud).
Minister of Religious Services: MICHAEL MALKIELI (Shas).
Minister of Innovation, Science and Technology: OFIR AKUNIS (Likud).
Minister of Strategic Affairs: RON DERMER (Likud).
Minister of the Development of the Periphery, Negev and Galilee: ISSAC SHIMON WASSERLAUF (Otzma Yehudit).
Minister of Tourism: HAIM KATZ (Likud).
Minister of Transportation and Road Safety: MIRI MIRIAM REGEV (Likud).
Minister within the Ministry of Education: HAIM BITON (Shas).
Minister within the Ministry of Jerusalem Affairs and Heritage: MEIR PORUSH (United Torah Judaism).

Note: The Prime Minister automatically assumes responsibility for any portfolio that becomes vacant, until a permanent or acting minister is appointed. However, as of late 2023 this provision did not apply to Prime Minister Netanyahu, owing to the fact that he remained under investigation on charges of corruption.

MINISTRIES

Office of the President: 3 Hanassi St, Jerusalem 92188; tel. 2-6707211; fax 2-5887225; e-mail public@president.gov.il; internet www.president.gov.il.

Office of the Prime Minister: POB 187, 3 Kaplan St, Kiryat Ben-Gurion, Jerusalem 91950; tel. 3-6109898; fax 2-5605000; e-mail pm_eng@pmo.gov.il; internet www.pmo.gov.il.

Ministry for the Advancement of the Status of Women: Tel Aviv.

Ministry of Agriculture and Rural Development: POB 30, Agricultural Centre, Beit Dagan 50200; tel. 3-9485800; fax 3-9485835; e-mail sarmoag@moag.gov.il; internet www.moag.gov.il.

Ministry of Aliyah and Integration: 6 Ester Hamalka St, Tel Aviv; tel. (3)9733333; fax (72) 3229697; e-mail sar@moia.gov.il; internet www.gov.il/he/departments/ministry_of_aliyah_and_integration.

Ministry of Communications: 23 Jaffa St, Jerusalem 91999; tel. 2-6706323; fax 2-6240029; e-mail dovrut@moc.gov.il; internet www.gov.il/he/Departments/ministry_of_communications.

Ministry of Construction and Housing: POB 18110, 3 Clermont Ganneau St, Kiryat Hamemshala (East), Jerusalem 91180; tel. 2-5847654; fax 2-5847530; e-mail pniot@moch.gov.il; internet www.gov.il/he/Departments/ministry_of_construction_and_housing.

Ministry of Culture and Sport: 2 Agudat Sport HaPoel St, Jerusalem 96951; tel. 3-452333; fax 3-452334; internet www.gov.il/he/Departments/ministry_of_culture_and_sport.

Ministry of Defense: POB 976, Kirya, Tel Aviv 64734; tel. 3-6975540; fax 3-7380619; e-mail pniot@mod.gov.il; internet www.mod.gov.il.

Ministry of Diaspora Affairs: 3 Kaplan St, Jerusalem 91919; tel. 2-5422100; fax 2-5422124; e-mail diaspora@pmo.gov.il; internet www.mda.gov.il.

Ministry of the Economy and Industry: 5 Bank of Israel St, Jerusalem 9195021; tel. 2-6662080; fax 2-6662293; internet www.gov.il/he/Departments/ministry_of_economy.

Ministry of Education: POB 292, 34 Shivtei Israel St, Jerusalem 91911; tel. 2-5602222; fax 2-5602238; e-mail info@education.gov.il; internet edu.gov.il.

Ministry of Energy: POB 36148, 7 Bank of Israel St, Jerusalem 91360; tel. 2-8644024; fax 4-8660189; e-mail pniot@energy.gov.il; internet www.gov.il/he/Departments/ministry_of_energy.

Ministry of Environmental Protection: POB 343370, 5 Kanfei Nesharim St, Givat Shaul, Jerusalem 95464; tel. 2-6553720; fax 2-6495892; e-mail pniot@sviva.gov.il; internet www.sviva.gov.il.

Ministry of Finance: POB 13195, 1 Kaplan St, Kiryat Ben-Gurion, Jerusalem 91950; tel. 2-5317111; fax 2-5695347; e-mail pniot@mof.gov.il; internet www.gov.il/he/departments/ministry_of_finance.

Ministry of Foreign Affairs: 9 Yitzhak Rabin Blvd, Kiryat Ben-Gurion, Jerusalem 91030; tel. 2-5303111; fax 2-5303367; e-mail pniot@mfa.gov.il; internet mfa.gov.il.

Ministry of Health: POB 1176, 39 Yirmiyahu St, Jerusalem 94467; tel. 8-6241010; fax 2-5655969; e-mail call.habriut@moh.health.gov.il; internet www.health.gov.il.

Ministry of Innovation, Science and Technology: POB 49100, Jerusalem 9149002; tel. 2-5411172; fax 2-5825581; e-mail pniyot_m@most.gov.il; internet www.gov.il/he/Departments/ministry_of_science_and_technology.

Ministry of Intelligence: Jerusalem; tel. 2-6663004; fax 2-6663005.

Ministry of the Interior: POB 6158, Kiryat Ben-Gurion, Jerusalem 91061; tel. 2-6701400; fax 2-4448800; e-mail pniot@moin.gov.il; internet www.gov.il/he/departments/ministry_of_interior.

Ministry of Jerusalem Affairs and Heritage: 3 Kaplan St, Jerusalem 91919; tel. 2-6587110; fax 2-6587140; e-mail mankalj@pmo.gov.il; internet www.gov.il/he/Departments/ministry_of_jerusalem_and_heritage/.

Ministry of Justice: POB 49029, 29 Salahadin St, Jerusalem 91490; tel. 2-6466666; fax 2-6285438; e-mail sar@justice.gov.il; internet www.justice.gov.il.

Ministry of National Missions: Jerusalem.

Ministry of National Security: Clermont-Ganneau St, Building C, Kiryat Hamemshala (East), Jerusalem 91181; tel. 2-5428502; fax 2-5428500; e-mail sar@mops.gov.il; internet www.gov.il/he/Departments/ministry_of_public_security.

Ministry of Public Diplomacy: Tel Aviv.

Ministry of Regional Co-operation: Jerusalem.

Ministry of Religious Services: POB 13059, 7 Kanfei Nesharim St, Jerusalem 95464; tel. 2-5311111; fax 2-5311308; e-mail contactus@dat.gov.il; internet www.gov.il/he/Departments/ministry_of_religious_services.

Ministry of Social Affairs and Social Services: POB 915, 2 Kaplan St, Kiryat Ben-Gurion, Jerusalem 91008; tel. 2-6752518; fax 2-5085590; e-mail pniot@molsa.gov.il; internet www.gov.il/en/departments/molsa.

Ministry of Social Equality and Pensioners: 3 Kaplan St, Kiryat Ben-Gurion, Jerusalem 91919; tel. 2-654702202; fax 2-6547034; e-mail pniot@mse.gov.il; internet www.gov.il/he/Departments/ministry_for_social_equality.

Ministry of Tourism: POB 1018, 5 Bank of Israel St, Jerusalem 91009; tel. 2-6664200; fax 2-6510358; e-mail webmaster@tourism.gov.il; internet www.gov.il/he/Departments/ministry_of_tourism.

Ministry of Transportation and Road Safety: POB 867, Government Complex A, 5 Bank of Israel St, Jerusalem 91008; tel. 2-6663004; fax 2-6663005; e-mail sar@mot.gov.il; internet www.gov.il/he/departments/ministry_of_transport_and_road_safety.

GOVERNMENT AGENCY

The Jewish Agency for Israel: POB 92, 48 King George St, Jerusalem 94262; tel. 2-6202222; fax 2-6202303; e-mail pniyottzibor@jafi.org; internet www.jewishagency.org; f. 1929; reconstituted in 1971 as a partnership between the World Zionist Org. and the fundraising bodies United Israel Appeal, Inc (USA) and Keren Hayesod; according to the Agreement of 1971, the Jewish Agency oversees the immigration and absorption of immigrants in Israel; Chair. of Executive DORON ALMOG (acting); Chair., Board of Governors MARK WILF; CEO and Dir-Gen. AMIRA AHARONOVICH.

Legislature

Knesset: Kiryat Ben-Gurion, Jerusalem 91950; tel. 2-6753333; fax 2-6753665; e-mail mshenkar@knesset.gov.il; internet www.knesset.gov.il.

Speaker: AMIR OHANA (Likud).

General Election, 1 November 2022

Party	Votes	%	Seats
Likud	1,115,336	23.41	32
Yesh Atid	847,435	17.79	24
Religious Zionist Party*	516,470	10.84	14
National Unity†	432,482	9.08	12
Shas	392,964	8.25	11
United Torah Judaism	280,194	5.88	7
Israel Beytenu	213,687	4.48	6
Ra'am (United Arab List)	194,047	4.07	5
Hadash-Ta'al	178,735	3.75	5
Israeli Labor Party	175,992	3.69	4
Total (incl. others)	4,764,742‡	100.00	120

Note: seats are allocated on a proportional basis to parties achieving more than 3.25% of the valid votes cast.

* Otzma Yehudit and Noam contested the election on the Religious Zionist Party's list, winning a respective six seats and one seat (of the total 14 secured by the list as a whole).

† An alliance comprising Kahol Lavan/Israeli Resilience Party and New Hope.

‡ Excluding 29,851 invalid votes.

Election Commission

Central Elections Committee: Knesset, Kiryat Ben-Gurion, Jerusalem 91950; tel. 2-6753407; fax 2-5669855; e-mail pniot.bechirot@knesset.gov.il; internet www.bechirot.gov.il; f. 1955; independent; Supreme Court elects a Justice as Chair; each parliamentary group nominates representatives to the Cttee in proportion to the group's level of representation in the Knesset; Chair. Justice NOAM SOHLBERG.

Political Organizations

Agudat Israel (Union of Israel): POB 513, Jerusalem; tel. 2-5385251; fax 2-5385145; f. 1912; mainly Ashkenazi ultra-Orthodox Jews; advocates the introduction of laws and institutions based on Jewish religious law (the Torah); forms part of the United Torah Judaism list (with Degel Hatorah); Leader YITZHAK GOLDKNOPF.

Arab Movement for Renewal (Tnua'a Aravit le'Hitkadshut—Ta'al): Jerusalem; tel. 2-6753333; fax 2-6753927; e-mail atibi@knesset.gov.il; f. 1996 following split from Balad; contested the Nov. 2022 elections in alliance with Hadash, as Hadash-Ta'al; Leader Dr AHMAD TIBI.

Balad (National Democratic Assembly): POB 2248, Nazareth Industrial Zone, Nazareth 16000; tel. 4-6455070; fax 4-6463457; f. 1995; united Arab party; Leader SAMI ABU SHEHADEH.

ISRAEL

Communist Party of Israel (Miflagah Kommonistit Yisraelit—Maki): POB 26205, 5 Hess St, Tel Aviv 61261; tel. 3-6293944; fax 3-6297263; e-mail info@maki.org.il; internet www.maki.org.il; f. 1948; Jewish-Arab party descended from the Socialist Workers' Party of Palestine (f. 1919); renamed Communist Party of Palestine 1921, Jewish and Arab sections split 1945, reunited as Communist Party of Israel (Maki) 1948; further split 1965: pro-Soviet predominantly Arab anti-Zionist group formed New Communist Party of Israel (Rakah) 1965, while predominantly Jewish bloc retained name Maki; Rakah joined with other leftist orgs as Hadash 1977; name changed to Maki 1989, as the dominant component of Hadash (q.v.); Gen. Sec. ADEL AMER.

Degel HaTorah (Flag of the Torah): 103 Rehov Beit Vegan, Jerusalem; tel. 2-6438106; fax 2-6418967; f. 1988 by Lithuanian Jews as breakaway faction from Agudat Israel; mainly Ashkenazi ultra-Orthodox (Haredi) Jews; forms part of the United Torah Judaism list (with Agudat Israel); Leader MOSHE GAFNI.

Derech Eretz: Tel Aviv; f. 2020; formed by fmr mems of Telem; Leaders YOAZ HENDEL, ZVI HAUSER.

Hadash (Hachazit Hademokratit Leshalom Uleshivyon—Democratic Front for Peace and Equality): POB 26205, Tel Aviv 38723; tel. 3-6292512; e-mail info@hadash.org.il; internet hadash.org.il; f. 1977 by merger of the New Communist Party of Israel (Rakah) with other leftist groups; party list, the principal component of which is the Communist Party of Israel (q.v.); Jewish-Arab membership; advocates a socialist system in Israel and a lasting peace between Israel, Arab countries and the Palestinian Arab people; favours full implementation of United Nations Security Council Resolutions 242 and 338, Israeli withdrawal from all Arab territories occupied since 1967, formation of a Palestinian Arab state in the West Bank and Gaza Strip (with East Jerusalem as its capital), recognition of national rights of State of Israel and Palestinian people, democratic rights and defence of working-class interests, and demands an end to discrimination against Arab minority in Israel and against oriental Jewish communities; formed part of the Joint List (with Balad, the Arab Movement for Renewal/Ta'al and the United Arab List/Ra'am), until the dissolution of the Joint List in September 2022; Leader AYMAN ODEH.

Israel Beytenu (Israel Is Our Home/Nash dom Izrail): 78 Yirmiyahu St, Jerusalem 91950; tel. 2280; internet www.beytenu.org.il; f. 1999; right-wing immigrant party; seeks resolution of the Israeli–Palestinian conflict through the exchange of territory and population with the Palestinians, incl. the transfer of Arab Israelis to territory under Palestinian control; membership largely drawn from fmr Union of Soviet Socialist Republics; Leader AVIGDOR LIEBERMAN.

Israeli Labor Party (Mifleget HaAvoda HaYisraelit): POB 62033, Tel Aviv 61620; tel. 3-7283609; fax 3-7946911; e-mail irgun@havoda.org.il; internet www.havoda.org.il; f. 1968 as a merger of the three Labor groups, Mapai, Rafi and Achdut HaAvoda; Am Ehad (One Nation) merged with Israeli Labor Party 2004; a Zionist democratic socialist party; Chair. MERAV MICHAELI.

Jewish Home (HaBayit HaYehudi): HaAvoda St, Rosh HaAyin; tel. 3-6093580; fax 3-6913640; e-mail ask.baityehudi@gmail.com; internet baityehudi.org.il; f. 2008 by merger of Nat. Religious Party (f. 1956), Moledet and Tkuma; however, Moledet and some Tkuma mems subsequently withdrew from new party; right-wing nationalist, Zionist; opposes further Israeli withdrawals from the West Bank and the creation of a Palestinian state; Chair. HAGIT MOSHE.

Kahol Lavan (Blue and White): internet kachollavan.org.il; f. 2019; formed before the 2019 elections as a political alliance between the Israeli Resilience Party (Chosen L'Yisrael), Yesh Atid and Telem; following March 2020 elections, Yesh Atid and Telem left the alliance after the Israeli Resilience Party's decision to form a government with Likud; Israeli Resilience Party retained the name Kahol Lavan; contested Nov. 2022 elections as member of National Unity alliance; Leader BENJAMIN (BENNY) GANTZ.

Likud (Consolidation): 38 Rehov King George, Tel Aviv 61561; tel. 3-6210666; internet www.likud.org.il; f. 1973; officially known as Likud-National Liberal Movement; fmrly a parliamentary bloc comprising Herut (f. 1948), the Liberal Party of Israel (f. 1961), Laam (For the Nation—f. 1976), Ahdut and Tami (f. 1981; joined Likud in 1987); Herut and the Liberal Party (together with the other, smaller members of the Likud bloc) officially merged in 1988 to form a single party; Israel B'Aliyah merged with Likud 2003; Chair. BENJAMIN NETANYAHU.

Meretz (Social Democratic Party of Israel): POB 20177, Yage'a Kapaim 1, Tel Aviv; tel. 3-6098998; fax 3-6961728; e-mail info@meretz.org.il; internet www.meretz.org.il; f. 1992 as a parliamentary bloc comprising Ratz, Shinui and the United Workers' Party; merged with Shahar (f. 2002; a breakaway faction of the Israeli Labour Party) in 2003 to form Yachad (Together—Social Democratic Israel); renamed Meretz-Yachad in 2005, and Meretz in 2006; Jewish-Arab social democratic party; advocates Palestinian self-determination and a return to the 1967 borders, with minor adjustments; a divided Jerusalem, but no right of return for Palestinian refugees to Israel; separation of religion from the state; Chair. ZEHAVA GAL-ON.

National Unity (State Camp): Tel Aviv; f. 2022 to contest the Nov. 2022 legislative elections; an alliance comprising Kahol Lavan/Chosen L'Yisrael and New Hope; Leader BENJAMIN (BENNY) GANTZ.

New Hope (Tikva Hadasha): Tel Aviv; e-mail info@newhope.org.il; internet www.newhope.org.il; f. 2020; advocates immigration to Israel, limiting tenure of Prime Minister to eight years and greater powers for local govt; contested Nov. 2022 elections as part of National Unity bloc; Leader GIDEON SA'AR.

New Right: Tel Aviv; e-mail join@newyamin.org; internet newyamin.org; f. 2018; a far-right, pro-settler party; leading mem. of Yemina alliance; Co-Chairs AYELET SHAKED, NAFTALI BENNETT.

Noam: internet noamparty.org.il; f. 2019; far-right Orthodox; contested Nov. 2022 elections on jt list with Religious Zionist Party and Otzma Yehudit; Spiritual Leader HANS (ZVI YISRAEL) THAU; Chair. AVI MAOZ.

Otzma Yehudit (Jewish Power): Jerusalem; tel. 3902323; e-mail oz.yehudit@gmail.com; internet 440.co.il; f. 2012; a far-right political party originally named Otzma LeYisrael; contested Nov. 2022 legislative elections on list of Religious Zionist Party; Leader ITAMAR BEN GVIR.

Religious Zionist Party (HaTzionut HaDatit): Beit HaShenhav Bldg, Jerusalem; e-mail office@zionutdatit.org.il; internet zionutdatit.org.il; f. 1998 as Tkuma, present name adopted 2021; far-right; Otzma Yehudit and Noam contested Nov. 2022 legislative elections on Religious Zionist Party's list; Leader BEZALEL SMOTRICH.

Ra'am (Reshima Aravit Me'uchedet) (United Arab List): Jerusalem; tel. 9-7997088; fax 9-7996295; e-mail amc@amc-a.com; internet www.a-m-c.org; f. 1996 by merger of the Arab Democratic Party and individuals from the Islamic Movement and Nat. Unity Front (left-wing Arab parties); supports establishment of a Palestinian state, with East Jerusalem as its capital, and equality for all Israeli citizens; Chair. MANSOUR ABBAS.

Shas (Hit'ahdut HaSefaradimShomrei HaTorah) (Sephardic Torah Guardians): POB 34263, Jerusalem 91341; tel. 2-5008888; fax 2-5380226; e-mail p@shas.org.il; internet shas.org.il; f. 1984 by splinter groups from Agudat Israel; ultra-Orthodox Sephardic party; Chair. ARYEH DER'I.

Telem: 1 Rotem St, Tel Aviv; tel. 3-6866800; e-mail office@telem-il.org; internet www.telem-il.org; f. 2019; contested 2019 and 2020 legislative elections as part of Kahol Lavan (with Chosen L'Yisrael and Yesh Atid); following March 2020 elections, Telem and Yesh Atid left the Kahol Lavan alliance after Chosen L'Yisrael's decision to form a government with Likud; Leader MOSHE YA'ALON.

United Torah Judaism (Yahadut HaTorah): f. prior to 1992 elections; electoral list of four minor ultra-Orthodox parties (Moria, Degel HaTorah, Poale Agudat Israel and Agudat Israel) established to overcome the increase in the election threshold from 1% to 1.5% and to seek to counter the rising influence of the secular Russian vote; contested 2003 elections as list composed of Degel HaTorah and Agudat Israel, into which constituent parties it split in early 2005; the two parties reunited in 2005 and contested March 2006 and Feb. 2009 legislative elections together; represents Ashkenazi ultra-Orthodox Jews and advocates the application of religious precepts in all areas of life and government; Chair. YITZHAK GOLDKNOPF.

Yemina: f. 2018; an religious, ultra right-wing alliance led by the New Right; formed to contest the Sept. 2019 legislative elections; Jewish Home left the alliance in July 2020 and the Religious Zionist Party left in Jan. 2021; Leader NAFTALI BENNETT.

Yesh Atid (There's a Future): Yigal Alon 157 Bet, Tel Aviv 67443; tel. 3-7715054; fax 3-7715041; e-mail contact@yeshatid.org.il; internet www.yeshatid.org.il; f. 2012; contested 2019 and 2020 legislative elections as part of Kahol Lavan (with Chosen L'Yisrael and Telem); following March 2020 elections, Yesh Atid and Telem left the Kahol Lavan alliance after Chosen L'Yisrael's decision to form a government with Likud; Founder and Leader YAIR LAPID.

Diplomatic Representation

EMBASSIES IN ISRAEL

Albania: Laz-Rom Bldg, 11 Tuval St, Ramat Gan 5252226; tel. 3-5465866; fax 3-6883314; e-mail embassy.telaviv@mfa.gov.al; internet www.ambasadat.gov.al/israel; Ambassador Dr BARDHYL CANAJ.

Angola: 14 Simtat Beit Hashoeva St, Tel Aviv 65814; tel. 3-6912093; fax 3-6912094; e-mail secretary@angolaembassy.org.il; internet www.angolaembassy.org.il/home; Ambassador OSVALDO DOS SANTOS VARELA.

ISRAEL

Argentina: 85 Medinat Hayehudim St, 2nd Floor, Herzliya Pituach, Tel Aviv 4676670; tel. 3-2520800; fax 9-9702748; e-mail eisra@mrecic.gov.ar; internet eisra.cancilleria.gov.ar; Chargé d'affaires a.i. FRANCISCO FABIAN TROPEPI.

Armenia: 29 HaMered St, Tel Aviv; tel. 3-5322124; fax 3-7191757; e-mail armisraelembassy@mfa.am; internet israel.mfa.am; Ambassador ARMAN AKOPIAN.

Australia: POB 29108, Bank Discount Tower, 28th Floor, 23 Yehuda Halevi St, Tel Aviv 6513601; tel. 3-6935000; e-mail telaviv.embassy@dfat.org.au; internet israel.embassy.gov.au; Ambassador Dr RALPH PETER KING.

Austria: Sason Hogi Tower, 12 Abba Hillel Silver St, 4th Floor, Ramat Gan 5250606; tel. 3-6120924; fax 3-7510716; e-mail tel-aviv-ob@bmeia.gv.at; internet www.bmeia.gv.at/en/austrian-embassy-tel-aviv; Ambassador NIKOLAUS LUTTEROTTI.

Azerbaijan: Tel Aviv; Ambassador MUKHTAR MAMMADOV.

Bahrain: Tel Aviv; Ambassador KHALID YUSUF AL-JALAHMA.

Belarus: POB 11129, 3 Reines St, Tel Aviv 64381; tel. 3-5231259; fax 3-5231273; e-mail israel@mfa.gov.by; internet israel.mfa.gov.by; Ambassador EVGENY SEMYONOVICH VOROBYEV.

Belgium: 12 Abba Hillel Silver St, 15th Floor, Ramat Gan 5250606; tel. 3-6138130; fax 3-6138160; e-mail telaviv@diplobel.fed.be; internet israel.diplomatie.belgium.be; Ambassador JEAN-LUC BODSON.

Bosnia and Herzegovina: Yachin Bldg, 10th Floor, 2 Kaplan St, Tel Aviv; tel. 3-6124499; fax 3-6124488; e-mail embtelaviv@bezeqint.net; Ambassador DUSKO KOVACEVIĆ.

Brazil: 23 Yehuda Halevi St, 30th Floor, Tel Aviv 6513601; tel. 3-7971500; fax 3-6916060; e-mail consular.telaviv@itamaraty.gov.br; internet telaviv.itamaraty.gov.br; Chargé d'affaires a.i. LINCOLN BERNARDES, Jr.

Bulgaria: Sderot Sha'ul HaMelech, Tel Aviv 64733; tel. 3-6961372; e-mail embassy.telaviv@mfa.bg; internet www.mfa.bg/embassies/israel; Ambassador RUMYANA BACHVAROVA.

Cameroon: 28 Moshe Sharet St, Ramat Gan 52425; tel. 3-5298401; fax 3-5270352; e-mail activ50@yahoo.fr; Ambassador JEAN-PIERRE BIYITI EL-ESSAM.

Canada: POB 9442, 3/5 Nirim St, Tel Aviv 6706038; tel. 3-6363300; fax 3-6363380; e-mail taviv@international.gc.ca; internet www.canadainternational.gc.ca/israel; Ambassador LISA ANNE STADELBAUER.

Chile: 32 Habarzel St, Entrance A, 5th Floor, Ramat Hahayal, Tel Aviv 6971047; tel. 3-5102751; fax 3-5100102; e-mail chile@chile-emb.co.il; internet chile.gob.cl/israel; Ambassador JORGE CARVAJAL.

China, People's Republic: POB 6067, 222 Ben Yehuda St, Tel Aviv 61060; tel. 3-5467312; fax 3-5467251; internet il.china-embassy.org; Ambassador CAI RUN.

Colombia: Sason Hogi Tower, 12 Abba Hillel Silver St, 8th Floor, Ramat Gan 52506; tel. 3-7163482; fax 3-6957847; e-mail eisrael@cancilleria.gov.co; internet israel.embajada.gov.co; Ambassador MARGARITA ELIANA MANJARREZ HERRERA.

Congo, Democratic Republic: 1 Rachel St, 2nd Floor, Tel Aviv 64584; tel. 3-5239860; fax 3-5295483; e-mail ambardc_il@yahoo.fr; Chargé d'affaires a.i. JEAN-MARIE NGAKALA.

Congo, Republic: POB 12504, 6 Galgalei HaPlada, Herzliya Pituach 46120; tel. 9-9577130; fax 9-9577216; e-mail ambacotlv@yahoo.fr; Chargé d'affaires a.i. EMMANUEL IKOGNE.

Costa Rica: Paz Tower, 5–7 Shoham St, 6th Floor, Ramat Gan 52521; tel. 3-6135061; fax 3-6134779; e-mail embcr-il@rree.go.cr; Chargé d'affaires ALFREDO JOSE PIZARRO CAMPOS.

Côte d'Ivoire: Atrium Bldg, 2nd Floor, 2 Jabotinsky St, Ramat Gan 52521; tel. 3-6126677; fax 3-6126688; internet israel.diplomatie.gouv.ci; Ambassador FENI KOUAKOU.

Croatia: 2 Weizman St, Migdal Amot, Tel Aviv 64239; tel. 3-6403000; fax 3-6438503; e-mail croemb.israel@mvep.hr; internet il.mvep.hr; Ambassador VESELA MRĐEN KORAĆ.

Cyprus: Top Tower, 14th Floor, Dizengoff Centre, 61 Dizengoff St, Tel Aviv 6433233; tel. 3-9273000; fax 3-6290535; e-mail ambassador@cyprusembassytelaviv.com; internet www.mfa.gov.cy/embassytelaviv; Ambassador THEODORA CONSTANTINIDOU.

Czech Republic: POB 16361, 23 Zeitlin St, Tel Aviv 6404629; tel. 3-6918282; fax 3-6918286; e-mail telaviv@embassy.mzv.cz; internet www.mzv.cz/telaviv; Ambassador VERONIKA K. SMIGOLOVA (designate).

Denmark: POB 21080, Museum Tower, 11th Floor, 4 Berkowitz St, Tel Aviv 64238; tel. 3-6085850; fax 3-6085851; e-mail tlvamb@um.dk; internet israel.um.dk; Chargé d'affaires a.i. RASMUS BØGH JOHANSEN.

Dominican Republic: 84 Ha'Hashmonaim St, Tel Aviv 6713203; tel. 3-6055592; fax 3-6055594; e-mail israel@embajadadominicana.net; Ambassador MICHEL COHEN (designate).

Ecuador: POB 34002, Asia House, 5th Floor, 4 Weizman St, Tel Aviv 64239; tel. 3-6958764; e-mail eecuisrael@mmrree.gob.ec; internet fb.com/embajadadeecuadorenisrael; Ambassador MARIA C. BARAHONA.

Egypt: 54 Basel St, Tel Aviv 62744; tel. 3-5464151; fax 3-5441615; e-mail egyptelaviv@hotmail.com; Ambassador KHALED MAHMOUD ABDUL MONIEM AZMI.

El Salvador: 6 Hamada St, Naor Bldg, 4th Floor, Herzliya Pituach 46733; tel. 9-9556542; fax 9-9556543; e-mail embajadaisrael@rree.gob.sv; internet www.fb.com/embajadaisraelsv; Ambassador MILTON EDUARDO UMAÑA.

Equatorial Guinea: Galgali Haplada 11, Herzliya, Tel Aviv; tel. 799121865; e-mail egembassy@eg-il-embassy.com; Ambassador EUSTAQUIO NSENG ESONO.

Eritrea: 3 Nirim St, 2nd Floor, Tel Aviv; tel. 3-6120039; fax 3-5750133; e-mail eritrea@bezeqint.net; Chargé d'affaires SOLOMON KINFE.

Estonia: POB 52057, 24th Floor, Menachem Begin Rd 125, 44 Kaplan St, HaYovel Tower, Tel Aviv 61071; tel. 3-7103910; fax 3-7103919; e-mail embassy.telaviv@mfa.ee; internet telaviv.mfa.ee; Ambassador VEIKKO KALA.

Ethiopia: 48 Petach Tikva Rd, Tel Aviv 66184; tel. 3-6397831; fax 3-6397837; internet www.ethioemb.org.il; Ambassador TESFAYE YETAYEH ANTENEH.

Finland: POB 9101, Adgar 360, 31st Floor, 2 Hashlosha St, Tel Aviv 6706054; tel. 3-7456600; fax 3-7440314; e-mail sanomat.tel@formin.fi; internet www.finland.org.il; Ambassador KIRSIKKA LEHTO-ASIKAINEN.

France: 112 Tayelet Herbert Samuel, Tel Aviv 63572; tel. 3-5208300; fax 3-5208340; e-mail diplomatie@ambafrance-il.org; internet il.ambafrance.org; Ambassador FRÉDÉRIC JOURNÈS.

Georgia: 3 Daniel Frisch St, Tel Aviv 64731; tel. 3-6093206; fax 3-6093205; e-mail israel.emb@mfa.gov.ge; internet israel.mfa.gov.ge; Ambassador LASHA ZHVANIA.

Germany: POB 16038, 2 HaShlosha St, Tel Aviv 6706054; tel. 3-6931313; fax 3-6969217; e-mail info@tel-aviv.diplo.de; internet www.tel-aviv.diplo.de; Ambassador STEFFEN SEIBERT.

Ghana: 15 Keren HaYesod St, Herzliya, Tel Aviv; tel. 3-5766000; fax 3-7520827; e-mail ghanaemb.il@gmail.com; internet telaviv.mfa.gov.gh; Ambassador LYDIA OFOSUA AMARTEY.

Greece: 3 Daniel Frisch St, Tel Aviv 64731; tel. 3-6953060; e-mail gremb.tlv@mfa.gr; internet www.mfa.gr/telaviv; Ambassador KYRIAKOS LOUKAKIS.

Guatemala: Derech Agudat Sport Hapoel 2, Tower Bldg, 11th Floor, Technology Park, Malha, Jerusalem 9695102; tel. 9-26307625; fax 9-26745945; e-mail embisrael@minex.gob.gt; internet israel.minex.gob.gt; Ambassador AVA ATZUM ARÉVALO TRIBOUILLIER DE MOSCOSO AGUILAR.

Holy See: POB 84151 Netiv Hamazalot, Old Jaffa 68037; tel. 2-6835658; fax 2-6835659; Apostolic Nuncio Most Rev. ADOLFO TITO CAMACHO YLLANA (Titular Archbishop of Montecorvino—also Apostolic Delegate to Jerusalem and Palestine).

Honduras: Technological Park Ltd, Derech Agudat, 4th Floor, Jerusalem 9695102; tel. 3-9660180; fax 9-9662555; e-mail honduras@netvision.net.il; Chargé d'affaires a.i. SERGIO ACOSTA.

Hungary: POB 21203, 18 Pinkas St, Tel Aviv 62661; tel. 3-5456666; fax 3-5467018; e-mail mission.tlv@mfa.gov.hu; internet telaviv.mfa.gov.hu; Ambassador LEVENTE BENKŐ.

India: POB 3368, 140 Hayarkon St, Tel Aviv 61033; tel. 3-7620700; fax 3-5291953; e-mail amb.telaviv@mea.gov.in; internet www.indembassyisrael.gov.in; Ambassador SANJEEV KUMAR SINGLA.

Ireland: Amot Atrium Tower, 2 Ze'ev Jabotinsky St, Ramat Gan 525051; tel. 3-6964166; fax 3-6964160; e-mail telavivembassy@dfa.ie; internet www.dfa.ie/irish-embassy/israel; Ambassador SONYA McGUINNESS (designate).

Italy: Trade Tower, 25 Hamered St, Tel Aviv 6812508; tel. 3-5104004; fax 3-5100235; e-mail amb.telaviv@cert.esteri.it; internet www.ambtelaviv.esteri.it; Ambassador SERGIO BARBANTI.

Japan: Museum Tower, 19th and 20th Floors, 4 Berkowitz St, Tel Aviv 6423806; tel. 3-6957292; fax 3-6910516; e-mail info@tl.mofa.go.jp; internet www.israel.emb-japan.go.jp; Ambassador MIZUSHIMA KOICHI.

Jordan: 10 HaSadot St, Herzlyia; tel. 3-7517722; fax 3-7517712; e-mail tel-aviv@fm.gov.jo; Ambassador GHASSAN MAJALI.

Kazakhstan: 52A Hayarkon St, Tel Aviv 63432; tel. 3-7417805; fax 3-5163437; e-mail tel-aviv@mfa.kz; internet www.gov.kz/memleket/entities/mfa-tel-aviv; Ambassador SATYBALDY BURSHAKOV.

Kenya: POB 3621, 15 Abba Hillel Silver St, Ramat Gan 52136; tel. 3-5754633; fax 3-5754788; e-mail telaviv@mfa.go.ke; internet kenyaembassyisrael.com; Ambassador Lt-Gen. (retd) SAMUEL N. THUITA.

ISRAEL

Korea, Republic: 6 Hasadna'ot St, Herzliya Pituach 46278; tel. 9-9596800; fax 9-9569853; e-mail israel@mofa.go.kr; internet overseas.mofa.go.kr/il-en/index.do; Ambassador KIM JIN-HAN.

Latvia: Amot Investments Tower, 15th Floor, 2 Weizman St, Tel Aviv 6423902; tel. 3-7775800; fax 3-6953101; e-mail embassy.israel@mfa.gov.lv; internet www.mfa.gov.lv/en/israel; Ambassador AIVARS GROZA.

Lithuania: Sason Hogi Tower, 12 Abba Hillel Silver St, Ramat Gan, Tel Aviv; tel. 3-6958685; fax 3-6958691; e-mail amb.il@urm.lt; internet il.mfa.lt; Ambassador AUDRIUS BRŪZGA (designate).

Malta: 28 S Tower, HaArbaa St, Tel Aviv; tel. 3-6295916; fax 3-6295917; e-mail maltaembassy.telaviv@gov.mt; internet foreignandeu.gov.mt/en/embassies/me_telaviv; Ambassador CECILIA ATTARD PIROTTA.

Mexico: Trade Tower, 5th Floor, 25 Hamered St, Tel Aviv 68125; tel. 3-5163938; fax 3-5163711; e-mail communication1@embamex.org.il; internet embamex.sre.gob.mx/israel; Ambassador MAURICIO ESCANERO FIGUEROA.

Moldova: 38 Rembrandt St, Tel Aviv 64045; tel. 3-5231000; fax 3-5233000; e-mail cons.tel-aviv@mfa.md; internet www.israel.mfa.md; Ambassador ALEXANDR ROITMAN.

Myanmar: Textile Centre, 12th Floor, 2 Kaufman St, Tel Aviv 68012; tel. 3-5170760; fax 3-5163512; e-mail myanmar@zahav.net.il; internet www.metelaviv.org; Ambassador MAUNG MAUNG LYNN.

Nepal: Textile Centre, 14th Floor, 2 Kaufman St, Tel Aviv 68012; tel. 3-5100111; fax 3-5167965; e-mail nepal.embassy@012.net.il; internet il.nepalembassy.gov.np; Ambassador KANTA RIJAL.

Netherlands: Beit Oz, 13th Floor, 14 Abba Hillel Silver St, Ramat Gan 52506; tel. 3-7540777; fax 3-7540751; e-mail tel@minbuza.nl; internet www.netherlandsworldwide.nl/countries/israel/about-us/embassy-in-tel-aviv; Ambassador HANS DOCTER.

Nigeria: POB 3339, 34 Gordon St, Tel Aviv 61030; tel. 3-5222144; fax 3-5248991; e-mail nigemb@zahav.net.il; internet www.nigerianembassy.co.il; Ambassador NART AUGUSTINE KOLO.

North Macedonia: Paz Tower, 9th Floor, 5 Shoham St, Ramat Gan 52136; tel. 3-7154900; e-mail telaviv@mfa.gov.mk; internet telaviv.mfa.gov.mk/mk; Chargé d'affaires MACIEJ KACZOROWSKI.

Norway: POB 17575, Canion Ramat Aviv, 13th Floor, 40 Einstein St, Tel Aviv 6910203; tel. 3-7401900; fax 3-7441498; e-mail emb.telaviv@mfa.no; internet www.norway.no/israel; Chargé d'affaires a.i. BJØRN KLOUMAN BEKKEN.

Panama: 31 Karlibach, Beit Lishkar Bldg, 5th Floor, Tel Aviv 6713225; tel. 7-4398589; e-mail embpanamaisrael@mire.gob.pa; internet www.mire.gob.pa/index.php/es/embajada-de-israel; Ambassador ADIS URRIETA.

Paraguay: 3rd Floor, 4 Shenkar St, Industrial Zone, Herzliya Pituach 46725; tel. 9-7732555; fax 9-7735999; e-mail embaparisrael@mre.gov.py; Chargé d'affaires a.i. LUCAS HERNAN FRANCO GODOY.

Peru: 89 Medinat Hayehudim St, 12th Floor, Herzliya Pituach, Tel Aviv 46766; tel. 9-9578835; fax 9-9568495; e-mail consulperu-telaviv@rree.gob.pe; Ambassador MANUEL JOSE ANTONIO CACHO SOUSA VELAZQUEZ.

Philippines: 18 Bnei Dan St, Tel Aviv 62260; tel. 3-6010500; fax 3-6041038; e-mail filembis@netvision.net.il; internet tel-avivpe.dfa.gov.ph; Ambassador PEDRO LAYLO.

Poland: 16 Soutine St, Tel Aviv 6468408; tel. 3-7253101; fax 3-5237806; e-mail telaviv.amb.sekretariat@msz.gov.pl; internet www.gov.pl/web/israel; Chargé d'affaires a.i. AGATA CZAPLIŃSKA.

Portugal: 32 HaArba St, S Tower, 26th Floor, Tel Aviv 6473925; tel. 3-6956373; e-mail telavive@mne.pt; internet www.telavive.embaixadaportugal.mne.gov.pt; Ambassador RUBEIRO DA SILVA BARROS.

Romania: 9 Israelis St, Tel Aviv 6438209; tel. 3-5229472; fax 3-5247379; e-mail telaviv@mae.ro; internet telaviv.mae.ro; Ambassador RADU IOANID.

Russian Federation: 120 Hayarkon St, Tel Aviv 6357308; tel. 3-5226736; e-mail embassy.israel@mid.ru; internet israel.mid.ru; Ambassador ANATOLII D. VIKTOROV.

Rwanda: 8 Maskit St, Herzliya, Tel Aviv; tel. 9-7997177; e-mail ambatelaviv@minaffet.gov.rw; internet www.rwandainisrael.gov.rw; Ambassador JAMES GATERA.

Serbia: 10 Bodenheimer St, Tel Aviv 62008; tel. 3-6045535; fax 3-6049456; e-mail srb.emb.israel@mfa.rs; internet www.telaviv.mfa.gov.rs; Chargé d'affaires a.i. MIHAJLO TRIPIĆ.

Slovakia: POB 16432, 37 Jabotinsky St, Tel Aviv 6116301; tel. 4-7585031; fax 4-7585042; e-mail emb.telaviv@mzv.sk; internet www.mzv.sk/web/telaviv; Ambassador IGOR MAUKŠ.

Slovenia: POB 23245, Top Tower, 19th Floor, 50 Dizengoff St, Tel Aviv 6433222; tel. 3-6293572; e-mail sloembassy.telaviv@gov.si; internet www.telaviv.embassy.si; Ambassador ANDREJA PURKRAT MARTINEZ.

South Africa: POB 7138, Sason Hogi Tower, 17th Floor, 12 Abba Hillel Silver St, Ramat Gan 52506; tel. 3-5252566; fax 3-5253230; internet www.safis.co.il; Chargé d'affaires T. B. CEKE.

South Sudan: 75 Ramat Yam St, Herzliya Pituah, Tel Aviv; tel. 9-9660691; fax 9-9660686; e-mail embassyrss.israel91@outlook.com; Ambassador WOL MAYAR ARIEC.

Spain: Dubnov Tower, 18th Floor, 3 Daniel Frisch St, Tel Aviv 64731; tel. 3-7697900; fax 3-6965217; e-mail emb.telaviv@maec.es; internet www.exteriores.gob.es/embajadas/telaviv; Ambassador ANA MARÍA SÁLOMON PÉREZ.

Sri Lanka: 4 Jean Jaurès St, Tel Aviv 63412; tel. 3-5277635; fax 3-5277634; e-mail slemb.telaviv@mfa.gov.lk; internet www.srilankaembassyil.com; Ambassador NIMAL BANDARA.

Sweden: Adgar 360 Bldg, 24th Floor, 2 HaShlosha St, Tel Aviv 6706054; tel. 3-7180000; fax 3-7180005; e-mail ambassaden.tel-aviv@gov.se; internet www.swedenabroad.se/sv/utlandsmyndigheter/israel-tel-aviv; Ambassador ERIK ULLENHAG.

Switzerland: 228 Hayarkon St, Tel Aviv 6340524; tel. 3-5464455; fax 3-5464408; e-mail telaviv@eda.admin.ch; internet www.eda.admin.ch/telaviv; Ambassador URS BUCHER.

Tanzania: 12 Abba Hillel Silver St, Sason Hogi Tower, 12th Floor, Ramat Gan 5250606; tel. 3-7761100; fax 3-7761101; e-mail telaviv@nje.go.tz; internet il.tzembassy.go.tz; Ambassador ALEX GABRIEL KALUA.

Thailand: POB 2125, 3 Maskit St, Herzliya Pituach 4673303; tel. 9-9548412; fax 9-9548417; e-mail consular.tav@mfa.go.th; internet www.thaiembassy.org/telaviv; Ambassador PANNABHA CHANDRARAMYA.

Türkiye (Turkey): 202 Hayarkon St, Tel Aviv 63405; tel. 3-7416900; fax 3-5241390; e-mail embassy.telaviv@mfa.gov.tr; internet telaviv.be.mfa.gov.tr; Ambassador ŞAKIR ÖZKAN TORUNLAR.

Ukraine: 50 Yirmiyahu St, Tel Aviv 62594; tel. 3-6273300; e-mail emb_il@mfa.gov.ua; internet israel.mfa.gov.ua; Ambassador YEVGEN KORNIYCHUK.

United Arab Emirates: Tel Aviv; e-mail telavivemb@mofaic.gov.ae; internet www.mofaic.gov.ae/en/missions/tel-aviv; Ambassador MOHAMMED MAHMOUD AL-KHAJA.

United Kingdom: 192 Hayarkon St, Tel Aviv 63405; tel. 3-7251222; fax 3-5249176; e-mail webmaster.telaviv@fco.gov.uk; internet ukinisrael.fco.gov.uk; Ambassador SIMON WALTERS.

USA: 14 David Flusser St, Jerusalem 9378322; tel. 2-6304000; e-mail nivtelaviv@state.gov; internet il.usembassy.gov; Ambassador THOMAS R. NIDES.

Uruguay: G.R.A.P. Bldg, 1st Floor, 4 Shenkar St, Industrial Zone, Herzliya Pituach 46725; tel. 9-9569611; fax 9-9515881; e-mail secretaria@emburuguay.co.il; Ambassador MANUEL ETCHEVARREN AGUERRE.

Uzbekistan: 31 Moshe Sharet St, Ramat Gan 52413; tel. 3-6722371; fax 3-6722621; e-mail il.uzembassy@mfa.uz; internet www.uzbembassy.org.il; Ambassador FERUZA MAKMUDOVA.

Viet Nam: Asia Bldg, 4th Floor, 4 Weizman St, Tel Aviv; tel. 3-6966304; fax 3-6966243; e-mail vnembassy.il@mofa.gov.vn; internet www.vietnamembassy-israel.org; Ambassador LY DUC TRUNG.

Zambia: Nirim St 3, 3rd Floor, Canada House, Tel Aviv; tel. 3-5174886; e-mail zamtel2015@gmail.com; Ambassador MARTIN C. MWANAMBALE.

Judicial System

The law of Israel is composed of the enactments of the Knesset and, to a lesser extent, of the acts, orders-in-council and ordinances that remain from the period of the British Mandate in Palestine (1922–48). The pre-1948 law has largely been replaced, amended or reorganized, in the interests of codification, by Israeli legislation. This legislation generally follows a very similar pattern to that operating in England and the USA. However, there is no jury system.

The Supreme Court: Sha'arei Mishpat St, Kiryat David Ben-Gurion, Jerusalem 91950; tel. 2-2703333; fax 2-6759648; e-mail pniyot@court.gov.il; internet supreme.court.gov.il; this is the highest judicial authority in the state. It has jurisdiction as an Appellate Court over appeals from the District Courts in all matters, both civil and criminal (sitting as a Court of Civil Appeal or as a Court of Criminal Appeal). In addition, it is a Court of First Instance (sitting as the High Court of Justice) in actions against governmental authorities, and in matters in which it considers it necessary to grant relief in the interests of justice and which are not within the jurisdiction of any other court or tribunal. The High Court's exclusive power to issue orders in the nature of *habeas corpus, mandamus*, prohibition and *certiorari* enables the court to review the legality of, and redress grievances against, acts of administrative authorities of all kinds; Pres. ESTHER HAYUT.

District Courts: There are five District Courts (Jerusalem, Tel Aviv, Haifa, Beersheba, Nazareth). They have residual jurisdiction as Courts of First Instance over all civil and criminal matters not within the jurisdiction of a Magistrates' Court (e.g. civil claims exceeding NIS 1m.), all matters not within the exclusive jurisdiction of any other tribunal, and matters within the concurrent jurisdiction of any other tribunal so long as such tribunal does not deal with them. In addition, the District Courts have appellate jurisdiction over appeals from judgments and decisions of Magistrates' Courts and judgments of Municipal Courts and various administrative tribunals.

Magistrates' Courts: There are 29 Magistrates' Courts, having criminal jurisdiction to try contraventions, misdemeanours and certain felonies, and civil jurisdiction to try actions concerning possession or use of immovable property, or the partition thereof, whatever may be the value of the subject matter of the action, and other civil claims not exceeding NIS 1m.

Labour Courts: Established in 1969. Regional Labour Courts in Jerusalem, Tel Aviv, Haifa, Beersheba and Nazareth, composed of judges and representatives of the public; a National Labour Court in Jerusalem; the Courts have jurisdiction over all matters arising out of the relationship between employer and employee or parties to a collective labour agreement, and matters concerning the National Insurance Law and the Labour Law and Rules.

Religious Courts: The Religious Courts are the courts of the recognized religious communities. They have jurisdiction over certain defined matters of personal status concerning members of their respective communities. Where any action of personal status involves persons of different religious communities, the President of the Supreme Court decides which Court will decide the matter. Whenever a question arises as to whether or not a case is one of personal status within the exclusive jurisdiction of a Religious Court, the matter must be referred to a Special Tribunal composed of two Justices of the Supreme Court and the President of the highest court of the religious community concerned in Israel. The judgments of the Religious Courts are executed by the process and offices of the Civil Courts. Neither these Courts nor the Civil Courts have jurisdiction to dissolve the marriage of a foreign subject; Jewish Rabbinical Courts have exclusive jurisdiction over matters of marriage and divorce of Jews in Israel who are Israeli citizens or residents. In all other matters of personal status they have concurrent jurisdiction with the District Courts; Muslim Religious Courts have exclusive jurisdiction over matters of marriage and divorce of Muslims who are not foreigners, or who are foreigners subject by their national law to the jurisdiction of Muslim Religious Courts in such matters. In all other matters of personal status they have concurrent jurisdiction with the District Courts; Christian Religious Courts have exclusive jurisdiction over matters of marriage and divorce of members of their communities who are not foreigners. In all other matters of personal status they have concurrent jurisdiction with the District Courts; Druze Courts, established in 1963, have exclusive jurisdiction over matters of marriage and divorce of Druze in Israel, who are Israeli citizens or residents, and concurrent jurisdiction with the District Courts over all other matters of personal status of Druze.

Attorney-General: GALI BAHARAV-MIARA.

Religion

JUDAISM

Judaism, the religion of the Jews, is the faith of the majority of Israel's inhabitants. In December 2021 Judaism's adherents totalled 6,928,200, equivalent to 73.9% of the country's population.

There are two main Jewish communities: the Ashkenazim and the Sephardim. The former are the Jews from Eastern, Central or Northern Europe, while the latter originate from the Balkan countries, North Africa and the Middle East.

There is also a community of Ethiopian Jews, the majority of whom have been airlifted to Israel from Ethiopia at various times since the fall of Emperor Haile Selassie in 1974.

The supreme religious authority is vested in the Chief Rabbinate, which consists of the Ashkenazi and Sephardi Chief Rabbis and the Supreme Rabbinical Council. It makes decisions on interpretation of the Jewish law, and supervises the Rabbinical Courts. There are eight regional Rabbinical Courts, and a Rabbinical Court of Appeal presided over by the two Chief Rabbis.

According to the Rabbinical Courts Jurisdiction Law of 1953, marriage and divorce among Jews in Israel are exclusively within the jurisdiction of the Rabbinical Courts. Provided that all the parties concerned agree, other matters of personal status can also be decided by the Rabbinical Courts.

There are over 170 Religious Councils, which maintain religious services and supply religious needs, and about 400 religious committees with similar functions in smaller settlements. The Religious Councils are under the administrative control of the Ministry of Religious Services. In all matters of religion, the Religious Councils are subject to the authority of the Chief Rabbinate. There are 365 officially appointed rabbis. The total number of synagogues is about 7,000, most of which are organized within the framework of the Union of Synagogues in Israel.

Head of the Ashkenazi Community: The Chief Rabbi DAVID LAU.

Head of the Sephardic Community: The Chief Rabbi YITZHAK YOSEF, Jerusalem; tel. 2-5313131.

Two Jewish sects still loyal to their distinctive customs are:

The Karaites: a sect which recognizes only the Jewish written law and not the oral law of the Mishna and Talmud. The community of about 12,000, many of whom live in or near Ramla, has been augmented by immigration from Egypt.

The Samaritans: an ancient sect mentioned in 2 Kings xvii, 24. They recognize only the Torah. The community in Israel numbers about 600; about one-half of this number live in Holon, where a Samaritan synagogue has been built, and the remainder, including the High Priest, live in Nablus, near Mt Gerazim, which is sacred to the Samaritans.

ISLAM

Muslims in Israel belong principally to the Sunni sect of Islam, and are divided among the four rites: the Shafe'i, the Hanbali, the Hanafi and the Maliki. Before June 1967 they numbered approximately 175,000; in 1971 some 343,900. At 31 December 2021 the total Muslim population of Israel was 1,690,100, equivalent to 18.0% of the country's population.

Mufti of Jerusalem: POB 17412, Jerusalem; tel. 2-283528; Sheikh MUHAMMAD AHMAD HUSSEIN (also Chair. Supreme Muslim Council for Jerusalem); appointed by the Palestinian (National) Authority (PA).

There was also a total of 147,700 Druzes in Israel at 31 December 2021. The official spiritual leader of the Druze community in Israel is Sheikh MUWAFAK TARIF.

CHRISTIANITY

The total Christian population of Israel (including East Jerusalem) at 31 December 2021 was 181,400.

Evangelical Alliance Israel (EAI): internet ea-israel.org; f. 1956 as United Christian Council in Israel; present name adopted 2009; member of World Evangelical Alliance; over 30 mems (evangelical churches and social and educational insts); Chair. Rev. CHARLES KOPP.

The Roman Catholic Church

Armenian Rite

The Armenian Catholic Patriarch of Cilicia is resident in Beirut, Lebanon.

Patriarchal Exarchate of Jerusalem and Amman: POB 19546, 36 Via Dolorosa, Jerusalem 91190; tel. 2-6284262; fax 2-6272123; e-mail acpejerusalem@yahoo.com; f. 1885; Exarch Patriarchal NAREG NAAMOYAN.

Chaldean Rite

The Chaldean Patriarch of Babylon is resident in Baghdad, Iraq.

Patriarchal Exarchate of Jerusalem: Chaldean Patriarchal Vicariate, POB 20108, 7 Chaldean St, Saad and Said Quarter, Jerusalem 91200; tel. 2-6844519; fax 2-6274614; e-mail kolin-p@zahav.net.il; Exarch Patriarchal (vacant).

Latin Rite

The Patriarchate of Jerusalem covers Palestine, Jordan and Cyprus.

Bishops' Conference: Conférence des Evêques Latins dans les Régions Arabes, Notre Dame of Jerusalem Center, POB 20531, Jerusalem 9120402; tel. 2-6288554; fax 2-6288555; e-mail bethbeth@faris.ps; f. 1962; Pres. His Beatitude PIERBATTISTA PIZZABALLA (Latin Patriarch of Jerusalem).

Patriarchate of Jerusalem: Latin Patriarchate of Jerusalem, POB 14152, Jerusalem 91141; tel. 2-6282323; fax 2-6271652; e-mail mediapj@lpj.org; internet www.lpj.org; Patriarch PIERBATTISTA PIZZABALLA; Auxiliary Bishops of Jerusalem WILLIAM SHOMALI (Patriarchal Vicar for Jerusalem and Palestine), RAFIC NAHRA (Patriarchal Vicar for Israel); Vicariat Patriarcal Latin, Street 6191/3, Nazareth 16100; tel. 4-6554075; fax 4-6452416; e-mail latinpat@rannet.com.

ISRAEL

Maronite Rite

The Maronite community is under the jurisdiction of the Maronite Patriarch of Antioch (resident in Lebanon).

Patriarchal Exarchate of Jerusalem: Maronite Patriarchal Exarchate, POB 14219, 25 Maronite Convent St, Jaffa Gate, Jerusalem 91141; tel. 2-6282158; fax 2-6272821; Exarch Patriarchal Mgr MOUSSA EL-HAGE (also the Maronite Archbishop of Haifa).

Melkite Rite

The Greek-Melkite Patriarch of Antioch and all the East, of Alexandria and of Jerusalem (GRÉGOIRE III LAHAM) is resident in Damascus, Syrian Arab Republic.

Patriarchal Vicariate of Jerusalem
Patriarcat Grec-Melkite Catholique, POB 14130, Porte de Jaffa, Jerusalem 91141; tel. 2-6282023; fax 2-6286652; e-mail gcpjer@p-ol.com; Protosyncellus Archim. Archbishop YASSER HANNA AYYASH.

Archbishop of Akka (Acre): YOUSSEF MATTA, Archevêché Grec-Catholique, POB 9450, 33 Hagefen St, 31094 Haifa; tel. 4-8508108; fax 4-8508106; e-mail chacoure@netvision.net.il.

Syrian Rite

The Syrian Catholic Patriarch of Antioch is resident in Beirut, Lebanon.

Patriarchal Exarchate of Jerusalem: Vicariat Patriarcal Syrien Catholique, POB 19787, 6 Chaldean St, Jerusalem 91197; tel. 2-6282657; fax 2-6284217; Exarch Patriarchal Mgr YAACOUB CAMIL AFRAM ANTOINE SEMAAN.

The Armenian Apostolic (Orthodox) Church

Patriarch of Jerusalem: Archbishop TORKOM MANOOGIAN, Armenian Patriarchate of St James, POB 14235, Jerusalem; tel. 2-6264853; fax 2-6264862; e-mail webmaster@armenianpatriarchate.org; internet www.armenian-patriarchate.org.

The Greek Orthodox Church

The Patriarchate of Jerusalem includes Israel, the Occupied Territories, Jordan, Kuwait, Saudi Arabia and the United Arab Emirates.

Patriarch of Jerusalem: THEOPHILOS III, POB 14518, Jerusalem 91145; tel. 2-6274941; fax 2-6282048; e-mail secretariat@jerusalem-patriarchate.info; internet www.jerusalem-patriarchate.info.

The Anglican Communion

Episcopal Diocese of Jerusalem and the Middle East: POB 19122, 65 Nablus Rd, Jerusalem 91191; tel. 2-6271670; fax 2-6273847; e-mail info@j-diocese.org; internet www.j-diocese.org; Archbishop The Most Rev. HOSAM NAOUM (Primate of the Province of Jerusalem and the Middle East and Anglican Archbishop in Jerusalem).

Other Christian Churches

Other denominations include the Coptic Orthodox Church, the Russian Orthodox Church, the Ethiopian Orthodox Church, the Romanian Orthodox Church, the Baptist Church, the Lutheran Church and the Church of Scotland.

The Press

DAILY NEWSPAPERS (PRINT AND ONLINE)

Calcalist: Tel Aviv; tel. 3-7350735; e-mail mail@calcalist.co.il; internet www.calcalist.co.il; f. 2008; Hebrew; business; publ. by Yedioth Ahronoth Group; Founder and Publr NOA ESTERON; Publr NOA TAMIR.

Globes: POB 5126, Rishon le Zion 75150; tel. 3-9538666; fax 3-9525971; e-mail feedback@globes.co.il; internet www.globes.co.il; f. 1983; evening; Hebrew; business and economics; owned by the Monitin Group; CEO ALONA BAR-ON; Editor-in-Chief NAAMA SIKULER.

Ha'aretz (The Land): 21 Schocken St, Tel Aviv 61590; tel. 3-5121333; fax 3-5121349; e-mail customer@haaretz.co.il; internet www.haaretz.co.il; f. 1919; morning; Hebrew and English; liberal; independent; 25% stake acquired by M. DuMont Schauberg (Germany) 2006; Man. Dir RAMI GUEZ; Editor-in-Chief ALUF BENN.

Hamodia (The Informer): 16A Petach Tikva St, Jerusalem 91012; tel. 2-5952888; fax 2-5696098; e-mail englishweekly@hamodia.com; internet www.hamodia.com; f. 1950; morning; Hebrew, English and French edns; Orthodox; organ of Agudat Israel; Editor HAIM MOSHE KNOPF.

Israel HaYom (Israel Today): 2 Hashlosha St, Tel Aviv; e-mail hayom@israelhayom.co.il; internet israelhayom.co.il; f. 2007; free daily publ. Sun.–Thur.; Hebrew; Publr Dr MIRIAM ADELSON; Editor-in-Chief OMER LACHMANOVITCH; CEO AMIR FINKELSTEIN.

Israel Post: 15 HaAchim MeSalvita, Tel Aviv; f. 2007 as Metro Israel; free daily; afternoon; Hebrew; publ. by Metro Israel Ltd; Co-owners ELI AZUR, DAVID WEISMAN; Editor-in-Chief GOLAN BAR-YOSEF.

Al-Itihad (Unity): 1 Hariri St, Haifa; tel. 4-8605400; e-mail aletihad.44@gmail.com; internet www.alittihad44.com; f. 1944; Arabic; organ of Hadash; Editor-in-Chief HISHAM NAFAA.

The Jerusalem Post: POB 81, The Jerusalem Post Bldg, Romema, Jerusalem 91000; tel. 2-5315666; fax 2-5389527; e-mail feedback@jpost.com; internet www.jpost.com; f. 1932 as The Palestine Post, renamed as above 1950; morning; English; independent; CEO INBAR ASHKENAZI; Editor-in-Chief YAAKOV KATZ; there is also a weekly international edn and a weekly French edn.

Novosti nedeli (The Week's News): 15 Ha-Ahim Mi-Slavita St, Tel Aviv; tel. 3-6242225; fax 3-6242227; Russian; Editor-in-Chief DMITRII LODYZHENSKII.

Al-Quds (Jerusalem): POB 19788, Jerusalem; tel. 2-6272663; fax 2-6272657; e-mail it@alquds.net; internet www.alquds.com; f. 1968; Arabic; Chair. ZIAD ABU AL-ZALAF; Editor WALEED ABU AL-ZALAF.

Yedioth Ahronoth (The Latest News): POB 7324, Tel Aviv 61072; tel. and fax 3-6082222; e-mail service@y-i.co.il; internet www.ynet.co.il; f. 1939; evening; Hebrew; independent; Editor-in-Chief NETA LIVNEH.

WEEKLY AND FORTNIGHTLY NEWSPAPERS (PRINT AND ONLINE)

Akhbar al-Naqab (News of the Negev): POB 426, Rahat 85357; tel. 8-9919202; fax 8-9917070; internet www.akhbarna.com; f. 1988; weekly; Arabic; educational and social issues concerning the Negev Bedouins; Editor-in-Chief MUHAMMAD YOUNIS.

Aurora: POB 57416, 6 Tushia, Tel Aviv 61573; tel. 3-5625216; fax 3-5625082; e-mail aurora@aurora-israel.co.il; internet www.aurora-israel.co.il; f. 1963; weekly; Spanish; Editor-in-Chief ARIE AVIDOR; circ. 20,000.

B'Sheva: POB 3631, Petach Tikva; tel. 3-9185553; fax 3-9237777; e-mail menashe@besheva.co.il; internet besheva.co.il; f. 2002; Hebrew; religious Zionist newspaper, distributed freely in religious communities; owned by Arutz Sheva (Channel Seven) media network; Editor EMANUEL SHILO.

Etgar (The Challenge): POB 35252, Ha'aliyah St, 2nd Floor, Tel Aviv 61351; tel. 3-5373268; fax 3-5373269; internet www.etgar.info; 2 a week; Hebrew; publ. by Hanitzotz Publishing House; Editor NATHAN YALIN-MOR.

The Jerusalem Post International Edition: POB 81, Romema, Jerusalem 91000; tel. 3-7619056; fax 3-5613699; e-mail subs@jpost.com; internet www.jpost.com/LandedPages/international.aspx; f. 1959; weekly; English; overseas edn of *The Jerusalem Post* (q.v.); circ. 60,000 to 80 countries; Editor LIAT COLLINS.

Jerusalem Report: POB 81, Jaffa 206, Jerusalem 9100002; tel. 2-5315414; e-mail jerusalemreport@gmail.com; internet www.jpost.com/Jerusalem-Report; f. 1990; bi-weekly; English; publ. under umbrella of *The Jerusalem Post*; Editor-in-Chief STEVE LINDE.

Laisha (For Women): POB 28122, 35 Bnei Brak St, Tel Aviv 66021; tel. 3-6386400; fax 3-6386904; internet xnet.ynet.co.il; f. 1949; Hebrew; women's magazine; Editor-in-Chief ILAN ITZHIK; circ. 100,000.

My Tour-Il Magazine: 15 Lamdan St, Tel Aviv 6941415; tel. 52-7747748; fax 3-6486622; e-mail ilan777@gmail.com; internet www.mytour-il.co.il; f. 1994; weekly; Hebrew and English; Publr and Editor ILAN SHCHORI; circ. 50,000.

Reshumot: 22 Beit Hadfus St, Jerusalem 9134301; tel. 73-3926750; fax 73-3926758; e-mail reshumot_p@justice.gov.il; internet www.gov.il/he/Departments/official_gazette; f. 1948; Hebrew, Arabic and English; official govt gazette.

OTHER PERIODICALS

Bitaon Heyl Ha'avir (Israel Air Force Magazine): Military POB 01560, Zahal; tel. 3-6063162; fax 3-6067735; e-mail iafm1948@gmail.com; internet www.iaf.org.il; f. 1948; bi-monthly; Hebrew and English; Dep. Editor LIOR ESTLINE; Editor-in-Chief Maj. DROR ALBUCHER; circ. 30,000.

Al-Bushra (Good News): POB 6228, Haifa 31061; tel. 4-8385002; fax 4-8371612; f. 1935; 12 a year; Arabic; organ of the Ahmadiyya movement; Editor MUSA ASA'AD O'DEH.

Diamond Intelligence Briefs: POB 68, Caesarea 30889; tel. 3-5750196; fax 3-5754829; e-mail office@tacy.co.il; internet www.diamondintelligence.com; f. 1985; English.

ISRAEL

HaMizrah HeHadash (The New East): Israel Oriental Society, The Hebrew University, Mount Scopus, Jerusalem 91905; tel. 2-5883633; e-mail meisai1949@gmail.com; internet www.meisai.org.il; f. 1949; annual of the Israel Oriental Society; Middle Eastern, Asian and African Affairs; Hebrew with English summary; Editors AMI AYALON, GAD GILBAR; circ. 400–500 (2020).

Harefuah (Medicine): POB 3566, 2 Twin Towers, 35 Jabotinsky St, Ramat Gan 52136; tel. 3-6100430; fax 3-7519673; e-mail harefuah@ima.org.il; internet www.ima.org.il/harefuah; f. 1920; 12 a year; journal of the Israel Medical Asscn; Hebrew with English summaries; also publishes *Israel Medical Asscn Journal*; Editor Prof. YEHUDA SHOENFELD; circ. 16,000.

Hed Hachinuch (Echoes of Education): 7 Ben Serok, Tel Aviv; tel. 3-6922939; fax 3-6928221; e-mail hed@morim.org.il; internet www.hedhachinuch.co.il; f. 1926; 12 a year; Hebrew; also publishes Arabic edn; educational; publ. by the Israel Teachers Union; Editor ISRAEL SOREK; circ. 40,000.

Hed Hagan (Echoes of Kindergarten): 8 Ben Saruk St, Tel Aviv 62969; tel. 3-6922958; e-mail contact@kranoth.org.il; internet www.itu.org.il; f. 1935; 4 a year; Hebrew; early education issues; publ. by the Israel Teachers Union; Editor ILANA MALCHI; circ. 9,000.

Historia: POB 10477, 2 Beitar St, Jerusalem 9110401; tel. 2-5650444; fax 2-6712388; e-mail historical@historical.org.il; f. 1998; bi-annual; Hebrew, with English summaries; general history; publ. by the Historical Society of Israel; Editors Prof. BILLIE MELMAN, Prof. YURI PINES, Prof. ALEXANDER YAKOBSON, Prof. JOSEPH ZIEGLER; circ. 1,000.

Israel Environment Bulletin: Ministry of Environmental Protection, POB 34033, 5 Kanfei Nesharim St, Givat Shaul, Jerusalem 95464; tel. 2-6553825; fax 2-6554823; e-mail shoshana@sviva.gov.il; internet www.sviva.gov.il; f. 1973; bi-annual; English; environmental policy, legislation and news; Editor SHOSHANA GABBAY; circ. 3,500.

Israel Exploration Journal: POB 7041, 5 Avida St, Jerusalem 9107001; tel. 2-6257991; fax 2-6247772; e-mail ies@vms.huji.ac.il; internet israelexplorationsociety.huji.ac.il/iej.htm; f. 1950; bi-annual; English; general and biblical archaeology, ancient history and historical geography of Israel and the Holy Land; Exec. Editor T. KUPER-BLAU; circ. 2,500.

Israel Journal of Chemistry: POB 34299, Jerusalem 91341; tel. 2-6522226; fax 2-6522277; e-mail info@israelsciencejournals.com; internet www.sciencefromisrael.com; f. 1951; 4 a year; English; publ. by Science from Israel; Editor Prof. EHUD KEINAN.

Israel Journal of Ecology and Evolution: POB 34299, Jerusalem 91341; tel. 2-6522226; fax 2-6522277; internet www.sciencefromisrael.com; f. 1951 as *Israel Journal of Zoology*; name changed 2006; 4 a year; English; publ. by Science from Israel; Editors LEON BLAUSTEIN, BURT P. KOTLER.

Israel Journal of Mathematics: The Hebrew University Magnes Press, POB 39099, Jerusalem 91390; tel. 2-6586656; fax 2-5633370; e-mail info@magnespress.co.il; internet www.ma.huji.ac.il/~ijmath; f. 1951; bi-monthly; English; Editor-in-Chief MICHAEL TEMKIN.

Israel Journal of Plant Sciences: POB 34299, Jerusalem 91341; tel. 2-6522226; fax 2-6522277; e-mail info@israelsciencejournals.com; internet www.sciencefromisrael.com; f. 1951 as *Israel Journal of Botany*; 4 a year; English; publ. by Science from Israel; Editor-in-Chief HAYA FRIEDMAN.

Israel Journal of Psychiatry and Related Sciences: Gefen Publishing House Ltd, 6 Hatzvi St, Jerusalem 94386; tel. 2-5380247; fax 2-5388423; e-mail raels@tauex.tau.ac.il; f. 1963; quarterly; English; Editor-in-Chief RAEL STROUS.

Israel Journal of Veterinary Medicine: POB 22, Ra'anana 43100; tel. 9-7419929; fax 9-7431778; e-mail ijvm10@gmail.com; internet www.ijvm.org.il; f. 1943; fmrly *Refuah Veterinarith*; quarterly of the Israel Veterinary Medical Asscn; English; Editor-in-Chief TREVOR WANER.

Israel Law Review: Minerva Center for Human Rights, Faculty of Law, Hebrew University of Jerusalem, Mt Scopus, Jerusalem 9190501; tel. 2-5881156; fax 2-5881379; e-mail ilr@savion.huji.ac.il; internet law.huji.ac.il/book/israel-law-review; f. 1966; 3 a year; English; Editors-in-Chief MALCOLM N. SHAW, YUVAL SHANY.

Israel Medical Asscn Journal (IMAJ): POB 3566, 2 Twin Towers, 11th Floor, 35 Jabotinsky St, Ramat Gan 52136; tel. 3-6100418; fax 3-7519673; e-mail imaj@ima.org.il; internet www.ima.org.il/imaj; f. 1999; 12 a year; English-language journal of the Israel Medical Asscn; also publishes *Harefuah*; Editor-in-Chief Prof. YEHUDA SHOENFELD.

Israel Travel News: Israel Travel News Ltd, POB 3251, Tel Aviv 61032; tel. 3-5251646; fax 3-5251605; e-mail office@itn.co.il; internet www.itn.co.il; f. 1979; 12 a year; English; Editor-in-Chief EYAL SHMUELI; circ. 19,250.

Journal d'Analyse Mathématique: The Hebrew University Magnes Press, POB 39099, Jerusalem 91390; tel. 2-6586656; fax 2-5633370; e-mail info@magnespress.co.il; internet www.ma.huji.ac.il/jdm; f. 1955; 3 vols a year; French; Exec. Editor DANIEL KRONBERG.

Leshonenu: Academy of the Hebrew Language, Givat Ram Campus, Jerusalem 9190401; tel. 2-6493555; fax 2-5617065; e-mail ivrit@hebrew-academy.org.il; internet hebrew-academy.huji.ac.il; f. 1929; 4 a year; Hebrew; for the study of the Hebrew language and cognate subjects; Editor MOSHE BAR-ASHER.

Leshonenu La'am: Academy of the Hebrew Language, Givat Ram Campus, Jerusalem 9190401; tel. 2-6493555; fax 2-5617065; e-mail ivrit@heberw-academy.org.il; internet hebrew-academy.huji.ac.il; f. 1945; 4 a year; Hebrew; popular Hebrew philology; Editor MOSHE FLORENTIN.

Lilac: Nazareth; f. 2000 for Christian and Muslim Arab women in the region; 12 a year; Arabic; Israel's first magazine for Arab women; Founder and Editor-in-Chief YARA MASHOUR.

MB-Yakinton (Yakinton): 157 Yigal Alon St, Tel Aviv 6744365; tel. 3-5164461; fax 3-5164435; e-mail info@irgun-jeckes.org; internet www.irgun-jeckes.org; f. 1932; 6 a year; journal of the Irgun Jotsei Merkaz Europa (Asscn of Israelis of Central European Origin); Hebrew and German; Editor MICHAEL DAK.

News from Within: POB 31417, Jerusalem 91313; tel. 2-6241159; fax 2-6253151; internet aicnews.org; 12 a year; joint Israeli-Palestinian publ.; political, economic, social and cultural; publ. by the Alternative Information Centre.

People and Computers: 53 Derech Hashalom, Givaatayim 54333; tel. 3-7330733; fax 3-7330703; e-mail info@pc.co.il; internet www.pc.co.il; f. 1981; online only; Hebrew; information on information technology; CEO DAHLIA PELED; CEO and Editor-in-Chief PELI PELLED.

Proche-Orient Chrétien: St Anne's Church, POB 19079, Jerusalem 91190; tel. 2-6281992; fax 2-6280764; e-mail mafrpoc@steanne.org; f. 1951; quarterly on churches and religion in the Middle East; publ. in asscn with St Joseph University, Beirut, Lebanon; French; circ. 1,000.

Terra Santa: POB 871, 2 Keren Hayesod St, Jerusalem 9100801; tel. 2-5639661; fax 2-5669553; e-mail info@cmc-terrasanta.com; internet www.cmc-terrasanta.org; f. 1973; bi-monthly; publ. by the Christian Information Centre, which is sponsored by the Custody of the Holy Land (the official custodians of the Holy Shrines); Italian, Spanish, French, English and Arabic edns publ. in Jerusalem by the Franciscan Printing Press, German edn in Munich, Maltese edn in Valletta.

WIZO Review: Women's International Zionist Organization, 38 Sderot David Hamelech Blvd, Tel Aviv 64237; tel. 3-6923824; fax 3-6923801; e-mail wreview@wizo.org; internet www.wizo.org; f. 1926; English (3 a year); Editors INGRID ROCKBERGER, TRICIA SCHWITZER; circ. 6,000.

PRESS ASSOCIATIONS

Daily Newspaper Publishers' Asscn of Israel: POB 51202, 74 Petach Tikva Rd, Tel Aviv 61200; fax 3-5617938; safeguards professional interests and maintains standards, supplies newsprint to dailies; negotiates with trade unions; mems all daily papers; affiliated to International Federation of Newspaper Publishers; Pres. SHABTAI HIMMELFARB; Gen. Sec. BETZALEL EYAL.

Foreign Press Asscn: 1 Agudat Hasport Hapoel St, Jerusalem 9695102; tel. 54-6311177; e-mail fpa.execsec@gmail.com; internet www.fpa.org.il; f. 1957; represents journalists employed by international news orgs who report from Israel, the West Bank and the Gaza Strip; private, non-profit org.; almost 500 mems from 30 countries; Chair. ANDREW CAREY.

Israel Association of Periodical Press (IAPP): 17 Keilat Venezia St, Tel Aviv 6940021; tel. 3-6449851; fax 3-6449852; e-mail iapp.organization@gmail.com; internet www.iapp.co.il; f. 1962; 300 mems; Chair. ALIZA ZEZAK.

Israel Press Council: 12 Kaplan St, Tel Aviv; tel. 3-6951437; fax 3-6951145; e-mail moaza@m-i.org.il; internet www.m-i.org.il; f. 1963; deals with matters of common interest to the press such as drafting the code of professional ethics, which is binding on all journalists; Chair. DALYA DONER; Gen. Sec. MOTI ROSENBLUM.

National Federation of Israeli Journalists (NFIJ): POB 585, 37 Hillet St, Jerusalem 91004; tel. 2-6254351; fax 2-6254353; e-mail office@jaj.org.il; internet www.jaj.org.il; affiliated to International Federation of Journalists; Chair. AHIA HIKA GINOSAR.

Publishers

Achiasaf Publishing House Ltd: 3, Bney Binyamin St, Netanya 4201959; tel. 9-8851390; fax 9-8851391; e-mail info@achiasaf.co.il; internet www.achiasaf.co.il; f. 1937; general; Pres. MATAN ACHIASAF.

Am Oved Publishers Ltd: 22 Mazeh St, Tel Aviv 65213; tel. 3-6288500; fax 3-6298911; e-mail info@am-oved.co.il; internet www.am-oved.co.il; f. 1942; fiction, non-fiction, children's books, poetry, classics, science fiction; Man. Dir HANITAL SWISA.

Amihai Publishing House Ltd: POB 8448, 19 Yad Harutzim St, Netanya Darom 42505; tel. 9-8859099; fax 9-8853464; e-mail ami1000@bezeqint.net; internet www.amichaibooks.co.il; f. 1948; fiction, general science, linguistics, languages, arts; Dir ITZHAK ORON.

Arabic Publishing House: 93 Arlozorof St, Tel Aviv; tel. 3-6921674; f. 1960; established by the Histadrut; periodicals and books; Gen. Man. GHASSAN MUKLASHI.

Ariel Publishing House: POB 3328, Jerusalem 91033; tel. 2-6434540; fax 2-6436164; e-mail arielpublishinghouse@gmail.com; internet www.arielp.co.il; f. 1976; history, archaeology, religion, geography, folklore; CEO ELY SCHILLER.

Astrolog Publishing House: POB 1231, Hod Hasharon 45111; tel. 3-9190957; fax 3-9190958; e-mail abooks@netvision.net.il; f. 1994; general non-fiction, religion, alternative medicine; Man. Dir SARA BEN-MORDECHAI.

Carta, The Israel Map and Publishing Co Ltd: POB 2500, 18 Rivka St, Talpiot, Jerusalem 9102401; tel. 2-6783355; fax 2-6782373; e-mail support@carta-jerusalem.com; internet www.carta-jerusalem.com; f. 1958; the principal cartographic publr; Pres. and CEO SHAY HAUSMAN.

Eliner Library—The World Zionist Organization: POB 10615, Jerusalem 91104; tel. 2-6202137; fax 2-6202552; e-mail eliner@wzo.org.il; internet www.eliner.co.il; f. 1945; education, Jewish philosophy, studies in the Bible, children's books publ. in Hebrew, English, French, Spanish, German, Swedish and Portuguese, Hebrew teaching material; Dir of Publication Division ITZCHACK SHTIGLITZ.

Gefen Publishing House Ltd: 6 Hatzvi St, Jerusalem 94386; tel. 2-5380247; fax 2-5388423; e-mail sales@gefenpublishing.com; internet www.israelbooks.com; f. 1981; largest publr of English-language books in Israel; also publishes wide range of fiction and non-fiction; Publr ILAN GREENFIELD.

Globes Publishers: POB 5126, Rishon le Zion 75150; tel. 3-9538611; fax 3-9525971; e-mail support@globes.co.il; internet www.globes.co.il; business, finance, technology, law, marketing; CEO ALONA BAR-ON; Editor-in-Chief NAAMA SIKULER.

Gvanim: POB 11138, 29 Bar-Kochba St, Tel Aviv 61111; tel. 3-5281044; fax 3-6202032; e-mail traklinm@zahav.net.il; internet gvanim-books.com; f. 1992; poetry, belles lettres, fiction; Man. Dir MARITZA ROSMAN.

Hakibbutz Hameuchad—Sifriat Poalim Publishing Group: POB 2104, Bnei Brak, Tel Aviv 51114; tel. 3-5785810; fax 3-5785811; e-mail info@kibutz-poalim.co.il; internet www.kibutz-poalim.co.il; f. 1939 as Hakibbutz Hameuchad Publishing House Ltd; subsequently merged with Sifriat Poalim; general; Gen. Dir UZI SHAVIT.

Hanitzotz Publishing House: POB 35252, Tel Aviv 61351; tel. 3-5373268; fax 3-5373269; internet www.hanitzotz.com; f. 1985; 'progressive' booklets and publications, incl. the periodicals *Challenge* (in English), *Etgar* (Hebrew), and *Al-Sabar* (Arabic); also produces documentary films on human and workers' rights; Contact RONI BEN EFRAT.

The Hebrew University Magnes Press: The Hebrew University, The Sherman Bldg for Research Management, POB 39099, Givat Ram, Jerusalem 91390; tel. 2-5633370; fax 2-5660341; e-mail ruhama.halevi@magnespress.co.il; internet www.magnespress.co.il; f. 1929; academic books and journals on many subjects, incl. biblical, classical and Jewish studies, social sciences, language, literature, art, history and geography; Dir JONATHAN NADAV.

Hed Arzi (Ma'ariv) Publishing Ltd: 3A Yoni Netanyahu St, Or-Yehuda, Tel Aviv 60376; tel. 3-5383333; fax 3-6343205; f. 1954 as Sifriat-Ma'ariv Ltd; later known as Ma'ariv Book Guild Ltd; general; Man. Dir ELI SHIMONI.

Hod-Ami—Computer Books Ltd: POB 6108, Herzliya 46160; tel. 9-9564716; fax 9-9571582; e-mail info@hod-ami.co.il; internet www.hod-ami.co.il; f. 1984; information technology, management; translations from English into Hebrew and Arabic; CEO ITZHAK AMIHUD.

Jerusalem Center for Public Affairs: 13 Tel Hai St, Jerusalem 92107; tel. 2-5619281; fax 2-5619112; e-mail info@jcpa.org; internet www.jcpa.org; f. 1976; Jewish political tradition; publishes *Daily Alert, Jerusalem Issue Brief, Jewish Political Studies Review* and other books; Dir-Gen. CHAYA HERSKOVIC; Chair. ARTHUR EIDELMAN.

The Jerusalem Publishing House: 2B HaGai St, Beit Hakerem, Jerusalem 96262; tel. 2-6537966; fax 2-6537988; internet jerpub.com; f. 1966; biblical research, history, encyclopedias, archaeology, arts of the Holy Land, cookbooks, guidebooks, economics, politics; CEO MOSHE HELLER.

Jewish History Publications (Israel 1961) Ltd: POB 1232, 29 Jabotinsky St, Jerusalem 92141; tel. 2-5632310; f. 1961; encyclopedias, World History of the Jewish People series.

Keter Publishing House Ltd: POB 7145, Givat Shaul B, Jerusalem 91071; tel. 8-9180000; fax 8-9221299; e-mail info@keterbooks.co.il; internet www.keter-books.co.il; f. 1959; original and translated works of fiction, encyclopedias, non-fiction, guidebooks and children's books; publishing imprints: Israel Program for Scientific Translations, Keter Books, Domino, Shikmona, Encyclopedia Judaica; Publr RONNIE MODAN.

Kinneret Zmora-Bitan Dvir Publishing House: 10 Hataasiya St, Or-Yehuda 60210; tel. 3-6344977; fax 3-6340953; internet www.kinbooks.co.il; f. 2002 following merger between Kinneret and Zmora Bitan-Dvir publishing houses; adult and children's fiction and non-fiction, history, science, sociology, psychology, current affairs and politics, dictionaries, architecture, travel; CEOs ERAN ZMORA, YORAM ROSE.

MAP-Mapping and Publishing Ltd (Tel Aviv Books): POB 56024, 17 Tchernikhovski St, Tel Aviv 61560; tel. 3-6210500; fax 3-5257725; e-mail info@mapa.co.il; internet www.mapa.co.il; f. 1985; maps, atlases, travel guides, textbooks, reference books; Man. Dir HEZI LEVY.

Ministry of Defense Publishing House: POB 916, Yaakov Dori Rd, Kiryat Ono 55108; tel. 3-7380738; fax 3-7380645; f. 1958; military literature, Judaism, history and geography of Israel; Dir JOSEPH PERLOVITZ.

M. Mizrachi Publishing House Ltd: 67 Levinsky St, Tel Aviv 66855; tel. 3-6870936; fax 3-6888185; f. 1960; children's books, fiction, history, medicine, science; Dirs MEIR MIZRACHI, ISRAEL MIZRACHI.

Mosad Harav Kook: POB 642, 1 Maimon St, Jerusalem 91006; tel. 2-6526231; fax 2-6526968; internet www.mosadharavkook.com; f. 1937; editions of classical works, Torah and Jewish studies; Exec. Chair. Rabbi YEHUDA LEIB RAFAEL.

Otsar Hamoreh: c/o Israel Teachers Union, 8 Ben Saruk, Tel Aviv 62969; tel. 3-6922983; fax 3-6922981; f. 1951; educational; Man. Dir JOSEPH SALOMAN.

People and Computers Ltd: POB 11438, 53 Derech Asholom St, Givatayim 53454; tel. 3-7330733; fax 3-7330703; e-mail info@pc.co.il; internet www.pc.co.il; f. 1981; information technology; Editor-in-Chief and Chair. PELI PELED; CEO DAHLIA PELED.

Rodney Franklin Agency: POB 37727, 53 Mazeh St, Tel Aviv 65789; tel. 3-5600724; fax 3-5600479; e-mail rodneyf@netvision.net.il; internet www.rodneyagency.com; f. 1974; exclusive representative of various British, other European and US publrs; e-marketing services for academic and professional journal publrs in 15 countries; Dir RODNEY FRANKLIN.

Rubin Mass Ltd: POB 990, 25 Ramban St, Jerusalem 9242226; tel. 2-6277863; fax 2-6277864; e-mail rmass@barak.net.il; internet rubinmass.net; f. 1927; Hebraica, Judaica, export of all Israeli books and periodicals; Man. OREN MASS.

Schocken Publishing House Ltd: POB 57188, 24 Nathan Yelin Mor St, Tel Aviv 61571; tel. 3-5610130; fax 3-5622668; e-mail gila_b@haaretz.co.il; internet www.schocken.co.il; f. 1938; general; Publr RACHELI EDELMAN.

Shalem Press: 3 Ha'askan St, Jerusalem 9378010; tel. 2-5605586; fax 2-5605565; e-mail shalempress@shalem.ac.il; internet www.shalempress.co.il; f. 1994; economics, political science, history, philosophy, cultural issues; Pres. DANIEL POLISAR.

Sinai Publishing: 24 Rambam St, Tel Aviv 65813; tel. 3-5163672; fax 3-5176783; e-mail sinaipub@zahav.net.il; internet www.sinaibooks.com; f. 1853; Hebrew books and religious articles; Dir MOSHE SCHLESINGER.

Steinhart Sharav Publishers Ltd: POB 8333, Netanya 42505; tel. 9-8854770; fax 9-8854771; e-mail mail@haolam.co.il; internet www.haolam.co.il; f. 1991; travel; Man. Dir OHAD SHARAV.

Tcherikover Publishers Ltd: 12 Hasharon St, Tel Aviv 66185; tel. 3-6396099; fax 3-6874729; education, psychology, economics, psychiatry, literature, literary criticism, essays, history, geography, criminology, art, languages, management; Man. Editor S. TCHERIKOVER.

Yavneh Publishing House Ltd: POB 4781, 4 Mazeh St, Tel Aviv 65213; tel. 3-6297856; fax 3-6293638; e-mail publishing@yavneh.co.il; internet www.yavneh.co.il; f. 1932; general; Man. Dir NIRA PREISKEL.

Yedioth Ahronoth Books: POB 445, 1 Noah Moses St, Industrial Area, Tel Aviv 61534; tel. 3-7683333; fax 3-7683300; e-mail mzkirut@yedbooks.co.il; internet www.ybook.co.il; f. 1952; non-fiction, politics, Judaism, health, music, dance, fiction, education; Man. Dir DOV EICHENWALD.

S. Zack: 31 Beit Hadfus St, Jerusalem 95483; tel. 2-6537760; fax 2-6514005; e-mail zackmt@bezeqint.net; internet www.zack.co.il; f. 1935; fiction, science, philosophy, Judaism, children's books,

ISRAEL

educational and reference books, dictionaries, languages; Dir MICHAEL ZACK.

PUBLISHERS' ASSOCIATION

The Israeli Association of Book Publishers: POB 20123, 29 Carlebach St, Tel Aviv 67132; tel. 3-5614121; fax 3-5611996; e-mail rights1@tbpai.co.il; internet www.tbpai.co.il; f. 1939; mems: 84 publishing firms; Chair. BINI TRIWAKS; Man. Dir SARIT OREN.

Broadcasting and Communications

TELECOMMUNICATIONS

Bezeq—The Israel Telecommunication Corpn Ltd: Azrieli Center 2, Tel Aviv 61620; tel. 3-7278199; e-mail ca-2@bezeq.co.il; internet www.ir.bezeq.co.il; f. 1984; privatized 2005; launched own mobile telephone network, Pelephone Communications Ltd, in 1986; Chair. GIL SHARON; CEO RAN GURON.

Pelephone Communications Ltd: 33 Hagvura St, Givatayim, Tel Aviv 53483; tel. (50) 7079630; internet www.pelephone.co.il; f. 1986; launched Esc brand 2003; CEO RAN GURON.

Cellcom Israel: POB 4060, 10 Hagavish St, Netanya 42140; tel. 52-9990052; fax 9-8607921; e-mail cellcom_pniyot@cellcom.co.il; internet www.cellcom.co.il; f. 1994; mobile telecommunications operator; Chair. DORON COHEN; CEO DANIEL SAPIR.

013 Netvision: POB 4060, 10 Hagavish St, Netanya 42140; fax 03-7255858; e-mail pniot-tzibur@013netvision.co.il; internet netvision.cellcom.co.il; f. 2007 after merger with 013 Barak and GlobCall.

Partner Communications Co Ltd: POB 435, 8 Amal St, Afeq Industrial Park, Rosh Ha'ayin 48103; tel. 54-7814888; fax 54-7814999; e-mail investors@partner.co.il; internet www.partner.co.il; f. 1999; provides mobile telecommunications and Wi-Fi internet services; represents about one-third of the mobile telecommunications market in Israel; operated under Orange brand name until 2016; SB Israel Telecom holds 29.4% stake; Chair. SHLOMO RONEN; CEO AVI GABAY.

Ribbon Communications Operating Co: POB 3038, 30 Hasivim St, Petach-Tikva, Tel Aviv 49517; tel. 3-9266555; internet ribboncommunications.com; acquired ECI Telecom Ltd in 2020; Chair. SHAUL SHANI; Pres. and CEO BRUCE MCCLELLAND.

BROADCASTING

Israel Public Broadcasting Corpn (KAN): 23 Kinnfei Nesharim, Jerusalem; tel. 76-8098000; e-mail info@kan.org.il; internet www.kan.org.il; f. 2017, following dissolution of Israel Broadcasting Authority; 8 radio stations: Kan Tarbut, Kan Reshet Bet, Kan C, MaKan, Kan Farsi, Kan REKA, Kan 88, Kan Kol HaMusica and Kan Moreshet; 3 television channels: Kan 11 (in Hebrew), MaKan 33 (Arabic) and Kan Educational; Chair. GIL OMER; CEO GOLAN YOCHPAZ.

Radio

Galei Zahal: POB 01005, 23 Dro St, Jaffa, Tel Aviv; tel. 3-5126666; fax 3-5126710; e-mail radio@galatz.co.il; internet glz.co.il; f. 1950; Israel Defence Force broadcasting station, Tel Aviv, with studios in Jerusalem; broadcasts 24-hour news, current affairs, music and cultural programmes in Hebrew on FM, medium and short waves; Dir GALIT ALTSTEIN.

Television

The Council of Cable TV and Satellite Broadcasting: 23 Jaffa Rd, Jerusalem 9199907; fax 2-6702273; e-mail pniyot_tv@moc.gov.il; f. 1982; Dir RONEN AVRAMSON.

Second Authority for Television and Radio: POB 3445, 20 Beit Hadfus St, Jerusalem 95464; tel. 2-6556222; fax 2-6556287; e-mail rashut@rashut2.org.il; internet www.rashut2.org.il; f. 1991; previously responsible for providing broadcasts through two principal television channels, Channel 2 and Channel 10 and Channel 10, plus some 14 radio stations; since broadcasting reforms implemented in 2017, charged with supervising the operations of private commercial television networks; Chair. EDEN BAR TAL.

Keshet International: POB 58151, 12 Raul Valenberg St, Tel Aviv 6971910; tel. (3) 7676085; e-mail info_keshetinter@keshet-tv.com; internet www.keshetinternational.com; f. 1993; owns and operates television channel Keshet 12; CEO ALON SHTRUZMAN.

Reshet: 23 Habarzel St, Tel Aviv; tel. (3) 7690000; fax (3) 7690069; e-mail operator@reshet.tv; internet 13tv.co.il; f. 1993 as operator of Channel 2; since 2017, owns and operates television channel Reshet 13; merged with Channel 10 in 2019; Chair. NADAV TOPOLSKI; CEO YORAM ALTMAN.

Finance

BANKING
Central Bank

Bank of Israel: POB 780, Bank of Israel Bldg, Kiryat Ben-Gurion, Jerusalem 91007; tel. 2-6552211; fax 2-6528805; internet www.boi.org.il; f. 1954 as Cen. Bank of the State of Israel; Gov. Prof. AMIR YARON.

Principal Commercial Banks

Bank Hapoalim: 50 Rothschild Blvd, Tel Aviv 66883; tel. 3-5673697; fax 3-7136146; internet www.bankhapoalim.co.il; f. 1921 as Workers' Bank; name changed as above 1961; mergers into the above: American-Israel Bank 1999, Maritime Bank of Israel 2003, Mishkan-Hapoalim Mortgage Bank and Israel Continental Bank 2004; privatized 2000; Chair. REUVEN KRUPIK; Pres. and CEO DOV KOTLER.

Bank of Jerusalem Ltd: POB 2255, 2 Herbert Samuel St, Jerusalem 91022; tel. 2-8096666; e-mail webmaster@bankjerusalem.co.il; internet www.bankjerusalem.co.il; private bank; Chair. ZEEV NAHARI; CEO YAIR KAPLAN.

Bank Leumi le-Israel BM: 34 Yehuda Halevi St, Tel Aviv 65546; tel. 3-9544333; e-mail pniot@bll.co.il; internet www.bankleumi.co.il; f. 1902 as Anglo-Palestine Co; renamed Anglo-Palestine Bank 1930; reincorporated as above 1951; 34.78% state-owned; Chair. SAMER HAJ YEHIA; CEO HANAN FRIEDMAN.

Bank Otsar Ha-Hayal Ltd: POB 3506, 11 Menachem Begin St, Ramat Gan 52136; tel. 3-5130038; fax 3-7964500; e-mail pniyot@mailotsar.co.il; internet www.bankotsar.co.il; f. 1946; owned by First Int. Bank of Israel; Chair. YOSSI LEVI; Man. Dir YAACOV MALKIN.

First International Bank of Israel Ltd (FIBI): 42 Rothschild Blvd, Tel Aviv 66883; tel. 3-5130031; e-mail support@fibi.co.il; internet www.fibi.co.il; f. 1972 by merger between Foreign Trade Bank Ltd and Export Bank Ltd; Chair. RON LEBKOWITZ; CEO ELI COHEN.

Israel Discount Bank Ltd: 38 Yehuda Halevi St, Tel Aviv 61003; tel. 76-8053900; fax 76-8890014; internet www.discountbank.co.il; f. 1935; name changed as above in 1957; Chair. SHAUL KUBRINSKY; Pres. and CEO AVI LEVI.

Mercantile Discount Bank Ltd: POB 1292, 132 Menachem Begin, Tel Aviv 61012; tel. (76)-8072000; fax (76)-8072020; e-mail fec@mdb.co.il; internet www.mercantile.co.il; f. 1971 as Barclays Discount Bank Ltd, to take over (from Jan. 1972) the Israel brs of Barclays Bank Int. Ltd; Barclays Bank PLC, one of the joint owners, sold its total shareholding to the remaining owner, Israel Discount Bank Ltd, in Feb. 1993, and name changed as above that April; Mercantile Bank of Israel Ltd became member of the above March 1997; Chair. ESTER DEUTSCH; Gen. Man. JOSHUA BURSHTEIN.

Mizrahi Tefahot Bank Ltd: POB 3450, 7 Jabotinsky St, Ramat-Gan 52136; tel. 76-8040770; fax 3-7552150; internet www.mizrahi-tefahot.co.il; f. 1923 as Mizrahi Bank Ltd; mergers into the above: Hapoel Hamizrahi Bank Ltd, as United Mizrahi Bank Ltd; Finance and Trade Bank Ltd 1990; Tefahot Israel Mortgage Bank Ltd 2005, when name changed as above; Adanim Mortgage Bank merged into above bank 2009; Chair. MOSHE VIDMAN; Pres. and CEO MOSHE LARY.

ONE ZERO Digital Bank Ltd: 1st Floor, 3 Aminadav St, Tel Aviv 6706703; e-mail talk2us@onezerobank.com; internet onezerobank.com; f. 2019; first digital bank in Israel; Chair. SHUKI OREN; CEO GAL BAR DA'A.

Union Bank of Israel Ltd: 6–8 Ahuzat Bayit St, Tel Aviv 65143; tel. 3-5191351; fax 3-5191421; e-mail info@ubi.co.il; internet www.unionbank.co.il; f. 1951; Chair. MOSHE LARY; CEO HAIM FREILICHMAN.

STOCK EXCHANGE

The Tel Aviv Stock Exchange: 2 Ahuzat Bayit St, Tel Aviv 65202; tel. 3-8160411; fax 3-5105379; internet tase.co.il; f. 1953; 541 listed cos, with a total domestic market cap. of US $362,118m. (2021); Chair. SALAH SAABNEH; CEO ITTAI BEN-ZEEV.

INSURANCE

Clal Insurance Enterprise Holdings Ltd: POB 326, 46 Petach Tikva Rd, Tel Aviv 66184; tel. 3-6387777; fax 3-6387676; e-mail avigdork@clal-ins.co.il; internet www.clalbit.co.il; f. 1962; 55% owned by IDB Group, 10% by Bank Hapoalim and 35% by the public; insurance, pensions and finance; Chair. SAMAT HAIM; CEO YORAM NAVEH.

Harel Insurance Investments and Financial Services Ltd: Tel Aviv; tel. 3-7547000; e-mail infonet@harel-group.co.il; internet www.harel-group.co.il; f. 1935 as Hamishmar Insurance Service; Harel

ISREAL

est. 1975, became Harel Hamishmar Investments Ltd 1982, Harel Insurance Investments Ltd 1998 and current name adopted 2007; acquired Dikla Insurance Co Ltd and Eliahu Insurance Co Ltd 2012; 46.49% owned by Hamburger family; Chair. YAIR HAMBURGER; CEO MICHEL SIBONI.

Menorah Mivtachim Insurance Co Ltd: POB 927, 15 Allenby St, Tel Aviv 61008; tel. 3-7107777; fax 3-7107402; e-mail anat-by@bezeqint.net; internet www.menoramivt.co.il; f. 1935; Chair. ARI KALMAN; CEO YEHUDA BEN ASSAYAG.

Phoenix Insurance Co Ltd: 53 Derech Hashalom, Givat Shmuel 53454; tel. 3-7332222; fax 3-5735151; e-mail ir@fnx.co.il; internet www.fnx.co.il; f. 1949; controlled by Delek Group; Chair. BENJAMIN GABBAY; CEO EYAL BEN SIMON.

Trade and Industry

GOVERNMENT AGENCIES

Foreign Trade Administration: 5 Bank Israel St, Jerusalem; tel. 4-7502629; e-mail foreign-trade@economy.gov.il; internet www.gov.il/en/departments/units/foreign_trade; Dir OHAD COHEN.

Israel Space Agency (ISA): 52 Derech Menachem Begin, Tel Aviv; tel. 3-7649600; fax 3-7649622; e-mail dovermada@most.gov.il; internet www.space.gov.il; f. 1983; Chair. Dr DAN BLUMBERG; Dir-Gen. URI ORON.

DEVELOPMENT ORGANIZATIONS

Galilee Development Authority: Bar-Lev Industrial Park, Misgav 20156; tel. 4-9552426; fax 4-9552440; e-mail judith@galil.gov.il; internet galil.gov.il; f. 1993; statutory authority responsible for the social and economic devt of the Galilee region; Dir-Gen. SHLOMI ATTIAS.

Israel Innovation Authority: Technology Park, Derech Agudat Sport, Ha'poel 2, Jerusalem 9695102; tel. (3) 7157900; e-mail hd@innovationisrael.org.il; internet innovationisrael.org.il; an independent publicly funded agency aimed at promoting technological, industrial and entrepreneurial innovation; Chair. Dr AMI APPELBAUM; CEO DROR BIN.

Jerusalem Development Authority (JDA): 2 Safra Sq., Jerusalem 91322; tel. 2-5890000; fax 2-6250875; e-mail eyal@jda.gov.il; internet www.jda.gov.il; f. 1988; statutory authority responsible for the economic devt of Jerusalem; CEO EYAL HAIMOVSKY.

Negev Development Authority: 84895 Negev; tel. 8-6239905; fax 8-6233176; e-mail youknow@negev.co.il; internet www.negev.co.il; f. 1991; statutory authority responsible for the economic and social devt of the Negev region, and co-ordination between govt offices; Chair BENNY BITTON; Man. Dir MOSHE MOORE YOSEF.

CHAMBERS OF COMMERCE

Federation of Israeli Chambers of Commerce: POB 20027, 84 Ha'Hashmonaim St, Tel Aviv 67132; tel. 3-5631010; fax 3-5619025; e-mail chamber@chamber.org.il; internet www.chamber.org.il; co-ordinates the Tel Aviv, Jerusalem, Haifa, Nazareth and Beersheba Chambers of Commerce; Pres. URIEL LYNN.

Israel Federation of Bi-National Chambers of Commerce and Industry with and in Israel: POB 50196, 29 Hamered St, Tel Aviv 61500; tel. 505234716; e-mail chambersofc@gmail.com; internet bi-national.org; Chair. MARIAN COHEN; Man. Dir YORAM ELDAR.

Beersheba Chamber of Commerce: POB 5278, 7 Hamuktar St, Beersheba 84152; tel. 8-6234222; e-mail office@negev-chamber.org.il; internet www.negev-chamber.org.il; Pres. MOSHE TRABELSI.

Chamber of Commerce and Industry of Haifa and the North: POB 33176, 53 Ha'atzmaut Rd, Haifa 31331; tel. 4-8302100; fax 4-8645428; e-mail main@haifachamber.org.il; internet www.haifachamber.org.il; f. 1921; Pres. DAVID CASTEL.

Israel-British Chamber of Commerce: POB 50321, Industry House, 13th Floor, 29 Hamered St, Tel Aviv 61502; tel. 3-5109424; fax 3-5109540; e-mail info@ibcc.org.il; internet ibcc.org.il; f. 1951; Chair. ANITA LEVIANT.

Jerusalem Chamber of Commerce: 10 Derech Hillel, Jerusalem 91020; tel. 2-6254333; fax 2-6254335; e-mail jerccom@inter.net.il; internet www.jerccom.co.il; f. 1908; 200 mems.

INDUSTRIAL AND TRADE ASSOCIATIONS

The Centre for International Agricultural Development Cooperation (CINADCO): POB 30, Beit Dagan 5025001; tel. 3-9485760; fax 3-9485761; e-mail cinadco@moag.gov.il; internet www.mashav.mfa.gov.il; a commercial org. within MASHAV (the Israeli Agency for Int. Devt Co-operation); shares agricultural experience through the integration of research and project devt; runs specialized training courses, advisory missions and feasibility projects in Israel and abroad, incl. those in co-operation with developing countries; Dir YACOV PELEG.

Israel Dairy Board (IDB): POB 97, 4 Derech Hahoresh, Yahud 56100; tel. 3-9564750; fax 3-9564750; e-mail office@milk.org.il; internet www.israeldairy.com; regulates dairy farming and the dairy industry; implements govt policy on the planning of milk production and marketing; CEO ITZHAK SHNAIDER.

Israel Diamond Exchange Ltd: 3 Jabotinsky Rd, Ramat Gan 52520; tel. 3-5760203; e-mail bursa_il@isde.co.il; internet www.isde.co.il; f. 1937; production, export, import and finance facilities; Pres. and Chair. BOAZ MOLDAVSKY; Man. Dir ERAN ZINI.

Israel Export and International Co-operation Institute: POB 50084, 29 Hamered St, Tel Aviv 6812511; tel. 3-5142800; fax 3-5162810; e-mail galit@export.gov.il; internet www.export.gov.il; f. 1958; jt venture between the state and private sectors; Chair. AYELET NAHMIAS VERBIN.

The Israeli Cotton Board: POB 384, Herzlia B 4610302; tel. 9-9604003; fax 9-9604030; e-mail cotton@cotton.co.il; internet www.cotton.co.il; f. 1956 as the Israel Cotton Production and Marketing Board; CEO YIZHAR LANDAU.

Kibbutz Industries' Asscn: POB 50441, 29 Hamered St, Tel Aviv 65100; tel. 3-6955413; e-mail kia@kia.co.il; internet www.kia.co.il; f. 1962; liaison office for marketing and export of the goods produced by Israel's *kibbutzim*; Chair. EDO RODOI; Man. Dir GIL LYNN.

Manufacturers' Asscn of Israel: POB 50022, Industry House, 29 Hamered St, Tel Aviv 6150001; tel. 3-5198832; fax 3-5103154; e-mail info@industry.org.il; internet www.industry.org.il; 1,700 mem. enterprises employing nearly 85% of industrial workers in Israel; Pres. Dr RON TOMER; Dir RUBY GINEL.

National Federation of Israeli Journalists: POB 585, Beit Agron, 37 Hillet St, Jerusalem 91004; tel. 2-6254351; fax 3-6254353; e-mail office@jaj.org.il; Chair. AHIYA GENOSAR.

Plants Production and Marketing Board: 40 Derech Ha'atzmaut, Yehud 5610102; tel. 3-9595666; fax 3-9502211; e-mail plants@plants.org.il; internet www.plants.org.il; includes fruit, citrus fruit, vegetable and olive board.

UTILITIES

Israel Electric Corporation Ltd (IEC): POB 58003, Halechi 17, Bnei-Brak IT School, Haifa 1200; tel. 3-6174944; fax 3-6174922; e-mail ucgia@iec.co.il; internet www.iec.co.il; state-owned; Chair. DOV BAHARAV; Pres. and CEO OFER BLOCH.

Mekorot (Israel National Water Co): POB 20128, 9 Lincoln St, Tel Aviv 61201; tel. 3-6230555; fax 3-6230833; e-mail m-doveret@mekorot.co.il; internet www.mekorot.co.il; f. 1937; state-owned; Chair. YITZHAK AHARONOVITCH; CEO AMIT LANG.

MAJOR INVESTMENT HOLDING COMPANIES

Delek Group: POB 2054, 19 Abba Eban Blvd, Herzliya 4612001; tel. 9-8638444; fax 9-8854955; e-mail info@delek-group.com; internet www.delek-group.com; f. 1951; est. as Israel Fuel Corpn; energy, infrastructure, financial services, automotive import and retail distribution; Chair. EHUD EREZ; CEO IDAN WALLACE.

Elco Holdings Ltd: Electra Tower, 50th Floor, 98 Yigal Alon St, Tel Aviv 978914; tel. 3-6939670; fax 3-6913256; e-mail tali@elco.co.il; internet www.elco.co.il; f. 1949; controls five business units: Electra Ltd, Electra Real Estate Ltd, Electra Consumer Products Ltd, Golan Telecom, and Elco Media and Entertainment; revenue US $4,764m. (2021); Co Man. Dirs. DANIEL SALKIND, MICHAEL SALKIND.

Israel Corpn: POB 20456, Millenium Tower, 23 Aranha St, Tel Aviv 61204; tel. 3-6844500; e-mail ir@israelcorp.com; internet israelcorp.com; f. 1968; privatized 1999; 55% owned by Ofer Group; chemicals, fertilizers, energy, transportation and shipping; sales US $6,955m. (2021); Chair. AVIAD KAUFMAN; CEO YOAV DOPPELT.

MAJOR COMPANIES

ADAMA Agricultural Solutions Ltd: Golan St, Airport City 7015103; tel. 3-2321000; e-mail office@adama.com; internet www.adama.com; generic mfr and distributor of crop protection products; owned by China National Agrochemical Corpn (CNAC—People's Republic of China); fmrly Makhteshim Agan Industries Ltd; present name adopted 2014; revenue US $4,128m. (2020); Chair. ERIK FYRWALD; Pres. and CEO STEVE HAWKINS; over 9,000 employees (2023).

Agricultural Export Co (Carmel Agrexco): Beit Ampa, 1 Sapir St, Herzliya 4685205; tel. 54-9708400; fax 9-9708433; e-mail head-office@agrexco.com; internet www.agrexco.com; owned by Ampa Group; Chair. SHLOMI FOGEL; Gen. Man. YOAV SHOR.

Elbit Systems Ltd: POB 539, Advanced Technology Centre, Haifa 3100401; tel. 7-2940000; e-mail corporate.int.marketing@elbitsystems.com; internet www.elbitsystems.com; f. 1996; 45.8% owned by Federman Enterprises; defence electronics co engaged in wide range of defence-related programmes worldwide; acquired Tadiran Communications (Israel's leading mfr of civil and military communications technology) in 2008; acquired state-owned IMI Systems Ltd in 2018 and renamed it as Elbit Systems Land Ltd; total revenue US $5,512m. (2022); Chair. of Bd MICHAEL FEDERMANN; Pres. and CEO BEZHALEL MACHLIS.

Israel Aerospace Industries Ltd (IAI): Ben Gurion International Airport, Tel Aviv 70100; tel. 3-9353111; fax 3-9353131; e-mail privacy@iai.co.il; internet www.iai.co.il; f. 1953; 100% state-owned; designers and mfrs of military and civil aerospace; Chair. AMIR PERETZ; Pres. and CEO BOAZ LEVY.

Israel Chemicals Ltd: Millenium Tower, 23 Aranha St, Tel Aviv 61070; tel. 3-6844400; fax 3-6844444; e-mail contactus@icl-group.com; internet www.icl-group.com; f. 1968; produces fertilizer, other chemicals and supplies phosphate products; Chair. YOAV DOPPELT; Pres. and CEO RAVIV ZOLLER.

Perrigo Israel Pharmaceuticals Ltd: 29 Lehi St, Bene Beraq 51200; tel. 3-5773800; fax 3-5797045; e-mail hr@perrigo.co.il; internet perrigo-pharma.co.il; mfrs of over-the-counter and prescription drugs; subsidiary of Perrigo (USA); Pres. JOSEPH C. PAPA.

Rafael Advanced Defense Systems Ltd: POB 2250, Haifa 3102102; tel. 3-3354444; e-mail intl-mkt@rafael.co.il; internet www.rafael.co.il; f. 2002; fmrly owned by the Ministry of Defence; designs and manufactures defence systems for air, land, sea and space applications; Pres. and CEO Maj.-Gen. (retd) YOAV HAR-EVEN; 8,000 employees (2021).

Soltam Systems Ltd: POB 13, Yokneam 20692; tel. 4-9896282; fax 4-9892045; e-mail headoffice@soltam.com; military manufacturer; owned by Elbit Systems.

Strauss Group Ltd: POB 194, 49 HaSivim St, Petach Tikva 49517; e-mail service@strauss-group.com; internet www.strauss-group.com; f. 2004 by merger of Strauss and Elite Industries Ltd; adopted present name 2007; produces, markets and distributes variety of food and drink products; operates in Israel and abroad; Chair. OFRA STRAUSS; Group CEO SHAI BABAD; CEO, Israel RAANAN KOVALSKY.

Suny Cellular Communications Ltd: Segula Industrial Park, Petach Tikva 49277; tel. 3-9057777; fax 3-9300424; e-mail service@scailex.com; internet www.samsungmobile.co.il; f. 1968 as Scitex Corpn; fmrly known as Scailex Corporation Ltd; imports Samsung mobile telephones and accessories; Chair. JACOB LUXENBERG.

Teva Pharmaceutical Industries Ltd: 5 Basel St, Petach Tikva 49131; tel. 3-9267267; fax 3-9234050; internet www.tevapharm.com; f. 1944; pharmaceuticals; Chair. Dr SOL J. BARER; CEO RICHARD FRANCIS.

The Histadrut

Histadrut (General Federation of Labour in Israel): 93 Arlozorof St, Tel Aviv 62098; tel. 3-6921511; fax 3-6921511; e-mail avitals@histadrut.org.il; internet www.histadrut.org.il; f. 1920; Chair. ARNON BAR-DAVID.

The Histadrut is the largest labour organization in Israel. Membership of the Histadrut is voluntary, and open to all men and women of 18 years of age and above who live on the earnings of their own labour without exploiting the work of others. These include the self-employed and professionals, as well as housewives, students, pensioners and the unemployed. Workers' interests are protected through a number of occupational and professional unions affiliated to the Histadrut.

In 2017 the Histadrut had a membership of 570,000. In addition, over 100,000 young people under 18 years of age belong to the Organization of Working and Student Youth, HaNoar HaOved VeHalomed, a direct affiliate of the Histadrut.

All members take part in elections to the Histadrut Convention (Veida), which elects the General Council (Moetsa) and the Executive Committee (Vaad Hapoel). The latter elects the 41-member Executive Bureau (Vaada Merakezet), which is responsible for day-to-day implementation of policy. Nearly all political parties are represented on the Histadrut Executive Committee.

OTHER TRADE UNIONS

Histadrut Haovdim Haleumit (National Labour Federation): 23 Sprintzak St, Tel Aviv 64738; tel. 3-6958351; fax 3-6961753; f. 1934; Chair. YOAV SIMCHI; 220,000 mems.

Histadrut Hapoel Hamizrachi (National Religious Workers' Party): 166 Ibn Gvirol St, Tel Aviv 62023; tel. 3-5442151; fax 3-5468942; 150,000 mems in 85 settlements and 15 *kibbutzim*.

Histadrut Poale Agudat Israel (Agudat Israel Workers' Organization): POB 11044, 64 Frishman St, Tel Aviv; tel. 3-5242126; fax 3-5230689; 33,000 mems in 16 settlements and 8 educational insts.

Transport

RAILWAYS

A rail route for freight traffic serves Haifa and Ashdod ports on the Mediterranean Sea, while a combined rail-road service extends to Eilat port on the Red Sea. Passenger services operate between the main towns: Nahariya, Haifa, Tel Aviv and Jerusalem. Construction of a high–speed rail link between Jerusalem and Tel Aviv commenced in 2001. Following severe delays, a section of the line between a newly-built terminus in Jerusalem and Ben Gurion International Airport opened in 2018; the remaining part of the line to Tel Aviv opened in December 2019. The first line of a light railway network in Jerusalem was inaugurated in 2011. The project was a source of considerable controversy owing to the incorporation within the 13.9-km Red Line of disputed Jewish developments in East Jerusalem. Extensions to the Red Line, totalling some 8.6 km, are expected to be completed by 2026. Two further lines are also under construction—the 19.6-km Green Line and the 23-km Blue Line. The 24-km first section of a light rail system in Tel Aviv was inaugurated, after numerous delays, in August 2023. Two further lines are under construction.

Israel Railways (IR): POB 18085, Central Station, Tel Aviv 61180; tel. 3-5774000; fax 3-6937443; e-mail israelrailways@tservice.co.il; internet www.rail.co.il; f. 2003 as an ind. govt-owned corpn; prior to that date IR had operated as a unit of the Ports and Railways Authority; Chair. MOSHE SHIMONI; CEO MICHAEL MAIXNER.

Underground Railway

Haifa Underground Funicular Railway: 122 Hanassi Ave, Haifa 34633; tel. 4-8376861; fax 4-8376875; e-mail orna@carmelit.com; internet www.carmelithaifa.co.il; opened 1959; 2 km in operation.

ROADS

Egged, Israel Co-operative Transport Society Ltd: POB 150, Egged Bldg, 5 Menachem Begin Blvd, Beit Dagan 5025002; tel. 3-9142000; fax 3-9142237; internet www.egged.co.il; f. 1933; operates 3,057 bus routes throughout Israel; Chair. GIDEON MIZRACHI.

SHIPPING

Haifa and Ashdod are the main ports in Israel. The former is a natural harbour, enclosed by two main breakwaters and dredged to 45 ft below mean sea level. There is a deep-water port at Ashdod, which was expanded to house a new container terminal, Eitan Port, in 2005. The privatization of the Port of Haifa was completed in January 2023, with the lease agreement due to run until 2054.

The port of Eilat, Israel's gateway to the Red Sea, has storage facilities for crude petroleum. It is a natural harbour, operated from a wharf.

Port Authority and Companies

Israel Ports Development and Assets Co Ltd (IPC): POB 20121, 74 Menachem Begin Rd, Tel Aviv 6721516; tel. 3-5657070; e-mail dovf@israports.co.il; internet www.israports.co.il; f. 1961 as the Israel Ports Authority (PRA); the IPC was established by legislation in 2005 as part of the Israeli Port Reform Program, whereby the PRA was abolished and replaced by four govt-owned cos: the IPC as owner and developer of port and infrastructure, and three port-operating cos responsible for handling cargo in each of Israel's three commercial seaports; responsible for devt and management of Israel's port infrastructure on behalf of the Govt and carries out some of the largest infrastructure projects in the country; CEO ISAAC BLUMENTHAL.

Ashdod Port Co Ltd: POB 9001, Ashdod 77191; tel. 8-8517799; fax 8-8517632; e-mail igalbz@ashdodport.co.il; internet www.ashdodport.co.il; provides full range of freight and passenger services; f. 1965; Chair. ORNA HOZMAN BECHOR; CEO MOSHE COHEN.

Eilat Port Company Ltd: Eilat; tel. (8) 6358332; internet www.eilatport.co.il; f. 2004; CEO GIDEON GOLBER.

Haifa Port Co Ltd: POB 33539, Haifa 3133401; tel. 4-8518666; fax 4-8667938; internet www.haifaport.co.il; 6.5-km dock, 10.5 m–15.2 m draught; f. 1933; CEO MENDI ZALTZMAN.

Principal Shipping Companies

XT Shipping: POB 15090, 9 Andre Saharov St, Matam Park, Haifa 31905; tel. 4-8610610; fax 4-8501515; e-mail mail@xtholdings.com; internet www.xtholdings.com; f. 1956 as shipping agency, Mediterranean Seaways; fmrly known as Ofer Shipping Group, renamed as above 2012; part of the XT Group; runs cargo and container services; Chair. UDI ANGEL.

ZIM Integrated Shipping Services Ltd: POB 1723, 9 Andrei Sakharov St, Matam Park, Haifa 31016; tel. 4-8652111; fax 4-8652956; internet www.zim.co.il; f. 1945; 100% owned by the Israel Corpn; international integrated transportation system providing

ISRAEL

door-to-door services around the world; operates about 85 vessels; Chair. of Bd YAIR SEROUSSI; Pres. and CEO ELI GLICKMAN.

CIVIL AVIATION

The principal airport is Ben Gurion International Airport, situated about 15 km from the centre of Tel Aviv. The busiest domestic airports are located at Timna, Haifa and Rosh Pina. Ramon International Airport, at Timna, north of Eilat, was inaugurated in January 2019. The facility replaced the existing airports at Eilat and Ovda for civilian traffic in March.

Israel Airports Authority: POB 137, Ben Gurion Airport, Tel Aviv 70150; tel. 3-9723333; fax 3-9752387; e-mail contactus@iaa.gov.il; internet www.iaa.gov.il; f. 1977; Chair. ELIEZER MARUM; Dir-Gen. YAAKOV GANOT.

Arkia Israeli Airlines Ltd: POB 39301, Dov Airport, Tel Aviv 61392; tel. 3-6903712; e-mail customer.service@arkia.co.il; internet www.arkia.co.il; f. 1980 by merger of Kanaf-Arkia Airlines and Aviation Services; scheduled passenger services linking Tel Aviv, Jerusalem, Haifa, Eilat, Rosh Pina, Kiryat Shmona and Yotveta; charter services to many European destinations, Türkiye (Turkey) and Jordan; CEO YARON AMZALEG.

El Al Israel Airlines Ltd: POB 41, Ben Gurion Airport, Tel Aviv 70150; tel. 3-9771111; fax 3-7602233; e-mail customer@elal.co.il; internet www.elal.co.il; f. 1948; over 42% owned by Eli Zachary Rozenberg; about 14% state-owned; regular services to many European cities, as well as to destinations in North and South America, Africa and Asia; Chair. of Bd (vacant); Pres. and CEO DINA BEN TAL GANANCIA.

Israir Airlines: POB 26444, 23 Ben Yehuda St, Tel Aviv 63806; tel. 3-7969213; fax 3-7954051; internet www.israir.co.il; f. 1996; domestic flights between Tel Aviv and Eilat, and international flights to destinations in Europe and the USA; Pres. and CEO URI SIRKIS.

Tourism

Ministry of Tourism: see Ministries; Dir-Gen. DANI SHAHAR.

Defence

As assessed at November 2022, the Israel Defense Forces comprised 169,500 personnel: army 126,000 (100,000 conscripts); navy 9,500 (2,500 conscripts); air force 34,000. There were also 465,000 reserves and a paramilitary force of 8,000. Military service is compulsory for Jewish and Druze citizens (with certain exceptions), while Christians, Circassians and Muslims may serve as volunteers. Officers are conscripted for regular service of 48 months, male soldiers for 30 months and female soldiers for 24 months. Annual reserve training is undertaken thereafter, up to 40 years of age for men (54 years for some specialists) and 38 years (with exemptions for marriage/pregnancy) for women.

Defence Budget: NIS 63,900m. in 2022.

Chief of Staff of the Israel Defense Forces: Maj.-Gen. HERZL 'HERZI' HALEVI.

Chief of Ground Forces Command: Maj.-Gen. TAMIR YADAI.

Commander-in-Chief of the Air Force: Maj.-Gen. TOMER BAR.

Commander-in-Chief of the Navy: Vice-Adm. DAVID SAAR SALAMA.

Education

Free, compulsory education is provided for all children between five and 15 years of age. Since 2012 pre-primary education has been provided free of charge in public institutions for children aged three and four years. Primary education is provided for all those between five and 10 years of age. There is also secondary, vocational and agricultural education. Post-primary education comprises two cycles of three years. According to UNESCO estimates, enrolment at primary schools in 2019/20 included 99.5% of children in the relevant age-group, while the comparable rate for lower secondary schools was 99.9%. Enrolment at upper secondary schools in 2018/19 included 98% of children in the relevant age-group. There are several universities, as well as the Technion (Israel Institute of Technology) in Haifa and the Weizmann Institute of Science in Rehovot. In 2020 expenditure on education was equivalent to 15.6% of total government spending, according to UNESCO figures.

OCCUPIED TERRITORIES

EAST JERUSALEM

LOCATION

Greater Jerusalem includes: Israeli West Jerusalem (99% Jewish); the Old City and Mount of Olives; East Jerusalem (the Palestinian residential and commercial centre); Arab villages declared to be part of Jerusalem by Israel in 1967; and Jewish neighbourhoods constructed since 1967, either on land expropriated from Arab villages or in areas requisitioned as 'government land'. Although the area of the Greater Jerusalem district is 627 sq km, the Old City of Jerusalem covers just 1 sq km.

DEMOGRAPHY

Immediately prior to the 1967 Arab–Israeli War, East Jerusalem and its Arab environs had an Arab population of approximately 70,000, and a small Jewish population in the old Jewish quarter of the city. By contrast, Israeli West Jerusalem had a Jewish population of 196,000. As a result of this imbalance, in the Greater Jerusalem district as a whole the Jewish population was in the majority. Israeli policy following the occupation of East Jerusalem and the West Bank consisted of encircling the eastern sector of the city with Jewish settlements. Official statistics for 31 December 2021 reported that Greater Jerusalem had a total population of 1,209,700, of whom 802,400 were Jews, 375,800 were Muslims and 17,100 were Christians. The Jerusalem Institute for Policy Research (JIPR—formerly the Jerusalem Institute for Israel Studies) estimated in 2021 that the population of Greater Jerusalem was 61% Jewish and 39% Arab; the growth rate for the Arab population was some 2.5%, compared with a rate of 1.2% for the Jewish population. The Old City, within the walls of which are found the ancient quarters of the Jews, Christians, Muslims and Armenians, is predominantly Arab. According to the JIPR, the Old City had a total population of 30,410 in 2021 (a decline of 2.3% from the previous year).

ADMINISTRATION

Until the 1967 Arab–Israeli War, Jerusalem had been divided into the new city of West Jerusalem—captured by Jewish forces in 1948— and the old city, East Jerusalem, which was part of Jordan. Israel's victory in 1967, however, reunited the city under Israeli control. On 28 June Israeli law was applied to East Jerusalem and the municipal boundaries were extended by 45 km (28 miles). Jerusalem had effectively been annexed. Israeli officials, however, still refer to the 'reunification' of Jerusalem.

Immediately following the occupation, all electricity, water and telephone grids in West Jerusalem were extended to the east. Roads were widened and cleared, and the Arab population immediately in front of the 'Wailing Wall' was forcibly evicted. Arabs living in East Jerusalem became 'permanent residents' and could apply for Israeli citizenship (in contrast to Arabs in the West Bank and Gaza Strip). However, few chose to do so. None the less, the Arab residents were taxed by the Israeli authorities, and their businesses and banks became subject to Israeli laws and regulations. Now controlling approximately one-half of all land in East Jerusalem and the surrounding Palestinian villages, the Israeli authorities allowed Arabs to construct buildings on only 10%–15% of the land in the city, and East Jerusalem's commercial district was limited to three streets.

In May 1999 the Israeli Government refused to grant Israeli citizenship to several hundred Arabs living in East Jerusalem, despite their compliance with the terms of the Citizenship Law. In October, however, Israel ended its policy of revoking the right of Palestinians to reside in Jerusalem if they had spent more than seven years outside the city. Moreover, the Israeli Government announced in March 2000 that Palestinian residents of Jerusalem whose identity cards had been revoked could apply for their restoration.

At the Camp David talks held between Israel and the Palestinian (National) Authority (PA) in July 2000, the issue of sovereignty over East Jerusalem in a future 'permanent status' agreement was the principal obstacle to achieving a peace deal. The Israeli Government had reportedly offered the PA municipal autonomy over certain areas (including access to the Islamic holy sites), although sovereignty would remain in Israeli hands; the proposals were rejected by PA President Yasser Arafat. In September the holy sites of East Jerusalem were the initial focal point of a renewed uprising by Palestinians against the Israeli authorities, which was called the al-Aqsa *intifada* (after Jerusalem's al-Aqsa mosque). The publication of the internationally sponsored 'roadmap' in April 2003 offered directions for peace talks on Jerusalem, but progress was halted by renewed Palestinian attacks on Israeli citizens and Israeli counter-attacks.

In November 2007 the Israeli Prime Minister, Ehud Olmert, and the PA President, Mahmoud Abbas, attended an international Middle East peace conference held in Annapolis, USA. In February 2008 the Israeli premier declared that the final status of Jerusalem, and the key demand by the Palestinians that East Jerusalem become their capital, would be the last 'core issue' to be negotiated. Meanwhile, the Israeli Government continued to contravene its roadmap obligations by issuing tenders for hundreds of new housing units in Jewish settlements in East Jerusalem and the West Bank.

The Administration of US President Barack Obama, who was inaugurated in January 2009, demanded a temporary halt to Israel's settlement building programme as a precondition for resuming negotiations. However, although in November the Israeli Government imposed a 10-month moratorium on settlement building in the West Bank, building activity in East Jerusalem was exempted. Upon the expiry of the moratorium in September 2010, the PA suspended its involvement in the peace process, demanding that the Israeli Government end both settlement construction and the blockade of Gaza.

Israel accelerated its settlement programme in East Jerusalem and the West Bank following the PA's admission in October 2011 as a full member of the United Nations Educational, Scientific and Cultural Organization (UNESCO), and, again, after the UN General Assembly's decision in November 2012 to upgrade the PA's status to that of a non-member observer state.

Following intense US diplomacy, formal discussions between Israel and the PA commenced in August 2013. However, in April 2014 Prime Minister Benjamin Netanyahu suspended Israel's participation in the peace process after the announcement of a national unity agreement between Hamas and Fatah (see Palestinian Territories).

In September 2014 the Jerusalem Municipality approved plans for the construction of a new settlement at Givat Hamatos, to the south of the city. This development would complete a band of Jewish settlement housing in East Jerusalem and thus obstruct any future Palestinian state from establishing a capital city there. Despite UN Secretary-General Ban Ki-Moon declaring the proposal 'a clear violation of international law', in October Israel announced further developments in Har Homa and Ramat Shlomo. In July 2016 the Cabinet approved plans to expand the number of homes at Ma'ale Adumim, Ramot and Har Homa. Construction of additional homes for Arab residents of Beit Jalala were also approved. These announcements came despite the international Quartet group (comprising the USA, the Russian Federation, the UN and the European Union) urging a halt to settlement construction in the Arab areas of East Jerusalem and in the West Bank.

UNESCO gave a preliminary endorsement in October 2016 to a PA-sponsored resolution which sought to remove the specific connection between Judaism and the Temple Mount/Haram al-Sharif compound; the decision was widely criticized within Israel. A landmark ruling by Israel's Supreme Court in March 2017 determined that a Palestinian who had been born in East Jerusalem but who had, as a child, moved to the USA and acquired US citizenship could legally have his or her right to reside in the city restored. The Court notably described such Palestinians as 'native-born residents' of Jerusalem. The ruling was expected to lead to similar court cases involving some of the more than 14,500 East Jerusalem Arabs whose residency rights had been removed, often because they had spent over seven years outside the city.

On 6 December 2017 US President Donald Trump, who had succeeded Obama in January, declared that the USA would henceforth recognize Jerusalem as Israel's capital and planned to move the US embassy to the city (it was inaugurated in May 2018). In response, Palestinians announced a general strike and protests took place in East Jerusalem; by 24 December 12 people had died in clashes with Israeli security forces. Meanwhile, on 21 December the UN General Assembly voted overwhelmingly to reject the USA's unilateral declaration, asserting that the final status of Jerusalem could only be decided as part of a comprehensive peace settlement. However, seven other countries backed the new US policy on Jerusalem (see Israel). On 24 December the Israeli Government announced plans to build a further 300,000 new homes in East Jerusalem. The USA's change of policy on Jerusalem led to a further expansion of Israel's settlement activity in East Jerusalem and the West Bank during 2018–20, prompting the UN Secretary-General, António Guterres, in January 2021 to insist that the Government 'halt and reverse' its settlement building in order to guarantee a 'just, lasting and comprehensive peace'. However, from mid-2023, two-and-a-half years after the inauguration of US President Joe Biden (who stated that he planned to keep the US embassy in Jerusalem), the Israeli settlement programme was actually to be accelerated.

The PA had firmly rejected a new US plan for ending the Israeli–Palestinian conflict and achieving peace in the Middle East, published in January 2020 (see Israel), partly because the plan described Jerusalem as 'Israel's undivided capital'. The long-awaited US proposals did, however, indicate that parts of East Jerusalem would constitute the capital of a future Palestinian state.

Following the formation of a new, right-wing Israeli Government under Netanyahu on 29 December 2022, a UN resolution was adopted on 31 December requesting the International Court of Justice (ICJ) to give its advisory opinion on the legal implications of Israel's occupation of Palestinian territories. The resolution also asked the ICJ to consider actions taken by Israel 'aimed at altering the demographic composition, character and status' of Jerusalem. There was an intensification of Israeli–Palestinian violence, including in East Jerusalem, in early 2023. Following several fatal incidents between Palestinians and Jewish settlers in the West Bank, tensions between the two communities remained high at the end of August.

In early September 2023 Papua New Guinea became the fifth country to open a full embassy in Jerusalem (see above), after the USA, Guatemala, Honduras and Kosovo.

THE GOLAN HEIGHTS

LOCATION AND CLIMATE

The Golan Heights, a mountainous plateau that formed most of the Syrian Arab Republic's Quneitra Province (1,710 sq km) and parts of Dar'a Province, was occupied by Israel after the Arab–Israeli War of June 1967. Following the Disengagement Agreement of 1974, Israel continued to occupy some 70% of the territory (1,176 sq km), valued for its strategic position and abundant water resources (the headwaters of the Jordan river have their source on the slopes of Mount Hermon). The average height of the Golan is approximately 1,200 m above sea level in the northern region and about 300 m above sea level in the southern region, near Lake Tiberias (the Sea of Galilee). Rainfall ranges from around 1,000 mm per year in the north to less than 600 mm per year in the south.

Demography

As a consequence of the Israeli occupation, an estimated 93% of the ethnically diverse Syrian population of 147,613, distributed across 163 villages and towns and 108 individual farms, was expelled. The majority were Arab Sunni Muslims, but the population also included Alawite and Druze minorities and some Circassians, Turkmen, Armenians and Kurds. Approximately 9,000 Palestinian refugees from the 1948 Arab–Israeli War also inhabited the area. At the time of the occupation, 64% of the labour force was employed in agriculture. Only one-fifth of the population resided in the administrative centres. By 1991 the Golan Heights had a Jewish population of about 12,000 living in 21 Jewish settlements (four new settlements had been created by the end of 1992), and a predominantly Druze population of some 16,000 living in the only six remaining villages, of which Majd al-Shams is by far the largest. According to official figures, on 31 December 2021 the Golan Heights had a total population of 53,700, of whom 24,800 were Jews, 2,800 were Muslims and 24,100 Druze.

Administration

Prior to the Israeli occupation, the Golan Heights were incorporated by Syria into a provincial administration of which the city of Quneitra, then with a population of 27,378, was the capital. The Disengagement Agreement mediated by US Secretary of State Henry Kissinger in 1974 (after the 1973 Arab–Israeli War) provided for the withdrawal of Israeli forces from Quneitra. Before withdrawal, however, Israeli army engineers destroyed the city. In December 1981 the Knesset enacted the Golan Annexation Law, whereby Israeli civilian legislation was extended to the territory of Golan, now administered by the Commissioner for the Northern District of Israel. The Arab-Druze community responded by declaring a strike and appealed to the UN Secretary-General to force Israel to rescind the annexation decision. At the seventh round of multilateral talks between Israeli and Arab delegations in Washington, DC, USA, in August 1992, the Israeli Government of Itzhak Rabin for the first time accepted that UN Security Council Resolution 242, adopted in 1967, applied to the Golan Heights. In January 1999 the Knesset approved legislation stating that any transfer of land under Israeli sovereignty (referring to the Golan Heights and East Jerusalem) must be approved by both an absolute majority of Knesset members and by the Israeli electorate at a national referendum. Following the election of Ehud Barak as Israel's Prime Minister in May, peace negotiations with Syria were resumed in December. However, in January 2000 the talks were postponed indefinitely after Syria demanded a written commitment from Israel to withdraw from the Golan. In July 2001 Ariel Sharon, the new Israeli premier, stated that Israel's occupation of the territory was 'irreversible'.

In May 2008 Israel and Syria confirmed that indirect negotiations aimed at concluding a 'comprehensive peace' were being held through Turkish intermediaries in Istanbul. By August four rounds of discussions had taken place. Yet despite subsequent claims by Syrian President Bashar al-Assad that Israel and Syria were within 'touching distance' of an agreement, a fifth round of the Turkish-mediated talks, scheduled for September, was delayed owing to the political uncertainty in Israel following Ehud Olmert's resignation as premier. Moreover, President Assad formally suspended the dialogue in December, following an Israeli military incursion into the Gaza Strip. In November 2009 the Knesset approved legislation stating that any Israeli withdrawal from the Golan Heights would require the prior endorsement of Israeli voters in a referendum.

Hopes of further progress towards a resumption of direct negotiations were put on hold following the onset of the popular uprising in Syria (q.v.) in early 2011. In May Israeli troops clashed with hundreds of pro-Palestinian protesters who had broken through a security fence to enter the Golan Heights from Syria. Syrian state media reported in June that 12 Palestinians and two Syrians had been killed when Israeli soldiers opened fire at another group of protesters. The Israeli authorities accused the Assad Government of orchestrating the violence to divert international attention from its harsh crackdown on Syrian opposition activists.

From late 2012, with the Syrian domestic unrest having descended into civil conflict, fears increased that the violence could spill over into the Golan Heights. In November a campaign by Syria against opposition fighters located near the border resulted in mortar shells landing close to Israeli army posts in the north of the territory, prompting Israeli retaliatory attacks on Syrian government positions. Similar incidents were reported during 2013, and several soldiers from the UN Disengagement Observer Force (UNDOF) were abducted by Syrian militant groups.

Exchanges of artillery, mortar and gunfire between Syrian and Israeli troops continued sporadically. In June 2014 Israel launched strikes against strategic targets inside Syria, in response to an attack that had caused the death of an Israeli teenager in the Golan Heights, while in April 2015 up to four people were reportedly killed in an Israeli air strike at the border between the territory and Syria. It was alleged that those targeted had been transporting an explosive device towards the border with the intent to kill Israeli military personnel. In September 2017 Israel claimed that its armed forces had shot down an unmanned aerial vehicle (drone) over the Golan Heights, alleging that it had been supplied by Iran to Hezbollah for espionage purposes. The situation deteriorated in February 2018, after Israel shot down another alleged Iranian drone and an Israeli fighter plane was subsequently brought down by Syrian anti-aircraft weaponry as it participated in air strikes against Syrian and Iranian targets inside Syria.

In another dramatic change of US foreign policy, on 25 March 2019 the Administration of US President Donald Trump formally recognized Israeli sovereignty over the Golan Heights (see Israel). This unilateral declaration prompted a strong response both internationally and from Syrian government officials, who called it 'irresponsible' and expressed their increased determination to return the territory to Syrian control. Meanwhile, amid heightened tensions across the region, in June Israel responded to rocket fire launched from Syria onto Mount Hermon by attacking Hezbollah and Iranian military positions in southern Syria; three Syrian soldiers and seven foreign fighters were reportedly killed in the Israeli air raids. In November 2020 Israel conducted renewed air strikes against Syrian and Iranian military targets within Syria, after the discovery of several roadside bombs along the Golan border. The number of fatalities in the raids was disputed by Syrian government officials and independent sources. Further such incidents in the area of the Golan Heights continued to be reported during 2021–23. In early April 2023 six rockets apparently fired from Syria towards the Golan prompted Israeli forces to launch air strikes against purported militant targets close to the Syrian capital, Damascus.

On 26 December 2021 the Israeli Government headed by Prime Minister Naftali Bennett approved a controversial plan to double the Israeli population of the Golan Heights to 100,000 by 2025. The proposals, which included the creation of two new Jewish settlements (each comprising some 2,000 homes), were denounced by both the Syrian Government and environmental protection groups.

Bibliography

General and Historical Context

Abu-Baker, Khawla, and Rabinowitz, Dan. *Coffins on Our Shoulders: The Experience of the Palestinian Citizens of Israel.* Berkeley, CA, University of California Press, 2005.

Adler, Emanuel (Ed.). *Israel in the World: Legitimacy and Exceptionalism.* Abingdon, Routledge, 2012.

Allon, Yigal. *The Making of Israel's Army.* London, Vallentine, Mitchell, 1970.

Atashe, Zeidan. *Druze and Jews in Israel: A Shared Destiny?* Eastbourne, Sussex Academic Press, 1995.

Ben-Porat, Guy, Feniger, Yariv, Filc, Dani, Kabalo, Paula, and Mirsky, Julia (Eds). *Routledge Handbook on Contemporary Israel.* Abingdon, Routledge, 2022.

Bentwich, Norman. *Fulfilment in the Promised Land 1917–37.* London, 1938.

Israel Resurgent. Ernest Benn, 1960.

Israel, Two Fateful Years 1967–69. London, Elek, 1970.

Bethell, Nicholas. *The Palestine Triangle: The Struggle Between the British, the Jews and the Arabs, 1935–48.* London, André Deutsch, 1979.

Black, Ian, and Morris, Benny. *Israel's Secret Wars: History of Israel's Intelligence Services.* New York, Grove Weidenfeld, 1992.

The Palestine Question. London, Croom Helm; New York, Methuen, 1987.

Breger, Marshall J., and Hammer, Leonard M. *The Contest and Control of Jerusalem's Holy Sites: A Historical Guide to Legality, Status, and Ownership.* Cambridge, Cambridge University Press, 2023.

Cohen, Mark R., and Udovitch, Abraham L. *Jews among Arabs: Contacts and Boundaries.* Princeton, NJ, The Darwin Press, 1994.

Crossman, R. H. S. *Palestine Mission.* London, 1947.

A Nation Reborn. London, Hamish Hamilton, 1960.

Davis, Moshe (Ed.). *Israel: Its Role in Civilisation.* New York, 1956.

Dayan, Shmuel. *The Promised Land.* London, 1961.

Dershowitz, Alan. *The Case for Israel.* Indianapolis, IN, John Wiley & Sons, 2004.

Dumper, Michael (Ed.). *Arab-Israeli Conflict.* Abingdon, Routledge, 2009.

El-Eini, Roza I. M. *Mandated Landscape: British Imperial Rule in Palestine, 1929–1948.* Abingdon, Routledge, 2006.

Ellis, Mark H. *Beyond Innocence and Redemption: Confronting the Holocaust and Israeli Power.* San Francisco, CA, Harper and Row, 1990.

Esco Foundation for Palestine. *Palestine: A Study of Jewish, Arab and British Policies.* 2 vols, New Haven, CT, 1947.

Gat, Moshe. *The Arab–Israeli Conflict, 1956–1975: From Violent Conflict to a Peace Process.* Abingdon, Routledge, 2017.

Grinberg, Lev Luis. *Politics and Violence in Israel/Palestine: Democracy versus Military Rule.* Abingdon, Routledge, 2009.

Heller, Joseph. *The Stern Gang: Ideology, Politics and Terror 1940–49.* London, Frank Cass, 1995.

Hersh, Seymour. *The Samson Option: Israel, America and the Bomb.* London, Faber and Faber, 1991.

Inbar, Efraim. *Israel's National Security Issues and Challenges Since the Yom Kippur War.* Abingdon, Routledge, 2008.

Jiryis, Sabri. *The Arabs in Israel.* Beirut, Institute for Palestine Studies, 1968.

Khalidi, Walid. *From Haven to Conquest: Readings in Zionism and the Palestine Problem until 1948.* Beirut, Institute for Palestine Studies, 1971.

Koestler, Arthur. *Thieves in the Night.* New York and London, 1946.

Promise and Fulfilment: Palestine, 1917–1949. London, 1949.

The Thirteenth Tribe. London, Random House, 1976.

Küntzel, M. *Nazis, Islamic Antisemitism and the Middle East: The 1948 Arab War against Israel and the Aftershocks of World War II.* London, Routledge, 2023.

Lochery, N. *View From the Fence: The Arab–Israeli Conflict from the Present to its Roots.* New York, Continuum, 2005.

Lomsky-Feder, Edna, and Orna Sasson-Levy. *Women Soldiers and Citizenship in Israel: Gendered Encounters with the State.* Abingdon, Routledge, 2017.

Lorch, N. *The Edge of the Sword: Israel's War of Independence 1947–49.* New York, Putnam, 1961.

Mahler, Gregory S. *Bibliography of Israeli Politics.* Abingdon, Routledge, 2022.

Marmorstein, Emile. *Heaven at Bay: The Jewish Kulturkampf in the Holy Land.* Oxford, Oxford University Press, 1969.

Ohana, David. *Birth-Throes of the Israeli Homeland: The Concept of Moledet.* Abingdon, Routledge, 2020.

Pappé, Ilan. *The Making of the Arab-Israeli Conflict 1947–1951*, Revised edn. London, I. B. Tauris, 2015.

Parfitt, Tudor (Ed.). *Israel and Ishmael: Studies in Muslim–Jewish Relations.* London, RoutledgeCurzon, 1999.

Parkes, J. W. *The Emergence of the Jewish Problem, 1878–1939.* Oxford, 1946.

A History of Palestine from AD 135 to Modern Times. London, Gollancz, 1949.

End of Exile. New York, 1954.

Whose Land? A History of the Peoples of Palestine. Harmondsworth, Pelican, 1970.

Patai, R. *Israel Between East and West.* Philadelphia, PA, 1953.

Culture and Conflict. New York, 1962.

Rabinovich, Itamar. *Yitzhak Rabin: Soldier, Leader, Statesman.* New Haven, CT, Yale University Press, 2017.

Rabinovich, Itamar, and Reinharz, Jehuda (Eds). *Israel in the Middle East: Documents and Readings on Society, Politics, and Foreign Relations, pre-1948 to the Present.* Waltham, MA, Brandeis University Press, 2007.

Rodman, David. *Israel in the 1973 Yom Kippur War: Diplomacy, Battle, and Lessons.* Brighton, Sussex Academic Press, 2017.

Royal Institute of International Affairs. *Great Britain and Palestine 1915–45.* London, 1946.

Sachar, Howard M. *The Peoples of Israel.* New York, 1962.

Safran, Alexandre. *Israël et ses racines.* Paris, Editions Albin Michel, 2001.

Schwarz, Tanya. *Ethiopian Jewish Immigrants in Israel.* London, RoutledgeCurzon, 1999.

Seikaly, May. *Haifa: Transformation of an Arab Society, 1918–1939.* London, I. B. Tauris, 2001.

Sheffer, Gabriel, and Barak, Oren (Eds). *Militarism and Israeli Society.* Bloomington, IN, Indiana University Press, 2010.

Stendel, Ori. *The Arabs in Israel.* Eastbourne, Sussex Academic Press, 1996.

Summerfield, Daniel. *From Falashas to Ethiopian Jews.* London, RoutledgeCurzon, 1999.

Zander, Walter. *Israel and the Holy Places of Christendom.* Weidenfeld and Nicolson, 1972.

Contemporary Political History

Achcar, Gilbert, and Warschawski, Michel. *The 33-Day War: Israel's War on Hezbollah in Lebanon and Its Aftermath.* London, Saqi Books, 2007.

Alimi, Eitan Y. *Israeli Politics and the First Palestinian Intifada: Political Opportunities, Framing Processes and Contentious Politics.* Abingdon, Routledge, 2009.

Alpher, Joseph. *Periphery: Israel's Search for Middle East Allies.* Lanham, MD, Rowman & Littlefield Publishers, 2015.

Arian, Asher. *Politics in Israel: The Second Republic* (2nd edn). Washington, DC, CQ Press, 2004.

Avi-hai, Avraham. *Ben Gurion, State Builder.* Israel Universities Press, 1974.

Badi, Joseph. *Fundamental Laws of the State of Israel.* New York, 1961.

Barak, Ehud. *My Life, My Country: Fighting for Israel, Searching for Peace.* London, Macmillan, 2018.

Barari, Hassan. A. *Israeli Politics and the Middle East Peace Process, 1988–2002.* London, RoutledgeCurzon, 2004.

Ben Gurion, D. *Rebirth and Destiny of Israel.* New York, 1954.

Israel: A Personal History. London, New English Library, 1972.

Ben-Porat, Guy, et al. *Israel Since 1980.* Cambridge, Cambridge University Press, 2009.

Bergman, Ronen. *Rise and Kill First: the Secret History of Israel's Targeted Assassinations.* New York, Random House, 2018.

Bialer, Uri. *Israeli Foreign Policy: A People Shall Not Dwell Alone.* Bloomington, IN, Indiana University Press, 2020.

Bickerton, Ian J., and Klausner, Carla L. *A History of the Arab–Israeli Conflict.* Abingdon, Routledge, 2022.

Bregman, Ahron. *A History of Israel*. New York, Palgrave Macmillan, 2003.

Cohen, Amichai, and Cohen, Stuart. *Israel's National Security Law: Political Dynamics and Historical Development*. Abingdon, Routledge, 2011.

Cohen, Samy (trans. Lehrer, Natasha, and Schoch, Cynthia). *Doves Among Hawks: Struggles of the Israeli Peace Movements*. London, C. Hurst & Co, 2019.

Cohen, Stuart, and Klieman, Aharon (Eds). *The Routledge Handbook on Israeli Security*. Abingdon, Routledge, 2018.

Cohen, Yoel. *The Whistleblower of Dimona: Israel, Vanunu, and the Bomb*. New York, Holmes and Meier, 2003.

Cohen-Almagor, Raphael (Ed.). *Israeli Democracy at the Crossroads*. Abingdon, Routledge, 2005.

De Gaury, Gerald. *The New State of Israel*. New York, 1952.

Del Sarto, Raffaella. *Israel under Siege: the Politics of Insecurity and the Rise of the Israeli Neo-revisionist Right*. Washington, DC, Georgetown University Press, 2017.

Dieckhoff, Alain (Ed.) (trans. Shread, Carolyn). *The Routledge Handbook of Modern Israel*. Abingdon, Routledge, 2013.

Doron, Gideon, Naor, Arye, and Meydani, Assaf (Eds). *Law and Government in Israel*. Abingdon, Routledge, 2010.

Eban, Abba. *The Voice of Israel*. New York, Horizon Press, 1957.

Eilam, Ehud. *Israel, the Arabs and Iran: International Relations and Status Quo, 2011-2016*. Abingdon, Routledge, 2017.

Enderlin, Charles. *Le rêve brisé, histoire de l'échec du processus de paix au Proche-Orient, 1995-2002*. Paris, Editions Fayard, 2002.

Faris, Hani A. (Ed.). *The Failure of the Two-State Solution: The Prospects of One State in the Israel-Palestine Conflict*. London, I. B. Tauris, 2013.

Filc, Dani. *The Political Right in Israel: Different Faces of Jewish Populism*. Abingdon, Routledge, 2009.

Fraser, T. G. *The Arab–Israeli Conflict*. London, Palgrave Macmillan, 2004.

Freedman, Robert O. (Ed.). *Contemporary Israel: Domestic Politics, Foreign Policy, and Security Challenges*. Boulder, CO, Westview Press, 2008.

(Ed.). *Israel Under Netanyahu: Domestic Politics and Foreign Policy*. London, Routledge, 2019.

Freilich, Charles D. *Zion's Dilemmas: How Israel Makes National Security Policy*. Ithaca, NY, Cornell University Press, 2012.

Israeli National Security: a New Strategy for an Era of Change. New York, Oxford University Press, 2018.

Gerstenfeld, Manfred, Sandler, Shmuel, and Frisch, Hillel (Eds). *Israel at the Polls 2009*. Abingdon, Routledge, 2010.

Ghanem, As'ad, and Mustafa, Mohanad. *Palestinians in Israel: The Politics of Faith After Oslo*. Cambridge, Cambridge University Press, 2018.

Gilboa, Eytan, and Inba, Efraim (Eds). *US-Israeli Relations in a New Era: Issues and Challenges after 9/11*. Abingdon, Routledge, 2008.

Gluska, Ami. *The Israeli Military and the Origins of the 1967 War: Government, Armed Forces and Defence Policy 1963-67*. Abingdon, Routledge, 2009.

Golan, Galia. *Israeli Peacemaking since 1967: Factors Behind the Breakthroughs and Failures*. Abingdon, Routledge, 2015.

Hirschhorn, Sara Yael. *City on a Hilltop: American Jews and the Israeli Settler Movement*. Cambridge, Harvard University Press, 2017.

Hollis, Rosemary. *Israel on the Brink of Decision: Division, Unity and Cross-currents in the Israeli Body Politic*. London, Research Institute for the Study of Conflict and Terrorism, 1990.

Hussein, Cherine. *The Re-Emergence of the Single State Solution in Palestine-Israel: Countering an Illusion*. Abingdon, Routledge, 2015.

Jamal, Amal. *Arab Minority Nationalism in Israel: The Politics of Indigeneity*. Abingdon, Routledge, 2014.

Janowsky, Oscar I. *Foundations of Israel: Emergence of a Welfare State*. Princeton, NJ, Anvil Nostrand Co, 1959.

Jones, Clive, and Catignani, Sergio (Eds). *Israel and Hizbollah: An Asymmetric Conflict in Historical and Comparative Perspective*. Abingdon, Routledge, 2009.

Kader, Razzak Abdel, and Karsh, Efraim (Ed.). *Israel: The First Hundred Years, Vol. 1. Israel's Transition from Community to State*. London, Frank Cass, 2000.

(Ed.). *Israel: The First Hundred Years, Vol. 2. From War to Peace?* London, Frank Cass, 2000.

(Ed.). *Israel: The First Hundred Years, Vol. 3. Israeli Politics and Society since 1948. Problems of Collective Identity*. London, Frank Cass, 2001.

Karsh, Efraim, and Miller, Rory (Eds). *Israel at Sixty: Rethinking the Birth of the Jewish State*. Abingdon, Routledge, 2008.

Karsh, Efraim, Kerr, Michael, and Miller, Rory (Eds). *Conflict, Diplomacy and Society in Israeli-Lebanese Relations*. Abingdon, Routledge, 2010.

Kaye, Dalia Dassa. *Beyond the Handshake: Multilateral Co-operation in the Arab-Israeli Peace Process, 1991-96*. New York, Columbia University Press, 2001.

Kober, Avi. *Israel's Wars of Attrition: Attrition Challenges to Democratic States*. Abingdon, Routledge, 2009.

The Israel-Arab Reader. London, Weidenfeld and Nicolson, 1969.

Laron, Guy. *The Six-Day War: the Breaking of the Middle East*. New Haven, Yale University Press, 2017.

Lazin, A., and Mahler, G. S. *Israel in the Nineties: Development and Conflict*. University Press of Florida, 1996.

Leshem, Noam. *Life after Ruin: the Struggles over Israel's Depopulated Arab Spaces*. Cambridge, MA, Cambridge University Press, 2017.

Leslie, Jonathan G. *Fear and Insecurity: Israel and the Iran Threat Narrative*. Oxford, Oxford University Press, 2023.

Levran, Aharon. *Israeli Strategy after Desert Storm: Lessons of the Second Gulf War*. London, Frank Cass, 1997.

Likhovski, Eliahu S. *Israel's Parliament: The Law of the Knesset*. Oxford, Clarendon Press, 1971.

Lucas, Noah. *The Modern History of Israel*. London, Weidenfeld and Nicolson, 1974-75.

Mazie, Steven V. *Israel's Higher Law: Religion and Liberal Democracy in the Jewish State*. Lanham, MD, Lexington Books, 2006.

Medding, Peter Y. *Mapai in Israel: Political Organization and Government in a New Society*. Cambridge, Cambridge University Press, 2010.

Meir, Golda. *This is our Strength*. New York, 1963.

Merhav, Peretz. *The Israeli Left: History, Problems, Documents*. Tantivy Press, 1981.

Morris, Benny. *1948: A History of the First Arab–Israeli War*. New Haven, CT, Yale University Press, 2008.

Netanyahu, Benjamin. *A Durable Peace: Israel and Its Place Among the Nations*. New York, Warner Books, 2000.

Nusseibeh, Sari, and Heller, Mark A. *No Trumpets, No Drums: A Two-State Settlement of the Israeli–Palestinian Conflict*. London, I. B. Tauris, 1992.

O'Ballance, E. *The Arab–Israeli War*. New York, Praeger, 1957.

The Third Arab–Israeli War. London, Faber and Faber, 1972.

Oren, Michael B. *Six Days of War: June 1967 and the Making of the Modern Middle East*. Oxford University Press, 2002.

Oren, Neta. *Israel's National Identity: The Changing Ethos of Conflict*. Boulder, CO, Lynne Rienner, 2019.

Orkibi, Eithan, and Gerstenfeld, Manfred. *Israel at the Polls 2015: A Moment of Transformative Stability*. Abingdon, Routledge, 2017.

Pappé, Ilan. *The Forgotten Palestinians: A History of the Palestinians in Israel*. New Haven, CT, Yale University Press, 2011.

Peleg, Ilan, and Waxman, Dov. *Israel's Palestinians: The Conflict Within*. Cambridge, Cambridge University Press, 2011.

Peters, Joel, and Geist Pinfold, Rob (Eds). *Understanding Israel Political, Societal and Security Challenges*. Abingdon, Routledge, 2018.

Penslar, Derek. *Israel in History: The Jewish State in Comparative Perspective*. Abingdon, Routledge, 2006.

Perlmutter, Amos. *Military and Politics in Israel, 1948-1967*. 2nd edn, London, Frank Cass, 1977.

Politics and the Military in Israel, 1967-1976. London, Frank Cass, 1977.

The Times and Life of Menachem Begin. New York, Doubleday, 1987.

Pinfold, Rob Geist. *Understanding Territorial Withdrawal: Israeli Occupations and Exits*. New York, Oxford University Press, 2023.

Plonski, Sharri. *Palestinian Citizens of Israel: Power, Resistance and the Struggle for Space*. London, I. B. Tauris, 2017.

Polakow-Rubenstein, Sasha. *The Unspoken Alliance: Israel's Secret Relationship with Apartheid South Africa*. New York, Pantheon, 2010.

Rabin, Yitzhak. *The Rabin Memoirs*. London, Weidenfeld and Nicolson, 1979.

Rabinovich, Itamar. *Waging Peace: Israel and the Arabs, 1948-2003*. Princeton, NJ, Princeton University Press, 2004.

Rothstein, Robert L., Ma'oz, Moshe, and Shikaki, Khalil (Eds). *The Israeli-Palestinian Peace Process: Oslo and the Lessons of Failure*. Eastbourne, Sussex Academic Press, 2002.

Rouhana, Nadim N., and Huneidi, Sahar S. *Israel and its Palestinian Citizens: Ethnic Privileges in the Jewish State*. Cambridge, Cambridge University Press, 2017.

Sachar, Howard M. *A History of Israel:* Vol. I: *From the Rise of Zionism to Our Time;* Vol. II: *From the Aftermath of the Yom Kippur War*. Corby, Oxford University Press, 1987.

Samaan, Jean-Loup. *Israel's Foreign Policy Beyond the Arab World: Engaging the Periphery*. Abingdon, Routledge, 2017.

Samsonov, Gil. *Netanyahu and Likud's Leaders: The Israeli Princes*. London, Routledge, 2020.

Sandler, Shmuel. *The Jewish Origins of Israeli Foreign Policy: a Study in Tradition and Survival*. Abingdon, Routledge, 2018.

Savir, Uri. *The Process: 1,100 Days that Changed the Middle East*. London, Random House, 1998.

Schiff, Ze'ev, and Ya'ari, Ehud. *Israel's Lebanon War*. New York, NY, Simon & Schuster, 1984.

Intifada: The Palestinian Uprising—Israel's Third Front. London, Simon & Schuster, 1990.

Segev, Tom. *One Palestine, Complete: Jews and Arabs Under the British Mandate*. New York, Metropolitan Books/Henry Holt & Co, 2000.

Shafir, Gershon. *A Half Century of Occupation: Israel, Palestine, and the World's Most Intractable Conflict*. Oakland, CA, University of California Press, 2017.

Shahak, Israel. *Open Secrets: Israeli Foreign and Nuclear Policies*. London, Pluto Press, 1997.

Shahak, Israel, and Mezvinsky, Norton. *Jewish Fundamentalism in Israel*. London, Pluto Press, 2004

Shamir, Michal, and Rahat, Gideon. *The Elections in Israel 2015*. Abingdon, Routledge, 2017.

Shindler, Colin. *A Modern History of Israel*. Cambridge, Cambridge University Press, 2008.

The Hebrew Republic: Israel's Return to History. Lanham, MD, Rowman & Littlefield Publishers, 2017.

Spyer, Jonathan. *The Transforming Fire: The Rise of the Israel-Islamist Conflict*. New York, Continuum, 2011.

Stein, Leslie. *The Making of Modern Israel: 1948–1967*. Cambridge, Polity Press, 2009.

Steinberg, Gerald M., and Rubinovitz, Ziv. *Menachem Begin and the Israel-Egypt Peace Process: Between Ideology and Political Realism* Bloomington, IN, Indiana University Press, 2019.

Tal, David (Ed.). *Israeli Identity: Between Orient and Occident*. New York, Routledge, 2014.

Timerman, Jacob. *The Longest War*. London, Chatto & Windus, 1982.

Yakobson, Alexander, and Rubinstein, Amnon. *Israel and the Family of Nations: The Jewish Nation-State and Human Rights*. Abingdon, Routledge, 2008.

Zionism

Attwell, Katie. *Jewish-Israeli National Identity and Dissidence: the Contradictions of Zionism and Resistance*. Basingstoke, Palgrave Macmillan, 2015.

Avishai, Bernard. *The Tragedy of Zionism*. Farrar, Strauss and Giroux, 1986.

Brenner, Michael. *In Search of Israel: the History of an Idea*. Princeton, NJ, Princeton University Press, 2018.

Cohen, Israel. *A Short History of Zionism*. London, Frederick Muller, 1951.

Engle, Anita. *The Nili Spies*. London, Frank Cass, 1997.

Fisch, Harold. *The Zionist Revolution: A New Perspective*. London, Weidenfeld and Nicolson, 1978.

Frankl, Oscar Benjamin. *Theodor Herzl: The Jew and Man*. New York, 1949.

Herzl, Theodor. *The Jewish State: An Attempt at a Modern Solution of the Jewish Question* (trans.). New York, Dover Publications, 1989.

Huneidi, Sahar. *A Broken Trust: Herbert Samuel, Zionism and the Palestinians*. London, I. B. Tauris, 2001.

Kedourie, Elie, and Kedourie, Sylvia. *Zionism and Arabism in Palestine and Israel (RLE Israel and Palestine)*. Abingdon, Routledge, 2015.

Laqueur, Walter. *A History of Zionism*. London, Weidenfeld and Nicolson, 1972.

Lowenthal, Marvin (Ed. and trans.). *Diaries of Theodor Herzl*. New York, Grosset and Dunlap, 1965.

Mandel, Daniel. *H. V. Evatt and the Establishment of Israel: The Undercover Zionist*. London, Taylor and Francis, 2004.

O'Brien, Conor Cruise. *The Siege: The Saga of Israel and Zionism*. London, Weidenfeld and Nicolson, 1986.

Prior, Michael. *Zionism and the State of Israel: A Moral Inquiry*. London, Routledge, 1999.

Rose, Norman. *Chaim Weizmann*. London, Weidenfeld and Nicolson, 1987.

Rubinstein, Amnon. *From Herzl to Rabin: The Changing Image of Zionism*. New York, Holmes and Meier, 2001.

Schama, Simon. *Two Rothschilds and the Land of Israel*. London, Collins, 1978.

Schechtman, J. *Rebel and Statesman: The Jabotinsky Story*. New York, Thomas Yoseloff, 1956.

Shindler, Colin. *The Triumph of Military Zionism: Nationalism and the Origins of the Israeli Right*. London, I. B. Tauris, 2006.

Sober, Moshe. *Beyond the Jewish State: Confessions of a former Zionist*. Toronto, ON, Summerhill Press, 1990.

Stein, Leonard, and Yogev, Gedilia (Eds). *The Letters and Papers of Chaim Weizmann; Volume I 1885–1902*. Oxford University Press, 1968.

Vital, David. *The Origins of Zionism*. Oxford University Press, 1975, reissued 1980.

Weisgal, Meyer, and Carmichael, Joel. *Chaim Weizmann—a Biography by Several Hands*. London, Weidenfeld and Nicolson, 1962.

Weizmann, Dr Chaim. *The Jewish People and Palestine*. London, 1939.

Trial and Error: The Autobiography of Chaim Weizmann. London, Hamish Hamilton, 1949; New York, Schocken, 1966.

Economy

Aharoni, Yair. *The Israeli Economy: Dreams and Realities*. London, Routledge, 1991.

Ashwarya, Sujata. *Israel's Mediterranean Gas: Domestic Governance, Economic Impact, and Strategic Implications*. New Delhi, Routledge India, 2019.

Haidar, Aziz. *On The Margins: The Arab Population in the Israeli Economy*. Hurst and Co, 1997.

Maman, Daniel, and Rosenhek, Zeev. *The Israeli Central Bank: Political Economy, Global Logics and Local Actors*. Abingdon, Routledge, 2011.

Razin, Assaf. *Israel and the World Economy: The Power of Globalization*. Cambridge, MA, The MIT Press, 2018.

Rubner, Alex. *Economy of Israel*. Abingdon, Routledge, 1960.

Senor, Dan, and Singer, Saul. *Start-Up Nation: The Story of Israel's Economic Miracle*. New York, Twelve Books, 2009.

Shatil, J. *L'économie collective du kibboutz israélien*. Paris, Les Editions de Minuit, 1960.

Official Publications

Annual Yearbook of the Government of Israel.

Government Survey of Palestine. 2 vols, 1945–46, Jerusalem. Supplement, July 1947, Jerusalem.

Jewish Agency for Palestine. Documents Submitted to General Assembly of UN, relating to the National Home, 1947.

The Jewish Plan for Palestine. Jerusalem, 1947.

Statistical Survey of the Middle East. 1944.

Report of the Anglo-American Committee of Enquiry. Lausanne, 1946.

Report of the Palestine Partition Commission, 1938. Cmd 5854, London.

Report of the Palestine Royal Commission, 1937. Cmd 5479, London.

Report of the UN Economic Survey Mission for the Middle East. December 1949, United Nations, Lake Success, NY; HM Stationery Office.

Report to the United Nations General Assembly by the UN Special Committee on Palestine. Geneva, 1947.

Statement of Policy by His Majesty's Government in the United Kingdom. Cmd 3692, London, 1930; Cmd 5893, London, 1938; Cmd 6019, London, 1939; Cmd 6180, London, 1940.

Statistical Abstract of Israel. Central Bureau of Statistics, annual.

Occupied Territories

Armstrong, Karen. *A History of Jerusalem: One City, Three Faiths*. London, HarperCollins, 1997.

El-Assal, Riah Abu (Bishop of Jerusalem). *Caught In Between: The Extraordinary Story of an Arab Palestinian Christian Israeli*. London, SPCK, 1999.

Cattan, Henry. *Jerusalem*. London, Saqi Books, 2000.

Dumper, Michael. *The Politics of Jerusalem since 1967*. New York, Columbia University Press, 1997.

Goldhill, Simon. *The Temple of Jerusalem*. London, Profile Books, 2006.

Klein, Menachem. *Jerusalem: The Contested City*. London, C. Hurst and Co, 2001.

Kollek, Teddy, and Pearlman, Moshe. *Jerusalem, Sacred City of Mankind*. London, Weidenfeld and Nicolson, 1968.

Lundquist, John M. *The Temple of Jerusalem: Past, Present, and Future*. New York, Praeger, 2007.

Pullan, Wendy, et al. *The Struggle for Jerusalem's Holy Places*. Abingdon, Routledge, 2013.

Sebag Montefiore, Simon. *Jerusalem: The Biography*. London, Weidenfeld and Nicolson, 2011.

Shlay, Anne B. *Jerusalem: The Spatial Politics of a Divided Metropolis*. Cambridge, Polity Press, 2015.

JORDAN

Geography

The Hashemite Kingdom of Jordan (previously Transjordan) came officially into existence under its present name in 1947, and was enlarged in 1950 to include the districts of Samaria and part of Judaea that had previously formed part of Arab Palestine. The country is bounded on the north by the Syrian Arab Republic, on the north-east by Iraq, on the east and south by Saudi Arabia, and on the west by Israel and the Palestinian territory in the West Bank. The total area of Jordan is 88,794 sq km (34,284 sq miles). The territory west of the Jordan river (the West Bank)—some 5,633 sq km (2,175 sq miles)—was occupied by Israel in June 1967, but since May 1994 the Palestinian (National) Authority has assumed jurisdiction for civil affairs in some areas. (Jordan severed all legal and administrative links with the territory in July 1988.)

PHYSICAL FEATURES

The greater part of the State of Jordan consists of a plateau lying some 700 m–1,000 m above sea level, which forms the north-western corner of the great plateau of Arabia (see Saudi Arabia). There are no natural topographical frontiers between Jordan and its neighbours Syria, Iraq and Saudi Arabia, and the plateau continues unbroken into all three countries, with the artificial frontier boundaries drawn as straight lines between defined points. Along its western edge, facing the Jordan Valley, the plateau is uptilted to give a line of hills that rise 300 m–700 m above plateau level. An old river course, the Wadi Sirhan, now almost dry with only occasional wells, fractures the plateau surface on the south-east and continues into Saudi Arabia.

The Jordanian plateau consists of a core or table of ancient rocks, covered by layers of newer rock (chiefly limestone) lying almost horizontally. In a few places (e.g. on the southern edge of the Jordan Valley) these old rocks are exposed at the surface. On its western side the plateau has been fractured and dislocated by the development of strongly marked tear faults that run from the Red Sea via the Gulf of Aqaba northwards to Lebanon and Syria. The narrow zone between the faults has sunk, to give the well-known Jordan rift valley, which is bordered both on the east and west by steep-sided walls, especially in the south near the Dead Sea, where the drop is often precipitous. The valley has a maximum width of 22 km and is now thought to have been produced by lateral shearing of two continental plates that on the east have been displaced by about 80 km.

The floor of the Jordan Valley varies considerably in level. At its northern end it is just above sea level; the surface of Lake Tiberias (the Sea of Galilee) is 209 m below sea level, with the deepest part of the lake over 200 m lower still. The greatest depth of the valley is at the Dead Sea (surface 400 m below sea level, maximum depth 396 m).

Dislocation of the rock strata in the region of the Jordan Valley has had two further effects: first, earth tremors are still frequent along the valley; and second, considerable quantities of lava have welled up, forming enormous sheets that cover wide expanses of territory in the State of Jordan and southern Syria, and produce a desolate, forbidding landscape. One small lava flow, by forming a natural dam across the Jordan Valley, has impounded the waters to form Lake Tiberias.

The Jordan river rises just inside the frontiers of Syria and Lebanon—a recurrent source of dispute between the two countries and Israel. The river is 251 km (156 miles) long, and after first flowing for 96 km in Israel, it lies within Jordanian territory for the remaining 152 km. Its main tributary, the Yarmouk, is 40 km long, and close to its junction with the Jordan forms the boundary between the State of Jordan, Israel and Syria. A few kilometres from its source, the Jordan river used to open into Lake Huleh, a shallow, marsh-fringed expanse of water that was previously a breeding ground of malaria, but which has now been drained. Lake Tiberias, also, like the former Huleh, in Israel, covers an area of 316 sq km and measures 22 km from north to south, and 26 km from east to west. Outflowing river water from the lake is used for the generation of hydroelectricity.

The river then flows through the barren, inhospitable country of its middle and lower valley, very little of which is actually, or potentially, cultivable, and finally enters the Dead Sea. This lake is 65 km long and 16 km wide. Owing to the very high air temperatures at most seasons of the year, evaporation from the lake is intense, and has been estimated as equivalent to 8.5m. metric tons of water per day. At the surface the Dead Sea water contains about 348 g of dissolved salts per litre, and at a depth of 110 m the water is chemically saturated (i.e. holds its maximum possible content). Magnesium chloride is the most abundant mineral, with sodium chloride next in importance, but commercial interest centres on the less abundant potash and bromide salts.

CLIMATE

Summers are hot, especially on the plateau and in the Jordan Valley, where temperatures of up to 49°C have been recorded. Winters are fairly cold, and on the plateau frost and some snow are usual, though not in the lower Jordan Valley. The significant element of the climate of Jordan is rainfall. In the higher parts (i.e. the uplands of Samaria and Judaea and the hills overlooking the eastern Jordan Valley) 380 mm–630 mm of rainfall occurs annually, enough for agriculture; but elsewhere as little as 200 mm or less may fall, and pastoral nomadism is the only possible way of life. Only about 25% of the total area of Jordan is sufficiently humid for cultivation.

POPULATION

According to the 2004 census, the population of Jordan stood at 5,103,639, compared with 4,139,458 in 1994. The census of November 2015 recorded a significant increase in the population, with the total reaching 9,531,712. This increase was attributed principally to the influx of foreign nationals from the region, particularly those fleeing the civil conflict in Syria. Jordanian nationals numbered 6,613,587, while there were 1,265,514 Syrians, 636,270 Egyptians, 634,182 Palestinians and 130,911 Iraqis. Official estimates put the total population at 11,302,000 at the end of 2022.

Following the outbreak of conflict in Syria in 2011 between government forces and groups opposed to the rule of President Bashar al-Assad, a significant number of Syrians fled that country, many of whom entered Jordan. At 31 July 2023 a total of 656,762 Syrian refugees were registered with the Office of the UN High Commissioner for Refugees (UNHCR) in Jordan. However, as indicated by the 2015 census, many unregistered Syrian migrants were also present in Jordan. At 31 December 2020 there were 2,307,011 Palestinian refugees registered with the UN Relief and Works Agency for Palestine Refugees in the Near East (UNRWA) in Jordan.

Arabic, the official language, is spoken everywhere, except in a small number of settlements inhabited by Circassians, who settled in Jordan as refugees during the 19th and 20th centuries. Over 90% of the population are Sunni Muslims, and King Abdullah can trace unbroken descent from the Prophet Muhammad. There is a Christian minority, as well as smaller numbers of Shi'a Muslims.

History

COURTNEY FREER

PREHISTORIC JORDAN

The Hashemite Kingdom of Jordan has a long and varied pre-independence history. Indeed, the first record of human activity in Jordan emerged in the Palaeolithic period, some 2m. years ago, with inhabitants of the area becoming more settled during the Neolithic period (10000–4300 BCE). Jordan became increasingly developed during the Chalcolithic era (4500–3200 BCE) and the Bronze Age (3300–1200 BCE), during which time inhabitants of the area started trading with present-day Egypt, Iran, Iraq, the Syrian Arab Republic and Türkiye (formerly Turkey); it had traditionally traded bronze tools primarily with present-day Israel, Lebanon, Palestine and western Syria. The biblical kingdoms of Ammon and Moab in central Jordan, Gilead in the north, and Midian and Edom in the south developed within the borders of present-day Jordan during the Iron Age (1200–539 BCE).

THE ASSYRIAN, GREEK, PERSIAN AND BYZANTINE ERAS

The Assyrians came to control the eastern portion of Jordan as far as Edom from 811 BCE, with a series of revolts leading to the eventual retaking of the country by Tiglath-Pileser III in 734–733 BCE. He divided the state into provinces under the control of Assyrian governors—a system that continued until the fall of the Assyrian Empire in 612 BCE. Present-day Jordan next came under the control of the Persian Empire, which absorbed the Assyrian and Babylonian empires in the fourth century BCE. In 333 BCE Alexander the Great defeated the Persian military in southern Turkey (officially redesignated as Türkiye in June 2022) and went on to conquer the remainder of that empire, launching a period of Greek rule in present-day Jordan.

In 64–63 BCE the Nabataean Kingdom, which had long been a client state of the Roman Empire, was conquered by the Romans under Pompey. He allowed the country to remain independent on the condition that it would pay imperial taxes. The Nabataeans in Jordan are best known for their construction of the city of Petra, which linked several major trade routes for spices. Nabataeans, who had been in the area east of the Jordan river known as Transjordan since 312 BCE, were absorbed into the Roman Empire formally in 106 CE as the province of Palaestina Tertia, during which time a series of new towns and villages were established. The entirety of Jordan, aside from Decapolis, became part of Arabia Petraea, which had its capital at Petra initially and later at Busra al-Sham in Syria.

Fighting between Byzantium and Sasanian Persia ravaged the area of present-day Jordan in the sixth and seventh centuries CE. The Byzantines controlled the region between 324 and 635 after the collapse of the Western Roman Empire. Byzantine rule fostered the development of infrastructure and a more settled population, although the region remained rather unstable politically.

ARAB RULE OF TRANSJORDAN

Arab Muslim rule over Transjordan began in 636 and lasted until 661. Muslims from the Arabian Peninsula, led by Khalid bin al-Walid, destroyed the Byzantine army at the Battle of the Yarmouk River, thereby placing most of Syria and Palestine under Muslim rule. This period is known as the time of the four 'rightly guided' or 'righteous' caliphs, signifying the first four rulers of the first caliphate (Abu Bakr, Umar bin al-Khattab, Uthman bin Affan and Ali bin Abi Talib). Muslim armies, under their rule, took control of large areas of present-day Egypt, Iran and northern Africa.

Rulers of the Umayyad Caliphate, or second caliphate, took control from 661 until 750, after the rule of the four righteous caliphs, and established Damascus as their capital, yet built palaces and rebuilt many Roman forts throughout Transjordan. Under Umayyad rule, Amman began housing the provincial governor, bringing Transjordan closer to the political epicentre of the caliphate.

The Abbasid Caliphate took over from the Umayyads from 750 until 969 and moved the capital city from Damascus to Kufa and then to Baghdad, again making Transjordan less politically and economically relevant and leading to its economic decline. From 969 until 1171 the Fatimid Caliphate, with its capital in Cairo, took control of the area of present-day Jordan. This proved prosperous for Transjordan and the Levant more generally, as its rulers established new trading routes.

THE CRUSADERS AND ADVENT OF OTTOMAN RULE

In 1099 Crusaders from Europe seeking to conquer the Holy Lands on behalf of the Catholic Church and Pope Urban II took control of Jerusalem; the Latin Kingdom of Jerusalem was expanded east of the Jordan river, and a principality known as Oultre Jourdain was created, with its capital at al-Karak (Kerak). The Crusaders' rule was short-lived; their forces were overthrown by the Ayyubids between 1187 and 1263 and by the Mamluk Sultanate between 1250 and 1516. Jordan finally became incorporated into the Ottoman Empire in 1516 as part of the province of Damascus. Agricultural towns in Jordan temporarily prospered during this period, but the area was later largely neglected by the Ottomans, apart from their visits for the purpose of tax collection.

As a result, Wahhabi forces were able to take control of the region from 1803 until 1812, until the Ottomans led by Ibrahim Pasha, son of the governor of the Egypt Eyalet, managed to expel the Wahhabis, at the request of the Ottoman sultan. In 1833 Ibrahim Pasha established his own rule independently of the Ottomans. However, he implemented such repressive tactics that the peasants revolted in Palestine in 1834; the cities of al-Salt and al-Karak were destroyed by his forces during the search for a leader of the Palestinian rallies. The population of Jordan remained largely nomadic during this period, with settled populations only at al-Salt, Irbid, Jarash (Jerash) and al-Karak; urban areas were often raided by Bedouins, whom city dwellers had to pay for protection, making the town centres less desirable places to live. The establishment of the Hejaz Railway linking Makkah (Mecca) and İstanbul in 1910 helped to revive the Jordanian economy to a limited extent.

Overall, during the four centuries of Ottoman rule (1516–1918) Jordan stagnated; people of the Transjordan also led major uprisings in 1905 and 1910 to protest against repressive Ottoman rule, which was only ended after the First World War (1914–18). During the First World War people living in present-day Jordan unsurprisingly chose to join with the British against the Ottomans, along with other Arabs under their rule. In a 1916 revolt, they severed the Hejaz Railway and in July 1917 the military of Prince Faisal bin Hussein of the Hashemite dynasty took control of al-Aqabah (Aqaba); by 1918 Amman and Damascus were under Allied control. After the war, the 1920 San Remo Conference led to the creation of a Palestinian mandate, under British control, and a Syrian mandate, which was under French authority. Although Prince Faisal's brother, Abdullah, had at first been intent on encouraging tribes to defeat French rule, by April 1921 the British made him ruler over what came to be known as the Kingdom of Transjordan. Thus, an Ottoman imperial power was replaced by a British authority, which was formally acknowledged by the League of Nations in July 1922 (Documents on Palestine, see p. 1203).

POST-FIRST WORLD WAR TRANSJORDAN

The British acknowledged the Kingdom of Transjordan's independence under Amir Abdullah in May 1923; however, the state remained under the control of the British Resident and the High Commissioner for Palestine and Transjordan for matters related to finance, the military and foreign policy, with complete independence granted only in 1946, after the Second World War. British rule helped to entrench Abdullah's authority over Transjordan. Indeed, Abdullah was threatened by repeated Wahhabi attacks into southern Jordan that required the establishment of a small British military base near Amman to help to ensure the protection of his regime, particularly between 1922 and 1924. Abdullah also used the forces to suppress local revolts in 1921 and 1923. With almost one-half of the population nomadic (about 103,000 people) in 1922, it proved difficult to control.

In 1928 the British granted Abdullah full autonomy in domestic administration, although the military still provided security. A British Resident also continued to control financial and foreign policy. This Anglo-Jordanian Treaty and the resulting Organic Law of 1928 also included a Constitution for Transjordan, promulgated in April 1928, which led to the first meeting of a Legislative Council in 1929. In 1934 a new agreement granted Transjordan the power to appoint its consular representatives to other Arab states, and in 1939 the British agreed to Transjordan's decision to transform the elected Legislative Council into a cabinet of ministers. Although it was unmistakably on the path to independence over the course of the 1920s and 1930s, this progress was stalled during the Second World War.

INDEPENDENCE AFTER THE SECOND WORLD WAR

The 1946 Treaty of London between the British Government and the Amir of Transjordan secured Transjordan's independence as the Hashemite Kingdom of Transjordan. When the country first applied for membership of the United Nations (UN), the Union of Soviet Socialist Republics (USSR) refused to acknowledge it, as it did not consider Transjordan sufficiently independent of British rule. As a result, another treaty in 1948 stripped Jordan of all limits on its sovereignty. Notably, the Transjordanian Government had taken action on the international scene prior to independence, in particular through its participation in the London Conference on Palestine held in May 1939 that led to the formation of the League of Arab States (Arab League, see p. 1146) in 1945, of which Transjordan was a founding member.

Following independence, Abdullah named himself King of Jordan, and the state's name was changed to the Hashemite Kingdom of Jordan in 1949. British financial assistance proved critical to the foundation of the Arab Legion inside Jordan, which consisted primarily of Bedouin troops, trained and commanded by British officers. These troops helped to ensure Abdullah's grip on power among outlying nomadic populations.

Since independence Jordan has existed as a parliamentary monarchy, wherein the King and his appointed cabinet of ministers (including the Prime Minister) retain primary political power. The bicameral National Assembly consists of an elected House of Representatives and a smaller Senate (House of Notables), the members of which are appointed by the King; both houses have four-year terms.

THE ESTABLISHMENT OF ISRAEL AND THE FIRST ARAB–ISRAELI WAR

The day after the proclamation of the independent State of Israel, in May 1948, Transjordan, along with neighbouring Egyptian, Iraqi, Lebanese and Syrian troops, embarked on the first Arab–Israeli War. King Abdullah hoped, secretly, to take control of the area allocated to Palestinian Arabs under UN Resolution 181 in November 1947. As a result, his troops were based in the present-day West Bank—the area he hoped to bring under his rule. Abdullah's troops successfully removed Jewish forces from East Jerusalem, thus playing a major role in the fighting. In the aftermath of the war, in September 1948, the All Palestine Government was established in the Gaza Strip, under the control of Egyptian troops occupying the area; Transjordan responded by naming Abdullah King of Arab Palestine (and Jordan) in December.

On 3 April 1949 Jordan signed an armistice with Israel, and the West Bank and East Jerusalem were placed under Jordanian control. This led to the formal annexation by Jordan, on 24 April 1950, of the West Bank, excepting East Jerusalem, following which all West Bank residents were given Jordanian citizenship. Only the United Kingdom, Iraq and Pakistan recognized this move, which more than doubled Jordan's population, as legal. Importantly, Jordan opposed the internationalization of Jerusalem at this time and instead set about resettling Palestinians, even bringing three Palestinians into the cabinet. Jordanian–Palestinian tensions persisted none the less.

ABDULLAH'S ASSASSINATION AND TALAL'S REIGN

It was a young Palestinian nationalist who killed King Abdullah at the al-Aqsa Mosque on 20 July 1951. The assassination may have been motivated by Abdullah's support for the Greater Syria policy—which would have united Transjordan, Syria and Palestine as a step towards further inclusion with Iraq—or by Abdullah's alleged co-operation with Israel.

Abdullah's eldest son, Talal, took power after his father's death and oversaw the promulgation of a new Constitution. The current Constitution was approved in 1952, with influences from the Constitution of 1947 and the Organic Law of 1928. Perhaps the only hallmark of Talal's brief rule is the promulgation of the Constitution, which granted the monopoly of political power to the King. Talal also, notably, showed some signs of opposing his father's pursuit of co-operation with Syria and Egypt; indeed, Jordan failed to sign the Arab Collective Security Pact in 1950. However, only one year after his coronation, Talal, who was judged mentally unfit to rule, ceded de facto power to his 18-year-old son, Hussein bin Talal, who was proclaimed as King on 11 August 1952, although he was not crowned until 2 May 1953.

KING HUSSEIN'S FIRST FOREIGN POLICIES IN THE 1950s

King Hussein largely continued with Abdullah's foreign policies, completing an economic agreement with Syria in 1953. Jordan also signed a financial aid agreement with the UK in December 1954, and in May 1955 King Saud of Saudi Arabia arrived for a series of state visits. However, Hussein refused to join either the Egyptian-Syrian-Saudi Arabian bloc or the Baghdad Pact, which would have granted Jordan a Western security umbrella and which he had initiated alongside the UK, Turkey, Iran and Iraq. Egyptian and West Bank resistance ultimately prevented Hussein from siding with the West, and in 1956 he agreed to join the Unified Arab Command, a mutual defence pact. Ties grew to such an extent that in 1957 Egypt, Saudi Arabia and Syria replaced the UK as the main providers of financial support to Jordan.

In 1956 King Hussein dismissed all British diplomats to demonstrate support for pan-Arab nationalism, led by Egypt and boosted during the Suez Crisis. A new cabinet was formed, and fresh legislative elections were followed by negotiations for the abrogation of the Anglo-Jordanian Treaty of 1948. Although financial aid then came mainly from Egypt, Saudi Arabia and Syria, in practice the shares from Egypt and Syria were never paid, owing to later political events.

In March 1957 the Anglo-Jordanian Treaty was formally abrogated, and the last British troops had left by early July. Prime Minister Sulayman Nabulsi's pro-Soviet leanings led to his resignation in April 1957 and to his replacement by Ibrahim Hashim. The USA hoped to maintain Jordan's independence from the USSR and, in fact, airlifted arms to Amman in September, as a pointed message to Syria, which had begun receiving military aid from the Soviets in 1955.

King Hussein's ties with his neighbours suffered somewhat, however, and this had domestic consequences. In May 1957 Syrian troops under the joint Syrian-Egyptian-Jordanian command withdrew from Jordanian territory at Jordan's request, leading to the partial rupture of diplomatic ties with Egypt. Also in 1957, members of the National Guard, mainly those from the West Bank, attempted to overthrow the King, who was protected by East Banker Bedouins. In the aftermath of this turmoil, Palestinian nationalists were banned from the legislature; political parties were made illegal; and more authoritarian policies were implemented at the executive level. In fact, multi-party legislative elections did not take place again until 1993.

Following the formation of the United Arab Republic (UAR—the union of Egypt and Syria) in February 1958, Iraq's King Faisal II persuaded his cousin Hussein to join a union, the Arab Federation, with Iraq. Five months later, when Faisal and his family were killed in a military coup (see Iraq), Hussein looked to the UK and the USA for protection, instead of forming a federation with neighbouring states. Both Western powers responded positively, as they hoped to have a pro-Western regime in place in Jordan. The British installed troops in the country until late 1958, and the USA granted additional military and economic aid; by the early 1960s the USA was providing some US $100m. in annual aid to King Hussein.

CHANGING REGIONAL ALLIANCES AND THE PLO

Palestinians who opposed closer ties with the West did not attempt an overthrow, although the new alliance completed Jordan's isolation from Iraq, Israel and the UAR. Relations with the UAR were severed in July 1958, to be restored only in August 1959. In January 1960 King Hussein and his Prime Minister publicly criticized Arab leaders' approach to the Palestinian issue, and in February Jordan offered citizenship to any Arab refugees who applied for it. As before, Jordan hoped to maintain the Palestinian territory west of the Jordan river, although the UAR and other Arab states were keen to establish an independent Palestinian state.

In August 1960 Prime Minister Hazza al-Majali, along with 12 others, was assassinated by a bomb allegedly planted by members of the Syrian secret intelligence services; he was succeeded by several replacements over the next five years. Relations with the rest of the Arab world remained uneasy, and in September 1963 the Arab League formally approved the creation of a 'Palestinian entity'—a move opposed by the Jordanian Government, as it hoped to maintain sovereignty over the West Bank. The first meeting of Palestinian Arab groups was hosted in the Jordanian sector of Jerusalem in May–June 1964 and resulted in the creation of the Palestine Liberation Organization (PLO) as 'the only legitimate spokesman for all matters concerning the Palestinian people'. The Arab League would finance the body and recruit, from among the refugee population, troops for a Palestine Liberation Army (PLA). King Hussein, who was opposed to this move, refused to allow the PLA's forces to train on his land and denied the PLO the right to collect taxes from Palestinian refugees living on his land.

In 1965, with Egyptian and Syrian support, the Fatah movement—established in 1959 as the Palestine National Liberation Movement under the leadership of Yasser Arafat—began to carry out raids against Israel from Jordanian territory, which led to deaths and property damage as well as to retaliatory raids into the West Bank from Israel. This also spurred a breakdown in relations between Palestinians and the Jordanian monarchy, leading Hussein to conduct private talks with Israel and to try to contain the Palestinian guerrillas, or *fedayeen* ('martyrs'). At the end of 1966 the Israeli army, however, made a particularly violent raid into Samu in the Jordanian-controlled West Bank, in retaliation for previous Fatah raids. Some 15 Jordanian soldiers, a fighter pilot and six villagers were killed, stoking Jordanian and Palestinian anger and tipping the balance towards the Palestinian guerrillas.

THE 1967 WAR

In early 1967, fearing the outbreak of war after escalations in Israeli–Arab violence, Jordan decided to sign a defence treaty with Egypt and Syria; as a result, when Israeli and Jordanian forces came to blows in East Jerusalem, King Hussein joined Egypt and Syria in a new Arab–Israeli War (known as the Six-Day War).

Two days after the start of the conflict, Israeli troops had taken over all land west of the Jordan river, including Jerusalem. The military defeat had shattering effects for Jordan: it suffered a high number of casualties and lost about one-third of its most fertile territory; tens of thousands of refugees also fled to Jordan after the war. King Hussein had entered the war to maintain his position, fearing Egyptian and Syrian co-operation against him, so although the loss of territory was certainly a disappointment, it was not the worst possible outcome for Hussein.

Jordan became increasingly reliant on foreign aid after the 1967 war—particularly from Kuwait, Libya and Saudi Arabia. US and British aid was also restored during this period. In addition, an arrangement with Israel, which allowed Jordanians to farm in the Jordan Valley in 1971, helped to revitalize the economy. King Hussein also pursued secret talks with the Israelis regarding the West Bank and East Jerusalem, largely to strengthen the Jordanian position at the expense of the PLO.

EMERGENCE OF THE FEDAYEEN AND 'BLACK SEPTEMBER'

In November 1968, marking the 51st anniversary of the Balfour Declaration of 1917 (see Documents on Palestine, see p. 1201), street fights broke out between Palestinian nationalists and the Jordanian army; violent confrontations also erupted in February and June 1970, leading King Hussein to make concessions to the Palestinians. King Hussein and PLO Chairman Yasser Arafat came to an agreement: Hussein dismissed his commander-in-chief and a cabinet member, both of whom were family members, as they were considered anti-*fedayeen*.

The new 1970 administration featured more Palestinians in key ministries, and Abd al-Munem Rifai, a Jordanian of Palestinian descent, became Prime Minister for the second time (he had served as premier from March to August 1969). None the less, the Government faced a major challenge from Palestinian guerrilla groups, mainly Fatah, under the control of Arafat. Such groups were able to mobilize support, particularly at increasingly large refugee camps and among the Palestinian majority inside Jordan. The *fedayeen* also benefited from backing and training from Syria, as well as financing from the Persian (Arabian) Gulf countries.

More than simply challenging the power of King Hussein, the *fedayeen* also diminished the likelihood of any settlement with Israel. Political strain remained, in particular when the USA released peace proposals for Palestine, which were almost universally rejected. In September 1970 the already tense relations between the PLO, under the control of Arafat, and the Jordanian Government deteriorated when the Popular Front for the Liberation of Palestine, a radical Marxist-Palestinian organization and traditionally the second largest group in the PLO behind Fatah, hijacked four international airliners and blew them up in a deserted airfield in the Jordanian desert. In response, King Hussein reinstated martial law, and the so-called Black September conflict began between the Hashemite regime and the PLO during 16–27 September 1970. Syria sent 250 tanks into Jordan in support of the PLO, and Hussein used US and British military aid, along with Israeli overflights, to overcome Syrian forces and the PLO by 27 September. By January 1971 the Jordanian military had taken more aggressive action against Palestinian groups, leading to protests from Algeria, Egypt and Syria. The Government had regained sufficient control by April, however, to mandate the withdrawal of the *fedayeen* from Amman.

The Black September organization was formed as a result in 1971, established by Fatah members to launch revenge attacks. Although the PLO guerrillas had been forced out of Jordan by July 1971, on 28 November members of Black September assassinated Prime Minister Wasfi al-Tal.

Eager to maintain a secure position in power, in August 1971 King Hussein created a new appointed council of tribal leaders, chaired by the Crown Prince, which was responsible for administering tribal regions of the country. In September, one month after the creation of the council, the Jordanian National Union (renamed the Arab National Union in March 1972) was created as the state's only legal political party; however, as the party was chaired by the King and Crown Prince and barred from membership anyone who supported 'imported ideologies', it was essentially a new means of supporting the regime.

Having, for the most part, secured control over tribal areas, King Hussein sought to gain Palestinian support by announcing plans for a 'United Arab Kingdom' in March 1972. This union would include both Jordanian and Palestinian regions in a federation, both under control of the King and a federal Council of Ministers, but for the most part would be autonomous. Israel and the Palestinian organizations strongly opposed this plan, and Egypt responded by severing diplomatic ties with Jordan. King Hussein none the less continued to pursue the federation to alleviate Jordan's isolation inside the region. It was not until September 1973 that Hussein met Egyptian leader Col Anwar Sadat and Syrian President Hafiz al-Assad for a reconciliation summit. King Hussein gained limited Palestinian support for granting amnesty to political prisoners, including many previously imprisoned Fatah members, as something of a peace offering.

THE 1973 WAR AND THE RABAT CONFERENCE

King Hussein did not join the Egyptian-Syrian surprise attack on Israel in October 1973, but instead sent tanks to help Syria in the Golan Heights largely as a symbolic measure. In negotiations following the war, he demanded the return of the West Bank and East Jerusalem to Jordanian control. Although Israel had proposed to withdraw its forces from Israeli-occupied Egyptian lands, it refused to extend the same offer to Jordan.

King Hussein still tried to stem the tide of PLO influence in his own favour. In October 1974, however, at the Arab Summit Conference in Rabat, Morocco, representatives from 20 Arab states unanimously granted to the PLO the responsibility of being sole representative of the Palestinians and gave the organization the right to establish national authority over Palestinian territory, forcing Hussein to acquiesce on the matter of incorporating the West Bank into Jordan.

After the disappointment of the Rabat conference, the National Assembly granted King Hussein greater authority to revise the Jordanian Constitution. He was also given the right to rule for one year without parliament and to reduce the number of Palestinians in the executive and legislative branches. After parliament was dissolved, Palestinian representation was decreased, and, in fact, the citizenship of some 800,000 Palestinians in Jordan became contested. Elections were not held in March 1975; when the legislature was in session in February 1976, a constitutional amendment was passed that allowed elections to be suspended for an indeterminate period.

Jordan and Syria created a supreme command in August 1975 to co-ordinate foreign and military activity, largely to contain the PLO. In 1977 Iraqi President Saddam Hussain, Anwar Sadat and US President Jimmy Carter spoke about a potential relationship between Jordan and a Palestinian 'entity', yet the PLO spoke out against any such arrangement. In May 1977 the election of right-wing Likud candidate Menachem Begin as Prime Minister of Israel further harmed Israeli-Jordanian relations. Begin stepped up the construction of Jewish settlements in the West Bank and Gaza to secure Israeli rule in those areas. The Camp David Accords of 1978 required Israel to give autonomy to the Palestinians and to negotiate the status of the occupied territories, but Hussein completely broke off secret ties with Israel from 1977 until 1984, owing to the new Government's intransigent stance. Israel's invasion of Lebanon in 1982 only fuelled Jordanian fears that Israel planned to transfer Palestinians to their country.

CAMP DAVID AND NEW ARAB-ISRAELI-JORDANIAN PURSUITS OF PEACE

After the Israeli-Egyptian peace treaty (a result of the Camp David Accords) was signed in March 1979, Jordan was the first Arab country to sever diplomatic ties with Egypt. Over time, however, bitterness towards Egypt became displaced to Syria, which accused Jordan of harbouring movements opposing Hafiz al-Assad's rule. Syria also supported Iran in the Iran-Iraq war (1980–88), and Jordan backed Iraq. This led to a build-up of troops on the Jordan–Syria border in December 1980 and finally, in February 1981, to the abrogation of a six-year economic and customs agreement with Syria after the Jordanian chargé d'affaires was abducted in the Lebanese capital, Beirut.

Following its expulsion from Lebanon the PLO restarted negotiations with King Hussein, and Arafat and Hussein's relationship improved considerably. In 1984 Hussein permitted the Palestine National Council (PNC) to meet in Amman, where it continued to serve as a de facto legislature for the Palestinians. Hussein also signed, in February 1985, an agreement with Arafat that committed him to co-operating with the PLO on a joint peace initiative. The King, at this point, harboured the impression that Arafat would accept a federation of the West and East Banks under Jordanian control. For his part, Arafat continued to demand an independent Palestinian state in the West Bank and would accede only to an eventual union with Jordan—a major disappointment to King Hussein.

Jordan re-established ties with Egypt in September 1984, despite its treaty with Israel. In February 1985 King Hussein and Arafat announced the terms of a joint Jordanian-Palestinian agreement on the framework for a peace settlement: peace talks had to involve an international conference with the five permanent members of the UN Security Council (the People's Republic of China, France, the UK, the USA and the USSR), as well as all parties to the conflict, including the PLO representing Palestinians in a Jordanian-Palestinian delegation. Palestinians would be granted the right to self-determination through a confederated Jordanian-Palestinian state. However, the PLO insisted that Palestine should have its own representative, separate from Jordan. Ultimately, then, Syria, Libya and portions of the PLO rejected the agreement as it stood.

For its part, Israel rejected Hussein's four-stage plan presented in May 1985 to guide Arab-Israeli negotiations, and instead hoped to enlist the help of the five permanent members of the Security Council and all parties to the conflict, aside from members of the PLO and the PNC. In November 1985 King Hussein conceded that Jordan had, unknowingly, sheltered members of the Syrian Muslim Brotherhood who hoped to overthrow Hafiz al-Assad. To secure Syrian involvement in peace talks, the Jordanian King apparently agreed to deport the Brotherhood members. Yasser Arafat, however, refused to accept UN Security Council Resolutions 242 and 338 (see Documents on Palestine) as the basis for peace negotiations, and so the Jordanian-Palestinian peace initiative crumbled.

Owing to such misunderstandings, in February 1986 Hussein nullified the Amman agreement with Arafat and ended negotiations with the PLO. He demanded that the PLO's Amman offices be shut, and many Fatah officials loyal to Arafat were deported, although the group was never completely banned. He also announced that the economy of the West Bank would be the responsibility of the Jordanian Government and that, as such, the West Bank would be added to a five-year plan for Jordan (which was granted US $1,300m. with support from Israel); he also increased the number of Palestinians to some 50% in an enlarged National Assembly. Hussein was going headlong into pursuing his goal of creating a Jordanian-Palestinian-Israeli administration to make the West Bank independent of the PLO, allowing him to regain at least some measure of control over the area.

In January 1985 King Hussein, frustrated with the USA's inability to slow the pace of Israeli settlements and unable to buy US arms, approved the purchase of a Soviet air defence system, having already agreed to purchase French anti-aircraft missiles in September 1984. The USA reacted, in June 1985, by offering extra economic aid of US $250m. over a period of 27 months.

By 1987 King Hussein and Israeli Minister of Foreign Affairs Shimon Peres had agreed to a UN-sponsored peace conference, with a united Jordanian-Palestinian delegation. When Israel demanded that only Jordan be included, Hussein held an Arab League meeting in Amman which led to the re-establishment of ties with Egypt, which had been severed after the signing of the peace treaty between Egypt and Israel in 1979 (see Documents on Palestine, see p. 1215).

OUTBREAK OF THE *INTIFADA*

The outbreak of Palestinian violence (*intifada* or 'uprising') targeted at Israeli occupation of the West Bank and the Gaza Strip in December 1987 drastically changed political priorities and regional alliances. King Hussein, worried that the *intifada* could threaten his rule, voiced support for the uprising and granted aid to the families of victims of Israeli counter-attacks. Indeed, substantial support for the *intifada* existed inside Jordan. Despite King Hussein's efforts, *intifada* leaders, particularly Yasser Arafat, decried moves by the Jordanian regime as insufficient. Israeli-Jordanian peace talks broke down, and Hussein halted the five-year plan for the West Bank. In April 1988 the Palestinian extremist group Black September claimed responsibility for several bombings in Amman, which the group said targeted the 'client Zionist regime in Jordan'.

The ongoing *intifada* attracted international attention and led to renewed efforts at reviving Israeli-Palestinian peace negotiations. The Arab League responded by hosting an extraordinary summit in the Algerian capital, Algiers, in June 1988. At the meeting King Hussein lent his support to the *intifada* and dismissed Jordanian ambitions to restore its rule in the West Bank, also insisting that the PLO must represent the Palestinians in future negotiations. The summit's concluding statement praised the 'heroic' *intifada*, reiterated support for Palestinian self-determination and an independent Palestinian state in the West Bank, and demanded that the PLO participate in future negotiations.

King Hussein thus had to begin to work under the condition that Jordan could not realistically take control of the West Bank. Indeed, in July 1988 Jordan cancelled its US $1,300m. development plan for the West Bank, which the PLO had opposed since its announcement in 1986. Shortly thereafter, King Hussein cut legal and administrative links with the West Bank and dissolved the elected house of parliament, as Palestinians from the West Bank had held 30 of the 60 seats. Palestinians in the West Bank were also no longer considered Jordanian citizens; although they could retain their Jordanian passports, in the future they would solely have travel documents.

On 15 November 1988 the PNC declared the establishment of an independent State of Palestine and, for the first time, accepted UN Security Council Resolution 242 as a basis for peace negotiations, thus implicitly accepting the existence of Israel. Jordan and 60 other countries recognized the state. After Yasser Arafat addressed a special session of the UN General Assembly in Geneva, Switzerland, in December and renounced violence for the PLO, the USA opened dialogue with the organization.

DOMESTIC DEMOCRATIC REOPENING OF 1989 AND EARLY 1990s

In April 1989 riots erupted in several Jordanian cities, following price rises on basic goods and services. To appease the population King Hussein did not change the prices but instead called the first general election in 22 years. The polls, held in November 1989, resulted in gains for opposition movements, mainly the political arm of the Muslim Brotherhood, the Islamic Action Front (IAF). The IAF won 20 of the 60 contested seats, and independent Islamists who supported the organization yet ran independently won 14 seats. Palestinians or Arab nationalists won seven seats, leftist candidates won four, with the remaining seats going to pro-Government candidates.

The rise of the opposition surprised the Government, especially because a disproportionate number of seats had been assigned to rural areas that had traditionally housed loyalist East Bank tribes. As a result, after the election King Hussein pressed to institute constitutional reforms, in particular to allow greater freedom for political parties and less leeway for political corruption. He appointed a 60-member Royal Commission, which included members of the Muslim Brotherhood and leftist parties, to draft a National Charter to regulate political life in Jordan. The King endorsed the resulting charter in June 1991 and it became law in 1992. This document was surprisingly progressive in its rhetorical support for democracy, pluralism, equality and tolerance. Notably, it removed the ban on political parties so long as they recognized the legitimacy of the Hashemite regime and the ultimate executive power of the King. Furthermore, in July 1991 the King revoked martial law, which had been in place since defeat in the 1967 war.

In 1992 a law legalizing political parties was passed in advance of the first multi-party elections since 1956, scheduled for November 1993. After unexpectedly dissolving parliament in August, however, King Hussein changed the voting laws, so that each citizen could cast only one vote, rather than the number equal to the number of candidates in the constituency. The elections went ahead as scheduled, with a 52% turnout rate among eligible voters. Many Palestinian Jordanians were reported to have abstained, as they felt excluded from the polls, owing to the new electoral laws that favoured the East Bank population. Of the 80 elected members of parliament (MPs), 50 were independent, demonstrating the weakness of the country's nascent political parties and the prevailing political strength of tribalism, particularly under the new electoral law. The IAF won 16 seats, the most of any party, yet this share represented a six-seat decrease from its share in 1989; 14 of the MPs elected were of Palestinian origin.

In March 1994 the National Assembly passed a law to allow municipal elections in Amman for two-thirds of the Greater Amman Municipality, which worried the Government, owing to Palestinian and Islamist sentiment in the capital. Municipal elections were held nationwide for the first time in July 1995. They yielded gains to pro-Government and independent candidates and losses for Islamist and left-wing groups. After the polls King Hussein publicly and repeatedly voiced his commitment to promoting pluralistic government.

Political reform could not stop economic discontent, however. In August 1996 riots took place in the southern parts of the country after the Government more than doubled bread prices as part of an austerity plan sponsored by the International Monetary Fund (IMF) to remove subsidies. Some one-third of Jordanians were estimated to be living below the poverty line at the time, and the unrest spread throughout the country. King Hussein responded by dissolving parliament and dispatching the military to re-establish control in al-Karak, where most of the unrest had taken place.

During the remainder of King Hussein's rule in the 1990s further reforms were not implemented. Instead, opposition parties were constricted, in an effort to bolster the monarchy and consolidate power in the hands of loyalists.

KING HUSSEIN AND IRAQ'S INVASION OF KUWAIT

In the wake of Iraq's invasion in August 1990 and occupation of Kuwait until February 1991, King Hussein took the side of President Saddam Hussain, although Jordan was officially neutral; the PLO also sided with Iraq. None the less, Jordan openly opposed a statement by the Organization of the Islamic Conference (now the Organization of Islamic Cooperation—OIC) that condemned the invasion and called for Iraq's immediate withdrawal. King Hussein also consistently voiced his support for a strictly Arab solution to the situation. In fact, after talks with Saddam Hussain in December 1990 in Baghdad, Hussein proposed a peace plan connecting the Iraqi–Kuwaiti dispute to the Arab–Israeli conflict. He travelled to the capitals of several European countries to dissuade them from going to war.

Once the US military became involved Jordan condemned its participation, and popular anti-Western and anti-Israeli demonstrations broke out inside Jordan. Following the liberation of Kuwait, King Hussein still publicly called for regional reconciliation. Kuwait's Western allies responded to Jordanian opposition to their involvement in Kuwait by suspending all aid to Jordan, as well as by imposing an air and sea blockade; some 200,000–300,000 Kuwaiti refugees also fled to Jordan around this time. Ties with the USA became normalized by the end of 1991, when the USA hoped to involve King Hussein in a joint US-Israeli peace initiative.

THE MADRID SUMMIT AND PEACE TALKS, 1991–94

King Hussein resolved to attend the Madrid summit of 1991, peace talks convened by the USA and USSR and attended by

Israeli, Jordanian, Lebanese, Palestinian and Syrian representatives; the PLO Central Council approved the formation of a joint Jordanian-Palestinian delegation. While negotiations in Washington, DC, USA, and Moscow, USSR, between Israeli and joint Jordanian-Palestinian teams remained deadlocked, secret talks between the PLO and the Israeli Government began in Oslo, Norway, in 1993, which led to the August 1993 Declaration of Principles (Documents on Palestine, see p. 1220), signed in Washington, DC, in September. King Hussein supported this declaration, even though he had been surprised to learn of the talks. The two sides concluded a 'common agenda' for later bilateral meetings, agreed to respect each other's security, and pledged to discuss future territorial and economic co-operation. This agreement was, notably, the first between an Arab state and Israel since 1979, even though it was nothing more than an outline of topics to be discussed at future negotiations.

The Madrid talks also led to the establishment, in 1994, of the Palestinian (National) Authority (PA) as governing body for the West Bank and Gaza Strip; it took on civic duties following Israeli withdrawals in 1994.

ISRAELI-JORDANIAN NEGOTIATIONS

In mid-1994 King Hussein unexpectedly began unilateral negotiations with Israel. These talks led to the Washington Declaration, formally ending the state of war that had existed between Jordan and Israel. Notably, this was the first public meeting between King Hussein and an Israeli Prime Minister. In October 1994 an Israeli-Jordanian peace treaty (see Documents on Palestine, see p. 1227) was formally signed, and full diplomatic relations were established in November. King Hussein was also recognized as custodian of the Muslim holy sites in East Jerusalem. Jordanian Islamists decried the declaration, while Yasser Arafat congratulated the Jordanian leadership on talks with Israel. None the less, he took issue with the declaration of King Hussein as guardian of the holy places of Jerusalem, as that city's status was yet to be determined.

After an Islamist-led rally against the treaty, the Jordanian Government banned all public meetings. This did not halt opposition, however. Regarding Jerusalem, in January 1995 a bilateral accord between the PLO and Jordan led the Palestinians to recognize the Israeli-Jordanian Peace Treaty, implicitly granting Jordan control over the Jerusalem shrines until Palestinian sovereignty, while Jordan reaffirmed support for Palestinian independence with a capital in East Jerusalem.

In January 1995 King Hussein signed a treaty with the PLO formally voicing his support for an independent Palestinian state including East Jerusalem. The Palestinians none the less remained sceptical, owing to the peace treaty with Israel. Despite some frustrations with Israeli policies, King Hussein was a key interlocutor between Israel and the PLO—helping to secure the Israeli withdrawal from Hebron in early 1997.

DOMESTIC POLITICS AFTER THE ISRAELI-JORDANIAN PEACE TREATY

The IAF boycotted the November 1997 parliamentary elections, following criticism that the National Assembly lacked meaningful authority to influence political and economic policies. The IAF, with nine smaller parties from left-leaning and nationalist orientations, complained that the electoral system favoured tribal representatives, yet the Government failed to change the system. Voter turnout fell as low as 26% in some parts of Amman. East Banker MPs with tribal links dominated the new Assembly, and the opposition was completely absent.

King Hussein had begun to undergo treatment for lymphatic cancer in July 1998 in the USA and, by August, had issued a royal decree transferring power to his brother, Crown Prince Hassan. After his return to the country in January 1999 the King made Hassan Deputy Crown Prince and named his eldest son, Abdullah, Crown Prince of Jordan. (Reportedly, Hussein had been unhappy with his brother's rule in his absence, particularly his attempts at intervening in military affairs.) King Hussein died on 7 February.

KING ABDULLAH'S INITIAL DOMESTIC REFORMS

Hussein's son Abdullah came to power in March 1999, yet faced domestic opposition, owing to Jordan's ties with the USA and Israel. He also had to contend with a fractious royal family and dismissed four senior army officers who were said to have pledged their loyalty to Hassan. Opposition groups were cautiously optimistic, and the Muslim Brotherhood hoped to meet the new King, largely to press for changes to electoral law. In April 1999 all censorship of Arab and foreign newspapers and magazines, in addition to imported audio and video cassettes, was removed in an amendment to the Press and Publications Law. In late March Abdullah also released some 500 political prisoners.

Municipal elections took place throughout Jordan in July 1999. Independent and tribal candidates gained the majority of seats, while the IAF won five of 20 elected seats in Amman and 70 of its 100 candidates won nationally. Relations between the Brotherhood and the new Government became contentious, however, when the offices of the Palestinian Islamic Resistance Movement (Hamas), a Sunni Islamist organization established in 1987, were closed by security forces, as the premises were reportedly being used for illegal political activities of non-Jordanian organizations. The home of Khalid Meshaal, a leading figure in Hamas, was raided, 15 Hamas officials were detained, and warrants for the arrest of five others were issued. The Government later released 24 Hamas officials, including four leaders who were deported to Qatar.

AL-AQSA INTIFADA

Following the outbreak of renewed Israeli–Palestinian violence in September 2000, the Jordanian Government withdrew its ambassador to Israel for four years. The official Jordanian position after the al-Aqsa *intifada* broke out in September 2000 was that Jordan would help the Palestinian cause by maintaining its diplomatic ties with Israel. None the less, on 7 October Jordan chose not to dispatch its new ambassador to Israel, and the Government tried to distance itself from the conflict. In the weeks between the collapse of the most recent Arab-Israeli negotiations and the start of the *intifada*, King Abdullah met Israeli Prime Minister Ehud Barak three times, making it clear that Jordan would not accept Israeli or international control of the Muslim holy sites in East Jerusalem.

In March 2001 Amman hosted the Arab League summit, which was meant to restore co-operation among Arab states, primarily by expressly backing the Palestinian cause. The meeting was the Arab League's first since Iraq's invasion of Kuwait in 1990. The summit resolved to transfer US $40m. per month to the PA; Egypt and Jordan retained diplomatic ties with Israel, but did not return their ambassadors to Tel Aviv and would not create new diplomatic ties or commercial links with Israel until it changed its treatment of the Palestinians. The Amman Declaration also resulted, which highlighted the need for Arab countries to be united, particularly in their demands for the removal of Israeli forces from all occupied Palestinian territories.

Powerful professional syndicates led the anti-normalization campaign inside Jordan, which, in 2000, released a list of Jordanian 'normalizers' with Israel. Tensions escalated to the extent that, on 27 January 2001, authorities raided the homes of prominent members of the associations' joint Anti-Normalization Committee and arrested seven people.

THE EARLY 2000s: DELAY OF PARLIAMENTARY ELECTIONS AND NEW ELECTORAL LAW

In April 2001 King Abdullah extended the term of the legislature for an additional two years, thereby bypassing the polls scheduled for November. This was probably due to the major opposition Abdullah faced from Islamist opposition groups, which were vocal in their criticism of his dealings with Israel.

The King also ratified a new electoral law in July 2001. Electoral districts were redrawn, and the number of constituencies increased from 21 to 44, raising the number of deputies in the House of Representatives from 80 to 104; the voting age was also reduced from 19 to 18 years. Although the Muslim Brotherhood welcomed the increase in the number of elected deputies, it lamented the lack of electoral lists, which had been part of the system before 1997 and had helped organized political parties, and so the group threatened a boycott of the polls.

King Abdullah, at least rhetorically, supported political reform and civil liberties. None the less, riots occurred sporadically. In January 2002 demonstrations took place in Ma'an after a local youth, Sulayman Ahmad al-Fanatseh, died in police custody, leading to claims of police brutality. Islamists also accused the Government of arresting Islamist activists to stem the tide of their opposition activity. Other riots expressed frustration with poverty and the high unemployment rate.

Although the Government had passed harsh legislation in 2000 restricting demonstrations after a series of large, pro-Palestinian, Islamist-led rallies, such events continued to take place. Israel's reoccupation of Palestinian-controlled parts of the West Bank in March 2002 served only further to increase tensions and provoked renewed street activity.

In May 2002 the cabinet granted King Abdullah the right to delay parliamentary elections indefinitely. Supported by the cabinet, the King postponed legislative elections until 2003, owing to instability throughout the region. In October the 'Jordan First' campaign was launched, with the aim of increasing popular support for the Government—particularly in its policies towards Iraq and Palestine; the Government had a unique opportunity to spread its message, owing to the absence of parliament and thus a general lack of public political opposition, yet voiced its support for democratic government. Aside from promoting greater national unity, the campaign also involved the arrest of three anti-Israeli activists from the Anti-Normalization Committee on charges of involvement with an illegal organization and distribution of anti-normalization materials, which were seen to harm the state economy. In late November a judicial ruling allowed for government dissolution of the Anti-Normalization Committee, which involved 14 professional associations, as a means of thwarting its members' political ambitions.

Riots broke out again in November 2002 after special police occupied Ma'an in a week-long operation that led to the deaths of three civilians and two police officers, as well as dozens of arrests. The operation had followed the assassination in October of US diplomat Laurence Foley in Amman. The resulting campaign of arrests and the crackdown (including the declaration of Ma'an an 'arms-free zone') was loudly criticized by Islamists, who considered it a means of targeting their opposition.

King Abdullah took steps to modernize the Jordanian economy and to appease domestic political opponents. In 2003 the Central Bank of Jordan rescinded an earlier decision to freeze the accounts of Hamas leaders. The opposition, largely members of the Palestinian Jordanian community, questioned the fairness of the 2003 polls, as they believed that they had been purposely disenfranchised. Parliamentary elections were eventually held on 17 June 2003 and led to major gains for tribes and families loyal to the regime, who won more than two-thirds of the 110 elected seats. The IAF, meanwhile, won 17 seats, having boycotted the previous 1997 polls. In general, the urban elite and professionals were under-represented, while tribal leaders made disproportionate gains. Questions abounded about the fairness of the elections.

At the behest of its ally the USA, Jordan cracked down severely on anti-American speech in September 2004, particularly in mosques and in statements made by clerics and members of the Muslim Brotherhood. Nine prominent Brotherhood *imams* and leaders were arrested, charged with preaching sermons without permission from the Ministry of Awqaf, Islamic Affairs and Holy Places, while the houses of other Brotherhood members were raided. Confrontation between the Brotherhood and the regime gradually dissipated, as the Prime Minister agreed to release all detainees and allow *imams* to return to their mosques so long as they followed the 'preaching and guidance law'. However, the Brotherhood continued to speak out against the US-led occupation of Iraq and the pro-Israeli policies of the regime.

In October 2004 a total of 11 pro-establishment parties merged into the Jordanian National Movement (JNM). The new organization hoped to unite all pro-regime forces and support the Government—particularly in its policies towards Iraq, Israel and the USA—as well as to confront the opposition bloc, which comprised 14 Islamist, pan-Arab nationalist and left-wing parties. The JNM had among its members many tribal leaders, as well as former government officials. Notably, in November King Abdullah removed the title of Crown Prince from his 24-year-old half-brother Prince Hamzah, who had held the position since Hussein's death in 1999.

FOREIGN POLICY DURING A TROUBLED TIME

The Jordanian regime chose to support US-led military operations in Iraq in 2003, further alienating it from Islamists inside Jordan. Despite its unpopularity, this move did help the Government to gain considerable support from the USA, amounting to some US $450m. of economic and military funding annually, which led to a short-lived economic boom. Jordan's General Intelligence Department (GID) became an important component of US operations, and the Central Intelligence Agency (CIA) even embedded some of its personnel at Amman's GID.

In April 2004 a Jordanian court sentenced Jordanian al-Qa'ida leader Abu Musab al-Zarqawi to death, *in absentia*, after he was convicted of the 2002 murder of Laurence Foley. Hoping to bolster its regional security, in February 2005 Jordan returned its ambassador to Tel Aviv, following his withdrawal in September 2000 in the aftermath of the *intifada*. On 9 November 2005 Amman was hit by suicide bomb attacks in three major hotels, killing 59 people. Al-Zarqawi, in an audio broadcast posted online, defended the hotel bombings yet made it clear that they were meant to target US and Israeli intelligence rather than Jordanians.

Security was seriously tightened, especially in Amman, as a result of the attacks. The overarching concern for security also led to greater authoritarianism in 2005 and 2006. Freedoms of media, public assembly and speech were threatened. The number of political prisoners also increased during this period. In February 2006 a riot broke out at Juwaidi prison in Amman, where many Islamist activists were being held. Riots also subsequently took place at Suwaiqa and Qafqafa prisons.

EFFORTS AT REGIONAL ECONOMIC ACCORDS

King Abdullah has made a concerted effort to modernize and liberalize the Jordanian economy. In 2001 he joined Syrian President Bashar al-Assad and Egyptian President Hosni Mubarak in opening a US $300m. electricity line to link the three countries' individual grids. In 2002 Jordan and Israel agreed to construct a water pipeline from the Red Sea to the Dead Sea, and in 2004 King Abdullah and President Assad launched the Wardah Dam project on the Yarmouk river.

In June 2006 Jordan signed up for several joint projects with Israel, and the creation of free trade zones and co-operation in quarry exploration were also discussed. Following Hamas's electoral victory in the PNC elections in 2006, Israel was unwilling to negotiate with the Palestinians, as Hamas had refused to acknowledge that state's legitimacy. Jordan also backed US-led efforts to alienate the Hamas Government unless it recognized Israel and halted attacks on Israeli settlers; Hamas was very critical in response.

CHAOS IN IRAQ AND ATTEMPTS AT ARAB-ISRAELI PEACE TALKS

As the situation in Iraq deteriorated in 2006–07, developments in that country increasingly came to influence Jordanian domestic policy. In 2004 King Abdullah had dubbed the area between Iran and Lebanon the 'Shi'a crescent', as a Shi'a-dominated regime had come to power in Baghdad, signalling the potential for destabilizing sectarianism to take over the region. Despite the presence of this threat, the Jordanian regime focused primarily on suppressing jihadist and *takfiri* organizations inside Jordan. (A *takfiri* is a Muslim who accuses another of being an unbeliever.)

Also during this period Jordan became home to some 750,000 Iraqi refugees. The economy suffered as a result, with unemployment soaring and an estimated 14% of Jordanians living in poverty amid rising housing costs.

In early 2007 the notion of a Jordanian option, or combining the West Bank and Jordan, was revived in Arab-Israeli peace talks. Jordan remained custodian of the holy cities in Jerusalem. By 2008 there were more than 2m. Iraqi refugees in the Middle East, mostly in Jordan and Syria. In late 2007 Jordan alone was estimated to be hosting almost 500,000 refugees, although officials claimed the figure to be 700,000–800,000. While the Jordanian authorities classified the Iraqis as 'guests' and thus not the responsibility of the state, the Office of the UN High Commissioner for Refugees (UNHCR) designated them as refugees. The border with Iraq was closed in 2007–08, but Jordanians continued to suffer from rising prices, as well as shortages of water and electricity. Iraqis legally could not work and when they did so illegally it was often under appalling conditions and for low pay; the UN did help to fund their education, however.

2007 ELECTIONS AND ONGOING DOMESTIC DISSENT

Municipal elections were held in July 2007 for the 93 councils nationwide and for one-half of the Greater Amman Municipality's membership. The Municipalities Law had been changed earlier that year, introducing a quota of 20% of the 965 seats for women. The IAF withdrew its candidates after voting had started, claiming that the Government was interfering in elections and that Amman's council was only half 'elected'. In August King Abdullah dissolved parliament ahead of polls scheduled for November. Despite opposition protests, parliament passed the Political Parties Law in 2007. Of the 36 existing parties, only 12, including the IAF, had filed for status by the deadline. The law required that a party have at least 500 members from at least five governorates. The 2007 elections confirmed the strength of pro-Government candidates and especially of tribal leaders, while the IAF suffered, taking only six seats, 11 fewer than in 2003. The new legislature comprised primarily members of the business elite, tribal leaders and former military personnel, and thus represented a major victory for pro-regime political forces.

By the end of 2008 inflation in Jordan had reached a new high with increased fuel prices and an unsuccessful harvest. Beginning in 2007 the Government gradually removed subsidies on fuel and food to decrease its budget deficit. The resulting price increases, however, negatively affected Jordanians and led to protests. In response, the Government increased public sector wages and delayed subsidy reductions on liquid petroleum gas for domestic use. Financial aid from the USA and Saudi Arabia helped the Government to stay afloat, and official figures showed that financial aid between 2004 and 2007 reached US $2,600m.

In July 2009 King Abdullah appointed, through royal decree, his 15-year-old eldest son, Prince Hussein, as Crown Prince. In that year, owing to the influx of Iraqi refugees and the global economic downturn, unemployment reached almost 30%; inflation rose above 9%; and national debt amounted to some US $11,000m.

In November 2009 King Abdullah dissolved parliament. Although the Constitution requires that a new parliament be formed within four months of its dissolution, the King failed to schedule a date for new elections until the cabinet produced a new electoral law. (Elections were eventually held in November 2010, with the Government ruling by emergency law in the interim.) In May 2010 the cabinet approved the new electoral law: the quota for female deputies was increased from six to 12 seats, with nine seats reserved for Christians and three seats for Circassians; 10 seats were also added, bringing the total for the lower house to 120 seats. Of the 10 new seats, four were in traditionally under-represented urban and Palestinian-dominated areas. The opposition still complained, nonetheless, about the one person, one vote system, which helped tribes to maintain their influence in the legislature.

Meanwhile, East Bank Jordanians felt that Palestinians inside Jordan were gaining too much power in senior government positions, possibly through the influence of King Abdullah's Palestinian wife, Queen Rania. A petition by 60 former army officers made such claims, in addition to criticizing Abdullah's attempts at economic liberalization, demanding disenfranchisement of Palestinians, urging anti-corruption measures and greater military strength against Israel, and calling for formalization in the Constitution of the 1988 disengagement with the West Bank, to prevent Israel from reviving a Jordanian option to the Palestinian question.

RELATIONS WITH THE NETANYAHU GOVERNMENT AND FAILURE OF PEACE TALKS

Relations with Israel deteriorated with the election of Benjamin Netanyahu as Prime Minister (his second term of office) at the head of a coalition Government in February 2009. His right-wing Likud party was far more confrontational with the Palestinian population and continued with the construction of settlements. King Abdullah remained supportive of US President Barack Obama's efforts at Israeli-Palestinian peace, and so was invited to Washington, DC, in September 2010, with Hosni Mubarak, for US-brokered negotiations between Netanyahu and PA President Mahmoud Abbas. This effort garnered little domestic support inside Jordan, with the IAF leading the opposition to the talks. Over the course of several rounds of negotiations basic principles were drawn up but lacked specificity. In September a 10-month moratorium on Israeli settlement construction in the West Bank lapsed, and Netanyahu could not be persuaded to extend it, despite US offers of increased aid if he did so. Abbas therefore stopped the talks—a move that the Arab League supported.

THE 2010 PARLIAMENTARY ELECTIONS

A new round of parliamentary elections was held in November 2010—a year after King Abdullah had unconstitutionally dissolved the body. International monitors observed the polls for the first time and concluded that they were fair; about 53% of eligible voters participated, with only 34% in Amman. Urban voters tended not to participate, as many of them supported the IAF, which had resolved to boycott the elections. The resulting composition of the parliament was much like previous iterations: even though 70% of the MPs were newly elected, they were still primarily loyalist tribal figures.

ARRIVAL OF THE 'ARAB SPRING' IN JORDAN

In January 2011, at the onset of the so-called Arab Spring, thousands of Jordanians, inspired by recent uprisings in Egypt and Tunisia, protested against high prices, unemployment, corruption and lack of representative government. Such rallies took place in Amman, Ma'an, al-Karak, al-Salt, Irbid and other, smaller cities. King Abdullah went through a series of three different prime ministers to try to stem the tide of the movements, with protesters directing most of their vitriol at government ministers rather than at the monarch himself.

The Government's initial effort to halt weekly protests involved the provision of economic benefits, in particular a decreased tax on petrol, higher subsidies on gas and some food items, and higher public sector salaries; this amounted to a US $230m. package. When such disbursements failed to mollify the population, Prime Minister Samir Rifai proposed a $550m. subsidy package for fuel and staple food products (requiring Jordan to rely more heavily on foreign grants to rebalance its budget), yet this still did not stem the popular protests. King Abdullah dismissed his cabinet in February 2011 and made Marouf al-Bakhit his new Prime Minister. The IAF accused al-Bakhit of corruption, but East Bankers were pleased with his appointment because, unlike Rifai, al-Bakhit was not Palestinian. King Abdullah demanded that al-Bakhit seriously consider enhancing the political reform process.

To demonstrate his commitment to reform, the King created a National Dialogue Committee, led by Speaker of the Senate and former premier Taher al-Masri, to recommend reforms—particularly to the electoral law that would advance party and parliamentary politics. The IAF and other opposition groups believed that reform should lie in the hands of elected MPs, rather than government elites, and assumed that these figures would not deliver major reforms. When reforms did not emerge, the protests continued in February and March 2011. On 18 February alleged pro-regime supporters attacked a peaceful protest, the first violence at such demonstrations.

On 25 February some 100,000 people protested in Amman, and weekly protests, on Friday after prayers, were held thereafter.

In February 2011 a group of 36 major East Banker tribal members, traditionally loyal to the regime, sent a letter to King Abdullah alleging that Queen Rania was interfering with politics, and in particular had installed family members in influential positions in order to enrich them and to extend Palestinian influence. It also warned that Jordan would face protests if democratic reforms were not introduced; the statement read: '[p]olitical reform is now an urgent matter that cannot be delayed'. Such an attack on a member of the royal family and such an urgent call for reform were unprecedented. In response, a petition, signed by 3,000 tribal leaders, denounced the letter and reiterated their loyalty to King Abdullah.

Two discontented factions had thus emerged: a pro-reform contingent, composed of leftists, youth and the Muslim Brotherhood; and East Banker tribes on whom King Abdullah had traditionally relied for political support. About 40% of Jordan's population is tribal, making it a very important demographic for the Government. The fact that even a small number of tribal members released a statement expressing political discontent was both surprising and worrying to the King. Further complicating relations with the tribes, at the beginning of January 2011 inter-tribal violence had broken out in southern Jordan, in particular in the cities of al-Salt and Ma'an.

On 22 May 2011 a pro-reform political coalition, including opposition parties and trade unionists, was formed to advocate for the 'rule of law' in Jordan. Constitutional amendments, government accountability, anti-corruption measures, new economic policies, redefining the role of security agencies, judicial reforms, press freedoms, and reforming the educational system were the main cornerstones of this National Front for Reform, according to a statement released by the coalition. The group united a disparate collection of parties, including the IAF, the Jordanian Communist Party, the Jordanian Democratic Popular Unity Party (Wihda), the country's two Baathist groups, the Jordanian People's Democratic Party (Hizb al-Shaab al-Dimuqrati), the National Current Party, the Social Left Movement and the Jordanian Women's Union. Other members included several professional associations and trade unions, in addition to independent figures. Such co-ordination was short-lived, however, as members of the coalition came to disagree on several topics, particularly after the fall of the Muslim Brotherhood-led Government in Egypt in 2013. None the less, it provided a new framework for opposition co-operation inside Jordan, which may be reignited in the future, and which was highly influential over the course of the 2011 protests.

The first protest-related death took place on 24 March 2011, when a youth-led organization, the 'Youth of March 24' organized a sit-in in front of the Interior Ministry Circle in Amman. Pro-Government supporters attacked the sit-in, provoking the involvement of security forces, who allegedly sided with the pro-regime protesters and attacked reformists. As a result, 62 civilians and 52 police officers were injured, and one man died.

GOVERNMENT EFFORTS AT REFORM

In his first televised speech since the outbreak of the protests, King Abdullah pledged on 12 June 2011 that the country's parliament would be reformed. He said that a new electoral law would create 'a parliament with active political party representation . . . that allows the formation of governments based on parliamentary majority . . . in the future'. He also reiterated that the National Dialogue Committee, established in March, was reviewing the country's Constitution and he promised to fight corruption and promote democracy.

The National Dialogue Committee proposed a new electoral law, which did not replace the one person, one vote system but recommended introducing 15 more seats to be contested at the national level, leaving in place existing governorates. Reformers, especially the IAF, were frustrated by this proposal. They were once again disappointed when, in August 2011, the Royal Committee on Constitutional Review recommended 42 amendments to empower parliament. Concessions included the end of military trials for civilians, outlawing torture, more accountability for ministers, and an independent judiciary; however, primary power remained in the hands of the King. He was allowed to rule without parliament for four years—as opposed to the two years granted by earlier legislation—and the parliament did not gain the right to appoint the Prime Minister (a key demand), with the King instead appointing him. The recommendations passed through the (mainly loyalist) parliament, yet the balance of power between King and legislature remained largely the same.

Opposition protests persisted. Violence erupted during a protest in central Amman in July 2011 led by the Center for Defending Freedom of Journalists, leading to accusations that security forces and loyalists were violently targeting protesters. Prime Minister al-Bakhit was accused of corruption and of passing an anti-corruption law that was held to be aimed at silencing the press. He also tried to restructure municipal boundaries in advance of municipal elections, leading some 70 MPs to write a letter to the Royal Court criticizing him.

King Abdullah replaced al-Bakhit with Awn Khasawneh, former Chief of the Royal Court, in October 2011. He, too, postponed the December elections, in the hope of re-establishing municipal borders in the interim. Abdullah promised that elections would be held within six months of the approval of a new municipalities law. None the less, the protests continued. Criticism of the police and of the regime intensified after loyalists clashed with Islamist protesters in Mafraq in December and the IAF's local headquarters was set on fire.

In March 2012 the new cabinet submitted a proposed new electoral law that took into account the National Dialogue Committee's recommendations by increasing the number of parliamentary seats to 138 (three for women and 15 by proportional representation). The remaining 120 would be elected on a constituency basis, in 45 constituencies wherein each voter would have two local votes and one national vote for the extra 15 seats. The draft legislation added that no party could win more than five of the 15 new seats. The opposition remained dissatisfied, as it hoped that people would be granted more than one vote at national level, making people less likely to vote based on tribal affiliation.

In June 2012 parliament approved the new electoral law, which was almost universally denounced by the opposition, leading to an IAF boycott of the 2013 polls. The new legislation was alleged by its opponents to grant more weight to areas of traditional government support. The January 2013 elections led to a loyalist parliament, and opposition complaints about an unfair election. The official rate of turnout was 56%—a figure that the opposition insisted was inflated.

THE SYRIAN CRISIS COMES TO JORDAN

As the region descended into increasing chaos and violence during the course of 2011, Jordan resolved to reach out to several new allies, both inside and outside the Middle East. It also became an attractive destination for foreign aid, as one of the only seemingly stable states in an ever more chaotic region. Saudi Arabia granted Jordan US $400m. in June 2011, and the US Agency for International Development gave $359m. in September. By the end of the year Jordan had been promised more than $1,400m. in grants—its stability had become more important in light of the outbreak of civil war in neighbouring Syria.

Political disintegration in Syria drastically altered the domestic economic, political and social situation inside Jordan. Anti-regime protests that had started in the southern city of Dar'a, near the Jordanian border, had transformed into a civil war by the end of 2011. Notably, King Abdullah became the first Arab leader to call on President Assad to step down from power, in November 2011, when his regime had begun responding violently to growing and persistent protests. Inside Jordan, the IAF was sympathetic to the Syrian opposition and arranged demonstrations outside Syria's embassy, urging the Jordanian Government to withdraw its ambassador from the Syrian capital, Damascus.

Thousands of Syrian refugees began fleeing to Jordan in 2011, reinforced by strong cross-border tribal linkages. In July

2012, in an effort to deal with the massive inflow of refugees, the Jordanian authorities began construction of the Zaatari camp; by 2013 it housed some 140,000 people, making it the fourth largest city in Jordan. Another camp was built near Zarqa in March 2013. Costs were crippling. In that year King Abdullah claimed that refugees were costing the Government US $550m. annually. Low-level riots broke out in April, owing to poor conditions inside the camps. A third refugee camp finally opened in Azraq in April 2014, following delays, owing to a lack of foreign funding.

Jordan became drawn into the violence in Syria through Jordanians' involvement. In October 2012 a group of 11 Jordanians, allegedly with connections to al-Qa'ida in Iraq, were arrested for plotting terrorist attacks in Jordan using weapons from Syria. The jihadist group Islamic State in Iraq and the Levant (subsequently renamed Islamic State), originally an offshoot of al-Qa'ida, proved to have broader ambitions of expanding its purview over Iraq, Syria, Lebanon, Israel and the Palestinian Territories, and Jordan. From 2011 up to 2,200 Jordanians went to fight in Iraq and Syria alongside Islamic State, with a Jordanian official estimating that 900 were fighting in those countries as of 2017. Legislation in April 2014 that broadened the scope of terrorist offences and increased penalties for the guilty, helped the authorities to crack down on terrorism.

The Jordanian military had become involved in skirmishes with Syrian troops, mainly when protecting refugees crossing the border. Reportedly, the Jordanian Government permitted Saudi Arabia to supply its rebel allies with arms through Jordan in exchange for aid, and the CIA was also said to be training Syrian rebel fighters in Jordan. In mid-2013 US missile launchers and fighter aircraft, as well as 1,000 troops, were sent to Jordan, but the Jordanian Government refused to allow the USA to launch an aerial bombardment from its territory. Indeed, Jordan maintained diplomatic ties with Syria, owing largely to the fact that many Jordanians lived in Syria. The Syrian ambassador was expelled only in May 2014, after speaking about Jordan providing refuge for the Syrian opposition.

The Jordanian economy has suffered under the weight of the new population, as have its infrastructure and public services. The census of November 2015 indicated that there were almost 1.3m. Syrians in Jordan at that time. More than 13m. people—one-half of Syria's pre-war population—had been killed or forced to leave that country as a result of the conflict. There had been a 9%–10% population increase in Jordan as a result, putting a severe strain on water resources that were already threatened. The rate of unemployment in Jordan was estimated, as of 2020, to stand at 23.2%, although youth unemployment was considerably higher. Economic issues that existed long before the Syrian conflict have only become further exacerbated, with no clear end in sight for the Syrian conflict. Indeed, an estimated two-thirds of Syrian refugees lived below the poverty line in 2020.

To help to relieve worsening economic pressures on Jordan, the World Bank announced plans in September 2016 to release US $300m. in loans to assist Syrian refugees to enter the Jordanian workforce. The funds were meant to attract investors and foster economic reforms to help Syrian refugees to gain access to work. In the same month, the UN denounced the living conditions of some 70,000 refugees at the border with Syria, where Jordan blocked both entry and the delivery of aid after a suicide bombing by Islamic State that killed seven Jordanian soldiers in June (see *The Rise of Islamic State and Jordan's New Alliances*).

Jordan has served as a key interlocutor in peace talks. In March 2018 Jordan hosted a meeting between US Secretary of State Rex Tillerson and the so-called moderate Syrian opposition, ahead of a meeting with the leaders of the Russian Federation. Russia invited Jordan to attend peace talks in Astana, Kazakhstan, and urged that the Jordanian–Syrian border be one of four proposed 'de-escalation zones'. In the interest of preserving Jordanian security and stability, King Abdullah urged the Government of Russia and the US Administration to reach agreement on this matter.

At the end of 2018 Jordan strengthened its ties with Syria in an attempt to end Syrian regional isolation and stabilize the Syrian state. In October Jordan facilitated the reopening of the Nasib border crossing, which had been closed since 2015, to help to revive trade and ease Syria's isolation. In November 2018 Jordan entered into talks with the USA and Russia about closing down Rukban refugee camp in Syria on the border with Jordan, which was housing some 50,000 displaced Syrians, in order to defuse regional security tensions. As of July 2023 the camp had not yet been closed and was facing shortages, owing to a halt in smuggling routes into the camp. Meanwhile, in January 2019 Jordan appointed a chargé d'affaires at its embassy in Damascus, and in the same month Jordanian civil aviation officials held talks with their Syrian counterparts about the resumption of passenger flights between the two countries.

THE RETURN OF MILITARY RULE IN EGYPT: FOREIGN POLICY AND DOMESTIC EFFECTS

Meanwhile, a changing political landscape in Egypt added to regional confusion. On 3 July 2013 the Egyptian armed forces, under the leadership of Gen. Abd al-Fatah al-Sisi, removed from power President Mohamed Mursi, who had been elected in June 2012 as the Muslim Brotherhood's candidate. This led to a suspension of the recently approved Egyptian Constitution and a violent crackdown on the Muslim Brotherhood, which seemed to spread throughout the region, with Saudi Arabia and the United Arab Emirates (UAE) both designating the Brotherhood as a terrorist organization. The Jordanian Government supported both the coup and the resulting crackdown on the Muslim Brotherhood; King Abdullah became the first foreign leader to make an official visit to President al-Sisi on 20 July 2013.

The IAF was outraged by the coup in Egypt and was angered by King Abdullah's public support for it, leading the Muslim Brotherhood and other Islamists to hold demonstrations in Jordan. Notably, in the aftermath of the coup, a division emerged inside the IAF itself, with more moderate Islamists breaking away to form the National Initiative for Building (Zamzam), which adopted a more conciliatory attitude towards the Government than the IAF.

By supporting al-Sisi, Jordan secured its alliance with Saudi Arabia, which had financially bolstered the Egyptian military regime. Saudi Arabia even offered Jordan its seat on the UN Security Council following its election to that body in 2013. Jordan had been particularly eager to forge strong links with Saudi Arabia as the US Administration of President Barack Obama became increasingly disengaged from the Middle East. Ties with the USA remained close, however: the latter committed to lend some US $1,000m. to Jordan in February 2014.

THE RISE OF ISLAMIC STATE AND JORDAN'S NEW ALLIANCES

In early 2014 Jordan agreed to the restoration of diplomatic ties with Iran. In March King Abdullah also received a visit from the Amir of Qatar, Sheikh Tamim bin Hamad Al Thani, and commercial ties with Russia increased. Jordan also came to a rapprochement with Hamas, with which there had been an uneasy relationship since its 1999 expulsion from Jordan. Khalid Meshaal met King Abdullah and Sheikh Tamim in Amman in January 2012, where Qatar offered Jordan up to US $1,000m. per year and a free supply of gas if it would agree to host Hamas. Jordan had also welcomed an invitation by the Cooperation Council for the Arab States of the Gulf (GCC, see p. 1131) to apply for membership in 2011, as this would strengthen its trade profile and ability to increase aid from the Gulf considerably.

These ties became increasingly important with the continued rise of Islamic State. From its base in Raqqa, Syria, Islamic State alarmed Jordan in January 2014 when it captured the Iraqi city of Fallujah, on the border with Jordan. Jordanian troops were deployed on the eastern border. In June, after Islamic State attacked several Iraqi targets and captured Mosul, Tikrit, Ramadi and Rutba, about 100 km from the Jordanian border, the Jordanian military became further alarmed. Shortly after the capture of Mosul, the authorities discovered that a group in Ma'an had planned to raise Islamic

State's flag there. In late September Jordan became involved in US-led air strikes on Islamic State in northern Syria; Bahrain, Saudi Arabia and the UAE also participated.

In December 2014 Jordanian military pilot Muath al-Kasasbeh was shot down over Syria and captured by Islamic State, which initially offered to exchange al-Kasasbeh for two Islamist militants imprisoned for their role in the 2005 Amman bombings. Negotiations proceeded, and the Jordanian Government demanded proof of life in late January 2015 before the exchange. In early February, however, Islamic State released footage of the pilot being burned to death. King Abdullah promised retaliation and authorized the execution of the two prisoners whose release Islamic State had demanded. On the same day, the Jordanian air force undertook additional air strikes in Mosul and launched an assault in Syria, targeting Raqqa. In February 2017 Jordan conducted aerial bombing raids on Islamic State positions in southern Syria.

In the most serious attack in recent years in Jordan, Jordanian Islamic State militants claimed responsibility for a gun attack that took place in December 2016 at a Crusader castle in al-Karak in which 14 people were killed—the first attack by Islamic State on Jordanian territory. Jordanian police reported that they had killed four gunmen in an exchange of fire that lasted for several hours. Jordanian security forces arrested a man suspected of funding the atrocity and claimed that further attacks had been planned across the country.

Islamic State claimed responsibility for a suicide attack on 21 June 2016 that killed seven soldiers at a military post in Rukban on the Syrian border. Shortly after the attack, the Jordanian army declared the country's desert regions bordering Syria in the north-east and Iraq in the east 'closed military zones'. The bombing came only two weeks after a gunman had killed five Jordanian intelligence officers in a Palestinian refugee camp north of Amman. The five suspected attackers were sentenced to death in January 2017 with 16 other Jordanians sentenced to prison terms of between three and 15 years for their part in the attacks. The militants were reported to have been part of an Islamic State cell that had been broken up in March 2016 through a large-scale security mission in Irbid.

An attack in August 2018 carried out by Jordanian adherents of Islamic State killed five members of the security forces in Fuheis, west of Amman; three suspects were killed and five arrested in a subsequent police raid in al-Salt, and large quantities of explosives were discovered buried near the suspects' hideout. In November a total of 10 Jordanians were sentenced to prison terms of between three years and life for their roles in the Islamic State attack in December 2016 in al-Karak.

Relations with Israel, which had been tense, owing to the 2014 break-up of Palestinian protests in Jerusalem by Israeli security forces, improved after the killing of al-Kasasbeh. Prime Minister Netanyahu personally called King Abdullah to express his condolences. The Israeli Minister of Foreign Affairs, Avigdor Lieberman, also publicly condemned the pilot's murder and praised the King's response of increasing military action against Islamic State. The relationship between the Israeli and Jordanian militaries remained deep, particularly as they faced a shared threat. However, in statements made in August 2016, after seven Jewish extremist protesters were detained by Israeli police for breaking into the al-Aqsa/Temple Mount compound, King Abdullah reiterated his commitment to remaining custodian of the holy sites in Jerusalem, and said that 'Jordan will fight Israeli aggression, which is manifested by the incursion of extremist Israelis into the [al-Aqsa] mosque compound'. He also stated that he would ensure that al-Aqsa's compound was not partitioned.

In September 2016 the Jordanian Government signed an agreement to import natural gas from Israel in order to lower energy costs and diversify sources of natural gas. Despite limited protests in October the agreement went ahead.

Relations with the new US Administration under President Donald Trump remained close, particularly with regard to combating Islamic State and achieving peace with Israel. In April 2017, following a US air strike on a Syrian air base, the Jordanian Government dubbed the action a 'necessary and appropriate response' to a chemical weapons attack blamed on the Syrian Government. In the following month Jordan and the USA engaged in annual military exercises, the seventh held since 2011 and the largest and most complex to date, involving some 6,000 Jordanian and US troops.

The threat of Islamic State-inspired attacks in Jordan remained. In November 2019 Jordanian intelligence officials foiled a plot by two suspected jihadist militants to carry out terrorist attacks against US and Israeli diplomats and US troops at a military base in southern Jordan. In January 2020 three Jordanians were charged with stabbing eight people at one of the country's most visited archaeological sites in Jerash, in an attack carried out in November 2019, which was apparently inspired by Islamic State. The three defendants, who had allegedly planned to conduct another attack on a church in northern Jordan, pleaded guilty. In January 2021 a Jordanian security court sentenced a man to death for the attack at Jerash; another man was sentenced to life imprisonment and a third to a prison term of seven years for allegedly aiding the attack.

King Abdullah received a telephone call in early October 2021 from Syrian President Bashar al-Assad, the first since the beginning of Syria's civil war. King Abdullah confirmed Jordan's support for 'efforts to preserve Syria's sovereignty, stability, territorial integrity and people'. The conversation also came days after Jordan had fully reopened its main border crossing with Syria, amid a region-wide move to work towards normalizing ties with the Syrian regime. Over the course of 2021 Jordan also issued a record number of 62,000 work permits to Syrian refugees entering its labour market. Syrian refugees had been permitted to work in several sectors of the Jordanian economy since 2016. In March 2022 Turkey and Jordan agreed to work together to ensure the voluntary return of Syrians living in the two countries. As of July 2023 Jordan was hosting 739,557 refugees and asylum seekers registered with the UNHCR; of these, 659,030 were from Syria, making Jordan the number two host (after Lebanon) of Syrian refugees per capita globally.

During the first half of 2022 Jordan worked to cement and diversify its regional security ties, particularly amid concerns about Iran's nuclear capabilities. In February the Jordanian and Egyptian armed forces conducted joint military drills called 'Aqaba 6'. In the same month the US Administration of President Joe Biden approved a US $4,200m. sale of F-16 fighter aircraft to Jordan. In March Jordan and Iraq signed a memorandum of understanding to increase security co-operation. King Abdullah also stated, in June, that he would support the formation of a Middle East military alliance, similar to the North Atlantic Treaty Organization. The establishment of such a body was discussed during President Biden's visit to the Middle East in July.

During 2022 Jordan became increasingly involved in efforts to resolve the ongoing Yemeni civil war, reflecting its strengthened ties with Saudi Arabia. In November King Abdullah met the head of Yemen's Presidential Leadership Council, Rashad al-Alimi, in Amman, whereupon he reiterated his country's support for efforts to end the conflict. Notably, the headquarters of the office of the UN Special Envoy for Yemen has been housed in Amman since 2017, and at late 2022 the Jordanian capital was home to around 14,000 Yemeni refugees. The Yemen conflict showed some signs of de-escalating in 2022, with the country coming under the control of the Presidential Leadership Council in April following the signing of a ceasefire, and in May Amman was the destination for the first Yemeni passenger plane to depart San'a (the capital of Yemen) in six years.

THE DOMESTIC LANDSCAPE AND 2016 ELECTIONS

King Abdullah dissolved parliament in October 2012 and called for new elections, two years ahead of schedule, as a means of showing his commitment to reform. The King also appointed Abdullah Ensour, seen as more moderate than his predecessor, as the new Prime Minister. The final electoral law produced by the Government was still unsatisfactory: it reserved 15 parliamentary seats for women, while 27 were to be chosen through party lists, with the remaining 108 decided by first-past-the-post local elections within gerrymandered constituency boundaries that were favourable to loyalists. The IAF boycotted the polls as a result. The elections took place in January 2013, attracting a turnout of 56%. Independents and tribal loyalists were reported to have received some three-quarters of the total number of votes. A newly created 'moderate' Islamist group, the Islamic Centrist Party, received the highest number of seats (16 in total).

Opposition continued to grow in 2013. None the less, the IAF and other opposition movements collectively known as 'Hirak' could not garner the level of popular support as enjoyed by similar movements in Egypt and Syria. The regime, aside from failing to make major changes to the electoral law, also increased censorship, making it even more difficult for the opposition to publicize its grievances. A new press law in September 2012 demanded that all media register with local authorities. None the less, opposition emerged in unexpected areas. In early 2013 members of the East Banker tribal youth population in southern Jordan resorted to violence, owing to a lack of economic opportunity and inability to influence the Government. Sporadic riots took place in Ma'an and in universities in the south such as Al-Hussein Bin Talal University and Mutah University—areas that were traditionally loyalist strongholds.

In June 2013 the Prime Minister suggested the revision of the electoral law to allow a system based on party lists, which would lessen tribal power; he also appointed former political activists to his cabinet to signal his commitment to reform. In addition, Ensour placed restrictions on the power of the State Security Court in September and introduced a National Integrity Charter in December in an attempt to stem the tide of corruption. Despite such progress, the IAF remained unimpressed, boycotting the August 2013 municipal elections, which had a turnout of only 37%.

New anti-terrorism laws were enacted in June 2014, and led to the arrest of several members of the Muslim Brotherhood, including deputy leader Zaki Bani Irshad. King Abdullah also stepped up his criticism of that organization, calling it a 'masonic cult ... run by wolves in sheep's clothing'. This anti-Brotherhood stance culminated, in April 2016, in the closure of its Amman headquarters. Jordanian authorities claimed that the Brotherhood had not obtained legal authorization to continue its activities, as its licence had not been renewed as stipulated in the Political Parties Law of 2014. For its part, the Brotherhood called the Government's decision 'illegal' and 'politically motivated'. Notably, the Government authorized the formation of the breakaway Zamzam in 2015 as the official Muslim Brotherhood party in Jordan, which took a more conciliatory stance towards the Government than did the IAF.

The IAF had boycotted the last two parliamentary polls, but it planned to participate in the elections to the 130-seat House of Representatives on 20 September 2016. The IAF formed a broad coalition with various groups representing Christians to the Circassian and Chechen communities to contest seats in 15 of the 23 electoral districts, and was expected to receive considerable popular support. At the elections, which took place as scheduled under the supervision of European Union observers, turnout was estimated at 36%, compared with more than 50% in the 2013 polls. Final results published by the Independent Elections Committee indicated that the IAF-led coalition, the National Coalition for Reform, had secured 15 seats in the new legislature, while Zamzam and the Islamic Centrist Party each took five seats. Candidates representing political parties—including the IAF—won 30 seats in total, while the majority of the others elected were independents representing either tribal or business interests. The new legislature had 74 first-time MPs, representing a significant turnover from the previous legislature.

Shortly after the elections, protesters called for the resignation of the Government, in particular Prime Minister Hani Mulki and Minister of the Interior Hammad, over its alleged failure to prevent the killing of Christian writer Nahed Hattar on 25 September 2016 outside an Amman court, where he was standing trial on charges relating to an anti-Islam cartoon.

In January 2017 King Abdullah reorganized the cabinet, but retained Prime Minister Mulki, in an effort to face down Islamist militants and continue with unpopular IMF-mandated economic reforms to decrease public debt. This was the second reorganization since Mulki was appointed in May 2016. Hammad was replaced as Minister of the Interior by Ghalib al-Zu'bi, after narrowly avoiding a parliamentary vote of no confidence over his handling of the Islamic State attack in al-Karak in December 2016. After the reorganization, Mulki defended the recent arrest of a group of prominent retired army and security officers who had criticized the monarch and blamed recent security breaches on official corruption, by claiming that 'we respect freedom of expression as long as it does not violate the higher national interest'.

Protests, led by the IAF and its coalition, took place in February 2017 over government decisions to impose new taxes on a variety of goods and services. While the rallies began in Amman, similar protests were reported in al-Salt, al-Karak and Madaba. The price increases were the result of Jordan's deal with the IMF to secure a US $723m. three-year line of credit.

THE GCC CRISIS

In June 2017 GCC members Bahrain, Egypt, Saudi Arabia and the UAE severed all ties with neighbouring Qatar over complaints about that state's funding of terrorist organizations and backing of the Al Jazeera media network. Although Jordan had traditionally maintained solid ties with both sides of this rift (indeed, the GCC considered allowing Jordan and Morocco to apply for membership in 2011), it initially seemed to side with Saudi Arabia in this latest row. One day after the quartet cut ties with Qatar, Jordan downgraded diplomatic relations with Qatar and revoked Al Jazeera's broadcasting licence.

None the less, Jordan did not consider either the Muslim Brotherhood (which had seats in parliament) or Hamas to be dangerous to the degree the anti-Qatar quartet did. Furthermore, the Qatari ambassador was the only Qatari who was asked to leave the country, and Royal Jordanian, the country's flagship airline, continued its flights to the Qatari capital, Doha. Jordan therefore appeared to be trying to maintain ties with both sides of the conflict.

Key GCC allies Kuwait, Saudi Arabia and the UAE failed to renew a five-year financial assistance programme with Amman worth US $3,600m. that ended in 2017; the $5,000m. GCC aid package that ended in 2016 was also not renewed. In June 2018, however, Kuwait, Saudi Arabia and the UAE pledged $2,500m. of aid to Jordan as renewed protests (discussed below) were spurred on by recently enacted austerity measures, specifically the introduction of a controversial income tax bill. The pledge included a deposit to Jordan's central bank, guarantees to the World Bank, annual budgetary support for five years, and a series of development projects. A few days after the new pledge of aid was announced, Qatar promised $500m. for infrastructure and tourism investments, while promising to open 10,000 jobs to Jordanian nationals in Qatar. It was hoped that these packages, although less generous than previous programmes, could help Jordan to achieve a politically viable austerity plan. Notably, in July 2019 King Abdullah issued a royal decree to appoint a new ambassador to Qatar, after the previous envoy had been withdrawn in June 2017 at the start of the GCC crisis, becoming the first state to restore its diplomatic presence in Qatar since the dispute began.

In July 2019 senior Jordanian officials held discussions in Amman with the Turkish Minister of Foreign Affairs, the Minister of National Defence and the chiefs of the Turkish intelligence services and armed forces; the two parties issued a joint statement proclaiming that the two countries had agreed to 'develop their ties and expand economic co-operation and deepen co-ordination on regional issues'. The move was seen as a snub to Saudi Arabia, particularly as it came shortly after Jordan's appointment of a new ambassador to Qatar, which Saudi Arabia, together with Bahrain, Egypt and the UAE, continued to blockade. Jordan had abrogated a free trade pact with Turkey in 2018, under pressure from Saudi Arabia, which sought to diminish Turkey's role in the region, but the Turkish President, Recep Tayyip Erdoğan, has been vocal in supporting the role of King Abdullah as custodian of Muslim religious sites in Jerusalem, and by mid-2021 the relationship between Turkey and Jordan appeared to have improved.

VIOLENCE IN PALESTINE

The Jordanian Government expressed its opposition to the USA's decision in December 2017 to move its embassy in Israel from Tel Aviv to Jerusalem. In May 2018, after the move led to protests, King Abdullah condemned 'the blatant acts of aggression and violence perpetrated by Israel' against Palestinian Arabs in Gaza and reiterated his criticism of the embassy relocation during a telephone call with French President Emmanuel Macron.

At the end of May 2018, a consultative meeting in Cairo, Egypt, brought together the Egyptian and Jordanian foreign affairs ministers, along with the Secretary-General of the Executive Committee of the PLO, and each country's heads of intelligence, to discuss developments in Palestine. All parties reiterated their condemnation of Israeli actions and warned of the danger of continued and escalating violence in the area. They also discussed means of obtaining more protection for Palestinians through the UN. The Palestinian Minister of Foreign Affairs requested that the International Criminal Court investigate Israel's settlements in the occupied Palestinian territories and human rights violations. This move signalled a worsening of ties between the PA and the Netanyahu Government. In July the Jordanian Government sent the Israeli Government a note protesting against settler raids on the al-Aqsa Mosque, signalling further disagreements between the two.

In the first half of 2019 the Trump Administration promoted its so-called deal of the century peace plan to ease Israeli–Palestinian tensions. In May King Abdullah met President Trump's senior adviser and son-in-law, Jared Kushner, in Amman, to discuss the plan, amid vociferous anti-US public protests. The King's statements at the meeting emphasized that negotiations should be based on a two-state solution and an independent Palestinian state with its capital in Jerusalem. Hundreds of Islamists marched in Amman in June to protest against Kushner's plan and the participation of the Jordanian Government at a workshop held in that month in Bahrain to promote a US $50,000m. 'peace to prosperity plan'; the PA boycotted the event. Although a Jordanian delegation attended the conference, it did not send ministerial-level representatives (it was represented by a civil servant from the Ministry of Finance) and emphasized that a plan based on economics should not replace a political solution to end the Israeli occupation of the West Bank and establish an independent Palestinian state.

EFFECTS OF REGIONAL DISORDER ON DOMESTIC POLITICS

Although the Jordanian Government has long fallen short of delivering its promised political reforms, there has been a general tightening of the domestic political sphere, particularly after the Arab Spring heightened security concerns. Most dramatically, 15 people were executed in March 2017—at that time the largest number to be executed in a single day in recent history; Amnesty International claimed that the executions had been carried out in 'secrecy and without transparency' and therefore represented 'a big step backwards on human rights protection in Jordan'. Ten of the 15 executed had been convicted on terrorism charges, and the other five were involved in an attack on security forces in the city of Irbid.

Beginning in June 2018, some of the largest protests seen in years took place over the implementation of IMF-backed price increases; the protests were organized under the banner of Al Hirak Al Shababi (The Youth Movement), in addition to involving 33 professional associations and civil society groups. Thousands of protesters called for the resignation of Prime Minister Mulki as a means of stopping a draft income tax bill which the Government had sent to parliament in May and which many believed would lead to a decline in living standards in Jordan. The protests resulted in Mulki's resignation and, more importantly, the withdrawal of the tax bill. Omar al-Razzaz, previously the Minister of Education, formed a new cabinet. Although the protests died down, austerity remained a major issue in Jordan.

In October 2018 Prime Minister al-Razzaz announced a cabinet reorganization in an effort to pursue austerity measures and spur economic growth. Several members of his new cabinet were political conservatives who had served in past governments, as well as tribal figures, some of whom had criticized the proposed income tax bill. In November parliament approved the controversial tax law and other legislation aimed at reducing public debt; notably, parliament also approved a series of amendments to the bill that included exemptions to ease the impact on middle-income taxpayers. Large protests against the bill took place in Amman, calling for the Prime Minister to resign over the issue and his failure to improve economic performance. Protests escalated in December, and security personnel dispersed demonstrators at an anti-austerity rally in Amman with tear gas and arrested 17 protesters, yet ultimately the Government sought to hold a dialogue with protesters. In February 2019 Prime Minister al-Razzaz reported that the economy was beginning to recover, and in June parliament announced that it had enacted further measures to reduce the effects of the new tax legislation on middle-income taxpayers.

Unrest in Syria has continued to destabilize Jordan, not least in terms of the influx of Syrians into Jordan seeking refuge from the conflict. Since 2018, when the Syrian military and pro-Iranian militias seized control of much of southern Syria, Jordan has struggled to stem the trade of illegal narcotics, particularly Captagon (fenethylline), from that territory into Jordan and Saudi Arabia. Despite repeated assurances from the Jordanian Deputy Prime Minister and Minister of Foreign and Expatriates Affairs, Ayman al-Safadi, that the Jordanian authorities were doing all that they could to stop the flow of drugs, diplomats in Amman and security officials across the region estimate that the trade of narcotics from Syria into Jordan is worth billions of dollars every year. Improved relations with the Syrian Government since 2021, as discussed above, do not appear to have diminished the flow of illegal drugs. In May 2023, days after Syria was readmitted to the Arab League and pledged to fight drug smuggling, Jordanian forces for the first time launched air strikes against a major drug smuggler based in southern Syria. Fears of possible further air strikes drove some drug smugglers to evacuate the area in the following weeks. Nevertheless, in a raid in June some 22,000 illicit Captagon pills and 75 pouches of hashish were seized.

In February 2023 al-Safadi visited Damascus and the Turkish capital, Ankara, in the wake of a massive earthquake that caused widespread devastation and loss of life in Syria and Türkiye. Al-Safadi's visit to Syria was the first such visit by a senior Jordanian official since the start of the Syrian civil war in 2011. In May al-Safadi announced that Jordan had 'exceeded its capacity' to manage Syrian refugees, although he also stated that they should not be forced to return home. Notably, this comment was the first to be made by a Jordanian official on the subject of refugees after Syria's readmittance to the Arab League earlier that month.

DETERIORATING RELATIONS WITH ISRAEL

Jordan recalled its ambassador to Israel in October 2019 in protest at Israel's refusal to release from detention two Jordanians of Palestinian origin, Hiba Labadi and Abdul Rahman Miri; the Jordanian Government claimed that its two citizens had been illegally detained in Israel for several months without charge. For its part, the Israeli Government maintained that the two Jordanians were being held as a result of committing 'security offences' after entering the West Bank in August–September—charges that the two Jordanians denied. In November the two Jordanians were released from detention and transferred to Jordan following negotiations between Israeli and Jordanian security officials. The Jordanian ambassador duly returned to Israel later that month.

In November 2019 King Abdullah announced that Jordan would regain 'full sovereignty' over two areas of land, Baqoura and al-Ghamr, which had been leased by Jordan to Israel for 25 years under the 1994 peace treaty. Hundreds of Jordanians had demonstrated in Amman urging the cancellation of the deal. In May 2020 the Jordanian Ministry of Foreign and Expatriates Affairs confirmed that Israeli farmers would no longer be allowed to cultivate their fields in Baqoura and al-Ghamr.

In January 2020 the Jordanian National Assembly unanimously approved draft legislation to ban imports of Israeli natural gas, several days after exports of the commodity had commenced, under an agreement made in 2016 that provoked vociferous opposition from many Jordanians. The matter was referred to the Jordanian cabinet for approval, although the Government had previously stated that the agreement was not a matter for government intervention, as the US $10,000m. supply deal was struck between a Jordanian state-owned utility company, National Electric Power Company, and a US-Israeli consortium led by Noble Energy. The deal, which was intended to provide gas to Jordan's power plants for electricity generation, had never been referred to parliament for approval.

Following the Trump Administration's formal announcement of its peace plan in January 2020, the Jordanian Government expressed its rejection of the proposals and reiterated that the only means of reaching a durable Middle East peace was through the creation of an independent Palestinian state based on 1967 borders, with East Jerusalem as its capital. The Jordanian Minister of Foreign and Expatriates Affairs, Ayman al-Safadi, called for direct negotiations with Israel to resolve final status issues in the Palestinian territories, including Jordanian interests. In July 2020 King Abdullah warned that any unilateral Israeli moves to annex territory in the occupied West Bank would fuel instability and make movement towards a settlement more difficult. In November King Abdullah met the Palestinian President Mahmoud Abbas, and both expressed the hope that the newly elected US President, Joe Biden, would revive peace talks towards a two-state solution to the Arab–Israeli conflict.

On 9 May 2021 Jordan urged Israel to halt what it called 'barbaric' attacks on worshippers at Jerusalem's al-Aqsa Mosque in the latest round of violence and pledged to increase international pressure on Israel. King Abdullah dubbed Israel's actions 'dangerous provocations'. On 23 May, after a ceasefire was reached, King Abdullah stressed the importance of translating the ceasefire into an extended truce, emphasizing that there was no alternative to a two-state solution between Israel and Palestine.

In November 2021 Israel and Jordan signed their largest-ever co-operation agreement, involving the construction by the UAE of a major solar power plant in Jordan to generate electricity for Israel, and a desalination plant in Israel to send water to Jordan. The agreement was brokered by the UAE, which had normalized ties with Israel in 2020, and was signed in Dubai. Although Israeli-Jordanian relations had cooled under Netanyahu, the new Israeli Prime Minister, Naftali Bennett, who came to power in June 2021, prioritized strengthening ties with Jordan, meeting with King Abdullah in Amman in July in the first summit between the leaders of the two countries in over three years. After this first meeting it was announced that Israel would sell 50m. cu m of water a year to Jordan, thereby doubling its annual supplies; the agreed amount was raised further at a meeting in October. Thousands of Jordanians marched in Amman in protest at the signing of the agreement in November, emphasizing their rejection of negotiating with the 'Zionist entity' and, in particular, opposing the use of Jordanian-generated electricity in illegal Israeli settlements.

In January 2022 Israeli Minister of Defense Benny Gantz and King Abdullah held a meeting in Amman to discuss bilateral ties and regional security. The Royal Court reported that during the meeting King Abdullah 'reiterated the need to maintain calm in the Palestinian Territories, and to take the necessary measures to create the horizon needed to achieve just and comprehensive peace, on the basis of the two-state solution'. In order to maintain ties with the PA as well, in late March King Abdullah met Palestinian President Mahmoud Abbas in Ramallah, in his first trip to the West Bank since 2017.

Riots broke out in April 2022 at the Temple Mount complex, when Israeli police stormed the al-Aqsa Mosque during Ramadan prayers, clashing with Palestinians, at least 152 of whom were injured. The Jordanian Ministry of Foreign and Expatriates Affairs summoned Israel's deputy ambassador to be reprimanded over Israeli actions on Temple Mount during the holy month of Ramadan. King Abdullah released a statement, urging Israel to 'cease illegal provocative measures' on the Temple Mount.

In October 2022 Netanyahu was re-elected as Israeli Prime Minister in the country's fifth election in four years. Shortly after Netanyahu took office, King Abdullah warned the new right-wing Israeli Government against increasing pressure on Palestinians in Jerusalem or undermining Jordanian influence in the city. In January 2023 the King met Netanyahu in Amman on the Israeli leader's first official trip abroad to discuss 'respecting the historical and legal status quo' at the al-Aqsa Mosque, three weeks after regional tension resurfaced over Israeli actions there. Indeed, on 3 January the new ultra-nationalist Israeli Minister of National Security, Itamar Ben Gvir, visited the Temple Mount compound, in a move condemned by the Jordanian Government as a breach of international law, prompting the Ministry of Foreign and Expatriates Affairs to summon the Israeli ambassador. Other Arab countries similarly condemned the visit, and a UN Security Council meeting was convened to defuse the ensuing tensions.

In a separate incident in January 2023, Israeli police intercepted Jordan's ambassador on his way to al-Aqsa, claiming that he had not co-ordinated with police officials prior to his visit; in response, the Jordanian foreign affairs ministry again summoned the Israeli ambassador, and issued a statement reiterating that Jordanian officials did not need permission to enter al-Aqsa due to Jordan's position as custodian over the mosque. In a meeting with Netanyahu following these incidents, King Abdullah was reported by the Jordanian Royal Palace to have 'reaffirmed Jordan's steadfast position in support of the two-state solution, which guarantees the establishment of an independent Palestinian state on the 1967 lines, with East Jerusalem as its capital'.

Also in January 2023, Egyptian President Abd al-Fatah al-Sisi hosted Jordanian and Palestinian leaders for talks on the Israeli–Palestinian conflict. In a joint statement, al-Sisi, King Abdullah and Mahmoud Abbas called for Israel to halt 'all illegitimate, unilateral measures' that undermined the creation of an independent Palestinian state and to maintain the status quo at the al-Aqsa Mosque.

In February 2023 Israel agreed to curb its settlement activity in the occupied Palestinian territories, representing a partial acquiescence to Arab demands during a meeting between Israeli and Palestinian security officials, as well as representatives from Egypt, Jordan and the USA, in Aqaba, which had been convened in response to a recent upsurge in violence in the West Bank. In a joint communique issued following the meeting, Israel and the PA 'reaffirmed the necessity of committing to de-escalation on the ground and to prevent further violence' and 'confirmed their joint readiness and commitment to immediately work to end unilateral measures for a period of 3–6 months', as well as to 'pursue confidence-building measures'. Regarding Jordan specifically, the declaration asserted that the five parties emphasized 'the Hashemite Custodianship/ special role of Jordan' in Jerusalem. However, Hamas, which governs the Gaza Strip, dismissed the meeting as 'worthless' and condemned the PA's participation. Similar statements emerged from a second round of talks held in Sharm el-Sheikh, Egypt, in March. Meanwhile, the violence continued.

During a meeting with US Secretary of Defense Lloyd Austin in Amman in March 2023, King Abdullah stated that the upsurge in West Bank violence threatened regional stability and asked for assistance in fighting the growing drug war along the border with Syria. In April a spokesperson for the Jordanian Ministry of Foreign and Expatriates Affairs blamed Israel for the recent escalation in violence, which it expected to worsen following a series of rocket attacks and Israeli air strikes in Gaza, Lebanon and Syria.

In May 2023 Jordanian MP Imad al-Adwan was charged by a state security court in Amman with four counts of illegally exporting weapons and 'carrying out actions that breach security and threaten community peace', having been apprehended in April at an Israeli-controlled border crossing, through which he was alleged to have smuggled rifles, handguns and gold into the West Bank. The alleged smuggling scandal threatened further to increase tensions between Israel and Jordan.

CONTINUED ECONOMIC CHALLENGES AND THE COVID-19 PANDEMIC

In early November 2019 more than 6,000 Jordanian employees of the UN Relief and Works Agency (UNRWA) commenced strike action, leading to the closure of schools and health care facilities, as well as a temporary halt of rubbish collection, in camps for Palestinian refugees in Jordan. Foreign affairs minister al-Safadi brokered an agreement between UNRWA and employees' trade unions in the following week to increase salaries to US $140 per month, effective from 2020, although the Agency continued to face financial challenges, owing to a loss of funding from the USA, after the Trump Administration suspended payments to it in August 2018.

Following the spread of the coronavirus disease (COVID-19) pandemic to the Middle East in March 2020, Jordan entered one of the world's strictest lockdowns from March until May, which included sealing the country's borders, the implementation of a state of emergency, a driving ban, a night-time curfew and the closure of the Amman Stock Exchange. As a result, by 21 July Jordan had officially recorded only 1,223 confirmed cases of COVID-19, including just 11 deaths, although its economy had been seriously harmed. Public debt had already increased by almost one-third in a decade to JD 30,100m. (about US $42,400m.) in 2019—equivalent to 97% of gross domestic product—but high levels of state expenditure, particularly on public sector salaries, continued. Indeed, Jordan's public spending was set to reach around $14,000m. in 2020—the world's highest level of government spending relative to the size of its economy. As a result of the pandemic Jordan also lost crucial income from the tourism sector, which had provided revenue of some $5,000m. annually in recent years.

In an effort to mitigate the effects of the COVID-19 pandemic on Jordan, in May 2020 the IMF approved a loan worth US $396m. The following month the UN Development Programme predicted that the rate of unemployment in Jordan would exceed 19%, as many businesses had made employees redundant or ceased operations altogether, and the financial position of many Jordanians had become precarious.

In July 2020 Prime Minister Omar al-Razzaz pledged to increase crackdowns on tax evasion, which was believed to have cost the country billions of dollars in recent years. In particular, the Government sought to prosecute senior businessmen and former politicians suspected of tax evasion and money laundering. The need to do so had become more urgent due to the exacerbation of existing economic problems by the COVID-19 pandemic, which had continued over the course of 2020 and into 2021, when a new spike in infections was recorded leading to the imposition of even stricter government restrictions.

In April 2022 Saudi Arabia provided Jordan with US $50m. to help fund its budget; this was the fourth of five instalments of economic aid that Saudi Arabia had agreed in 2018 to send to Jordan. In June 2022 Saudi Crown Prince and de facto ruler Mohammed bin Salman visited Amman in the first such official visit for more than five years. The visit signalled an important thaw in relations between the two kingdoms and a potential boon for the Jordanian economy, which continued to struggle with the impact of the COVID-19 pandemic and the Russian invasion of Ukraine in February. Jordanian business leaders hoped that the visit would lead to the instigation of at least $3,000m. worth of Saudi investment projects that had been announced in recent years but had not yet materialized.

Upon the conclusion of a visit in May 2023 to conduct the sixth review of Jordan's economic reform programme, the IMF stated that the country was still recovering from the impact of the COVID-19 pandemic, and stressed that the authorities would need to implement major economic and administrative changes to curb high unemployment, which stood at some 23%. As a result of the review, the organization's total funding for reforms in Jordan was increased to US $1,750m., up from $1,700m. in December 2022, when the previous review was conducted.

Also in May 2023, King Abdullah approved a cabinet decision to revoke the state of emergency that had remained in place since March 2020, during the early stages of the pandemic, which had granted authorities wide-ranging powers to impose curfews, ban gatherings and intervene in business activities.

CRACKDOWN ON RISING OPPOSITION, NEW ELECTIONS AND FISSURES IN THE ROYAL FAMILY

In July 2020 Jordan's Court of Cassation issued a final verdict dissolving the country's branch of the Muslim Brotherhood due to the group's failure to 'rectify its legal status under Jordanian law'. The organization pledged to appeal the ruling. Meanwhile, the IAF remained active and participated in the parliamentary elections in November 2020 (see below).

Also in July 2020, Jordanian security forces arrested leading members of the Jordanian Teachers' Syndicate (JTS), raided its offices and suspended its activities for two years. The previous year, the JTS, which has around 100,000 members, had undertaken industrial action, leading to a one-month closure of schools, in one of the country's longest and most disruptive public sector strikes. In July 2020 the teachers' union accused the Government of failing to honour a deal signed in October 2019 to end the strike, which included a 50% pay rise that the Government claimed was unaffordable due to the economic impact of the COVID-19 pandemic. Security forces arrested 13 leading members of the JTS on charges of incitement, corruption, criminal activities and financial irregularities. Following these arrests, Jordanian anti-riot police clashed with teachers who continued to protest in Amman, and several were injured and arrested. In late August 2020 the Government released the 13 detainees. In December, however, a Jordanian court sentenced five leaders of the JTS to one year's imprisonment on charges of incitement to hatred and unlawful gatherings. Following an appeal against the verdict, the five union members were released on bail.

On 27 September 2020 King Abdullah dissolved parliament in order to pave the way for elections in November, as opposition mounted over worsening economic conditions and curbs to freedoms imposed under emergency laws during the COVID-19 pandemic. In early October King Abdullah accepted the resignation of Prime Minister Omar al-Razzazz, who had been appointed in mid-2018 amid protests over tax increases sought by the IMF to decrease Jordan's substantial public debt. Days after al-Razzazz's resignation, King Abdullah appointed diplomat and palace adviser Bisher al-Khasawneh as the new Prime Minister. In October the King swore in a new cabinet that was mandated to implement IMF-backed economic reforms as Jordan's economy continued to struggle due to the impact of the ongoing pandemic.

On 10 November 2020 Jordanians voted in parliamentary elections; turnout was recorded at 29.9% of eligible voters, the lowest level for years. Fears about COVID-19 were suspected to have affected turnout, as people were not allowed to vote early or remotely. On the whole, wealthy businessmen and tribal independents gained seats, while reform-orientated candidates lost representation, with less than 10% of the 130 members coming from political parties. The number of female MPs decreased from 20 to 15 of the 130 members, which is the number reserved for women under a quota system, and no women were elected through competitive races. The Muslim Brotherhood-linked IAF won 10 seats compared with 15 in 2016, amid complaints that the electoral system was unfair.

In March 2021 Prime Minister Bisher al-Khasawneh reorganized the cabinet in order to accelerate IMF-recommended economic reforms to assist the country's recovery from the impact of the pandemic. Six new ministers were appointed, including those holding the interior and justice portfolios, after the previous incumbents were found to have violated the COVID-19 restrictions they were meant to enforce. Also in

March, the Minister of Health resigned after at least seven patients in a hospital COVID-19 ward died due to a shortage of oxygen supplies in the town of al-Salt. The Prime Minister ordered an investigation into the deaths, while King Abdullah ordered the suspension of the director of the hospital, as about 150 people gathered outside the hospital demanding answers. Protests erupted in other cities and towns after the scandal, in violation of a night curfew that had been imposed to curb the spread of the virus. Police used tear gas to disperse protesters in several cities, including Amman.

In early April 2021 a rare public rift emerged in the royal family, when King Abdullah placed his half-brother Prince Hamzah under house arrest and arrested more than a dozen others for allegedly conspiring with foreign supporters to destabilize Jordan. The Jordanian authorities imposed a sweeping gag order on media coverage of the feud after a recording indicated that the authorities (through the military Chief of Staff) had tried to silence Prince Hamzah after he attended meetings organized by critics of the regime. Hamzah denied the allegations of his involvement in a conspiracy via a video statement, insisting that he had, in fact, spoken out against years of official corruption and mismanagement and claiming that the Government was trying to silence him because of his criticisms. Mediation took place at Hassan's home at the Royal Hashemite Court, and ended with Hamzah making a statement in which he declared his loyalty to the King and to Jordan's Constitution. The US and Arab governments sided with King Abdullah in the matter, which was considered to pose a threat to the country's stability. The King stated that the sedition had been quashed and that the country was stable and secure. US President Joe Biden telephoned King Abdullah to declare that the USA supported Jordan's actions 'to preserve its security and stability'.

In mid-April 2021 Prince Hamzah made his first public appearance since he was placed under house arrest, reciting Quranic verses with King Abdullah at the graves of their forefathers in a show of unity on the occasion of the centenary of the establishment of the Emirate of Transjordan. At the end of April, in a sign of clemency during the holy month of Ramadan, the Jordanian authorities released 16 people detained earlier that month over the alleged foreign-backed conspiracy linked to Prince Hamzah. The 16 included tribal leaders and former senior officials; however, two of those arrested, former senior royal officials Bassem Awadallah and Sharif Hassan bin Zaid, remained in prison. In June the cases of the two officials were transferred to a national security court, where they were charged with sedition and incitement.

In March 2022 it was reported that Prince Hamzah had apologized publicly for his role in the palace feud that had taken place in 2021 and was seeking the King's forgiveness. However, in early April 2022, shortly after issuing his apology, Prince Hamzah announced that he had relinquished his royal title in protest at how the country was run. He posted the announcement on his Twitter account, stating that he was driven to make such a decision because his 'personal convictions' were at odds with the 'current approaches, orientations and method of our modern institutions'. The Royal Court made no immediate comment, but in May King Abdullah again placed the former Crown Prince under house arrest, citing his 'erratic behaviour and aspirations', and further stating that Hamzah 'will not have the space he once abused to offend the nation, its institutions, and his family, nor to undermine Jordan's stability'.

Amid the ongoing discord in Jordan's royal family, in January 2022 the Jordanian parliament passed a series of 30 constitutional amendments that critics feared would broaden the King's political authority. One amendment involved the creation of a National Security and Foreign Policy Council, composed of the Prime Minister, the Minister of Foreign and Expatriates Affairs, the Minister of the Interior, the heads of the armed forces and of the security and intelligence departments, and two individuals appointed by the King. The new body would be convened in a 'state of necessity' at the invitation of the King. The amendments also included an addition to article 40, expanding the King's 'exclusive powers' to give him responsibility for the appointment and dismissal of the President of the Supreme Court, the head of the *Shari'a* Judicial Council and other members of the judiciary.

Such centralization of political power was noted by international agencies. In its annual report for 2021, Freedom House, the US-based research organization that advocates for democracy and human rights, downgraded Jordan from 'partly free' to 'not free'. It cited 'harsh new restrictions on freedom of assembly, a crackdown on the teachers' union following a series of strikes and protests, and factors including a lack of adequate preparations that harmed the quality of parliamentary elections during the COVID-19 pandemic'. Further, in a press conference held in February 2022, activists said that up to 200 Jordanians, including several dissidents and journalists, had been targeted by the Pegasus spyware that is used to hack smartphones and harvest data from them. The reported hacking heightened concerns about increased government surveillance.

Further weakening public trust in the royal family, banking data leaked in February 2022 revealed that King Abdullah and Queen Rania had deposited hundreds of millions of dollars in at least six different Swiss bank accounts. Several of the accounts were opened during the Arab Spring period of unrest in 2011, leading many to believe that the royals had set up the accounts in case they were ousted. Lawyers for King Abdullah and Queen Rania insisted that there had been no wrongdoing and provided information about the source of the funds.

During 2022 the Government attempted to introduce reforms to enhance public sector and government efficacy. In July Prime Minister Bisher al-Khasawneh announced that the Ministry of Labour would be dissolved and that six other ministries would be merged over the next two years as part of efforts to curb Jordan's bloated public sector; in 2015 (the latest year for which employment data are available) around one-third of Jordan's 1.35m. employed population worked for the Government. However, the plan was subsequently revised to allow the Ministry of Labour to be restructured rather than abolished. Meanwhile, in October 2022 King Abdullah replaced eight cabinet ministers, in the fifth government reorganization since its appointment in 2020. Responsibility for the key portfolios of finance, foreign affairs and the interior, however, remained unchanged. Also in October 2022, King Abdullah appointed a new Senate, incorporating members with greater political and financial expertise. Around one-half of the new Senate were new appointees, including 26 former ministers (compared with 17 former ministers in the previous Senate).

International rights organization Human Rights Watch in September 2022 accused the Jordanian authorities of reducing civic space and of using vague and abusive legislation to criminalize free speech, association and assembly in order to persecute those engaging in political dissent. The organization further reported that the authorities detained, interrogated and harassed journalists, activists and members of political parties and trade unions, as well as their relatives, in addition to restricting their ability to work and travel.

Protests over worsening living conditions amid continued economic stagnation degenerated into riots in Ma'an and several other cities in Jordan in December 2022, during which a police officer was fatally shot in Ma'an. In a subsequent raid on the hideout of militants suspected of shooting the officer, three other police officers were killed, along with one suspect, while nine further militants were arrested and a cache of weapons was seized. The Government pledged to deploy more anti-riot police officers in response to those engaged in violent protests. According to police sources, more than 40 security personnel were injured in the clashes in December; 44 people were arrested in the immediate aftermath of the unrest, with a further 200 suspects wanted in connection with the troubles.

Economy

ROBERT E. LOONEY

Based on an original essay by ONN WINCKLER

INTRODUCTION

Jordan is one of the smaller countries in the Middle East and North Africa region with a gross domestic product (GDP) of US $48,400m. in 2022, making it slightly smaller than Sudan ($49,400m.) but larger than Tunisia ($46,600m.). The country's per capita income rose from $1,654 in 1980 to $1,703 in 2000, $3,737 in 2010 and $4,741 in 2022. Jordan's per capita income in 2022 was above that of Egypt ($4,563), Iran ($4,110) and the West Bank and Gaza ($3,502), but below that of Iraq ($6,400).

The country's economic growth has slowed down in recent years. After expanding at an average annual rate of 4.6% during 1980–2010, average annual GDP growth decelerated to 2.1% between 2011 (the year of the 'Arab Spring') and 2022. Average annual growth of 6.6% in the 2000s slowed to 2.7% in 2010–15 and further to 1.7% in 2016–22. Per capita growth averaged 0.6% per year between 1980 and 2010, and contracted at an average annual rate of 0.8% during 2011–22. The country's current account on the balance of payments averaged a deficit of 3.7% of GDP between 1980 and 2010, but this widened to an unsustainable 8.4% in 2011–22.

Jordan has several strengths that it can use to restore rates of growth to levels that can reduce unemployment. The country enjoys political stability, by Middle Eastern standards, and receives significant political and financial support from the USA, European countries and Gulf monarchies. It is a major producer and exporter of phosphate and potash, despite being resource poor.

However, the Government's efforts face several obstacles. Severe water and energy shortages plague the country, and its manufacturing base is small and underdeveloped in a relatively weak private sector. Jordan is also vulnerable to international economic conditions and regional political instability. The country depends heavily on foreign aid and capital inflows owing to its large current account and budget deficits. Unemployment is persistently high, particularly among the youth population and women; total unemployment averaged 13.3% in 1980–2010, increasing to 17.0% in 2011–22. In addition, the large number of Syrian refugees poses a potential threat to the country's stability.

EVOLUTION OF THE ECONOMY

After independence in 1946, the annexation of East Jerusalem and the West Bank in 1950 led to a doubling of Jordan's population. Despite gloomy predictions regarding the ability of the Jordanian economy to absorb the hundreds of thousands of Palestinian refugees, alongside the rapid growth of the East Bank population itself, many new members of the Jordanian workforce were well educated and highly skilled, and the economy expanded rapidly. During 1952–66 real GDP grew at an average annual rate of 6.9%. The standard of living improved markedly, while there was a steady decline in the death rate. The educational level of the population improved significantly, while the unemployment rate fell sharply to 5%–6% during the mid-1960s.

Jordan achieved impressive growth in the 1960s, thanks to advancements in agriculture, tourism, industry and infrastructure. The port development at Al-Aqabah (Aqaba) also played a significant role. Jordanians working in the Persian (Arabian) Gulf countries sent more money back home, boosting the economy. By 1967 Jordanians enjoyed a higher standard of living than other non-oil-exporting Arab nations.

A Five-Year Plan published by the Development Board for 1962–67 was later replaced with a Seven-Year Plan for 1964–1970. The primary goal was to achieve import substitution in various products, including processed food, refined sugar, textiles, ceramics, glass products, cosmetics, pharmaceuticals, cleaning products, paint and plywood. The plans also attempted to create more jobs, reduce the trade deficit and facilitate the shift from an agriculture-based economy to an industry-based one. In addition, the Government also promoted phosphates and cement production. Unlike in Egypt, the Syrian Arab Republic and Iraq, Jordan's private sector played a crucial role in developing industries and agriculture.

The Israeli occupation of East Jerusalem and the West Bank during the Six-Day War in 1967 had a severe impact on Jordan, causing political and security damage and greatly harming the economy. Jordan had to absorb 310,000 Palestinian refugees from the West Bank and Gaza Strip. This led to a loss of 90% of tourism sites, almost one-half of agricultural production and 20% of industrial production, and reduced the amount of fresh water available. As a result, Jordan's GDP contracted by 4.2% in 1968.

In September 1970 the 'Black September' conflict between the Palestine Liberation Organization (PLO) armed forces and Jordan's military exacerbated Jordan's economic woes. The clashes disrupted normal economic activities and created economic pessimism, leading to a decrease in private investment and consumption. The closure of Syria's border with Jordan, to support the PLO struggle against the Hashemite regime, also harmed Jordan's economy, since most of the country's exports were through Syrian ports. In 1970 Jordan's GDP contracted by an unprecedented 11.4%.

The PLO armed forces were deported in 1971, which helped the Jordanian economy to recover. GDP growth increased from 5.7% in 1971 to 6.7% in 1972. Arab aid increased after the Arab League summit held in Khartoum, Sudan, in August 1967. Syria's reopening of its border with Jordan in April 1972 allowed for the import of agricultural products and the export of phosphates and potash. Political and security stability also improved.

The Third Development Plan (1973–75) aimed to boost the economy. The plan's goals were to create 70,000 new jobs, reduce the trade deficit, expand exports of phosphates, potash and agricultural products, and increase tourism. Public services in education and health were also to be expanded. The plan aimed to achieve average annual GDP growth of 8%.

The Jordanian economy received a significant boost from the 'oil boom' in October 1973. Many Jordanian workers went to work in Arab oil-exporting countries, particularly Kuwait and Saudi Arabia, and by the early 1980s Jordan had become the largest Arab exporter of labour. Unemployment dropped from 14% in 1972 to less than 2% in 1976. From the mid-1970s workers' remittances became the country's largest source of foreign currency. Another benefit of the oil boom was the enormous increase in Arab aid, which peaked at US $1,300m. in 1980 (at current prices), following the Arab League summit held in Baghdad, Iraq, in March 1979. Overall, during the early 1980s foreign aid represented about one-half of government revenue.

Operations at Aqaba port were boosted by the reopening of the Suez Canal in 1975 and following the outbreak of the Iran–Iraq War in 1980, which paralyzed operations at the Iraqi port of Basra, Aqaba became an alternative route for transporting commodities to Iraq. Jordan's merchandise exports to Iraq increased, and in the 1980s Iraq supplied 80% of Jordan's oil requirements at a preferential price. Meanwhile, wealthy Arabs found Jordan a more appealing option for tourism and investments following the outbreak of civil war in Lebanon in 1975.

Other developments were also quite favourable to the economy. The prosperity of the West Bank economy led to a rapid increase in the scale of trade with Jordan (within the framework of the Israeli 'open bridges' policy). The rise in the price of phosphates in 1974 tripled Jordan's revenues from their export. By 1984 Jordan's exports amounted to US $644m., compared with $48m. in 1972. Imports increased at an even higher rate—from $267m. in 1972 to $2,566m. in 1984.

During a period of rapid economic growth, the Government created development plans for 1976–80 and 1981–86, which aimed to transform the economy from a service-rentier model to a commodity-producing one. This would allow foreign grants to be used for infrastructure projects instead of supporting the budget.

Jordan experienced high GDP growth rates during the 'oil decade' (1973–82), averaging over 8% per year (among the highest globally). However, oil prices declined in 1983, and by June 1986 the price of a barrel of oil (West Texas Intermediate—WTI) had fallen to US $10, which was only one-quarter of the 1981 price in real terms. Jordan was in the worst situation among all non-oil-exporting Arab countries because of its heavy dependence on financial aid and workers' remittances. As a result of the decline in their income from oil exports, financial aid from the Arabian Gulf oil-exporting countries to Jordan decreased from a peak of $1,300m. in 1980 to $500m. in 1989.

Labour immigration policy in the Arabian Gulf oil countries changed to favour non-Arab workers. This caused a decrease in the number of Jordanian workers and a decline in remittances. By the end of the 1980s remittances from Jordanian expatriates were equivalent to only one-half of their value at the start of the decade. The first Palestinian *intifada* ('uprising') in December 1987 led to a decline in exports to the Palestinian territories and a decrease in Palestinian investments in Jordan. The end of the Iran–Iraq War in August 1988 also affected the Jordanian economy, due to the close economic ties enjoyed between Jordan and Iraq during the conflict.

The Jordanian Government borrowed heavily, locally and internationally, to maintain public sector spending. As a result, the country recorded a record high budget deficit in 1988. To reduce the large deficit on the balance of payments, the Government adopted a number of measures, including banning vehicle and luxury goods imports, increasing duty fees and freezing new infrastructure projects. However, these measures proved insufficient. In early 1989 Jordan's financial situation was so dire that the Government suspended external debt repayments. GDP in that year contracted by 10.7%.

The recession forced the Government to adopt severe austerity measures, including a significant cut in subsidies on basic foodstuffs and energy products. In exchange, Jordan received a loan of US $125m. from the International Monetary Fund (IMF) and a loan of $100m. from the World Bank. During this period, inflation increased from –0.2% in 1987 to 6.6% in 1988 and 25.7% in 1989, before moderating to 16.2% in 1990.

In 1988 the Central Bank of Jordan almost ran out of US dollars. This led to public discontent and large-scale riots in Ma'an, a region traditionally loyal to the Hashemite regime, prompting the resignation of Prime Minister Zaid Rifai in April 1989, and the cancellation of some austerity measures by the Government. However, despite a good start, per capita incomes declined at an average annual rate of 1.0% during the 1980s.

King Hussein of Jordan refused to join the multinational anti-Iraqi coalition following Iraq's invasion of Kuwait in August 1990. As a result, Saudi Arabia restricted its economic relations with Jordan, halting financial aid and imports (mostly agricultural products). The Trans-Arabian Pipeline was closed, forcing Jordan to import oil at higher prices from Syria and Yemen. Saudi Arabia and Kuwait deported 300,000 Jordanian and Palestinian workers. This caused unemployment in Jordan to rise from 16.8% in 1990 to 18.8% by the end of 1991, and placed strains on health care and education services.

Meanwhile, the cost of subsidies on basic foodstuffs and energy products also rose sharply. Government debt reached some 227.5% of GDP by the end of 1990, remaining at 207.7% at the end of 1991. Jordan's adherence to United Nations (UN) sanctions against Iraq imposed further burdens on its economy. The economic downturn in the Palestinian territories following PLO leader Yasser Arafat's support for Iraq during the Gulf crisis, together with a decline in the Jordanian tourism industry, which relied mainly on the countries of the Cooperation Council for the Arab States of the Gulf (the Gulf Cooperation Council—GCC), also contributed to the overall economic recession in Jordan. In 1990 the economy contracted by 0.3%, and the fiscal deficit reached 7.5% of GDP. In 1991 the economy grew by only 1.6%.

The economy made a remarkable recovery in 1992, growing by 16.9%, driven by the injection of new capital from returnees from the GCC countries, who invested mainly in housing and local businesses. This trend continued in 1994 and 1995, with respective growth rates of 4.4% and 5.0%.

The October 1994 peace treaty between Jordan and Israel played a crucial role in supporting the economy through debt relief, external debt rescheduling and significant US financial aid. The treaty also led to an increase in foreign investment (mainly in the tourism sector, which expanded rapidly) and improvements in the water supply. Unlike Egypt, which was expelled from the Arab League following its peace treaty with Israel in 1979, Jordan faced no consequences. Iraq, which opposed any relationship with Israel, continued to provide Jordan with all its oil needs and remained the primary market for Jordanian exports. By 2000 Jordan had exported more than US $850m. worth of goods to Iraq under the UN's 'oil-for-food' agreement, which allowed Iraq to sell oil on the world market in exchange for imports of food and medical equipment, representing more than one-third of Jordan's non-mineral exports.

Prior to 2003, Jordan's economy was boosted by low oil prices, with an average price per barrel (WTI) of US $31.1. Improved relations with the Arabian Gulf oil-producing countries also helped. As a result, Jordanian workers' remittances significantly increased, reaching $1,900m. in 2000, compared with $500m. in 1990. Financial aid from these countries also increased. However, per capita growth remained negative, declining at an average annual rate of 0.3% during 1990–99.

Despite the detrimental impact on regional tourism of the second Palestinian *intifada* (the al-Aqsa *intifada*) in September 2000, followed by the al-Qa'ida attacks on the mainland of the USA on 11 September 2001, the Jordanian economy grew at an average annual rate of 6.8% in 2000–08. This was the highest growth rate among the non-oil Arab economies. Per capita income also increased at an average annual rate of 3.7% after declining in the 1980s and 1990s.

However, the global economic crisis in 2008, combined with high oil prices, caused an increase in commodity prices and halted Jordan's rapid economic growth. Subsidies on basic food and energy became unsustainable, leading to a budget deficit of 8.8% of GDP in 2009. By 2010 GDP growth was only 2.3%, contracting by 2.8% in per capita terms.

The Arab Spring began in Tunisia in December 2010 and rapidly spread to other Arab countries in the Middle East and North Africa. The economic repercussions of the upheaval severely impacted even the non-oil Arab nations that remained stable. Amid declining tourism and growing political unrest, the region recorded reductions in private investment and consumption. By the beginning of 2011 Jordan was facing economic stagnation and high public debt. Aside from the devastating economic consequences of the Arab Spring that were common to all the non-oil Arab economies, Jordan experienced three unique repercussions.

First, Jordan received many Syrian refugees, costing the country between US $1,500m. and $2,500m. per year. A deal concluded with the European Union in 2016 provided for the opening up of the Jordanian job market to Syrian refugees in exchange for financial aid. However, this effectively forced an increasing number of Jordanian workers into low-paid informal employment and caused unemployment rates to rise.

Second, the closure of Jordan's borders with Syria and Iraq also led to a decline in exports to these countries. The Karameh–Turaibil border crossing remained closed until 2017 because of the unsafe security situation in Iraq. Jordan's border with Syria finally reopened in September 2021, but as of mid-2023 bilateral trade had yet to return to its pre-closure level.

Finally, Jordan had been importing natural gas from Egypt through the Arab Gas Pipeline since 2003. However, in July 2013 the pipeline ceased operations owing to repeated insurgent attacks in Sinai. As a result, Jordan had to buy liquefied natural gas (LNG) at much higher prices, mainly from Qatar.

In response to the Arab Spring protests, the Jordanian Government raised subsidies on basic food and energy products. This caused the government budget deficit to increase to 9.8% of GDP in 2011 and 14.3% in 2012. Despite foreign aid, Jordan's economy remained stagnant, with per capita income contracting by 2.6% in 2011 and by 3.0% in 2022. Government expenditure on subsidies and salaries continued to increase. By 2015 the debt-to-GDP ratio was 78.4%, up from 59.3% in 2010. However, a positive factor was the decline in oil prices from mid-2014, resulting in lower food and energy subsidy costs. The price per barrel of oil fell from US $100 at the beginning of 2014 to $53 by the end of the year and to less than $40 by the end of 2015.

In August 2016 the IMF approved a loan of US $723m. to help Jordan implement reforms intended to narrow the budget deficit by reducing public sector spending and increasing tax revenue. This was necessary because rising debt was holding back economic growth. In October the World Bank signed a three-year $300m. loan agreement with Jordan.

To fulfill the IMF loan conditions, the Government lifted the subsidy on bread and increased taxes on various consumer and food products in May 2018; it also unified the sales tax at 16% and proposed new tax legislation to increase personal income tax and thus reduce government debt. The young middle class and professional unions protested against these measures in May and June. To defuse the situation, Prime Minister Hani Mulki and his cabinet resigned, and most of the measures were abandoned. During 2009–19 per capita income contracted at an average annual rate of 1.3%.

In March 2020 the coronavirus disease (COVID-19) was declared a global pandemic by the World Health Organization. By mid-July 2022 Jordan had reported over 1.7m. confirmed cases and 14,000 associated deaths. However, Jordan's economy was already in a deep stagnation in early 2020. In that year, GDP contracted by 1.6% and per capita income declined by 2.6%. The contraction stemmed from several factors, the most prominent being the effective cessation of tourism activity from March 2020; tourism receipts decreased from US $7,800m. in 2019 to $1,800m. in 2020.

Public sector expenditure increased by 4.5% in 2020, primarily owing to higher health spending, while public sector revenue fell by 9.4%. As a result, the fiscal deficit widened from 5.7% of GDP in 2019 to 8.5% in 2020. At the end of 2020 the debt-to-GDP ratio was 87.0%, compared with 74.3% at the end of 2018.

The disruption of many economic sectors in 2020 led to a sharp rise in unemployment. The unemployment rate increased to 19.2% from 16.8% in 2019. For those under the age of 25, the unemployment rate rose from 30.9% in 2015 to 42.4% in 2020. The pandemic had one positive impact on the Jordanian economy—the price of oil and related products decreased, leading to inflation of just 0.4% in 2020 (compared with 0.7% in 2019). In 2021 there was a partial rebound in the economy, but real GDP grew by only 1.6%, or 0.1% in per capita terms.

In February 2022 the invasion of Ukraine by the Russian Federation caused the prices of energy and grains to rise sharply. Oil prices increased by over 30%, peaking at more than US $130 per barrel in April 2022—five times higher than two years previously. As a result, inflation increased to 4.2% in 2022.

GDP growth increased to 2.7% in 2022, driven by 4.8% growth in the agriculture sector, reflecting a good harvest, and 3.2% growth in construction. Manufacturing expanded by 2.7%, while retail and hospitality grew by 2.6%. However, Jordan needs annual GDP growth of around 6% in order to address high unemployment and challenge rising poverty.

The underwhelming growth in hospitality will have a negative impact on job creation initiatives. The IMF has predicted a meagre 2.7% increase in Jordanian GDP in 2023. This will most likely aggravate social pressures stemming from poverty, the incidence of which was 15.7% in 2018—the latest year for which official data were available at mid-2023.

The COVID-19 pandemic revealed significant structural issues in the economy that will continue to hinder economic growth, such as a high dependency on imports, weak private sector investment, inadequate government spending and a persistent fiscal deficit. These issues exacerbated the impact of the pandemic on unemployment. Although unemployment had decreased to 18.4% by the end of 2021, International Labour Organization (ILO) estimates indicate that youth unemployment in Jordan reached some 42.3% in 2020, and remained high, at 39.4%, in 2022—the third highest rate in the Middle East and North Africa, after Libya and the West Bank and Gaza.

DEVELOPMENT PLANNING

Since 1989 Jordan has undergone significant economic liberalization by means of an IMF-supported stabilization programme. However, the Government has prioritized political stability and regional politics over economic development, providing jobs and heavily subsidized public services in exchange for political loyalty. The Government has limited the private sector to small and medium-sized industry and services, while state ownership has been prevalent. Despite this, the IMF programmes have gradually decreased the state's involvement in the economy. This has led to fiscal and monetary stability being restored since the 1990s.

King Abdullah II aimed to replicate the economic success of the GCC economies when he ascended to the Jordanian throne in 1999. His plans included simplifying bureaucracy, revamping business laws, improving the judiciary, promoting investments and upgrading education and vocational training.

Following consultations with over 500 academics, business people and civil servants, in June 2022 the Government announced the launch of a 10-year economic plan, the 'Economic Modernisation Vision', which targeted average annual real GDP growth of 5.6% between 2022 and 2033; the creation of 1m. jobs for young Jordanians entering the labour force; average real per capita income growth of 3% per year; and a 30% improvement in global rankings for the business and regulatory environment. The plan was to be implemented in three phases. Most of the initiatives were to begin in the first phase (2022–25); the second phase (2026–29) was to prioritize consolidation, while the final phase (2030–33) was to focus on future planning.

The Government will prioritize projects based on their contribution to GDP, employment, output per worker and export revenue. Industry is the largest sector in terms of output, employment and exports. The listed sub-sectors are food, chemicals, pharmaceuticals, textiles and engineering. These industries account for 17.4% of Jordan's current GDP, 13.6% of the workforce and almost one-half of merchandise exports. The plan aims for 7% average annual growth in industrial output, with 10% growth envisaged for textiles and pharmaceuticals.

The initiatives listed for industry include calls for greater investment, reductions in energy costs (notably through expanding the natural gas grid), encouraging small and medium-sized enterprises to improve productivity and price competitiveness, making use of scientific research to improve quality, better training, and a campaign to encourage women to work in industry (Jordan has a notably low level of female participation in the workforce).

The plan expects the highest growth rates to be in the information and communications technology (ICT) and tourism sectors. It projects 13% annual growth for ICT (which currently accounts for 3% of GDP), with a fourfold increase in the sector's labour force to over 100,000 and a 30% annual rise in exports. Initiatives include an early roll-out of fifth generation (5G) telephony, setting up a tech 'Sandbox' and creating a free zone for tech start-ups. The plan expects tourism to grow by 10% per year, its workforce to treble to 150,000 and tourism revenue to increase by 13.6% per year to JD 6,900m.

Unfortunately, the plan, like many before it, lacks details of specific strategies to accomplish its diverse goals. However, it does at least provide prospective investors with useful background about the current state of the economy and an assurance of the Government's commitment to changing regulations and the business culture in order to achieve its development goals.

The plan calls for total investment of JD 41,400m. (US $57,600m.), of which almost three-quarters is to come from private sources, principally through foreign direct investment (FDI) and international development finance. High-value industries and future industries are to receive more than one-half of the investment from investors.

The primary target audience for the plan is the governments and sovereign wealth funds of the Gulf Arab states. The recent surge in oil and gas prices has generated huge surpluses for Gulf exporters, which have announced several initiatives to step up investment in the region, with Jordan and Egypt at the top of the list of countries that could benefit. Gulf leaders have indicated that they regard investment as a more effective way of supporting their needy neighbours than the previous tendency to provide financial bailouts to cover chronic fiscal and external payment deficits.

The Jordanian Government is no doubt hoping that its vision document will help it to engage Gulf investors, while convincing its own citizens that it has an effective strategy for raising living standards. Given the dismal record of the past decade, and the perilous state of the global economy, this will be a hard sell. Jordan has launched several development strategies since the country went bankrupt in 1989, but the constant change of ministers and officials owing to political reasons has contributed to their failure.

SOCIOECONOMIC DEVELOPMENT

The UN Development Programme's Human Development Index (HDI) for 2021/22 ranked Jordan 102nd out of 191 countries, ahead of only Libya (104th), the Palestinian territories (106th), Lebanon (112nd), Iraq (121st) and Morocco (123rd) within the Middle East and North Africa.

The HDI represents an average achievement in key dimensions of human development: a long and healthy life, being knowledgeable and having a decent standard of living. In 2021 life expectancy in Jordan reached 74.3 years, while the mean years of schooling was 10.4. Jordan's per capita gross national income (GNI) was eight places lower than its HDI, suggesting that the country's limited resources had reached large segments of the population. However, Jordan's lacklustre economic performance has adversely affected its progress in improving the standard of living for large segments of the population. Jordan's HDI score increased at an average annual rate of 0.9% between 1990 and 2000, slowing to 0.7% between 2000 and 2010, and it contracted at a rate of 0.6% in 2010–21.

Jordan has a relatively well-distributed income, with a Gini coefficient of 33.7 in 2010 (the latest year for year data was available). During 2010–21 the income share of the poorest 40% of the population was 20.3%, while that of the top 10% was 27.5%. In 2021 the share of the richest 1% was 17.5%. As in many Arab countries, there is considerable gender inequality, with GNI per capita in 2021 (on a 2017 purchasing party basis) of US $15,631 for males and just $3,778 for females, while the labour participation rate was 63.2% for males but just 13.2% for females. However, there was less disparity in education, with the mean years of schooling at 10.8 years for males, compared with 10.1 years for females.

The Legatum Prosperity Index provides a broader picture of Jordan's socioeconomic progress. The index comprises 12 dimensions of prosperity, and in 2023 Jordan ranked 86th out of 167 countries—18 places lower than in 2011. In the 2023 index, Jordan ranked highest in enterprise conditions (41st), followed by investment environment (50th), living conditions (61st), infrastructure and market access (67th) and governance (68th). Jordan's lowest rating came in social capital (152nd), followed by natural environment (146th), economic quality (121st), personal freedom (116th), health (100th), education (90th) and safety and security (74th). The biggest improvement over the last decade has been in enterprise conditions.

Although Jordan's governance is relatively high by non-Gulf Arab standards, the World Bank's Worldwide Governance Indicators indicates a general pattern of decline from 1996 (when the series began) to around 2010. In recent years, there has been an improvement in some key areas relevant to the economy, while other areas have deteriorated. In terms of regulatory quality (a proxy for the business environment), Jordan improved from the 55th percentile in 1996 to the 58th in 2010, where it remained in 2021. Jordan scored lowest in voice and accountability (a rough measure of democracy), declining from the 42nd percentile to the 27th between 1996 and 2010, and was in the 26th percentile in 2021. For political stability/absence of violence, it declined from the 47th percentile in 1996 to the 35th in 2010, before improving to the 37th in 2021. There was gradual improvement in terms of government effectiveness, from the 56th percentile in 1996 to the 59th in 2010 and the 60th in 2021. Conversely, Jordan's performance in the rule of law governance dimension deteriorated, falling from the 61st percentile in 1996 to the 60th in 2010 and the 58th in 2021. Finally, in terms of control of corruption, Jordan improved from the 55th percentile in 1996 to the 60th by 2010, but had declined to the 58th by 2021.

The Economic Modernisation Vision does not prioritize improved governance. However, the plan will need increased foreign investment if it is to succeed. It is unclear whether the required volumes of investment will occur without significant improvements in areas such as the rule of law and control of corruption.

DEMOGRAPHICS

Between 1960 and 2022 Jordan's population increased from 847,936 to 11,285,869, growing at an average annual rate of 4.2%. Jordan's population is the sixth largest in the Middle East and North Africa, after Egypt, Iran, Iraq, Saudi Arabia and Yemen. Population growth has not been constant or even declining at a regular rate, as in most developing countries. Growth averaged 6.1% in the 1960s, 3.8% in the 1970s, 4.4% in the 1980s, 4.0% in the 1990s, 3.1% in the 2000s and 3.9% in 2010–22.

The growth of the local population has slowed down in recent years, but this has been offset by large numbers of refugees arriving from Syria and Iraq. The 2015 census in Jordan indicated a total population of 9.5m.; of these, 6.6m. were Jordanian nationals, of whom more than one-half were of Palestinian origin. The remaining 2.9m. included 1.27m. Syrians, 636,270 Egyptians and 634,182 Palestinians without Jordanian citizenship. According to the census, there were 130,911 Iraqis (far short of anecdotal estimates of up to 500,000), as well as 31,163 Yemeni and 22,700 Libyan nationals. Although significant numbers of refugees are expected to return to their home countries as the respective security situations stabilize, most are expected to remain in Jordan at least in the short term.

The age composition of the population has shifted considerably over time. Those in the working age group (15–64 years) increased from 46.8% of the total population in the 1970s to 49.4% in the 1980s, 55.3% in the 1990s, 58.1% in the 2000s and 62.0% in 2010–21; in 2022 64.1% of the population was in this age group. Conversely, the youth population (0–14 years) declined from 50.4% in the 1970s to 34.5% in 2010–22; in 2022 32.1% of the population was in this group.

With this age structure, Jordan is experiencing a 'demographic dividend', with a large working age population supporting a relatively small number of younger and older individuals. Demographers expect the working-age group to account for 65% of the population by 2025 and 67% by 2023, with a decrease expected from 2045. However, a demographic dividend can turn into a curse if the economy is unable to provide viable employment for the increasing numbers of people of working age. If the Economic Modernisation Vision fails to achieve its target of creating 1m. jobs for young Jordanians joining the labour force, the country will face growing levels of high youth unemployment and likely increased social discontent.

Many Jordanians work in neighbouring Saudi Arabia, which is now focusing on employing its own nationals. This trend could threaten the export of workers from Jordan to the Gulf Arab states. The Jordanian Government is working to align the education system and job market. Egypt has supplied many unskilled workers to Jordan, but a significant number end up in the informal economy. However, Jordan is making progress in integrating Syrian refugees into the labour force.

Jordan has a relatively high-quality health care system, but it has come under stress, owing to the Syrian refugee surge from 2011 and subsequently as a result of the COVID-19 pandemic from 2020. The stress on health facilities owing to the pandemic has led to a slight increase in Jordan's mortality rate since 2020.

LABOUR FORCE AND EDUCATION

Jordan's labour market is similar to that of the Gulf oil countries. It has a large public sector workforce, a high unemployment rate among nationals, a low labour force participation rate and a significant number of foreign workers. However, unlike the Gulf oil countries, Jordan is a significant exporter of labour.

In the 1950s Jordan encouraged labour emigration in order to ease unemployment and increase remittances. By 1961 15,901 Jordanian workers were employed in other Arab countries. In 1970 this increased to over 54,000. After the 1973 oil boom, Jordanian workers abroad rapidly increased to 271,200 in 1983, constituting over 30% of the civilian workforce—the highest rate among all Arab labour-exporting countries. During the early 1980s remittances from workers abroad became Jordan's largest source of foreign currency. These remittances amounted to an average of US $1,200m. per year in the mid-1980s, equivalent to 20% of total GDP.

In the late 1980s the number of Jordanian workers in GCC countries decreased owing to the economic recession caused by a drop in oil prices and a change in employment policies. Following the deportation of 300,000 Jordanian and Palestinian workers from Kuwait and Saudi Arabia during the Kuwait crisis (see *Evolution of the Economy*), annual workers' remittances fell to less than US $500m. in 1991, from $1,200m. in 1986. Jordanian workers gradually returned to GCC countries from 1992 onwards. As of 2019, there were about 800,000 Jordanian workers abroad, with the majority in GCC countries; foreign remittances in that year amounted to 11.4% of Jordan's GDP, decreasing to 9.8% in 2022.

Following the 1973 oil boom, Jordan adopted an open-door policy for foreign labour, in order to address the labour shortages caused by large numbers of Jordanian workers going to work in Arab oil countries. Low-cost foreign workers would replace highly educated Jordanian workers who had gone abroad. The benefit was that remittances from Jordanian workers abroad would be much higher than the salaries paid to foreign workers in Jordan. By 1975 the number of foreign workers in Jordan totalled 33,000; this figure steadily increased to reach 226,000 by 1988.

The foreign worker population continued to grow despite the country's struggling economy in the late 1980s and early 1990s. The arrival of refugees as a result of the unrest caused by the Arab Spring did not change this trend either. Experts estimated that around 1.5m. foreign workers were working in Jordan in 2020. Despite the high unemployment rate among Jordanians, the private sector preferred to hire foreign workers on lower wages. This resulted in a lack of investment in modern technology that could reduce labour costs.

The Government has focused on education to improve employment opportunities for new jobseekers. Educational outcomes like enrolment and literacy rates have improved, and Jordan has achieved near-universal literacy rates. However, the education system faces challenges, including integrating Syrian refugees and developing curricula focused on ICT literacy to prepare students for modern jobs.

Enrolment in primary and middle school education is compulsory (between six and 16 years of age), followed by two years of non-compulsory academic or vocational secondary education. For those attending government schools, tuition is free, with equal access to education for all. Completion of secondary education allows students to apply for university study, with Bachelor's degrees typically lasting four years, after which a student may enrol in a graduate programme. Tertiary enrolment rates are relatively low.

Low investment in research and development (R&D), the low number of research personnel and firms, and the limited ability to tap into the skills of highly educated females all serve to dampen the attractiveness of the country's R&D efforts. This will also impede efforts to develop Jordan into a knowledge-based economy.

AGRICULTURE

Despite its historic dominance and important cultural role, in 2021 the agricultural sector accounted for only 5.2% of GDP and 1.4% of employment. Jordan's monarchy gained support from Transjordanian tribes, who considered livestock keeping as a vital part of their identity. However, because of urbanization, these tribes now comprise only around one-third of the population. The country imports approximately 70% of its red meat, and government efforts to reverse this will struggle, owing to high input costs. Climate change and water scarcity (with agriculture accounting for over 50% of Jordan's water consumption) will further increase pressure on the sector.

Jordanian agriculture mostly takes place in the rain-fed highlands, between the Jordan Valley and the desert plains. The country's principal crops are cereals (corn, wheat and rice), olives, tobacco, grapes, apples and nuts. Cereal production fluctuates due to climatic conditions, with the highest yield, of 400,558 metric tons, recorded in 1964 and the lowest, of 14,460 tons, in 1999. Production totalled 133,241 tons in 2020 but fell to 92,521 tons in 2021.

A new strain of foot and mouth disease, which as of mid-2023 was untreatable, was first reported to be affecting Jordanian livestock in January of that year. To limit the spread of the disease, the Jordanian Ministry of Agriculture closed all livestock markets in the country for 14 days in February and again in May. According to the Ministry, 90% of infected cows were in Al-Dhuleil and Al-Hallabat in the north-east of Jordan, which is home to around 80% of Jordan's cattle. The affected farms were reported to have infection rates ranging between 60% and 100%.

Livestock losses will compound the existing socioeconomic pressures on small-scale farmers, who are already suffering from the long-term effects of climate change, such as drought and desertification. Protests in regions heavily affected by the foot and mouth outbreak, including the al-Zarqa and Irbid governorates, are likely to increase, following violent protests against the rising cost of living that have taken place in the country since late 2022.

WATER

Jordan has a Mediterranean climate in the north and desert conditions in the south. Annual precipitation varies widely, from 400 mm–500 mm in the north-west to less than 50 mm in the desert areas. Experts estimate the country's annual water supply at 1,054m. cu m. Of this, 288m. cu m comes from surface water sources, 619m. cu m from groundwater and 147m. cu m from treated wastewater.

Jordan is facing a severe water shortage, with less than 100 cu m of water per person per year. This makes it one of the most water-scarce countries in the world. Jordan qualifies as an 'absolute water-scarcity' country, which means that it has less than 500 cu m of water per person annually. High population growth and low rainfall is forecast to increase water scarcity by 1.0%–1.5% per year. By the end of the century, over 90% of households are expected to be vulnerable to critical water shortages, leading to increasing competition for water resources among agriculture, urban settlements and industry, as well as the vital tourism sector (which accounts for around 20% of GDP). As a result, economic development and political stability may be affected. Mindful of this risk, the Government has included improving water security in the 'Vision 2025' framework.

Population growth is not the sole factor in increased water scarcity. Water availability should have remained broadly stable, but political disputes with neighbouring economies over access to water and climate change have worsened the problem. Surface water, which provides 27% of Jordan's water, is most vulnerable to political issues. Jordan shares the Jordan River Basin, which has an annual water flow of 1,300m. cu m, with Israel, the Palestinian territories, Syria and Lebanon.

Tensions arose between Jordan and Israel as a result of the construction of the National Water Carrier in Israel during the 1950s. This system of canals, pipes and reservoirs carries water from the Sea of Galilee to coastal areas, resulting in reduced water flows in the lower Jordan river, which is essential to Jordan. In the 1994 peace treaty, Israel agreed to provide 50m. cu m per year from the Sea of Galilee to compensate. However, Jordan claims that it receives only 30m. cu m per year.

Water co-ordination with Syria has also been problematic. Syria has proved an unreliable neighbour, especially regarding the sharing of information on hydrological data and water use. The 1987 bilateral treaty between Syria and Jordan refers only to surface water resources. Because of Syria's over-exploitation of groundwater resources, Jordan has experienced lower than expected inflows into the Yarmouk river.

Jordan relies on groundwater for 60% of its water supply. About 500m. cu m are renewable resources, while 120m. cu m are non-renewable. Most of the non-renewable water comes from the Disi aquifer and is used to provide water to Amman. However, experts predict that the Disi aquifer, which is a fossil water source, will dry up within the next three decades.

The construction of camps for Syrian refugees in northern Jordan has placed increased pressure on water resources. Consequently, Jordan has attempted to treat increased amounts of wastewater in recent years, enabling farmers to use almost 150m. cu m in agriculture annually. However, farmers have complained about the quality of the treated water, which they claim has led to a decline in the quality of crops such as citrus fruits. Many wastewater treatment plants are being used beyond their capacity, adding to the quality concerns expressed by farmers.

Several strategies exist to mitigate the risk of long-term absolute water scarcity. Jordan's National Water Strategy for 2016–25 focuses on increasing freshwater supplies and using industrial wastewater for irrigation in agriculture. The European Investment Bank has provided a €200m. (US $220m.) concessional loan to the Jordanian Government for the Aqaba-Amman Water Desalination and Conveyance Project, marking the beginning of the transference of funds from the $1,830m. pledged by bilateral and multilateral donors at a donors' conference in April 2022. The project aims to deliver 300m. cu m of water to Jordan annually by 2027—more than one-quarter of the country's total consumption of 1,100m. cu m in 2022.

In 2022 Jordan and Israel signed a memorandum of understanding (MOU) on the implementation of a resource exchange agreement (brokered by the United Arab Emirates—UAE), which had been concluded in late 2021. The agreement envisages the generation of 600 MW of renewable power in Jordan for export to Israel in exchange for 200m. cu m per year of desalinated water. All parties pledged to begin the planning and development stage of the project by November 2023.

On the demand side, Jordan needs to adopt a strict water policy to manage its limited resources. The efficiency of water usage in the agricultural sector, which accounts for 45% of total water consumption despite its limited contribution to GDP, needs to be improved by adopting better irrigation technologies. Paradoxically, more efficient use of a resource can lead to increased usage when its cost falls. Thus, Jordan must take stock of its water resources before introducing new irrigation technologies.

Jordan could benefit from co-operation with Israel on strict water allocation. After taking stock of its water resources, Israel introduced a system of water quotas, particularly for farmers, coupled with draconian penalties if they disregarded the quotas. This has incentivized Israeli farmers to invest in efficient irrigation technologies. Such a policy in Jordan would require drastic measures to curb corruption in the water sector. Illegal pumping from wells consumes an unknown volume of water each year. Solutions must therefore address not only the supply side through large-scale investment but also the demand side through strict policies, including meticulous accounting and management.

MINING

Jordan possesses considerable reserves of phosphate and potash. The discovery of phosphate in Jordan in commercial quantities occurred in 1932. The mining sector has been a source of government revenue since the establishment in the 1950s of the Jordanian Phosphate Mines Company (JPMC) and Arab Potash Company (APC), which derive revenues both directly from the sale of mined or quarried raw materials and indirectly through associated manufactured goods such as fertilizers. In 2021 mining contributed 2.4% of GDP. Industries associated with phosphate production form a substantial part of the Jordanian industrial base. The APC and JPMC were privatized in 2003 and 2006, respectively, resulting in an increase in taxes and royalties.

JPMC operates four mines, at Eshidiya, Al-Hassa, Wadi al-Abiad and Al-Rusayfah (Russeifa). It is the world's sixth biggest producer of phosphate rock and the second largest exporter of phosphate. The company employs 5,280 people and has a fertilizer and chemical plant in Aqaba, which in 2021 produced 728,000 metric tons of fertilizer. JPMC's phosphate reserves at its mines amount to a combined total of approximately 1,250m. tons.

Phosphate production increased from 338,000 metric tons in 1959 to 557,000 tons in 1962, 1.8m. tons in 1968 and 6.8m. tons in 1987, before declining to 4.2m. tons by 1994. However, production subsequently increased to 7.1m. tons in 2002, 7.6m. tons in 2011 and 10.0m. tons in 2021.

In 1956 the Arab Potash Co (APC) was established as a pan-Arab project. The Jordanian Government awarded it a concession to extract and manufacture minerals from the Dead Sea until 2058. In 2022 the APC was the seventh largest potash producer in the world by volume. The company exported 2.3m. metric tons of potash to over 30 countries in 2021. The APC has 2,200 employees and is valued at around US $2,700m.

However, the Government is diversifying the mining sector away from potash and phosphates. There are metallic and mineral resources in the south of Jordan and exploration efforts have shown potential. Silica sand, feldspar and kaolin are other mineral and metallic resources that Jordan has not yet exploited.

Jordan has approximately 20m. metric tons of copper reserves. Proposed mining operations in the Dana Biosphere Reserve, the largest national park in the country and home to the largest concentration of copper deposits, have faced opposition from environmental activists. Nevertheless, the Government has signed MOUs with both local and foreign mining companies for copper exploration in recent years. The Manaseer Group, a large Jordanian holding company, became the first firm to begin exploration activities at the reserve in 2018. Industry specialists predict that copper extraction will begin soon.

Officials are optimistic about metallic resources such as gold, lead, arsenic, silver and lithium. Geologists from the Ministry of Energy and Mineral Resources discovered gold deposits at three of 12 test sites in the southern Wadi Araba area, and the Government has received expressions of interest for further exploration. The energy ministry has launched a programme for lithium exploration in Aqaba.

Although policymakers want to expand Jordan's mining sector, there are major obstacles. Some relate to the country's geography, with the discovery of copper and gold in remote, rugged or mountainous areas making potential extraction difficult and expensive. Other obstacles involve the business environment, with Jordan struggling to keep up with international best practices for mining and exploration. The legal framework for mining has changed little since the 1960s and 1970s. Land fees have increased, resulting in the closure of smaller mines and discouraging new investment. The rate of corporation tax has doubled in the past decade, to 24%. Energy tariffs are high compared with regional competitors, such as Saudi Arabia, which raises operating costs.

Finally, the Government lacks a coherent plan for development of the mining sector. Regulations are unstable and constantly changing. In 2014 the Government dissolved the Natural Resources Authority (NRA) and transferred some of its duties to the Energy and Minerals Regulatory Commission. Other responsibilities, such as mapping, surveying and exploration, are now held by the Ministry of Energy and Mineral Resources. This separation of responsibilities has made strategic planning difficult. Additionally, most employees in the energy ministry lack the technical skills of the former NRA staff.

MANUFACTURING

During the British mandate in Jordan (1922–46), there was little manufacturing. Only olive pressing and flour milling existed in Transjordan. After the 1948 Arab–Israeli War, the Jordanian Government developed light industries, including mechanical workshops, woodwork and furniture making, and established a development fund with the help of the UN Relief and Works Agency for Palestine Refugees in the Near East (UNRWA) in 1951 to finance small enterprises. Jordan did not create public sector industries, unlike socialist countries.

In 1959 there were only nine manufacturing establishments with more than 100 employees. The primary industry plants included a petroleum refinery, cement mills and a tannery that produced goods for local customers. Smaller industries made traditional products such as food, textiles, shoes, batteries, furniture, toothpaste, shaving cream and cigarettes, and construction-related items such as aluminium. In the 1960s entrepreneurs established small pharmaceutical plants for local customers. Until the 1970s Jordan focused on import substitution as a development strategy. In the 1980s, because of the Iran–Iraq War and the 'oil-for-food' programme, the country shifted to export-oriented industries. These mainly involved pharmaceuticals, textiles and food.

The 1994 peace treaty signed between Jordan and Israel led to the creation of Qualifying Industrial Zones (QIZs). In 1997 the USA, Jordan and Israel signed an agreement that allowed products made in the QIZs to enjoy duty-free access to the US market, provided that the value added to the product through joint Israeli-Jordanian input was at least 35%. As a result, Jordan's exports to the USA increased from US $8m. in 1998 to $660m. by 2003. Following the fall of Saddam Hussain's regime in Iraq in 2003, the USA became Jordan's largest export market.

In 2001 Jordan and the USA signed a free trade agreement—the first such agreement between the USA and an Arab country. As a result, many QIZ operations shifted from exporting to the USA under the QIZ agreement to exporting under the new trade deal.

Over time, manufacturing accounted for a larger share of Jordan's exports. In 1970 the sector's share of total exports was only 16.1%. This had increased to 50.8% by 1990 and to 72.0% by 2010. In 2021 it accounted for 75.0% of total exports. Most of Jordan's manufacturing exports are textile products, which are mostly sent to the USA. Medical and pharmaceutical products are also important exports.

Manufacturing expanded at an average annual rate of 5.8% in the 1980s, 7.7% in the 1990s and 9.9% in the 2000s, before growth slowed to 1.8% in 2010–22. The sector's share of total GDP averaged 10.3% in the 1970s, increasing to 11.8% in the 1980s, 16.1% in the 2000s and 18.2% in 2010–22.

The manufacturing sector was not severely affected by the COVID-19 pandemic, contracting by a relatively small 2.7% in 2020. The sector has since recovered, and expanded by 2.3% in 2021 and 3.3% in 2022. The principal products in 2022 included refined petroleum, food products, cement, fertilizer, textiles, and medical and pharmaceutical products.

ENERGY

Unlike neighbouring Iraq and Syria, Jordan does not have large reserves of oil or natural gas. As a result, around 95% of the country's energy requirements are imported. Prior to the fall of the Saddam Hussain regime, Iraq used to provide more than 80% of Jordan's oil at preferential prices; however, Saudi Arabia has since become Jordan's main oil supplier.

Jordan imported natural gas from Egypt between 2003 and 2013. In February 2014 the APC and Jordan Bromine, both located near the Dead Sea, signed an agreement with Israel's Tamar Petroleum Ltd to supply natural gas worth US $500m.–$700m. Gas supply to these companies began in January 2017. In October 2016 Jordan's National Electric Power Company signed a 15-year agreement with the USA's Noble Energy, the major owner of Israel's offshore Leviathan gasfield, for the supply of 45,000m. cu m of gas worth $10,000m. This deal ensured a stable supply of gas at a preferential price, which was expected to save Jordan around $1,000m. annually. Jordan received the first consignment of gas from the Leviathan gasfield in early 2020.

Experts have identified oil shale as a resource with significant potential in Jordan, with deposits of an estimated 70,000m.–100,000m. metric tons, and a good percentage of extractable oil. The deposits are mostly shallow, making them suitable for open-cast mining. This could provide the country with cheap and reliable energy in the long term, alongside projects to expand the use of renewables.

In May 2009 Jordan's NRA signed an agreement with Royal Dutch Shell to extract oil shale deposits. There are plans to use locally produced oil shale to fuel the 477-MW Attarat um Ghudran electricity plant, which is located 100 km southeast of Amman. This project—a joint venture between Jordan, Malaysia, the People's Republic of China and Estonia—will be the first oil shale power plant in Jordan, and is expected to generate some 3,700m. kWh of electricity, meeting nearly 20% of Jordan's power requirements.

Jordan has an extensive land area and experiences 10 months of sunshine annually, which has prompted the country to invest in solar energy development. The 2020–30 National Energy Strategy plan envisaged the generation of 30% of the kingdom's electricity from renewable sources such as solar and wind power by 2030.

BANKING AND FINANCE

Jordan has 23 banks, of which 16 are domestic. There is a high level of concentration in the banking system, with Arab Bank being the market leader. At the end of March 2023 Arab Bank had total assets of JD 27,810m., more than three times greater than those held by its nearest competitor.

Banks in Jordan mostly provide basic personal, retail and corporate banking, and there is potential for expansion in service offerings across the country. Islamic banking services are only available in specific Islamic banks. Jordanian banks mainly concentrate on the local market. However, Arab Bank is an exception, as it operates beyond Jordan.

Arab Bank dates back to 1930, when it became the first private sector financial institution in the Arab world. The bank continues to be a major economic engine in Jordan and throughout the Middle East and North Africa, providing innovative, modern banking services and facilitating development and trade throughout the region. The bank has the highest market capitalization of all companies listed on the Amman Stock Exchange. Its global network includes 600 branches (spanning five continents), of which 75 are in Jordan. The bank is present in key markets and financial centres such as London (United Kingdom), Dubai (UAE), Geneva (Switzerland), Frankfurt (Germany), Sydney (Australia), Manama (Bahrain) and Singapore.

In October 2021 Jordan was added to the 'grey list' drawn up by the Financial Action Task Force (FATF) of countries that have significant deficiencies in their ability to counter money laundering, terrorist financing and the financing of proliferation. Inclusion on this list increases the cost of cross-border financial transactions owing to higher monitoring costs. Although Jordan remained on the 'grey list' following the FATF's most recent review, in June 2023, the task force noted that the country had completed its action plan ahead of schedule. The FATF was to revisit Jordan to verify that implementation of the necessary reforms was under way and that the political will to ensure their sustained implementation remained in place; if this was found to be the case, Jordan could potentially be delisted.

TOURISM

The tourism industry is the largest private sector employer in Jordan, providing jobs for about 10% of the total workforce, mainly young people. In 2019 the industry supported over 160,000 jobs. It is also the largest source of foreign exchange revenue, which is especially critical within a context of declining foreign aid. Jordan boasts famous archaeological sites, including Petra, Wadi Rum, and Roman remains in Amman and Jerash. The country also has two unique tourism sites, the Dead Sea and Aqaba, which offer sea, sun and sand. These destinations compete with similar Israeli sites in the Dead Sea and Eilat.

In 2019 visitor numbers reached a record 5.36m., earning revenue of US $5,786m. (JD 4,100m.) and accounting for 13% of GDP. In 2020 arrivals declined to 1.24m. as a result of the

COVID-19 pandemic, and the hospitality and retail sectors were slower than other sectors to recover. Arrivals increased to 2.36m. in 2021, less than one-half of 2019's total. However, arrivals rebounded to 5.05m. in 2022, while travel receipts rose to $5,816m., buoyed by increased connectivity (see below).

The Government is pushing forward with investment in tourism, which could facilitate a wider economic recovery. The Economic Modernisation Vision aimed to create 99,000 new full-time employment opportunities, and prioritized an aggressive, government-funded incentive scheme intended to attract European low-cost carrier (LCC) airlines. The scheme, which was initiated in 2018, but put on hold during the pandemic, aims to attract more flights, increase their frequency and extend the tourism season. It provides marketing support and financial compensation. By 2022, following the resumption of the scheme, four LCCs were operating in Jordan: Ryanair, Wizz Air, easyJet and Vueling. These airlines connected Amman and Aqaba to 38 routes serving 15 countries. During 2022 some 26% of people arriving in Jordan by air travelled on LCCs.

The LCC incentive scheme has been controversial in Amman, not least because of reported negative impacts on the flag carrier airline, Royal Jordanian. There are also concerns about the type of tourists that the scheme is likely to encourage to visit the country, with LCC passengers typically considered to be more budget-conscious and therefore likely to spend less in the local economy than other tourists. However, a recent report by the Jordan Tourism Board indicated that the average LCC passenger spent nearly the same amount per day as other types of traveller and was in the country for longer. Such tourists are also more likely to travel to less mainstream sites, which helps to mitigate the problem of overcrowding at the more popular destinations, and to eat at local cafes and buy from local vendors, which benefits small-scale businesses and communities in these areas.

Jordan now faces the challenge of maintaining its competitiveness in an increasingly crowded market. Competition is rising from neighbouring countries, including new entrants such as Saudi Arabia. This presents a challenge not only in terms of attracting tourists but also in retaining the qualified workforce needed to sustain the industry. Many Jordanian professionals in a range of sectors, including hospitality, adventure tourism and even the film industry, have been lured to Saudi Arabia by attractive salaries and relocation packages.

Loss of skilled workers to Saudi Arabia and other countries was a point of major discussion at the National Economic Workshop launched in February 2022, under royal patronage. This workshop formed the basis for the country's Economic Modernisation Vision, one of the aims of which is a doubling of tourism revenues. The projected average annual growth rate of 10% during the next decade would make tourism one of the highest growth sectors in the economy.

To achieve these goals, the plan calls for the development of new products focusing on religious tourism, adventure tourism, medical tourism and film tourism, as well as meetings, incentives, conferences and exhibitions, and it mandates the improvement of existing infrastructure and services to enhance the overall visitor experience. The plan also emphasizes the importance of promoting sustainable tourism practices, preserving Jordan's cultural heritage and supporting local communities.

In order to attract increased investment, the plan aims to improve the regulatory environment for tourism businesses and to streamline visa and permit procedures. It calls for the establishment of a Tourism Investment Fund to support new projects, as well as the development of new tourism-related technologies and innovations.

FISCAL POLICY

Government finances in Jordan show several trends. Both revenue and expenditure have declined since 1985, with annual revenue falling from an average of 32.5% of GDP during 1985–89 to 33.2% in the 1999s, 30.4% in the 2000s and 24.6% in 2010–22, and annual expenditure falling from 41.0% of GDP during 1985–89 to 36.8% in 1990–99, 34.7% in 2000–09 and 32.3% in 2010–22. These movements produced persistent annual budget deficits, averaging 8.5% of GDP in 1985–89, 3.6% in 1990–99, 4.3% in 2000–09 and 7.7% in 2010–22.

Gross government debt fell steadily from a peak of 222.0% of GDP in 1990 to 54.2% of GDP by 2008. However, external events occasionally pushed the fiscal and current account deficits into double-digit territory. Public debt increased to 90.9% of GDP in 2021 before dipping to 89.4% in 2022. However, this understates the true position as the figures exclude Social Security Investment Fund debt; including this would cause the government debt level at the end of 2021 to be around 110% of GDP.

Since 1989 Jordan has been subject to several debt rescheduling agreements, which have entailed the support of the IMF, the World Bank and bilateral donors such as the USA, Japan and the Gulf states, as well as private sector lenders. However, the Jordanian Government's capacity to address the debt build-up is constrained by slow economic growth, high levels of current spending that is politically difficult to cut, and a strong commitment to the fixed exchange rate with the US dollar. The fixed exchange rate means that a devaluation to rebalance the current account is not an option. Strong foreign exchange reserves, the structure of the debt and the availability of donor support mitigate the risks to some extent.

In 2022 the IMF optimistically forecast that Jordan's fiscal deficit would fall to 1.6% of GDP by 2027; to achieve this, economic growth would need to be considerably stronger than the 1.7% average annual GDP growth registered since 2016. Moreover, the loss-making state-operated electricity and water sectors would have to be restructured, and the public sector wage bill (equivalent to 5.4% of GDP) and other current spending would have to be curtailed. However, the Government has been hesitant to act in these areas amid fears of widespread protests. The Government should take steps to improve tax collection. Taxes on income and profits account for only 3.3% of GDP, while sales tax brings in a further 12% of GDP. Finally, the Government will also have to ensure that it continues to attract economic assistance into the medium term, although reliance on aid reduces pressure for fiscal reform.

Foreign aid has been crucial in supporting government finances. The UK provided financial aid to Jordan from its establishment in 1921 until the early 1960s, after which most aid came from the USA. Before the Six-Day War in 1967, foreign aid to Jordan constituted 13% of GDP and about one-third of public sector revenue. However, following the war, the Arab League summit in Khartoum decided that Saudi Arabia, Kuwait and Libya would provide Jordan with US $112m. annually in place of the discontinued US grant.

During the late 1960s and early 1970s one-half of Jordan's public sector income originated from foreign aid. In March 1979 the Arab League summit in Baghdad resulted in a pledge of US $12,500m. in aid to Jordan from Gulf oil states over the next decade. In the early 1980s foreign aid averaged $1,300m. per year, accounting for one-half of total public sector revenue. This aid helped to offset a trade deficit of over $2,500m. at that time. However, from 1984 Arab aid to Jordan gradually declined amid lower export revenues; by 1989 it had fallen to $500m., representing less than one-half of the level of aid received at the beginning of the decade. Foreign aid to Jordan dried up almost completely following the refusal of King Hussein to support the anti-Iraqi coalition during the Kuwait crisis.

The peace treaty with Israel in 1994 led to an increase in foreign aid to Jordan. Western countries and the US increased aid to Jordan after the invasion of Iraq in 2003, and further aid came after the Arab Spring. These donors, including Western European countries, viewed Jordan as a stronghold against the spread of Sunni Islamist fundamentalism, and credited Jordan with keeping Syrian refugees from flooding into Western Europe.

Total financial aid to Jordan increased from US $550m. in 2000 to $1,700m. in 2011. The GCC countries gave Jordan $3,600m. in aid between 2012 and 2016. Meanwhile, US aid, which averaged $1,000m. annually during the first half of the 2010s, increased to an average annual of $1,500m. during 2015–17.

In February 2018 the USA and Jordan signed an MOU on the provision to Jordan of US $6,375m. in bilateral assistance over the next five years (2018–22). Hence, Jordan had become the second largest recipient of US aid globally, after Israel. In 2022 the USA pledged $1,450m. annually for the next seven years

In June 2018, after a series of large-scale strikes in Jordan in protest against a new income tax law, Saudi Arabia, Kuwait and the UAE announced US $2,500m. in aid to Jordan. Qatar subsequently pledged a further $500m. in assistance. In recent years, foreign aid has accounted for some 10%–12% of total Jordanian public sector revenue.

Jordan's 2023 budget increased spending by 8.3%, compared with the previous year's budget, to JD 11,400m. (US $16,100m.), well above the 3.8% inflation rate. The budget deficit was nevertheless forecast to narrow slightly in 2023, to 2.9% of GDP, with revenue projected to rise more strongly, to JD 9,600m. This was expected to be driven by an 11.7% increase in tax revenue, based on new efforts to curb smuggling and tax evasion. For the third consecutive year, the authorities neither raised taxes nor imposed new levies, reflecting ongoing concerns about widespread poverty and unemployment.

In the IMF's April 2023 review of its 2020 loan programme in Jordan, the Fund noted that the country's fiscal health still depended heavily on external aid, particularly from the USA and the wealthy Gulf states. The Fund acknowledged, however, that the international donor community should continue to provide Jordan with robust concessional support, contending that this would assist the country with its 'disproportionate burden' in supporting and hosting 1.3m. Syrian refugees. However, the Fund also observed that 'concessional support was becoming harder to attract in the face of global donor fatigue and competing crises'.

As highlighted by the COVID-19 pandemic, the economy remains vulnerable to external shocks, particularly core sectors such as trade and tourism. The Government is now seeking to balance its current IMF-supported fiscal rationalization programme, which includes the gradual elimination of a widespread subsidy system, with efforts to keep the economy afloat, save jobs and maintain living standards in order to prevent a breakdown of its hard-earned social and political stability.

BALANCE OF PAYMENTS

Since 2005 Jordan has been unable to address the structural difficulties of its current account deficit on the balance of payments. In part, this stems from the dinar's fixed peg to the US dollar, which means that the traditional route of devaluing a currency to rebalance the current account is out of the question. The trade balance is perpetually in deficit; imports were more than twice the level of exports in 2019. The trade deficit is partially offset by tourism revenues and remittances, as well as by grants (which were equivalent to 3.3% of GDP in 2020).

Jordan's reliance on imported energy renders the current account vulnerable at times of high oil prices, such as between 2010 and 2014, when oil prices averaged more than US $100 per barrel, and at present. To offset the current account deficit, the Government will have to encourage higher inflows of private sector capital. These could be in the form of FDI, which tends to be long-term but is difficult to attract, given Jordan's small population and low per capita income. Regional insecurity and a weak business environment also curtail these flows. FDI inflows totalled only $693m. in 2020, while the current account deficit was $3,700m.

The stock market is small and cannot meet international regulatory norms, resulting in low portfolio capital flows. In 2020 capital repatriation caused negative portfolio flows of US $93m. Weak investment inflows force Jordan to borrow in order to avoid depleting its foreign exchange reserves, a practice which contributes to the country's debt levels.

PROSPECTS

The country has recovered from the COVID-19 pandemic, but it is likely to face increasing social unrest, owing to high unemployment, an education system out of sync with job requirements, resource scarcity (particularly water), and high food and energy prices. The lack of government resources aggravates the situation. In December 2022 a lorry drivers' strike against fuel prices sparked a nationwide outbreak of protests. The current socioeconomic pressures may lead to further unrest and industrial action. The risk remains high because of enduring fiscal constraints.

In the longer term, without effective mitigation, global temperature increases and lower precipitation will cause major stress to Jordan's fragile natural resources by 2050. Greater incidence of droughts will increase disruptions to water and food supplies. This will play into existing economic problems of disrupted livelihoods, poverty and joblessness among youth, exacerbated by the existing education system, which does not meet market needs.

JORDAN

Statistical Survey

Source: Department of Statistics, POB 2015, Amman 11181; tel. (6) 5300700; fax (6) 5300710; e-mail stat@dos.gov.jo; internet www.dos.gov.jo.

Area and Population

AREA, POPULATION AND DENSITY

Area (sq km)	88,794*
Population (census results)	
1 October 2004	5,103,639
30 November 2015	
Males	5,046,827
Females	4,484,885
Total	9,531,712†
Population (official estimates at 31 December)‡	
2020	10,806,000
2021	11,057,000
2022	11,302,000
Density (per sq km) at 31 December 2022	127.3

* 34,284 sq miles.
† Of the total number enumerated, 6,613,587 were Jordanian nationals; the remainder included nationals of the Syrian Arab Republic (1,265,514), Egypt (636,270), the Palestinian territories (634,182 yet to receive Jordanian state accreditation) and Iraq (130,911).
‡ Rounded figures.

Note: According to UNHCR estimates, Jordan had a temporary refugee population totalling some 741,450 at 31 March 2023, largely comprising those fleeing conflict in the Syrian Arab Republic (some 660,646).

POPULATION BY AGE AND SEX
(estimated population at 31 December 2022)

	Males	Females	Total
0–14 years	1,991,120	1,891,410	3,882,530
15–64 years	3,782,005	3,220,515	7,002,520
65 years and over	210,875	206,075	416,950
Total	5,984,000	5,318,000	11,302,000

GOVERNORATES
(estimated population at 31 December 2022)

	Area (sq km)	Population ('000)	Density (per sq km)
Ajloun	420	208.5	496.4
Al-Aqabah (Aqaba)	6,905	222.8	32.3
Al-Balqa	1,120	582.1	519.7
Al-Karak (Kerak)	3,495	374.8	107.2
Al-Mafraq	26,551	651.1	24.5
Al-Tafilah	2,209	114.0	51.6
Al-Zarqa (Zarqa)	4,761	1,616.0	339.4
Amman	7,579	4,744.7	626.0
Irbid	1,572	2,095.7	1,333.1
Jarash (Jerash)	410	280.7	684.6
Ma'an	32,832	187.6	5.7
Madaba	940	224.0	238.3
Total	88,794	11,302.0	127.3

PRINCIPAL TOWNS
(population at 2015 census)

Amman (capital)	1,812,059	Wadi al-Sir	367,370
Al-Zarqa (Zarqa)	802,265	Tila' al-Ali (Tla' El-Ali)	251,000
Irbid	739,212	Khuraybat as-Suq (Khraibet Essoq)	186,158
Al-Quwaysimah	582,659	Al-Aqabah (Aqaba)	159,018
Al-Rusayfah (Russeifa)	481,900		

BIRTHS, MARRIAGES AND DEATHS*

	Registered live births		Registered marriages		Registered deaths	
	Number	Rate (per 1,000)	Number	Rate (per 1,000)	Number	Rate (per 1,000)
2018	207,917	22.3	70,734	6.7	27,753	2.7
2019	197,287	20.6	67,696	6.4	29,836	2.9
2020	176,557	17.4	67,389	6.2	32,653	3.1
2021	187,722	18.1	75,360	6.8	38,505	3.5
2022	181,991	16.1	63,834	5.6	30,075	2.7

* Data are tabulated by year of registration rather than by year of occurrence. Registration of births and marriages is reported to be complete, but death registration is incomplete. Figures exclude foreigners, but include registered refugees.

Life expectancy (official figures, years at birth): 73.3 (males 72.3; females 75.1) in 2021.

EMPLOYMENT
(public and private sectors)

	2020	2021	2022
Agriculture, forestry and fishing	13,187	15,870	17,013
Mining and quarrying	7,768	8,315	7,389
Manufacturing	118,825	129,240	133,552
Electricity, gas and water	16,921	14,008	13,877
Construction	40,989	42,843	39,833
Wholesale and retail trade; repair of motor vehicles and motorcycles and personal and household goods	125,422	134,410	143,349
Hotels and restaurants	36,092	36,499	47,849
Transport, storage and communications	74,680	83,813	83,500
Financial intermediation	26,617	25,195	24,927
Real estate, renting and business activities	51,021	51,596	53,874
Public administration and compulsory social security	360,331	350,141	364,623
Education	166,739	173,977	177,540
Health and social work	67,596	69,592	69,370
Other community, social and personal service activities	33,503	36,430	38,778
Extraterritorial organizations and bodies	5,985	6,998	7,256
Total employed	1,145,676	1,178,927	1,222,730
Males	904,958	930,957	969,474
Females	240,716	247,970	253,258

JORDAN

Health and Welfare

KEY INDICATORS

Total fertility rate (children per woman, 2021)	2.8
Under-5 mortality rate (per 1,000 live births, 2021)	14.6
HIV/AIDS (% of persons aged 15–49, 2018)	<0.1
COVID-19: Cumulative confirmed deaths (per 100,000 persons at 30 June 2023)	125.1
COVID-19: Fully vaccinated population (% of total population at 21 August 2022)	40.4
Physicians (per 1,000 head, 2019)	2.5
Hospital beds (per 1,000 head, 2017)	1.5
Domestic health expenditure (2020): US $ per head (PPP)	358.9
Domestic health expenditure (2020): % of GDP	3.7
Domestic health expenditure (2020): Public (% of total current health expenditure)	49.7
Access to improved water resources (% of persons, 2020)	99
Access to improved sanitation facilities (% of persons, 2020)	97
Total carbon dioxide emissions ('000 metric tons, 2019)	24,628
Carbon dioxide emissions per head (metric tons, 2019)	2.3
Human Development Index (2021): ranking	102
Human Development Index (2021): value	0.720

Note: For data on COVID-19 vaccinations, 'fully vaccinated' denotes receipt of all doses specified by approved vaccination regime (Sources: Johns Hopkins University and Our World in Data). Data on health expenditure refer to current general government expenditure in each case. For more information on sources and further definitions for all indicators, see Health and Welfare Statistics: Sources and Definitions section (europaworld.com/credits).

Agriculture

PRINCIPAL CROPS
('000 metric tons)

	2019	2020	2021
Apples	21.1	19.6	20.5*
Apricots	26.5	21.0	21.4*
Aubergines (Eggplants)	55.6	57.4	59.0*
Bananas	32.8	33.0	38.4*
Barley	66.6	86.6	35.0†
Beans, green	16.5	8.0	17.4*
Cabbages and other brassicas	35.1	52.6	46.8*
Cantaloupes and other melons	62.5	53.7	54.0*
Cauliflowers and broccoli	46.8	56.8	65.6*
Chillies and peppers, green	65.8	95.3	95.1*
Cucumbers and gherkins	163.5	141.4	191.8*
Dates	23.4	25.0	27.0*
Grapes	53.9	43.0	44.6*
Lemons and limes	39.2	30.6	28.7*
Lettuce and chicory	41.5	49.8	55.3*
Maize	20.9	19.0	25.0†
Olives	215.0	169.3	172.1†
Onions, dry	54.5	82.2	65.8*
Oranges	48.7	42.0	45.8*
Peaches and nectarines	79.4	87.6	79.4†
Potatoes	173.7	147.9	177.5*
Pumpkins, squash and gourds	53.0	85.5	82.0*
Tangerines, mandarins, etc.	27.2	24.7	23.0*
Tomatoes	496.2	577.3	629.2*
Watermelons	93.8	87.5	99.1*
Wheat	26.4	25.7	30.0†

* FAO estimate.
† Unofficial figure.

Aggregate production ('000 metric tons, may include official, semi-official or estimated data): Total cereals 114.2 in 2019, 133.2 in 2020, 92.5 in 2021; Total fruit (primary) 547.7 in 2019, 506.1 in 2020, 523.3 in 2021; Total oilcrops 215.0 in 2019, 169.3 in 2020, 172.1 in 2021; Total roots and tubers 173.7 in 2019, 147.9 in 2020, 177.5 in 2021; Total vegetables (primary) 1,178.1 in 2019, 1,374.0 in 2020, 1,489.7 in 2021.

Source: FAO.

LIVESTOCK
('000 head, year ending September)

	2019	2020	2021
Asses*	7.0	6.7	6.4
Camels*	14.1	14.2	13.6
Cattle	77.6	77.9	78.5
Chickens*	30,131	30,379	30,626
Goats	764.5	762.8	803.9
Sheep	3,008.8	3,002.3	3,085.3

* FAO estimate(s).
Source: FAO.

LIVESTOCK PRODUCTS
('000 metric tons)

	2019	2020	2021
Cattle hides, fresh*	5.1	5.6	6.0
Cattle meat	42.0	45.8	48.6*
Cattle offals, edible*	8.7	9.5	10.1
Cows' milk	346.9	299.8	309.1
Chicken meat	184.4	217.6	205.0†
Goat meat	8.7	4.2	6.5*
Goats' milk	14.4	9.3	11.3*
Sheep meat	19.1	28.4	27.3*
Sheep's (Ewes') milk	96.0	101.1	97.1*
Hen eggs	78.9*	71.6	n.a.
Wool, greasy*	4.4	4.5	4.5

* FAO estimate(s).
† Unofficial figure.
Source: FAO.

Forestry

ROUNDWOOD REMOVALS
('000 cu m, excluding bark, FAO estimates)

	2019	2020	2021
Industrial wood	4	4	4
Fuel wood	372	380	388
Total	376	384	392

Source: FAO.

Fishing

(metric tons, live weight)

	2019	2020	2021
Capture*	679	584	665
Freshwater fishes	430	400	410*
Tunas*	60	33	50
Aquaculture*	1,940	2,055	2,145
Common carp*	1,020	1,030	1,080
Tilapias*	920	1,025	1,065
Total catch*	2,619	2,639	2,810

* FAO estimate(s).
Source: FAO.

JORDAN

Mining

('000 metric tons unless otherwise indicated)

	2017	2018	2019
Crude petroleum ('000 barrels)	2,400	7,500	7,500
Phosphate rock	8,688	8,022	9,223
Potash salts*	2,230	2,436	2,486
Bromine	85	89	150†
Gypsum	344	191	260†

* Figures refer to the K_2O content.
† Estimate.

Source: US Geological Survey.

Industry

SELECTED PRODUCTS
(42-gallon barrels unless otherwise indicated)

	2017	2018	2019
Asphalt	1,344	1,000	1,066
Phosphatic fertilizers ('000 metric tons)	379	632	n.a.
Cement ('000 metric tons)	4,680	4,680*	5,050*
Liquefied petroleum gas	831	690	777
Motor spirit (petrol)	4,734	4,108	4,320
Jet fuel	2,902	2,568	2,934
Gas-diesel (distillate fuel) oils	6,304	5,508	5,950
Electrical energy (million kWh)	20,759	20,476	21,030

* Estimate.

Electrical energy (million kWh): 21,291 in 2020; 21,925 in 2021; 23,654 in 2022 (preliminary).

Sources: partly US Geological Survey.

Finance

CURRENCY AND EXCHANGE RATES

Monetary Units
1,000 fils = 1 Jordanian dinar (JD).

Sterling, Dollar and Euro Equivalents (31 May 2023)
£1 sterling = JD 0.878;
US $1 = JD 0.710;
€1 = JD 0.758;
JD 10 = £11.39 = $14.08 = €13.18.

Exchange Rate: An official mid-point rate of US $1 = 709 fils (JD1 = $1.4104) has been maintained since October 1995.

BUDGET
(JD million)*

Revenue†	2021	2022	2023‡
Taxation	5,626.9	6,047.9	6,633.0
Taxes on income and profits	1,179.6	1,548.2	1,545.0
Corporations	802.8	1,094.6	1,086.1
Individuals	276.8	328.2	337.8
National contribution account	100.0	125.3	121.0
Taxes on domestic transactions	4,038.7	4,167.5	4,587.0
Taxes on financial transactions	70.6	99.5	141.0
Taxes on foreign trade	338.0	232.7	275.0
Taxes on Grants	—	—	85.0
Other revenue	1,690.4	2,069.1	2,128.0
Fees	838.4	886.3	963.0
Interest and profits	357.9	458.6	497.3
Miscellaneous revenues	494.1	724.3	667.7
Repayment	26.7	17.0	31.0
Pensions	7.5	4.9	6.0
Total	**7,324.9**	**8,121.9**	**8,767.0**

Expenditure	2021	2022	2023‡
Current	8,720.6	8,954.3	9,839.5
Wages and salaries	1,595.0	1,669.7	1,810.0
Social security	176.3	179.1	214.1
Purchases of goods and services	441.7	417.3	498.0
Interest payments	1,403.4	1,427.6	1,577.0
Domestic	977.1	959.5	1,024.4
Foreign	426.3	468.1	552.6
Food and oil subsidies	238.1	240.4	477.3
Defence and security	2,749.6	2,845.9	2,998.7
Social assistance	287.9	347.7	378.7
Pensions	1,605.0	1,638.4	1,679.0
Grants	20.2	20.1	26.9
Other current expenditures	203.4	168.3	179.8
Capital	1,138.2	1,512.3	1,591.9
Total	**9,858.8**	**10,466.6**	**11,431.4**

* Figures represent a consolidation of the Current, Capital and Development Plan Budgets of the central Government. The data exclude the operations of the Health Security Fund and of other government agencies with individual budgets.
† Excluding foreign grants received (JD million): 803.3 in 2021; 792.2 in 2022; 802.0 in 2023 (budget figure).
‡ Budget figures.

Source: Ministry of Finance, Amman.

INTERNATIONAL RESERVES
(US $ million at 31 December)

	2014	2015	2016
Gold (national valuation)	744.7	1,407.5	1,521.2
IMF special drawing rights	178.9	136.6	95.6
Reserve position in the IMF	0.5	0.5	0.5
Foreign exchange	15,120.0	15,025.0	13,923.3
Total	**16,044.1**	**16,569.6**	**15,540.6**

2018: IMF special drawing rights 31.6; Reserve position in the IMF 0.5.
2019: IMF special drawing rights 15.7; Reserve position in the IMF 0.8.
2020: IMF special drawing rights 18.7; Reserve position in the IMF 0.8.
2021: IMF special drawing rights 15.2; Reserve position in the IMF 1.2.
2022: IMF special drawing rights 9.6; Reserve position in the IMF 1.1.

Source: IMF, *International Financial Statistics*.

MONEY SUPPLY
(JD million at 31 December)

	2020	2021	2022
Currency outside banks	5,939.4	6,225.4	6,037.4
Transferable deposits	8,959.5	9,869.9	9,971.2
Other deposits	20,628.3	21,931.4	24,063.3
Broad money	**35,527.1**	**38,026.7**	**40,072.0**

Source: IMF, *International Financial Statistics*.

COST OF LIVING
(Consumer Price Index; base: 2018 = 100)

	2020	2021	2022
Food (incl. beverages)	102.6	102.7	106.1
Clothing (incl. footwear)	97.5	96.3	96.6
Housing	99.7	101.2	108.0
All items (incl. others)	**101.1**	**102.5**	**106.8**

Source: Central Bank of Jordan, Amman.

JORDAN

NATIONAL ACCOUNTS
(JD million at current prices)

Expenditure on the Gross Domestic Product

	2019	2020	2021
Government final consumption expenditure	5,390.6	5,730.8	5,958.7
Private final consumption expenditure	28,720.7	29,787.9	30,973.4
Gross fixed capital formation	5,801.1	5,621.8	6,760.3
Change in inventories	1,010.5	989.7	1,073.8
Total domestic expenditure	**40,922.90**	**42,130.2**	**44,766.2**
Exports of goods and services	11,451.0	7,396.3	9,810.3
Less Imports of goods and services	15,489.4	12,993.3	16,460.0
Statistical discrepancy	−5,287.5	−5,508.2	−5,993.5
GDP in purchasers' values	**31,597.0**	**31,025.0**	**32,123.0**

Source: UN National Accounts Main Aggregates Database.

GDP in constant 2016 prices (preliminary): 29,615.8 in 2020; 30,274.1 in 2021; 31,032.1 in 2022 (Source: Central Bank of Jordan, Amman).

GROSS DOMESTIC PRODUCT BY ECONOMIC ACTIVITY
(preliminary)

	2020	2021	2022
Agriculture, hunting, forestry and fishing	1,425.9	1,488.3	1,572.6
Mining and quarrying	668.9	780.0	901.9
Manufacturing	5,311.2	5,496.7	5,864.6
Electricity and water	499.7	509.6	530.2
Construction	827.7	879.8	943.0
Wholesale and retail trade, restaurants and hotels	2,815.5	2,920.0	3,106.3
Transport, storage and communications	2,388.6	2,468.6	2,631.5
Finance, insurance, real estate and business services	6,001.5	6,216.5	6,485.4
Public administration, defence, and social security	4,348.6	4,451.5	4,584.2
Other services	2,736.9	2,745.8	2,804.5
GDP in basic prices	**27,024.5**	**27,956.8**	**29,424.2**
Taxes on products (net)	3,917.2	4,075.8	4,266.4
GDP in purchasers' values	**30,941.7**	**32,032.6**	**33,690.6**

Source: Central Bank of Jordan, Amman.

BALANCE OF PAYMENTS
(US $ million)

	2019	2020	2021
Exports of goods	8,317.3	7,943.2	9,357.5
Imports of goods	−17,052.4	−15,329.0	−19,229.6
Balance on goods	**−8,735.0**	**−7,385.8**	**−9,872.1**
Exports of services	7,852.8	2,501.1	4,506.6
Imports of services	−4,911.1	−3,095.1	−4,162.3
Balance on goods and services	**−5,793.4**	**−7,979.7**	**−9,527.7**
Primary income received	1,270.3	913.4	755.5
Primary income paid	−1,262.8	−1,037.8	−1,001.3
Balance on goods, services and primary income	**−5,785.9**	**−8,104.1**	**−9,773.5**
Secondary income received	5,611.8	6,007.5	6,304.2
Secondary income paid	−599.3	−408.9	−561.1
Current balance	**−773.4**	**−2,505.5**	**−4,030.4**
Capital account (net)	25.4	23.9	15.5
Direct investment assets	−43.4	−26.3	−15.9
Direct investment liabilities	729.7	760.3	621.8
Portfolio investment assets	−31.8	28.2	−50.4
Portfolio investment liabilities	−1,034.9	396.6	−182.0
Other investment assets	28.5	−892.0	−100.3
Other investment liabilities	2,242.7	2,995.9	3,474.6
Net errors and omissions	−325.4	−163.8	2,128.7
Reserves and related items	**817.3**	**617.3**	**1,861.5**

Source: IMF, *International Financial Statistics*.

External Trade

PRINCIPAL COMMODITIES
(distribution by HS, JD million)

Imports c.i.f.	2020	2021	2022
Live animals and animal products	681.3	762.5	925.2
Vegetable products	1,141.0	1,220.6	1,663.7
Cereals	555.1	667.1	1,002.8
Prepared foodstuffs; beverages, spirits and vinegar; tobacco and manufactured tobacco substitutes	1,043.6	1,092.7	1,330.0
Mineral products	1,358.3	2,481.3	3,686.5
Mineral fuels, oils, distillation products, etc.	1,318.6	2,403.9	3,575.6
Crude petroleum oils	411.9	747.1	962.2
Non-crude petroleum oils	552.6	869.7	1,595.8
Petroleum gases	319.2	716.4	896.7
Chemicals and related products	1,290.8	1,495.7	1,722.5
Plastics, rubbers, and articles thereof	515.6	654.6	763.2
Plastics and articles thereof	437.4	561.0	663.9
Textiles and textile articles	919.2	1,145.9	1,276.7
Pearls, precious or semi-precious stones, precious metals, and articles thereof	151.1	994.9	1,705.2
Base metals and articles thereof	759.3	837.7	1,161.4
Machinery and mechanical appliances	1,522.8	1,724.5	1,902.1
Machinery, boilers, etc.	803.0	921.1	1,029.1
Electrical, electronic equipment	719.8	803.4	873.0
Vehicles, aircraft, vessels and associated transport equipment	1,049.0	1,196.3	1,298.8
Vehicles other than railway, tramway	888.2	1,100.8	1,168.0
Motor cars and other passenger vehicles	556.4	720.8	799.2
Total (incl. others)	**12,235.4**	**15,295.1**	**19,428.5**

Exports f.o.b.*	2020	2021	2022
Live animals and animal products	186.7	168.8	213.3
Vegetable products	317.3	439.5	778.4
Edible vegetables, roots and tubers	145.5	140.6	273.0
Prepared foodstuffs; beverages, spirits and vinegar; tobacco and manufactured tobacco substitutes	307.2	336.2	755.8
Mineral products	370.0	485.2	919.8
Salt, sulphur, earth, stone, plaster, lime and cement	300.6	435.4	834.3
Natural calcium and aluminium phosphates, phosphatic chalk	243.1	377.0	759.7
Chemicals and related products	1,875.2	2,401.9	3,390.1
Inorganic chemicals	498.3	742.7	906.4
Pharmaceutical products	439.6	435.4	456.5
Medicaments put in doses	292.8	344.4	356.3
Fertilizers	644.3	938.8	1,669.5
Nitrogenous mineral or chemical fertilizers	163.2	287.2	444.6
Potassic mineral or chemical fertilizers	380.8	514.5	1,056.8

JORDAN

Statistical Survey

Exports f.o.b.*—continued	2020	2021	2022
Plastics, rubbers, and articles thereof	136.5	185.2	316.7
Plastics and articles thereof	132.3	178.2	309.5
Textiles and textile articles	1,229.3	1,352.1	2,952.8
Articles of apparel and clothing accessories, knitted or crocheted	1,117.6	1,232.8	2,734.7
Base metals and articles thereof	216.9	406.7	824.3
Machinery and mechanical appliances	266.8	316.3	603.0
Machinery, boilers, etc.	140.5	134.4	225.3
Electrical, electronic equipment	126.4	181.8	377.8
Vehicles, aircraft, vessels and associated transport equipment	115.6	121.0	134.7
Total (incl. others)	5,639.8	6,643.9	9,073.7

* Including re-exports.

PRINCIPAL TRADING PARTNERS
(countries of consignment, JD million)

Imports c.i.f.	2020	2021	2022
Argentina	188.7	265.6	325.0
Australia	73.6	48.4	195.1
Brazil	200.1	207.2	330.8
China, People's Republic	1,924.2	2,230.2	2,959.0
Egypt	424.2	505.9	556.0
France	216.6	211.2	242.8
Germany	522.9	544.3	565.1
India	347.5	420.2	992.5
Indonesia	85.8	233.9	420.7
Israel	314.4	453.1	543.2
Italy	363.7	456.2	460.0
Japan	234.4	256.1	246.8
Korea, Republic	305.8	356.7	379.1
Malaysia	75.5	158.8	117.7
Mexico	123.2	101.4	80.0
Netherlands	123.6	153.1	152.0
Romania	261.0	420.0	611.1
Russian Federation	187.6	163.0	110.4
Saudi Arabia	1,521.5	2,282.2	2,931.7
Spain	264.1	243.0	283.6
Switzerland	106.0	431.6	734.1
Taiwan	188.7	232.4	229.8
Türkiye	396.9	490.6	644.8
Ukraine	140.1	142.9	60.2
United Arab Emirates	448.9	1,014.1	1,520.6
United Kingdom	153.6	141.8	159.4
USA	976.2	988.0	1,065.2
Viet Nam	129.6	142.3	148.6
Total (incl. others)	12,235.4	15,295.1	19,428.5

Exports f.o.b.*	2020	2021	2022
Algeria	66.7	70.3	80.3
Bangladesh	42.0	35.2	129.3
Brazil	32.5	90.6	150.5
China, People's Republic	119.3	73.7	192.3
Egypt	100.6	146.8	201.7
India	615.2	910.1	1,281.2
Indonesia	89.7	119.9	241.0
Iraq	471.1	436.8	658.0
Israel	59.7	66.1	101.6
Kuwait	164.1	163.8	123.3
Malaysia	37.5	41.9	107.4
Netherlands	38.6	43.1	124.9
Palestinian territories	117.7	144.2	210.5
Qatar	81.2	93.8	115.2
Saudi Arabia	592.7	758.0	866.2
Switzerland	174.3	46.3	4.8
Syrian Arab Republic	45.3	84.0	104.6
Türkiye	66.0	74.3	73.7
United Arab Emirates	250.4	191.8	238.5
USA	1,245.4	1,641.3	2,026.5
Yemen	54.6	67.3	67.2
Total (incl. others)	5,639.8	6,643.9	9,073.7

* Including re-exports.

Transport

RAILWAYS
(domestic traffic)

	2018	2019	2020
Passenger-km ('000)	19.0	100.3	3.1

Freight ton-km: 3,920 in 2010.

Source: Ministry of Transport, Amman.

ROAD TRAFFIC
(motor vehicles in use)

	2020	2021	2022
Passenger cars	1,231,385	1,279,007	1,323,626
Buses	4,111	4,085	4,067
Trucks and tankers	197,261	202,067	206,105
Trailers and semi-trailers	29,218	29,577	30,129

Source: Ministry of Transport, Amman.

SHIPPING

Flag Registered Fleet
(at 31 December)

	2020	2021	2022
Number of vessels	38	36	38
Displacement ('000 grt)	102.5	87.1	87.1

Source: Lloyd's List Intelligence (www.bit.ly/LLintelligence).

International Seaborne Freight Traffic
('000 metric tons)

	2019	2020	2021
Goods loaded	6,195	6,148	6,650
Goods unloaded	10,904	9,857	10,075

CIVIL AVIATION
(domestic and international traffic)

	2020	2021	2022
Aircraft movements	29,486	52,730	75,622
Passengers carried ('000)	2,235	4,683	8,089
Freight carried (metric tons)	49,701	60,213	68,068
Mail carried (metric tons)	311	1,278	1,571

Source: Ministry of Transport, Amman.

Tourism

ARRIVALS BY NATIONALITY
('000)*

	2020	2021	2022
Egypt	47.2	285.3	173.9
Iraq	58.5	86.1	150.5
Israel	21.6	42.9	169.1
Palestinian territories	145.4	254.8	604.2
Saudi Arabia	184.5	296.5	899.4
Syrian Arab Republic	40.3	95.9	309.6
USA	34.3	49.5	160.0
Total (incl. others)	1,239.9	2,358.7	5,049.1

* Including pilgrims and excursionists (same-day visitors).

Source: Ministry of Tourism and Antiquities, Amman.

Tourism receipts (US$ million, excl. passenger transport): 1,409 in 2020; 2,758 in 2021 (provisional); 5,808 in 2022 (provisional) (Source: World Tourism Organization).

JORDAN

Communications Media

	2019	2020	2021
Telephones ('000 main lines in uses)	355.5	391.5	427.5
Mobile telephone subscriptions ('000)	7,778.8	6,987.9	7,275.6
Broadband subscriptions, fixed ('000)	457.5	630.5	719.0
Broadband subscriptions, mobile ('000)	7,778.8	6,987.9	7,275.6
Internet users (% of population)	70.1	75.4	82.8

Internet users (% of population): 65.2 in 2018.

Source: International Telecommunication Union.

Education

(2021/22 unless otherwise indicated)

	Schools	Teachers	Pupils
Pre-primary	1,702	7,848	140,928
Primary	3,860	104,297	1,827,154
Secondary: general	} 1,753	25,660	276,669
Secondary: vocational			
Higher*	62	11,983	310,019
of which universities	30*	10,921†	302,703†

* 2015/16.
† 2016/17.

Source: partly Ministry of Higher Education and Scientific Research, Amman.

Pupil-teacher ratio (qualified teaching staff, primary education, UNESCO estimate): 18.3 in 2020/21 (Source: UNESCO Institute for Statistics).

Adult literacy rate (UNESCO estimates): 98.4% (males 98.7%; females 98.1%) in 2021 (Source: UNESCO Institute for Statistics).

Directory

The Constitution

The revised Constitution was approved by King Talal I on 1 January 1952.

The Hashemite Kingdom of Jordan is an independent, indivisible sovereign state. Its official religion is Islam; its official language Arabic.

RIGHTS OF THE INDIVIDUAL

There is to be no discrimination between Jordanians on account of race, religion or language. Work, education and equal opportunities shall be afforded to all as far as is possible. The freedom of the individual is guaranteed, as are his dwelling and property. No Jordanian shall be exiled. Labour shall be made compulsory only in a national emergency, or as a result of a conviction; conditions, hours worked and allowances are under the protection of the state.

The press, and all opinions, are free, except under martial law. Societies can be formed, within the law. Schools may be established freely, but they must follow a recognized curriculum and educational policy. Elementary education is free and compulsory. All religions are tolerated. Every Jordanian is eligible for public office, and choices are to be made by merit only. Power belongs to the people.

THE LEGISLATIVE POWER

Legislative power is vested in the National Assembly and the King. The National Assembly consists of two houses: the Senate and the House of Representatives.

THE SENATE

The number of Senators is one-half of the number of members of the House of Representatives. Senators must be unrelated to the King, over 40 years of age, and are chosen from present and past Prime Ministers and Ministers, past Ambassadors or Ministers Plenipotentiary, past Presidents of the House of Representatives, past Presidents and members of the Court of Cassation and of the Civil and *Shari'a* Courts of Appeal, retired officers of the rank of General and above, former members of the House of Representatives who have been elected twice to that House, etc. They may not hold public office. Senators are appointed for four years. They may be reappointed. The President of the Senate is appointed for two years.

THE HOUSE OF REPRESENTATIVES

The members of the House of Representatives are elected by secret ballot in a general direct election and retain their mandate for four years. General elections take place during the four months preceding the end of the term. The President of the House is elected by secret ballot each year by the Representatives. Representatives must be Jordanians of over 30 years of age, they must have a clean record, no active business interests, and are debarred from public office. Close relatives of the King are not eligible. If the House of Representatives is dissolved, the new House shall assemble in extraordinary session not more than four months after the date of dissolution. The new House cannot be dissolved for the same reason as the last.

GENERAL PROVISIONS FOR THE NATIONAL ASSEMBLY

The King summons the National Assembly to its ordinary session on 1 November each year. This date can be postponed by the King for two months, or he can dissolve the Assembly before the end of its three-month session. Alternatively, he can extend the session up to a total period of six months. Each session is opened by a speech from the throne.

Decisions in the House of Representatives and the Senate are made by a majority vote. The quorum is two-thirds of the total number of members in each chamber. When the voting concerns the Constitution, or confidence in the Cabinet, 'the votes shall be taken by calling the members by name in a loud voice'. Sessions are public, though secret sessions can be held at the request of the Government or of five members. Complete freedom of speech, within the rules of either chamber, is allowed.

The Prime Minister places proposals before the House of Representatives; if accepted there, they are referred to the Senate and finally sent to the King for confirmation. If one chamber rejects a law while the other accepts it, a joint session of the House of Representatives and the Senate is called, and a decision made by a two-thirds' majority. If the King withholds his approval from a law, he returns it to the Assembly within six months with the reasons for his dissent; a joint session of the chambers then makes a decision, and if the law is accepted by this decision it is promulgated. The Budget is submitted to the National Assembly one month before the beginning of the financial year.

THE KING

The throne of the Hashemite Kingdom devolves by male descent in the dynasty of King Abdullah bin al-Hussein. The King attains his majority on his eighteenth lunar year; if the throne is inherited by a minor, the powers of the King are exercised by a Regent or a Council of Regency. If the King, through illness or absence, cannot perform his duties, his powers are given to a Deputy, or to a Council of the Throne. This Deputy, or Council, may be appointed by *Iradas* (decrees) by the King, or, if he is incapable, by the Cabinet.

On his accession, the King takes the oath to respect and observe the provisions of the Constitution and to be loyal to the nation. As Head of State he is immune from all liability or responsibility. He approves laws and promulgates them. He declares war, concludes peace and signs treaties; treaties, however, must be approved by the National Assembly. The King is Commander-in-Chief of the navy, the army and the air force. He orders the holding of elections; convenes, inaugurates, adjourns and prorogues the House of Representatives. The Prime Minister is appointed by him, as are the President and members of the Senate. Military and civil ranks are also granted, or withdrawn, by the King. No death sentence is carried out until he has confirmed it.

MINISTERS

The Cabinet consists of the Prime Minister and his or her ministers. Ministers are forbidden to become members of any company, to receive a salary from any company, or to participate in any financial act of trade. The Cabinet is entrusted with the conduct of all affairs of state, internal and external.

The Cabinet is responsible to the National Assembly for matters of general policy. Ministers may speak in either chamber of the legislature, and, if they are members of one chamber, they may also vote in that chamber. Votes of confidence in the Cabinet are cast in the House of Representatives, and decided by a two-thirds' majority. If a vote of no confidence is returned, the ministers are bound to resign. Every newly formed Cabinet must present its programme to the House of Representatives and ask for a vote of confidence. The House of Representatives can impeach ministers, as it impeaches its own members.

AMENDMENTS

Two amendments were passed in November 1974 giving the King the right to dissolve the Senate or to dismiss any of its members, and to postpone legislative elections for a period not exceeding one year, given circumstances in which the Cabinet considered that it was not possible to hold elections. A further amendment in February 1976 enabled the King to postpone elections indefinitely. In January 1984 two amendments were passed, allowing elections 'in any part of the country where it is possible to hold them' (effectively, only the East Bank) and empowering the National Assembly to elect deputies from the Israeli-held West Bank. In February 2003 the King ratified legislation according to which six seats in the House of Representatives were, from the next legislative elections, to be reserved for women; the number of seats reserved for women was raised to 12 in 2010 and 15 in 2012. Amendments adopted in April 2016 and January 2022 served further to consolidate the powers of the King (see History).

The Government

HEAD OF STATE

King: HM King ABDULLAH BIN AL-HUSSEIN (succeeded to the throne on 7 February 1999).

Deputy King: Prince FAISAL BIN AL-HUSSEIN (sworn in on 1 July 2022).

CABINET
(September 2023)

Prime Minister and Minister of Defence: Dr BISHER AL-KHASAWNEH.
Deputy Prime Minister and Minister of Local Administration: TAWFIQ KREISHAN.
Deputy Prime Minister and Minister of Foreign and Expatriates Affairs: AYMAN HUSSEIN ABDULLAH AL-SAFADI.
Deputy Prime Minister for Economic Affairs and Minister of State for Public Sector Modernisation: NASSER SHRAIDEH.
Minister of Agriculture: KHALED HNEIFAT.
Minister of Education, and of Higher Education and Scientific Research: AZMI MAHAFZAH.
Minister of Planning and International Co-operation: ZEINA TOUKAN.
Minister of Public Works and Housing, and of Transport: AHMAD MAHER ABUL SAMEN.
Minister of Political and Parliamentary Affairs: WAJIH AZAIZEH.
Minister of Tourism and Antiquities: MAKRAM MUSTAFA QUEISI.
Minister of Industry, Trade and Supply, and of Labour: YOUSEF SHAMALI.
Minister of the Interior: MAZEN FARAIAH.
Minister of Justice: AHMAD ZIADAT.
Minister of Energy and Mineral Resources: SALEH KHARABSHEH.
Minister of Finance: MOHAMAD AL-ISSISS.
Minister of Awqaf (Religious Endowments) and Islamic Affairs: Dr MOHAMMAD KHALAILEH.
Minister of Culture: HAIFA NAJJAR.
Minister of the Environment: MUAWIEH RADAIDEH.
Minister of Social Development: WAFAA BANI.
Minister of Health: FERAS AL-HAWARI.
Minister of Water and Irrigation: MOHAMMAD NAJJAR.
Minister of Youth: MOHAMMAD SALAMEH AL-NABULSI.
Minister of Digital Economy and Entrepreneurship: AHMAD HANANDEH.
Minister of Investment: KHOLOUD SAQQAF.
Minister of Government Communications: FAISAL SHBOUL.
Minister of State for Cabinet Affairs: IBRAHIM JAZI.
Minister of State for Legal Affairs: NANCY NAMROUQA.

Note: The Head of Intelligence and the Governor of the Central Bank also have full ministerial status.

MINISTRIES

Prime Ministry of Jordan: POB 80, Fourth Circle, Fas St, Bldg 1, Amman 11180; tel. (6) 4641211; fax (6) 4642520; e-mail info@pm.gov.jo; internet www.pm.gov.jo.

Ministry of Agriculture: POB 2099, Amman; tel. (6) 5686151; fax (6) 5686310; e-mail moa.mail@moa.gov.jo; internet moa.gov.jo.

Ministry of Awqaf (Religious Endowments) and Islamic Affairs: POB 659, al-Razi St, Jabal al-Hussein, Amman 11118; tel. (6) 5666141; fax (6) 5602254; e-mail awqaf@awqaf.gov.jo; internet www.awqaf.gov.jo.

Ministry of Culture: POB 6140, Amman; tel. (6) 5696218; fax (6) 5691640; e-mail info@culture.gov.jo; internet www.culture.gov.jo.

Ministry of Defence: POB 80, Amman 11190; tel. (6) 5000800; fax (6) 4642520; e-mail info@jaf.mil.jo; internet www.jaf.mil.jo.

Ministry of Digital Economy and Entrepreneurship: Amman.

Ministry of Education: POB 1646, Amman 11118; tel. (6) 5607331; fax (6) 5666019; e-mail moecs@moe.gov.jo; internet www.moe.gov.jo.

Ministry of Energy and Mineral Resources: Abdul Rahim al-Haj Mohammed St, Bldg 44, Amman 11118; tel. (6) 5803060; fax (6) 5865714; e-mail memr@memr.gov.jo; internet www.memr.gov.jo.

Ministry of the Environment: POB 1408, Amman 11941; tel. (6) 5560113; fax (6) 5516377; e-mail info@moenv.gov.jo; internet www.moenv.gov.jo.

Ministry of Finance: POB 85, King Hussein St, Amman 11118; tel. (6) 4636321; fax (6) 4618527; e-mail info@mof.gov.jo; internet www.mof.gov.jo.

Ministry of Foreign and Expatriates Affairs: POB 35217, Amman 11180; tel. (6) 5735150; fax (6) 5735163; e-mail inquiry@mfa.gov.jo; internet www.mfa.gov.jo.

Ministry of Health: POB 86, Amman 11118; tel. (6) 5200230; fax (6) 5688373; e-mail diwan@moh.gov.jo; internet www.moh.gov.jo.

Ministry of Higher Education and Scientific Research: POB 35262, Amman 11180; tel. (6) 5347671; fax (6) 5349079; e-mail mohe@mohe.gov.jo; internet www.mohe.gov.jo.

Ministry of the Interior: POB 100, Amman; tel. (6) 5691141; fax (6) 5606908; e-mail info@moi.gov.jo; internet www.moi.gov.jo.

Ministry of Justice: POB 6040, Amman 11118; tel. (6) 4603630; fax (6) 4643197; e-mail feedback@moj.gov.jo; internet www.moj.gov.jo.

Ministry of Labour: 11 Issa al-Naouri St, Amman; tel. (6) 5802666; fax (6) 5855072; e-mail info@mol.gov.jo; internet www.mol.gov.jo.

Ministry of Local Administration: POB 1799, Amman 11118; tel. (6) 4641393; fax (6) 4640404; e-mail dewan@moma.gov.jo; internet www.mma.gov.jo.

Ministry of Planning and International Co-operation: POB 555, Amman 11118; tel. (6) 4644466; fax (6) 4642247; e-mail mop@mop.gov.jo; internet www.mop.gov.jo.

Ministry of Political and Parliamentary Affairs: POB 841367, Amman 11180; tel. (6) 5501200; fax (6) 5542265; e-mail info@mopa.gov.jo; internet www.moppa.gov.jo.

Ministry of Public Sector Development: POB 2575, Amman 11821; tel. (6) 5502530; fax (6) 5502548; e-mail info@mopsd.gov.jo; internet www.mopsd.gov.jo.

Ministry of Public Works and Housing: POB 1220, Amman 11118; tel. (6) 3803580; fax (6) 5857590; e-mail mpwh@mpwh.gov.jo; internet www.mpwh.gov.jo.

Ministry of Social Development: POB 6720, Amman 11118; tel. (6) 5679327; fax (6) 5679961; e-mail contact@mosd.gov.jo; internet www.mosd.gov.jo.

Ministry of Tourism and Antiquities: POB 224, Amman 11118; tel. (6) 4603360; fax (6) 4648465; e-mail contacts@mota.gov.jo; internet www.mota.gov.jo.

Ministry of Transport: POB 35214, Amman 11180; tel. (6) 5518111; fax (6) 5527233; e-mail info@mot.gov.jo; internet www.mot.gov.jo.

Ministry of Water and Irrigation: POB 2412, Amman 11181; tel. (6) 5652265; fax (6) 5652287; e-mail mwiinfo@mwi.gov.jo; internet www.mwi.gov.jo.

Ministry of Youth and Sports: POB 1794, Amman; tel. (6) 5604701; fax (6) 5604717; e-mail web@moy.gov.jo; internet www.moy.gov.jo.

JORDAN

Legislature

NATIONAL ASSEMBLY

House of Representatives

Elections to the House of Representatives took place on 10 November 2020. According to the Independent Election Commission, around two-thirds of the outgoing members of the chamber lost their seats. Voter turnout was recorded at 29.9%.

House of Representatives: POB 72, Amman 11118; tel. (6) 5635200; fax (6) 5685970; e-mail info@representatives.jo; internet www.representatives.jo.

Speaker: AHMAD SAFADI.

General Election, 10 November 2020

Party/Group	Seats
Independents and tribal representatives	118
National Coalition for Reform (Islamic Action Front and allies)	10
Other parties	2
Total	130*

*In accordance with electoral legislation approved by the King in March 2016, 15 seats were reserved for female candidates, five seats for Christian candidates and three seats for Circassian/Chechen candidates.

Senate

The Senate (House of Notables) consists of 65 members, appointed by the King. The current Senate was appointed on 30 October 2022. (According to the Constitution, the number of seats in the upper chamber may not exceed more than one-half of that in the elected lower chamber.)

Senate: POB 72, Amman 11101; tel. (6) 5664121; fax (6) 5689313; e-mail info@senate.jo; internet www.senate.jo.

Speaker: FAISAL AL-FAYEZ.

Election Commission

Independent Election Commission: POB 375, Tlaa al-Ali Area, Ismail Hejazi St, Next to Audit Bureau Bldg, Amman 11953; tel. (6) 5531111; fax (6) 5504660; e-mail info@iec.jo; internet www.iec.jo; f. 2012; comprises Board of Commissioners and Executive apparatus; Chair. MUSA MAAYTAH.

Political Organizations

Arab Islamic Democratic Party (Dua'a): POB 104, Amman 11941; tel. and fax (6) 5514443; f. 1993; moderate Islamist party; Founder YOUSUF ABU BAKR.

Higher Co-ordination Committee for Opposition Parties: Amman; opposition bloc currently consisting of 7 leftist, pan-Arab and Islamist parties: Baath Arab Progressive Party, Jordanian Arab Socialist Baath Party, Islamic Action Front, Jordanian Communist Party, Jordan People's Democratic Party (HASHD), National Movement for Direct Democracy and Jordanian Democratic Popular Unity Party (leftist).

Hizb-ut-Tahrir al-Islami (Party of Islamic Liberation): e-mail info@hizb-ut-tahrir.org; internet www.hizb-ut-tahrir.org; f. 1953; transnational org. prohibited in Jordan and many other countries; aims to establish Islamic caliphate throughout the world; denies claims that it is a militant group; Leader in Jordan RAMZI SAWALHAH.

Islamic Action Front (Jabhat al-Amal al-Islami—IAF): POB 925310, Abdali, Amman 11110; tel. (6) 5696985; fax (6) 5696987; internet www.jabha.net; f. 1992; seeks implementation of *Shari'a* (Islamic law) and preservation of the *Umma* (Islamic community); mem. of Higher Co-ordination Committee for Opposition Parties; Sec.-Gen. MURAD AL-ADAYLA.

Islamic Centrist Party (Hizb al-Wasat al-Islami): POB 2149, Haswa Bldg, 3rd Floor, Amman 11941; tel. and fax (6) 5353966; e-mail alwasaat2001@gmail.com; internet www.wasatparty.org; f. 2001 by fmr mems of Islamic Action Front and Muslim Brotherhood; Sec.-Gen. MUSTAFA AL-AMAWI.

Jordanian Arab Socialist Baath Party (Hizb al-Baath al-Arabi al-Ishtiraki al-Urduni): POB 8383, Amman; tel. (6) 4658618; fax (6) 4658617; f. 1993; promotes pan-Arabism; mem. of Higher Co-ordination Cttee for Opposition Parties; Sec.-Gen. FOUAD DABOUR.

Jordanian Communist Party: POB 2349, Amman; tel. and fax (6) 5159428; e-mail jcplive@umniahlive.net; internet www.cpjo.org; f. 1951; merged with Communist Workers Party of Jordan 2008; Sec.-Gen. Dr FARAJ TMEIZEH.

Jordanian Democratic Popular Unity Party: POB 922110, Amman; tel. (6) 5692301; fax (6) 5692302; e-mail wihdaparty@gmail.com; f. 1990; publishes *Nida'a al-Watan* newspaper; Sec.-Gen. SAEED THIYAB.

Jordanian Social Democratic Party (JSPD): Amman; f. 2016; Sec.-Gen. JAMIL AL-NIMRI.

National Constitutional Party (Al-Hizb al-Watani al-Dusturi—NCP): POB 1825237, Amman 11118; tel. (6) 5696256; fax (6) 5686248; f. 1997 by merger of 9 parties; Sec.-Gen. AHMAD SHUNNAQ.

National Movement for Direct Democracy: POB 922478, Amman 11192; tel. (6) 5652125; fax (6) 5639925; f. 1997; Sec.-Gen. MUHAMMAD AL-QAQ.

People's Democratic Party (Hizb al-Shaab al-Dimuqrati—HASHD): POB 9966, Amman 11191; tel. (6) 5691451; fax (6) 5686857; e-mail ahali@go.com.jo; internet www.hashd-ahali.org.jo; f. 1989; leftist party, which seeks to establish legal and institutional processes to protect the people, instigate economic, social, democratic and agricultural reform, and organize, unify and protect the working classes; supports the Palestinian cause; mem. of Higher Co-ordination Cttee for Opposition Parties; Sec.-Gen. ABLA ABU ULBAH.

Renewal Current Movement: Amman; f. 2016; comprises of Stronger Jordan (Urdun Aqwa), Reform and Renewal Party (HASSAD), National Democratic Party, National Current Party, Al-Hayah Party and Al-Awn National Party; pro-democracy.

Stronger Jordan (Urdun Aqwa): Amman; f. 2013; list formed to contest Jan. 2013 parliamentary elections; Leader ROLA AL-FARRA HROUB.

Other licensed parties include: Baath Arab Progressive Party, Al-Hayat, Jordan National Party, Mission Party (Hizb al-Risala), Al-Ahd, Jordanian Future Party, Free Jordanians Party, Jordanian National Approach Party and the Unified Jordanian Front.

Diplomatic Representation

EMBASSIES IN JORDAN

Afghanistan: POB 144522, Abdul Rahman Zaarour St, Amman 11814; tel. (6) 5922757; fax (6) 5922595; e-mail afghanemb.jordan@gmail.com; Ambassador TARIQ SHAH BAHRAMI.

Algeria: POB 830375, Amman 11183; tel. (6) 4641271; fax (6) 4629075; Ambassador ABDULKARIM BEHHA.

Australia: POB 35201, 41 Kayed al-Armouti St, Abdoun, Amman 11180; tel. (6) 5807000; e-mail amman.austremb@dfat.gov.au; internet www.jordan.embassy.gov.au; Ambassador BERNARD LYNCH.

Austria: POB 830795, Mithqal al-Fayez St 36, Jabal Amman, Amman 11183; tel. (6) 4601101; fax (6) 4612725; e-mail amman-ob@bmeia.gv.at; internet www.bmeia.gv.at/en/embassy/amman.html; Ambassador OSKAR WÜSTINGER.

Azerbaijan: POB 851894, 13 al-Awabed St, al-Kursi, Amman 11185; tel. (6) 5935525; fax (6) 5932826; e-mail amman@mission.mfa.gov.az; internet amman.mfa.gov.az; Ambassador ELDAR SALIMOV.

Bahrain: POB 5220, Faris al-Khoury St, Shmeisani, Amman 11183; tel. (6) 5664148; fax (6) 5664190; e-mail amman.mission@mofa.gov.bh; internet www.mofa.gov.bh/amman; Ambassador AHMAD YOUSEF AL-ROWAIE.

Bangladesh: POB 5685, Um Uthaina, Ibrahim Ghazlani St, Villa 7, Amman 11183; tel. (6) 5529192; fax (6) 5529194; e-mail mission.amman@mofa.gov.bd; internet amman.mofa.gov.bd; Ambassador NAHIDA SUBHAN.

Belgium: POB 942, 17 Sa'ad Jumah St, Jabal Amman, Amman 11118; tel. (6) 4655730; fax (6) 4655740; e-mail amman@diplobel.fed.be; internet jordan.diplomatie.belgium.be; Ambassador SERGE DICKSCHEN.

Bosnia and Herzegovina: POB 850836, 67 Said al-Mufti St, Amman 11183; tel. (6) 5856921; fax (6) 5856923; e-mail amman@bhembassyjo.com; internet bhembassyjo.com; Ambassador SLAVKO MATANOVIĆ.

Brazil: 17 Suleiman Yousef ak-Sukar St, Amman 11183; tel. (6) 5923941; e-mail brasemb.ama@itamaraty.gov.br; internet ama.itamaraty.gov.br; Ambassador MARCIO FAGUNDES DO NASCIMENTO.

Brunei Darussalam: POB 851725, 5 Ali Sharif al-Zoubi, Abdoun, Amman 11185; tel. (6) 5928021; fax (6) 5928024; e-mail amman.jordan@mfa.gov.bn; Ambassador Haji MAHADI MAIDIN.

Bulgaria: POB 950578, 7 al-Mousel St, Amman 11195; tel. (6) 5529392; fax (6) 5539393; e-mail embassy.amman@mfa.bg;

JORDAN

internet www.mfa.bg/embassies/jordan; Ambassador DIMITAR MIHAYLOV.

Canada: POB 815403, 133 Zahran St, Amman 11180; tel. (6) 5901500; fax (6) 5901501; e-mail amman@international.gc.ca; internet www.international.gc.ca/country-pays/jordan-jordanie/amman.aspx; Ambassador TARIK ALI KHAN.

Chile: POB 830663, 28 Hussein Abu Ragheb St, Abdoun, Amman 11183; tel. (6) 5923360; fax (6) 5924263; e-mail echile@orange.jo; internet chile.gob.cl/jordania; Ambassador JORGE ALEJANDRO TAGLE CANELO.

China, People's Republic: POB 7365, 9 Jakarta St, Amman 11118; tel. (6) 5518896; fax (6) 5518713; e-mail chinaemb_jo@mfa.gov.cn; internet jo.china-embassy.org; Ambassador CHEN XIAODONG.

Cyprus: POB 5525, 17A Alexandria St, Abdoun, Amman 11183; tel. (6) 5657467; fax (6) 5657895; e-mail info@cyprusembassyamman.org; Ambassador MICHALIS IOANNOU.

Czech Republic: POB 2213, 34 Halab St, Abdoun, Amman 11181; tel. (6) 5927051; e-mail amman@embassy.mzv.cz; internet www.mzv.cz/amman; Ambassador ALEXANDR SPORÝŠ.

Egypt: POB 35178, 7 Muhammad Ali Bedier St, Amman 11180; tel. (6) 5929807; fax (6) 5929811; Ambassador MOHAMMED SAMIR MARZOUQ.

France: POB 5348, 40 al-Mutanabbi St, Amman 11183; tel. (6) 4604630; fax (6) 4659606; internet jo.ambafrance.org; Ambassador ALEXIS LE COUR GRANDMAISON.

Georgia: POB 851903, Villa No. 2, al-Saraha St, Abdoun, Amman 11185; tel. (6) 5926433; fax (6) 5923374; e-mail amman.emb@mfa.gov.ge; internet www.jordan.mfa.gov.ge; Ambassador ZAZA KANDELAKI.

Germany: POB 183, 25 Benghazi St, Jabal Amman 11118; tel. (6) 5901170; fax (6) 5901282; e-mail info@amman.diplo.de; internet www.amman.diplo.de; Ambassador BERTRAM VON MOLTKE.

Greece: POB 35069, 7 Suleiman Youssef Sukkar St, Amman 11180; tel. (6) 5922724; fax (6) 5927622; e-mail gremb.amm@mfa.gr; internet www.mfa.gr/amman; Ambassador ELEFTHERIA GALATHIANAKI.

Holy See: POB 142916, 14 Anton al-Naber St, Amman 11814; tel. (6) 5929934; fax (6) 5929931; e-mail nunciature.jordan@gmail.com; Apostolic Nuncio Most Rev. GIOVANNI PIETRO DAL TOSO (Titular Archbishop of Foratiana).

Hungary: POB 3441, 24 Hani al-Akasheh St, Abdoun, Amman 11181; tel. (6) 5934056; fax (6) 5930836; e-mail mission.amm@mfa.gov.hu; internet amman.mfa.gov.hu; Ambassador ATTILA KALI.

India: POB 2168, Jabal Amman, 1st Circle, Amman 11181; tel. (6) 4622098; fax (6) 5926735; e-mail amb.amman@mea.gov.in; internet indembassy-amman.gov.in; Ambassador ANWAR HALEEM.

Indonesia: POB 811784, 13 Ali Seedo al-Kurdi St, Sweifieh, Amman 11181; tel. (6) 5926908; fax (6) 5926796; e-mail amman.kbri@kemlu.go.id; internet www.kemlu.go.id/amman; Ambassador ADE PADMO SARWONO.

Iran: 7 Samir al-Rifai St, Amman 11118; tel. (6) 4641281; fax (6) 4641383; e-mail iranemb.amm@mfa.gov.ir; internet jordan.mfa.gov.ir; Chargé d'affaires a.i. ALI ASGHAR NASERI.

Iraq: POB 2025, Amman; tel. (6) 4623175; fax (6) 4628750; e-mail ammemb@mofa.gov.iq; internet www.mofa.iq/amman; Ambassador HAIDER AL-ATHARI.

Ireland: 15 Bashir Kheir St, Abdoun, Amman; tel. (6) 5903200; internet www.dfa.ie/irish-embassy/jordan; Ambassador MARIANNE BOLGER.

Israel: POB 95866, 47 Maysaloon St, Dahiat al-Rabieh, Amman 11195; tel. (6) 5503500; fax (6) 5503579; e-mail embassy@amman.mfa.gov.il; internet embassies.gov.il/amman; Ambassador ROGEL RAHMAN.

Italy: POB 9800, Jabal al-Weibdeh, 5 Hafiz Ibrahim St, Amman 11191; tel. (6) 4638185; fax (6) 4659730; e-mail info.amman@esteri.it; internet www.ambamman.esteri.it; Ambassador LUCIANO BIZZOTTI.

Japan: POB 2835, 7 Fa'eq Halazon St, Zahran, Abdun Shamali, Amman 11181; tel. (6) 5932005; fax (6) 5931006; e-mail culture@am.mofa.go.jp; internet www.jordan.emb-japan.go.jp; Ambassador JIRO OKUYAMA.

Kazakhstan: Abu Bakir al-Banany St, Amman; tel. (6) 5927953; fax (6) 5927952; e-mail amman@mfa.kz; internet www.gov.kz/memleket/entities/mfa-amman; Ambassador AIDARBEK TUMATOV.

Korea, Republic: POB 3060, 7 Bahjat Homsi St, Amman 11181; tel. (6) 5930745; fax (6) 5930280; e-mail jordan@mofa.go.kr; internet jor.mofa.go.kr; Ambassador KIM DONG-GI.

Kuwait: POB 2107, Queen Zain al-Sharaf St, Amman 11181; tel. (6) 5675135; fax (6) 5681971; e-mail amman.sec@mofa.gov.kw; Ambassador AZIZ DEHANI.

Lebanon: POB 811779, 17 Muhammad Ali Badir St, Abdoun, Amman 11181; tel. (6) 5929111; fax (6) 5929113; e-mail lebanon.embassy.amman@live.com; internet www.amman.mfa.gov.lb/amman; Chargé d'affaires YOUSSEF RAJI.

Libya: POB 2987, Amman; tel. (6) 5693101; fax (6) 5693430; e-mail lib-emb-Amman@hotmail.com; Ambassador ABDUL BASIT ABDUL QADER AL-BADRI.

Malaysia: POB 5351, 5 Hassan al-Kayed St, Abdoun, Amman 11183; tel. (6) 5902400; fax (6) 5934343; e-mail mwamman@kln.gov.my; internet www.kln.gov.my/web/jor_amman; Ambassador MOHAMMED NASRI ABDUL RAHMAN.

Mexico: POB 5313, 52 Port Sa'eed St, Abdoun al-Shamali, Amman 11183; tel. (6) 5939971; fax (6) 5929579; e-mail embjordania@sre.gob.mx; internet embamex.sre.gob.mx/jordania; Ambassador ROBERTO RODRÍGUEZ HERNÁNDEZ.

Morocco: POB 2175, Amman 11183; tel. (6) 5680591; fax (6) 5680253; e-mail ambmaroc@orange.jo; Ambassador (vacant).

Netherlands: POB 941361, 3 Abu Bakr Siraj al-Din St, Amman 11194; tel. (6) 5902200; fax (6) 5930161; e-mail amm-info@minbuza.nl; internet netherlandsandyou.nl/your-country-and-the-netherlands/jordan/about-us/embassy-in-amman; Ambassador HARRY VERWEIJ.

Nigeria: 15 Sataan al-Hassan St, Amman 11181; tel. (6) 5923481; e-mail nigeria.amman@foreignaffairs.gov.ng; internet amman.foreignaffairs.gov.ng; Ambassador MUKHTAR IBRAHIM BASHIR.

Norway: POB 830510, 25 Damascus St, Amman 11183; tel. (6) 5902450; fax (6) 5902479; e-mail emb.amman@mfa.no; internet www.norway.no/jordan; Ambassador ESPEN EVJENTH LINDBACK.

Oman: POB 20192, Amman 11118; tel. (6) 5686155; fax (6) 5689404; e-mail amman@mofa.gov.om; Ambassador Sheikh HILAL BIN MARHOON BIN SALEM AL-MAAMARI.

Pakistan: POB 1232, 17 Anwar al-Khateeb St, North Abdoun, Amman 11118; tel. (6) 444546; fax (6) 4611633; e-mail parepamman@mofa.gov.pk; internet pakembassyjordan.com; Ambassador SAJJAD ALI KHAN.

Panama: POB 851008, 19 Hussein Abu al-Ragheb St, Amman 11185; tel. (6) 5924616; e-mail embpanamajordania@mire.gob.pa; Chargé d'affaires a.i. ROLANDO HAMBLIN.

Philippines: POB 925207, Villa Nos 1 and 12, al-Sulayman al-Bilbeesi St, Amman 11190; tel. (6) 5901730; e-mail amman.pe@dfa.gov.ph; internet ammanpe.dfa.gov.ph; Ambassador WILFREDO C. SANTOS.

Poland: POB 942050, 3 Mahmoud Seif al-Din al-Irani St, Amman 11194; tel. (6) 5512593; fax (6) 5512595; e-mail amman.amb.sekretariat@msz.gov.pl; internet amman.msz.gov.pl; Ambassador LUCJAN KARPIŃSKI.

Qatar: POB 5098, Majid al-Hajj Hassan St, Amman 11183; tel. (6) 5902300; fax (6) 5902301; e-mail amman@mofa.gov.qa; internet amman.embassy.qa; Ambassador Sheikh SAOUD BIN NASSER AL THANI.

Romania: POB 2869, 35 Madina Munawwara St, Amman 11181; tel. (6) 5813423; fax (6) 5812521; e-mail amman@mae.ro; internet amman.mae.ro; Ambassador GEORGE CRISTIAN MAIOR.

Russian Federation: POB 2187, 22 Zahran St, 3rd Circle, Amman 11181; tel. (6) 4641158; fax (6) 4647448; e-mail rusembjo@mid.ru; internet www.jordan.mid.ru; Ambassador GLEB DESYATNIKOV.

Saudi Arabia: POB 2133, Prince Hashim bin al-Hussein St, Abdoun, Amman 11181; tel. (6) 5907070; fax (6) 5921154; e-mail joemb@mofa.gov.sa; internet embassies.mofa.gov.sa/sites/Jordan/AR/Pages/default.aspx; Ambassador NAIF BIN BANDAR AL-SUDAIRI.

South Africa: POB 851508, Sweifiyeh, Amman 11185; tel. (6) 5921194; fax (6) 5920080; e-mail amman.admin@dirco.gov.za; Ambassador EBRAHIM SALEY.

Spain: POB 454, 28 Zahran St, Amman 11118; tel. (6) 4614166; fax (6) 4614173; e-mail emb.amman@maec.es; internet www.exteriores.gob.es/embajadas/amman; Ambassador MIGUEL DE LUCAS GONZALEZ.

Sri Lanka: Bldg 7, al-Madina al-Munawara St, Amman 11183; tel. (6) 5820611; fax (6) 5820615; e-mail slemb.amman@mfa.gov.lk; Ambassador J. A. D. S. P. WIJEGUNASEKERA.

Sudan: POB 3305, 7th Circle, Abdullah Ghosheh St, Amman 11181; tel. (6) 5854500; fax (6) 5854501; Ambassador HASSAN SALEH HASSAN SIWAR AL-DAHAB.

Sweden: POB 830536, 6 Abdul Jabbar al-Rawi St, Abdoun, Amman 11183; tel. (6) 5901300; fax (6) 5930179; e-mail ambassaden.amman@gov.se; internet www.swedenabroad.com/amman; Ambassador ALEXANDRA RYDMARK.

Switzerland: POB 5341, Abd al-Jabbar al-Rawi, St No. 4, South Abdoun, Amman; tel. (6) 5931416; fax (6) 5930685; e-mail amm.vertretung@eda.admin.ch; internet www.eda.admin.ch/amman; Ambassador EMILIJA GEORGIEVA.

Syrian Arab Republic: POB 1733, Amman 11118; tel. (6) 5920684; fax (6) 5920635; Chargé d'affaires a.i. ISSAM NYAL.

Thailand: POB 144329, 8 Ahmad Awamleh St, Abdoun, Amman; tel. (6) 5903888; fax (6) 5903899; e-mail thaiamm@mfa.go.th; internet www.thaiembassy.org/amman; Ambassador SUPARK PRONGTHURA.

Tunisia: POB 17185, Fawzi al-Qawuqji St, Amman 11195; tel. (6) 5922743; fax (6) 5922769; e-mail atamman@go.com.jo; Ambassador KHALED AL-SUHAILI.

Türkiye (Turkey): POB 2062, 31 Abbas Mahmoud al-Aqqad St, Amman 11181; tel. (6) 5002325; fax (6) 5002351; e-mail consulate.amman@mfa.gov.tr; internet amman.emb.mfa.gov.tr; Ambassador ERDEM OZAN.

Ukraine: Bldg 8, Irbit St, Abdoun, Amman; tel. (6) 5922402; e-mail emb_jo@mfa.gov.ua; internet jordan.mfa.gov.ua; Ambassador MYROSLAVA SHCHERBATIUK.

United Arab Emirates: POB 2623, Bldg 65, 5th Circle, Boumedienne St, Amman 11181; tel. (6) 5934780; fax (6) 5932666; e-mail ammanemb@mofaic.gov.ae; internet www.mofaic.gov.ae/en/missions/amman; Ambassador Sheikh KHALIFA BIN MOHAMMED BIN KHALID AL NAHYAN.

United Kingdom: POB 87, Abdoun, Amman 11118; tel. (6) 5909200; e-mail amman.enquiries@fco.gov.uk; internet ukinjordan.fco.gov.uk; Ambassador BRIDGET BRIND.

USA: POB 354, Umawiyyeen St, Abdoun, Amman 11118; tel. (6) 5906000; fax (6) 5920163; e-mail webmasterjordan@state.gov; internet jo.usembassy.gov; Ambassador YAEL LEMPERT.

Venezuela: 8 al-Khandaq St, Amman; tel. (6) 5851704; fax (6) 5851781; e-mail embve.joamm@mppre.gob.ve; internet jordania.embajada.gob.ve; Ambassador OMAR VIELMA OSUNA.

Yemen: POB 3085, Prince Hashem bin Al-Hussain St, Abdoun, Amman 11181; tel. (6) 5923771; fax (6) 5923773; Ambassador JALAL IBRAHIM FAQIRA.

Judicial System

With the exception of matters of purely personal nature concerning members of non-Muslim communities, the law of Jordan was based on Islamic Law for both civil and criminal matters. During the days of the Ottoman Empire certain aspects of Continental law, especially French commercial law and civil and criminal procedure, were introduced. Owing to British occupation of Palestine and Transjordan from 1917 to 1948, the Palestine territory has adopted, either by statute or case law, much of the English common law. Since the annexation of the non-occupied part of Palestine and the formation of the Hashemite Kingdom of Jordan, there has been a continuous effort to unify the law. A Constitutional Court was formally inaugurated on 7 October 2012, to replace the Higher Council for the Interpretation of the Constitution.

Constitutional Court: POB 1122, Tlaa al-Ali, 12 al-Hatimiah St, Amman 11953; tel. (6) 5505777; fax (6) 5513248; e-mail dewan@cco.gov.jo; internet www.cco.gov.jo; f. 2012; The Constitutional Court, established by royal decree in October 2012, retains the authority to decide 'the constitutionality of laws and regulations in force and issue its judgements in the name of the King'. It also 'has the right to interpret the provisions of the Constitution if requested, either by virtue of a decision of the Council of Ministers or by a resolution taken by the Senate or the House of Representatives passed by an absolute majority.' The court comprises nine members, including the President, appointed by the King; Chair. MOHAMMAD MAHADIN.

Court of Cassation (Supreme Court): The Court of Cassation consists of seven judges, who sit in full panel for exceptionally important cases. In most appeals, however, only five members sit to hear the case. All cases involving amounts of more than JD 100 may be reviewed by this Court, as well as cases involving lesser amounts and those that cannot be monetarily valued. However, for the latter types of cases, review is available only by leave of the Court of Appeal, or, upon refusal by the Court of Appeal, by leave of the President of the Court of Cassation. In addition to these functions as final and Supreme Court of Appeal, the Court of Cassation also sits as High Court of Justice to hear applications in the nature of habeas corpus, mandamus and certiorari dealing with complaints of a citizen against abuse of governmental authority; Pres. MUHAMMAD ODEH SALEH GHAZO.

Courts of Appeal: There are three Courts of Appeal, each of which is composed of three judges, whether for hearing of appeals or for dealing with Magistrates Courts' judgments in chambers. Jurisdiction of the three Courts is geographical, with one each in Amman, Irbid and Ma'an. Appellate review of the Courts of Appeal extends to judgments rendered in the Courts of First Instance, the Magistrates' Courts and Religious Courts.

Courts of First Instance: The Courts of First Instance are courts of general jurisdiction in all matters civil and criminal except those specifically allocated to the Magistrates' Courts. Three judges sit in all felony trials, while only two judges sit for misdemeanour and civil cases. Each of the 11 Courts of First Instance also exercises appellate jurisdiction in cases involving judgments of less than JD 20 and fines of less than JD 10, rendered by the Magistrates' Courts.

Magistrates' Courts: There are 17 Magistrates' Courts, which exercise jurisdiction in civil cases involving no more than JD 250 and in criminal cases involving maximum fines of JD 100 or maximum imprisonment of one year.

Religious Courts: There are two types of religious court: the *Shari'a* Courts (Muslims); and the Ecclesiastical Courts (Eastern Orthodox, Greek Melkite, Roman Catholic and Protestant). Jurisdiction extends to personal (family) matters, such as marriage, divorce, alimony, inheritance, guardianship, wills, interdiction and, for the Muslim community, the constitution of *Awqaf* (Religious Endowments). When a dispute involves persons of different religious communities, the Civil Courts have jurisdiction in the matter unless the parties agree to submit to the jurisdiction of one or the other of the Religious Courts involved; Each *Shari'a* (Muslim) Court consists of one judge (*Qadi*), while most of the Ecclesiastical (Christian) Courts are normally composed of three judges, who are usually clerics. *Shari'a* Courts apply the doctrines of Islamic Law, based on the Koran and the *Hadith* (Precepts of Muhammad), while the Ecclesiastical Courts base their law on various aspects of Canon Law. In the event of conflict between any two Religious Courts or between a Religious Court and a Civil Court, a Special Tribunal of three judges is appointed by the President of the Court of Cassation, to decide which court shall have jurisdiction. Upon the advice of experts on the law of the various communities, this Special Tribunal decides on the venue for the case at hand; Chief of Islamic Justice ABDUL HAFEZ RABTAH; Dir of *Shari'a* Courts SAMIH SULEIMAN AL-ZOUBI.

Religion

Over 90% of the population are Sunni Muslims, and the King can trace unbroken descent from the Prophet Muhammad. There is a Christian minority, living mainly in the towns, and there are smaller numbers of non-Sunni Muslims.

ISLAM

Chief of Islamic Justice: ABDUL HAFEZ RABTAH.

Grand Mufti of the Hashemite Kingdom of Jordan: Sheikh ABDUL KARIM KHASAWNEH.

Imam of the Royal Court: AHMAD KHALAILEH.

CHRISTIANITY

The Roman Catholic Church

Chaldean Rite

The Chaldean Patriarch of Babylon is resident in Baghdad, Iraq.

Chaldean Patriarchal Vicariate in Jordan: Jabal al-Wabdeh, POB 910833, Amman 11191; tel. and fax (6) 4629061; e-mail chaldeanjordanian@gmail.com; internet www.chaldeanjordan.org; f. 2002; Patriarchal Exarch Rev. LOUIS RAPHAEL SAKO.

Latin Rite

Jordan forms part of the Patriarchate of Jerusalem (see Israel).

Vicar-General for Transjordan: JAMAL DAIBES, Latin Vicariate, POB 851379, Sweifiyeh, Amman 11185; tel. (6) 5929546; fax (6) 5920548; e-mail regina-pacis2000@yahoo.com.

Maronite Rite

The Maronite community in Jordan is under the jurisdiction of the Maronite Patriarch of Antioch (resident in Lebanon).

Patriarchal Exarchate of Jordan: Mgr MOUSSA EL-HAGE, St Charbel's Parish, Amman; tel. (6) 4202558; fax (6) 4202559; e-mail stcharbelparish@yahoo.com.

Melkite Rite

Jordan forms part of the Greek-Melkite archdiocese of Petra (Wadi Musa) and Philadelphia (Amman).

Archbishop of Petra and Philadelphia: JOSEPH GÉBARA, Archevêché Grec-Melkite Catholique, POB 2435, Jabal Amman 11181; tel. and fax (6) 5866673; e-mail fryaser@yahoo.com.

Syrian Rite

The Syrian Catholic Patriarch of Antioch is resident in Beirut, Lebanon.

Patriarchal Exarchate of Jerusalem (Palestine and Jordan): Mont Achrafieh, POB 510393, Rue Barto, Amman; tel. (2) 6282657; fax (2) 6284217; Exarch Patriarchal Mgr YAACOUB CAMIL AFRAM ANTOINE SEMAAN (Titular Bishop of Hierapolis in Syria dei Siri).

JORDAN

The Anglican Communion

Within the Episcopal Church in Jerusalem and the Middle East, Jordan forms part of the diocese of Jerusalem. The President Bishop of the Church is the Bishop in Cyprus and the Gulf (see Cyprus).

Other Christian Churches

The Coptic Orthodox Church, the Greek Orthodox Church (Patriarchate of Jerusalem) and the Evangelical Lutheran Church in Jordan are also active.

The Press

DAILIES

Al-Anbat: POB 962556, Amman 11192; tel. (6) 5200100; fax (6) 5200113; e-mail news@alanbatnews.net; internet www.alanbatnews.net; f. 2005; independent; Arabic; political; Chair. Dr RIAD HAROUB; Man. Editor BILAL AL-ABWAINI.

Al-Diyar (The Homeland): Al-Fanar Complex, Queen Rania Al-Abdullah St, Amman; tel. (6) 5166588; f. 2004; Arabic; Chair. of Bd OMAR AMRUTI.

Ad-Dustour (The Constitution): POB 591, Amman 11118; tel. (6) 5608000; fax (6) 5667170; e-mail advertis@addustour.com.jo; internet www.addustour.com; f. 1967; Arabic; publ. by the Jordan Press and Publishing Co Ltd; owns commercial printing facilities; Dir-Gen. HUSSEIN AL-AMOUSH; Chief Editor MUSTAFA AL-RIYALAT.

Al-Ghad (Tomorrow): POB 3535, Amman 11821; tel. (6) 5544000; fax (6) 5544055; e-mail editorial@alghad.jo; internet www.alghad.jo; f. 2004; independent; Arabic; Editor-in-Chief JUMANA GHNEIMAT.

The Jordan Times: POB 6710, Queen Rania Al-Abdullah St, Amman 11118; tel. (6) 5600800; fax (6) 5696183; e-mail editor@jordantimes.com; internet www.jordantimes.com; f. 1975; English; publ. by Jordan Press Foundation; Editor-in-Chief MOHAMMAD GHAZAL.

Al-Rai (Opinion): POB 6710, Queen Rania Al-Abdullah St, Amman 11118; tel. (6) 5600800; fax (6) 5676581; internet www.alrai.com; f. 1971; morning; independent; Arabic; publ. by Jordan Press Foundation; Editor-in-Chief RAKAN AL-SA'AIDA; circ. 90,000.

Al-Sabeel (The Path): POB 213545, Amman 11121; tel. (6) 5692852; fax (6) 5692854; e-mail info@assabeel.net; internet www.assabeel.net; f. 1993; fmrly weekly; became daily publ. 2009; Arabic; Islamist; Editor-in-Chief ATEF GOLANI.

WEEKLIES

Al-Ahali (The People): POB 9966, Amman 11191; tel. (6) 5691451; fax (6) 5686857; e-mail ahali@go.com.jo; internet www.hashd-ahali.org.jo; f. 1990; Arabic; publ. by the Jordan People's Democratic Party; Editor-in-Chief SALEM NAHHAS.

Akhbar al-Usbou (News of the Week): POB 605, Amman; tel. (6) 5677881; fax (6) 5677882; f. 1959; Arabic; economic, social, political; Chief Editor and Publr ABD AL-HAFIZ MUHAMMAD.

Al-Hadath: POB 961167, Amman 11196; tel. 70940894; fax (6) 5160810; e-mail info@alhadathnews.net; internet www.alhadathnews.net; Arabic; general news; Man. Editor FATEH MANSOUR.

Al-Haqeqa al-Duwalia (Fact International): POB 712678, Amman 11171; tel. (6) 5805500; fax (6) 4200229; e-mail info@factjo.com; internet www.factjo.com; f. 1996; independent; Arabic and English; aims to promote moderate image of Islam and to counter conflicts within the faith; Editor-in-Chief ABDUL KARIM AL-ZOUBEI.

Al-Majd (The Glory): POB 926856, Amman 11190; tel. (6) 5359466; e-mail almajd@almajd.net; internet www.almajd.net; f. 1994; online only; Arabic; political; Editor-in-Chief FAHD RIMAWI.

Shihan: POB 96654, Amman; tel. (6) 5603585; fax (6) 5696183; Arabic; Editor-in-Chief (vacant).

PERIODICALS

Anty Magazine: POB 3024, Amman 11181; tel. (6) 5820058; fax (6) 5855892; internet www.anty.jo; monthly; Arabic; publ. by Front Row Publishing and Media Services; fashion, culture and current affairs from a professional woman's perspective; Chief Editor SAHAR ALOUL.

Huda El-Islam (The Right Way of Islam): POB 659, Amman; tel. (6) 5666141; f. 1956; monthly; Arabic; scientific and literary; publ. by the Ministry of Awqaf (Religious Endowments) and Islamic Affairs; Editor Dr AHMAD MUHAMMAD HULAYYEL.

Jordan: POB 224, Amman; e-mail webmaster@jordanembassyus.org; internet www.jordanembassyus.org/new/newsletter.shtml; f. 1969; quarterly; publ. by Jordan Information Bureau, Embassy of Jordan, Washington, DC, USA; 3 a year; Editor-in-Chief MERISSA KHURMA.

Jordan Business: POB 3024, Amman 11181; tel. (6) 5820058; fax (6) 5855892; internet www.jordanbusinessmagazine.com; monthly; English; publ. by Front Row Publishing and Media Services.

Military Magazine: Army Headquarters, Amman; f. 1955; quarterly; dealing with military and literary subjects; publ. by Armed Forces.

Royal Wings: POB 3024, Amman 11181; tel. (6) 5820058; fax (6) 5855892; e-mail royalwingsmag@rj.com; internet www.rj.com/en/fly-rj/royal-wings-magazine; bi-monthly; Arabic and English; magazine for Royal Jordanian Airlines; publ. by Front Row Publishing and Media Services; Man. Dir DANA BARADEI.

Skin: POB 940166, ICCB Centre, Queen Rania Abdullah St, Amman 11194; tel. (6) 5163357; fax (6) 5163257; internet www.skin-online.com; f. 2006; quarterly; English; publ. by Near East Media Iraq; art, design, fashion, photography, film and music; Editor-in-Chief TARIQ AL-BITAR.

NEWS AGENCY

Jordan News Agency (PETRA): POB 6845, Amman 11118; tel. (6) 5609700; fax (6) 5682493; e-mail petra@petra.gov.jo; internet www.petra.gov.jo; f. 1965; independent entity since 2004; previously controlled by Ministry of Information prior to its disbandment in 2001; Dir-Gen. FAIROUZ MUBAIDEEN.

PRESS ASSOCIATION

Jordan Press Association (JPA): POB 4256, Amman 11953; tel. (6) 5372005; fax (6) 5372003; e-mail info@jpa.jo; internet www.jpa.jo; f. 1953; Pres. RAKAN SAAIDEH.

Publishers

Alfaris Publishing and Distribution Co: POB 9157, Amman 11191; tel. (6) 5605431; fax (6) 4631229; e-mail info@airpbooks.com; internet www.airpbooks.com; f. 1989; Dir MAHER SAID KAYYALI.

Aram Studies Publishing and Distribution House: POB 997, Amman 11941; tel. (6) 835015; fax (6) 835079; art, finance, health, management, science, business; Gen. Dir SALEH ABOUSBA.

Dar al-Manhal Publishers and Distributors: POB 926428, Amman 11190; tel. (6) 5698308; fax (6) 5639185; e-mail info@manhal.com; internet www.manhal.com; f. 1990; children's and educational publs; Exec. Man. KHALED BILBEISI.

Dar al-Nafa'es: POB 927511, al-Abdali, Amman 11190; tel. (6) 5693940; fax (6) 5693941; e-mail alnafaes@hotmail.com; internet www.al-nafaes.com; f. 1990; education, Islamic; CEO SUFYAN OMAR AL-ASHQR.

Dar al-Thaqafa: POB 1532, Amman 11118; tel. (6) 4646361; fax (6) 4610291; e-mail info@daralthaqafa.com; internet www.daralthaqafa.com; f. 1984; academic publr, specializes in law; Man. Editor KHALID MAHMOUD GABR.

Al Faridah for Specialized Publications: POB 1223, Amman 11821; tel. (6) 5630430; fax (6) 5630440; e-mail hakam@alfaridah.com.jo; internet arabia.group/al-faridah; f. 2003; publr of magazines incl. *Layalina*, *Ahlan!*, *JO*, *Viva*, *Venture*; Editors-in-Chief RANIA OMEISH, SHIRENE RIFAI; Man. Dir QAIS ELIAS.

Front Row Publishing and Media Services: POB 3024, Muhammad Baseem Khammash St, Villa 3, Amman 11181; tel. (6) 5820058; fax (6) 5855892; e-mail info@frontrow.jo; internet www.frontrow.jo; f. 1997; publr of magazines incl. *Jordan Business*, *Living Well*, *Home*, *Royal Wings*; CEO IYAD SHEHADEH.

Jordan Book Centre Co Ltd: POB 301, al-Jubeiha, Amman 11941; tel. (6) 5151882; fax (6) 5152016; e-mail info@jbc.com.jo; internet www.jbc.com.jo; f. 1982; fiction, business, economics, computer science, medicine, engineering, general non-fiction; Man. Dir J. J. SHARBAIN.

Jordan Distribution Agency: POB 3371, Amman 11181; tel. (6) 5355855; fax (6) 5337733; e-mail jda@aramex.com; f. 1951; history; subsidiary of Aramex; Chair. FADI GHANDOUR; Gen. Man. WADIE SAYEGH.

Jordan House for Publication: POB 1121, Basman St, Amman; tel. (6) 24224; fax (6) 51062; f. 1952; medicine, nursing, dentistry; Man. Dir MURSI AL-ASHKAR.

Jordan Press and Publishing Co Ltd: POB 591, Amman 11118; tel. (6) 5608000; fax (6) 5667170; e-mail dustour@addustour.com.jo; internet www.addustour.com; f. 1967 by *Al-Manar* and *Falastin* dailies; publishes *Ad-Dustour* (daily), *Ad-Dustour Sport* (weekly) and *The Star* (English weekly); Chair. MOHAMED DAOUDIA; Gen. Man. Dr HUSSEIN AL-AMOUSH.

Jordan Press Foundation: POB 6710, Amman 11118; tel. (6) 5667171; fax (6) 5661242; internet jpf.jo; f. 1971; publishes *Al-Rai*

JORDAN

(daily), *The Jordan Times* (daily) and *Hatem* (monthly); Chair. AYMAN MAJALI; Dir-Gen. FARID SILWANI.

Al-Tanwir al-Ilmi (Scientific Enlightenment Publishing House): POB 4237, al-Mahatta, Amman 11131; tel. and fax (6) 4899619; e-mail taisir@yahoo.com; internet www.icieparis.net; f. 1990; affiliated with the Int. Centre for Innovation in Education; education, engineering, philosophy, science, sociology; Gen. Dir Prof. Dr TAISIR SUBHI YAMIN.

Broadcasting and Communications

TELECOMMUNICATIONS

Jordan Mobile Telephone Services Co (Zain Jordan): POB 940821, 8th Circle, King Abdullah II St, Amman 11194; tel. (7) 97900900; fax (6) 5828200; e-mail info.jo@zain.com; internet www.jo.zain.com; f. 1994 as Jordan Mobile Telephone Services Co (JMTS—Fastlink); merged with Mobile Telecommunications Co (MTC—Kuwait) 2003, corpn renamed Zain Group 2007; Zain Jordan merged with PalTel (Palestinian Territories) in 2009; private co; has operated Jordan's first mobile telecommunications network since 1995; CEO, Jordan FAHAD AL-JASEM.

Jordan Telecom Group (Orange Jordan): Abdali, The Blvd, Black Iris St, Central 1&2, POB 1689, Amman 11118; tel. (6) 5630090; fax (6) 5630098; internet www.orange.jo; f. 1971; fmrly Jordan Telecommunications Corpn, Jordan Telecommunications Co and Jordan Telecom; present name adopted in 2006 following integration of the following cos' operations into a single management structure: Jordan Telecom, MobileCom (mobile telecommunications services), Wanadoo (internet services) and e-Dimension (information technology); in 2007 Jordan Telecom, MobileCom and Wanadoo were all rebranded as Orange Jordan; 51.0% owned by Joint Investment Telecommunications Co, 28.9% by Social Security Corpn, 9.3% by Noor Telecommunications Holding Co (at 31 Dec. 2019); 3.2m. subscribers (2020); Chair. SHABIB AMMARI; CEO THIERRY MARIGNY.

Petra Jordanian Mobile Telecommunications: POB 941477, Amman 11194; tel. (6) 5630090; fax (6) 5630098; e-mail business@orange.jo; internet www.orange.jo; subsidiary of Jordan Telecom Group; CEO THIERRY MARIGNY.

Umniah Mobile Co: POB 942481, Amman 11194; tel. 788001333; e-mail contact@umniah.com; internet www.umniah.com; awarded contract for Jordan's third GSM licence in 2004; commenced operations in June 2005; first provider of wireless broadband internet services in Jordan; subsidiary of Alghanim Group (Kuwait); 96% owned by Bahrain Telecommunications Co (Batelco); CEO FAISAL QAMHIYAH.

Regulatory Authority

Telecommunications Regulatory Commission (TRC): POB 850967, Al-Shaheed Mohamad al-Zoghoul St, Bldg 13, Amman 11185; tel. (6) 5501120; fax (6) 5690830; e-mail trc@trc.gov.jo; internet trc.gov.jo; f. 1995; Chair. and CEO Eng. BASSAM AL-SARHAN.

BROADCASTING

Regulatory Authority

Media Commission (MC): POB 142515, Amman 11814; tel. (6) 5549720; fax (6) 5650027; internet www.mc.gov.jo; f. 2002; Dir-Gen. BASHIR MOMANI.

Radio and Television

Jordan Radio and Television Corpn (JRTV): POB 1041, Amman; tel. (6) 4773111; fax (6) 4744662; e-mail jrtv@jrtv.gov.jo; internet www.jrtv.jo; f. 1968; state broadcaster; operates 4 TV channels and 6 radio channels broadcasting programmes in Arabic, English and French; advertising accepted; Chair. FAISAL SHBOUL (Minister of Government Communications); Dir-Gen. IBRAHIM BAWARID.

Radio Al-Balad: POB 20513, Amman 11118; tel. (6) 4601216; fax (6) 4630238; e-mail info@ammannet.net; internet ar.ammannet.net; f. 2000 as internet radio station AmmanNet; began broadcasting as an FM radio station 2005, renamed as above 2008; news, politics and community broadcasts; Gen. Man. DAOUD KUTTAB.

Sawt al-Madina (SAM): POB 1171, Amman 1953; tel. (6) 5500006; fax (6) 5500009; internet www.al-baddad.com; f. 2006; owned by Al-Baddad Media and Communications; radio station broadcasting news and politics programmes; Group Gen. Man. FATEEN H. AL-BADDAD.

Other independent radio stations include Mazaj FM, Amin FM, Al-Hayat FM, Rotana FM Jordan and Radio Fann FM.

Finance

BANKING

Central Bank

Central Bank of Jordan: POB 37, King Hussein St, Amman 11118; tel. (6) 4630301; fax (6) 4638889; e-mail info@cbj.gov.jo; internet www.cbj.gov.jo; f. 1964; Gov. and Chair. ADEL SHARKAS.

National Banks

Arab Bank PLC: POB 144186, Shmeisani, Amman 11814; tel. (6) 4600900; fax (6) 5670564; e-mail customer.care@arabbank.com.jo; internet www.arabbank.jo; f. 1930; Chair. SABIH TAHER MASRI; CEO RANDA SADIK.

Bank of Jordan PLC: POB 2140, Bldg 15, Abdul Hameed Sharaf St, Shmeisani, Amman 11181; tel. (6) 5609200; fax (6) 5696291; e-mail boj@bankofjordan.com.jo; internet www.bankofjordan.com; f. 1960; Chair. TAWFIK SHAKER FAKHOURI; CEO SALEH RAJAB HAMMAD.

Cairo Amman Bank: POB 950661, Arar St, Wadi Saqra, Amman 11195; tel. (6) 5007700; fax (6) 5007100; e-mail info@cab.jo; internet www.cab.jo; f. 1960; Chair. YAZID ADNAN AL-MUFTI; Gen. Man. KAMAL GHARIB AL-BAKRI.

Capital Bank of Jordan: POB 941283, 54 Issam Ajlouni St, Shmeisani, Amman 11194; tel. (6) 5100200; fax (6) 5692062; e-mail info@capitalbank.jo; internet www.capitalbank.jo; f. 1996 as Export and Finance Bank; name changed as above 2006; Chair. BASSEM KHALIL SALEM AL-SALEM; CEO DAWOD MOHAMMAD AL-GHOUL.

Jordan Ahli Bank: POB 3103, Queen Noor St, Shmeisani, Amman 11181; tel. (6) 5007777; e-mail info@ahli.com; internet www.ahli.com; f. 1955 as Jordan Nat. Bank; name changed as above 2006; Chair. Dr SAAD NABIL MOUASHER; CEO and Gen. Man. Dr AHMAD AWAD ABDULHALIM AL-HUSSEIN.

Jordan Commercial Bank: POB 9989, King Abdullah II St, Amman 11191; tel. (6) 5203000; fax (6) 5664110; e-mail jcb@jcbank.com.jo; internet www.jcbank.com.jo; f. 1977 as Jordan Gulf Bank; name changed as above 2004; Chair. MICHAEL FAIQ IBRAHIM AL-SAYEGH; CEO and Gen. Man. CAESAR QULAJEN.

Jordan Islamic Bank: POB 926225, Shmeisani, Amman 11190; tel. (6) 5677377; fax (6) 5666326; e-mail jib@islamicbank.com.jo; internet www.jordanislamicbank.com; f. 1978; fmrly Jordan Islamic Bank for Finance and Investment; current name adopted Oct. 2009; Chair. MUSA ABDELAZIZ MOHAMMED SHIHADEH; CEO and Gen. Man. Dr HUSSEIN SAID MOHAMMAD AMMAR SAIFAN.

Jordan Kuwait Bank: Amman; tel. (6) 5621310; fax (6) 5694105; e-mail info@jkbank.com.jo; internet www.jkb.com; f. 1976; Chair. NASSER A. LOZI; CEO HAETHUM S. BUTTIKHI.

Specialized Credit Institutions

Agricultural Credit Corporation: POB 77, King Hussein St, Abdali, Amman 11118; tel. (6) 5661105; fax (6) 5668365; e-mail info@acc.gov.jo; internet www.acc.gov.jo; f. 1959; Chair. KHALED HNEIFAT (Minister of Agriculture); Vice-Chair. and Dir-Gen. Eng. MUHAMMAD AL-DUJAN.

Arab Jordan Investment Bank: POB 8797, Arab Jordan Investment Bank Bldg, 200 Zahran St, Shmeisani, Amman 11121; tel. (6) 5003005; e-mail info@ajib.com; internet www.ajib.com; f. 1978; Chair. HANI AL-QADI.

Bank al Etihad: POB 35104, Prince Shaker Ben Zeid St, Shmeisani, Amman 11180; tel. (6) 5607011; fax (6) 5666149; e-mail info@bankaletihad.com; internet www.bankaletihad.com; f. 1978 as Arab Finance Corpn; name changed to Union Bank for Savings and Investment 1991; name changed as above 2011; Chair. ISAM SALFITI; Gen. Man. NADIA AL-SAEED.

Cities and Villages Development Bank (CVDB): POB 1572, Amman 11118; tel. (6) 5682690; fax (6) 5668153; e-mail cvdb100@hotmail.com; internet www.cvdb.gov.jo; f. 1979; 68% state-owned; Gen. Man. OSAMA AL-AZZAM.

Housing Bank for Trade and Finance (HBTF): POB 7693, Parliament St, Amman 11118; tel. (6) 5005555; fax (6) 5691675; e-mail info@hbtf.com.jo; internet www.hbtf.com; f. 1973; Chair. Dr ABDEL ELAH AL-KHATIB; CEO AMMAR AL-SAFADI.

INVESTBANK: POB 950601, Bldg 43, Abd al-Hamid Sharaf St, Shmeisani, Amman 11195; tel. (6) 5001500; fax (6) 5681410; e-mail info@investbank.jo; internet www.investbank.jo; f. 1982 as Jordan Investment and Finance Corpn; name changed 2009; Chair. FAHMI F. ABU KHADRA; CEO MUNTASER DAWWAS.

Safwa Islamic Bank: POB 1982, Sulaiman al-Nabulsi St, Abdali, Amman 11118; tel. (6) 4602100; fax (6) 4647821; e-mail info@safwabank.com; internet www.safwabank.com; f. 1965 as Industrial Devt Bank; renamed Jordan Dubai Islamic Bank in 2010; present name adopted in 2017; Chair. MOHAMMED NASSER ABU HAMMOUR; CEO SAMER AL-TAMIMI.

STOCK EXCHANGE

The Amman Stock Exchange Co (ASE Co): POB 212466, Amman 11121; tel. (6) 5664109; fax (6) 5664071; e-mail info@ase.com.jo; internet www.ase.com.jo; f. 1978 as Amman Financial Market; name changed as above 1999; 172 listed cos (2021); Chair. Prof. KAMAL AHMED AL-QUDAH; CEO MAZEN WATHAIFI.

INSURANCE

Jordan Insurance Co Ltd (JIC): POB 279, 3rd Circle, Jabal Amman, Amman 11118; tel. (6) 4634161; fax (6) 4637905; e-mail allinsure@jicjo.com; internet www.jicjo.com; f. 1951; Chair. OTHMAN BDEIR; Man. Dir JAWAD JANEB.

Middle East Insurance Co Ltd (MEICO): POB 1802, 3rd Circle, Jabal Amman, Amman 11118; tel. (6) 5004100; fax (6) 5004101; e-mail info@meico.com.jo; internet www.meico.com.jo; f. 1962; Chair. ZAID KAWAR; CEO Dr RAJAI SWEIS.

National Insurance Co (Watania): POB 6156, Bldg no. 29, Sayed Qotub St, Shmeisani, Amman 11118; tel. (6) 5681979; fax (6) 5684900; e-mail info@natinsurance.jo; internet natinsurance.jo; f. 1965 as present name; name changed to National Ahlia Insurance Co in 1986, following merger with Ahlia Insurance Co (f. 1975); reverted to original name 2007; Chair. MUNJED MUNIR SUKHTIAN; Gen. Man. MANAL JARRAR.

Social Security Corpn: POB 926031, Amman 11110; tel. (6) 5501880; fax (6) 5501888; e-mail webmaster@ssc.gov.jo; internet www.ssc.gov.jo; f. 1978; regulates and implements a social security system, incl. the provision of health insurance, life insurance and unemployment benefit, funded by both voluntary and employer contributions; Dir-Gen. Dr MUHAMMAD SALEH AL-TARAWNEH.

United Insurance Co Ltd: POB 7521, Bldg 188, Zahran St, Amman 11118; tel. (6) 2003333; fax (6) 2003334; e-mail uic@unitedjo.com; internet unitedjo.com; f. 1972; all types of insurance; Chair. ZIAD ABU JABER; Gen. Man. IMAD AL-HAJI.

Insurance Federation

Jordan Insurance Federation (JOIF): POB 1990, Amman 11118; tel. (6) 5689266; fax (6) 5689510; e-mail info@jif.jo; internet www.joif.org; f. 1956 as the Jordan Asscn for Insurance Cos; present name adopted in 1989; regulatory and management authority; Chair. Eng. MAJED SMAIRAT; Dir Dr MUAYYAD M. KLOOB.

Trade and Industry

GOVERNMENT AGENCIES

Energy and Minerals Regulatory Commission (EMRC): POB 1865, Amman 11821; tel. (6) 5805000; fax (6) 5805003; e-mail abedalraheem.akayle@emrc.gov.jo; internet www.emrc.gov.jo; f. 2014 by merger of Jordan Nuclear Regulatory Commission, Natural Resources Authority and Electricity Regulatory Commission; supervision and devt of minerals and nuclear and non-nuclear energy resources; Chair. and CEO Dr HUSSEIN AL-LABOON.

Jordan Atomic Energy Commission: Shafa Badran, Amman; tel. (6) 5200460; fax (6) 5200471; e-mail contact@jaec.gov.jo; internet www.jaec.gov.jo; f. 2007; devt of civil nuclear energy programme; Chair. Dr KHALED TOUKAN.

DEVELOPMENT ORGANIZATIONS

Aqaba Development Corpn (ADC): POB 2680, Chamber of Commerce Bldg, Aqaba 77110; tel. (3) 2039100; fax (3) 2039110; e-mail info@adc.jo; internet www.adc.jo; f. 2004 by Aqaba Special Economic Zone Authority and Govt of Jordan; devt and strategic management of infrastructure, industry, trade, transport, real estate, tourism and education within Aqaba Special Economic Zone; Chair. Eng. NAYEF AHMAD BAKHEET; CEO HUSSEIN AL-SAFADI.

Jordan Enterprise Development Corporation (JEDCO): POB 7704, Amman 11118; tel. (6) 5603507; fax (6) 5684568; e-mail jedco@jedco.gov.jo; internet www.jedco.gov.jo; f. 2003 to replace Jordan Export Devt and Commercial Centres Corpn; devt and promotion of industry, trade and exports; Chair. YOUSEF SHAMALI (Minister of Industry, Trade and Supply); CEO Dr BASHAR AL-ZOUBI.

Jordan Investment Council (JIC): POB 893, Amman 11821; tel. (6) 5608400; fax (6) 5608416; e-mail info@moin.gov.jo; internet www.moin.gov.jo/en/investment-council; f. 2014; Chair. Dr BISHER AL-KHASAWNEH (Prime Minister).

Jordan Valley Authority (JVA): POB 2769, Amman 11183; tel. (6) 5689400; fax (6) 5689916; e-mail jvainfo@mwi.gov.jo; internet www.jva.gov.jo; f. 1973 as Jordan Valley Comm.; renamed as above 1977; govt org. responsible for the integrated social and economic devt of the Jordan Valley, with particular emphasis on the utilization and management of water resources; responsible for construction of several major irrigation, hydroelectric and municipal water projects; other projects include housing, schools and rural roads, and the devt of tourism infrastructure; Sec.-Gen. Eng. MANAR MAHASNEH.

CHAMBERS OF COMMERCE AND INDUSTRY

Amman Chamber of Commerce: POB 287, Amman 11118; tel. (6) 5666151; fax (6) 5666155; e-mail info@ammanchamber.org.jo; internet www.ammanchamber.org.jo; f. 1923; c. 50,000 regd mems (2022); Chair. KHALIL EL-HAJ TAWFIQ; Dir-Gen. HISHAM DWEIK.

Amman Chamber of Industry: POB 1800, Zahran St, Jabal, Amman 11118; tel. (6) 4643001; fax (6) 4647852; e-mail aci@aci.org.jo; internet www.aci.org.jo; f. 1962; Chair. Eng. FATHI AL-JAGHBIR.

Aqaba Chamber of Commerce: POB 12, Aqaba 77110; tel. (3) 2012229; fax (3) 2013070; e-mail info@aqabacc.com; internet www.aqabacc.com; f. 1965; Chair. NAEL AL-KABARITI; Dir-Gen. AMER IBRAHIM AL-MASRY.

Jordan Chamber of Commerce: POB 7029, Amman 11118; tel. (6) 5902040; fax (6) 5902051; e-mail info@jocc.org.jo; internet www.jocc.org.jo; f. 1955 as Fed. of the Jordanian Chambers of Commerce; renamed as above in 2003; intended to promote co-operation between the various chambers of commerce in Jordan, and to consolidate and co-ordinate the capabilities of each; Chair. NAEL AL-KABARITI.

Jordan Chamber of Industry: POB 811986, Amman 11181; tel. (6) 4642649; fax (6) 4643719; e-mail jci@jci.org.jo; internet www.jci.org.jo; promotes competitiveness in the industrial sector and co-operation between the various chambers of industry in Jordan; Chair. Eng. FATHI JAGHBIR; Dir-Gen. MAHER AL-MAHROUQ.

Professional Associations Council (PAC): Professional Associations Complex, Amman; Pres. ABDUL HADI FALAHAT.

PETROLEUM AND GAS

Jordan Oil Shale Co: POB 140502, Siwar bin Amara St, Bayadir Industrial Area, Amman 11814; tel. (6) 5806333; fax (6) 5806444; internet www.josco.jo; f. 2009; wholly owned subsidiary of Royal Dutch Shell PLC (Netherlands/UK); exploration and exploitation of oil shale deposits.

National Petroleum Co PLC: POB 3503, Amman 11821; tel. (6) 5548888; fax (6) 5536912; e-mail management@npc.com.jo; internet www.npc.com.jo; f. 1995; petroleum and natural gas exploration and production; signed partnership agreement with BP (UK) for devt of Risha gasfield 2009; Chair. LAITH AL-QASSEM; Gen. Man. Eng. MOHAMMAD OQLAH ISMAIL.

UTILITIES

Electricity

Central Electricity Generating Co (CEGCO): POB 2564, Amman 11953; tel. (6) 5340008; fax (6) 5340800; e-mail cegco@cegco.com.jo; internet www.cegco.com.jo; part-privatized in Sept. 2007; 51% owned by ENARA Energy Arabia, 40% by Govt and 9% by Social Security Corpn; electricity generation; Chair. Dr MOAYAD SAMMAN.

Electricity Distribution Co (EDCO): Bldg No. 1 and 3, Wasfi al-Tal St Extension, al-Khalideen, Khalda Amman, Amman; tel. (6) 5331330; fax (6) 5341213; e-mail info@edco.com.jo; internet www.edco.jo; f. 1999; privatized 2007; wholly owned by Kingdom Electricity, a jt venture between Jordan, Kuwait and the UAE; electricity distribution for southern, eastern and Jordan Valley regions; Chair. SAMIR MURAD; Dir-Gen. REEM HAMDAN.

Irbid District Electricity Co (IDECO): POB 46, Irbid; tel. (2) 7201500; fax (2) 7245495; e-mail ideco@ideco.com.jo; internet www.ideco.com.jo; f. 1957; 55.4% stake acquired by Kingdom Electricity (see EDCO) in 2007; electricity generation, transmission and distribution for northern regions; Chair. AHMED MAHER HAMDI TAWFIQ ABU AL-SAMEN; Gen. Man. Eng. BASHAR AL-TAMIMI.

Jordanian Electric Power Co (JEPCO): POB 618, Amman 11118; tel. (6) 5503600; fax (6) 5503619; e-mail complaints@jepco.com.jo; internet www.jepco.com.jo; f. 1938; privately owned; electricity distribution for Amman, al-Salt, al-Zarqa and Madaba; Chair. OTHMAN MOHAMMED ALI BDEIR; Gen. Man. MARWAN BUSHNAQ.

National Electric Power Company (NEPCO): POB 2310, Amman 11118; tel. (6) 5858615; fax (6) 5818336; e-mail info@nepco.com.jo; internet www.nepco.com.jo; f. 1996; fmrly Jordan Electricity Authority; electricity transmission; govt-owned; Chair. Eng. OMAR ASHRAF AL-KURDI; Dir-Gen. Eng. AMJAD AL-RAWASHDEH.

Samra Electric Power Co (SEPCO): POB 1885, Um Al-Sumaq, Mecca St, Amman 11821; tel. (6) 5506510; fax (6) 5506520; e-mail samra@sepco.com.jo; internet www.sepco.com.jo; f. 2004; electricity generation, gas turbines supply and installation and plant construction; Chair. Dr MAHIR AL-MADADHAH; Dir-Gen. Dr SUFYAN AL-BATAYNEH.

Water

Aqaba Water: POB 252, Aqaba 77110; tel. (3) 2014390; fax (3) 2015982; e-mail info@aw.com.jo; internet aw.jo; f. 2004; successor to the Water Authority in Aqaba; water supply and wastewater services; Chair. MAHMOUD JARAD GHANEM AL-NUAIMAT; CEO KHALED AL-OBEIDIN.

Jordan Water Co (Miyahuna): POB 922918, Amman 11192; tel. (6) 5666111; fax (6) 5682642; e-mail info@miyahuna.com.jo; internet www.miyahuna.com.jo; f. 2007; owned by Water Authority of Jordan; operates as an independent commercial entity; management of water and sewage services in Amman; Chair. KHALDON KHASHMAN; CEO Eng. GHAZI KHALIL.

Water Authority of Jordan (WAJ): POB 2412, Amman 11183; tel. (6) 5680100; fax (6) 5679143; e-mail wajinfo@mwi.gov.jo; internet waj.gov.jo/sites/en-us/default.aspx; f. 1984; govt-owned; scheduled for privatization; Sec.-Gen. Eng. BASHAR BATAINEH.

MAJOR COMPANIES

Agricultural Marketing and Processing Co of Jordan (AMPCO): POB 7314, Bldg 22, Abd Al-Rahim Wakid St, Amman 11118; tel. (6) 5691961; fax (6) 5687155; e-mail info@ampcojordan.com; internet www.ampcojordan.com; f. 1984; govt-owned; Chair. Dr ABD AL-HADI ALAWEEN; Dir-Gen. ABD AL-HAMID AL-KAYED.

Arab Centre for Pharmaceuticals and Chemicals (ACPC): POB 22, King Abdullah II Industrial City, Sahab 11512; tel. (6) 4022470; fax (6) 4022473; e-mail info@acpc.com.jo; internet www.acpc.com.jo; f. 1984; mfrs of pharmaceuticals and chemicals; Chair. MAZEN SENESH.

Arab Investment and International Trade Co Ltd: POB 94, Sahab Old Rd, al-Raqim, Amman 11591; tel. (6) 4161191; fax (6) 4161504; e-mail aiit@go.com.jo; f. 1978; mfrs of toiletries; Chair. ABD AL-MALIK SAID; Gen. Man. Eng. MUHAMMAD S. ABU SALAH.

Arab Pharmaceutical Manufacturing Co Ltd (APM): POB 42, Amman 19110; tel. (5) 3491200; fax (5) 3491203; internet www.apm.com.jo; f. 1964; mfrs of pharmaceuticals; owned by Hikma; Chair. MAZEN SAMIH TALEB DARWAZEH; Man. Dir SALAH AL-SALAH AL-MAWAJDEH.

Arab Potash Co Ltd (APC): POB 1470, Amman 11118; tel. (6) 5200520; fax (6) 5200080; e-mail info@arabpotash.com; internet www.arabpotash.com; f. 1956; production of potash, with a by-product of salt; production 2.6m. tons, sales 2.6m. tons (2021); 28% owned by Man Jia Industrial Development Ltd (China), 26% owned by Government Investment Management Co (Jordan), 20% owned by Arab Mining Co (Jordan), 10% owned by the Social Security Corpn, 16% owned by various other investors; Chair. Eng. SHEHADAH ABU HDAIB; Pres. and CEO Dr MAEN F. NSOUR.

Elba House Co WLL: POB 3449, King Abdullah II St, Amman 11181; tel. (6) 5300600; fax (6) 5300624; e-mail elba@elbahouse.com; internet www.elbahouse.com; f. 1976; mfrs of prefabricated buildings, caravans, steel structures, vehicle bodies and construction plants.

Hikma Pharmaceuticals Ltd: al-Bayader, King Abdullah II St, Amman; tel. (6) 5802900; internet www.hikma.com; f. 1978; mfrs of over 360 pharmaceutical products; Chair. and CEO SAID DARWAZAH.

Industrial, Commercial and Agricultural Co Ltd (ICA): POB 6066, Amman 11118; tel. (6) 5533201; fax (6) 5548389; e-mail icacontactus@ica-jo.com; internet www.ica-jo.com; f. 1961; industrial, commercial and agricultural investment; operates factories producing (under licence) soap, detergents, toiletries, paints, biscuits, ice-cream and containers.

Jordan Cement Factories Co Ltd: POB 930019, Amman 11193; tel. (6) 5600600; fax (6) 5600610; e-mail jo-c-concrete-info@lafargeholcim.com; internet www.lafarge.com.jo; f. 1951; merged with South Cement Co 1985; 50.2% owned by Lafarge SA, France; CEO SAMAAN SAMAAN.

Jordan Petroleum Refinery Co (JPRC): POB 1097, Amman 11118; tel. (6) 4630151; fax (6) 4657939; e-mail addewan@jopetrol.com.jo; internet www.jopetrol.com.jo; f. 1956; petroleum refining and distribution of refined petroleum products (lube oil blending and canning; mfr of LPG cylinders); privatized in 2004; Chair. ALAA AREF BATAYNEH; CEO Eng. ABDUL KARIM ALAWIN.

Jordan Pharmaceutical Manufacturing Co (JPM): POB 94, Naour 11710; tel. (6) 5727207; fax (6) 5727641; e-mail jpm@go.com.jo; internet www.jpm.com.jo; f. 1978; mfrs of generic pharmaceutical products, natural medicines and diagnostic products; CEO Dr MAHMOUD JARWAN.

Jordan Phosphate Mines Co Ltd (JPMC): POB 30, 7 al-Shareef al-Radi St, Alluibdeh, al-Abdali, Amman 11118; tel. (6) 5607141; fax (6) 5661754; e-mail info@jpmc.com.jo; internet www.jpmc.com.jo; f. 1930; production and export of rock phosphate; absorbed Jordan Fertilizer Industries Co; 25.6% state-owned; production 11m. metric tons (2022); exported approx. 6.6m. tons in 2022 worldwide; Chair. MOHAMMAD THNEIBAT; CEO Eng. ABDEL WAHAB AL-ROWAD.

Jordan Steel Group: POB 35165, Amman 11180; tel. (6) 4619380; fax (6) 4619384; e-mail info@jordansteelplc.com; internet www.jordansteelplc.com; f. 1993; mfrs of steel bars, steel billets and wire mesh; Chair. Dr MUSTAFA YAGHI.

Kawar Group: POB 222, Kawar Keystone Bldg, al-Abdali Blvd, 14 Rafiq Baha'a al-Din Hariri Ave, Amman 11118; tel. (6) 5609500; internet www.kawar.com; f. 1926; Pres. KARIM KAWAR; CEO RUDAIN KAWAR.

Metal Industries Co Ltd (Metalco): POB 143109, Amman 11814; tel. (6) 4023015; fax (6) 4023621; e-mail export@metalco.com; internet www.metalco.com; f. 1965; mfrs of steel panel radiators and boilers.

TRADE UNIONS

General Federation of Jordanian Trade Unions: Amman; tel. (6) 5675533; e-mail gfjtu@go.com.jo; internet fb.com/gfjtujo; f. 1954; mem. of Arab Trade Unions Confed; Pres. MAZEN MA'AYTEH.

Jordan Engineers' Association (JEA): POB 940188, Professional Associations Center, Shmeisani, Amman 11118; tel. (6) 5000900; fax (6) 5676933; e-mail info@jea.org.jo; internet www.jea.org.jo; f. 1958 as Jordan Engineers' Society; present name adopted 1972; 142,000 mems (2017); Pres. Eng. AHMAD SAMARA ZU'BI.

Transport

RAILWAYS

Although the historic Hedjaz Railway that linked the Syrian capital, Damascus, with Medina in Saudi Arabia was effectively abandoned in 1920, a former section of the line, the Jordan Hedjaz Railway (JHR), remains in operation, crossing the Syrian border and entering Jordanian territory south of Dar'a. It runs for approximately 366 km to Naqb Ishtar in Ma'an, passing through Zarqa, Amman and Qatrana. An express rail link between Amman and Damascus was inaugurated in 1999. Meanwhile, in 1975 the JHR constructed a branch line from Ma'an to the Red Sea port of Aqaba. In 1979 the Aqaba Railway Corporation was incorporated and took over the section of the JHR connecting Al-Abyad (to the north of Ma'an) and Aqaba. Although the Aqaba Railway retains close links with the JHR, there is no regular through traffic between Aqaba and Amman. The line comprises 242 km of 1,050-mm gauge track and is used solely for the transportation of minerals from three phosphate mines in Ma'an governorate to Aqaba port.

In 2012 the Ministry of Transport announced ambitious plans to construct a new national railway network. Upon completion, a north–south line of 509 km would link the southern port city of Aqaba with Amman, Zarqa and Irbid in the north, while two smaller branches would extend from Zarqa to the borders with Iraq and Saudi Arabia, eventually linking with rail networks being developed in those countries. As part of the first phase of the proposed new network, in 2019 Aqaba Special Economic Zone Authority signed a memorandum of understanding with the Saudi Jordanian Investment Fund to build a railway link between Aqaba and a proposed dry port in Ma'an governorate. In late 2020 updated plans for the project sited the proposed dry port in Madouneh in Amman governorate, rather than in Ma'an.

Aqaba Railway Corpn (ARC): POB 50, Ma'an 7111; tel. (3) 2132114; fax (3) 2131861; e-mail arc@orange.jo; internet arc.gov.jo; f. 1975; privately owned; Chair. WALEED MOHIUDDIN AL-MASRI.

Jordan Hedjaz Railway (JHR): POB 4448, Amman 11118; tel. (6) 4895414; fax (6) 7411489; e-mail info@jhr.gov.jo; internet www.jhr.gov.jo; f. 1952 as Hedjaz Jordan Railway; administered by the Ministry of Transport; Chair. AHMAD MAHER ABUL SAMEN (Minister of Transport); Gen. Man. ZAHI KHALIL.

ROADS

Amman is linked by road with all parts of the kingdom and with neighbouring countries. All cities and most towns are connected by a two-lane, paved road system. In addition, several thousand kilometres of tracks make all villages accessible to motor transport.

Jordanian-Syrian Land Transport Co: POB 20686, Amman 11118; tel. (6) 4711545; fax (6) 4711517; f. 1975; jt venture between Govts of Jordan and Syrian Arab Repub; transports goods between ports in Jordan and Syria; operates 210 heavy-duty trailers; underwent restructuring in 2010; Dir-Gen. JAMIL ALI MUJAHID.

SHIPPING

The port of Aqaba, Jordan's only outlet to the sea, consists of a main port, container port (1 km in length) and industrial port. There is a ferry link between Aqaba and the Egyptian port of Nuweibeh. In 2008 the Government initiated a tendering process for a US $700m. project to relocate Aqaba's main port to the southern industrial zone. The new development, supervised by the Aqaba Development

Corporation, was significantly to increase overall capacity and was to comprise a general cargo terminal with roll-on roll-off (ro-ro) facilities, a dedicated grain terminal and a new ferry terminal. Once vacated, the existing port site was to be redeveloped as a major new commercial, residential and tourism centre. The new, expanded cargo terminal—with a total capacity of 1.3m. 20-ft equivalent units (TEUs) per year—opened in 2013, while a dedicated terminal for liquefied natural gas imports opened in 2015. A new phosphates terminal was completed in 2018. In January 2023 a cruise ship terminal was inaugurated at Marsa Zayed in Aqaba.

Port Authorities

Aqaba Container Terminal (ACT): POB 1944, King Hussein bin Talal St, Aqaba 77110; tel. (3) 2091111; e-mail customerservice@act.com.jo; internet www.act.com.jo; Chair. NAYIEF AL-BAKHEET; CEO SOREN KOFOED JENSEN.

Aqaba Ports Corpn: POB 115, Aqaba 77110; tel. (3) 2014031; fax (6) 2043962; e-mail info@aqabaports.gov.jo; internet www.aqabaports.com.jo; f. 1952 as Aqaba Port Authority; name changed as above 1978; Dir-Gen. MUHAMMAD AL-MUBAIDEN.

Principal Shipping Companies

Amman Shipping & Trading Co Ltd (ASTCO): POB 213083, 5th Floor, Blk A, Aqqad Bldg, Gardens St, Amman 11121; tel. (6) 5514620; fax (6) 5532324; e-mail sts@albitar.com; internet www.1stjordan.net/astco/index.html; f. 1990.

Arab Bridge Maritime Co: POB 989, Aqaba; tel. (3) 2092000; fax (3) 2092001; e-mail info@abmaritime.com.jo; internet www.abmaritime.com.jo; f. 1985; jt venture between Egypt, Iraq and Jordan; commercial shipping of passengers, vehicles and cargo between Aqaba and the Egyptian port of Nuweibeh; Chair. SALMAN SADDAM JASEM; Man. Dir ADNAN AL-ABADLEH.

T. Gargour & Fils (TGF): POB 419, 1st Floor, Bldg No. 233, Arar St, Wadi Saqra, Amman 11118; tel. (6) 4626611; fax (6) 4622425; e-mail info@tgf.com.jo; internet tgf.com.jo; f. 1928; shipping agents and owners; CEO Dr DUREID MAHASNEH.

Jordan National Shipping Lines Co Ltd (JNSL): POB 5406, Bldg No. 51, Wadi Saqra St, Amman 11183; POB 557, Aqaba; tel. (6) 5511500; fax (6) 5511501; e-mail contactus@jnslgroup.com; internet www.jnslgroup.com; f. 1976; 75% govt-owned; service from Antwerp (Belgium), Bremen (Germany) and Tilbury (United Kingdom) to Aqaba; daily passenger ferry service to Egypt; land transportation to various regional destinations; Chair. AHMAD ARMOUSH.

Amin Kawar & Sons Co WLL: 14 Rafiq Al Hariri Ave, Abdali Blvd, Amman; tel. (6) 5609500; e-mail kawar@kawar.com.jo; internet www.kawarshipping.com; chartering, forwarding and shipping line agents; Chair. TAWFIQ KAWAR; CEO RUDAIN T. KAWAR; Pres. KARIM KAWAR.

Naouri Group: Um Uthaina, Saad Bin Abi Waqqas St, Bldg No. 30, Amman 11118; tel. (6) 5004000; e-mail info@naouri.com; internet naouri.com; f. 1994; operates several cos in shipping sector incl. Ammon Shipping and Transport, Salam Shipping and Forwarding, Kareem Logistics; Chair. IBRAHIM NAOURI.

Orient Shipping Co Ltd: Jordan Insurance Bldg, Bldg (A), 3rd Floor, POB 207, Amman 11118; tel. (6) 4641695; fax (6) 4651567; e-mail marketing@orientshipping.jo; internet www.orientshipping.jo; f. 1965; shipping agency.

Petra Navigation and International Trading Co Ltd: POB 942501, Amman 11194; tel. (6) 5607021; fax (6) 5601362; e-mail info@petra.jo; internet www.petra.jo; f. 1977; general cargo, ro-ro and passenger ferries; Chair. MOHANNAD ARMOUSH; Man. Dir ANWAR SBEIH.

Red Sea Shipping Agency Co: POB 1248, 24 Sharif Abd al-Hamid Sharaf St, Shmeisani, Amman 11118; tel. (6) 5609501; fax (6) 5688241; internet www.redseashipping.com.jo; f. 1955.

Salam International Transport and Trading Co: POB 212955, Salam Trading Center, 240 Arar St, Wadi Saqra, Amman 11121; tel. (6) 5654510; fax (6) 5697014; e-mail sittco@aagroup.jo; internet www.sittcogroup.com; f. 1996; publicly listed; diversified shipping, logistics, and oil and gas group; Chair. MOHAMMAD ABU HAMMOUR.

PIPELINES

Two oil pipelines cross Jordan. The former Iraq Petroleum Co pipeline, carrying petroleum from the oilfields in Iraq to Israel's Mediterranean port of Haifa, has not operated since 1967. The 1,717 km (1,067 mile) Trans-Arabian Pipeline (Tapline), which traverses Jordan for a distance of 177 km (110 miles), was built in the 1940s to carry petroleum from the oilfields of Dhahran in Saudi Arabia to Sidon on the Mediterranean seaboard in Lebanon. The section of the pipeline between Jordan and Israel ceased operating in 1976. The remainder of the Tapline, between Jordan and Saudi Arabia continued to transport modest amounts of petroleum until 1990, after which Saudi Arabia took it out of service in response to Jordan's support for Israel in the Gulf War. Confronted with the challenge of meeting rising oil demands, the Jordanian Government has been considering plans to rehabilitate sections of the Tapline since 2005. In 2013 the Governments of Jordan and Iraq signed an agreement to construct a 1,600–km double pipeline to transport oil and natural gas from Basra province in Iraq to Aqaba. However, the project was subsequently shelved amid conflict and insecurity in Iraq and financing difficulties. In 2021 Jordan and Iraq revived talks on the proposed project, the projected cost of which was US $9,000m.

CIVIL AVIATION

There are three international airports, two serving Amman and one in Aqaba (King Hussein International Airport). A 25-year concession to expand and operate Queen Alia International Airport at Zizya, 40 km south of Amman, including the construction of a new terminal building, was awarded to an international consortium, Airport International Group, in 2007. The new terminal was officially opened in 2013. The second phase of the expansion project was inaugurated in 2016.

Jordan Civil Aviation Regulatory Commission (CARC): POB 7547, Amman 11110; tel. (6) 4892282; fax (6) 4891653; e-mail info@carc.gov.jo; internet www.carc.jo; f. 2007, to replace Civil Aviation Authority (f. 1950); Chief Commr and CEO Capt. HATHAM MISTO.

Aqaba Airports Co (AAC): POB 2662, King Hussein International Airport, Special Economic Zone, Aqaba 77110; tel. (3) 2034010; fax (3) 2034011; e-mail info@aac.jo; internet khiaops.com/aac; f. 2007; Dir NASSER MAJALI.

Jordan Aviation (JATE): King Faisal bin Abdulaziz St, Um Uthaina, Amman; tel. (6) 5501760; fax (6) 5538746; e-mail info@jordanaviation.jo; internet www.jordanaviation.jo; f. 2000; first privately owned airline in Jordan; operates regional and international charter and scheduled flights; Chair. and CEO Capt. MUHAMMAD AL-KHASHMAN.

Royal Jordanian Airlines: Bldg 37, Mohammad Ali Janah St, Abdoun, Amman; tel. (6) 5202000; fax (6) 5672527; e-mail ccsupport@rj.com; internet www.rj.com; f. 1963; privatized in 2007; regional and international scheduled and charter services; Chair. SAID SAMIH DARWAZAH; CEO SAMER MAJALI.

Tourism

Ministry of Tourism and Antiquities: see Ministries; Sec.-Gen. FAROUK AL-HADIDI.

Jordan Tourism Board (JTB): POB 830688, Amman 11183; tel. (6) 5678444; fax (6) 5678295; e-mail info@visitjordan.com; internet www.visitjordan.com; f. 1997; Man. Dir Dr ABED AL-RAZZAQ ISSAM ARABIYAT.

Defence

As assessed at November 2022, the Jordan Armed Forces totalled 100,500 active personnel: army 86,000; navy 500; air force 14,000. There were also 65,000 reserves (army 60,000, joint services 5,000), while paramilitary forces were estimated at 15,000.

Defence Budget: JD 1,370m. in 2022.

Supreme Commander of the Armed Forces: King ABDULLAH BIN AL-HUSSEIN.

Chairman of the Joint Chiefs of Staff: Maj.-Gen. YOUSEF HUNEITI.

Commander of the Royal Jordanian Navy: Col HISHAM KHALEEL AL-JARRAH.

Commander of the Royal Jordanian Air Force: Brig.-Gen. MOHAMMAD FATHI HIYASAT.

Education

Primary education, beginning at six years of age, is free and compulsory. This 10-year preparatory cycle is followed by a two-year non-compulsory secondary cycle. The UN Relief and Works Agency (UNRWA) provides educational facilities and services for Palestinian refugees. According to UNESCO estimates, the enrolment ratio at pre-primary level in 2020/21 was equivalent to 26.6% of children (boys 26.4%; girls 26.8%) in the relevant age-group, while primary enrolment included 79.5% of children (boys 80.0%; girls 79.1%) in the relevant age-group. In 2020/21 enrolment at lower secondary schools included 75.9% of children (boys 75.9%; girls 75.8%) in the relevant age-group, while enrolment at upper secondary schools included 62.7% of children (boys 60.8%; girls 64.7%) in the relevant age-group. According to UNESCO, budgetary expenditure on education by the Government in 2021 was equivalent to 9.7% of total government spending.

Bibliography

Abdullah I, King of Jordan. *Memoirs* (trans. G. Khuri, ed. P. Graves). London and New York, Jonathan Cape, 1950.

Abdullah II, King of Jordan. *Our Last Best Chance: The Pursuit of Peace in a Time of Peril*. London, Penguin, 2012.

Abidi, A. H. H. *Jordan, a Political Study 1948–1957*. Delhi, Asia Publishing House, 1966.

Abu Jaber, Kamel, Buhbe, Matthes, and Smadi, Mohammad (Eds). *Income Distribution in Jordan*. Abingdon, Routledge, 2019.

Abu Nowar, Maan. *The Struggle for Independence 1939–1947. A History of the Hashemite Kingdom of Jordan*. Reading, Ithaca Press, 1999.

—*The Jordanian–Israeli War, 1948–51: A History of the Hashemite Kingdom of Jordan*. Reading, Ithaca Press, 2002.

—*The Development of Trans-Jordan 1929–1939: A History of the Hashemite Kingdom of Jordan*. Reading, Ithaca Press, 2005.

Abu-Odeh, Adnan. *Jordanians, Palestinians and the Hashemite Kingdom*. Washington, DC, United States Institute of Peace Press, 1999.

Allinson, Jamie. *The Struggle for the State in Jordan: the Social Origins of Alliances in the Middle East*. London, I. B. Tauris, 2016.

Alon, Yoav. *The Making of Jordan: Tribes, Colonialism and the Modern State*. London, I. B. Tauris, 2009.

—*The Shaykh of Shaykhs: Mithqal al-Fayiz and Tribal Leadership in Modern Jordan*. Stanford, CA, Stanford University Press, 2016.

Anderson, Betty S. *Nationalist Voices in Jordan: The Street and the State*. Austin, TX, University of Texas Press, 2005.

El-Anis, Imad. *Jordan and the United States: The Political Economy of Trade and Economic Reform in the Middle East*. London, I. B. Tauris, 2010.

Ashton, Nigel. *King Hussein of Jordan: A Political Life*. New Haven, CT, Yale University Press, 2008.

Atzori, Daniel. *Islamism and Globalisation in Jordan: The Muslim Brotherhood's Quest for Hegemony*. Abingdon, Routledge, 2015.

Barakat, Sultan, and Leber, Andrew. 'Fortress Jordan: Putting the Money to Work', *Brookings Doha Center Policy Briefing*, February 2015. www.brookings.edu/wp-content/uploads/2016/06/Fortress-Jordan-English.pdf.

Baylouny, Anne Marie. *When Blame Backfires: Syrian Refugees and Citizen Grievances in Jordan and Lebanon*. Ithaca, Cornell University Press, 2020.

Blackwell, Stephen. *British Military Intervention and the Struggle for Jordan: King Hussein, Nasser and the Middle East Crisis, 1955–1958*. Abingdon, Routledge, 2009.

Boulby, Marion. *The Muslim Brotherhood and the Kings of Jordan 1945–1993*. Atlanta, GA, Scholars Press, 1999.

Brand, Laurie A. *Jordan's Inter-Arab Relations: The Political Economy of Alliance Making*. New York, Columbia University Press, 1995.

Buck, Keven, and McPherson, Tad J. (Eds). *Bahrain and Jordan: Unrest and Foreign Relations*. New York, Nova Science Publishers, 2012.

Dearden, Ann. *Jordan*. London, Hale, 1958.

Engelcke, Dörthe. *Reforming Family Law: Social and Political Change in Jordan and Morocco*. Cambridge, Cambridge University Press, 2019.

Glubb, John B. *Britain and the Arabs: A Study of Fifty Years 1908–1958*. London, Hodder and Stoughton, 1959.

—*Syria, Lebanon, Jordan*. London, Thames and Hudson, 1967.

Habib, Randa. *Hussein and Abdullah: Inside the Jordanian Royal Family*. London, Saqi Books, 2010.

Hamid, Shadi, and Freer, Courtney. 'How Stable is Jordan?: King Abdullah's Half-Hearted Reforms and the Challenge of the Arab Spring'. *Brookings Doha Center Policy Briefing*, November 2011. www.brookings.edu/wp-content/uploads/2016/06/10_jordan_hamid_freer.pdf.

Hawwari, Adli. *Democracy and Islam/ism*. London, Ud al-Nad, 2016.

Hupp, Clea Lutz. *The United States and Jordan: Middle East Diplomacy during the Cold War*. London, I.B. Tauris, 2014.

Hussein, His Majesty King. *Uneasy Lies the Head*. New York, Random House, 1962.

—*Ma guerre avec Israël*. Paris, Albin Michel, 1968.

—*Mon métier de roi*. Paris, Laffont, 1975.

Jevon, Graham. *Glubb Pasha and the Arab Legion: Britain, Jordan and the End of Empire in the Middle East*. Cambridge, Cambridge University Press, 2017.

Joffé, George (Ed.) *Jordan in Transition 1990–2000*. London, C. Hurst & Co, 2001.

Johnston, Charles. *The Brink of Jordan*. London, Hamish Hamilton, 1972.

Jonasson, Ann-Kristin. *The EU's Democracy Promotion and the Mediterranean Neighbours: Orientation, Ownership and Dialogue in Jordan and Turkey*. Abingdon, Routledge, 2013.

Joyce, Miriam. *Anglo-American Support for Jordan: The Career of King Hussein*. New York, Palgrave Macmillan, 2008.

Kandeel, Amal A. *Jordan's Struggle for Survival: War in the Middle East and Arab Economies' Underdevelopment*. London, Pluto Press, 2008.

Khader, Bichara, and Badran, Adnan. *The Economic Development of Jordan*. Abingdon, Routledge, 2015.

Khorma, Tamer. 'The Myth of the Jordanian Monarchy's Resilience to the Arab Spring'. *SWP Comments*, Issue 33, July 2014. www.swp-berlin.org/fileadmin/contents/products/comments/2014C33_kor.pdf

Knowles, Warwick. *Jordan Since 1989: A Study in Political Economy*. London, I. B. Tauris, 2005.

Konikof, A. *Transjordan: An Economic Survey*. 2nd edn, Jerusalem, 1946.

Layne, Linda. *Home and Homeland: The Dialogues of Tribal and National Identities in Jordan*. Chichester, Princeton University Press, 1994.

Legrand, Vincent. *Prise de décision en politique étrangère et géopolitique: Le triangle «Jordanie-Palestine-Israël» et la décision jordanienne de désengagement de Cisjordanie (1988)*. Bern, Peter Lang Verlagsgruppe, 2009.

Lucas, Russell E. *Institutions and the Politics of Survival in Jordan: Domestic Responses to External Challenges, 1988–2001*. Albany, NY, State University of New York, 2005.

Luke, Sir Harry C., and Keith-Roach, E. *The Handbook of Palestine and Transjordan*. London, Macmillan, 1934.

Maggiolini, Paolo, and Ouahes, Idir (Eds). *Minorities and State-Building in the Middle East: The Case of Jordan*. Cham, Palgrave Macmillan, 2021.

Marashdeh, Omar. *The Jordanian Economy*. Amman, Al-Jawal Corpn, 1996.

Massad, Joseph A. *Colonial Effects: The Making of National Identity in Jordan*. New York, Columbia University Press, 2001.

MercyCorps. 'Tapped Out: Water Scarcity and Refugee Pressures in Jordan', March 2014. www.mercycorps.org/sites/default/files/MercyCorps_TappedOut_JordanWaterReport_March2014.pdf

Milton-Edwards, Beverley, and Hinchliffe, Peter. *Jordan: A Hashemite Legacy*. London, Routledge, 2001, 2nd edn, 2009.

Mishal, Shaul. *West Bank/East Bank: The Palestinians in Jordan 1949–67*. New Haven, CT, and London, Yale University Press, 1978.

Moaddel, Mansoor. *Jordanian Exceptionalism*. Basingstoke, Palgrave, 2001.

Morris, James. *The Hashemite Kings*. London, Faber, 1959.

Nevo, Joseph, and Pappé, Ilan (Eds). *Jordan in the Middle East: The Making of a Pivotal State 1948-1988*. London, Frank Cass, 1994.

Nimier, Michael. *Nation Building in Islamic Societies: King Abdullah the 1st and the Founding of Jordan*. Brighton, Pen Press, 2014.

Al-O'ran, Mutayyam. *Jordanian-Israeli Relations: The Peacebuilding Experience*. Abingdon, Routledge, 2009.

Patel, David Siddhartha. 'The More Things Change, the More They Stay the Same: Jordanian Islamist Responses in Spring and Fall', *Brookings Institution* Rethinking Political Islam Series, August 2015. www.brookings.edu/wp-content/uploads/2016/07/Jordan_Patel-FINALE.pdf.

Peake, F. G. *History of Jordan and Its Tribes*. Oxford, OH, University of Miami Press, 1958.

Piro, Timothy J. *The Political Economy of Market Reform in Jordan*. Lanham, MD, Rowan and Littlefield, 1998.

Robins, Philip. *A History of Jordan*. Cambridge, Cambridge University Press, 2004.

Robinson, Glenn E. 'Defensive Democratization in Jordan', *International Journal of Middle East Studies* (pp. 387–410). Vol. 30, No. 2, August 1998.

Rogan, Eugene L., and Tell, Tariq (Eds). *Village, Steppe and State: The Social Origins of Modern Jordan*. London, British Academic Press, 1994.

Ryan, Curtis R. *Inter-Arab Alliances: Regime Security and Jordanian Foreign Policy*. Gainesville, FL, University Press of Florida, 2008.

Jordan and the Arab Uprisings: Regime Survival and Politics Beyond the State. New York, NY, Columbia University Press, 2018.

Salibi, Kamal. *The Modern History of Jordan*. London, I. B. Tauris, 1999.

Schwedler, Jillian. 'The Political Geography of Protest in Neoliberal Jordan', *Middle East Critique* (pp. 259–270), Vol. 21, No. 3, September 2012.

Shlaim, Avi. *Lion of Jordan: The Life of King Hussein in War and Peace*. London, Allen Lane, 2007.

Sosland, Jeffrey K. *Cooperating Rivals: The Riparian Politics of the Jordan River Basin*. Albany, NY, State University of New York Press, 2008.

Sparrow, Gerald. *Modern Jordan*. Sydney, Allen & Unwin, 1961.

Tal, Lawrence. *Politics, the Military and National Security in Jordan, 1955-1967*. New York, Palgrave Macmillan, 2002.

Tal, Nachman. *Radical Islam in Egypt and Jordan*. Brighton, Sussex Academic, 2005.

Tell, Tariq. *The Social and Economic Origins of Monarchy in Jordan*. Basingstoke, Palgrave Macmillan, 2013.

Toukan, Baha Uddin. *A Short History of Transjordan*. London, Luzac & Co, 1945.

Vatikiotis, P. J. *Politics and the Military in Jordan 1921–57*. New York, Praeger, 1967.

Wagemakers, Joas. *Salafism in Jordan: Political Islam in a Quietist Community*. Cambridge, Cambridge University Press, 2016.

The Muslim Brotherhood in Jordan. Cambridge, Cambridge University Press, 2020.

Walker, Bethany J. *Jordan in the Late Middle Ages: Transformation of the Mamluk Frontier*. Chicago, IL, Middle East Documentation Center, 2011.

Wilson, Rodney (Ed.). *Politics and Economy in Jordan*. London, Routledge, 1991.

Yefet, Bosmat. *The Politics of Human Rights in Egypt and Jordan*. Boulder, CO, Lynne Rienner Publishers, 2015.

KUWAIT

Geography

Kuwait lies at the head of the Persian (Arabian) Gulf, bordering Iraq and Saudi Arabia. The area of the State of Kuwait is 17,818 sq km (6,880 sq miles), including the Kuwaiti share of the Neutral or Partitioned Zone (see below) but without taking into account the increase in territory resulting from the adjustment to the border with Iraq that came into effect in January 1993.

Immediately to the south of Kuwait, along the Gulf, is a Neutral/Partitioned Zone of 5,700 sq km, which is divided between Kuwait and Saudi Arabia. Each country administers its own half as an integral part of the state. However, the oil wealth of the whole Zone remains undivided, and production from the onshore concessions in the Neutral/Partitioned Zone is normally shared equally between the two states.

Although, for some time, the Gulf was thought to extend much further north, geological evidence suggests that the coastline has remained broadly at its present position, while the immense bodies of silt brought down by the Tigris and Euphrates cause irregular down-warping at the head of the Gulf. Local variation in the coastline is therefore likely, with possible changes since ancient times. The development of Kuwait owed much to its zone of slightly higher, firmer ground (giving access from the Gulf inland to Iraq) and to its reasonably good and sheltered harbour, away from nearby sandbanks and coral reefs.

The territory of Kuwait is mainly flat desert with a few oases. An annual rainfall of 1 cm–37 cm falls almost entirely between November and April, and there is a spring 'flush' of grass. Summer shade temperature may reach 49°C (120°F), although in January, the coldest month, temperatures range between −2.8°C and 28.3°C (27°F–85°F), with a rare frost. There is little inland drinking water, and supplies are largely distilled from sea water and brought by pipeline from the Shatt al-Arab waterway, which runs into the Gulf.

According to census results, the population of Kuwait increased from 206,473 in February 1957 to 1,697,301 by April 1985. From 1965 non-Kuwaiti residents formed a majority of the inhabitants. By the time of the census of April 1995 non-Kuwaiti residents constituted 58.5% of the population, which totalled 1,575,570. At the census of April 2011 foreign nationals accounted for 64.4% of the total population, which was recorded at 3,065,850, and at the census of January 2022 they accounted for 66.1% of the total population, which stood at 4,385,717. Apart from other Arabs (predominantly Egyptians and Syrians), the non-Kuwaitis are mainly Indians, Pakistanis and Iranians. According to official estimates based on new methodology used by the Public Authority for Civil Information, the total population of Kuwait had increased to 4,793,568 by 1 January 2023.

According to the January 2022 census, Salmiya was the largest town in Kuwait, with 282,541 inhabitants. Other sizeable localities were Jaleeb al-Shuyukh (population 271,168), Farwaniya (250,676) and Hawalli (205,895). However, these settlements are contiguous with the capital, Kuwait City, and are sometimes described as suburbs of it. Indeed, United Nations estimates—which include suburbs—put the capital's population at 3.0m. in 2019.

Apart from the distinction between Kuwaiti citizens and immigrants, Kuwaiti nationals can be divided into six groups. These groups reflect the tribal origins of Kuwaiti society. The first tribe of settlers, the Anaiza (led by the Sabah family), and later settlers, including the Bahar, Hamad and Babtain families, originated in the Nejd (central Arabia). Another group, the Kenaat (including the Mutawa family and its offshoot, the Saleh), came to Kuwait from Iraq, and remain distinct from the Nejdi families. There are also a few large families of Persian (Iranian) origin, including the Behbehanis. The remaining citizens may be described as 'new Kuwaitis'; a few are former Palestinians, although most are Bedouin who have been granted second-class citizenship. The majority of Kuwaitis (including the ruling family) are Sunni Muslims, but most of the Persian families belong to the Shi'a sect. About 30% of the total population are thought to be Shi'a.

History

Revised by CLAIRE BEAUGRAND

The establishment of the present-day city of Kuwait is usually dated to the beginning of the 18th century, when families of the Anaiza tribe migrated from the interior to the Arabian shore of the Gulf. The foundation of the current al-Sabah ruling dynasty dates from about 1756, when the settlers of Kuwait took the protection of a sheikh against other tribal threats, and to administer their affairs, provide them with security, and represent them in their dealings with the Ottoman rulers of Iraq. The town prospered, and in 1765 it was estimated to contain some 10,000 inhabitants, possessing 800 vessels, engaged in trading, fishing and pearling.

Between 1775 and 1779, during the Persian occupation of Basra, the British East India Company moved the southern terminal of its overland Basra–Aleppo mail route to Kuwait, and much Basra trade was diverted there. This temporary relocation was repeated in 1793 and again in 1821–22, and many merchant families migrated from Basra to Kuwait. At around the same time Kuwait was repeatedly threatened by raids from the Wahhabis—tribesmen from central Arabia who practised a puritanical form of Islam—and the need for protection led to closer contacts with the East India Company. Conflict between British and Arab fleets over control of the sea trade caused a decline in prosperity during the early 19th century, but trade later expanded again under British-Indian ascendancy. The growth of production in the region and the expansion of trade in the second half of the century brought renewed prosperity.

Although Kuwait was not under direct Ottoman administration, the Sheikh of Kuwait recognized a general Ottoman suzerainty over his sheikhdom by the payment of tribute and the acceptance of the title *Qa'immaqam* (District Officer) under the supervision of the Ottoman *Vali* (Provincial Governor) of Basra in 1871. The reign of Sheikh Mubarak al-Sabah (1896–1915) was notable for the increase of British Indian dominance over Kuwait. Mubarak 'the Great', as he is known today, feared that the Ottomans would bring Kuwait under direct administration, and in 1899, in return for British protection, he signed an agreement with the British Government of India not to cede, mortgage or otherwise dispose of parts of his territories to anyone except the British Government, nor to enter into any relationship with a foreign government without British consent. In that year the British Government of India appointed Hajji Ali bin Mulla Ghulam Riza, a prominent local merchant with connections to Britain, as its political agent in Kuwait. In 1904 the Government replaced Hajji Ali with a British political agent, Capt. Stuart Knox. In 1909 the British and Ottoman Governments discussed proposals that, although never ratified because of the outbreak of the First World War (1914–18), in practice secured the status of Kuwait as a British protectorate (to remain thus until 1961).

Sheikh Mubarak died in 1915 and was succeeded by his eldest son, Sheikh Jaber, founder of the al-Jaber branch of the ruling family. Sheikh Jaber died just two years later. He was succeeded by his brother, Sheikh Salim, founder of the al-Salim branch of the family, beginning a pattern of succession—the alternating appointment of rulers from the al-Salim and al-Jaber branches of the ruling family. This pattern ceased de facto in 2006 in favour of the al-Jaber branch, a trend confirmed in 2020 with the accession to power of a third ruler in a row stemming from this branch and the nomination of yet another one as Crown Prince (all half-brothers).

Sheikh Salim incurred British censure during the First World War, when he attempted to sell supplies to the Ottomans in Syria. Sheikh Salim died in 1921 and was succeeded by his nephew, Sheikh Ahmad al-Jaber who, in stark contrast to his predecessors, was long-lived. His 29-year reign witnessed the collapse of Gulf pearling income during the Great Depression and the introduction of less expensive Japanese cultured pearls to the world market, which together destroyed the market for Gulf pearls. Kuwait adjusted to those shocks by benefiting from the growth of Iraqi trade and through payments received for oil exploration. By 1937 Kuwait was a relatively prosperous mercantile community, with a population of about 75,000. Just north, in the newly independent kingdom of Iraq, King Ghazi was seeking the port city's integration and the end of British protection for Kuwait. Some of these demands were echoed within Kuwait itself, reflecting conflict between the established merchant families, who were pushing for more representation, and the al-Sabah branch of the ruling family, particularly during the short-lived period of an elected representative assembly in 1938.

The foundations of Kuwait's petroleum industry were laid during the 1930s. A joint concession was granted in 1934 to the Gulf Oil Corporation of the USA and the Anglo-Persian Oil Company of Great Britain, which together formed the Kuwait Oil Company Limited. Deep drilling started in 1936, and was just beginning to show promising results when the Second World War began in 1939. The oil wells were plugged in 1942 and drilling was suspended until the end of the war in 1945.

THE FOUNDATIONS OF THE MODERN STATE: ECONOMIC DEVELOPMENT AND INDEPENDENCE IN 1961

After the Second World War the petroleum industry in Kuwait was revived on an extensive scale (see *Economy*), and within a few years the town of Kuwait had developed from a traditional dhow port to a thriving modern commercial city, supported by petroleum revenues. In 1950 Sheikh Ahmad al-Jaber al-Sabah died and was succeeded by his cousin Sheikh Abdullah al-Salim al-Sabah (from the al-Salim branch), whose policies focused on the use of petroleum revenues to improve public welfare. In 1951 he inaugurated a programme of public works and educational and medical developments, which transformed Kuwait into a territory with a modern infrastructure and a high level of consumption for the indigenous population. The two-way dependence relationship between the ruling al-Sabah family and the traditional merchant elite began to change and with it the relationship between the ruler and the general Kuwaiti population. Until then, the Sheikh provided representation with powers outside Kuwait and a measure of internal security, in return for a limited ability to tax local merchant activity. With incomes drawn from oil, the Sheikh became the main economic provider for the population, in addition to holding a much wider political, security, administrative and judicial role. Consequently, the Sheikh came also to rely more on his family, whose members thus held most of the decision-making positions, than on building alliances with the merchant elite and with other sections of the population. Being a small, wealthy entity in a turbulent region, many Kuwaitis seemed to accept their dependence on the ruling family as the price of a privileged economic position. Thus, domestic opposition was muted, despite the increased education of the population.

Kuwait gradually built comprehensive welfare services, which are for the most part free of charge to Kuwaiti nationals. Education and health services are largely free, and housing heavily subsidized. For a time, the state sector virtually guaranteed well-paid employment and retirement pensions to Kuwaiti citizens, while making minimal tax demands upon them. Citizens were also given advantageous positions in business, and for several decades the scale of petroleum revenues enabled the Government to guarantee widespread benefits, including huge subsidies on water, electricity and consumer products, while the ruling family continued to enjoy its own special privileges. However, over time, the financial viability of these benefits and privileges has increasingly become a matter for debate, as the need for Kuwait to diversify away from dependence upon oil revenues has intensified. Non-citizens who came to work in the economically booming emirate were mostly excluded from these advantages. With the rapid development of the country, their numbers grew exponentially, equalling those of Kuwaiti nationals in 1961 and outnumbering them as of the 1965 Census (when nationals comprised 36% of the population). Moreover, the arrival of labourers and tribesmen in Kuwait in search of job opportunities, and loopholes in the 1959 nationality law compounded with generous welfare advantages, all created circumstances for the emergence of a 'grey' category between citizens and foreigners—the *bidoun*—stateless Arabs, who claimed that they had applied for or were eligible for nationality but were never granted it.

The 1899 agreement under which Britain assumed responsibility for the conduct of Kuwait's foreign policy was terminated in 1961; Kuwait became an independent state on 19 June, although it remained under British protection until 1971. The ruling Sheikh took the title of Amir, and Kuwait was admitted to the League of Arab States (Arab League).

Iraq, under the leadership of Gen. Abd al-Karim Kassem (President in 1958–63), did not recognize Kuwait's independence and revived a longstanding claim to sovereignty over the territory. British troops landed in Kuwait to deter Iraq from taking military action in support of its claim. The Arab League agreed in July 1961 that an Arab League force should be provided to replace the British troops as a guarantor of Kuwait's independence. This force, composed of contingents from Saudi Arabia, Jordan, the United Arab Republic (UAR) and Sudan, arrived in Kuwait in September. The UAR contingent was withdrawn in December, and the rest before the end of February 1963, following the bloody coup by members of the Baath Party that overthrew Gen. Kassem.

In December 1961, for the first time in Kuwait's history, an election was held to choose 20 members of a Constituent Assembly (the other members being ministers). This Assembly drafted a new Constitution under which a National Assembly (Majlis al-Umma) of 50 members was elected in January 1963. Sheikh Sabah al-Salim al-Sabah, brother of the Amir and heir apparent, was appointed as Prime Minister and formed a new Council of Ministers, yet without drawing any of its members from the elected Assembly. (Government ministers are ex officio members of the National Assembly, alongside its elected members.) Several members and supporters of the Arab Nationalist Movement (founded in the 1950s by Palestinian Dr George Habash—later leader of the Popular Front for the Liberation of Palestine) were elected. This nationalist group, led by Dr Ahmad al-Khatib, was generally regarded as the principal opposition to the Government.

With the Baath Party now in power, in October 1963 the Iraqi Government announced its decision to recognize Kuwait's complete independence, in an attempt to dispel the tense atmosphere between the two countries. Kuwait was thought to have made a substantial grant to Iraq at this juncture.

In January 1965 a constitutional crisis, reflecting the friction between the ruling house and the National Assembly, resulted in the formation of a strengthened Council of Ministers under Crown Prince Sheikh Sabah al-Salim. Later that year opposition legislators resigned from the Assembly. In November the Amir died and was succeeded by Sheikh Sabah, whose post of

Prime Minister was assumed by Sheikh Jaber al-Ahmad al-Jaber al-Sabah, who became heir apparent in May 1966.

After the January 1967 legislative elections, which were generally seen as rigged and which saw the defeat of the Arab nationalist candidates, the ruling family, under pressure from public opinion, permitted the assembly elections of January 1971 to be held on the basis of a free vote, although women, illiterate males, members of the police and military, and all non-Kuwaitis were excluded. The election campaign involved 184 candidates contesting the 50 seats, within a legal framework banning political parties (which remain illegal to the present day). Several members and supporters of the Arab Nationalist Movement (founded in the 1950s by Dr George Habash—later leader of the Popular Front for the Liberation of Palestine) were elected. This nationalist group, led by Dr Ahmad al-Khatib, was generally regarded as the principal opposition to the Government.

After the 1971 elections the representation of the ruling family was reduced from five to three in the new cabinet; moreover, for the first time, the Council of Ministers included two ministers drawn from the elected members of the National Assembly.

In August 1976 the Amir, Sheikh Sabah al-Salim al-Sabah, suspended the National Assembly on the grounds that, among other things, it had been delaying legislation. A committee was ordered to be formed to review the Constitution. The episode highlighted the strength of political patronage and the limitations of Kuwait's democracy. The Kuwaiti rulers were determined to insulate the state from the popular nationalist trend that was still thriving in the Arab region.

Sheikh Sabah died on 31 December 1977; he was succeeded by his cousin, Crown Prince Sheikh Jaber al-Ahmad al-Jaber al-Sabah (from the al-Jaber branch). Sheikh Saad al-Abdullah al-Salim al-Sabah (from the al-Salim branch) became Crown Prince and Prime Minister. Both the Amir and the Prime Minister publicly reaffirmed the Government's intention to reconvene the National Assembly and to restore democratic government by August 1980. In response to increasing public pressure, a 50-member committee was established in early 1980 to consider constitutional amendments and a revised form of legislature. Following its recommendations, an Amiri decree provided for the election of a new assembly before the end of February 1981. Despite the uncertainty generated by the Iran–Iraq War (1980–88), the election campaign proceeded. The franchise was limited to 90,000 'first-class' (i.e. endowed with political rights) Kuwaiti citizens, and, of these, fewer than one-half (or about 3% of the population) registered to vote. A conservative assembly was returned, including 23 tribal leaders, sympathetic to the ruling sheikhs, and 13 young technocrats out of the 50 seats. The radical Arab nationalists, the fiercest opposition to the Government in the previous assembly, failed to win any seats, while the Shi'a minority's representation was reduced to four seats. However, five Sunni Islamist fundamentalists were elected.

EXTERNAL RELATIONS, 1973–81: THE SOURCES OF KUWAITI SECURITY

Despite recognition by Iraq in 1963, Kuwait's borders, including those with Iraq, remained unsettled. Of all the Gulf states, Kuwait has been the most vulnerable to regional disruption. Along with other Gulf states, Kuwait allocated larger sums for the expansion of its armed forces after 1973, and it established its own navy. Legislation to introduce conscription was approved in 1975, but it was generally accepted that Kuwait's security could not be guaranteed through its own armed strength. Conscription was eventually abolished in 2001, only to be reintroduced in 2017. Purchases of military equipment have remained at a high level since the 1970s (even increasing in the 1990s), largely for the political purpose of cementing relations with arms-supplying powers.

During the first two decades of Kuwait's independence the country sought to project a distinct foreign policy, and attempted to enhance its security by broadening its international relations—including relations with the communist states, with non-aligned countries and across the Arab world. Kuwait adopted a neutral role in inter-Arab conflicts during 1966–67. It declared its support for the Arab countries in the June 1967 war with Israel and joined in the oil embargo imposed against the USA and the United Kingdom. The Government donated KD 25m. to the Arab war effort. At the Khartoum Conference in September Kuwait joined Saudi Arabia and Libya in offering financial aid to Egypt and Jordan, to help their economies to recover from the conflict with Israel.

In 1968 the UK announced that the agreement of June 1961—whereby the British had undertaken to give military assistance to Kuwait if requested—would be terminated by 1971. This followed an earlier announcement that the UK would withdraw all troops from the Gulf region by the end of that year.

A new direction in Kuwaiti foreign policy was taken from May 1981, when Kuwait, with Saudi Arabia, the United Arab Emirates (UAE), Qatar, Oman and Bahrain, founded the Cooperation Council for the Arab States of the Gulf (Gulf Cooperation Council—GCC). The cement of the alliance was the perceived common threats, as well as the rulers' alliances with the USA and the UK. From the 1990s a more positive regional integration agenda started to make slow progress, with some co-ordination of trade policies and the resolution of border disputes among the member states themselves. The GCC implemented the freedom of movement, work and residence for all GCC nationals in 2001 and a customs union in 2003, despite its failure to adopt a common currency. This momentum towards establishing a degree of internal consultation and representation mechanisms, which at first improved relations between the ruling families of the Gulf, was nevertheless brought to a halt in the 2010s as a consequence of diverging stances towards the 'Arab Spring' and political Islam, and the deteriorating economic situation.

THE IRAN–IRAQ WAR, 1980–88

Kuwait's regional security position began to change with the sequence of events that started with the Iranian Revolution of 1979 and the war between Iran and Iraq, which began in September 1980. In that war, Kuwait supported Iraq, granting access to its strategic ports, exporting, with Saudi Arabia, up to 310,000 barrels per day (b/d) of petroleum on Iraq's behalf, and contributing to the substantial financial aid from the Gulf states, which by the end of the war, in 1988, was thought to have reached US $40,000m.

In May 1984 two Kuwaiti and several Saudi Arabian tankers were bombed in a series of attacks by unidentified aircraft on shipping in the Gulf. Although both Iran and Iraq were known to have been firing at shipping, Iran was blamed for the attacks on Kuwaiti tankers. The bombings were seen as a warning to Kuwait to reduce its aid to Iraq and to put pressure on Iraq to desist from attacking tankers carrying Iranian oil. Concern arose as to whether the GCC countries could defend themselves unaided, and at the GCC summit conference in November the member states agreed to form a joint military force, capable of rapid deployment and aimed at combating any spread of the Iran–Iraq War.

Kuwait's attempts to mediate in the Iran–Iraq War in 1984 were hampered by Iran's increasing suspicion about the result of outstanding border disputes between Iraq and Kuwait. Iran believed that Kuwait was about to transfer three strategically important islands (Bubiyan, Warba and Failaka) to Iraq. In January 1985, however, Kuwait announced plans to build its own military bases on Bubiyan and Warba, and two months later Bubiyan was declared an out-of-bounds war zone. Kuwaiti forces were put on alert in February 1986, when Iranian forces crossed the Shatt al-Arab waterway and captured the Iraqi port of Faw, near Kuwait's north-eastern border. Iran pledged that Kuwait would not become embroiled in its war with Iraq provided that it maintained its military neutrality.

Between October 1986 and April 1987 Iranian forces attacked merchant ships sailing to and from Kuwait and seized cargoes, in reprisal for loading petroleum sold on Iraq's behalf and for the use of Kuwait's ports for Iraqi imports. In an attempt to deter Iranian attacks in the Gulf, Kuwait re-registered most of its fleet of oil tankers under the flags of the USA, Liberia, the Union of Soviet Socialist Republics

(USSR) and the UK. Kuwait received help from the USA and Saudi Arabia in clearing mines from the channel leading to its main oil-loading facilities at Mina al-Ahmadi, later joined by France, the UK and other European states.

In September 1987 Iran started attacking Kuwaiti installations. Kuwait's main offshore oil-loading terminal was closed between October and December, after an Iranian missile attack in which three workers were injured. A summit meeting of the GCC in December urged the United Nations (UN) Security Council to enforce its Resolution 598, which ordered a ceasefire to be observed in the Iran–Iraq War.

In March 1988 Iranian and Kuwaiti armed forces clashed for the first time during the Iran–Iraq War when three Iranian gunboats attacked Bubiyan Island, situated 25 km from the southern coast of Iraq. The following month an Iranian missile landed at al-Wafra oilfield, 80 km south of Kuwait City. The missile attack was believed to represent an Iranian warning to Kuwait for allegedly permitting Iraqi armed forces to use Bubiyan Island to recapture the Iranian-occupied Faw peninsula.

The ceasefire in the Iran–Iraq War in August 1988 brought a revival of economic growth in Kuwait. Relations between Kuwait and Iran improved, and co-operation with Iraq also appeared to increase.

INTERNAL UNREST 1985–90: THE SPREAD OF SHI'A POLITICAL ISLAM

In May 1985 an Iraqi Shi'a militant member of the Islamic Jihad movement (who belonged to the then banned Hizb al-Da'wa al-Islamiyya—Islamic Da'wa Party—which originated in Iraq) attempted to assassinate the Amir of Kuwait with a car bomb. In June 1986 four simultaneous explosions occurred at Kuwait's main oil export refinery at Mina al-Ahmadi. A hitherto unknown organization, the 'Arab Revolutionaries Group', later claimed responsibility for the attacks, which had been intended to force Kuwait to reduce its petroleum output.

In 1985 and 1986 almost 27,000 expatriates, many of whom were Iranian, were deported. Concern about Iranian influence over the Shi'a minority (about 30% of the population) led to severe measures to curb political agitation. In June 1987 six Kuwaiti Shi'a Muslims were sentenced to death for their part in sabotaging oil installations and plotting against the Government. There were further explosions in May and July. In June 1989 a total of 22 people accused of plotting to overthrow the ruling family were sentenced to prison terms of up to 15 years. Another consequence of the crackdown on the Shi'a, which was compounded by a fall in oil prices, was a covert decision taken by the Government in December 1986 to exclude the *bidoun* from the citizenry and, as a consequence, from accessing state resources, in order to reduce budget spending.

The tension in and surrounding Kuwait was reflected in the general political atmosphere. Although the traditional Arab nationalist opposition was dealt a severe blow by the dissolution of the National Assembly in 1976, political demands came to be expressed through religious and tribal alliances formed within the new Assembly, elected in 1985 and presided over by Ahmed al-Saadoun. In July 1986, following 15 months of increasing confrontation with the Assembly, the Amir dissolved it for a second time, and failed to adhere to the constitutional stipulation that fresh elections subsequently be organized. The newly appointed Government was given greater powers of censorship, including the right to close down newspapers for up to two years.

In December 1989 a number of former members of the National Assembly launched a campaign to restore the parliament. A pro-democracy movement started in the private sphere of *diwaniyyat* (the reception area where a Kuwaiti man traditionally receives his business colleagues and male guests). In January 1990 the Amir appealed for political dialogue, and in March the Prime Minister declared that he would welcome the restoration of an elected legislature. However, the Government was only prepared to permit a partly elected body with severely limited powers, which the opposition rejected and urged all parties to boycott. On 10 June a total of 62% of the electorate voted at a general election for 50 members of this new and distinct National Council. The Council was to be an interim body, and its members were to hold office for four years. It comprised 75 members, of whom 25 were appointed by the Amir. With a Council of Ministers still dominated by the al-Sabah family and no prospect of the restoration of the National Assembly, political unrest continued.

IRAQ'S INVASION OF KUWAIT: THE GULF CRISIS, 1990–91

In July 1990 President Saddam Hussain of Iraq accused Kuwait of having 'stolen' Iraqi oil reserves valued at US $2,400m. from a field that straddles the unresolved border. The Iraqi Minister of Foreign Affairs, Tareq Aziz, declared that Kuwait should not only cancel Iraq's war debt, but also compensate it for losses of revenue incurred during the war with Iran and as a result of Kuwait's overproduction of oil, to which he attributed a decline in prices. Later in July Iraq began to deploy armed forces on the Kuwait–Iraq border, immediately before a meeting of the Organization of the Petroleum Exporting Countries (OPEC) ministerial council in Geneva, Switzerland.

On 2 August 1990 Iraq invaded Kuwait with 100,000 troops. The Amir and other members of the Government escaped to Saudi Arabia, together with many Kuwaiti citizens. The UN Security Council immediately adopted a series of resolutions that condemned the invasion, demanded the immediate and unconditional withdrawal of Iraqi forces from Kuwait, and appealed for a negotiated settlement of the conflict. A comprehensive economic blockade was also imposed on Iraq and Kuwait. Immediately after the invasion, the USA and the members of the then European Community froze all Kuwaiti assets to prevent their transfer by an Iraqi-imposed regime.

On 7 August 1990 US President George Bush ordered the deployment of US troops and aircraft in Saudi Arabia, with the declared aim of securing the country's borders with Kuwait in the event of an Iraqi attack. A number of European governments, together with some members of the Arab League, agreed to provide military support for the US forces. On 8 August the Iraqi Government announced the formal annexation of Kuwait, and at the end of the month most of Kuwait was officially declared to be the 19th governorate of Iraq, and a northern strip was incorporated into Basra governorate.

Following the Iraqi invasion, there were widespread reports of looting in Kuwait. Some installations were completely dismantled and removed to Iraq. There were also frequent reports of serious human rights violations, as Iraqi forces searched for Kuwaiti resistance fighters and Westerners in hiding. By October 1990 an estimated 430,000 Iraqi troops had been deployed in southern Iraq and Kuwait. Kuwait's population was estimated to have decreased from approximately 2m. to about 700,000; besides Kuwaiti nationals, the majority of those who left were foreign workers, who represented 73% of the total population before the Iraqi invasion.

In October 1990 a conference was held in Jeddah, Saudi Arabia, where the exiled Crown Prince and Prime Minister of Kuwait, Sheikh Saad al-Abdullah al-Salim al-Sabah, addressed approximately 1,000 Kuwaiti citizens, including members of the dissolved National Assembly. He agreed to establish committees to advise the Government on political, social and financial matters, and pledged that, after the liberation of Kuwait, the country's constitution and legislature would be restored, and that free elections would be held. This was seen as a necessary concession to maintain national unity, particularly given the emerging divide between Kuwait's wealthier citizens, most of whom were now living in exile, and those who remained in Kuwait.

In November 1990 a UN Security Council resolution authorized the use of 'all necessary means' to liberate Kuwait. Iraq was given until 15 January 1991 to start implementing the 10 resolutions that had so far been adopted, including that stipulating unconditional withdrawal from Kuwait. In the interim period, a massive build-up of around 600,000 US troops, together with further substantial forces from a coalition of more than 30 states, was assembled in Saudi Arabia and in other parts of the region in preparation for a military campaign against Iraq, as diplomatic attempts remained unsuccessful. On 17 January 1991 the UN-backed, US-led multinational force launched its military campaign with an intensive aerial bombardment of Iraq aimed at disabling that country's economic and military infrastructure. On 24 February US-led ground forces entered Kuwait, encountering little effective Iraqi opposition. Within three days the Iraqi Government had agreed to accept all resolutions of the UN Security Council, and on 28 February the US Government announced a suspension of military operations—but not before Iraqi troops and fleeing civilians were bombarded by US aircraft at Mutla Ridge, north of Kuwait Bay, resulting in heavy casualties. In March the UN Security Council set out the terms for a permanent ceasefire. These included the release of all allied prisoners of war and of Kuwaitis detained as potential hostages. They also required Iraq to repeal all laws and decrees concerning the annexation of Kuwait. Iraq promptly announced its compliance with these conditions. Another resolution, adopted in April, provided for the establishment of a demilitarized zone, supervised by the UN Iraq-Kuwait Observer Mission (UNIKOM), between the two countries. The UNIKOM mandate was subsequently renewed at six-monthly intervals until the mission ended in October 2003.

THE RETURN FROM EXILE AND HUMAN RIGHTS AFTER THE IRAQI WITHDRAWAL, 1991–92

In mid-January 1991 a conference in Jeddah was attended by members of the Kuwaiti Government-in-exile and opposition delegates. Islamist and Arab nationalist groups had collaborated in forming a 'National Constitutional Front' to press for an immediate return of parliamentary and press freedom; the more radical elements in the movement demanded the resignation of the al-Sabah family from all important positions in the Government and the establishment of a constitutional monarchy. In February, despite discontent among the exiled Kuwaiti community, the Government-in-exile excluded the possibility of early elections after Kuwait had been liberated, claiming that the need to rebuild and repopulate the country took precedence. The opposition parties were further frustrated by the stated aim of the UN resolutions to reinstate Kuwait's 'legitimate' government prior to the Iraqi invasion, namely the al-Sabah family. In late February the Amir decreed that martial law would be enforced in Kuwait for the subsequent three months; members of Kuwait's opposition-in-exile asserted that the legislature should reconvene first. In early March the opposition groups in exile made public their intention to form a coalition against the Government of the al-Sabah family. In the same month the Amir announced the formation of a committee to administer martial law and to supervise the state's security. The committee's objectives were to identify people who had collaborated with Iraq and those brought by the Iraqi authorities to settle in the emirate, as well as to prevent the formation of vigilante groups.

The Prime Minister and other members of the exiled Government returned to Kuwait in early March 1991, followed by the Amir. The country was in a condition of instability, largely because the destruction of infrastructure and the emigration of most of the non-national workforce had led to a collapse in services. Departing Iraqi forces had set fire to over 600 oil wells, which burned for nearly a year. Later in March the Government announced that elections would take place within six to 12 months, following the return of Kuwaiti exiles and the compilation of a new electoral roll. On 20 March the Council of Ministers resigned, apparently in response to public discontent at the Government's failure to restore supplies of electricity, water and food. In April a new Council of Ministers was formed with several technocrats appointed to important positions but the major portfolios—foreign affairs, defence and the interior—remained in the hands of the al-Sabah family, which led members of opposition groups to denounce it as unrepresentative.

There were reports in May 1991 that 900 people were under investigation in connection with crimes committed during the Iraqi occupation. Bitter resentment was felt by Kuwaiti citizens against members of the Palestinian community, who were obliged to stay in Kuwait, but who were suspected of having collaborated with Iraq and whose leadership had failed to condemn the Iraqi invasion of Kuwait. In late May the human rights organization Amnesty International alleged that trials were being conducted in Kuwait without the provision of adequate defence counsel, and that, in some cases, torture had been used to extract confessions from defendants. In the same month the Prime Minister admitted that the abduction and torture of non-Kuwaiti residents, including *bidoun*, who had been targeted on suspicion of being pro-Iraqi, was taking place, and promised that the matter would be investigated. It was reported in June that 29 out of some 200 defendants in trials for alleged collaboration during the occupation of Kuwait had been sentenced to death. The sentences were condemned by international human rights organizations. On 26 June the Government repealed martial law and quashed all the death sentences that had been imposed in earlier trials. Subsequent trials of those accused of collaboration were referred to civilian courts.

By July 1991 the Kuwaiti population had declined to an estimated 600,000, and in particular the Palestinian population was estimated to have decreased from about 400,000 to just 80,000 as a result of large-scale expulsions with airlifts to Jordan that continued until August. International human rights organizations criticized the continued deportation of non-Kuwaiti nationals, citing the 1949 Fourth Geneva Convention, which prohibits such action against civilians who are justified in fearing persecution for their political or religious beliefs.

The first half of 1992 was characterized by an unprecedented breakdown of law and order in Kuwait, with regular shootings and other incidents of violence. Many of these were directed against expatriates, especially Palestinians. There were widespread allegations that the Government was using the shootings, and the fear of further conflict with Iraq, as a pretext to restrict the press and opposition meetings. However, disaffection with the performance of the ruling family and Kuwait's traditional business elite was not allowed to evolve into a political challenge, and Kuwait's pre-war institutions were re-established with a more prominent role for the National Assembly and the business class. The restoration of elite politics prevented the rise of a new opposition movement from within the poorer sections of the Kuwaiti population, who had been politicized by their experience of war and occupation.

Against the background of the attempt by the al-Sabah family to regain its political control after the liberation, the Government implemented the policy towards the *bidoun* that had been formulated in 1986, which denied them citizenship and deprived them of all their rights. The al-Sabah flight and exile abroad following the Iraqi invasion was resented by the poorer sections of the population who had endured the war and occupation. The *bidoun* who had integrated in Kuwaiti society, often working in the police and military before 1990, were stigmatized as disloyal, as the Government argued that most of them had originally come from Iraq. Hundreds of thousands of *bidoun* did not or could not return to Kuwait after fleeing the conflict. The repressive measures against them became an instrument for exercising power over society, effectively forcing thousands of *bidoun* into deeper poverty and marginalizing the whole group.

In the aftermath of the Iraqi occupation, when the expatriate population returned to the country, the Kuwaiti Government vowed to reduce the number of foreign workers substantially. However, it ultimately proved unable to do so and the proportion of foreigners rose again, from 59% of the overall population in 1995 to 63% in 2000.

US PROTECTION AND US FORCES IN KUWAIT

In June 1991, with British and US armed forces scheduled to leave Kuwait in July and September, respectively, the Minister of Defence declared that an agreement had been reached for their replacement by a united Arab force. However, the Arab alliance of the six GCC states, Egypt and Syria—known as the Damascus Declaration—never materialized, and the USA continued to play the predominant direct military role in the region. When the bulk of US armed forces withdrew from Iraq they left behind vast quantities of military equipment, providing a foundation for the post-occupation Kuwaiti Land Forces.

KUWAIT

History

In September 1991 the Kuwaiti Minister of Defence signed a 10-year defence pact with the USA that was still in effect in 2023; another agreement was signed with the UK in February 1992; and one with France in August (which was amended and renewed in October 2009). The agreement with the USA included provisions for the stockpiling of US military equipment in Kuwait, the use of Kuwaiti ports by US troops, and joint training exercises. The cost of maintaining the US troops had increased to an annual sum of US $474m. by 2000. In 2003 Kuwait hosted the bulk of the 250,000 US troops of Operation Iraqi Freedom and contributed $266m. to support the US combat effort to remove the Iraqi regime. The agreements with major powers and the US military presence, supported by a 10-year programme of Kuwaiti military expenditure that at times exceeded 12% of annual gross domestic product (GDP), became the cornerstone of Kuwait's security strategy.

After the attacks on the US mainland of 11 September 2001, the USA paid greater attention to its own domestic security and, as part of its 'war on terror', the US Administration sought to oust the Iraqi regime. Radical opposition to the presence of US forces has been persistent and at times militant in Kuwait, so that the initial deployment of US and British forces in Kuwait from mid-2002, in preparation for the invasion of Iraq, was disrupted by a series of low-level attacks on US forces. Following the 2003 conflict in Iraq, the growing US military presence in the region and the continuing violence in Iraq overshadowed any possibilities for regional security co-operation. Designated as a Major Non-North Atlantic Treaty Organization (NATO) Ally in 2004, Kuwait hosted 14,000 US soldiers when the USA withdrew its forces from Iraq in 2011.

Regional alliances such as the GCC defence pact remained useful in providing political support for the main strategy of security reliance on the USA: Kuwait supported the GCC decision to form a joint military command in 2013. In 2014 Kuwait joined the coalition against Islamic State in Iraq and the Levant (subsequently renamed Islamic State) and hosted the headquarters for the US-led operation (Operation Inherent Resolve). In November 2017 Kuwait signed an agreement with France to strengthen their defence co-operation and opened a NATO regional centre as part of the 2004 Istanbul Co-operation Initiative.

MISSING KUWAITIS

In 1991 UN Security Council Resolutions 686 and 687 obliged Iraq, in co-operation with the International Committee of the Red Cross (ICRC), to release all Kuwaiti and third country nationals detained during the war, repatriate the remains of any deceased Kuwaitis, and return all seized Kuwaiti property. The Tripartite Commission, chaired by the ICRC and composed of representatives from Kuwait, Iraq, Saudi Arabia, the USA, the UK and France, was established as a means of ascertaining the fate of missing people. Iraq released many ICRC-registered Kuwaiti prisoners of war. However, in 1994 the Kuwait National Committee for Missing People and Prisoners of War stated that 605 Kuwaiti residents were still missing in Iraq.

From mid-1996 Iraqi and Kuwaiti officials held meetings under the auspices of the ICRC in their mutual border area to discuss the fate of those not accounted for. In 'highly confidential' discussions held in Geneva in 1998, the Iraqi Government demanded that the whereabouts of more than 1,000 Iraqi citizens allegedly missing in Kuwait since 1991 should be included in any negotiations on this issue.

In 2006 a joint Kuwaiti-Iraqi committee was established which, by August 2009, had identified the remains of 236 missing Kuwaitis from the 1990–91 war. The remains of Kuwaiti citizens were found within the framework of the Tripartite mechanism in 2005, while Iraqi remains were recovered in 2011. In 2013 UN Security Council Resolution 2107 transferred the responsibility of facilitating efforts regarding the repatriation of the remains of all Kuwaiti and third country nationals and the return of Kuwaiti property, including the national archives, seized by Iraq, to the head of the UN Assistance Mission to Iraq (UNAMI). In 2019 human remains were exhumed from two burial sites in Samawah in Iraq and transferred to Kuwait in 2020 and 2021. In March 2021 Iraq returned a batch of Kuwaiti archives, the third shipment since 2019. According to the ICRC, only 215 Kuwaitis out of the 605 unaccounted for and 85 Iraqis have been repatriated since 1991.

WAR COMPENSATION

In 1991 the UN Security Council established the UN Compensation Commission (UNCC) to adjudicate and pay claims for compensation arising from the 1990–91 Iraqi invasion. After the first disbursements were approved in May 1994, the rate of payments increased rapidly following the implementation in December 1996 of UN Security Council Resolution 986 (the 'oil-for-food' arrangement), and by mid-2004 about US $18,400m. had been paid—a substantial penalty against a sanctioned and impoverished Iraq, and the equivalent of almost two-thirds of the total value of merchandise received by Iraq during the years of the oil-for-food arrangement.

In June 2000 a contentious Kuwaiti claim for US $21,000m. to compensate for oil revenue lost as a result of the Iraqi occupation brought the controversial issue of the major corporate claims to the fore. These claims, initially totalling more than $350,000m., plus interest, were a continuing source of tension between Iraq and Kuwait. In September the UNCC approved a reduced Kuwaiti oil claim of $15,900m., while the UN Security Council reduced the proportion of Iraqi oil revenues set aside for compensation purposes from 30% to 25%. In mid-2001 the UNCC began to consider a Kuwait Investment Authority (KIA) claim of $86,000m., mostly for estimated lost interest earnings. In June 2003 the UNCC rejected all but $1,500m. of the claim, leaving some $69,200m. of environmental losses as the largest part of unresolved Kuwaiti claims. These were gradually resolved until the UNCC completed its deliberations in June 2005.

Kuwait continued to receive substantial payments from Iraqi petroleum sales, but the proportion set aside for compensation was reduced from 25% to 5% in accordance with UN Security Council Resolution 1483 of May 2003—to the disappointment of Kuwait. Following the 2003 conflict in Iraq, Kuwait made an additional demand, of US $1,200m., from Iraqi Airways as compensation for 10 Kuwait Airways aircraft that it had appropriated during the 1990–91 occupation. In May 2010 Kuwait forced Iraqi Airways into bankruptcy, after making several attempts to seize the company's aircraft overseas.

The establishment of a new Iraqi regime, albeit one that was amicable towards the USA and that sought good relations with Kuwait, raised a major issue for the Kuwaiti Government with regard to its compensation claims. Many Iraqis considered their country's debt from the Iran–Iraq War to have accumulated as a result of a Kuwaiti alliance with the Saddam Hussain regime acting against their interests and deemed that, together with the Iranians, they bore the brunt of a regional war to defend the regimes of privileged minorities in the Gulf. Kuwait rejected this view and remained intransigent: when the Iraqi debt was reduced by 80% by the 'Paris Club' of official creditors in 2004, Kuwait did not follow suit with any reductions or debt cancellations.

In 2009 Iraqi members of parliament urged a halt to reparation payments to Kuwait. The request, presented by the Iraqi Prime Minister, Nuri al-Maliki, during a visit to the UN headquarters in New York, USA, received backing from the UN Secretary-General, Ban Ki-Moon, and the US and British Governments. The Iraqi legislators also demanded the cancellation of US $15,000m. of debt owed to Kuwait from the Saddam Hussain era. In March 2012 Kuwait and Iraq reached an agreement to resolve the outstanding airways debt, which included the creation of a joint Iraqi-Kuwaiti airline group, but the rest of the wider debt remained a matter of contention. In December 2014 the UNCC agreed to allow Iraq to postpone payments for one year, citing the deteriorating security situation in Iraq and the related increase in government expenditure. Further extensions were granted in October 2015 and November 2016. In November 2017 Kuwait accepted a proposal from Iraq to pay 0.5% of its hydrocarbon revenues in 2018, 1.5% in 2019 and 3% in 2020 and thenceforth until the outstanding compensation had been paid in full.

On 21 December 2021 the Iraqi Ministry of Finance announced that it had paid the final instalment of compensation to Kuwait. On 22 February 2022 the UN Security Council unanimously adopted Resolution 2621 confirming that the UNCC had fulfilled its mandate, thereby terminating it. In total, the UNCC awarded US $52,400m. of compensation against Iraq as payment for direct losses, damage or injury suffered by 1.5m. claimants be they foreign governments, nationals or corporations. This represented approximately 15% of the 2.7m. claims submitted to the Commission to the value of $352,000m. in compensation. Iraq had fulfilled its obligations under international law; however, the issue of missing persons and property remained.

THE KUWAIT–IRAQ BORDER: ONGOING PROBLEMS

The UN Iraq–Kuwait Boundary Demarcation Commission adjudged on 16 April 1992 that the border should be set 570 m to the north of the position existing at that time. This had the effect of awarding part of the port of Umm Qasr and several of the Rumaila oil wells to Kuwait. The decision was controversial, as Kuwait had never laid claim to that territory. Iraq initially rejected the validity of the settlement.

In August 1992, after a dispute between the Iraqi Government and weapons inspectors (operating in Iraq under UN Security Council Resolution 687), the USA deployed missiles in Kuwait, and some 7,500 US troops participated in a military exercise in the emirate. On 26 August the UN Security Council adopted Resolution 773, which guaranteed the new land frontier between Kuwait and Iraq. Demarcation was to take place before the end of the year, and the new border was to come into force on 15 January 1993. However, in the week leading up to this deadline Iraqi forces made several incursions into disputed territory and recovered armaments left behind at the end of the Gulf crisis. At the same time, as US aircraft led air attacks against Iraq, more than 1,000 US troops were dispatched to Kuwait. Following the deadline for enforcement of the border, Iraqi operatives began to dismantle installations on what had been declared Kuwaiti territory. None the less the USA deployed further missiles in Kuwait, and in early February the UN Security Council agreed to strengthen UNIKOM by approving the dispatch of armed troops (in addition to the existing unarmed personnel) to patrol the Kuwaiti border with Iraq.

In March 1993 the UN Iraq–Kuwait Boundary Demarcation Commission announced that it had completed the process of defining the maritime border between the two countries along the median line of the Khor Abdullah waterway. The UN demarcation placed the shipping lane to Iraq's only deep-water port at Umm Qasr inside Kuwaiti territorial waters, thus enabling Kuwait to cut off Iraq's access to the Gulf. On 27 May UN Security Council Resolution 833 specified the precise co-ordinates of the border between Kuwait and Iraq on the basis of the agreement between the two countries in 1963. In the same month Kuwait announced that construction was to begin of a trench, to be protected by mines and a wall of sand, along the entire length of the land border. Allegations by Kuwait of Iraqi violations of the border intensified during the second half of 1993, and there were reports of exchanges of fire in the border region. In November some 300 Iraqi civilians had reportedly crossed the border in the Umm Qasr region to protest against the digging of the trench, and Iraqi troops were reported to have attacked a border post. These incursions coincided with the beginning of the evacuation, under UN supervision, of Iraqi nationals and property from the Kuwaiti side of the new border. In November a 775-strong armed UNIKOM reinforcement was deployed in northern Kuwait to assist the unarmed force in the demilitarized zone. The UN mission was terminated in October 2003.

Following the US-led occupation of Iraq in 2003 and the overthrow of the regime of Saddam Hussain, the border settlement again became problematic. With Iraqi government institutions largely paralysed, Kuwait unilaterally commenced the installation of a permanent physical barrier along the demarcated border. In mid-2005 construction reached the town of Umm Qasr, and many local people witnessed their private land and civilian facilities being cut off behind the Kuwaiti barrier. This led to mass protests in the town and a degree of disquiet elsewhere in both Iraq and Kuwait. The weak Iraqi Interim Government formed in May 2004 was anxious not to allow a new source of tension to develop, and therefore attempted to settle the issue by acquiring adequate Kuwaiti compensation for Iraqi farmers and others affected by the new border demarcation. In 2006 Kuwait and Iraq reached an agreement whereby Kuwait could create a border fence and no man's land to separate the two countries, and pay compensation to Iraqi farmers who lost land as a result. During a state visit to Kuwait in June 2008 the Iraqi Prime Minister, Nuri al-Maliki, announced that Iraq's border dispute with Kuwait had been settled. In June 2009, however, members of the Iraqi Council of Representatives called for the maritime border as demarcated by the UN in 1993 to be renegotiated. Kuwait expressed an interest in writing off a significant portion of Iraq's remaining war reparations to Kuwait, in return for Iraqi recognition of the UN-defined borders (Saddam Hussain's Government had granted them official recognition in 1994, but this endorsement had been abandoned by subsequent Iraqi administrations).

In January 2011 a Kuwaiti coastguard was killed in a shoot-out with Iraqi fishermen who had strayed into Kuwaiti waters. In April Kuwait commenced construction of the US $1,100m. Mubarak al-Kabir Port, on the east coast of Bubiyan Island. The Iraqi Government notified Kuwait in the following month that it objected to the port, which is situated directly opposite Iraq's Faw peninsula, where the Iraqi Government planned to commence building the Faw Grand Port complex (with 100 berths), at a cost of $60,000m. The Iraqi authorities feared that the increased levels of maritime traffic would lead to serious congestion in what is already a crowded waterway, and many Iraqis concluded that the Kuwaiti project was an attempt to restrict Iraq's access to the Gulf. Iraq insisted that the maritime border delineation should provide it with unhindered access to Gulf waters, a lifeline for its economy and oil exports.

Iraqi protests over Mubarak al-Kabir Port intensified in mid-2011. In August the Iraqi Shi'a militant group Kata'ib Hezbollah announced that it would attack Mubarak al-Kabir Port and the South Korean consortium undertaking its construction, if the Kuwaiti Government pressed ahead with the scheme. Kuwait dispatched security forces to defend the construction site and demanded that the Iraqi Government prevent the attack. Later in August Kuwait hosted an Iraqi technical delegation at Mubarak al-Kabir, in an effort to demonstrate that activity at the new port would in no way impinge on Iraq's shipping lanes.

Meanwhile in January 2011 Prime Minister Sheikh Nasser al-Mohammed al-Ahmad al-Sabah made a visit to Baghdad—becoming the first Kuwaiti Prime Minister to visit Iraq since 1989. During his visit it was agreed that a Kuwait-Iraq joint committee would be formed, chaired by the countries' respective premiers, to discuss all outstanding matters between them, including war reparations and the border issue. In April 2012, following a visit to Iraq by Kuwait's Amir, the two countries came to an agreement on land and maritime borders, and established a joint commission to oversee its implementation. The agreement included the creation of a 500-m no man's land on each side and the allocation of new homes, paid for by Kuwait, to Iraqi farmers affected by the positioning of the border line.

During an official visit to Iraq in late July 2023, the Kuwaiti Minister of Foreign Affairs, Sheikh Salem Abdullah al-Jaber al Sabah, reaffirmed the 'complete consensus' between the two countries to 'resolve outstanding problems [...], particularly the demarcation of maritime boundaries', adding that discussions had also touched upon the subject of oilfields held jointly by Kuwait and Iraq (see *A Relative Diplomatic Effacement*).

A RETURN TO POLITICAL LIFE, 1992–2003

Following the end of the Iraqi occupation, Kuwait resumed its quasi-democratic political life. The Government revoked pre-publication censorship of written media in January 1992, but retained the right to close publications responsible for 'objectionable' articles. Only 'first-class' Kuwaiti male citizens, who numbered about 81,400 (just under 15% of the total, predominantly non-national adult population), were eligible to vote in the elections to the National Assembly in October of that year. Women's groups protested against their exclusion from the political process. Anti-Government candidates, in particular representatives of Islamist groups, secured 31 of the Assembly's 50 seats, and several of those elected had been members of the legislature dissolved in 1986.

In January 1993, in an attempt to curb financial corruption, the National Assembly adopted a law requiring state companies and investment organizations to produce accounts for the Auditor-General, who was in turn required to pass them on to a commission of the Assembly. The law also provided for harsher penalties for the misuse of public funds. In February a delegation of members of the Assembly travelled to the UK to investigate allegations that millions of dollars had been embezzled via the Kuwait Investment Office (KIO) in London. In March the Assembly voted to rescind a law of secrecy, which had been regarded as a legal mechanism to facilitate corruption. In the same month there were reports of criticism from members of the Assembly after the Government estimated defence spending for 1992/93 at US $6,200m. In August 1993 the Prime Minister submitted a proposal to the National Assembly whereby future budgets would, for the first time, contain details of purchases of defence equipment.

In January 1994 the National Assembly abrogated an earlier decree requiring that government ministers be tried by a special court. Sheikh Ali al-Khalifah al-Sabah, a former Minister of Finance and of Oil, and Abd al-Fattah al-Bader, a former Chairman of the Kuwait Oil Tanker Co, were among five people brought to trial in connection with alleged embezzlement from the company. In November 1995 a criminal court ruled that the trial of the former minister would be held in a special court for cases involving ministers, despite the Assembly's earlier ruling. In July 1996 three of the four former executives tried by the criminal court were found guilty of corruption, receiving prison sentences of between 15 and 40 years. In addition, they were ordered to repay the embezzled funds, together with fines totalling more than US $100m. The charges against Sheikh Ali al-Khalifah were later withdrawn on procedural grounds. In August 1999 a senior official of the KIO, Sheikh Fahd Muhammad al-Sabah, was convicted *in absentia* by the High Court in London of a $460m. fraud against the KIO's Spanish subsidiary. In the late 1980s income from the KIO funds (including the Fund for Future Generations) had met or exceeded oil revenues, so that such major corruption in the management of these funds was, therefore, a highly sensitive political issue. Furthermore, the dramatic rise in oil prices and revenues following the US-led occupation of Iraq brought the management of the funds under particular scrutiny—especially as government spending had been cautious, and surpluses were mounting at a time when public services were perceived to be deteriorating.

Government attempts to pursue an agenda of economic reform encountered opposition in the National Assembly and within the ruling family. In April 1994 the Government resigned, and the new cabinet announced it would persevere with economic reforms, including privatization. Relations between the Government and the Assembly became increasingly strained during late 1994 and early 1995, not least because of the discord apparent between the Prime Minister, Crown Prince Sheikh Saad al-Abdullah al-Salim al-Sabah, and the then Speaker of the National Assembly, Ahmad al-Saadoun, who sought a government composed only of elected members, as opposed to the current situation whereby cabinet members vote in parliament.

In June 1995 the National Assembly approved legislation designed to increase the size of the electorate by amending the 1959 nationality law to allow sons of naturalized Kuwaitis to vote. In July 1995 the Assembly approved a bill reducing the minimum period after which naturalized Kuwaitis become eligible to vote from 30 years to 20. Pro-Government candidates were the most successful at the polls in October, securing an estimated 19 of the 50 legislative seats. A number of small demonstrations by women in support of female enfranchisement took place in the days preceding voting.

In June 1997 an assassination attempt was made on Abdullah al-Nibari, an opposition member of the National Assembly and a former Chairman of the Committee for the Protection of Public Funds. One of the five men charged in connection with the offence was discovered to be related to the Minister of Finance, Nasir al-Rodhan. Responding to suggestions that he should resign, al-Rodhan insisted that he had had no knowledge of the attack. In November an incendiary bomb attack destroyed al-Nibari's office. It was widely believed that a conspiracy linked to state corruption lay behind the attacks on al-Nibari, and these suspicions exacerbated tensions between the Government and the Assembly.

The National Assembly continued to monitor defence contracts and other matters concerning public services—including the alleged loss of KD 300m. as a result of speculation in stock options by the Public Institution for Social Security. In May 1998 the Assembly approved a bill requiring public officials to declare their finances, to aid transparency and to facilitate moves to counter corruption. The Assembly had thus begun to assert its authority across a range of issues, and had claimed an increasing share of decision-making powers in areas previously considered the preserve of the ruling family.

In April 1999 a confrontation between the National Assembly and the Government, arising from widespread consternation among Islamist legislators over errors that had appeared in copies of the Koran printed and distributed by the Ministries of Justice and of Awqaf (Religious Endowments) and Islamic Affairs, prompted the Amir to dissolve the Assembly. During the interval between the dissolution and the election of a new Assembly in July, the Government introduced some 60 Amiri decrees, including legislation to accelerate privatization and open up the economy to foreign investment, to reduce subsidies and social spending, and to rationalize the labour market. However, liberal members of the new Assembly blocked the decrees on constitutional grounds.

Among the most significant decrees was one proposing the extension of the franchise and eligibility to seek public office to women, for which women's groups had campaigned since the 1960s. Liberal Assembly members, although sympathetic in principle, objected to the decrees on constitutional grounds, and the measure was defeated by an alliance of conservatives and liberals in November 1999. Liberals did, however, introduce an identical bill that would permit the enfranchisement of women, and for the first time in the Assembly's history the issue was openly debated. The proposal was, however, defeated.

At the July 1999 legislative elections, government supporters retained only 12 of the 50 seats in the legislature (compared with 19 in 1996), behind Islamist candidates, with 20 seats, and liberals, with 14 seats. Independent candidates secured the remaining four seats. In the newly formed Council of Ministers, members of the ruling family retained control of the most important portfolios. Jasem al-Kharafi was elected Speaker of the National Assembly, replacing the more populist and opposition-leaning Ahmad al-Saadoun.

In January 2001 the Government submitted its resignation, amid growing disagreements among its members, apparently stemming from rivalry between two branches of the ruling family, the al-Salim and al-Jaber: the former led by the Crown Prince and Prime Minister, Sheikh Saad al-Abdullah al-Salim al-Sabah; and the latter by the Amir, Sheikh Jaber al-Ahmad al-Jaber al-Sabah, and his brother Sheikh Sabah al-Ahmad al-Jaber al-Sabah, the increasingly dominant First Deputy Prime Minister and Minister of Foreign Affairs. After two weeks of discussions, the Amir appointed a new Council of Ministers in which both Sheikh Saad and Sheikh Sabah retained their former positions.

EXTERNAL RELATIONS 1993–2001 AND THE REGIONAL IMPACT OF '9/11'

Following the Gulf War, Kuwait continued to urge the GCC states to maintain an uncompromising stance towards Iraq, and to persist in a full enforcement of the UN sanctions regime. Between 1998 and 2001, however, Iraq's regional isolation was easing, and it appeared that Kuwait was itself becoming more isolated in Arab and Islamic diplomatic circles. In 1993 Kuwait announced that it was willing to restore relations with Arab states that had supported Iraq during the Gulf War, with the exception of Jordan and the leadership of the Palestine Liberation Organization (PLO). Relations between Kuwait and Jordan began to improve from 1996. In 1997–98 Kuwait pardoned and released Jordanians imprisoned in 1991 for collaboration with the Iraqi forces and the Jordanian embassy in Kuwait reopened in March 1999.

In early 1998 there was a discernible change in the tone of Kuwaiti foreign policy, with the Minister of Foreign Affairs, Sabah al-Ahmad al-Jaber al-Sabah, declaring that Kuwait no longer opposed Iraqi participation in Arab summit meetings. Subsequently, the National Assembly hosted a seminar that discussed the future of Iraqi-Kuwaiti relations, with the participation of Iraqis opposed to the then Iraqi Government. Although Kuwait's policy towards Saddam Hussain's Government had not changed, there was an implicit recognition that Kuwait could not rely solely and indefinitely on the defence umbrella provided by the USA. The shift in Kuwait's policy tone continued, with the Minister of Foreign Affairs declaring, at the Arab League summit conference in Amman, Jordan, in March 2001, that sanctions against Iraq should be revoked. The new Kuwaiti position was usually prefaced with the stipulation that Iraq should comply with all pertinent UN resolutions, but the general perception that Iraq should be rehabilitated was gathering support in the Arab world, reinforced by heightened concerns about the humanitarian cost to Iraqi civilians of maintaining the sanctions regime, by mounting opposition to continuing US and British air strikes inside Iraq, and by renewed Arab unity in support of a second Palestinian *intifada* against Israeli occupation after September 2000. Attempts to repair relations between the Palestinian leadership and the Kuwaiti Government were under way before the *intifada* began, and a meeting between the President of the Palestinian (National) Authority (PA), Yasser Arafat, and the Kuwaiti Minister of Foreign Affairs had already taken place. However, Kuwait's relations with the Palestinian leadership remained cool, and Kuwait was the only Arab state not to be represented at Arafat's funeral in November 2004. None the less, relations appeared likely to improve after the PA Prime Minister, Mahmoud Abbas, on a landmark visit to the emirate in December, apologized for the stance that the PLO had taken during Iraq's invasion of Kuwait. The embassy of Palestine in Kuwait reopened in April 2013 after having been closed since 1990.

Following the Amir's attendance at the summit meeting of the Organization of the Islamic Conference (now the Organization of Islamic Cooperation, see p. 1155) in Tehran, Iran, in November 1997, relations between Kuwait and Iran improved significantly.

Following the attacks on the US mainland of 11 September 2001, the Kuwaiti Government expressed its readiness to take immediate action against individuals and groups suspected of involvement with those held responsible. The Kuwaiti-born spokesman for al-Qa'ida, Sulayman Abu Ghaith, was divested of his Kuwaiti citizenship in October. Kuwait expressed solidarity with the USA and facilitated the US military build-up in the region, falling short, though, of a commitment of troops. Formally, the Government, in common with other Arab states, expressed opposition to bilateral US-British action, but this position was not reflected in any apparent tension with the USA. At the Arab League summit held in Beirut, Lebanon, in March 2002, Arab leaders reiterated their opposition to any US-led military campaign in Iraq. The head of the Iraqi delegation thanked delegates for opposing US threats against Iraq and announced that Iraq would henceforth agree to respect the sovereignty of Kuwait, and guarantee its independence, stability and security within its internationally recognized borders.

After the US-led occupation of Iraq and the ousting of the regime of Iraqi President Saddam Hussain in 2003, the resumption of diplomatic relations between Kuwait and Iraq was announced in August 2004.

THE 2003 ELECTIONS AND THE 2006 SUCCESSION CRISIS

Significant political reforms were finally introduced after legislative elections in July 2003. The election campaign was overshadowed by the US-led military campaign in Iraq, which was largely conducted from Kuwaiti territory. The elections were mainly fought over the issue of patronage. Opposition political groups—both liberals and moderate Islamists—lost ground, while gains were made by independents and a small group of Salafi Islamists. The independents were perceived to be aligned with the Government, although that did not mean that the Government's agenda of market reform, privatization and foreign investment in petroleum operations would necessarily gain wide support. Opposition to this agenda was widespread and was expected to continue to some extent in the National Assembly.

Voter turnout in the elections was low, at 45% of the electorate. Indeed, the pattern of the gains and losses in the polls pointed to widespread disaffection with the entire political process, and gave impetus to proposals for electoral reform. The constituency system then in force was seen to have encouraged the rise of a fragmented personal style of politics, in which large numbers of candidates competed through a narrow personal and family following and through promises to individuals, rather than on general principles and public discourse. Moreover, the process was open to corruption, vote-buying and other irregularities, such as fictitious changes of voters' addresses.

Following the elections, the Crown Prince relinquished the position of Prime Minister. The appointment of Sheikh Sabah al-Ahmad as his replacement brought an unprecedented separation of the post of Prime Minister and the position of Crown Prince, and provided some encouragement to reformists after their heavy electoral losses. With Sheikhs Ahmad al-Fahd al-Ahmad and Muhammad Sabah al-Salim al-Sabah as members (the latter as Minister of Foreign Affairs), the Council of Ministers now included two of the main new generation of al-Sabah princes.

In May 2005 the National Assembly finally approved a bill giving women the right to vote, stand for election and take high public office, after the Amir lent his full support to the measure. Kuwait's first female minister, Dr Massouma al-Mubarak, was subsequently appointed (as Minister of Planning and Minister of State for Administrative Development Affairs). Discriminatory legislation governing areas such as women's employment, access to subsidized housing and ability to extend visas to a foreign husband continued to be debated, but enfranchisement was a major political transformation. Women took part in national elections for the first time in June 2006, both as voters and candidates, but it was not until 2009 that the first women, al-Mubarak, Aseel al-Awadhi and Salwa al-Jassar (all professors at Kuwait University) and Rola Dashti, were elected to the Assembly. Their election marked a major victory for civil rights and for liberal reform in general in Kuwait. In October of that year the Constitutional Court ruled that Kuwaiti women need not wear a *hijab* (headscarf) to vote or sit in the Assembly, overturning legislation introduced by conservative Islamist legislators in 2005. It also ruled that women had the right to obtain passports without their husbands' approval, thus amending the 1962 Constitution. The Court's rulings constituted a major defeat for conservative Islamists, who had sought to counter the women's rights agenda.

Meanwhile, the increasingly poor health of both the Amir and the Crown Prince motivated the activation of an al-Sabah family council. Great uncertainty over the future political leadership of Kuwait began with the hospitalization of the Amir in September 2001, following a cerebral haemorrhage that incapacitated him until January 2002. While the Amir subsequently recovered to maintain a light schedule of duties, the Crown Prince's own health continued to deteriorate. There followed frank discussion of the possibility of redefining the role of the ruling family and of restructuring its responsibilities. In late 2005 disputes within the ruling family erupted into the open, and there were demands for a more direct leadership role for the ruling family through an advisory panel. Meanwhile, by the end of the year the left-leaning National

Democratic Alliance and the Popular Action Bloc were together leading the campaign for electoral reform.

On 15 January 2006 the Amir, Sheikh Jaber, died, leaving an ailing Crown Prince who was incapable of discharging the duties of Amir. Sheikh Saad al-Abdullah al-Salim al-Sabah was initially unwilling to abdicate, but on 24 January the Prime Minister and de facto ruler of Kuwait, Sheikh Sabah, convened the National Assembly and forced the abdication of Sheikh Saad on medical grounds. Sheikh Sabah was then chosen as Amir by the same Assembly. This unprecedented event was seen by some Kuwaitis as a historic shift towards constitutional monarchy, because of the direct involvement of the Assembly in the succession process. The accession of Sheikh Sabah was followed by the announcement that the former First Deputy Prime Minister and Minister of the Interior and of Defence, Sheikh Nawaf al-Ahmad al-Jaber al-Sabah, was to become the new Crown Prince. Subsequently, the Amir's nephew, Sheikh Nasser al-Muhammad al-Ahmad al-Sabah, was appointed Prime Minister. These appointments consolidated the highest offices within the al-Jaber branch of the ruling family—and particularly in the hands of another elderly Amir—while keeping most of the younger al-Sabahs from the highest political echelons.

POLITICAL INFIGHTING: THE PREMIERSHIP OF SHEIKH NASSER AL-MUHAMMAD

The new Amir responded to demands for political reform by apparently reneging on an initial undertaking to reduce the number of constituencies from 25 to five. When members of the National Assembly expressed their intention to question the new Prime Minister on the matter, the Amir dissolved the Assembly and called new elections for the end of June 2006, based on the old system. However, the Amir's seeming bid to curb the demands for change failed, as reform became the main election issue. A group of 29 legislators formed an Alliance for Change that mitigated the usual antagonisms among Islamist, liberal, leftist and populist tendencies, instead concentrating on electoral reform and fighting corruption. The Alliance duly won 34 seats in the Assembly, and the electoral constituency reform received legislative approval three weeks later. The new Government, subsequently formed by Sheikh Nasser, complied with the momentum for electoral reform, but it was thought unlikely that a more radical political reform would have an easy passage. The Government secured the election of its preferred candidate, Jasem al-Kharafi, as Speaker of the National Assembly, despite the support of the majority of elected members for the opposition Popular Action Bloc leader and erstwhile Speaker, Ahmad al-Saadoun. The Council of Ministers resigned in March 2007, after eight months in office, to prevent a vote of no confidence against the former Minister of Health, Sheikh Ahmad Abdullah al-Sabah, over corruption allegations. The successor administration retained most of the key ministers (excluding Sheikh Ahmad) in the same posts. In June the Minister of Oil and the Minister of Communications and Minister of State for National Assembly Affairs both resigned shortly before they were due to appear before a special meeting of the Assembly convened to question them about corruption. In August the Minister of Health also stood down, following allegations of government mismanagement in the wake of a devastating fire at Jahra Hospital in which two patients died.

Further allegations of corruption against public figures followed in early 2008. The entire Council of Ministers tendered its resignation in March, protesting that the deteriorating relationship between the Government and the Islamist-dominated National Assembly was causing gridlock in the legislative process. The unpopularity of the Prime Minister, Sheikh Nasser, and his policies with the majority of legislators was cited as a main reason for the impasse. The Amir responded by dissolving the Assembly and calling elections for May. The elections were to be the first since the adoption into law of the new, five-constituency system in July 2006. The old system of 25 constituencies (in force since 1980) had encouraged voting along tribal or sectarian lines which, in recent years, had undermined national unity. Under the new system intended to stem the problem of vote-buying, each citizen was granted a maximum of four votes in each constituency, and candidates were required to obtain a greater number of votes to win. In April 2008 the Electoral Commission effectively banned the popular, albeit illegal, tribal primaries. In the following month Kuwaiti police detained a number of men from the al-Mutair tribe who were accused of holding such primaries. Thousands of people from the al-Mutair tribe protested outside the police station where the detainees were being held.

In the May 2008 elections, which attracted a turnout of 59.4% of the eligible electorate, Islamists fared better than they had done in 2006: Sunni Islamists secured 21 seats, the Popular Action Bloc won four seats, and other Shi'a candidates took five seats. Liberals and their allies won seven seats, and independent candidates 13. As in 2006, none of the female candidates was elected. Sheikh Nasser subsequently formed his fourth Council of Ministers since 2006, including two women.

As the opposition of Islamist and Popular Action Bloc legislators to the Government's legislative programme continued, in November 2008 three Salafi legislators demanded that the Prime Minister submit to parliamentary interpellation and a no confidence vote. Although Sheikh Nasser could have easily survived the motion, he chose instead to submit the resignation of his Government. The Amir rejected the idea of holding fresh elections, and invited Sheikh Nasser to form a new cabinet. The limited extent of the reorganization (only two new members were appointed) prompted a walkout by a group of 12 National Assembly members. By early 2009 the Government and the Assembly were once again in deadlock. In March 2009, after Assembly members again asked to question the Prime Minister and hold a no confidence vote, the Prime Minister resigned once again, triggering the Assembly's dissolution by the Amir. Elections—the third in three years—were subsequently held in May. Turnout was slightly reduced, at 58%. A large gain for the liberals apparently reflected voters' increasing exasperation with the Islamists' obstructionism. The new Council of Ministers, still headed by Sheikh Nasser, included few changes apart from the notable appointment to the cabinet of a member of the moderate Islamic Constitutional Movement (ICM), the Kuwaiti branch of the Muslim Brotherhood.

In December 2009 Prime Minister Sheikh Nasser agreed for the first time to answer questions in a closed session of the National Assembly about alleged corruption. After the questioning, 10 legislators submitted a motion of no confidence, which the Prime Minister survived by a vote of 35 to 13, with one abstention. A further attempt to question the Prime Minister in June 2010, this time concerning alleged negligence in his duties, was cancelled after National Assembly legislators were unable to agree on whether this should be in a public or private session.

In late 2009 a prominent former editor of the conservative *al-Watan* newspaper, Muhammad Abd al-Qader al-Jasem, publicly criticized the Prime Minister's governance of the country, and demanded his resignation. Sheikh Nasser filed a private lawsuit against al-Jasem for slander, which led to al-Jasem's arrest in December and detention (for 12 days). His six-month prison sentence, handed down in April 2010 (along with a US $17,500 fine), was suspended on appeal. In May al-Jasem was arrested again, this time on charges of defaming the ruling family and Government, undermining the Amir's status, spreading false information and damaging Kuwait's national interests. He was released on bail in June, following pressure from several international human rights organizations, sentenced again, in November, to one year's imprisonment for defaming the Prime Minister, and released again on appeal after two months.

Meanwhile, the Prime Minister also filed a lawsuit against the head of the liberal National Democratic Alliance, Khaled al-Fadalah, accusing him of money laundering. In June 2010 al-Fadalah was sentenced to three months' imprisonment, although he was released on appeal after 10 days. At a press conference in July, the Prime Minister and Minister of Information stated that public criticism of the Amir, the Prime Minister, government ministers and countries with which Kuwait had close relations undermined 'national unity', and that the Government intended to amend the press and publications law accordingly. In February 2011, under pressure from a growing number of legislators in the National Assembly, the Amir ordered that the 600 lawsuits filed by the Ministry of Information against the local media and other government critics be abandoned.

In February 2010 the National Assembly finally approved the Prime Minister's US $129,000m. five-year development plan, which had long been delayed by conservative opposition. The plan, which took effect in April, envisaged the development of Kuwait into a regional trade and financial centre, with the construction of a $77,000m. business hub at Subiya, linked to the capital by a new causeway; the new container port on Bubiyan Island (see *The Kuwait–Iraq Border: Ongoing Problems*); a 518-km railway network (part of a wider GCC railway project); and a 171-km metro system. The plan also aimed to expand the role of the private sector in developing the country's infrastructure and diversifying the national economy, both of which had hitherto been state-dominated.

REGIONAL TENSIONS WITH IRAN, 2004–10

As sectarian tensions grew regionally, Kuwait retained a relationship with Iran. In 2006 the Iranian President, Mahmoud Ahmadinejad, made an official visit to Kuwait to discuss issues including gas and water exports to Kuwait, as well as the two countries' shared maritime fields. The visit came at a time of rising international tension as a result of claims, particularly by the USA, that Iran's nuclear programme was not intended for peaceful purposes (see the chapter on Iran). The Kuwaiti Government opposed a military strike carried out against Iran and was unwilling to permit US forces to use Kuwait as a base of operations for such an attack. In February 2007 the Deputy Prime Minister and Minister of Foreign Affairs, Sheikh Dr Muhammad al-Sabah al-Salim, made an official visit to Tehran and held talks with the Iranian President about regional security and Iran's nuclear programme. He announced Kuwait's support for the programme, believing it to be peaceful, and stated that the stand-off between the USA and Iran could only be resolved by negotiation. However, the spirit of closer co-operation was marred by an assault on a Kuwaiti diplomat in Tehran soon afterwards. Sheikh Muhammad announced that the incident constituted an attack on Kuwait itself, and demanded a written apology. In July 2007, in an effort to gain support against Iran and strengthen regional security, the USA announced a US $20,000m. package of military aid and arms sales to Kuwait and the five other GCC states. Although Kuwait continued to oppose a military strike against Iran, it did support the UN's demands that Iran disclose the details of its nuclear programme and open its nuclear facilities to inspectors of the International Atomic Energy Agency (IAEA). In November 2010, however, as a result of Iran's persistent refusal to open its facilities to IAEA inspectors, Kuwait agreed to comply with UN sanctions on Iran designed to limit its nuclear programme. Meanwhile, in January 2008 Sheikh Muhammad attended the first meeting of the Kuwait-Iran Economic Commission in Tehran, where he met both his Iranian counterpart and President Ahmadinejad.

In November 2009 Prime Minister Sheikh Nasser al-Muhammad visited Tehran for talks with President Ahmadinejad, the first Kuwaiti prime ministerial visit to Iran since the fall of the Shah in 1979. In May 2010, however, the discovery and arrest of an alleged Iranian-led 'spy cell' of six men and one woman in Kuwait provoked a further dispute between the two countries, and members of the National Assembly immediately called for the expulsion of the Iranian ambassador. Later that month the Iranian ambassador returned to Tehran, having completed his tour of duty, but Tehran chose not to replace him (a move that was widely interpreted as a form of protest over the spying accusations). At the end of the trial of the seven accused, which took place in a closed court during August 2010–March 2011, two Iranians and a Kuwaiti national were sentenced to death; a Syrian man and a Kuwaiti *bidoun* were sentenced to life imprisonment (all five had been serving in the Kuwaiti army prior to their arrest); and an Iranian man and woman were acquitted. Iran continued to insist that the accusations were false. In April 2011 the Kuwaiti Government recalled its ambassador in Tehran and expelled three Iranian diplomats from Kuwait. Iran, in turn, expelled three Kuwaiti diplomats over the following weeks. In May 2011 the Iranian Minister of Foreign Affairs visited Kuwait in an attempt to improve relations. During his visit he announced that the two countries had agreed to exchange ambassadors again; the envoys were in place by late May. However, also in late May it was reported that an alleged joint Iranian-Hezbollah 'spy ring' had been discovered in Kuwait.

Kuwait welcomed the election of Hassan Rouhani to the Iranian presidency in June 2013. Kuwait has remained a supporter of a conciliatory approach with Iran—an approach that was particularly evident in its cautious response to the proposals made by the US Administration of President Donald Trump in mid-2018 for a new 'Strategic Alliance in the Middle East' that would explicitly seek to challenge Iran militarily. With the escalation of tensions between the USA and Iran in May 2019, the Amir called on the Kuwaiti population to 'be ready for any eventuality', including that of armed conflict. Kuwait reacted with caution in June 2021 to the election of the conservative Ebrahim Raisi as the new President of Iran.

POPULAR MOBILIZATIONS AND THE 'ARAB SPRING' (2010–12)

Kuwait was already in a state of political mobilization as what came to be known as the 'Arab Spring' spread across the region. In December 2010 Sheikh Nasser alienated many by attempting to deprive an Islamist legislator, Faisal al-Muslim, of his parliamentary immunity, in order to file a lawsuit against him for having accused the Prime Minister of corruption. Parliamentary immunity is a fundamental constitutional safeguard of Kuwait's democracy, and the Prime Minister's action prompted the establishment of a constitutional defence coalition comprising one-half of the legislators in the National Assembly. A popular movement was formed to demand Sheikh Nasser's removal from office, and five people were injured when security forces intervened, on the orders of the Prime Minister, to quell a public protest in Kuwait City. A vote of no confidence was subsequently held in the Assembly in late December, with 22 legislators opposing the Prime Minister, 25 supporting him, and one abstaining. This was the second motion of no confidence against Sheikh Nasser in just over a year.

In January 2011 Sheikh Nasser was questioned by legislators in the National Assembly over the police action in the previous month. Furthermore, the Deputy Prime Minister and Minister of the Interior, Sheikh Jaber Khaled al-Jaber al-Sabah, was forced to resign following reports that police had tortured to death a Kuwaiti citizen, Muhammad Ghazzai al-Mutairi. The Amir replaced Sheikh Jaber with Sheikh Ahmad al-Homoud al-Jaber al-Sabah, a senior member of the ruling family who had previously served as Minister of the Interior in 1991–92 and as Minister of Defence in 1994. In March 2011 a total of 18 police officers and two civilians were tried for the illegal detention, torture and murder of al-Mutairi. In the same month there was a renewal of demands by opposition legislators and political activists for the Prime Minister to step down. Opposition legislators filed a request for the Prime Minister and three other government ministers to appear before the National Assembly. A political crisis ensued, resulting in the resignation of the Prime Minister and the Government at the end of March in order to avoid questioning in the Assembly.

In April 2011 the Amir asked Sheikh Nasser to form a new government—his seventh in seven years. The Prime Minister reappointed five of six ministers to whom the opposition had earlier objected. Opposition legislators again filed a petition to question Sheikh Nasser, but the Government submitted a request to the National Assembly to postpone the questioning by a year while it referred the matter to the Constitutional Court, which the Assembly approved. As a result of the growing frustration with the Prime Minister and his Government, political activists and opposition legislators called for a 'Day of Rage' rally to be held outside the Assembly building in May. The Government arranged a heavy security presence in anticipation of the event, and the protest passed without incident. In November more than 50,000 protesters took to the streets—

with some briefly taking over the Assembly building—to demand the ouster of the Prime Minister on grounds of corruption. This followed the Government's successful efforts to block a further request by some members of the Assembly to summon Sheikh Nasser for questioning. Although Kuwaitis did not echo the call of revolutionaries elsewhere in the region for the overthrow of the regime, many did demand movement towards a constitutional monarchy. The protests led, on 28 November, to the resignation of the Prime Minister, who was replaced by Sheikh Jaber al-Mubarak al-Sabah, and in early December the Amir again dissolved the Assembly.

In February and March 2011 there were major protests by the *bidoun*, who numbered 106,000 in 2010, according to the figures of the institution in charge of the issue, the Central System for the Remedy of the Situations of the Illegal Residents (CSRSIR), which was established in November 2010. The *bidoun* demanded an end to the policy that deemed them illegal residents, deprived them of most of their rights and refused to consider their claim to Kuwaiti citizenship. The *bidoun* issue had remained unsolved for decades. In 2000 the Kuwaiti Government had adopted a law on 'gradual naturalization', which pledged to grant Kuwaiti citizenship and its associated privileges to 2,000 people a year. However, the annual quota of naturalizations has not been transparently handled. The committee in charge of the *bidoun* cited a figure of 3,517 individuals naturalized for the years 2000 and 2001.

In April 2006 another piecemeal measure to manage the issue of the *bidoun* was introduced, offering identity cards to 13,000 individuals and giving the card holders some basic access to social services. In 2007 it also issued temporary driving licences. The measure did not satisfy campaigners, including the National Assembly's Human Rights Committee. The Assembly elected in June 2006 established a new parliamentary committee for *bidoun* affairs, with the aim of alleviating what were regarded as inhumane government practices. In December 2009 an Assembly session that was due to approve a draft law granting full civil and social rights to some 100,000–120,000 *bidoun* living in Kuwait was cancelled when only five ministers and 26 legislators attended (two fewer than the required quorum).

With the onset of the Arab Spring, the *bidoun*, inspired by mass mobilization elsewhere, took to the streets, flouting Article 12 of the Public Gatherings Law of 1979 that forbade non-nationals from participating in demonstrations. In February 2011 more than 1,000 *bidoun* joined a three-day protest in a *bidoun*-majority district of the city of al-Jahra (north-west of Kuwait City) and other *bidoun*-populated locations, demanding that the Government address their grievances. Security forces broke up the protests using batons, smoke bombs, tear gas and water cannons, and made several arrests. A number of legislators responded to the protests by submitting a bill to the National Assembly that would grant the *bidoun* basic civil rights (such as access to free education, medical care and employment), but the Government did not permit debate of the proposals. In response, further protests broke out in al-Jahra in March, involving some 500 people.

In March 2011 the Council of Ministers granted the *bidoun* a set of 11 'benefits and civil, social, and humanitarian facilities'. The CSRSIR adopted a new system of identity cards giving access to these benefits and facilities (including education and health care): a two-year card was granted to those *bidoun* registered in the 1965 census or having proof of residence in the country from that year or before (the Government estimated that 34,000 *bidoun* met the eligibility requirements to be naturalized as Kuwaiti citizens), while a one-year card was granted to the rest of the *bidoun*. However, the length of validity of most of the cards was reduced, and in 2019 it was reported that most cards were valid for only three months.

In January 2012 the Ministry of the Interior issued a statement banning all rallies and protests by *bidoun*. None the less, the *bidoun*'s mobilization, similarly to campaigns for the right to education, continued in the following years, despite the ban and waves of arrests of leading *bidoun* activists. Legislation passed in March 2013 and August 2019 to naturalize 4,000 'foreigners' (rather than stateless citizens) prioritized children born to Kuwaiti mothers and foreign fathers.

Several cases of *bidoun* committing suicide in an act of desperation against being denied civil documentation and justice were reported in 2019. In August a number of *bidoun* started a hunger strike, which lasted 12 days, in protest at their detention for expressing their opinions peacefully. In January 2020 a court handed down prison sentences to three *bidoun* (including one imposed *in absentia*) and acquitted 13 others, who were released on bail but had their means of communication confiscated. In April 2019, at the request of the Government, Kuwaiti banks had suspended the accounts of *bidoun* individuals who could not provide the necessary documents to renew their identity cards or who did not acknowledge the foreign nationality attributed to them. In February 2021 the suicide of a 12-year-old *bidoun* boy sparked renewed outrage in Kuwait. The suicide of a *bidoun* teenager in December led to the resumption of *bidoun* protest action. Following sit-ins organized every week from February 2022 in 'Freedom Square' in the Tayma district of al-Jahra, six *bidoun* activists conducted a hunger strike from 28 March to 14 April in front of the Sulaibiya police station to demand recognition of their fundamental rights. The protests were suspended following promises made by political forces and civil society organizations to find a solution to the decades-long issue.

THE POLITICAL AFTERMATH OF THE 'ARAB SPRING'

The parliamentary elections held on 2 February 2012 resulted in a decisive victory for the opposition and produced a loose alliance between Sunni Islamist and tribal legislators—with the Sunni Islamists winning 14 seats and tribal candidates (about one-half of whom were also Islamists) taking 21 seats. Liberal candidates performed poorly, and none of the 23 female candidates was elected. The number of Shi'a legislators, generally pro-Government, fell from nine to seven. Ahmad al-Saadoun was subsequently elected as the Speaker of the Assembly. A predictably fiery clash between the National Assembly and the Government emerged in the following months—beginning with the opposition legislators' demand for one-half of the ministerial positions in Sheikh Jaber's new Government, and rejection of the counter-offer of four portfolios. The Minister of Finance and the Minister of Social Affairs and Labour resigned in May and June, respectively, under pressure from parliament.

With the inauguration of the new National Assembly, Islamist issues moved to the forefront of Kuwaiti politics. In March 2012 a court suspended publication of the *al-Dar* newspaper for three months for allegedly fomenting sectarian strife. In June a Shi'a, Hamad al-Naqi, was convicted and sentenced to 10 years' imprisonment for allegedly insulting the Prophet Muhammad and his wife via a social networking website. In May the Assembly approved legislation imposing the death penalty for persons convicted of blasphemy. In the same month the Amir blocked a proposal by 31 legislators requiring that all legislation should conform to *Shari'a* law.

These political tensions escalated into crisis in mid-June 2012, when the Government, invoking Article 106 of the Constitution, announced that it would suspend the National Assembly for one month. (The suspension would thus abut Ramadan, during which period the National Assembly is typically closed.) The Government's action occurred a day before the Minister of Interior, Sheikh Ahmad al-Homoud al-Jaber al-Sabah, was due to appear before parliament for questioning. Although Kuwaiti rulers had previously dissolved the National Assembly seven times (twice unconstitutionally), this was the first suspension of parliament in Kuwait's history. Two days after the suspension was announced, the Constitutional Court—ruling on a challenge to the decree that had dissolved parliament in December 2011—took unprecedented and still more dramatic action, declaring the February 2012 elections void and ordering the reinstatement of the National Assembly previously elected in 2009. However, more than one-half of the restored parliament's members immediately resigned, in protest against the decision. Fresh elections were subsequently scheduled for 1 December 2012.

In October 2012 the Amir issued a decree allowing voters to cast ballots for just one candidate (as opposed to four).

Opposition groups argued against the unilateral nature of the decree and its timing, and expressed concern that the restriction would inhibit their ability to form coalitions. Hundreds of thousands of Kuwaitis protested in a 'March of Dignity', said to be the largest demonstration in Kuwait's history. The opposition's appeal for a boycott resulted in a significantly low turnout, of 43%, at the elections. A notable outcome of voting was that Shi'a representation increased from seven seats to 17. Three women were elected. This new National Assembly proved no less confrontational, and several ministers resigned in May 2013 rather than submit to parliamentary questioning.

In June 2013 the Constitutional Court rejected an opposition challenge to the one voter, one vote decree. However, it again ordered the dissolution of the National Assembly on procedural grounds. This forced new elections, which were set for 27 July. Voting was thus to take place during Ramadan, in which period formal politics typically halts in Kuwait. While some voters, including many Islamists, continued the boycott, others did not. The brief coalition of Islamists, tribal members and liberals that had mobilized large numbers of demonstrators had by now collapsed. Voter turnout was recorded at 52.5% (still below historical levels). More than one-half of those elected were new to parliament. Tribal candidates won 10 seats, after leaders from the Ajman, Mutair and Awazim tribes publicly urged members to vote. Liberals, who had boycotted the previous elections, won three seats. Shi'a Islamists won only eight seats. Meanwhile, two women (one Shi'a, one liberal) were also elected, including Safa al-Hashem, the first woman to win a seat in consecutive elections. Marzouq al-Ghanim, an independent legislator from a powerful merchant family (and the nephew of Jasem al-Kharafi, a former Speaker of the National Assembly), was elected Speaker of the Assembly. Following the elections, the Amir reappointed Sheikh Jaber al-Mubarak as Prime Minister, and a new Government was sworn into office on 4 August 2013. The cabinet was reorganized in January 2014, with two more Islamists being added to its membership.

Contention in the Assembly, however, continued. By May 2014 five Assembly members had announced their resignations over the Speaker's decision to reject their demands to question the Prime Minister.

As public unrest grew, and against the background of the 'Arab Spring', Kuwait's rulers responded with increasing harshness, focusing in particular on social media. In June 2013 a Kuwaiti woman, Huda al-Ajami, was sentenced to 11 years' imprisonment for posting messages deemed insulting to the Amir and to a religious sect. This followed the sentencing of nine Kuwaiti men in the course of the previous year for views expressed via social media sites. However, seven activists, including al-Ajami, were released during customary Ramadan pardons. In December a court acquitted 70 defendants who had entered the National Assembly in November 2011 amid protests outside the building demanding the Prime Minister's resignation.

The Government also acted to stem dissent from other quarters. In August 2013 it cancelled the television show of a well-known cleric over comments that it regarded as inflammatory and promoting the al-Qa'ida-affiliated Jabhat al-Nusra (al-Nusra Front) rebel group in the Syrian Arab Republic. It also deported nine Egyptians who participated in pro-Muslim Brotherhood rallies. In April 2014 a Kuwaiti court temporarily suspended two newspapers, *al-Watan* (together with two television stations it owned) and *Alam al-Yawm*, over articles published about an alleged coup plot. In July the Government revoked the nationality of Ahmad Jaber al-Shammari, a naturalized Kuwaiti and owner of a pro-opposition television station and newspaper, as well as that of an Islamist former legislator, Abdallah al-Barghash, and his three siblings. A further 10 citizens were divested of their Kuwaiti nationality in August, among them a number of opposition figures, including a spokesman for the Popular Action Bloc. By late 2014 the Government had also become increasingly concerned about supporters of Islamic State, arresting 11 in September.

In 2015 the Government continued to arrest and detain political activists who engaged in dissent via social, print or broadcast media, as well as through public protest. In April the Government arrested a prominent Shi'a attorney and former parliamentary legislator, Khaled al-Shatti, for tweets on social media site Twitter that were critical of Saudi Arabia's military intervention in Yemen. The Government also continued to revoke dissidents' citizenship, and in May it dissolved the Kuwait Transparency Society, a human rights group. In June the Ministry of Information revoked the licence of the Kuwait Media Group, closing down three television stations linked to the newspaper *al-Watan*. Kuwait's Islamist groups, both the ICM and Salafi, in view of regional developments, tempered their demands for greater Islamization of Kuwaiti society, favouring closer ties with a wide range of opposition groups.

In June 2015 a Saudi citizen with ties to Islamic State launched a suicide attack on the Shi'a Imam al-Sadiq Mosque, killing 27 and wounding over 200. This was the worst terrorist attack in Kuwait's history. The Amir expressed his solidarity with the worshippers, attending a joint Sunni-Shi'a prayer at Kuwait's Grand Mosque shortly afterwards, together with many prominent Kuwaitis. In July the National Assembly passed a number of security measures including US $400m. in emergency spending for the Ministry of the Interior. In August the Government announced that it had uncovered a terrorist cell and arrested three Kuwaiti nationals. In the same month legislation was proposed to make it mandatory for all citizens and foreign residents to be included in a national DNA database, prompting international criticism; the proposals were subsequently abandoned after the Constitutional Court ruled them to be unconstitutional.

The authorities detained and prosecuted civil society activists and critics of the Government, including Kuwaiti nationals, under provisions in cyber-crimes legislation passed in 2016 and the penal code that criminalizes speech that is deemed to threaten state security, to offend the Amir or to criticize neighbouring countries and allies. Increasingly, the Government also targeted those citizens who criticized the actions of Kuwait's regional allies, whether the Saudi-led military action in Yemen, the Bahraini Government's continuing attack on dissidents, or in one case tweets deemed insulting to Dubai's Heir Apparent. The Government announced a 'zero tolerance' policy on criticism directed at other countries and their rulers which could harm Kuwait's foreign relations, following its accession (despite the absence of ratification by the National Assembly) to the GCC Internal Security Pact. A number of dissidents were arrested at the request of Saudi authorities, beginning with the Salafist Hakim al-Mutairi. On 5 July 2021 the prominent Kuwaiti poet and businessman Jamal al-Sayer was arrested and detained over comments he had made on his Twitter account that were critical of the ruling family. He was charged with insulting the Amir and spreading 'fake news'.

ECONOMIC AUSTERITY AND SOCIAL TENSIONS (2014–20)

Kuwait's ability to address its domestic problems through government spending continued, but these efforts were hindered by a sharp fall in oil prices from late 2014. In October 2015 the Minister of Finance announced the introduction of taxes beginning in 2016. In March of that year a 10% tax on corporate profits was announced. However, the austerity drive met with resistance when applied to citizens. In April the Kuwait Oil Company Workers' Union launched a three-day strike, following the announcement of changes in pay that would adversely affect oil workers. Protests, of which there had been few over the decades of economic prosperity, were generally led by the lowest-paid foreign workers, who were usually deported. In April 2010 Kuwait introduced a minimum wage of KD 60 per month for workers. New legislation approved in July 2016 also set up maximum working hours, overtime pay and a system for dispute resolution for the 660,000 domestic workers who constituted around one-quarter of the foreign labour force.

The economic downturn heightened tensions between foreigners and Kuwaiti nationals. In June 2013 the Government began to implement a pilot plan in al-Jahra to ban expatriates from attending public hospitals in the morning, with the intention eventually to extend the ban to other facilities. In the context of budget cuts approved in January 2015, there was a rise in populism, including hostility to the presence of foreigners. This was embodied in particular by the only female member of the National Assembly, Safa al-Hashem (elected in 2012), who defended the introduction of specific taxes for foreigners (such as value-added tax or road tax) and the end of free health care services for non-nationals. Economic austerity measures and subsidy reductions, such as the liberalization of water and electricity prices in April 2016 (multiplying the tariffs by up to sevenfold) primarily affected foreigners and foreign companies. Furthermore, from October 2017 the cost of health care for expatriates was increased.

On 26 November 2016 early elections were held, following the National Assembly's dissolution by the Amir in October. The Amir cited the profound security threat and widespread instability affecting the region, although disagreement between the Government and the Assembly over economic policy was widely considered to have played a role in the decision. Voter turnout was high (at a reported 70%) and opposition candidates, both Islamist and liberal, did well, winning 24 of the 50 seats. Their victory was seen as a protest against the Government's austerity measures and against citizenship revocations (they subsequently convinced the Amir to reinstate the citizenship of opposition figures). The Shi'a Islamist bloc fell from nine to six seats. Sheikh Sabah inaugurated a new Council of Ministers on 10 December 2016, retaining Sheikh Jaber as Prime Minister.

The Government's crackdown on the opposition continued. In November 2017 the Court of Appeal convicted more than 70 people, among them former and current members of the Assembly, for their involvement in the storming of the National Assembly in November 2011. (They had been acquitted in 2013 but the Government appealed against the verdicts.) They were sentenced on charges including protesting illegally and received prison terms of between one and nine years. In July 2018 the Court of Cassation handed down a final verdict in the case of the storming of the National Assembly: it sentenced eight parliamentarians to three-and-a-half years' imprisonment, two of whom were incumbent members of the Assembly, and handed down similar sentences to five activists, while acquitting 17 other defendants. In anticipation of these verdicts, a large number of Kuwaiti opposition figures, including a leading opponent of the Government, Musallam al-Barrak, went into exile in Turkey (officially known as Türkiye from June 2022), followed by many more after the announcement of the verdict.

In the National Assembly, opposition members (mainly tribal, Islamist and independent legislators) continued to oppose the Government's economic austerity measures. After 10 members of the Assembly prepared to instigate a vote of no confidence against the Minister of Information for alleged violation of budgetary and legislative rules, the cabinet resigned in October 2017. The Amir invited Sheikh Jaber to form a new government, which was announced in December; the Amir's eldest son, Sheikh Nasser Sabah al-Ahmad al-Sabah (hitherto the head of the Royal Court), was appointed as First Deputy Prime Minister and Minister of Defence. However, the appointment of a new cabinet did not appease the opposition.

Meanwhile, the Government launched the New Kuwait Vision 2035 strategy in January 2017, with the primary objectives of attracting foreign direct investment (FDI), encouraging economic diversification and investing in the education and training of a skilled workforce. It also planned to develop five islands into an economic free zone, linking Kuwait to Central Asia and Europe, in a project costing US $160,000m. The large infrastructure project, called 'Silk City', was to be overseen by First Deputy Prime Minister Nasser al-Sabah, who in his remit as Minister of Defence introduced a number of policies, including in July 2017 the reinstitution of mandatory military service, approved in 2015, which had been suspended in 2001. As part of the project's first phase, Kuwait inaugurated the Sheikh Jaber al-Ahmad al-Sabah Causeway, in May 2019.

Several high-level officials, including former ministers and members of the royal family, were tried on grounds of corruption in 2019. In June the former director of the Public Social Security Institution, Fahad al-Rajaan (who died in 2022), and his wife, who were both in exile in London, were sentenced *in absentia* to life imprisonment for embezzlement of public funds. Corruption scandals also affected the Port Fund, a private equity investment fund, which was accused of wasting US $1,600m. of public money in a case in which two members of the royal family could face US sanctions.

Corruption cases involving members of the Government led to the fall of Prime Minister Jaber al-Mubarak al-Sabah in mid-November 2019, two days before the Minister of Defence and son of the Amir, Nasser al-Sabah, accused his predecessor Khaled al-Jarrah al-Sabah (now the Minister of the Interior), of embezzling more than US $795m. from the Kuwaiti Army Fund. In the following week the Amir announced the appointment of outgoing Minister of Foreign Affairs Sheikh Sabah al-Khaled al-Sabah as the new Prime Minister. The new Government, which was formed on 17 December, immediately became the target of parliamentary scrutiny, leading to the resignation of the Minister of Social Affairs and Labour. Sheikh Nasser al-Sabah was left without a portfolio; a potential candidate for succession, he died in December 2020, aged 72. In January 2021 former Prime Minister Jaber al-Mubarak al-Sabah and his sons were accused of money laundering, owing to their relationship with Jho Low, a businessman implicated in a case of massive fraud relating to the Malaysian sovereign wealth fund, 1Malaysian Development Berhad (1MDB). In April the ministerial court ordered the pre-trial detention of Jaber al-Mubarak and prolonged the custody of Khaled al-Jarrah (imposed one month earlier); both of the defendants were accused of misappropriating funds from the Kuwaiti Army Fund.

The Government has since 2014/15 drawn on the liquidity of its sovereign wealth fund, the KIA, to finance its budget deficit, which reached 40% of the GDP in 2020. This option of depleting the General Reserve Fund is reaching its limits due to the lack of liquidity of most of its investments, raising fears of difficulties in covering current expenditure. Moreover, in 2021 the five fixed-term appointees of the KIA board, whose terms had expired in April, were not replaced until early August. It is believed that the delay was caused by the National Assembly's sensitivity to corruption issues and the caution of the new Crown Prince.

Kuwait reacted swiftly to the onset of the coronavirus disease (COVID-19) pandemic in the country in mid-March 2020, suspending international flights and imposing a series of full and partial curfews. By the end of August 2023, according to the World Health Organization, Kuwait had recorded a relatively low number of COVID-related deaths, at 2,570. By 27 June of that year 78.4% of the population had been fully vaccinated against the virus.

The COVID-19 pandemic in Kuwait initially affected expatriate workers in the country, who were in some instances blamed for importing the virus, and this only served to exacerbate xenophobic attitudes. As the crisis deepened, in June 2020 Prime Minister Sheikh Sabah Khaled al-Sabah set the target of reducing the number of foreigners to 30% (compared with the existing level of about 70%) over the coming years, an issue that was discussed in the National Assembly in October under the 'Demographic Law' but was watered down by the Government. In January 2022 the Government lifted a controversial ban, announced in 2020, on the renewal of work permits for those aged 60 years and over and for those who did not have a university degree.

EXTERNAL RELATIONS SINCE 2011 AND THE GULF CRISIS

Rising sectarian tensions in the region prompted the Kuwaiti Government to move closer to its GCC allies. In March 2011, during the crackdown on protests in Bahrain, Kuwait offered to mediate between the pro-democracy activists and the Bahraini Government. The Bahraini Government publicly denied that any such approach had been made, while privately rebuking Kuwait for interfering in Bahraini affairs. In May that year, after initially declining to participate, Kuwait sent a small coastguard reinforcement to join the predominantly Saudi Arabian GCC Peninsula Shield Force that had entered Bahrain in March to put down the protests. The suppression of Bahrain's pro-democracy movement was viewed very critically by liberal and Shi'a Kuwaitis. Although clearly in the GCC 'camp', Kuwait appeared more actively to resist the increasingly sectarian framing of regional conflict. It continued to work towards improving relations with Iraq and did not witness a high level of sectarian tension domestically. In response, the Government banned sectarian rallies, and the Amir appealed for national unity in an effort to defuse the situation.

The 'Arab Spring' prompted the Kuwaiti Government to re-examine the role of Islam and politics. One aspect of the 'Arab Spring' was a heightened sectarian tension across the region that reflected the larger power struggle between Saudi Arabia and Iran. This led Kuwait largely to lean, with some reluctance, towards Saudi Arabia but also to work to improve relations with Iran. The Kuwaiti authorities were concerned to avert the rekindling of sectarian tension in the country, where Shi'as were long integrated into the political system. The rise of Sunni Islamists in several countries also led to regional shifts in power. The Kuwaiti Government sided with Saudi Arabia in its support for the military leadership in Egypt that removed Mohamed Mursi from power in 2013. Although not as hostile to the Muslim Brotherhood groups, which had long been active in domestic Kuwaiti politics, the deepening Saudi hostility to such groups prompted Kuwait to keep a closer eye on its own Islamists. Concern over Muslim Brotherhood groups became a foreign policy issue after the coup in Egypt, pitting Saudi Arabia against Qatar, which had supported Mursi's Government. When Saudi Arabia, the UAE and Bahrain recalled their ambassadors to Qatar in March 2014 over that country's continued support for the Muslim Brotherhood, this placed Kuwait in a difficult position but also provided an opportunity to help to mediate in the conflict. The Government froze the assets of Muslim Brotherhood members and prohibited pro-Mursi demonstrations in the country. In an effort to stem the financing of *salafi-jihadi* groups abroad, restrictions on Islamic charities were also increased and new legislation was adopted to combat money laundering. In August the authorities detained a cleric, Shafi al-Ajmi, whom the USA suspected of financing militants.

Concern with *salafi-jihadi* groups was particularly an issue in Syria and Iraq, where some Kuwaitis had provided financial support to such radical groups, including both the al-Nusra Front (now Levant Conquest Front) and Islamic State. The issue entered into domestic politics in April 2014 when the Kuwaiti Minister of Justice and of Awqaf (Religious Endowments) and Islamic Affairs, Nayif al-Ajmi, resigned after being accused by a senior US official of involvement in funding terrorist groups in Syria—where the Kuwaiti Government avoided involvement. In late 2014 and 2015 the Government introduced new legislation that made such financing more difficult.

Kuwait contributed 15 fighter jets to the Saudi-led military coalition of Arab League states against al-Houthi rebels in Yemen in March 2015, prompting a rare protest by Shi'a members of the National Assembly.

In June 2017, when Saudi Arabia, backed by the UAE, Bahrain and Egypt, accused Qatar of supporting terrorism, severed ties with the country, imposed an air and land blockade and presented Qatar with a list of 13 demands (these included closing the Al Jazeera news station, curbing ties with Iran, ceasing support for the Muslim Brotherhood, and ending the Turkish military presence in the country), Kuwait declined to join the blockade. With Muslim Brotherhood representatives in its National Assembly and with a history of acting as a mediator in such disputes, Kuwait, which also had an interest in maintaining its own ties with Iran, attempted, together with Oman, to arbitrate between the other Gulf states and Qatar. In December 2017 Kuwait hosted an extraordinary GCC summit to try to resolve the dispute, which did not prove successful, thereby demonstrating its declining influence as a peace-brokering country. The dispute between Qatar and its Gulf neighbours was resolved instead on 5 January 2021 at the GCC summit in al-Ula, Saudi Arabia, when the blockade on Qatar was lifted and diplomatic relations resumed.

AFTER THE RULE OF SHEIKH SABAH

On 29 September 2020 the death of Amir Sheikh Sabah al-Ahmad al-Jaber, in the USA, was announced. Crown Prince Sheikh Nawaf, his ailing half-brother (born in 1937), was sworn in as the new Amir on the following day. While a race for the position of Crown Prince involving a new generation of princes was expected, another half-brother of Sheikh Sabah, Sheikh Meshal al-Ahmad al-Jaber (born in 1940), Deputy Chief of the National Guard, was appointed on 7 October, thereby putting two octogenarians in charge of the country. Unlike its Gulf neighbours, Kuwait adhered to traditional succession norms favouring seniority over patrilineality.

A new National Assembly was elected on 5 December 2020 with a 60% turnout. These elections were marked by a large renewal (two-thirds of the incumbents lost their seats, including the only female parliamentarian, Safa al-Hashem, known for her xenophobia); a rejuvenation (30 of the new legislators were under the age of 45); a decline in the representation of the Shi'a (to six seats); the absence of elected women; and the breakthrough of opposition candidates, who won 24 of the 50 seats. Marzouq al-Ghanim was re-elected Speaker of the National Assembly, while Prime Minister Sabah al-Khaled al-Sabah, in office since 19 November 2019, was also reappointed, despite criticism from the parliamentary opposition.

Faced with the latter's threats to subject several ministers to votes of no confidence, the Amir decided to suspend the National Assembly for one month from 18 February 2021. On 14 March the Constitutional Court revoked the mandate as a legislator of Bader al-Dahoum, the leader of the radical opposition. Several of al-Dahoum's supporters, who had visited him in violation of health regulations, were summoned by the judge and briefly detained before the charges were dropped. This prompted the opposition to announce the end of its co-operation with the executive. On 30 March it boycotted the swearing-in session of the new Government in protest against al-Dahoum's removal from office; only 18 legislators voted to swear in the new Government, but the National Assembly passed a law prohibiting any vote of no confidence against the Prime Minister until October 2022. This infuriated the opposition legislators, who filed interpellation requests for three ministers. From 27 April they occupied the benches reserved for government members, preventing them from sitting; this led to the adjournment of parliament until May, after Ramadan.

After this turbulent first session, the opposition legislators returned to the Assembly at the end of October 2021 and appeared willing to make concessions. As part of a 'national dialogue' aimed at breaking the political stand-off, the Amir, Nawaf al-Ahmad al-Sabah, prepared a royal decree, approved by the Council of Ministers, that would grant amnesty to dissidents, including those in self-exile in Turkey who were handed prison terms in relation to the storming of the parliament in 2011 and to the members of the so-called Abdali cell who were convicted for spying on behalf of Iran and the Shi'a-backed militant grouping Hezbollah. The amnesty, which affected 36 individuals (including 11 parliamentarians), was announced on 8 November 2021, the day chosen by the Prime Minister, Sabah al-Khaled al-Sabah, to tender the resignation of his Government for the second time in a year. Both gestures were widely regarded as a step towards the de-escalation of political tensions. The political exiles—notably including Musallam al-Barrak and Faisal al-Muslim—returned to the country. On 15 November the Amir, whose health was deteriorating, officially handed over many of his constitutional duties to his deputy, Crown Prince Sheikh Meshal al-Ahmad. The latter reappointed Sheikh Sabah al-Khaled al-Sabah as Prime Minister on 23 November, and asked him to form a new government, the second in 2021 and the fourth since November 2019.

The National Assembly remained hostile to the Government that was eventually formed on 28 December 2021, including three legislators. Opposition members of the Assembly resumed the interpellations against members of the Government (the Ministers of Defence and of Foreign Affairs), particularly those from the ruling family, whom they blamed for the contested reappointment of the Speaker of the Assembly, Marzouq al-Ghanim, in December 2020. Legislators' interpellations led to the resignation on 16 February 2022 of the Minister of Defence, Sheikh Hamad al-Jaber al-Ali al-Sabah, and the Minister of the Interior, Ahmad Mansour al-Ahmad al-Sabah, both of whom also held the post of Deputy Prime Minister; the two men declared in a joint statement that reforms were impossible to achieve under the prevailing political circumstances. The latter was replaced by the Amir's own son, Sheikh Ahmad Nawaf al-Ahmad al-Sabah, in March 2022, and the former by Sheikh Talal Khaled al-Ahmad al-Sabah; both of the new appointees were additionally allocated the post of Deputy Prime Minister.

After facing questions in the National Assembly regarding accusations of misappropriation of public funds and unconstitutional practices that would have led to a vote of no confidence, the Prime Minister again offered his resignation on 5 April 2022; it was accepted one month later, on 10 May. After a sit-in staged by 16 legislators in their offices demanding fresh elections, Crown Prince Sheikh Mishal al-Ahmad, acting for the Amir, delivered a solemn speech on 22 June calling for the dissolution of parliament and new parliamentary elections 'in accordance with the will of the people and the rule of the Constitution'. On 24 July the Amir appointed Sheikh Ahmad Nawafas the new Prime Minister and dissolved the National Assembly on 2 August.

The legislative elections held on 29 September 2022 resulted in considerable losses for pro-Government candidates, an increase in the number of Shi'a, Islamist and so-called 'opposition' legislators, and the election of two women. A total of 20 former legislators lost their seats, including three former cabinet ministers. At the opening of the parliamentary session on 18 October, Ahmed al-Saadoun, then aged 87, was elected Speaker of the Assembly, while Sheikh Ahmed Nawaf presented a cabinet that had already been reorganized before he was sworn in again as Prime Minister.

The Government was soon faced with motions of censure and parliamentary interpellations, including that of the Minister of Defence, who tendered his resignation on 15 December 2022, shortly followed by the early retirement of the Chief of Staff of the Armed Forces. The power struggle between the National Assembly and the Government crystallized over a debt relief bill which the executive deemed unreasonable. The bill was opposed by the Minister of Oil and the Minister of State for National Assembly Affairs, who expressed their opposition by walking out of the parliamentary session on 10 January 2023, arousing anger and indignation among legislators. The political turmoil led to the resignation of the Government on 23 January, barely three months after its inauguration. A notable breakthrough during this period of stalemate was the pardon granted on 18 January to 34 political figures, including a prominent member of the royal family, Sheikh Athbi al-Fahad al-Sabah. Former head of the State Security Service and brother of high-profile Kuwaiti sports administrator Sheikh Ahmad al-Fahad al-Sabah, Sheikh Athbi had been sentenced in May 2016 to five years in prison with hard labour for insulting the Amir and the judiciary on the messaging service WhatsApp, where he and the other members of the so-called Al-Fintas Group had posted a message about a plot to overthrow the ruling system.

On 5 March 2023 Sheikh Ahmad Nawaf was tasked with forming a new cabinet, but on 19 March the political impasse was seriously exacerbated when the Constitutional Court, citing the alleged invalidity of the electoral process, annulled the September 2022 legislative elections, in which the opposition had secured a majority of seats, and ordered that the previous Assembly (elected in 2020), in which the opposition had narrowly failed to achieve a majority, be reinstated with immediate effect.

On 17 April 2023 the Crown Prince announced the dissolution of the reinstated National Assembly and called for fresh legislative elections to be held on 6 June. With a lower turnout than the previous poll, the results of the 2023 elections confirmed those of September 2022, with 29 opposition-leaning legislators, including 12 Islamists, securing seats. Only one woman candidate (representing the opposition) won a seat in the National Assembly. Ahmed al-Saadoun was re-elected as Speaker, replacing Marzouq al-Ghanim, a long-term supporter of the executive. The new Government formed on 18 June was notable for the return to politics of Sheikh Ahmad al-Fahad al-Sabah, who was appointed as Deputy Prime Minister and Minister of Defence. A candidate for the succession to the throne, Sheikh Ahmad al-Fahad benefits from support in both tribal and Islamist circles, and is a very divisive figure: an influential sports power broker, he held various ministerial positions from 2001 until his resignation from the cabinet in 2011. Since then, he has been involved in a number of financial and political scandals, among which are the allegations propagated by the Al-Fintas Group that former Speaker Jassem al-Kharafi and former Prime Minister Sheikh Nasser had plotted a coup. In the case of the alleged coup plot, Sheikh Ahmad al-Fahad received a public apology from the public prosecutor in March 2015 after the investigations into the case were dropped, but—with regard to the same case—he was convicted of forgery (for creating a fake video) by a Swiss criminal court in September 2021 (subsequently appealing against the conviction). Sheikh Ahmad al-Fahad has also faced numerous allegations of bribery and corruption linked to his former roles as President of the Olympic Council of Asia; as a member of the International Olympic Committee (from which he was banned for three years in July 2023); and as an official on the executive committee of the Fédération Internationale de Football Association (FIFA).

Public anger over corruption cases involving high-profile figures has been growing. The ministerial court decided on 9 March 2022 to acquit all nine defendants in a scandal involving the Kuwaiti Army Fund, including former Prime Minister Jaber al-Mubarak al-Sabah (2011–19) and former Minister of the Interior and Defence Khaled al-Jarrah al-Sabah, of charges of embezzling approximately KD 240m. (US $795m.) in public money for personal use. In late May the Kuwaiti Government filed a lawsuit in the US Los Angeles County Superior Court to recover at least $100m. in allegedly misappropriated and embezzled public funds from Khaled al-Jarrah al-Sabah, his son Jarrah and 260 unnamed other defendants. In March 2023, in another case involving misappropriation of public funds, the Kuwait Criminal Court convicted five people, including Sheikh Sabah Jaber al-Mubarak, the son of Jaber al-Mubarak al-Sabah, on charges of involvement in the 1MDB money laundering scandal. The Court of Appeal upheld the 10-year sentence on 9 July.

The political paralysis fostered a climate of censorship and social conservatism, which led to the cancellation in March 2022 of performances of a play by the British-Kuwaiti playwright Sulayman al-Bassam, a critic of authoritarianism; the banning in June of the Disney-Pixar animated film *Lightyear*, which features a same-sex kiss; and the banning in August 2023 of the Australian horror film *Talk to Me*, which includes a same-sex embrace and features a transgender actor. However, in February 2022 the Constitutional Court overturned a 2007 law (amending Article 198 of the penal code) criminalizing transgender people for 'imitation of the opposite sex', and in June 2022 a Kuwaiti court rejected an attempt to block the US media provider Netflix from streaming in the country, following its broadcasting of the Egyptian film *Perfect Strangers*, deemed 'contrary to Islamic values'.

Despite the launch of a domestic #MeToo movement by Kuwaiti human rights activists in 2021, women's rights in the country have suffered several setbacks, with some legislators preventing the abolition of Article 153 of the Kuwaiti Penal Code permitting honour killings after the murder of Farah Hamza Akbar in April 2021, blocking the organization of a women's yoga retreat in the desert, and limiting the Government's decision to recruit women into the army (by subjecting female recruits to the male guardianship system, imposing the wearing of head coverings and banning them from carrying weapons).

Against the tense political backdrop, the economy is suffering from a lack of reform. After a sharp recession in 2020, when the economy contracted by 8.9% due to the pandemic, the Kuwaiti economy returned to positive growth, of 1.3%, in 2021 and rebounded strongly in 2022 with growth of 8.2%. The Government is facing opposition from legislators regarding its proposal to introduce new taxes as part of the 2022–26 fiscal programme, which was presented in November 2022. Moreover, it is unable to borrow on the financial markets in the absence of appropriate legislation. In the event of a downturn in the oil market, the Government would be forced to draw on the general reserve fund to balance the budget. A fall in crude petroleum prices prompted the Government to announce, in April 2023, a production cut of 128,000 b/d. While the al-Zour refinery came on stream in November 2022 (10 years later than scheduled), the poor state of other infrastructure caused a leak so large that the Kuwait Oil Company declared a state of emergency in the west of the emirate in March 2023.

To diversify the economy and attract FDI, in July 2023 the Government announced plans to establish a new sovereign wealth fund, the Ciyada Development Fund, alongside the KIA (which at that time had assets of US $803,000m.)

A RELATIVE DIPLOMATIC EFFACEMENT

Kuwait has largely been relegated to a secondary role in organizing negotiations between the Yemeni Government of Abd al-Rabbuh Mansour Hadi and the al-Houthi rebels, after the failure of the peace talks that Kuwait hosted under the aegis of the UN during April–August 2016. Kuwait continued to maintain good relations with Iran and refused to support the US withdrawal from the Joint Comprehensive Plan of Action (the agreement reached between Iran and the USA, the Russian Federation, the People's Republic of China, France, the UK and Germany, together with the European Union, in July 2015, under which Iran committed to eliminate its stockpile of enriched uranium in exchange for relief from economic sanctions), which President Trump announced in May 2018.

In September 2018 a visit by the Saudi Crown Prince, Mohammed bin Salman bin Abdulaziz Al Sa'ud, to Kuwait ended prematurely without leading to an agreement to resume oil production in the Neutral Zone, which had been disrupted since 2015. In early 2016 Saudi Arabia and Kuwait had agreed to resume limited production at the disputed Khafji field, without specifying a date. Only in December 2019 did the two countries sign a memorandum of understanding ending the dispute. Production, potentially amounting to some 500,000 b/d, resumed gradually, but was frozen as part of reductions agreed by members of OPEC to support international oil prices. Sheikh Meshal, who has a well-established relationship with Mohammed bin Salman, paid his first official visit as Crown Prince to Saudi Arabia on 1 June 2021, which paved the way for the two countries to move past their temporary disagreement. On 21 March 2022 Kuwait and Saudi Arabia signed an agreement to exploit the offshore Dorra oil- and gasfield in their shared Neutral Zone, sparking renewed opposition from Iran which declared it 'illegal'. Kuwait had entered unsuccessful negotiations with Iran on delimiting their respective rights to the continental shelf, after agreeing in 2000 the demarcation of their maritime borders with Saudi Arabia. Iran claimed ownership over part of the Dorra field (known as Arash in Iran) and threatened to pursue exploration. Both Kuwait and Iran escalated the dispute verbally in July 2023, with both sides stating that they were ready to drill and exploit the field without having reached an agreement. Kuwait had re-established diplomatic relations with Iran in August 2022, six years after they had been suspended.

In January 2020 Kuwait signed a liquefied natural gas supply agreement with Qatar Petroleum providing for the supply of 3m. metric tons per year over a 15-year period, instead of the annual contracts signed since 2010, which were for only about one-half as much. The agreement sealed a strategic partnership with the Qatari regime and streamlined Kuwait's energy mix for power generation; institutional blockages and a lack of expertise had been slowing down the Kuwait Oil Company's own projects both for gas exploitation and for the planned increase in crude oil production to 4m. b/d in 2020.

Although Bahrain and the UAE signed the Abraham Accords with Israel on 15 September 2020, Kuwait has remained firmly opposed to any form of normalization with the Jewish state and has committed to the Oslo peace process. A decree issued in December 2021 banned the entry of commercial ships carrying goods to and from Israel into Kuwaiti territorial waters, while earlier, in May, the Kuwaiti National Assembly passed a bill banning all Kuwaiti residents from visiting Israel. This stance enjoys wide support among Kuwaitis. Also in May several demonstrations were held in Kuwait to protest against Israeli attacks on the Gaza Strip, in the Palestinian territories.

Kuwait followed other GCC countries (Saudi Arabia, the UAE and Bahrain) by recalling its ambassador from Beirut in October 2021 over criticism by George Kordahi, the then Lebanese Minister of the Interior, regarding the Saudi-led intervention in Yemen. Kuwait took the lead in resolving the diplomatic crisis, and, together with Saudi Arabia, returned its ambassador to Lebanon in April 2022.

Kuwait's diplomacy, marked by the ageing of its leaders, has shown a relative effacement, with the country not taking part in an ad hoc summit of regional leaders in Abu Dhabi on 18 January 2023. Despite reservations, Kuwait did not object to the decision, in May, by members of the Arab League to readmit Syria, a move orchestrated by Saudi Arabia. Following the murder of a Philippine domestic worker in January, Kuwait became embroiled in a dispute with the Philippines over the protection of foreign workers. In May Kuwait announced an indefinite suspension of new visas for Philippine nationals.

Economy

MÁTÉ SZALAI

INTRODUCTION

Kuwait has experienced political and economic instability on multiple fronts during recent years. On the one hand, owing to a domestic power struggle between the executive and the legislative branches, the efficiency of governance has been severely undermined. In April 2023 Kuwait's seventh Government in three years was inaugurated, marking an extremely turbulent period, even in a country with a decades-long tradition of protracted political crises. On the other hand, internationally, significant instability in the world economy, dramatic oil price fluctuations, the coronavirus disease (COVID-19) pandemic crisis and the Russian Federation's invasion of Ukraine have had serious and far-reaching effects on Kuwait's petroleum-dependent economy.

Kuwait shares its most fundamental economic attributes with the five other members of the Cooperation Council for the Arab States of the Gulf (the Gulf Co-operation Council—GCC). With approximately 6%–8% of global oil reserves (the second largest share among the GCC member states) and a capacity to produce around 3m. barrels per day, the country's economy is based on a rentier system, with 50% of gross domestic product (GDP) and 90% of government revenues and exports originating from the energy sector. Kuwait's oil wealth is remarkable even in a regional comparison: given its current production rate, the emirate has more than 110 years of oil production remaining, much more than, for example, Saudi Arabia (with less than 80 years).

Moreover, Kuwait's tiny land area of just under 18,000 sq km and its relatively small population of 4.4m. (including non-Kuwaitis) place the country in the category of the most developed and wealthiest nations. The population is highly urbanized, with 98% living in urban areas located near the shores of the Persian (Arabian) Gulf. From a sectoral perspective, the labour market is very similar to those of other developed countries, with 74% of workers employed in services, 24% in industry and just 2% in agriculture, according to the Economic Research Forum (ERF).

While Kuwait was heavily associated with oil-driven development and prosperity during the 20th century, the current economic picture is more complicated and multiple factors have undermined the country's economic potential.

ECONOMIC CONSEQUENCES OF GEOPOLITICS AND A TROUBLED HISTORY

Located on the northern shores of the Persian Gulf, Kuwait's geopolitical and geoeconomic situation is considered a mixed bag. On the one hand, being squeezed between the two major regional powers of Iraq and Saudi Arabia, Kuwaiti elites have always feared their independence and sovereignty being encroached upon by Baghdad, Riyadh or by other political and economic power centres. On the other hand, access to international waters creates vital potential for Kuwait to increase its chances of survival, economic well-being and independent development.

The country has historically been deprived of natural resources, but because of its location it has benefited from engagement in regional and global trade networks. Discoveries of oil were made relatively early, in the 1930s, after which the country started its oil-based development path as a front runner, even before its independence in 1961. Consequently, many regarded Kuwait as the most promising Gulf state after the Second World War. Per capita income had already started to rise at an accelerated pace in the 1950s, and oil revenues were heavily invested not just in infrastructure but also in various development projects.

The front-runner status of Kuwait manifests itself in several economic endeavours. One clear example is that in 1953 Kuwait became the first country in the world to create a sovereign wealth fund (SWF), the Kuwait Investment Authority (KIA), a practice copied by all Gulf states from the 1970s. Initially, SWFs were created as financial instruments to counteract the potential fluctuations in government revenues caused by oil price volatility, but later they were transformed into strategic investment tools. In 2023 the Sovereign Wealth Fund Institute ranked the KIA as the fifth-largest SWF globally, with total assets of US $803,000m., just behind the Abu Dhabi Investment Authority ($853,000m.). The KIA includes, *inter alia*, the General Reserve Fund and the Future Generations Fund (FGF), key financial instruments for preserving fiscal stability in the country.

Another area where Kuwait had a quasi-pioneer role is Islamic banking. In 1977, during the first major wave of the creation of Islamic banks (and only three years after the establishment of the international Islamic Development Bank), the Kuwait Finance House (KFH) was founded in parallel with similar institutions in Saudi Arabia, Dubai (in the United Arab Emirates—UAE), Bahrain, Sudan and Egypt. The subsequent establishment of other Islamic financial institutions in the emirate led to a duality in the Kuwaiti banking sector that still exists today. Currently, five of the 11 local banks registered by the Kuwait Banking Association are Islamic, while the rest are traditional or specialized.

By the 1990s the generally positively viewed Kuwaiti model of development had been undermined by geopolitical developments, with the Iraqi invasion of 1990 and the ensuing conflict having a lasting impact on the country's economic situation. State reserves vanished, while economic output declined considerably; according to the World Bank, Kuwaiti GDP contracted to 60% of its previous value as a consequence of the war. For a short period, the country's military budget was larger than its GDP. In the early 1990s Kuwait lost its ranking as the second-biggest economy among the smaller Gulf states (behind the UAE), a position that it regained temporarily until 2010, when it was overtaken by Qatar.

Geopolitics continued to play a destabilizing role in the Kuwaiti economy throughout the 1990s, when economic development remained highly volatile (in terms of the standard deviation of annual growth rates). The state budget remained in deficit until 1996. Despite the need to address the country's various economic problems, military expenditure and arms imports understandably rose significantly in the early 1990s, taking funds away from other sectors and initiatives. The defence budget peaked in 1991, at 117% of GDP, after which it took half a decade for Kuwait to lower defence spending to the level of the other Gulf states.

The Kuwaiti Government tried to re-energize the economy primarily by attempting to attract foreign capital. In 1997 the Government announced the launch of a US $7,000m., 25-year plan entitled Project Kuwait, which aimed to get international companies involved in the development of the oil sector, with the explicit intention of increasing output. In 2004 a legal amendment adopted in the National Assembly (Majlis al-Umma) allowed foreign banks to establish branches in the country.

The issue of compensation became a highly politicized question from both economic and moral perspectives, not just between Kuwait and Iraq but within Kuwaiti society as well. In 1991 the United Nations (UN) Security Council established the UN Compensation Commission to regulate the management of public and private compensation claims for the damages caused by the Iraqi invasion and to oversee the payments made by the Iraqi Government. The Security Council mandated Iraq to cover the costs through 5% of its annual oil revenues. Since its creation, the UN Compensation Commission has overseen the payment of US $52,400m. for approximately 1.5m. claims, the final instalment of which was paid by Iraq on 13 January 2022. The conclusion of the process represented a significant milestone in the normalization of bilateral relations between Kuwait and Iraq, as well as a symbolic end to the era of post-war reconstruction in the emirate.

None the less, geopolitics continues to have crucial implications for the Kuwaiti economy. A clear example is the ongoing border disputes between Kuwait and Iraq. After the war, Kuwait and Iraq failed fully to demarcate their borders, a situation that is especially problematic regarding the maritime border. Although the two countries signed an accord regulating maritime navigation in 2013, a comprehensive border settlement has yet to be achieved. These tensions and the eventual outcome of the maritime border delineation process will directly affect the competing Iraqi and Kuwaiti port construction projects, both of which aim to dominate trade on the northern shores of the Gulf.

DOMESTIC POLITICAL DYNAMICS AND THEIR IMPACT ON THE ECONOMY

Similar to other GCC members, state-society relations in Kuwait are predominantly shaped by the 'rentier social contract', according to which the Government and other state institutions guarantee a high level of living standards in exchange for political leverage and the practical exclusion of wider layers of the society from decision-making. Consequently, economic problems such as unemployment, inflation and limited energy availability can rapidly transform into political challenges for the regime.

While the rentier social contract is the predominant feature of Kuwait's political economy, other elements also play a crucial role. Despite its small population, Kuwait has a uniquely heterogeneous society. Besides the traditional tribal and sectarian differences, several other cleavages divide the Kuwaiti people into smaller identity and interest groups. Moreover, as the country is located in the proximity of millennia-old trade routes, the commercial elite has developed over many centuries to become stronger than in other Gulf states.

Although these socioeconomic characteristics led to more fragmentation in Kuwaiti society, at the same time, they created a more colourful political spectrum and more liberal political traditions than in other Gulf states. The merchant elite did not lose its power after the discovery of oil, which is why there exists in Kuwait a more inherent tradition of the distribution of power among various interest groups and institutions. As a result, the consultative or legislative branch (known as the National Assembly since 1962) has been stronger than in most GCC states, representing a kind of counterweight to the Government.

Although Kuwait's relatively free political life does not itself undermine economic stability or the rentier social contract, it does, however, allow tensions to be expressed and political conflicts to be played out publicly by different actors. Besides leading to wide-ranging political movements such as those that emerged in 2011–12, this characteristic of the Kuwaiti political system often leads to slow and cumbersome decision-making and limitations on the ability of the Government to push through important economic measures. The members of the National Assembly use their legislative powers to protect the economic and social interests of certain segments of society, which practically translates into an almost automatic refusal by the legislature to accept fiscally conservative measures initiated by the Government. Relations between the legislative and executive branches became especially tense after 2006, which, coupled with growing tensions between the tribal elites and the al-Sabah ruling family, as well as with the majority of the populace gaining access to online information and news in the last few decades, led to a state of chronic political crisis by the 2010s.

One example of how Kuwait's unsettled political situation has affected the country's economy is the case of the New Kuwait Vision 2035 reform programme, which was launched by the Government in January 2017. Issuing such a document became standard practice in the Gulf states in the 1990s and 2000s as they raced to project their economic competitiveness and to attract foreign capital. Kuwait (together with the UAE) was the last of the states to issue its national vision document, which was drafted in 2010 under the supervision of Prime Minister Sheikh Nasser al-Muhammad al-Ahmad al-Sabah. The document was strongly criticized by different interest groups both inside and outside the National Assembly, and was practically forgotten over the next few years before being rewritten.

Another example of the impact that the country's political system has had on the economy can be seen in the area of fiscal policy, which has been heavily influenced by the nature of relations between the legislative and executive powers. The Government is not permitted to use the FGF's reserves without the National Assembly's authorization. Moreover, when legislation concerning debt expired in 2017, the Government and the National Assembly failed to reach agreement on its renewal, thereby undermining fiscal leverage during the COVID-19 crisis in 2020 (see *The Dual Shock of 2020*).

RENTIERISM AND THE DOMINANCE OF THE OIL AND GAS SECTORS

The hydrocarbons sector in Kuwait undoubtedly plays the most vital role in the country's economy. Most of Kuwait's oil reserves are located in the Great Burgan field in the south-east of the country, one of the largest oilfields in the world. The first discoveries were made in the late 1930s, but substantial oil production only started after the Second World War. Another important location of oil reserves is the 5,700-sq-km Neutral (Partitioned) Zone, immediately to the south of Kuwait, which is shared between Kuwait and Saudi Arabia. While the history of the Zone includes a series of disputes and conflicts between the two countries, the development and production of the area's oil reserves have generally been conducted in a co-ordinated and amicable manner.

Not surprisingly, Kuwait's oil industry is heavily centralized. Policies are developed and implemented by the Supreme Petroleum Council, headed by the Prime Minister; the other members of the Council are representatives of the Government and the private sector appointed by the Amir. The dominant actor in the oil sector is the Kuwait Petroleum Corporation (KPC), which controls all upstream and downstream activities through its subsidiaries (including the Kuwait Oil Company and the Kuwait National Petroleum Company).

In addition to oil, Kuwait also has significant reserves of natural gas, which, according to British Petroleum (BP) estimates, amount to almost 1% of total global gas reserves. Most of the gas reserves are located in the Jurassic and Dorra offshore fields. Since diversification was placed on the agenda, the Government has invested more money in the gas sector to ease the country's dependence on oil. While gas output has somewhat increased, it is still not sufficient to meet domestic consumption requirements, especially given the high levels of demand arising from the resources-intensive activities of water desalination, enhanced oil recovery techniques, and the production of electricity and petrochemicals. The deficit has been covered since 2009 by importing liquefied natural gas (LNG), mainly from Qatar and Nigeria. With the trade in LNG widely expected to increase in the future, the Al-Zour LNG terminal, near the border with Saudi Arabia, was officially opened in July 2021.

As electricity consumption has risen substantially in Kuwait (as in other GCC states), meeting the demand with sufficient supply is among the emirate's most significant energy challenges. While electricity production has been on an almost constant upwards trajectory (with the help of the private sector during the last decade), additional steps have been discussed in Kuwait. In the late 2000s the development of nuclear energy was placed on the agenda by the Government, and a National Nuclear Energy Committee was created in 2009. However, the Government abandoned plans to establish a nuclear industry after the serious accident at Japan's Fukushima nuclear plant in 2011. By 2013 the six GCC states had completed a project to connect their national power grids. This connectivity helped Kuwait to meet some of its energy deficits, especially during the summer heat. Notably, the Government has not launched any initiatives to boost electricity production through the implementation of renewable technologies, even though such measures would help to offset the country's over-reliance on the oil sector.

DISADVANTAGES OF THE RENTIER SYSTEM

While enjoying its benefits, the Kuwaiti economy at the same time suffers negative consequences from the rentier system. 'Dutch disease', in the form of the distorted effects of the development and dominance of the oil industry on other sectors of the economy, is clearly visible. Owing to the generally high living standards of Kuwaiti citizens, there are no major incentives for innovation or for establishing businesses. The total entrepreneurial activity indicator—which records the ratio of people launching economic enterprises—is only normally around 2% in Kuwait, according to the ERF, equivalent to just one-fifth of the global average.

Empirically, it is also clearly evident that the rentier system incentivizes corruption, which is a severe economic and political problem in Kuwait. According to the 2022 Corruption Perceptions Index published by Transparency International in early 2023, Kuwait had the highest ranking in the GCC. *Wasta*, the practice of using personal connections to receive a benefit or get a job, is widely observed in the region; a survey by the International Monetary Fund (IMF) indicated that Kuwaiti citizens mention the practice the most, even compared with the other GCC countries. Besides *wasta*, embezzlement, fraud, forgeries (degrees, official papers and medical documents) and money laundering are encountered, both among the general populace and within official systems. A widely reported court case ended in March 2022 with the acquittal of former Prime Minister Sheikh Jaber al-Mubarak al-Sabah on charges of embezzling military aid funds.

The taxation system is also strongly influenced by the rentier logic. According to the Heritage Foundation (a US think tank), Kuwait's overall tax burden amounted to 1.8% of GDP in 2023, the second lowest in the GCC (that of the UAE stood at only 0.7%). There is still no individual income tax for citizens or corporate income tax for national companies, although a 15% tax is levied on foreign businesses and joint ventures. That being said, all private companies listed on the Kuwait Stock Exchange must pay 2.5% of their annual net profits as an employment tax. Contrary to most other member states of the GCC, Kuwait has yet to introduce a value-added tax (VAT) on consumption. As of mid-2023 there were no taxes on property, excise, transfers or payrolls. However, employers and employees have to pay social security contributions, amounting to approximately 20% of their monthly salaries.

A significant effect of the rentier system in Kuwait is the imbalance between the private and public sectors, with the latter dominating the major economic sectors and employing four out of five Kuwaiti citizens. Such a system translates into a lack of innovation and an unfavourable business environment; it also represents a substantial fiscal burden for the Government. For example, in 2021/22 75% of the state budget was spent on salaries, allowances and subsidies.

Aside from the imbalance between the private and public sectors, another historical division in the labour force is observable between Kuwaiti nationals and expatriate workers. One of the most well-known challenges in the GCC states is the management of migrant workers, who have played a vital role in developing the oil sector in the Gulf (and, more broadly, the whole economy of the region). The high demand for and supply of expatriate workers have led to their large presence both in absolute and relative terms, basically dominating the labour market. Being deprived of legal means of obtaining citizenship, foreign workers are effectively second-class inhabitants, while the local population often perceive their presence as posing some form of threat. Among the Gulf states, Kuwait is a prime example of this problem, particularly since expatriates had become the majority before 1970, as in Qatar. Historically, however, Kuwait had no real alternative but to invite foreign workers into the country, especially given the rapid development of the oil sector during the 20th century. None the less, the dominance of non-Kuwaiti nationals in the labour market creates challenges for both the state and society, especially during times of high unemployment.

These problems lie in the overlap of political and economic activities, making it more difficult to introduce significant reforms. Redrawing relations between the private and public sectors or between Kuwaiti nationals and expatriates, or implementing tax reforms would necessarily alter the social contract between the state and citizens and could potentially rapidly undermine political stability. These considerations help us to understand the lack of political appetite on the part of the elite to move forward with substantial reforms

REFORM AND DIVERSIFICATION

Despite the associated political risks and its massive oil reserves, the Kuwaiti Government has felt the need to put the question of diversification on its agenda. The most critical reform programme to address this is the above-mentioned New Kuwait Vision 2035, which was first drafted in 2010 but was heavily revised in 2017 after the sharp decline in oil prices in 2014–16. The final document specifies a number series of 'aspirations', 'strategic development goals' and 'pillars', some of which are merely general economic and institutional aims (e.g. a more effective civil service and support for human and social development). Nevertheless, a number of clear priorities are delineated in the Vision 2035 strategy, including the following:

• restoring the regional leadership role of Kuwait as a financial and commercial hub (an aspiration whose inclusion in the document was basically an admission of the competition between the smaller Gulf states in these sectors and of Kuwait's damaged competitiveness);

• reviving the pivotal role of the private sector in the 'leadership of development';

• improving the business environment through infrastructure development, human resource development and increased productivity;

• developing the non-oil sectors and achieving a 'sustainable, diversified economy';

• preserving the identity and social stability of the country.

In practice, the most essential element in this raft of aims is arguably achieving diversification and effectiveness through incentivizing the domestic and international actors in the private sector while, at the same time, reducing the role of the public sector. The Government planned to achieve this goal by tripling the level of foreign direct investment (FDI), while helping local small and medium-sized enterprises (SMEs) to thrive. Although the Government is frequently criticized for failing to implement the diversification programme, several specific steps have been taken, mainly in these latter two areas. In fact, the liberalization of investment regulations was initiated in the 1990s, in the context of post-war reconstruction. The first significant milestone was Kuwait's accession to the World Trade Organization in 1995. New momentum was engendered nearly two decades later, in 2013, when a number of measures were adopted to attract foreign capital. A new law opened up most economic sectors to foreign investment, while the Kuwait Direct Investment Promotion Authority was established (replacing the Kuwait Foreign Investment Bureau) to advance further the inflow of FDI.

Kuwait was recognized by the World Bank in its *Doing Business 2020* report as one of the top 10 most improved countries in the world in terms of ease of doing business. The Bank referred to substantive improvements in the merger of administrative procedures, the simplification of the process of receiving construction and energy permits, the streamlining of the property registration and inspection process, improvements in access to credit information, and the easing of cross-border trade procedures. However, Kuwait remained far behind other GCC countries in most areas of doing business and was overall only ranked 83rd on the list.

Infrastructure development is a crucial area for the reform programme, not only in terms of improving the business environment but also in the context of competition among the smaller Gulf states. According to international observers and comparisons, Kuwait lags behind other GCC member states in the field of infrastructure development. Cumbersome bureaucracy and slow decision-making undermine the Government's ability to implement projects and follow up on specific plans. The Madinat al-Hareer new city scheme (also known as Silk City), on the Subiya peninsula, is the Government's flagship infrastructure initiative. With a total budget of US $85,000m., the New Kuwait Vision 2035 includes at least a dozen separate projects focusing on tourism, maritime transport and logistics. One of the most important of these projects is the development of the Mubarak al-Kabir port on Bubiyan island, which is expected to contribute to the diversification and the development of Kuwait's less wealthy regions.

Strengthening the private sector and reducing the role of state institutions in the labour market appears to be proving an uphill battle. The Government is attempting to raise the ratio of Kuwaiti nationals in the workforce and to decrease the ratio of foreigners in the country to 30% of the population (a process often labelled as 'Kuwaitization'). Both aims would entail an increase in the employment of citizens by private entities. However, the majority of Kuwaitis prefer public sector jobs over those in the private sector because of higher salaries, more perks and benefits, a more stable outlook and a less demanding working environment. In response to this problem, the Government has initiated several measures, including a wage support programme to help to close the gap between private and public salaries. The National Labour Support Tax was introduced in 2000 to this end, although, to date, its effectiveness has been questionable. Indeed, a major breakthrough has yet to be achieved by the Government in the Kuwaitization process.

Developing the private sector is unachievable without supporting SMEs. According to the Gulf International Forum, there are approximately 25,000 such companies in Kuwait, constituting less than 3% of national economic activity and only 10% of the country's non-oil GDP. SMEs employ about one-quarter of the total workforce, predominantly migrant workers. According to the ERF, Kuwait has one of the lowest ratios of SMEs per capita in the Middle East and North Africa—there are only 12 such companies per 1,000 people, which is equivalent to only one-fifth of the European average and to just over one-half of the average in the Arab region.

The taxation system is also under review within the framework of fiscal diversification. In order to avoid regional competition and foster economic integration, the GCC states signed an agreement in 2017 to introduce VAT nationally. However, the agreement was not fully implemented by the six states. Unlike Saudi Arabia, the UAE, Oman and Bahrain (all of which introduced VAT between 2018 and 2021), Kuwait and Qatar postponed doing so. The Kuwaiti Ministry of Finance set a target date of 2023 for implementing the tax, at a rate of either 10% or 25%, although most observers did not expect its introduction in the near future.

Two factors might undermine the plan to introduce VAT. First, any significant change in the taxation system needs parliamentary approval, which could prove problematic for the Government to secure. Second, under the current inflationary environment, the introduction of VAT might be highly disadvantageous. Consequently the Government is also exploring alternatives—for example, levying more taxes on specific goods (e.g. tobacco, soft drinks or luxury items).

KUWAIT

FOREIGN ECONOMIC RELATIONS

The rentier system determines Kuwait's foreign economic relations. Trade accounts for more than 80% of the country's GDP, driven mainly by the energy sector. As mentioned earlier, oil and gas products account for some 80%–90% of all exports. According to data provided by the UN Conference on Trade and Development (UNCTAD), the ratio of hydrocarbons in Kuwait's overall exports had become the highest in the GCC by 2015 (the import structure being more balanced). This phenomenon is especially concerning since all of the other small GCC states have achieved considerable success in diversifying their exports in the last two decades. Moreover, in the same period, unlike its neighbours, Kuwait has also failed to reduce its commodity dependence ratio.

Traditionally, crude petroleum has accounted for approximately two-thirds of Kuwait's total exports, according to the Observatory of Economic Complexity. Refined petroleum and natural gas have contributed a further 13%–17% and 3%–4%, respectively. Since 2010 other products have provided between 6% and 16% of the country's total exports, although many of these goods are still connected to the oil and gas industry (e.g., chemical products and plastics).

As with the other oil-producing Gulf monarchies, most of Kuwait's trade is conducted with Asian countries, particularly the People's Republic of China, Japan, the Republic of Korea (South Korea) and India. China became Kuwait's primary export partner in 2018, when it surpassed South Korea. China's share of Kuwait's exports increased almost threefold between the early 2010s and the early 2020s, growing from 10.3% in 2010 to 27.4% in 2021, while that of the USA declined from 7%–10% to 1%–2%. Kuwait's main European export markets are the Netherlands, the United Kingdom, France and Italy, each of which accounted for less than 2% of Kuwait's total exports in 2021.

China has provided the largest share of Kuwait's annual imports over the last decade, with its contribution rising to approximately 15% by 2021, while the USA's share has been stagnating or even declining.

Kuwait has become one of China's top 10 energy partners. In 2021 Kuwait provided more than 6% of China's crude petroleum imports, surpassing the UAE. Chinese exports to Kuwait are more varied: according to the Observatory of Economic Complexity, exports from China include machinery, textiles and clothing, automobiles and various metals (notably iron products).

India is another Asian market closely connected to the Kuwaiti economy. India's share of Kuwaiti exports (currently around 14%–15%) surpassed even that of China in the early 2010s. Moreover, crude petroleum, natural gas, refined petroleum and other petrochemicals 'only' accounted for two-thirds of Kuwaiti exports to India in 2020, being supplemented by transportation goods, other chemical products and metals, among other things. India's share of Kuwait's total imports has declined to below 5% in the last decade (one-third of China's share); the list of imported goods from India includes vegetable products (primarily rice and coffee), machines, textiles and metal products.

The immediate environment of the Kuwaiti economy is the GCC. Political and social connections, geographic proximity, and the economic integration process of the GCC are the primary reasons for the deep embeddedness of the Kuwaiti economy in the Gulf economic space. In the 2010s the five other GCC member states accounted for 29%–40% of Kuwait's total exports and 16%–17% of the country's imports. Recent trade data indicate an increasing role for the GCC, although this might be due to the decline in oil prices and the subsequent reduction in the value of Kuwait's oil exports to east Asia. Trade between Kuwait and other members of the GCC is quite diverse: in both directions, it includes chemical products, metals, vegetable and animal products, paper products, plastics and machinery. Kuwait also exports cars and other vehicles to its neighbours.

While the GCC is not primarily an economic body, several of its key projects have profoundly determined the outlook of the Kuwaiti economy. The six member states successfully created a customs union in 2003 and a common market in 2008, and significantly lowered (though did not completely eliminate) non-tariff barriers. Goods can travel freely in the GCC, while a 5% duty is levied on all imports. However, the GCC allows for each member state to control substantial leverage over its own foreign trade and economic policy. According to the Heritage Foundation, among the GCC member nations, Kuwait ranks higher than only Saudi Arabia in terms of freedom of trade, while Kuwait's general tariff rate (4.7%) is the fourth lowest in the bloc (after the UAE, Qatar and Oman).

Kuwait's trade with other Middle Eastern and North African countries has been limited. As the largest Arab nation, Egypt has traditionally played an important role in Kuwait's foreign economic relations, accounting for 1%–3% of the country's exports and imports. Neighbouring Iraq accounts for a similar proportion, with goods exported from Kuwait to Iraq including cars and other vehicles, animal and vegetable products, and machinery. However, Iraqi exports (primarily refined petroleum) have not constituted a significant share of Kuwait's total imports over the last decade.

There is also a significant imbalance in Kuwait's trade with the USA. The USA has provided 8.5%–10.7% of Kuwaiti imports over the last decade, while accounting for only 1%–2% of Kuwait's exports, with a clear downward tendency. Kuwaiti exports to the USA are dominated by crude and refined petroleum; therefore, the small US share of Kuwait's exports is not surprising, given the USA's growing domestic energy production. The main US exports to Kuwait during the early 2020s included cars and other vehicles, machinery, chemicals and liquefied petroleum gas (LPG).

Kuwait has signed bilateral investment agreements with a considerable number of countries, including many members of the European Union (EU), Middle Eastern and North African states (including Egypt, Turkey—now Türkiye, Yemen and the UAE) and Asian countries (including China, Tajikistan and South Korea). One of the most important of these accords is the Trade and Investment Framework Agreement concluded with the USA in 2004, which was considered to be the first step in deepening US-Kuwaiti ties. However, while discussions between the two sides have taken place recently, no tangible results have yet been achieved.

Generally, FDI has played a much more limited role in the Kuwaiti economy than in the other GCC states. Inflows have slowed considerably in the last decade, decreasing from US $1,340m. in 2010 to $198m. in 2021, according to UNCTAD data. The overall inward stock reached approximately 10% of GDP in 2019, a ratio that was much higher in the case of Saudi Arabia (30%) and Bahrain (78%). In absolute terms, Kuwait's total cumulative FDI stock by 2021 ($15,000m.) was substantially less than the total FDI attained by Bahrain, Qatar or Oman ($27,000m.–$40,000m.), and was equivalent to only 8.7% of the value of FDI accumulated by the UAE ($171,000m.) and 6.0% of that accrued by Saudi Arabia.

Chinese investments in Kuwait gradually increased until 2017, when they reached a cumulative total of US $5,000m., after which there was a decline in terms of Chinese inflows. The growing Chinese role in the Kuwaiti market resulted in, *inter alia*, the organization of the first-ever Kuwait China Investment Forum in 2018 and a growing number of Chinese expatriate workers, amounting to almost 13,000 in that year. According to the ChinaMed project, China's FDI stock in Kuwait amounted to $853.6m. in 2021.

Annual FDI outflows have traditionally been much larger (twofold or threefold) than inflows. According to UNCTAD data, by 2021 the total cumulative outward stock of Kuwaiti FDI was more than US $36,000m. That being said, the KIA has much larger assets through its nine subsidiary companies, which are present in 125 countries. The primary destination for Kuwaiti FDI has been Western economies, primarily those of the USA, the EU and the UK. The KIA's investment policy has traditionally been conservative in the sense that it primarily builds on broad portfolios that focus on profit-seeking and not on political goals, especially in comparison with Qatar's investment policy.

However, the Kuwaiti Government does capitalize on its oil wealth to enlarge its international footprint both economically and politically. Similar to the UAE and Qatar, it provides humanitarian and development assistance amounting to approximately 2%–3% of its GDP annually. The primary institution in terms of aid policy is the Kuwait Fund for Arab Economic Development, founded in 1961, which, contrary to its name, has invested in more than 100 countries both within and outside of the Arab region. According to its 2020/21 report, the Fund's total assets amounted to US $19,000m. During that year it funded a total of 19 projects, focusing on water and sewerage (which received 39% of the funding), energy (25.5%), society (17%), transportation and communication (12%) and agriculture (6.5%), with most commitments being made to Arab countries (71.4%) and African countries (17.5%). According to most observers, humanitarian and development aid plays multiple roles in Kuwaiti foreign policy. On the one hand, it is connected to the troubled history of the emirate and its identity of focusing on reconstruction and social peace. On the other hand, it is also used as a soft power policy tool in international politics.

Such a duality was observable in the emirate's policies with regard to Iraq. In the wake of the devastating consequences of the rise of Islamic State in Iraq and the Levant (renamed Islamic State in mid-2014) in its northern neighbour, Kuwait hosted the International Conference for Reconstruction of Iraq in 2018 (in co-operation with the EU). In addition to helping Iraq to secure funding from international donors, Kuwait itself also pledged US $2,000m. worth of investments and loans. Through these various efforts, the emirate contributed towards the stabilization of its northern neighbour, while at the same time pursuing profit-maximization and economic influence in the country.

CLIMATE POLITICS

Sustainability is not a primary focus of the Kuwaiti Government's economic strategy. Climate-related topics have been only marginally discussed in the political circles of the emirate and have attracted less attention from among the elite compared with even Saudi Arabia or the UAE. Such a lack of political will manifests itself in several different ways. Besides general commitments aiming to achieve carbon neutrality by the second half of the 21st century, the emirate has yet to publish a tangible national climate change strategy (as Qatar and Saudi Arabia have done). According to the Grantham Research Institute at the London School of Economics and Political Science, of the 41 climate change-related laws and policies introduced by GCC member states to date, Kuwait has been responsible for just three of them, and only one of these— the New Kuwait Vision 2035 reform programme—was formulated in the last decade. Another telling figure is that Kuwait was responsible for only two of the 27 projects conducted in the six GCC states as part of the Clean Development Mechanism of the Kyoto Protocol framework.

None the less, a few steps have been taken to make economic activity more climate friendly. The Government has set official targets of attaining by 2030 a 15% renewable energy share in the country's energy mix, a 15% increase in energy efficiency and a 30% reduction in energy consumption (although the seriousness of these aims is questionable owing to the fact that baselines were not initially available for the latter two goals). In the framework of the Kuwait National Adoption Plan 2019–30, the Government aimed to reduce greenhouse gas emissions by shifting electricity production from the use of oil to natural gas and supporting a number of green infrastructure programmes. Moreover, the KPC has pledged to develop 2.5 GW of solar energy capacity. Although Kuwait signed the Paris Agreement on climate change in 2015, the country did not commit to any quantitative targets in its nationally determined contributions (NDCs) set in that year; instead, it merely referred to national efforts to diversify the economy and to maintain the current levels of emissions.

In 2021 Kuwait was among those countries that updated their NDCs in response to the intensification of international climate diplomacy, even without a legal obligation to do so. The Government introduced new baselines, pledging to keep greenhouse gas emission rates at the pre-pandemic level until 2035. Moreover, a novel reference was made to the circular carbon energy approach. The process of addressing climate change, therefore, is moving forward in Kuwait, albeit at a very slow pace.

CRISIS MANAGEMENT IN THE ECONOMY

In the 21st century to date, Kuwait's economy has experienced extreme fluctuations. According to the World Bank, the country's average annual GDP growth rate (which is mainly dependent on oil market tendencies) varied between an expansion of 17.3% (in 2003) and a contraction of 8.7% (in 2020). Three, or potentially four, distinct periods can be outlined, each with different dynamics. First, during 2000–09 Kuwait enjoyed high incomes and rapid economic growth, which came to an end with the global economic crisis. During this period the Kuwaiti economy grew at a slightly faster rate than the GCC average, at least until 2006. In the second period, between 2009 and 2017, a quick recovery led to a moderately expanding but relatively stable economic situation, which was brought to an end by the oil price crisis of the mid-2010s. During 2009–17 the Kuwaiti growth rate generally remained below the GCC average (except for 2011 and 2012), indicating a relative loss of competitiveness. The economic problems caused by the collapse in the price of oil on international markets from 2014 were compounded by domestic political and economic problems, which undermined the agency of the Government in economic affairs. Third, after 2017 the constrained Government was confronted with new threats to the economy, including large budget deficits, financial instability and the economic effects of the COVID-19 pandemic. It is possible that 2022 marked the start of a fourth period, characterized by renewed short-term stability without the Government addressing the country's most significant structural problems.

Kuwait after the Global Financial Crisis: Domestic Turmoil and Fluctuating Oil Prices

With regard to the Kuwaiti economy, the decade of the 2010s was dominated by three interlinked challenges: mitigating the adverse effects of the global financial crisis (2007–08), managing the political and social unrest in 2011–12 with economic tools, and accommodating fluctuations in the price of oil.

As the Kuwaiti financial sector (which, among the GCC states, has one of the largest shares in the national economy) had been integrated into global markets quite profoundly, the economic crisis that started in 2007 had a massive effect on the country. On the one hand, the sudden increase in the price of oil was beneficial, but the subsequent decline in mid-2008 and the spillover of international instability represented a considerable risk to the emirate. According to the IMF, Kuwait was one of three GCC countries (along with the UAE and Bahrain) that suffered the most during the crisis, given their embeddedness in global equity and credit markets.

The Government acted quickly to protect the banking sector. When in October 2008 one of the major lenders, the Gulf Bank, announced losses, the Central Bank of Kuwait suspended trading in its shares. In addition, the Government created a task force to monitor the effects of the financial crisis. The Government subsequently offered deposit guarantees to commercial banks (following in the footsteps of the UAE), and injected money into financial institutions and the stock market. In 2008 at least US $30,000m. were accessed from the reserves of the Kuwaiti sovereign funds.

Regarding monetary policy, the Kuwaiti authorities realized quite early that the problems in the USA might lead to inflationary pressures. Traditionally, GCC countries follow US monetary policy dynamics in terms of both exchange rate policy and interest rates; therefore, US decisions and tendencies have a determinant effect on the Gulf states' monetary environment. That being said, the Kuwaiti authorities perceived that on this occasion such an exposure (and dependence) would not help their country's economic stability, which is why they abandoned the dollar peg quite early, in May 2007, replacing it with a peg to an undisclosed mix of currencies. Moreover, between 2008 and 2011 the Central Bank of Kuwait decreased its key discount rate from above 6% to between 2% and 3%, at which level it remained (with only minimal fluctuations) until 2020. While US monetary policy is still closely monitored by the Kuwaiti Government and the Central Bank, Kuwait has become more independent of the USA in this respect than other GCC states (except for Oman). During 2008–11 Kuwait also engaged in monetary easing and central bank liquidity support in co-ordination with its neighbours.

While the Government's crisis management was generally adequate, some negative effects were not mitigated. Inflation reached almost 12% in 2008, the highest level since 1974, which meant that for a short period prices rose at a faster pace than they did after the Iraqi invasion in 1990. An estimated 2,000 Kuwaitis lost their jobs in the initial stages of the global economic crisis. During the crisis Kuwait had the largest share of non-performing loans (NPLs) in the GCC, at 3.1%–3.2%, and the worst annual decline in terms of banking sector profitability, according to IMF data. Two of the largest investment companies in Kuwait (the Global Investment House and Investment Dar) had to conclude restructuring agreements with their creditors. The IMF estimated that by the end of 2009 US $44,000m. worth of projects had been put on hold, the third-largest amount in the GCC (although fewer than 10% of the emirate's projects were suspended). Between 2008 and 2010 Kuwait registered the largest current account deficit among the GCC states, reaching almost 45% of GDP in 2008. Fearing additional problems, the emirate was the only GCC member whose budget in 2009 was smaller than in the previous year.

The global economic crisis was followed by another turning point in the history of Kuwait. During the era of the 'Arab Spring' (2011–12) the emirate witnessed substantial political upheaval, albeit relatively peaceful. Opposition movements had been founded and consolidated even before 2011, having their roots in the so-called Orange Movement, comprising a network of activists established in the 2000s. In late 2010 protests gained momentum, and in November 2011 pro-reform campaigners and opposition deputies stormed the National Assembly building and forced Prime Minister Sheikh Nasser al-Sabah to resign. Members of the opposition and other activists returned to the streets in late 2012 to protest against the dissolution of the National Assembly by the Amir, Sheikh Sabah al-Ahmad al-Sabah. It was only in 2013 that legitimate elections were held that were supported and recognized by most of the relevant political stakeholders, paving the way for a period of relative calm.

Owing to their organic connection to the decades-long political crisis in Kuwait, most analysts agree that the events of 2011–12 in that country should be considered separately from the wider Arab Spring. Another vital factor that differentiates Kuwait is that, unlike in many other affected countries, the protesters in Kuwait City and other cities were not primarily driven by economic problems. The World Bank estimates that the official unemployment rate was only around 1%–2% before 2011—although it must be said that among the youth the rate was significantly higher (at slightly above 10% since 2005), and inflation had also risen considerably after the global financial crisis. However, the general economic situation in Kuwait was much better than in Egypt, the Syrian Arab Republic or Yemen.

Nevertheless, the Kuwaiti authorities felt under pressure to use economic tools in an attempt to stabilize the country's political and social situation. In 2011 the Government announced the direct transfer of approximately US $3,600 in cash to each Kuwaiti citizen and practically free commodities for 14 months; in addition, the debts of many families were cancelled. Such measures directly led to fiscal expansion and budgetary overstretch in the following years, with the largest annual budgets in the history of Kuwait, including substantial increases in subsidies and salaries. Despite these actions, however, Kuwait's budget remained stable, with substantial surpluses (for the time being).

That being said, the events of 2011–12 had long-lasting consequences, resulting in a political deadlock that undermined the Government's ability to implement economic initiatives. In 2017 the activists who had participated in the storming of the National Assembly in 2011 were given harsh sentences by the judiciary, leading to many of them leaving the country. After 2017 the opposition deputies in the legislature attempted to secure amnesties for the protesters by blocking government initiatives that required parliamentary approval. Such action proved especially problematic during the COVID-19 pandemic (see *The Dual Shock of 2020*). In an attempt to end the political impasse, the newly inaugurated Amir, Sheikh Nawaf al-Ahmad al-Jaber al-Sabah, issued a royal decree in 2021 granting amnesty to several key activists and opposition politicians. Moreover, in December a new Government was announced, including several senior members of the National Assembly.

While tensions between the legislature and the Government subsequently appeared to ease somewhat, optimism about Kuwait's political situation ultimately proved to be misplaced. Through a non-co-operation motion and constant interpellations about corruption, members of the National Assembly forced the Government to resign in April 2022. In the following year three successive Governments were appointed. In an attempt to alleviate the political instability in the country and end the legislative deadlock, the Government offered amnesty to jailed political prisoners in January 2023 and fresh elections were held in June. Nevertheless, analysts deemed it unlikely that these steps would ease political tensions to any significant extent.

Together with these domestic challenges and the spillover effects of the global financial crisis, Kuwait has also had to manage the consequences of sudden decreases in energy prices. As a rentier economy, Kuwait is highly vulnerable to fluctuations in oil prices. From the second half of the 2000s, except for a brief period after 2008, the emirate enjoyed a significant increase in revenue owing to historically high oil prices, which reached more than US $110 per barrel. However, from mid-2014 the price of oil rapidly decreased, declining to around $25 per barrel in early 2016. Although there was a period of market consolidation during 2018–19 (when oil prices recovered to around $65–$70 per barrel), the economic atmosphere in the GCC changed substantially. Since the mid-2010s diversification and related reforms have dominated the agenda, spurring competition among the six member states.

The decline in oil revenues significantly undermined fiscal stability and represented a threat to the maintenance of policies aimed at keeping living costs low for the Kuwaiti population. This phenomenon was most apparent in the area of domestic fuel prices. In 2016 the Kuwaiti people enjoyed the lowest price for oil in the GCC. However, in that year the Government decided to increase it, following all the other GCC states. Moreover, although the emirate is estimated by the World Bank to be the sixth-highest per capita energy consumer in the world, as of 2016 domestic electricity prices had been unchanged since 1990. The Government attempted to decrease state subsidies and increase residential and commercial electricity prices, but the National Assembly blocked this initiative. In early 2017 the Assembly proposed that residential units inhabited by Kuwaiti citizens be excluded from electricity prices increases, meaning that effectively only expatriates would be obliged to pay more. In the event, the Government managed to engineer the introduction of a general (but differentiated) increase, thereby contributing to the tense relationship between the legislative and executive branches.

Although the changes effected by the Government were insufficient to retain a balanced budget, no significant economic reforms were implemented by the Kuwaiti authorities. There were no substantial reductions in expenditure (which declined by only 1.5% in 2016/17), although foreign assets were drawn down. The five-year economic development plan covering 2015/16–2019/20 focused on improving public financial management, privatization, legal reforms and supporting SMEs, but the political will was still lacking to initiate any major economic restructuring. Public investment in the energy sector remained high during this period, amounting to a cumulative total of US $100,000m. by 2020.

The Dual Shock of 2020

The outbreak of the COVID-19 pandemic in early 2020 and the subsequent decline in oil prices represented a dual shock for GCC countries. The crisis arose during a vulnerable period for the Gulf monarchies as their attempts at diversification, modernization and fiscal consolidation had already started but had yet to yield substantive results. Therefore, the Gulf states were under dual pressure in 2020—on the one hand, they had to continue their efforts at fiscal consolidation and restructuring government incomes, while, on the other hand, they had to provide financial support to their populations based on the rentier social contract.

While the vastness of its oil resources might appear to constitute an advantage for Kuwait during such a crisis, in practice, the country's extreme dependence on oil exports made the economy more exposed to the decline in oil prices. In a report published in October 2020, the IMF stated that Kuwait was the second worst affected economy in the Gulf (after Oman) in terms of GDP decline. Moreover, as growth in the non-oil sector is still based on government spending, in practice budgetary problems disincentivize any kind of diversification attempts.

In an effort to ease the fiscal pressure, the Government abandoned or suspended the implementation of several of its larger initiatives. In July 2020 the construction of the Al-Dabdaba solar plant—which would have been one of the most extensive solar energy facilities in the region—was cancelled. Moreover, in October the Mubarak al-Kabir port project, a cornerstone of the Silk City initiative (and, thus, the development of the non-oil sector), was put on hold.

The private sector suffered considerably during the first period of the COVID-19 crisis. According to a business impact survey conducted by the independent Kuwait-based firm Bensirri PR, 45% of business owners either suspended or completely shut down their business, while another 26% experienced a nearly 80% reduction in revenues. Expatriates, who constitute some four-fifths of private sector employees, were disproportionately affected; according to the same survey, the greater number of non-Kuwaiti employees that a company had, the more likely it was to have shut down during the pandemic.

The crisis also affected the financial sector. According to Markaz, a Kuwaiti asset management group, the ratio of NPLs to total loans rose to almost 5%, a rapid increase from less than 2% in 2019. The National Bank of Kuwait (NBK) reported a 36% decrease in profit in 2020, compared with the previous year.

Since 2020 Kuwait has mainly followed the GCC playbook of crisis management. First, the IMF assessed that the Government had reacted 'swiftly and decisively' to the health crisis in the country, with social restrictions and curfews, and, later, with a successful vaccination campaign against COVID-19. Although these measures did cause severe economic and social hardship, they managed to keep the pandemic relatively at bay.

Second, according to an assessment published by The Arab Gulf States Institute in Washington, DC, USA, all of the GCC Governments reacted similarly to the challenges arising from COVID-19 and the new oil price shock, using these five tools: providing direct economic support to citizens in order to mitigate the economic effects of the pandemic; reassessing state benefits and the social safety net; reducing expenditure in order to balance state budgets; raising domestic revenue by introducing selective taxes and fees; and balancing new debt issuances.

More specifically, the Kuwaiti Government temporarily reduced or waived fees for businesses and, in March 2020, provided additional funding of US $1,600m. to counter the economic and social consequences of the pandemic; however, this package mostly helped public sector employees. To cover the costs of the emergency funding, the budgets of government institutions were reduced by 20%. Even with such a radical step, 2020 was the first year to register a national budget deficit since the late 1990s, amounting to 9.4% of GDP, according to Trading Economics. The Central Bank had already decreased its key discount rate in late 2019; however, in 2020 the rate was reduced further by one-half of a percentage point to 1.5%, a rate at which it remained until March 2022.

A substantially smaller emergency funding package of US $780m., focusing on the private sector, was not introduced until July 2020 and did not, in practice, cover any support for non-Kuwaiti citizens. At the same time, the Government took several steps to attempt to ease the burden on SMEs, including reducing risk rating, providing long-term loans, postponing due instalments, and collecting social security contributions. In practice, however, the relevant information did not reach many SMEs, which resulted in larger companies receiving more support than their smaller counterparts. Moreover, the eligibility criteria for applying for crisis loans included a specific quota for the employment of Kuwaiti citizens, which deepened the existing divide between nationals and expatriates in the Kuwaiti workforce.

As a member of the Organization of the Petroleum Exporting Countries (OPEC), Kuwait was deeply involved in the discussions between the major oil producers during early 2020. The 'oil price war' between Saudi Arabia and Russia, which broke out in March, caused a further decline in energy prices, which represented another considerable threat to the emirate. It is not surprising that Kuwait was the first among the GCC countries to agree to reduce its production of oil after a deal was reached in April within the OPEC+ format.

During this period co-operation between the National Assembly and the Government was ambiguous and tense. After the legislature approved the annual budget with a considerable imbalance between revenue and expenditure, the finance and economic committee of the National Assembly rejected a proposal in August 2020 that would have allowed the Government to cover the budgetary deficit by borrowing US $65,000m. domestically and internationally, referring to 'the lack of clear and real reform'. This decision made it temporarily impossible for the Government to borrow more money from the markets, which is why it was forced heavily to draw on the assets of the General Reserve Fund. At the same time, the committee approved the suspension of the legal obligation to allocate 10% of annual state revenues to the FGF, which slightly expanded the Government's fiscal leverage.

Without the legal right to access the assets of the FGF, the Government changed its tactics. In parallel with fighting a political battle with the National Assembly, it started to transfer its performing assets to the Fund in exchange for cash, a temporary solution that enabled the Government to stay afloat and plug the budget deficit for the time being. The dangerous depletion of Kuwait's liquid assets caused severe economic problems, which led to international credit rating agencies downgrading the country's sovereign debt rating. In September 2020 Moody's credit rating agency cited the 'fractious relationship between parliament and the government' and the 'lower quality of legislative and executive institutions' as key determinants in its decision.

Post-COVID Consolidation and the Impact of the Russian–Ukrainian Conflict

The Russian invasion of Ukraine in late February 2022 represented another turning point in recent economic developments in Kuwait. The price of oil had already started to recover in 2021, but it rose dramatically after the Russian invasion, pushing Kuwaiti production levels to the pre-pandemic level. Such developments not only affected the emirate's oil companies but also its financial sector. In the first quarter of 2022 the NBK and the KFH reported a 38%–39% increase in profits, compared with the same period of 2021, while another major financial institution, Al-Ahli Bank of Kuwait, registered a 17% increase. In light of such figures, the credit rating agency S&P Global predicted that Kuwait's banks would fully recover their lost earnings in 2022. Indeed, the Egyptian financial services company EFG Hermes Holding predicted that the annual profits of the Kuwaiti banking sector would grow by 30% in 2022, an improvement twice the size of that forecast for the Saudi banking sector and one-third larger than that forecast for the banking sectors of the UAE and Qatar.

Kuwait's economic and financial situation had begun gradually to improve even before February 2022. The financial sector had remained liquid and stable during the pandemic in spite of decreasing profits, and from the second half of 2021 observers became more optimistic. In parallel with energy prices, domestic consumption and oil production also began to increase in Kuwait, especially in the second half of 2021. By the end of the fiscal year in March 2022, government revenues and expenditures had started to reach a balance. In October 2021 the IMF predicted that fiscal balance or even a budgetary surplus would be achieved in 2022/23, given the growth of oil revenues and the reduction in COVID-related expenditure. In August 2021 the Government instructed all state entities to reduce spending by at least 10%, a target that the IMF deemed as unattainable, but it was, nevertheless, praised as a step in the right direction.

Perhaps the most important indicator of fiscal stability was that the Government managed to lower the budget deficit in 2021/22. Defying most predictions, the deficit narrowed to 8.5% of GDP, mostly owing to unexpectedly high oil prices. In parallel, the recapitalization of the nearly depleted General Reserve Fund has begun. The outlook for 2022/23 is positive, although optimism can encourage expansionary spending practices. Indeed, the parliamentary budget and closing accounts committee have proposed increasing governmental spending by 5%.

In such a market environment when oil prices are high, it is not only the fiscal leverage of Gulf states that grows significantly but also their political weight in international relations. Together with Saudi Arabia and the UAE, Kuwait is a member of OPEC and also of OPEC+, through which oil producers co-ordinate their policies to control the supply side of the trade in oil. When energy prices are elevated, the major consumers try to pressure OPEC+ to increase production, and scarce capacity is currently primarily available in the Gulf region.

Besides rising oil prices, other developments and measures are a source of optimism among domestic and international observers alike. For instance, the dynamics of the real estate market in Kuwait are very promising; activity in the sector reached pre-pandemic levels in 2021 and continued to grow in 2022. The Government's willingness to invest heavily in projects resurfaced in 2021, with almost three times the amount being spent as in the previous year. None the less, total expenditure still fell short of the pre-2020 average, and most of it was still directed towards the oil and gas sector.

The Kuwaiti Government has also taken modest steps to combat corruption, an issue that has historically caused tensions between the executive and the National Assembly. The current 2019–24 Integrity and Anti-Corruption Strategy is being implemented primarily through executive decrees focusing on transparency, although further steps could be taken to increase the role of private and civil organizations.

FUTURE OUTLOOK

From a general perspective, the short-term crises of the last decade have been managed by the Kuwaiti authorities adequately. The Government's fiscal and monetary initiatives to mitigate the harmful effects of the global financial crisis, oil price fluctuations and the COVID-19 pandemic were sufficient to maintain economic and political stability. While the domestic political situation remains tense, it is noteworthy that the succession of the new Amir, Sheikh Nawaf al-Ahmad al-Jaber al-Sabah, in 2020 was conducted relatively smoothly.

Based on these tendencies, one can come to the conclusion that the prospects for the Kuwaiti economy over the medium term are positive. It is telling that two out of the three key risks to the country's financial well-being identified by the World Bank in a report published in October 2021 have subsided—a new pandemic in the short term is unlikely, while the Russian invasion of Ukraine pushed up oil prices and created fiscal leverage for the Government. That being said, the third key risk, namely the political impasse that weakens the ability of the Government to implement critical economic policies, has not receded, and has arguably even strengthened since the publication of the report.

Several additional problems need to be addressed over the short-to-medium term. First, the question of renewing the country's debt legislation has still not been resolved. Enabling the Government to access credit from domestic and international markets would provide the authorities with additional fiscal leverage, even in times of crisis. While the depletion of the General Reserve Fund was avoided, the current situation is sustainable only as long as oil prices remain high.

Second, while inflation remains low in Kuwait compared with the international average, it has been gradually rising over the last few years, reaching 4.4% by mid-2022. The prices of food and beverages rose at a much greater rate, peaking at 10%–12% on a year-to-year basis in the first half of 2021. Besides fiscal measures, the monetary policy of the Central Bank of Kuwait—especially the utilization of the current exchange rate peg to an undisclosed basket of currencies—seems adequate to tackle price rises, especially given the recent decrease in international food prices. All of these factors reduced annual food inflation to 7%–8% in 2022. While inflation is not currently a direct threat, decision-makers should recognize the potential risks posed by rising prices, especially given the political instability in the country. Moreover, macro-economic indicators (including GDP growth) were expected to moderate in 2022, owing primarily to the trends in the international oil market and the higher basis values.

Third, amid the series of economic crises experienced in the last couple of years, the initiatives of the Government actually led to a decrease in economic freedom. According to the Heritage Foundation's Index of Economic Freedom, Kuwait experienced a severe decrease in its ranking for respecting property rights and judicial effectiveness, declining from the 'moderately free' category to the 'mostly unfree' category. In 2023 Kuwait was ranked as the ninth freest economy in the Middle East and North Africa region and the 108th freest economy globally, a decline when compared with 2022. Kuwait was also ranked as the least free economy in the GCC, which could be a major disadvantage in the competition for FDI.

Fourth, infrastructure development is urgently required to maintain economic development and social stability. Heavy rains cause severe problems in Kuwait's cities; roads often need to be reconstructed. On a more pressing note, the Government must also address the deepening housing crisis. Citizens applying for an apartment, house or land often have to wait 15–20 years to acquire the necessary approval, compared with approximately five years in past decades. While the Public Authority for Housing Welfare, in co-operation with other government agencies, is endeavouring to keep pace with increasing demand through major construction plans (including the South Al-Mutlaa City and East Taima projects), slow implementation and poor co-operation between the various agencies undermine these efforts. Proposed regulatory changes, which would allow greater utilization of residential spaces, might have a positive impact, although this could lead to an increase in housing prices.

Fifth, there is definitely scope for improvement in terms of socioeconomic development. While the level of GDP per capita is outstanding in the case of Kuwait, and the country's massive oil wealth enables the Government to maintain high living standards, the overall picture is not entirely positive. Although Kuwait was ranked 50th out of the 191 countries and territories covered in the 2022 UN Development Programme's Human Development Index (HDI), and was designated as a state with very high human development, it had the second lowest ranking in the GCC, surpassing only Oman. Perhaps the most visible decline since 2000 has been in gender inequality, for which Kuwait's ranking had decreased below the global average by 2005. Moreover, there is insufficient data to measure several key indicators with any certainty, including the Gini coefficient (a measure of income inequality) and the general poverty rate.

Sixth, the diversification of the economy should be given a much higher priority by all branches of government. While officially Kuwait aims to decrease its dependence on the oil and gas sectors, in practice, it lags behind its neighbours, and political will seems to be lacking. The longer it takes for the Kuwaiti elites to decide to implement serious action, the less competitive the country's economy will be in the post-oil environment.

Finally, Kuwait needs to take urgent steps to combat climate change. At the Conference of the Parties to the UN Framework Convention on Climate Change held in Egypt in November 2022, Minister of Foreign Affairs Sheikh Salem Abdullah al-Jaber al-Sabah announced that the Government aimed to reach climate neutrality in the oil and gas sector by 2050 and in all sectors by the subsequent decade. While every commitment is important, this designated goal could be more ambitious, especially given the known obstacles in implementing green transition policies and the practice of 'green washing' inside and outside of the region. Mitigation will also be important for Kuwait, where temperatures are projected to rise by 1.8°C–2.6°C over the next three decades.

KUWAIT

CONCLUSION

Resolving all of these problems will require long-term strategic thinking and bold and ambitious leadership by the Kuwaiti authorities. However, the lack of co-operation between the legislative and executive branches continues to undermine both the Kuwaiti state's economic and fiscal leverage and its capacity to manage crises and confront strategic challenges. Reforming the rentier economic structure would necessarily involve multiple and co-ordinated strategies, including (but not limited to) diversification, 'Kuwaitization', finding a proper balance between the private and public sectors, maintaining fiscal stability, combating climate change, fostering human development, and tax reform.

In the coming years, as in the other Gulf states, generational change will likely accelerate in Kuwait, which will shape the future political dynamics in the country, although it is unclear in which direction. Growing dissatisfaction with the political elites can only be reversed if the authorities confront the existing challenges facing the country and provide a well-co-ordinated policy response.

Statistical Survey

Sources (unless otherwise stated): Economic Research Department, Central Bank of Kuwait, POB 526, 13006 Safat, Kuwait City; tel. 22403257; fax 22440887; e-mail cbk@cbk.gov.kw; internet www.cbk.gov.kw; Central Statistical Bureau, Arabian Gulf St, Sharq, Kuwait City; tel. 22428200; fax 22437048; e-mail csb@csb.gov.kw; internet www.csb.gov.kw.

Area and Population

AREA, POPULATION AND DENSITY

Area (sq km)	17,818*
Population (census results)†	
21 April 2011	3,065,850
1 January 2022	
Males	2,671,266
Females	1,714,451
Total	4,385,717‡
Population (official estimates at 1 January)	
2023	4,793,568
Density (per sq km) at 1 January 2023	269.0

* 6,880 sq miles.
† Figures include Kuwaiti nationals abroad.
‡ Comprising 1,488,716 Kuwaitis and 2,897,001 non-Kuwaitis.

POPULATION BY AGE AND SEX
(official estimates at 1 January 2023)

	Males	Females	Total
0–14 years	462,457	441,597	904,054
15–64 years	2,399,395	1,354,490	3,753,885
65 years and over	71,205	64,424	135,629
Total	2,933,057	1,860,511	4,793,568

GOVERNORATES
(at 2021 census)

Governorate	Area (sq km)*	Population	Density (per sq km)
Capital	199.8	574,839	2,877.1
Hawalli	}	926,170	}
Mubarak al-Kabir	368.4	279,666	6,285.7
Farwaniya	}	1,109,819	}
Al-Jahra	11,230.2	566,861	50.5
Al-Ahmadi	5,119.6	923,784	180.4
Total	16,918.0	4,385,717†	259.2

* Excluding the islands of Bubiyan and Warba (combined area 900 sq km).
† Including population of areas not officially demarcated (4,578 persons).

Source: Public Authority for Civil Information.

PRINCIPAL TOWNS
(at 1 January 2022 census)

Salmiya	282,541	Mangaf	112,548
Jaleeb al-Shuyukh	271,168	Fahaheel	96,660
Farwaniya	250,676	Sabah al-Salim	88,904
Hawalli	205,895	Sabahiya	79,702
Khitan	173,538	Salwa	77,284
Mahbula	142,145	Jabriya	73,448
Saad al-Abdulla	114,897	Jahra	68,023

Source: Public Authority for Civil Information.

BIRTHS, MARRIAGES AND DEATHS

	Registered live births		Registered marriages		Registered deaths	
	Number	Rate (per 1,000)	Number	Rate (per 1,000)	Number	Rate (per 1,000)
2017	59,172	14.7	13,932	7.1	6,679	1.7
2018	56,121	13.6	14,400	7.0	6,807	1.7
2019	53,565	12.1	13,886	6.2	7,306	1.6
2020	52,463	11.7	13,071	5.8	10,569	2.4
2021	51,585	12.2	16,393	7.9	10,938	2.6

2022: Registered marriages 13,656 (marriage rate 5.5 per 1,000 persons).

Life expectancy (years at birth, estimates): 78.7 (males 77.2; females 81.5) in 2021 (Source: World Bank, World Development Indicators database).

ECONOMICALLY ACTIVE POPULATION
(persons aged 15 years and over, at 2021 census)

	Kuwaitis	Non-Kuwaitis	Total
Agriculture, hunting and fishing	154	44,628	44,782
Mining and quarrying	11,406	9,103	20,509
Manufacturing	12,073	123,220	135,293
Electricity, gas and water	16,298	666	16,964
Construction	20,586	321,038	341,624
Wholesale and retail trade	18,825	382,064	400,889
Hotels and restaurants	2,532	102,966	105,498
Transport, storage and communications	18,390	65,654	84,044
Finance, insurance, real estate and business services	31,566	165,800	197,366
Public administration	51,041	190,909	241,950

KUWAIT

—continued	Kuwaitis	Non-Kuwaitis	Total
Education	101,175	49,537	150,712
Health and social work	13,910	47,361	61,271
Other community, social and personal service activities	4,426	61,305	65,731
Private households with employed persons	—	636,132	636,132
Extraterritorial organizations and bodies	25	479	504
Sub-total	442,275	2,060,994	2,503,269
Activities not adequately defined	2,499	40,331	42,830
Total employed	444,774	2,101,325	2,546,099
Unemployed	20,412	3,580	23,992
Total labour force	465,186	2,104,905	2,570,091

Source: Public Authority for Civil Information.

Health and Welfare

KEY INDICATORS

Total fertility rate (children per woman, 2021)	2.1
Under-5 mortality rate (per 1,000 live births, 2021)	8.7
HIV/AIDS (% of persons aged 15–49, 2018)	<0.1
COVID-19: Cumulative confirmed deaths (per 100,000 persons at 30 June 2023)	60.2
COVID-19: Fully vaccinated population (% of total population at 27 June 2023)	78.4
Physicians (per 1,000 head, 2020)	2.3
Hospital beds (per 1,000 head, 2017)	2.0
Domestic health expenditure (2020): US $ per head (PPP)	2,627.2
Domestic health expenditure (2020): % of GDP	5.7
Domestic health expenditure (2020): public (% of total current health expenditure)	89.9
Total carbon dioxide emissions ('000 metric tons, 2019)	92,648
Carbon dioxide emissions per head (metric tons, 2019)	20.9
Human Development Index (2021): ranking	50
Human Development Index (2021): value	0.831

Note: For data on COVID-19 vaccinations, 'fully vaccinated' denotes receipt of all doses specified by approved vaccination regime (Sources: Johns Hopkins University and Our World in Data). Data on health expenditure refer to current general government expenditure in each case. For more information on sources and further definitions for all indicators, see Health and Welfare Statistics: Sources and Definitions section (europaworld.com/credits).

Agriculture

PRINCIPAL CROPS
('000 metric tons)

	2019	2020*	2021*
Aubergines (Eggplants)	39.4	36.1	35.2
Cabbages and other brassicas	9.5	8.9	9.0
Cauliflowers and broccoli	7.8	7.3	8.4
Chillies and peppers, green	19.0	18.5	17.4
Cucumbers and gherkins	96.4	88.9	88.1
Dates	105.6	112.0	108.1
Lettuce	12.2	11.8	13.6
Onions, dry	7.1	7.7	6.8
Potatoes	34.8	43.2	47.3
Pumpkins, squash and gourds	19.2	21.2	23.0
Tomatoes	132.2	126.6	122.3

* FAO estimates.

Aggregate production ('000 metric tons, may include official, semi-official or estimated data): Total cereals 31.4 in 2019, 26.7 in 2020, 17.5 in 2021; Total fruit (primary) 116.9 in 2019, 126.3 in 2020, 120.2 in 2021; Total roots and tubers 34.8 in 2019, 43.2 in 2020, 47.3 in 2021; Total vegetables (primary) 388.5 in 2019, 371.7 in 2020, 374.8 in 2021.

Source: FAO.

LIVESTOCK
('000 head, year ending September)

	2019	2020*	2021*
Camels	17.8	17.1	14.6
Cattle	34.7	31.5	31.8
Chickens	53,530	55,430	57,371
Goats	235.3	214.3	219.8
Sheep	714.3	724.2	748.5

* FAO estimates.

Source: FAO.

LIVESTOCK PRODUCTS
('000 metric tons)

	2019	2020*	2021*
Cattle meat	2.9	2.2	2.3
Cows' milk	70.1	67.4	68.0
Chicken meat	61.2	62.5	64.6
Goats' milk	6.4	6.0	6.1
Sheep meat*	52.2	51.6	52.0
Sheep offals, edible*	9.9	9.7	9.8
Sheepskins, fresh*	11.8	11.7	11.8
Hen eggs	72.9†	80.2	n.a.

* FAO estimates.
† Unofficial figure.
Source: FAO.

Fishing

(metric tons, live weight)

	2019	2020*	2021*
Capture	3,016	3,095	3,525
Groupers	122	120	135
Hilsa shad	99	100	115
Klunzinger's mullet	346	340	390
Narrow-barred Spanish mackerel	116	100	115
Natantian decapods	918	1,005	1,155
Silver pomfret	92	115	130
Tigertooth croaker	265	240	275
Yellowfin seabream	194	180	205
Aquaculture	458	450	450
Nile tilapia	458	450	450
Total catch	3,474	3,545	3,975

* FAO estimates.
Source: FAO.

Mining

	2020	2021	2022
Crude petroleum (million tons)	131.2	129.9	145.7
Natural gas ('000 million cu m)	12.2	12.1	13.4

Source: Energy Institute, *Statistical Review of World Energy*.

Industry

SELECTED PRODUCTS
('000 metric tons unless otherwise indicated)

	2017	2018	2019
Bran and flour	497.2	503.2	527.3
Sulphur (by-product)*†	850	850	850
Chlorine	46.2	27.0	30.3
Caustic soda (Sodium hydroxide)	31.0	29.4	34.8
Salt*	58.2	58.2†	58.2†
Nitrogenous fertilizers*‡	546	250†	n.a.
Motor spirit (petrol) (million barrels)*§	13	13	22
Kerosene (million barrels)*§	52	52	50
Gas-diesel (distillate fuel) oils (million barrels)*§	62	62	61
Residual fuel oils (mazout—million barrels)*§	56	56	54
Cement*†	3,400	3,300	3,500
Electrical energy (million kWh)§	72,787	74,107	75,082

* Source: US Geological Survey.
† Estimate(s).
‡ Production in terms of nitrogen.
§ Including an equal share of production with Saudi Arabia from the Neutral (Partitioned) Zone.

Finance

CURRENCY, EXCHANGE RATES AND FISCAL YEAR

Monetary Units
1,000 fils = 10 dirhams = 1 Kuwaiti dinar (KD).

Sterling, Dollar and Euro Equivalents (31 May 2023)
£1 sterling = 380.01 fils;
US $1 = 307.35 fils;
€1 = 328.34 fils;
10 Kuwaiti dinars = £26.32 = $32.54 = €30.46.

Average Exchange Rate (fils per US $)
2020 306.23
2021 301.64
2022 306.25

From 1 January 2003 the official exchange rate was fixed within the range of US $1 = 289 fils to $1 = 310 fils (KD 1 = $3.2258 to KD 1 = $3.4602), but this 'peg' to the US dollar was abandoned in May 2007 in favour of a basket of currencies including the pound sterling, the euro and the yen.

Fiscal Year
The fiscal year ends on 31 March.

GENERAL BUDGET
(KD million, fiscal year)

Revenue	2020/21	2021/22	2022/23
Tax revenue	473.5	462.4	564.7
International trade and transactions	297.3	306.9	388.7
Non-tax revenue	10,046.8	18,150.5	22,834.4
Petroleum revenue	8,789.7	16,217.0	21,321.5
Total operating revenue of government enterprises	1,257.1	1,933.5	1,513.0
Total	**10,520.3**	**18,612.9**	**23,399.1**

Expenditure	2020/21	2021/22	2022/23
Current expenditure	19,550.0	19,740.5	21,216.7
Compensation of employees	7,445.8	7,990.4	8,537.6
Use of goods and services	2,873.6	3,190.7	4,081.7
Subsidies	556.6	620.3	797.9
Grants	5,432.5	5,550.9	5,629.1
Social benefits	847.2	1,037.5	736.2
Other current expenditure	2,394.3	1,350.9	1,434.2
Capital expenditure	1,742.7	1,862.5	2,306.3
Total	**21,292.7**	**21,604.0**	**23,523.0**

* Budget figures.

INTERNATIONAL RESERVES
(US $ million at 31 December)

	2020	2021	2022
Gold (national valuation)	104.7	104.9	103.6
IMF special drawing rights	1,924.1	4,463.9	4,252.0
Reserve position in IMF	697.7	750.1	726.3
Foreign exchange	45,495.3	39,689.9	42,882.0
Total	**48,221.8**	**45,008.8**	**47,963.9**

Source: IMF, *International Financial Statistics*.

MONEY SUPPLY
(KD million at 31 December)

	2020	2021	2022
Currency outside depository corporations	1,899.0	1,775.2	1,670.3
Transferable deposits	10,775.3	11,155.8	10,543.2
Other deposits	22,335.0	23,314.5	26,269.4
Broad money	**35,009.3**	**36,245.5**	**38,482.9**

Source: IMF, *International Financial Statistics*.

COST OF LIVING
(Consumer Price Index; base: 2013 = 100)

	2020	2021	2022
Food and non-alcoholic beverages	114.1	124.9	134.2
Clothing and footwear	110.9	117.7	124.4
Housing	115.0	115.5	118.0
All items	**116.6**	**120.6**	**125.4**

NATIONAL ACCOUNTS
(KD million at current prices)

Expenditure on the Gross Domestic Product

	2019	2020	2021
Government final consumption expenditure	10,429.0	8,358.6	9,448.7
Private final consumption expenditure	17,100.4	14,304.1	15,981.3
Increase in stocks	126.1	n.a.	n.a.
Gross fixed capital formation	10,218.8	8,185.1	9,557.1
Total domestic expenditure	**37,874.4**	**30,847.7**	**34,987.2**
Exports of goods and services	22,036.5	14,351.7	21,676.9
Less Imports of goods and services	18,561.5	12,754.4	15,446.9
GDP in purchasers' values	**41,349.3**	**32,445.0**	**41,217.1**
GDP at constant 2015 prices	**34,441.2**	**31,391.9**	**31,802.5**

Source: UN National Accounts Main Aggregates Database.

Gross Domestic Product by Economic Activity

	2018	2019*	2020*
Agriculture, hunting, forestry and fishing	186.7	159.0	148.4
Mining and quarrying	19,849.4	18,909.8	11,179.3
Manufacturing	3,109.6	2,966.0	2,143.7
Electricity, gas and water	1,086.0	1,069.3	738.8
Construction	1,127.4	1,194.7	676.8
Trade	1,694.3	1,723.0	1,550.2
Restaurants and hotels	367.7	360.3	274.1
Transport, storage and communications	2,747.8	2,832.6	2,653.8
Finance and insurance	3,725.9	3,844.9	4,134.0
Public administration and defence	4,302.6	4,778.5	4,949.7
Education	2,577.5	2,648.1	2,704.4

KUWAIT

—continued	2018	2019*	2020*
Health and social work	1,510.2	1,601.3	1,646.8
Households with employed persons	529.7	549.3	597.3
Other services	4,210.1	4,289.6	3,895.7
Sub-total	47,024.9	46,926.4	37,292.9
Indirect taxes (net)	−2,550.9	−2,808.5	−1,981.1
Less Imputed bank service charges	2,742.9	2,768.6	2,866.8
GDP in purchasers' values	41,731.1	41,349.3	32,445.0

* Provisional.

BALANCE OF PAYMENTS
(US $ million)

	2020	2021	2022
Exports of goods f.o.b.	40,248.2	68,415.6	100,314.3
Imports of goods f.o.b.	−24,835.9	−27,866.1	−28,364.3
Balance on goods	15,412.4	40,549.6	71,950.1
Exports of services	7,168.2	8,705.6	10,608.6
Imports of services	−19,179.4	−21,087.9	−27,544.9
Balance on goods and services	3,401.2	28,167.2	55,013.7
Primary income received	39,482.4	27,718.2	31,089.1
Primary income paid	−3,255.4	−2,342.4	−5,116.0
Balance on goods, services and primary income	39,628.1	53,543.0	80,986.8
Secondary income received	4.5	6.0	5.7
Secondary income paid	−17,602.9	−18,605.7	−17,910.4
Current balance	22,029.7	34,943.3	63,082.2
Capital account (net)	994.8	1,521.2	540.3
Direct investment assets	−3,153.9	2,241.0	−25,532.2
Direct investment liabilities	−558.1	−272.3	752.3
Portfolio investment assets	−50,174.7	−29,915.3	−46,515.7
Portfolio investment liabilities	1,059.2	−926.8	−4,338.6
Financial derivatives and employee stock options (net)	−245.1	1,007.9	−11.8
Other investment assets	42,109.6	−20,965.7	4,633.1
Other investment liabilities	−2,527.1	11,719.9	9,457.0
Net errors and omissions	−1,267.6	−2,568.2	1,639.0
Reserves and related items	8,266.9	−3,215.2	3,705.5

Source: IMF, *International Financial Statistics*.

External Trade

PRINCIPAL COMMODITIES
(distribution by HS, KD million)

Imports c.i.f.	2019	2020	2021
Live animals and animal products	482.5	504.2	501.8
Vegetables and vegetable products	556.8	554.8	546.4
Prepared foodstuffs; beverages, spirits, vinegar; tobacco and articles thereof	593.2	587.8	504.6
Chemicals and related products	1,046.9	1,017.6	1,114.4
Pharmaceutical products	422.1	460.5	502.6
Plastics, rubber, and articles thereof	408.9	301.6	345.0
Textiles and textile articles	465.3	571.5	639.2
Pearls, precious or semi-precious stones, precious metals, and articles thereof	333.0	294.0	691.1
Iron and steel, other base metals and articles of base metal	1,085.0	706.2	803.1
Articles of iron or steel	581.9	343.9	296.8
Machinery and mechanical appliances; electrical equipment and parts thereof	2,304.7	1,682.0	1,661.1
Machinery and mechanical appliances	1,187.8	794.2	783.4
Electrical machinery and equipment and parts thereof	1,116.8	887.2	877.6
Vehicles, aircraft, vessels and associated transport equipment	1,382.6	1,013.9	1,216.6
Road vehicles	1,336.1	1,003.1	1,199.7
Optical, medical apparatus, etc.; clocks and watches; musical instruments and parts thereof	343.2	328.0	305.4
Miscellaneous manufactured articles	295.2	260.6	337.1
Total (incl. others)	10,164.6	8,507.2	9,616.3

Exports f.o.b.†	2019	2020	2021
Live animals and animal products	52.8	34.4	34.4
Vegetables and vegetable products	43.4	25.3	24.4
Prepared foodstuffs; beverages, spirits, vinegar; tobacco and articles thereof	74.4	48.2	52.0
Chemicals and related products	603.0	411.9	586.0
Organic chemicals	506.3	338.4	502.0
Plastics, rubber, and articles thereof	192.5	173.1	126.8
Plastics and articles thereof	190.4	171.3	124.4
Pearls, precious or semi-precious stones, precious metals, and articles thereof	40.8	20.2	17.0
Iron and steel, other base metals and articles of base metal	76.3	80.5	130.8
Machinery and mechanical appliances; electrical equipment; parts thereof	159.8	110.1	125.7
Vehicles, aircraft, vessels and associated transport equipment	291.6	250.0	336.6
Road vehicles	290.5	242.6	324.4
Total (incl. others)	1,712.8	1,271.3	1,599.6

† Excluding petroleum exports (KD million): 17,827.4 in 2019; 10,958.0 in 2020; 19,000.4 in 2021.

PRINCIPAL TRADING PARTNERS
(KD million)*

Imports c.i.f.	2019	2020	2021†
Australia	116.0	89.9	134.9
Bahrain	140.3	158.4	138.6
China, People's Republic	1,818.1	1,574.3	1,727.7
Egypt	113.4	98.8	101.0
France	236.8	198.3	217.4
Germany	531.6	397.2	424.1
India	578.1	417.2	500.6
Iran	69.1	58.3	123.1
Italy	440.4	322.0	367.3
Japan	641.6	511.3	554.0
Korea, Republic	273.7	154.8	126.7
Netherlands	135.8	115.9	111.5
Poland	55.4	86.2	83.1

KUWAIT

Statistical Survey

Imports c.i.f.—continued	2019	2020	2021†
Saudi Arabia	629.6	504.7	508.8
Spain	121.9	110.2	113.5
Switzerland	163.9	187.3	215.3
Thailand	136.7	110.5	128.4
Türkiye	197.3	192.1	227.8
United Arab Emirates	855.6	715.3	1,143.7
United Kingdom	266.9	187.2	228.7
USA	921.2	730.2	768.7
Viet Nam	118.2	110.2	118.9
Total (incl. others)	10,164.6	8,507.2	9,616.3

Exports f.o.b.‡	2019	2020	2021
Bahrain	20.1	15.1	17.3
China, People's Republic	276.6	175.3	215.0
Egypt	13.9	8.7	23.5
India	244.6	152.8	211.7
Iraq	247.9	112.7	152.3
Jordan	31.2	29.2	39.1
Malaysia	7.5	5.9	17.1
Nigeria	8.1	21.4	4.4
Oman	62.0	52.4	44.0
Pakistan	57.1	50.5	94.2
Qatar	109.2	86.1	84.3
Saudi Arabia	197.2	199.6	219.7
Singapore	9.5	8.0	25.5
Türkiye	25.9	15.4	20.0
United Arab Emirates	170.5	163.7	243.1
USA	15.6	17.5	12.1
Viet Nam	18.4	19.6	7.5
Total (incl. others)	1,712.8	1,271.3	1,599.6

* Imports by country of production; exports by country of last consignment.
† Provisional.
‡ Excluding petroleum exports.

Transport

ROAD TRAFFIC
(motor vehicles in use at 31 December)

	2019	2020	2021
Passenger cars	1,793,739	1,841,727	1,887,834
Buses and coaches	40,344	40,385	39,036
Motorcycles and mopeds	28,069	32,235	34,443

SHIPPING

Flag Registered Fleet
(at 31 December)

	2020	2021	2022
Number of vessels	213	226	234
Displacement ('000 grt)	2,660.0	2,837.8	2,777.9

Source: Lloyd's List Intelligence (www.bit.ly/LLintelligence).

CIVIL AVIATION
(traffic on scheduled services)

	2013	2014	2015
Kilometres flown (million)	54	57	60
Passengers carried ('000)	3,245	3,531	3,655
Passenger-km (million)	8,193	8,655	8,950
Total ton-km (million)	246	268	276

Source: UN, *Statistical Yearbook*.

2021 (domestic and international): Departures 20,436; Passengers carried 2.2m.; Freight carried 200m. ton-km (Source: World Bank, World Development Indicators database).

Tourism

VISITOR ARRIVALS BY COUNTRY OF ORIGIN
(incl. excursionists)

	2019	2020	2021
Bahrain	230,247	42,578	22,674
Bangladesh	156,272	38,832	32,408
Egypt	969,087	264,779	249,728
India	1,315,109	318,356	290,185
Jordan	142,913	42,548	42,304
Lebanon	127,814	30,560	27,103
Pakistan	185,111	77,232	72,368
Philippines	246,959	50,060	56,612
Saudi Arabia	3,664,146	893,950	498,852
Syrian Arab Republic	212,454	84,130	82,818
USA	128,949	38,474	42,662
Total (incl. others)	8,565,065	2,160,854	1,605,597

Tourism receipts (US $ million, excl. passenger transport): 700 in 2019; 397 in 2020; 470 in 2021 (provisional) (Source: World Tourism Organization).

Communications Media

	2019	2020	2021
Telephones ('000 main lines in use)	583.5	583.5	n.a.
Mobile telephone subscriptions ('000)	7,327.0	6,770.3	6,918.2
Broadband subscriptions, fixed ('000)	84.6	73.9	70.5
Broadband subscriptions, mobile ('000)	5,584.5	5,442.6	5,807.6
Internet users (% of population)	99.5	99.1	99.7

Source: International Telecommunication Union.

Education

(state-controlled schools, 2021/22 unless otherwise indicated)

	Schools	Teachers	Students
Kindergarten	200	7,086	43,346
Primary	281	26,776	160,745
Intermediate	226	23,438	129,832
Secondary	146	16,035	91,578
Religious institutes	9	746	3,230
Special training institutes*	15	1,387	1,803

* 2019/20.

Private education (2021/22 unless otherwise indicated): 124 kindergarten schools (1,508 teachers (2020/21), 26,056 students); 156 primary schools (5,284 teachers (2020/21), 105,458 students); 159 intermediate schools (2,961 teachers (2020/21), 74,251 students); 136 secondary schools (3,122 teachers (2020/21), 48,090 students).

Pupil-teacher ratio (primary education, qualified teaching staff, UNESCO estimate): 10.9 in 2019/20 (Source: UNESCO Institute for Statistics).

Adult literacy rate (UNESCO estimates): 96.5% (males 97.1%; females 95.4%) in 2020 (Source: UNESCO Institute for Statistics).

Directory

The Constitution

The principal provisions of the Constitution, promulgated on 16 November 1962, are set out below. On 29 August 1976 the Amir suspended four articles of the Constitution dealing with the Majlis al-Umma (National Assembly). On 24 August 1980 the Amir issued a decree ordering the establishment of an elected legislature before the end of February 1981. The new National Assembly was elected on 23 February, and fresh legislative elections followed on 20 February 1985. The Assembly was dissolved by Amiri decree in July 1986, and some sections of the Constitution, including the stipulation that new elections should be held within two months of dissolving the legislature (see below), were suspended. A new Assembly was elected on 5 October 1992 and convened on 20 October. In 2005 the Assembly approved legislation allowing women to vote in and stand as candidates for parliamentary and local elections.

SOVEREIGNTY

Kuwait is an independent sovereign Arab State; its sovereignty may not be surrendered, and no part of its territory may be relinquished. Offensive war is prohibited by the Constitution.

Succession as Amir is restricted to heirs of the late Mubarak al-Sabah, and an Heir Apparent must be appointed within one year of the accession of a new Amir.

EXECUTIVE AUTHORITY

Executive power is vested in the Amir, who exercises it through the Council of Ministers. The Amir will appoint the Prime Minister 'after the traditional consultations', and will appoint and dismiss ministers on the recommendation of the Prime Minister. Ministers need not be members of the National Assembly, although all ministers who are not members of parliament assume membership ex officio in the legislature for the duration of office. The Amir also formulates laws, which shall not be effective unless published in the *Official Gazette*. The Amir establishes public institutions. All decrees issued in these respects shall be conveyed to the National Assembly. No law is issued unless it is approved by the Assembly.

LEGISLATURE

A National Assembly of 50 members is elected for a four-year term by all natural-born Kuwaitis over the age of 21 years, except servicemen and police, who may not vote. (Unelected cabinet ministers also sit in the Assembly, bringing the total membership to around 65.) Candidates for election must possess the franchise, be over 30 years of age and literate. The Assembly will convene for at least eight months in any year, and new elections shall be held within two months of the last dissolution of the outgoing legislature.

Restrictions on the commercial activities of ministers include an injunction forbidding them to sell property to the Government.

The Amir may ask for reconsideration of a bill that has been approved by the National Assembly and sent to him for ratification, but the bill would automatically become law if it were subsequently adopted by a two-thirds' majority at the next sitting, or by a simple majority at a subsequent sitting. The Amir may declare martial law, but only with the approval of the legislature.

The National Assembly may adopt a vote of no confidence in a minister, in which case the minister must resign. Such a vote is not permissible in the case of the Prime Minister. However, the Assembly may adopt a vote of non-cooperation with a Prime Minister; if such a vote is passed, the matter is then submitted to the Amir, who shall subsequently either dismiss the Prime Minister or dissolve the Assembly.

CIVIL SERVICE

Entry to the civil service is confined to Kuwaiti citizens.

PUBLIC LIBERTIES

Kuwaitis are equal before the law in prestige, rights and duties. Individual freedom is guaranteed. No one shall be seized, arrested or exiled except within the rules of law.

No punishment shall be administered except for an act or abstaining from an act considered a crime in accordance with a law applicable at the time of committing it, and no penalty shall be imposed more severe than that which could have been imposed at the time of committing the crime.

Freedom of opinion is guaranteed to everyone, and each has the right to express himself through speech, writing or other means within the limits of the law.

The press is free within the limits of the law, and it should not be suppressed except in accordance with the dictates of law.

Freedom of performing religious rites is protected by the state according to prevailing customs, provided it does not violate the public order and morality.

Trade unions will be permitted and property must be respected. An owner is not banned from managing his or her property except within the boundaries of law. No property should be taken from anyone, except within the prerogatives of law, unless a just compensation be given.

Houses may not be entered, except in cases provided by law. Every Kuwaiti has freedom of movement and choice of place of residence within the state. This right shall not be controlled except in cases stipulated by law.

Every person has the right to education and freedom to choose his or her type of work. Freedom to form peaceful societies is guaranteed within the limits of law.

The Government

HEAD OF STATE

Amir of Kuwait: His Highness Sheikh NAWAF AL-AHMAD AL-JABER AL-SABAH (acceded 30 September 2020).

COUNCIL OF MINISTERS
(September 2023)

Prime Minister: Gen. (retd) Sheikh AHMAD NAWAF AL-AHMAD AL-SABAH.

First Deputy Prime Minister and Minister of the Interior: Sheikh TALAL AL-KHALED AL-AHMAD AL-SABAH.

Deputy Prime Minister and Minister of Defence: Sheikh AHMAD AL-FAHAD AL-AHMED AL-SABAH.

Deputy Prime Minister and Minister of State for Cabinet Affairs and for National Assembly Affairs: ESSA AHMAD MOHAMMAD AL-KANDARI.

Deputy Prime Minister, Minister of Oil, and Minister of State for Economic Affairs: SAAD AL-BARRAK.

Minister of Foreign Affairs: Sheikh SALEM ABDULLAH AL-JABER AL-SABAH.

Minister of Finance: FAHD AL-JARALLAH.

Minister of Information and of Awqaf (Religious Endowments) and Islamic Affairs: ABDULRAHMAN BEDAH AL-MUTAIRI.

Minister of Education, and of Higher Education and Scientific Research: HAMAD ABDULWAHAB HAMAD AL-ADWANI.

Minister of Justice and Minister of State for Housing Affairs: FALEH AL-RGUBA.

Minister of Health: Dr AHMAD ABDULWAHAB AL-AWADHI.

Minister of Public Works: AMANI SULEIMAN ABDEL-WAHAB BUQAMAZ.

Minister of Commerce and Industry, and Minister of State for Youth Affairs: MOHAMMAD OTHMAN MOHAMMAD AL-AIBAN.

Minister of Electricity, Water and Renewable Energy: JASSEM AL-OSTAD.

Minister of Social Affairs, Family and Childhood Affairs: Sheikh FERAS SAUD AL-MALEK AL-SABAH.

Minister of State for Municipal Affairs and for Communications: FAHAD ALI ZAYED AL-SHULA.

MINISTRIES

Diwan of the Prime Minister: POB 2, 15015 Kuwait City; tel. 22000000; fax 22223048; e-mail contact@pm.gov.kw; internet www.pm.gov.kw.

Ministry of Awqaf (Religious Endowments) and Islamic Affairs: POB 13, 13001 Safat, Kuwait City; tel. 22487225; fax 22262407; e-mail contact_us@islam.gov.kw; internet islam.gov.kw.

Ministry of Commerce and Industry: POB 2944, 13030 Safat, Kuwait City; tel. 2248000; fax 22451088; e-mail office@moci.gov.kw; internet moci.gov.kw.

Ministry of Communications: POB 318, 11111 Safat, Kuwait City; tel. 24819033; fax 24814448; internet moc.gov.kw.

Ministry of Defence: POB 1170, 13012 Safat, Kuwait City; tel. 24848300; fax 24836444; e-mail mod_info@mod.gov.kw; internet mod.gov.kw.

Ministry of Education: POB 7, 13001 Safat, Hilali St, Kuwait City; tel. 24848586; fax 24810970; e-mail agent-1@moe.edu.kw; internet www.moe.edu.kw.

KUWAIT

Ministry of Electricity, Water and Renewable Energy: POB 12, South al-Sourra St, Ministries Area, Al Assimah, 13001 Safat, Kuwait City; tel. 25371000; fax 25384522; e-mail info@mew.gov.kw; internet www.mew.gov.kw.

Ministry of Finance: POB 9, 13001 Safat, al-Morkab St, Ministries Complex, Kuwait City; tel. 22480000; fax 22446361; e-mail minoff@mof.gov.kw; internet www.mof.gov.kw.

Ministry of Foreign Affairs: POB 3, 13001 Safat, Gulf St, Kuwait City; tel. 1800777; fax 22447350; internet www.mofa.gov.kw.

Ministry of Health: POB 5, 13001 Safat, Jamal Abd al-Nasser St, Kuwait City; tel. 24878168; fax 24863589; e-mail health@moh.gov.kw; internet www.moh.gov.kw.

Ministry of Higher Education: POB 27130, 13132 Safat, Kuwait City; tel. 22906103; fax 22906102; e-mail undersecretary@mohe.edu.kw; internet www.mohe.edu.kw.

Ministry of Information: POB 193, 13002 Safat, al-Sour St, Kuwait City; tel. 22326000; fax 22437551; e-mail info@media.gov.kw; internet www.media.gov.kw.

Ministry of the Interior: POB 11, 13001 Safat, Kuwait City; tel. 22430500; fax 22496570; e-mail info@media.gov.kw; internet www.moi.gov.kw.

Ministry of Justice: POB 6, 13001 Safat, al-Morkab St, Ministries Complex, Kuwait City; tel. 22480000; fax 22442257; e-mail info@moj.gov.kw; internet www.moj.gov.kw.

Ministry of Oil: POB 5077, 13051 Safat, Kuwait City; tel. 22406990; fax 24995408; e-mail alnaft@moo.gov.kw; internet www.moo.gov.kw.

Ministry of Public Works: POB 8, 13001 Safat, Kuwait City; tel. 25381750; fax 25385424; e-mail undersecretary@mpw.gov.kw; internet www.mpw.gov.kw.

Ministry of Social Affairs, Family and Childhood Affairs: POB 563, 13006 Safat, Kuwait City; tel. 22480000; fax 22406318; internet www.mosal.gov.kw.

Legislature

At elections to the National Assembly held on 6 June 2023, opposition candidates won an outright majority of 29 of the chamber's 50 elective seats, representing a gain of one seat on the opposition's tally of 28 seats in the elections of 29 September 2022 (annulled by the Constitutional Court on 19 March 2023). A total of 38 of those who secured representation in the September 2022 elections were re-elected to the legislature in June 2023. Only one woman candidate (representing the opposition) won a seat in the National Assembly, while Shi'a candidates took seven seats and the Islamic Constitutional Movement three. According to official estimates, the electoral turnout was around 51% of eligible voters.

National Assembly: POB 716, 13008 Safat, Kuwait City; tel. 22002000; e-mail media@kna.kw; internet www.kna.kw.

Speaker: AHMED ABDULAZIZ AL-SAADOUN.

Political Organizations

Political parties are not permitted in Kuwait. However, several quasi-political organizations are in existence. Among those that have been represented in the Majlis since 1992 are:

Islamic Constitutional Movement (Hadas): internet www.icmkw.org; f. 1991; Sunni Muslim; political arm of the Muslim Brotherhood; Sec.-Gen. NASSER AL-SSHY;AL-SANE.

Islamic Salafi Alliance: Sunni Muslim.

Justice and Peace Alliance: Shi'a Muslim; Leader HASSAN NASIR.

Kuwait Democratic Forum: internet www.alminbarkw.org; f. 1991; loose assen of secular, liberal and Arab nationalist groups; campaigned for the extension of voting rights to women; Sec.-Gen. ABDUL HADI AL-SANAFI.

National Action Bloc: liberal, nationalist.

National Democratic Alliance (NDA): Nuzha St, al-Nuzha Area, Kuwait City; tel. 5551212; e-mail info@altahalof.org; internet altahalof.org; f. 1997; secular, liberal; Sec.-Gen. BASHAR AL-SAYEGH.

National Islamic Alliance: Shi'a Muslim; Leader HUSSAIN AL-MA'TOUQ.

Popular Action Bloc: loose assen of nationalists and Shi'a Muslims; Leader AHMAD AL-SAADOUN.

Diplomatic Representation

EMBASSIES IN KUWAIT

Afghanistan: POB 33186, 73452 Rawdah, Block 6, Surra St, across from Surra Co-op Society, House 16, Kuwait City; tel. 25328156; fax 25326274; e-mail kuwait@mfa.af; Ambassador SAYED JAWAD HASHEMI.

Algeria: POB 578, 13006 Safat, Istiqlal St, Kuwait City; tel. 22519984; e-mail ambalg.kw@gmail.com; Ambassador NOUREDDINE MERYEM.

Argentina: POB 429, 47455 al-Sadiq, 47455 Kuwait City; tel. 25213202; fax 25216202; e-mail ekuwa@mrecic.gov.ar; internet www.cancilleria.gob.ar/es/representaciones/ekuwa; Ambassador CLAUDIA ALEJANDRA ZAMPIERI.

Armenia: Jabriya District, Blk 8, St 3, Villa 8, Kuwait City; tel. 25322175; fax 25314656; e-mail embassy.kuwait@mfa.am; internet kuwait.mfa.am; Ambassador SARMEN BAGHDASARYAN.

Australia: Dar al-Awadi Bldg (Level 12), Ahmad al-Jaber St, Sharq, Kuwait City; tel. 22322422; fax 22322430; e-mail austemb.kuwait@dfat.gov.au; internet kuwait.embassy.gov.au; Ambassador MELISSA KELLY.

Austria: POB 15013, Daiyah, Block 3, Ahmed Shawki St, House 10, 35451 Kuwait City; tel. 22552532; fax 22563052; e-mail kuwait-ob@bmeia.gv.at; internet bmeia.gv.at/oeb-kuwait; Ambassador MARIAN WRBA.

Azerbaijan: Block 2, Villa 15, Yarmouk, Kuwait City; tel. 25355247; fax 25355246; e-mail kuwait@mission.mfa.gov.az; internet kuwait.mfa.gov.az; Ambassador EMIL KARIMOV.

Bahrain: POB 1108, Plot 5, Villa 27, Area 1, Daiya, 13002 Kuwait City; tel. 25318530; fax 25330882; e-mail kuwait.mission@mofa.gov.bh; internet www.mofa.gov.bh/kuwait; Ambassador SALAH ALI AL-MALIKI.

Bangladesh: House 11, St 29, Khaldiya, Kuwait City; tel. 23900913; fax 23900912; e-mail ambassador.kuwait@mofa.gov.bd; internet kuwait.mofa.gov.bd; Ambassador Maj.-Gen. MD ASHIKUZZAMAN.

Belgium: POB 3280, Bayan, Blk 13, St 4, Villa 8, Safat, 13033 Kuwait City; tel. 25389755; fax 25384583; e-mail kuwait@diplobel.fed.be; internet kuwait.diplomatie.belgium.be; Ambassador CHRISTIAN DOMS.

Bhutan: POB 1510, 13016 Safat, Kuwait City; tel. 25213601; fax 25213603; e-mail rbe.kuwait@mfa.gov.bt; internet fb.com/Royal-Bhutanese-Embassy-in-Kuwait-102710328038620; Ambassador CHITEM TENZIN.

Bosnia and Herzegovina: Bayan, Blk 13, Plot 9, St 1, Villa 15, Kuwait City; tel. and fax 25392106; e-mail bhembkwt@yahoo.com; Ambassador SANJIN HALIMOVIĆ.

Brazil: Mubarak al-Abdullah al-Jaber Area, St 116, Blk 1, Villa 47, Kuwait City; tel. 25378561; fax 25378560; e-mail consular.kuaite@itamaraty.gov.br; internet kuaite.itamaraty.gov.br; Ambassador RODRIGO D'ARAUJO GABSCH (designate).

Brunei Darussalam: St 611, Blk 6, al-Siddeeq, Kuwait City; tel. 25234561; fax 25234564; e-mail missions.kuwait@mfa.gov.bn; internet www.mfa.gov.bn/kuwait-kuwaitcity; Ambassador Haji AHMAD BIN HAJI JUMAT.

Bulgaria: POB 12090, 71651 Shamiya, Jabriya, Area 11, St 107 and St 1, Kuwait City; tel. 25314458; fax 25321453; e-mail embassy.kuwait@mfa.bg; internet www.mfa.bg/embassies/kuwait; Ambassador DIMITAR DIMITROV.

Cambodia: St 1, Blk 1, Villa 25, Surra, Kuwait City; tel. 25310029; fax 25310026; e-mail camemb.kwt@mfaic.gov.kh; Ambassador SAMAN MANAN.

Canada: POB 25281, 13113 Kuwait City; tel. 22563025; fax 22560173; e-mail kwait@international.gc.ca; internet www.canadainternational.gc.ca/kuwait-koweit; Ambassador ALIYA MAWANI.

Chad: Villa 10, Block 3, 310 St, W Mishref, Kuwait City; tel. 25377660; e-mail info@ambatchadkuwait.org; internet ambatchadkuwait.org; Ambassador TAHER AL-NADIF.

China, People's Republic: POB 2346, St 1, Villa 82, 13024 Kuwait City; tel. 25333340; fax 25333341; e-mail chinaemb_kw@mfa.gov.cn; internet kw.chineseembassy.org; Ambassador ZHANG JIANWEI.

Croatia: Villa 32, St 301, Blk 3, Mubarak al-Abdullah al-Jaber, West Mishref, Kuwait City; tel. 25388705; e-mail croemb.kuwait@mvep.hr; Ambassador AMIR MUHAREMI.

Cuba: POB 1604, House 74, Abu Hayyan Al-Tawhidi St, Block 3, Rawda, Surra, 45711 Kuwait City; tel. 25356634; fax 25356638; e-mail embajada@kw.embacuba.cu; internet misiones.minrex.gob.cu/en/kuwait; Ambassador JOSÉ LUIS NORIEGA SÁNCHEZ.

Czech Republic: House 31B, Ghazza St, Blk 1, Khaldiya, Kuwait City; tel. 24926034; fax 24926044; e-mail kuwait@embassy.mzv.cz; internet www.mzv.cz/kuwait; Ambassador JAROSLAV SIRO.

Djibouti: Villa 60, St 1, Blk 4, Al Surra Area, Kuwait City; tel. 25351671; fax 25351690; e-mail ambdjibouti.kow@diplomatie.gouv.dj; internet djiboutiembassykuwait.net; Ambassador ABDOULKADER HOUSSEIN OMAR.

Egypt: POB 11252, Istiqlal St, Dasmah, 35153 Kuwait City; tel. 22519955; fax 22563877; e-mail embassy.kuwait@mfa.gov.eg; Ambassador OSAMA HUSSEIN SHALTOUT.

Eritrea: POB 53016, House 9, Block 9, St 21, Kuwait City; tel. 25317427; Chargé d'affaires HAMAD YAHYA HALI.

Eswatini: POB 632, Villa 69, Block 7, St 101, Jabriya, 46307 Kuwait City; tel. 25313306; fax 23513307; e-mail swazikuwait@gmail.com; Ambassador NKOOLIKO HORACE DLAMINI.

Ethiopia: Villa 12, Block 4, St 16, al-Fintas, Kuwait City; tel. 65614756; e-mail ambassador.kuwait@mfa.gov.et; internet fb.com/ethiopianembassyinkuwait; Ambassador Dr SIED MOHAMMED JIBRIL.

France: POB 1037, al-Hamra Tower, 40th Floor, al-Shuhada, Sharq, Kuwait City; tel. 22058900; fax 22571058; e-mail cad.koweit-amba@diplomatie.gouv.fr; internet kw.ambafrance.org; Ambassador CLAIRE LE FLÉCHER.

Georgia: Villa 6, Blk 2, St 1, Ave 3, Kuwait City; tel. 25621441; fax 25646454; e-mail kuwait.emb@mfa.gov.ge; internet kuwait.mfa.gov.ge; Ambassador KONSTANTINE ZHGENTI.

Germany: POB 805, al-Hamra Tower, 40th Floor, al-Shuhada St, Safat, Sharq, 13009 Kuwait City; tel. 22058955; fax 22058966; e-mail info@kuwa.diplo.de; internet www.kuwait.diplo.de; Ambassador HANS-CHRISTIAN FREIHERR VON REIBNITZ.

Ghana: Blk 12, St 4, Villa 44, Salwa, Kuwait City; tel. 25621159; e-mail kuwait@mfa.gov.gh; internet ghanaembassy-kuwait.com; Ambassador MOHAMMED HABIB IDRIS (designate).

Greece: POB 23812, Villa 4, Khaldiya, Block 4, St 44, Safat, 13099 Kuwait City; tel. 24817100; fax 24817103; e-mail gremb.kuw@mfa.gr; internet www.mfa.gr/kuwait; Ambassador KONSTANTINOS PIPERIGOS.

Holy See: POB 757, Villa 1, St 2, Blk 1, Yarmouk, 72658 Kuwait City; tel. 25337767; fax 25327776; e-mail nuntiuskuwait@gmail.com; Apostolic Nuncio Archbishop EUGENE MARTIN NUGENT.

Honduras: House 517, Blk 5, Ahmad bin Mohamed Salama St, Surra, Kuwait City; tel. 25310357; Ambassador LUIS ALONZO VELÁSQUEZ.

Hungary: POB 23955, Villa 381, Bayan, Blk 13, St 30, Safat, 13100 Kuwait City; tel. 25379351; fax 25379350; e-mail mission.kwi@mfa.gov.hu; internet kuvait.mfa.gov.hu; Ambassador ESZTER TORDA.

India: POB 1450, Diplomatic Enclave, Arabian Gulf St, Safat, 13015 Kuwait City; tel. 65806158; internet www.indembkwt.gov.in; Ambassador Dr ADARSH SWAIKA.

Indonesia: POB 21560, Bldg 2, Daiya Blk 1, Rashed Ibn Ahmed al-Roumi St, Kuwait City; tel. 22531021; fax 22531024; e-mail kuwait.kbri@kemlu.go.id; internet www.kemlu.go.id/kuwaitcity; Ambassador LENA MARYANA.

Iran: Isteghlal St, Diplomatic Zone, Kuwait City; tel. 22570156; fax 22529868; internet kuwait.mfa.ir; Ambassador MOHAMMAD TOTONCHI.

Iraq: al-Da'ia Area, Aden St, Kuwait City; internet www.mofa.gov.iq/kuwait; Ambassador AL-MANHAL AL-SAFI.

Italy: POB 4453, Jabriya, Villa 84, Blk 9, St 1, Safat, 13045 Kuwait City; tel. 25356010; fax 25356030; e-mail ambasciata.alkuwait@esteri.it; internet www.ambalkuwait.esteri.it; Ambassador CARLO BALDOCCI.

Japan: POB 2304, Plot 57, Blk 7A, Diplomatic Zone, Mishref, Safat, 13024 Kuwait City; tel. 25309400; fax 25309401; internet www.kw.emb-japan.go.jp; Ambassador YASUNARI MORINO.

Jordan: POB 39891, 73059 Kuwait City; tel. 25312293; fax 25312291; e-mail kujor@qualitynet.net; internet mfa.gov.jo/ar/embassy/kuwait; Ambassador SAQR ABU SHATTAL.

Kazakhstan: Villa 19, Blk 3, St 4, Kuwait City; tel. 22256186; fax 25625816; e-mail kuwait@mfa.kz; internet www.gov.kz/memleket/entities/mfa-kuveyt; Ambassador AZMAT BERDEBAYE.

Korea, Democratic People's Republic: Villa 473, 22 Ali Jassar St, Kuwait City; tel. 25217299; Chargé d'affaires JU MYONG CHOL.

Korea, Republic: POB 4272, Plot 6, Blk 7A, Diplomatic Zone 2, St 303, Safat, Mishref, 13043 Kuwait City; tel. 25378621; fax 25378628; e-mail kuwait@mofa.go.kr; internet kwt.mofa.go.kr; Ambassador CHUNG BYUNG-HA.

Kyrgyzstan: Villa 34, Blk 6, St 13, Surra, Kuwait City; tel. 25359951; fax 25359981; e-mail kyrgyzembkw@gmail.com; Ambassador AZAMAT KARAGULOV.

Lebanon: POB 253, al Da'ia Diplomatic Area, Plot 6, Safat, 13003 Kuwait City; tel. 22562103; fax 22571682; e-mail info.lebanonembassy.kw@gmail.com; internet www.kuwait.mfa.gov.lb; Chargé d'affaires a.i. BASIL OWEIDAT.

Libya: POB 21460, 27 Istiqlal St, Safat, 13075 Kuwait City; tel. 22575183; fax 22575182; Ambassador SULEIMAN AL-SAHALI.

Malawi: Villa 34, Blk 5, St 512, al-Shuhadaa St, Kuwait City; tel. 25235416; fax 25235418; e-mail info@malawiembkuwait.com; internet malawigulf.com; Ambassador YOUNOS ABDUL KARIM.

Malaysia: POB 4105, Plot 5, Daiya, Diplomatic Enclave, Area 5, Yemen St, Safat, 13042 Kuwait City; tel. 22550394; fax 22550384; e-mail mwkuwait.kln@1govuc.gov.my; internet www.kln.gov.my/web/kwt_kuwait; Ambassador ALAA ALDEEN BIN MOHAMMAD NOOR.

Malta: Villa 2, St 105, Blk 1, Mubarak Abdulla al-Jaber Area, New Mishref, Kuwait City; tel. 25388045; fax 25388047; e-mail maltaembassy.kuwaitcity@gov.mt; Ambassador GEORGE A. SAID-ZAMMIT.

Mauritania: POB 23784, al Zahra, Blk 8, St 809, Villa 119, Safat, 13098 Kuwait City; tel. 25245767; fax 25245953; e-mail ambarimkoweit@diplomatie.gov.mr; Ambassador MOHAMED LAMINE OULD CHEIKH.

Mexico: Cliffs Tower, Suite 6, Baghdad St, Blk 9, Salmiya, Kuwait City; tel. 22261980; fax 25731952; e-mail embkuwait@sre.gob.mx; internet embamex.sre.gob.mx/kuwait/index.php; Ambassador EDUARDO PATRICIO PEÑA HALLER (designate).

Mongolia: Villa 35, Block 8, Moutaz St, Salwa, Kuwait City; tel. 25646020; fax 25648030; e-mail kuwait@mfat.gov.mn; internet www.kuwait.embassy.mn; Ambassador P. SERGELEN.

Morocco: Villa 14, Yarmouk, Blk 2, St 2, Kuwait City; tel. 25312980; fax 25317423; e-mail amb.maroc.kw@gmail.com; internet www.moroccanembassykw.org; Chargé d'affaires a.i. SUJANI RANA.

Nepal: Villa 514, Blk 8, St 13, Jabriya, Kuwait City; tel. 25321603; fax 25321628; e-mail eonkuwait@mofa.gov.np; internet kw.nepalembassy.gov.np; Ambassador GHANSHYAM LAMSAL (designate).

Netherlands: House 7, Blk 6, St 11, Jabriya, Kuwait City; tel. 25312650; fax 25326334; e-mail kwe@minbuza.nl; internet www.netherlandsandyou.nl/your-country-and-the-netherlands/kuwait; Ambassador LAURENS WESTHOFF.

Nicaragua: Kuwait City; Ambassador MOHAMMED FERRARA LASHTAR.

Niger: POB 44451, Villa 183, Salwa Blk 12, St 6, Hawalli, 32059 Kuwait City; tel. 25652943; Ambassador TINNI OUSSEINI.

Nigeria: POB 6432, Blk 1, St 14, Hawalli, Surra, 32039 Kuwait City; tel. 25379540; e-mail conseckuwait@yahoo.com; internet kuwait.foreignaffairs.gov.ng; Ambassador JAZULI IMAM GALADANCI.

Oman: POB 21975, al-Odeilia Block 3, St 3, Villa 25, Safat, 13080 Kuwait City; tel. 25215875; fax 25215878; e-mail kuwait@fm.gov.om; Ambassador Dr SALEH BIN AMER AL-KHAROUSI.

Pakistan: POB 988, Villa 46, Jabriya, Plot 5, Blk 11, Police Station Rd, St 101, Safat, 13010 Kuwait City; tel. 25327649; fax 25327648; e-mail parepkuwait@mofa.gov.pk; internet www.mofa.gov.pk/kuwait; Ambassador MALIK MUHAMMAD FAROOQ.

Peru: Ahmed al-Jaber St, Kuwait City; tel. 22267250; e-mail embassy.peru.kw@gmail.com; internet fb.com/embajadaperuenkuwait; Ambassador CARLOS MANUEL ALFREDO VELASCO MENDIOLA.

Philippines: POB 26288, Villa 15, Masjid al-Aqsa St, Blk 1, Salwa Area, Safat, 13123 Kuwait City; tel. 69902188; internet kuwaitpe.dfa.gov.ph; Ambassador JOSE ALMODOVAR CABRERA, III.

Poland: POB 5066, Jabriya, Villa 20, Blk 7, St 3, Safat, 13051 Kuwait City; tel. 25311571; fax 25311576; e-mail kuwejt.amb.sekretariat@msz.gov.pl; internet kuwejt.msz.gov.pl; Chargé d'affaires ANNA GODOJ-CISZKOWKA.

Romania: POB 13574, Villa 34, Keifan, Blk 4, Moona St, Dasmah, 35152 Kuwait City; tel. 24845079; fax 24848929; e-mail kuwait@mae.ro; internet kuweit.mae.ro; Ambassador MUGUREL IOAN STĂNESCU.

Russian Federation: Da'ia Diplomatic Area, Plot 17, Blk 5, Kuwait City; tel. 22560427; fax 22524969; e-mail rusposkuw@mail.ru; internet www.kuwait.mid.ru; Ambassador VLADIMIR ZILTOV.

Saudi Arabia: Diplomatic Area, Arabian Gulf St, Kuwait City; tel. 22550021; fax 22551858; e-mail kwemb@mofa.gov.sa; internet embassies.mofa.gov.sa/sites/kuwait; Ambassador Prince SULTAN BIN SAAD BIN KHALID AL SA'UD.

Senegal: Villa 364, Plot 1, St 13, al-Rawadah, Kuwait City; tel. 22573477; e-mail senegal_embassy@yahoo.com; Ambassador AWADH AL-KAREEM BLAH MOUSA.

Serbia: Bayan, Villa 18, Blk 13, St 1, Safat, 13066 Kuwait City; tel. 25375042; fax 25375049; e-mail embrskw@gmail.com; internet kuwait.mfa.gov.rs; Chargé d'affaires a.i. FILIP KATIĆ.

Sierra Leone: POB 176, al-Zahra, Kuwait City; tel. 25243234; internet kw.slembassy.gov.sl; Ambassador Haja ISHATA THOMAS.

Somalia: POB 22766, Bayan, St 1, Block 7, Villa 25, Safat, 13088 Kuwait City; tel. 99168821; e-mail kuwaitembassy@mfa.gov.so; internet www.fb.com/somaliainkuwait; Ambassador MOHAMED ABDULLAHI ADWA.

KUWAIT

South Africa: POB 2262, Villa 91, Salwa Blk 10, St 1, Unit 3, Mishref, 40173 Kuwait City; tel. 25617988; fax 25617917; e-mail kuwait.political@dirco.gov.za; internet www.dirco.gov.za/kuwait; Ambassador MANELISI PAULOS GENJI.

South Sudan: Kuwait City; Ambassador Gen. THOMAS DUOTH GUET.

Spain: POB 22207, Villa 19, Surra, Blk 3, St 14, Safat, 13083 Kuwait City; tel. 25325828; fax 25325826; e-mail emb.kuwait@maec.es; internet www.exteriores.gob.es/embajadas/kuwait; Ambassador MIGUEL JOSÉ MORO AGUILAR.

Sri Lanka: POB 44650, Jabriya, Blk 10, St 107, Bldg 1, Kuwait City; tel. 25354611; e-mail slemb.kuwait@mfa.gov.lk; internet kuwait.embassy.gov.lk; Ambassador KAANDEEPAN BALASUBRAMANIAM.

Sudan: Blk 1, St 8, Villa 303, Surra, Kuwait City; tel. 25347294; fax 25347219; Ambassador AWADAL-KARIM AL-RAYAH BALLA.

Switzerland: POB 23954, House 122, Qortuba, Blk 2, St 1, Safat, 13100 Kuwait City; tel. 25340172; fax 25340176; e-mail kuwait@eda.admin.ch; internet www.eda.admin.ch/countries/kuwait/en/home/representations/embassy.html; Ambassador TIZIANO BALMELLI.

Tajikistan: House 72, Blk 2, St 101, Salwa, Kuwait City; tel. 25615152; fax 25617174; e-mail tajembkuwait@mfa.tj; internet mfa.tj/kuwait; Ambassador ZUBAYDULLO ZUBAYDZODA.

Tanzania: POB 8311, House 16, Blk 3, St 35, 22054 Kuwait City; tel. 22575368; fax 22575371; e-mail kuwait@nje.go.tz; internet kw.tzembassy.go.tz; Ambassador (vacant).

Thailand: POB 66647, Villa 3, St 21, Blk 6, Bayan, 43757 Kuwait City; tel. 25385050; fax 25381695; e-mail royalthaiembassykuwait@gmail.com; internet kuwait.thaiembassy.org; Ambassador EKAPOL POOLPIPAT.

Tunisia: POB 5976, Villa 45, Nuzha, Plot 2, Nuzha St, Safat, 13060 Kuwait City; tel. 22526261; Ambassador HASHMI AGILI.

Türkiye (Turkey): POB 20627, Blk 5, Plot 16, Istiqlal St, Safat, 13067 Kuwait City; tel. 22277400; fax 22560403; e-mail embassy.kuwait@mfa.gov.tr; internet kuwait.emb.mfa.gov.tr; Ambassador TUBA NUR SÖNMEZ.

Ukraine: Villa 37, Blk 5, St 1, Surra, Kuwait City; tel. 25318507; fax 25318508; e-mail emb_kw@mfa.gov.ua; internet kuwait.mfa.gov.ua; Ambassador Dr OLEKSANDR BALANUTSA.

United Arab Emirates: POB 1828, Blk 5, Yemen St, Bldg 7, Safat, 13019 Kuwait City; tel. 22528544; fax 22526382; e-mail kuwait@mofa.gov.ae; internet www.mofaic.gov.ae/en/missions/kuwait; Ambassador Dr MATAR HAMED AL-NEYADI.

United Kingdom: POB 2, Arabian Gulf St, Safat, 13001 Kuwait City; tel. 22594320; fax 22594339; internet www.gov.uk/world/kuwait; Ambassador BELINDA LEWIS.

USA: POB 77, Bayan, al-Masjed al-Aqsa St, Plot 14, Block 14, Safat, 13001 Kuwait City; tel. 22591001; fax 25380282; e-mail paskuwaitm@state.gov; internet kw.usembassy.gov; Ambassador KAREN SASAHARA (designate).

Uzbekistan: Villa 18A, Blk 2, St 5, Mishref, Kuwait City; Ambassador BAKHROMJON ALOEV.

Venezuela: POB 24440, Block 5, St 7, Area 356, Surra, Safat, 13105 Kuwait City; tel. 25324367; fax 25324368; e-mail embavene@qualitynet.net; Ambassador RON ALFREDO.

Viet Nam: Villa 96, St 19, Blk 10, Jabriya, Kuwait City; tel. 25311450; fax 25351592; e-mail vnemb.kw@mofa.gov.vn; Ambassador NGO TOAN THANG.

Yemen: POB 7182, al-Jabriya St, Kuwait City; tel. 25349416; Ambassador ALI MANSOUR BIN SAFA.

Zimbabwe: POB 36484, Salmiya, 24755 Kuwait City; tel. 25651517; fax 25621491; e-mail zimkuwait@zimfa.gov.zw; Ambassador CRISPEN TOGA MAVODZA.

Judicial System

Supreme Judicial Council: comprises heads of each branch of the judiciary. Oversees work of the courts, recommends candidates for judicial appointments and reviews appointment, promotion and transfer of judges at the request of Minister of Justice. Also advises the Minister of Justice and parliament on budgetary issues; Pres. MOHAMMAD BIN NAJI.

Constitutional Court: Fahad al-Salem St, Qibla, Kuwait City; tel. 22418395; fax 22410070; Comprises 5 judges. Interprets the provisions of the Constitution; considers disputes regarding the constitutionality of legislation, decrees and rules; has jurisdiction in challenges relating to the election of members, or eligibility for election, to the Majlis al-Umma; Pres. MOHAMMAD BIN NAJI.

Court of Cassation: Comprises 5 judges. Is competent to consider the legality of verdicts of the Court of Appeal and State Security Court; Chief Justice MOHAMMAD BIN NAJI.

Court of Appeal: Comprises 3 judges. Considers verdicts of the Court of First Instance; Pres. MOHAMMAD ABU SULAIB.

Court of First Instance: Comprises the following divisions: Civil and Commercial (1 judge), Personal Status Affairs (1 judge), Lease (3 judges), Labour (1 judge), Crime (3 judges), Administrative Disputes (3 judges), Appeal (3 judges), Challenged Misdemeanours (3 judges).

Summary Courts: Each governorate has a Summary Court, comprising one or more divisions. The courts have jurisdiction in the following areas: Civil and Commercial, Urgent Cases, Lease, Misdemeanours. The verdict in each case is delivered by one judge.

There is also a **Traffic Court**, with one presiding judge.

Prosecutor-General: SAAD AL-SAFRAN.

Religion

ISLAM

The majority of Kuwaitis are Muslims of the Sunni or Shi'a sects. The Shi'a community comprises about 30% of the total.

CHRISTIANITY

The Roman Catholic Church

Latin Rite

For ecclesiastical purposes, Kuwait forms part of the Apostolic Vicariate of Northern Arabia (see Bahrain).

Melkite Rite

Exarch Patriarchal: Rev. BOUTROS GHARIB, Vicariat Patriarchal Greek-Melkite, POB 1205, Salwa Block 12, St 6, House 58, Salmiya, 22013 Kuwait City; tel. and fax 25652802; e-mail greekcatholickuwait@yahoo.com.

Syrian Rite

The Syrian Catholic Patriarch of Antioch is resident in Beirut, Lebanon. The Patriarchal Exarchate of Basra and the Gulf is based in Basra, Iraq.

The Anglican Communion

Within the Episcopal Church in Jerusalem and the Middle East, Kuwait forms part of the diocese of Cyprus and the Gulf. The Anglican congregation in Kuwait is entirely expatriate. The Bishop in Cyprus and the Gulf is resident in Cyprus, while the Archdeacon in the Gulf is resident in Bahrain.

Other Christian Churches

National Evangelical Church in Kuwait: POB 80, 13001 Safat, Kuwait City; tel. 22407195; fax 22431087; e-mail info@neckkuwait.com; internet www.neckkuwait.com; Chair. Rev. AMMANUEL GHAREEB; an independent Protestant Church founded by the Reformed Church in America; services in Arabic, English, Korean, Malayalam and other Indian languages; comprises 80 separate congregations.

The Armenian, Greek, Coptic and Syrian Orthodox Churches are also represented in Kuwait.

The Press

DAILY NEWSPAPERS (PRINT AND ONLINE)

Al-Anbaa (The News): POB 23915, 13100 Safat, Kuwait City; tel. 22272727; fax 22272830; e-mail editorial@alanba.com.kw; internet www.alanba.com.kw; f. 1976; Arabic; general; Editor-in-Chief YOUSEF KHALED AL-MARZOOQ.

Arab Times: POB 2270, Airport Rd, Shuwaikh, 13023 Safat, Kuwait City; tel. 24849144; fax 24818267; e-mail arabtimes@arabtimesonline.com; internet www.arabtimesonline.com; f. 1977; English; political and financial; no Fri. edn; Editor-in-Chief AHMAD ABD AL-AZIZ AL-JARALLAH.

Al-Jarida (The Newspaper): POB 29846, 13159 Safat, Kuwait City; tel. 22257036; fax 22257035; e-mail info@aljarida.com; internet www.aljarida.com; f. 2007; Arabic; affiliated with the Nat. Democratic Alliance; Editor-in-Chief KHALID HILAL AL-MUTAIRI.

Kuwait Times: POB 1301, 13014 Safat, Kuwait City; tel. 24833199; fax 24835621; e-mail info@kuwaittimes.net; internet www.kuwaittimes.net; f. 1961; English, Malayalam and Urdu; political; Editor-in-Chief ABD AL-RAHMAN ALYAN.

Al-Qabas (Firebrand): POB 21800, 13078 Safat, Kuwait City; tel. 24812822; fax 24834355; e-mail editor@alqabas.com.kw; internet alqabas.com; f. 1972; Arabic; independent; Editor-in-Chief WALEED ABD AL-LATIF AL-NISF.

KUWAIT

Al-Rai (Public Opinion): Muhammed Abu al-Qasim St, Kuwait City; tel. 22244500; fax 22244638; e-mail editor@alraimedia.com; internet www.alraimedia.com; f. 1961; Arabic; political, social and cultural; Editor-in-Chief WALID JASIM AL-JASEM.

Al-Seyassah (Policy): POB 2270, Shuwaikh, Kuwait City; tel. 24813566; fax 24818267; e-mail alseyassah@alseyassah.com; internet www.al-seyassah.com; f. 1965; Arabic; political and financial; Editor-in-Chief AHMAD ABD AL-AZIZ AL-JARALLAH.

Al-Watan (The Homeland): POB 1142, 13012 Safat, Kuwait City; tel. 24840950; fax 24818481; e-mail online@alwatan.com.kw; internet www.alwatan.com.kw; f. 1962; Arabic; political; Editor-in-Chief Sheikh KHALIFA ALI AL-KHALIFA AL-SABAH.

WEEKLIES AND PERIODICALS

Al-Balagh (Communiqué): POB 4558, 13046 Safat, Kuwait City; tel. 24818820; fax 24812735; e-mail albalagh5@yahoo.com; internet www.al-balagh.com; f. 1969; weekly; Arabic; general, political and Islamic affairs; Editor-in-Chief ABD AL-RAHMAN RASHID AL-WALAYATI.

Byzance: Kuwait City; f. 2007; bimonthly; Arabic and French; lifestyle magazine, incl. features on fashion, jewellery, furniture and art; Man. Editor JEAN-PIERRE GUEIRARD; Exec. Editor-in-Chief ANTOINE DAHER.

Al-Dakhiliya (The Interior): POB 71655, 12500 Shamiah, Kuwait City; tel. 22410091; fax 22410609; e-mail moipr@qualitynet.net; monthly; Arabic; official reports, transactions and proceedings; publ. by Public Relations Dept, Ministry of the Interior; Editor-in-Chief Lt-Col AHMAD A. AL-SHARQAWI.

Dalal Magazine: POB 6000, 13060 Safat, Kuwait City; tel. 24840680; fax 24832039; internet www.dalal-kw.com; f. 1997; monthly; Arabic; family affairs, beauty, fashion; Editor-in-Chief AHMAD YOUSUF BEHBEHANI.

Friday Times: POB 1301, 13014 Safat, Kuwait City; tel. 24833199; fax 24835627; e-mail info@kuwaittimes.net; internet www.kuwaittimes.net; f. 2005; weekend edn of *Kuwait Times*.

Al-Hadaf (The Objective): al-Sahafa St, Airport Rd, al-Shuwaikh; tel. 1838281; fax 24911307; e-mail alhadafmag@hadafnet.com; internet alhadafmag.com; f. 1964; weekly; Arabic; social and cultural; Editor-in-Chief AHMAD ABD AL-AZIZ AL-JARALLAH.

Al-Iqtisadi al-Kuwaiti (Kuwaiti Economist): POB 775, 13008 Safat, Kuwait City; tel. 22423555; fax 22300074; e-mail kcci@kcci.org.kw; internet kuwaitchamber.org.kw; f. 1960; monthly; Arabic; commerce, trade and economics; publ. by Kuwait Chamber of Commerce and Industry; Editor MAJED B. JAMALUDDIN.

Journal of the Gulf and Arabian Peninsula Studies: POB 17073, 72451 Khaldiya, Kuwait University, Kuwait City; tel. 24984066; fax 24833705; e-mail jgaps@ku.edu.kw; internet pubcouncil.kuniv.edu.kw/jgaps; f. 1975; quarterly; Arabic and English; publ. by Academic Publication Council of Kuwait Univ; Editor-in-Chief Prof. OTHMAN HAMMOUD AL-KHADER.

Kuwait Medical Journal (KMJ): POB 1202, 13013 Safat, Kuwait City; tel. 1881181; fax 25317972; e-mail kmj@kma.org.kw; internet www.kma.org.kw/kmj.aspx; f. 1967; quarterly; English; publ. by the Kuwait Medical Asscn; original articles, review articles, case reports, short communications, letters to the editor and book reviews; Editor-in-Chief Prof. FOUAD ABDULLAH M. HASSAN; provides open online access.

Kuwait al-Youm (Kuwait Today): POB 193, 13002 Safat, Kuwait City; tel. 24911991; fax 24829868; e-mail kuwait_alyawm_cont@media.gov.kw; internet kuwaitalyawm.media.gov.kw; f. 1954; weekly; Arabic; statistics, Amiri decrees, laws, govt announcements, decisions, invitations for tenders, etc.; publ. by the Ministry of Information.

Al-Kuwaiti (The Kuwaiti): Information Dept, POB 9758, 61008 Ahmadi, Kuwait City; fax 23981076; e-mail info@kockw.com; f. 1961; monthly journal of the Kuwait Oil Co; Arabic; Editor-in-Chief QUSAY NASSER AL-AMER.

The Kuwaiti Digest: Information Dept, POB 9758, 61008 Ahmadi, Kuwait City; tel. 23982747; fax 23981076; e-mail kocinfo@kockw.com; f. 1972; quarterly journal of the Kuwait Oil Co; English; Editor-in-Chief KHALED AL-KHAMEES.

Al-Majaless (Meetings): POB 5605, 13057 Safat, Kuwait City; tel. 24841178; fax 24847126; weekly; Arabic; current affairs; Editor-in-Chief QASIM ABD AL-QADIR.

Al-Nahdha (The Renaissance): POB 695, 13007 Safat, Kuwait City; tel. 24813133; fax 24849298; f. 1967; weekly; Arabic; social and political; Editor-in-Chief THAMER AL-SALAH.

Osrati (My Family): POB 2995, 13030 Safat, Kuwait City; tel. 24813233; fax 24838933; internet www.osratimagazine.com; f. 1964; weekly; Arabic; women's magazine; publ. by Fahad al-Marzouk Establishment; Editor GHANIMA F. AL-MARZOUK.

NEWS AGENCY

Kuwait News Agency (KUNA): POB 24063, 13101 Safat, Kuwait City; tel. 22271800; fax 24813424; e-mail feedback@kuna.net.kw; internet www.kuna.net.kw; f. 1979; public corporate body; independent; also publishes research digests on topics of common and special interest; Chair. and Dir-Gen. Sheikh MUBARAK AL-DUAIJ AL-SABAH.

PRESS ASSOCIATION

Kuwait Journalists' Association: POB 5454, 13055 Safat, Kuwait City; tel. 24843351; fax 24842874; e-mail kja@kja-kw.com; internet www.kja-kw.com; Chair. FATIMA HUSSAIN AL-ESSA.

Publishers

Al-Abraj Translation and Publishing Co WLL: POB 26177, 13122 Safat, Kuwait City; tel. 22442310; fax 22407024; Man. Dir Dr TARIQ ABDULLAH.

Dar al-Seyassah Publishing, Printing and Distribution Co: POB 2270, 13023 Safat, Kuwait City; tel. 24813566; fax 24833628; internet www.dar-al-seyassah.com; publ. *Arab Times*, *Al-Seyassah* and *Al-Hadaf*.

Gulf Centre Publishing and Publicity: POB 2722, 13028 Safat, Kuwait City; tel. 22402760; fax 22458833; Propr HAMZA ISMAIL ESSLAH.

Kuwait National Advertising and Publishing Co (KNAPCO): Al-Shaha Complex, 5th Floor Salem Aal-Mubarak St, Salmiya, Kuwait City; tel. 25745770; fax 25745779; e-mail support@knapco.com; internet www.knapco.com; f. 1995; publ. annual commercial business directory, *Teledymag*; Founder NAWAF ABD AL-RAZAK.

Kuwait Publishing House Co: POB 1446, 13015 Safat, Kuwait City; tel. 22449686; fax 22436956; f. 1970; Dir ESAM AS'AD ABU AL-FARAJ.

Kuwait United Co for Advertising, Publishing and Distribution WLL: POB 29359, 13153 Safat, Kuwait City; tel. 24817111; fax 24817797.

Al-Talia Printing and Publishing Co: POB 1082, Airport Rd, Shuwaikh, 13011 Safat, Kuwait City; tel. 24840470; fax 24815611; Man. AHMAD YOUSUF AL-NAFISI.

GOVERNMENT PUBLISHING HOUSE

Ministry of Information: see Ministries.

Broadcasting and Communications

TELECOMMUNICATIONS

Ooredoo Kuwait: POB 613, Ooredoo Tower, Safat, 13007 Kuwait City; tel. 1805555; fax 22423369; internet www.ooredoo.com.kw; f. 1999 as National Mobile Telecommunications Co (Wataniya Telecom); Ooredoo QSC (Qatar) acquired 51% stake 2007; present name adopted in 2014; Chair. Sheikh MOHAMMED BIN ABDULLAH AL THANI; CEO ABDULAZIZ AL-BABTAIN.

stc Kuwait: POB 181, Salmiya, 22002 Kuwait City; tel. 55670000; fax 55676666; internet www.viva.com.kw; f. 2008 as VIVA; present name adopted in 2019; mobile communications; commercial brand of Kuwait Telecom Co; 52% owned by Saudi Telecom Co (stc); Chair. Dr MAHMOUD AHMAD ABDULRAHMAN; CEO Eng. MAZIAD BIN NASSER AL-HARBI.

Zain Kuwait: POB 22244, Safat, 13083 Kuwait City; tel. 24644444; fax 24644506; e-mail cust_care@kw.zain.com; internet www.kw.zain.com; f. 1983 as Mobile Telecommunications Co; in Sept. 2007 began operating under new global brand, Zain; group operates in 24 countries in the Middle East and Africa; Group Chair. OSAMA OTHMAN AL-FRAIH; Group Vice-Chair. and CEO BADER NASSER AL-KHARAFI.

BROADCASTING

Radio

Radio Kuwait: POB 397, Safat, 13004 Kuwait City; tel. 22423774; fax 22456660; e-mail info@media.gov.kw; internet www.media.gov.kw; f. 1951; broadcasts daily in Arabic, Farsi, English and Urdu; Dir of Radio SAAD AL-FINDI.

Television

Kuwait Television: POB 193, Safat, 13002 Kuwait City; tel. 22451288; fax 22438403; internet www.moinfo.gov.kw; f. 1961; transmission began privately in Kuwait in 1957; transmits in Arabic;

colour television service began in 1973; has a total of 9 channels; Head of TV Broadcasting MUHAMMAD AL-WASMI.

Al-Rai: Kuwait City; tel. 22244500; fax 22244638; internet www.alraimedia.com/TV; f. 2004; first private satellite television station in Kuwait; admin. offices in Kuwait and transmission facilities in Dubai (United Arab Emirates); owned by Al-Rai Media Group; Editor-in-Chief WALEED JASSIM AL-JASSIM.

Finance

BANKING

Central Bank

Central Bank of Kuwait: POB 526, Abdullah al-Ahmad St, Safat, 13006 Kuwait City; tel. 1814444; e-mail cbk@cbk.gov.kw; internet www.cbk.gov.kw; f. 1969; Gov. Dr BASEL AL-HAROUN.

National Banks

Al-Ahli Bank of Kuwait KSC (ABK): POB 1387, Ahmad al-Jaber St, Safat, 13014 Kuwait City; tel. 1866877; e-mail marketing@abkuwait.com; internet abk.eahli.com; f. 1967; wholly owned by private Kuwaiti interests; Chair. TALAL MOHAMED REZA BEHBEHANI; Group CEO GEORGE RICHANI.

Ahli United Bank KSC: POB 71, Safat, 12168 Kuwait City; tel. 1802000; fax 22461430; e-mail contact@ahliunited.com; internet www.ahliunited.com; f. 1971; fmrly Bank of Kuwait and the Middle East KSC; current name adopted April 2010 after acquiring Kuwaiti brs of British Bank of the Middle East; 75% owned by Ahli United Bank (Bahrain); became *Shari'a*-compliant 2010; Chair. MESHAL ABDULAZIZ ALOTHMAN; Group CEO and Man. Dir ADEL A. EL-LABBAN.

BBK: POB 24396, Ahmad al-Jaber Ave, Safat, 13104 Kuwait City; tel. 22233600; fax 22440937; e-mail customerservice@bbkonline.com; internet www.bbkonline.com.kw; f. 1971 as Bank of Bahrain and Kuwait BSC; name changed as above in 2005; Chair. MURAD ALI MURAD; Chief Exec. YASER MOHAMED AL-SAAD (acting).

Boubyan Bank KSC: POB 25507, Safat, 13116 Kuwait City; tel. 22282000; e-mail info@bankboubyan.com; internet www.bankboubyan.com; f. 2004; Chair. ABDULAZIZ ABDULLAH AL-SHAYA; CEO ADEL ABDUL WAHAB AL-MAJID.

Burgan Bank SAK: POB 5389, Abdullah al-Ahmad St, Blk 1, Safat, 12170 Kuwait City; tel. 1804080; e-mail info@burgan.com; internet www.burgan.com; f. 1975; 33.9% owned by Kuwait Projects Co (Holding), Safat; Chair. ABDULLAH NASSER SABAH AL-AHMAD AL-SABAH; CEO TONY DAHER.

Commercial Bank of Kuwait SAK: POB 2861, Mubarak al-Kabir St, Safat, 13029 Kuwait City; tel. 22990000; fax 22464870; e-mail cbkinq@cbk.com; internet www.cbk.com; f. 1960 by Amiri decree; Chair. Sheikh AHMAD DUAIJ JABER AL-SABAH; CEO ELHAM YOUSRY MAHFOUZ.

Gulf Bank KSC: POB 3200, Mubarak al-Kabir St, Safat, 13032 Kuwait City; tel. 22449501; e-mail complaintsunit@gulfbank.com.kw; internet www.e-gulfbank.com; f. 1960; Chair. JASEM MUSTAFA BOODAI; CEO ANTOINE DAHER.

Industrial Bank of Kuwait KSC (IBK): POB 3146, Joint Banking Complex, Ahmad al-Jaber St, Safat, 13032 Kuwait City; tel. 22337000; fax 22406595; e-mail ibk@ibkuwt.com; internet www.ibkuwt.com; 31.4% state-owned; f. 1973; Chair. MUSAB S. AL-NISF.

Kuwait Finance House KSC (KFH): POB 24989, Abdullah al-Mubarak St, Safat, 13110 Kuwait City; tel. 22445050; fax 22409414; e-mail kfh@kfh.com; internet www.kfh.com; f. 1977; 45% owned by the Future Generations Fund; Islamic banking and investment co; Chair. HAMAD ABDUL MOHSEN AL-MARZOUQ; Group CEO KHALID YOUSEF AL-SHAMLAN.

Kuwait International Bank (KIB): POB 22822, West Tower, Joint Banking Centre, Darwazzat Abd al-Razaq, Safat, 13089 Kuwait City; tel. 1866866; fax 22402611; internet www.kib.com.kw; f. 1973 as Kuwait Real Estate Bank KSC; name changed as above upon conversion into an Islamic bank 2007; wholly owned by private Kuwaiti interests; Chair. Sheikh MUHAMMAD JARRAH AL-SABAH; CEO RAED JAWAD BUKHAMSEEN.

National Bank of Kuwait SAK (NBK): POB 95, Abdullah al-Ahmad St, Safat, 13001 Kuwait City; tel. 22248361; internet www.nbk.com; f. 1952; Chair. HAMAD AL-BAHAR; Group CEO ISAM J. AL-SAGER; CEO, Kuwait SALAH Y. AL-FULAIJ.

INSURANCE

Al-Ahleia Insurance Co SAK: POB 1602, Bldg No. 21, Ahmad al-Jaber St, Safat, 13017 Kuwait City; tel. 1888444; fax 22430308; e-mail aic@alahleia.com; internet www.alahleia.com; f. 1962; all forms of insurance; Chair. AYMAN ABDULLATIF AL-SHAYEA; CEO YOUSEF SAAD AL-SAAD.

Arab Commercial Enterprises WLL (Kuwait): POB 2474, Safat, 13025 Kuwait City; tel. 22463610; fax 22424912; e-mail info.kuwait@acebrokers.com; f. 1952; Group Pres. and CEO NAGIB M. BAHOUS.

First Takaful Insurance Co (FTIC): POB 5713, 1st Floor, Souq al-Safat Bldg, Abdullah al-Mubarak St, Safat, 13058 Kuwait City; tel. 1880055; fax 22444599; e-mail info@firsttakaful.com.kw; internet firsttakaful.com.kw; f. 2000; Islamic insurance; Chair. ABDULLA ABDUL RAZAQ AL-ASFOUR; CEO HUSSAIN ALI AL-ATTAL.

Gulf Insurance Group KSCP: POB 1040, KIPCO Tower, Floor 40, Khaled bin Alwaleed St, Sharq, 13011 Kuwait City; tel. 1802080; fax 22961826; e-mail contacts@gig.com.kw; internet www.gulfinsgroup.com; f. 1962 as Gulf Insurance Co KSC; all forms of insurance; Chair. FARKAD ABDULLAH AL-SANE; Group CEO KHALED SAOUD AL-HASAN.

Kuwait Insurance Co SAK (KIC): POB 769, Abdullah al-Salem St, Safat, 13008 Kuwait City; tel. 1884433; fax 22428530; e-mail info@kic-kw.com; internet www.kic-kw.com; f. 1960; all life and non-life insurance; Chair. ALI M. BEHBEHANI; CEO SAMI SHARIF.

Kuwait Reinsurance Co KSCC: Kuwait Re Tower, al-Shuhada St, Kuwait City; tel. 22299666; e-mail kuwaitre@kuwaitre.com; internet www.kuwaitre.com; f. 1972; Chair. SULAIMAN AL-DALALI; CEO DAWOUD S. AL-DUWAISAN.

New India Assurance Co: POB 370, Behbehani Bldg, 19th Floor, Jaber al-Mubarak St, Sharq, Safat, 13004 Kuwait City; tel. 22412085; fax 22412089; e-mail info@newindiakuwait.com; internet newindiakuwait.com; f. 1919; Chair. and Man. Dir ATUL SAHAI.

The Oriental Insurance Co Ltd: POB 22431, Safat, 13085 Kuwait City; tel. 22267486; fax 22267487; e-mail insurance@almullagroup.com; internet www.orientalinsurancekw.com; f. 1947; Chair. and Man. Dir ANJAN DEY.

Sumitomo Marine & Fire Insurance Co (Kuwait Agency): POB 3458, Safat, 13035 Kuwait City; tel. 22433087; fax 22430853; Contact ABDULLAH BOUDROS.

Warba Insurance & Reinsurance: Ahmad al-Jaber St, Sharq, 13103 Kuwait City; tel. 1808181; fax 22451974; e-mail info@warbaonline.com; internet www.warba.insure; f. 1976; all forms of insurance; Chair. ANWAR JAWAD KHAMSEEN; CEO ANWAR F. AL-SABEJ.

Wethaq Takaful Insurance Co: Khaled bin al-Waleed St, City Tower, Sharq, Kuwait City; tel. 1866662; fax 22491280; e-mail contact-us@wethaq.com; internet www.wethaq.com; f. 2000; Islamic insurance; Chair. NASSER AL-ENEZI; CEO FAWAZ SAAD AL-MAZROUI.

STOCK EXCHANGE

Boursa Kuwait (Kuwait Stock Exchange): POB 22235, Mubarak al-Kabir St, Safat, 13083 Kuwait City; tel. 22992000; fax 22440476; e-mail info@boursakuwait.com.kw; internet www.boursakuwait.com.kw; f. 1983; 155 cos and 47 mutual funds listed (2023); Chair. HAMAD MISHARI AHMAD AL-HUMAIDHI; CEO MOHAMMAD SAUD AL-OSAIMI.

Markets Association

Kuwait Financial Markets Association (KFMA): 6th Floor, Deema Bldg, POB 25228, 13113 Safat, Block 3, St 64, Kuwait City; tel. 22498560; fax 22498561; e-mail kfma@kfma.org.kw; internet www.kfma.org.kw; f. 1977; represents treasury, financial and capital markets and their mems; Pres. HUSSEIN AL-ARYAN; Sec.-Gen. ABD AL-WAHAB AL-BANNA.

Trade and Industry

GOVERNMENT AGENCY

Kuwait Investment Authority (KIA): POB 64, Safat, 13001 Kuwait City; tel. 22485600; fax 22454059; e-mail information@kia.gov.kw; internet www.kia.gov.kw; oversees the Kuwait Investment Office (London, UK); sovereign wealth fund; responsible for the Kuwaiti General Reserve; Chair. FAHD AL-JARALLAH (Minister of Finance); Man. Dir GHANEM AL-GHUNAIMAN.

DEVELOPMENT ORGANIZATIONS

Arab Planning Institute (API): POB 5834, Safat, 13059 Kuwait City; tel. 24843130; fax 24842935; e-mail api@api.org.kw; internet www.arab-api.org; f. 1966; 15 Arab mem. states; publishes *Journal of Development and Economic Policies* (twice yearly) and proceedings of seminars and discussion group meetings; offers research, training programmes and advisory services; Dir-Gen. BADER MALALLAH.

Industrial and Financial Investments Co (IFIC): POB 26019, Safat, Joint Banking Complex, 8th Floor, Industrial Bank Bldg, Derwaza Abd al-Razak, 13121 Kuwait City; tel. 22429073; fax 22448850; internet www.ific.net; f. 1983; privatized in 1996; invests

KUWAIT   Directory

directly in industry; Chair. and Man. Dir ABD AL-LATIF MUHAMMAD JANAHI.

Kuwait Fund for Arab Economic Development (KFAED): POB 2921, Safat, cnr Mubarak al-Kabir St and al-Hilali St, 13030 Kuwait City; tel. 22999000; fax 22999090; e-mail info@kuwait-fund.org; internet www.kuwait-fund.org; f. 1961; state-owned; provides and administers financial and technical assistance to developing countries; Chair. Sheikh SALEM ABDULLAH AL-JABER AL-SABAH (Minister of Foreign Affairs); Dir-Gen. MARWAN ABDULLAH AL-GHANIM.

Kuwait International Investment Co SAK (KIIC): POB 22792, Safat, 13088 Kuwait City; tel. 22438273; fax 22454931; e-mail info@kiic.com.kw; internet kiic.com.kw; 31% state-owned; domestic real estate and share markets; Chair. and Man. Dir HAMED MOHAMMED AL-AIBAN.

Kuwait Investment Co SAK (KIC): POB 1005, Safat, 5th Floor, al-Manakh Bldg, Mubarak al-Kabir St, 13011 Kuwait City; tel. 22967000; fax 22444896; internet www.kic.com.kw; f. 1981; 88% state-owned, 12% owned by private Kuwaiti interests; international banking and investment; Chair. and Man. Dir Dr YOUSEF MOHAMMAD AL-ALI; CEO BADER N. AL-SUBAIEE.

Mega Projects Agency (MPA): c/o Ministry of Public Works, POB 8, Safat, 13001 Kuwait City; tel. 25385520; fax 25385234; f. 2005; supervises the progress of Failaka and Bubiyan island devts; Chair. BADER AL-HUMAIDI.

Public Authority for Industry (PAI): POB 4690, Safat, 13047 Kuwait City; POB 10033, Shuaiba; tel. 25302222; fax 25302190; e-mail indust@pai.gov.kw; internet www.pai.gov.kw; f. 1997; successor to Shuaiba Area Authority (f. 1964); develops, promotes and supervises industry in Kuwait; CEO MOHAMMAD OTHMAN MOHAMMAD AL-AIBAN (Minister of Commerce and Industry); Dir-Gen. ABDUL KARIM TAQI ABDUL KARIM.

CHAMBER OF COMMERCE

Kuwait Chamber of Commerce and Industry: POB 775, Safat, Commercial Area 9, al-Shuhadaa St, 13008 Kuwait City; tel. 22423555; fax 22300074; e-mail kcci@kcci.org.kw; internet www.kuwaitchamber.org.kw; f. 1959; 44,000 mems; Chair. MUHAMMAD JASSIM AL-HAMAD AL-SAQR; Dir-Gen. RABAH AL-RABAH.

STATE HYDROCARBONS COMPANIES

Supreme Petroleum Council (SPC): Kuwait City; f. 1974; highest energy decision-making body, responsible for national oil policy; Chair. Sheikh AHMAD NAWAF AL-AHMAD AL-SABAH (Prime Minister).

Kuwait Petroleum Corpn (KPC): POB 26565, Safat, 13126 Kuwait City; tel. 1858585; fax 22467159; internet www.kpc.com.kw; f. 1980; co-ordinating org. to manage the petroleum industry; Chair. SAAD AL-BARRAK (Minister of Oil); CEO NAWAF S. AL-SABAH; subsidiaries include:

Kuwait Aviation Fuelling Co KSC (KAFCO): POB 1654, Safat, 13017 Kuwait City; tel. 1835000; fax 23828505; e-mail airfuel@kafco.com; internet www.kafco.com; f. 1963; Chair. GHANIM NASSER AL-OTAIBI; Vice-Chair. and Gen. Man. MESHAL ABDULLAH AL-TANAIB.

Kuwait Foreign Petroleum Exploration Co KSC (KUFPEC): POB 5291, Safat, 13053 Kuwait City; tel. 1836000; fax 24921818; e-mail kufpec@kufpec.com; internet www.kufpec.com; f. 1981; state-owned; overseas oil and gas exploration and devt; Chair. QASEM A. AL-MAJADI; CEO Sheikh SAEED AL-SHAHEEN (acting); 169 employees.

Kuwait Gulf Oil Co KSC (KGOC): POB 9919, 61010 Ahmad; tel. 25454254; e-mail info@kgoc.com; internet www.kgoc.com; f. 2002 to take over Kuwait's interest in the Neutral (Partitioned) Zone's offshore operator, Khafji Joint Operations, and all of Kuwait's other offshore exploration and production activities; Chair. FUAD E. A. AL-ABBASI; CEO KHALED AL-OTAIBI.

Kuwait National Petroleum Co KSC (KNPC): POB 70, Safat, Ali al-Salem St, 13001 Kuwait City; tel. 23989900; fax 23986188; internet www.knpc.com; f. 1960; oil refining, production of liquefied petroleum gas, and domestic marketing and distribution of petroleum by-products; Chair. HAMZA ABDULLAH BAKHASH; CEO WADHA AL-KHATEEB; 5,611 employees.

Kuwait Oil Co KSC (KOC): POB 9758, 61008 Ahmadi; tel. 23989111; fax 23983661; e-mail kocinfo@kockw.com; internet www.kockw.com; f. 1934; state-owned; Chair. SANAD AL-SANAD; CEO AHMAD AL-EIDAN.

Kuwait Petroleum International (Q8): POB 1819, Safat, 13019 Kuwait City; tel. 22332800; fax 22332776; e-mail info-kuwait@q8.com; internet www.q8.com; marketing division of KPC; controls 4,000 petrol retail stations in Europe, and European refineries with a capacity of 235,000 b/d; Chair. FAHAD F. AL-AJMI; Pres. and CEO SHAFI AL-AJMI.

UTILITIES

The Government planned to create regulatory bodies for each of Kuwait's utilities, with a view to facilitating their privatization.

Ministry of Electricity, Water and Renewable Energy: see Ministries; provides subsidized services throughout Kuwait.

MAJOR COMPANIES

ACICO Industries Co KSC: al-Hamra Business Tower, 34th Floor, Sharq, Kuwait City; tel. 1888811; e-mail info@acicogroup.com; internet www.acicogroup.com; f. 1990; state-owned; cement, concrete, construction, etc.; Chair. EMAD ABDULLAH ABDUL RAHMAN AL-ISSA; Group CEO MOHAMED YAHYA YASSIN.

Agility Logistics: POB 25418, Safat, 13115 Kuwait City; tel. 1809222; e-mail marketing@agility.com; internet www.agility.com; f. 1979; logistics; Chair. HENADI ANWAR AL-SALEH.

Alghanim Industries: POB 24172, al-Hamra Tower, Blk 8, Sharq, Safat, 13102 Kuwait City; tel. 24962000; e-mail compliance@alghanim.com; internet www.alghanim.com; f. 1932; trading, contracting, manufacturing, shipping, travel and financial services; Chair. KUTAYBA Y. ALGHANIM; CEO SAMIR KASEM; over 14,000 employees (2022).

Boubyan Petrochemical Co KSC: POB 2383, KIPPCO Tower, 33rd Floor, Khalid bin al-Waleed St, Sharq, Safat, 13024 Kuwait City; tel. 22020100; fax 22010101; e-mail info-boubyan@boubyan.com; internet www.boubyan.com; f. 1995; manufacture, import and distribution of petrochemical products; Chair. DABBOUS MUBARAK AL-DABBOUS.

Contracting and Marine Services Co SAK (CMS): POB 22853, Safat, 13089 Kuwait City; tel. 22410270; e-mail info@cms-kw.com; internet cms-kw.com; f. 1973; associated with Nat. Industries Group; marine construction works and services; Chair. and CEO ALI D. AL-SHAMMARI.

Efad Real Estate: POB 616, Safat, 13007 Kuwait City; tel. 22427060; fax 22405093; e-mail info@efadholding.com; 12 subsidiaries, incl. Investment Dar; operates in real estate, contracting, general trading, hospitality, engineering, transportation and logistics, IT, investment banking; CEO REZAM MUHAMMAD AL-ROUMI.

Gulf Cable and Electrical Industries Co KSC: POB 1196, Safat, 13012 Kuwait City; tel. 24645500; fax 24675305; e-mail info@gulfcable.com; internet www.gulfcable.com; f. 1975; manufacture of cables and electrical equipment; Chair. and Man. Dir ASAAD AL-BANWAN; CEO BASEL OMRAN ABDULLAH KANAAN.

Independent Petroleum Group SAK (IPG): POB 24027, Safat, 13101 Kuwait City; tel. 22276222; fax 25329953; e-mail general@ipg.com.kw; internet www.ipg.com.kw; f. 1976; industrial, commercial and consulting role in hydrocarbons industry; Chair. ALI M. AL-RADWAN; CEO WALEED J. HADEED.

Kuwait Aluminium Co KSC: POB 5335, Safat, al-Rai Industrial Area, Plot 1636, St No. 13, 13054 Kuwait City; tel. 24734000; fax 24710475; e-mail kalu@kuwaitaluminium.com; internet www.kuwaitaluminium.com; f. 1968; design, manufacture, erection and maintenance of aluminium and glass works for construction industry; Chair. NASSER NAKI; 200 employees.

Kuwait Cement Co KSC: Cement House Bldg, al-Shuhadaa St, Blk 6, al-Sawaba, Kuwait City; tel. 22401700; fax 22440896; e-mail info@kuwaitcement.com; internet www.kuwaitcement.com; f. 1968; manufacture and marketing of cement; Chair. RASHID ABDULAZIZ AL-RASHID; CEO MISHAL ABDUL MOHSEN AL-RASHID.

Kuwait Livestock Transport and Trading Co KSC (KLTT): POB 23727, Kuwait City; tel. 22969600; fax 22969799; e-mail info@kltt.com.kw; internet almawashi.com.kw; f. 1973; trade in livestock and livestock products; Chair. NAEL MOHAMMED AL-HOMOUD; CEO OSAMA KHALED BOODAI.

Kuwait Pipe Industries and Oil Services Co KSC (KPIOS): POB 3416, Safat, 13035 Kuwait City; tel. 24675622; fax 24675897; e-mail makjpme@kpios.com; internet www.kpios.com; f. 1966; 16.6% govt-owned; mfrs of various pipes, tanks and coatings; Chair. and CEO Eng. MOHAMMED KHALAF.

Kuwait Portland Cement Co KSC: POB 42191, Shuwaikh, 70652 Kuwait City; tel. 24835615; fax 24846152; e-mail info@portlandkwt.com; internet portlandkw.co; f. 1976; imports, exports and trades in construction materials; Chair. ALI ABDEL RAHMAN AL-OMAR.

Kuwait Projects Co KSC (KIPCO): POB 23982, Khalid bin al-Waleed St, Sharq, Safat, 13100 Kuwait City; tel. 1805885; e-mail kipco@kipco.com; internet www.kipco.com; f. 1975; investment holding co; operates in the financial services and media and technology sectors; Chair Sheikh HAMAD SABAH AL-AHMAD AL-SABAH; Group CEO Sheikha DANA NASSER SABAH AL-AHMAD AL-SABAH.

Kuwait United Poultry KSC (KUPCO): POB 1236, Safat, 13013 Kuwait City; tel. 22085662; e-mail info@kupco.net; internet www.kupco.net; f. 1974; breeding and distribution of poultry and poultry products.

Mabanee Co: Sheikh Zayed bin Sultan Al Nahyan Rd, 2nd Avenue, al-Rai, Kuwait City; tel. 22244444; fax 22244440; e-mail info@mabanee.com; internet www.mabanee.com; real estate, investments and construction; Chair. and Man. Dir MUHAMMAD A. AL-SHAYA; CEO WALEED AL-SHARIAN.

Mohammed Saleh & Reza Yousuf Behbehani Co: POB 341, Safat, 13004 Kuwait City; tel. 1801010; fax 24761166; e-mail info@e-behbehani.com; internet www.e-behbehani.com; f. 1963; Pres. MUHAMMAD SALEH YOUSUF BEHBEHANI.

Mushrif Trading and Constructing Co KSCC: POB 32514, Rumaithya, 25556 Kuwait City; tel. 22052620; fax 24741423; e-mail info@mushrif.com; internet www.mushrif.com; f. 1968; part of Al-Wazzan Trading Group; construction; Chair. AHMED ALI ABDULAZIZ AL-WAZZAN; CEO SAAD ABDULAZIZ AL-WAZZAN.

Packaging and Plastic Industries Co: POB 1148, al-Shorouq Tower, Jaber al-Mubarak St, Sharq, Dasman, 15462 Kuwait City; tel. 22435841; fax 22435839; e-mail ppic@ppickw.com; internet www.ppickw.com; f. 1974; production of polypropylene woven bags for packaging fertilizers, polyethylene agricultural sheets, co-extruded flexible film packaging.

United Industries Co KSC (UIC): POB 25821, Safat, 13119 Kuwait City; tel. 22943236; fax 22943237; e-mail uic@uickw.com; internet www.uickw.com; f. 1979; member of Kuwait Projects Co (KIPCO); Chair. Sheikh KHALIFA AL-ABDULLAH AL-JABER AL-SABAH; CEO Sheikh SABAH MOHAMMED ABDULAZIZ AL-SABAH (acting).

TRADE UNIONS

Federation of Petroleum and Petrochemical Workers: Kuwait City; f. 1965; Chair. MOHAMMED MASHAAN AL-OTAIBI.

KOC Workers' Union: Kuwait City; f. 1964; Chair. ABBAS AWAD.

Kuwait Trade Union Federation (KTUF): POB 5185, Safat, 13052 Kuwait City; tel. 25636389; fax 25627159; f. 1967; central authority to which all trade unions are affiliated; Sec.-Gen. AHMED AL-ENEZI.

Transport

RAILWAYS

There are currently no railways in Kuwait. However, plans for a 518-km national rail network, which would be linked to a proposed regional rail network (the Gulf Railway or GCC Railway), connecting Kuwait with other member countries of the Cooperation Council for the Arab States of the Gulf (or Gulf Cooperation Council—GCC), were announced in 2008. The procurement process for both the trans-Kuwait rail network and for a proposed metro system in Kuwait City began in 2016; both projects were subject to delays, however. Plans for the Kuwait Metropolitan Rapid Transit System project were finally published in 2020: three lines, totalling 160 km in length and including 68 stations, were to be built in five phases. The first phase envisaged the construction of a 50-km line from Kuwait City to Kuwait International Airport, with 27 stations.

ROADS

Roads in the towns are metalled, and the most important are motorways or dual carriageways. There are metalled roads linking Kuwait City to Ahmadi, Mina al-Ahmadi and other centres of population in Kuwait, and to the Iraqi and Saudi Arabian borders. In 2019 a major causeway project in Kuwait Bay, including the construction of two artificial islands, was completed at a cost of around US $3,000m. The Sheikh Jaber al-Ahmad al-Sabah Causeway comprises two sections: the 36-km Main Link, connecting Kuwait City with northern Kuwait, including Madinat al-Hareer (Silk City—a new development under construction in Subiya), and the 13-km Doha Link, connecting Kuwait City with the Doha Peninsula.

Kuwait Public Transport Co SAK (KPTC): POB 375, Murghab, Safat Sq., Safat, 13004 Kuwait City; tel. 22328866; fax 22328870; e-mail info@kptc.com.kw; internet www.kptc.com.kw; f. 1962; state-owned; provides internal bus service; regular service to Mecca, Saudi Arabia; CEO MANSOOR AL-SAAD.

Public Authority for Roads and Transportation (PART): POB 420, Kuwait City; tel. 24728800; fax 24763725; e-mail info@part.gov.kw; internet www.part.gov.kw; Dir-Gen. Eng. SUHA ASHKANANI.

SHIPPING

Kuwait has three commercial seaports—Shuwaikh, Shuaiba (which, since 2003, has been used by the US Army as a base for supplying its troops in Iraq) and Doha. An oil port situated at Mina al-Ahmadi, 40 km south of Kuwait City, is the main export terminal for the country's oil industry.

In 2019 a contract for the construction of a new international port at Bubiyan island was awarded to China Communications Construction Co. The first phase of Mubarak al-Kabir Port—involving the construction of four berths—was completed in April 2021.

Port Authority

Kuwait Ports Authority: Kuwait Ports Authority Complex, Jamal Abdul Nasser St, Shuwaikh, Kuwait City; tel. 24619313; e-mail contact@kpa.gov.kw; internet www.kpa.gov.kw; f. 1977; Dir-Gen. Sheikh YUSUF AL-SABAH AL-NASSER AL-SABAH.

Principal Shipping Companies

Arab Maritime Petroleum Transport Co (AMPTC): POB 22525, Safat, 13086 Kuwait City; tel. 24959400; fax 24842996; e-mail amptc.kuwait@amptc.net; internet www.amptc.net; f. 1973; 6 crude petroleum tankers, 4 LPG carriers and 1 product carrier; owned by Algeria, Bahrain, Egypt, Iraq, Kuwait, Libya, Qatar, Saudi Arabia and the UAE; Gen. Man. AHMED EL-DEMERDASH.

Hapag-Lloyd Shipping Co KSCC: POB 20722, UASC Bldg, Old Airport Rd, Safat, 13068 Kuwait City; tel. 22022505; fax 24943000; e-mail ir@hlag.com; internet www.hapag-lloyd.com; CEO ROLF HABBEN JANSEN.

Heavy Engineering Industries and Shipbuilding Co (Heisco): POB 21998, Safat, 13080 Kuwait City; tel. 24835488; fax 24830291; e-mail heisco@heisco.com; internet www.heisco.com; f. 1974 as Kuwait Shipbuilding and Repairyard Co; name changed as above 2003; ship repairs and engineering services, underwater services, maintenance of refineries, power stations and storage tanks; maintains floating dock for vessels up to 35,000 dwt; synchrolift for vessels up to 5,000 dwt with transfer yard; 7 repair jetties up to 550 m in length and floating workshop for vessels lying at anchor; Chair. ADNAN AL-KHARAFI.

KGL Ports Int. Co (KGL PI): POB 42438, Shuwaikh, 70655 Kuwait City; tel. 22245155; fax 22245166; e-mail info@kglpi.com; internet www.kgl.com; f. 2004; subsidiary of Kuwait and Gulf Link Transport Co; port management and stevedoring; operates Shuaiba Commercial Port Container Terminal; also operations and management contracts with ports in the UAE and Saudi Arabia; Chair. MAHER ABDULLAH MARAFIE.

Kuwait Oil Tanker Co SAK (KOTC): POB 810, Shuwaikh Administrative Sector (P), Gamal Abdel Nasser St, Safat, 13009 Kuwait City; tel. 24625050; fax 24913597; e-mail ho-email@kotc.com.kw; internet www.kotc.com.kw; f. 1957; state-owned; operates 8 crude oil tankers, 11 product tankers and 5 LPG vessels; sole tanker agents for Mina al-Ahmadi, Shuaiba and Mina al-Abdullah and agents for other ports; LPG filling and distribution; Chair. BADER N. ALKHASHTI; CEO ABDULNASER Y. AL-FULAIJ (acting).

CIVIL AVIATION

Kuwait International Airport opened in 1980. The airport has undergone a major programme of expansion in recent years, with total potential overall capacity forecast eventually to reach 25m.–50m. passengers per year.

Directorate-General of Civil Aviation (DGCA): POB 17, Safat, 13001 Kuwait City; tel. 24310400; fax 24316830; e-mail president@dgca.gov.kw; internet www.dgca.gov.kw; Pres. (vacant); Dir-Gen. (vacant).

Jazeera Airways: POB 29288, Safat, 13153 Kuwait City; tel. 24333304; fax 24339432; e-mail feedback@jazeeraairways.com; internet www.jazeeraairways.com; f. 2005; low-cost airline owned by Boodai Group; serves 26 destinations in the Middle East, North Africa, Europe and Asia; Chair. MARWAN BOODAI; CEO ROHIT RAMACHANDRAN.

Kuwait Airways Corpn (KAC): POB 394, Kuwait International Airport, Safat, 13004 Kuwait City; tel. 24345555; e-mail web@kuwaitairways.com; internet www.kuwaitairways.com; f. 1954; scheduled and charter passenger and cargo services to the Arabian peninsula, Asia, Africa, the USA and Europe; sale of 25% stake approved by Govt in 2015; Chair. ALI M. AL-DUKHAN; CEO MAAN AL-RAZOUKI.

Tourism

Department of Tourism: Ministry of Information, Tourism Affairs, POB 193, al-Sour St, Safat, 13002 Kuwait City; tel. 22457591; fax 22401540.

Kuwait Tourism Services Co: POB 21774, Safat, 13078 Kuwait City; tel. 2451734; fax 2451731; e-mail kts@kts-kuwait-tourism.com; internet www.kts-kuwait-tourism.com; f. 1997; Chair. KHALID AL-DUWAISAN.

Touristic Enterprises Co (TEC): Al-Jahra St, Shuwaikh, Kuwait City; tel. 1806806; e-mail info@tec.com.kw; internet www

.kuwaittourism.com; f. 1976; 92% state-owned; manages 23 tourist facilities; Chair. BADER AL-BAHAR; Vice-Chair. SHAKER AL-OTHMAN.

Defence

As assessed at November 2022, the total strength of the Kuwaiti armed forces was 17,500: army 13,000 (incl. 1,500 Emiri Guard); navy est. 2,000; and air force 2,500. There were also 23,700 reserves, as well as a paramilitary force of 7,100 (national guard est. 6,600; coast guard 500).

All male citizens are required to complete 12 months' compulsory military service at the age of 18 years. All conscripts must remain in the reserve forces thereafter until the age of 40 years, and must complete 30 days' service each year during that period.

Defence Budget: KD 2,780m. (est.) in 2022.

Supreme Commander of the Armed Forces: HH Sheikh NAWAF AL-AHMAD AL-JABER AL-SABAH.

Chief of Staff of the Armed Forces: Lt-Gen. KHALED SALEH AL-SABAH.

Commander of the Air Force: Air Vice-Marshal SAIF AL-HUSSEINI.

Commander of the Navy: Brig.-Gen. HAZZA AL-ALATI.

Education

Compulsory education for children between six and 14 years of age was introduced in 1966–67. However, many children spend two years prior to this in a kindergarten, and go on to complete their general education at the age of 18 years. It is government policy to provide free education to all Kuwaiti children from the kindergarten stage to university.

Primary education lasts for five years between the ages of six and 10, after which the pupils move on to an intermediate school for another four years. Secondary education, which is optional and lasts between the ages of 14 and 18, is given mainly in general schools. There are also commercial institutes, a Faculty of Technological Studies, a health institute, religious institutes (with intermediate and secondary stages) and 11 institutes for disabled children. In 2019/20, according to UNESCO estimates, enrolment at pre-primary schools was equivalent to 60.3% of children (boys 58.5%; girls 62.1%) in the relevant age-group. In 2020/21 enrolment at primary schools included 80.8% of children (boys 75.5%; girls 87.0%) in the relevant age-group, while in 2014/15, secondary enrolment was equivalent to 97.8% of children in the relevant age-group.

Kuwait University was founded in 1966 and comprises 17 colleges across six campuses. A KD 1,000m. project to build a new university campus—Sabah al-Salem University City—and to integrate the institution's dispersed facilities in one site was expected to be completed by 2025. Scholarships are granted to students to pursue courses not offered by Kuwait University. Such scholarships are mainly used to study in Egypt, Lebanon, the United Kingdom and the USA. There are also pupils from Arab, African and Asian states studying in Kuwait schools on scholarships provided by the Kuwaiti Government. In 2020 expenditure on education by the central Government amounted to 11.9% of total government expenditure, according to UNESCO figures.

Bibliography

Ahmad, Attiya. *Everyday Conversions: Islam, Domestic Work, and South Asian Migrant Women in Kuwait*. Durham, NC, Duke University Press, 2017.

Azoulay, Rivka. *Kuwait and Al-Sabah: Tribal Politics and Power in an Oil State*. London, I. B. Tauris, 2020.

Bacik, Gökhan. *Hybrid Sovereignty in the Arab Middle East: the Cases of Kuwait, Jordan and Iraq*. Basingstoke, Palgrave Macmillan, 2008.

Bazoobandi, Sara. *Political Economy of the Gulf Sovereign Wealth Funds: A Case Study of Iran, Kuwait, Saudi Arabia and the UAE*. Abingdon, Routledge, 2013.

Beaugrand, Claire. *Stateless in the Gulf: Migration, Nationality and Society in Kuwait*. London, I. B. Tauris, 2015.

Boghardt, Lori Plotkin. *Kuwait Amid War, Peace and Revolution: 1979–1991 and New Challenges*. Basingstoke, Palgrave Macmillan, 2006.

Boutros-Ghali, Boutros (Ed.). *The United Nations and the Iraq–Kuwait Conflict, 1990–96* (UN Blue Books Series, V. 9). New York, United Nations Publications, 1996.

Casey, Michael S. *The History of Kuwait*. Westport, CT, Greenwood Press, 2007.

Chisholm, A. H. T. *The First Kuwait Oil Concession: A Record of the Negotiations 1911–1934*. London, Frank Cass, 1975.

Cordesman, Anthony H. *Kuwait*. Boulder, CO, Westview Press, 1997.

al-Dekhauel, Abdulkarim. *Kuwait: Oil, State and Political Legitimation*. London, Ithaca Press, 2000.

Dickson, H. R. P. *Kuwait and her Neighbours*. London, Allen and Unwin, 1956.

Fandy, Mamoun. *Kuwait and a New Concept of International Politics*. Basingstoke, Palgrave Macmillan, 2003.

Finnie, David. *Shifting Lines in the Sand*. London, I. B. Tauris, 1992.

Gardiner, Stephen, and Cook, Ian. *Kuwait: The Making of a City*. London, Longman, 1983.

González, Alessandra L. *Islamic Feminism in Kuwait: The Politics and Paradoxes*. New York, Palgrave Macmillan, 2013.

Hakima, Abu A. M. *The Modern History of Kuwait: 1750–1966*. St Ives, Westerham Press, 1983.

Hassan, Hamdi A. *The Iraqi Invasion of Kuwait: Religion, Identity and Otherness in the Analysis of War and Conflict*. London, Pluto Press, 1999.

Herb, Michael. *The Wages of Oil: Parliaments and Economic Development in Kuwait and the UAE*. Ithaca, NY, Cornell University Press, 2014.

al-Hijji, Yacoub Yusuf. *Kuwait and the Sea: A Brief Social and Economic History* (trans.). London, Arabian Publishing, 2010.

International Bank for Reconstruction and Development. *The Economic Development of Kuwait*. Baltimore, MD, Johns Hopkins Press, 1965.

Ismail, Raihan. *Rethinking Salafism: The Transnational Networks of Salafi 'Ulama in Egypt, Kuwait, and Saudi Arabia*. Oxford, Oxford University Press, 2022.

Joyce, Miriam. *Kuwait, 1945–1996: An Anglo-American Perspective*. London, Frank Cass, 1999.

Khouja, M. W., and Sadler, P. G. *The Energy of Kuwait: Development and Role in International Finance*. London, Macmillan, 1978.

Kuwait Oil Co Ltd. *The Story of Kuwait*. London, Kuwait Oil Co Ltd, 1963.

el Mallakh, Ragaei. *Economic Development and Regional Co-operation: Kuwait*. Chicago, IL, University of Chicago Press, 1968.

Marlowe, John. *The Persian Gulf in the 20th Century*. London, Cresset Press, 1962.

al-Mdaires, Falah Abdullah. *Islamic Extremism in Kuwait: From the Muslim Brotherhood to Al-Qaeda and Other Islamic Political Groups*. Abingdon, Routledge, 2010.

Mezerik, Avraham G. *The Kuwait–Iraq Dispute, 1961*. New York, International Review Service, 1961.

al-Mughni, Haya. *Women in Kuwait: The Politics of Gender*. London, Saqi Books, 2001.

al-Nakib, Farah. *Kuwait Transformed: a History of Oil and Urban Life*. Stanford, CA, Stanford University Press, 2016.

Panaspornprasit, Chookiat. *US–Kuwaiti Relations, 1961–1992: An Uneasy Relationship*. Abingdon, Routledge, 2005.

Rahman, H. *The Making of the Gulf War*. Reading, Garnet, 1997.

Rizzo, Helen M. *Islam, Democracy and the Status of Women: The Case of Kuwait*. Abingdon, Routledge, 2005.

Rush, Alan. *Al-Sabah History and Genealogy of Kuwait's Ruling Family 1752–1987*. London, Ithaca Press, 1987.

Al-Sabah, Meshal. *Gender and Politics in Kuwait: Women and Political Participation in the Gulf*. London, I. B. Tauris, 2013.

Al-Sabah, Souad M. *Mubarak Al-Sabah: The Foundation of Kuwait*. London, I. B. Tauris, 2014.

Abdullah Mubarak Al-Sabah: The Transformation of Kuwait. London, I. B. Tauris, 2015.

Saldanha, J. A. *The Persian Gulf: Administration Reports 1873–1957*. London, Archive Editions, 1986.

Sandwick, John A. *The Gulf Co-operation Council: Moderation and Stability in an Interdependent World*. London, Mansell Publishing Ltd, 1987.

Slot, Ben J. (Ed.). *Kuwait: The Growth of a Historic Identity*. London, Arabian Publishing Ltd, 2003.

Tetreault, Mary Ann. *Stories of Democracy: Politics and Society in Contemporary Kuwait*. New York, Columbia University Press, 2000.

Winstone, H. V. F., and Freeth, Z. *Kuwait: Prospect and Reality*. London, Allen and Unwin, 1972.

Yanai, Shaul. *The Political Transformation of Gulf Tribal States: Elitism and the Social Contract in Kuwait, Bahrain and Dubai, 1918-1970s*. Eastbourne, Sussex Academic Press, 2015.

LEBANON

Geography

The creation, after 1918, of the modern state of Lebanon, first under French mandatory rule and then as an independent territory, was designed to recognize the nationalist aspirations of a number of Christian groups that had lived for many centuries under Muslim rule along the coast of the eastern Mediterranean and in the hills immediately adjacent. At least as early as the 16th century CE there had been particularist Christian feeling that ultimately resulted in the granting of autonomy, though not independence, to Christians living in the territory of 'Mount Lebanon', which geographically was the hill region immediately inland and extending some 30 km–45 km north and south of Beirut. The territory of Mount Lebanon was later expanded, owing to French interest, into the much larger area of 'Greater Lebanon' with frontiers running along the crest of the Anti-Lebanon mountains, and reaching the sea some miles north of Tripoli to form the boundary with the Syrian Arab Republic. In the south there is a frontier with Israel, running inland from Ras al-Naqoura to the head of the Jordan Valley. In drawing the frontiers so as to give a measure of geographical unity to the new state, which now occupies an area of 10,452 sq km (4,036 sq miles), large non-Christian elements of Muslims and Druzes were included, so that today the Christians of Lebanon form less than 40% (and possibly as little as 30%) of the total population.

PHYSICAL FEATURES

Structurally, Lebanon consists of an enormous simple upfold of rocks that runs parallel to the coast. There is, first, a very narrow and broken flat coastal strip—hardly a true plain—then the land rises steeply to a series of imposing crests and ridges. The highest crest of all is Qurnet al-Sauda, just over 3,000 m high, lying south-east of Tripoli; Mount Sannin, north-east of Beirut, is over 2,700 m high. A few miles east of the summits there is a precipitous drop along a sharp line to a broad, trough-like valley, known as the Beqa'a (Biqa), about 16 km wide and some 110 km–130 km long. The eastern side of the Beqa'a is formed by the Anti-Lebanon mountains, which rise to 2,800 m, and their southern continuation, the Hermon Range, of about the same height. The floor of the Beqa'a valley, though much below the level of the surrounding mountain ranges, lies in places at 1,000 m above sea level, with a low divide in the region of Ba'albek. Two rivers rise in the Beqa'a—the Orontes, which flows northwards into Syria and the Gharb depression, ultimately reaching the Mediterranean through the Turkish territory of Antioch; and the Litani (Leontes) river. This latter river flows southwards, and then, at a short distance from the Israeli frontier, makes a sudden bend westwards and plunges through the Lebanon mountains by a deep gorge.

There exists in Lebanon an unusual feature of geological structure not present in either of the adjacent regions of Syria and Israel. This is the occurrence of a layer of non-porous rocks within the upfold forming the Lebanon mountains; and, because of this layer, water is forced to the surface in considerable quantities, producing large springs at the unusually high level of 1,200 m–1,500 m. Some of the springs have a flow of several thousand cu ft per second and emerge as small rivers; hence the western flanks of the Lebanon mountains, unlike those nearby in Syria and Israel, are relatively well watered and cultivation is possible up to a height of 1,200 m or 1,500 m.

CLIMATE

Given the country's great contrasts of relief, and the configuration of the main ranges, which lie across the path of the prevailing westerly winds, there is a wide variety in climatic conditions. The coastal lowlands are moderately hot in summer, and warm in winter, with complete absence of frost. Yet only 10 km or so away in the hills there is a heavy winter snowfall, and the higher hills are covered from December to May, giving the unusual vista for the Middle East of snow-clad peaks. From this the name Lebanon (*laban*—Aramaic for 'white') is said to originate. The Beqa'a has a moderately cold winter with some frost and snow, and a distinctly hot summer, as it is shut off from the tempering effect of the sea.

Rainfall is generally abundant but it decreases rapidly towards the east, so that the Beqa'a and Anti-Lebanon are definitely drier than the west. On the coast, between 750 mm and 1,000 mm fall annually, with up to 1,250 mm in the mountains, but only 380 mm in the Beqa'a. As almost all of this annual total falls between October and April (there are three months of complete aridity each summer), rain is extremely heavy while it lasts, and storms of surprising intensity sometimes occur. Another remarkable feature is the extremely high humidity of the coastal region during summer, when no rain falls.

POPULATION

The population of Lebanon was officially estimated at 3,759,137 in 2007. By mid-2023 this figure had reached 5,353,930, according to United Nations (UN) estimates. Owing to the civil conflict in neighbouring Syria, large numbers of Syrian refugees have crossed the border into Lebanon since 2011. As of July 2023 there were 795,322 Syrian refugees registered with the Office of the United Nations High Commissioner for Refugees (UNHCR) in Lebanon, although there were thought to be many more unregistered Syrians living in the country. According to the UN Relief and Works for Palestine Refugees in the Near East (UNRWA), the total number of registered Palestinian refugees in Lebanon was 490,687 at mid-2023. Beirut is the capital. At mid-2023 the city and its suburbs had a total population of 2,421,354, according to UN estimates.

Arabic, the official language, is current throughout the whole country. French was the leading European language in use in Lebanon. However, English has recently become more prevalent in commerce and education. Kurdish and Armenian are spoken by small ethnic minorities. In addition, Aramaic is used by some religious sects, but only for ritual—there are no Aramaic-speaking villages, unlike in Syria.

History

NATÁLIA CALFAT

Revised for this edition by the editorial staff

CENTURIES-OLD SECTARIAN INSTITUTIONS

In Lebanon, the division of state power and resources among different sects, as well as the judicial power belonging to religious authorities, date back to Ottoman times. Under the *millet* system, religious communities of different Muslim, Christian and Jewish sects enjoyed freedom of religious practice and administrative autonomy, with their leaders locally managing communal affairs and self-governing service provision. During the French mandate for Syria and Lebanon (1923–43), sectarian rule was reinforced, and confessional identity continued to be politicized and incorporated into the state's structure. Privileges unevenly granted were inherited by the modern Lebanese state structure and are the foundational building blocks of confessionalism. Such a power-sharing system—although partly conceived as a compromise solution between different religious affiliations—prompted tensions, communal loyalties and patronage networks that dominate Lebanese politics to this day.

The ethnically and religiously diverse Ottoman Empire came to depend on local feudal elites and communal entrenched dynasties to control its wide domains. The *zu'ama* (local political leaders providing protection, security and patronage) traded loyalty for access to services and power brokerage. To this day, some of these major families constitute the ruling sectarian elites in Lebanon. As a province of the Empire, Mount Lebanon was divided into districts under the control of different notable families. Elite families provided each region, under its inherited sphere of influence and autonomous administration, with a sense of identity. Religious affiliation and loyalty narrative became intertwined.

Given that the political balance in Mount Lebanon was biased in favour of Maronite Christians, disowning Muslims (and Druze, who were treated as Muslims for official purposes by the Empire) from their traditional privileges, hostilities emerged against Druze and Muslims during the 19th century, assuming the character of an intermittent religious civil war. Concerned, representatives of the European powers proposed in 1842 that Mount Lebanon be partitioned into two administrative units, each with a deputy governor: a Christian in the northern district; and a Druze in the southern district. Maronite Christians were supported by France, while the Druze were supported by Britain. However, the interference of outside power only fostered conflict. This 'Double Qaimaqamate', divided by the route of the road between Beirut and Damascus, had naturally mixed Maronite and Druze populations, which only exacerbated animosities.

Discontented peasants, overburdened by heavy taxes, revolted against the feudal practices of landlords in Mount Lebanon. The Maronite–Druze battles were mainly over the possession, use and rent of agricultural land and the equitable distribution of political power and benefits. Mount Lebanon's traditional economy and market were also faced with disturbance by modern influences, including European industrial products, which contributed to worsening social tensions in the region. In fact, scholars argue that peasant uprisings and sociopolitical crises were 'transmuted into sectarian denominational conflicts'. Christian religious affiliations as political identities were mobilized to divide, arm and rule against the Druze.

Ottoman *Tanzimat* reforms, seeking greater centralization of the Empire, increased control over provinces and forced Muslims and Christians to react and forge their own nationalisms. Through Ottoman modernization reforms and European colonial influence, the literature points out that 'politics of notability were replaced by political sectarian identity', reinforcing communal belonging in Mount Lebanon.

The Lebanese Emirs who ruled 19th-century Ottoman Lebanon encouraged the latent tension and aroused antagonism between Muslim and Christian sects, alienating the political power and authority of Druze feudal families. After the 1860 massacre of Maronites by the Druze, France intervened on behalf of the former, and an international committee formed by Great Britain, Austria, Prussia, Russia and the Ottoman Empire recommended a new judicial and administrative system. A semi-autonomous Mount Lebanon, now separated and independent from Syria, inaugurated the *mutasarrifiyah* system (1861–1915). The *mutasarrif* (administrative unit) was governed by a non-Arab Ottoman Christian and served as a refuge and protection for the 'Christian legacy' in the Middle East. Still constituting a significant two-thirds majority of the population, and with strong francophone ties, Levantine Christians prospered politically and economically. The law also provided for Mount Lebanon's autonomy, and assured the Maronite elite's loyalty to France.

Recognizing confessional diversity, the organic statute of 1861 established a 12-member Administrative Representative Council, with two representatives of each of the six major communities—Maronite, Greek Orthodox and Catholic Christians, Druze, and Sunni and Shi'a Muslims. However, the Council was the subject of confessional grievances and representation readjustments, and it was eventually modified to comprise seven Christians and five Muslims.

Under Ottoman rule, religious communal belonging was for the first time formally shaped under the sectarian system. Demographic partition schemes and geographical reorganizations of administrative divisions also had the purpose of rearranging and institutionalizing confessional representation and power. Most importantly, the Ottoman practices of the 19th century gave birth to the consociational power-sharing principles that prevailed and would further be reinforced and institutionally formalized during the following century.

By the end of the 19th century and during the First World War, the Lebanese differed on the best political course for the region. Conflicting visions emerged, including aspirations for a pan-Islamic Turkish state, for secession from the Empire, for Lebanon as a province in an independent Syria, and for an independent nation. After the First World War, Arab nationalists opposed the 1916 Sykes-Picot Agreement, which partitioned the Arab territory between France and Britain, and frustrated the British promise of Arab independence to Hussein bin Ali, the Sharif of Mecca. Arabs also disapproved of the Balfour Declaration of 1917, which promised British support for the creation of a Jewish national home in Palestine.

With the end of the war, Allied forces occupied Lebanon and the territory was placed under French military administration. Until the first half of the 20th century, the French military presence in Syria and in Lebanon strengthened France's position as a Mediterranean and world power, and Lebanon served as a route to its Empire in Indochina. In 1920, under the French mandate bestowed by the League of Nations, parts of Greater Syria were annexed to Mount Lebanon. Regions such as the Beqa'a Valley, Akkar and Beirut and other coastal cities such as Tripoli, Saida (Sidon) and Sur (Tyre) were added to the former autonomous territory of Mount Lebanon.

After the fall of the Ottoman Empire, the state established in Lebanon by the French mandate was composed of diverse confessional communities, but the power-sharing political system established by the French continued to favour Maronite Christians. In addition, the expansion of Mount Lebanon into the State of Greater Lebanon (in 1920–26) changed the demographic balance, with Muslims now becoming almost one-half of the population. By then, also due to the 'silk crisis' (when cheaper and better quality Chinese silk and silk products flooded Europe—the main market for Lebanese silk), around one-third of Mount Lebanon's population had emigrated. Mount Lebanon residents, for example, paid lower taxes compared with newly annexed areas, becoming the source of Sunni and Shi'a grievances. Additionally, Maronites profited unevenly from education and infrastructure projects. Meanwhile, in Greater Lebanon Maronites became the leading social group in the social private sphere, as well as securing key government and bureaucratic positions in state institutions. Notably, their political identity in the Middle East was increasingly dependent on the French.

The early days of French occupation in Lebanon were not received without struggle, and the concepts of 'resistance' and 'martyrdom' dominate the popular imagination in several regions to this day, particularly among the Shi'a. The French mandate over Lebanon was a 'regime of direct rule' and an Administrative Commission with mainly consultative powers continued the *mutasarrif* status quo to some extent. The initial proportion of the population who were Christians (67%) later fell to 60%. A partially elected Representative Council replaced the Commission, despite boycotts by the Muslim population.

Shi'a and Sunni Muslims, some of whom wanted to join with a larger Syrian state and were reluctant to identify with the new state, eventually had their participation incrementally obtained, including by the use of co-option through patronage. Fiscal, education and administrative reform attempts were made to reduce inequalities between the Mount Lebanon Maronites and the Muslims from the newly annexed territories. Such efforts were blocked, including under pressure from the Maronite Church. Eventually, Muslims were encouraged to help maintain the state with a considerable share of power in the government.

The Constitution unifying Lebanon was promulgated in 1926, under the French mandate, consolidating the sectarian power-sharing arrangement. Despite being opposed by the majority of Sunni and Shi'a leaders, the Constitution entered into effect in May, with the Republic of Greater Lebanon becoming the Lebanese Republic, and the Representative Council being replaced by a parliament (National Assembly). Remaining in force today (with subsequent amendments), the Constitution stipulated that each religious community would be proportionally represented in public offices and administrative posts. The President should be a Christian (usually Maronite), the Prime Minister a Sunni Muslim, and the speaker of parliament a Shi'a Muslim. The President of the Republic was granted extensive executive powers. Between 1926 and 1943 a total of 17 of the 30 seats in parliament were allocated to Christians and 13 to Muslims.

The French mandate for Lebanon reinforced the politics of confessional representation, as well as the religious domain of personal and civil status law, covering areas such as marriage, divorce and inheritance. Civil and family law remains exclusively under religious courts. Sectarian social welfare institutions also developed under the colonial state, enforcing communal solidarity and, in the long run, would serve to undermine the legitimacy of the national state and its provision of services.

The electoral laws of 1926 established that local electoral districts would have multiple seats allocated on a communal basis. By advancing agricultural development and land ownership, and by favouring candidates from most prominent local families in the north, the Beqa'a Valley and the south, the electoral power of powerful local landlords and dynasties was entrenched. Most elements of this system continue to be perpetuated in municipal elections in the 21st century, fostering local clientelist factional disputes and control of state resources. Patron–client relationships exchanging service provision for loyalty further entrench traditional notables' dominance in local politics and electoral lists.

With France at war and regional and domestic pressures to form part of a larger Syrian or Arab state, on the one hand, or to bring to fruition nationalist aspirations, on the other, independence for Lebanon was the solution to guarantee the country's controlled autonomy without bringing about substantive national integration. The French opted for considering Lebanon a 'land of religious minorities'—with the political supremacy of Maronites now ensured as the largest numerical minority. Maronites claimed that the historical territories of Greater Lebanon—which previously belonged to the Vilayets (administrative areas) of Beirut and Damascus—had a singular social and historical character, and that their independence from Syria was of vital importance.

However, Maronite Christians, who dominated the political and ruling establishment, faced opposition from Sunni Muslims, who were not as confident that a cohesive national identity would flow from a newly created artificial state, as well as from Shi'a Muslims, who in the late 1930s believed that as the second largest population in the country their jurisdictions were being widely neglected, and who sought therefore to increase their political rights and share in Greater Lebanon. In practice, the Shi'a were heavily under-represented in high-ranking civil servant positions, occupying 3.6% of appointments in 1955—a ratio that remained largely unchanged until 1975.

Meanwhile, in 1924 the Parti Communiste Libanais (PCL) was created, and in 1932 Antoun Saadeh's Syrian Social Nationalist Party (SSNP) was established, supporting the creation of a 'Greater Syrian' state and secular nationalism. Opposing Ottoman rule, Christians, mainly the Orthodox, also played an important role in developing Arab nationalist political thought. With the eventual return of many Lebanese from abroad, these new ideas and dialogue with the diaspora helped to give birth to Arab nationalist movements. In 1936 demonstrations and deadly riots led to the French imprisonment of Sunni activists. Young Maronites in Beirut responded by joining paramilitary organizations. In the same year, inspired by European fascism, Pierre Gemayel helped to establish the Maronite Phalangist Party (Phalanges Libanaises, or Al-Kataeb).

The Lebanese 'hybrid identity' had to come to terms with a leading Maronite role, with strong ties to the West, as well as with the country being part of the Arab and Muslim world. Nevertheless, local traditional elites and external players were able to satisfy their economic interests and leverage power in the form of an apparent 'political accommodation'.

During the Second World War the Allied Forces opposed Vichy control over French mandate territories in 1940, and fought a Syrian–Lebanese campaign the following year. Under domestic and international pressure, a French general proclaimed Lebanon's independence in November 1941. Under British supervision, Maronite and Sunni elites converged over sectarian shares of power in a newly independent state, principally benefiting the interests of the Christian and the Sunni Muslim business elites of Beirut, who had been profiting from industrial expansion and capital investment. The loyalty of traditional landlord notables from annexed territories was won through favouritism, and they became the main beneficiaries of government investment and support for agricultural development, mostly in Beqa'a, Akkar and the south. The continuance of a system of sectarian quotas also guaranteed the prominence of landed elites and patron–client politics. The 'liberal merchant Republic' status quo of Mount Lebanon and Beirut favoured the British, French, Maronites and conservative Arabs, blocking pro-Syrian or pan-Arab projects, at least in the short term.

A Franco-Lebanese Treaty proclaimed the independence of Lebanon on 22 November 1943, ending the French mandate over Lebanon, after 23 years. Nationalists of the Constitutional Bloc party had won elections in August–September of that year, electing Maronite Christian Bishara el-Khoury as President (1943–52). Riyad al-Solh was nominated Prime Minister, forming the first Government of independent Lebanon. With some resistance and having effected the arrest of several high-level politicians, French and British troops only fully left the country in 1946, completing the process of de facto independence on 31 December 1946, when the Treaty was ratified.

A NEW STATE, AN OLD SYSTEM

From the late Ottoman and pre-independence period, Lebanon's history was marked by privilege and land disputes, demographic as well as power imbalances, foreign intervention in domestic affairs, and continuing sectarianism. After independence, the new state—a parliamentary democracy—inherited the fragile power-sharing system that reserved the presidency and army command for a Maronite Christian, the prime ministerial office for a Sunni Muslim, the presidency of parliament for a Shi'a Muslim, and the vice-presidency for a Greek Orthodox Christian. Important amendments were made to the 1926 Constitution. The unwritten National Pact of 1943 established a ratio of political representation of 6:5 between Christians and Muslims in the National Assembly. The covenant established the terms of independence by trying to balance a Christian ideological alignment, as well as cultural and intellectual ties with the West, with Muslim identities and co-operation with Arab states and the use of the Arabic language. In addition, the National Pact determined that public offices and the civil service should be allocated proportionally among the recognized confessional groups.

The proportional formula was based on the results of the 1932 census, conducted following Sunni pressure, which recorded a total population of 785,543 Lebanese, of whom 49.9% were Christian and 48.8% were Muslim. Maronite Christians constituted 28.8% of the population, Greek Orthodox 9.7%, Greek Catholics 5.9%, Orthodox Armenians 3.2% and other Christian minorities 2.3%. Sunni Muslims made up 22.4% of the population, Shi'a 19.6% and Druze 6.8%; other minorities accounted for 1.2% of the population. Fearing that the power-sharing formula could be disrupted, an official census has never been conducted since in Lebanon.

Bishara el-Khoury was elected for a second six-year term in 1949, but he was opposed by Camille Chamoun, Kamal Joumblatt, Emile Bustani and Pierre Gemayel for his alleged corruption, elite manipulation, communal manoeuvring and favouritism. In fact, the pre-civil war period was dominated by prominent family networks, communal loyalties and patron-client relationships, with each sectarian circle loyal to and relying on their respective notable family.

Following clashes with Al-Kataeb, the SSNP attempted a (failed) coup in 1949, which led to the execution of Antoun Saadeh, on the orders of the Prime Minister, Riyad al-Solh. In retaliation, al-Solh was assassinated by the SSNP in 1951. Rallies and general strikes were organized. Facing growing antagonism to his Government, el-Khoury resigned in 1952. His administration was followed by the Chamoun presidency (1952–58), which was also eventually criticized by its political opponents for alleged accommodation to 'traditional Lebanese sectarian politics'.

The power-sharing balance established under the National Pact was tenuous and Muslims claimed that they now held a demographic superiority, calling for the seat allocations to be revised. Muslims protested that Christians dominated the executive and legislative branches, and occupied the highest offices in the state (filling a disproportionate number of civil service positions and high-level diplomatic posts), and repeatedly called for a new census from as early as the late 1930s. Christians, for their part, claimed that they contributed more than three-quarters of the country's tax revenue, providing the country with much-needed infrastructure, and demanded that a new census be conducted to include Lebanese emigrants (who were mainly Christians).

Domestic tensions in Lebanon were accompanied by the approval by the United Nations (UN) of a plan to partition Palestine into Arab and Jewish states in November 1947, despite Arab rejection. After the British Mandate of Palestine was ended and the State of Israel was officially declared in May 1948, an Arab military campaign mounted by Egypt, Syria, Lebanon, Iraq and Transjordan (later Jordan) was defeated by the newly formed Israeli military. The mass flight or expulsion of Palestinian Arabs from their homes during the war led to the arrival of 120,000–150,000 Palestinian Arab refugees in Lebanon, particularly in coastal cities such as Tyre and Sidon.

During the 1950s and the 1960s calls for Arab nationalism and independence from foreign powers, as well as social, land and educational reforms that would lead towards a decrease in inequalities, became increasingly influential in the region. Taking pan-Arabism a step further, Egyptian President Gamal Abdel Nasser stated not only that Arabs shared a common struggle against colonial powers, but also that the liberation of Palestine should be an 'Arab duty' (his political ideology becoming known as Nasserism).

In 1956 Nasser nationalized the Suez Canal, a waterway which controlled the passage of two-thirds of the oil used by Europe. The move was followed by a tripartite invasion of Egypt by Israel, the United Kingdom and France. The Suez Crisis is considered one of the last major efforts by the British and the French to reaffirm their rule in the Arab countries, and paved the way for Cold War disputes between the USA, the Union of Soviet Socialist Republics (USSR) and Arab nationalists. Calls for pan-Arab unity defied the fragile balance provided for by the Lebanese National Pact. Lebanese President Chamoun refused to dissolve diplomatic ties with the UK and France, indirectly siding with Israel.

Chamoun was re-elected and supposedly manipulated the parliamentary electoral law of 1957. In the following year the United Arab Republic (UAR) was formed by the political union of Egypt and the Syrian Arab Republic. (Syria left the Union in 1961, but Egypt retained the designation until 1971.) A considerable number of Lebanese Muslims petitioned for the country to become part of the UAR, whereas for Christians Lebanese independence and autonomy relied on co-operation and friendly ties with the West. In direct opposition to several prominent Sunni leaders, Chamoun favoured neither Nasserism nor pan-Arabism. Al-Kataeb and the SSNP also regarded pan-Arabism as a threat, while Druze of the Parti Socialiste Progressiste (PSP) joined the opposition against the President's ideological alignment. In the south, Tyre demonstrated support for the UAR, providing a base for the Shi'a opposition. Since the 1943 National Pact, Shi'a Muslims had been disaffected by not being reserved a leading government office, and in the late 1950s they became more disadvantaged, occupying only four of 115 senior posts and having a low proportion of university graduates among their population.

Regional ideological disputes added a layer to domestic rivalry among Lebanese political leaders and their respective confessional loyalty networks. General strikes, pan-Arab demonstrations and Muslim armed insurrections during the 1950s ultimately crystallized Maronite fears and narratives: that destabilizing Arab interventions and external Arab nationalists could potentially 'manipulate Lebanese Muslims as political leverage' and condemn the country to permanent instability. Conversely, Maronites were blamed for the disruption of the 'Greater Syria' project and for surrendering to Western economic, cultural and strategic interests in the country.

Since the emergence of the state, Muslims and Christians had disagreed over the meaning of Lebanese nationality and cultural identity. While Christians, who were responsible for heading the efforts for a national state, identified themselves with a Mediterranean Phoenician heritage, Muslims claimed to be part of a broader Arab history, eventually siding with Arab nationalists who held that Lebanon should integrate into a greater Arab homeland—additionally comprising the lands of Syria, Palestine, Transjordan, Iraq and the Persian (Arabian) Gulf.

Narratives of pan-Arabism and reinforcement of close ties to the Islamic heritage conflicted with accounts that emphasized the defence of Lebanese independence, sovereignty and freedom. These two opposing ideals helped to create a wedge between communities and prevented Lebanon, throughout the entire 20th century, from forging a sense of national political unity and identity.

The assassination in May 1958 of Nassib Metni, a Maronite anti-Chamoun and outspoken pan-Arabist figure, who was editor of the daily newspaper *Al-Talagraph*, intensified the popular unrest. Commander-in-Chief of the army Gen. Fouad Chehab refused to act against the armed insurgents, fearing divisions within the pluri-religious army. Chamoun accused the UAR of intervention in Lebanon by supplying Soviet arms via Syria and conveyed the matter to the UN Security Council; as a result, observers were sent to Lebanon. The USA's (mostly symbolic) three-month intervention was requested by President Chamoun in July upon the ousting of the pro-Western royal family in Iraq. Invoking the 1957 Eisenhower Doctrine, requesting assistance against armed aggression from 'international communism', Chamoun pleaded that the independence of Lebanon was at risk.

The period from the National Pact to the first civil war (1943–58) consolidated economic liberalism in the country's growing economy under the 'merchant Republic'. Beirut's free-market, deregulated and service-based economy was a prosperous regional centre for the financial and banking sectors. The city consolidated itself as the capital of the Arab world for education, publishing and tourism. The period provided stability and freedom of enterprise. Elites embraced an 'outward-looking and non-interventionist' economy resulting from post-independence debate, forging a country ruled by a Maronite and Sunni duopoly, composed of merchants, bankers and landowners. Over time, income inequalities and disparities became more salient, the industry sector was heavily damaged and the agricultural sector stagnated. Service sector returns were skewed towards Christians, and benefits and privileged access to credits concentrated with big landowners. High growth rates during the 'Lebanese Miracle' of reconstruction were unevenly spread. The merchant liberal Republic, however, did not meet the aspirations of many Sunni Muslims, the majority of the Shi'a and Druze, nor many rural Maronite Christians. Nasserism fuelled existing discontents.

The first civil war, in 1958, continued for three months and killed 2,000–4,000 Lebanese, mostly from Muslim areas, acting as a kind of 'sectarian rehearsal' for the following decades. The rift between Christians and Muslims, inspired by their rival visions of 'Lebanese particularism' and pan-Arab unity, respectively, would, years later, turn into open conflict. By then, the parties would also be disputing the right of Palestinian refugees and guerrillas to operate freely from and within the country against Israel.

Gen. Chehab was nominated as President by parliament as a compromise neutral candidate and Rashid Karami, a Sunni leader from Tripoli, was appointed as Prime Minister, helping to form a reconciliation Government that promoted national unity. The Cabinet sought a compromise under the slogan 'no victor, no vanquished'. Al-Kataeb responded by opposing a Cabinet composed of several Muslim leaders, fearing that by advocating Arabism the 'Christian community hegemony' would be compromised. The Cabinet was rebalanced and an electoral reform increased the size of the National Assembly from 66 to 99 seats. The withdrawal of US troops was requested in September 1958.

President Chehab (1958–64) inaugurated a somewhat progressive period of moderate social welfare interventionism (which continued until 1975), by trying to decrease the power of the traditional zu'ama leaders and empowering the state bureaucracy and the executive power, as well as improving infrastructure and provision of public goods. Chehab attempted to address some of the Muslim grievances concerning access to administrative offices by promoting communal equity and by assisting predominantly Muslim neglected and deprived areas, as well as addressing social and economic inequalities. Chehab also promoted public infrastructure investment in areas such as road systems, water, health care and electricity provision in the country's peripheries, particularly in the Shi'a south and the Beqa'a Valley and the Sunni north. In 1958 the Shi'a clerical leader Musa al-Sadr came to Lebanon from Iran and became the Mufti of Tyre. Chehab favoured the charismatic young activist, who was involved with social work, improvement of the rural population and fund-raising activities against poverty.

The Chehab period is said to have instigated a 'proto-awakening of Lebanese nationalism' and a foreign policy of Arab neutrality, maintaining good relations with the UAR and Nasser (until his death in 1970), as well as with the West. President Chehab continued to profit from the stability and economic boom that started under Chamoun's Government. However, Chehab's social reforms and efforts to restrain patronage in the bureaucracy endangered traditional patronage networks and faced resistance from both Christian and Sunni elites and political chiefs. In practice, Chehab was not able to sustain reform and free the state from patronage politics and elite co-optation, promoting traditional figures such as Rashid Karami, Kamal Joumblatt and Pierre Gemayel.

Charles Hélou (1964–70) succeeded Chehab as President and continued his policies in a 'softer version'. Hélou promoted socioeconomic changes and increased social mobility, but his reforms also faced obstruction from the traditional political class. Economic growth and urbanization deepened social and economic inequalities, contrasting wealthier urban classes in Beirut and Christian commercial bourgeoisie with unintegrated migrants, the mainly jobless, and the impoverished Shi'a. Rapid urbanization and constrained industrial development populated the Beirut suburbs of poor working class residents with large numbers of rural workers fleeing the agricultural crisis. The deprived 'poverty belt' also incorporated several Palestinian refugee camps, where much of the political base of the Palestine Liberation Organization (PLO) was located.

The Shi'a were affected greatly. Mostly rural in the post-independence period, by the 1970s more than three-quarters of the Shi'a population had been urbanized. With growing influence in southern Lebanon, al-Sadr pleaded for a Shi'a authority akin to the Supreme Islamic Council of the Sunnis and the Druze Communal Council. The Lebanese Parliament and Presidents Chehab and Hélou backed the establishment of the Higher Shi'a Islamic Council in 1967. The Council demanded not only improvement of the defence of the south but also the allocation of public funds for socioeconomic development, education, health care and an increase in the number of Shi'a officials appointed to senior government positions. Then considered a 'regional protector of the Shi'a', the Iranian Shah promoted them domestically and in Lebanon as a bulwark against both Marxism and pan-Arabism (ideologies that represented threats to his rule)—something that largely explains, in the context of the Cold War, the close alliance that emerged between the USA, Israel and pre-revolutionary Iran. Although Shi'a political discourse had always focused on social justice and the dispossessed, by confronting the left and opposing secularism, Musa al-Sadr endorsed the Lebanese sectarian framework, urging his followers to abide by the Lebanese state and citizenship as a means of institutionalizing Shi'a clerical guidance. Ultimately, by the end of the civil war, the rise of the Shi'a was able to disperse the leftist opposition in Lebanon.

In the south, after the creation of Israel in 1948, the Shi'a suffered in particular from the ongoing aggressions between Palestinian guerrillas, or *fedayeen*, the PLO (after its foundation in 1964) and Israeli forces. Also due to displacements caused by Israeli retaliation against the villages, the scenario resulted in the collapse of the economy in the regions of Jabal Amil and southern Beqa'a, prompting an exodus of the population from rural areas. Particularly in the south, the PLO was accused of building 'a state within a state', with military freedom and the health care infrastructure of which also served the Lebanese. With the abandonment and neglect of several different rural areas, the areas surrounding Sidon and Tyre were also sites for the emergence of slum-like suburbs. Such a mass of sub-proletarians living in poor sanitary and health conditions provided fertile conditions for forces and narratives across the political spectrum, with their plight being manipulated variously to explain the sources of inequalities and to idealize potential change.

Increasingly, Beirut's territory was physically divided by communal and religious affiliation. The inability to balance and integrate different segments of the population triggered social and political instability and polarization, becoming one of the key reasons for the second and more deadly civil war. In 1968 cabinet formation disputes and disagreements were aggravated by an Israeli raid on the International Airport of Beirut, fostering a government crisis in the following years until the 1973 and 1975 wars.

In the June 1967 war Israel was simultaneously attacked by the Egyptian, Syrian and Jordanian armies, but rapidly brought about their defeat. The war significantly altered the region's map and geopolitics. Pre-emptive air strikes followed by a ground offensive by the Israel Defense Forces (IDF) led to the Israeli annexation of the Sinai Peninsula and the Gaza Strip from Egypt, the West Bank and East Jerusalem from Jordan, and the Golan Heights from Syria. Even though Lebanon did not take part in the 1967 war, it had a great impact on the country. A sense that Arabs had been humiliated inspired the mostly secular Palestinian military mobilization in Lebanon, intensifying domestic tensions. The so-called Six-Day War helped put an end to the politics of the Chehab presidency—setting the stage for the civil war by disputing the confessional balance.

Palestinian refugee camps in Lebanon operated as bases and trenches for cross-border attacks against Israel. Meanwhile, in an initial attempt to prevent the army from formally becoming involved in clashes in the south, in 1970 the Lebanese Government announced a plan to 'fortify villages in the south, as well as to train and arm civilians against Israeli incursions'. Palestinian guerrilla movements joined the rising Lebanese militant left against the so-called 'Maronite hegemony', mobilizing youths living on the fringes of Beirut, in the Shi'a and Palestinian 'belt of misery' circling the capital. In the late 1960s the SSNP moved to the hard left. In the years leading up to the war, thousands of Israeli violations and attacks were registered in Lebanese territory. Maronite party leaders mobilized their own youths accordingly, and resisted the idea of the Lebanese being held hostage to both the Israeli offensive and Palestinian demands for the regime to support their cause and to reform the sectarian allocations. Severe clashes between commandos and the Lebanese army intensified. Musa al-Sadr called a nationwide general strike in 1970.

In 1971, following the 'Black September' conflict in Jordan, the PLO was expelled from that country and moved its headquarters to Lebanon. By 1973 10%–15% of the population of Lebanon (400,000) consisted of landless and mostly impoverished Palestinians living in refugee camps under rigorous police controls or scattered among the Lebanese population. This body of people, comprising mostly Sunni Muslims, was also politically disfranchised within the consociational power-sharing arrangement, sparking socioeconomic and political unrest in Lebanon. The presidency was still concentrated in the hands of Christians, as were privileged political positions. With significant numbers of Christians emigrating from the country and with a high birth rate among Muslims, it became clear to Sunni, Shi'a and Druze that the 1932 census ratio no longer reflected the demographic reality of the country. In 1972 the last parliament was elected in Lebanon until the 1989 ceasefire; it would not be until then when the formula would be re-examined.

During the 1970s intense Israeli retaliation to PLO guerrilla warfare in Lebanese territory and cross-border hostilities resulted in deep polarization of opinion within Lebanon. For an important segment of the population, who objected to the Palestinian military use of Lebanon and who feared Muslim dominance and subordination, the presence of Palestinians in the country was viewed as a potential threat to the already precarious sectarian and political balance.

A more conservative President, Suleiman Franjiya, took office in 1970 (remaining in post until 1976); he was said to embody an 'impossible combination' of policies: the liberation of the bourgeoisie from the statism of the Chehab presidency, an allegiance with Syria supported by the left and the Palestinians, and the protection of Lebanese sovereignty and of the Maronites' privileges. Under Franjiya, the Sunni-established elites perceived their leaders as being disenfranchised, with the Prime Minister's role diminished, and social grievances went unaddressed. In addition to guerrilla actions and retaliations, increasing inflation, popular demonstrations and unemployment prompted the Government to declare martial law in some areas. There were violent protests in the streets, where radical PLO factions challenged the Lebanese army and clashed with Al-Kataeb, increasingly fostering the perception that the interests of the Christian population were being disregarded. Disputing the Christian-Sunni balance of power, both the Druze and Musa al-Sadr urged a revision of the power-sharing ratio and of the National Pact. Israeli bombings also increased the number of displaced Shi'a peasants arriving in Beirut, strengthening the left's ranks.

In early 1975 Maarouf Saad, founder of the Popular Nasserist Organization, was killed during a demonstration of fishermen, becoming a symbol of popular martyrdom. Civil war commenced on 13 April, after 28 Palestinians bus passengers were shot dead by Al-Kataeb personnel, in retaliation for the assassination of several members of the paramilitary organization in a church in the district of Ain el-Rammaneh, in east Beirut. Four Phalangists were killed by PLO militants, including two of Pierre Gemayel's personal bodyguards. Killings spread through the suburbs of Beirut. Arab nationalists, leftists, Joumblatt and other members of the Lebanese National Movement coalition called for the dissolution of the Al-Kataeb party and the dismissal of its two ministers from the Cabinet, declaring a boycott of any government containing Al-Kataeb members.

THE CIVIL WAR: A MICROCOSM OF REGIONAL BATTLES

During the Lebanese civil war (1975–1990) 70,000–170,000 people died; nearly 900,000, or one-third of the country's population, were displaced; and 17,000 disappeared. Drawing into question the very meaning of sovereignty and national identity of the country, the civil war, which was initially fought between Lebanese Christians and recently settled Palestinians allied with poor rural Lebanese Muslims, assumed a deceptively sectarian appearance. In practice, socioeconomic alienation and disparities, calls for political reform, and the role of the army in guaranteeing security intersected with confessional grievances.

Diverse and multi-layered dimensions were quickly taken on after the outburst of violence. The sides soon started operating as a microcosm of a wider dispute between pan-Arabists and Nasserists against pro-Western nationalists. Old grievances arose again, without the mediation and arbitration that strong French and British forces had once supplied. The domestic conflict in Lebanon also internalized the broader disputes of not only the Arab–Israeli conflict, but also the Cold War. The 1973 Yom Kippur Arab–Israeli war also reverberated in Lebanon. In an effort to reverse the humiliating defeats of the Six-Day War, Egypt and Syria, backed by the Soviet military, were not able to regain control of the territories that the now US-backed Israel had occupied since 1967.

As the civil conflict escalated, Lebanese resentment that the PLO's presence in the country exposed its citizens to massive Israeli military pressure increased, extending beyond the political right. The perception that the PLO was yet another regional power that protected its own interests by operating in Lebanese territory, at the expense of those of the Lebanese, became increasingly widespread.

Hostilities between different Muslim and Christian paramilitaries continued, as militias gained control of parts of the country, with some of them assuming the functions of the state, including tax and custom duties collection, welfare programmes and the guarantee of some level of public order locally. All political parties—including Gemayel's Al-Kataeb, Joumblatt's PSP, the SSNP and Chamoun's National Liberation Party—mobilized paramilitary support. Filling the void left by the absence of the state, the militias enjoyed autonomy in providing public and social services and profited both politically and financially from war, contributing to the further undermining of state capacity. Repeating and intensifying the territorial split resulting from the 1958 civil war, Beirut was again divided primarily into a Christian zone in the east and a Muslim zone in the west. The so-called 'green line' that separated both territories and the confessionally divided city blocks could not be drawn without killings and mass expulsions. As the war spread within the country, forced internal migration was registered from mixed areas to villages where only one religious group prevailed. The Lebanese army followed suit, showing signs both of factionalization and of division between Muslim and Christian units.

The civil war can be divided into four phases: 1975–78, 1978–82, 1982–83 and 1984–90. During the first four years of the civil war, the diffuse Lebanese National Movement comprised anti-Government and confessionally mixed groups, including Joumblatt's Druze PSP, the SSNP, the Popular Nasserist Organization and the PCL. They promoted support for the PLO, left-wing ideology, secularism and the dismantling of confessionalism. The alliance established a paramilitary and armed wing, known as the Common Forces (Al-Quwwat al-Mushtaraka). Led by Chamoun and Bashir Gemayel (the son of Pierre Gemayel), Christian Maronites established the opposing Lebanese Front, composed of Al-Kataeb, the Parti National Libéral, the El-Marada Movement, the Al-Tanzim militia and the Guardians of the Cedars. This alliance, led by successors of the traditional Christian *zu'ama*, unified the Maronite militias under the Lebanese Forces (LF—Al-Quwwat al-Lubnaniyya), which fought the presence of the PLO in Lebanon, promoted the 'preservation of the country's identity and independence', the securing of state power and the preservation of the political system status quo. The LF even considered a partition of the country, including the potential creation of an autonomous Mount Lebanon as a sovereign Maronite state with a distinct culture and identity.

Maronite Christians rejected calls for a redistribution of the balance of confessional powers, and allied internationally with the USA, Syria and Israel. Aiming to guard Lebanon from partition and to prevent being dragged into a possible war with Israel, in 1976, at President Franjiya's request, Syria promoted a large-scale intervention in Lebanon on behalf of the Christians. In turn, this prompted a more active Israeli involvement in Lebanese affairs (despite the continuing absence of formal diplomatic relations between the two countries) as Israel's main ally against the PLO. Syria, having in the past supported Joumblatt and the PLO against the Christians, in 1977 again approached the PLO to the dissatisfaction of the LF, which found a new ally in Israel, which supported Maronite Christians by providing arms, logistics and financing their initiatives in the south. Under the authority of Maj. Saad Haddad, the South Lebanon Army (SLA) worked as a proxy militia, securing a buffer zone north of the Israeli–Lebanese border.

Syria maintained 27,000 troops in Lebanon as part of the Arab Deterrent Force established by the Arab League. Under the administration of President Elias Sarkis (1976–82), by trying to confine PLO operations and disarm Christian militias, Syrian relations with Lebanon deteriorated and the country fought the Lebanese Army and bombed Christian districts in east Beirut in 1978. In the early 1980s Syria carried out significant action against Bashir Gemayel's Phalangist militia. Fearing for the Christians under threat, Israel intervened on their behalf.

In June 1978 a base of the El-Marada militia, formed by former President Franjiya, in Ehden, in the north, was attacked by Al-Kataeb and the LF, under the orders of Samir Geagea and Bashir Gemayel. Antoine Franjiya, the son of the former President, together with his wife and daughter and dozens of supporters were assassinated. The Syrian army and Christian forces engaged in clashes, and internal Christian strife prompted El-Marada to change sides and ally with the Syrian forces, choosing Arab identity over an alliance with Israel. That year saw a split within the Christians, which has persisted. Disputes also revolved around financial resources in specific regions, opposing the clientelist family-based approach of the traditional political elites against rising powers, popular parties' leaderships and militias.

Throughout the civil war, several ceasefires and mediation efforts were negotiated. However, these attempts were frustrated or curtailed mainly due to increasing interference by external actors and the arising of sectarian power struggles profiting—financially, politically and symbolically—from the chaos.

Following the 1967 and 1973 wars, the Camp David Accords of 1978 normalized diplomatic relations between Israel and Egypt, which became the first Arab country to recognize Israel. In 1979 Israel agreed to withdraw from the Sinai Peninsula, and Egypt opened the Suez Canal to Israeli shipping. Additionally, Egypt officially left the Soviet sphere of influence. The PLO rejected the Accords, which weakened Palestinian voices in Lebanon and strengthened the position of those who favoured the normalization of relations with Israel. Meanwhile, since the 1970s Shi'a clerical elites had increasingly engaged in Lebanese sociopolitical arenas, as part of the wider re-emergence of Shi'a political activism, which was subsequently institutionalized by the 1979 Islamic Revolution in Iran.

Musa al-Sadr was the most prominent Shi'a spiritual and political leader in Lebanon. In 1974 al-Sadr inaugurated the 'movement of the deprived' (Harakat al-Mahrumin) gathering tens of thousands of Shi'a in the eastern city of Baalbek. The movement would eventually transform into the paramilitary organization and party Amal, which sought to end Shi'a underrepresentation in the political system.

In August 1978, while in Libya, Musa al-Sadr disappeared under circumstances that remain mysterious. His disappearance increased his status as a popular spiritual leader, 'archetypically reinforcing the circular esoteric dimension of Shi'ism'. This sense of deep loss was partially filled by Grand Ayatollah Muhammad Hussain Fadlallah, who was the target of an assassination attempt in 1985 in Beirut. He would later be considered a spiritual adviser to Hezbollah.

In the context of the Cold War, both Marxism and pan-Arabism were perceived as threats by the Shi'a clergy. In particular, the Baathist Iraqi President Saddam Hussain's form of Arab nationalism was framed in anti-Shi'a rhetoric, ultimately leading to the Iran–Iraq war (1980–88), reflecting territorial and hegemony disputes between Baathism and Shi'a revivalism. The Iran–Iraq War, as well as some degree of US and Western European support for Saddam Hussain, was of crucial importance in strengthening the Iranian Revolution as an anti-Western event, but also in allowing the presentation of a narrative of 'defence martyrdom' and the notion that Shi'a revivalism was under threat. Syria supported Iran during the war, resulting in the forging of long-lasting strategic alliances—even though Syria's support for Lebanese Shi'a militias during the 1980s was ambivalent.

Financial and military support from foreign powers, which sided with one camp or the other—and supported larger projects for the region—have always formed part of Lebanon's history. While, for example, the PLO was backed by the Gulf States, Iraq and the USSR, the LF was encouraged by Israel. Later, Syria and Iran supported Amal and Hezbollah.

The disaffected Shi'a community in the south was subject to growing PLO control and Lebanese army presence, as well as to Israeli military hostility. Calling for the moderation of PLO military action against Israel from Lebanon, during the 1980s Amal clashed with Fatah (the Palestine National Liberation Movement—the main guerrilla faction within the PLO) in the south. From 1985 to 1988, backed by the Syrians, Amal fought the 'War of the Camps' against Palestinian factions and the PLO 'state within a state'.

Supported by Israeli forces, Christian militias also fought for control of south Lebanon. Since 1977 Israel had forged ties with Lebanese officers as part of its 'good fence' policy. Attempting to restrain guerrilla attacks and the Palestinian presence near its northern border, as well as to limit Syria's increasing influence in the region, after systematically bombing the area in March 1978 Israel launched Operation Litani. Establishing a buffer zone, more than 25,000 Israeli forces occupied southern Lebanon for three months between the Israeli border and the Litani River. One consequence of Operation Litani was to bring about a rapprochement between Syria and the PLO.

The Lebanese Government protested against the Israeli invasion to the UN Security Council. Shortly afterwards, the Council adopted Resolutions 425 and 426 calling upon Israel immediately to cease its military action and withdraw its forces from all Lebanese territory, and for the respect of sovereignty, political independence, territorial integrity and internationally recognized boundaries. Composed of multinational troops, the UN Interim Force in Lebanon (UNIFIL) arrived in the country around 10 days later. The gradual withdrawal of Israeli forces was accepted by the deployment of the SLA under its command.

In June 1982 Israel again invaded Lebanon, launching Operation Peace for Galilee. Israeli forces reached as far as the suburbs of Beirut, from where they laid siege to the capital and, in what was widely regarded as a heavy defeat for the Palestinians, forced the evacuation of the PLO and its leader, Yasser Arafat, from its Beirut headquarters. UN Security Council Resolutions 508 and 509 (1982) recalled Resolutions 425 and 426 and urged a cessation of the conflict. In 1985 Israel carried out a partial withdrawal, but the IDF retained southern Lebanon as a 'control belt'. Lebanon repeatedly denounced the Israeli presence as illegal and in contravention of UN resolutions. In order to prevent a recurrence of hostilities across the border, and in response to requests of the Government of Lebanon and at the recommendation of the UN Secretary-General, UNIFIL's mandate in the country has been repeatedly extended to the present day.

The 1982 Israeli siege of west Beirut led to the subsequent emergence of a number of insurgent Shi'a groups, the most prominent of which was Hezbollah, which relied upon Iranian support. Formed through a split from Amal, the group emerged as a militia to respond to the Israeli invasion. Its militants sought to emulate the forces of the Islamic Revolution in Iran and to oppose a foreign military presence in Lebanon. During the 1980s Hezbollah's military actions included the use of suicide bombing, including against targets of the US, French and Israeli militaries, as well as against pro-Israeli Lebanese militias. Car and truck bombings targeting US and French troops and installations eventually led to the USA and France withdrawing their forces from Lebanon in 1983.

The role of the PLO in Lebanon diminished as the conflict unfolded. It was expelled from Beirut and southern Lebanon in 1982 by Israel (establishing its new headquarters in Tunisia), and was then dislodged from Tripoli and the Beqa'a Valley by Syria in 1983–84. It maintained a presence in Palestinian camps in Beirut and Sidon, as well as acting as an 'underground force' in south Lebanon against Israel. The SLA, which mainly fought against forces opposed to the Israeli presence in Lebanon such as Amal, leftist groups and Hezbollah, was disbanded in 2000.

Bashir Gemayel, the son of Pierre Gemayel, was elected President in 1982. Three weeks later, on 14 September, Phalangist headquarters were bombed and President Gemayel was assassinated. In the following days Israeli forces completed the occupation of west Beirut and surrounded the Sabra and Chatila refugee camps. The Israeli army was accused of allowing Phalangist militiamen, under the command of Elie Hobeika, to enter the camps, where they massacred civilians in retaliation. Defined as an act of genocide by UN General Assembly Resolution 37/123, the estimated number of civilians killed (mainly Palestinians and Shi'a) ranged from 700 to 3,500. The PLO, which had protected Palestinian camps in Lebanon for years, had evacuated the country shortly before.

Following international and domestic pressure, Israel withdrew its forces from Beirut. During the later stages of the war, Amal allied with Syria and the PSP and took control of west Beirut. In 1985 Israel removed its forces from Sidon, Tyre and Nabatiyah. A frontier strip along the southern border with Israel was occupied as a 'security zone'.

Amin Gemayel (1982–88), brother of Bashir Gemayel, was elected President in September 1982, but in the so-called 'war of the mountain', fighting continued between PSP Druze and LF Christians in the Chouf region. In 1986 the 'war of the flag' marked the dispute between Druze and Amal for territorial control of the capital; Syria intervened on behalf of Amal. In 1988 the 'war of brothers' erupted between Amal and Hezbollah.

The last phase of the civil war was marked by intracommunal conflict, infighting and increasing fragmentation within the various militias. Maronite Christians were caught between the fractured Phalangist-LF, pro-Franjiya militias in the north and Chamoun militias in the south. Muslims were divided between fundamentalist groups, Fatah and PLO factions, with Amal and Hezbollah in competition for the Shi'a support. Once enjoying populist legitimacy, the various militias were now involved in smuggling, drugs and arms trading. State institutions and the army were by now almost dismantled, and the country faced profound economic hardship and inflation. By usurping state revenues and collecting heavy taxes, militias became 'major business enterprises', controlling import trade and establishing partnerships with private companies in highly profitable sectors such as food supply and fuel-trading.

Political disputes followed Amin Gemayel's succession in 1988. In spite of the political instability, however, efforts to establish a ceasefire were successful, bringing an end to the war. In the presence of Lebanese parliamentary deputies, an agreement was brokered in September 1989 in Ta'if, Saudi Arabia, by a Tripartite Committee comprising the heads of state of Saudi Arabia, Algeria and Morocco. The agreement was signed on 22 October and approved by the Lebanese National Assembly on 4 November.

THE CHANCE OF A NEW SOCIAL CONTRACT: DIFFERENT RATIOS, SAME FORMULA

The Ta'if Accord helped to end 15 years of civil war in Lebanon, by transferring many of the former Maronite presidential powers to the Sunni Prime Minister, the Council of Ministers and the President of the National Assembly and his chamber. Cabinet portfolios, parliamentary seats and senior administrative positions, hitherto distributed according to the 6:5 ratio, were now to be equally divided between Christians and Muslims. The powers of the Shi'a President of the National Assembly were also expanded and his term was increased by three years. The National Assembly now comprised 128 seats, which were divided proportionately between the 11 politically represented denominations (out of 18 that were officially recognized), as well as proportionately between the electoral districts. Thus, within each electoral district, a confessional distribution of seats was pre-established.

In the National Assembly, 64 seats were reserved for Muslims and 64 for Christians, resulting in the following percentages of seats: Maronites were allocated 26.56% of the total seats (34); Greek Orthodox 10.94% (14); Greek Catholics 6.25% (eight); Armenian Orthodox 3.91% (five); Armenian Catholics 0.78% (one); Protestants 0.78% (one); other Christians and Jews 0.78% (one); among Muslims, Sunnis were to hold 21.09% of seats (27); Shi'as 21.09% (27); Druze 6.25% (eight); and Alawites 1.56% (two).

For civil service, judiciary, army and police posts, sectarian quotas were abolished. A 'rotation and parity system' was adopted for senior-level offices. The President lost most of his executive powers, such as the rights to vote in cabinet meetings, to nominate the Prime Minister, who was instead to be appointed by majoritarian consultation with the National Assembly and its President, and to dissolve parliament (a right that was now transferred to the Cabinet); decrees promulgating laws were henceforth to be signed jointly by the President, the Prime Minister and the minister concerned. Among several other state, judicial, educational, and administrative reforms, the Accord provided for the disbanding of all Lebanese and non-Lebanese militias within six months, the election of a new President of the Republic, and the formation of a national unity Cabinet.

Consociationalism was thereby reinstated in the country with minor reforms, again with the caveat that the framework, as a temporary remedy, would be gradually abandoned. The abolition of political sectarianism in the country was established as a 'fundamental national objective', inaugurating a future Third Republic. A Senate representing 'all the spiritual families' was also to be created, with its powers confined to crucial issues. The Ta'if Accord also urged against fragmentation and partition, and for the Lebanese not to be categorized on the basis of any affiliation. The repatriation of the Palestinians in Lebanon was not permitted.

By strengthening the state's armed forces, the Ta'if Accord had the objective of regaining and extending the country's sovereignty across the entire internationally recognized territory of Lebanon. The terms of the agreement called for the end of Israeli occupation in the south. Syrian personnel were to assist, for no longer than two years, in the extension of the state's legitimate authority. Relations with Syria were considered special and fraternal, and Lebanon's Arab identity and its ties with all Arab countries were pronounced. Syria agreed not to permit 'any act that poses a threat to Lebanon's security, independence, and sovereignty'.

Yet political instability was far from over. Christian Gen. Michel Aoun had been named acting Prime Minister in 1988 by President Amin Gemayel. However, his Cabinet was not recognized by Muslim forces, which established a rival government in west Beirut. René Moawad was elected President in 1989 but was assassinated within days of taking office. He was replaced by Elias Hrawi (1989–98). Aoun, who strongly opposed the Ta'if Accord because of its curtailment of presidential prerogatives and his concern that it would maintain a Syrian presence in the country, refused to step down and denounced both presidential elections as invalid. After resigning, Selim al-Hoss declared himself as Prime Minister. In September 1989 Aoun dissolved parliament, dismissed Prime Minister al-Hoss and declared himself to be the leader of the sole legitimate authority in Lebanon. From 1988 to 1990 the country had a vacant presidency and two competing Prime Ministers. The two parallel governments violently struggled for supremacy and legitimacy. In 1989 Aoun launched an offensive against the LF and declared a 'war of liberation', attacking Syrian positions in west Beirut.

With intense militarism, Aoun's movement rejected the revised terms of representation of Christians, seeking to guarantee the Lebanese identity as Christian, and strongly opposing any expansion of Syrian or Arab influence. Dismissed as head of the Lebanese armed forces, in 1990 Aoun was involved in intense intra-Maronite clashes with Samir Geagea's LF, resulting in some 1,500 casualties at the core of the traditionally Christian enclave of east Beirut. On 13 October Syrian troops launched an intensive assault against Aoun in the Baabda Palace, forcing him into exile in France until 2005, when Syria completed its full withdrawal from Lebanon. Syrian forces helped to implement Ta'if terms for the disbandment and the disarmament of militias, including those of the Palestinians. The army and state bureaucracy incorporated many of the former militia members. An exception was made for Hezbollah, which was allowed to retain its arms, in view of its role in the combat against the occupying Israeli forces. The reconstruction and reorganization of the Lebanese armed forces and the full demobilization of all militias in the country remained major challenges.

The Ta'if Accord did try to address and accommodate political reforms, national identity and state sovereignty, being hailed by some—in rather optimistic terms—as 'innovative and groundbreaking'. However, it did not represent a radical or paradigm shift away from earlier efforts. Rather, it welcomed, once again, 'ingrained and customary solutions for conflict resolution and state reform: consociationalism and the ethos of "no victor and no vanquished"'. Sectarianism continued to 'single out religious affiliation' and communal identity as the one—and only—defining political element of citizens. By simplifying intricate political, socioeconomic and communal aspects, it reduced the Lebanese identity to one distinctive and exclusive form.

The Ta'if Accord deeply rooted consociationalism in Lebanese political life, establishing the arrangement of a Maronite, Sunni and Shi'a troika de facto ruling the country. In spite of adjustments in the parity between several communities, the sectarian element of Lebanese politics was further entrenched and power-sharing and consultation dynamics tightened, fomenting instability and deadlock. The Accord renewed a national covenant that had been accused of being responsible for a top-down and secretive elite politics that facilitated corruption and a lack of transparency, and a parliament that had frequently been accused of rubber-stamping cabinet decisions.

THE SECOND REPUBLIC: PAX SYRIANA AND ENDEMIC CHALLENGES

After the first post-war parliamentary elections, in 1992, Rafiq Hariri was appointed as Prime Minister and led an extensive programme of infrastructure reconstruction. The Lebanese rentier model enabled a return to monetary stability and an economic revival. At high rates of return, European bonds flooded the market and capital investment was made in foreign currency. At the expense of the productive sector, the post-war economy was mainly based on tertiary and rentier activities. Capital investment was particularly oriented towards speculation in real estate. The Lebanese construction consortium Solidere extensively renovated parts of Beirut, while deepening its ties with Saudi Arabia. The post-war period saw increasing integration between the economic and sectarian political elites, with the prominence in politics of billionaires such as Rafiq Hariri, his son, Saad Hariri, Najib Miqati and many others.

Still a decisive player in Lebanon, Syria designated 40 members of the transitional parliament, greatly influencing the 1992 elections and ensuring that a majority of deputies were pro-Syrian. Over time, different political groups were accommodated within the revised political framework. The Maronites, who had initially boycotted the elections, gradually reintegrated into the electoral process. For the first time, Hezbollah participated in elections. Some of its members, however, inspired by the concept of the guardianship of the jurist or vicegerency (*wilayat al-faqih*) and the Islamic Revolution in Iran, demanded the establishment of an Islamic state in Lebanon. Following an intense internal debate, more integrationist figures, such as Mohammad Fadlallah, as well as the organization's Secretary-General Hassan Nasrallah, defended pragmatic compromise and Hezbollah's participation in national political life.

With the end of the war, most militias were disarmed and dismantled, and the intense communal conflict was transferred to the political arena. The formation of the first Cabinet after the civil war included many former militia leaders, warlords and the sons of the traditional entrenched political elites.

Following the presidential term of Hrawi, Gen. Emile Lahoud (1998–2007) was elected President, and Selim al-Hoss succeeded Saad Hariri as Prime Minister. The country's political, economic and infrastructure reconstruction was very gradual, reflecting continuing major problems in terms of state legitimacy, provision of public goods, corruption, inequality, clientelism and patronage, while adherence to sectarian affiliations was strengthened and deepened.

The National Pact and the Ta'if Accord both represented the pragmatic compromise reached by Lebanese political and economic elites. Riding on the economic growth and development that followed both agreements, a myth of confessional coexistence and national integration under a 'liberal merchant democracy' was sustained. In spite of the strong resilience shown by Lebanon's institutional framework over the decades, the civil wars and the ongoing institutional instability proved that the compromise was extremely frail, and in need of periodical renovation.

The type of deeply entrenched consociationalism that prevails in Lebanon has been subject to heavy criticism for numerous reasons: it engenders state weakness, institutional instability and perpetual deadlock; it leads to the distribution of power among traditional elites; generates feudalism, representative immobility and elitism; and ultimately consolidates sectarian divides. The democratic character of the regime itself is thereby seriously brought into question. Particularly by rewarding loyalty to ancestral family villages and religious sects, it fosters the maintenance of networks based on family and clientelist ties, which, while compensating for state absence, impairs actual state-building. The highly corrupt disputes over state services and social wealth undermine state centralization efforts and the adequate distribution of public welfare and goods. The virtual non-existence of state-provided basic goods reinforces communal disputes over the delivery of public services and the building of state legitimacy.

To different extents, the Sunni, Shi'a and Christian parties all distribute social benefits within their respective religious communities. Naturally, cross-cutting cleavages do exist, and Lebanon is frequently celebrated as a multicultural heaven and birthplace of innumerable civilizations, with cross-sectarian marriages and enterprises and secularist thought. However, it is also true that the century-long politicization of religious identities has been crystallized in the form of sectarian state institutions. Such a cycle is self-reinforcing, given that communities are encouraged to resort to so-called 'primordial identities', which in turn tend to outperform other forms of identification and association (such as class, ideology or political beliefs). As a result, both identity and politics are reduced to questions of religion.

In addition, consociational power-sharing recommendations, especially in the form of pre-determined representation, reinforce ethnic and religious identities. Inelasticity, disproportionalities and distortions in representation engendered by the confessional system are present, together with under-represented and over-represented electoral constituencies. Given that confessional groups and voting districts are allocated on the basis of the family ancestral village, as registered during the 1932 census, such rule reifies communal bonds and entrenches the electoral power of regionally based family elites. In practice, such an arrangement takes no account of the internal migrations that have occurred since that time, ideological changes or even anti-sectarian sentiment within the Lebanese social fabric. Such a scenario is highly problematic in a country where the sectarian balance is maintained only very tenuously. Confessionalism, by reinforcing and rewarding such a pattern, fosters service provision, legitimacy and symbolic discourse exclusively in sectarian terms, as well as anchoring traditional elites.

Post-war reconstruction efforts were additionally accompanied by regional instability and foreign engagement. During the 1980s and 1990s Hezbollah, the PCL and other forces struggled against the continuing presence of Israel in southern Lebanon. In 1996 the bombing of a UN compound by Israeli forces near the southern village of Qana killed at least 106 civilians and injured four Fijian soldiers serving in the UNIFIL mission. As a result of the increasing cost of operations and in accordance with the 1978 UN resolutions, in May 2000 the IDF withdrew from Lebanon. The Israeli withdrawal was subsequently celebrated in Lebanon on 25 May as 'Resistance and Liberation Day'. The official line of withdrawal between Lebanon and Israel became known as the 'Blue Line'.

After the Israeli withdrawal, pressures increased for Syria also to disengage its troops from Lebanon, and incremental redeployments and phased withdrawals began. The Syrian army presence of around 30,000 during the 1990s was reduced by around one-half. In a post-Cold War scenario, as during the previous decades, however, the Syrian presence and patronage was linked to different national and regional projects, opposing and polarizing domestic forces that would contest further political representation in the following decade.

With US support, in 1993 Israel and the PLO signed the Oslo Accords. Moreover, in 1994 Jordan also signed a peace treaty with Israel, despite the continuing Israeli occupation of the West Bank. Israel's disengagement from the Gaza Strip, involving the withdrawal of around 8,500 Jewish settlers, was achieved in 2005. On the side opposing the normalization of relations with Israel, under the Baathist ideology and President Bashar al-Assad's dynasty, Syria represented an alternative political enterprise for the region, aligning with Iran in forging an anti-Western and anti-Zionist narrative.

In 2002, following the attacks against the USA of 11 September 2001 perpetrated by the Islamist al-Qa'ida organization, Iran was included by US President George W. Bush in his so-called 'axis of evil'; Undersecretary of State John Bolton subsequently associated Syria with the group of what the USA termed 'rogue states'. As part of the USA's declared 'war on terror', both countries were accused of sponsoring terrorism and seeking weapons of mass destruction. In response, Iran, Syria and Hezbollah in Lebanon formed a so-called 'axis of resistance', opposing the USA, Saudi Arabia and Israel's policies for the region. The alliance drew heavily on the Shi'a revivalism that had been present in the Middle East for the previous four decades. In 2004 US economic sanctions against Syria were increased. In the aftermath of the US-led invasion of Iraq in 2003, which fostered divisive sectarian policies in that country, the Shi'a majority in Iraq was greatly empowered through Western-supported Prime Minister Nuri al-Maliki, eventually nurturing a sense of deprivation that would in turn fuel the militancy of the (Sunni) Islamic State organization. Iraq, an important cradle of the Shi'a revival, under Grand Ayatollah Ali al-Husaini al-Sistani would attach itself to the so-called 'Shi'a crescent' and disrupt the sectarian balance and regional political status quo, something that was further aided by the growth of Hezbollah's political influence inside Lebanon, particularly after 2006.

Former Prime Minister Rafiq Hariri was assassinated on 14 February 2005, as his convoy travelled through Beirut, in a bomb attack that killed a further 23 people. The Syrian Government and Hezbollah were accused of complicity in the attack, but denied any involvement. Hundreds of thousands of people gathered in the streets of Lebanon. The 'Cedar Revolution' of popular protests called for the withdrawal of Syrian troops from Lebanon and for an international commission to investigate the murder of the former premier. The anti-Syria coalition became known as the March 14 Alliance. In response, demonstrations on 8 March, organized by different parties, expressed support for Syria's role in helping to end the Lebanese civil war and for stabilizing the country, as well as for supporting Lebanese resistance to Israeli occupation. As a result of the protests, in April, after 29 years, Syria withdrew its military presence from Lebanon, officially ending the so-called Pax Syriana.

Importantly, after the Syrian withdrawal, Hezbollah, which had only contested parliamentary elections since 1992, decided to participate in compromise efforts and to join the Cabinet. Thenceforth, several disputes and outside pressures have revolved around its participation and its armed strength. A Special Tribunal for Lebanon (STL) was inaugurated in March 2009 to conduct a trial of those accused of organizing the assassination of Rafiq Hariri.

The events of 2005 polarized the country. In general terms, the country was divided between the March 8 Alliance, led by Hezbollah, comprising, among others, Amal, the Free Patriotic Movement (FPM), the SSNP, El-Marada, and the Armenian Revolutionary Federation (ARF), supported by Iran and Syria, and the March 14 Alliance, led by Saad Hariri, supported by Saudi Arabia and the USA, and composed of, among others, the Future Movement, the LF, Al-Kataeb and the Independence Movement. The Druze PSP took a more ambivalent stance between the two sides.

Israel and Hezbollah launched mutually retaliatory hostilities on numerous occasions and engaged in clashes in southern Lebanon. In July 2006 Hezbollah forces crossed the border and ambushed an Israeli military vehicle, capturing two soldiers and killing another three. Refusing to release Lebanese prisoners held in Israel in exchange for the two captured soldiers, Israel retaliated by launching a major military offensive against Hezbollah and Lebanon, including a large-scale air and ground attack and the imposition of an air and naval blockade on Lebanon; Hezbollah also launched extensive rocket attacks against Israel. Known as the 34-day war, around 1,200 Lebanese, mostly civilians, were killed in the conflict, and significant destruction was inflicted upon the Lebanese infrastructure, including the International Airport in Beirut, and 1m. people were displaced. In southern Lebanon, Hezbollah engaged Israeli forces in guerrilla warfare and ultimately expelled them; 120 Israelis were killed and 450,000 displaced in northern Israel.

The offensive against civilians was harshly condemned by the international community. UN Security Council Resolution 1701 ordered the deployment of 15,000 UN peacekeepers to help Lebanese troops retake control of southern Lebanon by establishing a buffer zone, and called for the immediate and full cessation of hostilities; full respect for the Blue Line by both parties; the full implementation of Resolutions 1559 (2004) and 1680 (2006) that required the disarmament of all armed groups in Lebanon; and the handing over to the UN of all remaining maps of landmines in Lebanon in Israel's possession.

Resolution 1680 was in accordance with the Lebanese Cabinet's decision of 27 July 2006, stating that 'there will be no weapons or authority in Lebanon other than that of the Lebanese State'. Hezbollah's disarmament in Lebanon remains a highly sensitive topic and divides the Lebanese between those who consider the organization's forces to be a necessary complement to the army in the fight with Israel, and those who think they are a liability in the south and east, given that Hezbollah had deployed several thousand of its fighters to the Syrian war since its beginning in early 2011. At the intersection of Syrian and Lebanese borders, but considered to be part of Lebanon, the Shebaa Farms area is a further source of dispute. Annexed by Israel (which states that it captured the territory from Syria, rather than from Lebanon, in 1967) in 1981, the ongoing occupation of the land is considered justification for the arming of Hezbollah.

The establishment of a strong and capable Lebanese army is a continuing challenge. One of the key arguments used by foreign countries to object to the arming of Hezbollah is that it breaks the state monopoly on the use of force. Between 2005 and 2019 the Lebanese army received military assistance from the USA amounting to US $2,290m. Hezbollah, however, claims that without its presence and its anti-Israeli activity in southern Lebanon, the region would have remained under Israeli occupation. Hezbollah also engaged in joint efforts with the Lebanese army to defeat Islamic State and the Syrian jihadist group Jabhat Fatah al-Sham (Levant Conquest Front) in cities along the eastern border with Syria.

Notably, Hezbollah has been significantly empowered since its foundation. Enjoying social and political protagonism, the group is one of the most important regional actors in the Middle

East and one of the most influential military, political and social forces in post-war Lebanon. The organization has not only capitalized on two major military victories against Israel, in 2000 and 2006—now with mutual deterrence fully established—but also enjoys political support across the Lebanese sectarian spectrum. Like virtually all political parties in Lebanon, Hezbollah also operates an extensive network of charity and welfare organizations.

With significant socioeconomic ties to Lebanon, until 2005 Syria acted as an external arbiter, mediating domestic conflicts and guaranteeing security with its troops in the country. Moreover, the Ta'if Accord granted Saudi Arabia and Syria the role of 'regional patrons' in post-war Lebanon, with President Assad exerting decisive mandatory power. By siding with either bloc, the Lebanese would endorse—even if unwittingly—different macro-endeavours. This Pax Syriana exerted a strong influence over domestic politics, and there was some debate over whether, in the absence of such an adjudicator, Lebanese confessionalism would be able to endure. Soon after the Syrian withdrawal, Lebanon was again the stage of intense political instability and foreign interference.

THE DOHA AGREEMENT: BROADENING THE GRAND COALITION AND ENTRENCHING CONFESSIONALISM

Following the 2006 war with Israel, the March 14 Alliance increasingly pleaded for the disarmament of Hezbollah and its exclusive dedication to Lebanese politics. In November 2006, in protest at demands by the governing majority for the investigation of Syrian participation in the murder of Rafiq Hariri, five Shi'a members and one Christian member resigned from the Cabinet. Up to 800,000 protesters were mobilized in support of demands for Western-backed premier Fouad Siniora to resign, for an end to corruption and for a more representative Cabinet. The President of the National Assembly, Nabih Berri, refused to convene the legislature and allow a vote for the establishment of the STL. After the refusal of President Lahoud to agree, Siniora bypassed government opposition through the UN Security Council and approved the statute for the Tribunal despite the calls for a national unity government and the absence of all Shi'a ministers. A peaceful sit-in in the central district of Beirut was organized, and was maintained continuously for 18 months. Denouncing the Tribunal as a political tool, protesters supporting the March 8 Alliance denounced what they referred to as the automatic implication of Syria in the assassination, the normalization of relations with Israel, and US influence over Lebanon.

The expiry of President Lahoud's term was followed by renewed political instability and deadlock. By the end of 2007 the required two-thirds' quorum had not been obtained in parliament to appoint a consensus candidate as the next President. Seeking a greater share of power, the March 8 Alliance boycotted the sessions, leading to a stalemate. From December 2007 to May 2008 19 voting attempts were made to elect a President. In total, the presidential office remained vacant for seven months.

Hezbollah and the March 8 Alliance were willing seriously to exert pressure on the Government to consider their demands for equitable participation. However, it was only after the Government's moves to close what it considered an 'illegal and unconstitutional telecommunications network', and to remove airport security chief Wafiq Shukair, that the Alliance's strategy of non-violent protests and parliamentary votes adapted to include the use of political violence. The disputes largely revolved around the question of what form the power sharing should take, who should participate and the type of international engagement. Clashes between pro-Government and opposition militias began on 7 May 2008. After months of political deadlock and eight days of violence, which resulted in the death of 65 people, the Government reversed its decision and an agreement was reached, allowing the election of a President.

Since 2006 the opposition led by Hezbollah had pressed for a so-called 'guaranteeing third vote', and a cabinet minority veto was finally obtained under the Doha Agreement, signed in the Qatari capital, Doha, on 21 May 2008. This narrative constructed by the opposition nurtured enhanced autonomy and empowerment for the Shi'a, ultimately establishing the March 8 Alliance and Hezbollah as major players with the power of veto. Regionally, this rebalancing of power reflected the rise of the Shi'a 'axis of resistance'—the anti-Israeli and anti-Western alliance comprising Iran, Syria, Hezbollah, Al-Hashd a-Sha'bi in Iraq and Ansar Allah (or the al-Houthi movement) in Yemen.

Importantly, the opposition, although headed by Hezbollah, also included Aoun's FPM, the Shi'a Amal and minority Sunnis, in addition to other Christian and leftist parties. After the FPM transferred its allegiance to the March 8 Alliance, in 2006 Aoun and Hezbollah signed a memorandum of understanding. A section of the Maronites found in the Shi'a parties pragmatic allies to safeguard the power of Christians in Lebanon. Despite having very different histories and backgrounds, both groups share a somewhat common ground of exclusion and disempowerment, especially given the ongoing diminution of Maronite prominence.

The Doha Agreement called for the formation of a national unity or consensus government, in which the Cabinet would be composed of 30 posts: 16 to be held by the majority, 11 by the opposition and three neutral candidates to be nominated by the President. The allocation of seats was a key demand of the opposition, given that since the conclusion of the Ta'if Accord the political system had remained essentially Maronite-Sunni dominated. With 11 cabinet seats (one-third of the total plus one) awarded to the opposition, the March 8 Alliance obtained the capacity to veto any future laws that required Hezbollah disarmament, a concession that dramatically increased its power in the Government. Most importantly, confessionalism was now deeply institutionalized, through a Sunni-Shi'a-Maronite executive troika. The grand coalition was once again widened to include important new players, with the three religious pillars having bargaining, compromise and decision-making power in the executive.

On 25 May 2008 Gen. Michel Suleiman was elected President (2008–14); he reappointed Siniora as Prime Minister. In 2008 a new electoral law was adopted, restructuring voting districts, and elections were held in June 2009, in which the March 14 Alliance won the majority of votes. After Saad Hariri was named Prime Minister, a national unity Government was finally formed in November. A total of 15 posts in the Cabinet were allocated to the March 14 Alliance governmental majority, 10 to the March 8 Alliance and five to candidates nominated by the President.

In 2010 new political instability and tensions dominated the country. The STL announced that members of Hezbollah would be indicted for the assassination of Rafiq Hariri. The March 8 Alliance called for the rejection of the STL. An agreement was attempted with the intermediation of Syria and Saudi Arabia, but this failed. As a result, formally using Doha prerogatives for the first time, 11 ministers from the opposition resigned, dismantling the national unity Government. The original indictment was filed by the STL on 17 January 2011, implicating four Hezbollah figures in Hariri's assassination.

The STL was the subject of both legal and political contestation, not least as it had several particularities, notably being the first international court with jurisdiction over acts of terrorism, and also the first to allow trial hearings and proceedings *in absentia*. Because it broke with existing conventions concerning international criminal tribunals, the STL was accused of being established as a 'permanent tool of political pressure' in Lebanese internal affairs.

Najib Miqati was nominated as Prime Minister in January 2011. Former premier Saad Hariri opposed Miqati's nomination and refused to participate in his administration, claiming that it would be Hezbollah-led. Hariri's supporters rioted, blaming Syrian and Iranian intervention for the collapse of his Government. Again, Lebanese society was divided between pro- and anti-Syrian forces, a rift that would be further enforced when the 'Arab Spring' of anti-Government protests spread across the region.

After five months of negotiations, in June 2011 a new Government was formed, one not of broad national unity but of coalition. The governing majority was allocated 18 seats, the minority nine seats (mostly independents and representatives of the PSP), and three members were neutral and nominated by the President. The March 8 Alliance became the majority force in the new Cabinet. No representatives of the Future Movement, Al-Kataeb or of the LF participated in the Government. Many claimed that the Doha Agreement had come to an end, as the 'Iranian-Syrian proxy Hezbollah dominated Lebanese politics'.

In 2011 pro-democracy popular movements erupted in Syria, demanding political and economic reforms; the unrest rapidly degenerated into a civil war. In 2010 and 2011 US economic sanctions were further tightened. Having initially called for political dialogue to resolve the conflict, in May 2013 Hezbollah's fighters officially entered Syria to fight against Sunni Islamist extremists and in order to protect Lebanon's eastern borders. In August the Roueiss neighbourhood in south Beirut was the target of a terrorist attack, which killed 27 people. The war in Syria rapidly ceased to be purely a civil conflict, with several countries actively participating in air strikes and bombings. The Russian Federation, Hezbollah and Iran allied with the Syrian Government, while European powers, the USA and Gulf countries financed the more or less radical opposition to the regime. The ramifications of the rise and strengthening of Islamic State and al-Qa'ida are closely linked to the international funding of such organizations and the promotion of Sunni Wahhabism to counterbalance rival powers and to confront the so-called 'axis of resistance'.

Lebanon was directly affected by the conflict in Syria, and both sides of the political spectrum accused each other of 'covertly providing or facilitating the influx of funds, weapons and fighters to respective allied forces in Syria'. As a key element of Shi'a revivalism, the Hezbollah presence in Syria came at the expense of losses among its combatants. Dozens of terrorist attacks took place on Lebanese territory dduring 2013–17, with Islamic State and Jabhat Fatah al-Sham claiming responsibility. Extremist groups operated in Tripoli, in Palestinian camps, and in areas close to the border with Syria, amid mutual recriminations over who was responsible for the Lebanese instability. Hezbollah, criticized for being a 'state within a state' that undermined the central Lebanese Government, just as the PLO had been, was accused of being responsible for Lebanese insecurity in the aftermath of its entrance into Syria. For its part, Hezbollah claimed that its presence and action in Syria, together with the activities of the Lebanese army, were crucial in precluding further terrorist attacks on Lebanese soil, defending Shi'a villages across the Lebanese–Syrian border and defending Christian and Yazidi minorities persecuted by Islamic State in Syria.

Lebanon was the country that received the largest number of Syrian refugees per head of population: in 2014 over 1m. Syrian refugees lived in the country (according to the UN High Commissioner for Refugees), although the total later reached 1.5m. (according to government estimates). A further 475,075 Palestinian refugees were officially registered. As a consequence, nearly one-quarter of the Lebanese population was composed of mostly Sunni Muslim refugees, who were ultimately deprived of basic rights and existed outside the confessional power-sharing quota. Like Palestinians, Syrians in the country were victims of scapegoating and anti-refugee rhetoric.

In a highly polarized context, Miqati resigned as Prime Minister in March 2013 and was replaced by Tammam Salam. Salam finally formed a Government in February 2014, when the March 14 Alliance returned as the majority in the Cabinet, with 11 seats. The March 8 Alliance opposition held eight seats. Citing security concerns over the war in Syria, parliament's term was extended three times: on 31 May 2013 (for 17 months), on 5 November 2014 (for 31 months), and on 14 June 2017 (until 6 May 2018, when new elections took place). Debates on a new electoral law and the adjustment of representation arose again.

In July 2015, after the Naameh landfill site, near Beirut, was closed and the Lebanese authorities, lacking a President, failed to implement a waste management contingency plan, piles of refuse mounted in Beirut. Facing constant electricity cuts, the crises echoed broader problems and state deficiencies that had long challenged the country. A series of popular protests took place and a number of emerging grassroots movements contested the 2018 municipal elections alongside the traditional parties.

After President Suleiman's term ended in May 2014, a protracted deadlock and presidential vacuum ensued until Gen. Michel Aoun was elected as President on 31 October 2016. A total of 40 attempts made by the National Assembly to elect Aoun between May 2014 and October 2016 had failed, due to boycotts by both the March 14 and March 8 blocs that had prevented the necessary two-thirds' quorum of votes from being achieved. Eventually, Aoun was agreed upon as a compromise candidate, with Saad Hariri returning as Prime Minister. In December 2016 a national unity Government was formed, with the March 8 Alliance holding the majority, with 16 seats, and the March 14 Alliance, mostly representatives of the Future Movement and the LF, the other 11 seats. As the minority group, the March 14 Alliance still had the veto power of one-third plus one, thus guaranteeing the continuity of the Doha Agreement for the opposing forces. The President in effect remained in control of the neutral and potential swing candidates.

On 4 November 2017, during a visit to Saudi Arabia, Prime Minister Hariri unexpectedly presented his resignation. He declared that both Hezbollah, as a coalition partner in the national unity Government, and Iran had 'spread strife across the region and destabilized Lebanon'. The unprecedented overseas announcement sparked accusations that the premier was being held hostage by Saudi Arabia and had been forced to resign. The announcement was suspended two weeks later, after Hariri returned to Lebanon (with mediation efforts by Egypt and France), and his resignation was officially reversed on 5 December. Hariri declared that he would continue in office, as all political components of the Government had agreed to 'dissociate themselves from the disputes and internal affairs of brother Arab states' in order to preserve Lebanon's economic and political relations (a similar commitment had been made under the 2012 Baabda Declaration). The Saudi Government had been pressurizing Hariri to promote a more assertive opposition to Hezbollah and to end normal relations with the group. In 2016 Saudi Arabia had halted a US $4,000m. military financing package to Lebanon, in protest against the activities of Hezbollah. Other Gulf partners issued a travel warning advising their citizens against visiting Lebanon.

The first parliamentary elections in Lebanon since the outbreak of conflict in Syria were held in May 2018, and were the first to be held using an element of proportional representation. The first-past-the-post system was substituted with a preferential ranking vote system. However, the confessional quota was maintained for the 15 electoral constituencies (which were reduced in number from 26). Diaspora voting overseas was also permitted. While enabling some new groups to enter into the legislature, the new electoral system also raised several undemocratic discrepancies and allowed for the promotion of privileged candidates.

In April 2018, prior to the elections, a conference for international donors and investors to support the Lebanese economy was held in Paris, France. Lebanon received pledges of US $10,200m. in loans and $860m. in grants. Hariri agreed to reduce the budget deficit by 5% of gross domestic product (GDP) in the following five years, while the Government was to undertake intensive reforms, approve anti-corruption laws, diversify the country's productive sectors and reform public sector spending—above all with regard to the subsidized electricity utility, Electricité du Liban. With public debt at over 150% of GDP, Lebanon had the world's third highest public debt-to-GDP ratio.

A new national unity Government was only formed in January 2019, with Saad Hariri again as Prime Minister, renewing the 2016 compromise arrangement. Amid the delay prior to the formation of the Cabinet, the ongoing debt crisis worsened and confidence in the economy decreased, with consumer and investor spending dropping substantially. Thirteen ministerial portfolios were allocated to the March 8 Alliance, and 10 to the March 14 Alliance. Seven posts were occupied by neutral or independent candidates.

Obtaining the public health, sports and youth, and parliamentary affairs portfolios, Hezbollah was once again denounced for controlling the small March 8 Alliance majority in the Cabinet and National Assembly—although it had secured 13 seats in the May 2018 elections, having obtained 12 in 2009—and for effectively 'taking the Government hostage'. The USA immediately called upon the Government to deprive Hezbollah of all official funding. Further adding to Lebanon's severe banking and economic crisis amid a halt in funding from the Gulf states, in 2019 the US Administration of President Donald Trump inaugurated a 'maximum pressure strategy' against Iran, Syria and Hezbollah, intensifying sanctions against the latter group and institutions linked to it. The act was a direct response to the territorial and political gains that Syrian President Assad had achieved in the civil war there in recent years, as well as a sign of opposition to some Gulf and European countries attempting to normalize relations with Assad.

The executive balance of power in Lebanon tilted slightly in 2019, reflecting the 2018 election results and 2016 proportional electoral law. The LF, which competed for the Maronite vote with the FPM and El-Marada, and which had doubled its support in the 2018 parliamentary elections, demanded more than one-third of the cabinet posts reserved for Christians. Eventually, it settled for four portfolios. A further dispute centred on Sunni representation, with Hassan Mourad of the Sunni opposition eventually being allocated a ministerial post as a presidential nominee. The one-third veto power was not guaranteed for the March 14 Alliance. None the less, the vetoing dynamics were greatly thematic and closely linked to the agenda presented, and, in practice, in such a confessional regime of national coalition, highly informal genres of veto were equally applied by the various religious minorities as an instrument of representation, identity leverage and protection of their vital interests.

Gen. Aoun and his FPM played a key role in the balance of power between forces in Lebanese politics. However, the March 8 and March 14 Alliances were more than simply sectarian forces: Maronite Christians participated in both blocs, as did Sunni Muslims. The divide reflected a wider division over different political projects concerning both domestic and regional issues. The Druze, even though they were neither numerically significant nor as politically powerful as they had been under Ottoman rule or the French mandate, still played an important swing vote role in the country, as they were not allied to either major bloc. Undoubtedly, the post-Doha scenario reframed the patronage of Syria and Saudi Arabia over its local counterparts, deepening the already polarized pro- and anti-Western disputes in Lebanon. The practice of external powers exploiting discord and manipulating Lebanon's factional and sectarian rivalries was familiar to the country. However, it was hardly a simple mirroring of a 'Sunni–Shi'a divide'. Therefore, even though Shi'a revivalism was paramount to the rise and establishment of the March 8 Alliance, there was a strong Christian and cross-sectarian element to the coalition (namely the FPM, El-Marada and the ARF), as well as one that went far beyond sectarian underpinnings, with the constituent parties referring to their social, economic and geopolitical stances regarding the country and the region (including, but not limited to, their stance on the Palestinian issue).

THE OCTOBER 2019 UPRISINGS AND THE BEIRUT PORT EXPLOSION

After eight years of civil war in Syria, by 2019 the Lebanese economy, strongly dependent on bilateral trading with its neighbour, had begun to suffer from its impact. The massive influx of refugees had overwhelmed the already debilitated infrastructure in the country. The enforced fixed exchange rate between the national currency (the Lebanese pound) and the US dollar, in place since 1999, was increasingly difficult to maintain. Eurobonds and foreign debt payments from the postwar reconstruction period mounted, with the country unable to manage the burden of debts, and debt servicing amounted to nearly one-half of the Government's revenues and one-third of its total spending. Large-scale institutionalized corruption and constant deadlock further exacerbated the country's structural weaknesses.

Saad Hariri's newly appointed Cabinet faced difficulties addressing the debt, and popular frustration grew over the Government's unrestrained corruption and inability—or unwillingness—to curb it. With mobile telephone services already costly, and extensive public reliance upon internet telecommunications services, the Government announced a US \$0.20/day tax on the use of voice over Internet Protocol (VoIP) communications. In response, large-scale protest demonstrations erupted in October 2019. The new tax was suspended, but the protests continued and the demands took on a much broader scope, incorporating demands for the abolition of other recently introduced taxes; the full dissolution of the Government; new national elections; the formation of a new technocratic government; the adoption of a modern, civil and non-sectarian electoral law; measures to hold the corrupt accountable; an independent and impartial judiciary; the suspension of banking secrecy; environmental protection, sustainable development and waste management; solutions for 'stateless' and 'under analysis' individuals; and support for women's citizenship rights.

Despite the Cabinet's approval of an emergency reform package, the resignation of the entire Government was demanded. In the aftermath of the popular protests, Prime Minister Hariri presented his resignation on 29 October 2019, only nine months after his Cabinet had been formed. Eventually, following massive popular pressure, the other government members followed suit and the Cabinet was dissolved. Hassan Diab, an independent and former Minister of Education, was nominated as Prime Minister on 19 December. Diab formed a coalition Government on 21 January 2020, which was described as comprising technocrats and independent politicians. A record number of six women were appointed to the Cabinet. The public, however, claimed that quite a few new ministers were endorsed by and loyal to traditional political parties and leaders. Although several figures were unknown to the general public, mostly being university professors or specialists, many were accused of having ties to conventional political forces, banks or the business sector.

In spite of Diab's reform efforts while the Government was struggling to cope with a severe financial, monetary and economic crisis, the Lebanese pound suffered rampant depreciation, with banks limiting US dollar withdrawals. On 9 March 2020, for the first time in the country's history, Lebanon defaulted on a sovereign debt payment, for a US \$1,200m. Eurobond, after public debt had reached 170% of GDP. The Lebanese authorities began negotiations with the International Monetary Fund (IMF), seeking a multi-billion-dollar bailout to avoid bankruptcy. The crisis also deepened the incidence of poverty among the population, widening income inequalities and raising levels of unemployment, especially among the youth. The concurrent coronavirus disease (COVID-19) pandemic and ensuing lockdown severely exacerbated the economic crisis, with many more businesses suspending operations or closing and the national currency depreciating further. These simultaneous crises galvanized networks of patronage that provided health care to constituents.

Many longstanding factors contributed to the economic and financial crisis of 2020, such as rampant tax evasion; a decline in Lebanese diaspora remittance flows; over-reliance on imports; the virtual absence of investment in infrastructure; real estate speculation; a decline in tourism; and state looting. Financial support packages demand severe austerity measures and deep fiscal adjustment. However, the very basis on which the confessional elites retain power lies partly in their ability to distribute state spoils and patronage, favouring and benefiting their own constituencies. Clientelist co-optation strategies are strongly based on public spending, pensions and wages, and any structural reform agenda is therefore directly confrontational to their interests. Hence, political sectarian leaders across the spectrum refrain from posing direct threats to the arrangement, fearing for their political and symbolic capital and resource allocations.

On 4 August 2020 there was a massive explosion at the port of Beirut, caused by the ignition of some 2,750 metric tons of ammonium nitrate that had been stored unsafely in a port warehouse since 2014. The blast killed 218 people and left

300,000 immediately displaced. Large parts of the capital were devastated, and the collective value of losses was estimated at up to US $15,000m. Outraged protesters clashed with the police for several nights following the blast, and Prime Minister Diab presented his own resignation and that of his Cabinet on 10 August 2020. In his resignation statement, Diab blamed endemic corruption and neglect for the explosion. Emergency humanitarian aid was received from countries around the world, but funds were conditional on any new transitional government's commitment to sweeping political and economic reforms. The French President, Emmanuel Macron, arrived in Lebanon immediately after the explosion, and during a second visit in September he presented an initiative comprising 34 reform measures. On 31 August Mustapha Adib was named Prime Minister-designate and asked to form a new Cabinet. Adib presented his resignation on 26 September amid a political impasse over the Cabinet's composition, mainly revolving around the finance ministry, which had been controlled by Amal since 2014.

Meanwhile, on 18 August 2020 the STL issued its sentence on the assassination of Prime Minister Rafiq Hariri. After 15 years and at a cost of approximately US $1,000m., a Hezbollah member, Salim Jamil Ayyash, was convicted of the attack, but the Tribunal exonerated three other defendants and stated that there was no proof of the involvement of the Hezbollah leadership or of Syria. However, following an appeal, in March 2022 the acquittals of two of the three other defendants were overturned, and they were convicted *in absentia* of acting as accomplices in the attack. Meanwhile, in September the USA expanded its sanctions against Lebanon, blacklisting former finance and transport ministers for their ties with Hezbollah, and appending an explicit threat to include others close to President Aoun. The sanctions also came in a context of several Arab countries normalizing relations with Israel, including the Gulf states of the United Arab Emirates and Bahrain. In November Gebran Bassil, President of the FPM and son-in-law of Aoun, was sanctioned by the US Department of the Treasury for alleged corruption.

Saad Hariri was reappointed as Prime Minister-designate on 22 October 2020. However, after months of consultations with President Aoun (who held the prerogative to confirm the composition of the cabinet), on 15 July 2021 Hariri abandoned his efforts to form a government. Disputes mainly concerned the total number of seats in the new government, with Aoun demanding 30—instead of the 24 seats proposed by Hariri—and that one-third of ministries be held by Christians, who would thereby secure a minority veto. Hariri was accused of not supporting this proposal and of disregarding the results from consultations with different parliamentary blocs, and was criticized for not ceding the interior and justice portfolios to Aoun and Gebran Bassil. By a majority of 72 votes, binding parliamentary consultations led to the designation of former premier Najib Miqati as the new Prime Minister on 26 July. Against a backdrop of US sanctions and competing foreign interests over regional affairs attached to any eventual financial aid, Miqati was tasked with forming a new Cabinet, implementing the French initiative and securing an international bailout package. Until the new government was formed, Hassan Diab remained as caretaker Prime Minister. As Lebanon faced shortages of fuel, power, medicine and basic products, as well as the threat of civil unrest, a donor conference was held on 4 August, the first anniversary of the port explosions. Co-hosted by France and the UN, the International Conference in Support of the Lebanese People raised around US $370m. in aid donations, including nearly $100m. from the USA and $118m. from France. By early September agreement on a new administration had been reached, and Miqati was sworn in as Prime Minister on 10 September. His new 24-member Government was described as technocratic, and comprised 12 Christian representatives (of various denominations), five Sunni Muslims, five Shi'a and two Druze. The largest single political faction represented was the FPM, with six ministers.

In mid-October 2021 members of Hezbollah, Amal and El-Marada staged a demonstration in Tayyouneh, a predominantly Christian neighbourhood in Beirut, to protest against Tarek Bitar, the judge leading the investigations into the Beirut port blast, whom they accused of representing US interests and of having indicted suspects before they had testified. Snipers belonging to the Lebanese Forces opened fire on the crowd, killing seven protesters and wounding dozens more. Meanwhile, Amal and Hezbollah ministers refused to attend cabinet sessions for three months, demanding Bitar's dismissal.

In late October 2021 a diplomatic dispute arose over comments made by Lebanon's Minister of Information, George Kordahi, prior to his nomination to the Cabinet but broadcast on television shortly after his appointment. Kordahi criticized the Saudi-led coalition's military campaign in Yemen, contesting that the Iranian-backed al-Houthi rebels were 'defending themselves against an external aggression'. Saudi Arabia fiercely denounced the implication that it was the aggressor and ordered the Lebanese ambassador to leave the Kingdom, banned its citizens from travelling to Lebanon and halted imports from the country. The Cooperation Council for the Arab States of the Gulf (Gulf Cooperation Council) also condemned the minister's remarks, with Bahrain and Kuwait recalling their respective ambassadors from Beirut. In May the Minister of Foreign Affairs and Expatriates, Charbel Wehbe, had resigned after suggesting in an interview that Gulf states had 'supported the rise of Islamic State in Syria and Iraq'. Besides claiming that Hezbollah weapons served as an 'insurance policy' against foreign occupation, Wehbe argued that funds should not come at the expense of Lebanese sovereignty.

With Saudi Arabia more reluctant than in the past to provide financial aid to its neighbour, Saudi–Lebanese ties were further hampered by the announcement, in January 2022, that Saad Hariri was to withdraw from political life. The premier's exit left a vacuum within the Sunni leadership and also paved the way for the Gulf nations, whose envoys returned to Lebanon one month prior to national elections, to support other more fiercely anti-Hezbollah leaders.

Amid negotiations for a deal to transport natural gas from Egypt to Lebanon via the Arab Gas Pipeline, the Russian invasion of Ukraine in February 2022 drove up fuel prices in Lebanon, as elsewhere, as well as the cost of subsidized imports of wheat and other grains.

In April 2022 the IMF reached a staff-level agreement with the Lebanese authorities on a Four-Year Extended Fund Facility worth around US $3,000m., with the funding contingent on the implementation of a multi-pronged fiscal and legislative reform programme (see Economy). In the run-up to the legislative elections, the authorities were able to achieve stabilization of the Lebanese pound and direct cash transfers, as well as improved energy supply.

THE 2022 ELECTIONS AND SUBSEQUENT POLITICAL IMPASSE

The general election was held on 15 May 2022 (from 6 May for voters resident overseas). A total of 142,041 of the 225,277 non-resident Lebanese nationals who had registered to vote cast their ballots, representing a turnout of 63.1% among the diaspora (considerably higher than the overall turnout of 41.0%), with the dire economic situation among the principal concerns incentivizing people to engage in the electoral process.

The March 8 Alliance, which had secured 70 seats in the 2018 elections, lost its parliamentary majority. While Hezbollah retained 13 seats and Amal secured 15 seats, the FPM (previously the largest Christian party in the legislature) lost 12 seats, taking its tally to 17 seats. As in 2018, the LF increased its representation, to 19 seats, from 15 seats previously, thereby becoming the largest Christian party in the National Assembly. Important gains were made by independent forces and grassroots movements, with the result that one-10th of the legislature (13 seats) was now occupied by independents, while a record eight women were elected. On 20 May 2022 the Cabinet approved a financial recovery plan, including the restructuring of the banking system, which would eventually permit Lebanon to receive the financial aid pledged by the IMF and other international lenders. (However, in March 2023 the Fund assessed that there had been only 'limited progress' in the Government's implementation of the reforms agreed in April 2022.)

Following the elections, on 31 May 2022 Nabih Berri was re-elected Speaker of the House for a seventh consecutive term. Orthodox Christian Elias Bou Saab (of the FPM) replaced Elie Ferzli as Deputy Speaker, while Maronite Christian Alain Aoun (also of the FPM) was re-elected as Secretary of the legislature. In the following month, after consultations with members of the National Assembly (54 of whom voted to re-elect Miqati as Prime Minister), President Aoun re-appointed Miqati as acting Prime Minister and asked him to form a new government. However, the ensuing negotiations between the various political parties and blocs proved to be protracted, and in the following months parliamentary deputies also repeatedly failed to agree on nominating a presidential candidate to replace Aoun, increasing political uncertainty and exacerbating the economic situation. Aoun left office on 30 October, one day before his mandate expired and without a designated successor in place. In accordance with the Constitution's provisions in the event of a presidential vacuum, on 31 October presidential powers were assumed by the Cabinet, and Prime Minister Miqati was appointed as acting head of state. However, as Miqati and his Government themselves held office in acting capacity, their executive powers were limited. Eleven further attempts made by the National Assembly between November and January 2023 to elect a new President all proved unsuccessful. Although the leading candidate for the presidency, Michel Moawad (the son of former President René Moawad), who was supported by the LFP, consistently received the most votes in the Assembly, he failed to secure the support of more than about one-third of deputies. In February—by which time Berri had decided to halt the parliamentary sessions to elect a new President—the crisis prompted the Governments of France, the USA, Saudi Arabia, Qatar and Egypt to warn Miqati that they would reconsider 'all ties' with Lebanon, if it failed to elect a new head of state. Besides a lack of consensus among Christian political parties, Hezbollah and Amal had joined forces to oppose the candidacy of anybody whom they deemed to threaten the 'resistance' to Israel.

Meanwhile, in a rare positive development for the Lebanese Government, in October 2022 it ratified an historic, US-brokered agreement with the Israeli Government regarding the demarcation of their shared maritime border, thereby opening the possibility for both countries of offshore hydrocarbons exploration within the formerly disputed area of the Mediterranean and the potential for exporting oil and gas to Europe as it sought to wean itself of Russian supplies following the Russian invasion of Ukraine. However, sovereignty over a short stretch of the maritime border (from the point where the northern coast of Israel and the southern coast of Lebanon meet, 5 km out to sea) remained unresolved as of September 2023. Nevertheless, in August Lebanon began gas and oil exploration in its Exclusive Economic Zone.

However, tensions with Israel rose again in early April 2023 after a wave of rockets was launched into northern Israel by Hamas militants in southern Lebanon and the Gaza Strip, prompting the IDF to retaliate with air and artillery strikes on alleged Hamas positions in Lebanon and Gaza. The rocket attack on Israel from southern Lebanon was the largest since the 2006 war between Israel and Hezbollah. In May 2023 Hezbollah conducted a high-profile military exercise (the group's first publicized military exercise in almost a decade) in southern Lebanon, apparently to demonstrate its armed capabilities to its internal and external rivals.

In early June 2023 Israeli soldiers constructing a barrier in the Shebaa Farms area were confronted by Lebanese protesters and local farmers, who claimed that the Israeli activities were a violation of Lebanese sovereignty as they were taking place across the UN's Blue Line demarcation between Israel, Lebanon and the occupied Golan Heights. Following the protests, Hezbollah erected a tent near Kfar Saba in an area of no man's land between Israeli territory and Lebanese territory. In late June tensions between Lebanon and Israel rose further after the latter announced that it had seized millions of dollars in digital wallets linked to Iran's Islamic Revolutionary Guard Corps–Quds Force and its proxy, Hezbollah. In the following days Lebanese media reported that Hezbollah had shot down an Israeli reconnaissance unmanned aerial vehicle (drone) over southern Lebanon near the Israeli border; the Israeli media claimed that the drone had crashed, owing to a technical problem.

In March 2023 the French Government proposed Suleiman Franjiya (the grandson of former President Franjiya, the leader of El-Marada and a Hezbollah ally) as a candidate for the presidency and Nawaf Salam, a judge and former Lebanese diplomat, as prime minister, but the USA, Saudi Arabia, Qatar and Egypt expressed their preference for a candidate more deeply committed to structural reforms. The Chinese-brokered rapprochement between Saudi Arabia and Iran in March (see Iran), when the two traditional rivals restored diplomatic ties, sparked hopes for progress being made in electing a president in Lebanon and a reduction in sectarian tensions among the country's rival political blocs following the rapprochement between their two major supporters.

In an absurd episode underlining how the Lebanese ruling elite has sought to divert attention away from more pressing issues, a decision in late March 2023 to postpone the country's transition to daylight savings time led to different confessional groups in the small nation briefly operating in two different time zones. Prime Minister Mikati and the parliamentary Speaker, Berri, had apparently decided arbitrarily to postpone putting forward the clocks by one hour to late April, after the end of the holy Muslim month of Ramadan. The decision ignited sectarian tensions as Lebanese Christians sharply criticized the delay imposed by the two Muslim leaders, viewing it as an attempt to 'Islamize' the country and refusing to accept the postponement, unilaterally putting forward their clocks by one hour in their Maronite strongholds. At a special cabinet session at the end of March to discuss the matter, ministers voted to put the clock forward at the end of March, as was customary, but the episode underscored the fundamental weaknesses that were driving Lebanon closer to complete collapse—specifically, failing to confirm the appointment of a president and cabinet, and to approve economic and fiscal reforms in order to unlock international support.

In April 2023 the National Assembly voted to postpone by one year the country's municipal elections, which were due to be held in May, citing a shortage of funding to organize the polls.

A 12th attempt by the National Assembly to elect a president was held in June 2023 and, not surprisingly, proved fruitless. In that month the USA declared that it was considering imposing sanctions on individuals who were obstructing the selection of a head of state in Lebanon (although it remained unclear how such a judgement could be made, in practice). In July Qatar hosted a summit attended by the USA, France, Saudi Arabia and Egypt in an attempt to find a resolution to Lebanon's extended political and economic crisis, including selecting a new head of state and a successor to Riad Salameh, who was to retire as Governor of the central bank at the end of that month. Also in July, the European Parliament approved a resolution calling for the sanctioning of parties found responsible for obstructing the election of a new president in Lebanon and explicitly criticizing Hezbollah and Amal, as well as the FPM. As of mid-September, however, no breakthrough in the political stalemate had been achieved.

In the mean time, the economic crisis continued, notably the issue of how an estimated US $70,000m. of losses would be shared between the central bank, private banks and depositors (see Economy). Hitherto considered untouchable, in March 2022 the Governor of the central bank, Salameh, was charged—together with his brother—with illegal enrichment and money laundering. It was reported in June that Salameh and his brother had filed a lawsuit against the Lebanese state, citing 'grave mistakes' in the investigation into their alleged crimes. In February 2023 both men were, nevertheless, formally charged with, *inter alia*, embezzlement, money laundering and tax evasion; they denied all the charges. Salameh stepped down from his position at the end of July upon the expiry of his term and was replaced, on an acting basis, by his deputy, Wassim Mansouri.

In Lebanon, endemic corruption has led to the absence of a functioning state and widespread mismanagement and deficiencies in service and infrastructure provision, including of electricity (daily power cuts in the country are ordinary events), water supply, sanitation, transport, waste management, telecommunications and other public services. Four years after the October 2019 protests, demonstrators—although having lost much of their momentum and with decreased capacity to enforce changes in the status quo—were continuing to demand that the Government implement anti-sectarian structural reform programmes.

The August 2020 port explosion further illustrated the blatant negligence and mismanagement in the country, and further intensified popular outrage—not least as by mid-2023 nobody had yet been held formally accountable, despite the detention of more than 20 port and customs officials. Notwithstanding anti-establishment protests, sectarianism permeates most aspects of life in the country. Even if sectarianism were to be formally abandoned, not only would its loyalty networks be hard to remove overnight, but what has been described as one of the worst economic crises in centuries might push citizens to rely on those very local leaders for support and patronage. There were numerous allegations of vote buying (through cash payment or access to fuel, electricity, basic services or assurances of protection against potential outbreaks of violence) during the 2022 general election campaign. Additionally, a number of nominally independent candidates were previously linked to the established parties. The relatively low voter turnout suggests that the public may have felt little reason to expect major changes from the political process. Another contributing factor was the boycott of the poll by the Future Movement following Saad Hariri's decision to retire from politics, and the consequent decision by many Sunni voters not to vote, although many party members had resigned from the organization in order to contest the elections at the head of their own Future Movement-affiliated bloc.

Facing a collapse in governmental provision, niche authoritarian rule and service support from sects across the religious spectrum might be the only alternative. Tacitly, Christians fear that both their political rights and cultural identity in Lebanon would be erased if official sectarianism came to an end. Regardless of the real demographic composition of the country (and suggestions that Christians now comprise only 25% of the population), there is a national consensus that respects the 50% share of Christian representation as constitutive of the Lebanese identity, culture and history.

Confessionalism is widely criticized for promoting state weakness, community-oriented elite politics and the entrenchment of old political dynasties and sectarian identities, as well as promoting a long history of an electoral system that does not stimulate cross-cutting cleavages, and which can be hostage to gerrymandering by different communities and regions. It is also highly questionable if the country is dependent on an external player to guarantee its domestic political stability. In addition, Lebanon's national unity governments are prone to secretive executive negotiation as well as informal decision-making. Frequently, the country is either under deadlock and paralysis or a cartel-like compromise. In any minority-majority scenario, securing a two-thirds' majority in the Cabinet is hardly an easy enterprise, and paralysis and deadlock are highly likely, especially after the Doha Agreement and the Syrian withdrawal, given the different formal and informal mechanisms of minority veto at hand. Surprisingly, however, despite abundant political instability, foreign interference, several regional wars and violent domestic episodes, the system has survived nearly one-and-a-half centuries under an extremely impaired and debilitated national state. In a sense, Lebanese political history is a history of continuity and a deeper entrenchment of a power-sharing design introduced as a response to the continuous political mobilization of confessional identities and manipulation of sectarian rhetoric to fill representative voids and oppose competing forces and ideologies. The constant need for compromise and to accommodate different interests is a widely established reality in daily politics.

The Lebanese duality between a 'pluri-religious and tolerant model', on the one hand, and institutional instability and sectarian deadlock, on the other, is the result of its institutional framework. It is as if the Lebanese state were characterized by a permanent condition of 'restless stability'. In addition, there is at all times a tension between the polarization fostered by the sectarian system itself and the political or ideological positioning of the different forces in the country, creating an overlap or traction between these different postures and combinations. Since the beginning of the Syrian war, the clashes between the regional powers Saudi Arabia and Iran have turned Lebanon into an important microcosm of the region's dispute for supremacy as a whole. This takes the form not of a 'Shi'a–Sunni divide', reflecting longstanding sectarian grievances, but rather of a clash between two contrasting utopias, as pan-Arabism and 'Lebanism' (arising from Maronite particularism) once were. As happened during the Ottoman and French periods, domestic elites—not merely proxies—have pragmatically allied themselves with regional players and foreign powers to strengthen their own interests and agendas, accommodating them strategically and symbolically, forging narratives and capitalizing from them.

It is certainly true that for a long time sectarianism has neither responded to nor reflected real cleavages in society, while the political system has shown signs of complete depletion. However, clientelism and patron–client networks are highly diffuse, institutionally and economically, and bureaucratically ingrained in a variety of realms of micro-politics. Sectarianism in Lebanon is embedded not only within but also outside of state institutions. Furthermore, as the results of the 2022 general election indicated, the political class shows significant resilience and endurance. Accordingly, even though civil society and protesters consistently demand an end to the system and the current scenario appears to provide a 'window of opportunity' for structural change, the formal abolition of confessional politics would be unlikely immediately to dismantle the existing fabric of daily life. The feasibility of effectively extinguishing sectarianism remains a medium-term challenge for future generations.

Economy

ALI NOUREDDEEN

INTRODUCTION: DEMOGRAPHIC BACKGROUND AND RECENT DEVELOPMENTS

Lebanon is one of the most densely populated countries in the Middle East, with an area of just 10,452 sq km and a total estimated population of 5.4m. people at mid-2023, according to the United Nations (UN) Population Division.

After the eruption of the Syrian civil war in 2011, Lebanon became the country hosting the largest number of refugees per capita and per square km in the world, and at mid-2023 about 1.5m. Syrian refugees and 13,715 refugees of other nationalities were living in Lebanon, according to Lebanese government data. It should be noted that only an estimated 55% of the resident Syrian refugees were officially registered with the UN High Commissioner for Refugees. According to the UN Relief and Works Agency for Palestine Refugees in the Near East, Lebanon was also host to 490,687 Palestinian refugees at mid-2023. the Palestinian refugees are long-term residents of the country, and around two-thirds of them live in Palestinian refugee camps. As a result, more than 36% of Lebanon's current population are either Palestinian or Syrian nationals, and they constitute the primary source of low-wage labour in the Lebanese economy.

Despite the massive influx of Syrian refugees over the past decade, Lebanon lost 14% of its overall population between 2015 and 2022, according to the UN Population Division. This trend was caused mainly by the recent wave of emigration of Lebanese nationals, more than 900,000 of whom have left the country over the past decade. In fact, emigration is not a new phenomenon to Lebanese society, as the country has witnessed several large waves of outward population flows since the beginning of the 20th century. However, the recent emigration wave, which was triggered by the ongoing economic and financial crisis (see *The Banking Sector and Financial Crisis*), is believed to be the largest in more than 45 years.

As a result of this recent demographic shift, Lebanon is currently facing a 'brain drain', which is depriving the country of its skilled human resources. The proportion of individuals who are fit to work and contribute to the economy, and the number of employees in critical sectors such as health care, nursing, engineering and education, have both been negatively affected by the outward flow of migrants. Owing to the importance of these sectors, the current outflow of human capital will have severe consequences in the coming years. Notably, the Staff Concluding Statement of the Article IV Mission published by the International Monetary Fund (IMF) in June 2023 warned that 'emigration, particularly of skilled workers, would accelerate undermining future growth prospects even further'.

From 2019 the pre-existing economic slowdown in Lebanon evolved into devastating financial, economic and monetary crises, which were ranked by the World Bank as one of 'the top 10, possibly top three, most severe crises episodes globally since the mid-nineteenth century'. As a result of the economic crisis, the Lebanese Government ceased making repayments on its outstanding foreign currency debt from March 2020, and the Lebanese pound has lost about 98% of its value since 2019. At the same time, Lebanese banks have imposed informal capital controls, which have restricted depositors' access to foreign currency savings. The consequences of the crisis were exacerbated by the economic impact of the coronavirus disease (COVID-19) pandemic from early 2020 and the massive explosion at the Port of Beirut in August of that year.

These developments compounded existing structural problems, such as weak infrastructure, insufficient water supplies, a dysfunctional electricity sector, unreliable wastewater management and solid waste management problems. The widening of the fiscal balance, as a result of the current economic crisis, has limited the Government's ability to deal with such challenging issues.

The evolvement of the current crisis is reflected in a cumulative four-year contraction of 37.2% in real gross domestic product (GDP) between 2018 and 2021, although the rate of economic contraction slowed to 2.6% in 2022 (compared with 25.9% in 2020 and 10.5% in 2021), according to the World Bank. In 2023 real GDP is expected to continue to shrink, by 0.5%, owing to the absence of necessary reforms. According to World Bank forecasts, nominal GDP will total US $17,950m. in 2023, compared with $54,900m. in 2018, which means that over this period the total economic output of the country is predicted to decrease by more than two-thirds. In fact, World Bank data indicate that total economic output in 2023 will fall to below the level of 2002, reversing all gains made over the intervening period.

World Bank data indicate that Lebanon's GDP per capita decreased by 36.5% between 2019 and 2021. In July 2022 the country was reclassified as a lower-income country, down from upper middle-income status. Between 2019 and 2021, owing to the current economic crisis, Lebanon lost all the accumulated gains in GDP per capita that had been achieved between 2007 and 2018.

Meanwhile, Lebanon's population is still suffering from the consequences of the financial meltdown, in the form of high levels of unemployment, loss of access to savings held in commercial banks, loss of purchasing power as a result of the devaluation of the local currency and a very high rate of inflation. At the same time, the collapse of the social safety net and the paralysis of governmental institutions has placed the most vulnerable groups in the population in a precarious position.

Owing to all these factors, the rate of multidimensional poverty almost doubled from 42% of the population in 2019 to 82% in 2021, according to ESCWA's report *Multidimensional Poverty in Lebanon*, published in September 2021. The report also stated that the percentage of households with no access to health care services increased from 9% in 2019 to 33% in 2021, while the percentage of residents who were unable to obtain necessary medicines increased to over 50%. Notably, the assets of the National Social Security Fund—the primary provider of social insurance coverage to private sector workers and their dependants in Lebanon—have deteriorated sharply since 2019, as a result of the sharp depreciation in the value of the Lebanese pound.

The UN World Food Programme (WFP) reported that at April 2023 some 1.46m. Lebanese and about 800,000 Syrian refugees—42% of the total population—were facing acute food insecurity, owing to the worsening economic crisis and sharply rising food prices. In addition, the Vulnerability Assessment of Syrian Refugees found that 90% of Syrian refugee families were in need of humanitarian assistance in order to survive and could not afford most essential goods.

THE BANKING SECTOR AND FINANCIAL CRISIS

Understanding the financial crisis and current state of the financial system and banking sector is essential in order to evaluate the problems that are hindering the growth of other productive sectors in the Lebanese economy. The financial sector's accumulated and unresolved losses are deeply interconnected with the monetary problems—and thus inflationary problems—that the country is currently facing, in addition to a lack of lending and credit activities. Meanwhile, a lack of trust in Lebanon's financial institutions is one of the main reasons for the decrease in incoming foreign currency transfers, which is exacerbating the decline in the country's foreign reserves. In the absence of even the most basic financial services, any economic recovery will be impossible.

Before the onset of the current financial crisis, Lebanon had received massive inflows of US dollar deposits following the end of the Lebanese civil war in 1990. To attract these deposits, the Lebanese banking sector offered absolute banking secrecy, which was protected by a special law adopted in 1956. The sector also provided very generous interest rates, compared with the rates offered in Western financial markets.

The Lebanese diaspora has traditionally represented a major source of incoming foreign currency deposits, and residents of neighbouring Arab countries have also benefited from the banking secrecy provided by the Lebanese financial system. For all of these reasons, the volume of foreign currency deposits rose massively over the years and by 2019 was worth more than 2.4 times the value of Lebanon's GDP.

However, all these massive inflows of capital, which were accumulated as deposit liabilities in the banking sector, were not used to provide beneficial credit or lending for Lebanon's productive sectors. Instead, commercial banks' liquidity was used excessively to finance the Government's budget deficit and the central bank, the Banque du Liban (BdL). Until 2019, Lebanese banks used 70% of their depositors' liquidity to provide credit for the Government and the BdL. This pattern allowed commercial banks to benefit from high interest rates, but it risked using depositors' liquidity to make unsafe investments.

In 2019 the Government's stock of public debt, financed mainly by the banking sector, rose to 171% of GDP, which clearly represented an unsustainable level of indebtedness. At the same time, the BdL was draining its foreign reserves, which were obtained from the commercial banks' deposits, in an attempt to uphold the value of the local currency. Ultimately, both the Government and the BdL were unable to meet their liabilities, which created a financial bubble that exploded in 2019 in the form of a meltdown in the financial sector.

In late 2019, after the onset of the financial crisis, commercial banks imposed informal rules on their customers that restricted cash withdrawals and outgoing transfers. Consequently, these banks were unable to attract new deposits or liquidity, and the banking sector could not provide its usual financial services for the rest of the economy. Depositors, who had placed their funds in the banking sector, are currently unable to benefit from their savings or pension funds. Lebanese companies have lost a huge share of their working capital, which was being held in their current accounts in the banking sector.

According to the consolidated balance sheet of Lebanon's commercial banks, at June 2023 the sector's liabilities in the form of deposits in foreign currency were valued at around US $91,900m., while the Government estimated that the total cumulative losses of the financial sector amounted to around $73,000m., owing to the Government's default in March 2020 on a repayment of €1,200m. on a Eurobond (the first sovereign default in the country's history) and the BdL's virtual collapse. In other words, cumulative losses in the banking sector were equivalent to 77.7% of depositors' liquidity, which explains the current liquidity crisis in the sector.

Despite the severity of the problem, only limited progress has been made in the past four years to restore the financial soundness of the banking sector. To date, the Lebanese National Assembly has neither considered or approved the legislation necessary to restructure the banking sector and resolve the problem of its accumulated losses. Moreover, the BdL has failed to take the requisite action to audit the balance sheets of each commercial bank on an individual basis, a step that is needed in order to plan for the essential mergers and acquisitions that will have to take place during the restructuring process. This inaction over the past several years reflects both the lack of political leadership and the continuing arguments about the nature of the reforms that should be implemented.

Moreover, from 2020 the Governor of the BdL, Riad Salameh, was subject to forensic investigations in Lebanese courts and in several other European countries. This undermined the reputation and credibility of the BdL, the main regulator of the Lebanese banking sector. In May 2023 Lebanon received two international arrest warrants for Salameh, from the International Criminal Police Organization (Interpol), which were issued at the request of judges in France and Germany. However, Salameh remained in his post until the end of July, when his term as Governor expired. The various Lebanese and European investigations and indictments were related to accusations of money laundering, embezzlement of the BdL's funds, forgery, illegal enrichment and other suspected offences connected to Salameh's erstwhile responsibilities as the chief regulator of the banking sector.

In April 2022—when the Lebanese state was declared bankrupt—a preliminary, four-year Extended Fund Facility agreement (worth US $3,000m.) was reached with the IMF, as the Government prepared a comprehensive economic recovery plan aimed primarily at restoring stability to the financial sector. The loan was subject to approval by the Fund's management and Executive Board, after the timely implementation by the Lebanese authorities of certain previously agreed measures. These measures included the approval of a bank restructuring strategy that recognized and addressed directly the large losses in the sector, and the National Assembly's approval of the legislation required to implement the strategy. However, these measures were not implemented fully by the Lebanese authorities, with the result that the IMF did not provide the anticipated funds to introduce the reform programme.

MONETARY POLICY AND INFLATION

Between 1999 and 2019, before the economic and financial crises, the BdL maintained a fixed official exchange rate of US 1 = £L1,507.5. The central bank had to take the necessary measures to enforce and maintain the rate in the market using traditional monetary policy tools, including open market operations, controlling interest rates and modifying the obligatory minimum reserve requirements for commercial banks. As a result, during this period the BdL did not allow free market forces to determine the value of the local currency. The policy also obliged the central bank to provide the necessary liquidity, from its own reserves, to finance foreign exchange operations for outgoing transfers, if demand and supply balances in the market required such interventions to maintain the fixed exchange rate.

In order to make this model work, the BdL adopted a tight monetary policy, which was characterized by high interest rates. This was necessary for the central bank to absorb the excess liquidity in local currency and to attract the commercial banks' liquidity in foreign currency, to boost the BdL's foreign currency reserves. Maintaining a high level of foreign currency reserves was essential to preserve the BdL's ability to intervene in the exchange market and protect the fixed exchange rate. The central bank was also able to use its accumulated reserves to finance the Government's fiscal deficit, which widened rapidly from 1993.

This monetary policy helped the BdL to contain inflation and boosted consumption, yet it discouraged private investment in the productive sectors. Extremely high interest rates over a period of 26 years raised the cost of borrowing for productive projects, which limited the utilization of the banks' credit in such projects. At the same time, tight monetary policy absorbed liquidity into the financial system, instead of injecting it into new projects in productive sectors.

The BdL's monetary policy also encouraged a high level of dollarization in the banking sector, as it relied increasingly on attracting foreign currency deposits. At the end of August 2018 deposits in foreign currency, particularly of the US dollar, accounted for 68.8% of total bank deposits, while more than 67.6% of cheques traded between banks were denominated in foreign currency, according to the BdL. This phenomenon made the financial sector and commercial banks dependent on constantly attracting new foreign currency inflows, to preserve their liquidity and keep financing the central bank's stock of foreign reserves. As subsequent events illustrated, this model was unsustainable.

During 2011–19 the country's entire monetary model was being challenged, and the balance of payments recorded a deficit every year from 2011, except in 2016. It should be noted that the balance of payments summarizes the net financial transfers between a specific country and its foreign counterparts over a particular period. Owing to the fixed exchange rate that was in place, these deficits depleted the reserves of the BdL, which was defending the fixed exchange rate by providing the dollars required to intervene in the market and compensate for the liquidity that left the country. The central bank was also financing foreign exchange operations for outgoing transfers.

Consequently, between 2011 and 2019 the BdL witnessed an expanding foreign currency mismatch (i.e. a gap between liabilities and assets held in foreign currency); and these developments were, as mentioned earlier, a key reason for the crisis in the financial system from 2019, as the central bank lost its ability to repay its foreign currency liabilities to the commercial banks. The Lebanese Government estimated that the central bank's currency mismatch amounted to around US $60,000m. in 2022, which was some 2.6 times larger than the country's GDP in that year.

For all these reasons, since 2019 the BdL has lost its ability to defend the fixed exchange rate in the parallel market (also known as the black market). The Lebanese pound weakened dramatically, from US $1 = £L1,507.5 in 2019 to around US $1 = £L89,500 in August 2023; in February 2023 worsening economic conditions had forced the Government to introduce a currency devaluation of some 90%, resetting the official exchange rate to 15,000 Lebanese pounds to the US dollar. The central bank and the Lebanese Government utilized other exchange rates for special operations such as taxation and loan settlements, which normalized the multiple exchange rate system. A parallel unofficial exchange rate in excess of 100,000 Lebanese pounds per US dollar was widely reported by mid-2023. However, according to the World Bank, multiple exchange rate systems are expensive, highly distortionary for all market participants, drive high inflation, impede private sector development and foreign investment, and lead to lower growth.

As Lebanon depends on imports for more than 80% of its food requirement, the prices on the local market have increased in line with the sharp depreciation of the Lebanese pound since 2019. There was a significant rise in food prices on the local market following the sudden removal of foreign exchange subsidies for food imports in 2020 (except for wheat imports). In addition, the gradual removal of foreign exchange subsidies for energy imports in 2021 contributed to further increases in the consumer price index (CPI), as the price of energy affects the cost of transporting and selling all goods. From late 2021 global inflationary pressures also played a role in pushing inflation in the local market even higher.

For all these reasons, according to the Central Administration for Statistics, the CPI grew by some 4,250% between January 2019 and August 2023, and although inflationary pressures affected all regions of the country, the intensity of inflation varied depending on each region's distance from Beirut, reflecting the cost of transporting goods from the commercial centre and largest port. As a result, remote areas of Lebanon, which usually suffer from higher rates of poverty in any case, were hit hardest by inflationary pressures in the market.

According to the *Lebanon Economic Monitor* published by the World Bank in early 2023, the main contributors to inflation in 2021 and 2022 were higher prices for food and non-alcoholic beverages, followed by transportation, water, electricity and gas. As a result, since basic consumer items were the primary drivers of overall inflation, the report described inflation in Lebanon as a 'highly regressive tax, disproportionately affecting the poor vulnerable and more generally people living on fixed incomes like pensioners'.

PUBLIC FINANCES AND FISCAL POLICY

Between 1993 and 2019 the Lebanese budget was never in balance or surplus in any year, and the average annual budget deficit during this period was 12.2% of GDP. The deficit widened from 9% of GDP in 1993 to 26% in 2000, before narrowing steadily over the succeeding years to reach 6% in 2011. The deficit widened in the following years, to 11% in 2019. The chronic annual deficit in the Lebanese budget was always a result of weak tax compliance, poor governance, the cost of repaying interest on the huge stock of public debt and the loss-making electricity sector.

In fact, during the period 1993–2019 Lebanon registered an overall deficit of a cumulative £L123,000,000, equivalent to around US $82,000m., according to the fixed exchange rate that was in place at the time. However, it should be noted that the Government would have registered a cumulative surplus of £L22,000,000m. ($14,700m.) during the same period, without the burden of interest payments, which accumulated as a result of the mounting public debt. This fact highlights the critical role played by interest payments in draining Lebanese government resources.

Owing to the accumulated fiscal deficit, total public debt as a percentage of GDP increased from 48% in 1993 to 171% in 2019, just before the financial crisis. The burden of public debt repayments limited to a large extent the Lebanese Government's manoeuvrability and restricted its ability to finance the country's much-needed social safety net. By the beginning of 2020 total public debt amounted to about US $90,000m. Of this, some $32,000m. were in the form of foreign currency international bonds (Eurobonds), while the remaining $58,000m. were in the form of local Treasury bills, predominantly in Lebanese pounds.

After the onset of the financial crisis in October 2019, the depreciation of the Lebanese pound led to a sharp decline in fiscal revenues, from 13.1% of GDP in 2020 to less than 6% in 2022, one of the lowest rates globally. As a result, the Government had significantly to reduce its spending, which decreased from 20.1% of GDP in 2020, according to the IMF, to an estimated 9.1% in 2021 and an estimated 11.5% in 2022. Continuing pressure on the Lebanese pound threatens to trigger further decreases in the overall budget. The unfavourable fiscal environment caused paralysis in most public sector institutions as revenues were not sufficient to cover current expenditure, including wages.

As mentioned earlier, the sudden halt in capital inflows, along with the continuing depletion of the BdL's reserves, forced the Government in March 2020 to suspend the payment of a Eurobond. Since that time, Lebanon has been excluded from global and local foreign currency debt markets, as the Government is unable to issue or sell any new Eurobonds.

As of September 2023 no negotiations between the Government and its creditors had commenced with a view to restructuring Lebanon's outstanding foreign currency debt, by amending the maturities and other terms. Accordingly, the BdL remained the sole available source of foreign currency borrowing for the Government, which is further draining the central bank's dwindling reserves of foreign currency.

Owing to the sovereign debt default, between 2019 and 2022 interest payments on sovereign debt rose by 97%. Despite there being no debt restructuring plan in place, the budget registered a surplus of 0.9% of GDP in 2022. It should be noted that the Lebanese Treasury incurred huge losses in revenue between 2019 and 2022, owing to the low and unrealistic exchange rates that were used to collect value-added tax and customs tariffs. In addition, tax administration capacity was considerably weakened, owing to a rising rate of employee absenteeism, which increased sharply after the collapse in the real value of wages as the local currency depreciated.

REMITTANCES

According to World Bank estimates, Lebanon received remittances worth a record 31.7% of GDP in 2022, the second highest ratio of any country. The dependence on remittances is a historical phenomenon in Lebanon, where these inflows averaged US $6,500m. annually between 2012 and 2021. Owing to a fall in the nominal value of GDP since 2019, the sum of remittances as a percentage of GDP increased from an average of 13.0% in 2012–19, to 19.8% in 2020, 26.4% in 2021 and 31.7% in 2022. This factor made stability in the foreign exchange market highly dependent on the inflow of remittances.

In addition to their monetary significance, remittances are currently considered an essential component of the remaining social safety net in the country. A large proportion of Lebanese families depend on transfers from the diaspora to finance household consumption, which supports the domestic economy. As the financial crisis has prompted a sizeable new exodus of highly skilled labour, the value and role of remittances are expected to increase in the coming years.

Prior to 2019, most remittances were transferred directly from the diaspora to Lebanese commercial banks, to remain there as deposits and earn interest or to be paid to local beneficiaries. A proportion of incoming remittances was formerly used to fund purchases in the real estate sector. However, since the onset of the economic crisis, and owing to the financial situation in the country, most remittances are now received by non-banking financial services companies, and the funds are used almost entirely to fund essential needs.

The excessive reliance on remittances from the diaspora raises many questions among the general public and economists alike. This reliance has forced Lebanon into a vicious cycle of exporting its skilled workers, in order to earn wages in hard currency, rather than investing in the local economy to employ these well-qualified workers. Many observers consider this phenomenon to be a key part of the failing economic model, which eventually entered into crisis in 2019 and which has negatively affected the competitiveness of the domestic economy.

THE CHALLENGES FACED BY THE ELECTRICITY SECTOR

According to data from the BdL, between 2010 and 2021 over US $24,500m. was transferred from the country's foreign currency reserves to the Ministry of Energy and Electricity. Of this sum, $18,400m. was allocated as advances to the Treasury for fuel purchases by Electricité du Liban (EdL, the state-owned electricity company), as well as $543m. in direct transfers to the company. In addition, $5,600m. was disbursed to the energy and water ministry for various expenditures, including maintenance, service provider payments and project planning, further illustrating the deep-rooted crisis in the electricity sector. The data show that the electricity sector was responsible for 31% of the accumulated losses in the central bank's balance sheet between 2010 and 2021.

Despite the transfer of huge sums, the electricity sector is still suffering from major problems, which is hindering the growth of all Lebanese productive sectors. Since February 2021 the average electricity supply provided by EdL has fallen to less than four hours per day, owing to insufficient cash flow, operating inefficiency, challenges in obtaining hard currency and low production capacity at the country's power plants.

Lebanon's energy demand currently stands at approximately 3,000 MW, but the country's power plants' maximum production capacity is only about 1,600 MW (about 13 hours of coverage a day). However, power outages extend to more than 20 hours a day, owing to liquidity issues relating primarily to challenges in converting the sector's revenues in local currency to foreign currency, in order to purchase fuel. The accumulation of problems in the sector—and the lack of solutions—is due mainly to political disputes about alternatives and ongoing discussions about the sites of new proposed facilities.

According to the Ministry of Energy and Water, the main challenge facing the sector is the fact that its governance structure, its inability to recruit new employees, operational unsustainability and political interventionism all combine to cripple decision-making and progress in the sector. For example, the Ministries of Energy and Water and of Finance have administrative and financial oversight of EdL, respectively, but overall responsibility and reform of the sector rests with the Cabinet.

The Ministry of Energy and Water has warned that the sector is on the verge of collapse, owing to its inability to supply electricity or independently to meet most of its operating costs, thereby accumulating arrears with most of its suppliers. In short, the sector, which was already suffering from historical structural inefficiencies, is now facing challenges that have been exacerbated by the ongoing financial crisis.

According to Human Rights Watch, 20% of the population do not have the financial means to obtain electricity from private generators. These families are, accordingly, limited to receiving only four hours of electricity per day provided by EdL. As subscriptions for private generators are now denominated in US dollars, and as the Lebanese pound has weakened so much, nine out of 10 Lebanese households claim that the cost of electricity has affected their ability to pay for other basic services.

AGRICULTURE

Lebanon benefits from fertile soil, temperate weather and plentiful water resources, which are all considered key elements to building a competitive and sustainable agricultural sector. According to the UN Food and Agriculture Organization, 65% of Lebanon's total land area is agricultural land, comprising an area of 6,697 sq km. According to World Bank data, Lebanon is ranked 31st globally and first in the Middle East region in terms of the proportion of its land that is allocated to agriculture.

Despite all these positive factors, the Lebanese market is dependent on imports to satisfy up to about 80% of the country's food needs in any given year. The agricultural sector has historically been neglected in governmental economic policies and plans, and spending on the sector has reached barely 0.5% of the total government budget in recent years, leaving farmers heavily dependent on international aid, private sector spending and foreign investment.

For these reasons, Lebanese farmers have historically faced challenges related to quality control and standards, in addition to a high exposure to external events in international markets. The lack of active co-operation and government support has exacerbated the problems facing the agricultural sector, especially in terms of the high cost of transport, marketing, packaging and other logistics. These difficult conditions are reflected in the sector's inability to meet the domestic demand for food.

According to figures from the Lebanese Customs Administration, the value of agricultural imports fell by 33% between 2018 and 2021, owing to a deterioration in Lebanon's purchasing power following the sharp depreciation of the local currency. During the same period, the value of food exports increased by 59%, reflecting the benefits of the local currency depreciation and the concomitant rise in the competitiveness of Lebanon's exports on foreign markets. Despite these developments, Lebanon registered a deficit in terms of trade in agricultural products (i.e. the difference in value between imports and exports of agricultural products) of US $1,310m. in 2021, equivalent to 56% of revenue from agricultural products imports in that year.

These data reflect the persistence of Lebanon's dependence on imported food products, despite the depreciation of local currency. The major factor leading to these circumstances is the effect of the collapse of infrastructure sector activity since 2019 on agricultural output, especially in terms of water and electricity supplies. As a result, local agricultural activity could not offset the increase in prices of imported food items, owing to the depreciation of the local currency. Lebanon is fully dependent on imports to meet local demand for sugar, seeds, tea, cocoa beans, sesame, spices, rice and sunflower oil.

According to data from the Ministry of Agriculture, 32% of cultivated land is planted with fruit trees, 23% with olive trees, 20% with cereals, 16% with vegetables and 4% with industrial crops.

According to the Lebanese Customs Administration, in 2022 exports of coffee accounted for 11.7% of total revenue from agricultural exports, followed by grapes (7.6%), potatoes (7.6%), bananas (6.6%), live sheep and goats (6.1%), ginger and thyme (6%), lettuce and chicory (5.9%), apple and pears (5.6%), and citrus fruit (also 5.6%).

The major export destinations for Lebanon's agricultural products are concentrated in neighbouring Arab countries. According to the Lebanese Customs Administration, in 2022 the United Arab Emirates (UAE) and the Syrian Arab Republic were the top export destinations for Lebanese agricultural products, taking 18% and 14% of total agricultural exports, by value, respectively. Other major destinations were Iraq (5.5% of total agricultural exports), Türkiye/Turkey (4%), Switzerland (4%), Qatar (4%) and the USA (3%).

According to World Bank data, the agriculture sector's share of GDP has fallen in recent years, from 4.9% in 2007 to just 1.4% in 2021. Meanwhile, the percentage of the total workforce employed in the sector decreased from 5% in 2007 to 4% in 2021.

INDUSTRY

In recent decades, the industrial sector has been negatively affected by the deteriorating economic situation in the country. High interest rates have discouraged investment, and weak infrastructure and an unstable security situation have both contributed to limited growth in the sector. As a result, the sector's share in the country's total GDP has fallen sharply, from 23.7% in 1998 to just 2.8% in 2021. The percentage of the total workforce employed in the sector has also decreased, from 25% in 2000 to 21% in 2021. Since 2019 the sector has been negatively affected by long electricity outages, with the high operating costs of private electricity generators undermining the competitiveness of local production. A lack of suitable financial services, notably credit facilities, has also deprived the sector of the resources that it needs for growth.

According to the Lebanese Customs Administration, Lebanon's major industrial exports in 2022 were precious metals and jewellery, including processed gold and silver. These items represented the country's top export commodity, with a total annual export value of around US $190m. The country benefits from its good reputation in the field of jewellery craftsmanship and design, and jewellery products are exported principally to Switzerland, Saudi Arabia, the UAE and the USA. The value of pharmaceuticals exports in 2022 amounted to about $75m. Fertilizers, pesticides and industrial chemicals are exported principally to Saudi Arabia, Iraq and Syria. Textiles and apparel exports amounted to some $40m. in 2022, and the major markets were Saudi Arabia, Iraq and the UAE. Exports of tobacco and cigarettes amounted to about $30m. in 2022, sent principally to markets in Syria, Iraq and Jordan. Exports of plastic products amounted to some $25m. in that year, and exports of cement and construction materials totalled $20m.

TOURISM

Historically, tourism has been a leading economic sector in Lebanon, representing a major source of income and employment. The sector's direct contribution to the national and local economy includes expenditure by foreign tourists, consumption by domestic tourists and purchases by tourism providers, and its indirect contribution includes the domestic supply chain, capital investment and collective government spending on tourism and imported goods for indirect spending.

However, according to the Office of the Minister of State for Administrative Reform, Lebanon is not among the countries that have developed and currently implement a comprehensive strategy for the tourism sector. Although there have been sporadic initiatives in the past, a lack of political and economic stability has deprived the Government and Lebanese businesses of administrative, co-operative and inclusive policy orientation in the long term.

Lebanon's competitive advantages in the tourism sector include its many historical and archaeological sites, reflecting thousands of years of history. The country's most famous historical sites include the old towns of Tripoli, Batroun, Zahleh, Tyre, Sidon and Rachaya, as well as Byblos Castle, Sidon Sea Castle, Mseilha Fort and Baalbek temple complex. In addition, Lebanon benefits from the presence of a large diaspora, which represents a strong source of regular visitors. The country's moderate climate also makes it an attractive destination for tourists from neighbouring Arab countries.

According to the Ministry of Tourism, Lebanon expected to earn revenue from the tourism sector totalling about US $9,000m. in 2023, which would represent about 40% of nominal GDP in that year. The ministry estimated that tourist arrivals totalled some 1.7m. in 2022, with foreign tourists accounting for some 25% of arrivals and the remainder coming from the Lebanese diaspora. The ministry's data indicate that most foreign tourists come from Arab countries, including Egypt, Jordan, Iraq and Kuwait, while non-Arab tourists come principally from France, Germany, the USA and Australia.

A strong performance by the tourism sector in 2022 and 2023, as indicated by data from the Ministry of Tourism, followed a slump in the sector in 2020–21, as a result of the restrictions that were imposed during the COVID-19 pandemic as well as the disruption caused by the devastating explosion at the Port of Beirut in August 2020.

THE LABOUR MARKET

The labour market is characterized by a high level of fragility; in 2022 77.8% of total employment was in the informal sector, and thus lacked any social protection or entitlements, such as paid annual leave or sick leave. Accordingly, the benefits of the National Labour Law and the National Social Security Fund apply only to the minority of employees who work in the formal labour market. Notably, the number of Syrian and Palestinian workers in the informal sector in 2022 amounted to 95% and 93.9% of the total, respectively.

Owing to the ongoing economic crisis, the unemployment rate rose from 11.4% in 2018 to an estimated 29.6% in 2022, according to a labour force survey conducted by the International Labour Organization (ILO) and the Central Administration for Statistics. The data revealed that during that period the unemployment rate approximately doubled (to 47.8% in 2022) among young people, compared with adults (25.6%). The unemployment rate among women also surged, to 32.7% in 2022.

The Lebanese labour market has suffered historically from a limited social protection system with a low level of coverage, and about 80% of Lebanese citizens above the age of 65 years lack social benefits, health care coverage and retirement compensations. The labour market also lacks mechanisms to compensate workers who lose their jobs, and while the social assistance programmes that do exist are fairly numerous, there is no comprehensive system that co-ordinates benefits in order to reach the widest range of beneficiaries.

The Syrian refugee crisis has exacerbated the phenomenon of child labour in Lebanon, and many minors work in unsafe and unhealthy conditions. Recent data indicate that 72% of Syrian children in Lebanon do not benefit from primary education, and only 2% of Syrian children benefit from secondary education. As a result, there are currently more than 300,000 Syrian children not attending school in Lebanon, who are exposed to various forms of abuse, including unsafe employment. Although the Ministry of Labour drew up a national plan to combat the worst forms of child labour, it has failed to keep pace with the expansion of the phenomenon, owing to the scale of the Syrian refugee crisis and the repercussions of the economic crisis in Lebanon.

There has been no increase in the minimum wage for private sector employees since 2012. Between 2012 and 2019 the CPI increased by 25%, but since 2019 it has soared by 4,250%, owing mainly to local currency deterioration. These developments contributed to the erosion of purchasing power for employees on fixed salaries.

Despite the worsening economic conditions, Lebanon has not yet developed a national employment policy or strategy, nor has the Government devised a plan to address the impact of the economic crisis on the national labour force. The World Bank, the ILO and the WFP have worked with the Lebanese authorities to draft strategies aimed at protecting the most vulnerable segments of the workforce, but most of these programmes have not been put into effect, owing to limited available resources.

TRADE AND THE BALANCE OF PAYMENTS

Lebanon has suffered historically from a chronic trade deficit, owing to the weak output of its productive sectors and the excessive reliance on imported items. The overvalued local currency exchange rate before 2019 boosted the level of consumption, which amplified the demand for imports even further.

In 2020, according to IMF figures, the trade deficit more than halved from US $13,378m. in 2019 to $6,499m. in 2020. This decrease was caused mainly by the devaluation of the local currency from late 2019, which led to a decrease in imports. In addition, the consequences of the COVID-19 pandemic contributed to a slump in consumption in the domestic market.

The trade deficit widened by 26.6% in 2021, according to IMF estimates, to US $8,226m. and by a further 66.3% in 2022 to $13,677m. The sharp increase in the trade deficit in 2022 was due mainly to a 40.8% increase in imports, to pre-crisis levels, to an estimated $18,051m. As a result, the deficit on the current account of the balance of payments widened from $3,539m. (equivalent to 17.3% of GDP) in 2021, according to IMF estimates, to $6,479m. (29.0%) in 2022, which contributed to a substantial demand for foreign currency in the local market. As a result, gross foreign currency reserves held by the central bank decreased by about $2,600m. in 2022.

The steady increase in the value of imports in 2021 and 2022 was due mainly to rising prices of food items and petroleum and its derivatives on the international market. In addition, the lifting of COVID-related restrictions led to a gradual increase in demand for imported items, which caused a further widening of the trade deficit. Meanwhile, the demand for hard currency to finance the trade deficit remains a major challenge for the BdL in terms of its monetary policy.

MARITIME BORDER AGREEMENT WITH ISRAEL AND EXPLORATION FOR HYDROCARBONS

In October 2022 Lebanon and Israel concluded an historic agreement to end an long-running dispute over their shared maritime border, which paved the way for offshore hydrocarbons exploration in the Lebanese Exclusive Economic Zone (EEZ) in the Mediterranean Sea. Lebanon saw the deal as an opportunity to attract foreign investment and reduce the foreign currency costs of importing petroleum and its derivatives. However, it had not been ascertained whether sufficient quantities of natural gas reserves actually existed to make extraction economically viable.

In August 2023 the Ministry of Public Works and Transportation announced the arrival in Lebanese waters of the Trans-Ocean Barents drilling rig, which was to begin gas exploration activities by drilling an exploratory well in Lebanon's offshore

Block 9 before the end of the year. TotalEnergies of France was in charge of the project.

In the coming years, Lebanon will have to construct the necessary legislative framework for an oil and gas sector, including the establishment of a sovereign wealth fund to manage and invest the revenues earned from activity in the sector.

PROSPECTS

Lebanon is in dire need of a comprehensive financial rescue plan, in order to arrest the rapid economic decline that began in 2019. The plan must include urgent monetary policy measures to unify the multiple exchange rates and restore stability to the local foreign exchange market. In addition, the required reforms should be complemented by suitable emergency legislation, to restructure the banking system and resolve the issue of accumulated losses in the balance sheets of the BdL and the country's beleaguered commercial banks. In parallel, Lebanon's sovereign debt needs to be restructured, after a fair and 'in good faith' negotiation process with the country's creditors.

The financial recovery roadmap should not neglect the required adoption of a transparent and credible anti-corruption framework, to enhance accountability in the public sector. Reforming the country's state-owned enterprises, particularly its public utilities, is a prerequisite to limit the depletion of public resources. Improving the quality of public services is also required to enhance the performance of productive sectors, notably agriculture and industry. Tax policy and revenue administration reforms are also needed to broaden the tax base and limit and reduce the persistent budget deficit.

There is a consensus within the international community and international institutions, including the IMF and the World Bank, that since the onset of the financial crisis in 2019 Lebanon has achieved very little in terms of introducing the necessary reforms. In its concluding statement following its Article IV Mission to Lebanon in June 2023, the IMF stated explicitly that 'despite the severity of the situation, which calls for immediate and decisive action, there has been limited progress in implementing the comprehensive package of economic reforms'.

Without rapid emergency measures and long-term reforms, Lebanon could descend into a prolonged economic and social crisis that will leave permanent scars. Without urgent action, the rates of poverty and unemployment will remain high, and state structures will disintegrate completely. Owing to the crisis in the formal economic sector, the size of the informal economy could grow even further, thus increasing the risks of money laundering and other illicit activities. The continued weakening of the local currency could further deplete the real value of Lebanese wages, which would exacerbate the cost-of-living crisis, and there is a risk that the country's modest official social safety net could collapse altogether.

An alternative path, leading to prosperity and economic growth, requires political courage and leadership to overcome the traditional sectarian divisions and disputes that have prevented agreement about a comprehensive package of reforms since the economic crisis began in 2019. In this regard, it is important to remember that the World Bank described the Lebanese financial crisis as a 'deliberate depression', in reference to the absence of adequate policy responses. The World Bank judged that this reality did not result from a lack of informed advice, but rather from 'a lack of [...] political consensus in defense of a bankrupt economic system, which benefited few for so long'. Therefore, Lebanon's economic and financial recovery requires determination from the political class to reform the central features of the country's public policy.

Statistical Survey

Sources (unless otherwise stated): Central Administration for Statistics, Beirut; tel. (1) 373169; internet www.cas.gov.lb; Lebanese Customs Administration, Ministry of Finance, Beirut; tel. (1) 700115; e-mail info@customs.gov.lb; internet www.customs.gov.lb.

Area and Population

AREA, POPULATION AND DENSITY

Area (sq km)	10,452*
Population (official estimate)	
15 November 1970†	
Males	1,080,015
Females	1,046,310
Total	2,126,325
Population (UN estimates at mid-year)‡	
2021	5,592,631
2022§	5,489,740
2023§	5,353,930
Density (per sq km) at mid-2023§	512.2

* 4,036 sq miles.
† Figures are based on the results of a sample survey, excluding Palestinian refugees in camps. According to UNRWA, the total number of registered Palestinian refugees in Lebanon was 490,687 at mid-2023. In the first six months of 2013 UNHCR estimated that the number of refugees fleeing to Lebanon from the ongoing crisis in Syria increased by more than 400,000, to some 570,000; by the end of 2021 the Lebanese Government estimated a Syrian refugee population of around 1.5m., although the authorities suspended registration of Syrian refugees in 2015. In July 2023 795,322 Syrian refugees in Lebanon were registered with UNHCR.
‡ Source: UN, *World Population Prospects: The 2022 Revision*.
§ Projection.

POPULATION BY AGE AND SEX
('000, UN projections at mid-2023)

	Males	Females	Total
0–14 years	749.7	710.1	1,459.8
15–64 years	1,606.0	1,737.7	3,343.6
65 years and over	239.3	311.2	550.5
Total	2,595.0	2,759.0	5,353.9

Note: Totals may not be equal to the sum of components, owing to rounding.
Source: UN, *World Population Prospects: The 2022 Revision*.

PRINCIPAL TOWNS
(population in 2003)*

Beirut (capital)	1,171,000	Jounieh	79,800
Tarabulus (Tripoli)	212,900	Zahle	76,600
Saida (Sidon)	149,000	Baabda	58,500
Sur (Tyre)	117,100	Ba'albak (Ba'albek)	29,800
Al-Nabatiyah al-Tahta (Nabatiyah)	89,400	Alayh	26,700

* Figures are rounded.
Source: Stefan Helders, *World Gazetteer*.

Mid-2023 (incl. suburbs, UN projection): Beirut 2,421,354 (Source: UN, *World Urbanization Prospects: The 2018 Revision*).

LEBANON

BIRTHS, MARRIAGES AND DEATHS

	Live births	Marriages	Deaths
2017	103,931	41,889	26,953
2018	115,229	39,840	26,829
2020*	93,520	31,538	29,097
2021	86,613	36,287	35,621
2022	79,212	31,707	29,630

* Data for 2019 were not available.

Birth rate (UN estimates, rates per 1,000): 15.8 in 2019; 15.3 in 2020; 14.9 in 2021 (Source: UN, *World Population Prospects: The 2022 Revision*).

Death rate (UN estimates, rates per 1,000): 5.2 in 2019; 6.3 in 2020; 8.3 in 2021 (Source: UN, *World Population Prospects: The 2022 Revision*).

Life expectancy (years at birth, estimates): 75.0 (males 72.8; females 77.3) in 2021 (Source: World Bank, World Development Indicators database).

ECONOMICALLY ACTIVE POPULATION
(labour force and household living condition survey, persons aged 15 years and over, 2018)

	Males	Females	Total
Agriculture, forestry and fishing	49,079	7,512	56,591
Mining and quarrying	400	49	449
Manufacturing	144,967	28,032	172,999
Electricity, gas and water supply	11,315	576	11,891
Construction	137,170	3,625	140,795
Wholesale and retail trade; repair of motor vehicles and motorcycles	245,023	70,414	315,437
Hotels and restaurants	58,846	10,633	69,479
Transport, storage and communications	92,660	11,102	103,762
Financial intermediation	21,408	17,594	39,002
Real estate, renting and business activities	84,705	29,912	114,617
Public administration and defence; compulsory social security	137,092	20,446	157,538
Education	37,834	99,378	137,212
Human health and social work activities	26,916	42,661	69,577
Other community, social and personal service activities	41,865	23,097	64,962
Households with employed persons	9,110	115,116	124,226
Extraterritorial organizations and bodies	5,322	4,340	9,662
Sub-total	1,103,712	484,487	1,588,199
Not classified by economic activity	1,656	546	2,202
Total employed	1,105,368	485,033	1,590,401
Unemployed	122,399	81,247	203,646
Total labour force	1,227,767	566,279	1,794,047

Health and Welfare

KEY INDICATORS

Total fertility rate (children per woman, 2021)	2.1
Under-5 mortality rate (per 1,000 live births, 2021)	8.2
HIV/AIDS (% of persons aged 15–49, 2021)	<0.1
COVID-19: Cumulative confirmed deaths (per 100,000 persons at 30 June 2023)	199.2
COVID-19: Fully vaccinated population (% of total population at 22 December 2022)	44.0
Physicians (per 1,000 head, 2019)	2.6
Hospital beds (per 1,000 head, 2017)	2.7
Domestic health expenditure (2020): US $ per head (PPP)	350.7
Domestic health expenditure (2020): % of GDP	2.6
Domestic health expenditure (2020): public (% of total current health expenditure)	33.1
Access to improved water resources (% of persons, 2020)	93
Total carbon dioxide emissions ('000 metric tons, 2019)	27,947
Carbon dioxide emissions per head (metric tons, 2019)	4.8
Human Development Index (2021): ranking	112
Human Development Index (2021): value	0.706

Note: For data on COVID-19 vaccinations, 'fully vaccinated' denotes receipt of all doses specified by approved vaccination regime (Sources: Johns Hopkins University and Our World in Data). Data on health expenditure refer to current general government expenditure in each case. For more information on sources and further definitions for all indicators, see Health and Welfare Statistics: Sources and Definitions section (europaworld.com/credits).

Agriculture

PRINCIPAL CROPS
('000 metric tons, FAO estimates unless otherwise indicated)

	2019	2020	2021
Almonds, with shell	29	27	26
Apples	252	243	233
Apricots	33	34	34
Aubergines (Eggplants)	29	27	27
Avocados	17	18	19
Bananas	83	83	84
Barley*	32	30	30
Beans, green	14	14	14
Cabbages and other brassicas	55	55	54
Cantaloupes and other melons	17	18	18
Carrots and turnips	5	5	5
Cauliflowers and broccoli	17	17	16
Cherries, sweet	32	34	34
Cucumbers and gherkins	123	122	121
Figs	4	3	3
Garlic	3	3	3
Grapefruit and pomelos	8	9	9
Grapes	62	61	59
Lemons and limes	106	106	106
Lettuce and chicory	19	16	17
Olives	145	160	144
Onions, dry	81	81	82
Oranges	164	165	164
Peaches and nectarines	53	50	48
Pears	32	33	32
Plums and sloes	37	39	40
Potatoes	618	645	659
Pumpkins, squash and gourds	28	28	28
Tangerines, mandarins, etc.	27	26	26
Tobacco, unmanufactured	10	10	10
Tomatoes	271	271	271
Watermelons	62	61	60
Wheat*	140	100	100

* Unofficial figures.

Aggregate production ('000 metric tons, may include official, semi-official or estimated data): Total cereals 176 in 2019, 134 in 2020, 134 in 2021; Total fruit (primary) 1,049 in 2019, 1,037 in 2020, 1,024 in 2021; Total oilcrops 154 in 2019, 170 in 2020, 154 in 2021; Total roots and tubers 619 in 2019, 645 in 2020, 660 in 2021; Total vegetables (primary) 700 in 2019, 693 in 2020, 692 in 2021.

Source: FAO.

LEBANON

LIVESTOCK
('000 head, year ending September, FAO estimates)

	2019	2020	2021
Asses	14	14	14
Cattle	86	86	87
Chickens	71,828	68,047	67,770
Goats	522	527	531
Sheep	431	432	431

Source: FAO.

LIVESTOCK PRODUCTS
('000 metric tons, FAO estimates)

	2019	2020	2021
Cattle meat	49.3	46.0	45.5
Cows' milk	350.0	322.1	337.4
Chicken meat	121.0	116.6	114.0
Goats' milk	28.7	28.9	29.1
Sheep meat	5.6	4.8	4.5
Sheep's (Ewes') milk	18.8	18.7	18.2
Hen eggs	39.8	42.2	41.6

Source: FAO.

Forestry

ROUNDWOOD REMOVALS
(cubic metres, excluding bark, FAO estimates)

	2019	2020	2021
Sawlogs, veneer logs and logs for sleepers*	7,150	7,150	7,150
Fuel wood	18,577	18,546	18,546
Total	25,727	25,696	25,696

* Figures assumed to be unchanged since 1992.
Source: FAO.

SAWNWOOD PRODUCTION
('000 cubic metres, including railway sleepers, FAO estimates)

	2019	2020	2021
Total (all broadleaved)	9.1	9.1	9.1

Note: Figures assumed to be unchanged from 1993.
Source: FAO.

Fishing

(metric tons, live weight)

	2019	2020*	2021*
Capture	2,620	2,455	2,580
Bogue	128	140	175
Spinefeet (Rabbitfishes)	153	150	190
White seabream	297	265	265
Axillary seabream	85	140	140
Barracudas	16	75	75
Mullets	0	0	0
Clupeoids	27	50	100
Little tunny	270	200	200
Aquaculture	936*	828	778
Rainbow trout	900*	800	750
Total catch	3,556*	3,283	3,358

* FAO estimate(s).
Source: FAO.

Mining

('000 metric tons unless otherwise indicated)

	2017	2018	2019
Gold (kg)*	8,600	8,100	12,000†
Lead (secondary)†	12	6	2
Phosphate for fertilizers	187	215	182†
Other phosphates, compounds, phosphoric acid	80	120	120†
Stone, crushed, limestone, for cement†	7,000	7,000	6,000

* Refinery output, Au content.
† Estimate(s).

Gypsum: 110 in 2013.
Salt (unrefined): 15 in 2014.
Source: US Geological Survey.

Industry

SELECTED PRODUCTS
('000 metric tons unless otherwise indicated)

	2020	2021	2022
Cement (deliveries)	1,958.2	1,950.7	2,124.3
Wine	3*	n.a.	n.a.
Electrical energy (million kWh)	12,324	7,856	2,821

* FAO estimate.

Cigarettes: 6,266 metric tons in 2019.

Finance

CURRENCY AND EXCHANGE RATES

Monetary Units:
100 piastres = 1 Lebanese pound (£L).

Sterling, Dollar and Euro Equivalents (28 April 2023):
£1 sterling = £L18,695.3;
US $1 = £L15,000.0;
€1 = £L16,471.5;
£L10,000 = £0.53 sterling = $0.67 = €0.61.

Exchange Rate: The official exchange rate was maintained at US $1 = £L1,507.5 from September 1999 until February 2023, when worsening economic conditions forced the Government to introduce a currency devaluation of some 90%, resetting the official exchange rate to 15,000 Lebanese pounds to the US dollar. Despite this drastic measure, a parallel unofficial exchange rate in excess of 100,000 pounds per dollar was widely reported by mid-2023. Data in local currency in the foregoing tables have not yet been adjusted to reflect the February 2023 devaluation.

BUDGET
(excl. treasury transactions, £L '000 million)

Revenue	2018	2019	2020
Tax revenue	12,765.7	12,534.7	10,473.9
Customs revenues	2,024.9	1,800.3	1,289.9
Value added tax	3,840.9	3,258.3	1,864.1
Miscellaneous tax revenue	6,900.0	7,476.1	6,219.4
Real estate registration fees	n.a.	n.a.	1,100.5
Non-tax revenue	3,423.4	3,355.5	3,211.7
Telecommunications revenues	1,614.1	1,428.0	1,520.0
Total	16,189.1	15,890.2	13,685.6

LEBANON

Statistical Survey

Expenditure	2018	2019	2020
General expenditures	16,206.7	15,236.6	14,070.4
Transfers to Électricité du Liban	2,647.3	2,269.2	1,393.5
Commitments carried over	2,064.5	2,841.5	2,390.1
Interest payments	8,156.0	8,067.8	2,917.0
Interest on foreign debt	3,381.2	3,226.5	233.2
Repayment on foreign debt	301.3	298.1	189.2
Total	24,664.0	23,602.4	17,176.6

Source: Banque du Liban, Beirut.

INTERNATIONAL RESERVES
(US $ million at 31 December)

	2020	2021	2022
Gold (national valuation)	17,324.2	16,596.4	16,651.4
IMF special drawing rights	282.0	4.4	1.7
Reserve position in IMF	182.1	177.0	168.3
Foreign exchange	24,536.6	18,272.8	15,629.4
Total	42,324.8	35,050.6	32,450.8

Source: IMF, *International Financial Statistics*.

MONEY SUPPLY
(£L '000 million at 31 December)

	2015	2016	2017
Currency outside banks	4,013.8	4,592.3	4,889.0
Demand deposits at commercial banks	4,906.9	5,436.9	5,628.8
Total money (incl. others)	9,042.4	10,159.1	10,654.6

Source: IMF, *International Financial Statistics*.

COST OF LIVING
(Consumer Price Index; base: December 2013 = 100)

	2020	2021	2022
Food and non-alcoholic beverages	416.5	1,632.9	5,551.9
Clothing and footwear	823.9	2,471.3	6,331.1
Housing and utilities	115.8	173.3	332.5
All items (incl. others)	202.9	516.8	1,401.6

NATIONAL ACCOUNTS
(£L '000 million at current prices)

Expenditure on the Gross Domestic Product

	2018	2019	2020
Government final consumption expenditure	12,693	12,534	14,996
Private final consumption expenditure	73,597	75,090	101,441
Gross fixed capital formation	18,611	9,882	9,138
Changes in stocks			
Total domestic expenditure	104,901	97,506	125,575
Exports of goods and services	17,177	16,599	26,891
Less Imports of goods and services	39,315	33,909	56,766
GDP in purchasers' values	82,764	80,196	95,700

Gross Domestic Product by Economic Activity

	2018	2019	2020
Agriculture, hunting, forestry and fishing	2,675	2,541	8,556
Mining and quarrying	340	243	317
Manufacturing	6,162	5,655	11,724
Electricity, gas and water	1,988	2,156	2,106
Construction	2,936	1,970	2,733
Wholesale, retail trade, vehicle maintenance and repair	10,685	9,668	14,665
Hotels and restaurants	2,474	2,398	1,947
Transport, storage and communications	4,089	4,042	5,058
Finance and insurance	7,043	7,378	8,379
Real estate, professional, scientific and technical services	18,387	18,536	20,811
Public administration and defence	9,434	9,732	12,397
Education	6,146	6,428	6,466
Health and social care	3,068	2,999	1,872
Personal and community services	2,396	2,425	6,186
Sub-total	77,822	76,171	103,216
Indirect taxes (net)	4,942	4,025	−7,517
GDP in purchasers' values	82,764	80,196	95,700

BALANCE OF PAYMENTS
(US $ million)

	2019	2020	2021
Exports of goods	4,535.2	3,819.0	4,299.7
Imports of goods	−17,989.5	−10,403.3	−12,642.4
Balance on goods	−13,454.4	−6,584.2	−8,342.7
Exports of services	13,673.3	4,954.2	5,847.2
Imports of services	−13,157.2	−4,802.4	−4,740.6
Balance on goods and services	−12,938.3	−6,432.4	−7,236.0
Primary income received	3,095.2	1,590.3	703.6
Primary income paid	−4,344.7	−2,633.4	−1,601.5
Balance on goods, services and primary income	−14,187.8	−7,475.6	−8,133.8
Secondary income received	8,312.4	7,710.9	7,679.6
Secondary income paid	−5,389.2	−3,230.8	−2,531.0
Current balance	−11,264.6	−2,995.5	−2,985.2
Capital account (net)	1,447.8	1,671.3	943.4
Direct investment assets	−339.0	−10.5	−28.0
Direct investment liabilities	1,906.4	1,623.3	597.2
Portfolio investment assets	1,239.5	844.0	−280.0
Portfolio investment liabilities	−2,345.7	1,361.5	812.6
Other investment assets	7,801.4	403.0	2,431.0
Other investment liabilities	−4,722.1	−8,538.9	−6,413.8
Net errors and omissions	3,886.3	−8,478.2	−3,569.6
Reserves and related items	−2,390.1	−14,120.0	−8,492.5

Source: IMF, *International Financial Statistics*.

LEBANON

External Trade

PRINCIPAL COMMODITIES
(distribution by HS, £L '000 million)

Imports c.i.f.	2020	2021	2022
Live animals and animal products	934.3	752.4	1,389.6
Vegetables and vegetable products	1,201.6	1,260.9	2,557.6
Prepared foodstuffs; beverages, spirits and vinegar; tobacco and articles thereof	1,130.1	1,211.5	2,532.2
Mineral products	4,951.7	6,067.0	14,518.0
Mineral fuels, mineral oils and products thereof	4,866.4	5,928.7	14,299.9
Petroleum oils, not crude	4,663.6	5,617.3	13,586.3
Chemicals and related products	2,543.8	2,204.9	3,076.6
Pharmaceutical products	1,785.9	1,357.6	1,471.4
Medicament mixtures	1,076.0	767.0	1,036.5
Plastics, rubber and articles thereof	525.2	744.7	1,631.6
Plastics and articles thereof	465.5	616.4	1,280.9
Textiles and textile articles	401.5	510.6	1,315.8
Pearls, precious or semi-precious stones, precious metals, and articles thereof	1,348.3	1,867.4	3,685.6
Gold	885.0	1,003.9	2,246.7
Iron and steel, other base metals and articles of base metal	588.1	890.1	2,103.7
Iron and steel	290.7	464.8	1,093.8
Machinery and mechanical appliances; electrical equipment; parts thereof	1,459.9	1,878.9	5,573.1
Boilers, machinery and mechanical appliances	971.9	901.4	2,132.6
Electrical machinery and equipment and parts thereof	488.0	977.5	3,440.5
Vehicles, aircraft, vessels and associated transport equipment	607.6	1,678.2	4,000.8
Vehicles other than railway	545.9	1,591.8	3,676.8
Total (incl. others)	17,122.8	20,896.2	46,672.4

Exports f.o.b.	2020	2021	2022
Vegetables and vegetable products	365.6	790.9	996.4
Prepared foodstuffs; beverages, spirits and vinegar; tobacco and articles thereof	595.9	644.8	1,056.9
Edible fruit and nuts	183.1	610.6	477.5
Chemicals and related products	501.9	530.5	973.2
Plastics, rubber and articles thereof	166.1	179.9	708.4
Plastics and articles thereof	158.1	175.5	696.7
Pulp of wood, paper and paperboard and articles thereof	139.5	143.7	263.4
Pearls, precious or semi-precious stones, precious metals, and articles thereof	2,226.0	1,577.1	2,328.3
Gold	1,644.7	681.4	664.3
Iron and steel, other base metals and articles of base metal	473.0	732.4	1,211.0
Iron and steel	142.7	266.4	372.7
Ferrous waste and scrap; remelting scrap ingots	130.4	244.4	344.0
Copper and articles thereof	112.0	166.4	269.8
Copper waste and scrap	102.1	154.3	254.3
Machinery and mechanical appliances; electrical equipment; sound and parts thereof	698.0	724.3	1,513.0
Boilers, machinery and mechanical appliances	324.1	288.4	474.5
Electrical machinery and equipment and parts thereof	374.0	435.8	1,038.5
Electric generating sets and rotary converters	192.6	235.5	503.6
Total (incl. others)	6,159.5	7,016.7	12,234.0

Source: Lebanese Customs Administration, Ministry of Finance, Beirut.

PRINCIPAL TRADING PARTNERS
(£L '000 million)

Imports c.i.f.	2020	2021	2022
Azerbaijan	1.0	46.5	504.7
Belgium	308.6	383.4	486.8
Brazil	267.8	213.8	513.0
China, People's Republic	1,128.0	1,914.8	6,511.5
Cyprus	158.6	514.3	513.1
Egypt	482.4	548.6	1,887.4
France	578.3	522.2	899.7
Germany	850.4	934.7	1,496.3
Greece	1,301.3	2,063.8	4,754.0
India	226.0	397.5	1,706.9
Italy	984.7	977.7	2,262.4
Japan	150.4	255.4	647.8
Netherlands	382.5	216.4	714.0
Romania	229.7	199.9	392.6
Russian Federation	779.1	917.9	627.9
Saudi Arabia	276.7	261.5	710.1
Spain	484.4	438.6	835.5
Switzerland	488.1	494.3	1,355.7
Türkiye	1,259.5	2,290.8	6,190.1
Ukraine	410.7	520.7	756.0
United Arab Emirates	955.7	1,156.5	1,358.7
United Kingdom	403.3	503.2	776.1
USA	1,409.0	1,159.9	2,106.8
Venezuela	25.4	215.4	488.7
Total (incl. others)	17,122.8	20,896.2	46,672.5

LEBANON

Statistical Survey

Exports f.o.b.	2020	2021	2022
Algeria	33.3	19.0	31.7
Congo, Republic	49.9	70.4	174.3
Côte d'Ivoire	68.0	103.9	198.9
Egypt	194.9	279.9	462.9
France	88.4	124.4	563.7
Germany	62.8	58.3	107.1
Greece	120.0	143.6	208.6
Iraq	274.2	258.3	577.9
Italy	68.6	73.2	190.4
Jordan	131.2	137.7	259.4
Korea, Republic	72.6	136.0	231.6
Kuwait	116.7	140.1	218.6
Nigeria	46.9	46.9	76.1
Qatar	238.6	318.8	386.7
Saudi Arabia	346.4	203.6	0.6
South Africa	3.7	3.2	9.2
Spain	66.6	100.0	146.7
Switzerland	1,596.4	646.5	565.2
Syrian Arab Republic	189.0	165.4	665.4
Türkiye	190.7	172.2	643.3
United Arab Emirates	880.5	1,568.2	2,576.9
United Kingdom	52.9	46.4	84.0
USA	243.9	232.5	444.1
Total (incl. others)	6,159.5	7,016.7	12,234.0

Source: Lebanese Customs Administration, Ministry of Finance, Beirut.

Transport

SHIPPING

Flag Registered Fleet
(at 31 December)

	2020	2021	2022
Number of vessels	38	40	45
Total displacement ('000 grt)	210.8	208.5	230.6

Source: Lloyd's List Intelligence (www.bit.ly/LLintelligence).

International Seaborne Freight Traffic
('000 metric tons)

	2020	2021	2022
Goods loaded	803	862	960
Goods unloaded	3,728	3,785	4,559

Source: Banque du Liban, Beirut.

CIVIL AVIATION
(traffic on scheduled services)

	2013	2014	2015
Kilometres flown (million)	40	40	41
Passengers carried ('000)	2,241	2,419	2,583
Passenger-km (million)	3,981	4,288	4,544
Total ton-km (million)	70	60	54

Source: UN, *Statistical Yearbook*.

2021 (domestic and international): Departures 13,934; Passengers carried 1.6m.; Freight carried 22m. ton-km (Source: World Bank, World Development Indicators database).

Tourism

FOREIGN TOURIST ARRIVALS
('000)*

Country of nationality	2019	2020	2021
Australia	75.6	8.3	3.2
Canada	113.1	22.7	25.1
Egypt	92.5	23.4	19.0
Ethiopia	23.1	5.4	7.0
France	181.1	46.2	42.6
Germany	106.4	30.1	52.9
Iraq	196.3	52.9	77.7
Jordan	87.4	13.2	11.7
Kuwait	43.3	4.1	4.6
Saudi Arabia	88.1	6.8	1.4
Sweden	47.2	12.0	24.3
Türkiye	33.9	9.3	9.7
United Kingdom	74.2	17.0	14.7
USA	192.7	38.1	63.3
Total (incl. others)	1,936.3	414.2	470.7

* Figures exclude arrivals of Syrian nationals, Palestinians and students.

Tourism receipts (US $ million, excl. passenger transport): 8,593 in 2019; 2,353 in 2020; 3,135 in 2021 (provisional) (Source: World Tourism Organization).

Communications Media

	2019	2020	2021
Telephones ('000 main lines in use)	882.2	875.5	875.5
Mobile telephone subscriptions ('000)	4,238.0	4,288.2	4,288.2
Broadband subscriptions, fixed ('000)	420.0	432.1	432.1
Broadband subscriptions, mobile ('000)	2,934.9	4,348.5	4,348.5
Internet users (% of population)	79.8	83.1	86.6

Source: International Telecommunication Union.

Education

(2020/21 unless otherwise indicated)

	Institutions	Teachers	Students
Pre-primary	1,938[1]	13,009	187,343
Primary	2,160[1]	12,788	509,734
Secondary:			
general	n.a.	50,049[2]	424,028
vocational	275[3]	11,022[4]	62,551[5]
Higher	n.a.	45,916[6]	242,642[7]

[1] 1996/97 figure.
[2] 2015/16 figure.
[3] 1994 figure.
[4] 2010/11 figure.
[5] 2017/18 figure.
[6] 2013/14 figure.
[7] 2018/19 figure.

Sources: UNESCO Institute for Statistics; Banque du Liban, *Annual Report*.

Pupil-teacher ratio (qualified teaching staff, primary education, UNESCO estimate): 17.8 in 2020/21 (Source: UNESCO Institute for Statistics).

Adult literacy rate (UNESCO estimates): 95.3% (males 97.0%; females 93.6%) in 2019 (Source: UNESCO Institute for Statistics).

Directory

The Constitution

The Constitution was promulgated on 23 May 1926 and amended by the Constitutional Laws of 1927, 1929, 1943, 1947 and 1990.

According to the Constitution, the Republic of Lebanon is an independent and sovereign state, and no part of the territory may be alienated or ceded. Lebanon has no state religion. Arabic is the official language. Beirut is the capital.

All Lebanese are equal in the eyes of the law. Personal freedom and freedom of the press are guaranteed and protected. The religious communities are entitled to maintain their own schools, on condition that they conform to the general requirements relating to public instruction, as defined by the state. Dwellings are inviolable; rights of ownership are protected by law. Every Lebanese citizen over 21 is an elector and qualifies for the franchise.

LEGISLATIVE POWER

Legislative power is exercised by one house, the National Assembly, with 108 seats (raised, without amendment of the Constitution, to 128 in 1992), which are divided equally between Christians and Muslims. Members of the National Assembly must be over 25 years of age, in possession of their full political and civil rights, and literate. They are considered representative of the whole nation, and are not bound to follow directives from their constituencies. They can be suspended only by a two-thirds' majority of their fellow members. Secret ballot was introduced in a new election law of April 1960.

The National Assembly holds two sessions yearly, from the first Tuesday after 15 March to the end of May, and from the first Tuesday after 15 October to the end of the year. The normal term of the National Assembly is four years; general elections take place within 60 days before the end of this period. If the Assembly is dissolved before the end of its term, elections are held within three months of dissolution.

Voting in the Assembly is public—by acclamation, or by standing and sitting. A quorum of two-thirds and a majority vote is required for constitutional issues. The only exceptions to this occur when the Assembly becomes an electoral college, and chooses the President of the Republic or Secretaries to the National Assembly, or when the President is accused of treason or of violating the Constitution. In such cases voting is secret, and a two-thirds' majority is needed for a proposal to be adopted.

EXECUTIVE POWER

With the incorporation of the Ta'if agreement into the Lebanese Constitution in August 1990, executive power was effectively transferred from the presidency to the Cabinet. The President is elected for a term of six years and is not immediately re-eligible. He is responsible for the promulgation and execution of laws enacted by the National Assembly, but all presidential decisions (with the exception of those to appoint a Prime Minister or to accept the resignation of a government) require the co-signature of the Prime Minister, who is head of the Government, implementing its policies and speaking in its name. The President must receive the approval of the Cabinet before dismissing a minister or ratifying an international treaty. The ministers and the Prime Minister are chosen by the President of the Republic in consultation with the members and President of the National Assembly. They are not necessarily members of the National Assembly, although they are responsible to it and have access to its debates. The President of the Republic must be a Maronite Christian, and the Prime Minister a Sunni Muslim; the choice of the other ministers must reflect the level of representation of the communities in the Assembly.

Note: In October 1998 the National Assembly endorsed an exceptional amendment to Article 49 of the Constitution to enable the election of Gen. Emile Lahoud, then Commander-in-Chief of the Army, as President of the Republic: the Constitution requires that senior state officials relinquish their responsibilities two years prior to seeking public office. In September 2004 the National Assembly voted in favour of a constitutional amendment extending President Lahoud's term of office for a further three years.

The Government

HEAD OF STATE

President: Najib Miqati (acting).

Following four unsuccessful attempts (on 29 September 2022 and 13, 20 and 24 October) by the National Assembly to elect a new President to succeed the incumbent, Michel Aoun, the latter left office on 30 October, one day before his mandate officially expired and without a designated successor. In accordance with the Constitution, in the event of the presidency falling vacant, presidential powers were to be assumed by the Cabinet, with the Prime Minister becoming acting head of state. However, since Prime Minister Najib Miqati and his Government held office in an acting capacity, their executive powers were limited. On 10 November the National Assembly failed in a fifth attempt to elect a new President; seven further attempts, on 17 and 24 November, on 1, 8 and 15 December and on 19 January and 14 June 2023, also proved unsuccessful.

INTERIM CABINET
(September 2023)

Prime Minister: Najib Miqati.
Deputy Prime Minister: Saade Chami.
Minister of Education and Higher Education: Abbas Halabi.
Minister of Finance: Youssef Khalil.
Minister of Youth and Sports: George Kallas.
Minister of Foreign Affairs and Expatriates: Abdullah Bou Habib.
Minister of Industry: George Pushkian.
Minister of Information: Ziad al-Makari.
Minister of the Interior and Municipalities: Bassam Mawlaoui.
Minister of National Defence: Maurice Selim.
Minister of Public Works and Transportation: Ali Hamieh.
Minister of Tourism: Walid Nassar.
Minister of Justice: Henri Khoury.
Minister of Economy and Trade: Amin Salam.
Minister of Public Health: Firas Abiad.
Minister of Labour: Mustapha Beyram.
Minister of Social Affairs: Hiktor el-Hajjar.
Minister of Agriculture: Abbas Hajj Hasan.
Minister of Telecommunications: Johnny Qorm.
Minister of the Environment: Nasser Yassine.
Minister of the Displaced: Issam Sharaf Eddine Shuhayeb.
Minister of Culture: Mohammed Wissam Murtada.
Minister of Energy and Water: Walid Fayyad.
Minister of State for Administrative Development Affairs: Najla Riachi.

MINISTRIES

Presidency of the Republic of Lebanon: Presidential Palace, Baabda, Beirut; tel. (5) 900900; fax (5) 900919; e-mail president_office@presidency.gov.lb; internet www.presidency.gov.lb.

Office of the President of the Council of Ministers: Grand Sérail, place Riad el-Solh, Beirut; tel. (1) 746800; fax (1) 983065; e-mail conseilm@pcm.gov.lb; internet www.pcm.gov.lb.

Ministry of Agriculture: Embassies St, Bir Hassan, Beirut; tel. (1) 849600; fax (1) 849620; e-mail ealawiea@agriculture.gov.lb; internet www.agriculture.gov.lb.

Ministry of Culture: Immeuble Hatab, rue Madame Curie, Verdun, Beirut; tel. (1) 744250; fax (1) 756322; internet www.culture.gov.lb.

Ministry of the Displaced: POB 9150, Minet el-Hosn, Starco Centre, Beirut; tel. (1) 366373; fax (1) 366087; e-mail modbeirut@hotmail.com; internet www.ministryofdisplaced.gov.lb.

Ministry of Economy and Trade: 5th Floor, Azarieh Bldg, rue Riad el-Solh, Hamra, Beirut; tel. (1) 982360; fax (1) 982293; e-mail info@economy.gov.lb; internet www.economy.gov.lb.

Ministry of Education and Higher Education: Unesco Quarter, Habib Abi Chahla, Beirut; tel. (1) 772500; fax (1) 772529; e-mail info@higher-edu.gov.lb; internet www.higher-edu.gov.lb.

Ministry of Energy and Water: Beirut River Highway, Beirut; tel. (1) 565040; fax (1) 449639; e-mail minister@energyandwater.gov.lb; internet www.energyandwater.gov.lb.

Ministry of the Environment: POB 11-2727, 7th and 8th Floors, Lazarieh Centre, Beirut; tel. (1) 976555; fax (1) 976535; e-mail webmaster@moe.gov.lb; internet www.moe.gov.lb.

Ministry of Finance: MOF Bldg, place Riad el-Solh, Beirut; tel. (1) 981001; fax (1) 982189; e-mail infocenter@finance.gov.lb; internet www.finance.gov.lb.

Ministry of Foreign Affairs and Expatriates: POB 9180, Bustros Palace, Achrafieh, Beirut; tel. (1) 213511; fax (1) 204895; e-mail mfa@foreign.gov.lb; internet mfa.gov.lb.

LEBANON

Ministry of Industry: Ministry of Industry and Petroleum Bldg, ave Sami Soleh, Beirut; tel. (1) 427006; fax (1) 429337; internet www.industry.gov.lb.

Ministry of Information: rue Hamra, Beirut; tel. (1) 351038; fax (1) 343370; e-mail dghassanf@nna-leb.gov.lb; internet www.ministryinfo.gov.lb.

Ministry of the Interior and Municipalities: Grand Sérail, place Riad el-Solh, Beirut; tel. (1) 751602; fax (1) 750084; e-mail admin@moim.gov.lb; internet www.moim.gov.lb.

Ministry of Justice: rue Sami Solh, Adlieh, Beirut; tel. (1) 422944; fax (1) 611142; internet www.justice.gov.lb.

Ministry of Labour: al-Baraj Bldg, Shiah, Beirut; tel. (1) 556804; fax (1) 556806; e-mail ministry@labor.gov.lb; internet www.labor.gov.lb.

Ministry of National Defence: Yarze, Beirut; tel. (5) 420000; fax (5) 951014; e-mail difaa@mod.gov.lb; internet www.mod.gov.lb.

Ministry of Public Health: Bir Hassan, Jnah, Beirut; tel. (1) 830300; fax (1) 615773; e-mail info@moph.gov.lb; internet www.moph.gov.lb.

Ministry of Public Works and Transportation: 3rd Floor, Starco Center, Georges Picot St, Beirut; tel. (1) 371644; fax (1) 371647; internet www.transportation.gov.lb.

Ministry of Social Affairs: rue Badro, Beirut; tel. (1) 611260; fax (1) 611245; e-mail info@socialaffairs.gov.lb; internet www.socialaffairs.gov.lb.

Ministry of State for Administrative Development Affairs: 5th Floor, Immeuble Starco, rue Omar Daouk, place Minet el-Hosn 2020 3313, Beirut; tel. (1) 371510; fax (1) 371599; e-mail info@omsar.gov.lb; internet www.omsar.gov.lb.

Ministry of State for Parliamentary Affairs: Beirut.

Ministry of State for Women and Youth Economic Empowerment Affairs: Beirut.

Ministry of Telecommunications: Ministry of Telecom Bldg, 1st Floor, place Riad el-Solh, Beirut; tel. (1) 979979; fax (1) 979316; e-mail webmaster@mpt.gov.lb; internet www.mpt.gov.lb.

Ministry of Tourism: POB 11-5344, rue Banque du Liban 550, Beirut; tel. (1) 340940; fax (1) 340945; e-mail info@destinationlebanon.gov.lb; internet mot.gov.lb.

Ministry of Youth and Sports: rue Sami Solh, Beirut; tel. (1) 424388; fax (1) 426658; internet www.minijes.gov.lb.

Legislature

The equal distribution of seats among Christians and Muslims is determined by law, and the Cabinet must reflect the level of representation achieved by the various religious denominations within that principal division. Deputies of the same religious denomination do not necessarily share the same political or party allegiances. The distribution of seats is as follows: Maronite Catholics 34; Sunni Muslims 27; Shi'a Muslims 27; Greek Orthodox 14; Druzes 8; Greek-Melkite Catholics 8; Armenian Orthodox 5; Alawites 2; Armenian Catholics 1; Protestants 1; Others 1.

The 2022 elections were contested under a hybrid system, combining proportional representation for party lists and the above quotas as determined by religious denomination.

National Assembly: place de l'Etoile, Beirut; tel. (1) 955000; e-mail info@lp.gov.lb; internet www.lp.gov.lb.

President: NABIH BERRI.

General Election, 15 May 2022

Party	Seats
Lebanese Forces Party (LFP)	21
Free Patriotic Movement (FPM)	18
Amal	15
Hezbollah	13
Parti Socialiste Progressiste	8
Pro-Hezbollah independents	8
Ex-Future Movement blocs*	7
Al-Kataeb (Lebanese Social Democratic Party)	5
Armenian Revolutionary Federation—Dashnaktsutiun	3
El-Marada Movement	2
Independence Movement	2
Independents and others	26
Total	**128**

* Although the Future Movement officially boycotted the poll, many of its members resigned from the party in order to contest the election at the head of their own Future Movement-affiliated blocs.

Political Organizations

Amal (Hope—Afwaj al-Muqawamah al-Lubnaniyyah—Lebanese Resistance Detachments): internet www.amal-movement.com; f. 1975 as a politico-military organization; Shi'a political party; contested 2009 legislative elections as part of March 8 Alliance; Leader NABIH BERRI.

Armenian Revolutionary Federation—Dashnaktsutiun (ARF—D): rue Spears, Beirut; internet www.arfd.am; f. 1890; principal Armenian party; historically the dominant nationalist party in independent Armenia 1918–20; prohibited in Armenia under Soviet rule, but continued to operate among the diaspora, incl. in Lebanon; socialist ideology; part of March 8 Alliance; Gen.-Sec. HAGOP PAKRADOUNIAN.

Azm Movement (Tayar al-Azm): e-mail info@azmtayyar.org; internet www.azmtayyar.org; Leader NAJIB MIKATI.

Al-Baath (Baath Arab Socialist Party): Beirut; f. 1948; local branch of secular pro-Syrian party with policy of Arab union; contested 2009 legislative elections as part of March 8 Alliance; Sec.-Gen. ALI HIJAZI.

Bloc National Libanais (Lebanese National Bloc): 291 rue Gouraud, Gemmayzeh, Beirut; tel. (1) 445554; e-mail info@nationalbloc.org; internet nationalbloc.org; f. 1943; right-wing Lebanese party with policy of power sharing between Christians and Muslims and the exclusion of the military from politics; Sec.-Gen. MICHEL HÉLOU.

Free Patriotic Movement (FPM) (Tayar al-Watani al-Horr): Beirut; tel. (3) 122858; e-mail info@tayyar.org; internet www.tayyar.org; aims to recover sovereignty and complete independence for Lebanon; majority of leaders and supporters are from the Christian community, although party is officially secular; largest party in the Change and Reform parliamentary bloc; contested 2009 legislative elections as part of March 8 Alliance; Leader GEBRAN BASSIL.

Future Movement (Tayar al-Mustaqbal): POB 123, Koraytem, Hamra, Beirut; tel. (3) 375442; fax (1) 375442; e-mail info@almustaqbal.org; internet www.almustaqbal.org; opposed to Syrian influence in Lebanese affairs; contested 2009 legislative elections as largest party of the March 14 Alliance.

Hezbollah (Party of God): Beirut; e-mail info@moqawama.org; internet www.moqawama.org; f. 1982 by Iranian Revolutionary Guards who were sent to Lebanon; militant Shi'a faction, which has become the leading organization of Lebanon's Shi'a community and a recognized political party; demands the withdrawal of Israeli forces from the occupied Shebaa Farms area of what it considers to be southern Lebanon (but which is designated by the UN as being part of Syria) and the release of all Lebanese prisoners from Israeli detention; contested 2009 legislative elections as part of March 8 Alliance; Chair. MOHAMMED RA'D; Leader and Sec.-Gen. Sheikh HASAN NASRALLAH; Spiritual Leader Ayatollah MUHAMMAD HUSSAIN FADLALLAH.

Hizb-ut-Tahrir al-Islami (Party of Islamic Liberation): e-mail info@hizb-ut-tahrir.org; internet www.hizb-ut-tahrir.org; f. 1953; transnational org. granted a political parties licence in Lebanon in 2006; aims to establish Islamic caliphate throughout the world; denies claims that it is a militant group; Global Leader Sheikh ABU YASIN ATA BIN KHALIL ABU RASHTA, (Sheikh Ata Abu Rashta).

Independence Movement (Harakat al-Istiklal): Beirut; internet www.michelmoawad.com; Pres. MICHEL MOAWAD.

Al-Kataeb (Lebanese Social Democratic Party): POB 992, place Charles Hélou, Beirut; tel. and fax (1) 325535; e-mail info@kataeb.org; internet kataeb.org; f. 1936 as the Phalangist Party (Phalanges Libanaises); nationalist, reformist, democratic social party; largest Maronite party, although is officially secular; contested 2009 legislative elections as part of March 14 Alliance; Pres. SAMI GEMAYEL.

Lebanese Democratic Party (LDP): Beirut; e-mail webmaster@ldparty.org; internet www.ldparty.org; f. 2001; contested 2009 legislative elections as part of March 8 Alliance; Leader TALAL ARSLAN; Sec.-Gen. WALID BARAKAT.

Lebanese Forces Party (LFP): Beirut; tel. and fax (9) 212989; e-mail contact@lebanese-forces.com; internet www.lebanese-forces.com; political successor to the **Lebanese Forces** (f. 1976; coalition of Maronite Christian militias); launched as political party in 1989; proscribed by the Government in 1994; resumed activities as a legal party in 2005; contested 2009 legislative elections as part of March 14 Alliance; Leader SAMIR GEAGEA.

Lebanese Option Gathering: POB 45-489, Hazmieh, Mar Takla, La Diva Bldg, Beirut; tel. (5) 957257; e-mail info@lebaneseoption.org; internet www.lebaneseoption.org; f. 2007; aims to contest Hezbollah's monopoly over Shi'a political representation in Lebanon, and to reform and develop the south of the country; Leader AHMAD AL-ASSAD.

El-Marada Movement: Zgharta; e-mail info@elmarada.org; internet elmarada.org; f. as the Marada Brigade, relaunched in

LEBANON

1996 as a political party; advocates Lebanese unity, sovereignty and independence; contested 2009 legislative elections as part of March 8 Alliance; Leader SULAYMAN TONY FRANJIYA.

National Dialogue Party: POB 15-5060, Immeuble Marj el-Zouhour, 1st Floor, rue Donna Maria, Ras el-Nabeh, Beirut; tel. (1) 637000; fax (1) 6311234; e-mail info@alhiwar.com; internet www.alhiwar.com; f. 2004; advocates a comprehensive national dialogue to bring about political, social and judicial reforms; also seeks to target corruption and to ensure that the State has authority over the whole of Lebanon; Founder and Chair. FOUAD MUSTAFA MAKHZOUMI.

Parti Communiste Libanais (PCL) (Lebanese Communist Party): rue al-Bahatri, al-Watuat, Beirut; tel. and fax (1) 739616; internet www.lcparty.org; f. 1924; officially dissolved 1948–71; Marxist, with much support among intellectuals; Sec.-Gen. HANNA GHARIB.

Parti National Libéral (PNL) (Al-Wataniyin al-Ahrar): POB 165576, rue du Liban, Beirut; tel. (1) 338000; fax (1) 200335; e-mail ahrar@ahrar.org.lb; internet www.ahrar.org.lb; f. 1958; liberal reformist secular party, although has traditionally had a predominantly Maronite Christian membership; contested 2009 legislative elections as part of March 14 Alliance; Pres. CAMILLE CHAMOUN.

Parti Socialiste Progressiste (PSP) (Al-Takadumi al-Ishteraki): POB 11-2893, Beirut 1107 2120; tel. (1) 309123; fax (1) 318119; e-mail internationalrelation@psp.org.lb; internet www.psp.org.lb; f. 1949; progressive party, advocates constitutional road to socialism and democracy; mainly Druze support; contested 2009 legislative elections as part of March 14 Alliance; Pres. TAYMOUR JUMBLATT.

Syrian Social Nationalist Party (al-Hizb al-Suri al-Qawmi al-Ijtima'i): internet www.ssnp.net; f. 1932 in Beirut; banned 1962–69; seeks creation of a 'Greater Syrian' state, incl. Lebanon, the Syrian Arab Republic, Iraq, Jordan, the Palestinian Territories, Kuwait, Cyprus and parts of Egypt, Iran and Türkiye (Turkey); advocates separation of church and state, the redistribution of wealth and a strong military; supports Syrian involvement in Lebanese affairs; contested 2009 legislative elections as part of March 8 Alliance; Leader ASAAD HARDAN.

Al-Wa'ad (National Secular Democratic Party—Pledge): Beirut; tel. (2) 4360340; e-mail parti.pds@gmail.com; f. 1986 by the late Elie Hobeika; pro-Syrian splinter group of Lebanese Forces; officially secular, although most supporters are Maronite Christians; aligned with March 8 Alliance; did not achieve parliamentary representation in June 2009 legislative elections.

Other parties include the **Independent Nasserite Movement** (Murabitoun; Sunni Muslim Militia; Leader IBRAHIM QULAYAT) and the **Lebanese Popular Congress** (Pres. KAMAL SHATILA). The **Nasserite Popular Organization** and the **Arab Socialist Union** merged in January 1987, retaining the name of the former. The **Islamic Amal** is a breakaway group from Amal, based in Ba'albek (Leader HUSSEIN MOUSSAVI). **Islamic Jihad** is a pro-Iranian fundamentalist guerrilla group. The **Popular Liberation Army** (f. 1985 by the late MUSTAFA SAAD) is a Sunni Muslim faction, active in the south of Lebanon. **Tawhid Islami** (the Islamic Unification Movement; f. 1982; Sunni Muslim) and the **Arab Democratic Party** (or the Red Knights; Alawites; pro-Syrian; Leader ALI EID) are based in Tripoli.

Diplomatic Representation

EMBASSIES IN LEBANON

Algeria: POB 4797, face Hôtel Summerland, 1 rue Jnah, Sector 8, Beirut; tel. (1) 826712; fax (1) 826711; Ambassador ABDEL KARIM RAKAYBI.

Argentina: Residence des Jardins, Immeuble Moutran, 2e étage, 161 rue Sursock, Achrafieh, Beirut; tel. (1) 210803; fax (1) 210802; e-mail elbno@mrecic.gov.ar; internet www.elbno.mrecic.gov.ar; Ambassador MAURICIO ALICE.

Armenia: rue Jasmin 23/20, Mtaileb, Beirut; tel. (4) 418860; fax (4) 402952; e-mail armlebanonembassy@mfa.am; internet lebanon.mfa.am; Ambassador VAHAGN ATABEKYAN.

Australia: Embassy Complex, Sérail Hill, Beirut; tel. (1) 960600; e-mail consular.beirut@dfat.gov.au; internet www.lebanon.embassy.gov.au; Ambassador ANDREW BARNES.

Austria: POB 11-3924, 812 Immeuble Tabaris, 8e étage, 812 ave Charles Malek, Achrafieh, Beirut 2071 1606; tel. (1) 213017; fax (1) 217772; e-mail beirut-ob@bmeia.gv.at; internet www.bmeia.gv.at/en/embassy/beirut; Ambassador RENÉ AMRY.

Bangladesh: Immeuble al-Riyadh, rue Safara al-Kuwaiti, Bir Hassan, Beirut; tel. (1) 842586; fax (1) 842588; internet beirut.mofa.gov.bd; Ambassador Air Vice-Marshal JAVED TANVEER KHAN (designate).

Belgium: Immeuble Lazarie, 10e étage, rue Emir Béchir, Beirut; tel. (1) 976001; fax (1) 976007; e-mail beirut@diplobel.fed.be; internet lebanon.diplomatie.belgium.be; Ambassador KOEN VERVAEKE.

Brazil: POB 11-562, rue de l'Armée, Colline du Sérail, Beirut; tel. (1) 982161; fax (1) 982159; e-mail brasemb.beirute@itamaraty.gov.br; internet beirute.itamaraty.gov.br; Ambassador TARCISIO DE LIMA FERREIRA FERNANDES COSTA.

Bulgaria: POB 11-6544, Sector 6, Mar-Takla, Hazmieh, Beirut; tel. (5) 452883; fax (5) 452892; e-mail embassy.beirut@mfa.bg; internet www.mfa.bg/embassies/lebanon; Chargé d'affaires a.i. ALEXANDRINA GIGOVA.

Canada: POB 60163, Immeuble Coolrite, 1er et 2e étage, Autoroute Jal el-Dib 43, Beirut; tel. (4) 726700; fax (4) 726702; e-mail berut@international.gc.ca; internet international.gc.ca/world-monde/lebanon-liban/beirut-beyrouth.aspx; Ambassador STEFANIE MCCOLLUM.

Chile: Nouvelle Naccache, Sector 2, rue 64, Immeuble Antoine Boukather, 1er étage, Beirut; tel. (4) 418670; fax (4) 418672; e-mail echile.ellibano@minrel.gob.cl; internet chile.gob.cl/libano; Ambassador CARLOS MORÁN LÉON.

China, People's Republic: POB 11-8227, 72 rue Nicolas Ibrahim Sursock, Ramlet el-Baida, Beirut 1107 2260; tel. (1) 850315; fax (1) 822492; e-mail chinaemb_lb@mfa.gov.cn; internet lb.china-embassy.org; Ambassador QIAN MINJIAN.

Colombia: Immeuble Sarkis Group, 8e étage, Zalka Highway, Amaret Chalhoub, Beirut; tel. (1) 895381; fax (1) 895380; e-mail ebeirut@cancilleria.gov.co; internet libano.embajada.gov.co; Chargé d'affaires a.i. EDWIN OSTOS ALFONSO.

Cuba: 43 Immeuble Raymond Nouhra, 1e étage, 44 rue des Officiers, Mar-Takla, Hazmieh, Beirut 2901 6727; tel. (1) 459925; fax (1) 950070; e-mail libancub@cyberia.net.lb; internet misiones.minrex.gob.cu/es/libano; Chargé d'affaires a.i. JORGE P. LEON CRUZ.

Cyprus: 6 Immeuble Yarzeh Pine, rue 15, Baabda, Beirut; tel. (5) 929006; fax (5) 922643; e-mail beirutembassy@mfa.gov.cy; internet www.mfa.gov.cy/embassybeirut; Ambassador (vacant).

Czech Republic: POB 40195, 17, 419th Rd, Mount Lebanon, Baabda, Beirut 21007; tel. (5) 929010; fax (5) 922120; e-mail beirut@embassy.mzv.cz; internet www.mzv.cz/beirut; Ambassador JIŘÍ DOLEŽEL.

Denmark: POB 11-5190, rue de l'Armée, Colline du Sérail, Beirut; tel. (1) 991001; fax (1) 991006; e-mail beyamb@um.dk; internet www.libanon.um.dk; Ambassador KRISTOFER VIVIKE.

Egypt: POB 5037, rue Dr Mohamad el-Bezri, Bir Hassan, Beirut; tel. (1) 825566; fax (1) 859988; Ambassador YASSER ALLAWI.

Finland: POB 16-5513, Immeuble Tabaris 812, Bloc A, 4e étage, rue Charles Malek, Achrafieh, Beirut; tel. (1) 218860; fax (1) 218861; e-mail sanomat.bei@formin.fi; internet finlandabroad.fi/web/lbn/mission; Ambassador ANNE MESKANEN.

France: rue de Damas, Espace des Lettres, Ras el-Nabaa, Beirut; tel. (1) 420000; fax (1) 420013; e-mail cad.beyrouth-amb@diplomatie.gouv.fr; internet www.ambafrance-lb.org; Ambassador ANNE GRILLO.

Germany: POB 55-464, Sin el-Fil, Beirut 1107 2110; tel. (1) 504600; fax (1) 504601; e-mail info@beirut.diplo.de; internet www.beirut.diplo.de; Ambassador (vacant).

Greece: POB 70-319, Immeuble Boukhater, Nouvelle Naccache, rue des Ambassades, Antelias, Beirut; tel. (4) 521700; fax (4) 418774; e-mail gremb.bei@mfa.gr; internet www.mfa.gr/beirut; Ambassador CATHERINE FOUNTOULAKI.

Holy See: POB 1061, Apostolic Nunciature, Jounieh, Beirut; tel. (9) 263102; fax (9) 264488; e-mail anlebanon@gmail.com; Apostolic Nuncio PAOLO BORGIO.

Hungary: POB 113-5259, Immeuble BAC, 9e étage, rue Justinien, Sanayeh, Beirut; tel. (1) 730083; fax (1) 741261; e-mail mission.bej@mfa.gov.hu; internet bejrut.mfa.gov.hu; Ambassador FERENC CSILLAG.

India: POB 113-5240, 239 rue Ibrahim Abed el-Aal, Hamra, Beirut; tel. (1) 735922; fax (1) 741283; e-mail amb.beirut@mea.gov.in; internet www.indianembassybeirut.gov.in; Ambassador MOHD NOOR RAHMAN (designate).

Indonesia: POB 40007, ave Palais Presidential, rue 68, Secteur 3, Baabda, Beirut; tel. (5) 924676; fax (5) 924678; e-mail beirut.kbri@kemlu.go.id; internet www.kemlu.go.id/beirut; Ambassador HAJRIYANTO Y. THOHARI.

Iran: POB 11–5355, Bir Hassan, rue des Ambassades, Beirut; tel. (1) 821224; fax (1) 821229; e-mail iranemb.bey@mfa.gov.ir; internet lebanon.mfa.gov.ir; Ambassador MOJTABA AMANI.

Iraq: Ramlet el-Baida, St No. 77 Dr Philippe Hitti, Beirut; tel. (1) 780006; fax (1) 799916; internet www.mofa.gov.iq/beirut/; Ambassador HAIDER SHIAA AL-BARRAK.

LEBANON

Italy: POB 40057, rue du Palais Présidentiel, Baabda, Beirut 2902 2633; tel. (5) 954955; fax (5) 959616; e-mail amba.beirut@esteri.it; internet www.ambbeirut.esteri.it; Ambassador NICOLETTA BOMBARDIERE.

Japan: POB 11-3360, rue de l'Armée, Zkak al-Blat, Colline du Sérail, Beirut; tel. (1) 989751; fax (1) 989754; internet www.lb.emb-japan.go.jp; Ambassador MASAYUKI MAGOSHI.

Jordan: POB 109, Beirut 5113; tel. (5) 922500; fax (5) 922502; e-mail beirut@fm.gov.jo; Ambassador ZAID ZUREIKAT.

Kazakhstan: Immeuble Abboud Abdel Razzak, 2 étage, rue Abdul Hamid Karami, Bab Idriss, Beirut 1316; tel. (1) 982152; fax (1) 982151; internet www.gov.kz/memleket/entities/mfa-beirut; Ambassador RASUL BEREKETULY.

Korea, Republic: POB 40-290, Immeuble Diplomat 2F, rue Palais Presidentiel, Baabda, Beirut; tel. (5) 922846; fax (5) 922851; e-mail lbkor@mofa.go.kr; internet overseas.mofa.go.kr/lb-ko/index.do; Ambassador PARK IL.

Kuwait: POB 4580, Rond-point du Stade, Bir Hassan, Beirut; tel. (1) 792901; fax (1) 792823; e-mail kw@kuwaitembassy-lb.com; Chargé d'affaires a.i. ABDULLAH SULEIMAN AL-SHAHEEN.

Malaysia: Immeuble Halwani, 5e & 6e étage, rue Salah el-din al-Ayyoubi, Beirut; tel. (1) 787144; fax (1) 787344; e-mail mwbeirut@kln.gov.my; internet www.kln.gov.my/web/lbn_beirut; Ambassador AZRI MAT YACOB.

Mexico: Villa Achkar 6, rue Sabil, Dik el-Mehdi, Metn, Beirut; tel. (4) 927394; fax (4) 926600; e-mail emblibano@sre.gob.mx; internet embamex.sre.gob.mx/libano; Ambassador JOSÉ IGNACIO MADRAZO BOLIVAR.

Morocco: rue Michel Chiha, Baabda, Yarzeh, Beirut; tel. (1) 05924751; fax (1) 05924750; e-mail sifmar@cyberia.net.lb; Ambassador MUHAMMAD GRINE.

Netherlands: POB 167190, Netherlands Tower, ave Charles Malek, Achrafieh, Beirut 2073 0802; tel. (1) 211150; e-mail bei@minbuza.nl; internet www.netherlandsworldwide.nl/countries/lebanon; Ambassador HANS PETER VAN DER WOUDE.

Norway: Immeuble Stratum, 4 rue Omar Dauk, Mina el-Hosn, Beirut; tel. (1) 763200; fax (1) 763298; e-mail emb.beirut@mfa.no; internet norway.no/lebanon; Ambassador MARTIN YTTERVIK.

Oman: Ramlet el-baida, rue Sabah Salem Al Sabah, Immeuble al-Taissir, Beirut; tel. (1) 855757; fax (1) 855454; e-mail beirut@fm.gov.om; Ambassador AHMED AL-SAEEDI.

Pakistan: Immeuble Taiseer, 4e & 5e étage, rue Phillip Hatti, Mosaytbeth, Beirut; tel. (1) 843971; fax (1) 843973; e-mail parepbeirut@mofa.gov.pk; internet www.mofa.gov.pk/lebanon; Ambassador SALMAN ATHAR.

Paraguay: Immeuble La Rosa, Rez-de-chaussée, rue Farid Zeidan, Mar-Takla, Hazmieh, Beirut; tel. (5) 5458502; fax (5) 458503; Chargé d'affaires a.i. FERNANDO AGUSTIN PARISI MORENO.

Philippines: POB 136631, Immeuble W, rue Mar Geries, Hadath, Baabda, Beirut; tel. (5) 953522; fax (5) 953521; e-mail beirut.pe@dfa.gov.ph; internet beirutpe.dfa.gov.ph; Ambassador RAYMOND REYES BALATBAT.

Poland: POB 40-215, Immeuble Khalifa, ave Président Sulayman Franjiya 52, Baabda, Beirut; tel. (5) 468152; fax (5) 924882; e-mail beirut.embassy@msz.gov.pl; internet bejrut.msz.gov.pl; Ambassador PRZEMYSŁAW NIESIOŁOWSKI.

Qatar: rue Bir Hassan, Beirut; tel. (1) 835111; fax (1) 835444; e-mail beirut@mofa.gov.qa; internet beirut.embassy.qa; Ambassador Sheikh SAUD BIN ABDULRAHMAN BIN FAISAL THANI AL THANI (designate).

Romania: rue du Palais Présidentiel, Baabda, Beirut; tel. (5) 924848; fax (5) 924747; e-mail beirut@mae.ro; internet beirut.mae.ro; Ambassador RADU CĂTĂLIN MARDARE.

Russian Federation: POB 5220, rue Mar Elias el-Tineh, Wata Mseitbeh, Beirut; tel. (1) 300041; fax (1) 303837; e-mail embassyofrussia@gmail.com; internet www.lebanon.mid.ru; Ambassador ALEXANDER N. RUDAKOV.

Saudi Arabia: POB 136144, rue Bliss, Hamra, Beirut; tel. (1) 762722; fax (1) 762706; e-mail lbemb@mofa.gov.sa; internet embassies.mofa.gov.sa/sites/Lebanon; Ambassador WALID BUKHARI.

Slovakia: Immeuble Tabco, 4e étage, rue Omar Daouk, Minet el-Hosn, Beirut; tel. (1) 367422; fax (1) 367423; e-mail emb.beirut@mzv.sk; internet www.mzv.sk/web/bejrut; Ambassador MAREK VARGA.

Spain: POB 11-3039, Palais Chehab, Hadath Antounie, Baabda, Beirut 1107 2120; tel. (5) 464120; fax (5) 464030; e-mail emb.beirut@maec.es; internet www.exteriores.gob.es/embajadas/beirut; Ambassador IGNACIO SANTOS AGUADO.

Sri Lanka: POB 175, Hazmieh, Beirut; tel. (5) 769585; fax (5) 769584; e-mail slemb.beirut@mfa.gov.lk; internet www.srilankaembassybeirut.com; Ambassador KAPILA SUSANTHA JAYAWEERA.

Sudan: POB 2504, Hamra, Beirut; tel. (1) 350057; fax (1) 353271; Ambassador ALI AL-SADIQ.

Sweden: POB 11-4883, Riad el-Solh, Beirut; tel. (1) 951200; fax (1) 951201; e-mail ambassaden.beirut@gov.se; internet www.swedenabroad.se/en/embassies/lebanon-beirut; Ambassador ANN DISMORR.

Switzerland: POB 11-172, Immeuble Bourj al-Ghazal, ave Fouad Chehab, Achrafieh, Beirut 1107 2020; tel. (1) 324129; fax (1) 324167; e-mail bey.vertretung@eda.admin.ch; internet www.eda.admin.ch/beirut; Ambassador MARION WEICHELT KRUPSKI.

Syrian Arab Republic: rue Makdessi, Hamra, Beirut; tel. (5) 922581; fax (5) 922589; internet mofaex.gov.sy/beirut-embassy; Ambassador ALI ABDEL KARIM ALI.

Tunisia: Immeuble Haddad, rue Georges Feghali, Mar-Takla, Hazmieh, Beirut; tel. (5) 457431; fax (5) 950434; e-mail at.beyrouth@diplomatie.gov.tn; Ambassador BOURAOUI LIMAM.

Türkiye (Turkey): POB 70-666, Zone II, rue 1, Rabieh, Beirut; tel. (4) 528061; fax (4) 407557; e-mail ambassade.beyrouth@mfa.gov.tr; internet beirut.emb.mfa.gov.tr; Ambassador ALI BARIŞ ULUSOY.

Ukraine: POB 40268, rue Antoine el Rayes, Mount Lebanon, Casa Baabda, Baabda, Beirut; tel. (5) 921975; fax (5) 921974; e-mail emb_lb@mfa.gov.ua; internet lebanon.mfa.gov.ua; Chargé d'affaires a.i. VALERY HRYHORASH.

United Arab Emirates: rue Zayed bin Sultan Al Nahyan, Jnah, Beirut; tel. (1) 829999; fax (1) 828498; e-mail beirutemb@mofaic.gov.ae; internet www.mofaic.gov.ae/en/missions/beirut; Ambassador FAHAD SALEC SAEED MOHAMED AL-KAABI.

United Kingdom: POB 11-471, Embassies Complex, rue de l'Armée, Colline du Sérail, Zkak al-Blat, Beirut; tel. (1) 960800; fax (1) 960855; e-mail ukinlebanon@fcdo.gov.uk; internet www.gov.uk/world/lebanon; Ambassador HAMISH COWELL.

USA: POB 70-840, Antélias, Beirut; tel. (4) 542600; fax (4) 554019; e-mail beirutpd@state.gov; internet lb.usembassy.gov; Ambassador DOROTHY CAMILLE SHEA.

Uruguay: POB 2051, Centre Stella Marris, 7e étage, rue Banque du Liban, Jounieh; tel. (9) 636529; fax (9) 636531; internet www.embauruguaybeirut.org; Ambassador CARLOS GUITTO.

Venezuela: POB 11-603, autoroute Jal el-Dib, Immeuble Bourj el-Hajal, 2e étage, Zalka, Beirut; tel. (4) 718612; fax (4) 718614; e-mail embajadora@embavenelibano.com; Ambassador JESÚS GREGORIO GONZÁLEZ.

Yemen: Bir Hassan, face au Golf Club, Beirut; tel. (1) 852688; fax (1) 821610; e-mail yemb-beirut@mofa.gov.ye; Ambassador ABDUL KARIM AL-DOUIS.

Judicial System

Law and justice in Lebanon are administered in accordance with the following codes, which are based upon modern theories of civil and criminal legislation:

Code de la Propriété (1930).

Code des Obligations et des Contrats (1932).

Code de Procédure Civile (1933).

Code Maritime (1947).

Code de Procédure Pénale (Code Ottoman Modifié).

Code Pénal (1943).

Code Pénal Militaire (1946).

Code d'Instruction Criminelle.

Court of Cassation: comprises the First President and the Presidents of its 11 chambers.

Courts of First Instance: 56 courts, each consisting of a single judge, and dealing in the first instance with both civil and criminal cases; there are 17 such courts in Beirut and 7 in Tripoli.

Courts of Appeal: 11 courts, each consisting of three judges, including a President and a Public Prosecutor, and dealing with civil and criminal cases; there are 5 such courts in Beirut.

State Consultative Council: deals with administrative cases; Pres. FADI ELIAS.

Court of Justice: a special court consisting of a President and 4 judges, deals with matters affecting the security of the State; there is no appeal against its verdicts.

Constitutional Council: 239 ave Camille Chamoun, Hadath; tel. (5) 466184; fax (5) 466191; e-mail info@cc.gov.lb; internet www.cc.gov.lb; considers matters pertaining to the constitutionality of legislation; Pres. TANNUS MASHLAB.

LEBANON   *Directory*

Higher Judicial Council: considers matters involving mems of the executive branch; Pres. SUHAIL ABBOUD.

Military Court: competent to try crimes and misdemeanours involving the armed and security forces; Chief of the Military Court Brig.-Gen. KHALIL ALI JABER.

In addition, Islamic (*Shari'a*), Christian and Jewish religious courts deal with affairs of personal status (marriage, death, inheritance, etc.).

Religion

Of all the countries of the Middle East, Lebanon probably presents the closest juxtaposition of sects and peoples within a small territory. The Maronites, a uniate sect of the Roman Catholic Church, inhabited the old territory of Mount Lebanon, i.e. immediately east of Beirut. In the south, towards the Israeli frontier, Shi'a villages are most common, while between the Shi'a and the Maronites live the Druzes (divided between the Yazbakis and the Joumblatis). The Beqa'a valley has many Greek Christians (both Roman Catholic and Orthodox), while the Tripoli area is mainly Sunni Muslim.

CHRISTIANITY
The Roman Catholic Church
Armenian Rite

Patriarchate of Cilicia: Patriarcat Arménien Catholique, rue de l'Hôpital orthodoxe, Jeitawi, Beirut 2078 5605; tel. (1) 570555; fax (1) 570562; e-mail nerbed19@magnarama.com; internet www.armeniancatholic.org; f. 1742; est. in Beirut since 1929; includes patriarchal diocese of Beirut, with an estimated 12,000 adherents; Patriarch RAPHAËL BEDROS XXI MINASSIAN.

Chaldean Rite

Diocese of Beirut: POB 373, Evêché Chaldéen de Beyrouth, Baabda, Brazilia, Beirut; tel. (5) 457732; fax (5) 457731; e-mail chaldepiscopus@hotmail.com; an estimated 10,000 adherents (31 December 2007); Bishop of Beirut MICHEL KASSARJI.

Latin Rite

Apostolic Vicariate of Beirut: Vicariat Apostolique, POB 11-4224, Riad el-Solh, Beirut 1107 2160; tel. (9) 236101; e-mail vicariat.latin@gmail.com; f. 1954; an estimated 18,000 adherents (31 December 2021); Vicar Apostolic CÉSAR ESSAYAN (Titular Bishop of Mareotes).

Maronite Rite

Patriarchate of Antioch and all the East: Patriarcat Maronite, Bkerké; tel. (9) 915441; fax (9) 933501; includes patriarchal dioceses of Jounieh, Sarba and Jobbé; the Maronite Church in Lebanon comprises 4 archdioceses and 6 dioceses; Patriarch Cardinal BÉCHARA BOUTROS RAÏ.

Archbishop of Antélias: ANTOINE FARÈS BOU NAJEM, Archevêché Maronite, POB 70400, Antélias; tel. (4) 410020; fax (4) 415872.

Archbishop of Beirut: Most Rev. PAUL ABDEL SATER, Archevêché Maronite, 10 rue Collège de la Sagesse, Achrafieh, Beirut; tel. (1) 561980; fax (1) 561930; e-mail maronitebeyrouth@yahoo.fr; also representative of the Holy See for Roman Catholics of the Coptic Rite in Lebanon.

Archbishop of Tripoli: Most Rev. YOUSSEF ANTOINE SOUEIF, Archevêché Maronite, POB 104, rue al-Moutran, Karm Sada, Tripoli; tel. (6) 624324; fax (6) 629393; e-mail rahmat@inco.com.lb.

Archbishop of Tyre: Most Rev. CHARBEL YUSEF ABDALLAH, Archevêché Maronite, Tyre; tel. (7) 740059; fax (7) 344891; e-mail abounacharbel@cyberia.net.lb.

Melkite Rite

Patriarch of Antioch: Patriarcat Grec-Melkite Catholique, POB 22249, 12 ave al-Zeitoon, Bab Charki, Damascus, Syrian Arab Republic; tel. (11) 5441030; fax (11) 5417900; e-mail info@pgc-lb.org; internet www.pgc-lb.org; f. 1724; the Melkite Church in Lebanon comprises 7 archdioceses, with an estimated 393,000 adherents (31 December 2009); Patriarch of Antioch and all the East, of Alexandria and of Jerusalem His Beatitude YOUSSEF (JOSEPH) ABSI.

Archbishop of Ba'albek: Most Rev. ELIAS RAHAL, Archevêché Grec-Catholique, Ba'albek; tel. (8) 370200; fax (8) 373986.

Archbishop of Baniyas: Most Rev. GEORGES NICOLAS HADDAD, Archevêché de Panéas, Jdeidet Marjeyoun; tel. and fax (3) 830007.

Archbishop of Beirut and Jbeil: GEORGES BACOUNI, Archevêché Grec-Melkite-Catholique, POB 11-901, 655 rue de Damas, Beirut; tel. (1) 616104; fax (1) 616109; e-mail agmcb@terra.net.lb.

Archbishop of Saida (Sidon): Most Rev. ELIE BÉCHARA HADDAD, Archevêché Grec-Melkite-Catholique, POB 247, rue el-Moutran, Sidon; tel. (7) 720100; fax (7) 722055; e-mail info@melkitessaida.com; internet melkitessaida.com.

Archbishop of Tripoli: Most Rev. EDOUARD GEORGES DAHER, Archevêché Grec-Catholique, POB 72, rue al-Kanaess, Tripoli; tel. (6) 415937; fax (6) 416056.

Archbishop of Tyre: Most Rev. GEORGES ISKANDAR, Archevêché Grec-Melkite-Catholique, POB 257, Tyre; tel. (7) 740015; fax (7) 349180; e-mail pbacouni@yahoo.com.

Archbishop of Zahleh and Furzol: Most Rev. IBRAHIM MICHAEL IBRAHIM, Archevêché Grec-Melkite-Catholique, Saidat el-Najat, Zahleh; tel. (8) 800333; fax (8) 822406; e-mail info@catholiczahle.org; internet www.catholiczahle.org.

Syrian Rite

Patriarchate of Antioch: Patriarcat Syrien Catholique d'Antioche, POB 116-5087, rue de Damas, Beirut 1106 2010; tel. (1) 615892; e-mail psc_lb@yahoo.com; jurisdiction over about 150,000 Syrian Catholics in the Middle East; Patriarch Most Rev. IGNACE JOSEPH III YOUNAN.

The Anglican Communion

Within the Episcopal Church in Jerusalem and the Middle East, Lebanon forms part of the diocese of Jerusalem (see Israel).

Other Christian Groups

Armenian Apostolic Orthodox Church: Armenian Catholicosate of Cilicia, POB 70317, Antélias; tel. (4) 410001; fax (4) 419724; e-mail info@armenianorthodoxchurch.org; internet www.armenianorthodoxchurch.org; f. 301 CE in Armenia, re-established in 1293 in Cilicia (now in Türkiye), transferred to Antélias, Lebanon, 1930; Leader His Holiness ARAM KESHISHIAN I (Catholicos of Cilicia); jurisdiction over an estimated 3.5m. adherents in Lebanon, Canada, Cyprus, Greece, Iran, Kuwait, Qatar, South America, the Syrian Arab Republic, the USA and the UAE.

National Evangelical Synod of Syria and Lebanon: POB 70890, Antélias; tel. (4) 525030; e-mail info@synod-sl.org; internet www.synod-sl.org; f. 1959; Gen. Sec. Rev. JOSEPH KASSAB.

Patriarchate of Antioch and all the East (Greek Orthodox): Patriarcat Grec-Orthodoxe, POB 9, Damascus, Syria; tel. (11) 5424400; fax (11) 5424404; e-mail secretary@antiochpatriarchate.org; internet antiochpatriarchate.org; Patriarch His Beatitude JOHN X.

Supreme Council of the Evangelical Community in Syria and Lebanon: POB 70/1065, rue Rabieh 34, Antélias; tel. (4) 525036; fax (4) 405490; Pres. Rev. JOSEPH KASSAB.

Union of the Armenian Evangelical Churches in the Near East: POB 11-0377, Beirut; tel. (1) 565628; fax (1) 565629; e-mail secretary@uaecne.org; internet www.uaecne.org; f. 1846 in Turkey (now known as Türkiye); comprises about 30 Armenian Evangelical Churches in the Syrian Arab Republic, Lebanon, Egypt, Cyprus, Greece, Iran, Türkiye and Australia; Chair. Rev. PAUL HAIDOSTIAN.

ISLAM

Shi'a Muslims: Leader Imam Sheikh SAYED MOUSSA AL-SADR (went missing during visit to Libya in August 1978); Vice-Pres. of the Supreme Islamic Council of the Shi'a Community of Lebanon Sheikh ALI AL-KHATIB; Beirut.

Sunni Muslims: Grand Mufti of Lebanon, Dar el-Fatwa, rue Ilewi Rushed, Beirut; tel. (1) 422340; Leader Sheikh ABD AL-LATIF DERIAN.

Druzes: Supreme Spiritual Leader of the Druze Community, Beirut; Supreme Spiritual Leader Sheikh SAMI ABI AL-MUNA; Political Leader WALID JOUMBLATT.

Alawites: a schism of Shi'a Islam; there are an estimated 50,000 Alawites in northern Lebanon, in and around Tripoli.

JUDAISM

A small Jewish community, thought to number fewer than 100 people, remains in Lebanon.

Jewish Community: Pres. ISAAC ARAZI (Beirut).

The Press

DAILY NEWSPAPERS (PRINT AND ONLINE)

Al-Akhbar (The News): POB 5963-113, Concorde Centre, 6th Floor, rue Verdun, Beirut; tel. (1) 759500; fax (1) 759597; e-mail online@

LEBANON

Directory

al-akhbar.com; internet www.al-akhbar.com; f. 2006; Arabic; ind; Editor-in-Chief IBRAHIM AL-AMIN.

Al-Anwar (Lights): c/o Dar Assayad, POB 11-1038, Hazmieh, Beirut; tel. (5) 456374; fax (5) 452700; internet www.alanwar.com; f. 1959; Arabic; ind; supplement, Sun.; cultural and social; publ. by Dar Assayad SAL; Editors-in-Chief MICHEL RAAD, RAFIK KHOURY; circ. 24,508.

Aztag: POB 80-860, Shaghzoyan Cultural Centre, Bourj Hammoud; tel. (1) 258526; fax (1) 258529; e-mail info@aztagdaily.com; internet www.aztagdaily.com; f. 1927; Armenian; Editor-in-Chief SHAHAN KANDAHARIAN; circ. 6,500.

Daily Star: Markaziah Centre, 3rd Floor, Umm Gelias St, Beirut Central District, Beirut; tel. (1) 985313; fax (1) 561333; e-mail editorial@dailystar.com.lb; internet www.dailystar.com.lb; f. 1952; English; online only from 2020; Publr SALMA EL-BISSAR; Editor-in-Chief NADIM LADKI.

Al-Diyar (The Homeland): al-Nahda Bldg, Yarze, Beirut; tel. (3) 293010; fax (5) 923773; internet www.aldiyaronline.com; f. 1987; Arabic; Propr and Editor-in-Chief CHARLES AYYUB.

Al-Liwaa (The Standard): POB 11-2402, Beirut; tel. (1) 735745; fax (1) 735749; e-mail info@aliwaa.com.lb; internet www.aliwaa.com; f. 1963; Arabic; Propr ABD AL-GHANI SALAM; Editor SALAH SALAM; circ. 26,000.

Al-Mustaqbal: POB 14-5426, Beirut; tel. (1) 746301; fax (1) 746312; e-mail salayli@almustaqbal.com.lb; internet mustaqbalweb.com; f. 1999; Dir SAAD AL-AYLI; Editor-in-Chief HANI HAMMOUD.

An-Nahar (The Day): Immeuble An-Nahar, place des Martyrs, Marfa', Beirut 2014 5401; tel. (1) 994888; fax (1) 996777; internet www.annahar.com; f. 1933; Arabic; ind; publ. by Editions Dar an-Nahar SAL; Editor-in-Chief NAYLA TUENI; circ. 50,000.

L'Orient-Le Jour: POB 11-2488, Route de Damas, montée Fiyaddiyé, 200m après station Total, Beirut; tel. (5) 956444; fax (5) 957444; e-mail administration@lorientlejour.com; internet www.lorientlejour.com; f. 1970 by merger of two newspapers, *L'Orient* and *Le Jour*; French; ind; Pres. and CEO NAYLA DE FREIGE; Editors-in-Chief MICHEL TOUMA, ELIE FAYAD, EMILIE SUEUR; circ. 23,000.

As-Safir: POB 113-5015, Immeuble as-Safir, rue Monimina, Hamra, Beirut 1103-2010; tel. and fax (1) 350001; internet www.assafir.com; f. 1974; Arabic; political; Publr and Editor-in-Chief TALAL SALMAN; circ. 45,000.

Zartonk: POB 11-617, rue Nahr Ibrahim, Beirut; tel. and fax (1) 566709; internet www.zartonkdaily.com; f. 1937; Armenian, Arabic and English; official organ of the Armenian Liberal Democratic Party; Man. Editor BAROUYR H. AGHBASHIAN.

WEEKLY NEWSPAPERS (PRINT AND ONLINE)

Achabaka (The Net): c/o Dar Assayad SAL, POB 11-1038, Said Freiha St, Hazmieh, Beirut; tel. (5) 456376; fax (5) 452700; e-mail achabaka2008@gmail.com; internet www.achabaka.com; f. 1956; Arabic; society and features; Founder SAID FREIHA; Editor ELHAM FREIHA; circ. 139,775.

Al-Anwar Supplement: c/o Dar Assayad, POB 11-1038, Hazmieh, Beirut; tel. (5) 450406; fax (5) 452700; internet www.alanwar.com; cultural and social; every Sun.; supplement to daily *Al-Anwar*; Editor ISSAM FREIHA; circ. 90,000.

Attamaddon: POB 90, Aljmizzat St, Tripoli; tel. (6) 441164; fax (6) 435252; e-mail attamaddon@hotmail.com; internet www.attamaddon.com; f. 1972; political; Editor-in-Chief FAWAZ SANKRI.

Al-Bayan: 5th Floor, Karim Centre, Tripoli; tel. and fax (3) 158015; e-mail info@albayanlebanon.net; internet albayanlebanon.net; f. 1923; political.

Ad-Dabbour: place du Musée, Beirut; tel. and fax (3) 895949; e-mail addabbour@gmail.com; internet www.addabbour.net; f. 1922; Arabic; CEO JOSEPH RICHARD MOUKARZEL; Editor-in-Chief ANTOINE ABU JOUDA.

L'Hebdo Magazine: POB 11-1404, Immeuble Sayegh, rue Sursock, Beirut; tel. (1) 202070; fax (1) 202652; e-mail info@ediori.com.lb; internet www.magazine.com.lb; f. 1956; French; political, economic and social; publ. by Editions Orientales SAL; Pres. CHARLES ABOU ADAL; Editor-in-Chief PAUL KHALIFEH; circ. 18,000.

Al-Hiwar (Dialogue): rue Donna Maria, Beirut; tel. (1) 637000; fax (1) 631282; e-mail info@alhiwar.info; internet www.alhiwar.info; f. 2000; Arabic; publ. by the National Dialogue Party; Chair. FOUAD MAKHZOUMI; Editor-in-Chief SAM MOUNASSA.

Al-Kifah al-Arabi (The Arab Struggle): POB 5158-14, Immeuble Rouche-Shams, Beirut; tel. (1) 809300; fax (1) 808281; e-mail editor@kifaharabi.com; internet www.kifaharabi.com; f. 1974; Arabic; political, socialist, pan-Arab; Publr WALID HUSSEINI.

Al-Moharrer (The Liberator): POB 136702, rue Hamra, Beirut; tel. (1) 750516; fax (1) 750515; e-mail almoharrer@almoharrer.net; f. 1962; Arabic; Gen. Man. WALID ABOU ZAHR; circ. 87,000.

Al-Ousbou' al-Arabi (Arab Week): POB 11-1404, Immeuble Sayegh, rue Sursock, Beirut; tel. (1) 202070; fax (1) 202663; e-mail editing@arabweek.com.lb; internet www.arabweek.com.lb; f. 1959; Arabic; political and social; publ. by Editions Orientales SAL; Chair. CHARLES ABOU ADAL; Editor-in-Chief ELIAS MAALOUF.

La Revue du Liban (Lebanon Review): POB 165612, Immeuble Dimitri Trad, rue Issa Maalouf, Achrafieh, Beirut; tel. (1) 200961; fax (1) 338929; e-mail editors@rdl.com.lb; internet www.rdl.com.lb; f. 1928; French; political, social, cultural; publ. by Dar Alf Leila wa Leila; Publr MELHEM KARAM; Gen. Man. MICHEL MISK; circ. 22,000.

Al-Shiraa (The Sail): POB 13-5250, Beirut; tel. (1) 817870; fax (1) 703000; internet www.alshiraa.com; Arabic; Chief Editor HASSAN SABRA; circ. 40,000.

OTHER PERIODICALS

Alam Attijarat (Business World): POB 11-7007, 8th Floor, Noura Center, Sin el-Fil, Beirut; tel. and fax (1) 485560; e-mail beirut@rlpgroup.com; internet www.alamattijarat.com; f. 1965; monthly; commercial; Editor DALIA AL-QADI; international circ. 17,500.

Al Computer, Communications and Electronics (ACCE): c/o Dar Assayad, POB 1038, Hazmieh, Beirut; tel. (5) 450935; fax (5) 452700; internet www.accemagazine.com; f. 1984; monthly; computer technology; publ. by Dar Assayad Int; Chief Editor ANTOINE BOUTROS.

Arab Defence Journal: c/o Dar Assayad, POB 11-1038, Hazmieh, Beirut; tel. (2) 456374; fax (5) 450609; e-mail info@dar-assayad.com; internet www.arabdefencejournal.com; f. 1976; monthly; military; publ. by Dar Assayad Int; Editor-in-Chief NAZEM AL-KHOURI; circ. 30,000.

The Arab World: POB 567, Jounieh; tel. and fax (9) 935096; internet www.naamanculture.com; f. 1985; 24 a yr; publ. by Dar Naamān lith-Thaqāfa (Maison Naaman pour la Culture); Editor NAJI NAAMAN.

BusinessWeek Al-Arabiya: POB 11-4355, Beirut; tel. (1) 739777; fax (1) 749090; f. 2005; monthly; Arabic edn of US weekly business publ; publ. by InfoPro SARL; distributed across 22 countries; Regional Dir SYLVIE GYURAN.

Le Commerce du Levant: POB 45-332 Baabda, Route de Damas, Immeuble l'Orient-Le Jour, 3e étage, Hazmieh, Beirut; tel. (1) 952259; fax (1) 453644; e-mail redaction@lecommercedulevant.com; internet www.lecommercedulevant.com; f. 1929; monthly; French; commercial and financial; publ. by Société de la Presse Economique; Chief Editor SAHAR AL-ATTAR; circ. 15,000.

construction HQ: POB 13-5121, Chouran, Beirut 1102 2802; tel. and fax (1) 748333; e-mail info@constructionhq.world; internet www.constructionhq.world; f. 1983; monthly; English; publ. by CPH World Media; Publr and Gen. Man MUHAMMAD RABIH; circ. 4,965.

Déco: POB 11-1404, Immeuble Sayegh, rue Sursock, Beirut; tel. (1) 202070; fax (1) 202663; e-mail info@decomag.com.lb; internet www.decomag.com.lb; f. 2000; quarterly; French; architecture and interior design; publ. by Editions Orientales SAL; Editor-in-Chief CHRISTIANE TAWIL; circ. 14,000.

Fairuz International: c/o Dar Assayad, POB 11-1038, Hazmieh, Beirut; tel. (5) 456376; fax (5) 452700; internet www.fairuzmagazine.com; f. 1982; monthly; Arabic; publ. by Dar Assayad Int; Chief Editor ELHAM FREIHA; circ. 98,790 (2014).

Al-Fares: c/o Dar Assayad, POB 11-1038, Hazmieh, Beirut; tel. (5) 450406; fax (5) 450609; internet www.alfaresmagazine.com; f. 1991; monthly; Arabic; publ. by Dar Assayad Int; Chief Editor ELHAM FREIHA.

Al-Idari (The Manager): c/o Dar Assayad, POB 11-1038, Hazmieh, Beirut; tel. (5) 450406; fax (5) 450609; internet www.alidarimagazine.com; f. 1975; monthly; Arabic; business management, economics, finance and investment; publ. by Dar Assayad Int; Pres. BASSAM FREIHA; Gen. Man. ELHAM FREIHA; circ. 31,867.

Lebanese and Arab Economy: POB 11-1801, Sanayeh, Beirut; tel. (1) 353390; fax (1) 353395; e-mail iktissad@infopro.com.lb; internet www.ccib.org.lb; f. 1951; monthly; Arabic, English and French; publ. by Chamber of Commerce, Industry and Agriculture of Beirut and Mount Lebanon; Editor RAMZI AL-HAFEZ.

Lebanon Opportunities: c/o InfoPro SARL, POB 11-4355, 2nd Floor, rue Hamra, Piccadilly Center, Beirut; tel. (1) 739777; fax (1) 749090; e-mail infopro@infopro.com.lb; internet www.opportunities.com.lb; monthly; English; real estate, business and general finance and economy; publ. by InfoPro SARL; Publr and Editor-in-Chief RAMZI EL-HAFEZ.

Al-Mar'a: POB 11-1404, Immeuble Sayegh, rue Sursock, Beirut; tel. (1) 202070; fax (1) 202663; e-mail info@almara.com.lb; internet www.almara.com.lb; f. 2000; monthly; Arabic; publ. by Editions Orientales SAL; Dir MOUNA BÉCHARA; Chief Editor PAUL KHALIFEH; circ. 20,000.

food HQ: POB 13-5121, Chouran, Beirut 1102 2802; tel. and fax (1) 748333; e-mail content@mefmag.com; internet www.foodhq.world;

LEBANON

f. 1985; monthly; publ. by CPH World Media; Pres. and CEO MUHAMAD RABIH CHATILA; Editor-in-Chief ROLA HAMDAN GHUDMI; circ. 4,735.

healthHQ: POB 13-5121, Barouk St, Chatila Bldg, Beirut 1102 2802; tel. (1) 748333; e-mail info@healthhq.world; internet www.healthhq.world; f. 1986 as Arab Health World magazine; monthly; English and Arabic; publ. by CPH World Media SARL; CEO MOHAMAD RABIH CHATILA; Editor-in-Chief Dr RAJAA CHATILA.

Siyassa was Strategia (Politics and Strategy): POB 567, Jounieh; tel. and fax (9) 935096; e-mail naamanculture@lynx.net.lb; internet www.naamanculture.com; f. 1981; 36 a year; Arabic; publ. by Dar Naamān lith-Thaqāfa (Maison Naaman pour la Culture); Editor NAJI NAAMAN.

Takarir Wa Khalfiyat (Background Reports): c/o Dar Assayad, POB 11-1038, Hazmieh, Beirut; tel. (5) 456374; fax (5) 452700; f. 1976; monthly; Arabic; political and economic bulletin; publ. by Dar Assayad SAL; Editor-in-Chief HASSAN EL-KHOURY.

Al-Tarik (The Road): Beirut; monthly; Arabic; cultural and theoretical; publ. by the Parti Communiste Libanais; circ. 5,000.

Travaux et Jours (Works and Days): Rectorat de l'Université Saint-Joseph, rue de Damas, Beirut; tel. (1) 421000; fax (1) 421005; e-mail travauxetjours@usj.edu.lb; internet www.usj.edu.lb; f. 1961; 2 a year; French; political, social and cultural; Editor ANTOINE COURBAN.

water HQ: POB 13-5121, Chouran, Beirut 1102-2802; tel. (1) 748333; fax (1) 352419; e-mail info@waterhq.world; internet waterhq.world; f. 1977 as Arab Water World; present name adopted 2018; monthly; English and Arabic; publ. by CPH World Media; Editor-in-Chief NIZAR AKER; circ. 4,020.

NEWS AGENCY

National News Agency (NNA): Hamra, Beirut; tel. (1) 754400; fax (1) 745776; e-mail news@nna-leb.gov.lb; internet www.nna-leb.gov.lb; state-owned; Dir ZIAD HARFOUSH; Chief Editor ALI LAHHAM.

PRESS ASSOCIATION

Lebanese Press Order: ave Saeb Salam, Beirut 2039-5801; tel. (1) 350800; fax (1) 519865; e-mail info@pressorderlebanon.com; internet pressorderlebanon.com; f. 1911; 18 mems; Pres. AOUNI AL-KAAKI; Sec. ABDUL KARIM EL-KHALIL.

Publishers

Dar al-Adab: POB 4123, Beirut; tel. (1) 795135; fax (1) 861633; e-mail rana@daraladab.com; internet daraladab.com; f. 1953; dictionaries, literary and general; Man. RANA IDRISS; Editor-in-Chief SAMAH IDRISS.

Arab Institute for Research and Publishing (Al-Mouasasah al-Arabiyah Lildirasat Walnashr): POB 11-5460, Beirut; tel. (1) 707892; fax (1) 707891; e-mail info@airpbooks.com; internet www.airpbooks.com; f. 1969; works in Arabic and English; Dir MAHER KAYYALI.

Arab Scientific Publishers BP: POB 13-5574, Immeuble Ein al-Tenah Reem, rue Sakiet al-Janzir, Beirut; tel. (1) 786233; fax (1) 786230; e-mail asp@asp.com.lb; internet www.asp.com.lb; computer science, biological sciences, cookery, travel, politics, fiction, children's; Pres. BASSAM CHEBARO.

Dar Assayad Group (SAL and International): POB 11-1038, Hazmieh, Beirut; tel. (5) 456376; fax (5) 452700; internet www.dar-assayad.com; Dar Assayad SAL f. 1943; Dar Assayad Int. f. 1983 and provides publishing, advertising and distribution services; publishes in Arabic *Al-Anwar* (daily), *Assayad* (weekly), *Achabaka* (weekly), *Background Reports*, *Arab Defense Journal* (monthly), *Fairuz* (international monthly edition), *Al-Idari* (monthly), *Al Computer, Communications and Electronics* (monthly), *Al-Fares* (monthly); also publishes monthly background reports; has offices and correspondents in Arab countries and most parts of the world; Chair. ISSAM FREIHA; CEO BASSAM FREIHA; Man. Dir ELHAM FREIHA.

CPH World Media SARL: Barouk St, Hamra, Beirut; tel. (1) 748333; fax (1) 352419; e-mail info@cph.world; internet cph.world; f. 1977 as Chatila Publishing House; adopted present name in 2008; magazine publishing, events and research; publishes *Arab Construction World* (monthly), *Arab Water World* (monthly), *MENA Health World* (monthly), *Middle East Food* (monthly); Pres. and Publr FATHI CHATILA; CEO MUHAMMAD RABIH CHATILA.

Edition Française pour le Monde Arabe (EDIFRAMO): POB 113-6140, Immeuble Elissar, rue Bliss, Beirut; tel. (1) 862437; Man. TAHSEEN S. KHAYAT.

Editions Dar an-Nahar SAL: BP 11-226, Immeuble an-Nahar, rue Banque du Liban, Hamra, Beirut; tel. (1) 747620; fax (1) 747623; internet www.darannahar.com; f. 1967; pan-Arab publishing house; Pres. GHASSAN TUÉNI; Dir JANA TAMER.

Editions Orientales SAL: POB 11-1404, Immeuble Sayegh, rue Sursock, Beirut; tel. (1) 202070; fax (1) 202663; e-mail info@ediori.com.lb; internet www.ediori.com.lb; political and social newspapers and magazines; Pres. and Editor-in-Chief CHARLES ABOU ADAL.

GeoProjects SARL: POB 11-8375, Immeuble Barakat, Zahia Salman St, Beirut; tel. (1) 830620; fax (1) 830616; e-mail info@geo-publishers.com; internet www.geo-publishers.com; f. 1978; cartographers, researchers, school textbook publrs; Dir-Gen. RIDA ISMAIL.

Dar el-Ilm Lilmalayin: POB 1085, Centre Metco, rue Mar Elias, Beirut 2045 8402; tel. (1) 306666; fax (1) 701657; e-mail info@malayin.com; internet www.malayin.com; f. 1945; dictionaries, encyclopedias, reference books, textbooks, Islamic cultural books; CEO TAREF OSMAN.

InfoPro SARL: POB 11-4355, Centre Piccadilly, rue Hamra, Beirut; tel. (1) 739777; fax (1) 749090; e-mail infopro@infopro.com.lb; internet www.infopro.com.lb; f. 1997; information-based magazines, incl. *BusinessWeek Al-Arabiya* and *Lebanon Opportunities*, as well as reference books; Pres. RAMZI EL-HAFEZ.

Institute for Palestine Studies, Publishing and Research Organization (IPS): POB 11-7164, rue Anis Nsouli, Verdun, Beirut 1107 2230; tel. (1) 868387; fax (1) 814193; e-mail library@palestine-studies.org; internet www.palestine-studies.org; f. 1963; independent non-profit Arab research org., which promotes better understanding of the Palestine problem and the Arab–Israeli conflict; publishes books, reprints, research papers, etc.; Chair. Dr TAREK MITRI.

The International Documentary Center of Arab Manuscripts: POB 2668, Immeuble Hanna, Ras Beirut, Beirut; f. 1965; publishes and reproduces ancient and rare Arabic texts; Propr ZOUHAIR BAALBAKI.

Dar al-Kashaf: POB 11-2091, rue Assad Malhamee, Beirut; tel. (1) 249952; e-mail dakashaf4@yahoo.com; f. 1930; publrs of *Al-Kashaf* (Arab Youth Magazine), maps, atlases and business books; printers and distributors; Propr M. A. FATHALLAH.

Dar al-Kitab al-Lubnani: POB 11-8330, Beirut; tel. (1) 735731; fax (1) 351433; e-mail info@daralkitabalmasri.com; internet www.daralkitabalmasri.com; f. 1929; publr of books on Islamic studies, history, sciences and literature; Pres. and Gen. Dir Dr HASSAN EL-ZEIN.

Dar Alf Leila wa Leila: BP 165612, rue Issa Maalouf, Immeuble Dimitri Trad, Achrafieh, Beirut; tel. (1) 200961; fax (1) 338929; internet www.rdl.com.lb; publishes *Al-Bayraq* (Arabic, daily), *Al-Hawadeth* (Arabic, weekly), *La Revue du Liban* (French, weekly), *Monday Morning* (English, weekly); Editor-in-Chief MELHEM KARAM.

Librairie du Liban Publishers: POB 11-9232, Beirut; tel. (9) 217944; fax (9) 217734; e-mail info@ldlp.com; internet www.ldlp-dictionary.com; f. 1944; publr of children's books, dictionaries and reference books; distributor of books in English and French; Man. Dirs HABIB SAYEGH, PIERRE SAYEGH.

Dar al-Maaref Liban SARL: POB 2320, Riad el-Solh, Beirut; tel. (1) 931243; f. 1959; children's books and textbooks in Arabic; Man. Dir Dr FOUAD IBRAHIM; Gen. Man. JOSEPH NACHOU.

Dar al-Machreq SARL: POB 166778, Beirut 1100 2150; tel. (1) 202423; fax (1) 202424; e-mail info@darelmachreq.com; internet www.darelmachreq.com; f. 1848; religion, art, Arabic and Islamic literature, history, languages, science, philosophy, school books, dictionaries and periodicals; Man. Dir SALAH ABOUJAOUDE.

Dar Naamān lith-Thaqāfa (Maison Naaman pour la Culture): POB 567, Jounieh; tel. and fax (9) 935096; e-mail info@najinaaman.org; internet www.najinaaman.org; f. 1979; publishes books in several languages; Propr NAJI NAAMAN; Exec. Man. MARCELLE AL-ASHKAR.

Naufal Group SARL: POB 11-2161, Immeuble Naufal, rue Sourati, Beirut; tel. (1) 354898; fax (1) 354394; f. 1970; encyclopedias, fiction, children's books, history, law and literature; subsidiary cos: Macdonald Middle East Sarl, Les Editions Arabes; Man. Dir TONY NAUFAL.

Publitec Publications: POB 16-6142, Beirut; tel. (1) 495401; fax (1) 493330; f. 1965; publishes *Who's Who in Lebanon* and *Who's Who in the Arab World* (both bi-annual); Pres. CHARLES GEDEON; Man. KRIKOR AYVAZIAN.

Rihani Printing and Publishing House: 13-5378, Beirut; tel. (1) 838281; fax (1) 868384; f. 1963; Propr ALBERT RIHANI; Man. DAOUD STEPHAN.

Sader Publishers: POB 55530, Immeuble Sader, Dekwaneh, Beirut; tel. (1) 488776; e-mail info@sadergroup.com; internet sadergroup.com; f. 1863; legal publr; Chair. JOSEPH SADER.

Samir Éditeur: POB 175132, rue Gouraud Gemmayzé, Sin el-Fil, Beirut; tel. (1) 448181; fax (1) 448799; e-mail edition@samirediteur.com; internet www.samirediteur.com; children's books in Arabic, English and French.

LEBANON
Directory

World Book Publishing: POB 11-3176, rue al-Khansa, Rifai Bldg, Beirut; tel. and fax (1) 659894; e-mail info@wbpbooks.com; internet www.wbpbooks.com; f. 1926; literature, education, philosophy, current affairs, self-help, children's books; Chair. M. SAID EL-ZEIN; Man. Dir RAFIK EL-ZEIN.

Broadcasting and Communications

TELECOMMUNICATIONS

OGERO (Organisme de Gestion et d'Exploitation de l'ex Radio Orient): POB 11-1226, Bir Hassan, Beirut 1107 2070; tel. (1) 840000; fax (1) 826823; internet www.ogero.gov.lb; f. 1972; 100% state-owned; plans for the incorporation of OGERO and 2 depts of the Ministry of Telecommunications into a single operator, Liban Télécom, were announced in 2005; however, no progress has since been made; fixed-line operator; Dir-Gen. IMAD KRAYDIEH.

Alfa: Parallel Towers, Dekwaneh, Beirut; tel. (3) 391111; fax (3) 391109; e-mail alfa.customercareteam@alfamobile.com.lb; internet www.alfa.com.lb; managed by the Ministry of Telecommunications; operates the state-owned MIC1 mobile telephone network under licence; offers 4G LTE services; Chair. and CEO JAD NASSIF.

touch: POB 17-5051, Bashoura 1526, Immeuble Central Beirut-Touch, ave Fouad Chehab, Beirut; tel. (3) 800111; e-mail info@touch.com.lb; internet www.touch.com.lb; f. 2004 as MTC Touch; present name adopted 2012; managed by Zain Group (fmrly Mobile Telecommunications Co—Kuwait); operates the state-owned MIC2 mobile telephone network under licence; Chair. and CEO SALEM ITANI.

Regulatory Authority

Telecommunications Regulatory Authority (TRA): Marfaa Bldg 200, 2nd Floor, Beirut Central District, Beirut; tel. (1) 964300; fax (1) 964341; e-mail info@tra.gov.lb; internet www.tra.gov.lb; f. 2007; Gen. Man. AMINE MOUKHEIBER (acting).

BROADCASTING
Radio

Al-Nour: POB 197/25, Beirut; tel. (1) 543555; e-mail info@alnour.com.lb; internet www.alnour.com.lb; f. 1988; owned by Lebanese Communication Group; affiliated to Hezbollah; broadcasts on 91.7 FM, 91.9 FM and 92.2 FM.

Radio Liban: rue Emile Edée, Sanayeh, Hamra, Beirut; tel. (1) 743529; internet www.radioliban.gov.lb; run by the Ministry of Information in conjunction with Radio France International; f. 1937; Arabic programmes broadcast on 98.1 FM and 98.5 FM; scheduled for privatization; Dir-Gen. HASSAN FALHA; Dir of Programmes RITA NAJIM AL-ROUMI.

The Home Service broadcasts in Arabic on short wave, and the Foreign Service broadcasts in Portuguese, Armenian, Arabic, Spanish, French and English.

Television

Lebanese Broadcasting Corpn (LBC) Sat Ltd: POB 111, Zouk, Beirut 165853; tel. and fax (9) 850850; e-mail support@lbcgroup.tv; internet www.lbcgroup.tv; f. 1985 as Lebanese Broadcasting Corpn Int. SAL; name changed 1996; operates satellite channel on Arabsat 2C, Arabsat 3A and Nilesat 102; programmes in Arabic, French and English; broadcasts to Lebanon, the Middle East, Europe, the USA and Australia; Chair. Sheikh PIERRE EL-DAHER.

Al-Manar (Lighthouse): Bir Hassan, Beirut; tel. (1) 276000; fax (1) 555953; e-mail info@almanar.com.lb; internet www.almanar.com.lb; f. 1991; owned by Lebanese Communication Group; broadcasts to Arab and Muslim audiences worldwide; has operated satellite channel since 2000; affiliated to Hezbollah; Chair. of Bd IBRAHIM FARHAT.

Murr Television: Naccache, Beirut; tel. (4) 444000; internet www.mtv.com.lb; f. 1991; closed down in 2002 for contravening electoral laws; relaunched 2009; privately owned; CEO MICHEL GABRIEL EL-MURR.

Finance

BANKING
Central Bank

Banque du Liban: POB 11-5544, rue Masraf Loubnane, Beirut; tel. (1) 750000; fax (1) 738195; internet www.bdl.gov.lb; f. 1964 as successor in Lebanon to the Banque de Syrie et du Liban; Gov. WASSIM MANSOURI (acting).

Principal Commercial Banks

Bank Audi SAL: POB 11-2560, Riad el-Solh, Beirut 1107 2808; tel. (1) 994000; fax (1) 990555; e-mail contactus@bankaudi.com.lb; internet www.bankaudi.com.lb; f. 1962 as Bank Audi; acquired Orient Credit Bank 1997 and Banque Nasr 1998; absorbed into Audi Saradar Group in 2004; Chair. and CEO SAMIR N. HANNA.

Bank of Beirut SAL: POB 11-7354, Bank of Beirut SAL Bldg, Foch St, Beirut Central District, Beirut; tel. (5) 955262; e-mail bobdirect@bankofbeirut.com.lb; internet www.bankofbeirut.com.lb; f. 1973; acquired Transorient Bank 1999, Beirut Riyad Bank 2002; Chair. and CEO SALIM G. SFEIR.

BankMed SAL: POB 11-0348, Centre Groupe Méditerranée, 482 rue Clémenceau, Beirut 2022 9302; tel. (1) 373937; fax (1) 362706; internet www.bankmed.com.lb; f. 1944 as Banque Naaman et Soussou; name changed to Eastern Commercial Bank 1955, Banque de la Méditerranée SAL 1970 and as above 2006; acquired Allied Bank SAL in 2006; Chair. RAYA HAFFAR EL-HASSAN; Gen. Man. MICHEL ACCAD.

Banque BEMO SAL: BEMO Bldg Elias Sarkis Ave, Ashrafieh, Beirut; tel. (1) 200505; fax (1) 217860; e-mail bemo@bemobank.com; internet www.bemobank.com; f. 1964 as Future Bank SAL; name changed to BEMO (Banque Européenne pour le Moyen-Orient) SAL 1994 and as above 2006; Chair. and Gen. Man. RIAD BECHARA OBEGI; Vice-Chair. and Gen. Man. SAMIH H. SAADEH.

Banque Libano-Française SAL: POB 11-0808, Tour Liberty, rue de Rome, Beirut 1107 2804; tel. (1) 791332; fax (1) 440118; e-mail info@eblf.com; internet www.eblf.com; f. 1967; Chair. and Gen. Man. WALID RAPHAËL.

Banque Misr-Liban SAL: rue Riad el-Solh, Beirut 2011 9301; tel. (4) 727400; fax (1) 964296; e-mail mail@bml.com.lb; internet www.bml.com.lb; f. 1929 as Banque Misr Syrie Liban; name changed as above 1958; Chair. MUHAMMAD EL-ETREBI; Exec. Gen. Man. GABY KASSIS.

BBAC (Bank of Beirut and the Arab Countries) SAL: POB 11-1536, Immeuble de la Banque, 250 rue Clémenceau, Riad el-Solh, Beirut 1107 2080; tel. (1) 360460; fax (1) 365200; e-mail contactus@bbac.com.lb; internet www.bbacbank.com; f. 1956; Chair. and Gen. Man. GHASSAN T. ASSAF.

BLC Bank SAL: POB 11-1126, BLC Bldg, Adlieh Intersection, Beirut 2064 5809; tel. (1) 429000; fax (1) 616984; e-mail info@blcbank.com; internet www.blcbank.com; f. 1950; 74.8% owned by Fransabank SAL; Chair. and Gen. Man. NADIM KASSAR; Gen. Man. and CEO BASSAM HASSAN.

BLOM Bank SAL: POB 11-1912, Immeuble BLOM Bank, rue Rachid Karameh, Verdun, Beirut 1107 2807; tel. (1) 758000; fax (1) 737218; e-mail callcenter@blom.com.lb; internet www.blom.com.lb; f. 1951 as Banque du Liban et d'Outre-Mer; name changed as above 2000; Chair. and Gen. Man. SAAD AZHARI.

Byblos Bank SAL: POB 11-5605, ave Elias Sarkis, Achrafieh, Beirut 1107 2811; tel. (1) 335200; fax (1) 339436; e-mail byblosbk@byblosbank.com.lb; internet www.byblosbank.com; f. 1959; merged with Banque Beyrouth pour le Commerce SAL 1997; acquired Byblos Bank Europe SA 1998, Wedge Bank Middle East SAL 2001 and ABN AMRO Bank Lebanon 2002; Chair. and Gen. Man. Dr SEMAAN BASSIL.

Creditbank SAL: POB 16-5795, Freeway Center, Sin el-Fil blvd, Dekwaneh, Beirut 1100 2802; tel. (1) 501600; fax (1) 485245; e-mail info@creditbank.com.lb; internet www.creditbank.com.lb; f. 1981 as Crédit Bancaire SAL; name changed as above following merger with Crédit Lyonnais Liban SAL 2002; Chair. and Gen. Man. TAREK JOSEPH KHALIFÉ.

Crédit Libanais SAL: POB 16-6729, Immeuble Crédit Libanais, Corniche el-Nahr, Adlieh Intersection, Beirut 1100 2811; tel. (1) 607100; fax (1) 608126; e-mail info@creditlibanais.com.lb; internet www.creditlibanais.com.lb; f. 1961; Chair. and Gen. Man. Dr JOSEPH M. TORBEY.

Fenicia Bank SAL: POB 113-6248, Immeuble Fenicia Bank, rue Foch, Beirut Central District, Beirut 1103 2110; tel. (1) 957857; e-mail info@feniciabank.com; internet www.feniciabank.com; f. 1959; as Bank of Kuwait and the Arab World SAL; name changed as above 2010; 74% owned by Achour Group, 15% by Maacaron Group, 10% by Merhi Group and 1% by Dr Cheaib; Chair. and Gen. Man. ABDUL RAZZAK ACHOUR.

First National Bank SAL: POB 11-0435, Marfaa 147, rue Allenby, Riad el-Solh, Beirut 2012 6004; tel. (1) 963000; fax (1) 973090; e-mail fnb@fnb.com.lb; internet www.fnb.com.lb; f. 1994; acquired Société Bancaire du Liban SAL 2002; Chair. RAMI R. EL-NIMER; Gen. Mans. ELIAS S. BAZ, NAJIB M. SEMAAN.

Fransabank SAL: POB 11-0393, rue Hamra, Riad el-Solh, Beirut 1107 2803; tel. (1) 340180; fax (1) 341413; e-mail fsb@fransabank.com; internet www.fransabank.com; f. 1921; acquired Banque Tohmé SAL 1993, Universal Bank SAL 1999, United Bank of Saudi and Lebanon SAL 2001 and Banque de la Beka'a SAL 2003; Banque de la Beka'a was subsequently sold to Bank of Sharjah Ltd (United Arab Emirates) in July 2007; Chair. ADNAN KASSAR.

IBL Bank SAL: POB 11-5292, Immeuble Ittihadiah, ave Charles Malek, Beirut 1107 2190; tel. (1) 200350; fax (1) 204524; e-mail ibl@ibl.com.lb; internet www.ibl.com.lb; f. 1961 as Intercontinental Bank of Lebanon SAL; Chair. and Gen. Man. SALIM Y. HABIB.

Lebanese Swiss Bank SAL: POB 11-9552, Immeuble Hoss, 3–6e étage, rue Emile Eddé, place Hamra, Ras Beirut, Beirut; tel. (1) 732000; e-mail info@lebaneseswissbank.com; internet www.lebaneseswissbank.com; f. 1962; Chair. and Gen. Man. Dr TANAL SABBAH.

Lebanon and Gulf Bank SAL: POB 11-3600, 124 Allenby St, Beirut Central District, Beirut; tel. (1) 965000; fax (1) 965199; e-mail info@lgbbank.com; internet www.lgbbank.com; f. 1963 as Banque de Crédit Agricole; name changed as above 1980; Chair. and Gen. Man. SAMER A. H. ITANI.

MEAB Bank: POB 14-5958, Immeuble Hejeij, ave Adnan al-Hakim, Beirut 1105 2080; tel. (1) 826740; fax (1) 841190; e-mail meab@meabank.com; internet www.meabank.com; f. 1991 as Middle East and Africa Bank SAL; name changed as above 2003; Chair. ALI HEJEIJ; Gen. Man. VINCENT NABIH HADDAD.

Société Nouvelle de la Banque de Syrie et du Liban SAL (BSL): POB 11-957, rue Riad el-Solh, Beirut; tel. (1) 980080; fax (1) 980991; e-mail info@bslbank.com; internet www.bslbank.com; f. 1963; Chair. RAMSAY A. EL-KHOURI; Gen. Man. NICOLAS SALIBY.

Syrian Lebanese Commercial Bank SAL: SLCB Bldg, Makdessi St, Beirut; tel. (1) 741666; fax (1) 738214; e-mail info@slcb.com.lb; internet www.slcb.com.lb; f. 1974; Gen. Man. Dr ALI MOHAMMED YOUSSEF.

Supervisory Body

Banking Control Commission of Lebanon: POB 11-5544, rue Masraf Loubnane, Beirut; tel. (1) 750000; fax (1) 750040; internet www.bccl.gov.lb; f. 1967; Chair. MAYYA DABBAGH.

Banking Association

Association of Banks in Lebanon: POB 976, Gouraud St, Saifi, Beirut; tel. (1) 676167; e-mail abl@abl.org.lb; internet www.abl.org.lb; f. 1959; serves and promotes the interests of the banking community in Lebanon; mems: 69 banks and 7 foreign rep. offices; Chair. SALIM SFEIR; Sec.-Gen. FADI KHALAF.

STOCK EXCHANGE

Beirut Stock Exchange (BSE): POB 11-3552, Immeuble Azareih, 4e étage, Bloc 01, Beirut; tel. (1) 993555; fax (1) 993444; e-mail bse@bse.com.lb; internet www.bse.com.lb; f. 1920; recommenced trading in Jan. 1996; 10 cttee mems; Vice-Chair. GHALEB MAHMASSANI.

INSURANCE

Allianz SAL: POB 16-6528, Immeuble Allianz SAL, Hazmieh, Beirut 1100 2130; tel. (1) 422000; fax (1) 956624; e-mail info@allianz.com.lb; internet www.allianzsna.com; f. 1963 as Société Nationale d'Assurances SAL; renamed as above 2008; part of Allianz Group; Chair. ANTOINE ISSA.

Arabia Insurance Co SAL: POB 11-2172, Arabia House, rue de Phénicie, Beirut; tel. (1) 360893; e-mail careers@arabiainsurance.com; internet www.arabiainsurance.com; f. 1944.

Bankers Assurance SAL: POB 11-4293, 4th Floor, Immeuble Asseily, rue El Mir Bechir, Riad el-Solh Sq., Beirut; tel. (1) 962700; fax (1) 984004; e-mail mail@bankers-assurance.com; internet www.bankers-assurance.com; f. 1972; Chair. GINO NADER; CEO RAMI SABBAGH.

Commercial Insurance Co (Lebanon) SAL: POB 11-4351, Centre Starco, North Block, 9th Floor, Beirut; tel. (1) 373070; fax (1) 373071; e-mail comins@commercialinsurance.com.lb; internet www.commercialinsurance.com.lb; f. 1962.

Al-Ittihad al-Watani: POB 11-1270, Jisr al-Wati, Area 66, Road 99, Immeuble Al-Ittihad al-Watani, Beirut; tel. (1) 426480; fax (1) 426486; e-mail webmaster@alittihadalwatani.com.lb; internet www.alittihadalwatani.com.lb; f. 1947; Chair. and Gen. Man. TANNOUS FEGHALI.

Libano-Suisse Insurance Co SAL: POB 11-3821, Immeuble Commerce and Finance, 2nd Floor, Beirut 1107 2150; tel. (1) 374900; fax (1) 368724; e-mail libano-suisse@libano-suisse.com; internet www.libano-suisse.com; f. 1959; Chair. MICHEL PHARAON; Gen. Man. PIERRE PHARAON.

Al-Mashrek Insurance and Reinsurance SAL: POB 16-6154, Immeuble Al-Mashrek, Antélias Main Rd, Rabieh, Beirut 1100 2100; e-mail almashrek@almashrek.com.lb; internet www.almashrek.com.lb; f. 1962; Chair. and CEO ALEXANDRE MATOSSIAN.

'La Phénicienne' SAL: POB 11-5652, Immeuble Hanna Haddad, rue Amine Gemayel, Sioufi, Beirut; tel. (1) 425484; fax (1) 424532; e-mail info.ph@laphenicienne.net; internet www.laphenicienne.net; f. 1964.

Insurance Association

Association des Compagnies d'Assurances au Liban: POB 45-237, Immeuble ACAL, Hazmieh, Beirut; tel. (5) 956957; fax (5) 458959; e-mail acal@acal.org.lb; internet www.acal.org.lb; f. 1971; Pres. ELIE TORBEY; Sec.-Gen. JAMIL HARB.

Trade and Industry

DEVELOPMENT ORGANIZATIONS

Council for Development and Reconstruction (CDR): POB 11–3170, Tallet el-Serail, Beirut 2023–9201; tel. (1) 980096; fax (1) 981252; e-mail infocenter@cdr.gov.lb; internet www.cdr.gov.lb; f. 1977; an autonomous public institution reporting to the Cabinet, the CDR is charged with the co-ordination, planning and execution of Lebanon's public reconstruction programme; it plays a major role in attracting foreign funds; Pres. NABIL ADNAN EL-JISR.

Investment Development Authority of Lebanon (IDAL): POB 113-7251, Azarieh Tower, 4th Floor, Emir Bechir St, Riad el-Solh, Beirut; tel. (1) 983306; fax (1) 983302; e-mail invest@idal.com.lb; internet investinlebanon.gov.lb; f. 1994; state-owned; Chair. and Gen. Man. Dr MAZEN SOUIED.

Société Libanaise pour le Développement et la Reconstruction de Beyrouth (Solidere): POB 11-9493, 149 rue Saad Zaghoul, Beirut 2012-7305; tel. (1) 980650; fax (1) 980662; e-mail info@solidere.com.lb; internet www.solidere.com; f. 1994; real estate co responsible for reconstruction of Beirut Central District after the civil war; Chair. and Gen. Man. NASSER CHAMMAA.

CHAMBERS OF COMMERCE AND INDUSTRY

Federation of the Chambers of Commerce, Industry and Agriculture in Lebanon: POB 11-1801, Immeuble CCIAB, rue Justinien, Sanayeh, Beirut; tel. (1) 744702; e-mail fccial@cci-fed.org.lb; internet www.cci-fed.org.lb; f. 1996; Pres. MUHAMMAD CHOUCAIR.

Chamber of Commerce, Industry and Agriculture of Beirut and Mount Lebanon: POB 11-1801, 1 rue Justinien, Sanayeh, Beirut; tel. (1) 353190; fax (1) 353395; e-mail dg-office@ccib.org.lb; internet www.ccib.org.lb; f. 1898; 16,000 mems; Pres. MUHAMMAD NIZAR CHOUCAIR.

Chamber of Commerce, Industry and Agriculture in Sidon and South Lebanon: POB 41, rue Maarouf Saad, Sidon; tel. (7) 720123; fax (7) 722986; e-mail chamber@ccias.org.lb; internet www.ccias.org.lb; f. 1933; Pres. MUHAMMAD HASSAN SALEH.

Chamber of Commerce, Industry and Agriculture of Tripoli and North Lebanon: POB 47, rue Bechara Khoury, Tripoli; tel. (6) 425600; fax (6) 442042; e-mail mail@cciat.org.lb; internet www.cciat.org.lb; f. 1870; Chair. TOUFIC DABBOUSSI.

Chamber of Commerce, Industry and Agriculture of Zahleh and Beqa'a: POB 100, Zahleh; tel. (8) 802602; fax (8) 800050; e-mail info@cciaz.org.lb; internet www.cciaz.org.lb; f. 1939; 2,500 mems; Pres. EDMOND JREISSATI.

EMPLOYERS' ASSOCIATION

Association of Lebanese Industrialists: POB 11-1520, Chamber of Commerce and Industry Bldg, 5e étage, rue Justinien, Sanayeh, Beirut; tel. (1) 350280; fax (1) 351167; e-mail ali@ali.org.lb; internet www.ali.org.lb; Pres. SALIM ZEENNI; Gen. Man. TALAL HIJAZI.

UTILITIES

Electricity

Electricité du Liban (EDL): POB 131, Immeuble de l'Electricité du Liban, 22 rue du Fleuve, Beirut; tel. (1) 442720; fax (1) 443828; e-mail info@edl.gov.lb; internet www.edl.gov.lb; f. 1954; state-owned; Chair. and Dir-Gen. KAMAL F. HAYEK.

Water

The Water Establishment of Beirut and the Mount of Lebanon: Immeuble Chedrawi, rue Sami Solh, Beirut; tel. (1) 386760; e-mail info@ebml.gov.lb; internet www.ebml.gov.lb; f. 2000; Chair. JEAN GIBRAN.

The Water Establishment of the Beqa'a: Zahleh; f. 2000; Gen. Dir Eng. MAROUN MOUSSALLEM.

The Water Establishment of North Lebanon: Georges Nassif Bldg, Koura; tel. (1) 651011; internet eeln.gov.lb; f. 2000; Chair. JAMAL KRAYYEM.

The Water Establishment of South Lebanon: Sidon; f. 2000; Chair. and Dir-Gen. WASSIM DAHER.

LEBANON

Litani River Authority: rue Bechara el-Khoury, Beirut; tel. (1) 662112; fax (1) 660476; e-mail webmaster@litani.gov.lb; internet www.litani.gov.lb; f. 1954; responsible for water resources management, irrigation, and the devt of dams and hydroelectric facilities; Dir-Gen. Dr SAMI ALAWIEH; Commr GHASSAN NOUREDDINE.

MAJOR COMPANIES

Arabian Construction Co SAL: POB 114–5175, 1st and 2nd Floor, Bloc C, Gefinor, Ras Beirut; tel. (1) 355910; fax (1) 355917; e-mail beirut@accsal.com; internet www.accsal.com; f. 1971; construction of multi-storey buildings, hotels, houses, etc.

Château Ksara SAL: Sin el-Fil, Beirut; tel. (1) 488054; fax (1) 488084; e-mail info@ksara.com.lb; internet www.chateauksara.com; f. 1857; wines and spirits (incl. Ksarak); Chair. and CEO ZAFER CHAOUI.

Consolidated Contractors International Co SAL (CCC): POB 11-2254, Bir Hassan, Nicolas Sursock St, Riad el-Solh, Beirut 1107-2100; tel. (1) 847777; fax (1) 856857; internet www.ccc.net; general construction and engineering projects incl. infrastructure and heavy industry; subsidiary of Consolidated Contractors Co (Greece); Group Chair. SAMER KHOURY.

Contracting and Trading Co (CAT) Group: POB 11-1036, Immeuble CAT, rue al-Arz, Saifi, Beirut; tel. (1) 449910; fax (1) 446931; e-mail catgroup@catgroup.net; internet www.catgroup.net; main subsidiaries: Mothercat Ltd, CAT Int. Ltd, Contracting and Trading Co (CAT) Lebanon SAL; Pres. and CEO JOSEPH GEBARA; 12,000 employees (2023).

Fonderies Ohannes H. Kassardjian SAL: POB 11-4150, Beirut; tel. (5) 462462; fax (5) 464645; f. 1939; production of brass and gun-metal valves, ferrules, saddles and fittings for water-service house connections, cast-iron fittings for pipes, manhole covers and gratings, urban furniture, etc.; Pres. JOSEPH O. KASSARDJIAN.

Hamra Engineering SARL: POB 11-6040, Dekwaneh, Main St, Beirut; tel. and fax (1) 688747; f. 1966; part of the Al-Hamra Group; civil, electrical and mechanical engineering; construction work on industrial projects, etc.; steel structures, offshore works; production and trading in building materials, etc.; Chair. HANNA AYOUB.

Industrial Development Co (INDEVCO) SAL: POB 11-2354, Tellat al-Ansafir, Ajaltoun, Beirut; tel. (9) 230130; fax (9) 235541; e-mail info@indevcogroup.com; internet www.indevcogroup.com; f. 1955; private co; mfrs of plastic and paper flexible packaging, corrugated containers, tissue rolls, personal hygiene products and other disposables; CEO NEEMAT FREM.

Karoun Dairies SAL: POB 11-9150, Immeuble Baghdassarian, Cité Industrielle, Bauchrieh, Beirut; e-mail info@karoundairies.com; internet www.karoun.com; f. 1931; dairy products; Pres. and CEO ARA BAGHDASSARIAN.

Lahoud Engineering Co Ltd: POB 114-5175, Gefinor Center, Beirut; tel. (1) 355910; fax (1) 355917; e-mail mail@lahoudeng.com; internet www.lahoud.com; f. 1972; construction of industrial plants.

M1 Group: Immeuble Starco, Bloc B, rue Omar Daouk, Beirut 2020 3313; tel. (1) 356666; fax (1) 356635; internet www.m1group.com; investment holding co with interests in various sectors, incl. oil and energy, real estate, retail and travel; Chair. TAHA A. MIKATI; CEO AZMI T. MIKATI.

Mothercat Ltd: POB 11-1036, Immeuble CAT, rue al-Arz, Saifi, Beirut; tel. (1) 49910; fax (1) 446931; f. 1994; civil, mechanical, electrical, pipeline, storage tanks and district cooling contractors; subsidiary of C.A.T. Holding SA (Luxembourg).

Société Nationale d'Entreprises: POB 11-7101, Beirut; tel. (1) 892805; fax (1) 892806; civil engineering incl. road construction and water contracting; Chair. JOSEPH KHOURY.

TRADE UNION FEDERATION

Confédération Générale des Travailleurs du Liban (CGTL): POB 4381, Beirut; f. 1958; 300,000 mems; only national labour centre in Lebanon and sole rep. of working classes; comprises 18 affiliated feds, incl. all 150 unions in Lebanon; Pres. BÉCHARA ASMAR.

Transport

RAILWAYS

Office des Chemins de Fer et des Transports en Commun (OCFTC): POB 11-109, Gare St Michel, Nahr, Beirut; tel. (1) 587211; fax (1) 447007; from 1961 all railways in Lebanon were state-owned; the network, which at its peak totalled some 412 km, largely ceased functioning in the 1970s owing to the civil war and the last remaining routes were taken out of service for economic reasons during the 1990s; although several proposals to reconstruct and revive sections of the rail system have been discussed, none have, as yet, come to fruition (largely owing, in recent years, to the conflict in the Syrian Arab Repub.); Dir-Gen. and Pres. RADWAN BOU NASSER EL-DIN.

ROADS

The two international motorways are the north–south coastal road and the road connecting Beirut with Damascus in Syria. Among the major roads are those crossing the Beqa'a and continuing south to Bent-Jbail and the Shtaura–Ba'albek road.

SHIPPING

In the 1990s a two-phase programme to rehabilitate and expand the port of Beirut commenced, involving the construction of an industrial free zone, a fifth basin and a major container terminal; the container terminal became operational in 2005 and was extended in 2013. Tripoli, the northern Mediterranean terminus of the oil pipeline from Iraq, is also a busy port, with good equipment and facilities. A further two sea ports are located at Saida and Tyr, in southern Lebanon.

On 4 August 2020 large sections of the port of Beirut and its infrastructure were destroyed by a massive explosion, caused by the ignition of some 2,700 metric tons of ammonium nitrate stored in one of the port's warehouses. The port was forced to close, with cargo being redirected to the country's other, smaller ports.

Port Authorities

Gestion et Exploitation du Port de Beyrouth: POB 1490, Beirut; tel. (1) 580211; fax (1) 585835; e-mail info@portdebeyrouth.com; internet www.portdebeyrouth.com; Pres., Dir-Gen. and Man. Dir OMAR ITANI; Harbour Master AYMAN KARKAR.

Office d'Exploitation du Port de Tripoli: rond point Tripoli, rue Mina, Tripoli; tel. (6) 620800; e-mail info@oept.gov.lb; internet www.oept.gov.lb; f. 1959; Dir AHMED TAMER.

Principal Shipping Companies

Ademar Shipping Lines: POB 175-231, rue Shafaka, al-Medawar, Beirut; tel. (1) 444100; fax (1) 444101; e-mail admin@adelmarservices.com; internet www.ademarlb.com; f. 1992.

Consolidated Bulk Inc (CBI): POB 70-152, Centre St Elie, Blk A, 6e étage, Antélias, Beirut; tel. (4) 410724; fax (4) 402842; e-mail trading@bulkgroup.com; internet www.bulkgroup.com; f. 1993; Gen. Man. SAMI P. ZACCA.

O. D. Debbas & Sons: POB 3, blvd Corniche du Fleuve, Achrafieh, Beirut; tel. (1) 585253; fax (1) 587135; e-mail oddebbas@oddebbas.com; internet www.oddebbas.com; f. 1892; Man. Dir WADIH ELIE DEBBAS.

Freight Leader SARL: POB 175530, Immeuble Medawar, 5e étage, rue Pasteur, Saifi, Beirut; tel. (1) 581870; fax (1) 564387; e-mail info@freightleader.com; internet www.freightleader.com; f. 2001; transportation services and logistics; Exec. Man. MOUSSA SALAMOUN.

Navigators Co SARL: POB 175179, Immeuble Medawar 1200, 6e étage, Achrafieh, Beirut; tel. (1) 570571; fax (1) 575730; e-mail navigators@navigators-lb.com; internet www.navigators-lb.com; Man. Dir ANTOINE MOUHAYAR.

Orient Shipping and Trading Co SARL: POB 11-2561, Immeuble Saab 5, rue Phoenicia, Ain-Almraisseh, Beirut; tel. (1) 364455; fax (1) 365570; e-mail ortship@inco.com.lb; internet ortship.com; CEO HABIB ELIE ZAROUBY.

CIVIL AVIATION

A major expansion project at Beirut International Airport was completed in 2001; facilities included a new terminal building and two new runways. In May 2005 the airport was renamed Beirut Rafiq Hariri International Airport, in honour of the former Prime Minister who had been killed in February of that year. In June 2019 the airport's newly renovated and expanded departures and arrivals terminals were opened and in that year the number of passengers totalled 8.7m.

MEA (Middle East Airlines, Air Liban SAL): POB 11-206, blvd de l'Aéroport, Beirut 1107 2801; tel. (1) 629999; fax (1) 629260; e-mail callcenter@mea.com.lb; internet www.mea.com.lb; f. 1945; acquired Lebanese International Airways in 1969; regular services throughout Europe, the Middle East, North and West Africa, and the Far East; Chair. and Dir-Gen. MUHAMMAD A. EL-HOUT.

Tourism

Destination Lebanon: POB 11-5344, 550 Central Bank St, Hamra, Beirut; tel. 1-340940; fax 1-340945; e-mail info@destinationlebanon.gov.lb; internet destinationlebanon.gov.lb; part of the Ministry of Tourism.

Defence

As assessed at November 2022, the total strength of the Lebanese Armed Forces was 60,000 (army 56,600; navy 1,800; air force 1,600). Paramilitary forces included an estimated 20,000 members of the Internal Security Forces, attached to the Ministry of the Interior and Municipalities.

Following conflict in Lebanon between Hezbollah and Israeli armed forces in July–August 2006, the United Nations (UN) Security Council unanimously adopted Resolution 1701, calling for a full cessation of hostilities, upon which Lebanon was to deploy government forces in southern Lebanon and the presence there of the UN Interim Force in Lebanon (UNIFIL) was to be expanded to a maximum authorized strength of 15,000 troops (reduced to 13,000 in August 2020), while Israel was to commence the parallel withdrawal of all its forces from that region. A formal ceasefire entered into effect on 14 August. At the end of November 2022 there were some 10,000 UNIFIL military personnel deployed in Lebanon.

Defence Budget: £L2,900,000m. in 2020.
Commander-in-Chief of the Army: Gen. JOSEPH AOUN.
Chief of Staff of Armed Forces: (vacant).
Commander of the Air Force: Brig.-Gen. ZIAD HAYKAL.
Commander of the Navy: Rear Adm. HAISSAM DANNAOUI.
Director-General of State Security Forces: Maj.-Gen. TONY SALIBA.

Education

Education is compulsory for a period of nine years between six and 15 years of age. Primary education has been available free of charge in state schools since 1960, but private institutions still provide the main facilities for secondary and university education. Private schools enjoy almost complete autonomy, except for a certain number that receive government financial aid and are supervised by inspectors from the Ministry of Education and Higher Education. In 2020 government spending on education was equivalent to 9.9% of total budgetary expenditure, according to UNESCO figures.

Primary education begins at six years of age and lasts for six years, comprising two cycles of three years each. Secondary education, beginning at the age of 13, lasts for up to six years, comprising two cycles of three years each. Technical education is provided mainly at the National School of Arts and Crafts, which offers four-year courses in electronics, mechanics, architectural and industrial drawing, and other subjects. There are also public vocational schools providing courses for lower levels. In 2017 enrolment at primary schools included 86% of children (boys 89%; girls 84%) in the relevant age-group, while the comparable rate for secondary schools in 2012 was 65% (boys 65%; girls 65%).

Bibliography

Abboud, Samer Nassif. *Rethinking Hizballah: Legitimacy, Authority, Violence*. Farnham, Ashgate, 2012.

Abisaab, Rula Jurdi, and Abisaab, Malek. *The Shi'ites of Lebanon: Modernism, Communism, and Hizbullah's Islamists*. Syracuse, NY, Syracuse University Press, 2014.

Abouchdid, E. E. *Thirty Years of Lebanon and Syria (1917–47)*. Beirut, Sader-Rihani Print. Co, 1948.

Aboultaif, Eduardo Wassim. *Power Sharing in Lebanon: Consociationalism Since 1820*. London, Routledge, 2019.

Agwani, M. S. (Ed.). *The Lebanese Crisis, 1958: A Documentary Study*. London, Asia Publishing House, 1965.

Ajami, Fouad. *The Vanished Imam: Musa al-Sadr and the Shi'a of Lebanon*. London, I. B. Tauris; New York, NY, Cornell University Press, 1986.

Alamuddin, Amal, Nabil Jurdi, Nidal, and Tolbert, David (Eds). *The Special Tribunal for Lebanon: Law and Practice*. Oxford, Oxford University Press, 2014.

Andeweg, Rudy. 'Consociational Democracy'. *Annual Review of Political Science*, Vol. 3, No. 1, 2000, pp. 509–536.

Assi, Abbas. *Democracy in Lebanon: Political Parties and the Struggle for Power since Syrian Withdrawal*. London, I. B. Tauris, 2016.

Arsan, Andrew. *Lebanon: a Country in Fragments*. London, C. Hurst & Co, 2018.

Attie, Caroline. *Struggle in the Levant: Lebanon in the 1950s*. London, I. B. Tauris, 2003.

Azani, Eitan. *Hezbollah: The Story of the Party of God*. Basingstoke, Palgrave Macmillan, 2008.

Barak, Oren. *The Lebanese Army: A National Institution in a Divided Society*. Albany, NY, State University of New York Press, 2009.

Barry, Brian. 'The Consociational Model and Its Dangers'. *European Journal of Political Research*, Vol. 3, No. 4, 1975, pp. 393–412.

The Beirut Massacre: The Complete Kahan Commission Report. New York, Karz-Cohl, 1983.

Blanford, Nicholas. *Killing Mr Lebanon: The Assassination of Rafik Hariri and its Impact on the Middle East*. London, I. B. Tauris, 2006.

Bonsen, Sabrina. *Martyr Cults and Political Identities in Lebanon: "Victory or Martyrdom" in The Struggle of the Amal Movement*. Wiesbaden, Springer VS, 2020.

Bulloch, John. *Death of a Country: The Civil War in Lebanon*. London, Weidenfeld and Nicolson, 1977.

Final Conflict: The War in Lebanon. London, Century Publishing Co, 1983.

Burckhard, C. *Le Mandat Français en Syrie et au Liban*. Paris, 1925.

Calfat, Natalia, and Nahas, C. M. 'The Frailties of Lebanese Democracy: Outcomes and Limits of the Confessional Framework'. *Contexto Internacional*, Vol. 40, No. 2, 2018, pp. 269–293.

Cammett, Melani. *Compassionate Communalism: Welfare and Sectarianism in Lebanon*. New York, Cornell University Press, 2014.

Chamie, Joseph. *Religion and Fertility: Arab Christian-Muslim Differentials*. Cambridge, Cambridge University Press, 1981.

Chamoun, C. *Les Mémoires de Camille Chamoun*. Beirut, 1949.

Chehabi, H. E. (Ed.). *Distant Relations: Iran and Lebanon in the Last 500 Years*. London, I. B. Tauris, 2006.

Comaty, Lyna. *Post-Conflict Transition in Lebanon: The Disappeared of the Civil War*. London, Routledge, 2019.

Constitute Project (trans. Fouad Fahmy Shafik and Abed Awad. 'Lebanon's Constitution of 1926 with Amendments through 2004'. www.constituteproject.org/constitution/Lebanon_2004.pdf?lang=en.

Daher, Joseph. *Hezbollah: the Political Economy of Lebanon's Party of God*. London, Pluto Press, 2016.

Dib, Kamal. *Warlords and Merchants: The Lebanese Business and Political Establishment*. London, Ithaca Press, 2004.

Di Peri, Rosita, and Meier, Daniel. *Lebanon Facing the Arab Uprisings: Constraints and Adaptation*. Basingstoke, Palgrave Macmillan, 2017.

El Khazen, Farid. *The Breakdown of the State in Lebanon, 1967–76*. Cambridge, MA, Harvard University Press, 2000.

Firro, Kais. *Inventing Lebanon: Nationalism and the State Under the Mandate*. London, I. B. Tauris, 2002.

Metamorphosis of the Nation (al-Umma): The Rise of Arabism and Minorities in Syria and Lebanon, 1850–1940. Eastbourne, Sussex Academic Press, 2009.

Gaspard, Toufic K. *A Political Economy of Lebanon, 1948–2002: The Limits of Laissez-faire*. Leiden, Brill, 2004.

Gaunson, A. B. *The Anglo–French Clash in Lebanon and Syria, 1940–45*. London, Macmillan, 1987.

Geha, Carmen. *Civil Society and Political Reform in Lebanon and Libya: Transition and Constraint*. Abingdon, Routledge, 2016.

Geukjian, Ohannes. *Lebanon After the Syrian Withdrawal: External Intervention, Power-sharing and Political Instability*. Abingdon, Routledge, 2017.

Haddad, Simon. *The Palestinian Impasse in Lebanon: The Politics of Refugee Integration*. Brighton, Sussex Academic Press, 2003.

Haddad, Tania N. *International and Local Actors in Disaster Response: Responding to the Beirut Explosion*. Abingdon, Routledge, 2022.

Hafeda, Mohamad. *Negotiating Conflict in Lebanon: Bordering Practices in a Divided Beirut*. London, I. B. Tauris, 2019.

Hage Ali, Mohanad. *Nationalism, Transnationalism, and Political Islam: Hizbullah's Institutional Identity*. Cham, Springer, 2017.

Hakim, Carol. *The Origins of the Lebanese National Idea, 1840–1920*. Berkeley, CA, University of California Press, 2013.

Halawi, Majed. *A Lebanon Defied: Mosa al-Sadr and the Shi'a Community*. Oxford, Westview Press, 1993.

Hamzeh, Ahmad Nizar. *In the Path of Hizbullah*. Syracuse, NY, Syracuse University Press, 2004.

Harel, Amos, and Issacharoff, Avi. *34 Days: Israel, Hezbollah, and the War in Lebanon*. New York, Palgrave Macmillan, 2008.

Harik, Iliya F. *Politics and Change in a Traditional Society—Lebanon 1711–1845*. Princeton, NJ, Princeton University Press, 1968.

Harik, Judith P. *Hezbollah: The Changing Face of Terrorism*. London, I. B. Tauris, 2004.

Harris, William. *Lebanon: A History, 600–2011*. New York, Oxford University Press, 2012.

Hashemi, Nader, and Postel, Danny (Eds). *Sectarianization: Mapping the New Politics of the Middle East*. London, C. Hurst & Co, 2017.

Hazran, Yusri. *The Druze Community and the Lebanese State: Between Confrontation and Reconciliation*. Abingdon, Routledge, 2014.

Helou, Joseph P. *Activism, Change and Sectarianism in the Free Patriotic Movement in Lebanon*. Cham, Palgrave Macmillan, 2020.

Hirst, David. *Beware of Small States: Lebanon, Battleground of the Middle East*. London, Faber and Faber, 2010.

Hitti, Philip K. *Lebanon in History*. London, Macmillan, 3rd edn, 1967.

Hollis, Rosemary, and Shehadi, Nadim (Eds). *Lebanon on Hold: Implications for Middle East Peace*. London, Royal Institute for International Affairs, 1996.

Hourani, Albert K. *Syria and Lebanon*. London, Oxford University Press, 1946.

A History of the Arab Peoples. Cambridge, MA, Harvard University Press, revised edn, 2002.

Hudson, Michael C. *The Precarious Republic: Political Modernization in the Lebanon*. New York, Random House, 1968.

Husayn, Abdul Rahim Abu. *The View from Istanbul: Ottoman Lebanon and the Druze Emirate*. London, I. B. Tauris, 2002.

El-Husseini, Rola. *Pax Syriana: Elite Politics in Postwar Lebanon*. Syracuse, NY, Syracuse University Press, 2012.

Johnson, Michael. *All Honourable Men: The Social Origins of War in Lebanon*. London, I. B. Tauris, 2001.

Jones, Clive, and Catignani, Sergio (Eds). *Israel and Hizbollah: An Asymmetric Conflict in Historical and Comparative Perspective*. Abingdon, Routledge, 2009.

Kalawoun, Nasser M. *The Struggle for Lebanon. A Modern History of Lebanese-Egyptian Relations*. London, I. B. Tauris, 2000.

Karam, Jeffrey G., and Majed, Rima (Eds). *Lebanon Uprising of 2019: Voices From the Revolution*. London, I. B. Tauris, 2022.

Karsh, Efraim, Kerr, Michael, and Miller, Rory (Eds). *Conflict, Diplomacy and Society in Israeli-Lebanese Relations*. Abingdon, Routledge, 2010.

Kassir, Samir. *La guerre du Liban. De la dissension nationale au conflit régional*. Paris, Karthala and CERMOC, 1994.

Histoire de Beyrouth. Paris, Fayard, 2003.

Kerr, Michael, and Knudsen, Are J. *Lebanon: After the Cedar Revolution*. London, C. Hurst & Co, 2012.

Khalaf, Samir. *Civil and Uncivil Violence: The Internationalization of Communal Conflict in Lebanon*. New York, Columbia University Press, 2002.

Lebanon Adrift: From Battleground to Playground. London, Saqi Books, 2012.

Khalidi, Rashid. 'Lebanon in the Context of Regional Politics'. *Third World Quarterly*, Vol. 7, No. 3, 1985, pp. 495–514.

Kingston, Paul. *Reproducing Sectarianism: Advocacy Networks and the Politics of Civil Society in Postwar Lebanon*. New York, SUNY Press, 2013.

Kisirwani, Maroun. 'Foreign Interference and Religious Animosity in Lebanon'. *Journal of Contemporary History*, Vol. 15, No. 4, 1980, pp. 685–700.

Klaushofer, Alex. *Paradise Divided: A Portrait of Lebanon*. Oxford, Signal Books, 2007.

Leenders, Reinoud. *Spoils of Truce: Corruption and State-Building in Postwar Lebanon*. Ithaca, NY, Cornell University Press, 2012.

Llewellyn, Tim. *Spirit of the Phoenix: Beirut and the Story of Lebanon*. London, I. B. Tauris, 2010.

Longrigg, S. H. *Syria and Lebanon under French Mandate*. Oxford, Oxford University Press, 1958.

Mackey, Sandra. *Lebanon: A House Divided*. New York, W. W. Norton & Co, 2006.

Mirror of the Arab World: Lebanon in Conflict. New York, W. W. Norton & Co, 2008.

Makdisi, Samar. *Lessons of Lebanon: The Economics of War and Development*. London, I. B. Tauris, 2004.

Makdisi, Ussama. 'Reconstructing the Nation-State: The Modernity of Sectarianism in Lebanon'. *Middle East Report*, No. 200, 1996, pp. 23–30.

The Culture of Sectarianism: Community, History, and Violence in Nineteenth-Century Ottoman Lebanon. Los Angeles, CA, University of California Press, 2000.

Mikdashi, Maya. *Sextarianism: Sovereignty, Secularism, and the State in Lebanon*. Stanford, Stanford University Press, 2022.

Marron, Rayyar. *Humanitarian Rackets and their Moral Hazards: the Case of the Palestinian Refugee Camps in Lebanon*. Abingdon, Routledge, 2016.

Meier, Daniel. *Shaping Lebanon's Borderlands: Armed Resistance and International Intervention in South Lebanon*. London, I. B. Tauris, 2016.

Mishal, Shaul. *Understanding Shiite Leadership: The Art of the Middle Ground in Iran and Lebanon*. New York, Cambridge University Press, 2014.

Mohseni, Payam, and Kalout, Hussein. 'Iran's Axis of Resistance Rises: How It's Forging a New Middle East'. *Foreign Affairs*, Vol. 24, 2017.

Monroe, Kristin V. *The Insecure City: Space, Power, and Mobility in Beirut*. New Brunswick, NJ, Rutgers University Press, 2016.

Moumneh, Nader. *The Lebanese Forces: Emergence and Transformation of the Christian Resistance*. Lanham, MD, Hamilton Books, 2019.

Nagle, John, and Clancy, Mary-Alice (Eds). *Power-Sharing after Civil War: Thirty Years since Lebanon's Taif Agreement*. Abingdon, Routledge, 2021.

Najem, Tom. *Lebanon: The Politics of a Penetrated Society*. Abingdon, Routledge, 2011.

Nasser, Salem Hikmat. 'International Law and Politics: International Criminal Courts and Judgments—The Case of the Special Tribunal for Lebanon'. *Gonzaga Journal of International Law*, Vol. 15, 2012, pp. 146–171.

Norton, Augustus Richard. *Hezbollah: A Short History*. Princeton, NJ, Princeton University Press, 2007.

'Hizballah: From Radicalism to Prgmatism?'. *Middle East Policy*, Vol. 5, No. 4, 1998, pp.147–158.

'The Role of Hezbollah in Lebanese Domestic Politics'. *The International Spectator*, Vol. 42, No. 4, pp. 475–491.

Nucho, Joanne Ramda. *Everyday Sectarianism in Urban Lebanon: Infrastructures, Public Services, and Power*. Princeton, NJ, Princeton University Press, 2017.

O'Ballance, Edgar. *Civil War in Lebanon, 1975–1992*. New York, St Martin's Press, 1998.

Osoegawa, Taku. *Syria and Lebanon: International Relations and Diplomacy in the Middle East*. London, I. B. Tauris, 2013.

Pape, Robert. 'The Strategic Logic of Suicide Terrorism'. *American Political Science Review*, Vol. 97, No. 3, 2003, pp. 343–361.

Pellegrin, Paolo, Smith, Patti, and Anderson, Scott. *Double Blind: Lebanon Conflict 2006*. London, Trolley, 2007.

Picard, Elizabeth. *Lebanon: A Shattered Country*. New York and London, Holmes and Meier, revised edn, 2002.

Presidency of the Council of Ministers. 'Previous Governments and Ministerial Statements'. pcm.gov.lb/arabic/charts.aspx?pageid=266.

Qubain, Fahim I. *Crisis in Lebanon*. Washington, DC, Middle East Institute, 1961.

Rabil, Robert G. *Religion, National Identity, and Confessional Politics in Lebanon: The Challenge of Islamism*. New York, Palgrave Macmillan, 2011.

The Syrian Refugee Crisis in Lebanon: the Double Tragedy of Refugees and Impacted Host Communities. Lanham, MD, Lexington Books, 2016.

Reilly, James A. *The Ottoman Cities of Lebanon: Historical Legacy and Identity in the Modern Middle East*. London, I. B. Tauris, 2016.

Rougier, B. *Everyday Jihad: The Rise of Militant Islam Among Palestinians in Lebanon*. Cambridge, MA, Harvard University Press, 2007.

Rubin, Barry. *Lebanon: Liberation, Conflict, and Crisis*. Basingstoke, Palgrave Macmillan, 2009.

Saad-Ghorayeb, Amal. *Hizbullah: Politics and Religion*. London, Pluto Press, 2002.

Saade, Bashir. *Hizbullah and the Politics of Remembrance: Writing the Lebanese Nation*. Cambridge, Cambridge University Press, 2016.

Salam, Nawaf A. (Ed.). *Options for Lebanon*. London, I. B. Tauris, 2005.

Salamey, Imad. *The Government and Politics of Lebanon*. Abingdon, Routledge, 2013.

Salibi, K. S. *The Modern History of Lebanon*. New York, Praeger, and London, Weidenfeld and Nicolson, 1964.

Cross Roads to Civil War: Lebanon 1958–76. New York, Caravan Books, 1976.

A House of Many Mansions: The History of Lebanon Reconsidered. London, I. B. Tauris, 2003.

Salloukh, Bassel F., Barakat, Rabie, Al-Habbal, Jinan S., Khattab, Lara W., and Mikaelian, Shoghig. *Politics of Sectarianism in Postwar Lebanon*. Chicago, IL, University of Chicago Press, 2015.

Samii, Abbas William. 'The Shah's Lebanon Policy': The Role of SAVAK. *Middle Eastern Studies*, Vol. 33, No. 1, 1997, pp. 66–91.

Saouli, Adham. *Hezbollah: Socialisation and its Tragic Ironies*. Edinburgh, Edinburgh University Press, 2019.

Sbaity Kassem, Fatima. *Party Politics, Religion, and Women's Leadership: Lebanon in Comparative Perspective*. Basingstoke, Palgrave Macmillan, 2013.

Shaery-Eisenlohr, Roschanack. *Shi'ite Lebanon: Transnational Religion and the Making of National Identities*. New York, Columbia University Press, 2008.

Shanahan, Rodger. *The Shi'a of Lebanon: Clans, Parties and Clerics*. London, I. B. Tauris, 2005.

Sogge, Erling Loretzen. *Palestinian National Movement in Lebanon: A Political History of the 'Ayn al-Hilwe Camp*. London, I. B. Tauris, 2021.

Soueid, Mahmoud. *Israël au Liban. La fin de 30 ans d'occupation?* Paris, Revue d'études Palestiniennes, 2000.

Stocker, James R. *Spheres of Intervention: US Foreign Policy and the Collapse of Lebanon, 1967-1976*. Ithaca, NY, Cornell University Press, 2016.

Stel, Nora. *Hybrid Political Order and the Politics of Uncertainty: Refugee Governance in Lebanon*. Abingdon, Routledge, 2022.

Suleiman, M. W. *Political Parties in Lebanon*. Ithaca, NY, Cornell University Press, 1967.

Thuselt, Christian. *Lebanese Political Parties: Dream of a Republic*. London, Routledge, 2021.

Traboulsi, Fawwaz. *A History of Modern Lebanon*. London, Pluto Press, 2nd edn, 2012.

United Nations Peacemaker. 'Taif Accords'. 22 Oct. 1989. peacemaker.un.org/lebanon-taifaccords89.

Wählisch, Martin. *Update: The Special Tribunal for Lebanon (STL)—An Introduction and Research Guide*. Hauser Global Law School Program, New York University School of Law, Nov./Dec. 2015. www.nyulawglobal.org/globalex/Special_Tribunal_Lebanon1.html.

Wehrey, Frederic M. (Ed.). *Beyond Sunni and Shia: The Roots of Sectarianism in a Changing Middle East*. Oxford, Oxford University Press, 2017.

Wiegand, Krista. 'Reformation of a Terrorist Group: Hezbollah as a Lebanese Political Party'. *Studies in Conflict & Terrorism*, Vol. 32, No. 8, 2009, pp. 669–680.

Wilkins, Henrietta. *The Making of Lebanese Foreign Policy: Understanding the 2006 Hezbollah–Israeli War*. Abingdon, Routledge, 2013.

Wilson, Anna (Ed.). *Lebanon, Lebanon*. London, Saqi Books, 2006.

Yadav, Stacey Philbrick. *Islamists and the State: Legitimacy and Institutions in Yemen and Lebanon*. London, I. B. Tauris, 2013.

Young, Michael. *The Ghosts of Martyrs Square: An Eyewitness Account of Lebanon's Life Struggle*. New York, Simon and Schuster, 2010.

Zamir, Meir. *The Foundation of Modern Lebanon*. London, Croom Helm, 1985.

Lebanon's Quest: The Road to Statehood 1926–1939. London, I. B. Tauris, 1998.

Ziadeh, Hanna. *Sectarianism and Inter-Communal Nation Building in Lebanon*. London, C. Hurst & Co, 2006.

Zisser, Eyal. *Lebanon: The Challenge of Independence*. London, I. B. Tauris, 2000.

LIBYA

Geography

Libya is bounded on the north by the Mediterranean Sea, on the east by Egypt and Sudan, on the south and south-west by Chad and Niger, on the west by Algeria and on the north-west by Tunisia. The three component areas of Libya are Tripolitania, in the west; Cyrenaica, in the east; and the Fezzan, in the south—giving an approximate total for Libya of 1,676,198 sq km (647,189 sq miles).

The independence of Libya was proclaimed in December 1951; before that date, following conquest by the Italians, Tripolitania and Cyrenaica had been ruled by a British administration (at first military, then civil), while the Fezzan had been administered by France. The revolutionary Government that came to power in September 1969 renamed the three regions: Tripolitania became known as the Western provinces, Cyrenaica the Eastern provinces, and the Fezzan the Southern provinces. Tarabulus (Tripoli) was formerly the administrative capital of the country, but under a decentralization programme announced in 1988 most government departments and the legislature were relocated to Surt (Sirte), while some departments were transferred to other principal towns.

In August 2011 the National Transitional Council, which was widely recognized as the de facto governing body for Libya following the outbreak of conflict between opposition forces and those loyal to Muammar al-Qaddafi earlier that year, issued an interim constitutional declaration, which redesignated Tripoli as the country's capital. A new legislature, the House of Representatives, was inaugurated in Tobruk in August 2014. The chamber was eventually to be based in Banghazi (Benghazi).

PHYSICAL FEATURES

The whole of Libya may be said to form part of the vast plateau of North Africa, which extends from the Atlantic Ocean to the Red Sea; however, there are certain minor geographical features that give individuality to the three component areas of Libya. Tripolitania consists of a series of regions at different levels, rising in the main towards the south, and thus broadly comparable with a flight of steps. In the extreme north, along the Mediterranean coast, there is a low-lying coastal plain called the Jefara. This is succeeded inland by a line of hills, or rather a scarp edge, that has several distinguishing local names, but is usually alluded to merely as the Jebel. Here and there in the Jebel occurs evidence of former volcanic activity—old craters, and sheets of lava. The Jefara and adjacent parts of the Jebel are by far the most important parts of Tripolitania, since they are better watered and contain most of the population, together with Tripoli.

South of the Jebel there is an upland plateau—a desert landscape of sand, scrub and scattered irregular masses of stone. After several hundred kilometres the plateau gives way to a series of east–west running depressions, where artesian water, and hence oases, are found. These depressions make up the region of the Fezzan, which is merely a collection of oases on a fairly large scale, interspersed with areas of desert. In the extreme south the land rises considerably to form the mountains of the central Sahara, where some peaks reach 3,500 m in height.

Cyrenaica has a slightly different physical pattern. In the north, along the Mediterranean, there is an upland plateau that rises to 600 m in two very narrow steps, each only a few kilometres wide. This gives a bold, prominent coastline to much of Cyrenaica, and so there is a marked contrast with Tripolitania where the coast is low-lying, and in parts fringed by lagoons. The northern uplands of Cyrenaica are called the Jebel Akhdar (Green Mountain), and here, once again, are found the bulk of the population and the two main towns, Benghazi and Darna. On its western side the Jebel Akhdar drops fairly steeply to the shores of the Gulf of Sirte; on the east it falls more gradually, and is traceable as a series of ridges, about 100 m in altitude, that extend as far as the Egyptian frontier. This eastern district, consisting of low ridges aligned parallel to the coast, is known as Marmarica, and its chief town is Tobruk.

South of the Jebel Akhdar the land falls in elevation, producing an extensive lowland, which, except for its northern fringe, is mainly desert. Oases occur sporadically at Aujila (or Ojila), Jalo and Jaghbub in the north, and Jawf, Zighen and Kufra (the largest of all) in the south. These oases traditionally supported only a few thousand inhabitants and were less significant than those of the Fezzan, though some are now in petroleum-producing areas and, consequently, are increasing in importance. In the same region, and becoming more widespread towards the east, is the Sand Sea—an expanse of fine, mobile sand, easily lifted by the wind into dunes that can sometimes reach about 100 m in height and more than 150 km in length. Finally, in the far south of Cyrenaica, lie the central Saharan mountains—the Tibesti Ranges, continuous with those to the south of the Fezzan.

CLIMATE

The climate of Libya is characterized chiefly by its aridity and by its wide variation in temperatures. Lacking mountain barriers, the country is subject to the climatic influence of both the Sahara and the Mediterranean Sea, and, as a result, there can be abrupt transitions in climatic conditions. In winter it can be fairly raw and cold in the north, with sleet and even light snow on the hills. In summer it is extremely hot in the Jefara of Tripolitania, reaching temperatures of 40°C–45°C. In the southern deserts, conditions are hotter still; Gharian has recorded temperatures in excess of 49°C. Several feet of snow can also fall here in winter. Northern Cyrenaica has a markedly cooler summer of 27°C–32°C, but with high air humidity near the coast. A special feature is the *ghibli*—a hot, very dry wind from the south that can raise temperatures in the north by 15°C or even 20°C in a few hours, sometimes resulting in temperatures of 20°C or 25°C in January. This sand-laden, dry wind (which can cause considerable crop damage) may blow at any time of the year, but spring and autumn are the usual seasons.

The hills of Tripolitania and Cyrenaica annually receive as much as 400 mm–500 mm of rainfall, but in the remainder of the country the rainfall is usually 200 mm or less. Once every five or six years there is a pronounced drought, sometimes lasting for two successive seasons.

POPULATION

In 2012 a national census conducted by the Ministry of Planning indicated that the population had grown by a negligible amount since the last such exercise in 2006, to 5,363,369. However, many external organizations contended that the actual figure was much higher. By mid-2023 the United Nations (UN) estimated that the population totalled 6,888,388. According to UN estimates, Tripoli was the country's largest city, with a population of 1,183,292 at mid-2023. Other major cities included Misurata (984,193) and Benghazi (859,209).

Arabic, introduced by the 10th century invaders, is the sole official language of Libya, but a few Tamazight-speaking Berber villages remain. English and Italian are also used in commerce.

History
Revised by RONALD BRUCE ST JOHN

PRE-COLONIAL AND COLONIAL PERIODS

Both the Phoenicians and the Greeks colonized the coastlands of what is now called Libya before the area came under the control of Rome in 96 BCE, inaugurating a period of great prosperity that lasted until the decline of the Roman Empire in the early fifth century CE. Arab invaders from the east swept across Libya in the mid-seventh century, and most of the Berber inhabitants were subsequently Islamized and Arabized. In the early 16th century Tripoli was captured by Spain, but in 1551 the city was seized by the expanding Ottoman Empire and Libya remained under Ottoman sovereignty until the early 20th century. For much of this time real power was exercised by professional soldiers, the Janissaries, in the name of the Ottoman Sultan. The activities of pirate corsairs also expanded, attracting reprisals from the European naval powers. In 1835, probably owing to concerns about French expansion in Algeria and the British occupation of Malta, the Ottoman Sultan decided to bring Libya once more under direct rule. The years that followed were marked by corruption, oppression and revolts, and by the rise of the Senussi religious brotherhood, which attracted many adherents, especially among the tribesmen of Cyrenaica.

In 1911 Italy declared war on Ottoman Turkey (officially redesignated as Türkiye in June 2022) and with a large military force quickly occupied Tripoli and other coastal towns, but the invading troops met stiff resistance when they pressed inland. In October 1912 the Sultan signed a peace treaty with Italy, under which he gave up his rights in Libya; however, he did not recognize Italian sovereignty. Instead, he granted Libyans 'full autonomy'. The Italians, who had already proclaimed their sovereignty over the country, ignored this provision and continued their military occupation. The outbreak of the First World War (1914–18) greatly weakened Italy's position, and the Senussi, supplied with arms and ammunition by Turkey and its ally Germany, began to engage Italian forces, which by the end of the war held only Tripoli and a few other coastal towns. The Libyans continued to press for self-government and agreed to join forces under Said Muhammad Idris, the Senussi leader, but negotiations with the Italians came to nothing. The advent of fascism in Italy in 1922 brought a new impetus to the Italian conquest of Libya. During the next decade Italian forces subdued first Tripolitania, then Fezzan and finally Cyrenaica in a series of military campaigns. Success was achieved by forcing the civilian population into concentration camps in order to deprive the Senussi resistance of supplies and auxiliaries. Such a policy resulted in a heavy death toll among Libyans and caused bitterness that persists even into the 21st century.

INDEPENDENCE

During the Second World War (1939–45) Italian rule was overthrown by the Allied armies and Libya was placed under British and French military administration. However, its political future remained uncertain and in 1945 the Great Powers were unable to agree on a settlement. The USA favoured a United Nations (UN) Trusteeship, the Union of Soviet Socialist Republics (USSR) asked for the trusteeship of Tripolitania for itself and France recommended the return of all the Italian colonies to Italy. This was opposed by the United Kingdom, which had pledged to its ally Muhammad Idris, head of the Senussi order, that Cyrenaica would never be returned to Italian rule. Eventually, the UN took responsibility for Libya, and in 1949 the General Assembly voted in favour of independence, which was proclaimed in 1951 with Idris as King. Initially, the new kingdom had a cumbersome federal structure of government, but this was abolished in 1963 in favour of a unitary state.

During the first 10 years of independence Libya remained desperately poor and heavily dependent on foreign funds for its economic survival. In particular, Libya signed agreements under which the UK and the USA were allowed to maintain military bases in Libya in return for substantial economic aid. The discovery of petroleum in 1959 transformed Libya into a prosperous country, but also played an important part in unleashing social and political forces that within a decade were to expose the fragility of the monarchy.

These domestic developments coincided with the rise of political consciousness in the wider Arab world, and Libya's newly urbanized population was particularly receptive to political influences, especially from neighbouring Egypt. As Arab nationalism in the region grew, Libya, which remained a client state of the West, became more isolated, and divisions between the monarchy and the populace widened. There was widespread speculation that the monarchy would be overthrown; when a military coup took place on 1 September 1969, the only surprise was that the leaders were drawn from the junior rather than the senior officer ranks.

THE 1969 COUP: MUAMMAR AL-QADDAFI BECOMES LIBYAN LEADER

The military coup staged in Tripoli in 1969 was organized by young army officers led by a 27-year-old captain, Muammar al-Qaddafi (who subsequently promoted himself to the rank of colonel). In a matter of hours, the young officers overthrew the Government and seized control of the state with relatively few arrests, virtually no fighting and no deaths being reported. King Idris refused to abdicate but accepted exile in Egypt, where he remained until his death in 1983.

Most of the new men of the revolution were from poor families from the interior who had joined the army because there were no other opportunities for them. Qaddafi himself was born in Sirte, in the desert that reaches to the coastline between Tripolitania and Cyrenaica, and he spent his formative years in the oasis town of Sabha in the Fezzan. From the outset supreme power lay with a 12-man Revolution Command Council (RCC), which proclaimed the Libyan Arab Republic. Its Chairman, Qaddafi, also became head of government and the Commander-in-Chief of the army. With his gift for communication with the Libyan people and a talent for conducting mass meetings, Qaddafi quickly established himself as chief spokesman and ideologist of the new regime.

Motivated by the principles of Arab nationalism, Libya's new leaders set to work with great enthusiasm and energy. Foreign businesses were nationalized, the property of all Jews and Italians still living in Libya was sequestered by the Government, and both communities were encouraged to leave. Furthermore, both the USA and the UK were required to close their military bases in Libya. Emphasis was placed on the Arabic language and a return to the fundamental precepts of Islam in everyday life. All street signs and public notices were to be in Arabic only, alcohol was forbidden, and bars and nightclubs were closed.

In negotiations with the international oil companies operating in Libya, the new regime quickly achieved notable success, spearheading an early push for price increases by the Organization of the Petroleum Exporting Countries (see p. 1161). This allowed Libya to achieve continuous oil revenue growth, despite reducing production in order to conserve reserves. A large number of oil companies held concessions in Libya, including many small independent oil companies, some of which were heavily dependent on Libya for the bulk of their supplies. One of the leading independents, Occidental, obtained almost all its output from Libya. The independent operators were therefore extremely vulnerable, and in 1970–71 they gave in one after the other to pressure from the new regime for greater control over its hydrocarbon resources. This forced the major oil companies to follow suit for fear of losing their concessions. The Libyan Government subsequently acquired a 51% share in the Libyan operations of some of the oil companies and completely nationalized the holdings of others.

THE 'CULTURAL REVOLUTION' AND THE CREATION OF THE SOCIALIST PEOPLE'S LIBYAN ARAB JAMAHIRIYA

Despite the dominance of the new regime, Qaddafi's efforts to institutionalize his ideology and build a participatory political culture proved difficult. Firm control over the state's administrative and military apparatus was easily accomplished, and the early actions of the regime generated a degree of popular support and laid the foundations for Qaddafi's growing authority, primarily on account of his strong personal charisma. None the less, as Qaddafi sought to extend his authority further, he encountered growing resistance from established interests, including bureaucrats, the tribal elite and the Westernized bourgeoisie. In April 1973, therefore, he launched the so-called Popular or Cultural Revolution to broaden his personal support base, as well as popular backing for his vision of a new revolutionary community. The 'Cultural Revolution' called for the destruction of imported ideologies, whether Eastern or Western, and the creation of a society based on the tenets of Islam. Officials and business executives who failed to show the required revolutionary fervour were dismissed, and books and magazines deemed to be offensive were destroyed. At the same time Qaddafi presented his 'third international theory', which claimed to be 'an alternative to capitalism, materialism and communist atheism'. Qaddafi's own personal leadership was firmly established by 1975, and with the publication of the first volume of his *Green Book* in 1975—a blueprint for the social and economic transformation of Libya—he emerged as the country's sole ideological authority. By the end of the 1970s a new political system had been established based on a 'popular democracy' organized through a series of assemblies and committees, from the grass-roots 'popular committees' through the 'basic people's congresses' and 'popular congresses' to the General People's Congress (GPC), a type of national assembly, the General People's Committee, corresponding to the cabinet, and the General Secretariat, the supreme political leadership, replacing the RCC. A separate network of 'revolutionary committees' responsible for political leadership within the popular committee structure was also created.

In March 1977 the official name of the country was changed to the Socialist People's Libyan Arab Jamahiriya (the prefix 'Great' was added in 1986), with power vested in the people through the GPC and the groups represented in it. Qaddafi claimed that this system removed the barriers between people and leaders; however, the exercise of 'popular democracy' was firmly controlled from above. Recruitment to political office, major areas of policymaking and the actual implementation of policies were clearly determined by the leadership. Qaddafi appeared to have been genuine in his desire for popular participation in decision making, yet was unwilling to accept 'popular' views that differed from his own. At the same time Qaddafi became convinced that a more radical transformation of the country along socialist lines was required. Land was nationalized, no one was allowed to own more than one house, state-run supermarkets replaced private shops and demonetization eliminated many assets of the rich. Such measures, more radical than those attempted anywhere else in the Arab world, resulted in a massive levelling of the social structure. Those groups badly hit by the reforms, principally the upper and middle classes, were alienated and in some cases scarce skills were lost, making Libya more dependent on foreigners. In the post-Qaddafi era, the resolution of property rights issues arising from these sweeping redistribution policies would hamper the reconstruction of Libya.

ARAB UNITY BY MERGER OR SUBVERSION

Foreign affairs remained one major area of policy always closely controlled by Qaddafi. When he came to power, the Arab world was more deeply divided than ever. Egypt had been defeated in the 1967 war with Israel, more Arab lands had been occupied and Arab ranks were in disarray. It was Qaddafi's deeply held belief that every reverse for the Arab cause arose from Arab disunity. The Arab world had to be united to win the battle for Palestine. Therefore, the vision of one Arab nation from the Gulf to the Atlantic, and opposition to Zionism and to its ally, Western imperialism, became the dominant themes of Libyan foreign relations.

Almost immediately Qaddafi suggested that Libya form an alliance with Egypt and Sudan in a revolutionary front to consolidate three 'progressive' revolutions. The Tripoli Charter linking the three countries was signed in December 1969. Qaddafi pressed for complete unity between the three states, but President Gamal Abdel Nasser of Egypt was more cautious. After Nasser's death, Egypt and Libya—now joined by the Syrian Arab Republic—created the Federation of Arab Republics on the principles of no negotiated peace with Israel and no abandoning support for the Palestinian cause.

In July 1972 Qaddafi appealed for an immediate merger of Egypt and Libya, and an agreement was signed to take effect in September 1973. As the date for union drew nearer, Nasser's successor, Anwar Sadat, appeared to hesitate. Qaddafi became increasingly impatient and in July 1973 dispatched 40,000 Libyans towards Cairo, Egypt, on a 'unity march' designed to pressure Sadat into bringing about immediate fusion of the two countries. The marchers were turned back at the Egyptian frontier. Despite Egyptian suspicion of the Libyan revolution, the union came into effect in September but soon fell apart, wrecked by Qaddafi's opposition to Egypt's conduct of the Arab–Israeli war of October 1973.

When Egypt and Syria declared war on Israel in October 1973, Qaddafi, who had been the strongest supporter of the Palestinian movements, one of the chief paymasters of the *fedayeen* (martyrs or freedom fighters) and the leading advocate of war with Israel, was not consulted. He was deeply offended and refused to attend the Algiers (Algeria) meeting of Arab heads of state after the war, declaring that it would only ratify Arab capitulation.

Qaddafi's enthusiasm for Arab unity continued unabated, but the failure of political mergers led him to embark on a new course. His speeches attacked Arab leaders who blocked unity and failed to 'liberate' Palestine, and he spoke of providing Libyan aid for revolutionary movements and of the need for popular pressure on North African governments as a means of attaining Arab unity. For some time Libya had been providing money, arms and training for 'liberation' groups in Ireland, Eritrea, the Philippines, Rhodesia (now Zimbabwe), Portuguese Guinea (now Guinea-Bissau), Morocco and Chad, as well as providing aid for sympathetic countries such as Pakistan, Uganda, Zambia and Togo. Now it appeared that Libya was supporting subversion in Egypt and Sudan. Attempted coups in Egypt in April 1974 and in Sudan in the following month were believed to have had Libyan support.

Relations with Egypt deteriorated when, in November 1977, President Sadat launched his peace initiative with Israel. Qaddafi condemned Sadat's move and was a leading instigator of the Tripoli summit of 'rejectionist' states which formed a 'front of steadfastness and confrontation' against Israel in December. Meanwhile, relations with the mainstream Palestine Liberation Organization (PLO) became strained and Qaddafi accused the PLO Chairman, Yasser Arafat, of abandoning the armed struggle in favour of a strategy of diplomacy and moderation. It was not until early 1987 that Qaddafi was reconciled with Arafat and the PLO.

Qaddafi, who had been repeatedly accused of supporting plots to topple the Government of Col Gaafar Muhammad al-Nimeri in Sudan, visited its capital, Khartoum, in May 1985 to endorse Lt-Gen. Abd al-Rahman Swar al-Dahab, who had overthrown al-Nimeri in a bloodless coup the previous month. Qaddafi urged the rebels of the Sudan People's Liberation Army in southern Sudan, who had received Libyan support under al-Nimeri, to begin negotiations with the new Government. A military protocol was signed with Sudan in July, and Libya became Sudan's principal supplier of armaments. Following a military coup in Sudan in June 1989, Qaddafi discussed the possible merger of the two countries with the new Sudanese leader, Lt-Gen. Omar Hassan Ahmad al-Bashir, but little significant progress was made.

Following Iraq's invasion of Kuwait in August 1990, Libya voted against a motion put forward at a League of Arab States (Arab League, see p. 1146) emergency summit meeting condemning the Iraqi action and advocating the deployment of a pan-Arab force for the defence of Saudi Arabia and other states from possible Iraqi aggression. Libya announced that its ports were at Iraq's disposal for the purpose of importing food supplies, and anti-war demonstrations took place in Libya when the US-led Operation Desert Storm began the liberation of Kuwait in January 1991.

RELATIONS WITH LIBYA'S MAGHREB NEIGHBOURS

The coup that brought Qaddafi to power initially reoriented Libya away from the Maghreb, and in 1970 Libya withdrew from the Maghreb Permanent Consultative Committee. In 1971 relations with Morocco were severed after Libya prematurely gave its support to an unsuccessful attempt to overthrow King Hassan. After two failed attempts at union with Tunisia in 1972 and 1974, relations with Libya's western neighbour remained uneasy and were often strained for over a decade.

There was widespread surprise when, in August 1984, Libya and Morocco signed a treaty of union creating the Arab-African Federation. It was an unlikely partnership given Morocco's pro-Western orientation. The union, which Qaddafi envisaged as the first step towards the creation of a politically united Great Arab Maghreb or Greater Maghreb, proved short-lived. Already angered by Qaddafi's announcement of a treaty between Libya and Iran, King Hassan abrogated the union in August 1986.

Relations with Tunisia improved, and in April 1988 the two countries signed a co-operation pact encompassing political, economic, cultural and foreign relations. In June the leaders of Algeria, Morocco, Tunisia, Libya and Mauritania held a meeting in Algiers—the first of its kind since they had achieved independence—to discuss the prospects for 'a Maghreb without frontiers'. A Maghreb commission was created, which led to a treaty signed in February 1989 by the five countries proclaiming the formation of the Union du Maghreb Arabe (UMA—Union of the Arab Maghreb, see p. 1169). However, the union had few practical results owing to divisions between Algeria and Morocco over Western Sahara, the Algerian civil war and UN sanctions against Libya.

QADDAFI'S AFRICAN POLICY

Like his appeal for Arab unity, Qaddafi's much publicized African policy formed part of his scheme to liberate Arab lands from Zionist aggression. He believed that Israel's presence in Africa threatened the Arab states through their own back door. Employing a policy of religious propaganda and promises of financial assistance and aid, Libya appealed to its black African, largely Muslim, neighbours to sever their diplomatic relations with Israel. This policy achieved some notable success, but it also led to a costly military intervention in Chad.

In 1973 Libya occupied the Aozou strip in northern Chad, basing its action on an unratified treaty of 1935 whereby Italy and France altered the frontiers between their two colonies. According to Libya, sovereignty over the strip passed to Italy and subsequently to Libya, when it achieved independence in 1951. The Government of Chad challenged these claims and referred the dispute to the Organization for African Unity (OAU, now the African Union—AU, see p. 1119), which set up a committee of reconciliation, although Libya consistently refused to attend its sessions. For many years Libya had been supporting the predominantly Muslim Front de Libération Nationale du Tchad (FROLINAT) in its rebellion against the Chad Government, but in 1979, when the mainstream of FROLINAT severed their links with Libya over its annexation of the Aozou strip, Libyan army units invaded northern Chad.

During the 1980s an increasing number of Libyan troops were engaged in Chad and Libyan military aid was offered to first one faction and then another in a country caught up in a bitter civil war. As the Libyan army supported rebel forces in the north of Chad, France sent troops to help the beleaguered Government in the capital, N'Djamena. Despite an agreement between France and Libya providing for the evacuation of both countries' forces, Libya continued to support those rebel forces who had not declared allegiance to the Government in N'Djamena, while publicly denying any involvement in the fighting.

However, in 1987 Libyan forces suffered heavy losses as forces loyal to the Chadian Government captured Libyan bases in the north and advanced into the Aozou strip. Libya responded by bombing towns in northern Chad and succeeded in recapturing Aozou. In September Libya and Chad agreed to observe a ceasefire proposed by the OAU, and in October 1988 diplomatic relations between the two countries were resumed. In August 1989 a peace accord was signed in Algiers, which provided for an end to fighting over the Aozou strip, the withdrawal of all forces from the disputed region and an agreement that both parties should attempt to resolve their dispute by means of a political settlement. In August 1990 Libya and Chad agreed to refer the dispute over the Aozou strip to the International Court of Justice in The Hague, Netherlands, which ruled against Libya's claim in February 1994. Libyan forces completed their withdrawal from the disputed region in May.

ATTEMPTS TO QUELL OPPOSITION AT HOME AND ABROAD

In February 1980 the third meeting of the revolutionary committees, responsible for ensuring the progress of the revolution at the popular level (and in practice for imposing Qaddafi's will on the people's committees), appealed for the 'physical liquidation' of opponents of the revolution who were living abroad and of 'elements obstructing change' inside Libya. An extensive anti-corruption campaign was launched in the same month, ostensibly to eradicate 'economic' crime. Between February and April more than 2,000 people were arrested, mainly on charges of bribery, to be tried by members of the revolutionary committees. However, the arrests of several senior military officers introduced political overtones. In April Qaddafi issued an ultimatum to Libyan exiles abroad to return to Libya by 10 June, beyond which date he could not undertake to protect them from the revenge of the revolutionary committees. According to the human rights organization Amnesty International (based in London, UK), Libya ordered the assassinations of at least 25 of its political opponents abroad in 1980–87. The National Front for the Salvation of Libya (NFSL), formed in 1981 and led by Muhammad Yousuf Magariaf, was only one of several opposition groups based abroad, which the Libyan leader accused foreign governments of nurturing.

Inside Libya, Qaddafi's opponents were active during 1984. In May as many as 20 commandos belonging to the NFSL attacked Qaddafi's residence in a heavily fortified barracks in the suburbs of Tripoli. According to the NFSL, 15 of its commandos were killed, but heavy casualties were inflicted on Libyan soldiers. The actions of Qaddafi's opponents were the signal for a wave of arrests of suspected dissidents in the first half of 1984.

RUMOURS OF AN ABORTIVE ARMY COUP AND INTERNAL DISSENT, 1993–99

During the second week of October 1993 rumours began to circulate in the Western media that a revolt by army units had been crushed by the Libyan air force, which had remained loyal to Qaddafi. There were unconfirmed reports that Libya had closed its borders and that after three days of unrest 2,000 people had been arrested and 12 officers executed. Qaddafi's second-in-command, Maj. Abd al-Salam Jalloud, was reported to have been placed under house arrest. There was speculation that the coup, described in the media as the most serious challenge to the Libyan leader since 1986, had arisen as a result of differences between Qaddafi and Jalloud over the handling of the Lockerbie crisis (see below), and that the armed forces were divided along tribal lines. Throughout the Lockerbie affair, Jalloud, who belonged to the al-Magaraha tribe, was firmly opposed to surrendering the two suspects, both of whom were members of his tribe.

In December 1993 Mansour al-Kikhia, a former Secretary for Foreign Liaison and, since the early 1980s, leader of the opposition Libyan National Alliance, disappeared while attending a meeting of the Alliance in Cairo. It was widely assumed that he had been abducted by Libyan security agents. The affair proved particularly embarrassing as al-Kikhia had been living in the USA, had an American wife and had agreed to attend the meeting in Cairo only after receiving personal assurances from senior Egyptian officials about his safety there.

In March 1994 Libyan television broadcast 'confessions' by three army officers and a student, all members of the Warfallah tribe, who had been arrested in the Bani Walid region during the army revolt in October 1993. It was the first official acknowledgement of the attempted coup. The NFSL claimed that, after calls for the execution of the four men, demonstrations erupted in the Bani Walid region, where several protesters were arrested after setting fire to government buildings.

Despite reports of continued dissent within the armed forces and the destabilizing effects of tribal rivalries, some observers argued that the Islamist opposition was the most dangerous threat to Qaddafi. In June 1995 there were several armed confrontations between police and Islamist militants in and around Benghazi. The Government blamed the unrest on 'extremist infiltrators' from Egypt and Sudan. There were reports of further clashes between the security services and Islamist militants in September in Benghazi, Darna and al-Bayda. In response to these incidents, thousands of Sudanese and Egyptian workers were expelled, the Government tightened its control over the country's mosques and hundreds of suspected Islamist militants were arrested. It also made moves to re-Islamize Libyan society, adopting laws based on *Shari'a* (Islamic law).

In February 1996 it was reported that Islamist militants calling themselves the Jama'ah al-Islamiyah al-Muqatila (Libyan Militant Islamic Group—MIG) had attempted to assassinate Qaddafi in Sirte. In March, following a mass escape from the al-Kuwaifiyya prison near Benghazi, during which police shot dead many of the prisoners, unrest erupted once again in and around Benghazi, Darna and al-Bayda. Several other prison breakouts occurred at this time, as Abu Salim prison in particular became dangerously overcrowded owing to the security forces' crackdown on Islamists. In June the prisoners protested against the deteriorating conditions at the prison, in an uprising that was violently quashed by the authorities; it was reported that some 1,200 inmates had been killed.

Meanwhile, at the end of April 1996 the MIG issued a statement claiming to have killed 15 security officers in Sirte during the previous month, and to have seized weapons from police stations in Ras al-Hilal and al-Qubba. In May violent clashes were reported in Benghazi between security forces and supporters of a new opposition group, the Islamic Martyrs' Movement, which claimed responsibility for the assassinations of several high-ranking government officials. In the following month a third Islamist group, the Libya Islamic Group (LIG), claimed responsibility for the murders of eight police officers during an attack on a police training centre in Darna. Reports of clashes between Islamist groups and government forces continued throughout the second half of 1996.

The threat from militant Islamist groups was accompanied by continued unrest within the armed forces and the alienation of tribal support for the Government. In July 1996 it was reported that an attempted coup organized by Khalifa Haftar, a military officer who had taken part in the overthrow of the monarchy in 1969, had been quashed after fierce fighting in the Jebel Akhdar, near Darna. Also in July 1996, bodyguards of Qaddafi's son Saadi opened fire on crowds at Tripoli's football stadium, after fans chanted anti-Government slogans following a decision by the referee that ruled in favour of a team sponsored by Saadi. In August another coup attempt was uncovered, involving some 45 army officers, and said to include members of the Libyan leader's own tribe, the Qadhafa. Officers from the powerful Warfallah tribe, purportedly accused of leading the abortive coup of 1993, were put on trial at the Supreme Military Court in 1996. Following their conviction, six senior army officers and two civilians were executed in January 1997. In the same month Muhammad al-Senussi, the grandson of the late King Idris and the heir to the Libyan throne, who was living in exile in the UK, claimed to have received death threats from Qaddafi's agents. He later condemned the Government for threatening Libyan exiles and accused the security forces of having used chemical weapons in attacks against insurgents in the Jebel Akhdar in August 1996.

ISLAMIST OPPOSITION IN THE 21ST CENTURY

Towards the end of the 1990s Libyan officials began to make conciliatory gestures to the opposition in exile, offering its members financial inducements if they agreed to return to Libya. Although there were claims that some prominent opposition figures based in the USA were prepared to continue the dialogue, the London-based NFSL completely rejected any rapprochement with Qaddafi. In June 2005 around 300 exiled Libyans met in London at a National Conference for the Libyan Opposition. The very fact that they managed to meet and, indeed, to issue a joint declaration at the close of the event was surprising, given that prior to the conference the opposition was notable for its differences. The joint declaration urged the removal of Qaddafi and the resurrection of the country's 1951 Constitution. A subsequent conference took place in London in early 2008, but few details emerged from its deliberations.

Conspicuous by its absence from both London meetings was the Muslim Brotherhood, the umbrella grouping for Libya's various Islamist organizations and associations, including the LIG, the Libyan Islamic Fighting Group (LIFG—as the MIG had been renamed) and the Libya Brothers. Rumours abounded at the time that the Muslim Brotherhood was in secret negotiations with the Government, through the Qaddafi International Foundation for Charity Associations (QIFCA—renamed the Qaddafi International Charity and Development Foundation in 2006), run by Qaddafi's son, Seif al-Islam, to secure the release of some of its members from Libyan gaols. These rumours gained substance, when, in March 2006, 85 members of the group were released in an 'amnesty'.

Despite such reports, the Government continued to face threats from Islamist groups. In May 2007 the security forces launched an operation to round up suspected Islamist militants in the Benghazi area. The detentions appeared to have been a pre-emptive measure against Islamist mobilization, following the announcement earlier that year that the international terrorist al-Qa'ida network had established the al-Qa'ida Organization in the Land of the Islamic Maghreb (AQIM), in neighbouring Algeria. Meanwhile, two of the LIFG's leaders, Abu-al-Layth al-Libi and Abu-Yahya al-Libi, were prominent in the al-Qa'ida organization in Afghanistan (the former was reported to have been killed in a US air strike in February 2008, and the latter to have been killed in a US drone attack in June 2012). Prior to his death, Abu-al-Layth al-Libi in November 2007 announced that the LIFG had joined AQIM.

In July 2009 it was reported that substantive talks between key members of the LIFG within Libya and the Libyan Government had been ongoing since late 2007. In July 2009 the LIFG renounced its affiliation to AQIM, and in the following month it published a *Book of Correctional Studies*, in which it denounced Salafism and the pursuit of violent *jihad* to achieve its Islamic goals. In September the LIFG issued a public apology, seeking forgiveness from Qaddafi for the violent actions that it had perpetrated in the 1990s, leading to the early release from prison of 88 LIFG members in October. Three prominent LIFG leaders were among a further 214 prisoners released in March 2010 and by the end of the year almost all the members of the LIFG had been freed. In February 2011 the Government arrested Fathi Terbil, the lawyer representing the families of the victims of the Abu Salim prison massacre. His arrest proved to be one of the catalysts for the Libyan revolution, which began in earnest later that month (see *Revolution and Civil War*).

In March 2012 the Muslim Brotherhood announced the creation of the Justice and Construction Party (JCP), one of several newly formed Islamist parties and groupings. In elections for a General National Congress (GNC) in July, however, the JCP won only 17 of the 80 seats available to political parties. The poor performance of the JCP and other Islamist parties in the July 2012 elections was due to several interrelated factors. Historically, the Libyan people have never shown any real appetite for radical Islam, as advocated by the Taliban, al-Qa'ida or AQIM. Moreover, Qaddafi had long suppressed all Islamist movements, especially the Muslim Brotherhood, which meant that there was little in the way of an organized base in Libya for the JCP to build upon. In addition, Libyans in the post-Qaddafi era were highly suspicious of any potential effort by the Muslim Brotherhood or others to impose a new ideology or political agenda on them, and there was also concern that Islamist parties like the JCP could be influenced by outside forces. After 42 years of isolation under Qaddafi's rule, most Libyans longed for a more open socioeconomic and political system and feared that Islamist politicians would again close them off from the outside world.

None the less, militant Islamist elements continued to challenge sources of authority and sovereignty in Libya. In August 2012 Salafists attacked a Sufi mosque in Tripoli, razing it to the ground. In September an attack on the US consulate in Benghazi, believed to have been instigated by a radical Islamist group, Ansar al-Sharia, resulted in the death of the US ambassador, J. Christopher Stevens, and three other Americans. In December a Coptic Christian building in Dafiniyya was attacked, resulting in the deaths of two Egyptians. In March 2013 a Catholic priest was shot outside a Tripoli church, and a major Sufi shrine was destroyed by Salafists. In April Islamist militants attacked the French embassy in Tripoli, apparently to protest against the French military mission to combat Islamist militants in Mali.

In late April 2014 acting Prime Minister Abdallah al-Thani classified Ansar al-Sharia and other, unnamed, radical Islamist groups in eastern Libya as terrorist organizations. Previous post-revolution governments had blamed 'unknown armed groups' for the violence around the country, but this was the first time one had identified Ansar al-Sharia by name as a terrorist organization. In mid-May 2014 Haftar, who had led an attempted coup in 1996, took direct action against radical Islamist elements in Benghazi, attacking Ansar al-Sharia and affiliated militias, with the stated aim of ridding the city of extremist groups. On the following day forces loyal to Haftar and his self-styled Libyan National Army (LNA) stormed the GNC in Tripoli, detaining Islamist deputies and officials. Haftar and his supporters accused the GNC and its Speaker, the Islamist-leaning Nuri Ali Abu Sahmain, of allowing extremist Islamist forces to exert considerable influence throughout the country. Several regular military units, irregular militias and prominent government officials supported Operation Dignity, Haftar's offensive against Ansar al-Sharia and other Islamist groups, believing that this would bring stability to the country. In March 2015 the internationally recognized House of Representatives, which was based in Tobruk, and its Government (the Government of Libya; see *Revolution and Civil War*) appointed Haftar as chief of the armed forces.

Haftar's offensive against Islamist elements contributed to the political and religious polarization that characterized Libya after 2011. His attack on militant Islamic units in a religiously conservative country also helped to create the conditions that led to the emergence in mid-2014 of Islamic State in eastern Libya. Given the large number of Libyans who had joined Islamic State in Syria and Iraq, it was always a question of when, not if, an affiliate organization would emerge in Libya. In mid-October Islamic State announced that it was launching a satellite television channel, which would broadcast propaganda from Sirte, and in the following week the Shura Council of Islamic Youth in Darna moved to establish an Islamic court, based on *Shari'a* law.

Libya's proximity to Europe was a major attraction for Islamic State, which conducted a series of violent attacks in Libya in 2015 and 2016 to gain media attention, including one on the Corinthia Hotel in Tripoli and several on oil facilities south of Sirte. It also beheaded 21 Egyptian Copts near Sirte and occupied state institutions in the town. According to UN reports, by November 2015 Islamic State had largely consolidated its control over central Libya, carrying out summary executions, beheadings and amputations. As Islamic State continued to attack oil terminals and other soft targets, it denounced key figures in the two competing governments in Libya as apostates, thereby turning the political crisis into a three-way war. In March 2016, following the creation of a Government of National Accord (GNA), militia units from Misurata in the north-west of the country attacked Islamic State forces in Sirte, and in April Islamic State was forced out of Darna. By 2018 the threat posed by Islamic State and AQIM had been greatly reduced but not entirely eliminated. At the end of 2019 a UN report acknowledged that counter-terrorism efforts by the GNA, the LNA and the US African Command (AFRICOM) had disrupted the structure and reduced the operational capacity of Islamic State and AQIM. However, both terrorist organizations, especially Islamic State, remained a threat to the long-term stability and security of Libya, as well as to neighbouring states in the Sahel and West Africa. In a small victory in a long war, in June 2022 Mustafa Abdel Hamid bin Dallah, a senior Islamic State commander reportedly responsible for the security of other important leaders, turned himself in to Libyan army forces in Bani Walid. In December a Libyan court sentenced to death 17 former members of Islamic State who had been convicted of participating in the killing of 53 people in the western Libyan city of Sabratha. Two defendants were sentenced to life imprisonment and another 16 were given lesser prison sentences. In May 2023 a Libyan court sentenced 23 people to death and another 14 to life imprisonment for their role in a deadly Islamic State campaign that included the beheading of 21 Egyptian Coptic Christians and the occupation of Sirte in 2015.

At the same time the fundamentalist Madkhalis slowly increased their influence in many parts of the country. The Madkhalis are an ultraconservative Salafist movement founded by a Saudi Arabian sheikh, Rabi al-Madkhali. The Qaddafi regime invited the Madkhalis to Libya in the 1990s to oppose jihadists and the Muslim Brotherhood. With an ideological aversion to political participation, the Madkhalis despise Western traditions and democracy and have taken advantage of the post-war chaos in Libya to impose their hardline interpretation of Islam often through force and coercion. Active in major armed groups in both eastern and western Libya, they wield considerable military influence and significant political leverage over the two rival governments. However, the Madkhalis are more closely associated with the LNA in eastern Libya, and in 2018 al-Madkhali publicly endorsed that body. Furthermore, the movement is explicitly opposed to the Islamist movement the Muslim Brotherhood, to which some senior GNA figures are sympathetic. Although there is no single explicitly and fully pro-LNA Madkhali militia or battalion (the LNA commander, Haftar, disbanded such a battalion, Tawhid, in 2016), Madkhalis dominate several eastern-based core LNA units, including those commanded by Haftar's sons, as well as some pro-LNA western forces. Having taken control of several important religious institutions, notably the eastern branch of the General Authority of Religious Endowments and Islamic Affairs (the state body that administers mosques), their anti-democratic agenda and rejection of cultural and religious pluralism have prompted growing apprehension among many Libyans. Concern was especially great in areas of the country where Madkhalis formed anti-vice patrols to combat activities they considered un-Islamic, leading to Madkhali norms-based policing that relied on a combination of elite co-optation and coercion to achieve local acceptance and compliance.

In May 2023 the General Authority of Awqaf and Islamic Affairs (GAAIA) launched the so-called Guardians of Virtue programme, which it referred to as an 'awareness' scheme aimed at protecting and guarding Islamic virtues and values in what had long been only a moderately conservative Muslim country. Supporters of the GAAIA defended the new programme, pointing to allegations that foreign non-governmental organizations (NGOs) disguised as aid organizations were proselytizing and helping young Libyans convert to Christianity, religious conversion being a serious crime in Libya that is potentially punishable by the death penalty. However, opponents considered the GAAIA to be an extremist organization controlled by radical Islamists and described the Guardians of Virtue as a form of secret police without constitutional or other legal authority. Under the surface, the controversy reflected the mounting influence within post-Qaddafi Libya of conservative Muslim movements, including the Muslim Brotherhood and affiliated bodies, and more radical Islamist elements, such as Ansar al-Sharia, Islamic State and the

Madkhalis. These groups brought differing interpretations of Islam to a country most of whose inhabitants belonged to the Sunni branch of Islam and had a history of rejecting radical Islam in any form.

REVOLUTION AND CIVIL WAR

In January 2011 revolutions broke out in neighbouring Tunisia and Egypt, and the contagion quickly spread to Libya, with civil unrest erupting there later in the month. A heavy-handed government response to a demonstration in Benghazi on 17 February, a so-called day of rage, proved the tipping point, and from thereon the country rapidly descended into civil war. In the process, the focus of protests shifted from complaints about inadequate housing, social services and unemployment to demands for regime change. As fighting erupted throughout the country, especially in eastern Libya, it soon became apparent that the rebel militias were ill-equipped to take on the better-armed, better-organized government forces. The rebels were gradually forced back, leaving the road open to rebel-held Benghazi. As government troops advanced to the outskirts of the city, concern increased inside and outside Libya that Qaddafi would take ruthless measures to crush the rebellion.

In late February 2011 the UN Security Council unanimously adopted Resolution 1970, imposing sanctions on Qaddafi and his inner circle and calling on the International Criminal Court (ICC) to investigate government attacks on Libyan civilians. On 17 March the UN Security Council adopted Resolution 1973, imposing an air exclusion zone over Libya and authorizing member states to take 'all necessary measures' to protect civilians. One week later the North Atlantic Treaty Organization (NATO) agreed to enforce the UN-mandated air exclusion zone. Owing in large part to the air support provided by NATO forces, rebel militias were able to halt the advance of government forces, forcing them to retreat from Benghazi.

On the political front, Mustafa Muhammad Abd al-Jalil, who had served as Secretary for Justice under Qaddafi, announced on 26 February 2011 the establishment of the Transitional National Council of the Libyan Republic (subsequently National Transitional Council—NTC). The Council—which was largely staffed by technocrats from so-called Free Libya (the eastern part of the country) and senior defectors from the Government, including the former Secretary of Public Security, Gen. Abd al-Fattah Yunis, the former head of National Planning, Mahmoud Jibril, and Ali al-Essawi, a former Libyan ambassador to India—declared that it would draw up a new constitution that would allow for a free, democratic Libya. At the end of June, the NTC proclaimed itself to be the sole legitimate representative of the Libyan people, and by the end of September it had secured the official recognition of 94 countries. As the fighting intensified, the NATO mission transgressed its original remit to protect Libyan civilians and began to target Qaddafi himself. Government circles in Europe openly admitted that there was no question of allowing Qaddafi to stay in power and that the unstated Western policy in Libya was regime change.

As his apparatus of control slowly collapsed around him, Qaddafi became increasingly defiant, declaring that he would never leave Tripoli. At the end of March 2011 Musa Kusa, the Secretary for Foreign Liaison and International Co-operation and one of Qaddafi's closest lieutenants, fled to the UK. In late May eight senior army officers arrived in the Italian capital, Rome, where they denounced Qaddafi, and a month later Shokri Muhammad Ghanem, head of the National Oil Corporation (NOC) and a key reformist, appeared in Athens, Greece, announcing his defection. At the end of June, the ICC issued arrest warrants for Muammar al-Qaddafi, Seif al-Islam and Abdullah al-Sanoussi, the head of intelligence. Meanwhile, after breaking the siege of Misurata, rebel forces made further advances on all fronts, encircling Tripoli.

Militarily, August 2011 marked the effective end of Qaddafi's rule. Early in that month rebel forces consolidated their hold on Zlitan, and later in August they occupied Tripoli. At the end of August, the Algerian Government confirmed that it had allowed members of Qaddafi's family, including his wife, his daughter, Aisha, and two of his sons, Muhammad and Hannibal, to cross the border into Algeria, citing humanitarian concerns. (All four were subsequently granted asylum in Oman.) A third son, Seif al-Arab, was killed in an air strike in April, and a fourth son, Khamis, was killed at the end of August. In early September a fifth son, Saadi, fled into exile in Niger, but he was later extradited to Libya. Qaddafi himself was captured and killed outside Sirte on 20 October, together with another son, Muatassim. After being put on public display for several days, the bodies of both men were buried in a secret location in the Sahara desert. On 19 November Seif al-Islam Qaddafi was captured by rebel fighters near the town of Obari and transferred to Zintan, where he was incarcerated, pending trial. On 20 November Libya's intelligence chief al-Sanoussi was captured, also near Obari. In July 2015 Seif al-Islam Qaddafi and al-Sanoussi were sentenced to death, together with seven other senior officials from the former Qaddafi regime, including Dr al-Baghdadi Ali al-Mahmoudi, who had been premier at the time Qaddafi's regime collapsed. They were charged with, *inter alia*, war crimes and crimes against humanity, including recruiting mercenaries, and ordering attacks on civilians from the air, and the firing of live rounds on public demonstrations. Seif al-Islam was released in June 2017, under an amnesty law adopted by the House of Representatives; however, he remained subject to an ICC arrest warrant. In early January 2023 Seif al-Islam issued a statement arguing that he should be eligible to run for the presidency if and when long delayed presidential and parliamentary elections were held.

Following the capture of Tripoli, the Chairman of the NTC, Abd al-Jalil, indicated that the Council would move its operations from Benghazi to Tripoli. In early September 2011 interim Prime Minister Jibril became the most senior NTC official to take up residence in Tripoli, and in mid-September Abd al-Jalil gave a televised address in the city's former Green Square—renamed Martyr's Square following Qaddafi's ouster—in which he outlined the plans for the transition to a multi-party democracy. On 16 September the UN General Assembly approved, by 117 votes to 17, a motion to accredit NTC-appointed representatives, in effect recognizing the NTC as the legitimate governing authority in Libya.

On 3 August 2011 the NTC released a Draft Constitutional Charter for the Transitional Stage, which outlined a workable political process leading to elections for a GNC in June 2012. Following the release of a draft election law in early February 2012, the NTC decided that, of the 200 GNC seats, 80 would be allocated to political parties, and 120 would be reserved for independent candidates. At the beginning of March, a meeting of eastern leaders in Benghazi called for Libya to adopt a federal system similar to the one in place in 1951–63. Bowing to federalist pressure, the NTC on 15 March 2012 amended the Draft Constitutional Charter to specify that the GNC would choose a 60-member constitutional committee based on the model of the 1951 constitutional committee, with 20 representatives each from Cyrenaica, Fezzan and Tripolitania.

On 7 July 2012 a general election—the first national poll involving political parties since 1952—took place in Libya to establish a 200-member GNC, which was to appoint a new interim government, oversee the drafting of a constitution and supervise elections based on provisions in the new constitution. Widely recognized as both free and fair, the elections were doubly remarkable in that they took place only nine months after the fall of Qaddafi, and the Libyan electorate strongly supported moderate, mainstream parties, reversing a trend elsewhere in North Africa in favour of Islamist groups.

The National Forces Alliance (NFA), a coalition of political parties and civil society groups, won 39 of the 80 party seats. Led by Jibril, who was not a candidate because former members of the interim Government were barred from participating in the election, the NFA was most often described in the Western press as a liberal political party. In contrast, the NFA, recognizing the important role of Islam in Libyan society, presented itself to voters as a moderate Islamist movement. The JCP—the political arm of the Muslim Brotherhood—secured the second largest representation among political parties, with 17 seats. Collectively, moderate parties, such as the NFA, won over 60% of the party seats in the GNC.

Election results for the 120 independent seats were not as clear-cut as those for the 80 party seats. Genuinely independent candidates and individual candidates with ties to parties other than the NFA won a majority of the GNC seats reserved for independents. With many of these independent candidates elected on the basis of local connections, tribal affiliation or social standing, the composition of the GNC reflected the extent to which politics in Libya tended to focus on local concerns and issues. On 8 August 2012 Abd al-Jalil formally announced the dissolution of the NTC, symbolically transferring its power to the oldest member of the newly elected GNC. On the following day Magariaf, the leader of the National Front Party, was elected Speaker of the GNC and de facto head of state.

On 12 September 2012 the GNC narrowly elected Mustafa Abu Shagur, Deputy Prime Minister in the outgoing administration of Abd al-Rahim al-Keib, as Prime Minister with 96 votes in the second round of voting, defeating Jibril, who received 94 votes. On 7 October Prime Minister Abu Shagur was defeated in a vote of no confidence, and was subsequently replaced by Ali Zidan.

On 6 February 2013 the GNC upheld an earlier NTC decision that the constitutional committee would be elected in a general election, as opposed to being appointed by the GNC. Meanwhile, the GNC approved a three-member committee representing Libya's three historical regions, Cyrenaica, Fezzan and Tripolitania, to draft a law for the election of the 60-member constitutional committee. No timeline was set for the completion of the election law or the holding of the general election. On 5 May the GNC, under pressure from heavily armed Islamist militants, approved a political isolation law, which appeared to ban from government anyone linked to the Qaddafi era, even those who had been actively involved in his removal from power. In response, Magariaf, who had been the Libyan ambassador to India until his defection in 1980, resigned from his position as Speaker of the GNC. With the support of the JCP, the GNC elected Abu Sahmain, a political independent and member of the Amazigh (Berber) minority, to replace Magariaf on 25 June 2013.

Tensions between the Zidan Government and rebel militias increased during 2013, with the assassination of individuals tied to Qaddafi and the current Government commonplace. The Government took steps to rebuild the military and the police force, as well as to disband the militias; however, Zidan made little progress in restoring national security, his stated goal. Moreover, oil and natural gas production was often disrupted by violent industrial action. In addition, the prevailing sense of entitlement among the general population was conducive to widespread graft and corruption, undermining the policies necessary to bring about much needed political and economic reform. After Zidan was forced to step down in March 2014, the GNC appointed the Minister of Defence, Abdallah al-Thani, as acting Prime Minister; he announced that security would be the main priority of his administration.

There was limited support in the eastern and southern regions of Libya for a return to federalism, owing to the deteriorating security situation, the slow progress of reform, the lack of co-operation among politicians, and a widespread perception of marginalization. In both regions, federalist supporters allied themselves with local notables, tribal groups, Islamist elements and militias, weakening the national Government and prolonging the constitution-drafting process. These disparate groups had major policy differences but shared a common goal of preventing the Government from extending its authority to their areas of influence. Although federalism remained a minority movement, a survey conducted in May 2013 by the Ministry of Higher Education and Scientific Research found that 57% of respondents hoped to see some form of decentralization in the new constitution. A similar poll conducted by the University of Benghazi found that only 8% of Libyans nationwide and 15% of those in the east favoured a federal state, but that 47% supported at least limited local legislative and executive powers.

The factors that resulted in the weak showing of the JCP and other Islamist parties in the GNC election of July 2012 also contributed to their poor performance in the February 2014 constitutional committee poll. The results of the election suggested that the Libyan people were strongly opposed to Islamists dominating the constitution-drafting process. Frustrated with the failure of the GNC to recognize their cultural, linguistic and economic demands, the Amazigh minority boycotted the election. In an indication of the low esteem in which Islamist politicians were held, Ali Tarhuna, regarded as a liberal, was elected to head the constitutional committee. After the election, in which women were allocated only six of the 60 seats, Tarhuna pledged that women would be an integral part of the constitution-drafting process.

The Draft Constitutional Charter of August 2011 presented a relatively liberal vision and an inclusive approach to the rights and freedoms of all Libyans. Article 1 described Islam as 'the religion of the state', but stipulated that *Shari'a* would be 'the principal source of legislation' as opposed to the only source. Article 6 stated that all 'Libyans shall be equal before the law' and 'enjoy equal civil and political rights', 'the same opportunities', and 'be subject to the same public duties and obligations, without discrimination owing to religion, belief, race, language, wealth, kinship or political opinions or social status'. It concluded by affirming that the 'state shall guarantee for woman all opportunities which shall allow her to participate entirely and actively in political, economic and social spheres'.

The results of the public opinion surveys conducted in late 2013 indicated that Libyans continued to favour a new constitution that expressed the democratic values outlined in the Draft Constitutional Charter. An overwhelming majority of respondents believed that legal experts and civil society representatives should be included in the constitutional committee, but a majority opposed the inclusion of tribal leaders and political parties. The vast majority of Libyans also believed that basic civil, economic and political rights should be enshrined in the constitution, including the right to education, employment, health and medical care, and housing. Strong majorities also supported provisions to guarantee the right to a fair trial and freedom from torture. Finally, 70% of the Libyans polled viewed equal rights for women as very important.

In mid-May 2014, as Haftar's forces continued their offensive against Islamist militias in eastern Libya, a new round of political infighting commenced in Tripoli. Prime Minister al-Thani refused to hand over power to Ahmad Maitig, who had been recently elected by the GNC, until the Supreme Court ruled on the legitimacy of the latter's election. The political crisis reflected the divide between the Islamists and more moderate forces, as well as regional and tribal divisions. Maitig was supported by the Islamist bloc within the GNC in a contested election that critics argued lacked a quorum; he then took control of the Prime Minister's office under the protection of Islamist militias. The crisis ended in June, when the Supreme Court ruled that Maitig's election was unconstitutional, and he resigned, leaving al-Thani for a time as the undisputed Prime Minister.

Elections to a new 200-member interim parliament, the House of Representatives, to replace the GNC were held on 25 June 2014. The House of Representatives was inaugurated on 4 August in the eastern city of Tobruk, owing to political uncertainty in Tripoli and ongoing clashes between pro-Islamist militias and Haftar's forces in Benghazi. However, 12 seats remained unallocated after security concerns prompted the closure of polling stations. Several elected deputies, moreover, refused to travel to Tobruk, citing concerns for their safety.

In July 2014 the Muslim Brotherhood and allied Islamist elements in Tripoli joined forces with diverse tribal and regional interests to form Libya Dawn, a direct competitor to Haftar's Operation Dignity. By August Libya Dawn units, which continued to recognize the GNC as the legitimate legislature, had taken control of much of the capital city. The conflict between Libya Dawn and Operation Dignity increased the polarization of the country along communal, ideological and regional lines that had emerged following the overthrow of the Qaddafi regime. In mid-August Abu Sahmain denied that the GNC was no longer in existence, arguing that all decisions taken by the House of Representatives were therefore illegal. Shortly afterwards, some members of the former GNC reconvened in Tripoli, appointed Omar al-Hassi as a rival prime minister and directed him to form a Government of National Salvation. With Libya Dawn in control of

Tripoli, al-Hassi occupied the official offices of the Prime Minister in mid-September and other members of his rump government moved into other official buildings in the capital. In late September, after the House of Representatives had approved a new Government with a slimmed-down, 13-member cabinet, Prime Minister al-Thani announced that his newly constituted administration would operate from al-Bayda until it was possible to return to Tripoli. Amid criticism from several fronts, not least after his description of Ansar al-Sharia as 'a beautiful idea', al-Hassi was dismissed by the GNC in March 2015, and replaced by his deputy, Khalifa al-Ghweil.

In September 2014 UN-brokered talks began in the western Libyan town of Ghadames in an effort to find a political solution to the conflict engulfing Libya. Bernardino León, the Special Representative of the UN Secretary-General, proclaimed the opening of talks as a great day for Libya; however, UN-sponsored talks aimed at forming a government of national reconciliation continued for many months. The efforts of the UN to broker a power-sharing agreement, first by León and, as of November 2015, by Martin Kobler, culminated in the signing of the Libyan Political Agreement (LPA) in Skhirat, Morocco in December. The LPA made the House of Representatives the sole legislative authority in Libya and transformed the GNC, representing what was left of Libya Dawn, into the High Council of State. The functions of head of state were to be exercised by a Presidency Council composed of nine people, representing various political factions. Fayez al-Sarraj, the Prime Minister and head of the Presidency Council, arrived in Tripoli in late March 2016 amid much tension, establishing his headquarters at the Bu Setta naval base.

Chief among the many challenges that confronted the GNA was the failure of the UN Support Mission in Libya (UNSMIL) and the LPA that it brokered to take full advantage of the political culture that had traditionally served as a source of state legitimacy in Libya. The extended family, village, clan and tribe remained the basic elements of contemporary Libyan society, and any agreement that was not grounded in them threatened to worsen, rather than alleviate, factional violence and divide, rather than unite, Libya. Presented as a peace accord, the top-down power-sharing agreement brokered by UNSMIL was based on the groups, factions and individuals that mismanaged the country after 2011. As a result, the GNA experienced considerable difficulty after March 2016 in taking up residency in Tripoli and establishing state legitimacy throughout the country.

The Constitutional Assembly, which was elected in February 2014 with a mandate to write the country's first constitution since 1951, released a second draft on 3 February 2016, which was intended to reconcile conflicting views and clashing interests, including the place of federalism, decentralization, women, ethnic minorities and *Shari'a* law in post-Qaddafi Libya. Although consensus existed that *Shari'a* should be a reference for future legislation, there was no agreement about whether it should be the only source, a principal source or one source among many. The issues of federalism and decentralization were interconnected and central to the question of how to distribute the country's hydrocarbon revenues. Women, who were struggling to retain the rights and responsibilities that they thought that they had earned during the revolution, were guaranteed a minimum of 25% of the total seats in elected councils for three electoral cycles under a special provision in the second draft. The revised document also attempted to address the demands of the Berber, Tebu and Tuareg ethnic minorities. In the end, the second draft constitution, in seeking to accommodate the wishes and demands of many interest groups, was a masterpiece of compromise and concession that risked pleasing nobody.

After 2016 Prime Minister al-Sarraj, the Presidency Council and the GNA were unable to extend their authority much beyond their base in Tripoli, and they also failed to establish a working relationship with important state institutions, such as the Central Bank and the NOC. Instead of the single unity government that had been called for in the LPA, Libya continued to be divided by major power blocs in the east and west that were unable to find common ground. In Tripoli, one group of militias supported the GNA, and another supported the rump Government led by al-Ghweil. In turn, the al-Thani Government in al-Bayda, the House of Representatives in Tobruk and newly promoted Field Marshal Haftar and his LNA controlled most of eastern and southern Libya. Officially, the international community supported the GNA; unofficially, it added to the confusion by supporting militant militias from Misurata in their fight against Islamic State in Sirte, while covertly supporting Haftar and his associates in their attempt to expel militant Islamists from Benghazi. First proposed in October 2017, the idea of holding parliamentary and presidential elections by the end of 2018 gained traction in the coming months. However, the involved parties failed to establish the constitutional basis and commitments required for the passage of electoral laws by September 2018, and parliamentary and presidential elections, scheduled for 10 December, were thus not able to be held.

In January 2019 Haftar and the LNA launched a military operation to capture the Fezzan region in south-western Libya, with the stated objective of securing petroleum facilities, halting migrant flows and purging jihadists and criminal gangs. By employing diplomacy, exploiting ethnic and tribal ties and distributing largesse, as opposed to relying on military force, Haftar's militias swept through southern Libya, and by early April they were on the verge of capturing Tripoli. However, Haftar's advance on the capital stalled after a disparate group of militias rallied around the GNA; none the less, his march on the capital proved to be a paradigm-shifting episode. Haftar's advance on Tripoli occurred just before a proposed UN-sponsored National Conference, which was postponed as a result, thereby reducing the chances of the LPA being amended or ultimately implemented. Consequently, the political institutions of the LPA (the House of Representatives and the GNA), together with the framework for power-sharing that it defined, no longer reflected the military and political realities in Libya.

In an often chaotic and volatile political environment, the military dynamics around Tripoli changed dramatically in the first half of 2020. Politically, peace-making initiatives in Moscow (Russian Federation), Berlin (Germany), Cairo and elsewhere produced little in the way of positive results, as both Prime Minister al-Sarraj and Haftar were unwilling to compromise. Militarily, both sides continued to flout the UN-mandated arms embargo, with Turkey and Qatar on the GNA's side matching whatever armaments Egypt, Russia, the United Arab Emirates (UAE) and others provided to Haftar and the LNA. The insertion of Russian mercenaries into the theatre of combat in late 2019, combined with the extensive use of UAE-supplied Chinese combat aerial unmanned vehicles (drones), boosted the LNA's prospects for a while in early 2020, but Turkish-backed mercenaries returned the momentum to the GNA in the following month. By June GNA forces had pushed the LNA back from Tripoli and other key bases in western Libya and were threatening the strategically important town of Sirte. In response, the LNA, supported by Egypt, France, Germany and Italy, among other interested parties, including the UN, called for a ceasefire and the suspension of the ongoing military build-up throughout Libya. The GNA rejected the appeal to cease fighting, and the LNA eventually repelled the assault, which led to the GNA suffering heavy casualties.

With a military solution to the conflict increasingly unlikely, UNSMIL promoted a three-track process (economic, military, political) under the umbrella of the 2020 Berlin Conference. The economic track called for a solution to the political crisis that also addressed the deepening economic crisis. The military track hoped to establish a lasting ceasefire, restore security to civilian areas and incorporate all militias into a national army and police force. The political track sought to draft a new constitution and hold elections leading to a new government. After months of relative inactivity, the 5+5 Joint Military Commission (JMC) agreed on 23 October 2020 to a countrywide and permanent ceasefire. The agreement was intended to set in motion steps to unify the security forces and disarm, demobilize and reintegrate the numerous armed factions operating in Libya. It also called for all foreign fighters to leave Libya within 90 days. Three weeks later UNSMIL facilitated the creation of the Libyan Political Dialogue Forum (LPDF), 75 Libyans that the UN said represented the full social and political spectrum of Libya. As to whether the LPDF was truly representative of Libya's political and military landscape, almost one-half of its participants were members of the GNC or House of Representatives and the remainder were handpicked by the UN to ensure certain powerbrokers or constituencies were represented or to accommodate the foreign interests invested in Libya. In November 2020 the LPDF agreed to hold parliamentary and presidential elections on 24 December 2021, 70 years to the day after Libya declared independence in 1951.

On 5 February 2021 the LPDF appointed Abdul Hamid Mohammed Dbeibah as Prime Minister, together with a three-person Presidency Council, headed by Mohammad Younes Menfi. In March the House of Representatives approved a Government of National Unity (GNU) chosen by Dbeibah to replace the GNA. The GNU consisted of 32 ministers and two Deputy Prime Ministers. While five women were named to the cabinet, including Najla Mohamed el-Mangoush as Minister of Foreign Affairs and International Co-operation, these five women represented only 15% of all ministers and thus fell far short of the 30% quota promised by the LPDF. Nevertheless, the GNU did represent a power-sharing formula with cabinet positions distributed among disparate interest groups and locales, most notably the three regions of Cyrenaica, Fezzan and Tripolitania. Both Khalifa Haftar and the Muslim Brotherhood, influential forces in post-Qaddafi Libya, were poorly represented in the new government, suggesting a shift in the Libyan political landscape. Thereafter, progress slowed, with Russia and Turkey refusing to withdraw their troops from Libya and the LPDF unable to agree on a legal basis for the elections on 24 December.

In June 2021 the 17 countries that met in Berlin in January 2020 reconvened to consider implementation of the peace process agreed to by the LPDF. The most important outcomes of the Berlin II Conference (see *Relations with the EU Improve*) were a fresh commitment to hold national elections on 24 December 2021 and a renewed demand that all foreign forces, including those of Russia and Turkey (officially known as Türkiye from June 2022), leave Libya. Nevertheless, as 2021 ended, most foreign forces remained in Libya and the December elections had been postponed due to disputes over the basic rules governing them. Türkiye later announced, in June 2022, that it was extending its troop deployment for another 18 months.

Meanwhile, the House of Representatives voted to replace the Dbeibah Government, alleging that its term of office had ended with the postponement of elections on 24 December 2021. On 10 February 2022 the House of Representatives replaced Dbeibah with Fathi Bashagha, hitherto Minister of Interior in the GNA, without any input from the High Council of State. The manner in which the newly formed Government of National Stability (GNS) was formed on 1 March, together with its composition, were controversial from the start. Most of the GNS ministers were either relatives or allies of important members of the House of Representatives, leading to charges that the GNS was the product of House of Representatives patronage networks, to the detriment of the High Council of State and other political elites. In response, the UN issued a statement attributed to Secretary-General António Guterres, which said that the Bashagha cabinet 'fell short of the expected standards of transparency and procedures and included acts of intimidation prior to the session'.

The creation of the GNS parallel to the existing GNU initiated a new period of economic, military and political instability as the rival governments competed for power and legitimacy. Powerful militias controlling Tripoli and most of western Libya split, with some supporting Dbeibah and others supporting Bashagha. When Prime Minister Bashagha in mid-May 2022 tried to enter Tripoli to assert his authority, for example, militias supporting Prime Minister Dbeibah prevented him from doing so. Moreover, the support of the Western international community, including France, Germany, Italy, the UK, the USA and the European Union (EU), was also in doubt as they agreed to follow the lead of UNSMIL and the Special Adviser to the Secretary-General on Libya, Stephanie Turco Williams (a US diplomat). Russia, on the other hand, quickly issued a statement saying that it looked forward to establishing relations with the GNS. In the end, Peter Millett, a former British ambassador to Libya, best captured the moment when he argued that the division in Libya was not an east–west split but a division 'between the Libya people—who want elections—and the political elite, who don't'.

In a statement issued in July 2022 to mark her departure from the role of Special Adviser, Williams criticized the Libyan political elite, arguing that the only way forward from the stalemate that had persisted since the 2011 revolution was through the holding of elections. In September 2022 the UN Secretary-General appointed Senegalese diplomat Abdoulaye Bathily as the Special Representative for Libya and head of UNSMIL.

The JMC convened in January 2023, for the first time in seven months, to discuss a variety of issues, including the ongoing ceasefire, and in early February—together with liaison committees from Libya, Niger and Sudan—it approved the establishment of an integrated mechanism for joint coordination and data exchange to facilitate the full withdrawal of all mercenaries and foreign fighters from Libya. The representatives from Niger and Sudan participated in the meeting amid concerns that the return of foreign fighters to their countries of origin might potentially destabilize the region.

In late February 2023 Bathily announced a much anticipated new plan for Libya, which had taken six months to formulate, and which was aimed at adopting a legal framework and detailed roadmap for the holding of elections before the end of 2023, as well as achieving consensus on election security and approving a code of conduct for candidates. The plan called for the establishment of a High-level Steering Panel for Libya (HSPL) within UNSMIL, comprising an unspecified number of key Libyan stakeholders, including major political leaders, representatives of political institutions, tribal leaders, civil society organizations, security actors, women and youth representatives. The problem with Bathily's plan was that it looked a lot like the previous plan that created the LPDF in late 2020. Granted, the proposed composition of the HSPL appeared wider in scope than that of the LPDF, the composition of which had compromised its legitimacy, goals and conduct. However, the failure to disclose the anticipated number of HSPL members, let alone their names, led observers to question the real differences between the two initiatives and whether the UN had learned from the errors of the LPDF.

In May 2023 the 6+6 Committee, which comprised six members from the House of Representatives and six from the High Council of State and was charged with drafting electoral laws for the planned elections, met in Bouznika, Morocco. A week before the meeting, the House of Representatives unexpectedly replaced Bashagha as GNS Prime Minister, citing his failure to enter Tripoli and oust Dbeibah's GNU as the grounds for his removal. At the same time the House of Representatives announced plans to investigate Bashagha's conduct; however, suggestions that financial irregularities were another reason behind his dismissal were given little credibility. The House of Representatives appointed Osama Hamada, hitherto the GNS Minister of Finance, as acting Prime Minister. With all parties positioning themselves in advance of possible elections in 2023, and amid rumours that the House of Representatives and the High Council of State were discussing the formation of an interim government to oversee the elections, the elimination of the polarizing Bashagha appeared connected to the work of the 6+6 Committee.

For elections to succeed, whenever they are eventually held, a number of unresolved issues will first need to be addressed, including the lack of a constitutional and legal basis for elections, a complete lack of trust in the political elite, an aggrieved and vulnerable youth population, which constitutes more than one-half of the total populace, meddlesome external actors and the persistent threat of violence. In this context, it is of no surprise that some of the most perceptive articles on Libya published in the first half of 2023 carried titles such as 'Libya faces the same old problems in the new year', 'The U.N.'s Libya Mission Needs a Reset', 'Libya elections: Has the UN lost the plot?', and 'Beyond Elections: Libya Needs Unified Institutions and Reconciliation'. Since 2011, Libya has been locked in a complex conflict in which rival governments in the east and west, an uncompromising political elite and a host of external actors have exacerbated longstanding regional and local conflicts between various tribes, ethnic and religious minorities, armed organizations and other marginalized groups. In this Byzantine conflict, elections in themselves will not create a stable and secure state. Doing the same thing over and over again has clearly not worked. Instead, the UN would be wise to focus more of its efforts on areas in which it can make a difference, such as local government, which has proven itself able to get things done that the central Government cannot, and civil society, which offers expertise and practical experience to overwhelmed municipalities.

THE OPPOSITION AND HUMAN RIGHTS

Human rights abuses were widespread in Qaddafi's Libya, particularly against opponents of the Government. These were chronicled in an Amnesty International report in 1998, which listed extensive human rights violations, including the torture of Libyans suspected of opposition activities. In September 2001 Amnesty International reported that Libya's longest serving political prisoner, Ahmed al-Zubayr Ahmed al-Senussi, had been released after 31 years' incarceration, but it expressed concern about hundreds of other political prisoners detained for more than 10 years without trial. In the wake of Amnesty International's first visit to Libya in 2004, Qaddafi announced that the emergency laws imposed by the people's courts would be abolished and that Libya would adopt 'normal criminal law procedures'.

In May 2005 Qaddafi sanctioned a visit by the US-based NGO Human Rights Watch (HRW), which commended Libya for implementing some of Amnesty International's recommendations, including the abolition of the People's Prosecution Bureau—the so-called exceptional court, in which due process was notoriously absent. Shortly after HRW published its report, the Government claimed that it was prosecuting at least 48 security officials on charges of torture and was reforming the penal code to minimize the use of the death penalty. None the less, an article by a senior HRW official published soon after the report stated that Libya remained a closed and tightly controlled society with no independent press, civil society, or political groups that were not officially sanctioned; Libyans were not allowed to criticize the Government, the political system or the Leader; the state security apparatus was pervasive; and cases of forced disappearances remained unresolved.

Amnesty International published a new report on Libya in May 2009, stating that continued violations of human rights in Libya 'cast a shadow over its improved international diplomatic standing'. It also asserted that basic human freedoms in the country, including those of expression, association and assembly, remained severely restricted. In December the Government granted permission to HRW to launch its annual human rights report on Libya at a public press conference in Tripoli. However, the meeting was disrupted by hardliners who shouted down members of the public who had come to speak out against the Government.

Libya's human rights credentials gained international legitimacy in May 2010, when the country was elected to the UN Human Rights Council. Although 30 international NGOs lobbied against its accession, the vote was considered a formality, as Libya had already secured its regional nomination unopposed. After the outbreak of conflict in Libya in mid-February 2011, reports of serious human rights abuses by the security forces began to emerge. By the end of the month all 192 members of the UN had voted unanimously to suspend Libya's membership of the UN Human Rights Council for 'gross and systematic violations of human rights'. In the aftermath of the revolution, evidence surfaced of human rights abuses committed by both Government and rebel forces. Moreover, violations of human rights—including threats to freedom of speech, association and assembly, and the use of intimidation and politically motivated violence—continued in the years after the fighting had ended.

Having played an important role in the overthrow of Qaddafi, Libyan women in particular struggled to retain recent gains in gender equality. Prominent political leaders and influential clerics adopted a more conservative stance on the status of women, challenging their right to education, work, freedom of thought and speech, and human dignity. In response, women's rights advocates launched creative new programmes in an effort to retain existing social and legal rights; at the same time, many of them recognized that a further erosion of their rights might be inevitable. Salwa Bugaighis, a prominent lawyer and human rights activist who had fled into exile after her life was threatened by Islamist extremists, was assassinated in June 2014, shortly after she had returned to Libya to vote in parliamentary elections. In the following month, Ariha al-Berkawi, a former GNC member and a leader of the women's movement, was assassinated in Darna, and in February 2015 Intisar al-Hasiri, a prominent civil rights activist, was found murdered in her car in Tripoli, together with the body of her aunt. A UN Development Programme report, published in late 2015 highlighted the limited participation of women in the security sector and politics, the widespread opposition of men to greater female participation in these areas, and the extremely weak legal framework in place to protect the rights of women to physical security and health care.

With defenders of human rights in general and advocates for women's rights in particular continuing to suffer abuse, harassment and even murder, many human rights activists retreated to the shadows or left the country. Others remained active, launching new initiatives at home and asserting their rights with the support of international groups abroad. Women found some respite in 'families only' cafes; none the less, Libya remained a dangerous place for anyone advocating women's rights. In January 2018 social media blogger and activist Maryam al-Tayeb, known as Dushka al-Harbi, was detained and beaten by militia members because she advocated the rights of women in post-Qaddafi Libya. In June Amnesty International issued a report that concluded in part that the insufficient response of Libyan authorities to gender-based violence against women who fought for political inclusion 'demonstrates a tolerance for this violence, while conservative social norms further protect those who commit such crimes'. Symptomatic of the ongoing challenges that women face, when the GNU was formed in March 2021 it included only five women, or 15% of the total number of ministers, even though Prime Minister Dbeibah—in line with the Roadmap for the Preparatory Phase of a Comprehensive Solution—had promised a quota of 30% in his new Government.

In March 2023 the UN-appointed independent Fact-Finding Mission (FFM) on Libya reported that women continued to be 'systematically discriminated against' and their overall situation had 'markedly deteriorated' during the previous three years due to 'the proliferation of armed groups whose powers continuously increase and the weakening of state institutions'. Domestic violence against women, which is not punishable by any comprehensive law, also increased, including a spate of honour-related femicides in July 2022 referred to as 'the bloody week'. In addition, the FFM report asserted that Libya's fledgling civil society was under an intensifying crackdown. Militias and other armed groups frequently targeted media professionals and other social media users for expressing critical views or simply carrying out their work. An anti-cybercrime law passed by the House of Representatives in September attracted particular attention, with UN experts arguing that this highly restrictive law infringed the rights of free expression, privacy and freedom of association. In March 2023 the head of the Law Department of the Supreme Judicial Council (SJC) in Tripoli issued a legal opinion calling into question the legal status of many, if not most, NGOs in Libya. The SJC attempted to frame its legal opinion as a move to protect Libya from foreign or national influence through NGOs; however, it was widely seen as an attempt to exert tighter control over civil society in western Libya to prevent activism that could undermine the authority of the GNU. The timing of the issuance of the legal opinion was notable, coming as the electoral process was gaining momentum and civil society was poised to raise potentially embarrassing questions on key issues and concerns.

Violence against migrants and asylum seekers in government-controlled detention centres also remained a serious problem. In a report published in June 2013, Amnesty International documented cases of violence by guards in three migrant detention centres, and in June 2014 HRW released detailed findings from its investigation into nine detention centres, reporting that cruel, inhumane and degrading practices, including torture, were widespread. In January and April 2015 HRW visited government-controlled detention facilities in eastern Libya, interviewing detainees who complained of the use of torture to coerce false confessions, lack of due process, absence of medical care, and other poor conditions. In February 2016 the Office of the UN High Commissioner for Human Rights (UNHCHR) on Libya published a detailed report that concluded that there were 'widespread violations of international human rights law and international humanitarian law, and abuses of human rights in Libya throughout 2014 and 2015', including against migrants and asylum seekers. With three governments in competition for legitimacy and control of territory in 2016–17, armed militias on all sides continued to be guilty of arbitrary detention, torture, unlawful killings, disappearances and the forceful displacement of people. In addition, the tens of thousands of migrants and asylum seekers passing through Libya en route to Europe remained subject to torture, sexual assault and forced labour from traffickers, prison guards and members of the coastguard. In April 2018 UNHCHR released a report stating that Libyan militias, including some affiliated with the authorities, continued to hold thousands of prisoners in prolonged arbitrary and unlawful detention that often included torture. Migrants and asylum seekers also continued to suffer as a result of the extension of Italy's deal with the Libyan coastguard to return migrants to Libya who had been intercepted crossing the Mediterranean, drawing sharp criticism from humanitarian groups. According to the International Organization for Migration, 32,425 migrants were rescued at sea and returned to Libya in 2021—almost triple the number recorded the previous year. In addition, in that year 655 migrants died trying to reach Europe and another 897 were reported as missing. In September 2022 the World Organisation Against Torture (OMCT) noted that law enforcement officials, militias and other armed groups collectively killed at least 581 civilians in Libya, both local citizens and foreign migrants, between January 2020 and March 2022. The March 2023 FFM report concluded that security forces and armed groups in Libya may have committed 'a wide array of war crimes and crimes against humanity' targeting Libyan citizens and foreign migrants alike. The report also documented sweeping abuses, including 'repression of civic groups, arbitrary detention, murder, rape, enslavement, extrajudicial killing, and enforced disappearance'.

DOMESTIC REFORM

In 1988 Qaddafi implemented a limited number of liberalizing economic and political reforms. In March he began to encourage the reopening of private businesses, in recognition of the failure of the state-controlled supermarkets to satisfy demand for even the most basic commodities. At the same time all prisoners (including foreigners), except those convicted of violent crimes or of conspiring with foreign powers, were released; Libyan citizens were guaranteed freedom of travel abroad; and the revolutionary committees were deprived of their powers of arrest and imprisonment, which had often been used indiscriminately and arbitrarily.

In June 1988 the GPC approved a charter of human rights, guaranteeing freedom of expression and condemning violence. Earlier in the year the GPC had created a people's court and a people's prosecution bureau to replace the 'revolutionary courts'. In August Qaddafi announced the abolition of the army and the police force. The army was to be replaced by a force of Jamahiri Guards, comprising conscripts and members of the existing army and police force. A new policy of decentralization was announced, and in September the decision was taken to relocate all but two of the secretariats of the General People's Committee (ministries) away from Tripoli, mostly to Sirte, Qaddafi's birthplace. In January 1989 Qaddafi announced that all state institutions, including the state intelligence service and the official Libyan news agency, were to be abolished. Despite much official rhetoric, the practical consequences of these pronouncements proved limited and were non-existent as far as human rights were concerned.

At the annual meeting of the GPC held in Sirte in March 2000, Qaddafi announced that most of the central government secretariats were being abolished and their functions devolved to the municipal and provincial level. The move continued a decentralization policy introduced in the late 1980s, but was interpreted in part as a means of deflecting popular criticism away from central government by ensuring that any complaints would have to be dealt with by the relevant commune or provincial council. Significantly, however, the Libyan leader declared that the Secretariats for Foreign Liaison and International Co-operation, for Finance and for Justice and Public Security would be retained and that two new secretariats would be created (African Unity, and Information, Culture and Tourism), thus ensuring that key areas of government remained centralized. Policy on hydrocarbons was transferred to the NOC following the abolition of the energy secretariat, ensuring that this vital area also remained under central control.

In June 2003 another reorganization took place, amid press reports that Qaddafi had demanded the total privatization of key economic sectors, including the petroleum industry, arguing that the public sector was uncompetitive and had failed. Ghanem, who had been appointed as Secretary of the General People's Committee in the reorganization, reportedly favoured economic openness and was keen to encourage greater foreign investment in Libya.

At the GPC meeting held in Sirte in March 2004, a reorganization of the General People's Committee was announced that appeared to strengthen the position of 'reformers' and gave the Libyan Government a more orthodox appearance. Ghanem retained his post as Secretary, indicating Qaddafi's continued commitment to reform. Five new secretariats were created, relating to the portfolios of Energy (revived after having been abolished in 2000), National Security, Youth and Sport, Culture, and Training and Labour. New legislation was adopted to facilitate the transfer of state corporations to private management, to increase immigration controls and ban illegal immigration, and to promote tourism.

A further reorganization of the GPC was announced in March 2006. Ghanem was replaced by his Deputy, al-Mahmoudi, and was himself appointed as Chairman of the NOC. Senior officials had strongly criticized Ghanem's pursuit of liberal economic policies, in particular the privatization of state-owned companies, the freezing of salaries and the removal of subsidies for several essential products. Al-Mahmoudi insisted that Ghanem's programme of reforms would continue; however, although he refrained from attacking the policies of his predecessor, he did little to support them. He also affirmed his commitment to opening the banking sector to investment from private and foreign banks.

In January 2006 it was reported that Qaddafi had given Seif al-Islam permission to proceed with a plan to permit privately-owned newspapers and radio and television news organizations to operate in the country. Seif al-Islam announced that preparations were under way to create a satellite television channel and contracts had been signed to distribute over 50 international and Arab publications in Libya without censorship. The Al-Ghad Foundation was duly set up and its various media organs gained notoriety for openly criticizing government officials and policies. However, in June 2009 the Government abruptly announced that Al-Ghad was to be nationalized and placed under the control of the National Centre for Media Services, which was to redraft the group's editorial policy.

The weakening of Seif al-Islam's position was emphasized in December 2010, when the board of trustees of his foundation, the Qaddafi Development Foundation, announced that it would no longer include advocacy for political and human rights reform in Libya among its activities. Both the Foundation and Al-Ghad were the two vehicles through which Seif al-Islam promoted reform in Libya, and the curtailment of the domestic activities of both organizations pointed to the growing ascendancy of the hardliners.

In March 2008 Qaddafi announced at the annual GPC meeting in Sirte his plan to abolish almost all of the government secretariats. He also declared his intention to disburse the country's hydrocarbons revenues directly to the people and railed against the 'octopus' of government, stating that the 'administration had failed'. His proposals would have effectively abolished the executive arm of government, with only some ministerial departments remaining (reportedly foreign affairs, defence, internal security, justice and finance). A reorganization of the General Secretariat of the GPC and of the General People's Committee was also announced at the annual meeting. There was speculation that the new appointments mostly served to concentrate power more closely within the tight clique of Qaddafi's family and trusted friends—a trend that had become increasingly characteristic of the Libyan leader in the 2000s.

In September 2008 Qaddafi reiterated his plans to dismantle the majority of secretariats and to redistribute oil revenues, stating that the reforms would come into effect at the beginning of 2009. However, rather than implementing the proposed reforms directly, Qaddafi referred them to the Basic People's Congresses (BPCs). At the annual GPC meeting in March 2009, the Conference rejected the proposed package of reforms, after the BPCs had themselves voted against it. The BPCs did not reject the scheme completely, saying that they endorsed it in principle, but 'supported the postponement of direct distribution (of oil revenue) until the relevant procedures have been completed', and in the intervening period 'supported continuing providing services through executive institutions'. None the less, Qaddafi did carry out a reorganization of the General People's Committee. Kusa, hitherto the head of the Libyan intelligence service, was appointed as Secretary for Foreign Liaison and International Co-operation, while Abd al-Hafid Mahmoud Zlitni assumed responsibility for the newly merged Secretariat for Finance and Planning. Several other secretariats were merged, and the post of Secretary for Manpower, Training and Employment was abolished. In January 2010 the number of secretariats was reduced from 12 to seven and Muhammad Aboulghasem al-Zwai, a former ambassador to the UK and to Morocco, was appointed as Secretary of the GPC.

WORSENING RELATIONS WITH THE WEST: LIBYA ACCUSED OF 'STATE-SPONSORED TERRORISM'

Qaddafi's policies in the Middle East and Africa and the actions of his people's bureaux in Europe and the USA increasingly antagonized Western governments during the late 1970s and 1980s. Early in 1984, following renewed official calls for Libyans to liquidate enemies of the revolution, seven bombs exploded in Manchester and London, in the UK. It was believed that these attacks were aimed at Libyan dissidents whom Qaddafi had recently accused the UK of harbouring. On 17 April, during a demonstration outside the Libyan people's bureau in London by Libyans opposed to Qaddafi's rule, a female police officer, Yvonne Fletcher, was killed, and 11 people were injured by shots fired from inside the bureau. A 10-day siege of the building ensued, during which the UK severed diplomatic relations with Libya and ordered Libyan diplomats to leave the country. Qaddafi denied responsibility for the murder of the police officer, but, after the UK broke off diplomatic relations, he was understood to have ordered so-called hit squads to suspend their activities in Europe for fear of economic or other sanctions.

By the late 1970s relations with the USA had already become strained. In December 1979 a mob protesting against the presence in the USA of the exiled Shah of Iran sacked the US embassy in Tripoli, and it was closed in January 1980. As Libya drew closer to the Eastern Bloc by signing agreements with the USSR (already Libya's major arms supplier), Czechoslovakia, Poland, Bulgaria and Romania in the early 1980s, relations with the USA deteriorated further. When Ronald Reagan became US President in 1981, Qaddafi was quickly elevated to the status of 'international enemy number one', and the US campaign against Qaddafi moved swiftly from covert action to military confrontation. In August of that year US aircraft shot down two Soviet-made Libyan fighter aircraft over the Gulf of Sirte, which Libya claimed as its territorial waters, and in November Reagan alleged that Libya had sent a group to assassinate him. Details of a plan by the US Central Intelligence Agency (CIA) to undermine Qaddafi were revealed in the US press in November 1985. In the following month the US Government accused Libya of harbouring and training members of the pro-Palestinian Fatah Revolutionary Council, led by Abu Nidal, who were believed to be responsible for simultaneous attacks on passengers at the departure desks of the Israeli airline, El Al, at Rome (Italy) and Vienna (Austria) airports on 27 December, and of being a centre for international terrorism. On 7 January 1986 President Reagan ordered the severance of all economic and commercial relations with Libya, and on the following day he froze Libyan assets in the USA. He was unsuccessful, however, in persuading the USA's European allies to impose economic sanctions against Libya.

In December 1985 Qaddafi had drawn a notional 'line of death' across the north of the Gulf of Sirte, along latitude 32°30′N, which he warned US and other foreign vessels not to cross. In January 1986, ostensibly in the exercise of its right to navigation in the area under international law, the Sixth Fleet was deployed off the Libyan coast, although no US vessel was believed to have crossed the 'line of death'. On 24 March—the day after the Sixth Fleet had begun its fourth set of manoeuvres in the area since January (and the 18th since 1981)—Libya fired recently installed Soviet SAM-5 missiles at US fighter aircraft flying over the Gulf of Sirte and inside the 'line of death'. In two retaliatory attacks—on 24 and 25 March 1986—US fighter aircraft destroyed missile and radar facilities at Sirte and sank four Libyan patrol boats in the Gulf. On 15 April US F-111 bombers flying from bases in the UK, together with aircraft from the Sixth Fleet, bombed military installations (including the Aziziya barracks where Qaddafi and his family were living), airports, government buildings and suspected terrorist training camps and communications centres in Tripoli and Benghazi. Reliable estimates suggested that 39 people were killed, many of them civilians (reportedly including Qaddafi's adopted daughter), and almost 100 people were injured. The US Administration justified the raids as 'self-defence' against 'state-sponsored terrorism' on the part of Libya, claiming to have proof that Libya was responsible for a bomb attack on a discotheque in West Berlin, Germany on 5 April, in which a US soldier and a Turkish woman were killed.

Conflict with the USA erupted again in January 1989, when US aircraft shot down two Libyan fighter aircraft in 'self-defence' over international waters in the Mediterranean. In March 1990 the USA and the Federal Republic of Germany (West Germany) claimed that Libya had commenced production of mustard gas at a plant near Rabta, south of Tripoli. When a fire broke out at the plant during the same month, Libya accused those countries, together with Israel, of involvement in sabotage, allegations that all three countries denied. In September, following an official investigation, France alleged that Qaddafi, together with President Hafiz al-Assad of Syria and the leader of the Popular Front for the Liberation of Palestine, Ahmad Jibril, had been responsible for planning the bombing of a French Union des Transports Aériens (UTA) passenger aircraft over Niger in September 1989, in which 171 people were killed. In June 1991 a Libyan proposal aimed at restoring diplomatic relations with the UK was rejected by the British Foreign and Commonwealth Office, which stated that there could be no possibility of a resumption in relations until there was convincing evidence that Libya had renounced its support for groups engaged in international terrorism, including the Irish Republican Army (IRA), and was prepared to co-operate fully in bringing to justice those responsible for the death of Yvonne Fletcher. In June 2010 Qaddafi agreed to pay US $2,000m. in compensation to the relatives of victims of IRA violence. However, in an attempt to prevent further claims against it, the Libyan Government refused to acknowledge specific liability.

THE LOCKERBIE AFFAIR AND THE IMPOSITION OF UN ECONOMIC SANCTIONS

In December 1988 all 259 people aboard a Pan Am Boeing 747, en route for New York, USA, died when the aircraft exploded over Lockerbie, Scotland. Eleven people on the ground also died. The plane had been flying from Frankfurt am Main, Germany, where it was believed that a suitcase containing a bomb had been loaded on board. Investigations also revealed that this suitcase had arrived at Frankfurt on a flight from Malta, where an employee of Libyan Arab Airlines, Al-Amin Khalifa Fhimah, was stationed. On 13 November 1991 international warrants were issued for the arrest of Fhimah and the former security chief of the Libyan airline, Abd al-Baset al-Megrahi, accusing them both of responsibility for the bombing of the Pan Am aircraft; Libya denied any involvement in the bombing.

Libya resisted pressure for the extradition of the two Lockerbie suspects and also for the arrest of four other Libyans sought by France in connection with the 1989 UTA airliner bombing, mounting a campaign among its Arab neighbours to enlist their support in countering the allegations. On 5 December 1991 the Arab League Council, meeting in Cairo, expressed solidarity with Libya and urged the avoidance of sanctions. However, on 26 December US President George Bush extended economic sanctions, which the USA had imposed on Libya in January 1986, for a further year. A unanimous resolution (No. 731), adopted by the UN Security Council on 21 January 1992, demanded the extradition of the Lockerbie suspects to the USA or the UK, as well as Libya's full co-operation with France's inquiry into the 1989 UTA airliner bombing.

On 31 March 1992 the UN Security Council adopted Resolution 748, imposing mandatory economic sanctions against Libya. From 15 April all civilian air links and arms trade with Libya were prohibited and its diplomatic representation abroad reduced. However, an embargo on the sale of Libyan petroleum was not imposed. Qaddafi responded with a threat to cut off oil supplies to, and withdraw all business from, those countries that complied with Resolution 748. Arab diplomats and the more pragmatic members of Qaddafi's circle urged a compromise, fearing that the imposition of further UN sanctions, particularly an embargo on the sale of petroleum, would be disastrous.

Despite the USA's efforts to secure a tightening of the economic embargo, the main European importers of Libyan petroleum, in particular Germany, Italy and Spain, remained firmly opposed to an oil embargo. In August 1993 the USA, the UK and France, increasingly frustrated at Qaddafi's defiance, issued an ultimatum to Libya stating that if the two suspects were not surrendered for trial by 1 October, they would propose a new UN Security Council resolution imposing tougher sanctions. When Libya failed to comply, on 11 November the Security Council adopted Resolution 883, which provided for the freezing of all Libyan assets abroad, with the exception of earnings from hydrocarbon exports, placed a ban on the sale to Libya of certain equipment for the 'downstream' oil and gas sectors, and placed further restrictions on Libyan civil aviation.

In April 1995 Qaddafi successfully defied UN sanctions by ordering a Libyan aircraft carrying 150 pilgrims to leave Tripoli for Jeddah in Saudi Arabia. The UN immediately condemned the Libyan action as a 'flagrant violation of the UN air embargo' and criticized Egypt and Saudi Arabia for their involvement. However, it rejected persistent US demands for stronger sanctions, including an oil embargo, and merely renewed existing sanctions. In June Qaddafi once again flouted UN sanctions by flying to Cairo to attend an Arab League summit, which urged the UN to lift sanctions against Libya, and appealed to the UK and the USA to accept an Arab proposal that the two Libyan suspects in the Lockerbie affair should be given a neutral and fair trial in The Hague, rather than the UK, but with Scottish judges in session and in accordance with Scottish law.

USA IMPOSES SECONDARY SANCTIONS

In July 1996 the US Congress unanimously approved the controversial Iran and Libya Sanctions Act (ILSA), which aimed to weaken further the Libyan economy as a penalty for that country's alleged support of international terrorism. The legislation had originally targeted only Iran, but was amended to include Libya, and involved the imposition of sanctions on any company investing more than US $40m. (subsequently revised to $20m.) in Iran or Libya in any one year. European governments protested vociferously against the legislation, and promptly lodged a protest with the World Trade Organization (WTO). European oil companies, particularly those of Italy and Spain, were heavily involved in the Libyan petroleum industry, and EU countries were, therefore, most likely to suffer as a result of the new sanctions. In April 1997 the EU and the USA reached a compromise: the US Administration promised to protect European companies from the adverse effects of the legislation, and in return the EU agreed to withdraw its complaint to the WTO regarding an earlier US law, the Helms-Burton Act, which imposed sanctions on non-US companies involved in business with Cuba.

Qaddafi tried to take advantage of the divisions between the USA and the EU by working to improve European relations, particularly with France. He praised France for its pursuit of an independent foreign policy and allowed the French judge investigating the 1989 bombing of the UTA airliner over Niger unprecedented access to Libyan evidence during his visit to Tripoli in July, which led to the judge's decision to try *in absentia* the Libyans suspected of the attack. A declaration by German authorities in October that clear evidence was available to prove the Libyan Government's direct involvement in the 1986 bomb attack on a Berlin discotheque was also a major setback. Shortly thereafter, arrest warrants were issued for the three Libyans believed to have been involved in the attack. In March 1997 Libya achieved a rare success in foreign policy when the Vatican resisted US pressure and established formal diplomatic relations with Libya.

FURTHER DEVELOPMENTS IN THE LOCKERBIE AFFAIR

In July 1997 the Arab League, which had previously been criticized by Qaddafi for its lack of support, formally proposed that the two Libyan suspects in the Lockerbie affair be tried by Scottish judges under Scottish law in a neutral country. At an Arab League meeting in September the member states urged a relaxation of the air embargo on Libya and in October the President of South Africa, Nelson Mandela, visited Libya, despite US disapproval, and publicly expressed support for the proposals to hold a trial of the Lockerbie suspects in a third country. Later that month the UK requested that the UN send envoys to examine the Scottish legal system, and in December the UN issued a report concluding that the Libyan suspects would receive a fair trial under the Scottish system.

In August 1998 the USA and the UK, under mounting diplomatic pressure, agreed to a trial of the two Libyan suspects in the Netherlands before a panel of Scottish judges and in accordance with Scottish law. Soon after the offer was made the UN Security Council unanimously approved Resolution 1192, allowing the lifting of the UN sanctions against Libya as soon as the two suspects were surrendered for trial. By the time Kofi Annan, the UN Secretary-General, visited Libya in December, Qaddafi had agreed to a trial in the Netherlands under Scottish law.

In early March 1999 the six Libyans accused of the 1989 UTA bombing were found guilty *in absentia* after a three-day trial in Paris, France, and were sentenced to life imprisonment. The French authorities proceeded to issue international warrants for the arrest of the six men and demanded that the Libyan authorities should punish them. It appeared very unlikely that Libya would impose prison sentences on the men, who included Qaddafi's brother-in-law. In July 1999 Libya paid more than US $31m. in compensation to the families of the 70 people killed in the bombing of the French airliner.

In mid-March 1999, following further diplomatic efforts by South Africa, President Nelson Mandela announced that Libya would release the two men accused of the Lockerbie bombing for trial by 6 April. On 5 April Fhimah and al-Megrahi arrived at Valkenburg airport in the Netherlands, accompanied by the UN's chief legal counsel, Hans Corell. With the surrender of the two suspects, the UN Security Council immediately suspended the sanctions imposed on Libya in 1992, but, under pressure from the USA, avoided a vote on whether to approve a permanent lifting of sanctions. US sanctions against Libya—some of which dated from 1981—remained in place despite opposition from US business groups. In contrast, in September 2000 the EU removed most of its remaining sanctions against Libya, and Libya was invited to participate in the Euro-

Mediterranean partnership programme initiated in Barcelona, Spain, in 1995.

Several European countries moved quickly to strengthen political and economic links with Libya in the hope of gaining lucrative investment opportunities there. In July 1999 the UK announced that it was resuming full diplomatic relations with Libya after a rupture of 15 years. The decision followed a statement by Qaddafi in which he accepted Libya's 'general responsibility' for the murder of British police officer Yvonne Fletcher outside the Libyan people's bureau in London in 1984. Qaddafi expressed his 'deep regret' for the incident and offered to pay compensation to the woman's family. In November 1999 the British authorities confirmed that compensation (estimated at £250,000) had been paid, and a British ambassador arrived in Tripoli in the following month. In December the Italian Prime Minister, Massimo D'Alema, became the first EU premier to visit Libya in more than eight years. During the visit the two countries issued a joint statement appealing for greater international co-operation to eradicate terrorism. Efforts by relatives of victims of the 1989 UTA airliner bombing to begin legal action against Qaddafi for complicity in the attack were not supported by the French Government, which considered the matter closed and was also anxious to strengthen links with Libya.

In October 2000 the French Court of Appeal ruled that Qaddafi could be prosecuted in France for complicity in the 1989 UTA airliner bombing, but this was overturned in March 2001 by the Court of Cassation in Paris, on the grounds that as head of state Qaddafi had immunity from such action. The families of victims of the bombing pledged to take their case to the European Court of Human Rights.

Libya's relations with the EU suffered a reversal at the beginning of 2000. Although Libya had agreed to accept the terms for joining the Euro-Mediterranean partnership programme, it insisted that both Israel and the Palestinian (National) Authority should be excluded. This demand was unacceptable to the EU, and in January the President of the European Commission, Romano Prodi, withdrew an invitation to Qaddafi, originally made in December 1999, to visit Brussels, Belgium. In April 2000 the Libyan leader used his main speech to the EU-OAU summit in Cairo to castigate Africa's former colonizers. However, a private meeting with Prodi was described as more positive, and Libya was courted by several European leaders eager to capitalize on the country's rehabilitation. In October all EU member states supported a resolution proposed by Libya in the UN General Assembly criticizing unilateral sanctions, and in November Libya was invited as an observer to the Euro-Mediterranean meeting of foreign affairs ministers in Marseille, France.

In February 2000 the US authorities had for the first time granted a visa to Libya's ambassador to the UN, enabling him to travel from the UN headquarters in New York to Washington, DC, USA. In the following month several US Department of State officials visited Libya to determine whether security arrangements were satisfactory for US citizens to travel there; a ban on Americans visiting Libya had been in place since 1981 and was renewed in November 1999. Although the US Government strenuously denied that it planned to lift unilateral sanctions, the visit angered the 'Lockerbie lobby' group of relatives of US victims of the 1988 bombing. In July 2000 the US Department of Defense stated that Libya was no longer engaged in acts of terrorism and that there was no evidence that it was pursuing a chemical weapons programme.

Meanwhile, during a visit to Russia by the Libyan Secretary for Foreign Liaison and International Co-operation in July 2000, President Vladimir Putin called for a definitive end to UN sanctions. A month earlier Russia had indicated that it was resuming arms sales to Libya, with the first contracts reported to be worth US $100m. Other high-level political contacts followed.

THE LOCKERBIE TRIAL

The trial of the two Libyans accused of the Lockerbie bombing began on 3 May 2000. Fhimah and al-Megrahi were charged on three counts: murder; conspiracy to murder; and contravention of the 1982 Aviation Security Act. The prosecution alleged that the two accused were members of the Libyan intelligence service and had planted a bomb in a suitcase on an Air Malta flight which was then transferred to Pan Am flight 103 at Frankfurt. The two defendants pleaded not guilty, and their defence team alleged that a small Palestinian guerrilla group, the Popular Front for the Liberation of Palestine—General Command (PFLP—GC), acting as agents of the Iranian Government, had planted the bomb in revenge for the shooting down of an Iranian civilian airliner over the Gulf by a US warship in 1988.

In November 2000, after 73 days of evidence and submissions from more than 230 witnesses, the prosecution concluded its case. Much of the evidence was highly circumstantial, and several key witnesses proved unreliable or offered testimonies that appeared to undermine the prosecution's case. The defence case began in December, when lawyers sought an adjournment to give them more time to gather new evidence, which they claimed was held by the Syrian Government and which purportedly implicated the Syrian-backed PFLP—GC and the obscure Palestinian Popular Struggle Front in the bombing. However, at the beginning of January 2001 the court was told that the Syrian authorities had refused to co-operate or hand over any documents. In the end, lawyers for the defence focused on undermining the evidence presented by the prosecution's principal witness, Abd al-Majid Giaka, a Libyan double agent who had worked for both the Libyan intelligence services and the CIA.

On 31 January 2001 the three Scottish judges unanimously found al-Megrahi guilty of the murder of 270 people and sentenced him to life imprisonment, with a recommendation that he serve a minimum of 20 years. However, Fhimah was acquitted, owing to a lack of evidence, and immediately freed. In an 82-page judgment, the judges accepted that al-Megrahi was a member of the Jamahiriya Security Organization (the Libyan intelligence services), 'occupying posts of fairly high rank', and, although they acknowledged their awareness of 'uncertainties and qualifications' in the case, they concluded that the evidence against him combined to form 'a real and convincing pattern' that left them with no reasonable doubt as to his guilt. The judges ruled out any involvement of the PFLP—GC and the Palestinian Popular Struggle Front in the bombing, stating that they inferred from the evidence that the planning and execution of the plot was of Libyan origin.

For many, al-Megrahi's conviction pointed clearly to Libyan state-sponsored terrorism and to the highest level in the Libyan leadership. Others continued to maintain that Libya had been made a scapegoat by the West and remained convinced that suspicions should still focus on Iran, Syria and the PFLP—GC. British relatives of the victims stated that they intended to renew their campaign for a public inquiry into the atrocity, insisting that serious questions remained unanswered. A British government spokesman stated that the UK expected the Libyan authorities to take full responsibility for the actions of their official. US relatives pledged to pursue a civil case for damages from the Libyan Government. US President George W. Bush, who had taken office in early 2001, assured them that his Administration would maintain sanctions against Libya until the Libyan authorities accepted responsibility for the bombing and agreed to compensate the families.

The day after the judgment was announced, Qaddafi indicated that he would shortly reveal evidence that proved al-Megrahi's innocence. Four days later the Libyan leader made a long speech in Tripoli in which he repeated his claim that Libya was not to blame for the bombing; however, he failed to produce the new evidence, asserting only that US and British investigators had planted evidence at Lockerbie to incriminate Libya.

RELATIONS WITH THE WEST AFTER THE LOCKERBIE VERDICT

Qaddafi immediately condemned the September 2001 suicide attacks on New York and Washington, DC. He was swift to recall that, some six years earlier, he had issued a warrant for the arrest of Osama bin Laden, whom the USA held principally responsible for the attacks, and who, at that time, had been accused of financing a radical Islamist movement in Libya intending to assassinate the Libyan leader. Shortly after the attacks the LIFG appeared on a list published by the US Federal Bureau of Investigation (FBI) of alleged terrorist organizations linked to the al-Qa'ida network whose assets were to be frozen. In October and again in January 2002 the US Assistant Secretary of State for Near Eastern Affairs, William Burns, met the head of Libyan intelligence services, Kusa, in London. Kusa also held meetings with members of the CIA and the British security intelligence agency, MI5, regarding the combating of international terrorism. The Libyan team was reported to have provided US officials with information about the al-Qa'ida network. The Libyans, for their part, requested co-operation in securing the extradition of Libyan militant Islamists living in Europe, particularly members of the LIFG.

The 'war on terror' was one of the main topics discussed during a visit to Tripoli in October 2001 by the French Minister for Co-operation, Charles Josselin. In February 2002 daily flights between Paris and Tripoli were resumed after a 14-year hiatus. Meanwhile, in November 2001 a German court sentenced a German woman, two Palestinians and a Libyan national to prison terms of 12–18 years' duration for carrying out a bomb attack on a West Berlin discotheque in April 1986. On the basis of new evidence from East German intelligence files, the prosecution stated that the Libyan intelligence services were implicated in the bombing, which was seen as a revenge attack for the sinking of two Libyan patrol boats in the Mediterranean by the US Navy in the previous month. The prosecution was, however, unable to prove that the Libyan leader had ordered or approved the attack.

Al-Megrahi's appeal began in January 2002 before a panel of five Scottish judges at the Scottish Court in the Netherlands, Camp Zeist. At the centre of the appeal was new evidence from a former security guard at London's Heathrow Airport, who claimed that on the night that the Pan Am flight departed a door giving access to the loading area of Terminal 3 had been tampered with—suggesting that the bomb could have been planted in London and not in Malta, as the trial judges had concluded, thus casting doubt on the original judgment. On 16 March the five Scottish judges ruled that none of the grounds put forward by the defence was well founded, and al-Megrahi's appeal was unanimously rejected. Meanwhile, diplomatic contacts aimed at improving relations with the USA continued. US oil companies, which had assets exceeding US $2,000m. in Libya, lobbied the Administration of President George W. Bush, apparently concerned that unless relations improved Tripoli might terminate their concessions and allocate them to European companies. None the less, relations remained strained with the US Administration in late 2001 renewing the ban on US passport holders visiting Libya for another year, and naming Libya as one of several potentially hostile states trying to establish a nuclear capability.

In August 2002 Mike O'Brien, a minister in the British Foreign and Commonwealth Office, visited Libya for talks with Qaddafi. After the meeting O'Brien stated that Libya was considering making an announcement whereby it would accept 'general responsibility' for the Lockerbie bombing, and the Secretary for Foreign Liaison declared that Libya was ready 'in principle' to take steps to compensate the relatives of victims. Qaddafi had also expressed his willingness to co-operate with the international community on issues such as weapons of mass destruction and the 'war on terror'. O'Brien welcomed these statements but emphasized that there had to be clear proof that the Libyan leader intended to fulfil his undertakings.

The French Minister of Foreign Affairs, Dominique de Villepin, visited Tripoli in October 2002 and reported that progress had been made regarding compensation for the families of victims of the 1989 UTA airliner bombing. Libya was ready to consider compensation for those French victims who had not been compensated and to consider additional compensation once a French court had ruled on the issue. Thus far Libya had paid some €32.5m., and families of 57 of the 171 victims (53 of whom were French nationals) had been compensated. On 22 October 2002 the first meeting in 20 years of the Franco-Libyan Commission took place in Paris, presided over by the two countries' foreign affairs ministers, a clear sign that bilateral relations were back on track.

After long and protracted negotiations, on 16 August 2003 Libya finally delivered a letter to the President of the UN Security Council stating that it accepted responsibility for the actions of its officials in the Lockerbie bombing; agreed to pay compensation to the families of the victims; pledged co-operation in any further Lockerbie inquiry; and agreed to continue its co-operation in the 'war on terror' and to take practical measures to ensure that such co-operation was effective. The UK and the USA declared that they were prepared to allow the formal lifting of UN sanctions against Libya once the US $2,700m. in compensation had been transferred to the Bank for International Settlements.

France, however, demanded a similar level of compensation for families of victims of the 1989 UTA bombing, who had received a mere US $35m., and there were fears that France might veto the resolution unless Libya agreed to additional compensation. After intense negotiations between the UK, France and the USA, de Villepin announced on 11 September 2003 that a framework agreement had been reached between the relatives of the victims of the 1989 UTA bombing and the QIFCA providing for additional compensation, and that France had no objection to the UN Security Council vote taking place. On 12 September 2003 the Security Council voted formally to adopt Resolution 1506, which lifted the sanctions imposed against Libya; the USA and France abstained from the vote. Meanwhile, the Bush Administration confirmed that bilateral US sanctions would remain in place until Libya had addressed US concerns over its poor human rights record and lack of democratic institutions, its destructive role in perpetuating regional conflicts in Africa, and its continued pursuit of weapons of mass destruction and their related delivery systems.

In October 2003 Seif al-Islam Qaddafi appealed to President Jacques Chirac of France to lift the obstacles preventing the implementation of the framework agreement between the QIFCA and the families of victims of the UTA bombing. He stated that the Foundation would pay a maximum of US $1m. to each family and that the French had agreed to accept this offer. The victims' relatives, however, responded that the level of compensation proposed was unacceptable and that the framework accord was simply an agreement to pursue further negotiations. An agreement between Libya and France was finally signed in January 2004, according to which the QIFCA would pay $170m. in compensation to the families of victims, in addition to the $35m. already paid.

In June 2003 the Italian Prime Minister, Silvio Berlusconi, caused diplomatic embarrassment when he announced that Italy was close to signing an agreement with Libya that would allow Italian troops to patrol Libyan ports and Italian ships to sail in Libyan territorial waters, as part of a campaign to combat illegal immigration into Italy. Addressing the Italian Senate, he referred to the 'return' of Italian forces to Libya, a direct reference to the Italian colonial period. In return for Libyan co-operation, Italy, which assumed the presidency of the EU in July, promised the Libyan authorities that it would use its influence to persuade the EU to relax its arms embargo on Libya. The Libyan authorities, however, denied that any discussions with Italy had taken place and Libya's Secretary for Foreign Liaison and International Co-operation stated that his country would not allow such measures, although it was willing to co-operate in the curbing of illegal immigration, but not at the expense of its sovereignty.

The Spanish Prime Minister, José María Aznar, arrived in Libya for talks with Qaddafi in September 2003 that focused on Iraq and the Middle East peace process, as well as Libya's role as a key transit point for illegal immigration from Africa to southern Europe. During talks held in February 2004 at the extraordinary AU summit in Sirte, Qaddafi told the President of the European Commission that Libya was ready to start working towards membership of the 'Euro-Med' trade and aid partnership. It was subsequently reported that Italy and the UK favoured the lifting of the remaining EU sanctions against Libya, notably the arms embargo, but that Germany would continue to oppose this measure until Libya had agreed to pay compensation for the 1986 bombing in Berlin. Reports in September 2004 stated that Libya had agreed to pay

US $35m. to compensate more than 150 non-US victims of the Berlin bombing.

LIBYA AGREES TO ABANDON WEAPONS OF MASS DESTRUCTION

On 19 December 2003 the UK and the USA announced that, after nine months of clandestine negotiations, Libya had agreed to disclose and destroy all its weapons of mass destruction, end all programmes to develop them and limit the range of its missiles to no more than 300 km. Libya would allow international inspectors to oversee the elimination of chemical, biological and nuclear weapons to ensure that the process was transparent and verifiable. The initiative for these talks came from Qaddafi and was widely attributed to the 'Iraq effect'. US President Bush stated that the decision would allow Libya to begin the process of rejoining the community of nations and pledged that if Libya fulfilled its promises 'its good faith would be returned'. Within days a delegation from the International Atomic Energy Agency (IAEA) had visited the country and in late December the Director-General of the IAEA, Muhammad el-Baradei, stated that after visits to four secret nuclear sites he could confirm that Libya had been in the very early stages of a weapons programme.

In early February 2004 Berlusconi visited Tripoli for talks with Qaddafi. At the same time the USA announced that a US diplomat had been posted to Tripoli—the first for 25 years. In mid-February the Secretary for Foreign Liaison and International Co-operation, Abd al-Rahman Muhammad Shalgam, was invited to London, where he held talks with the British Prime Minister, Tony Blair, and the Secretary of State for Foreign and Commonwealth Affairs, Jack Straw. Both sides agreed to enhance co-operation in resolving the issue of the murder of British police officer Yvonne Fletcher. Libya had accepted 'general responsibility' for her murder, but no one had been arrested. British families of victims of the Lockerbie bombing stated that they felt 'let down' by the British Government, suggesting that the UK and the USA wanted to ingratiate themselves with Qaddafi in order to take advantage of developments within the Libyan petroleum industry.

Meanwhile, Dr Abdul Qadeer Khan, Pakistan's leading nuclear scientist responsible for developing Pakistan's nuclear bomb, admitted to selling nuclear expertise to several countries including Libya. Shortly afterwards, it was reported in the US press that documents obtained from Libya contained proof that the People's Republic of China had played a key role in the transfer of nuclear technology to Pakistan in the early 1980s and that technology from China had entered the international nuclear black market via the intermediary of Pakistan. Meanwhile, information leaked from a confidential IAEA report alleged that Libya had started a programme to develop nuclear weapons in the 1980s, beginning with exports to an unnamed nuclear weapons state in 1985 of uranium ore concentrate, which were then returned to Libya in the form of uranium compounds that could be used in the uranium enrichment process. Later, according to the report, Libyan scientists at the Tajura nuclear reactor succeeded in extracting small quantities of plutonium from uranium. In January 2004 Libya signed the Chemical Weapons Convention, and teams from the Organization for the Prohibition of Chemical Weapons later visited Libya to oversee the dismantling of the country's chemical weapons programme. In January 2018 Germany announced that it had completed the destruction of the components from Libya's chemical weapons programme 'in an environmentally sustainable manner'.

In February 2004, in a radio interview with the British Broadcasting Corporation, Ghanem caused controversy when he implied that Libya did not accept responsibility for the Lockerbie bombing, nor for the murder of Yvonne Fletcher. He stated that he did not see Libya's decision to pay compensation as an admission of guilt and that it had been done 'to buy peace with the West'. Following Ghanem's remarks, the UK announced that it had obtained assurances from Shalgam that Libya stood by the commitments it had made in relation to the Lockerbie bombing and the shooting of Fletcher. The USA, for its part, proceeded to lift the travel ban on US citizens visiting Libya, in place for 23 years, and stated that it would expand its diplomatic presence in Tripoli. The Bush Administration also announced that US oil companies operating in Libya before US sanctions were imposed would be allowed to begin negotiating their return, pending the lifting of sanctions.

In March 2004 William Burns held talks with Qaddafi in his capacity as US Assistant Secretary of State for Near Eastern Affairs—the highest-level visit to Libya by a US official for more than 30 years. Shortly afterwards, Blair became the first British Prime Minister to visit Libya since Qaddafi came to power. British officials announced that British police investigating the shooting of Yvonne Fletcher would visit Libya in April and hoped to talk directly to those suspected of involvement in her murder. At the same time the Royal Dutch Shell group announced an agreement, estimated to be worth US $1,000m., to develop Libya's gas resources, and BAE Systems, a major British aerospace and defence manufacturer, was reported to be about to sign a major deal with Libya on civil aviation.

On 22 April 2004—the date by which the USA was required to have lifted US sanctions on Libya for the next tranche of compensation payments to be made to families of Lockerbie victims under the 2003 agreement—Libya announced that it had extended the deadline by three months. On the following day, however, the USA announced that it was lifting the majority of sanctions against Libya, including those imposed under ILSA; would no longer oppose Libya's accession to the WTO; and would work to rebuild diplomatic ties. The USA was to set up a liaison office in Tripoli as a step towards restoring normal diplomatic relations broken in 1981, and Libyan envoys would open a liaison office in Washington, DC. Certain US sanctions would remain in place while Libya continued to be designated a 'state sponsor of terrorism', and frozen Libyan assets valued at hundreds of millions of dollars would not be released. In June 2004 the USA formally re-established diplomatic relations with Libya with the opening of a US liaison office in Tripoli. In September President Bush issued a presidential executive order formally abolishing the US embargo against Libya and releasing frozen Libyan assets in the USA.

Qaddafi made an official visit to Brussels in April 2004, at the invitation of European Commission President Prodi. It was his first visit to Europe in more than 15 years. At a joint press conference Qaddafi stated that in the past Libya had led liberation movements in Africa and developing countries but had now decided to lead the peace process all over the world. He claimed that all states, including the USA, should follow Libya's example and give up weapons of mass destruction, saying that the country wanted to be a bridge between Europe and Africa, and to participate in reviving the Barcelona Process to bring peace and co-operation to the Mediterranean region. Qaddafi also urged the EU to help Libya and Algeria to control illegal immigration into Europe via North Africa. Prodi stated that after discussions with Germany and Bulgaria he was confident that issues between these countries and Libya could be solved 'within weeks'.

In August 2004 the Italian Minister of Foreign Affairs, Franco Frattini, stated that he was involved in strenuous diplomatic negotiations to seek to gain the EU's acquiescence to a partial lifting of its arms embargo. During a visit to Libya later that month by Frattini and Berlusconi, talks with Qaddafi focused on the problem of illegal immigration, with Berlusconi urging Libya to place stricter border controls on the country's northern coastline. In September, following the EU's announcement that it would lift the arms embargo and economic sanctions imposed on Libya since 1986 (a decision ratified by EU ministers of foreign affairs in October 2004), Italy and Libya signed a new agreement on immigration. The agreement provided for joint patrols of Libya's coastline, the training of Libyan police by Italian officers, and the establishment of transit camps for immigrants on Libyan territory. In October Italy began deporting to Libya more than 1,000 illegal immigrants who had recently arrived on the Italian island of Lampedusa.

Meanwhile, EU foreign affairs ministers stated that an improvement in human rights in Libya was an essential element for progress in relations with Europe, pointing to serious obstacles to freedom of speech and association, inhumane conditions of detention, and credible reports of detainee torture. They also underlined their opposition to the death penalty. In September 2004 an agreement was signed between the QIFCA and the lawyers representing German victims of the 1986 bomb attack on a Berlin discotheque, under which Libya was to pay US $35m. in compensation. In October 2004 Gerhard Schröder became the first German Chancellor to visit Libya. He welcomed the process of normalization in relations between Libya and the international community and praised both the policy of openness and especially the decision to abandon weapons of mass destruction. In the following month President Chirac became the first French head of state since 1951 to visit Tripoli, where he expressed his wish to begin afresh with Libya after many years of tensions.

THE BULGARIAN MEDICAL STAFF HIV CASE

In May 2004 EU officials expressed deep disquiet when six Bulgarian medical personnel (five nurses and a Palestinian-born doctor who was granted Bulgarian citizenship during his detention), who had been arrested in 1999 and charged with deliberately infecting several hundred Libyan children at a Benghazi hospital with blood products contaminated with the HIV virus, were convicted and sentenced to death by a Libyan court. At an international conference on AIDS held in Nigeria in May 2001, Qaddafi had declared that the Bulgarians were acting on the orders of Western intelligence services and demanded an international 'Lockerbie-style' trial. However, in the absence of a motive for the alleged crimes, some observers argued that the Bulgarians had been made scapegoats by the Libyan authorities, who were faced with a growing number of cases of HIV/AIDS in the country and were being used to cover up inadequate sterilization of instruments at the hospital before the Bulgarian medics began working there. In December 2005 the Supreme Court, which had been due to hear the final appeal of the six medics, ordered a retrial. A former Bulgarian government minister subsequently claimed that Libya had sought to exchange the nurses for al-Megrahi.

Despite a wealth of data that strongly suggested that the children had already been infected with the HIV virus prior to the arrival in Libya of the accused in 1998, the judge upheld the original verdict in December 2006, following a retrial, and reinstated the six death sentences. The death sentences were upheld by the Supreme Court in July 2007 and were commuted to life imprisonment shortly afterwards, with the families of those infected accepting a compensation deal reportedly worth US $1m. per child. Bulgaria formally requested that the medics be allowed to serve out their sentences on Bulgarian soil, and later that month Benita Ferrero-Waldner, the European Commissioner responsible for External Relations and European Neighbourhood Policy, and Cécilia Sarkozy, the wife of the French President, Nicolas Sarkozy, arrived in Libya in order to procure the release of the detained medical staff into Bulgarian custody. The six medics were released from Libyan detention and transferred to Bulgaria, where they were pardoned immediately by Bulgarian President Georgi Parvanov. In August the Bulgarian Government announced its decision to waive Libya's debt of $56.6m., accrued during the Soviet era, and to divert the funds into providing treatment for the children infected by HIV and compensation for their families. Meanwhile, both the EU and France denied having made any financial deals to procure the medics' release. In April 2013 a Dutch court ordered Libya to pay the Palestinian-born doctor, Ashraf al-Hajuj, €1m. in damages for his eight years' false imprisonment.

RELATIONS WITH THE EU IMPROVE

On a visit to Tripoli in January 2006, the French Minister of Foreign Affairs, Philippe Douste-Blazy, praised the development in relations between the two countries and declared that France would provide treatment for the HIV-infected children. In March France and Libya signed an agreement to co-operate in the development of peaceful nuclear technology, the first such agreement since Libya abandoned its programme to develop weapons of mass destruction in 2003. In July 2007 France and Libya signed a deal providing for the sale to Libya of anti-tank missiles as part of a broader bilateral military agreement, the first arms contract to be signed between Libya and a Western nation since the international arms embargo was lifted in 2004. Considerable anger greeted the news in France, where many linked the culmination of the deal with the release of the Bulgarian medics, in which the French presidency had played a central role; President Sarkozy firmly denied any correlation between the two events. None the less, Sarkozy attracted further criticism when he invited the Libyan leader to Paris on a state visit. In his first trip to a major Western state since the imposition of sanctions, Qaddafi pitched his Bedouin tent in the French capital in December 2007 and spent five days signing contracts amounting to US $10,000m. Many senior French officials refused to meet the Libyan leader, and the French press was critical of the trip, accusing President Sarkozy of subordinating public morals to the quest for commercial gain. From Paris, Qaddafi flew to Madrid, making his first ever trip to Spain, where he signed further commercial deals.

Libya signed a memorandum of understanding (MOU) with the British Government in October 2005 to allow the deportation of Libyan nationals held in the UK on suspicion of involvement in terrorist activities. The agreement included a written assurance from Libya that deportees would be treated in a humane manner. (British law forbids the deportation of foreign nationals to countries suspected of practising inhumane treatment.) In response, Amnesty International noted that torture and suspicious deaths in custody were still commonly reported in Libya, and that it would be misguided to assume that Libya would honour such an agreement. In March 2007 Libya and the UK signed an MOU agreeing to enhance scientific and technical co-operation. In May Blair visited Libya shortly before his resignation as British premier, where he signed an agreement with Qaddafi pledging closer co-operation on defence matters. Blair hailed the former pariah of the West as a 'transformed' nation, and an example to Iran and other 'outcasts' in the international community.

In June 2007 the Scottish Criminal Cases Review Commission granted al-Megrahi the right to a second appeal, having identified six points during his 2001 trial that it believed might have constituted a miscarriage of justice. The decision was based on the contents of an 800-page report detailing the findings of an inquiry, lasting nearly four years, into the investigation and trial. Several relatives of the victims of the bombing expressed doubts about the conviction of al-Megrahi, and the view that Iran or Syria might have been behind the incident was attracting increasing levels of support.

The EU sought to follow up on its success over negotiating the release of the Bulgarian medics by deepening its dialogue with Qaddafi. In February 2008 Ferrero-Waldner announced that the European Commission was looking to create a formal framework for the development of relations with Libya. According to Ferrero-Waldner, the framework would be built around EU support for Libya's economic and social reforms and would be aimed at the ultimate establishment of a free trade agreement. The renewed negotiations with Libya took place outside the EU's existing framework for relations with the southern Mediterranean countries, the Euro-Mediterranean Partnership, or the Barcelona Process. With the lifting of sanctions, the EU tried to entice Libya into this scheme, but Qaddafi remained reluctant because of the human rights and good governance conditions attached to membership. In June Qaddafi derided plans by President Sarkozy for a Union for the Mediterranean to deepen economic ties between the EU members and southern Mediterranean rim states, branding the initiative an 'insult to Arabs and Africans', and contending that the EU was 'taking us for fools'. In January 2009, following the Israeli incursion into Gaza, Qaddafi declared the Union defunct, stating that it had been 'killed by Israel's bombs'.

Relations between Libya and Italy appeared to improve with the commencement of joint marine operations to help to counter illegal immigration in May 2009. In August 2008 relations between Italy and Libya were further consolidated when Berlusconi apologized for the 'damage inflicted on Libya by Italy during the colonial era' and signed an agreement to invest US $5,000m. in Libya over the next 25 years as a form of compensation. Under the Friendship, Partnership and Co-operation Treaty, formally ratified during a visit to Libya by Berlusconi in March 2009, Italy was to disburse a total of

$5,000m. to Libya, in annual instalments of $250m. until 2028. The money was to finance numerous infrastructure projects to be carried out by Italian companies. In June 2009, further cementing the deal, Qaddafi visited Rome for the first time. During his trip he assured Italian companies that they would have priority access to a Libyan Government investment scheme worth some €11,800m., as well as special commercial benefits, which would give Italian firms an advantage over other foreign competitors and, acknowledging Italy's dependence on Libyan oil, guaranteed that Libya would not 'favour supplying gas and petrol to other countries if it is at Italy's expense'. At the end of 2010 the Italian oil and gas company Eni agreed to help Libya to build a port and related infrastructure along the Gulf of Sirte, as part of the 2008 agreement to invest in social projects.

As relations with Italy improved, those with Switzerland deteriorated. In July 2008 Hannibal Qaddafi (the fifth son of the Libyan leader and the fourth by his second wife) and his wife were arrested at a hotel in Geneva, Switzerland, and later charged with assaulting two members of their domestic staff. Although the case against them was dismissed when the charges were dropped, the Libyan Government responded angrily, claiming that their treatment was a serious case of 'abuse of Libyan diplomats'. In the immediate aftermath of the incident, Libya detained two Swiss nationals; stopped issuing visas to Swiss travellers; cancelled its oil exports to Switzerland; prohibited flights by Swissair into Tripoli; and threatened to remove all the money it held in Swiss bank accounts. In April 2009 Libya filed a lawsuit against the civil authorities in Geneva for damages suffered by Hannibal and his wife.

During a visit to Tripoli in August 2009 the President of the Swiss Confederation, Hans-Rudolf Merz, apologized for the arrests, in return for the release of the two Swiss citizens who had previously been refused permission to leave Libya. However, Merz was left embarrassed when Libya failed to honour its side of the bargain. As a consequence, the Swiss Government prohibited the entry into Switzerland of 188 Libyans, including Qaddafi, his family, and senior members of his Government. In retaliation, a Libyan court in December sentenced the two detained Swiss men to 16 months' imprisonment for overstaying their visas. Following a successful appeal, the conviction of one of the defendants was overturned in January 2010, and he was allowed to leave the country; the conviction of the second defendant was upheld, although his gaol term was reduced to four months. At the same time, the Libyan Government announced that it was suspending visas for citizens residing in those countries adhering to the EU's Schengen Agreement on relaxed border controls, in effect including 25 European countries in the dispute, in an apparent attempt to apply diplomatic pressure on Switzerland. Intense mediation, most notably by the Italians, finally resolved the impasse; the second Swiss detainee returned home in June, and the two countries signed a formal accord agreeing to normalize relations.

In August 2009 it was reported that the Scottish Cabinet Secretary for Justice, Kenny MacAskill, was considering a request for the release of al-Megrahi on compassionate grounds after it was revealed that he was suffering from terminal prostate cancer. On 20 August MacAskill announced that al-Megrahi would be allowed to return to Libya; al-Megrahi had withdrawn an appeal against his conviction on the previous day. The celebrations that marked al-Megrahi's arrival in Tripoli and his subsequent meeting with Qaddafi provoked an angry reaction from the US Administration. It also prompted allegations that the British Government had secretly agreed to the release in order to secure commercial advantages for British companies in Libya. Both countries denied the allegations, but suspicions over al-Megrahi's release persisted as he survived well beyond the period that doctors had given him to live, eventually passing away in May 2012. Al-Megrahi's family, together with some of the relatives of the bombing victims, announced in June 2014 that they were filing an application with the Scottish Criminal Cases Review Commission (SCCRC), in a fresh effort to exonerate al-Megrahi. In July 2015 a Scottish court ruled that the relatives of the victims could not launch an appeal on al-Megrahi's behalf because the law did not 'allow victims or relatives of victims to be direct participants in criminal proceedings'. In May 2018 the SCCRC announced that it would fully review al-Megrahi's conviction to determine whether the case should be referred for a fresh appeal. After the SCCRC ruled in March 2020 that a miscarriage of justice might have occurred, in June lawyers representing the al-Megrahi family formally appealed his conviction of 2001 for the Lockerbie bombing. In January 2021 the Scottish Appeal Court in Edinburgh rejected an appeal by the al-Megrahi family, based on a possible misconduct of justice, and in April the same court refused permission for them to appeal the case to the UK Supreme Court. An attempt by al-Megrahi's relatives to have this ruling overturned was also rejected in July 2022.

Two years after Abu Agila Mohammad Masud was formally charged with involvement in the Lockerbie bombing, the US authorities announced in December 2022 that he was now in US custody. Prosecutors claimed that Masud had played a central role in the Lockerbie bombing, travelling to Malta and delivering the bomb that was used in the attack. The circumstances surrounding the capture of Masud were initially shrouded in mystery; however, the Dbeibah Government eventually admitted that it had played a role in the extradition of the former intelligence officer, sparking a backlash against the administration. In January 2023 the House of Representatives ordered the judiciary to assign a legal team to defend Masud.

Meanwhile, the speed with which the EU member states moved to condemn Qaddafi and offer support to the rebels reflected their deep ambivalence towards him prior to the outbreak of the civil war. The French Government, together with that of the UK, was instrumental in forging a military alliance against Qaddafi and both countries took a lead in the campaign. By September 2011 all 27 EU member states had officially recognized the NTC as the legitimate governing authority in Libya. By establishing an air exclusion zone over Libya, individual European states, through NATO, played a key role in the success of the revolution; however, the EU assumed a more limited role in post-Qaddafi Libya. The NATO intervention resurrected debates throughout the Arab world and Africa about the intentions of the Western powers in a region of considerable strategic importance. Consequently, the issue of the appropriate level and form of EU engagement dominated dialogue inside and outside Libya regarding the pace and objectives of political transformation. In response, the EU and individual European countries mostly limited their assistance to training and equipment to enhance security, together with information, training and support for democratic governance.

Libyan officials attended a meeting of the Western Mediterranean Forum (5+5 Dialogue) in October 2012, comprising Algeria, Libya, Mauritania, Morocco and Tunisia on the southern side of the Mediterranean, and France, Italy, Malta, Portugal and Spain on the northern side. In its first meeting since the 'Arab Spring', the Forum agreed to establish a humanitarian task force to combat illegal migration across the Mediterranean. In December the European Commission approved a €25m. package to support education, health care, security and rule of law reforms in Libya. The EU announced in January 2013 that it was prepared to assist Libya in developing an integrated border management plan, and in May that it would deploy a 110-member monitoring team, comprising European border security experts and costing €30.3m. over two years. In November the EU granted Libya two financial support packages, totalling €15m., the first aimed at supporting small and medium-sized business development and the second intended to ensure that detainees in Libya were housed and treated according to international standards.

In July 2014 the EU agreed to fund a €2.4m. programme to address the needs of vulnerable and marginalized groups in Libya, including internally displaced persons. At a ministerial conference on stability and development held in Libya in September, the EU joined African and European partners in unanimously rejecting military intervention as a means to restore stability in Libya, and in October the EU issued an 11-point statement underlining the importance of dialogue but emphasizing that the House of Representatives was the only legitimate parliamentary assembly in Libya.

Areas of sustained EU interest in Libya included energy supply, illegal migration, investment and trade, and security. Europe remained the principal market for Libyan oil and natural gas, and EU member states were well placed to take advantage of commercial opportunities in Libya. The EU and certain of its member states also were well placed to assist Libya to secure its borders, suppress illegal trafficking and reduce terrorist-related concerns through training, advanced equipment and co-ordinated strategies with contiguous states. Immigration was an area of policy evolution as the GNA promised to be more co-operative in restraining illegal immigration than either the Qaddafi regime or the interim governments that succeeded it. In June 2018 the UN Security Council voted unanimously to authorize the EU maritime task force operating off the coast of Libya, known as Operation Sophia, to continue to enforce an arms embargo and to seize migrant-smuggling vessels. In April 2020 Operation Irini succeeded Operation Sophia as the EU's task force in the area. Whereas the main objective of Operation Sophia was to reduce the flow of illegal immigration to Europe, the main task of Operation Irini was to use aerial, satellite and maritime assets to enforce the UN arms embargo in the eastern Mediterranean. More recently, the EU supported efforts to create a peaceful, stable Libya, but it was not a major player in the political process that led to the formation of the GNU.

In early 2022 a confidential EU report leaked to the press called for the continuation of the EU programme to train and equip the Libyan coastguard and navy, despite ongoing criticism of their treatment of migrants. The report acknowledged the 'excessive use of force' by Libyan authorities, behaviour that had already led to at least three petitions to the ICC requesting that EU and Libyan officials be investigated for possible crimes against humanity. Shortly thereafter, an EU official reported that three new search and rescue vessels and two refurbished patrol boats would be delivered to Libya before the summer of 2022, when illicit sea crossings were expected to rise. As concerns over Libya's treatment of migrants increased, Germany announced at the end of March that it would no longer provide training to the Libyan coastguard.

Individual European states, many of which had long-standing interests in Libya, moved quickly to re-establish bilateral diplomatic, economic, military and other ties. In November 2012 the British Government announced that it would not seek compensation from the Libyan Government for the cost of its intervention in the Libyan civil war, estimated at €200m., and in early December a large British trade mission, led by Minister without Portfolio Kenneth Clarke, arrived in Tripoli. In June 2014 a contingent of 325 Libyan army cadets arrived in the UK for six months of military training; however, they were sent home in November before completing their training, after three of them were charged with sexual assault on a British citizen. In July the UK Government announced that it would support the efforts of British victims of Libyan-sponsored terrorism to obtain compensation, but it reversed the decision in March 2015 when it announced that the victims—principally of terrorist attacks perpetrated by the IRA using plastic explosives supplied by Libya—would not get government assistance in their legal case against Libyan authorities.

In May 2017 the British Secretary of State for Foreign and Commonwealth Affairs, Boris Johnson, made a one-day visit to Tripoli to discuss with the Presidency Council areas of potential co-operation, including education, energy, health care and infrastructure projects. Later that month a British citizen of Libyan descent, Salman Abedi, detonated a suicide bomb in the British city of Manchester, killing more than 20 people and injuring many others. In January 2020 the survivors of IRA terrorist attacks and bereaved relatives of those killed in them launched a fresh attempt to sue Libya for supplying the IRA with plastic explosives. In July 2021 the UK Government announced that it would not seek access to frozen Libyan funds to compensate victims of IRA attacks conducted decades earlier. The UK Government also indicated that it would not create a fund for victims of Qaddafi-sponsored terrorism, suggesting that it was up to the Libyan Government to pay any compensation owed. Following the formation of the GNU in March 2021, Johnson, who was now British Prime Minister, called Prime Minister Dbeibah to offer his support. At the end of 2021 the House of Representatives threatened to declare the British ambassador to Libya, Caroline Hurndall, *persona non grata*, after she used social media to express her support for the GNU and opposition to the creation of parallel governments and institutions in Libya. With the creation of the GNS in March 2022, the UK joined other Western powers in releasing a joint statement calling for peace and expressing support for UNSMIL's mediation efforts. The Royal Navy's amphibious landing ship HMS *Albion* paid a goodwill visit to Libya in September.

The German Government hosted a one-day summit in Berlin in January 2020 with the expressed aim of encouraging Libya to become a sovereign and peaceful state. Sixteen states and international organizations endorsed a 55-point declaration at the end of the meeting that committed them to redouble efforts to achieve a permanent ceasefire, to uphold the UN arms embargo, to end military backing for warring factions in Libya and to support UN-backed negotiations with financial, military and political tracks. The first Berlin Conference was the basis for the three-track process that led to a countrywide, permanent ceasefire agreement on 23 October 2020 and to a subsequent agreement in November 2020 to hold parliamentary and presidential elections on 24 December 2021. Berlin I was followed by Berlin II in June 2021. Core issues at the second Berlin Conference included the withdrawal from Libya of some 20,000 foreign fighters and mercenaries who were supposed to be gone within 90 days of the conclusion of the permanent ceasefire agreement and the composition of the December 2021 elections. Berlin II concluded with a 58-page communiqué and 'hopes' for the withdrawal of foreign forces, a critical step for consolidating peace in Libya, but with no mechanism for implementation. Germany reopened its embassy in Tripoli in September 2021, and despite its central role in international efforts to mediate a resolution of the Libyan conflict, it has since remained a more or less neutral actor. As the largest country in Europe, Germany's interests are closely tied to those of the EU, which centre on stemming the flow of migrants coming from Libya. Therefore, it was significant when Germany announced at the end of March 2022 that it would no longer provide training for the Libyan coastguard due to concerns about its treatment of migrants.

At the end of May 2014, when al-Thani and Maitig were competing for the premiership, Russia affirmed its support for the al-Thani Government. During a visit to Moscow in April 2015 al-Thani accused Western governments of supporting the Muslim Brotherhood and called on Russia and China to support Libyan appeals to lift the arms embargo. In mid-June 2016 Russia announced that it would veto any UN Security Council resolution approving another NATO intervention in Libya, and at the end of the month Haftar visited Moscow to discuss military co-operation, including arms deliveries. Although Russia continued its public support for Haftar, it appeared to recognize the limited capabilities of his LNA. Therefore, the Russian Government also continued its support for the GNA, hosting an official delegation led by Prime Minister al-Sarraj in March 2017. In November 2018 Prime Minister Dmitrii Medvedev reiterated Russia's longstanding position that the US-led NATO alliance had deceived the international community before its intervention in Libya in 2011, and in December 2018 the Russian Government expressed support for a future political role for Seif al-Islam Qaddafi after he had expressed interest in running for the presidency.

Russia has remained flexible in its approach to ending the Libya conflict as part of a wider strategy of increasing its presence and influence across the Middle East and Africa. Russian foreign affairs ministry officials remained cordial towards Haftar, who visited Moscow in November 2018 and again in April 2019, and in that month Russia pledged to veto a draft UN Security Council resolution that called on Haftar to halt his advance on Tripoli and participate in a ceasefire. At the same time, Russia was careful not to commit itself to Haftar to the exclusion of other Libyan actors. Instead, Russian officials continued to meet Libyans representing a range of groups and interests to ensure that whichever party eventually ended up in control of the country would support Russia's policy objectives in the region. At the end of 2019 Russian mercenaries linked to the Russian Government emerged on the front lines of the battle for Tripoli, temporarily shifting the conflict in favour of Haftar's forces. Concurrent with Russia's deployment of mercenaries, President Putin hosted abortive peace talks between the GNA and Haftar in mid-January 2020 and supported the Berlin peace conference later that month. In addition to fresh troops on the ground, Russian military assets, including anti-tank guided missiles, electronic warfare, reconnaissance drones and precision-guided artillery, contributed to rapid LNA gains in early 2020. None the less, Turkish-backed GNA forces had put Haftar on the defensive again by the middle of the year, repelling him from Tripoli. Even as Russia continued to support Haftar with military hardware, at the same time it continued to call for a political solution to the conflict—one that Russia hoped would deliver geopolitical returns. At the same time Russia ignored the stipulation in the permanent ceasefire agreement calling for all foreign fighters, including the Wagner Group of private military contractors, to depart Libya within 90 days.

Russia later embraced the GNU and supported Libyan plans for national elections in December 2021; however, after the elections were postponed, it played something of an obstructionist role. Russia opposed the appointment of Stephanie Turco Williams as a UN special adviser to Libya, calling instead for the appointment of a special envoy, a position over which Russia enjoyed veto power. It also rejected an extension of UNSMIL's mandate to September 2022, eventually accepting shorter-term extensions. When the House of Representatives approved the creation of the GNS on 1 March 2022, Russia applauded the move, arguing that it was an important step forward in resolving the political crisis in Libya. Following Russia's invasion of Ukraine in February 2022, there were reports that some of the Russian mercenaries in Libya were redeployed to Ukraine; however, the majority were believed to remain in Libya to help maintain Russia's political influence there. Increasingly focused on the protracted conflict in Ukraine, Russia relied on the Wagner Group to support its goals in Libya and elsewhere in Africa. In addition to securing legitimate contracts for the provision of security services to oil and gas companies operating in central and southern Libya, the Wagner Group used Libya as a forward base for its activities in the Sahel, notably in Chad, Mali and Niger, as well as in Sudan. In response to charges by France, other European countries and the USA that the Wagner Group was committing 'humanitarian crimes' in Mali and elsewhere in Africa, in April 2023 Russia's Permanent Representative to the UN claimed that the instability in the Sahel was the product of the 'reckless Western adventure in Libya'.

France was increasingly concerned about terrorist activities in the Sahara and Sahel, and in August 2014 President François Hollande appealed to the UN to organize 'exceptional' support for Libya for fear that a failure to do so could lead to terrorism spreading across the region. Throughout the first half of 2015 French foreign affairs ministry officials continued to express concern about the state of lawlessness in Libya, but stopped short of openly supporting the military intervention for which regional powers in the Sahel region were appealing, including Niger and Mali. In November 2015 the French Government acknowledged for the first time that it was conducting aerial reconnaissance and intelligence missions over Libya, including areas controlled by Islamic State. By early 2016 French special forces were active on the ground, assisting Libyan troops in their fight against the Islamist organization; however, the French Government continued to rule out air strikes, fearing that direct military intervention could worsen the political situation. Although President Hollande supported the GNA, even as French forces worked closely with Operation Dignity to eliminate militant Islamist forces in Cyrenaica, the newly elected Government of President Emmanuel Macron signalled a shift in French policy when in May 2017 it called for the inclusion of Field Marshal Haftar in a unified national Libyan army. In July French efforts to broker a peace deal in Libya appeared to make some progress: at a meeting in Paris, Prime Minister al-Sarraj and Haftar signed an agreement to begin a conditional ceasefire and to enable elections to take place in 2018. However, no other groups were involved in the talks.

In the first half of 2018 the Macron Government dealt with two corruption cases involving Libya. In March former President Sarkozy was taken into police custody for questioning over allegations that he received millions of euros in illegal campaign contributions from the Qaddafi regime. In June 2020 the appeal court in Paris announced that it would rule in September on a legal challenge by Sarkozy and former aides against an investigation into the claims that Libyan money was used in Sarkozy's presidential election campaign in 2007. In June 2018 Société Générale SA agreed to pay US $860m. in criminal penalties for bribing Qaddafi-era officials and manipulating the London Interbank Offered Rate (LIBOR—an interest rate based on the average interest rates at which a large number of international banks in London lend money to one another). In the interim, France hosted a summit in Paris at the end of May which brought together the leaders of the four principal competing groups in Libya, together with representatives from 20 other countries and the UN. The Paris meeting concluded by fixing the dates for establishing the constitutional basis and commitments needed for the passage of the requisite electoral laws by 6 September in order to hold parliamentary and presidential elections by 10 December 2018. Ultimately, December came and went without elections, and by March 2019 France was commending the LNA for its success in occupying southern Libya.

While France tried to position itself as a mediator in the Libyan civil war, the preservation of French economic interests in Libya and the strengthening of France's political influence in North Africa and the Sahel appeared to depend largely on the elimination of extremist groups, and Haftar appeared best placed to support that goal. In early 2020 a dispute arose between President Macron and Turkish President Recep Tayyip Erdoğan, in which the French president accused his Turkish counterpart of hostile acts to stop the enforcement of the Libyan arms embargo, declaring Turkey to be an 'obstacle' to securing a ceasefire in Libya. At the same time the French Government joined other Mediterranean states in rejecting a maritime boundary accord that had been concluded by Libya and Turkey in late 2019. In March 2021 France reopened its embassy in Tripoli after a seven-year closure in a demonstration of support for the GNU. Meanwhile, it continued to press Turkey to remove its forces from Libya. Following the formation of the GNS in March 2022, France joined Germany, Italy, the UK and the USA in calling for the parallel GNU and GNS governments to avoid violence. In a joint statement, the Western powers also expressed their support for the mediation efforts of UNSMIL and the Special Adviser to the Secretary-General on Libya, Stephanie Turco Williams. When fighting broke out in Tripoli in May, the Macron Government issued a statement calling for all sides to refrain from violence and to find a peaceful solution to their differences. Anti-French sentiment subsequently increased in North Africa and the Sahel over the following 12 months, largely owing to misguided and ill-fated military interventions by France.

Given its long association with Libya, Italy continued to be a major source of cultural, economic and military assistance. In February 2013 the Italian Government presented Libya with 20 armoured vehicles, and later in the year an Italian consortium announced that it was ready to begin construction work on the first section of a new coastal highway between Tunisia and Egypt. In April 2014 the initial contingent of some 2,000 Libyan soldiers began basic training in Italy, and Libya requested Italian assistance in creating a satellite surveillance system to assist in securing its borders. Even as Italy, Libya and the EU continued joint efforts to manage the surge of refugees crossing the Mediterranean Sea, Europe's worst immigration crisis since the Second World War entered its third year with little sign of any slowing in the flow of people coming from North Africa to Italy. In December 2015 Italian Prime Minister Matteo Renzi declared Libya to be the 'keystone' of Italy's Mediterranean policy and pledged Italy's full support for the GNA. At the same time, Italy joined other EU states in continuing to reject Western military intervention in Libya. In 2017 less than half as many migrants reached Europe by sea in comparison with 2016, following the introduction of curbs that reduced traffic of vessels carrying migrants from

Libya to Italy. However, illicit migration remained the central issue in bilateral affairs between Libya and Italy.

In April 2018 Libya and Italy agreed to increase co-operation on training and for combating illegal migration, and in June Italy's new populist Government refused for the first time to allow a rescue boat with more than 600 immigrants to dock. In conjunction with its crackdown on immigration Italy also called for the establishment of immigrant reception centres on the southern borders of Libya. Meanwhile, the EU agreed to explore a plan for 'regional disembarkation platforms' to be established around the Mediterranean where immigrants could be held outside the EU until it was decided whether to admit them. Libyan officials immediately opposed the idea of immigrant reception centres or regional disembarkation platforms on Libyan soil. Meanwhile, Libya and Italy agreed to reactivate the Friendship, Partnership and Co-operation Treaty signed in 2008, and Italy called for an end to the international arms embargo on Libya, arguing that weapons dealers and migrant traffickers were ignoring it in any case. In November 2018 the Italian Government hosted an international conference in Palermo, Sicily, to advance the UN-sponsored stabilization process in Libya; unfortunately, the conference made only limited progress towards stabilization. Although this was the first occasion on which Italy had formally legitimized Haftar of the LNA as a party in peace negotiations since the formation of the GNA in 2016, Italy failed in its attempt to use the conference to reassert its role as the leading EU player in terms of the bloc's relations with Libya. Consequently, the divergent strategies pursued by France and Italy were increasingly at odds. Where France viewed support for Haftar as a counterweight to the threat from Islamist terrorism while advancing French prestige on the world stage, Italy argued that the French approach was flawed and misguided, as it relied on the unrealistic notion that a military victory would bring peace to Libya.

Thereafter, Italy adopted a policy of 'equidistance' from the GNA and the LNA that did little to help it achieve its strategic objectives in Libya, which ranged from managing migrant flows to accessing energy markets. In April 2021 Prime Minister Mario Draghi visited Libya, his first trip abroad since taking office, where he met with Prime Minister Dbeibah. Draghi said his brief visit was an opportunity to 'rebuild an ancient friendship' and to start 'a new future', adding that the 2020 ceasefire must be observed. Later in the month Minister of Foreign Affairs and International Co-operation Najla el-Mangoush announced that Libya had agreed with Italy to reopen airspace between the two countries and for Italy to open a consulate in Benghazi and an honorary one in Sabha. In early May Libya and Italy reactivated their Joint Economic Committee in conjunction with beginning a review of Italian investments past, present and future in Libya. In the second half of 2021 Italy joined other Western powers in pushing for the national elections scheduled for 24 December 2021 but later postponed. When the House of Representatives approved the creation of the GNS in March 2022, Italy joined interested European powers and the USA in supporting mediation efforts by UNSMIL.

In early December 2022 newly elected Italian Prime Minister Giorgia Meloni presented a long-term strategy for closer co-operation between Europe and Africa—the so-called the Mattei Plan, which was named after Enrico Mattei, the founding chairman of Italian energy company Eni. Russia's war against Ukraine accelerated Italy's shift towards African hydrocarbons suppliers, and during a visit to Tripoli by Meloni in January 2023 Eni and the NOC signed a US $8,000m. agreement providing for the development of Libya's offshore natural gas deposits, the largest single investment in Libya's energy sector for more than two decades. The 40-year agreement provided for the development of two gasfields, production at which was scheduled to commence in 2026, and ultimately reaching 750m. cu ft of gas daily. The gas was to supply the domestic Libyan market as well as ensuring export supply to Europe. In May 2023 Meloni met with Haftar in Rome to discuss initiatives to stabilize Libya and North Africa. During a series of meetings with various Libyan officials, the Meloni Government reiterated its support for UN efforts to facilitate the staging of parliamentary and presidential elections by the end of 2023. The arrival in Italy by sea of an increasing number of migrants and refugees from North Africa, and from Libya in particular, was also discussed, but no official statement on the matter was subsequently released. An important factor in Meloni's election as Prime Minister had been the strength of her pledge to solve Italy's migration problems, and her inability effectively to tackle the issue in the initial months of her administration provoked both domestic and foreign criticism.

THE USA RESTORES FULL DIPLOMATIC RELATIONS

In May 2006 the US Secretary of State, Condoleezza Rice, announced that the USA would re-establish full diplomatic relations with Libya, including the opening of an embassy in Tripoli, and in the following month Libya was removed from the US list of states deemed to support terrorism and from the list of states that refused to co-operate with US anti-terrorism activities. Despite Rice's announcement, diplomatic ties were not forthcoming, owing to a continuing impasse over the final Lockerbie compensation payment. The first two instalments had been paid in 2003 and 2004, but Libya withdrew the remaining US $536m. from the holding account in February 2005, arguing that the time limit on the deal had expired. Even though the USA removed Libya from its terrorism list in June 2006, the Qaddafi Government continued in its refusal to pay the outstanding balance, prompting the US Congress in June 2007 to block the release of funds requested by the Bush Administration to develop ties with Libya. Further to blocking the funds, Congress also refused to confirm the nomination of Gene Cretz as US ambassador to Libya.

In January 2008 President Bush signed into law a bill permitting the victims of state-sponsored terrorism to sue the foreign governments believed to be responsible and to have their assets in the USA seized. Although Bush sought to have Libya exempted from the law, Congress refused to ratify the presidential waiver. Ali Aujali, the Libyan ambassador to the USA, subsequently claimed that ties were becoming 'increasingly strained'. A meeting between representatives of the two countries held in London in May, culminated in an announcement in August that Libyan and US officials had signed a deal agreeing to provide full compensation to all victims of bombings involving the two countries—although, notably, the agreement precluded any admission of fault by either state. Then, in a significant step, Rice visited Libya in September, the first US Secretary of State to do so since 1953. Following Libya's deposit in October 2008 of the final instalment of the Lockerbie compensation payments, in November Congress finally gave its approval for Cretz, the US ambassador-designate, to take up his post in Tripoli.

Following the online publication of secret US Department of State correspondence by the WikiLeaks organization, in January 2011 Cretz was recalled after complaints by the Libyan Government. WikiLeaks exposed numerous cables written by Cretz to his superiors in Washington, DC, providing details about Qaddafi's private life. Following the outbreak of civil war, the Administration of US President Barack Obama roundly condemned the Libyan leader. In mid-July the USA accepted the NTC as Libya's 'legitimate governing authority', and in September Cretz returned to his post upon the reopening of the US embassy in Tripoli.

Following the overthrow of Qaddafi, the US Administration actively supported the political process that led to the GNC elections in July 2012, the constitutional committee polls in February 2014 and the elections to the House of Representatives in June. Working through NGOs and the UN, the USA joined the EU in providing extensive support, training and materials prior to all three elections, focusing on creating a functioning legal system, developing an independent media and promoting women's rights. The USA also facilitated the return of Libyan assets seized abroad. In concert with EU efforts to establish border security, curtail arms trafficking and limit illegal migration, the USA also revisited several regional initiatives, such as AFRICOM and the Trans-Sahara Counterterrorism Partnership, which had been opposed by Qaddafi.

Bilateral relations were effectively put on hold following the death of US Ambassador J. Christopher Stevens and three other US citizens on 11 September 2012, during an attack on the US consulate in Benghazi. The fatalities caused a political controversy in the USA, with the opposition Republican Party seeking to gain political advantage from the incident while security concerns in Libya hampered a thorough investigation into the parties responsible for the attack. In November 2013 A. Elizabeth Jones, the acting US Assistant Secretary of State for Near Eastern Affairs, met with Prime Minister Zidan; both parties agreed that security and defence were Libya's main priorities. At the same time the USA adopted an ambiguous policy towards Haftar's attempts to rid eastern Libya of Islamist extremists. Trapped between support for the democratic process in Libya and a desire to see militant Islamist forces eliminated, US officials supported the resolution of political problems through established institutions on the one hand, while contending that combating militant groups like Ansar al-Sharia was essential to the creation of a free and democratic Libya on the other. In early October 2013 US special forces entered Libya and captured Nazih Abdul-Hamed Nabih al-Ruqai, known as Abu Anas al-Libi, a Libyan militant indicted in 2000 for his alleged role in the 1998 bombings of the US embassies in Kenya and Tanzania. In January 2015 US officials announced that al-Libi had died in captivity from complications arising from longstanding medical problems. In another raid inside Libya, US special forces in June 2014 seized Ahmed Abu Khattala, who was suspected of leading the September 2012 attack on the US consulate in Benghazi. In June 2018 he was sentenced to 22 years in prison for his role in the attack during which four Americans were killed.

Following consultations with the al-Thani Government, in mid-June 2015 the USA carried out an air strike in Libya against Mokhtar Belmokhtar, the mastermind of the seizure by extremist Islamist terrorists of an Algerian gas complex at In Amenas in January 2013. Belmokhtar was reported to have been killed. With Libyan officials continuing to deny the need for any form of international intervention to cope with security threats, including terrorism, photographs of US special forces operating in Libya were posted on Facebook in December 2015, and in the following months, US officials confirmed that special operations units were active in Libya on intelligence and training missions. In the second half of 2016 the USA conducted nearly 500 air strikes in support of Misurata-based militias seeking to oust Islamic State from the coastal city of Sirte, and in January 2017 the USA launched new air strikes against Islamic State units attempting to regroup south of Sirte. In June 2019 a federal jury in Washington, DC, found Mustafa al-Imam—a second suspect in the attack on the US consulate in Benghazi in September 2012—guilty of two terrorism charges relating to the incident. In January 2020 al-Imam was sentenced to more than 19 years in prison for his role in the attack in Benghazi.

The inauguration of US President Donald Trump in January 2017 led to a change in US policy in Libya. After AFRICOM released a 2017 statement describing instability in Libya as the 'most significant near-term threat' facing the USA in the region, in April President Trump stressed that the USA had no role in Libya beyond suppressing Islamic State. During the following year the USA continued to participate in multilateral discussions about Libya but generally avoided taking a leadership role. In February 2018 the USA signed bilateral agreements with Libya covering cultural property protection and in April it concluded a second agreement covering airport security and support for policing, prisons and justice sector development. Throughout this period, AFRICOM continued to launch 'precision air strikes' against Islamic State and AQIM targets in southern Libya. In April 2019 President Trump appeared to endorse Haftar during a telephone conversation with the militia leader, recognizing his 'significant role in fighting terrorism and securing Libya's oil resources'. The conversation appeared to signal a major shift in US foreign policy; however, the Trump Administration rapidly downplayed the significance of the conversation, reiterating US support for a diplomatic solution to Libya's problems. When Haftar's offensive to against the UN-backed Government in Tripoli stalled in mid-2020, the Trump Administration called on the former CIA asset to suspend his attack but not to withdraw or to surrender, as the US Department of State continued to see a useful political role for Haftar at the negotiating table.

In early 2021 the newly installed Administration of US President Joe Biden hit the reset button on Libya when it signalled a willingness to get more involved in the country in support of efforts to resolve the political crisis. In May Acting Assistant Secretary of State Joey Hood visited Libya, where he emphasized that the aim of the USA was 'a sovereign, stable, unified Libya with no foreign interference, and a state capable of combating terrorism'. The Biden Administration had supported the GNU upon its formation in March 2021, and when the House of Representatives appointed the rival GNS in March 2022, the White House joined other Western governments in continuing to support the ongoing efforts of UNSMIL to mediate a peaceful resolution to the political transition in progress. William Burns, who had been appointed as director of the CIA in 2021, and Barbara Leaf, the Assistant Secretary of State for Near Eastern Affairs, both met separately with Dbeibah and Haftar during visits to Libya in early 2023, in January and March, respectively. Transcripts of the meetings were not publicly released, but US officials were thought to have discussed three policy concerns: first, Russian influence in Libya via the Wagner Group; second, the need to secure the Libyan energy sector from significant disruptions; and third, the re-emergence of terrorist threats in southern and western Libya.

In April 2023 the Biden Administration submitted to the US Congress a 10-year strategic plan through which the USA was to prioritize engagements and partnerships with Libya (as well as separate plans for US relations with other priority countries) under the remit of the United States Strategy to Prevent Conflict and Promote Stability (SPCPS—also known as the Global Fragility Strategy), which had first been announced in 2020 and was intended to facilitate inclusive political processes, peacebuilding and the creation of the conditions necessary for long-term regional stability. (Libya had been included as one of the Administration's priority countries in a prologue added to the strategic plan in April 2022.) More a framework for a plan than a detailed plan itself, the SPCPS was criticized for being too vague and focusing on southern Libya instead of on Tripoli and Benghazi. Nevertheless, the SPCPS had some real strengths. First, it incorporated extensive civil society input. Second, it focused on a 'grass-roots' approach, emphasizing the importance of 'engagement with and support for subnational, local municipal, and civil society actors'. Third, it stressed the importance of inclusion, in order 'to increase the participation and representation of women, youth, and other groups traditionally marginalized and underrepresented in Libya's polity'. Finally, the SPCPS adopted a long view, recognizing that it could take 10 years (or more) to achieve a Libya that is 'governed by a democratically elected, unified, representative, and internationally recognized authority that is able to secure human rights, deliver public service, promote inclusive and sustainable economic growth, secure its border, and partner with the United States and international community on shared priorities'.

The USA's commitment to play a more direct role in Libya clearly increased in 2023. However, while other foreign embassies reopened or were in the process of reopening, US diplomats continued to operate from the US embassy in Tunisia with no date being announced for the reopening of the embassy in Tripoli. The USA will need to go beyond its current day-trip diplomacy, limited to hasty meetings in heavily guarded facilities in Tripoli or elsewhere in Libya, if it is to play a more meaningful role in resolving the protracted conflict in Libya.

WIDER RELATIONS WITH THE ARAB STATES

Egypt firmly opposed the UN sanctions imposed on Libya and made strenuous diplomatic efforts to mediate between Libya and the West over the Lockerbie affair. Qaddafi was seen as a bulwark against the spread of militant Islam in the region and offered the prospect of much needed economic opportunities for Egypt, especially the employment of surplus Egyptian manpower. For Libya, which had become increasingly isolated internationally through the efforts of the USA and the UK,

Egypt served as a valuable intermediary with the outside world. Consequently, the close relationship between the two countries survived the embarrassment resulting from Libya's condemnation of the Israel-PLO accord signed in September 1993 and the disappearance of Libyan opposition leader al-Kikhia in Cairo at the end of that year. In November 1994 Libya supported Egypt's application to join the UMA; however, fresh political differences emerged during 1995, largely owing to Libyan opposition to the normalization of relations between a growing number of Arab states and Israel. Qaddafi was critical of Egypt's role in promoting economic co-operation between Israel and its Arab neighbours, and Libya's expulsion of Egyptian workers during the second half of 1995 further soured relations.

Egypt had long been suspicious of Libya's close relations with Sudan, which supported Libyan opposition to the peace process and offered shelter to Islamist militants from Egypt. In April 1995 a Libyan delegation attended the Popular Arab and Islamic Conference in Khartoum, together with representatives of Islamist opposition groups from Algeria, Morocco and Tunisia. The meeting avoided any criticism of the Libyan Government's harsh repression of its Islamist opposition and appealed for the lifting of UN sanctions against Libya. In the second half of 1995 relations between Libya and Sudan deteriorated owing to Libya's expulsion of large numbers of Sudanese workers; none the less, Sudanese President al-Bashir attended the 26th anniversary of the Libyan revolution in September 1995 as an honoured guest.

Although Libya joined the UMA and Qaddafi assumed the presidency of the organization for a period of six months on 1 January 1991, the Libyan leader showed little interest in further integration with his country's western neighbours, preferring to look east to Egypt. Of the UMA leaders, only the Algerian President, Liamine Zéroual, attended the celebrations marking the 25th anniversary of the Libyan revolution held in Tripoli in September 1994. At the beginning of 1995 Libya announced that it would not, in future, take over the presidency of the UMA nor chair any of its institutions, although it continued to attend UMA meetings.

Relations with Tunisia, often strained and sometimes hostile, improved after the imposition of UN sanctions. Libya came to depend increasingly on transit facilities through Tunisia as the air embargo imposed by the UN tightened. Tunisia profited greatly from this transit traffic, and remittances from the 20,000 Tunisians working in Libya also represented a valuable source of foreign exchange. Despite Tunisia's strict implementation of UN sanctions and the large profits that it made out of its role as Libya's main transit route to Europe, relations remained cordial for most of 1995.

Despite misunderstandings with Algeria over Qaddafi's attitude towards the Front Islamique du Salut (FIS), a fundamentalist Islamist opposition movement, Algeria continued to support Libya in the UN and the Arab League. In April 1995 Qaddafi visited Algeria for talks with President Zéroual, which concluded with a joint statement reviewing bilateral and economic relations and urging the UN to end sanctions against Libya. In April 1996 the two countries signed a security agreement to co-operate in the struggle against the threat posed by militant Islamist groups, and shortly afterwards there was speculation that Libya had handed over some 500 Algerian members of the FIS who had taken refuge in Libya. In January 1997 relations were again strained when the FIS asked Libya to mediate in its conflict with the Algerian authorities, as Libya had ostensibly severed ties with the FIS in 1994 when Qaddafi had pledged to cease all support for the Islamist opposition in Algeria.

Morocco supported Libya in the UN by abstaining during the vote in the Security Council in November 1993 to impose tougher sanctions on Libya. After Libya criticized Morocco for its moves towards normalizing its relations with Israel, relations improved in 1995 when King Hassan, on a visit to Washington, DC, in March, urged the US Administration to re-examine its position on sanctions against Libya. During 1996 both countries appealed for a revival of the UMA.

In November 1995, after Mauritania had established diplomatic relations with Israel, Libya expelled some 10,000 Mauritanian workers, withdrew its ambassador to the country, severed economic links and threatened Mauritania's status as a member of the UMA and the Arab League. In March 1997, however, diplomatic relations between the two countries were restored, despite accusations by the Mauritanian authorities earlier in the year that Libya had maintained links with several opposition leaders, ostensibly for the purpose of destabilizing the Mauritanian leadership.

In October 2000 Qaddafi embarked on a tour of the Arab world, visiting Jordan, Syria and Saudi Arabia, during which he presented a strategic proposal for Arab unity with Africa, urging the Arab states to 'wake up from their long sleep and be part of the African space'. Qaddafi was due to end his tour by attending the Arab League summit in Cairo called in response to renewed violence between Israel and the Palestinians; however, after prematurely revealing the Egyptian draft of the final declaration of the summit, denouncing it as a betrayal and challenging Arab leaders 'to take steps that would satisfy the angry Arab masses', Qaddafi decided not to attend the summit. In March 2002 the Secretary-General of the Arab League, Amr Moussa, visited Tripoli after Qaddafi threatened to withdraw from the organization in protest against what he condemned as its ineptitude with regard to the Israeli-Palestinian conflict.

In March 2003 Libyan and Saudi Arabian officials exchanged angry threats at the Arab League summit in Sharm el-Sheikh, Egypt, after Crown Prince Abdullah, the de facto Saudi ruler, took exception to comments made by Qaddafi in a speech. Abdullah accused Qaddafi of lying and left the meeting. In response, Libya recalled its ambassador to Saudi Arabia, and Qaddafi again announced his determination to withdraw from the Arab League. At the end of March Kuwait expelled the Libyan chargé d'affaires and reduced the Libyan mission to three diplomats, after demonstrators attacked Kuwait's embassy in Tripoli.

Libya closed its embassy in Beirut, Lebanon, in September 2003, after the Speaker of the Lebanese Parliament, Nabih Berri, and Sheikh Hasan Nasrallah, the leader of the Lebanon-based Shi'a Islamist group, Hezbollah, demanded that Qaddafi provide information about Imam Mousa al-Sadr, the spiritual leader of Lebanon's Shi'a population, who had disappeared in Libya in 1978. Relations between Libya and Lebanon continued to deteriorate as Lebanon's Shi'a political leaders demanded that Qaddafi reveal al-Sadr's whereabouts. In 2013 the family of al-Sadr complained in the Lebanese media that the NTC was not doing enough to investigate al-Sadr's disappearance. In July 2014 the Libyan Government agreed to co-operate with Lebanon in clarifying al-Sadr's fate. In December 2015 Hannibal Qaddafi was abducted by a Shi'a militia in the Lebanese city of Baalbek and briefly detained by Lebanese security forces in connection with al-Sadr's disappearance. In June 2019 a civil court in Lebanon suspended legal proceedings against Hannibal, citing a lack of jurisdiction (as the case fell under the competence of a military court), but he remained in custody.

Qaddafi attended the opening session of the Arab League heads of state summit held in Tunis in May 2004, but left during the opening speeches. In a press conference Qaddafi stated that he was 'disgusted' by the summit's agenda, felt slighted that the League had ignored his repeated appeals for Israel and the Palestinian territories to be merged into a single, non-religious state, and again threatened to withdraw Libya from the organization. In June the US media reported allegations that in the second half of 2003 Qaddafi had ordered the assassination of Crown Prince Abdullah of Saudi Arabia, following their clash at the Arab League summit in March. In December 2004 Saudi Arabia recalled its ambassador to Libya and expelled the Libyan ambassador to Saudi Arabia, but in December 2005 Prime Minister Ghanem confirmed that normal relations had been re-established.

Qaddafi met President Zine al-Abidine Ben Ali of Tunisia and President Abdelaziz Bouteflika of Algeria on a visit to Tunis in November 2005 to examine ways to strengthen co-operation and solidarity between the Maghreb states. In June the UMA foreign affairs ministers met in Tripoli and declared their support for plans to reinvigorate the institution. This desire to relaunch the UMA was reiterated in April 2008, during celebrations in Tangier, Morocco, in honour of the 50th anniversary of the summit at which the idea of a union of Arab Maghreb states was first proposed. In spite of residual tension between Moroccan and Algerian officials, the event ended peacefully with renewed appeals for regional collaboration. In 2010 UMA officials decided to establish a Maghreb Customs Co-operation Council in Algiers and a training centre in Casablanca, the most notable and concrete steps toward regional reconciliation in many years. In December 2012 Libya and Mauritania concluded an agreement aimed at reinforcing bilateral commercial ties. In January 2013 Libya joined its UMA partners in creating an investment bank with capital of US $100m. to finance infrastructure projects in the region, and a few days later Libya, Algeria and Tunisia met in Ghadames, whereupon they agreed to enhance border security in an effort to reduce the flow of illegal drugs and arms and the regional impact of organized crime.

Prominent Libyan dissident al-Kikhia, who disappeared in Cairo in 1993, was finally laid to rest in December 2012 after his body was found in a Libyan intelligence services morgue. In March 2013 the Libyan embassy in Cairo temporarily suspended operations after Egyptian demonstrators burned a Libyan flag in front of the embassy to protest against the death in prison of an Egyptian citizen detained by Libyan authorities for allegedly spreading Christianity in Libya. On the following day Egyptian police arrested three former Qaddafi loyalists (Gen. Ahmad Qaddaf al-Dam, a cousin and special envoy of Qaddafi, former Libyan ambassador to Egypt Ali Maria, and Muhammad Ibrahim Mansour, the brother of a Libyan spokesperson, Moussa Ibrahim) who had been living openly in Egypt despite being wanted for trial in Libya. In April Libya and Egypt signed a military co-operation agreement pertaining to training, combating illegal immigration, illicit fishing operations and drug trafficking. In May Libya, Sudan and Egypt agreed to work together to develop their border triangle, to establish free trade zones and to link electricity and alternative energy networks.

In February 2013 Prime Minister Zidan visited Turkey to award diplomas to 817 Libyan police graduates who had successfully completed a 30-month training programme at a training centre in the Turkish capital, İstanbul. Two days later, in a deal conditioned on Turkish firms completing suspended projects in Libya, Zidan announced that Libya would pay Turkish contractors US $10,000m., about one-half of what they were owed, with the remainder to be paid in two instalments upon completion of projects suspended during the civil war. In May Turkish officials indicated that Turkey was ready to provide greater support in boosting border security, stepping up military training and rebuilding military institutions, and in April 2014 the first group of Libyan soldiers trained in Turkey returned to Libya. In September Libya recalled its ambassador to Turkey after Turkish President Erdoğan termed the establishment of the House of Representatives in Tobruk 'unacceptable'. His comments followed earlier reports that Turkey was supporting the Muslim Brotherhood and allied Islamist elements that had taken control of the GNC. In February 2015 Prime Minister al-Thani accused Turkey of arming the rump government in Tripoli and in December 2018 customs officials at the Libyan port of Al-Khams seized illicit arms shipments originating in Turkey.

Following Haftar's advance on Tripoli in April 2019, Turkey continued to provide weapons to the GNA, in violation of the UN arms embargo. In November Turkey announced that it had reached accords with the GNA covering the delineation of the Turkish–Libyan maritime boundary and had expanded security and military co-operation. The MOU on the maritime boundary, which determined the co-ordinates of the Turkish–Libyan continental shelf and exclusive economic zone, was immediately denounced by neighbouring states, notably Cyprus, Egypt, Greece and Israel. Greece and Turkey have long made competing claims to oil and gas deposits off the island of Cyprus. After the Turkish parliament approved the security accord, in December Turkey began deploying mercenaries in the form of Syrian rebel forces to Tripoli in support of the GNA. In January 2020 the foreign affairs ministers of Cyprus, Egypt, France and Greece issued a joint statement declaring 'null and void' the two accords signed between the GNA and Turkey in November 2019. The build-up of Turkish mercenary forces, when combined with the ongoing supply of sophisticated weapons including armed drones, enabled the GNA to seize the initiative in early 2020. A string of military victories by Turkish-backed forces in western Libya in May–June dealt a heavy blow to the aspirations of Haftar and the LNA.

Turkey supported the ceasefire announced in October 2020, but it refused to withdraw its forces from Libya, as called for in the agreement, on the grounds they were not foreign mercenaries but military trainers deployed under an accord for military co-operation with the GNA. Turkey supported the GRU when it was formed in March 2021, and when a high-level Libyan delegation visited Turkey in April, several MOUs were signed, covering projects in education, energy, media and reconstruction. In addition, Prime Minister Dbeibah and President Erdoğan reaffirmed their commitment to the controversial November 2019 MOU covering delimitation of the Libyan-Turkish maritime area. When the House of Representatives approved the rival GNS in March 2022, Turkey continued to support the GNU, joining other states in calling for the postponed national elections to be held. In June Türkiye (as Turkey was now officially called) extended its troop deployment in Libya for another 18 months, suggesting that Libya was still far from reaching a political solution to its decade-long crisis.

In early October 2022 a high-level Turkish delegation visited Tripoli, meeting with the leadership of the GNU and signing several MOUs related to security training, oil and natural gas, and the media. Like those concluded in November 2019 the new MOUs—notably the agreement related to the hydrocarbons industry, which gave Türkiye the right to prospect for oil and gas in Libya's territorial waters—were of dubious legality and were greeted with widespread domestic and international opposition. For one thing, the political roadmap produced by the LPDF specifically prohibited the interim GNU administration from signing such deals with other countries. The GNS, the House of Representatives and the High Council of State were among those to condemn the MOUs, while, outside Libya, Egypt, France and Greece, inter alia, also questioned whether the GNU had the legal right to conclude such agreements. In January 2023 a Libyan court suspended the hydrocarbons exploration deal concluded by the GNU and Türkiye in October 2022, highlighting the difficulty that Türkiye experienced in navigating the shifting dynamics among Libya's political elite and the vagaries of regional diplomacy.

With cross-border smuggling, arms trafficking and infiltration concerns for both Egypt and Libya, Prime Minister Zidan met his Egyptian counterpart in September 2013 to discuss a co-ordinated approach to improved security in the border region. In December Zidan also met his Jordanian counterpart, concluding a strategic agreement covering a wide range of fields, including military and security concerns. Following reports in August 2014 that the UAE, with the support of Egypt, had carried out air strikes against Islamist militants vying for control of Tripoli, Prime Minister al-Thani flew to Abu Dhabi to solicit financial and political support from the UAE. During his visit al-Thani denied reports of Egyptian and UAE involvement in bombing attacks but offered no suggestion of an alternative actor that could have been responsible.

In May 2014 Egyptian President al-Sisi described Libya as 'one of the security threats Egypt is facing, especially with regards to terrorism', and in October al-Thani visited Cairo where he met President al-Sisi and Egyptian Prime Minister Ibrahim Mehleb, concluding a military co-operation agreement. In February 2015, after Islamic State beheaded 21 Egyptian workers, all of whom were Coptic Christians, the Egyptian air force bombed Islamic State facilities around Darna and instructed Egyptian nationals living in Libya to return to Egypt; more than 45,000 Egyptians reportedly fled Libya over the next month. In April King Abdullah of Jordan pledged his country's support for Libyan efforts to confront terrorist organizations. Rejecting international intervention in Libya, Egypt in 2017–18 continued to affirm its support for the GNA, arguing that the international community needed to recognize Haftar and the LNA, and lift the arms embargo against Libya so that it could be more effective in fighting terrorism. In April 2019 President al-Sisi met Haftar less than two weeks after the latter began his advance on Tripoli. A statement issued by al-Sisi's office did not mention Haftar's offensive directly but 'confirmed Egypt's support for efforts to combat terrorism and extremist groups' in order to achieve security and stability in Libya. Over much of the next year Egypt affirmed support for the GNA but also provided political and military assistance to Haftar and the LNA. Concerned about security on its long western border with Libya, the Egyptian Government distrusted the GNA and viewed Turkey's involvement in Libya as a threat. In line with this thinking, Egypt worked with Cyprus, France, Greece and the UAE to counter Turkish moves in the eastern Mediterranean.

In early 2020 Egypt faced new Turkish assertiveness in Libya, as exemplified by Haftar's strategic retreat from the western part of the country in the face of a resurgent GNA. After announcing a 'red line' in June 2020 regarding western militia advances toward the Egyptian border, the Egyptian Government accepted the ceasefire proposed by the GNA in August and backed the permanent ceasefire announced on 23 October. In an ongoing recalibration of its Libyan strategy, Egypt supported efforts by UNSMIL to resume a national dialogue between the rival parties, recognized the GNU and reopened its embassy in Tripoli. It also signed several MOUs with Libya, covering key sectors such as communications, energy, infrastructure, investments and transport. Egypt refused to recognize the rival GNS when it was formed in March 2022, but continued to support efforts to broker a settlement that would bring both peace and stability to Libya and security to the Egypt–Libya border. In November President al-Sisi issued a presidential decree demarcating Egypt's maritime borders with Libya, which appeared to cut off thousands of square kilometres of Libya's maritime zone, in a direct challenge to the MOUs concluded between Libya and Türkiye. In a rare moment of agreement between opposing parties in Libya, both the GNU in the west and Haftar in the east condemned al-Sisi's decree. Greece, meanwhile, welcomed Egypt's decision to encroach on Libya's maritime borders.

Libya also worked with Sudan to secure their common border in conjunction with efforts to reduce arms trafficking and illegal migration. In late June 2014, after Sudan joined a long list of countries offering training for the Libyan armed forces, gunmen attacked the Sudanese embassy in Tripoli, and in September a Sudanese military aircraft was detained at Kufrah airport in south-eastern Libya after a consignment of weapons was found on board. Sudan claimed that the arms were intended for a joint Libyan-Sudanese border force; however, the al-Thani administration concluded that they were destined for Libya Dawn. In October Sudan recognized the House of Representatives as Libya's sole legitimate legislature, but it also emphasized that it was neutral regarding the conflict in Libya. Two weeks later, the Presidents of Egypt and Sudan agreed to foster stability in Libya and to support the al-Thani administration's fight against terrorism. In May 2016 Sudan proposed the creation of a joint force to monitor the border area between Libya and Sudan, and when UN envoy Kobler visited Khartoum in May 2017, Sudan reiterated its commitment to the territorial integrity of Libya. In March 2018 UNSMIL expressed its concern over the ongoing violence around Sabha in southern Libya, supporting an earlier GNA statement that foreign mercenaries from Chad and Sudan were active in the area. Reports from Sabha later confirmed that at least two Darfuri rebel groups, the Sudanese Liberation Army and the Justice and Equality Movement, maintained a presence in the south of Libya, allegedly in Haftar's employ. In February 2021 a UN report alleged the UAE had established direct contact with Sudanese fighting groups in Libya, bypassing Haftar's forces. At the time, observers viewed the UAE move as a sign that the UAE was adopting a more hands-on role in the conflict because of its growing mistrust of Haftar and his LNA. Subsequently, tentative evidence emerged suggesting that the UAE was reducing its role in the Libyan conflict.

In April 2023 fighting broke out between the Sudanese army, led by military leader Abdel Fattah al-Burhan Abdelrahman, and the paramilitary Rapid Support Forces (RSF), led by Lt-Gen. Mohamed Hamdan Dagalo, commonly known as Hemedti. The fighting did not have an immediate impact on political developments in Libya; however, it was expected to have ramifications in the coming months as the fallout from the fighting became clearer. Although the border between Libya and Sudan is relatively short, at less than 400 km, policing a harsh and arduous desert ideally suited for smugglers and human traffickers has long been a problem. Add to the mix the involvement of Sudanese mercenaries in Libya's internal wars, supporting Haftar's army in the east, and the situation becomes highly complex. Before the fighting broke out, media reports indicated that the LNA was preparing the RSF for battle, sharing intelligence, increasing arms and fuel deliveries, and possibly training RSF fighters. There were also reports that Haftar and Hemedti were collaborating in a range of highly profitable smuggling operations. Following the outbreak of fighting, media reports suggested that the LNA was facilitating the movement of supplies to Hemedti's forces in Sudan as well as allowing Wagner Group forces to use LNA-controlled airbases and other assets as staging posts for providing tactical support to the RSF. Highlighting the complexity of the situation, Egypt supported al-Burhan while the UAE aided Hemedti. A consolidation of Hemedti's position in Sudan would not only solidify lucrative smuggling networks controlled by the LNA, it would also strengthen Haftar's ability to call on the RSF, as well as the Wagner Group, to assist the LNA in expanding its control of eastern and central Libya. At the same time, a Hemedti victory could jeopardize the political support that Egypt has long afforded Haftar.

By mid-2014 tension among the Gulf states had spilled over into a proxy war in Libya, with Qatar and the UAE supporting competing militias. As a result of its policies in Libya and elsewhere (notably Syria, where Islamist militants had been engaged in a conflict with the regime of President Bashar al-Assad since 2011), Qatar in late 2014 found itself under attack from a most unlikely alignment of interests—including Egypt, Israel, Saudi Arabia and the UAE—all of which considered Qatar to be a major sponsor of militant Islamist organizations. Over the next two years Qatar appeared to reduce its official involvement in Libya; however, individual Qatar-based donors were suspected of continuing to support militant Islamist movements. At the same time, the UAE continued its support for Haftar and the LNA. In June 2017 the al-Thani Government joined Saudi Arabia, the UAE and other Arab states in suspending diplomatic relations with Qatar over its alleged support of militant Islamist groups. In 2017–18 Qatar and the UAE continued to be involved in negotiation efforts; however, regional mediations like these did little to further the legitimacy of the UN negotiation process. In an effort to maintain lines of communication, Minister of Foreign Affairs and International Co-operation el-Mangoush travelled to the Qatari capital, Doha, in May 2023, where she met with Prime Minister and Minister of Foreign Affairs Sheikh Mohammed bin Abdulrahman bin Jassim Al Thani. The two discussed closer bilateral co-operation, as well as the current political situation in Libya, especially preparations for parliamentary and presidential elections.

In early 2019 Saudi Arabia joined the UAE in supporting Haftar's offensive on Tripoli, and to counter Turkey's intervention on the side of the GNA, the Saudi Arabian Government increased its diplomatic and financial support to Haftar in the first half of 2020. At the same time, the UAE also increased its military and political footprint in Libya. Disappointed with the lack of US leadership in the region and especially afraid of the spread of political Islam, which puts it at odds with Qatar and Turkey in Libya, the Emirati Government took a more aggressive role in Libya, supplying large quantities of weaponry and conducting hundreds of drone and air strikes on behalf of Haftar and the LNA. That said, the UAE in March 2021 declared its support for the newly formed GNU, and by the end of the year it appeared to be scaling back its role in overseas conflicts, notably Libya. Going forward, UAE policy in Libya will likely be heavily influenced by its relationship with the USA. Policy differences over the war in Yemen, the US approach to Iran and US conditions on arms sales have strained that bilateral relationship. At the same time, the UAE and other Gulf states have tried to maintain a neutral stance between Russia and the West because of UAE state investments in Russian companies and its sovereign fund, as well as their partnership in the Organization of Petroleum Exporting Countries (OPEC).

In December 2013, following the discovery by Algerian troops of a large arms cache on the Libyan border, the Algerian Prime Minister, Abdelmalek Sellal, visited Libya to discuss enhanced security co-ordination with Libyan officials. In September 2014 Algeria joined Tunisia in rejecting the option of international intervention in Libya, advocating instead a diplomatic approach based on neighbouring states launching a national dialogue between the warring factions. During 2017 Algeria and Tunisia joined Egypt in tripartite talks aimed at mediating the political crisis in Libya. Diplomatic efforts by Algeria sought to balance Egyptian influence in Libya, as Algerian officials feared that a more forceful intervention by Egypt in Libya on the part of Haftar would exacerbate existing security challenges on the Algerian border with Libya. In December 2018 the Algerian Government criticized Turkey for shipping arms to Libya, describing them as a potential threat to Algerian security, and in June 2019 Algeria joined Egypt and Tunisia in calling for a ceasefire in Libya. Increasingly preoccupied with the deteriorating security situation in its eastern neighbour, in the first half of 2020 Algeria abandoned its strict military doctrine of non-intervention outside its borders. After declaring the siege of Tripoli 'a red line no one should cross' President Abdelmadjid Tebboune declared his Government ready to act as a mediator in any Libyan ceasefire talks. In doing so, Algeria hoped to recover a diplomatic role in the region both by condemning foreign interference in Libyan affairs and promoting a political solution to the Libyan crisis. Subsequently, statements by the Algerian Government revealed closer co-ordination with Qatar and Turkey, belying claims of neutrality over the years. In response, Haftar closed the southern border with Algeria in June 2021 in a move intended to demonstrate his political relevance following the creation of the GNU in March. In January 2022 Sonatrach, Algeria's state petroleum company, announced plans to resume oil operations in Libya. Later in the month the Algerian Government opened a consulate in Tripoli, ending an eight-year absence. In September Tebboune reiterated his support for the GNU, again rejecting the parallel administration of Bashagha. In May 2023 Minister of Foreign Affairs and International Co-operation el-Mangoush held a meeting with her Algerian counterpart in Algiers, during which Algeria pledged its full support for achieving consensus in Libya in order to move forward with the holding of parliamentary and presidential elections.

In June 2015 the Tunisian Government announced that the two Tunisian gunmen who killed 22 people at the Bardo National Museum in Tunis in March and the lone Tunisian gunman who killed 38 people at a tourist hotel in Sousse in June had all received training at a militant Islamist camp in Libya. In response, the six UMA member states expressed their concern at the ongoing political instability in Libya but continued to oppose international intervention. In February 2016 Tunisia announced the completion of 196-km barrier along its border with Libya the first stage in a complex system of border obstacles designed to keep Islamist militants from entering the country. One month later extremists attacked the Tunisian border town of Ben Gardane, killing dozens of people and leaving many more injured. Shortly afterwards, the Moroccan Government announced that it had dismantled a terrorist cell linked to Islamic State in Libya that was in the final stages of terrorist operations in Morocco. In April the UMA interior ministers announced that regional security co-ordination was their top priority, and in June Algerian Prime Minister Sellal called for the developed states to initiate development assistance programmes, arguing that military intervention alone would not solve Libya's problems.

Throughout this period, the Moroccan Government pursued a policy of active neutrality, which included stronger bilateral relations with Libya, an improved international image as a regional security provider, and a check on what Morocco viewed as Algeria's plans to become a regional hegemon. In January 2020 the Moroccan Minister of Foreign Affairs, African Co-operation and Moroccan Expatriates, Nasser Bourita, again reaffirmed his Government's opposition to foreign intervention in Libya, arguing that inter-Libyan dialogue was the optimum path to a peaceful political position. In March 2022 Bourita met with his Libyan counterpart, el-Mangoush, and announced his Government's 'full and unlimited support' for the return of CEN-SAD (see *Changing Relations with Africa*) to its official headquarters in Tripoli, a move welcomed by Libyan officials. Following a meeting with UN Special Representative for Libya and head of UNSMIL Bathily in January 2023, Bourita expressed his Government's firm support for the newly appointed UN envoy and stressed Morocco's willingness to work with Libya to achieve a lasting political settlement. At the meeting of the 6+6 Committee held in Morocco in May 2023, the committee members held discussions aimed at resolving differences ahead of the planned elections and to reach consensus on electoral legislation.

Meanwhile, Tunisia was primarily concerned with threats emanating from its shared border with Libya and the effect that those threats could have on its struggling economy and fragile political system. The Libyan conflict reduced remittances from Tunisians working in Libya, contributed to a sharp drop in tourism and led to an influx of Libyan refugees, all of which placed a strain on the Tunisian economy. The regional political scene was complicated by the policies of the Turkish–Muslim Brotherhood axis in Libya and the manoeuvres of Ennahdha, an Islamist party, in Tunisia. In response, the Tunisian Government attempted to remain 'equidistant' from the warring factions in Libya; however, that policy had its limits. Turkish use of Tunisian territory and air space to transfer aid to the GNA in western Libya during the siege of Tripoli, for example, exacerbated tensions between Tunisia and Turkey. In May 2021 the GNU granted Tunisia €1,000m. to help bolster its struggling economy and to aid in restoring economic and political ties. Libya and Tunisia are so interlinked that the success of the democratic process in Tunisia as well as its economic recovery are largely dependent on political developments in Libya. In November 2022 Libya and Tunisia signed several bilateral agreements, including on economic, trade and transport co-operation, during a visit to Tripoli by a high-level Tunisian ministerial delegation. During a visit to Tunisia two weeks later, President Dbeibah announced that Libya would pay its outstanding debt to Tunisia by the end of the year.

CHANGING RELATIONS WITH AFRICA

After some 30 years of promoting the virtues of Arab unity, Libya announced in October 1998 that it was downgrading its representation at the Arab League in Cairo, and in December the GPC abolished the Secretariat for Arab Unity. The official Libyan news agency emphasized that Libya belonged to the African continent, and from October the country's state-controlled radio station, 'Voice of the Greater Arab Homeland', changed its name to 'Voice of Africa'. Instead of his customary pan-Arab rhetoric, Qaddafi began to champion African self-determination, stating that he wished Libya to become a 'black' country and urging Libyans to marry black Africans. For years Libya had promoted closer relations with countries south of the Sahara, using financial assistance as an incentive, and in early 1998 it initiated the Community of Sahel-Saharan States (CEN-SAD), comprising Burkina Faso, Chad, Mali, Niger and Sudan, to promote economic, social and cultural exchanges.

Qaddafi attended the OAU summit in Algiers in July 1999, and in September, on the occasion of the 30th anniversary of his seizure of power, he hosted an extraordinary OAU summit in Sirte. Qaddafi presented his vision of a 'United States of Africa' and demanded that Africa be given veto power in the UN Security Council. The Sirte Declaration, which was adopted by the 43 attending heads of state and of government, appealed for the strengthening of the OAU, the establishment of a pan-African parliament, African monetary union and an African court of justice. Qaddafi's proposal for a United States of Africa was officially adopted at the OAU summit in Lomé, Togo, in July 2000; however, it required ratification by two-thirds of OAU members before implementation, and key states such as South Africa and Nigeria expressed their reservations, preferring a more cautious approach.

The Libyan leader's African ambitions suffered a reverse in September 2000, when Libyans attacked black African migrant workers, killing more than 50 and forcing thousands of others to leave the country. African-owned businesses were destroyed and Niger's embassy in Tripoli was looted. It remained unclear exactly what triggered the violence, which began in Zuwara, west of Tripoli, but it quickly spread to other parts of the country. Deep-rooted racism, fear that the migrants posed a threat to Libyan culture and were responsible for a range of social problems, such as crime, drugs and prostitution, and a widespread misperception that migrants competed with Libyans for low-paid jobs were among the factors apparently contributing to this hostility.

At the beginning of March 2001 some 40 African heads of state were invited by the Libyan leader to a second summit meeting at Sirte. In place of Qaddafi's ambitious project for a United States of Africa, more modest plans were approved to replace the OAU with a new AU, incorporating a range of pan-African institutions, including a parliament, a central bank and a court of justice, but without supranational executive powers. Sceptics questioned the viability of an African parliament, noting that many African states were embroiled in armed conflicts, and the democratic credentials of others were questionable. The proposal for equal representation was opposed by states such as Nigeria and Egypt, which were concerned that such an arrangement would diminish their regional influence, and questions were also raised about the funding of the proposed African central bank, given the combined debt of the sub-Saharan region.

In May 2001, following mediation by Qaddafi, Uganda and Sudan agreed to restore diplomatic relations severed in 1995. (Twelve years later the director of Sudan's National Intelligence and Security Services accused Qaddafi of being responsible for many of the internal and external crises that Sudan had confronted over the years, charging him with having incited partisanship and strife instead of peace and reconciliation.) At the end of May 2001 Libya sent some 100 troops to support President Ange-Félix Patassé of the Central African Republic (CAR) after an attempted coup, and in November it dispatched another 80 soldiers to the CAR when there was another coup attempt. In early 2002 the Libyan troops were reinforced by military personnel from Sudan and Djibouti as part of a CEN-SAD peacekeeping force. In October Libyan troops and military aircraft were engaged in fighting in the CAR capital, Bangui, against forces loyal to rebel leader Gen. François Bozizé. The threat was repulsed, but in March 2003, after the withdrawal of Libyan troops in December 2002, Patassé was overthrown and Gen. Bozizé seized power.

Qaddafi travelled to Durban, South Africa, in July 2002 for the final summit of the OAU, which saw the formal creation of the new AU. Although South African President Thabo Mbeki's speech focused on the need for democracy, good government, the eradication of corruption, respect for human rights and peace and stability, the Libyan leader addressed his comments to the West, declaring that those who wanted to assist Africa were welcome, but that those who insisted on imposing their conditions upon African states were not. He heralded the birth of the AU as his 'African dream'. During the summit Mbeki and numerous other African heads of state tried to persuade Qaddafi to abandon his hostility towards the New Partnership for Africa's Development (NEPAD), a contract between Africa and the international community under which, in exchange for aid and investment, the African states agreed to strive towards democracy and good governance. The Libyan leader criticized the programme for imposing a Western model of development on Africa and ignoring the continent's traditions and religions.

HRW criticized the appointment of Qaddafi to the steering group of NEPAD in August 2002, noting that although the new initiative was committed to promoting human rights and good governance, Libya had a long record of human rights abuses. In January 2003, after the USA had taken the unprecedented step of demanding a vote on Libya's nomination to the UN Commission on Human Rights (UNCHR), 33 of the 55 members of UNCHR voted in Libya's favour, 17 (including seven European countries) abstained and only three (including the USA) voted against Libya. Libya's election provoked growing demands for reform, and some UN officials voiced concern about UNCHR's credibility.

The fifth ordinary summit of the AU was held in Sirte in July 2005. In his opening remarks Qaddafi stated that in order to tackle the big challenges of economic development and to fight poverty, African states needed to unite and become one country. The summit ended with appeals for a substantial increase in aid from the West and the cancellation of Africa's entire debt, despite comments by the Libyan leader that they should not 'beg' for money from rich states. In February 2006 Qaddafi helped to broker a peace accord between Sudan and Chad after President Deby accused Sudan of supporting a rebel group that sought to overthrow him. On a visit to Mali in April 2006 Qaddafi appealed to the Tuareg tribes of the Sahel region to unite and form a 'Greater Sahara', a statement that caused disquiet among neighbouring countries, most notably Algeria and Niger.

In mid-2007 Qaddafi conducted a tour of West Africa, which included visits to Côte d'Ivoire, Guinea, Mali and Sierra Leone. The final leg of his tour was a visit in early July to the Ghanaian capital, Accra, for the ninth ordinary session of the AU, where Qaddafi continued to champion the idea of a pan-Africa government, declaring on the eve of the summit that Africa must 'unite or die'. However, other AU heads of state and prominent figures proved reluctant to allow the summit to afford primacy to the issue of continental unity, concerned that energy divested therein would result in the neglect of more pressing issues, such as the humanitarian crises in the Darfur region, Somalia and Zimbabwe. In the end, the attendant heads of state reached a largely non-committal agreement on the unity issue, pledging to establish a committee to consider the move towards a pan-African government, without establishing any time frame for this; Qaddafi was reported to have stormed out of the session when a majority of those present rejected his appeal for the immediate creation of a 'United States of Africa'.

In February 2009, at the annual AU summit meeting in Addis Ababa, Ethiopia, Qaddafi was elected Chairman of the organization. He used the occasion to hector African leaders on the failings of African democracy, insisting that, as Chairman, he would prioritize the creation of a 'United States of Africa'. Indeed, his plan overshadowed the meeting's entire agenda, and discussions eventually continued into an unscheduled third day. As it turned out, the majority of the heads of state were opposed to full political union and only minor changes to existing AU institutions were agreed. At the AU summit in January 2010, Qaddafi defied the grouping's stipulation that the chairmanship should rotate annually by seeking re-election as Chairman for a second consecutive year. Despite gaining the support of several smaller African states, whose membership fees Qaddafi had paid, 53 other African countries voted for Malawi to assume the chairmanship, thwarting the Libyan leader's ambitions.

The African response to the revolution that broke out in Libya in January 2011 reflected the diplomatic support that Qaddafi had generated in previous years, when many African states benefited considerably from Libyan aid and investment. In April, and again in July, the AU presented a peace plan to both sides, and South African President Jacob Zuma flew to Tripoli in order to persuade Qaddafi to accept it. Qaddafi did so, declaring that it was the only plan that he would countenance; however, the plan was rejected by both the rebels and the international coalition, as it would have allowed Qaddafi to remain in power during a transitional period. The AU did not formally recognize the NTC as the official representative authority of the Libyan people until 20 September—several weeks after most European states, the USA and several prominent African states, including Ethiopia, Côte d'Ivoire, Nigeria and Senegal, had granted recognition.

The future role that post-Qaddafi Libya could play in Africa remains unclear, in part because events in the Sahara and Sahel regions have left little time for Libyan politicians to consider a wider policy for sub-Saharan Africa. However, the disruption of regional alliances and the weakening of governments previously supported by Qaddafi set the stage for a policy reorientation away from the African continent upon which Qaddafi lavished financial aid in an effort to secure influence. As early as February 2013 Prime Minister Zidan, at the opening of the CEN-SAD summit, captured the ongoing reorientation of Libyan policy towards Africa when he declared that 'Libya intends to be actively involved in African affairs, but not in the interfering way of the Qaddafi regime'. In August 2013 Libya hosted a two-day workshop on border security co-operation, which was attended by delegates from 11 neighbouring states, as well as interested regional and international bodies. Following the meeting, the Libyan Government launched several initiatives with neighbouring states to increase stability and improve security in its borderlands.

As Libya descended into civil war, African leaders at the end of 2014 called for Western intervention to check the flow of arms from Libya to militant groups in the Sahel region. Reflecting similar concerns, the AU's International Contact Group for Libya in early 2015 stated that Libya had become a safe haven for local and international Islamist extremists. At a two-day summit in Addis Ababa in January 2016, the AU again expressed concern that Islamic State was gaining ground in Libya, but warned against military intervention, appointing a task force to seek a political solution to the crisis to include the formation of the GNA. In January 2018 Prime Minister al-Sarraj indicated that the GNA was keen to resume normal ties with 'African countries'. In June 2019 the AU and CEN-SAD both called for a ceasefire in Libya, warning of the consequences of prolonged conflict. In the first half of 2020 the AU continued its efforts sporadically to broker peace talks in Libya; however, the bloc's limited initiatives were overshadowed by simultaneous diplomatic efforts in Berlin, İstanbul and Moscow. Representatives of the AU attended both the Berlin I and Berlin II conferences on Libya, and the AU immediately recognized the GRU when it was created in March 2021. At the AU Extraordinary Summit in Malabo, Equatorial Guinea, in May 2022, AU officials once again called for a peaceful resolution to the Libyan crisis, noting that it had resulted in an increase in terrorist groups and foreign mercenaries active in Africa. In June Libyan Minister of Foreign Affairs and International Co-operation el-Mangoush, in something of an overstatement, hailed the 'massive role' that the AU had played in supporting national reconciliation efforts in Libya, assuring the AU that the GNU was working to hold elections and achieve peace and security.

After lobbying for years for the UN to appoint an African diplomat to head its mission in Libya, the AU welcomed the appointment in September 2022 of Senegal's Bathily as the UN's Special Representative for Libya and head of UNSMIL. His appointment immediately raised expectations in Africa of the AU assuming a more significant role in resolving the Libyan conflict and related issues in the Sahel. As a first step, AU officials announced in February 2023 that they were organizing a national reconciliation conference for Libya. However, at mid-2023 it remained to be seen whether or not the AU had the requisite will and capacity to contribute in a meaningful fashion to a lasting settlement in Libya.

Economy

AMIR MAGDY KAMEL

INTRODUCTION

Libya's strategic location and abundance of resources provide the fundamentals for economic prosperity. With a population of 6.9m. at mid-2023, according to United Nations (UN) estimates, and gross domestic product (GDP) per head of US $6,716 in 2022 at current prices (one of the highest in Africa), Libya's economic status is underpinned by rentier petroleum and natural gas revenues, representing a combined 61% of GDP and 94% of trade exports in 2022. This is made possible by Libya's consistently high global ranking in terms of proven reserves of oil (in the top 10) and natural gas (top 25). The value of these resources is recognized in the country, where the control and management of hydrocarbons facilities have been contested by political actors and have been the source of national disagreements and outside interest. Notably, Libya's natural gas is transferred through the 545-km (340-mile) Greenstream pipeline, which runs across the Mediterranean Sea and into Europe via Sicily, Italy, tethering European interests to Libyan natural gas. In the political realm, Libya's geographical location has seen it play host to several actors and forces that include, on the one hand, regional and global security threats, migratory pressures and refugee concerns; on the other hand, it is an integral country with which co-ordination is necessary to tackle regional and global concerns. In addition, Libya hosts five UN Educational, Scientific and Cultural Organization World Heritage sites, including Roman, Ancient Greek and North African tribal ruins, alongside natural deserts, lakes and coastal attractions.

While Libya's economic indicators provide a strong foundation for growth, the political environment continues to thwart the achievement of prosperity targets. This has resulted from the contextual make-up of Libya; the policies and practices of former and current competing regimes; attempts by external actors to maintain strategic and local influence; the 2011 uprising and removal of Muammar al-Qaddafi as the long-serving 'Brotherly Leader and Guide of the Revolution' and the subsequent civil conflict. These factors combine to exacerbate tensions between various internal and external actors in Libya—to the detriment of the goal of establishing a fully functioning and stable economy. It is of note that fluctuations—often extreme in nature—in the country's GDP, inflation, current account balance, and levels of public and private investment have occurred amid political upheaval over the past half-century. Furthermore, Libya is currently experiencing a political impasse that has, at times, descended into violence. As of mid-2023 the executive and legislative elections had been indefinitely postponed, having initially been scheduled for December 2021 (presidential) and January 2022 (parliamentary), despite elections having already taken place after the fall of Qaddafi. This political uncertainty has a negative impact on the economic conditions for Libyans, with overall unemployment in 2022 standing at 19.6% of the working-age population, according to the World Bank, and with unemployment rates of 52% for those under the age of 25 years and 70% for female youths (see *Demographics*). All these factors have resulted in a volatile economic performance and investment pattern, demonstrating how the health and outlook of the economy are inextricably linked to contextual forces that drive or undermine economic performance. While the spike in global oil prices following the emergence of the coronavirus disease (COVID-19) pandemic in early 2020 had a positive impact on growth and public accounts, the subsequent inflationary pressures and decrease in oil prices had a negative effect. Importantly, the level of oil revenue is dependent on the security of production facilities, which have been subject to political disputes and weigh heavily on Libya's future prospects.

This context is linked to the country's location on the southern coast of the Mediterranean Sea. Nomadic tribes travelled through and settled in Libya, as well as the neighbouring regions, for several thousand years. Combined with the country's position in the far north of the African continent, this led to Libya becoming host to several interests, actors and conflicts. Each of these are complicated by regional differences within the country's modern-day borders, and can be divided into three internal regions: Tripolitania in the north-west, Fezzan in the south-west and Cyrenaica in the east.

More broadly, following the Ottoman Empire's initial control over Libya in 1551, the Ottomans took the country's tribal complexities seriously enough to leave domestic actors to preside over their own governance practices, on condition that they remained part of the Ottoman Empire. Following the 1911–12 Italo–Turkish War, control over Tripolitania and Cyrenaica shifted to Italy and eventually the anti-German Allies in the Second World War from 1943. It was during this period and up to the eventual independence of Libya in 1951 that the Italians and Allies attempted to forge a united Libyan state containing all three regions. This unification initiative was met with hostility against the occupying forces and infighting among tribes and culminated in the UN-forged independence mandate that recognized the kingdom of Libya in 1951. The King, Muhammad Idris, head of the Cyrenaican Senussi order, was reluctant to co-operate with the rival Tripolitanian and Fezzani tribes, having fought against them previously (as well as the Italians and the Allies). King Senussi's disinclination manifested itself in the form of favourable tax policies for his allies and eventually foreign energy firms, after the discovery of hydrocarbons in Libya in 1959. Popular resentment towards the monarch's abuse of power and the preferential treatment afforded to tribal and economic actors prompted a *coup d'état* in 1969 led by Qaddafi and the Free Officers Movement, in which the King was overthrown.

During Qaddafi's rule as Libyan leader from 1969 to 2011, he pursued a new system of governance that funnelled public interests and conflicts through a tiered structure of committees and congresses. This system—termed the 'Third Universal Theory' in the *Green Book*, which Qaddafi authored in 1975—provided a forum for Libyans to present any governance disputes or discrepancies direct to their local congress in the first instance, which could then be escalated to the next tier. The logic and structure therefore catered for a new 'direct democracy' system that resolved domestic issues through this bottom-up approach; meanwhile, independent media organizations, political parties and opposition movements were banned. Qaddafi's new system governed all aspects of Libya's society, with the exception of the energy and defence sectors, which remained under Qaddafi's control as the 'Brotherly Leader and Guide of the Revolution'. Under Qaddafi, Libya experienced an influx of private investment (particularly in the hydrocarbons sector), an increased reliance on energy revenue, links to and support for causes across the Arabic-speaking world (including terrorist groups), the pursuit of a weapons of mass destruction (WMD) programme and the subsequent imposition of sanctions by the international community until their dismantlement in 2003, as well as attempts to introduce economic reforms in the 21st century.

Despite these intentions and the unique system of governance, Qaddafi's tenure replicated the same preferential practices of his predecessor—this time in favour of his own tribe and allies. This ultimately precipitated the 2011 revolution that brought Qaddafi's rule to an end. Since then, the country has experienced ongoing conflict between rival tribes and groups, some of whom have had the support of foreign states and actors. Furthermore, some Libyan actors have used the control of hydrocarbons production and trading facilities to force political concessions from transitional and competing local governments. By October 2020 the two rival governing bodies that had fiercely vied for control in Libya agreed on a ceasefire. From that point the interim Government of National Accord (GNA) in Tripoli, Tripolitania, and the House of Representatives (HoR) in Tobruk, Cyrenaica (along with the support of the Libyan National Army—LNA—commanded by Gen. Khalifa Haftar) agreed to oversee the period of transition. This was made possible after almost five years of disagreements following the signing of the 2015 Libyan Political Agreement (LPA) which attracted varying degrees of support from different factions within the rival camps. This transition forged the Government of National Unity (GNU) in March 2021 which superseded the GNA and sought to oversee elections by the end of the year. By September, however, the HoR had passed a no-confidence motion against the GNU, pushing back the elections from December 2021 to June 2022, and thereafter indefinitely. In May 2023 the 6+6 committee—comprising representatives from the rival governments in Tobruk and Tripoli—held a meeting in Morocco in an attempt to agree on a schedule for fresh elections. The ensuing discussions, however, highlighted the fact that both sides remained far apart on key issues. These divisions illustrate the differences among Libyan actors, as well as how external actors have sought to influence domestic affairs. The multiple fragile ceasefires exposed the difficulties encountered in dealing with recent concerns surrounding migration pressures (particularly those exerted by European-bound refugees from Sub-Saharan Africa) and the disunited response to the COVID-19 pandemic from early 2020 and the economic pressures that subsequently arose as a result of the health crisis. Throughout a largely unstable preceding decade, Libya's economy has failed to reach its full potential in terms of delivering growth and prosperity, while demonstrating how the country's contextual make-up plays a pivotal role in its economic affairs.

ECONOMIC CONTEXT AND CONFLICT

Libya's competing political actors and varying governance structures have resulted in a number of laws, policies and practices that have derailed a previously sought-after liberal economy. This has led to the country being unable to qualify for certain foreign aid, loan and investment programmes. Concurrently, Libya's unique political systems and practices have led to frequent bouts of political and economic sanctions, isolation and instability. The Qaddafi regime's WMD programme and support for causes that involved acts of violent terrorism prompted the imposition of stringent sanctions, notably by the USA and the UN. This followed the bombings of a nightclub in West Berlin, Federal Republic of Germany, in April 1986, of a US airliner over Lockerbie, Scotland, in December 1988 and of a French airliner over Chad in September 1989—all of which were later revealed to have involved Libyan connivance (see History). The sanctions sought to isolate Libya, including through the USA's 1996 Iran and Libya Sanctions Act (ILSA), which focused on penalizing third-party states for trading or otherwise co-operating with Qaddafi's Government, to the detriment of the Libyan economy. Meanwhile, domestic actors sought to further their own interests in Libya against Qaddafi's regime.

By the time the 2011 revolution took place, an estimated 140 tribal networks were operating in Libya, each with their own histories and rivalries. Since then, a number of growing (and sometimes shrinking) actors have controlled and competed in Libya, the country's three regions and various aspects of the economy, including but not limited to: the General National Congress (GNC), the HoR, the GNA, the GNU, the High Council of State, the National Transitional Council (NTC), the Muslim Brotherhood's Justice and Construction Party and Haftar (a military officer who had taken part in the Qaddafi-led 1969 revolution), together with his allied forces (including the LNA). All of these actors are (or were) connected to tribal and regional interests and have received support from foreign actors, including the UN, the Arab League, the USA, the United Kingdom, France, Egypt, Qatar, Turkey (officially known as Türkiye from June 2022), the Russian paramilitary Wagner Group, al-Qa'ida in the Islamic Maghreb and a branch of Islamic State. This complex and constantly shifting network of actors has weighed heavily on the economy, as Libya has been riven by disputes and armed clashes among these and other actors ever since the ousting of Qaddafi in 2011.

It is also important to treat the country's economic data with caution. Owing to Libya's resource-rich and rentier nature, conventional economic assessments paint an optimistic picture of the country's economic affairs. This is aside from any issues surrounding data availability and accuracy that are inevitable in countries that experience such disruption and changes in leadership. An examination of Libya's economic indicators alongside the geopolitical context is therefore necessary to draw out the detail, which in turn demonstrates the above point.

Libya's GDP performance is strongly influenced by and correlated to the geopolitical landscape. The WMD-related sanctions meant that Libya's GDP at current prices averaged US $30,330m. per year between 1990 and 2002 while the average GDP per capita stood at $6,081. At the end of that period Qaddafi sought to implement several economic reforms that were required for sanctions relief and for access to foreign markets and finances, and to help fulfil Libya's economic potential. Examples of this came in the form of the creation of the new post of Prime Minister, first held by Shukri Muhammad Ghanem, who decided to abolish the two parallel rates of the national currency, the Libyan dinar, by ensuring that the commercial and official rates were the same, obliging foreign firms to employ Libyans and reviewing existing salaries, alongside calls for reform by Qaddafi's son, Seif al-Islam. Although al-Islam held no official role in Qaddafi's Government, he was widely seen as second in command, demonstrating how the sentiment of family and tribal fidelities continued in the country well into the 21st century. This was reflected by the fact that al-Islam was involved in negotiations with the International Monetary Fund (IMF) and other financial agencies to secure loans and assistance to help develop Libya after 2003. Ghanem's successor, Baghdadi al-Mahmoudi, continued this momentum by launching Libya's Economic Development Board and the Libyan Investment Authority, while simultaneously encouraging Libyan entrepreneurial activity by offering Libyan businesses similar economic incentives to those that were offered to their foreign counterparts from 2007.

Following the removal of WMD-related sanctions in 2003 and the implementation of economic reform programmes and initiatives, Libya's GDP grew by 13.0% year on year in 2003 to reach US $26,270m. having shrunk by 1.0% in 2002. In addition, Libya's GDP recorded an average yearly growth rate of 5.2% and an average annual nominal output of $61,130m. from 2004 until Qaddafi's removal in 2011—an output value that was more than double that recorded during the pre-sanctions period (1990–2000). The annual GDP per capita growth rate switched from a 2.5% contraction in 2002 to an 11.2% year-on-year expansion in 2003 to reach $4,673. This figure more than doubled to reach an average of $10,189 per year between 2004 and the 2011 fall of Qaddafi, and the average annual GDP growth rate during this period was 3.7%.

The removal of Qaddafi exposed domestic cleavages in Libya as internal and external actors pursued their various interests in the country after 2011. This took a heavy toll on the country and resulted in volatile economic indicator performances. The revolution led to a 62.1% contraction in GDP in 2011, to US $34,700m. In 2012 GDP rebounded by an annualized figure of 123.1%, to reach $81,870m. GDP per capita declined by 62.4% year on year in 2011, to $5,554, before jumping by 121.8% in 2012 to $13,025. Following this initial rebound, Libya's GDP swung between contraction (hitting a low of 23.0% in 2014) and growth, which peaked at 32.5% in 2019—resulting in an average annual contraction rate of 2.0% between 2013 and 2019. Over the same period GDP per capita recorded an even steeper average annual rate of contraction, of 3.6%, and totalled $10,102 per year on average, with a peak of $12,589 in 2013 and a low of $7,867 in 2015. The COVID-19 pandemic engendered further fluctuations in Libya's GDP performance—much like in other countries around the world—initially contracting by 29.8% in 2020, rebounding to grow by 31.4% in 2021 and then contracting once again, by 1.2%, in 2022; the GDP per capita growth rate followed a similar pattern over these three years. In nominal terms, GDP gradually declined from a high of $76,686m. in 2018 to an average annual of $50,403m. over the succeeding four years and amounting to $45,752m. in 2022. This decline illustrates how unresolved political discord coupled with global pressures represent barriers to the achievement of a stable economy and growth (see Outlook)

Libya's volatile economic performance came in the context of ongoing disagreements and often violent disputes between the various actors in the country. This, in turn, meant there was a disunited front in place to counter universal concerns such as the COVID-19 crisis, which, according to data from the World Health Organization (WHO), had infected 507,266 Libyans and caused 6,437 fatalities by July 2023. While the country deployed several COVID-19 vaccines, the vaccination programme only started in April 2021 and, according to Johns Hopkins University and Our World in Data, by mid-January 2023 only 18.2% of the total population had been fully vaccinated against the disease. Moreover, compounding Libya's political infighting and the associated governance concerns was the fact that as of early 2023, according to the International Organization for Migration, Libya was playing host to some 706,000 migrants of more than 44 different nationalities who intended to cross the Mediterranean to seek refuge in Europe (see Demographics). This situation further highlights how broader regional interests in Libya extend beyond hydrocarbons stability. The country's reliance on hydrocarbons and its lack of economic diversification has meant that control of these natural resources has been used to achieve political influence and secure concessions. The fact that external states and actors also have vested interests in the security of refineries, and the delivery of oil in particular, makes for a complex picture in terms of how the energy sector affects Libya's economic affairs.

HYDROCARBONS AND UTILITIES

The first oil discovery in Libya was reported during water well drillings in 1914. After stop-start development during and between the two World Wars, mass oil exploration and production took place following the passage of the 1955 Libyan Petroleum Law. Under the legislation, 12.5% of production and storage royalties went to the Libyan state and profits were shared equally with the exploration companies. This disproportionate allocation of profit to private companies led to criticism and a legislative amendment in 1961 that imposed more stringent conditions and ensured that all royalties as well as profits were shared equally between Libya and the respective oil companies. Although more equitable, Libya under King Senussi was still ceding a significant amount of rent and control over the oil industry to foreign actors.

In 1962 Libya joined the Organisation of the Petroleum Exporting Countries (OPEC), having begun exporting the resource one year earlier. This marked a turning point for the Libyan economy, as oil and eventually gas had a lasting impact on the way that the state was governed, where revenues and wealth were distributed, and how foreign states and actors sought to secure the resources for their own interests. Following the Qaddafi-led revolution in 1969, there was significant growth in the production of crude oil as the figure breached the 3m. barrels per day (b/d) level, reaching 3.1m. b/d in 1969, up from 2.6m. b/d in 1968. Concurrently, Libya's petroleum exports increased in value from US $1,860m. in 1968 to $2,160m. in the following year.

In 1970 the National Oil Corporation (NOC) was established to oversee the country's oil sector, succeeding the Libyan Petroleum Corporation. In that year crude oil production reached 3.3m. b/d; production since that time has never exceeded 3m. b/d (with the second highest annual output of 2.1m. in 1989 and all subsequent production below 2m. b/d). The oil boom provided an insight into Libya's economic potential, should the resource be capitalized on. In 1979 the NOC was given greater governance powers over the hydrocarbons sector, including increased jurisdiction over Libya's petroleum stock, as well as a mandate to contribute to the national economy, manage reserves and exploration initiatives, and work with international partners. This had a positive impact on petroleum exports, which grew steadily throughout the 1970s to reach a then record high of US $21,910m. in 1980.

The 1980s marked a further shift in how hydrocarbons contributed to the Libyan economy. During this period Qaddafi's decisions to pursue a WMD programme and to support internationally recognized terrorist causes (including the attack on a West Berlin nightclub in 1986 and the airliner bombings of Pan Am flight 103 in 1988 and of UTA flight 772 in 1989) led to a raft of international sanctions that curtailed Libya's economy, including the hydrocarbons sector. Libya's oil production fell from 1.3m. b/d in 1986 to 1.0m. b/d in 1987 and remained low right up until the dismantlement of the WMD programme in 2003 and subsequent international sanctions relief, averaging 1.3m. b/d annually between 1987 and 2002. This was the case even though Libya's proven crude oil reserves increased from 22,800m. barrels in 1987 to 36,000m. in 2002.

One of the most stringent sanctions imposed on Libya during this period came in the form of the 1996 ILSA, implemented by the USA, which sought to punish US and other companies (and countries) for conducting business with Libya and Iran. The rationale behind the ILSA cited Qaddafi's support for international terrorism and development of the WMD programme, and remained in place until 2003, despite calls from the European Union (EU) to suspend the sanctions from the outset. The EU reached an agreement with the USA in 1997 to exempt European countries and companies from being subject to the ILSA, and the UN suspended support for the act in 1998 after the suspected perpetrators of the Lockerbie bombing were extradited to stand trial for their alleged crimes.

Following the dismantlement of the WMD programme in 2003 and co-operation, including admissions of involvement and investigations into the Berlin nightclub attack as well as the airliner bombings, crude oil production increased to an average of 1.6m. b/d in 2003–10 (an 82% increase from the comparable figure for 1987–2002). This 2003–10 period, during which economic reforms were implemented, witnessed significant development in the oil and gas sectors. Total revenue from natural resources peaked at 67.7% of Libya's GDP in 2006 (with oil accounting for 99.7% of this figure). The country recorded petroleum exports of US $61,495m. in 2008 (the highest ever annual sum), and crude oil reserves increased from 39,100m. barrels in 2003 to 47,100m. barrels in 2010. However, the fall of Qaddafi in 2011 led to a period of marked instability for hydrocarbons production, exploration and trade.

The high value of and reliance on hydrocarbons for the country's income meant that oil and gas facilities were often targeted for financial and political gain by rival actors in Libya following the ousting of Qaddafi. In turn, this led to a decline in the contribution of hydrocarbons to the economy after the 2011 revolution, as oil revenue fell to 44.4% of GDP in that year (with petroleum exports recorded at US $18,620m., marking a year-on-year decrease of 39.4%). This was a result of oil production falling from 1.5m. b/d in 2010 (Qaddafi's last full year in power) to just 0.5m. b/d in 2011. The industry recovered in 2012, as oil revenue rose to constitute 60.8% of Libya's GDP and petroleum exports increased to $60,188m., with production of 1.5m. b/d. However, oil and gas facilities continued to be targeted by warring factions as a means of gaining political and financial control over the country. For example, in June 2012 the Cyrenaica Federalists (who were seeking greater autonomy for their region) blocked routes between the east and Tripolitania, and halted production in the facilities of the Sirte Basin, Ras Lanuf, Sidra, Brega, Zuweitina and Al-Hreigaarea. This action lasted two days before the Tripolitania-based NTC bowed to the Cyrenaica Federalists' demand for their region (as well as for Fezzan) to be given equal representation in the transition process. In the same year, the Petroleum Defence Force was set up by the first GNC parliament to protect the country's oil industry, and was led by a former anti-Qaddafi leader in Cyrenaica, Ibrahim al-Jathran. After being frustrated by the slow pace of operations and by corruption concerns surrounding the GNC, al-Jathran took control of Cyrenaica's hydrocarbons facilities and closed the oil facilities at the ports of Sidra and Ras Lanuf. These developments demonstrated how political power could be wielded through the control of hydrocarbons, while simultaneously suppressing activities in the sector. In 2013 crude oil production fell by 68.3% year on year to 1m. b/d, and decreased by more than one-half to 0.5m. b/d in 2014, as the country experienced continued infighting.

In 2014 there was hope for improved political progress, as elections took place that led to the establishment of a new legislative body, the HoR. However, the GNC did not recognize the new HoR, which set the scene for two rival parliaments: one in Tripoli (the new GNC) and the other in Tobruk (the HoR), resulting in differences of interest between their two divergent sets of policies. This led to a decrease in oil production to just 400,000 b/d in 2015 and 389,000 b/d in 2016—the lowest level since 1962, when production was 180,000 b/d. The hydrocarbons sector's contribution to Libyan GDP also fell as a result of the instability, to a low of 21.0% in 2016—the lowest level since 1999, shortly before the lifting of the WMD-related sanctions. In 2016 petroleum exports amounted to US $9,310m., rising to $15,010m. in 2017, and saw an approximately two-thirds' increase in 2018 and 2019 to $25,386m. and $24,197m., respectively. The pandemic and subsequent fall in demand led to this figure declining to just $5,724m. in 2020 before rebounding to $27,485m. in 2021. Production rose to 811,000 b/d in 2017, and to 951,000 b/d in 2018, and breached the 1m. b/d mark, to hit 1,097,000 b/d in 2019 and 1,207,000 b/d in 2021, following a dip to 389,000 b/d in 2020 during the height of the pandemic.

In December 2018 local tribes halted about one-third of the country's output by closing the Al-Sharara oilfield, demanding that poor economic conditions be addressed. Many of the developments that took place following the revolution of 2011 disrupted oil exploration, with Libya's proven crude oil reserves estimated at 48,363m. barrels during 2013–21 (an increase of just 2.6% from 2010). The disruption continued, and oil production fell to a monthly average of 1.08m. b/d in January 2022 (the lowest level since October 2020), following shutdowns by armed groups, maintenance issues and more port closures than usual amid adverse weather conditions. The first six months of 2023 saw oil revenue fall to US $6,950m. (with output averaging 1.16m. b/d), compared with $7,800m. in the first six months of 2022 (during which output averaged 1.17m. b/d, despite production in May falling to a monthly low of 0.71m. b/d).

Natural gas has played an increasingly important role in Libya's economic affairs. In 1969 the country's proven natural gas reserves were recorded at 850,000m. cu m, up from 570,000m. cu m in 1968, the year before the Qaddafi-led revolution. However, production remained a fraction of proven reserves. There was no production between 1960 and 1969, and it averaged just 5,100m. cu m per year during 1970–2002, peaking at 6,800m. cu m in 1989. Between 1990 and 2002 revenue from natural gas contributed an average of just 0.3% to Libya's GDP. Following the removal of sanctions in 2003, natural gas production rose from 5,900m. cu m in 2002 to a record 16,814m. cu m in 2010, while revenue as a contribution to GDP increased to an average of 1.0% between 2003 and 2010.

The 2011 revolution disrupted exploration in the natural gas sector, much as it did in the oil sector. Proven natural gas reserves increased to 1,505,000m. cu m during 2014–21—an increase of just 0.01% from the level in 2010. Production also fell markedly, to 7,855m. cu m in 2011 (with revenue contributing 1.9% to GDP in that year), before a surge to 18,118m. cu m in 2012 (contributing 1.3% to GDP) and again in 2013 to the highest level of production in the post-Qaddafi era, of 18,463m. cu m (contributing 1.9% to GDP). Local actors used the control of gas facilities as a way of gaining political influence in Libya during this period. An example of this is when an anti-GNC Berber tribe in western Libya closed the Melitah complex and the Greenstream pipeline that connects Libyan gas to European buyers, in an attempt to secure greater constitutional recognition. This led to a year-on-year decrease of 10.5% in natural gas production to 16,523m. cu m in 2014, although natural gas revenue's contribution to GDP peaked at 2.6% in that year (as oil's contribution to total output had fallen much more sharply in relative terms). Natural gas production decreased to 15,150m. cu m in 2015, before resuming an upward trajectory to reach 26,830m. cu m in 2019; this figure dropped amid the pandemic to 20,930m. cu m in 2020 before recovering to 24,244m. cu m. in 2021. Despite steadily rising output, natural gas continued to contribute only a minor and fluctuating share of Libya's GDP compared with the oil industry. Natural gas revenue contributed 2.6% to GDP in 2014, 2.2% in 2016 and a post-Qaddafi low of 1.0% in 2019 (averaging 1.8% between 2011 and 2020).

However, Libya's gas industry had an increasing role in meeting demand for electricity, replacing the leading role of oil. The available data from 1970 to 2015 show how all of the country's electricity production was generated from oil and gas sources. Between 1970 and 1994 the entirety of the country's electricity production came from oil sources. In 1995 this balance began to shift as natural gas accounted for 22.8% of electricity production and remained at a stable average of 21.7% between 1995 and 2004. Qaddafi's economic reforms and incentive programmes led to natural gas producing an average 38.4% of Libya's electricity between 2005 and 2009. The year 2010 was the final year that oil resources contributed more to electricity production than gas (which then accounted for 47.2% of production). The switch from a greater reliance on oil to gas for electricity production came in 2011, when gas accounted for 59.8%. Gas's contribution to electricity production reached a record high of 60.5% in 2012, before declining to

58.4% in 2013 and to 53.7% in 2014 and 2015. This demonstrates how attempts to diversify the Libyan economy away from oil were successful, even after the ouster of Qaddafi. However, the dominant role of oil and gas in Libya illustrates just how much the country depends on hydrocarbons for its economic health. This in turn means that the security and maintenance of oil and gas facilities and deliveries plays a vital role in determining Libya's economic affairs.

EXTERNAL TRADE AND INVESTMENT

Libya's foreign economic ties have been subject to the varying interests of local and global actors, internationally imposed sanctions, and the internal and external reliance on hydrocarbons. For most of the country's history, trade exports have mostly been made up of petroleum and crude oil and have outweighed imports, resulting in a significant trade surplus. In theory, this provided the potential and means to develop Libya's economy, particularly during Qaddafi's time as leader. However, the undertakings of local actors, including Qaddafi, meant that this was not the case, as several sectors of the economy remained underdeveloped, and the level of GDP per capita remained relatively low with revenue being unevenly shared among Libyans (see *Economic Context and Conflict*).

There were some notable exceptions to Libya's maintenance of a consistent trade surplus, the first of which occurred when the country was still developing its oil industry; the value of imports outweighed exports by US $160m. in 1960, $130m. in 1961 and $70m. in 1962. This trade deficit was minor compared with the only other two years in which imports outweighed exports, when the deficit reached $9,590m. (in 2014) and $5,040m. (in 2015), following the removal of Qaddafi and amid ongoing instability, halts to oil and gas production and violent conflict in many parts of the country. Apart from these two periods, Libya enjoyed a healthy trade surplus, although it narrowed during the WMD-related sanctions era before 2003 and during the 2008–09 global financial crisis.

From the 1969 revolution until 2002, before the sanctions were lifted, Libya's imports averaged US $4,530m. and exports $9,190m. (with petroleum making up $8,990m. of this figure). In the period between the lifting of sanctions and the removal of Qaddafi (2003–10) the average import level increased more than threefold to reach $15,980m., while exports increased more than fourfold to $38,350m. ($37,580m. of which comprised petroleum products). Notably, this period included a steep drop in exports, from $61,950m. (of which $61,495m. was from petroleum) in 2008 to $37,060m. (of which $35,600m. was from petroleum) in 2009, owing to the slump in demand triggered by the global financial crisis, before a rebound to $48,940m. (of which $47,245m. was from petroleum) in 2010. The country's largest recorded trade surplus, of $40,750m., was recorded in 2008, just before the international economic downturn.

Following the fall of Qaddafi, Libya witnessed infighting between local actors, which in turn disrupted any sense of external trade stability while simultaneously suppressing import and export levels. This volatility was felt as imports decreased from US $25,167m. in 2010 to $11,200m. in 2011, while exports decreased from $48,935m. ($47,245m. of which comprised petroleum products) in 2010 to $19,060m. (of which $18,615m. was from petroleum) in 2011. During 2011–21 imports averaged $18,236m. and exports averaged $25,239m. (94% of which comprised hydrocarbons products). In 2016 imports and exports reached a post-Qaddafi low of $8,667m. and $9,446m. (of which $9,313m. was from petroleum), respectively, as infighting continued. Libya's imports reached a record high in 2013, of $34,050m., while exports reached their second highest ever level in 2012, at $61,026m. (of which $60,188m. was from petroleum products)—second only to the $61,950m. (of which $61,495m. was from petroleum) recorded in 2008 and resulting in the second highest ever trade surplus of $35,440m. being registered in 2012 (again, behind the peak achieved in 2008). The pandemic saw imports slump from $17,184m. in 2019 to $13,748m. in 2020, before recovering to $18,972m. in 2021; export figures saw an even greater fluctuation, from $27,722m. in 2019 ($24,197m. from petroleum), to $7,345m. in 2020 ($5,724m. in petroleum) and back up to $28,986m. in 2021 ($27,485m. in petroleum). The fact that the country registered a record high trade deficit (of $18,788m.) in 2014 before returning to surplus from 2017 onwards (except for the pandemic deficit of $9,451m. in 2020) to reach $5,177m. in 2021 demonstrated how, although parts of the economy had suffered during the ongoing conflict, the production and delivery of hydrocarbons were mostly protected. This illustrates how external partners (notably in Europe) strive to ensure that Libya's oil and gas sectors are maintained as well as possible, which has a knock-on effect of limiting economic diversification, and which also requires a hydrocarbons-dependent economy to work overtime to compensate for other sectors during periods of instability and conflict.

Libya's primary regional trade partner for exports is Europe. Based on the available data covering the period from 2012 to 2021, Libya exported an average of 730,758 b/d of petroleum per year to foreign trade partners, 76.5% of which went to European buyers. This latter figure fluctuated from an average annual high of 90.6% in 2013–15 to a low of 66.9% in 2019, indicating that European partners have a vested interest in upholding and securing Libya's hydrocarbons industry.

Net inflows of foreign direct investment (FDI) measured in the balance of payments at current US dollar levels show how the sanctions regime before 2003, the 2008–09 global financial crisis, the 2011 revolution and post-Qaddafi instability all weighed on this economic indicator. The available data record FDI stock averaging US $34,000m. per year between 1972 and 2002. After the lifting of sanctions in 2003 FDI net inflows increased more than fivefold to an average of $1,830m. per year during 2003–10, including a drop from an all-time high of $5,888m. in 2008 to $1,165m. in 2009 as the global financial crisis undermined the international economy. The revolution of 2011 led FDI net inflows to decline from $2,722m. in 2010 to $131m. in 2011. Following the fall of Qaddafi, FDI inflows fluctuated dramatically, rising to $2,508m. in 2012, before declining to $707m. in 2013 amid the ongoing unrest and instability. A negative net inflow of FDI, of $77m., was recorded in 2014. This was the first time that a negative net inflow had been recorded since 2002 (before sanctions were lifted), when a negative net inflow of $136m. was registered. FDI net inflows recovered to $394m. in 2015 and to $440m. in 2016, before dipping to a negative net inflow in 2017, of $295m., marking the second largest deficit in this indicator on record (after the $479m. recorded in 1993). FDI recovered to a net inflow of $275m. in 2018, decreasing to $101m. in 2019, before rebounding to $205m. in 2020. This volatility again demonstrates how the policies of Qaddafi, sanctions, domestic and foreign actors and interests, as well as the global (recession) and regional (revolution) developments led to economic uncertainty. It is clear that Libya's ties with the world in recent decades paint a picture of a heavy reliance on hydrocarbons and a lack of economic diversification. Taken together with the contextual factors that drove instability and violence, Libya's foreign economic relations have been unable to reach their full potential. This is reflected in the country's public finances.

PUBLIC FINANCES AND THE CURRENT ACCOUNT

Prior to the lifting of the WMD-related international sanctions in 2003, Libya's current account balance averaged a surplus of US $879m. during 1977–2002. It peaked at $8,214m. in 1980 and hit a low point in 1981, recording a deficit of $3,963m. The surplus jumped from $694m. in 2002 to a post-sanctions high of $35,701m. in 2008, before the global economic downturn took hold, and the surplus fell to $9,380m. in 2009 prior to recovering in 2010, to $16,800m.; the average surplus was $16,941m. during 2003–10. This demonstrated once more the potential and capacity for the economy of Qaddafi's Libya to develop and grow, even during a global economic downturn. The 2011 revolution led to a further period of volatility for the current account balance. The surplus fell to $3,192m. in 2011, but recovered to $23,836m. in 2012, reflecting fluctuations in oil output. Revised World Bank figures then show a narrowing of the surplus to just $10.0m. in 2013, which shifted to a deficit of $18,788m. in 2014 (the first such negative balance since a deficit of $209m. in 1998). The deficit declined to $9,233m. in 2015 and further to $4,610m. in 2016, before the current account returned to surplus in 2017–18. Revised figures show deficits of $1,600m. in 2019 and $6,600m. in 2020 amid the pandemic, before the current account recovered to record a surplus of $7,400m. in 2021. The IMF estimated that the surplus would widen to $8,800m. in 2022, and then narrow to $3,500m. in 2023. The fluctuations of the current account between surplus and deficit were caused by the instability that followed the fall of Qaddafi, the ensuing conflict, the impact of the pandemic, and the economic crisis arising from the Russian Federation's invasion of Ukraine in February 2022, which led to an increase in the price of essential commodities.

In 2002, before the international sanctions were lifted, inflation, measured as a GDP deflator percentage year on year, hit a high of 27.3%, up from 7.2% in 2001 and 13.3% in 2000. Following the lifting of sanctions, according to revised figures from the World Bank, inflation averaged 13.2% between 2003 and 2010, including a high of 28.6% in 2005 and the first instance of deflation on record, of 24.8% in 2009, in the context of the global financial crisis. Consumer prices rebounded by 19.3% in 2010. The removal of Qaddafi and instability in 2011 led to a rise in inflation in that year, to 24.3%, although it fell to 6.0% in 2012 and to just 0.1% in 2013. Then, after two years of prices contracting, by 1.0% in 2014 and 7.0% in 2015, inflation returned, at 4.7% in 2016, 1.8% in 2017, 3.6% in 2018 and 4.2% in 2019. The pandemic saw deflationary pressures leading to a contraction in consumer prices of 5.1% in 2020, before surging back to an inflationary figure of 110.4% in 2021, which moderated to 24.1% in 2022. The Central Bank of Libya took the decision to integrate the Libyan dinar into market exchanges, by agreeing to a new floating exchange rate from January 2021. While this points to a reason behind the spike in inflation in 2021 (along with the pandemic context), the rationale behind the bank's action was to achieve a Libyan currency that was in harmony with its counterparts. As of mid-2023 the inflationary pressures appeared likely to persist, as the Russia–Ukraine crisis continued to constrain trade in essentials, thus causing global rises in the price of staple foods and goods.

The fluctuating nature of the public finances and current account made it very difficult for public institutions to set economic policies and allocate funds efficiently. This was exacerbated by the often violent clashes between domestic actors, including the threats to and blockades of oil and gas facilities. An example of this occurred in 2012 when the Central Bank of Libya was only able to spend about one-half of its allocated budget, owing to the instability that followed the removal of Qaddafi. Furthermore, the elections in 2014 and the continuing disputes between the GNC and the HoR created an environment where the NOC was unable effectively to manage the hydrocarbons sector. Attacks on oil facilities made it difficult for the industry to attract foreign investors and to protect existing tenders. This also led to divisions within the NOC, based on the geographical location of the oil and gas production sites. For example, in January 2017 the Cyrenaican branch of the NOC granted 29 foreign contracts for oil production, without the consent of the Tripoli-based headquarters. This led to the Cyrenaican-based Government (the HoR) supporting Haftar's forceable control over the Sirte Basin and rejecting attempts to unify all branches of the NOC. The head of the NOC, Mustafa Sanalla, cited concerns about how different groups were controlling the country's oil infrastructure in that year. This once again demonstrates how the control of hydrocarbons had a debilitating impact on the ability of Libyan public institutions to govern efficiently. This pattern was replicated in the private sector.

The capacity of Libyan businesses to stimulate economic activity was aided by the domestic credit provided to the private sector, mostly by financial companies in the first instance. Between 1990 (when the World Bank's records on Libya were first compiled) and 2002, before the removal of the WMD-related international sanctions, domestic credit to the private sector as a percentage of Libya's GDP averaged 25.9% (with the finance sector providing 80.4% of the total). Between 2003 and 2010 this value decreased to an average of 8.8% (as the financial sector became a net consumer of credit, taking 35.2% of the total credit granted), indicating how the source of credit shifted to come from external sources as the economy opened up and Qaddafi's reforms took effect in the 2000s. Following the removal of the Qaddafi regime, revised figures show that the provision of domestic credit to the private sector as a share of GDP increased from 9.3% in 2010 to 14.2% in 2011. This figure fell to 9.3% in 2012, before increasing to 21.5% in 2015. Domestic credit to the private sector subsequently steadied to 18.9% of GDP in 2016, 14.8% in 2017, 12.8% in 2018 and 14.6% in 2019. This figure registered a high of 21.9% of GDP in 2020, reflecting the provision of support during the pandemic, before moderating to 9.8% in 2021 and 10.1% in 2022. The fluctuating figures demonstrate how instability undermined the supply of domestic credit to the private sector and how a lack of economic diversification, despite oil and gas revenue being sufficient to provide the funds to do so, meant that the hydrocarbons sector had to be bailed out on a number of occasions. This, in turn, had a negative impact on quality of life for many.

DEMOGRAPHICS

Despite being the 16th largest country in the world, with a land mass of 1.68m. sq km, Libya had an estimated population of just 6.89m. at mid-2023 (according to UN estimates) and an average growth rate of 1.1% per year during 2012–21. The relatively small population size is partly due to the fact that 91% of the country's land area is rural, mostly made up of the Sahara Desert; agricultural land comprises just 8.7% of the total area, and Libya's arable land covers only about 17,200 sq km (just over 1% of the national territory). In addition, the population has been adversely affected by the policies of former regimes, international sanctions and the ongoing instability that has blighted the country since the 2011 revolution. All of these factors contributed to a net outflow in migration in 2017, of 9,997, which followed a record net outflow of 300,002 in 2012; the most recent positive net migration figure was recorded in 1992 (of just 3,962). These data do not take into account the large numbers of migrants from other Arab countries and Sub-Saharan Africa who have, since the fall of Qaddafi, used Libya as a base from which to attempt to cross the Mediterranean.

Libya's labour force amounted to 2.3m. people in 2022 (nearly 50% of Libyans aged 15 years and over). In that year 34.4% of the labour force were female. Labour force participation rate as a share of the total population has fluctuated between 42% and just under 50% since 1990. Libya's unemployment rate did not change much in the 2000s, according to World Bank statistics, despite the introduction of economic reforms in that decade. Between 1990 and 2002 the rate of unemployment as a measure of the total labour force averaged 19.0% and declined slightly following the implementation of reforms to 18.8% during 2003–10. After the fall of Qaddafi, the rate averaged 19.7% in 2011–22 and stood at 19.6% in 2022, according to the World Bank. The problem is particularly acute for Libyans aged between 15 and 24 years, among whom the unemployment rate averaged 50.4% in 2011–21 (up from 47.6% during 2003–10 and 45.5% in 1991–2002). The total youth unemployment rate was 51.5% in 2022. Breaking this figure down by gender reveals an even starker state of affairs: 70.1% of the female Libyan youth population (aged 15–24) were unemployed in 2022, up from an average of 65.2% during 2003–10 and 59.2% during 1991–2002 (with the figure standing at 55.9% in 1991). These data show how economic liberalization reforms coincided with falling employment levels among Libya's female youths.

Libya's access to power and electricity has been falling steadily since 2000. In that year 99.8% of the population had access to electricity—100.0% of Libyans living in urban areas and 99.2% in rural areas. This indicator then commenced a steadily downward trend, resulting in only 70.2% of the population having access to electricity in 2021, although 100% of Libyans living in urban areas still had access at that time. However, data from 2012 point to an increasing disparity between urban and rural residents, with just 0.8% of rural Libyans having access to electricity in that year. Since 2011 there have been regular power outages as a result of unrest in the country, which has damaged essential infrastructure, including power generation facilities and hospitals (with only 17.5% functioning fully in 2018), and water supplies have been intermittent (with 43% of the population relying on vehicle-transported water rather than a mains supply). This demonstrates how the actions of the Qaddafi regime, together with the ongoing disputes and differences between the various tribal groups and competing governments, had a detrimental impact on the Libyan population. Although electricity production was diversified away from being solely reliant on oil and now relies chiefly on gas (see *Hydrocarbons and Utilities*), the lack of diversification to other sources has contributed to this negative outcome. Indeed, a more diversified energy source base, e.g. including renewables, would counteract some of the access problems, especially when coupled with the fact that rival actors in Libya have targeted the only two energy sources (oil and gas) in order to achieve political gain. This issue is another product of Libya's geoeconomic status, which highlights how external interests are in play and weigh heavily on the country's domestic consumption and broader economic performance. While the October 2020 ceasefire agreement provided some respite, the indefinite delay in holding elections originally scheduled for December 2021 and subsequent protests posed challenges to Libya's economy.

Furthermore, owing to the political impasse and its geographic location, Libya has become a natural hub for migrants and would-be refugees seeking to enter Europe. The UN High Commissioner for Refugees estimated that as of July 2023 there were some 803,000 people in Libya who were in need of humanitarian assistance (with 44,468 officially registered as refugees or asylum seekers). The COVID-19 pandemic and the domestic political environment have meant that co-ordination of policies to address the humanitarian situation, both internally and with international organizations, is difficult. Moreover, the situation has placed significant strains on the country's already overstretched resources and poses a policy problem for the Libyan authorities to work towards solving in the future.

OUTLOOK

Libya's resources and geoeconomic status have afforded the country a number of opportunities to drive prosperity and growth. The wealth accrued from hydrocarbons resources has meant that foreign states and companies have long sought to develop and benefit from the associated profits. However, the actions and policies implemented by former Libyan leaders, specifically the Petroleum Law of 1955 and its subsequent amendments, have led to a historically disproportionate amount of resource-based profits leaving the country. In addition, the nature of the political system adopted by Qaddafi meant that domestic opposition to his actions was muted and led to the ring-fencing of the hydrocarbons industry, preventing any interference from those outside the regime's elite. The pursuit of WMDs and Qaddafi's support for foreign terrorist groups compounded the risks to Libya's economy, owing to the international sanctions that were imposed on the country as a result. Set against these circumstances, the historical context and make-up of Libya's society has witnessed often violent clashes among different local actors (some with external support). This was particularly the case in the 2011 revolution that unseated Qaddafi as Libya's leader and ushered in a period of sustained economic volatility.

In 2023 Libya's economy still relied heavily on hydrocarbons resources for energy and revenue. The LPA of 2015, the 2020 ceasefire and the establishment of the GNU appeared to promise some respite in the ongoing conflict between the competing governments and actors on either side of the east–west divide in the country. However, the past failures to abide by the LPA's commitment to peace and reach a lasting settlement, along with the indefinite delay to the parliamentary and presidential elections scheduled to be held in late 2021 and early 2022, point to a number of challenges for Libya's stability in both economic and political terms. While the World Bank and the African Development Bank continued with their optimistic outlooks in mid-2023, the suspension of elections, owing to political disagreements, and the instability arising from oil blockades and humanitarian problems pointed to short-term pressures. Furthermore, global inflationary pressures and constricted growth posed a problem for Libya's rentier economy, as demand for oil looked to remain subdued well into the latter half of 2023.

Linked to this are the effects of the COVID-19 pandemic and Russia–Ukraine conflict which continue to weigh heavily on Libya. While the pandemic caused a slowdown in global commercial activity and thus suppressed demand for hydrocarbons, the post-2020 global rebound and the imposition of international sanctions on exports of Russian hydrocarbons have bolstered oil and gas prices, propping up Libya's economic prospects. However, this also means that the stability and security of oil refineries are even more important. Indeed, a dispute in mid-2022 over how the NOC should be run (including the possibility of it being broken up into smaller organizations) threatened the functioning of the hydrocarbons sector and added to global pressure on energy prices. The prospect of uninterrupted exports from Libya of hydrocarbons at elevated prices goes some way in assuaging the current uncertainty surrounding the supply of staples—mainly wheat—from Eastern Europe and in particular from Ukraine. At the same time, however, the continuing political impasse in Libya places a significant burden on the economy and has adverse effects for both macro- and individual-level economic activity.

Policymakers, businesses and analysts frequently point to how Libya's hydrocarbons resources offer an incentive to resolve disagreements and conflicts within the country and to foster economic growth. The fact that domestic differences and rivalries—often supported by and tied to external interests (see History)—continue despite this, demonstrates how heavily the Libyan context determines the country's stability and trajectory of its economy. As a consequence, although other areas present opportunities for growth and development in the long term, including the potential for tourism (in view of Libya's impressive Roman remains and long Mediterranean coast) and increased hydrocarbons exploration, the tribal and regional actors and interests in the country and abroad show only intermittent signs of coming together to achieve lasting stability. The Libyan economic outlook therefore depends very much on resolving local differences in terms of governance and political representation, effectively handling external pressures on demand for hydrocarbons, ensuring the security of domestic oil and gas facilities, and managing external interference and support for clashing domestic actors.

Statistical Survey

Sources (unless otherwise stated): Bureau of Statistics and Census, 17 February Street, Tripoli; tel. and fax (21) 8213605636; e-mail info@bsc.ly; internet www.bsc.ly; Central Bank of Libya, POB 1103, Sharia al-Malik Seoud, Tripoli; tel. (21) 3333591; fax (21) 4441488; e-mail info@cbl.gov.ly; internet www.cbl.gov.ly.

Area and Population

AREA, POPULATION AND DENSITY

Area (sq km)	1,676,198*
Population (census results)†	
August 1995	4,404,986
August 2006	
Males	2,610,639
Females	2,687,513
Total	5,298,152
Population (UN estimates at mid-year)	
2021	6,735,277
2022‡	6,812,341
2023‡	6,888,388
Density (per sq km) at mid-2023‡	4.1

* 647,184 sq miles.
† Excluding non-Libyans: 409,326 in 1995 and 359,540 in 2006.
‡ Projection.

Note: In October 2013 the Ministry of Planning announced the result of a population census conducted in 2012, however considerable doubt was expressed about the credibility of the recorded total population, at 5,363,369, given the much higher estimates presented by several international statistical agencies.
Sources: National Authority for Information and Authentication; UN, *World Population Prospects: The 2022 Revision*.

POPULATION BY AGE AND SEX
('000, UN projections at mid-2023)

	Males	Females	Total
0–14 years	979.9	928.7	1,908.6
15–64 years	2,350.7	2,286.7	4,637.4
65 years and over	153.1	189.2	342.4
Total	3,483.8	3,404.6	6,888.4

Note: Totals may not be equal to the sum of components, owing to rounding.
Source: UN, *World Population Prospects: The 2022 Revision*.

ADMINISTRATIVE DISTRICTS
(official population estimates, 2020)

	Area (sq km)	Population	Density (per sq km)
Al-Butnan	84,996	195,088	2.3
Banghazi (Benghazi)	11,372	807,255	71.0
Darnah (Darna)	31,511	201,639	6.4
Ghat	68,482	27,675	0.4
Al-Jabal al-Akhdar	11,429	250,020	21.9
Al-Jabal al-Gharbi	76,717	374,911	4.9
Al-Jifarah	2,666	548,855	205.9
Al-Jufrah	139,038	60,853	0.4
Al-Kufrah	433,611	55,495	0.1
Al-Marj	13,515	286,045	21.2
Al-Marqab	6,796	532,227	78.3
Marzuq	356,308	94,088	0.3
Misratah (Misurata)	29,172	663,853	22.8
Nalut	67,191	113,886	1.7
Al-Nuqat al-Khams	6,089	349,755	57.4
Sabha	17,066	153,454	9.0
Surt (Sirte)	86,399	170,869	2.0
Tarabulus (Tripoli)	835	1,293,016	1,548.5
Wadi al-Hayat	31,485	91,749	2.9
Wadi al-Shati	90,244	95,294	1.1
Al-Wahah	108,523	213,728	2.0
Al-Zawiyah (Zawia)	2,753	351,306	127.6
Total	1,676,198	6,931,061	4.1

Note: After 2013 local administration was carried out through loosely instituted governorates and around 100 districts. In March 2022 it was announced that new administrative powers would be transferred to 18 newly created provinces: Al-Akhdar, Benghazi, East Coast, Gheryan, Al-Hizam, Al-Jifarah, Al-Khaleej, Al-Kufrah, Al-Marqab, Marzuq Basin, Nalut, Sabha, Tripoli, Al-Wadi, Al-Wahah, West Coast, Al-Zawiyah and Zintan.

PRINCIPAL TOWNS
(population at 2006 census)

Tarabulus (Tripoli, the capital)	997,065	Al-Nuquat al-Khams	269,553
Banghazi (Benghazi)	622,148	Al-Jabal al-Akhdar	192,689
Misratah (Misurata)	511,628	Al-Marj	175,455
Al-Jifarah	422,999	Al-Wahah	164,718
Al-Marqab	410,187	Darnah (Darna)	155,402
Al-Jabal al-Gharbi	288,944	Al-Butnan	150,353
Al-Zawiyah (Zawia)	270,751	Surt (Sirte)	131,786

Source: National Authority for Information and Authentication.

Mid-2023 (incl. suburbs, UN projections): Tarabulus (Tripoli) 1,183,292; Misratah (Misurata) 984,193; Banghazi (Benghazi) 859,209 (Source: UN, *World Urbanization Prospects: The 2018 Revision*).

BIRTHS, MARRIAGES AND DEATHS

	Registered live births		Registered marriages		Registered deaths	
	Number	Rate (per 1,000)	Number	Rate (per 1,000)	Number	Rate (per 1,000)
2007	128,337	23.7	59,583	11.0	20,045	3.7
2008	132,826	24.6	65,326	12.1	21,481	4.0
2009	134,682	24.9	66,551	12.3	22,859	4.2
2010	151,762	28.1	56,396	10.4	26,426	4.9
2011	151,638	28.0	59,286	11.0	30,403	5.6

Birth rate (UN estimates, rates per 1,000): 18.7 in 2019; 18.3 in 2020; 17.8 in 2021 (Source: UN, *World Population Prospects: The 2022 Revision*).

Death rate (UN estimates, rates per 1,000): 5.5 in 2019; 5.6 in 2020; 6.0 in 2021 (Source: UN, *World Population Prospects: The 2022 Revision*).

Life expectancy (years at birth, estimates): 72.8 (males 69.4; females 76.4) in 2021 (Source: World Bank, World Development Indicators database).

LIBYA

ECONOMICALLY ACTIVE POPULATION
('000 persons)

	2012	2013
Agriculture, forestry and fishing	13.0	13.9
Mining and quarrying	35.9	20.1
Manufacturing	61.6	74.9
Electricity, gas and water	44.2	42.7
Construction	27.6	27.3
Trade, restaurants and hotels	91.4	82.7
Transport and communications	69.3	76.0
Financing, insurance and real estate	42.9	39.9
Public administration	526.8	632.8
Education	488.0	532.3
Health services	104.3	125.4
Other services	19.3	20.0
Total employed	1,524.2	1,688.0
Unemployed	358.3	355.3
Total labour force	1,882.4	2,043.3

2022 (labour force survey, preliminary): Total employed 1,956,430 (males 1,207,873, females 748,557); Unemployed 354,265 (males 185,201, females 169,064); *Total labour force* 2,310,695 (males 1,393,074, females 917,621).

Health and Welfare

KEY INDICATORS

Total fertility rate (children per woman, 2021)	2.5
Under-5 mortality rate (per 1,000 live births, 2021)	10.8
HIV/AIDS (% of persons aged 15–49, 2021)	0.2
COVID-19: Cumulative confirmed deaths (per 100,000 persons at 30 June 2023)	94.5
COVID-19: Fully vaccinated population (% of total population at 16 January 2023)	18.2
Physicians (per 1,000 head, 2017)	2.1
Hospital beds (per 1,000 head, 2017)	3.2
Domestic health expenditure (2011): US $ per head (PPP)	397
Domestic health expenditure (2011): % of GDP	3.8
Domestic health expenditure (2011): public (% of total current health expenditure)	63.3
Access to improved sanitation facilities (% of persons, 2020)	92
Total carbon dioxide emissions ('000 metric tons, 2019)	56,800
Carbon dioxide emissions per head (metric tons, 2019)	8.4
Human Development Index (2021): ranking	104
Human Development Index (2021): value	0.718

Note: For data on COVID-19 vaccinations, 'fully vaccinated' denotes receipt of all doses specified by approved vaccination regime (Sources: Johns Hopkins University and Our World in Data). Data on health expenditure refer to current general government expenditure in each case. For more information on sources and further definitions for all indicators, see Health and Welfare Statistics: Sources and Definitions section (europaworld.com/credits).

Agriculture

PRINCIPAL CROPS
('000 metric tons, FAO estimates unless otherwise indicated)

	2019	2020	2021
Almonds, with shell	34.6	34.6	34.6
Apricots	25.9	25.9	25.9
Barley*	70.0	70.0	70.0
Cantaloupes and other melons	26.5	26.5	26.5
Carrots and turnips	35.1	34.5	34.7
Chillies and peppers, green	26.3	26.4	26.7
Dates	177.4	178.5	179.6
Figs	10.4	10.3	10.3
Grapes	31.5	31.4	31.3
Groundnuts, with shell	16.4	16.4	16.4
Lemons and limes	21.4	21.4	21.4
Olives	174.5	173.8	173.3
Onions and shallots, green	55.6	55.9	56.3

—continued	2019	2020	2021
Onions, dry	188.7	189.1	189.5
Oranges	53.7	52.8	53.0
Peaches and nectarines	14.0	14.0	14.1
Plums and sloes	54.8	54.5	54.7
Potatoes	329.2	326.4	328.9
Pumpkins, squash and gourds	34.8	35.0	35.2
Tangerines, mandarins, etc.	10.3	10.4	10.4
Tomatoes	217.5	218.5	219.5
Watermelons	233.6	233.7	233.9
Wheat*	140.0	130.0	130.0

* Unofficial figures.

Aggregate production ('000 metric tons, may include official, semi-official or estimated data): Total cereals 219.4 in 2019, 209.5 in 2020, 209.5 in 2021; Total fruit (primary) 683.3 in 2019, 682.1 in 2020, 683.5 in 2021; Total oilcrops 240.4 in 2019, 239.6 in 2020, 239.0 in 2021; Total roots and tubers 329.2 in 2019, 326.4 in 2020, 328.9 in 2021; Total treenuts 34.6 in 2019, 34.6 in 2020, 34.6 in 2021; Total vegetables (primary) 686.6 in 2019, 688.5 in 2020, 691.2 in 2021.

Source: FAO.

LIVESTOCK
('000 head, year ending September, FAO estimates)

	2019	2020	2021
Asses	30.0	30.3	27.2
Camels	58.9	60.5	62.5
Cattle	198.8	199.2	199.6
Chickens	35,035	35,593	36,155
Goats	2,619.1	2,627.9	2,636.8
Horses	45.7	45.7	45.7
Sheep	7,304.9	7,341.7	7,378.6

Source: FAO.

LIVESTOCK PRODUCTS
('000 metric tons, FAO estimates)

	2019	2020	2021
Camel meat	5.6	5.7	5.8
Cattle meat	6.0	5.9	5.8
Cows' milk	135.1	135.5	135.8
Chicken meat	125.8	126.7	127.6
Goat meat	11.9	11.9	11.9
Goats' milk	20.6	20.6	20.7
Sheep meat	30.2	29.9	29.6
Sheep's (Ewes') milk	60.3	60.5	60.8
Sheepskins, fresh	6.6	6.5	6.4
Hen eggs	70.0	70.9	71.9
Wool, greasy	10.1	10.2	10.3

Source: FAO.

Forestry

ROUNDWOOD REMOVALS
('000 cubic metres, excl. bark, FAO estimates)

	2019	2020	2021
Sawlogs, veneer logs and logs for sleepers*	63.0	63.0	63.0
Other industrial wood†	53.0	53.0	53.0
Fuel wood	1,051.6	1,061.9	1,072.2
Total	1,167.6	1,177.9	1,188.2

* Annual output assumed to be unchanged since 1978.
† Annual output assumed to be unchanged since 1999.

Source: FAO.

LIBYA

Statistical Survey

SAWNWOOD PRODUCTION
('000 cubic metres, incl. railway sleepers, FAO estimates)

	2019	2020	2021
Total (all broadleaved)	31	31	31

Note: Annual output assumed to be unchanged from 1978.
Source: FAO.

Fishing

(metric tons, live weight, FAO estimates unless otherwise indicated)

	2019	2020	2021
Capture	32,335	31,804	31,951
Common pandora	4,295	4,295	4,300
Bogue	1,325	1,325	1,350
Surmullets (Red mullets)	3,745	3,745	3,750
Atlantic bluefin tuna*	2,052	2,228	2,234
Jack and horse mackerels	1,835	1,835	1,835
Round sardinellas	6,060	5,500	5,500
Dogfish sharks	3,850	3,850	3,850
Common cuttlefish	1,240	1,199	1,250
Aquaculture	10	10	10
Total catch	32,345	31,814	31,961

* Official figures.
Source: FAO.

Mining

('000 metric tons unless otherwise indicated, estimates)

	2017	2018	2019
Salt	40	50	100
Gypsum (crude)	225	225	210

Source: US Geological Survey.

Crude petroleum ('000 metric tons, estimates): 20,000 in 2020; 59,600 in 2021; 51,000 in 2022 (Source: Energy Institute, *Statistical Review of World Energy*).

Natural gas (excl. flared, million cu m, estimates): 12,400 in 2020; 14,500 in 2021; 14,800 in 2022 (Source: Energy Institute, *Statistical Review of World Energy*).

Industry

SELECTED PRODUCTS
('000 metric tons unless otherwise indicated)

	2019	2020	2021
Jet fuels (incl. kerosene)	547	168	485
Motor spirit (petrol)	368	139	346
Naphthas (raw)	872	275	708
Gas-diesel (distillate fuel) oil	1,388	543	1,233
Residual fuel oils	1,859	730	1,473
Electrical energy (million kWh)*	34,629	29,499	n.a.

* Source: UN Energy Statistics Database.

Cement ('000 metric tons, hydraulic): 4,500 in 2017; 4,500 in 2018 (estimate); 4,200 in 2019 (estimate) (Source: US Geological Survey).

Finance

CURRENCY AND EXCHANGE RATES

Monetary Units:
1,000 dirhams = 1 Libyan dinar (LD).

Sterling, Dollar and Euro Equivalents (31 March 2023):
£1 sterling = 5.917 dinars;
US $1 = 4.781 dinars;
€1 = 5.199 dinars;
100 Libyan dinars = £16.90 = $20.92 = €19.23.

Average Exchange Rate (Libyan dinars per US $):
2020 1.3887
2021 4.5144
2022 4.8132

BUDGET
(LD million)

Revenue	2020	2021	2022
Hydrocarbon budget allocation	5,280	103,369	130,535
Non-hydrocarbon	2,281	2,251	3,841
Non-hydrocarbon tax revenue	765	1,110	1,592
Taxes on income and profits	633	799	1,381
Taxes on international trade	132	311	211
Non-hydrocarbon non-tax revenue	1,516	1,141	2,249
Other revenue	15,257	—	—
Total	22,818	105,620	134,376

Expenditure	2020	2021	2022
Current	30,982	61,894	94,149
Administrative expenditure	25,382	41,064	74,111
Subsidies and other current transfers	5,600	20,830	20,038
Capital	1,801	17,390	33,725
Emergency expenditure	4,527	6,491	—
Total	37,310	85,776	127,874

Note: In 2020 a loan of LD 26,706m. was made by the Libyan central bank to cover extraordinary budget expenses.

INTERNATIONAL RESERVES
(US $ million at 31 December)

	2020	2021	2022
Gold (national valuation)	158	158	158
IMF special drawing rights	2,393	4,450	4,242
Reserve position in IMF	588	571	543
Foreign exchange	69,584	70,415	75,102
Total	72,723	75,594	80,045

Source: IMF, *International Financial Statistics*.

MONEY SUPPLY
(LD million at 31 December)

	2020	2021	2022
Currency outside depository corporations	39,732.1	31,799.8	31,353.3
Transferable deposits	86,282.1	68,498.1	78,039.6
Other deposits	2,420.1	2,110.9	1,683.8
Broad money	128,434.4	102,408.7	111,076.7

Source: IMF, *International Financial Statistics*.

LIBYA

COST OF LIVING
(Consumer Price Index; base: 2008 = 100)

	2020	2021	2022
Food and beverages	302.5	314.0	327.8
Clothing and shoes	407.0	416.6	434.6
Housing and utilities	174.6	177.3	191.3
All items (incl. others)	268.2	275.7	288.3

NATIONAL ACCOUNTS
(LD million at current prices)

Expenditure on the Gross Domestic Product

	2019	2020	2021
Government final consumption expenditure	38,569.9	25,029.3	66,706.1
Private final consumption expenditure	37,326.0	24,243.0	64,505.7
Changes in inventories	−7,583.2	−1,103.8	−2,531.3
Gross fixed capital formation	15,336.8	10,428.3	28,141.3
Total domestic expenditure	83,649.5	58,596.8	156,821.9
Exports of goods and services	41,479.6	23,774.1	69,846.8
Less Imports of goods and services	34,254.6	17,323.0	50,580.1
Statistical discrepancy	5,961.0	−0.1	−0.2
GDP in purchasers' values	96,835.5	65,047.8	176,088.3
GDP at constant 2015 prices	84,184.4	59,370.4	76,166.9

Gross Domestic Product by Economic Activity

	2019	2020	2021
Agriculture, forestry and fishing	3,959.4	2,520.3	6,822.5
Mining and utilities	40,771.0	25,536.5	73,472.3
Manufacturing	2,821.0	1,847.7	5,021.7
Construction	3,182.9	2,312.3	5,813.3
Trade, restaurants and hotels	6,626.3	5,479.1	12,813.9
Transport, storage and communications	2,492.5	2,782.0	7,202.8
Other services	44,881.7	29,534.3	78,797.9
Sub-total	104,734.8	70,012.2	189,944.4
Net taxes on products*	−7,899.3	−4,964.4	−13,856.1
GDP in purchasers' values	96,835.5	65,047.8	176,088.3

*Figures obtained as residuals.

Source: UN National Accounts Main Aggregates Database.

BALANCE OF PAYMENTS
(LD million)

	2019	2020	2021
Exports of goods	40,640.2	12,942.9	145,982.4
Imports of goods	−24,791.4	−12,715.7	−76,646.5
Balance on goods	15,848.8	227.2	69,335.9
Exports of services	375.0	306.6	374.3
Imports of services	−10,688.0	−7,202.0	−38,190.4
Balance on goods and services	5,535.8	−6,668.2	31,519.8
Income (net)	2,558.5	1,164.1	−2,426.3
Balance on goods, services and income	8,094.3	−5,504.1	29,093.5
Current transfers (net)	−1,357.2	−1,140.5	−3,441.1
Current balance	6,737.1	−6,644.6	25,652.8
Direct investment (net)	376.5	−487.1	−1,706.8
Portfolio investment (net)	1,097.9	244.2	−4,126.3
Other investment (net)	−6,150.9	−6,466.3	−26,596.1
Net errors and omissions	−2,776.5	2,206.3	−2,610.3
Reserves and related items	−716.9	−11,147.2	−5,973.6

External Trade

PRINCIPAL COMMODITIES
(LD million)

Imports c.i.f.	2020	2021	2022
Live animals and animal products	1,018.9	3,906.3	3,853.4
Vegetables and vegetable products	1,156.0	5,559.1	6,132.8
Prepared foodstuffs; beverages, spirits, vinegar; tobacco and articles thereof	2,280.0	8,241.5	8,851.0
Mineral products	2,635.0	14,661.8	26,701.1
Chemicals and related products	1,328.3	6,113.6	5,794.4
Plastics, rubber, and articles thereof	715.1	3,448.3	3,925.9
Textiles and textile articles	1,028.5	3,739.6	4,124.9
Articles of stone, plaster, cement, asbestos; ceramic and glass products	446.0	2,195.6	2,328.5
Iron and steel, other base metals and articles of base metal	765.8	3,834.9	4,126.3
Machinery and mechanical appliances; electrical equipment; parts thereof	2,458.5	13,682.3	13,594.1
Vehicles, aircraft, vessels and associated transport equipment	1,215.0	4,940.8	4,920.8
Miscellaneous manufactured articles	740.5	3,055.5	3,830.3
Total (incl. others)	17,216.8	79,989.0	96,033.0

Exports f.o.b.*	2020	2021	2022
Mineral products	10,078.9	142,483.9	180,979.1
Chemicals and related products	20.6	935.7	1,089.0
Pearls, precious or semi-precious stones, precious metals, and articles thereof	2,306.3	1,073.9	1,320.7
Iron and steel, other base metals and articles of base metal	610.9	3,771.2	3,906.2
Total (incl. others)	13,127.6	148,589.7	187,996.5

*Including re-exports.

PRINCIPAL TRADING PARTNERS
(LD million)

Imports c.i.f.	2020	2021	2022
China, People's Republic	2,614.0	9,614.4	11,405.8
Cyprus	227.5	965.0	624.3
Egypt	796.2	3,595.6	3,364.1
France (incl. Monaco)	238.1	940.2	1,103.4
Germany	556.6	3,086.6	2,688.9
Greece	1,000.0	5,373.0	9,240.3
Italy	1,397.1	6,476.7	10,906.0
Korea, Republic	469.8	1,935.1	1,763.3
Netherlands	798.0	2,419.6	1,784.4
Spain	482.1	1,656.0	2,114.6
Tunisia	629.4	2,901.5	3,407.4
Türkiye	2,297.8	12,506.3	13,654.0
Ukraine	357.0	1,919.3	2,403.0
United Arab Emirates	1,412.4	7,706.4	8,650.6
USA	439.9	1,336.3	1,398.5
Total (incl. others)	17,216.8	79,989.0	96,033.0

LIBYA

Exports (incl. re-exports) f.o.b.	2020	2021	2022
China, People's Republic	1,128.7	14,773.8	14,097.6
France (incl. Monaco)	732.9	9,825.7	10,906.5
Germany	1,180.8	16,527.7	18,093.3
Greece	81.0	4,620.7	12,195.0
Italy	2,739.6	33,734.2	50,308.6
Netherlands	168.2	7,644.1	10,107.3
Singapore	275.2	773.1	961.2
Spain	980.2	15,476.9	19,043.3
Thailand	454.3	5,219.9	9,419.1
Türkiye	2,327.3	3,711.2	3,686.1
United Arab Emirates	1,350.1	4,318.1	4,325.3
United Kingdom	123.4	6,992.0	7,639.0
USA	312.6	10,114.3	10,793.1
Total (incl. others)	13,127.6	148,589.7	187,996.5

Transport

ROAD TRAFFIC
(new registrations of motor vehicles)

	2015
Passenger cars	243,019
Transportation vehicles	52,469
Motorcycles	222
Taxis	1,800
Buses	19
Tractors and trailers	26,657

SHIPPING
Flag Registered Fleet
(at 31 December)

	2020	2021	2022
Number of vessels	97	100	113
Total displacement ('000 grt)	910.7	911.6	958.3

Source: Lloyd's List Intelligence (www.bit.ly/LLintelligence).

CIVIL AVIATION
(traffic on scheduled services)

	2013	2014	2015
Kilometres flown (million)	39	41	39
Passengers carried ('000)	2,745	2,677	2,566
Passenger-km (million)	3,698	3,789	3,616
Total ton-km (million)	4	4	4

Source: UN, *Statistical Yearbook*.

2021 (domestic and international): Departures 9,046; Passengers carried 1.0m.; Freight carried 14m. ton-km (Source: World Bank, World Development Indicators database).

Tourism

VISITOR ARRIVALS*

Country of origin	2002	2003	2004
Algeria	70,416	71,657	73,459
Egypt	354,189	429,220	441,230
Morocco	19,076	19,120	20,803
Tunisia	329,145	346,331	366,871
Total (incl. others)	857,952	957,896	999,343

* Including same-day visitors (excursionists).

Tourism receipts (US $ million, excl. passenger transport): 85 in 2019; 28 in 2020.

Source: World Tourism Organization.

Communications Media
(ITU estimates)

	2019	2020	2021
Telephones ('000 main lines in use)	1,576.0	1,576.0	1,576.0
Mobile telephone subscriptions ('000)	3,718.0	2,922.0	2,922.0
Broadband subscriptions, fixed ('000)	318.0	332.0	332.0
Broadband subscriptions, mobile ('000)	1,453.0	1,142.0	1,142.0

Internet users (% of population): 21.8 in 2017.

Source: International Telecommunication Union.

Education
(2005/06 unless otherwise indicated)

	Teachers	Students
Pre-primary	2,486	22,246
Primary	148,476	755,338
Secondary	152,338	732,614
Tertiary*	15,711	375,028

* 2002/03.

Source: UNESCO Institute for Statistics.

Institutions: Primary and preparatory: general 2,733 (1993/94), vocational 168 (1995/96); Secondary: vocational 312 (1995/96); Universities 13 (1995/96).

2010/11 (public schools only): *Primary and Preparatory (General):* Institutions 3,245; Teachers 116,791; Students 951,636. *Secondary (General):* Institutions 785; Teachers 28,274; Students 169,993.

2014/15 (Universities): *Teaching assistants, staff and technicians:* 46,252; *Students enrolled:* 374,705; *Postgraduate students:* 13,132.

Adult literacy rate (UNESCO estimates): 91.4% (males 97.0%; females 85.8%) in 2015 (Source: UNESCO Institute for Statistics).

Directory

The Constitution

Following the capture of the capital, Tripoli, in August 2011 by forces loyal to the opposition National Transitional Council (NTC), all constitutional decrees approved during the rule of Muammar al-Qaddafi were suspended. A 37-article Constitutional Declaration had been published by the NTC on 3 August. The Declaration states that Libya is an independent democratic state, with Tripoli as its capital and Islam as its state religion. The country is to be organized as a multi-party democracy, with the principles of Islamic law (*Shari'a*) as the principal source of legislation. Under the terms of the Declaration, an interim government was to be installed no more than 30 days after the defeat of Qaddafi, and elections for a 200-member national assembly were to take place no more than 240 days after Qaddafi's ouster.

Elections to a 60-member body tasked with drafting a new, permanent constitution were held in February 2014. However, the de facto division of the country and resurgence of conflict from 2014 impeded the workings of the Constitution Drafting Assembly (CDA). It was not until July 2017 that the CDA formally approved, by more than a two-thirds' majority, a final draft constitution, which defined a presidential system of government, with considerable powers being assigned to the head of state and limited decentralization. As stipulated in the Constitutional Declaration, the draft constitution was to be put to a national referendum. In February 2018, however, the Tobruk-based House of Representatives (HoR) announced that it refused to recognize the Tripoli-based CDA, calling instead for the formation of a committee of experts to draw up a new charter based on the 1951 Constitution. As of April 2023 a national referendum on the CDA's draft constitution had yet to take place. In February 2022, meanwhile, the HoR (reportedly with the support of the High Council of State in Tripoli) approved an amendment to the 2011 Constitutional Declaration which would enable the formation of a 24-member committee to draw up a new draft constitution to replace the document proposed by the CDA.

The Government

PRESIDENCY COUNCIL

Presidency Council: Tripoli.
Chairman: MOHAMMAD YOUNES MENFI.
Vice-Chairmen: ABDULLAH AL-LAFI, MOSSA AL-KONI.

GOVERNMENT OF NATIONAL UNITY
(September 2023)

Prime Minister: ABDUL HAMID MOHAMMED DBEIBAH.
Deputy Prime Minister and Acting Minister of Agriculture and Livestock Resources: HUSSEIN ATIYA ABDUL HAFEEZ AL-QATRANI.
Deputy Prime Minister and Minister of Health: RAMADAN AHMED BOUJENAH.
Minister of Defence: held jointly by the three members of the Presidency Council.
Minister of Foreign Affairs and International Co-operation: (vacant).
Minister of the Interior: IMAD MUSTAFA TRABELSI.
Minister of Education: MOUSSA MUHAMMAD AL-MAGARIEF.
Minister of Labour and Rehabilitation and Acting Minister of Civil Service: ALI AL-ABED.
Minister of Culture and Knowledge Development: MABROUKA TOGHI.
Minister of Economy and Trade: MOHAMMED AL-HUWIJ.
Minister of Environment: IBRAHIM AL-ARABI MOUNIR.
Minister of Finance: KHALED AL-MABROUK ABDULLAH.
Minister of Higher Education and Scientific Research: IMRAN MUHAMMAD ABDUL NABI AL-QEEB.
Minister of Housing and Construction: ABUBAKER MOHAMED AL-GHAWI.
Minister of Industry and Minerals: AHMED ABUHISA.
Minister of Justice: HALIMA IBRAHIM ABDEL RAHMAN.
Minister of Local Government: BADR AL-DIN AL-SADIQ AL-TOUMI.
Minister of Oil and Gas: MUHAMMAD AHMAD MUHAMMAD AOUN.
Minister of Planning: MOHAMED AL-ZAIDANI.
Minister of Social Affairs: WAFAA ABU BAKR MUHAMMAD AL-KILANI.
Minister of Sports: ABDUL SHAFI' HUSSEIN MUHAMMAD AL-JUIFI.
Minister of Technical and Vocational Education: SAEED SIFAW.
Minister of Tourism and Handicrafts: ABD AL-SALAM ABDULLAH AL-LAHI TIKI.
Minister of Transportation: MUHAMMAD SALEM AL-SHAHOUBI.
Minister of Water Resources: TAREK BOUTEFLIKA.
Minister of Youth: FATHALLAH ABD AL-LATIF AL-ZANI.
Minister of State for Affairs of the Displaced and Human Rights: AHMED FARAJ MAHJOUB ABU KHUZAM.
Minister of State for Communication and Political Affairs: WALID AMMAR MUHAMMAD AMMAR AL-LAFI.
Minister of State for Economic Affairs: SALAMA IBRAHIM AL-GHWAIL.
Minister of State for Immigration Affairs: (vacant).
Minister of State for Prime Minister and Cabinet Affairs: ADEL JUMAA AMER.
Minister of State for Women's Affairs: HOURIA AL-TARMAL.

MINISTRIES

The internationally recognized Presidency Council and Government of National Unity (GNU) are both based in Tripoli. It was reported in April 2016 that the Presidency Council had taken control of several ministry buildings in the capital from the Libya Dawn alliance of militias. At that time, the headquarters of other ministries remained under the control of the 'Government of National Salvation' led by Khalifa al-Ghweil. Following its formation on 15 March 2021, the GNU was expected to take control of all ministries in Tripoli, pending the holding of legislative elections in December (which, in the event, did not take place).

Legislature

Elections to a new, 200-seat House of Representatives (HoR) were held on 25 June 2014, the results of which were confirmed by the High National Elections Commission on 22 July. Some 12 seats remained unallocated, owing to boycotts and the closure of polling stations following concerns over security. All 200 seats were reserved for individual candidates; none the less, it was thought that many of those contesting the elections were affiliated to political organizations. The new chamber was inaugurated on 4 August in Tobruk. The HoR was due to have its permanent base in Benghazi; however, the new legislature was unable to establish its operations there, owing to the intensification of conflict between Islamist militia groups and their opponents in that city.

On 6 November 2014 the Supreme Court ruled that the procedure under which the HoR had been created was illegal, and ordered the chamber's dissolution. The ruling was issued amid an ongoing dispute between the Tobruk-based HoR and the General National Congress (GNC), which remained in de facto operation in Tripoli under the direction of pro-Islamist groups. The mandate of the HoR formally expired on 20 October. However, it remained in place, amid UN-led discussions over the formation of a 'national unity' administration.

Members of the Tobruk and Tripoli parliaments signed the Libyan Political Agreement at a meeting in Skhirat, Morocco, on 17 December 2015. Under the terms of the Agreement, a High Council of State (HCS) was to be created as an upper, consultative chamber to the HoR in a bicameral legislature. In April 2016 the GNC announced its own dissolution and in September the HCS, comprising 70 former GNC members, took office in the capital.

House of Representatives (HoR): Tobruk.
President: AGEELA SALAH ISSA.
High Council of State (HCS): Tripoli; e-mail info@hcs.gov.ly; internet www.hcs.gov.ly.
President: MOHAMMED MOFTAH TAKALA.

Election Commission

High National Elections Commission: Sidi al-Masri, Tripoli; tel. (21) 3623512; e-mail info@hnec.ly; internet hnec.ly; f. 2013; Chair. IMAD AL-SAYEH.

Political Organizations

In 1971 the Arab Socialist Union (ASU) was established as the country's sole authorized political party. The General National Congress of the ASU held its first session in 1976 and later became the General People's Congress. Following the ouster of Muammar al-Qaddafi, a number of new political organizations were formed, the most prominent among which are listed below:

Central National Current: f. 2012.
Justice and Construction Party (JCP): Tripoli; tel. (21) 7154443; fax (21) 7154447; e-mail info@ab.ly; f. 2012; Leader IMAD AL-BANANI.
National Forces Alliance (NFA): Tripoli; tel. (21) 4782593; f. 2012; comprises 58 political parties; Leader KHALED AL-MARIMI.
National Front Party: al-Sikka Rd, Tripoli; tel. 8910023099; e-mail info@jabha.ly; internet www.jabha.ly; f. 2012; offshoot of National Front for the Salvation of Libya; Leader ABDULLAH AL-RAFADI.
Union for Homeland: Tripoli; tel. (21) 4445315; fax (21) 4443805; f. 2012; Leader ABDURRAHMAN SEWEHLI.
Wadi Al-Hayat Gathering: f. 2012.

Diplomatic Representation

EMBASSIES IN LIBYA

Afghanistan: POB 4245, Sharia Mozhar al-Aftes, Tripoli; tel. (21) 4841441; fax (21) 4841443; Ambassador (vacant).

LIBYA

Argentina: POB 932, Gargaresh, Madina Syahia, Tripoli; tel. (21) 916139817; fax (54) 572777; e-mail elbia@mrecic.gov.ar; internet elbia.cancilleria.gov.ar; currently operating from Tunis, Tunisia; Ambassador José Maria Arbilla.

Austria: POB 3207, Sharia Khalid bin al-Walid, Garden City, Tripoli; tel. (21) 4443379; fax (21) 4440838; e-mail tripolis-ob@bmeia.gv.at; internet www.bmeia.gv.at/tripolis; Ambassador Christoph Meyenburg.

Bangladesh: POB 5086, Hadba el-Khadra, Tripoli; tel. (21) 4911198; e-mail bdtripoli@yahoo.com; internet www.bangladeshembassylibya.com; Ambassador Abu al-Hasanat Muhammad Khair al-Bishr.

Bosnia and Herzegovina: POB 6946, Hasi Masoud, Siyahiya, Tripoli; tel. (21) 4844383; fax (21) 4844387; Ambassador Nermin Mešinović.

Brazil: POB 2270, Sharia Ben Ashour, Tripoli; tel. (21) 3614894; fax (21) 3614895; currently operating from Tunis, Tunisia; Ambassador Afonso Carbonar.

Bulgaria: POB 2945, Sharia Madinet el-Hadeek-Muhammad Farid, Dahra, Tripoli; tel. (21) 3346630; fax (21) 3346633; e-mail embassy.tripoli@mfa.bg; internet www.mfa.bg/embassies/libya; currently operating from Tunis, Tunisia; Chargé d'affaires Margarita Isaeva.

Burkina Faso: POB 81902, Route de Gargaresh, Tripoli; tel. (21) 4771221; fax (21) 4778037; e-mail ambafasolibye@yahoo.fr; Ambassador Ibrahim Taruari.

Canada: POB 93392, al-Fateh Tower Post Office, Tripoli; tel. (21) 3351633; fax (21) 3351630; e-mail trpli@international.gc.ca; internet www.canadainternational.gc.ca/libya-libye; currently operating from Tunis, Tunisia; Ambassador Isabelle Savard.

Chad: POB 1078, Sharia Muhammad Mussadeq 25, Tripoli; tel. (21) 4443955; Ambassador Daoussa Déby.

China, People's Republic: POB 5329, Sharia Menstir, Andalus, Gargaresh, Tripoli; tel. (21) 27167924; fax (21) 4831877; e-mail chinaemb_ly@mfa.gov.cn; internet ly.china-embassy.org; Chargé d'affaires Wang Qimin.

Czech Republic: POB 1097, Sharia Rewaifaa bin Thabet, Ben Ashour, Tripoli; tel. (21) 3615436; fax (21) 3615437; e-mail tripoli@embassy.mzv.cz; internet www.mzv.cz/tripoli; currently operating from Tunis, Tunisia; Ambassador Jan Vyčítal (concurrent ambassador to Tunisia).

Egypt: Sharia Omar el-Mokhtar, Tripoli; tel. and fax (21) 3345119; e-mail eg.emb_tripoli@mfa.gov.eg; Chargé d'affaires a.i. Tamer Mustafa.

Eritrea: POB 91279, Tripoli; tel. (21) 4773568; fax (21) 4780152; Ambassador Issa Ahmed Issa.

France: POB 312, Sharia Ben Khafaja, Hay Andalus, Tripoli; tel. (21) 4770452; fax (21) 4770450; internet www.ambafrance-ly.org; Ambassador Mostafa Mihraje.

Germany: POB 302, Palm City, Jansour, Tripoli; tel. (21) 4423930; fax (21) 4844564; e-mail info@tripolis.diplo.de; internet www.tripolis.diplo.de; Ambassador Michael Ohnmacht.

Ghana: Hay al Andalus, Tripoli; tel. (21) 4772534; e-mail tripoli@mfa.gov.gh; internet www.ghanaembassy-libya.com; Ambassador Marc Michael Antsi.

Greece: POB 5147, Sharia Jalal Bayar 18, Tripoli; tel. (21) 3336978; fax (21) 4441907; e-mail gremb.tri@mfa.gr; internet www.mfa.gr/tripoli; Chargé d'affaires Agapios Kalognomi.

Guinea: POB 10657, Hay Andalus, Tripoli; tel. (21) 4772793; fax (21) 4773441; e-mail embaguitp@yahoo.fr; Ambassador Abdul Aziz Soumah.

Hungary: POB 4010, Sharia Talha Ben Abdullah, Tripoli; tel. (21) 3618218; fax (21) 3618220; consular activities based in Tunis, Tunisia; Chargé d'affaires Gabriel Babb.

Indonesia: POB 5921, Amaama al-Saraaj, Tripoli; tel. (21) 5596366; e-mail tripoli.kbri@kemlu.go.id; internet kemlu.go.id/tripoli; Chargé d'affaires a.i. Dede Achmad Rifai.

Iran: POB 6185, Tripoli; tel. (21) 3609552; fax (21) 3611674; e-mail iran_em_tripoli@hotmail.com; Ambassador Mohammadreza Ra'ouf Sheybani.

Italy: POB 912, Sharia Vahran 1, Tripoli; tel. (21) 3334131; fax (21) 3331673; e-mail ambasciata.tripoli@esteri.it; internet www.ambtripoli.esteri.it; Ambassador Gianluca Alberini.

Japan: POB 3265, Sharia Jamal al-Din al-Waeli, Hay Andalus, Tripoli; tel. (21) 4781041; fax (21) 4781044; internet www.ly.emb-japan.go.jp; currently operating from Tunis, Tunisia; Chargé d'affaires Masaaki Amadera.

Korea, Democratic People's Republic: Tripoli; Ambassador Zoo Jin-Hyuk.

Korea, Republic: POB 4781, Abounawas Area, Sharia Gargaresh, Tripoli; tel. (21) 4831322; fax (21) 4831324; e-mail libya@mofa.go.kr; internet overseas.mofa.go.kr/ly-ko; currently operating from Tunis, Tunisia; Ambassador Lee Sang-Soo.

Kuwait: POB 2225, Beit al-Mal Beach, Tripoli; tel. (21) 4440281; fax (21) 607053; Ambassador Ziad al-Mashan.

Lebanon: POB 927, Malek Ben Auss, Al Noflyeen St, Tripoli; tel. (21) 3615744; fax (21) 3611740; e-mail emblebanon_ly@hotmail.com; Ambassador Muhammad Skeine.

Lesotho: POB 5771, Hay Andalus, Tripoli; tel. (21) 4840900; fax (21) 4840901; e-mail esothotripoli@yahoo.com; Ambassador (vacant).

Mali: POB 2008, Sharia Jaraba Saniet Zarrouk, Tripoli; tel. (21) 4444924; fax (21) 4844380; e-mail maliambatrp@yahoo.fr; Ambassador Amadou Toré.

Malta: POB 2534, Sharia al-Asbagh Ben Omar, Ben Achour, Tripoli; tel. (21) 3115882; fax (21) 3611180; e-mail maltaembassy.tripoli@gov.mt; internet foreign.gov.mt; Ambassador Charles Saliba.

Mauritania: POB 4664, Sharia Aïssa el-Wakwak, Tripoli; tel. (21) 4443223; fax (21) 4443223; Chargé d'affaires Athomar Ould Mohamed el-Amine.

Netherlands: POB 3801, Sharia Jalal Bayar 20, Dahra, Tripoli; tel. (21) 4441549; fax (21) 4440386; e-mail tri@minbuza.nl; internet libya.nlembassy.org; Ambassador Joost Clarenbeek.

Niger: POB 2251, Fachloun Area, Tripoli; tel. (21) 4443104; fax (21) 4781639; e-mail antripoli12@yahoo.fr; Ambassador Isid Kato.

Nigeria: POB 4417, Sharia Narjis, Hai al-Zuhoor, Tripoli; tel. (21) 4443036; e-mail nigeria@nigeriantripoli.org; internet tripoli.foreignaffairs.gov.ng; Chargé d'affaires Kabiru Musa.

Oman: Tripoli; tel. (21) 4772879; fax (21) 4773849; e-mail tripoli@mofa.gov.om; Ambassador Dr Qasim bin Muhammad bin Salem al-Salehi.

Pakistan: POB 2169, Sharia al-Jamei, Abu Zaid Dorda Area, Tripoli; tel. (21) 3610937; fax (21) 3600412; e-mail pareptripoli@gmail.com; internet www.mofa.gov.pk/libya; Ambassador Maj.-Gen. Rashad Javeed.

Philippines: POB 12508, Sharia Gargaresh, Km 7, Seyahiya, Tripoli; tel. (91) 8244208; e-mail tripoli.pe@dfa.gov.ph; internet tripolipe.dfa.gov.ph; Chargé d'affaires Dr Juan E. Dayang, Jr.

Poland: POB 519, Sharia Ben Ashour 61, Tripoli; tel. (21) 3608569; fax (21) 3615199; internet www.gov.pl/web/libya/embassy; Chargé d'affaires a.i. Dariusz Niderla.

Portugal: Zaid Bem Thabet, Sharia Ben Ashour, Tripoli; tel. (21) 3621352; fax (21) 3621351; Ambassador Nunu Belo.

Qatar: POB 6312, Libay, Tripoli; tel. (21) 3360300; fax (21) 3360310; e-mail tripoli@mofa.gov.qa; Ambassador Khalid Mohammed Zabin al-Zabin al-Dosari.

Romania: POB 5085, Sharia Ali bin Talib, Ben Ashour, Tripoli; tel. (71) 749-986; fax (71) 749-291; e-mail tripoli@mae.ro; internet tripoli.mae.ro; Ambassador Nicolae Marin.

Russian Federation: POB 4792, 10 Sharia Mustapha Kamel, Tripoli; tel. (21) 3330545; fax (21) 4446673; e-mail embr@mail.ru; Ambassador Aydar Aghanin.

Senegal: POB 6392, el-Arabia Gotchalle 246/5, Gargaresh, Tripoli; tel. (21) 4836090; fax (21) 4838955; Chargé d'affaires a.i. Baboucar Sambe.

Serbia: POB 1087, Abdalla Ben Salam St, Ben Achour, Tripoli; tel. (21) 3623205; fax (21) 3623207; e-mail serbianembassy_tripoli@yahoo.com; internet www.tripoli.mfa.gov.rs; Chargé d'affaires Gradimir Gajić.

Sierra Leone: Tripoli; Ambassador Al-Haji Abubakarr Jalloh.

Somalia: POB 4512, Tripoli; tel. (21) 4781368; fax (21) 4747764; e-mail tripoliembassy@mfa.gov.so; internet www.fb.com/SomaliainLibya.

Spain: POB 23302, Sharia al-Hawana, Ben Achour, Tripoli; tel. (21) 3620051; fax (21) 3620061; e-mail emb.tripoli@maec.es; internet www.maec.es/embajadas/tripoli; Ambassador Francisco Javier García-Larrache.

Sudan: POB 1076, Sharia Gargaresh, Tripoli; tel. (21) 4775387; fax (21) 4774781; e-mail sudtripoli2005@yahoo.com; Ambassador Ibrahim Mohammed Ibrahim.

Switzerland: POB 439, Sharia el-Moussawer Ben Maghzamah, off Sharia Ben Ashour, Tripoli; tel. (21) 3614118; fax (21) 3614238; e-mail tripoli@eda.admin.ch; internet www.eda.admin.ch/tripoli; temporarily closed since end of July 2014; Ambassador Josef Renggli.

Tunisia: POB 613, Sharia el-Bashir Ibrahimi, Medinat el-Hadaik, Tripoli; tel. (21) 3331051; fax (21) 4447600; Ambassador Al Asad al-Ajili.

Türkiye (Turkey): POB 947, Sharia Zaviya Dahmani, Tripoli; tel. (21) 3401140; fax (21) 3401146; e-mail embassy.tripoli@mfa.gov.tr; internet tripoli.emb.mfa.gov.tr; Ambassador Kenan Yilmaz.

LIBYA

Ukraine: POB 4544, Sharia Dhil, Ben Ashour, Tripoli; tel. 94127342; e-mail emb_ly@mfa.gov.ua; internet libya.mfa.gov.ua; presence in Libya suspended; currently operating from Tunis, Tunisia; Ambassador VOLODYMYR A. KHOMANETS (concurrent ambassador to Tunisia).

United Arab Emirates: Sharia Gargaresh, Tripoli; e-mail tripoli@mfa.gov.ae; Ambassador MOHAMMED ALI AL-SHAMSI.

United Kingdom: Tripoli; tel. (71) 108-700 (preceded by int. dialling code for Tunisia); e-mail britishembassy.tripoli@fcdo.gov.uk; internet www.gov.uk/world/libya; presence in Libya suspended in 2014; currently operating from Tunis, Tunisia; Ambassador CAROLINE HURNDALL.

USA: Sidi Slim Area, Sharia Wali al-Ahed, Tripoli; e-mail tripolipao@state.gov; internet ly.usembassy.gov; presence in Libya suspended in 2014; currently operating from Tunis, Tunisia; Chargé d'affaires LESLIE ORDEMAN.

Venezuela: POB 2584, Sharia Ben Ashour, Jamaa al-Sagaa Bridge, Tripoli; tel. (21) 3600408; fax (21) 3600407; e-mail embavenezlibia@hotmail.com; Ambassador CARLOS FEO ACEVEDO.

Viet Nam: POB 587, Sharia Gargaresh, Tripoli; tel. (21) 4901456; fax (21) 4901499; e-mail dsqvnlib@gmail.com; concurrent ambassador to Egypt; Ambassador NGUYEN HUY DUNG.

Yemen: POB 4839, Sharia Ubei Ben Ka'ab 36, Tripoli; tel. (21) 376533; fax (21) 376532; e-mail yementripoli@mfa.gov.ye; currently operating from Tunis, Tunisia; Ambassador HASSAN AL-HARD.

Judicial System

The Judicial Organization Law promulgated in 1973, under the rule of Muammar al-Qaddafi, was still largely in place at mid-2019. The legislation created a court system comprising, in order of seniority, of the Supreme Court, Courts of Appeal, and Courts of First Instance and Summary Courts.

Supreme Judicial Council: Tripoli; comprises 13 members; supervises work of the judicial bodies; studies and proposes laws related to judicial systems; Chair. MUFTAH AL-QAWI.

Supreme Court: The judgments of the Supreme Court are final. It is composed of the President and several Justices. Its judgments are issued by circuits of at least three Justices (the quorum is three). The Court hears appeals from the Courts of Appeal in civil, penal, administrative and civil status matters; Pres. ABDULLAH ABU RAZIZAH.

Courts of Appeal: These courts settle appeals from Courts of First Instance; the quorum is three Justices. Each court of appeal has a Court of Assize.

Courts of First Instance and Summary Courts: These courts are first-stage courts in the Jamahiriya, and the cases heard in them are heard by one judge. Appeals against summary judgments are heard by the appellate court attached to the Court of First Instance, the quorum of which is three judges.

Attorney-General: SIDDIQ AL-SOUR.

Religion

ISLAM

The vast majority of Libyan Arabs follow Sunni Muslim rites.

Grand Mufti of Libya: Sheikh SADEQ AL-GHARIANI.

CHRISTIANITY

The Roman Catholic Church

Libya comprises three Apostolic Vicariates and one Apostolic Prefecture.

Apostolic Vicariate of Benghazi: POB 248, Benghazi; tel. and fax (61) 9081599; e-mail apostvicar@yahoo.com; Vicar Apostolic Mgr SANDRO OVEREND RIGILLO.

Apostolic Vicariate of Tripoli: POB 365, Dahra, Tripoli; tel. (21) 8927715; e-mail bishoptripolibya@hotmail.com; internet www.catholicinlibya.com; Vicar Apostolic Mgr GEORGE BUGEJA (Titular Bishop of San Leone).

The Anglican Communion

Within the Episcopal Church in Jerusalem and the Middle East, Libya forms part of the diocese of Egypt (q.v.).

Other Christian Churches

The Coptic Orthodox Church is represented in Libya.

The Press

DAILIES

Al-Fajr al-Jadid (The New Dawn): POB 91291, Press Bldg, Sharia al-Jamahiriya, Tripoli; tel. (21) 3606393; fax (21) 3605728; e-mail info@alfajraljadeed.com; f. 1969; also publishes bimonthly English version; Editor AOUN ABDULLAH MADI.

Al-Jamahiriya: POB 4814, Tripoli; tel. (21) 3605731; f. 1980; Arabic; political.

Al-Shams: POB 82331, Al-Sahafa Bldg, Sharia al-Jamahiriya, Tripoli; tel. (21) 4442524; fax (21) 609315; e-mail info@alshames.com; Editor MUHAMMAD M. IBRAHIM.

Az-Zahf al-Akhdar (The Green March): POB 14273, Al-Sahafa Bldg, Sharia al-Jamahiriya, Tripoli; tel. (21) 4776890; fax (21) 4772502; f. 1980; Editor-in-Chief HAMID ABU SALIM.

PERIODICALS

Al-Amal (Hope): POB 4845, Tripoli; monthly; social, for children; publ. by the Press Service.

Al-Daawa al-Islamia (Islamic Call): POB 2682, Sharia Sawani, Km 5, Tripoli; tel. (21) 4800294; fax (21) 4800293; f. 1980; weekly (Wed.); Arabic, English, French; cultural; publ. by the World Islamic Call Society; Eds MUHAMMAD IMHEMED AL-BALOUSHI, ABDULAHI MUHAMMAD ABD AL-JALEEL.

Economic Bulletin: POB 2303, Tripoli; tel. (21) 4773901; e-mail ecorestat@cbl.gov.ly; monthly; publ. by JANA.

Al-Jarida al-Rasmiya (The Official Newspaper): Tripoli; irregular; official state gazette.

Libyan Arab Republic Gazette: Tripoli; weekly; English.

Risalat al-Jihad (Holy War Letter): POB 2682, Tripoli; tel. (21) 3331021; f. 1983; monthly; Arabic, English, French; publ. by the World Islamic Call Society.

Scientific Bulletin: POB 2303, Tripoli; tel. (21) 3337106; monthly.

Al-Thaqafa al-Arabiya (Arab Culture): POB 4587, Tripoli; f. 1973; weekly; cultural; circ. 25,000.

Al-Usbu al-Thaqafi (The Cultural Week): POB 4845, Tripoli; weekly.

Al-Watan al-Arabi al-Kabir (The Greater Arab Homeland): Tripoli; f. 1987.

Publishers

Al-Dar al-Arabia Lilkitab (Maison Arabe du Livre): POB 3185, Tripoli; tel. (21) 4447287; f. 1973 by Libya and Tunisia.

Al-Dar al-Hikma Publishing House: Tripoli; tel. (21) 3606571; fax (21) 3606610.

Al-Fatah University, General Administration of Libraries, Printing and Publications: POB 13543, Tripoli; tel. (21) 4628034; fax (21) 4625045; f. 1955; academic books.

General Co for Publishing, Advertising and Distribution: POB 921, Sirte (Surt); tel. (54) 63170; fax (54) 62100; general, educational and academic books in Arabic and other languages; makes and distributes advertisements throughout Libya.

Ghouma Publishing: POB 80092, Tripoli; tel. (21) 3630864; e-mail ghoumapub@hotmail.com; f. 1993; book publishing, distribution and art production; Gen. Man. MUSTAFA FETOURI.

Broadcasting and Communications

TELECOMMUNICATIONS

Libya Post, Telecommunications and Information Technology Co (LPTIC): Bab Tajoura, al-Nawflin, Tripoli; tel. (21) 7131939; fax (21) 5800549; e-mail info@lptic.ly; internet lptic.ly; f. 2005; holding co for state-owned entities in telecommunications and information technology sector; subsidiaries include Libyana Mobile Phone Co, Al-Madar Al-Jadeed (mobile telecommunications operators), and Libya Telecom and Technology; Chair. MUHAMMAD BIN AYYAD.

Hatif Libya Co (HLC): Tripoli; tel. (21) 3622104; fax (21) 3622102; e-mail info@hlc.ly; internet hlc.ly; f. 2008 to operate and maintain the national fixed-line telephone network; also internet service provider.

Libyana Mobile Phone Co: POB 90071, Tripoli; tel. (21) 3406555; internet www.libyana.ly; f. 2004.

The Libyan International Telecom Co: Tripoli; tel. (21) 3660366; e-mail info@litc.ly; internet litc.ly; f. 2009.

LIBYA

Libya Telecom & Technology: Abu Seta, near al-Furusia, Sharia al-Shutt, Tripoli; tel. (21) 3400020; e-mail support@ltt.ly; internet www.ltt.ly; f. 1997.

Al-Madar Al-Jadeed: POB 83792, Tripoli; tel. 919190500; fax 919190537; e-mail info@almadar.ly; internet www.almadar.ly; f. 1997; mobile telecommunications network operator; CEO ABDUL KHALEK ASHOUR.

REGULATORY AUTHORITY

General Authority for Communications and Informatics: POB 81686, Tripoli; tel. (21) 3619811; fax (21) 3622452; e-mail info@cim.gov.ly; internet cim.gov.ly; Chair. ABDUL BASIT AL-BAOUR (acting).

BROADCASTING
Radio

Libya Radio and Television Network: POB 80237, Tripoli; tel. (21) 3402107; fax (21) 3403468; e-mail info@en.ljbc.net; f. 2011 as successor to the Great socialist People's Libyan Arab Jamahiriya Broadcasting Corpn (f. 1968); broadcasts in Arabic.

Voice of Africa: POB 4677, Sharia al-Fateh, Tripoli; tel. (21) 4449209; fax (21) 4449875; f. 1973 as Voice of the Greater Arab Homeland; adopted current name 1998; broadcasts in Arabic, French, English, Swahili and Hausa; Dir-Gen. ABDULLAH AL-MEGRI.

Television

People's Revolution Broadcasting TV: POB 80237, Tripoli; tel. (21) 3402107; fax (21) 3403468; e-mail info@en.ljbc.net; internet www.ljbc.net; f. 1957; broadcasts in Arabic; additional satellite channels broadcast for limited hours in English; Dir ABDULLAH MANSOUR.

Finance
BANKING
Central Bank

Central Bank of Libya (CBL): POB 1103, Sharia al-Malik Seoud, Tripoli; tel. (21) 3333591; fax (21) 4902148; e-mail website.dep@cbl.gov.ly; internet www.cbl.gov.ly; f. 1955 as National Bank of Libya; name changed to Bank of Libya 1963, to Central Bank of Libya 1977; state-owned; bank of issue and central bank carrying govt accounts and operating exchange control; commercial operations transferred to Nat. Commercial Bank 1970; Gov. and Chair. SADDEK OMAR ALI ELKABER.

Other Banks

Alwafa Bank: POB 84212, Sharia Alfallah, Tripoli; tel. (21) 4845351; fax (21) 4845352; e-mail info@alwafabank.com; internet www.alwafabank.com; f. 2003; private bank; Chair. AHMED ASHTEIWI MOHAMMED.

Alwaha Bank: Bab Tajoura, Tripoli; tel. (21) 3513490; fax (21) 3513491; e-mail info@alwahabank.com; internet alwahabank.ly; f. 2005; 80% owned by Banque Sahélo-Saharienne pour l'Investissement et le Commerce, and 20% by Libyan Investment and Development Fund; Dir-Gen. SALEM AL-TARJMANI.

Banque Sahélo-Saharienne pour l'Investissement et le Commerce (BSIC): POB 93221, Tripoli; tel. (21) 4842150; fax (21) 4842152; internet bsicbank.com; f. 1999 as an organ of the Community of Sahel-Saharan States; Chair. and Gen. Man. ALI OMAR AL-MOKTAR.

Jumhouria Bank: POB 685, Sharia Omar el-Mokhtar, Tripoli; tel. (21) 3334031; fax (21) 4442476; e-mail info@jbank.ly; internet www.jbank.ly; f. 1969 as successor to Barclays Bank International in Libya; originally known as Masraf al-Gumhouria; present name adopted 2000; merger with Umma Bank SAL completed 2008; Chair. Dr KHALID AL-MABROUK ABDULLAH; Gen. Man. ABDUL RAZZAQ AL-TARHOUNI.

Libyan Foreign Bank: POB 2542, Tower 2, Dat al-Imad Complex, Tripoli; tel. (21) 3350160; fax (21) 3350169; e-mail info@lafbank.com; internet www.lfb.ly; f. 1972 as Libyan Arab Foreign Bank; present name adopted 2005; offshore bank wholly owned by Central Bank of Libya; Chair. MOHAMMED ALI ADDARRAT; Gen. Man. KHALED AMR ALGONSEL.

National Commercial Bank SAL: POB 543, Aruba Ave, al-Bayda; tel. (21) 3345542; fax (21) 3345455; e-mail ncb.hq@ncb.ly; internet www.ncb.ly; f. 1970 to take over commercial banking division of Central Bank (then Bank of Libya) and brs of Aruba Bank and Istiklal Bank; 74% owned by Central Bank; Chair. ABDUL WAHAB AHMED AL-MUKHTAR; Gen. Man. AL-SEDIG MOHAMED KHANFAR.

Sahara Bank SPI: POB 70, Sharia 1 September, Tripoli; tel. (21) 3340663; fax (21) 4443836; internet saharabank.ly; f. 1964 to take over br. of Banco di Sicilia; the Govt sold a 19% stake to BNP Paribas (France) 2007; Chair. and Gen. Man. Prof. MUHAMMAD ABU KHUDAIR; CEO ABUBAKER AL-WADAN.

Wahda Bank: POB 452, Sharia Gamal Abd al-Nasser, Benghazi; tel. 2224256; e-mail wahda@wahdabank.com; internet www.wahdabank.com.ly; f. 1970 to take over Bank of North Africa, Commercial Bank SAL, Nahda Arabia Bank, Société Africaine de Banque SAL, and Kafila al-Ahly Bank; 19% stake acquired by Arab Bank PLC (Jordan) 2008; remainder owned by Central Bank of Libya; Chair. ABDUL KARIM MUHAMMAD AL-SHAHATI; Gen. Man. MAREI MOFTAH AL-BARASI (acting).

SOVEREIGN WEALTH FUND

Libyan Investment Authority (LIA): Omar bin al-Khattab St, Abu Nuwas, Qaraqarsh, Tripoli; tel. (21) 4843505; e-mail info@lia.ly; internet www.lia.ly; f. 2006, operations commenced 2007; sovereign wealth fund managing state-allocated assets, including Oil Reserve Fund; Chair. Dr ALI MAHMOUD HASSAN.

STOCK EXCHANGE

Libyan Stock Market: Sharia Omar el-Mokhtar, Tripoli; tel. (21) 3365026; fax (61) 9091097; e-mail info@lsm.gov.ly; internet www.lsm.ly; f. 2007.

INSURANCE

Libya Insurance Co: POB 80087, Aman Bldg, Sharia Sanaa, Tripoli; tel. (21) 4444150; fax (21) 4444176; internet libtamin.ly; f. 1964; merged with Al-Mukhtar Insurance Co in 1981; all classes of insurance; Chair. HAFEZ MOHAMMED OMRAN; Man. Dir AHMED MOHAMMAD ENKISSA.

Trade and Industry
GOVERNMENT AGENCIES

Council for Oil and Gas Affairs: f. 2006; holds ultimate responsibility for all matters involving oil, gas and their by-products; Chair. AL-MABROOK BUSEIF.

Great Man-made River Water Utilization Authority (GMRA): POB 7217, Benghazi; tel. (61) 2230392; fax (61) 2230393; internet www.gmrwua.com; supervises construction of pipeline carrying water to the Libyan coast from beneath the Sahara desert, to provide irrigation for agricultural projects; Sec. for the Great Man-made River Project ABD AL-MAJID AL-AOUD.

National Economic and Social Development Board (NEDB): Tripoli; tel. 210000000; e-mail info@nesdb.ly; internet www.nesdb.ly; f. 2007; charged with the drafting and execution of reform campaigns, and the facilitation of decision-making and action on critical economic issues; Pres. ABDUL HAMID MOHAMMED DBEIBAH (Prime Minister).

DEVELOPMENT ORGANIZATIONS

Arab Organization for Agricultural Development: POB 12898, Zohra, TripoliPOB 474, 7 Amarat St, Khartoum; tel. and fax (21) 3471374; e-mail info@aoad.org; internet www.aoad.org; f. 1972; responsible for agricultural devt projects; Gen. Dir IBRAHIM ELDUKHERI.

General National Organization for Industrialization: Sharia San'a, Tripoli; tel. (21) 3334995; f. 1970; public org. responsible for the devt of industry.

Kufra and Sarir Authority: Council of Agricultural Development, Benghazi; f. 1972 to develop the Kufra oasis and Sarir area in south-eastern Libya.

CHAMBERS OF COMMERCE

Benghazi Chamber of Commerce, Trade, Industry and Agriculture: POB 208 and 1286, Benghazi; tel. (61) 3372319; fax (61) 3380761; internet bencci.com; f. 1956; Pres. Dr BADIA; Gen. Man. Dr TAREK TARBAGHIA; 150,000 mems.

Tripoli Chamber of Commerce and Industry: POB 2321, Sharia Najed 6–8, Tripoli; tel. (21) 3336855; fax (21) 3332655; f. 1952; Chair. MUHAMMAD KANOON; Dir-Gen. ABD AL-MONEM H. BURAWI; 30,000 mems.

UTILITIES

Electricity

General Electricity Co of Libya (GECOL): POB 668, Tripoli; tel. (21) 4800956; e-mail gecol@gecol.ly; internet www.gecol.ly; Dir-Gen. Mohammed Ismaiel.

STATE HYDROCARBONS COMPANIES

Since March 2000, the National Oil Corporation has been responsible for Libya's oil policy.

National Oil Corpn (NOC): POB 2655, Sharia Assekka, Tripoli; tel. (21) 4446181; fax (21) 4446181; internet noc.ly; f. 1970 to: undertake jt ventures with foreign cos; build and operate refineries, storage tanks, petrochemical facilities, pipelines and tankers; take part in arranging specifications for local and imported petroleum products; participate in general planning of oil installations in Libya; market crude and refined petroleum and petrochemical products; and establish and operate oil terminals; Chair. Farhat Omar Bengdara.

Arabian Gulf Oil Co (AGOCO): POB 263, Benghazi; tel. (61) 28931; fax (22) 29006; internet agoco.ly; wholly owned subsidiary of the NOC; Chair. Salah al-Qatrani.

Azzawiya Oil Refining Co (ARC): POB 6451, Tripoli; tel. (21) 3610539; fax (21) 3610538; e-mail info@arc.com.ly; internet arc.com.ly; f. 1976; Chair. Sadiq Muhammad al-Jurmi.

Brega Oil Marketing Co: POB 402, Tripoli; tel. (21) 4803015; f. 1971; Chair. Ibrahim Boubreedia.

National Oil Wells Drilling and Workover Co: POB 1106, Tripoli; tel. (21) 3368740; fax (21) 4446743; e-mail info@nwd.ly; internet nwd.ly; f. 1986; Chair. Mahmud Abusrewil.

Ras Lanouf Oil and Gas Processing Co (RASCO): POB 1971, Ras Lanouf, Benghazi; tel. (21) 3605177; fax (21) 3605174; f. 1978.

Sirte Oil Co: POB 385, Marsa el-Brega, Tripoli; tel. (21) 361037690; fax (21) 4800937; e-mail info@sirteoil.com.ly; internet www.sirteoil.com.ly; f. 1955 as Esso Standard Libya, taken over by Sirte Oil Co 1982; absorbed National Petrochemicals Co in Oct. 1990; exploration, production of crude petroleum, gas and petrochemicals, liquefaction of natural gas; Chair. Massoud Suleiman.

Waha Oil Co: POB 395, Tripoli; tel. (21) 3601122; e-mail info@wahaoil.net; internet www.wahaoil.ly; Chair. Ahmed Ammar.

Zueitina Oil Co (ZOC): POB 2134, Tripoli; tel. (21) 4440956; fax (21) 3339109; e-mail info@zueitina.com; internet zueitina.com.ly; f. 1986.

TRADE UNION

General Federation of Producers' Trade Unions: POB 734, Sharia Istanbul 2, Tripoli; tel. (21) 4446011; f. 1952; Sec.-Gen. Bashir Ihwij; 17 trade unions with 700,000 mems.

General Union for Oil and Petrochemicals: Tripoli; Chair. Muhammad Mithnani.

Pan-African Federation of Petroleum Energy and Allied Workers: Tripoli; affiliated to the Organisation of African Trade Union Unity.

Transport

RAILWAYS

There are, at present, no railways in Libya. In 1998 the Government invited bids for the construction of a 3,170-km railway system, comprising one branch, 2,178 km in length, running from east to west along the north coast (between Emsaed on the Egyptian border and Ras Ajdir on the Tunisian border), and another branch, 992 km in length, running from north to south (between Sirte and Sabha). Construction of the railway commenced in 2008, but following the onset of civil conflict in 2011, the project was reported to have been halted. As of mid-2023 it appeared unlikely that work on the proposed network would be resumed in the near future, owing to continuing instability in Libya.

Railway Executive Board: POB 82376, Swani Rd, Tripoli; tel. and fax (21) 4801401; e-mail railwayslibya@lttnet.net; oversees the planning and construction of railways; Chair. Ali Rashaida.

ROADS

The most important road is the 1,822-km national coast road from the Tunisian border to the Egyptian border, passing through Tripoli and Benghazi. Another national road runs from Abu Qurayn, on the coastal road 120 km south of Misurata, through Sabha to Ghat near the Algerian border (total length 1,250 km). A 690-km road, connecting Tripoli and Sabha, and another of 626 km in length, from Ajdabiya in the north to Kufra in the south-east, were opened in 1983. There are roads crossing the desert from Sabha to the frontiers of Chad and Niger. As part of a wide-ranging agreement signed by Libya and Italy in 2008, the latter agreed to fund construction of a new, 1,700-km coastal highway between Libya's Tunisian and Egyptian borders. Construction work on the project commenced in 2009. Following lengthy delays owing to the outbreak of civil war in Libya in 2011, it was announced in December 2020 that work would be resumed in the first quarter of 2021. In November 2022 it was reported that Italy was inviting tenders for the project.

SHIPPING

The principal ports are Tripoli, Benghazi, Marsa Brega, Misurata and al-Sider. Zueitina, Ras Lanouf, Marsa al-Hariga, Marsa Brega and al-Sider are predominantly oil ports. A pipeline connects the Zelten oilfields with Marsa Brega. Another pipeline joins the Sarir oilfield with Marsa al-Hariga, and the port of Tobruk, and there is a pipeline from the Sarir field to Zueitina. A small port has been developed at Darna, and plans are under way for the expansion of the port of Sirte. Libya also has the use of Tunisian port facilities at Sand Gabès, to alleviate congestion at Tripoli. In January 2019 it was announced that the Government of National Accord in Tripoli and the House of Representatives in the east had reached agreement jointly to support the construction of a deep-sea port near the north-eastern town of Susah, which, upon completion, would be one of the largest in North Africa. In May a contract was signed with the Guidry Group of the USA to develop the port, which was to include a logistics facility integrated with a free trade zone, at an estimated cost of US $1,500m.

Principal Shipping Companies

General National Maritime Transport Co (GNMTC): POB 80173, el-Shaab Terminal, Tripoli; tel. and fax (21) 4843324; e-mail info@gnmtc.com; internet www.gnmtc.com; f. 1975 to handle all projects dealing with maritime trade; state-owned; Chair. Capt. Ali Belhag Ahmed.

Libya Shipping Agency: POB 4288, Abu Seta area, nr Abokmisha Mosque, Tripoli; tel. (21) 3402528; fax (21) 3403496; e-mail info@libyashipping.com; internet www.libyashipping.com; provides chartering, land transportation and customs clearance services; Gen. Man. Imad Fellah.

CIVIL AVIATION

Following the ousting from power of Muammar al-Qaddafi in 2011, it was reported that Tripoli International Airport had incurred severe damage. During 2012–18 the airport suffered intermittent closures amid conflict between various factions competing for control of the country, and most international and domestic flights were transferred to Mitiga International Airport, located some 8 km to the east of central Tripoli. Benina International Airport, situated 19 km (12 miles) from Benghazi, reopened in 2017, having been closed for some three years due to the ongoing conflict.

Civil Aviation Authority: POB 14399, Imam Malek St, Althahra, Tripoli; tel. (21) 3330256; fax (21) 3605322; e-mail info@caa.gov.ly; internet www.caa.gov.ly; f. 1954; Dir-Gen. Dr Mohamed Shlebic.

Afriqiyah Airways: POB 83428, Alnassar St, Tripoli; tel. (21) 4442622; fax (21) 4449128; e-mail customerservices@afriqiyah.aero; internet www.afriqiyah.aero; f. 2001; state-owned; flights to 8 destinations in Africa, Asia, Europe and the Middle East; Chair. Mustafa Maatouq.

Buraq Air: Mitiga International Airport, Tripoli; tel. (21) 3509807; e-mail info@buraq.aero; internet www.buraq.aero; f. 2001; first privately-owned Libyan airline; scheduled international passenger and cargo flights to Egypt, Morocco, the Syrian Arab Republic and Türkiye (Turkey); domestic flights from Tripoli, Benghazi and Sabha; Chair. and Man. Dir Capt. Muhammad A. Bubeida.

Libyan Airlines: POB 2555, Ben Fernas Bldg, Sharia Haiti, Tripoli; tel. (21) 3614102; fax (21) 3614815; internet www.libyanairlines.aero; f. 1964 as Kingdom of Libya Airlines; reorg. in 1975 as Libyan Arab Airline; present name adopted 2006; passenger and cargo services from Tripoli, Benghazi and Sabha to destinations in Europe, North Africa, the Middle East and Asia; domestic services throughout Libya; Chair. Abdelati el-Meshkhi.

Tourism

General Authority for Tourism: Tripoli; Pres. Khaider Malik.

General Board of Fairs: POB 891, Sharia Omar Mukhtar, Tripoli; tel. (21) 3365115; e-mail info@libyafairs.com; internet www.libyafairs.com; Head of Fairs Gamal N. A. al-Amoushi.

Defence

The Libyan National Army (LNA) was founded in 2011 by the National Transitional Council after the overthrow of Muammar al-Qaddafi. However, following the formation of the Government of National Accord (GNA) in early 2016, the LNA's Chief of Staff, Gen. (now Field Marshal) Khalifa Haftar, remained loyal to the Tobruk-based House of Representatives and the administration led by Abdullah al-Thani. (Under the terms of the Libyan Political Agreement, signed in December 2015, the Tripoli-based Presidency Council was to act as the collective Commander-in-Chief of the Armed Forces.) As assessed at November 2013, the LNA's total strength was just 7,000. After the formation of the interim Government of National Unity (GNU) in March 2021 the GNA transferred power to the new administration. The extent of the forces loyal to the GNU was unknown at November 2022. There were also a significant number of independent militia groups operating in the country at that time. The personnel listed below are those of the GNU:

Estimated Defence Expenditure: LD 6,000m. in 2013.

Chief of Staff of Ground Forces: Maj.-Gen. MOHAMMED AL-HADDAD.

Commander of Air Force: Maj.-Gen. AMHIMMID QOUJEEL.

Commander of Navy, Coast Guard and Port Security: Cdre SHUAIB AL-SABER.

Education

Education is officially compulsory for nine years between six and 15 years of age. Primary education begins at the age of six and lasts for nine years. Secondary education, beginning at 15 years of age, lasts for a further three or four years. Libya also has institutes for agricultural, technical and vocational training.

In 1958 the University of Libya opened in Benghazi with Faculties of Arts and Commerce, followed the next year by the Faculty of Science, near Tripoli. Faculties of Law, Agriculture, Engineering, Teacher Training, and Arabic Language and Islamic Studies have since been added to the University. In 1973 the University was divided into two parts, to form the Universities of Tripoli and Benghazi, later renamed Al-Fateh and Ghar Younis universities. The Faculty of Education at Al-Fateh University became Sabha University in 1983. There is a University of Technology (Bright Star) at Mersa Brega and the Al-Arab Medical University at Benghazi. The Government's budget for 2012 allocated LD 4,600m. (equivalent to 6.7% of total spending) to the Ministry of Education.

Bibliography

Ahmida, Ali Abd al-Latif. *Forgotten Voices: Power and Agency in Colonial and Postcolonial Libya*. London, Routledge, revised edn, 2005.

The Making of Modern Libya: State Formation, Colonization and Resistance. Albany, NY, State University of New York Press, 2nd edn, 2011.

Allan, J. A. *Libya since Independence: Economic and Political Development (RLE Economy of Middle East)*. Abingdon, Routledge, 2014.

Libya: The Experience of Oil. Abingdon, Routledge, 2022.

Anderson, Lisa. *The State and Social Transformation in Tunisia and Libya: 1830-1980*. Princeton, NJ, Princeton University Press, 2014.

Baldinetti, Anna. *The Origins of the Libyan Nation: Colonial Legacy, Exile and the Emergence of a New Nation-State*. Abingdon, Routledge, 2009.

Bowen, Wyn Q. *Libya and Nuclear Proliferation: Stepping Back from the Brink*. Abingdon, Routledge, 2006.

Bradley, Megan, Fraihat, Ibrahim, and Mzioudet, Houda. *Libya's Displacement Crisis: Uprooted by Revolution and Civil War* (Georgetown Digital Shorts). Washington, DC, Georgetown University Press, 2016.

Chivvis, Christopher S. *Toppling Qaddafi: Libya and the Limits of Liberal Intervention*. New York, Cambridge University Press, 2014.

Chorin, Ethan. *Exit the Colonel: The Hidden History of the Libyan Revolution*. New York, PublicAffairs, 2012.

Cole, Peter, and McQuinn, Brian. *The Libyan Revolution and its Aftermath*. New York, NY, Oxford University Press, 2016.

Craig Harris, Lillian. *Libya: Qadhafi's Revolution and the Modern State*. Abingdon, Routledge, 2022.

De Bona, Giacomina. *Human Rights in Libya: The Impact of International Society Since 1969*. Abingdon, Routledge, 2012.

Deeb, Mary-Jane. *Libya's Foreign Policy in North Africa*. Boulder, CO, Westview Press, 1991.

Engelbrekt, Kjell, Mohlin, Marcus, and Wagnsson, Charlotte. *The NATO Intervention in Libya: Lessons Learned from the Campaign*. Abingdon, Routledge, 2014.

Erdağ, Ramazan. *Libya in the Arab Spring: From Revolution to Insecurity*. New York, Palgrave Macmillan, 2017.

Fraihat, Ibrahim. *Unfinished Revolutions: Yemen, Libya, and Tunisia after the Arab Spring*. New Haven, CT, Yale University Press, 2016.

Geha, Carmen. *Civil Society and Political Reform in Lebanon and Libya: Transition and Constraint*. Abingdon, Routledge, 2016.

Gurney, Judith. *Libya: The Political Economy of Oil*. Oxford, Oxford University Press, 1996.

Hehir, Aidan, and Murray, Robert (Eds). *Libya, the Responsibility to Protect and the Future of Humanitarian Intervention*. Basingstoke, Palgrave Macmillan, 2013.

Henriksen, Dag, and Larssen, A. K. *Political Rationale and International Consequences of the War in Libya*. Oxford, Oxford University Press, 2016.

Lacher, Wolfram. *Libya's Fragmentation: Structure and Process in Violent Conflict*. London, I. B. Tauris, 2020.

Laessing, Ulf. *Understanding Libya Since Gaddafi*. London, C. Hurst & Co, 2020.

Layish, A. *Legal Documents on Libyan Tribal Society and the Process of Sedenterization: Part 1*. Wiesbaden, Harrassowirz Verlag, 1998.

Lewis, A. M. *Humanitarian and Military Intervention in Libya and Syria: Parliamentary Debate and Policy Failure*. London, Routledge, 2022.

Marcuzzi, Stefano. *The EU, NATO and the Libya Conflict: Anatomy of a Failure*. Abingdon, Routledge, 2022.

Martel, André. *La Libye des Ottomans à Da'ech: 1835–2016*. Paris, L'Harmattan, 2016.

Monzali, L., and Soave, P. (Eds). *Italy and Libya: From Colonialism to a Special Relationship (1911–2021)*. London, Routledge, 2023.

Mundy, Jacob. *Libya*. Cambridge, Polity Press, 2018.

Obeidi, Amal. *Political Culture in Libya*. Richmond, Curzon, 2001.

O'Sullivan, Susannah. *Military Intervention in the Middle East and North Africa: The Case of NATO in Libya*. Abingdon, Routledge, 2017.

Otman, Waniss, and Karlberg, Erling. *The Libyan Economy: Economic Diversification and International Repositioning*. Berlin, Springer-Verlag Berlin, 2007.

Pack, Jason. *Libya and the Global Enduring Disorder*. Oxford, Oxford University Press, 2022.

Pack, Jason (Ed.). *The 2011 Libyan Uprisings and the Struggle for the Post-Qadhafi Future*. Basingstoke, Palgrave Macmillan, 2013.

Pargeter, Alison. *Libya: The Rise and Fall of Qaddafi*. New Haven, CT, Yale University Press, 2012.

Pelt, Adrian. *Libyan Independence and the United Nations*. New Haven, CT, Yale University Press, 1970.

Pichou, Jean. *La Question de Libye dans le règlement de la paix*. Paris, 1945.

al-Qaddafi, Col Muammar. *The Green Book*. 3 vols; Tripoli, 1976–79; Vol. I: 'The Solution of the Problem of Democracy', Vol. II: 'The Solution of the Economic Problem', Vol. III: 'The Social Basis of the Third Universal Theory'.

Ronen, Yehudit. *Qaddafi's Libya in World Politics*. Boulder, CO, Lynne Rienner Publrs, 2008.

Roumani, Maurice M. *The Jews of Libya: Coexistence, Persecution, Resettlement*. Eastbourne, Sussex Academic Press, 2008.

Sarihan, A. *The Role of the Military in the Arab Uprisings: The Cases of Tunisia and Libya*. London, Routledge, 2023.

St John, Ronald Bruce. *Historical Dictionary of Libya* (5th edn). Lanham, MD, Rowman & Littlefield, 2014.

Libya: Continuity and Change (2nd edn). Abingdon, Routledge, 2015.

Libya: From Colony to Revolution (3rd edn). Oxford, Oneworld Publications, 2017.

Simons, Geoff. *Libya and the West: From Independence to Lockerbie.* London, I. B. Tauris, 2004.

Vandewalle, Dirk. *Libya Since Independence: Oil and State-Building.* Ithaca, NY, Cornell University Press, 1998.

A History of Modern Libya. Cambridge, Cambridge University Press, 2006.

(Ed.). *Libya Since 1969: Qadhafi's Revolution Revisited.* London, Palgrave Macmillan, 2008.

Villard, Henry S. *Libya: The New Arab Kingdom of North Africa.* Ithaca, NY, 1956.

Wehrey, Frederic. *The Burning Shores: Inside the Battle for the New Libya.* New York, NY, Farrar, Strauss & Giroux, 2018.

Weighill, Rob, and Gaub, Florence. *The Cauldron: NATO's Campaign in Libya.* London, C. Hurst & Co, 2018.

al-Werfalli, Mabroka. *Political Alienation in Libya: Assessing Citizens' Political Attitude and Behaviour.* Reading, Ithaca Press, 2011.

Wester, Karin. *Intervention in Libya: The Responsibility to Protect in North Africa.* Cambridge, Cambridge University Press, 2020.

Wright, John. *The Emergence of Libya.* London, Society for Libyan Studies, 2008.

Libya: A Modern History. Abingdon, Routledge, 2022.

MOROCCO

Geography

The Kingdom of Morocco is the westernmost of the three North African countries known to the Arabs as Jeziret al-Maghreb or 'Island of the West'. It occupies an area of 458,730 sq km (177,117 sq miles), excluding Western (formerly Spanish) Sahara (252,120 sq km), a disputed territory under Moroccan occupation. Morocco has an extensive coastline on both the Atlantic Ocean and the Mediterranean Sea. However, owing to its position and intervening mountain ranges, Morocco remained relatively isolated from the rest of the Maghreb and served as a refuge for descendants of the native Berber-speaking inhabitants of north-western Africa.

PHYSICAL FEATURES

The physical geography of Morocco is dominated by the highest and most rugged ranges in the Atlas Mountain system of north-western Africa. They are the result of mountain-building in the Tertiary era, when sediment deposited beneath an ancestral Mediterranean Sea was uplifted, folded and fractured. The mountains remain geologically unstable and Morocco is liable to severe earthquakes.

In Morocco the Atlas Mountains form four distinct massifs, which are surrounded and partially separated by lowland plains and plateaux. In the north, the Rif Atlas comprise a rugged arc of mountains that rise steeply from the Mediterranean coast to heights of more than 2,200 m above sea level. There, limestone and sandstone ranges form an effective barrier to east–west communications. They are inhabited by Berber farming families who live in isolated mountain villages and have little contact with the Arabs of Tétouan (estimated population 444,713 at mid-2023, according to United Nations—UN—figures) and Tangier (1,314,178) at the north-western end of the Rif chain.

The Middle Atlas lie immediately south of the Rif, separated by the Col of Taza, a narrow gap that affords the only easy route between western Algeria and Atlantic Morocco. They rise to about 3,000 m and form a broad barrier between the two countries. They also function as a major drainage divide and are flanked by the basins of Morocco's two principal rivers, the Oum el-Rbia, which flows west to the Atlantic, and the Moulouya, which flows north-east to the Mediterranean. Much of the Middle Atlas consists of a limestone plateau dissected by river gorges and capped here and there by volcanic craters and lava flows. The semi-nomadic Berber tribes spend the winter in villages in the valleys and move to the higher slopes in summer to pasture their flocks.

To the south the Middle Atlas chain merges into the High Atlas, the most formidable of the mountain massifs, which rises to about 4,000 m and is heavily snow-clad in winter. The mountains extend from south-west to north-east, and rise precipitously from both the Atlantic lowland to the north and the desert plain of Saharan Morocco to the south. There are no easily accessible routes across the High Atlas, but numerous mountain tracks allow the exchange of goods by pack animal between Atlantic and Saharan Morocco. A sizeable Berber population lives in the mountain valleys in compact, fortified villages.

The Anti-Atlas is the lowest and most southerly of the mountain massifs. Structurally, it forms an elevated edge of the Saharan platform which was uplifted when the High Atlas was formed. It consists largely of crystalline rocks and is joined to the southern margin of the High Atlas by a mass of volcanic lava, which separates the valley of the river Sous, draining west to the Atlantic at Agadir, from that of the upper Draa, draining south-east towards the Sahara. On the southern side of the chain, barren slopes are trenched by gorges from which cultivated palm groves protrude.

Stretching inland from the Atlantic coast is an extensive area of lowland, enclosed on the north, east and south by the Rif, Middle and High Atlas. It consists of the Gharb plain and the wide valley of the River Sebou in the north, and of the plateaux and plains of the Meseta, the Tadla, the Rehamna, the Djebilet and the Haouz farther south. Most of the Arabic-speaking people of Morocco live in this region.

CLIMATE AND VEGETATION

Northern and central Morocco experience a 'Mediterranean' climate, with warm, wet winters and hot, dry summers, but to the south this gives way to semi-arid and eventually to desert conditions. In the Rif and the northern parts of the Middle Atlas mean annual rainfall exceeds 750 mm and the summer drought lasts only three months, but in the rest of the Middle Atlas, in the High Atlas and over the northern half of the Atlantic lowland rainfall is reduced to between 400 mm and 750 mm and the summer drought lasts for four months or more. During the summer intensely hot winds from the Sahara, known as the Sirocco or Chergui, occasionally cross the mountains and desiccate the lowland. Summer heat on the Atlantic coastal plain is tempered, however, by sea breezes.

Over the southern half of the Atlantic lowland and the Anti-Atlas semi-arid conditions prevail and rainfall decreases to 200 mm–400 mm per year, becoming very variable and generally insufficient for the regular cultivation of cereal crops without irrigation. East and south of the Atlas Mountains, which act as a barrier to rain-bearing winds from the Atlantic, rainfall is reduced still further and regular cultivation becomes entirely dependent on irrigation.

The chief contrast in the vegetation of Morocco is between the mountain massifs, which support forest or open woodland, and the surrounding lowlands, which tend to be covered only by scrub growth of low, drought-resistant bushes. The natural vegetation has been depleted, and in many places actually destroyed, by excessive cutting, burning and grazing. The middle and upper slopes of the mountains are often quite well wooded, with evergreen oak dominant at the lower and cedar at the higher elevations. The lowlands to the east and south of the Atlas Mountains support distinctive species of steppe and desert vegetation, among which esparto grass and the argan tree (which is unique to south-western Morocco) are conspicuous.

POPULATION

According to census results, the population at 1 September 2014 was 33,848,242, compared with 29,680,069 at September 2004. By mid-2023, official projections put the total population at 37,022,385. The official languages are Arabic and Amazigh, the latter of which is spoken by the Berber population. Spanish is widely spoken in the northern regions, and French in the rest of Morocco. Berber-speaking peoples, living mainly in mountain villages, are thought to comprise a significant minority within the population, while the Arabic-speaking majority is concentrated in the low-lying towns, particularly in Casablanca (with a population estimated by the UN at 3,892,837 at mid-2023), Rabat (the modern administrative capital—1,959,388), Fez (1,290,039) and Marrakesh (1,049,690).

THE ANNEXED TERRITORY OF WESTERN SAHARA

After independence the Moroccan Government claimed a right to administer a large area of the western Sahara, including territory in Algeria and Mauritania, and the whole of Spanish Sahara. The claim was based on the extent of Moroccan rule in medieval times. The existence of considerable deposits of phosphates in Spanish Sahara and of iron ore in the Algeria–Morocco border region further encouraged Moroccan interest in expansion. After Spain's withdrawal from the Sahara in 1976, Morocco and Mauritania divided the former

Spanish Sahara (now known as Western Sahara) between them, with Morocco annexing the northern part of the territory, including the phosphate mines of Bou Craa. In August 1979 Mauritania renounced its share, which was immediately annexed by Morocco and incorporated as a new province, Oued Eddahab.

At the census of September 2014 the population of Western Sahara was 510,713. The principal towns in the area are el-Aaiún (Laâyoune), el-Smara (formerly Smara) and Dakhla (Villa Cisneros). As part of a reorganization of local government in 2010, Morocco was divided into 12 administrative regions, two of which—Laâyoune-Sakia El Hamra and Eddakhla-Oued Eddahab—lay wholly within Western Sahara. (A third, Guelmim-Oued Noun, incorporates a small part of Western Sahara in its territory.) At mid-2023 official projections put the population of the region of Laâyoune-Sakia El Hamra at 417,756 and that of Eddakhla-Oued Eddahab at 200,847.

The relief of most of the area is gentle. The coast is backed by a wide alluvial plain overlain in the south by extensive sand dunes aligned from south-west to north-east and extending inland over 250 km (155 miles). Behind the coastal plain the land rises gradually to a plateau surface broken by sandstone ridges that reach 300 m in height. In the north-east, close to the Mauritanian frontier, isolated mountain ranges, such as the Massif de la Guelta, rise to over 600 m. There are no permanent streams and the only considerable valley is that of the Saguia el-Hamra which crosses the northernmost part of the area to reach the coast at el-Aaiún north of Cape Bojador. The whole region experiences an extreme desert climate. Nowhere does mean annual rainfall exceed 100 mm and over most of the territory it is less than 50 mm. Vegetation is restricted to scattered desert shrubs and occasional patches of coarse grass in most depressions. Along the coast, summer heat is tempered by air moving inland after it has been cooled over the waters of the cold Canaries current, which flows off shore from north to south.

History

NEIL PARTRICK

Based on an original essay by RICHARD I. LAWLESS

THE PRE-COLONIAL AND COLONIAL PERIODS

The Phoenicians and Carthaginians established trading posts on Morocco's coasts, and later the Romans took control in the north, creating the province of Mauritania Tingitana. By the eighth century CE Arab invaders from the east had conquered most of the country. The Berber (or 'Amazigh') tribes of Morocco quickly rallied to Islam, and new Arab invaders in the 11th and 12th centuries contributed greatly to Arabization, but significant segments of the population remained Berber speakers. In the 12th century a religious movement, the Almoravids, established control over Morocco and much of Algeria and annexed Muslim lands in Spain, but their power rapidly declined. A new religious force, the Almohads, replaced them, conquering much of the Maghreb including Libya, and brought Muslim Spain under their control, but from the early 13th century their empire also began to decline. In the following centuries successive regimes strove to maintain their power in the face of tribal dissidence and the threat of foreign intervention, especially from the Spanish and Portuguese, who were able to establish outposts along the Moroccan coasts. The dynasty of the Alaouites came to power in 1666 and has remained at least nominally in control to the present day. By the beginning of the 20th century Morocco was one of the few African states to remain independent, and competition among the great powers to control the country was increasing. In 1904 France and Spain concluded a secret agreement that divided Morocco into two zones of influence: a Spanish zone in the north and a French zone in the south. In 1912 France established a protectorate over Morocco, and later in the year an agreement was signed with Spain over the limits of its zone. An international regime was established in Tangier in 1923.

The first French Resident-General, Gen. Hubert Lyautey, quickly established effective control over the plains and lower plateaux of Morocco from Fez to the Atlas Mountains south of Marrakesh, but it was not until 1934 that the French established control over the Middle Atlas, the Tafilalt, the Anti-Atlas and the deep south. A major rebellion against Spanish rule in the north during the 1920s had been crushed by the Spanish military, aided by French troops.

INDEPENDENCE

By the early 1930s a clandestine Moroccan nationalist movement had emerged. The Second World War gave a new impulse to the development of Moroccan nationalism, and in 1943 the Istiqlal (Independence) party was formed, demanding independence under the rule of Sultan Mohammed bin Yousuf. In the years following the Second World War the nationalist movement gained in strength and won international support. In August 1953 France moved to depose bin Yousuf, who was exiled to Madagascar, and replaced him as Sultan with another royal prince, Mohammed bin Arafa. Urban violence continued, and with the outbreak of the Algerian war in 1954 the French Government urgently needed to find a settlement in Morocco. After a successful conference between French and Moroccan representatives in August 1955, bin Arafa abdicated and bin Yousuf returned from exile as the legitimate ruler. In March 1956 the French Government recognized the independence of Morocco. At the same time Spain relinquished its protectorate over northern Morocco, although it retained the enclaves of Ceuta and Melilla. The Spanish-controlled territories of Tarfaya and Ifni in the south became part of Morocco under agreements signed in 1958 and 1969, respectively. Tangier was restored to Morocco in 1956.

KING HASSAN REFUSES TO SHARE POWER

Mohammed bin Yousuf, who had assumed the title of King Mohammed V after independence, died in 1961 and was succeeded by his son, Hassan II. The close association of the monarchy with the nationalist movement had strengthened the position of the King, who also claimed traditional religious authority as *amir al-mouminin* (Commander of the Faithful). Istiqlal remained the leading political party, but its efforts to curb the power of the monarchy had been hampered by internal divisions and a split in 1959 resulted in the creation of a breakaway party, the Union Nationale des Forces Populaires (UNFP), led by Mehdi Ben Barka. In 1962 a new Constitution—establishing a constitutional monarchy with the King as head of state, supported by an elected parliament—was approved by referendum. In elections to the new National Assembly in May 1963 the Front pour la Défense des Institutions Constitutionnelles, a new coalition of monarchist parties, won the largest number of seats but failed to gain an overall majority. This situation gave rise to a period of ineffective government, and unemployment and rising prices led to riots in the capital, Rabat, and Casablanca in 1965. The King proclaimed a state of emergency, suspended parliament, and assumed full legislative and executive powers. After the 1963 elections repressive actions against the opposition Istiqlal and UNFP resulted in numerous arrests, and in October 1965 the UNFP leader, Ben Barka, disappeared in France and was presumed to have been assassinated. At a subsequent French trial Gen. Mohamed Oufkir, one of the King's closest supporters, was found guilty *in absentia* of complicity in Ben Barka's disappearance (see *The King Moves to Redress Human Rights Grievances*).

In July 1971 a group of army officers attacked the King's summer palace at Skhirat, south of Rabat, but Hassan, together with Oufkir, escaped and with loyal forces foiled the attempted coup. A second unsuccessful attempt on Hassan's life, in 1972, had apparently been planned by Oufkir, the King's erstwhile defender, who was found shot dead. Bomb attacks by armed groups in several cities in March 1973 prompted the arrest of several UNFP leaders, some of whom were later executed. Hassan quickly moved to regain control of the situation, reconstructing the security forces, dividing the opposition parties and using the Western Sahara issue to divert the army from domestic politics.

ANNEXATION OF WESTERN SAHARA

The independence agreement of 1956 did not define Morocco's boundaries. As the pre-protectorate nation also had no formal boundaries in the Sahara, the possibilities for territorial expansion were considerable. Prior to independence the Istiqlal party had envisaged the creation of a 'Greater Morocco', to include certain areas in south-western Algeria, the Spanish Sahara (the northern Saguia el-Hamra and the southern Río de Oro) and Mauritania, and Morocco reiterated these claims in the following years. In July 1962 Moroccan troops entered the region south of Colomb-Béchar in Algeria, a region never officially demarcated, and the Moroccan press also launched a strong campaign in support of Morocco's claims to the mineral-rich Tindouf area in Algeria, proximate to the border with Morocco and with the Western Sahara. In February 1964 an agreement was reached to establish a demilitarized zone, but a 1972 treaty on the demarcation of the joint border was not ratified by Morocco until 1989. Morocco abandoned its claim to Mauritania in 1969, and full diplomatic recognition followed in 1970.

In 1974 Morocco stepped up its claims to the Spanish Sahara, where massive reserves of phosphates had been discovered and developed in the late 1960s. Its claim was essentially based on the past recognition of the spiritual and temporal authority of the Sultan by the people of the region. Hassan's initiative was supported by all the country's political parties. After resisting United Nations (UN) demands for decolonization of the territory, in mid-1974 Spain declared its readiness to withdraw from its Saharan territories, and in October Morocco and Mauritania reached a secret agreement on the division of the territories and the joint exploitation of their phosphate resources. A year later the International Court of Justice in The Hague, Netherlands, ruled in favour of self-determination for the people of Spanish Sahara. In response, King Hassan ordered a march of 350,000 unarmed civilians to take possession of the Spanish territories. The so-called Green March began in November, and the Spanish authorities allowed the marchers to progress a short distance across the border before halting their advance. Shortly afterwards, a tripartite accord was signed in Madrid, Spain, whereby the Spanish Government undertook to withdraw from Western Sahara (as the territory was redesignated) in early 1976 and transfer the territory to a joint Moroccan-Mauritanian administration. Algeria, however, opposed the agreement and increased its support for the Frente Popular para la Liberación de Saguia el-Hamra y Río de Oro (the Polisario Front), founded in 1973, which sought independence for Western Sahara. Moroccan troops swiftly occupied the territory and entered the capital, el-Aaiún, in December 1975. They encountered fierce resistance from Polisario guerrillas, and many Sahrawis fled across the Algerian border. The last Spanish troops left in January 1976, and Moroccan and Algerian troops subsequently clashed within Western Sahara. However, the prospect of war between the two countries receded as Algeria contented itself with arming and training Polisario guerrillas and providing refugee camps. In February, in the Algerian capital, Algiers, Polisario proclaimed the Sahrawi Arab Democratic Republic (SADR), and in March Morocco severed diplomatic relations with Algeria.

In April 1976 Morocco and Mauritania reached agreement on the division of Western Sahara. The greater part of the territory, containing most of the known mineral wealth, was allocated to Morocco, which subsequently divided it into three provinces and absorbed these into the kingdom. By placing army garrisons in the territory's few urban centres, the Moroccans were able to secure them against guerrilla attacks, but incursions by Polisario forces into the surrounding desert areas could not be prevented. Morocco also took increasing responsibility for the defence of the Mauritanian sector. France favoured the expansion of Moroccan, rather than Algerian, interests in this area and launched several air attacks on Polisario forces. Following a military coup in Mauritania in July 1978, Mauritania signed a peace treaty with Polisario, renouncing its territorial claims to Western Sahara. King Hassan immediately claimed the former Mauritanian sector of Western Sahara and proclaimed it a province of Morocco. Polisario forces continued their attacks, some of these inside Morocco's original borders, and in 1980 Morocco resorted to defensive tactics, protecting a *triangle utile*, between el-Aaiún, Bou Craa and el-Smara, containing most of the population and the most important phosphate mines.

In November 1979 the UN General Assembly adopted a resolution confirming the legitimacy of the Polisario Front's struggle for independence, and a year later it urged Morocco to end its occupation of Western Sahara. At a summit meeting of the Organization of African Unity (OAU, now African Union—AU) in 1980 a majority of members approved the admission of the SADR, and Morocco subsequently became the first state to withdraw from the organization. By 1981 the SADR had been recognized by 45 governments. In May 1982 Morocco and the USA signed a military co-operation accord providing for the establishment of US military airbases on Moroccan territory in the event of crises in the Middle East or Africa.

GROWING SOCIAL AND POLITICAL UNREST

The Saharan takeover won King Hassan considerable domestic prestige and popularity, and in 1977 he held national elections originally envisaged under the 1972 Constitution. With the exception of the UNFP, the opposition parties agreed to participate. The election of the new Chamber of Representatives, in which independent pro-monarchy candidates won 141 of the 264 seats, ended 12 years of direct rule.

Although there appeared to be solid popular support for the war effort, signs of social discontent did emerge, which could be partly attributed to the financial burden of the Western Sahara conflict. In June 1981 at least 66 people were killed in Casablanca during a general strike against reductions in food subsidies. In January 1984 violent street protests erupted in several towns after the Government announced imminent increases in the prices of basic foodstuffs and in education fees.

Following parliamentary elections in September 1984, the legislature was again controlled by centre-right parties. King Hassan named a new coalition Government of four centre-right parties, which excluded both Istiqlal and the Union Socialiste des Forces Populaires (USFP—established in 1972 following a split in the UNFP). Meanwhile, the Government mounted a campaign against organizations deemed to pose a threat to internal security, particularly left-wing and Islamist movements. In the 1970s left-wing militancy had been the gravest threat to the regime, and Hassan had sought to counter the rise of the left by appealing to religious elements in society. However, the tactics had backfired when Sheikh Abdessalam Yassine, founder and leader of the Islamist movement Al-Adl wal-Ihsan (Justice and Charity), accused the King of ruling illegitimately and not abiding by religious teachings. For this, he was arrested and confined in a psychiatric hospital for more than two years. During the 1980s Islamism began to grow. In 1982 Al-Adl wal-Ihsan was refused official registration, and in 1989 24 of its members were arrested for threatening state security. In January 1990 the Government ordered the dissolution of Al-Adl wal-Ihsan, and arrested and imprisoned members of its executive committee. In May 1991 Al-Adl wal-Ihsan and other opposition groups participated in a rally in Casablanca in which 100,000 demonstrators demanded measures to

EFFORTS FAIL TO DRAW THE OPPOSITION INTO GOVERNMENT

In June 1992 the Chamber of Deputies, in the absence of opposition parties which boycotted the session, adopted a new electoral law. The legislation reduced the minimum voting age to 20 years and the minimum age for election candidates to 23. It also made provision for equal funding and media exposure for all parties. The opposition parties—Istiqlal, the USFP, the Parti de l'Avant-garde Démocratique Socialiste (PADS—a breakaway organization from the USFP) and the Parti du Progrès et du Socialisme (PPS)—had earlier formed the Bloc Démocratique. On 4 September a revised Constitution was endorsed at a national referendum by almost 100% of voters. The opposition claimed that the result destroyed any credibility that the democratic process may have had. The revised Constitution required the composition of the Government to reflect that of the Chamber of Deputies and to submit its programme to a vote in the legislature.

Parliamentary elections proceeded in June and September 1993. The number of seats in the Chamber of Representatives was increased from 306 to 333. The five loyalist parties secured 195 seats in the new Chamber and the Bloc Démocratique 120 seats, with independents winning the remaining 18.

Having failed to draw the opposition into government, in January 1995 King Hassan reappointed Abdellatif Filali, a member of his inner circle, as Prime Minister, and once again selected a Government from among the loyalist Union Constitutionelle (UC), the Mouvement Populaire (MP) and the Parti National Démocrate (PND).

CONSTITUTIONAL CHANGES

In a referendum held on 13 September 1996, voters overwhelmingly supported the creation of a second, directly elected parliamentary chamber, the Chamber of Advisers. Its members were to be chosen by electoral colleges representing mainly local councils. The Chamber of Advisers could initiate legislation, issue 'warning' motions to the Government and, by a two-thirds' majority vote, force its resignation. Moroccan officials denied that the new upper house was intended to neutralize the Chamber of Representatives.

In February 1997 a total of 11 political parties, including five from the opposition, signed a political pact with Minister of State for the Interior Driss Basri, with the aim of 'strengthening the democratic regime based on the monarchy'. The Bloc Démocratique announced that it would present joint candidates in some 25,000 municipal districts. The 'loyalist' parties (including the UC, the MP and the PND), which held a majority of seats in the Chamber of Representatives, also formed a common front, the Entente Nationale (or Wifaq), and adopted the same strategy. Several radical Islamist groups demanded the right to form political parties and to contest the forthcoming elections. However, although Al Islah wa Attajdid acquired legal status in January 1997 as a result of its merger with the Mouvement Populaire Constitutionnelle et Démocratique (MPCD), the authorities rejected Al-Adl wal-Ihsan's claim for recognition as a political party.

THE 1997 LOCAL AND LEGISLATIVE ELECTIONS

The political pact signed in February 1997 had its first test at local elections held in June. Although the opposition Bloc Démocratique won 31.7% of the seats, overall control of local councils was retained by the right-wing Entente Nationale and the centrist grouping led by the Rassemblement National des Indépendants (RNI), which took 30.3% and 26.4% of the seats, respectively. As the MPCD boycotted the poll, members of Al Islah wa Attajdid contested the elections as independent candidates.

In August 1997 King Hassan appointed a new Cabinet, primarily comprising technocrats. Voting for the wholly elected Chamber of Representatives in the new bicameral parliament took place on 14 November. The Bloc Démocratique won 102 of the 325 seats, the Entente Nationale secured 100 seats and parties of the centre-right took 97 seats. The Bloc Démocratique won 34.3% of the vote, compared with 27.3% by the centre-right parties and 24.8% by the Entente Nationale. The MPCD, the PPS and the FFD each won nine seats. Indirect elections for the new Chamber of Advisers took place on 5 December 1997. The right and centre-right parties secured a dominant position in the upper house, winning 166 of the 270 seats.

MOROCCO'S FIRST USFP-LED GOVERNMENT

With the three main political groupings holding roughly the same number of seats in the Chamber of Representatives, on 4 February 1998 King Hassan named el-Youssoufi, the veteran leader of the USFP, as Prime Minister. In March el-Youssoufi formed a coalition Government in which 23 of the 41 members were from the USFP and its allies. Although officially hailed as the country's first 'gouvernement d'alternance' in the transition to democracy, with opposition parties taking charge of key areas of economic and social policy, the ministers with responsibility for the interior, foreign affairs, justice, and religious endowments and Islamic affairs, together with the Secretary-General of the Government and the Minister-delegate in charge of the Administration of National Defence, were direct appointees of the King. The security services and important networks of economic influence were outside the new premier's control.

The Minister of Justice, Omar Azzimane, began a reform of the justice system, initiating disciplinary proceedings against 30 magistrates, mainly on the grounds of corruption. By the end of 1998 nine judges had been dismissed, and others suspended.

THE ACCESSION OF KING MOHAMMED

King Hassan died of a heart attack on 23 July 1999, and was succeeded by his eldest son, who took the throne as Mohammed VI. The new King immediately demonstrated his enthusiasm for change, introducing a more informal style of interaction with his advisers, elected politicians and visiting foreign officials.

In his first address as King, Mohammed pledged to support the multi-party system, the rule of law, and respect for human rights and individual liberties. He travelled widely throughout the kingdom (notably undertaking a 10-day visit to the isolated and impoverished northern Rif region, which had been virtually ignored by King Hassan), pledged to help the poor and reduce unemployment, and advocated for equal rights for women. Shortly after his succession, the King granted an amnesty to thousands of prisoners and established a body to determine compensation for the families of 'disappeared' political opponents or victims of arbitrary detention. In September 1999 he granted permission for Abraham Serfaty, the country's most prominent dissident, to return from exile in France.

In July 2001 King Mohammed expressed his desire to eliminate nepotism and corruption in the administration, and to establish what he called a new social contract between unions, employers and government. At a time of violent unrest among Berbers in neighbouring Algeria, the King also announced a royal institute to 'protect, revive and promote Berber culture' and explore ways of integrating Tamazight (the principal Berber language) into Morocco's education system.

While modernizing the monarchy, King Mohammed continued to dominate the political sphere, making appointments to all key posts and formulating political strategy. There was also disquiet in some circles at the appearance of several senior army officers in prominent positions in the King's entourage.

THE KING MOVES TO REDRESS HUMAN RIGHTS GRIEVANCES

In June 2001 it was reported that the Moroccan authorities had for the first time given permission for a French judge to carry out inquiries in Morocco into the disappearance of opposition leader Mehdi Ben Barka in Paris in 1965. At the end of June 2001, a former member of the Moroccan special services, Ahmed Boukhari, purportedly confessed that the Moroccan special services had kidnapped Ben Barka in Paris, where he died under torture, and named those allegedly responsible. In August 2001 Boukhari was sentenced to three months' imprisonment on unrelated charges of fraud, and after being released was rearrested and imprisoned for 'defamation'.

The new King's approach encouraged many to test the limits of the state's beneficence. Berber groups, long denied a voice, attacked plans for the introduction of Berber language courses in schools and universities, insisting that they lacked proper preparation and were intended to fail. However, it was the press that most pushed the new boundaries. None the less, comments on the monarchy, the army and Western Sahara remained subject to censure.

In March 2002 the lower house approved controversial new press legislation granting the courts, rather than the Prime Minister, authority to close down newspapers but retaining tough prison sentences for offending the monarchy, Islamic values or Morocco's 'territorial integrity'.

THE LEGISLATIVE ELECTIONS OF SEPTEMBER 2002

Al-Adl wal-Ihsan and the Parti de l'Avant-garde Démocratique Socialiste (PADS) both boycotted the national elections on 27 September 2002. The USFP enjoyed the greatest success, retaining 50 seats (down from 57 in 1997), while Istiqlal went from 32 seats in 1997 to 48. In third place was the Parti de la Justice et du Développement (PJD—previously the MPCD), which went from nine in 1997 to 42.

The King had been expected to choose a new Prime Minister from the USFP leadership. There was some surprise, therefore, when the King appointed Minister of the Interior Driss Jettou to the post. The new Government comprised representatives of six political parties: the USFP (eight ministers), Istiqlal (eight), the RNI (six), the MP (three), the PPS (two) and the Mouvement National Populaire (two). Two leaders of political parties were included in the Government, albeit in relatively minor posts: Istiqlal's Secretary-General, Abbas el-Fassi, was promoted to Minister of State without portfolio, and MP leader Mohand Laenser became Minister of Agriculture and Rural Development.

SUICIDE BOMBINGS IN CASABLANCA AND THE RISE OF ISLAMISM

The Islamist movement, the influence of which extended over wide sections of society, had become more visible since 2000. Notably, the officially recognized PJD and the unauthorized Al-Adl wal-Ihsan had increased in prominence. In February 2000 the leader of Al-Adl wal-Ihsan, Abdessalem Yassine, posted on his website an 18-page letter, addressed to King Mohammed, in which he launched a vitriolic attack on the reign of Hassan II. In it, he appealed to King Mohammed to relinquish his father's assets abroad—estimated at US $400m.—in order to pay off the national debt, and condemned the ceremony of allegiance to the monarch (*baia*) as a sacrilegious abomination. Yassine also stated that the current political system was the principal reason for Morocco's backwardness and that only genuine democratic reforms would save the country. In March Al-Adl wal-Ihsan, together with the PJD and the League of Ulama, organized a rally in Casablanca in which 500,000 Islamists protested against social reforms proposed by the Secretary of State for Social Affairs, which would vastly improve the social status and legal rights of Moroccan women. The proposals included allocating women one-third of parliamentary seats; raising the minimum age of marriage for women from 15 to 18 years; bans on polygamy and on 'repudiation' as a form of divorce; and equal rights for women under a divorce settlement. The plan was regarded by Islamists as a serious assault on the religious code underpinning personal law. The protests forced the Government to establish a special panel to review the planned reforms, and a new law on personal status was not promulgated until 2003, following the personal intervention of the King and the unexpected turnaround in the fortunes of Al-Adl wal-Ihsan. In May 2001 Yassine was released from house arrest, although Al-Adl wal-Ihsan technically remained prohibited. At the same time the organization's newspaper was banned, as were marches planned near the border with Algeria.

On the evening of 16 May 2003 a series of suicide bomb attacks in central Casablanca targeted restaurants and hotels frequented by foreigners, and a Jewish cultural centre; 45 people were killed and 100 injured. The authorities announced that the 12 Moroccan suicide bombers were linked to a small extremist Islamist group. However, the police also insisted that the attacks had been orchestrated by an international terrorist network operating in Europe, possibly al-Qa'ida. The attacks were not only a challenge to the Moroccan state but to the Islamist leadership of the PJD and Al-Adl wal-Ihsan. Leaders of several political parties accused the PJD of spreading radicalism, and there were demands that all Islamist organizations be banned.

Following the suicide bomb attacks, the parliament swiftly approved uncompromising new anti-terrorism legislation, giving the security forces increased powers. By July 2003 more than 200 people had reportedly been arrested in connection with the attacks. Meanwhile, the trial began of the first 16 defendants, including three alleged suicide bombers. In August four men, including two surviving suicide bombers, were sentenced to death for their part in the Casablanca attacks. Meanwhile, the Moroccan authorities issued international arrest warrants for several members of Groupe Islamique Combattant Marocain (GICM) for their alleged involvement in the bombings.

During 2005 the King pardoned 285 Islamist prisoners who had been convicted under anti-terrorism legislation, including 164 members of Salafia Jihadia, a small group suspected of being involved in the suicide bomb attacks in Casablanca in May 2003. Ennassir, a support association for Islamist prisoners in Morocco, estimated that more than 2,000 were incarcerated, the majority of whom were members of Salafia Jihadia and the GICM. In November 2005 police arrested 17 Islamists suspected of planning attacks on US and Jewish targets in Morocco and on the parliament. In late May and early June 2006 500 Al-Adl wal-Ihsan activists were arrested. The threat from Islamist militants resurfaced in April 2007 when several attempts by suicide bombers to attack sensitive sites such as the US consulate in Casablanca were thwarted by the security forces.

The security forces announced in February 2008 that they had uncovered a large Islamist network, resulting in the arrest of 35 suspects and the discovery of a significant cache of arms. The suspected leader of the group was Abdelkader Belliraj, who ordinarily resided in Belgium. The Belgian media subsequently reported that Belliraj was on the payroll of the Belgian intelligence services as an informer, thus raising bilateral diplomatic tensions. In July 2009 Belliraj was convicted of 'disturbing the state's internal security and premeditated murder', and sentenced to life imprisonment.

In late 2006 an Algerian Islamist group, the Groupe Salafiste Pour la Prédication et le Combat, announced that it was aligning itself with al-Qa'ida, changing its name in early 2007 to al-Qa'ida Organization in the Land of the Islamic Maghreb (AQIM). The new group stated that its remit covered the whole of North Africa. Attuned to the threat, in May 2008 Moroccan security forces arrested 11 people suspected of recruiting fighters on behalf of al-Qa'ida to join the insurgency in Iraq. Some of their number were also accused of planning attacks in Morocco, suggesting that AQIM was slowly gaining a foothold in the country.

Another 15 arrests took place in August 2008. The Government stated that its security operations were designed to be 'preventative' and that it was particularly concerned about the activities of Moroccans in Europe. As a consequence, during Ramadan the Government sent Moroccan preachers abroad, mainly to France, to promote moderate spiritual guidance. Later that month the King announced reforms to Islamic jurisprudence in Morocco. These included the restructuring of local *ulama* councils; the establishment of an *ulama* council for the Moroccan community in Europe; and the creation of a new and separate body with the power to issue *fatwas* (religious edicts). The Government's concerns over the involvement of Moroccan expatriates in militant activity were borne out in December, when several radical Moroccan Islamists were arrested in separate raids in Belgium and Italy. In April 2010 a total of 24 alleged members of AQIM, suspected of seeking to target Moroccan-based foreigners, were arrested in Morocco, and arms and ammunition were seized. This action was followed in August by the arrest of an additional 18 suspected Islamist militants, who were believed to have been plotting to attack foreign targets in Morocco.

In April 2011 a bomb attack on a café in Marrakesh killed 17 people and injured 20 more. AQIM denied responsibility for the attack, which appeared to be the work of an independent Islamist group.

REFORM OF THE FAMILY CODE

The new, relatively liberal era ushered in by King Mohammed highlighted differences, probably as an intentional form of state political management, between moderates and conservatives. The differences were most noticeable over women's rights. After the King met representatives of women's groups in March 2001, he announced the establishment of a royal commission, led by Driss Dahak, President of the Supreme Court, and including leading Islamic scholars and jurists, to revise the country's laws on personal rights and responsibilities.

In October 2003 King Mohammed announced the main outlines of a controversial new family code (*moudawana*). The family was to become the joint responsibility of both spouses, rather than just the father. A wife's obligation to obey her husband was to be replaced by equality between the two partners. A woman would no longer require the permission of her father or brother to marry, and the minimum age of marriage for girls was to be raised from 15 to 18 years. Although there was to be no formal ban on polygamy, it was proposed that the practice be made extremely difficult. Similarly, the act of repudiation would require legal authorization. If a couple separated, the mother would normally be granted guardianship of the children. The bill was adopted unanimously by both upper and lower chambers in January 2004. The new *moudawana* was seen as the most important of King Mohammed's reforms since taking the throne. Aside from Tunisia, the code remains the most progressive in North Africa.

Meanwhile, in July 2005 Nadia Yassine, spokesperson for Al-Adl wal-Ihsan (and daughter of the organization's founder), was put on trial for insulting the monarchy after she advocated for a republic. The international publicity prevented the courts from pursuing the matter further, although restrictions were placed on her movements. In December the Ministry of Justice created a unit to monitor the press. Several journalists were subject to charges of defamation and fines for reporting on sensitive topics, exemplifying the limits that continued to be placed on freedom of expression. The practice of imposing heavy fines on newspapers and magazines had become an effective substitute for closing them down, as very rarely can these publications afford such costs.

FURTHER POLITICAL REFORM AND THE EMERGENCE OF THE PAM

In October 2004 King Mohammed announced details of a bill designed to reform the regulation of political parties, notably imposing stringent rules supposedly upholding democratic practices and transparent financial management. The bill received parliamentary approval a year later. However, critics claimed that the new law was designed to limit the right of association and to strengthen state control over political discourse. The law proscribed any party based on religion, ethnicity, language or region or that had the aim of impugning Islam, the monarchy or Morocco's territorial integrity.

Elections were conducted on 8 September 2006 to renew one-third of the seats in the Chamber of Advisers. The largest number of seats went to Istiqlal, which took 17 of the 90 seats contested. Legislative elections were held on 7 September 2007. Istiqlal emerged as the largest party in the Chamber of Representatives, with 10.7% of the vote and 52 seats. The PJD surpassed Istiqlal in the popular vote, achieving 10.9% of the valid votes cast; however, it only won 46 seats. The discrepancy was attributed to the inequalities of the electoral system, which favoured rural, conservative constituencies over urban ones. The USFP lost 12 of its 50 seats, and was outperformed by both the MP and the RNI, which won 41 and 39 seats, respectively. Voter turnout was reported as 37%. Later that month King Mohammed appointed el-Fassi, Secretary-General of Istiqlal, as Prime Minister. The new premier established a ruling four-party coalition consisting of Istiqlal, the USFP, the PPS and the RNI, together with several independents.

The governing coalition was challenged by a new political association established in January 2008, the Mouvement pour Tous les Démocrates, which positioned itself to the left of centre and was clearly acting as a pro-Government organization. By mid-2008 the new group had co-opted five other small parties and established itself as the Parti de l'Authenticité et de la Modernité (PAM), which controlled 11% of the seats in parliament. In September the PAM announced that it had agreed to join the RNI, in effect taking the new party into government.

In February 2009 a former Minister of Health, Muhammad Cheikh Biadillah, was chosen as the PAM's first leader. In May, following simmering differences with the governing coalition, the PAM announced its withdrawal from the RNI, effectively denying the Government a majority in parliament. Despite internal tensions, the PAM came first in the municipal elections in June, winning nearly 22% of the seats. The PAM further consolidated its position in October, when Biadillah was elected as President of the Chamber of Advisers.

PROTESTS AND CONSTITUTIONAL REFORM

The fervour for political reform that swept across much of North Africa and parts of the wider Middle East in early 2011 inevitably gained traction in Morocco, fuelled by longstanding political and socioeconomic disaffection. On 20 February protests took place in urban areas, including Rabat, Casablanca, Marrakesh and Tangier. They brought together a whole range of diverse groups and interests, under the banner of the February 20th Movement for Change. They demanded constitutional reform and a shift in the structure of government from an absolute to a constitutional monarchy. The protesters were clear that they did not challenge the legitimacy of the King, but that they wanted sufficiently far-reaching reform to ensure a clear separation and balance of power within the Moroccan political system. The demonstrations were peaceful and only attracted about 40,000 participants, which in part reflected the widespread support for King Mohammed VI, as well as public concerns over instability.

Although the protests failed to rouse the mass public support seen in Tunisia and Egypt, they were large enough to force the King into responding to the protesters' demands. In March 2011 he announced a constitutional reform committee, and that reforms based on its findings would be put to a national referendum. Protesters claimed this did not go far enough because the King retained control over the appointment of the committee and the scope of its deliberations. The demonstrators' demands became more specific: they sought the dismissal of the Government and the dismantling of the *makhzen* (ruling elite), and demanded that public officials be tried for corruption. Although further protests failed to gain any real critical mass of public support, the King responded with further concessions in April, ordering the release of numerous political prisoners, raising public sector salaries and increasing the minimum wage.

The constitutional committee delivered its report in June 2011. In the subsequent referendum, approval of the proposed constitutional reforms, according to the official results, was near unanimous, based on a turnout given as about three-quarters of total registered voters. The envisaged reforms did not go nearly as far as the protesters had demanded, and although they granted the Government executive authority and gave wider legislative authority to parliament, the King retained wide-ranging powers, allowing him to intervene in almost all areas of state. The February 20th Movement for Change organized another set of protests, but, in recognition of the support for the King, demands were more focused on corruption and human rights.

THE 2011 LEGISLATIVE ELECTIONS

In legislative elections held on 25 November 2011, the PJD emerged as the strongest party in the Chamber of Representatives, winning 107 of the 395 seats. Istiqlal obtained 60 seats, followed by the RNI with 52, the PAM with 47 and the USFP with 39. Having failed to secure an outright majority, the PJD was obliged to form a coalition Government that included the centre-right MP (which controlled 32 seats) and the socialist PPS (18 seats). PJD Secretary-General Abdelilah Benkirane was appointed as Prime Minister. Voter turnout was modest, at 45%, partly owing to a boycott urged by the February 20th Movement. In theory, Benkirane could exploit the powers granted to the Chamber of Representatives under the 2011 Constitution to ensure that his Government determined domestic policy, as opposed to the palace. In practice, however, the King's approval was still needed to advance policy. Authority over foreign affairs also remained under the King's prerogative power. The PJD did not directly oppose the ruling authorities, reflecting the party's philosophy, which was rooted in pragmatism and a rejection of the harder-line approach of other Moroccan Islamists.

Despite the greater authority that had ostensibly been bestowed upon the elected Government, the reform process continued to be criticized as inadequate. In May 2012 several judges alleged government failure to carry out promised judicial reforms, while trade unions organized a mass demonstration in Casablanca against the Government's failure to implement reforms.

Allegations of human rights abuses continued to be levelled at a state machinery that remained tough on Islamist militancy and resistant to substantive political reform. In May 2014 an influential and popular trade union leader in the Rif area, Karim Lachkar, died in police custody in al-Hoceima. In September 2013, meanwhile, the editor of the online news site *Lakome*, Ali Anouzla, was arrested after publishing an article discussing an AQIM video that was particularly critical of King Mohammed and which urged *jihad*; Anouzla was subsequently charged with aiding terrorism, and he remained under threat of a lengthy custodial sentence.

There was a broad protest in Rabat in March 2013, supported by trade unionists, human rights activists, members of the February 20th Movement and representatives of civil society. Protesters urged economic and social reforms, and denounced the high level of unemployment and increased living costs; some also demanded Benkirane's resignation.

In July 2013 Istiqlal withdrew from the coalition Government, claiming that Benkirane had monopolized decision-making and criticizing his economic policies. Benkirane held discussions with other prospective partners, and in October the RNI joined the coalition.

RENEWED POPULAR PROTESTS

In early November 2015 ordinary Moroccans took to the streets in Tangier to protest against price rises for water and electricity implemented by Amendis, a sister company of France's Veolia. The main Moroccan union federations held a series of strongly supported 24-hour strikes in November and December over several grievances, chief of which were proposed changes to the state pension scheme, but trade union rights were also asserted, as were tax cuts, and there were some demands for the Prime Minister to resign. In late November the Government argued that the economic necessity of pension reform could not be avoided, and this meant that the union protests were not legitimate. A further 24-hour general strike in February 2016 was once again primarily about economic issues, but had heavily political overtones. The unions focused on securing legally guaranteed freedoms and increased salaries, and, once again, resisting the planned pensions reform.

Popular discontent continued periodically to be expressed over corruption and unemployment, which still bedevilled Moroccan political and economic life, despite the political upheaval that brought about reforms in 2011. However, in August 2016 the remnants of the February 20th Movement could muster only a small demonstration over corruption, despite accusations that state officials had access to heavily subsidized land in prime real estate locations. None the less, the authorities took no chances when in the same month hundreds of qualified teachers, objecting to being defined as private contract labour under new government 'privatization' measures, took to the streets demanding that their employment status be regularized, or that they be given guaranteed public sector jobs. Police used force to break up the demonstration.

Teachers, however, continued to stage protests, which often took on a political form beyond the original grievance. In February 2019, for example, several thousand teachers demonstrated in Rabat against the imposition of short-term contracts. Although relatively peaceable, some of the protesters chanted 'death to the dictatorship' and moved to blockade a bridge between the capital and Salé. In March an estimated 10,000 teachers, who argued that they were being 'forcibly (privately) contracted', protested in Rabat.

THE 2016 LEGISLATIVE ELECTIONS

The outcome of the October 2016 parliamentary elections was an improved performance by the PJD, which won 125 of the 395 seats in the Chamber of Representatives, although this was a long way short of an overall majority. It could be argued that the PJD had suffered from a perceived failure to tackle endemic economic problems, including ongoing corruption. Both the PJD and its nearest rival, the PAM, which secured 102 seats, ruled out forming a coalition with each other, prompting negotiations between the PJD and several small parties, including Istiqlal (46 seats) and the PPS (12), which both agreed to back a PJD-led government, although their support was still insufficient to secure a majority. In the event, the required 45-day period allowed for the formation of a new government was exceeded, and so the King used his constitutional powers to oblige the former, and putative, Prime Minister, Benkirane, to step aside in favour of PJD Secretary-General Saadeddine el-Othmani. The UFSP (20 seats), an opponent of the PJD, formed a four-party tactical alliance with the RNI (37), the MP (27) and the UC (20), in coalition negotiations that resulted in the RNI receiving the most prominent cabinet roles, including the interior, foreign affairs, and economy portfolios. Arguably, the PJD had been outmanoeuvred by the King's representatives in that, despite holding a parliamentary plurality, it ended up with fewer important cabinet portfolios than the RNI, which had less than one-third of the PJD's seat total, and the PJD had barely more responsibilities than its much smaller PPS ally.

STATE EFFORTS TO INSTITUTIONALIZE ISLAMIC PRACTICE

In a measure of how the PJD's public position had, paradoxically, been weakened by the outcome of the elections, in November 2016 Ahmed Touafiq, the Minister of Religious Endowments and Islamic Affairs, was authorized by the Supreme Council of Religious Affairs to remove PJD-affiliated teachers from *madrassas* (religious schools) if they were judged to have insufficient knowledge of the Koran. The Supreme Council is part of the King's formal religious institutions, and is one of the instruments used to vouch for the monarch's claimed legitimacy as the leader of the Muslim community in Morocco, the *amir al-mouminin*. The decision appeared to be an attempt by the King to use his own religious credentials against, in this case, hundreds of mostly female teachers, in order to move against the PJD's toehold on the institutionalized political life of the country, and to enhance, via Islamic means, his own political authority.

These royal decisions to, in effect, more closely nationalize Islamic life in Morocco were expected to continue to be studiously implemented under the enforcement of a Ministry of the Interior whose ministerial portfolio in April 2017 was handed to an independent, Abdelouafi Laftit, who was unlikely to change its role. Since the terrorist attacks in Casablanca in 2003, the Higher Council of *Ulema* (religious scholars) had been used by the monarchy to ensure greater unanimity and state institutionalization of Islamic practice, in accordance with Morocco's adherence to the Maliki school of Islamic law. To this effect, the Higher Council was vetting all mosque sermons for 'correct' content. The more recent moves concerning PJD teachers (see above) were in accordance with this practice.

In September 2016 the PJD had already come under attack from the state when the Ministry of the Interior declared that it was shutting down al-Awn wa al-Ighathah (Help and Assistance), the charitable division of the PJD's umbrella organization Tawhid wa al-Islah (Monotheism and Reform). The PJD charity, believed to be a key form of outreach for the party in northern Morocco, was in receipt of donations from Muslim Brotherhood supporters in the Gulf states, according to reports in the Moroccan newspaper *Assabah*. The ministry's decision in early December to train some 100 imams to instruct members of the armed forces in the perceptibly 'correct' understanding of Islam appeared to be part of the authorities' attempt to counter any PJD, or more radical Islamists', influence in the public sphere or in wider society.

ECONOMIC PROTESTS GATHER STRENGTH

Compounding popular dissatisfaction with the authorities was the death in November 2016 of the man dubbed 'Morocco's Bouazizi', the 31-year-old fish seller Mohsen Fakri. The latter, like Mohamed Bouazizi, a market trader whose suicide sparked the Tunisian uprising in 2011 (see Tunisia), became the subject of public demonstrations in Morocco after he was crushed to death in the back of a refuse truck in the northern coastal city of al-Hoceima, located in the (mostly Berber) Rif region. In a heavily contested sequence of events, it appeared that a policeman confiscated Fakri's freshly caught fish after he allegedly refused to pay a bribe, and that Fakri then jumped into the back of a refuse truck to try to retrieve his fish.

Public and social media anger did not manifest itself in a popular uprising. However, the view that the lives of individuals near the bottom of the economic pecking order were not valued was widely felt and overlapped with popular frustration with the political class. The February 20th Movement was able to mobilize more than 1,000 demonstrators in February 2017, the anniversary of the original Moroccan uprising in 2011, and the issue of Fakri continued to be a highly symbolic one for those expressing discontent. The so-called Hirak al-Shaabi (Popular Movement) grew in strength and was focused on economic deprivation, and challenged what it considered the corrupt operation of officialdom—interlinked issues raised by the treatment of Fakri and strongly resonant throughout the Rif area. The unofficial leader of Hirak al-Shaabi, Nasser Zefzafi, was arrested in late May 2017 after he had reportedly interrupted Friday prayers at a mosque in al-Hoceima. Hirak-style demonstrations took place in Casablanca, Nador, Beni, Tangier, Imzouren and at the National Assembly building in Rabat at the end of May to protest against his arrest. In June the February 20th Movement organized a march on Rabat. To the surprise of many observers, Al-Adl wal-Ihsan announced that it was joining the demonstration, after having earlier split from the February 20th Movement.

In early July 2017 a Berber activist group, Izerfan, announced that it would be joining the Hirak al-Shaabi demonstration planned for al-Hoceima later in that month. Berbers already dominated the protests, but a formal endorsement of political dissent as being on behalf of the broader Berber community was usually avoided. There were reports that demonstrations on 8 July were violently dispersed. Unconventional protests, including demonstrators banging pots and pans throughout the Rif region in June, and by male youths on the beach in Safi, continued in mid-2017. Meanwhile, water shortages in the southern city of Zagora led to demonstrations being staged in September, dubbed the 'Hirak al-Atach' ('thirst protest').

In December 2017 the accidental deaths of two brothers collecting coal in an abandoned mine in the impoverished north-eastern town of Jerada ignited protests and led to solidarity Hirak demonstrations in the Rif area, echoing demonstrations in al-Hoceima one year earlier. Jerada had been neglected since a mines closure programme of the 1990s transformed a major industrial site into an economic backwater. Local representatives of national political parties joined the 'black bread loaf' march—so called because of local hardships. Unrest continued in Jerada throughout January 2018. In February anger increased when another local man died in similar circumstances to the two unofficial miners, and 50 local people were arrested when they protested. The King responded by dispatching Prime Minister el-Othmani to talk to the discontented former miners and the wider community. The premier promised action to ease the plight of the unemployed in Jerada—promises that were dismissed by some as empty rhetoric. In contrast, in April four activists involved in the protest were sentenced to gaol terms by a court in the north-eastern city of Oujda; their alleged offences included that three of them had assaulted and disrespected police officers and hidden a suspected criminal, while a fourth was charged with seemingly unrelated offences following a traffic accident.

Rif activists were also found guilty of offences related to demonstrations in their region, including a renowned female activist, Nawal ben Eissa, who received a suspended sentence in mid-February 2018. Trade unions also continued to be angered by economic conditions, and a specific proposal that would arguably constrain their constitutional right to strike led the leading union federation, the Union Marocaine du Travail, in late January to announce a month-long series of protests and to assert that it was opposed to a Government that it said was pushing up prices and was responsible for policies and legislation intended to 'deepen hostility to the working class'.

In early February 2018 angry demonstrations broke out in Tendrara—an eastern town near the Algerian border—after a small child was killed in a traffic accident. The protesters' anger seemed to be about far more than this tragic death, and was vented on the local authorities. Seven protesters received gaol terms of several months.

In July 2018 the King delivered his annual Throne Day speech in al-Hoceima—the city in which the protests had originally begun—in an attempt to show that the poorer Berber community was not being ignored and, paradoxically perhaps, that the state remained strong despite the internal dissent. In a populist move, the King used the occasion to dismiss Mohamed Boussaid, the unpopular finance minister and a leading RNI figure. The King also appealed for better and more efficient socioeconomic programmes, using his supposed 'above politics' role to blame politicians for the country's economic problems.

Further upset occurred in June 2018, when lengthy gaol terms were handed to 53 Rif protest activists and a journalist. The most prominent organizer, Zefzafi, and three others were given sentences of 20 years each. Hamid El-Mahdaoui, the editor of an opposition website, Badil.info, was sentenced to three years in prison for not writing about alleged attacks on state forces. In August the King granted amnesties to 184 of those detained during the protests. In the previous month the Government had announced that it would introduce a fuel price cap in an apparent effort to reduce popular frustrations, albeit one with a high fiscal cost.

In April 2019 a court decision (following an appeal) to uphold the prison sentences given to 42 of those convicted in June 2018 of involvement in the Hirak protests prompted several thousand people to hold a demonstration in Casablanca against the alleged injustice of the ruling and to protest against unemployment. The USFP announced its support for the demonstrators.

The particular grievances of the Rif Berber community were partly addressed in July 2019 when it was announced that Tamazight (the standardized version of 'Berber') would be designated as an official language. However, this move, although useful symbolically as it implied state acceptance of this long-disadvantaged community, failed to address the Berbers' economic grievances.

Morocco recovered from the 2011 protests owing to the ability of the monarchy to accommodate reform without relinquishing its power over the strategic direction of the country, including over its foreign and defence relations and national security. The King and the royal family seemingly still retained relatively strong support at the popular level, even though the monarchy's inevitable role was not as widely accepted as in the past, given that, as a 2019 British Broadcasting Corporation (BBC) News Arabic poll revealed, Moroccans were becoming less conservative. In short, many

Moroccans favoured both the monarchy and significant political change—an apparent paradox that suggested that a constitutional monarchy was desired, not the ongoing use of executive powers by the King and the *makhzen* to control the overall direction and security of the country.

MEDIA CONTROVERSY

Taoufik Bouachrine, the publishing director of the Moroccan newspaper *Akhbar al Yaoum al Maghribiya*, was arrested in February 2018. He was accused by the authorities of a sexual assault, something that he denied and about which his lawyers pointed out was not clearly defined as a crime under Moroccan law (meaning that his arrest on this basis would have questionable legality). Although the veracity of charges (also including 'human trafficking'), which appeared to lack detail, was difficult to establish one way or the other, it was of political interest that, in the increasingly confrontational political climate, a journalist whose newspaper was sympathetic to the PJD had come under pressure from the state. Notably, however, in June Bouachrine's newspaper did not shy away from criticizing the prison sentences for the Rif protest organizers nor from casting the decision in the context, as the newspaper saw it, of intended constitutional reforms that had failed to separate the judiciary from the executive (or *makhzen*). In November a court in Casablanca found Bouachrine guilty on charges of sexual assault and sentenced him to 12 years in prison. Rassani claimed that the King might issue a pardon to offset the court's response to assumed *makhzen* pressure. However, in October 2019 the appeal court in Casablanca increased Bouachrine's sentence to 15 years.

The idea of the *makhzen* continuing to run the country almost autonomously from the King, even if it constituted part of the monarchical regime, appeared to be underscored during Mohammed's long absences from Morocco in the first half of 2018 (see *Relations with Europe—France*). The King continued to be periodically out of view, sometimes owing to matters of his health. In June 2020 he underwent successful heart surgery in Rabat.

By 2023 the King's periodic lengthy absences from Morocco and his disengagement from state leadership were attracting greater attention. It was also widely noted in Morocco that, whether he was at home or abroad, Mohammed was increasingly spending his time with three controversial German-Moroccan brothers, one of whom had served time in German gaols, prompting even parts of the *makhzen* subtly, but publicly, to raise their concerns. In May *The Economist*, a British news publication, reported that Mohammed had resided outside of Morocco for the majority of 2022.

Meanwhile, the state's interest in targeting journalists who criticized the authorities, by focusing on their private lives, continued, with the imprisonment of a young journalist from *Akhbar al-Youm al-Maghribiya*, Hajjar Raissouni. In September 2019 she was convicted of having an abortion and conducting an extra-marital relationship. She denied the former charge. In the following month she received a pardon from the King, suggesting that, although illegal, these practices for which she had been convicted were not the real reasons for gaoling her. In May 2020 Raissouni's uncle, Suleiman Raissouni, the editor of *Akhbar al-Youm al-Maghribiya*, was arrested on a charge of harassment of a homosexual man in the journalist's own home. Given the reputation of the newspaper and Suleiman for writing about subjects with which the Government was uncomfortable, this once again appeared to constitute a political arrest.

In December 2019 Mohamed Sekkaki, a prominent broadcaster on social media, was sentenced to a four-year gaol term for posting a video in which he criticized the King. Criticizing the monarch is unambiguously a criminal offence under Moroccan law, and social media activists are an increasing focus of the local authorities. Among other individuals who were arrested and sentenced for posting criticism of the Government on social media was Abdelali Bahmad, who criticized the King and expressed support for the Hirak protests in the Rif; he was imprisoned for a year as a consequence. The Moroccan Association for Human Rights (Association Marocaine des Droits Humaine) estimated in March 2020 that 110 people were in prison for publishing material that was considered politically offensive.

Among a significant proportion of Morocco's burgeoning young population, the local rap music scene is as important as the conventional media. For this reason, the imprisonment of a rap artist, Simo Gnawi, in December 2019 was significant. Gnawi's hugely popular song 'Long Live The People' implied that the King was responsible for the disappearance of public money while accumulating wealth for himself. The song also subverted King Mohammed's official title, *amir al-mouminin* (Commander of the Faithful) to *amr al-mudminin* (Commander of the Addicts), in reference to the large number of Moroccan youths who, often without a job, engage in drug use (itself a major illicit Moroccan export industry). Gnawi was not convicted of political offences as such (even though insulting the monarch is a criminal offence), but for an earlier offence of allegedly insulting a policeman. The Ministry of Culture, Youth and Sports banned all rap concerts after Gnawi's imprisonment.

Nabila Mounib, the leader and sole parliamentary representative of a relatively radical socialist grouping, the Parti Socialiste Unifié, proposed a national amnesty law in mid-April 2022 that would, if passed, seek a parliamentary means of nullifying the application of sentences on the Hirak leaders and activists over the largely Amazigh protests in the Rif region (see above). Mounib, the first female head of a Moroccan political party, was, however, by definition, a solo operator. Furthermore, the proposed legislation, while theoretically removing the issue of de facto political prisoners from the judicial process, could not avoid the fact that under the law the King is the ultimate arbiter of what would ultimately be a royal pardon. Notably, Zefzafi continued in principle to reject a royal pardon, if proffered, on the basis that its acceptance would be an admission of guilt for what he argued was his right to protest against injustice.

In February 2022 something of a seeming latter-day Moroccan tradition of targeting public figures who speak out against officialdom by accusing them of alleged sexual misdemeanours apparently claimed another victim. The former Minister of Human Rights, Mohamed Ziane, had angered the authorities in December 2020 with his sharply worded criticism of national security organs. His fall from grace, however, allegedly rested in part on what he claimed was the role of the General Directorate of Territorial Surveillance in leaking a video of him in a compromising situation with a married policewoman. He was formally charged with, *inter alia*, insulting state institutions, defaming people on social media and setting a bad example to minors, and was sentenced to three years' imprisonment.

CANNABIS PRODUCTION AND EXPORTATION LEGALIZED

One of the more suspect claims made by some elected legislators was that their success in May 2021 in securing the support of the lower house for the legalization of Morocco's foreign cannabis trade, for either medical or what was termed 'industrial' use, would help tackle economic hardship among Rif farmers. Supporters of the move, approved via a vote that actively involved only a minority of elected representatives (votes cast were 125 to 49 in favour), claimed that it would raise Rif farmers' income by approximately one-third within seven years. This was the supposed financial gain that they said would come from a managed cannabis export scheme that the law proposed would be operated by cannabis farmers in partnership with the Moroccan Government. The formal approval of the bill attracted significant international attention—not least as it legitimized the export of cannabis at a time when many foreign countries continued to ban it outright. The PJD rather piously expressed its opposition to legalizing a recreational drug renowned for its use in the West that had long been a staple of Moroccan export revenue, albeit traditionally on an illicit basis. The PJD legislators, who were largely running the Government, may have been opposed in principle to legalizing the production of cannabis for export, but only 49 members actively voted against the proposed law.

In March 2022 the RNI-led Government took what appeared to be the final step in introducing the proposed cannabis legalisation when it approved a draft (executive) decree—tabled by the interior minister—to implement the new law. According to Morocco World News (MWN), the decree identified legalization of production in three provinces only: al-Hoceima, Chefchaouen and Taounate (all in the Rif region), although it held open the possibility of extending the 'right' to other provinces. The cabinet decree enabled production in these provinces for export and, according to MWN, for medical use. The latter suggested the possibility of production for domestic consumption in strictly medical circumstances. The newly legalized industry was to be closely monitored, partly to ensure co-operative relations with recipient countries, and the Government hoped to make considerable financial gains through export taxes and large-scale investment. In October the Government issued the first 10 licences to Moroccan businesses to produce cannabis for medicinal or 'industrial' use and for export. However, critics noted that the promised government body for oversight and regulation of the cannabis industry had still not been created. Furthermore, some analysts suggested that without careful regulation the profits of the legal trade could get confused with the large illicit trade that would inevitably remain for recreational use and export, making criminal detection much harder.

POLITICAL DEVELOPMENTS FAIL TO BREAK IMPASSE

King Mohammed had marked Throne Day in July 2019 with an appeal for 'new blood' to be injected into the Cabinet in the form of 'elite' appointments based purely on merit. This looked like another typical example of political expediency on the part of the Moroccan monarch: responding to popular political discontent by implying that this was resolvable by a reorganization of the Cabinet and wider administration. The King also went some way to accommodating frustration with the repression of the Hirak movement (see above) by pardoning 4,764 prisoners, several of whom had been involved in the Rif protests. In a further indication that he was attempting to be seen as responsive to the popular grievances that had motivated the Hirak movement and the subsequent boycott movements, King Mohammed also used his speech to announce the formation of a new Special Commission to investigate and reduce social and regional inequalities, to be known as the Special Commission for the Development Model (SCDM). In December the SCDM's 35-strong membership was announced, with the former interior minister, Chakib Benmoussa, as chair of a body comprising individuals with extensive public sector and private sector experience. Its remit was to present a report to the King in mid-2020 about the social, political and economic development of the country; what had been achieved and what was lacking; and to encompass in its analysis the expectations of the Moroccan population. Perhaps surprisingly, it was reported that the SCDM's analysis would include the kingdom's international relations. Members of the SCDM consulted a wide range of people, including representatives of business and even minor political parties. It was stressed upon its foundation that the SCDM was not to be considered as a 'shadow' or alternative government, although it seemed plausible that some of its findings would have an influence within the palace and wider *makhzen*, whether its recommendations for changes in the existing 'development model' were directly followed or not. It was not clear whether the elite nature of the SCDM's leading members, and their close association with the palace, would give the new body much room for bold thinking and or whether it would have credibility among the politically disaffected sections of Moroccan society.

In the event, the publication of the SCDM's report, on 26 May 2021, was delayed, owing to the coronavirus disease (COVID-19) pandemic—the tackling of which by government bodies became one of the key focuses of the inquiry. In the event, however, the report's conclusions were very generalized in terms of how they re-envisaged governmental administration. The SCDM's conclusions seemed little different to an array of medium- and long-term 'national visions' that over the previous decade had been issued by governments throughout the Middle East and North Africa. In an analysis provided by the Qatari-owned Arabic news website *Arabi21* on 31 May, it was noted that, after directly consulting nearly 10,000 Moroccans and receiving more than 6,000 individual submissions, the SCDM's consequent report had urged the creation of a productive, diversified economy that would ensure good-quality jobs for all Moroccans by 2035. *Arabi21*'s analysis of the SCDM emphasized that its content fell short of the type of criticism of Moroccan governance and political economy that the King himself had been making. *Arabi21* argued that, in drawing up the report, the SCDM had decided to avoid stating what were the causes of the malaise that it was addressing or to recommend any of the 'radical solutions' needed to address them.

In October 2019 Prime Minister el-Othmani announced a cabinet reorganization. On the one hand, it markedly reduced the total number of ministers (including junior ministers) from 41 to 24. On the other, many of the most powerful and sought-after cabinet positions were left unchanged: the ministers for foreign affairs, finance, industry, energy, education, and agriculture remained in post, as did the ministers for human rights and for logistics, while many of the portfolios that changed hands were primarily about political party machinations in the distribution of the spoils. However, the politically controversial health minister, Annas Doukali (who had been disowned by his PSP colleagues after he remained in office following their withdrawal from the Government in 2018) was replaced by a renowned health care professional, Khalid Aït Taleb, apparently on the orders of the King. This appointment later appeared prescient given the scale of the challenge from the COVID-19 pandemic. The meritocratic nature of the other new appointments was unclear, however. Mohamed Aujar of the RNI was replaced as the Minister of Justice by the UFSP's Mohamed Ben Abdelkader. The overall political balance that had favoured the PJD, which held the plurality of parliamentary seats, was consolidated. Mohamed Amkraz of the PJD replaced fellow party member Mohammed Yatim as Minister of Employment and Professional Integration, while the PJD's Nezha El-Ouafi replaced the UFSP's Abdelkarim Benatiq as the Minister-Delegate in charge of Moroccan Expatriates. Perhaps the greatest personal beneficiary was Hassan Abyaba of the UC, who was appointed as Government Spokesman and Minister of Culture, Youth and Sports. However, in April 2020 the King overrode Prime Minister el-Othmani's prerogative and dismissed Abyaba from the Cabinet. Abyaba had proven to be less than competent and was replaced as culture minister by Othmane el-Ferdaous, while Minister for National Education Saïd Amzazi assumed the post of Government Spokesman.

In an indication that the *makhzen* realized that these relatively minor rearrangements were too insubstantial to appease the disaffected sections of the population, in June 2020 the Government introduced legislation to give the National Anti-Corruption Commission more powers. The issue of corruption was central to the motivation for the 2011 protests in Morocco and the wider Arab uprisings and was a large part of the disaffection expressed in the kingdom in the following years. The popular call for *nazaha* (integrity) remains a potent one in demonstrations in Morocco and more widely. Created in early 2019 under Mohammed Rashidi, the National Commission for Integrity, Prevention and Combating Bribery (NCIPCB) was initially only allowed to investigate reports of alleged corruption that were submitted to other parts of the state apparatus, although the Government claimed that the Commission would eventually be able to act autonomously and instigate its own investigations. Rashidi had reportedly been pushing for these police-like powers for some time. In a profile of Rashidi in *Al-Araby al-Jadeed* in June 2020, it was noted that he had stated in February 2019 that he was urging a legal refounding of the Commission to ensure that it was a wholly independent body, although not in terms of being entirely separate from other public bodies with which it needed to collaborate to ensure corruption was combatted. Rashidi stressed that the Commission's findings would enable proper legal pursuit of the allegedly corrupt. However, he also emphasized that the body was as much about education as it was about encouraging the prosecution of corrupt individuals—a position that attracted some criticism. The legislation received final approval in February 2021, but until the new powers began to take effect, it was expected to be difficult to assess how effective the Commission could be and whether it could assuage popular frustration. It was not clear whether the NCIPCB had, in practice, begun autonomously to address vested interests where alleged corruption lay. However, a German think tank, the International Relations and Politics Foundation (Stiftung Wissenschaft und Politik), reported in June 2021 that, according to the 'Global Perceptions Index' on corruption, Morocco only had an 'intermediate ranking' of 86th out of 160 countries surveyed.

PANDEMIC POLITICS

At the same time as his intervention in April 2020 to reorganize the Cabinet, the King announced that a further 5,654 prisoners would be pardoned—a move that seemed genuinely to be motivated by concerns about public health in the context of the COVID-19 pandemic. However, the planned releases would not offset the more than 50,000 Moroccans arrested during the month following the announcement on 19 March of the state of emergency for not complying with COVID-19 regulations. Based on official statistics, however, Morocco was coping comparatively well with the pandemic, perhaps in part because of the toughness of the enforcement measures that the Government had introduced since the beginning of the crisis.

Expressions of public discontent were reported not long after the lockdown was introduced. On 22 March 2020 large numbers of protesters took to the streets in Fez, Tétouan, Tangier and Salé in demonstrations involving the chanting of religious slogans and in which three Islamist figures played a controversial role: Ashraf Hayani, Radwan Ben Abdulsalim and El-Munshed Tetouani. The principal focus of the protest was the economic impact of the lockdown on the poorer sections of society, including seasonal workers and street traders, for whom food shortages were common. However, many other ordinary Moroccans were angry with the three Islamist preachers and others for encouraging popular protests that created a danger to public health, given the participants' blatant lack of regard for social-distancing. Furthermore, a renowned preacher known as Abu Naim had already been arrested for urging popular disregard for government strictures against attending mosque. There were demands in the media and elsewhere for the Government to combine more effective emergency food relief measures to address the protesters' plight with tougher policing of behaviour that undermined the lockdown and risked spreading COVID-19. At the end of June taxi drivers in Rabat protested about the impact on their livelihood of new measures that allowed them to operate but only at 50% capacity, without being allowed to raise their prices to offset losses, which other transport providers had been allowed to do.

Protest and upheaval continued to be a feature of Moroccan political life. While it appeared that the Rif-based Hirak movement did not have the same weight on the streets that it once possessed, it still had the ability to unsettle the authorities. For example, it was reported in February 2021 that its leader, Nasser Zafzafi, who had been sentenced to prison for 20 years from May 2017, had collapsed in his cell for well over an hour due to his pursuit of a hunger strike. In a precursor to Morocco's dispute with Spain over the reception given to the Polisario chief (see *Talks Founder Amid Morocco–UN Tensions*), demonstrations were held in Madrid in support of the Hirak leader.

ELECTORAL REFORM PROVES DIVISIVE

In February 2021 the Cabinet decided, with the backing of four of its constituent seven parties, to support a number of electoral reforms intended to be applied in the elections scheduled for September (which in turn would determine who, as leader of the majority party, became Prime Minister). The most significant proposed change—from national to regional determination of party candidate lists—was rejected by the PJD, which also voted against the revision of electoral legislation that was successfully passed by the lower house on 6 March with the support of almost all of the political parties, including all of the other governing coalition parties. The Islamist PJD saw the proposed change as calculated to reduce its representative strength in the lower house and to thus, potentially, remove its majority and, therefore, its leadership in government. The greatest enthusiasm for the change came, unsurprisingly, from parties that anticipated gains, such as the main opposition party PAM. The change created the impression of introducing greater democracy to the elected part of the Moroccan political system. From national party-managed electoral lists that had awarded a share of seats in the lower house, and a minority of the seats in the upper chamber, based on each party's share of the national vote, Morocco was set to transition to an electoral system designed both to decentralize the determination of the order of parties' candidate lists (and thus the determination of potential seats) in favour of a provincially determined process, and to ensure that women and, potentially via the decentralization process, minorities, i.e. Berber (Amazigh), were better represented among legislators. However, critics observed that ensuring regional representation in a national parliament on the basis of the number of people within a given province registered to vote, as opposed to actual votes cast, was undemocratic. The apparent anomaly was due to the proposed determination of a region's representation being effectively according to its electoral population size; actual votes cast would, under the legislation's proposed changes, determine how much a given political party obtained from any region's allocated seats. The alleged greater democraticness of increased female representation was on the relatively contentious basis of the new law determining that two-thirds of seats from any region had to go to women. However, it was not clear how exactly the consequent presumably fairly top-heavy weighting in both order and proportionality in favour of women in each party's regional list of candidates would guarantee that the two-thirds' proviso was either reached, or not excessively exceeded. Additionally, it was not clear if the gender make-up of the upper house would have to be similarly managed with respect to the determination of the indirectly chosen seats, which formed the majority of members of this chamber, nor how this would be achieved.

In tandem with the above change to existing election legislation, was the introduction in February 2021 of two new bills into the lower house that sought to streamline, so their proponents claimed, the conduct of elections at all levels of society, including those to (national) chambers of agriculture, fishing and commerce. Like the approved two-thirds' requirement for women's representation in parliament, these instituted specific moves to increase the female quotient in professional and trade bodies, but, according to press reports, without setting a fixed threshold. One of the bills also emphasized ensuring that all those with identity cards would be registered to vote, albeit that, reportedly, this was described as a national process (in contradistinction with the regionalization described above).

2021 LEGISLATIVE ELECTIONS SEE ISLAMISTS ROUTED

In the legislative elections held on 8 September 2021, support for the PJD declined from 125 seats in 2016 to just 13. The RNI emerged as the leading party, with 102 seats, a gain of 65 seats compared with 2016. The PAM secured 87 seats and Istiqlal won 81 seats. On 10 September the leader of the RNI, Aziz Akhannouch, was invited by the King to form a new government. Assuming that his new coalition (comprising the RNI, the PAM and Istiqlal) remained stable, the new Prime Minister commanded a parliamentary majority of 270 out of the 395 seats in the lower chamber.

While the RNI's gain of 65 seats was phenomenal, the biggest story of the 8 September 2021 poll was the near total collapse of the PJD, which secured barely 10% of its 2016 tally. Popular disfavour for a party affiliated to the Muslim Brotherhood had not happened in isolation; in Tunisia, prior to the July 2021 coup, there had also been a weakening of support for the Islamist Ennahdha party. Arguably, however, the PJD's extreme electoral misfortune was primarily a specific consequence of its infighting and to an extent dissolution over its then leader's major public role in what had effectively been a *makhzen*-driven normalization of relations with Israel (see *Relations with the Middle East*).

Two parties of a moderately socialist hue made significant gains: the USFP gained 14 seats and the PPS 10, bringing their respective tallies to 34 and 22. That these two left-of-centre parties should perform well suggests that Moroccan popular support for relatively secular and moderate reform trends had a firm, albeit still decidedly minority, position in the lower chamber. Despite proceeding to form part of the governing coalition, the PAM's tally actually declined, although not significantly. The PAM's weakened position may have reflected voter frustration with the party's internal divisions.

Following the PJD's dire electoral performance, the party's politically disgraced leader, el-Othmani, who had himself lost his parliamentary seat, announced his resignation. His predecessor, Benkirane, was re-elected as party leader at a PJD congress in October 2021. The PJD's electoral collapse had occurred in the context of its transition from a partially pro-establishment party (as almost by definition it needed to be in Morocco's system of managed competition) to being fully co-opted. This suggested that moderate Islamism, or any form of modest political dissent, could find a meaningful outlet in the post-2011 Moroccan political system.

Following his reassumption of the leadership of the PJD, Benkirane attempted to bolster the party's 'anti-Zionist' credentials by adopting a tough rhetorical stance against the normalization of Morocco's relations with Israel (a process that the PJD under el-Othmani had been involved in). Benkirane sought to capitalize on popular discontent, especially when senior Israeli representatives visited Morocco, including in October 2021 when a defence agreement was signed during a visit by the Israeli Minister of Defense, Benny Gantz (see *Relations with the Middle East*).

Benkirane also continued his party's periodic sparring with the socialist USFP, despite the opposition in general ostensibly being committed to participating in a Co-ordination Committee on budgetary and other legislative matters. However, the USFP stated in November 2022 that it was withdrawing from the Co-ordination Committee in response to the attacks on the party and its leader by Benkirane.

In October 2021 the new Government was sworn in under the leadership of a new Prime Minister, Aziz Akhannouch. Having served as agriculture minister in the previous administration, this represented a major promotion for Akhannouch. Nasser Bourita, a familiar individual who had seemingly proven successful in playing hardball with the Europeans (see below), remained foreign affairs minister. Significantly, given the institutional power of the security services in the Moroccan state, the interior minister post, held by Abdelouafi Laftit, was unchanged too. Nadia Fettah Alaoui was elevated from the position of tourism minister, to economy and finance minister, and was one of seven women in the 25-member Cabinet, including the former mayor of Marrakech, Fatima Ezzahra el-Mansouri, who was appointed as Minister of National Planning, Urban Planning, Housing and Urban Policy. The leader of the PAM, Abdellatif Ouahbi, was appointed justice minister, while the Istiqlal leader, Nizar Baraka, was given responsibility for the infrastructure and water portfolio. The composition of the new Government obviously in part reflected the parliamentary arithmetic underpinning the coalition and the balance of forces within the latter. However, the King and senior officials within the *makhzen* likely played a role in the ministerial appointments (as well as, no doubt, in the formation of the actual coalition in the first place).

In November 2021 Minister of the Economy and Finance Alaoui succeeded in getting the new Government's budget for 2022 through the Chamber of Representatives by a healthy margin of 206 votes to 67. Alaoui emphasized to the lower chamber that, despite spending constraints, the Government attached importance to making progress with the ongoing regional development plans—a seeming nod to continuing Amazigh and other regional discontent over unemployment and low incomes amid rising prices.

In late February 2022 popular protests took place in Rabat and in many other parts of Morocco as the rising cost of living, particularly of food and of many essential imported products, fuelled discontent across the kingdom. Some of this unrest overlapped with political disquiet in the Amazigh (Berber) areas, especially in the Rif, but the February protests were essentially a national expression of discontent that seemingly united Arab and Amazigh, region with region, and employed and unemployed. Alaoui's deputy, Faouzi Lekjaa (the minister responsible for the budget at the Ministry of the Economy and Finance), stressed that in response to global pressure on grain supplies and prices, and amid a drought in Morocco (see Economy), the Government was having to help farmers as well as the general populace. However, he also admitted to the media on 21 February that these government responses were 'insufficient'.

Public protests against the rising cost of food and other staple goods continued during 2022–23, with the Government being criticized for inadequately addressing the problem. In April 2023 demonstrations were held outside the parliament building in Rabat in protest against expensive food imports. The agriculture minister responded by blaming global factors and inclement weather conditions, in addition to a drought that had disrupted domestic agricultural production.

In March 2023 the PAM and the PPS demanded that the Government take action to address the rising cost of living. The PAM urged the governing parties to meet immediately to resolve the 'domestic crisis', while the PPS advocated for price control measures.

Morocco's political system continued to attract domestic and international criticism, particularly the inability of elected officials to take decisions freely to address popular concerns. Freedom House (a US non-governmental organization), in its 2023 global assessment of political and civil freedom, continued to define Morocco as only 'partly free'. Given the ongoing imprisonment of government critics and the detention of those seen as politically troublesome, this was unsurprising. However, it was noted by Freedom House that the religious and academic spheres were relatively liberal, but not in terms of political expression, which was strongly curtailed. Freedom House drew attention to the arrest of Saida el-Alami of Women Against Political Detention, who had criticized the Government online. In September 2022 el-Alami's April conviction was upheld and her sentence was increased to three years.

Meanwhile, in January 2022 the *Al-Quds Al-Arabi* news outlet reported that the Moroccan League for the Defense of Human Rights had warned that the disconnect between the practical reality and what it referred to as the 'constitutional' position on issues such as the Tamazight (Berber) language could mean that the Government was unwittingly fomenting Amazigh discontent. The League stated that the limited progress made regarding the promised introduction of the teaching of Tamazight in government schools was an indicator of the problem. It also called for the declaration of Amazigh New Year's day as a paid official national holiday, and a review of the dedicated Amazigh television channel in order to avoid it becoming a cultural ghetto, as opposed to what it argued would be a preferable policy of introducing more Amazigh-oriented programming on the main television channels.

In March 2022 the Government banned a scheduled annual conference of Amazigh groups. The conference's planning committee argued that the ban was illegal and told the Middle East Monitor, a UK-based independent media research institution, that they had co-ordinated all their preparations according to the law. On the face of it, such an event was not inherently illegal; however, the precise legal reason for not allowing the event to proceed was not made clear.

In May 2023 the Government announced that the Amazigh New Year would be recognized as an official state holiday, suggesting that the authorities were making a genuine, if thus far limited, attempt at projecting Morocco as more than a uniform 'Arab' country. The government budget for 2023 had also increased by 50% the allocation for supporting the use of the Tamazight language, although Amazigh activists remained frustrated by the limited amount of teaching of their language in government schools. In June the Government announced that it would ensure that 4m. schoolchildren would be taught in Tamazight at primary school level by 'the end of the decade'. Education minister Chakib Benmoussa stated that a large increase in teachers able to conduct this role would be required and that more recruitment would begin from the start of the next school year.

TERRORIST THREATS CONTINUE

Throughout 2015–16 the Moroccan authorities arrested terrorist suspects—often described as foreign Arabs, principally Algerians and Libyans, as well as Moroccan nationals—primarily for involvement in the extremist Islamic State group. In August 2015 the Ministry of the Interior announced the arrest of a '13-member cell' (presumably Moroccan) who were apparently involved in recruiting Moroccans to fight for Islamic State abroad. In September a three-member—presumably Moroccan—Islamic State cell was arrested, accused by the ministry of planning attacks in Morocco, prior to travelling to Iraq and the Syrian Arab Republic. In November, in another ambiguous statement, the authorities reportedly claimed to have arrested 140 terrorist cells since 2002, many of whom would, by definition, have been AQIM-related; from 2014 Islamic State had attracted the allegiance of many AQIM followers. In December 2015 the Moroccan authorities announced the arrest of members of three armed cells, ranging from eight to 11 members, who, it was believed, were planning to travel to join Islamic State in Libya, Syria or Iraq. In March 2016 the Moroccan authorities reportedly arrested a nine-member Islamic State cell that was supposedly part of a Libyan Islamic State unit and had been plotting attacks in Morocco. However, arrests earlier in that month of members of a seven-person cell were not directly linked to neighbouring countries, other than the apparent intention of these Moroccans to head to Libya. The cell's members were described as being active in the southern Moroccan city of Smara and in the towns of Belfaa and Aït Amira.

The Libyan Islamic State connection was demonstrated again in July 2016 when the authorities stated that, in a series of raids across Morocco, they had arrested a cell consisting, reportedly, of six Moroccans who had spent time with Islamic State in Libya and who were allegedly intent on joining a nascent Islamic State operation in Morocco. Periodic arrests of Islamic State suspects continued to be made, including, unusually, three women in Tangier in October. The authorities proved efficient at intercepting plots, and, consequently, Morocco has been relatively immune from actual attacks. Proactive tactics such as heavy policing of clerical activity, including the advanced vetting of religious sermons by the Ministry of Religious Endowments and Islamic Affairs, appears to have paid dividends, and contrasts with the more *laissez-faire* approach to Islamic activity in Tunisia. In January 2017 the Moroccan authorities announced that they had arrested seven people who were part of a cell plotting to attack tourist sites in El-Jadida. The alleged Islamic State-linked operation apparently involved commanders stationed in Iraq, Syria and Libya. In October the head of the Bureau Central d'Investigations Judiciaires (BCIJ), Abdulhak el-Khiame, told British newspaper *The Financial Times* that in the previous two years 42 such cells had been broken up by his organization. His confidence, just two months after the involvement of Moroccans in a terrorist attack in Spain (see *Relations with Europe—Spain*), was such that he offered to train imams in 'Western countries'. In February 2018 the BCIJ arrested seven members of a cell they claimed was affiliated with Islamic State in Tangier and Meknès, and whom they accused of plotting terrorist attacks in Moroccan nightclubs and public facilities, and of planning to assassinate officials. In late 2018 el-Khiame claimed that the BCIJ had dismantled eight terrorist cells between January and October. Judging by official claims at least, Morocco's counterterrorism campaign appeared to have been successful. However, the killing of two Scandinavian tourists in December in an unprovoked knife attack in the Atlas Mountains allegedly carried out by three Moroccans affiliated with Islamic State emphasized how much the threat from Islamic State and other terrorist groups could undermine Morocco's foreign relations and economic interests. (The trial of 24 suspects charged with the attack in the Atlas Mountains commenced in Salé in May 2019, and in July the three apparent leaders of the group received death sentences, while another defendant was sentenced to life in prison.) In October the BCIJ reported that it had been successful in dismantling Islamist State cells in Casablanca, Ouezzane and Chefchaouen. The seven Moroccan men arrested in the action were part of an advanced plot that, in tandem with foreign Islamic State operatives, was reportedly targeting strategic sites and economic infrastructure. The BCIJ also found chemicals, rifles and pistols. The Moroccan cells were aided by a Syrian national who had based himself in Morocco and who facilitated the illicit import of the arms from the Sahel region. Periodic BCIJ operations to dismantle such cells were reportedly relatively frequent. Islamic State continued to cite the kingdom as a target for future attacks, and the organization (together with allied groups) remained a threat in the Maghreb and neighbouring countries.

Reports at the beginning of June 2021 indicated that the Morocco's battle with Islamist militants was continuing. In an operation that the authorities claimed had intercepted planned actions against Moroccan military and other key targets, it was said that two suspects were detained in the villages of Tamdafelt and Beni Khalled. According to regional press reports, the two suspects professed allegiance to the current Islamic State head, Abu Ibrahim al-Hashimi al-Qurashi. Moroccan security forces stated that they also discovered a cache including electronic devices, uniforms and weapons. The authorities regarded the return to Morocco of militants who had been involved in armed combat in Libya, Syria and Iraq as the most dangerous terror threat.

Morocco was praised by the Australian-based international think tank the Institute of Economics and Peace (IEP) in March 2022 when it published its annual Global Terrorism Index. The IEP ranked Morocco 76th on the global list of countries affected by terrorism, two places lower than in 2021. The IEP claimed that this relatively good position was due to the success and interconnectedness of Morocco's hard and soft counterterrorism methods, nationally and internationally. In a press report on the issue, MWN said that although terrorists 'would have Morocco on their radar' (mindful, it could be interpreted, of active Islamist elements in some neighbouring territories, whether Libya or the Sahel), the kingdom had made great progress in countering armed militants.

None the less, in May 2023 the Washington Institute for Near East Policy (WINEP) reported that there had only been seven arrests in Morocco during that year of individuals suspected of terrorism—markedly fewer than in Algeria and Tunisia. Claims of attacks by Islamic State in Libya had not, according to WINEP, occurred for more than a year, while branches of AQIM in Algeria and Tunisia had not claimed any attacks since 2018 and 2019, respectively. It was a reasonable assumption, however, that ongoing instability in Libya would continue to facilitate cross-border terrorist threats in those countries, and therefore potentially in Morocco. A revived home-grown terrorist threat in Morocco was also possible, especially if the displaced persons' camps in north-eastern Syria were closed and the Moroccans among their number returned home.

UN PEACE PLAN FOR WESTERN SAHARA—1988

As fighting between Moroccan troops and Polisario forces continued, the UN and the OAU made a concerted effort to settle the conflict in Western Sahara. In August 1988 the UN Secretary-General announced that a detailed peace plan had been drafted. The plan contained proposals for a ceasefire and a referendum to determine the status of the territory, and a UN representative, with wide-ranging powers, and a 2,000-strong UN monitoring force were to oversee their implementation. Prior to the referendum, Morocco was to reduce its presence in Western Sahara from 100,000 to 25,000 troops, who would then be confined to barracks, and Polisario forces (totalling an estimated 8,000) were to withdraw to their bases. The referendum was to offer a choice between complete independence for the territory and its integration into Morocco; it was hoped that a further option would be added, offering a large measure of autonomy for the Sahrawi people under the Moroccan crown. Both Morocco and the Polisario Front formally accepted the UN peace plan, although both sides expressed reservations. However, the UN's expectation that a ceasefire could be secured within one month, and the referendum held within six months, proved wholly unrealistic.

In October 1988 the UN General Assembly agreed that direct talks should be held, to be followed by a ceasefire and a referendum. Morocco abstained in the voting, claiming that, as both sides had accepted the UN proposal for a ceasefire, there was no need for direct talks. Polisario stepped up its attacks, but King Hassan refused to 'negotiate with his own subjects' and announced his readiness to order his troops across international borders in pursuit of Polisario forces. Morocco, meanwhile, continued its massive development programme in Western Sahara, where Moroccan settlers, able to relocate as a result of attractive financial packages, now outnumbered the Sahrawi population. It was not until April 1991 that the UN Security Council approved Resolution 690, authorizing the establishment of the UN Mission for the Referendum in Western Sahara (MINURSO), which was to implement the plan for a referendum of self-determination with a UN peacekeeping force to supervise the operation. The ceasefire came into effect in September, and deployment of MINURSO personnel began at el-Aaiún. Each side swiftly accused the other of violating the ceasefire, and disagreements over exactly who was entitled to vote resulted in the postponement of the referendum, originally scheduled for January 1992.

In March 1993 UN Security Council Resolution 809 decreed that the referendum should take place before the end of the year. Both Morocco and Polisario accepted the resolution, but continued disputes over the process of identification of voters meant that the referendum was repeatedly delayed.

In March 1997 the new UN Secretary-General, Kofi Annan, appointed former US Secretary of State James Baker as his personal envoy to Western Sahara. Between June and September Baker chaired a series of direct talks between the Moroccan Government and representatives of Polisario. In September a compromise agreement ('the Houston accords') was reached on voter eligibility in the referendum, now scheduled for December 1998.

However, disputes continued over the voter registration process, and a new date, December 1999, was set for the referendum. In January 1999 the UN warned Morocco that if it did not co-operate fully, MINURSO's mandate would not be renewed and the UN would withdraw from the region. Polisario declared that if the referendum did not take place, the alternative was war. The referendum was subsequently postponed until July 2000.

Following his accession in 1999, King Mohammed created a Royal Commission for Sahrawi Affairs and proposed the establishment of an elected autonomous assembly for the territory. Polisario condemned these initiatives, asserting that Morocco was attempting unfairly to influence the population in advance of the referendum.

AUTONOMY PLAN FOR WESTERN SAHARA

In December 1999 Annan conceded that the referendum was unlikely to take place before 2002, and in early 2000 he expressed doubts that the referendum would be held at all. In February the leader of Polisario warned that renewed hostilities were possible if the referendum were not held before the end of the year.

It was against this unhopeful background that Annan asked Baker to resume his role as personal envoy. The UN's favoured option appeared to be autonomy for Western Sahara under Moroccan sovereignty, and there were reports that both the USA and France preferred the widest possible autonomy for the territory. However, several meetings in mid-2000 between Baker and representatives of the Moroccan Government and Polisario failed to make any progress, and neither side was prepared to discuss Baker's suggestion of an alternative political solution to the referendum plan. At a meeting chaired by Baker in September, Morocco indicated its willingness to begin talks on autonomy for Western Sahara. Prime Minister el-Youssoufi subsequently stated that his Government was looking at models of 'regionalization' adopted by other countries, and was preparing plans to allow the inhabitants of the territory to administer their own affairs; however, Polisario continued to reject any alternative to the referendum, which it remained confident of winning. None the less, Polisario suffered from declining diplomatic support in Africa, and there were reports of unrest among Sahrawi civilians under its control.

In June 2001 the UN Security Council unanimously approved a compromise resolution encouraging Morocco and Polisario to discuss an autonomy plan for Western Sahara, as proposed by Annan, but without abandoning the delayed referendum. Under the autonomy proposal, the inhabitants of Western Sahara would have the right to elect their own legislative and executive bodies, and to have control over some areas of local government administration—including budget and taxation, law enforcement, internal security, local economy, infrastructure and social affairs—for at least five years, during which Morocco would retain control over defence and foreign affairs. It also provided for the holding of a referendum on the final status of the territory within that five-year period. Polisario categorically rejected the autonomy plan, and continued to demand that the referendum should proceed. Earlier in June it had been reported that Polisario had rejected a Moroccan plan for the autonomy of Western Sahara, whereby the territory would be administered by a senior official appointed by the Moroccan Government.

Meanwhile, Polisario lodged a legal challenge at the UN when Morocco granted the first oil permits in Western Sahara. In February 2002 the UN's legal counsellor stated that although the oil permits were not illegal per se, exploration work and production that was not in the interests of, or according to the wishes of, the Sahrawi people would represent a violation of the principles of international law. In May Polisario signed an agreement with Fusion Oil of Australia to undertake at its own cost a 16-month integrated study of all relevant geological and geophysical data available on 'Sahrawi territorial waters'.

In a new report to the UN Security Council in February 2002, Annan stated that the future of the peace process in Western Sahara was rather depressing, and that in his opinion there were only four options available: that the Security Council insist on proceeding with the long-delayed referendum on self-determination; that Western Sahara become a semi-autonomous province of Morocco—an option rejected by both Polisario and Algeria; that the UN end its peace mission in the territory and withdraw its military observers, risking possible confrontation between Algeria and Morocco; and, the most controversial proposal, that Western Sahara be divided between Morocco and Polisario. However, the Secretary-General pointed out that although Algeria and Polisario might be willing to discuss this last option, Morocco was firmly opposed to it. The UN Security Council subsequently adopted a resolution rejecting the option of a UN withdrawal from the disputed territory and setting a deadline of 30 April for the UN to decide which of the remaining three options should be pursued. In late April and early May US diplomats failed to persuade members of the Security Council to accept the autonomy option favoured by Morocco. Polisario had declared that if US efforts were successful, it would demand the withdrawal of the UN troops from Western Sahara (which could lead to the renewal of hostilities between Polisario and Moroccan forces).

BAKER PRESENTS REVISED PLAN

In early 2003 Polisario rejected revised proposals presented by Baker for a political solution for Western Sahara, stating that these were simply a reformulation of the plan to integrate Western Sahara into Morocco. In May, however, at celebrations marking Polisario's 30th anniversary, the SADR 'President', Muhammad Abdelaziz, stated that Polisario had made fundamental concessions concerning the UN peace plan and would now accept all voters willing to participate in the referendum, provided that they were registered by MINURSO. The UN Secretary-General subsequently urged Morocco, Polisario and Algeria to accept a new peace plan, which proposed immediate self-government for the territory for a period of four to five years, followed by a referendum providing all bona fide residents with an opportunity to determine the future for themselves. The Security Council approved the Secretary-General's proposals at the beginning of June, and at the end of the month Polisario, under strong pressure from Algeria, accepted the Baker plan as a basis for negotiation. Morocco, however, refused to accept any 'imposed decision' on Western Sahara.

In July 2003 the UN Security Council unanimously adopted Resolution 1495 on Western Sahara. This supported the Baker plan and appealed to parties and states of the region to co-operate fully with the Secretary-General and his personal envoy in working towards its implementation. Negotiations on specific elements of the peace plan were expected to ensue, in an attempt at progress towards implementation before the end of the year. Morocco expressed satisfaction with Resolution 1495 because it accepted the principle that any solution should be negotiated and accepted by all parties. However, it reiterated its rejection of Baker's latest proposals, arguing that they drew inspiration from the 1991 settlement plan and moved away from the principle of a political solution.

In April 2004, shortly before the UN Security Council was due to meet to discuss Western Sahara, Morocco's government spokesman announced that Morocco had given its response to the UN on the Baker plan, emphasizing that Morocco was seeking an agreed and lasting political solution but ruled out the independence option and the transitional period. Morocco was willing to discuss other aspects of the plan and to negotiate on the basis of a lasting autonomy for Western Sahara. Morocco expressed strong reservations about the Baker plan, but insisted that it did not reject it 'either in part or parcel', while emphasizing that there were red lines that the plan could not cross. In his report to the Security Council, Secretary-General Annan stated that there were two options from which to choose: either to withdraw the peacekeeping force, or to seek once again to get the parties to work towards accepting and implementing the revised Baker plan. Polisario and Algeria both welcomed UN Security Council Resolution 1541, adopted at the end of the month, emphasizing that it reiterated the Security Council's commitment to respect the Sahrawi people's right to self-determination. Morocco's permanent representative to the UN stated that it was now clear to the international community that dialogue between Algeria and Morocco was the only way to achieve progress in finding a political solution to the conflict.

In June 2004 Baker resigned from his post as personal envoy of the UN Secretary-General, apparently frustrated by his failure to break the political stalemate. Annan asked Alvaro de Soto to take over the role.

THE IMPASSE CONTINUES: UNREST ERUPTS

In October 2004, in Resolution 1570, the UN Security Council reaffirmed its commitment to achieving a mutually acceptable political solution that would provide for the self-determination of the people of Western Sahara. Morocco stated that the new resolution clearly asked both sides to find an alternative political solution to the Baker plan and insisted that a 'compromise' must take into account Morocco's inalienable right to preserve its territorial integrity. It announced that it was willing to enter UN-sponsored talks to formulate a suitable arrangement whereby the inhabitants of the region could manage their own affairs. Algeria strongly supported the resolution, maintaining that this emphasized the validity of the Baker plan as the most suitable political solution and reaffirmed the right of the Sahrawi people to self-determination.

In August 2005 Alvaro de Soto was succeeded as the Secretary-General's personal envoy for Western Sahara by Peter van Walsum, of the Netherlands. Also in August, Polisario released the remaining 404 Moroccan prisoners of war (some of whom had reportedly been held for more than 20 years). In October, however, following his first visit to the region, van Walsum concluded that the positions of the main parties in the dispute were 'quasi-irreconcilable'. Meanwhile, in May a large pro-independence demonstration in el-Aaiún led to violent clashes between protesters and Moroccan security forces that quickly spread to other towns. By October there were reports of daily clashes between Sahrawi youths and police.

In February 2006 Abdelaziz reaffirmed Polisario's rejection of the proposal for autonomy, as advocated by Morocco, and the Algerian Government insisted that the revised Baker plan remained viable. During a six-day visit to Western Sahara in March, King Mohammed pardoned 216 Sahrawi prisoners. A local human rights organization reported that several Sahrawi political activists had been arrested before and during the visit.

ANNAN PROPOSES DIRECT TALKS

With the revised Baker plan seemingly abandoned, and Morocco expected to reject any new plan that did not rule out the prospect of independence for Western Sahara, van Walsum determined that direct negotiations between Morocco and Polisario, without preconditions, were the sole remaining option. However, as the Security Council insisted that any solution must be reached within the framework of the UN and under its auspices, the Secretary-General urged the Security Council to invite Algeria and Mauritania to participate in the negotiations and appealed to Security Council members that had previously supported Morocco's stance to do everything possible to ensure the talks' success. As Polisario had reiterated its opposition to any proposal of autonomy under Moroccan sovereignty, van Walsum had pointed out that negotiations 'without preconditions' meant that there was no requirement for Polisario to recognize Morocco's sovereignty before discussing the 'granting' of autonomy. Annan urged the Security Council and its individual member states 'to do all in their powers to help negotiations to get off the ground', before the Western Sahara question became a threat to international peace and security.

Polisario immediately rejected these proposals as 'unacceptable and unfeasible' and threatened to resume its armed struggle if the report's recommendations were adopted. Algeria also rejected the report, stating that any negotiations should be between Morocco and Polisario and should concern the implementation of the revised Baker plan. Morocco stated that a solution to the conflict required a change of attitude from Algeria, insisting that Polisario acted on the instructions of the Algerian Government. In late April 2006 the UN Security Council unanimously adopted Resolution 1675, affirming its commitment to finding a lasting solution to the dispute. Polisario declared that the resolution represented 'an outstanding victory for the Sahrawi cause and for international legitimacy', in that it rejected the Secretary-General's report and confirmed the right of the Sahrawi people to self-determination and the commitment of the UN to the revised Baker plan. The Moroccan Ministry of Foreign Affairs and Co-operation also welcomed the resolution, stating that Morocco wished to continue with a series of internal negotiations and urging other parties to join these talks.

In July 2006 Morocco's Minister of Foreign Affairs and Co-operation, Muhammad Benaïssa, attended the AU summit meeting in Banjul, The Gambia. Morocco had withdrawn from the OAU in 1985 and had not applied to join the successor AU. The meeting declared that Western Sahara merited greater attention from the international community, and appealed for urgent action to allow the Sahrawi people to exercise their right to self-determination. In March 2007 Algeria's President Abdelaziz Bouteflika stated forcefully that the Sahara issue would 'never constitute a *casus belli* between Algeria and Morocco'. Furthermore, increased bilateral co-operation in combating terrorism reduced tensions with regard to Polisario and Western Sahara.

In April 2007 Morocco presented to the UN Security Council a comprehensive plan for autonomy in Western Sahara. Later that month the Security Council adopted Resolution 1754, which referred to Morocco's proposal in favourable terms and encouraged both sides to begin direct talks without preconditions. In June the new Secretary-General of the UN, Ban Ki-Moon, confirmed that both parties would attend talks, together with Algeria and Mauritania, at the invitation of the UN. The first round of negotiations, held in New York, USA, in that month, yielded little; but at further talks in August both Morocco and Polisario apparently agreed that the status quo was unacceptable and that the process of negotiations would continue. The new framework was given a boost when the European Union (EU) called the talks 'substantive', and the USA endorsed the Moroccan view that 'meaningful autonomy is a promising and realistic way forward'. In Resolution 1783, adopted in October, the UN Security Council welcomed Morocco's 'serious and credible' efforts to seek a resolution. The third round of talks eventually proceeded in January 2008, but no tangible progress was made.

Western backing for Morocco's plan was further emphasized in April 2008, when van Walsum informed the UN Security Council that an independent Western Sahara was 'not a realistic goal'. It was his belief that further talks should be based on two 'realities': that the UN would not force a referendum on Morocco, but nor would it recognize Moroccan sovereignty without an agreement. The personal envoy's statement clarified the UN Security Council's long-held position that it was unwilling to impose a solution to the Western Sahara question. With the exception of an agreement to meet again, a fourth round of talks, held in March 2008, achieved little in the way of significant progress.

In January 2009 Christopher Ross, a former US diplomat, was appointed as the UN Secretary-General's personal envoy for Western Sahara. A fifth round of talks between representatives of the Government and Polisario finally took place in February 2010 in the USA, but ended without agreement. In November 2009 the King had given a speech reiterating the Government's plan for autonomy for Western Sahara, under a new 'regionalization' process that would devolve authority to Morocco's provinces. Many European states quietly supported this plan, and, during a visit to Morocco in that month, the US Secretary of State, Hillary Clinton, had intimated that the USA also endorsed the Government's policy of regional autonomy. However, Polisario continued to demand full independence and the redress of human rights grievances.

MINURSO's mandate continued to be extended on an annual basis. Further talks were held during 2010–11, although no progress was reported. In May 2012 Morocco blamed Ross for the failure of the talks, claiming that he was biased against Moroccan interests.

TALKS FOUNDER AMID MOROCCO–UN TENSIONS

In June 2012 Wolfgang Weisbrod-Weber, of Germany, was appointed Special Representative of the UN Secretary-General and MINURSO Chief of Mission in place of Hany Abdel Aziz (of Egypt, who had held the post since 2009). Following intervention by Ban, Ross resumed the role of mediator, and later that year made his first visit to Western Sahara. In April 2013, in his annual report to the UN Security Council regarding the territory, Ban noted that Ross had secured the continued commitment of both the Moroccan Government and Polisario, as well as neighbouring states, to remain engaged in the UN-sponsored effort. In July 2014 Kim Bolduc, of Canada, succeeded Weisbrod-Weber as Special Representative of the UN Secretary-General and head of MINURSO.

In March 2016 Morocco asked the 84 UN staff deployed as part of MINURSO to leave the country after Ban described the kingdom as an 'occupying' force in Western Sahara, during his visit to refugee camps there. In June there were signs that Morocco would allow the UN staff to return amid speculation in the Moroccan press of a compromise formula whereby MINURSO would be officially designated by the UN as a 'visiting' rather than 'permanent' mission—the latter being the usual term adopted by the UN in its missions to territories that under international law it judges to be occupied as opposed to the more diplomatic term 'disputed'. In May the death of the Polisario Secretary-General and President of the SADR, Abdelaziz, was announced. At an extraordinary congress held by Polisario in early July, Brahim Ghali was elected to succeed Abdelaziz as the organization's Secretary-General and, therefore, as SADR President.

In a striking development in July 2016, at the AU summit in Kigali, Rwanda, Morocco announced that it would seek to return to the AU, which, in its incarnation as the OAU, it had left in 1984 in a dispute over the organization granting the SADR representation. The King argued that Morocco was losing influence as a result of its absence from the AU and sought support for its re-admission without, officially at least, demanding that the SADR's membership be rescinded as a prior condition. Later in July 2016 Moroccan government representatives travelled to Algeria and other neighbouring states to rally support. Algeria later publicly criticized the drawing-up of a petition by 28 African countries, presumably encouraged by Morocco, which called on the SADR's membership of the bloc to be rescinded, stating that Morocco would be permitted to rejoin the bloc only if its readmission was 'unconditional'. In January 2017 Morocco officially rejoined the AU, when 39 of the 54 members voted in favour of the proposal. While being a part of the AU framework was perhaps considered by the Moroccan authorities as a way of trying to settle, or maybe circumvent, the Western Sahara issue, the latter continued to be a point of conflict and dispute between Morocco and some of its neighbours, particularly Algeria. However, the SADR welcomed Morocco's readmission and expressed hope that an AU committee would be created to address the dispute over Western Sahara.

In April 2018 the Moroccan Government issued the Laayoune Declaration, named after the city in which Morocco's political parties met to reject the alleged further movement by the SADR of military assets from Algeria into the disputed Western Sahara. Morocco attended an AU meeting in Mauritania in July, itself a sign of improved relations with its Sahel neighbour (see Relations with the Sahel). However, it emphasized that the AU's decision to form a commission of inquiry to try to find a resolution to the Western Sahara dispute was outside of its responsibilities. Morocco stressed that the AU should defer to the UN over the conflict. Another disputed responsibility issue regarding Western Sahara had occurred earlier, in February, when the European Court of Justice (ECJ) effectively, and controversially, ruled in the SADR's favour by declaring that the EU's fisheries agreement with Morocco did not apply to Western Sahara (see also Relations with Europe—The EU, Other Member States and NATO), compounding the SADR's success a few weeks earlier when a South African court had ruled that importing Western Saharan phosphates via the Moroccan company OPC was illegal.

Having played a role in restarting (for the first time in over six years) UN-hosted talks between the direct and indirect parties to the Western Sahara dispute in December 2018, the UN Secretary-General's Personal Envoy for Western Sahara, Horst Köhler, resigned in May 2019, owing to poor health. Köhler had served in this role since August 2017.

In a reflection of the determination of Morocco to exercise sovereignty over Western Sahara, in January 2020 the Chamber of Representatives approved by a unanimous majority two legal measures that brought the entire 1,000-km maritime border of the territory under full Moroccan jurisdiction. Foreign affairs minister Bourita described the move as a welcome upgrading of Morocco's 'full national legal arsenal' with the 'full sovereignty of the kingdom over its land and maritime borders'. The measures apparently complemented existing legislative measures regarding sovereignty over the land with those affecting the maritime waters of the disputed territory. Although the latest instance of Morocco's fisheries agreement with the EU in February 2019 (see Relations with Europe—The EU, Other Member States and NATO) overcame the bloc's political and legal difficulties with any such agreement applying to Western Sahara, it appeared that the latest Moroccan measure was intended to remove any legal loopholes or ambiguities, at least as far as the kingdom's sovereignty claims were concerned.

In November 2020 the military situation on the ground in Western Sahara reflected deteriorating diplomatic expectations. According to Polisario, on 21 October it had successfully blocked a road 'illegally' used by the Moroccan military to connect the Western Sahara via a crossing at Guerguerat to Mauritania; in other words, a strategic and, in Polisario's eyes, 'illegal' gateway from the kingdom to the rest of Africa had been successfully obstructed. However, on 10 November the Moroccan armed forces announced that they had successfully taken control of the road and of the crossing south; independent observers stated that Moroccan heavy weapons had been used to attack the border buffer zone. A significant Moroccan military victory led Polisario to declare that its observance of the ostensible ceasefire was over. It was against this backdrop that Morocco decided to embrace a peace deal with Israel that in the eyes of the US Government (and Israel) would legitimize its claimed sovereignty over the Western Sahara.

Events that resulted from the peace deal in December 2020 through to mid-2021 made the situation in the Western Sahara, and relations between Morocco and Algeria, even more sensitive. On 22 December 2020 Morocco and Israel signed a declaration, along with the USA, that included a Moroccan-Israeli shared commitment 'to move toward full diplomatic, peaceful and friendly relations'. The *quid pro quo* for this, written into the same document, was that the USA, the facilitator of the agreement, recognized Moroccan sovereignty over Western Sahara; a move that, arguably at a stroke, up-ended decades of the US Administration's, if not the UN's, promotion of a negotiated settlement between the two parties. Compounding Polisario's anger and sense of disempowerment at this development was the secondary but not insignificant recognition of Moroccan sovereignty throughout all of its territory by Israel and by the latter's new Gulf Arab allies: the United Arab Emirates (UAE) and Bahrain. The sovereignty recognition, and its obvious underlining that even talk of compromise was redundant, undermined Moroccan attempts to gain greater acceptance in sub-Saharan circles, including its desired full membership of the Economic Community of West African States (ECOWAS). Algeria was quick to exploit the Moroccan deal with Israel as having been made at, perceptibly, the Sahrawi people's expense. However, this did not prevent two ECOWAS member states, and two other sub-Saharan states, from recognizing Moroccan sovereignty over the Western Sahara by opening diplomatic missions there (see *Relations with Sub-Saharan Africa*).

Just as Morocco was enjoying greater acceptability in US and Gulf Arab circles for what some still saw as an 'occupation', its relations with Europe and, in particular, Spain suffered. It was as if Morocco had gained kudos from one important Western ally at the expense of its relations with all of its immediate neighbours, Arab, sub-Saharan and European. It was difficult to not view this as the background to a spiral of events that in mid-May 2021 saw the Spanish Government provide medical treatment to Polisario head and SADR President, Brahim Ghali. Spain, the former colonial power in a disputed territory that Morocco had annexed without warning, had long seen itself as a mediator in an important territorial dispute directly connected to relations between Morocco and Algeria. While wishing to keep relations with Morocco co-operative, Spain would not have wanted to deny Ghali any urgently needed medical help. That said, its willingness to do this at a time when Morocco had succeeded in effectively neutralizing Spanish and other efforts at mediation, gave its hosting of the Sahrawi leader added import.

Morocco's response to Ghali's perceptibly official hosting in Spain was dramatic and arguably no less effective (see *Relations with Europe—Spain*). The country's playing politics with migration flows into 'Europe'—specifically the Spanish enclave, Ceuta—only served to emphasize that the Sahrawi issue, already damaged by the US shift, would struggle to get beyond the Moroccan Government's now reinforced policy posture of offering autonomy or nothing. Morocco's move towards Israel, following in the footsteps of the UAE and Bahrain, and the reconciliation between the member nations of the Cooperation Council of the Arab States of the Gulf (Gulf Cooperation Council—GCC) in January 2021, helped to reinforce the country's Gulf Arab flank, and probably ended for good Gulf Arab ambiguity towards Morocco's claims over Western Sahara that the Government's 'non-aligned' approach to the GCC spat had engendered (see *Relations with the Middle East*).

Periodic skirmishing in Western Sahara continued during 2021–22. In January 2022 Polisario claimed that its fighters had successfully targeted Moroccan troops in four areas—Al Mahbes Hawza, Farsia and Awsard—although they likely only had a modest impact. Shortly afterwards the Algerian authorities accused Morocco of using heavy weapons to the east of the 'Berm' (a 2,700-km-long structure, mostly comprising a sand wall, that runs through Western Sahara and the south-western portion of Morocco and separates the Moroccan-controlled areas from the Polisario-controlled areas), claiming that Morocco had thereby crossed 'over international boundaries' and was targeting what Polisario and its Algerian backers considered occupied territory. In many senses, the shift in perspective in 2022 of Spain and other Western countries (see below), as well as the resumption of a firmer supportive stance for Morocco by the major Gulf Arab states, was having an impact on the once lively battlefield. According to a report in March by *The Economist*, Polisario fighters were 'getting hammered' by Moroccan forces. The report noted that Israel was playing an important role in this, both in helping to establish the 'Berm' barrier and in providing Morocco with drones (unmanned aerial vehicles), which were proving highly effective against the Polisario troops on the ground.

Meanwhile, in October 2021 Staffan de Mistura had been appointed as the UN Secretary-General's new Personal Envoy for Western Sahara. In July 2022 de Mistura visited both Rabat and Polisario-held territories to hold talks with representatives of both sides. However, with international diplomatic attention focusing increasingly on Morocco's longstanding autonomy plan, it appeared as if the UN process was losing relevance and receiving only rhetorical support from Western and Arab states, which effectively accepted Moroccan sovereignty over Western Sahara. Nevertheless, the fact that Polisario still controlled 20% of Western Sahara's overall territory confirmed that the de facto realities were largely unchanged.

RELATIONS WITH THE USA

Morocco was swift to capitalize on the goodwill that it had generated in the USA by sending a small detachment of Moroccan troops to Saudi Arabia after Iraq's invasion of Kuwait in August 1990. It benefited from bilateral aid and credits from US-dominated agencies, receiving more from the World Bank than any other country in the Middle East or North Africa. Morocco also appeared to have secured US support for its policy on Western Sahara. In return, it supported the US peace initiative in the Middle East and hosted several meetings with key representatives.

The Moroccan authorities strongly condemned the suicide attacks on New York and Washington, DC, USA, of 11 September 2001, but many ordinary Moroccans held Osama bin Laden, who was responsible for the attacks, in the highest esteem for his defiance of the USA. The Moroccan security services co-operated with the US Federal Bureau of Investigation in tracking down alleged terrorists of Maghreb origin based in Europe.

In response to the Israeli military incursions into Palestinian-controlled areas of the West Bank, US Secretary of State Colin Powell began a regional tour in Morocco in April 2002. More than 1m. protesters, including Islamists as well as representatives of the main political parties, took to the streets of Rabat on the day before Powell's visit to express solidarity with the Palestinian people. Moroccan secret service agents were reported to have taken part with the US Central Intelligence Agency (CIA) in interrogating detainees held in Guantánamo Bay. In June the Moroccan authorities announced that at the beginning of May they had arrested three Saudi nationals and several Moroccans who were alleged to be members of an Islamist cell, linked to al-Qa'ida, that had been preparing terrorist attacks on US and British warships in the Strait of Gibraltar. Morocco's Minister of the Interior attributed the success in discovering and dismantling this terrorist cell to close co-operation between Morocco's security services and their Saudi and US counterparts. In February 2003 a young Moroccan, Mounir al-Motassadek, became the first person to be convicted in connection with the September 2001 attacks on the mainland USA, when a German court found him guilty of being an accessory to murder and of membership of a terrorist organization and sentenced him to 15 years in prison. (In August 2005 al-Motassadek was acquitted of involvement in the September 2001 attacks; he was none the less convicted of belonging to a terrorist organization and sentenced to seven years' imprisonment.)

Thousands of people marched through the streets of Rabat in January 2003 to protest against a likely US-led war against the regime of Saddam Hussain in Iraq, denouncing the impotence of Arab governments in the face of US policy. Anti-war protests continued, and in March, in the biggest demonstration in the region since the Iraq crisis began, some 160,000 Moroccans marched in Casablanca to condemn 'US imperialist aggression'. The Moroccan Government, which had appealed for diplomatic efforts through the UN to resolve the crisis, avoided open criticism of the USA.

In March 2004 Morocco and the USA announced that they had concluded negotiations for a free trade agreement—only the second to be made by the USA with an Arab state. The agreement entered into effect on 1 January 2006.

Tens of thousands of demonstrators, mainly Islamists, marched in Rabat in November 2004 to protest against the continuing US-led military occupation of Iraq and to express support for the Palestinians. There were further anti-US demonstrations in December when Morocco hosted the first 'Forum of the Future', part of the USA's Greater Middle East Initiative to promote democracy and economic reform in the region, which was attended by finance and foreign affairs ministers of the Group of Eight (G8) industrialized nations and Middle East and North African countries. In August 2005 it was reported that the USA had been involved in discreet but intense diplomatic efforts that helped to secure the release of the remaining Moroccan prisoners of war held by Polisario. In December the Moroccan authorities denied allegations that the CIA had transferred detainees suspected of involvement in terrorist activities to secret detention centres in Morocco, where they were subjected to torture.

In the mid-2000s support grew within US political circles for Morocco's position on Western Sahara. This chiefly arose out of a growing belief that it was in the security interests of the USA to push for a resolution of the Western Sahara conflict and that meaningful autonomy, under Moroccan sovereignty, was the most feasible solution. The US Administration became increasingly concerned about the emergence of AQIM and believed that rapprochement between Algeria and Morocco would do much to counter the threat from the organization. Relations with the USA remained firm following the political changes in Morocco, owing partly to the King's ongoing control of foreign policy.

The rise of Islamic State, to which some parts of AQIM pledged allegiance and which was apparently behind attacks against foreign tourists in Tunisia in March and June 2015, as well as existing AQIM threats throughout the Maghreb, continued to underline the importance of Morocco's relationship with the USA. In this context, residual bilateral tension over the Western Sahara issue, and the fact that a small but not insignificant number of Moroccans were fighting for Islamic State, took second place.

In February 2016 the US Under Secretary of State for Political Affairs, Thomas Shannon, visited Morocco and praised what he called its 'mature and balanced' approach regarding the Sahara issue—a stance in keeping with the USA's established position on the dispute, which lacked the ambiguity of some EU states, and its attempt to work with Morocco on wider issues.

The inauguration of Donald Trump as US President in January 2017 led to a more polarizing foreign policy stance from the US Administration, which emphasized the need for alliances with states judged to be proactive in countering Islamist terrorism, and reduced US interest in pursuing human rights issues abroad. Although bilateral relations were already strong, Trump's foreign policy, for all its contradictions, served the Moroccan leadership fairly well. It was feared that there might be difficulties for Morocco over the President's insistence on all US allies 'paying their way' in terms of security guarantees. However, in practice, this did not prove to be a major obstacle. In April Princess Lalla Joumala Alaoui, King Mohammed's cousin, met Trump when being sworn in as Morocco's new ambassador to the USA. She emphasized the historic relationship that included Morocco's designation in 2002 as a major non-North Atlantic Treaty Organization (NATO) US ally and Morocco's commitment to combating terrorism and extremism.

Given the increasing attention that the King had given to the Alaouite monarchy's self-defined role as *amir al-mouminin*, Morocco's chairmanship of the Al-Quds (Jerusalem) Committee of the Organization of Islamic Cooperation (OIC, see p. 1155) and the residual importance of the Israeli–Palestinian issue in Moroccan politics, it was hardly surprising that President Trump's announcement in December 2017 that he would be moving the US embassy in Israel from Tel Aviv to the contested city of Jerusalem would cause tension in Morocco's relations with the USA. In that month Morocco, partly because Saudi Arabia and Egypt did not want to antagonize the USA and had arguably accepted the downgrading of the Jerusalem issue, hosted an emergency Arab summit that was attended largely by lower-level officials. To Morocco's frustration, in May 2018 the US Administration followed through on its decision to move the embassy. In June Morocco hosted the fifth incarnation of the UN-supported International Conference on the Question of Palestine. As was the case with the December 2017 meeting on Jerusalem, the King's sense of gravitas meant that he did not attend the meeting. However, a letter of support from the King stated that Trump's decision was 'unacceptable', although, in keeping with expectations, it gave a nod to the religious dimension while also firmly asserting the primary importance of a political resolution regarding Jerusalem's future by the Palestinians and the Israelis (see *Relations with the Middle East*). This was itself arguably an acknowledgement of how the Jerusalem issue was no longer seen by most Arab leaders as an existential Arab–Israeli question.

In March 2019 King Mohammed met Jordan's King Abdullah in Casablanca to affirm their shared commitment to Jerusalem and their opposition to any attempt (by Israel or the USA) to alter its political, religious or cultural status. This could be seen as a significant rebuttal of both President Trump's decision to move the US embassy in Israel to Jerusalem and Saudi Arabia's alleged interest in contesting Jordanian custodianship of Jerusalem's Islamic sites. It was reported in the Jordanian media that King Mohammed had explicitly affirmed his support for the extant Hashemite custodianship of Jerusalem's Islamic holy places.

Although King Mohammed and the Moroccan Government disapproved of President Trump's pro-Israeli stance, bilateral diplomatic and intelligence relations remained strong. Although the Israeli–Palestinian issue presented Morocco with periodic challenges, it did not threaten to destabilize the fundamentals of Morocco's relationship with the USA, including counterterrorism co-operation.

A short declaration of Moroccan-Israeli intent to establish full diplomatic relations signed on 22 December 2020 included the imprimatur of the US Administration, emphasizing how much the USA was a direct party to the unexpected agreement. Given the prior reticence of the *makhzen* to submit to the Trump Administration's mounting pressure on the Moroccan Government, it was a formal peace that, while not totally shocking, could be understood in terms of the importance of Western Sahara to Morocco and almost its entire political class. The USA's acceptance of Moroccan sovereignty over the territory—and thus by a number of ECOWAS countries too (see *Relations with the Sahel and Sub-Saharan Africa*)—was sufficient to allow Prime Minister el-Othmani to sign up to normalization with Israel without, arguably, a politically fatal loss of face (although he later sought to burnish his Palestinian credentials—see *Relations with the Middle East*). Given that the signed document made plain the constitutional and political fact that el-Othmani was signing on behalf of the King, and following the latter's own understanding with President Trump, then the perceptible 'trading' of the Moroccan monarchy's focus on both the need for a Palestinian state and for the securing of Palestinian and Muslim rights in Jerusalem for acceptance of Moroccan sovereignty in Western Sahara obviously seemed like a worthwhile gamble. In January 2021 Morocco's foreign affairs minister hosted the US diplomat David Schenker in the Western Saharan 'capital' of Laayoune for the opening of the new US consulate.

An unprecedented visit by a US Chairman of the Joint Chiefs of Staff, Mark Milley, to Rabat occurred in early March 2023. With the Russian Federation having reportedly signed a 10-year military partnership agreement with Algeria, it seemed that Morocco was more overtly aligning itself with its traditional Western allies. However, media reports suggested that the Moroccan Government was dissatisfied with the USA's failure formally to recognize Western Sahara as sovereign Moroccan territory. During a visit to Morocco in late March US

Secretary of State Anthony Blinken reaffirmed the USA's longstanding support for Morocco's autonomy plan, albeit with the usual US condition that any permanent resolution of the conflict must be led by the UN.

Morocco continued to view the USA as its primary strategic and military ally, but it was also prepared to engage with the People's Republic of China on military purchases, even though the wider economic relationship with China remained underdeveloped. Milley's visit was arguably an expression of US concern regarding potential Chinese and Russian penetration into north-west Africa and adjacent parts of the Sahel. Moroccan analysts often argued that balancing the country's international partnerships made sense as Morocco sought leverage over the USA. A longstanding US reluctance to supply certain arms to Morocco frustrated the Moroccan authorities, especially as Russia was becoming increasingly involved in strengthening Algeria's military.

MOROCCAN-CHINESE RELATIONS DEEPEN

Moroccan-Chinese economic relations have grown significantly in recent years, and King Mohammed has courted China's highly active business presence throughout Africa. Proposals were tabled for a Chinese economic zone to be built in Tangier; the visa requirement for Chinese nationals visiting Morocco was abolished in 2016; and in May of that year the King made a state visit to China. Morocco was actively trying to position itself as China's gateway to West Africa, and Casablanca's status as a financial centre was an important part of this. Morocco appreciated the fact that China, despite being hitherto closer to Algeria, to which it was a significant arms supplier, had not taken a public stance on the Western Sahara dispute. Meanwhile, Morocco appealed to China as a business-friendly African country proximate to Europe, which was itself a highly desirable Chinese export market. In September 2018 Prime Minister el-Othmani met his Chinese counterpart at the triennial Forum on China-Africa Cooperation, held in China. Chinese investment in, and trade with, Morocco had been growing strongly, and the kingdom had attracted Chinese involvement in its Mohammed VI Tangier Tech City project. As with so many of Morocco's burgeoning relations outside of the West, however, the Western Sahara issue, often compounded by the greater international importance of Algeria, arguably placed limits on the extent to which the Moroccan-Chinese relationship was likely to grow.

RELATIONS WITH EUROPE

France

Morocco has long relied on France for diplomatic support in the UN Security Council and within the EU. In July 1994 the new French President, Jacques Chirac, visited Morocco. This was his first foreign visit in his capacity as head of state. Chirac pledged to assist Morocco in combating Islamist extremism, and his administration subsequently strengthened relations by assisting with Morocco's external debt and increasing project aid to the country. The Socialist administration of Prime Minister Lionel Jospin, which assumed office in France in May 1997, sought to demonstrate that Morocco remained an important partner in France's Mediterranean strategy. During Prime Minister el-Youssoufi's visit to Paris in October 1998 Morocco and France signed several co-operation agreements, and the French Government announced additional aid amounting to US $765m. and plans for a second debt swap agreement between the two countries.

King Mohammed's first official overseas visit was to Paris in March 2000. During the visit the French Government announced emergency aid worth 100m. French francs to help Morocco to deal with the impact of the recent drought. The French Minister of Foreign Affairs, Hubert Védrine, and President Chirac visited Rabat in October and December 2001, respectively, as part of their tours of Maghreb capitals, and declared that there was full agreement with the Moroccan Government on the 'war on terror'. Moreover, the French President delighted his hosts by referring to Western Sahara as the 'southern provinces of Morocco'.

In February 2006 the French Government reiterated its view that only direct political dialogue between Morocco and Algeria would allow a permanent solution to the Western Sahara conflict. In April President Chirac stated that France supported a political 'situation' in Western Sahara acceptable to the UN.

During a visit to the Maghreb in July 2007 shortly after his election as President of France, Nicolas Sarkozy reiterated that he was 'very satisfied' with the state of relations between France and Morocco. He expressed the wish that Morocco would take very seriously his proposal regarding the creation of a 'Mediterranean Union'. Morocco responded favourably to the initiative, envisaging for itself a leading role in the development of closer co-operation among the Mediterranean states.

In January 2008 Morocco hosted a meeting of Union of the Arab Maghreb (Union du Maghreb Arabe—UMA, see p. 1169) foreign affairs ministers in preparation for President Sarkozy's summit for the Union for the Mediterranean (UfM). Morocco intensified its diplomatic activity in the months leading up to the summit, in an effort to demonstrate its desire to play a prominent role in the proceedings and ensure progress in ongoing discussions over the 'advanced status' agreement. In May a new think tank focusing on EU-Maghreb co-operation was opened in Rabat, and in June, reflecting its strong backing, the Government convened a second large conference to discuss the forthcoming summit. Given his support for the initiative, there was some surprise that, when the UfM was officially inaugurated in Paris in July, King Mohammed did not attend, choosing instead to send his brother, Prince Moulay, as the country's representative.

Under French President François Hollande, who assumed office in 2012, bilateral relations deteriorated, although they improved markedly following King Mohammed's 10-day official visit to Paris in February 2015. Morocco had suspended judicial and legal co-operation agreements with France in early 2014 in protest against an attempt by a French investigating magistrate to summon Abdellatif Hammouchi, the head of the Moroccan domestic intelligence service, for questioning in connection with allegations of torture made by Moroccan human rights activists. In January 2015 the two countries resumed limited co-operation, although the Moroccan Government denied that it had requested legal immunity for its officials operating in France in future as a precondition. The fatal shooting by terrorists—reportedly affiliated to al-Qa'ida in Yemen—of staff at the offices of the satirical journal *Charlie Hebdo* in Paris in January (and the subsequent terrorist attacks in Paris later in that week) arguably encouraged Morocco to take some steps of reconciliation in relations with France, as one of the attackers had apparently spent time in Morocco. However, the Moroccan Minister of Foreign Affairs and Co-operation, Salaheddine Mezouar, did not attend the solidarity march in Paris on the weekend after the attacks, ostensibly owing to concerns that the cartoons originally published by *Charlie Hebdo* (which had apparently enraged the assailants) would be on display.

In September 2015 President Hollande visited Morocco, having described relations as 'exceptional' prior to flying to Rabat. During his visit he requested that Morocco help France to tackle domestic Islamist extremism by providing training of French imams. More predictably, intelligence co-operation continued to be a key and growing part of this bilateral relationship. In the wake of the Islamic State-linked terrorist attacks in Paris in November, Moroccan intelligence aided the French capacity to track down one of the assailants and to reduce the risk of further attacks in France and in Belgium. In late November Belgium's Minister of the Interior and Public Security and, separately, its ambassador to Morocco praised Moroccan efforts to this end. Notably, the Belgian Minister of Defence, Steven Vandeput, met the Moroccan Chief of the Defence Staff in Rabat in October to discuss defence co-operation.

Despite periodic Moroccan sensitivity over perceived criticism by France, or positive French engagement with Algeria, Moroccan-French relations remained broadly positive. In October 2016 Ghali, leader of the SADR, accused France of retaining a 'colonial mentality' towards Western Sahara and the wider North African region and of having a common interest with Morocco in such schemes as a planned motorway connecting Western Sahara with Morocco as a means to deliver French goods to Africa. In a highly symbolic move, in June 2017 the newly elected French President, Emmanuel Macron, made a brief visit to Morocco to enjoy the *iftar* evening meal with King Mohammed during Ramadan and later spoke in Rabat of the two countries' 'common policies' regarding Africa, while praising Morocco's growing role in the affairs of the continent.

France under President Macron continued to be a firm supporter of Morocco in international fora during 2019, including over the Western Sahara issue. Indeed, the Algerian uprising in early 2019, with its overtones of anti-French sentiment (given France's ties to the incumbent regime), led to an apparent increase in French support for Algeria's North African rival. This was the case, even though the importance of Morocco's economic relations with France had diminished compared with those with Spain (see below).

France stated on 10 June 2021 that its overt role in countering Islamist militants in the Sahel would be reduced in favour of allowing the sub-Saharan African states to take action on their own, or jointly. At the same time, however, it also announced that it would continue to work with African allies in ensuring the protection of 'the southern flank of the Sahara'. This ongoing, if somewhat tarnished, French role in Saharan security was still important for Morocco, and implied that Morocco's de facto operation on that strategic flank via the Western Sahara was something that France would continue to value and assist, even if it could not officially legitimize Morocco's 'occupation'. The main contribution that France continued to make to Moroccan security was via the sale of arms and the associated military training that such defence packages often involved.

A diplomatic crisis between the two states arose in 2022 when a judicial process was begun in France against the former director of Moroccan intelligence over the alleged torture of three French nationals of apparent Moroccan/Maghreb heritage. However, this case was subsequently withdrawn, possibly with presidential encouragement. Bilateral relations were also strained as a result of allegations that Morocco had used Israeli 'spyware' to monitor French officials. In January 2023 tensions increased further when Morocco in effect recalled its ambassador to France. Ostensibly, this was to appoint him to another governmental post in Morocco, but it reflected badly on the two countries' relations. More generally, it appeared as if France was no longer prepared to prioritize Morocco over Algeria (the two countries being France's primary North African partners) as generational shifts in the French establishment and the changing geostrategic energy calculus following Russia's invasion of Ukraine in February 2022 had resulted in Algeria becoming more important. Meanwhile, foreign affairs minister Bourita had given expression to Morocco's frustration with France's unwillingness publicly and overtly to support Morocco's autonomy plan for Western Sahara. Moroccan-Spanish relations, by contrast, had improved following Spain's endorsement of the plan (see below).

Spain

Although Morocco and Spain signed a treaty of friendship in 1991, and Spain overtook France as the principal foreign investor in the kingdom, diplomatic relations became strained as a result of disputes over the EU fisheries accord, sovereignty of the Spanish enclaves of Ceuta and Melilla, the problem of illegal immigration into Spain from Morocco and the situation of Moroccans working in Spain. In September 1994 Morocco criticized Spain at the UN General Assembly for its autonomy plans for Ceuta and Melilla, and, after the Spanish parliament gave final approval to the statutes of autonomy for the two enclaves in February 1995, Morocco intensified its diplomatic campaign to obtain sovereignty over the two territories. Spanish concerns about illegal immigration from Morocco was discussed at a meeting between the Spanish and Moroccan interior ministers in Tangier in August 1998. However, after Morocco refused to renew the EU fisheries accord, which expired in December 1999, an agreement that largely affected Spanish fishing vessels, relations with Spain deteriorated sharply. Spain closed its ports to Moroccan vessels, and on a visit to Ceuta and Melilla in January 2000 Prime Minister José María Aznar described them as constant parts of Spain's future, emphasizing the 'Spanishness' of the two. In February many people were injured during violence resulting from attacks on Moroccan migrant labourers at El Ejido in southern Spain. King Mohammed made an official visit to Spain in September, when it was agreed that the two countries would work together to settle their differences. None the less, relations remained strained, particularly owing to Morocco's lack of flexibility over the proposed new EU fisheries accord and attacks by angry Spanish fishermen on vehicles carrying Moroccan exports through Spanish ports.

In October 2001 Morocco unprecedentedly recalled its ambassador to Spain for consultations, provoking a diplomatic crisis. The Moroccan Minister of Foreign Affairs and Cooperation stated that the Spanish Government was out of step with the EU on certain 'Moroccan national issues'—a clear reference to Western Sahara—and criticized recent border controls introduced by the Spanish authorities for Moroccans entering the Spanish enclaves of Ceuta and Melilla. He stated that since the September suicide attacks in the USA Spain had implied that there was a link between illegal immigration and terrorist networks (several Islamist cells active in Spain had recently been dismantled by Spanish police). The breakdown in April of talks about renewing the EU fisheries accord also contributed to strained bilateral relations. A new disagreement erupted in December over maritime boundaries between the Spanish Canary Islands and Morocco's Atlantic coast after the Spanish Government granted petroleum exploration rights around the Canary Islands to a Spanish company, Repsol.

Relations deteriorated further in July 2002 when a small detachment of Moroccan troops occupied the uninhabited rocky islet of Perejil (called Laila by Morocco), west of the Spanish enclave of Ceuta and close to the Moroccan coastline. Morocco claimed that it was establishing a surveillance post on the island as part of its campaign against illegal emigration and drug-trafficking. Spain rejected this explanation, describing the Moroccan occupation as a 'serious incident'. The Spanish Government insisted that since 1990 there had been an agreement that neither Morocco nor Spain would occupy the island, whereas the Moroccan authorities claimed to have held full sovereignty over it since 1956 and the end of the Spanish protectorate over northern Morocco, maintaining that Moroccan troops had been deployed there in the past when it was deemed necessary. Spain, which proceeded to reinforce its military presence in Ceuta and Melilla, stated that it did not make a formal claim to sovereignty over Perejil, but demanded the immediate evacuation of Moroccan troops from the island and a return to the *status quo ante* whereby neither Spain nor Morocco occupied it permanently—a demand supported by the EU and NATO.

A week before Moroccan troops landed on Perejil, Morocco had protested to the Spanish ambassador after five Spanish warships approached the Moroccan coast near al-Hoceima during a naval exercise. Some analysts suggested that the occupation of Perejil was Morocco's response to this incident, while others believed that it was designed to draw international attention to Morocco's claims to Ceuta and Melilla and perhaps to put pressure on Spain to change its position with regard to Western Sahara. A few days later Spain's ambassador to Morocco was recalled for an indefinite period, and Spanish special forces intervened and removed Moroccan troops from Perejil without casualties on either side. While Spanish officials underlined the sensitivity of the situation, they insisted that Spanish troops would be withdrawn if King Mohammed gave assurances that his forces would not reoccupy the island. They also suggested joint use of the island in the campaign against drug trafficking. Morocco denounced the Spanish action as equivalent to a declaration of war, but maintained that it sought a diplomatic solution to the crisis.

Morocco's stance regarding Perejil was supported by all political parties and the Islamist organizations, and several popular demonstrations were held in northern Morocco to protest against the Spanish assault on Perejil. Both the League of Arab States (Arab League, see p. 1146) and the OIC expressed support for Morocco. Following mediation by the US Secretary of State, Colin Powell, Spanish forces withdrew from the island, and talks in Rabat between the Spanish and Moroccan foreign affairs ministers towards the end of July 2002 (the first at this level since October 2001) resulted in an accord whereby both states agreed to return to the *status quo ante*. A meeting to discuss some of the other issues causing friction between the two countries was, however, cancelled by Morocco, which claimed that a Spanish military helicopter had landed on the disputed islet on the eve of the talks. The Moroccan Ministry of Foreign Affairs and Co-operation described the incident as an unacceptable violation of Morocco's airspace and territory. Talks finally proceeded in early December 2002, when the Moroccan Minister of Foreign Affairs and Co-operation met his Spanish counterpart in Madrid. Both sides agreed to normalize relations, although no date was set for the return of their respective ambassadors to their posts.

In late December 2002, following widespread oil pollution along the Galician coastline resulting from the sinking of the oil tanker *Prestige* in November, Morocco offered to allow 67 Spanish fishing vessels to operate in Moroccan territorial waters. The offer, made by King Mohammed himself, was welcomed by the Spanish Government as a clear sign of a change in attitude on the part of Morocco.

In mid-January 2003 a Spanish delegation travelled to Rabat to set up three working groups on immigration, delimitation of territorial waters and political issues. Two other groups, on economic co-operation and the rapprochement of civil society, would be established at a later date. When the Moroccan and Spanish foreign affairs ministers met in Agadir at the end of January both countries announced the return of their ambassadors (this took place in February). The meeting was extremely cordial, but it was clear that Spain had not changed its position on Ceuta and Melilla or on Western Sahara. In April talks on Moroccans working in Spain took place in Rabat between the Moroccan Minister of the Interior and the Spanish interior ministry's delegate in charge of foreigners' affairs and immigration, and an agreement was reached on readmission procedures to Morocco for Moroccans illegally resident in Spain.

In March 2004, after a series of co-ordinated bomb attacks on commuter trains in Madrid, which killed more than 190 people and injured some 1,900, Spanish police arrested 18 men, most of them Moroccans. The Spanish security services suspected that the extremist GICM, which the Moroccan authorities believed to have been involved in the Casablanca bomb attacks in May 2003, was behind the Madrid attacks and had links with al-Qa'ida. King Mohammed and leaders of Morocco's political parties, including the Islamist PJD, immediately condemned the Madrid bomb attacks and expressed their solidarity with the Spanish people. After the Spanish general election, which took place three days after the bombings, King Mohammed sent a message of congratulation to the leader of the Spanish Socialist Party and Prime Minister-elect, José Luis Rodríguez Zapatero, assuring him that Morocco was willing to co-operate fully with Spain against extremism and terrorism. Zapatero responded by stating that a priority of his foreign policy would be to begin a new era of good relations with Morocco. In late April, soon after becoming premier, Zapatero visited Morocco for talks with King Mohammed and Prime Minister Jettou. At a news conference Zapatero stated that it had been agreed to intensify co-operation in the fight against terrorism. On Western Sahara, the Spanish premier stated that Spain would adopt 'a constructive and positive position to reach a broad agreement on the issue'. In May Spain's new Minister of Foreign Affairs stated that Spain would support the plan for the self-determination of the Sahrawi people based on all UN resolutions.

The Spanish Minister of Foreign Affairs and Co-operation held talks with King Mohammed in Tangier in October 2004, and in an interview stated that a final solution to the Western Sahara conflict that was acceptable to all parties was vital for the Maghreb and for future relations between the Maghreb and EU. The Spanish Government's legalization of 'illegal' foreign workers in 2005 pleased the Moroccan authorities, as a significant number of these foreign workers were from Morocco and could now have legal status in Spain.

In January 2005 King Juan Carlos made a three-day official visit to Morocco—his first since 1979—and congratulated King Mohammed on a series of important political and social reforms, stating that Spain advocated privileged links between Morocco and the EU. In June 2005, however, relations became strained over Western Sahara after the Moroccan authorities refused to allow several Spanish delegations to enter the territory to carry out fact-finding missions after demonstrations in el-Aaiún and other towns. At a meeting in Madrid with his Moroccan counterpart in July, the Spanish premier stated that Spain would try to contribute to resolving the conflict in Western Sahara but that agreement had to be reached within the UN framework.

In September and early October 2005 hundreds of illegal immigrants, mostly from sub-Saharan Africa, made repeated attempts to breach security barriers that had been constructed to protect the borders between Morocco and Ceuta and Melilla. Violent clashes with the Moroccan security forces and the Spanish civil guard followed, in which 11 immigrants were killed (four were shot dead by Moroccan troops). Prime Ministers Jettou and Zapatero agreed to open an inquiry into the events. Morocco subsequently announced plans to increase police operations in areas surrounding the enclaves. Some 2,500 illegal immigrants were subsequently repatriated to sub-Saharan African countries. During talks in Rabat in early October the Spanish Minister of Foreign Affairs and Co-operation and his Moroccan counterpart agreed to increase bilateral co-operation and to study further measures to combat illegal immigration. However, they insisted that illegal immigration was a problem that required close co-operation between all EU member states and the countries of the Maghreb and Africa. A Euro-Africa ministerial conference on illegal immigration was held in Rabat in July 2006.

Tensions between the two countries flared up again in October 2006 when Spanish anti-terrorism judge Baltasar Garzón announced that he would convene an inquest into allegations of suspected Moroccan atrocities, including genocide, in Western Sahara. On the following day a Spanish court handed down prison sentences to two Moroccans who had been convicted of carrying out the 2004 Madrid train bombings.

Relations were further strained in November 2007 when King Juan Carlos paid a visit to Ceuta and Melilla—the first of his reign. The visit drew fierce criticism from the Moroccan Government and, as a result, Morocco recalled its ambassador to Spain. Following a visit by Zapatero to Rabat in January 2008, however, Morocco returned its ambassador to Spain, and, signalling a further rapprochement, in December a high-level Moroccan delegation visited Madrid and signed a three-year bilateral investment agreement worth €520m.

In November 2010 Spain criticized Morocco over the deaths of protesters at the Gdaim Izyk protest camp. As a result, Morocco's Chamber of Representatives took the decision of referring the status of the Spanish enclaves of Ceuta and Melilla to the UN Special Committee on Decolonization. A mass demonstration took place in Casablanca protesting against Spanish 'interference'.

In June 2012 the visit of the Spanish crown prince, Felipe de Borbón, to a bilateral economic conference in Morocco helped to improve relations. However, Spain's willingness to raise contentious issues such as the Western Sahara question continued to strain ties, as did the attack on a Moroccan consulate in Spain in May of that year, which was alleged to have been carried out by elements formerly connected to Polisario. None the less, Spain persisted in seeking to mediate in what it considered to be a Moroccan–Algerian dispute focused on Western Sahara. Morocco continued to find this irritating, not least as Spain did not suggest that Ceuta and Melilla should also be part of the discussion.

Despite residual tensions over territorial and other issues, at the beginning of June 2015 Moroccan Prime Minister Benkirane reported that Moroccan-Spanish relations were 'better than ever before'. Benkirane added that he wanted Spain to continue to play an active role in mediating over Western Sahara. As the Mediterranean refugee crisis greatly increased throughout the first half of 2015, albeit more focused on African (including North African) and Middle Eastern migrants attempting to seek refuge in Europe via Libya, this problem, coupled with related and shared anti-terrorism and anti-criminality concerns, underlined the need for what remained a close relationship. The Spanish-Moroccan summit in June produced an accord in which an exploration of whether fellow nationals could vote in each other's municipal elections was raised, together with a possible easing of Moroccan migrants' access to the labour market in Spain.

On 17 August 2017 12 Moroccan youths were involved in a plot that killed 16 people when a van was driven into people on a street in Barcelona's popular tourist area Las Ramblas. Although stressing the appalling nature of the crime, Moroccan officials claimed that the 12 men were not connected to Morocco. However, 11 of them had been born there and appeared to have been influenced by Abdelbaki el-Satti—a militant Moroccan imam based in Spain. None the less, bilateral relations were not unduly damaged. In fact, in what appeared to be a piece of political chutzpah designed to emphasize Morocco's grip on domestic and foreign-linked Islamist radicalism, on 17 October the director of the BCIJ, Abdulhaq Khiame, gave an interview with *The Financial Times* in which he offered to organize Moroccan training of imams in 'Western countries', essentially meaning Spain and France, with whom there had been close co-operation following the terrorist attacks in Paris in 2015 (see also *Terrorist Threats Continue* and *Relations with the Sahel*).

Immigration into Europe from Morocco and the wider Maghreb, principally via Spain, but also via Italy, remained a source of political and security tension between the southern European nations and Morocco. According to official EU data, the number of Moroccans who had reached the EU by sea (virtually all Moroccan migrants used this method) in 2017 almost doubled compared with the previous year (rising to 28,349, reflecting a largely upward trend since 2012). In Spain specifically, Moroccans were the largest immigrant group in the first half of 2018, representing 12% of the overall total. The Spanish Prime Minister, Pedro Sánchez, visited Rabat in November to discuss immigration and other issues. Although rising immigration remained a point of controversy in Morocco's relations with its immediate European neighbours, some believed that the issue could conceivably give the kingdom a degree of bargaining power as it attempted to control and reduce emigration in exchange for European assistance in addressing Moroccan concerns. As the main entry point for African immigrants travelling to Europe, Spain played a major role in the EU's security efforts to control this influx. Spain had also been Morocco's primary European economic trading partner for the five years up to the end of 2017, compounding the importance of Sánchez's visit. Sánchez had earlier stated that Spain's relations with Morocco were of 'the highest importance' because of the need for bilateral 'security, immigration and economic co-operation'. Moroccan immigration to Spain more than doubled in 2018, to 65,383, which, although not large in global terms, was enough to encourage Spain to push for a new one-off disbursal of EU financial support (€140m.) for the maintenance of more effective border controls. Spain also promoted EU-Moroccan talks in 2019 as part of an attempted reinvigoration of the Association Agreement between the two.

Spanish-Moroccan relations reached a serious nadir in April–June 2021 following the admittance of the Polisario chief to Spain for medical treatment. It appeared that Ghali's arrival had necessitated co-ordination between the Spanish and Algerian Governments, compounding the anger felt in Morocco over a perceived alignment with a leader and an aspirant state whom Morocco had arguably defeated via US and wider recognition of Moroccan sovereignty over Western Sahara. A war of words ensued that involved both countries' leading government figures. The Spanish political class was not united in its enthusiasm to host an, in effect, leader of a national liberation movement and in the process upset a bilateral relationship that the Spanish foreign affairs minister was still calling 'strategic', before noting that legal action against Ghali could be brought by complainants if a Spanish court would hear them. However, the controversial decision to treat Ghali, who was reported to have had COVID-19, led in mid-May to the Moroccan leadership effectively waging a war of migration: the arguable 'Achilles heel' in southern European—especially Spanish—relations with North Africa. Morocco was plainly a valued controller of economic migration from Africa to Europe and so, in a decision that almost certainly involved the King, an estimated 8,000–9,000 migrants, including many women and children, were released from Morocco into the Spanish enclave of Ceuta. The latter territory, while considered an 'occupied (Moroccan) outpost' by the Moroccan Government was an easy way to put pressure on Spain to refrain from any such future *de facto* siding with the SADR. Calling the hosting of Ghali a 'transgression', the Moroccan premier said on 24 June that the 'crisis of trust' needed addressing if relations were to be rebuilt.

Relations deteriorated further in 2022 when accusations were aired in some Spanish and international media, although not by the Spanish Government itself, that Morocco's burgeoning relationship with Israel had enabled Rabat's intelligence services to target the telephone of Spanish premier Sánchez. Sánchez and the Spanish defence minister, Margarita Robles, both stated that their personal mobile telephones were hacked in 2021, a time when the diplomatic crisis between the two countries was at its height. In early June 2022 Arancha González Laya, Spain's former foreign affairs minister from January 2020 until July 2021 (when relations had reached a nadir), told a Spanish newspaper that Morocco had been actively 'eavesdropping' on Spanish officials. (The Government had merely said that Israeli software had been used, but without identifying exactly by whom.) She identified the hosting of Ghali as a major reason for the eavesdropping and the objective as being to discredit Spain for its hospitable gesture.

In January 2022 King Felipe of Spain called on Morocco to 'walk together, with Spain to begin to materialise a new relationship, on the basis of stronger and more solid pillars', Spain's *El Espanol* reported. The Spanish king was addressing a gathering in Madrid of diplomats accredited to Spain at which Spanish Prime Minister Sánchez and foreign affairs minister José Manuel Albares were present. There have been suggestions that the energy crisis had compounded Spanish caution in its relations with Morocco as Madrid engaged more with Algeria (as were a number of other European countries, in their quest to secure longer-term natural gas supply arrangements). Morocco's normalization with Israel was arguably a US initiative that the Administration of President Joe Biden was cooler towards than the Trump authors of the process, and Algerian anger over Israel's 'presence' next door may have added caution to the Spaniards' stance. However, the King's message in January seemed to suggest that Madrid had resolved to turn a new page with Rabat. In March Spain then made it clear that it backed the Moroccan proposals for Western Saharan autonomy. Although it could be argued that this stance did not represent a total contradiction of the traditional Spanish position that had sought a mutually acceptable arrangement, the Sahrawi leadership position (as also articulated by Algeria) remained in favour of territorial self-determination. Spain stated via Prime Minister Sánchez, that it '[R]ecognises the importance of the Sahara issue for Morocco' and that 'Spain considers the autonomy initiative presented by Morocco in 2007 as the most serious, realistic and credible for resolving the dispute'. This suggested that the Prime Minister also desired a 'new relationship' with Morocco following the tensions of recent years. Appeasing Algeria for the sake of gas imports appeared out of the window, at least for now. That this shift should be expressed, in spite of European sensitivities over the USA's stance on Western Sahara in the context of Morocco's agreed normalization with Israel, was striking. The shift in Spanish policy received a very positive response in Rabat.

Germany too conducted a more or less total diplomatic volte-face with regard to Western Sahara and backed Morocco's autonomy plan in March 2022. Bourita used the Spanish and German conversions to Morocco's 'expanded autonomy' proposals for Western Sahara to try to encourage other European states to do likewise, arguing that it was '[T]ime for Europe to leave its comfort zone in connection with this conflict'. Morocco resumed ambassadorial-level diplomatic representation in Madrid and Berlin. Given that these two European states would have been mindful of the dangers of even greater

Moroccan–Algerian tension in the wake of Morocco's moves toward Israel and given their greater energy vulnerability following Russia's invasion of Ukraine in February, it is perhaps surprising that Spain and Germany seemed to focus only on rekindling their suspended bilateral relations with Morocco. The risk of Algeria carrying out a strongly implied threat of using some form of force, as the country's President, Abdelmadjid Tebboune, suggested, appears to have encouraged their siding with Rabat. That said, Morocco accompanied its mending of relations with Europe with the return of its ambassador to Algiers. However, it was unclear if this move would be of any help at all in assuaging growing Algerian–Moroccan tensions.

In March 2022 Morocco was also reportedly taking strong steps to block any further movement of migrants into Melilla from its own territory. Arguably it had leveraged the earlier mass movement of migrants into the Spanish enclave precisely in order to get Spain on side (which presumably precluded any future humanitarian gestures such as that made to the Polisario leader). In May there were reports by the BBC and other media that additional measures against migrant movement into Melilla had been implemented by Morocco that also affected the Spanish enclave of Ceuta.

Moroccan-Spanish relations had improved to such an extent in relation to the Western Sahara question that in early 2023 the two countries stated that their joint forum would include discussions on air and maritime management and border demarcation in Western Sahara. Morocco hoped that the improved bilateral relationship would result in Spain relinquishing its exclusive Western Saharan airspace authority. It also appeared as if the two countries would delineate their maritime border; if a future border agreement acknowledged that the former Spanish territory was now under Moroccan maritime sovereignty, then this would constitute *de jure* Spanish recognition of Western Sahara as Moroccan.

The EU, Other Member States and NATO

In February 1996 Morocco signed an economic Association Agreement with the EU, as part of the EU's plan for a 'Euro-Mediterranean partnership' leading to the gradual introduction of free trade in manufactured goods with the EU. When the European Parliament ratified the agreement in June, it inserted a clause allowing for the accord's suspension should concerns arise regarding the violation of human rights in Morocco. Furthermore, despite Morocco's desire for closer ties with Europe, its major trading partner, several problems, notably fisheries, illegal immigration and drug-trafficking, remained sources of friction. Relations became strained at the end of 1999 when Morocco refused to renew its fisheries agreement with the EU, under which Morocco received annual compensation for allowing fishing boats from EU countries (mainly Spain) to operate in its territorial waters.

Morocco and the EU signed an 'advanced status' agreement in October 2008, building upon their 1996 Association Agreement. This integrated Morocco into an EU plan to create a 'common economic space' (together with other countries such as Norway, Liechtenstein and Iceland) in advance of the establishment of a wide-ranging free trade agreement. Morocco was expected to be invited to join various EU agencies, mainly in the defence and security sphere.

The EU and Morocco held their first bilateral summit in Granada, Spain in March 2010. The meeting focused on accelerating Morocco's progress on its 'advanced status', and to this effect trade liberalization and regulatory convergence were discussed. In July 2013 a new common fisheries agreement was reached between the EU and Morocco, the European Parliament having rejected the previous accord in 2011.

A decision by the ECJ in December 2015 to annul an extension to the 2012 agricultural agreement with Morocco led the latter to threaten to end security co-operation with the EU—something that was valued by France and Belgium especially. However, although Moroccan Minister-delegate to the Minister of Foreign Affairs and Co-operation Mbarka Bouaida declared in mid-December 2015 that the ECJ ruling was 'incoherent and incomprehensible', she noted that it would not prevent continued agricultural (and other) trade under the existing rules. In February 2016 Morocco threatened to break off all formal relations with the EU after expressing frustration with the lack of 'transparency' over the ECJ's decision. The EU Commission made clear that it opposed the ECJ's judgment. A visit to Morocco by Federica Mogherini, the EU's High Representative for Foreign Affairs and Security Policy, in mid-March restored normal diplomatic relations. However, the dispute over the agricultural agreement remained unresolved.

The ECJ further complicated Moroccan-EU relations in February 2018 when it judged that the joint fisheries agreement did not apply to Western Sahara. It could be argued that this was the ECJ venturing into a highly controversial matter best left to the UN. Either way, it was plainly a victory for the SADR, which had only a few weeks earlier successfully persuaded a South African court to reject Moroccan phosphate exports on the same basis, opening up the possibility that EU phosphate imports from Morocco could in the future also be ruled illegal by the ECJ.

Despite the controversy over the issue, in February 2019 Morocco and the EU agreed a new fishing deal that included Western Sahara; the Moroccan parliament ratified the agreement in June. The accord defined the precise location and conditions affecting fishing in the applicable zones and stipulated that EU payments to the Moroccan state for the right to fish in its waters would rise by 30%—to just over US $45m. a day.

In June 2019 Morocco and the EU held their first Association Council meeting in four years, which was officially presented as a 'reinvigoration of relations'. Short on specific policies, the joint statement sought to push the discussion from the usual focus on aid and development and talked of the need for common efforts to improve Morocco's education and training capacity and its ability to contribute to the knowledge economy. Morocco was also presented as pursuing political reforms; this was true to an extent but arguably an over-simplistic and optimistic appraisal, given the constraints to reform applied by the *makhzen* and the marked inequalities and non-transparency in how the Moroccan economy functions. The EU's ambitions for a 'deep and comprehensive free trade agreement' (see Economy) with Morocco was overtly emphasized and, in the face of Moroccan resistance, seems to have encouraged a broader EU focus on the kingdom's social economy needs, as well as vaguer language on political reform.

In September 2021 the General Court of the EU in Luxembourg struck down the 2019 fisheries deal with Morocco after assiduous lobbying by the Polisario Front. The court said that exporting fish from the whole of Moroccan-controlled territory without Morocco having obtained the proven consent of the people of Western Sahara was unacceptable. The 2019 deal remained in operation, however, pending Morocco's right of appeal. Polisario argued that the Court's annulment of the deal effectively meant that the EU had accepted that the movement was a legitimate representative of the 'sovereign' Sahrawi people. However, Josep Borrell, the High Representative of the EU for Foreign Affairs and Security Policy, in a joint declaration with Bourita, stated 'We remain fully mobilised to continue co-operation between the EU and Morocco'.

It appears that Morocco has felt able to play hardball with its European neighbours. The country has a major role in incoming European immigration and used it effectively to bring Spain into a more politically compliant position. Having mass-settled Western Sahara with Moroccans, Morocco presumably felt able to hold out for de facto European recognition of its sovereignty there even if it could not secure *de jure* recognition, even seemingly from its close US and Israeli allies. In the mean time, building a highway that crossed through Western Sahara to the 'Moroccan' border with Mali and developing the port city of Dakhla, and via these actions possibly even becoming an alternative (to Algeria) energy hub for Europe by transporting renewable energy from sub-Saharan Africa, may have bolstered Rabat's confidence. There remain difficulties, however, with Europe. The migration issue is not easy to manage, while Morocco's development projects proximate to Spanish-held territory have caused periodic disquiet.

King Mohammed declared in August 2022 that the 'Sahara issue is the prism through which Morocco views the world' and measures the 'truthfulness' of its 'friendships' and the 'efficiency' of its 'partnerships'. This was interpreted by Moroccan analysts as being directed at EU member states in advance of the July 2023 renewal of the EU-Morocco fisheries agreement and a decision over the key issue of whether the deal would include Western Sahara. Moroccan frustration with France's relatively newfound desire to balance its relations with Algeria and Morocco (see below) contrasted with Spain and Germany's accommodation of Morocco's Western Sahara stance. In addition, Portugal hosted a round of bilateral meetings with Prime Minister Akhannouch and foreign affairs minister Bourita in Lisbon in May, at which it also endorsed the Moroccan autonomy plan.

In terms of Morocco's co-operation with Western security structures, it continued to be an active part of NATO's Istanbul Cooperation Initiative (ICI)/Mediterranean Dialogue, and as such it was a valued part of NATO's partnership and joint operations with its so-called southern periphery. This situation was valued by Rabat even though the kingdom was mindful of how much its national and regional security concerns were not able fully to be addressed within this framework (although the USA, the de facto head of NATO, and leading NATO member France remained pre-eminent security partners of Morocco). The ICI, launched in 2004, brings Morocco and most of its north African neighbours together in dialogue and, in a more ad hoc form, military co-operation with two of its Near Eastern (Levantine) allies. Morocco, Algeria, Mauritania, Tunisia and Egypt are part of the ICI, together with Jordan and Morocco's new ally (after years of discreet co-operation), Israel.

Ultimately, Morocco was in the Western orbit, as an ally of Western countries and now of Israel, too. While this did not preclude good Moroccan relations with the West's rivals Russia and China, it emphasized that Algeria was effectively in a different camp (despite being party to NATO's ICI). The Ukraine conflict had seen Algiers try deftly to balance its military alignment with Russia with increased Western interest in Algeria's gas resources. However, heightened tension between Algeria and Spain over the latter's effective siding with Morocco against Algeria over Western Sahara, and constraints on Algeria's additional gas production capacity, further emphasized how much Rabat appeared to be a more natural political partner for Western countries than Algeria.

RELATIONS WITH MOROCCO'S MAGHREB NEIGHBOURS

At a summit meeting of heads of state in Marrakesh in February 1989 the UMA was inaugurated, grouping Morocco with Algeria, Libya, Mauritania and Tunisia. The new body aimed to promote unity by allowing free movement of goods, services and labour, but the Western Sahara dispute, civil war in Algeria and UN sanctions against Libya prevented any real progress, with the result that by the mid-1990s the organization was virtually moribund. At a meeting of UMA foreign affairs ministers, referring to the acutely sensitive issue of Western Sahara, Benaïssa stated that there was no question of Morocco sacrificing its 'national cause to build a Greater Maghreb'. Attending a meeting of UMA foreign affairs ministers in Algiers in January 2003, Benaïssa appealed for renewed efforts to overcome differences between members, but added that the strength of the UMA lay 'in the territorial integrity and strength of its individual states'.

Relations with Algeria improved during 1992 while Muhammad Boudiaf, who had lived in exile in Morocco for more than 20 years, was Algerian head of state, but after Boudiaf's assassination relations quickly deteriorated; the frontier was closed, and Algerian supplies to the Polisario Front were resumed. In January 1993 there was a reconciliation, when ambassadors were exchanged and the border was reopened. However, in 1994 relations reached their lowest ebb for many years. At his trial in Algiers, the alleged leader of the Algerian Groupe Islamique Armée stated that, before his extradition from Morocco, senior Moroccan army officers had asked him to eliminate certain members of the Moroccan opposition living in Algeria, together with Polisario Secretary-General Muhammad Abdelaziz. In August, after the murder of two Spanish tourists in Marrakesh, the Moroccan Ministry of the Interior issued a public statement alleging that two of the suspects were in the pay of the Algerian secret services. The Algerian Government strongly denied that it was sponsoring terrorism against its neighbour, and sealed the border with Morocco. By mid-September, however, bilateral tensions had eased, and in a gesture of goodwill Algeria appointed a permanent ambassador to Morocco. Despite a meeting between the respective ministers responsible for the interior in late 1996, relations remained strained, with Algeria accusing Morocco of providing covert assistance to armed opposition groups in Algeria, and Morocco accusing Algeria of attempting to destabilize Morocco as preparations were made for the referendum on Western Sahara.

The election of Abdelaziz Bouteflika as President of Algeria in April 1999 raised hopes of a rapprochement. However, the improvement in relations with Algeria proved short-lived. The Western Sahara dispute and Algeria's support for Polisario continued to prevent any significant improvement in relations. In September 2003 King Mohammed and President Bouteflika were reported to have agreed to establish a joint task force to improve co-operation on issues such as illegal immigration and security. However, when Algeria failed to respond to Morocco's unilateral decision in July to abolish visa requirements imposed in 1994 on Algerians visiting Morocco, the Moroccan press accused President Bouteflika of 'slamming the door on reconciliation'.

King Mohammed attended the summit meeting of heads of state of the Arab League in Algiers in March 2005—his first visit to Algeria since his accession and the first visit by a Moroccan monarch since 1991. Morocco welcomed Algeria's decision in April 2005 to reciprocate and abolish visa requirements for Moroccans visiting Algeria. However, in May, just before the UMA heads of state summit was due to be held in Tripoli, King Mohammed announced that he would not be attending, owing to recent comments by President Bouteflika in which he reaffirmed Algeria's support for Polisario. The summit was postponed indefinitely.

Following Polisario's release, in August 2005, of the remaining Moroccan prisoners of war, there were reports of a rapprochement between Morocco and Algeria. However, after attempts by illegal immigrants to enter the Spanish enclaves of Ceuta and Melilla in September and October, Morocco insisted that many of the immigrants involved had entered the country via Algeria and criticized the Algerian authorities for their failure to prevent the immigrants from crossing the border. In November Algeria rejected Morocco's proposal of autonomy for Western Sahara under Moroccan sovereignty and reiterated its support for the Sahrawis' right to self-determination. However, concerns about security related to the threat of terrorism led to an increase in co-operation between Morocco and Algeria, as the start of direct talks over Western Sahara demonstrated.

In June 2007 King Mohammed announced that Morocco and Algeria had agreed to co-ordinate more closely on security matters, particularly over issues relating to the rise of radical Islamism in North Africa. However, this consensus failed to break either the ongoing deadlock over the border closure or the impasse over Western Sahara. In May 2008 Algeria rejected further overtures from Morocco to collaborate on either issue, despite Morocco's announcement that the Western Sahara problem was impossible to resolve without Algeria's involvement.

Relations between Morocco and Algeria were also marred by alleged Algerian efforts to undermine Moroccan interests elsewhere in the Maghreb and in Africa more widely, as well as by Algeria's maintenance of the closure of its side of the border.

In October 2015 Morocco marked the imminent Green March anniversary by promoting its self-rule proposals 'for the south'—a 'decentralization' that it said was going to go ahead as part of a further national redistribution of power (some national decentralization had occurred under the 2011 Constitution). In a seeming deflection of its support for Polisario, in the same month Algeria's semi-official newspaper *Echorouk El-Youmi* accused Morocco of 'now overtly' backing Ferhat Mehenni and his separatist Mouvement pour l'Autonomie de la Kabylie in Algeria—a stance that it said Morocco shared with 'Zionists', i.e. Israel. In April 2016 the Algerian news website *El Khabar* reported that Algeria had decided on a security plan that included erecting a fence along the entire 170-km border with Morocco and the active use of the Algerian air force there. The report stated that the fence would counter criminal smuggling from its Moroccan neighbour, but that it would also be used to prevent the alleged movement of terrorists from inside Morocco to Algeria.

For their part, semi-official Moroccan media outlets often linked military mobilization reports to an Islamist terrorist threat in Morocco seen principally as coming from the ongoing civil conflict in Libya and, in the Moroccan view, often involving radicalized militants based in Libya, including Libyan nationals and those of other Arab countries, who were accused either of entering or attempting to enter Moroccan territory to commit acts of violence. The rise of Islamic State added to Moroccan concerns about foreign-related domestic threats, with Algerians and Tunisians identified as part of the threat from that group, whether related to the conflict in Libya or not. In April 2015 an Algerian national was charged by the Moroccan authorities with attempting to recruit Moroccans to Islamic State, and later that month two Algerians were arrested for allegedly planning a terrorist attack in Skhirat. In September 2014 several Tunisians were reportedly arrested by the Moroccan authorities for supposedly plotting terrorist operations in Morocco.

In June 2015 the General Director of the Moroccan National Office for Hydrocarbons and Mining, Amina Benkhadra, was reported in *Echorouk El-Youmi* as having told the Moroccan publication *Aujourd'hui le Maroc* that drilling for oil shale reserves had begun in the south-east of Morocco, and that the country had permitted foreign companies the right to do so 'across border areas' between Morocco and Algeria. The territories in question included parts of Tarfaya province, in the far south-west of Morocco, and were in certain parts located close to water channels, for which the companies had provided the necessary guarantees to proceed under Moroccan environmental protection legislation.

In May 2016 Morocco accused Algeria of not doing enough to combat Islamic State. In June the Moroccan security service arrested 10 Islamic State suspects in and around Oujda, close to the Algerian border. The implication of the report was that the suspects were Algerian, although this was unclear. Arrests of each other's nationals for alleged Islamic State activity were commonplace. For example, in two separate incidents in February, Algeria announced the arrest of 15 Moroccans, who, it claimed, had either flown into Algeria or been caught on the Algerian side of the border with the intention of travelling on to Libya. In July the Algerian authorities reportedly announced that they were raising the threat level attached to Moroccans entering their territory illegally, arguing that such foreign nationals could mingle among legal foreigners in their efforts to conduct illicit activity. In July 2015 Morocco admitted that, since 2013, some 1,350 Moroccan nationals had joined Islamic State, of whom 286 had died fighting.

The Moroccan decision in July 2016 to seek re-admission to the AU led to something of a rapprochement with Algeria. Although hostile words were still exchanged through their respective official and semi-official media channels, Morocco's foreign affairs minister-designate Bourita travelled to Algiers with a Moroccan intelligence official, Yassine Mansouri, in July. Algeria's backing for Morocco's AU membership was being sought, but so was badly needed intelligence co-operation. Bourita and Mansouri held a meeting with Algerian Prime Minister Abdelmalek Sellal and the new Algerian intelligence chief, Gen. Bachir Tartag, at which the two sides concluded an agreement to increase co-operation in security and operations to combat Islamist militant groups operating in the Sahel region. Intelligence co-operation had effectively stalled over several years amid mutual accusations of a lack of seriousness about dealing with a regional Islamist militancy problem that did not respect borders. Now it seemed that both sides wanted to at least try to work together more efficiently.

Tensions remained high, with each side accusing the other of taking inadequate measures to address the threat from Islamic State in North Africa. In August 2016 Morocco commenced construction of a 100-km section of a fence on its side of the border in the far north, while Algeria began digging a 700-km trench on its side, reportedly to prevent illicit trafficking and terrorism. In November 2018 King Mohammed proposed a bilateral mechanism for frank discussion of all subject areas. However, this was dismissed by Algeria. The King's initiative should be viewed in the context of it being proposed during a speech commemorating the Green March into Western Sahara. Reopening the land border would, from Algeria's perspective, require Moroccan respect for its view that the territorial conflict was a 'colonial' issue—a position that was anathema to Morocco. None the less, in the same month Morocco and Algeria agreed to hold talks with Polisario and Mauritania, under UN auspices, to discuss the territorial conflict for the first time since 2012. However, Moroccan-Algerian relations remained tense, and the prospect of a breakthrough in the Western Sahara dispute appeared unlikely.

Morocco maintained an official position toward Algeria of being open to dialogue—a position that King Mohammed reiterated in his Throne Speech in July 2019. On the face of it, this was a more diplomatic position than that of Algeria and even suggestive of possible Moroccan initiatives regarding the Western Sahara question. However, autonomy for the territory remained the Moroccan Government's maximum concession. Algeria maintained a relatively hostile stance towards Morocco via semi-official media as well as official platforms, while Morocco, although generally more judicious, was not above semi-official criticism of Algeria. It has been suggested that Morocco would have been wiser to frame the issue as a border dispute between itself and Algeria or to question how representative the Algerian-supported SADR really was. The issue remained at an impasse in much the same way as did Moroccan-Algerian relations—something reinforced by the centrality of perceived regime interests on either side, regardless of the popular uprising in Algeria from February 2019 and sporadic popular discontent in Morocco.

Moroccan relations with Algeria suffered in the wake of the recognition by the USA, Israel and some sub-Saharan states of Western Sahara as sovereign Moroccan territory at the end of 2020 and beginning of 2021 (see above). Relations further declined when the SADR President's emblematic medical sojourn in Spain from April 2021 and eventual return to Algeria were facilitated by secret Spanish-Algerian discussions. Morocco's moves toward formalizing its relationship with Israel may have taken place in too public a form given domestic and regional Arab discontent; however, the Government seemed to be signalling that it had options, including Arab ones, outside of the Maghreb and the AU with their susceptibility to Algerian influence.

On 9 June 2021 Algeria's President Tebboune stated that his country had no problems with Morocco, rather vice versa. Morocco could perhaps have been forgiven for finding the President's words more than a little disingenuous given that in his interview with Qatar-based broadcaster Al-Jazeera he reiterated his opposition to Moroccan sovereignty over Western Sahara, saying that the Moroccan King (with US support) had presented a fait accompli on the Western Sahara question. Tebboune also told French publication *Le Point*, in relation to the USA's recognition of Morocco's sovereignty, 'How can you think of offering a monarch an entire territory, with all its population?' Algeria stated that it remained open to dialogue, but on the question of reopening the two countries' long border the President said that being under 'attack' by Morocco made this impossible at present.

In late August 2021 Algeria broke off all formal diplomatic relations with Morocco. Algiers stated that the Moroccan authorities' alleged use of Israeli-supplied Pegasus cyber (spy) ware against Algerian state officials was one of the reasons for the two countries' poisoned relations. Algeria also claimed that Morocco had been covertly aiding the separatist ambitions of Algeria's Amazigh (Berber) minority; Morocco did periodically publicly raise the issue of the Algerian Amazigh as a seeming riposte to Algeria's strong support for the Sahrawi people within Moroccan-controlled territory. Algeria even alleged that Morocco had been behind a spate of wildfires in Algeria that summer.

In July 2021 allegations of Moroccan use of Israeli spyware in Algeria had surfaced via a third-party investigation undertaken by the non-profit organization Forbidden Stories. These allegations obviously compounded Algeria's fears about (Arab) normalization with Israel that it had already fulminated against and that some (possibly erroneous) media reports had further fuelled (see Relations with Europe). Whether some of the reported claims of the extent of the Israeli-Moroccan partnership were true or not, Algeria's comments reflected genuine concerns about Israeli penetration, via Morocco, of the Maghreb and specifically of Algeria's national security. When announcing the severance of diplomatic relations, the Algerian foreign affairs minister stated that Morocco was now a 'secondary base' for what he called 'a series of dangerous aggressions against Algeria'. Whatever wider geostrategic leverage Algeria had possibly been expecting in the wake of its enhanced importance in terms of energy provision to the West following Russia's invasion of Ukraine, it did not materialize as forecast with the southern European states. Perhaps Algeria was still viewed by the Europeans as being too firmly in Russia's orbit and too impenetrable for the Western investment and technical expertise that they perceived as being required by Algeria.

In November 2021 Algeria accused Morocco of being responsible for a bomb explosion that killed three Algerian lorry drivers close to the border between Moroccan-held Western Sahara and Mauritania. President Tebboune stated that Morocco would 'pay the price' for its alleged involvement in the attack, while Morocco denied all responsibility for or knowledge of who was behind the attack. In the same week Algeria announced that it would cut Morocco out of its gas supply to Spain via the Maghreb–Europe Gas Pipeline; 10% of the gas that flowed through the pipe had been diverted to Morocco. It was not clear whether Algeria could maintain its commercial commitment to supply Spain by switching to its announced smaller pipeline alternative (see Economy), although in early June 2022 Algeria seemed to put future, non-contracted, gas supply to Spain in doubt (and therefore, once again, the diverted supply to Morocco) by suspending its 20-year-old 'friendship' treaty with Spain. Spain's support for the Moroccan position over Western Sahara was pivotal in this move.

In a further indication of the poor state of Moroccan-Algerian relations, in February 2022 Morocco established what it called a 'new military zone' situated close to the kingdom's eastern border with Algeria. An official Moroccan armed forces publication announced that this development would ensure effective 'command and control' of the kingdom's different armed forces branches and their integrated operations there. Notably, around this time it was also reported that Morocco had resumed full diplomatic representation in Algiers; however, Algeria's ambassador had not returned to Rabat. Tension continued over the Western Sahara question. In September the Algerian Minister of Foreign Affairs, Ramtane Lamamra, met with de Mistura and publicly urged Morocco to negotiate directly with Polisario. However, Morocco appeared increasingly confident that the diplomatic and military realities regarding the territory were in its favour. Nevertheless, without a final resolution to the dispute, Morocco's relations with Algeria would continue to be strained.

Morocco's relations with Libya were strengthened following the collapse in 2011 of the regime of Muammar al-Qaddafi, who had been distrusted in Morocco. The political transformations improved bilateral relationships across the Maghreb, in turn prompting proposals to revitalize the UMA. However, Tunisia's republican tradition, Libya's highly unstable political development, and the longstanding resistance among the Maghreb states to fundamental compromises of national sovereignty were expected to restrict the likelihood of a meaningful union. Although there were good economic and security reasons to co-operate more closely, including intra-Maghreb concerns over AQIM and, to a lesser extent Islamic State, prospects for greater union remained limited. Algeria regarded the longstanding problem of Islamist extremism in its territory as something that it alone (albeit in collaboration with the USA and the EU) was best placed to address. Morocco's King congratulated the newly appointed UMA head, Taïeb Baccouche, a Tunisian national, in early May 2016. Moreover, Morocco's Minister of Foreign Affairs and Co-operation, Mezouar, attended a gathering of UMA foreign affairs ministers in Tunis, the Tunisian capital, in that month amid speculation that the meeting confirmed the Maghreb countries' mutual desire to reactivate the UMA's institutions and to ensure deeper co-operation. In late April the UN Security Council called on the Maghreb countries to work more closely together via the UMA in order to resolve the Western Sahara issue—an optimistic gambit, given how diametrically opposed the interests of Morocco and Algeria were over the issue—and to contribute to stability in the Sahel. Progress on intra-UMA co-operation remained slow, however, owing to ongoing and fundamental national differences. Notably, Morocco's PJD joined the other leading Islamist parties of the Maghreb in late April to promote closer intra-Maghreb political co-operation. The gulf between this apparently genuine stance and that of the actual states concerned emphasized these parties' relative powerlessness, even when, like the PJD, they were formally leading the Moroccan Government.

Morocco hosted UN-brokered Libyan peace talks in Skhirat during 2015, albeit without representatives of one of Libya's two rival governments (see Libya) being represented until June. Morocco's interest in progress from such talks was underlined by an attack, albeit without casualties, at the entrance to the Moroccan embassy in Tripoli in mid-April, which was claimed by Islamic State. In December the key Libyan parties concluded agreement in Skhirat on the formation of a Libyan Presidency Council, which was firmly welcomed, as might be expected, by the Moroccan Government when it was actually put in place in February 2016. However, in April Morocco reiterated its concern, in common with practically the entire international community, that the legislature in Tobruk had not yet expressed support for the Presidency Council or for its proposed Government of National Accord (GNA).

An integrated government structure in Libya was emerging as the precondition for an expanded Western—and probably NATO-led—military intervention in Libya, this time to counter Islamic State. Mezouar agreed with his Tunisian counterpart, Khmaïyes Jhinaoui, in a joint press conference in late February 2016 that such a planned action should not happen as it would be counter-productive in Libya. Periodic US air strikes and French military action were already encouraging Islamic State fighters in Morocco's direction (via Tunisia and Algeria), Jhinaoui said. To some extent Morocco's stance was surprising. In July 2015 the semi-official Moroccan press had reported, sourcing a plausible article in the US publication The Wall Street Journal, that Morocco was in discussion with the USA about its territory being used for the drone component of a US-led counter-Islamic State military operation in the Maghreb that would include drone strikes on Libya. The Skhirat process continued to be the basis for Arab League and AU efforts to promote a solution to the Libyan conflict. Morocco shared the official position of Egypt, expressed in January 2017, of rejecting foreign military intervention in the crisis by Western powers, and of urging the warring parties to become fully supportive of the GNA. Libya remained a source of sensitivity for Moroccan national security, in view of the apparent influence of senior Islamic State commanders there on the activities of affiliated terrorist cells operating in Morocco.

Morocco's proprietorial defence of the Skhirat agreement created a significant gap between its outlook on the Libya question and that of some of the key foreign Arab interlocutors in the Libyan civil war. This was exemplified by an emergency Arab League meeting of foreign affairs ministers in June 2020. Egypt had called the meeting to garner Arab support for the position of the Egyptian President, Abd al-Fatah al-Sisi, that if the Turkish-backed GNA forces entered the strategic Libyan coastal city of Sirte, then he would deploy Egyptian troops to defend both western Egypt and 'Arab national security'. Egypt's own Libyan peace plan included the disarming of GNA-aligned militias in favour of the eastern-based rebel general Khalifa Haftar and his Libyan National Army. To Morocco's displeasure, Egypt, together with the UAE, had long intervened in the conflict as an arms—and presumably intelligence—supplier, as well as a political backer of Haftar's forces, just as Qatar had backed the Turkish military intervention in support of GNA forces. This breaking of an official

UN arms embargo put Morocco at discreet odds with France too; Paris had backed support for the official embargo but continued to support Haftar, as well as Egypt's response to the Turkish intervention. Such Arab interventions were described by Morocco as 'cynical' and 'hypocritical'. In response to what Egypt considered as the purpose of the Arab League meeting, Bourita said that Morocco rejected any direct Arab intervention in the Libyan conflict and tabled a Moroccan proposal for an Arab 'task force' to support wider international efforts to find a solution to the conflict. He conceded that the Skhirat process might need updating, but stressed that its emphasis on an inclusive Libyan-focused process, with international backing, was the proper basis for a solution when there was no alternative process. The Libyan House of Representatives, based in Tobruk, and which was only loosely associated with the General National Congress under the GNA in Tripoli, had suggested in May that Morocco had the neutrality and the commitment to be a mediator in the conflict. Without this being the view of those Arab states that were still backing Haftar, despite the weakening of his hold in eastern Libya, it appeared unlikely that this Moroccan role could substantively be put into action.

Morocco's relations with Libya arguably benefited from the latter's attempted domestic political reconciliation in March 2021, when a new, inclusive, coalition Government of National Unity (GNU) was established, drawn from the previously disputatious parties. However, this latest Libyan political process did not substantively involve Morocco. The latter's previous disdain for Gulf Arab and Egyptian support for rebel general Haftar was presumably eased by improved Moroccan relations with all of the Gulf Arab states, and thus Egypt, even if the long-held Moroccan concern about Haftar's potential to upset political arrangements remained as relevant as ever.

Egyptian opposition media and the Italian media company Nova were among those reporting in early June 2022 that Morocco had hosted a meeting in Bouznika of rival Libyan political actors, including two sons of the rebel Libyan military leader Gen. Haftar, whose strongholds were located in various parts of the east of Libya, and political figures from Tripoli, Misrata, Zawiya and Briga. Other media sources disputed that the dialogue was as senior or as broadly-based. What political role, if any, the Moroccan Government played in the talks was unclear, other, that is, than the still important job of facilitating the holding of the talks (albeit following an earlier meeting in Switzerland). Morocco had an obvious interest in events in Libya, and was relatively trusted across the Libyan political spectrum given its past record of fair-minded attempts at mediation.

Moroccan-Tunisian relations have become more unpredictable since the uprising in Tunisia that led to the ouster of President Ben Ali in early 2011. Parliamentary and presidential elections in 2014 returned a 'secular' leadership in Tunis instead of the Muslim Brotherhood-affiliated administration that came to power immediately after Ben Ali was ousted. Although the participation of the Brotherhood-affiliated PJD in government in Rabat had chimed with more radical Tunisian developments in 2010–11 and thus helped to improve bilateral relations for a while, the *makhzen* had not had comfortable relations with the Brotherhood generally. In part, this was a function of Morocco's foreign relations, not least with Gulf Arab states, where sensitivity to militant Islamist activity was generally high (with the exception of Qatar), and sensitivity on the part of the royal establishment about the Brotherhood establishing itself as a rival in terms of embodying Islamic legitimacy in Morocco. As a result, the change in the elected Tunisian leadership in 2014 was, broadly speaking, positive for bilateral relations. In June 2015 the two countries signed eight co-operation agreements covering areas such as education and housing.

In 2015 a rise in the terrorist threat in Tunisia, after two murderous attacks on foreign tourists, carried out by agents inspired by Islamic State, raised already growing concerns in Morocco about the potential for this to affect its territory. However, the Tunisian authorities and media generally reacted positively to Morocco's subsequent attempted crackdown on Islamic State and its sympathizers on Moroccan territory. Morocco had, earlier in 2015, continued to take precautions against an AQIM attack, mindful of the dangers inherent in the collapse of the Libyan state, as well as concerns about perceived failings in the security capabilities of the Tunisian state. Tunisia backed Morocco's application for re-entry to the AU (see *Western Sahara*), which was made in July 2016 and took effect in January 2017. Despite ongoing Moroccan concerns about Tunisia's capacity to control its borders, Moroccan re-entry into the AU encouraged an improved Moroccan-Tunisian economic relationship, symbolized by the two countries concluding an agreement in June to facilitate better customs arrangements. At the time of the deal Moroccan premier el-Othmani reported that bilateral relations were 'excellent' and urged cordial political relations to be reflected in improved economic ties. Tunisia continued to encourage Moroccan-Algerian reconciliation. In November 2018 the Tunisian Minister of Foreign Affairs, Khmaïyes Jhinaoui, commented on the importance of this and announced that he was seeking to reconvene intra-Maghreb talks on reviving the UMA.

The election of a new Tunisian President in October 2019 was an opportunity for Morocco to emphasize its goodwill toward Tunisia, and a large, high-level Moroccan delegation was dispatched to Tunis for the inauguration of Kaïs Saïed as head of state. On the question of the Libyan conflict, Morocco and Tunisia continued to agree, and Tunisia endorsed Morocco's Skhirat process. In May 2020 President Saïed told Libya's Fayez al-Sarraj (Prime Minister of the GNA) that Tunisia considered the process as the only basis for any permanent solution to the conflict. When Bourita visited Tunis to meet Saïed in late June, the two men reaffirmed this common position. It appeared as if the principles that had underpinned Skhirat continued to be applicable to the arrangements for the March 2021 GNU.

The head of the upper chamber of the Moroccan legislature, Naam Miyara, held a meeting with the Tunisian ambassador, Mohamed Ben Abbad, on 31 January 2022, during which Ben Abbad said that the two countries' relations were 'indefectible'. However, closer analysis suggests that while the Moroccan *makhzen* was never wholly comfortable with Tunisia's seeming democratic path from 2011, especially when it resulted in governments dominated by the Muslim Brotherhood, the severity of the authoritarian centralization of power under Tunisian President Kaïs Saïed from July 2021 did not sit well with Rabat either. The ongoing potential for political destabilization and radicalization (including among Tunisian Islamists) in Tunisia, was likely to have raised fears in Rabat that there could be consequences for Moroccan national security. Furthermore, Tunisia's traditionally mediatory role in Moroccan-Algerian relations, and regarding Libya, had been largely appreciated in Rabat; a Tunisia that was being strongly criticized by Western allies and that was politically and economically struggling, would likely witness a weakening of its normally positive regional role.

President Saïed hosted the Tokyo International Conference on African Development in Tunis in August 2022 and caused consternation in Moroccan governmental and wider civil societal circles by not only inviting Ghali, but also meeting with the Polisario leader. The Tunisian Government defended itself by declaring that its actions were in accordance with its desire for compromise between the various parties involved in the Western Sahara dispute, that it had always been neutral on this issue, and that the AU had also invited Ghali to attend similar events as the SADR was an AU member. Nevertheless, Moroccan officials refused to attend the Conference in protest, and Morocco subsequently withdrew its ambassador from Tunisia.

RELATIONS WITH THE SAHEL AND SUB-SAHARAN AFRICA

A highly symbolic visit by King Mohammed to Mauritania in September 2001, intended to inaugurate an era of improved relations between the two countries, was cut short as a result of the suicide attacks on the US mainland. In March 2002 it was reported that the land frontier between Morocco and Mauritania, which had been closed for 23 years, would be reopened. In November 2005 Col Ely Ould Mohamed Vall—the new Mauritanian leader following a coup there—visited Morocco at the invitation of King Mohammed and signed three agreements on bilateral co-operation. In April 2006 King Mohammed received the Mauritanian Prime Minister, Sidi Mohamed Ould Boubacar, for talks in Meknès.

The second Regional Ministerial Conference on Border Security, attended by representatives of all the countries bordering the Sahel-Sahara region, together with delegates from the wider international community, took place in Rabat in November 2013. Although the conference suffered notably from only low-level Algerian participation, it was agreed, *inter alia*, to establish a permanent secretariat in Tripoli. King Mohammed congratulated the Mauritanian President, Mohamed Ould Abdel Aziz, on his re-election in June 2014 and helped to facilitate the signing of a bilateral security agreement when the Mauritanian Minister of the Interior and Decentralization visited Rabat to meet his counterpart in October. The visit was reciprocated later that month when Minister of Foreign Affairs and Co-operation Mezouar visited Nouakchott, the Mauritanian capital, for talks with his counterpart. In subsequent years relations deteriorated as Morocco considered Mauritania to be unable to secure its northern border with Morocco and more interested in fostering good relations with Western Sahara, in an effort to undermine Moroccan influence in the region. Mauritania's hosting of the annual Arab League summit in Nouakchott in July 2016 included a presentation in which the map of Morocco did not include Western Sahara—a major break with Arab norms. At that point in time King Mohammed had not visited Mauritania in over a decade, and Morocco's Mauritanian diplomatic presence was meagre: it had not appointed an ambassador to Rabat since 2012. In August 2016, after a Moroccan military operation against an alleged Mauritanian trafficking operation along their mutual border, President Abdel Aziz ordered a military state of alert and deployed missiles at the border. However, a breakthrough occurred in September 2017 when Morocco announced that it would not be providing a haven for Mauritanian opposition figures—something that Nouakchott had long accused it of doing deliberately as a form of political leverage. For the first time in five years a Moroccan ambassador was appointed to the Mauritanian capital.

Also in September 2017, Morocco committed itself to aiding the border security and troop training of Mauritania and to the rest of the (Francophone) so-called G5 Sahel countries: Burkina Faso, Mali, Niger and Chad. In that month the Moroccan foreign affairs minister, Bourita, talked of this effort in the context of wanting to expand the role of Francophone countries in international peacekeeping and policing. Bourita praised the countries of the Organisation Internationale de la Francophonie, but said that the Francophone contribution to peacekeeping could be higher. He also picked up on a theme deployed elsewhere that the kingdom's experience of training imams and *murcheds* (guides) could make a huge and constructive contribution to countering the radicalization that undermined security in the Sahel.

In March 2018 Morocco continued its drive to improve relations with Sahel countries. Malian Prime Minister Soumeylou Boubèye Maïga conducted a two-day official visit to Morocco, putting relations on an improved footing, after five years during which they, like Moroccan-Mauritanian relations, had been tense. Transport and livestock deals with Mali were signed in Rabat.

Morocco also sought to forge closer relations with West Africa and, in particular, to join ECOWAS as a step towards deeper economic integration with the rest of the continent. Morocco had rejoined the AU in 2017 (see *Relations with Morocco's Maghreb Neighbours*), a move that symbolized the kingdom's supposed 'African pivot' at a time of ongoing intra-Maghreb tensions, and also reflected the King's close relations with the heads of state of Côte d'Ivoire and Gabon. Moroccan banks had expanded their presence throughout West Africa, as had key Moroccan industries such as the phosphate sector. However, this Moroccan economic advance encountered resistance from powerful business interests in Nigeria. The Nigerian President, Muhammadu Buhari, had been courted by King Mohammed, who hosted him in Rabat in June 2018, but Nigeria's full recognition of Polisario was a source of bilateral tension, as it was in Morocco's relations with several other ECOWAS states sympathetic towards the Sahrawi people.

In June 2019 the Moroccan parliament moved to ratify the kingdom's membership of the African Continental Free Trade Area (AfCFTA), another part of Morocco's economic pivot towards sub-Saharan Africa. The AfCFTA did not exclude Morocco from Maghreb tensions, as the SADR acceded to AfCFTA membership at a meeting of the nascent economic bloc in Niger in July. Speaking at a meeting of the AU in July, foreign affairs minister Bourita said that Morocco's membership of the AfCFTA was in no way a recognition of the SADR and that the membership of this 'entity' was an 'aberration', as it did not control any territory. However, Bourita suggested that 'it' (referring to the SADR) could trade via Tindouf in Algeria, which appeared to allow for an anomaly in terms of the conventions of sovereign statehood. Morocco ratified the AfCFTA treaty on 19 April 2022.

Following the USA's recognition of Moroccan sovereignty over Western Sahara on 22 December 2020, as part of the Morocco-Israel commitment to full diplomatic relations, four sub-Saharan states set up diplomatic missions to Morocco in Western Sahara (in addition to their existing embassies in Rabat). Despite Algerian (and Mauritanian) efforts, two ECOWAS member states—The Gambia and Guinea-Bissau—opened a consulate in Dakhla, more or less simultaneously with the USA, while Gabon and the Comoros Islands (located off Tanzania) did likewise in Laayoune in mid-January 2021. The controversy of this act by four sub-Saharan African states, whether in or out of ECOWAS, if anything complicated Morocco's stalled full membership bid regarding the West African bloc and underscored opposition to Morocco in the AU, especially among the SADR's supporters, including Algeria, South Africa and Nigeria. In April 2022 the head of the ECOWAS Parliament, Sidie Mohamed Tunis, expressed his optimism during a meeting with Bourita about Morocco's 'future accession' to the organization and stated that ECOWAS members were very positive about Morocco becoming a member. According to a report on their meeting published on the website Atalayer (a Spanish/French/English language site on Mediterranean affairs), Morocco's accession was supported by ECOWAS as it was expected to boost the organization's economic and political influence; however, the site also noted Nigeria's opposition in previous ECOWAS fora.

RELATIONS WITH THE MIDDLE EAST

Morocco was the first Arab state to condemn Iraq's invasion of Kuwait in August 1990 and voted for the resolutions at the Arab League summit held in Cairo, Egypt, denouncing Iraq's action. King Hassan agreed to send 1,200 Moroccan troops to Saudi Arabia and a further 5,000 were stationed in Abu Dhabi, the UAE. However, faced with strong pro-Iraqi feelings among the Moroccan people and hostility towards US military intervention in the region, the King quickly adopted a more neutral stance in the conflict and attempted to act as mediator in the dispute. Prior to the outbreak of hostilities, King Hassan sent a letter to Saddam Hussain, urging him to accept the deployment of a North African military force in Kuwait to replace the Iraqi army and avoid conflict with the US-led multinational force. In January 1991 opposition parties appealed for the withdrawal of the Moroccan contingent, and all parties in parliament demanded a negotiated solution to the crisis. Several pro-Iraqi demonstrations took place despite a government ban on street protests, and the Government also allowed the opposition parties to hold a march of solidarity with Iraq in Rabat. King Hassan stated that an agreement to send Moroccan troops to Saudi Arabia had been made before the Cairo summit, that their role was to be purely defensive, and that they were totally independent of coalition forces.

In January 1992 Arab foreign affairs ministers met in Marrakesh to agree a common strategy for the forthcoming Moscow session of the Middle East peace talks. In October, just before the seventh round of talks (held in Washington, DC), King Hassan made his most extensive tour of the Middle East in 30 years, visiting Jordan, Syria, Saudi Arabia, the Gulf states and Egypt. In December 1994 Morocco hosted a summit meeting of the OIC at the request of Saudi Arabia; however, despite lengthy negotiations, King Hassan failed to bring about any reconciliation between Iraq and Saudi Arabia and Kuwait.

King Hassan made an official visit to Egypt in May 1998 in order to strengthen bilateral relations. The King and President Hosni Mubarak signed several economic agreements, and, in a joint statement, expressed support for the Palestinian people and urged the USA to continue its efforts to revive the Middle East peace process. In July Morocco again hosted a meeting of the OIC's Al-Quds (Jerusalem) Committee, of which King Hassan was the Chairman, to discuss the stalled Middle East peace process.

In September 1993, following the mutual recognition and signature of a peace accord between Israel and the Palestine Liberation Organization, the Israeli Prime Minister, Itzhak Rabin, and the Minister of Foreign Affairs, Shimon Peres, visited Rabat for talks with King Hassan. Apart from Egypt, Morocco was the only Arab state to receive the two Israeli leaders. In October a group of Moroccan industrialists, including King Hassan's economic adviser, visited Israel to attend a business conference: this was the first official Moroccan delegation to visit the country. Commercial links developed rapidly, and tourism was expected to expand: the Moroccan-Jewish community constitutes more than 10% of the Israeli population, and large numbers visit their country of origin every year. After talks with King Hassan in June 1994, Peres announced that the two countries had agreed to establish telecommunications links and, at a later date, to establish 'representations of some kind'. In September, as the peace process gained momentum, Morocco and Israel agreed to open 'liaison offices' in Rabat and Tel Aviv. King Hassan had maintained discreet contacts with Israeli leaders since the 1970s. The latest move towards a normalization of relations with Israel was criticized by the opposition parties, which urged caution until a comprehensive Middle East peace settlement had been achieved. In October 1994, during an historic appearance on Israeli television, King Hassan declared that the peace process would lead to the establishment of full diplomatic relations between Morocco and Israel, but carefully avoided stating when this would take place. He reiterated Morocco's stance on the restoration of Arab lands and rights, while insisting that the unconditional recognition of Israeli sovereignty within internationally agreed borders was essential. In early 1995 Morocco opened an economic bureau in Tel Aviv, making it the third Arab state after Egypt and Jordan to have a representative office in Israel. In February 1996 an Israeli-Moroccan chamber of commerce was opened in Tel Aviv.

The King organized a meeting in Rabat of the OIC's Jerusalem Committee in March 1997. The committee demanded that the Israeli Government stop construction of a Jewish settlement on the outskirts of Arab East Jerusalem and appealed to Arab states that had begun to establish relations with Israel to reconsider these links. A threat by Morocco in April to close the Moroccan-based Bureau for Economic Development in the Middle East, established to promote economic relations between the Arab states and Israel, was withdrawn in May after US intervention. Morocco did not close its liaison office in Tel Aviv, despite King Hassan's continued refusal to have any contact with the administration of Binyamin Netanyahu. However commercial and business links between Morocco and Israel remained strong.

In August 2000 King Mohammed chaired a meeting of the OIC's Jerusalem Committee, which reaffirmed that the city should be the capital of a Palestinian state. Following renewed violence between Israel and the Palestinians in September–October, there was growing criticism within Morocco of the country's links with Israel. In late October Morocco closed Israel's liaison office in Rabat and its own interest section in Tel Aviv. However, in December Israel's Deputy Prime Minister and Minister of Foreign Affairs, Peres, visited Rabat to discuss US peace proposals with King Mohammed, suggesting that Morocco was continuing its role as mediator between the Arab states and Israel.

There was widespread outrage in Morocco in response to the Israeli military offensive in Palestinian-controlled areas of the West Bank from March 2002. A national march in solidarity with the Palestinian people, which took place in Rabat in April, attracting more than 1m. people, was the biggest demonstration in the Arab world. Meanwhile, there were reports in the Moroccan press that an apparent resurgence of anti-Jewish sentiment since the onset of the second *intifada*, a renewed uprising by Palestinians against Israeli occupation, was causing disquiet among members of Morocco's Jewish community. The Moroccan authorities remained silent on this subject, but arrested several radical imams for criticizing the Moroccan and other Arab governments' alleged quiescence with regard to the situation in the Palestinian Territories.

In April 2005 Morocco's Minister of Agriculture, Rural Development and Maritime Fisheries denied reports that Morocco had trade links with Israel. In February 2006 King Mohammed received the new (Moroccan-born) leader of the Israel Labour Party, Amir Peretz, and in April the PA President, Mahmoud Abbas, visited Rabat for talks with King Mohammed. In early July Morocco condemned Israeli military incursions into the Gaza Strip. In July 2007 Benaïssa and the Israeli Vice-Prime Minister and Minister of Foreign Affairs, Tzipi Livni, held the first such official meeting for four years in order to discuss the Middle East peace process. Arab outrage at the Israeli–Gaza war of 2008–09 prevented further high-level meetings for some time. In December 2013 a Moroccan parliamentary bill proposed the cutting of residual Moroccan ties with Israel. The proposal apparently had the blessing of the royal court, as a means to assuage the strength of public feeling in Morocco about the Palestinian question. Parliamentary intentions did not lead to any significant shift in official Moroccan policy, however, controlled as it is by the King.

Moroccan-Israeli relations remained distinctly cool after the re-election of Netanyahu as Israeli Prime Minister in March 2015. Allowing a large 'anti-normalization' demonstration to be held in Casablanca in October both symbolized the *makhzen*'s ongoing detachment toward Israel and the popular pressure to maintain it. Despite a modest improvement in Saudi and Emirati relations with Israel based on the perception that they shared a common enemy in Iran—a situation compounded by the intra-Gulf state crisis (see below)—Morocco showed no indication of wanting to warm relations with Israel. In fact, a measure of domestic hostility to doing so was the response given to the former Israeli Minister of Defence and Labour Party leader Peretz, when in October 2017 he led the Israeli delegation to a conference on Mediterranean trade held, under the auspices of the Parliamentary Assembly of the Mediterranean, at the Moroccan Chamber of Representatives. Peretz and his delegation were obliged to leave the parliamentary building, and even the country, after an angry response from Moroccan anti-normalization activists had followed a PJD boycott. In March 2018 Israeli participation at an international judo tournament in Agadir proved too much for some Moroccans, who walked out after the Israeli national anthem was played and the Israeli flag raised. The decision to hold the sporting event, which, like the regional parliamentary gathering, inevitably meant an obligation to host Israeli representatives, was a sign of a Moroccan willingness to allow a modest form of engagement, but also confirmed the difficulty of moving much further.

In December 2017 and May 2018 Turkey (officially redesignated as Türkiye in June 2022) organized extraordinary OIC summits on Jerusalem. These gatherings, like King Mohammed's subsequent meeting with the Jordanian monarch in March 2019, were intended both to rebut President Trump's decision to move the US embassy in Israel to the city and to challenge Saudi Arabia, which was perceived as positioning itself more closely with the USA on the Israeli–Palestinian issue (see *Relations with the USA*). Morocco's participation was at a senior level, not to stand overtly against Saudi Arabia, but instead reflecting its own historical projection of Islamic leadership and its ongoing chairmanship of the OIC's Al-Quds (Jerusalem) Committee.

Thousands of protesters demonstrated in Rabat (as in many other Arab capitals) in June 2019 in opposition to a US-organized 'workshop' in Bahrain that focused on economic measures to aid the Palestinians. The meeting was criticized for ignoring the political context of the Israeli–Palestinian conflict and for not advocating a final settlement in line with established Arab (including Moroccan) positions. Palestinian officials boycotted the event. The sizeable Moroccan Jewish population in Israel and Morocco's engagement with both parties to the conflict afforded King Mohammed some leverage with Israel. However, the lack of a political process supported by the Palestinians made it difficult, if not impossible, for the King to adopt a stance that could in any way be perceptibly sympathetic to the Israeli position. Reflecting this, the Moroccan Government dispatched a relatively junior official to the Bahrain workshop. The anticipated launch of the Trump's so-called 'Deal of the Century' (officially known as 'Peace to Prosperity') led to consultation with Morocco by several other Arab states that were pivotal in any possible normalization of relations with Israel, as well as by the USA. In August 2019 the Jordanian foreign affairs minister, Ayman al-Safadi, visited Morocco to consult Bourita. Both countries, drawing on their monarchies' strong Islamic credentials and, arguably, legitimacy, were especially alarmed that the right of Palestinians to have control over East Jerusalem (or any part of that city) did not feature in the US-Israeli co-ordinated proposals, as well as being disconcerted by periodic reports of Saudi Arabia's interest in taking over the custodianship of Islamic holy sites in Jerusalem. The eventual Peace to Prosperity launch in January 2020 was preceded by Morocco (and Jordan) sending a clear message to the USA that what was about to be promoted would fall far short of what it could support diplomatically.

That the King and *makhzen* agreed to the US-orchestrated peace deal with Israel in December 2020 came as a surprise, despite the fact that Morocco and Israel had had diplomatic relations before, albeit more limited than what was expected under this fully fledged 'normalization'. Not surprisingly it also created problems for the PJD's base specifically. While the King could partly distance himself from what was inevitably a controversial decision in Morocco and in the wider Arab world, it was Prime Minister el-Othmani who was delegated to sign the agreement. Arguably protocol made it necessary: the USA was only represented by the 'special adviser to the President', Jared Kushner; and Israel by the National Security Chief, Meir Ben-Shabbat, and by Alon Ushpiz, the director-general of the Israeli foreign affairs ministry (and the Israeli Government's *de facto* normalization 'guru'). However, as head of government, el-Othmani was carrying responsibility for something that he would subsequently imply he was not happy with, but which he had little choice but to execute. The agreement referred to the 'coherent, constant and unchanged position of the Kingdom of Morocco on the Palestinian question, as well as the position expressed on the importance of preserving the special status of the sacred city of Jerusalem for the three monotheistic religions in His Majesty the King's capacity as Chairman of the Al-Quds Committee'. However, this could be seen as a fig leaf intended to spare the Arabist and Islamic blushes of the *amr al-mouminin*. After all, in practical terms it could be argued that 'preserving the special status' of the Holy City constituted little more than an expressed wish akin to that which the UAE had written into the so-called Abraham Accords, which were signed in September 2020 by the UAE and Bahrain with Israel and the USA. The city's 'special status' had arguably not been ended even by Israel's occupation of the eastern half of Jerusalem, including the Islamic sites subject to the authority of the *Awqaf* (literally 'trust'; the traditional and long-established Islamic authorities in Jerusalem), but the practical expression of this 'special status' was routinely subject to Israeli security and political considerations, and a *de jure* annexation under Israeli law of the eastern half of the city, that continued to include the de facto erosion of the Palestinian national presence proximate to the holy sites. Notably, the above quote from the normalization agreement contains the only nod in the document to Palestinian national claims, and, furthermore, it is made as an almost passing and ambiguous reference without even asserting its equation with Palestinian sovereignty in the half of the city that includes the said holy sites.

Visible, tangible signs of normalization had been slim after the receipt by Morocco's King of what was billed as an 'American-Israeli delegation to Morocco' on the day of the signing of the peace deal on 22 December 2020. In late June 2021 there were reports from the kingdom that Moroccan landlords were unwilling to grant Israel either the land or the buildings on which to open its planned embassy in Rabat.

El-Othmani's hosting of Hamas leader Ismael Haniyeh in late June 2021 (as part of a brief regional trip to Egypt, Qatar, Lebanon and Mauritania), the month after the Palestinian Islamist movement had perceptibly 'won the peace' following an armed confrontation with Israel, brought the wrath of Western anti-Zionists against Haniyeh for fraternizing with a supposed friend of Israel. However, in Morocco and in much of the region it was largely seen as a deft move by the Prime Minister designed to restore some credibility to his and the PJD's image for their role in normalization with Israel at a time when the party's political fortunes were flagging at home. It also helped both Morocco generally and the King, who had, after all, given the deal with Israel an Islamic imprimatur with, arguably, little having been gained in exchange.

In the assessment of Moroccan academic Aziz Chahir, writing for the UK online site *Middle East Eye*, 'The professed religious authority of the Moroccan monarch has thus been seriously undermined by the new agreement'. Chahir, presumably France-based, was none the less a consultant and senior researcher at a Moroccan institute, the Jacques-Berque Centre in Rabat. Comment made in a domestic Moroccan context had, by definition, to be more circumspect. However, the May 2021 Israeli–Palestinian violence, which included Palestinian–Israeli clashes on Jerusalem's Haram Al-Shareef holy compound that the King continued to put such store in being a defender of, was uncomfortable for the Moroccan political leadership.

Following the electoral trouncing of the PJD, however, and the assumption of formal governmental control by a centre-right alliance in November 2021, Morocco pursued more open and more developed relations with Israel. Moroccan intelligence relations with Israel were nothing new at the semi-covert level. However, Morocco's signing of a defence co-operation memorandum of understanding (MOU) with Israel on 24 November was a reflection of a symbolic, as well as a likely practical, shift.

However, reservations about too deep and too high-level a diplomatic engagement persisted on the Moroccan side owing in part to the lack of US and Israeli follow-through on the transactional peace deal overseen by the Trump Administration. Biden didn't follow through on the promised US recognition of Western Sahara as Moroccan—and nor did Israel, perhaps itself wary of being too out of step with the USA (and a large swathe of Western and, to a degree, Arab opinion). This did not prevent ongoing bilateral normalization, however. In February 2022 Israel and Morocco signed a trade co-operation agreement. By March three of the most senior officials in the Israeli Defense Forces, including the head of military intelligence, were in Rabat for meetings that included one with the Moroccan Inspector General of the armed forces and another with the head of the Moroccan intelligence service. The Israeli media reported that the Israeli officials stated that the two sides had signed an accord confirming their shared objective of greater military collaboration.

The Negev Forum, first convened in Israel in 2022, brought together Morocco, Israel and the other signatory nations to the Abraham Accords to discuss regional issues. However, a second meeting of the Forum, originally scheduled to be held in Morocco in March 2023, was repeatedly postponed. Moroccan popular opinion of Israel had never been sympathetic, and thus the prospect of hosting such a public expression of 'normalization' proved difficult for Morocco. The formation in December 2022 of an Israeli Government that was perceptibly the most hard-line nationalist in the country's history only compounded the difficulty for Morocco. In June 2023 Israeli media reported that Morocco had postponed a prospective July Negev Forum meeting after a settlement expansion announcement by Israel. Arguably, the Accords had left their Arab signatories looking like regional outliers given popular Arab, and to some extent international, antipathy towards the Israeli Government and given the nascent Gulf Arab rapprochement with Iran. Morocco had seemingly secured US support for its sovereignty claims over Western Sahara and perhaps did not feel the need to be too overtly engaged with Israel. However, it was probably also the case that the USA did not want to 'reward' a particularly nationalist Israeli Government with which it had significant disagreements.

In January 2023 the first Monitoring Committee for Moroccan-Israeli Defence Co-operation was inaugurated, and a commitment to deepening bilateral military co-operation was agreed, with a particular focus on logistics, training and the acquisition and modernization of defence equipment, according to MWN. Senior Israeli military officers also travelled to Morocco in early 2023 for talks with Moroccan defence officials.

Local and international media reported in mid-2023 that Israel was considering formally recognizing Morocco's sovereignty claims over Western Sahara. During an official visit to the kingdom in early June the Speaker of the Israeli parliament, Amir Ohana, stated that he thought that Prime Minister Netanyahu would announce a decision on recognition shortly. Ohana declared that he was 'aware' of the 'full importance' of Israel recognizing the 'Moroccan Sahara'. Indeed, Reuters reported on 8 June that Ohana had affirmed that Israel 'will announce its support for' Morocco's claims of sovereignty over Western Sahara.

Prime Minister el-Youssoufi led a delegation of ministers and business representatives to Iran in January 2001, with the aim of preparing for closer political relations. Several commercial agreements were signed during the visit. (No senior Moroccan politician had visited Iran since the Islamic Revolution in 1979, and in 1981 Iran had severed diplomatic relations with Morocco after King Hassan allowed the deposed Shah to take refuge in Morocco.) In May 2003 the Iranian Minister of Foreign Affairs visited Rabat at the head of a high-ranking delegation, and at a meeting with his Moroccan counterpart there were appeals for closer economic, political and cultural ties between the two countries. In June 2006 Benaïssa visited the Iranian capital, Tehran, for talks with Iranian President Mahmoud Ahmadinejad, whereupon an agreement was concluded to create a joint political committee. However, relations deteriorated abruptly in March 2009, when Morocco severed diplomatic relations with Iran following remarks made by a senior Iranian official appearing to claim Iranian sovereignty over Bahrain.

Relations with Iran showed some signs of improving following the election in June 2013 of Hassan Rouhani, considered a relative moderate, as Iranian President. However, events in the wider Middle East had pitted Morocco more overtly on the side of the Gulf Arab states against Iranian interests. Morocco was a natural ally of Saudi Arabia in this matter, particularly as Riyadh has sought to strengthen support for Arab hereditary monarchies since the uprisings and civil unrest of 2011. Despite this, in 2014 formal Moroccan relations with Iran were restored, owing in part to modest signs that Saudi Arabia wanted to test the diplomatic water with Rouhani. However, even though Moroccan relations on the Arab side of the Gulf were negatively affected by the Gulf states' own divisions, Morocco remained sensitive to Gulf distrust of Iran, especially on the part of Saudi Arabia and the UAE. In May 2018 Morocco again severed relations with Iran, this time alleging that Iran was aiding Polisario via the Lebanese Shi'a group Hezbollah. Morocco accused the latter of providing missiles to Polisario and of doing so via Iran's embassy in Algeria. The Moroccan break with Iran had the effect of uniting an otherwise divided Gulf Arab bloc as Saudi and Qatar competed to congratulate Morocco. The Arab League—long a platform for the interests of its host, Egypt, which had become closely aligned with Saudi and UAE interests—joined in the accusation against Iran and expressed 'solidarity' with Morocco; Algeria, meanwhile, made plain its discontent. The more united Gulf front, following the signing of the Al-Ula Accord in January 2021, if anything only emphasized that for Morocco relations with Iran would necessarily remain difficult. Iran's election of a hard-line conservative as formal head of government in June appeared to underscore the difficulty in relations improving. In October 2022 it seemed as if Moroccan-Iranian relations had reached a new low when Bourita publicly accused Iran of meddling in Yemen and providing Polisario with drones, while Iran condemned Morocco's rapprochement with Israel. Morocco expressed concern that Iran was arming Polisario as part of a wider intervention strategy in Algeria, Mauritania and the Sahel. Indeed, Moroccan, and US, concern about Iran had contributed to Morocco joining the Abraham Accords and normalizing its relations with Israel.

Ties with Saudi Arabia have been strengthened under King Mohammed. In May 2007 Morocco and Saudi Arabia signed a co-operation accord that included a Saudi pledge of US $50m. to promote Morocco's development. This brought total Saudi aid to the kingdom to $170m. over eight years. As the regional turmoil of 2011 intensified, Morocco (and Jordan) received an unexpected invitation in May from Saudi Arabia's King Abdullah to join the GCC. The invitation, which was clearly designed to bring the Arab monarchies closer together and to close ranks against the democratizing forces within the region, provoked widespread bemusement in Morocco, and subsequent discussions over Morocco's membership proved tentative. After indications from the UAE and Kuwait that they opposed the inclusion of Morocco and Jordan in the GCC, and that they had not been consulted over King Abdullah's invitation, the Saudi Minister of Foreign Affairs, Prince Sa'ud al-Faisal Al Sa'ud, declared in December that the two countries' 'applications' would need further consideration. In January 2012 Kuwait proposed 'full integration' after two years of partnership with Morocco and Jordan. In the event, the GCC's pledge to provide dedicated funding to the two countries seemed to replace the fading and barely formed 'commitment' to their GCC membership.

In May 2014 Saudi Arabia formally designated the Muslim Brotherhood a terrorist organization in a move that was a counterpart to the UAE's deeply held hostility to the regional movement. This followed the role of Saudi Arabia and the UAE in encouraging the overthrow of the Government of Muhammad Mursi in Egypt in July 2013. Despite the leading role of Prime Minister Benkirane's PJD in the Moroccan Government, neither the declaration concerning the Brotherhood nor the change of administration in Egypt harmed Moroccan relations with Saudi Arabia and the UAE. In any case, the Saudi adjustment to a more pragmatic attitude towards the Brotherhood and its affiliated groups after the death of King Abdullah in January 2015 suggested that individuals not engaged in violence and loyal to the regime were wholly exempt from the previous Saudi stance. Nor, seemingly, did the turn of events in Cairo have an especially negative effect on Moroccan relations with Egypt under the rule of President al-Sisi. At the time of Mursi's overthrow, however, there had been some criticism of the Egyptian military's action by the Moroccan Ministry of Foreign Affairs and Co-operation; and a PJD member was later accused, but then acquitted, of planning to attack the Egyptian ambassador to Rabat. Relations subsequently fluctuated. On the one hand, Morocco was lauded in Egypt's annual anniversary celebration of the 1973 Arab–Israeli War. On the other, residual Egyptian resentment of any Arab criticism of what it liked to describe as the July 2013 'revolution' (rather than some observers' description of it as a coup) led to periodic media briefing against Morocco, which none the less alternated with more positive coverage. By March 2015 the two countries had seemingly put their differences behind them when Benkirane held a private meeting with President al-Sisi during a summit of the Arab League in Sharm el-Sheikh—much to the displeasure of the Brotherhood in Egypt.

Morocco joined the Saudi-led Arab military and political coalition (which included Egypt and the Gulf Arab states) against the al-Houthi rebels and their allies in Yemen, who took over large parts of that country from late 2014 and prompted the collapse of the Saudi-backed Government in the capital, San'a. At least six Moroccan air force fighter jets, together with military personnel, were deployed to the action in Yemen from March 2015. Following reports in May of a Moroccan military aircraft having been shot down by al-Houthi fighters, it was not clear if Morocco continued to play an active part in the military coalition. However, in early December the Moroccan press, including the privately owned Moroccan newspaper *Assabah*, reported that the kingdom was about to dispatch 1,500 army paratroopers to support the forces of the Saudi-backed coalition in Yemen fighting the al-Houthis and their allies. In a reflection of the growing strength of Moroccan-

Saudi relations, in mid-December Morocco signed a military technology co-operation agreement with Saudi Arabia.

By March 2016 Saudi Arabia's attempted negotiations with the al-Houthis, alongside ongoing intra-Yemeni peace talks and a partly holding Kuwaiti-brokered ceasefire, made the involvement of countries like Morocco less important from a warfare point of view. In June *Assabah* reported that Morocco had withdrawn 1,500 troops from Yemen in what was described as a tactical withdrawal of men not material, intended to respond to efforts to secure an intra-Yemeni peace deal and to offset prospective Algerian activation of Polisario while such 'elite units' were absent. The latter statement appeared calculated to offset any embarrassment about the perceptible softening of Morocco's commitment to the Saudi-led war, even though Morocco was likely to have consulted the kingdom before announcing its decision. In any case, Morocco remained politically firmly supportive of the Saudi and wider GCC position against the al-Houthis. This largely reflected its increasingly close (and relatively dependent) relationship with Saudi Arabia and, to some extent, a similar relationship with the UAE and Qatar. The latter's generous donations of financial aid reflected its competition with Saudi Arabia and the UAE for influence among less wealthy Arab nations. Furthermore, the Qatari leadership's traditional sympathy for political Islamism helped to underpin good Moroccan-Qatari relations, owing to the continued presence in the Moroccan Government of the PJD.

In a further sign of the Arab Gulf states' firm embrace of Morocco, on 20 April 2016 a Moroccan-GCC summit took place in the Saudi capital, Riyadh. This was preceded in early April by a Saudi national commitment to US $230m. of 'soft' financing for Moroccan infrastructure projects, and was followed later that month by the signing of three Moroccan-Bahraini taxation agreements. Saudi King Salman bin Abdulaziz Al Sa'ud made a public statement during the Moroccan-GCC joint summit in support of the Moroccan position over Western Sahara, thereby worsening sometimes difficult Algerian-Saudi relations, while Morocco's King Mohammed made a statement saying that Moroccan-Jordanian-GCC states' security was being targeted by common enemies and that their countries' security interests were 'interdependent'. Jordan's absence from the summit was surprising, as, ever since the Arab uprisings of 2011, Saudi Arabia had sought to deepen the GCC's partnership with Morocco and Jordan. Shortly after the GCC summit, Morocco's premier Benkirane and his Jordanian counterpart, Abdullah Ensour, met in the Jordanian capital, Amman, to try to promote their countries' bilateral higher committee. At the end of April 2016 King Mohammed visited Bahrain and Qatar.

The outbreak of an intra-GCC political and economic dispute in June 2017, pitting Saudi Arabia, the UAE and Bahrain (with Egyptian support) against Qatar, with Kuwait trying to mediate and Oman remaining on the sidelines, created a problem for Morocco in trying to remain on good terms with all parties. The ostensible focus of the dispute—Qatar's alleged support for Islamist militants and radicals, and its relatively cordial relations with Iran—were issues on which King Mohammed took an opposing view, even if he had adopted a relatively gentle line in constraining the activities of Islamists in the Moroccan political system. Morocco's most favoured option in the Gulf was to work towards a negotiated compromise, which reduced intra-Gulf tension and ended any obligation on Morocco to take one side or the other. Although Morocco's backing for the Saudi-led military coalition in Yemen and its minimal (then later terminated—see above) relations with Iran granted it effective political credit in Saudi Arabia (and in the USA), the King saw no political or economic advantage in Morocco alienating either side in the Gulf conflict.

However, Moroccan neutrality seemingly upset Saudi Arabia and its close partner on the Qatar issue, the UAE. In mid-June 2017 state media in Saudi Arabia broadcast a short programme that deviated from the hitherto official Saudi line by describing what was normally referred to as the Moroccan Sahara, as Western Sahara. The UAE used the same reference in a separate broadcast in the same month. Reports of increased Moroccan food exports to Qatar from June, amid the Saudi-led blockade of that country, were unlikely to have endeared Morocco to Saudi Arabia, the UAE or their Egyptian and Bahraini allies, either. Morocco continued to try to tread an awkward path between rival Gulf states, mindful of its need to please the key ones, not least because of their economic and financial strength. Notably, however, in September Qatar, seeking to ensure its own options amid the blockade, opportunistically relaxed visa requirements for Moroccan nationals, irritating the Saudi-led anti-Qatar alliance. However, King Mohammed made sure that Morocco did not become too estranged from Saudi Arabia and the UAE. The King attended the opening of Abu Dhabi's branch of the Louvre Museum in November, albeit partly to please France's President Macron, who was also in attendance. King Mohammed then, in effect, broke the blockade by flying direct from Abu Dhabi to Qatar as he sought, unsuccessfully, to mediate in the intra-Gulf crisis. This suggested that the UAE understood Morocco's need to appear as neutral as possible. The visit of King Hamad bin Isa Al Khalifa of Bahrain—a very close ally of Saudi Arabia—to Morocco in May 2018 emphasized how mindful the Moroccan King was of the need to maintain cordial relations with Qatar's (current) Gulf Arab enemies.

Moroccan-Qatari relations were boosted in March 2018 when Qatar's Prime Minister, Sheikh Abdullah Nasser al-Thani, travelled to Rabat and signed 11 agreements and MOUs, including on education, farming and anti-money-laundering. The international outrage over the murder of Saudi journalist Jamal Khashoggi in Turkey in October by Saudi state officials reportedly linked to a senior aide to Saudi Arabia's Crown Prince Mohammed bin Salman seemed to encourage Morocco to abstain from joining in with some Arab states' expressions of support for the Saudi regime. Morocco's response to this controversy, together with its known disapproval of Saudi Arabia's military intervention in Yemen and of Mohammed bin Salman's reported flexibility towards Israel over the Jerusalem issue, apparently prompted Saudi Arabia to broadcast another critical television programme on the Western Sahara dispute in February 2019, souring bilateral relations again. The programme reportedly once again questioned Moroccan sovereignty over Western Sahara and presented Polisario as the legitimate representative of the Sahrawi people and the disputed territory. Shortly afterwards, Morocco announced formally that it was withdrawing from the Saudi-led coalition in Yemen—a move prefigured by the withdrawal of its fighter jets in April 2018 and the reduction of its military involvement in the conflict. In March 2019 Morocco's Minister of Foreign Affairs and International Co-operation, Bourita, informed the media that relations with Saudi Arabia and the UAE were 'close, important and strategic', but that Morocco would not be taken for granted. In April the Moroccan ambassador to Saudi Arabia, who had been recalled after the broadcast of the controversial television programme in February, returned to Riyadh.

The Moroccan Government also apparently disapproved of Saudi and Emirati military and economic ambitions in Morocco's neighbour, Mauritania. Bourita declined to visit the UAE during his Gulf tour in April 2019 (although he did visit the more powerful Saudi Arabia in May). This apparent snub to the UAE followed a statement by Bourita earlier that month that emphasized the importance of 'reciprocal loyalty' between Saudi Arabia and the UAE on the one side and Morocco on the other. Bourita seemed, in part, to be referencing Saudi and Emirati ambitions in Mauritania. The Gulf states' interest in Mauritania could economically threaten Morocco's Tanger Med and Dakhla development projects, while the military aspect of Saudi and Emirati interest in Mauritania was unwelcome in light of the aforementioned political differences. More significantly, perhaps, for Morocco, was that Libya was becoming an increasing focus for the UAE's military and political ambitions, reflected in the periodic air force engagement in Libya by the UAE and its close ally Egypt and their strong support for the Libyan rebel leader, Haftar. In May Morocco withdrew its ambassador to the UAE, who had also reportedly been recalled in February; the recall in May followed the withdrawal of the Emirati ambassador from Morocco a month earlier, seemingly in response to Bourita's snub.

Difficulties in Moroccan-Emirati relations were further confirmed by Morocco's engagement with Qatar (the UAE had arguably been the most determined of all of Qatar's Arab opponents to maintain the blockade, pending a de facto Qatari capitulation). In February 2020 Morocco declared its willingness to assist Qatar with logistical preparations for the International Federation of Association Football (Fédération Internationale de Football Association) 2022 World Cup. In early March 2020 Morocco confirmed that it would shortly be taking part in a military exercise in Qatar called 'Impregnable Guard 2020'. Although this would not have been welcomed by the UAE (or Saudi Arabia, for that matter), it should be noted that the USA and France were among the international participants in the exercise, together with Pakistan, a close Saudi Arabian ally. The exercise followed an announcement that a working meeting of Moroccan and Qatari interior ministry officials had recently taken place. Also in March, it was reported that Morocco had withdrawn its ambassador and several other embassy officials from the UAE, and the latter's ambassador to Rabat was absent from his position, although neither side had made these absences the subject of official statements.

In April 2020 the UAE proposed restrictions on future employment in the Emirates for nationals of countries that had not repatriated their residents; this would include Morocco. Some unemployed Moroccan nationals were stranded in Gulf Arab states following the imposition of lockdowns to contain the COVID-19 pandemic, including in the UAE—the host of the largest Moroccan expatriate population in the Middle East. Although bilateral tensions on this issue were partly about the two countries' different approaches to managing the pandemic—Morocco reportedly offered aid and assistance to its stranded nationals—it also reflected an existing high level of bilateral distrust, largely driven by the issue of the boycott of Qatar. In May allegations were made in the Moroccan media that Emirati-based 'bots' (autonomous agents on social media that seek to influence the course of an online discussion) were targeting the social media accounts of Morocco's senior political leaders by making negative comments.

Moroccan-Saudi relations had, however, improved in May 2019 when, in the context of Bourita's visit, the Saudi Government confirmed that, contrary to the implication of its media broadcasts, it regarded Western Sahara as Moroccan. Confirming the determination of Morocco and Saudi Arabia to place their relations on a more stable footing, a Saudi delegation led by the head of the Saudi Arabian Majlis al-Shura (Consultative Council), Abdullah al-Sheikh, met Prime Minister el-Othmani in Rabat in February 2020. El-Othmani's assertion, following the meeting, that Saudi Arabia had never backed the SADR and that it fully supported the Moroccan plan for Sahrawi autonomy and respected Morocco's territorial integrity was an indication of improved relations.

The ending of the intra-GCC spat with the convening of the GCC summit in Al-Ula, Saudi Arabia, on 5 January 2021 occurred alongside the six member states stating clearly their shared commitment to Morocco with whom they said the GCC had a 'special strategic relationship'. The UAE had arguably begun to re-evaluate its relationship with Morocco because Algeria had proven so resistant to Emirati efforts to persuade it to take a strong oppositional stance toward Turkey's role in Libya. The interconnection between the Morocco-Israeli peace deal and Moroccan sovereignty in Western Sahara was emphasized by the fact that the UAE and Bahrain, which had only a few months earlier made peace with Israel, bought into the 'exchange' by also opening consulates in Laayoune, the 'capital' of Western Sahara. Morocco had arguably played a good game in what had been a complex intra-GCC dispute. Now, by joining the UAE and Bahrain in normalizing relations with Israel, Morocco had reasserted its so-called eastern strategic flank with the Gulf countries at a time when they, and especially the Saudis, had proven ready for a compromise 'peace' within Gulf ranks too. The ongoing deepening of the two Gulf states' normalization deals with Israel during the first half of 2022 was in tandem with Morocco's own deepening accord with Israel. If anything, the security aspect of the Moroccan-Israeli accord went deeper, at least at the public level, than those of the Emirati and Bahraini deals. However, this did not appear to create any tensions between Morocco on the one hand, and the UAE, Bahrain and, indirectly, Saudi Arabia on the other.

Economy

NEIL PARTRICK

Based on an original essay by ALAN J. DAY

Morocco's economy is highly dependent on agriculture, which is in turn highly dependent on weather conditions, leading to a large degree of volatility in economic output. According to the World Bank, GDP growth in 2013 was 4.5% (owing to heavy rainfall), fell to 2.7% in 2014 and rose to 4.6% in 2015 (owing to high revenues from cereal production). A drought in 2016 led to a sharp decline, with GDP growth falling to 1.2%. After 2017, however, Morocco recorded an economic upturn with growth of 4.2% according to the International Monetary Fund (IMF), owing mainly to an increase in agricultural GDP of 15.1%. According to the IMF, GDP growth in 2018 fell to 3.1% amid lower output and a dip in foreign direct investment (FDI), and to 2.9% in 2019, owing chiefly to a contraction that year of 5.0% in the agricultural sector as a result of a drought (see below).

The Fund reported that the fiscal deficit fell to 3.5% of GDP in 2017. Although this was in line with the Moroccan Government's commitment to reducing the deficit to 3% of GDP in 2019–21 and to reduce public debt to 60% by 2021, it had been made easier by the size of GDP growth in 2017. According to the IMF, the fiscal deficit was equivalent to 3.4% of GDP in 2018 and 3.6% in 2019. The devastating impact of the coronavirus disease (COVID-19) pandemic from March 2020 resulted in a sharp contraction in the Moroccan economy from the second quarter of that year. The pandemic led to the Government drawing on the whole of its loan funding under an arrangement with the IMF in April (see *Budget*). In that month the IMF stated that the decline in exports, tourist arrivals, remittances from migrant workers, and what it hoped would be only a 'temporary freeze' in economic activity generally, would cause the economy to contract. The IMF added that the deficit on the balance of payments would widen, amid a decline in capital inflows, but assumed that the Fund's loan financing would prevent a balance-of-payments crisis. In April 2023 the IMF reported that the Moroccan economy had shrunk by 7.2% in 2020, although real growth of 7.9% was recorded in 2021 as the effects of the drought and the pandemic eased. It might be added that the lifting of pandemic-related lockdowns and greater global economic confidence, owing to the gradual availability of the vaccine against COVID-19, also played a part in the rebound. The IMF estimated that real GDP growth in 2022 was a more modest 1.1%. The impact of sharply rising prices for imported commodities and energy supplies following the Russian Federation's invasion of Ukraine in February was a major contributor to sluggish growth internationally. The IMF reported that the fiscal deficit had widened to 7.1% of GDP in 2020, before decreasing to 5.9% in 2021 and an estimated 5.1% in 2022.

The inflation rate has been relatively low since the 2000s, and between 2004 and 2014, according to the IMF, it did not rise above 3.9%, with an average annual increase in consumer prices of 1.8%. The rate remained mostly unchanged over the following years, although in 2019 it almost flatlined at only

0.2%, according to the IMF, seemingly in line with that year's modest real growth and the contraction in the agricultural sector. In 2020, amid economic contraction, the annual average inflation rate rose slightly to 0.7%, according to the Fund. Consumer prices increased by an annual average of 1.4% in 2021 and by an estimated 6.6% in 2022. The shifting story reflected a recovering Moroccan and global economy in 2021 and, relatedly, imported inflation via rising energy costs as global oil prices increased substantially. This was compounded in 2022, when the conflict in Ukraine began to underpin even higher oil prices and rising prices for imported foodstuffs. That said, the IMF noted positively that the Government had taken measures to offset imported inflation, such as by increasing wheat and gas price subsidies, fixing electricity tariff rates, and providing additional funding to the transportation and agricultural sectors. However, as of February 2023, the official year-on-year inflation rate reportedly exceeded 10%, including a food inflation rate of over 20%. Rising food prices precipitated popular protests in the capital, Rabat, in April (see History).

Morocco has relatively few natural resources, of which phosphate is the most important. After agriculture, manufacturing—especially automotive industries, food processing, leather processing and textiles—has the greatest significance for the Moroccan economy. The energy industry, telecommunications, computers and electronics and aerospace have also become important in recent years. According to official figures, the industrial sector (including mining, manufacturing, power and construction) contributed 28.2% of GDP in 2022. In 2020, according to official data, the services sector employed 45.8% of the total employed population, the agricultural sector 31.3% and the industrial sector 23.0%.

In 2018 the services sector, with tourism performing especially well, accounted for the largest share of GDP, at 56%. According to the IMF's most recent annual Article IV report on Morocco, issued in January 2023, the value of tourism receipts in 2020, despite being the first year of the COVID-19-related tourism downturn, was equivalent to 16% of total export revenue. While, according to IMF data, tourism receipts remained at the same, comparatively low, level (around US $3,800m.) in 2021, they declined to the equivalent of 12% of total export revenue. However, based on data for the first 10 months of 2022, the IMF projected a doubling of tourism receipts in that year, representing an estimated 22% of the value of total export revenue.

According to official figures, Moroccan exports totalled a provisional 428,612m. dirhams in 2022 (up from 329,405m. dirhams in 2021), the principal commodities including fertilizers, clothing and textiles, citrus fruits, vegetables and fish, crude mineral products (including phosphates), and electric wire and cable. The main export destinations were Spain and France (19.6% and 18.8%, respectively), India (6.4%) and Italy (4.5%).

Morocco's commitment to an IMF-advocated structural adjustment from 1998 included the privatization of state assets, which became more pronounced in the 2000s. While this led to an improved economic performance in data terms, social problems, including significant socioeconomic inequality, persisted. Unemployment was a major difficulty, particularly among young people, including university graduates.

Following criticism of the Government over high unemployment, in July 2015 it announced the introduction of a national employment strategy intended to create 200,000 new jobs each year. However, unemployment remained stubbornly high—at 9.4% at the end of 2018, according to the IMF, and, specifically, 27% of young people and 20% of university graduates. In addition, according to the African Development Bank (AfDB), there was a high illiteracy rate and large social and regional disparities, affecting the health care and education systems and the labour market. These inequalities fuelled social unrest, which increased sharply in 2017/18, especially in the Amazigh (Berber)-dominated northern Rif Mountains. Although in January 2022 the IMF stated that Morocco had 'recovered most of the jobs lost in 2020', in April 2023 the Fund estimated that Morocco's unemployment rate stood at 12.9%, still above pre-pandemic levels.

Numerous social programmes have attempted to narrow social disparities and boost economic development. At the same time, in line with the structural adjustment measures, the Moroccan Government has reduced subsidies for gasoline and basic necessities, which has fuelled public protests.

Economic strategies have included extensive public investment activities, including the Tangier-Med 2 and Nador West-Med port projects and Morocco's strategic orientation towards Africa. Morocco returned to the African Union (see p. 1119) in January 2017, submitted an application to the Economic Community of West African States (ECOWAS) in March and created the post of Minister-delegate for African Co-operation in October. In June 2019 Morocco joined the African Continental Free Trade Area.

In June 2022 the World Bank agreed to issue a US $500m. loan to Morocco to assist with protection against health risks, infant mortality, poverty in old age and 'climate change risks'. The Bank suggested that some of its funding could be used for schemes to aid the victims of a protracted drought in the country. Harsh weather and rising imported inflation from food essentials made costly due to the Ukraine conflict, were noted by the World Bank as inducing greater suffering across the kingdom. In March 2023 the World Bank approved a third tranche of development funding, totalling $450m., to support financial and digital inclusion initiatives.

AGRICULTURE AND FISHERIES

Morocco's principal crops are cereals (especially wheat, barley and maize), citrus fruit, tomatoes, potatoes, olives, beans and chickpeas. Canary seed, cumin, coriander, linseed and almonds are also grown. Sugar beet and cane are cultivated on a large scale to substitute for imports; sugar is one of Morocco's principal food imports, reflecting the high level of domestic consumption. According to the Canadian Ministry of Agriculture, Morocco imports about 40% of its grain consumption as well as fish, vegetables and fruits, and high-quality agricultural products are exported to Europe.

Climatic conditions cause substantial annual variations in agricultural output. These fluctuations, moreover, have a significant impact on the economy, affecting the level of GDP growth or decline and the rate of unemployment. According to official figures, in 2022 agriculture, hunting, forestry, fishing and aquaculture contributed 11.4% of GDP at current prices.

As a result of favourable climatic conditions, the agricultural sector alone experienced strong growth in 2017, with sectoral GDP rising by 13.0%. In the same year, according to the United Nations (UN) Development Programme, an estimated 36.5% of the working population were employed in agriculture, forestry and fishing. In 2018 the sector's GDP increased by only 4.0% as the level of rainfall fell, which also affected the harvest in early 2019. The IMF reported that agricultural GDP contracted by 5.8% in 2019, as drought conditions limited cereal yields. The agricultural sector contracted by 8.6% in real terms in 2020, according to the IMF in its January 2022 Article IV report. However, the IMF reported overall real GDP growth of 7.9% in 2021. In that year real agricultural growth was 17.8%, according to the IMF. This was attributed to what, at the time of the IMF's visit in January 2022, was considered a strong harvest, following the drought in 2019 and 2020. By February 2022, however, the Moroccan Government was faced with another, even worse, drought after there had been little rainfall since the preceding September. It was reported by Al-Monitor in March as the worst drought for 40 years, with the country's reservoirs having received only 11% of what they should have over the previous 12 months. The Government put together an emergency relief aid package worth the equivalent of €1,000m. for the agricultural sector.

Reflecting ongoing drought conditions, real agricultural GDP was estimated by the IMF to have contracted by 14.0% in 2022, and these conditions continued into 2023. Rising public dissatisfaction was expressed over food inflation in the country, which was partly imported but also, some argued, a result of domestic and structural factors. In May 2023 Prime Minister Aziz Akhannouch argued that state support for the agricultural sector was reflected in contracts that the Government had signed with Moroccan agricultural 'professionals', amounting to US $4,300m. He pledged a further $17,500m. of such support over the next decade via public-private contracts.

Optimism about Moroccan wheat production in the second half of 2023 was reflected in an April forecast by the US Department of Agriculture that Moroccan wheat output in 2023/24 would increase by 41% over the previous year, reaching 3.8m. metric tons. According to Standard & Poor's, reporting in April 2023, the Moroccan Government was planning to impose a 135% tariff on imported wheat in an attempt to stabilize local prices and incentivize increased local production. The Government also subsidizes the price of wheat flour to keep bread prices down.

In 2015 Morocco was the fourth largest exporter of agrifood products in Africa and the world's largest exporter in some product sectors (capers, green beans and argan oil). Food exports represented 21.5% of the overall value of Moroccan exports in 2021, according to the IMF, having risen in value, according to the World Trade Organization (WTO), by around 7% annually during 2015–19.

A major problem for Morocco's agricultural sector is water supply. According to the WTO, about one-half of government investment in the sector goes to projects intended to modernize, refurbish and expand irrigation systems and promote water-saving irrigation techniques. The WTO estimated that 16% of agricultural land was irrigated, but that this land produced almost 75% of agricultural exports and 50% of the agricultural value added in an average year.

As of early 2022 an estimated 80% of the kingdom's constrained water supply was being used for agricultural irrigation. Better irrigation techniques, better conservation of stocks, and, controversially, greater access to desalinated water would help the situation. According to the IMF, Morocco's National Water Plan (2020–50) aimed to invest the equivalent of 33% of GDP as of 2021 over 30 years to enhance Morocco's capacity to meet future water demand This was to be achieved via new dams, irrigation systems and desalination plants. However, as of mid-2023 Morocco's desalination plants programme was very behind schedule. Furthermore, desalination plants consume large amounts of energy and usually involve the pumping of brine back into the Atlantic or the Mediterranean. In May the Minister of Infrastructure and Water, Nizar Baraka, claimed that the ongoing drought conditions, which had continued to undermine agricultural output, would be alleviated within a few months by a significant increase in imported potable water and the expected completion of a pipeline connecting the Sebou dam to the Moulay Abdallah dam. However, it was unclear how realistic these goals were, as well as the minister's commitment to commence construction of the planned desalination plant in Sidi Rahal, near Casablanca, at the end of 2023, which was scheduled to be completed in 2027.

Fishing is one of the most important economic sectors and was the subject of an intensive development programme named the Halieutis Plan, which was initiated in 2009 to run until 2020. The Moroccan coast is about 3,500 km long with an exclusive economic zone of 1.1m. sq km and an annual fishing potential estimated at 1.5m. metric tons. Fish production off the Moroccan coast increased sharply from about 1.1m. tons in 2010 to about 1.4m. tons in 2014, and it remained at around this level during 2015–21. According to the Food and Agriculture Organization (FAO) of the UN, the net value of Morocco's fish trade was US $2,009m. in 2019, a slight increase on the figure for 2017. According to derived FAO data, the net value of the fruit and vegetable trade (fresh, dried, dehydrated, prepared and preserved) in 2021 was $1,640m., while cereals (largely barley, maize, malt and wheat) recorded a net deficit of $1,700m. Food exports represented 4.8% of GDP in 2021, according to the IMF, and agriculture and processed agricultural products together represented 4.1% of exports by value as of March 2022, according to the central bank, Bank Al-Maghrib (BAM).

Following an initial agreement in 1995, the fourth fisheries agreement between Morocco and the European Union (EU) was signed in 2005 and entered into force in 2007, since when it has been renewed several times. The status of the waters off the coast of Western Sahara is disputed. In 2015 the agreement provided for fishing opportunities for 100 EU vessels without maximum catches (with some exceptions). In return, the EU made an annual payment of €40m. In 2018 the EU and Morocco started negotiations over a new fisheries agreement which would increase the EU's annual payment to Morocco. However, negotiations were hindered in February when the European Court of Justice (ECJ) ruled that the existing fisheries agreement did not apply to Western Sahara, as the Sahrawi population in the disputed territory had not been consulted. In February 2019 the European Parliament none the less ratified the new EU-Morocco Sustainable Fisheries Partnership Agreement (including the waters off Western Sahara) in apparent defiance of the ECJ, following vigorous lobbying on the part of the Moroccan Government. In a blow to the Moroccan fishing industry, in September 2021 the EU General Court in Luxembourg struck down the 2019 Sustainable Fisheries Partnership Agreement on the basis that the Sahrawi people had not been consulted over fishing in the disputed Western Sahara region. However, Spain and the EU's chief diplomat effectively argued that the deal would continue regardless (see History). In November 2022 the European Commission stated that the fourth EU-Morocco joint commission under the SFPA had made excellent progress, and argued that EU support for the Moroccan fisheries sector had particularly benefited small-scale businesses, as well as fostering the formation of fishing co-operatives and helping to improve working conditions and safety measures.

MINING AND HYDROCARBONS

Mining is a significant contributor to Morocco's non-agricultural GDP. According to derived IMF data, exports of phosphates and derived products represented 6.2% of GDP in 2021 (just behind automobile exports, which represented 6.5%). Mineral substances extracted from Morocco's subsoil include, according to the WTO, precious metals (gold and silver), base metals (principally copper, lead, zinc, cobalt, manganese and iron) and industrial substances and rocks (barite, salt, fluorite, bentonite and fuller's earth).

Phosphate is Morocco's most important mining product. Phosphate exploitation began in 1921 and has since been subject to a monopoly implemented by the state-owned Office Chérifien des Phosphates (OCP—Moroccan Phosphates Board). Major deposits are located at Khouribga, Youssoufia and Ben Guerir. Morocco also controls production at Bou Craa in Western Sahara. Including its contested control of the latter territory, Morocco holds over 72% of world phosphate deposits (according to an analysis published by *The Atlantic* magazine, a US publication, in November 2016—a figure broadly in line with that published by the OCP. By 1997 Morocco had become the world's leading exporter, overtaking the USA and accounting for almost one-third of world trade—at mid-2022 the OCP stated that the country's share stood at 31%. At that time the OCP stated that Morocco was producing 37.6m. metric tons annually (of which about one-third was assumed to be exported). Morocco is the world's second largest producer of phosphate, second only to the People's Republic of China. As of April 2022 export earnings from phosphates constituted 25% of Morocco's total export earnings, according to the Moroccan trade information service the Office des Changes (OC). The OC also stated that the OCP's annual earnings as of April had risen by 99% year on year to reach 34,160m. dirhams (US $3,600m.). Russia's invasion of Ukraine increased demand for ammonia-based products, and thus the value of Moroccan fertilizer exports rose dramatically during 2022. However, a subsequent global market adjustment resulted in fertilizer prices weakening, and Morocco's phosphate earnings consequently declined significantly in early 2023.

Morocco has invested heavily in the 'downstream' phosphates industry, with processing plants in operation at Safi and Jorf Lasfar producing phosphoric acid, fertilizers and sulphuric acid. In 1987 the value of exports of phosphate derivatives surpassed that of phosphate rock for the first time, and by 1988 the combined value of phosphoric acid and fertilizers accounted for almost two-thirds of total exports of phosphates and phosphate derivatives. The Government intends to capitalize on Morocco's phosphate resources by processing more domestically rather than sending output for export and by exploiting the fertilizers produced for domestic agricultural use. In February 2016 the OCP began production at a new fertilizer plant in Jorf Lasfar, which had the capacity to produce up to 1m. metric tons of fertilizer, 1.4m. tons of sulphuric acid and 450,000 tons of phosphoric acid per year destined for African markets. In August 2020 the OCP announced that a new plant at Jorf Lasfar would double its existing phosphoric acid production capacity from 140,000 tons to 280,000 tons a year.

As successor to the Office National de Recherches et d'Exploitations Pétrolières, the Office National des Hydrocarbures et des Mines (ONHYM—National Hydrocarbons and Mining Board) is the public agency responsible for research and exploration, improving geological surveys and managing the transportation system more efficiently. In mid-2013 the Government announced that it would increase investment in the non-phosphates mining industry to 4,000m. dirhams, in an effort to triple the sector's annual revenues, to 15,000m. dirhams, by 2025.

The upstream petroleum sector has been little developed in Morocco for many years. Exploitation is strictly regulated, and surveys and exploitation are subject to state permits and concessions, although the Hydrocarbons Code provides for incentives for exploration and exploitation. In 2001 the Government signed two controversial exploration agreements, both off shore, in Western Sahara, which is believed to be potentially rich in oil reserves. These were with TotalFinaElf (now Total) of France for the Dakhla zone and with the USA's Kerr-McGee for an area in the Boujdor region, near el-Aaiún. The Polisario Front (a group campaigning for independence for Western Sahara) protested to the UN, which determined that Morocco would be in violation of international law if it allowed foreign firms to produce oil from the disputed territory without taking into account the interests of its inhabitants. Total was reported to have ceased all petroleum exploration in Western Sahara in 2004. Political sensitivities over Western Sahara have mostly deterred large oil companies from entering Morocco, and the country attracted interest only from small independent companies. However, high oil prices and a growing conviction within the industry that Morocco offers considerable offshore potential resulted in Chevron signing an exploration deal in January 2013. Exploration continued apace in 2014, with additional new licences being awarded, and the Government announced that it would drill up to 30 new wells in that year. In addition, interest was growing in Morocco's potential oil shale resources, located in some 10 deposits throughout the country. In early 2017 Qatar Petroleum, which had acquired a 30% stake from Chevron Morocco Exploration in August 2016 in three deep-water offshore leases located 200 km north-west of Agadir in the Atlantic Ocean, announced plans to carry out exploration for oil and gas in the country. British-based Chariot Oil & Gas Plc began drilling at the Rabat Deep Offshore exploration prospect in mid-2018, with Eni of Italy having acquired operatorship and a 40% equity interest. In June 2019 Chariot reported that drilling for natural gas off shore was technically highly feasible. Chariot was also exploring potential reserves of natural gas in Larache on the Atlantic coast, and Sound Energy (United Kingdom) was performing exploration drills in Tendrara in the east of the country. In February 2020 Sound Energy finalized a gas sales agreement with the Moroccan Government in the Tendrara concession. In January 2022 Chariot announced a significant gas find off Larache at an offshore site (Anchois) covering 2,390 sq km where it held 75% ownership; the remainder was held by ONHYM, which was less effusive and only said that the find was promising. That said, in the context of a European desire to increase the importation of North African gas to replace Russian supplies, Anchois could take on greater importance. In July Standard & Poor's reported that the initial estimates of the recoverable resources at Anchois had since doubled, while the estimated value had more than tripled owing to rising gas prices. Another site has also shown some positive indicators: that of the onshore Guercif basin where another UK company, Predator, has led the drilling work. In 2019 Predator was awarded the licence to develop gas production at Guercif, which is proximate to a gas pipeline to Spain that could potentially enable Morocco to become an exporter of domestically produced gas. Predator estimated that the site potentially contained 11,000m. cu m of natural gas. However, feasibly and economically utilizing such a resource is, as yet, another matter. None the less, Morocco appears to be on the point of reducing its level of dependency on imports of hydrocarbons. According to the IMF, fuel imports accounted for 16.3% of Morocco's total import bill in 2021, well below the 26% average annual share recorded during 2016–20.

Morocco's aspirations to become a gas export hub were arguably reflected in the Government's regasification agreement with Spain in 2022 (see *Power and Water*), under which Morocco would buy liquefied natural gas (LNG) on the international market and export it to Spain via the Maghreb–Europe gas pipeline, while Spain would export regasified LNG back to Morocco. These ambitions were further invigorated by the sharp increase in energy prices following Russia's invasion of Ukraine. Meanwhile, in September Morocco signed a number of memorandums of understanding with Nigeria, a major gas exporter, regarding the proposed construction of a 7,000-km gas pipeline between the two countries at an estimated cost of US $23,000m. and involving the participation of a total of 13 West African countries, in an effort to compete with an Algerian alternative (a deterioration in Moroccan-Algerian relations had accelerated Morocco's energy integration with southern Europe). Morocco enjoys access to the Maghreb–Europe gas pipeline owing to its LNG arrangement with Spain. However, according to Agence France-Presse, in February 2023 the agreement with Nigeria, which could potentially establish Morocco as a gas hub linking West Africa with Europe, was at the feasibility study stage only.

Morocco has two oil refineries: at Mohammedia and Sidi Kacem. The Government began to sell its holdings in the two companies in 1996. In 1997 a Saudi Arabian-owned company, Corral Petroleum Holdings, purchased majority stakes in both companies, and the two entities were merged in 1999. In 2002 the Mohammedia refinery, producing 80%–90% of the country's refined products, was badly damaged following a severe flood and massive fire; a contract to rehabilitate and upgrade the refinery was awarded to an Italian-Turkish consortium in 2005. In 2006 a consortium led by Terminals Ltd (United Arab Emirates—UAE) was awarded a 25-year concession to build and operate an international petroleum storage terminal at the port of Tangier.

Natural gas is not yet a major industry in Morocco, despite a number of discoveries. The exploitation is in the hands of national and international private operators, in co-operation with ONHYM. In 1992 Morocco and Spain signed a 25-year agreement to build the Maghreb–Europe gas pipeline, to run from Hassi R'Mel in Algeria, across Morocco and the Strait of Gibraltar to Spain. Despite concerns over the security situation in Algeria and rising tensions between Morocco and Algeria, work on the pipeline began formally in 1994. The pipeline became operational in November 1996, when the first gas supplies were delivered to Spain, and a link to Portugal was completed in early 1997. In January 2020 Sound Energy received environmental impact assessment approval from the Moroccan Government to construct a 120-km (75-mile) gas pipeline to connect a gas treatment plant and compression centre to the Maghreb–Europe pipeline.

In 2007 the Government announced that it was planning to build an LNG terminal and combined-cycle power plant with a capacity of 2,400 MW at Jorf Lasfar, as part of a drive to diversify energy supply. The project, estimated to cost US $4,500m., was formally launched in December 2014. In late 2018 the Ministry of Energy, Mining and the Environment was reportedly inviting bids for the project from international firms to build and operate the facility, which was expected to have the capacity to process up to 7,000m. cu m of gas a year by 2025. However, as of August 2023 no further progress had been made on the project.

S&P Global Platts reported in May 2021 that Predator was preparing a bid to build a Floating Storage and Regasification Unit in the north of Morocco with an initial annual scope of 1,100m. cu m by 2025, rising to 1,700m. cu m in 2030 and 3,000m. cu m in 2040. The report stated that Morocco's gas storage needs were expected to rise as the kingdom sought further to diversify consumption in favour of gas and renewables and away from coal-fired power.

Despite its strong external dependency on fuel imports, Morocco is also a fuel exporter, albeit a modest one. At the end of 2019 the country's fuel exports accounted for 1.8% of the overall total by value, up from 0.9% in 2017.

POWER AND WATER

Morocco's rising population and continued economic development have caused a rapid increase in demand for electricity, and severe droughts have exacerbated power shortages. An important focus of Moroccan energy policy is the renewable energy sector. The Moroccan Agency for Solar Energy (MASEN)—later renamed the Moroccan Agency of Sustainable Energy—was established in 2009. In late 2011 Morocco was awarded loans totalling US $300m. by various World Bank agencies to construct a network of solar and wind power plants that would be able to supply Europe with energy.

According to the IMF's Article IV Report of January 2020, the Government aimed to expand renewable energy—wind, solar and hydroelectric—to 63% of the country's total installed capacity by 2030. The IMF believes that Morocco's obviously favourable climate for the development of solar power means that it has the potential to become an exporter of renewable energy to Europe. The IMF report noted that there was a project proposal for linking the kingdom's solar and wind producers with 7m. homes in the UK. This was reported by the site *Powermag* in June 2022 as a 10.5-GW solar and wind power project involving a UK subsea cables company, XLCC, which from a yet-to-be-built facility would produce subsea cables for a UK renewables company, XLinks, to undertake the linking of the UK to a Moroccan solar and wind facility. Powermag reported that the first phase was scheduled to be connected between 2025 and 2027. According to XLinks, the project would bring electricity from a 1,500-sq-km solar and wind facility in Guelmim Oued Noun, via subsea cables, to Devon, England.

Morocco also has a direct pipeline linking it to Spain that could make a more attractive and efficient source of 'green hydrogen' than its Maghreb neighbours Algeria and Libya, which are less 'friendly' to foreign investors and politically more problematic for Europe. Following an improvement in Moroccan-Spanish relations, in February 2022 Spain agreed to allow Morocco to use the Maghreb–Europe pipeline, after Algeria had stopped supplying gas to the kingdom. In the context of Morocco's increasingly acute energy needs, Spain allowing Morocco to transport LNG (bought internationally) for regasification in Spain and then for return to Morocco via the pipeline was obviously appealing. The acute global energy crisis caused by the conflict in Ukraine made these efforts even more important, but it also made buying the LNG problematic, and Morocco had to build (at some expense) a floating LNG terminal for importing the product.

In April 2022 UAE-based AMEA Power agreed with Morocco to build two solar power stations, at Taroudant and El-Hajeb, each with a capacity of 36 MW. The UAE has skills in renewable, as well as more traditional, sources of power and its diplomatic relationship with Morocco has solidified, with both countries having signed normalization agreements with Israel in 2020. Israel's NewMed Energy (formerly Delek Drilling) signed an agreement with ONHYM in December 2022 to conduct offshore hydrocarbons exploration in the Atlantic over an initial period of eight years.

In 2009 the Moroccan Solar Energy Plan was initiated with the ambitious objective of 2,000 MW of electricity being produced by solar energy by 2020. The first contract under the plan, worth US $1,500m., was awarded in 2012 to an international consortium, ACWA Power Ouarzazate (comprising Saudi Arabia's ACWA Power International, MASEN and two Spanish firms, Aries IS and TSK EE), for the design, finance, construction, operation and maintenance of a 160-MW concentrated solar power plant. The first phase, the construction of the Noor 1 Concentrated Solar Power Independent Power Project, was completed in February 2016. Five plants were to supply solar power by 2020, and Noor was to form one of the world's largest solar energy complexes. The EU pledged to invest $69.6m. in solar power projects in Morocco in December 2018 to support the bloc's Southern Neighbourhood programme. According to the Office National de l'Electricité (ONE), the second and third phases of the Noor project had commenced by mid-2020. As part of the Noor Tafilalt photovoltaic project to generate 120 MW of solar power, in 2018 construction work began on building three photovoltaic power plants—in Zagora, Erfoud and Missur. A similar project focused on the Atlas (Noor Atlas), aiming to generate 200 MW, was also under way. According to ONE, prequalification for contracts for seven photovoltaic plants was conducted in 2018 following the completion of an environmental and social impact assessment. In the Spring 2021 edition of the *Middle East Report*, published by the Middle East Research and Information Project (MERIP), it was stated, in a dedicated analysis of the project, that all four of Noor's stages at different 'farm' locations were under way, including a photovoltaic plant at Noor IV. *MERIP*'s report was critical of the project's impact, especially with regard to the environment and the costs (over the short term at least) for the local farming community. It also argued that Noor had failed to deliver the job opportunities of which MASEN had boasted.

A wind energy development strategy (Plan Eolien Intégré) aimed to increase the share of wind energy to 2,000 MW (26% of annual production). This would enable annual savings of about 5.6 metric tons of carbon dioxide. Development of the Tanger II (100 MW), Jbel Lahdid (200 MW), Midelt (150 MW), Tiskrad (300 MW) and Boujdour (100 MW) wind farms was under the management of the Office National de l'Electricité et de l'Eau Potable (ONEE), which was founded in 2011.

At mid-2020 hydropower accounted for the largest share of Moroccan renewable energy production. According to MASEN, the quantity of hydroelectric power in operation in 2020 was 1,770 MW, while plans to expand production by a further 350 MW were 'in development'.

A 400-kV undersea electricity link between Spain and Morocco (the first power link between North Africa and Europe) was inaugurated in 1998. The project was partly funded by the European Investment Bank (EIB), which approved a €120m. loan in 2002 to finance a doubling of the capacity of the undersea link and terminals.

The water sector is key to Morocco's economic and social development. Water scarcity poses a major risk to the country's agricultural sector. According to Germany Trade & Invest, the agricultural sector accounts for 87.3% of water consumption in Morocco, compared with 9.8% for households and 2.9% for industry. Among the policy priorities of the World Bank's Country Partnership Framework for Morocco for 2019–24 is better management of water resources and strengthening resilience to climate change shocks.

Morocco officially aims to introduce civil nuclear power 'after 2030'. According to the International Atomic Energy Agency (IAEA), Morocco has uranium within its (ample) phosphate deposits, and this could in theory be utilized in the planned Moroccan nuclear power industry. Various research deals with foreign nuclear power specialists continue to be signed, and as of 2023 the nuclear option appeared to remain of interest to the kingdom.

INDUSTRY

In 2022, according to official figures, the industrial sector (comprising mining, manufacturing, power and construction) provided 28.2% of real GDP and employed 23.0% of the working population. According to World Bank data, the GDP of the industrial sector, at constant 2015 prices, increased by 3.6% in 2017, 3.0% in 2018 and 3.5% in 2019, before contracting by 5.5% during the 2020 global demand slump, and then rebounding to record growth of 6.4% in 2021. BAM's 2021 annual report stated that the GDP of the extractive industries declined by 0.2% in 2020.

According to the World Bank, manufacturing GDP, at constant 2015 prices, expanded by 2.5% in 2017, 3.5% in 2018 and 2.8% in 2019, before contracting by 5.3% in 2020 and recovering to grow by 7.7% in 2021. The Moroccan manufacturing industry is closely linked to the European market. Morocco is one of the world's largest producers of automotive sector products, which have become the country's most important export, owing in particular to European direct investments. Other important sectors are the food, phosphate processing and clothing industries.

The national Industrial Acceleration Plan (PAI) was implemented between 2014 and 2020. Some 500,000 new jobs were envisaged as being created in the industrial sector under the PAI, one-half of them on the basis of FDI and the other half by restructuring the sector. The core element of the plan was the creation of a network of 'ecosystems' consisting of small and large companies. The aim was to create industrial hubs nationwide, which offered industrial land for rent and equipment and services. The programmes were funded by a €2,000m. Industrial and Investment Development Fund. To the extent that such plans have relied on steady and growing FDI, beyond the initial investment boost that the Government envisaged, they were partly stymied by net FDI remaining modest prior to the COVID-19 pandemic (US $600m in 2019, according to the IMF). Inward FDI then deteriorated sharply, even though overall (or 'net') FDI remained steady, as outward investment fell less sharply than inward. The IMF assumed in its January 2021 Article IV report that further government 'pro-private sector' reforms (together with an envisaged recovery in the real estate and tourism sectors as the impact of the pandemic eased) would enable greater net FDI. The decision by PSA Peugeot Citroën (of France) to invest in Morocco, under an agreement signed in June 2015, was presented by the Moroccan Government and its French partner as a mark of PAI's progress (see below).

The main industry historically, in terms of investment and foreign exchange earnings, is the processing of phosphates, which is undertaken by the state-controlled OCP (see *Mining and Hydrocarbons*).

Cement production is one of Morocco's major import substitution industries. Annual cement production totalled 14m.–15m. metric tons in 2015–17. Cement production capacity had reached nearly 25m. tons by 2018, but production was still only 15.3m. tons. According to the Moroccan Professional Association of Cement Manufacturers, 'domestic cement deliveries' totalled 14m. tons in 2021, while cement production capacity was 25.8m. tons per year. In 2022 cement deliveries declined to 12.5m. tons. In December *Cement News* reported that Nova-Cim's new 1.4m. tons-per-year cement plant at Ouled Ghanem, near El Jadida, had started production. Full commissioning of the facility was scheduled for 2023.

Morocco's textile industry focuses on ready-made clothing and knitwear, as textile production is relatively low in the country. Textile exports are thus closely linked to textile imports, especially of cotton and synthetic-fibre fabrics. Most textile exports go to the EU. According to the OC, exports of manufactured garments increased by 24.9% year on year to reach 22,645m. dirhams in 2021 and by a further 21.9% in 2022 to a provisional 27,611m. dirhams.

In 2014 the automotive sector overtook phosphate production as the largest source of Moroccan exports. In 2021 automotive exports contributed 6.5% to overall GDP, according to the IMF. The car assembly market has been dominated by the French companies Renault Maroc and PSA Peugeot Citroën, which hold significant stakes in the Société Marocaine de Constructions Automobiles. In 2007 Renault and Nissan of Japan announced joint plans to locate a car manufacturing plant in Meloussa in the Tangier free zone, mainly serving the European export market and creating some 6,000 jobs. The plant opened in February 2012, with an initial production capacity of 170,000 vehicles and employing some 7,000 people. In 2021 Renault produced 230,002 vehicles at its plant in Meloussa and 73,589 at its plant in Casablanca.

The automotive sector received a significant boost in June 2015 when PSA signed an agreement to invest €557m. in a new car plant in Kénitra, in the newly designated 'Atlantic Free Zone'. The plant commenced production in June 2019, with initial annual output of 100,000 vehicles for the local and regional market, a figure which, according to PSA, would rise to 200,000 vehicles per year by 2023. The company claimed that the plant would create about 2,500 jobs.

According to BAM, the value of automobile exports (including construction and related products) was 27.5% of the export total in 2020, rising to 28.3% in 2021. As of October 2022, measured by value, automotive exports were reported by the IMF to have increased by 25% year on year. In the four months to the end of April 2023 automotive exports increased in value by 40.4% over the same period in 2022, according to the OC.

BAM data show that exports of phosphates in 2021 rose by more than 54% (by value) compared with 2020, representing 24.5% of total export revenue in that year. The IMF estimated that phosphate exports rose by a further 23.3% in 2022 and constituted 32% of the overall export total by value. According to OC data, however, exports of phosphates and phosphate derivatives declined by 30.5% in value in the first four months of 2023, compared with the same period in 2022. This coincided with a decrease in the OCP's reported profits in the first quarter of 2023, compared with the first quarter of 2022, which the company attributed to a reduction in fertilizer prices globally, a decline in the price of raw materials such as sulphur and ammonia, as well as lower demand generally (despite exceptions such as Brazil and India).

According to the OC, exports of foodstuffs, beverages and tobacco accounted for 19.1% of total export revenue in 2021; they increased in value by 19.4% in 2022, representing 17.5% of total estimated export revenue.

Government plans to spend heavily on infrastructure development, particularly social housing, were expected to stimulate growth in the construction sector from 2013. However, construction output rose by only 0.7% in 2015 and 1.7% in 2016, although growth accelerated to 6.2% in 2017, before slowing to 1.4% in 2018. According to BAM data, the construction sector expanded by 1.7% in 2019 and by 10.8% in 2021. According to the OC, in 2021 construction accounted for 5.9% of overall real GDP and for 6.1% in 2022.

BALANCE OF PAYMENTS AND TRADE

Morocco's main sources of revenue are earnings from the export of phosphate rock and phosphate derivatives, agricultural products and manufactured goods, receipts from tourism and workers' remittances from abroad. Expenditure is mainly on imports of capital equipment, food and crude petroleum.

Morocco's external transactions have been characterized since the early 1980s by a large annual merchandise trade deficit, which has tended to be offset, at least partially, by tourism earnings and expatriate remittances. According to the IMF, the trade deficit narrowed from US $20,300m. in 2018 to $19,800m. in 2019, aided by a a relative decline in average oil prices and despite below-average phosphate prices, while an increase in tourism revenue helped to lower the current account deficit from $6,200m. in 2018 (equivalent to 4.9% of overall GDP) to $4,400m. in 2019 (3.4% of GDP). In spite of a huge decline in tourism revenue owing to the pandemic, lower energy costs helped to reduce the trade deficit to $15,500m. in 2020 and the current account deficit to $1,400m. (1.2% of GDP). The trade deficit widened to $19,900m. in 2021. Although increased revenues from, principally, phosphates and automobiles helped total export revenue to rise by $8,100m., offsetting this were sharp increases in the cost of imported food, energy and capital goods, which underpinned a $12,400m. overall rise in imports. The current account deficit increased to $3,200m. in 2021, equivalent to 2.3% of GDP. The stronger balance of payments outcome than that of the balance of trade was reflected in a $6,900m. services inflow (albeit only $200m. more than in 2020) and robust levels of worker remittances (which at $10,300m. were $3,200m. higher than the total of $7,100m. in 2020). The current account deficit in 2021 was financed by a combination of foreign investments, loans and IMF financing. However, IMF support in 2021 amounted to $800m. (much smaller than the $3,000m. extended by the Fund in 2020 amid the onset of the pandemic).

According to IMF estimates, the current account deficit increased by US $2,800m. in 2022 to reach $6,000m., despite the fact that the services surplus rose by an estimated $5,000m. in that year, owing primarily to the restoration of tourism receipts to pre-COVID-19 levels. However, the cost of energy imports was estimated to have risen by $5,600m. in 2022 owing to global shortages caused by the Ukraine conflict and the consequent upturn in fuel prices, while, relatedly, the cost of

Morocco's food imports increased by over $2,000m. As a result, the trade deficit in 2022 rose by an estimated 36% to $27,000m. The consequent sharp rise in the current account deficit was assumed by the IMF to have been mostly met by increased private and public loans.

BAM data (given in its May 2023 *Weekly Reports*) for the first quarter of 2023 show that, year on year, the trade deficit had increased by 13.5%. Exports by value in the first quarter of 2023 rose strongly, by 8%, largely driven by a 44.5% increase in the value of automotive exports. Set against this were further increases in imported energy costs (which were up by nearly 16% year on year), consumer goods (up by 15%) and equipment (up by 22%), presumably reflecting rising domestic demand owing to stronger economic growth. BAM reported a huge year-on-year increase in Moroccans' 'travel earnings', of 141%, sharply outstripping the value of the rise in workers' remittances over the same period. No services data were provided by BAM in its May 2023 *Weekly Reports*, but the current account deficit would presumably have mostly been matched by the above-mentioned increased overseas' receipts.

According to the IMF, in 2022 the principal source of Morocco's imports was Spain (15.9%). Other major suppliers in that year included France (12.3%), China (11.4%), the USA (8.3%), Saudi Arabia (7.0%) and Türkiye/Turkey (6.8%). France was the principal market for Morocco's exports in 2022, accounting for an estimated 26.2%, followed by Spain (21.6%) and Brazil (19.8%). In 2022 the euro area (i.e. 20 of the 27 EU member states) provided the majority of Morocco's imports. In 2020, according to BAM's 2021 Annual Report, Europe received 63.4% of Morocco's exports. The principal three export categories in 2022 were phosphates, automobiles and food, according to the IMF, while the principal imports were capital goods, energy products and foodstuffs.

Morocco's trade is likely to remain dependent on Europe, and, in view of this, Morocco has continually sought more favourable trade agreements. (In the 1980s Morocco twice made unsuccessful applications for full membership of the European Community—EC, now EU.) A formal Association Accord with the EU was signed in 1996, including an agreement for the eventual creation of a Euro-Mediterranean free trade zone. The Association Accord came into effect in 2000. In early 2012 Morocco and the EU extended their longstanding agreement to cover a wider range of agricultural products. Under the revised arrangement, up to 70% of EU agricultural exports were to be permitted duty-free entry into Morocco by 2022. In return, all duty was, with a few minor exemptions, to be removed from 55% of Moroccan agricultural products with immediate effect. In an effort to consolidate relations with North African states following the outbreak of civil unrest across the Middle East and North Africa region in 2011, the EU and Morocco launched a fresh round of talks in 2013, with the intention of further liberalizing trade in services, improving market access and easing visa regulations, to establish a 'deep and comprehensive free trade area (DCFTA)'. Negotiations progressed into 2014, but were undermined by EU changes to its import pricing system for fruit and vegetables, which, most notably, threatened Morocco's exports of tomatoes. However, in June 2019, following a meeting of the EU-Morocco Association Council in Brussels, Belgium, a communiqué was issued promising the swift resumption of talks on, *inter alia*, a DCFTA between the two parties and the possibility of visa-free access for Moroccan nationals to the EU. Morocco was reportedly keen to access some of the EU's new development-related private finance initiatives, while the EU required assistance to control the flow of migrants from sub-Saharan Africa, many of whom attempt to cross the Mediterranean Sea from Morocco. In February 2021 the European Commission published its revised strategy for trade. It included an objective to 'work to advance negotiations' on a DCFTA with Morocco.

FDI inflows rose to 39,910m. dirhams in 2015, falling slightly to an estimated 33,010m. dirhams, or 3.2% of GDP, in 2016. France remained the leading investor in Morocco in that year, with a share of 26.4%, followed by the UAE (12.2%) and Saudi Arabia (8.4%). In 2017 the net FDI inflow decreased to 25,996m. dirhams, but rose to 33,314m. dirhams in 2018 as investment in finance and the automotive sector rose significantly. According to the World Bank, in 2019 FDI inflows fell by more than one-half compared with 2018 (from US $3,540m. to just under $1,600m.). Or, put differently, FDI inflows accounted for 0.5% of GDP in 2019, according to the IMF, down from 2.4% in 2018. Although Moroccan investment abroad was continuing to accelerate, it was evident that the Government's new programme to provide five-year corporate tax breaks to industrial companies in order to attract foreign investors to Morocco (see *Budget*) had not proven to be an effective incentive. In 2020 FDI inflows fell further, in part owing to the COVID-19 pandemic and the consequent reduction in international trade. According to the IMF's Article IV report published in January 2023, in 2022 FDI accounted for 1.5% of GDP, representing a slight increase over 2021.

Morocco has been a member of the WTO since 1995. The country's trade with the other Maghreb countries remains limited. From the late 1990s bilateral trade accords were negotiated in an attempt to offset Morocco's dependence on Europe, including with China and Thailand. Most notably, in 2004 Morocco concluded a free trade agreement with the USA. Under the agreement, more than 95% of industrial tariff lines would become duty-free immediately, with the remainder phased out over nine years.

In the years that followed, Moroccan trade with sub-Saharan states increased significantly. Trade agreements were signed with Guinea and Senegal. Morocco concluded public-private and private-private agreements with Côte d'Ivoire in January 2015, and in 2017 Morocco began to seek membership of ECOWAS, after it was readmitted to the AU in January of that year, despite the fact that Nigeria had reportedly resisted the idea. Nigeria was concerned that Morocco, as the beneficiary of free trade agreements with the EU and the USA, could be used by those two blocs as a tariff-free 'back door' into West Africa by foreign companies seeking to dump their products. As of mid-2023 Morocco's bid to gain membership of ECOWAS appeared to have stalled, in part owing to the country's arguably increasingly contentious occupation of Western Sahara (see *History*). This situation prompted the kingdom's continental adversaries to exert pressure on ECOWAS member states to resist Morocco's full inclusion.

TOURISM

Tourism is of crucial importance to the Moroccan economy and is the most important source of foreign currency, above even transfers made by Moroccan nationals resident abroad. The sector accounted for 6.4% of overall GDP in 2019. Pre-COVID, the number of arrivals had been rising for many years, but the profits of the sector had not increased to the same extent. For example, in 2018 tourist arrivals rose by 8.0%, while tourism receipts rose by only 1.4%. This was due to the growing number of cheap internet bookings, falling hotel prices, especially as a result of unrest in 2011, and the preference for short breaks in cities such as Marrakesh rather than longer visits in resorts in places such as Agadir.

In 2011 the Government announced a new 10-year tourism plan, Vision 2020, superseding the extended Vision 2010. This anticipated increasing tourist arrivals to 18.6m., expanding hotel room capacity by an additional 200,000 beds and boosting annual tourism receipts to 140,000m. dirhams. The Government's plans suffered a serious reverse when a bomb exploded in the centre of Marrakesh in April 2011, killing 17 people, mostly French tourists. At this time tourist arrivals from France comprised 36% of the total, and this event, combined with the regional political turmoil and the economic downturn in Europe, severely damaged the tourism industry. Overnight stays by non-residents fell by 11% in 2011, although total tourist arrivals remained largely unchanged, at 9.3m. (including Moroccans resident abroad). The persistent economic recession in the EU meant that the number of tourist arrivals remained at much the same level in 2012, but the sector picked up in 2013, boosted by Royal Air Maroc's decision to expand its fleet in order to improve air connections with Morocco. By the end of 2013 the number of air passengers had risen by 9.2%, supporting a 7.2% increase in the number of tourists, which totalled 10.0m. for the year. In 2014 tourist arrivals rose to 10.3m. and tourism receipts to US $7,060m. However, violent attacks on tourists in Tunisia in the first half of 2015, in Fez in

November and in Imlil in December 2018 hindered the Government's aim to increase the number of tourist arrivals to 20m. by 2020 (which would place Morocco among the top 20 global tourist destinations). Tourist arrivals declined to 10.2m. in 2015, but rose to 10.3m. in 2016, 11.3m. in 2017, 12.3m. in 2018 and 12.9m. in 2019.

Tourist inflows and outflows were drastically reduced from March 2020, owing to the COVID-19 pandemic, and in May Royal Air Maroc announced the suspension of all flights. As the pandemic eased, tourism revenues were supposed to aid a recovery in inward FDI, assisted by focused government support, including tax relief and a direct financial assistance scheme. However, the IMF reported that in 2021 tourism receipts had improved only slightly on the total of US $3,800m. recorded in 2020 (compared with $8,200m. in 2019). From 6.4% of GDP in 2019, the tourism sector's contribution fell to 3.2% in 2020 and 2.7% in 2021. Tourism minister Fatim-Zahra Ammor told the Middle East Monitor website in early February 2022 that annual tourist arrivals had decreased by 71% year on year in 2020 and by 79% in 2021. However, international flights resumed in February 2022, after having been halted by the Government in December 2021 as part of an anti-COVID drive. According to the IMF, tourism receipts more than doubled in 2022 to an estimated $7,900m. In a sign that the tourism sector was continuing to recover, tourist arrivals in the first quarter of 2023 reached 2.9m. according to *Morocco World News (MWN)*, 17% more than in the first quarter of 2019 (i.e. pre-COVID-19). *MWN* also stated that by the end of February 2023 tourist arrivals totalled 1.9m., a 464% increase over the same period of 2022.

TRANSPORT

According to a 2022 analysis by the US Department of Commerce, Morocco has 27 commercial ports, including Casablanca, Safi, Mohammedia, Agadir, Kénitra, Jorf Lasfar, Tan Tan along its Atlantic coast, and Tangier (in the north-west) and Nador (in the north-east) on the Mediterranean. Dakhla and el-Aaiún are in the disputed territory of Western Sahara. In 2014 the country's ports handled an estimated 115.1m. metric tons of cargo. This was due mainly to the expansion of container shipping and Morocco's rising trade.

The largest harbour is Tangier-Med. Since the opening of the first part in 2007 Tangier-Med has developed into a central transshipment hub, owing mainly to a specific tax regime and its central location on the Strait of Gibraltar. Tangier-Med is an important location for petroleum product storage and is, according to the WTO, Morocco's fourth largest port for import-export. The Tangier-Med 2 port expansion was opened in June 2019, tripling Tangier's port capacity and making it the largest facility for maritime cargo in the Mediterranean basin; Maersk (of Denmark) operated the new facility. Mohammedia port specializes in oil, Agadir in fishing, Safi and Jorf Lasfar in minerals and Nador in the steel, mining and food-processing industries. From 1985 the major ports were controlled by the Office d'Exploitation des Ports (ODEP). In December 2006, to comply with international security and safety standards, ODEP was divided into two separate agencies—the Agence Nationale des Ports as regulator and the Société d'Exploitation des Ports as manager and operator. Tangier-Med port is managed by the Tangier-Med Port Authority. Moroccan port traffic continued to increase, even during the COVID-19 pandemic. According to the Ministry of Infrastructure, Transport and Logistics, traffic rose by 12.0% in 2020 and by a further 10.4% in 2021, to reach a total of 192.1m. metric tons.

Moroccan ports served about 3.5m. passengers in 2022, according to the website *MaritimeAfrica*, an almost fourfold increase on 2021 (when the global pandemic-related downturn was at its most severe). In 2015 goods handling at Moroccan ports was controlled by three major multinational companies, including Maersk at Tangier-Med's first container terminal. Work on Tangier-Med 2 commenced in June 2019—a new container port terminal to be constructed by Maersk that would, upon completion, add 3.3m. twenty-foot equivalent units (TEUs) of capacity, 1m. TEUs of which were scheduled to be available by mid-2020. Tangier-Med 2's new container terminal, described by the main port operator, Marsa Maroc, as the project's third terminal, began operating in January 2021.

Morocco's railways are operated by the Office National des Chemins de Fer (ONCF). The rail network covers around 2,300 km and, according to the US Department of Commerce, 135 stations, making it one of the largest in Africa. The network was modernized between 2010 and 2015, the work included the construction of a high-speed line from Tangier to Casablanca.

The ONCF offers local services between Casablanca, Rabat, Kénitra and el-Jadida and some long-distance services to other major cities. Following more than 20 years of on-off consultations, the Governments of Morocco and Spain announced plans in 2003 to build a 39-km train tunnel link (27.7 km of which would be submarine) between their two countries. The tunnel would connect Punta Malabata in Morocco with Punta Paloma, to the west of Gibraltar. The Transport Sector Reform Programme envisaged the acquisition of multi-unit trains and the doubling of the rail network to Fez, Settat and Jorf Lasfar. Construction work subsequently began on several projects, including the extension of the network to Tangier port and modernization of the Casablanca–Marrakesh main line. In 2015 an agreement was signed between the ONCF and the French National Railway Company (SNCF) for the construction and operation of a high-speed rail service, the Ligne à Grande Vitesse. The high-speed Tangier–Casablanca line ('Al-Boraq') opened in November 2018, and reduced the journey time between the two cities by more than one-half. According to provisional official figures, the ONCF transported 45.8m. passengers and 20.8m. metric tons of freight on its principal railways in 2022. Further development of rail transport, especially of long-distance routes such as Casablanca–Marrakesh, was planned under the 2040 Rail Strategy. In July 2022 it was reported that the ONCF had completed a feasibility study into a planned high-speed 'Maghreb Line' that would link Rabat to Fez in the east, beginning with a Rabat–Meknès connection. Further impact assessments were due to be conducted. In March 2023 the ONCF stated that the Al-Boraq line was expected to transport 5.0m. passengers in 2023, up from 4.2m. in 2022. The ONCF also announced that the examination of funding and other practicalities regarding the planned southerly extension of the Al-Boraq line to Agadir via Marrakesh was continuing.

Road transport is the most important form of freight transport in Morocco, with about 75% of domestic freight being transported by truck. The highway network covers 1,511 km and is managed and financed by the state and by tolls. The Casablanca–Rabat highway was completed in 1986. The Rabat–Fez highway was completed in 1999 and opened in three phases (Fez–Meknès, Meknès–Khemisset and Khemisset–Rabat). The Rabat–Kénitra section of the Rabat–Tangier highway was opened in 1995, the section to Larache in 1996 and the section to Asilah in 2002. In 1998 the Government announced that it was proceeding with the construction of a Mediterranean coastal highway linking Tangier with Saidia, near the border with Algeria. Much of the construction costs would be financed by the state, but certain stretches were to be privately financed on a build-operate-transfer basis. A 30-km section of the highway linking Tangier and Laksar S'ghir opened in 2000. In 1998 work began on the construction of a motorway between Casablanca and Settat. In 1999 Autoroutes du Maroc (ADM)—a public-private partnership—announced new investment of US $100m. to develop the country's road network, including highways linking Sidi el-Yamani to Tangier and Khemisset to Fez. During 2004 ADM issued a tender for the construction of a 240-km highway between the southern tourist resorts of Marrakesh and Agadir; the Hassan II Fund was partly to finance the project, providing $166m. of the estimated $690m. cost. The Kuwait Fund for Arab Economic Development (KFAED), meanwhile, approved a $149m. loan to finance the construction of a 62-km section of highway linking Settat and Skhour Rhamna in the south and a 28-km highway section between Tétouan and Fnideq in the north. The EIB approved a €110m. loan to construct a section of highway between Marrakesh and Settat. The KFAED was also co-funding a project to connect the port of Tangier to the national highway; the planned 54-km highway was scheduled to open for traffic by the time that the new port of Tangier became operational. In 2005 the Government announced that ADM was to receive funding from the Hassan II Fund for a 320-km highway between Fez, Taza and Oujda. The $700m. project would extend the existing Rabat–Meknès–Fez road and form a major new east–west link. The Asilah–Tangier highway was completed in 2005. In 2006 the Arab Fund for Economic and Social Development agreed to finance the Fez–Oujda highway and part-finance the project to link Marrakesh and Agadir. During 1995–2005 the World Bank provided funding for a national programme to upgrade 10,000 km of rural roads. In 2006 the Bank approved a $60m. loan for a second national programme of rural road building. The EIB contributed to the project in 2008, with a €60m. grant to build 700 km of roads in isolated areas. The second national programme aimed to build 15,560 km of roads at a rate of 2,000 km per year. The Moroccan Ministry of Infrastructure, Transport and Logistics website states that the 'second rural roads programme' was completed in 2014, 'adding 2,500 km of rural roads' and expanding rural access in the process. Ensuring that at least 80% of the country's populated areas are connected by road has long been an objective of the Government. In an online report published in July 2019, the US Department of Commerce indicated that the Moroccan Government's ambitions might have become more modest than suggested by the above targets. The US Government website stated that the Moroccan ministry intended to build 'an additional 2,100 miles [3,360 km] of expressway and 1,300 miles [2,080 km] of highway by 2030, at an expected cost of $9.6 billion'. The ministry's website stated that, as of 2020, 62.7% of Morocco's roads were either in what it called acceptable or good condition; this was up from 60.9% in 2018.

According to the Office National des Aéroports (ONDA), Morocco has 18 international airports. The most important are located at Casablanca, Marrakesh and Agadir. El-Aaiún in Western Sahara also has an airport. According to official figures, Morocco's airports handled some 25.1m. passengers in 2019. The first cases of individuals infected with COVID-19 in Morocco were reported in early March 2020, and the partial suspension of flights in and out of the country began shortly afterwards, before all flights were formally suspended in May. In 2020 as a whole only 7.2m. passenger transited in and out of Morocco by air, but, following the gradual resumption of international civilian flights to and from the country from mid-June 2021, this figure rose to 9.9m. in 2021 and a preliminary 20.6m. in 2022.

Royal Air Maroc, established in 1953, is the national airline, operating services to European and African countries, as well as to the USA. However, since the liberalization of the sector Royal Air Maroc has increasingly struggled against foreign competition. It shut down subsidiary company Atlas Blue in 2010, and by 2012 it was aiming to implement an emergency recovery plan entailing extensive restructuring. Although the airline escaped bankruptcy, it was forced to cut 20 routes as part of its restructuring. By 2013 Royal Air Maroc appeared to have overcome its difficulties; as of 2020 it was renewing its fleet and introducing new routes, but it faced renewed competition, notably from Qatar Airways, which in May 2019 commenced thrice-weekly flights to Rabat from the Qatari capital, Doha (adding to its existing services to Casablanca and Marrakesh). In April 2019 Royal Air Maroc began operating three flights a week from Casablanca to Miami, USA, and in June it started operating three flights a week from Casablanca to Boston, USA, complementing its already developed North American routes. Owing to the COVID-19 pandemic, all domestic and international flights to and from Morocco were suspended in May 2020, but in June domestic flights were allowed to resume on a controlled basis. Some international flights were resumed in mid-2021, although further COVID-19 restrictions temporarily affected some flights from late 2021. In March 2022 Royal Air Maroc announced that it would shortly commence operating four flights a week between Casablanca and Tel Aviv.

COMMUNICATIONS

Legislation providing for the liberalization of the fixed-line and mobile telecommunications sector was adopted in 1997. In the following year the functions of the state-owned Office National des Postes et Télécommunications were divided between a new Agence Nationale de Réglementation des Télécommunications (ANRT), responsible for telecommunications regulation, and Itissalat al-Maghrib (Maroc Télécom), which was granted a monopoly of telecommunications services until 2001. The sale of the second Global System for Mobile Communications (GSM) licence took place in 1999. The 15-year licence was awarded to Médi Télécom (Méditel)—a consortium led by Telefónica of Spain together with Portugal Telecom and Moroccan investors, which pledged investment of US $660m. in the first four years. The network became operational in 2000. Later that year the Government announced that a 35% stake in Maroc Télécom had been sold to Vivendi Universal (now Vivendi SE) of France. Having completed a contract for the expansion of the GSM network in the main northern cities, in 2001 Maroc Télécom signed a further agreement with the US company Motorola to expand its network infrastructure.

In 2004 the Government sold a further 16% stake in Maroc Télécom to Vivendi, giving the French group a 51% holding. A further 14.9% stake in the company was sold on the Casablanca and Paris stock exchanges that year. In 2005 and 2007 another 17% of the company was sold via an initial public offering (IPO). In 2013 Vivendi announced that it was looking to sell its stake in Maroc Télécom. The UAE-based Etisalat bought it in May 2014. The Moroccan Government retained 30%, with the remaining 17% owned by minority shareholders. The sale was expected to result in the expansion and consolidation of Maroc Télécom's presence in Francophone sub-Saharan Africa. In July 2019 the Government reduced its stake in Maroc Télécom once again: 6% was sold to institutional investors and 2% as an IPO issued on the Casablanca Stock Exchange.

In early 2005 ANRT invited applications for three new types of telecommunications licence, covering the local network, with a maximum of two licences available for each region, two licences for the national system and two international licences. In July Méditel was awarded the country's second fixed-line licence. In late 2005 ANRT completed the liberalization of fixed-line services with the award of a third licence to local operator Maroc Connect, controlled by the Omnium Nord Africain (now Société Nationale d'Investissement). In May 2006 ANRT launched the tender for the third GSM licence. To meet increased demand for access to broadband connections, in July Maroc Télécom and Alcatel of France signed a contract to install a submarine cable network linking Asilah in north-western Morocco with Marseille in southern France. Also in July three domestic operators—Maroc Télécom, Méditel and Maroc Connect (since rebranded as Wana)—were awarded national 3G licences. In 2008 Maroc Télécom commenced high-speed phone services using 3G technology in the major cities, and Wana launched its 3G mobile service. By the end of 2008 the number of subscribers in Morocco had risen by 13.9%, to 22.8m., according to ANRT. Maroc Télécom was the dominant operator, with a 63.4% share of the mobile market; Méditel held a 34.7% share, and Wana just 1.9%.

Reflecting the global decline in fixed telephone line usage, in 2022, according to official figures, there were only about 2.6m. fixed-line subscribers in Morocco, compared with 53.0m. mobile subscribers (up from 23.7m. in 2019). According to the International Telecommunication Union (ITU), the internet was used by 88.1% of the population in 2021, while the ANRT reported that the number of internet users exceeded 26m. in 2019. The kingdom's fixed broadband users totalled 2.3m. in 2021, up from 2.1m. in 2020, while over the same period mobile broadband subscriptions increased from 27.7m. to 30.6m.

ANRT is responsible for processing licence requests and authorizations for private networks and regulating competition in the telecommunications market. It also manages development projects in the information and communication technologies sector, including the implementation of e-government infrastructure, the digitalization of small and medium-sized enterprises (SMEs) and overall IT expansion. The focus is on export industries such as mobile services, e-money, web design, computer graphics and multimedia. Specialized funds, including the Maroc Numeric Fund, and several IT clusters, including the Technoparks in Casablanca, Rabat and Tangier and the Rabat Technopolis offshore zone, were set up to finance the project.

In November 2017 Morocco successfully launched an earth observation satellite, named Mohammed VI-A, which was manufactured by Thales Alenia Space of France and Airbus; it launched the Mohammed VI-B satellite in November 2018, becoming the first African country to possess a constellation of earth surveillance satellites. The satellites will be used primarily for mapping and land surveillance, agricultural monitoring, the management of natural disasters, monitoring changes in the environment, and border and coastal surveillance.

In February 2019 the World Bank approved a new Country Partnership Framework for Morocco for 2019–24, and in March 2019 the Bank approved US $700m. in loan funding to accelerate Morocco's adoption of digital technology, in an effort to establish the country as a digital hub in North Africa. In August, following the latest phase of its privatization of Maroc Télécom, the Government signed a $1,000m. deal with the company to develop mobile broadband and fixed-line access across the country.

However, Morocco's digital development is lagging in some ways. In 2020 about one-third of the country's population still did not have access to the internet or to financial services, reflecting the fact that nearly 40% of the population lived in rural areas often with limited or no access to mobile banking and in places that often did not have fixed-line communications or physical banking in the first place. However, financial technology has expanded, and Morocco is relatively well placed in terms of digital services: the UN Educational, Scientific and Cultural Organisation has ranked it among the top three countries in this respect in the Middle East and North Africa (excluding the member states of the Gulf Cooperation Council).

BANKING AND FINANCE

The banking and financial sector is important to the Moroccan economy, as a large proportion of economic activity is financed by bank loans, and the sector plays a significant role in the export of services, particularly on the African continent. Three Moroccan banks (Attijariwafa Bank, the Banque Marocaine du Commerce Extérieur—BMCE—and the Banque Centrale Populaire—BCP) have branches in 22 African countries, according to the WTO.

The sector has undergone profound changes. By the early 1980s Morocco's foreign debt had reached unmanageable proportions, necessitating difficult economic restructuring, extensive IMF and World Bank support and the rescheduling of repayments to its international creditors over the rest of that decade. However, Morocco's economic prospects improved significantly when, in late 1991, Saudi Arabia and other Gulf states cancelled bilateral debts estimated at about US $3,600m. In early 1992 the IMF approved a new standby credit to support the Government's economic programme to March 1993. 'Paris Club' governments, meanwhile, rescheduled further official debt worth $1,500m., and the World Bank approved a $275m. structural adjustment loan.

In 1992 Morocco became a major recipient of concessionary development financing from France, and Spain agreed to provide a new five-year credit programme worth US $1,056m. The EU also agreed to lend Morocco a total of ECU 438m. in 1992–96, together with funds for structural adjustment and EIB loans for the Maghreb–Europe gas pipeline. In 2001 the Ministry of Finance announced a 5% devaluation in the dirham—a move regarded by some analysts as overdue and not of a scale to have a significant effect on the economy.

In 1998 Moody's Investors Service and Standard & Poor's awarded Morocco its first international credit ratings—a positive development that would help the Government to raise additional funds on the market.

By 2014 the IMF estimated that external debt had risen to the equivalent of 33.4% of GDP, at some US $36,000m. The debt was 33.9% of GDP in 2015, 34.6% in 2016, 33.5% in 2017, 40.5% in 2018 and 42.5% in 2019. Notably, the IMF's previous assumption that external debt as a proportion of the economy would plateau for four years, and then fall to 27% of GDP in 2024, was greatly upset by increased borrowing following the pandemic and, in 2020 at least, a shrinking economy. For instance, the Government took up its full IMF Precautionary and Liquidity Line (PLL) loan allocation in April 2020 (see *Budget*). In its January 2023 Article IV report, the IMF estimated that Morocco's external debt at the end of 2022 was 40.7% of GDP, down from 45.4% in 2021 and 54.1% in COVID-afflicted 2020.

The IMF reported in January 2021 that gross foreign currency reserves were 'comfortably above' the level seen at the end of 2019, owing to the recent allocation of PLL funding and additional Moroccan external borrowing (including two fresh bond issues in 2020). The IMF estimated that gross foreign reserves amounted to some US $36,000m. (equivalent to 7.2 months of imports of goods and services) in December 2020, up from $26,419m. (6.9 months) at the end of 2019. According to the IMF, gross foreign reserves decreased only slightly in 2021, totalling $35,600m. (5.8 months of imports of goods and services) at the end of that year. Notably, in December BAM injected 78,200m. dirhams into the Moroccan banking system. IMF funding (measured as a percentage of GDP) fell significantly in 2021, compared with 2020, although it was still approaching $1,000m. The IMF did not make available fresh financing in 2022. According to IMF estimates, foreign reserves had decreased to $31,800m. by the end of 2022 (equivalent to 5.5 months of import cover).

Morocco's central bank, BAM, is the sole issuer of currency; it holds and administers the state's foreign currency reserves, regulates the commercial banking sector and advises the Government on financial policy. The financial sector has undergone a period of liberalization, reflected in reforms supported by a series of World Bank initiatives that began in the early 1990s. The main reforms have included the elimination of credit ceilings, interest rate liberalization, overhaul of the legislative framework governing lending institutions (under a 1993 banking law), gradual elimination of mandatory holdings of government securities and the strengthening of prudential regulation of banks in accordance with international standards. A revised banking law and new central bank statutes were adopted in 2005, establishing the central bank's independence in monetary policy and clarifying its role in determining exchange rate policy in relation to that of the Ministry of Finance and Privatization. The central bank was also given greater powers to supervise banks and diversify its policy instruments to ensure efficient functioning of the money market. The new statutes prohibited the central bank from giving finance facilities to the Government and state-owned institutions.

By the end of 2004 there were 17 approved commercial banks, the largest of which were the BMCE, Crédit du Maroc, the BCP and Attijariwafa Bank. Commercial banks are permitted to have foreign majority ownership. In 1993 the Banco Exterior de España had become the first wholly owned foreign company authorized to open a subsidiary in Morocco since independence. In 1995 the Minister of Privatization sold most of the state's 50.4% holding in the BMCE. In 2022 BAM (according to its annual report) had supervisory control of 90 credit institutions and similar bodies, including 19 conventional banks, five participatory banks, 29 finance companies, six offshore banks, 11 microcredit associations, 18 payment institutions specializing in money transfer, the Caisse de Dépôt et de Gestion (Deposit and Management Fund) and the Société Nationale de Garantie et du Financement de l'Enterprise (National Company for Guarantee and Financing of Business), which operates under the brand name TAMWILCOM.

From 1999 the central bank authorized all Moroccan banks to invest up to 10% of their equity in the euro, which became the major currency for Morocco's external transactions in January 2002. Transactions would continue to be carried out in British sterling, Swiss francs, Danish krone and Norwegian krone, with separate rates for these currencies. In 2004 the Banque Commerciale du Maroc purchased 36.4% of the capital and 47.7% of the voting rights of Wafabank and 70.5% of Wafa Assurance. The merger of the two banks created one of the largest banks in Africa—Attijariwafa Bank—with more than 1m. clients and 460 branches.

Prudent management and modernization of the financial sector by BAM enabled the banking system to remain resilient through the international financial crisis. The central bank raised the capital adequacy ratio of banks and maintained a cautious monetary policy. However, the economy slowed in response to declining external demand and foreign investment. By the end of 2009 the sector had managed to reduce its portfolio of non-performing loans (NPLs) to 5.5%, from 6.0% in 2008. The proportion of NPLs fluctuated thereafter and fell to a historic low of 4.7% in December 2011. However, by 2019 they stood at 7.6%, and at June 2022 NPLs represented 8.5% of the loan stock.

Meanwhile, plans to promote Morocco's position and status as a financial sector hub and gateway to West Africa progressed in 2012, with the inauguration of the Casablanca Financial City (CFC). The Moroccan Government issued a decree providing for tax concessions for companies setting up in the zone and defining clear legal and regulatory frameworks. By mid-2016 more than 100 companies had joined the scheme, including many leading multinational firms.

In September and December 2020 Morocco issued two separate bonds on the international market (see *Budget*); the first, a €1,000m. issuance, occurred in two tranches; the second was the kingdom's first US dollar bond issue in seven years—its three tranches totalling US $3,000m. Given Morocco's ongoing financing pressures, the Government returned to the bond market from February 2023 to raise further international debt, issuing over $8,000m. in two tranches.

A review of Morocco's economic outlook by Fitch Ratings in April 2023 resulted in a 'BB+' rating, with the agency arguing that Morocco's macroeconomic indicators were sound, that its institutional capacity had provided the country with shock resilience, and that government debt continued to have only a moderate foreign currency element.

In a boost to Morocco's financial standing internationally, in May 2023 the EU removed the country from its money-laundering and terrorism-financing watchlist. The European Commission stated that Morocco had abided by a plan to address the EU's concerns about apparent illicit financial activity in Morocco, and noted the anti-money-laundering and counter-terrorism-financing measures that the kingdom had undertaken. Three months earlier, Morocco had also been removed from a similar 'grey list' maintained by the Financial Action Task Force (FATF); Morocco had been on the FATF's list for two years.

Two new indices were launched on the Moroccan stock exchange in 2002—the Most Active Shares Index (MADEX), monitoring the 10 most liquid stocks on the exchange, and the Moroccan All-Share Index (MASI), replacing the benchmark Casablanca Stock Exchange (CSE) index covering all stocks listed. The performance of the indices improved in 2010, when MASI grew by 23%. The rally in the CSE was short-lived, however: both indices declined by 13% in 2011, and MASI fell by 15.1% in 2012. The Government was concerned that the poor performance of the exchange would affect its plans to develop the CFC and was considering ways of deepening the market's liquidity—such as by establishing a futures market and by permitting transactions in foreign currency as well as by developing the regulatory framework needed for a derivatives market. These plans gathered pace in early 2013, after the bourse registered its lowest trading levels for several years, with volumes on the CSE falling by 30% (and on MASI by 19%). However, the Government's intentions suffered a major reverse in June, when the Morgan Stanley Capital International index downgraded the CSE from 'emerging market' to 'frontier' status. By the end of June the overall index had fallen by 7%, with a steeper decline expected following the downgrade. The market had recovered slightly by the end of 2013, but still recorded a 2.6% decline for the year as a whole. The MASI index rallied in 2014, growing by 5.6%. In 2016 MASI registered a substantial increase of 30.5% (the largest since 2007), following a contraction of 7.2% in 2015. It rose by 6.4% in 2017, fell by 8.3% in 2018 and rose by 6.8% in 2019. Market capitalization increased to 58% of GDP in 2016 and 59% in 2017, although it fell to 52.6% in 2018, rising to 55.5% at the end of 2019. As of the end of the day's trading on 14 June 2021 the MASI index rose by 11.3% during the year to 14 June 2021, but fell by 9.7% in the year ending 29 June 2022. By the end of May 2023 the MASI index had declined by a further 6.0% over the previous 12 months.

At about US $65,000m. at the end of 2019, the CSE's market capitalization had not altered much in a decade, although the number of traded companies had risen to 81 by 2016. In practice, the market remained illiquid, and its contribution to financing the economy was still marginal. In April 2020 the CSE reported that the bourse's market capitalization had fallen by 22% from its level at the end of 2019, as some investors pulled out of the market following the downturn engendered by the onset of the COVID-19 pandemic in early 2020. At the end of 2020 the CSE's market capitalization was more or less back at its December 2019 figure, registering $65,651m., and by 14 June 2021 had risen to $72,576m. While at this date the number of traded companies was down a little, at 76, the capitalization figure suggested that the CSE was not only recovering from the 2020 economic contraction but that the bourse was in better shape than before the pandemic. However, during January–May 2022 the bourse's market capitalization followed a broadly downward trend, declining from $71,928m. at the start of the year to $64,496m. by May. The CSE's market capitalization fell further to $51,482m. in October, but had recovered somewhat by June 2023 when it stood at $60,573m.

BUDGET

Wages and subsidies dominate the 2012 budget, which aimed to alleviate social stresses. Some 32,500m. dirhams were allocated to the subsidy fund, representing a significant increase compared with the previous year's budget, but a decline against the 2011 out-turn. The wage bill showed a steady rise, as the Government agreed to raise both public sector wages and the minimum wage. The deficit widened to 8.3% of GDP in 2012, but despite this the 2013 budget projected a much-reduced deficit of 4.7%.

The Government expected to reduce the deficit in 2013 through further subsidy reforms—a policy supported by the IMF, which extended a US $6,200m. precautionary credit line to Morocco in August 2012 and renewed it for two further years in July 2013. In the event, the Government was forced, halfway through the fiscal year, to raise its deficit forecast to 5.5% of GDP. It did, however, push ahead with subsidy reform, announcing a rise in petrol and diesel prices. The 2014 budget planned for further subsidy reductions—on gas, sugar and flour. The Government succeeded in reducing the budget deficit to 4.9% of GDP by the end of that year, although the announcement in May that the minimum wage would be raised again extended the public sector wage bill. By 2015 the energy subsidy bill was estimated to have been reduced to 3% of GDP, down from 6.6% in 2012, but the Government was still reluctant to remove the subsidy for butane—the cooking fuel of choice for the majority of Moroccans. However, determined to push ahead with its fiscal consolidation programme, the Government announced plans in late 2014 to raise the retirement age from 60 to 65 over a period of 10 years, while reducing the final salary pension entitlement and increasing paid contributions from employees. A full liberalization of liquid fuel products took place in December 2015, which, helped by falling international oil prices, resulted in a reduction in subsidy spending of 2.3 percentage points of GDP between 2014 and 2016, according to the IMF. Despite significant resistance, the reform of the civil service pension system was adopted in June 2016. Meanwhile, most of the provisions of an organic budget law intended to strengthen the regulatory framework entered into force in January. The Financial Law 2016 implemented extensive tax reforms, including new 'progressive' corporate tax rates and increased tax penalties.

Morocco's budget deficit fell further in 2015, to 4.2% of GDP (from 4.9% in 2014), with the Government's stated objective being to reduce the deficit to 3.0% by 2017. However, in 2016 the budget deficit only declined slightly, to 4.1% of GDP, and total government debt rose to 65.1% of GDP. The budget for 2017 projected an overall surplus of some 20,000m. dirhams. The country's general government gross debt was 690,376m. dirhams in 2017, equivalent to 65.1% of GDP. Morocco's total external debt in 2017 was US $49,752m., of which $33,314m. was public and publicly guaranteed debt. The budget for 2018 included measures to promote investment and entrepreneurship, for example through tax breaks for companies. The budget deficit fell to 3.4% of GDP in 2018. In March 2018 the IMF published its final review of Morocco's finances under a new, two-year loan agreement concluded in July 2016: the PLL arrangement was worth $3,420m. The Fund commended Morocco's strong monetary and financial performance, while urging fiscal reforms. The loan agreement expired in July 2018 (although Morocco had in fact not drawn upon the loan funding and the Government had stated earlier in that year that it would not seek its renewal). However, in December the IMF approved a new loan facility (under the PLL arrangement) worth $2,970m. to support fiscal reforms, a reduction in debt and protection against external vulnerabilities. The budget for 2019 included subsidies of 17,676m. dirhams on wheat, cooking gas and sugar (an increase of 4,650m. dirhams from the previous year), while social spending increased by 5,400m. dirhams to 68,000m. dirhams. Firms with annual net profits above 40m. dirhams were to be subject to a 2.5% 'solidarity tax' on their net profit from 2019, in order to fund social welfare spending and reduce the budget deficit. In January 2019 the Government announced a five-year corporate tax break for newly established industrial companies in an effort to attract foreign investment.

The fiscal outcome for 2019 was a modest rise in the deficit as a proportion of GDP, to 3.6% of GDP. The Government had been hoping that its sale of 8% of its shares in Maroc Télécom in July 2019 would have eased fiscal pressures more significantly, but strong public sector wage pressure continued to feed rising expenditure. In its budget for 2020, the Government projected that the overall deficit would be about 3.5% of GDP. A marked rise in public sector wage settlements was envisaged, together with a significant rise in dedicated payments to Moroccans on low incomes. Offsetting these pressures would be some 3,000m. dirhams in receipts from further privatizations and a planned cut of 4,400m. dirhams in the cost of food subsidies. However, the Government was also committed to large increases in spending on education and health care. The Government's budget assumptions for 2020 were premised on a higher level of economic growth than achieved in 2019 (2.9%) and a fall in average international oil prices. In the event, however, the onset of the COVID-19 pandemic in early 2020 upended all assumptions about government revenues, as a number of revenue streams weakened, together with receipts from tourism and foreign remittances. At the same time, overall expenditure increased owing to money allocated for economic stimulus measures. Despite the overall impact of the collapse in oil prices offsetting some government costs, the budget deficit inevitably rose sharply. In late January 2021 Morocco's finance ministry announced that tax revenues in 2020 had actually risen by 13m. dirhams, compared with 2019, helping, it was said, to offset the fall in other revenues caused by the pandemic. According to the IMF, the 2020 fiscal out-turn was a deficit of 53,600m. dirhams, and an overall budget deficit equivalent to 7.1% of GDP. Revenue had actually increased year on year by just under 16,000m. dirhams, while 'other revenues' had risen by nearly 30,000m. dirhams. This 'other revenues' category in 2020 included income from the emergency COVID-19 Fund. However, spending in 2020 rose by more than 4 0,000m. dirhams, largely due to a 20,000m. dirhams increase in social spending as the solidarity fund and other measures were used to support business and individuals. IMF figures showed that, contrary to the Government's claim of an increase in tax revenues, overall tax revenues did indeed fall in 2020 (by 6.5%), as would have been expected under the circumstances. Thus, the overall deficit in 2020 was nearly 36,000m. dirhams larger than in 2019. Financing in 2020 was partly provided by increasing Morocco's foreign debt burden, including two bond issues on the international market.

On 9 December 2020 Morocco issued a US $3,000m. bond, in three tranches, representing its first US currency-denominated bond in 12 years. In late September that year, Morocco had issued a €1,000m. bond, in two tranches (see above).

The impact of the COVID-19 pandemic also changed the Government's perspective regarding drawing on the IMF's PLL arrangement, and in April 2020 the Government took up all of the available loan financing of just under US $3,000m. (about 3% of GDP) in order to ensure that there were adequate foreign reserves to offset pressure on the balance of payments.

From spending-led attempts to offset economic recession in 2020, including via a dedicated COVID-19 Fund to utilize both public and private sector donations for discretionary spending, the IMF described Morocco's 2021 budget as prioritizing investment-led growth stimulation. This, it argued, would happen via the Mohammed VI Investment Fund (MVIIF) and via other forms of state subsidized or guaranteed credit. (The 15,000m. dirham MVIIF was created in the Government's 2020 Supplementary Budget. It was envisaged, according to the IMF, as eventually being, in effect, privatized and as attracting private investment in infrastructure and aiding SME development, including via private equity investment.)

The 2021 budget prioritized easing the fiscal deficit amid the ongoing domestic and global economic pressure related to the COVID-19 pandemic. The IMF noted that Morocco's fiscal 'space' was tight—indicated by both the growth in the deficit and, consequently, in public debt as a percentage of GDP (central government debt rose from 60.3% to 72.2% in 2020). The COVID-19 Fund and the MVIIF were seen by the IMF as aids both to growth and a consequent easing of the deficit.

The IMF's assessment in its Article IV report issued in January 2021, was that the fiscal deficit in 2021 would ease only slightly in terms of its share of projected GDP, albeit that the latter was projected to rise rather than contract (as it had in 2020). The IMF's projection for the Moroccan fiscal deficit for 2021 seemed to be more or less based on assumptions similar to those of the Government when it issued the budget at the end of 2020. However, the IMF assumed that low interest rates, the long maturity of public debt, and what it called possible 'domestic fiscal savings' could make managing and funding the deficit possible. Measures to tackle more strategically the consequent large public debt should, stated the IMF, be delayed until the economic recovery stabilized. The Fund expected that over the longer term revenues would be boosted by further privatization, including divestment of real estate and, it was hoped, by an improved tax collection system.

In the event, the 2021 budgetary deficit out-turn, at 49,200m. dirhams, did not declined significantly from the deficit in 2020 (but did, however, represent, at 5.9% of GDP, a smaller proportion of an enlarged economy). Total revenue in 2021 rose by a modest 3.6%, with income from taxes on goods and services more than covering the small decrease in 'other revenue'. The 8.8% rise in overall tax income in 2021 was largely due to strong value-added tax receipts as sales picked up as the economy recovered. The IMF January 2022 Article IV report implied that in 2021 the COVID-19 Fund was no longer operational—or not on the same scale—and that therefore this had reduced income under the 'other revenue' category. According to the IMF, budgetary spending in 2021 fell slightly, by about 0.4%, as the pandemic eased and 'social benefits' expenditure was consequently reduced by about 12,500m. dirhams; none the less, overall spending was still much higher than before the pandemic. In order to finance the still-large deficit, the Government continued to draw on foreign debt.

In its budget for 2022 the Government forecast that tax revenues would increase further and that aspects of spending would contribute to this higher revenue (solidarity spending, for instance). The tax rise projection was partly based on changes to corporate tax that were expected to increase overall tax revenue. The Government predicted that expenditure in 2022 would rise by about the same amount as revenue, with priority being given to job creation measures, state-owned enterprise transfers, and higher spending on education and health care. In the longer term, the objective was to extend what IMF referred to as 'social protection' to greater portions of the population. According to the IMF, the 2022 budget out-turn included a fiscal deficit that was, at 5.1% of GDP, actually smaller than the 6.3% that the Fund had forecast. Both revenue and expenditure had risen—the former by 36,800m. dirhams and the latter by 49,500m.—but the resultant deficit was a smaller percentage of a growing economy.

MOROCCO

Statistical Survey

The IMF's analysis of the Government's budget for 2023, announced in October 2022, was that it continued a welcome focus on achieving debt reduction commensurate with the social and economic spending necessary to stimulate the economy and thus provide the capacity to reduce the deficit. The 2023 budget included a three-year fiscal framework that the IMF commended as providing an institutional basis for taxation and expenditure considerations. The budget was based on the assumption that the deficit would be equivalent to 4.5% of GDP. The Government intended to target outlays on the most needy under a national register scheme, and to increase health expenditure, while claiming that tax collection would improve. In April 2023 the IMF predicted that the fiscal deficit would, at 4.9% of GDP, not be significantly smaller than the 2022 out-turn, with both revenue and expenditure continuing to rise. Financing would presumably include ongoing access to both public and private debt, including external financing, despite the Government's stated objective to reduce the country's debt. The World Bank's pledge in May 2023 to provide further support for government programmes aimed at increasing small businesses' access to finance would constitute part of the fiscal deficit financing.

Statistical Survey

Sources (unless otherwise stated): Haut Commissariat au Plan, Direction de la Statistique, rue Muhammad Belhassan el-Ouazzani, BP 178, Rabat 10001; tel. (53) 7773606; fax (53) 7773217; e-mail contact@hcp.ma; internet www.hcp.ma; Bank Al-Maghrib, 277 ave Muhammad V, BP 445, Rabat; tel. (53) 7702626; fax (53) 7706667; e-mail webmaster@bkam.ma; internet www.bkam.ma.

Note: Unless otherwise indicated, the data exclude Western (formerly Spanish) Sahara, a disputed territory under Moroccan occupation

Area and Population

AREA, POPULATION AND DENSITY

Area (sq km)	710,850*
Population (census results)†	
2 September 2004	29,680,069
1 September 2014	
Males	16,978,075
Females	16,870,167
Total	33,848,242
Population (official projections at mid-year)	
2021	36,313,189
2022	36,670,216
2023	37,022,385
Density (per sq km) at mid-2023	52.1

* 274,461 sq miles. This area includes the disputed territory of Western Sahara, which covers 252,120 sq km (97,344 sq miles).
† Including Western Sahara, with a population of 510,713 at the 2014 census.

POPULATION BY AGE AND SEX
(official projections at mid-2023)

	Males	Females	Total
0–14 years	4,711,249	4,511,595	9,222,844
15–64 years	12,256,451	12,507,131	24,763,582
65 years and over	1,471,263	1,564,696	3,035,959
Total	18,438,963	18,583,422	37,022,385

REGIONS
(official projections at mid-2023)

	Population
Béni Mellal-Khénifra	2,656,384
Drâa-Tafilalet	1,721,357
Eddakhla-Oued Eddahab*	200,847
Fez-Meknès	4,486,674
Grand Casablanca-Settat	7,688,562
Guelmim-Oued Noun	452,529
Laâyoune-Sakia El Hamra*	417,756
Marrakech-Safi	4,896,681
Oriental	2,532,440
Rabat-Salé-Kénitra	5,008,353
Souss-Massa	3,018,226
Tangier-Tétouan-Al Hoceima	3,942,576
Total	37,022,385

* Regions situated in Western Sahara.

PRINCIPAL TOWNS
(UN projections at mid-2023)

Casablanca	3,892,837	Agadir	979,248
Rabat (capital)*	1,959,388	Oujda	593,968
Tanger (Tangier)	1,314,178	Kénitra	507,848
Fès (Fez)	1,290,039	Tétouan	444,713
Marrakech (Marrakesh)	1,049,690	Safi	335,853

* Including Salé and Temara.

Source: UN, *World Urbanization Prospects: The 2018 Revision*.

BIRTHS, MARRIAGES AND DEATHS

	2019/20	2020/21	2021/22
Birth rate (per 1,000)	16.7	16.5	16.2
Death rate (per 1,000)	5.0	5.1	5.1

Registered marriages: 275,477 in 2019; 194,480 in 2020; 269,978 in 2021.

Life expectancy (years at birth, estimates): 74.0 (males 71.9 females 76.4) in 2021 (Source: World Bank, World Development Indicators database).

ECONOMICALLY ACTIVE POPULATION
('000 persons aged 15 years and over, 2020)

	Males	Females	Total
Agriculture, hunting, forestry and fishing	2,281	1,015	3,295
Mining and quarrying	44	1	45
Manufacturing	854	316	1,169
Electricity, gas and water	60	6	66
Construction	1,128	11	1,139
Wholesale and retail trade; repairs	1,683	155	1,838
Hotels and restaurants	303	69	372
Transport, storage and communications	529	27	556
General administration and community services	748	370	1,118
Financial intermediation, real estate and business services	643	293	936
Sub-total	8,273	2,263	10,534
Activities not adequately defined	5	3	8
Total employed	8,278	2,265	10,542
Unemployed	991	438	1,429
Total labour force	9,269	2,703	11,971

2023 (January–March, '000): Total employed 10,418; Unemployed 1,549; Total labour force 11,967.

Note: Totals may not be equal to the sum of components, owing to rounding.

Health and Welfare

KEY INDICATORS

Total fertility rate (children per woman, 2021)	2.3
Under-5 mortality rate (per 1,000 live births, 2021)	18.0
HIV/AIDS (% of persons aged 15–49, 2021)	<0.1
COVID-19: Cumulative confirmed deaths (per 100,000 persons at 30 June 2023)	43.5
COVID-19: Fully vaccinated population (% of total population at 14 May 2023)	62.8
Physicians (per 1,000 head, 2017)	0.7
Hospital beds (per 1,000 head, 2017)	1.0
Domestic health expenditure (2020): US $ per head (PPP)	196.6
Domestic health expenditure (2020): % of GDP	2.6
Domestic health expenditure (2020): public (% of total current health expenditure)	43.5
Access to improved water resources (% of persons, 2020)	90
Access to improved sanitation facilities (% of persons, 2020)	87
Total carbon dioxide emissions ('000 metric tons, 2019)	71,479
Carbon dioxide emissions per head (metric tons, 2019)	2.0
Human Development Index (2021): ranking	123
Human Development Index (2021): value	0.683

Note: For data on COVID-19 vaccinations, 'fully vaccinated' denotes receipt of all doses specified by approved vaccination regime (Sources: Johns Hopkins University and Our World in Data). Data on health expenditure refer to current general government expenditure in each case. For more information on sources and further definitions for all indicators, see Health and Welfare Statistics: Sources and Definitions section (europaworld.com/credits).

Agriculture

PRINCIPAL CROPS
('000 metric tons)

	2019	2020	2021
Almonds, with shell	102.2	134.4	169.3
Anise, badian, fennel and coriander*	27.7	27.7	27.8
Apples	809.8	778.9	889.7
Apricots	109.8	93.0	78.4
Artichokes	44.8	45.0	40.5
Aubergines (Eggplants)	68.3	60.9	81.0
Avocados	54.6	69.9	82.4
Bananas	349.9	341.0	336.1
Barley	1,161.2	645.0	2,780.3
Beans, green*	212.3	231.0	227.8
Broad beans, dry	72.7	49.0	131.2
Cauliflowers and broccoli	50.8	57.5	58.2
Chillies and peppers, green	247.6	143.9	213.1
Cantaloupes and other melons	390.6	504.9	540.6
Carobs*	22.0	22.0	22.0
Carrots and turnips	412.2	403.4	387.5
Cucumbers and gherkins	57.4	46.4	59.9
Dates	101.5	143.2	150.3
Figs	153.5	144.2	144.2
Garlic	10.3	12.0	11.1
Grapes	459.5	396.9	420.1
Groundnuts, with shell	39.7	36.7	36.8
Lemons and limes	44.9	34.6	41.2
Lupin beans*	56.6	57.0	56.9
Maize	40.5	29.9	48.6
Olives	1,912.2	1,409.3	1,590.5
Onions, dry	880.4	828.9	855.3
Oranges	1,182.5	806.3	1,039.4
Peaches and nectarines	158.8	159.5	169.0
Peas, green	107.1	96.9	78.4
Peppermint	66.6	40.4	30.0
Plums and sloes	151.5	143.5	178.8
Potatoes	1,956.7	1,707.1	1,641.9
Pumpkins, squash and gourds	198.9	154.0	329.2
Quinces	39.6	57.7	54.6

—continued	2019	2020	2021
Rice, paddy	64.6	65.7	50.9
Strawberries	167.8	167.0	141.1
String beans	119.9	109.4	127.5
Sugar beet	3,692.9	3,631.6	2,574.0
Sugar cane	519.0	792.5	613.3
Sunflower seeds	29.5	22.4	24.6
Tangerines, mandarins, etc.	1,374.6	926.6	1,248.4
Tomatoes	1,347.1	1,398.8	1,311.1
Watermelons	674.8	677.3	824.1
Wheat	4,025.3	2,561.9	7,543.8

* FAO estimates.

Aggregate production ('000 metric tons, may include official, semi-official or estimated data): Total cereals 5,316.3 in 2019, 3,325.7 in 2020, 10,447.7 in 2021; Total fruit (primary) 6,382.2 in 2019, 5,592.3 in 2020, 6,502.7 in 2021; Total oilcrops 1,985.9 in 2019, 1,473.8 in 2020, 1,657.3 in 2021; Total pulses 290.1 in 2019, 218.4 in 2020, 340.8 in 2021; Total roots and tubers 1,966.2 in 2019, 1,714.6 in 2020, 1,651.3 in 2021; Total sugar crops (primary) 4,211.8 in 2019, 4,424.0 in 2020, 3,187.2 in 2021; Total vegetables (primary) 4,212.0 in 2019, 3,995.5 in 2020, 4,218.4 in 2021.

Source: FAO.

LIVESTOCK
('000 head, year ending September)

	2019	2020	2021
Asses	927	925	925
Camels*	61	62	62
Cattle	3,328	3,167	3,179
Chickens*	209,287	213,375	217,462
Goats	5,993	5,961	6,207
Horses	191	190	190
Mules	385	387	387
Pigs	8	8	8
Sheep	21,591	22,089	22,726
Turkeys*	12,417	12,602	12,788

* FAO estimates.

Source: FAO.

LIVESTOCK PRODUCTS
('000 metric tons)

	2019	2020	2021
Camels' milk*	8.8	8.9	9.0
Cattle hides, fresh*	44.3	44.2	44.2
Cattle meat	283.0	282.0	282.0
Cattle offals, edible*	53.4	53.2	53.2
Cows' milk	2,550.0	2,500.0	2,500.0
Chicken meat	625.0	535.0	525.0
Game meat*	52.3	53.2	54.0
Goat meat	32.1	31.0	31.0
Goats' milk*	45.9	45.8	47.0
Sheep meat	178.8	179.0	179.0
Sheep offals, edible*	45.6	45.7	45.7
Sheep's (Ewes') milk*	36.4	36.9	37.5
Sheepskins, fresh*	25.5	25.5	25.5
Hen eggs*	414.0	415.0	415.0
Honey (natural)	8.0	8.0	8.0
Wool, greasy*	60.6	61.3	62.7
Snails (other than sea snails)*	16.8	17.0	17.4

* FAO estimates.

Source: FAO.

MOROCCO

Forestry

ROUNDWOOD REMOVALS
('000 cubic metres, excl. bark, FAO estimates)

	2019	2020	2021
Sawlogs, veneer logs and logs for sleepers	65.0	11.0	43.0
Pulpwood	220.0	98.0	196.0
Fuel wood	6,595.8	6,575.2	6,557.5
Total	6,880.8	6,684.2	6,796.5

Source: FAO.

SAWNWOOD PRODUCTION
('000 cubic metres, incl. railway sleepers, FAO estimates)

	2019	2020	2021
Coniferous (softwood)	43	43	43
Broadleaved (hardwood)	40	12	12
Total	83	55	55

Source: FAO.

Fishing

('000 metric tons, live weight)

	2019	2020	2021
Capture	1,458.6	1,375.3	1,411.8
European pilchard (sardine)	968.5	843.3	788.2
Chub mackerel	211.0	186.0	254.7
Jack and horse mackerels	28.8	31.1	33.8
European anchovy	19.6	50.1	48.2
Octopuses	42.4	51.9	63.5
Aquaculture	1.3	1.4	1.9
Total catch (incl. others)	1,459.9	1,376.7	1,413.7

Source: FAO.

Mining

('000 metric tons)

	2019	2020	2021
Iron ore*	19.9	39.2	24.6
Copper concentrates*	109.3	113.0	179.2
Lead concentrates*	46.5	54.2	44.5
Manganese ore*	71.2	84.1	82.5
Zinc concentrates*	85.9	70.6	79.4
Phosphate rock†	35,277	37,442	38,122
Fluorspar (acid grade)	73.2	83.8	189.0
Barytes	1,119.8	501.9	840.5
Salt (unrefined)	854.4	490.9	295.7
Bentonite	188.1	92.4	134.3

* Figures refer to the gross weight of ores and concentrates.
† Including production in Western Sahara.

2022: Phosphate rock 30,456,000 metric tons.

Industry

SELECTED PRODUCTS
('000 metric tons unless otherwise indicated)

	2015	2016	2017
Wine*	39	33	34
Olive oil (crude)†	135	135	131
Motor spirit—petrol	186	131	161
Naphthas	204	103	109
Distillate fuel oils	1,120	2,341	2,332
Residual fuel oils	422	640	717
Jet fuel	412	n.a.	n.a.
Petroleum bitumen—asphalt	247	n.a.	n.a.
Cement	14,460	14,260	14,850
Electrical energy (million kWh)	31,217	32,141	33,192

* Estimated figures.
† Unofficial figures.

Cement ('000 metric tons): 15,300 in 2018.

Liquefied petroleum gas ('000 barrels): 1,114 in 2013; 9,915 in 2014; 5,453 in 2015.

Wine ('000 metric tons, FAO estimates): 40.8 in 2018; 47.4 in 2019; 40.9 in 2020.

Refined sugar ('000 metric tons): 1,748.8 in 2019; 1,841.4 in 2020; 1,810.5 in 2021.

Olive oil ('000 metric tons): 145 in 2018/19; 145 in 2019/20; 160 in 2020/21.

Electrical energy (million kWh): 38,372 in 2020; 40,512 in 2021; 42,317 in 2022.

Sources: partly FAO; US Geological Survey, UN Industrial Commodity Statistics Database; UN Energy Statistics Database.

Finance

CURRENCY AND EXCHANGE RATES

Monetary Units:
100 centimes (santimat) = 1 Moroccan dirham.

Sterling, Dollar and Euro Equivalents (28 April 2023):
£1 sterling = 12.559 dirhams;
US $1 = 10.077 dirhams;
€1 = 11.066 dirhams;
100 Moroccan dirhams = £7.96 = $9.92 = €9.04.

Average Exchange Rate (dirhams per US $):
2020　9.497
2021　8.988
2022　10.161

GENERAL BUDGET
('000 million dirhams)

Revenue*†	2022	2023‡	2024‡
Tax revenue	294.2	307.6	322.6
Taxes on income and profits	116.3	119.7	128.0
Taxes on property	14.3	14.9	15.9
Taxes on goods and services	143.3	152.8	158.1
Taxes on international trade	14.5	14.0	14.0
Other tax revenues	5.7	6.2	6.6
Non-tax revenue	63.6	92.7	99.5
Total	359.2	402.2	423.1

MOROCCO

Expenditure§	2022	2023‡	2024‡
Wages and salaries	147.8	155.8	161.3
Use of goods and services	37.8	39.4	44.0
Grants	74.9	93.8	99.5
Interest	28.6	34.2	36.4
Subsidies	42.1	26.6	8.9
Social benefits	11.4	12.5	24.1
Other expense	34.1	41.3	44.9
Total	**376.7**	**403.4**	**419.1**

* Excluding grants (million dirhams): 1.5 in 2022; 1.9 in 2023 (projection); 1.0 in 2024 (projection).
† Includes tariffs destined for food subsidies and road fund revenues.
‡ Projections.
§ Excluding net lending.

Source: IMF, *Morocco: Request for an Arrangement Under the Flexible Credit Line—Press Release; Staff Report; and Statement by the Executive Director for Morocco* (April 2023).

INTERNATIONAL RESERVES
(US $ million at 31 December)

	2020	2021	2022
Gold (national valuation)	1,346	1,294	1,292
IMF special drawing rights	743	2,048	1,914
Reserve position in IMF	212	206	196
Foreign exchange	33,698	32,100	28,916
Total	**35,999**	**35,648**	**32,318**

Source: IMF, *International Financial Statistics*.

MONEY SUPPLY
(million dirhams at 31 December)

	2020	2021	2022
Currency outside depository corporations	300,626	320,111	354,734
Transferable deposits	679,245	729,059	793,140
Other deposits	402,091	409,615	428,720
Securities other than shares	29,632	28,915	25,117
Broad money	**1,411,595**	**1,487,700**	**1,601,710**

Source: IMF, *International Financial Statistics*.

COST OF LIVING
(Consumer Price Index for urban areas; base: 2017 = 100)

	2020	2021	2022
Food and non-alcoholic beverages	101.6	102.2	113.7
Clothing and footwear	102.7	104.7	109.7
Housing, water, electricity, gas and other fuels	101.8	102.6	103.6
All items (incl. others)	**102.5**	**103.9**	**110.8**

NATIONAL ACCOUNTS
(million dirhams at current prices)

Expenditure on the Gross Domestic Product

	2020	2021	2022
Government final consumption expenditure	223,638	242,213	255,627
Private final consumption expenditure	680,810	761,419	824,362
Change in inventories	27,597	51,484	39,746
Acquisition of valuable objects	1,807	2,089	2,521
Gross fixed capital formation	302,245	335,620	360,825
Total domestic expenditure	**1,236,097**	**1,392,825**	**1,483,081**
Exports of goods and services	354,895	423,003	596,039
Less Imports of goods and services	438,514	541,101	748,962
GDP in purchasers' values	**1,152,478**	**1,274,727**	**1,330,158**

Gross Domestic Product by Economic Activity

	2020	2021	2022
Agriculture, hunting and forestry	117,094	143,963	130,299
Fishing and aquaculture	5,802	8,948	7,127
Mining and quarrying	16,659	24,298	38,297
Manufacturing	174,916	192,034	199,747
Electricity and water	44,343	45,360	28,101
Construction	64,229	67,183	72,741
Commerce; repairs of motorcycles and automobiles	111,643	129,930	151,084
Hotels and restaurants	23,416	26,501	41,736
Transport and storage	33,754	37,264	36,820
Information and communications	32,727	32,112	32,950
Finance and insurance	51,956	56,578	59,809
Real estate activities	86,599	89,957	93,209
Research and development; business services	51,623	56,924	64,472
Public administration and social security	119,152	126,029	132,153
Education, health and social service activities	87,739	91,233	96,469
Other services	14,397	15,183	15,932
Sub-total	**1,036,049**	**1,143,497**	**1,200,946**
Taxes, less subsidies, on imports	116,428	131,230	129,212
GDP in purchasers' values	**1,152,478**	**1,274,727**	**1,330,158**

BALANCE OF PAYMENTS
(US $ million)

	2020	2021	2022
Exports of goods	23,678.5	31,674.7	36,574.8
Imports of goods	−39,218.1	−51,641.9	−63,037.2
Balance on goods	**−15,539.6**	**−19,967.3**	**−26,462.4**
Exports of services	13,866.8	15,415.6	21,981.0
Imports of services	−7,140.2	−8,573.2	−10,746.0
Balance on goods and services	**−8,812.9**	**−13,124.9**	**−15,227.4**
Primary income received	777.0	921.0	785.1
Primary income paid	−1,985.5	−2,960.3	−2,632.3
Balance on goods, services and primary income	**−10,021.4**	**−15,164.2**	**−17,074.6**
Secondary income received	9,229.3	12,365.4	12,951.0
Secondary income paid	−576.3	−549.9	−651.7
Current balance	**−1,368.4**	**−3,348.7**	**−4,775.2**
Capital account (net)	0.3	—	2.2
Direct investment assets	−459.3	−642.8	−612.6
Direct investment liabilities	1,418.7	2,264.1	2,177.8
Portfolio investment assets	−155.2	−38.1	−101.3
Portfolio investment liabilities	2,491.4	−247.7	−930.4
Financial derivatives and employee stock options (net)	−65.0	32.6	−40.6
Other investment assets	−1,251.7	126.9	7.9
Other investment liabilities	−874.3	4,377.5	1,968.7
Net errors and omissions	1,734.0	897.7	2,122.5
Reserves and related items	**1,470.5**	**3,421.6**	**−180.9**

Source: IMF, *International Financial Statistics*.

MOROCCO

External Trade

PRINCIPAL COMMODITIES
(million dirhams)

Imports c.i.f.	2020	2021	2022*
Foodstuffs, beverages and tobacco	55,220	59,868	86,734
Corn	13,505	14,294	n.a.
Energy and lubricants	49,878	75,792	153,187
Petroleum gas and other hydrocarbons	11,944	17,433	26,302
Refined petroleum products	23,316	35,980	76,369
Crude products	19,454	29,526	44,257
Semi-finished products	93,224	115,854	169,685
Chemical products	9,670	12,500	16,873
Plastics and article thereof	12,947	16,133	21,677
Finished capital goods	108,330	118,471	141,303
Finished consumer products	96,754	128,908	142,006
Pharmaceutical products	7,656	13,124	8,616
Textile and cotton fabrics	6,527	8,966	11,364
Vehicle spare parts	15,801	19,727	24,138
Total (incl. others)	422,861	528,571	737,441

Exports f.o.b.	2020	2021	2022*
Foodstuffs, beverages and tobacco	56,796	62,990	75,218
Crustaceans and molluscs	8,026	11,493	10,753
Prepared and preserved fish	7,910	7,310	8,750
Energy and lubricants	1,355	2,317	4,327
Crude mineral products	12,176	16,493	22,138
Phosphates	7,338	8,943	13,390
Semi-finished products	58,516	90,895	125,047
Natural and chemical fertilizers	32,148	51,511	79,266
Finished industrial capital goods	52,860	55,216	69,612
Electric wire and cable	27,970	28,570	37,350
Finished consumer products	74,837	93,712	123,235
Manufactured garments	18,131	22,645	27,611
Hosiery	5,804	7,529	8,475
Total (incl. others)	263,089	329,405	428,612

* Provisional.

Source: Office des Changes, Rabat.

PRINCIPAL TRADING PARTNERS
(million dirhams)*

Imports c.i.f.	2020	2021	2022†
Algeria	4,012	5,869	1,694
Argentina	5,782	7,445	12,546
Belgium	6,918	9,507	10,564
Brazil	7,292	7,632	13,128
Canada	5,012	5,145	7,211
China, People's Republic	51,537	61,941	74,007
Egypt	5,521	7,366	10,378
France	50,656	55,570	78,058
Germany	22,367	23,113	30,167
India	6,356	9,632	13,952
Italy	21,952	26,719	33,405
Kazakhstan	240	2,080	6,969
Korea, Republic	3,811	3,745	6,432
Netherlands	6,282	8,144	8,480
Poland	4,465	6,226	7,604
Portugal	11,163	14,732	13,628
Romania	5,189	6,818	10,508
Russian Federation	15,411	18,250	22,880
Saudi Arabia	8,517	16,502	47,624
Spain	64,935	82,965	103,996
Trinidad and Tobago	1,777	2,549	9,068
Türkiye	23,074	30,501	37,980
United Arab Emirates	4,850	9,577	14,488
United Kingdom	5,357	6,541	8,205
USA	26,556	33,571	54,713
Total (incl. others)	422,861	528,571	737,441

Exports f.o.b.	2020	2021	2022†
Bangladesh	1,064	5,265	8,856
Belgium	3,790	4,975	8,120
Djibouti	2,362	2,313	5,447
Brazil	10,856	18,244	17,220
France	57,523	67,238	80,523
Germany	8,571	9,681	13,531
India	11,299	16,242	27,286
Italy	11,587	14,025	19,107
Netherlands	8,391	8,360	8,946
Pakistan	2,993	4,905	8,145
Portugal	3,459	4,640	6,007
Spain	62,909	70,856	84,122
Türkiye	5,711	7,192	11,150
United Kingdom	5,378	10,859	16,297
USA	9,369	9,924	14,355
Total (incl. others)	263,089	329,405	428,612

* Imports by country of production; exports by country of last consignment.
† Provisional.

Source: Office des Changes, Rabat.

Transport

RAILWAYS
(traffic)*

	2020	2021	2022†
Passengers carried ('000)	22,368	34,482	45,751
Passenger-km (million)	2,721	4,464	6,059
Freight ('000 metric tons)	24,888	25,487	20,832
Freight ton-km (million)	3,122	3,148	2,672

* Figures refer to principal railways only.
† Provisional.

ROAD TRAFFIC
('000 motor vehicles in use at 31 December)

	2019	2020	2021
Passenger cars	3,090.1	3,194.3	3,290.8
Buses and lorries	1,225.9	1,271.7	1,329.0
Motorcycles and mopeds	236.4	266.0	291.7

SHIPPING

Flag Registered Fleet
(at 31 December)

	2020	2021	2022
Number of vessels	456	461	491
Total displacement ('000 grt)	324.2	329.1	352.3

Source: Lloyd's List Intelligence (www.bit.ly/LLintelligence).

International Seaborne Freight Traffic
('000 metric tons)

	2020	2021*	2022*
Goods loaded	33,450	33,086	28,270
Goods unloaded	54,841	54,841	58,857

* Provisional.

CIVIL AVIATION
(commercial traffic)

	2019	2020	2021*
Aircraft movements	210,572	73,251	104,036
Passenger arrivals ('000)	12,436.9	3,489.5	4,793.9
Passenger departures ('000)	12,638.2	3,665.4	5,063.2
Passengers in transit ('000)	119.8	51.4	81.5
Freight (metric tons)	97,516	61,732	70,724

* Preliminary.

Non-commercial traffic: *Aircraft movements:* 25,053 in 2019; 14,163 in 2020; 22,155 in 2021. *Passengers* ('000): 86.2 in 2019; 40.8 in 2020; 72.5 in 2021. *Freight* (metric tons): 1,395 in 2019; 327 in 2020; 743 in 2021.

2022 (commercial traffic, preliminary): Aircraft movements 174,820; Total passengers 20,592,000; Freight 69,751 metric tons.

Tourism

FOREIGN TOURIST ARRIVALS*

Country of nationality	2019	2020	2021
Belgium	272,328	40,603	64,996
France	1,990,813	412,179	493,933
Germany	413,384	79,077	38,894
Italy	351,916	57,105	52,588
Netherlands	241,065	40,909	34,591
Spain	880,818	200,136	99,495
United Kingdom	551,499	113,258	56,435
Maghreb countries	227,281	49,240	46,265
USA	346,702	54,103	66,991
Total (incl. others)	7,043,006	1,407,994	1,284,335

* Excluding Moroccans resident abroad: 5,889,254 in 2019; 1,369,808 in 2020; 2,437,367 in 2021.

Cruise ship passengers: 319,353 in 2009; 475,915 in 2010; 441,629 in 2011.

Source: Ministry of Tourism, Rabat.

Receipts from tourism (US $ million, excl. passenger transport): 3,839 in 2020; 3,817 in 2021 (provisional); 8,985 in 2022 (provisional) (Source: World Tourism Organization).

Communications Media

	2019	2020	2021
Telephones ('000 main lines in use)	2,054.5	2,357.3	2,511.4
Mobile telephones ('000 subscriptions)	46,666.7	49,421.0	51,333.9
Broadband subscriptions, fixed ('000)	1,751.3	2,102.4	2,271.3
Broadband subscriptions, mobile ('000)	23,677.2	27,743.1	30,621.2
Internet users (% of population)*	74.4	84.1	88.1

* Persons aged 5 years and over, in at least one year.

Source: International Telecommunication Union.

2022 ('000, provisional): Telephones 2,645 main lines in use; Mobile telephones 52,959 subscriptions.

Education

(2021/22 unless otherwise indicated)

			Pupils/Students		
Institutions	Teachers	Males	Females	Total
Pre-primary	27,168	31,832	464,034	451,457	915,491
Primary	11,911	175,292	2,429,768	2,245,718	4,675,486
public	8,131	141,529	2,015,237	1,859,361	3,874,598
private	3,780	33,763	414,531	386,357	800,888
Secondary	6,618	149,099*	1,605,811	1,538,571	3,144,382
public college	2,144	62,895	948,835	832,212	1,781,047
private college	1,923	n.a.	104,612	98,084	202,696
public qualifying	1,394	57,489	487,887	547,635	1,035,522
private qualifying	1,157	n.a.	64,477	60,640	125,117
Tertiary	432	21,416†	553,793	617,043	1,170,836
public universities	157	15,830†	502,519	558,737	1,061,256

* 2019/20.
† Permanent teaching staff.

Sources: partly Ministry of Higher Education, Scientific Research and Management Training, Rabat.

Pupil-teacher ratio (qualified teaching staff, primary education, UNESCO estimate): 26.5 in 2020/21 (Source: UNESCO Institute for Statistics).

Adult literacy rate (UNESCO estimates): 75.9% (males 84.8%; females 67.4%) in 2021 (Source: UNESCO Institute for Statistics).

Directory

The Constitution

The following is a summary of the main provisions of the Constitution, as approved in a national referendum on 1 July 2011.

PREAMBLE

The Kingdom of Morocco is founded on the principles of participation, pluralism and good governance, and is a sovereign Islamic state. Acknowledging its diverse heritage and peoples, the Kingdom aims to preserve its singular national identity and territorial integrity. It adheres to the principles, rights and obligations of those international organizations of which it is a member, reaffirms its respect for human rights as they are universally recognized, and works for the preservation of peace and security in the world.

GENERAL PRINCIPLES

Morocco is a constitutional, democratic, parliamentary and social monarchy. Sovereignty pertains to the nation and is exercised directly by means of the referendum and indirectly by the constitutional institutions. The territorial organization of the Kingdom is decentralized. All Moroccans are equal before the law, and all adults enjoy equal political rights including the franchise. Islam is the religion of the state, which guarantees freedom of worship for all. Arabic is the official language of the state. Tamazight also constitutes an official language. There shall be no one-party system.

LIBERTIES AND FUNDAMENTAL RIGHTS

Men and women enjoy, equally, the fundamental civil, economic, political, social, cultural and environmental rights as stipulated by the Constitution. The Kingdom of Morocco strives to achieve equality between men and women, and to fight against discrimination in all forms.

The right to life is the most fundamental right of all human beings, and is protected by the law. No person may be subject to treatment that is cruel, inhuman, degrading or otherwise damaging to their dignity. The use of torture, no matter by whom it is committed, is a crime punishable by law. Arbitrary or secret detention are crimes of the utmost severity and those responsible will be subject to the most severe punishment.

Freedoms of movement, opinion and speech and the rights of assembly and non-violent protest are guaranteed. The freedom of the press and the right of citizens to publish ideas and opinions are inviolable.

All Moroccans shall have equal access to social welfare, health care, education, housing, employment and water. The right to strike, and to private property, is guaranteed. All Moroccans contribute to the defence of the Kingdom and to public costs.

THE MONARCHY

The King, as Commander of the Faithful, ensures respect for Islam and guarantees freedom of worship for all. As head of state, supreme representative, symbol of the unity of the nation, he safeguards the Constitution and guarantees the durability and continuity of the state. The Crown of Morocco and its attendant constitutional rights shall be hereditary in the line of HM King Muhammad VI, and shall be transmitted to the oldest son, unless during his lifetime the King has appointed as his successor another of his sons. The person of the King is inviolable. The King appoints as Prime Minister the leader of the party with the largest representation in the Chamber of Representatives. Upon the Prime Minister's recommendation, the King appoints government ministers, and presides over the Cabinet. The King may, on his own initiative and after consultation with the head of government, dismiss one or more ministers. He shall promulgate adopted legislation within a 30-day period, and has the power to dissolve the Chamber of Representatives and/or the Chamber of Advisers. The sovereign is the Commander-in-Chief of the Armed Forces; makes appointments to civil and military posts; appoints Ambassadors; signs and ratifies treaties; presides over the Supreme Council of Security, the Supreme Council of the Magistracy, the Supreme Council of Education and the Supreme Council for National Reconstruction and Planning; and exercises the right of pardon. In cases of threat to the national territory or to the action of constitutional institutions, the King, having consulted the President of the Chamber of Representatives, the President of the Chamber of Advisers and the Chairman of the Constitutional Council, and after addressing the nation, has the right to declare a State of Emergency by royal decree. The State of Emergency shall not entail the dissolution of Parliament and shall be terminated by the same procedure followed in its proclamation. The fundamental liberties and rights as stipulated by the Constitution shall remain guaranteed under the State of Emergency.

LEGISLATURE

The legislature consists of a bicameral parliament: the Chamber of Representatives and the Chamber of Advisers. The Opposition is an integral component of both chambers. Members of the Chamber of Representatives are elected by direct universal suffrage for a five-year term. Members of the Chamber of Advisers, of whom there shall be no fewer than 90 and no more than 120, are elected for a six-year term. Three-fifths of the members of the Chamber of Advisers are elected by electoral colleges of local councils; the remainder are elected by electoral colleges representing chambers of commerce and trade unions. Deputies in both chambers shall not be arrested or convicted for opinions or votes expressed during the exercise of their functions, except if said opinion represents an attack on the system of monarchy, the religion of Islam or the person of the King. Parliament shall adopt legislation, which may be initiated by members of either chamber or by the Prime Minister. Draft legislation shall be examined consecutively by both parliamentary chambers. If the two chambers fail to agree on the draft legislation the Government may request that a bilateral commission propose a final draft for approval by the chambers. If the chambers do not then adopt the draft, the Government may submit the draft (modified, if need be) to the Chamber of Representatives. Henceforth the draft submitted can be definitively adopted only by absolute majority of the members of the Chamber of Representatives. Parliament holds its meetings during two sessions each year, commencing on the second Friday in October and the second Friday in April.

GOVERNMENT

The Government, composed of the Prime Minister and his or her Ministers, is responsible to the King and Parliament and ensures the execution of laws. After its appointment by the King, the Prime Minister must submit his or her Government's programme to a debate in each of the parliamentary chambers. The Government shall be sworn in to office only after having gained an absolute majority in a vote by the members of the Chamber of Representatives. The Prime Minister is empowered to initiate legislation and to exercise statutory powers except where these are reserved to the King. He or she is responsible for co-ordinating ministerial work.

RELATIONS BETWEEN THE AUTHORITIES

The King may request a second reading, by both Chambers of Parliament, of any draft bill or proposed law. In addition, he may submit proposed legislation to a referendum by decree; and dissolve either Chamber or both if a proposal that has been rejected is approved by referendum. He may also dissolve either Chamber by decree after consulting the President of the Constitutional Court, and addressing the nation, but the succeeding Chamber may not be dissolved within a year of its election, except in the absence of a governing majority. The head of government may also dissolve the Chamber of Representatives by decree, having consulted the King and the Presidents of the Chamber of Representatives and the Constitutional Court. The Chamber of Representatives may force the collective resignation of the Government either by refusing a vote of confidence or by adopting a censure motion. The election of the new Parliament or Chamber shall take place within two months of its dissolution. In the interim period the King shall exercise the legislative powers of Parliament, in addition to those conferred upon him by the Constitution. A censure motion must be signed by at least one-quarter of the Chamber's members, and shall be approved by the Chamber only by an absolute majority vote of its members. The Chamber of Advisers is competent to issue 'warning' motions to the Government and, by a two-thirds' majority, force its resignation.

JUDICIARY

The judiciary is independent. Judges are appointed on the recommendation of the Supreme Council of the Magistracy presided over by the King.

THE CONSTITUTIONAL COURT

The Constitutional Court consists of 12 members, of whom six are appointed by the King, and six members appointed for the same period—three elected by a two-thirds' majority of each parliamentary chamber. The King appoints the Chairman from among the members of the Court. One-third of each category of the Council are renewed every three years. The Council is empowered to judge the validity of legislative elections and referendums, as well as that of organic laws and the rules of procedure of both parliamentary chambers, submitted to it.

REGIONS AND TERRITORIAL COLLECTIVITIES

The territorial collectivities of the Kingdom comprise the regions, governorships, provinces and communes. The governing Councils of the regions and communes are elected by universal suffrage.

THE HIGH AUDIT COUNCIL

The High Audit Council exercises the general supervision of the implementation of fiscal laws. It ensures the regularity of revenues and expenditure operations of the departments legally under its jurisdiction, as it assesses the management of the affairs thereof. It is competent to penalize any breach of the rules governing such operations. Regional audit councils exercise the supervision of the accounts of local assemblies and bodies, and the management of the affairs thereof.

THE ECONOMIC, SOCIAL AND ENVIRONMENTAL COUNCIL

An Economic, Social and Environmental Council shall be established to give its opinion on all matters of an economic, social or environmental nature. Its constitution, organization, prerogatives and rules of procedure shall be determined by an organic law.

GOOD GOVERNANCE

Public services shall be organized according to the principles of equal access for all citizens, of even coverage of the national territory and of continuity of provision. The bodies and organizations in charge of ensuring good governance are independent. The following institutions shall be established: a National Council for Human Rights; a Council for the Moroccan Community Abroad; a Council for Competition; National Institute for Financial Probity and the Prevention of Corruption; a Superior Council for Education, Professional Training and Scientific Research; a Consultative Council for the Family and Children; a Council for Youth Affairs and Associations. An independent Mediator shall defend citizens' rights in their interaction with public bodies, contribute to efforts to uphold the law and promote transparency in the administration of public affairs. All of the above institutions shall present a report to parliament annually.

REVISION OF THE CONSTITUTION

The King, the head of government, the Chamber of Representatives and the Chamber of Advisers are competent to initiate a revision of the Constitution. The King has the right to submit the revision project he initiates directly to a national referendum. A proposal for a revision by either parliamentary chamber shall be adopted only if it receives a two-thirds' majority vote by the chamber's members. Revision projects and proposals shall be submitted to the nation for referendum by royal decree; a revision of the Constitution shall be definitive after approval by referendum. Neither the state, system of

MOROCCO

monarchy, liberties and fundamental rights, nor the prescriptions related to the religion of Islam may be subject to a constitutional revision.

The Government

HEAD OF STATE

Monarch: HM King MOHAMMED VI (acceded 23 July 1999).

CABINET
(September 2023)

A coalition of the Rassemblement National des Indépendants (RNI), Parti de l'Authenticité et de la Modernité (PAM) and Istiqlal.

Prime Minister: AZIZ AKHANNOUCH.
Minister of the Interior: ABDELOUAFI LAFTIT.
Minister of Foreign Affairs, African Co-operation and Moroccan Expatriates: NASSER BOURITA.
Minister of Justice: ABDELLATIF OUAHBI.
Minister of Habous (Religious Endowments) and Islamic Affairs: AHMED TOUFIQ.
Secretary-General of the Government: MOHAMED EL-HAJJOUI.
Minister of the Economy and Finance: NADIA FETTAH ALAOUI.
Minister of Infrastructure and Water: NIZAR BARAKA.
Minister of National Education, Pre-schools and Sports: CHAKIB BENMOUSSA.
Minister of Health and Social Protection: KHALID AÏT TALEB.
Minister of National Planning, Urban Planning, Housing and Urban Policy: FATIMA EZZAHRA EL-MANSOURI.
Minister of Agriculture, Fisheries, Rural Development, Waterways and Forests: MOHAMED SADIKI.
Minister of Economic Inclusion, Small Businesses, Employment and Skills: YOUNES SEKKOURI.
Minister of Industry and Trade: RYAD MEZZOUR.
Minister of Tourism, Handicrafts, and Social and Solidarity Economy: FATIM-ZAHRA AMMOR.
Minister of Higher Education, Scientific Research and Innovation: ABDELLATIF MIRAOUI.
Minister of Energy Transition and Sustainable Development: LEILA BENALI.
Minister of Transport and Logistics: MOHAMED ABDELJALIL.
Minister of Youth, Culture and Communications: MOHAMED MEHDI BENSAID.
Minister of Solidarity, Social Inclusion and Family: AOUATIF HAYAR.
Minister-delegate to the Prime Minister, in charge of the Administration of National Defence: ABDELLATIF LOUDIYI.
Minister-delegate to the Prime Minister, in charge of Investment, Convergence and the Evaluation of Public Policies: MOHCINE JAZOULI.
Minister-delegate to the Minister of the Economy and Finance, in charge of the Budget: FAOUZI LEKJAA.
Minister-delegate to the Prime Minister, in charge of Relations with Parliament, and Government Spokesperson: MUSTAPHA BAITAS.
Minister-delegate to the Prime Minister, in charge of Digital Transition and Administrative Reform: GHITA MEZZOUR.

MINISTRIES

Office of the Prime Minister: Palais Royal, Touarga, Rabat; tel. (53) 7219400; fax (53) 7768656; e-mail courrier@pm.gov.ma; internet www.pm.gov.ma.

Ministry in charge of the Administration of National Defence: Rabat.

Ministry of Agriculture, Fisheries, Rural Development, Waterways and Forests: ave Muhammad V, Quartier Administratif, pl. Abdellah Chefchaouni, BP 607, Rabat; tel. (53) 7665300; internet www.agriculture.gov.ma.

Ministry of Civil Service and the Modernization of the Public Sector: Quartier Administratif, rue Ahmed Cherkaoui, Agdal, BP 1076, Rabat; tel. (53) 7679930; fax (53) 7778438; e-mail info@mmsp.gov.ma; internet www.mmsp.gov.ma.

Ministry of Crafts, Social Economy and Solidarity: Rabat; internet www.artisanat.gov.ma.

Ministry of Culture and Communication: 1 rue Ghandi, Rabat; tel. (53) 7209494; fax (53) 7209400; e-mail contact@minculture.gov.ma; internet www.minculture.gov.ma.

Ministry of the Economy and Finance: blvd Mohammed V, Quartier Administratif, Chellah, Rabat; tel. (53) 7677501; fax (53) 7677526; e-mail internet@finances.gov.ma; internet www.finances.gov.ma.

Ministry of Employment and Social Affairs: rue al-Jommayz, Hay Riad, Rabat; tel. (53) 7760521; fax (53) 7750192; e-mail communication@emploi.gov.ma; internet www.emploi.gov.ma.

Ministry of Energy, Mining, Water and the Environment: rue Abou Marouane Essaadi, BP 6208, Agdal, Rabat; tel. (53) 7688400; fax (53) 7688863; e-mail webmaster@mem.gov.ma; internet www.mem.gov.ma.

Ministry of Foreign Affairs and International Co-operation: ave Franklin Roosevelt, Rabat; tel. (53) 7761125; fax (53) 7765508; internet www.diplomatie.ma.

Ministry in charge of General Affairs and Governance: Quartier Administratif, Agdal, BP 412, Rabat; tel. (53) 7687300; fax (53) 7771697; internet www.affaires-generales.gov.ma.

Ministry of Habous (Religious Endowments) and Islamic Affairs: al-Mechouar Essaid, Rabat; tel. (53) 7766801; fax (53) 7666037; e-mail contact@mhai.gov.ma; internet www.habous.gov.ma.

Ministry of Health: 335 ave Mohammed V, Rabat; tel. (53) 7761025; fax (53) 7763895; e-mail contact@sante.gov.ma; internet www.sante.gov.ma.

Ministry of Higher Education, Scientific Research and Management Training: rue Idriss Al Akbar-Hassan, BP 4500, Rabat; tel. (53) 7217501; fax (53) 7217547; e-mail enssup@enssup.gov.ma; internet www.enssup.gov.ma.

Ministry of Housing and Urban Policy: rues al-Jouaze and al-Joumaize, Hay Riad, Secteur 16, 10000 Rabat; tel. (53) 7577372; fax (53) 7577078; e-mail contact@mhpv.gov.ma; internet www.mhpv.gov.ma.

Ministry of Industry, Trade, Investment and the Digital Economy: Quartier administratif, Rabat; tel. (53) 7765227; fax (53) 7766265; e-mail ministre@mcinet.gov.ma; internet www.mcinet.gov.ma.

Ministry of Infrastructure, Transport and Logistics: Quartier Administratif, Chellah, Rabat; tel. (53) 7684151; fax (53) 7764825; e-mail sg@mtpnet.gov.ma; internet www.mtpnet.gov.ma.

Ministry of the Interior: Quartier Administratif, Chellah, Rabat; tel. (53) 7761868; fax (53) 7762056.

Ministry of Justice and Liberties: pl. Mamounia, BP 1015, Rabat; tel. (53) 7213737; internet www.justice.gov.ma.

Ministry in charge of Moroccans Resident Abroad and Migration: angle ave de France et rue Oum Erbii, Agdal, Rabat; tel. (53) 7776588; fax (53) 7770006; e-mail info@mcmre.gov.ma; internet marocainsdumonde.gov.ma.

Ministry of National Education and Vocational Training: Bab Rouah, Rabat; tel. (53) 7771822; fax (53) 7687255; e-mail contact@men.gov.ma; internet www.men.gov.ma.

Ministry in charge of Relations with Parliament and Civil Society: Nouveau Quartier Administratif, Agdal, Rabat; tel. (53) 7683440; fax (53) 7777719; e-mail contact@mcrpsc.gov.ma; internet www.mcrp.gov.ma.

Ministry of Solidarity, Women, Family and Social Development: 47 ave ibn Sina, Agdal, Rabat; tel. (53) 7684062; fax (53) 7671967; internet www.social.gov.ma.

Ministry of Tourism: Centre d'Affaires-Aile Sud, Lot 1 C17, ave Ennakhil-Hay Riad, Rabat; tel. (53) 7577800; fax (53) 7577901; e-mail webmaster@tourisme.gov.ma; internet www.tourisme.gov.ma.

Ministry of Youth and Sports: ave ibn Sina, Agdal, Rabat; tel. (53) 7271482; e-mail secgen@mjs.gov.ma; internet www.mjs.gov.ma.

Legislature

CHAMBER OF REPRESENTATIVES

Chamber of Representatives: POB 431, Rabat; tel. (53) 7679500; fax (53) 7767726; e-mail parlement@parlement.ma; internet www.parlement.ma.

President: RACHID TALBI ALAMI.

MOROCCO

General Election, 8 September 2021

Party	Seats
Rassemblement National des Indépendants (RNI)	102
Parti de l'Authenticité et de la Modernité (PAM)	87
Istiqlal	81
Union Socialiste des Forces Populaires (USFP)	34
Mouvement Populaire (MP)	28
Parti du Progrès et du Socialisme (PPS)	22
Union Constitutionnelle (UC)	18
Parti de la Justice et du Développement (PJD)	13
Mouvement Démocratique et Social (MDS)	5
Front des Forces Démocratiques (FFD)	3
Fédération de la Gauche Démocratique (FGD)	1
Parti Socialiste Unifié (PSU)	1
Total	**395***

* Of the total number of seats, 305 seats are reserved for candidates from local party lists, while the remaining 90 seats are allocated to candidates from national lists. Each party must allocate two-thirds of its share of those 90 seats to women and the remaining one-third to men under 40 years of age.

CHAMBER OF ADVISERS

Chamber of Advisers: POB 432, Rabat; tel. (53) 7218304; fax (53) 7733192; e-mail info@conseiller.ma; internet www.chambredesconseillers.ma.

President: NAAM MIYARA.

Election, 2 October 2015*

Party	Seats
Istiqlal	24
Parti de l'Authenticité et de la Modernité (PAM)	23
Parti de la Justice et du Développement (PJD)	12
Mouvement Populaire (MP)	10
Rassemblement National des Indépendants (RNI)	8
Union Socialiste des Forces Populaires (USFP)	8
Union Constitutionnelle (UC)	3
Mouvement Démocratique et Social (MDS)	3
Parti du Progrès et du Socialisme (PPS)	2
Parti Al Ahd Démocratique	1
Parti de la Réforme et du Développement (PND)	1
Trade unions	20
Independents	8
Total	**120**

* Of the chamber's 120 members, 72 were elected by regional councils, 20 by an electoral college at regional level by members of professional associations in the agriculture, arts and crafts, commerce, industry and services, and marine fisheries sectors, 20 by trade unions and eight by regional employers' associations.

Political Organizations

Fédération de la Gauche: Rabat; f. 2022; created as a merger of Congrès National Ittihadi and Parti de l'Avant-Garde Démocratique et Socialiste, and Gauche Unioniste; Sec.-Gen. ABDESLAM EL-AZIZ.

Front des Forces Démocratiques (FFD): 13 ave Tariq ibn Ziad, Hassan, Rabat; tel. (53) 7661625; fax (53) 7660621; f. 1997 after split from PPS; Sec.-Gen. MUSTAPHA BENALI.

Istiqlal (Independence): 4 ave Ibn Toumert, Bab el-Had, 50020 Rabat; tel. (53) 7730951; fax (53) 7725417; e-mail istiqlal.info2018@gmail.com; internet www.istiqlal.info; f. 1944; aims to raise living standards and to confer equal rights on all; emphasizes the Moroccan claim to Western Sahara; Sec.-Gen. NIZAR BARAKA.

Mouvement Démocratique et Social (MDS): 4 ave Imam Malik, route des Zaërs, Rabat; tel. (57) 7631552; fax (53) 7658253; f. 1996 as Mouvement National Démocratique et Social after split from Mouvement National Populaire; adopted current name Nov. 1996; Sec.-Gen. ABDESSAMAD ARCHANE.

Mouvement Populaire (MP): 66 rue Patrice Lumumba, Rabat; tel. (53) 7766431; fax (53) 7767537; e-mail parti_mp@hotmail.fr; internet www.alharaka.ma; f. 1958; merged with the MNP and Union Démocratique 2006; liberal; Sec.-Gen. MOHAMMED OUZZINE.

Parti de l'Action (PA): 113 ave Allal Ben Abdallah, Rabat; tel. (53) 7206661; f. 1974; advocates democracy and progress; Sec.-Gen. MUHAMMAD EL-IDRISSI.

Parti Al Ahd Démocratique: 14 rue Idriss al-Akbar, rue Tafraout, Hassan, Rabat; tel. (53) 7204816; fax (53) 7204786; f. 2002; Sec.-Gen. ABDELMOUNAIM EL-FATTAHI.

Parti de l'Authenticité et de la Modernité (PAM): 33 rue Mohammed VI, Souissi, Rabat; tel. (53) 7756900; fax (53) 7751910; e-mail communication@pam.ma; internet www.pam.ma; f. 2008; Founder FOUAD ALI EL-HIMMA; Sec.-Gen. ABDELLATIF OUAHBI.

Parti Démocrate National (PDN): f. May 2009 by fmr members of Parti National Démocrate, following that party's merger into PAM; Sec.-Gen. MOUSSA SAÏDI.

Parti Démocratique et de l'Indépendance (PDI): 9 Lalla Yakout, rue Araar, Apt 11, 2ème étage, blvd d'Anfa, Casablanca; tel. (52) 2200949; fax (52) 2200928; f. 1946; Sec.-Gen. AHMED BELGHAZI.

Parti de l'Environnement et du Développement Durable (PEDD): 25 ave Muhammad Abdou, Agdal, Rabat; tel. and fax (53) 7670620; internet www.pedmaroc.ma; f. 2002 as Parti de l'Environnement et du Développement; merged with PAM 2008; relaunched as above 2009; environmentalist; Sec.-Gen. Dr KARIM HRITANE.

Parti de l'Equité (PEQ): 16 rue Sebou, Apt 5, Agdal, Rabat; tel. (53) 7777266; fax (53) 7777452; e-mail partipre@yahoo.fr; internet www.peq.ma; f. 2002; Pres. CHAQUIR ACHEHBAR.

Parti des Forces Citoyennes (PFC): 353 blvd Mohammed V, 9ème étage, Casablanca; tel. (52) 2400608; fax (52) 2400613; f. 2001; Sec.-Gen. (vacant).

Parti de la Justice et du Développement (PJD): ave Abdelwahed Elmorakechi, rue Elyafrani, 4 les Orangers, Rabat; tel. (53) 7208862; fax (53) 7208854; e-mail pjdcontact@gmail.com; internet www.pjd.ma; f. 1967 as Mouvement Populaire Constitutionnel et Démocratique; breakaway party from MP; formally absorbed mems of the Islamic asscn Al Islah wa Attajdid June 1996; present name adopted 1998; Sec.-Gen. ABDELILAH BENKIRANE.

Parti Marocain Libéral (PML): 114 ave Allal Ben Abdallah, 2ème étage, Rabat; tel. (53) 7733604; fax (53) 7734452; internet www.pml.ma; f. 2002; Nat. Co-ordinator ISAAC CHARIA.

Parti du Progrès et du Socialisme (PPS): 29 ave Muhammad VI, Youssoufia, Rabat; tel. (53) 7540999; fax (53) 7540992; e-mail contact@pps.ma; internet www.ppsmaroc.com; f. 1974; successor to Parti Communiste Marocain (banned 1952) and Parti de la Libération et du Socialisme (banned 1969); left-wing; advocates modernization, social progress, nationalization and democracy; 35,000 mems; Sec.-Gen. MUHAMMAD NABIL BENABDELLAH.

Parti de la Réforme et du Développement (PRD): 34 ave Pasteur, Rabat; tel. and fax (53) 7703801; internet www.prd.ma; f. 2001 by fmr mems of RNI; Sec.-Gen. ABDUL RAHMAN AL-KOHEN.

Parti de la Renaissance et de la Vertu: Bouznika; f. 2005; national democratic party based on the principles of Islam; Sec.-Gen. MOHAMED KHALIDI.

Parti Socialiste Unifié (PSU): 9 rue d'Agadir, Immeuble Maréchal Ameziane, Casablanca; tel. (52) 2485902; fax (52) 2278442; e-mail psumaroc@yahoo.fr; internet psu.ma; f. 2005 by merger of Parti de la Gauche Socialiste Unifieé and Fidélité à la Démocratie; created Fédération de la Gauche Démocratique with the Congrès National Ittihadi and the Parti de l'Avant-garde Démocratique Socialiste Jan. 2014; Sec.-Gen. NABILA MOUNIB.

Rassemblement National des Indépendants (RNI): 6 rue Laos, ave Hassan II, Rabat; tel. (53) 7716168; fax (53) 7563402; internet www.rni.ma; f. 1978 from the pro-Govt independents' group that then formed the majority in the Chamber of Representatives; Sec.-Gen. AZIZ AKHANNOUCH.

Union Constitutionnelle (UC): 158 ave des Forces Armées Royales, Casablanca; tel. (52) 2441145; fax (52) 2441141; e-mail belmkadem99@gmail.com; internet www.possible.ma; f. 1983; Sec.-Gen. MOHAMED JOUDAR.

Union Marocaine pour la Démocratie (UMD): Rabat; f. 2006; Sec.-Gen. JAMAL EL-MANDRI.

Union Socialiste des Forces Populaires (USFP): 9 ave al-Araâr, Hay Riad, Rabat; tel. (53) 7565511; fax (53) 7565510; e-mail usfp@usfp.ma; internet www.usfp.ma; f. 1959 as Union Nationale des Forces Populaires (UNFP); became USFP in 1974 after UNFP split into 2 separate entities; merged with Parti Socialiste Démocratique 2005; merged with Parti Travailliste and Parti Socialiste 2013; democratic socialist and progressive party; First Sec. DRISS LACHGAR.

The following movement is not authorized as a political party by the Government, but is generally tolerated:

Al-Adl wal-Ihsan (Justice and Charity): fax (53) 7810519; e-mail tawassol@aljamaa.net; internet www.aljamaa.net; advocates an Islamic state based on *Shari'a* law; rejects violence; Sec.-Gen. MUHAMMAD ABBADI.

The following group is active in the disputed territory of Western Sahara:

Frente Popular para la Liberación de Saguia el-Hamra y Río de Oro (Frente Polisario) (Polisario Front): BP 10, el-Mouradia, Algiers, Algeria; fax (2) 747206; f. 1973 to gain independence for Western Sahara, first from Spain and then from Morocco and Mauritania; signed peace treaty with Mauritanian Govt 1979; supported by Algerian Govt; in February 1976 proclaimed the Sahrawi Arab Democratic Republic (SADR); admitted as the 51st mem. of the OAU Feb. 1982; recognized by more than 80 countries worldwide in 2023; its main organs are a 33-mem. Nat. Secretariat, a 101-mem. Sahrawi Nat. Assembly (Parliament) and a 13-mem. Govt; Pres. of the SADR and Sec.-Gen. of the Polisario Front BRAHIM GHALI; Prime Minister of the SADR BUCHARAYA HAMUDI BEYUN.

Diplomatic Representation

EMBASSIES IN MOROCCO

Angola: km 5, 53 Ahmed Rifaï, BP 1318, Souissi, Rabat; tel. (53) 7659239; fax (53) 7653703; e-mail amb.angola@menara.ma; internet www.embaixada-angola-marrocos.org; Ambassador BERNARDO MBALA DOMBELE.

Argentina: 4 ave Mehdi Ben Barka, Souissi, 10170 Rabat; tel. (53) 7755120; fax (53) 7755410; e-mail emarr@mrecic.gov.ar; internet emarr.mrecic.gov.ar; Ambassador RAUL IGNACIO GUASTAVINO.

Australia: 66 ave Mehdi Ben Barka, Souissi, 10000 Rabat; tel. (53) 7543366; e-mail rabat@dfat.gov.au; internet morocco.embassy.gov.au; Ambassador MICHAEL GRAEME BRUCE CUTTS.

Austria: 2 rue Tiddas, BP 135, 10000 Rabat; tel. (53) 7761698; fax (53) 7765425; e-mail rabat-ob@bmeia.gv.at; internet www.bmeia.gv.at/oeb-rabat; Ambassador Dr ANNA JANKOVIĆ.

Azerbaijan: 50 ave Ould Saïd, Souissi, Rabat; tel. (53) 7751325; fax (53) 7751201; e-mail rabat@mission.mfa.gov.az; internet rabat.mfa.gov.az; Ambassador NAZIM SAMADOV.

Bahrain: Villa 318, rue Béni Hassan, BP 1470, Souissi, Rabat; tel. (53) 7633500; fax (53) 7630732; e-mail rabat.mission@mofa.gov.bh; internet www.mofa.gov.bh/rabat; Ambassador KHALID BIN SALMAN BIN JABR AL-MUSALLAM.

Bangladesh: 25 ave Tarek ibn Ziad, BP 1468, 10010 Rabat; tel. (53) 7766731; fax (53) 7766729; e-mail mission.rabat@mofa.gov.bd; internet rabat.mofa.gov.bd; Ambassador MD SHAHDAT HOSSAIN.

Belgium: rue Mohammed Ben Hassan El Ouazzani et rue Mejjat, Souissi, Rabat; tel. (53) 7268060; fax (53) 7767003; e-mail rabat@diplobel.fed.be; internet morocco.diplomatie.belgium.be; Ambassador VÉRONIQUE PETIT.

Benin: 30 ave Mehdi Ben Barka, BP 5187, Souissi, 10105 Rabat; tel. (53) 7754158; fax (53) 7754156; e-mail ambassey.rabat@gouv.bj; internet ambaben.ma; Ambassador SERGE DAGNON.

Brazil: 38 rue Mohamed Bahraoui, Souissi, 10220 Rabat; tel. (53) 7572730; fax (53) 7714808; e-mail brasemb.rabat@itamaraty.gov.br; internet rabat.itamaraty.gov.br; Ambassador ALEXANDRE GUIDO (designate).

Bulgaria: 4 ave Ahmed el-Yazidi, BP 1301, 10000 Rabat; tel. (53) 7765477; fax (53) 7763201; e-mail embassy.rabat@mfa.bg; internet www.mfa.bg/embassies/morocco; Ambassador PLAMEN STOYANOV TZOLOV.

Burkina Faso: 7 rue al-Bouziri, BP 6484, Agdal, 10101 Rabat; tel. (53) 7675512; fax (53) 7675517; e-mail burkinafasoambassade@yahoo.fr; internet ma.ambaburkina.org; Ambassador MAMADOU COULIBALY.

Burundi: 11 rue Ait Hani, Souissi, 10000 Rabat; tel. (53) 7753497; Ambassador NESTOR BANKUMUKUNZI.

Cameroon: 20 rue du Rif, BP 1790, Souissi, Rabat; tel. (53) 7758818; fax (53) 7750540; e-mail ambacam_rabat@ymail.com; internet www.ambacamrabat.ma; Ambassador MOUHAMADOU YOUSSIFOU.

Canada: 66 ave Mehdi Ben Barka, BP 2040, Souissi, Rabat; tel. (53) 7544949; fax (53) 7544853; e-mail rabat@international.gc.ca; internet www.morocco.gc.ca; Ambassador NELL STEWART.

Central African Republic: 65, rue 29 Youssoufia est-ext. de l'etat, BP 770, Agdal, 10000 Rabat; tel. (53) 7658970; e-mail centrafriquemaghreb1@yahoo.fr; internet fb.com/centrafrique.diplomatie; Chargé d'affaires a.i. JEAN WENZOUÏ.

Chad: angle rue Ouled Farès et rue Ihou Derrane, Souissi-Bir Kacem, 10170 Rabat; tel. (53) 7632102; e-mail ambassade.tchad@menara.ma; internet www.fb.com/ambatchadrabat; Ambassador HASSAN ADOUM BAKHIT HAGGAR.

Chile: 66 rue Beni Arouss et rue Ain Seghrouchen, Souissi, 10170 Rabat; tel. (53) 7636065; fax (53) 7636067; e-mail echile.marruecos@minrel.gob.cl; internet chile.gob.cl/marruecos; Ambassador RAFAEL PUELMA CLARO.

China, People's Republic: 16 ave Ahmed Balafrej, 10000 Rabat; tel. (53) 7754056; fax (53) 7757519; e-mail chinaemb_ma@mfa.gov.cn; internet ma.china-embassy.org; Ambassador LI CHANGLIN.

Colombia: 66 rue Beni Aarousse et Aït Seghrouchen, Souissi, Rabat; tel. (53) 7751768; fax (53) 7754283; e-mail erabat@cancilleria.gov.co; internet marruecos.embajada.gov.co; Ambassador JOSÉ SALAZAR ACOSTA.

Comoros: 204 rue N. Dee, Rabat; Ambassador YAHAYA MOHAMED ILLIAS.

Congo, Democratic Republic: 34 ave de la Victoire, BP 553, 10000 Rabat; tel. (53) 7262280; Ambassador HENRI MANGAYA.

Congo, Republic: 197 ave Général Abdendi Britel, Souissi II, Rabat; tel. (53) 7262280; fax (53) 7207407; e-mail ambardcrabat60@yahoo.fr; Ambassador JEAN MARIE MOWELLE.

Côte d'Ivoire: 7 rue Ould Said, BP 192, Souissi, Rabat; tel. (53) 7655770; fax (53) 7655637; e-mail ambci_maroc@yahoo.fr; internet www.maroc.diplomatie.gouv.ci; Ambassador IDRISSA TRAORE.

Croatia: 73 rue Marnissa, Souissi, Rabat; tel. (53) 7638824; fax (53) 7638827; e-mail vrhrabat@mvep.hr; internet ma.mvep.hr; Ambassador JASNA MILETA.

Cuba: 44 angle rue Massa et Ait Baha, Souissi, Rabat; tel. (53) 7753392; e-mail embajada@ma.embacuba.cu; internet misiones.minrex.gob.cu/es/marruecos; Ambassador JAVIER DOMOKOS RUIZ.

Czech Republic: Villa Merzaa, km 4.5, ave Muhammad VI, rue Zankat Aït Melloul, BP 410, Souissi, 10000 Rabat; tel. (53) 7755420; fax (53) 7754393; e-mail rabat@embassy.mzv.cz; internet www.mzv.cz/rabat; Ambassador LADISLAV SKEŘÍK.

Denmark: 14 rue Tiddas angle rue Roudana, Quartier Hassan, 10020 Rabat; tel. (53) 7665020; fax (53) 7660581; e-mail rbaamb@um.dk; internet marokko.um.dk; Ambassador JASPER KAMMERSGAARD.

Djibouti: 28 rue Bani Boufrah, Ghandouri, Souissi, Rabat; tel. (53) 7754900; e-mail djibmaamb@gmail.com; internet fr.ambassadedjibma.com; Ambassador MOHAMED DOUHOUR HERSI.

Dominican Republic: 1 ave Mohammed Bel Hassan El Ouazzani, Souissi, 10105 Rabat; tel. (53) 7715905; fax (53) 7715957; e-mail embdomrabat@gmail.com; internet republiquedominicaine.ma; Ambassador AMAURY JUSTO DUARTE.

Egypt: 31 rue al-Jazair, 10000 Rabat; tel. (53) 7731833; fax (53) 7706821; e-mail embegypt@mtds.com; Ambassador YASSER OTHMAN.

El Salvador: Rabat; Ambassador IGNACIO DE COSSÍO PEREZ DE MENDOZA.

Equatorial Guinea: ave President Roosevelt, angle rue d'Agadir 9, Rabat; tel. and fax (53) 7660337; Ambassador SALOMON NFA NDONG NSENG.

Eswatini: Rabat; tel. (53) 7656595; internet mae eswatini-embassy.ma; Chargé d'affaires a.i. SIPHELELE W. DLUDLU.

Ethiopia: 10 rue Mernissa, rue Mohamed el-Ghazi, Souissi, Rabat; tel. (53) 7653619; fax (53) 7673628; e-mail ethembrabat@gmail.com; internet www.rabat.mfa.gov.et; Ambassador ISAIAS GOTA.

Finland: 6 rue Beni Ritoune, Souissi, 10002 Rabat; tel. (53) 7658775; fax (53) 7658904; e-mail sanomat.rab@formin.fi; internet www.finlande.ma; Ambassador PEKKA HYVÖNEN.

France: 1 rue Ibn Hajar, BP 577, Agdal, 10190 Rabat; tel. (53) 7689700; fax (53) 7276711; internet www.ambafrance-ma.org; Ambassador CHRISTOPHE LE COURTIER.

Gabon: 72 ave Mehdi Ben Barka, Souissi, 10170 Rabat; tel. (53) 7751950; fax (53) 7757550; e-mail chancellerie@ambagabon.ma; internet www.ambagabon.ma; Ambassador SYLVER MINKO MI-NSEME.

The Gambia: 6 rue Jabal al-Ayachi, Agdal, Rabat; tel. (53) 7638045; fax (53) 7752908; Ambassador SAFFIE LOWE CEESAY.

Germany: 7 Zankat Madnine, BP 235, 10000 Rabat; tel. (53) 7218600; fax (53) 7706851; e-mail info@rabat.diplo.de; internet www.rabat.diplo.de; Ambassador ROBERT DÖLGER.

Ghana: 27 rue Ghomara, La Pinede, Souissi, Rabat; tel. (53) 7757620; e-mail rabat@mfa.gov.gh; internet ghanaembassy-morocco.com; Ambassador SAMUEL JOJO EFFAH-BRONI.

Greece: 18 rue Aït Hdidou, Souissi, Rabat; tel. (53) 7638964; fax (53) 7638990; e-mail gremb.rab@mfa.gr; internet www.mfa.gr/missionsabroad/morocco; Ambassador NICOLAS ARGYROS.

Guatemala: 78 rue Tafilalte, Souissi-Rabat, 10100 Rabat; tel. (53) 7639947; e-mail ambaguatemalarabat@gmail.com; internet www.marruecos.minex.gob.gt; Ambassador ERICK ESTUARDO ESCOBEDO AYALA.

Guinea: 15 rue Hamzah, Agdal, 10000 Rabat; tel. (53) 7674148; fax (53) 7675070; e-mail ambaguirabat@mae.gov.gn; Ambassador ABOUBACAR DIONE.

Guinea-Bissau: Villa 31, rue Attarajil, Secteur 11, Hay Ryad, Rabat; tel. (53) 7572144; e-mail embaguibismamaroc@gmail.com; Ambassador FILOMENA MENDES MASCARENHAS TIPOTE.

Haiti: Rabat; Chargé d'affaires JOSUÉ JEAN.

Holy See: rue Béni M'tir, BP 1303, Souissi, Rabat (Apostolic Nunciature); tel. and fax (53) 7653536; Apostolic Nuncio (vacant).

Hungary: route des Zaêrs, 17 Zankat Aït Melloul, BP 5026, Souissi, Rabat; tel. (53) 7750757; fax (53) 7754123; e-mail mission.rba@mfa.gov.hu; internet rabat.mfa.gov.hu; Ambassador MIKLÓS TROMLER.

India: 88 rue Oulad Tidrarine, Souissi, Rabat; tel. (53) 7635801; fax (53) 7634733; e-mail amb.rabat@mea.gov.in; internet indianembassyrabat.gov.in; Ambassador RAJESH VAISHNAW.

Indonesia: 63 rue Béni Boufrah, km 6, route des Zaêrs, BP 576, 10000 Rabat; tel. (53) 7757860; fax (53) 7757859; e-mail rabat.kbri@kemlu.go.id; internet www.kemlu.go.id/rabat; Ambassador HASRUL AZWAR.

Iraq: 39 blvd Mehdi Ben Barka, 10100 Rabat; tel. (53) 7754466; fax (53) 7759749; Chargé d'affaires BOTAN DIZAYEE.

Ireland: Rabat Mahaj Ryad Centre, 8 ave Attine Bâtiment, Hay Ryad, Rabat; internet www.dfa.ie/irish-embassy/morocco/; Ambassador JAMES MCINTYRE.

Israel: ave Mehdi Ben Barka, Souissi, Rabat; tel. (53) 7631976; e-mail info@rabat.mfa.gov.il; Ambassador ALONA FISHER.

Italy: 2 rue Idriss al-Azhar, BP 111, 10001 Rabat; tel. (53) 7219730; fax (53) 7706882; e-mail ambassade.rabat@esteri.it; internet www.ambrabat.esteri.it; Ambassador ARMANDO BARUCCO.

Japan: 39 ave Ahmed Balafrej, Souissi, 10170 Rabat; tel. (53) 7631782; fax (53) 7750078; internet www.ma.emb-japan.go.jp; Ambassador HIDEAKI KURAMITSU.

Jordan: 25 Villa Dhahr Tamae, ave Mohamed Belhassane el-Ouazzani, Souissi, Rabat; tel. (53) 7751125; fax (53) 7658198; e-mail jo.am@iam.net.ma; Ambassador JUMANA GHUNAIMAT.

Kazakhstan: 3 rue Beni Mtir, Souissi, 10170 Rabat; e-mail kazembmar@gmail.com; Ambassador SAULEKUL SAILAUKYZY.

Korea, Republic: 41 ave Mehdi Ben Barka, Souissi, 10100 Rabat; tel. (53) 7751767; fax (53) 7750189; internet overseas.mofa.go.kr/ma-ko/index.do; Ambassador CHUNG KEE-YONG.

Kuwait: 28 rue Beer-Qasim, BP 11, Souissi, Rabat; tel. (53) 7631111; fax (53) 7753591; e-mail mofa.gov.kw@al-rabat; Ambassador ABDULLATIF ALI ABDULLAH AL-YAHYA.

Lebanon: 114 ave Abd el-Malek Ben Marouane, Rabat; tel. (53) 7656949; fax (53) 7657195; Ambassador ZIAD ATALLAH.

Liberia: 23 rue Qadi Ben Hamadi Senhaji, Souissi, 10170 Rabat; tel. and fax (53) 7638426; Ambassador (vacant).

Libya: km 5.5, route de Zaêrs, ave Imam Malik, Souissi, Rabat; tel. (53) 7631871; fax (53) 7631877; Chargé d'affaires ABU BAKR AL-TAWEEL.

Malaysia: 307 rue Bani Yidder, Souissi, Rabat; tel. (53) 7658324; fax (53) 7658363; e-mail mwrabat@kln.gov.my; internet www.kln.gov.my/web/mar_rabat; Ambassador Dato ASTANAH ABDULAZIZ.

Mali: 7 rue Thami Lamdouar, Souissi, Rabat; tel. (53) 7759121; fax (53) 7754742; e-mail ambamalirabat@gmail.com; Ambassador MOHAMED MAHAMOUD BEN LABBAT.

Mauritania: 6 rue Thami Lamdouar, BP 207, Souissi, 10000 Rabat; tel. (53) 7656678; fax (53) 7656680; internet www.ambarimrabat.ma; Ambassador MOHAMED HANANI.

Mexico: Villa B2, ave Abderrahim Bouabid, Secteur 22, Hay Ryad, 10100 Rabat; tel. (53) 7631969; fax (53) 7631971; e-mail infomexmar@sre.gob.mx; internet embamex.sre.gob.mx/marruecos; Ambassador MABEL DEL PILAR GÓMEZ OLIVER.

Netherlands: 40 rue de Tunis, BP 329, Hassan, 10001 Rabat; tel. (53) 7219600; fax (53) 7219665; e-mail rab-cdp@minbuza.nl; internet www.paysbasetvous.nl/votre-pays-et-les-pays-bas/maroc; Ambassador JEROEN ROODENBURG.

Niger: A4 ave al-Haour, Secteur 7, Hay Ryad, Rabat; tel. (53) 7566839; fax (53) 7566840; e-mail contact@embassyniger-ma.org; internet ambassadeniger-ma.org; Ambassador SALISSOU ADA.

Nigeria: 70 ave Omar ibn al-Khattab, BP 347, Agdal, Rabat; tel. (53) 7671857; fax (53) 7672739; e-mail nigerianrabat@menara.ma; internet rabat.foreignaffairs.gov.ng; Ambassador ALBASHIR IBRAHIM SALEH AL-HUSSAINI.

Norway: 6 rue Beni Ritoune, BP 757, Agdal, Souissi, 10106 Rabat; tel. (53) 7664200; fax (53) 7664291; e-mail emb.rabat@mfa.no; internet www.norway.no/morocco; Ambassador SJUR LARSEN.

Oman: 21 rue Hamza, Agdal, 10000 Rabat; tel. (53) 7673788; fax (53) 7674567; Ambassador Dr SAEED BIN MUHAMMAD AL-BARAMI.

Pakistan: 37 ave Ahmed Balafrej, Souissi, Rabat; tel. (53) 7631192; fax (53) 7631243; e-mail pareprabat@mofa.gov.pk; internet mofa.gov.pk/rabat-morocco; Ambassador HAMID ASGHAR KHAN.

Panama: 7 rue Eulophia, Secteur 15, Bloc 7, Hay Ryad, Rabat; tel. (53) 7715404; e-mail embpanamarabat@mire.gob.pa; Ambassador TOMÁS A. GUARDIA.

Paraguay: 51 rue Ibrahim Tadili, Souissi, 10170 Rabat; tel. (53) 7632350; fax (53) 7656743; e-mail embparaguay@menara.ma; Ambassador VICTOR HUGO RAMON PANIAGUA FRETES.

Peru: 16 rue d'Ifrane, 10000 Rabat; tel. (53) 7723236; fax (53) 7702803; e-mail leprurabat@menara.com; Ambassador FÉLIX ARTURO CHIPOCO CACEDA.

Philippines: 23 rue Bani Ritoune, Souissi, 10170 Rabat; internet rabatpe.dfa.gov.ph; Ambassador LESLIE J. BAJA.

Poland: 23 rue Oqbah, Agdal, BP 425, 10000 Rabat; tel. (53) 7771173; fax (53) 7775320; e-mail rabat.amb.sekretariat@msz.gov.pl; internet www.gov.pl/web/maroc; Ambassador KRZYSZTOF KARWOWSKI.

Portugal: 5 rue Thami Lamdouar, Souissi, 10100 Rabat; tel. (53) 7756446; fax (53) 7756445; e-mail rabat@mne.pt; internet www.rabat.embaixadaportugal.mne.pt; Ambassador CARLOS JOSÉ DE PINHO E MELO PEREIRA MARQUES.

Qatar: 20 al-Zarhoon, BP 1220, Souissi, 10001 Rabat; tel. (53) 7544544; fax (53) 7544500; e-mail rabat@mofa.gov.qa; internet rabat.embassy.qa; Ambassador ABDULLAH BIN THAMER BIN MOHAMMED BIN THANI AL THANI.

Romania: 10 rue d'Ouezzane, Hassan, 10000 Rabat; tel. (53) 7724694; fax (53) 7700196; e-mail rabat@mae.ro; internet rabat.mae.ro; Ambassador MARIA CIOBANU.

Russian Federation: km 4, ave Mohammed VI, Souissi, Rabat; tel. (53) 7753509; fax (53) 7753590; e-mail ambrusmaroc@inbox.ru; internet www.marocco.mid.ru; Ambassador VLADIMIR BAYBAKOV.

Rwanda: 6 rue Midelt, Hassan, Rabat; e-mail ambassaderabat@minaffet.gov.rw; Ambassador SHAKILA KAZIMBAYA UMUTONI (designate).

Saudi Arabia: 322 ave Imam Malik, km 3.5, route des Zaêrs, Rabat; tel. (53) 7633000; fax (53) 7639696; e-mail maemb@mofa.gov.sa; internet embassies.mofa.gov.sa/sites/Morocco; Ambassador ABDULLAH BIN SAAD AL-GHURAIRI.

Senegal: 17 rue Cadi Ben Hamadi Senhaji, Souissi, BP 365, 10000 Rabat; tel. (53) 7754171; fax (53) 7754149; e-mail ambassene@menara.ma; Ambassador SEYNABOU DIAL.

Serbia: 24 rue el Kadi Ahmed Mouline, BP 5014, Souissi, 10105 Rabat; tel. (53) 7752201; fax (53) 7753258; e-mail ambrsrabat@gmail.com; internet rabat.mfa.gov.rs; Ambassador IVAN BAUER.

Sierra Leone: Rabat; Ambassador ATUMANNI DAINKEH.

South Africa: 34 rue Saâdiens, Quartier Hassan, 10100 Rabat; tel. (53) 7689159; fax (53) 7724550; e-mail sudaf@mtds.com; Ambassador EBRAHIM EDRIES.

South Sudan: Rabat; Ambassador RIEK PUOK RIEK.

Spain: 3 rue Aïn Khalouiya, ave Mohammed VI, km 5.3, route des Zaêrs, Souissi, 10000 Rabat; tel. (53) 7633900; fax (53) 7630600; e-mail emb.rabat@maec.es; internet www.exteriores.gob.es/embajadas/rabat; Ambassador RICARDO DÍEZ-HOCHLEITNER RODRÍGUEZ.

Sudan: 5 ave Ghomara, Souissi, 10000 Rabat; tel. (53) 7752864; fax (53) 7752865; Ambassador MAWADDA EL-BADAWI.

Sweden: 159 ave Mohammed VI, BP 428, Souissi, 10001 Rabat; tel. (53) 7633210; fax (53) 7758048; e-mail ambassaden.rabat@gov.se; internet www.swedenabroad.com/rabat; Ambassador JÖRGEN KARLSSON.

Switzerland: sq. de Berkane, BP 169, 10000 Rabat; tel. (53) 7268030; fax (53) 7268040; e-mail rabat@eda.admin.ch; internet www.eda.admin.ch/rabat; Ambassador GUILLAUME SCHEURER.

Thailand: 10 rue Kadib Addahab, Secteur 6, Bloc G, Hay Ryad, Rabat; tel. (53) 7634603; fax (53) 7634607; e-mail thaima@menara.ma; internet www.thaiembassy.org/rabat; Ambassador FABIO JINDA.

Togo: 1000 Rabat; e-mail ambassadeatogorabat@hotmail.com; Chargé d'affaires a.i. MESSAN AMAKOÉ KLUTSE.

Tunisia: 6 ave de Fès et 1 rue d'Ifrane, 10000 Rabat; tel. (53) 7730636; fax (53) 7730637; Ambassador MOHAMED BEN ABBAD (recalled Aug. 2022).

Türkiye (Turkey): 7 ave Abdelkrim Benjelloun, 10010 Rabat; tel. (53) 7661522; fax (53) 7660476; e-mail ambassade.rabat@mfa.gov.tr; internet rabat.emb.mfa.gov.tr; Ambassador GÖREV EŞLENMEMİŞ.

Ukraine: 212 rue Mouaouya Ben Houdaig, Cité OLM, Souissi II, 10020 Rabat; tel. (53) 7657840; fax (53) 7754679; e-mail emb_ma@mfa.gov.ua; internet morocco.mfa.gov.ua; Ambassador SERGEY SAENKO.

United Arab Emirates: 11 ave des Alaouines, 10000 Rabat; tel. (53) 7707070; fax (53) 7724145; e-mail rabatemb.amo@mofaic.gov.ae;

MOROCCO

internet www.mofaic.gov.ae/en/missions/rabat; Ambassador AL ASRI SAEED AHMED AL-DHAHERI.

United Kingdom: 28 ave S. A. R. Sidi Muhammad, BP 45, Souissi, 10105 Rabat; tel. (53) 7633333; fax (53) 7758709; e-mail ukinmorocco.ambassador@fcdo.gov.uk; internet www.gov.uk/world/morocco; Ambassador SIMON MARTIN.

USA: km 5.7, ave Mohammed VI, Souissi, 10170 Rabat; tel. (53) 7637200; fax (53) 7637201; internet ma.usembassy.gov; Ambassador PUNEET TALWAR.

Viet Nam: 9 rue Beni MTIR, Souissi, Rabat; tel. (53) 7639174; fax (53) 7639174; e-mail vnambassade@yahoo.com.vn; Ambassador DANG THI THU HA.

Yemen: ave Mohamed VI, km 6.6, rue Beni Tajit, Quartier des Ambassadeurs, Souissi, Rabat; tel. (53) 7631220; fax (53) 7631267; e-mail yemen@menara.ma; Ambassador EZZEDINE SAÏD AHMED AL-ASBAHI.

Zambia: 54 rue Bani Ouaryaghel, Rabat; Ambassador ELIPHAS CHINYONGA.

Judicial System

Court of Cassation: Hay Riad, Ave al-Nakhil, Rabat; tel. (53) 7714931; fax (53) 7715106; internet www.coursupreme.ma; the Court of Cassation replaced the Supreme Court in 2011; responsible for the interpretation of the law and regulates the jurisprudence of the courts and tribunals of the Kingdom. The Court sits at Rabat and is divided into multiple Chambers; First Pres. MOHAMED ABDENNABAOUI.

Courts of Appeal: The 21 courts hear appeals from lower courts and also comprise a criminal division.

Courts of First Instance: The 65 courts pass judgment on offences punishable by up to five years' imprisonment. These courts also pass judgment, without possibility of appeal, in personal and civil cases involving up to 3,000 dirhams.

Communal and District Courts: composed of one judge, who is assisted by a clerk or secretary, and hear only civil and criminal cases.

Administrative Courts: The seven courts pass judgment, subject to appeal before the Supreme Court pending the establishment of administrative appeal courts, on litigation with government departments.

Commercial Courts: The nine courts pass judgment, without the possibility of appeal, on all commercial litigations involving up to 9,000 dirhams. They also pass judgment on claims involving more than 9,000 dirhams, which can be appealed against in the commercial appeal courts.

Permanent Royal Armed Forces' Court: tries offences committed by the armed forces and military officers.

Attorney-General: MOULAY EL-HASSAN DAKI.

Religion

ISLAM

About 99% of Moroccans are Muslims (of whom about 90% are of the Sunni sect), and Islam is the state religion.

CHRISTIANITY

There is a small Christian population in Morocco, mostly comprising Roman Catholics.

The Roman Catholic Church

Morocco (excluding the disputed territory of Western Sahara) comprises two archdioceses, directly responsible to the Holy See. The Moroccan archbishops participate in the Conférence Episcopale Régionale du Nord de l'Afrique (f. 1985).

Bishops' Conference: Conférence Episcopale Régionale du Nord de l'Afrique, 1 rue Hadj Muhammad Riffaï, BP 258, 10001 Rabat; tel. (53) 7709232; e-mail secretariatarchev@yahoo.fr; f. 1985; Pres. Cardinal CRISTÓBAL LÓPEZ ROMERO (Archbishop of Rabat).

Archbishop of Rabat: Cardinal CRISTÓBAL LÓPEZ ROMERO, Archevêché, 1 rue Hadj Muhammad Riffaï, BP 258, 10001 Rabat; tel. (53) 7709239; fax (53) 7706282; e-mail landel@wanadoo.net.ma.

Archbishop of Tangier: (vacant), Archevêché, 55 rue Sidi Bouabid, BP 2116, 9000 Tangier; tel. (53) 9932762; fax (53) 9949117; e-mail agrelomar@hotmail.com.

Prefect Apostolic of Western Sahara: Fr MARIO LEÓN DORADO, Misión Católica, BP 31, 70001 el-Aaiún; tel. (52) 8893270; e-mail omisahara@menara.ma.

The Anglican Communion

Within the Church of England, Morocco forms part of the diocese of Gibraltar in Europe. There are Anglican churches in Casablanca and Tangier.

Protestant Church

Evangelical Church: 33 rue d'Azilal, 20000 Casablanca; tel. (66) 9371513; fax (52) 2444768; e-mail casaipc@gmail.com; internet www.casablancachurch.org; f. 1920; established in 8 towns; Lead Pastors CHRIS MARTIN, CAROL MARTIN.

JUDAISM

It is estimated that there are fewer than 3,000 Jews in Morocco, most of whom live in Casablanca.

Conseil des Communautés Israélites du Maroc: 52 Béni Snassen, Souissi, Rabat; tel. (53) 222861; fax (53) 266953; Pres. SERGE BERDUGO.

The Press

DAILY NEWSPAPERS (PRINT AND ONLINE)

Al-Ahdath al-Maghribia (Moroccan Events): 5 rue Saint-Emilion, Casablanca; tel. (52) 2443070; fax (52) 2442932; e-mail ahdath@ahdath.info; internet ahdath.info; f. 1998; Arabic; Dir EL-MOKHTAR LARHZIOUI; Editor-in-Chief ABDUL MAJEED HACHADI; circ. 30,000 (2013/14).

Al-Alam (The Flag): ave Hassan II, Lot Vita, BP 141, Rabat; tel. (53) 7292642; fax (53) 7291784; internet www.alalam.ma; f. 1946; Arabic; literary supplement on Sat; organ of the Istiqlal party; Dir ABD AL-JABBAR SUHEIMAT; Editor-in-Chief HASSAN ABDELKHALEK.

Assabah (The Morning): Groupe Ecomedia, 70 blvd al-Massira al-Khadra, Casablanca; tel. (52) 2953660; fax (52) 2364358; e-mail assabah@assabah.press.ma; internet assabah.ma; f. 2000; Arabic; sister publication of *L'Economiste*; Pres. ABDELMOUNAÏM DILAMI; Dir-Gen. KHALID BELYAZID; Editor-in-Chief Dr KHALED ALHARI.

Assahra al-Maghribia: 17 rue Othman Ben Affan, Casablanca; tel. (52) 2489100; fax (52) 2203048; e-mail support@lematin.ma; internet www.almaghribia.ma; f. 1989; Arabic; Pres. MUHAMMAD HAYTAMI; Dir-Gen. KAMAL ALAMI; Editor HASSAN AL-ATAFI.

Aujourd'hui le Maroc: 20–26 rue Bassatine, Immeuble Myr, 5e étage, blvd de la Résistance, 20400 Casablanca; tel. (52) 2457560; fax (52) 2542009; internet aujourdhui.ma; f. 2001; French; Dir and Editor SAÂD BENMANSOUR; circ. 12,000 (2017).

Al-Bayane (The Manifesto): 119 blvd Emile Zola, 8ème étage, BP 13152, Casablanca; tel. (52) 2307882; fax (52) 2308080; internet albayane.press.ma; f. 1972 as weekly; daily since 1975; Arabic and French; organ of the Parti du Progrès et du Socialisme; Dir MAHTAT REKAS; Editor NAJIB EL-AMRANI; circ. 2,329 (2010).

L'Economiste: Groupe Ecomedia, 70 blvd al-Massira al-Khadra, Casablanca; tel. (52) 2953600; fax (52) 2365926; e-mail courrier@leconomiste.com; internet www.leconomiste.com; f. 1991; French; Pres. and Dir-Gen. ABDELMOUNAÏM DILAMI; Editor-in-Chief MUHAMMAD BENABID.

Al-Haraka (Progress): 66 rue Patrice Lumumba, BP 1317, Rabat; tel. (53) 7768620; fax (53) 7766383; e-mail achiban59@hotmail.fr; internet www.harakamp.ma; Arabic; organ of the Mouvement Populaire; Dir ALI ALAOUI.

Al-Ittihad al-Ichtiraki (Socialist Unity): 33 rue Amir Abdelkader, BP 2165, Casablanca; tel. (52) 2619404; fax (52) 2622810; e-mail jaridati1@gmail.com; internet www.alittihad.info; Arabic; f. 1983; organ of the Union Socialiste des Forces Populaires; Dir ABD AL-HADI KHAYRAT; Editor MUSTAPHA LAÂRAKI.

Libération: 33 rue Amir Abdelkader, BP 2165, Casablanca; tel. (52) 2619404; fax (52) 2620972; e-mail liberation@libe.ma; internet www.libe.ma; f. 1964; French; organ of the Union Socialiste des Forces Populaires; Dir HABIB EL-MALKI; Editorial Dir MOHAMED BENARBIA.

Al-Massae (The Evening): 10 ave des Forces Armées Royales, 2ème étage, Casablanca; tel. (52) 2275918; fax (52) 2275597; internet www.almassaepress.com; f. 2006; Arabic; independent; Dir RACHID NINI.

Annahar Al Maghribia (The Moroccan Day): 12 pl. des Alaouites, 2ème étage, Rabat; tel. (53) 7737547; e-mail annahar30@gmail.com; internet annahar-press.com; f. 2002; Arabic; Man. Editor ABDEL HAKIM BADIE.

Le Matin: 17 rue Othman Ben Affane, Casablanca; tel. (52) 2489100; fax (52) 2203048; e-mail s.badri@lematin.ma; internet lematin.ma; f. 1971 as Le Matin du Sahara et du Maghreb; later name adopted as above; French; royalist; Dir-Gen. MUHAMMAD HAITAMI; Editor-in-Chief BADRI SOUAD.

L'Opinion: ave Hassan II, Lot Vita, Rabat; tel. (53) 7293002; fax (53) 7293997; e-mail redaction@lopinion.ma; internet www.lopinion.ma; f. 1962; French; organ of Istiqlal; Dir MAJDOULINE EL-ATOUABI; Editor-in-Chief AHMAD NAJI.

Rissalat al-Oumma (The Message of the Nation): 152 ave des Forces Armées Royales, BP 20005, Casablanca; tel. (52) 2901925; fax (52) 2901926; Arabic; weekly edn in French; organ of the Union Constitutionnelle; Dir MUHAMMAD TAMALDOU.

SELECTED PERIODICALS

Achamal 2000: 7 rue Omar Ibn Abdel Aziz, Tangier; tel. (53) 9943008; fax (53) 9944216; e-mail contact@achamal.ma; internet www.achamal.ma; weekly; Arabic; Editor-in-Chief KHALID MECHBAL.

Al-Alam al-Amazighi: Editions Amazigh, 5 rue Dakar, BP 477, Rabat; tel. 66-1767073; fax (53) 7727283; weekly; Berber; Pres. AMINA BEN SHEIKH.

Al-Ayam (The Days): Espace Paquet, 5th Floor, 508 rue Mohamed Smiha, cnr rue Mohammed VI, Casablanca; tel. (52) 2449889; fax (52) 2441173; e-mail contact@alayam24.com; internet www.alayam24.com; f. 2001; Arabic; weekly; Editor NOUREDDINE MIFTAH.

Asdae (Echoes): 30 ave Okba, Rabat; tel. and fax (53) 7773706; e-mail asdae@asdae.com; internet www.asdae.com; weekly; Arabic; Editor-in-Chief MOULAY TOHAMI BHATT.

CGEM Mag: 23 blvd Muhammad Abdou, Palmiers, 20340 Casablanca; tel. (52) 2997000; fax (52) 2983971; e-mail mustaphamoulay@cgem.ma; internet www.cgem.ma; monthly; French; organ of the Confédération Générale des Entreprises du Maroc; Dir MIRIEM BENSALAH-CHAQROUN; Editor-in-Chief MUSTAPHA MOULAY.

Challenge Hebdo: 58 ave des Forces Armées Royales, Tour des Habous, 13ème étage, Casablanca; tel. (52) 2548150; fax (52) 2318094; e-mail contact@challenge.ma; internet www.challenge.ma; weekly; French; business; Dir ADIL LAHLOU; Editor ADAMA SYLLA.

Femmes du Maroc: 18 blvd Massira al-Khadra, Maârif, Casablanca; tel. (52) 2584595; fax (52) 2973929; e-mail courrier@femmesdumaroc.com; internet femmesdumaroc.com; monthly; French; lifestyle magazine; Dir and Editor-in-Chief ZINEB TIMOURI.

Le Journal de Tanger: 7 bis, rue Omar Ben Abdelaziz, Tangier; tel. (53) 9943008; fax (53) 9945709; e-mail lejournaldetanger@gmail.com; internet www.lejournaldetanger.com; f. 1904; weekly; French, English, Spanish and Arabic; Dir ABDELHAK BAKHAT; Editor-in-Chief MUHAMMAD ABOUABDILLAH.

Maroc Hebdo International: 4 rue des Flamants, Casablanca 20410; tel. (52) 2238176; fax (52) 2982161; e-mail mhi@maroc-hebdo.press.ma; internet www.maroc-hebdo.press.ma; f. 1991; weekly; French; Editor-in-Chief MUHAMMAD SELHAMI.

Al-Mountakhab (The Team): 42 bis rue de Madagascar, Rabat; tel. (52) 2264638; fax (53) 7201776; e-mail almountakhab86@gmail.com; internet www.almountakhab.com; f. 1986; fortnightly; Arabic; sport; Dir MUSTAFA BADRI; Editor-in-Chief BADREDDINE IDRISSI.

La Nouvelle Tribune: 320 blvd Zerktouni, angle rue Bouardel, Casablanca; tel. (52) 2424670; fax (52) 2200031; e-mail lanouvelletribune@gmail.com; internet lnt.ma; f. 1996; weekly (Thur.); French; Dir FAHD YATA; circ. 15,000 (2017).

Le Reporter: 1 Sahat al-Istiqlal, 2ème étage, 20000 Casablanca; tel. (52) 2541103; fax (52) 2541105; e-mail lereporter@gmail.com; internet www.lereporter.ma; f. 1998; weekly; French; Dir BAHIA AMRANI.

TelQuel: 28 ave des Forces Armées Royales, Casablanca; tel. (52) 2270827; fax (52) 2251331; e-mail contact@telquel.ma; internet telquel.ma; f. 2001; weekly; French; Dir REDA DALIL; Editor-in-Chief YASSINE MAJDI.

La Vie éco: 5 blvd Abdallah Ben Yacine, 20300 Casablanca; tel. (52) 2450555; fax (52) 2449421; e-mail a.guendouli@lavieeco.com; internet www.lavieeco.com; f. 1921; weekly; French; economics; Dir NABILA FATHI; Editor-in-Chief ALIÉ DIOR NDOUR; circ. 24,158 (2017).

NEWS AGENCY

Maghreb Arabe Presse (MAP): 122 ave Allal Ben Abdallah, BP 1049, 10000 Rabat; tel. (53) 7279400; fax (53) 7765005; internet www.map.ma; f. 1959; Arabic, French, English and Spanish; state-owned; Dir-Gen. KHALIL HACHIMI IDRISSI.

PRESS ASSOCIATIONS

Fédération Marocaine des Editeurs de Journaux (FMEJ): Groupe Ecomedia, 70 blvd al-Massira al-Khadra, Casablanca; tel. (52) 2953600; fax (52) 2365926; f. 2005; Pres. NOUREDDINE MIFTAH.

Organisme de Justification de la Diffusion (OJD Maroc): 4 rue des Flamants, Casablanca; tel. (52) 2238176; fax (52) 2981346; e-mail asmaehassani@gmail.com; internet www.ojd.ma; f. 2004; compiles circ. statistics; Pres. MUHAMMAD SELHAMI; Dir ASMAE HASSANI.

Publishers

Afrique Orient: 159 rue Ali Ibn Taleb, Casablanca; tel. (52) 2296753; fax (52) 2440080; f. 1983; sociology, philosophy and translations; Dir MUSTAPHA CHAJII.

Dar el-Kitab: 1 ave Imperiale, Quartier des Habous, BP 4018, Casablanca; tel. (52) 2305419; fax (52) 3026630; e-mail espacedarelkitab@gmail.com; f. 1948; Arabic and French; philosophy, history, Africana, general and social sciences; state-controlled; Dir BOUTALEB ABDOU ABD AL-HAY; Gen. Man. KHADIJA EL-KASSIMI.

Editions Le Fennec: 91 blvd d'Anfa, 14ème étage, Casablanca; tel. (52) 2209314; fax (52) 2277702; e-mail info@lefennec.com; internet www.lefennec.com; f. 1987; fiction, social sciences; Dir LAYLA B. CHAOUNI.

Editions La Porte: 281 blvd Muhammad V, BP 331, Rabat; tel. (53) 7709958; fax (53) 7706476; law, guides, economics, educational books.

Les Editions Maghrébines: Quartier Industriel, blvd E, N 15, Sin Sebaâ, Casablanca; tel. (52) 2351797; fax (52) 2357892; f. 1962; general non-fiction.

Les Editions Toubkal: Immeuble I. G. A, pl. de la Gare Voyageurs, Bélvèdere, 20300 Casablanca; tel. and fax (52) 22342323; e-mail contact@toubkal.ma; internet www.toubkal.ma; f. 1985; economy, history, social sciences, literature, educational books; Dir MUHAMMAD DIOURI.

Malika Editions: 60 blvd Yacoub el-Mansour, 20100 Casablanca; tel. (52) 2235688; fax (52) 2251651; e-mail edmalika@connectcom.net.ma; internet www.malikaedition.com; art publications.

Tarik Editions: 321 blvd Brahim Roudani, 20390 Casablanca; tel. (52) 2252357; fax (52) 2232550; e-mail tarik.edition@gmail.com; internet www.tarikeditions.com; f. 2000; history and social sciences; Dir BICHR BENNANI.

Yomad: Résidence Oasis, Villa 62, Tamesna, Rabat; tel. (66) 1193536; e-mail yomadeditions@gmail.com; internet www.yomadeditions.net; f. 1998; children's literature; Dir NADIA ESSALMI.

GOVERNMENT PUBLISHING HOUSE

Imprimerie Officielle: ave Yacoub el-Mansour, Rabat-Chellah; tel. (53) 7765024; fax (53) 7765179.

Broadcasting and Communications

TELECOMMUNICATIONS

inwi: Lot la Colline II, Sidi Maârouf, 20190 Casablanca; tel. (52) 2900000; e-mail drh.info@inwi.ma; internet www.inwi.ma; f. 2009 as Wana following award of third GSM licence; mobile telephone and internet services launched 2010; Dir-Gen. AZZEDINE EL-MOUNTASSIR BILLAH.

Itissalat al-Maghrib—Maroc Télécom: ave Annakhil Hay Riad, Rabat; tel. (53) 7719000; fax (53) 7710600; e-mail support_mt@iam.ma; internet www.iam.ma; f. 1998; part-privatized 2004; Emirates Telecommunications Corpn (Etisalat—UAE) holds a 53% stake, the Moroccan Govt 30% and individual investors 17%; CEO ABDESLAM AHIZOUNE.

Orange Maroc: Twin Centre, angle blvd Zerktouni et blvd Massira al-Khadra, Casablanca; tel. (63) 121121; internet orange.ma; f. 1999 as Médi Telecom; rebranded in 2016; provides national mobile telecommunications services; Dir-Gen. HENDRIK KASTEEL.

Regulatory Authority

Agence Nationale de Réglementation des Télécommunications (ANRT): Centre d'Affaires, blvd al-Riad, BP 2939, Hay Riad, 10100 Rabat; tel. (53) 7718400; fax (53) 7203862; e-mail com@anrt.ma; internet www.anrt.ma; f. 1998; Dir-Gen. MOHAMED EL-HAJJOUI.

BROADCASTING

Morocco can receive broadcasts from Spanish radio stations, and the main Spanish television channels can also be received in northern Morocco.

Radio

Radio Casablanca: c/o Loukt s.a.r.l, BP 16011, Casa Principal, 20001 Casablanca; internet www.maroc.net/rc; f. 1996; Gen. Man. AMINE ZARY.

Radio Méditerranée Internationale (Médi1): Zone Franche de Tanger, Lot 31, BP 2397, Tangier; tel. (53) 9936363; fax (53) 9949037; e-mail info@medi1.com; internet www.medi1.com; Arabic and French.

Voice of America Radio Station in Tangier: c/o US Consulate-General, chemin des Amoureux, Tangier.

Television

Société Nationale de Radiodiffusion et de Télévision: 1 rue el-Brihi, BP 1042, 10000 Rabat; tel. (53) 7685100; fax (53) 7733733; internet www.snrt.ma; govt station; transmission commenced 1962; 45 hours weekly; French and Arabic; carries commercial advertising; Pres. and Dir-Gen. FAYÇAL LARAÏCHI.

SOREAD 2M: Société d'Etudes et de Réalisations Audiovisuelles, km 7.3, route de Rabat, Aïn-Sebaâ, Casablanca; tel. (52) 2667300; internet www.2m.ma; f. 1988; transmission commenced 1989; public television channel; owned by Moroccan Govt (72%) and by private national foreign concerns; broadcasting in French and Arabic; Man. Dir SALIM CHEIKH.

Regulatory Authority

Haute Autorité de la Communication Audiovisuelle (HACA): Ave Annakhil, Espace les Patios, Hay Riad, BP 20590, Rabat; tel. (53) 7714385; fax (53) 7572112; e-mail info@haca.ma; internet www.haca.ma; f. 2002; Pres. LATIFA AKHARBACH.

Finance

BANKING

Central Bank

Bank Al-Maghrib: 277 ave Mohammed V, BP 445, Rabat; tel. (53) 7574383; e-mail accueil@bkam.ma; internet www.bkam.ma; f. 1959 as Banque du Maroc; name changed as above 1987; bank of issue; Gov. ABDELLATIF JOUAHRI; Dir-Gen. ABDERRAHIM BOUAZZA.

Other Banks

Attijariwafa Bank: 2 blvd Moulay Youssef, BP 11141, 20000 Casablanca; tel. (52) 2298888; fax (52) 2294125; e-mail crc@attijariwafa.com; internet www.attijariwafabank.com; f. 2004 by merger between Banque Commerciale du Maroc SA and Wafabank; 46.5% owned by Groupe Al Mada, 5.1% by Grupo Santander (Spain); Pres. and Dir-Gen. MOHAMED EL-KETTANI.

Bank of Africa (BMCE): 140 ave Hassan II, BP 13425, 20000 Casablanca; tel. (52) 2462424; e-mail relationsinvestisseurs@bankofafrica.ma; internet www.bankofafrica.ma; f. 1959; transferred to majority private ownership 1995; Pres. and Dir-Gen. OTHMAN BENJELLOUN.

Banque Centrale Populaire (Crédit Populaire du Maroc): 101 blvd Muhammad Zerktouni, 20100 Casablanca; tel. (52) 2469087; internet www.cpm.co.ma; f. 1961; 51% state-owned, 49% privately owned; merged with Société Marocaine de Dépot et Crédit 2003; Pres. and Man. Dir MOHAMED KARIM MOUNIR.

Banque Marocaine pour le Commerce et l'Industrie SA (BMCI): 26 pl. des Nations Unies, 20000 Casablanca; tel. (52) 22461000; fax (52) 22299406; e-mail adiba.lahbabi@africa.bnpparibas.com; internet www.bmci.ma; f. 1964; 65.05% owned by BNP Paribas (France); Chair. PHLIPPE DUMEL; Man. Dir RACHID MARRAKCHI.

Citibank-Maghreb: Zénith Millenium, Immeuble 1, Lot Attaoufik, Sidi Maârouf, BP 13362, Casablanca; tel. (52) 2489600; e-mail hasna.boufkiri@citi.com; f. 1967; Pres. TAOUFIK RABBAA.

Crédit Agricole du Maroc SA: pl. des Alaouites, BP 49, 10000 Rabat; tel. (53) 7208219; fax (53) 7208218; e-mail m_kettani@creditagricole.ma; internet www.creditagricole.ma; f. 1961 as Caisse Nationale de Crédit Agricole; became a limited co and adopted present name 2003; 78% owned by Ministry of the Economy and Finance; Chair. NOURREDDINE BOUTAYEB.

Crédit Immobilier et Hôtelier: 187 ave Hassan II, 20019 Casablanca; tel. (52) 2479000; fax (52) 2479363; internet www.cihbank.ma; f. 1920; transferred to majority private ownership 1995; Pres. and CEO LOTFI SEKKAT.

Crédit du Maroc SA: 48–58 blvd Mohammed V, 20000 Casablanca; tel. (52) 2477477; fax (52) 2477127; e-mail mohammadine.menjra@ca-cdm.ma; internet www.cdm.co.ma; f. 1963 as Crédit Lyonnais Maroc; name changed as above 1966; 78.7% owned by Groupe Holmarcom; Chair. of Supervisory Bd MOHAMED HASSAN BENSALAH; Chair. of Exec. Bd ALI BENKIRANE.

Société Générale Marocaine de Banques SA: 55 blvd Abdelmoumen, BP 13090, 21100 Casablanca; tel. (52) 2438888; e-mail contact.sgmaroc@socgen.com; internet www.sgmaroc.com; f. 1962; Pres. LAURENT GOUTARD; Dir-Gen. AHMED EL-YACOUBI.

STOCK EXCHANGE

Bourse de Casablanca: angle ave des Forces Armées Royales et rue Mohamed Errachid, Casablanca; tel. (52) 2452626; fax (52) 2452625; e-mail contact@casablanca-bourse.com; internet www.casablanca-bourse.com; f. 1929; 75 listed cos (2019); Chair. KAMAL MOKDAD; CEO TARIK SENHAJI.

INSURANCE

Allianz Maroc: 166 angle Zerktouni et rue Hafid Ibrahim, 20000 Casablanca; tel. (52) 2436200; fax (52) 22491733; e-mail client@allianz.com; internet www.allianz.ma; f. 1953 as Zurich Assurances Maroc; present name adopted in 2017 following an acquisition by Allianz Group (Germany); all kinds of insurance; Pres. ABDERRAHIM DBICH.

AtlantaSanad Assurance: 181 blvd d'Anfa, BP 13685, 20050 Casablanca; tel. (52) 2957676; e-mail info@atlanta.ma; internet www.atlanta.ma; f. 2020 by the merger of Atlanta Assurance and Sanad Assurance; wholly owned by Groupe Holmarcom; Dir-Gen. JALAL BENCHEKROUN.

AXA Assurance Maroc: 120–122 ave Hassan II, 20000 Casablanca; tel. (52) 2889292; fax (52) 2889189; internet www.axa.ma; Pres. and Dir-Gen. PHILIPPE ROCARD.

La Marocaine Vie: 37 blvd Moulay Youssef, Casablanca; tel. (52) 2263636; internet www.lamarocainevie.ma; f. 1978; 83% owned by Société Générale Marocaine de Banques SA; Dir-Gen. TAOUFIK LACHKER.

Mutuelle Agricole Marocaine d'Assurances et Mutuelle Centrale Marocaine d'Assurances (MAMDA et MCMA): angle ave Mohammed VI et rue Houmane el-Fatouaki, 10200 Rabat; internet www.mamda-mcma.ma; f. 1968; MAMDA and MCMA are two separate insurers that use the same resources.

Mutuelle d'Assurances des Transporteurs Unis (MATU): 215 blvd Muhammad Zerktouni, Casablanca; tel. (52) 2954501; fax (52) 2954504; e-mail info@matu-assurance.ma; internet matu-assurance.ma; Pres. and Dir-Gen. KHALID ABDELBAKI.

Royale Marocaine d'Assurance (RMA): 83 ave des Forces Armées Royales, 20000 Casablanca; tel. (52) 2312163; fax (52) 2313884; e-mail contact@rmawatanya.com; internet www.rmaassurance.com; f. 2005 as RMA Watanya by merger of Al-Wataniya and La Royale Marocaine d'Assurances; present name adopted in 2016; Chair. OTHMAN BENJELLOUN; CEO (vacant).

Sanlam: 216 blvd Muhammad Zerktouni, 20000 Casablanca; tel. (52) 2474040; fax (52) 2206081; internet www.sanlam.ma; f. 2009 as CNIA Saada Assurance; present name adopted in 2022; 100% owned by Sanlam (South Africa); Pres. SAÏD EL ALJ; Dir-Gen. YAHIA CHRAÏBI.

Société Centrale de Réassurance (SCR): Tour Atlas, pl. Zallaqa, BP 13183, Casablanca; tel. (52) 2460400; fax (52) 2460460; e-mail scr@scrmaroc.com; internet www.scrmaroc.com; f. 1960; Dir-Gen. YOUSSEF FASSI FIHRI.

Société Marocaine d'Assurance à l'Exportation (SMAEX): 24 rue Ali Abderrazak, BP 15953, 201000 Casablanca; tel. (52) 2982000; e-mail smaex@smaex.com; internet www.smaex.com; f. 1988; insurance for exporters in the public and private sectors; assistance for export promotion.

WAFA Assurance: 1 blvd Abdelmoumen, 20100 Casablanca; tel. (52) 22545555; e-mail consultation-net@wafaassurance.co.ma; internet www.wafaassurance.ma; subsidiary of Attijariwafa Bank; Pres. and Dir-Gen. BOUBKER JAÏ.

Insurance Association

Fédération Marocaine des Sociétés d'Assurances et de Réassurances: 154 blvd d'Anfa, Casablanca; tel. (52) 2391850; fax (52) 2391854; e-mail contact@fmsar.ma; internet www.fmsar.org.ma; f. 1958; 21 mem. cos; Pres. MUHAMMAD HASSAN BENSALAH.

Trade and Industry

GOVERNMENT AGENCIES

L'Agence Marocaine de Développement des Investissements et Exportations (AMDIE): Mahaj Riad Centre, ave Attine, Bâtiment Business 5 & 8, Hay Riad, Rabat; tel. (53) 7226400; fax (53) 7673417; internet www.morocconow.com; state org. for promotion of exports and foreign investments; established by the merger of L'Agence Marocaine de Developpement des Investissements (AMDI), Centre Marocain de Promotion des Exportations (CMPE), and L'Office des Foires et Expositions de Casablanca (OFEC); Dir-Gen. ALI SEDDIKI.

MOROCCO

L'Agence Marocaine pour l'Energie Solaire (Moroccan Agency for Solar Energy—MASEN): Immeubles A-B, Zénith, Souissi, Rabat; tel. (53) 7574550; fax (53) 7571474; e-mail recrutement@masen.ma; internet www.masen.ma; f. 2010; Pres. and CEO MUSTAPHA BAKKOURY.

L'Agence Nationale pour la Promotion de Petite et Moyenne Entreprise (Maroc PME): 3 ave Annakhil, 457 Lot 11, Parcelle No. 3, Hay Riad, Rabat; tel. (53) 7574444; fax (53) 7707695; e-mail marocpme@marocpme.ma; internet marocpme.gov.ma; f. 1973 as the Office pour le Développement Industriel; name changed as above 2002; state agency to develop industry; Dir-Gen. BRAHIM AREJDAL.

Direction des Entreprises Publiques et de la Privatisation (DEPP): rue Haj Ahmed Cherkaoui, Quartier Administratif, Agdal, Rabat; tel. (53) 7689303; fax (53) 7689347; e-mail odp@depp.finances.gov.ma; part of the Ministry of the Economy and Finance; in charge of regulation, restructuring and privatization of state enterprises; Dir ABDERRAHMANE SEMMAR.

Office National des Hydrocarbures et des Mines (ONHYM): 5 ave Moulay Hassan, BP 99, 10050 Rabat; tel. (53) 7239898; fax (53) 7709411; e-mail presse@onhym.com; internet www.onhym.com; f. 2003 to succeed Bureau de Recherches et de Participations Minières and Office National de Recherches et d'Exploitations Pétrolières; state agency conducting exploration, valorization and exploitation of hydrocarbons and mineral resources; Dir-Gen. AMINA BENKHADRA.

DEVELOPMENT ORGANIZATIONS

L'Agence pour le Développement Agricole (ADA): ave Annakhil et Mehdi Benbarka, Bâtiments 2 & 3, Hay Riad, Rabat; tel. (53) 7573826; fax (53) 7573739; e-mail daf@ada.gov.ma; internet www.ada.gov.ma; f. 2009; state agricultural devt org.; Dir-Gen. MAHDI ARRIFI.

Al Mada: 60 rue d'Alger, BP 38, 20070 Casablanca; tel. (52) 2224102; fax (52) 2484303; internet almada.ma; f. 1966 as Société Nationale d'Investissement; transferred to majority private ownership 1994; name changed in 2018; Pres. and Man. Dir HASSAN OURIAGLI.

Caisse de Dépôt et de Gestion: pl. Moulay el-Hassan, BP 408, 10001 Rabat; tel. (53) 7669000; fax (53) 7763849; e-mail cdg@cdg.ma; internet www.cdg.ma; f. 1959; finances small-scale projects; Dir-Gen. KHALID SAFIR.

Finéa: 101 blvd Abdelmoumen, 4e étage, 20100 Casablanca; tel. (52) 2264483; fax (52) 2472554; e-mail info@finea.ma; internet www.finea.ma; f. 1950 as Caisse Marocaine des Marchés; name changed in 2013; Pres. LATIFA ECHIHABI; Dir-Gen. MOHAMMED BELMAACHI.

CHAMBERS OF COMMERCE

Fédération des Chambres Marocaines de Commerce, d'Industrie et de Services (FCMCIS): 6 rue Erfoud, BP 218, Hassan, Rabat; tel. (53) 7767078; fax (53) 7767896; e-mail fcmcisdirecteur@gmail.com; internet www.fcmcis.ma; f. 1962; unites the 12 Chambers of Commerce and Industry; Pres. LHOUCINE ALIOUA; Dir-Gen. NARJISS LOUBARIS.

Chambre de Commerce, d'Industrie et de Services Casablanca-Settat: 98 blvd Mohammed V, 20250 Casablanca; tel. (52) 2264371; fax (52) 2268436; e-mail contact@cciscs.ma; internet www.cciscs.ma; Pres. HASSANE BERKANI.

Chambre de Commerce, d'Industrie et de Services de la Wilaya de Rabat-Salé Kénitra: 1 rue Gandhi, BP 131, Rabat; tel. (53) 7706444; e-mail sinfo@ccirabat.ma; internet www.ccirabat.ma; Pres. HASSAN SAKHI.

INDUSTRIAL AND TRADE ASSOCIATIONS

Office National Interprofessionnel des Céréales et des Légumineuses (ONICL): 3 ave Moulay Hassan, BP 154, Rabat; tel. (53) 7217300; fax (53) 7709626; e-mail contact@onicl.org.ma; internet www.onicl.org.ma; f. 1937; Dir-Gen. MOHAMED SEBGUI.

Office National des Pêches: 15 rue Lieutenant Mahroud, BP 16243, 20300 Casablanca; tel. (52) 2240551; fax (52) 2242305; e-mail info@onp.ma; internet www.onp.ma; f. 1969; state fishing org.; Man. Dir AMINA FIGUIGUI.

EMPLOYERS' ORGANIZATIONS

Association Marocaine des Exporteurs (ASMEX): 2 rue Jbel el-Aroui, Sidi Abderrahmane, 20203 Casablanca; tel. (52) 2949305; fax (52) 2949473; e-mail asmex@asmex.org; internet www.asmex.org; f. 1982; Pres. HASSAN EL-IDRISI.

Association Marocaine des Industries du Textile et de l'Habillement (AMITH): 11 Immeuble A2, al-Mawlid, Sidi Maarouf, Casablanca; tel. (52) 2780470; e-mail contact@textile.ma; internet www.textile.ma; f. 1960; 850 mems; textiles, knitwear and ready-made garment mfrs; Pres. ANASS EL-ANSARI; Dir-Gen. FATIMA ZAHRA ALAOUI.

Association des Producteurs d'Agrumes du Maroc (ASPAM): 283 blvd Zerktouni, Casablanca; tel. (52) 2363946; fax (52) 2364041; f. 1958; links Moroccan citrus growers; has its own processing plants; Pres. ABDELLAH JRID.

Association Professionnelle des Agents Maritimes, Consignataires de Navires, et Courtiers d'Affrètement du Maroc (APRAM): 219 ave des Forces Armées Royales, 5ème étage, 20000 Casablanca; tel. (52) 2541112; fax (52) 2541415; e-mail apram@wanadoopro.ma; internet www.apram.ma; f. 1999; 53 mems; Pres. ABDELAZIZ MANTRACH.

Association Professionnelle des Cimentiers (APC): Lotissement California Garden, Immeuble B, Sidi Maarouf, Casablanca; tel. (52) 2589999; e-mail contact@apc.ma; internet www.apc.ma; 4 mems; cement mfrs; Pres. KHALID CHEDDADI.

Confédération Générale des Entreprises du Maroc (CGEM): 23 blvd Mohamed Abdou, Quartier Palmiers, 20100 Casablanca; tel. (52) 2997000; fax (52) 2983971; e-mail cgem@cgem.ma; internet www.cgem.ma; 27 affiliated feds; Pres. CHAKIB ALJ.

UTILITIES

Electricity and Water

Office National de l'Electricité et de l'Eau Potable (ONEE): ave Belhassan el-Ouazzani, 20000 Rabat; tel. (53) 7759600; fax (53) 7650649; internet www.onep.ma; f. 2012 by merger of Office National de l'Eau Potable and Office National de l'Electricité; Dir-Gen. ABDERRAHIM EL-HAFIDI.

Taqa Morocco: BP 99 Sidi Bouzid, El Jadida; tel. (52) 3389000; fax (52) 3345375; internet www.taqamorocco.ma; f. 1997; Chair. ABDELMAJID IRAQUI HOUSSAINI.

Gas

Afriquia Gaz: 139 blvd Moulay Ismail, Aïn Sebaâ, 20700 Casablanca; tel. (52) 22639600; fax (52) 22639666; e-mail afriquiagaz@akwagroup.com; internet www.afriquiagaz.com; f. 1992; Morocco's leading gas distributor; Dir-Gen. TAWFIK HAMOUMI.

MAJOR COMPANIES

Charbonnages du Maroc: Centre Minier, 60550 Jerada; tel. (5) 5821048; fax (5) 5821158; f. 1946; coal mining.

Ciments du Maroc: 621 blvd Panoramique, 20150 Casablanca; tel. (52) 2859450; e-mail presse-contact@cimar.co.ma; internet www.cimentsdumaroc.com; f. 1992; created by the merger of Cimasfi and Société des Ciments d'Agadir (SCA); acquired by HeidelbergCement Group in 2016; Dir-Gen. MATTEO ROZZANIGO.

Compagnie Générale Immobilière (CGI): Espace Oudayas, ave Mehdi Ben Barka, BP 2177, Hay Riad, Rabat; tel. (53) 7239494; fax (53) 7563225; e-mail contact@cgi.ma; internet www.cgi.ma; f. 1960; real estate devt.

COSUMAR: 8 rue el Mouatamid Ibnou Abbad, BP 3098, 20300 Casablanca; tel. (52) 5678300; fax (52) 2241071; internet www.cosumar.co.ma; f. 1967; sugar refining and trading; Pres. and Dir-Gen. HASSAN MOUNIR.

Les Grandes Marques et Conserveries Chérifiennes Réunies (LGMC): Immeuble California Garden, 3 étage, Casablanca; tel. (52) 2687272; e-mail contact@lgmc-mutandis.com; internet www.lgmc-industrie.com; f. 1946; fish and food processing and canning; fully acquired by Mutandis in 2016.

Groupe Addoha: km 7, autoroute de Rabat, Ain Sebaâ, 20600 Casablanca; tel. (52) 2343435; e-mail contact@groupeaddoha.com; internet www.groupeaddoha.com; f. 1988; real estate devt; Pres. and Dir-Gen. ANAS SEFRIOUI.

Groupe des Boissons du Maroc: 38 blvd Ain Ifrane, Alamia, Sidi Moumen, Casablanca; tel. (52) 2769000; e-mail contact@gbm-ma.com; internet www.boissons-maroc.com; f. 1919 as Brasseries du Maroc; distillery, brewery and producer of soft drinks; Man. Dir SÉBASTIEN YVES-MÉNAGER.

LafargeHolcim Maroc: 6 blvd de Mekka, Quartier les Crêtes, Casablanca; e-mail mar-communication@lafargeholcim.com; internet www.lafargeholcim.ma; f. 1928; mfrs of cement and building materials; Pres. SAID EL-HADI; Dir-Gen. JOSÉ ANTONIO PRIMO.

Office Chérifen des Phosphates (OCP): blvd al-Abtal, BP 5196, Casablanca; e-mail contact@ocpgroup.ma; internet www.ocpgroup.ma; f. 1921; state co producing and marketing rock phosphates and derivatives; Chair. and CEO MUSTAPHA TERRAB.

Phosphates de Boucraa SA (PHOSBOUCRAA): ave Hassan II, BP 101, Laâyoune; tel. (52) 8893628; internet www.phosboucraa.ma; f. 1962; production and processing of phosphate rock; Chair. MAOULAÏNINE MAOULAÏNINE.

Société d'Exploitation des Mines du Rif (SEFERIF): 30 Abou-Faris el-Marini, BP 436, Rabat; tel. (7) 7766350; nationalized 1967;

MOROCCO

open and underground mines produce iron ore for export and for the projected Nador iron and steel complex.

Société Marocaine de Constructions Automobiles (SOMACA): km 12, autoroute de Rabat, BP 2628, Ain Sebaâ, Casablanca; tel. (52) 2754848; f. 1959; assembly of motor vehicles; owned by Renault; 1,575 employees (2022).

Société Nationale de Sidérurgie (SONASID): Twin Centre, angle blvd Zerktouni et blvd Massira al-Khadra, Tour A, 18ème étage, Casablanca; tel. (52) 2954100; fax (52) 2958643; e-mail consultation@sonasid.ma; internet www.sonasid.ma; f. 1974; mfrs of construction and building materials; transferred to private ownership 1997; Pres. SAID EL HADI; Dir-Gen. ISMAIL AKALAY.

Société Nouvelle des Conduites d'Eau (SNCE): Résidence Kays Sahat Rabia, Al Adaouiya Agdal, 10090 Rabat; tel. (53) 7776714; e-mail contact@snce.ma; internet www.snce.ma; f. 1961; manufacture of steel and cast-iron pipes and materials.

Winxo: rond Point des Sports, blvd Abdellatif Benkaddour, BP 6180, Casablanca; tel. (52) 2424300; fax (52) 2207955; e-mail info@winxo.com; internet winxo.com; fmrly Cie Marocaine des Hydrocarbures; name changed 2014; distribution of petroleum and oil products; CEO HASSAN AGZENAI.

TRADE UNIONS

Confédération Démocratique du Travail (CDT): 64 rue al-Mourtada, Quartier Palmier, BP 13576, Casablanca; tel. (52) 2994470; fax (52) 2994473; internet cdtmaroc.ma; f. 1978; Sec.-Gen. ABDELKADER ZAËR.

Fédération Démocratique du Travail (FDT): 12 rue Muhammad Diouri, Sidi Belyoute, Casablanca; tel. (52) 2446362; fax (52) 2446365; e-mail bcffdt@gmail.com; internet www.fdtmaroc.com; f. 2003 by fmr mems of CDT associated with USFP; Sec.-Gen. ABDELHAFID ABOUMAAZA.

Union Générale des Travailleurs du Maroc (UGTM): 43 rue Mansour Eddahbi, blvd Allal Ben Abdellah, Rabat; tel. (53) 7702396; fax (53) 7736192; e-mail info@ugtm.ma; internet www.ugtm.ma; f. 1960; associated with Istiqlal; supported by unions not affiliated to UMT; Sec.-Gen. MAYARA ENAÂM.

Union Marocaine du Travail (UMT): Bourse du Travail, 232 ave des Forces Armées Royales, 20000 Casablanca; tel. (22) 5300118; fax (22) 5307854; e-mail umt.secretariatgeneral@gmail.com; internet umt.ma; f. 1955; left-wing; most unions are affiliated; Sec.-Gen. MILOUDI MOUKHARIK.

Union Nationale du Travail du Maroc (UNTM): 23 Immeuble Fleuri, ave Mohammed V, 10000 Rabat; tel. (53) 7263545; internet untm.org.ma; f. 1976; Islamist, associated with the PJD; Sec.-Gen. MOHAMED ZOUITEN.

Transport

Société Nationale des Transports et de la Logistique (SNTL): ave al-Fadila, Quartier Industriel, BP 114, Chellah, Rabat; tel. (53) 7289317; fax (53) 7797850; internet sntlgroup.ma; f. 1958; Dir-Gen. AZIZ ALAMI GOUREFTI.

RAILWAYS

All services are nationalized. Plans for a four-line, 76-km tram system in Casablanca were approved in 2008. Lines 1 and 2 were inaugurated in 2012 and 2019, respectively. Meanwhile, a feasibility study into plans for the construction of a 39-km railway tunnel under the Strait of Gibraltar linking Morocco and Spain was completed in 2009. In February 2023 the Moroccan and Spanish Governments resolved to relaunch the project and planned to start construction of the tunnel in 2030. A 323-km high-speed train link between Casablanca and Tangier was inaugurated in 2018. The line—the first of its kind in Africa—was intended eventually to form part of a 1,500-km high-speed network called the Maghreb Line, serving other major Moroccan cities.

Office National des Chemins de Fer (ONCF): 8 bis rue Abderrahmane el-Ghafiki, Rabat-Agdal; tel. and fax (53) 7774747; e-mail ketary@oncf.ma; internet www.oncf.ma; f. 1963; administers all Morocco's railways; Dir-Gen. MUHAMMAD RABIE KHLIE.

ROADS

Autoroutes du Maroc (ADM): BP 6526, Hay Ryad, Rabat; tel. (53) 7579700; fax (53) 7711059; e-mail naitbrahim.ismail@adm.co.ma; internet www.adm.co.ma; responsible for the construction and upkeep of Morocco's highway network; Dir-Gen. ANOUAR BENAZZOUZ.

Compagnie de Transports au Maroc (CTM—SA): km 13.5, autoroute Casablanca–Rabat, Casablanca; tel. (52) 2762100; fax (52) 2765428; internet www.ctm.ma; f. 1919; 18 agencies nationwide;

privatized in 1993, with 40% of shares reserved for Moroccan citizens; Pres. and Dir-Gen. EZZOUBEIR ERRHAIMINI.

SHIPPING

The most important ports, in terms of the volume of goods handled, are Tanger Med, Jorf Lasfar, Casablanca, Safi, Mohammedia and Agadir. Tangier is the principal port for passenger services. In August 2021 a contract was awarded to Société Générale des Travaux du Maroc (SGTM) and SOMAGEC for the construction of Dakhla-Atlantic port at a projected cost of some US $1,200m.; the port was expected to be completed by 2029.

Port Authorities

Agence Nationale des Ports (ANP): 300 lotissement Mandarona, Sidi Maârouf, 20270 Casablanca; tel. (52) 0121314; fax (52) 2786102; internet www.anp.org.ma; f. 2006, following division of Office d'Exploitation des Ports; regulator of port activity; also responsible for development and maintenance of port facilities; Dir-Gen. NADIA LARAKI.

Société d'Exploitation des Ports (Marsa Maroc): 175 blvd Zerktouni, 20100 Casablanca; tel. (52) 2776794; fax (52) 2999652; e-mail investors@marsamaroc.co.ma; internet www.sodep.co.ma; f. 2006, following division of Office d'Exploitation des Ports; responsible for management of port terminals and quayside facilities; Pres. MUHAMMAD ABDELJALIL.

Tanger Med Special Agency: Rte de Rabat, 90000 Tangier; tel. (53) 9349250; fax (53) 9943427; e-mail contact@tangermed.ma; internet tangermed.ma; CEO MEHDI TAZI RIFFI.

Principal Shipping Companies

Agence Med SARL: 3 rue ibn Rochd, 90020 Tangier; tel. (53) 9935875; fax (53) 9932118; e-mail agencemed@mhbland.com; internet uat.blandgroup.com/agencemed; f. 1904; owned by the Bland Group; also at Agadir, Casablanca, Jorf Lasfar, Nador and Safi; Operations Man. CHAFIK ABAROUDI.

Compagnie Marocaine de Navigation (COMANAV): 7 blvd de la Résistance, BP 628, Casablanca 20300; tel. (52) 2464470; fax (52) 2303771; internet www.comanav.ma; f. 1946 as Cie Franco-Chérifienne de Navigation; name changed as above 1959; privatization pending; subsidiary of CMA CGM Group; regular services to European, Middle Eastern and West African ports; tramping; Pres. and Dir-Gen. TOUFIQ IBRAHIMI; 12 agencies.

CIVIL AVIATION

The main international airports are at Casablanca (King Mohammed V), Rabat, Tangier, Marrakesh, Agadir Inezgane, Fez, Oujda, al-Hocima, el-Aaiún, Ouarzazate, Agadir al-Massira and Nador. In January 2020 the Office National des Aéroports announced plans for the construction of a new airport to serve Marrakesh and a third terminal at King Mohammed V, both of which were scheduled to be completed by 2025.

Jet4you: 4 Lot la Colline, Sidi Maârouf, 20270 Casablanca; fax (52) 2584228; internet www.jet4you.com; f. 2006; wholly owned by TUI Travel PLC (United Kingdom); low-cost airline; services to destinations in 5 European countries; Pres. KARIM BAINA; CEO JAWAD ZIYAT.

Office National des Aéroports (ONDA): Siège Social Nouasseur, BP 8101, Casablanca; tel. (52) 2437863; fax (52) 2539901; e-mail communication@onda.ma; internet www.onda.ma; f. 1990; Dir-Gen. HABIBA LAKLALECH.

Royal Air Maroc (RAM): Aéroport de Casablanca-Anfa; tel. (52) 2912000; fax (52) 2912087; e-mail callcenter@royalairmaroc.com; internet www.royalairmaroc.com/corporate; f. 1953; 53.9% state-owned; 44.1% owned by Fonds Hassan II; scheduled for partial privatization; domestic flights and services to Western Europe, Scandinavia, the Americas, North and West Africa, and the Middle East; Chair. and CEO ABDELHAMID ADDOU.

Tourism

Office National Marocain du Tourisme (ONMT): angle rue Oued el-Makhazine et rue Zalaga, BP 19, Agdal, Rabat; tel. (53) 7278300; fax (53) 7674015; e-mail contact@onmt.org.ma; internet www.visitmorocco.com; f. 1918; Dir-Gen. ADEL EL-FAKIR.

Defence

As assessed at November 2022, the total strength of the Royal Moroccan Armed Forces was 195,800: army 175,000; navy 7,800 (including 1,500 marines); air force 13,000. There was also a reserve force of 150,000. Paramilitary forces numbered 50,000: royal gendarmerie 20,000; auxiliary force 30,000. Compulsory military service was abolished in 2006 but was re-introduced in 2018. Conscript liability is for 12 months for men aged between 19 and 25 years.

Defence Budget: 63,500m. dirhams in 2023.

Commander-in-Chief of the Armed Forces: HM King MOHAMMED VI.

Inspector General of the Royal Moroccan Armed Forces: Lt-Gen. MOHAMMED BERRID.

Inspector General of the Royal Moroccan Air Force: Maj.-Gen. MOHAMED GADIH.

Inspector General of the Royal Moroccan Navy: Rear-Adm. MOHAMMED TAHIN.

Commander of the Royal Moroccan Gendarmerie: Maj.-Gen. MOHAMED HARAMOU.

Education

A decree of November 1963 made education compulsory for children between the ages of seven and 13 years, and this has now been applied in most urban areas; from September 2002 children were to be educated from six years of age. In 2020/21, according to UNESCO estimates, enrolment at pre-primary level was equivalent to 59.9% of children (boys 60.1%; girls 59.6%) in the relevant age-group, while primary level included 99.6% of children in the relevant age-group. Instruction is given in Arabic for the first two years and in Arabic and French for the next four years, with English as the first additional language. Teaching in the principal Berber language, Tamazight, began in primary schools in the 2003/04 academic year.

Secondary education, beginning at the age of 13, lasts for up to six years (comprising two cycles of three years). Lower secondary enrolment in 2020/21 included 93.8% children (males 95.0%; females 92.5%) in the relevant age-group, while the comparable rate at upper secondary level was 74.8% of children (males 74.8%; females 74.8%). Under the 2022 budget, spending on education by the central Government was projected at 56,199m. dirhams (23.2% of total general government expenditure).

There are eight universities in Morocco, including the Islamic University of al-Quarawiyin at Fez (founded in 859), the Muhammad V University at Rabat (opened in 1957), and an English-language university, inaugurated at Ifrane in 1995. In addition, there are institutes of higher education in business studies, agriculture, mining, law, and statistics and advanced economics.

Bibliography

Abourabi, Yousra. *La politique africaine du Maroc: Identité de role et projection de puissance*. Leiden and Boston, MA, Brill, 2021.

Agnaou, F. *Gender, Literacy, and Empowerment in Morocco*. Abingdon, Routledge, 2012.

Ashford, D. E. *Political Change in Morocco*. Princeton, NJ, Princeton University Press, 1961.

Badran, Sammy Zeyad. *Killing Contention: Demobilization in Morocco During the Arab Spring*. Syracuse, Syracuse University Press, 2022.

Bergh, Sylvia I. *The Politics of Development in Morocco: Local Governance and Participation in North Africa*. London, I. B. Tauris, 2017.

Bernard, Stéphane. *Le Conflit Franco-Marocain 1943–1956*, 3 vols. Brussels, 1963; English translation, New Haven, CT, Yale University Press, 1968.

Boukhars, Anouar. *Politics in Morocco: Executive Monarchy and Enlightened Authoritarianism*. Abingdon, Routledge, 2010.

Buasriyah, Abd al-Ilah. *Sufism and Politics in Morocco: Activism and Dissent*. Abingdon, Routledge, 2014.

Cherkaoui, Mohamed. *Morocco and the Sahara: Social Bonds and Geopolitical Issues*, revised 2nd edn. Oxford, The Bardwell Press, 2007.

Cohen, Shana, and Jaidi, Larabi. *Morocco: Globalization and its Consequences*. Abingdon, Routledge, 2006.

Dawson, Carl. *EU Integration with North Africa: Trade Negotiations and Democracy Deficits in Morocco*. London, Tauris Academic Studies, 2009.

Fernández-Molina, Irene. *Moroccan Foreign Policy Under Mohammed VI, 1999-2014*. Abingdon, Routledge, 2016.

Gershovich, Moshe. *French Military Rule in Morocco: Colonialism and its Consequences*. London and Portland, OR, Frank Cass, 2000.

Gilson Miller, Susan. *A History of Modern Morocco*. Cambridge, Cambridge University Press, 2013.

Glacier, Osire. *Universal Rights, Systemic Violations and Cultural Relativism in Morocco*. New York, Palgrave Macmillan, 2013.

Halstead, John P. *Rebirth of a Nation: The Origins and Rise of Moroccan Nationalism*. Cambridge, MA, Harvard University Press, 1967.

El Hamel, Chouki. *Black Morocco: A History of Slavery, Race, and Islam*. Cambridge, Cambridge University Press, 2013.

Hannoum, Abdelmajid. *Living Tangier: Migration, Race, and Illegality in a Moroccan City*. Philadelphia, PA, University of Pennsylvania Press, 2020.

Hassan II, King of Morocco. *Le Défi*. Paris, Albin Michel, 1976.

Hughes, Stephen O. *Morocco Under King Hassan*. Reading, Ithaca Press, 2006.

Landau, Rom. *Morocco Independent under Mohammed V*. London, Allen & Unwin, 1961.

Loudiy, Fadoua. *Transitional Justice and Human Rights in Morocco: Negotiating the Years of Lead*. Abingdon, Routledge, 2014.

McDougall, James, and Parks, Robert P. *Global and Local in Algeria and Morocco: The World, The State and the Village*. Abingdon, Routledge, 2015.

Maddy-Weitzman, Bruce, and Zisenwine, Daniel (Eds). *Contemporary Morocco State: Politics and Society under Mohammed VI*. Abingdon, Routledge, 2012.

El Mansour, Mohamed. *The Power of Islam in Morocco: Historical and Anthropological Perspectives*. Abingdon, Routledge, 2021.

Marglin, Jessica M. *Across Legal Lines: Jews and Muslims in Modern Morocco*. New Haven, CT, Yale University Press, 2016.

Marzok, Mokhtar Mohatar. *La contestation au Maroc à l'epreuve du politique: Le cas du Rif, 1980–2008*. Algiers, Editions Bouchène, 2009.

Moore, Sharlissa. *Sustainable Energy Transformations, Power and Politics: Morocco and the Mediterranean*. Abingdon, Routledge, 2019.

El Ouali, Abdelhamid. *Saharan Conflict: Towards Territorial Autonomy as a Right to Democratic Self-Determination*. London, Stacey International, 2008.

Park, Thomas Kerlin, and Boum, Aomar. *Historical Dictionary of Morocco*. 3rd edn, Lanham, MD, Rowman & Littlefield, 2016.

Pennell, C. R. *Morocco since 1830: A History*. New York, New York University Press, 2001.

Porch, Douglas. *The Conquest of Morocco*. New York, Farrar, Straus and Giroux, 2005.

Sandberg, Eve Nan. *Moroccan Women, Activists, and Gender Politics: An Institutional Analysis*. Lanham, MD, Lexington Books, 2014.

Sandberg, Eve, and Binder, Seth. *Mohammed VI's Strategies for Moroccan Economic Development*. Abingdon, Routledge, 2019.

Sater, James N. *Civil Society and Political Change in Morocco*. Abingdon, Routledge, 2007.

— *Morocco: Challenges to Tradition and Modernity*. 2nd edn, Abingdon, Routledge, 2016.

Spiegel, Avi. *Young Islam: The New Politics of Religion in Morocco and the Arab World*. Princeton, NJ, Princeton University Press, 2015.

Stenner, David. *Globalizing Morocco: Transnational Activism and the Postcolonial State*. Stanford, CA, Stanford University Press, 2019.

Stock, Inka. *Time, Migration and Forced Immobility: Sub-Saharan African Migrants in Morocco*. Bristol, Bristol University Press, 2019.

Storm, Lise. *Democratization in Morocco: The Political Élite and Struggles for Power in the Post-independence State*. Abingdon, Routledge, 2007.

Terem, Etty. *Old Texts, New Practices: Islamic Reform in Modern Morocco*. Redwood City, CA, Stanford University Press, 2014.

Thobhani, Akbarali. *Western Sahara Since 1975 Under Moroccan Administration: Social, Political and Economic Transformation.* Lewiston, NY, Edwin Mellen Press, 2002.

Vairel, Frédéric. *Politique et Mouvements Sociaux au Maroc: La Révolution Désamorcée.* Paris, Presses de Sciences Po, 2014.

Wainscott, Ann Marie. *Bureaucratizing Islam: Morocco and the War on Terror.* Cambridge, Cambridge University Press, 2017.

Wegner, Eva. *Islamist Opposition in Authoritarian Regimes: The Party of Justice and Development in Morocco.* Syracuse, NY, Syracuse University Press, 2011.

White, Gregory. *A Comparative Political Economy of Tunisia and Morocco: On the Outside of Europe Looking In.* Albany, NY, State University of New York Press, 2001.

Willis, Michael J. *Politics and Power in the Maghreb: Algeria, Tunisia and Morocco from Independence to the Arab Spring.* London, Hurst & Co, 2014.

Wyrtzen, Jonathan. *Making Morocco: Colonial Intervention and the Politics of Identity.* Ithaca, Cornell University Press, 2015.

Zeghal, Malika. *Islamism in Morocco: Religion, Authoritarianism, and Electoral Politics.* Princeton, NJ, Markus Wiener Publishers, 2008.

OMAN

Geography

The Sultanate of Oman occupies the extreme east and south-east of the Arabian peninsula. It is bordered by the United Arab Emirates (UAE) to the north and west, by Saudi Arabia to the west, and by Yemen to the south-west. A detached area of Oman, separated from the rest of the country by UAE territory, lies at the tip of the Musandam peninsula, on the southern shore of the Strait of Hormuz. Oman is separated from Iran by the Gulf of Oman, and has a coastline of some 1,700 km (1,056 miles) on the Indian Ocean. The total area of the country is 309,980 sq km (119,684 sq miles). Disputes over the demarcation of Oman's frontiers often complicated the country's foreign relations in the past; however, in mid-1995 Oman completed the demarcation of its joint borders with both Yemen and Saudi Arabia (in May 1997 Oman and Yemen signed international border demarcation maps in Muscat), and in June 2002 it was reported that agreement had also been reached with the UAE on the demarcation of common international borders.

In Muscat average annual rainfall is 100 mm and the mean temperature varies between 21°C and 35°C (70°F and 95°F). Rainfall on the hills of the interior is somewhat heavier, and the south-western province of Dhofar is the only part of Arabia to benefit from the summer monsoon.

Oman may be divided into nine topographical areas. The largest urban area in the country is the capital region, around Muscat. Although most of the country is arid, the al-Batinah plain, which lies between the Gulf of Oman and the Hajar al-Gharbi range of mountains, comprises a fertile coastal region, and is among the most densely populated areas of the country. Another such plain is found between Raysut and Salalah, on the south-west coast in the Dhofar region, which, in total, occupies one-third of the country's area and extends northwards into the Rub al-Khali, or 'empty quarter', on Oman's western border: a rainless, unrelieved wilderness of shifting sand, almost entirely without human habitation.

Irrigation has been developed in some parts of the country, including the Dhahira area, a semi-desert plain between the south-western Hajar mountains and the Rub al-Khali, which also provides clusters of cultivable land near the Dank and Ain *wadis* (river valleys) and the Buraini oasis. From Jebel al-Akhdar, at the southern tip of the Hajar al-Gharbi range, towards the desert in the south, lies the country's central hill region and the most densely populated zone. The area has four main valleys, two of which (Halafein and Samail) provide the traditional route to Muscat.

The less hospitable regions are sparsely populated by groups of tribal settlers. The Hajar al-Gharbi, running parallel to the coast southwards from Oman's border with the UAE, is the home of the Rostaq, Awabi and Nakhe tribes. To the east of the Hajar range, the Sharqiya area extends south towards the Arabian Sea. It is an area of sandy plains and the home of the various Bani tribes. Musandam, separated from Oman by the UAE, is a mountainous area inhabited by the al-Shahouh tribes. Around the eastern coast of the Arabian Sea, the Barr al-Hekkman, a group of islands and salt-plains of 650 sq km (250 sq miles), is inhabited by fishing communities.

The first full census in Oman was held in 1993 and recorded the total population at 2,018,000. Previous estimates of the country's population varied widely between official Omani figures and those of independent international organizations. According to the census of December 2010, the population totalled 2,773,479, comprising 1,957,336 Omani nationals (70.6%) and 816,143 non-Omanis (29.4%), compared with a total of 2,340,815 at the 2003 census. At the census of December 2020 the total population had increased to 4,471,148, comprising 2,731,456 Omani nationals (61.1%) and 1,739,692 non-Omanis (38.9%). According to official estimates, at 31 December 2022 the total population was 4,933,850. The country's official language is Arabic. Islam is the official religion. Some 50% of the population are Ibadi Muslims and another 35% Sunni Muslims; there are also Hindu and Christian minorities. Following the creation of seven new governorates in October 2011, the Sultanate is divided into 11 governorates, subdivided into 61 *wilayat* or provinces, each under the jurisdiction of a *wali*, or provincial governor. The capital, Muscat, and its suburbs had a population of 1,302,440 at the 2020 census. Other significant provinces included al-Seeb (population 478,517), Bawshar (382,184), Salalah (331,949), Sohar (232,849) and Mutrah (230,881). (Bawshar and Mutrah provinces are both part of the Governorate of Muscat.)

History

Revised by MARC VALERI

Oman was probably the land of Magan (mentioned in Sumerian tablets) with which cities such as Ur of the Chaldees traded in the third millennium BCE. The territory of the modern province of Dhofar also produced frankincense in vast quantities, which was shipped to markets in Iraq, Syria, Egypt and the Mediterranean. Oman, at various times, came under the influence of the Himyaritic kingdoms of southern Arabia and of Iran, which are believed to have been responsible for the introduction of the falaj irrigation systems.

The tribal people of Oman come from two main ethnic groups, the Qahtan, who migrated from southern Arabia, and the Nizar, who arrived from the north. According to tradition, the first important invasion from southern Arabia was led by Malik bin Faham, after the final collapse of the Marib dam in Yemen in the second century CE. Oman was one of the first territories to be converted to Islam by Amr bin al-As, who later converted Egypt. Omanis of the tribe of al-Azd played an important part in the early days of Islam in Iraq. They subsequently embraced the Ibadi doctrine, which holds that the caliphate in Islam should not be hereditary or confined to any one family, and established their own independent Imamate in Oman in the eighth century. Subsequently, although subject to invasions by the Caliphate, Iranians and others, Inner Oman largely maintained its independence. During the 10th century Omani mariners sailed as far afield as China.

When Afonso de Albuquerque and the Portuguese forces arrived in 1507, on their way to India, the Omani coast was under the suzerainty of the King of Hormuz, himself of Omani stock. They established themselves in the already prosperous Omani ports, concentrating principally on Sohar and Muscat. British and Dutch traders followed in the wake of the Portuguese, although they did not establish themselves by force of arms in Oman. In 1650 the Imam Nasir bin Murshid of the Yaariba dynasty expelled the Portuguese from Muscat and the rest of Oman. By 1730 the Omanis had conquered the Portuguese settlements on the east coast of Africa. Oman was, however, ravaged by civil war in the first half of the 18th century, when the authority of the Imam diminished. During this period the Iranians were summoned to assist one of the contenders for the Imamate, but they were subsequently ousted by Ahmad bin Said, who was elected Imam in 1749 and founded the al-Bu-Said dynasty, which still rules Oman. Under the new dynasty, the country's maritime influence revived.

Ahmad bin Said's grandson Said bin Sultan ruled Oman from 1804 until 1856. Although officially an independent state, Oman had been under British imperial influence since the 1798 Anglo-Omani Treaty, which declared that a British political agent should reside in Muscat and, as a result, bound the Omani ruler to the British side in the Anglo-French contest. Further treaties providing for the establishment of consular relations were negotiated with the USA in 1833 and with France in 1844.

Said bin Sultan revived Omani interest in Zanzibar (now part of Tanzania) and made it his capital in 1832. As part of his imperial conquest, Said bin Sultan encouraged the settlement of Omani people on the eastern African coast, a process that did not cease until the mid-20th century. In 1829 Said claimed suzerainty over the region of Dhofar. The territory was eventually annexed to Oman in 1879. During Said's reign, Omani dominions expanded to their greatest extent, covering the whole north-western edge of the Indian Ocean, from contemporary Mozambique to Baluchistan.

After Said's death, the inability of his sons to regulate the succession led, under British pressure, to the dismemberment of the Omani possessions into two political entities of Muscat and Zanzibar in 1861. Moreover, a series of treaties with the United Kingdom to curb the slave trade also brought about a decline in the local economy, as Muscat had been an important port for this lucrative traffic. Omani rulers had become dependent on British support by the 1900s; this was illustrated by the 1891 treaty, under which Sultan Faisal bin Turki committed himself never to cede a part of his territory without British agreement. From that time on, Britain enjoyed a quasi-protectorate in Oman. Oman's foreign affairs were managed by the UK, except for relations with the USA, France and (after 1947) India, but only after prior British approval. This arrangement continued until 1971, when the UK withdrew its military forces from the Gulf.

The economic difficulties, linked in people's minds to the British tutelage over Muscat, led to several tribal and religious insurrections towards the end of the 19th century. In 1913 a new Imam was elected in the interior, in defiance of the Sultan, who ruled from Muscat. An agreement was reached under the supervision of the British political agent between Sultan Taimur bin Faisal (who had ruled since 1913) and the leaders of the Imamate in 1920. It provided for free movement of persons between the interior and the coast, and non-interference by the government of the Sultan in the internal affairs of the signatory tribes. A Treaty of Friendship with the UK, signed on 20 December 1951, recognized that the Sultanate, officially called Muscat and Oman, had certain rights, although in reality the British kept the upper hand over a divided and weakened territory.

In 1949 Ibn Saud awarded a concession to the Arabian American Oil Company (Aramco) south of Al-Buraymi oasis. In May 1954 Imam Muhammad al-Khalili, who had agreed to join forces with Sultan Said bin Taimur (who had succeeded his father in 1932) to expel the Saudis from Al-Buraymi, died. The political line of the Imamate changed in favour of a rapprochement with the Saudis. In the face of the Saudi-US threat, the British's Trucial Oman Scouts, based in Abu Dhabi, contemporary United Arab Emirates (UAE), launched a head-on attack on the Imamate in October 1955, leading to its collapse. However, no strategy of development and political stabilization had been implemented by the British, except for the building of a road to the interior, to provide access to the Fahud oil wells. This led to the proclamation of the Imamate's swift rebirth in June 1957 in the Jebel Akhdar (the Green Mountain), north-west of Nizwa. The Trucial Oman Scouts, with the support of the British Royal Air Force, regained control in January 1959. From then on, the Imamate resorted to intimidation (such as mines and sabotage) and the establishment of a government in exile, supported by the League of Arab States (Arab League). Even though the 'question of Oman' was regularly discussed in United Nations (UN) commissions, the Imamate authorities in exile were slowly marginalized in the 1960s and Oman (as Muscat and Oman was renamed in 1970) became a member of the UN in October 1971.

DOMESTIC DEVELOPMENTS UNDER QABOOS, 1970–2020

In 1958 Sultan Said retired to Salalah, in the south of Oman. The features of his mode of government that emerged in the 1940s—deep suspicion towards the Omanis, aversion to social and economic reforms, and entrustment of the daily running of the country to foreign experts—were to be exacerbated. By the end of the 1960s more than 50,000 Omanis had migrated to other Gulf emirates, where they sought better living conditions. Under the impulse of the revolution in neighbouring Yemen, a Dhofar Liberation Front formed in 1965 became the Popular Front for the Liberation of the Occupied Arabian Gulf (PFLOAG) in 1968, and declared itself Marxist-Leninist. It wanted nothing short of the elimination of monarchy from Arabia and was supported by the People's Democratic Republic of Yemen (PDRY—formerly South Yemen), the People's Republic of China, the German Democratic Republic (East Germany), the Union of Soviet Socialist Republics (USSR) and Iraq.

When the rebellion spread to northern Oman in 1970, the British forced Sultan Said to abdicate in favour of his son Qaboos in July. This change enjoyed the support of the other Gulf rulers as well as the Shah of Iran, all of whom were worried by potential revolutionary contagion. Sultan Qaboos appointed his uncle, Tarik bin Taimur, as Prime Minister. Qaboos's unwillingness to question British influence in Oman and his own inclination to personal power led to Tarik's resignation in December 1971. From that time Qaboos himself acted as Prime Minister until his death in January 2020. After taking power, Sultan Qaboos increased defence expenditure to 50% of the state budget and decided to use part of the oil income (exploited since 1967) in pursuing development programmes in education, health care and agriculture. In addition, a number of prisoners were released and many Omanis returned from abroad.

Foreign assistance to the Sultan in the conflict in Dhofar increased dramatically in mid-1972, with the arrival of Iranian troops, in addition to more British personnel. The Sultan also received support from Jordan, Saudi Arabia, Pakistan and India. In 1974 the PFLOAG's Omani and non-Omani branches separated: the Omani branch renaming itself the Popular Front for the Liberation of Oman (PFLO). In 1975 joint offensives by the Sultan's Armed Forces (SAF) and Iran overcame the most secure of the rebel positions, although at a very heavy human and material cost. On 11 December 1975 Sultan Qaboos proclaimed the official end of the insurrection. None the less, small PFLO groups continued to fight until the early 1980s. British and Iranian forces officially withdrew in 1977, but several hundred officers and non-commissioned officers (NCOs) seconded from the British armed forces, and former British officers and NCOs on private contract (as military and intelligence advisers), remained in the SAF.

A 45-member State Consultative Council (SCC—appointed by the Sultan) was created in October 1981. Its role, however, was confined to commenting and making recommendations on economic and social development. In 1991 the SCC was replaced by a new Consultative Council (Majlis al-Shura), composed of 60 members, who were appointed by the President and who were to serve three-year terms of office. Some 500 prominent figures met to nominate three candidates for each of the country's *wilayat* (provinces). From these three, one was chosen by the ruler himself. The Council had no legislative power. Membership of the Council was increased to 80 in 1995. Women were permitted, for the first time, to be nominated as candidates in the capital area governorate (*muhafadha*). In early 1995 two women were appointed to the Council.

In August 1994 the security forces announced the arrest of 430 members of an allegedly foreign-sponsored Islamist organization. Some 150 people, including two ministers and businessmen, were tried before a special Security Court. In November several detainees were sentenced to death, having been found guilty of fomenting sedition; the Sultan subsequently commuted the death sentences to life imprisonment. In the following year, he announced that he would grant royal pardons to every prisoner.

In November 1996 Sultan Qaboos issued a decree promulgating a Basic Statute of the State defining, for the first time, the organs and guiding principles of the State. The Sultan of Oman has all the prerogatives of executive and legislative power. Articles 44 to 55 established that the Sultan would be helped and advised by the Council of Ministers, to which was given the task of implementing general state policies. Article 58 of the Statute provided for a Council of Oman (Majlis Oman), to be composed of the Consultative Council and a new State Council (Majlis al-Dawlah). The latter was to be appointed by the Sultan for three years from among prominent Omanis (including tribal leaders, businessmen, former senior military officers and ambassadors). In December a Defence Council was established by royal decree, comprising the Minister of the Royal Court and the heads of all the branches of the internal and external security forces (all officials who do not belong to the al-Said royal family). The process of succession to the Sultan, as defined by the Basic Statute, required the ruling family to choose a successor from within the family within three days, failing which the Defence Council would open a sealed letter containing the name of the Sultan's preferred successor.

Voting was organized in October 1997 to select candidates for appointment to the Consultative Council. The electorate amounted to 51,000 people, 10% of whom were women. Women were also given the right to vote and to stand for election throughout Oman. In the elections of September 2000, the candidates to the Consultative Council with the highest numbers of votes were automatically elected, and the Sultan no longer intervened in a discretionary second round. Although the number of people eligible to vote was extended to some 150,000 (i.e. one adult in four), only 65% had registered to vote.

In the elections to the Consultative Council held in October 2003, voting rights were for the first time granted to all Omani citizens over 21 years of age—a total of some 820,000 people. Only 32% of Omani citizens registered to vote. Tribal loyalties guided the decision-making of most voters. Two female candidates secured election to the Council. The term of office for members of both the Consultative Council and the State Council was extended to four years. In the elections to the Consultative Council in October 2007, only 28% of Omanis eligible to vote actually cast their ballot.

A key element of Sultan Qaboos's legitimization rested on the nation-building process implemented since 1970, which linked the country's economic and social development to the modernizing state (as the administrator of the oil rent), on the one hand, and to the person of the Sultan on the other. The Sultan portrayed himself as the embodiment of modern Oman in general and of the post-1970 renaissance (nahda) ideology in particular. Since the early 2000s Oman has faced a series of social and economic challenges, calling into question the order established in the 1970s. Growing sectors of society, particularly the younger generations, feel excluded from political and economic decisions that determine the future of their country. This has created fertile ground for the development of political grievances. In April 2005 31 Islamist Ibadis were tried before the State Security Court, following waves of arrests in relation to a plot to attack a festival coinciding with the Id al-Adha celebration. The prosecution alleged that those arrested belonged to an underground organization that sought to establish an Imamate in Oman. The defendants, who were sentenced to prison terms ranging from one to 20 years, denied that the organization had a political dimension. A further 43 members of the military, including senior officers, were also found guilty in a second, secret trial. The Sultan pardoned all 74 men in June. In July a former member of the Consultative Council, Tayyibah al-Mawali, was sentenced to 18 months' imprisonment for publicly criticizing human rights violations in Oman.

Inspired by a wave of anti-regime demonstrations that had spread across the Middle East and North Africa region since December 2010, on 17 January 2011 about 200 people assembled in Muscat, the capital, to protest against government corruption and economic hardship. This was followed in February by a series of nationwide protests against low salaries, high unemployment and the Consultative Council's lack of legislative powers.

Security forces shot dead one protester in Sohar. In response, Sultan Qaboos announced the introduction of a jobseeker's allowance and the creation of 50,000 new jobs for Omanis. He also dismissed two of his most unpopular ministers: the Minister of the Diwan of the Royal Court, Sayyid Ali bin Hamoud al-Busaidi, and the Minister of the Royal Office, Gen. Ali bin Majid al-Maamari. They were replaced by Sayyid Khalid bin Hilal al-Busaidi and Lt-Gen. Sultan bin Muhammad al-Numani, respectively.

In March 2011 there was an expansion of the unrest across the country. Many workers went on strike, and a growing number of protesters pitched tents outside government buildings. Sultan Qaboos responded on 7 March by dismissing 10 ministers (one-third of his cabinet).

On 1 April 2011 riot police, supported by the armed forces, cleared protesters participating in a sit-in from the Globe Roundabout in Sohar, resulting in the death of one protester. None the less, Friday protests continued in other cities, with the overall number of arrests increasing after each event. On 13 May police raided a protest camp outside the Consultative Council in Muscat and the sit-in of protesters in front of the office of Salalah's Governor. During the same month Sultan Qaboos expanded the powers of the police, allowing them to arrest individuals without an arrest warrant from the public prosecution. The Sultan did not address the population directly during the crisis; only government ministers spoke to the people.

A total of 1,133 candidates (including 77 women) stood in the elections to the Consultative Council in October 2011. Three men who had taken part in the protests earlier in the year were elected, as well as one woman. Some 46% of eligible people cast their ballot. Five days after the elections, Sultan Qaboos issued a decree amending the Basic Statute in relation to the succession process. Chairmen of both the Consultative Council and State Council, along with three Supreme Court members and Defence Council members, were henceforth to confirm the appointment to the throne of the person designated by the former ruler in his letter to the Ruling Family Council. The Consultative Council was also granted the ability to elect its own Chairman and to draft laws on its own initiative. At the opening session of the Council on 31 October, the Sultan made his first public address since the protests, promising to combat unemployment and corruption.

In October 2011 a royal decree announced the creation of municipal councils in all 11 governorates, composed of members representing provinces and elected by universal suffrage (all Omanis over 21 years of age registered on the voting lists) for a four-year renewable term, in addition to ex officio members representing ministries. All the municipal councils are chaired by the head of the governorate, who is appointed by the Sultan, but enjoy advisory powers only. They provide recommendations on the development of systems and municipal services in the governorate (such as infrastructure, health care, environment, and local taxes). On 22 December 2012 Oman held its first ever municipal elections. At least 50 applications for candidacies submitted by individuals who took part in the 2011–12 protests were rejected by the election committee 'for security reasons'. Only 50% of the total 447,500 registered voters cast their ballot.

Popular frustration with the slow pace of reform resurfaced in May–June 2012. Oil workers went on strike, demanding better pay and working conditions. In early June the Public Prosecutor announced that anyone who publicly criticized the Government would be charged with sedition. Between July and December some 30 writers, human rights activists and lawyers—who were subjected to practices of mistreatment amounting to torture—were sentenced to gaol terms (of up to 18 months) on charges related to incitement to cause riot and defamation of the Sultan. However, in March and July 2013 Sultan Qaboos pardoned (and ordered the release of) all individuals sentenced and imprisoned since 2011 for their role in the protests. The Sultan also ordered those dismissed from private and public sector jobs after the 2011–12 protests to be reinstated. In another attempt by the Government to show its attentiveness to popular demands, several government officials and businessmen were charged in 2013 and 2014 with various types of abuse of office, money laundering and corruption. However, they received a royal pardon in June 2016.

Meanwhile, arbitrary arrests by special security forces and incommunicado detentions without charge of bloggers and human rights activists have remained common practice. In August 2013 renewed demonstrations in the Sohar industrial area led to several arrests, including of a Consultative Council representative, Talib al-Maamari. Despite theoretically enjoying parliamentary immunity from prosecution, he was sentenced to three years in gaol on charges of 'undermining the prestige of the state'. He was released in May 2016.

In October 2013 teachers from government schools held a four-week strike, the longest and largest on record, demanding the ability to form an elected union. The following month the Minister of Manpower issued a resolution prohibiting industrial action by staff employed by essential public services, including oil refineries, ports and airports. A new Nationality Law (promulgated in August 2014) gave the state the power to strip Omani nationals of their citizenship if they 'engage in a group...that adopts principles or doctrines that can harm the interests of Oman' or 'worked for a foreign country...and failed to fulfil the Omani Government's order to abandon such a work'.

The Sultan travelled to Germany to receive medical care in July 2014. His return to Oman in March 2015 failed to suppress rumours that he was suffering from cancer.

In October 2015 the Ministry of the Interior banned 174 candidates, including three incumbent Council members, from taking part in the elections for the Consultative Council, reportedly for filing inaccurate information in their registration documents. Voter participation was recorded at only 57%—a drop of almost 20 percentage points compared with 2011. Only one woman secured a seat. In December 2016 only 40% of registered voters cast their ballot in the country's second set of municipal elections.

During 2015–16 all independent Omani newspapers and magazines were closed. In January 2016 the independent online magazine *Muwatin* ceased publication in order to protect the safety of its journalists. In September a Muscat court ordered the permanent closure of independent newspaper *al-Zaman* and three of its journalists were sentenced to gaol terms (of up to three years) on charges including 'undermining the prestige of the state'. The last independent Omani newspaper in operation, *al-Balad* (available only online), announced its definitive closure in October 2016, explaining that several of its journalists had been threatened with criminal proceedings in the preceding weeks. At least 15 human rights activists, journalists and writers have fled Oman to seek political asylum in Western countries since 2014—the largest reported exodus from the country since the 1980s.

A leading Omani writer, Abdullah Habib, who had called for Sultan Qaboos to reveal the whereabouts of the Omanis killed in the Dhofar war in the 1970s, was sentenced to three years in prison in November 2016. In April 2018 a former diplomat and online activist, Hassan al-Balushi, died while serving a three-year prison sentence on charges related to 'insulting the Sultan' and 'public blasphemy of God's holiness'.

In January 2018 Sultan Qaboos promulgated a new, more restrictive Penal Law. Article 116 stated that anyone who establishes, administers or finances a body that is 'aimed at combating the political, economic, social or security principles of the State' can be punished with a gaol term of up to 10 years. Article 118, moreover, provided for prison terms of up to three years for anyone who has 'obtained or edited editorials or publications containing a promotion of anything provided for in Article 116'. Hundreds of unemployed Omanis demonstrated in several cities against a lack of job opportunities in January 2018 and January 2019. In October 2018 four activists from Musandam who had called for reforms in the governorate, were sentenced to life imprisonment for 'prejudicing the security and unity of the country and its territories by using information technology'. They received a royal pardon in November 2020.

A total of 637 candidates, including 40 women, contested elections to the expanded 86-member Consultative Council in October 2019. About 713,000 people were registered to vote, but turnout fell to 49%. Two women were elected. The election campaign was marked by the excitement created by a lawyer and human rights activist, Basma Mubarak, who was a candidate in Bawshar (Muscat Governorate), who had been convicted to six months in prison in August 2012. A few days before the elections, she was charged by the Public Prosecutor with 'disrupting public order'.

In mid-December 2019, while Sultan Qaboos was in Belgium to undergo medical treatment, the local media announced that he had returned to Oman earlier than planned, knowing that he was terminally ill. By the end of the month unsubstantiated reports had emerged that the Sultan was clinically dead and that al-Numani had called on the royal family to make a decision on the succession. On 11 January 2020 the Oman News Agency announced that Sultan Qaboos had died the previous day. A few hours later, in a heavily choreographed ceremony, the Royal Family Council met and opened the sealed envelope in which Qaboos had reportedly named his cousin, Haitham bin Tarik al-Said, as his successor.

DOMESTIC DEVELOPMENTS UNDER SULTAN HAITHAM, 2020–

Born in 1954, Haitham had served as Secretary-General in the Ministry of Foreign Affairs, before being appointed as Minister of National Heritage and Culture in 2002. One of the first Omani royals to pursue a career as a businessman, with mixed results, since December 2013 he had also been the head of the committee responsible for developing the long-term national strategy, 'Oman Vision 2040'.

Sultan Haitham's first decree, after the 40-day official mourning period for the late ruler ended, amended the national anthem to remove the reference to Qaboos. Unlike his predecessor, who had largely excluded his family from office, Sultan Haitham quickly appointed close relatives to key positions: his brother Sayyid Shihab bin Tarik al-Said was named Deputy Prime Minister for Defence Affairs in March 2020. In the same month, his paternal cousins, Sayyid Fatik bin Fahr and Sayyid Mansur bin Majid, were appointed as Special Envoy to the Sultan and Special Adviser to the Sultan, respectively, both with the rank of minister.

This trend continued in August 2020, when the new ruler formed his first full Council of Ministers. Sultan Haitham's 31-year-old son, Theyazin (who married his cousin, Sayyid Shihab's daughter Miyan, in November 2021), was appointed as Minister of Culture, Sports and Youth and third most senior member of the administration. While retaining the roles of Prime Minister, Minister of Defence and Chief of Staff of the Armed Forces, as had been the case under Qaboos since 1971, Sultan Haitham appointed a Minister of Foreign Affairs, a Minister of Finance and a Chairman of the Central Bank of Oman—titles that he had inherited from Qaboos but which he now relinquished. Yousuf bin Alawi, who had served as Minister of Foreign Affairs since 1982, was replaced by his deputy since 2000, Sayyid Badr bin Hamad al-Busaidi. The son of Sultan Haitham's half-brother Asa'ad, Taimur bin Asa'ad bin Tarik al-Said, was appointed as Chairman of the Central Bank.

Notably, the Ministry of Economy was re-established (albeit with a limited remit), after it had been abolished following the protests in 2011; meanwhile, the erstwhile Ministries of Justice and of Legal Affairs were merged into one; the Ministry of Oil and Gas was renamed the Ministry of Energy and Minerals, and the Ministry of Labour was formed from the erstwhile Ministries of Manpower and of the Civil Service. The Ministry of Regional Municipalities and Water Resources was abolished, and most of its duties were redistributed to the governorates, whose heads (except those of Muscat, Dhofar and Musandam, who have the rank of Minister of State) exercise their prerogatives under the supervision of the Minister of the Interior.

A number of key ministers retained their positions, including Minister of the Diwan of the Royal Court, Sayyid Ali bin Hamoud al-Busaidi, and the Minister of the Royal Office, al-Numani, despite the establishment in June of a Special Office, which was independent from the other two bodies and reported directly to the Sultan. Former Minister of Justice Abdulmalik bin Abdullah al-Khalili was appointed as Chairman of the State Council.

In September 2020 a request by the last Sultan of Zanzibar, Sayyid Jamshid bin Abdullah al-Said (who ruled in 1963–64), to return to Oman, was accepted, after 56 years of living in exile in the UK.

On his first anniversary as ruler, on 11 January 2021, Sultan Haitham abrogated the existing Basic Statute of the State and promulgated a new statute by royal decree. The new text, which was substantially similar to the previous version, ratified a paternalistic conception of a state whose guide is the Sultan, defined as 'the symbol of national unity' (Article 48). The ruler promulgates and ratifies laws and can grant pardons and commute sentences. Respecting him is a duty, and his orders must be obeyed. The major new contribution of the text relates to the creation of the position of Crown Prince (Article 7) and the succession process. The principle of male primogeniture becomes the rule, which guarantees that Haitham's elder son should succeed him.

The Council of Oman Law, which was promulgated in mid-January 2021, further restricted the already largely consultative role of the bicameral institution. The Council of Oman can propose laws, which must be referred to the Council of Ministers, but the latter has the right to reject them. Draft legislation prepared by the Council of Ministers should be referred to the Council of Oman (for approval or amendment only) before being submitted to the ruler for promulgation. Laws 'which the public interest requires' must be submitted directly to the ruler by the Council of Ministers, and the Consultative Council is permitted only to provide recommendations (which the Council of Ministers is free to ignore) concerning development projects and the annual state budget. Moreover, the Consultative Council cannot question the heads of sovereign ministries, and the opinion of the two chambers is not binding on the Sultan, who can dissolve both chambers.

In terms of policies regarding internal security and civil liberties, Sultan Haitham showed strong continuity with his predecessor. A new law issued by royal decree in March 2020 gave the Internal Security Service (ISS) broader grounds to exercise police powers of search and arrest and granted the head of the ISS power to issue the regulations necessary to implement the provisions of the law. In June a television presenter, Adel al-Kasbi, and a former member of the Consultative Council, Salim al-Awfi, whose application to stand as a candidate in the 2019 elections had been rejected, were sentenced to one year in prison on charges of 'using information technology to spread harm to public order', after posting critical statements on social media about government tyranny, corruption and a lack of justice in Omani courts. In the same month, Sultan Haitham established the Cyber Defence Centre (CDC) by royal decree. Affiliated to the ISS, the CDC has control over internet users and their devices, effectively leading to the suppression of dissenting opinions. In March 2021 the social media app Clubhouse was blocked. In December, after Consultative Council member Muhammad al-Zadjali criticized the Council's Chairman on a private radio station, the Ministry of Information instructed media outlets that the hosting of Consultative Council members would henceforth be subject to the prior approval of the authorities.

In scenes reminiscent of the protests of 2011–12, Omanis took to the streets again in May 2021, one month after the Government introduced a value-added tax of 5% on most goods and services. Originating in Sohar, protests quickly spread across the whole country, including the normally peaceable interior. The protesters' demands revolved around proactive measures to curb high youth unemployment, rising prices and economic inequality, while granting legislative powers to the elected Consultative Council. The Sultan promptly ordered the creation of some 32,000 public sector jobs, including in the military, but several dozen protesters and online activists were arrested before being released within a week. In early June security forces barricaded a number of royal palaces, major roads and the central districts of several towns to prevent protesters from gathering again.

In March 2022 criminal charges were filed against journalist Mukhtar al-Hinai, in reprisal for him disclosing information, via Twitter, on a corruption case involving officials who had been found guilty of embezzlement and falsification of documents; the Ministry of Information had previously prohibited the media from publishing anything about this subject. Al-Hinai, who had been imprisoned in 2012, having been convicted of lese-majesty, was acquitted in July 2022 of the charges brought against him in March.

In May 2022, in an effort to pre-empt popular protests about increasing economic hardship, the Government announced a series of discretionary measures, including the writing-off of the outstanding debts of all Housing Loans Programme beneficiaries. In June social media activists Maryam al-Nuaimi and Ali al-Ghafri, who had been arrested and held incommunicado in July 2021 following online discussions about the right to hold atheist views and to criticize Oman's Islamic heritage, were sentenced to prison terms of three and five years, respectively, on charges of blasphemy and the misuse of information technology.

In a minor cabinet reorganization in June 2022 the Minister of Energy and Minerals, Muhammad bin Hamad al-Rumhy, who had held the position since 1997, was replaced by his undersecretary Salem al-Oufi. Hilal al-Sabti and Muhammad al-Maamari were appointed as Minister of Health and Minister of Awqaf (Religious Endowments) and Religious Affairs, respectively. Also in June 2022, Sultan Haitham reconstituted by royal decree the Supreme Judicial Council, to incorporate and assume the responsibilities of the Administrative Affairs Council for the Judiciary, the Administrative Court and the Public Prosecution Department. Sultan Haitham appointed himself as Chairman of the new body and named as its Deputy Chairman the former Governor of Dhofar, Muhammad bin Sultan al-Busaidi, who was the subject of a complaint by citizens in 2021 regarding the unlawful distribution of lands to influential individuals in the governorate. Following the dismissal of the case against al-Busaidi by Dhofar's Administrative Court in February 2022, online activist Ahmad al-Kathiri was arrested and detained incommunicado, after he posted a message on Twitter stating that 'after the court ruling today, it is clear that the political power is still in control of the judiciary'. Three entrepreneurs were arrested in August while holding a sit-in in Bawshar (Muscat Governorate) to protest against government corruption and to call for urgent economic reforms. In October one of the entrepreneurs was sentenced to one year's imprisonment for 'calling for a gathering' and 'undermining the prestige of the state'.

As a result of the surge in the number of cases of citizens criticizing the lifestyle of the ruler's family on social media, in October 2022 Sultan Haitham amended the Penal Law by royal decree. According to the amendment, anyone who 'commits, publicly or through publication, a challenge to the rights of the Sultan, His prerogatives, or disgraces His person' would be punished with a gaol term of three to seven years. In addition, whoever published similar content about the wife of the Sultan and/or his children would receive the same punishment.

The third set of municipal elections, scheduled for 2020 but postponed owing to the outbreak of the coronavirus disease (COVID-19) pandemic in March of that year, took place in December 2022. All of the votes were cast via the Intekhab mobile telephone app—in a trial run for elections to the Consultative Council scheduled to take place in October 2023—but the turnout remained low (39.5%). Also in December 2022, internet activist Majid al-Ruhili was arrested after he had tweeted 'The non-democratic power ... uses a lot of election propaganda to create fake positions for the winner to sell illusion to society' and 'They wreaked havoc with public money and told the people to pay the price'. He was released after being held incommunicado for three weeks.

In March 2023 the National Centre for Statistics and Information announced that the total population of Oman had passed 5m. (57% of whom were Omani nationals), an increase of 80% since 2010. In 2021 47% of all Omani nationals were aged under 20 years. In April 2023 Sultan Haitham issued a royal decree allowing Omanis to marry foreign nationals without having first to obtain approval from the Ministry of Interior. However, it stated that such marriages should not contravene Islamic law and that the ruling did not apply to Omanis who held positions in 'public offices of special importance or nature'. In May the Sultan announced plans for the development of a new city named Sultan Haitham City in Seeb (Muscat Governorate), which was to house 100,000 residents. Covering 14.8m. sq km, the city was to be built in four phases and was scheduled for completion in 2045. The first phase of construction would take place during 2024–30.

In July 2023 new social protection and labour laws, scheduled to come into force in January 2024, were issued by royal decree. Also in July 2023, the Ministry of the Interior announced the final list of 843 candidates (including 32 women) for the 10th elections to the Consultative Council. Several candidates, including former Vice-Chairman of the Council's economic committee (2015–19) Ahmed al-Haddabi and internet activists Majid al-Rahili and Awad al-Sawafi, were banned from taking part, although reasons for this decision were not provided.

Meanwhile, the beginning of Sultan Haitham's rule was marked by the COVID-19 pandemic. In January 2020 Oman's Public Prosecution Department warned that spreading misinformation about the virus on social media would be punishable by a prison term of up to three years. In May 2022 all COVID-related restrictions were lifted, including the requirement to wear a face mask in public. As of July, Oman had registered 4,628 deaths associated with COVID-19 infection—the highest death rate per capita among members of the Cooperation Council for the Arab States of the Gulf (Gulf Cooperation Council—GCC, see p. 1131). Furthermore, the percentage of Oman's population who had been fully vaccinated against COVID-19 by that date, at about 60%, was lower than in the other GCC member states.

FOREIGN RELATIONS UNDER QABOOS AND HAITHAM, 1970–

Omani dependence on British military force to suppress the revolts in Jebel Akhdar and Dhofar were condemned by Egypt, the Syrian Arab Republic and Saudi Arabia, among others, increasing Oman's isolation in the Arab world. However, since the 1970s Saudi Arabia, Kuwait and the UAE have supplied much-needed financial aid to Oman. Oman's support for the Israeli-Egyptian peace treaty of 1979 threatened to damage relations with several members of the Arab League, but promised closer ties with the USA and with Egypt, which, at that time, undertook to respond to any request from Oman for military aid. Concern over regional security prompted Oman to join the GCC, which was founded in May 1981.

Under Sultan Haitham, who was the UK's preferred choice as Qaboos's successor, Oman is unlikely to lose its title of 'Britain's oldest friend in Arabia' (according to a correspondent of a British newspaper, *The Times*, in 1974). In his accession speech, Sultan Haitham stated that he intended to continue Qaboos's foreign policy. The corollary of the desire to perpetuate an independent policy towards its regional neighbours has been that Oman has never been able—and has certainly not wanted—to question the strategic and economic privileged partnership with the UK and the USA. Following the withdrawal of British forces from Masirah island in 1977, Oman and the USA signed in April 1980 a 'facilities access agreement' that allowed US troops use of Omani military facilities, but only with the agreement of the Omani Government. The renewal of the facilities (in 1985, 1990, 2000 and 2010) and of military co-operation agreements with the UK in 1985 and 1995 confirmed Oman's dependency on the USA and the UK.

In September 1985 Oman established diplomatic relations with the USSR. The move was encouraged by the peaceful relations that had been maintained between Oman and the PDRY since the resumption of diplomatic contact in October 1982.

After the invasion of Kuwait by Iraqi troops in August 1990, Oman, together with the other members of the GCC, gave its support to the deployment of a US-led defensive force in Saudi Arabia. In November Oman attempted to mediate in the crisis, and the Iraqi Minister of Foreign Affairs, Tareq Aziz, made the first official Iraqi visit to a GCC state, other than Kuwait, since the invasion. However, it wasn't until May 2019 that Oman announced its intention to reopen its embassy in Baghdad, which had been closed in August 1990, and to re-establish full diplomatic ties with Iraq.

Following the terrorist attacks perpetrated on the US mainland on 11 September 2001 ('9/11'), the US military presence in Oman increased to more than 4,300 personnel in support of Operation Enduring Freedom in Afghanistan. In March 2003, as the US-led forces began assaults on targets in Saddam Hussain's Iraq, Sultan Qaboos appealed for a swift curtailment of the conflict, which he described as 'unjustified' and 'illegitimate'. There were frequent anti-war protests in Oman at this time, as had been the case in relation to the conflict in Afghanistan. None the less, Oman was a close military ally of the USA. It hosted up to three US Air Force Expeditionary Wings supporting military operations in the GCC and Afghanistan, although the presence of these units was not commonly known in Oman. A few hundred US military personnel have been stationed in Oman since then, and each year Omani and US forces participate in joint exercises.

In 2006 the USA and Oman signed a bilateral free trade agreement, which came into force on 1 January 2009. Since June 2015 the USA has transferred at least 30 detainees from Guantanamo Bay, Cuba, to Oman for resettlement. Oman officially joined the US-led coalition against the Islamic State in Iraq and the Levant (subsequently renamed Islamic State) in 2014, but did not actively participate in military operations. In March 2019 Oman and the USA signed a 'Strategic Framework Agreement' that expanded the 1980 military agreement by allowing US forces to use the ports of Duqm and Salalah and to upgrade storage facilities, with the construction of new runways at Musannah airbase. In August 2021, after the Taliban seized the Afghan capital, Kabul, and prompted the rapid withdrawal of US and other Western troops, Grand Mufti Ahmed bin Hamad al-Khalili praised on Twitter the 'victory of the brotherly Muslim people of Afghanistan against the aggressive invaders', in a notable instance of a senior Omani departing from the country's general alignment on US policy in West Asia.

Confidential US National Security Agency documents released in 2013 revealed the existence of the British intelligence and security agency GCHQ's Middle East base at Seeb, near Muscat, which extracts communications information from undersea cables. In October 2018 a British Joint Logistics Support Base was opened in Duqm. This joint venture between British defence company Babcock International and the Oman Drydock Company provides the UK with a permanent training facility (at Ras Madrakah, south of Duqm) and key logistics centre in the Gulf. It supported the third British-Omani joint military exercise in October–November 2018, the UK's largest military exercise in the Middle East in 20 years. In February 2019 a new British-Omani joint defence agreement, allowing the UK to maintain a permanent military presence in Oman for the first time since the 1970s, was signed in Muscat by British Secretary of State for Defence Gavin Williamson and Oman's Minister responsible for Defence Affairs Sayyid Badr bin Saud al-Busaidi. In May 2019 the Minister responsible for Foreign Affairs, Yousuf bin Alawi, and the British Secretary of State for Foreign and Commonwealth Affairs, Jeremy Hunt, signed a British-Omani Comprehensive Agreement in London, UK. Referring to the 'spirit of' the 1798 Anglo-Omani treaty, this text aimed to reinforce bilateral political, economic, scientific and cultural ties between the two countries. The British heir to the throne, Prince Charles, and the British Prime Minister, Boris Johnson, visited Oman on the first day of mourning after Qaboos's death in January 2020. In response to written parliamentary questions in June 2021, the British Minister for Defence Procurement, James Heappey, confirmed that 'the UK currently has 230 military personnel based in Oman' and that they 'are in regular contact with the Omani authorities ... to share ideas and experience on all aspects of security'. In December Sultan Haitham made a 10-day visit to the UK, where he met Prime Minister Johnson, who acknowledged 'the strategic importance of the Duqm base in Oman for the UK'. Sultan Haitham was hosted by the head of state Queen Elizabeth II at Windsor Castle, in one of the few official audiences that the 95-year-old British monarch gave in late 2021.

Following Queen Elizabeth II's death on 8 September 2022, Sultan Haitham ordered Omani flags to be flown at half-mast in public and private sectors and in Omani embassies abroad.

He attended the reception hosted by the new King, Charles III, at his London residence, Buckingham Palace, on 18 September, while Minister of Foreign Affairs Sayyid Badr bin Hamad al-Busaidi represented Oman at the Queen's funeral the following day. Sayyid Theyazin represented his father at King Charles III's coronation in London in May 2023. In November 2022, during a UK Defence Committee hearing, British Secretary of State for Defence Ben Wallace announced that the British Army would increase its presence in Oman, as the use of the Duqm base for advanced brigade combat team training would be expanded from around six weeks per year to more than eight months per year.

Oman joined the other GCC states in voting for the UN General Assembly resolution adopted in early March 2022 condemning the invasion of Ukraine by the Russian Federation and calling for Moscow to withdraw its troops. During a visit by Russia's Minister of Foreign Affairs, Sergei Lavrov, to Muscat in May, Sultan Haitham 'stressed the need to adhere to the rules of international law and to intensify efforts to reach political and diplomatic solutions through dialogue'. In an interview with a French newspaper in the same month, foreign affairs minister Badr bin Hamad al-Busaidi stated that Oman was 'neutral ... Mistakes were made on both sides', and that Oman did not 'want to be dragged into' the imposition of international sanctions on Russia. The sixth joint ministerial meeting of the Russia-GCC strategic dialogue was held in July 2023 in Moscow. Badr bin Hamad al-Busaidi chaired the GCC side. A joint action plan for 2023–28 was adopted, focusing on increasing trade and investment, as well as elevating co-operation in the fields of energy, agriculture and food security, and health care.

In July 2022 Sultan Haitham made a three-day official visit to Germany and held meetings with President Frank-Walter Steinmeier and Chancellor Olaf Scholz. The two countries signed a declaration of intent for co-operation in the fields of renewable energy technologies, smart networks and energy efficiency.

Oman officially demarcated its common borders with Saudi Arabia and the UAE in July 1995 and July 2008, respectively. However, relations with the UAE deteriorated significantly in 2004, after the UAE armed forces dismissed the large number of Omani soldiers that it employed. This was followed by the UAE's construction of an extensive fence and border posts between Al-Ain (UAE) and Al-Buraymi. In January 2011 the Omani security forces claimed that they had uncovered a UAE spy ring within the Omani Government and military; the UAE denied the allegations. However, Oman fully supported the decision by Saudi Arabia and the UAE to send troops to Bahrain in March to suppress peaceful protests. In the same month Oman also accepted GCC plans for an aid package worth more than US $10,000m. over 10 years to help Oman to cope with anti-Government protests. In January 2014 Sultan Qaboos ratified the GCC security pact signed in November 2012, which allowed for the integration of the security apparatuses of signatory states to provide support during times of unrest.

Like Kuwait, Oman did not join the diplomatic and economic blockade imposed on Qatar by Saudi Arabia, Bahrain, the UAE and Egypt in June 2017. Oman was used by Qatar to circumvent the economic blockade. Relations between Oman and the UAE have also been affected by the political situation in al-Mahrah governorate, in eastern Yemen, where Oman, the UAE and Saudi Arabia have been competing for influence for about a decade. In November 2018 Oman issued a decree prohibiting GCC nationals from owning property in several areas of the country (including governorates bordering Saudi Arabia and the UAE), reflecting tensions with its two neighbours.

Sultan Haitham's accession to the throne was welcomed by Abu Dhabi's Crown Prince, Sheikh Mohammed bin Zayed Al Nahyan, whose investment vehicle, Mubadala, was associated with Haitham's business assets. In May 2022 Haitham visited Abu Dhabi to offer his condolences to Mohammed bin Zayed Al Nahyan, the new President of the UAE, following the recent death of his predecessor in the post, Sheikh Khalifa bin Zayed Al Nahyan. In September Mohammed bin Zayed Al Nahyan made a two-day state visit to Muscat during which the establishment of a joint venture, the Oman-Etihad Rail Company, which was to build and operate a cross-border freight and passenger rail link between Abu Dhabi and Sohar, was signed. Abu Dhabi's sovereign wealth fund ADQ and the Oman Investment Authority also announced that they were in discussions regarding joint investment opportunities (valued at US $8,000m.) in Oman, in the fields of hydrogen, solar and wind power, food and agriculture, health care, and water and electricity networks. Along with the rulers of Bahrain, Egypt, Jordan and Qatar, Sultan Haitham attended a summit in Abu Dhabi in January 2023 on 'Prosperity and Stability in the Region', which focused on deepening economic co-operation among the countries.

Following the signature by GCC member states of the Al-Ula agreement in January 2021 restoring ties between blockading countries and Qatar, Saudi-Omani relations took a notable turn. In July Sultan Haitham made a two-day visit to the new economic city of NEOM, Saudi Arabia—his first official trip abroad since assuming power—and held meetings with Saudi King Salman bin Abdulaziz Al Sa'ud and Crown Prince Mohammed bin Salman bin Abdulaziz Al Sa'ud, the de facto ruler of the kingdom. The two countries' leaders reportedly discussed means of 'strengthening fraternal ties between the two brotherly Omani and Saudi peoples'. In November Haitham made a two-day visit to Qatar and held a meeting with Amir Sheikh Tamim bin Hamad Al Thani. The two leaders witnessed the signing of an investment co-operation agreement between the Qatari and Omani sovereign wealth funds.

Crown Prince Mohammad bin Salman Al Sa'ud was received by Sultan Haitham in Muscat in December 2021. A total of 13 memorandums of understanding (MOUs) concerning petrochemicals, renewable energy, green hydrogen, real estate, mining and fisheries, and valued at a combined total of US $30,000m., were signed between companies from the two countries. During the Crown Prince's visit, a direct road link through the Rub Al-Khali desert, which skirts the UAE and gives Saudi Arabia more direct access to the Indian Ocean, was officially opened. In a further sign of warming bilateral ties, Saudi Arabia's Chief of the General Staff, Gen. Fayyadh bin Hamid al-Ruwaili, and Royal Saudi Air Force Commander Lt-Gen. Prince Turki bin Bandar Al Sa'ud visited Muscat for talks with senior Omani security officials, in January and July 2022, respectively. In December the Muscat Stock Exchange and the Saudi Stock Exchange (Tadawul) signed an agreement to enable dual listings, allowing companies to gain access to both financial markets. Two months later, during the Saudi-Omani Investment Forum in Riyadh, Saudi Arabia, the Saudi Fund for Development announced that it would provide $320m. for a joint project to build the infrastructure of a new special economic zone in Oman's Al-Dhahirah Governorate, 20 km from the new border checkpoint in the Rub Al-Khali desert.

Sultan Qaboos maintained diplomatic relations with Tehran after the Islamic Revolution in 1979, not wanting to present Iran as the sole source of regional tensions. In early 1987 Oman tried to convince Tehran to approve the UN resolution putting an end to the war against Iraq but later supported the Arab League's condemnation of Iran for prolonging hostilities. In March 1991 Oman hosted a meeting at which diplomatic relations between Saudi Arabia and Iran were restored.

Oman's increasing dependence on Iran for natural gas has given the Government a particular interest in maintaining good relations with the Islamic Republic since the mid-2000s. In August 2009 Sultan Qaboos paid a state visit to Tehran to promote trade between the two countries. This was his first visit to Iran since 1974. In the following year, the two countries agreed to hold joint military exercises and to increase co-operation in protecting common borders and in tackling the trafficking of drugs and people. In August 2013 Sultan Qaboos returned to Tehran. President Hassan Rouhani visited Oman in March 2014 (his first official visit to an Arab country since his election in 2013) and signed an agreement for Iran to supply Oman with gas via a pipeline linking southern Iran to northern Oman. A comprehensive agreement to expand Oman-Iran economic co-operation was signed in January 2015. In September of the following year the two countries exchanged the final documents of an agreement delineating a 450-km section of their maritime border which had not previously been defined.

Since the early 2010s Oman has also acted as mediator in securing the release of US and UK nationals held by Iran, as well as Iranian nationals detained by the UK and the USA. Oman supports Iran's use of nuclear energy for peaceful purposes and opposes the use of force against Iran. However, Oman does not support Iran's claims to sovereignty over Abu Musa and the Tunb islands (all of which are claimed by the UAE). Oman also facilitated the back channel that helped to lead to the conclusion of the Iran–E3/EU+3 nuclear agreement in July 2015. The US Government's reimposition of sanctions on Iran from August 2018, following its withdrawal from the Joint Comprehensive Plan of Action (JCPOA), considerably slowed Oman-Iran economic co-operation. Minister responsible for Foreign Affairs Yousuf bin Alawi, who was received by President Rouhani in Tehran in July 2019, clarified that Oman was not undertaking any mediation efforts around tensions in the Gulf but was 'in contact with all parties'.

In March 2022 the Omani Government assisted in securing the release of two British-Iranian nationals, Nazanin Zaghari-Ratcliffe and Anoosheh Ashoori, who had been held in Iranian prisons since 2016 and 2017, respectively. Iranian President Ebrahim Raisi visited Oman in May 2022 to discuss developing closer bilateral commercial ties. Eight MOUs and four co-operation programmes were signed in fields including energy, higher education, transport and agriculture, and the two countries confirmed their commitment to revive plans for an underwater pipeline to deliver Iranian gas to Oman. In December Oman voted against a US resolution at the UN Economic and Social Council to remove Iran from the Commission on the Status of Women for the remainder of its four-year term ending in 2026. In March 2023, when Saudi Arabia, Iran and China issued a statement announcing an agreement to resume diplomatic relations between Riyadh and Tehran, it was revealed that Oman, like Iraq, had hosted lower-level direct talks between Saudi Arabia and Iran since 2021.

In May 2023 Sultan Haitham visited Egypt to meet President Abd al-Fatah al-Sisi, before travelling to Tehran, where he informed Supreme Leader Ayatollah Seyed Ali Hosseini Khamenei of Egypt's interest in restoring relations with Iran. Several MOUs on investments and free zone developments were signed between Iran and Oman, as well as an agreement jointly to explore and develop the shared Hengam-Bukha gasfield. In the same month, US media revealed that rounds of indirect talks were to take place in Oman in June between US National Security Council Co-ordinator for the Middle East and North Africa Brett McGurk and Iran's chief nuclear negotiator, Ali Bagheri Kani. Also in May, as part of a prisoner swap mediated by Oman, four Europeans were released by Iran in return for the release of Asadollah Assadi, an Iranian diplomat detained in Belgium.

The agreement between Oman and Yemen (the Yemen Arab Republic and the PDRY were unified in May 1990) to establish the demarcation of their border was completed in June 1995. In July 1996 Oman withdrew its troops from the last of the disputed territories on the Yemeni border. Saudi claims that the border agreement violated sovereign Saudi territory were rejected by both Oman and Yemen. Out of concern for the consequences that the instability in Yemen could have on its own territory, Oman contracted an Indian state-run company in 2013 to build a fence along its Yemeni border; the work on this project was expected to continue until at least 2024. Oman, which considers Yemen's Ansar Allah (Supporters of God) Shia group, otherwise known as the al-Houthis, as a faction representing a part of Yemeni society that cannot be ignored in the establishment of a post-conflict order, was the only GCC state not to join Saudi Arabia's military campaign against the al-Houthis in March 2015, and made efforts to bring the warring parties to the negotiating table. Omani-Saudi relations deteriorated further in September 2015 when the Omani ambassador's residence in San'a, the Yemeni capital, was hit in air strikes conducted by the Saudi air force. Saudi Arabia denied targeting the Omani embassy.

The Sultanate has hosted regular meetings since 2019 between al-Houthi delegations and UN Special Envoys to Yemen in efforts to resolve the conflict. The Saudis strengthened their positions in al-Mahrah governorate in eastern Yemen during the first half of 2020, effectively turning the governorate into the site of a power struggle between Saudi Arabia and Oman. An Omani delegation travelled to San'a in June 2021 to meet al-Houthi leaders—the first such trip since the conflict began in 2014. During the visit an online meeting was arranged between Sultan Haitham and the al-Houthis' leader Abdulmalik al-Houthi. Saudi Arabia's decision to withdraw its forces from al-Mahrah governorate in November 2021 was welcomed by Oman, which views the region as part of its sphere of influence. However, the Saudi withdrawal was expected to place more pressure on Muscat to prevent violations of the arms embargo imposed by the UN on the al-Houthis. In April 2022 Oman negotiated the release of 15 foreign nationals (including crew members of a UAE-flagged cargo ship), who had been kidnapped and held in al-Houthi custody. In September and October UN Special Envoy to Yemen Hans Grundberg held further meetings with the al-Houthis' chief negotiator, Muhammad Abdel Salam, in Muscat. In April 2023 talks between Saudi officials and al-Houthi representatives in San'a were co-ordinated by Oman, but did not result in a major breakthrough.

Oman, which had only in 1988 recognized the existence of the Palestinian leadership, established relations with Israel in 1993. In April 1994 the Israeli Deputy Minister of Foreign Affairs, Yossi Beilin, made the first official visit by an Israeli minister to a GCC state since Israel's declaration of independence in 1948. In September 1994 Oman and the other GCC member states announced the partial ending of their economic boycott of Israel. The Israeli Prime Minister, Itzhak Rabin, made an official visit to the Sultanate in November, and in February 1995 it was announced that low-level diplomatic relations were to be established between the two countries. Israel opened its trade office in Muscat in May 1996. Oman opened its trade office in Tel Aviv in August. However, in April 1997, in accordance with an Arab League resolution adopted in March, Oman officially resumed the economic boycott of Israel. In July Oman announced the opening of a representative office in the Palestinian (National) Authority (PA)-administered city of Gaza, and in June 1998 Yasser Arafat, the President of the PA, visited Oman. In October 2000, after the start of the second *intifada* (uprising), Oman closed both its trade office in Tel Aviv and the Israeli trade office in Muscat.

Less than one week after Palestinian President Mahmoud Abbas's visit to Oman, the Israeli Prime Minister, Benjamin Netanyahu, was invited to Muscat for talks with Sultan Qaboos in October 2018. This official visit led many Omanis to express support for the Palestinian cause via social networks, leading to waves of arrests until March 2019. In an interview with an Israeli newspaper in April, Yousuf bin Alawi emphasized that Oman would not normalize relations with Israel until a Palestinian state had been established, but stated that 'as Arabs, we must see how we can eliminate Israel's feeling that it has enemies in the region'. In June 2020 Oman announced its decision to open an embassy in Palestine, in the West Bank city of Ramallah.

Following the Israeli-Emirati normalization agreement in August 2020, Oman issued an official statement celebrating the deal as 'a step towards the achievement of peace in the Middle East', prompting many Omanis to express their disagreement. The Grand Mufti warned on social media that the liberation of Jerusalem from Israeli occupation remained a sacred duty, and if the circumstances did not allow the Muslims to achieve it, then they should not compromise it in any way. In May 2021 hundreds of Omanis rallied in Muscat's embassy district to demand that the international community order Israel to cease air strikes on the besieged Gaza Strip. In July Minister of Foreign Affairs Badr bin Hamad al-Busaidi confirmed, in an interview with the British-based newspaper *Asharq Al-Awsat*, that Oman was satisfied with the current level of bilateral relations with Israel and 'will not be the third Gulf state to normalise ties'. Oman joined Saudi Arabia in opening its airspace to the national carriers of Israel in February 2023. The Grand Mufti expressed his 'surprise' on social media, saying 'We had hoped that our proud authority would continue its steadfast position against any relationship with that entity [Israel] ... We fear that this step will be followed by other steps.'

In October 2020 the new Omani ambassador to Syria took up his post in Damascus—the first GCC ambassador to resume residence in the Syrian capital, as Oman was one of the few Arab states to have maintained ties with Damascus since 2011. In May 2021 Sultan Haitham was the first GCC leader to congratulate Bashar al-Assad on being re-elected as President of Syria. In January 2022 Badr bin Hamad al-Busaidi visited Syria and was received by al-Assad, and in February 2023 the Syrian President visited Oman—his second such trip to an Arab state since 2011. Bashar al-Assad and Haitham discussed regional issues and bilateral ties.

Sultan Haitham welcomed Tanzanian President Samia Suluhu Hassan to Muscat in June 2022. In a sign of growing interest in expanding historical ties, several MOUs were signed, including on energy and tourism, and the establishment of a joint investment fund was discussed.

Oman's relations with India have strengthened considerably since the 1990s. In December 2005 Oman and India signed an MOU on defence co-operation—the first agreement of its type that India had signed with a GCC state. This was followed in March 2006 by the establishment of the India-Oman Joint Military Co-operation Committee—the first such agreement that India had established with a Muslim state. In November 2008 the US $100m. Oman-India Investment Fund was established to promote Omani investment in India. In February 2018, during an official visit to Oman by Prime Minister Narendra Modi, the two countries signed eight co-operation agreements relating to defence, health care, tourism and legal and judicial matters.

Oman also significantly strengthened its economic ties with several East Asian countries in the 2010s. Oman is part of a GCC free trade agreement with Singapore, which entered into force in September 2013. Since 2018 Oman has held the status of 'strategic partner' for China, which is the largest investor in the Special Economic Zone at the port of Duqm. In May 2016 an agreement regarding the construction of an industrial park, called the Sino-Oman Industrial City, in Duqm, was signed between a consortium of Chinese companies and the Special Economic Zone Authority at Duqm. Various installations, including an oil refinery, a heavy petrochemicals complex, an aluminium smelter and a seawater desalination facility, were planned, as part of a total investment of US $10,700m. by 2023. Meanwhile, in July 2017 the Government of Oman signed a $3,550m. five-year maturity loan from three Chinese banks—the largest such loan for a Middle Eastern borrower in the Chinese market. In December 2019 the Omani Government sold a 49% stake in its electricity transmission network operator to State Grid Corporation of China for about $1,000m. Moreover, Oman supported China in a vote at the UN Human Rights Council in Geneva, Switzerland, in July 2020 on the introduction of China's new national security law in Hong Kong. In April 2022 Chinese Minister of National Defence Lt-Gen. Wei Fenghe held talks in Muscat with Badr bin Hamad al-Busaidi and Sayyid Shihab about enhancing joint military co-operation and potential investment by China in the Omani energy and food security sectors.

Meanwhile, in March 2019 Minister responsible for Defence Affairs Badr bin Saud al-Busaidi and his Japanese counterpart, Takeshi Iyawa, signed an MOU in Tokyo, the Japanese capital, on military co-operation between the two countries.

Economy

FRANCIS OWTRAM

INTRODUCTION

It is a central assertion of the academic field of political economy that the realms of politics and economics are inevitably closely linked. Perhaps this is the case no more so than in the monarchies of the Cooperation Council for the Arab States of the Gulf (Gulf Cooperation Council—GCC, see p. 1131). The economies of these states are often referred to as rentier economies in that the greatest part of their gross domestic product (GDP) accrues from the sale of a single commodity—oil—on the world market. These oil revenues accrue to the state without needing to extract other revenue from the populace by means of taxation, and so the government does not offer meaningful representation. This has been termed the 'rentier social contract'; other typical features include a relatively low population of indigenous citizens, a high proportion of whom are employed in the public sector with generous subsidies, and a high dependence on expatriate labour to undertake most of the productive work. Oman shares some of these characteristics with its neighbours but also exhibits a number of notable differences. It has a much larger population of indigenous citizens, a diversity of geographical terrain and a tradition of political community on the south-eastern corner of the Arabian Peninsula, which extends back over several millennia. Crucially, it has much more limited oil and gas reserves in comparison with its neighbours Saudi Arabia and the United Arab Emirates (UAE), and therefore the need to diversify away from oil is that much more pressing for Oman.

This essay surveys the historical development and key sectors of the economy of Oman from independence in 1970 to the present day, utilizing a political economy approach. Following the introduction, the essay first sketches the historical context of Oman's economic development up to the coup that brought Sultan Qaboos bin Said al-Said to power in 1970. This coup, it is claimed, constitutes the founding moment of modern Oman. It then proceeds to analyse the development of the rentier economy as it took place during the time of the Dhofar War (1963–76) in Oman's far south-western governorate. This is placed in the context of fluctuations in global oil prices. Tracking the five-year development plans, the first of which was introduced in 1976, the essay traces the development of the national infrastructure in roads, education and health care, identifying the state as a motor of economic growth using revenues from the export of oil. After Sultan Qaboos was involved in a near-fatal car crash in 1995, substantive plans for diversification (Vision 2020 and later Vision 2040) were proposed. However, it is possible to surmise that Qaboos envisaged the implementation of this vision to be attempted only in earnest once he had departed from the scene, thus a task for his successor. The final section of the essay is concerned with developments since 2020: the death of Qaboos and the coronavirus disease (COVID-19) pandemic, the accession of Sultan Haitham bin Tarik al-Said and measures to diversify the economy.

OMAN'S ECONOMY OVER THE MILLENNIA

In contrast to many of the other GCC states, which owe their existence largely to the establishment of a relationship of their ruling families with the British in the 19th century, Oman has a history over several millennia of a community exploiting the economic possibilities for subsistence and indeed prospering on the south-east corner of the Arabian Peninsula. In the 17th, 18th and 19th centuries an Indian Ocean-focused economy developed, based on trade in enslaved peoples, ivory and cloves, which was so valuable that the ruling sultans from the Al Bu-Said dynasty eventually moved their capital from Muscat to the island of Zanzibar, having first ousted the Portuguese from the Arabian and East African coastlines. The British-sponsored separation of the Zanzibar and Muscat sultanates in the mid-19th century led to the impoverishment of the Arabian branch of the Al Bu-Said dynasty. (As an historical footnote, the Zanzibar-based sultans were overthrown in 1964, and the last sultan lived in the United Kingdom until being allowed to return to Oman in 2020.) It suited British strategic interests to keep the capital, Muscat, isolated as a quiet stopover on the route to India. In the late Victorian age of British dominance in the Gulf, Oman remained nominally an independent state, but the country can be considered as part of the UK's informal empire in the Gulf in which the British managed all of the Sultanate's foreign relations through special treaty relations.

In the 1920s the outside world and the developing needs of a global capitalist economy impinged on the isolation of the Arabian littoral through oil concessions and the concomitant need to establish sovereign frontiers. As it was supporting the Al Bu-Said sultans, the UK sought to restructure the administration and economy of 'Muscat State' through the provision of a financial adviser, Bertram Thomas, although he actually focused more on his passion for desert exploration.

In 1932 Said bin Taimur became Sultan and, perceiving that Omani debts to British-Indian merchants was the basis for his dependence on the British Government, he embarked on a programme of cost-cutting. He abolished the Regency Council and cut subsidies to members of the ruling family. His aversion to starting projects, including those related to economic development, until he had all the funds in hand for the completion of the scheme, was an approach that he continued until near the end of his reign, as articulated in his 1968 declaration, 'The Word of Said bin Taimur'.

The date of 23 July 1970, when Qaboos bin Said removed his father, Sultan Said bin Taimur, in a palace coup in Salalah, is arguably the founding moment of the modern Omani state and the point from which Oman began to emerge from the embrace of British informal imperialism. This is the point from which this essay will trace the development of the Omani (political) economy. As this development has been based on oil revenues it is first necessary to set this in brief historical context.

THE DISCOVERY OF OIL IN OMAN AND THE DEVELOPMENT OF A RENTIER ECONOMY

Following the award of a concession in the 1920s and a number of oil exploration expeditions including a near-miss, oil was discovered at Fahud in 1964. Oil revenues began to accrue in the Sultanate's coffers after oil exports commenced in 1967. At this point Sultan Said gave his only ever statement to the Omani people on his approach to economic development in 'The Word of Said bin Taimur' declaration. He explained his cautious approach to economic development and his restrictive approach to letting the outside world intrude, which included a ban on radios and emigration, as well as a mistrust of education.

However, for the people of Oman, who had to emigrate illegally to partake in the oil-fuelled expansion taking place at Kuwait (Graz has written that the word used in Kuwait for a labourer in the 1950s was 'Omani') this was too late, and in particular for the populace of Dhofar, who had to bear the continual presence of Said in his palace in Salalah, the Dhofari capital. Rebellion had broken out in Dhofar in 1963, and, upon the establishment of the Marxist People's Democratic Republic of South Yemen that followed the British withdrawal from Aden in 1967, Dhofar subsequently took a Marxist-Leninist turn when in 1968, at the Second Congress of the Dhofar Liberation Front, the organization changed its name to Popular Front for the Liberation of the Occupied Arabian Gulf. Qaboos, who had remained under virtual palace arrest since his return from officer training at the military academy in Sandhurst, UK, sought the help of his Sandhurst classmate, Tim Landon. The UK, concerned about a potential loss of influence, organized the 1970 Salalah palace coup which brought Qaboos to the throne.

Immediately, Qaboos sought to leverage the newly flowing oil revenues both to fight the war in Dhofar (some 50% of the national budget was allocated to the Ministry of Defence) and embark on an ambitious programme of modernization in economic infrastructure to move beyond subsistence agriculture and fishing. The amount of arable land as a proportion of the total land area in Oman was estimated at just 1%. Large-scale agriculture has historically been confined to two coastal strips, the Batinah plain (in the al-Batinah region) and the Salalah plains (in Dhofar governorate), where dates, limes, tomatoes, onions are grown in rich alluvial soil. Fish is an essential part of the diet of the Omani people, including the people of the interior desert regions, where fish is desiccated and salted for year-round consumption.

ECONOMIC DEVELOPMENT SINCE 1970

The period of modernization since 1970 is often referred to by the sultanate authorities as the Omani renaissance (al-nahda). For Qaboos and his British backers, the immediate priority was to win the war in Dhofar. In this effort, the recently flowing oil revenues were a critical asset which increased by fourfold as a result of the 1973 Arab–Israeli War and again after the Islamic revolution in Iran in 1979. It is thus important to note that between Qaboos's ascension to power in July 1970 until the end of the Dhofar War (in effect in 1975), oil profits were essential to fund defence and a war economy before Oman was stable enough to consider the typical welfare rentier model of the Gulf. An examination of the historical record relating to Middle East oil revenue indicates that such revenues suddenly increased in the first period of high oil prices from 1973 to 1983 and 'flooded' the entire region, engulfing all states in the process of rent circulation. However, this was a limited experience, which was not repeated in the second period of high prices (2004–14): the major oil-exporting states were already rentier, in the sense of being independent of domestic taxation, before 1973, and continue to be so. As the state does not have to compromise with society, there is a distinct authoritarian tendency in which the provision of wide-ranging benefits and state employment for citizens obviates the need for the state to make concessions in terms of political participation. Hence, Qaboos's early years were punctuated by a heavy reliance on oil for political and military survival amid a conflict that posed questions around his legitimacy from the start of his reign. This reliance would also feed into state development, and will be discussed below.

Sultan Qaboos, with British strategic support, pursued a 'hearts and minds' campaign in which the 'legitimate' grievances of the people were met through health care and employment provision, alongside the gradual military elimination of the resistance to the British-backed sultanate regime. In this, the sultanate forces (which were staffed by British officers) were supported by other monarchies, financially and militarily, by the Shah of Iran and by Jordan. Through the construction of a series of defensive military lines after each monsoon, the Dhofari rebels were gradually pushed back until in 1975 the war was declared to be over. In 1977 the British flag at Oman's airfields was lowered for the last time as the facilities were handed over officially to the Omani authorities. It should be noted that until 1990 the Commander of the Royal Air Force of Oman was a seconded British officer. Even in 2023 a number of seconded British military personnel still provide important services to the Omani armed forces.

In addition to the expansion and upgrading of the Omani armed forces, massive construction programmes in transport infrastructure, hospitals and health care facilities and educational establishments at all levels were initiated as part of a series of five-year plans that commenced in 1976. As elsewhere in the Gulf, this involved the 'importation' of many expatriate staff from the Asian sub-continent as construction workers. The provision of employment for Omani nationals as civil servants accelerated, and eventually almost 80% of Omanis were employed in the public sector. In this process, a delicate balance was pursued between the various social components of the Sultanate on the coast and the powerful tribes of the interior.

DEVELOPMENT OF THE OIL AND GAS SECTOR

In the early years of Sultan Qaboos's rule the price of oil increased from US $2 per barrel in 1971 to $35 per barrel in 1980. Oil was initially found in Yibal in 1962, and fields were subsequently discovered in Natih and Fahud in the following two years. After the construction of a power plant in Fahud, commercial exploitation became viable, and in 1967 the first oil tanker left with about 500,000 barrels of Omani oil for export 30 years after the first concession agreement had been inked.

More fields were brought online in the central and southern regions of Oman, requiring additional pipelines and refinery capacity: the Mina' al-Fahal and Sohar refineries were brought into service in 1982 and 2007, respectively. Overseen by the Ministry of Energy and Minerals, Petroleum Development Oman (PDO—a hydrocarbons exploration and production company) has progressively increased its investment and activity in the oil sector, and by late 2020 it managed 67% of total reserves. The Ministry of Energy and Minerals' 2019 *Annual Report,* which was published in July 2020, reported that reserves of crude oil and condensates in the Sultanate totalled 4,843m. barrels at the end of 2019. Total reserves of natural gas at the end of 2019 were estimated to be 23,800,000m. cu ft—53.7% were held by the PDO, followed by BP with 41.0% (the Khazzan and Ghazeer fields) and 5.3% was held by other companies. The Government of Oman retains a majority shareholding of 60% in the PDO, Royal Dutch Shell holds 34%, and the French companies Total (4%) and Partex (2%) own the remainder. The Sultanate's average daily production of crude oil in June 2020 was 683,625 barrels per day, according to the ministry's monthly report.

Oman exports more than 90% of its oil to the Far East, and the People's Republic of China is the major customer of Omani crude. Oman declined to join the Organization of the Petroleum Exporting Countries or the Organization of Arab Petroleum Exporting Countries, so it can pursue an independent oil policy. Oman's revenues from oil increased in line with global oil prices before the 2014 crash. Omani oil is relatively expensive to produce in comparison with Saudi Arabia, as Omani fields are more dispersed, and the terrain is more challenging; as a result the production costs of Omani oil are about seven times those of Saudi Arabia's. Furthermore, Oman's reserves are far more limited.

Over the past four decades global oil prices have fluctuated, including crashes in 1986 and 2014. Based on the revenues from oil exports, a series of five-year development plans starting in 1976 sought to modernize Oman, with the state as the motor of economic development. The first metalled road linked Muscat with Sohar in 1973, and gradually the road network was developed, and by 2013 the metalled road network extended to some 32,600 km. The development of a construction sector was promoted to meet the needs of this infrastructure building. The early profits from petroleum exports allowed the Government to tender out projects for massive infrastructure projects to build roads, bridges, ports and airports, water supply to consultants, international organizations and foreign companies.

By the 1980s Oman had experienced an oil boom, and Qaboos had established himself as the founder of modern Oman. This notion of Qaboos as the father of the nation was summed up by a comment made several years after the 1970 coup: 'Before him there was nothing, now there is everything'. It was time to focus on development, with an emphasis on increasing government capabilities. Although the 1970s witnessed a steadier flow of oil profits, it was not until after the end of the Dhofar War in 1975 that more resources could be devoted to increasing the reach and competency of government services. Not only had the civil war drained state resources, but it had also hindered centralized planning, construction and the expansion of infrastructure. The first five-year development plan (1976–80) sought to include Dhofar in such expansion in order to minimize potential grievances after the war, as well as developing Muscat as modern Oman's capital, with the aim of the city hosting marine ports and airports, emphasizing Oman's desire to be globally connected. However, the 1986 oil glut and concomitant oil price crash threw off Qaboos's third five-year plan (1986–90). Muscat received some upgrades, but many such projects in Dhofar were suspended—a reminder that Oman's modernization was inextricably linked to and fuelled by the state's hydrocarbons sector. Qaboos was only too aware of this fact, illustrated by outside observations that he avoided the ostentatious projects of some of his Gulf neighbours, preferring instead 'carefully planned development' that shunned extravagance.

The volatility of oil wealth encouraged Oman to establish the State General Reserve Fund (SGRF) in 1980, into which oil revenue was channelled. The Fund partly cushioned the impact of the 1986 oil glut, when revenue collapsed. Simultaneously, a separate Contingency Fund was established to meet expenses in unforeseen circumstances. The rationale was to ensure that a second fund was available to prevent ad hoc rather than planned use of the SGRF during financial emergencies. However, the SGRF did not perform as expected and, in the event, became an emergency fund that was drawn upon to cushion the effect of price spikes in the very resource that it was funded by. Oil price fluctuations and rising state debt in the 1980s led to declining contributions to the SGRF.

In August 1990 Kuwait was invaded by Iraqi troops on the orders of President Saddam Hussain. The consequent instability and disruption to oil supplies briefly led to an increase in prices for oil-importing states. With Kuwait under siege, its customers turned to other Gulf states, including Oman, to meet their hydrocarbons demands. Oil funded the expansion of the Omani education and health care sectors at a time when oil prices exceeded state expenditure on such expansion—a reminder that five-year plans seeking to reform education to meet labour market demands away from oil were still funded by Oman's sole commodity.

A report published by the World Bank in 1994 included the observation that the 'use of the SGRF as an oil revenue stabilization fund has pre-empted its potential as a vehicle for long-term public savings and investment. The planned allocation of most of the money flowing into the [. . .] Fund to the financing of planned public sector deficits means that funds are not available to deal with genuine emergencies'. The reality of using oil revenue to plug public sector deficits reflected Oman's dependence on oil to maintain its generous welfare state.

CORRUPTION IN THE OIL AND GAS SECTOR

In 2004 a series of arrests were made, including of oil company officials. Corruption has been especially rampant in the oil industry, which is an ongoing concern, as it is through oil that Oman has financed its development, including social services and the attraction of foreign investment. Corruption has traditionally been linked to (international) dealings with the political and business elite, risking a negative effect on foreign investment by enforcing the image of pervasive corruption. As with other Arab states, corruption not only affected international trade but also domestic stability. In 2011 the so-called 'Arab Spring' protests affected Oman's hydrocarbons sector. In January and February of that year, demonstrations began to take place in Muscat and Sohar, a strategic port town. However, the protests were relatively small, and demonstrators broadly respected Sultan Qaboos while demanding that corruption be addressed. Demonstrators included domestic employees from Oman's hydrocarbons sector, who protested about low wages and poor working conditions. No doubt, such demands were more acrimonious within the context of perceived corruption within the business and political elite.

In 2014, when oil prices fell sharply, a range of corruption charges were made against high-profile business and political figures. After the 2011 protests, Qaboos had ordered an anti-corruption campaign to address popular grievances. Prosecutions targeted senior figures in the hydrocarbons sector. Heavy sentences sent a message that corruption in the hydrocarbons sector would no longer be tolerated. In February 2014 Omani Ahmad al-Wahaibi, the CEO of state-owned Oman Oil company was found guilty of accepting bribes, abuse of office and money laundering and sentenced to 23 years in prison. The same trial also found Adel al-Raisi, a former adviser in the economy ministry, guilty of organizing a bribe from a senior official at a firm based in the Republic of Korea (South Korea) to al-Wahaibi. Al-Raisi was sentenced to 10 years in gaol. His South Korean counterpart, Myung Jao Yoo, received the same sentence.

Further high-profile cases targeting corruption the oil and gas sector took place in March 2014. Adel al-Kindi, the CEO of Omani Oil Refineries and Petroleum Industries received a three-year sentence and 1m.-rial fine after being found guilty of accepting a bribe. As a former member of the appointed State Council, he was also banned from government service for 30 years. In the same case, Oman's Director-General of Ports, Qasim al-Shizawi, was found guilty of accepting a bribe of

RO 200,000. He received a three-year prison sentence and a fine of RO 750,000. These cases illustrate a hardened stance towards corruption after Oman's brush with the Arab Spring protests. Furthermore, it is interesting to note that each trial sentenced not only members of the business elite who managed state enterprises but also targeted government officials and even foreign business executives, as exemplified by the sentencing of Myung. The imprisonment of government officials on corruption charges alongside business officials no doubt emphasized that there would be no distinction between members of the business elite and members of the more traditional political elite. As for the imprisonment of a senior official representing a South Korean conglomerate, this stance also sent a message indicating that although Oman was open for global business, it would not tolerate bribery in exchange for international trade—even though expansion of public services since 1970, especially health care and education, had been reliant on this international trade.

HEALTH CARE AND EDUCATION

In July 1970, when life expectancy in Oman was just 49 years, there were only two hospitals (both run by a US Mission) and 10 clinics and dispensaries in the whole country. By 1973 later there were nine fully operational hospitals—in Ruwi, Salalah, Tan'am, Matrah, Muscat, Nizwa, Al-Rustaq, Sohar and Sumail—and a rising number of health care centres and dispensaries in each region.

The Ministry of Health developed the system in three main stages. Between 1976 and 1990 the focus was mainly on building up health care infrastructure, and between 1991 and 2005 new strategies were adopted to establish a system of decentralized health care centres, spread across 11 health care administrative divisions throughout the country. In such a way, the right to free primary health care services could rapidly be guaranteed to Omani citizens almost everywhere, from urban areas to the most isolated rural and Bedouin areas, and from the mountains to the desert and the coasts. From 1987 onwards an emphasis was placed on specific infrastructure that would feed into social services such as health care. In 1987 the Royal Hospital in Muscat was opened, specializing in curative (rather than preventive) medicine. The construction of this facility and other hospitals under the mobilization of the military aimed to create an extensive health care system that could tackle 'immunization, diarrhoeal disease, tuberculosis, trachoma, acute respiratory infections, and other issues'.

Between 2006 and 2010 more comprehensive plans were conceived to involve both central health care institutions and local structures in the various administrative divisions, in order to address the new challenges more effectively. Health initiatives based on prevention became a top priority: although malaria and other infectious diseases had been eradicated in a short period of years, non-communicable diseases had started increasing as the process of modernization progressed.

However, although there have been significant investments in health care infrastructure, the quality of health care in Oman does not necessarily meet the standards of economically developed countries. According to a Gallup survey in 2012, 43% of Omanis would prefer to receive medical treatment abroad. That is particularly evident when it comes to non-communicable diseases, in which treatment is also influenced by the quality of research. At the same time, a recent study notes that Oman, together with the other GCC states, is 'currently experiencing an increased demand for health care services due to an immense population growth, increasing life expectancy and higher incidence of non-communicable diseases'. To meet these expanding needs the role of migrant workers in the health care sector, as in other parts of the economy, has been critical.

Expansion of the education sector took place as part of Oman's third five-year development plan (1986–90). It should be noted that from 1970 onwards, expanding education was a priority. At the start of Qaboos's reign in 1970, Oman had fewer than 20 schools. By 1975 this had increased to 207 and by 1985 to 373. The third five-year development plan sought to enhance and diversify existing educational services. This included ensuring that the education system was aligned with labour market needs (an element that could parallel Vision 2040's demands of a competitive economy—see below) that educational services reach remote places and the 'Omanization' of teaching posts. Under the fourth five-year development plan (1991–95), education was developed further, with the establishment of a Ministry of Higher Education distinct from the existing Ministry of Education, the widespread foundation of teacher training colleges and the simultaneous upgrading of some institutions to university status. Education and the development of human resources is essential for economic diversification when a state is reliant on one commodity.

ECONOMIC DIVERSIFICATION: OMAN'S VISION 2020 AND VISION 2040

It should be noted that official statements discussing Vision 2020, first announced in 1995, described the plan as relying on 'oil and gas revenues to achieve economic diversification' and that such diversification would still be achieved in conjunction with 'optimal exploitation of the natural resources of the Sultanate'. This context implies that Vision 2020 assumed a reliance on hydrocarbons profits and that laying the groundwork for economic diversification was not the same as achieving such diversification independent of hydrocarbons income. This fact foreshadows the notion that Vision 2040 (a repackaging of Vision 2020) would not replace the oil rentier model that bolstered Qaboos's rule, and that any serious economic diversification would not be undertaken in his lifetime, but by a successor. Before he died, Sultan Qaboos entrusted the development of Vision 2040 to his cousin and eventual successor as head of state, Haitham bin Tarik.

Vision 2020's forward-looking framework was influenced by a car crash in September 1995 in which Sultan Qaboos was injured and his close adviser, Qais Abdel-Munem al-Zawawi, was killed. This incident was a significant turning point, as Qaboos lost an adviser who had helped him to forge links with the outside world in the early days of his reign. The loss of an essential figure in his Government no doubt made Qaboos question his own mortality and assess how to ensure Oman's stability after he had gone. A year after the car accident Qaboos promulgated by royal decree the Basic Law—the nearest document that Oman has to a constitution.

The fact that the Basic Law, including articles addressing the Sultan's succession, was issued a year after Vision 2020 was published is striking. Vision 2020's scant references to economic diversification (which assumed equal development of optimal natural resources exploitation) already implied that true economic diversification was not the Vision's goal. Rather, the groundwork for such diversification would be laid without altering the oil rentier model. By issuing a law formalizing the succession shortly after Vision 2020 was published, it would seem that Sultan Qaboos was planning that core economic reforms and diversification away from the oil sector as the engine of the Omani economy would be the responsibility of the next Sultan. The Vision 2020 conference took place in 1996, shortly after a World Bank report commissioned by the Omani Government had been published, which noted that Oman's oil reserves would run out after 18 years—that is, by 2012. Since then, the perpetual refrain seems to have been '18 more years', as new oil discoveries have added to the reserves.

Thus, although Vision 2020 laudably called for additional investment in a wide range of industries such as the mining of copper, zinc and bauxite, together with expanding production of aluminium, plastics, petrochemicals and fertilizers, its main aim was to transform the economy to nurture employment and wealth-creating opportunities for the country's expanding youth population in a post-oil future. However, one of the core economic reforms that was not explicitly mentioned in Vision 2020 was the need to tackle corruption. In late 2019 a member of the Supreme Council for Planning stated that some 70% of the goals of Vision 2020 had been achieved.

2020: DEATH OF QABOOS AND THE COVID-19 PANDEMIC

While Omanis were still coming to terms with the death of Sultan Qaboos on 10 January 2020, a world-shaking pandemic emerged from China. The novel coronavirus emanating from Wuhan in the Chinese province of Hubei spread around the world apparently unchecked, forcing governments to impose lockdown measures on their populations, leading to economic shutdown in most of them.

It is not an exaggeration to state that this situation can be likened to a seismic shock: to the death of Sultan Qaboos and the undoubted challenges of diversifying the economy away from oil was added the catastrophe of COVID-19, combining the obvious and direct threats to public health and associated pandemic containment measures with a concomitant massive economic impact and the related political implications. As Amin Mohseni-Cheraghlou assessed, writing for the Middle East Institute: 'Facing this new reality, Oman's new ruler, Sultan Haitham, who ascended to the throne in January 2020 following the death of Sultan Qaboos, needs to act quickly. He only has a short timeframe in which to aggressively diversify the country's economy and reduce its dependency on hydrocarbon exports. Moreover, this already difficult task is further complicated by the twin challenges of the global coronavirus pandemic and low oil prices, both of which limit the government's fiscal room for manoeuvre.'

A sobering analysis outlining the scale of the task faced is to be found in a report of an economic consultant, John Davis of Castlereagh Associates, published in June 2020, in which he notes that: 'The severity of the economic challenge facing Oman will persist long after the COVID-19 pandemic has receded, requiring the country to rethink its long-term approach to economic development. Vision 2040 remains a top priority for the leadership under Sultan Haitham but with insufficient funds to carry out legacy spending commitments, it will have to rely on the private sector to drive diversification, including further dismantling of foreign investment restrictions, privatisation, closer ties with China and a new tourism strategy.'

Davis goes on to outline the 'challenging new normal for Oman's economy' and notes that it was already on 'shaky foundations' at the beginning of 2020 before being hit by the virus and associated oil price collapse precipitating an 'economic reckoning'. The International Monetary Fund (IMF) forecast the worst recession in Oman in two decades (predicting a contraction of 2.8% in GDP in 2020), with only minimal economic growth thereafter, as oil prices, which were still the main driver of the economy, were expected to remain low in the medium term. Concomitantly, the non-oil economy was expected to 'take years to recover from the surge in bankruptcies accompanying COVID-19'.

Thus, in a strange echo of the wartime circumstances of Qaboos's ascent to power in 1970, the newly installed Sultan Haitham found himself in a very short time in charge of the Omani front of what has been likened to a world war against an invisible enemy: the battle against the COVID-19 pandemic.

As in the other Gulf oil monarchies, a large percentage of Omani citizens are directly employed in the public sector, and the Government was thus able to order them to work from home and support it in its effort to contain the COVID-19 pandemic, thereby helping to reduce the spread of the virus. However, for most non-Omani migrant workers, who make up about 45% of the country's population, this choice was not available. There were reports of rioting by expatriate workers at sites operated by Al Tasnim Enterprises, after some 2,000 workers were laid off for demanding immediate repatriation, which the company argued it could not provide, in view of recent economic hardships. Further compounding its financial challenges, Oman has a comparatively large population and does not have the vast hydrocarbons reserves of Saudi Arabia, Kuwait, Qatar or the UAE. Accordingly, a mid-rent state such as Oman has a smaller level of oil revenue per capita, compared with a high-revenue state such as Kuwait. In March 2021 Oman's government bonds were downgraded by three international credit ratings agencies, owing to the COVID-19-related decrease in international oil prices and the increased demands on government finances, which, as Omani analyst Hatem al-Shanfari described it, represented an intensification of what was already 'a perfect storm'.

However, in the same way that it would be difficult to predict the onset of a global pandemic, it was also perhaps difficult to predict the decision made by the Russian Federation to invade Ukraine in February 2022. As a result of the ensuing conflict, the price of Brent crude oil increased from US $70 per barrel in 2021 to $100 in 2022 and was expected to remain at around the mid-$70 mark in 2023 and 2024, according to the US Energy Information Administration. The rise in global oil prices has given Oman's economy an unexpected fiscal boost, by enabling it to move in the direction of diversification and economic reform.

SULTAN HAITHAM, VISION 2040 AND THE DRIVE FOR DIVERSIFICATION

Vision 2040 was developed by Sultan Haitham, who had been given that remit in 2013 by Sultan Qaboos while Minister of National Heritage and Culture. Since ascending to the throne in January 2020, Sultan Haitham has implemented a raft of new policy measures in an attempt to address pressing questions of dependence on oil and issues concerning unemployment and participation in the workforce for a largely youthful population. The measures have included forcing the retirement of most civil servants with over 30 years' employment, rationalizing Oman's sovereign wealth funds, abolishing the No Objection Certificate (NOC) for migrant workers, and acceding to a range of international conventions on human rights, as well as reconsidering the powers of the Consultative Council.

In June 2020 Sultan Haitham ordered the formation of a committee to study the pandemic's economic impact; its first measures including offering interest-free loans to struggling Omani businesses suffering from the effects of the lockdown. None the less, despite these actions, in August Fitch Ratings downgraded Oman's credit rating for the second time that year, taking into account the 'continued erosion of Oman's fiscal and external balance sheets, which have accelerated amid low oil prices and the coronavirus shock, despite some progress on underlying fiscal consolidation'.

The IMF estimated that Oman's fiscal deficit widened in 2020, to 19.3% of GDP, from 7.0% in 2019, and forecast that the Government's capacity to fund deficits through borrowing would decline. Notwithstanding a 10% reduction in 2020 public spending commitments, from the start of 2020 Oman's credit rating was downgraded to sub-investment grade or 'junk' status, as assessed by all three major ratings agencies: Fitch Ratings, Moody's and Standard and Poor's. As a result, Oman's Vision 2040, according to Davis, would have to 'rely more on the private sector to invest in diversifying the economy over the coming years'. He notes a number of routes for attracting foreign capital, which would include relaxing foreign ownership restrictions, privatization and deepening ties with China.

Attracting private capital might require incentives and the relaxing of restrictions is a better option for the cash-strapped Omani Government than offering subsidies and financial perks. In January 2020 a new Foreign Capital Investment Law permitted 100% foreign ownership in a range of industries in which this was previously prohibited, including defence, hydrocarbons and hospitality. However, total foreign ownership is still not allowed in transportation, vehicle maintenance, personnel services and social care. These sectors could be a target for further liberalization.

Meanwhile, the trend of privatizing state assets is likely to continue. The Government sold a 49% stake in the state-owned Oman Electricity Transmission Company to the State Grid Corporation of China for US $1,000m. in December 2019. There are reports that Oman is considering privatizing Muscat International Airport, and future transport infrastructure, such as the Salalah-Thumrait toll road, could be financed on a public-private partnership model.

The oil and gas sector is the largest sector that could be privatized, and near-term financing needs might necessitate privatization sooner rather than later. Chinese investment in Oman could materialize in return for petrochemicals products from the Duqm refinery and natural gas from the Khazzan-Makarem field.

OMAN AND CHINA'S 'BELT AND ROAD' INITIATIVE

Of note in Oman's diversification plans has been China's ambitious Belt and Road Initiative (BRI), a global infrastructure development strategy, which includes a section across the Persian (Arabian) Gulf. This initiative has led to Chinese state and private sector firms becoming increasingly involved in business partnerships across the Gulf, including in the energy sector. For Oman, this has meant Chinese investment for transportation projects such as railway infrastructure and the construction of the port at Duqm. This includes construction of a high-capacity oil refinery and a high-capacity petrochemicals complex. For China, investment in Oman is part of a larger plan to accelerate oil flow from the Gulf to China, with the port of Duqm regarded as having the potential to become a vital energy hub along the new Silk Road. Chinese media outlets have presented the BRI as means of constructing a Chinese-Arab community with a shared future. Despite this statement of apparent mutual equality, there are concerns that promises of Chinese funding for mega-projects could lead to dependence on Beijing. It would appear that China has become central to Oman's economic diversification. This seems especially true, as such projects as Duqm port are set to create much-needed jobs for Omanis; and as oil prices take a hit, Oman is viewing co-operation with the China as a potential source of future dependence. At the same time, Oman has launched independent projects, including a large-scale solar power field—a partnership between Japanese Marubeni Corporation, Qatari Nebras Power and Oman Gas Company. However, the reach of such a project could be limited; it is estimated that such a solar field could meet 21% of Oman's energy needs by 2030. Meanwhile, China National Petroleum Corporation entered advanced talks in mid-2020 to purchase a 10% stake in Oman's Khazzan-Makarem gasfield, which would be worth some US $1,500m. and dilute BP's current 60% ownership of the field. The increasing involvement of China in Oman's diversification plans, including (part-)ownership of Omani energy assets appears to be feeding into China's strategy to increase oil and gas flow between the Gulf and Beijing, prompting the question of who benefits most from the BRI in Oman and to what extent the Chinese-Omani partnership will contribute to Oman's hopes for long-term diversification away from oil and gas.

Chinese investment in the port of Duqm is a key aspect of the linking of the Sultanate to developing global networks of trade in the 21st century. The Oxford Business Group noted in late 2019 that the Sultanate 'had a strong commitment to diversification, beginning in earnest in 2014'. While the country was still largely dependent on oil and gas at 2019, Oman's non-oil sector had achieved average real GDP growth of 7% and the country's strategic position near global trade routes and a history of political neutrality was opening up opportunities in transport, trade and tourism. The report by the Oxford Business Group noted that, in addition to real GDP growth of 1.8% in 2018, the fiscal deficit narrowed to 9% of GDP.

TRANSPORT AND INDUSTRIAL INFRASTRUCTURE

Port infrastructure is being developed to exploit Oman's geostrategic position close to major sea lanes and connecting major markets in Asia and Africa. The Sultanate has until now targeted luxury tourism aboard cruise liners arriving at Port Sultan Qaboos, Muscat, which was designated as a tourist hub while diverting commercial and import/export activities to Sohar Industrial Port. Since 1999 construction work has been ongoing in Port Sohar on one of the world's largest port development projects. Supported by US investment and proceeding in phases at a cost of US $15,000m., the Sohar port will eventually handle 3m. containers annually. The development at Duqm port consists of a massive new city with fish-processing plants, dry-dock facilities and a massive container port terminal. Oman's air transport sector was bolstered by the opening in March 2018 of a new $1,800m. passenger terminal at Muscat International Airport. It was expected to double capacity at the capital city's airport, to accommodate 12m. passengers annually.

TOURISM AND THE TRANSITION TO A SUSTAINABLE ECONOMY

An integral part of Vision 2040 is to achieve sustainable development goals in the context of Oman's limited hydrocarbons reserves. Mohseni-Cheraghlou noted that in just under 50 years Sultan Qaboos was able to transform Oman into a modern economy with the associated infrastructure of modern roads, ports, rapid internet speeds and the provision of health care facilities. In terms of gross national income per capita (recorded by the World Bank at US $15,030 in 2020) Omanis enjoy today living standards at about the level of the citizens of France and the UK, average life expectancy was 75.1 years in 2021, and the literacy rate exceeds 96%. However, Mohseni-Cheraghlou emphasized the fact that Oman's oil and natural gas reserves-to-production ratios were only 15 and 18.5 years, respectively, much lower than those of its neighbours in the GCC. With the planet facing a climate emergency as average temperatures increase, and as a signatory to the Kyoto Protocol to reduce emissions of carbon dioxide, the Omani Government is obliged, as other governments globally, to move towards a low-carbon future. An example of this intention is that the world's largest solar project is being developed in Oman's West Amal oilfield.

Mohseni-Cheraghlou went on to outline salient points about a sector that, arguably, could flourish in a post-oil economy: its tourism industry. The country has five United Nations Educational, Scientific and Cultural Organization (UNESCO) World Heritage sites, namely, the *aflaj* irrigation systems, the port of Qalhat, the archaeological sites of Bat, Al-Khutum and Al-Ayn, Bahla Fort and the Land of Frankincense. Combined with the fact that Oman is one of the few demonstrably safe destinations for tourists wishing to experience authentic Arab culture, this would seem to provide a useful opportunity for economic development. However, although tourism became a priority sector, together with manufacturing, logistics, fisheries and mining, in the ninth five-year development plan (2016–20), the tourism sector contributed only 2.9% of GDP in 2018. Mohseni-Cheraghlou contended that this figure needed to rise to at least 10%–15% and highlighted that in Bahrain, tourism constituted 10.3% of GDP in 2019, achieved without the undoubtedly much richer geographical and heritage resources of the Sultanate. Oman could also relax tourism restrictions. To date, Oman has targeted the luxury tourism market as a way of maximizing revenue while minimizing the impact and disruption from foreign visitors on the local population. Now, however, the country is presenting itself as a multifaceted tourist and heritage destination.

Taking into account the Omani Government's limited resources, expansion of the tourism industry would require eliciting foreign direct investment and public-private partnership schemes in the form of possible link-ups with corporations with substantial funds to invest, such as Qatar's Katara Hospitality Group, which was involved in the development of a hotel resort in Tangier, Morocco, for example. About one-half of tourists visiting Oman are GCC nationals and possibly more could be done to promote Oman to the wider world. Furthermore, the tourism strategy must include the expansion of employment opportunities. Although Oman's fertility rate has declined in recent years, in 2019 approximately 60% of Oman's population was under the age of 34, and 40% was in the 15–34 age category.

'OMANIZATION': EMPLOYING AN OMANI WORKFORCE

'Omanization' refers to the requirement of firms to increase the rate of employment of Omani nationals. According to Davis, in line with trends elsewhere in the Gulf, the economic shock since early 2020 will act as a drag on foreign investment in the country, in view of the scarcity of local skilled labour, and the policy of 'Omanization' will increase the costs for foreign businesses to operate in Oman and therefore make investment less attractive. The Government has recently introduced a mix of 'prescriptive nationalization policies' through quotas and prohibitions, as well as policies based on market incentives, concerning migrant workers. Most notably, the NOC has been abolished, which had banned non-Omanis from re-entering the country for two years if they left their employer without permission, inviting debate from Omani economists and entrepreneurs. Some argued that the abolition of the NOC would be detrimental to Omani businesses, while others hailed it as a step in the right direction that would increase competitiveness and eventually lead to higher salaries.

Research on the 'Gulfization' of the labour market and proposed reform of the policy indicates that a healthy competitive economy depends greatly on mobility rights that allow foreigners and citizens alike to compete on an even playing field (which would eventually lead to greater employment of Omani nationals in the private sector). Closing this gap would encourage citizens to compete more actively to appeal to employers, which in turn would improve productivity and the acquisition of skills. To this end, the abolition of the NOC, which allows migrant workers to transfer sponsorships without permission from their sponsor after completing a two-year contract, is the type of market-incentive policy that deals with the core issue of market segmentation.

However, the Omani Government has simultaneously introduced quotas and prohibitions on the renewal of work-permit licences for some expatriate workers in a number of sectors, including urging the 'Omanization' of delivery services and other 'work that can be easily [carried out by] Omanis'. However, at the same time, some sectors that had been reserved for Omani nationals, such as the construction industry and brick factories, have been allowed to hire expatriate workers.

Administrative micro-interventionist policies such as these, which place quotas and controls on businesses, are likely to be more prone to 'widespread evasion' and 'political wrangling'. As Steffen Hertog suggests, experiences of past 'Gulfization' policies 'underline the need to address the underlying causes of labour market segmentation, instead of trying to alleviate them after the fact. A more flexible regime would aim to avoid micro-interventions but instead narrow the gap in labour prices and labour rights between nationals and foreigners.' Such measures may be required if Oman is to move on from its oil-based rentier economy.

OMAN LOOKS TO THE FUTURE

On becoming Sultan in 2020 Haitham cancelled the public holiday on Oman's 'Renaissance Day'—23 July—the date in 1970 when Qaboos had assumed power. Having weathered the restrictions necessitated by the global pandemic in 2020–22, the year 2023 saw the implementation of a number of new measures which indicated the balancing act that the Omani Government was pursuing as it attempted to navigate away from an oil-based economy. Social welfare measures included plans to construct Sultan Haitham City, a city on the outskirts of Muscat to house people on low incomes. New taxes such as an amended value-added tax (VAT) were introduced and a personal income tax was also likely to be rolled out (for wealthy individuals initially). In April 2023 credit agencies revised their view of Oman to positive. A US $5,200m. investment fund, the Oman Future Fund, was established in June to help the economy diversify away from oil. The consensus of international financial institutions is that, with the Medium-Term Fiscal Plan for 2020–24, Haitham has placed Oman on a path towards a fiscally more robust and sustainable economy and has used the unexpected windfall of higher oil prices resulting from the Russian invasion of Ukraine prudently to pay off some of the country's costly debt and to record budget surpluses.

CONCLUSION

Sultan Qaboos built the economy of a modern welfare state through reliance on oil production and exports. Throughout his reign, hydrocarbons revenues were the central plank of Oman's economic vitality, and although he acknowledged the vulnerability of oil prices, none of the five-year development plans, nor indeed Vision 2020, really pushed structural diversification away from oil.

Since January 2020 Sultan Haitham has implemented a raft of new policy measures in an attempt to address pressing questions of dependence on oil and issues concerning unemployment and participation for a young population. These have included forcing the retirement of most civil servants with over 30 years' employment, rationalizing the country's sovereign wealth funds, abolishing the NOC for migrant workers and acceding to a range of international conventions on human rights, as well as reconsidering the powers of the Consultative Council. Although these are difficult waters for Oman, this might also prove to be an opportunity to move in the direction of diversification and economic reform, in order to capitalize on the country's much-vaunted geostrategic position to maximize emerging economic opportunities. The increase in oil prices following Russia's invasion of Ukraine allowed the Government of the Sultanate to pay off a sizeable amount of public debt and improve its credit rating.

During the Omani manifestation of the Arab Spring protests, with demonstrators massing in Sohar and Dhofar, the GCC provided loans to Oman worth several billion US dollars in order that the authorities could attempt to 'buy off' social discontent with government jobs and subsidies. Seeking regional assistance now, however, would be a last resort, as it could impinge on Oman's longstanding independent foreign policy. Such independence has allowed Oman to maintain strong diplomatic and economic ties with the GCC on the one hand and with Qatar and Iran on the other. Omani foreign policy is often characterized as independent or neutral (Oman is sometimes referred to as the 'Switzerland of the Middle East'), but it is slightly more nuanced than this. Oman has assiduously maintained a close relationship with a core Western power, the USA, as a guarantor of regime survival, while balancing this relationship with other Western and global powers. Furthermore, through its policy of not taking sides in regional conflicts (it remained neutral in the Saudi-led boycott of Qatar—see Saudi Arabia and Qatar), combined with its facilitation of dialogue between conflicting states and groups, Oman does not expose itself to the risks of incurring dangerous enmities which, given its smaller economy, could leave it vulnerable to external pressures exerted by economic means.

Sultan Qaboos refused to countenance any fundamental debate on widening popular participation in the political process. Since 2020 Sultan Haitham has introduced a wide range of reforms which will inevitably further affect the social contract between the rulers and ruled in Oman. Questions therefore remain about whether the reform measures taken so far will be sufficient to address the reality of dwindling oil reserves and meet the expectations of Omanis of all generations as they transition to a more diversified economic base.

OMAN

Statistical Survey

Sources (unless otherwise stated): National Center for Statistics and Information, Supreme Council for Planning, POB 881, Muscat 100; tel. 24698900; fax 24698467; e-mail info@ncsi.gov.om; internet www.ncsi.gov.om; Central Bank of Oman, POB 1161, 44 Mutrah Commercial Centre, Ruwi 112; tel. 24777777; fax 24777723; e-mail CBOPortalServices@cbo.gov.om; internet www.cbo.gov.om.

Area and Population

AREA, POPULATION AND DENSITY

Area (sq km)	309,980*
Population (census results)	
12 December 2010	2,773,479†
12 December 2020	
Males	2,739,954
Females	1,731,194
Total	4,471,148‡
Population (official estimates at 31 December)	
2021	4,527,446
2022	4,933,850
Density (per sq km) at 31 December 2022	15.9

* 119,684 sq miles.
† Comprising 1,957,336 Omani nationals and 816,143 non-Omanis.
‡ Comprising 2,731,456 Omani nationals and 1,739,692 non-Omanis.

Note: For breakdown of census data, the number of non-Omanis was believed to have been reduced significantly by the proximity of the census to the Christmas holiday season.

POPULATION BY AGE AND SEX
(official estimates at 31 December 2022)

	Males	Females	Total
0–14 years	641,590	617,084	1,258,674
15–64 years	2,357,472	1,185,549	3,543,021
65 years and over	63,570	68,585	132,155
Total	3,062,632	1,871,218	4,933,850

ADMINISTRATIVE DIVISIONS
(official estimates at 31 December 2022)

	Area (sq km)	Population	Density (per sq km)
Al-Batinah North Governorate	8,000	872,014	109.0
Al-Batinah South Governorate	5,323	518,026	97.3
Al-Buraymi Governorate	8,068	125,761	15.6
Al-Dakhliya Governorate	32,000	533,694	16.7
Al-Dhahirah Governorate	35,881	232,858	6.5
Dhofar Governorate	99,062	486,369	4.9
Musandam Governorate	2,000	53,224	26.6
Muscat Governorate	4,000	1,401,456	350.4
Al-Sharqiya North Governorate	21,136	301,232	14.3
Al-Sharqiya South Governorate	12,039	349,748	29.1
Al-Wosta Governorate	82,471	59,468	0.7
Total	309,980	4,933,850	15.9

PRINCIPAL TOWNS
(population by *wilayat* at 2020 census)

Muscat (capital)	1,302,440	As-Suwayq	184,561
Al-Seeb	478,517	Barka	181,630
Bawshar	382,184	Ibri	163,179
Salalah	331,949	Saham	150,057
Sohar	232,849	Nizwa	131,763
Mutrah	230,881	Amarat	121,103

BIRTHS, MARRIAGES AND DEATHS
(Omani nationals only, official estimates)

	Live births		Registered marriages		Deaths	
	Number	Rate (per 1,000)	Number	Rate (per 1,000)	Number	Rate (per 1,000)
2020	77,272	28.2	18,762	n.a.	8,668	3.2
2021	76,457	27.3	n.a.	n.a.	10,108	3.6
2022	71,464	n.a.	n.a.	n.a.	8,377	3.0

Life expectancy (official estimates, Omani nationals only, years at birth): 75.1 (males 72.2; females 76.5) in 2021.

EMPLOYMENT
(persons aged 15 years and over, 2003 census)

	Omanis	Non-Omanis	Total
Agriculture and fishing	14,210	43,904	58,114
Mining and quarrying	11,998	8,117	20,115
Manufacturing	13,831	45,661	59,492
Electricity, gas and water	1,826	2,219	4,045
Construction	10,128	108,129	118,257
Trade, hotels and restaurants	24,999	84,158	109,157
Transport, storage and communications	17,202	10,472	27,674
Finance, insurance and real estate	12,657	12,543	25,200
Public administration and defence	144,699	18,043	162,742
Other community, social and personal services	54,923	83,299	138,222
Sub-total	306,473	416,545	723,018
Activities not adequately defined	5,973	7,633	13,606
Total employed	312,446	424,178	736,624
Males	258,655	364,337	622,992
Females	53,791	59,841	113,632

Mid-2015 (estimates in '000): Agriculture, etc. 470; Total labour force 1,779 (Source: FAO).

2020 (excluding Royal Court): Omanis employed 430,605 (males 280,781, females 149,824); non-Omanis employed 1,429,052 (males 1,244,970, females 184,082); Total employed 1,859,657 (government 204,015, private sector 1,402,961, domestic service 252,681).

2020 census: Manufacturing 231,083 (Omanis 61,949, non-Omanis 169,134); Construction 442,547 (Omanis 70,926, non-Omanis 371,621); Wholesale and retail trade 252,434 (Omanis 52,765, non-Omanis 199,669); Transportation and storage 102,358 (Omanis 44,274, non-Omanis 58,084); Accommodation and food service activities 113,359 (Omanis 13,704, non-Omanis 99,655); Other 1,017,026 (Omanis 508,213, non-Omanis 508,813); *Total* 2,158,807 (Omanis 751,831, non-Omanis 1,406,976).

Health and Welfare

KEY INDICATORS

Total fertility rate (children per woman, 2021)	2.6
Under-5 mortality rate (per 1,000 live births, 2021)	10.1
HIV/AIDS (% of persons aged 15–49, 2021)	0.1
COVID-19: Cumulative confirmed deaths (per 100,000 persons at 30 June 2023)	101.1
COVID-19: Fully vaccinated population (% of total population at 25 October 2022)	66.6
Physicians (per 1,000 head, 2020)	1.9
Hospital beds (per 1,000 head, 2017)	1.5
Domestic health expenditure (2020): US $ per head (PPP)	1,637.6
Domestic health expenditure (2020): % of GDP	4.8
Domestic health expenditure (2020): public (% of total current health expenditure)	90.3
Access to improved water resources (% of persons, 2020)	92
Total carbon dioxide emissions ('000 metric tons, 2019)	76,027
Carbon dioxide emissions per head (metric tons, 2019)	16.5
Human Development Index (2021): ranking	54
Human Development Index (2021): value	0.816

Note: For data on COVID-19 vaccinations, 'fully vaccinated' denotes receipt of all doses specified by approved vaccination regime (Sources: Johns Hopkins University and Our World in Data). Data on health expenditure refer to current general government expenditure in each case. For more information on sources and further definitions for all indicators, see Health and Welfare Statistics: Sources and Definitions section (europaworld.com/credits).

Agriculture

PRINCIPAL CROPS
('000 metric tons)

	2019	2020	2021
Bananas	18.4	18.4	18.4
Cabbages and other brassicas	19.2	30.0	26.0
Carrots and turnips	18.3	12.5	19.3
Cauliflowers and broccoli	28.3	13.4	22.6
Cucumbers and gherkins	74.0	102.7	93.1
Dates	376.9	368.6	374.2
Eggplants (aubergines)	30.9	39.2	36.3
Lemons and limes	7.2	8.4	8.3
Mangoes, mangosteens and guavas	16.0	16.0	16.1
Okra	16.8	13.1	19.6
Onions, dry	9.2	14.4	14.7
Papayas	5.8	5.8	5.8
Potatoes	15.8	16.1	12.5
Pumpkins, squash and gourds	10.6	15.7	15.4
Sorghum	49.8	148.9	107.4
Tomatoes	201.3	340.2	283.3
Watermelons	56.6	37.1	44.6

Aggregate production ('000 metric tons, may include official, semi-official or estimated data): Total cereals 65.7 in 2019, 183.9 in 2020, 130.1 in 2021; Total fruit (primary) 514.8 in 2019, 505.2 in 2020, 514.4 in 2021; Total roots and tubers 15.8 in 2019, 16.1 in 2020, 12.5 in 2021; Total vegetables (primary) 633.8 in 2019, 837.8 in 2020, 782.8 in 2021.

Source: FAO.

LIVESTOCK
('000 head, year ending September)

	2019	2020	2021
Asses*	23	22	22
Camels	273	279	285
Cattle	405	413	422
Chickens*	4,747	4,801	4,860
Goats	2,348	2,395	2,443
Sheep	617	630	642

* FAO estimates.

Source: FAO.

LIVESTOCK PRODUCTS
('000 metric tons)

	2019	2020	2021
Camel meat*	16.0	16.4	16.9
Cattle meat*	15.0	15.3	15.6
Cows' milk	100.0	215.3	219.6
Chicken meat*	6.6	6.7	6.8
Goat meat*	17.5	17.8	18.2
Goats' milk*	111.3	112.9	114.6
Sheep meat*	30.6	31.4	32.2
Sheep's (Ewes') milk*	23.6	23.9	24.3
Hen eggs*	25.1	25.1	n.a.

* FAO estimates.

Source: FAO.

Fishing

('000 metric tons, live weight)

	2019	2020	2021
Capture	579.2	793.4	922.1
Sea catfishes	7.4	8.8	17.6
Emperors (Scavengers)	17.0	29.0	33.7
Hairtails and scabbardfishes	15.2	21.7	17.5
Indian oil sardine	275.2	430.1	440.2
Anchovies	17.5	13.6	21.5
Longtail tuna	14.7	27.2	28.2
Yellowfin tuna	37.1	68.6	71.7
Jacks, crevalles	38.6	25.9	71.8
Aquaculture	1.0	1.3	1.7
Total catch	580.2	794.7	923.8

Source: FAO.

Mining

('000 metric tons unless otherwise indicated)

	2019	2020	2021
Crude petroleum (million barrels)	354,393	347,949	354,498
Natural gas (million cu m)	46,190	46,396	50,191
Marble	1,128.5	1,130.5	1,005.4
Salt	15.0	11.7	10.1
Gypsum	10,982.9	11,120.2	12,290.2

Gold (kg): 102 in 2015; 67 in 2016; 3 in 2017 (Source: US Geological Survey).

Chromium ('000 metric tons): 453 in 2017; 885 in 2018; 608 in 2019 (Source: US Geological Survey).

Industry

SELECTED PRODUCTS
('000 barrels unless otherwise indicated, estimates)

	2017	2018	2019
Jet fuel and kerosene	7,175	13,327	14,018
Motor spirit (petrol)	25,502	27,072	28,143
Gas-diesel (distillate fuel) oils	24,847	27,248	25,038
Residual fuel oils	2,459	1,833	1,840
Electrical energy (million kWh)	35,673	37,192	37,534

Electrical energy (million kWh): 36,995 in 2020; 39,537 in 2021; 41,698 in 2022 (preliminary).

Source: mainly US Geological Survey.

Finance

CURRENCY AND EXCHANGE RATES

Monetary Units
1,000 baiza = 1 rial Omani (RO).

Sterling, Dollar and Euro Equivalents (31 May 2023)
£1 sterling = 475.4 baiza;
US $1 = 384.5 baiza;
€1 = 410.8 baiza;
10 rials Omani = £21.04 = $26.01 = €24.35.

Exchange Rate: Since January 1986 the official exchange rate has been fixed at US $1 = 384.5 baiza (1 rial Omani = $2.6008).

BUDGET
(RO million)

Revenue	2019	2020	2021
Petroleum revenue (net)	6,098.5	3,937.5	5,613.0
Gas revenues	1,900.5	1,860.2	2,628.5
Other current revenue	2,331.5	2,087.1	2,874.1
Taxes and fees revenue	1,442.7	1,199.2	1,492.7
Income tax on enterprises	624.8	468.4	446.0
Customs duties	234.4	185.7	187.4
Fees on licences and others	583.5	545.1	859.3
Non-tax revenue	888.7	887.9	1,381.4
Surplus from public authorities	10.7	9.5	21.1
Income from government investments	260.6	237.5	833.2
Capital revenue	70.9	132.9	49.4
Capital repayments	187.3	485.5	29.9
Total	**10,588.7**	**8,503.2**	**11,194.9**

Expenditure	2019	2020	2021
Current expenditure	9,506.3	9,458.9	9,388.3
Defence and national security	3,358.5	2,834.8	2,785.2
Civil ministries	4,486.8	4,580.6	4,415.8
Investment expenditure	2,673.9	2,461.5	1,983.9
Share of PDO expenditure*	885.5	905.9	779.6
Participation and subsidies	1,031.0	1,005.3	1,045.6
Total	**13,211.2**	**12,925.7**	**12,417.8**

* Referring to the Government's share of current and capital expenditure by Petroleum Development Oman.

2022 (preliminary): Total revenue 14,477.0; total expenditure 13,294.0.

INTERNATIONAL RESERVES
(US $ million at 31 December)

	2020	2021	2022
Gold (national valuation)	1.2	1.2	110.5
IMF special drawing rights	142.2	968.5	976.5
Reserve position in IMF	188.2	182.9	173.9
Foreign exchange	14,675.7	18,578.3	16,346.1
Total	**15,007.3**	**19,730.9**	**17,607.1**

Source: IMF, *International Financial Statistics*.

MONEY SUPPLY
(RO million at 31 December)

	2020	2021	2022
Currency outside depository corporations	1,378.6	1,307.1	1,243.0
Transferable deposits	5,138.7	5,540.3	5,566.6
Other deposits	12,808.6	13,373.4	13,525.8
Broad money	**19,326.0**	**20,220.8**	**20,335.5**

Source: IMF, *International Financial Statistics*.

COST OF LIVING
(Consumer Price Index; base: 2012 = 100)

	2020	2021	2022
Food, beverages and tobacco	104.9	105.7	111.2
Clothing and footwear	97.6	97.8	99.0
Rent, electricity, water and fuel	104.2	104.6	105.8
All items (incl. others)	105.1	106.7	109.7

NATIONAL ACCOUNTS
(RO million in current prices)

Expenditure on the Gross Domestic Product

	2019	2020	2021
Final consumption expenditure	20,527.9	20,472.8	22,534.5
General government	7,824.4	7,607.9	7,507.7
Households	12,675.4	12,836.7	14,997.6
Non-profit institutions serving households	28.2	28.2	29.2
Gross capital formation	9,096.4	8,061.7	7,598.8
Gross fixed capital formation	9,803.4	9,215.7	8,687.5
Changes in inventories	−707.1	−1,154.0	−1,088.7
Statistical discrepancy	1,448.8	1,780.0	1,321.9
Total domestic expenditure	**31,073.1**	**30,314.5**	**31,455.2**
Exports of goods and services	15,309.0	11,954.3	16,489.7
Less Imports of goods and services	12,522.6	13,081.6	14,035.1
GDP in purchasers' values	**33,859.4**	**29,187.2**	**33,909.8**
GDP at constant 2018 prices	**34,786.7**	**33,611.2**	**34,650.5**

Gross Domestic Product by Economic Activity

	2020	2021	2022*
Agriculture and fishing	720.7	719.2	811.5
Mining and quarrying	7,937.6	10,506.0	16,881.1
Crude petroleum	6,248.7	8,749.1	14,490.9
Natural gas	1,478.8	1,538.4	2,128.8
Non-petroleum	210.1	218.5	261.4
Manufacturing	2,438.9	3,093.9	4,627.6
Electricity and water	801.4	909.7	948.5
Construction	2,583.2	2,660.2	2,664.4
Wholesale and retail trade	2,627.2	2,928.6	3,520.5
Hotels and restaurants	434.0	522.9	635.0
Transport, storage and communications	1,689.3	1,803.5	2,909.8
Financial intermediation	2,276.3	2,467.7	2,683.8
Real estate	1,951.0	2,096.7	2,148.7
Public administration and defence	3,441.1	3,442.4	3,533.9
Education	1,874.1	3,871.6	4,180.7
Health	1,184.0		
Other community, social and personal services	403.2		
Private households with employed persons	179.7		
Sub-total	**30,541.7**	**35,022.4**	**45,545.5**
Less Financial intermediation services indirectly measured	813.7	829.0	907.1
Gross value added in basic prices	**29,728.1**	**34,193.4**	**44,638.5**
Taxes, less subsidies, on products	−541.0	−283.6	−549.1
GDP in purchasers' values	**29,187.2**	**33,909.8**	**44,089.5**

* Provisional.

OMAN

BALANCE OF PAYMENTS
(US $ million)

	2019	2020	2021
Exports of goods	38,685.3	33,483.3	44,590.9
Imports of goods	−20,456.8	−25,845.2	−28,048.8
Balance on goods	18,228.5	7,638.1	16,542.1
Exports of services	4,898.2	2,236.6	1,733.4
Imports of services	−12,111.8	−8,177.2	−8,453.4
Balance on goods and services	11,014.9	1,697.5	9,822.0
Primary income received	1,187.6	727.4	1,378.8
Primary income paid	−7,089.3	−5,959.2	−7,371.4
Balance on goods, services and primary income	5,113.3	−3,534.3	3,829.5
Secondary income paid	−9,133.6	−8,772.2	−8,117.7
Current account	−4,020.3	−12,306.6	−4,288.2
Capital account (net)	93.6	179.7	39.5
Direct investment assets	465.3	696.5	396.8
Direct investment liabilities	4,237.7	2,888.9	4,019.5
Portfolio investment assets	−2,390.6	−725.1	−1,263.6
Portfolio investment liabilities	2,725.1	3,158.6	4,957.3
Other investment assets	−4,830.4	1,933.6	−2,134.5
Other investment liabilities	2,882.2	2,521.5	2,291.5
Net errors and omissions	−515.1	−406.3	−910.4
Reserves and related items	−1,352.5	−2,059.1	3,108.1

Source: IMF, *International Financial Statistics*.

External Trade

PRINCIPAL COMMODITIES
(RO million)

Imports c.i.f. (distribution by HS)*	2019	2020	2021†
Live animals and animal products	511.9	521.0	577.4
Vegetables and vegetable products	434.4	599.7	677.5
Prepared foodstuffs; beverages, spirits, vinegars; tobacco and related products	540.5	533.3	605.4
Mineral products	582.2	1,286.8	2,181.6
Chemicals and related products	760.2	989.3	1,150.1
Plastics, rubber, and articles thereof	429.6	406.1	466.1
Iron and steel; other base metals and articles thereof	1,370.5	1,406.4	1,511.2
Machinery and mechanical appliances; electrical equipment; parts thereof	2,058.7	2,440.1	1,990.6
Vehicles, aircraft, vessels and associated transport equipment	1,020.6	1,452.0	1,224.2
Total (incl. others)	9,038.3	10,961.0	11,917.5

Exports f.o.b.	2019	2020	2021†
Petroleum and natural gas	10,195.1	6,997.9	10,031.5
Crude petroleum	7,555.9	5,053.6	7,184.8
Refined petroleum	929.1	632.1	1,182.1
Natural gas	1,710.1	1,312.2	1,664.6
Non-hydrocarbon exports	4,699.1	5,876.4	7,113.6
Live animals and animal products	220.6	279.8	325.4
Mineral products	448.8	498.5	880.9
Chemicals and related products	902.0	775.1	1,286.1
Plastics, rubber, and articles thereof	224.7	530.4	915.0
Iron and steel; other base metals and articles thereof	920.8	986.0	1,356.0
Total‡	14,894.2	12,874.3	17,145.1

* Excluding unrecorded imports (RO million): 296.1 in 2019; 142.3 in 2020; 132.5 in 2021.
† Provisional.
‡ Excluding re-exports (RO million): 1,464.2 in 2019; 1,780.0 in 2020; 1,322.0 in 2021 (provisional).

2022 (provisional): Total recorded imports 14,831.0; total exports 25,397.0.

PRINCIPAL TRADING PARTNERS
(RO million)

Imports c.i.f.	2019	2020	2021
Australia	101.6	91.2	136.7
Bahrain	159.1	154.8	278.4
Belgium	83.0	121.4	139.4
Brazil	379.1	312.8	579.1
China, People's Republic	605.4	770.6	832.3
Germany	201.8	189.8	173.0
India	444.8	725.7	782.1
Iran	100.9	84.0	98.8
Italy	149.5	151.0	138.7
Japan	127.2	523.0	473.7
Korea, Republic	116.8	234.7	106.2
Luxembourg	163.7	131.1	85.4
Netherlands	110.1	127.2	101.1
Pakistan	62.3	101.0	148.9
Qatar	243.7	546.4	764.9
Saudi Arabia	352.7	536.0	561.3
Türkiye	77.9	186.3	185.0
United Arab Emirates	3,641.6	4,033.2	4,238.3
United Kingdom	163.7	99.7	95.9
USA	254.4	263.2	275.2
Total (incl. others)	9,038.3	10,961.0	11,917.5

Exports f.o.b.*	2019	2020	2021
Brazil	13.4	36.4	114.3
China, People's Republic	245.7	326.5	393.3
Egypt	51.1	68.7	158.3
India	341.0	388.7	510.0
Indonesia	20.7	22.2	65.8
Iran	217.5	94.1	155.6
Iraq	39.1	52.6	45.8
Korea, Republic	41.7	51.5	89.9
Kuwait	77.9	104.9	123.6
Malaysia	55.9	146.8	63.0
Netherlands	102.9	45.7	87.6
Pakistan	48.2	43.7	60.1
Qatar	542.0	808.4	381.9
Saudi Arabia	616.5	572.2	664.7
Singapore	172.1	102.8	164.7
Somalia	89.4	96.6	101.4
South Africa	6.9	33.3	118.9
United Arab Emirates	1,037.8	1,415.0	1,477.7
United Kingdom	61.1	58.7	61.4
USA	247.6	367.7	653.7
Viet Nam	50.7	46.7	57.3
Yemen	66.5	217.0	300.3
Total (incl. others)	4,701.3	5,876.4	7,113.6

* Data for non-petroleum exports and including re-exports.

OMAN

Statistical Survey

Transport

ROAD TRAFFIC
(vehicles registered)

	2020	2021	2022
Private cars	1,221,302	1,233,109	1,273,791
Taxis	29,931	28,480	28,117
Commercial and rented vehicles	263,817	256,935	267,145
Government	12,695	12,206	12,167
Motorcycles	6,466	6,306	6,765
Diplomatic	857	845	839
Other	22,385	14,784	14,552
Total	1,557,453	1,552,665	1,603,376

SHIPPING

Flag Registered Fleet
(at 31 December)

	2020	2021	2022
Number of vessels	78	77	79
Total displacement (grt)	92,189	104,985	108,264

Source: Lloyd's List Intelligence (www.bit.ly/LLintelligence).

International Seaborne Freight Traffic
('000 metric tons unless otherwise indicated)

	2014	2015	2016
Port Sultan Qaboos:			
Vessels entered (number)	1,545	n.a.	n.a.
Goods loaded	586	n.a.	n.a.
Goods unloaded	2,391	977	996
Salalah Port:			
Vessels entered (number)	863	n.a.	n.a.
Goods loaded	8,986	n.a.	n.a.
Goods unloaded	1,774	1,815	2,182
Mina al-Fahal Coastal Area			
Vessels entered (number)	379	312	323
Petroleum loaded	41,667	41,709	43,684
Petroleum products unloaded	1,773	2,524	2,839

2018: *Port Sultan Qaboos:* Goods unloaded 824; *Salalah Port:* Goods unloaded 1,525; *Mina al-Fahal Coastal Area:* Vessels entered 247, Petroleum products unloaded 219.

2019: *Port Sultan Qaboos:* Goods unloaded 859; *Salalah Port:* Goods unloaded 2,013; *Mina al-Fahal Coastal Area:* Vessels entered 279, Petroleum products unloaded 683.

2020: *Port Sultan Qaboos:* Goods unloaded 830; *Salalah Port:* Goods unloaded 2,957; *Mina al-Fahal Coastal Area:* Vessels entered 238, Petroleum products unloaded 132.

2021: *Port Sultan Qaboos:* Goods unloaded 805; *Salalah Port:* Goods unloaded 5,245; *Mina al-Fahal Coastal Area:* Vessels entered 244, Petroleum products unloaded 22.

CIVIL AVIATION
(aircraft movements, passengers and cargo handled at Muscat International Airport)

	2020	2021	2022
International flights:			
flights (number)	32,897	28,580	60,621
passengers ('000)	3,897	3,156	7,634
goods handled ('000 metric tons)	95.9	109.1	n.a.
Domestic flights:			
flights (number)	7,284	11,966	8,116
passengers ('000)	727	1,414	969
goods handled ('000 metric tons)	0.4	1.1	n.a.

Tourism

FOREIGN TOURIST ARRIVALS BY NATIONALITY
(arrivals of non-resident tourists at national borders)

Country of nationality	2019	2020	2021
China, People's Republic	109,520	32,406	7,965
Egypt	53,274	12,996	18,173
France	74,710	22,458	12,976
Germany	176,769	46,605	17,000
India	437,030	96,373	106,042
Italy	76,179	29,017	3,893
Pakistan	91,143	17,050	19,326
Philippines	61,522	14,060	4,564
United Kingdom	157,351	37,739	13,955
USA	69,900	14,855	7,179
Yemen	120,136	24,916	41,823
Total (incl. others)	3,506,441	868,571	651,633

Tourism receipts (US $ million, excl. passenger transport): 1,811 in 2019; 455 in 2020; 362 in 2021 (provisional).

Source: mainly World Tourism Organization.

Communications Media

	2019	2020	2021
Telephones ('000 main lines in use)	592.1	594.6	572.2
Mobile telephone subscriptions ('000)	6,383.5	6,276.5	6,115.5
Broadband subscriptions, fixed ('000)	475.1	511.0	526.6
Broadband subscriptions, mobile ('000)	4,604.3	5,385.6	5,096.6

Education

(state schools, 2022/23 unless otherwise indicated)

			Pupils/Students		
	Institutions	Teachers	Males	Females	Total
Pre-primary*	554	4,048	44,912	42,757	87,669
Basic:					
First cycle	337	16,505	113,994	111,889	225,883
Second cycle	303	14,831	124,753	94,550	219,303
Continuing schools	493	21,675	92,379	126,998	219,377
School grades 10–12	87	4,644	37,299	25,898	63,197
Post basic:					
School grades 11–12	21	1,049	6,029	7,545	13,574
Higher†	69‡	7,174§	14,762‖	16,192‖	30,954‖
University	1	1,235‡	1,690‖	1,883‖	3,573‖

* Private schools.
† Including private universities and colleges.
‡ 2015/16.
§ 2019/20.
‖ 2020/21.

Source: mostly Ministry of Education, Muscat.

Pupil-teacher ratio (qualified teaching staff, primary education, UNESCO estimate): 12.3 in 2020/21 (Source: UNESCO Institute for Statistics).

Adult literacy rate (UNESCO estimates): 95.7% (males 97.0%; females 92.7%) in 2018 (Source: UNESCO Institute for Statistics).

Directory

The Constitution

The Basic Statute of the State was promulgated by royal decree on 6 November 1996, as Oman's first document defining the organs and guiding principles of the State. A series of amendments to the Basic Statute were promulgated by royal decree on 13 October 2011, most notably including changes to the jurisdiction and terms of the Majlis Oman (Council of Oman—see below).

Chapter 1 defines the State and the system of government. Oman is defined as an Arab, Islamic and independent state with full sovereignty. Islamic law (*Shari'a*) is the basis for legislation. The official language is Arabic. The system of government is defined as Sultani (Royal), hereditary in the male descendants of Sayyid Turki bin Said bin Sultan. Article 6 determines the procedure whereby the Sultan is designated.

Chapter 2 defines the political, economic, social, cultural and security principles of the State. Article 11 (economic principles) includes the stipulation that 'All natural resources and revenues therefrom shall be the property of the State which will preserve and utilize them in the best manner taking into consideration the requirements of the State's security and the interests of the national economy'. The constructive and fruitful co-operation between public and private activity is stated to be the essence of the national economy. Public property is inviolable, and private ownership is safeguarded. Article 14 (security principles) provides for a Defence Council to preserve the safety and defence of the Sultanate.

Chapter 3 defines public rights and duties. Individual and collective freedoms are guaranteed within the limits of the law.

Chapter 4 concerns the Head of State, the Council of Ministers, Specialized Councils and financial affairs of the State. Article 41 defines the Sultan as Head of State and Supreme Commander of the Armed Forces. The article states that 'His person is inviolable. Respect for him is a duty and his command must be obeyed. He is the symbol of national unity and the guardian of its preservation and protection'. The Sultan presides over the Council of Ministers, or may appoint a person (Prime Minister) to preside on his behalf. Deputy Prime Ministers and other Ministers are appointed by the Sultan. The Council of Ministers and Specialized Councils assist the Sultan in implementing the general policy of the State.

Chapter 5 defines the jurisdiction, terms, sessions, rules of procedure, membership and regulation of the legislature. This states that the Council of Oman shall consist of the Majlis al-Shura (Consultative Council) and the Majlis al-Dawlah (State Council). The Consultative Council shall consist of elected members representing all *wilayat* (provinces) of the Sultanate. All *wilayat* with a population of less than 30,000 shall be entitled to elect one representative to the Consultative Council and those with a population over 30,000 two representatives. The election of the Consultative Council members shall be conducted through general secret ballot and according to the provisions of the electoral law. Following the election of a new Consultative Council, its Chairman shall be elected by an absolute majority of the members. The State Council consists of a chairman and members not exceeding the total number of Consultative Council members, appointed by royal decree. Members of both Councils shall serve for a term of no more than four years. The government must submit draft legislation to the Council of Oman for amendment or approval prior to promulgation by the Sultan. The Council may propose draft legislation and refer it to the government for consideration.

Chapter 6 concerns the judiciary. Articles 59 and 60 state that the supremacy of the law shall be the basis of governance, and enshrine the dignity, integrity, impartiality and independence of the judiciary. Article 66 provides for a Supreme Council of the judiciary.

Chapter 7 defines the general provisions pertaining to the application of the Basic Statute.

The Government

HEAD OF STATE

Sultan: HAITHAM BIN TARIK AL-SAID (acceded to the throne on 11 January 2020).

COUNCIL OF MINISTERS
(September 2023)

Prime Minister and Minister of Defence: Sultan HAITHAM BIN TARIK AL-SAID.

Minister of Culture, Sports and Youth: Crown Prince Sayyid THEYAZIN BIN HAITHAM BIN TARIK AL-SAID.

Deputy Prime Minister for the Council of Ministers: Sayyid FAHD BIN MAHMOUD AL-SAID.

Deputy Prime Minister for Defence Affairs: Sayyid SHIHAB BIN TARIK BIN TAIMUR AL-SAID.

Minister of the Diwan of the Royal Court: Sayyid KHALID BIN HILAL BIN SAUD AL-BUSAIDI.

Minister of the Royal Office: Gen. SULTAN BIN MUHAMMAD AL-NUMANI.

Minister of the Interior: Sayyid HAMOUD BIN FAISAL BIN SAID AL-BUSAIDI.

Minister of Foreign Affairs: Sayyid BADR BIN HAMAD AL-BUSAIDI.

Minister of Finance: SULTAN BIN SALIM BIN SAID AL-HABSI.

Minister of Awqaf (Religious Endowments) and Religious Affairs: Dr MUHAMMAD AL-MAAMARI.

Minister of Energy and Minerals: SALEM AL-OUFI.

Minister of Health: Dr HILAL AL-SABTI.

Minister of Education: Dr MADIHA BINT AHMAD BIN NASSER AL-SHIBANIYAH.

Minister of Justice and Legal Affairs: Dr ABDULLAH BIN MUHAMMAD BIN SAID AL-SAEEDI.

Minister of Information: Dr ABDULLAH BIN NASSER BIN KHALIFA AL-HARRASI.

Minister of State and Governor of Dhofar: Sayyid MARWAN BIN TURKI BIN MAHMOUD AL-SAID.

Minister of Heritage and Tourism: SALIM BIN MOHAMMED BIN SAID AL-MAHROUQI.

Minister of Agriculture, Fisheries and Water Resources: Dr SAUD BIN HAMOUD BIN AHMED AL-HABSI.

Minister of Housing and Urban Planning: Dr KHALFAN BIN SAID BIN MUBARAK AL-SHU'AILI.

Minister of Higher Education, Research and Innovation: Dr RAHMA BINT IBRAHIM BIN SAID AL-MAHROUQI.

Minister of Transport, Communications and Information Technology: Eng. SAEED BIN HAMOUD AL-MAAWALI.

Minister of Economy: Dr SAID BIN MOHAMMED BIN AHMED AL-SAQRI.

Minister of Commerce, Industry and Investment Promotion: QAIS BIN MOHAMMED BIN MOOSA AL-YOUSEF.

Minister of Social Development: LAILA BINT AHMED BIN AWADH AL-NAJAR.

Minister of Labour: Dr MAHAD BIN SAID BIN ALI BA'OWAIN.

MINISTRIES

Diwan of the Royal Court: POB 632, Muscat 113; tel. 24738711; fax 24739427.

Ministry of Agriculture, Fisheries and Water Resources: POB 467, RB 100, Muscat; tel. 24952000; fax 24692434; e-mail cs@maf.gov.om; internet www.maf.gov.om.

Ministry of Awqaf (Religious Endowments) and Religious Affairs: POB 4, Bidiyah 421, Muscat; tel. 24644999; fax 24693339; e-mail info@mara.gov.om; internet www.mara.gov.om.

Ministry of Commerce, Industry and Investment Promotion: POB 550, Way 3505, Muscat 113; tel. 80000070; e-mail info@tejarah.gov.om; internet tejarah.gov.om.

Ministry of Culture, Sports and Youth: POB 211, Muscat 113; tel. 24755112; fax 24704558; e-mail info@mosa.gov.om; internet mosa.gov.om.

Ministry of Defence: POB 113, Muscat 113; tel. 24333361; fax 24333369; e-mail jundoman@mod.gov.om; internet www.mod.gov.om.

Ministry of Economy: Muscat.

Ministry of Education: POB 3, Muscat 113; tel. 24255552; e-mail moe@moe.om; internet www.moe.gov.om.

Ministry of Energy and Minerals: POB 551, Muscat 100; tel. 24640555; fax 24691046; e-mail info@mog.gov.om; internet www.mog.gov.om.

Ministry of Finance: POB 506, Muscat 100; tel. 24746000; fax 24737028; e-mail info@mof.gov.om; internet www.mof.gov.om.

Ministry of Foreign Affairs: POB 252, Muscat 112; tel. 24699500; fax 24696141; e-mail inquiries@mofa.gov.om; internet www.mofa.gov.om.

Ministry of Health: POB 393, Muscat 113; tel. 22357111; fax 22358003; e-mail webmaster@moh.gov.om; internet www.moh.gov.om.

Ministry of Heritage and Tourism: POB 668, Muscat 113; tel. 24641300; fax 24641331; e-mail mhc.web@mhc.gov.om; internet www.mhc.gov.om.

Ministry of Higher Education, Research and Innovation: POB 82, Ruwi 112; tel. 24340900; fax 24340172; e-mail public.services@mohe.gov.om; internet www.mohe.gov.om.

Ministry of Housing and Urban Planning: POB 173, Ruwi 100; tel. 24693333; e-mail dept.infopr@housing.gov.om; internet eservices.housing.gov.om.

Ministry of Information: POB 600, Muscat 113; tel. 24941582; fax 24693770; e-mail info@omaninfo.om; internet www.omaninfo.om.

Ministry of the Interior: POB 127, Ruwi 112; tel. 24686000; fax 24696660; e-mail info@moi.gov.om; internet www.moi.gov.om.

Ministry of Justice and Legal Affairs: POB 354, Ruwi 112; tel. 24697699; fax 24607716; e-mail info@moj.gov.om; internet www.moj.gov.om.

Ministry of Labour: POB 3994, Ruwi 112; tel. 24689999; fax 24692459; internet www.mol.gov.om.

Ministry of the Royal Office: POB 2227, Ruwi 112; tel. 24600841.

Ministry of Social Development: Muscat; tel. 24602742; e-mail mosd@mosd.gov.om; internet www.mosd.gov.om.

Ministry of Transport, Communications and Information Technology: POB 684, Ruwi 112; tel. 24685000; fax 24685757; e-mail info@motc.gov.om; internet www.motc.gov.om.

Legislature

CONSULTATIVE COUNCIL

The Consultative Council (Majlis al-Shura) was established by royal decree in November 1991. Initially, members of the Council were appointed by the Sultan from among nominees selected at national polls, but from the September 2000 elections members were directly elected. Two representatives are elected in each *wilaya* (district) of more than 30,000 inhabitants, and one in each *wilaya* of fewer than 30,000 inhabitants. Members of the Council are elected for a single four-year term of office. The Council elected on 25 October 2019 comprised 86 members. The duties of the Council include the approval and amendment of all social and economic draft laws prior to their enactment by the Sultan; public service ministries are required to submit reports and answer questions regarding their performance, plans and achievements. A decree issued by Sultan Qaboos bin Said al-Said on 19 October 2011 granted members of both chambers of the Council of Oman the right to propose draft legislation, while members of the Consultative Council may issue a request to question government ministers. The President of the Council is elected by an absolute majority of its members.

Consultative Council: POB 981, 111 Muscat; tel. 24510444; fax 24855042; e-mail info@shura.om; internet www.shura.om.

President: Sheikh KHALID BIN HILAL BIN NASSER AL-MA'AWALI.

STATE COUNCIL

The State Council (Majlis al-Dawlah) was established in December 1997, in accordance with the terms of the Basic Statute of the State. Like the Consultative Council, it is an advisory body, the function of which is to serve as a liaison between the Government and the people of Oman. Its members are appointed by the Sultan for a four-year term. A new State Council, comprising 86 members, was appointed in November 2019.

State Council: POB 59, Muscat; tel. 24855777; fax 24698719; e-mail statecouncil@statecouncil.om; internet www.statecouncil.om.

President: Sheikh ABDULMALIK BIN ABDULLAH BIN ALI AL-KHALILI.

Political Organizations

There are no political organizations in Oman.

Diplomatic Representation

EMBASSIES IN OMAN

Algeria: Madinat al-Sultan Qaboos, POB 116, Muscat 115; tel. 24694945; fax 24694419; e-mail algeria1@omantel.net.om; internet algerianembassy.gov.om; Ambassador Dr FILALI GUENNI.

Austria: Villa 1605, Way 3019, Shatti al-Qurum, Muscat 103; tel. 24091600; fax 24699265; e-mail maskat-ob@bmeia.gv.at; internet www.bmeia.gv.at/en/austrian-embassy-muscat; Ambassador (vacant).

Bahrain: Villa 2421, Way 3030, 66 Madinat al-Sultan Qaboos, POB 115, Shatti al-Qurum, Muscat; tel. 24605074; fax 24605072; e-mail muscat.mission@mofa.gov.bh; internet www.mofa.gov.bh/muscat; Ambassador JUMA BIN AHMAD AL-KA'ABI.

Bangladesh: Villa 4207, Way 3052, POB 3959, Shatti al-Qurum, Muscat; tel. 24698660; fax 24698789; e-mail info@bdembassyoman.org; internet muscat.mofa.gov.bd; Ambassador MD NAZMUL ISLAM.

Brazil: al-Khuwair, Villa 1424, Way 1521, POB 1149, Madinat al-Ilam, Muscat; tel. 24640100; fax 24640181; e-mail brasemb.mascate@itamaraty.gov.br; internet www.gov.br/mre/pt-br/embaixada-mascate; Ambassador (vacant).

Brunei Darussalam: POB 91, Villa 4062, Shatti al-Qurum, Ruwi, Muscat 112; tel. 24603533; fax 24605910; e-mail muscat.oman@mfa.gov.bn; internet mfa.gov.bn/oman-muscat; Ambassador NORALIZAN ABDUL MOMIN.

China, People's Republic: House 1368, Shatti al-Qurum, POB 315, Ruwi, Muscat 112; tel. 24958000; fax 24958068; e-mail chinaemb_om@mfa.gov.cn; internet om.chineseembassy.org; Ambassador LI LINGBING.

Cyprus: House 1798, Way 3021, Shatti al-Qurum, Muscat 103; tel. 24699815; fax 24698812; e-mail muscatembassy@mfa.gov.cy; Ambassador ANDREAS NIKOLAIDES.

Egypt: Jamiat al-Dowal al-Arabiya St, Diplomatic City, al-Khuwair, POB 2252, Ruwi, Muscat 112; tel. 24600411; fax 24603626; e-mail eg.emb_muscat@mfa.gov.eg; Ambassador KHALED MOHAMED ABDEL HALIM RADHI.

Ethiopia: Villa 3900, Way 3048, As Saruj St, POB 148, Shatti al-Qurum, Muscat 103; tel. 24956487; fax 24956496; e-mail ethembaoman@gmail.com; internet fb.com/ethiopianembassyinoman/?ref=page_internal&mt_nav=0; Ambassador (vacant).

France: Diplomatic City, al-Khuwair, POB 208, Madinat al-Sultan Qaboos, Muscat 115; tel. 24681800; fax 24681843; e-mail contact@ambafrance-om.org; internet om.ambafrance.org; Ambassador VÉRONIQUE AULAGNON.

Germany: POB 337, Shatti al-Qurum, Muscat 103; tel. 24691218; fax 24691278; e-mail info@maskat.diplo.de; internet www.maskat.diplo.de; Ambassador THOMAS FRIEDRICH SCHNEIDER.

Holy See: Muscat; Apostolic Nuncio Archbishop NICOLAS HENRY MARIE DENIS THEVENIN.

Hungary: 209 al-Rawaq Bldg, 2nd Floor, POB 1272, Shatti al-Qurum, Muscat 116; tel. 22507468; fax 22579930; e-mail mission.mct@mfa.gov.hu; internet muscat.mfa.gov.hu; Ambassador FODOR BARNABÁS.

India: Diplomatic Area, Jamiat al-Dowal al-Arabiya St, al-Khuwair, POB 1727, Ruwi, Muscat 112; tel. 24684500; fax 24698291; e-mail indembassy.muscat@mea.gov.in; internet www.indemb-oman.gov.in; Ambassador AMIT NARANG.

Indonesia: Bldg 1091, Way 3015, POB 642, Shatti al-Qurum, Muscat 115; tel. 24691050; fax 24691243; e-mail muscat.kbri@kemlu.go.id; internet www.kemlu.go.id/muscat; Ambassador MOHAMAD IRZAN DJOHAN.

Iran: Diplomatic Area, Jamiat al-Dowal al-Arabiya St, POB 3155, Ruwi, Muscat 112; tel. 24696944; fax 24696888; e-mail iranembassy@hotmail.com; internet oman.mfa.gov.ir; Ambassador ALI NAJAFI KHOSHROUDI.

Iraq: House 1073, Way 3015, POB 262, Shatti al-Qurum, Muscat 115; tel. 24695559; fax 24602026; internet www.mofa.gov.iq/muscat; Ambassador QAIS SAAD AL-AMIRY.

Italy: POB 520, House No. 2697, Way 3034, Shatti al-Qurum, Ruwi, Muscat 115; tel. 24693727; fax 24694721; internet www.ambmascate.esteri.it; Ambassador PIERLUIGI D'ELIA.

Japan: Villa 760, Way 3011, Jamiat al-Dowal al-Arabiya St, POB 3511, Shatti al-Qurum, Ruwi, Muscat 112; tel. 24601028; fax 24698720; e-mail embjapan@mc.mofa.go.jp; internet www.oman.emb-japan.go.jp; Ambassador GOTA YAMAMOTO.

Jordan: Diplomatic City, Arab League St, POB 70, al-Adhaiba, Muscat 130; tel. 24692760; fax 24692762; e-mail muscat.consular@fm.gov.jo; Ambassador AMJAD JAMIL AL-QUHAIWI.

Kazakhstan: Villa 4076, Way 3050, POB 88, Shatti al-Qurum, Muscat 103; tel. 24692418; fax 24692485; e-mail muscat@mfa.kz; internet www.gov.kz/memleket/entities/mfa-muscat; Ambassador NAJMEDIN MUHAMETALI.

Kenya: Villa 4074, Way 3050, POB 173, Shatti al-Qurum, Muscat 103; tel. 24697664; fax 24697366; e-mail muscat@mfa.go.ke; internet www.kenyaembassymuscat.com; Ambassador AMINA ALI ABDULLAH.

Korea, Republic: POB 377, Madinat al-Sultan Qaboos, Muscat 115; tel. 24691490; fax 24691495; e-mail emboman@mofa.go.kr; internet overseas.mofa.go.kr/om-ko/index.do; Ambassador KI-JOO KIM.

Kuwait: Diplomatic Area, Bldg 58, al-Khuwair, Arab League St, Blk 13, POB 1798, Ruwi, Muscat 112; tel. 8699626; Ambassador MOHAMMED AL-HAJRI.

Lebanon: Villa 1613, Way 3019, al-Harthy Complex, POB 67, Shatti al-Qurum, Muscat 118; tel. 24695844; fax 24695633; e-mail lebanon1@omantel.net.om; internet www.muscat.mfa.gov.lb; Ambassador ALBERT SAMAHA.

Libya: Villa 2994, Way 3038, POB 134, Shatti al-Qurum, Muscat 118; tel. 24699729; fax 24601662; tel. 2460 1662; Ambassador HAGER AMRU KHALIFA AL-NAMY.

Malaysia: Villa 1611, Way 3019, POB 51, Shatti al-Qurum, Bareeq al-Shatti, Muscat 112; tel. 24698329; fax 24605031; e-mail mwmuscat.kln@1govuc.gov.my; internet kln.gov.my/web/omn_muscat; Ambassador SHAIFUL ANWAR MOHAMMED.

Mauritania: Shatti al-Qurum, Muscat; tel. 24607051; fax 24607091; Ambassador MOHAMED VALL OULD AHMED.

Morocco: Villa 2443, Way 3030, POB 1054, Shatti al-Qurum, Muscat 133; tel. 24696152; fax 24601114; e-mail sifamarmusc@gmail.com; Ambassador TARIQ LAHSSISNE.

Nepal: Villa 2294, Way 2830, POB 517, Shatti al-Qurum, Muscat 116; tel. 24696177; fax 24696772; e-mail eonmuscat@mofa.gov.np; internet om.nepalembassy.gov.np; Ambassador DORNATH ARYAL.

Netherlands: Villa 1366, Way 3017, POB 3302, Shatti al-Qurum, Ruwi, Muscat 112; tel. 24603706; fax 24603778; e-mail mus@minbuza.nl; internet www.netherlandsworldwide.nl/countries/oman; Ambassador STELLA KLUTH.

Pakistan: Way 2133, POB 1302, Madinat al-Sultan Qaboos, Ruwi, Muscat 112; tel. 24603439; fax 24697462; e-mail parepmuscat@mofa.gov.pk; internet mofa.gov.pk/muscat-oman; Ambassador MOHAMMED IMRAN ALI CHAUDHARY.

Philippines: Bldg 4067, Way 3050, Plot 813, Sarooj, Shatti al-Qurum, Muscat; tel. 24605335; fax 24605179; e-mail muscat.pe@dfa.gov.ph; internet muscatpe.dfa.gov.ph; Chargé d'affaires a.i. JACQUELINE JOAN S. ARQUIZA.

Qatar: Diplomatic City, Jamiat al-Dowal al-Arabiya St, al-Khuwair, POB 802, Muscat 100; tel. 24697247; e-mail muscat@mofa.gov.qa; internet muscat.embassy.qa; Ambassador Sheikh JASSIM BIN ABDUL RAHMAN BIN MOHAMMED AL THANI.

Romania: Villa 2990, Way 2840, POB 161, Shatti al-Qurum, Bareeq al-Shati, Muscat 103; tel. 24953871; e-mail muscat@maec.ro; internet muscat.mae.ro; Ambassador FLORIN MARIUS TACO.

Russian Federation: Way 3032, Surfait Compound, POB 745, Shatti al-Qurum, Muscat 115; tel. 24602894; fax 24604189; e-mail rusemboman@mid.ru; internet www.oman.mid.ru; Ambassador ILYA MORGUNOV.

Saudi Arabia: Diplomatic City, Jamiat al-Dowal al-Arabiya St, POB 1411, Ruwi, Muscat 112; tel. 24699507; fax 24601708; e-mail omemb@mofa.gov.sa; internet embassies.mofa.gov.sa/sites/oman; Ambassador ABDULLAH BIN SAUD AL-ANZI.

Senegal: POB 702, Shatti al-Qurum, Muscat 130; tel. 24949496; fax 24602423; e-mail ambasene@omantel.net.om; Ambassador SERINE ALI DAM.

Singapore: POB 57, Way 2840, Hay al-Sarooj, Muscat; tel. 24607760; fax 24607322; e-mail singemb_mct@mfa.sg; internet www.mfa.gov.sg/muscat; Chargé d'affaires SYED NOUREDDIN BIN SYED HASSIM.

Somalia: Villa 2254, Way 2830, POB 1767, Shatti al-Qurum, Muscat 112; tel. and fax 24697977; e-mail muscatembassy@mfa.gov.so; internet fb.com/SomaliainOman; Ambassador Dr OSMAN AHMED MOHAMED.

South Africa: Villa 1384, Way 3017, POB 231, Shatti al-Qurum, Muscat 118; tel. 24647300; fax 24694792; e-mail shogolem@dirco.gov.za; internet www.dirco.gov.za/Oman; Ambassador (vacant).

Spain: Villa 2573, Way 2834, POB 3492, Shatti al-Qurum, Ruwi, Muscat 112; tel. 24691101; fax 24698969; e-mail emb.mascate@maec.es; internet www.exteriores.gob.es/embajadas/mascate; Ambassador MARÍA LUISA HUIDOBRO MARTÍN-LABORDA.

Sri Lanka: Villa 701, Way 2114, POB 95, Madinat al-Sultan Qaboos, Muscat 115; tel. 24697841; fax 24697336; e-mail info@slemb.org.om; internet www.slemb.org.om; Ambassador AHMED LEBBE SABARULLAH KHAN.

Sudan: Jamiat al-Duwal al-Arabia St, al-Khuwair, POB 3971, Ruwi, Muscat 112; tel. 24697875; fax 24699065; Ambassador SALAH AL-DIN AL-HAJJ MUHAMMAD AL-KANDO.

Switzerland: Villa 1366, Way 3017, POB 210, Shatti al-Qurum, Muscat 103; tel. 24603267; fax 24603298; e-mail muscat@eda.admin.ch; internet www.eda.admin.ch/muscat; Ambassador THOMAS OERTLE.

Syrian Arab Republic: Diplomatic Area, al-Khuwair, Muscat 115; tel. 24392661; fax 24392646; internet www.mofaex.gov.sy/muscat-embassy; Ambassador Dr IDRIS MAYA.

Tanzania: POB 1170, al-Khuwair, Muscat 133; tel. 24601174; fax 24604425; e-mail muscat@nje.go.tz; internet om.tzembassy.go.tz; Ambassador FATMA MOHAMMED RAJAB (designate).

Thailand: Villa 1339, Way 3017, POB 60, Shatti al-Qurum, Ruwi, Muscat 115; tel. 24602684; fax 24605714; e-mail thaimct@omantel.net.om; internet www.thaiembassy.org/muscat; Ambassador SUWAT KAEWSOOK.

Tunisia: Bldg 1446, Way 1522, POB 220, Muscat 115; tel. 24603486; fax 24607778; Ambassador EZZEDINE ALTIS.

Türkiye (Turkey): Bldg 3270, Way 3042, POB 47, Shatti al-Qurum, Muscat 115; tel. 24697050; fax 24697053; e-mail embassy.muscat@mfa.gov.tr; internet muskat.be.mfa.gov.tr; Ambassador MUHAMMET HEKIMOĞLU.

United Arab Emirates: Diplomatic City, al-Khuwair, Muscat; tel. 24400000; fax 24400055; e-mail muscatemb@mofaic.gov.ae; internet www.mofaic.gov.ae/en/missions/muscat; Ambassador MUHAMMAD NAKHIRA JUMA AL-DHAHERI.

United Kingdom: POB 185, Mina al-Fahal, Muscat 116; tel. 24609000; fax 24609010; e-mail muscat.enquirieswebsite@fcdo.gov.uk; internet www.gov.uk/world/oman; Ambassador LIANE SAUNDERS.

USA: Bldg 32, Jamiat al-Dowal al-Arabiya St, POB 202, Madinat al-Sultan Qaboos, Muscat 115; tel. 24643400; fax 24643740; e-mail answersom@state.gov; internet om.usembassy.gov; Chargé d'affaires a.i. JUNAID MUNIR.

Uzbekistan: Villa 3900, Way 3048, Shatti al-Qurum, Muscat 103; tel. 26601360; e-mail uzembassyinoman@gmail.com; Ambassador (vacant).

Yemen: POB 105, Madinat al-Sultan Qaboos, Muscat 115; tel. 24600815; fax 24605008; e-mail muscat@mofa-ye.org; Ambassador Dr KHALED SALEH SHOTEIF.

Judicial System

Oman's Basic Statute guarantees the independence of the judiciary. The foundation for the legal system is *Shari'a* (Islamic law), which is the basis for family law, dealing with matters such as inheritance and divorce. Separate courts have been established to deal with commercial disputes and other matters to which *Shari'a* does not apply.

Courts of the First Instance are competent to try cases of criminal misdemeanour; serious crimes are tried by the Criminal Courts; the Court of Appeal is in Muscat. There are district courts throughout the country. Special courts deal with military crimes committed by members of the armed and security forces.

The Basic Statute provides for a Supreme Judicial Council to supervise the proper functioning of the courts.

The office of Public Prosecutor (or Attorney-General) was established in 1999, and the first appointment to the post was made in June 2001.

Supreme Judicial Council: Muscat; f. 2022; established by royal decree to incorporate the Administrative Affairs Council for the Judiciary, the Administrative Court (f. 2001 and comprising two circuits, namely the Trial Chamber and the Appeals Chamber) and the Public Prosecution Department; Chair. Sultan HAITHAM BIN TARIK AL-SAID; Deputy Chair. Sayyid MUHAMMAD BIN SULTAN BIN HAMOUD AL-BUSAIDI.

Supreme Court: Muscat; Chair. Sayyid KHALIFA BIN SAID BIN KHALIFA AL-BUSAIDI.

Attorney-General: NASR BIN KHAMIS BIN MOHAMMED AL-SAWA'EE.

Religion

ISLAM

In 2015 some 91% of the population were Muslims—50% of the population belonged to the Ibadi sect, 35% were Sunni and 6% Shi'a.

Grand Mufti of Oman: Sheikh AHMAD BIN HAMAD AL-KHALILI.

HINDUISM

According to 2015 estimates, 2.9% of the population are Hindus.

CHRISTIANITY

In 2015 an estimated 4.0% of the population were Christians, including Roman Catholics (2.8% of the total population), Orthodox Christians (0.7%) and Protestants (0.5%).

Protestantism

The Protestant Church in Oman: POB 1982, Ruwi 112; tel. 24702372; e-mail officesec@churchinoman.com; internet www.churchinoman.com; joint chaplaincy of the Anglican Church and the Reformed Church of America; four inter-denominational churches in Oman, at Ruwi and Ghala in Muscat, at Sohar, and at Salalah.

OMAN

The Roman Catholic Church

Oman forms part of the Apostolic Vicariate of Southern Arabia. The Vicar Apostolic is resident in the United Arab Emirates.

The Press

NEWSPAPERS

Oman: POB 3002, Ruwi 112; tel. 24649444; fax 24697443; e-mail info@omandaily.om; internet www.omandaily.om; daily; Arabic; publ. by the Ministry of Information; Editor-in-Chief SAIF BIN SAUD AL-MAHROUQI.

Al-Shabiba (Youth): POB 2998, Ruwi 112; tel. 24726604; fax 24726660; e-mail online@shabiba.com; internet www.shabiba.com; f. 1993; daily; Arabic; culture, leisure and sports; publ. by Muscat Media Group (MMG); Editor-in-Chief AHMAD BIN ESSA AL-ZEDJALI.

Al-Watan (The Nation): POB 463, Muscat 113; tel. 24491919; fax 24491280; e-mail alwatan@omantel.net.om; internet alwatan.com; f. 1971; daily; Arabic; Editor-in-Chief MUHAMMAD BIN SULAYMAN AL-TAI.

English Language

Oman Daily Observer: POB 947, Muscat 100; tel. 24649444; fax 24699643; e-mail editor@omanobserver.om; internet www.omanobserver.om; f. 1981; daily; publ. by the Ministry of Information; Chair. IBRAHIM AHMAD AL-KINDI; Editor ABDULLAH SALIM AL-SHUELLI.

Oman Tribune: POB 463, Muscat 113; tel. 24491919; fax 24498938; internet www.omantribune.com; f. 2004; Chair. MUHAMMAD BIN SULAYMAN AL-TAI; Editor-in-Chief ABD AL-HAMID BIN SULAYMAN AL-TAI.

Times of Oman: POB 770, Ruwi 112; tel. 24726666; fax 24813153; e-mail webeditor@timesofoman.com; internet timesofoman.com; f. 1975; daily; publ. by Muscat Media Group (MMG); Founder, Chair. and Editor-in-Chief ESSA BIN MUHAMMAD AL-ZEDJALI.

TheWeek: POB 2616, Ruwi 112, Muscat; tel. 24799388; fax 24785951; e-mail info@apexmedia.co.om; f. 2003; weekly; free; publ. by Apex Press and Publishing; CEO and Man. Editor MARK RIX.

PERIODICALS

Al-Ain al-Sahira (The Vigilant Eye): Royal Oman Police, POB 302, Mina al-Fahal 116; tel. 24600654; fax 24567161; e-mail info@rop.gov.om; internet www.rop.gov.om; quarterly magazine of Royal Oman Police; Editor-in-Chief HILAL BIN MOHAMMAD AL-HARASI.

Alam Aliktisaad Wala'mal (AIWA) (World of Economy and Business): POB 3305, Ruwi 112; tel. 24700896; fax 24707939; e-mail avi@umsoman.com; f. 2007; monthly; Arabic; business magazine; publ. by United Media Services Group (UMS); Business Head AVI TITUS.

Al-'Aqida (The Faith): POB 1001, Ruwi 112; tel. 24701000; fax 24709917; weekly illustrated magazine; Arabic; political; Editor SAID AL-SAMHAN AL-KATHIRI.

Business Today: POB 2616, Ruwi 112; tel. 24799388; fax 24785951; e-mail editorial@apexmedia.co.om; monthly; publ. by Apex Press and Publishing.

The Commercial: POB 2002, Ruwi 112; tel. 24704022; fax 24795885; e-mail omanad@omantel.net.om; f. 1978; monthly; Arabic and English; business news; Man. MUHAMMAD AYOOB; Chief Editor ALI BIN ABDULLAH AL-KASBI.

Al-Ghorfa (The Chamber): POB 1400, Ruwi 112; tel. 24763754; fax 24708497; e-mail alghorfa@chamberoman.com; internet omanchamber.om; f. 1978; 6 a year; English and Arabic; business; publ. by Oman Chamber of Commerce and Industry; Editor-in-Chief SAID BIN SALEH AL-KIYUMI; Man. Editor HAMOOD BIN HAMAD AL-MAHROUQI.

Al-Jarida al-Rasmiya (Official Gazette): POB 578, Ruwi 112; tel. 24605802; fax 24605697; f. 1972; fortnightly; publ. by govt.

Jund Oman (Soldiers of Oman): Ministry of Defence, POB 113, Muscat 113; tel. 24613615; fax 24613369; f. 1974; monthly; Arabic; illustrated magazine of the Ministry of Defence; Supervisor Chief of Staff of the Sultan's Armed Forces.

Al-Mar'a (Woman): United Media Services, POB 3305, Ruwi 112; tel. 99715390; fax 24707939; e-mail ghalib@umsoman.com; internet www.almaraonline.com; monthly; Arabic; publ. by United Press and Publishing LLC; Editor GHALIB BIN ABDALLAH AL-FORI.

Al-Markazi (The Central): POB 1161, Ruwi 112; tel. 24791212; fax 24702253; e-mail haider.allawati@cbo.gov.om; internet www.cbo.gov.om; f. 1975; bi-monthly economic magazine; Arabic and English; publ. by Cen. Bank of Oman; Editor-in-Chief MOHAMMED ISSA AL-BALUSHI.

Al-Nahda (The Renaissance): POB 979, Muscat 113; tel. 24563104; fax 24564106; weekly illustrated magazine; Arabic; political and social; Editor-in-Chief WADHAH AL-MEAWALY.

Nizwa: POB 855, 117 Wadi Kabir; tel. 24601608; fax 24694254; e-mail nizwam2020@hotmail.com; internet www.nizwa.com; f. 1994; quarterly; Arabic; literary and cultural; publ. by the Ministry of Information; Editor-in-Chief SAIF AL-RAHBI.

Oman Economic Review: POB 3305, Ruwi 112; tel. 24700896; fax 24707939; e-mail mayank@umsoman.com; internet www.oerlive.com; f. 1998; monthly; English; business news; publ. by United Media Services Group; Group Editor MAYANK SINGH.

Oman Today: POB 2616, Ruwi 112; tel. 24799388; fax 24793316; e-mail editorial@apexmedia.co.om; f. 1981; monthly; English; leisure and sports; publ. by Apex Press and Publishing; Man. Editor MOHANA PRABHAKAR.

Al-Omaniya (Omani Woman): POB 3303, Ruwi 112; tel. 24792700; fax 24707765; f. 1982; monthly; Arabic; Editor AIDA BINT SALIM AL-HUJRI.

Risalat al-Masjid (The Mosque Message): POB 3066, Ruwi 112; tel. 24832940; fax 24830921; issued by Diwan of the Royal Court Protocol Dept (Schools and Mosques Section); Editor JOUMA BIN MUHAMMAD BIN SALEM AL-WAHAIBI.

Al-Usra (The Family): POB 440, Mutrah 114; tel. and fax 24703539; f. 1974; monthly; Arabic; socioeconomic illustrated magazine; Gen. Man. MOHAMAD SAAD; Chief Editor SADEK ABDOWANI.

NEWS AGENCY

Oman News Agency: Ministry of Information, POB 3659, Ruwi 112; tel. 24944700; fax 24944703; e-mail ona@omannews.gov.om; internet www.omannews.gov.om; f. 1986; Dir-Gen. and Editor-in-Chief Dr MOHAMMED BIN MUBARAK AL-ARAIMI.

Publishers

Apex Press and Publishing: POB 2616, Ruwi 112, Muscat; tel. 24799388; fax 24793316; e-mail muscatdaily@apexmedia.co.om; internet www.apexmedia.co.om; f. 1980; art, history, trade directories, maps, leisure and business magazines, and guidebooks; publs incl. *TheWeek* (English weekly), *Business Today* (business monthly), *Oman Today* (leisure monthly); Exec. Chair. SALEH M. TALIB AL-ZAKWANI; CEO MARK RIX.

Muscat Media Group (MMG): POB 770, Ruwi 112; tel. 24726666; fax 24813153; e-mail contact@mmg.om; internet mmg.om; publs incl. *Times of Oman* (English daily) and *Al-Shabiba* (Arabic daily); owns Shabiba FM and T FM (radio stations); Chair. MUHAMMAD BIN ESSA AL-ZEDJALI; CEO AHMAD BIN ESSA AL-ZEDJALI.

Oman Establishment for Press, News, Publication and Advertising (OEPNPA): POB 974, al-Qurum, Muscat 113; tel. 24649458; fax 24649469; f. 1996 as Oman Newspaper House; publs include *Oman* (Arabic daily), *Oman Daily Observer* (English language) and *Nizwa* (Arabic quarterly); three regional offices in Dhofar, Nizwa and Sohar; CEO Dr IBRAHIM AL-KINDI; Editor-in-Chief FAHMI BIN KHALID AL-HARTHI.

United Media Services LLC (UMS): POB 3305, Ruwi 112; tel. 24700896; fax 24707939; e-mail contact@umsoman.com; internet www.umsoman.com; f. 1989; part of Muscat Overseas Group (MOG); publishes *Alam Aliktisaad Wala'mal* (Arabic monthly) and *Oman Economic Review* (English monthly); CEO ATULYA SHARMA.

Broadcasting and Communications

TELECOMMUNICATIONS

Oman Telecommunications Company SAOC (Omantel): POB 789, Ruwi 112; tel. 24242424; fax 24240112; e-mail dpo@omantel.om; internet www.omantel.om; f. 1999 as successor to Gen. Telecommunications Org.; provider of fixed-line, mobile and internet services; held a monopoly on fixed-line services until 2008; 70% stake owned by the Government of Oman; Chair. MULHAM AL-JARF; CEO TALAL SAID MARHOON AL-MAMARI.

Omani Qatari Telecommunications Co SAOC (Ooredoo): POB 874, Muscat 111; tel. 22002200; fax 95104094; e-mail customerservice@ooredoo.om; internet ooredoo.om; f. 2004 as Nawras; present name adopted 2014; awarded Oman's second mobile telecommunications licence 2004; awarded Oman's second fixed-line licence 2009; jt venture between Qatar Telecommunications Corpn (Q-Tel) and several Omani investors; Chair. AMJAD MUHAMMAD AL-BUSAIDI; CEO BASSAM YOUSEF AL-IBRAHIM.

OMAN

Regulatory Authority

Telecommunications Regulatory Authority: POB 3555, Ruwi 111; tel. 24222222; fax 24222000; e-mail traoman@tra.gov.om; internet tra.gov.om; f. 2002 to oversee the privatization of Omantel and to set tariffs and regulate the sale of operating licences; Chair. Eng. SALEM BIN NASSER AL-AWFI; CEO OMAR BIN HAMDAN AL-ISMAILI.

BROADCASTING

Radio

Sultanate of Oman Radio: Ministry of Information, POB 1130, Madinat al-Ilam, Muscat 133; tel. 24602058; fax 24601393; e-mail customer.service@part.gov.om; internet part.gov.om/omanradio; f. 1970; operates four services: General Arabic Channel, Al-Shabab Channel (youth service), English-language FM service, Holy Koran Channel.

Television

Sultanate of Oman Television: Ministry of Information, POB 1130, Madinat al-Ilam, Muscat 133; tel. 24603222; fax 24605032; e-mail customer.service@part.gov.om; internet part.gov.om/ar/web/omantv; began broadcasting in 1974; programmes broadcast via Arabsat and Nilesat satellite networks.

Finance

BANKING

At the end of December 2019 there were 16 commercial banks (7 local and 9 foreign) and two specialized banks operating throughout Oman. The country's first *Shari'a*-compliant bank was established in 2012 and by December 2019 two locally-incorporated Islamic banks were in operation.

Central Bank

Central Bank of Oman: POB 1161, 44 Mutrah Commercial Centre, Ruwi 112; tel. 24777777; fax 24777723; e-mail cboportalservices@cbo.gov.om; internet cbo.gov.om; f. 1974; 100% state-owned; Chair. of the Bd TAIMUR BIN ASA'AD BIN TARIK AL-SAID; Exec. Pres. TAHIR BIN SALIM BIN ABDULLAH AL-AMRI.

Commercial Banks

Ahli Bank SAOG: POB 545, Mina al-Fahal 116; tel. 24577177; e-mail info@ahlibank.om; internet ahlibank.om; f. 1997 as Alliance Housing Bank; renamed as above 2008; Chair. HAMDAN ALI NASSER AL-HINAI; CEO SAID ABDULLAH MOHAMMED AL-HATMI.

Bank Dhofar SAOG: POB 1507, Ruwi 112; tel. 24790466; fax 24797246; e-mail info@bankdhofar.com; internet www.bankdhofar.com; f. 1990 as Bank Dhofar al-Omani al-Fransi SAOG; renamed as above 2004 after merger with Majan Int. Bank SAOC; Chair. Eng. ABDUL HAFIDH SALIM RAJAB AL-AUJAILI; CEO ABDUL HAKEEM OMAR AL-OJAILI.

BankMuscat SAOG: POB 134, Ruwi 112; tel. 24795555; e-mail care@bankmuscat.com; internet www.bankmuscat.com; f. 1993 by merger as Bank Muscat Al-Ahli Al-Omani; renamed Bank Muscat Int. 1998, and as above 1999; merged with Commercial Bank of Oman Ltd SAOG 2000 and with Industrial Bank of Oman 2002; 88.8% owned by Omani shareholders; Chair. Sheikh KHALID BIN MUSTAHAIL AL-MASHANI; Chief Exec. Sheikh WALEED KHAMIS AL-HASHAR.

Bank Nizwa: POB 1423, al-Khuwair; tel. 24950500; fax 24649038; e-mail customercare@banknizwa.om; internet banknizwa.om; f. 2013; first dedicated Islamic bank in the country, offering *Shari'a* compliant products and services; Chair. Sheikh KHALID ABDULLAH ALI AL-KHALILI; CEO KHALID JAMAL AL-KAYED.

Bank Sohar SAOG: POB 44, Hay al-Mina, Muttrah 114; tel. 24730000; e-mail customerservice@soharinternational.com; internet soharinternational.com; f. 2007; 32.5% owned by Oman Govt, 12% by Al Ghadir Al Arabia LLC, 55.5% by various Omani shareholders; Chair. MUHAMMAD MAHFOUDH AL-ARDHI; CEO AHMED JAFAR AL-MUSALMI.

HSBC Bank Oman SAOG: POB 240, Ruwi 112; tel. 80074722; internet www.hsbc.co.om; merged with Oman International Bank SAOG 2012; Chair. Sir SHERARD COWPER-COLES.

National Bank of Oman SAOG (NBO): POB 751, Ruwi 112; tel. 24770000; e-mail ask@nbo.co.om; internet www.nbo.om; f. 1973; 100% Omani-owned; Chair. AMAL SUHAIL BAHWAN; CEO ABDULLAH ZAHRAN AL-HINAI.

Oman Arab Bank SAOC: POB 2240, Ruwi 130; tel. 24754000; fax 24797736; e-mail contactus@oman-arabbank.com; internet www.oman-arabbank.com; f. 1984; purchased Omani European Bank SAOG in 1994; 49% owned by Arab Bank PLC (Jordan), 31.6% by Oman International Development and Investment Co (OMINVEST); Chair. RASHAD MUHAMMAD AL-ZUBAIR; CEO SULAIMAN AL-HARTHI.

Development Banks

Oman Development Bank SAOC: POB 3077, Ruwi 112; tel. 80007888; e-mail info@odb.om; internet odb.om; f. 1977; absorbed Oman Bank for Agriculture and Fisheries in 1997; provides finance for devt projects in industry, agriculture and fishing; state-owned; Chair. Eng. MOHAMMED BIN ABU BAKR BIN SALEM AL-SAIL AL-GHASSANI; CEO ABDULAZIZ BIN MUHAMMAD AL-HINAI.

Oman Housing Bank SAOC: POB 2555, Ruwi 112; tel. 24775800; fax 24704071; e-mail ohb@ohb.co.om; internet www.ohb.co.om; f. 1977; long-term finance for housing devt; 100% state-owned; Chair. SALAM BIN SAEED AL-SHAQSI; CEO MOUSA MASOUD AL-JADIDI.

SOVEREIGN WEALTH FUND

Oman Investment Authority (OIA): POB 188, Muscat 100; tel. 24745100; e-mail info@oia.gov.om; internet oia.gov.om; f. 2020; combining all state-owned assets previously held by State General Reserve Fund and Oman Investment Fund; Chair. SULTAN BIN SALIM BIN SAID AL-HABSI (Minister of Finance).

STOCK EXCHANGE

Muscat Stock Exchange (MSX): POB 3265, Muscat 112; tel. 24823600; fax 24823706; e-mail info@msx.om; internet www.msx.om; f. 2021; took over the functions of Muscat Securities Market; Chair. MOHAMMED BIN MAHFOUD AL-ARDHI; Dir-Gen. HAITHAM BIN SALEM AL-SALMI.

Supervisory Body

Capital Market Authority (CMA): POB 3359, Ruwi 112; tel. 24823224; fax 24817471; e-mail info@cma.gov.om; internet www.cma.gov.om; f. 1998 to regulate capital market and insurance sector; Chair. Eng. SULTAN BIN SALIM BIN SAID AL-HABSI (Minister of Finance); Exec. Pres. ABDULLAH BIN SALEM AL-SALMI.

INSURANCE

Al-Ahlia Insurance Co SAOC: Muscat; tel. 24766808; e-mail aaic@om.rsagroup.com; internet www.alahliaoman.com; f. 1985; part of Royal and Sun Alliance Group (United Kingdom); Man. Dir HANAA AL-HINAI.

Arabia Falcon Insurance Co SAOC (AFIC): POB 2279, Ruwi 112; tel. 24660900; e-mail complaints@afic.om; internet afic.om; f. 2017 through the merger of Arabia Insurance Co and Falcon Insurance Co; Chair. MAROUN KYRILLOS.

Dhofar Insurance Co SAOC: POB 1002, Ruwi 112; tel. 80007777; e-mail dhofar@dhofarinsurance.com; internet www.dhofarinsurance.com; f. 1989; Chair. MAJID BIN SULTAN AL-TOQI; CEO SUNIL KOHLI.

Al Madina Insurance Co SAOC: POB 80, Offices 301–302, 3rd Floor, Muscat Grand Mall, Muscat 136; tel. 22033888; fax 22033833; e-mail reachus@almadinatakaful.com; internet almadinatakaful.com; f. 2006; Chair. MUHAMMAD ALI AL-BARWANI; CEO USAMA AL-BARWANI.

Muscat Insurance Co SAOC: POB 72, Ruwi 112; tel. 22364400; fax 22364500; e-mail info@muscatinsurance.com; internet www.misaog.com; f. 1995 as Muscat Insurance Co SAOG; restructured 1999 as Muscat Nat. Holding Co SAOG (parent co), Muscat Insurance Co SAOC and Muscat Life Assurance Co SAOC; subsidiary of Omar Zawawi Establishment (OMZEST); Chair. MOHAMED AMER MOHAMED EL-METWALY SATUR.

National Life and General Insurance Co SAOC: POB 798, Wadi Kabir 117; tel. 24730999; e-mail info@nlicgulf.com; internet www.nlg.om; f. 1983; subsidiary of Oman Nat. Investment Corpn Holding SAOG; Chair. KHALID MUHAMMAD AL-ZUBAIR.

Oman Qatar Insurance Co SAOC: POB 3660, Ruwi 112; tel. 24765333; fax 24765399; e-mail contact@oqic.com; internet oqic.com; subsidiary of Qatar Insurance Co; Chair. KHALAF AHMED AL-MANNAI; CEO HASAN AL-LAWATI.

Oman United Insurance Co SAOC: POB 1522, Ruwi 112; tel. 24477300; fax 24477334; e-mail info@omanutd.com; internet www.omanutd.com; f. 1985; CEO R. MUTHUKUMAR.

Trade and Industry

CHAMBER OF COMMERCE

Oman Chamber of Commerce and Industry: POB 1400, Ruwi 112; tel. 24763700; fax 24708497; e-mail s.mughairi@chamberoman.com; internet chamberoman.om; f. 1973; Chair. Eng. READH JUMA MOHAMMED ALI AL-SALEH.

STATE HYDROCARBONS COMPANIES

National Gas Co SAOG: ONEIC Bldg, al-Khuwair, Muscat; tel. 24446073; fax 22084901; e-mail info@nationalgasco.net; internet www.nationalgasco.net; f. 1979; bottling of LPG; Chair. Sheikh ABDULLAH SULEIMAN AL-HARTHY; CEO NALIN CHANDNA.

Oman LNG LLC: POB 560, Mina al-Fahal 116; tel. 24609999; fax 24609900; e-mail info@omanlng.co.om; internet www.omanlng.com; f. 1994; 51% state-owned; Royal Dutch Shell 30%; manufacturing, shipping and marketing of liquefied natural gas; Chair. TALAL HAMID AL-AWFI; CEO HAMED AL-NAAMANY.

OQ: POB 261, Grand Mall, Muscat 118; tel. 22143999; internet oq.com; f. 2018 as Oman Oil and Orpic Group by merger of Duqm Refinery and Petrochemical Industries Co, Oman Oil Co Exploration and Production, Oman Gas Co, Oman Oil Co, Oman Trading Intl, Orpic, OXEA, Salalah LPG and Salalah Methanol Co; name changed to OQ in 2019; Chair. Dr MULHAM BASHEER AL-JARF; CEO TALAL HAMID AL-AWFI.

Petroleum Development Oman LLC (PDO): POB 81, Muscat 100; tel. 24678111; e-mail external-affairs@pdo.co.om; internet pdo.co.om; incorporated in Sultanate of Oman by royal decree as an LLC since 1980; 60% owned by Oman Govt, 34% by Royal Dutch Shell; exploration and production of crude petroleum and gas; crude petroleum production (2018) averaged 610,170 b/d from 209 fields, linked by a pipeline system to terminal at Mina al-Fahal, near Muscat; gas supply (2018) totalled 64.8m. cu m/d; Chair. SALEM AL-OUFI (Minister of Energy and Minerals); Man. Dir RAOUL RESTUCCI.

UTILITIES

As part of its privatization programme, the Omani Government is divesting the utilities on a project-by-project basis. Private investors have already been found for several municipal wastewater projects, desalination plants and regional electricity providers.

Supervisory Bodies

Authority for Public Services Regulation (APSR): POB 954, Ominvest Business Centre, 1st Floor, Madinat al-Erfan, al-Khuwair 133; tel. 24609700; fax 24609701; e-mail enquiries@apsr.om; internet www.apsr.om; f. 2004 as Authority for Electricity Regulation; present name adopted in 2020; responsible for the regulation of several public utility sectors, including electricity, natural gas and water; Chair. SALEM AL-OUFI (Minister of Energy and Minerals).

Public Authority for Water (Diam): POB 1889, al-Azaiba, Muscat 130; tel. 24611100; fax 24611133; e-mail info@paew.gov.om; internet diam.om; f. 2007 as Public Authority for Electricity and Water following restructuring of fmr Ministry of Housing, Electricity and Water; present name adopted 2018 following privatization of electricity and water sector; Chair. MOHAMMED ABDULLAH AL-MAHROUQI.

Electricity

NAMA Holding: Muscat; tel. 24559200; e-mail info@holding.nama.om; internet www.nama.om; f. 2002 as Electricity Holding Co SAOC; name adopted as above later; state-owned; established to hold Govt's ownership in 9 utility cos and to facilitate the commercial restructuring of the sector; Al-Rusail Power Co was privatized in 2007; of the remaining 8 successor cos, 6 are currently scheduled for privatization; Chair. HAMDAN BIN AHMAD AL-SHAQSI; CEO Eng. OMAR AL-WAHAIBI.

Principal subsidiaries of the EHC include:

Muscat Electricity Distribution Co SAOC (MEDC): POB 3732, al-Ghubrah 112; tel. 24588600; e-mail koopidadmin@medcoman.com; internet www.medcoman.com; f. 2005; responsible for all distribution in the Governorate of Muscat; Chair. SALEEM AHMED ALI ABDULLATIFF; CEO SALMAN BIN ALI BIN ABDULLAH AL-HATALI (acting).

Oman Electricity Transmission Co SAOC (OETC): POB 1389, al-Khoud, Muscat 132; tel. 24283000; e-mail info@omangrid.com; internet www.omangrid.com; f. 2003; owns and operates the Main Interconnected System, which covers the north of Oman and accounts for 90% of the Sultanate's electricity transmission; scheduled for privatization; Chair. Eng. AHMED AMUR AL-MAHRIZI; CEO Eng. SALEH BIN NASSER AL-RUMHI.

Oman Power and Water Procurement Co SAOC: POB 1388, Ruwi 112; tel. 24508400; fax 24399946; e-mail info@omanpwp.com; internet www.omanpwp.com; f. 2003; responsible for forecasting and managing the supply and demand of electricity and water; CEO YAQOUB BIN SAIF AL-KIYUMI.

Rural Areas Electricity Co (Tanweer): POB 1166, Seeb 133; tel. 24250800; fax 24250963; e-mail info@tanweer.nama.om; internet tanweer.om; f. 2005; Chair. AHMED AMUR NASSER AL-MAHRIZI; CEO AHMED AL-HARTHI (acting).

Other subsidiaries of the EHC are: Al-Ghubrah Power and Desalination Co, Majan Electricity Co, Mazoon Electricity Co, Rural Areas Electricity Co and Wadi Jizzi Power Co.

Water

Ministry of Agriculture, Fisheries and Water Resources: (see Ministries); assesses, manages, develops and conserves water resources.

Oman Power and Water Procurement Co SAOC: see Electricity.

Haya Water: POB 1047, al-Khuwair 133; tel. 24611100; e-mail customerservice@haya.om; internet haya.om; f. 2002; fmrly Oman Wastewater Services Co; devt and operation of a wastewater system in the Governorate of Muscat; govt-owned; Chair. Eng. OMAR AL-WAHAIBI; CEO QAIS SAUD AL-ZAKWANI.

MAJOR COMPANIES

Construction Materials Industries SAOG: POB 1791, Sohar 112; tel. 26752247; fax 26750867; e-mail info@cmioman.com; internet cmioman.com; f. 1977; manufacture and supply of calcium silicate bricks, paving and hydrated lime and limestone products; Chair. KHALED ABDULLAH MUHAMED AL-JABRI; Gen. Man. TALAL NASER QASIM OQLAH.

National Detergent Co SAOG: POB 3104, Ruwi 112; tel. 24493824; fax 24492145; e-mail ndcoman@omantel.net.om; internet www.ndcoman.com; f. 1980; manufacture and marketing of detergents; CEO DEEPAK JAIN (acting); 461 employees (2022).

Oman Cement Co SAOG: POB 560, Ruwi 112; tel. 24437070; fax 24437777; e-mail admin@omancement.com; internet occ.om; f. 1978; partially privatized 1994; development and production of cement; Chair. LI YEQING.

Oman Chromite Co SAOG: POB 346, Tareef Sohar 321; tel. 26845115; e-mail info@omanchromite.com; internet www.omanchromite.com; f. 1991; production of chromite; Chair. HUMAID MASOUD ALI AL-MAQBALI; CEO ABDULMONEM AL-MURSHIDI.

Oman Fisheries Co SAOG: POB 2900, Ruwi 112; tel. 24509500; fax 24597804; e-mail info@omanfisheries.com; internet omanfisheries.com; f. 1980 as Oman Nat. Fisheries Co; renamed as above 1989; Oman Govt holds 24% share of capital; responsible for commercial devt of fishing, processing and marketing of marine products; operates nine deep-sea trawlers, a processing and freezing plant, and an on-board fishmeal plant; Chair. HAITHAM MOHAMMED ALI AL-FANNAH; CEO NABEEL SALIM RWIDI.

Oman Flour Mills Co SOAG: POB 566, Ruwi 112; tel. 24717300; fax 24714711; e-mail info@omanflourmills.com; internet www.omanflourmills.com; f. 1977; 51% state-owned; produces 800 metric tons per day (t/d) of various flours and 1,500 t/d of animal feedstuffs; CEO HIATHAM AL-FANNAH.

Oman Mining Co LLC: POB 758, Ruwi, Muscat 100; tel. 25669430; fax 25669407; e-mail info@omanmining.net; internet oman-mining.com; f. 1978; state-owned; devt of copper, gold and chromite mines; Chair. NASSER AL-MAQBALI; Gen. Man. RASHID SALIM ABDULLAH AL-TOQI.

Oman Refreshment Co Ltd SAOG: POB 30, Central Post Office, Muscat 111; tel. 24589100; fax 24589099; e-mail info@pepsioman.com; internet www.pepsioman.com; f. 1974; bottling and distribution of soft drinks, water, juices and snacks; Chair. BUTI OBAID AL-MULLA; CEO YOUSSEF EZZIKHE.

Poly Products LLC (Raha): POB 2561, Ruwi 112; tel. 24448100; e-mail info@rahaoman.com; internet www.rahaoman.com; f. 1979; manufacture of flexible and rigid polyurethane foam and spring mattresses, divans and upholstered beds, sofas, sofa seats and polyester fibre.

Raysut Cement Co SAOG: POB 1020, Salalah 211; tel. 23220600; e-mail info@raysutcement.com.om; internet raysutcement.om; f. 1982; production of cement; Chair. HAMDAN AHMED AL-SHAQSI; CEO KHALID AL-RAWAS.

Shell Oman Marketing Co SAOG: POB 38, Mina al-Fahal 116; tel. 24570200; fax 24570164; e-mail feedbackandissues-om@shell.com; internet www.shelloman.com.om; f. 1997 by merger of Shell Marketing (Oman) Ltd and Oman Lubricants Co LLC; supply and marketing of petroleum products; Chair. WALID HADI; Man. Dir MUHAMMAD MAHMOOD AL-BALUSHI.

Sohar Aluminium: POB 80, Sohar Industrial Estate, Sohar 327; tel. 26863000; fax 26883001; e-mail info@sohar-aluminium.com; internet www.sohar-aluminium.com; f. 2004 to undertake US $2,400m. Greenfield Aluminium Smelter project in Sohar; inaugurated April 2009; 40% stake owned by OQ Group, 40% by TAQA (United Arab Emirates) and 20% by Rio Tinto Alcan (Canada); Chair. AYAD ALI AL-BALUSHI; CEO SAID MUHAMMAD AL-MASOUDI.

Yahya Construction LLC: POB 286, Muscat 100; tel. 24115656; fax 24115677; e-mail inquires@yahyagroupholding.com; internet yahyagroupholding.com; f. 1977 as Yahya Costain LLC; civil and building engineering, furniture manufacture and joinery; Chair. YAHYA MUHAMMAD NASIB; Man. Dir NASEEB YAHYA NASIB.

Transport

RAILWAYS

There are currently no railways in Oman. Plans for a regional rail network, connecting Oman with the five other member countries of the Cooperation Council for the Arab States of the Gulf (or Gulf Cooperation Council—GCC), were finalized in late 2009. On completion, the network was to total some 2,177 km in length, and the section in Oman was to run from the southern port city of Salalah to Buraimi, on the border with the United Arab Emirates (UAE). However, in 2016 the Omani Government placed the project on hold, following similar temporary suspensions in other GCC countries. In mid-2021 the Government announced plans to build a metro rail network connecting Muscat International Airport (located in the coastal city of Seeb) with Ruwi (the main business area of the capital). At the same time plans were drawn up for the country's first passenger rail service, connecting Seeb with the port city of Sohar, about 120 km north-west of Muscat. This train line would form part of a 2,135-km national network, as envisaged under the National Railway Project, linking Oman with the UAE in the north and Yemen in the south.

Oman Rail: POB 470, Madinat al-Sultan Qaboos, Muscat 115; tel. 22308900; e-mail info@omanrail.om; internet www.omanrail.om; f. 2014 to develop a 2,135-km passenger and freight railway network in Oman; Chair. Eng. SAEED BIN HAMOUD AL-MAAWALI (Minister of Transport, Communications and Information Technology); CEO ABDULRAHMAN AL-HATMI.

ROADS

A network of adequate graded roads links all the main centres of population, and only a few mountain villages are inaccessible by off-road vehicles. There are three expressways—the 54-km Muscat Expressway, the 256-km Batinah Expressway (which was opened in 2018 and runs from Halban to the UAE border at Khatmat Malaha) and the 246-km al-Sharqiyah Expressway.

Directorate-General of Roads: Ministry of Transport, Communications and Information Technology, POB 338, Ruwi 112; tel. 24221611; fax 24221612; e-mail fathiyar@motc.gov.om; Dir-Gen. of Roads Sheikh MUHAMMAD BIN HILAL AL-KHALILI.

Mwasalat: POB 620, Muscat 113; tel. 24121500; internet mwasalat.om; f. 1972 as Oman National Transport Co SAOG; re-established in 1984; renamed as above 2015; operates local, regional and long-distance bus services; Chair. NABIL AL-BIMANI; CEO BADAR AL-NADABI (acting).

SHIPPING

Salalah Port, formerly known as Mina Raysut, is Oman's largest transshipment terminal and serves as a major transshipment centre for the region. Other major ports include Port Sultan Qaboos (Mina Sultan Qaboos), located at the entrance to the Persian (Arabian) Gulf, and Duqm Port, on the Gulf of Masirah. The oil terminal at Mina al-Fahal can also accommodate the largest super-tankers on offshore loading buoys.

Port Authorities and Regulatory Body

Directorate-General of Ports and Maritime Affairs: POB 684, Ruwi 113; tel. 24685900; fax 24685909; e-mail seafarers@motc.gov.om; Dir-Gen. Dr TAHER AL-BUSAIDI (acting).

Port Services Corpn SAOG (PSC): POB 133, Muscat 113; tel. 24711205; fax 24714007; internet www.pscoman.com; f. 1976; jointly owned by the Govt of Oman and private shareholders; responsible for management and operation of Port Sultan Qaboos; CEO SAUD BIN AHMAD AL-NAHARI.

Salalah Port Services Co SAOG (SPS): POB 369, Salalah 211; tel. 23220000; fax 23219520; e-mail info@salalahport.com; internet www.salalahport.com; f. 1997; holds a 30-year concession to manage and develop Salalah Port; Chair. Sheikh BRAIK MUSALLAM AL-AMRI; CEO MARK HARDIMAN.

Principal Shipping Companies

National Ferries Co SAOG: Bldg 218, Blk 236, 18th November St, al-Ghoubra, Muscat; tel. 80072000; fax 24711333; e-mail reservation@nfc.om; internet www.nfc.om; f. 2006; govt-owned; operates a high-speed, passenger and vehicle ferry service between Muscat and Khasab, on the Strait of Hormuz; Chair. MEHDI MUHAMMAD AL-ABDUWANI.

Oman Shipping Co SAOC (OSC): Bldg 1/171, Bawsher St, Muscat 118; tel. 24400900; fax 24400922; e-mail info@omanship.co.om; internet www.omanship.co.om; f. 2003; govt-owned (Ministry of Finance 80%, Oman Oil Co SAOC 20%); owns and operates a fleet of over 49 vessels; transportation of LNG, crude petroleum and petrochemical products; subsidiaries include: Oman Charter Co, Oman Charter Management Co, Oman Container Line; Dep. Chair. Eng. SAEED BIN HAMOUD AL-MAAWALI (Minister of Transport, Communications and Information Technology); CEO IBRAHIM AL-NADHAIRI.

CIVIL AVIATION

Domestic and international flights operate from Muscat International Airport (known as Seeb International Airport prior to Feb. 2008). Oman has three other international airports—located at Salalah, Duqm and Sohar.

Civil Aviation Authority (CAA): POB 1, Muscat International Airport, Muscat 111; tel. 24354433; e-mail info@caa.gov.om; internet www.caa.gov.om; f. 2012 as Public Authority for Civil Aviation; present name adopted in 2020; responsible for legal and regulatory aspects of civil aviation; CEO Eng. NAYEF BIN ALI BIN HAMAD AL-ABRI.

Oman Air SAOC: POB 58, Muscat International Airport, Muscat 111; tel. 24531111; fax 24153300; e-mail webbooking@omanair.com; internet www.omanair.com; f. 1993 as a subsidiary of Oman Aviation Services Co (f. 1981); whole corpn renamed Oman Air 2008; state-owned; air charter, maintenance, handling and catering; operators of Oman's domestic and international commercial airline; operates a fleet of 21 aircraft; Chair. SULTAN BIN SALIM BIN SAID AL-HABSI (Minister of Finance); CEO ABDULAZIZ AL-RAISI.

Oman Airports Management Co SOAC: POB 1707, Muscat 111; tel. 24351234; fax 24250004; e-mail feedback@omanairports.com; internet www.omanairports.co.om; f. 2002; originally 75% owned by private investors; 100% owned by Oman Govt since 2004; manages all of Oman's state-owned civil airports; Chair. Eng. KHAMIS MOHAMMED MAHNA AL-SAADI; CEO AIMEN AHMED AL-HOSNI.

Tourism

Directorate-General of Tourism: POB 200, Madinat al-Sultan Qaboos, Muscat 115; tel. 22088000; fax 22088252; e-mail info@omantourism.gov.om; internet mht.gov.om; Dir-Gen. SALIM ADI AL-MAMARI.

Oman Tourism Development Co (Omran): Bldg 305, Way 3, Complex 303, POB 991, Madinat al-Irfan, Seeb 130; tel. 24391111; fax 24391112; internet omran.om; f. 2005; Chair. Eng. MOHAMMED SALIM AL-BUSAIDI; CEO HASHIL AL-MAHROUQI.

Defence

As assessed at November 2022, the total strength of the Sultan's Armed Forces was 42,600: army 25,000; navy 4,200; air force 5,000; plus 2,000 expatriate personnel. There was also a 6,400-strong Royal Guard. Paramilitary forces numbered 4,400: tribal Home Guard (*Firqat*) 4,000; police coastguard 400.

Defence Budget: RO 2,470m. in 2022.

Chief of Staff of the Sultan's Armed Forces: Vice-Adm. ABDULLAH KHAMIS AL-RAISI.

Commander of the Royal Army of Oman: Maj.-Gen. MATAR BIN SALIM AL-BALUSHI.

Commander of the Royal Air Force of Oman: Air Vice-Marshal KHAMIS BIN HAMMAD AL-GHAFRI.

Commander of the Royal Navy of Oman: Rear Adm. SAIF BIN NASSER AL-RAHBI.

Commander of the Royal Guard of Oman: Maj.-Gen. SALEM ALI BADER AL-HOSANI.

Education

Although education is not compulsory, it is provided free to Omani citizens from primary to tertiary level. Primary education begins at six years of age and lasts for six years. The next level of education, divided into two equal stages (preparatory and secondary), lasts for a further six years. In 1998/99 a new system, comprising 10 years of basic education and two years of secondary education, was introduced in 17 schools; it was to be implemented gradually throughout the country. According to UNESCO estimates, pre-primary enrolment in 2020/21 was equivalent to 27.4% of children (male 27.8%; female 27.0%) in the relevant age-group, while primary enrolment included 99.9% of children in the relevant age-group. In 2020/21 enrolment at lower secondary secondary schools included 95.7% of children (male 94.0%; female 97.5%) in the relevant age-group, while upper secondary enrolment in 2018/19 included 90.1% of children in the relevant age-group. Oman's first national university, named after Sultan Qaboos, was opened in 1986. In 2020 government spending on education amounted to 12.2% of total government expenditure, according to UNESCO figures.

Bibliography

Akehurst, John. *We Won a War: The Campaign in Oman 1965–75.* London, Michael Russell, 1982.

Allen, Calvin H., and Rigsbee, W. Lynn. *Oman Under Qaboos: From Coup to Constitution, 1970–1996.* London, Frank Cass, 2000.

Alston, Robert and Stuart Laing. *Unshook Till The End of Time: A History of Britain and Oman, 1650-1970.* Reading, Gilgamesh Publishing, 2012.

Arkless, David C. *The Secret War: Dhofar 1971/72.* London, W. Kimber, 1988.

al-Azri, Khalid M. *Social and Gender Inequality in Oman: The Power of Religious and Political Tradition.* Abingdon, Routledge, 2012.

Baabood, Abdullah. 'Oman's Independent Foreign Policy' in *The Small Gulf States: Foreign and Security Policies Before and After the Arab Spring*, (ed. Almezaini, Khalid S., and Rickli, Jean-Marc.), pp. 107–123. London, Routledge, 2017.

Badger, G. P. *The History of the Imams and Sayyids of Oman, by Salilbin-Razik, from AD 661 to 1856.* London, Hakluyt Society, 1871, reprint 1967.

Bailey, Ronald (Ed.). *Records of Oman 1867–1960.* Slough, Archive Editions, 1988 (12 vols).

Bhacker, M. *Trade and Empire in Muscat and Zanzibar.* London, Routledge, 1992.

Clark, Sir Terence. *Underground to Overseas: The Story of Petroleum Development Oman.* London, Stacey International, 2008.

Davis, John. 'Oman's New Economic Reality Calls for Vision 2040 Strategy Rethink'. *Castlereagh Associates*, 9 June 2020. castlereagh.net/omans-new-economic-reality-calls-for-vision-2040-strategy-rethink/.

'Oman: Challenges to limit pace of diversification', *Castlereagh Associates*, 10 January 2020. castlereagh.net/oman-challenges-to-limit-pace-of-diversification/.

Due-Gundersen, Nicolai. 'Patriotism from Fragmentation: the Personal Nationhood of Oman' openDemocracy.net, 5 June 2017. www.opendemocracy.net/en/north-africa-west-asia/patriotism-from-fragmentation-personal-nationhood-of-om/.

'Father of Oman: the Fragile Legacy of Sultan Qaboos,' *Albawaba.com*, 1 May 2019. www.albawaba.com/insights/father-oman-fragile-legacy-sultan-qaboos-1283394.

'The Two Sultans of Oman', *albawaba.com*, 19 February 2020. www.albawaba.com/opinion/two-sultans-oman-qaboos-haitham-bin-tariq-1340223.

Due-Gundersen, Nicolai, and Owtram, Francis. 'The Foundation, Development and Future of the Omani Rentier State: from the Dhofar War to Vision 2040', *Arabian Humanities*, Thematic Issue 15. Spring 2021.

Al-Farsi, Sulaiman. *Democracy and Youth in the Middle East: Islam, Tribalism and the Rentier State in Oman.* London, I. B. Tauris, 2013.

Ghubash, Hussein. *Oman—The Islamic Democratic Tradition.* Abingdon, Routledge, 2005.

Government of Oman. *Oman Vision 2040.* www.2040.om/en.

Graz, Liesl. *The Omanis: Sentinels of the Gulf.* London, Longman, 1980.

Hawley, Donald. *Oman and its Renaissance.* London, Stacey International, 6th edn, 2012.

Jones, Jeremy, and Rideout, Nicholas. *A History of Modern Oman.* Oxford, Oxford University Press, 2015.

Joyce, Miriam. *The Sultanate of Oman.* Westport, CT, Praeger Publrs, 1995.

Kelly, J. B. *Great Britain and the Persian Gulf, 1793–1880.* London, 1968.

Manea, Elham. *Regional Politics in the Gulf: Saudi Arabia, Oman and Yemen.* London, Saqi Books, 2005.

Maurizi, Vincenzo. *History of Seyd Said.* Cambridge, Oleander Press, 1984.

Mohseni-Cheraghlou, Amin. 'Linking the Past to the Future: Economic Diversification and Tourism in Oman', *Middle East Institute*, 23 July 2020. www.mei.edu/publications/linking-past-future-economic-diversification-and-tourism-oman.

Morris, Jan. *Sultan in Oman.* London, Faber, 1957.

Oman Studies Centre, *Oman Studies Bibliographic Info.* Pforzheim, Germany.

Owtram, Francis. *A Modern History of Oman: Formation of the State Since 1920.* London, I. B. Tauris, 2004.

'Skull Measuring, Oil Seepages and Desert Crossings: Bertram Thomas and the Exploration of the Arabian Peninsula.' *Qatar Digital Library*, 30 April 2019. www.qdl.qa/en/skull-measuring-oil-seepages-and-desert-crossings-bertram-thomas-and-exploration-arabian-peninsula.

'Oman After Qaboos: Continuities, Challenges and Choices.' *LSE Middle East Centre Blog*, 24 January 2020. blogs.lse.ac.uk/mec/2020/01/24/oman-after-qaboos-continuities-challenges-and-choices.

'The Lesser-Known Early Years of Sultan Qaboos.' *British Library Untold Lives* blog, 23 July 2020. blogs.bl.uk/untoldlives/2020/07/the-lesser-known-early-years-of-sultan-qaboos.html.

Owtram, Francis, and Hayek, Malak. 'Oman in the COVID-19 Pandemic: People, Policy and Economic Impact.' *LSE Middle East Centre Blog*, 23 July 2020. blogs.lse.ac.uk/mec/2020/07/23/oman-in-the-covid-19-pandemic-people-policy-and-economic-impact.

Owtram, Francis, Profanter, Annemarie, and Maestri, Elena. 'In Oman, No Security for the Migrant Health Workers Fighting the Pandemic' openDemocracy.net, 23 July 2020, www.opendemocracy.net/en/north-africa-west-asia/in-oman-no-security-for-the-migrant-health-workers.

Pappas Funsch, Linda. *Oman Reborn: Balancing Tradition and Modernization.* Basingstoke, Palgrave MacMillan, 2015.

Peterson, J. E. *Oman in the Twentieth Century.* London, Croom Helm, 1978.

Oman's Insurgencies: The Sultanate's Struggle for Supremacy. London, Saqi Books, 2008.

Plekhanov, Sergey. *A Reformer on the Throne.* London, Trident Press, 2004.

Pridham, Brian R. 'Oman: Change or Continuity', in *Arabia and the Gulf: From Traditional Society to Modern States*, (ed. Netton, Ian R.). London, Croom Helm, 1986, pp. 132–155.

(Ed.). *Oman: Economic, Social and Strategic Developments.* London, Croom Helm, 1987.

Rabi, Uzi. *The Emergence of States in a Tribal Society: Oman Under Sa'id Bin Taymur, 1932–1970.* Eastbourne, Sussex Academic Press, 2006.

al-Rawas, Isam. *Oman in Early Islamic History.* Reading, Ithaca Press, 2000.

Reda Bhacker, M. *Trade and Empire in Muscat and Zanzibar: The Roots of British Domination.* London, Routledge, 1992.

Risso, Patricia. *Oman and Muscat: An Early Modern History.* London, Croom Helm, 1986.

Sachedina, Amal. *Cultivating the Past, Living the Modern: The Politics of Time in the Sultanate of Oman.* Ithaca, Cornell University Press, 2021.

Al-Sahiri, Aisha. 'Post-coronavirus: The Future of Economic Diversification and Climate Action in the GCC.' *Fifth Issue: Report on the Regional and International Impacts of Coronavirus* (Ed. al-Sarhan, Saud, and Thompson, Mark C.), 4 May 2020. www.kfcris.com/en/view/post/279.

Al-Salimi, Abdulrahman, and Staples, Eric. *Oman: A Maritime History.* Hildesheim, Georg Olms Verlag, 2017.

Sheriff, Abdul. *Slaves, Spices and Ivory in Zanzibar: Integration of an East African Commercial Empire into the World Economy, 1780–1873.* Oxford, James Currey, 1987.

Sirhan, Sirhan ibn Said ibn. *Annals of Oman.* Cambridge, Oleander Press, 1985.

Skeet, Ian. *Oman before 1970: The End of an Era.* London, Faber, 1985.

Oman: Politics and Development. London, Macmillan, 1992.

el-Solh, Raghid (Ed.). *Oman and the South-Eastern Shore of Arabia.* Reading, Ithaca Press, 1997.

Takriti, Abdul Razzaq. *Monsoon Revolution: Republicans, Sultans, and Empires in Oman, 1965–76.* Oxford, Oxford University Press, 2013.

Thesiger, Wilfred. *Arabian Sands.* London, Longman, 1959.

Townsend, John. *Oman: The Making of the Modern State.* London, Croom Helm, 1977.

Valeri, Marc. *Oman: Politics and Society in the Qaboos State.* London, C. Hurst & Co, 2nd edn, 2017.

Vine, Peter. *The Heritage of Oman.* London, Immel, 1995.

Ward, Philip. *Travels in Oman: On the Track of the Early Explorers.* Cambridge, Oleander Press, 1986.

Wikan, U. *Behind the Veil in Arabia: Women in Oman.* London, The Johns Hopkins University Press, 1982.

Wilkinson, John C. *The Imamate Tradition of Oman*. Cambridge, Cambridge University Press, 1987.

Wippel, Stefan (Ed.). *Regionalizing Oman: Political, Economic and Social Dynamics*. Dordrecht, Springer, 2013.

World Bank. 'Oman's Economic Update', 16 April 2020. www.worldbank.org/en/country/gcc/publication/oman-economic-update-april-2020#:~:text=Oman's%20economy%20is%20expected%20to,low%20oil%20and%20gas%20prices.

Worrall, James. *Statebuilding and Counterinsurgency in Oman: Political, Military and Diplomatic Relations at the End of Empire*. London, I. B. Tauris, 2014.

Worthington, Joe. *British Diplomacy in Oman and Bahrain: 50 Years of Change*. London, Routledge, 2022.

al-Yousuf, Muhammad bin Musa. *Oil and the Transformation of Oman 1970–1995*. London, Stacey International, 1995.

PALESTINIAN TERRITORIES

Geography

The West Bank lies in western Asia, to the west of the Jordan river and the Dead Sea. To the north and south is the State of Israel, to the west the State of Israel and the Gaza Strip. The Israeli-Palestinian Interim Agreement on the West Bank and the Gaza Strip of September 1995 (Documents on Palestine, see p. 1230) provides for the creation of a corridor, or 'safe passage', linking the Gaza Strip with the West Bank. A 'southern' safe passage between Hebron and Gaza was opened in October 1999 (although it has been closed since October 2000). Including East Jerusalem, the West Bank covers an area of 5,655 sq km (2,183 sq miles). The West Bank can be divided into three major sub-regions: the Mount Hebron massif, the peaks of which rise to between 700 m and 1,000 m above sea level; the Jerusalem mountains, which extend to the northernmost point of the Hebron-Bethlehem massif; and the Mount Samaria hills, the central section of which—the Nablus mountains—reaches heights of up to 800 m before descending to the northern Jenin hills, of between 300 m and 400 m. The eastern border of the West Bank is bounded by the valley of the Jordan river, leading to the Dead Sea (part of the Syrian–African rift valley), into which the Jordan drains. The latter is 400 m below sea level. Precipitation ranges between 600 mm and 800 mm on the massif and averages 200 mm in the Jordan valley; 36% of the area is classified as cultivable land, 32% grazing land, 27% desert or rocky ground and 5% natural forest.

The Gaza Strip, lying beside the Mediterranean Sea and Israel's border with Egypt, covers an area of 365 sq km (141 sq miles). Crossed only by two shallow valleys, the Gaza Strip is otherwise almost entirely flat, and has no surface water. Average annual rainfall is 300 mm. Gaza City is the main city and the centre of administration, with a total population of 778,187 at mid-2023, according to United Nations (UN) estimates. Israel completed the implementation of its Disengagement Plan (Documents on Palestine, see p. 1250), which involved principally the withdrawal of Israeli armed forces and settlers from the Gaza Strip, during August–September 2005 (see Recent History).

According to a census conducted in December 2017, the total population of the Palestinian territories was 4,781,248. At 31 December 2022, official estimates put the population at 5,419,053, giving a population density of 900.2 people per sq km. Apart from the urban centres of Bethlehem (Beit Lahm—population 28,591 at the 2017 census), Hebron (al-Khalil—201,063) and Yatta (63,511) to the south, the majority of the Palestinian population is concentrated in the northern localities around Nablus (156,906), Qalqilya (51,683) and Tulkarm (64,532). The Palestinian (National) Authority's administrative centre is in Ramallah (38,998).

In November 1988 the Palestine National Council proclaimed Jerusalem as the capital of a newly declared independent State of Palestine. In fact, West Jerusalem has been the designated capital of the State of Israel since 1950. In 1967 East Jerusalem was formally annexed by the Israeli authorities, although the annexation has never been recognized by the UN (Occupied Territories, see p. 374). Under the terms of the Declaration of Principles on Palestinian Self-Rule, concluded by Israel and the Palestinians in September 1993 (Documents on Palestine, see p. 1220), negotiations on the 'final status' of the city were scheduled to begin no later than the beginning of the third year of the five-year transitional period following the completion of Israel's withdrawal from the Gaza Strip and the Jericho (Ariha) area. However, despite the signing of the Wye River Memorandum (Documents on Palestine, see p. 1237) in October 1998, 'final status' negotiations did not commence until November 1999, and are currently stalled. The future of Jerusalem is probably the most bitterly contentious of all the issues subject to 'final status' talks, and, in the opinion of some observers, may elude agreement by negotiation. UN estimates put the population of East Jerusalem at 275,086 at mid-2018.

The official language of the Palestinians in the West Bank and the Gaza Strip is Arabic; Hebrew and English are also widely spoken. The majority of the Palestinian population are Muslims, with a Christian minority representing about 1%–2% of the Palestinian population of the territories. This minority, in turn, represents about 45% of all Palestinian Christians.

Recent History

Updated by NIGEL PARSONS

Revised for this edition by VAUGHN SHANNON

Until the end of the 1948 Arab–Israeli War, the West Bank formed part of the British Mandate of Palestine, before becoming part of the Hashemite Kingdom of Jordan under the Armistice Agreement of 1949. It remained under Jordanian sovereignty, despite Israeli occupation in 1967, until King Hussein of Jordan formally relinquished legal and administrative control on 31 July 1988. Under Israeli military occupation, the West Bank was administered by a military government, which divided the territory into seven sub-districts. The Civil Administration (as it later became known) did not extend its jurisdiction to the many Jewish settlements that were established under the Israeli occupation; these remained subject to the Israeli legal and administrative system. The Interim Agreement of September 1995 divided the West Bank into three zones: Areas A, B and C. By October 2000 approximately 17.2% of the West Bank (Area A) was under sole Palestinian jurisdiction and security control, but Israel retained authority over movement into and out of the zone; about 23.8% of the West Bank (Area B) was under Israeli military control, with responsibility for civil administration and public order transferred to the Palestinian authorities; the remaining 59% of the territory (Area C) was under Israeli military occupation.

An administrative province under the British Mandate of Palestine, Gaza was transferred to Egypt after the 1949 armistice and remained under Egyptian administration until June 1967, when it was invaded and occupied by Israel. Following Israeli occupation, the Gaza Strip also became an 'administered territory'. Until the provisions of the Declaration of Principles on Palestinian Self-Rule (signed in 1993) began to take effect, the management of day-to-day affairs was the responsibility of the area's Israeli military commander. In 2001 an estimated 42% of the Gaza Strip was under Israeli control, including Jewish settlements, military bases, bypass roads and a 'buffer zone' along the border with Israel. However, under the terms of the Disengagement Plan (Documents on Palestine, see p. 1250) formulated by the Government of Ariel

Sharon, Israel implemented a unilateral withdrawal from the territory in mid-2005.

TOWARDS AN INDEPENDENT STATE

In accordance with the Declaration of Principles on Palestinian Self-Rule of 13 September 1993 (Documents on Palestine, see p. 1220), and the Cairo Agreement on the Gaza Strip and Jericho of 4 May 1994 (Documents on Palestine, see p. 1223), the Palestine Liberation Organization (PLO) assumed control of the Jericho area of the West Bank, and of the Gaza Strip on 17 May 1994. In November and December 1995, under the terms of the Israeli-Palestinian Interim Agreement on the West Bank and the Gaza Strip (the third 'Oslo Accord'—a term referring to the role played by Norwegian diplomacy in their negotiation) signed by Israel and the PLO on 28 September 1995 (Documents on Palestine, see p. 1230), Israeli armed forces withdrew from the West Bank towns of Nablus, Ramallah, Jenin, Tulkarm, Qalqilya and Bethlehem. In late December the PLO assumed responsibility in 17 areas of civil administration in the town of Hebron. Under the terms of the Oslo Accords, the PLO was eventually to assume full responsibility for civil affairs in the 400 surrounding villages, but the Israeli armed forces were to retain freedom of movement to act against potential hostilities there. In Hebron Israel effected a partial withdrawal of its troops in January 1997, but retained responsibility for the security of some 400 Jewish settlers occupying about 15% of the town. Responsibility for security in the rest of Hebron (excluding access roads) passed to the Palestinian police force. Israel was to retain control over a large area of the West Bank (including Jewish settlements, rural areas, military installations, and the majority of junctions between Palestinian roads and those used by Israeli troops and settlers) until July. Following the first phase of the redeployment and the holding, on its completion, of elections to a Palestinian Legislative Council (PLC) and for a Palestinian executive president, Israel was to effect a second redeployment from rural areas, to be completed in that month. The Israeli occupation was to be maintained in Jewish settlements, military installations, East Jerusalem and the Jewish settlements around Jerusalem until the conclusion of 'final status' negotiations between Israel and the Palestinians, scheduled for May 1999.

Subsequent postponements, and further negotiations within the context of the Oslo peace process, resulted in a new timetable for Israeli redeployment, which envisaged two phases, subsequent to the Hebron withdrawal, to be completed by October 1997 and August 1998. 'Final status' discussions on borders, the Jerusalem issue, Jewish settlements and Palestinian refugees were to commence within two months of the signing of the agreement on Hebron. As guarantor of the agreements, the USA undertook to obtain the release of some Palestinian prisoners, and to ensure that Israel continued to engage in negotiations for the establishment of a Palestinian airport in the Gaza Strip and for safe passage for Palestinians between the West Bank and Gaza. The USA also undertook to ensure that the Palestinian (National) Authority (PA—appointed in May 1994) would continue to combat terrorism, complete the revision of the Palestinian National Charter (or PLO Covenant), adopted in 1964 and amended in 1968 (Documents on Palestine, see p. 1209), and consider Israeli requests to extradite Palestinians suspected of involvement in attacks perpetrated on Israeli territory. By July 1998, however, conflicting interpretations of the extent of both the phased and total final redeployment of Israeli armed forces (90% of the West Bank, according to the Palestinians; less than 50%, according to the Israelis) had resulted in a seemingly intractable impasse in the Oslo peace process. Those within the wider Palestinian movement who had never accepted the peace process argued that an essential weakness of the Oslo Accords was that they failed to stipulate the precise area of the territory over which the PA should assume control. The implementation of the Oslo Accords was further complicated by the election, in May 1996, of Benjamin Netanyahu as Israeli Prime Minister. Netanyahu formed a new coalition Government, in which his party, Likud, was the dominant force. Likud had never sought to conceal its opposition to the Oslo Accords negotiated by the previous Labour Government.

A significant paralysis of the peace process emerged from the decision of the Israeli Government, announced in February 1997, to begin the construction of a new Jewish settlement on Jabal Abu Ghunaim (Har Homa in Hebrew), near Beit Sahur. Construction in this area was particularly controversial because, if completed, the new settlement would make it impossible to reach East Jerusalem from the West Bank without crossing Israeli territory, thereby prejudicing 'final status' negotiations concerning Jerusalem. In response, the Palestinians withdrew from 'final status' discussions that had been scheduled to commence on 17 March. The beginning of construction work at Jabal Abu Ghunaim on the following day provoked rioting among the Palestinian population and a resumption of attacks by the military wing of the Islamic Resistance Movement (Hamas) on Israeli civilian targets. The Israeli Cabinet responded by ordering a general closure of the Palestinian areas.

Both the Jabal Abu Ghunaim (Har Homa) construction and Israel's unilateral decision to redeploy its armed forces from only 9% of West Bank territory (announced in March 1997) were regarded by many observers as a vitiation of both the Oslo and the subsequent post-Hebron agreements. These were further undermined by the publication, in the Israeli daily newspaper Ha'aretz, of the results of a US study that claimed that more than 25% of Jewish settlers' homes in the Gaza Strip and the West Bank were uninhabited (a claim rejected by the Israeli Central Bureau of Statistics, which cited a figure of only 12%). The same newspaper later reported that Netanyahu's original plan, evolved within the framework of the Oslo Accords, eventually to relinquish 90% of the West Bank, had been revised in a new proposal—the so-called 'Allon plus' plan—to a 40% redeployment.

In June 1997 the US House of Representatives voted in favour of recognizing Jerusalem as the undivided capital of Israel and of transferring the US embassy to the city from Tel Aviv. US President Bill Clinton was reported to have strongly disapproved of the vote, owing to its possible implications for the peace process. The decision coincided with violent clashes between Palestinian civilians and Israeli troops in Gaza and Hebron. On 28 July, following US mediation, the PA and the Israeli Government announced that peace discussions were to be resumed in early August. However, on 30 July, on the eve of a scheduled visit by Dennis Ross, the US Special Co-ordinator to the Middle East, to reactivate the discussions, Hamas carried out a suicide bomb attack at a Jewish market in Jerusalem, in which 14 civilians were killed. Ross cancelled his visit, and the Israeli Government immediately halted the payment of tax revenues to the PA and closed the Gaza Strip and the West Bank. In the aftermath of the suicide bombing, the PA commenced a campaign to detain members of Hamas and another militant group, Islamic Jihad. In late August, however, President Yasser Arafat convened a Palestinian national dialogue conference in Gaza, in response to the Israelis' imposition of sanctions. On this occasion, representatives of Hamas, who had boycotted a similar conference held in the previous year, agreed to participate, on the condition that the Palestinian authorities would address the issue of the Hamas members whom they were holding in detention. During the conference Arafat publicly embraced Hamas leaders and urged them, and representatives of Islamic Jihad, to unite with the Palestinian people against Israeli policies. On 26 August Hamas rejected a request from Palestinian leaders to suspend its attacks on Israeli targets.

At the beginning of September 1997, in anticipation of a visit to the Middle East by the US Secretary of State, Madeleine Albright, the Israeli authorities relaxed the closure they had imposed on the West Bank and Gaza on 30 July. On 4 September, however, a further suicide bomb attack in Jerusalem, in which eight people died, led to the reimposition of Israeli sanctions. Hamas claimed responsibility for the attack, and the Israeli Prime Minister immediately renewed his demand that the PA should take effective action against the 'terrorist infrastructure'. During her visit in mid-September Albright reportedly stated that Israel should halt the construction of Jewish settlements on Arab lands, cease confiscations of land

and the demolition of Arab dwellings, and end its policy of confiscating Palestinian identity documents. At the same time she endorsed Netanyahu's demand that the Palestinian leadership should take more effective measures to suppress the military wing of Hamas. Impatience within the US Administration at the Israeli Government's apparent provocation was demonstrated by Albright's criticism of Netanyahu's decision, announced in late September, to permit the construction of 300 new homes for Jewish settlers at Efrat in the West Bank.

On 28 September 1997 it was announced that, as a result of US diplomacy, Israeli and Palestinian officials had agreed to recommence negotiations in October. The first round of discussions, scheduled to begin on 6 October, would reportedly focus on the outstanding issues of the Oslo Accords, in particular the opening of an airport and seaport facilities in the Gaza Strip, the establishment of a safe corridor linking Gaza with the West Bank, and the release of Palestinian prisoners from Israeli detention. A second round of discussions was to commence on 13 October, at which the participants were to address the issues of security co-operation between the Palestinian and the Israeli authorities; the long-delayed redeployment of Israeli armed forces from the West Bank; Israeli expansion and construction of settlements; and questions pertaining to 'final status' negotiations.

There were reports in late September 1997 that the PA had closed 16 institutions—mainly providers of social welfare services—with links to Hamas, and arrested 'scores' of its officials since the recent suicide bombing in Jerusalem. Hamas officials who remained at liberty, however, insisted that the organization's campaign against Israeli civilian targets would continue. In particular, the attempted assassination in the Jordanian capital, Amman, of Khalid Meshaal, the head of the Hamas political bureau in Jordan, provoked warnings of retaliation both before and after official confirmation that agents of the Israeli security service, Mossad, had been responsible for the attack. In order to secure the release of its agents by the Jordanian authorities, Israel was obliged, on 1 October, to free (together with other Arab political prisoners) Sheikh Ahmad Yassin, the founder and spiritual leader of Hamas, who had been sentenced to life imprisonment in Israel in 1989 for complicity in attacks on Israeli soldiers. As had been widely predicted, Israel's release of Sheikh Yassin into Jordanian custody was swiftly followed by his return, on 6 October 1997, to Gaza.

On 7 October 1997 discussions resumed between Palestinian and Israeli negotiators on the outstanding issues of the Oslo Accords, and on the following day the Palestinian President and the Israeli Prime Minister held their first meeting for eight months at the Erez checkpoint between Israel and the Gaza Strip. In December, following further US pressure, the Israeli Cabinet reportedly agreed in principle to withdraw troops from an unspecified area of West Bank territory, although it remained uncertain whether Netanyahu would be able to persuade intransigent elements within his Government to endorse this decision. In early January 1998 Dennis Ross visited Israel in a further attempt to break the deadlock regarding the redeployment of Israeli armed forces from the West Bank. However, in the second week of January the Israeli Government declared that it would not conduct such a redeployment until the PA had fulfilled a series of conditions. Among these were requirements that: the Palestinian leadership should make a 'systematic and effective' effort to counter terrorism; it should reduce the strength of its security forces from 40,000 to 24,000; and the Palestinian National Charter should be revised to recognize explicitly Israel's right to exist. Palestinian officials maintained that these conditions had already been met when the agreement regarding the withdrawal of Israeli forces from Hebron was concluded one year earlier. There was further evidence of a hardening of the Israeli position prior to a summit meeting, scheduled to take place in Washington, DC, USA, in the third week of January. The Israeli Cabinet issued a communiqué detailing 'vital and national interests' in the West Bank that it was not prepared to relinquish: in total this amounted to some 60% of all West Bank territory, including that surrounding the Jerusalem region.

On 20 January 1998 President Clinton held discussions with the Israeli Prime Minister in Washington, DC. It was reported that the USA was seeking to persuade Israel to affect a second withdrawal of its armed forces from 12% of the West Bank over a period of 80 days, in exchange for increased co-operation on security issues by the PA. On 25 January, however, Mahmoud Abbas, the Secretary-General of the PLO Executive Committee, reported that direct contacts between the Palestinian delegation and the Israeli premier had collapsed.

In March 1998 Ross arrived in Jerusalem in order to present details of the latest US initiative, which, it appeared, would involve an Israeli withdrawal from slightly more than 13% of West Bank territory, and a suspension of settlement construction in return for further efforts by the PA to combat Palestinian organizations engaged in campaigns of violence against Israeli targets. President Arafat sought an Israeli withdrawal from a further 30% of the West Bank, but there were indications that he might be prepared to accept an initial withdrawal from 13% of the territory. In any case, the Israeli Cabinet rejected the reported details of the new US initiative.

Meanwhile, the European Union (EU) was seeking to play a greater role in the stalled Middle East peace process. On 20 April 1998 it was reported that, during a visit to Gaza City, the British Prime Minister, Tony Blair, had obtained the agreement of President Arafat to attend a conference in London, United Kingdom, based on the most recent US peace proposals. A summit meeting, hosted by Blair and attended by Netanyahu, Arafat and US Secretary of State Albright, took place in early May. However, the adoption by the Israeli Cabinet, in June, of a plan to extend the boundaries of Jerusalem and construct homes there for a further 1m. people prompted accusations by PA officials that the proposal amounted to a de facto annexation of territories that were officially subject to 'final status' discussions.

On 7 July 1998 the United Nations (UN) General Assembly, in defiance of objections from the USA and Israel, approved a resolution, by a vote of 124–4, to upgrade the status of the PLO at the UN. The new provision allowed the PLO to participate in debates, to co-sponsor resolutions and to raise points of order during discussions on Middle Eastern affairs.

On 19–22 July 1998 Israeli and Palestinian delegations held direct negotiations for the first time since March 1997. They discussed the most recent US initiative to reactivate the peace process, but the proposal was deemed unacceptable by the Israelis. In late August 1998 Netanyahu was reported to have presented a compromise plan to his Cabinet, whereby Israel would effect a full redeployment from a further 10% of the West Bank and a partial withdrawal from 3% of the Judaean desert. Arafat cautiously welcomed the plan. In September Netanyahu and Arafat met at the White House in Washington, DC, and agreed to participate in a peace conference in the USA in the following month. The summit meeting, also attended by US President Clinton, began at the Wye Plantation, Maryland, on 15 October 1998 (see Israel), and culminated in the signing, on 23 October, of the Wye River Memorandum (Documents on Palestine, see p. 1237), which was intended to facilitate the implementation of the Interim Agreement of September 1995.

Under the terms of the Wye River Memorandum, which was to be implemented within three months of its signing, Israel was to transfer a further 13.1% of West Bank territory from exclusive Israeli control (Area C) to joint Israeli-Palestinian control (Area B). An additional 14% of the West Bank was to be transferred from joint Israeli-Palestinian control to exclusive Palestinian control (Area A). The Wye River Memorandum also stipulated that: negotiations with regard to a third Israeli redeployment (under the terms of the Oslo Accords) should proceed concurrently with 'final status' discussions; the PA should reinforce anti-terrorism measures under the supervision of the US Central Intelligence Agency (CIA); the strength of the Palestinian police force should be reduced by 25%; the Palestinian authorities should arrest 30 suspected terrorists; Israel should carry out the phased release of 750 Palestinian prisoners (including political detainees); the Palestine National Council (PNC) should annul those clauses of the PLO Covenant deemed to be anti-Israeli; Gaza International Airport should become operational, with an Israeli security presence; and an access corridor linking the West Bank to the Gaza Strip should be opened.

The Memorandum was endorsed by the Israeli Cabinet on 11 November 1998, and was approved by the Knesset (parliament) on 17 November. Three days later Israel redeployed its armed forces from about 500 sq km of the West Bank. Of this area, some 400 sq km came under exclusive Palestinian control for both civil and security affairs. In the remaining 100 sq km the PA assumed responsibility for civil affairs, while Israel retained control over security. At the same time Israel released some 250 Palestinian prisoners (although a majority were non-political detainees) and signed a protocol for the opening of Gaza International Airport. Israel retained the right to decide which airlines could use the airport, which was officially inaugurated by President Arafat on 24 November. However, implementation of the Wye River Memorandum did not proceed smoothly, with mutual accusations of failure to observe its terms.

In the weeks prior to a visit to Israel and the Gaza Strip by the US President on 12–15 December 1998, violent clashes erupted in the West Bank between Palestinians and Israeli security forces. One cause of the unrest was a decision by the Israeli Cabinet to suspend other releases of Palestinian prisoners under the terms of the Wye River Memorandum, and its insistence that Palestinians convicted of killing Israelis, together with members of Hamas and Islamic Jihad, would not be freed. On 14 December, meanwhile, in the presence of President Clinton, the PNC voted to annul articles of the Palestinian National Charter deemed to be anti-Israeli. While the Israeli Prime Minister welcomed the vote, he insisted that several other conditions had to be met before Israel would further implement its commitments under the Wye River Memorandum. At a summit meeting between the US President, Netanyahu and Arafat at the Erez checkpoint on 15 December, Netanyahu reiterated Israel's stance regarding the release of Palestinian prisoners. He further demanded that the Palestinians should cease incitement to violence and formally relinquish plans unilaterally to declare Palestinian statehood on 4 May 1999, the original deadline established by the Oslo Accords. At the conclusion of the meeting Netanyahu announced that Israel would not proceed with the second scheduled redeployment of its armed forces (under the Wye River agreement) on 18 December 1998, claiming once again that the Palestinians had failed to honour their commitments. On 20 December the Israeli Cabinet voted to suspend implementation of the Wye River Memorandum.

At a summit meeting in Berlin, Germany, on 26 March 1999, EU leaders issued a commitment to support the creation of an independent Palestinian state. The 'Berlin Declaration' appealed to Israel to conclude 'final status' discussions with the Palestinians within one year, insisting that Israel's security would best be assured through the establishment of a viable Palestinian state.

As the deadline for a final decision regarding the 4 May 1999 declaration approached, it became increasingly apparent that Arafat would be forced to capitulate under the weight of both international and domestic opinion. In late April PLO chief negotiators Abbas and Saeb Erekat (the Minister of Local Government) visited Washington, DC, in order to secure certain assurances from the USA in return for an extension of the Oslo deadline. On 27 April the Palestinian Central Council (PCC), together with Hamas representatives, met in Gaza for final discussions. On 29 April the Council announced a postponement of any declaration on statehood until after the Israeli elections. The announcement was welcomed by Israel, the USA, and EU and Arab states; however, Palestinians in the Occupied Territories held violent protests against the decision.

Palestinians extended a cautious welcome to Ehud Barak's victory over Netanyahu in the Israeli premiership elections of 17 May 1999. PA officials immediately urged Barak to break the deadlock in the Middle East peace process. However, in his victory address the new Israeli Prime Minister insisted that he would not offer the Palestinians any fundamental concessions. After the elections there was a Palestinian consensus that a halt to Israel's programme of settlement expansion in the Occupied Territories must be a precondition for any meaningful resumption of the peace process. On 3 June Palestinians in the West Bank declared a 'day of rage' against continuing settlement expansion there; the mass demonstrations, which were particularly violent in Hebron, followed an announcement in late May that the population of the West Bank's largest Jewish settlement, Ma'aleh Adumim, was to be expanded from 25,000 to 50,000 settlers.

The first direct meeting between Prime Minister Barak and President Arafat was held at the Erez checkpoint on 11 July 1999. Although both leaders repeated their commitment to restarting the peace process, Arafat was said to have been alarmed by Barak's apparent opposition to full implementation of the Wye River Memorandum, his evasiveness on the issue of settlements and his seeming preoccupation with the Syrian track of the peace process. During the second meeting between the Israeli and Palestinian leaders, on 27 July at Erez, Barak angered Palestinians by seeking to win Arafat's approval to postpone implementation of the Wye agreement until it could be combined with 'final status' negotiations (thereby implying a 15-month delay in further redeployments of Israeli armed forces). On 1 August Barak promised to bring forward the release of 250 Palestinian prisoners if Arafat agreed to a postponement. On the same day, however, discussions between the Israeli and PA delegations broke down after Arafat rejected the Israeli position. Discussions were resumed in mid-August, when Israel agreed to pursue implementation of the Wye River Memorandum, and on 4 September Barak and Arafat signed the Sharm el-Sheikh Memorandum or Wye Two accords (Documents on Palestine, see p. 1239), in the presence of US Secretary of State Albright and President Hosni Mubarak of Egypt. Under the terms of the Memorandum (which outlined a revised timetable for implementation of the outstanding provisions of the Wye agreement), on 9 September Israel released some 200 Palestinian 'security' prisoners; on the following day Israel effected the transfer of a further 7% of the West Bank to PA control.

'FINAL STATUS' NEGOTIATIONS WITH ISRAEL

A ceremonial opening of 'final status' discussions between Israel and the PA took place at the Erez checkpoint on 13 September 1999; shortly afterwards details emerged of a secret meeting between the Israeli and Palestinian leaders to discuss an agenda for such discussions. However, on 8 October the Palestinians' chief negotiator and Minister of Culture and Information, Yasser Abd al-Rabbuh, warned that the PA would boycott 'final status' discussions unless Israel ended its programme of settlement expansion. In mid-October Barak, also under pressure from left-wing groups in Israel, responded by dismantling 12 'settlement outposts' in the West Bank, which he deemed to be illegal. Meanwhile, on 15 October Israel released a further 151 Palestinian prisoners, under the terms of Wye Two. The inauguration of the first 'safe passage' between the West Bank and Gaza Strip took place on 25 October. The opening had been delayed by almost a month owing to a dispute between Israel and the PA over security arrangements for the 44-km route, which linked the Erez checkpoint in Gaza to Hebron in the West Bank. Israel asserted that it would maintain almost complete control over the so-called 'southern' route, including decisions on which Palestinians would be permitted to use it.

'Final status' negotiations between Israel and the PA commenced in Ramallah on 8 November 1999, following a summit meeting held on 2 November in Oslo, Norway, between Arafat, Barak and US President Clinton. On the day before the discussions opened, three bombs had exploded in northern Israel; the Israeli authorities claimed that Hamas was responsible. A further redeployment of Israeli troops from 5% of the West Bank, scheduled for 15 November, was postponed owing to disagreement over the areas to be transferred (see Israel). Relations between the two sides worsened when on 6 December PA negotiators walked out of 'final status' discussions after demanding that Israel should end immediately its policy of settlement expansion. The announcement came amid reports that settlement activity had intensified under Barak's premiership. On the following day the Israeli Prime Minister, apparently in response to US pressure, announced a halt to settlement construction while the negotiations regarding a

Framework Agreement on Permanent Status (FAPS) were proceeding. However, the PA continued to demand the complete cessation of Jewish settlement building. On 21 December Barak held discussions in Ramallah with Arafat—becoming the first Israeli premier to hold peace discussions in Palestinian territory.

On 6–7 January 2000 Israeli armed forces withdrew from a further 5% of the West Bank, under the terms of Wye Two; 2% of the land was transferred from partial Palestinian control (Area B) to complete Palestinian control (Area A), while 3% shifted from Israeli control (Area C) to Area B. However, Israel announced on 16 January that a third redeployment from 6.1% of the territory (scheduled to take place on 20 January) would be postponed by three weeks until Barak had returned from peace discussions with the Syrian Arab Republic in the USA. The delay was apparently due to disagreements over Arab villages on the outskirts of Jerusalem. Meanwhile, the explosion of a bomb in northern Israel appeared to be a further attempt by Palestinian militants to disrupt the peace process.

The approval by the Israeli Cabinet of a withdrawal of its troops from only a sparsely populated area of the West Bank led Palestinian negotiators to break off the discussions in early February 2000. On 3 February peace discussions held between Arafat and Barak at Erez broke down acrimoniously, after Arafat had reportedly been angered by an Israeli map showing the proposed redeployment from a further 6.1% of the West Bank. The map included none of the Arab villages situated near East Jerusalem (as Arafat had anticipated), but instead showed various pockets of land in the north and south of the territory. On 6 February the PA announced that it was suspending peace discussions with Israel. Mediation by US Special Middle East Co-ordinator Dennis Ross later in that month failed to break the deadlock, and both sides acknowledged that the 13 February deadline to reach a framework agreement would elapse. On 2 March four members of Hamas's military wing were killed in the Israeli Arab town of Tayibbah by Israeli security forces, who claimed that the men were plotting suicide bombings inside Israel. 'Final status' discussions resumed between Israel and the PA on 21 March, and on the same day the redeployment of Israeli troops from a further 6.1% of the West Bank was carried out, including villages near Ramallah, Hebron, Jericho and Jenin.

On 15 February 2000 an 'historic' agreement was signed between the Vatican and the PLO, with the intention of strengthening relations between the Roman Catholic Church and a future Palestinian state. The Vatican reiterated its view that Jerusalem should be granted a special international status so that the rights of Christians, Jews and Muslims (especially the right of access to their holy sites) were protected. It also implicitly criticized Israel for its 'Judaization' of Arab East Jerusalem, its settlement expansion in and around the city, and its gradual expulsion of the city's Palestinian inhabitants. In March Pope John Paul II undertook a five-day visit to Israel and the Palestinian self-rule areas. The Pope's visit, which the Vatican insisted was purely spiritual in nature, was accorded unprecedented importance by Palestinian and Israeli leaders. The pontiff paid a symbolic visit to Dheisheh refugee camp, south of Bethlehem. Speaking at the camp, which houses some 10,000 Palestinian refugees expelled from their homes in 1948, the Pope expressed his support for justice for the refugees and indicated that they had a 'natural right to a homeland'.

Following further discussions between Barak and President Clinton in Washington, DC, on 11 April 2000, it was announced that the Israeli premier had agreed to PA demands for a greater US presence in future Israeli-Palestinian negotiations. The third round of 'final status' negotiations opened at the Israeli port of Eilat on 30 April. On 7 May Barak and Arafat held a crisis meeting in Ramallah, in the presence of Dennis Ross, to discuss 'sticking and interim phase issues'. The discussions were unsuccessful, however, and led to a further suspension of the peace process.

On 15 May 2000 al-Rabbuh resigned his post as Chief Negotiator after discovering that 'secret' informal discussions between the PA and Israel had been proceeding in Stockholm, Sweden, without his knowledge. The establishment of an alternative negotiating channel appeared to reflect Israel's dissatisfaction with the progress being made through the official process. The Stockholm discussions, which began in early May, were led by Ahmad Quray, Speaker of the PLC, and Shlomo Ben-Ami, the Israeli Minister for Public Security.

On 21 May 2000 Barak ordered the suspension of the Stockholm discussions, following the worst outbreak of violence to occur in the West Bank and Gaza Strip since the rioting provoked by the Israeli decision to reopen the Hasmonean tunnel in Jerusalem in 1996. On 1 May 2000 as many as 1,000 of the 1,650 Palestinian prisoners held in Israeli gaols began a hunger strike. A few days later mass demonstrations were initiated by Palestinians throughout the self-rule areas in support of the prisoners. By 15 May, a date declared by Palestinians to be a 'day of rage' (marking *al-Nakba* or 'the Catastrophe'—the anniversary of the foundation of the State of Israel in 1948), the protests had escalated into extreme violence. By the time the clashes between stone-throwing Palestinians and the Israeli security forces subsided on 18 May 2000, seven Palestinians were reported to have been killed and about 1,000 injured; some 60 Israelis were also injured. The Palestinian prisoners ended their hunger strike at the end of May.

THE CAMP DAVID SUMMIT

US Secretary of State Albright began a tour of Israel and the Palestinian areas in early June 2000, in an attempt to reinvigorate the peace discussions. The US Administration was seeking to increase its diplomatic efforts in preparation for hosting a summit meeting between Barak and Arafat prior to the expiry of President Clinton's term of office in the autumn. On 21 June it was reported that the PA had agreed to a delay in the latest Israeli withdrawal from the West Bank, scheduled to take place two days later. On 2 July the PCC convened and, after two days of discussions, announced that the PLO would unilaterally declare statehood on or before 13 September, with Jerusalem as its capital.

On 11 July 2000 peace discussions between Barak and Arafat were inaugurated by President Clinton at Camp David, Maryland, USA, in a renewed attempt to reach a FAPS. An official news blackout was imposed, and thus few details emerged about the discussions. However, on 13 July it was reported that Barak and Arafat had held their first discussions in private. Nevertheless, despite round-the-clock diplomatic efforts, the discussions failed to break the deadlock regarding future arrangements for Jerusalem; the PA refused to accept anything less than full Palestinian sovereignty over the city's Islamic holy sites (notably the Dome of the Rock and the al-Aqsa Mosque), with East Jerusalem as the capital of a Palestinian state. The Camp David summit ended, without agreement, on 25 July. Despite the failure of the summit, both sides, under the guidance of President Clinton, pledged to continue their diplomatic efforts and promised not to pursue 'unilateral actions' (apparently referring to Arafat's threat to declare Palestinian statehood). On his return to the Middle East Arafat was hailed by Palestinians as the 'hero of Jerusalem' for his refusal to grant concessions to Israel over the future of the city.

Amid growing international pressure, it emerged in August 2000 that Arafat had agreed, in principle, to a postponement of his declaration of Palestinian statehood. (The PCC announced on 10 September that it would postpone indefinitely such a declaration, although 15 November was reportedly designated as the target date.) Meanwhile, Israeli and PA negotiators continued to meet during August and September in the hope of achieving a breakthrough regarding the third redeployment of Israeli armed forces from the West Bank, as well as further prisoner releases. On 26 September Arafat and Barak held their first direct discussions since the Camp David summit. However, tensions between the two communities remained high, especially in Jerusalem, where several clashes were reported between Palestinians and the Israeli security forces.

RELATIONS WITH OTHER ARAB STATES

After Barak's electoral victory in Israel in May 1999, one of Arafat's principal concerns was the Israeli concentration of efforts on the Lebanese and, especially, Syrian tracks of the Middle East peace process. Any shift of focus away from Israeli-Palestinian discussions was likely to leave the Palestinian leadership in an acutely vulnerable and isolated position. In

June Arafat was reported to have accused both the Jordanian and Syrian leaders of having turned their backs on the PA. In August a political crisis developed after the Syrian Deputy Prime Minister and Minister of Defence, Maj.-Gen. Mustafa Tlass, allegedly made highly insulting remarks about Arafat—including a claim that Arafat had 'sold Jerusalem and the Arab nation' in peace deals concluded with Israel since 1993—leading to Palestinian demands for Tlass's resignation, and the issuing, by Fatah, of a death warrant against him. Following the resumption of the Israeli-Syrian track of the peace process in December 1999, US and Israeli officials sought to reassure Arafat that negotiations on the Palestinian track would not be sidelined. When President Hafiz al-Assad of Syria died on 10 June 2000, Arafat declared three days of mourning in the Palestinian self-rule areas for the man who had once accused him of making the 'peace of cowards' with Israel. On 13 June Arafat attended President Assad's funeral in Damascus, Syria, despite his poor relations with the Syrian regime.

Palestinians reacted to the death of King Hussein of Jordan on 7 February 1999 with great sorrow. (Of the kingdom's more than 4m. inhabitants, about 65% are believed to be of Palestinian origin.) Three days of mourning were declared in the Palestinian territories, and Arafat travelled to Amman to pay his last respects to the man he once called a 'Zionist agent', but later praised as 'the wise man of the Arabs'. Public grief was particularly apparent in the West Bank, which King Hussein had ruled for 15 years until June 1967. For Arafat, the death of Hussein was a political disaster; the King had frequently supported Arafat in times of crisis, especially when the peace process with Israel appeared to be on the verge of collapse. Hamas leaders also paid tribute to King Hussein, recalling his efforts in September 1997 to free Sheikh Ahmad Yassin from an Israeli gaol after the assassination attempt on Meshaal.

INTERNAL AFFAIRS

Elections to a PLC took place on 20 January 1996. A total of 79% of the estimated 1m. eligible Palestinian voters were reported to have participated in the elections, returning 88 deputies to the 89-seat Council. (One seat was automatically reserved for the president of the PLC's executive body—the Palestinian President.) The election of a Palestinian Executive President was held at the same time. Arafat, who was opposed by one other candidate, Samiha Khalil, received 88.1% of the votes cast and took office as President on 12 February. Deputies returned to the PLC automatically became members of the PNC, the existing 483 members of which were subsequently permitted to return from exile by Israel. The PLC held its first session in Gaza City on 7 March, electing Quray as Speaker.

On 22–24 April 1996 the PNC held its 21st session in Gaza City. At the meeting the PNC voted to amend the Palestinian National Charter by annulling all of the clauses that sought the destruction of the State of Israel. The PNC also voted to amend all clauses that were not in harmony with the agreement of mutual recognition concluded by Israel and the PLO in September 1993. On the final day of its meeting the PNC elected a new Executive Committee. In May 1996 it was reported that President Arafat had appointed the members of a Palestinian Cabinet. The appointments were approved by the PLC in July.

In April 1997 President Arafat's audit office reported the misappropriation by PA ministers of US $326m. of public funds. PA General Prosecutor Khalid al-Qidra promptly resigned in response to the findings and was reportedly placed under house arrest in June. At the end of July a parliamentary committee, appointed by Arafat to conduct an inquiry into the affair, concluded that the Cabinet should be dissolved and some of its members prosecuted. In August the Cabinet submitted its resignation, but this was not accepted by Arafat until December. Arafat's long-awaited new Cabinet was announced on 5 August 1998 and was promptly denounced by all sides. Only one prominent minister of the former administration had been removed, many others assuming alternative responsibilities or becoming ministers of state without portfolios. (The size of the Cabinet was increased significantly by the appointment of several PLC members to minister-of-state status.) Despite the immediate resignations of the newly appointed Ministers of Higher Education (Hanan Ashrawi) and Agriculture (Abd al-Jawad Saleh), on 10 August the new administration was approved by the PLC. Although the Cabinet was criticized by officials of the principal international organizations granting funds to the PA, in November donors agreed to grant the PA more than $3,000m., to be disbursed over the next five years.

In addition to persistent allegations of corruption within the PA, President Arafat himself was frequently accused of autocracy. In March 1998 the PLC threatened to organize a vote of no confidence in Arafat's leadership, in protest against alleged corruption, the long delay in approval of the budget and the failure to hold local elections. The PLC renewed its threat in mid-1998 in an ultimatum to the President and the Cabinet, demanding that they respond to allegations of corruption and mismanagement and approve the budget proposals within two weeks. In September the PA chief negotiator at the peace discussions and Minister of Local Government, Erekat, and the PA Minister of State for the Environment, Yousuf Abu Saffieh, were both persuaded by Arafat to withdraw their resignations, tendered in protest against alleged inefficiency and incompetence within the PA.

In August 1998 the Palestinian Ministry of the Interior dissolved the Palestinian Ahd Party, the Palestinian Labour Party, the Ahrar Party and the Popular Forces party, claiming that, as small individual entities that were unsuccessful in the previous legislative elections, the groups were not financially viable. According to a spokesman at the Ministry of the Interior, it was planned to merge small parties with similar ideologies.

Shortly after the signing of the Wye River Memorandum, on 24 October 1998 the PA detained 11 journalists for attempting to obtain an interview with the spiritual leader of Hamas, Sheikh Ahmad Yassin (who was placed under house arrest on 29 October). On the same day the Palestinian authorities arrested outspoken al-Aqsa cleric Sheikh Hamid Bitawi and Islamic Jihad's chief spokesman for publicly criticizing the Wye agreement. In the weeks following the agreement there was a steady erosion of press freedom in the West Bank and Gaza: several radio and television stations, as well as press offices, were closed down by the PA, and journalists and cameramen were imprisoned for crimes ranging from 'endangering the national interest' to reporting 'illegal' demonstrations.

The PA's human rights record remained a major concern for Palestinians. In January 1999 the PLC approved a motion urging an end to political detention and the release of all those imprisoned on exclusively political charges. The PA responded by releasing 37 political prisoners (36 Islamists and one member of the Popular Front for the Liberation of Palestine—PFLP). However, on 24 January scores of detainees linked to Hamas and Islamic Jihad began a hunger strike in Jericho and Nablus, in protest against their continued detention without trial by the Palestinian authorities. During February thousands of Palestinians—mostly Hamas supporters—demonstrated in support of the detainees. On 6 February some 3,000 protesters marched to the PA headquarters, chanting slogans criticizing the PA's alleged 'subservience to Israel and the CIA'.

Also in February 1999 the Gazan-based chief of police, Ghazi al-Jabali, alleged that Hamas had received some US $35m. from Iran to carry out suicide bomb attacks against Israeli targets that would undermine the prospects of Israeli moderates and assist Netanyahu's May 1999 election campaign. Both Iranian and Hamas leaders vehemently denied the allegations. Relations between the PA and Hamas were further strained following the murder of a Palestinian intelligence officer in Rafah on 1 February. On 10 March a security agent and former member of Hamas's military wing was sentenced to death for the attack, and two accomplices received lengthy prison sentences. The verdict provoked serious clashes between Palestinian police and protesters in the Gaza Strip, during which two teenagers were shot dead by police.

Security surrounding Arafat was intensified in June 1999, after a group of Palestinian dissidents calling themselves 'the Free Officers and the Honest People of Palestine' released a statement in which they accused leading Palestinian officials of corruption and of collaboration with Israel, and indirectly threatened to assassinate the President. Nine arrests were made by the security forces following the issuing of the statement.

There was considerable criticism by Palestinian opposition groups of the Sharm el-Sheikh Memorandum signed with Israel on 4 September 1999. Palestinians in East Jerusalem observed a general strike in protest against the agreement, and dozens staged a sit-in at Orient House, the de facto headquarters of the Palestinian administration in East Jerusalem, to denounce concessions on the release of political prisoners. However, the PA continued to encourage meetings among opposition groups to seek agreement on a unified Palestinian position on 'final status' issues. On 1 August a Palestinian national dialogue had been held in Cairo, Egypt, with the participation of officials from Fatah and the PFLP. At the end of August representatives of nine political factions agreed on an agenda for a comprehensive national dialogue. Three meetings were held in the West Bank town of Ramallah to discuss the convening of such a dialogue. The first, hosted by the PLO Executive Committee on 31 August, was attended by the Arab Liberation Front (ALF), the Democratic Front for the Liberation of Palestine (DFLP), Fatah, the Palestinian Democratic Union (FIDA) and the PFLP. Hamas and Islamic Jihad both declined an invitation to attend; in late August the PA had arrested several suspected activists of these two organizations. The second meeting, on 14 September, was held among FIDA, the Palestinian People's Party (PPP) and the Palestinian Popular Struggle Front (PPSF). The third, on 12 October, was attended by all seven of the political organizations, as well as Hamas and the Palestine Liberation Front (PLF). The Damascus-based opposition groups held a similar meeting in late September.

In discussions in Cairo on 22–23 August 1999, Arafat and the DFLP Secretary-General, Nayef Hawatmeh, agreed to set aside their differences and co-ordinate their positions on the 'final status' issues; it was their first meeting since 1993. The head of the PLO Political Department, Faruq Qaddumi, conducted further discussions with DFLP officials in Damascus on 2 November 1999. Meanwhile, it was reported in early September that the leader of the PFLP, George Habash, had decided to resign. (Habash resigned the leadership on 27 April 2000 and was replaced by his deputy, Abu Ali Moustafa, on 8 July.) On 28 September 1999 representatives of Fatah and the PFLP met in Amman. Although the two parties failed to reach an agreement on the PFLP's participation in 'final status' discussions, they issued a joint statement appealing to all PLO factions to take part in an upcoming Central Council session to discuss organizational matters. Qaddumi continued discussions with PFLP leaders in Damascus on 2 November. At Arafat's request, on 16 September Israel agreed to allow the PFLP Deputy Secretary-General, Abu Ali Moustafa, to return to PA-controlled areas after more than 30 years in exile, in order to participate in reconciliation discussions; he returned to the West Bank on 30 September. However, although the Israeli Government had also reportedly granted an entry permit to Nayef Hawatmeh of the DFLP on 25 October, Hawatmeh's right of return was rescinded on 29 October, after he stated in an interview that armed struggle was legitimate as long as Jewish settlements remained in the Occupied Territories. On 12 October the Israeli Supreme Court ruled that PLF head Muhammad 'Abu' Abbas was immune from trial in Israel for the 1985 *Achille Lauro* hijacking (see Israel).

A series of protests staged during November 1999 prompted the Chairman of the PLC, Azmi Shuaybi, to criticize publicly the PA's lack of fiscal monitoring and accountability. Shuaybi claimed that the Administration was afraid of instituting a monitoring process because it 'would reveal the extent of public funds that are going missing'. He noted that the US $126m. that the Minister of Finance, Muhammad Zohdi al-Nashashibi, claimed to have transferred to various ministries could not be accounted for. Shuaybi added that several PA-run companies that received several million dollars in public funding did not report their profits to the PLC's budget committee, claiming to be private companies, yet at the same time did not pay taxes, claiming to be government enterprises. His report was followed on 27 November by a petition signed by 20 leading Palestinian academics, professionals and members of the PLC that not only accused the PA of corruption, mismanagement and abuse of power, but also implicated Arafat personally. Between 28 and 30 November PA security services arrested, interrogated or placed under house arrest 11 of the document's signatories; the other nine (all Fatah officials) were immune from prosecution because of their status as members of the PLC. At an emergency session, convened on 1 December by Arafat in Nablus, PLC members voted to condemn their nine colleagues for seeking to divide the Palestinian people, but did not act on Arafat's reported wish to deprive them of their immunity. Outside the meeting thousands of Arafat supporters marched in solidarity with the PA. Returning from the session, one of the nine PLC members who had signed the anti-corruption manifesto, Mouawiyyah al-Masri, was shot and injured by unidentified gunmen. Another legislator was reportedly detained by the General Intelligence Service and severely beaten for participating in a sit-in supporting the signatories. Between 19 December and 6 January 2000 Arafat released the 11 detainees on bail. The PA's draconian reaction to the anti-corruption petition prompted international condemnation: statements in solidarity with the anti-corruption campaigners were signed by hundreds of Palestinians worldwide, and demonstrations were organized, including a rally of 5,000 protesters in Ramallah on 4 December. The DFLP, Hamas, Islamic Jihad and the PFLP also held a 'solidarity' meeting in Gaza on 29 November to condemn the PA response.

On 10 January 2000 the PA established a Higher Council for Development, to be chaired by Arafat. The Council's role would be to ensure the transparency of the public finance system: it would handle the general revenue administration, reporting all revenue collected into a single treasury account; oversee management of all commercial and investment operations of the PA; develop a privatization strategy; and oversee the handling of internal and external debt policy and the repayment of loans. The International Monetary Fund (IMF) and foreign donors praised the Council as a major step towards ending corruption and mismanagement. In mid-January Arafat ratified the Non-Governmental Organization (NGO) law, delineating the relationship between the PA and the Palestinian NGOs, which broadly welcomed the new legislation.

On 2–3 February 2000 the Central Council finally convened in Gaza with 96 of the 126 members attending. Participants represented the ALF, the DFLP, Fatah, FIDA, the PPP, the PPSF, the Islamic Salvation Party and the National Salvation Party. The PFLP presented its positions prior to the meeting but did not participate. Hamas also boycotted the session, although its spiritual leader, Sheikh Yassin, attended as an observer. Invited but not attending were Islamic Jihad, the Popular Front for the Liberation of Palestine—General Command (PFLP—GC) and al-Saiqa. The Council's final communiqué urged Arafat to declare an independent Palestinian state by September at the latest, outlined consensus positions on interim and 'final status' issues, and appealed for the reactivation of dormant PLO committees. The DFLP accepted an invitation by the PLO to join the Palestinian delegation attending the Camp David discussions with Israel in July, although many opposition organizations decried the summit.

It was announced on 3 April 2000 that a new PNC was to be established, including the PLO Executive Committee and other leading public figures; the new council's considerations were to include the issue of the Palestinian diaspora, of refugee camps in other Arab countries, and the possible participation of the Palestinians concerned in elections in those countries. In June there were reports that the first draft of the constitution for a Palestinian state was complete and had been submitted to the President for approval.

THE AL-AQSA UPRISING: THE FATAH TANZIM AND INTRA-PALESTINIAN CO-ORDINATION

In September 2000 the West Bank and Gaza became engulfed in the most serious violence seen in the territories for many years, as Palestinians demonstrated their frustration at the lack of progress in the peace process. On 28 September Sharon, leader of Israel's right-wing Likud party, visited Temple Mount/Haram al-Sharif in Jerusalem—the site of the al-Aqsa Mosque and the Dome of the Rock—flanked by Israeli security guards. Sharon's visit to the Islamic holy sites provoked violent protests by stone-throwing Palestinians, to which Israeli security forces responded with force. The clashes spread rapidly to other Palestinian towns; by the end of October more than 140 people had died—all but eight of them Palestinians—and thousands were reportedly injured. The Palestinians received considerable international support, and there were widespread protests in Arab capitals. Arafat and Barak visited Paris, France, on 4 October for discussions led by US Secretary of State Albright. However, no agreement was reached on the composition of an international commission of inquiry into the causes of the clashes. Arafat and Albright continued discussions at the Egyptian resort of Sharm el-Sheikh on the following day. The Israeli authorities subsequently closed the borders of the West Bank and Gaza. On 7 October the UN Security Council issued a resolution condemning the 'provocation carried out' at Temple Mount/Haram al-Sharif and the 'excessive use of force' employed by the Israeli security forces. Israeli officials, meanwhile, accused Arafat of failing to halt the violence, as members of his own organization, Fatah, joined Hamas and other militant groups in what swiftly became known as the 'al-Aqsa *intifada*'. In mid-October Israel launched rocket attacks against Arafat's headquarters in the territories, following the murder, on 12 October, of two Israeli army reservists by a Palestinian crowd in Ramallah.

In an attempt to prevent the latest Middle East crisis from developing into a major regional conflict, a US-brokered summit meeting between Barak and Arafat was convened on 16–17 October 2000 at Sharm el-Sheikh. President Clinton announced that Israel and the PA had agreed a 'truce' to halt the spiralling violence. The two sides were also said to have agreed on the establishment of a US-appointed committee to investigate the violence. (The five-member international commission of inquiry was appointed by Clinton in early November, to be chaired by former US senator George Mitchell.) Barak, meanwhile, insisted that Arafat re-arrest about 60 Islamist militants who had been released by the PA in early October. Amid renewed clashes in the Palestinian self-rule areas, the League of Arab States (the Arab League) held an emergency summit meeting in Cairo on 21–22 October and strongly condemned Israeli actions. Barak responded by announcing that Israel was calling a 'time-out' on the peace process.

The al-Aqsa *intifada* marked a new phase in the Palestinian struggle for independence. The leading political and military forces behind the revolt appeared to be grassroots cadres belonging to the backbone of Arafat's Fatah organization, the Tanzim. These consisted mainly of Fatah's 'inside' leadership, which emerged before and during the first *intifada*, and included fighters who had been members of the PA's myriad intelligence services. It was this legacy and role that increasingly bestowed on Fatah the contradictory function of being at once the military basis of the PA's government and also its most steadfast political opposition. The Tanzim were concerned by the PA's increasingly incompetent performance and the seepage of popular support away from Fatah, as well as the very terms of the Oslo process, whereby Palestinian national aspirations had been subject to a negotiating strategy based on US-led diplomacy and security co-operation with Israel. Fatah Tanzim leaders increasingly advocated other options aside from negotiation and diplomacy, including popular and armed resistance against Israeli military 'outposts' and Jewish settlements in order to augment the cost of the occupation to Israel. The new Palestinian uprising led to armed attacks being routinely deployed against Israeli soldiers, settlements and bypass roads in or near Palestinian areas throughout the Occupied Territories, including East Jerusalem. It was this armed dimension that most distinguished the al-Aqsa revolt from the first *intifada*.

A second dimension was the shifting of the Palestinian struggle away from the perceived tutelage of US diplomacy and Israeli hegemony to the forum of the UN and the Arab world. In particular, there was a reassertion of the principle that an end to the current conflict must be conditional upon Israel's full withdrawal from the territories occupied in 1967 (including East Jerusalem), the dismantlement of Jewish settlements and Israel's acknowledgment of the right of return of Palestinian refugees. The Israeli air strikes of mid-October 2000 (see Israel) resulted in an escalation of Palestinian outrage. Certainly, when Palestinian debate on the forthcoming Sharm el-Sheikh summit began, there was a groundswell of Palestinian anger towards Arafat that had not been seen previously. Hundreds of Palestinians immediately rallied in Gaza on 13 October to denounce the PA; the subsequent announcement of the Sharm el-Sheikh meeting was followed by another Gaza demonstration attended by thousands of Hamas supporters who urged Arafat not to attend the meeting. While the summit was taking place, during 16–17 October, Fatah and Hamas again organized demonstrations condemning Arafat's participation. When the 'ceasefire' arrangements between Israel and the PA were announced on 17 October, various organizations, including Fatah, Hamas, Islamic Jihad, the DFLP and the PFLP, denounced them and vowed to continue the *intifada*.

At the end of October 2000 there was an upsurge in violence against Israeli targets by militant Islamist groups opposed to the Oslo peace process. Israel responded by launching air strikes against Fatah military targets in the Palestinian enclaves and announced a new policy of targeting leaders of militant Islamist organizations deemed to be involved in 'terrorist' actions. On 1 November Arafat and the Israeli Minister for Regional Co-operation, Shimon Peres, held crisis discussions in Gaza, at which they were reported to have agreed a 'ceasefire' based on the truce brokered at Sharm el-Sheikh in October; however, violence between Israelis and Palestinians intensified during November. Nevertheless, bilateral negotiations were resumed later in that month, partly as a result of Russian diplomatic efforts. At the end of November a partial peace plan, announced by the Israeli Government, was rejected by the PA.

Although the Palestinian demonstrations during the early days of the al-Aqsa *intifada* appeared to be spontaneous, within the first two weeks highly localized, though apparently unco-ordinated, leaderships did emerge in the West Bank and Gaza. While many of the local organizers were Fatah officials—most famously Marwan Barghouthi, who was said to attract considerable support among Palestinians in Ramallah and other parts of the West Bank, Fatah and the Tanzim, groups much vilified by Israel, seemed not to be operating on a mass scale. Claims that Fatah radiated instructions to the Palestinian masses ignored the divisions that existed within Fatah. Throughout the first two months of the al-Aqsa *intifada*, Arafat and the PA were in many ways non-present, neither organizing protests nor making a concerted effort to prevent them. Hamas and Islamic Jihad were similarly inactive as organizations. On 8 October 2000 Arafat met the PLO Executive Committee and representatives of Hamas and Islamic Jihad to co-ordinate a joint response to Barak's threats to escalate military action. Arafat held similar meetings in November, but these seemed more directed towards gauging consensus and keeping Islamist groups within the fold than towards drafting battle plans.

However, an important dimension of the al-Aqsa *intifada* did emerge in the first few weeks, and was reflected in moves towards a national unity among all the Palestinian factions, including the non-PLO members Hamas and Islamic Jihad. Prior to the outbreak of the *intifada*, nationalist and Islamist groups had generally limited their joint discussions and co-operation efforts to achieving a broad consensus on fundamental issues: whether and how to continue the peace process, fundamental positions on 'final status' issues, and the timing of a declaration of Palestinian statehood. From late September 2000, however, this national unity was reflected in the formation of an umbrella movement comprising all the Palestinian factions—the Palestinian National and Islamic Forces (PNIF), which laid down a calendar of mass protests and actions. The PNIF included members of the PLO, Hamas and Islamic Jihad. From its inception, the driving force behind the al-Aqsa revolt remained Arafat's Fatah movement and, in particular, its grassroots organization. However, the direction of the organization's policy remained determined by the decisions of local leaders rather than by orders 'from above'. The basic strategy behind Fatah's local leadership was expressed less by PA officials than by grassroots leaders such as Marwan Barghouthi in the West Bank and Saqr Habash. Modelling themselves on the final phase of Hezbollah's resistance in southern Lebanon, these two leaders described the al-Aqsa uprising as 'peaceful civilian' protests combined with 'new forms of military actions against soldiers and settlers in the Occupied Territories'. Moreover, the longer the revolt continued, the more the 'military actions' by Palestinians took precedence over peaceful ones and stemmed in the view of many from the fractured, atomized geography that the Oslo Accords had imposed on the West Bank and Gaza.

A major element of the al-Aqsa *intifada* was the importance of unity between the contending 'nationalist' and 'Islamist' groupings within Palestinian politics. Although lending a certain religious imagery to the al-Aqsa *intifada*—owing mainly to the role that Jerusalem's al-Aqsa Mosque had played in its ignition—the initial role of Hamas and Islamic Jihad in the uprising was merely supportive. The two groups did not challenge Fatah's leading role on the political, diplomatic or military levels, and granted the PLO unprecedented legitimacy by attending, for the first time, sessions of its leadership and by joining the PNIF. In return for this alliance, the uprising saw the release of most Hamas and Islamic Jihad detainees from Palestinian gaols; this was the clearest evidence of the breakdown in the PA's security co-operation with Israel and the CIA. On 2 November 2000 a car bomb attack in West Jerusalem left two Israelis dead; on 22 November another car bomb exploded in the Israeli town of Hadera, killing another two civilians. Islamic Jihad claimed responsibility for the first attack, and the second bore a resemblance to Hamas's operations. The response to both attacks by Fatah and the PNIF as a whole was a resounding silence.

The encirclement of Palestinian towns by the Israeli army and the obstruction of roads in the West Bank and Gaza, combined with Israel's escalation of military reprisals against residential areas, added a new dynamic to the conflict. The larger demonstrations of the first few weeks of the Palestinian uprising—which led to clashes with the Israeli army at checkpoints and major crossings, particularly near Jewish settlements—became more difficult and more costly. Given the new situation, it was no coincidence that the PNIF, comprising all nationalist and Islamist parties but separate from the PA, began issuing weekly leaflets on 23 October 2000 appealing for non-violent demonstrations and co-ordinated social activities, such as olive picking. However, the leaflets also urged Palestinians to organize themselves locally and suggested general strategies, such as focusing attacks on Israeli soldiers and settlers, which became standard after this period. By mid-November the PNIF was still a nascent body that was far from having well-delineated networks on the ground, although it heralded a new chapter in intra-Palestinian co-ordination.

Prior to the outbreak of the al-Aqsa *intifada*, the PA had begun to place more emphasis on state-building activities. For example, on 27 August 2000 the Ministry of Local Government had begun planning elections for 350 villages and municipal councils in the West Bank and Gaza Strip. The PA had originally planned to hold local elections in June 1996, but Arafat had postponed them indefinitely and appointed Fatah loyalists as new council heads, replacing longstanding elected and popular figures. On 20 September 2000 the PA's Minister of Planning and International Co-operation, Dr Nabil Shaath, began forming a team to draft plans to transform the ministry into a foreign ministry, to appeal to foreign countries to upgrade the diplomatic status of PLO offices to that of embassies, and to otherwise standardize the Palestinian diplomatic network. PLC deputy Azmi Shuaybi announced on 28 September the formation of a new anti-corruption coalition (consisting of PLC members, intellectuals and representatives of leading institutions), aimed at promoting and enforcing the rule of law. After the al-Aqsa clashes erupted, however, the PA shifted to crisis management. The PCC was unable to meet in full session, owing to economic closures, demonstrations and Israel's revocation of VIP passes. PA ministries shifted from regular project work to monitoring the damage to their sectors caused by the Israeli blockade and by Israeli air strikes and shelling.

In November 2000 PA officials began stating repeatedly that there could be no return to the old Oslo formula, in which the promise of nominal 'statehood' was traded for very significant Palestinian concessions on issues like settlements, refugees and Jerusalem. Similarly, Arafat himself increasingly opted for the 'internationalization' of the diplomatic process. Like the majority of Palestinians, he wanted the Oslo process unshackled from what he deemed the pro-Israeli bias imposed by the USA's monopoly of the negotiations, and balanced by the participation of countries such as Egypt and the Russian Federation and international bodies such as the UN and EU. An offshoot of the same strategy was the public Palestinian appeal for 2,000 UN peacekeeping troops to be dispatched to Gaza and the West Bank in order to ensure protection for the Palestinian people.

By November–December 2000 the al-Aqsa *intifada* was rapidly escalating into armed combat between Israel and the Palestinians. One trend was the slow decline of popular Palestinian protests in deference to armed actions, usually in reaction to Israeli military attacks. A second trend was the clear shift in power within the Palestinian national leadership, with grassroots Fatah leaders such as Marwan Barghouthi becoming major players. Moreover, institutions such as the PLC and the PA ministries—which drew their authority from the Oslo Accords—in effect ceased to function or were relegated to the subsidiary role of service providers. In their stead, there was a revival in legitimacy and public loyalty towards the PLO and, above all, Fatah—the latter as a national liberation movement rather than as the 'ruling party of the PA'. This development enabled a new Palestinian unity, with Hamas openly participating in Fatah-dominated bodies like the PNIF, the 'field' organization that determined the time-scale and nature of *intifada* activities. None the less, this 'unity' remained largely tentative. For example, there was a broad agreement among the PLO factions that resistance should be confined to the West Bank and Gaza Strip, as the strategic aim was to end the Israeli occupation on the basis of international legitimacy. It was less clear whether this consensus was shared by the Islamist groups. Arafat himself refused to consider the idea of a Palestinian national unity administration. As for the transformation of PA institutions into state institutions, the response was that the goal was not a formal declaration of statehood but to sustain the *intifada* to end the occupation.

In December 2000 a court in the West Bank town of Nablus passed a death sentence on a Palestinian who had been found guilty of collaborating with Israeli secret services in the assassination of a Hamas commander. This signalled a change in policy by the PA, which in January 2001 carried out the executions by firing squad of two alleged collaborators. In the same month Hisham Mekki, the Chairman of Palestinian Satellite Television, Director of the state broadcasting corporation and a close associate of Arafat, was killed by unidentified gunmen in Gaza. A militant Palestinian group, the al-Aqsa Martyrs Brigades, claimed responsibility for the attack, and accused Arafat of failing to end official corruption. Israel denied PA claims that Palestinian collaborators with Israel were behind the assassination.

In the run-up to the end of Bill Clinton's presidency in the USA in January 2001 and to the Israeli premiership election in February, a further round of peace negotiations opened in mid-December 2000. The outgoing US President was reported to have proposed a peace settlement that included plans for a future Palestinian state covering the Gaza Strip and about 95% of the West Bank, as well as granting Palestinian sovereignty over the Islamic holy sites in Jerusalem. However, the US proposals also required that the Palestinians renounce the right of return to Israel for 3.7m. refugees, which the PA deemed unacceptable. In late December the discussions ended after two Israelis were killed by Palestinian bombings in Tel Aviv and Gaza. Arafat travelled to Washington, DC, in early January 2001 to seek official clarification of the Clinton proposals, and Israel was reported to have cautiously accepted the peace initiative as a basis for further discussions.

From its outbreak, there existed a rift between the 'field' leadership of the *intifada* and the PA. Several months into the uprising—and with the arrival of an Israeli Government under Ariel Sharon in early February 2001—the rift was beginning to show signs of political confusion and internal breakdown. Violent demonstrations by Palestinians in the Occupied Territories followed the election of Sharon, whom they held responsible for the massacre of Palestinian refugees in Lebanese camps in 1982 (at which time he was Israel's Minister of Defence). The Palestinian authorities, under strong pressure from their European and Egyptian allies, had gone to inordinate lengths, if not to get Barak re-elected, then at least not to be blamed for bringing Sharon to power. This had been the main motivation for the PA to attend the Israeli-Palestinian negotiations, which began on 21 January 2001 in Taba, Egypt, as they apparently knew that no agreement would be reached. Indeed, the discussions ended without settlement soon afterwards, following the killing of two Israeli civilians in the West Bank for which Hamas claimed responsibility. The drift into disarray and popular resentment was compounded by the absence of the PA in every public sphere except education and health care and its apparent inability to alleviate Palestinian suffering. In Gaza there were simmering clashes between Palestinian refugees and the PA's Preventive Security Force (PSF), ostensibly over the arrest of a Hamas activist.

By this time, a dynamic of action and reaction had developed between armed Palestinian resistance and the Israeli army that was now perilously close to being beyond control. On 17 April 2001, in response to a Palestinian mortar attack on the southern Israeli town of Sderot, the Israeli army moved tanks to the PA-controlled town of Beit Hanoun in the Gaza Strip. However, as was to occur frequently in the Palestinian territories in subsequent months, Israeli forces were soon withdrawn from the town. On 26 April four Fatah activists were killed in an explosion on Gaza's border with Egypt, including Raad Azzam, the leader of the Popular Resistance Committee (PRC), which had led the armed resistance and defence of southern Gaza since the start of the uprising. The Palestinian police chief based in Gaza, Ghazi al-Jabali, insisted that the four 'police officers' had been assassinated by a remote-controlled Israeli device. Palestinians responded by renewing mortar attacks on Gaza's Jewish settlements of Gush Qatif and Kfar Darom on 28–29 April. Convening a session of the PA's National Security Council (which represented all the Palestinian police and intelligence forces) on 29 April, Arafat appealed to his followers to curb all 'security breaches', especially the mortar attacks. According to Palestinian sources, he also disbanded the PRC, appealing to its members to return to their original security institutions. In addition, the Palestinian President arrested Hamas official Abd al-Aziz al-Rantisi, following a recent speech during which al-Rantisi urged Palestinians to reject the Egyptian-Jordanian initiative, while brandishing a Kalashnikov, as the 'only way to liberate Palestine'.

The PA leadership now seemed to view engagement in any diplomatic process—no matter how futile in practical terms—as a crucial part of the struggle for sheer survival that it was now reduced to waging. However, the PA needed something to show for the Palestinians' suffering and sacrifices, hence the authorities' insistence on the settlement-building moratorium as part of the 'ceasefire', a demand that the Israeli Government continued to reject.

The PA agreed in early June 2001 to implement the recommendations contained in the report of the international fact-finding committee led by George Mitchell (the 'Mitchell Committee'), which had been published on 20 May (Documents on Palestine, see p. 1240). The report's recommendations included a freeze on Israeli settlement activity; a clear statement by the PA leadership demanding an end to the violent protests; an 'immediate and unconditional' end to the violence and the disengagement of forces by both sides; and the resumption of security co-operation. The report failed to support Palestinian demands for a UN peacekeeping force to be stationed in the West Bank and Gaza (a request which had been consistently rejected by the Israeli Government and which had been blocked by a US veto at the UN Security Council vote in March). On 12 June the PA also approved an extended 'ceasefire', negotiated by CIA Director George Tenet. The reaction of Hamas to the tentative ceasefire between Israel and the PA was rather conflictual. Hamas had claimed responsibility for a suicide bomb attack on a Tel Aviv disco on 1 June that killed 21 Israelis. On 5 June a senior Hamas official in Gaza, Dr Mahmud al-Zahar, had stated that Hamas would attack Israelis 'everywhere, by all means', thereby casting doubt on the viability of the recent ceasefire. Al-Zahar declared that earlier reports that Hamas was willing to abide by the truce were due to 'miscommunications' between the group's military and political wings. In early July both Islamic Jihad and Hamas formally declared an end to the ceasefire.

During August 2001 several Palestinians were sentenced to death and at least 100 others were detained by the authorities, on charges of having collaborated with Israeli security services in recent attacks on senior Hamas officials. Meanwhile, the PA rejected a request by the Israeli Government that it arrest seven alleged Islamist militants, who headed a 'most wanted' list of about 100 Palestinians. On 10 August, in response to a suicide bomb attack on a restaurant in central Jerusalem (in which at least 15 Israelis died), Israel ordered its forces to occupy several official PA buildings, including Orient House. On 14 August Israeli armed forces entered the town of Jenin in the West Bank; this was the first time that Israel had ordered its military onto land that had been transferred to full PA control under the terms of the Oslo peace process initiated in 1993. PA officials described the Israeli action as a 'declaration of war'. On 27 August 2001 the leader of the PFLP, Abu Ali Moustafa, was assassinated by Israeli troops in the West Bank. Moustafa was the highest-ranking Palestinian official to be killed by Israel under its so-called policy of 'targeted killings'. (Ahmad Saadat later assumed the PFLP leadership.)

IMPROVEMENT IN RELATIONS WITH SYRIA

The expected reconciliation between Arafat and the Syrian leadership, under the effect of the al-Aqsa *intifada* and after some 20 years of estrangement, was achieved during sessions of the Arab League summit held in Amman in March 2001. Arafat met Syrian President Bashar al-Assad on the sidelines of the summit. President Assad demanded the liberation of all Palestinian territory occupied by Israel in 1967 (including East Jerusalem), the unconditional return of all 3.7m. Palestinian refugees to their homeland and the creation of an independent Palestinian state (with Jerusalem as its capital). The meeting indicated that the Palestinian leader had met Syria's condition that the PA commit itself to the borders of 4 June 1967. The two sides agreed on the 'unity of the tracks' in the peace process and pledged to co-ordinate and to maintain bilateral contacts.

THE *INTIFADA* IN THE AFTERMATH OF 11 SEPTEMBER 2001

The unprecedented scale of the suicide attacks launched by the Islamist al-Qa'ida organization against the World Trade Center in New York and the Pentagon in Washington, DC, on 11 September 2001 led to a further escalation of tensions between Israel and the PA. As the US Administration sought to gain support for an international 'coalition against terror', President George W. Bush placed considerable pressure on the two sides to end the fighting in the West Bank and Gaza. In mid-September Arafat, who had strongly condemned the attacks in the USA, announced that he had given militant Palestinian groups 'strict orders for a total ceasefire', and the Israeli Government agreed to withdraw from PA-controlled territory in the West Bank. However, Sharon prevented a planned meeting between Arafat and Peres from taking place, stating that Israel required 48 hours without violence prior to the convening of peace discussions. On 26 September Arafat and Peres finally met in the Gaza Strip, in an attempt to consolidate the 'ceasefire' arrangements outlined in the Mitchell Report. However, retaliatory attacks soon resumed between Israelis and Palestinians. According to the Palestinian Red Crescent Society (PRCS), by the end of September 2001 at least 690 Palestinians had been killed and more than 16,000 injured since the start of the al-Aqsa *intifada* one year earlier. An estimated 170 Israelis had reportedly died as a result of the violence, and many more had been injured. The USA's launch of its 'war on terror' in the aftermath of the 11 September attacks appeared to encourage Israel to step up assaults on PA targets and ultimately to reoccupy six major Palestinian cities.

On 17 October 2001 PFLP militants assassinated Israeli Minister of Tourism Rechavam Ze'evi in East Jerusalem. In response, Israel escalated its military campaign in PA-controlled areas of the West Bank. Although Arafat denounced Ze'evi's murder, ordered Palestinian security forces to arrest the perpetrators and outlawed the armed wing of the PFLP, Sharon issued an ultimatum to the PA that it arrest and extradite Ze'evi's killers and other leading PFLP militants or face a harsh response.

The USA urged Sharon to show restraint. It still wanted Israel to resume discussions with the PA and for the two sides to implement previous ceasefire agreements, which would facilitate US coalition-building for the 'war on terror' and the US-led military campaign in Afghanistan. In an attempt to revitalize the ceasefire arrangements, US Secretary of Defense Donald Rumsfeld toured the Middle East in early October 2001, and President Bush declared on 2 October that the creation of a Palestinian state 'has always been a part of our vision, so long as the right of Israel to exist is respected'. This public US support for a Palestinian state apparently angered Sharon, as did the fact that Rumsfeld had not come to Israel during his regional consultations on the 'war on terror'. Furthermore, the USA had not supported Israel's demand for the extradition of Ze'evi's assassins. Together with the EU and Russia, the USA continued to put pressure on both the PA and Israel to adhere to the ceasefire arrangement of 29 August, which had been mediated by the EU's High Representative for the Common Foreign and Security Policy, Javier Solana.

Sharon rejected personal appeals by President Bush and US Secretary of State Colin Powell to resume discussions with the PA, on 18 October 2001 suspending all contacts with the PA and giving the Israeli military the 'green light' to step up assassinations of Palestinian activists. Some right-wing Israeli politicians even demanded the expulsion of Arafat from the West Bank and Gaza. In mid-October Israel deployed helicopter gunships over Palestinian cities and moved troops to the outer fringes of Jenin. On 18 October Israeli forces reoccupied Jenin, Nablus and Ramallah, Bethlehem and Beit Jala were taken on 19 October, and Qalqilya and Tulkarm on 20 October. Two days later, the USA condemned the Israeli invasion of PA-controlled cities in Area A as 'unacceptable' and demanded Israel's immediate withdrawal. Israel was forced to withdraw from the cities, but its army continued to occupy large sectors of territory belonging to the PA and to carry out 'targeted killings' of senior members of Hamas. The violence continued throughout late 2001, and Arafat reportedly expressed his disappointment at the lack of international pressure on the Israeli Government. Mounting internal opposition to Arafat's policy of arresting Palestinian militants did little to strengthen his position in the Occupied Territories.

THE *KARINE A* AFFAIR

As the US special envoy, Anthony Zinni, returned to the region in an effort to broker an Israeli-Palestinian ceasefire, on 3 January 2002 Israeli naval commandos captured a freighter ship, the *Karine A*, in the Red Sea, which was alleged to be carrying weaponry destined for the PA. The Israelis argued that the smuggling operation had been devised by the PA leadership and approved by Arafat, and accused Iran of involvement. Although the Palestinian authorities and Iran denied any responsibility, the Israeli interrogation of the ship's crew apparently indicated direct PA involvement. The US Administration accepted the Israeli position regarding the affair. For months after the seizure of the *Karine A*, US and Israeli intelligence officials continued to claim that the affair was part of a broader relationship and accused Arafat of personally forging an alliance with Iran that included imports of Iranian heavy weapons and millions of US dollars to Palestinian guerrilla organizations in the Occupied Territories. This PA-Iranian alliance, they claimed, was conceived at a meeting in Moscow, Russia, in May 2001 between some of Arafat's senior aides and Iranian government officials. Palestinian spokesmen dismissed the claims and argued that the allegations were part of an attempt by Israel to justify its 'aggressive' military operations in the West Bank and Gaza Strip.

THE RISE OF THE AL-AQSA MARTYRS BRIGADES

The first three months of 2002 witnessed the rise of the al-Aqsa Martyrs Brigades, a militant offshoot of the mainstream Fatah Tanzim, which had been purposely built as a loose network of regional 'cells'. The Brigades pursued a campaign of gun attacks against Israeli soldiers at military roadblocks in the West Bank and Gaza, and dispatched suicide bombers deep into Israel. On 21 March, after suicide bombers from the al-Aqsa Martyrs Brigades killed three Israelis and injured dozens more in West Jerusalem, the US Department of State branded the Palestinian militia a 'terrorist organization'.

In January 2002 a volunteer for the PRCS in Ramallah became the first female suicide bomber. The following month the al-Aqsa Martyrs Brigades claimed joint responsibility for a raid on a West Bank checkpoint, in which six Israeli soldiers died, and in early March some 10 Israelis (most of them soldiers) were shot dead by a sniper from the Brigades at a West Bank checkpoint. The Brigades' success encouraged a belief that Israel could be driven out of the Occupied Territories, just as Hezbollah had forced Israeli troops from southern Lebanon. The doggedness of the Brigades also served as a counterpoint to Arafat's compromises and efforts to regain US approval by vowing to punish those responsible for the 21 March bombing and continuing discussions concerning a US-mediated ceasefire. The commanders of the al-Aqsa Martyrs Brigades answered to no higher authority and certainly not to Arafat, who made several attempts to disband the militia. This autonomy produced a curious hybrid: although the fighters remained part of the mainstream, secular Fatah movement, they adopted the strategies of radical Islamists. The Brigades' suicide bombings in early 2002 broke two Palestinian taboos: they defied Fatah's policy of confining the uprising to the West Bank and Gaza, and, for the first time, they employed women as suicide bombers. In late 2001 and early 2002, after Israel had deployed its air force, navy, tanks and ground forces against Palestinian refugee camps and cities in the biggest military offensive carried out by Israel in a generation, the al-Aqsa Martyrs Brigades decided to concentrate its attacks inside Israel itself. The Jerusalem bombing of 21 March, in particular, encapsulated the limits of Arafat's influence over his mainstream Fatah militia, let alone his radical Islamist opponents such as Hamas and Islamic Jihad.

THE RAMALLAH INCURSION OF MARCH 2002

Only after the Palestinians were beaten, Sharon reportedly stated in early March 2002, would negotiations be possible. According to a report by the human rights organization Amnesty International, the scale of Israeli attacks on Palestinian cities and refugee camps in the West Bank and Gaza was 'disproportionate and often reckless'. Amnesty estimated that in the six weeks from 1 March to mid-April more than 600 Palestinians had been killed and over 3,000 injured by Israeli soldiers. A major escalation occurred on 11 March 2002, when the Israeli army entered Ramallah (the Palestinians' commercial and political hub in the West Bank), in what Israel said was part of a general sweep for activists and militants. The massive incursion involved some 150 tanks and was part of Israel's largest military offensive in the West Bank and Gaza Strip since the Israelis captured these territories in 1967. The incursion took place while US envoy Anthony Zinni was engaged in a renewed effort to broker a ceasefire between the two sides.

The Israelis' short-lived incursion into Ramallah resulted in huge damage to Palestinian infrastructure, affecting water and electricity supplies, the sewerage system and roads, and was estimated by PA officials as costing tens of millions of US dollars. Twelve Palestinians were killed during the assault on Ramallah. On 16 March 2002 Israeli tanks withdrew from the West Bank city, ending their brief reoccupation of President Arafat's power base. The Israeli army, meanwhile, announced that its forces had left positions in two other West Bank cities but that they remained on the outskirts of Bethlehem, Nablus, Jenin and Hebron. Israeli forces also formed a cordon around Ramallah.

THE USA'S 'WAR ON TERROR' AND THE FAILURE OF US MEDIATION

As Zinni pressed ahead with ceasefire discussions between the PA and Israel, the Bush Administration demanded a complete withdrawal of all Israeli forces from PA-controlled areas. However, at the same time, both Israel and the USA continued to repeat their demand that Arafat 'must do more' to rein in Palestinian militants and halt attacks on Israelis. Zinni convened the joint Israeli-Palestinian security committee for discussions on how to move into the security plan prepared by CIA Director George Tenet.

The joint Israeli-Palestinian security committee met on 20 and 21 March 2002, with Zinni in attendance; however, no agreement was reached on the terms of a ceasefire. Representing the Palestinians in the meetings were Col Jibril Rajoub, the head of the PSF in the West Bank, and his Gaza counterpart, Muhammad Dahlan. Disagreement focused on the length of time to be allocated to the Tenet ceasefire plan before the resumption of the diplomatic process, and the arrest of Palestinian militants wanted by Israel. Israel demanded the arrests of those involved in past attacks, but the Palestinians replied that they would only detain those who intended to launch future attacks.

Meanwhile, the PA continued to demand that Israel withdraw its troops to their positions as at September 2000, and lift all sieges and remove all checkpoints around Palestinian towns and villages, as stated by the Tenet plan; the Palestinians also demanded that international observers be placed in the Occupied Territories. PA representatives insisted that they would co-operate provided they could prove to the Palestinian public that there would be an immediate response from Israel, and provided that the security arrangements would result in a renewal of the political negotiations. Israel, however, wanted the Palestinians first to take action against militant groups, including arrests, dismantling militias and collecting weapons.

ISRAELI REOCCUPATION OF PA-CONTROLLED AREAS

On 29 March 2002 Israel launched Operation Defensive Shield—a large-scale military offensive in the West Bank in response to a series of suicide attacks by Palestinian militants and, more specifically, to a suicide bombing two days previously in Netanya (in which 29 Israelis celebrating Passover died). This was the bloodiest attack since the start of the Palestinian uprising against Israeli occupation in September 2000. As part of its military campaign, Israeli forces broke into Arafat's presidential compound in Ramallah, where the Palestinian leader remained inside his office, in effect cut off from the rest of the city. Although Israel stated that it had no intention of harming Arafat personally, PA officials insisted that Arafat's life was in danger. On 1 April 2002 Israeli tanks entered the town of Betunya, near Ramallah, surrounding the PSF compound of West Bank security chief Rajoub and causing considerable damage to the complex. The PSF apparatus had been the strongest and most prominent of all PA forces on the West Bank.

Israeli tanks also entered Beit Jala, Bethlehem, Qalqilya, Salfeet, Tulkarm, Nablus and Jenin, patrolling the streets and enforcing strict curfews that confined hundreds of thousands of Palestinians to their homes. In addition, Israeli troops laid siege to Jenin's refugee camp, resulting in battles with Palestinian residents of the camp who retaliated with bombs and gunfire. Israeli soldiers also encircled hundreds of Palestinian gunmen who had barricaded themselves in the Church of the Nativity in Bethlehem. Arafat, meanwhile, confined to his Ramallah headquarters, remained defiant, stating that he would prefer to die rather than be forced into exile.

It was apparent that Sharon now wanted to expel Arafat from the Territories, publicly suggesting on 2 April 2002 that he be exiled. However, although the US Administration offered Sharon tacit support for Israel's military operation in the West Bank, US officials were not prepared to allow the Israeli Government to expel the PA President, to destroy the PA or to completely retake the areas under nominal Palestinian control. Yet, the Israeli offensive prevented the PA from taking effective control of the security situation in the Palestinian self-rule areas because vital Palestinian installations, including its West Bank security headquarters, had been destroyed.

The heaviest fighting between the Israeli army and Palestinian militias occurred in the refugee camp at Jenin, home to some 13,000 Palestinians. Israeli tanks had entered Jenin and surrounded the adjacent refugee camp on 3 April 2002, provoking fierce opposition from Palestinian gunmen. Many of the camp's inhabitants fled during the fighting and heavy bombardment by Israeli tanks and helicopters. The fighting in the Jenin camp lasted until 11 April. Palestinians subsequently estimated that more than 100 Palestinians had died as a result of the Israeli invasion of the camp. The UN's special envoy to the Middle East, Terje Rød-Larsen, was strongly critical of Israel's actions at Jenin. However, an exact tally of the number of fatalities was not possible because Israel initially barred reporters and medical personnel from the camp. After the siege of early April the Palestinians came to embrace Jenin as a symbol of wider resistance to the Israeli occupation.

THE ARREST OF MARWAN BARGHOUTHI

On 15 April 2002 Marwan Barghouthi, one of the most influential Fatah leaders in the West Bank, was detained by Israeli armed forces in Ramallah. Israel presented Marwan Barghouthi's detention as a major achievement of its reoccupation of the city, using it to counter strong international pressure against its military offensive in the West Bank. Israel accused Marwan Barghouthi of being the leader of the al-Aqsa Martyrs Brigades, despite the fact that he had never acknowledged a formal relationship with the group. In recent years Marwan Barghouthi had attained the status of a 'folk hero' among most young Palestinians. His fiery speeches and almost daily media interviews, including several that he had given to Israeli television in Hebrew, had made him a defining face of the Palestinian *intifada*. Since September 2000 Marwan Barghouthi had at times appeared to disagree publicly with Arafat over the direction of the Palestinian uprising. However, Marwan Barghouthi's acumen—he never mentioned the Palestinian leader by name when criticizing his policies—and popularity had ensured his political survival. Trial proceedings against Marwan Barghouthi began on 5 September 2002.

ENDING THE STAND-OFFS IN RAMALLAH AND BETHLEHEM

The stand-off at the Church of the Nativity began on 2 April 2002, when Israel invaded Bethlehem and about 200 Palestinians (including militiamen, policemen, officials, clerics and church workers) sought refuge in the shrine. By 23 April Israeli forces had withdrawn from most West Bank cities, but still surrounded Arafat's compound in Ramallah and the Bethlehem church. In Ramallah, Israel demanded that Arafat hand over five men suspected of involvement in the October 2001 assassination of Rechavam Ze'evi, as well as the alleged mastermind of the *Karine A* arms shipment to the PA. Although Arafat had initially refused this request, he now took preemptive legal action by putting the suspected assassins of Ze'evi on trial in a makeshift court, using Palestinian policemen in the Ramallah compound as judges. On 25 April 2002 the 'military field court' handed out gaol terms of between one and 18 years to four men convicted of involvement in Ze'evi's assassination. The sentences were ratified by Arafat. On 28 April the Israeli Cabinet approved a US proposal aimed at ending the siege of Arafat's compound. The US plan required US and British personnel to guard six Palestinians wanted by Israel, and, in turn, Arafat was allowed to leave his headquarters and to move freely in the Palestinian areas of the West Bank and Gaza. Finally, an accord based on proposals to offer militants wanted by Israel and stranded in the Church of the Nativity a choice of exile or trial in Israel, or transfer to the Gaza Strip, was devised, with US mediation. Arafat approved the dispatch of 13 Palestinians to Europe and of a further 26 to Gaza, despite strong Fatah and Hamas criticism of the agreement. On 12 May the 13 Palestinian militants were flown initially to Cyprus after leaving the Bethlehem church, on their way to permanent exile.

REOCCUPATION OF THE WEST BANK

On 23 June 2002, after two suicide bombings in Jerusalem had killed 26 Israelis, the Israeli military reinvaded all West Bank cities, keeping at least 600,000 Palestinians under effective house arrest with round-the-clock curfews and largely barring the media from covering its military operations. This military offensive encountered minimal Palestinian resistance and limited international criticism. Israeli tanks again surrounded Arafat's shell-damaged compound, with the President and his aides inside. As Israeli forces clamped down harder on security in the West Bank, Sharon pledged to widen the Israeli offensive against the Palestinians to the Gaza Strip. The reoccupation of the West Bank and the prolonged curfews imposed by Israel brought about a major humanitarian crisis for the Palestinians, with UN and aid agencies having trouble getting assistance to hundreds of thousands of Palestinians there.

GENERAL ELECTION AND PA REFORM ANTICIPATED

In mid-May 2002 Arafat decided to hold presidential and parliamentary elections within a year, which, according to PA officials, would be part of a broader reform package of the administration. Longstanding Palestinian complaints about widespread corruption and nepotism in the PA had intensified during the months of Israeli closures and invasions, which had severely disrupted everyday life. Previous attempts to reform the administration had led to few significant changes, with Arafat disregarding laws adopted by the PLC as well as decisions by the judiciary. However, despite widespread Palestinian dissatisfaction with the PA, Arafat continued to be seen as a symbol of the Palestinian people and was not expected to face a strong challenge for leadership. Nevertheless, Israel's six-week reoccupation of the West Bank towns during April–May had strengthened a sense among many Palestinians that the PA was ineffective and unable to protect them against the Israeli military. Thus, Arafat may have decided to hold elections as a way of ensuring renewed legitimacy. PA officials emphasized that polling would be conducted on the condition that Israeli troops first withdrew to positions they had held before September 2000.

The elections would be the first time that Arafat faced voters since he was overwhelmingly elected as President of the PA in 1996. The parliament's list of demands was drafted by a committee of eight legislators from Arafat's Fatah movement, who had requested that a post of prime minister be created, with the premier to be in charge of day-to-day government operations. The planned reforms also urged a streamlining of the Palestinian security services. However, al-Rantisi, leader of the Hamas movement, dismissed the planned administrative changes as cosmetic.

On 27 May 2002 Arafat, following demands for reform by ordinary Palestinians and Western governments alike, named a new, smaller Cabinet that included a new minister to oversee the security forces. Notably, he named Abd al-Razzak al-Yahya, a former PLO commander, as the new Minister of the Interior. Amid accusations of financial corruption in his administration, Arafat also named a new Minister of Finance, Dr Salam Fayyad, who had recently been employed by the IMF in Jerusalem and had urged greater financial accountability in the Palestinian administration.

ARAFAT'S DISMISSAL OF WEST BANK SECURITY CHIEF

In early July 2002, while the Israeli army continued its offensive in the West Bank, Arafat dismissed his most powerful security chief, Rajoub, the commander of the PSF in the West Bank. Although Arafat's motives were unclear, Rajoub had evidently lost credibility following the Israeli military takeover of the PSF's headquarters in Betunya four months earlier. Moreover, several Palestinian leaders, including some of Arafat's closest aides, had insinuated that Rajoub had handed over Fatah and Hamas fighters to Israel. On 5 July a terse formal statement from the PA stated that Arafat had decided to 'relieve' Rajoub of his responsibilities and to appoint in his place Zuheir Manasra, a former governor of Jenin. Gen. Ghazi al-Jabali, the Palestinian police chief, was dismissed by Arafat in a similar fashion, also in early July, and his deputy, Col Salim Bardini, was nominated to replace him. The tumult of the al-Aqsa *intifada* prompted a period of sustained upheaval within the upper ranks of the PA's security forces, precipitating structural reform.

The entire Palestinian Cabinet resigned on 11 September 2002, in order to prevent a vote of no confidence being brought against it in the PLC. (On the same day Arafat had issued a decree setting 20 January 2003 as the date of the presidential and legislative elections.) Although a new cabinet was expected to be announced within two weeks, Arafat subsequently declared that he was unable to form a new administration while his compound in Ramallah was under Israeli occupation. Following a further Palestinian suicide bombing in Tel Aviv, on 19 September 2002 Israel had ordered its troops into Ramallah and demolished Arafat's presidential buildings, where several 'wanted' militants were believed to be sheltering. Amid strong international pressure, Israeli forces redeployed to the outskirts of the Ramallah compound on 29 September. The incumbent Palestinian ministers were to remain in office pending the formation of a new cabinet.

POWER STRUGGLE BETWEEN ARAFAT AND ABBAS

On 26 November 2002 the Secretary-General of the PLO's Executive Committee and Arafat's deputy, Mahmoud Abbas, urged Palestinian militants fighting the Israeli occupation to halt suicide attacks in Israel 'to avoid giving Israel the pretext to reoccupy more Palestinian land'. Abbas (who had been the key PLO figure behind the secret discussions with the Israelis in Oslo, which eventually led to the signing of the Declaration of Principles in 1993) had consistently criticized the use of arms by Palestinians during the al-Aqsa *intifada*. Meanwhile, a poll conducted by Birzeit University and released in late 2002 showed that almost two-thirds of Palestinians in the Occupied Territories disapproved of the way in which the *intifada* had evolved and supported immediate reform of the PA.

The power struggle between Arafat and Abbas dominated PA politics at this time. Both were co-founders of Fatah and the clash reflected the depth of the Palestinian crisis. Following the Oslo agreements, a kind of Palestinian mini-entity had come into being, consisting of several small enclaves on the West Bank and the Gaza Strip. However, the Palestinian national vision of 'a viable, independent and sovereign state in all the West Bank and Gaza Strip, including East Jerusalem' was far from being realized. Consequently, two different, and even contradictory, structures had emerged side by side in the West Bank and Gaza: a national liberation movement, defined by its assortment of militant groups and requiring direction, and a micro-entity in need of a transparent administration. Arafat remained the symbol of the national liberation movement, with his charisma and authoritarian leadership. Abbas, by nature a man of compromise and a diplomat, represented the second reality of small fragmented enclaves, surrounded by and dependent on Israel. Abbas had little influence over the Palestinians, but did have the support of the USA and Israel.

The conflict between the two leaders centred on diverging assessments of the al-Aqsa *intifada*. By mid-2003 some 2,500 Palestinians had been killed, some 10,000 disabled and injured, and the Palestinian economy debilitated. Abbas appealed for the cessation of the 'armed *intifada*' and maintained that the Palestinians could achieve more in negotiations with the USA and Israel. Relying on mainstream Israeli politicians such as former Labour Party minister Yossi Beilin in his assessment of the *intifada*, Abbas believed that the military confrontation with Israel undermined the Oslo process and harmed Palestinian interests. Abbas's Palestinian critics (including Arafat loyalists), meanwhile, argued that the *intifada* had achieved important results: first, the Israeli economy was in deep crisis; second, social and political cleavages within Israeli society had widened; third, Israel's image in the world had been severely harmed; fourth, Israeli security had worsened to the point where there was a conspicuously ubiquitous public security presence; and fifth, Israeli casualties were high.

THE NATIONAL DIALOGUE IN CAIRO

In late 2002 and early 2003 both the PA and the Fatah movement were facing a mounting challenge from Hamas, the armed wing of which, the Izz al-Din al-Qassam Brigades, spearheaded anti-Israeli attacks in the Occupied Territories, thus gaining increasing support among the Palestinians. By mid-2002 the Israeli army had destroyed the PA's security infrastructure in the West Bank, although the PA still maintained control in many areas in the Gaza Strip, which had been heavily targeted by the Israeli army but had not been reoccupied. The rise of Hamas provided the background for the Palestinian national dialogue in Cairo. In November representatives of Fatah and Hamas launched a new round of discussions in Cairo, sponsored by President Hosni Mubarak, aimed at agreeing on a common Palestinian strategy in the face of escalating Israeli attacks and the reoccupation of Palestinian territories. The delegations to the Cairo discussions were initially led by Fatah representative Zakaria al-Agha and Hamas politburo chief Meshaal.

Arafat himself had repeatedly appealed to all Palestinian factions to agree to halt suicide attacks within Israel and had voiced his condemnation of all attacks perpetrated against both Palestinian and Israeli civilians. However, the Cairo discussions yielded little except a commitment to continue dialogue. Subsequently, PA Minister of External Affairs Shaath elaborated by saying that Fatah would 'maintain its demands, namely a halt to all operations against civilians as a first step towards a ceasefire to allow Israel to pull back its forces from the territories to the September 2000 lines'. He stated that 'civilians' meant all unarmed Israelis 'including unarmed settlers' in the West Bank and Gaza Strip.

The national dialogue in Cairo was resumed in mid-January 2003 and involved 12 Palestinian factions, with delegates from across the political spectrum. However, the delegates failed to agree on an Egyptian draft proposal for a Palestinian-Israeli ceasefire that also upheld the right to resist Israeli occupation through civil disobedience. Delegates fell into three broad camps concerning the Egyptian proposal: those who accepted it unconditionally; those who agreed only to halting attacks against civilians inside Israel; and those who would agree only to halting attacks if Israel gave reciprocal guarantees to stop 'targeted killings' of leading Palestinian militants.

POSTPONEMENT OF ELECTIONS AND REFORM OF THE PA

In late 2002 PA officials began arguing that they had been hampered in their reforms, including the holding of elections, by the Israelis' reoccupation of the West Bank and their regular incursions into the Gaza Strip. In December PLC Speaker Quray announced that it would not be practical to proceed with the presidential and legislative elections scheduled for 20 January 2003 until Israel withdrew from the reoccupied PA areas. PA officials argued that the Israeli blockades made it impossible for the Palestinian population to move around, crippling the economy and undermining hopes that voters could get to polling stations. Meanwhile, the USA and Israel, which both demanded that the PA undertake sweeping 'democratic and security reforms', requested that the Palestinian presidential election be delayed for fear that Arafat could win a new term as President.

In January 2003 the PCC met for the first time in two years to ratify the draft of a Palestinian constitution, including a clause establishing the post of prime minister—one of the conditions of the peace plan known as the 'roadmap', drafted by the Quartet group (comprising the USA, the EU, the UN and Russia). Meanwhile, the European Commission praised PA efforts to achieve transparency in its finances, although Israel claimed that money was being used to finance 'terrorism'. The PA's first complete budget, submitted by Minister of Finance Fayyad to the PLC in December 2002, received widespread praise. In late January 2003 PA officials in Ramallah reacted with dismay to Sharon's re-election to the Israeli premiership.

THE ABBAS CABINET

On 14 February 2003 Arafat finally yielded to pressure from the EU, Israel and the USA, and announced that he would create a prime ministerial post as part of efforts to reform his administration. Abbas was immediately considered the most likely candidate. Arafat, whose power was largely unchecked, made the announcement after a meeting with special representatives from the UN, Russia and the EU. However, the Palestinian President gave no indication as to when a new prime minister might be appointed.

The power struggle between Arafat and Abbas continued throughout early 2003. In mid-April Abbas's efforts to form a new cabinet ran into trouble, when several leading PA figures and Arafat loyalists remained highly critical of Israeli and US pressure on the PA. On 22 April Abbas announced that discussions with Arafat had broken down over the latter's refusal to accept his nomination of Dahlan, who had long-term relations with both the USA and Israel, and who had clashed with Arafat while serving as the PA President's security chief.

Meanwhile, the USA, which firmly supported Abbas, declared that he had until midnight on 23 April 2003 to name a new cabinet or step aside, thereby jeopardizing the chances for the Quartet-sponsored roadmap, which US President George W. Bush had said he would release when Abbas had announced his cabinet. With world leaders urging him to back down, Arafat bowed to key cabinet demands from Abbas. Dahlan was appointed a Minister of State for Security Affairs, while Abbas himself would become Prime Minister and Minister for the Interior. On 29 April the Cabinet comfortably won a vote of confidence in the PLC. The new Cabinet marked a major victory for Abbas and a severe blow for Arafat, who had been struggling to maintain control of the key Palestinian security forces in the most serious challenge to his leadership for two decades. Abbas had promised the Quartet that he would root out corruption, crack down on Palestinian militants and open the way for renewed peace discussions with Israel.

THE ROADMAP PEACE PLAN

On 30 April 2003, four months after it had been finalized by the Quartet group, the roadmap to peace in the Middle East was formally placed on the diplomatic agenda and presented to the PA and Israel (Documents on Palestine, see p. 1248). The presentation of the roadmap took place in Ramallah within hours of the swearing in of the new Palestinian Cabinet. The roadmap was the first major international diplomatic initiative in three years aimed at resuming negotiations between Israel and the Palestinians. The document urged an end to the Israeli–Palestinian conflict and the establishment of a Palestinian state by 2005. From the point of view of PA officials, the roadmap, at the very least, was supposed to create the diplomatic pressure necessary to end Israel's policy of 'creating facts on the ground' by its military actions in the West Bank and Gaza.

The roadmap focused upon a Palestinian renunciation of efforts to use force and 'terror' to change the status quo. The plan offered the option of the 'possible creation of an independent Palestinian state with provisional borders in 2005' and demanded a complete cessation of Israeli settlement expansion in the West Bank and Gaza and the evacuation of settlements established after March 2001. Under the terms of the roadmap, Israel was also required to end its prohibition on Palestinian travel on most roads in the Palestinian territories. The PA endorsed the roadmap almost immediately. Israel, however, rejected the demand for an effective settlement freeze, referring instead to a policy permitting the 'natural growth' of settlements. Israeli officials opposed the removal of the approximately 70 new settlement 'outposts' established since March 2001.

On 16 May 2003 Erekat resigned as Minister for Negotiation Affairs. Erekat had previously led Palestinian teams in negotiations with Israel prior to the al-Aqsa *intifada* and had been considered closer to Arafat than to Abbas. While the Minister of State for Security Affairs, Dahlan, and the PLC Speaker, Quray, had been invited to join Abbas in discussions with Sharon the following day, Erekat had not been invited and he appeared to have resigned in order to express his displeasure at this perceived snub. In late May Sharon's vague acceptance of the roadmap and the seemingly conflicting messages to the Palestinians and Israelis by the Bush Administration in the USA were cautiously welcomed by the PA. After the USA had, in late May, declared that it would consider 'fully and seriously' Israeli concerns relating to the roadmap, the Palestinian leadership emphasized the importance of implementing the roadmap without any change to its detail, and insisted that it should be dealt with as a 'package'.

THE AQABA SUMMIT

Soon after Israel had announced its qualified acceptance of the roadmap, President Bush declared that he was calling a three-way summit, to take place in Aqaba, Jordan, between himself, Sharon and Abbas, in what would mark the US President's first major involvement in the Middle East peace process. Although the USA had been the senior partner in the Quartet group that had drafted the peace plan, Bush had been slow to engage in this process. His Administration had had no serious dialogue with the Palestinians for more than a year. Prior to the Aqaba summit, Abbas stated that he expected to reach an agreement with Hamas whereby the organization would halt its campaign of attacks against Israelis. Hamas had rejected the roadmap but its spokesman disclosed that the group was considering a temporary ceasefire. Since November 2002 Egypt had hosted several rounds of inter-Palestinian discussions in a bid to stop attacks against Israelis, with Hamas and Islamic Jihad rejecting a truce unless Israel stopped its 'targeted killings' of Palestinian activists and withdrew its army from the West Bank and Gaza. Israel had earlier ruled out the prospect of a ceasefire agreement at this stage, stating that 'terrorist organizations would take advantage of it to rebuild their infrastructure'.

On 4 June 2003 the Aqaba summit formally launched the roadmap. Bush held separate meetings with the summit's host, King Abdullah, followed by discussions with Sharon and Abbas before the three-way summit began at King Abdullah's summer residence of Beit al-Bahr. Separate statements were issued after the discussions, as the Israelis and Palestinians failed to agree on a joint communiqué.

On the same day Israeli forces pushed into the West Bank towns of Nablus and Jenin, prompting clashes with inhabitants that left several Palestinians injured. Israeli troops in Hebron demolished three houses owned by Palestinian fighters in the southern district and imposed a curfew on the area. More critically, however, the decision to target Hamas leader al-Rantisi for assassination on 10 June 2003 threatened to derail the efforts of Abbas to negotiate a ceasefire with Hamas representatives. From Sharon's perspective, Hamas had invited the assault on al-Rantisi with its deadly attack on Israeli soldiers in Gaza two days earlier, and he had never favoured the idea of Abbas negotiating a ceasefire with the militant group. Following the Aqaba summit, the Israeli policy of 'targeted assassination' of Hamas militants continued.

On 14 June 2003, after a particularly violent week in Israel and the Palestinian territories, there was a growing chorus of voices, led by UN Secretary-General Kofi Annan, demanding the deployment of an armed force of peacekeepers to keep the two sides apart and enable them to begin implementing the roadmap. Palestinians had long maintained that an international peacekeeping force could reduce tensions and end the curfews, roadblocks and travel restrictions that put severe constraints on life in the West Bank and Gaza. However, Israel remained vehemently opposed to such a force, stating that it would not relinquish control over its security to a third party. Meanwhile, on the same day Israel and the Palestinians resumed discussions concerning the withdrawal of Israeli troops from parts of the Gaza Strip and Bethlehem. In late June Hamas and other militant organizations declared a ceasefire, which they said was conditional upon Israel ending its policy of killing Palestinian militants and upon the release of Palestinian prisoners.

In July 2003 the Israeli Cabinet 'reluctantly' agreed to free several hundred Palestinian prisoners, but Sharon ruled out releasing members of Hamas and Islamic Jihad involved in attacks on Israeli targets. Abbas, who had made the prison releases a key demand, urged Sharon to free several prominent detainees, including Marwan Barghouthi, who was on trial in Israel, accused of perpetrating terrorism against Israeli citizens. Marwan Barghouthi had played a crucial role in persuading Hamas, Islamic Jihad and Fatah to agree to the ceasefire announced in late June.

On 25 July 2003 President Bush received Abbas at the White House in Washington, DC, for the first time, in a visit designed to hasten the implementation of the roadmap and to reinforce Abbas's authority. The visit came at a critical time for Abbas, a month after he had coaxed Palestinian militants into ending their attacks on Israel; Abbas was also under pressure to demonstrate that the ceasefire had achieved concrete results for the Palestinians. During the meeting Bush appeared to side with Abbas on one key issue, the demand for a halt to construction of the 'security fence' that Israel was building along the length of the West Bank, which appeared in effect to annex areas of Palestinian land. At the same time, however, Bush was equivocal on a demand by Abbas for Israel to release substantial numbers of the 6,000 Palestinian prisoners it held.

By early June 2003 the number of people killed since the outbreak of the al-Aqsa *intifada* in September 2000 had risen to 3,278, including 2,476 Palestinians and 742 Israelis. In early May 2003 the UN Relief and Works Agency for Palestine Refugees in the Near East (UNRWA) reported that the total number of Palestinians made homeless by the Israeli military demolition campaign had risen to above 12,000 following a rapid acceleration of the demolition policy in Gaza during the first quarter of the year.

Abbas resigned as Prime Minister at the beginning of September 2003; it was widely believed that his resignation was the culmination of his ongoing dispute with Arafat regarding ultimate authority over the Palestinian security apparatus. Arafat moved quickly to nominate Quray, the Speaker of the PLC, as the new Prime Minister. Quray accepted the post shortly afterwards. Also in early September Erekat was reappointed as the Minister for Negotiation Affairs.

NEW PALESTINIAN CABINET AND EGYPTIAN MEDIATION OF TRUCE NEGOTIATIONS

On 12 November 2003 Arafat inaugurated the long-awaited new Palestinian Cabinet, led by Prime Minister Quray. The latter immediately vowed to seek a ceasefire with Israel and to bring an end to the al-Aqsa *intifada*. In mid-November Egyptian intelligence chief Omar Suleiman held discussions in Ramallah with Arafat and Quray, aimed at facilitating a new, durable and mutually acceptable ceasefire. Both Suleiman and his PA hosts hoped that this time the ceasefire would hold, unlike the previous *hudna* (truce) unilaterally declared by the Palestinian resistance groups in June. On 18 November Suleiman also dispatched some of his aides to Gaza to meet with the leaders of local Fatah, Hamas and Islamic Jihad organizations to discuss the proposed truce.

Following this round of Egyptian mediation, Hamas's founder and spiritual leader Sheikh Ahmad Yassin publicly welcomed the Egyptian efforts, calling Egypt an 'older brother'. Yassin indicated that Hamas was willing in principle to accept a new ceasefire, provided that Israel refrained from assassinating Palestinian leaders and al-Aqsa *intifada* activists, and ended its repeated incursions into Palestinian population centres in the Gaza Strip. Hamas also demanded that Israel end its policy of demolishing Palestinian homes and destroying orchards and farms, and removed all travel restrictions throughout the West Bank and Gaza Strip. In response, the Egyptian mediators and PA officials alike declared that Hamas's demands were reasonable, as no lasting ceasefire agreement would be sustained without ending Israeli 'targeted killings' of Palestinians.

However, the anticipated meeting between Sharon and Quray did not take place, despite renewed US pressure; the PA and Israel blamed each other for not holding the meeting. In the period between 4 October 2003 and 31 January 2004 the Israeli army was reported to have killed 113 Palestinians, the majority of them civilians (including 25 children). In January Palestinian guerrillas and suicide bombers killed four Israeli soldiers, two settlers and 11 civilians. After a series of bloody incursions by the Israeli army into Palestinian population centres in Gaza which left scores of Palestinians dead or injured, Hamas responded on 14 January by carrying out a suicide bombing against Israel at the Erez border crossing; three Israeli soldiers and a security guard were killed. On 28 January Israeli armed forces stormed the al-Zaytoun neighbourhood in central Gaza, killing at least eight Palestinians. Two weeks later, on 11 February, the Israeli army invaded the Shujaiya neighbourhood, to the east of Gaza. At least 15 Palestinians, including five civilians, were killed in the eight-hour incursion. The Israeli operation began as an undercover attempt to assassinate Sheikh Yassin.

More crucially, however, there were few signs that Israel was prepared to abandon its 'targeted killings' policy. On 25 December 2003 an Israeli helicopter gunship fired several missiles at a car travelling in the Sheikh Radwan neighbourhood of Gaza, killing five people. Among the victims was the head of Islamic Jihad's military wing. Israel also continued to demand that the PA dismantle the Palestinian 'terror organizations' and collect all illegal weapons; Sharon insisted on a 'total defeat' of the *intifada* as a *sine qua non* for the resumption of peace discussions with the Palestinians. In late November PLC Speaker Rafiq al-Natsheh had ruled out the possibility of any real breakthrough with Israel as long as Sharon stayed in power and the USA remained 'at Israel's beck and call'. Al-Natsheh, who stated that the PA was still committed to 'true peace and reconciliation' with Israel, dismissed Israel's purported willingness to reach a ceasefire with the Palestinians as 'tactical in nature and motivated by public relations considerations'. Hamas, on the other hand, realizing that a new truce with Israel was unrealistic, continued to advocate armed resistance.

THE RIGHT OF RETURN AND PALESTINIAN OPPOSITION TO THE GENEVA ACCORDS

On 1 December 2003 a group of Palestinian politicians and Israeli opposition figures signed and launched the 'Geneva Accords' (named after the Swiss city in which they were signed). The document, which had been concluded two months earlier by Palestinian and Israeli political figures including Abd al-Rabbuh and Yossi Beilin, laid out a plan for a peace agreement between Israel and the Palestinians. The PA did not officially adopt the Geneva Accords, but the 50-member Palestinian delegation, which signed the document in their personal capacity, were closely associated with the PA and President Arafat. As the new initiative was being launched, thousands of Palestinians took to the streets in the Palestinian territories to protest against and condemn the 'treacherous document'. In the Gaza Strip, home to more than 800,000 refugees, thousands of angry Palestinians called Palestinian signatories to the document 'traitors'. Palestinian opposition and Islamist leaders were particularly angered by the renunciation of the right of return. In Gaza City itself, hundreds of political leaders representing major Palestinian political strata, including key PLO figures, denounced the Geneva Accords and urged Arafat to reject them outright.

Palestinian opposition to the Geneva declaration centred on the following: first, the perception that the document nullified the right of return, both as a collective national right and as an individual right, of Palestinians to their homeland; second, the perception that the document provided a Palestinian cover for the exclusive nature of the Israeli polity as a 'Jewish State', thus failing to recognize the rights of the 1.2m. Arab citizens of Israel to live in a democratic state for all its citizens; third, that it accepted the reconfiguration of Jerusalem based on Israeli annexation plans, and that it granted Palestinian legitimacy to Israeli 'colonial' processes that altered the Arab character of Jerusalem; fourth, that it permanently accepted the presence of the vast majority of Israeli settlements in the West Bank; fifth, that it provided a Palestinian endorsement of a truncated and demilitarized Palestinian entity devoid of real sovereignty; and finally, that it left open all Israeli claims to the West Bank's water resources and airspace.

Faced with strong public opposition to the Geneva Accords, Arafat found himself in an unenviable position for, although it was reported that he had encouraged the Palestinian signatories, he was reluctant to speak out in support of the document for fear of losing stature, or even legitimacy. Arafat reportedly called it 'a brave initiative that would push the peace process forward', but refused to adopt it officially. Earlier, on 22 November 2003, Arafat loyalist Rafiq al-Natsheh denied that the PA had endorsed the document. Al-Natsheh stated that any final peace agreement with Israel would have to be approved by the Palestinian people both at home and abroad through a referendum. None the less, there was a general unanimity within Palestinian political circles that PA official al-Rabbuh would not have signed the document had he not received a 'green light' from Arafat. The latter's public hesitation was the outcome of the overwhelming opposition among Palestinians to the agreement, especially those parts tacitly conceding the right of return. Another reason explaining Arafat's equivocation was Sharon's 'total rejection' of the Accords on 1 December, having described them as 'amounting to suicide' for the Jewish state.

PALESTINIAN REACTIONS TO SHARON'S UNILATERAL GAZA PLAN

In his 'Herzliya speech' on 18 December 2003, Prime Minister Sharon presented the plan that Israel officially dubbed as 'disengagement from the Palestinians'. He vowed to take far-reaching unilateral measures against the Palestinians if they did not meet Israeli conditions for 'peace' within the next six or nine months. He stated that Israel would tighten its already firm grip on the Palestinian population centres in the West Bank, complete the construction of the 'separation barrier' (or 'security fence') and eventually redeploy the Israeli army to new lines, all for the purpose of 'disengaging from the Palestinians'. Sharon's 'disengagement plan' also envisaged the 'evacuation of all Jewish settlers' from the Gaza Strip, of which there were some 7,000 in more than 70 settlements. The Israeli Ministry of the Interior, however, reported on 30 December a 16% increase in the number of West Bank and Gaza settlers since Sharon came to power.

Sharon's 'unilateral' designs inevitably elicited strong Palestinian reactions. The PA leadership declared that a more appropriate name for Sharon's plan should be 'suffocating the Palestinians', as the plan would encircle Palestinian population centres in the West Bank with the security fence and Israeli military watchtowers, checkpoints and roadblocks. Inevitably, Palestinian leaders and media strongly condemned the plan, calling it 'another Israeli ploy to steal more Palestinian land'. They thought that if Sharon's designs were implemented, at least 58% of the West Bank area would in effect become part of Israel: the State of Israel would be in control of 90% of the land between the Mediterranean Sea and the river Jordan. The disjointed remaining 10% would be left to the Palestinians, who would be enclosed in a series of isolated enclaves behind a security barrier.

ISRAELI ASSASSINATIONS OF HAMAS LEADERS YASSIN AND AL-RANTISI

On 22 March 2004 Sheikh Ahmad Yassin, the founder and spiritual leader of Hamas, was killed by Israeli forces in the Gaza Strip by rockets fired from an Israeli helicopter as he was leaving a mosque in Gaza City. Sheikh Yassin was the most prominent Palestinian leader to be killed since the outbreak of the al-Aqsa *intifada*. According to the Israeli daily *Ha'aretz*, the Israeli Security Cabinet took the decision to target Yassin following a double suicide bombing at the Ashdod port earlier in March, in which at least 10 Israelis were killed. Sharon, who oversaw the operation, dismissed international condemnation and vowed to continue the war against Hamas.

As Hamas and other Palestinian resistance groups warned of an immediate upsurge in violence in the Middle East, an estimated 200,000 mourners poured onto the streets of Gaza for Yassin's funeral procession. Political leaders across the Arab world and beyond condemned Israel's action. Hamas threatened, for the first time, revenge on the USA as well as Israel, claiming that US backing of Israel had made Yassin's assassination possible. The USA, however, denied any prior knowledge of the operation. After Yassin's assassination, his successor as leader of Hamas in the Gaza Strip, Abd al-Aziz al-Rantisi, became a principal Israeli target. On 18 April 2004 al-Rantisi, his son and a bodyguard were also killed in an Israeli helicopter missile attack.

Meanwhile, on 29 January 2004 Israel released 400 Palestinian prisoners into the West Bank and Gaza Strip as part of a German-mediated prisoner swap agreement reached earlier in the week with Hezbollah; many were students from the Hebron region imprisoned for their affiliation with Islamist student blocs in local colleges. However, there were reportedly still as many as 7,500 Palestinian prisoners in Israeli gaols and detention centres, a large number of whom were interned without charge or trial.

THE TRIAL OF MARWAN BARGHOUTHI

On 20 May 2004 a Tel Aviv court convicted imprisoned Fatah leader Marwan Barghouthi on five counts of murder and of commanding a 'terrorist organization', relating to Palestinian militant attacks on Israeli forces and settlers. Marwan Barghouthi, who was viewed by many Palestinians as a potential successor to Arafat, had always rejected Israel's right to try him, arguing that Israel was an occupying power and that the Palestinians were victims of a military occupation that dehumanized them and denied them basic human rights. During a court hearing in the previous year Marwan Barghouthi reportedly told Israeli prosecutors that resistance was not 'terror' but rather a personal, human and national duty upon the oppressed. The PA strongly denounced the conviction of Marwan Barghouthi, calling it 'illegal, immoral and unjust'. According to the Palestinian Human Rights Monitoring Group, from the outset of the al-Aqsa *intifada* to 5 February 2004, a total of 2,826 Palestinians and 952 Israelis had been killed.

DEMOLITION OF PALESTINIAN HOUSES IN RAFAH, MAY–JUNE 2004

The Rafah area, a small strip of land at the southern edge of the Gaza Strip, became the target of a major military assault by the Israeli army during 17–20 May 2004, in which 43 Palestinians were killed, mostly civilians (among them nine children). On 19 May an Israeli helicopter gunship fired at a peaceful demonstration against Israel's campaign in Rafah, resulting in the deaths of some two dozen people. Israel declared that its operation in Rafah was in response to the killing of 13 of its troops at the hands of Palestinian militants, who had earlier deployed landmines against Israeli soldiers.

Following the escalation of the Rafah clashes, and the intensification of Israel's policy of demolishing houses along the Gaza–Sinai border, Egyptian intelligence chief Omar Suleiman returned on 25 May 2004 to hold extensive discussions with Palestinian and Israeli leaders for the purpose of reactivating the ceasefire plan. His discussions came as Israeli tanks were withdrawing from Rafah, ending a 10-day operation and home demolitions, in which dozens of Palestinian civilians were killed and hundreds of homes were destroyed. According to Israeli sources, Suleiman informed Israeli leaders of Egypt's willingness to play a more active role along the Rafah–Sinai borders in the event of an Israeli military withdrawal from Gaza. Suleiman also told Israeli leaders that if Israel carried out an 'honest and complete withdrawal from Gaza', Egypt would make serious efforts to maintain security on the borders and prevent the smuggling of weapons from Sinai to the Gaza Strip—a message that he later relayed to the Palestinian leadership. However, the Egyptian official made clear that his Government's commitments to that effect would be honoured only if Israel stopped all assassinations, incursions and attacks in Gaza.

Following the discussions with Suleiman, the PA leadership restated its readiness to 'assume its responsibilities' in the Gaza Strip following the 'presumed' Israeli withdrawal. The PA also undertook to present a workable plan for the Gaza Strip, which would include the unification of Palestinian security agencies, as well as a readiness to prevent security violations. Suleiman reportedly proposed the formation of a committee, comprising the USA, Israel, Egypt and the PA, to oversee the implementation of the Gaza withdrawal plan.

However, PA officials dismissed Sharon's purported willingness to negotiate with the PA as a 'public relations' exercise.

THE INTERNATIONAL COURT OF JUSTICE'S RULING ON THE 'SEPARATION BARRIER'

In December 2003 the UN General Assembly (UNGA) approved a resolution asking the International Court of Justice (ICJ) in The Hague, Netherlands, to consider the legality of the controversial 'separation barrier' that Israel was building inside the West Bank in an attempt to prevent Palestinian militants from infiltrating Israeli territory. (In October the UNGA had adopted a resolution demanding that Israel halt construction of the barrier.) The Palestinians argued that the barrier, which cut into West Bank territory, was designed to redraw borders ahead of any future peace settlement. On 23 February 2004 the ICJ, which has the power to issue legal opinions but does not have any power to impose rulings or sanctions, began examining the barrier issue. On the same day thousands of Palestinians and international peace activists took to the streets throughout the West Bank and Gaza Strip to protest against its construction. Palestinian representatives argued that Israel's barrier made the creation of a viable Palestinian state impossible.

On 9 July 2004 the ICJ gave its long-awaited advisory opinion, ruling that Israel's separation barrier in the West Bank contravened international law; that it must be dismantled; and that compensation must be paid by Israel to the Palestinian owners of property confiscated for its construction. The ICJ found that the construction of the first 200 km of the planned 700-km barrier was causing widespread confiscation and destruction of Palestinian property, and the disruption of the lives of thousands of civilians. The ICJ decision branded Israel's vast concrete and steel barrier through the West Bank a political rather than a security measure. The court concluded that the barrier severely impeded the Palestinian right to self-determination, in breach of the Geneva Convention and international humanitarian law. It appealed to the UN to consider measures against Israel and stated that signatories to the Geneva Convention, including the UK and the USA, were obliged to ensure that Israel upheld the ruling.

The Palestinian leadership hailed the ruling as a landmark judgment that could mobilize international opinion. Israel rejected the ruling, but on 20 July 2004 the UNGA voted to demand that Israel comply with the ICJ ruling and remove the barrier. The UK supported the resolution, but the USA opposed it.

ONGOING CRISIS WITHIN FATAH

In February 2004 more than 350 low- and medium-ranking members resigned from Fatah in protest against the lack of political and organizational reform, corruption, and the leadership's enduring failure to challenge effectively the Israeli occupation. Fatah's constitution required leadership elections every five years, but none had been held since 1989. This chronic malaise created deep disenchantment among younger grass-roots members. Fatah was also plagued by its unclear and overlapping relationship with the PA, in which many Fatah leaders from the Central Committee and Revolutionary Council held key positions. Moreover, the uprising had greatly strained whatever semblance of ideological homogeneity Fatah had possessed. Some factions of the movement, particularly in the northern part of the West Bank, had in effect 'converted' to the Islamist camp, with many field guerrillas and activists joining, either formally or practically, Hamas and Islamic Jihad.

The internal Fatah crisis escalated in July 2004 amid rebellion in the Gaza Strip against PA corruption and incompetence, and a threat by Prime Minister Quray to bring down the administration if he were not given more powers. On 17 July, in a desperate attempt to stem growing anarchy in the Strip, Arafat dismissed two senior security commanders, Ghazi al-Jabali (national police chief) and Abd al-Razek al-Majaydeh (Commander of the General Security Services), declared a state of emergency, and sent loyal troops to protect government buildings. In a highly controversial move, the deeply unpopular Musa Arafat, the head of the Palestinian intelligence service and President Arafat's cousin, replaced al-Majaydeh. Furthermore, under Egyptian pressure, Arafat promised to amalgamate the overlapping groups of rival security forces in Gaza into a more coherent three-branched model. On 18 July Arafat rejected the 'resignation' of Quray, who stated that he was appalled at the chaos reigning in Gaza.

However, Fatah dissenters dismissed Arafat's 'reforms' as inadequate. They also criticized Quray for being part of the corrupt PA system. The al-Aqsa Martyrs Brigades directed their criticism against Musa Arafat, accusing him of personal corruption. On 18 July 2004 the head of the Gaza coastguard resigned in protest against the appointment of Musa Arafat, as did other security officials in Gaza; these resignations appeared to persuade the PA leader to change his mind, and on 20 July Quray agreed to stay in office as 'caretaker' Prime Minister. (Musa Arafat eventually retired in April 2005, but was assassinated by Palestinian gunmen in September at his home in Gaza City.)

REFRAMING GAZA

On 29 September 2004 the Israeli military launched Operation Days of Penitence, the most extensive incursion into the Gaza Strip since the beginning of the al-Aqsa *intifada* and the largest Israeli offensive within the Occupied Territories since the 2002 reoccupation of the West Bank. The backdrop for the incursion was Sharon's Gaza redeployment plan and the need to prevent Palestinian fighters from using northern Gaza as a launching pad for rocket attacks on Israeli border towns. Sharon rejected the concept of a Palestinian negotiating partner, owing to the territorial concessions that any negotiated agreement would entail. The Gaza redeployment plan became popular in Israel partly because the Labour Party had failed to conclude a viable agreement with the Palestinians under the framework of the Oslo Accords. The resulting four years of violent conflict saw a growing majority of the Israeli public prepared once again to consider 'unilateral disengagement'. In December 2004 the Labour Party, led by Peres, joined Likud in a unity Government committed to the Gaza redeployment plan.

From an Israeli point of view, the redeployment plan had the advantage of not relinquishing physical control of the Gaza Strip, while freezing any discussion on the peace process, the creation of a Palestinian state, refugees and borders. Although Sharon was determined to act unilaterally, his Government sought Palestinian partners in Gaza to implement the plan. Rather than seeking to scuttle Sharon's plan, former Gaza security chief Dahlan and his erstwhile patron Abbas (who had succeeded Arafat in November 2004 as leader of the politically dominant Fatah movement) believed that redeployment could establish the basis for renewed international engagement leading to an Israeli-Palestinian settlement. Dahlan held that the ability of Fatah to ensure stability in the Gaza Strip in the wake of an eventual Israeli redeployment would both place it at the helm of the political system and mark it out as a 'reliable partner' for Israel and the international community. Dahlan's faction of Fatah contended for influence in the Gaza Strip with a rival grouping encompassing Hamas and a broad array of Islamist and nationalist militants. In contrast with Dahlan's faction, the radical trend saw Israeli redeployment, through the prism of Hezbollah's success in Lebanon, as vindication of the strategy of armed struggle to force Israel to withdraw under fire. Hamas's tactics had included bold attacks on Israeli positions and the launching of home-made missiles into Israel. Dahlan's strategy, on the other hand, was predicated on his ability to neutralize the radical Islamists and promote a Palestinian ceasefire. His other urgent priority had been to establish control over the Palestinian security forces and Fatah itself in Gaza.

ARAFAT'S DEATH

In mid-October 2004, after enduring prolonged ill health at his Ramallah headquarters (the *muqata'a*), Arafat fell seriously ill. On 25 October the Israeli Government granted Arafat permission to leave the *muqata'a* to visit a Ramallah hospital, but on 29 October he was flown with his wife to a military hospital in Paris. Arafat's condition continued to deteriorate; according to hospital sources, the Palestinian leader had fallen into a deep coma and was brain-dead.

Arafat's failing health left Palestinians in a state of political crisis. In Ramallah Palestinian security chiefs held an emergency meeting at the *muqata'a* to discuss how to handle the likely event of Arafat's imminent death. The PLO leadership in the West Bank agreed to cede more of Arafat's powers to Quray, the Prime Minister. Quray and his Minister of Foreign Affairs, Shaath, travelled to the Gaza Strip to press Palestinian factions there to avoid internal conflict during the crisis. After meeting representatives of all 13 Palestinian factions, including Hamas and Islamic Jihad, in Gaza City on 6–7 November 2004, Quray announced that agreement had been reached to avoid in-fighting. Meanwhile, in Ramallah, former premier Abbas was named by the Fatah Revolutionary Council as the new head of the PLO, and PLC Speaker Rawhi Fattouh was sworn in as caretaker President of the PA.

On 10 November 2004 Palestinian officials announced that Arafat was close to death after having suffered a brain haemorrhage; his death was announced on 11 November. Palestinians gave credence to rumours of poisoning by Mossad; however, this theory was ruled out following a PA investigation in 2005. However, after the reported emergence of new evidence, which led his widow to initiate legal proceedings in France in July 2012, it was announced that French prosecutors were to launch an inquiry into whether the former Palestinian leader had in fact died as a result of radioactive poisoning.

Arafat had previously stated that he wished to be interred at the Haram al-Sharif, inside Jerusalem's Old City. However, Israel attempted to force a burial in the Gaza Strip, saying that it was making preparations for Arab leaders and foreign dignitaries to travel there without passing through Israel. Nevertheless, Erekat of the PA announced that the burial would take place at the wrecked *muqata'a*, 'the symbol of the steadfastness of the Palestinian people, the President's place of siege'. On 12 November 2004, after a funeral in Cairo attended by Arab leaders and world dignitaries, Arafat's body was buried in Ramallah. Some of the tens of thousands of Palestinians in attendance wore the black masks of Hamas or the al-Aqsa Martyrs Brigades, and carried guns or swords.

PRESIDENTIAL ELECTION

A presidential election was scheduled for 9 January 2005. Although the new head of the PLO, 69-year-old Mahmoud Abbas, was favoured by Fatah's Central Committee, the family and political associates of the much younger Marwan Barghouthi declared that he was interested in contesting the presidency. The incarcerated Marwan Barghouthi had strong appeal on the Palestinian street as the former head of Fatah's Tanzim in the West Bank. He also had widespread support as one of a younger generation of leaders committed to political reform and had been at the forefront of the al-Aqsa *intifada*. In early December 2004 Marwan Barghouthi reversed his initial decision not to challenge Abbas, and unexpectedly threw open the Palestinian ballot by registering as an independent candidate just hours before the deadline. Marwan Barghouthi's break with Fatah, however, drew stiff criticism from allies and other Fatah reformers who argued that dividing the movement played into Israel's hands. On 12 December Marwan Barghouthi, under intense pressure, dropped out of the race. In an open letter from gaol, he remained critical of the Fatah leadership for apparently abandoning armed resistance, but indicated that he would support Abbas.

Abbas won by a clear majority in the 9 January 2005 presidential election, which was restricted to Palestinians inside the West Bank and Gaza Strip; final results gave Abbas 62.5% of the vote, and his nearest rival, Mustafa Barghouthi, 19.5%. The Central Elections Commission (CEC) reported that 45.6% of the 1.8m. Palestinians who were eligible to vote had participated. The EU observer team asserted that the election represented 'a genuine effort to conduct a regular electoral process. However, the [Israeli] occupation and continuing violence, as well as restrictions on freedom of movement, meant that a truly free election was always going to be difficult to achieve'. Hamas, which had boycotted the poll, declared that it would work with Abbas but complained of electoral irregularities.

Abbas was sworn in as PA President on 15 January 2005. He stated that he was extending the hand of peace to Israel and that he denounced violence. However, prior to the inauguration ceremony, Israel had severed ties with Abbas in response to an attack by Palestinian fighters on a Gaza cargo crossing in which six Israeli workers were killed, announcing that it would only renew contacts with him once he reined in the militants. In his first speech to the PLC as President in Ramallah, Abbas identified his priorities as: national liberation; ending Israeli occupation and establishing a Palestinian state within the 1967 borders, with Jerusalem as its capital; and reaching a 'just and agreed solution to the refugee problem on the basis of international resolutions', including UN Resolution 194 of December 1948 and the resolution approved at the March 2002 Arab summit in Beirut, Lebanon. He also emphasized his commitment to the roadmap as a 'matter of Palestinian national interest'. In return, he expected Israel to implement its obligations.

On 8 February 2005 Abbas met Israeli Prime Minister Sharon in the Red Sea resort of Sharm el-Sheikh, at a summit hosted by Egyptian President Hosni Mubarak. It was the Palestinian leader's first meeting with Sharon since succeeding Arafat. Abbas and Sharon agreed a ceasefire and pledged to 'end violence' after more than four years of confrontation. As part of the Sharm el-Sheikh agreement, Israel agreed to hand over control of five West Bank towns to the PA within three weeks and to release 500 Palestinian political prisoners. The two sides also agreed to set up several joint committees, and their leaders reiterated that future negotiations would be conducted under the aegis of the roadmap. Hamas reacted to the summit by saying that, although it was not bound by the ceasefire declaration, it had no intention of being the first to break it.

NEW PALESTINIAN CABINET

On 23 February 2005 the PLC approved a new line-up of ministers proposed by Abbas, in a Cabinet in which 'technocrats' replaced several Arafat loyalists. The vote was a key test for Abbas. Initially, Prime Minister Quray had proposed to the PLC a cabinet consisting largely of the ministers who had been in office under Arafat, but the PLC had rejected this. Fatah's Central Committee was forced to produce new candidates, to the delight of PA reformists. The new Cabinet, again led by Quray, committed itself to reform. The most important new ministers were: Dr Nasser al-Kidwa, Arafat's nephew and for many years Palestinian Permanent Observer to the UN, who became Minister of Foreign Affairs; Dahlan, Minister of Civil Affairs, whose job entailed dealing with Israel; and Maj.-Gen. Nasser Yousuf, Minister of the Interior and National Security. Yousuf's main role would be to reorganize the security forces and 'maintain the ceasefire'. Yousuf had been responsible for a crackdown on Hamas in 1997 following a spate of suicide bombs in Israel. Shaath, the former Minister of Foreign Affairs, was appointed Deputy Prime Minister.

MUNICIPAL ELECTIONS: HAMAS'S ELECTORAL BREAKTHROUGH

Following Arafat's death, a series of elections was held: local elections in the West Bank (December 2004); the presidential poll (January 2005); local elections in Gaza and the remainder of the West Bank (May 2005); and finally legislative elections (January 2006). In conjunction with the unilateral Israeli withdrawal from Gaza in September 2005, these polls would do much to shape PA politics in the post-Arafat era.

The first municipal elections were held on 23 December 2004. Palestinians in 26 West Bank towns and villages cast their votes. Turnout was reported at 81% of the 144,000 eligible voters. Fatah secured 136 of the 306 council seats, representing 44.4% of the vote, closely followed by Hamas, with a total of 109 seats (35.6%). Independent candidates won 40 of the remaining seats, and 21 were split between representatives of local tribes and left-wing groups. Of the 887 local council candidates, one in six were women, all of whom won seats, owing partly to a clause in the Palestinian electoral laws that stipulates that women candidates must constitute at least 16% of elected representatives.

Following the presidential election, held on 9 January 2005, polls were conducted on 5 May to elect municipal council representatives in both the West Bank and Gaza. There had been no municipal elections in Gaza since the end of the British Mandate in 1948; in recent years all the previous Gaza town officials had been Fatah appointees. Municipal elections had last been held in the West Bank in 1976. Some 3,000 Palestinian security officers ensured public order at the polling stations. Israel had informed the CEC that its army would not enter any of the areas where elections were scheduled to be held from the evening of 4 May until the morning of 6 May 2005. Nevertheless, voting in several localities in the northern part of the West Bank was disrupted by Israeli army incursions. One serious violation also occurred when masked men stormed two polling stations in the West Bank village of Attarah and destroyed three ballot boxes. Although officially Fatah won a majority of the seats (56%), Hamas took at least 33% and the PFLP received a large share of the remaining seats, with some seats going to independent candidates and left-wing factions. This meant that 45 out of 84 municipal councils had a majority of Fatah representatives, 23 had a majority of Hamas representatives and 16 had a majority from left and independent lists. However, Hamas's leader in Gaza, Mahmud al-Zahar, subsequently disputed the official results. He claimed that Hamas had won 34 municipalities, including 11 municipalities that were officially categorized as having been won by independent candidates but were in practice Hamas affiliates who had concealed their true identities fearing persecution and arrest by Israel.

Hamas's full participation in the local elections and its declared intention to take part in the PLC elections appeared to represent a major victory for the democratic process in the Palestinian territories. Moreover, Hamas and other militant groups had earlier committed themselves to a de facto ceasefire, in order to allow Abbas some negotiating power. If Hamas could translate its street popularity and municipal success into an effective political campaign, then institutional power would be within its reach. For Fatah, the local elections sent a clear signal that it could not afford to isolate itself from the electorate or take power for granted. The municipal elections also suggested that, despite the international media attention given to the presidential election, the democratic priorities of the Palestinian people in the West Bank and Gaza centred on local matters. The high voter turnout further suggested that legitimization of political power could be found at the grassroots level of Palestinian civil society; however, the challenge remained to translate local democracy into national institutions such as the PLC and PA ministries.

HAMAS GAINS LEGISLATIVE MAJORITY

In May 2005 the CEC signalled its intention to postpone the parliamentary elections, scheduled for 17 July, for several months, ostensibly to allow time for further preparations. It was not entirely clear whether Abbas himself had originally sought the postponement. 'Democratic elections' were the cornerstone of the agreements he had signed with all the political factions in Cairo in March and a condition for the ceasefire. Nevertheless, he appeared swayed by the advice given by the USA, the EU and Egypt: to defer all elections so that the PA could consolidate its rule in Gaza and 'win back' the popular support that was now flowing to Hamas. Fatah's electoral standing had been seriously damaged by a long history of corruption and inefficiency, especially during its exclusive control of the PA throughout its 11-year existence. Abbas issued a presidential decree in June confirming the postponement, until further notice. The delay allowed Fatah to capitalize on Israel's withdrawal from the Gaza Strip, scheduled to take effect in mid-August.

The Palestinian public was largely hostile to the postponement, and the move increased the already heightened tensions between Fatah and Hamas as a result of the dispute over local election results. The situation degenerated into the worst period of fighting in the Occupied Territories since the

Palestinian factions had committed themselves to a ceasefire in March 2005. This further undermined the Abbas regime's legitimacy, which had already been damaged by the apparent lack of diplomatic progress with Israel and the perceived inadequacy of the reform of the security forces and other PA institutions. In early June officers from PA Military Intelligence attacked the PLC building in Gaza City, closed roads in Rafah and briefly abducted a PA diplomat en route to Egypt. The officers feared that proposed reforms would deprive them of some of their privileges and autonomy. Meanwhile, on 5 June militiamen from Fatah's al-Aqsa Martyrs Brigades laid siege to the governor's house in Nablus in protest against the PA's failure to provide the Brigades with protection and salaries commensurate with their status as the 'armed resistance'. The Ministry of the Interior pacified the two revolts by in effect yielding to their demands. These challenges to law and order were exacerbated by other developments. Despite a court decision annulling election results in three Gaza municipalities where Hamas had won majorities, Hamas officials had taken up PA offices, creating a situation of de facto dual power. New elections were postponed indefinitely in order to defuse the tension.

The legislative elections were subsequently rescheduled for 25 January 2006. Hamas had earlier stated that, in return for acquiescing to the postponement of the poll, Abbas had promised an amendment to the election laws that could favour the Islamist movement. Hamas had wanted one-half of the legislators to be chosen on the basis of district constituencies and the other half on the basis of party lists. Apparently, Abbas had agreed to such a system in early 2005 when he brokered an informal Hamas ceasefire with Israel, but had subsequently stated that he would prefer all legislators to be chosen from party lists. Meanwhile, Palestinians in the Gaza Strip held large celebrations to mark the completion of the Israeli military's withdrawal from the territory on 12 September 2005.

Sixteen constituencies in the West Bank and Gaza Strip were scheduled to elect 132 deputies to the PLC. Under the new system, one-half of the 132 seats would be chosen by proportional representation, with the rest being contested by individual candidates in a 'first-past-the-post' system. The Palestinian Elections Law stipulated that at least one woman should be among the first three names on any party list, at least one woman among the next four names, and at least one woman among each five names after that. Six seats were guaranteed to Palestinian Christian candidates. Palestinian residents in the West Bank, Gaza Strip and East Jerusalem were allowed to vote, and there were about 1.34m. eligible voters. The 100,000 eligible voters living in occupied East Jerusalem had their own special arrangements. Initially, Israel had threatened to ban voting there, but, after international pressure, it decided to allow Palestinian residents to vote through an 'absentee ballot' at five city post offices, as had happened in 1996. In reality, however, only 6,300 residents were allowed to vote in this way; the remainder had to travel outside the (Israeli-defined) city boundaries. Israel also refused to allow Hamas to campaign in Jerusalem.

Hamas ran an effective campaign centred on government corruption, under the title of the Change and Reform list, in order to avoid a ban on its direct participation. Hamas's manifesto combined an established social welfare programme and generally pragmatic Islamic principles with a 'pro-resistance' stance towards Israel. Conspicuous in its exclusion from the manifesto was Hamas's commitment, enshrined in its charter, to destroy Israel through *jihad* and replace it with an Islamic state; however, the manifesto did pledge to use any means necessary to defend the Palestinian nation and establish a state with Jerusalem as its capital.

Hamas won a majority in the new PLC, securing 74 of the 132 parliamentary seats and earning the right to form the next administration under President Abbas. Fatah, a dominant force in Palestinian politics since the late 1960s, suffered a historic defeat, emerging with 45 seats. The strategic failure of the Oslo process and a record of poor governance through the PA contributed to the defeat. Internal divisions also played a role, as a younger and more radical grouping (the 'new guard'), led by the gaoled Marwan Barghouthi, had registered its own list of candidates for the elections, although the group had agreed to rejoin a unified list shortly before the deadline for registration. A collection of nationalist, leftist and independent parties claimed the remainder of the seats.

Hamas's spectacular victory stunned the Israelis, their US allies and the EU. All three reacted by repeatedly stating that they would not work with or fund a PA that included Hamas, which they classified as a terrorist organization. Meeting on 30 January 2006, the Quartet group announced that financial assistance to a future Palestinian administration would depend on the extent to which Hamas as a partner fulfilled the following conditions: that it renounce violence; respect agreements approved under the Fatah regime; and recognize Israel's right to exist. Hamas rejected the conditions, asserting that the Quartet group should have demanded an end to Israeli 'occupation and aggression' and arguing that the Oslo process had not benefited the Palestinians. Following the inauguration of the new Cabinet, led by Ismail Haniya, on 28 March, the USA and the EU declared the withdrawal of all direct aid to the PA until Hamas complied with the terms. Sanctions and a funding boycott resulted in Palestinian public revenues declining by 40%–50%.

Fatah adjusted poorly to forfeiting its dominant position in both the PLC and the PA. The Palestinian electorate's switch of support to Hamas was widely interpreted as a form of popular protest against Fatah's endemic corruption and authoritarianism. Competition for jobs and access to limited resources intensified after the elections, with occasional violent clashes between the armed militias and security forces. Fatah resisted attempts by Hamas to tempt it into an administration of national unity. Instead, Abbas tried to maintain his role determining Palestinian national policy and controlling the PA security services, although he still needed PLC approval for his budget and legislative proposals. Hamas's victory undermined Abbas's efforts to seek negotiations with Israel, with Hamas repeatedly refusing to recognize Israel and renounce violence. Abbas also publicly quarrelled with Hamas's Minister of the Interior over control of the security forces in Gaza.

Neighbouring Jordan supported international efforts to isolate and undermine the Hamas administration. In April 2006 the Jordanian authorities accused Hamas of stockpiling arms on Jordanian territory—allegations that Hamas officials denied—and cancelled a visit by the Palestinian Minister of Foreign Affairs, Dr Mahmoud al-Zahar, to Amman. In July the Jordanian Arab Bank turned back remittances intended for PLC members, saying that it was not prepared to deal with PLC members affiliated with Hamas.

THE 'PRISONERS' DOCUMENT'

On 27 June 2006 representatives of Fatah and Hamas agreed to a joint political platform, which contained implicit recognition of Israel's existence. The representatives approved a document drawn up in early May by several Palestinian political prisoners in Israeli gaols, led by Marwan Barghouthi and fellow prisoner Sheikh Abd al-Khaleq Natshe of Hamas. Setting out 18 points for a return to negotiations with Israel, the document demanded the creation of a Palestinian state, with Jerusalem as the capital, on all land occupied by Israel in 1967. It did not explicitly recognize Israel's right to the territories that it controlled prior to the 1967 war. Moreover, it did not renounce violence, as demanded by the Quartet group, but advocated that 'resistance' be limited to the Occupied Territories under a 'unified resistance front'. It also appealed for the formation of a national unity administration in which the major parliamentary blocs, especially Hamas and Fatah, but also other parties that supported the document's principles, would be represented. Israel was to recognize the Palestinian 'right of return' and release all Palestinian prisoners and detainees.

President Abbas seized on the prisoners' document and issued an ultimatum to Hamas to announce its recognition of Israel within 10 days or face a referendum on the matter. Hamas's senior leadership initially discounted the document as an untenable compromise on its own position regarding Israel, but came under intense Palestinian pressure to accept it, reinforced by the crippling economic sanctions imposed by foreign donors. An opinion poll carried out in June 2006 revealed that 77% of Palestinians supported the prisoners' document. In late June Hamas endorsed the document and agreed in principle to a power-sharing administration with Fatah, committed to a negotiated two-state settlement and negotiations with Israel on the basis of an independent Palestinian state on territories occupied in 1967. Nevertheless, Hamas emphasized that its acceptance of the document did not constitute explicit recognition of Israel, while the group's military wing and its political leaders in exile continued to oppose the agreement, an opposition likely to complicate any attempt to implement it.

THE KIDNAP OF CORPORAL GILAD SHALIT

The Israeli Government of Ehud Olmert, formed in May 2006, adopted the former Cabinet's policy of insisting that the Hamas-led Palestinian administration recognize Israel's right to exist before it would allow peace negotiations to be restarted, and continued to advocate plans to annex large parts of the West Bank and fix Israel's border unilaterally. The Gaza Strip remained under siege; Gazan targets were routinely attacked; and Palestinian fighters fired homemade *Qassam* missiles into Israel in response, mainly towards the town of Sderot. Tensions escalated in June after shelling killed a family of Palestinians on a beach in northern Gaza. On 25 June eight Hamas fighters from Gaza launched a raid into Israel: after a gun battle that left two dead on either side, an Israeli corporal, Gilad Shalit, was kidnapped and taken to Gaza. The Palestinian fighters stated that the kidnapping had been carried out in a bid to secure an exchange of prisoners. Israel reacted by shelling bridges and a power plant in the Strip, and by reinvading southern and northern Gaza. Operation Summer Rain was ostensibly ordered to free Shalit. Water and electricity were cut off to one-half of the Strip and supplies of food halted.

On 29 June 2006 Israel arrested 64 senior Palestinian officials, including one-third of the Palestinian Cabinet (eight Hamas ministers) and 20 other parliamentarians. The Palestinian Deputy Prime Minister, Dr Nasser al-Shaer, went into hiding to avoid capture, and an Israeli minister hinted that even Prime Minister Haniya would not be exempt from arrest or possible assassination. The Israeli Government's undeclared objective appeared to be the ousting of the democratically elected administration of Hamas. The next day an Israeli missile destroyed the offices of the Palestinian Ministry of the Interior and Civil Affairs in Gaza City. On 2 July another strike destroyed Haniya's office. On 6 July Israeli forces and Palestinian fighters fought a fierce battle, with reports of at least 25 Palestinian deaths, mostly civilian. In the period between late June and 23 July Israeli troops killed more than 160 Palestinians, the majority of whom were women and children, and injured hundreds more. Israel arrested a further member of the Hamas regime, Speaker of the PLC Aziz Duweik, on 5 August.

THE MECCA AGREEMENT AND 'COALITION GOVERNMENT'

In December 2006 the continuing political deadlock between the PA-dominated presidency and the Hamas administration compelled Abbas to call for the holding of early presidential and parliamentary elections. However, he lacked the authority to enforce such a demand; early elections held with the dissent of Hamas and other factions would have been politically unsustainable. Consequently, in January 2007 Abbas met the head of Hamas's political bureau, Meshaal, in Damascus to discuss the formation of a 'coalition government'. However, no agreement was reached. On 6 February the two men embarked on another attempt to form a 'unity government', at a meeting hosted by King Abdullah of Saudi Arabia in the holy city of Mecca. Two days of intensive negotiations produced an agreement. The symbolism of holding the discussions at Islam's holiest site seemed to have some effect, with the promise of US $1,000m. in Saudi aid acting as a further incentive. In the Gaza Strip, people took to the streets to cheer the signing of the deal, which had ended months of violence between Fatah and Hamas. The 'national unity Government' was formed in March, led by Ismail Haniya of Hamas. Hamas received nine posts, while Fatah was allotted six and other smaller parties four. Independents were given responsibility for key portfolios. Fayyad, a respected technocrat, became the Minister of Finance—a position he had held previously during 2002–05. For the long-suffering Palestinians, the real value of a 'national unity Government' was the expectation that international aid would be resumed. However, the West had demanded much more: Hamas still had to recognize Israel, renounce violence and formally accept existing agreements with Israel. This partly explained the USA's muted response to the Mecca agreement.

HAMAS TAKES CONTROL OF GAZA

Throughout the first half of 2007 growing Israeli and Western pressures had disastrous consequences for internal Palestinian affairs. Israel and the USA seemed determined to undermine the Hamas-led 'coalition Government', and they facilitated a marked increase in the military capability of the Fatah-controlled Special Presidential Guard. Gaza witnessed renewed internecine violence between Hamas and Fatah, as the PA remained largely incapable of governing the Strip.

Lawlessness and the proliferation of armed groups in the Strip extended to the spread of militant Salafism, influenced by the al-Qa'ida network. This was exemplified by the kidnapping at gunpoint in Gaza City of a reporter for the British Broadcasting Corporation, Alan Johnston, in March 2007. The Army of Islam, a Salafi group centred around the powerful Dughmush clan, was held responsible and was also suspected of being behind the kidnappings of other foreigners in Gaza. The clan's activities were described by PA officials as being largely criminal, involving extortion, smuggling and arms-dealing. In May the group issued an audio tape demanding the release of Muslim preacher Abu Qatada, who was held in prison in the UK on suspicion of being a key al-Qa'ida figure in Europe. In July, following the military takeover of the Gaza Strip by Hamas, the Army of Islam was forced, under threat of military action from Hamas, to release Johnston.

Despite the formation of the national unity administration in March 2007, the power struggle between Hamas and Fatah in Gaza continued and the spectre of an open civil war was much in evidence. Fighting in Gaza continued to escalate, and around 80 Palestinians were killed in factional clashes between mid-May and mid-July. The immediate cause of friction was the struggle for control of the security services, but the conflict was not totally detached from the abysmal social and economic conditions in Gaza, exacerbated by international sanctions.

On 5 June 2007 gunmen from Hamas and Fatah fought each other in the Strip, and President Abbas himself warned that the Palestinians were now on the brink of civil war. On 11 June at least 13 Palestinians were killed in factional fighting in Gaza, three of whom died in a gun battle inside a hospital. In Gaza City government offices were fired upon and the killings became increasingly brutal. Heavy gun battles erupted in several locations in the Gaza Strip on 12 June, as better organized and better disciplined Hamas fighters captured positions from Fatah supporters. Hamas militants launched a successful attack on the headquarters of the Fatah-controlled security forces in northern Gaza. Hamas issued an ultimatum to Fatah supporters to abandon their posts in the Strip, prompting President Abbas to accuse Hamas of attempting to stage a military coup. Meanwhile, the head of the Egyptian mediation team in the Strip, Lt-Col Burhan Hamad, announced that neither side had responded to his appeal to hold truce discussions.

The Gaza battles were won decisively by Hamas. By 13 June 2007 hundreds of Fatah fighters had surrendered to Hamas, which systematically took control of security positions in the north and south of Gaza, leaving the main battle for the Strip's security and political nerve centre, in Gaza City, until last. At the same time, however, across the West Bank hundreds of Fatah gunmen stormed Hamas-controlled institutions, seeking revenge for the Islamist movement's takeover of the Strip. Dozens of terrified Fatah officials and fighters tried to flee the Strip via Israel and Egypt. Abbas dismissed Prime Minister

Haniya and dissolved his 'unity Government'. Haniya, in a bid to consolidate control over the Strip, sought to reorganize the previously Fatah-dominated National Security Forces; he appointed a new security chief, Maj.-Gen. Said Fanouna. Hamas also accused Dahlan, formerly the Fatah 'strongman' in Gaza (who had been in Cairo for medical treatment during most of the fighting), of attempting a coup against the Hamas leadership.

FATAH RETRENCHMENT IN THE WEST BANK AND THE EMERGENCY GOVERNMENT OF SALAM FAYYAD

Fatah continued to exercise influence in Palestinian cities of the Israeli-occupied West Bank, even though the PA remained without any real power in the territory. Yet, with two separate Palestinian administrations, the separation between the West Bank and Gaza was widening and consequently endangering further the prospect of future Palestinian political unity. Abbas continued to reject pleas from the Arab League to meet with Hamas's exiled leader in Syria, Meshaal. He refused to conduct dialogue with Hamas until the Islamist movement withdrew its forces from former Fatah positions in Gaza. To the delight of Western donors, Abbas installed former Minister of Finance Salam Fayyad as the new Prime Minister in Ramallah. Fayyad had worked at the World Bank in Washington, DC, in 1987–95 and had then served as the IMF's representative to the Palestinian territories until 2001.

Abbas was supported by the USA, the EU and most Arab regimes, and, in a major boost for the Palestinian President, the US consul-general in Jerusalem, Jacob Walles, announced that the US Administration would end its 15 months of sanctions once the new Palestinian administration was in place. Fayyad moved quickly to form an 'emergency government'. On 17 June 2007 his administration was sworn in at the presidential compound in Ramallah; it comprised 12 ministers, most of them from the West Bank. Fayyad himself held three portfolios: Prime Minister, Minister of Finance, and briefly Minister of Foreign Affairs (Riyad al-Maliki assumed the foreign affairs portfolio in July). The administration included two Christians and two women. Fayyad announced that his main priority was restoring law and order. Earlier, Abbas had signed a decree granting himself, as President, the power to make decisions without PLC approval (Hamas still held an elected majority in the PLC). A second decree issued by Abbas outlawed the paramilitary force of Hamas and other 'militias' linked to the Islamist group. In reality, however, the ban could not be enforced.

On 18 June 2007 the USA and the EU rewarded Abbas's 'West Bank government' by lifting their economic and political boycott of the Palestinian administration. On 24 June Israel also agreed to release some of the US $350m. in blocked tax revenues to Fayyad's administration. Palestinian officials, however, insisted that Israel owed the PA as much as $700m. The Israeli move was announced on the eve of a summit in Sharm el-Sheikh between Israeli Prime Minister Olmert, President Abbas, President Mubarak of Egypt and King Abdullah of Jordan. The meeting was aimed at bolstering the 'West Bank government' of Fayyad, leaving Hamas isolated in Gaza. On 4 July, three days after Israel began transferring $117m. of withheld Palestinian taxes to the 'West Bank government', thousands of Palestinian civil servants began receiving their first full salaries for 16 months. An estimated 170,000 employees on the PA's books had received only partial pay packets since March 2006. However, the Fayyad administration refused to pay civil servants hired by Hamas in Gaza.

On 27 November 2007 the Annapolis International Conference was held at the US Naval Academy in Annapolis, Maryland, and was attended by 40 leaders, including Abbas, Israeli Prime Minister Olmert and US President George W. Bush. The conference aimed ostensibly to relaunch serious negotiations between Israel and the PA for the first time in seven years, but was devised partly to strengthen the standing of Abbas. In the event, Annapolis ended inconclusively. The six core issues at the heart of the conflict (the 'final status' issues—Jerusalem, refugees and their right of return, borders, settlements, water, and security) remained unresolved, and Israel and the PA had agreed only to hold new discussions, which were to begin on 12 December. The Israeli Government appeared unwilling to make concessions on any of the fundamental questions, and the USA did not seem prepared to exert serious pressure on the Israelis. The Israeli Government continued its construction of the 'separation barrier' that bisected Palestinian territory on the West Bank, and continued to expand Israeli settlements there.

None the less, Abbas's position was strengthened through other developments. On 1 October 2007, as part of its strategy to support the PA President in his power struggle with Hamas, Israel freed 57 Palestinian prisoners, most of whom belonged to Abbas's Fatah movement; none belonged to Hamas. To bolster further the administration in the West Bank, Israel cracked down on charitable organizations associated with Hamas. On 17 December Israeli troops arrested 24 Hamas activists in Nablus and other West Bank cities. Many of those arrested were politicians and intellectuals rather than fighters. Among those rounded up was Ahmad al-Hajj Ali, a member of the PLC. His arrest brought to 46 the number of Palestinian parliamentarians held in Israeli gaols. At the same time a Hamas spokesman in Gaza, Fawzi Barhoum, accused Abbas and Fayyad of collaboration with Israel in pursuing Hamas fighters and politicians in the West Bank.

ISRAELI BLOCKADE OF THE GAZA STRIP

Following Hamas's seizure of the Strip in June 2007, Israel tightened its blockade of coastal Gaza; supplies of food, fuel and aid were strictly limited. In addition, Israel continued a series of military incursions and air strikes in response to the firing of rockets and mortars into Israel. Egypt also sealed its border with Gaza after June 2007, reopening the border only occasionally on humanitarian grounds. In January 2008, under pressure from UN agencies and international human rights organizations, Israel agreed to allow humanitarian food and medical supplies to enter Gaza at the rate of 50 lorries a day. Following a 10-day embargo, Israel also agreed to deliver about 500,000 litres of diesel oil and petrol a day for vehicles, industry and power stations. However, this action fell short of meeting international demands or preventing a humanitarian crisis; electricity was still being cut for hours every day.

On 31 December 2007 hundreds of Palestinian pilgrims returning from Saudi Arabia to Gaza went on the rampage in temporary desert camps in northern Sinai, after the Egyptian authorities insisted that they return via Gaza border crossings controlled by the Israeli army. The Palestinian protesters demanded to enter Gaza via the Egyptian terminal at Rafah—the main Egyptian terminal through which the pilgrims had left for the *Hajj* (pilgrimage) in Mecca. The Rafah crossing had become Gaza's main gateway to the outside world. An elderly woman died during a scuffle between the protesting pilgrims and Egyptian policemen. Egypt had allowed a few thousand pilgrims to leave via its Rafah crossing because it did not want to be accused of stopping Muslims making the *Hajj*. However, Egyptian President Hosni Mubarak had subsequently decided to yield to Israeli demands to send the pilgrims back via two Israeli-controlled crossings: Kerem Shalom and Erez. The Israeli army had intended to arrest Hamas activists among the returning pilgrims.

Hamas fighters blew up the Egypt–Gaza border wall on 23 January 2008 in a bid to end the siege of Gaza. Thousands of Gazans surged into the Egyptian territory in northern Sinai. On the following day dozens of Egyptian police gathered at the border and directed traffic away from the destroyed frontier wall, while the Egyptian Government sought to assure its US ally that it would soon reseal its border with Gaza. Egypt at this point was more interested in bringing Hamas and the West Bank administration together and was no longer pretending to boycott Hamas. However, the PA persisted in refusing to recognize the authority of Hamas in Gaza.

On 27 January 2008 President Abbas met Israeli Prime Minister Olmert in Jerusalem partly to discuss Hamas's demolition of the Gaza–Egyptian border fence and the collapse of their joint strategy of isolating Hamas. However, Israel was sceptical of the suggestion that the PA share control of the Rafah crossing with Egyptian and EU monitors, with the

Israeli Ministry of Defence expressing its concern that Hamas would retain effective control of the crossing. On 3 February the Gaza border was finally sealed by Egyptian forces; the Rafah crossing would henceforth be opened occasionally on humanitarian grounds.

On 4 February 2008 a Palestinian suicide bomber blew himself up at a shopping centre in the southern desert town of Dimona, killing one Israeli. Hamas claimed responsibility for the bombing, the first Hamas militant attack inside Israel since 2004. On 8 February 2008 Israeli troops supported by tanks, helicopter gunships and warplanes killed seven Palestinians in a raid in the Strip. In Ramallah the PLO Executive Committee, at a meeting chaired by President Abbas, issued a statement demanding that Israel halt its operation in Gaza. The statement also expressed its opposition to rocket fire being launched against Israel from Gaza. On 6 March an attack by a lone Palestinian gunmen on a Jewish religious college in Jerusalem killed eight students.

YEMENI MEDIATION

On 23 March 2008 Hamas and Fatah signed up to the 'San'a Declaration', a Yemeni-brokered agreement designed to reconcile the two rival factions. The statement was signed, after a week of discussions, by Fatah's parliamentary leader, Azzam al-Ahmad, and Hamas leader Musa Abu Marzuk. The Yemeni initiative envisaged new Palestinian elections, the creation of a 'government of national unity' and the restructuring of the security forces along national rather than factional lines. However, only hours after the signing of the agreement, an apparent dispute broke out over just what was included in the deal. Abbas's chief negotiator, Erekat, insisted that Hamas must agree to end its control of Gaza, allow the PA back into the Strip, accept the PLO 'obligations' towards the 1993 Oslo Accords and accept the principle of negotiation with Israel for a two-state solution. Meanwhile, Hamas demanded that Abbas restore the 'national unity government' led by Hamas's Haniya. Furthermore, Hamas argued that long-term peace depended not on endorsing the Oslo Accords, but on ending Israeli occupation of the West Bank, dismantling Jewish settlements and opening the crossing points into the Strip.

EGYPTIAN-BROKERED HAMAS-ISRAEL TRUCE

Following months of indirect negotiations brokered by Egyptian intelligence officers, a preliminary six-month truce between Israel and Hamas came into effect on 19 June 2008. It was primarily aimed at bringing an end to fighting that had resulted in the deaths of more than 600 Palestinians, many of them civilians, and 18 Israelis since the last Hamas-Israel ceasefire collapsed in April 2007. The terms required Hamas to halt attacks on Israel; the latter was to cease military incursions into the Gaza Strip. If the cessation of hostilities lasted for three days, Israel would then ease its blockade of Gaza, allowing vital supplies into the territory. If further progress were achieved in the Egyptian-mediated negotiations, Israel would then allow more commodities into Gaza and Egypt would open the Rafah crossing for two to three days per week. Moreover, a week after the ceasefire took hold, Egypt would host indirect negotiations between Hamas and Israeli representatives to broker a prisoner deal that would swap Shalit—captured by Palestinian fighters in mid-2006—for Palestinian prisoners being held in Israeli gaols. Hamas had earlier conditioned the release of Shalit on the freeing of 450 Palestinian prisoners, of whom Israel had publicly stated that it would release only 70.

However, the ceasefire deal reached in June 2008 in effect constituted no more than promises from both Hamas and Israel to Egypt. Consequently, on 26 June, barely a week into the ceasefire, Israel declared that its border crossings with Gaza would remain closed. This prompted Hamas spokesman Sami Abu Zuhri to accuse Israel of breaching the truce. He added that the commitment of Hamas to the deal hinged on Israel's lifting of the siege of Gaza and the opening of all the crossings. Israel claimed that it had reinstated the blockade on 25 June in response to rockets fired from Gaza by Islamic Jihad fighters, apparently in retaliation for the Israeli army's killing of an Islamic Jihad commander in the West Bank. Israel maintained that the truce covered only Gaza and not the West Bank. On 1 July Israel closed all its cargo crossings with Gaza, accusing Hamas of firing a rocket at southern Israel the previous night.

Meanwhile, both Israel and the PA continued to combat the growing support for Hamas across the West Bank. On 7 July 2008 Israeli troops raided the offices of the Tadamun association, a Palestinian charity in Nablus with links to Hamas. Similar raids were carried out around Ramallah, Hebron and Qalqilya.

OPERATION CAST LEAD

On 27 December 2008 Israeli forces began a bombing campaign on the Gaza Strip, as part of Operation Cast Lead, the stated aim of which was to prevent further rocket attacks into Israel by Hamas militants. The scale and intensity of the Israeli attacks were unprecedented. More Palestinians were killed and more properties destroyed in the 22-day military campaign than in any previous Israeli offensive against Gaza; according to Amnesty International, some 1,400 Palestinians were killed and 5,000 injured. Palestinian human rights NGOs estimated that nearly two-thirds of those killed were civilians. Targeted institutions included police stations, schools, clinics, mosques, welfare organizations and the Islamic University of Gaza, as well as a range of media outlets. On 6 January 2009 Israeli shelling killed 46 people at the UN-operated al-Fakhoura school in the Jabalya refugee camp.

However, the aerial campaign failed to decapitate Hamas, defeat it militarily or even prevent the intensification of rocket-fire into Israel. Senior Hamas leader Nizar Rayyan was killed on 31 December 2008 during the bombing of a residential building, which also resulted in the deaths of over a dozen women and children. On 15 January 2009 Said Siam, the Minister of the Interior in the de facto Hamas administration, was assassinated when Israeli warplanes attacked his brother's home in Gaza City. Siam was thought to be Hamas's number three in command in Gaza, behind Haniya and the group's political chief in Gaza, Dr Mahmoud al-Zahar. None the less, the Damascus-based Meshaal remained de facto leader of Hamas. In April Meshaal was re-elected head of the political bureau in a secret vote conducted over several days. It was reported that some 50 senior members of Hamas inside and outside the Palestinian territories (including some of those in Israeli gaols) had taken part in the vote. There was no report of any significant challenge to Meshaal's leadership.

The Gaza campaign took place before an Israeli general election, scheduled for 10 February 2009. Israeli leaders appeared to believe that they could weaken Hamas militarily and transform the situation on the ground while boosting their electoral prospects and the fortunes of the Ramallah-based PA. The Gaza campaign also presented an opportunity to restore Israeli military prestige, much tarnished following the offensive against Hezbollah in 2006. In the Arab world, the 22-day campaign prompted pro-Palestinian demonstrations targeting Egyptian embassies in Beirut, Amman, and elsewhere in protest against Egypt's perceived complicity in the Israeli blockade of Gaza. The official Arab response was deeply divided, with Syria and Hezbollah urging a full Arab boycott of Israel. The PA issued tough statements condemning the Israeli attacks, while at the same time cracking down on anti-Israeli protests in the West Bank—partly in order to deflect attention from its support for the Israeli siege of Gaza and its desire that Hamas would finally be weakened by Israel.

FATAH-HAMAS MEDIATION IN CAIRO

Arab efforts to broker Fatah-Hamas reconciliation recommenced in April 2009 in Cairo. Hamas was represented by al-Zahar, and Shaath, a senior Fatah leader, represented the PA. The discussions focused on the formation of a transitional 'unity government', based on power-sharing, which would remain in place until the 2010 parliamentary elections.

The first round of unity discussions, which had been arranged by Saudi Arabia in February 2007, had collapsed and the factions had reverted to internal fighting until Hamas seized full control of Gaza in June of that year. The second round of discussions between the two factions began in November 2008 under Egyptian auspices. Egyptian officials had produced proposals for an agreement, including the formation of a government of national unity, an end to the economic blockade, the reform of the security forces, and the holding of presidential and legislative elections. Hamas, for its part, had demanded an end to the blockade of Gaza and membership of a reformed PLO.

The legal mandate and term of President Abbas was due to expire on 9 January 2009, but the prospect of a new presidential election being held seemed unlikely, leaving Abbas without democratic legitimacy. The work of the PLC had been frozen since 2006, and the Governments of Fayyad in Ramallah and Haniya in Gaza both confronted isolation. Abbas's mandate topped the agenda of the Cairo negotiations in November 2008, and Hamas initially insisted on the illegality of an extension of his mandate. However, Hamas's subsequent concession for Abbas to keep his position beyond January 2009 only underscored the fact that the PA was on the verge of institutional breakdown.

By early April 2009 the third round of unity discussions had broken down, mainly over the issue of the PA's previous accords with Israel. Egypt pressed for persevering with further such discussions, arguing that an agreement was vital in order for the US $4,500m. of aid pledged by international donors to be paid out to help to rebuild Gaza. Many donor countries refused to channel their aid through Hamas, insisting that disbursal of the money should be the responsibility of a unity government. The Quartet group continued to state that it would deal only with Hamas if the Islamist organization recognized Israel, accepted previous Israeli-PA agreements and laid down its arms. However, Ali Barakeh, a senior Hamas official based in Damascus, claimed that Fatah's co-operation with Israel and the USA represented the main obstacle to reconciliation.

The fourth round of power-sharing discussions between Hamas and Fatah again ended without a deal, and the two factions agreed to resume negotiations in May 2009. However, divisions remained on key issues such as the electoral system, reform of the Palestinian police and security services (including the role of Jordan and the USA in training), and possible Hamas participation in the PLO. The Cairo discussions came just two weeks after Hamas had accused Fatah of attempting to assassinate one of its leaders in the West Bank. Further discussions in October also failed to produce an agreement.

Throughout the first half of 2009 both the PA and Israel continued to detain senior Hamas figures on the West Bank. On 19 March the Israeli security forces arrested 10 leaders of Hamas in the West Bank, including al-Shaer, the Deputy Prime Minister and Minister of Education and Higher Education in the Government formed by Hamas in early 2006. Three others, including a member of the Legislative Council and a local mayor, were arrested in Ramallah, and a Hamas member of the PLC was detained near Jenin. The arrests followed the failure of Egyptian-mediated negotiations between Hamas and Israel over a proposal for the release of Shalit in exchange for hundreds of Palestinians held in Israel. By late March 2009 more than 40 Hamas members of the PLC from the West Bank were imprisoned in Israel.

THE 13TH PA CABINET

In May 2009 the PA Cabinet was reorganized for the first time since the appointment of the 'emergency government' in 2007. A total of 12 new ministers entered an expanded PA executive, most of whom were members of Fatah. Expansion allowed Abbas to retain the technocratic core of Fayyad's administration while placating restless elements within Fatah. Saeed Abu Ali, of Fatah, remained Minister of the Interior and was joined by a further eight Fatah ministers. Fayyad remained Prime Minister and Minister of Finance. Representatives of three other PLO factions also entered the Cabinet: the DFLP, FIDA and the PPSF. They joined several independents, among them Riyad al-Maliki (formerly of the PFLP), who had held the role of Minister of Foreign Affairs since July 2007.

PA SECURITY REFORM IN THE WEST BANK

The USA had been involved in training the PA's security forces since the 1990s. Following the Wye negotiations in 1998, the CIA increased its support for the PA, to bolster it against Hamas. However, in the post-Arafat, post-al-Aqsa *intifada* era, the scale and ambition of US involvement deepened considerably, increasing further following the electoral ascent of Hamas. The US 'security co-ordination' programme, led by Lt-Gen. Keith Dayton, was launched by the Bush Administration in 2005 to help the PA to reform its security services. In effect, Dayton was, controversially, given overall responsibility for the PA security forces. It was reported that the Dayton programme planned to train seven battalions totalling 4,700 troops, in addition to training and supplying equipment for an additional 15,000 troops. It was estimated that the total cost of the programme would reach US $1,300m., although by 2009 costs amounted to just $161m. However, overall US investment in training, arming and financing the PA's Presidential Guard and National Security Forces was thought to be much higher.

PA security forces reorganized into three main branches: police, intelligence and military. The primary goal was to provide the PA leadership with the capacity to contain resistance on the part of Hamas or other opposition factions; to that end, forces engaged in a series of offensives against members of Hamas across the West Bank. The PA claimed that the 'Dayton force' had made discoveries of arms and explosives across the West Bank, and President Abbas insisted that he had been the target of a Hamas assassination plot.

However, the Dayton initiative attracted criticism. The equipment used was vetted and approved by Israel, leaving the force largely under-resourced (but not underfunded). Israel had refused to allow body armour, which meant that recruits risked their lives in every operation. Some critics within the PA complained that the amount of funding the 'Dayton force' received was disproportionate compared with other sections of the PA, such as the neglected judicial system. The Dayton programme posed deeper questions about Palestinian national security. The PA had opted to embrace security co-operation with Israel, but it remained subject to Israeli influence, and as a result it ran the risk of further weakening the PA's standing with the public. The Dayton mission came under severe criticism from Hamas as a major barrier to the establishment of a Palestinian unity government and as an unjustified US intrusion into internal Palestinian affairs. The programme had already forced Hamas to seek support from regional powers in the Middle East to counter the US-sponsored security forces.

THE SIXTH FATAH GENERAL CONFERENCE

Security sector reform facilitated an incremental re-extension of PA territorial reach. PA police returned to Nablus in late 2007, to Jenin and Hebron during 2008, and by mid-2009 were on patrol in Bethlehem as the city prepared to host the long-delayed sixth Fatah General Conference. The conference was held on 4–11 August 2009, with over 2,300 delegates in attendance. Some 400 delegates from Gaza were prevented from travelling to the conference by Hamas in retaliation for PA detention of Hamas members in the West Bank. Abbas continued to eschew armed struggle, but did link the resumption of direct negotiations with Israel to a settlement freeze. The PA President was re-elected unopposed to the post of Fatah Chairman. Of the 18 members of the Central Committee, only five were re-elected.

Capitalizing on Fatah's organizational momentum, the PNC convened on 26–27 August 2009 in Ramallah, and six new members were added to the Executive Committee. Two of the new members were prominent figures within Fatah: Quray and Erekat. They were joined by the first woman to take a seat on the Committee, Ashrawi.

PROGRESS UNDER FAYYAD

The bifurcation of the Palestinian territories persisted into 2010; with the absence of fresh elections or a restoration of national unity, Hamas continued to preside over the economically devastated Gaza Strip, but in the West Bank the uneasy partnership of Fayyad and Fatah steered in a different direction. Favoured by the West for his independence, technical expertise, commitment to reform and political moderation, the technocrat Fayyad stood apart from the established Palestinian political factions and culture. However, echoing the criticism of Abbas's expired presidency, Hamas could reasonably contest the legality of Fayyad's premiership, as the PLC, in which Hamas still enjoyed a technical majority, had not been afforded a vote on the appointment. Fayyad combined administrative competence with a surprising degree of nationalist combativeness, emerging as a political force in his own right.

Like Abbas, Fayyad eschewed armed struggle, instead focusing on the construction of political and economic infrastructure and systematic institutional capacity-building, to lay the foundations of an independent Palestinian state. Fayyad's constructive agenda attracted the attention of external parties including the USA and the EU, while a peaceful method of implementation was more difficult for Israel to oppose forcibly. Launched in August 2009, the Fayyad plan, officially entitled 'Ending the Occupation, Establishing the State', proposed to create the basis for Palestinian independence by 2011. Meanwhile, PLO and PA officials set out to secure international support for the plan, although Israel objected to this new Palestinian unilateralism as a breach of the Oslo Accords.

In December 2009 Fayyad launched a PA boycott of settlement produce, sale of which was estimated to be worth up to US $200m. per year to the settler economy. In January 2010 Fayyad followed this up with a 'National Honour Fund', intended to replace settlement products with Palestinian goods and to strengthen Palestinian exporters. Subsequent measures during that year aimed to ban Palestinian labourers from working in the settlements, while making provision for their systematic reintegration into the national economy. Meanwhile, improvements in the PA's security forces in the West Bank expedited a modest reduction in Israeli military checkpoints and raids.

THE PROLONGED CRISIS OF THE ABBAS PRESIDENCY

In April 2009 the UN appointed South African judge Richard Goldstone to head an independent inquiry into alleged human rights violations committed during Operation Cast Lead. On 15 September Goldstone published his report, in which he was heavily critical of the Israeli military campaign, but also careful to highlight Hamas's transgressions. Israel was censured for the use of disproportionate force and laying siege to the Strip, and Hamas was criticized for firing indiscriminately at civilian targets in southern Israel. Under US pressure, on 2 October Abbas backed down from an earlier plan to refer the report to the UN Human Rights Council, which in theory would have opened up the possibility of trials for war crimes and crimes against humanity at the International Criminal Court (ICC). The presidential *volte-face* prompted a furious backlash from Gaza, and Abbas admitted that the reversal in policy had been a mistake.

Reeling from the Goldstone affair and cognizant that his diplomatic strategy had failed to generate results, on 5 November 2009 Abbas revealed that he would not seek re-election to the presidency. The immediate consequences were limited, however, because elections under the prevailing conditions were simply not viable, on account of Hamas opposition and uncertainty over the Israeli position on a poll in East Jerusalem. The constitutional term of the PLC expired on 25 January 2010. Plans were announced in April for a fresh round of local elections in July, but the idea was abandoned owing to the inability of some Fatah branches to agree on a list of candidates, and the refusal by Hamas to permit the poll in Gaza or to participate in elections in the West Bank.

RESUMPTION OF DIRECT NEGOTIATIONS

While Fayyad's Government pursued the practicalities of state-building, which could—at least in part—be carried out independently of discussions with Israel, the PLO had a remit to pursue negotiations, albeit in the context of the discredited Oslo framework and subsequent attempts to resuscitate it. However, by late 2009 the Fatah leadership was proving to be uncharacteristically obdurate in resisting US pressure to return to bilateral negotiations. More than 15 years of attrition at the negotiating table seemed to have prompted a rethink among mainstream secular Palestinian nationalists. The re-election of Benjamin Netanyahu as Israeli Prime Minister in March 2009 was regarded as a further obstacle to a negotiated settlement. Mindful of the resolutions of the Sixth General Conference earlier in the year, the Fatah-led PLO began to hold out for a comprehensive Israeli settlement freeze and clarification of the purpose of negotiations, including assurances of statehood within 1967 borders subject to minor amendments.

On 25 November 2009 Netanyahu yielded to US pressure and agreed to a limited 10-month settlement freeze. However, as with the roadmap, the Israeli Government appended a series of exceptions, including work on existing projects, public buildings, and the full range of construction under way in East Jerusalem. Consequently, Israel's settlement freeze failed to meet Abbas's preconditions for a resumption of direct negotiations. US-proposed 'proximity discussions', whereby both parties agreed to negotiate separately with the USA rather than with each other, did finally commence in May 2010, and on 2 September direct negotiations between Abbas and Netanyahu began in Washington, DC, but with little hope of substantial success.

HAMAS AND GAZA, WITHIN AND WITHOUT

Largely isolated from the West Bank and subject to close surveillance by the authorities, local Fatah elements struggled to mount an effective challenge to Hamas in Gaza. However, an altogether different challenge arose in the form of a Salafi insurrection in Rafah. A commitment to resistance had led Israel to designate Hamas-controlled Gaza as a 'hostile entity' since September 2007. However, for radical critics of Hamas, ceasefire arrangements in place since the end of Operation Cast Lead and Hamas's efforts to prevent the launching of rockets into southern Israel brought this commitment into question. In August 2009 an 'Islamic Emirate' was declared in Rafah by the Jund Ansar Allah, led by Abd al-Latif Musa. The group was one of several small Salafi movements established amid Gaza's isolation and poverty. This direct challenge to Hamas was short-lived, however, and the 'Emirate' was quickly subjugated. Hamas's effective suppression of resistance in the Strip led to a period of relative calm for southern Israel, although this was interrupted in July 2010 by a rocket strike on the port of Ashkelon. Israel struck back at Hamas, even though it was thought that the Islamist movement was not responsible, echoing Israeli policy during the al-Aqsa *intifada*, when PA security forces were routinely attacked in reprisal for independent acts. In April 2011 alleged Salafis kidnapped and murdered an Italian peace activist in Gaza, prompting Hamas security forces to pursue and kill those responsible.

Meanwhile, on 19 January 2010 a leading figure from Hamas's military wing, Mahmoud al-Mabhouh, was assassinated in Dubai, United Arab Emirates (UAE). It was alleged by Dubai police that Israeli agents had carried out the killing, travelling on false or stolen third-country passports. Israel refused to comment on the assassination, but found itself exposed to official criticism and diplomatic censure from around the world.

Even more controversial than the assassination of al-Mabhouh were the events surrounding the so-called 'Gaza Freedom Flotilla' at the end of May 2010. The flotilla was organized by a group of humanitarian organizations in an attempt to breach the blockade of Gaza to bring aid and other supplies into the territory. The Israeli armed forces undertook to intercept the flotilla, and paratroopers boarded the lead ship, the MV *Mavi Marmara*. In the subsequent skirmish, nine activists—all of whom were Turkish citizens—were killed. The incident put tremendous strain on Israeli-Turkish relations (which were downgraded in August 2011) and prompted the formation of a UN panel of inquiry, which published its findings in September 2011. Pro-Gaza activists were deeply disappointed to find the Israeli naval blockade deemed 'a legitimate security measure', but noted that the military's actions were found to be 'excessive and unreasonable'. Mindful of this diplomatic and public relations disaster, in mid-2011 Israel took a series of pre-emptive steps against a planned second flotilla, in effect neutralizing the initiative.

THE PLO, ISRAEL AND THE USA: STAGNANT NEGOTIATIONS

The PLO-Israeli negotiations briefly recommenced in September 2010, with the opening session in Washington, DC, followed by a further round in Sharm el-Sheikh and Jerusalem, but the momentum proved short-lived. Israel declined to extend the West Bank settlement freeze at the end of the month, and, consistent with the platform agreed by Fatah during its 2009 General Conference, the Palestinians withdrew from the discussions. PLO officials directed unusually harsh criticism at the USA for its failure to secure an additional settlement freeze. This more resolute political stance resonated well with domestic constituents; local Fatah leaders understood that a clear policy, firmly adhered to, would help to bolster the movement's tentative but still precarious rehabilitation in the West Bank. The USA responded by announcing that it would continue to work towards a solution with both parties separately, although visits by US diplomats became less frequent, and US President Barack Obama's special envoy to the region, George Mitchell, resigned in May 2011.

While the US-sponsored negotiations stalled, Abbas escalated an international diplomatic campaign aimed at securing recognition, on a bilateral basis (in contrast to the unilateral declaration of independence issued in 1988), of a Palestinian state in the West Bank, the Gaza Strip and East Jerusalem. PLO diplomacy quickly registered several bilateral successes, including recognition from Brazil and a number of other Latin American states, and upgraded diplomatic relations with several European nations, and the PLO General Delegation to the USA was permitted to fly the Palestinian flag at its premises in Washington, DC. As the annual session of the UNGA scheduled for September 2011 approached, Abbas announced that 122 nations already recognized a Palestinian state within the 1967 borders. To admit that state as a full member of the UN required a two-thirds' majority in the General Assembly, but first a recommendation from the Security Council was needed, and the USA predictably threatened to use its veto. (In February 2011 the USA had vetoed a draft resolution on the illegality of Israeli settlement construction in the West Bank and East Jerusalem, despite all 14 of the other Security Council members voting in favour.) Israel dismissed this initiative as a Palestinian attempt to delegitimize it amid plans for mass violence. The PLO retained the option of submitting an alternative resolution to the General Assembly, which would bypass the US veto, to upgrade the Permanent Observer Mission of Palestine to the UN to non-member observer state, comparable in status to the Holy See. Approval would require a simple majority among the UN's 193 member states and would result in important privileges being granted, including membership rights in UN agencies; the prospect of Palestinian leverage at the ICC was of particular concern to Israel. The Arab League supported a move to seek full UN membership for a Palestinian state. Despite confirmation by the US Administration that it would use its veto, Abbas duly submitted the application on 23 September. The President's uncharacteristically resolute stance was welcomed by many within the Palestinian territories. However, the application itself, even before it could meet the US veto, was shunted to the margins via a Committee on the Admission of New Members.

FATAH POLITICS FOLLOWING THE SIXTH GENERAL CONFERENCE

Fatah's Central Committee announced in December 2010 that it was suspending the membership of spokesman and former Gazan security chief Dahlan, pending an internal investigation into charges of Dahlan conspiring against Abbas and establishing a heavily armed personal militia. Dahlan was regarded with suspicion by many Palestinians, owing to his perceived closeness to Israel and the USA. Popular opinion held that he was being punished for accusing Abbas's two sons, Tariq and Yasir, of accruing wealth improperly. Dahlan's organizational network and media interests were closed down, and in June 2011 it was reported (although disputed) that Dahlan had been expelled from Fatah altogether. Dahlan remained in exile in the UAE, although rumours subsequently persisted of an imminent return to the Palestinian territories.

Away from the divisions in the higher echelons of the movement, local Fatah leaders focused on maintaining the momentum from the 2009 General Conference. Adhering to principle on the settlement freeze issue was popular with the public, but maintaining the organization itself required enthusiasm among the lower and middle ranks. The conference had produced mixed results in this respect: on the one hand, it had generated a great deal of activity and excitement, but, on the other hand, the limited number of seats available on the Revolutionary Council had left many aspirants disappointed and a corresponding decline in commitment ensued. In response, Fatah planned fresh elections at district and regional level; the movement hoped that this would keep internal political life healthy while also serving as preparation for proposed local council elections. The prospect of mobilizing behind the PLO at the UN offered another opportunity for action; both Abbas and, from prison, Marwan Barghouthi appealed for mass demonstrations.

PALESTINIAN FACTIONAL POLITICS DURING THE 'ARAB SPRING'

In the short term, the 'Arab Spring'—the series of anti-Government protests that spread throughout the Middle East and North Africa from December 2010—reversed the usual state of affairs in the region, as turmoil in neighbouring Arab states contrasted with relative calm in the Palestinian territories. Although the Fayyad Government formally resigned on 14 February 2011, the move was seen as a superficial attempt to mollify public opinion with little practical effect. However, the dramatic changes occurring near its borders inevitably crossed into the Palestinian factional landscape. In Egypt, the fall of longstanding President Mubarak at first seemed to benefit Hamas; Mubarak's ouster removed a stalwart opponent of political Islam and opened up the possibility of a much higher profile for the Muslim Brotherhood in politics and government. However, the Islamists' early optimism faded into uncertainty; the Egyptian military, at least initially, remained steadfast at the helm of a transitional administration, and the Brotherhood exercised its new-found freedom with caution. When a similar, but more violent, upheaval affected Syria, the Damascus-based Hamas leadership itself appeared exposed, particularly when the influential Egyptian cleric Sheikh Yusuf al-Qaradawi declared his support for the anti-Government protesters in March. The Assad regime subsequently deployed Hamas chief Meshaal to bolster Syria's pro-Palestinian credentials, although the intervention sat uneasily with Syrian protesters and the Palestinian public.

The conjunction of PLO diplomacy, the destabilization of Syria and the lure of better relations with Egypt precipitated a fresh attempt at Palestinian national reconciliation. A surprise agreement between Fatah and Hamas, mediated by Egypt, was announced in late April 2011 and signed by Abbas and Meshaal on 4 May. The terms stipulated that a unity government, comprised of independents, be formed, with elections to the PLC and the presidency to follow within a year; the contentious issue of security arrangements was finessed in the short term as Egypt planned to send technical support to Gaza. However, implementation of the deal stalled when the two sides could not agree on who should serve as Prime Minister, with Hamas rejecting Abbas's choice of Fayyad. The process also exposed the lingering disagreements within the Hamas leadership, as the Gaza-based al-Zahar expressed surprise at the April agreement brokered by Mousa Abu Marzuk on Meshaal's behalf. Like the earlier momentum, the subsequent stall owed much to regional events, specifically the end of a tentative rapprochement between Egypt and Iran, owing to Saudi pressure on the former. In retaliation, Iran might have urged Hamas to distance itself from a reformed unity government, to deprive the Egyptian administration of its diplomatic success.

Meanwhile, Israel expressed its dissatisfaction with the Fatah-Hamas agreement by withholding tax receipts collected on the PA's behalf, forcing Fayyad temporarily to halve public sector salaries in July 2011, in an echo of the 2007 crisis.

Palestinian officials also linked Israel's response to their leadership's diplomatic moves.

THE INTERNAL AND EXTERNAL BORDERS OF ISRAEL/PALESTINE

Conditions in the West Bank enclaves of Area A and Area B improved during the first half of 2011. The PA continued the construction of extensive new government offices in the Ramallah suburb of Masyun, the town assuming the appearance of state administrative (if not political) permanence. PA and NGO opportunities attracted migrants, prompting a construction boom. Reforms implemented by the Palestine Monetary Authority increased the availability of credit, encouraging consumption, and the PA was correspondingly able to accumulate limited tax revenues. However, pressure on Palestinians outside the urban enclaves increased: the Jordan Valley population struggled against restrictions on zoning and planning; military measures against Bedouin were intensified; and settler violence rose sharply.

Meanwhile, Hamas continued its efforts to curb rocket attacks launched from the Gaza Strip, as the PA worked to limit Hamas's influence in the West Bank. Nevertheless, there was an increase in violence around Gaza in early April 2011, after a rocket hit an Israeli school bus. Further south, the post-Mubarak Government in Egypt opened the Rafah crossing in late May. However, to the dissatisfaction of Hamas and residents in Gaza, it quickly became clear that the new transit procedures were merely a limited relaxation of existing restrictions. Meanwhile, lax security in Sinai led to a rise in the transfer of goods via the Rafah tunnels, with Israel expressing concern at an increased flow of arms, especially from eastern Libya (where a popular uprising was taking place against the regime of Libyan leader Muammar al-Qaddafi).

Online groups inspired by the 'Arab Spring' demonstrations tried to mobilize support for protests at Israel's frontiers to mark the anniversary of *al-Nakba* in mid-May 2011. In the West Bank, turnout at the Qalandiya checkpoint was limited, and Gazan protesters attempting to march to the Erez checkpoint were fired upon by Israeli troops. More significant were the protests at the Syrian and Lebanese borders, which apparently went ahead with the support of Syria and Hezbollah, respectively. In Syria, dozens of Palestinian refugees breached the border fence and crossed into the Golan Heights. In the south of Israel, near Eilat, a series of gun and bomb attacks perpetrated by suspected Palestinian militants on 18 August left eight Israelis dead and more than 30 injured; five of the attackers were killed and several more Palestinians later died as the result of Israeli air strikes on Gaza. The deaths of three Egyptian security personnel in Sinai during subsequent Israeli military action added to the strain on relations between the two increasingly unenthusiastic allies.

'STATE OF PALESTINE' ADMITTED TO UNESCO

The PLO's diplomatic initiative may have stalled at the UN Security Council in New York, but progress did extend to entry into the UN Educational, Cultural and Scientific Organization (UNESCO) in Paris. 'The state of Palestine' secured a comfortable vote in favour of membership on 31 October 2011, and became the 189th state party to the World Heritage Convention in December. Elias Sanbar was appointed as the Permanent Delegate of Palestine to UNESCO from January 2012. Membership of UNESCO afforded the PA a new diplomatic tool: accession to the World Heritage Convention permitted nomination of sites of cultural or natural significance for inscription on the World Heritage List. During 2012 the PA successfully nominated the Church of the Nativity in Bethlehem and the associated Pilgrimage Route; 13 additional sites were put forward on a Tentative List for possible consideration 12 months later. They included the Jerusalem Southern Terraced Landscape, centred on the village of Battir, which had hoped to secure the original nomination on account of imminent danger from Israel's 'separation barrier'. Supporters of Battir chastised the Palestinian leadership for allegedly bowing to external intervention: the case was made that UNESCO protection of Battir, in Area C, might have been deemed more confrontational than the listing of an established international landmark in Area A. The PA, however, disputed that view. Independent of domestic politics, controversy at home was preceded by fallout abroad: Israeli-US objections to the admission of 'the state of Palestine' to UNESCO triggered another temporary freezing by Israel of customs revenue transfer to the PA during November 2011 and, in line with established congressional legislation, the withdrawal of US contributions to UNESCO's budget.

PALESTINIAN PRISONERS BEGIN HUNGER STRIKE

In late 2011 Hamas and Israel agreed to exchange large numbers of Palestinian prisoners in return for kidnapped Israeli soldier Shalit. The agreement stipulated that a total of 1,027 Palestinian prisoners be released in exchange for Shalit. The initial release, on 18 October, included a tranche of 477 prisoners, the first of them being 27 women; some 40 Palestinians were released into exile overseas.

In 2012 Palestinian prisoners again attracted international attention, with a major cross-factional and lengthy hunger strike. Action initiated in February gained momentum from 17 April, when the Jerusalem-based prisoner support and rights association, Addameer, estimated that around 1,200 prisoners had launched a major strike; the number of participants subsequently rose by several hundred as protests peaked. Addameer reported that Israel held 4,706 political prisoners at mid-2012, of whom 285 were administrative detainees (a technical measure preceding the occupation through which suspects could be detained without charge or trial for up to six months and their detention renewed indefinitely); 18 administrative detainees were members of the PLC. The hunger strikers' demands included the restoration of family visiting rights for Gazan prisoners: suspended in the wake of Shalit's abduction, Israel had been expected to restore these rights upon the soldier's release but then demurred. Other complaints included the use of administrative detention and solitary confinement, as well as a ban on academic studies and access to books. Pressure on the Israel Prison Service (IPS) increased, as leading hunger strikers Bilal Diyab and Tahir Halahleh approached and then exceeded the recorded limit for endurance of a fast. On hunger strike for 77 days before reaching terms with IPS on 14 May, both prisoners were objecting to the prospective renewal of their terms in administrative detention; they were following the lead of Khader Adnan, an administrative detainee who had successfully forced the hand of the IPS with a 66-day hunger strike ending in mid-April. Israel was said to have agreed to multiple concessions: Palestinians claimed that administrative detainees would no longer have their terms renewed without the presentation of fresh evidence; there would be an end to long-term solitary confinement; and family visits for Gazans and West Bankers denied the right would be reinstated.

Keeping prisoners in the news, Akram Rikhawi undertook a 102-day fast, ending on 22 July 2012; he ultimately secured a revised release date on medical grounds. Rikhawi was preceded by renowned Palestinian footballer Mahmud Sarsak, who had been held in administrative detention for almost three years; Sarsak was ultimately released and permitted to return to Gaza after a 96-day hunger strike. Meanwhile, Israel released the remains of 91 Palestinians to the PA on 31 May; some of the bodies had been held in Israeli custody for almost four decades.

NEW CABINET IN RAMALLAH

The PA had presided over a period of relative calm for much of the 'Arab Spring', but the future remained unpredictable. The authoritarian side of the PA was clearly revealed at the end of June 2012. In an attempt to reopen communications with Israel, Abbas had extended an invitation to Shaul Mofaz, head of the Kadima list in the Knesset and the Chief of Staff during Operation Defensive Shield, to visit Ramallah. The invitation prompted a substantial public outcry and was hastily rescinded. However, the simmering discontent precipitated street protests, and PA security forces responded with considerable violence.

Meanwhile, in an attempt to provide some fresh momentum to the PA in Ramallah, Abbas installed a new Cabinet on 16 May 2012, the first major government reorganization for three years. Ministers were tasked first and foremost with preparing the ground for local elections that were supposed to have been held in 2009. The most significant change affected Fayyad, who remained as Prime Minister, but relinquished the finance portfolio; he was replaced in that post by the independent academic and technocrat Nabil Qassis. Two primary issues drove the reorganization: the PA's looming financial crisis and the persistent failure to expedite reconciliation with Hamas. Rising indebtedness and a major shortfall in the PA's annual budget cost Fayyad the portfolio, despite his favour with Western donors. Besides the occupation and related limits on economic growth and tax collection, the PA had to deal with a reduction in donor aid compounded by a failure to meet pre-existing pledges. Hamas complained that the unilateral formation of a new PA Cabinet in the West Bank was in breach of the Doha agreement reached in February 2012 and had no electoral mandate; Abbas responded that longevity and attrition—including the resignation of two ministers charged with corruption—required that he act, while also pointing out that the Cabinet could be dissolved in an instant, should national unity be realized.

HAMAS ON THE MOVE

The Palestinian polity remained divided at mid-2012: Fatah and Fayyad wrestled with one set of dilemmas, as well as each other, in Ramallah; Hamas remained dormant under repression throughout the West Bank but continued to rule in Gaza, from where it surveyed a rapidly changing neighbourhood. Building on the *rapprochement* of May 2011, inter-factional reconciliation took another tentative step forward during December and January 2012. By way of preparing the ground for elections, negotiations between the Damascus-based head of Hamas's political bureau, Meshaal, and Fatah's Abbas led to a public revision of tactics by the Islamists: Hamas would reserve the right to use force in defence, but otherwise turn away from armed struggle. The move did not sit well with some in the Gazan-based leadership; both Hamas premier Haniya and senior leader al-Zahar contested the shift in policy. Fissures became apparent again following a more substantive step forward; the Doha agreement concluded on 6 February 2012 was signed by Abbas for Fatah, Meshaal for Hamas, and the Amir of Qatar, Sheikh Hamad bin Khalifa Al Thani.

Denied a secure base on Palestinian soil, events in the wider region afforded Meshaal a different perspective that would have been familiar to the historic PLO leadership; deteriorating conditions in host country Syria left him struggling to reconcile loyalty to the Assad regime with solidarity towards his Sunni brethren. Mindful of the disagreement with Qaradawi earlier in the crisis and encouraged by agitated supporters back home, Hamas's Damascus-based leadership declined to offer any further public support to the minority Alawi regime. The Damascus headquarters were eventually abandoned and the leadership team in exile dispersed: Meshaal joined Qaradawi in Doha during February 2012; Abu Marzuk opted for Cairo; and other Hamas officials scattered across the region. The diminution of the alliance with Hamas was a clear setback for Syria's strategic ally, Iran, and as a result, Hamas forfeited substantial financial support from the Islamic Republic. The distance between the two parties was underlined in March, when senior Hamas figures let it be known that in the event of an Israeli attack on Iran's nuclear facilities, the Islamist movement could not be expected to open up a southern front that did not serve Palestinian national interests. Regional upheaval appeared to undermine Meshaal's standing in the movement, but he continued to lead, holding meetings with King Abdullah of Jordan in June and with Egypt's new President, Mohamed Mursi, in July. Meanwhile, a skirmish on the Israel–Egypt border on 18 June drew fresh attention to the security vacuum in Sinai and prompted a rare military escalation between Hamas and Israel: dozens of rockets were fired by Hamas militants in exchange for Israeli air strikes being carried out on the Strip.

OPERATION PILLAR OF DEFENSE

In November 2012 Israel launched a series of heavy strikes on the Gaza Strip under the codename Operation Pillar of Defense. The precise reason for this action was disputed, but the intensive bout of conflict that ensued appeared to be prompted by an incursion into the Gazan town of Khan Yunis by the Israeli Defence Forces on 8 November, in the course of which a Palestinian child was killed. Hamas responded by firing an anti-tank missile two days later; a fierce escalation in violence involving Israeli air strikes and Palestinian rocket fire left over 170 Palestinians dead in an eight-day campaign briefly reminiscent of the 2008/09 assault codenamed Operation Cast Lead. The most prominent Palestinian fatality occurred on 14 November 2012 with the targeted assassination of Ahmad al-Jabari, head of Hamas's military wing the Izz al-Din al-Qassam Brigades. Al-Jabari, a former Fatah activist, was alleged to have been on the brink of concluding a truce with Israel immediately prior to his assassination. In the event, the bout of hostilities that cost al-Jabari his life was brought to an end through Egyptian mediation. Israel reported five citizens among its dead, along with injuries to many more.

HAMAS GOVERNS GAZA

Beneath the ever-present threat of aerial assault, life continued in much the same vein in Gaza during 2012–13 as it had done since the schism of 2007. On the domestic front, two contrasting developments made headline news in this period. Internal to Hamas, Qatar-based political chief Meshaal crossed from Egypt via Rafah to make his first visit to the Palestinian territories in almost four decades; besides one short visit in the mid-1970s, Meshaal had been in exile from his home near Jerusalem since the 1967 Six-Day War. During his two-day visit in December 2012 Meshaal paid his respects at the homes of prominent Hamas martyrs, including the group's spiritual guide and founder Sheikh Ahmad Yassin and the more recently assassinated al-Jabari. Meshaal then attended a rally to commemorate the 25th anniversary of the founding of Hamas during the early days of the first *intifada*. Taking note, Fatah activists followed this with a huge demonstration of their own on 4 January 2013. The demonstration was organized to mark Fatah's 48th anniversary (and to recall the launch by Arafat of the armed struggle under the name of al-Asifa in 1965), and was attended by hundreds of thousands of Fatah supporters gathered in Gaza City's Saraya Square. That they were permitted to mobilize on this scale—the first time since 2007—was taken as evidence of goodwill between Fatah and Hamas.

On a regional level, the ouster of Egypt's elected, if controversial, President Muhammad Mursi on 3 July 2013 deprived Hamas of a kindred spirit at the helm in a major Arab state. Cairo's Muslim Brotherhood-led Government had overseen a modest extension of support for the Palestinians in Gaza: movement through the Rafah crossing had been eased and a visit—amid Operation Pillar of Defense—from Prime Minister Hisham Qandil. Rafah's tunnels had long been a target of the Egyptian authorities, but following Mursi's removal from office, efforts to curb tunnel traffic were redoubled. Gaza was seemingly caught up in the Egyptian national goal of re-securing Sinai for the state. Matters deteriorated further when it was announced later in July that Mursi was under investigation for collusion with Hamas. The charge was levelled that during the internal upheaval in Egypt in January 2011 Mursi, together with other Muslim Brotherhood leaders and inmates, had escaped from Wadi al-Natrun prison with the assistance of Hamas (and Hezbollah). It was further alleged that Hamas had then joined Brotherhood forces in violent attacks on Egyptian security facilities in a campaign against the state. Hamas denied any such involvement and claimed that the allegations were the result of attempts by Fatah and the PA to besmirch its reputation in Egypt. The apparent loss of Egyptian support compounded a fast-moving regional change of attitude towards Hamas: Egypt joined Syria and Iran on a lengthening list of states withdrawing support from the

Islamist movement in Gaza. To make matters worse, sectarian fallout from the Syrian civil war put Hamas in opposition to Hezbollah, a previously valued, respected and potent ally.

PALESTINE ACKNOWLEDGED AT THE UN

In lieu of meaningful negotiations, the PLO pursued an independent diplomatic campaign to secure an upgrade in status at the UN. Circumventing the US veto at the Security Council, focus fell on the General Assembly. Besides pressuring Israel and the USA, the vote to secure non-member state standing was one of the few means available to try and revive the fortunes of the secular-nationalist mainstream in Palestinian politics. The moment arrived on 29 November 2012, when 'the state of Palestine' was duly granted an upgrade to non-member observer status by the General Assembly. The pertinent UN document recounted a list of resolutions underpinning the decision, including: UNGA Resolution 181 (1947), which sought to partition Palestine into separate, 'Independent Arab and Jewish States'; UN Security Council (UNSC) Resolution 242 (1967) calling on Israel to withdraw from 'territories occupied' (which included the West Bank and the Gaza Strip); UNSC Resolution 338 (1973), which reiterated that demand; UNGA Resolution 3236 and UNGA Resolution 3237 (1974), which respectively recognized the Palestinian people's right to self-determination and first granted the PLO observer status; and UNSC Resolution 1397 (2002), in which the USA signed up to 'a vision of a region where two States, Israel and Palestine, live side by side within secure and recognized borders'. The upgrade in UN standing of 2012 built on the decision one year earlier to admit 'the state of Palestine' as a full member of UNESCO.

A total of 138 members of the General Assembly cast their ballot in support of the upgrade; nine cast a vote against and 41 abstained. The minority against included Israel, North American allies Canada and the USA, Panama and a cluster of minor Pacific island states dependent on US aid (the Marshall Islands, Micronesia, Nauru and Palau). Among the European members, only the Czech Republic's centre-right and pro-USA Government cast one isolated ballot against the motion.

WEST BANK ADMINISTRATION IN CRISIS

Technical progress at the UN stubbornly refused to translate into substantive progress on the ground; in fact it would actually feed into a downward spiral. In lieu of an end to occupation, colonization and any prospect of sustainable development, economic stagnation and deepening fiscal crisis generated social tension that fuelled long-established political frustrations. Furthermore, in the moribund political environment overseen by the PA, the tension lacked any obvious procedural outlet. Local elections held unevenly across the West Bank in October 2012 generated limited renewal; the polls were banned by Hamas in the Gaza Strip and boycotted by the Islamists in the West Bank. Reflecting protest elsewhere in the Arab world, discontent surfaced, ostensibly in response to an increase in the cost of living. West Bank anger was compounded by an increase in the rate of value-added tax. Trade unions led a succession of strikes that did not spare PA institutions. Fleeting success at the UN then added to the stress: demonstrations drew renewed vigour towards the end of the year as Israel revisited the sanction earlier imposed for success at UNESCO. Customs revenues collected on the PA's behalf in accord with the Oslo-era Paris Protocol were suspended. Consequently, the PA proved unable to meet salary commitments and the anomie besetting the national project deepened. There was a resurgence of demonstrations during early 2013, with fresh mobilization behind the issue of prisoners. The immediate trigger was the death (following his alleged torture) of Palestinian detainee Arafat Jaradat in Israeli custody in February; fellow prisoners launched a mass hunger strike in protest.

Fiscal pressures and social unrest gradually eased over the following weeks; Israeli-held revenues and US aid were transferred, the PA drew on renewed liquidity and a semblance of calm resumed during April 2013. The relief had been timed to coincide with a brief visit to Ramallah by US President Obama on 21 March. Following meetings in Israel the previous day, Obama met Abbas at the presidential compound. During an ensuing press conference the US President said little to lift Palestinian spirits, particularly regarding the PLO's position that settlement construction needed to halt prior to any resumption of negotiations. The press conference was emblematic of a visit that generated little enthusiasm and a modicum of protest among a deeply jaded Palestinian public.

NEW PA PRIME MINISTER IN RAMALLAH

Deficits in representation, purpose and legitimacy continued seriously to erode the standing of the PA into 2013, with consequences for the executive. Buffeted by popular discontent, amid the evident failure to build a state, and undermined by Fatah, PA Prime Minister Fayyad finally resigned on 13 April 2013. This was the second cabinet portfolio that Fayyad had relinquished in less than a year, having stepped down as Minister of Finance in May 2012. In early June 2013 President Abbas announced Fayyad's replacement to be the respected but politically inexperienced Dr Rami Hamdallah, an independent with a reputation for sound administration forged during his long tenure as president of the Nablus-based Al-Najah National University. However, on 20 June Hamdallah tendered his resignation just two weeks after being appointed. Surrounded by members of Fatah in cabinet, Hamdallah's political independence had appeared further compromised following the President's appointment of two Deputy Prime Ministers. Constitutionally, these appointments should have been the Prime Minister's prerogative. In lieu of an immediate replacement, Hamdallah acceded to the President's request to remain in the premiership on a caretaker basis. On 13 August Hamdallah accepted a request from Abbas to form a new government. That Government, the composition of which was the same as that appointed in June, duly took office on 19 September.

US-BROKERED PEACE NEGOTIATIONS FAIL

Mindful of the unsustainable status quo in the Palestinian territories and hopeful of a second-term foreign policy legacy in the Middle East, the Obama Administration increased efforts to restart PLO-Israeli negotiations. Intense diplomacy by US Secretary of State John Kerry throughout the first half of 2013 culminated in a tentative revival of dialogue at the end of July. Kerry appointed former US ambassador to Tel Aviv, Martin Indyk, as the special envoy with the task of overseeing progress; preparatory meetings between the two sides were held in Washington, DC on 30 July 2013 and negotiations resumed in Jerusalem on 14 August.

However, it became increasingly apparent during early 2014 that the deadline for the discussions to end by April could not be met, whereupon Israel urged the Palestinians to extend them. The Palestinians, cognizant of how little two decades of negotiations had delivered since the signing of the Oslo Accords, demurred. Before discussions broke down, Palestinian participation had secured Israel's agreement on the release of 104 long-term prisoners in four stages: the first group was released in August, a second group followed at the end of October and 26 prisoners in a third group were set free at the end of December. Israel refused to release a fourth and final group scheduled for 28 March 2014, however. In April dozens of Palestinians subject to administrative detention commenced a hunger strike. Israel considered forced feeding of the inmates to end the impasse. The inmates suspended their hunger strike in June—although they remained in administrative detention, they obtained concessions, including being returned to their original place of imprisonment (having previously been moved between prisons) and an end to solitary confinement. Failure to expedite the fourth stage of prisoner release, combined with the announcement of the construction of hundreds of new homes in illegal settlements in the West Bank, suggested that further discussions would be fruitless. Israel blamed Palestine for refusing to extend the negotiations, and the PLO held Israel responsible for failing to honour previous agreements. News of a breakthrough in reconciliation between Fatah and Hamas in late April prompted Israel to end negotiations decisively, as it refused to engage with Hamas, which it considered a terrorist organization. In this context the second track of Kerry's diplomacy become merely hypothetical—assembling a 'framework agreement' to which both parties might adhere as they navigated core issues including the Jerusalem issue, the right of return of Palestinian refugees, final borders, security and diplomatic recognition. Israel's lack of enthusiasm to make an agreement had been apparent in late 2013 when it announced settlement expansion in the West Bank, despite appeals from Kerry to exercise restraint, a vote in a ministerial committee of the Knesset to support annexation of the Jordan Valley in December, and an ad hominem attack on Kerry by the Minister of Defence, Moshe Ya'alon in January 2014. Addressing the foreign relations committee of the US Senate in the wake of his failed mission, Kerry placed primary responsibility for the failure of the negotiations with Israel.

THE PLO AND PALESTINE PURSUE UNILATERAL DIPLOMACY

Responding to an apparent lack of progress in January 2014, PLO Secretary-General Abd al-Rabbuh dismissed the framework agreement as a 'worthless' initiative. In the same vein, the PLO executive committee called on Abbas to end negotiations and resume unilateral diplomacy. The PLO had a certain degree of influence in this respect: Palestine had obtained the right to accede to several UN treaties and conventions through its admission as a non-member observer state of the UN in November 2012. The exercise of this right had been held in abeyance in order to give Kerry's initiative a chance; as the Kerry mission unravelled in April, Abbas signed up to an additional 15 UN instruments attending to human and social rights. He stopped short of exercising all the rights accrued in 2012, however, including an appeal to the ICC to consider war crimes and crimes against humanity committed by Israel during Operation Cast Lead in 2008–09, among other incursions. However, momentum for such an appeal gained ground as Israel pursued its ferocious assault on Gaza—Operation Protective Edge—during July–August 2014. On 5 August the Minister of Foreign Affairs al-Maliki visited the ICC in The Hague, Netherlands, specifically to consult on Palestine's position in this regard.

In the mean time, Palestinian and Arab frustrations were evident at the 25th Arab League summit held in Kuwait in March 2014. Abbas presented a long list of grievances with Israel, including its construction of new homes for Jewish settlers in the West Bank, the destruction of existing homes belonging to Palestinians and the ongoing death toll exacted by the Israeli military occupation. The summit closed with a unanimous refusal by member states to countenance recognition of Israel as a Jewish state.

The PA received encouragement of sorts in May 2014 when Pope Francis visited Bethlehem. The pontiff referred explicitly to the state of Palestine and also referred to Abbas as its President. Francis made a similar point with the logistics of his trip, travelling from Amman to the West Bank and on to Israel rather than rather than flying directly to Tel Aviv, as previous pontiffs had done. Prior to celebrating mass in Manger Square in Bethlehem, the Pope stopped to say a prayer at the separation barrier. He then met Palestinian refugees at the Dheisheh refugee camp, before meeting Israeli President Peres in Tel Aviv and Prime Minister Netanyahu in Jerusalem. A further, modest diplomatic success was achieved in June 2014 when UNESCO accorded World Heritage site status to the Jerusalem Southern Terraced Landscape in Battir. The site's stone terraces, which were located in an Israeli-controlled area and had been threatened by construction work on the separation barrier, joined the Church of the Nativity in Bethlehem as the second World Heritage site registered by the PA.

ISOLATION OF HAMAS PRECEDES ASSAULT IN GAZA

Besides ruling out recognition of Israel as a Jewish state, the closing statement at the Arab League summit in Kuwait in March 2014 also applauded the Doha Declaration of 2012; based on the unfulfilled promise of the 2011 Cairo Agreement, it held out the prospect of the renewal of Palestinian national unity. By 2014 circumstances were such that both Hamas and Fatah had an interest in making this happen. Most importantly for Hamas, the military coup in Egypt in July 2013 deprived the Palestinian Islamists of their main regional ally, President Muhammad Mursi. Former military chief and current President, Abd al-Fatah al-Sisi, oversaw a systematic crackdown on the Muslim Brotherhood, prohibiting the group in September 2013; the group's electoral wing, the Freedom and Justice Party, was banned in August 2014. The al-Sisi regime proved equally ill-disposed to the Muslim Brotherhood's affiliated group in the Palestinian territories, and Hamas was banned from operating in Egypt in March. Besieged to the west, north and east by Israel, Gaza under Hamas now found itself hemmed in from the south by Egypt. By way of restoring state power over an increasingly lawless Sinai, Egypt cracked down on the tunnel network that existed along its 12-km border with Gaza, and which had allowed a degree of commerce to be conducted between Gaza and the outside world. This in turn deprived Hamas of tax revenues levied on the tunnel trade and left tens of thousands of civil servants waiting for their salaries to be paid. Travel from Gaza to Egypt was severely curtailed and the population of Gaza grew increasingly desperate.

Hamas's loss proved Fatah's gain, as President al-Sisi restored the pro-Fatah policy pursued under Mubarak with the help of Egyptian intelligence officers who had experience of dealing with Fatah. As Hamas looked to end its isolation, Fatah sought to enhance its weakening legitimacy as a representative of Palestinians, which led both parties to consider an attempt at national reconciliation.

FATAH-HAMAS NATIONAL RECONCILIATION GOVERNMENT

In parallel with the steady breakdown in the discussions overseen by Secretary of State Kerry during 2013–14, April 2014 marked the signing of the Gaza Agreement, an attempt at restoring Palestinian national unity for the first time since the bloody fallout and rift of 2007. Veteran negotiators Azzam al-Ahmad for Fatah and the Egypt-based Abu Marzuk for Hamas played the principal role in concluding an agreement that was reached with surprising rapidity. The agreement resulted in a national reconciliation government, sworn in on 2 June 2014, comprising a Cabinet of nominally neutral technocrats, whom both Fatah and Hamas (in practice, mainly the former) could legitimately claim represented them. The besieged Prime Minister Haniya of Hamas stepped down in favour of Hamdallah, who had been the Fatah-recognized Prime Minister since 2013. Elections to the presidency and the moribund PLC were to follow within six months. The reconciliation agenda extended to reform of the PLO, alongside other issues negotiated in previous agreements.

If reaching the agreement proved straightforward, implementing it proved significantly more difficult. In the West Bank the tension between Fatah's agenda of co-operation with Israel and Hamas's agenda of confrontation became evident in Hebron. When Hamas organized a demonstration in June 2014 in support of the hunger-striking prisoners (see above), PA security forces confronted the demonstrators with force and confiscated recording equipment from journalists, and when Israel launched a massive operation to recover three missing teenagers in the West Bank in June, PA security forces assisted the Israel Defence Forces (IDF) in its search. In the Gaza Strip in June, public sector workers under Hamas queued alongside colleagues on the official PA payroll to withdraw wages paid from Ramallah; it soon became apparent that deposits were reaching only the latter, and altercations between the workers were reported to have taken place.

Noting that the unity Government as a whole—if not Hamas as a party—subscribed to three of the conditions established by the Quartet group in 2006 (disavowal of armed struggle, respect for previous agreements and recognition of Israel), the international community cautiously accepted the development. Israel rejected it outright, ruling that negotiations were impossible as long as the PA had a government claiming to represent an unreformed Hamas.

UNREST IN THE WEST BANK AND EAST JERUSALEM

Unrest in the West Bank escalated following the abduction of three Israeli teenagers on the outskirts of the settlement block of Gush Etzion on 12 June 2014. Israel quickly blamed Hamas—a charge the group denied—and Israel was unable to present compelling evidence to support the claim. The abductions prompted a massive search operation in which six Palestinians were killed and about 350 more were arrested, including most of the leading members of Hamas in the West Bank and several individuals who had been released in previous agreements, such as the prisoner exchange involving Shalit (see above). The boys' bodies were found near Hebron on 30 June. About 400 Palestinians were arrested. Hamas personnel and institutions bore the brunt of Israel's crackdown and the homes of two suspects in Hebron were demolished in August. On 2 July in East Jerusalem a Palestinian teenager, Muhammad Abu Khdeir, was kidnapped and burned to death, apparently in revenge for the killing of the three Israeli teenagers in Hebron; three Israelis, two of them teenagers, were charged with murder. The killing provoked demonstrations and riots across the West Bank, East Jerusalem and inside Israel. Protests in solidarity with Gaza during Operation Protective Edge led to the killing of more than a dozen Palestinians by the IDF in the second half of July. The ongoing security co-ordination between the PA and Israel did little to increase support for the West Bank leadership. When Prime Minister Hamdallah organized a transfer of medical supplies to Gaza in July, the PA representatives supervising delivery were attacked by the local population.

OPERATION PROTECTIVE EDGE

The ceasefire that ended Operation Pillar of Defense in November 2012 had proved largely successful, particularly for Israel. Sporadic breaches of the border had occurred, but these were typically small in scale and initiated by Islamist radicals generally understood to be beyond the control of Hamas. None the less, Israel held Hamas accountable. Israeli firepower was relatively restrained during the ceasefire, but Gaza was by no means immune from occasional air strikes and incursions. Meanwhile, the siege of Gaza continued. The fatal shooting of an Israeli worker by a Palestinian sniper at the border fence in December 2013 marked a brief escalation of tension and Israeli air strikes on Gaza, but this was dwarfed by the launch on 8 July 2014 of Operation Protective Edge. The death and destruction wrought over the next seven weeks and more would exceed even that of Operation Cast Lead in 2008–09.

The pressure of events in the West Bank, compounded by an Israeli air strike on 7 July 2014 that killed several of its members in Khan Yunis in Gaza, prompted Hamas to launch several rockets from Gaza into southern Israel. The Israeli military response appeared to be premeditated, thorough to the point of being described as 'disproportionate' by some observers, and reflective of a political mood that meant pressure on Netanyahu (who had been in office since 2009), came less from the centre or the left of his coalition than from the hard right. Israeli military goals included a sharp reduction in Gaza's capacity to launch rockets, demolition of tunnels extending from beneath Gaza into Israel and a major weakening of the Islamist movement in general. However, Israel stopped short of demolishing Hamas entirely; this was partly a question of battlefield dynamics, but might also have reflected an acknowledgement that more radical elements would likely emerge in its place. Netanyahu for his part sought to restore political capital on the radical right of his administration, which had been vocal in calling for Hamas to be severely weakened or even destroyed.

The assault from land, sea and air began on 8 July 2014 and initially targeted rocket-launching sites before escalating into a ground invasion on 17 July focused on tunnels. The collection of rockets at Hamas's disposal gave the group unprecedented range to strike Israel, but the majority of launches were rendered ineffective by Israel's warning and shelter network, together with the 'Iron Dome' anti-missile defence system. One of the most notable effects of the rockets was to alarm international airlines sufficiently that many briefly suspended flights to Israel in late July, after Hamas warned that it would target Ben-Gurion International Airport in Tel Aviv. The ground invasion afforded different opportunities. The IDF remarked on the professionalism and sophisticated tactics on the part of Hamas's military wing, the Izz al-Din al-Qassam Brigades, which it attributed to Iranian training. The fighting appeared to empower the military commander of Hamas, Muhammad Deif. The toll of the conflict on Gaza's civilian population was enormous.

Egyptian President al-Sisi brokered a 72-hour ceasefire that began on 5 August 2014, when all IDF soldiers withdrew from Gaza. Violence flared briefly, however, and Israel withdrew from negotiations before a 72-hour extension could be agreed from 9 August. The ceasefire was then renewed for five days from 13 August; brief rocket fire, reportedly launched by marginal elements in Gaza, did not disrupt the discussions. Palestinian demands focused on the lifting of the Israeli siege of Gaza, the opening of its borders and reconstruction. Israel repeatedly emphasized the necessity of its security and urged the demilitarization of Gaza.

On 19 August 2014 it was reported that Israel had agreed to lift certain elements of the blockade, in exchange for a commitment to demilitarization from Hamas. However, the ceasefire was broken later that day when Hamas was reported to have fired rockets into southern Israel, and fighting ensued for another week, during which Israel killed three leading members of Hamas in Rafah, and Hamas subsequently executed at least 17 Palestinians who were accused of collaboration, including informing Israel of the whereabouts of senior Hamas personnel. On 24 August rockets were reported to have been fired into northern Israel from Lebanon and the Golan Heights, although the latter case was reported to have been unintentional stray fire from the civil conflict in Syria. A month-long ceasefire was accepted by Hamas (and Islamic Jihad) and Israel on 26 August. The terms of the ceasefire were similar to those proposed on 5 August. Israel committed to open crossings on its border to allow humanitarian aid and construction materials to enter Gaza, and would extend the limits afforded to Gaza's fishing fleet from 5.5 km off the coast of Gaza to 11 km. Egypt agreed to open its border with Gaza at the Rafah border crossing. Indirect negotiations between the two parties were scheduled for September and were reported to include Hamas's demands for an airport and modern marine port in Gaza and the release of Palestinian prisoners, while Israel insisted on the disarmament of militant groups in Gaza and the return of the remains of two IDF soldiers who had been killed in the fighting.

By the time the month-long ceasefire had been agreed in late August 2014 the local Ministry of Health reported that more than 2,100 Palestinians had been killed. According to figures subsequently reported by the UN, 2,220 had been killed, 1,492 (over two-thirds) of whom were civilians, including more than 500 children. More than 11,000 Palestinians were believed to have been injured and more than 200,000 had been rendered homeless and were living in UN shelters. Around one-quarter of Gaza's population—almost half a million people—were thought to have been internally displaced at one stage of the conflict. A total of 71 Israelis, including 66 soldiers, as well as one foreign national were killed. Many of the civilian casualties were incurred during the bombing of several schools operated by UNRWA, which were serving as designated shelters. Israel alleged that the schools had been used by Hamas to store missiles. The IDF action devastated infrastructure and left Gaza without sufficient supplies of water or electricity and the threat of communicable disease was substantial. Acting on a request from the PA, on 23 July the UN Human Rights Council had voted in favour of an investigation into allegations that Israeli actions in Gaza were in breach of international law. There were 17 abstentions and only the USA voted against the motion. In early August UN Secretary-General Ban Ki-moon condemned the latest in a series of Israeli air strikes on UNRWA-operated schools as a 'moral outrage and a criminal act'. The Obama Administration issued condemnation of Israel's targeting of UN facilities and expressed its frustration that the Department of Defense appeared to be able to meet Israeli requests for armaments without its prior consultation. The US Congress approved some US $225m. worth of funding to Israel to maintain its 'Iron Dome' anti-missile defence system in early August.

Meanwhile, the war in Gaza had undermined the stability of the recently formed unity Government, with reports of Hamas having harassed members of Fatah in Gaza during the conflict, while Abbas and Israel accused Hamas of planning to overthrow the PA in August 2014. Popular support for Hamas was reported to have risen following the end of hostilities, to the detriment of Fatah. In September the PA announced its intention to appeal to the ICC to open an investigation against Israel for war crimes and crimes against humanity.

LACK OF RECONCILIATION AND RECONSTRUCTION IN GAZA

One year after Operation Protective Edge, the situation in Gaza was little changed: the technocratic unity Government remained unable to function effectively, and pledges of aid, small in any case, were not realized as actual relief for civilians. Inter-factional reconciliation also failed to gain appreciable momentum following the conflict, and the two main movements were occupied by disputes about ministerial remits, public sector salaries, security and the right to raise taxes on goods passing through border crossings. Hamas appeared to foster discord within Fatah, arresting certain of its members in Gaza, while quietly encouraging supporters of former antagonist Dahlan. The Government's decision to withhold the salaries of over 200 Dahlan-affiliated security personnel only increased dissent. In May 2015 Hamas spokesman in Gaza Ahmed Yousef blamed Fatah for not integrating the two administrations, criticizing, in particular, the failure to pay Hamas appointees their salaries and a lack of preparation for elections. On 16 June President Abbas informed the Fatah leadership that the Cabinet would be dissolved. Prime Minister Hamdallah began to reorganize his administration (rather than dissolve it, as previously announced), and Hamas complained about a lack of consultation. A security crackdown on Hamas in the West Bank also exacerbated relations. A reorganized Cabinet, in which five portfolios had been reallocated, eventually took office in Ramallah at the end of July.

Hamas faced a challenge in a different sphere from affiliates of fundamentalist militia group Islamic State in Iraq and the Levant (renamed Islamic State in June 2014) among Gaza's Salafist underground. On 2 June 2015 Hamas forces killed an alleged Islamic State member. Islamic State threatened to remove Hamas, then appeared to instigate a series of car bombings on 20 July, targeting figures in the armed wing of Hamas, the Izz al-Din al-Qassam Brigades, and its Islamic Jihad counterpart, the al-Quds Brigades.

HAMAS IN REGIONAL AND INTERNATIONAL AFFAIRS

Under attack in the Palestinian territories, Hamas sought to restore its standing in the Middle East. It retained a diaspora base in Doha, an asset for the Amir of Qatar, Sheikh Tamim bin Hamad Al Thani. The road out of isolation also led back to Iran; following preliminary meetings in Beirut, normal relations between Hamas and the Iranian administration were reported to have been restored by December 2014. Elsewhere in the Gulf, in July 2015 Hamas political bureau chief Meshaal met the new Saudi monarch, King Salman bin Abd al-Aziz Al Sa'ud. Relations with Saudi Arabia were typically cool in light of the kingdom's unease with the affiliated Muslim Brotherhood, together with Hamas's record of sponsorship by Iran. However, the meeting appeared to open up the prospect of Saudi support for Egypt in a regional effort to reduce tensions between Fatah and Hamas.

The relationship between Hamas and Egypt under President al-Sisi remained one of strategic hostility subject to tactical adjustment. In January 2015, following a violent assault against government forces in Sinai, the Izz al-Din al-Qassam Brigades were judged to be a terrorist organization; a similar ruling against Hamas followed in a separate court the next month. Charges focused on Hamas's alleged role in fomenting instability in northern Sinai. Yet the al-Sisi regime itself prompted legal controversy in June when a court of appeal overturned the previous decision. A new ruling aligned the legal situation with the actual practice of Egyptian intelligence; legal or not, officers routinely negotiated with Hamas members in Cairo and Gaza. In this context, it was reported that the Dubai-based Dahlan might constitute a useful conduit.

Hamas also reached out to the north. In January 2015, several months after apparently surviving an Israeli assassination attempt in which his wife, two children and several bystanders were killed, Hamas's military commander Deif was reported to have issued an appeal to Hezbollah to unite against Israel: relations between the two Islamist groups had suffered since the Hamas leadership withdrew from Damascus and distanced the group from the Syrian President, Assad.

Further afield, Hamas received an unanticipated boost when the EU General Court ruled that the group be taken off the list of terrorist groups on account of alleged procedural errors in the original listing. The Izz al-Din al-Qassam Brigades had been on the list from the outset in 2001, and Hamas added in 2003. The European Council challenged the General Court's decision in what appeared likely to be a lengthy process. Meanwhile, Meshaal met longstanding Russian Minister of Foreign Affairs Sergei Lavrov in early August, in Doha, when he was granted an invitation to visit Moscow for the first time since 2010.

PALESTINIAN DIPLOMACY AT THE UN AND THE ICC

In December 2014 the UN Security Council considered a Jordanian-led attempt to advance Palestinian diplomacy through the international body. The draft resolution's key themes were twofold: harnessing progress to a timetable, first for negotiations with Israel to be concluded within 12 months, and then for Israeli withdrawal from the occupied Palestinian territories by the end of 2017; and for a further upgrade of Palestine's standing to full membership of the UN as an independent state. Reprising a bid in 2011, this draft could not overcome US opposition. The PA failed to muster the nine votes necessary to pass a resolution, although it did secure eight, including two from Europe, namely Luxembourg and France, the latter joining Russia and the People's Republic of China as three of five permanent members to support the attempt. Among the rotating members, the decisions of Nigeria and Australia were unexpected: a fellow-member of the Organization of the Islamic Conference, Nigeria had been expected to provide the ninth vote in favour but instead ceded to intense US-Israel lobbying to abstain. The capitulation rendered the US veto a moot point; the US ambassador to the UN, Samantha Power, was joined by the Australian representative in casting just two votes against the resolution.

Disappointment at the UN Security Council led the PA immediately to escalate its diplomatic campaign via the ICC. Abbas adopted a tranche of 19 international commitments the next day, foremost among them a renewed approach to the ICC. In 2009 the PA had attempted to lodge notification of acceptance of ICC jurisdiction under article 12/3 of the Rome Statute; as the Statute was open only to states, the ICC had scrutinized the bid for three years before passing it on for the UN to determine Palestine's standing. The upgrade to non-member observer state recorded in UNGA resolution 67/19 of November 2012 resolved the ambiguity; that the situation had been clarified to the satisfaction of the ICC was indicated earlier in December, when the Assembly of States Parties to the Rome Statute agreed to admit the PA as an observer. Now Abbas could repeat the 2009 attempt, successfully submitting to ICC jurisdiction, in addition to depositing an instrument of accession to the statute with the UN Secretary-General. The ICC reported that the PA, as the state of Palestine, had acceded to the Rome Statute on 2 January 2015.

Acting on the PA's initiative, ICC Chief Prosecutor Fatou Bensouda opened a preliminary investigation on 16 January 2015. Palestinian acceptance of ICC jurisdiction had been backdated to 13 June 2014—the date on which Israel launched its crackdown on the West Bank, with a view to strengthening the investigation into Operation Protective Edge. The Rome Statute entered into force for Palestine on 1 April 2015. The

ICC now had jurisdiction to investigate war crimes, crimes against humanity and genocide committed on Palestinian-controlled territory. Palestinian politicians were aware that the ICC's attention could be directed the other way, on perpetrators of violence in their own ranks, most obviously (but not exclusively) Hamas and Islamic Jihad on account of civilian casualties from rocket and mortar attacks. Hamas leaders had indicated their consent to the ICC move during the latter stages of Operation Protective Edge and appeared confident in their ability to argue that the Izz al-Din al-Qassam Brigades now focused effectively on military targets. The Palestinian public appeared to approve the decision, even though many believed it to be long overdue, and it helped to restore some of the eroded legitimacy to Abbas and the PA. Following the murder of 18-month old Ali Dawabsheh in July 2015 (see *Repression in the West Bank*), the PA now had an institutional outlet of sorts and promptly presented a case on Jewish 'settler terrorism' to the Chief Prosecutor.

REPRESSION IN THE WEST BANK

The destruction in Gaza was accompanied by a parallel increase in the pressure administered across the West Bank by Israel and the PA. During Operation Protective Edge, the UN reported that 23 West Bank Palestinians had been killed, among them three children. Reporting on the year overall, the Office for the Coordination of Humanitarian Affairs (OCHA) recorded that Israel killed more Palestinian civilians during 2014 than in any year since the occupation began in 1967. Public anger, coupled with the effective demobilization of organized resistance by the PA, prompted a spate of what were termed 'lone wolf' attacks, typically using domestic items such as knives or vehicles. The colonial context was underlined when, shortly after the end of Operation Protective Edge in August 2014, Israel announced the confiscation of almost 1,000 acres of land between Hebron and Bethlehem. Estimated by NGO Peace Now to be the largest single act of confiscation in decades, the move delimited the development of five Palestinian villages, while connecting the Gush Etzion settlement block near Bethlehem to Israel beyond the provisions of the 1949 armistice or 'Green Line'. Meanwhile, in the Jordan Valley Israel consolidated the settlement enterprise by deploying the IDF to remove Palestinians through the revocation of residency rights, on the grounds that land had to be used for military training; at the same time, IDF units were ordered to sink new wells for settlements. The decisive re-election of Israeli Prime Minister Netanyahu in March 2015 continued Israel's rightward trajectory.

On 10 December 2014 a PA minister with responsibility for settlements and the separation wall (and a popular member of the Fatah Revolutionary Council), Ziad Abu Ein, died following a confrontation with Israeli soldiers. Abu Ein had been part of a protest group planting trees at the village of Turmusiya, in an effort to defend village land against encroaching Jewish settlement. Under pressure to respond, Abbas called future security co-operation with Israel into question. Eventually, and amid the further interruption of customs revenue by Israel in retaliation for the PA joining the ICC, the PLO Central Council voted to suspend security co-ordination on 6 March 2015; the ruling could be implemented only by the Executive Committee, and although it drew the attention of the UN Secretary-General, the precise implications remained unclear. In part owing to external pressure, Israel agreed to transfer customs revenue during March and April, but only after informing that it would subtract large sums for overdue electricity bills, much to the indignation of the unity Government.

In late March 2015 the IDF decreed that aspects of the Israeli penal code be formally applied to Palestinians in the West Bank, while precluding them from a right to self-defence against home invasion, a right that was accorded to Jewish settlers. Towards the end of July settler activism provoked fresh clashes in East Jerusalem, when a party of religious nationalists under police escort visited the al-Aqsa mosque compound. Shortly afterwards, in the village of Duma, near Nablus, a family home was set alight by unknown assailants, resulting in the death of Dawabsheh and later of his parents. The fire, which appeared to be part of an escalating campaign of settler violence against Palestinians, fuelled additional clashes at al-Aqsa. In August the PA lodged the case of Dawabsheh, under the broader case of Jewish 'settler terrorism', at the ICC.

Under attack from by Israel, alienated from Gaza, and with West Bank police observing rising levels of intra-societal violence, Abbas became increasingly authoritarian. In November 2014, following strike action, the Civil Servants' Union was banned and two union senior leaders arrested. Reflecting the dominance of the public sector, the union was the largest in Palestine, with some 40,000 members; an appeal was lodged with the courts regarding the union's status, and its leaders released after a week. Around the same time, the West Bank media were instructed to intensify a campaign against Hamas, emphasizing responsibility for the latest Gaza war, alleging plans for another coup, highlighting the harassment of Fatah members in Gaza, and holding Hamas responsible for the failure of the unity Government. This pressure, and further rumours that Abbas might resign, revealed new cracks in the Palestinian political elite. The antagonism of Dahlan-affiliated officers in Gaza drew criticism from senior Fatah member Tawfiq al-Tirawi. PLO Secretary-General Abd al-Rabbuh was dismissed in June 2015; he had been critical of the handling of the union issue and of the split with Gaza, advocating the inclusion of Hamas into the organization. al-Rabbuh, who was replaced by Erekat, was sharply critical of the perceived centralization of power under Abbas but rejected any suggestion that he had been conspiring with Dahlan or former premier Fayyad. Meanwhile, Fayyad's Future for Palestine group was harassed, and its funds frozen, apparently owing to allegations of a connection with Dahlan.

THIRD INTIFADA FAILS TO ERUPT IN EAST JERUSALEM AND THE WEST BANK

In 2015 the number of overall casualties in the West Bank at the hands of the IDF more than doubled from the previous year, to 136. The statistical data showed that the conflict dynamics of Israeli settlement, decentralized resistance, demonstrations and further casualties were clearly escalating.

In the context of increasing settlement and settler violence, along with heightened Palestinian anxiety about Israeli behaviour regarding the al-Aqsa mosque complex, decentralized, individual knife or vehicular attacks by Palestinians in and around East Jerusalem continued. Among the incidents during October and November 2015: a youth was shot dead after a knife attack in East Jerusalem; another was killed during an attempted knife attack outside Nablus; further vehicular assaults were staged against Israeli pedestrians, including outside West Bank settlements; clashes between Israeli forces and Palestinian youths occurred across the territory; and a Palestinian baby was killed by teargas inhalation near Bethlehem. In November the death toll approached some 80 Palestinians and nearly 20 Israelis. UN Secretary-General Ban Ki-Moon visited the territory in October, in an attempt to calm tensions, just as US Secretary of State Kerry was reported to have intervened in regard to the governance of the al-Aqsa complex.

PALESTINE'S FLAG FLIES AT THE UN

Developments in Palestinian diplomacy advanced through two sessions of the UNGA. On 30 September 2015, subsequent to a vote by the General Assembly, the Palestinian flag, as that of a non-member observer state (together with the flag of the Vatican City), was officially raised at the UN headquarters in New York. The ceremony was preceded by a speech by President Abbas, in which he expressed pride at witnessing the raising of the flag, while lamenting the failure of the peace process since the Oslo Accords to the point that he was no longer willing to abide by them. In contrast, UN Secretary-General Ban expressed his hope that the symbolic act would lift Palestinian spirits (although circumstances seemed to render that unlikely). The flag initiative, besides the symbolic gain, represented a limited victory for unilateral Palestinian diplomacy; the hoisting ceremony was achieved despite resolute Israeli and US opposition. In this respect, Abbas remained consistent, pursuing symbolic objectives through unilateral diplomacy while rejecting a return to negotiations with Israel (which had been suspended since April 2014, the Palestinian authorities maintaining that they would not provide Israel with a pretext for further encroachment on the West Bank in parallel with futile talks).

During his speech to the UNGA in September 2015, Abbas called for the international recognition of Palestine as a state under occupation—an analogy being drawn with the countries occupied by Nazi Germany during the Second World War, which was not favourably received by Israel. In September 2016 he followed this by asserting that Israeli settlement construction had virtually destroyed the possibility of a two-state solution, a goal with which he himself had been closely associated for many years. Noting that 2017 would mark the 50th anniversary of the occupation, Abbas then suggested that it be known as the year in which it would end. Referring to an episode a further 50 years in the past, he demanded that the UK apologize for the 1917 Balfour Declaration, a letter in which the British Secretary of State for Foreign Affairs promised British support for the 'establishment in Palestine of a national home for the Jewish people'.

In a further denunciation, Abbas blamed Israel for its negative response to an international conference that had been proposed by France in an attempt to revive the peace process. The proposed summit would follow discussions at a conference convened by the French Government in June 2016; with at least four permanent members of the UN Security Council in favour of the initiative, and the EU constituting the PA's key financial support and Israel's principal trading partner, the participants were, at least in theory, of significant influence. Meanwhile, the Obama Administration in September finalized a 10-year US $38,000m. arms deal with Israel. This record amount was generally regarded in part as compensation for the agreement negotiated with Iran during 2015 on its nuclear programme.

Meanwhile, in a further symbolic act, the Palestinian flag was flown above a delegation of Palestinian athletes at the 2016 Summer Olympic Games staged in Rio de Janeiro, Brazil. Under a treaty that entered into force in January, the Vatican City extended formal recognition of the state of Palestine.

FATAH–HAMAS TENSIONS PREVENT MUNICIPAL ELECTIONS

Planned municipal elections in the West Bank and Gaza, which were announced in June 2016 and scheduled for 8 October, were to constitute the first full local polls in a decade, with the exception of limited local polling, boycotted by Hamas, in 2012. The elections were, however, suspended shortly beforehand by order of the Supreme Court in Ramallah. The formal grounds for the decision were two-fold: echoing political practices in Iran (where electoral candidates are vetted by Islamic authorities and frequently disqualified), a predictable dispute arose over the authority of local courts in Gaza which barred certain Fatah candidates from standing. The Supreme Court further ruled that Israel's exclusion of East Jerusalem from the process precluded a legitimate vote (only two Jerusalem districts voted in 2012).

The decision to suspend the polls was interpreted by Hamas and many independent observers as a means of protecting Fatah in the West Bank. There were several possible reasons for this. First, with the PA serving a major conduit for international donor funds, it would be against the interests of many people for Fatah to lose the elections. Second, Fatah and the established elite continued to endure a profound and ongoing crisis of political legitimacy, with no presidential election since 2005 and no legislative elections since 2006, together with local opinion polls that showed ever decreasing faith in 80-year-old President Abbas, a two-state solution, or the peace process. Third, Palestinian political history contained an unnerving precedent for Fatah: Hamas had performed fairly well in the first local elections of 2004–05, and had then secured victory in the legislative elections of 2006. Local polls, as well as student council elections, could serve as a test of the political climate, and Hamas had just defeated Fatah twice at Birzeit University, near Ramallah, in April 2016, as well as in the previous year. Fourth, Israel contributed to Hamas's suspicions by preventing its members in the Central Election Commission from carrying out their duties, placing them under arrest through the much loathed mechanism of administrative detention (see *Palestinian Prisoners Begin Hunger Strike*).

DISSENT IN NABLUS

During August 2016 the West Bank's volatile northern hub and potential financial centre, Nablus, experienced fierce Palestinian infighting, this time between the PA's security services and Fatah. Two PA security officers were killed on 18 August. Less than one week later, three local suspects were dead, most prominent among them Fatah leader Ahmad Izzat Halawa, who was reportedly beaten to death while in PA custody in Junayd prison, after other officers unsuccessfully tried to protect him. Halawa had been a renowned leader of the al-Aqsa Martyrs Brigades now serving as the military wing of Fatah, which had been formed during the second *intifada* in order to offset the rising popularity of Hamas and its military wing, the Izz al-Din al-Qassam Brigades (see above).

Halawa's death prompted a wave of protest that extended to resignations within Fatah. Hamas spokesman Sami Abu Zuhri accused the PA of adopting a policy of execution. The event had a particular impact, not just on account of Halawa's seniority and prominence, but also due to the location of his death: Junayd prison had long constituted a feared symbol of Israeli repression prior to its handover to the PA some two decades previously. Now it carried similar associations under Palestinian jurisdiction. This latest death of a Palestinian in PA custody reinforced longstanding and popular misgivings concerning the PA security apparatus, its remit for security co-operation with Israel, and its role in policing dissent in the territory. Public anger had been evident in January 2016, when it was revealed that the Commander of General Intelligence, Maj.-Gen. Faraj, had claimed that the PA had thwarted some 200 attacks against Israelis in the previous few months. Apparently supporting this claim, in May the Israeli media reported data showing the PA to be responsible for detaining up to 40% of suspects. For Abbas, his officers and the PA in general, this was regarded as an effort to encourage Israel to reduce or halt routine military incursions into Area A. For much of the Palestinian public, however, it only increased their suspicion towards the PA. Meanwhile, in Nablus demonstrators demanded resignations, not least those of Hamdallah and of the local governor and security chief. PA police dispersed the crowds of protesters with tear gas.

DETERIORATION IN THE GAZA STRIP

After nearly a decade of blockade and three major Israeli military operations, conditions in Gaza had deteriorated to critical levels by 2016. As the population rose to nearly 1.8m., almost 1.3m. held refugee status. Data collected by various UN agencies reported colossal damage to society, infrastructure and productivity: almost one-half of the population (many of whom were displaced) were dependent on food aid, including that from the severely overstrained UNRWA; the growing population suffered from a persistent crisis in potable water; electricity was scarce; mass unemployment appeared to be reaching record levels; and psychological trauma was widespread. OCHA reported decreased movement in and out of the Gaza Strip during 2016, owing primarily to a tightening of restrictions by Egypt on exit through the southern border at Rafah. OCHA further reported that 16 heads of UN agencies operating in the Palestinian territories in August called for the 'uninterrupted and predictable flow of material and increased funding to address humanitarian needs and boost economic prospects'.

In circumstances such as this, militancy flourished, some of it to the detriment of Hamas. In September 2015, and reportedly for the first time since the heavy bombardment of mid-2014 (see *Operation Protective Edge*), rockets fired from Gaza landed in the southern Israeli town of Sderot and were also aimed at Ashkelon. A Salafist group believed to be affiliated with Islamic State claimed responsibility for the Ashkelon attack; amid hostility between the Palestinian nationalist Hamas and the jihadist Islamic State, the local Salafis were protesting at repression by Hamas, as well as drawing attention to the ongoing tension at the al-Aqsa mosque complex in Jerusalem. Sporadic rocket fire continued through 2016, to which Israel responded with air strikes and tank shells.

Beyond Gaza, in October 2015 the Hamas leadership secured a diplomatic victory with an official visit to South Africa led by its political bureau chief, Meshaal, and his deputy, Abu Marzuk. The high-level delegation was welcomed formally by the representatives of ruling African National Congress (ANC), and afforded a reception that included a meeting with South African President Jacob Zuma. Much irritation emanated from the Israeli authorities at the prospect of a close Hamas-ANC network. In a further success for Hamas, an Advocate-General of the European Court of Justice in September 2016 upheld a 2014 ruling of the lower General Court to recommend removal of the movement from the EU's list of terrorist organizations.

PROGRESS FOR PALESTINE AT THE UN

On 23 December 2016 the UN Security Council supported Resolution 2334. The text of the resolution was unambiguously critical of the ongoing development of settlements in occupied territories; in key sections, the Security Council:

1. Reaffirms that the establishment by Israel of settlements in the Palestinian territory occupied since 1967, including East Jerusalem, has no legal validity and constitutes a flagrant violation under international law and a major obstacle to the achievement of the two-State solution and a just, lasting and comprehensive peace;

2. Reiterates its demand that Israel immediately and completely cease all settlement activities in the occupied Palestinian territory, including East Jerusalem, and that it fully respect all of its legal obligations in this regard.

Frustrated during two presidential terms by Israeli intransigence, outgoing Obama Administration instructed the US delegation on the Security Council to withhold its customary veto against any Resolution critical of Israel, and the Resolution passed, with 14 votes in favour (and the one US abstention). Alarmed by the implications for the settlement project and frustrated by the readiness of the USA to withhold its veto, the provoked undisguised anger in Israeli Prime Minister Netanyahu, who described the Resolution as 'shameful'. The short-term diplomatic fallout was considerable and included the recall of Israel's ambassadors from New Zealand and Senegal, after the Governments of the two countries defended their decision, as temporary members of the Security Council, to co-sponsor Resolution 2334, along with Malaysia and Venezuela (with which Israel does not have diplomatic relations). Netanyahu also announced that he had suspended some US $6.3m. in funding to five UN bodies which he described as 'especially hostile' to Israel.

In further notable developments, in March 2017 the UN's Economic and Social Commission for Western Asia published a report entitled *Israeli Practices towards the Palestinian People and the Question of Apartheid*. The question posed—broadly, whether Israel was comparable to South Africa under the policy of apartheid, where one particular racial or religious group was treated preferentially in law—was answered in the affirmative, and the authors of the report concluded that Israel was, in their opinion at least, indeed an 'apartheid state'—a charge that the Israeli Government vociferously rejected, comparing the report to anti-Semitic propaganda from the era of Nazi rule in Germany. In July UNESCO voted to add the Old City of Hebron and the Ibrahimi mosque to its list of World Heritage sites (the third site under the control of the PA to be registered). The Israeli Government expressed its outrage at the decision, as it officially deemed the site to be the Tomb of the Patriarchs, as described in the Old Testament of the Bible, and one of the holiest sites for followers of the Jewish faith. Netanyahu, who had failed to have the motion on Hebron blocked, despite the intervention of the US delegation to the UN, immediately announced a US $1m. cut in Israeli funding to the UN.

The annual round of speeches on the Palestinian question at the UNGA took place in September 2017. The tone surrounding Abbas's presence on this occasion was gloomy, even by recent standards: recent opinion polling in the Palestinian territories had found that some two-thirds of respondents urged Abbas to resign as PA President; at the same time, support for a one-state solution to the Israeli-Palestinian conflict surpassed the 50% mark. Mindful of ongoing Israeli settlement-building in the West Bank and hostile Palestinian public opinion, Abbas remarked at the Assembly that the two-state solution had been rendered all but impossible, in consequence of which, the Palestinian struggle for self-determination might now evolve into a rights-based struggle within a single territory.

PALESTINE CONTEMPLATES PRESIDENT DONALD TRUMP

In contrast to the typically supportive forums of the UN, the advent of the Trump presidency held uncertain consequences for Palestine. As President-Elect, Donald Trump publicly disagreed with the US abstention permitting UN Security Council Resolution 2334 to pass in December 2016 and promised to act in defence of Israeli interests following his inauguration. Upon taking office on 20 January 2017, Trump quickly appointed a range of Jewish, pro-Israeli figures to his Administration, notably his son-in-law Jared Kushner as a senior policy adviser and hard-right pro-Israeli settlement lawyer David Friedman as US ambassador to Israel. During the election campaign, Trump had threatened to approve transfer of the US embassy in Israel from Tel Aviv to Jerusalem, although in practice he did not rush to do so once in office, and by September the embassy remained in Tel Aviv. At a press conference in February Trump appeared ambivalent towards the two-state solution, although he met Abbas in Washington, DC, in early May, and again in Bethlehem later in that month. Items on Trump's agenda included: encouraging the PA in its containment of armed resistance; a cessation of incitement to violence against Israelis; and perhaps, most sensitively of all, the end of welfare support from the PA to the casualties, prisoners and families of those affected by resistance to Israeli occupation. Opinion polls suggested that less than 10% of the Palestinian public had faith in Trump as a potential peacemaker.

POLITICKING WITHIN FATAH: THE SEVENTH GENERAL CONFERENCE AND BEYOND

Late November 2016 heralded the opening of Fatah's seventh general conference, convened in Ramallah and attended by just over 1,300 delegates—the first such gathering since 2009. The event produced a new Revolutionary Council of around 130 members and a Central Committee of some 20 members, which continued to be chaired by Abbas. Among the three heavyweights for the post-Abbas succession, Marwan Barghouthi reportedly came top of the local opinion polls, burnishing his credentials as the Palestinian version of Nelson Mandela, seemingly destined for greatness while languishing in Israeli custody. Rajoub came in second place, while Abbas's one-time ally and subsequent arch rival Dahlan, himself a former PSF chief in Gaza, had been expelled from the movement in 2011. His supporters were prevented from attending the conference at all and Dahlan's expulsion from Fatah was confirmed. Headquartered in the UAE since 2012, the ambitious Dahlan cultivated close relations with regional powers including his hosts and Egypt; since September 2016, both states had led efforts to resolve the two major schisms in the Palestinian body politic: within Fatah itself (essentially between the Dahlan and Abbas camps) and of course between Fatah and Hamas. Jordan and Saudi Arabia contributed to this regional initiative.

Local elections in several West Bank municipalities were held in May 2017. Boycotted by Hamas, Islamic Jihad and the PFLP, the polls were in effect reduced to another internal Fatah affair and did little to legitimize the moribund Abbas regime.

POLITICKING WITHIN HAMAS: IMPLICATIONS FOR GAZA AND THE WIDER REGION

The year 2017 was a busy one for the internal politics of Hamas. Two major changes took place. In February Yahya Sinwar was elected as the new head of the movement in the Gaza Strip.

Sinwar was among the founders of Hamas's military wing, the Izz al-Din al-Qassam Brigades, and much respected. He had spent more than 20 years in prison in Israel until his release in 2011 as part of the prisoner exchange for Israeli soldier Shalit—a deal of which Sinwar disapproved on account of it being too favourable to Israel. Born into a refugee family in the Khan Yunis refugee camp, Sinwar was considered a man of the people; his roots were very similar to those of Dahlan, and the two had known each other as students, even though their trajectories went on to diverge markedly. Sinwar's rise to prominence had been preceded by quiet manoeuvering—in particular the appointment of key ally Tawfiq Abu Naim to head of the police and intelligence services in 2015. Abu Naim would go on to play an important role in negotiations between Hamas and the Egyptian regime under President al-Sisi.

In May 2017, upon completion of a turbulent two terms in office, Meshaal, now resident in Qatar, could no longer run for election as the overall head of Islamist movement's executive, the political bureau. He was succeeded by the Gazan-based former prime minister Haniya. The joint ascent of Haniya and Sinwar marked a decisive shift in Hamas's centre of gravity from the diaspora to Gaza.

Just days before the installation of Haniya, Hamas published a new charter. It was the culmination of a process of many years, which had been often interrupted: by the elections in 2006, Hamas's pre-emptive coup in 2007 and three major Israeli operations against Gaza in 2008–09, late 2012 and mid-2014. The original charter dated back to 1988 and was beset with unhelpful, violent rhetoric against Israel. The new version sought to update the manifesto and the message that Hamas projected to its followers, as well as to the outside world. It was much more nuanced in its political assessment and programme. Features of note included a clarification that Hamas's struggle was with 'Zionism as a colonizing power', rather than with Jews per se, and that its struggle was strictly confined to Palestine. The commitment to armed struggle remained as a strategic choice in pursuit of Palestinian rights, but at the same time the group accepted a two-state solution, even as it continued to withhold recognition from Israel.

The change in Hamas leadership and especially Sinwar's ascent were interpreted in some quarters as a prelude to improved relations with Iran. Following a period of hedging, the Hamas leadership under Meshaal had opted decisively to side with their co-religionists in Syria's Sunni Muslims rather than adhere to the Alawi-led regime of Bashar al-Assad in Damascus. This placed some stress on Hamas's relationship with pro-Assad Iran. That relationship was never ruptured, but was certainly downgraded. Sinwar's background in the Izz al-Din al-Qassam Brigades—the wing of Hamas to which Iran had been most consistently committed—was thought to help to facilitate the repair in relations. One such indication of the rapprochement came in August 2017, when a Hamas delegation was invited to attend the inauguration of President Hassan Rouhani for a second term as head of state in Tehran, Iran. Meanwhile, Hezbollah was reported to be mediating between Iran and Hamas.

Elsewhere, Sinwar and Abu Naim held meetings with Egyptian intelligence officials; the Saudi-led effort to exclude Qatar diplomatically, which was initiated in June 2017 and to which Egypt was party, appeared to nudge Egypt and Hamas towards rapprochement. Under regional pressure, Qatar asked senior Hamas military commander Salah Aruri to leave the country. Supported by alternative sources of Gulf funding, Egypt stood well-placed to expedite an improvement in conditions in the coastal enclave that it bordered.

ECONOMIC AND SOCIAL CONDITIONS IN THE GAZA STRIP

The demand for development aid in Gaza was substantial, wherever it might come from. Labouring through over a decade of Israeli blockade from 2006, and punctuated by three wars, conditions were grim. Gaza no longer had a real economy or even much of a tunnel-based trafficking substitute; some two-fifths of Gazans scratched out an existence below the poverty line. Many relied on tiny incomes from extended family and social networks in what was beginning to resemble a cashless society, where useful goods and services were exchanged, rather than formal salaries paid. Neither Egypt nor Israel wished to oversee famine, and yet food insecurity became endemic; as many as eight out of 10 Gazans were thought to be dependent on food aid, much of it provided by UNRWA. Restricted access to agricultural land and the sea amplified the problem, and mass unemployment reinforced poverty. Sanitation and public health continued to deteriorate as reconstruction proceeded at a frustratingly slow pace. It was reported that the UN took at least a year to rebuild the first house in Gaza, partly on account of Israeli guidelines that classified cement as a dual-use resource: it was indeed needed for housing, but the Israeli authorities considered that it could also be used to reinforce tunnels and bunkers. Tens of thousands of Gazans without homes relied on generous hosts or temporary accommodation for shelter. In conditions reminiscent of southern Lebanon, unexploded munitions killed or mutilated local civilians as they moved through the rubble left by recent conflicts.

During his final trip to the Palestinian territories in June 2016, outgoing UN Secretary-General Ban Ki-Moon reiterated the UN's judgement that the siege constituted a form of (illegal) collective punishment. His successor, António Guterres, on a visit to Gaza in August 2017, lamented the humanitarian crisis and appealed for an end of the siege.

The Fatah–Hamas rift led the PA, at least in the short term, to exacerbate rather than relieve conditions. In a series of coordinated moves during the first half of 2017, the PA added to Gaza's electricity crisis, first by eliminating tax exemptions on fuel for the Strip's only power plant and then by reducing payments for already limited electricity supplies provided by Israel. Highly contentious, the move did eventually bear fruit as Hamas agreed to meet part of the bill. Others measures targeted Gaza's dysfunctional public sector. Having lost to Hamas's pre-emptive coup in 2007, President Abbas ordered the majority of the PA's civil servants and security officers in Gaza to strike in protest, as a requirement of continuing to receive a salary. Hamas administrators then filled the vacancies and services were resumed, even if those workers frequently went unpaid. In April 2017 the PA then imposed pay cuts on its loyalists and followed up in July by imposing compulsory early retirement on more than 6,000 of them.

PALESTINIAN PROTESTS IN PRISON, EAST JERUSALEM AND ACROSS THE WEST BANK

Launched in mid-April 2017, a hunger strike by Palestinian prisoners held by Israel concluded on 26 May, the first day of Ramadan. Supported by demonstrations across the West Bank, the striking prisoners demanded a list of improvements to their conditions, including increased family visits, access to education, television and telephones. Led by Fatah's most high-profile prisoner, Marwan Barghouthi, the affair elevated his profile in prison and beyond still further (even if, allegedly, he was caught on camera eating a chocolate bar).

In East Jerusalem, following a shooting incident on 14 July 2017 that left two Israeli police officers dead, Israel installed metal detectors at the Lions' Gate entrance to the al-Aqsa mosque compound, which remains a site of unparalleled symbolic importance to secular and religious Palestinians alike. President Abbas ordered an immediate cessation of security cooperation with Israel until the measures were reversed. Protests against the measures escalated quickly and spread as far as Türkiye and Yemen. In clashes between Palestinian protesters and the IDF following Friday prayers on 21 July, three Palestinians were killed in East Jerusalem. Later that day clashes unfolded with Israeli forces across the West Bank, and in the evening a Jewish family in the settlement of Halamish suffered three fatalities in a knife attack by a Palestinian attacker. Israel eventually removed the metal detectors from the compound on 25 July, in addition to the accompanying surveillance cameras. Violence flared up again in late September in the Jewish settlement of Har Adar on the border between East Jerusalem and the West Bank, where a Palestinian from nearby Beit Surik in the West Bank shot three Israelis dead— one soldier and two security guards—before being shot dead himself by the Israeli armed forces. Hamas appeared to endorse the attack, without formally claiming responsibility.

LOOMING SHIFTS WITHIN FATAH

Not for the first time, the 82-year-old Abbas showed signs of ill health in early 2018. Most notably, he was hospitalized in May suffering from an ear infection. The prospect of the end of the Abbas era provoked conjecture about who might succeed to the presidency of the state of Palestine, as well as the Palestinian Authority, in addition to the chairmanship of the PLO and Fatah. Potential successors politicked behind the scenes, but a single front-runner had yet to emerge from a pack that included two former PSF chiefs: Rajoub, a prominent official in the West Bank who served as Secretary-General of Fatah's Central Committee as well as director of the Palestinian Football Association and the Palestinian Olympic Committee. His rival Dahlan, with roots in Gaza, remained in exile as a guest of the UAE. Other possible candidates included al-Aqsa intifada leader Marwan Barghouthi, who remained in Israeli custody (alongside an estimated 5,700 of his compatriots in late 2018), and chief negotiator Erekat, who appeared to be recovering from lung transplant surgery in October 2017. The PNC held its first regular session since 2009 in April 2018 and elected 103 new members to replace those who had died since the last session. Abbas was re-elected as PNC President in May.

HAMAS IN NEGOTIATIONS

Reconciliation between Fatah and Hamas remained more of a goal than a reality in 2017–18. Even though a Hamas delegation led by Saleh Arouri had signed a reconciliation deal Fatah, represented by central committee member Azzam al-Ahmad in Cairo in October 2017, and Hamas had agreed to dismantle its temporary Administrative Committee and made provisions to hold legislative elections by the end of 2018, thornier questions remained unanswered, including: which faction would take charge of security in the Gaza Strip? What would become of Hamas civil servants, and could Hamas be brought under the umbrella of the PLO? Reconciliation suffered another blow in March 2018, when a convoy including the Palestinian Prime Minister Hamdallah and intelligence chief Maj-Gen. Faraj was bombed during a short visit by a Fatah delegation to Gaza.

Independently of key Palestinian institutions, in August 2018 Hamas found itself part of an international effort to calm tensions along the fractious Gaza-Israel border fence. This international effort pitted Hamas on one side, supported by Qatar and Türkiye, and Israel, Egypt and the USA on the other. The absent PA and PLO looked on, somewhat frustrated, from the sidelines.

Hamas and its allies continued to suffer casualties both within and beyond the Strip in 2018. Imad al-Alami, a former member of the political bureau of Hamas, died of a gunshot to the head in January, reportedly a self-inflicted accident, although observers suggested that it could have been an attempted assassination. Another senior member of Hamas, Fadi al-Batsh, a university lecturer and engineer at the University of Kuala Lumpur in Malaysia, was assassinated in April. The operation apparently bore all the hallmarks of an execution by Mossad. Batsh was an expert in drone (unmanned aerial vehicle) technology; the skies over Gaza and southern Israel would become increasingly and innovatively contested as the year progressed (see *The Great March of Return and US Embassy Protests*). Also in April, four members of Islamic Jihad died in Gaza near the border with Israel in what was reported to have been an explosives accident.

THE GREAT MARCH OF RETURN AND US EMBASSY PROTESTS

Protests flared in the Gaza Strip following the launch of the Great March of Return on 30 March 2018. A total of 18 Palestinian protesters were shot dead by the IDF on the first day of the protest, reportedly after entering the Israeli-imposed border zone and shooting at Israeli troops, although the IDF provided no evidence that the protesters had been armed. The march represented the will of the population of Gaza to return to the homes that they and their ancestors had occupied prior to the creation of the state of Israel in 1948. The project, which enjoyed broad public support, had not been initiated by Hamas, but the Islamist group was quick to assert its authority, to offer support to marchers and to use it to pressurize Israel into granting concessions. The protests and clashes that followed brought the much-neglected Gaza Strip to international attention. The demonstrations were invigorated each Friday, upon the occasion of the main weekly prayers. The human toll was considerable; demonstrations reached a climax in mid-May 2018, to coincide with the anniversary of the *al-Nakba* on 15 May. President Trump's highly contentious decision to inaugurate the move of the US embassy to Jerusalem from Tel Aviv on the day before (Israel's Independence Day) provoked enormous Palestinian anger, and contrasting images played on international news channels showing on the one hand US and Israeli dignitaries attending a solemn ceremony at the US embassy in Jerusalem and on the other images of Palestinian protesters at the Israeli border lying injured or dead at the hands of the IDF in Gaza. An estimated 60 Palestinian protesters were reported to have been killed by the IDF on 14 May alone. The protests escalated from June after Israel suspended the supply of fuel and gas to the Strip; Palestinian protesters began to launch kites and balloons carrying incendiary material across the border, which caused large fires that damaged several thousand hectares of Israeli farms, parks and forests, although no injuries were reported. Israel closed its only border crossing to Gaza in July in response. Skirmishes escalated in early August when Hamas launched an estimated 150 rockets into southern Israel from Gaza, to which Israel responded with limited air strikes. In mid-August Egyptian officials in Cairo mediated a ceasefire between Israel and Palestinian representatives in Gaza (with the notable exclusion of officials from Fatah), to last for one year and which included the lifting of some economic restrictions on the Strip. Sporadic Palestinian protests at the border nevertheless continued on a small scale, drawing a violent response from the IDF. Palestinian medical services reported at the end of September that since 30 March almost 190 Palestinians had been killed by Israeli soldiers, and an estimated 18,000 people had been injured.

PALESTINE, THE PLO, DIPLOMACY AND AID

Meanwhile, Palestine achieved a useful if modest gain when the international policing body Interpol voted in favour of admitting Palestine to the organization in September 2017. Israel had made strenuous efforts to prevent Palestine's accession to the body and roundly condemned the outcome of the vote, which was a convincing approval for Palestine by 75 votes to 24. In the same month Palestinian and Arab diplomacy, in conjunction with that of a robustly pro-Palestinian South Africa, exerted sufficient pressure on the West African state of Togo to cancel hosting a much-publicized Israeli-Africa summit at short notice. Domestic upheaval also played its part in the Togolese Government's decision, but it was a triumph for Palestine and pro-Palestine advocates such as the Boycott, Divestment and Sanctions movement (BDS—a Palestinian-led movement, which had attracted some success in Western nations, promoting various forms of boycott against Israel until it meets what the campaign describes as Israel's obligations under international law, defined as withdrawal from the occupied territories, the removal of the separation barrier in the West Bank, full equality for Arab-Palestinian citizens of Israel, and 'respecting, protecting, and promoting the rights of Palestinian refugees to return to their homes and properties'). On the domestic front, a new educational and cultural centre, the A. M. Qattan Foundation, opened in Ramallah in June 2018. Also in that month the Duke of Cambridge (then second in line to the British throne) made an official visit to the Palestinian territories (as part of a tour of the region including Israel), where he met Abbas in Ramallah. The Duke assured Palestinians in a public speech that 'you have not been forgotten'.

PLO-US relations regressed sharply in 2018, primarily as a result of Trump's decision in January to recognize Jerusalem as the capital of Israel and to move the US embassy there from

Tel Aviv. To some observers, Trump's proposed plan to bring peace to the Middle East appeared to involve accommodating Israel at almost every turn while tightening the screws on the much weaker Palestinian side. As Abbas declared that the USA no longer had a legitimate role to play in brokering peace between Palestine and Israel, it appeared that the peace process under the Trump Administration was irrevocably stalled. Kushner visited several countries in the region in June (although the Palestinian territories were not on his itinerary) to discuss the peace plan. His proposals were reported to include providing aid to Palestinians via Gulf monarchies and Egypt, circumventing the PA and UNRWA, which drew the ire of the Abbas administration; the PA also criticized US envoys for removing the issue of the right of return for Palestinian refugees from negotiations. Moreover, at a meeting of the PLO Central Committee convened in January, an angry Abbas had mocked Trump's so-called 'deal of the century' by declaring it 'the slap of the century', and he described the openly pro-Israel US ambassadors to Israel and the UN, David Friedman and Nikki Haley, a 'disgrace'. The US response to Abbas's criticism was to punish the PA and the Palestinian public, especially refugees, by cutting the US aid budget for Palestine by some US $200m. in August, including ending all funding of UNRWA. (US funding of the agency had already been cut in January, from a scheduled $125m. to just $60m.) Increasing pressure again, the Trump Administration closed the office of the General Delegation of the PLO to the USA in Washington, DC, in mid-September, and expelled the PLO's representative and his family later in the month.

NEW PRIME MINISTER AND ADMINISTRATION

PA Prime Minister Hamdallah submitted his resignation, and that of his national unity Cabinet, to President Abbas in January 2019. In April a new Palestinian Prime Minister was sworn in, with Fatah Central Committee member and experienced technocrat Mohammad Shteyyeh replacing Hamdallah. With ample academic qualifications (from the Palestinian territories and the UK), as well as credibility within Fatah, Shteyyeh had a solid reputation earned as a senior official at the Palestinian Economic Council for Development and Reconstruction—an infrastructure agency that had been established in 1993 to prepare for and then work as part of the emergent PA. A new Fatah-dominated Cabinet, which excluded representatives of Hamas and Islamic Jihad, was sworn in on 13 April; the PFLP and the DFLP declined to join the new administration. Some observers interpreted the elevation of Shteyyeh as a move by the ailing Abbas to prepare the way for a potential successor as his own rule appeared to be nearing its end.

Precisely how successful the refreshed cabinet might be was open to question. The almost total lack of popular legitimacy afforded to the PA had been illustrated just a few months earlier in a very public dispute over a social security plan, which the PA implemented in December 2018; it culminated in PNC President Abbas eventually backing down and withdrawing the scheme in January 2019, prompting Hamdallah's resignation as premier. The intentions of the plan included the establishment of a basic social insurance scheme for private sector workers. Although apparently mundane and well intentioned on the surface, the proposed scheme aroused enormous civic opposition in the West Bank on the grounds that many people simply did not trust the PA to make appropriate use of their taxes. The Fatah Revolutionary Council publicly supported the President's decision to concede, in another apparent example of the Palestinian nationalist establishment desperately trying to remain in touch with its popular roots.

This round of protests and concessions raised deeper questions about the future of politics and the PA. It had been clear for some time that younger Palestinians (including employees of the PA and the PLO) were abandoning hope of a two-state solution; instead, they were diverting their efforts to a civil rights-style struggle with greater relevance to their life circumstances and, perhaps, greater prospects for success, even if such a campaign was likely to provoke a significant political response from Israel. Linked with the relative success of the BDS campaign, momentum within Palestinian politics appeared to be moving in a new direction, and the role of the PA in such a scenario appeared to be increasingly ambiguous.

TRUMP'S 'DEAL OF THE CENTURY' MAKES INAUSPICIOUS DEBUT

The mysteries of the Trump peace plan became a little clearer in early 2019. The specifics of the economic dimension, titled 'Peace to Prosperity', received as much press attention as they did mockery at a glitzy official debut for Trump's peace plan, convened in Manama, the Bahraini capital, in June. In the run-up to the event, Kushner had travelled widely in the Middle East region in an attempt to drum up enthusiasm. The results of his efforts were modest at best, not least on account of the official Palestinian boycott of the event. Kushner's efforts culminated in an economic summit, which opened on 25 June, hosted by the Bahraini Government, which enjoyed a particularly close relationship with the Trump Administration. The results were understood by most informed observers as a cynical and misguided attempt to buy off Palestinians' political aspirations in return for US $50,000m. to fund improvements to their standards of living. The financing would form part of an investment fund for some 180 infrastructure and business projects, funded mostly by Arab states and wealthy private investors. More than one-half of the funding would be spent in the West Bank and Gaza, with $9,000m. allocated to Egypt, $7,000m. to Jordan and $6,300m. to Lebanon.

The likely political dimensions of the Trump peace plan remained nebulous, although outlines gradually began to emerge. Such information as could be gleaned revealed a set of proposals with almost no prospect of success, primarily on account of a near-total failure to accommodate the most basic of Palestinian national aspirations: East Jerusalem as the capital of an independent Palestinian state, recognition of the Palestinian refugees' right of return and an adequate compromise on territorial sovereignty over the West Bank. Israel's relentless settlement project in the West Bank, coupled with a fierce determination to retain its existing illegal settlements (combined with US complicity in that endeavour), effectively rendered meaningful Palestinian sovereignty a moot point. During a fiercely contested election campaign that he eventually failed to win in September 2019, Netanyahu rather underlined this point by promising to annex about 30% of the West Bank constituted by the Jordan Valley and northern Dead Sea area, if he was returned as Prime Minister.

THE POLITICS OF AID TO PALESTINE REVISITED

The objectives of US aid with regard to Palestine became increasingly clear as twin initiatives unfolded under the Trump Administration. Subsequent to the withdrawal of funding for UNRWA in August 2018, in September 2019 legislation was put before the US Senate granting US $75m. in aid to the PA for the specific use of the security apparatus. The goal of denying funding to UNRWA was a fairly transparent attempt to frustrate its work, which had been a long-term goal of successive Israeli governments, particularly those that were led by Likud and hence on the nationalist right of the political spectrum. UNRWA prompted Israeli anger for several reasons, among them its habit of documenting and publicizing the consequences of IDF operations in Palestinian refugee camps, such as routine damage to UNRWA facilities and casualties among camp inhabitants and UNRWA staff. A second and deeper issue was the role played by UNRWA in supporting a very substantial portion of the Palestinian population with education, health care and dietary support; in so doing, UNRWA helped to maintain both a sense of refugee status among Palestinians in the West Bank and Gaza and of Palestinian national identity, which Israel had long hoped might diminish over time. Israel's attempt to undermine the agency unfolded just at the same time as Trump's peace plan appeared to evaporate any hope of progress with implementation of the right of return of Palestinian refugees. For the Palestinians' part, several aspects of the operations of the PA's security forces (such as the PSF and related intelligence agencies) were engineered specifically in order to keep a tight lid on Palestinian resistance as Israel's settlement project proceeded around Palestinians in the West Bank. The proposed legislation, included in the US Government's State and Foreign Operations Funding Bill for 2020, represented more than a doubling of the typical level of support afforded to the Palestinian security services. Meanwhile, with regard to funding for civic purposes, the oil-rich Gulf state of Qatar appeared to be coming forward to meet at least some of the deficit left by Trump's policies and lack of crucial international funding for Palestine.

DISSENT, ATTRITION AND THE PALESTINIAN BODY POLITIC

Not surprisingly, given the circumstances outlined above, dissent remained rampant across the Gaza Strip and the West Bank; as with the demonstrations over social insurance, dissent might be aimed at Palestinian institutions as often as it was at Israel. In the West Bank, the PA struggled to cope with pressure from Israel as it deducted tax revenues in lieu of stipends paid to the families of Palestinian prisoners; the cancellation of such payments was a politically inconceivable demand for the PA to meet, akin to any routine government being forced to abandon its war veterans. In February 2019 the PA began to refuse any payments from Israel until normal service was resumed. On the surface, this appeared to be one struggle that the PA had won, at least in the short term, as Israel relented in August. The move might also have helped to dampen rising discontent among Palestinian prisoners housed in the expansive and volatile Israeli penal system. Addameer reported that at August 2023 Palestinian political prisoners held in Israeli gaols numbered some 5,100, including 1,200 in administrative detention and about 165 children.

Meanwhile, residents of the embattled Gaza Strip continued to endure a constant campaign of attrition with Israel; besieged, impoverished and angry, Gazans persisted in putting their lives at risk, particularly along the border with Israel, and the casualty rate grimly and predictably rose. In September 2019 OCHA reported that between the end of March 2018 and July 2019 more than 7,000 Palestinians had received injuries from live ammunition fired by members of the IDF; the demand for limb reconstruction services in Palestinian clinics and hospitals was overwhelming, and about 1,200 cases were under consideration at the time of OCHA's report. Local health care providers simply could not provide treatment for the enormous number of people in need of medical attention, and this was exacerbated by the suspension of non-security-related aid from the Trump Administration.

Besides the confrontation with Israel, and perhaps more worrying for the ruling Hamas movement, protests in the Gaza Strip sometimes targeted Hamas officials, particularly over the rising cost of living and desperate measures by the local authorities to raise revenue by increasing taxes. The sporadic pressure on the PA in the West Bank was mirrored in Gaza as fuel supplies were disrupted by the alternate periods of limited hostilities followed by temporary ceasefires; the limits imposed on Gazan fishermen similarly expanded and contracted with the circumstances. This all combined to leave the Palestinian body politic in the West Bank and the Strip very weak but not yet dead; that outcome, deemed liberating by some, would inevitably lead to chaos at the expense of Israeli security. In December 2019 Abbas announced that all of the principal Palestinian factions, including Fatah and Hamas, had agreed to hold both presidential and legislative elections in 2020. According to the President, the PA had formally requested that Israel allow Palestinians resident in East Jerusalem to participate in the polls. Some reports suggested that Abbas was reluctant to agree an exact time frame for the staging of the elections and used the issue of East Jerusalem as an excuse.

In the event, neither the presidential nor the legislative elections were held in 2020, owing to the onset of the coronavirus disease (COVID-19) pandemic. However, an apparent breakthrough occurred following talks between the two main factions in Istanbul, Türkiye, in September, when Abbas agreed a deal regarding the sequencing of the polls with Fatah representatives and Haniya on behalf of Hamas: elections to the PLC (the first since 2006) were scheduled for 22 May 2021, and a presidential election was set for 31 July. However, intra-Palestinian solidarity waned, particularly after the defeat of President Trump in the US election in November 2020 (his avowedly pro-Israeli stance had the side effect of giving Fatah and Hamas common cause in opposing it), and tensions grew from early 2021. In April of that year Abbas announced the indefinite postponement of the elections to the PLC and the presidency, blaming the delay on Israel's failure to guarantee permission for the approximately 350,000 Palestinians living in East Jerusalem to vote. However, observers suggested that the primary cause for the delay was probably the creation of competing electoral lists that threatened to split the vote for Fatah and potentially to hand Hamas a majority in parliament. The postponement prompted demonstrations across the West Bank and Gaza against Abbas's rule and the PA's ongoing failure to improve economic conditions or address perceived corruption.

ARAB WORLD OVERLOOKS THE PALESTINIAN CAUSE TO SEEK CLOSER TIES WITH ISRAEL

A significant development for Arab-Israeli relations occurred in September 2020, when Israel signed the US-sponsored Abraham Accords Peace Agreement with the UAE and Bahrain at a ceremony in Washington, DC. According to the terms of the Abraham Accords, which had been drafted partly in response to growing concerns about Iran in both Israel and the Gulf Arab states, the UAE and Bahrain would normalize their political and economic relations with Israel, in exchange for a pledge by the Israeli Government to suspend its planned annexation of parts of the West Bank. In addition, in December Morocco agreed to re-establish diplomatic relations with Israel and in January 2021 also signed the Abraham Accords. The PA and all political factions in the Palestinian territories denounced the Accords in the strongest terms, describing them as a 'betrayal' in the Palestinians' long quest for statehood. This stance received support from other regional governments, many of which emphasized that the Palestinian question should remain the focus for Arab nations. In December, for example, the Egyptian and Saudi Arabian Ministers of Foreign Affairs issued a joint statement reaffirming their support for an 'independent viable Palestinian state', with East Jerusalem as its capital. Jordanian officials also expressed concern that the normalization agreements signalled an erosion of the traditional linkage between Arab recognition of Israel and the latter's withdrawal from occupied Palestinian territory.

Meanwhile, the Israeli Government accelerated its programme of settlement expansion in East Jerusalem and the West Bank during 2020. According to Peace Now, Israeli settlement activity was at its highest level since the organization had begun monitoring the situation in 2012.

THE NEW BIDEN ADMINISTRATION AND US POLICY TOWARDS PALESTINE: CONTINUATION AND CHANGE

Joe Biden succeeded Trump as US President in January 2021 (having won the presidential election in November 2020), but his Administration did not immediately reverse the key foreign policy decisions taken by its predecessor regarding Israeli-Palestinian affairs. In February 2021 the US Senate voted overwhelmingly for the country's embassy to remain in Jerusalem, and in March the US Department of State announced its opposition to the ICC's decision to launch a formal investigation into whether Israel had committed war crimes in the West Bank and Gaza since June 2014; the Court was also to investigate alleged war crimes, such as the use of human shields, committed by Hamas.

Nevertheless, there was a significant change of US policy in late January 2021 (in the week after President Biden was inaugurated), when it was announced that the new Administration was to reopen diplomatic missions and restore US aid to the Palestinian territories, almost two years after Trump had withdrawn this support. However, UNRWA faced an extremely challenging financial situation, as a result of the additional medical, economic and social costs incurred during the COVID-19 pandemic. Meanwhile, the imminent withdrawal of Trump from the global stage following his election defeat had prompted an improvement in relations between the Palestinians and Israel. In mid-November 2020 the PA had agreed to resume civil and security co-operation with the Israeli Government, having suspended it in May in protest at Israel's planned annexation of West Bank territory. In view of these positive developments, in March 2021 the Quartet group called for new negotiations between the two sides. However, events soon scuppered the prospects of any rapprochement.

RENEWED CONFLICT BETWEEN HAMAS AND ISRAEL IN GAZA

In early May 2021 violent clashes between Palestinians and Israeli police at Temple Mount/Haram al-Sharif in Jerusalem prompted a sharp escalation of violence elsewhere in Israel and a wider conflict between Hamas and Israel. The clashes had been prompted by controversial Israeli police tactics preventing Palestinians from accessing the al-Aqsa mosque, along with plans by Israeli religious-nationalist groups to march into predominantly Muslim areas of the city in celebration of the Jerusalem Day holiday and tensions surrounding an ongoing court hearing over the forced eviction of Muslim families from the Sheikh Jarrah area of the city. Inter-communal riots erupted in Jerusalem, as well as in other cities in Israel. On the afternoon of 10 May Hamas gave Israel an ultimatum to withdraw security forces from the Temple Mount and Sheikh Jarrah by evening. When the ultimatum expired without a response, Hamas and Palestinian Islamic Jihad began to launch rockets into southern Israel. This prompted the IDF to carry out air strikes against alleged Hamas targets in Gaza and to station troops on the border between Israel and the Strip. Over the next 11 days at least 242 Palestinians, including 66 children, were killed in IDF air strikes, and almost 2,000 more were injured. In Israel, at least 12 people were killed, and some 700 were injured. About 4,350 rockets were fired from Gaza towards Israel from Gaza, of which some 90% bound towards populated areas were intercepted by the 'Iron Dome' defence system. Israel conducted about 1,500 air, land and naval strikes on the Strip. Hamas proposed a ceasefire on 13 May, but Netanyahu rejected it. On 18 May France, Egypt and Jordan filed a resolution with the UN Security Council for a ceasefire. This came into effect on 21 May. During the conflict in Gaza, incidents of riots broke out in 'mixed' towns and cities in Israel between Jews and Israeli Arabs, causing serious injuries to several dozen people from the two communities and damage to synagogues, as well as to Jewish and Arab houses.

In an attempt to strengthen the ceasefire, in late May 2021 US Secretary of State Antony Blinken visited both Israel and Palestine and announced an additional US $75m. in aid to the PA, as well as aid for immediate disaster relief and for UNRWA, to fund the repair of critical infrastructure that was destroyed during the brief conflict and the planned reopening of the US consulate in East Jerusalem (which has historically acted as an office for diplomatic relations with Palestine). In the previous week Egypt and Qatar had each pledged $500m. to rebuild Gaza after the conflict. The episode of intense violence reinforced the image of Abbas as weak and ineffective in protecting Palestinian interests and bolstered Hamas's reputation as the main advocate of Palestinian claims against Israel.

Tensions remained high in Jerusalem following the Gazan conflict. This was highlighted by the incursion in mid-July 2021 by right-wing Jewish activists into the courtyard of the al-Aqsa mosque in Jerusalem, violating an understanding between Jordan and Israel that Jews were not allowed to pray there. Palestinians living in Jerusalem responded by calling for a pilgrimage to the al-Aqsa mosque on the day of Arafat (the final day of the Hajj pilgrimage) on 19 July. Jewish activists none the less entered the al-Aqsa mosque compound, protected by Israeli police, for prayers on 18 July, further stoking already high tensions and leading to renewed violent clashes between Palestinians and Israeli police. The formation of a new Israeli Government in June, led by the right-wing Prime Minister Naftali Bennett, augured poorly for more cordial relations; he had supported the right of Jews to visit the disputed area in Jerusalem, before clarifying that this did not include prayer at the site.

Meanwhile, low-level violence between Palestinian militants and the IDF continued, constraining the easing of border restrictions and provision of humanitarian and financial aid to Palestine. In June 2021 incendiary balloons were launched from Gaza into Israel, prompting air strikes by the IDF on the Strip, and similar incidents took place in late August, after Israeli forces killed four Palestinian protesters in the West Bank in the previous week and injured several more. On 19 August Israel had nevertheless approved the release of a Qatari aid package for Gaza, under which around 100,000 Palestinian families were each to receive US $100. This followed an announcement by Israel in late July, permitting the import of electronic products, agricultural goods and food into Gaza. At the end of August Israel offered the PA a loan of $156m. and permits for 16,000 more Palestinians to work in Israel, bringing the total to nearly 100,000. However, Prime Minister Bennett ruled out resuming peace process talks with the PA.

THE PA'S CRISIS OF LEGITIMACY AND THE COVID-19 PANDEMIC

By late 2021 the PA was facing a crisis of legitimacy and was riven by ongoing sectarian tensions, low-level violent incidents with Israel in both the West Bank and Gaza, ongoing settlement-building, including expansion in Jerusalem, as well as the burden of the COVID-19 pandemic. Under international law and under Israeli public law, as interpreted by the Israeli Supreme Court, the Israeli Government has a duty to ensure that the population in the territories is vaccinated against potentially fatal diseases. For its part, Israel cited the Oslo Accords, claiming that responsibility for distributing vaccines in Gaza and the West Bank was explicitly given to the PA. Critics of Israel conceded that although Israel had no legal obligation to distribute vaccines, as the occupying power and the much wealthier neighbour, it had a moral and epidemiological obligation to do so, once effective vaccines had been manufactured. Hamas and the PA signed up to the World Health Organization's COVAX Facility (aimed at supplying COVID-19 vaccines to vulnerable and low-income populations) in early 2021. At that time Amnesty International demanded that Israel provide vaccines to Palestinians living in the West Bank, but the PA itself did not ask for Israeli assistance, and the Israeli Ministry of Health stated that Israeli citizens must receive the vaccine as a priority. On 1 February Israel nevertheless confirmed that it had authorized the transfer of 5,000 doses of vaccine to the PA, and the first consignment of vaccines via COVAX was made later that month, followed by sizeable donations of vaccines from Russia, China and the UAE in March.

However, when the first consignment of Russian-made vaccines intended for frontline health workers in the Strip arrived at the Israeli–Gazan border on 15 February 2021, it was blocked by Israeli border officials. The Gazan authorities eventually received a small proportion of the consignment, two days later. Palestine's public vaccination programme began in March. Meanwhile, in the same month Israel began vaccinating the approximately 120,000 Palestinian workers with permits to enter and work in Israel. In June the Israeli Government announced that it had agreed with the PA to transfer at least 1m. vaccine doses to the PA, although it was quickly reported that these were scheduled to expire imminently, and later that day the PA cancelled the deal, also opposing the Israeli demand that none of the doses be transferred to Hamas in Gaza. By October 2022, according to Johns Hopkins University, only 38% of the population of Palestine had been fully vaccinated against the virus (compared with about 70% in Israel by that time). By early September 2023 over 700,000 confirmed cases of COVID-19 had been recorded in the Palestinian territories, including 5,708 reported deaths.

Discussions held between Israeli Prime Minister Bennett and Egyptian President al-Sisi in Sharm el-Sheikh in September 2021 (without any Palestinian participation) reportedly focused on the process of resuming Israeli-Palestinian peace negotiations, as well as on ways to maintain the recent cease-fire agreed between Israel and Hamas in Gaza.

Despite the indefinite postponement of the legislative and presidential elections, municipal elections took place, in two stages, in December 2021 (in villages and smaller towns) and March 2022 (in larger urban conurbations), but only in the West Bank. Although Hamas officially boycotted the elections—and refused to hold them in Gaza—Hamas members were able to stand as independents or in alliances (often with the PFLP). Candidates from non-affiliated lists secured 64.4% of the contested local council seats, in a clear sign of public discontent with the ruling Fatah, owing to its failure to stop the construction of Jewish settlements in the West Bank and East Jerusalem. (Notably, in May 2022 the Israeli high court rejected a petition against the forced displacement of about 1,200 Palestinian residents from Masafer Yatta in the southern West Bank, amounting to the single largest displacement of Palestinians in several decades; and in July a further 1,446 Jewish settlement units to the south-east of Jerusalem were approved.) The legitimacy of the elections was undermined by a relatively low turnout, with only about 55% of eligible voters participating.

Meanwhile, on 1 January 2022 former intelligence chief Ziad Hab al-Reeh was appointed as the PA Minister of the Interior, becoming the first incumbent of that post for seven years. Hatem al-Bakri was named as the Minister of Awqaf and Religious Affairs. Both cabinet positions had hitherto been held by Prime Minister Shtayyeh since he assumed office in April 2019. During the 31st session of the PCC, in February 2022, Rawhi Fattouh was elected to replace Salim al-Za'nun as Chairman and Speaker of the PNC and of the PCC. Fahmi al-Za'arir was elected as Secretary-General of the two bodies, while Hussein al-Sheikh (who had served for several years as the PA's Minister for Civil Affairs and thus responsible for civil co-ordination with Israel) was appointed as the new Secretary-General of the PLO Executive Committee (following the death of Erekat in November 2020), as concerns grew about the health of the ageing Abbas, who turned 87 years old in March 2022. Demonstrations in Ramallah in July called for Abbas to resign, as the popularity of al-Sheikh, his likely successor, increased. Marwan Barghouthi, who continued to be a popular senior figure in Fatah, remained in an Israeli prison as of late 2023.

TENSIONS AT THE AL-AQSA MOSQUE AND FURTHER CONFLICT IN GAZA

Meanwhile, on 1 March 2022 Israel's Supreme Court halted the eviction of four Palestinian families from the Sheikh Jarrah neighbourhood, but protests about Israeli settlement activity and forced evictions nevertheless continued. In the West Bank, Israeli security forces clashed with Palestinians protesting about Israeli settlements and forced evictions of Palestinians and carried out raids to arrest suspected Palestinian militants. There was a serious escalation in violence from the middle of the month. Four Israelis were fatally stabbed in Beersheba on 22 March, and two Israeli border police officers were shot dead by two gunmen in Hadera on 27 March. Both attacks were reportedly carried out by Israeli Arab gunmen (who were eventually killed by Israeli forces) and claimed by Islamic State. On 29 March five Israelis were killed by a Palestinian gunman in Bnei Brak, east of Tel Aviv; the gunman, from the West Bank, was later shot dead by Israeli security forces. Several other non-fatal attacks on Israelis took place in that month, as well as killings of suspected Palestinian militants by Israeli security forces across the West Bank. Abbas publicly denounced the attack in Bnei Brak, despite his recent apparent unwillingness to condemn Palestinian attacks against Israelis. In early April Israel further tightened its security measures, after a Palestinian gunmen killed three Israelis at a bar in Tel Aviv. A number of Palestinians in the West Bank were shot dead by Israeli forces over the subsequent days, and on 15 April more than 150 were reportedly injured when riot police entered the al-Aqsa mosque, apparently in order to stop stone-throwing by Palestinians and to make arrests, crossing what many Palestinians regard as a red line. Tensions had escalated over the preceding days following reports that members of an extremist Israeli religious-nationalist group were planning to perform rituals to mark Passover at the Temple Mount/Haram al-Sharif compound. On 20 April Israeli police prevented hundreds of ultra-nationalist Israelis from entering the Damascus Gate, which had become a particular flashpoint for unrest. Israeli police raided the al-Aqsa mosque on two further occasions in late April during the holy month of Ramadan, injuring over 70 Palestinians. Meanwhile, earlier that month Palestinians in Nablus vandalized the sacred Jewish site of Joseph's Tomb. About 600 Israeli settlers stormed the al-Aqsa mosque compound in early May, despite a large deployment of Israeli police around the compound. In mid-May more than 70 Palestinians were injured in clashes with Israeli police during a funeral procession for a Palestinian man who had died of injuries sustained during the violent unrest at the Al-Aqsa mosque in the previous month. Hundreds of Israeli ultra-nationalists entered the al-Aqsa mosque compound on 29 May during a march to commemorate Jerusalem Day (the date of the city being 'reunified' following the Six-Day War). Low-level violence continued in June and July, and a small number of rockets were fired from Gaza towards Israel (most of them being intercepted) after Israeli incursions into or air strikes on the Strip.

Meanwhile, Fatah, Hamas and other Palestinian factions denounced a summit meeting held in the Negev desert in southern Israel in March 2022, which was attended by the foreign affairs ministers of Israel, Egypt, Bahrain, the UAE and Morocco, as well as by US Secretary of State Blinken. An announcement by the Israeli foreign affairs minister that it was envisaged that the summit would become a permanent regional security co-operation forum caused particular concern among Palestinians.

In June 2022 the EU agreed to release funding to the Palestinian territories for 2021 that it had withheld over concerns about the anti-Israeli content of Palestinian school textbooks, and in August flights from Ramallah via Israel to İstanbul began, making it easier for Palestinians to travel abroad.

Meanwhile, in an attempt to effect political reconciliation between the two major Palestinian groups, in early July 2022 the Algerian Government hosted President Abbas and Hamas leader Haniya for their first meeting in person since 2016. In the following week US President Biden met President Abbas in Bethlehem (after meeting acting Israeli Prime Minister Yair Lapid and President Isaac Herzog in Jerusalem, where he reaffirmed US commitment to Israeli security). Biden pledged aid to Palestinians, including US $100m. in assistance to the PA and $201m. of funding for UNRWA, although he failed to address Palestinian demands that the USA reopen its consulate in East Jerusalem and remove the PLO from its list of terrorist organizations.

Tensions flared up again in Gaza in early August 2022, after the IDF launched a series of air strikes on the territory that killed Tayseer al-Jaabari, a senior commander of Islamic Jihad, several other jihadi fighters and two civilians and destroyed some of the group's facilities in the Strip. The air strikes came several days after Israel had arrested another senior Islamic Jihad leader in the West Bank. The subsequent retaliatory Islamic Jihad rocket attacks against Israeli civilian population centres (most of which Israel blocked with its 'Iron Dome' anti-missile system) exposed differences among the various resistance factions in Gaza, primarily between Hamas and the more hard-line Islamic Jihad. The latter group's Iranian-based secretary, Ziad Nakhaleh, called on other Gazan factions to join the fray, following al-Jaabari's killing, but Hamas declined to become involved, limiting itself to statements of support. Hamas was perhaps aware that Gazans could not afford yet another protracted, damaging conflict with the territory being in such a poor economic state—the unemployment rate was estimated at about 47% in mid-2022 and there were ongoing fuel and electricity shortages. Indeed, Haniya urged Egypt to pressurize Israel into a ceasefire to spare Gaza from all-out conflict. An Egyptian-mediated ceasefire came into effect after about 48 hours of fighting, which left 49 Palestinians dead, including 17 children, and about 350 injured, many of them seriously. Israeli sources claimed that 34 Israelis were injured. Observers suggested that the outgoing Government of Israeli Prime Minister Lapid was adopting a hard line against Palestinian militants in the run-up to legislative elections in Israel in November following the collapse of the coalition administration in June, after acknowledging that there was no chance of obtaining approval for emergency legislation that would extend Israeli civil law to Jewish settlers in the West Bank.

Meanwhile, the IDF raided the offices of seven human rights organizations in the West Bank in August 2022, six of which the Israeli Government had categorized as 'terrorist organizations' in October 2021. Also in August 2022 Israel continued to carry out security raids in the West Bank and East Jerusalem, arresting over 300 Palestinians. Notably, Israeli security forces killed three Palestinians from the al-Aqsa Martyrs Brigades in Nablus.

In September 2022 Israel released revised guidelines for foreign nationals entering the West Bank, removing several of the most controversial clauses, including one that required visitors to report romantic relationships with Palestinians and another relating to limits placed on the number of foreign academics (100) and international students (150) studying at Palestinian universities in the West Bank. The changes came following US and European pressure, but the revised rules nevertheless further tightened Israel's control over the West Bank. Similarly, the US Administration pressurized Israel to initiate an investigation into the killing of a Palestinian-US journalist, Shireen Abu Aqla, during an incursion by IDF forces in Jenin in May. An investigation into Abu Aqla's death continued for several months, and Israel's final report into the incident indicated that she had probably been shot unintentionally but also could have been struck by Palestinian forces (although no other reports indicated that any armed Palestinians were engaged at the time and place of the shooting). In June 2023 US Senator Chris Van Hollen called for the declassification of the assessment of the US Security Coordinator for Israel and the Palestinian Authority on the death of the journalist. The Committee to Protect Journalists supported his call in the name of transparency and accountability, but there was little indication of Israel or the USA disclosing any more than they already had. Abu Aqla was the 48th journalist to have died at the hands of the IDF since 2000.

Meanwhile, the West Bank, Jenin and Nablus witnessed the rise of new armed groups in 2022—notably the Nablus Brigades, the Balata Brigades, the Tubas Brigades and the Yabad Brigades—inspired by the creation in 2021 of the Jenin Brigades in the city's refugee camps in response to Israel's killing of a member of Palestinian Islamic Jihad, Jamil al-Amouri. The new armed groups provoked a firm Israeli response in the form of 'Operation Break the Wave' from March 2022, leading to an escalation of deadly violence that would escalate in 2023.

In November 2022 Netanyahu was re-elected as Israeli Prime Minister, leading a coalition Government comprising the Likud Party and five far-right parties, including the Religious Zionist Party, whose leader, Israeli settler Bezalel Smotrich, in return for supporting the new administration, secured two highly controversial political promises from Netanyahu—judicial reform and an expansion of settlements in the West Bank. The judicial reform process, which sought to reduce the powers of the Israeli Supreme Court to the benefit of the Knesset, was a largely domestic affair within Israel but led to instability in Israeli politics and civil unrest (see Israel). Meanwhile, hard-line policies on settlements exacerbated violence between Israel and the Palestinian territories: in the first half of 2023 a total of 137 Palestinians were killed by the IDF and 24 Israelis were killed in attacks by Palestinians. In mid-June the Israeli Cabinet approved plans to build some 5,000 new homes in Israeli settlements in the West Bank, despite international pleas to refrain from doing so, including from the USA. Two days later Palestinian gunmen killed four Israelis and injured several others in the illegal West Bank settlement of Eli, prompting yet another cycle of revenge attacks by settlers against Palestinians living nearby, as well as their homes and farms. Tor Wennesland, the UN Special Co-ordinator for the Middle East Peace Process and envoy of the UN Secretary-General, condemned the settler attacks on Palestinian civilians, asserting that Israel's 'relentless expansion' of settlements fuelled violence and threatened 'the viability of a future Palestinian state'.

As the frequency of attacks by Palestinians on Israelis increased in the West Bank, East Jerusalem and Israel, in early July 2023 the IDF carried out a large-scale incursion into the refugee camp in Jenin, in which 12 Palestinians were killed, including three civilians, and more than 100 injured, and which led to an estimated 3,000 Palestinians fleeing the area. While the incursion in Jenin was under way, a Palestinian assailant carried out a car ramming and stabbing attack in Tel Aviv, which was claimed by Hamas. Further IDF raids took place in Nablus and Jericho in the following weeks, in which several Palestinian militants were killed.

In an attempt to secure regional and international attention, in January 2023 the PLO's Anti-Discrimination and Apartheid Department partnered with the Palestinian Human Rights Organizations Council, the Palestinian Ministry of Justice, the Palestinian NGO Network and the BDS Movement in hosting the First Anti-Apartheid Palestinian National Conference Call Towards a Global Front to Dismantle Israel's Regime of Settler-Colonialism and Apartheid.

Meanwhile, the PA sought to avert the normalization of diplomatic ties between Israel and further Arab states. In August 2023 Saudi Arabia named its ambassador to Jordan as 'Non-resident ambassador to the State of Palestine and Consul General in Jerusalem', in an apparent move to strengthen the recognition of the Palestinian territories as a sovereign state. However, observers claimed that Saudi Arabia may have made the appointment to appease the Palestinians ahead of pending Saudi plans finally to recognize Israel. Meanwhile, Israel refused to allow the Saudi diplomatic representation to reside in Jerusalem, which Israel continued to assert as its own capital.

Also in August 2023, in an apparent attempt to reassert his authority amid growing domestic criticism, the ageing Abbas dismissed 12 of the territories' 15 governors, including the governor of Jenin, where the recent incursion by the IDF had led to awkward questions about the effectiveness of the PA's leadership and legitimacy in the governorate. The PA announced that a committee would be formed to appoint replacements for the 12 governors. According to a survey conducted in June by the Palestine Center for Policy and Survey Research, 80% of Palestinians wanted Abbas to resign. By late 2023 there was no indication that presidential or legislative elections were likely to be held soon, further antagonizing the Palestinian population. Notably, Fatah's armed wing, the al-Aqsa Martyrs Brigades, had strengthened ties with the Palestinian Islamic Jihad in cities including Jenin and Nablus, causing frictions within Fatah and threatening the PA's security services and their monopoly (officially, at least) over security in the West Bank.

Economy

HABIB HINN, RAJA KHALIDI and ISLAM RABEE

INTRODUCTION

Human Development Index (HDI) in the Palestinian Territories—Key Economic Drivers

The United Nations (UN) Human Development Index (HDI) is used as an indicator for assessing long-term progress, focusing on three fundamental aspects of human development: a long and healthy life, access to knowledge and a decent standard of living. A long and healthy life is measured by life expectancy. Access to learning and knowledge is measured by mean years of schooling among the adult population and by expected years of schooling for children of school-entry age. Standard of living is measured by gross national income (GNI) per capita, expressed in US dollars at constant 2017 prices converted using purchasing-power parity (PPP) conversion rates.

The HDI does not provide a comprehensive aggregation of the state of human development in the Palestinian territories as it does not include crucial indicators that reflect the particular and structurally constrained conditions of Palestinian human development, including denial of access to natural resources and sovereignty. However, it does provide a general understanding of the progress made towards human development in the Palestinian territories, to make cross-country comparisons. Since the HDI provides a simplified snapshot of human development in the Palestinian territories, this essay will also include an analysis of other relevant socioeconomic indicators that play a role in the complex realities on the ground.

The HDI value for the Palestinian territories in 2021 was 0.715—placing it just within the 'high' human development category, and positioning the Palestinian territories at 106th out of 190 countries and territories. Between 2014 and 2021 the Palestinian territories' HDI increased from 0.699 to 0.715, life expectancy at birth increased by 0.9 years (to 73.5 years), expected years of schooling increased by 0.2 years, mean years of schooling increased by 0.2 years (to 13.4 years), and GNI per capita (on a PPP basis at constant 2017 prices in US dollars) decreased by $28.

Overall, the Palestinian territories had maintained an incrementally positive HDI growth trajectory since 2014 (except for decreases in 2020 and 2021) and, at face value, their HDI scoring shows that improvement was possible even under the ongoing constraints. However, compared regionally, in 2021 the Palestinian territories found themselves well behind Israel (0.919), the United Arab Emirates (0.910), Saudi Arabia (0.875), Qatar (0.855), Oman (0.816) and Egypt (0.731). The Palestinian territories' HDI was around the level of Jordan (0.720) and better than Lebanon (0.706), Iraq (0.686), the Syrian Arab Republic (0.577), Sudan (0.508) and Yemen (0.455).

Regarding gender inequality in the HDI, the Gender Development Index (GDI) for the Palestinian territories in 2021 was 0.891, a slight increase from 0.877 in 2014. This value indicates a significant difference between male and female human development in the Palestinian territories. Life expectancy at birth and expected years of schooling in 2021 were both higher for females than for males (75.9 and 14.3 versus 71.1 and 12.5, respectively). However, GNI per capita (on a PPP basis at constant 2017 prices in US dollars) was considerably lower for females than for males ($2,250 versus $10,937) and mean years of schooling was higher for males than for females (8.9 versus 8.4). The drastic difference in GNI per capita is likely what pushed the overall HDI for females to be significantly lower than males in 2021, at a value of 0.655 versus 0.735. Further indicators of inequality, gender based and non-gender based, are discussed below.

The following section examines several conventional empirical indicators. Without a doubt, changes in the political context have depressed growth and the development of the Palestinian economy. These factors have increased uncertainty and further destabilized the expansion of the Palestinian economy due to cuts in aid and tax payments, and have hindered progress towards Palestinian sovereignty. Furthermore, the coronavirus disease (COVID-19) pandemic that began in 2020 shocked the world (including the Palestinian territories) into an economic recession. The recovery that took place in 2021 slowed in 2022. Heightened regional political tensions following the Israeli legislative elections in late 2022, after which ultra-far-right parties formed part of a new governing coalition, together with disruption to international supply chains caused by the Russian Federation's invasion of Ukraine in February and the ensuing conflict, and rising prices of basic commodities, all hampered growth trajectories.

Multidimensional Poverty

In 2010 the global Multidimensional Poverty Index (MPI) was introduced in the UN Human Development Report in acknowledgement of the non-monetary factors that also contribute to poverty. Since 2018 the MPI estimates have been jointly produced by the Human Development Report Office (HDRO) and the Oxford Poverty and Human Development Initiative, and they have been adopted officially by the Palestinian (National) Authority (PA) as its framework for analysing and combating poverty. The MPI includes multiple overlapping deprivations suffered by individuals across three dimensions: health, education and standard of living. The most recent survey conducted by the HDRO with data that are publicly available for the Palestinian territories' MPI estimates was for 2019/20. According to this data, 0.6% of the population are multidimensionally poor, while 1.3% are classified as vulnerable. The intensity of deprivation, which is the average deprivation score experienced by people in multidimensional poverty, is 35.0%. The MPI value for the Palestinian territories, which is the share of the population that is multidimensionally poor, was 0.004 in 2014.

However, owing to the specific context of the Palestinian territories and the different contextual non-monetary factors that contribute to multidimensional poverty in different places, in 2020 the Palestinian Central Bureau of Statistics (PCBS) developed a national multidimensional poverty profile in the Palestinian territories. This built on the global MPI, with the inclusion of additional categories of indicators relevant to the Palestinian territories, including safety, housing and personal freedom. This new framework includes rights-based analysis and the monetary poverty statistics as part of the index.

The data by region shows the extent of the differences in levels of poverty between the West Bank and Gaza Strip. While 24% of people in the West Bank live in poverty according to their level of income, a shocking 67.6% of people in the Gaza Strip fall under this category. Furthermore, 15% of people in the West Bank are categorized as living in deep poverty, while more than one-half of the population in the Gaza Strip suffer such extreme deprivation (53.9%). The numbers according to consumption show a similar trend. Where 13.9% and 5.8% of people in the West Bank live in poverty and deep poverty, respectively, 53% and 33.8% fall under those categories in the Gaza Strip (PCBS, 2018). These structural discrepancies between the two regions are not represented in the traditional MPI analysis or in the HDI, as both of these sources combine the data from the two regions.

Since the establishment of the PA, the incidence of poverty in the Palestinian territories (as measured by relative and absolute household expenditure) has remained relatively high in the West Bank and risen significantly in Gaza and East Jerusalem. Incidence of poverty is more widespread than previously believed. Between 2011 and 2017, alongside a 3% increase in national poverty, there was a significant change in regional poverty trends. By 2017 the incidence of poverty was much higher in the Gaza Strip (53.0%) than in the West Bank (13.9%). Significantly, from a policy perspective the Gaza Strip contains a larger share of the overall poor population than the West Bank: 71.2% of the poor population are found there, compared with 28.8% in the West Bank (PCBS, 2018).

The increase in poverty in the Gaza Strip between 2011 and 2018 was accompanied by an alarming decline in access to essential services, especially severe shortages of water and electricity. Following the impact of the COVID-19 pandemic, the World Bank estimated that the share of poor households increased to 64% in Gaza and to 30% in the West Bank. The West Bank and Gaza differ significantly in terms of natural resources, wealth of infrastructure, size of markets, population density, rural-urban composition and refugee status, among other things. These variations inform the likelihood of households being poor in each area.

An official Palestinian definition of poverty was developed in 1997 for the West Bank and Gaza, with two poverty lines based on family expenditure (a family of two adults and three children used as the reference) for measuring poverty among Palestinians in the two areas: the first, termed 'deep poverty line', was calculated to reflect a budget for food, clothing and housing; and the second line incorporates other necessities, including health care, education, transportation, personal care and housekeeping supplies. The two lines are adjusted to reflect the different consumption needs of households based on their composition (household size and the number of children). A spatial price deflator is used covering the three regions: the West Bank, East Jerusalem and Gaza. Recently, poverty has come to be viewed as a multifaceted phenomenon, encompassing deprivations along dimensions that include not only expenditure or consumption but also education and health. The usefulness of such tools in the Palestinian context has to be questioned, if they exclude dimensions such as individual security (against arrest, being killed or injured, or house demolition, collective punishment, land confiscation and besiegement), and the ability as a people to exercise self-determination, to have a sovereign statehood, and freedom of movement and expression.

Palestinians in East Jerusalem also experience significant poverty levels. Although completely under Israeli administration, Palestinians in Jerusalem are socially and economically marginalized. The poverty rate among Palestinians in East Jerusalem is considerably higher than among the Israelis. Using the Israeli poverty line, in 2019 72% of the Palestinians in East Jerusalem (and 81% of their children) lived in poverty, compared with 26% of Israelis (and 36% of their children); around one-half of the Palestinians in East Jerusalem are Palestinian-Arab citizens of Israel (ACRI, 2019).

A significant portion of the poor is composed of those who work. Hence, while a policy of creating employment might alleviate poverty and its severity, it would not on its own eradicate deprivation. For this to happen, it would be necessary to create conditions that enhanced decent job security, raised minimum wages above the poverty line and provided a comprehensive social security system that catered to the needs of the poor.

Economy and Employment

Since 2014 the economic and employment performances in the Palestinian territories have deteriorated substantially. Against the backdrop of a worsening political and fraught governance environment, the average annual rate of economic growth declined from 5.2% in 2011–14 to 2.6% in 2015–18. In 2020 the COVID-19 pandemic and other adverse impacts led to a year-on-year decline of some 12% in gross domestic product (GDP), and by mid-2023 recovery to pre-pandemic levels of growth had not yet been achieved.

Since 2007 the Gaza Strip has been on a downward spiral of denied economic opportunities, poor governance and deteriorating services. Its productive base has been hollowed out, and its population has been subjected to four wars, with thousands of casualties and billions of dollars in lost capital stock. Over one-half of the labour force is unemployed and has fallen into poverty. The humanitarian consequences of this relentless degradation call for emergency measures.

Yet prospects for the coming years point to a further deterioration caused by a number of structural factors. These include an expected decline in external support (from 12.0% to 3.8% of GDP between 2015 and 2022; World Bank, 2018) and progressively larger deductions from the tax revenues that Israel collects on behalf of the PA (which amounted to some US $450m. in 2022). A law passed by the Knesset (Israeli parliament) in 2018 requires the Israeli Government to deduct Government of Palestine budgetary expenditures on prisoners, martyrs and their families from Government of Palestine tax receipts collected by Israel under the clearance mechanism, leading to a reduction of clearance revenues and a consequent loss of 2% of GDP. Other negative factors include a deepening of the separation of Gaza from the West Bank; riing prices; further fragmentation of Palestinian territory, due to settlement expansion in Area C and East Jerusalem; and private sector retrenchment from new investments in an uncertain climate.

The unemployment rate in the Palestinian territories in 2022 was 24.4% of the labour force (13.1% in the West Bank and 45.3% in the Gaza Strip); the overall figure had increased from 23.0% in 2014. Labour force participation increased from 41.7% in 2014 to 45.0% in 2022. It is important to note that labour force participation in the Palestinian territories is dominated by men—the labour force participation rate was 70.7% for males and 18.6% for females in 2022. These figures had increased from 66.8% and 15.4%, respectively, in 2014 (World Bank, 2018).

Youths and women are disproportionately affected by unemployment (Morrar and Syed Zwick, 2021). The youth unemployment rate (aged 15–29) was 35.0% in 2022, down from 36.1% in 2014, while the percentage of youth not in school or employment was 22.3% in 2022, down from 32.2% in 2014. Almost one-half (45.9%) of women (with 13 years of education) and over one-half (57.0%) of young women (aged 15–24) were unemployed in 2022 (PCBS, 2023). The high rate of unemployment among educated females discourages participation in the labour force, while unemployed youth risk being marginalized, exacerbating social fragmentation. This calls for targeted employment programmes and training, proactive reintegration into the labour market, the creation of new jobs, and access to finance and business development opportunities.

The employment situation in Palestine is dire. With approximately one-quarter of persons aged 15 and above (and 36.0% of those aged 15–24) unemployed, it is clear that unemployment is one of the Palestinian territories' worst performing indicators in terms of the state of human development. This is even more true for the Gaza Strip, where these numbers run significantly higher.

Furthermore, 23.9% of employed individuals in the Palestinian territories are categorized as being 'vulnerably' employed. Vulnerable employment is defined by the International Labour Organization (ILO) as a measure of what are deemed to be the more vulnerable statuses of employment, namely own-account workers and contributing family workers as a proportion of total employment. While the number of those in vulnerable employment has decreased from 25.9% in 2014, it is still relatively high. The Palestinian economy is largely a service economy with the services sector accounting for 62% of total employment in 2022. Furthermore, nearly 17% of employed individuals were employed in Israel or Israeli settlements in 2022, a flow that is inherently vulnerable to Israeli security and other restrictions (PCBS, 2023).

Oslo-Paris Accords Policy Constraints

Volumes of international, Palestinian and Israeli scholarly and policy literature have documented how the occupation impacts the movement of people and goods, fragments the territory geographically and socio-politically, stunts economic growth, and restricts Palestinian use of critical resources such as land, water and minerals (UN 2016, ILO 2018, World Bank 2015, MAS 2019). With the very same instruments, the occupation hinders policymaking, governance and service delivery by the PA (UN 2016). Most of the literature concurs that the 1994 Paris Protocol on Economic Relations between Israel and the Palestine Liberation Organization deprives the Palestinian territories of sovereign economic policy space or tools and has appended the Palestinian economy to Israel's in a colonial dependency framework.

The PA was established in 1994 as part of the 'interim, self-governing arrangements' agreed under the Oslo Accords, supposedly for only five years. The PA has no control over its borders—land, air or sea—or of its customs revenues. It does not have its own currency or authority to print money. It lacks access and policy jurisdiction over Area C, which is administered by Israel and comprises some 60% of the West Bank. It lacks influence over the Gaza Strip, owing to territorial fragmentation and internal Palestinian division that prevent the operationalization of a government of national consensus in the Palestinian territories as a whole. The PA fiscal space is restricted. A major part of the PA's revenue (60%–70%) comes from the clearance revenues system, in which all taxes and revenues payable at borders, seaports and by air on Palestinian goods and services are collected by the Israeli fiscal authorities on behalf of the PA in return for a 3% administrative charge to Israel.

The PA also has limited space for the development of effective regional or local government and local development policies. Israel's planning regime in Area C and East Jerusalem is discriminatory and restrictive. It is not designed for the benefit of the protected population. Palestinian local governance and service delivery are limited by increasing territorial fragmentation. For example, movement restrictions and lack of of jurisdiction in large parts of the Occupied Territories hamper the rule of law, the maintenance of security and the delivery of justice services.

Restrictions on movement, access and trade have been identified as the main impediments to economic growth in the Palestinian territories. Restrictions are implemented through a complex system of checkpoints, permits, military roadblocks, settlements, a bypass road system, parallel legal regimes and the 'separation barrier' in the West Bank. Such restrictions have fragmented the Palestinian landscape. They have created isolated communities, undermined social cohesion, ruptured a common identity and reduced economic activity within and among the fractured Palestinian populations of the territory. The United Nations Conference on Trade and Development (UNCTAD) estimated the fiscal cost of occupation to the Palestinian people during 2000–2017 at US $47,700m. UNCTAD argues that, had that amount instead been pumped into the Palestinian economy through expansionary fiscal policies, thousands of additional jobs could have been created.

Therefore, under the prevailing Israeli matrix of control, the Palestinian territories' ability to determine their development fate remains highly circumscribed. A government that does not control its borders, its revenue and its monetary policy, and cannot access much of its natural resources is embarking on the UN 2030 Agenda for Sustainable Development with an overwhelming handicap.

Given international acquiescence with the political stasis, the option of changing the failing paradigm of 'aid for peace' has not been politically feasible at the global level, while Palestinian disunity and internal weaknesses have prevented the accumulation of any weight in rapidly changing regional and global power balances. Even with the rise in the past decade of the most extreme, pro-settlement, anti-Palestinian state forces ever to lead Israel, donors and Palestinians are trying to conduct business as usual. Hence, considerable donor resources have been ploughed into addressing Israeli occupation constraints on the economy, trade, finances and the private sector through a range of micro-measures. This amounts to tinkering with solutions inside the box, rather than challenging the continued validity and functionality of the bygone Oslo-era 'interim self-governing arrangements'.

Recent soul-searching by aid agencies and donor representatives on aid effectiveness has questioned the viability and morality of sustaining support that ultimately perpetuates Israeli occupation while propping up what observers and domestic public opinion see as a sclerotic governing authority (Wildeman, 2019, PMA 2011). The estimated US $36,200m. of aid funnelled into institution building and good governance between 1993 and 2017 has been most successful in creating a securitized PA, serving both domestic and international security functions (Wildeman, 2019). Meanwhile, the efficiency and quality of the basic services provided to some 4.5m. Palestinians by the PA is patchy, especially after a limited performance in responding to the fallout from the COVID-19 pandemic.

Under the current scenario, it is likely that the fundamental condition for human development in the Palestinian territories, namely freedom, will remain elusive for the coming years. This can only change if once more, as in some previous epochs, the collective strength and human capacities of millions of Palestinians around the world, deprived of their basic rights for generations, can coalesce around legitimate common goals coherent with international law, and project a credible narrative of dispossession and liberation.

TWO DECADES OF MACROECONOMIC DYSFUNCTION

This section analyses the most conspicuous trends in the performance of the Palestinian economy over the past two decades under the management of the PA and highlights issues that should be duly considered in devising the development and trade policies that would allow it to move onto a path of growth-enhancing transformation, guaranteeing a sustainable improvement in the well-being of the population.

Lost Development Decades

There is ample and well-documented consensus on the four main defining features of the Palestinian macroeconomic growth path during the last decades.

First, there is wide accord that the Palestinian economy has significantly underperformed, both in terms of its potential and in relation to relevant comparator countries. Different estimates have shown that the growth rate of the Palestinian economy could have been significantly higher—up to two or three times higher—than those historically achieved (Gal and Rock, 2018). Furthermore, the Palestinian economy's per capita income long-term growth rate has failed to match that of its non-oil-exporting Arab comparators by a significant margin. Perhaps more telling is the fact that the Palestinian GDP per capita, adjusted for PPP, stands at less than one-half of that of relevant comparator countries (World Bank, 2017). In this regard, the average PPP GDP per capita of the Palestinian territories during the period 2011–15 was less than one-third of that of Lebanon, a country that has also suffered conflict and political instability, and around 40% of that of Jordan, a country with which the Palestinian territories share many features (USAID, 2017). In 2022, according to the World Bank Development Indicators Database, the GDP in PPP terms of Palestine (at constant 2017 US dollars) was equivalent to only 27.4% of Jordan's, 39.7% of Lebanon's and 6.8% of Israel's.

In terms of trade, a gravity model estimate suggests that, based on its size, income level and proximity to large markets, the Palestinian economy's exports and imports could be a multiple of their current levels, by a factor of at least two, and possibly more (World Bank, 2017). It is also well established that the performance of the Palestinian economy, even in the presence of a significantly low labour participation rate, has not been able to generate the necessary number of decent jobs for its growing labour force, thereby maintaining a high structural unemployment rate (World Bank, 2019; ILO, 2018).

The Perverse Impact of Prolonged Occupation

Second, there is agreement among analysts in acknowledging that the dismal performance of the Palestinian economy is a direct consequence of the multi-layered system perpetuating occupation. The constraints on access to resources, on the movement of goods and people, and other measures that increase transaction costs and distort investment decisions continue to be the main impediment to sustainable economic growth and development in the Palestinian territories. The enormous magnitude of the economic cost of occupation has been substantiated in numerous reports and studies. The cost of occupation is an important aspect of assessing the perverse impact of occupation on Palestinian human development prospects and has been examined from many angles.

The IMF reported in 2016 that if there had been no occupation, real GDP per capita in the Palestinian territories would have been, depending on the methodology utilized, 40%–83% higher. Furthermore, the Fund reported that if the growth rates of the period 1968–87 had been sustained, real GDP per capita would have been 130% higher. The World Bank (2014a) estimated that the total potential additional value added from just alleviating restrictions on access to, and activity and production in, Area C would have amounted to around 35%

of Palestinian GDP in 2011. A study assessing the impact of restrictions on movement concluded that checkpoints alone cost the West Bank economy a minimum of 6% of GDP (Calì and Miaari, 2013). A more recent analysis by the World Bank, in 2017, suggests that alleviating some restrictions quantified in the study could raise real GDP by some 36% in the West Bank and by 40% in the Gaza Strip by 2025. Only relaxing the 'dual-use list'—which bans the importation of technology and critical inputs and contains 56 items requiring 'special approval' to enter Gaza and the West Bank and an additional 61 items that only apply to Gaza—would bring additional cumulative growth of 6% to the West Bank and about 11% in the Gaza Strip (World Bank, 2019). It is estimated that easing the restrictions on the Gaza Strip would result in a 39% increase in GDP, a 55% increase in households' purchasing power, a 23% drop in unemployment, a 625% increase in exports and a 105% increase in imports (Gal and Rock, 2018).

Distorted and Dysfunctional Markets
Third, most analyses underscore the fact that by distorting prices and investment decisions, and by seriously limiting the degree of freedom of the private and public sectors to act, the measures imposed to sustain the occupation have had a significant impact on the structure of the Palestinian economy, engendering a 'malformed economy', signalled by profound deformations and abnormalities (Roy, 2001; Abu Ghattas, 2017; Khalidi, 2019; UNCTAD, 2012; UNCTAD, 2017; World Bank, 2017). Occupation-imposed measures continuously feed into a pattern of behaviour by economic agents that tends to perpetuate and progressively deepen the structural distortion of the economy. The structural distortions are multiple: hypertrophy of the non-tradable sectors and the concomitant underdevelopment of tradables; a significantly underdeveloped private sector; a fragmented domestic market; a high level of informality; population displacement; and a distorted spatial allocation of economic activity and labour market segmentation, among other factors. Their harsh effects reinforce each other, and they together embody the long-term underperformance of the Palestinian territories' growth and development.

Geographic Fragmentation and Smallness
Finally, a defining feature of the long-term trajectory of the Palestinian economy is the fact that the growth and development patterns of the West Bank and Gaza Strip have differed significantly following the major political events of 2006. The two regions have evolved into a situation in which they function essentially as separate territorial entities, both in economic as well as in political terms. The fragmentation of the two territories has magnified the various and critical constraints that all small, resource-poor economies experience, undermining the development prospects of both territories. Most attention has been given to the plight of the Gaza Strip, while the impact of the splintering of the two main territories has not received enough attention. For firms in the West Bank, losing 33% of their potential market is definitely not a trivial issue.

The limitations arising from smallness have been further amplified by the fact that because of occupation-imposed restrictions the economy of the West Bank is itself also severely fragmented, engendering what the World Bank has called an 'archipelago economy' with poor economic links between 'islands'. Firms are confined to isolated small segments of the market, where they experience different conditions and constraints depending on their location. This situation has had a significant adverse effect on the dynamics of private sector development, and therefore on the economy as a whole. The economy of the Gaza Strip has effectively collapsed, amid an acute deterioration in humanitarian conditions, and has essentially become functionally unviable (UNCTAD, 2019).

Growth Trajectory—Fragility and Volatility
The long-term annual compound real growth rate (ACGR) of the Palestinian economy since 1994 has been 4.65%. Given the high rate of population growth there has been a modest long-term growth rate of real GDP per capita of only 1.45%. Growth has been highly volatile, making any point-to-point comparison inadequate. Growth has displayed boom and bust cycles and significant yearly variance. During the period 2013–19, growth significantly slowed to an average annual real rate of only 2.6%. In 2020 the COVID-19 pandemic had a notable impact on growth; in consequence, real GDP per capita (at 2015 prices) in that year was 7.4% lower than in 2013. Real GDP per capita in 2022 was 6.9% less than in 2013.

Some general observations are in order regarding the Palestinian growth trajectory. First, it should be underscored that the main driver of economic growth has been total final consumption, which in a sustained manner through time has exceeded the level of GDP by a substantial margin. Consumption is fuelled by remittances and other components of gross national disposable income (GNDI), and is essentially furnished by imports. Consumption-induced growth as experienced by the Palestinian territories does not lead to the development of domestic production, neither does it lead in any significant way to job creation—either in the short or long term.

Second, as noted above, the growth paths of the West Bank and Gaza Strip have diverged considerably since the fragmentation of the territories. Since 2006, when the two territories were divided between competing political authorities and several Israeli military assaults against the Gaza Strip took place, the West Bank economy has achieved an ACGR of 6.4%, while that of the Gaza Strip is only 0.38%. Consequently, the latter's weight in the overall Palestinian economy has continued to decline. In 2022 the Gaza Strip contributed only 17% of total Palestinian GDP, down from 32% in 2006. Different growth performance and population growth rates have broadened the disparity in GDP per capita between the two territories. While in 1994 GDP per capita in both regions was almost the same, in 2022 GDP per capita in the Gaza Strip was equivalent to only 28.2% of the West Bank's.

Third, in examining the long-term growth trajectory of the Palestinian economy the fact that economic volatility is inimical to sustained economic growth and development needs to be emphasized. It has been shown that countries experiencing such trends tend to grow over time at a lower rate, and that volatility's indirect welfare cost through reduced economic growth is magnified in countries that are poor, financially and institutionally underdeveloped, or unable to conduct countercyclical fiscal policies, as is the case with the Palestinian territories. Severe growth oscillations engender an unpredictable business environment beset with uncertainty, discouraging long-term investment, leading to asset destruction when firms cannot weather the downturns, and affects business decisions leading to sub-optimal outcomes (Amodio and Di Maio, 2017). In the case of the Palestinian territories, the unsettled political situation intensifies the degree of uncertainty permeating all economic activity.

Growth volatility in the Palestinian territories has been the outcome of different factors. A decisive factor has been the impact of exogenous non-economic shocks. Conflict has been a major source of growth volatility, generating boom and bust cycles, with overwhelming effects on GDP (World Bank 2011; Abu-Eideh, 2014). A study has estimated that severe conflict can reduce Palestinian GDP by 46% (RAND Corporation, 2015). There is evidence suggesting that growth volatility due to conflict blights the economy's long-term performance to a larger extent than volatility generated by normal business fluctuations, and that the effects are significantly more persistent (Rodrik, 1999; Novta and Pugacheva, 2020).

Besides major conflict events, yearly growth rates in the Palestinian territories are strongly linked to the relative intensity of unrest prevalent in a given period; the status of relations between the PA and Israel, on which the transfer of fiscal revenue and the easing of some restrictions depends; and the particular nature of the restricting measures applied by Israel. Another important source of growth volatility has been major fluctuations in the level of incoming factor income, mainly wages of Palestinian workers in Israel, and of unrequited transfers, essentially remittances and, very importantly, foreign aid, which, as pointed out above, buttresses the levels of household and government consumption that are the main drivers of economic growth in the Palestinian territories. Finally, given the extreme dependence on the Israeli economy, during periods of relative calm the growth rates in the Palestinian territories reflect Israel's business cycles, which are transmitted primarily through foreign trade and employment of Palestinian workers.

A Structurally Underdeveloped Economy

Since 1994 the composition of the Palestinian economy has experienced a significant transformation, both in terms of the relative contribution of the different sectors of economic activity to total value added, as well as in terms of the share of the different institutional sectors. In the latter case, there has been a progressive increase in the participation of the enterprise sector at the expense of the other institutional sectors—i.e. households (26.7%) and non-profit institutions serving households (3.5%) in 2019, down from 45.2% and 6.6% in 2004, respectively. (The PCBS attributes all agricultural value added to the household sector.)

In 2021 the non-financial enterprise sector generated 47.4% of the total value added produced by the Palestinian economy, up from 22.3% in 2004. Including financial enterprises, the formal private enterprise sector generated 53.2% of GDP in 2021, up from 26.4% in 2004. There has been a notable decline in the share of the general government in GDP, from 21.8% in 2004 to 16.6% in 2021. It must be noted, however, that non-enterprise sectors still represent a sizeable share of the Palestinian GDP.

The increased share of the enterprise sector in the Palestinian economy does not necessarily indicate the emergence of a robust modern private sector. The sector in the Palestinian territories comprises mainly family-owned small and micro-enterprises, with low capital accumulation and technological absorption capabilities, where the informal sector is predominant. Informality undermines labour productivity and indicates the ill health of the economy. A study found that during 1995–2012 the shadow economy—composed of informal activities—accounted for 58%–89% of Palestinian GDP (Sabra, Eltalla and Alfar, 2015). A more recent study estimates that the informal sector represents around one-third of Palestinian GDP (Awad and Alazzeh, 2020).

According to the definition of the ILO (2018), the informal sector includes jobs without legal and social protection, whether carried out in formal firms or otherwise. On this basis, in 2018 informality accounted for 64.3% of non-agriculture employment in Palestine: 31.2% in informal activities; 30.8% in informal employment in the formal sector; and 2.3% in household employment. Entrepreneurial activity in the Palestinian territories is principally driven by necessity (Morrar et al., 2022), being a resilience mechanism aimed at the creation of self-employment and jobs for family members in the absence of wage employment opportunities, feeding into informality. Such a pattern does not augur, in a business-as-usual scenario, a very auspicious future for the private sector.

Because of the conditions prevailing under occupation, private investment in commodity production activities and modern technology-intensive services remains far from what would be necessary to engender a robust modern private sector, capable of spurring adequate rates of growth and generating the needed employment for a growing labour force (Morrar and Gallouj, 2016). The Palestinian territories fare relatively well in relation to comparator countries in terms of total gross fixed capital formation, and in many years this has been above the 25% identified in the World Bank Growth Report (2008) as the minimum rate required for sustaining growth. However, investment in the Palestinian territories is channelled mostly into buildings, and the share of non-building investment, which is in productive assets, has been exceptionally low. Since 2012 total non-buildings investment, both private and public, has amounted to just 7.9% of GDP, only 33.2% of total gross fixed capital formation.

This is not because of insufficient investment capital but is mainly due to the absence of profitable investment opportunities in the territories, and the prevailing uncertainty that defines the business environment. This is corroborated by the behaviour of the financial system that consistently has the necessary liquidity to provide investment funds, but these are mostly channelled to other undertakings (further discussed below). Moreover, banks' credit facilities are permanently significantly lower than total deposits, and excess liquidity is deposited with the Palestinian Monetary Authority (PMA), which is ultimately available to help finance the government budget deficit. The significant investments of Palestinians abroad also attest to the availability of investment capital that is not contributing to growth and development in the territories.

Since the signing of the Oslo Accords the composition of the Palestinian economy in terms of economic activities has also changed considerably. A defining feature has been the hypertrophy of the services sector at the expense of the commodity-producing sectors. (In this section we are using the World Trade Organization General Agreement on Trade in Services definition of services, which includes all activities except agriculture, fishing and forestry, mining and quarrying, and manufacturing. We include the distribution of electricity and water and sewerage services within services.) The Palestinian economy has emerged as essentially a services economy (Shikaki, 2021; Morrar and Gallouj, 2016; Morrar and Abdelhadi, 2016; Al-Falah, 2013). In 2022 services activities, in both the West Bank and the Gaza Strip, accounted for around 80% of GDP, while in 1994 services contributed only 67.7% of Palestinian GDP. In parallel, commodity-producing sectors have progressively lost ground. The contribution of agriculture to total value added declined from 12.0% in 1994 to 6.0% in 2022, while that of manufacturing fell from 19.5% to 12.0% over the same period. Mining and quarrying, concentrated in the West Bank, has traditionally made an insignificant contribution to GDP—0.3% in 2022, down from 0.7% in 1994. Commodity-producing activities have not been able to unleash all of their potential, being seriously impacted by shocks and stifled by the myriad of protracted restrictions imposed by Israel, which has hindered their productive capacity and competitiveness.

The shift towards services is a normal drift as economies develop and per capita GDP increases (Chenery and Syrquin, 1975; Herrendorf, Rogerson and Valentinyi, 2014). However, the Palestinian case is an anomaly and does not reflect a typical country transitioning towards higher economic complexity and economic development. In the Palestinian territories the share of services in GDP is significantly higher than might be expected from the level of GDP per capita. International comparison clearly signals that the Palestinian territories stand out as an outlier, showing perhaps one of the highest contributions of services to GDP in the world, and even higher than in some highly developed countries (Abu Ghattas, 2017; World Bank, 2017; USAID, 2017).

The disproportionate growth of services activities is one of the main abnormalities engendered by the measures imposed to sustain occupation. The forces set in motion by occupation have restructured the Palestinian economy and made its growth performance driven mainly by low productivity non-tradable services—those that Shikaki (2021) terms 'occupation-circumventing' economic activities. According to the analysis of Indian economist Kunal Sen, the Palestinian territories exhibit a structurally underdeveloped economy, where labour has been progressively reallocated from agriculture to low-productivity non-business services.

Commodity-producing Sectors—Neglected Engines of Growth and Development

Agriculture and manufacturing have underperformed since 1994 and are producing well below their potential. As discussed above, their contribution to GDP has declined considerably, and in relation to comparator countries it is significantly lower than what could be expected, given the level of Palestinian income per capita. These activities have been particularly emasculated by occupation. Examining the post-1994 period we can clearly observe that both sectors experienced a prolonged period of stagnation. In the case of agriculture, the ACGR during 1994–2005 was only 1.38%, and the 1994 GDP level was not exceeded until 2004. In the case of manufacturing, the performance was even worse: the ACGR for 1994–2008 was only 0.21%, and the 1994 GDP level was recovered only 14 years later, in 2008. Agriculture experienced some dynamism after the al-Aqsa intifada (uprising), which began in 2000, growing at an average annual rate of 4.6% during 2004–09; however, it has reverted to stagnation during the past decade, when GDP showed practically no growth. Manufacturing since

2008 has fared relatively better, registering an average annual growth rate of 4.4%.

The agriculture and manufacturing sectors have experienced higher growth volatility than that of overall GDP, which would appear to indicate that services activities are relatively more resilient to shocks. This suggests that the negative effect of growth volatility might have had a greater impact on agricultural and manufacturing activities and would explain in part their observed performances. Even though quarrying plays a relatively important role in exports, its contribution to GDP has been marginal. The Palestinian territories have not been able to exploit the full potential of this activity because since 1994 Israel has refused to issue new permits to Palestinian stone mining and quarrying companies, while operating some 11 quarries, including a number in Area C, for Israeli use.

Farming has traditionally been the mainstay of the Palestinian economy and society, and the dominant economic activity for the majority of the population. However, since occupation began, agriculture has been squeezed by limitations on access to water and land. Access to and distribution of water are among the most critical and sensitive issues emerging from occupation. It is important to highlight that the average yearly per capita availability of water in the Palestinian territories is one of the lowest in the world, and that Palestinians in the West Bank have access to only about 15%–20% of the water availability in the area, the rest being allocated to Israel's settlements and for use within Israel itself. In the Gaza Strip, water scarcity and degradation led the UN to predict in 2012 that the area would be uninhabitable in the near future.

Palestinian water supplies are insufficient to satisfy demand, both for households that consume below the minimum internationally recommended levels, as well as for economic activities. In the Palestinian territories only 5.5% of available agricultural land is irrigated. Israel's confiscation and control of Palestinian water resources undermine any possibility of the sustainable development of agriculture or, indeed, of manufacturing.

Agricultural land availability is another major constraint confronting the Palestinian territories. Land is taken over by Israeli authorities under different justifications: declaration of state land; designated military areas; nature reserves; construction of settlements; declaration of land as fallow if not cultivated for three years; and the application of the absentee landlord law in order to take over privately owned land. Land has been appropriated by Israel for the construction of bypass roads and other infrastructure to serve settlers. Farmland is governed under a complex legal-bureaucratic mechanism, designed to facilitate the transfer of land to settlers (Smith, 2020). State land is allocated exclusively to Jewish-Israeli citizens—according to the Israeli Peace Now organization, in 2018 99.8% of state lands allocated in the West Bank were given to Israelis—and land requisitioned for military purposes is given to the settlements (Hass, 2019).

Without access to agricultural land and sufficient water, the prospects for agricultural development in the Palestinian territories are without doubt quite grim. Moreover, besides these restrictions, the structure of the Palestinian agricultural sector itself is another factor inhibiting its development. The sector is characterized by the prevalence of family-owned micro-landholdings, mostly oriented to self-consumption, where agriculture, in a significant proportion of cases, is not the main occupation of the landowner. A high proportion of landowners lack title over their properties, which limits access to finance. Agriculture has emerged as the employment of last resort that still occupies, mostly informally, around 10% of the working population.

Labour and total factor productivity is relatively low in Palestinian agriculture (FAO, 2019). Yields per area in the Palestinian territories are about one-half of those in Jordan and around 40% of those in Israel (UNCTAD, 2015), two countries that have similar climate and soil conditions. Productivity is also hampered by the restrictions imposed by the dual-use list, prohibiting access to quality fertilizers, and by the high cost of other imported inputs on which it extensively depends. Agricultural production has also been increasingly affected by settler violence and land confiscation involving the uprooting of olive trees and orchards, which are the main staples of Palestinian agriculture.

The manufacturing sector does not fare much better. This sector is populated by micro- and small enterprises with limited capital accumulation and technological absorption capabilities, and it has not shown any noticeable transition towards modernization and upgrading during recent decades. The sector's structure has remained for the most part unchanged, and there are some indicators that even suggest a regression in terms of its underlying potential to achieve higher productivity and efficiency. Manufacturing activity is concentrated in the West Bank, a trend that has deepened as a result of the devastation wrought on the manufacturing sector in the Gaza Strip, which hosts 76% of all manufacturing establishments and 95% of manufacturing employment. Micro-enterprises (consisting of four workers or fewer) represent 77.6% of all establishments in the Palestinian territories, while those with between five and nine workers account for 14.2%. Therefore, only around 8% of manufacturing firms have 10 or more workers, while 107 firms—0.5% of the total—have 50 or more workers.

In the Palestinian territories' manufacturing sector the 'middle-size' firms are missing; this is a segment that, as shown by various studies, is a major driver of employment and innovation and its absence constitutes a significant hurdle for the development of the sector (Tybout, 2000; Morrar and Arman, 2020). Firms in the Palestinian territories, for the most part, do not expand; micro and small firms tend to remain as such, and therefore economies of scale go unexploited (World Bank, 2014). Although manufacturing has shown some dynamism during the past decade, growing at an ACGR of 3.3%, job creation has not followed suit, with employment in the sector growing at a rate of 1.6%, indicating low employment elasticity.

Palestinian manufacturing generates, in general, low value added and is highly dependent on imported inputs and capital goods. Overall, labour productivity in manufacturing is relatively low, and a study examining firm-level productivity in the Palestinian territories suggested that physical capital and labour input are significant factors in determining the level of output, while technology exhibits diminishing returns to scale (Kashiwagi, 2016). A deteriorating pattern in capital intensity has prevailed since the early 1990s. A defining trait of the evolution of manufacturing in the Palestinian territories is that growth, both in terms of number of establishments and of employment, has mainly taken place in the types of enterprise and in those activities exhibiting relatively lower productivity, which diminishes the aggregate productivity level of the sector.

There are, none the less, 'pockets of excellence' in the Palestinian light industry sector, such as pharmaceutical firms, some in the food and beverage sector, and others in furniture, metal and plastics production. These do not, however, add up to a critical mass with the potential of having an overall impact on the entire economy, either through their technological spillovers, or by means of their integration with firms in other sectors of economic activity in value chains; with the notable exception perhaps of agro-business. However, the development of agro-business is restricted by the poor overall performance of the agricultural sector and by marketing constraints. Overall, the absence of any significant foreign direct investment in the sector has deprived Palestinian manufacturing of the benefits usually associated with its historical role in economic development, including, *inter alia*, through know-how spillovers and integration into international value chains.

The premature de-industrialization of the Palestinian economy is one of the enduring legacies of occupation and inappropriate Palestinian development policy. Firms in the Palestinian territories are confronted by high transaction costs, resulting from Israeli security policy, undermining their competitiveness while operating in an open market. In an import-dependent economy, firms face higher costs due to longer waiting times, limitations caused by security inspection infrastructure, increased transportation costs, high storage fees and security inspection costs (Fesen, 2021; World Bank, 2019; UNCTAD, 2014). These factors equally undermine firms' export possibilities, impeding a process of 'learning by exporting', which is reportedly an important source of productivity improvements for firms.

International Competitiveness and Growth-reducing Structural Change

The distortion of two basic prices in the Palestinian economy, exchange rate and wages, has a significant impact on its tradable production sectors. The exchange rate is a determining factor of firms' competitiveness, both in the domestic market as well as in third markets, and therefore on trade flows (IMF, 2015). An appreciation of the exchange rate increases the price of exports expressed in the target market's currency and lowers the price of imports expressed in national currency in the domestic market, intensifying competition with domestic production.

The behaviour of the new Israeli shekel against other currencies reflects the performance of the Israeli economy and the country's monetary policies, without any connection to the realities of the Palestinian economy. For a prolonged period the shekel has experienced a significant and sustained appreciation against the major international currencies (Friedman and Galo, 2015; Palatnik, et al., 2019; IMF, 2021. This means that domestic prices in the Palestinian territories, including those of non-tradables, labour costs and domestic inputs for production, expressed in US dollars have significantly increased, hindering the competitiveness of firms, which are increasingly subject to strong competition from imports. Overvaluation of the exchange rate has also impaired export growth. By curtailing investment opportunities in tradables, overvaluation of the currency has negatively hampered the long-term growth prospects of the Palestinian territories. What might be good for Israeli trade is generally not good for the Palestinian territories.

The cost of labour is another factor affecting the international competitiveness of the Palestinian producers. Wages are high enough, relative to those in competing countries, substantially to restrict competitiveness in labour-intensive activities, in particular in the manufacturing sector. Besides the impact of exchange rate overvaluation on the cost of labour expressed in dollar terms, employment of Palestinians in Israel and the settlements exercises an upward pressure on the wages prevailing in the Palestinian private sector. This effect is reinforced by the public employment wage premium, which constitutes a major distortion in the labour market, limiting job creation in the private sector (World Bank, 2019).

The pull factor of employment in the countries of the Gulf Cooperation Council for highly-skilled workers and the level of the minimum wage also place pressure on formal private sector wages. The minimum wage is a right stipulated in the Palestinian Labour Law and it was adopted for the first time for the West Bank in October 2012 and entered into force in January 2013. It was set at NIS 1,450 per month (roughly around US $375 at the time) and was raised to NIS 1,800 on 1 January 2022. (This is comparatively high in relation to other lower middle-income countries.) However, a significant proportion of Palestinian workers receive wages below the minimum level, mostly in micro and small firms and in the informal sector. The inflow of income earned in Israel and in the settlements increases the relative price of non-tradables relative to the price of tradable goods in the Palestinian territories, an effect analogous to that of real exchange rate appreciation, weakening the competitiveness of exports and of domestic production competing against importable goods.

Economic growth and inclusive development are the outcome of a process where investible surplus and the labour force are progressively shifted towards higher productivity activities with greater technological spillovers, increasing returns and higher demand elasticities. What is produced and exported matters. For this process to take place the system of economic signals has to be such that the private sector is compelled to invest in upgrading and diversifying production, continuously shifting resources towards products that would contribute to supply-upgrading along a learning curve, and adapting a country's export productive capacity to meet ever-changing international demand. In the case of small economies like the Palestinian territories, in which the size of the domestic market constitutes a significant limitation for unleashing a process of this type, foreign trade needs to play a leading role in making it possible to achieve higher economic complexity and the required economies of scale. However, in the Palestinian territories exports have not contributed to achieving these objectives.

As McMillan and Rodrik (2011) point out, increasing aggregate productivity in the economy can be the outcome of two processes: either as the result of reallocating labour from lower productivity activities to higher productivity ones, the structural change effect; or by increasing productivity in each of the sectors of economic activity, the within effect. The Palestinian territories have experienced a process of growth-reducing structural change.

During 1998–2022 the bulk of employment generation took place in those activities with the lowest relative labour productivity, those with productivity of only one-fifth or even lower than that of the best performing sector. Manufacturing activities that employ the bulk of workers are among the worst performers, as is the case with textile and apparel production and the food products industry. Positive rates of long-term productivity growth can be observed in public utilities and a few other services activities, but these employ a tiny fraction of workers in the non-agriculture enterprise sector.

The overall dismal productivity performance during 1998–2022, in particular of manufacturing, is notable. Except for tobacco and leather products, basic metals and furniture, all other manufacturing sectors saw insignificant or negative rates of productivity growth.

Dysfunctional Integration into the Global Trading System

The Palestinian economy is a relatively open one, in which exports and imports of goods and services represented 81.2% of GDP in 2022 (at current prices). Two main features define the integration of the Palestinian territories into the global trading system. First, the territories have a predominantly import economy, in which imports of goods and services account for most of the observed degree of openness. The Palestinian territories have not been able to develop export activities to any significant extent, either in goods or services. Second, the trade integration of the Palestinian territories is characterized by a high and asymmetrical dependence on the Israeli economy, which has diminished in time but which is still predominant. Bilateral trade data are not very reliable, but it has been estimated that Israeli-Palestinian trade flows are significantly larger than predicted by gravity trade models and that there is little correspondence between the Palestinian territories' imports from Israel and what Israel exports to the world, indicating that there is significant trade diversion. This attests to the dysfunctionality of the trade arrangements included in the Oslo Agreements, which have engrained the Palestinian territories' dependency and render them a captive market for Israel, with significant economic costs (World Bank, 2017).

Analysis of the performance of Palestinian total trade, goods and services, demonstrates that there has been no improvement during the last two decades. Even though the total trade deficit as a percentage of GDP has declined, it still stood at 48.8% in 2022, one of the highest deficits recorded in the world. The coverage ratio, exports over imports, for total trade declined from 31.0% in 2000 to 27.5% in 2022, indicating a slightly higher growth rate for imports than for exports. The coverage ratio for trade in goods decreased from 28% in 2000 to 25% in 2022, indicating higher growth rates of exports compared with imports. This trend is concerning, because if it persists, it will aggravate the already extremely fragile external position of the Palestinian economy. The coverage ratio for trade in services increased significantly between 2000 and 2022, from 47% to 61%. A forecast based on past trends indicates that even with a higher growth rate of exports the deficit will continue rising in absolute terms for a prolonged period, and it would take decades before the deficit could finally be reversed.

As result of the high and persistent combined deficit in trade in goods and services, the Palestinian territories have presented over time a very fragile external position with a sustained current account deficit. This has been partly financed by net factor income, essentially earnings of Palestinians in

Israel; private transfers, mainly remittances of Palestinian workers in third countries; and official transfers, mainly government aid from bilateral donors. In a business-as-usual scenario, the current account deficit is expected to remain high over the medium to long term. In such a scenario the volatility of current account financing sources coupled with the absence of policy space on the part of the PA to confront external disequilibria has led many observers to entertain serious doubts about the overall long-term sustainability of the Palestinian macroeconomy in the absence of a significant policy shift.

The Palestinian territories have experienced a large and persistent deficit on trade in goods, which in 2022 was equivalent to 48.8% of GDP. The deficit on trade in goods as a percentage of GDP has declined from the levels registered in the late 1990s, where it stood at a yearly average of around 60% of GDP. However, this has not been the result of major export dynamism, but of the hypertrophy of non-tradable economic activities in the Palestinian economy. In fact, exports of goods as a percentage of GDP have declined from a yearly average of 9.6% in the second half of the 1990s to only 6.6% during the last five years. The Palestinian territories exhibit a very low exports-to-GDP ratio in comparison with other small economies and with the average for all lower middle-income countries—the category to which the Palestinian territories belong—for which the ratio is around 17%. Given the low valued added of production in the Palestinian territories and the weight of re-exports, which constituted 30% of total exports during 2018/19, it would be safe to conclude that exports of goods have made an insignificant contribution to the Palestinian economy.

The West Bank accounts for almost all Palestinian goods exports. The Gaza Strip effectively ceased exporting some years ago, accounting for only 6% of total exports in 2022. Despite having preferential market access to the European Union (EU), the USA, MERCOSUR, and to members of the Greater Arab Free Trade Area (GAFTA), the Palestinian territories have not been able to reap benefits from these arrangements owing to the multiple restrictions and distortions in place. The Palestinian territories have not experienced any significant trade diversification, either in terms of goods exported or markets served.

Export growth has taken place mainly in the intensive margin, exporting the same goods to the same markets. Analysis of an eight-digit disaggregation of the Harmonized System shows a high concentration of exports in the 10 main products, which represented 62.5% of total domestic exports in 2019. Primary and labour-intensive products, such as stone, metals waste and scrap, olive oil, shoes and furniture, among a few other products, constitute the bulk of exports. There are only a small number of technologically advanced domestic exports, as is the case with pharmaceuticals, but they only make up a miniscule fraction of total exports. Most of the products register a significantly low yearly export value, and there is high export instability, as few products register exports in a good number of years of the series.

Even though the Palestinian economy is dominated by services, trade in services has not been a major engine of economic growth or of structural transformation of the economy. Exports of services represented 3% of GDP in 2022, while imports accounted for 5%. As is the case with trade in goods, the weight of services trade in the economy has declined since 2000, and the Palestinian territories have recorded a persistent deficit on trade in services, which has been widening over time, as exports have registered an ACGR of 5.7% since 2000 while imports grew by 7.0%. Since 2014 imports have grown at an average annual rate of 11.6% while exports have grown by only 2.2%, which suggests that if the pattern persists the deficit might grow exponentially. Travel (i.e. incoming tourists), construction and telecommunications services represented almost 80% of total services exports during recent years. Imports of services are more diverse, but travel, accounting for 50% of the total, predominates; international transport—on which the Palestinian territories are almost totally dependent—accounts for around 22% and other business services for an additional 13.5%. Bilateral trade in services with Israel has a relatively significant weight.

ECONOMIC PERFORMANCE IN 2022: SLOWING RECOVERY AND DEEPENING STRUCTURAL IMBALANCES

In 2022 the economic recovery from the ramifications of the COVID-19 pandemic slowed, with rate of growth of real GDP decelerating from 7.0% in 2021 to 3.9% in 2022. Despite what appears to be a strong performance, economic growth in 2022 was driven by external influences more than by expansion in productive activities. Growth resulted mainly from a large increase in the collection of customs duties and value-added tax (VAT) on imports (as a direct result of the value of imports rising by 25.7% year on year). Customs duties contributed 1.14 percentage points of real GDP growth and VAT 1.72, followed by the industrial and trade sectors, which contributed 0.61 and 0.57 percentage points, respectively. However, 2022 witnessed a decline in the value added of several major sectors, such as agriculture (which contracted by 5.7%), construction (1.0%) and information and communications (6.9%). If the increase in the collection of customs and import taxes was not taken into account and the increase in value added in the production and service sectors looked at alone, GDP growth in 2022 (from the production side) would be only 1.1% (compared with the headline rate of 3.9%).

Key sectors and subsectors have not yet returned to their pre-pandemic levels of output, and in 2022 production in some sectors was even less than the low levels recorded in 2020 (agricultural and communications values added in 2022 were 6.3% and 0.8% lower than in 2020, respectively). The values added of the agricultural, commerce and transportation sectors in 2022 were still more than 10% below the pre-pandemic levels registered in 2019, while the values added of hospitality and restaurant services, professional activities and construction were more than 20% below their pre-pandemic levels.

At the level of spending, despite the discernible increase in exports, private consumption and investment, recovery possibilities in 2022 were undermined by a decrease in public spending and a growing dependency on imports of goods and services. This, in turn, led to a widening of the current account deficit, despite increases in compensation to workers in Israel, income from investments abroad and current transfers to non-governmental sectors. Notably, Israel's continued and increasing deductions from the tax revenues that it collects on behalf of the PA prompted the latter to introduce more austerity measures, as well as leading to an ever-increasing accumulation of arrears to private sector and public sector employees. This placed greater downward pressure on recovery opportunities in 2022, with the PA paying only partial wages to over 150,000 public servants from late 2021. In addition to this predicament, limited sources of growth and development, heightened political tension and fears about rising prices at both global and local levels (in the latter case owing to the depreciation of the new Israeli shekel against the US dollar) continue to restrain the prospects for recovery in 2023.

Aggregate values hide the discrepancy in economic performance between the West Bank and the Gaza Strip. In the besieged Strip in 2022, the value added of all major economic sectors increased, except for the information and communications sector (where it decreased by 7.9%), which led to overall real GDP growth of 5.6%. This increase coincided with the issuance of permits for about 18,000 workers and merchants from Gaza to work in Israel, in addition to an increase in imports of goods from Egypt, an increase in exports to Israel and the easing of restrictions on movement for Palestinians leaving Gaza. However, reconstruction efforts in Gaza have not made any tangible progress, and there are still thousands of damaged or destroyed housing units as a result of the successive wars in the Strip, as the local authorities await the arrival of aid and permits from Israel to import the necessary materials. The Israeli military assault on Gaza in August 2022 undermined the prospects of faster economic growth. Gaza's contribution to overall Palestinian GDP remained limited and amounted to an estimated 17.4% in 2022—almost one-half of its historical contribution.

In the West Bank, growth in 2022 in the sectors of industry (5.1%), commerce (2.4%), transportation (2.7%), finance (4.2%) and services (0.3%) was offset by declines in the sectors of agriculture (10.2%), construction (3.2%), information and communications (6.9%) and public administration (0.2%). Overall, the West Bank economy grew by 3.6%, in real terms, in 2022. The political situation in the West Bank worsened in conjunction with a rise in settler attacks on and Israeli military operations in Palestinian towns and cities during the latter half of 2022 and into 2023, while the imposition of more restrictions on the movement of people and goods weakened growth opportunities.

KEY MACROECONOMIC INDICATORS

The structural distortions discussed in the preceding section of this essay entail, *inter alia*, an adverse path of dependency on external sources of income and a fragility to external shocks. These are vividly depicted by the fact that the Palestinian economy produces from domestic sources only 75% of total national income, with net factor income, remittances and international aid comprising the rest. (Most of the statistics quoted in this section originate from the PCBS—especially the national accounts statistics. Other sources are indicated where they are used. Unless otherwise stated, all change ratios are measured at constant prices, using a base year of 2015.)

Gross Domestic Product

Preliminary data from the PCBS indicate a slowdown in the economic recovery, as real GDP grew by 3.9% in 2022, compared with 7.1% in 2021. This growth was driven by an increase of 3.6% in GDP in the West Bank and of 5.6% in the Gaza Strip. However, growth in 2021 and 2022 was not sufficient to restore GDP to its pre-pandemic level; in 2022 overall GDP was still 1.4 percentage points less than in 2019 (lower by 0.8 of a percentage point in the West Bank and by 3.8 percentage points in the Gaza Strip). It nevertheless exceeded the official projections for 2022 (which forecast growth of about 3%, according to the baseline scenario). At current prices, GDP stood at US $19,112m. in 2022.

In terms of expenditure, private consumption remained the main catalyst for growth in 2022, accounting for 102.0% of GDP, followed by investment (26.9%) and government spending (20.3%). Inhibiting economic growth prospects, the trade balance deficit stood at 47.8% of GDP. In 2022 private final consumption expenditure grew by 20.5%, compared with the previous year. (Private consumption expenditure includes final consumption by households and final consumption by non-profit enterprises serving households.) Total investment (gross capital formation) also rose, by 11.3%, in 2022, driven by an increase in the gross fixed capital formation in non-buildings (31.7%) and in inventory (4.4%); gross fixed capital formation in buildings decreased by 1.7%. Public final consumption expenditure decreased by 10.5%, and the trade balance deficit widened by 35.4%, owing to a surge in imports (which totalled US $2,121.2m., representing an increase of 25.7%) compared with exports ($171.0m., representing an increase of 6.2%).

The value added of all major service sectors increased in 2022, compared with the previous year, with the exception of the information and communications sector (the value added of which decreased by 6.9%). The value added of the industrial sector grew by 5.1%, while those of the agricultural and construction sectors, declined by 5.7% and 1.0%, respectively. The construction and commerce sectors showed the weakest recovery towards their pre-pandemic levels, as their values added in 2022 were still 21.3% and 17.6% lower than in 2019, respectively. However, some sectors recovered fully and their values added in 2022 actually exceeded their pre-pandemic levels, including financial activities (15.5% larger than in 2019), health care and social work (31.3% larger) and public administration (16.8% larger).

GDP per Capita

The upward curve in GDP in 2022—at a rate exceeding annual population growth—led to a rise of 1.2% in real GDP per capita: by 0.9% in the West Bank and by 2.7% in the Gaza Strip. Although GDP per capita reached US $3,779 at current prices in 2022 in the Palestinian territories, the overall performance figures in the economy conceal an alarming gap in economic performance between the West Bank ($5,477) and the Gaza Strip ($1,514).

Gross National Income

GNI refers to the sum market value of all finished products and services produced by a nation's economy through the means of production owned by its citizenry over a specific period, whether within the country's border or beyond. The difference between GDP and GNI lies in the income citizens receive from abroad plus non-residents' income within the country. In the Palestinian territories this flow is generated by the 190,000 Palestinian dayworkers in the Israeli market, adding significant net factor income to a fragile GDP. Real GNI increased by 4.2% between 2021 and 2022, driven by a 6% rise in net receipts from abroad, in addition to the 3.6% increase in real GDP. GNI in current prices reached US $23,100m. in 2022.

GNI reflects the resources available to Palestinians better than GDP does. Totalling about US $4,000m. at current prices in 2022, the substantial value of net earnings from Palestinian factors of production outside the domestic economy, equivalent to 20.9% of GDP, lends credence to this notion. The mainstay (about 97.3% in 2022) of this net factor income is attributed to the compensation of Palestinian workers in Israel and the settlements, while the rest is generated from net property income abroad.

Gross National Disposable Income

Gross national disposable income (GNDI) is the sum of the disposable incomes of all the citizenry of a country. In addition to GNI, this indicator includes net current transfers receivable from abroad—including aid and gifts sent by expatriates overseas to their families and friends in the Palestinian territories, and support and grants from abroad to private and public institutions and bodies. This means that GNDI provides further insight into the resources available to the Palestinian economy—especially since current transfers constitute an important source of income for Palestinians. In 2022 the value of net current transfers from abroad amounted to about US $2,500m. at current prices (12.9% of GDP). Gross national disposable income rose by 8.0% between 2021 and 2022, due to a 13.9% increase in final consumption and a 36.6% decrease in savings. During the same period net current transfers from abroad increased by 60.2%.

Sectoral Performances

Even though the value added of productive sectors increased in 2022 by 0.8%, compared with the previous year, it was still 13.5% below the level recorded in 2019. The contribution of the productive sectors to GDP fell from 23.2% in 2021 to 22.5% in 2022, which was also below the 2019 share (25.7%). These figures reflect the persistent fragile growth and distortion throughout the Palestinian economic structural transformation. (The source of figures for this section is the PCBS National Accounts Quarterly Statistics, 2000–2022 (PCBS, 2023.)

Overall, 2022 was marked by the recovery of the industrial sector—while agriculture and construction lagged behind. The value added of agriculture, forestry and fishing decreased by about 5.7%, compared with 2020—and by nearly 14.8%, compared with 2019. In the same vein, the sector's contribution to GDP fell from 7.0% in 2019 to 6.6% in 2021 and 6.0% in 2022.

The value added of the industrial sector in 2022 was 5.1% higher than in 2021. As a result, the sector's contribution to GDP rose from 11.9% to 12.0% over the same period. The industry sector's value added in 2022 remained 9.3% lower than in 2019—mainly because the output of manufacturing industries was still lower than its pre-pandemic level. Manufacturing industries contributed 85.7% of the value added of the industrial sector in 2022.

In 2022 the value added of the construction sector decreased by 1.0%, compared with 2021. As a result, the sector's contribution to GDP fell slightly, from 4.7% in 2021 to 4.5%. The construction industry has been the slowest sector to recover from the effects of the pandemic; its value added in 2022 was still lower, by 21.3%, than in 2019, while the sector's contribution to GDP remained 1.1 percentage points lower than in 2019.

The scale of growth of the commercial, financial and services sectors in 2022 (1.5%) was greater than that of productive sectors in general (0.8%). None the less, the contribution of the former sectors to GDP decreased slightly in 2022, to 60.5%, owing to significant increases in customs duties (by 12.2%) and in import VAT (25.8%). The increase in the value added of economic activities involving the commercial, financial and services sectors was a result of the recovery in most subsectors, except for communications and telecommunications (which declined by 6.9%), professional, scientific and technical services activities (which declined by 1.4%), hospitality and food services (which declined by 0.4%), education (which declined by 0.6%) and other services (which declined by 0.1%).

Balance of Payments, International Investment Position and External Debt

The Palestinian territories suffer from a chronic trade balance deficit, as the value of imports is usually more than three times the value of exports. Compensation to workers in Israel, foreign aid, remittances and income from investments abroad partly offset the deficit. However, they are insufficient to cover domestic consumption. Therefore, the Palestinian territories suffer from a structural current account deficit that is usually financed through borrowing. In order to address this deficit, the obstacles and restrictions imposed by the occupation on the sources of production and movement need to be surmounted—including, but not limited to, investment in Area C, land use, economic infrastructure development, and control over borders and crossings. The existing restraints limit the Palestinian economy's productivity, hinder the access of Palestinian products to global markets, and deepen the territories' dependence on the Israeli economy as a supplier of a substantial part of private and public consumption and which accounts for about one-half of Palestinian imports.

In 2022 the current account deficit increased by 61.2% year on year to reach US $2,900m., or 15% of GDP at current prices. The widening of the current account deficit can be attributed to a 34.2% increase in the trade deficit and a 38.3% decline in donor support for non-governmental sectors. Increases in compensation to workers in Israel (11.1%), in investment income (16.5%), in donor support for the government sector (33.0%) and in current transfers to non-governmental sectors (excluding donor support) (35.8%) were not enough to compensate for the increase in the trade deficit. As a result, net borrowing from abroad increased by 87.1% in 2022, compared with 2021.

At the end of 2022 the total investments of Palestinians residing outside the Palestinian territories (i.e. total assets invested abroad) exceeded non-resident investments in the territories (total foreign liabilities) by about US $3,400m. Net foreign investment in the Palestinian territories decreased by about 8.1% in 2022, compared with 2021. The decrease resulted from lower domestic deposits in offshore banks and a 4.3% decline in foreign exchange circulating in the Palestinian economy, despite a 5.2% increase in net direct investment and a 13.1% increase in net portfolio investment. About 62.8% of total assets invested abroad were in the form of currency and deposits ($5,900m.).

Total (accumulated) external debt was approximately US $2,191m. at the end of 2022—1.5% higher than in 2021. This situation is attributable to increases in the long-term external debt of the non-financial private sector (141.9%), in government short-term external debt (15.7%) and in the banks' short-term external debt (9.3%). The long-term external debt of the Government and of the banks decreased by 4.2% and 17.7%, respectively, in 2022. Government debt is essentially long term and constituted 49.3% of the total Palestinian external debt in 2022.

Prices

The Consumer Price Index (CPI) is the average price of a selection of basic goods and services that reflects the consumption patterns of the average household in a given country. The CPI reached around 105.9 points in the Palestinian territories in 2022, up from 102.1 in 2021—and 100 in the base year, 2018. (The source of figures in this section is the PCBS Index Surveys, 2010–2022.)

Driven by the upturn in economic activity and import prices fuelled by global inflationary pressures arising from the Russia–Ukraine war, the inflation rate for 2022 as a whole reached 3.7%, resulting from increases in prices of food and non-alcoholic beverages (6.7%), hospitality and restaurant services (6.7%), and recreational and cultural goods and services (5.1%). The year 2022 also witnessed an increase in the prices of alcoholic beverages and tobacco (3.5%), clothing and footwear (3.4%), furniture, house equipment and routine home maintenance (3.3%), education services (3.2%) and transportation (3.0%). There were, in addition, increases in housing prices (2.7%), communications (1.9%), financial services (1.4%) and medical services (1.3%).

The increase in inflation in 2022 indicates a decrease in the purchasing power of the new Israeli shekel by the same value during that year. It is perhaps fitting to note that the trends of the shekel's purchasing power are inversely proportional to the increase in consumer prices. In 2022 the average exchange rate of the US dollar relative to the shekel increased by 3.8%, compared with 2021. As a result, the purchasing power of those whose income is in US dollars but whose expenses are entirely covered in shekels rose by 0.1%, compared with 2021. Because the Jordanian dinar is pegged to the dollar at a fixed exchange rate, the dinar's purchasing power also increased, by 0.4%.

Public Finance

(In this section the data are preliminary and may be adjusted and revised—Ministry of Finance, 2023). Domestic revenue collection during 2022 amounted to NIS 5,940.1m, marking a remarkable increase of 19.3%, compared with the previous year. This growth was owing to a 19.2% rise in tax revenues to a total of NIS 3,840.2m., and an 18.3% rise in non-tax revenues to NIS 1,537.9m. In 2022 the allocated collections amounted to NIS 561.7m., compared with NIS 458.2m. in 2021, while clearance revenues increased by 17.6%, reaching about NIS 10,571.3m. Grants and foreign aid remained at a very low level, albeit increasing from NIS 1,026.0m in 2021 to NIS 1,174.0m in 2022. In the final analysis, in 2022 net public revenues and grants increased by 14.9%, compared with 2021, to reach a total of NIS 16,889.7m., mainly as a result of the upturn in economic activity.

Wages and salaries paid (on a cash basis) rose by 6.8% in 2022, compared with 2021, amounting to NIS 6,872.6m. and constituting 84.7% of the wages and salary bill due in that year. Net lending (to cover unpaid utility bills owed to Israeli suppliers) also increased in 2022, by 1.4%, to a total of NIS 1,224.6m. Non-wage expenses increased by 3.9% year on year, to reach NIS 5,458.0m. (constituting 76.1% of non-wage due expenses), while development expenditure increased by 12.1% to NIS 605.9m. (constituting 66.8% of total development expenditure committed). In the final analysis, actual public expenditure increased by 7.4% in 2022, compared with the previous year, to reach a total of NIS 14,609.4m. (equivalent to 81.2% of total public expenditure scheduled for that year).

The total budget deficit, after grants and aid based on commitment, amounted to NIS 593.6m. in 2022, compared with a deficit of some NIS 3,000m. in 2021. However, the total balance on a cash basis generated a surplus of NIS 2,280.3m. in 2022 (equivalent to 4.4% of GDP), compared with a surplus of about NIS 1,400m. in 2021. In 2022 gross arrears amounted to NIS 3,458.9m., compared with NIS 4,488m. in 2021, representing a decrease of 22.9%. Total arrears included non-wage expenditure (NIS 1,718.9m.), wages and salaries arrears (NIS 1,241.5m.), development expenditure arrears (NIS 300.9m.), and arrears of allocated payments and tax returns (about NIS 200m.). The Government paid about NIS 1,900m. from the previous year's arrears to bring net arrears in 2022 to about NIS 1,600m.

By the end of 2022 dollar-denominated government public debt had fallen by 7.9% year on year to a total of US $3,542.7m. (some NIS 12,500m.), equivalent to about 18.5% of nominal GDP. Over the same period domestic government debt fell by 11.3% to $2,184.6m. In comparison, external government debt in 2022 stabilized at around the level of the previous year, with just a slight decrease, of 0.4%, to about $1,300m. The interest paid on public debt in 2022 amounted to some NIS 106.5m.

PALESTINIAN TERRITORIES

Banking Sector

(Data source in this section are from PMA, 2023.) At the end of 2022 the number of bank branches and offices licensed to operate in the Palestinian territories stood at 378, of which 248 were branches and offices of domestic banks, and 130 were branches of foreign banks (five Jordanian banks and one Egyptian bank).

The consolidated budget data for banks at the end of 2022 indicate a decline in the assets/liabilities of banks by 1.2%, compared with those of 2021, bringing the total to US $21,404.4m. (The 13.6% rise in the exchange rate of the dollar against the new Israeli shekel had a clear impact on the growth of the consolidated budget items, of which the shekel constitutes a large part.)

Data indicate an increase in credit facilities by 2.8% in 2022, compared with 2021, bringing the total to US $11,045.0m. This increase was driven by a 6.9% growth in facilities extended to the private sector, while public sector facilities decreased by 11.0%. These developments led to the public sector's share of total credit facilities decreasing to 19.9%, compared with 23.0% in 2021. The facilities granted in US dollars grew significantly, by 15.9%, while the facilities granted in Jordanian dinars and Israeli new shekel decreased, by 7.8% and 5.0%, respectively.

Balances with the PMA and banks decreased by 8.5% in 2022 to a total of US $5,500m., driven by a 2.2% decline in balances with offshore banks. The value of cash and precious metals fell by about 4.0%, compared with their value in 2021. This decrease was primarily owing to the 13.6% rise in the exchange rate of the dollar against the new Israeli shekel.

Customer deposits stabilized in 2022 at about the same level as in 2021, amounting to about US $16,500m., constituting 77% of banks' liabilities. The private sector acquired the majority of these deposits, with a share of about 96% (some $15,800m.), while the public sector's share amounted to about 4%.

In 2022 net banking income after taxes reached US $229.2m., representing a year-on-year increase of 28.5%. This remarkable growth was driven by a 15.3% increase in total revenues of the banking sector to $886m. However, expenditures increased by 11.3%, to reach $656.8m. in 2022.

Non-banking Financial Sector

According to the Palestine Capital Market Authority (PCMA—the source of the figures in this section), the Palestine Exchange's (PEX) Al-Quds Index closed at 639.7 points at the end of 2022, representing an increase of 5% over its closure at the end of 2021. However, the market value at the end of 2022 was significantly higher, by 11%, compared with at the end of 2021, reaching US $4,896.1m., which was equivalent to 25.6% of GDP at current prices (a year-on-year increase of nearly 1.3 percentage points). The total trading volumes and values at the end of 2022 were 21% and 13% larger, respectively, compared with at the end of 2021. The total number of dealers on the PEX had risen to 71,407 by the end of 2022, some 7% of whom were foreign dealers, the majority being from Jordan.

As of the end of 2022 there were eight financial leasing companies licensed by the PCMA. Their performance witnessed improvement in that year, concluding about 2,800 contracts with a total investment value of US $143m. This represented an increase in the number and value of contracts of 47% and 40%, respectively, compared with 2021.

At the end of 2022 there was still a high concentration in the number of financial leasing contracts in the city of Ramallah, where the percentage of the total stood at 36%, followed by the cities of Nablus and Hebron, with 13% and 11%, respectively. The distribution of these percentages among cities has remained relatively constant over the years, as a result of factors related to the economy's structure and the concentration of business in certain governorates.

Vehicles still accounted for the largest share (93%) of the financial leasing portfolio in 2022. This was due to the ease of registering the ownership of vehicles in traffic services and the low risks of having a secondary market and repossessing them. Trucks, heavy vehicles and commercial vehicles accounted for 3% of the financial leasing portfolio, and money in transit (equipment, production lines, etc., not including vehicles) accounted for the remaining 4%.

The number of insurance companies licensed by the PA in 2022 stood at 10 companies. The total insurance portfolio in that year amounted to about US $396m. The total investments of insurance companies amounted to about $290m., while the net compensation incurred in the sector amounted to $228m.

The insurance sector's contribution to GDP is still modest, despite its growth over the past four years, reaching 2.2% in 2022. The 'insurance penetration ratio' refers to the total insurance portfolio attributable to GDP at current prices. In terms of insurance density, which refers to the individual's share of the total insurance portfolio, it reached US $73.1 in 2022.

SPECIAL FOCUS: THE ECONOMIC SITUATION IN THE GAZA STRIP AFTER ALMOST 20 YEARS OF SIEGE, WAR AND POLITICAL DIVISION

Since 2005 the economy of the Gaza Strip has endured exceptionally challenging economic conditions, due to the stifling Israeli blockade and devastating assaults—aside from the persistent Palestinian political rift.

This section of the essay first looks at the status of Gaza's economy before 2005 and its contribution to the Palestinian economy. It then tracks the decline that the economy went through over the past two decades and the subsequent impact on the Palestinian economy as a whole.

The Gaza Strip is considered a major part of the Palestinian economy: before 2005 the Gaza Strip accounted for 40% of the population of the Occupied Territories. Its economy was one-third of the Palestinian economy, contributing 36% to Palestinian GDP. The political and economic challenges that the Palestinian territories have been confronted by, especially in the Gaza Strip, have impacted overall Palestinian economic growth and worsened the economic position in the Gaza Strip in particular. This debilitation unfolded at all levels owing to the siege and wars of 2008, 2012, 2014, 2021 and 2022. Since mid-2007 political division as hindered economic development and the exchange of benefits between the northern and southern governorates. Moreover, since the political split, the Islamic Resistance Movement (Hamas) has had de facto control over the Gaza Strip, even though it is still *de jure* under the jurisdiction of the PA.

This division has caused the Gaza Strip to lose out on huge aid and investments, with donors reluctant to provide support after the USA, the EU and some Arab Gulf states designated Hamas a terrorist organization (Morrar and Sultan, 2020; Morrar and Baba, 2022). This label cast deep shadows over Gaza's commercial and productive capabilities. It also restricted imports and exports, reducing Gaza's contribution to Palestinian GDP to an average annual rate of 25% during 2006–13. The share further declined, notably in 2014, averaging 19.6% between 2014 and 2019. The coronavirus pandemic exacerbated the economic decline in the Gaza Strip, lowering its contribution to overall Palestinian GDP to 17.7% in 2020 (PCBS, 2021a).

The biggest challenges faced by the productive sectors in the Gaza Strip are the prolonged blockade, economic and trade restrictions, movement restrictions and repeated Israeli bombardments (UNCTAD, 2020). Since 2007 Israel has prevented most of the trade inside and outside the Gaza Strip through its almost total control over sea, air and land borders. This has led to a significant reduction in trade revenues and impeded the sectors' ability to develop their markets and revenues. In addition, trade and production factors (particularly resources and production inputs) have been severely restricted since 2007, owing to the Israeli blockade.

These constraints have reduced the ability of factories to produce regularly and effectively, expand and maintain competitive prices, and create jobs. This situation can be attributed to the fact that most of the raw materials and equipment needed for production in all industries (e.g. fertilizers, pesticides and seeds, spare parts, hardware, telecommunications equipment, steel pipes, chemicals, building materials, water pumps, medical equipment and gas) fall under the dual-use goods category, by which Israel prevents Palestinians from importing certain items on the grounds that they may be used for military purposes (UNCTAD, 2020). In addition, Israel's control of borders prevents the Gaza Strip from benefiting from the West Bank market, which is considered one of its most important markets.

All these factors led to a slowdown in the real growth of the industrial sector in the Gaza Strip (the average annual growth rate between 1994 and 2022 was only about 1%). The value added of the sector, which was once one of the most important components of overall GDP, fell from 25.8% in 1994 to just 7.2% in 2022. The deceleration in the value added growth of the industrial sector was greater than in other sectors, such as the wholesale and retail trade sector, which registered average annual growth of 4.4% between 1994 and 2022 (PCBS, 2023).

The massive decline in the productive sectors led to a fall in the contribution of the Gaza Strip to overall Palestinian GDP—from 37.0% in 1994 to 17.4% in 2022. This was reflected in a 50% decrease in GDP per capita in the sectors over the same period, from US $2,328.2 in 1994 to $1,256.8 in 2022. The economic downturn in the productive sectors intensified unemployment, which stood at 44.1% in 2022 (PCBS, 2023)—one of the highest rates in the world.

Bibliography

Abu-Eideh, O. M. 'Factors of Economic Growth in Palestine: An Empirical Analysis During the Period of 1994–2013'. *International Journal of Business and Economic Development*, Vol. 2, No. 2, July 2014.

Abugattas, L. *Palestine: Macroeconomic Performance and Development Challenges and Policies*. EU Support to the Palestinian Ministry of National Economy for Trade Policy Formulation and WTO Accession (EU-TSP), Ministry of National Economy, Ramallah, 2017.

Amodio, F., and Di Maio, M. 'Making Do with What You Have: Conflict, Input Misallocation and Firm Performance'. *The Economic Journal*, Vol. 128, Issue 615, August 2018, pp. 2559–2612.

Awad, I. M., and Alazzeh, W. 'Using currency demand to estimate the Palestine underground economy: An econometric analysis'. *Palgrave Communications*, Vol. 6, 2020.

Cali, M., and Miaari, S. H. *The Labor Market Impact of Mobility Restrictions Evidence from the West Bank*. Policy Research Working Paper 6457, The World Bank Poverty Reduction and Economic Management Network, International Trade Department, 2013.

Chenery, H., and Moshe, S. *Patterns of Development, 1950–1970*. Delhi, Oxford University Press, 1975.

The economic cost of the Israeli occupation of the occupied Palestinian Territories. The Applied Research Institute, Jerusalem 2015.

Al-Falah, B. *Structure of the Palestinian Services Sector and Its Economic Impact*. MAS Palestine Economic Policy Research Institute, Ramallah, 2013.

Fesen, Z. T. 'A Barrier to Prosperity? Analysing the Impact of Israeli Security Policy on Palestinian Manufacturing Productivity'. *Inquiries Journal*, Vol. 13, No. 1, 2021.

Food and Agriculture Organization. *Context Analysis of the Country Programming Framework for Palestine 2018–2022*. Jerusalem, 2019.

Fridman, A., and Liar, G. *Effective Exchange Rate in Israel*. Bank of Israel, Tel Aviv, 2015.

Gal, Y., and Rock, B. *Assessing the Economic Impact of Easing Measures for the Gaza Strip*. Tony Blair Institute for Global Change, Jerusalem, 2018.

Gal, Y., and Rock, B. *Israeli Palestinian Trade: In-depth Analysis*. Tony Blair Institute of Global Change, Jerusalem, 2018.

Hass, A. 'How the Israeli Army Takes Palestinian Land and Hands It to Settlers'. *Haaretz*, 12 March 2019.

Herrendorf, B., Rogerson R., and Valentinyi, A. 'Growth and Structural Transformation', in *Handbook of Economic Growth* 2. 2014, pp. 855–941.

International Labour Organization. *The Occupied Palestinian Territory: An Employment Diagnostic Study*. Beirut, 2018.

International Monetary Fund. 'Exchange Rate and Trade Flows: Disconnected?', in *World Economic Outlook 2015: Adjusting to Lower Commodity Prices*. Washington DC, 2015.

International Monetary Fund. *West Bank and Gaza*. Report to the Ad Hoc Liaison Committee meeting, 26 August 2016.

International Monetary Fund. *Israel: 2020 Article IV Consultation*. Staff Report, January 2021.

Kashiwagi, K. 'Productivity Growth and Technological Progress in the Palestinian Economy: Empirical Evidence from the West Bank'. *Advances in Management and Applied Economics*, Vol. 6, Issue 1, 2016, pp. 1–4.

Khalidi, R. 'The Structural Transformation of the Palestinian Economy after Oslo', in Turner, M. (Ed.). *From the River to the Sea: Palestine and Israel in the Shadow of "Peace"*. London, Lexington Books, 2019.

Morrar, R., and Abdelhadi, M. 'Obstacles of Innovation in Palestine'. *Journal of Inspiration Economy*, Vol. 3, Issue 2, 2016, pp. 53–64.

Morrar, R., and Arman, H. 'The Transformation Role of a Third Actor Within the Triple Helix Model-the Case of Palestine'. *Innovation: The European Journal of Social Science Research*, 2020.

Morrar, R., and Sultan, S. 'The Donor-Driven Model and Financial Sustainability: A Case Study from Palestinian Non-Government Organizations'. *Cosmopolitan Civil Societies: An Interdisciplinary Journal*, Vol. 12, No. 2–3, 2020, pp. 144–159.

Morrar, R., and Syed Zwick, H. 'Determinants and Wage Penalty of Qualification Mismatches: The Case of Palestine'. *Journal of Education and Work*, Vol. 34, No. 4, 2021, pp. 504–517.

Morrar, R., and Baba, S. 'Social Innovation in Extreme Institutional Contexts: The Case of Palestine'. *Management Decision*, Vol. 60, No. 5, 2022, pp. 1387–1412.

Morrar, R., Amara, M., and Syed Zwick, H. 'The Determinants of Self-Employment Entry of Palestinian Youth'. *Journal of Entrepreneurship in Emerging Economies*, Vol. 14, No. 1, 2022, pp. 23–44.

Morrar, R., and Khalidi, R. 'The Role of Inclusive, Rapid and Responsive Governance in Mitigating the Consequences of the COVID-19 Pandemic'. *Journal of Economic and Development Policies*, Arab Planning Institute, Vol. 23, Issue 3 2022, pp. 87–112.

Morrar, R., and Gallouj, F. 'The growth of the service sector in Palestine: the productivity challenge'. *Journal of Innovation Economics & Management*, Vol. 19, Issue 1, 2016, pp. 179–204.

Ministry of Finance of Palestine. 'Financial Operations - Revenue, Expenditure and Funding Sources. (December, 2021)'. *Monthly Financial Reports 2021*, Ramallah, 2022.

Palatnick, R. R., Tavor, T., and Voldman, L. 'The Symptoms of Illness: Does Israel Suffer from Dutch Disease?'. *Energies*, Vol. 12, No. 14, 2019, p. 2752.

Palestinian Central Bureau of Statistics. *Poverty Profile in Palestine, 2017*. Ramallah, 2018. www.pcbs.gov.ps/Document/pdf/txte_poverty2017.pdf?date=16_4_2018_2.

Palestinian Central Bureau of Statistics. *Multi-dimensional Poverty Profile in Palestine, 2017: Main Results*. Ramallah, 2018. mppn.org/wp-content/uploads/2020/06/book2524-Palestine-28-48.pdf.

Palestinian Central Bureau of Statistics. *Palestinian Labour Force Survey (January–March 2023)*. Ramallah, 2023. www.pcbs.gov.ps/portals/_pcbs/PressRelease/Press_En_LFSQ012023E.pdf.

Palestinian Central Bureau of Statistics. 'On the occasion of the International Youth Day, PCBS issues a press release demonstrating the situation of youth in the Palestinian society'. Ramallah, 2020. www.pcbs.gov.ps/site/512/default.aspx?lang=en&ItemID=3787.

Palestinian Central Bureau of Statistics. *Foreign Trade Statistics*. Ramallah, 1994–2022.

Palestinian Central Bureau of Statistics. *National Accounts Statistics*. Ramallah, 1994–2022.

Palestinian Central Bureau of Statistics. *National Accounts Quarterly Statistics*. Ramallah, 2000–2022.

Palestinian Central Bureau of Statistics. *Consumer Price Index Survey*. Ramallah, 2016–2022.

Palestinian Central Bureau of Statistics and Palestine Monetary Authority. *International Investment Status and External Debt Statistics*. Ramallah, 2010–2022.

Palestine Monetary Authority. Combined bank balance sheet, profit and loss list, and Monetary Authority database.

Smith, R. *Freedom is a Place: The Struggle for Sovereignty in Palestine*. University of Georgia Press, 2020.

Rand Corpn. *The Costs of the Israeli-Palestinian Conflict*. 2015. www.rand.org/content/dam/rand/pubs/research_reports/RR700/RR740-1/RAND_RR740-1.pdf.

Rodrik, D. 'Where Did All the Growth Go? External Shocks, Social Conflict, and Growth Collapses'. *Journal of Economic Growth*, Vol. 4, December 1999, pp. 385–412.

Roy, S. 'Palestinian Society and Economy: the Continued Denial of a Possibility'. *Journal of Palestine Studies*, Vol. 30, No. 4, 2001, pp. 5–20.

Sabra, M. M., Eltalla, A. H. A., and Alfar, A. R. 'The Shadow Economy in Palestine: Size and Causes'. *International Journal of Economics and Finance*, Vol. 7, No. 3, 2015, pp. 98–108.

Shikaki, I. 'The Demise of Palestinian Productive Sectors: Internal Trade as a Macrocosm of the Impact of Occupation'. *Policy Brief*, The Palestinian Policy Network—Al-Shabaka, February 2021. al-shabaka.org/briefs/demise-of-palestinian-productive-sectors/.

Tybout, J. R. 'Manufacturing firms in Developing Countries: How Well Do They and Why?'. *Journal of Economic Literature*, Vol. 38, 2000, pp. 11–44.

United Nations Development Programme. *Human Development Report 2020: The Next Frontier Human Development and the Anthropocene*. 2020. hdr.undp.org/sites/default/files/hdr2020.pdf.

United Nations. *Leave No One Behind: A Perspective on Vulnerability and Structural Disadvantage in Palestine*. 2016.

United Nations Economic and Social Commission for Western Asia. *Measuring the Cost of Israeli Restrictions on the Palestinian Economy: A Computable General Equilibrium (CGE) Approach*. 3 December 2015.

United Nations General Assembly. *Economic costs of the Israeli occupation for the Palestinian people: the Gaza Strip under closure and restrictions*. Note by the Secretary-General, Seventy-Fifth Session, Item 37 of the Provisional Agenda: Question of Palestine, 2020. unctad.org/system/files/official-document/a75d310_en_1.pdf.

United Nations Conference on Trade and Development. *The Palestinian Economy: Macroeconomic and Trade Policymaking Under Occupation*. 2012. unctad.org/system/files/ official-document/gdsapp2011d1_en.pdf.

United Nations Conference on Trade and Development. *Trade Facilitation in the Occupied Palestinian Territory: Restrictions and Limitations*. New York and Geneva, 2014. unctad. org/system/files/official-document/gdsapp2014d1_en.pdf.

United Nations Conference on Trade and Development. *The Besieged Palestinian Agricultural Sector*. 2015. unctad.org/system/files/ official-document/gdsapp2015d1_en.pdf.

United Nations Conference on Trade and Development. *Reports on UNCTAD assistance to the Palestinian people: Developments in the economy of the Occupied Palestinian Territory*. 1 September 2016.

United Nations Conference on Trade and Development. *The Occupied Palestinian Territory: Twin Deficits or an Imposed Resource Gap?*. New York and Geneva, 2017.

United Nations Conference on Trade and Development. *The Economic Costs of the Israeli Occupation for the Palestinian People: Cumulative Fiscal Costs*. 2019. unctad.org/system/files/official-document/gdsapp2019d2_en.pdf.

United Nations Conference on Trade and Development. *Reports on UNCTAD assistance to the Palestinian people: Developments in the economy of the Occupied Palestinian Territory*. 22 July 2019. unctad.org/system/files/official-document/tdbex68d4_en.pdf

United Nations Conference on Trade and Development. *Reports on UNCTAD assistance to the Palestinian people: Developments in the economy of the Occupied Palestinian Territory*. 2020.

United States Agency for International Development. *West Bank and Gaza Inclusive Growth Diagnostic*. April 2017.www.usaid.gov/sites/default/files/documents/1865/West_Bank_and_Gaza_IGD_2017_v9a.pdf.

Wildeman, J. *Donor Perceptions of Palestine: Limits to Aid Effectiveness*. The Palestinian Policy Network—Al-Shabaka, June 2019.

World Bank. *West Bank and Gaza Coping with Conflict: Poverty and Inclusion in the West Bank and Gaza*. Report No. 61293-GZ, July 2011.

World Bank. *Area C and the Future of the Palestinian Economy*. 2014. documents1.worldbank.org/curated/en/257131468140639464/pdf/Area-C-and-the-future-of-the-Palestinian-economy.pdf.

World Bank. *West Bank and Gaza Investment Climate Assessment: Fragmentation and Uncertainty*. 2014.

World Bank. *Unlocking the Trade Potential of the Palestinian Economy: Immediate Measures and a Long-Term Vision to Improve Palestinian Trade and Economic Outcomes*. Report No. ACS22471, 2017.

World Bank. *Palestine—Prospects for Growth and Jobs: A General Equilibrium Analysis*. Washington, DC, December 2017.

World Bank. *Economic Monitoring Report to the Ad Hoc Liaison Committee*. 6 September 2018.

World Bank. *Enhancing Job Opportunities for Palestinians*. West Bank and Gaza, 2019. documents1.worldbank.org/curated/en/523241562095688030/pdf/West-Bank-and-Gaza-Jobs-in-West-Bank-and-Gaza-Project-Enhancing-Job-Opportunities-for-Palestinians.pdf.

World Bank. *Palestinian Economy Struggles as Coronavirus Inflicts Losses*. 2020. www.worldbank.org/en/news/press-release/2020/06/01/palestinian-economy-struggles-as-coronavirus-inflicts-losses.

World Bank. *Gaza Rapid Damage and Needs Assessment*. 2021.

PALESTINIAN TERRITORIES

Statistical Survey

Source (unless otherwise indicated): Palestinian Central Bureau of Statistics (PCBS), POB 1647, Ramallah; tel. (2) 2982700; fax (2) 2982710; e-mail diwan@pcbs.gov.ps; internet www.pcbs.gov.ps.

Note: Unless otherwise indicated, data include East Jerusalem, annexed by Israel in 1967

Area and Population

AREA, POPULATION AND DENSITY

Area (sq km)	6,020*
Population (census results)	
1 December 2007	3,767,549
1 December 2017†	
Males	2,433,196
Females	2,348,052
Total	4,781,248
Population (official estimates at 31 December)	
2020	5,164,173
2021	5,290,925
2022	5,419,053
Density (per sq km) at 31 December 2022	900.2

* 2,324 sq miles. The total comprises: West Bank 5,655 sq km (2,183 sq miles); Gaza Strip 365 sq km (141 sq miles).
† Includes the enumerated population (4,705,855), and an adjustment for underenumeration of 1.7% (75,393), estimated in accordance with a post-enumeration survey. Figures include an estimate for Palestinian residents of East Jerusalem, but exclude Jewish settlers.

Note: Official projected estimates of a total worldwide Palestinian population of 14,320,369 at 31 December 2022 included 1,709,811 Palestinians resident in Israel and 6,430,820 resident in Arab countries.

POPULATION BY AGE AND SEX
(official estimates at 31 December 2022)

	Males	Females	Total
0–14 years	1,037,391	992,820	2,030,211
15–64 years	1,628,218	1,573,513	3,201,731
65 years and over	87,926	99,185	187,111
Total	2,753,535	2,665,518	5,419,053

GOVERNORATES
(official population estimates at 31 December 2022)

	Area (sq km)	Population	Density (per sq km)
West Bank			
Ariha (Jericho) and Al-Aghwar	593	54,779	92.4
Beit Lahm (Bethlehem)	659	242,222	367.6
Janin (Jenin)	583	349,375	599.3
Al-Khalil (Hebron)	997	812,303	814.7
Nabulus (Nablus)	605	427,578	706.7
Qalqilya	166	125,678	757.1
Al-Quds (Jerusalem)	345	487,202	1,412.2
Ram Allah (Ramallah) and Al-Birah	855	366,316	428.4
Salfeet	204	84,960	416.5
Tubas	402	68,059	169.3
Tulkarm	246	204,174	830.0
Gaza Strip			
Deir al-Balah	58	315,014	5,431.3
Gaza	74	740,156	10,002.1
Khan Yunus (Khan Yunis)	108	432,307	4,002.8
North Gaza	61	437,479	7,171.8
Rafah	64	271,451	4,241.4
Total	6,020	5,419,053	900.2

PRINCIPAL LOCALITIES
(population at 2017 census, excluding Jewish settlers)

West Bank			
Al-Quds (Jerusalem)	281,163*	Dura	39,336
Al-Khalil (Hebron)	201,063	Ram Allah (Ramallah)	38,998
Nabulus (Nablus)	156,906	Al-Dhahiriya	35,924
Tulkarm	64,532	Beit Lahm (Bethlehem)	28,591
Yattah (Yatta)	63,511	Halhul	27,031
Qalqilya	51,683	Beituniya	26,604
Janin (Jenin)	49,908	Al-Samu	26,011
Al-Birah	45,975	Idhna	26,009
Gaza Strip			
Ghazzah (Gaza)	590,481	Al-Nuseirat	54,851
Khan Yunus (Khan Yunis)	205,125	Beit Hanoun	52,237
Jabalyah (Jabalia)	172,704	Jabalyah Camp	49,462
Rafah	171,899	Bani Suhaylah	41,439
Beit Lahya	89,838	Khan Yunus Camp	41,182
Deir al-Balah	75,132	Al-Shati Camp	40,734

* The figure refers only to the eastern sector of the city.

Mid-2018 (incl. suburbs, UN estimates): Al-Quds (Jerusalem) 275,086; Gaza 673,638. *Mid-2023* (projection): Gaza 778,187 (Source: UN, *World Urbanization Prospects: The 2018 Revision*).

BIRTHS, MARRIAGES AND DEATHS
(West Bank only, official estimates)*

	Live births		Marriages†		Deaths	
	Number	Rate (per 1,000)	Number	Rate (per 1,000)	Number	Rate (per 1,000)
2017	80,544	28.1	29,977	10.5	7,123	4.0
2018	83,815	28.0	28,378	9.7	7,227	4.0
2019	82,943	27.7	27,280	9.1	7,741	3.9
2020	82,953	27.5	20,493	6.7	9,087	3.9
2021	82,822	27.2	24,443	7.8	9,948	3.9

* Excluding Jewish settlers.
† Registered marriages.

Gaza Strip (2021): Live births 58,270 (32.9 per 1,000); Registered marriages 20,575 (9.8 per 1,000); Deaths 6,807 (3.4 per 1,000).

2022 Registered marriages 24,263 (7.6 per 1,000) in West Bank, and 19,167 (8.8 per 1,000) in Gaza Strip.

Life expectancy (years at birth, official estimates): 74.3 (males 73.2; females 75.4) in 2022.

PALESTINIAN TERRITORIES

ECONOMICALLY ACTIVE POPULATION
('000 persons aged 15 years and over)

	2020	2021	2022
Agriculture, hunting, forestry and fishing	61	69	70
Mining and quarrying and utilities	10	12	110
Manufacturing	122	124	141
Construction	161	194	213
Trade, transport, accommodation and administrative services	293	319	265
Public administration, community, social and other services	310	318	337
Total employed	957	1,036	1,136
Unemployed	334	372	366
Total labour force	1,291	1,408	1,503
Males	1,040	1,132	1,197
Females	251	276	306

Note: Totals may not be equal to the sum of components, owing to rounding.
Source: ILO.

Health and Welfare

KEY INDICATORS

Total fertility rate (children per woman, 2021)	3.5
Under-5 mortality rate (per 1,000 live births, 2021)	14.8
COVID-19: Cumulative confirmed deaths (per 100,000 persons at 30 June 2023)	108.7
COVID-19: Fully vaccinated population (% of total population at 18 October 2022)	33.9
Physicians (per 1,000 head, 2021, official estimate)	2.7
Hospital beds (per 1,000 head, 2021, official estimate)	1.5
Access to improved water resources (% of persons, 2020)	98
Access to improved sanitation facilities (% of persons, 2020)	99
Total carbon dioxide emissions ('000 metric tons, 2016)	3,234.3
Carbon dioxide emissions per head (metric tons, 2016)	0.7
Human Development Index (2021): ranking	106
Human Development Index (2021): value	0.715

Note: For data on COVID-19 vaccinations, 'fully vaccinated' denotes receipt of all doses specified by approved vaccination regime (Sources: Johns Hopkins University and Our World in Data). For more information on sources and further definitions for all indicators, see Health and Welfare Statistics: Sources and Definitions section (europaworld.com/credits).

Agriculture

PRINCIPAL CROPS
('000 metric tons, FAO estimates)

	2019	2020	2021
Almonds, with shell	4.0	3.9	3.9
Aubergines (Eggplants)	48.6	48.5	48.4
Barley	20.0	20.1	20.3
Beans, green	7.4	7.5	7.6
Cabbages and other brassicas	19.1	18.0	18.7
Cantaloupes and other melons	5.3	5.5	5.1
Cauliflowers and broccoli	30.9	31.3	31.6
Chillies and peppers, green	11.9	12.2	11.4
Cucumbers and gherkins	106.8	99.8	98.7
Dates	7.6	8.2	8.2
Figs	4.2	4.3	4.2
Grapes	40.3	40.4	40.1
Lemons and limes	13.3	13.1	14.3
Maize, green	9.9	9.8	9.8
Okra	3.3	3.3	3.3
Olives	177.6	76.6	67.6
Onions, dry	22.0	23.2	22.0

—continued	2019	2020	2021
Oranges	11.7	11.8	11.5
Poppy seed	1.5	1.5	1.5
Potatoes	59.8	60.3	60.5
Pumpkins, squash and gourds	47.2	47.3	47.4
Spices	2.6	2.7	2.6
Spinach	4.1	4.1	4.1
Strawberries	3.2	3.2	3.2
Tomatoes	116.8	98.2	104.3
Watermelons	10.6	10.8	10.3
Wheat	34.4	34.4	34.4

Aggregate production ('000 metric tons, may include official, semi-official or estimated data): Total cereals 55.4 in 2019, 55.5 in 2020, 55.7 in 2021; Total fruit (primary) 119.6 in 2019, 120.9 in 2020, 120.4 in 2021; Total oilcrops 179.4 in 2019, 78.4 in 2020, 69.4 in 2021; Total pulses 11.1 in 2019, 10.9 in 2020, 10.9 in 2021; Total roots and tubers 57.8 in 2019, 63.9 in 2020, 64.2 in 2021; Total vegetables (primary) 455.6 in 2019, 430.4 in 2020, 434.7 in 2021.

Source: FAO.

LIVESTOCK
('000 head, FAO estimates unless otherwise indicated)

	2019	2020	2021
Cattle	45.6	48.2	67.8*
Chickens	11,290	7,329	6,544
Goats	212.3	213.8	240.0*
Sheep	764.7	769.4	771.2*

* Official figure.
Source: FAO.

LIVESTOCK PRODUCTS
('000 metric tons, FAO estimates)

	2019	2020	2021
Cattle meat	9.0	9.1	18.3
Cows' milk	63.4	64.7	66.4
Chicken meat	65.2	42.0	37.3
Goats' milk	20.4	20.5	22.3
Sheep meat	12.0	12.0	12.0
Sheep's (Ewes') milk	53.2	53.4	53.5
Hen eggs	25.0	25.0	25.0

Source: FAO.

Fishing

GAZA STRIP
(metric tons, live weight)

	2019	2020	2021
Capture	3,943	4,662	4,661
Bogue	21	17	32
Jack and horse mackerels	204	186	148
Sardinellas	790	1,285	999
Chub mackerel	136	513	153
Little tunny	262	209	148
Aquaculture	630	600*	687
Total catch	4,573	5,262*	5,348

*Estimate.
Source: FAO.

PALESTINIAN TERRITORIES

Finance

CURRENCY AND EXCHANGE RATES

Monetary Units:
At present, there is no domestic Palestinian currency in use. The Israeli shekel, the Jordanian dinar and the US dollar all circulate within the West Bank and the Gaza Strip.

GOVERNMENT FINANCE
(general government transactions, non-cash basis, US $ million)

Summary of Balances

	2019	2020	2021
Revenue	4,427.2	4,444.8	5,166.4
Less Expense	4,577.4	4,894.4	5,233.0
Net operating balance	−150.2	−449.6	−66.6
Less Net acquisition of non-financial assets	234.2	170.0	142.0
Net lending/borrowing	−384.4	−619.6	−208.6

Revenue

	2019	2020	2021
Taxes	3,251.6	3,316.2	3,955.8
Taxes on income, profits, and capital gains	197.3	152.8	225.9
Taxes on payroll and work force	72.3	66.2	73.0
Taxes on property	80.1	81.5	71.4
Taxes on goods and services	1,757.3	1,701.9	1,874.1
Taxes on international trade and transactions	1,144.6	1,313.7	1,711.5
Social security contributions	0.8	4.3	—
Grants and aids	520.6	524.1	346.4
Other revenue	654.1	600.2	864.2
Sales of goods and services	554.2	473.3	756.3
Total	4,427.2	4,444.8	5,166.4

Expense

Expense by economic type	2019	2020	2021
Compensation of employees	2,236.0	2,380.7	2,754.6
Use of goods and services	957.0	989.6	1,150.5
Consumption of fixed capital	11.5	9.4	25.0
Interest	65.3	122.2	124.5
Subsidies and grants	49.3	22.6	10.7
Social benefits	1,147.8	1,279.8	1,113.7
Other expense	110.5	89.9	54.0
Total	4,577.4	4,894.4	5,233.0

Source: Ministry of Finance, Ramallah.

COST OF LIVING
(Consumer Price Index; base: 2018 = 100)

	2020	2021	2022
Food and non-alcoholic beverages	100.8	101.6	108.5
Textiles, clothing and footwear	94.1	93.6	96.8
Housing	100.5	104.2	107.0
All items (incl. others)	100.8	102.1	105.9

NATIONAL ACCOUNTS*
(US $ million at current prices)

Expenditure on the Gross Domestic Product

	2020	2021	2022†
Final consumption expenditure	17,418.4	20,338.1	23,483.6
Households	13,268.6	15,500.5	19,042.6
Non-profit institutions serving households	510.2	527.8	549.2
General government	3,639.6	4,309.8	3,891.8
Gross capital formation	3,774.8	4,609.0	5,066.5
Gross fixed capital formation	3,528.6	4,323.5	4,778.4
Changes in inventories	246.2	285.5	288.1
Total domestic expenditure	21,193.2	24,947.1	28,550.1
Exports of goods and services	2,385.3	3,140.3	3,543.7
Less Imports of goods and services	8,065.7	10,094.4	12,873.6
Net errors and omissions	18.9	116.0	−108.3
GDP in purchasers' values	15,531.7	18,109.0	19,111.9
GDP at constant 2015 prices	14,037.4	15,021.7	15,612.5

Gross Domestic Product by Economic Activity

	2019	2020	2021
Agriculture and fishing	1,208.6	1,103.0	1,143.9
Mining and quarrying	66.6	49.1	55.1
Manufacturing	1,924.9	1,715.8	2,027.0
Electricity and water supply	212.1	182.7	232.9
Construction	954.6	697.2	887.6
Wholesale and retail trade	3,948.9	3,009.9	3,450.7
Transport, storage and communications	818.0	755.2	836.5
Financial intermediation	685.5	690.9	871.6
Real estate activities	773.3	744.5	860.4
Professional, scientific and technical activities	204.6	157.5	165.3
Administrative and support service activities	117.4	103.0	108.7
Hotels and restaurants	304.7	289.0	289.7
Education	1,133.4	1,045.5	1,132.8
Health and social work	593.0	660.5	824.5
Public administration and defence	1,404.8	1,531.4	1,891.2
Households with employed persons	8.7	6.9	8.3
Other services	477.9	410.4	439.3
Sub-total	14,837.0	13,152.5	15,225.5
Customs duties	1,258.0	1,271.3	1,648.2
Net taxes on imports	1,038.5	1,107.9	1,235.3
GDP in purchasers' values	17,133.5	15,531.7	18,109.0

* Referring to the West Bank and the Gaza Strip, but excluding that part of Jerusalem annexed in 1967.
† Preliminary.

BALANCE OF PAYMENTS
(US $ million)

	2020	2021	2022
Exports of goods f.o.b.	1,715.1	2,288.4	707.7
Imports of goods f.o.b.	−6,498.0	−8,312.4	−2,825.6
Trade balance	−4,782.9	−6,024.0	−2,117.9
Exports of services	670.2	851.7	261.9
Imports of services	−1,567.3	−1,781.7	−605.3
Balance on goods and services	−5,680.1	−6,953.9	−2,461.3
Primary income received	2,651.6	3,770.6	1,023.1
Primary income paid	−159.3	−143.4	−53.9
Balance on goods, services and income	−3,187.9	−3,326.6	−1,492.1
Secondary income received	1,700.2	2,193.4	681.7
Secondary income paid	−415.2	−644.8	−95.2
Current balance	−1,902.8	−1,777.9	−905.6

PALESTINIAN TERRITORIES

Statistical Survey

—continued

	2020	2021	2022
Capital account (net)	431.4	472.0	107.7
Direct investment assets	59.0	−57.8	0.0
Direct investment liabilities	79.7	353.4	127.8
Portfolio investment (net)	69.2	86.7	−73.6
Other investment assets	635.4	1,014.2	550.0
Other investment liabilities	96.6	159.1	−32.9
Net errors and omissions	568.7	−75.2	118.9
Overall balance	37.2	174.4	−107.7

Source: Palestine Monetary Authority, Ramallah.

External Trade

PRINCIPAL COMMODITIES
(distribution by SITC, US $ million)

Imports c.i.f.	2018	2019	2020
Food and live animals	1,449.5	1,571.8	1,604.3
Beverages and tobacco	339.2	333.0	363.1
Animal and vegetable oils and fats	47.6	62.3	53.1
Crude materials (inedible) except fuels	161.1	112.0	127.0
Mineral fuels, lubricants, etc.	1,260.0	1,245.7	1,020.8
Chemicals and related products	633.4	765.1	696.1
Basic manufactures	1,226.2	1,160.5	1,030.2
Machinery and transport equipment	1,048.5	981.4	800.1
Miscellaneous manufactured articles	373.9	381.6	368.9
Total (incl. others)	6,539.6	6,613.5	6,063.4

Exports f.o.b.	2018	2019	2020
Food and live animals	177.4	162.5	150.7
Beverages and tobacco	46.3	23.6	26.8
Animal and vegetable oils and fats	49.4	57.0	43.5
Crude materials (inedible) except fuels	121.1	98.2	95.8
Mineral fuels, lubricants, etc.	0.8	1.0	1.1
Chemicals and related products	73.9	70.6	72.9
Basic manufactures	404.1	388.8	354.3
Machinery and transport equipment	42.1	48.2	55.8
Miscellaneous manufactured articles	240.5	253.9	253.8
Total	1,155.6	1,103.8	1,054.6

PRINCIPAL TRADING PARTNERS
(US $ million)

Imports c.i.f.	2017	2018	2019
China, People's Republic	428.7	424.9	447.3
Egypt	69.5	93.8	72.8
France (incl. Monaco)	79.3	110.2	88.1
Germany	214.6	209.3	181.3
India	46.1	66.2	67.8
Israel	3,234.8	3,605.8	3,636.2
Italy	107.0	110.3	112.6
Jordan	153.2	199.0	296.4
Saudi Arabia	77.3	87.6	80.5
Spain	70.5	81.9	78.1
Türkiye	579.2	657.8	669.1
Ukraine	66.4	88.6	59.6
USA	61.6	68.1	79.1
Total (incl. others)	5,853.9	6,539.6	6,613.5

Exports f.o.b.	2017	2018	2019
Israel	878.6	967.5	897.6
Jordan	77.2	74.0	71.4
Kuwait	8.8	9.1	11.1
Saudi Arabia	15.2	21.0	19.4
United Arab Emirates	26.7	26.4	32.4
USA	13.9	14.5	19.8
Total (incl. others)	1,064.9	1,155.6	1,103.8

2020: Total imports 6,063.4 (Israel 3,342.7); total exports 1,054.6 (Israel 886.1).

2021: Total imports 6,420.4 (Israel 3,475.2); total exports 1,458.4 (Israel 1,296.3).

2022 (provisional): Total imports 8,197.0 (Israel 4,638.3); total exports 1,584.7 (Israel 1,395.3).

Transport

ROAD TRAFFIC
(registered motor vehicles holding Palestinian licence)

	West Bank (2021)	Gaza Strip (2012)
Private cars	256,248	38,981
Taxis	9,315	2,160
Buses	1,925	650
Trucks and commercial cars	26,189	11,091
Motorcycles and mopeds	1,119	16,735
Tractors	762	720

Tourism

ARRIVALS OF VISITORS AT HOTELS*
(West Bank only)

	2019	2020	2021
Total	746,911	109,870	180,632

* Including Palestinians.

2019: Total guest nights in hotels 2,009,934 (Palestinians 146,290; EU members 965,864; Israelis 131,237; Asians 356,772).

2020: Total guest nights in hotels 297,629 (Palestinians 47,694; EU members 133,130; Israelis 25,938; Asians 36,653).

2021: Total guest nights in hotels 338,596 (Palestinians 136,104; EU members 3,363; Israelis 193,442; Asians 1,445).

Communications Media

	2019	2020	2021
Telephones (main lines in use) .	467,189	466,283	485,830
Mobile telephone subscriptions ('000)	4,300.2	4,062.3	4,053.0
Broadband subscriptions, fixed .	364,881	376,911	415,492
Broadband subscriptions, mobile ('000)	960.5	962.7	1,030.8
Internet users (% of population) .	70.6	74.6	n.a.

Source: mostly International Telecommunication Union.

Education

(2021/22)

	Institutions	Teachers	Students
Pre-primary	2,167	8,198	160,737
Primary	1,900	} 60,552	} 1,092,572
Secondary	1,242		265,838
Higher:			
universities . . .	34*	6,870	214,081
community colleges . .	17	497	11,894

* Figure includes 15 university colleges, but excludes two universities for open education.

Pupil-teacher ratio (qualified teaching staff, primary education, UNESCO estimate): 32.1 in 2020/21 (Source: UNESCO Institute for Statistics).

Adult literacy rate (persons aged 15 and over): 97.8% (males 98.9%; females 96.7%) in 2022.

Directory

Administration

PALESTINIAN NATIONAL AUTHORITY

Appointed in May 1994, the Palestinian National Authority, generally known internationally as the Palestinian Authority (PA), has assumed some of the civil responsibilities formerly exercised by the Israeli Civil Administration in the Gaza Strip and parts of the West Bank.

Executive President: MAHMOUD ABBAS (assumed office 15 January 2005).

CABINET
(September 2023)

The administration is formed by Fatah and independents.
Prime Minister: Dr MOHAMMAD SHTAYYEH.
Deputy Prime Minister: ZIAD ABU AMR.
Deputy Prime Minister and Minister of Information: NABIL ABU RUDEINEH.
Minister of the Interior: ZIAD HAB AL-REEH.
Minister of Culture: ATEF ABU SEIF.
Minister of National Economy: KHALED OSSAILI.
Minister of Finance and of Planning: SHUKRI BISHARA.
Minister of Foreign Affairs: Dr RIYAD NAJIB AL-MALIKI.
Minister of Local Government: MAJDI SALEH.
Minister of Tourism and Antiquities: ROLA MA'AIYA.
Minister of Education: MARWAN AWARTANI.
Minister of Higher Education: MAHMOUD ABU MOUEIS.
Minister of Health: MAI KAILEH.
Minister of Telecommunications and Information Technology: ISHAQ SADR.
Minister of Transport: ASSEM SALEM.
Minister of Women's Affairs: AMAL HAMAD.
Minister of Justice: MOHAMMAD SHALALDEH.
Minister of Labour: NASRI ABU JISH.
Minister of Agriculture: RIAD ATARI.
Minister of Social Affairs: AHMAD MAJDALANI.
Minister of Public Works and Housing: MOHAMMAD ZIYARA.
Minister of Jerusalem Affairs: FADI HIDMI.
Minister of Awqaf and Religious Affairs: HATEM AL-BAKRI.
Minister of State for Entrepreneurship and Empowerment: USAMA SADAWI.
Secretary-General of the Government: Dr AMJAD GHANEM.

MINISTRIES

Office of the President: Ramallah; internet president.ps.
Ministry of Agriculture: POB 197, Ramallah; tel. (2) 2403360; fax (2) 2403361; e-mail info@moa.pna.ps; internet www.moa.pna.ps.
Ministry of Awqaf (Religious Endowments): POB 17412, Jerusalem; tel. (2) 6282085; fax (2) 2986401.
Ministry of Culture: POB 147, Ramallah; tel. (2) 2986205; fax (2) 2986204; e-mail moc@moc.pna.ps; internet www.moc.pna.ps.
Ministry of Education and Higher Education: POB 576, al-Masioun, Ramallah; POB 5285, al-Wihda St, Gaza; tel. (2) 2983200; fax (2) 2983222; e-mail siteadmin@moehe.gov.ps; internet moehe.pna.ps.
Ministry of Finance: POB 795, Sateh Marhaba, al-Birah/Ramallah; POB 4007, Gaza; tel. (8) 2832750; fax (2) 2848900; e-mail mof@mof.ps; internet www.mof.gov.ps.
Ministry of Foreign Affairs: POB 1336, Ramallah; tel. (2) 2405040; fax (2) 2403772; e-mail mofa@gov.ps; internet www.mofa.gov.ps.
Ministry of Health: POB 14, al-Mukhtar St, Nablus; POB 1035, Abu Khadra Center, Gaza; tel. (9) 2384772; fax (9) 2384777; e-mail info@moh.ps; tel. (8) 2829173; fax (8) 2826295; internet www.moh.ps.
Ministry of the Interior: POB 641, Ramallah; tel. (2) 2429244; fax (2) 224298; e-mail info@moi.pna.ps; internet www.moi.pna.ps.
Ministry of Jerusalem Affairs: POB 20479, Jerusalem; tel. (2) 6273330; fax (2) 6286820.
Ministry of Justice: POB 267, Ramallah; POB 1012, Gaza; tel. (2) 2987661; fax (2) 2974491; e-mail info@moj.gov.ps; internet www.moj.gov.ps.
Ministry of Labour: POB 350, al-Salq St, Ramallah; tel. (2) 2982800; fax (2) 2982801; e-mail info@mol.pna.ps; internet www.mol.pna.ps.
Ministry of Local Government: POB 731, Albaloo, al-Birah/Ramallah; Gaza; tel. (2) 2401092; fax (2) 2401091; tel. (8) 2820272; fax (8) 2828474; e-mail info@molg.gov.ps; internet www.molg.pna.ps.
Ministry of National Economy: POB 1629, Umm al-Sharayet, Ramallah; POB 4023, Maqqusi Bldg, al-Nasser St, Gaza; tel. (2) 2981218; fax (2) 2981207; tel. (8) 2874146; fax (8) 2874145; e-mail info@met.gov.ps; internet www.mne.gov.ps.
Ministry of Public Works and Housing: Gaza; tel. (8) 2829232; fax (8) 2823653.
Ministry of Social Development: Ramallah 00972; tel. (2) 2405641; fax (2) 2405642; e-mail info@mosa.gov.ps; internet www.mosa.pna.ps.
Ministry of Telecommunications and Information Technology: Ramallah; Gaza; tel. (2) 2943333; fax (2) 2419348; e-mail info@mtit.gov.ps; internet www.mtit.pna.ps.
Ministry of Tourism and Antiquities: Jamal Abdul Naser St, Bethlehem; Gaza; tel. (2) 2741581; fax (2) 2743753; internet travelpalestine.ps.
Ministry of Transport: POB 399, Ramallah; tel. (2) 2951297; fax (2) 2951318; e-mail webmaster@mot.gov.ps; internet www.mot.gov.ps.
Ministry of Women's Affairs: Makka Bldg, al-Birah/Ramallah; tel. (2) 2403315; e-mail info@mowa.pna.ps; internet www.mowa.pna.ps.

President

Presidential and legislative elections had been due to take place by 25 January 2010; however, the polls were postponed indefinitely owing to the ongoing dispute between the Palestinian (National) Authority Cabinet and the de facto Hamas administration in the Gaza Strip. Following the signature of a unity agreement by the main Palestinian factions in early May 2011, it had been expected that elections would take place later that year. A government of national reconciliation, with jurisdiction over Gaza and the West Bank, was formed in June 2014. Following further talks, President Mahmoud Abbas announced in late 2019 that presidential, legislative and municipal elections would take place by mid-2020. A decree finalizing the dates of elections in the territories controlled by the Palestinian Authority was finally published in January 2021. Legislative elections were scheduled to take place on 22 May 2021 and presidential elections on 31 July. However, in April 2021 Abbas announced that the elections would be postponed indefinitely, ostensibly owing to the refusal of Israel to allow voting to take place in East Jerusalem.

Election, 9 January 2005

Candidate	Votes	%
Mahmoud Abbas (Fatah)	501,448	62.52
Mustafa Barghouthi (Ind.)	156,227	19.48
Tayseer Khalid (DFLP)	26,848	3.35
Abd al-Halim al-Ashqar (Ind.)	22,171	2.76
Bassam el-Salhi (PPP)	21,429	2.67
Al-Said Baraka (Ind.)	10,406	1.30
Abd al-Karim Shbeir (Ind.)	5,717	0.71
Invalid votes	57,831	7.21
Total	**802,077**	**100.00**

Legislature

Palestinian Legislative Council: POB 1930, Ramallah; tel. (2) 2984301; fax (2) 2984652; internet www.pal-plc.org.

Speaker: Dr Aziz Duwaik.

General Election, 25 January 2006

Parties, Lists and Coalitions	Seats		
	Majority system	Proportional system	Total
Change and Reform*	29	45	74
Fatah	28	17	45
Martyr Abu Ali Moustafa†	3	0	3
The Third Way	2	0	2
The Alternative‡	2	0	2
Independent Palestine§	2	0	2
Independents	0	4	4
Total	**66**	**66**	**132**

* The Islamic Resistance Movement (Hamas) contested the elections as Change and Reform.
† The Popular Front for the Liberation of Palestine contested the elections as Martyr Abu Ali Moustafa.
‡ Electoral list comprising the Palestinian Democratic Union, the Coalition of the Democratic Front (representing the Democratic Front for the Liberation of Palestine) and the Palestinian People's Party.
§ Coalition comprising independents and representatives of the Palestinian National Initiative.

Election Commission

Central Elections Commission (CEC): POB 2319, Qasr al-Murjan Bldg, Al-Balou, nr Jawwal Circle, Ramallah; tel. (2) 2969700; fax (2) 2969712; e-mail info@elections.ps; internet www.elections.ps; f. 2002; independent; comprises 9 mems, appointed by the Exec. Pres. of the PA; Chair. Dr Hanna Nasser; Sec.-Gen. Dr Lamis al-Alami.

Political Organizations

Alliance of Palestinian Forces: f. 1994; comprises representatives of the PLF, the PPSF, the PRCP and the PFLP—GC; opposes the Declaration of Principles on Palestinian Self-Rule signed by Israel and the PLO in September 1993, and subsequent agreements concluded within its framework (the Oslo accords). The PFLP and DFLP left the Alliance in 1996. The **Fatah Revolutionary Council**, headed by Sabri Khalil al-Banna, alias 'Abu Nidal', split from Fatah in 1973. Its headquarters were formerly in Baghdad, Iraq, but the office was closed down and its staff expelled from the country by the Iraqi authorities in November 1983; a new base was established in Damascus, Syria, in December. Al-Banna was readmitted to Iraq in 1984, having fled Syria. With 'Abu Musa' (whose rebel Fatah group is called **Al-Intifada** or 'Uprising'), Abu Nidal formed a joint rebel Fatah command in February 1985, and both had offices in Damascus until June 1987, when those of Abu Nidal were closed by the Syrian Government. Forces loyal to Abu Nidal surrendered to Fatah forces at the Rashidiyeh Palestinian refugee camp near Tyre, northern Lebanon, in 1990. Abu Nidal was reportedly found dead in Baghdad in August 2002.

Arab Liberation Front (ALF): Ramallah; f. 1969; fmrly supported by Iraq's Arab Baath Socialist Party under the leadership of former President Saddam Hussain; member of the PLO; opposes Oslo accords; Sec.-Gen. Rakad Salim (imprisoned in 2002).

Democratic Front for the Liberation of Palestine (DFLP) (Al-Jabha al-Dimuqratiyya li-Tahrir Filastin): Damascus, Syria; tel. (11) 4448993; fax (11) 4442380; Ramallah; tel. (2) 2954438; fax (2) 2980401; e-mail dflp-palestine@dflp-palestine.net; internet www.dflp-palestine.net; f. 1969 following split with PFLP; Marxist-Leninist; contested Jan. 2006 leg. elections on The Alternative electoral list as the Coalition of the Democratic Front; Sec.-Gen. Nayef Hawatmeh (Damascus).

Fatah (Harakat al-Tahrir al-Watani al-Filastin—Palestine National Liberation Movement): POB 1965, Ramallah; tel. (2) 2411832; e-mail info@fatahmedia.ps; internet www.fatehmedia.ps; f. 1957; militant group that became the single largest Palestinian org. and strongest faction in both the administration and Palestinian Legislative Council until the leg. elections of Jan. 2006; leadership is nominally shared by the mems of the Cen. Cttee, who were elected at Fatah's Sixth Gen. Conference on 10 Aug. 2009; Chair. of Cen. Cttee Mahmoud Abbas.

Islamic Jihad (Al-Jihad al-Islami): Damascus, Syria; f. 1979–80 by Palestinian students in Egypt; militant Islamist; opposed to the Oslo accords; Sec.-Gen. Ziad al-Nakhalah.

Islamic Resistance Movement (Hamas—Harakat al-Muqawama al-Islamiyya): Gaza; Damascus, Syria; internet hamas.ps; f. 1987; originally welfare organization Mujama (f. 1973) led by the late Sheikh Ahmad Yassin (killed by Israeli forces in March 2004); militant Islamist; opposes the Oslo accords; following the killing by Israeli forces of Hamas's leader in the Gaza Strip, Abd al-Aziz al-Rantisi, in April 2004, the group announced that it was adopting a policy of 'collective leadership'; contested Jan. 2006 legislative elections as Change and Reform; Head of Political Bureau Ismail Haniya; Gen. Commdr of military wing, Izz al-Din al-Qassam Brigades, Muhammad Deif (in hiding from the Israeli authorities since 1992, though presumed to be in Gaza).

Palestine Liberation Front (PLF): f. 1977 following split with PFLP—GC; the PLF split into three factions in the early 1980s, all of which retained the name PLF; one faction (Leader Muhammad 'Abu' Abbas) was based in Tunis, Tunisia, and Baghdad, Iraq, and remained nominally loyal to Yasser Arafat; the second faction (Leader Talaat Yaqoub) belonged to the anti-Arafat National Salvation Front and opened offices in Damascus, Syria, and Libya; a third group derived from the PLF was reportedly formed by its Central Cttee Secretary, Abd al-Fattah Ghanim, in June 1986; the factions of Yaqoub and Ghanim were reconciled in early 1985; at the 18th session of the PNC a programme for the unification of the PLF was announced, with Yaqoub (died November 1988) named as Secretary-General and Abu Abbas appointed to the PLO Executive Committee, while unification talks were held. The merging of the two factions was announced in June 1987, with Abu Abbas becoming Deputy Secretary-General. Abu Abbas was apprehended by US-led coalition forces in Iraq in April 2003, and reportedly died of natural causes in March 2004 while still in US custody; Sec.-Gen. Wassel Abu Yusuf.

Palestine Liberation Organization (PLO) (Munazzimat al-Tahrir al-Filastiniyya): Negotiations Affairs Dept, POB 4120, Ramallah; tel. (2) 2963741; fax (2) 2963740; f. 1964; the supreme legislative and policy-making organ of the PLO is the Palestine Nat. Council (PNC; Chair./Speaker Rawhi Fattouh, Sec.-Gen. Fahmi al-Za'arir), while the PLO Exec. Cttee (Chair. Mahmoud Abbas; Sec.-Gen. Hussein al-Sheikh) deals with day-to-day business. Fatah (the Palestine Nat. Liberation Movement) joined the PNC in 1968, and all the guerrilla orgs joined in 1969. In 1973 the Palestinian Cen.

PALESTINIAN TERRITORIES

Council (PCC; Chair./Speaker RAWHI FATTOUH, Sec.-Gen. FAHMI AL-ZA'ARIR) was established to act as an intermediary between the PNC and the Exec. Cttee. The PCC meets when the PNC is not in session and approves major policy decisions on its behalf; Chair. MAHMOUD ABBAS.

Palestine Revolutionary Communist Party (PRCP) (Al-Hizb al-Shuyu'i al-Thawri al-Filastini): principally based in Lebanon; promotes armed struggle in order to achieve its aims.

Palestinian Democratic Union (FIDA): POB 247, Ramallah; tel. 2954072; fax (2) 2954071; f. 1990 following split from the DFLP; contested Jan. 2006 legislative elections on The Alternative electoral list; Sec.-Gen. SALEH RAAFAT.

Palestinian National Initiative (Al-Mubadara): Ramallah; tel. (5) 9293006; e-mail almubadara@almubadara.org; internet www.almubadara.org; f. 2002; seeks peaceful resolution of conflict with Israel through establishment of an independent, unified, viable and democratic Palestinian state, with East Jerusalem as its capital; advocates reform of internal political structures, and aims to fight corruption and injustice, and to uphold citizens' rights; contested Jan. 2006 legislative elections as part of the Independent Palestine coalition; Sec.-Gen. Dr MUSTAFA BARGHOUTHI.

Palestinian People's Party (PPP) (Hezb al-Sha'ab): Ramallah; tel. (2) 2963593; fax (2) 2963592; e-mail web@ppp.ps; f. 1921 as Palestine Communist Party; adopted current name in 1991; admitted to the PNC at its 18th session in 1987; contested Jan. 2006 legislative elections on The Alternative electoral list; Sec.-Gen. BASSAM AL-SALHI.

Palestinian Popular Struggle Front (PPSF) (Jabhat al-Nidal al-Sha'biyya al-Filastiniyya): f. 1967; has reportedly split into two factions which either support or oppose the PA; the pro-PA faction (Leader AHMAD AL-MAJDALANI) is based in the West Bank; the anti-PA faction (Leader KHALID ABD AL-MAJID) is based in Damascus, Syrian Arab Republic.

Popular Front for the Liberation of Palestine (PFLP) (Al-Jabha al-Sha'biyya li-Tahrir Filastin): Damascus, Syria; internet pflp.ps; f. 1967; Marxist-Leninist; publr of *Democratic Palestine* (English; monthly); contested Jan. 2006 legislative elections as Martyr Abu Ali Moustafa; Sec.-Gen. AHMAD SAADAT (imprisoned in 2002).

Popular Front for the Liberation of Palestine—General Command (PFLP—GC): Damascus, Syria; f. 1968 following split from the PFLP; pro-Syrian; Leader TALAL NAJI.

Popular Front for the Liberation of Palestine—National General Command: Amman, Jordan; split from the PFLP—GC in 1999; aims to co-operate with the PA.

Al-Saiqa (Thunderbolt, or Vanguard of the Popular Liberation War): f. 1968; Syrian-backed; pan-Arab; opposed to the Oslo accords; Sec.-Gen. Dr MUHAMMAD QAIS.

The formation of the **Right Movement for Championing the Palestinian People's Sons** by former members of Hamas was announced in April 1995. The movement, based in Gaza City, was reported to support the PA. The **Al-Aqsa Martyrs Brigades**, consisting of a number of Fatah-affiliated activists, emerged soon after the start of the al-Aqsa *intifada* in September 2000, and have carried out attacks against Israeli targets in Israel, the West Bank and the Gaza Strip.

Diplomatic Representation

On 29 November 2012 an application to the UN General Assembly by the PLO (as Palestine) for non-member observer status was approved. Of the 193 member states, 138 voted in favour of the application, while nine voted against. A further 46 countries abstained from the vote or were absent.

Countries with which the PLO maintains diplomatic relations include:

Afghanistan, Albania, Algeria, Angola, Argentina, Austria, Azerbaijan, Bahrain, Bangladesh, Belarus, Belize, Benin, Bolivia, Bosnia and Herzegovina, Brazil, Brunei Darussalam, Bulgaria, Burkina Faso, Cambodia, Cameroon, Chad, Chile, China (People's Rep.), the Comoros, Congo (Rep.), Costa Rica, Côte d'Ivoire, Cuba, Cyprus, Djibouti, Dominican Republic, Ecuador, Egypt, El Salvador, Eswatini (Swaziland), Ethiopia, Gabon, The Gambia, Georgia, Ghana, Grenada, Guinea, Guinea-Bissau, Guyana, Haiti, the Holy See, Honduras, Hungary, Iceland, India, Indonesia, Iran, Iraq, Jordan, Kazakhstan, Kenya, Korea (Dem. People's Rep.), Kuwait, Lao People's Democratic Rep., Lebanon, Libya, Malawi, Malaysia, Maldives, Mali, Malta, Mauritania, Mauritius, Mongolia, Montenegro, Morocco, Mozambique, Namibia, Nicaragua, Niger, Nigeria, Norway, Oman, Pakistan, Papua New Guinea, Paraguay, Peru, Philippines, Poland, Qatar, Romania, Russian Fed., Saint Lucia, Saudi Arabia, Senegal, Serbia, Seychelles, Slovakia, Somalia, South Africa, Sri Lanka, Sudan, Sweden, Syrian Arab Republic, Tajikistan, Tanzania, Timor Leste, Thailand, Tunisia, Türkiye (Turkey), Uganda, Ukraine, the United Arab Emirates, Uruguay, Uzbekistan, Vanuatu, Venezuela, Viet Nam, Yemen, Zambia and Zimbabwe.

The following states, while they do not recognize Palestine, allow the PLO to maintain a regional office: Australia, Belgium, Canada, Colombia, Denmark, Estonia, Finland, France, Germany, Greece, Ireland, Korea (Rep.), Italy, Japan, Latvia, Lithuania, Luxembourg, Mexico, the Netherlands, New Zealand, Portugal, Slovenia, Spain, Switzerland and the United Kingdom.

Judicial System

In the Gaza Strip, the West Bank towns of Jericho, Nablus, Ramallah, Jenin, Tulkarm, Qalqilya, Bethlehem and Hebron, and in other, smaller population centres in the West Bank, the PA has assumed limited jurisdiction with regard to civil affairs. However, the situation is confused owing to the various and sometimes conflicting legal systems that have operated in the territories occupied by Israel in 1967: Israeli military and civilian law; Jordanian law; and acts, orders-in-council and ordinances that remain from the period of the British Mandate in Palestine.

As of mid-2023 the judicial system under the auspices of the Palestinian (National) Authority (PA) comprised the Court of First Instance, the Court of Conciliation, the Constitutional Court, the Court of Cassation, the High Court of Justice, the Electoral Court and the Courts of Appeal. There were also a number of religious and military courts under the control of the PA, as well as a Higher State Security Court in Gaza under the control of Hamas.

A decree issued by President Mahmoud Abbas in January 2021 amended the 2002 Judicial Authority Act, giving him the power to appoint the heads of the various courts, including the Constitutional Court; the judges were previously nominated by the High Judicial Council for approval by the President. A further presidential decree, issued in October 2022, established a Supreme Council of Judicial Bodies and Authorities, which was to have full supervisory power over the judicial system and was to be appointed and headed by Abbas.

Supreme Council of Judicial Bodies and Authorities: Ramallah; f. 2022; headed by the President of the Palestinian National Authority; the other members include the heads of the various courts and judicial bodies (incl. the Constitutional Court and the High Judicial Council), the Minister of Justice, the Attorney-General and the President's legal advisor; according to the decree by which the new body was established, its members are appointed by the President on a personal rather than institutional basis—meaning that they serve in the body at the President's discretion; Pres. MAHMOUD ABBAS.

High Judicial Council: Ramallah; f. 2002; Pres. ISSA ABU SHARAR.

Constitutional Court: Ramallah; f. 2016; Pres. ALI MUHANNA.

Higher State Security Court: Gaza; f. 1995; decides on security offences both inside and outside the PA's area of jurisdiction; and implements all valid Palestinian laws, regulations, rules and orders in accordance with Article 69 of the Constitutional Law of the Gaza Strip of 5 March 1962.

Attorney-General: AKRAM AL-KHATIB.

Religion

The vast majority of Palestinians in the West Bank and Gaza are Muslims, while a small (and declining) minority are Christians of the Greek Orthodox and Roman Catholic rites.

ISLAM

The PA-appointed Grand Mufti of Jerusalem and the Palestinian Lands is the most senior Muslim cleric in the Palestinian territories.

Grand Mufti of Jerusalem and the Palestinian Lands: Sheikh MUHAMMAD AHMAD HUSSEIN.

CHRISTIANITY

The Roman Catholic Church

Latin Rite

The Patriarchate of Jerusalem covers Israel and the Occupied Territories, the Palestinian territories, Jordan and Cyprus.

Patriarchate of Jerusalem: Patriarcat Latin, POB 14152, Jerusalem 91141; tel. (2) 6282323; fax (2) 6271652; e-mail latinvic@latinpat.org; internet www.lpj.org; Patriarch PIERBATTISTA PIZZABALLA; Vicar-General for Jerusalem WILLIAM SHOMALI (Titular Bishop of Lydda); Vicar-General for Israel RAFIC NAHRA (Titular Bishop of Verbe).

PALESTINIAN TERRITORIES

Melkite Rite

The Greek-Melkite Patriarch of Antioch and all the East, of Alexandria, and of Jerusalem (GRÉGOIRE III LAHAM) is resident in Damascus, Syrian Arab Republic.

Patriarchal Vicariate of Jerusalem: Patriarcat Grec-Melkite Catholique, POB 14130, Porte de Jaffa, Jerusalem 91141; tel. (2) 6282023; fax (2) 6286652; e-mail gcpjer@p-ol.com; Protosyncellus Archim. Archbishop YASSER HANNA AYYASH; about 3,762 adherents (31 Dec. 2020).

The Greek Orthodox Church

The Patriarchate of Jerusalem covers Israel and the Occupied Territories, the Palestinian territories, Jordan, Kuwait, the UAE and Saudi Arabia.

Patriarchate of Jerusalem: POB 14518, Jerusalem 91145; tel. (2) 6271657; fax (2) 6282048; e-mail patriarch@jerusalem-patriarchate.info; internet www.jerusalem-patriarchate.info; Patriarch THEOPHILOS III.

The Press

NEWSPAPERS

Al-Ayyam: POB 1987, al-Ayyam St, Commercial Area, Ramallah; tel. (2) 2987341; fax (2) 2987342; e-mail news@al-ayyam.ps; internet www.al-ayyam.ps; f. 1995; weekly; Arabic; publ. by Al-Ayyam Press, Printing, Publishing and Distribution Co; Editor-in-Chief AKRAM HANIYA.

Al-Hadaf (The Target): e-mail alhadaf@alhadafmagazine.com; internet www.alhadafmagazine.com; f. 1969 in Beirut, Lebanon; weekly; Arabic; organ of the Popular Front for the Liberation of Palestine.

Al-Hayat al-Jadidah: POB 1822, Ramallah; tel. (2) 2407251; fax (2) 2407250; e-mail alhaya-news95@alhaya.ps; internet www.alhaya.ps; f. 1994; weekly; Arabic; Gen. Man. MAJID AL-RIMAWI; Editor MAHMOUD ABU AL-HIJA.

Al-Hourriah (Liberation): POB 11488, Damascus, Syria; tel. (1) 6319455; fax (1) 6319125; e-mail sahli56@hotmail.com; internet www.alhourriah.org; Arabic; organ of the Democratic Front for the Liberation of Palestine; publ. in Beirut (Lebanon) and Damascus; Dir SAMI MISHAQO; Editor-in-Chief MUHAMAD AL-SAHLI.

Al-Istiqlal (Independence): al-Thawra St, Gaza City; e-mail alesteqlal@p-i-s.com; weekly; Arabic; organ of Islamic Jihad; Sec. TAWFIQ AL-SAYYID SALIM.

Palestine Times: POB 10355, London, NW2 3WH, UK; internet www.ptimes.org; f. 2006; monthly; English; privately owned; independent; Editor-in-Chief AHMAD KARMAWI.

Al-Quds (Jerusalem): POB 19788, Jerusalem; tel. (2) 5833501; fax (2) 5856937; e-mail it@alquds.net; internet www.alquds.com; independent; pro-PA; supports peace negotiations; online (Arabic and Hebrew) and print (Arabic) edns; daily; Chair. ZIAD ABU AL-ZULF; Editor-in-Chief WALEED ABU AL-ZULF; circ. (print edn) c. 30,000 (2023).

Al-Risala (Letter): Gaza City; weekly; Arabic; affiliated with the Islamic Resistance Movement (Hamas); Editor-in-Chief GHAZI HAMAD.

Al-Watan: Gaza City; weekly; Arabic; supports Hamas.

PERIODICALS

Filastin (Palestine): Gaza City; e-mail falasteenfalasteen@gmail.com; internet www.falasteen.com; f. 1998; ceased operations during 2005–2010; revived April 2010; weekly; Arabic; pro-Hamas, banned from publication and distribution in the West Bank; Editor ADEL SALEM.

The Jerusalem Times: POB 20185, 19 Nablus Rd, Jerusalem; tel. (2) 2961078; fax (2) 2961079; e-mail tjt@yahoo.com; f. 1994; weekly; English; independent; Publr HANNA SINIORA; Man. Editor SAMI KAMAL.

Al-Karmel Magazine: POB 1887, Ramallah; tel. (2) 2965934; fax (2) 2987374; e-mail editor@alkarmel.org; internet www.alkarmel.org; f. 1981 in Beirut, Lebanon; literature.

Madar: Madar—al-Markaz al-Filastini lil-Dirasat al-Israiliyah, Ramallah; publ. by Madar—The Palestinian Centre for Israeli Studies; political; Editor SALMAN NATOUR.

Raise Your Voice: Jaba, Jerusalem; tel. (2) 2346710; fax (2) 2346715; e-mail pyalara@pyalara.org; internet www.pyalara.org; f. 1998; online; Arabic and English; publ. by the Palestinian Youth Association for Leadership and Rights Activation; Editor-in-Chief HANIA BITAR.

NEWS AGENCY

Wikalat Anbaa Filastiniya (WAFA, Palestine News Agency): Al-Rasal, Al-Masayif, Binayat Mkat 2, Ramallah; tel. (2) 2413628; fax (2) 2413589; e-mail edit@wafa.ps; internet www.wafa.ps; f. 1972; official PLO news agency; Editor KHOLOUD ASSAF.

Publishers

Al-Ayyam Press, Printing, Publishing and Distribution Co: POB 1987, Ramallah; tel. (2) 2987341; fax (2) 2987342; e-mail news@al-ayyam.ps; internet www.al-ayyam.ps; f. 1995; publishes Al-Ayyam al-Arabi daily newspaper, Al-Ayyam weekly newspaper, books and magazines.

Beit Al-Maqdes for Publishing and Distribution: Ramallah; history, politics, fiction, children's.

Centre for Palestine Research and Studies (CPRS): POB 132, Nablus; tel. (9) 2380383; fax (9) 2380384; f. 1993; history, politics, strategic studies and economics; Dir SAID KANAAN.

Ogarit Centre for Publishing and Distribution: Ramallah; non-fiction, children's.

Broadcasting and Communications

TELECOMMUNICATIONS

A monopoly on fixed-line services is held by the Palestine Telecommunications Co PLC (PalTel). However, a second mobile telephone licence was awarded to Wataniya Mobile (now Ooredoo Palestine) in 2006.

Ooredoo Palestine: POB 4236, al-Birah/Ramallah; tel. (2) 2415000; fax (2) 2423044; internet www.ooredoo.ps; f. 2009 as Wataniya Mobile; present name adopted in 2018; 48.45% owned by Ooredoo Group (Qatar), 34.03% owned by Palestine Investment Fund; Chair. MUHAMMAD ABU RAMADAN; CEO Dr DURGHAM MARAEE.

Palestine Telecommunications Co PLC (PalTel): POB 3999, al-Birah/Ramallah; tel. (9) 2300000; fax (2) 2350469; e-mail paltel@palnet.net; internet www.paltel.ps; f. 1995; following acquisition of 56% stake by Zain Kuwait in May 2009, PalTel was merged with Zain Jordan; provider of fixed-line, mobile and internet services; Chair. SALIH MASRI; CEO ABDUL MAJEED MELHEM.

Palestine Cellular Co (Jawwal): POB 3999, al-Birah/Ramallah; tel. (2) 2968000; fax (2) 2968636; internet www.jawwal.ps; f. 1999; wholly owned subsidiary of PalTel; CEO (vacant).

BROADCASTING

Palestinian Broadcasting Co (PBC): POB 984, al-Birah/Ramallah; tel. (2) 2967921; fax (2) 2967920; e-mail pbcnews1@hotmail.com; internet www.pbc.ps; f. 1994; state-controlled; Chair. AHMED ASSAF.

Sawt Filastin (Voice of Palestine): c/o Police HQ, Jericho; tel. (2) 2984731; fax (2) 2959891; internet vop.ps; f. 1994; official radio station of the PA; broadcasts in Arabic from Jericho and Ramallah.

Palestine Television: tel. (2) 2967921; fax (2) 2967920; internet www.pbc.ps; f. 1994; broadcasts from Ramallah and Gaza City; broadcasts online on JumpTV.

Finance

BANKING

The Palestine Monetary Authority (PMA) is the financial regulatory body in the Palestinian territories, and is expected to evolve into the Central Bank of Palestine. Three currencies circulate in the Palestinian economy—the Jordanian dinar, the Israeli shekel and the US dollar—and the PMA currently has no right of issue. According to the PMA, there were 13 licensed banks operating in the West Bank and Gaza in 2022.

Palestine Monetary Authority (PMA): POB 452, al-Irsal St, Ramallah; POB 4026, al-Sayaden Port, Gaza; tel. (2) 2415251; fax (2) 2415310; tel. (8) 2825713; fax (8) 2844487; e-mail info@pma.ps; internet www.pma.ps; f. 1994; began licensing, inspection and supervision of the Palestinian and foreign commercial banks operating in the Gaza Strip and the Jericho enclave in the West Bank in July 1995; assumed responsibility for 13 banks in the Palestinian territories over which the Central Bank of Israel had hitherto exercised control in Dec. 1995; Gov. FIRAS MILHEM.

PALESTINIAN TERRITORIES

Banks

Arab Islamic Bank: al-Nuzha St, Ramallah; tel. (2) 2407060; fax (2) 2407065; e-mail aib@aib.ps; internet aib.ps; f. 1995; Chair. RUSHDI GHALAYINI; Gen. Man. HANI NASER.

Bank of Palestine PLC (BOP): POB 471, Court St, Ain Misbah, Ramallah; tel. (2) 2946700; fax (2) 2964703; e-mail cs@bankofpalestine.com; internet www.bankofpalestine.com; f. 1960; Chair. HASHIM SHAWA; Gen. Man. MAHMOUD SHAWA.

Palestine Investment Bank PLC: POB 3675, Irsal St, al-Birah/Ramallah; tel. (2) 2943500; fax (2) 2973558; e-mail info@pibc.ps; internet www.pibbank.com; f. 1995 by the PA; some shareholders based in Jordan and the Gulf states; provides full commercial and investment banking services throughout the West Bank and Gaza; Chair. ABDUL AZIZ ABU DAYYEH.

Palestine Islamic Bank: POB 2106, al-Masyoun, Ramallah; tel. (2) 2949797; fax (2) 2979787; e-mail info@islamicbank.ps; internet www.islamicbank.ps; f. 1996; Chair. MAHER AL-MASRI; Gen. Man. EMAD AL-SAADI.

Al-Quds Bank for Development and Investment (Quds Bank): POB 2471, Ramallah; tel. and fax (2) 2979555; e-mail quds@qudsbank.ps; internet www.qudsbank.ps; f. 1995; merchant bank; Chair. AKRAM ABDUL LATIF; CEO SALAH HIDMI.

STOCK EXCHANGE

Palestine Exchange (PEX): POB 128, ASAL Bldg, 7th Floor, Rafedya St, Nablus; tel. (9) 2390999; fax (9) 2390998; e-mail pex@pex.ps; internet www.pex.ps; f. 1995; 49 listed cos (Dec. 2022); Chair. SAMIR OTHMAN MAHMOUD HULILEH; CEO NIHAD TALAL.

INSURANCE

A very small insurance industry exists in the West Bank and Gaza.

Ahleia Insurance Group Ltd (AIG): POB 1933, 17 Nizar Qabbani St, Masyoun Heights, Ramallah; tel. (2) 2986634; e-mail info.ramallah@ahlia.ps; internet www.aig.ps; f. 1994; Chair. and CEO Dr MUHAMMAD AL-SABAWI.

Arab Insurance Establishment Co Ltd (AIE): POB 166, al-Qasr St, Nablus; tel. (9) 2341040; fax (9) 2341033; f. 1975; Chair. WALID ALOUL.

Al-Mashreq Insurance Co: Al-Mashreq Insurance Co Bldg, al-Idressi St, al-Nahda District, 1600 Ramallah; tel. (2) 2958090; fax (2) 2958089; e-mail info@mashreqins.com; internet www.mashreqins.com; f. 1992; life and non-life; Chair. JALAL KAZEM NASEREDDIN; CEO AYUB WAEL AYUB ZEARAB.

National Insurance Co: POB 1819, 34 Municipality St, al-Birah/Ramallah; tel. (2) 2983800; fax (2) 2407460; e-mail nic@nic-pal.com; internet www.nic-pal.com; f. 1992; Chair. AZIZ MAHMOUD ABDEL-GAWAD.

DEVELOPMENT FINANCE ORGANIZATIONS

Arab Palestinian Investment Co Ltd: Palestinian Automobile Co Bldg, al-Ayyam St, Ramallah; tel. (2) 2977040; fax (2) 2977044; e-mail apic@apic.com.jo; internet www.apic.ps; f. 1995; headquarters in Amman, Jordan; Chair. and CEO TAREK OMAR AGGAD.

Jerusalem Real Estate Investment Co: POB 1876, Ramallah; tel. (2) 2965215; fax (2) 2965217; e-mail jrei@palnet.com; f. 1996; Chair. AWNI ALSAKET.

Palestine Development & Investment Co (PADICO): POB 666, Rawabi; tel. (2) 2948222; fax (2) 2948223; e-mail info@padico.com; internet www.padico.com; f. 1993; 12 subsidiary and affiliate cos; Chair. BASHAR AL-MASRI.

Palestine Real Estate Investment Co: Rawabi; tel. (2) 2948233; e-mail prico@prico.ps; internet www.prico.ps; f. 1994; Chair. NIMR ABDUL WAHID.

Palestinian Economic Council for Development and Reconstruction (PECDAR): POB 54910, Dahiyat al-Barid, Jerusalem; tel. (2) 2974300; fax (2) 2974331; e-mail info@pecdar.pna.net; internet www.pecdar.ps; privately owned; Chair. MOHAMMAD ABU AWAD.

Trade and Industry

CHAMBERS OF COMMERCE

Federation of Palestinian Chambers of Commerce, Industry and Agriculture: Ramallah; tel. (2) 2985556; e-mail info@pal-chambers.org; internet www.pal-chambers.org; f. 1989; Pres. OMAR HASHEM.

Bethlehem Chamber of Commerce and Industry: POB 59, Bethlehem; tel. (2) 2742742; fax (2) 2764402; e-mail info@bethlehem-chamber.org; internet www.bethlehem-chamber.org; f. 1952; Chair. of Bd SAMIR HAZBOUN.

Gaza Chamber of Commerce, Industry and Agriculture: POB 33, Sabra Quarter, Gaza; tel. (8) 2864588; fax (8) 2866149; e-mail gazacham@palnet.com; internet www.gazacham.ps; f. 1954; Chair. WALID KHALID AL-HOSARY.

Hebron Chamber of Commerce and Industry: POB 272, Hebron; tel. (2) 2228218; fax (2) 2227490; e-mail info@hebroncci.org; internet www.hebroncci.org; f. 1953; Dir ABDO HAMZA IDRIS; over 3,000 mems.

Jenin Chamber of Commerce, Industry and Agriculture: Jenin; internet www.jenincci.org; f. 1953; Chair. AMMAR ABU BAKAR.

Jericho Chamber of Commerce, Industry and Agriculture: POB 91, Jericho 00970; tel. (2) 2323313; e-mail jericho.chamber@gmail.com; internet fb.com/jccia; f. 1953; Chair. Haj TISSER AL-HAMIDI.

Jerusalem Arab Chamber of Commerce and Industry: POB 19151, Jerusalem 91191; tel. (2) 2344923; fax (2) 2344914; e-mail info@jacci.org; internet www.jacci.org; f. 1936; 2,050 mems; Chair. AHMAD HASHEM ZUGHAYAR; Dir FADI ARAFAT HIDMI.

Nablus Chamber of Commerce and Industry: POB 35, Nablus; tel. (9) 2380355; fax (9) 2377605; e-mail nabluschamber@gmail.com; internet nablus-chamber.org; f. 1943; Pres. OMAR HASHEM; Dir ISAM ABU ZAID; 5,223 mems (2022).

Palestinian-European Chamber of Commerce: Jerusalem; tel. (2) 894883; Chair. HANNA SINIORA.

Qalqilya Chamber of Commerce, Industry and Agriculture: POB 13, Qalqilya; tel. (9) 2941473; fax (9) 2940164; e-mail chamberq@hally.net; internet www.pal-chambers.org/chambers/qalqilya.html; f. 1972; 1,068 mems.

Ramallah Chamber of Commerce and Industry: POB 256, al-Birah/Ramallah; tel. (2) 2955052; fax (2) 2984691; e-mail info@ramallahcci.org; internet www.ramallahcci.org; f. 1950; Chair. ABED AL-GHANI AL-ATARI; Dir-Gen. SALAH HUSSIN; 3,566 mems.

Salfeet Chamber of Commerce, Industry and Agriculture: Salfeet; e-mail salfeetchamber@yahoo.com; internet fb.com/salfitchamber; f. 1997; Chair. FAWAZ SHAHADA.

Tulkarm Chamber of Commerce, Industry and Agriculture: POB 51, Tulkarm; tel. (9) 2671010; fax (9) 2675623; e-mail tulkaremchamber@gmail.com; f. 1945; 2,000 mems; Chair. IBRAHIM MUSTAFA ABU HASSIB.

TRADE AND INDUSTRIAL ORGANIZATIONS

Palestinian General Federation of Trade Unions (PGFTU): POB 102, Nablus; tel. (9) 2385136; fax (9) 2384374; e-mail pgftu@pgftu.org; internet www.pgftu.org; f. 1965; Sec.-Gen. SHAHER SAED.

Union of Industrialists: POB 1296, Gaza; tel. (8) 2866222; fax (8) 2862013; Chair. MUHAMMAD YAZIJI.

UTILITIES

Electricity

Palestinian Energy Authority (PEA): POB 3591, Nablus St, al-Birah/Ramallah; POB 3041, Gaza; tel. (2) 2986190; fax (2) 2986191; tel. (8) 2821702; fax (8) 2824849; internet pea-pal.tripod.com; f. 1994; Chair. Dr ABDUL RAHMAN HAMAD; Dir-Gen. SULIMAN IYADA ABDALLA SAMHADANEH.

Jerusalem District Electricity Co (JDECO): POB 19118, 15 Salah el-Din St, Jerusalem; tel. (2) 6269333; fax (2) 6282441; e-mail info@jdeco.net; internet www.jdeco.net; Gen. Man. HISHAM AL-OMARI.

Palestine Electric Co (PEC): POB 1336, Gaza; tel. (8) 2888600; fax (8) 2888607; e-mail info@pec.ps; internet www.pec.ps; f. 1999; 33% state-owned; Chair. SAMER KHOURY; CEO RAFIQ MALIHA.

Water

Palestinian Water Authority (PWA): POB 2174, Baghdad St, Ramallah; tel. (2) 2429022; fax (2) 2429341; e-mail pwa@pwa.ps; internet www.pwa.ps; f. 1995; Dir Dr MAZEN GHONEIM.

Transport

CIVIL AVIATION

Palestinian Civil Aviation Authority (PCAA): Yasser Arafat International Airport, POB 8007, Rafah, Gaza; tel. and fax (8) 2827844; e-mail abuhalib@gaza-airport.org; internet www.gaza-airport.org; f. 1994; Gaza International Airport (renamed as above after Arafat's death in Nov. 2004) was formally inaugurated in 1998 to operate services by Palestinian Airlines (its subsidiary), EgyptAir and Royal Jordanian Airline; the airport was closed by the

Israeli authorities in Feb. 2001 and the runway was seriously damaged by Israeli air strikes in late 2001 and early 2002; Dir-Gen. SALMAN ABU HALIB; Admin. Man. JAMAL AL-MASHHARAWI.

Tourism

Ministry of Tourism and Antiquities: see Administration.
NET—Near East Tourist Agency: POB 19015, 17 Mount of Olives Rd, Jerusalem 91190; tel. (2) 5328720; fax (2) 5328701; e-mail jerusalem@netours.com; internet netours.com; f. 1964; CEO SAMI ABU DAYYEH; Man. STEVE USTIN.

Defence

As assessed at November 2022, the strength of paramilitary forces operating in the Gaza Strip and in the areas of the West Bank where the Palestinian (National) Authority has assumed responsibility for security totalled an estimated 28,200; however, figures for personnel strength in the various forces were impossible to confirm, owing to the uncertain situation in the Palestinian territories. Active forces included, inter alia, a Presidential Security Force (est. 3,000 personnel), a Special Force (est. 1,200), a National Security Force (est. 10,000), a Preventative Security Force (est. 4,000), a Civil Defence Force (est. 1,000) and a Police Force (est. 9,000). There were also two paramilitary organizations allied to the main political factions within the Palestinian territories: the al-Aqsa Martyrs Brigades (affiliated to Fatah) and the Izz al-Din al-Qassam Brigade (linked to Hamas; est. 15,000–20,000 personnel). In 2013 the defence budget was reported to account for 28% of total current budgetary expenditure.

Public Security and Order Budget: US $433.9m. (est.) in 2004.
Commander of the Palestinian National Security Forces: Maj.-Gen. NIDAL ABU DUKHAN.
Commander of the Presidential Guard: Brig.-Gen. MUNIR AL-ZOUBI.
Commander of the Interior Forces and the Civil Police: Maj.-Gen. YOUSEF AL-HELOU.
Commander of General Intelligence: Maj.-Gen. MAJID FARAJ.

Education

The Palestinian Authority's Ministry of Education and Higher Education is responsible for providing and managing public education services from the pre-primary to the higher level, as well as overseeing services provided by the UN Relief and Works Agency for Palestine Refugees in the Near East (UNRWA) and private (mainly charitable) organizations. At 1 January 2022 UNRWA operated 96 schools in the West Bank and 284 in the Gaza Strip, providing education to 46,022 pupils in the West Bank and to 294,086 pupils in Gaza. UNRWA education personnel in that year numbered 2,215 in the West Bank and 9,443 in Gaza. In addition, UNRWA operated four vocational training centres (two in the West Bank and two in Gaza), as well as an educational sciences centre in the West Bank. In 2021 UNRWA budgeted some US $465.8m. for expenditure on education in the Palestinian territories.

Bibliography

A very large literature on the Palestinian question exists and many of these works are included in the bibliography concluding the chapter on Israel. The following are mainly volumes that have appeared since the signing of the Declaration of Principles on Palestinian Self-Rule by Israel and the PLO in September 1993.

Abu-Amr, Ziad. *Islamic Fundamentalism in the West Bank and Gaza: Muslim Brotherhood and Islamic Jihad*. Bloomington, IN, Indiana University Press, 1995.

Abu Sharif, Bassam. *Arafat and the Dream of Palestine: An Insider's Account*. Basingstoke, Palgrave Macmillan, 2009.

Achilli, Luigi. *Palestinian Refugees and Identity: Nationalism, Politics and the Everyday*. London, I. B. Tauris, 2015.

Aruri, Naseer. (Ed.). *Palestinian Refugees: The Right of Return*. London, Pluto Press, 2001.

Baconi, Tareq. *Hamas Contained: the Rise and Pacification of Palestinian Resistance*. Stanford, CA, Stanford University Press, 2018.

Bar-Siman-Tov, Yaacov. *Justice and Peace in the Israeli-Palestinian Conflict*. Abingdon, Routledge, 2014.

Blumenthal, Max. *The 51 Day War: Ruin and Resistance in Gaza*. London, Verso, 2015.

Bouris, Dimitris. *The European Union and Occupied Palestinian Territories: State-Building without a State*. Abingdon, Routledge, 2014.

Brenner, Björn. *Gaza under Hamas: from Islamic Democracy to Islamist Governance*. London, I. B. Tauris, 2017.

Buchanan, Andrew S. *Peace with Justice: A History of the Israeli-Palestinian Declaration of Principles on Interim Self-Government Arrangements*. London, Macmillan, 2001.

Cohen, Michael J. *The British Mandate in Palestine: A Centenary Volume, 1920–2020*. Abingdon, Routledge, 2020.

El Kurd, Dana. *Polarized and Demobilized: Legacies of Authoritarianism in Palestine*. New York, Oxford University Press, 2020.

Erakat, Noura. *Justice For Some: Law and the Question of Palestine*. Stanford, CA, Stanford University Press, 2019.

Farsoun, Samih K., and Aruri, Naseer. *Palestine and the Palestinians: A Social and Political History*. Boulder, CO, Westview Press, 2nd edn, 2006.

Filiu, Jean-Pierre. *Gaza: A History*. London, Hurst & Co, 2014.

Friedman, Yaron. *The Shi'is in Palestine: From the Medieval Golden Age Until the Present*. Leiden, Brill, 2020.

Gelber, Yoav. *Palestine, 1948: War, Escape and the Emergence of the Palestinian Refugee Problem*. Brighton, Sussex Academic Press, 2001.

Ghanem, As'ad. *The Palestinian Regime: A 'Partial Democracy'*. Brighton, Sussex Academic Press, 2002.

Gunning, Jeroen. *Hamas in Politics: Democracy, Religion, Violence*. London, C. Hurst & Co, 2007.

Hanafi, Sari, and Tabar, Linda. *The Emergence of a Palestinian Globalized Elite: Donors, International Organizations and Local NGOs*. Institute for Palestine Studies, 2005.

Hilal, Jamil. *Where Now for Palestine? The Demise of the Two-State Solution*. London, Zed Books, 2007.

Hroub, Khaled. *Hamas: A Beginner's Guide*. London, Pluto Press, 2009.

Hussein, Cherine. *The Re-Emergence of the Single State Solution in Palestine-Israel: Countering an Illusion*. New York, Routledge, 2015.

Israeli, Raphael. *Palestinians Between Nationalism and Islam*. Portland, OR, Vallentine Mitchell, 2008.

Jamal, Amal. *The Palestinian National Movement: Politics of Contention, 1967–2005*. Bloomington, IN, Indiana University Press, 2005.

Jones, Clive, and Pedahzur, Ami. (Eds). *Between Terrorism and Civil War: The Al-Aqsa Intifada*. Abingdon, Routledge, 2004.

Kabha, Mustafa. *The Palestinian People: Seeking Sovereignty and State*. Boulder, CO, Lynne Rienner Publishers, 2014.

Kamrava, Mehran. *The Impossibility of Palestine: History, Geography, and the Road Ahead*. New Haven, CT, Yale University Press, 2016.

Karayanni, Michael Mousa. *Conflicts in a Conflict: A Conflict of Laws Case Study on Israel and the Palestinian Territories*. New York, Oxford University Press, 2014.

Karmi, Ghada, and Cotran, Eugene (Eds). *The Palestinian Exodus, 1948–98*. Reading, Ithaca Press, 1999.

Kear, Martin. *Hamas and Palestine: The Contested Road to Statehood*. Abingdon, Routledge, 2018.

Khalidi, Rashid. *Palestinian Identity: The Construction of Modern National Consciousness*, revised edn. New York, Columbia University Press, 2010.

The Hundred Years' War on Palestine: A History of Settler Colonialism and Resistance, 1917–2017. New York, Metropolitan Books, 2020.

Khalili, Laleh. *Heroes and Martyrs of Palestine: The Politics of National Commemoration.* Cambridge, Cambridge University Press, 2007.

Khan, Mushtaq (Ed.). *State Formation in Palestine: Establishing Good Governance and Democracy Through Social Transformation.* London, RoutledgeCurzon, 2004.

Kimmerling, Baruch and Migdal, Joel S. *The Palestinian People: A History.* Cambridge, MA, Harvard University Press, 2003.

Koensler, Alexander. *Israeli-Palestinian Activism: Shifting Paradigms.* Farnham, Ashgate, 2015.

Kurz, Anat N. *Fatah and the Politics of Violence: The Institutionalization of a Popular Struggle.* Eastbourne, Sussex Academic Press, 2005.

Le More, Anne. *International Assistance to the Palestinians after Oslo: Political Guilt, Wasted Money.* Abingdon, Routledge, 2008.

Lia, Brynjar. *Building Arafat's Police: The Politics of International Police Assistance in the Palestinian Territories After the Oslo Agreement.* Reading, Ithaca Press, 2006.

Masalha, Nur. *Palestine: A Four Thousand Year History.* London, Zed Books, 2018.

Migdal, Joel S. *Palestinian Society and Politics.* Princeton, NJ, Princeton University Press, 2014.

Milton-Edwards, Beverley, and Farrell, Stephen. *Hamas: The Islamic Resistance Movement.* Cambridge, Polity Press, 2010.

Niksic, Orhan. *Area C and the Future of the Palestinian Economy.* Washington, DC, The World Bank, 2014.

Norman, Julie M. *The Second Palestinian Intifada: Civil Resistance.* Abingdon, Routledge, 2010.

Pace, Michelle, and Sen, Somdeep. *The Palestinian Authority in the West Bank: The Theatrics of Woeful Statecraft.* Abingdon, Routledge, 2019.

Pappe, Ilan. *A History of Modern Palestine: One Land, Two Peoples.* Cambridge, Cambridge University Press, 2004.

Parsons, Nigel. *The Politics of the Palestinian Authority: From Oslo to Al-Aqsa.* Abingdon, Routledge, 2006.

Peleg, Ilan. *Human Rights in the West Bank and Gaza: Legacy and Politics.* Syracuse, NY, Syracuse University Press, 1995.

Porath, Y. *The Palestinian Arab National Movement, 1929-1939: From Riots to Rebellion.* London, Routledge, 2015.

Roberts, Nicholas E. *Islam under the Palestine Mandate: Colonialism and the Supreme Muslim Council* London, I.B. Tauris, 2017.

Robinson, Glenn E. *Building a Palestinian State: The Incomplete Revolution.* Bloomington, IN, Indiana University Press, 1997.

Roy, Sara. *The Gaza Strip: The Political Economy of De-Development.* Institute for Palestine Studies, 1995.

Hamas and Civil Society in Gaza: Engaging the Islamist Social Sector. Princeton, NJ, Princeton University Press, 2011.

Said, Edward W. *The End of the Peace Process: Oslo and After.* New York, Granta Books, 2000.

Al-Salim, Farid. *Palestine and the Decline of the Ottoman Empire: Modernisation and the Path to Palestine Statehood.* London, I. B. Tauris, 2015.

Schanzer, Jonathan. *Hamas vs. Fatah: The Struggle For Palestine.* Basingstoke, Palgrave Macmillan, 2008.

Seliktar, Ofira. *Doomed to Failure?: The Politics and Intelligence of the Oslo Peace Process.* Santa Barbara, CA, Praeger, 2009.

Shachar, Nathan. *The Gaza Strip: Its History and Politics—From the Pharoahs to the Israeli Invasion of 2009.* Eastbourne, Sussex Academic Press, 2010.

Shehadeh, Raja. *Where the Line is Drawn: Crossing Boundaries in Occupied Palestine, 1951-2017.* London, Profile Books, 2017.

Skare, Erik. *A History of Palestinian Islamic Jihad: Faith, Awareness, and Revolution in the Middle East.* Cambridge, Cambridge University Press, 2021.

Palestinian Islamic Jihad: Islamist Writings on Resistance and Religion. London, I. B. Tauris, 2021.

Smith, Charles D. *Palestine and the Arab-Israeli Conflict: A History with Documents.* Basingstoke, Palgrave Macmillan, 8th edn, 2013.

Stamatopoulou-Robbins, Sophia. *Waste Siege: the Life of Infrastructure in Palestine.* Stanford, CA, Stanford University Press, 2020.

Tartir, Alaa, and Seidel, Timothy (Eds). *Palestine and Rule of Power: Local Dissent vs. International Governance.* Cham, Palgrave Macmillan, 2019.

Tovy, Jacob. *Israel and the Palestinian Refugee Issue: The Formulation of Policy, 1948–1956.* Abingdon, Routledge, 2014.

Turner, Mandy, and Shweiki, Omar. *Decolonizing Palestinian Political Economy: De-Development and Beyond.* Basingstoke, Palgrave Macmillan, 2014.

Zahlan, Rosemarie Said. *Palestine and the Gulf States: The Presence at the Table.* Abingdon, Routledge, 2009.

QATAR

Geography

The State of Qatar occupies a peninsula (roughly 160 km long, and between 55 km and 90 km wide), projecting northwards from the Arabian mainland, on the west coast of the Persian (Arabian) Gulf. Its western coastline joins onto the shores of Saudi Arabia, and to the east lie the United Arab Emirates and Oman. The total area is 11,493 sq km (4,437 sq miles).

The climate of Qatar is hot and humid in summer, with temperatures reaching 44°C between July and September, and humidity exceeding 85%. There is some rain in winter, when temperatures range between 10°C and 20°C. Qatar is stony, sandy and barren; limited supplies of underground water are unsuitable for drinking or agriculture because of high mineral content. More than one-half of the water supply is now provided by seawater distillation processes.

At the census of 16 March 1986 the population was 369,079, of whom fewer than one-third were native Qataris. The census of March 1997 enumerated a total population of 522,023. About 60% of the total were concentrated in the capital, Doha, on the east coast. Since then the population of Qatar has risen rapidly, principally owing to an influx of foreign workers. (Non-Qatari nationals accounted for 94.3% of the employed population in 2021, according to official figures.) According to the census of 2015, the population (including resident workers from abroad) was 2,404,776, giving a significantly increased population density of 209.2 persons per sq km. By the time of the next census, in 2020, the population had risen to 2,846,118 and the population density to 247.6 persons per sq km. Official estimates put the total population at 2,658,311 at mid-2022. At the 2020 census, Doha had a population of 1,186,023.

History

DAVID ROBERTS

THE DEVELOPMENT OF MODERN QATAR

Although there is evidence of human activity on the Qatari peninsula dating back thousands of years, there is no meaningful historical record before the mid-18th century. Without abundant natural water supplies and with limited tillable soil for agriculture, the Qatari peninsula was not an ideal location for a settled community, particularly as other nearby locations were regarded as more hospitable. None the less, migratory routes of roaming Bedouins and sporadic settlements along the coasts appear to have been the norm and it is from these beginnings that the modern state of Qatar emerged.

In the 1760s large sections of the Bani Utub tribal confederation moved to Qatar from Kuwait. Initially, these groups attempted to settle in Bahrain—well-known for its rich pearling banks—but land there had been taken by tribes loyal to Persia. Therefore, the Bani Utub settled in Zubara (al-Zubara) on Qatar's west coast. This Bani Utub grouping included the Al Khalifa family, whose descendants now include the royal family of Bahrain.

At that time there were existing tribes on the Qatari peninsula. Although the records are far from complete, the Al Musallam, for example, are thought to have been pre-eminent at that time. In turn, the Al Musallam paid a tribute to the much larger Bani Khalid confederation, whose notional area of control included the Qatari peninsula.

Either through initial conflict or through the sheer number of them arriving in Qatar, the Bani Utub (led by the Al Khalifa) came to dominate the west coast of Qatar. Another section of the confederation—the Al Jalahima—was relegated to second place in the pecking order, a situation that did not sit well with this group. Indeed, after having their demands for a greater share of profits dismissed by the Al Khalifa, the Al Jalahima retreated to the south of Zubara. Although they were soon comprehensively defeated in battle, the threat persisted as the Al Jalahima allied with a range of actors in an attempt to regain their prestige.

Indeed, this resort to seeking alliances was the basis of local and regional relations. Like the Al Musallam, the Al Khalifa (and the other Bani Utub tribes) were not numerous enough to ensure their own survival. They, therefore, needed to come to arrangements with larger regional groupings (such as groups based in Persia, the Wahhabis from central Arabia, and the Sultan of Muscat) for a wider guarantee of protection.

This was not an academic desire to ensure a wider array of allies, but an immediate practical and perhaps existential need. A plague in 1773 and the subsequent blockage in 1775–79 of the great port of Basra diverted a substantial amount of maritime traffic to Zubara, which had recently become a working port. Zubara thus quickly became a rich settlement, and attracted wider attention. The Persians and their proxies in Bahrain attacked sporadically from 1777 onwards. With the assistance of other tribes in Qatar, the Al Khalifa managed to defend Zubara and themselves; they then attacked Bahrain, taking control of those islands during 1782–83, although they still ruled from Zubara for a time.

From the 1790s the Qatari peninsula was subjected to repeated raids by Wahhabi tribesmen, often aided by the Al Jalahima. By 1797 the Al Khalifa were forced to relocate to Bahrain, leaving the Qatari peninsula to the Wahhabis. Only two years later the Al Khalifa were attacked by the Sultan of Muscat's forces in Bahrain. After attempts to persuade Persian forces to protect them failed, the Al Khalifa ceded Bahrain to the Sultan in 1800. Displaced to the Wahhabi-controlled Qatar peninsula, the Al Khalifa reached an agreement with the Wahhabis and, with their support, having promised to promote a Wahhabi 'tribal commonwealth', regained control of Bahrain in 1802. However, the Al Khalifa grew to resent Wahhabi suzerainty shortly thereafter. After the United Kingdom refused in 1805 to help the Al Khalifa extract themselves from their agreements with the Wahhabis, they turned to the Sultan of Muscat for protection in 1811 and the cycle of rotating allegiance continued.

The Ottoman and British Empires became increasingly involved as the 19th century progressed. The Ottomans maintained a presence for half a century in Qatar until 1916. The British, using their naval fleet and a series of agents stationed around the Persian (Arabian) Gulf region, corralled and persuaded various Gulf sheikhdoms into joining treaties to preserve the peace. Far from being an external imposition, this complemented existing arrangements that had existed in the region for centuries.

The UK's interest in the Gulf was primarily to maintain peace in the region to protect its trading and communication routes to India. When, therefore, in 1867, the Al Khalifa—who were still dominant in Qatar—joined with forces from Abu Dhabi to raid Qatar, explicitly breaking their treaty obligations to the UK, the British authorities reacted harshly. In 1868 the British Political Resident in the Gulf, Lt-Col Lewis Pelly, removed Muhammad bin Khalifa from power in Bahrain and demanded reparations. Meanwhile, Pelly met with

Muhammad bin Thani, the representative of the people of Qatar, and signed a treaty with him. Although this treaty did not independently recognize Al Thani as the legitimate power in Qatar, for it still included provisions for the payment of tribute to the Al Khalifa, it is regarded as the de facto starting point of the Al Thani's rule. Muhammad Al Thani paid the tribute until 1872, when he signed an agreement with the Ottoman Empire for the stationing of its troops in Qatar, ending his reliance on the Al Khalifa.

Like all rulers in the region, the Al Thani resisted attempts at meaningful control and oversight by the Ottomans and ruled the east of the peninsula as autonomously as possible, while maintaining wider links and potential guarantees of protection. The bilateral relationship was typically fractious. Agitation for less Ottoman control led to a battle in Wajbah in 1892 and an unlikely Qatari victory, which heralded the end of de facto Ottoman power in Qatar and which is considered a landmark event in Qatari history.

The Ottoman presence in Qatar finally ended in 1915 and in the following year Abdullah Al Thani, the successor to Jassim, signed an agreement with the UK. Abdullah was officially recognized as the ruler of Qatar, under the auspices of the wider British agreements in the Gulf. However, Qatar was still far from united. Tribes in the west retained their loyalty to the Al Khalifa until a decisive final battle in 1937, when Zubara was captured and the peninsula was finally brought under a single ruler in Abdullah Al Thani. None the less, the weakness of the Qatari state was evident until the late 1940s, when Saudi Arabian geologists with armed guards travelled into the centre of the peninsula, exploring for petroleum deposits. While this was conducted under the notion that roaming Al Murra tribes in Qatar's interior were loyal to the Saudi King, Abdulaziz Al Sa'ud, it served as an example of the Al Thani's continued lack of control over parts of Qatar's territory.

The discovery of petroleum deposits in Qatar in the late 1930s came too late for immediate exploitation as the outbreak of the Second World War (1939–45) intervened. This came at a critical time for Qatar. Its existing economic difficulties were exacerbated by a decline in the market for pearls, the over-running of fertile, rice-producing areas by warring troops in south-east Asia and the sinking of food-laden ships, which led to severe food shortages. Some estimates suggest that up to one-third of Qatar's population left during that period, leaving only 10,000 people living on the peninsula by the end of the Second World War. The eventual beginning of petroleum exports in 1949 was much needed and the rudimentary institutions of state were established in the 1950s and 1960s.

The UK surprised its dependants in the Gulf in 1968 by announcing its intention to withdraw British forces from the region by 1971. Initial attempts by Qatar, Bahrain and the Trucial States (now the United Arab Emirates—UAE) to form a federation of Gulf Arab states failed, with Qatar's relations with Bahrain hindering an agreement. Qatar became a fully independent nation state on 1 September 1971, and although ruler Sheikh Ahmad Al Thani did not return from Geneva, Switzerland, for the official independence ceremony, he took the title of Amir.

However, arguably the first ruler to concentrate meaningfully on state-building was Sheikh Khalifa bin Hamad Al Thani, a cousin of Sheikh Ahmad, who proclaimed himself as Amir after a bloodless coup in February 1972. Sheikh Khalifa's first act was to attempt to create wider sources of legitimacy and support beyond the Al Thani family. He began with widespread programmes to build housing, create jobs, increase pension payments and social aid for ordinary Qataris, while he also promoted Qatar in foreign media outlets. Meanwhile, foreign archaeologists were invited to the country to uncover its history, as Sheikh Khalifa attempted to create a national identity. Embassies were opened and Qatar positioned itself as a donor of financial aid to developing countries when its finances allowed.

Qatar's economy remained wholly reliant upon revenues from petroleum, and thus the country's financial security ebbed and flowed with the oil price on the international market. The 1970s were a period of great wealth for Qatar, but modern budget deficits were recorded for the first time in the 1980s, prompted by the fall of the price of oil. Although the world's largest gasfield was discovered in 1971 in the waters between Qatar and Iran, at that time gas was seen as merely a by-product of the discovery and processing of petroleum. It was, therefore, largely ignored until the early 1990s.

THE ACCESSION OF SHEIKH HAMAD

Just as Sheikh Ahmad had spent increasingly less time in Qatar towards the end of his rule, so did Sheikh Khalifa, producing the same result: he was ousted in a bloodless coup in 1995. Hamad bin Khalifa Al Thani, the Heir Apparent, Minister of Defence and Commander-in-Chief of the Armed Forces, assumed power from his father. Sheikh Hamad had been building a power base of his own in the late 1980s and had begun taking Qatar's foreign policy in new directions. In 1988, for example, he oversaw the opening of diplomatic relations with the Union of Soviet Socialist Republics (USSR) and the People's Republic of China without waiting for Saudi Arabia to do so first, which was an unusual move.

His ascent to power was further aided by a government reorganization in 1989. This represented the first large-scale change in government since independence. Sheikh Hamad's closest political ally, Sheikh Hamad bin Jassim Al Thani, crucially took responsibility for the municipalities portfolio. Meanwhile, Sheikh Hamad had begun to form 'Supreme Councils' under his direct control, with oversight of policy in key areas such as planning, education and health. During the following years these Councils would become a mechanism through which Sheikh Hamad and his allies could bypass the ministries and develop policies after their own vision.

While changes were taking place within Qatar, external developments also had a profound effect. The Iraqi invasion of Kuwait in 1990 prompted particular concern. Much like Kuwait, Qatar was a small, intrinsically defenceless country which was exceedingly wealthy and was surrounded by larger countries with which it had historically been in conflict. For many influential people in Qatar, the analogies between the two were clear and concerning.

Qatar used this opportunity to guarantee its long-term security. Rejecting any would-be protection by Saudi Arabia, Sheikh Hamad, like others in the region at that time, turned to the USA. The shock of the Kuwait invasion negated existing reticence to closer relations with the USA, whose support of Israel made it an unpalatable ally. The breaking of Qatari-US relations in the late 1980s over Qatar's refusal to return illegally purchased missiles to the USA was overcome, and the first of a series of bilateral defence agreements was signed in June 1992. Part of this relationship included the expansion of the US military presence in Qatar. In the mid-1990s the Qatari Government invested around US $1,000m. in building and upgrading an air force base at al-Udaid, 30 km from the capital, Doha. Within a decade, Qatar was hosting one of the largest US pre-positioning bases in the world and was a central hub of a key command centre for an entire regional force. Although the US-Qatari agreements may not have compelled the USA to defend Qatar in the event of a deep crisis, Qatari elites felt such a significant US presence in Qatar considerably boosted the country's deterrence.

Qatar's arrangements with the USA came at a time when its relations with Saudi Arabia were deteriorating markedly. The exact point at which this began is impossible specifically to define, but it is notable that they appeared to decline as Sheikh Hamad's influence on Qatar increased. Partly it seems that Hamad had displeased the authorities in the Saudi capital, Riyadh, as he sought to carve an independent policy for Qatar and increasingly avoided following the Saudi line. While there was something of a détente between Iran and the Arab Gulf states in the early 1990s, after Ali Akbar Hashemi Rafsanjani took office as President of Iran in 1989 and sought a more conciliatory relationship, Qatar took this even further, much to the Saudis' displeasure.

Relations between Qatar and Saudi Arabia declined still further in the early 1990s. The years 1992, 1993 and 1994 each were marked by border skirmishes between the two countries' forces. Moreover, during this time Qatar began to augment its relations with Israel, a policy opposed to that of Saudi Arabia. When, in June 1995, Sheikh Hamad replaced his father as

Amir while Khalifa was out of the country, this proved to be a step too far. The young Heir Apparent had not only been leading an independent and controversial foreign policy, but he had now usurped his father, which was an unpopular move among conservative, monarchical neighbours. Sheikh Khalifa returned to the region after the coup and was received as the legitimate ruler by both the UAE and Saudi Arabia. At least two attempts were subsequently launched by Sheikh Khalifa to regain power, with, it was believed, the support of Saudi Arabia. However, these attempts failed and Saudi Arabia reluctantly gave its recognition to the new Amir, Sheikh Hamad. Saudi-Qatari relations were, however, difficult from there on. Indeed, after something of a 'cold war' between the two states, Saudi Arabia withdrew its ambassador from Doha in 2002. The ambassador's return after elite-level talks in 2008 signalled a new and more co-operative era in bilateral relations that lasted until the ascent of Hamad's son, Tamim bin Hamad Al Thani, in June 2013.

Qatar, a significantly smaller country than Saudi Arabia in both geographical and political terms, understandably struggled to counter Saudi influence. However, the reanimation of an existing idea—to create a Qatar-based television news network—in 1996 was to prove to be an important method through which Qatar burnished its image, and presented a challenge to Saudi Arabia's dominance of the region.

BURGEONING 'SOFT' POWER UNDER SHEIKH HAMAD'S RULE

Arguably the single most effective tool used to enhance Qatar's reputation was Al Jazeera. The broadcaster's antecedents went back into the early 1990s under the rule of Sheikh Khalifa, but it was in 1996 that Al Jazeera was finally launched. It was staffed by a cadre of Western-trained journalists, lending it a degree of credibility and a professional approach from the beginning.

Al Jazeera first gained wider prominence in 1998, when it sold exclusive footage of Operation Desert Fox conducted by the USA in Iraq (see Iraq) to a number of foreign channels. Early in 1999 Al Jazeera began 24-hour broadcasting, and by 2000 it had become the pre-eminent Arab news broadcaster. The suicide attacks in New York, Pennsylvania and Washington, DC, USA in September 2001 and their aftermath increased Al Jazeera's notoriety outside the Middle East, as it broadcast video messages from Osama bin Laden, the leader of the Islamist militant group al-Qa'ida that claimed responsibility for the attacks. Despite the apparent disapproval of the USA, Al Jazeera continued to expand. An English-language channel, Al Jazeera English, was founded in 2006, in an attempt to compete in terms of depth and breadth of coverage with international rivals. In 2013 a new US-based channel, Al Jazeera America, began broadcasting, although viewing figures were disappointing, and Qatar's search for cost savings was so great that in 2016 the channel was closed down.

It is difficult to grasp the importance and novelty of Al Jazeera in the Middle East from an outside perspective. The channel's programming amounted to little less than a revolution in the region's media. In contrast with the partisan state broadcasters, Al Jazeera offered criticism of government, talk-shows discussing subjects never broached in such a public manner, and interviews with opposition figures, all in a modern, vibrant setting. It can rightly be seen as the vanguard of Qatar's efforts to define itself as a modern state on the international stage.

Almost all countries in the region have complained to the Qatari Government about Al Jazeera's coverage at certain times. The complaints have included banning Al Jazeera from operating in the countries in question, deporting journalists, expelling Qatari diplomats, and even cutting off diplomatic ties with Qatar altogether. In 1999, for example, the Algerian Government was alleged to have cut electricity supplies to that country's capital city, Algiers, in an attempt to prevent the inhabitants from watching the broadcast of a debate with anti-Government figures.

Qatar has consistently promoted culture as a way to boost its 'soft' power. The founding of The Museum of Islamic Art in Doha in 2008 and the hosting of an annual film festival from 2009–12 in conjunction with the New York-based Tribeca organization are a few of Qatar's endeavours to position itself as a mature, cultured country. Meanwhile, during the 2000s Qatar became increasingly keen to host regional and global sporting events. From staging Asian and world championships in sports such as handball, wrestling, sailing and fencing, Qatar progressed to hosting large-scale events, including the Asian Games in 2006 and the Asian Cup association football tournament in 2011. Additionally, annual tournaments in tennis, golf, motor racing and athletics all take place in the country. The biggest achievement of this strategy to date came in December 2010, when Qatar was awarded the right to host the world's second largest sporting tournament, the International Federation of Association Football (Fédération Internationale de Football Association—FIFA) World Cup in 2022. In 2014 Doha was awarded the right to stage the International Association of Athletics Federations World Championships in 2019.

Moreover, Qatar began to involve itself in international diplomacy under the leadership of Sheikh Hamad, particularly in the 2000s, with a range of mediation efforts in both the Middle East and beyond: for example, in Yemen, the disputed territory of Western Sahara, the Sudanese region of Darfur, Ethiopia and Eritrea, and Somalia. Additionally, Qatar hosted negotiations between the Lebanese militant organization Hezbollah and the Lebanese Government in 2008, and between the Palestinian political movements Hamas and Fatah in 2012. Qatar's active diplomacy became a hallmark of Sheikh Hamad's rule and was usually associated with his Prime Minister and Minister of Foreign Affairs, Sheikh Hamad bin Jassim.

Qatar's recent history has also been marked by financial generosity. The Government donated US $100m. to the US city of New Orleans in the aftermath of Hurricane Katrina in 2005, allegedly paid around $460m. to secure the release of a group of Bulgarian nurses and a Palestinian doctor held in Libya in 2007, and pledged at least $50m. to Hamas following its victory in the 2006 Palestinian legislative elections. Elsewhere, its munificence was often channelled through the Qatar Foundation, which was established in 1995 to fund community projects, scientific research and educational programmes in Qatar and abroad.

Qatar paid for these initiatives with revenues from the largest gasfield in the world, the North Field, which was first discovered in 1971. However, it was not developed until the early 1990s due to political instability in the region and domestic indifference to the economic potential of gas.

Sheikh Hamad's political ascent in the late 1980s coincided with an upsurge in Qatar's interest in exploiting its natural gas reserves. Although discussions had been ongoing for more than a decade, Sheikh Hamad gave a new focus to the process. Despite a range of issues, including the invasion of Kuwait scattering foreign workers, technical difficulties, and the withdrawal of BP from the programme in 1992, the production of liquefied natural gas (LNG) eventually began in 1997, helped by Japanese finance and guarantees of demand from Japanese consumers.

Qatar's vast reserves and growing demand, especially in East Asia and Europe, enabled it to become the world's largest producer of LNG after only one decade of its entrance into the market. Although petroleum continued to be a major source of revenues for Qatar, it was LNG that transformed it, according to some per capita measurements, into the richest country in the world, and was the main facilitating factor that allowed Sheikh Hamad to pursue the policies that defined his rule.

It is possible to discern a range of motives for the pursuit of such expansionist policies. In supporting and hosting a variety of cultural events, Qatar is not only seeking to increase visitor numbers to aid economic diversification, but it is fundamentally advertising Qatar worldwide. In this, and its desire to host global sports events, Qatar seeks to promote itself as a modern and attractive state with which to do business. Indeed, one must not forget the regional competitive context. The Emirati cities of Abu Dhabi and Dubai are two similar territories within the same region, and Qatar needs to find ways to differentiate itself from them, not just in order to compete for foreign direct investment, but so that Qataris can foster a distinct national identity among regional competitors with a similar tribal, cultural, social, political and economic history.

Meanwhile, high-profile exercises in international diplomatic mediation, such as in Darfur and Lebanon, foster the notion of Qatar as a quasi-neutral, peace-promoting actor. The fact that Qatar is willing to deal with both Israel and Hezbollah, while also trying to establish relations with Iran, underlines this notion of quasi-neutrality.

There are also more security-oriented reasons as to why Qatar has chosen to pursue such internationally directed actions. Qatar's colonial experiences offer today's leaders a bleak view of international relations. From its modern-day inception in the late 18th century, Qatar's leaders have found themselves in need of alliances for formal protection. The Al Khalifa of Bahrain, the Wahhabis of (Saudi) Arabia, the Persians, the Sultan of Muscat from modern-day Oman, the Ottoman Empire and the UK were all suzerains at one stage. However, those suzerains and alliances changed frequently: allies could become enemies within a short period of time. Leaders, therefore, had to be dextrous in international affairs.

Aside from the consistent vacillation of allies and rivals, it is worth highlighting the potential effect of the dissolution of the Ottoman Empire and the world-spanning British Empire as suzerains on future Qatari leaders. Having enjoyed the support of such large entities at one stage would have been comforting. Yet, these empires eventually disappeared. Overall, therefore, Qatar's historical predicament in its international relations evokes the dictum that states have neither permanent friends nor allies, only permanent interests.

While, just as before, Qatar is largely reliant upon one key ally—the USA—for its security, its recent policies have reduced this dependency to a degree. The fact that Qatar exports a significant proportion of the energy required by the UK, the Republic of Korea (South Korea), China and Japan, among others, means that Qatar's continued prosperity is critical to these countries. Whether they hold formal defensive agreements with Qatar is almost irrelevant to their interests: given the dependence of many countries on Qatar's gas, they were always likely to be supportive to the Qatari state when it came under duress, as with the 2017–21 Gulf blockade (see below).

Qatar is also courting support within the region, seeking to boost the popularity of the country by way of providing the Middle East's leading source of information, or playing to the 'Arab street' as some observers would put it. Given the popularity of Al Jazeera throughout much of its initial decade and a half, this part of the plan appears to have been remarkably effective, although, as discussed below, Al Jazeera became less an asset than a liability during the 'Arab Spring'.

QATAR AND THE 'ARAB SPRING'

The fundamental trait of Qatar's foreign policy from the late 1980s to 2011—its desire to be regarded as relatively neutral—was at odds with its prominent role in fostering the popular uprisings in the Middle East and North Africa, collectively known as the 'Arab Spring'. In Libya and the Syrian Arab Republic, Qatar supported the removal from power of those countries' respective leaders, Muammar al-Qaddafi and President Bashar al-Assad. Qatari forces participated directly in the North Atlantic Treaty Organization (NATO) action against Qaddafi in March–October 2011, and from early 2012 to 2014 Qatar was sporadically supplying aid to forces opposed to Assad's rule in Syria.

However, while Qatar's tactics changed during the 'Arab Spring', the overall strategy stayed the same. The main aim of foreign policy has been to make Qatar as important as possible to as many international actors as possible. Previously, Qatar's relations with Libya and Egypt were insignificant. The revolutions of 2011 allowed a small but prosperous state such as Qatar to contribute to effecting great changes in the region, many of which proved, initially at least, to be beneficial to Qatar's own geopolitical position.

In Libya, Tunisia and especially Egypt, Qatar tended to direct its support largely via the local incarnation of the Muslim Brotherhood or groups associated with moderate Islam more generally. Partly this was because exiles resident in Doha provided influential contacts with such organizations. Also, given the coherence of the Muslim Brotherhood as a structured organization with popular support, it was regarded as an effective vehicle to use. Indeed, with the comparative lack of an opposition comprising secular or liberal groups, Qatar had little choice but to support the Brotherhood if it wanted to take a leading role in the uprisings from the beginning.

While such a move may have bolstered Qatar's popularity among sections of the Arab world, supporting the Brotherhood was more of a tactic to allow Qatar to support the new governments in those countries themselves. In the case of Egypt, Qatar became its most significant financial supporter prior to the removal from power of Muslim Brotherhood President Mohamed Mursi in July 2013. In April of that year Qatar had agreed to increase its total financial aid to Egypt to some US $8,000m. This was not directly due to any kind of ideological affiliation with the Brotherhood, but more to do with the prestige and influence of a centrally important state like Egypt.

Previously, Qatar's relations with Egypt had been strained. This was problematic for Qatar, particularly as it sought to involve itself in diplomatic affairs in which Egypt held considerable influence, such as Sudan and the League of Arab States (Arab League, see p. 1146). Indeed, according to a secret US diplomatic cable published by the WikiLeaks organization, in 2010 the Egyptian Minister of Foreign Affairs, Ahmad Aboul Gheit, had threatened to 'thwart every single initiative' proposed under Qatar's presidency of the Arab League. However, with the development of elite-to-elite relations following the removal of President Hosni Mubarak from power in February 2011 and with the credit that Qatar was building with its financial and diplomatic support of the new Egyptian leadership, it was a reasonable assumption that Qatar could expect greater co-operation in the future.

These policies were driven by members of Qatar's ruling elite, who were relatively unencumbered in their decision-making and who felt profoundly secure both domestically, facing little or no evident local opposition, and internationally, given Qatar's close relations with the USA. Moreover, the elite-led nature of the policies allowed Qatar to make decisions quickly, while maintaining consistency by virtue of continuity among the members of that elite. Equally, however, the lack of institutionalization of foreign policy was potentially concerning. It meant that Qatar's implementation of foreign policy decisions was inconsistent, and the lack of an experienced and trusted cadre of diplomats meant that the state's foreign policy was reliant on interlocutors of varying degrees of reliability.

Qatar's foreign policy under Sheikh Hamad proved remarkably successful for many years. However, the change of tactics following the 'Arab Spring' ultimately saw the country's image tarnished. As the groups that it supported fractured across the region and little progress was made, at best Qatar was seen as a state out of its depth, unable to cope with the array of complex decisions it had taken upon itself. At worst, it was seen as actively seeking to support militant, uncontrollable Islamist factions and making a bad situation worse.

QATAR UNDER SHEIKH TAMIM

This was the difficult situation that Qatar's new Amir inherited in 2013. With no apparent motive, Sheikh Hamad abdicated as Amir on 25 June 2013, transferring power to the 33-year-old Heir Apparent, Sheikh Tamim bin Hamad Al Thani. Sheikh Tamim effected a substantial reorganization of the Council of Ministers on the following day, most notably replacing Sheikh Hamad bin Jassim as Prime Minister and Minister of Foreign Affairs. Sheikh Hamad bin Jassim was also replaced as CEO of the Qatar Investment Authority and as Chairman of Qatar's national airline.

The transition marked a profound change in Qatar's political governance, as both Sheikh Hamad, as Amir, and Sheikh Hamad bin Jassim, as Prime Minister and Minister of Foreign Affairs, had been pivotal in building Qatar's contemporary wealth and prestige. The reasons behind the changes are difficult to discern. One explanation proposed by observers was that serious concerns for his health had prompted Sheikh Hamad to consider his future. Rather than leaving Qatar in an uncertain position in the event of an abrupt end to his rule, he decided to act early. This would allow Sheikh Tamim a period to adapt to leadership, with Sheikh Hamad (who was awarded the title of Father Amir) in an informal, ad hoc advisory role, while also breaking a regional taboo in abdicating in favour of a son, thus once more distinguishing Qatar from other Gulf states and showing that a smooth transition of power was possible.

Initially, Tamim's rule in Qatar focused on internal reform and the professionalization of government institutions. The previous Prime Minister was also the Minister of Foreign Affairs, but the new Prime Minister, Sheikh Abdullah, took the interior portfolio, reflecting Sheikh Tamim's focus on domestic affairs.

All ministries, with the exception of the Ministry of Defence, were subject to stringent budget cuts of around 30%. This was designed to cut back on ever-increasing spending plans across the state and to prepare Qatar for a more uncertain fiscal future. This prepared Qatar fortuitously well for the dramatic fall in international oil and gas prices that began in mid-2014. Overall, from 2014 to 2015, Qatar's budget revenue contracted by around 40% as a result of lower prices. Although the oil price was expected to dip, nobody quite expected the dramatic drop that transpired. Despite cuts being keenly felt in the education sector (particularly in the foreign universities in Qatar's 'Education City' in Doha) and in the museum sector, ordinary Qataris citizens were broadly unaffected by the drop in public spending.

Sheikh Tamim's immediate domestic focus was derailed in early 2014 when Qatar's three closest Arab neighbours—Bahrain, Saudi Arabia and the UAE—withdrew their ambassadors from Qatar in an unprecedented attempt to force policy change in Qatar under the recently installed Amir. Leaders of the three countries opposed Qatar's long-time policy of channelling support to and through groups and individuals associated with political Islam, particularly the Muslim Brotherhood. The troika of states increasingly believed that political Islam as a concept and groups linked to it (such as the Muslim Brotherhood) posed a clear and present threat to their interests.

This move deeply shocked Qatar's new leaders. It was accompanied by headlines in Saudi-controlled newspapers referring to potential escalation, including blockading the Qatari–Saudi border (Qatar's only and crucial land border) or banning Qatar Airways from entering Saudi airspace. While these notions seemed far-fetched at the time, the idea of all three ambassadors being embarrassingly and unprecedentedly withdrawn in unison seemed equally unlikely until it happened.

Ultimately, relations were mended. Indeed, from relatively early in the dispute Saudi Arabia seemed to develop a mediating role between Qatar and the UAE. For Saudi Arabia, preserving the unity of the Cooperation Council for the Arab States of the Gulf (Gulf Cooperation Council, see p. 1131) was more important than putting pressure on Qatar for longer than a few months. This unity was soon tested when Saudi Arabia and the UAE launched Operation Decisive Storm, a multinational military operation in Yemen in 2015. Qatar contributed a small number of fighter jets to take part in the air campaign and also sent some troops to Yemen itself. However, media reports that Qatar sent 1,000 troops, helicopters and armour overstate the Qatari deployment, which was ultimately more a political decision to keep Saudi Arabia appeased than a wholehearted contribution to the mission.

Meanwhile, a campaign led by Western-based human rights organizations increasingly drew attention to the situation of migrant workers in Qatar, particularly among those constructing facilities for the 2022 FIFA World Cup. The now former President of FIFA, Sepp Blatter, visited Qatar in November 2013 and received an assurance from Sheikh Tamim that his Government was committed to improving the conditions of migrant workers. In March 2014 the International Labour Organization renewed its criticism of Qatar's treatment of migrant workers, particularly the abuse of the *kafala* system by which foreign workers were contracted and upheld a complaint from the International Trade Union Confederation on the right of migrant workers to join trade unions in Qatar. The Prime Minister, Sheikh Abdullah, subsequently announced that the Government was proposing changes to the *kafala* system. However, such changes were slow in coming and this is part of the tragedy of this issue in Qatar. After winning the right to host the World Cup, it was obvious that the state would have to reform these employment practices substantially. Instead of getting on and doing it, however, the state delayed and obfuscated, which served only to increase international pressure and gave the impression that Qatar only reacted under abject duress.

One other strand of international censure in Qatar stems from the groups with which the state associated itself during the Arab Spring. In particular, Qatar appeared to develop a pragmatic relationship with the al-Qa'ida affiliate Jabhat al-Nusra (al-Nusra Front; renamed Jabhat Fatah al-Sham—Levant Conquest Front—in July 2016) in Syria. Lengthy interviews with its leader on Al Jazeera in 2014 and 2015 were, it seems, part of a plan to attempt to rehabilitate the group's reputation in the wider international community. As Qatar seldom explains its logic, it attracts harsh criticism in the Western press for helping such groups. This is unfortunate, as Qatar's Government believes that there is little to be gained by ignoring them. Just as the British Government eventually negotiated with the Irish Republican Army, so too does Qatar want to eschew the years of isolation, given that groups such as the al-Nusra Front are not likely to disappear any time soon. Moreover, Qatar appears to believe that the al-Nusra Front is, irrespective of its beliefs, a useful ally in the wider struggle against Syria's President Assad. Qatar considers him to be the root of the problems in Syria and passionately believes that a coalition is needed to force him from power. Equally, there are more direct uses for such groups and associations. As a result of Qatar's links in Syria and Iraq, dozens of Fijian, Lebanese and US hostages have been released from captivity. To some extent, therefore, Sheikh Tamim is echoing the policies of his father, seeking to boost relations even with undesirable sides in a conflict to provide such niche services.

DETERIORATION IN REGIONAL RELATIONS

Qatar was profoundly blindsided yet again by its closest neighbours (Saudi Arabia, Bahrain and the UAE) and Egypt in June 2017. This time, however, rather than just withdrawing their ambassadors, this quartet launched a diplomatic, air, and land blockade against Qatar without prior indication. Those countries' air spaces were closed to Qatari aircraft, transhipping through the critical port of Dubai's Jebel Ali was suspended, the Qatari land border with Saudi Arabia was closed, and all Qatari nationals were given just two weeks to leave the four states. Fearing some kind of military escalation, Qatar placed its military on high alert as it worked out how to deal with the situation, which was unprecedented in the region's history.

Interestingly, the blockade was launched after the internet site of Qatar's official news agency was hacked in April 2017, which led to the publication of falsified stories about a speech given by Sheikh Tamim at a military graduation ceremony, in which he was supposed to have praised Iran, while condemning the USA. In hindsight, it appears that the hack was a fake *casus belli*, used by Qatar's antagonists as a reason to take action against it.

In terms of the reasons for launching the blockade, as well as a long-term disapproval of Qatar's engagement with groups on the Islamist spectrum, there were two proximate events to note. At the time of the announcement in June 2017, Qatar was in the process of paying for the release of 26 Qatari hostages (including members of the ruling family) from Shi'a militias in southern Iraq. This issue likely reminded the Gulf 'troika' of Qatar's connections to such Shi'a groups and its Government's willingness to pay ransoms to hostile groups, both of which actions Qatar was supposed to have abrogated under the terms of its agreements with its neighbours in 2014. The timing of the blockade, mere days after US President Donald Trump's visit to Saudi Arabia—which was, unprecedentedly for a US President, his first destination abroad since taking office—suggests that Trump's robust support for Saudi and UAE leaders to control policy in their region emboldened Qatar's neighbours. They took this opportunity to settle old scores, confident that there was an unusual President in the White House who would, to a large degree, ignore the institutional advice of the US Department of State and Department of Defense, and back the troika.

Initially, the quartet (the Gulf troika and Egypt) did not publish any demands as to how Qatar could rectify the situation. They seemed to hope that the severity of their actions and the element of surprise would induce Qatar to capitulate. When this did not happen, after 10 days they submitted to the Qatari Government a list of 13 demands that the vast majority of analysts regarded as impossibly onerous. These included that Qatar shut down Al Jazeera, close its diplomatic representation in Iran, evict a growing Turkish military mission in Qatar, and submit itself to frequent audits of its foreign affairs spending. The quartet also sought to isolate Qatar internationally, but was largely unsuccessful. Only an irrelevant few smaller states such as the Maldives joined in their blockade of Qatar.

Both the US Secretary of Defense, James Mattis, and the US Secretary of State, Rex Tillerson, men with vast experience in the Gulf region, found the demands to be excessive. President Trump, however, initially indicated his support for the quartet via social media. This bifurcation in the US approach prevented the Trump Administration from taking a unified position from which to press all sides to come to a resolution. In July 2017, none the less, the quartet reduced its demands to six principles that harked back to the 2014 agreements. This curious climb-down in the face of Qatari stoicism indicates how badly misjudged their initial 13 points were.

After the initial fury and fear of escalation, the Qatari state rallied. After a downgrade of Qatar's economy by international ratings agencies at the outset of the crisis, its ratings had bounced back to their previous high levels by early 2018. The Qatari population appeared to be deeply offended by the treatment of their country by their neighbours, which they considered unfair, and rallied around the leadership of Sheikh Tamim. Alternative trading relations were established, and Qatar strengthened its defensive relations with key states including Turkey (officially redesignated as Türkiye in June 2022), the USA, France and the UK. Overall, the blockade galvanized Qatari nationalism as never before. Although the blockade incurred extra costs for the Qatari state, those proved to be easily affordable.

COVID-19, THE END OF THE BLOCKADE AND AFTER

All Gulf monarchies were brutally exposed to the coronavirus disease (COVID-19) pandemic that spread across the world in early 2020, not least because of their extensive use of foreign workers who live and work in cramped, often less than sanitary conditions, and their world-spanning airlines making their states into global transportation hubs. In per capita terms, Qatar suffered heavily. Within six months of its first recorded case of COVID-19, in late February 2020, Qatar accounted for around 120,000 cases in total and nearly 200 related deaths. The Government compelled citizens and residents to use its own contact tracing app (imposing large fines or potential prison terms for those who failed to comply), but it was launched with serious security flaws that, though swiftly corrected, put at risk details of up to 1m. people. Otherwise, the authorities responded with robust measures to help local businesses, notably with a financial aid package worth up to 13% of national gross domestic product and six-month exemptions on utility payments and some rent agreements. Internationally, a pan-GCC meeting of finance ministers in March 2020 marked Qatar's first inclusion at such a high level since the outset of the 2017 blockade. However, no breakthrough was forthcoming, and a disagreement emerged between Qatar and Bahrain. A minor issue regarding Qatar's repatriation of Bahraini citizens from Iran during the COVID-19 crisis took on unexpected importance, leading to the Bahraini Minister of Foreign Affairs offering a fiery denunciation of Qatar's actions, confounding those following the incident, to many of whom the level of anger displayed seemed disproportionate. However, this seemed to mirror the current state of the Gulf dispute, where each side was ever more solidifying the assumption of perfidy on the part of the other as a norm of regional engagement.

Against this simmering backdrop, in early 2021 the blockade of Qatar finally concluded. Analysts argue that consistent Kuwaiti mediation incrementally inched the sides closer together, enabling the resolution. However, it is equally plausible that Saudi decision-makers, who had never been as invested in the blockade as their Emirati counterparts, decided to cut their losses. On 5 January 2021 Sheikh Tamim arrived in Al-Ula, Saudi Arabia, for a summit meeting of the GCC heads of state. At the meeting, the Amir and representatives from Bahrain, Saudi Arabia and the UAE, as well as Egypt, signed the Al-Ula Declaration, which formalized the terms of resolution. In due course, borders were reopened, trade was resumed and a level of normality returned to relations among the GCC countries, although tensions remained.

Qatar's citizens and leaders feel quite sure that they 'won' the blockade, in that they did not capitulate but stood firm. A slew of international friends and allies exerted pressure on the antagonists. Qatar pursued its case in myriad international jurisdictions (e.g. before sporting tribunals, telecommunications bodies, trade organizations, etc.) and won various small victories. While these various bodies typically found in favour of Qatar, none landed anything like a 'knockout blow'. Equally, it is plausible to argue that Qatar's fastidious approach in proving its case in myriad arenas further exerted pressure on the antagonists.

Qatar's positioning in international affairs only increased in importance in the fallout of the invasion of Ukraine by the Russian Federation in February 2022. With many European countries subsequently seeking to diversify their energy supplies away from Russia, Qatar was one of the few countries that could, at least in the medium term, provide an alternative source. Back in 2017, Qatar had announced that it was lifting the moratorium on exploration in the enormous gasfield that it shares with Iran. Its rationale at the time concerned regaining market share that was being reduced by significant US and Australian supplies, as well as a desire not to have stranded assets left in the ground in the longer term. Most notably, this resulted in two 27-year gas supply agreements with China and a 15-year agreement with Germany. By the end of the 2020s, Qatar is expected to account for up to 40% of all new LNG coming to market, even as the state seeks to address climate targets and reduce greenhouse gas emissions by 25%.

CROWNING GLORY: THE 2022 FIFA WORLD CUP

Over a decade after being awarded the rights to host the men's 2022 FIFA World Cup, Qatar's moment in the sun finally arrived in November and December 2022. Over 1m. people visited Qatar for the tournament, which was watched and 'engaged with' by around 5,000m. people worldwide. Perhaps partly because it was the first World Cup ever held in an Arab state, the final match achieved a 67.8% share of the potential audience of some 242.8m. viewers. The Qatari football team lost all their matches in a poor show, but otherwise, the tournament was a tremendous success. The event proceeded smoothly overall, the state's newly finished infrastructure coped with the influx of tourists, and the France-Argentina final is widely considered one of the great finals of the modern era. For the presentation of the winners' trophy, the Argentinian captain and one of football's greatest ever players, Lionel Messi, was enrobed in the traditional Qatari black *bisht* (cloak) by the Qatari Amir, Sheikh Tamim, an iconic moment captured forever for posterity.

Certainly, the tournament was highly controversial in a small number of European states such as the UK, Denmark, Germany and the Netherlands. Newspapers ran report after report attacking—and often lambasting—Qatar's human rights record with regard to migrant workers and the state's laws on social issues such as those related to sexual minorities. Before the tournament, Qatari organizers vociferously defended their state, arguing that a range of laws and positive changes had been implemented. Although this is perfectly true, problems persisted regarding the implementation of these laws. Indeed, Qatari citizens remained generally opposed to any such changes, and the Qatari state proved unwilling to push too far against the wishes of its own people and businesses.

Economy

FRANCIS OWTRAM

INTRODUCTION

In late 2022 the eyes of the world were on Qatar as it hosted the International Federation of Association Football/Fédération Internationale de Football Association (FIFA) World Cup, culminating in Qatar's ruler Amir Tamim bin Hamad Al Thani draping the captain of the victorious Argentinian team, Lionel Messi, in a black and gold Arabic *bisht* (cloak) as he received the trophy. The success of the tournament from a footballing and logistical perspective undoubtedly came as a great relief for Qatar's elite, after a decade of investment in building infrastructure from scratch and repeated negative headlines in the months ahead of the spectacle centring on the exploitation of labourers and project overruns. It will likely be several years before any meaningful assessment can be made as to whether the colossal investment has been worthwhile; but it is worth noting that while many have shaken their heads at the erection of multiple stadia that will perhaps never be filled regularly, much of the work centred on transport links and accommodation. The gains in terms of soft power are impossible to calculate, but there is a widespread consensus that Qatar emerged from the tournament with its credentials very much burnished, at least among consequential actors that shape commercial activity.

The authorities will also take heart from initial headline economic data. Real growth in gross domestic product (GDP) was recorded at 8.0% year on year in the fourth quarter of 2022, surpassing consensus expectations and resulting in GDP growth of 4.8% over the year as a whole. The hydrocarbons sector was a key driver of this strong performance, and the desperation of gas-importing countries to renew and extend import agreements with Qatar in the wake of sanctions against the Russian Federation stemming from its invasion of Ukraine from February 2022 will be of much more enduring utility than much of the new infrastructure. However, preparation for the tournament, the influx of fans and media rights—especially for Qatar's beIN Sports—had a clearly discernible effect on output, as the non-hydrocarbons component of GDP expanded by 6.8%, its fastest pace since 2015.

In the first quarter of 2023 GDP growth slowed to 2.7% year on year, with construction exerting an understandable drag (contracting by 12.5% year on year). However, the authorities will have taken heart from resilient visitor arrivals, boding well for hopes that Doha could come to serve as an alternative winter holiday destination to Dubai for well-heeled European visitors. Indeed, this post-World Cup resilience stretched further into 2023, as the country welcomed 1.75m. visitors in the first five months of the year, an increase of 58,000 on the same period of 2022, according to Qatar's Planning and Statistics Authority.

The aim of this essay is to provide a succinct overview and analysis of Qatar's economy and its political underpinnings: the historical context of its development prior to independence from the UK in 1971, and the development of the economy and its key sectors up to the contemporary period. The essay then breaks down this contemporary period into key and noteworthy developments, ranging from the blockade of Qatar by Saudi Arabia and other fellow Arab nations, the global coronavirus disease (COVID-19) pandemic and a tentative assessment of the post-World Cup outlook.

ACADEMIC LITERATURE ON QATAR AND ITS ECONOMY

A number of notable scholars of Gulf Studies have observed that Qatar is the state in the Gulf and indeed the Middle East on which the least has been written. Given the relative paucity of literature, key works (notably those by Gray, Fromherz, Kamrava, Ulrichsen, Wright, Zweiri and Qawasmi) are listed in the Bibliography at the end of this essay. The essay draws primarily on the existing literature, including the author's own initial historical work on the development of Qatar in the 1940s at the start of the oil era. It is beyond the scope of this essay to investigate in detail arguments relating to the nature and conceptualization of Qatar's economy: interested readers can refer to the debates between Steven Wright, who articulates a preference for an interpretation rooted in the developmental state literature, which argues for the primacy of politics, and those whose work is grounded in the rentier state literature (most notably Matthew Gray's excellent characterization of Qatar as a late-rentier state).

HISTORICAL CONTEXT OF BRITISH INVOLVEMENT AND PEARLING

Michael Quentin Morton recounts how 'in 1863 Muhammed Al Thani told an English visitor, William Palgrave, we are all from the highest to the lowest, slaves of one master: Pearl.' Although British recognition of the Al Thani family in 1868 was instrumental in the creation of Qatar as an independent and distinct political entity, Britain's main concern at that time was the suppression of maritime warfare. As in other Gulf sheikhdoms during that period, Britain had little involvement in the internal affairs of Qatar. Ottoman influence in Qatar's internal affairs had been recognized by the British up to the 1913 Anglo-Ottoman Convention. During the course of the First World War, the Sheikh of Qatar, Abdullah Al Thani, and the Political Resident in the Persian Gulf, Percy Cox, signed the 1916 Qatar Treaty. This contained a provision for Britain to post an agent in Doha, but this clause had still not been implemented by 1946, and British relations with the Ruler of Qatar continued to be conducted via the Political Agency in Bahrain. British officials reviewing the Treaty in the 1930s had found that, due to an 'oversight', the Treaty had been specific to Sheikh Abdullah personally, and that it had omitted the usual article binding his successor. In addition, Qatar's economy was severely impacted in the 1930s by the Great Depression and the introduction of synthetic Japanese pearls to the world market. It was only upon the start of the exploration for oil in 1935 that hopes emerged for Qatar's prosperity; however, the Second World War curtailed these initial activities. Nonetheless, by the late 1940s it was clear that the oil era was starting in earnest for Qatar.

OIL AND THE TRANSFORMATION OF QATAR

Writing in 1990, political scientist Jill Crystal noted that at the beginning of the 20th century Qatar's settled population numbered only 27,000; by the mid-1980s it had grown to over 350,000 and Doha had been transformed from a quiet pearling village into an urban conglomeration. By the 2020s the skyline had become unrecognizable, made up of state-of-the-art high-rise concrete and glass buildings. Oil was at the centre of this change. By the mid-20th century Qatar's dependence on oil had replaced its earlier dependence on pearling. Oil production rose rapidly, from 2,000 barrels per day (b/d) in 1949, the first year of exports, to 570,000 b/d by 1973. As described by Mirabella (2014), 'The first license for oil exploration was granted to the Anglo-Persian Oil Company (A.P.O.C.) by the ruler of Qatar, Shaikh Abdullah bin Jasim Al Thani, in 1932... Qatar's exploratory wells were drilled relatively late, especially considering that oil exploration had already begun in the 1920s, and earlier in some cases, in most other countries in the Middle East. For example, by that time, exploration had already concluded in Bahrain with the discovery of oil in 1931... In 1922, Major Frank Holmes, a British-New Zealander known as 'the Father of Oil', started seeking an exploratory lease in Qatar. A lease was granted by the Shaikh in 1926 to the British owned D'Arcy Exploration Company, a subsidiary of A.P.O.C. and early predecessor of British Petroleum (BP) ... the A.P.O.C. agreed to undertake a geological exploration of the country in return for the sole right to submit an application for a concession. The importance of oil as a resource in Qatar only grew after the crisis of the pearling industry, which was partially brought about by the introduction of cultured pearls by the Japanese into the market. The fall in value of luxury goods after the Wall Street Crash of 1929 also played its role in realigning the Qatari economy towards oil.'

After the end of the First World War and the collapse of the Ottoman Empire, Qatar came under the British sphere of influence and in 1935 Qatar's first onshore oil concession was awarded to the Anglo-Iranian Oil Company (AIOC). Because of its obligations under a 1928 agreement, AIOC transferred the concession to an associate company of the Iraq Petroleum Company, Petroleum Development (Qatar) Ltd, which was later renamed the Qatar Petroleum Company (QPC). In October 1938 drilling of the Dukhan oilfield commenced and by January 1940 it was yielding 4,000 b/d. However, exploration and development was suspended during the Second World War. The suspension of concession revenue, justified by the British as a result of a 'force majeure', combined with the collapse in pearling, placed Sheikh Abdullah in dire financial straits, even forcing him to mortgage his own home. With the resumption of oil activities after the end of the war, the Political Agent in Bahrain, C. J. Pelly, while disparaging about the conditions in Qatar, was of the view that it was 'highly important that we make a beginning really to get into Qatar'. The question remained as to the specific administrative arrangement to achieve this. Pelly initially argued against the appointment of an Assistant Political Agent for Qatar, and instead suggested the establishment of a Rest House in Doha that would be 'furnished with camp crockery ... [and] a car with it suitable for desert travel'. This would allow the Political Agent in Bahrain to keep abreast of matters in Qatar by means of monthly visits. He added that 'an officer there without a car will lose at least half of his value and about as much of his prestige'.

Sheikh Abdullah expressed concerns over increased British presence in Qatar. Pelly reported to Sir Rupert Hay, the British Political Resident in the Persian Gulf, that the Sheikh was worried that the establishment of a Rest House would impact on the assurances given to him by the British in 1916 concerning non-interference in matters of 'slavery'. According to Pelly, Sheikh Abdullah had concerns that 'if the Political Agent was going to stay 4 or 5 days at a time in Doha ... every slave in the place would be at his door clamouring to leave his master; and this would be very difficult for the Shaikh's people'.

Following this meeting, British officials discussed how to formulate the wording of any agreement with Sheikh Abdullah over the delicate matter of 'slaves in Qatar'. The Political Agent in Bahrain advanced a draft in which Britain recognized that Sheikh Abdullah had 'not conceded to His Majesty's Government the right of the manumission of slaves, and any Agent appointed to Qatar will not, therefore, attempt to exercise such a right except in cases where definite cruelty by a master towards a slave seeking manumission has been proved, and then only after consultation with Your Excellency'. Full co-operation, however, was expected in the event of any recent abductions or in the future if it concerned the territory of the Ruler. The Persian Gulf Residency inserted certain phrases that gave more leeway for British manoeuvre but authorized the Political Agent in Bahrain to negotiate the best terms possible 'so worded as to give the least handle for criticism should its contents become known'.

On 23 August 1949 Sir John Wilton arrived to take up his post as the first Political Agent in Qatar. He was advised on the order of precedence of his calls—he should visit the new Ruler, Sheikh Ali Al Thani, 'on the first day and postpone calling on Sheikh Abdullah and others until the second day'. The British Government could now better assess and manage issues of imperial involvement on the Qatar peninsula which were escalating with every new oil well sunk. In 1916 the Qatar Treaty envisaged the establishment of a Political Officer in Qatar. For more than 30 years this had not been implemented due to a combination of lack of British interest and Sheikh Abdullah's subtle negotiating skills, but now the UK had gained access to Doha.

Exports of crude petroleum commenced in 1949. Also in 1949 the first offshore concessions were granted to the International Marine Oil Company (IMOC), a subsidiary of Superior Oil and the British-registered Central Mining and Investment Corporation. In 1952, after the withdrawal of IMOC, the Shell Company Qatar (SCQ) acquired exploration rights to much offshore territory. The Idd al-Shargi and Maydan Mahzam oilfields were discovered in 1960 and 1963, respectively; the largest offshore field, Bul Hanine, was discovered in 1970 and came on stream in 1972

LABOUR UNREST

However, in the 1950s and 1960s there were several significant protests by workers in the petroleum industry. Conditions and hours of work, as well as wages, varied widely before the introduction of labour regulations. The payment of overtime was inconsistent, workers could be summarily dismissed and the majority earned a low salary compared with high-ranking members of the Al Thani family and foreign officials. Initial strikes focused on wages and conditions, and the Amir himself encouraged strike action when negotiating new contracts to pressurize the oil company into granting concessions. After strike action in 1951, the Government deported Omani workers who had come into conflicts with Qatari workers; meanwhile, in July of that year nearly 900 workers refused to return to work after the arrest of strike leaders. Ultimately, markets in the capital Doha ceased to function in a demonstration of solidarity, so the authorities were pressurized into making concessions in response to the workers' demands. Eventually, in mid-July the detained workers were released and the minimum wage was increased, albeit by a small amount. Nevertheless, strikes continued throughout 1951. Subsequently, in August 1952 a coalition of workers presented demands to the Amir's son Ahmad Al Thani, which again centred around the desire for improved working conditions, as well as a reduction in the number of foreigners holding senior positions and increased wages.

As the 1950s progressed, workers' protests became linked with other issues, particularly as Qatari workers became influenced by Arab nationalists employed from other countries, such as Iraq and Yemen. Pan-Arabism, anti-colonialism and general discontent with the ruling family came to the fore. At a major strike in 1955 the Amir ordered the police forcibly to quash the unrest. Eventually, following a very large protest in 1956 which attracted up to 2,000 participants (among them many high-ranking Qataris sympathetic to Arab nationalists and the dissatisfied petroleum-industry workers), the Government decided to include a clause in contracts of employment that prohibited political activity. However, disputes continued. In 1957 the SCQ and Ahmad Al Thani came into conflict after he ordered an additional oil refinery to be constructed with company funds. In 1959, a labour department was established by the Government and four years later, in 1963, a labour group was established, known as the National Unity Front. One of the National Unity Front's principal demands was increased rights for Qatari workers in the petroleum industry.

QATAR'S ECONOMY SINCE INDEPENDENCE: DEVELOPMENT OF OIL AND GAS

Qatar became an independent state on 3 September 1971 following the British decision, announced in 1968, to withdraw from the Gulf. Simon C. Smith notes that following independence, Qatar immediately took the opportunity in the 1970s to diversify away from British companies if better deals in terms of delivery times, quality and price for the development could be achieved for its post-independence infrastructure; this included its oil and gas sector. Even if the Qatari Amir and ruling family were favourably inclined to award a contract to a British company, if the terms offered were not sufficiently attractive, the contract would likely be placed with countries such as France or the USA.

In 1973, the state acquired 25% of both the QPC's onshore concessions and the SCQ's offshore concessions. Under the associated agreement, the Government's stake was to increase by 5% annually, until it was intended to reach 51% by 1981. However, in early 1974 the agreement was repealed, after the QPC agreed to a new arrangement allowing the Government to increase its stake in both companies to 60%. In December of that year the Government announced its intention officially to acquire the remaining stake in SCQ and QPC, and this decision was confirmed by a government decree which was passed in 1975. Later negotiations concluded in the Government assuming full ownership of the QPC's onshore concessions and the SCQ's offshore activities in September 1976 and February 1977, respectively. In this way, the oil sector was fully nationalized.

In 1991 the state-owned company Qatar Petroleum (QP—which became QatarEnergy in 2021) began to upgrade oil production capabilities, bringing the Diyab structure (Dukhan) online and increasing oil recovery, particularly at Dukhan. QP hoped to increase capacity at Dukhan to 350,000 b/d by 2008, and initiated work at other, smaller fields, including Bul Hanine and Maydam Mahzam. Prospects for new discoveries remained limited, although QP encouraged foreign operators to apply for exploration licenses, and the number of wells drilled increased towards the end of the 1980s, albeit with little success. Exploration and production (E&P) was largely carried out offshore by large multinational energy companies, such as US-registered ExxonMobil and Chevron, and the French multinational Total. Until 2017 the al-Shaheen field was operated by Denmark's Maersk Oil, in a production-sharing agreement with QP. In June 2016 Total won a tender for a 30% stake in a new joint-venture contract to operate the al-Shaheen field, with QP retaining 70%. Total oil production from al-Shaheen gradually increased from some 240,000 b/d at the beginning of 2006. By July 2017, when Total and QP officially took over operations at al-Shaheen for a 25-year period, production was some 300,000 b/d. In August 2019 Total signed deals transferring some of its assets in Kenya, Guyana and Namibia to QP. In 2021 Qatar's total oil production averaged some 1,746,000 b/d.

The Economist Intelligence Unit (EIU) reported that in June 2023 QatarEnergy signed an agreement with the China National Petroleum Company (CNPC) to supply 4m. metric tons of liquified natural gas (LNG) per year to the CNPC for 27 years. This was a similar agreement to one signed previously with another Chinese state-owned firm, Sinopec. The effect will be to make Qatar the single largest supplier of LNG to China over the period 2023–27. A further notable aspect of QatarEnergy's activity was its international expansion with proven partners in the oil and gas industry, which the EIU noted was 'aimed at diversifying risk and income away from its vast domestic gas resources'. This was achieved by making participation in international ventures a factor in the award of contracts for the further development of the vast North Field LNG expansion project beginning in 2026. QatarEnergy is now a partner with TotalEnergies, ExxonMobil, Shell (UK) and Eni (Italy) in a number of oil and gas exploration ventures in different parts of the world.

QATAR'S OIL PIPELINE AND REFINERY NETWORK

Qatar's oil pipeline network is operated by QatarEnergy, carrying supplies to the refineries and export terminals. An extensive offshore pipeline network transports crude oil from offshore oil fields to processing facilities at Halul Island or onshore to the country's first refinery at Umm Said (also known as Mesaieed), which commenced operations in 1958, and was upgraded in 1974. The primary export terminals are located at Umm Said, Halul Island and Ras Laffan. Exports have been predominantly sent to Asia, with Japan the single largest purchaser.

Refining is carried out at the Umm Said Refinery and at the two Laffan Refineries in Ras Laffan. The Umm Said Refinery has a refining capacity of some 137,000 b/d. Laffan Refinery 1 came onstream in September 2009, with a processing capacity of 146,000 b/d. Laffan Refinery 2 started production in 2016, bringing overall processing capacity at Ras Laffan to 292,000 b/d. In the early 2000s QP also launched joint ventures with Sasol of South Africa (Oryx Gas to Liquid Fuels—GTL) and British-Dutch Shell (Pearl GTL) for the production of synthetic petroleum products from natural gas.

The Dolphin Gas Project

QP participated in the Dolphin gas project, established in 1999, which aimed to connect the natural gas networks of Oman, the United Arab Emirates (UAE) and Qatar through the region's first cross-border natural gas pipeline. The project was developed by Dolphin Energy, a consortium currently comprising the Mubadala Investment Company, owned by the Government of the UAE (51%), TotalEnergies of France (24.5%) and the US company Occidental Petroleum (24.5%). The initial phase of the 420-km pipeline project was completed in mid-2007. The Dolphin Energy Pipeline is able to transport some 2,000m. cu ft per day of natural gas to markets in the UAE and Oman.

QatarGas

QatarGas was established in 1984 and through its production of LNG Qatar has become an extremely important player in the global energy market. Wright (2011) noted that Qatar had become the largest global supplier of LNG as well as GTL fuels, and at that time anticipated that by 2014 the European Union (EU) member states would account for up to 40% of Qatar's gas exports from the state-owned companies RasGas and QatarGas. A further 23% was expected to go to the USA, although by 2020 Japan, the Republic of Korea (South Korea) and India remained the most significant purchasers of Qatari LNG. Notably, in January 2020 QP signed a 15-year agreement with Kuwait for the supply of 3m. metric tons of LNG each year, with effect from 2022.

THE QATAR INVESTMENT AUTHORITY: QATAR'S SOVEREIGN WEALTH FUND

The Qatar Investment Authority (QIA) is a sovereign wealth fund, founded in 2005 to bolster the national economy through diversification into new asset classes. In 2021 the QIA had assets worth an estimated US $450,000m., according to estimates by the International Monetary Fund. The QIA's structure and methods of decision-making have, however, been widely described as non-transparent, with investments linked to the Amir and the Prime Minister. Qatar's acquisition of leading French football club Paris St Germain, and an overall focus on investment in the UK and other European countries, indicate that the QIA is keen to establish the Qatari state as a key and visible player in Europe. In his book *AngloArabia*, David Wearing outlines in detail the importance of Qatari investment for the UK, much of it made by the QIA. In 2022 the QIA helped US entrepreneur Elon Musk in his purchase of social media platform Twitter.

QATAR'S NATIONAL VISION 2030

In July 2008 the Government published a formal outline of Qatar's National Vision 2030 (QNV 2030), which was launched in October that year to 'transform Qatar into an advanced society capable of achieving sustainable development' by 2030. The QNV 2030 constituted a broad strategy for the future, promoting reduced dependence on hydrocarbons, with a focus on human, social, economic and environmental development, while at the same time emphasizing planned and regulated growth.

The QNV 2030 seeks to address challenges presented in a series of human development reports published by the General Secretariat for Development Planning since 2006. Challenges in the first report ranged from long-term demographic imbalances to a loss of cultural heritage, and it served as the foundation for the National Development Strategy 2011–16 and the Second National Development Strategy 2018–22. Much remains, however, to achieve in terms of the declared aim of transitioning to a low-carbon economy.

QNV 2030's economic development strategy involves ensuring the efficient management of the national economy, the responsible management of natural resources and the development of a knowledge-based economy. It also outlines the need for a reduction in the number of unskilled foreign workers, who constitute around 75% of the country's expatriate population, which is considered to create a dependency on non-national labour.

The Qatari authorities encourage following Islamic philosophy and adopting humanitarian values, and the Government has implemented various social programmes. Other initiatives include the promotion of sporting activities, and a focus on the family and on cultural heritage. The low rate of Qatari citizens joining the workforce is considered to represent a major challenge to human development. 'Qatarization' is an initiative intended to increase the proportion of Qatari nationals employed in both the public and private sectors. The energy and industrial sectors are aiming for one-half of their workforce to be composed of Qatari citizens by 2030, in line with prevailing policy in the rest of the country, particularly the government sector.

DIVERSIFICATION AND INDUSTRIAL POLICY

Steven Wright has noted that efforts towards economic diversification in Qatar have become a priority for state economic policy. As in other Gulf states, the majority of Qatar's GDP is derived from energy, with the natural gas sector being the most important focus of attention. The huge North Field, discovered in 1971, was identified as the world's largest non-associated gasfield (with gas produced by natural gas wells, rather than by oil wells). Qatar is estimated to hold slightly less than 10% of global natural gas deposits. Although, within the region, Iran has higher reserves of natural gas, they are dispersed over a significantly greater area, making them more costly to exploit.

In June 2022 TotalEnergies took a US $2,000m. stake in the North Field East project, which aims to help Qatar increase its LNG production by more than 60% by 2027. Qatar's Minister of State for Energy Affairs Saad bin Sharida al-Kaabi described the joint venture as 'a marriage more than an engagement', since it will last until 2054.

As noted above, Qatar has become the largest supplier of LNG products, in addition to GTL products, worldwide. A trend towards increased exports to EU countries and the USA may begin to signify a break with the past, with the majority of Qatar's gas exports having traditionally been sold to Asian buyers, such as Japan, the Republic of Korea and India. The benefit of engaging with Qatar for the EU countries is that it allows them to diversify their energy imports away from dependency on Russian fuel, of particular importance following the Russian invasion of Ukraine in February 2022. Nevertheless, it is important to note that Qatar has increasingly begun to incorporate diversion clauses into its supply agreements, a significant development that gives the country the ability to direct shipping to the most attractive markets, limited only by the need for a suitable port facility to load cargo.

Qatar's economy has benefited from revenue generated from pipeline supply and consumption, as well as tanker-based supply. The Dolphin project, discussed earlier, was the first gas export-based project within the Gulf Cooperation Council (GCC), and had potential as a precursor to any GCC gas grid with supply coming from Qatar. The UAE imports some 2,000m. cu ft from Qatar each day, supplied to Abu Dhabi and Dubai by Dolphin Energy.

Stimulating a Knowledge Economy

Record GDP growth has given confidence to policy-makers in Qatar. Qatar is seeking to emulate the UAE's successful diversification efforts by promoting a 'knowledge economy' sector that could de-couple the country from the overwhelming predominance of the oil and gas sector. A notable example of this is Qatar's 'Education City' in Doha, which has a large number of campuses of top Western universities providing undergraduate, taught postgraduate and PhD research degrees.

Economic Diversification and the Environment

Qatar's efforts to moderate its reliance on the hydrocarbons sector indicate a recognition of the need to rebalance the country's economy, including the proposals discussed above for seeking a transformation into a knowledge-based economy. The successful expansion of Qatar's economy from the mid-1990s was based on exploitation of its massive North Field gas reserves. But the country's leaders inevitably realize that hydrocarbons resources are finite. In 2021 Qatar had reserves of 25,000m. barrels. Its proven reserves are equivalent to 402.1 times its annual consumption: this means that, without net exports, there would be about 402 years of oil left (at current consumption levels and excluding unproven reserves).

The Government is preoccupied with issues relating to the North Field gas reserve and in 2022 was receiving investment to develop a massive new gas field, North Field East. As part of its efforts towards diversification, the Government has also been gradually increasing its industrial investments, which may reduce vulnerabilities in the energy sector, but also help to create employment in a country where around one-quarter of the population are below the age of 25.

The Government has means of support available that are not directly related to its hydrocarbons base. The QIA has an array of foreign assets that provide a valuable source of capital diversification, mainly held offshore in foreign currency instruments, including 'blue chip' equities, bonds and property. In May 2022 the ratings agency Moody's assigned a foreign currency senior unsecured programme rating of P(Aa3) to the Government of Qatar's global medium-term note programme, reflecting a long-term issuer rating of Aa3, owing to Qatar's high income per-head and its immense energy reserves.

The much-discussed growth in the knowledge economy may help in diversifying the economy. But Qatar needs to improve the performance of significant non-oil sectors too, such as steel and aluminium. Qatar Aluminium Co (Qatalum—jointly owned by QP and Hydro of Norway) was inaugurated in April 2010. The smelter had an annual capacity of 585,000 metric tons per year. Industry is not the only driver of economic growth, however. There have also been substantial efforts made towards the development of Qatar as an air-route hub, and Qatar has also made efforts to expand its financial sector. Nevertheless, in the short term at least, the country's energy resources continue to drive the economy, especially as even apparently non-hydrocarbons sectors, such as manufacturing, are dependent to some extent on the oil and gas sector.

According to Oxford Economics, Qatar and most of the Middle East and North Africa region as a whole have the financial and natural resources to enable them to undertake the transition towards low-carbon energy sources. By building on existing plans for economic diversification, the region could bridge the investment gap with more environmentally sound capital stock. By these means, some countries in the GCC have the potential to become leaders in the fight against climate change. Oxford Economics stated that the region overall held significant potential for developing solar and wind energy, which could be further expanded with improvements in storage technology. Notably, in 2017 the Qatari Government, together with the Qatar General Electricity and Water Corporation (Kahramaa) and others, commenced work on the development of Qatar's first large renewable energy project, Siraj 1 (the Al Kharsaah Solar PV Independent Power Producer Project). Nevertheless, since the Russian invasion of Ukraine, Qatar—previously berated by the West for not doing enough to curb oil and gas production to combat climate change—has been exhorted to exploit more gas, as the West seeks to limit Russian energy imports in order to restrict the funds available to Russian President Vladimir Putin to finance his war in Ukraine.

A further sector targeted as part of diversification efforts is tourism. In early September 2022 Qatar Tourism announced that the number of visitors had reached 151,000 in July—the largest number of summer arrivals recorded since 2017, representing an increase of 297% year on year. Qatar had also eased its COVID-19 requirements for incoming travellers, by removing its 'red travel list' and mask mandate, although visitors to Qatar were required to present a negative antigen test result. A new large-scale advertising campaign was launched to promote Qatar as a stopover destination, as it prepared to admit some 1.2m. visitors for the World Cup in November–December 2022. Qatar was to add over 100 new hotels and apartments to its portfolio of tourist properties. New hotels included the Pullman Doha West and Hilton's Double Tree Doha Downtown Hotel, as well as plans for the opening of luxury eco-hotel The Outpost Al Barari in November and the construction of the new Katara Hills LXR Hotels and Resorts, to comprise 15 luxury villas together with private pools.

In the short term, the World Cup was expected to stimulate both recovery and diversification and play a significant role in the Government's diversification strategy, covering six principal areas: diversification and private sector development; fiscal management and innovation; digitization; globalization and talent attraction; value creation; and energy transition and sustainability.

QNV 2030 has outlined several distinct challenges facing Qatar's environment, which include the rapidly growing population, increased air pollution and damage to natural habitats. One method employed by Qatar to address environmental issues was through the acquisition of more advanced technology. Government reports claimed that gas flaring (the burning of natural gas associated with oil extraction) was reduced by nearly one-half during 2008–12 through the adoption of new technology. Other strategies implemented to further environmental development included conducting environmental awareness campaigns and promoting sustainable urban growth.

KEY DEVELOPMENTS IN THE CONTEMPORARY PERIOD

This section examines some key developments in the contemporary period, including the blockade of Qatar by some of its neighbouring states, the COVID-19 pandemic and preparations for the 2022 World Cup.

The Blockade of Qatar

The blockade of Qatar that was implemented from 5 June 2017 by Saudi Arabia, the UAE, Bahrain and Egypt was not only a political event but had immense economic ramifications, as outlined by Kristian Ulrichsen. During a hacking attack on Qatari news websites in May, fake comments were inserted in support of Iran and the Palestinian Islamic Resistance Movement (Hamas) and attributed to Amir Tamim of Qatar. This provided the pretext for Saudi Arabia, the UAE, Bahrain and Egypt to announce the closure of Qatar's land border and surrounding sea and air space, representing an immediate economic shock. Qatar, which denied the reports, implemented various remedial measures to minimize economic risks and sought to introduce economic and financial measures to reassure foreign investors and create opportunities for local businesses by re-routing trade through other countries, including Oman and Iran, and expanding both domestic food production and manufacturing. Qatar announced its decision to leave the Organization of Petroleum Exporting Countries (OPEC) in December 2018, stating that its exit was the result of its increasing focus on natural gas as its main export (Qatari petroleum represented only some 2% of OPEC's output). Qatar had been a member of OPEC since 1961, and some observers regarded the move as a result of the rift between Qatar and its erstwhile Arab allies. The blockade was finally lifted on 5 January 2021 with the signing of the Al-Ula Declaration, which also restored travel links between Qatar and the blockading countries. However, another shock had hit in the mean time: the COVID-19 pandemic.

Qatar's Economy Recovers from COVID-19

With the impact of the COVID-19 pandemic, which spread around the world in early 2020, together with a steep drop in oil and gas prices, Qatar's economy experienced challenges throughout 2020 and the first half of 2021, resulting in a recession and GDP contracting by 3.6% in 2020. However, recovery was aided by several factors, not least a spectacular rebound in energy prices from the second half of 2021.

By July 2021 the Purchasing Managers' Index (PMI), a measure of economic activity calculated from a monthly survey of major companies, showed expansionary trends in private sector non-petroleum-orientated GDP. GDP rebounded to record growth of 1.5% in 2021 and 4.0% in 2022. Growth in non-oil sectors such as construction, transportation and real estate led the expansion, which was, however, offset by declines in mining and manufacturing. The PMI indicated an ongoing improvement in the non-oil sector, suggesting that its strong performance would continue to offset weaknesses in the oil sector and contribute to overall annual growth.

Oil Prices Increase following Outbreak of Conflict in Ukraine

The significant increase in oil prices that followed Russia's invasion of Ukraine in February 2022 was of great benefit to Qatar's budget. The conflict in Ukraine helped Qatar to increase its influence over global energy flows, as the West searched for alternative sources of energy in wake of the invasion. The subsequent imposition of sanctions on Russia by Western nations gave the Gulf state a boost in revenues as it was embarking on the North Field East development project. There was greatly increased demand from the EU for Qatari gas, as many EU member states sought to reduce their dependence on Russian gas supplies over a relatively short time frame. Meanwhile, Russia demonstrated its willingness to use the supply of gas as a political weapon, after halting exports to several states, as well as ceasing transmission via a key European pipeline. Over the longer term, however, trends are moving towards the decarbonization of the global economy in order to combat climate change, the effects of which are becoming ever more apparent.

Impact of FIFA 2022 World Cup and Its Aftermath

The rise in oil prices following Russia's invasion of Ukraine was one major factor that boosted the economy of Qatar in that year, another was the FIFA World Cup. The World Cup hosted by Qatar in 2022 was the most expensive ever held, with a total of US $220,000m. being spent after the tournament was awarded to Qatar in 2010. However, as noted by the EIU, the money spent by Qatar on projects was not just for the World Cup per se. Rather, this investment fed into a long-term development strategy, which encompassed a massive upgrading of Qatar's infrastructure, including the construction of a metro and railway network, roads and airport expansion, residential units and hotel accommodation. Some visitors during the World Cup stayed on Pearl Island, an artificial island incorporating a mixed-use complex, including residential apartments and hotels, built on the site of a former major pearling area. The vast majority of international visitors to the World Cup travelled to Qatar by air.

Of particular note for the establishment of Qatar as an aviation transport hub is that in March 2022 the UN's International Civil Aviation Authority granted Qatar's request (made in 2018) for its own Flight Information Region (FIR) rather than being subsumed under the one controlled by Bahrain. The latter country was among those that had imposed a blockade on Qatar between 2017 and 2021 at the behest of Saudi Arabia. The acquisition of a FIR has increased Qatar's sovereign control of its airspace.

All of this had the potential to raise Qatar's profile as an international business hub and tourist destination as envisaged in the Government's economic development plan. Central to the achievement of this is the country's flag carrier, Qatar Airways, which in 2023 expanded its range of destinations and in August of that year signed an agreement to establish a cargo hub in Rwanda. This will support the airline's operations in East Africa and further afield as it endeavours to become the Middle East's leading air hub for both passenger and cargo, capitalizing on the geographical centrality of the Gulf region in global transport logistics and sub-Saharan Africa's status as a crucial global provider of natural resources.

The World Cup was not without its controversies which had the potential to impact on Qatar's economy in the future in terms of the country's status as a destination for international tourism. LGBT (lesbian, gay, bisexual and transgender) football fans around the world expressed reservations about travelling to a place where judicial penalties for homosexuality range from imprisonment of one to three years to the death penalty for Muslims tried and found 'guilty' in a *shari'a* (Islamic law) court. Furthermore, in terms of human rights, the employment practices connected to the construction of the new stadia were brought into sharp focus, especially as international media began to hone in on the country in the run-up to the tournament. In mid-August 2022, as Qatar made final preparations for the World Cup, some 60 migrant workers protested about unpaid wages outside the offices of the Al Bandary International Group, a construction and engineering company, in Doha. Some workers had reportedly not been paid for seven months. The Qatari Government told the British Broadcasting Corporation (BBC) that a number of workers had been found to be in breach of public security laws and detained, with those 'who failed to remain peaceful' being deported. The Qatari Government pledged to pay all delayed salaries and benefits to the affected workers, and asserted that the Al Bandary group was under investigation for non-payment of salaries to workers, and that further action was being taken after a deadline to settle payments had been missed. Despite the Government's pledge, many observers expressed their concern that wealthy company owners should apparently deem it acceptable business practice not to pay workers recruited from some of the most impoverished regions of the world, who were effectively exploited victims caught in a form of modern-day slavery.

CONCLUSION

After withstanding one of the most testing economic blockades in modern history during 2017–21, Qatar has benefited from renewed vast revenues as oil prices increased to around US $100 per barrel following the Russian invasion of Ukraine in 2022 and then settled at around the $70–$80 mark. In September 2023 the respected *Gulf States Newsletter* felt able to conclude that the Qatari Amir had 'entered into his second decade as ruler in a strong position, having dealt with the regional blockade, the Covid pandemic and the Fifa World Cup'. Qatar has sought to leverage the impact of its successful hosting of the FIFA 2022 World Cup and has achieved some measure of success in diversification across a range of sectors, including cultural tourism, sports broadcasting and tourists travelling for sporting events, but oil and gas revenues will continue to constitute the Government's main source of income well beyond the short to medium term. Beyond the repercussions generated by Russia's invasion of Ukraine and associated hydrocarbon power plays, the world remains largely poised to wean itself off its dependence on oil and gas, so the challenge still stands for Qatar to demonstrate that it has the capacity to cope with this transition as set out in QNV 2030.

Given that the country's vast sovereign wealth fund will accrue sufficient income into the foreseeable future, the more salient question may be whether Qataris will maintain their support for the Al Thani family over the long term and remain quiescent on matters of politics and power. It would appear that provided that Qatari citizens remain prosperous, and given a tendency to outsource work to migrant workers from South Asia, the answer is likely to remain in the affirmative. More pertinent perhaps is the question of how long the imported workforce is prepared to remain quiet should its conditions of work and pay in Qatar be consistently undermined. Ultimately, however, Qatar maintains the capacity to suppress any such manifestations of imported migrant labour discontent and there are numerous public relations agencies vying for lucrative contracts to spin away negative optics and deflect reputational costs.

Bibliography

Abu Omar, A. 'Qatar's Economy Stalls After Last Year's World Cup and Gas Boom', 31 August 2023, www.bloomberg.com/news/articles/2023-08-31/qatar-s-economy-stalls-after-last-year-s-world-cup-and-gas-boom.

Crystal, Jill. *Oil and Politics in the Gulf: Kuwait and Qatar*. Cambridge, Cambridge University Press, 2011.

Davidson, Christopher. *The Persian Gulf and Pacific Asia: From Indifference to Interdependence*. London, Hurst, 2010.

Davidson, Christopher (Ed.). *Power and Politics in the Persian Gulf States*. London, Hurst, 2011.

Economist Intelligence Unit.

FIFA World Cup 2022 is a game changer for Qatar, 1 November 2022.

Qatar seals second LNG delivery deal with Chinese importer, 12 July 2023.

Qatar Airways expands aviation co-operation with Rwanda, 29 August 2023.

Qatar Energy accelerates its international expansion drive, 18 January 2023.

FinancialAdvice.co.uk. 'Is the Economy Becoming Something of a Financial Football?', www.financialadvice.co.uk/news/12/ukeconomy/10379/is-the-economy-becoming-something-of-a-political-football.html.

Fromherz, Allen James. *Qatar: A Modern History*. London, I.B. Tauris, 2012.

Gray, Matthew. *Qatar: Politics and the Challenges of Development*. Boulder, CO, Lynne Rienner, 2013.

Gray, Matthew. *The Economy of the Gulf States*. Newcastle, Agenda Publishing, 2018.

Gulf States Newsletter. 'Qatar Searches for a New Strategy After World Cup and Tamim's First Decade in Power', 1 September 2023.

Gulf Times. 'Qatar's non-oil sector strength to counterbalance oil sector weakness in 2022: Oxford Economics', July 2022, www.gulf-times.com/story/720738/Qatar-s-non-oil-sector-strength-to-counterbalance-oil-sector-weakness-in-2022-Oxford-Economics.

Hanieh, Adam. *Money, Markets and Monarchies: The Gulf Cooperation Council and the Political Economy of the Contemporary Middle East*. Cambridge, Cambridge University Press, 2018.

Hobbs, Mark. 'Twilight of Pearl Trade Sees "Slave" Divers Seek Freedoms', Qatar Digital Library, 11 October 2017, www.qdl.qa/en/twilight-pearl-trade-sees-%E2%80%98slave%E2%80%99-divers-seek-freedoms.

Kamrava, Mehran. *Qatar: Small State, Big Politics*. Cornell, Cornell University Press, 2013.

Lucente, Adam. 'Qatar's sovereign wealth fund, Dubai's Vy Capital help Elon Musk buy Twitter', May 2022, www.aldmonitor.com/originals/2022/05/qatars-sovereign-wealth-fund-dubais-vy-capital-help-elon-musk-buy-twitter.

Middle East Economic Digest. 'Creating a Knowledge Economy in Qatar', 30 May 2008, www.meed.com/creating-a-knowledge-economy-in-qatar.

Mirabella, Valentina. 'The Qatar Oil Concession Ushers in a New Era for British Relations with Doha', Qatar Digital Library, 14 October 2014, www.qdl.qa/en/qatar-oil-concession-ushers-new-era-british-relations-doha.

Mogielnicki, Robert. *A Political Economy of Free Zones in Arab Gulf States*. Basingstoke, Palgrave, 2021.

Morton, Michael Quentin. *Masters of the Pearl: A History of Qatar*. London, Reaktion, 2020.

Oh, Wonee. 'Small State Diplomacy and Branding of Qatar', Georgetown University Qatar, 2014, blogs.commons.georgetown.edu/sabr-034-summer2014/2014/05/23/small-state-diplomacy-and-branding-of-qatar.

Owtram, Francis. 'Petroleum and the Politics of Non-Interference: The First Political Officer in Qatar', Qatar Digital Library, 24 March 2021, www.qdl.qa/en/petroleum-and-politics-non-interference-first-political-officer-qatar.

Owtram, Francis. 'A Dispensary for Doha: Healthcare, Subterfuge and External Political Influence in late 1940s Qatar'. Qatar Digital Library, 18 October 2021, www.qdl.qa/en/dispensary-doha-healthcare-subterfuge-and-external-political-influence-late-1940s-qatar.

Peterson, John E. *Qatar and the World: Branding for a Micro-State*. Washington, DC, Middle East Institute, 2006.

PriceWaterhouseCooper, 2021, www.pwc.com/m1/en/media-centre/2021/qatar-economy-emerges-from-covid19-in-position-of-strength.html.

Rahman, Hussein. *The Emergence of Qatar*. London, Keegan Paul, 2005.

Smith, Simon C. 'Imperialism After Empire? Britian and Qatar in the aftermath of the withdrawal from East of Suez'. *Middle Eastern Studies*, 58:6, pp. 843–858, 2022.

Thomas, Merlyn. 'Qatar deports migrant workers after wage protest', BBC, 23 August 2022, www.bbc.co.uk/news/world-middle-east-62645350.

Ulrichsen, Kristian. *The International Political Economy of Arab Gulf States*. Basingstoke, Palgrave, 2016.

Ulrichsen, Kristian. *Qatar and the Blockade: A Study in Resilience*. London, Hurst, 2020.

Ulrichsen, Kristian. *The Blockade of Qatar and Lessons for Small States*, National University of Singapore, Middle East Institute, 19 October 2020, mei.nus.edu.sg/think_in/the-blockade-of-qatar-and-lessons-for-small-states.

Wearing, David. *AngloArabia: Why Gulf Wealth Matters to Britain*. Cambridge, Polity Press, 2018.

Wikipedia. *Qatar Energy*. Available at: en.wikipedia.org/wiki/QatarEnergy.

Wright, Steven 'Qatar' in Davidson, Christopher (Ed.), *Power and Politics in the Persian Gulf States*. London, Hurst, 2011.

Wright, Steven. 'Conceptualising Qatar's Political Economy as a Developmental State' in Zweiri, Mahjoob and Al Qawasmi, F. (Eds), *Contemporary Qatar: Examining State and Society*, Singapore, Springer Nature, 2021.

Zweiri, Mahjoob and Al Qawasmi, Farah (Eds). *Contemporary Qatar: Examining State and Society*. Singapore, Springer Nature, 2021.

Statistical Survey

Sources (unless otherwise stated): Dept of Economic Policies, Qatar Central Bank, POB 1234, Doha; tel. 4456456; fax 4318346; e-mail fssd@qcb.gov.qa; internet www.qcb.gov.qa; Planning and Statistics Authority, POB 1855, Doha Tower, Doha; tel. 4958888; fax 4839999; e-mail info@psa.gov.qa; internet www.psa.gov.qa.

Area and Population

AREA, POPULATION AND DENSITY

Area (sq km)	11,493*
Population (census results)†	
20 April 2015	2,404,776
1 December 2020	
Males	2,034,518
Females	811,600
Total	2,846,118
Population (official estimates at mid-year)‡	
2021	2,504,910
2022	2,658,311
Density (per sq km) at mid-2022	231.3

* 4,437 sq miles.
† Including resident workers from abroad.
‡ Estimates not adjusted to take account of results of 2020 census.

POPULATION BY AGE AND SEX
(official estimates at mid-2022)

	Males	Females	Total
0–14 years	152,923	146,971	299,894
15–64 years	1,819,474	501,953	2,321,427
65 years and over	22,721	14,269	36,990
Total	1,995,118	663,193	2,658,311

PRINCIPAL TOWNS
(population of municipalities at 2020 census)

Al-Dawha (Doha)	1,186,023	Umm Slal	149,701
Al-Rayyan	826,786	Al-Khor–Al-Thakhira	140,453
Al-Wakra	265,102	Al-Daayan	100,083
Al-Sheehaniya	161,240	Al-Shamal	16,730

BIRTHS, MARRIAGES AND DEATHS

	Registered live births		Registered marriages		Registered deaths	
	Number	Rate (per 1,000)	Number	Rate (per 1,000)	Number	Rate (per 1,000)
2017	27,906	10.2	3,719	1.4	2,294	0.8
2018	28,069	10.2	3,765	1.4	2,385	0.9
2019	28,412	10.8	3,621	1.3	2,200	0.8
2020	29,014	10.2	4,247	1.5	2,811	1.0
2021	26,319	9.6	4,390	1.6	2,841	1.0

2021 Registered marriages 4,390.

Life expectancy (years at birth, estimates): 79.3 (males 78.3; females 80.9) in 2021 (Source: World Bank, World Development Indicators database).

ECONOMICALLY ACTIVE POPULATION
(labour force surveys, population aged 15 years and over, 2021)

	Qatari	Non-Qatari	Total
Agriculture, hunting, forestry and fishing	33	26,686	26,719
Mining and quarrying	5,877	27,807	33,684
Manufacturing	1,868	104,396	106,264
Electricity, gas and water	2,944	12,007	14,951
Construction	1,561	666,480	668,041
Wholesale and retail trade; repair of motor vehicles, motorcycles and personal and household goods	1,608	244,045	245,653
Hotels and restaurants	1,903	73,248	75,151
Transport and storage	2,445	133,472	135,917
Information and communications	3,426	17,464	20,890
Financial intermediation	4,226	17,449	21,675
Real estate, renting and business activities	948	15,164	16,112
Public administration	63,332	47,866	111,198
Professional, scientific and technical activities	612	48,392	49,004
Administrative and support service activities	1,506	177,527	179,033
Education	13,282	44,126	57,408
Health and social work	7,828	67,957	75,785
Arts, entertainment and recreation	1,680	3,821	5,501
Other community, social and personal service activities	164	10,551	10,715
Private households with employed persons	—	160,786	160,786

QATAR

—continued	Qatari	Non-Qatari	Total
Extraterritorial organizations and bodies	262	6,835	7,097
Total employed	115,505	1,906,079	2,021,584
Unemployed	427	2,323	2,750
Total labour force	115,932	1,908,402	2,024,334
Males	70,445	1,644,497	1,714,942
Females	45,487	263,905	309,392

Health and Welfare

KEY INDICATORS

Total fertility rate (children per woman, 2021)	1.8
Under-5 mortality rate (per 1,000 live births, 2021)	5.3
HIV/AIDS (% of persons aged 15–49, 2021)	0.2
COVID-19: Cumulative confirmed deaths (per 100,000 persons at 30 June 2023)	25.6
COVID-19: Fully vaccinated population (% of total population at 7 May 2023)	105.8
Physicians (per 1,000 head, 2018)	2.5
Hospital beds (per 1,000 head, 2017)	1.3
Domestic health expenditure (2020): US $ per head (PPP)	3,108.1
Domestic health expenditure (2020): % of GDP	3.3
Domestic health expenditure (2020): public (% of total current health expenditure)	79.1
Total carbon dioxide emissions ('000 metric tons, 2019)	91,970
Carbon dioxide emissions per head (metric tons, 2019)	32.5
Human Development Index (2021): ranking	42
Human Development Index (2021): value	0.855

Note: For data on COVID-19 vaccinations, 'fully vaccinated' denotes receipt of all doses specified by approved vaccination regime (Sources: Johns Hopkins University and Our World in Data). Data on health expenditure refer to current general government expenditure in each case. For more information on sources and further definitions for all indicators, see Health and Welfare Statistics: Sources and Definitions section (europaworld.com/credits).

Agriculture

PRINCIPAL CROPS
('000 metric tons)

	2019	2020	2021
Aubergines (Eggplants)	5.4	5.8	6.2
Barley	0.2	0.3	0.1
Cabbages and other brassicas	2.0	2.3	2.3
Cantaloupes and other melons	2.0	0.9	0.3
Cauliflowers and broccoli	1.9	1.7	1.4
Chillies and peppers, green	2.4	3.4	4.1
Dates	25.8	26.6	28.7
Maize, green*	1.0	1.0	1.0
Onions, dry	2.5	2.7	1.5
Pumpkins, squash and gourds	10.5	7.2	9.6
Tomatoes	28.3	31.8	39.5

* FAO estimates.

Aggregate production ('000 metric tons, may include official, semi-official or estimated data): Total cereals 1.0 in 2019, 1.5 in 2020, 3.3 in 2021; Total fruit (primary) 28.9 in 2019, 28.3 in 2020, 30.4 in 2021; Total vegetables (primary) 84.8 in 2019, 96.5 in 2020, 92.0 in 2022.

Source: FAO.

LIVESTOCK
('000 head, year ending September)

	2019	2020	2021
Camels	131.1	125.9	119.6
Cattle	43.1	44.7	50.7
Chickens*	2,718	3,000	3,000
Goats	441.3	458.8	384.7
Horses	9.7	10.9	12.0
Sheep	1,009.0	1,021.7	921.4

* FAO estimates.
Source: FAO.

LIVESTOCK PRODUCTS
('000 metric tons, FAO estimates unless otherwise indicated)

	2019	2020	2021
Camel meat	1.9	1.0	1.4
Camels' milk	20.2	19.6	18.9
Cows' milk	7.5	7.5	7.5
Chicken meat	27.0*	34.8	35.3
Goat meat	1.6	0.9	1.1
Goats' milk	10.5	10.7	9.6
Sheep meat	9.4	9.3	8.2
Sheep offals, edible	1.8	1.7	1.5
Sheep's (Ewes') milk	13.0	13.1	12.4
Hen eggs	7.9	9.1	9.4

* Unofficial figure.
Source: FAO.

Fishing

(metric tons, live weight)

	2019	2020	2021
Capture	17,130	15,087	16,555
Groupers	1,331	1,039	1,583
Grunts and sweetlips	162	194	258
Emperors (Scavengers)	3,794	3,087	2,712
Narrow-barred Spanish mackerel	1,905	2,507	2,598
King soldier bream	452	346	426
Spinefeet (Rabbitfishes)	1,159	929	1,066
Aquaculture	22	23	114
Total catch	17,152	15,109	16,668

Source: FAO.

Mining

	2020	2021	2022
Crude petroleum ('000 metric tons)	71,651	72,821	74,084
Natural gas (million cu m)*	174,935	176,980	178,411

* Excluding gas flared or recycled.
Source: Energy Institute, *Statistical Review of World Energy*.

QATAR

Industry

SELECTED PRODUCTS
(000 metric tons unless otherwise indicated)

	2018	2019	2020
Ammonia (for fertilizer)	3,724.0	3,771.0	3,786.0
Urea (for fertilizer)	5,655.0	5,772.0	5,801.0
Cement*†	4,800	4,500	n.a.
Liquefied natural gas (million metric tons)*	76	78	n.a.
Ethylene	779.5	1,424.0	1,351.0
Methanol	1,091.0	932.0	1,067.0
Electrical energy (million kWh)	47,913	49,873	49,259

* Source: US Geological Survey.
† Estimates.

2014 (million barrels): Petrol (motor spirit—gasoline) 16.9; Naphtha 30.2; Jet fuel (incl. kerosene) 24.6; Gas oil 16.4; Diesel 32.0.

Finance

CURRENCY AND EXCHANGE RATES

Monetary Units
100 dirhams = 1 Qatar riyal (QR).

Sterling, Dollar and Euro Equivalents (31 May 2023)
£1 sterling = 4.500 riyals;
US $1 = 3.640 riyals;
€1 = 3.889 riyals;
100 Qatar riyals = £22.22 = $27.47 = €25.72.

Exchange Rate
Since June 1980 the official mid-point rate has been fixed at US $1 = QR 3.64.

BUDGET
(QR million, year ending 31 December)

Revenue	2020	2021	2022
Petroleum and natural gas	134,080	156,342	253,209
Miscellaneous transferable	37,895	37,384	44,580
Total	171,975	193,726	297,789

Expenditure	2020	2021	2022
Current expenditure	115,922	119,635	208,742
Wages and salaries	57,997	58,730	62,873
Capital expenditure	3,510	3,528	4,846
Development expenditure	63,022	68,972	70,527
Total	182,454	192,135	284,115

INTERNATIONAL RESERVES
(US $ million at 31 December)

	2020	2021	2022
Gold (national valuation)	3,453.9	3,309.7	5,382.2
IMF special drawing rights	396.6	1,374.0	1,308.8
Reserve position in IMF	291.7	283.5	281.6
Foreign exchange	36,836.2	37,235.4	40,451.2
Total	40,978.5	42,202.6	47,423.8

Source: IMF, *International Financial Statistics*.

MONEY SUPPLY
(QR million at 31 December)

	2020	2021	2022
Currency outside depository corporations	13,791	12,708	13,264
Transferable deposits	164,168	175,042	199,986
Other deposits	421,928	420,750	501,232
Broad money	599,887	608,500	714,482

Source: IMF, *International Financial Statistics*.

COST OF LIVING
(Consumer Price Index; base: 2018 = 100)

	2020	2021	2022
Food and non-alcoholic beverages	100.2	102.9	107.1
Clothing and footwear	94.5	91.9	92.6
Housing, water, electricity and gas	92.7	88.0	93.6
All items (incl. others)	96.6	98.8	103.7

NATIONAL ACCOUNTS
(QR million at current prices)
Expenditure on the Gross Domestic Product

	2020	2021	2022
Government final consumption expenditure	115,410	108,921	110,480
Private final consumption expenditure	136,549	143,122	167,280
Gross capital formation	230,497	239,898	258,936
Total domestic expenditure	482,455	491,942	536,695
Exports of goods and services	258,197	385,313	601,213
Less Imports of goods and services	214,995	223,230	274,158
GDP in purchasers' values	525,657	654,025	863,750
GDP at constant 2018 prices	648,027	658,338	690,125

Gross Domestic Product by Economic Activity

	2020	2021	2022
Agriculture and fishing	1,781	1,951	2,201
Mining and quarrying*	152,343	240,752	380,079
Manufacturing	41,586	57,323	80,255
Electricity, gas and water	6,053	6,517	6,805
Construction	75,112	87,839	99,542
Trade, restaurants and hotels	48,807	53,593	61,711
Transport and communications	30,970	36,861	48,087
Finance, insurance, real estate and business services	112,337	121,315	137,096
Public administration	48,255	44,945	45,588
Education	11,559	11,243	11,467
Health	13,771	13,310	13,352
Other services	11,553	11,421	13,131
Sub-total	554,127	687,070	898,314
Import duties	3,087	3,391	4,231
Less Imputed bank service charge	31,556	36,436	39,795
GDP in purchasers' values	525,657	654,025	863,750

* Including services incidental to mining of petroleum and natural gas.

BALANCE OF PAYMENTS
(QR million)

	2020	2021	2022*
Exports of goods f.o.b.	187,474	317,420	476,711
Imports of goods f.o.b.	−88,695	−97,786	−122,012
Trade balance	98,779	219,634	354,699
Exports of services	70,723	66,780	111,851
Imports of services	−126,300	−124,998	−149,241
Balance on goods and services	43,202	161,416	317,309
Other income received	38,140	37,730	51,629
Other income paid	−49,222	−47,787	−81,800
Balance on goods, services and income	32,120	151,359	287,138
Current transfers (net)	−42,988	−55,557	−57,389
Current balance	−10,868	95,802	229,749
Capital account (net)	−613	−526	−808
Financial account (net)	18,071	−85,203	−196,686
Net errors and omissions	−4,725	−6,027	−7,163
Overall balance	1,865	4,046	−25,092

* Preliminary.

External Trade

PRINCIPAL COMMODITIES
(distribution by HS, QR million)

Imports	2020	2021	2022
Live animals and animal products	3,888.4	3,937.8	5,330.2
Vegetables and vegetable products	3,822.1	3,550.4	4,253.1
Prepared foodstuffs; beverages, spirits, vinegar; tobacco and articles thereof	3,355.4	3,270.1	4,621.1
Mineral products	2,115.5	2,987.1	4,268.7
Chemicals and related products	8,934.5	9,893.8	11,269.3
Plastics, rubber, and articles thereof	3,049.4	3,505.5	3,936.3
Textiles and textile articles	3,700.0	3,676.1	4,453.6
Iron and steel; other base metals and articles of base metal	8,526.7	9,207.3	9,958.4
Articles of iron and steel	4,283.5	4,184.5	4,652.3
Machinery and mechanical appliances; electrical equipment; parts thereof	25,716.3	27,653.3	30,181.6
Boilers, machinery, etc.	17,596.6	17,960.1	19,800.9
Electrical machinery and equipment; sound and television recorders and reproducers	8,119.7	9,693.2	10,380.7
Vehicles, vessels, aircraft and other transport equipment	11,701.6	11,093.1	12,048.7
Vehicles other than trains, vessels and air and spacecraft	4,434.4	6,942.8	8,071.8
Aircraft, spacecraft, etc.	3,431.8	2,870.6	3,499.2
Ships, boats and floating structures	3,213.4	981.9	408.4
Optical, medical apparatus, clocks, watches; musical instruments	2,959.3	3,414.1	3,815.1
Arms, ammunition and parts thereof	2,558.9	1,407.9	6,908.2
Pearls, precious or semi-precious stones, precious metals, and articles thereof	2,329.9	4,897.0	4,380.9
Miscellaneous manufactured articles	3,270.5	3,971.1	5,062.0
Works of art, collectors' pieces and antiques	3,311.3	3,542.0	4,067.0
Total (incl. others)	94,039.0	101,866.9	121,863.6

Exports*	2020	2021	2022
Mineral products	153,520.7	269,970.9	419,482.7
Mineral fuels and oils, and products thereof	153,382.0	267,914.8	416,126.7
Petroleum oil and oils from bituminous minerals, etc. (crude)	26,402.8	44,981.0	68,171.3
Petroleum oils and oils obtained from bituminous minerals (excluding crude)	11,832.0	28,605.9	37,088.6
Petroleum gases and other gaseous hydrocarbons	115,145.6	194,317.4	310,865.9
Chemicals and related products	10,720.9	17,743.6	24,483.7
Plastics, rubber and articles thereof	7,582.0	11,597.2	12,442.3
Plastics and articles thereof	7,552.8	11,557.3	12,373.3
Iron and steel, other base metals and articles of base metal	5,514.0	8,153.2	10,370.5
Total (incl. others)	187,475.1	317,420.0	476,710.7

*Including re-exports (QR million): 9,534.5 in 2020; 10,244.2 in 2021; 10,277.6 in 2022.

PRINCIPAL TRADING PARTNERS
(QR million)

Imports	2020	2021	2022
Australia	1,753.1	1,920.7	2,383.5
Belgium	615.9	1,252.5	785.1
Brazil	1,018.4	749.3	1,384.7
China, People's Republic	14,014.9	16,562.2	19,796.3
France	3,068.5	2,712.3	3,265.5
Germany	5,759.6	5,888.0	6,048.2
India	4,885.1	6,468.7	7,533.7
Indonesia	707.4	1,290.9	794.0
Italy	4,085.0	5,112.9	6,936.7
Japan	3,043.8	3,310.6	3,134.1
Korea, Republic	1,089.5	1,445.3	1,866.7
Malaysia	1,043.8	1,098.7	1,128.8
Netherlands	1,267.3	1,121.1	1,544.4
Norway	126.4	162.2	2,049.9
Oman	2,194.6	2,221.5	3,680.2
Russian Federation	1,038.8	1,025.9	548.0
Singapore	1,118.6	1,906.6	1,764.9
Spain	1,452.1	1,744.5	1,947.2
Sweden	867.7	1,248.8	780.4
Switzerland	2,030.4	3,828.6	3,871.5
Thailand	1,003.9	1,281.8	1,462.8
Türkiye	3,937.7	3,980.2	5,294.8
United Arab Emirates	1.5	225.2	1,609.0
United Kingdom	6,588.7	5,756.5	4,812.9
USA	14,749.8	12,045.4	17,816.6
Viet Nam	1,819.8	836.0	1,097.9
Total (incl. others)	94,039.0	101,866.9	121,863.6

Exports*	2020	2021	2022
Bangladesh	3,521.1	5,176.7	9,971.0
Belgium	813.3	1,681.9	26,066.7
China, People's Republic	28,449.2	49,041.6	75,647.2
France	1,786.4	3,414.4	13,050.7
Germany	492.3	5,155.8	605.6
India	26,764.3	40,756.9	55,139.4
Italy	3,661.5	8,926.4	23,481.1
Japan	29,106.9	43,111.1	45,755.1
Korea, Republic	24,119.2	40,738.6	51,974.5
Kuwait	3,259.0	6,194.8	7,153.6
Oman	2,721.3	2,237.6	2,596.7
Pakistan	4,940.9	9,501.8	14,294.3
Poland	1,923.4	3,853.2	8,301.1
Singapore	12,532.8	19,460.9	24,259.1
Taiwan	6,476.5	8,240.6	11,409.5
Thailand	6,160.9	9,886.9	13,381.0
Türkiye	2,861.2	2,757.3	2,607.3
United Arab Emirates	3,956.6	12,644.6	20,844.8
United Kingdom	4,169.3	10,640.0	31,146.5
USA	4,450.5	6,150.5	6,290.8
Total (incl. others)	187,475.1	317,420.0	476,710.7

*Including re-exports (QR million): 9,534.5 in 2020; 10,244.2 in 2021; 10,277.6 in 2022.

Transport

ROAD TRAFFIC
(registered vehicles)

	2018	2019	2020
Private cars	998,987	998,987	1,083,377
Other private transport	415,178	428,668	441,651
Heavy equipment	67,555	69,254	71,259
Motorcycles and mopeds	22,972	26,233	29,938
Total (incl. others)	1,587,815	1,655,700	1,731,284

QATAR

SHIPPING

Flag Registered Fleet
(at 31 December)

	2020	2021	2022
Number of vessels	187	185	186
Total displacement ('000 grt)	827.7	614.1	590.4

Source: Lloyd's List Intelligence (www.bit.ly/LLintelligence).

INTERNATIONAL SEABORNE FREIGHT TRAFFIC
(excl. Ras Laffan, 2022)

	Traffic
Doha Port	
Vessels entered and cleared	57
Containers	—
Capacity ('000 grt)	3,868
Umm Said (Mesaieed) Port	
Vessels entered and cleared	1,534
Tankers	463
Containers	346
Capacity ('000 grt)	42,978
Halul Port	
Vessels entered and cleared	77
Tankers	77
Capacity ('000 grt)	12,022
Hamad Port	
Vessels entered and cleared	1,588
Tankers	3
Containers	1,031
Capacity ('000 grt)	56,731
Rowais Port	
Vessels entered and cleared	1,487
Capacity ('000 grt)	830
Total	
Vessels entered and cleared	4,743
Tankers	543
Containers	1,377
Capacity ('000 grt)	116,429

CIVIL AVIATION
(Hamad International Airport)

	2018	2019	2020
Aircraft arrivals	110,322	116,462	66,287
Passenger arrivals ('000)*	17,262	19,376	6,189
Cargo and mail received (metric tons)	1,218,364	1,217,844	1,192,087
Cargo and mail dispatched (metric tons)	979,946	997,961	983,205

* Excluding private aircraft and including transit passengers.

Tourism

TOURIST ARRIVALS
(arrivals of non-resident tourists in hotels and similar establishments)

Region of residence	2019	2020	2021
Asia	1,413,516	889,269	1,777,774
Europe	1,430,636	468,352	599,914
Middle East	873,398	582,702	666,977
Total (incl. others)	6,595,582	3,835,039	7,512,087

Tourism receipts (US $ million, excl. passenger transport): 3,563 in 2020; 4,263 in 2021 (provisional); 7,262 in 2022 (provisional) (Source: World Tourism Organization).

Communications Media

	2019	2020	2021
Telephones ('000 main lines in use)	461.3	454.7	460.2
Mobile telephone subscriptions ('000)	3,917.6	3,798.5	3,876.5
Broadband subscriptions, fixed ('000)	284.7	296.1	311.9
Broadband subscriptions, mobile ('000)	3,535.0	3,466.3	3,871.8
Internet users (% of population)	99.7	99.7	100.0

Source: International Telecommunication Union.

Education

(2020/21)

	Institutions	Teachers	Students Males	Females	Total
Private schools*	864	13,498	109,119	96,176	205,295
Pre-primary	426	3,355	21,560	19,489	41,049
Primary	199	6,157	54,351	48,727	103,078
Preparatory	132	1,920	19,229	16,488	35,717
General secondary	107	2,066	13,979	11,472	25,451
Independent schools†	318	14,237	60,627	65,629	126,256
Pre-primary	68	988	3,843	4,328	8,171
Primary	114	6,920	28,036	30,471	58,507
Preparatory	67	3,068	14,527	15,571	30,098
General secondary‡	69	3,261	14,221	15,259	29,480
Total	1,182	27,735	169,746	161,805	331,551
Pre-primary	494	4,343	25,403	23,817	49,220
Primary	313	13,077	82,387	79,198	161,585
Preparatory	199	4,988	33,756	32,059	65,815
General secondary‡	176	5,327	28,200	26,731	54,931
University of Qatar§	—	1,832	12,857	28,568	41,425

* Including the Qatar Foundation for Education, Science and Community Development (including the Qatar Academy and the Qatar Leadership Academy and Learning Centre) and the Academy for Sports Excellence (Aspire).
† Including government schools.
‡ Including specialized secondary schools.
§ Including Qatar Community College.

Pupil-teacher ratio (qualified teaching staff, primary education, UNESCO estimate): 12.5 in 2020/21 (Source: UNESCO Institute for Statistics).

Adult literacy rate (UNESCO estimates): 93.5% (males 94.7%; females 93.1%) in 2017 (Source: UNESCO Institute for Statistics).

Directory

The Constitution

According to the provisional Constitution adopted on 2 April 1970, executive power was vested in the Amir, as head of state, and exercised by the Council of Ministers, appointed by the head of state. The Amir was assisted by the appointed Advisory (*Shura*) Council of 20 members (increased to 30 in 1975 and to 35 in 1988), whose term was extended regularly thereafter. All fundamental democratic rights were guaranteed. In 1975 the Advisory Council was granted the power to summon individual ministers to answer questions on legislation before promulgation. In March 1999 elections took place, by universal adult suffrage, for a 29-member Central Municipal Council, which was to have a consultative role in the operations of the Ministry of Municipal Affairs and Agriculture.

The Amir formally adopted a new Constitution following a referendum held on 29 April 2003. Under this Constitution, the Amir was to remain head of the executive, while a reformed 45-member Advisory Council, of which two-thirds was to be directly elected (the remainder being appointed by the Amir), was to have the power to legislate, review the state budget, monitor government policy and hold ministers accountable for their actions. The new body was to have a four-year mandate. Suffrage was to be extended to all citizens, including women, aged 18 years and above. Elections to the partially elective Advisory Council were initially expected to be conducted in 2004; however, owing to alleged difficulties pertaining to the electoral roll, they were repeatedly postponed. In June 2013 the Amir issued a decree extending the term of the existing Advisory Council for an indeterminate period. The Council's term was further extended in June 2016 and again in July 2019. Meanwhile, in November 2017 the Advisory Council was expanded to 45 members (including, for the first time, women members, of whom four were appointed). Following the approval of new electoral legislation in May 2021, on 22 August the Amir issued a decree providing for the first-ever elections to the Advisory Council to be held on 2 October. Qatari citizens were to vote for 30 of the Council's 45 members, while the remaining 15 members were to be appointed by the Amir.

The Constitution guarantees freedom of association, expression and religious affiliation, and provides for the establishment of an independent judiciary; however, it does not authorize political parties.

The Government

HEAD OF STATE

Amir and Commander-in-Chief of the Armed Forces: Sheikh TAMIM BIN HAMAD AL THANI (assumed power 25 June 2013).

COUNCIL OF MINISTERS
(September 2023)

Prime Minister and Minister of Foreign Affairs: Sheikh MOHAMMED BIN ABDULRAHMAN BIN JASSIM AL THANI.

Deputy Prime Minister and Minister of State for Defence Affairs: Dr KHALID BIN MOHAMED AL-ATTIYAH.

Minister of the Interior: Sheikh KHALIFA BIN HAMAD BIN KHALIFA AL THANI.

Minister of Finance: Sheikh ALI BIN AHMED AL-KUWARI.

Minister of Awqaf (Religious Endowments) and Islamic Affairs: Maj.-Gen. (retd) GHANEM BIN SHAHEEN BIN GHANEM AL-GHANEM.

Minister of Culture: Sheikh ABDULRAHMAN BIN HAMAD BIN JASSIM BIN HAMAD AL THANI.

Minister of the Environment and Climate Change: Dr FALEH BIN NASSER BIN AHMED BIN ALI AL THANI.

Minister of Justice: MASOUD BIN MOHAMED AL-AMERI.

Minister of Education and Higher Education: BUTHAINA BINT ALI AL-JABR AL-NUAIMI.

Minister of Transport: JASIM BIN SAIF AHMAD AL-SULATI.

Minister of Public Health: Dr HANAN MOHAMED AL-KUWARI.

Minister of Commerce and Industry: Sheikh MOHAMMED BIN HAMAD BIN QASSIM AL-ABDULLAH AL THANI.

Minister of Municipality: ABDULLAH BIN ABDULAZIZ BIN TURKI AL-SUBAIE.

Minister of Labour: ALI BIN SAEED BIN SMAIKH AL-MARRI.

Minister of Communications and Information Technology: MOHAMMED BIN ALI BIN MOHAMMED AL-MANNAI.

Minister of Social Development and Family: MARYAM BINT ALI BIN NASSER AL-MISNAD.

Minister of Sports and Youth: SALAH BIN GHANEM AL-ALI.

Minister of State for Cabinet Affairs: MOHAMMED BIN ABDULLAH BIN MOHAMMED AL-YOUSEF AL-SULAITI.

Minister of State for Energy Affairs: SAAD BIN SHARIDA AL-KAABI.

MINISTRIES

Ministry of Awqaf (Religious Endowments) and Islamic Affairs: POB 422, Doha; tel. 44700000; fax 44470700; e-mail info@islam.gov.qa; internet www.islam.gov.qa.

Ministry of Commerce and Industry: 1st Floor, Lucille City; tel. 16001; fax 44945308; e-mail info@moci.gov.qa; internet www.moci.gov.qa.

Ministry of Communications and Information Technology: Doha.

Ministry of Culture: POB 2511, Doha; tel. 8000002; fax 44022222; e-mail info@mcs.gov.qa; internet www.mcs.gov.qa.

Ministry of Defence: Qatar Armed Forces, POB 37, Doha; tel. 44614111.

Ministry of Education and Higher Education: POB 35111, al-Dafna, Doha; tel. 44044444; fax 44044586; e-mail info@edu.gov.qa; internet www.edu.gov.qa.

Ministry of the Environment and Climate Change: Doha.

Ministry of Finance: al-Corniche St, al-Souq, Doha; tel. 44461444; fax 44431177; e-mail info@baladiya.gov.qa; internet www.mof.gov.qa.

Ministry of Foreign Affairs: al-Mirqab Tower, West Bay, Doha; tel. 440111111; fax 44324131; e-mail webmaster@mofa.gov.qa; internet www.mofa.gov.qa.

Ministry of the Interior: Doha 8895; tel. 2366666; fax 44323339; e-mail minister@moi.gov.qa; internet www.moi.gov.qa.

Ministry of Justice: POB 917, Doha; tel. 40215555; fax 40216550; e-mail info@moj.gov.qa; internet www.moj.gov.qa.

Ministry of Labour: al-Faisal Tower, Doha; tel. 40288888; e-mail info@adlsa.gov.qa; internet www.adlsa.gov.qa.

Ministry of Municipality: POB 22332, al-Corniche St, Doha; tel. 44348038; fax 44437993; e-mail info@mme.gov.qa; internet www.mme.gov.qa.

Ministry of Public Health: POB 42, Doha; tel. 44070000; fax 44070899; e-mail ghcc@moph.gov.qa; internet www.moph.gov.qa.

Ministry of Social Development and Family: Doha.

Ministry of Sports and Youth: Doha.

Ministry of Transport: West Conference Center St, Doha; tel. 40451111; fax 44994655; e-mail info@motc.gov.qa; internet www.motc.gov.qa.

Legislature

ADVISORY COUNCIL

The Advisory or *Shura* Council was established in 1972, with 20 nominated members. It was expanded to 30 members in 1975, and to 35 members in 1988. Under the terms of the new Constitution, promulgated in 2003, the wholly nominated Advisory Council was to be reformed to comprise 45 members, two-thirds of whom were to be directly elected and the remaining 15 members appointed by the Amir. The reformed Council, which would have a four-year mandate, was to have the power to legislate, review the state budget, monitor government policy and hold ministers accountable for their actions. However, elections to the new body were repeatedly postponed; prior to his abdication as Amir in June 2013, Sheikh Hamad bin Khalifa Al Thani issued a decree extending the term of the existing Advisory Council for an indeterminate period. Amir Sheikh Tamim bin Hamad Al Thani further extended the term of the Advisory Council in June 2016 and again in July 2019. Meanwhile, in November 2017 the Advisory Council was expanded to 45 members (including, for the first time, women members, of whom four were appointed). Following the passage of new electoral legislation in May 2021, on 22 August the Amir issued a decree providing for the first-ever elections to the Advisory Council to be held on 2 October. In accordance with the 2003 Constitution, Qatari citizens were to vote for 30 of the Council's 45 members, while the remaining 15 members were to be appointed by the Amir. The elections attracted a turnout of 63.5% of registered voters. A total of 233 candidates contested the 30 directly elective seats, none of which was won by any of the 26 women candidates. Two women, however, were among the 15 members of the reformed

Advisory Council who were nominated by the Amir on 14 October. The new Council held its first ordinary session on 26 October.
Advisory Council: POB 2034, Doha; tel. 44221222; fax 44425526; e-mail info@shura.gov.qa; internet www.shura.qa.
Speaker: HASSAN BIN ABDULLAH AL-GHANIM.

Political Organizations

There are no political organizations in Qatar.

Diplomatic Representation

EMBASSIES IN QATAR

Afghanistan: POB 22104, West Bay, al-Haditha Rd, al-Dafna, Doha; tel. 44932319; fax 44932330; e-mail qatar@afghanistan-mfa.net; Ambassador MOHAMMAD NAEEM.
Albania: POB 22659, Doha; tel. 40027413; e-mail embassy.doha@mfa.gov.al; internet www.ambasadat.gov.al/qatar; Ambassador Dr NURI DOMI.
Algeria: New Diplomatic Area, West Bay, Doha; tel. 44835880; e-mail info@embalgdoha.com.qa; internet fb.com/embalgeria.doha; Ambassador SALAH ATTIA.
Angola: Doha; Ambassador ANTONIO COELHO RAMOS DA CRUZ.
Argentina: 6 Rawdat Ehraish St, Zone 66, West Bay, Doha.; tel. 44173601; fax 44273609; e-mail eqatr@mrecic.gov.ar; internet eqatr.cancilleria.gov.ar; Ambassador GUILLERMO LUIS NICHOLAS.
Armenia: POB 7734, Villa 5, St 501, Zone 67, al-Dafna, Doha; tel. 44919232; fax 44279025; e-mail armqatarembassy@mfa.am; internet www.mfa.am/en/embassies/qa; Ambassador ARMEN SARGSYAN.
Australia: Tornado Tower, Majlis al-Taawon St, Doha; tel. 40078500; fax 40078503; internet qatar.embassy.gov.au; Ambassador SHANE FLANAGAN.
Austria: POB 12011, Palm Tower B, Level 33, West Bay, Doha; tel. 40337300; fax 40337373; e-mail doha-ob@bmeia.gv.at; internet www.bmeia.gv.at/en/austrian-embassy-doha; Ambassador KARIN FICHTINGER-GROHE.
Azerbaijan: POB 23900, St 66, Saha 41, West Bay, Doha; tel. 44932450; fax 44931755; e-mail azembassy@qatar.net.qa; internet doha.mfa.gov.az; Ambassador MAHIR ALIYEV.
Bangladesh: POB 2080, Bldg No. 153, St 820, Zone 43, Doha; tel. 44671927; e-mail info@bdembassydoha.org; internet doha.mofa.gov.bd; Ambassador MOHAMMED NAZRUL ISLAM.
Belarus: POB 22283, Villa 8, St 538, Zone 66. Legtaifiya, West Bay, Doha; tel. 44690989; fax 44862579; e-mail qatar@mfa.gov.by; internet qatar.mfa.gov.by; Chargé d'affaires ALEKSEY V. MALAFEY.
Belgium: POB 24418, al-Sanaa St, District 64, Doha; tel. 44931542; fax 44930151; e-mail doha@diplobel.fed.be; internet qatar.diplomatie.belgium.be; Ambassador WILLIAM ASSELBORN.
Benin: POB 24210, Villa No. 6, Onaiza 65, Saha 256, Doha; tel. 44930128; fax 44115713; e-mail ambabenin-doha@hotmail.com; internet www.benin-qa.com; Ambassador MUHAMMAD BARE.
Bosnia and Herzegovina: POB 876, al-Funduq St, Salam Tower, 14th Floor, West Bay, Doha; tel. 44113828; fax 44113234; e-mail info@bhembassyqatar.com; internet bhembassyqatar.com; Ambassador SEMIR HALILOVIĆ (designate).
Brazil: POB 23122, Bldg 20, Wadi al-Hadab St, al-Dafna, Doha; tel. 44838227; fax 44838087; e-mail brasemb.doha@itamaraty.gov.br; internet www.gov.br/mre/pt-br/embaixada-doha; Ambassador LUIZ ALBERTO FIGUEIREDO MACHADO.
Brunei Darussalam: POB 22772, Villa 6, St 540, Umm al-Saneem, West Bay, Doha; tel. 44831956; fax 44836798; e-mail doha.qatar@mfa.gov.bn; internet www.mfa.gov.bn/qatar-doha; Ambassador MOHAMED BAHRIN ABU BAKAR.
Bulgaria: POB 23812, Villa 98, Waraqa bin Nawfal St 848, Zone 66, al-Dafna, Doha; tel. 44120023; fax 44120024; e-mail embassy.doha@mfa.bg; internet www.mfa.bg/embassies/qatar; Ambassador PLAMEN STANKOV DELEV.
Burkina Faso: POB 5038, Bldg No. 7, Zone 66, St 539, al-Dafna, Doha; tel. 44728915; fax 44215495; e-mail amba.burkina.doha@gmail.com; internet www.fb.com/Ambassade-du-Burkina-Faso-au-Qatar-1826589400981057/; Chargé d'affaires a.i. TIHNGO SIDIKI TRAORÉ.
Burundi: Bldg 14, 567 St, District 66, al-Dafna, Doha; tel. 44328116; fax 44156096; e-mail brdiembassy.qa@gmail.com; Ambassador ISIDORE NTIRAMPEBA.
Canada: POB 24876, Tornado Tower, West Bay, Doha; tel. 44199000; fax 44199035; e-mail dohag@international.gc.ca; internet www.canadainternational.gc.ca/qatar; Ambassador ISABELLE MARTIN.
Central African Republic: POB 23653, Doha; tel. 44817695; fax 44817693; e-mail ambrcadoha@gmail.com; Chargé d'affaires HAMMOUDI AL-SHEIKH.
Chad: POB 24386, Area 66, al-Dafna, West Bay, Doha; tel. 44829852; fax 44760119; e-mail ambtchadqatar@gmail.com; Ambassador DAUSA IDRISS DEBY ITNO.
China, People's Republic: POB 17200, St 801, District 66, Doha; tel. 44934203; fax 44934201; e-mail chinaemb_qa@mfa.gov.cn; internet qa.china-embassy.org; Ambassador ZHOU JIAN.
Congo, Democratic Republic: Doha; Ambassador VALERIE LUSAMBA KABEYA.
Costa Rica: POB 23313, Villa 40, Street 834, Zone 64, Jebilat, Doha; tel. 44980094; fax 44980106; e-mail embcr-qa@rree.go.cr; internet fb.com/CRenCatar; Chargè d'affaires a.i. JAIRO FRANCISCO LÓPEZ-BOLAÑOS.
Côte d'Ivoire: POB 5846, House 24, Zone 66, St 821, al-Dafna, Doha; tel. 40381695; fax 44673090; e-mail ambaci.doha@gmail.com; Ambassador ABDUL KARIM CISSÉ.
Croatia: POB 23150, Bldg 3, Wadi al-Humra 807 St, Saha 96, al-Dafna, Doha; tel. 44835224; fax 44835175; e-mail croemb.doha@mvep.hr; internet qa.mvep.hr; Ambassador DRAGO LOVRIĆ.
Cuba: POB 12017, 802 St, Zone 66, West Bay Lagoon, New Dafna, Doha; tel. 44110714; fax 44110387; e-mail embajada@qa.embacuba.cu; internet misiones.minrex.gob.cu/es/qatar; Ambassador (vacant).
Cyprus: POB 24482, Bldg 3, Saba Saha 12 St, District 63, West Bay, Doha; tel. 44934390; fax 44933087; e-mail kyprosdoha@cyprusembassy.org.qa; internet www.mfa.gov.cy/embassydoha; Ambassador NICHOLAS MANOLIS.
Czech Republic: 953 Ibn Roshd, Villa 60, Onaiza, Doha; e-mail doha@mzv.cz; internet www.mzv.cz/doha; Ambassador PETR CHALUPECKY.
Djibouti: POB 23796, Doha; tel. 44934657; fax 44839245; e-mail ambdji.sec@gmail.com; Ambassador TAYEB DBD ROBLEH.
Dominican Republic: POB 23545, Salam Tower, 9th Floor, al-Corniche St, Doha; tel. 44113868; fax 44113267; e-mail info@domrepemb-qatar.com; internet www.domrepemb-qatar.com; Ambassador GEORGES BAHSA HAZIM.
Ecuador: POB 23501, Villa 14, St 502, Zone 66, West Bay, Doha; tel. 40161800; fax 40161803; e-mail eecucatar@cancilleria.gob.ec; internet www.cancilleria.gob.ec/map_maps/qatar; Ambassador PASCUAL DEL CIOPPO.
Egypt: POB 2899, Diplomatic Area, al-Dafna, Doha; tel. 44832116; e-mail embassy.doha@mfa.gov.eg; internet fb.com/egyptianembassyindoha; Ambassador Dr AMR EL-SHERBINI.
El Salvador: Villa 54, al-Riyad St, West Bay, Doha; tel. 44110195; e-mail esvq@rree.gob.sv; internet embajadaqatar.rree.gob.sv; Ambassador MILTON ALCIDES MAGANA HERRERA.
Eritrea: POB 4309, Doha; tel. 44667934; fax 44664139; e-mail info@eritreanembassyqa.org; internet eritreanembassyqa.org; Ambassador ALI IBRAHIM AHMED.
Eswatini: POB 24322, Villa 41, Lusail Expressway, West Bay, Doha; tel. 44933145; fax 44933216; e-mail swaziqa@gmail.com; Ambassador SOTJA MPHUKUCO DLAMINI.
Ethiopia: POB 24856, Bldg 26, St 847, Area al-Seylan 66, al-Dafna, Doha; tel. 40207000; fax 44719588; e-mail dohaembassy@mfa.gov.et; internet www.fb.com/EthiopiainQatar; Ambassador FAISAL ALI IBRAHIM.
France: POB 2669, Diplomatic Area, West Bay, Doha; tel. 44021777; fax 44021731; e-mail contact@ambafrance-qa.org; internet www.ambafrance-qa.org; Ambassador JEAN-BAPTISTE FAIVRE.
The Gambia: POB 21629, Villa 11, Saha 254, Ibn Batouta St, al-Dafna, Doha; tel. 44652002; fax 44719145; e-mail gambiaembassydoha@gmail.com; internet www.fb.com/people/Embassy-of-the-Republic-of-The-Gambia-in-Qatar/100064778256208/; Ambassador FODAY MALANG.
Georgia: POB 24118, Villa 9, St 835, Zone 66, West Bay, Doha; tel. 44739499; fax 44739495; e-mail doha.emb@mfa.gov.ge; internet qatar.mfa.gov.ge; Ambassador NICOLOZ REVAZISHVILI.
Germany: POB 3064, Doha; tel. 44082300; fax 44082333; e-mail info@doha.diplo.de; internet www.doha.diplo.de; Ambassador LOTHAR FREISCHLADER.
Ghana: POB 5931, Villa 7, St 576, Zone 66, al-Dafna, Doha; tel. 44364486; fax 44986094; e-mail doha@mfa.gov.gh; internet dohaembassy.gov.gh; Ambassador MOHAMMED NURUDEEN ISMAIL.
Greece: POB 15721, Bldg 5, St 530, Zone 66, Doha; tel. 44128150; fax 44128160; e-mail gremb.doha@mfa.gr; internet www.mfa.gr/doha; Ambassador ELENI MICHALOPOULOU.

Guinea: Bldg 40, Oued al-Haddad St, Zone 66, Doha; tel. and fax 44416224; e-mail ambaguidoha@gmail.com; internet www.fb.com/ambaguineeqatar/; Chargé d'affaires a.i. ABOUBACAR CAMARA.

Guinea-Bissau: POB 23557, Bldg 5, Sq. 64, St 534, District 66, West Bay, Doha; tel. 55403100; e-mail embaguinebissaudoha@gmail.com; Ambassador UMARO DJAU.

Guyana: Doha; Ambassador SAFRAAZ AHMAD SHADOOD.

Haiti: POB 10812, Doha; tel. 31332215; e-mail ambhaiti.qatar@diplomatie.ht; internet www.fb.com/haitiembassyqatar; Ambassador FRANCOIS GUILLAUME, II.

Hungary: POB 23525, Bldg 15, Zone 66, West Bay, Doha; tel. 44932531; fax 44932537; e-mail mission.doh@mfa.gov.hu; internet doha.mfa.gov.hu; Ambassador FRANS CORUM.

India: POB 2788, Villas 86 & 90, 941 al-Eithra St, Zone 63, Onaiza, Doha; tel. 44255777; fax 44655471; e-mail amboff.doha@mea.gov.in; internet indianembassyqatar.gov.in; Ambassador Shri VIPUL.

Indonesia: POB 22375, 21 al-Salmiya St, Zone 66, Onaiza, Doha; tel. 44657945; fax 44657610; e-mail doha.kbri@kemlu.go.id; internet kemlu.go.id/doha; Ambassador MUHAMMAD RIDWAN HASSAN.

Iran: POB 1633, Diplomatic Area, West Bay, Doha; tel. 44831550; fax 44831665; e-mail iranemb.doh@mfa.gov.ir; internet doha.mfa.ir; Ambassador HAMID REZA DEHGHANI.

Iraq: POB 1526, House 156, al-Muntzah St, al-Hilal District, Doha; tel. 44216146; fax 44216152; e-mail dohemb@mofa.gov.iq; internet www.mofa.gov.iq/doha; Ambassador OMAR AHMED KARIM AL-BARAZANCHI.

Italy: POB 4188, al-Fardan Office Tower, 23rd Floor, 61 al-Funduq St, West Bay, Doha; tel. 44831828; fax 44831909; e-mail ambasciata.doha@esteri.it; internet www.ambdoha.esteri.it; Ambassador PAOLO TOSCHI.

Japan: POB 2208, New Diplomatic Area, al-Shabab St, Onaiza, Doha; tel. 44409000; fax 40293655; e-mail eojqatar@dh.mofa.go.jp; internet www.qa.emb-japan.go.jp; Ambassador SATOSHI MAEDA.

Jordan: POB 2366, Diplomatic Area, al-Dafna, Doha; tel. 44832202; fax 44832173; e-mail doha@fm.gov.jo; Ambassador ZAID MUFLEH AL-LAWZI.

Kazakhstan: POB 23513, Bldg 2, Zone 66, Doha; tel. 44128015; fax 44128014; e-mail doha@mfa.kz; internet www.gov.kz/memleket/entities/mfa-doha; Ambassador ARMAN ISAGALIEV.

Kenya: POB 23091, Bldg 10, St 840, Zone 66, West Bay, Doha; tel. 44931870; fax 44831730; e-mail information@kenyaembassydoha.com; internet www.kenyaembassydoha.com; Ambassador BONIFACE N. MWILU.

Korea, Republic: POB 3727, New Diplomatic Area, al-Shabab St, Onaiza, Doha; tel. 44930809; fax 44833264; e-mail koemb_qa@mofa.go.kr; internet qat.mofa.go.kr; Ambassador HAM SANG-WOOK.

Kosovo: al-Fardan Tower, 25th Floor, al-Funduq St, Zone 61, al-Dafna, Doha; tel. 403737701; fax 403737702; e-mail embassy.qatar@rks-gov.net; Ambassador FUAD MORINA.

Kuwait: POB 1177, Bldg 510, St 233, Zone 66, al-Dafna, Doha; tel. 44832111; fax 44832042; e-mail doha.sec@mofa.gov.kw; Ambassador KHALED AL-MUTAIRI.

Kyrgyzstan: Villa 4, 75 Umm al-Seneem St, Zone 66, West Bay, Doha; tel. 44131519; fax 44131123; e-mail kgembassy.qa@mfa.gov.kg; Ambassador CHYNGYZ ESHIMBEKOV.

Lebanon: POB 2411, 63 United Nations St, al-Haditha Area, Doha; tel. 44114127; fax 44114129; e-mail embleb@qatar.net.qa; Ambassador FARAH BERRI.

Liberia: POB 23810, Zone 501, Saha 63, al-Dafna, Doha; tel. 44125672; fax 44125675; e-mail libemg.doha@yahoo.com; Chargé d'affaires a.i. ALI SYLLA.

Libya: POB 574, House 6, St 503, Area 63, Doha; tel. 44831231; fax 44839407; e-mail embassy.qa@mofa.gov.ly; Ambassador MOHAMMED MUSTAFA AL-SAGHIR AL-LAFI.

Malawi: POB 17302, Doha; tel. 44415419; fax 44121498; e-mail malawiembassyqatar@gmail.com; Ambassador ROY AKAJUWE KACHALE.

Malaysia: POB 23760, Bldg 6, 821 Dawhat Zekreet St, Zone 66, Onaiza, Doha; tel. 44836463; fax 44836453; e-mail mwdoha@kln.gov.my; internet www.kln.gov.my/web/qat_doha/home; Ambassador ZAMSHARI SHAHARAN.

Mali: POB 23686, Villa 10, 511 West Bay Lagoon St, Doha; tel. 44515970; fax 44922607; e-mail ambamali.doha@gmail.com; Ambassador AMADOU DIEM.

Malta: Bldg 20, Amal Tower, 14th Floor, 850 St, Zone 60, West Bay, Doha; tel. 33460573; e-mail maltaembassy.doha@gov.mt; internet foreign.gov.mt/en/Embassies/Me_Doha/Pages/ME_Doha.aspx; Ambassador SIMON POLICHINO.

Mauritania: POB 3132, al-Rabiah St 71, al-Dafna, Doha; tel. 44836003; fax 44836015; Chargé d'affaires a.i. MOHAMED OULD ABDEL AZIZ.

Mexico: POB 22534, Bldg 14, Saha St 512, Saba 12, District 63, al-Dafna, West Bay, Doha; tel. 44508000; e-mail consularqat@sre.gob.mx; internet embamex.sre.gob.mx/qatar; Ambassador GUILLERMO ORDORIK.

Moldova: POB 22528, Villa 151, al-Mabahej St 826, Area 66, al-Dafna, Doha; tel. 44421303; fax 44935700; e-mail doha@mfa.gov.md; internet www.qatar.mfa.gov.md; Ambassador IULIAN GRIGORITĂ.

Morocco: POB 3242, Diplomatic Area, West Bay, Doha; tel. 44831885; fax 44833416; e-mail moroccoe@yahoo.com; Ambassador MOHAMED SETRI.

Mozambique: Doha; Ambassador ISAC MAMUDO MASSAMBY.

Nepal: POB 23002, 810 Rawdat Umm al-Theyab St, Abu Hamour Area, Zone 66, Doha; tel. 44675681; fax 44675680; e-mail eondoha@mofa.gov.np; internet qa.nepalembassy.gov.np; Ambassador NARESH BIKRAM DHAKAL.

Netherlands: POB 23675, al-Fardan Office Tower, 18th Floor, 16 al-Funduq St, West Bay, Doha; tel. 44954700; fax 44836340; e-mail doh@minbuza.nl; internet www.nederlandwereldwijd.nl/landen/qatar; Ambassador FERDINAND LAHNSTEIN.

Niger: POB 23068, Bldg 12, Zone 67, West Bay, Doha; tel. 44219045; fax 44423680; e-mail amb.qa@diplomatie.gouv.ne; internet ambnigerqatar.com; Ambassador ABDULKARIM SOUMANA.

Nigeria: POB 9687, Bldg 39, 941 Istiqbal St, Zone 63, Dafna, Doha; tel. 44485013; e-mail nigerianembassy.doha@gmail.com; internet doha.foreignaffairs.gov.ng; Chargé d'affaires a.i. KIMIEBI EBIENFA.

North Macedonia: POB 24262, Villa 54, 941 al-Ithar St, Diplomatic Area, al-Dafna, Doha; tel. 44931374; e-mail doha@mfa.gov.mk; internet doha.mfa.gov.mk; Ambassador SHABAN JASHARI.

Oman: POB 1525, Bldg 18, Area 66, New Diplomatic Area, al-Dafna, Doha; tel. 44931514; fax 44932278; e-mail office.omanembassy@gmail.com; Ambassador NAJEEB BIN YAHYA AL-BALUSHI.

Pakistan: POB 334, Diplomatic Area, Plot 30, West Bay, Doha; tel. 44832525; fax 44832227; e-mail parepqat@qatar.net.qa; internet www.mofa.gov.pk/qatar; Ambassador Dr MOHAMMED EJAZ.

Panama: POB 17427, Villa 30, Zone 66, St 828, Onaiza, al-Dafna, Doha; tel. 44837740; fax 44837477; e-mail embpanamaqatar@mire.gob.pa; Ambassador MOUSA ABDELHAE ASVAT KASU.

Paraguay: POB 23885, Bldg 14, Zone 66, St 505, al-Mebahej St, West Bay, Doha; tel. 44935218; fax 44148247; e-mail embapar.qatar@mre.gov.py; Ambassador ANGEL BARCHINI CIBILS.

Peru: POB 24062, Bldg 42, St 835, Lejbailat Zone 64, Doha; tel. 44915944; fax 44915940; e-mail info@peruembassy.com.qa; internet www.fb.com/embajadaperuqatar; Ambassador JOSÉ ARSENIO BENZAQUEN PEREA.

Philippines: POB 24900, Villa 7, 860 al-Eithar St, Zone 68, Jelaiah, Doha; tel. 44831585; fax 44831595; e-mail doha.pe@dfa.gov.ph; internet dohape.dfa.gov.ph; Ambassador RAUL HERNANDEZ (designate).

Poland: POB 23380, al-Qutaifiya 66, St 519, Saha 49, West Bay, Doha; tel. 44113230; fax 44110307; e-mail doha.amb.sekretariat@msz.gov.pl; internet doha.msz.gov.pl; Ambassador JANUSZ JANKE.

Portugal: POB 24854, Bldg 31, St 803, Zone 67, al-Dafna, Doha; tel. 44864691; fax 44189545; e-mail doha@mne.pt; internet www.doha.embaixadaportugal.mne.pt; Ambassador PAULO NEVES POCINHO.

Romania: POB 22511, St 953, Zone 65, al-Dafna, Doha; tel. 44934848; fax 44934747; e-mail doha@mae.ro; internet doha.mae.ro; Ambassador NICUSOR DANIEL TANASE.

Russian Federation: POB 15404, Bldg 193, St 804, Zone 66, Doha; tel. 44836231; fax 44836243; e-mail rusemb@qatar.net.qa; internet www.qatar.mid.ru; Ambassador DMITRY DOGADKIN.

Rwanda: Bldg 74, St 803, Zone 66, al-Dafna, Doha; tel. 40398447; e-mail ambadoha@minaffet.gov.rw; internet www.rwandainqatar.gov.rw; Ambassador IGOR MARARA KAYINAMURA.

Saudi Arabia: POB 1255, Diplomatic Area, al-Dafna, Doha; tel. 44832712; fax 44832720; e-mail qaemb@mofa.gov.sa; internet embassies.mofa.gov.sa/sites/qatar; Ambassador Prince MANSOUR BIN KHALID BIN FARHAN AL SA'UD.

Senegal: POB 8291, Bldg 1, St 593, Zone 65, Saha 252, al-Dafna, Doha; tel. 44837644; fax 44838872; e-mail embassysenegal@yahoo.com; Ambassador Dr MOHAMMED HABIBO DIALLO.

Serbia: POB 22195, Zone 66, West Bay, Um al-Seneem 5, Doha; tel. 44175181; fax 44439656; e-mail embsrbqat@gmail.com; internet www.doha.mfa.gov.rs; Chargé d'affaires a.i. SLOBODAN RADEKA.

Singapore: POB 24497, New West Bay Area, Doha; tel. 44128082; fax 44128180; e-mail singemb_doh@mfa.sg; internet www.mfa.gov.sg/doha; Ambassador WONG CHOW MING (designate).

QATAR

Somalia: POB 1948, Diplomatic Area, West Bay, Doha; tel. 44832771; fax 44935751; e-mail somaliaembassydoha@yahoo.com; Ambassador ABDUL RAZZAQ FARAH ALI.

South Africa: POB 24744, Saha 100, West Bay, Doha; tel. 44857111; fax 44835961; e-mail doha.admin@dirco.gov.za; internet www.dirco.gov.za/doha; Ambassador GHULAM HUSSEIN ASMAL.

Spain: POB 24616, Villa 9, 563 St, Saha 93, West Bay, Doha; tel. 44290555; fax 44835887; e-mail emb.doha@maec.es; internet www.exteriores.gob.es/embajadas/doha; Ambassador JAVIER CARBAJOSA SANCHEZ.

Sri Lanka: POB 19075, St 860, Zone 47, Doha; tel. 44998660; fax 44674788; e-mail slemb.doha@mfa.gov.lk; internet www.slembassy-qatar.com; Ambassador MOHAMED MAFAZ MOHIDEEN.

Sudan: POB 2999, Diplomatic Area, Onaiza, Doha; tel. 44831474; fax 44833031; e-mail suemdoha@yahoo.com; Ambassador AHMED AL-DAHAB.

Sweden: POB 22649, Palm Tower B, Suite 1301, West Bay, Doha; tel. 44449500; fax 44443350; e-mail ambassaden.doha@gov.se; internet www.swedenabroad.com/doha; Ambassador GAUTAM BHATTACHARYA.

Switzerland: POB 23745, Villa 60, 807 Wadi al-Humra St, Zone 66, al-Dafna, Doha; tel. 40203400; fax 40203402; e-mail doha@eda.admin.ch; internet www.eda.admin.ch/doha; Chargé d'affaires a.i. PETER HAFNER.

Syrian Arab Republic: POB 6537, Bldg 75, St 908, Zone 66, Doha; tel. 40208222; fax 40208295; e-mail info@syrembassy.com; internet syrembassy.com; Chargé d'affaires a.i. Dr BILAL TOURKIYA.

Tajikistan: POB 22395, 64 Dafna Zone, 810 St, Doha; tel. 44123906; fax 44984694; e-mail tajemqatar@gmail.com; internet tajembqatar.tj; Ambassador KHOSROW SAHIBZADEH.

Tanzania: POB 36302, Bldg 7, Ibn Batouta St 591, al-Onaiza 65, Doha; tel. 40360860; fax 40294067; e-mail doha@nje.go.tz; internet www.qa.tzembassy.go.tz; Ambassador HABIBU AWESI MOHAMED (designate).

Thailand: POB 22474, Villa 122, Saha 3 al-Eithar St, West Bay, Doha; tel. 44934426; fax 44930514; e-mail thaidoh@qatar.net.qa; internet www.thaiembassy.org/doha; Ambassador SIRA SWANGSILPA.

Tunisia: POB 21185, Doha; tel. 40162222; fax 44128938; e-mail at.doha@qatar.net.qa; Ambassador FARHAD KHALIF.

Türkiye (Turkey): POB 1977, 310 al-Rabwa St, Diplomatic Area, al-Dafna, Doha; tel. 44951300; fax 44951320; e-mail embassy.doha@mfa.gov.tr; internet doha.emb.mfa.gov.tr; Ambassador Dr MUSTAFA GÖKSU.

Uganda: POB 5503, Bldg 9, Saha 74, St 544, Zone 66, West Bay, Doha; tel. 44277339; internet doha.mofa.go.ug; Ambassador STEPHEN CHEBROT.

Ukraine: POB 22539, Bldg 11, St 552, Zone 66, West Bay, Qatifiya, Doha; tel. 44147298; e-mail emb_qa@mfa.gov.ua; internet qatar.mfa.gov.ua; Ambassador ANDRIY KUZMENKO.

United Arab Emirates: POB 3099, 22 al-Markhiyah St, Diplomatic Area, Khalifa Northern Town, Doha; tel. 44838880; fax 44836186; e-mail doha@mofa.gov.ae; Ambassador Sheikh ZAYED BIN KHALIFA BIN SULTAN BIN SHAKHBOOT AL NAHYAN (designate).

United Kingdom: POB 3, al-Shabab St, Zone 66, West Bay, al-Dafna, Doha; tel. 44962000; fax 44962086; e-mail embassy.doha@fcdo.gov.uk; internet www.gov.uk/world/qatar; Ambassador JONATHAN WILKS.

Uruguay: POB 23237, Villa 1, Area 64, University Rd, al-Jabeilath, Doha; tel. 44113833; fax 44113540; e-mail uruqatar@gmail.com; Ambassador JORGE ANTONIO SERE STURZENEGGER.

USA: POB 2399, 22nd February St, al-Luqta District, Doha; tel. 44966000; fax 44884298; e-mail pasdoha@state.gov; internet qa.usembassy.gov; Ambassador TIMMY T. DAVIS.

Venezuela: POB 24470, Villa 36, Samra bin Jandab St, West Bay, Doha; tel. 44932730; fax 44932729; e-mail embve.qadoh@mppre.gob.ve; internet qatar.embajada.gob.ve; Ambassador CARLOS JOSÉ MATA FIGUEROA.

Viet Nam: POB 23595, Villa 8, West Bay, Doha; tel. 44128480; fax 44128370; e-mail vnemb.qa@mofa.gov.vn; internet vietnamembassy-qatar.org; Ambassador NGUYEN DINH THAO.

Yemen: POB 3318, 23 Fareeq bin Mahmoud al-Jazeera St, opp. Moshaireb Complex, Doha; tel. 44432555; fax 44429400; e-mail yemb-doha@mofa.gov.ye; Ambassador RAJEH HUSSAIN FARHAN BADI.

Judicial System

The independence of the judiciary was guaranteed by the provisional Constitution and further augmented in the Constitution formally adopted by the Amir in April 2003. All aspects pertaining to the civil judiciary are supervised by the Ministry of Justice, which organizes courts of law through its affiliated departments. The *Shari'a* judiciary hears all cases of personal status relating to Muslims, other claim cases, doctrinal provision and crimes under its jurisdiction. Legislation adopted in 1999 unified all civil and *Shari'a* courts in one judicial body, and determined the jurisdictions of each type of court. The law also provided for the establishment of a court of cassation; this was to be competent to decide on appeals relating to issues of contravention, misapplication and misinterpretation of the law, and on disputes between courts regarding areas of jurisdiction. In addition, the law provided for the establishment of a supreme judiciary council, to be presided over by the head of the court of cassation and comprising, *inter alia*, the heads of the *Shari'a* and civil courts of appeal. The legislation came into effect in 2003. An Amiri decree published in June 2002 provided for the establishment of an independent public prosecution system. A Supreme Constitutional Court was established in 2008 to adjudicate on the constitutionality of laws and to arbitrate in disputes between different branches of the judiciary.

Supreme Judiciary Council: POB 9673, Doha; tel. 44591166; fax 44833939; e-mail pr@sjc.gov.qa; internet www.sjc.gov.qa; f. 2003; Pres. Dr HASSAN BIN LAHDAN AL-HASSAN AL-MOHANADI.

Court of Cassation: judgments are issued by a five-member panel; Pres. Dr HASSAN BIN LAHDAN AL-HASSAN AL-MOHANADI.

Courts of Appeal: judgments are issued through a three-member panel.

Courts of First Instance: members include a president and other judges; judgments are issued by a three-member panel, but law allows the Supreme Judicial Council to form circuits that can deliver judgments through a single judge.

Public Prosecution Office: POB 705, Doha; tel. 4843333; fax 44843149; e-mail info@pp.gov.qa; internet www.pp.gov.qa; Attorney-Gen. Dr ISSA BIN SAAD AL-JAFALI AL-NUAIMI.

Religion

The indigenous population are Muslims of the Sunni sect, most being of the strict Wahhabi persuasion. Qatar does not appoint a Grand Mufti or official Islamic legal and religious authority. In March 2008 the first official Christian church (of the Roman Catholic branch) was consecrated in Doha; open worship among Christians had previously been prohibited. Other Christian places of worship have since opened to cater for adherents of the Anglican and Greek Orthodox branches.

CHRISTIANITY

The Anglican Communion

Within the Episcopal Church in Jerusalem and the Middle East, Qatar forms part of the diocese of Cyprus and the Gulf. The Anglican congregation in Qatar is entirely expatriate. The Bishop in Cyprus and the Gulf is resident in Cyprus, while the Archdeacon in the Gulf is resident in Doha.

Archdeacon in the Gulf: Ven. Canon MICHAEL MBONA, The Church of the Epiphany, POB 3210, Doha; tel. 44165728; fax 44165729; e-mail secretary@epiphany-qatar.org; internet www.anglicanchurchinqatar.org.

The Roman Catholic Church

An estimated 200,000 adherents in Qatar, mainly expatriates, form part of the Apostolic Vicariate of Northern Arabia. The Vicar Apostolic is resident in Bahrain.

The Greek Orthodox Church

There is a small Greek Orthodox community in Qatar, which congregates at the Church of St Isaac and St George in Doha and forms part of the Patriarchate of Jerusalem.

The Press

NEWSPAPERS

Al-'Arab (The Arabs): POB 22612, Doha; internet www.alarab.qa; f. 1972; ceased publication in 1996, but recommenced following relaunch in 2007; daily; Arabic; publ. by Dar al-Sharq Media Group; Editor-in-Chief FALEH HUSSEIN AL-HAJRI.

Gulf Times: POB 533, Doha; tel. 44350478; fax 44350474; e-mail editor@gulf-times.com; internet www.gulf-times.com; f. 1978; daily and weekly edns; English; political; publ. by Gulf Publishing and Printing Co; Chief Editor FAISAL ABDULHAMEED AL-MUDAHKA.

The Peninsula: POB 3488, Doha; tel. 44557739; e-mail editor@pen.com.qa; internet www.thepeninsulaqatar.com; f. 1995; daily; English; political; publ. by Dar al-Sharq Printing, Publishing and

Distribution; Chair. Sheikh THANI BIN ABDULLAH AL THANI; Editor-in-Chief Dr KHALID AL-SHAFI.

Qatar Tribune: POB 23493, Doha; tel. 40002222; fax 40002235; e-mail editor@qatar-tribune.com; internet www.qatar-tribune.com; f. 2006; daily; English; Editor-in-Chief Dr HASSAN MUHAMMAD AL-ANSARI.

Al-Rayah (The Banner): POB 3464, Doha; tel. 44466566; fax 44350476; e-mail editor@raya.com; internet www.raya.com; f. 1979; daily and weekly edns; Arabic; political; publ. by Gulf Publishing and Printing Co; Editor ABDULLAH BIN GHANIMA AL-BINALI AL-MUHANNADI.

Al-Sharq (The Orient): POB 3488, Doha; e-mail social@al-sharq .com; internet www.al-sharq.com; f. 1985; daily; Arabic; political; publ. by Dar al-Sharq Printing, Publishing and Distribution; Editor-in-Chief JABER AL-HARAMI.

Al-Watan: POB 22345, Doha; tel. 40002222; fax 40002225; e-mail news@al-watan.com; internet www.al-watan.com; f. 1995; daily; Arabic; political; publ. by Dar al-Watan Printing, Publishing and Distribution; Editor-in-Chief MUHAMMAD HAMAD AL-MERRI.

PERIODICALS

Glam: POB 3272, Doha; tel. 44550983; fax 44550982; e-mail glam@ oryxpublishing.com; internet www.glamqatar.com; monthly; English; fashion and lifestyle; publ. by Oryx Advertising Co; f. 2008; Editor-in-Chief YOUSUF BIN JASSIM AL-DARWISH.

Al-Jawhara (The Jewel): POB 2531, Doha; tel. 44414575; fax 44671388; f. 1977; monthly; Arabic; magazine covering watches and jewellery; publ. by al-Ahd Establishment for Journalism, Printing and Publications Ltd; Editor-in-Chief ABDULLAH YOUSUF AL-HUSSAINI.

Al-Ouroba (Arabism): POB 663, Doha; tel. 44325874; fax 44429424; f. 1970; weekly; Arabic; political; publ. by Dar al-Ouroba Printing and Publishing; Editor-in-Chief YOUSUF NAAMA.

Qatar Al-Yom: POB 3272, Doha; tel. 44672139; fax 44550982; internet omsqatar.com/qatar-alyom.html; f. 2005; Arabic; news, business and lifestyle; publ. by Oryx Advertising Co; Editor-in-Chief YOUSUF JASSEM AL-DARWISH.

Qatar Today: POB 3272, Doha; tel. 44672139; fax 44550982; e-mail info@oryxpublishing.com; internet qatartoday.online; f. 1978; monthly; English; news, business and lifestyle; publ. by Oryx Advertising Co; Editor-in-Chief YOUSUF JASSIM AL-DARWISH.

Al-Tarbiya (Education): POB 9865, Doha; tel. 44044596; fax 44044557; f. 1971; quarterly; publ. by Qatar Nat. Comm. for Education, Culture and Science; Editor-in-Chief MUHAMMAD SIDDIQ.

Al-Tijara Wal A'amal: POB 272, Doha; tel. 44478042; fax 44478063; e-mail info@mashaheermedia.com; internet www.mashaheermedia .com; f. 2003; English; business and industry; publ. by Mashaheer Media Qatar.

Al-Ufuq: POB 3488, Doha; tel. 44602844; fax 44601294; f. 2002; monthly; Arabic; business; publ. by Dar al-Sharq Printing, Publishing and Distribution.

Al-Ummah: POB 893, Doha; tel. 44447300; fax 44447022; e-mail m_dirasat@islam.gov.qa; f. 1982; bi-monthly; Islamic thought and affairs, current cultural issues, book serializations.

NEWS AGENCY

Qatar News Agency (QNA): POB 3299, Doha; tel. 44450321; fax 44438316; internet www.qna.org.qa; f. 1975; affiliated to Ministry of Foreign Affairs; Dir-Gen. AHMED SAID JABER AL-RUMAIHI.

Publishers

Ali bin Ali Media and Publishing: POB 75, Doha; tel. 44432045; fax 44015031; e-mail advertise@alibinali.com; internet www .abamediapublishing.com; part of Ali bin Ali Group; publrs of *Qatar Telephone Directory* and *Yellow Pages*; Chair. and Pres. ADEL ALI BIN ALI; Gen. Man. ANTOINE CHERFANE.

Dar al-Sharq Printing, Publishing and Distribution: POB 3488, Doha; tel. 44557866; fax 44557871; e-mail alsharq@al-sharq .com; internet www.al-sharq.com; publrs of *Al-Sharq* and *The Peninsula* newspapers, and *Al-Ufuq* magazine; distributor for various foreign newspapers; Editorial Dir SADIQ MOHAMMED AL-AMMARI; Editor-in-Chief SADIQ MOHAMMED AL-AMARI.

Gulf Publishing and Printing Co: POB 2888, Doha; tel. 44350475; fax 44350474; e-mail editor@gulf-times.com; internet www.gulf-times.com; f. 1978; publrs of *Gulf Times* and *Al-Rayah*; Chair. ABDULLAH BIN KHALIFA AL-ATTIYA.

Hamad bin Khalifa University Press: POB 34110, Education City Student Center, Doha; tel. 44542433; e-mail hbkupcomms@ hbkupress.com; internet hbkupress.com; f. 2009 as Bloomsbury Qatar Foundation Publishing; present name adopted in 2016; publr of fiction and non-fiction in English and Arabic, including educational, academic, reference and children's books; owned by Qatar Foundation; Dir KATHY ROONEY.

Oryx Advertising Co WLL: POB 3272, Doha; tel. 44550983; fax 44550982; e-mail info@oryxpublishing.com; internet oryxpublishing .com; f. 1973; publs include *Qatar Today*, *Qatar Al-Yom*, *Glam*, *T Qatar* and *SME Connect*; Publr and Editor-in-Chief YOUSUF JASSEM AL-DARWISH.

Qatar National Printing Press (QNPP): POB 355, Doha; tel. 44448452; fax 44360950; e-mail info@qnpp.net; internet www.qnpp .net; f. 1958; books, magazines, promotional materials, business forms, stationery, screenprinting, etc.; Gen. Man. JOSEPH DORLIAN.

Broadcasting and Communications

TELECOMMUNICATIONS

Communications Regulatory Authority (CRA): POB 23404, al-Nasr Tower B, al-Corniche St, Doha; tel. 44995535; fax 44995515; e-mail info@cra.gov.qa; internet www.cra.gov.qa; f. 2014 as ind. regulatory body for telecommunications sector; Pres. MUHAMMAD ALI AL-MANNAI.

Ooredoo QSC: POB 217, West Bay, Doha; tel. 44400400; fax 44476231; e-mail customer.service@ooredoo.qa; internet www .ooredoo.qa; f. 1987; majority state-owned; fmrly Qatar Telecommunications Corpn—Qatar Telecom; provides telecommunications services within Qatar; Chair. Sheikh FAISAL BIN THANI AL THANI; Man. Dir AZIZ AL-UTHMAN FAKHROO; CEO, Qatar ALI BIN JABOR AL THANI.

Vodafone Qatar QSC: POB 27727, Qatar Science & Technology Park, Doha; tel. 44069938; e-mail care.qa@vodafone.com; internet www.vodafone.qa; f. 2008; majority shareholders Vodafone Group PLC (United Kingdom) and Qatar Foundation for Education, Science and Community Devt; initial public offering for Qatari nationals of 40% of shares conducted 2009; awarded Qatar's second mobile telephone operating licence 2008; Chair. ABDULLAH BIN NASSER AL-MISNAD; CEO Sheikh HAMAD BIN ABDULLAH BIN JASSIM AL THANI.

BROADCASTING

Regulatory Authority

Qatar Media Corpn (QMC): POB 1836, Doha; tel. 44894444; fax 44885463; e-mail info@qmc.qa; internet www.qmc.qa; f. 2009; Chair. HAMAD BIN THAMER AL THANI; CEO Sheikh ABDULAZIZ BIN THANI AL THANI.

Radio

Qatar Broadcasting Service (QBS): POB 3939, Doha; tel. 44894466; fax 44882888; e-mail info@qbsradio.qa; internet www .qbsradio.qa; f. 1968; govt service transmitting in Arabic, English, French and Urdu; programmes include Holy Quran Radio and Doha Music Radio.

Sout al-Khaleej: POB 1414, Doha; tel. 44030000; e-mail infoskr@ skr.fm; internet www.soutalkhaleej.fm; f. 2002; Arabic arts broadcasting.

Television

Al Jazeera Media Network: POB 23123, Doha; tel. 44896666; e-mail advertising@aljazeera.net; internet www.aljazeera.net; f. 1996; 24-hr broadcasting of news and current affairs in Arabic; English-language service launched 2006; documentary channel launched 2007; also operates channels broadcasting sports, children's programmes and live coverage of political conferences; Al Jazeera Balkans, based in Bosnia and Herzegovina, began transmission in 2011; Al Jazeera America, based in the USA, began operations 2013; a Turkish-language channel, Al Jazeera Türk, began online operations 2014; Chair. Sheikh HAMAD BIN THAMER AL THANI.

Qatar Television Service (QTV): POB 1836, Doha; tel. 44894444; fax 44874170; internet www.qtv.qa; f. 1970; operates 2 channels (of which 1 broadcasts in English); 24-hr broadcasting.

Finance

STATE FINANCIAL AUTHORITIES

In March 2005 the Government established the Qatar Financial Centre (QFC), which was intended to attract international financial institutions and multinational corporations to Qatar, 'to establish business operations in a best-in-class international environment'. The QFC comprised the QFC Authority and the QFC Regulatory

Authority (QFCRA), as well as two legal bodies—the QFC Regulatory Tribunal and the QFC Civil and Commercial Court—which were charged with upholding the rule of law and ensuring the transparency of QFC transactions.

Qatar Financial Centre Authority (QFC): POB 23245, Doha; tel. 44967777; fax 44967676; e-mail contact@qfc.qa; internet qfc.qa; f. 2005; charged with promoting Qatar as an attractive location for international banking, insurance and financial services; Chair. Sheikh MOHAMMED BIN HAMAD BIN QASSIM AL-ABDULLAH AL THANI (Minister of Commerce and Industry); CEO YOUSUF AL-JAIDA.

Qatar Financial Centre Regulatory Authority (QFCRA): POB 22989, Level 14, Qatar Financial Centre Tower, Doha; tel. 44956888; fax 44956868; e-mail info@qfcra.com; internet www.qfcra.com; f. 2005; charged with the regulation and supervision of a wide range of financial activities, incl. banking, insurance, asset management and financial advisory services; Chair. Sheikh BANDAR BIN MOHAMMED BIN SAUD AL THANI; CEO MICHAEL RYAN.

Qatar Financial Markets Authority (QFMA): POB 25552, Doha; tel. 44289999; fax 44441221; e-mail media@qfma.org.qa; internet www.qfma.org.qa; f. 2007 to supervise the stock exchange and securities industry; Chair. Sheikh BANDAR BIN MOHAMMED BIN SAUD AL THANI; Chief Exec. TAMI AHMAD AL-BUTAMI AL-BINALI.

BANKING
Central Bank

Qatar Central Bank: POB 1234, Doha; tel. 44456456; internet www.qcb.gov.qa; f. 1966 as Qatar and Dubai Currency Bd; became Qatar Monetary Agency 1973; renamed Qatar Cen. Bank 1993; state-owned; Gov. Sheikh BANDAR BIN MOHAMMED BIN SAUD AL THANI.

Commercial Banks

Ahlibank QSC: POB 2309, Suhmin bin Hamad St, al-Sadd Area, Doha; tel. 44205222; e-mail info@ahlibank.com.qa; internet www.ahlibank.com.qa; f. 1984 as Al-Ahli Bank of Qatar QSC; name changed as above in 2004; announced plans to merge with Al-Khalij Commercial Bank and Int. Bank of Qatar 2016; Chair. and Man. Dir Sheikh FAISAL BIN ABDULAZIZ BIN JASSEM AL THANI; CEO HASSAN AHMED AL-EFRANGI.

Commercial Bank of Qatar QSC (CBQ): POB 3232, Grand Hamad Ave, Doha; tel. 44490000; fax 44490070; e-mail info@cbq.com.qa; internet www.cbq.com.qa; f. 1975; Chair. Sheikh ABDULLAH BIN ALI BIN JABER AL THANI; Man. Dir OMAR HUSSAIN IBRAHIM AL-FARDAN; CEO JOSEPH ABRAHAM.

Doha Bank: POB 3818, Grand Hamad Ave, Doha; tel. 44456000; fax 44416631; e-mail hellodoha@dohabank.com.qa; internet www.dohabank.com.qa; f. 1979; Chair. Sheikh FAHAD BIN MUHAMMAD BIN JABER AL THANI; Group CEO GUDNI STIHOLT ADALSTEINSSON (acting).

Dukhan Bank: Grand Hamad St, Doha; tel. 44100888; e-mail groupcommunications@barwabank.com; internet www.dukhanbank.com; merged with International Bank of Qatar in 2019; Chair. and Man. Dir Sheikh MOHAMMED BIN HAMAD BIN JASSIM AL THANI; Group CEO AHMED HASHEM (acting).

Lesha Bank: POB 28028, Suhaim bin Hamad St, Doha; tel. 44483333; fax 44483560; e-mail information@qfb.com.qa; internet www.qfb.com.qa; f. 2008; est. as Qatar First Bank; present name adopted 2022; offers *Shari'a*-compliant investment banking services; Chair. Sheikh FAISAL BIN THANI AL THANI; CEO ABDULRAHMAN TOTONJI.

Masraf Al Rayan: POB 28888, Doha; tel. 44253333; e-mail info@alrayan.com; internet www.alrayan.com; f. 2006; merged with Al-Khalij Commercial Bank in June 2021; offers *Shari'a*-compliant banking services; Chair. MOHAMMED BIN HAMAD BIN QASSIM AL-ABDULLAH AL THANI; Group CEO FAHAD AL-KHALIFA.

Qatar Development Bank (QDB): POB 22789, Doha; tel. 44300000; fax 44316613; internet www.qdb.qa; f. 1996 as Qatar Industrial Devt Bank; inaugurated Oct. 1997; relaunched under above name in 2007 with expanded capital provision to facilitate private sector involvement in national economic devt; state-owned; provides long-term, low-interest industrial loans; finances wide range of industrial and social projects; broadened consultancy services following relaunch; Chair. ALI AHMED AL-KUWARI; CEO ABDULRAHMAN HESHAM AL-SOWAIDI (acting).

Qatar International Islamic Bank: POB 664, Grand Hamad St, Doha; tel. 44840000; fax 44444101; e-mail info@qiib.com.qa; internet www.qiib.com.qa; f. 1990; Chair. and Man. Dir KHALID BIN THANI BIN ABDULLAH AL THANI; CEO ABDULBASIT AL-SHAIBEI.

Qatar Islamic Bank SAQ (QIB): POB 559, Grand Hamad St, Doha; tel. 40333333; fax 44412700; e-mail info@qib.com.qa; internet www.qib.com.qa; f. 1982; Chair. Sheikh JASIM BIN HAMAD BIN JASIM BIN JABER AL THANI; CEO BASSEL GAMAL.

Qatar National Bank SAQ: POB 1000, Doha; tel. 44407777; fax 44413753; e-mail ccsupport@qnb.com.qa; internet www.qnb.com.qa; f. 1964; owned 50% by Govt of Qatar and 50% by Qatari nationals; Chair. ALI BIN AHMED AL-KUWARI (Minister of Finance); Group CEO ABDULLA MUBARAK AL-KHALIFA.

SOVEREIGN WEALTH FUND

Qatar Investment Authority (QIA): POB 23224, Doha; tel. 44995919; e-mail contactus@qia.qa; internet www.qia.qa; f. 2005 to develop, invest and manage state reserve funds; Chair. Sheikh BANDAR BIN MOHAMMED BIN SAUD AL THANI; CEO Sheikh MANSOUR BIN EBRAHIM AL-MAHMOUD.

STOCK EXCHANGE

Qatar Exchange (QE): POB 22114, al-Dana Tower, West Bay, Doha; tel. 44333666; fax 44319233; e-mail info@qe.qa; internet www.qe.com.qa; f. 2009 to replace fmr Doha Securities Market (f. 1997); 80% stake owned by Qatar Holding, 20% owned by NYSE Euronext; 50 cos listed (April 2021); Chair. Sheikh MOHAMMED BIN HAMAD BIN QASSIM AL-ABDULLAH AL THANI (Minister of Commerce and Industry); CEO TAMIM HAMAD AL-KAWARI.

INSURANCE

Doha Insurance Co: POB 7171, Doha; tel. and fax 44292777; e-mail info@dig.qa; internet www.dicqatar.com; f. 1999 as public shareholding co; Chair. Sheikh NAWAF BIN NASSER BIN KHALID AL THANI; CEO JASSIM ALI AL-MOFTAH.

Al-Khaleej Takaful Insurance Co (SAQ): POB 4555, Grand Hamad St, Doha; tel. 44041111; e-mail cs@alkhaleej.com; internet www.alkhaleejtakaful.com; f. 1978; all classes except life; Chair. Sheikh ABDULLAH BIN MUHAMMAD JABER AL THANI; CEO ABDULLAH BIN ALI AL-ASSIRI.

Qatar General Insurance and Reinsurance Co SAQ: POB 4500, A Ring Rd, al-Asmakh Area, Doha; tel. 44282222; fax 44437302; e-mail info@qgirco.com; internet www.qgirco.com; f. 1979; all classes; Chair. KHALIFA BIN JASSIM BIN MOHAMMAD AL THANI; CEO SAEED ABU GHARBIEH.

Qatar Insurance Co SAQ: POB 666, Tamin St, West Bay, Doha; tel. 44962222; e-mail info@qic-insured.com; internet www.qic-insured.com; f. 1964; all classes; the Govt has a majority share; Chair. and Man. Dir Sheikh KHALIFA A. AL-SUBAEY; Group CEO SALEM KHALAF AL-MANNAI.

Qatar Insurance Services LLC (Qatarlyst): 6th Floor, QFC Tower, POB 23245, Doha; tel. 44968301; fax 44968310; e-mail enquiries@qatarlyst.com; internet www.qatarlyst.com; f. 2008 by the QFCA, with the aim of establishing Qatar as a regional hub for the insurance industry; launched internet-based insurance trading and processing service (Qatarlyst) 2009; CEO KHALID AL-MUGHESIB; Chair. ABD AL-RAHMAN AHMAD AL-SHAIBI.

Qatar Islamic Insurance Co: POB 22676, Doha; tel. 44658888; fax 44550111; e-mail qiic@qiic.com.qa; internet www.qiic.com.qa; f. 1993; Chair. Sheikh KHALID BIN THANI AL THANI; CEO ALI IBRAHIM ABDUL GHANI.

Trade and Industry

DEVELOPMENT ORGANIZATIONS

Department of Industrial Development: POB 2599, Doha; tel. 44846444; fax 44832024; a div. of the Ministry of Commerce and Industry; conducts research, licensing, devt and supervision of new industrial projects.

General Secretariat for Development Planning: POB 1588, Doha; tel. 44958888; internet www.gsdp.gov.qa; f. 2006; responsible for co-ordination of the emirate's long-term devt strategy; monitors progress of Qatar's Nat. Vision 2030 and Nat. Devt Strategy; Sec.-Gen. Dr SALIH BIN MUHAMMAD AL-NABIT.

Public Works Authority (Ashghal): POB 22188, Doha; tel. 44950000; fax 44950900; e-mail customerservice@ashghal.gov.qa; internet www.ashghal.gov.qa; f. 2004; responsible for the management and devt of public infrastructure projects; Chair. ABDULLAH BIN ABDULAZIZ BIN TURKI AL-SUBAIE (Minister of Municipality); Pres. SAAD BIN AHMED BIN IBRAHIM AL-MUHANNADI.

CHAMBER OF COMMERCE

Qatar Chamber of Commerce and Industry: POB 402, Doha; tel. 44559111; fax 44661693; e-mail info@qcci.org; internet qatarchamber.com; f. 1963; 17 elected mems; Chair. Sheikh KHALIFA BIN JASIM BIN MUHAMMAD AL THANI; Gen. Man. SALEH BIN HAMAD AL-SHARQI.

QATAR

STATE HYDROCARBONS COMPANIES

Qatar Fuel (WOQOD): POB 7777, WOQOD Tower, West Bay, Doha; tel. 40217777; fax 44309215; e-mail customerservice@woqod.com.qa; internet www.woqod.com; f. 2002; distributor of petroleum products and LPG; operates a network of branded service stations throughout Qatar; Chair. AHMAD SAIF AL-SULAITI; CEO SAAD RASHID AL-MUHANNADI.

Qatar Petrochemical Co SAQ (QAPCO): POB 756, Doha; tel. 40338000; fax 44324700; e-mail info@qapco.com.qa; internet www.qapco.com.qa; f. 1974; 80% owned by Industries Qatar, 20% by Total Petrochemicals (France); operation of petrochemical plant at Mesaieed; Chair. ABDULAZIZ JASSIM M. AL-MUFTAH; Man. Dir and CEO MUHAMMAD YOUSUF AL-MULLA.

Qatofin Co Ltd: POB 55013, Doha; tel. 40338000; fax 44324700; e-mail info@qatofin.com.qa; internet www.qatofin.com.qa; f. 2009; 63% owned by Qatar Petrochemical Co, 36% by Total and 1% by QatarEnergy; capacity to produce 450,000 metric tons of low-density polyethylene annually; Chair. ABDULAZIZ JASSIM M. AL-MUFTAH; Man. Dir and CEO MUHAMMAD YOUSUF AL-MULLA.

QatarEnergy: POB 3212, Doha; tel. 40134895; fax 44831125; e-mail webmaster@qp.com.qa; internet www.qatarenergy.qa; f. 1974 as Qatar Gen. Petroleum Corpn (QGPC), name changed 2001 to Qatar Petroleum; present name adopted in 2021; the State of Qatar's interest in cos active in petroleum and related industries was passed to QP; has responsibility for all phases of oil and gas industry both onshore and offshore, incl. exploration, drilling, production, refining, transport and storage, distribution, sale and export of oil, natural gas and other hydrocarbons; Oryx gas to liquids (GTL) plant became operational in 2006, with capacity for 34,000 b/d of GTL products; Chair. and Man. Dir Sheikh ABDULLAH BIN HAMAD AL THANI; Pres. and CEO SAAD BIN SHERIDA AL-KAABI (Minister of State for Energy Affairs); 5,500 employees.

Qatar Liquefied Gas Co (Qatargas): POB 22666, Doha; tel. 44736000; fax 44736666; e-mail infos@qatargas.com.qa; internet www.qatargas.com; f. 1984 to develop the North Field of unassociated gas; 65% owned by QatarEnergy, 10% each by ExxonMobil (USA) and Total, and 7.5% each by Marubeni Corpn and Mitsui & Co of Japan; merged with RasGas in 2018; annual production capacity 77m. metric tons of gas; Chair. SAAD SHERIDA AL-KAABI; CEO KHALID BIN KHALIFA AL THANI.

QatarEnergy also wholly or partly owns: Industries Qatar (IQ) and its subsidiaries, Qatar Gas Transport Co (Nakilat), Gulf Helicopters Co Ltd (GHC), Qatar Vinyl Co (QVC), Qatar Chemical Co (Q-Chem), Qatar Clean Energy Co (QACENCO), Qatar Electricity and Water Co (QEWC), Qatar Shipping Co (Q-Ship), Arab Maritime Petroleum Transport Co (AMPTC), Arab Petroleum Pipelines Co (SUMED), Arab Shipbuilding and Repair Yard Co (ASRY), Arab Petroleum Services Co (APSC) and Arab Petroleum Investments Corpn (APICORP).

UTILITIES

Qatar General Electricity and Water Corpn (Kahramaa): POB 41, Doha; tel. 44845555; fax 44845496; e-mail contactus@km.com.qa; internet www.km.qa; f. 2000; state authority for planning, implementation, operation and maintenance of electricity and water sectors; Pres. ISSA HILAL AL-KUWARI.

Qatar Electricity and Water Co (QEWC): POB 22046, Doha; tel. 44858585; fax 44831116; e-mail welcome@qewc.com; internet qewc.com; f. 1990; 48% privately owned; devt and operation of power generation and water desalination facilities; Chair. SAAD BIN SHARIDA AL-KAABI; Gen. Man. MOHAMED NASSER AL-HAJRI.

MAJOR INVESTMENT HOLDING COMPANIES

Qatar Investment and Projects Development Holding Co (QIPCO Holding): POB 8612, Doha; tel. 44058800; fax 44341115; e-mail enquiries@qipco.com.qa; internet qipco.com.qa; f. 1999; privately owned; investment holding; subsidiaries in real estate devt and management, construction, oil and gas and services sectors; Chair. and CEO Sheikh ABDULLAH BIN KHALIFA AL THANI.

Qatari Diar Real Estate Investment Co: POB 23175, Lusail, Doha; tel. 44974444; fax 44974333; e-mail customerservice@qataridiar.com; internet www.qataridiar.com; f. 2005; real estate investment holding, land acquisition and devt; owned by QIA and Govt of Qatar; Chair. Sheikh KHALID BIN KHALIFA AL THANI; CEO Eng. ABDULLAH BIN HAMAD AL-ATTIYAH.

Salam International Investment Ltd (SIIL): POB 15224, Salam Tower, Corniche Rd, Doha; tel. 44830439; fax 44833576; e-mail info@salaminternational.com; internet www.salaminternational.com; f. 1952; investments in, *inter alia*, energy and information technology sectors; Chair. ISSA ABDULSALAM ABU ISSA; CEO ABDULSALAM ABU ISSA.

Zad Holding Co: POB 1444, Doha; tel. 44415000; fax 44438137; e-mail info@zad.qa; internet zad.qa; f. 1969; operations include manufacturing and distributing FMCG, real estate, contracting and logistics services, etc.; subsidiaries include Qatar Flour Mills, Qatar Foods Industries, Gulf Unified Real Estate Investments Co; Chair. Sheikh NASSER BIN MOHAMMED BIN JABOR AL THANI; Man. Dir Sheikh NAWAF BIN MOHAMMAD BIN JABOR AL THANI.

MAJOR COMPANIES

Aamal Co QSC: POB 22477, Doha; tel. 44223870; fax 44223840; e-mail info@aamal.com.qa; internet www.aamal.com.qa; f. 2001; property devt, industrial manufacturing, retail, managed services and pharmaceuticals; Chair. Sheikh FAISAL BIN QASSIM AL THANI; CEO RASHID ALI AL-MANSOORI.

AKC Contracting & Supply: al-Tadamon Complex, D Ring Service Rd, Doha; tel. 44146319; fax 44601720; internet akcqatar.com; f. 1975; building, plumbing, joinery, landscaping, etc.; Gen. Man. MOHAMED MOHSEN.

Arab-Qatari Co for Dairy Production (Ghadeer): POB 8324, Doha; internet fb.com/ghadeerdairy; f. 1985; production of dairy products, ice creams and fruit juices.

Arab-Qatari Co for Poultry Production (al-Waha): POB 3606, Doha; tel. 44729042; fax 44729028; e-mail info@aqpoultry.com.qa; internet www.aqpoultry.com.qa; subsidiary of Hassad Food.

Barwa Real Estate Co: POB 27777, Suhaim bin Hamad St, C Ring Rd, Doha; tel. 44088888; fax 44088885; e-mail info@barwa.com.qa; internet www.barwa.com.qa; f. 2005; real estate devt; Chair. ABDULLA HAMAD AL-ATIYYA; CEO ABDULLAH JUBARA AL-RUMAIHI.

Ezdan Holding Group: POB 30503, Doha; tel. 44332333; e-mail info@ezdanholding.qa; internet www.ezdanholding.qa; f. 1960; real estate devt and trading; Chair. Sheikh THANI BIN ABDULLAH THANI AL THANI.

Industries Qatar Co (IQ): POB 3212, Doha; tel. 40132080; fax 40139750; e-mail iq@qatarenergy.qa; internet www.iq.com.qa; f. 2003 as part of the Govt's programme of privatization; 51% stake owned by QatarEnergy; controls Qatar Petrochemical Co, Qatar Fertilizer Co, Qatar Fuel Additives Co and Qatar Steel; Chair. and Man. Dir SAAD SHERIDA AL-KAABI.

Kassem Darwish Fakhro & Sons (KDS): POB 92, Doha; tel. 44422781; fax 44417599; e-mail mktg@darwish-tdg.qa; internet www.darwish-tdg.qa; f. 1911; corporate group est. 1971; electrical, mechanical and civil contractors, general trading, mfrs.

Mesaieed Petrochemical Holding Co (MPHC): POB 3212, Doha; tel. 40132080; fax 40139750; e-mail mphc@qatarenergy.qa; internet www.mphc.com.qa; f. 2013; established by Qatar Petroleum by combining Qatar Chemical Company Ltd, Chemical Company II Ltd and Qatar Vinyl Company (QVC) Ltd QSC; Chair. AHMAD SAIF AL-SULAITI.

National Industrial Gas Plants (NIGP): POB 1391, Doha; tel. 44411351; fax 44435030; e-mail nigp@qatar.net.qa; internet www.mhalmanagroup.com; f. 1954; part of the Mohammed Hamad Al Mana Group; production of industrial gases (oxygen, carbon dioxide, nitrogen, argon and acetylene), liquid gases (oxygen, nitrogen and argon), and dry ice, hydrostatic pressure testing of high-pressure cylinders; Pres. M. H. AL-MANA.

Qatar Fertilizer Co SAQ (QAFCO): POB 50001, Umm Said (Mesaieed); tel. 44227777; fax 44770347; e-mail pr@qafco.com.qa; internet www.qafco.qa; f. 1969; owned by Industries Qatar (IQ); Chair. AHMED HELAL AL-MOHANNADI; CEO ABDULRAHMAN AL-SUWAIDI.

Qatar Flour Mills Co SAQ (QFM): POB 1444, Doha; tel. 44415000; fax 44438137; e-mail feedback@qfm.qa; internet www.qfm.qa; f. 1969.

Qatar Industrial Manufacturing Co (QIMC): POB 16875, al-Corniche St, West Bay, Doha; tel. 44344222; fax 44837878; e-mail qimc@qimc.com.qa; internet www.qimc.com.qa; f. 1989 to establish domestic and international industrial ventures; 20% state-owned; subsidiaries and associated cos include Qatar Nitrogen Co, Qatar Metal-Coating Co, National Paper Industries Co, Qatar Sand-Treatment Plant, Qatar Acids Co, National Food Co, Qatar Jet Fuel Co, Qatar-Saudi Gypsum Industries Co, Qatar Paving Stones; Chair. and Man. Dir Sheikh ABDUL RAHMAN BIN MUHAMMAD JABER AL THANI; CEO ABDUL RAHMAN AL-ANSARI.

Qatar National Cement Co SAQ (QNCC): POB 1333, Doha; tel. 44711811; fax 44711432; e-mail qncc@qatarcement.com; internet www.qatarcement.com; f. 1965; CEO ESSA MUHAMMED ALI KALADARI.

Qatar National Plastic Factory (QPLAST): POB 5615, Bldg No. 135, St No. 4, Zone 81, New Industrial Area, Doha; tel. 44689977; fax 44689922; e-mail info@qnplast.com; internet qnplast.com; f. 1977; production of UPVC pipes & fittings, PE pipes, construction sheet and tapes; Gen. Man. DOMINIC MAJENDIE.

Qatar Steel Co (QASCO): POB 50090, Mesaieed; tel. 44778778; fax 44771424; e-mail webmaster@qatarsteel.com.qa; internet www.qatarsteel.com.qa; plant completed in 1978; 100% govt-owned;

QATAR

Chair. SAAD RASHID AL-MUHANNADI; Man. Dir and CEO ABDULRAHMAN ALI A. AL-ABDULLA.

Readymix Qatar Ltd: POB 5007, Doha; tel. 44536600; fax 44328056; e-mail rmq.sales@holcim.com; internet www.readymixqatar.com.qa; f. 1978; production of ready-mixed concrete; Gen. Man. JON BROOKS.

Qatar Quarry Co LLC: POB 5007, Doha; tel. 44653071; fax 44651534; f. 1983; production of aggregates, road materials and armour rock; Gen. Man. SALIM KUTTY.

United Development Co: Doha; tel. 44098400; e-mail info@udcqatar.com; internet udcqatar.com; f. 1999; businesses include real estate, property management, district cooling, hospitality and maritime, infrastructure and utilities; Chair. TURKI MOHAMED AL-KHATER; Pres. and CEO IBRAHIM JASSIM AL-OTHMAN.

Transport

RAILWAYS

In 2009 the Qatar Railways Development Co (QRDC), a joint venture comprising Qatari Diar Real Estate Investment Co and Deutsche Bahn AG (Germany), was established to supervise the development of a national rail network, which would be linked to a regional rail network, connecting Qatar with the other member countries of the Cooperation Council for the Arab States of the Gulf (Gulf Cooperation Council—GCC). In 2011 QRDC established the Qatar Railways Co (Qatar Rail) to oversee the implementation of plans to develop the national rail network. Three lines of a planned 124-km, four-line metro system in Doha opened for passengers during 2019. The fourth line was expected to become operational in 2026. The first section of a 34-km light rail network to serve the new, planned city of Lusail, some 23 km north of Doha, was inaugurated in January 2022.

Qatar Railways Co (Qatar Rail): Qatar Rail Tower, 231 Suhaim bin Hamad St (C-Ring Rd), al-Sadd Area 38, POB 29988, Doha; tel. 44331111; fax 44331110; internet corp.qr.com.qa; f. 2011; fully owned by Qatar Railways Development Co (QRDC); Chair. Sheikh KHALID BIN KHALIFA BIN ABDULAZIZ AL THANI; CEO Dr ABDULLA BIN ABDULAZIZ TURKI AL-SUBAIE.

ROADS

A major upgrade of the national road network was planned for the early decades of the 21st century. Work on the QR 15,000m., Doha Expressway project, involving the construction of a dual carriageway linking the north and south of the country and a Doha ring road, commenced in 2007 and was ongoing in early 2023. The planned construction of a 40-km causeway linking Ras Ishairij in Qatar with Askar in eastern Bahrain (the Qatar Bahrain Friendship Bridge) was approved in 2004; the causeway was to carry both motor vehicles and trains and, when completed, would be the longest fixed causeway in the world. However, as a result of various issues including financial problems and diplomatic disputes between Qatar and Bahrain, the project suffered serious delays and as of early 2023 construction work had not yet commenced.

SHIPPING

The North Field gas project has increased the demand for shipping facilities. A major new industrial port was inaugurated at Ras Laffan in 1995, providing facilities for LNG and condensate carriers and ro-ro vessels. Ras Laffan port was subsequently expanded and now incorporates the world's largest LNG export facility, with more than 1,000 LNG tankers calling at the port annually.

Hamad Port, located near Mesaieed industrial city to the south of Doha, is Qatar's main seaport. It was officially opened in September 2017 (replacing Doha's existing port) and was expected to become fully operational by 2025.

Port Authority

Qatar Ports Management Co (Mwani): St 201, Mesaieed; tel. 40453333; fax 40453302; e-mail info@mwani.com.qa; internet www.mwani.com.qa; CEO Capt. ABDULLA AL-KHANJI.

Principal Shipping Companies

Qatar Gas Transport Co Ltd (Nakilat): POB 22271, Shoumoukh Towers B, C Ring Rd, Doha; tel. 44998111; fax 44483111; e-mail smedia@qgtc.com.qa; internet www.nakilat.com.qa; f. 2004; specializes in the shipment of LNG, LPG and petroleum products; owns 69 vessels; Chair. MUHAMMAD BIN SALEH AL-SADA; Man. Dir ABDULLAH FADHALAH AL-SULAITI.

Qatar Navigation QSC (Milaha): POB 153, 60 al-Tameen St, West Bay, Doha; tel. 44949666; fax 44833244; internet www.milaha.com; f. 1957 as Qatar Nat. Navigation and Transport Co Ltd; changed name as above 2013; acquired Qatar Shipping Co in 2010; 92.2% owned by Qatari nationals; shipping agents, stevedoring, chandlers, forwarding, repairs, construction, etc.; Chair. Sheikh JASSIM BIN HAMAD BIN JASSIM JABER AL THANI; Pres. and CEO MOHAMED ABDULLA SWIDAN (acting).

Qatar Shipping Co QSC (Q-Ship): POB 22180, Doha; tel. 44949666; fax 44315793; e-mail rahul@qship.com; internet www.qship.com; f. 1992; subsidiary of Qatar Navigation QSC; oil and bulk cargo shipping; wholly owns 7 vessels; Chair. and Man. Dir SALEM BIN BUTTI AL-NAIMI; CEO JOSEPH COUTINHO.

CIVIL AVIATION

Hamad International Airport, which was constructed some 4 km to the east of the existing Doha International Airport, commenced operations in 2014, when it replaced the latter as the country's provider of scheduled commercial passenger services.

Civil Aviation Authority: POB 3000, Doha; tel. 44557333; fax 44557103; e-mail caaqatar@caa.gov.qa; internet www.caa.gov.qa; Pres. MOHAMED FALEH AL-HAJRI.

Hamad International Airport: POB 24844, Doha; tel. 44656666; e-mail hiamedia@hamadairport.com.qa; internet dohahamadairport.com; CEO AKBAR AL-BAKER.

Gulf Helicopters Co (GHC): POB 811, al-Areesh St, Ras Abu Aboud Rd, Doha; tel. 44333888; fax 44411004; e-mail ghc.social@gulfhelicopters.com; internet www.gulfhelicopters.com; f. 1970; owned by Qatar Petroleum; owns a fleet of 41 helicopters; CEO MUHAMMAD AL-MOHANNADI.

Qatar Airways: POB 22550, Qatar Airways Tower 1, Airport Rd, Doha; tel. 40230023; fax 44621533; internet www.qatarairways.com; f. 1993; state-owned; services to more than 80 international destinations; CEO AKBAR AL-BAKER.

Tourism

Katara Hospitality: POB 2977, Marina District, Lusail City, Doha; tel. 44237777; fax 44237860; internet www.katarahospitality.com; f. 1993 as Qatar National Hotels Co; develops and manages hotels and other tourist facilities; govt-owned; Chair. ALI BIN AHMED AL-KUWARI; CEO ANDREW HUMPHRIES (acting).

National Tourism Council: POB 24624, Doha; tel. 44997499; fax 44991919; internet www.visitqatar.qa/NationalTourismCouncil; f. 2000 as Qatar Tourism Authority; rebranded as National Tourism Council in 2018; oversees the operations of three cos: Qatar Tourism Promotion Co, Qatar Tourism Development Co and Qatar Business Events Co; Chair. Sheikh MOHAMMED BIN ABDULRAHMAN BIN JASSIM AL THANI (Prime Minister); Sec.-Gen. AKBAR AL-BAKER.

Defence

As assessed at November 2022, the strength of the Qatar Armed Forces totalled 16,500: army 12,000; navy 2,500 (incl. marine police); air force 2,000. There was also an Internal Security Force numbering up to 5,000.

Defence Budget: QR 30,600m. (est.) in 2022.

Commander-in-Chief of the Armed Forces: Maj.-Gen. Sheikh TAMIM BIN HAMAD AL THANI.

Chief of Staff of the Armed Forces: Lt-Gen. SALEM BIN MOHAMMED BIN AQEEL AL-NABIT.

Commander of the Qatar Emiri Air Force: Maj.-Gen. JASSEM MOHAMED AL-MANNAI.

Commander of the Qatar Emiri Navy: Rear Adm. ABDULLAH BIN HASSAN AL-SULAITI.

Education

All education within Qatar is provided free of charge, although it is not compulsory, and numerous scholarships are awarded for study overseas. Primary schooling begins at six years of age and lasts for six years. The next level of education, beginning at 12 years of age, is divided between a three-year preparatory stage and a further three-year secondary stage. There are specialized religious, industrial, commercial and technical secondary schools for boys; the technical school admitted its first students in 1999/2000, as did two scientific secondary schools (one for girls). According to UNESCO estimates, enrolment at pre-primary level in 2020/21 was equivalent to 54.0% of children (boys 53.8%; girls 54.2%) in the relevant age-group, while enrolment at primary schools in that year included 98.6% of children in the relevant age-group. In 2020/21 the ratio for lower secondary enrolment was 90.0% (boys 89.8%; girls 90.1%).

There are two public universities in Qatar. The Qatar University, which was established in 1977, comprises 11 colleges, with a total of more than 23,000 students in 2023. Hamad bin Khalifa University was established in 2010 by the Qatar Foundation for Education, Science and Community Development, and is located at Education City Qatar (which also hosts branch campuses of eight foreign universities, as well as a range of other educational and research institutions). Qatar's first national private university, Lusail University, was officially inaugurated in 2020. According to UNESCO, in 2021 expenditure on education was equivalent to 8.9% of total government spending.

Bibliography

al-Abdulla, Yousof Ibrahim. *A Study of Qatari-British Relations 1914–1945*. Doha, Orient Publishing and Translation, 1981.

Al Thani, Mohamed A. J. *Jassim the Leader: Founder of Qatar*. New York, Profile Books, 2012.

al-Arayed, Jawal Salim. *A Line in the Sea: The Qatar Versus Bahrain Border Dispute in the World Court*. Berkeley, CA, North Atlantic Books, 2003.

Battaloğlu, Çihat. *Political Reforms in Qatar: From Authoritarianism to Political Grey Zone*. Berlin, Gerlach Press, 2018.

Coates Ulrichsen, Kristian. *Qatar and the Arab Spring*. London, Hurst & Co, 2014.

Qatar and the Gulf Crisis. London, Hurst & Co, 2020.

Fromherz, Allen. *Qatar: Rise to Power and Influence*. London, I. B. Tauris, 2017.

Galeeva, Diana. *Qatar: The Practice of Rented Power*. Abingdon, Routledge, 2022.

Gillespie, Frances. *Hasharat Qatar*. London, Bloomsbury, 2015.

Gray, Matthew. *Qatar: Politics and the Challenge of Development*. Boulder, CO, Lynne Rienner Publishers, 2013.

Harkness, Geoff. *Changing Qatar: Culture, Citizenship, and Rapid Modernization*. New York, New York University Press, 2020.

Kamrava, Mehran. *Qatar: Small State, Big Politics*. Ithaca, NY, Cornell University Press, 2013.

Luomi, Mari. *The Gulf Monarchies and Climate Change: Abu Dhabi and Qatar in an Era of Natural Unsustainability*. London, Hurst & Co, 2012.

al-Mallakh, Ragaei. *Qatar, Energy and Development*. London, Croom Helm, 1985.

Miles, Hugh. *Al Jazeera: How Arab TV News Challenged the World*. London, Abacus, 2005.

Nafi, Zuhair Ahmed. *Economic and Social Development in Qatar* (new edn). London, Bloomsbury Academic, 2013.

al-Othman, Nasser. *With Their Bare Hands: The Story of the Oil Industry in Qatar*. London, Longman, 1984.

Rahman, Habibur. *The Emergence of Qatar: The Turbulent Years 1627–1916*. London, Kegan Paul International, 2005.

Rahman, H., al-Sulaiti, M. E., and al-Jaber, J. *The Changing Face of Qatar: From the Age of the Pearl to the 21st Century*. London, Kegan Paul International, 2007.

Roberts, David B. *Qatar: Securing the Global Ambitions of a City-State*. London, Hurst & Co, 2017.

(Ed.). *Reflecting on the GCC Crisis: Qatar and it Neighbours*. Abingdon, Routledge, 2022.

Seib, Philip (Ed.). *Al Jazeera English: Global News in a Changing World*. Basingstoke, Palgrave Macmillan, 2012.

Smith, Simon C. *Britain's Revival and Fall in the Gulf: Kuwait, Bahrain, Qatar, and the Trucial States, 1950–71*. London, Routledge, 2004.

Ulrichsen, Kristian Coates. *Qatar and the Gulf Crisis*. Oxford, Oxford University Press, 2020.

Vora, Neha. *Teach for Arabia: American Universities, Liberalism, and Transnational Qatar*. Stanford, CA, Stanford Univeristy Press, 2018.

Zweiri, Mahjoob, and al-Qawasmi, Farah (Eds). *Contemporary Qatar: Examining State and Society*. Singapore, Springer, 2021.

For further titles of relevance to Qatar, see the Bibliography sections for Bahrain and the United Arab Emirates.

SAUDI ARABIA

Geography

The Arabian peninsula is a distinct geographical unit, delimited on three sides by sea—on the east by the Persian (Arabian) Gulf and the Gulf of Oman, on the south by the Indian Ocean, and on the west by the Red Sea—while its remaining (northern) side is occupied by the deserts of Jordan and Iraq. This isolated territory, extending over some 2.5m. sq km (about 1m. sq miles), is divided politically into several states. The largest of these is Saudi Arabia, which occupies 2,240,000 sq km (864,869 sq miles); to the east and south lie much smaller territories where suzerainty and even actual frontiers are disputed in some instances. Along the shores of the Persian Gulf and the Gulf of Oman there are, beginning in the north, the State of Kuwait, with two adjacent zones of 'neutral' territory; then, after a stretch of Saudi Arabian coast, the islands of Bahrain and the Qatar peninsula, followed by the United Arab Emirates and the much larger Sultanate of Oman. Yemen occupies most of the southern coastline of the peninsula, and its south-western corner.

PHYSICAL FEATURES

Structurally, the whole of Arabia is a vast platform of ancient rocks, once continuous with north-east Africa. Subsequently, a series of great fissures opened, as a result of which a large trough, or rift valley, was formed and later occupied by the sea, to produce the Red Sea and Gulf of Aden. The Arabian platform is tilted, with its highest part in the extreme west, along the Red Sea, and it slopes gradually down from west to east. Thus the Red Sea coast is often bold and mountainous, whereas the Persian Gulf coast is flat, low-lying and fringed with extensive coral reefs which make it difficult to approach the shore in many places.

Dislocation of the rock strata in the west of Arabia has led to the upwelling of much lava, which has solidified into vast barren expanses, known as *harras*. Volcanic cones and flows are also prominent along the whole length of the western coast as far as Aden, where peaks rise to more than 3,000 m above sea level. The mountains reach their highest in the south, in Yemen, with summits at 4,000 m, and the lowest part of this mountain wall occurs roughly half-way along its course, in the region of Jeddah, Mecca and Medina. A principal reason for the location of these three Saudi Arabian towns is that they offer the easiest route inland from the coast, and one of the shortest routes across Arabia.

Further to the east the ancient platform is covered by relatively thin layers of younger rocks. Some of the strata have been eroded to form shallow depressions; others have proved more resistant, and now stand out as ridges. This central area, relieved by shallow vales and upstanding ridges and covered in many places by desert sand, is called the Najd, and is considered to be the homeland of the Wahhabi sect, which now rules the whole of Saudi Arabia. Further east, practically all the land lies well below 300 m in altitude, and both to the north and to the south are desert areas. The Nefud in the north has some wells, and even a slight rainfall, and therefore supports a few oasis cultivators and pastoral nomads. South of the Najd, however, lies the Rub al-Khali, or Empty Quarter, a rainless, unrelieved wilderness of shifting sand, too harsh for occupation even by nomads.

Most of the east coast of Arabia (al-Hasa) is low-lying, but an exception is the imposing ridge of the Jebel al-Akhdar ('Green Mountain') of Oman, which also produces a fjord-like coastline along the Gulf of Oman. Another feature is the large river valleys, or *wadis*, cut by river action during an earlier geological period, but in modern times almost, or entirely, dry and partially filled with sand. The largest is the Wadi Hadramout, which runs parallel to the southern coast for several hundred km; another is the Wadi Sirhan, which stretches north-westwards from the Nefud into Jordan.

CLIMATE

Owing to its landlocked nature, the winds reaching Arabia are generally dry, and almost all the area is arid. In the north there is a rainfall of 100 mm–200 mm annually; further south, except near the coast, even this fails. The higher parts of the west and south do, however, experience appreciable precipitation—rather sporadic in some parts, but copious and reliable in areas adjacent to the Red Sea.

As a result of aridity, and hence relatively cloudless skies, there are great extremes of temperature. The summer is overwhelmingly hot, with maximum temperatures of more than 50°C, which are intensified by the dark rocks, while in winter there can be general severe frost and even weeks of snow in the mountains. Another result of the wide variations in temperature is the prevalence of violent local winds. Also, near the coast, atmospheric humidity is particularly high, and the coasts of both the Red Sea and the Persian Gulf are notorious for their humidity. Average summer temperatures in Saudi Arabia's coastal regions range from 38°C to 49°C (100°F–120°F), sometimes reaching 54°C (129°F) in the interior, or falling to a minimum of 24°C (75.2°F) in Jeddah. The winters are mild, except in the mountains. Winter temperatures range from 8°C (46.4°F) to 30°C (86°F) in Riyadh, and reach a maximum of 33°C (91.4°F) in Jeddah.

Owing to the tilt of the strata eastwards, and their great elevation in the west, rain falling in the hills near the Red Sea apparently percolates gradually eastwards, to emerge as springs along the Persian Gulf coast. This phenomenon, borne out by the fact that the flow of water in the springs greatly exceeds the total rainfall in the same district, suggests that water may be present underground over much of the interior. Irrigation schemes to exploit these supplies have been developed, notably in the Najd at al-Kharj, but results have been fairly limited.

POPULATION

A recent result of the rapid economic growth in the petroleum-producing countries has been the influx of large numbers of migrants from the developed countries of the Western world, and from developing countries further east. At the national census of May 2022, the population of Saudi Arabia was recorded at 32,175,224, including 13,382,962 foreign nationals (41.6% of the total). The royal and financial capital, Riyadh, is situated in the centre of the country. Its population was estimated at 6,924,566 at the census of 2022. Jeddah (population 3,712,917), located on the Red Sea coast, is also a significant commercial hub. Other large cities included Mecca (population 2,385,506), Medina (1,411,599) and Dammam (1,386,166). The official language of Saudi Arabia is Arabic, which is spoken by almost all of the population.

As its borders enclose the holy cities of Mecca and Medina, Saudi Arabia is considered the centre of the Islamic faith. About 85% of Saudi Muslims belong to the Sunni sect of Islam, the remainder being Shi'a. Except in the Eastern region, Sunni rites prevail.

History

BRANDON FRIEDMAN

INTRODUCTION

Since the 1990s, senior Saudi elites have recognized that the kingdom's oil revenues cannot continue to provide for the large-scale patronage that the state used politically to co-opt a fast-growing population in the 1970s and 1980s. The state received a reprieve when oil prices were high between September 2005 and November 2014, but the stark challenge of declining oil income and a large population struck when King Salman bin Abdulaziz Al Sa'ud succeeded King Abdullah in 2015. The Vision 2030 economic reform programme is the roadmap presented in 2016 by Crown Prince Mohammed bin Salman bin Abdelaziz (colloquially known by his initials MBS) to create jobs for a young and educated Saudi population. About 4.5m. Saudis are expected to join the job market by 2030, which means that the state will face enormous pressure to foster a growth-oriented, market-driven private sector that generates attractive jobs. While the Government had touted its initial public offering (IPO) of Saudi Aramco, the massive state oil company, to raise capital for Vision 2030, Saudi planners recognized that in order to create a 'knowledge-based economy', there needs to be substantial foreign investment in the private sector to generate consistent growth. Yet there are two sides to a prospective new Saudi political economy. On the one hand, the Government needs to create new jobs for the Saudi population. On the other, young Saudis will need to *participate* in building this prospective new economy, something that the kingdom has never asked of its citizens.

In order for this economic transformation to succeed, young Saudis, including young women, will need to be mobilized to work. This mobilization will demand important social change in the kingdom, which has historically been controlled by the strict Wahhabi social norms enforced by the country's religious leadership. For example, since 2016 the state has taken unprecedented steps to allow Saudi women greater social freedoms, such as the ability to drive and travel abroad without male consent or guardianship. In this area and others, the Crown Prince has directly challenged the religious leadership's control over the social sphere in the kingdom.

The result of this top-down economic and social reform is a new formula for political legitimacy in the kingdom based on nationalism. Instead of legitimizing the kingdom through its historical partnership between monarchy and religious leadership—the pact between the *ulama* (Wahhabi religious leaders) and the *umara* (senior Saudi princes), Crown Prince Mohammed is attempting to legitimize the Al Sa'ud monarchy as the sole embodiment and protector of the Saudi nation.

The new Saudi nationalism is also intended to mobilize the Saudi masses to confront security challenges by framing them as threats to the nation. In this way, Crown Prince Mohammed was forging a link between internal threats to regime security and external threats against the state. Saudi Arabia has faced four major security challenges since the 1990–91 Gulf War. First, the Salafi-*jihadi* challenge to the Saudi state, initially from Osama bin Laden's al-Qa'ida and later from Islamic State (IS, also known as ISIS, or the Islamic State in Iraq and al-Sham). Second, the post-Saddam Hussain challenge of Iranian-backed Shi'a ascendancy and expansion in the eastern Arab world, which threatened to alter the status quo of a US-backed Sunni primacy in the region. Iranian-backed Shi'a dominance in Iraq and Lebanon (and later in the Syrian Arab Republic and Yemen), along with the potential threat of an Iranian nuclear weapons programme, were considered signs of a dangerous and unfavourable revision to the regional balance of power. Third, the post-'Arab Spring' threat of a Muslim Brotherhood inspired revolution within the kingdom. Fourth, the threat to Saudi Arabia's leading position in global oil markets, owing first to the shale oil revolution in the USA and later to the growing global drive to energy transition as a result of the climate crisis.

At the heart of these external challenges is the core tension in Saudi Arabia's foreign policy: MBS views the kingdom as a rising global power, and seeks to play that role on the international stage, but it remains vulnerable within the region as it has not yet developed the military power successfully to project force or protect itself from external threats. Saudi Arabia has moved from a trial period of security self-help between 2015 and 2019 to a protection-seeking strategy.

THE END OF THE RENTIER SOCIAL CONTRACT: HISTORICAL BACKGROUND

This section will briefly explain the rise and fall of the rentier system of patronage in the Saudi kingdom, from the 1970s to the 1990s. It will also explain how, during the same period, the religious sphere in the kingdom diversified, leading to a new form of political dissent that challenged Saudi authority and security on religious grounds. This, in turn, led some senior Saudi elites to recognize that the Wahhabi religious establishment no longer dominates the religious sphere in the kingdom and therefore the founding pact between the *ulama* and the *umara* can no longer fully guarantee the regime's legitimacy and stability. These two historical developments—the erosion of rentier patronage and the rise of an activist religious opposition—account for MBS's Vision 2030 plan, which, beyond its restructuring of the Saudi economy, represents an attempt first to mobilize the Saudi population to work, and, second to generate a form of Saudi solidarity rooted in nationalism. The rest of this section explains the rise and fall of rentierism, as well as the emergence of political dissent rooted in new forms of religious opposition.

The modern kingdom of Saudi Arabia was established in 1932. In practice, the modern Saudi monarchy's authority took hold in stages, and the social contract, or modern state order, has evolved as the state matured, modernized and bureaucratized.

In the first stage, during and after the First World War, the Saudi state operated as a chieftaincy, based on ad hoc arrangements between settled and nomadic populations. It lacked a fully articulated central government and only began to acquire the key attributes of modern 'stateness'—defined borders, a central government and sociopolitical cohesiveness—as it faced the challenges of the post-war period: the collapse of the Ottoman Empire, the British dominance and the new Arab state system. King Abdulaziz bin Abd al-Rahman, known in the West as Ibn Sa'ud, created new state institutions but maintained his authority through the tribal practices of a traditional chieftaincy: a royal biological elite of senior princes, which was the product of the Saudi family's practice of intermarrying with notable religious and merchant families; and a system of patron-client networks emanating from senior princes, which formed a state structure bound to the monarchy.

Oil wealth led to the establishment of a rentier social contract in the 1970s, which characterized the second stage of Saudi state-formation. The kingdom was able to obtain the political consent and loyalty of the majority of its citizens by channelling externally derived wealth (oil revenues) through state networks of patronage that ultimately provided secure government employment, free health care and education, and subsidized fuel and energy to its citizens.

The order of King Faisal bin Abdulaziz (1964–75) prevailed over two alternative visions of the Saudi state. King Sa'ud bin Abdulaziz (1953–64) wanted to maintain his father's state order in the post-Second World War era, despite the challenges of revolutionary Arab nationalism and a rapidly growing population that needed welfare, health care and education. Prince Talal bin Abdulaziz favoured a constitutional monarchy, while Faisal's vision was based first and foremost on a strong monarchy that preserved traditional religious and social norms. 'Faisal's Order' consolidated the monarchical structures of the Saudi state. Yet Faisal also pursued institutional and technological development. He created 20 government ministries and expanded the state civil service, which grew from about 62,000 to 336,000 between 1960 and 1980. A unified educational system and national economy took root in the kingdom, and every part of Saudi society experienced some contact with the state.

'Faisal's Order' sought a balance between social change and tradition, seeking to maintain economic and social stability within the existing religious and social framework. In addition to preserving Wahhabi religious norms, King Faisal also cemented the patrimonial kinship networks that formed the state elites. His state order incorporated tribalism into the Government's bureaucracy. Faisal created a new social contract between the ruler and ruled by redistributing the state's oil wealth to the population through the patrimonial networks, guaranteeing Saudis a standard of living that included no income tax, free education and health care services, and heavily subsidized food, electricity and water. This rentier bargain—the kingdom's second stage—defined the state order until the mid-1980s.

From the mid-1980s to the mid-1990s the kingdom's declining oil revenues undermined the rentier social contract and opened the door to an Islamist challenge to Saudi authority. Per capita gross domestic product (GDP) in Saudi Arabia almost doubled between 1968 and 1978, but in the early 1980s it lost around one-half of its value and then remained stagnant from 1987 to 2002. In the 1960s Faisal championed 'Islamic solidarity' as an alternative to the revisionist vision of Arab unity of Lt-Col Gamal Abd al-Nasir (Nasser), the Egyptian President, as embodied in the ideology of secular-socialist Arab nationalism. Faisal mobilized the Muslim Brotherhood intellectuals to whom he had given refuge in the kingdom during the 1950s and 1960s, after they fled the persecution of the Arab nationalist regimes in Egypt and, later, Syria. These Islamist thinkers became Faisal's instruments to counter the Nasserist narrative in the region. In the 1970s the Muslim Brotherhood consolidated its influence in the Saudi educational system. This process led to the institutionalization of Islamic activism in Saudi Arabia. The intellectuals of the al-Sahwa al-Islamiyya ('Islamic Awakening') introduced a Muslim Brotherhood world view into the kingdom, which was reformulated to fit the Wahhabi tradition. With the rise of the revolutionary Islamic Republic of Iran, following the Iranian Revolution in 1979, it was *Sahwi* intellectuals who provided the sophisticated response to Ayatollah Khomeini's revolutionary discourse. During the 1970s, with the largesse of unprecedented state oil revenues, the Wahhabi religious establishment (the Committee of Senior Scholars, established in 1971) institutionalized its religious authority. Yet it also funded and encouraged the new streams of religious opposition that were increasingly beyond its control. When 'Faisal's Order' began to erode, owing to weak leadership and an economic downturn from the mid-1980s to the mid-1990s, challenges to the state came from these new religious opposition groups.

The 1991 Gulf War (see Iraq) gave rise to another serious challenge to the regime's legitimacy. *Sahwi* activists rejected the Wahhabi establishment's religious decision to allow US forces to use Saudi soil as a base for coalition military operations to roll back Saddam Hussain's invasion of Kuwait. While the radical group that seized the Grand Mosque in Mecca in 1979, al-Jamaa al-Salafiyya al-Muhtasiba, and its leader, Juhayman al-Utaybi, could be written off as deviant radicals, the '*Sahwi* insurrection' between 1991 and 1994, which challenged the authority of the Wahhabi Committee of Senior Scholars and issued demands for reforming governance, lay at the very heart of Islamist political dissent in Saudi Arabia. The state responded to dissent with repression and then co-option. In September 1994 Salman al-Awda, a leading *Sahwi* scholar, was arrested, together with hundreds of others.

In June 1999 the *Sahwi* dissidents were released from prison. Their release was conditioned on not openly challenging Saudi leadership. In effect, the *Sahwi* intellectuals were co-opted by the state and enlisted by authorities to de-legitimize more revolutionary challengers to the Saudi state. Osama bin Laden and al-Qaida's global jihad, particularly in the aftermath of the attacks on the USA (involving 15 Saudi hijackers) on 11 September 2001, supplanted the *Sahwis* as the primary Islamist challenge to the Saudi state order. Between 2001 and 2011 the *Sahwis* became allies of the Saudi state in combating the revolutionary jihadi ideology among the Saudi population. This was not a theoretical exercise; Saudi security forces waged a domestic campaign against al-Qaida in the Arabian Peninsula between May 2003 and 2007, during which the terrorist network carried out between 20 and 25 violent operations in the kingdom. Therefore, in the 20 years between 1991 and 2011 the Saudi state faced a dual challenge: rentier networks were weakening at the same time that religious opposition was growing.

As the state faced growing socioeconomic challenges, Saudi authority was more vulnerable to Islamist dissent as an expression of popular discontent. However, the economic recovery that came with rising oil prices in the late 1990s eased the pressure on the Saudi state and provided it with enough resources to continue to co-opt major sources of dissent. When Crown Prince Abdullah officially succeeded Fahd as King in 2005, he tried implementing reforms to address these challenges. However, the price of oil remained high between 2005 and November 2014 and breathed new life into the fraying rentier order in the kingdom. Thanks to a boom in oil revenues (owing in part to robust economic growth in India and the People's Republic of China), real per capita GDP grew by about 40% in Saudi Arabia between 2003 and 2014, postponing any drive to reform the system. At the same time, the founding generation of senior Saudi princes sought to reaffirm the dominant place of Islam in the state's legitimacy. In 2008 Prince Salman (King since January 2015) delivered a lecture at Umm al-Qura University in Mecca, publicly reinforcing his belief that the Saudi state was based on Islam—the Qur'an (Koran) and the Sunna—and called on subjects 'not to allow anyone to damage this basis'.

There were five important developments that prompted Saudi leadership to take a new approach eight years later, in 2016. First, the 2008 global financial crisis brought about a worldwide economic slowdown and renewed pressure on the rentier-patronage system. Second, the shale oil revolution in the USA between 2007 and 2013 led to that country becoming a major oil producer and challenging the Saudi share of the global oil market. Third, the Arab uprisings of 2010–11 (popularly known as the 'Arab Spring' protests) led to renewed religious opposition to Saudi authority within the kingdom, particularly from Muslim Brotherhood-influenced intellectuals, who wanted to reduce the power of the Saudi monarchy. Fourth, the 'Middle East cold war' between Iran and Saudi Arabia intensified following the Saudi-led Gulf Cooperation Council intervention in Bahrain in the wake of anti-monarchy protests in that country in 2011. Fifth, the Islamic State in Iraq and Syria emerged as revolutionary force in the latter half of 2014 and was viewed as both an internal and external threat to the kingdom's security.

But perhaps the most important change for the Saudi state was King Abdullah's death at the end of 2014. He was succeeded in January 2015 by King Salman, who delegated much of his authority to his youngest son, Mohammed bin Salman, who at the time was just 30 years old. Crown Prince Mohammed prioritized the enormous challenge of transforming the kingdom's economy away from its dependence on oil.

SAUDI NATIONALISM IN VISION 2030

Vision 2030, announced in April 2016, was MBS's plan to transform Saudi Arabia from a commodity-dependent economy to a diverse, market-driven economy. The core idea of the Vision 2030 plan was to diversify the economy, reducing the state's dependency on the export of crude oil and downstream refined products and petrochemicals. In 2017 oil revenues accounted for about 40% of Saudi GDP, some 70% of government revenues, and almost 80% of export profits. In a report published in 2018 discussing Saudi Arabia, the World Bank noted that with the prospect of a sustained period of low oil prices, 'the old social contract—one based on government employment, generous subsidies and free public services—is no longer sustainable'. By mid-2022, with the price of oil having generally remained at more than US $100 per barrel since the Russian invasion of Ukraine in February of that year, these concerns appeared to be unfounded. (In the following year prices declined, but remained high, at an estimated average of more than $80 per barrel.) However, in 2016 the Saudis were legitimately focused on planning for the possibility of global oil demand reaching its peak in the near future, leaving untapped Saudi oil wealth stranded underground.

Given that oil revenues will not be able to sustain Saudi rentier patronage in the long term, Vision 2030 aims to create jobs for a young and educated population. What makes Vision 2030 a potentially transformative step for the kingdom are not its plans for government restructuring or budget benchmarks, or even its ability to convert oil assets into multiple streams of wealth. Rather, it is the way the plan attempts to reshape the relationship between the Saudi state and society. Vision 2030 is a distinctly modern vision, conferring agency on Saudis as individuals, with each individual, including women, being asked to play their part in the framework of a reformulated Saudi national identity.

Crown Prince Mohammad bin Salman, in the foreword of the 86-page Vision 2030 document, declares that the plan will unlock the country's *human* potential (emphasis in the original), declaring that Saudi Arabia's 'real wealth lies in the ambition of our people and the potential of our younger generation. They are our nation's pride and the architects of our future'. Indeed, the Vision 2030 document includes a section on 'Taking Pride In Our National Identity', which affirms a collective identity that includes Islam but is not limited to it: 'We take immense pride in the historical and cultural legacy of our Saudi, Arab, and Islamic heritage'. The document also commits individual Saudis to taking personal responsibility for their futures, and in doing so delivers the implicit message that they are not to leave it in God's hands. Notably, in referring to how this will be done, Vision 2030 does not distinguish between the responsibilities of the rulers versus those of the ruled, but instead refers, in the first-person plural, to a collective realization of a shared obligation to Saudi society: 'As such, we will develop ourselves and will work to become independent and active members of society, developing new skills in the process'. Enjoining Saudis to become 'independent' and 'active' individuals is a radical break from a system of social and political behaviour historically circumscribed by collectivist Wahhabi and tribal norms. This new nationalizing and modernist framework is repeated, when the plan promises: 'This will all be achieved by adhering closely to Islamic principles, Arab values and our national traditions'.

Vision 2030 is a programme to mobilize state and society and in the process reinvent the Saudi social contract along national lines. However, this is no rentierism. Saudis are not being bought out. They are not being offered additional rentier welfare to increase household spending. Instead, they are being encouraged to buy in; they are being encouraged by the Saudi state to generate their own private resources to create economic growth. This requires not only reforming the public sphere to allow women in the workplace, but also calls for fostering values such as individual enterprise and risk-taking, entrepreneurship, and individual travel and leisure. One of the least appreciated aspects of Vision 2030 is the Crown Prince's tacit assumption that these changes to longstanding Saudi social and cultural norms will be embraced by the kingdom's younger generations.

GLOBALIZATION AND THE SAUDI KINGDOM

Overlapping the recent state-driven reform process have been longer-term bottom-up processes of *social* and *cultural* change that were catalyzed by globalization, beginning in the 1970s. At the heart of globalization were processes that led to the sense of an increasing compression of time and space. The economic historian Anthony G. Hopkins notes that 'Globalization involves the extension, intensification and quickening velocity of flows of people, products and ideas that shapes the world. It integrates regions and continents; it compresses time and space; it prompts imitation and resistance'.

Saudi Arabia was very much linked to the global flows of people, products and ideas that was compressing time and space during the 20th century. It happened in an organic way, in part as a result of the Saudi state pursuing its interests and the accompanying second- and third-order social and cultural effects. However, globalization also reached the kingdom through changes in technology and the flow of ideas that occurred independent of the state and its interests.

The USA's role in the kingdom's oil industry was one of the earliest and most powerful globalizing forces in Saudi Arabia. Aramco brought the West to the kingdom, even if its influence was closely circumscribed and contained, introducing new technologies, business practices, engineering standards and professional culture. Aramco was also the force integrating Saudi Arabia into global capital markets. In the early 1970s Saudi Arabia contributed to the global oil price revolution that changed the structure of the global oil market and transferred wealth from the countries of the industrial West to the oil-producing states.

After the Six-Day War of June 1967, Saudi Arabia increased its financial support for the spread of Islam outside of the kingdom. Saudi Arabia established transnational organizations such as the Muslim World League (in 1962), the Organization of Islamic Conferences (in 1969) and the World Assembly of Muslim Youth (in 1972) in order to counter Arab nationalism and promote Islamic solidarity through Saudi religious leaders. These organizations played an important role in the spread of Salafi religious practice to places such as Ethiopia, Indonesia and India.

Muslims from across the Arab world, South Asia and Africa were brought to the kingdom to work during the construction boom of the 1970s. Pakistanis, Bangladeshis and mainly Muslim Indians, as well as Sri Lankans and Filipinos were exposed to Saudi religious influence during their time in the kingdom. Teachers, doctors and engineers from Egypt, Jordan and elsewhere in the Arab world also spread Saudi religious teachings when they returned home.

However, the flow of people and ideas was not one-directional. Saudi religious ideology and national and transnational institutions were also reshaped by the flow of Muslim Brotherhood intellectuals into the kingdom, beginning in the 1950s. The synthesis of Salafism and Muslim Brotherhood ideas in the kingdom from the 1950s to the 1980s contributed to the popularity of a variety of new hybrid Salafist ideologies, including the al-Sahwa al-Islamiyya and al-Qaida in the 1980s and 1990s and Islamic State in the first two decades of the 21st century.

In the 1970s and 1980s new oil wealth and rentier wealth created a new mass consumer society. Yet the initial wave of mass consumerism in the 1970s and 1980s, targeted by global and local marketing ('glocal') forces, served only to reinforce traditional patriarchy, tribal values and Islamic morality. It would take another 15 years and the spread of new communication technologies to create domestic consumer consumption in the kingdom that was linked to global brands.

Two principal developments have catalyzed the social and cultural effects of globalization in the kingdom during the past 25 years. First, Saudi Arabia experienced the information revolution and the diffusion of new communications technologies. Widespread internet access in Saudi Arabia began in 1999 and quickly increased the speed in which ideas and information flowed into and across the kingdom. Second, the role of education in the exchange of ideas and people also played a critical role in driving social and cultural change.

This process occurred on two levels. As noted above, beginning in the 1960s and 1970s Islamic institutions played an important role in creating flows of people and ideas to and from the kingdom related to the spread of various streams of Salafi and Islamist ideas and intellectuals. This was in part encouraged by the state, which was attempting to mobilize Islamist intellectuals to compete with and neutralize the ideological appeal of Arab nationalism in the region. Later, the number of Saudis travelling and studying abroad, particularly in the West, dramatically increased, especially during the first decade of the 21st century. In 1982 there were slightly fewer than 12,000 Saudis studying abroad; 30 years later the number had grown to nearly 200,000. The King Abdullah Scholarship Program (KASP), launched in 2005, led to a huge increase in the number of Saudis pursuing a higher education degree abroad. In 2012/13 the total number of Saudis studying abroad was nearly 200,000, with more than 165,000 receiving scholarships through the KASP. In less than a decade the KASP increased the number of Saudis studying in the USA from 5,000 to more than 100,000.

The flow of ideas and information through education and new communication technologies opened up the world to Saudis and Saudi Arabia to the world and, at the same time, provided the means for a new generation of Saudi elites to experience life outside the kingdom during their formative years.

SAUDI CULTURE: AGENTS OF CHANGE

The compression of time and space that was accelerated by the internet and greater circulation of Saudi men and women abroad has prompted a transformation of the standing of women in the kingdom. The status of women began to change in the early 21st century owing to a combination of domestic and global factors. The state attempted to use the status of women, which was viewed as a symbol of the kingdom's social and religious conservatism, as a means to reduce international pressure in the wake of Saudi involvement in the 11 September 2001 terrorist attacks (colloquially referred to as '9/11') in the USA. The state attempted to showcase cosmopolitan Saudi women and a series of gender-related social reforms in an attempt to demonstrate the modernizing face of the kingdom. However, greater international and local media scrutiny also focused on the historical marginalization of Saudi women, their segregation and their surveillance, control and restriction in the public sphere.

Social anthropologist Madawi al-Rasheed notes that an active discourse on gender roles in Saudi Arabia was not new. It was a topic addressed by a small circle of intellectuals dating back to the 1960s. However, post-'9/11' the issue was amplified, owing to a combination of greater media attention given to Saudi society and enlarged virtual space for public discourse on these issues. Rasheed also argues that the Saudi state allowed this discourse to flourish, believing that it would serve to counterbalance the media attention given to radicalization and jihadism in the kingdom. As a result, in the decade following the '9/11' attacks there were fierce public debates between Saudi religious leaders and Saudi liberals about the question of gender-mixing in educational institutions and in the workplace.

The ferocity of these public debates, some of which continue to rage, has been dramatically overtaken by the swift tide of change in three critical gender areas of great consequence. First, women were given the right to drive in the kingdom from June 2018; second, in 2019 the kingdom removed major restrictions that were at the heart of the 'guardianship system' that restricted individual freedoms for females, particularly with respect to obtaining civil documents, accessing the labour market and travelling abroad; and, third, the state has allowed gender-mixing at entertainment events.

The grassroots campaign for women to be allowed to drive in Saudi Arabia began on 6 November 1990, when 47 women independently drove in Riyadh, breaking a taboo and prompting the state to make it illegal for women to drive. More than 20 years later, in June 2011 Manal al-Sharif breathed new life into the 'Women2Drive' movement when she publicly drove, challenging the law in the kingdom. On 26 October 2013 women publicly drove throughout the kingdom, filming themselves and uploading the videos to YouTube to highlight their struggle. Nevertheless, it was the change in leadership from King Abdallah to King Salman and his son Mohammed bin Salman in 2015 that led to the breakthrough that granted women the right to drive after nearly 25 years of activism. And it was a substantial change. It provides women with the freedom of mobility, which allows them more easily to join the work force.

The 2019 changes to the laws of 'guardianship' largely dismantled the legal basis for the system and granted women even more autonomy and mobility. In particular, the changes have permitted divorced or separated women access to family documents for the first time, allowing them to reassert control over their lives and care for their children. The changes allow women to register births, deaths and divorces, and to obtain family cards that document their relationship to their children. Furthermore, they permit Saudi women to live independently as guardians of their children. Perhaps most consequentially, the amended laws allow Saudi women over the age of 21 years to apply for a passport and travel abroad without a male guardian's permission. Although women still require a male guardian's permission to marry, Saudi activist Dr Maha al-Muneef stated that the changes to the guardianship system 'takes the dependency on men out of women's lives. We feel very strong and empowered, and it is completing me as a woman'.

In the past few years, the kingdom has witnessed unprecedented public gender-mixing or gender integration (ikhtilat). In January 2018 the kingdom permitted women to attend a soccer match in a Jeddah stadium for the first time. In May a government 'Quality of Life Program 2020' outlined plans to amend Saudi laws legally to permit gender-mixing. In December 2018 a mixed-gender crowd publicly danced together for the first time in the kingdom during the Diriyah music festival. In the following month the kingdom's first-ever mixed-gender theatrical performance took place at the King Fahad Cultural Center in Riyadh. Although the pace of change can largely be attributed to the Crown Prince Mohammed's Vision 2030 reforms, grassroots activists in the kingdom have pushed for change since the turn of the century. Perhaps the most meaningful indication of official support for change on this issue was the statement made by a former Imam of the Grand Mosque in Mecca, Adil al-Kalabani, who said on Saudi television that gender segregation amounted to a 'phobia' or fear of women and that it must end. Admittedly, there has also been popular resistance to the changes, particularly among female religious leaders (al-da'iyat al-muthaqqafat). A mixed-gender suhoor (pre-dawn meal during Ramadan) in May 2019, an event indicating just how much the kingdom has changed in recent years, generated public outrage on social media over the fact that such an ostentatious 'party' was held during Ramadan. Nevertheless, official royal support for gender segregation has largely minimized public resistance.

The cultural opening up of the kingdom has been a top-down project imposed on society by the Crown Prince, but this abrupt social and cultural change also reflects a genuine popular demand among an important segment of the Saudi population. Saudi youths want more entertainment and recreation opportunities, whether they are comedy shows, international pop star performances, night clubs or music festivals. Of course, Saudi youths are not one undifferentiated bloc of society. There is still a strong wellspring of mass support for the kingdom's anti-modern Salafi social and cultural norms, and this drives a largely repressed reactionary backlash to the process of cultural change in the kingdom. Nevertheless, it might still be fair to say that the 32-year-old Crown Prince Mohammed reflected the popular sentiment of the new generation of Saudi youth when he said in 2018, 'Saudis don't want to lose their identity but we want to be part of the global culture. We want to merge our culture with global identity'.

If globalization has catalyzed cultural change in Saudi Arabia, what are the new implicit assumptions and understandings that are contributing to the reconstitution of Saudi culture? First, a critical mass of Saudis now sees the potential for living lives that hold possibilities beyond the fixed social roles and norms they were born into. In other words, one's family, clan or patrimony is not necessarily one's destiny. Young people see the potential to seek and define their own individual horizons. Second, these Saudis view themselves as belonging to a wider collective that transcends family, clan or tribe. There is the opportunity to forge new identities that are not bound by circumstances of birth. The idea of a distinctive Saudi collective identity has firmly taken root during the last generation. Third, there is a tacit belief in the autonomy of humankind, which can be seen in new Saudi visual art and popular entertainment. Fourth, Saudis view themselves as consciously contributing to shaping the social order and cultural norms of the kingdom through human activity. This is most clearly given expression in the more than 20 years of grassroots activism on behalf of women's emancipation in Saudi society.

Perhaps the most important challenge to Saudi Arabia's programme of reforms continues to come from Salafist and Islamist intellectuals and activists. Salafists reject the emergence of a reconstituted globalized Saudi culture, but appear loathe to challenge Saudi authority. While Salafi jihadists believe in an anti-modern revolution to prevent change, activist *tanwiri* Islamic thinkers, such as the reformist cleric Salman al-Awda, embrace the idea of a *dawla madaniyya* ('civil state') in an Islamic framework, which would mean, by definition, the end of the Saudi state as a kingdom. However, for now, the religious opposition to change in the kingdom is divided among themselves and there is little consensus about how best to challenge Saudi primacy. Saudi leadership exploits those divisions, and in combination with repression, co-opts sympathetic members of the Saudi religious leadership.

STATE SECURITY: BETWEEN SELF-HELP AND PROTECTION

The security challenges Saudi Arabia faced during the first two decades of the 21st century have shaped its response to events over the past four years. This section focuses on Saudi foreign affairs since 2019, explaining chronologically how Saudi Arabia has responded to US retrenchment, the coronavirus pandemic and the Ukraine war during this period.

While this section of the essay is focused on 2020-23, it is rooted in changes to Saudi strategic thinking and behaviour that evolved over the previous two decades. During the first decade of the 21st century the Saudis tried to rehabilitate their relationship with the USA in the aftermath of the terrorist attacks of '9/11', in which 15 of the 19 hijackers were Saudi nationals. In the aftermath of '9/11' the Saudis became a valued counter-terror partner for the USA, and announced the Arab Peace Initiative in 2002 to address the Israeli–Palestinian conflict. However, by the end of the decade Saudi Arabia had begun to doubt the efficacy of the US security commitment to the kingdom and the Middle East region.

For Saudi Arabia there were three major regional developments during 2001–10. The US invasions of Afghanistan (2001) and Iraq (2003) deposed the Taliban and Saddam Hussain, respectively, thereby removing two principal threats to the Islamic Republic of Iran. Iran's ability to project its influence through a Shi'a-dominated Government in Iraq, and undermine the credibility of the US occupation there, began to tip the balance of power against the traditional Sunni dominance in Iraq and the Middle East region. Moreover, the rise of a Sunni *jihadi* insurgency in Iraq, and that country's descent into civil war between 2005 and 2007, destabilized the region and threatened Saudi Arabia. The second challenge the Saudis faced was internal, with the emergence of al-Qa'ida in the Arabian Peninsula (AQAP) in the kingdom between 2005 and 2007. The militant group's campaign of terror shed light on the extent of *jihadi* support within Saudi Arabia and exposed the kingdom's vulnerability to the *jihadi* threat. Third, in 2002 Iran was discovered to have built an advanced uranium enrichment facility at Natanz. Throughout the remainder of the decade Iran's nuclear programme and its potential to produce nuclear weapons was perceived by Saudi Arabia as a threat to the security and stability of the Gulf and the broader region.

During 2011–14 Saudi attention was focused on containing and countering the spread of popular revolution triggered by the 2010–11 Arab uprisings. The Saudis, in partnership with the United Arab Emirates (UAE), intervened in Bahrain to suppress the uprising there and provide security support to the ruling Al Khalifa dynasty. In addition to using coercion and co-option to prevent any popular unrest at home, the Saudis also sought to influence the trajectory of the uprisings in Egypt, Libya, Syria and Yemen. In Egypt the Saudis backed the 2013 military coup led by Gen. Abd al-Fatah al-Sisi, while in Libya in 2014 the Saudis, alongside Egypt and the UAE, provided support to Khalifa Haftar's Libyan National Army, which opposed pro-General National Congress Islamist militias in Libya's civil war. In September 2014 the al-Houthi-led Ansar Allah rebels unseated the Government of Abd al-Rabbuh Mansour Hadi in Yemen, which ultimately found refuge in exile in Saudi Arabia. In Syria, unlike elsewhere, the Saudis supported the uprising against the regime of Bashar al-Assad. The Saudis feared that Iran would turn Syria into another Iraq, using the uprising to establish 'Alawi-Shi'a dominance over the Sunnis, further shifting the regional balance of power in Iran's favour. The Saudis were also frustrated by the USA's reluctance to intervene in Syria and were concerned that it indicated a US detente with Iran. A turning point for Saudi Arabia was a decision by the Administration of US President Barack Obama in September 2013 not to enforce its 'red line' policy in the aftermath of Assad's chemical weapons attacks against Syrian rebels. Saudi concerns intensified in January 2014 following President Obama's remarks that he would like to see an equilibrium of power between Iran and the Arab Gulf states, which for the Saudis would represent a return to the post-1979 US-led security order in the region.

At the end of 2014 the price of oil declined sharply in response to a combination of a marked growth of oil supply resulting from the shale oil revolution in the USA, and a similarly marked decline in oil demand from countries that were not members of the Organisation for Economic Co-operation and Development. The USA perceived the fracking revolution, which took place between 2007 and 2014, as reducing its dependence on the Gulf oil producers, prompting US policy-makers increasingly to call into question the high costs of the country's security commitment to the Gulf. For Saudi Arabia, US shale oil production threatened the Saudi market share and, perhaps more importantly, the Saudi position as the 'swing producer' in global oil markets. The net effect of this change began to transform the very essence of the relationship between the USA and Saudi Arabia from one of security interdependence to one of competition over the share of global oil markets. The interdependency between the USA and Saudi Arabia had been the basis for the 'oil-for-security' bargain struck between US President Franklin D. Roosevelt and King Abdulaziz at the end of the Second World War, and was now being eroded and tested by US shale oil production in the 21st century.

At the end of 2014 as oil prices abruptly declined, Islamic State succeeded in shattering the border between Iraq and Syria, and establishing its sovereignty in western Iraq and eastern Syria. Abu Bakr al-Baghdadi declared himself Caliph and explicitly attacked the legitimacy of the Saudi regime, declaring it a target in a video message issued in late 2014. The Saudis, in turn, became the lynchpin in encouraging Arab participation in the US-led military operation against Islamic State in late 2014 and early 2015. Saudi defence minister and brother of MBS, Khalid bin Salman, was among those piloting the Saudi warplanes participating in the operation in 2014. In late March 2015 the Saudis, who were frustrated by US inaction in Yemen following the al-Houthi coup, initiated a military operation to roll back al-Houthi gains. As one headline put it in May 2015, it was the Saudis' first real attempt to be a military power. However, by mid-2015, after some initial success, the Saudi war in Yemen began to turn ugly when the Saudi air force struggled to target the enemy successfully with its airstrikes, leading to errors and heavy civilian casualties. Moreover, Saudi ground forces proved unable to engage in combined operations to defend the kingdom's southern border. In July the USA and Iran reached a preliminary agreement on a nuclear deal, and in September Russia and Iran jointly intervened in the civil war in Syria to prop-up the Assad regime. For the Saudis, the Iranian escalation in Syria highlighted the central weakness of the new nuclear deal: it did not address Iran's regional expansion.

Under MBS's influence, a new assertive approach to Saudi leadership emerged in 2015 to confront these new threats. One well-informed Saudi observer, Nawaf Obaid, claimed that Saudi Arabia 'had no choice but to lead more forcefully'. In 2017 the Administration of US President Donald Trump legitimized and emboldened the more assertive Saudi approach under the leadership of MBS, which led to the blockade and isolation of Qatar in June of that year and the failed attempt to strong-arm Lebanese Prime Minister Saad al-Hariri into resigning in November. These heavy-handed Saudi initiatives weakened unity in the Sunni Arab world. However, they were mitigated in May 2018 when Trump decided to abrogate the nuclear deal with Iran as part of his policy of 'maximum pressure' on Iran.

However, by late 2018 MBS's attempts to implement an assertive foreign policy ultimately foundered on Saudi military failure in Yemen and the assassination of US-based Saudi journalist Jamal Khashoggi at the Saudi consulate in İstanbul, Turkey. Khashoggi's murder turned the US Congress against Saudi Arabia and weakened international consensus for increased pressure on Iran, undermining the Trump strategy.

Saudi military failure was felt most acutely on the Saudi home front, exposing the country's vulnerability to Iran's regional partners in 2018 and 2019, when Saudi civilians and infrastructure were targeted by al-Houthi drones (unmanned aerial vehicles) and missiles. Ultimately, the strategic evolution from Saudi assertiveness to vulnerability culminated on 14 September 2019 in the Iranian drone and cruise missile attacks on two of Saudi Aramco's major oil facilities, at Abqaiq and Khurais. In the aftermath of the attacks, Trump's statement that it was an attack on Saudi Arabia and not on the USA underscored Saudi vulnerability and isolation. If the Saudis suspected that they could no longer rely on US protection, Trump's decision not to respond to the September 2019 attack confirmed their worst fears.

The Pandemic Crisis, 2020
In late 2019 MBS sought to rehabilitate his damaged image in the international arena and searched for a way out of the Yemen war. Meanwhile, in March 2020 the coronavirus pandemic began to spread throughout the Gulf and oil prices declined sharply, triggering a major economic crisis for Saudi Arabia.

It is important to emphasize that MBS had increased confidence in Saudi policy to unprecedented levels between 2015 and 2018. One might even go so far as to say it ventured into hubris, as David Ottaway argued in a trenchant new book on MBS, which described him in terms of an Icarus syndrome. However, the combination of Western condemnation and Saudi economic crisis generated what could be viewed as a crisis of confidence for MBS in 2020 and early 2021. It did not help that, even as the Saudis searched for a way out of the Yemen war, the al-Houthis escalated their attacks against Saudi Arabia, even targeting Riyadh, which the Saudis were powerless to prevent. Thus, despite Trump's decision to order the assassination of the commander of the elite Quds Force of the Iranian Islamic Revolutionary Guard Corps, Qassem Soleimani, in January 2020, the Saudis remained vulnerable to Iranian power.

The coronavirus pandemic delivered a painful blow to Saudi Arabia. In early 2020 the Saudis experienced a serious outbreak of the disease that led to a series of lockdowns in the kingdom and curfews imposed during Ramadan and Eid. Mosques were closed for worship, and the *Umrah* and the July *Hajj* pilgrimages were cancelled. Plummeting oil prices (which fell from US $65 per barrel in December 2019 to $25 per barrel in May 2020) added to the economic pain of a crippled consumer economy and reduced tourism revenue. A $9,000m. budget deficit in the first quarter of 2020 prompted the introduction of austerity measures, which included tripling the country's value-added tax (VAT). The success of MBS's Vision 2030 plan to diversify the kingdom's economy and reduce its dependence on oil seemed in jeopardy, and Saudi Arabia's reputation in the Islamic world was damaged.

The pandemic-induced economic crisis and declining oil prices led Saudi Arabia to take aggressive steps to defend its share of the global oil market. This tested an already fragile Saudi-US relationship in the aftermath of the Khashoggi murder. When the Saudis flooded the market with oil in April 2020, they unleashed a price war for market share between Russia and Saudi Arabia. The price war threatened to destroy US shale oil producers, who could not turn a profit if the price of oil dropped too low (it stood at US $21.65 per barrel on 30 March). Facing political pressure from within his party, Trump personally intervened to stabilize markets. He threatened to cut Saudi Arabia off from US military protection unless MBS agreed to a moderate floor on oil prices that would not drive US oil producers out of business. If the price of oil fell too low, it would not allow US companies to cover the higher costs of pumping shale oil. Saudi Arabia's strategy had wreaked havoc in the oil industry, demonstrating the continued power of Saudi oil in the global economy. However, it was a decision driven by fear of losing market share during the uncertainty of the pandemic economic slowdown.

Saudi Arabia's actions attracted the ire of the USA, which under the Trump Administration, had backed the kingdom's regional leadership until the Khashoggi murder. The Riyadh Summit in May 2017, which was Trump's first presidential visit abroad, symbolized this strong support by the USA. MBS cultivated close ties with the Administration by forging a personal relationship with Trump's son-in-law, Jared Kushner. Trump had protected MBS during the Khashoggi affair in 2018, but he did not hesitate to bring pressure on Saudi Arabia to end the oil price war, demonstrating the kingdom's limited strategic autonomy and continued sense of dependency on US protection.

On 15 September 2020 the UAE and Bahrain signed the Abraham Accords with Israel, normalizing relations with Israel. Saudi Arabia's public reaction was to reaffirm its commitment to the 2002 Arab Peace Initiative, and to reiterate that 'relations' with Israel would be possible when peace between Israel and a Palestinian state was achieved on the basis of the 1967 borders. Privately, however, Saudi Arabia was believed to be supportive of the Abraham Accords. In October 2020 Faisal Al Farhan acknowledged that the Accords 'helped to lay the groundwork' for peace between Israel and the Palestinians. Bahrain, many argue, would not have signed the Accords without Saudi approval. The discrepancy between the Saudi public and private attitudes towards the Accords reflects the different positions of MBS and his father King Salman. It is, in part, a generational issue linked to the nature of the living memory of the conflict. The relatively young MBS believes that the Israeli–Palestinian conflict should be subordinate to Saudi national interests, while his elderly father views support for the Palestinian cause and the status of Jerusalem as a core Saudi obligation as custodian of Islam's two holiest mosques (in Mecca and Medina).

The UAE, in contrast to Saudi Arabia, immediately went 'all in' with normalization. It viewed normalization with Israel as providing strategic gains in four key areas. First, it helped the UAE cope with the threat of Iran, given the evolving US commitment to protection in the Gulf; second, it blunted US criticism of the UAE's policies, particular its role in the Yemen war; third, it provided the UAE with a partner on a range of new technologies that it viewed as crucial to its future success in both new modes of warfare and the 'fourth industrial revolution' (machine learning, artificial intelligence, biotech, quantum, big data, etc.); and fourth, it provided the UAE with a powerful economic partner to drive intra-regional trade and inter-regional connectivity at a time when recovery from the pandemic was in doubt.

Saudi Arabia began to resent the new leadership role that the UAE assumed in the aftermath of signing the Abraham Accords. It feared that the UAE would eclipse the kingdom as the Arab world's regional co-ordinator; it also triggered a competitive dynamic, in which the Saudis sought to lead their own multilateral regional initiatives. Similar to the UAE strategy, the Saudis turned to regionalism to provide alternative sources of protection, in light of doubts about the USA's commitment to Gulf security; and, to advance economic diversification as a means to manage the manifold challenges of the pandemic-induced economic contraction and the energy transition. The key difference between the UAE and Saudi approaches to regionalism was that for the Saudis it was a tactical, temporary measure until they became self-reliant in terms of security (if indeed they will ever achieve such self-reliance). For the UAE, regionalism was strategic, in that it viewed greater regional integration as the means to greater security and self-reliance.

More broadly, there was a real sense of alarm in the Gulf in 2020; decision-makers believed that the global economy was in crisis. Saudi Arabia hosted the Group of 20 (G20) summit in November 2020, and the disagreements between economists about the nature of any future economic recovery were not academic. In September, with oil prices at US $41 per barrel, Saudi Arabia required $76 per barrel to balance its budget. The kingdom's budget deficit was equivalent to 11.4% of GDP in 2020. The price war that Saudi Arabia had unleashed earlier in the year had protected Saudi market share, but it also set a ticking 'time bomb' for the economies of most of the region's energy producers. The lower price of oil meant that the region's hydrocarbon-dependent economies would struggle to fund government spending. If prices remained low, these countries faced even greater pressure to diversify their economies at an accelerated rate.

In November 2020 Joe Biden was elected US President, denying Trump a second term. Later that month, Israeli Prime Minister Benjamin Netanyahu secretly visited Saudi Arabia to meet MBS and US Secretary of State Mike Pompeo. Ostensibly, the meeting was about how to co-ordinate their policies on Iran, anticipating a different approach from the incoming Biden Administration. However, in the background was the possibility of expanding the Abraham Accords to include Saudi Arabia, which many suggested could be used by the kingdom to reduce Biden's hostility towards MBS and Saudi Arabia's war in Yemen.

Between the Pandemic Crisis and Ukraine War, 2021–22

Saudi Arabia was in crisis mode in 2020. This continued into the first half of 2021. It was unclear when and how the global economy would recover from the pandemic, leading to fears in Saudi Arabia that it would be facing an extended period of austerity, due to low oil prices. This threatened to put major parts of MBS's Vision 2030 reform programme at risk. The Saudis also faced a new US President who was openly critical of the kingdom and its Crown Prince.

Saudi Arabia faced three principal challenges in 2021: a hostile Biden Administration seeking to reduce US military commitments in the Middle East; escalating al-Houthi attacks on the Saudi home front; and the pandemic-induced economic crisis. Biden had promised to turn Saudi Arabia into 'a pariah', and one of his first initiatives after taking office in January was to announce a temporary freeze on arms deals with Saudi Arabia and the UAE. In response, Saudi Arabia tactically embraced regionalism to avoid isolation; to reduce the direct and indirect costs of regional conflicts during the pandemic; to shape regional security arrangements as the USA increasingly focused on its sharpening rivalry with China in Asia; and, to pursue intra-regional economic integration.

Saudi Arabia's political and economic vulnerability drove its efforts to rebuild its regional relationships in 2021. Yet these initiatives did not offer greater protection from the primary threat to Saudi security: al-Houthi missile and drone attacks on Saudi territory, which escalated throughout the year. In February the Biden Administration removed the al-Houthis from its list of foreign terrorist organizations as part of a diplomatic offensive to end the war in Yemen. However, the al-Houthis doubled the number of attacks on the kingdom (relative to 2020), averaging 78 attacks per month during the first nine months of 2021. In March the al-Houthis rejected a Saudi ceasefire proposal and attempted to launch an attack on Ras Tanura, Saudi Aramco's largest oil refinery. US diplomatic efforts to end the war were failing to progress, yet in June the USA announced it was withdrawing anti-missile defence systems from Saudi Arabia that had been deployed by the Trump Administration following the September 2019 attacks on Abqaiq and Khurais. These developments confirmed Saudi fears that the USA was abandoning its security commitment to the kingdom, as did the abrupt and poorly co-ordinated US withdrawal from Afghanistan in August 2021.

Paradoxically, at the same time that the USA was withdrawing military systems from Saudi Arabia and placing limits on weapons sales to it, the Biden Administration began to ask the kingdom to increase its oil production. In November 2021 US petrol prices had risen to US $3.40 per gallon (a high that had not seen for more than a decade), for three reasons: increased demand, as Americans returned to the roads after pandemic lockdowns; decreased supply, as US oil production declined in 2021 as a result of the pandemic and oil price war; and the imposition by OPEC+ of limits on production due to concerns that the increased demand was temporary and a recession was on the horizon. In November the Saudis and other OPEC+ producers rebuffed US demands to increase output.

Saudi-US relations were at a delicate junction at the end of 2021. The Saudis needed greater US air defence assistance, while the USA needed greater Saudi oil production. The Saudis agreed to implement moderate oil production increases in early 2022, and the USA resupplied the Saudis with more *Patriot* anti-missile interceptors between December 2021 and March 2022. However, the Saudis did not believe that pumping more oil served their interests, and they began to explore how they could supplement US air defence systems, particularly given the US Congress's continued opposition to arms sales to the kingdom.

The seeds of a multilateral regional air defence system were planted in 2021. US missile defence systems did not address the full range of threats against the kingdom. The *Patriot* and the Terminal High Altitude Area Defense (Thaad) systems were able to intercept missiles, but they were not built to defend against al-Houthi drone attacks. The Saudis needed a multi-layered air defence system with early warning radar that would provide a shield against cruise and ballistic missiles, as well as a means of defence against more unsophisticated, but deadly drones. The Saudis approached Israel in September when the USA began withdrawing anti-missile systems from the kingdom, expressing interest in Israel's 'Iron Dome' and *Barak-MX* defence systems. For Saudi Arabia, Israeli technology offered a potential alternative to the limits that the US Congress was placing on arms supplies to Saudi Arabia, while US co-ordination provided an umbrella for discreet Saudi-Israel air defence co-operation, in the absence of Saudi-Israeli normalization.

The Ukraine war, which began at the end of February 2022, led to a dramatic increase in the price of oil and provided a substantial boon to the Saudi economy. In March oil prices peaked at a 14-year high of US $139 per barrel. Energy was weaponized through the war, which underscored the strategic value of Gulf oil and gas production to the stability of the global economy. The International Monetary Fund predicted that the Middle East's oil producers would benefit from $1,000,000m. in additional oil revenues over four years, as a result of the conflict.

These developments helped to restore Saudi Arabia's sense of power and standing in the international community. On the other hand, the Saudis watched the West weaponize the global financial system by freezing Russian assets abroad and locking Russia out of the Swift system that processes financial transactions between banks across the world. The Saudis feared that the decision by the Group of 7 (G7) to embargo and cap the price on Russian oil was creating a buyer's cartel, which would lead to a bifurcated oil market, reducing Saudi influence on oil prices. The Saudis were concerned that they were vulnerable to this kind of economic warfare, which incentivized the kingdom to invest its war-driven oil windfall in regional economic development, rather than in the West.

The ambitious new economic zone dubbed NEOM is the cornerstone project of MBS's Vision 2030 development plan to reinvent Saudi Arabia. the Crown Prince's ambition is to use NEOM to transform the kingdom into a regional hub for trade connectivity, luxury tourism, the high-tech economy and green energy. It is a US $500,000m. project that encompasses 26,500 sq km in the Tabouk region in the north-west corner of the country, on the Red Sea coast. In 2021 the kingdom rolled out its plans for the Line, a 174 km-long (34 sq km) green, linear city in NEOM, based on advanced smart-city technologies. It also introduced Oxagon, a floating eight-sided industrial city and port on the Red Sea. Ultimately, the trilateral agreement between the Egypt, Israel and Saudi Arabia, which was brokered by the USA in 2017, will transfer control of the formerly Egyptian-owned Tiran and Sanafir islands to the Saudis, and allow the kingdom to connect NEOM's tourism and industrial sectors to Egypt by building a bridge or causeway across the Red Sea. NEOM, at this stage, is still more vision than reality. However, Vision 2030 is MBS's biggest development priority, and the stability of Egypt, in particular, and the Red Sea more broadly are crucial to NEOM's success. In the short to medium term, Saudi Arabia will lean on Egypt's (and through it, Israel's) military power in the Red Sea to protect its interests. US military power in the region continues to play a vital role in facilitating this regional defence co-operation.

Saudi Arabia's regional economic initiatives are competing with the UAE's bid to promote greater regional economic integration. The Abraham Accords with Israel have also provided the UAE with more opportunities for multilateral engagement, which have been bolstered by support from the Biden Administration, which backed the Negev Summit in Israel in March 2022 and the inaugural summit of the I2U2 Group (comprising India, Israel, the UAE and the USA) in July. In early 2022 the USA became increasingly desperate for Saudi co-operation in limiting ballooning oil prices. The Biden Administration was concerned that runaway inflation would damage the Democratic Party's performance in the November mid-term congressional elections. In return, the Saudis sought to rehabilitate MBS's international image and to reassert their regional leadership role, at the expense of the UAE.

The Saudis were unhappy with the UAE's phased withdrawal from Yemen in 2019 and early 2020, and the UAE's support for southern separatists in Yemen is at odds with the Saudi desire to maintain Yemen's unity, even if the al-Houthis control the north of the country. Egypt, for its part, was uncomfortable with the UAE's unilateral decisions in the Israeli-Palestinian sphere. In exchange for help in stabilizing oil markets, MBS wanted the USA to give its stamp of approval for Saudi regional leadership and co-ordination. The Crown Prince saw Saudi Arabia as the 'balance-maker' between Egypt and Türkiye, and believed that the kingdom could seal a reconciliation between the two countries. MBS sought to engineer this trilateral strategic regional partnership, supplanting the UAE as the US instrument to reshape regional security. On the one hand, Biden justified his visit to Saudi Arabia in July 2022 in terms of a broad vision of advancing peace through diplomacy. The USA promoted the trip in terms of a potential breakthrough for Saudi normalization with Israel and an expansion of the Abraham Accords. However, from the Saudi perspective, the Jeddah Summit was intended to reaffirm the US commitment to Saudi security and to demonstrate that the USA viewed MBS and Saudi Arabia as a regional power.

During this period global and regional circumstances were driving the Saudis reluctantly towards regionalism, but the Saudis wanted it to be a Saudi-led regionalism. The Saudis did not want to be an addendum to the Abraham Accords. They wanted credit for delivering, at least in some modest way, on their own Israeli-Palestinian initiative, which is why they revived the 2002 Arab Peace Initiative on the sidelines of the September 2022 UN General Assembly, organizing a closed ministerial meeting under the auspices of the Arab League and the European Union.

Saudi geopolitical strength as a result of the effects of the Ukraine war have offset the kingdom's security vulnerabilities, at least for the time being. The achievement in April 2022 of a ceasefire (albeit fragile) in Yemen also contributed to a greater sense of Saudi confidence. Major Saudi civilian infrastructure and oil facilities have not been targeted by the al-Houthis since early 2022. However, Saudi Arabia has continued to be at loggerheads with the Biden Administration on oil production cuts, prompting a renewal of the bilateral tensions that preceded the Biden's visit in July 2022.

From Saudi-Iranian Detente to Saudi-Israeli Normalization, 2023

On 10 March 2023 Saudi Arabia and Iran announced an agreement (brokered by China) to re-establish diplomatic ties. Saudi Arabia severed relations with Iran following an attack by an Iranian mob on the Saudi embassy in Tehran in January 2016. Riyadh viewed the attack as having been choreographed by the Islamic Republic in response to the kingdom's execution of dissident Saudi Shi'a religious leader Nimr al-Nimr.

It remains to be seen whether the 2023 agreement results in more than the reopening of the two countries respective embassies in Tehran and Riyadh, but it is potentially significant for three reasons. First, it may herald compromises in the political deadlocks in Lebanon and Yemen, in which both Iran and Saudi Arabia have been deeply involved. Greater political stability in Lebanon and Yemen might facilitate economic development in the Eastern Mediterranean and Red Sea sub-regions, both of which have been the focus of much greater regional investment since 2020. Second, it symbolizes a new diplomatic role for China in the Gulf, supplanting Russia as the great power alternative to the USA in the region. Third, it raises questions about Saudi Arabia's confidence in the ability of the USA (and to a lesser extent of Israel) to contain and deter Iran's nuclear development and protect the kingdom from what it perceives as Iranian encirclement.

The Saudi–Iranian rivalry was born out of the 1978–79 Iranian Revolution and the Iran–Iraq War in the 1980s. The US-led invasion that toppled the Taliban in Afghanistan in 2001 and Saddam Hussain in Iraq in 2003, removed threats along Iran's eastern and western borders and empowered pro-Iranian Shi'a politicians in Iraq. When Iraq descended into civil war in 2006 and 2007, Saudi Arabia grew concerned that Iran was using the Sunni–Shi'a violence in Iraq to alter the regional balance of power in its favour, upending the regional status quo based on Sunni supremacy. These fears were exacerbated by Hezbollah's armed takeover of Beirut in May 2008 and Iran's rapid nuclear development between 2005 and 2009.

The 2010–11 Arab uprisings intensified the rivalry. Saudi Arabia rejected Iran's characterization of the uprisings as an 'Islamic Awakening'. It argued that Iran was using the uprisings as a pretext to export its revolutionary politics to the Shi'a communities in the Gulf and beyond. In Bahrain, the Saudis saw Iran as directly meddling in the uprising that ultimately challenged the authority of the ruling Al Khalifa dynasty. The Saudis, with support from the UAE, intervened to support the Sunni ruling family in Bahrain against the Bahraini protesters under the banner of the Gulf Cooperation Council (GCC). In Syria, Iran provided direct military and economic assistance to the minority-dominated 'Alawi Government of Bashar al-Assad, helping it to suppress the largely Sunni popular uprising there. Saudi Arabia saw Iran's role in Syria in 2011–12, and in Yemen, following the 2014 al-Houthi coup, as reiterations of Iran's interference in Iraq following the 2003 US invasion.

Between April and September 2021, four rounds of talks took place between Iranian and Saudi officials in Baghdad. The talks focused on the war in Yemen and the political and financial crisis in Lebanon. The final round of talks before China's involvement, took place on 21 September 2021, and they were the first talks between Saudi Arabia and Ebrahim Raisi's new Government in Iran, which had taken office in August.

The Saudi-Iranian dialogue broke down between October 2021 and March 2022. In late October 2021 an al-Houthi offensive made significant gains in Ma'rib and Shabwa in Yemen, threatening to seize Yemen's most valuable gas and oil infrastructure. International efforts to stop the fighting and mediate between the al-Houthis and Saudis foundered. The al-Houthis were on the march, and seizing valuable resources in Ma'rib and Shabwa would make their state-building project more permanent. The Saudis believed that Hezbollah and Iran were encouraging and lending support to the al-Houthis in their push to capture Ma'rib. At the end of October the Saudis abruptly banned imports from Lebanon and expelled the Lebanese ambassador from Riyadh. The Saudis were ostensibly responding to comments by the Lebanese Minister of Information, George Kordahi, who, in a televised interview, said that the al-Houthis were defending themselves against 'foreign aggression' in Yemen, alluding to the Saudi military intervention. The Saudi ban denied Lebanon US $250m. in export revenue during a period in which the Lebanese economy was in the midst of a two-year-long systemic economic crisis. There was some suggestion that the 2021 Saudi-Iranian dialogue included a quid pro quo: in exchange for Iran reining in the al-Houthis in Yemen, the Saudis would provide Lebanon with an economic lifeline and facilitate a political compromise. When the al-Houthis escalated their push towards Ma'rib and Shabwa's energy infrastructure in mid-October, the Saudis retaliated in Lebanon, leading to a breakdown in the Saudi-Iranian dialogue that lasted until April 2022, when the dialogue was renewed for a fifth round.

In October 2022 Iran's Supreme Leader, Ayatollah Khamenei, again called for a reopening of Saudi and Iranian embassies, but there was a new Government in Baghdad that was less interested in mediating between the two sides. It was Chinese President Xi Jinping's visit to Saudi Arabia in December that reportedly opened the door to China's role in facilitating the deal. Iran may have also been more receptive to reconciling with the Saudis in late 2022, given the domestic uprising that it had contended with since September, and the increasing isolation that it faced as a result of its military aid to Russia in Ukraine during the past six months.

The deal also helped to advance the process of Bashar al-Assad and Syria's re-normalization into the Arab fold. Iran and China had much to gain from Saudi Arabian support for the re-integration of the Assad regime into the Arab League, particularly in the wake of the devastating earthquake that rocked Türkiye and Syria in February 2023. Syria's re-normalization could facilitate the permanent lifting of UN sanctions against the country (in place since 2011), which could stabilize the Assad regime and allow China to play a role in reconstructing Syria through its Belt and Road Initiative. With Russia preoccupied with Ukraine and reducing its presence in Syria, Saudi Arabia may be hoping that re-normalizing Assad's regime will limit or contain Iran's influence in Syria.

After the USA withdrew from the nuclear deal on Iran in May 2018 (the Joint Comprehensive Plan of Action—JCPOA), there was some measure of strategic convergence between Iran's regional rivals. The September 2020 Abraham Accords were an expression, in part, of a more open strategic alignment between Israel and the UAE and Bahrain. Saudi Arabia was also believed to support working more closely with Israel in containing Iran's nuclear programme and actively resisting Iran's regional expansion. To some degree, Saudi Arabia's detente with Iran suggests that Riyadh is no longer confident the USA and/or Israel will be able to limit Iran's nuclear development and contain that country's regional expansion. The Saudi-Iranian detente appears to signal a parallel strategy to the Saudi strategic alignment with Israel against Iran, and may represent an attempt on the part of Saudi Arabia to reduce the threat posed by Iran by building greater economic interdependence through investment and trade flows between the two countries.

However, the deal remains fragile and contingent on continued efforts at regional de-escalation. In mid-2023 Iran threatened to take military action to prevent Saudi Arabia and Kuwait from jointly developing an offshore gasfield (known as Durra in Saudi Arabia and Kuwait, and Arash in Iran) that Iran has claimed as its own. The two sides in the dispute had failed to demarcate an offshore boundary in March. The field is believed to have proven reserves of 310m. barrels of oil and 20,000,000m. cu m of gas, which means it potentially has great economic value. How the Saudis and Kuwaitis choose to respond to these Iranian threats may be an early test of the durability of the detente.

Saudi-Israeli Normalization, 2023
In May 2023 the Biden Administration began promoting a US initiative to normalize ties between Saudi Arabia and Israel. The deal would be part of a 'grand bargain' between Saudi Arabia and the USA that would provide the Saudis with greater protection and enhanced security co-operation. While the obstacles to such a deal are considerable, it also has the potential to revive the bilateral US-Saudi security partnership, which was historically based on US military protection in exchange for secure Saudi oil security in line with US interests. Saudi-Israeli normalization would also provide Biden with a historic foreign policy achievement during an election year.

For the Saudis, a US-backed normalization deal with Israel would be an opportunity to achieve three vital interests. First, it would revive the USA's commitment to Saudi security, which has been eroded over the previous 15 years. Second, in combination with the China-brokered detente with Iran, a 'grand bargain' with the USA would convey the message that Saudi Arabia was the principal regional power, facilitating the design of a new regional security architecture, in co-ordination with all of the so-called great powers (China, Russia and the USA). Third, Saudi normalization with Israel would deliver political and economic gains for the Palestinians, which would provide MBS with both prestige and popular support among Saudis and wider Arab and Muslim communities.

Saudi Arabia was reportedly seeking US partnership and co-operation for its civilian nuclear programme (a 'nuclear Aramco' was proposed, alluding to the historical US-Saudi partnership in the establishment of the Saudi national oil company), including the fuel-cycle; a NATO-style mutual security treaty that would commit the USA to respond to an attack on Saudi Arabia as if it were an attack on its own soil; and, permission to purchase the USA's most advanced anti-ballistic missile defence systems (such as the Thaad system). In exchange, the USA was asking the Saudis to end its involvement in the war in Yemen; to make an unprecedented financial contribution to Palestinian governing institutions; and to limit its relations with China. There was also an expectation that the USA and Saudi Arabia could settle their two-year feud over the price of oil and Saudi production cuts. Israel, for its part, would be expected to make significant concessions to the Palestinians that would preserve the prospect of a two-state solution, presumably under the general auspices of Saudi Arabia's 2002 Arab Peace Initiative.

The obstacles to such a 'grand bargain' are considerable. The Biden Administration would have to secure bipartisan support in the US Senate for a security pact, nuclear co-operation and major arms sales with Saudi Arabia. It would also have to secure unprecedented concessions to the Palestinians from Israel, which would likely require Israel's Prime Minister Netanyahu to form a new governing coalition while Israel is in the midst of a polarizing political crisis. The Saudis, for their part, would have to risk alienating the biggest customer for Saudi oil (China); withdraw from the war in Yemen, just as separatist violence in the south becomes a real possibility; and, make concessions to the USA on oil pricing that could have significant repercussions for the stability of the Saudi budget and MBS's development plans. The timing of this initiative was important: the Biden team wanted to put the principles of the deal together in advance of its 2024 re-election campaign.

Alongside Saudi-Israeli normalization, the US Administration expended considerable diplomatic effort in the first of half of 2023 in attempting to prevent Iran's nuclear programme from becoming a destabilizing factor in the Middle East during Biden's re-election campaign in 2024. Success in this aim would also, in theory, allow Biden to continue to focus his Administration's diplomatic and military resources on Russia and China, rather than on Iran. To that end, the Biden Administration has pursued an informal understanding with Iran that is intended to prevent Iran's development of nuclear weapons in exchange for Iran's limited access to sanctioned assets abroad (dubbed 'Plan C' by two US analysts). In addition to preventing an Iranian nuclear breakout, this informal understanding would also serve to avoid regional military escalation with Iran, while at the same time, leaving open the door to a more formal diplomatic agreement in the future. An informal agreement would allow Iran's nuclear programme to advance, while reducing Iran's economic and political isolation. In practice, it would also recognize Iran's status as a nuclear weapons threshold state.

Israeli media reports have suggested that the Biden Administration has pursued Saudi-Israeli normalization and its 'Plan C' agreement with Iran in parallel. The implication for regional security is that Saudi-Israeli normalization is intended to create a regional balance between a threshold nuclear Iran and normalized Saudi-Israeli security co-operation. Israeli critics of these two tracks argue that the Biden Administration has tried to earn Saudi and Israeli silence on the US understanding with Iran in exchange for the 'grand bargain' on Saudi-Israeli normalization. The Biden Administration appears to be hoping that these parallel diplomatic tracks will reduce the risk of conflict in the Middle East during the presidential campaign.

Saudi Arabia: From Protection to Autonomy and Back
The security of the Saudi kingdom has been bound to the USA since the end of the Second World War. Since the Arab Spring uprisings in 2010–11, the Saudis have perceived the US security commitment to the region as waning, and, as result, the Saudis have sought to become more self-reliant in terms of security. The Saudi role in the GCC intervention in the 2011 uprising in Bahrain was a good example of that ambition.

However, Saudi security self-help has foundered on its failed intervention in Yemen since 2015. Moreover, in September 2019 Saudi Arabia's inability to protect itself was exposed during the Iranian and al-Houthi combined drone and missile attacks on critical Saudi oil infrastructure at Abqaiq and Khurais. In July 2022 the Saudi ambassador to the USA, Princess Reema bint Bandar bin Al Sa'ud, declared the oil for security paradigm between the USA and Saudi Arabia as 'long gone'. However, the above-mentioned potential 'grand bargain' between Saudi Arabia, Israel and the USA, raises the question of whether a prospective US-Saudi reset will be based on a modified and more robust oil for security partnership.

Saudi Arabia and the USA are experiencing the biggest crisis in their relationship in 20 years. Global inflation and high petrol prices in the USA forced the Biden Administration to plead for increased Saudi oil production in 2021 and 2022, only to be repeatedly and publicly rebuffed by the Saudis. The October 2022 production cut was the most embarrassing for the Biden Administration, coming before US congressional elections and after Biden's trip to Riyadh in July. There was also a strong sense that the OPEC+ production cuts were an explicit expression of economic support for Russia as it fought against US-backed Ukraine. However, from the Saudi perspective, Russia is an important partner in OPEC+. Without Russia's co-operation, the cartel's ability to influence the price of oil in global markets would be diminished.

Continued Saudi production cuts into 2023 and ongoing increases in the price of petrol in the USA served as reminders to the Biden Administration that it would need Saudi assistance in 2024 if it wanted to keep oil prices down during its re-election campaign. Therefore, it might be reasonable to view Saudi oil production as an extension of Saudi statecraft and MBS may continue to use it as a means to bargain for a renewed security commitment from the USA.

The key difference for Saudi Arabia in a potential new protection relationship with the USA would be the nuclear component of the 'grand bargain'. If the US Senate permits the USA to partner with Saudi Arabia in creating an 'Arabian American Nuclear Power Company', along the lines of the early Aramco oil partnership, then it would provide Saudi Arabia with a new horizon for eventually achieving strategic autonomy. In the mean time, it would appear that the Saudis have recognized they are not quite ready to retire the oil-for-security paradigm in negotiating the future of their vital relations with the USA.

Bibliography and Sources

Abir, Mordechai. *Saudi Arabia: Society, Government, and the Gulf Crisis*. Abingdon, Routledge, 1993, pp. 51–98.

Abu Nasr, Donna, and Jefferson, Rodney. 'Liberated Saudi Youth Wonder Where Have All the Wahhabis Gone'. *Bloomberg Businessweek*, 19 November 2019.

Ahmed, Manail Anis. 'Outward Mobility of Saudi Students Abroad: An Overview'. *International Higher Education*, Vol. 83, 2015, pp. 19–20.

Al Hurra. 'Saudis discuss benefits of 'gender-mixing' [Arabic]. 29 March 2017.

Alhussein, Eman. *Saudi Changes to Guardianship System Ease Restrictions on Women*. Arab Gulf States Institute in Washington, 9 August 2019.

Almashabi, Deema, Carey, Glen, and Hamade, Riad. 'Saudi Arabia's Deputy Crown Prince Outlines Plans: Transcript'. *Bloomberg*. 4 April 2016.

Amgar, Samir. 'The Muslim World League in Europe: An Islamic Institution to serve Saudi Strategic Interests?'. *Journal of Muslims in Europe*, Vol. 1, No. 2, 2012, pp. 127–141.

Arabic21. 'Saudi Arrests Known Preacher after Criticism of General Entertainment Authority' [Arabic]. 11 September 2019.

Al Arabiya. 'How Saudi women interacted with the first mixed public sporting event'. 13 January 2018. english.alarabiya.net/en/News/gulf/2018/01/13/-How-Saudi-women-interacted-with-the-first-mixed-public-sporting-event.html.

Al Arabiya. 'Full Transcript of Al Arabiya's Interview with Saudi Finance Minister'. 2 May 2020.

Arab News. 'Senior Saudi cleric slams 'paranoia' over segregation between men and women'. 27 May 2019.

El-Ariss, Tarek. *Leaks, Hacks, and Scandals: Arab Culture in the Digital Age*. Princeton and Oxford, Princeton University Press, 2019, pp. 100–106.

Baker, Razan. 'Role of Saudi Women in Sport is Expanding to a Whole New Degree'. *Arab News*, 19 November 2019. www.arabnews.com/node/1586186.

Beblawi, Hazem. 'The Rentier State in the Arab World'. *Arab Studies Quarterly*, 1987, pp. 383–398.

Biden, Joe. 'Why I am going to Saudi Arabia'. *The Washington Post*, 9 July 2022.

Blas, Javier. 'How Did the Oil Price War End?'. *Bloomberg*, 13 April 2020.

BP Statistical Review of World Energy. BP, 2019.

Brewer, Eric, and Rome, Henry. 'Biden's Iran Gamble'. *Foreign Affairs*, 9 June 2023.

Browner, Derek, Manson, Katrina, England, Andrew, Wilson, Tom, and al-Atrush, Samer. 'Opec+ sticks with oil supply increase after US overture to Saudi Arabia'. *Financial Times*, 2 December 2021.

Brubaker, Rogers. *Nationalism Reframed: Nationhood and the National Question in the New Europe*. Cambridge University Press, 1996, pp. 19–21.

Bunzel, Cole. *The Kingdom and the Caliphate: Duel of the Islamic States*. The Carnegie Endowment for International Peace, February 2016.

Bunzel, Cole. 'The Kingdom and the Caliphate: Saudi Arabia and the Islamic State', in Wehrey, Federic (Ed.). *Beyond Sunni and Shia: The Roots of Sectarianism in a Changing Middle East*. Oxford, Oxford University Press, 2018, pp. 239–264.

Byman, Daniel. *The U.S.-Saudi counterterrorism relationship*. Brookings Institution, 24 May 2016.

Carey, Glen. 'Saudi Arabia Is Making Its First Real Attempt to Be a Military Power'. *Bloomberg News*, 13 May 2015.

Chulov, Martin. 'We feel empowered': Saudi women relish their new freedoms'. *The Guardian*, 3 August 2019.

Cioffoletti, Michelle. *Restructuring of Saudi Arts and Entertainment*. Arab Gulf States Institute in Washington, 8 August 2019.

Dadouch, Sarah. 'Saudi body appears to retract call to end gender segregation'. *Reuters*, 5 May 2018.

Al-Dakhil, Turki. 'Saudi Arabia: A kingdom full of youth'. *Al Arabiya*, 4 October 2017.

Determann, Jörg Matthias. *Historiography in Saudi Arabia: Globalization and the State in the Middle East*. London, I. B. Tauris, 2013, pp. 205–214.

Egozi, Arie. 'Saudi Arabia Considering Israeli-Made Missile Defense Systems'. *Breaking Defense*, 14 September 2021.

Eisenstadt, S. N. 'The Civilizational Dimension of Modernity'. *International Sociology*, Vol. 16, No. 3, 2001, pp. 320–340.

Elaph. 'Prince Bandar bin Sultan breaks his silence' [Arabic]. 5 February 2016.

Elliot House, Karen. *Profile of a Prince: Promise and Peril in Mohammed bin Salman's Vision 2030*. Harvard Kennedy School, Belfer Center for Science and International Affairs, April 2019.

Entous, Adam, and Barnes, Julian E. 'Deal With Saudis Paved the Way for Syrian Airstrikes'. *The Wall Street Journal*, 24 September 2014.

Erlanger, Steven. 'Saudi Prince Criticizes Obama Administration, Citing Indecision in the Middle East'. *The New York Times*, 15 December 2013.

Erlich, Haggai. *Saudi Arabia and Ethiopia: Islam, Christianity, and Politics Intertwined*. Boulder, CO, Lynne Rienner, 2007.

Eum, Ikran. 'New Women for a New Saudi Arabia?: Gendered Analysis of Saudi Vision 2030 and Women's Reform Policies'. *Asian Women*, Vol. 35, No. 3, September 2019, pp. 115–133.

Al-Faisal, Turki. *Keynote Remarks to the 31st Annual Arab-U.S. Policymakers Conference*. National Council on US-Arab Relations, 3 November 2022.

Foley, Sean. *Changing Saudi Arabia: Art, Culture, and Society in the Kingdom*. Boulder, CO, Lynne Rienner, 2019.

Foley, Sean. 'Legitimizing Transformation Without Calling it Change: Tajdid, Islah and Saudi Arabia's Place in the Contemporary World'. *Contemporary Review of the Middle East*, Vol. 2, Nos 1–2, March 2015, pp. 55–70.

Freer, Courtney. *Concerts, Cinemas and Comics in the Kingdom: Revising the Social Contract after Saudi Vision 2030*. The London School of Economics and Political Science, 26 May 2017.

Freer, Courtney. 'Hyper-Rentierism? Saudi Arabia's Vision 2030 and the Social Contract in 2017'. *Eurasia Review*, 15 June 2017.

Friedman, Brandon. 'Battle for Bahrain: What one uprising meant for the Arab States and Iran'. *World Affairs*, Vol. 174, No. 6, March 2012, pp. 74–84.

Friedman, Brandon. 'The Imperative of Saudi Reform: Conspiracy or Necessity?', in Friedman, Brandon, and Maddy-Weitzman, Bruce (Eds). *Inglorious Revolutions: State Cohesion in the Middle East After the Arab Spring*. The Moshe Dayan Center for Middle Eastern and African Studies, Tel Aviv, 2014, pp. 151–170.

Friedman, Brandon. 'Saudi Arabia: A Future Interrupted'. *Tel Aviv Notes*, Vol. 12, No. 19, 18 December 2018.

General Authority for Statistics. 'Population Estimates 2018, 2020'. www.stats.gov.sa/en/43.

Goldberg, Jeffrey. 'Saudi Crown Prince: Iran's Supreme Leader "Makes Hitler Look Good"'. *The Atlantic*, 2 April 2018.

Goldberg, Jeffrey. 'The Obama Doctrine'. *The Atlantic*, April 2016.

Haboush, Joseph. 'Saudi Arabia has always envisioned normalization with Israel would happen: FM'. *Al-Arabiya*, 15 October 2020.

Al-Hamad, Turki. 'The Unification of Arabia: The Role of Ideology and Organization in the Breaking of Social Structures that Hinder Unity' [Arabic]. *Al-Mustaqbal Al-Arabi*, Vol. 9, No. 3, November 1986, pp. 28–40.

Hamidaddin, Abdullah. *ma hi al-huwiyatu al-wataniya al-saudiya?* (What is Saudi national identity?). 31 December 2012.

Hamidaddin, Abdullah. 'Re-inventing Saudi Arabia'. *Al Arabiya*, 24 September 2013.

Hamidaddin, Abdullah. *Tweeted Heresies: Saudi Islam in Transformation*. London and New York, Oxford University Press, 2019, pp. 23–27.

Hegghammer, Thomas. 'Jihad, Yes, But Not Revolution: Explaining the Extraversion of Islamist Violence in Saudi Arabia'. *British Journal of Middle Eastern Studies*, Vol. 36, No. 3, 2009, pp. 395–416.

Hertog, Steffen, *Princes, Brokers, and Bureaucrats: Oil and State in Saudi Arabia*. Ithaca, NY, Cornell University Press, 2010.

Hertog, Steffen. 'Challenges to the Saudi Distributional State in the Age of Austerity', in Al-Rasheed, Madawi (Ed.). *Salman's Legacy: The Dilemmas of a New Era in Saudi Arabia*. London, Hurst & Co, 2018, pp. 73–96.

Hopkins, A. G. (Ed.). *Global History: Interactions between the Universal and the Local*. Palgrave Macmillan, p. 3, 2006.

i24 News. 'Report: U.S. offers Israel-Saudi Arabia normalization for silence on Iran deal'. 1 June 2023.

Jarbou, Rana. 'Know your enemy: the Saudi women's driving campaign from flyers and faxes to Youtube and hashtags'. *Feminist Media Studies*, Vol. 18, No. 2, 2018, pp. 321–325.

Jawhar, Sabria S. 'Red line is gone; welcome to the age of chemical warfare'. *Arab News*, 16 September 2013.

Johnsen, Gregory D. *The Growing Battle for South Yemen*. Arab Gulf States Institute in Washington, 18 July 2023.

Jones, Seth G., Thompson, Jared, Ngo, Danielle, McSorley, Brian, and Bermudez Jr., Joseph S. *The Iranian and Houthi War Against Saudi Arabia*. Center for Strategic and International Studies, December 2021.

Jordan, Frank, and Batrawy, Aya. 'Saudi Arabia cautiously welcomes UAE, Israel normalization'. *The Washington Post*, 19 August 2020.

Juergensmeyer, Mark. 'Thinking Sociologically about Religion and Violence: The Case of ISIS'. *Sociology of Religion: A Quarterly Review*, Vol. 79, No. 1, 2018, pp. 20–34.

Kane, Frank. 'Coronavirus pandemic a turning point in business history, says leading Saudi executive'. *Arab News*, 16 May 2020.

Kazimi, Nibras. 'Stations Along the Rim'. *Talisman Gate*, 31 August 2018.

Kechichian, Joseph A. *Legal and Political Reforms in Sa'udi Arabia*. Abingdon and New York, Routledge, 2013.

Kemp, John. 'Saudi Arabia's dwindling oil revenues and the challenge of reform'. *Reuters*, 21 January 2016.

Al-Khamri, Hana. 'The 'Right' to Drive for Women of Saudi Villages'. *Journal of Middle East Women's Studies*, Vol. No. 2, 2019, pp. 256–259.

Khorsheed, Mohammad S., 'Saudi Arabia: From Oil Kingdom to Knowledge Based Economy'. *Middle East Policy*, Vol. 22, No. 3, Fall 2015.

Kinninmont, Jane. *Vision 2030 and Saudi Arabia's Social Contract: Austerity and Transformation*. Chatham House, July 2017.

Kostiner, Joseph, and Teitelbaum, Joshua. 'State Formation and the Saudi Monarchy', in Kostiner, Joseph (Ed.). *Middle East Monarchies: The Challenge of Modernity*. Boulder, CO, Lynne Rienner, 2000, pp. 132, 134, 136–137.

Kostiner, Joseph. *The Making of Saudi Arabia, 1916–1936: From Chieftancy to Monarchical State*. Oxford University Press, 1993.

Krane, Jim. 'Saudi Arabia's Oil Strategy in a Time of Glut'. *Foreign Affairs*, 24 May 2016.

Krane, Jim. *Energy Governance in Saudi Arabia: An Assessment of the Kingdom's Resources, Policies, and Climate Approach*. Center for Energy Studies, Baker Institute for Public Policy, January 2019.

Lacroix, Stephane. *Awakening Islam: The Politics of Religious Dissent in Contemporary Saudi Arabia*. Cambridge, MA, Harvard University Press, 2011, pp. 52, 60, 103.

Levallois, Agnes and Therme, Clement. 'Iran and Saudi Arabia: Cold War'. *Confluences Méditerranée*, Vol. 97, No. 2, 2016, pp. 9–13.

Luciani, Giacomo. 'Allocation vs. Production States', in Beblawi, Hazem and Luciani, Giacomo (Eds). *The Rentier State*. London, Croom Helm, 1987.

Luciani, Giacomo. 'OPEC+ versus the United States and World Democracies'. *Cairo Review of Review of Global Affairs*, December 2022.

Makboul, Laila. 'Beyond Preaching Women: Saudi Da'iyat and Their Engagement in the Public Sphere'. *Die Welt Des Islams*, Vol. 57, 2017, pp. 303–328.

Maksad, Firas. 'Riyadh May Have Unleashed More Change than It Can Handle'. *Foreign Policy*, 22 April 2019.

Meijer, Roel. 'Reform in Saudi Arabia: The Gender Segregation Debate'. *Middle East Policy*, Vol. 17, No. 4, Winter 2010.

Meisel, Sebastian. 'The New Rise of Tribalism in Saudi Arabia'. *Nomadic Peoples*, Vol. 18, No. 2, 2014, pp. 100–122.

Menoret, Pascal. 'Development, Planning, and Urban Unrest in Saudi Arabia'. *Muslim World*, Vol. 101, No. 2, 2014, pp. 269–285.

Menoret, Pascal. 'The Suburbanization of Islamic Activism in Saudi Arabia'. *City & Society*, Vol. 29, No. 1, 2017, pp. 162–186.

Menoret, Pascal. 'Learning from Riyadh: Automobility, Joyriding, and Politics'. *Comparative Studies of South Asia,*

Africa, and the Middle East, Vol. 39, No. 1, May 2019, pp. 131–142.

Migdal, Joel S. *State in Society: Studying How States and Societies Transform and Constitute One Another*. Cambridge University Press, 2001, pp. 49–52.

Mills, Robin. 'Price cap on Russian oil signals an attempt by buyers' group to set terms in the market'. *The National*, 12 December 2022.

Mohamed, Arsalan. 'Saudi Arabia's Contemporary Art Scene is Suddenly Buzzing, With the Crown Prince's Blessing—and His Backing', *artnet*, 27 February 2018. news.artnet.com/art-world/saudi-arabia-art-scene-survey-1231676.

Mouline, Nabil. 'Enforcing and Reinforcing the State's Islam: The Functioning of the Committee of Senior Scholars', in Haykel, Bernard, Hegghammer, Thomas, and Lecroix, Stéphane (Eds). *Saudi Arabia in Transition*. Cambridge University Press, 2015, pp. 56–57.

Murphy, Carlyle. 'Questioning the Faith in the Cradle of Islam'. *Foreign Policy*, 29 October 2014.

Nagel, Jacob. 'Israel must oppose the Iran understandings with all it's got'. *Israel Hayom*, 16 June 2023.

The National. 'Saudi preacher says "phobia of women" must end'. 28 May 2019.

Nereim, Vivian. 'Saudi Program Calls for Gender Mixing, No Prayer Closure'. *Bloomberg*, 5 May 2018.

Nereim, Vivian. 'Saudi Arabia Quietly Revises Prince's Transformation Plan'. *Bloomberg*, 1 November 2018.

Nereim, Vivian. 'Party Time in Saudi Arabia Ends a Year of Fear'. *Bloomberg*, 19 December 2018.

Nonnemon, Gerd. 'Determinants and Patterns of Saudi Foreign Policy: 'Omnibalancing' and 'Relative Autonomy' in Multiple Environments', in Aarts, Paul, and Nonnemon, Gerd (Eds). *Saudi Arabia in the Balance: Political Economy, Society, Foreign Affairs*. New York, New York University Press, 2006, pp. 315–51.

Nuttall, Phillipa. 'Saudi Arabia is the biggest beneficiary of the war in Ukraine'. *The New Statesman*, 16 May 2022.

Obaid, Nawaf. 'A new generation of Saudi leaders — and a new foreign policy'. *The Washington Post*, 25 March 2015.

Al-Omran, Ahmed. 'Saudis Wrangle Over How to Have Fun'. *The Wall Street Journal*, 23 January 2017.

Ottaway, David. *MbS: The Icarus of Saudi Arabia?*. Boulder, CO, Lynne Rienner Publishers, 2021.

Pfeffer, Anshel. 'How Israel and Saudi Arabia Plan to Down Iranian Drones Together'. *Haaretz*, 13 June 2022.

Podeh, Elie. 'The emergence of the Arab state system reconsidered'. *Diplomacy & Statecraft*, Vol. 9, No. 3, 1998, pp. 50–82.

Qasemi, Farzad. 'Iran ignores Kuwait and imposes a fait accompli in al-Durra'. *Al-Jarida*, 3 July 2023.

Al-Quds Al-Arabi. 'Foreign Affairs: The coronavirus suspends Saudi ambitions and damages Saudi influence in the Islamic world ' [Arabic]. 16 April 2020.

Quilliam, Neil. 'The Saudi Dimension: Understanding the Kingdom's Position in the Gulf Crisis', in Krieg, Andreas. (Ed.). *Divided Gulf: The Anatomy of a Crisis*. Singapore, Palgrave Macmillan, 2019, pp. 109–126.

Quilliam, Neil. *Russia and Saudi Arabia Power Risk OPEC+ Break-Up*. Chatham House, 24 November 2020.

Radman, Hussam. *Local Deadlock and Regional Understandings: Analyzing the Houthi-Saudi and Islah-UAE Talks*. Sana'a Center for Strategic Studies, 16 December 2022.

Ramsay, Gilbert, and Fatani, Sumayah. 'The New Saudi Nationalism of the New Saudi Media', in Mellor, Noha, and Rinnawi, Khalil (Eds). *Political Islam and Global Media: The Boundaries of Religious Identity*. London and New York, Routledge, 2016, pp. 187–202.

Al-Rasheed, Madawi. *Muted Modernists: The Struggle over Divine Politics in Saudi Arabia*. London, Hurst & Co, 2015.

Al-Rasheed, Madawi. *A Most Masculine State: Gender, Politics, and Religion in Saudi Arabia*. Cambridge, Cambridge University Press, 2013, pp. 153, 159–160.

Ravid, Barak. 'U.S. working on normalization 'road map' for Saudi Arabia and Israel'. *Axios*, 22 June 2022.

Remnick, David. 'Going the Distance'. *The New Yorker*, 19 January 2014.

Riedel, Bruce. *Why are Yemen's Houthis attacking Riyadh now?*. Brookings Institution, 30 March 2020.

Saab, Bilal. *Rebuilding Arab Defense: US Security Cooperation in the Middle East*. Boulder, CO and London, Lynne Rienner Publishers, 2022, pp. 62–77.

Saghie, Hazim. 'Individualism in the Arab Middle East: An Overview', in Saghie, Hazim (Ed.). *The Predicament of the Individual in the Middle East*. London, Saqi Books, 2001, pp. 51–58.

Salah, Ehsan, and Tharwat, Hazem. 'US push for new regional cooperation sets off Gulf jockeying, MBS eyes Egypt-Turkey rapprochement, managing Brotherhood to bolster position'. *Mada Masr*, 28 June 2022.

Salame, Ghassan. '"Strong" and "Weak" States: A Qualified Return to the Muqaddimah', in Salame, Ghassan (Ed.). *The Arab State*. London, Routledge, 1990, pp. 205–240.

Saleh, Mahmoud Abdullah. 'The development of higher education in Saudi Arabia'. *Higher Education*, Vol. 15, 1986, pp. 17–23.

Samin, Nadav. *Of Sand and Soil: Genealogy and Tribal Belonging in Saudi Arabia*. Princeton, N.J., Princeton University Press, 2015.

Al-Sanosi, Rahaf, and Bukhari, Eman. 'Saudi Arabia: An Identity at a Crossroads'. *Jawazdiblomasy*, 3 July 2012. jawazdiblomasy.wordpress.com/2012/07/03/saudi-arabia-an-identity-at-a-crossroads.

Al-Sarhan, Saud. 'The Struggle for Authority: The Shaykhs of Jihadi-Salafism in Saudi Arabia, 1997–2003', in Haykel, Bernard, Hegghammer, Thomas, and Lecroix, Stéphane (Eds). *Saudi Arabia in Transition*. Cambridge University Press, pp. 184, 205, 2015.

Saudi Vision 2030.

Saudi Women's Driving School. HBO documentary, 2019.

Shield, Ralph. 'The Saudi air war in Yemen: A case for coercive success through battlefield denial'. *Journal of Strategic Studies*, 41 (3), pp. 461–489.

Sikkand, Yogindar. 'Stoking the Flames: Intra-Muslim Rivalries in India and the Saudi Connection'. *Comparative Studies of South Asia, Africa and the Middle East*, Vol. 27, No. 1, 2007, pp. 95–108.

Smith Diwan, Kristin. *Let Me Entertain You: Saudi Arabia's New Enthusiasm for Fun*. Arab Gulf States Institute in Washington, 9 March 2018.

Solomon, Jay. 'The Saudis want the US to help build a 'nuclear Aramco''. *Semafor*, 2 June 2023. www.wsj.com/articles/u-s-saudi-arabia-agree-to-broad-terms-for-israel-normalization-ac6d549c.

Stroul, Dana, Lippman, Thomas, and Feierstein, Gerard. 'The United States-Saudi Arabian Relationship'. *Middle East Policy Journal*, 26 (3), Fall 2019, pp. 5–29.

Tarmy, James. 'Saudi Arabia is Planning a Massive, New Arts Center'. *Bloomberg*, 29 January 2018. www.bloomberg.com/news/articles/2018-01-29/saudi-arabia-is-planning-a-massive-new-arts-center.

Teitelbaum, Joshua. 'Saudi Arabia Faces a Changing Middle East'. *Middle East Review of International Affairs*, Vol. 15, No. 3, 2011.

Thompson, Mark C. 'Saudi Women Leaders: Challenges and Opportunities'. *Journal of Arabian Studies*, Vol. 5, No. 1, 2015, pp. 15–36.

Thompson, Mark C. 'The Impact of Globalization on Saudi Male Millennials' Identity Narratives'. *Asian Affairs*, Vol. 50, No. 3, 2019, pp. 323–343.

Time. 'Crown Prince Mohammed Interview Transcript'. 5 April 2018.

Toumi, Habib. 'Saudi Arabia to stage first mixed-gender play'. *Gulf News*, 9 January 2019.

Tzoreff, Mira. 'The Quiet Revolution: Saudi Women Are Leading Change from Within' [Hebrew]. *The New East*, special issue, 2018, pp. 115–149.

The Ukraine Crisis and the Gulf: A Saudi Perspective: An Interview with Abdulaziz Al Sager. Institute Montaigne, 18 October 2022.

United Nations Conference on Trade and Development. *State of Commodity Dependence, 2014.* p. 182.

United Nations Conference on Trade and Development. *State of Commodity Dependence, 2019.* p. 178.

Vitalis, Robert. *America's Kingdom: Mythmaking on the Saudi Oil Frontier.* Stanford, Stanford University Press, 2007.

Wald, Ellen R. 'Signs Point To Trouble Ahead For Saudi Economy'. *Forbes*, 25 July 2018.

Al Watan. '72 percent of Saudi youth are interested in entertainment and culture' [Arabic]. 25 September 2019.

Woodward, Mark. 'Resisting Salafism and the Arabization of Indonesian Islam: A contemporary Indonesian didactic tale by Komaruddin Hidayat'. *Contemporary Islam*, Vol. 11, No. 3, 2017, pp. 237–258.

Young, Karen E. *Spending to Grow in Saudi Arabia.* The Arab Gulf States Institute of Washington, 10 August 2018.

Young, Karen E. *Saudi Economic Reform Update: Saudization and Expat Exodus.* The Arab Gulf States Institute in Washington, 28 February 2018.

Young, Karen E. 'The MBS Economy'. *Foreign Affairs*, 27 January 2022.

Al-Zaid, Saleh. 'Qiddiya Lays the Foundation for World's Largest Entertainment Project'. *Asharq Al-Awsat*, 25 July 2019.

Ze'evi, Dror. 'Back to Napoleon: Thoughts on the Beginning of the Modern Era in the Middle East'. *Mediterranean Historical Review*, 2004, pp. 73–94.

Economy

NEIL PARTRICK

Based on an original essay by MOIN SIDDIQI

The economy of Saudi Arabia—the largest among the Arab countries and the powerhouse of the Persian (Arabian) Gulf—is dominated by petroleum, of which the country is by far the largest producer within the Organization of the Petroleum Exporting Countries (OPEC, see p. 1161). Saudi Arabia has received massive revenue from petroleum exports (particularly since the dramatic increase in international petroleum prices in 1973–74), which it has used, in part, to finance an ambitious programme of infrastructural development and modernization and far-reaching programmes for health care, social and educational purposes. Substantial budgetary allocations have also been made to the country's armed forces and the purchase of sophisticated weaponry from abroad.

Conservative and traditionally strictly Islamic in orientation, the Saudi ruling family has consistently favoured a pro-Western, market-oriented economic strategy and placed great reliance on Western and Japanese expertise for the development of the country's petroleum and other sectors. There remains a substantial expatriate contribution to the management of various economic sectors, although Saudi nationals have come increasingly to the fore, especially in the hydrocarbons industries. Expatriates form the majority of the workforce. Emphasis has been placed, under recent development plans, on the promotion of 'downstream' oil industries, such as refining and petroleum derivatives, and progress has also been made in developing the country's non-oil industries.

The economy grew at a sluggish pace during 1980–99. Having achieved average annual growth of 10.6% in 1968–80, Saudi Arabia's gross domestic product (GDP) declined, in real terms, at an annual average rate of 1.2% in 1980–90, largely because petroleum output declined from a peak of almost 10m. barrels per day (b/d) in 1980 to 3.6m. b/d in 1985. Although production rose to more than 5m. b/d in 1988 and 1989, depressed international prices resulted in substantially reduced revenue, with adverse consequences for the current account and national budget, which both moved into deficit. According to the International Monetary Fund (IMF), real GDP growth expanded at an average annual rate of 1% during 1990–99, which lagged behind a population increase of 2.7% per year. Overall, GDP totalled US $160,960m. in 1999, compared with $104,670m. in 1990. GDP per capita, which exceeded $16,000 in the early 1980s, had fallen sharply by 1999, to $7,497.

Fuelled by strong global petroleum markets, the Saudi economy in the early 21st century entered a new period of healthy economic growth, coupled with burgeoning budget and current account surpluses. In 2013, according to the Saudi Central Bank (known by the acronym SAMA, referring to its previous title, the Saudi Arabian Monetary Authority), the kingdom's national output amounted to SR 2,791,000m. (US $744,000m.), equivalent to GDP per capita of $24,816), compared with $10,095 in 2006. With oil revenues in decline following the global oil price collapse of late 2014–early 2015, national output rose only slightly, to SR 2,827,000m. ($754,000m. or $23,915 per capita). SAMA reported that in 2015 national output fell to SR 2,453,000m. ($627,000m. or $21,180 per capita), owing to sustained lower revenue from oil as prices remained relatively low. This persisted in 2016, with oil (as measured by the price of Brent crude) averaging $44 per barrel, compared with $99 per barrel in 2014. The price of Brent crude rose to $71 per barrel in 2018, but fell to $64.20 in 2019. In the first five months of 2020 the price of Brent averaged $39.80 per barrel, principally owing to the negative impact of the coronavirus disease (COVID-19) pandemic on global economic activity—and thus demand—from March of that year. In April the average monthly price fell to a low of $23.30 per barrel, reflecting weak global demand and a surplus of oil on the market. However, the agreement of Saudi Arabia and other OPEC and associated producers to oil output reductions (see *Petroleum*) helped to arrest the plummeting price, and then encouraged a steady rise in the average monthly price to May 2021, when it averaged $68 per barrel. The Russian Federation's invasion of Ukraine in February 2022, and the consequent imposition of Western-led sanctions against Russia, including on its energy and related exports, contributed to an oil price that at certain points from late February was more or less double that of May 2021, and in mid-June 2022 stood at around $120 per barrel. During the first five months of 2022 Saudi Arabia resisted calls to lead an OPEC expansion of output in order to ease oil price pressure, but in early June agreed to increase production in July and August. Nevertheless, Saudi Arabia and some independent oil analysts argued that the upward global price pressure was not just an issue of the West's sanctions on Russian supplies (see *Petroleum*), and the kingdom was equally prepared to increase output should sufficient Russian oil and natural gas exports be taken offline.

Although Saudi Arabia was not 'decoupled' from the global financial crisis of 2007–08, the effects were less severe than elsewhere, reflecting low, manageable external (private) debt, a strongly capitalized banking system (not reliant on external funding) and the Government's pledge to spend US $400,000m. to bolster economic activity and diversify into new areas. Despite this, real GDP growth in 2009 was estimated at just 0.1%—its slowest rate since 2002. Real GDP grew (at producer prices) by 5% in 2010 and 10% in 2011, driven mainly by higher petroleum output and increased government consumption and investment. Growth decelerated to 5.4% in 2012, and further to 2.7% in 2013, before rising to 3.7% in 2014, due to relatively flat oil output and the removal of some illegal expatriate workers in 2012–13. In 2015 real growth of 4.1% was recorded as state stimuli remained high and oil output rose firmly. According to SAMA data, real growth slowed to 1.7% in 2016, despite rising oil output, as oil prices remained low and state spending fell significantly. Following a cut in oil production under a November 2016 OPEC agreement, real GDP contracted by 0.7% in 2017, reflecting the oil output constraint and weak government sector growth.

In 2018 real GDP growth was 2.5%, supported by rising oil prices during that year. Such growth was notable, given the knock to investor confidence caused by the widely reported semi-public detention of several members of the Saudi royal family and senior businessmen in November 2017 and the even more negative publicity generated by the murder of dissident Saudi journalist Jamal Khashoggi in October 2018. A contraction in the oil sector in 2019 reflected the 'OPEC+' agreement (including Russia) at the beginning of the year to cut output. The oil sector shrunk by 3.6% in real terms, despite some easing of the OPEC-agreed constraints in August, when Saudi Arabia increased its oil output modestly. However, over 2019 as a whole output fell markedly from 2018. Oil prices decreased sharply in the second half of 2019, undermining investment in the energy sector. However, the non-oil sector expanded by 3.3% in real terms, largely reflecting real growth of 3.8% in the private sector. The relatively strong performance in the private sector was in part a reflection of strong government demand for most of the year, although this waned in response to falling oil revenues in the second half of 2019. In December a new OPEC+ agreement was concluded in an effort to reduce output and support prices. Overall real growth in 2019 was a negligible 0.3%, according to the Government's General Authority for Statistics (GASTAT). According to GASTAT, real GDP in 2020 contracted by 4.1%, largely driven by a fall in real oil GDP of 6.7%, albeit partly offset by a more modest decline in the non-oil sector of 2.3%. Notably, the government sector registered a fall in real GDP of 0.5%, in part reflecting the oil GDP contraction and growth of only 0.4% in government services relating to the low oil output. This, in turn, contributed to a decline in the private sector of 3.1%. In 2021 the IMF reported a rebound in terms of real growth, of 3.2%. According to GASTAT, real GDP grew by 8.7% in 2022 as the Saudi economy continued to recover from pandemic-related demand constraints. The expansion was driven by significant increases in Saudi oil production, implemented over the year in order to ease global price pressures and thus maintain demand, as well as by robust non-oil GDP growth (estimated by the IMF at 4.8%). Non-oil growth in 2022 was driven by rising private consumption and private investment in gigaprojects, as well as greater public expenditure in the construction and transport sectors. In the first quarter of 2023 real overall GDP grew by 3.8% year on year, reflecting non-oil growth of 5.4%, fuelled by continuing investment in infrastructure projects, whereas real oil growth more or less flatlined.

Despite strong domestic demand and a high level of liquidity, inflationary pressures have traditionally remained subdued, owing largely to generous subsidies for essential goods and services and prudent monetary policy. The state provides implicit subsidies for petrol, electricity and water utilities. Annual rises in the consumer price index averaged just 1.0% during 2002–06. Inflation accelerated during 2007 to 4.1% and reached a historic high of 9.9% in 2008, fuelled by strong domestic demand.

The Government approved ad hoc measures to mitigate the effects of higher inflation, including providing a cost of living allowance for all state employees and pensioners, equivalent to 5.0% of their income for three years; increasing its social security contributions by 10.0%; and extending subsidies on basic commodities. Inflation decreased to 5.1%, 5.4% and 3.9%, respectively, in 2009, 2010 and 2011, according to the IMF, owing to lower import prices, rents and domestic demand. Inflation fell to 2.9% in 2012, but, according to official and IMF data, it increased to 3.5% in 2013 before falling to 2.7% in 2014 and 2.2% in 2015, reflecting the fall in oil revenue. The Economist Intelligence Unit (EIU) reported that inflation in 2016 decreased to 1.7%, despite a cut in government subsidies on certain essential items, including fuel, electricity and meat, as oil prices remained at a historic low. Although energy and electricity subsidies were further reduced in 2017, the pressure of shrinking incomes amid policies of fiscal constraint led to deflation in that year of 1.1%, according to the EIU. Amid higher oil revenues and the expectation of rising government expenditure in 2018, consumer prices rose by 2.4%. In 2019, according to SAMA, Saudi consumer prices fell by 2.1% as demand decreased sharply amid strongly falling oil revenues, lower government spending and a decline in business activity. However, in 2020 consumer price inflation rose, on average, by 3.5%, in part owing to higher prices of food and beverages. Average annual inflation declined to 3.1% in 2021. In 2022, according to the IMF, inflation fell to 2.5%, as state price subsidies and caps and the strength of the US dollar-pegged riyal provided a cushion from the rising cost of imports (caused primarily by the conflict in Ukraine).

Despite its economic development in recent decades, the kingdom still faces considerable demographic challenges, notably a burgeoning indigenous population (two-thirds of whom are under 30 years of age), a rapidly growing labour force (an estimated 150,000 young nationals enter the labour market annually), high unemployment and immense pressure on housing, public services and utilities.

POPULATION AND LABOUR FORCE

According to GASTAT, at mid-2022 the total population was an estimated 32.2m. At that time, expatriates, numbering some 13.4m., represented 41.6% of the total. The majority of non-nationals are from South Asia (especially Pakistan and India), South-East Asia, the Middle East and North Africa. The Eastern region, Jeddah, Mecca and Riyadh contain about two-thirds of the kingdom's population.

The structure of the indigenous population is expected to change markedly, with rising numbers of over-65-year-olds requiring higher social and health care spending. About 70% of the population is under the age of 32 years, indicating the importance of job creation, especially given that the total Saudi population is forecast to double by 2050.

Following the Nitaqat ('Saudization') Initiative, which was originally launched in 2011 and sought to increase the number of nationals employed in the private sector, GASTAT figures indicated a progressive reduction in the foreign workforce. According to GASTAT, the Labour Force Survey conducted in the first quarter of 2020 showed that total employment was 13.1m.—down from the estimated 13.4m. two years earlier when expatriate labour comprised 10.2m. workers and Saudi national labour was put at 3.2m. (a figure that according to GASTAT excluded the many Saudis employed in the military and security services). The decline in total employment was in line with Western media accounts of some legal foreign workers leaving the country owing to rising costs, and a clampdown on illegal workers, although the overall impact of the outflow would have been mitigated by the number of new expatriate labour visas still being granted.

GASTAT, citing the Labour Force Survey, recorded the overall employment rate in the first quarter of 2020 at 88.2% of the Saudi national workforce. The unemployment rate of 11.8%—though only marginally down from 12.0% in the previous quarter—implied a downward trend from the figure of 12.7% officially recorded at the end of 2018. Notably, however, male unemployment increased from 4.8% in the final quarter of 2019 to 5.6% in the first quarter of 2020, while female unemployment fell from 30.9% to 28.2%. The entry of Saudi women into the workforce (conceivably partly at the expense of some Saudi males), aided by a royal decree of 2018 giving them the legal right to drive, had produced the overall decline in unemployment. Unemployment among young Saudis continued to be a feature: 62.9% of the unemployed as of 31 March 2020 were between the ages of 20 and 29. According to GASTAT, 55.7% of new Saudi entrants to the job market at the end of 2022 were under 30, 29.3% were under 25 and 24% aged 20–24. Although official Saudi unemployment was on a downward trajectory in early 2023, providing sufficient sustainable jobs, especially in the private sector, for the burgeoning population of young Saudis remained a major challenge.

GASTAT data accessed in mid-June 2022 showed the overall official Saudi unemployment rate as having resumed its pre-pandemic modestly downward trend, recorded at 11% at the end of 2021. However, it was not clear that this suggested relative policy success. The real rate of unemployment among those Saudis (both men and women) who were officially classified as available for work was probably closer to one-third, if the number of Saudis claiming unemployment assistance was taken into account. Significantly, at 31 March 2020 the overall Saudi female labour force participation rate was 25.9%, compared with 65.8% for men, suggesting that part of the discrepancy between official unemployment figures and unofficial estimates is that, despite the legal and social changes and the consequent increase in Saudi females working, a large number of Saudi females were choosing not to enter the labour market. At the end of 2021 it was also evident that the apparent modest downward trend in overall Saudi unemployment disguised an indeterminate trend among women. According to IMF data published in June 2023, overall unemployment at the end of 2022 had fallen markedly, to a historic low of 4.8%, having declined from 9.0% during the pandemic, owing to higher employment of Saudi nationals in the private sector (long a frustrated goal of government policy). The IMF also noted a sharp reduction over two years in youth unemployment to 16% and a rise in female employment to 37%.

At 31 March 2021 the proportion of Saudi unemployed who were graduates had fallen, but still represented 47.1% of the total unemployed, implying that there had been additional engagement of graduates, although it was unclear if this was in the relatively dormant private sector or whether some graduates were being absorbed by the Saudi state, including in its essentially informal security-related workforce.

In the fourth quarter of 2018 the proportion of the overall workforce employed in the construction sector was 40.6%, trade 27.2%, services 12.2%, manufacturing 10.8%, post and telecommunications 4.5%, mining and quarrying 2.2%, utilities 1.2% and agriculture 1.1%. Expatriates were mostly employed in private companies, while jobs in the civil service, autonomous government institutions and parastatal organizations were largely reserved for Saudi nationals. More than 90% of the indigenous workforce was employed by the state. According to GASTAT, at the end of 2018 non-nationals comprised 85% of the total estimated private sector workforce of 11.1m. (including those foreigners classified as 'domestic workers'—the 'domestic workers' category represented a total of 2.5m. in the fourth quarter of 2018).

From 1996 the Government began to enforce quotas for the employment of Saudi nationals in various sectors of the economy, including certain types of manual and clerical work. The minimum Saudi element that the affected industries were required to employ varied from 5% to 40% of the company workforce. In July 1998 the Saudi Government restricted the duration of public sector employment contracts for expatriates to a maximum of 10 years in most categories of work, and a policy of 'Saudizing' the workforce brought to 36 the total number of occupations to which expatriate access was restricted or denied. The Human Resources Development Fund, financed partly by more expensive expatriate work permits and visas, was launched in April 2002 to subsidize skills training for nationals. In February 2003 the Minister of the Interior announced plans to reduce the number of expatriate workers and their dependants in the kingdom to 20% of the population by 2013—an incredible target, given that this would have required the removal of around 4m. foreign nationals. In the event, around 1.4m. illegal workers were removed between the beginning of 2013 and mid-2014. Nevertheless, the proportion of foreigners remained in excess of one-third. In January 2018 it was announced that all public sector employees (presumably, in practice, applying only to Saudi nationals) would receive a SR 1,000 monthly supplement because of the rising cost of living and the state's role in the increase. However, the marked outflows of expatriate workers in the wake of intensifying 'Saudization' pressures, the imposition of new financial charges on them and on each additional family member they bring to Saudi Arabia and other increases in the cost of living have made the kingdom less attractive to the less affluent expatriate labour demographic. Compounding this was the tripling of value-added tax (VAT) to 15% in July 2020, in response to falling government revenue amid the COVID-19 crisis, although it risked further imperilling economic demand, especially as the Government also suspended the subsidy that had been payable to all Saudi state employees to offset the rising cost of governments fees and utilities.

The impact of COVID-19 on the Saudi labour market deepened the overall outflow of expatriate labour. In the first three quarters of 2019, amid shrinking oil revenues, the number of private sector jobs, whether for Saudis or non-Saudis, fell by some 200,000. After the introduction of lockdown measures in March 2020, the Government introduced a subsidy for private sector Saudi employment equivalent to 60% of salary in an effort to contain the negative effect of the pandemic on Saudi employment, while maintaining public sector employment levels.

At the end of March 2021 the proportion of Saudis who worked in the state sector was recorded as 53.8% of total employment, whereas the private sector provided employment for 44.0% of the total (and 2.2% were described as 'other'). The anticipated shift to private sector employment was plainly still a 'work in progress'—a structural problem that had been noted by the Government and external observers around the time of the launch of the programme of economic and social reform, Saudi Vision 2030 (SV 2030—see *Saudi Vision 2030*), in 2016, and which did not appear to have changed five years later. The GASTAT data for the end of March 2021 showed that 26.4% of all Saudis in public or private employment were working in the sub-sector 'public administration and defence, and compulsory social security'—i.e. approximately 800,000 were employed in state administration, the military (including presumably its administrative components) or the General Organization for Social Insurance.

GASTAT data accessed in June 2022 indicated that public sector employment was continuing on a downward trend, accounting for 52.0% of total employment at the end of 2021, compared with 61.6% at the end of 2019. However, since the public sector employment share was not categorized according to Saudi national or non-national status, it was not apparent whether the officially desired proportional transfer of Saudi nationals to the private sector had actually been making progress.

In January 2021 a meeting of the Public Investment Fund (PIF—the Saudi sovereign wealth fund) led to an announcement by Crown Prince Mohammed bin Salman that due to a planned PIF investment in the Saudi economy of a huge US $267,000m. over the 'next five years', when, it was claimed, assets would exceed $1,000,000m., some 1.8m. jobs would be created. In keeping with such statements relating to SV 2030, it was not explained how the funds (on fiscal revenue projections) would be provided by the beginning of 2026, nor how such a seemingly arbitrary new number of jobs would be realized and nor what proportion of these jobs would be taken up by Saudi nationals.

SAUDI VISION 2030

From 1970 until 2016 the development of the Saudi economy was supposedly guided by a series of five-year plans. They were often highly ambitious in terms of projected infrastructure and business development, and the supposedly related expansion of skilled jobs for Saudis. Although the model of five-year plans was abandoned in 2016, much of the statist direction remained, albeit with a host of new state bodies created to carry it out. The Council for Economic and Development Affairs (CEDA) was established by King Salman in January 2015 to replace the Supreme Economic Council, under the title 'Saudi Vision 2030' (SV 2030). Within this framework, the National Transformation Programme (NTP) would, it was claimed, identify particular measures that would need to be taken by government bodies to realize the overall vision, as well as specific goals and steps. In effect, the NTP is the new 10th Development Plan, but in practice it will benefit from greater executive empowerment, as it will be an expression of what the CEDA intends to do.

SV 2030 emphasized that a fundamental and economically crucial ambition was to increase the private sector's contribution to the country's GDP. The NTP launch document claimed that the private sector had already funded 40% of the cost of the initiatives undertaken by the different programmes set up to realize such goals as expanding the 'local contribution' to the economy and streamlining government procedures important to private business. The 'digital transformation' of the Saudi economy was also proposed under the NTP.

Particularly striking was the claim made in April 2016 by the head of the CEDA, Prince Mohammed bin Salman (Crown Prince from June 2017) that at the end of the NTP, Saudi Arabia could end its reliance on oil revenues. Perhaps part of the explanation behind the claim was simply that oil revenues and other state income from industrial holdings will seemingly be converted into shares, whose dividends will be paid into the existing PIF of the Saudi Government. The PIF would be transformed into a formal sovereign wealth fund that would be funded, like those in neighbouring GCC states, to invest its income across all parts of the economy and abroad. In theory, this would mean that the state's earnings would be from a portfolio of holdings and not simply an appropriation of the profits of the state-run oil Saudi Arabian Oil Company (Saudi Aramco), which are conventionally estimated at about 90% of government revenue. It was also intended that in the process of making domestic investments (unusually for a sovereign wealth fund), the PIF would be able to stimulate domestic economic activity and aid diversification, which could increase the take-up of Saudi nationals in the workforce.

A target of increasing the value of the PIF's holdings by 25% to US $400,000m. in 2030 was announced, apparently including a planned transfer to the PIF of $69,100m. as Aramco was obliged to buy the former's majority stake in the state-owned chemicals company Saudi Basic Industries Corpn (SABIC) for this amount (itself a move intended to offset the postponing of an initial public offering—IPO—in Aramco). Apparently impatient to boost the PIF's activity and revenue-earning potential, the Saudis announced a total of $21,000m. worth of borrowing in the first eight months of 2019. A bond issue of $11,000m. was successfully conducted in April, and a loan of $10,000m. from three international banks was announced in July. However in mid-June 2020 the scheduled payment by Aramco to the PIF of the $69,100m. was extended over a period of eight years as oil prices had weakened. In addition, it was agreed that Aramco would have to make compensatory additional payments for a weakened SABIC share price.

As positive as the planned transparent and regularized way of managing revenue streams was, the announcement that 'up to 5%' of Aramco would be sold off in an IPO, itself necessitated that the balance of up to 95% would have to be converted into shares held in some form of state fund such as the PIF. This perhaps explains how the PIF might reach the SR 3,000,000m. target that the Government had set for it. Set against this ambition, however, was the hitherto highly politically expedient practice of appropriating undeclared amounts of Aramco profit, formally estimated at 90%, to meet both budget and off-budget revenue streams—the latter in part meeting defence and royal family expenditure. The Aramco IPO was indefinitely postponed in August 2018, despite significant progress having been made by that time in seeking a listing on the London Stock Exchange. In May 2019 the Ministry of Petroleum and Mineral Resources claimed that the IPO was still going ahead, but not before 2021 (see *Finance*).

SV 2030 also proposed several new bodies to sit alongside and under the CEDA in order to meet its targets and those of the NTP. In its proposals and accompanying graphics, this was plainly a very top-down structure. Sitting alongside the CEDA itself, at what is formally designated as Level One, is a financial committee of which the primary objective is to secure funding for the necessary projects. At Level Two in the SV 2030 plan the CEDA Strategy Committee will define the overall goals and how they will be realized. In doing this it will utilize the Strategic Management Office (SMO), which will be tasked with drawing up plans that will be relayed upwards to CEDA itself. A Project Management Office (PMO) will assess the plans, the risks involved in implementing them and the likely costs and benefits. A Delivery Unit was set up to oversee the realization of the overall plans and targets. In support of all of this is the body that holds overall responsibility for past Five-Year Plans—the Ministry of Economy and Planning. Its role appears to have been reduced to providing back-up support and data for the tasks that the CEDA is undertaking. At Level Three, according to SV 2030, are the execution bodies. These are chiefly the regular government ministries (including the economy and planning ministry, but with obvious implications for the labour and interior ministries too), but there is vague reference to other execution bodies. In addition, there is reference to the National Performance Management Centre; it is proposed that the Centre will monitor and publicize projects under the NTP to ensure that the Saudi public can see that goals are being realized.

Due to an apparent recognition that expecting the NTP's specific goals to be realized by 2020 across a wide range of criteria had been excessively ambitious, several revised and more modest targets were issued in November 2018. In January 2019 the National Industrial Development and Logistics Programme (NIDLP) was launched. This was reportedly intended to be the main driver of SV 2030. The NIDLP's focus was apparently on expanding domestic and foreign investment in manufacturing, mining, energy and logistics sectors in particular. The target set for additional investment was US $450,000m. by 2030—an objective reportedly recognized as difficult, given the limited growth in the global economy and what were referred to as domestic investment pressures. The flagship project to attract FDI and specifically to release money to the PIF for Saudi Arabia to make both domestic and foreign investment of its own, was the long-planned but much-delayed IPO of Aramco. In the event, a scaled-back version of the IPO was launched during December 2019–January 2020, with about 1.5% of shares, as measured by value, being sold compared with the original plan of about 5%. The smaller option came about as a result of the overall company valuation being estimated variously as between $1,100,000m. and $1,700,000m., i.e. potentially only a little over one-half of what had been expected. This led to the Saudi Government's decision to issue the IPO only via the Saudi Stock Exchange (the Tadawul), rather than on foreign stock markets, and to sell it to individual or corporate national share buyers or company purchasers from other GCC countries. In other words, those who would either feel an incentivized, or even cajoled commitment to buy or, in the case of an Emirati state purchaser, a politically sympathetic one. This raised almost $30,000m. following the unexpected issuing of a second tranche of shares in January 2020: a further 450m. shares were issued on the basis that the individual share price had remained within an acceptable range. This was still the world's largest ever IPO, but very far from raising the $100,000m. in revenue, based on a $2,000,000m. company valuation, that had first been envisaged.

Equally importantly, the revenues were, as planned, placed in the PIF, which proceeded to focus on international investments—a tendency compounded by the global downturn that accompanied the coronavirus pandemic. The global recession was, in turn, made worse for Saudi and other oil producers by Saudi oil policy (see *Petroleum*). In the context of the downturn, an IPO that was supposed to help the PIF to promote 'national champions' as part of a planned transformation of the private sector, instead largely further facilitated the PIF's statist collection of international trophies at relatively bargain prices. It was notable that, as a percentage of GDP, the private sector at the end of 2019 constituted only 40.7% of GDP; it was just under 39% in 2016 when SV 2030 was launched. A report by the US think tank Atlantic Council said that at the interim 2020 stage, SV 2030 suffered from a top-down approach that made the desired influx of foreign capital all the more unlikely, while demanding greater accountability from the Saudi leadership in order for foreign investors to risk investing in the country. At the end of 2022, according to GASTAT, the private sector represented 44% of overall real GDP (down from the 51.7% recorded at the end of March 2021, as the economy was expanding, boosted by high demand in the state oil sector). At the end of March 2023 the contribution of the private sector to the overall real economy stood at 46%. This rise suggested that progress was finally being made, although there was little sign that the identified top-down approach had altered that much and thus doubt remained as to how vibrant and self-sustaining the seemingly growing Saudi private sector really was.

The Atlantic Council approved of the proposal in the SV 2030 for the PIF to provide a 'seeding' role to promote the private sector, if the state is just the 'enabler' of the private sector rather than the latter being (as is traditional) the 'servicer' of the state. However, so far, the PIF, just like the wider SV 2030 and its emphasis on mega-projects like NEOM (see *Industry, Gas and Mining*), seems excessively focused on state-driven, grandiose, high-technology ambitions or on using finance for diplomacy. Given the insufficient decentralization and transparency of decision-making that might make SV 2030 more responsive to variable ground-level domestic needs, and given the limited regulatory focus, when the transparent resolution of business disputes including to the advantage of smaller enterprises was needed, it seemed as though SV 2030 would continue to struggle to meet an overall objective that was supposed to boost a non-oil-reliant and self-sustaining private sector.

Perhaps out of recognition of Saudi Arabia's difficulty in attracting FDI, a dedicated body, the Ministry of Investment was created in February 2020. The new ministry apparently incorporated the Saudi Arabian General Investment Authority (SAGIA), and its 'InvestSaudi' virtual platform presented itself as the online shopfront for non-Saudis wishing to do business in the kingdom, albeit linking to SAGIA for enquiries.

In April 2021 the CEDA published a review of progress made after five years of SV 2030. After a nebulous summary featuring terms such as 'empowering infrastructure' and 'building institutional and legislative structures', it declared that the next phase would be about the 'continuation of implementation' and 'ensuring greater participation by citizens and the private sector'. It was added in the conclusion that this would include additional steps to support 'promising sectors' of the economy. These vague objectives, past and future, lacked any clear definition or measure by which progress on them could be assessed. However, the CEDA assessment also provided a range of data intended to create the impression of economic progress, beginning with the claim that access to emergency health services 'within four hours' was now available for 'more than 86%' of people, compared with 36% 'when SV 2030 began'. How the improvement had been made, whether it applied to all residents in all parts of the kingdom, what its relevance was to the five years that SV 2030 had existed, and what the relationship of obtaining emergency medical treatment 'within four hours' was to a Saudi resident's medical health or mortality was not explained.

Separately, the PIF, which had become a de facto SV 2030 'ministry', one that branded itself as a 'leading global impactful investor', and that consequently arguably had more weight than the existing Ministry of Economy and Planning, in 2021 issued its own five-year plan, or 'programme' presenting its objectives for 2025. Fitting within the SV 2030 state economic direction model, and advertising its centrality to SV 2030, it set out 13 sectors that were to be the emphasis of its interventionist strategy.

An original key conception of the PIF's role was promoting indigenous private sector development. However, in 2017 the National Development Fund (NDF) was specifically tasked with advancing Saudi private sector development including, the NDF said, the development of Saudi banks. This seemed to fit with the SV 2030 rhetoric of the state providing 'seed money' for promising businesses. However, measuring the NDF's success, or failure, was difficult. I

The PIF, in practice, was a highly ambitious sovereign wealth fund, and, regardless of the needs of Saudi private sector development, it continued to focus on high-profile foreign acquisitions or stakes useful perhaps to global branding and intra-Gulf competition. However, such stakes were not always in the most promising companies or sectors, and were literally far from previous talk of the PIF's intended role in indigenous economic development likely to generate significant local Saudi knowledge capacity and related jobs. In June 2022 the PIF's alternative golf tournament, the LIV, began in Hertfordshire, UK, after controversially seeking to attract players from the established professional body and then each taking out costly lawsuits against the other. (In June 2023 the two rival international golf bodies agreed to merge, to the presumed benefit of Saudi ambitions, given the PIF's commitment to invest enormous sums of money into the new body.) Earlier in 2022 the PIF had acquired Newcastle Football Club, a British Premier League team. Mohammed bin Abdullah bin Abdulaziz al-Jaadan, the Minister of Finance, told the UK newspaper the *Financial Times* in May that any fiscal surplus that year would be directed into both the PIF and the NDF. The Saudi state's leading, if paradoxical, role in the private sector promotion envisaged in SV 2030 appeared set to continue. The ultimate aim of the ostensible commitment in SV 2030 to Saudi private sector development in terms of entrepreneurialism regarding small and medium-sized enterprises (SMEs) seemed to be addressed more with the creation of, paradoxically, another state entity: Monsha'at ('enterprises'; or 'The General Authority for SMEs'). Monsha'at, in turn, set up another state body to promote private sector development: the Saudi Venture Capital Company. According to a SAMA report on 'Financial Sector Development', the deployment of venture capital (traditionally seen as supporting SME development) rose significantly in 2021. In 2021 there were 76 investors in 'Saudi start-ups'—representing a 52% increase on the number in 2020. FinTech predominated among the start-ups. However, it was not clear how many of the 76 investors were in some way linked to Monsha'at's Saudi Venture Capital Company, or how many were genuine private investors (or how many were, for that matter, genuinely Saudi private business people).

The IMF's annual assessment of the Saudi economy, published in interim form in June 2023, contained guarded but still clear criticism of Saudi statism or 'intervention', in particular by the PIF, given the ongoing pressing need for the development of a non-state reliant private sector and the related requirement for more Saudi employment in the private sector. The Fund noted that the rise in oil revenue had not led to an increase in foreign reserves. In fact, it identified a US $30,000m. decrease in foreign reserves in the year to April 2023. The implication was that there had been continued use of US dollar reserves to fund the PIF's ongoing purchase of (sometimes questionable) foreign assets. This, when coupled with the IMF contesting that state direction, including the Special Economic Zones (SEZs), should be sensitive to private sector development on the ground, including training needs, suggested that the Fund continued to have reservations about various state-driven efforts to develop a self-reliant and Saudi-employing private sector. The IMF emphasized the need for the SEZs to aid skills training and for the state-run Human Capability Development Program to facilitate greater training of nationals for private sector work and thereby boost economic development.

PETROLEUM

The origins of Saudi Arabia's oil power date back to the early 1930s. In 1933 a concession was granted to Standard Oil Co of California, USA to explore for hydrocarbons reserves in the new desert kingdom. The operating company, the Arabian-American Oil Co (Aramco) began exploration in that year, and discovered crude oil in commercial quantities in 1938. Other US companies gradually acquired shares in Aramco, and by 1948 Standard Oil, Texaco and Exxon each owned a 30% share, with Mobil accounting for the remaining 10%. In November 1962 the Government created the General Petroleum and Mineral Organization (Petromin) as the instrument for increasing state participation in the petroleum and gas industries. In line with the actions of other Arab petroleum-producing states, the Saudi Government acquired a 25% share in Aramco in January 1973. A 100% takeover of the company was agreed in 1980.

The expansion of Saudi Arabia's petroleum output in the 1960s and 1970s was spectacular. Production increased from about 62m. metric tons (equivalent to 1.3m. b/d) in 1960 to 178m. tons (3.8m. b/d) in 1970, and to 412m. tons (8.5m. b/d) in

1974. This growth in output was accompanied by rising prices for petroleum, culminating in the huge increases of October and December 1973, which almost quadrupled the price per barrel. The Government's petroleum revenue increased dramatically, from US $1,214m. in 1970 to $22,573m. in 1974.

In April 1989 Saudi Aramco was formed to take control of the nationalized Aramco assets. In addition, a new Supreme Oil Council was established to take responsibility for the country's petroleum industry. The council's members included private businessmen and government ministers, and it was seen as an indication of the Government's desire to involve the private sector in the management of the economy. In January 2015 a new oil decision-making committee was formed, led by the then Deputy Crown Prince Mohammed bin Salman, as part of CEDA.

The hydrocarbons industry has long formed the bedrock of the Saudi economy, providing 43% of real GDP and 88% of total state revenues in 2014. At the end of 2020, according to GASTAT, 'the oil sector' represented just 23% of real GDP; this figure, published without comparative data for this defined sector in 2019, is hard to reconcile with the above historic data, even allowing for the OPEC+ production constraint agreement made in response to the COVID-19 pandemic in March (see below), which began to have a severe impact in the second quarter of 2020. Notably, the same GASTAT report stated that the more specific category of 'crude petroleum and natural gas' represented as little as 19.7% of GDP in 2020, markedly down from 27.4% in 2019. According to the US Energy Information Administration (EIA), average Saudi crude oil output fell from just under 10m. b/d in the first quarter of 2020 to just under 9m. b/d in the third quarter, before rising slightly, to an average of 9.2m. b/d, in the fourth quarter. The substantive reduction in overall output in 2020 provided a partial explanation at least for the Saudi economic performance apparently being less dependent on hydrocarbons, which was an objective of SV 2030. However, that hydrocarbons should fall so markedly, even as a percentage of what, overall, was a shrinking economy in 2020, was still unexpected. Notably, the EIA stated that Saudi crude oil output in the first quarter of 2021 fell slightly, to average 8.7m. b/d (Aramco reported that it had decreased to 8.6m. b/d). According to GASTAT, in the first quarter of 2022 the hydrocarbons sector constituted 32.4% of nominal GDP, a position in part reflecting the sharp increase in oil revenues.

The stability of global energy markets has relied heavily on Saudi Arabia (the world's largest oil exporter), which acts as a 'swing producer' within OPEC, underpinned by a large excess production capacity, estimated at 4m. b/d (equivalent to the total output of the People's Republic of China). According to the EIA, Saudi Arabia's total production (crude oil, natural gas liquids—NGLs—and condensates) averaged 10.8m. b/d in 2020. This was down from 11.8m. b/d, according to BP data, in 2019, when it accounted for 12.4% of the global total—a proportion that the kingdom is likely to have maintained in 2020 given overall output reductions in that year.

The quality of Saudi petroleum ranges from medium-and-heavy 'sour' crude, containing higher sulphur levels and derived from offshore fields, to 'extra-lighter' grades (i.e. super light), mainly produced from onshore fields. An estimated 65% of total output is considered of light gravity. Most Saudi crude petroleum is exported from the Persian Gulf via the huge Abqaiq processing facility. Major export terminals are situated at Ras Tanura Facility, which can handle over 6m. b/d, Yanbu (4.5m. b/d), Ras al-Ju'aymah (3.6m. b/d) on the Gulf coast and Ras Tanura Port (2.5m. b/d). Together, these terminals are capable of handling a combined 16.6m. b/d. Saudi Aramco employs more than 5,000 armed guards to protect its petroleum installations from possible terrorist attacks. The Ministry of the Interior operates the Facilities Protection Force, which was founded in 2007 with the objective of protecting all energy facilities nationally. It began operations with about 9,000 personnel (which was reported to include Saudi Aramco's own force of some 5,000 or more armed guards) and aimed to reach 35,000 personnel by the end of 2011, trained and advised by US instructors. However, ascertaining the current number of serving security guards is difficult.

The kingdom might hold as many as 1,200,000m. barrels of 'ultimately' recoverable oil. According to Saudi Aramco, original-oil-in-place is 735,000m. barrels, while incremental probable and possible reserves are about 103,000m. barrels. According to Aramco's *Annual Report 2022* (published in March 2023), proven oil reserves (including one-half of the Neutral/Partitioned Zone) totalled 338,434m. barrels at the end of 2022 (approximately 20% of the world's total). BP assessed the ratio of reserves-to-production (R/P) in 2019 at 61 years. The authorities claim that, through new discoveries and an aggressive exploration and development programme, provable reserves could reach more than 461,000m. barrels by 2025. That, in turn, would increase the kingdom's R/P ratio to more than 100 years. The International Energy Agency, based in Paris, France, estimates that Saudi Arabia still has about 70 'undeveloped' oilfields, mainly in the Rub al-Khali (Empty Quarter) and the Red Sea basin, which could hold an estimated 100,000m. barrels of reserves.

Although the kingdom has about 100 major oil- and gasfields, with 320 reservoirs (and 1,849 wells), more than two-thirds of proven reserves are deposited in eight 'ultra-giant' oilfields. These include Ghawar (with reserves of 70,000m. barrels), offshore Safaniya (35,000m. barrels), Manifa (22,800m. barrels), Abqaiq (17,000m. barrels), Shaybah (15,000m. barrels) and Khurais (16,800m. barrels). The Najd fields, south of Riyadh, contain about 30,000m. barrels of liquids and substantial natural gas reserves. The Ghawar oilfield (at 3,263 sq km, the world's largest) holds more than 80% of the level of the total reserves of Russia (87,100m. barrels) and accounts for about one-half of total Saudi output capacity.

Together with Kuwait, Saudi Arabia shares equal exploitation and production rights to 5,000m. barrels of proven reserves within the 6,200-sq-m Neutral Zone, the total output of which was about 520,000 b/d in 2014. However, a contract dispute between the two countries dating back to 2009 halted production (ostensibly for environmental reasons) in one of the zone's fields, Khafji, in October 2014, and in May 2015 they both agreed temporarily to cease output at another field, Wafra. In December 2016 the British-based news agency Reuters reported that both countries had, seemingly once again, agreed a restart that would affect both fields and whose implementation was expected to be 'gradual'. A complicating factor in terms of resumption of the physical production of oil in the Neutral Zone was the OPEC agreement reached in November 2016 concerning oil production cuts. As long as this agreement held, any fresh production at Wafra or Khafji would have needed to be accompanied by further reductions elsewhere. In June 2018 OPEC reached a general consensus that all member countries would adhere to their individual official production quotas. This had the possible consequence that Saudi Arabia would increase its output, albeit probably not significantly. In December 2019 agreement was finally reached on a basis for restarting output in Wafra and Khafji, arguably reflecting the more buoyant oil prices at the time which made prospective additional oil output more logical. In addition, the mutually appealing prospect of jointly developing the Neutral Zone's offshore Dorra gasfield, with its estimated 10,000,000m.–11,000,000m. cu ft of gas and 300m. barrels of oil, also provided an incentive for agreement over the shared oil facilities. In January 2020 a deal concerning gas production at Dorra was reportedly reached, with the prospect of the first joint NGL production taking place in 2024. However preparations for joint gas production had not been undertaken by June 2023, obstructed by the need for Saudi-Kuwaiti agreement on technical issues as well as on whether they would conduct operations via their own national firms or via foreign companies. Moreover, the situation was made difficult, if not potentially confrontational, by the acknowledged need since April 2022 for an agreement to be reached on maritime boundaries with Iran, with particular regard to how any delineation would affect production at what the Iranians call the Arrash field. The much-vaunted Saudi-Iranian political rapprochement (see History) brokered by China in March 2023 increased speculation that a tripartite political breakthrough over Dorra/Arrash might be made to the benefit of the three countries' shared, even if not joint, gas production there.

SAUDI ARABIA

Economy

With oil prices collapsing again following the Saudi–Russian price war (see below) and the negative impact on demand caused by the pandemic, oil output at the Neutral Zone, which resumed in February 2020, was even slower than expected. By April total oil production from the Neutral Zone was reportedly only about 20,000–30,000 b/d. Storage constraints at a time of low demand meant that even reaching about two-thirds of the total production capacity of 500,000 b/d was delayed. As of February 2023, however, total oil output from the Neutral Zone was reportedly at least 300,000 b/d.

The kingdom claimed a 'sustainable' production capacity of 12.5m. b/d in mid-2012 (a figure based on crude oil production alone) and has not used or acknowledged a markedly different figure since then. Saudi Aramco has identified another 2.5m. b/d for future projects, if required. Any projected oil and gas capacity increases need, however, to take account of the rising proportion of production being absorbed domestically. Saudi Arabia is the largest energy consumer in the Middle East and North Africa, especially of transportation fuels. Measured in terms of million metric tons per year, the *Statistical Review of World Energy 2023* (now published by Energy Intelligence—EI—rather than BP) reported that Saudi domestic oil consumption (apparently excluding NGLs and condensates) in 2022 was equivalent to 3.88m b/d, and had been on an upward trajectory since 2020, when it was 3.44m b/d (consumption having declined steadily during 2015–20). However, given assumptions, despite greener alternatives, of rising, if presently unsteady, global demand, the Saudis would arguably need to make faster progress on reducing domestic consumption in order to meet fiscal pressures caused by a growing population (which itself, in a highly subsidized environment, helps to drive consumption pressure upwards) In July 2019 Aramco signed contracts with several international partner companies (see *Industry, Gas and Mining*) to expand existing oil production in the Gulf. The Marjan Increment Project at Tanajib was intended to add 300,000 b/d of crude oil capacity. A separate contract with Italy's Saipem for the Berri Increment facility envisaged creating an additional 200,000 b/d of oil production capacity at the field located near Ras Tanurah. The projects were scheduled to be completed by 2025. In early 2020 the Saudi Government stated that it would increase sustained oil production capacity to 13m. b/d (from 12m. b/d, excluding the Neutral Zone). Aramco CEO Amin Nasser announced in March 2021 that capacity would be increased in stages 'over the next few years'. In May 2022 Nasser, in an interview with the *Financial Times*, stated that Saudi Arabia was aiming for a sustainable 13m. b/d output capacity by 2027 and that its aim was to boost gas output by 60% by the end of 2030. It was not clear what work had been done as of mid-2023 to help realize the additional 1m. b/d capacity (even though some Aramco estimates at the time put established sustainable capacity at 12.5m. b/d). In August 2022 Aramco forecast that average oil output would rise only gradually, reaching 12.3m. b/d at some point in 2025.

The long-planned Aramco IPO took place in December 2019–January 2020 (see *Saudi Vision 2030*), but not before the ambitions for it were lowered, leaving the external ownership portion at just 1.5%, confined to individual Saudi nationals and companies and wider Gulf interests, and therefore it was much less likely to affect the company's operations.

Despite slackening global demand even before the economic constraints caused by worldwide COVID-related lockdown measures from March 2020, Russia's refusal to collaborate with Saudi Arabia on a further OPEC+ deal led to Saudi Arabia substantially increasing its oil output. This drove prices down further, and seemed to be a bid both to drive out US shale producers and to pressurize Russia into agreeing output restraint. However, after several weeks of a de facto price war between Saudi and Russia, while a mutual economic and fiscal need to put a floor under oil prices remained imperative, the two countries eventually agreed to try once again to underwrite an OPEC+ deal for a reduction in oil output. A deal in principle was made among major oil producers in April to remove 10m. b/d from the market. However, widespread adherence proved sketchy, and the Saudi commitment to the deal required public declarations from Iraq, among others, that it would maintain what had been a much-tightened quota.

When in July there was talk of easing output cuts from August, this proved difficult to agree, as Iraq and other producers under very tight budgetary pressures were reluctant to take actions that could undermine a recovery in prices. In the first half of 2021 the OPEC+ commitment to restraining production, due principally to low demand in the wake of the pandemic, continued to motivate Saudi Arabia as the effective swing producer and leader in the cartel's formal decision-making and liaison with Russia. A policy of maintaining output constraint until April had been accepted, upheld by Saudi Arabia, but operated under some duress. Resentment had been brewing between Saudi Arabia and the United Arab Emirates (UAE) as the latter increasingly exceeded its tight quota, believing that a lifting of economic recession necessitated more oil—its oil—on the market. The UAE considered that constraint was damaging it disproportionately, and undermined Saudi efforts to tighten supply in order to curtail the drop in global prices—something that was a much greater fiscal need for the populous Saudi kingdom than the comparatively tiny Emirati national population. In July OPEC+ oil ministers met virtually; the UAE made clear its opposition to the seemingly otherwise accepted Saudi policy of extending quota constraint to the end of 2022, and it was agreed to raise total OPEC+ output by 2m. b/d in August–December 2021, with expected increased demand held to justify the rise.

In the context of the Russian invasion of Ukraine in February 2022 and the ensuing conflict, the West (particularly the USA) placed pressure on Saudi Arabia to lead an OPEC+ increase in oil output to try to bring down the price of oil. This was resisted for more than three months until early June, when planned OPEC+ quota increases for August and September were brought forward. However, the impact on global oil prices of these relatively modest production increases was itself modest. Minister of Energy Prince Abdulaziz bin Salman told the *Financial Times* in May that Saudi Arabia's assessment was born not of geopolitical calculations but of a desire to work with Russia on the basis of existing co-operation among (major) oil producers. While this could have been interpreted as in itself a partly political siding with Russia in the context of US pressure to ramp up oil output, the Prince made clear that, in his opinion, it was a question of global supply and demand. The real issue for him was Western reluctance, given environmental considerations, to invest in more refining capacity. Sufficient oil to meet demand was being undermined by insufficient refining, he argued. 'Backwardation'—the lower price at which future supplies of oil were being traded than the price of currently produced volumes—seemed to support the Saudi assessment that there was, at that point at least, enough oil on the market to meet expected demand in the relatively short term. According to US news site *Politico* (in an article published in mid-June), Crown Prince Mohammed bin Salman had told US National Security Advisor Jake Sullivan that the USA was partly responsible for what it perceived to be a tight oil market after the Administration of President Joe Biden (again for environmental reasons) abandoned key oil production projects inherited from the Administration of Donald Trump. This may have partly been a geopolitical ploy ahead of an assumed eventual improvement in relations (with a visit by Biden to Saudi Arabia in July). However, it was consistent with Aramco CEO Amin Nasser's comments at a meeting in Davos, Switzerland, in late May, when he stated that global oil production spare capacity was tight but that environmental sensitivities were responsible (and certainly not Saudi Arabia). The Saudi willingness to compromise a little in bringing forward extant OPEC+ plans to raise output may have been a small geopolitical concession to the USA. However, it seemed that Saudi Arabia's strategic energy assessment was firmly linked to working with Russia as a fellow major oil (and in Russia's case) gas exporter. Russia's desire for high oil prices at a time of conflict in Ukraine fitted with the Saudi view. These energy producers shared a desire to avoid a price collapse similar to the one that they had brought about in 2020, and not significantly to increase output when global demand was unsteady and when more refined oil would genuinely push prices down.

Average Saudi oil output in 2022 was 10.5m. b/d, according to the *Statistical Review of World Energy 2023*. Although this was

SAUDI ARABIA

Economy

12% more than the average for 2021, Saudi Arabia, as the lead OPEC+ actor, was in disagreement with many countries (and with the USA in particular) for much of the year and into early 2023 about what consumer-orientated, election-sensitive Western countries viewed as insufficient global oil supply, which, in turn, led to higher fuel prices for the consumer. Despite strong US opposition, in October 2022 OPEC+ agreed to take 2m. b/d off the market from November until the end of 2023—a decision that largely reflected a desire to ensure that member countries' budget-dependent oil revenues were not undermined by a price collapse amid possible oversupply. In April 2023 OPEC+ agreed to a further (voluntary) cut of 1.66m. b/d from May until the end of the year, prompting a stark warning from the IEA that the Saudi-led cartel risked undermining global demand by keeping oil prices high and driving wider inflation. The IEA also claimed that Saudi and other producers were ultimately weakening demand for oil at a time when green alternatives were becoming more attractive and receiving greater investment. OPEC+ was unbowed and in June extended the cuts from the end of 2023 to the end of 2024. In the same month the Saudi Ministry of Energy stated that the country's output of oil would decrease to 9m. b/d in July, down from around 10m. b/d in May.

Aramco's own financial position, post-IPO, had been tighter, partly owing to the Government's determination that the oil company's new shareholders be adequately rewarded, despite the damage to oil revenues globally in the wake of the pandemic. Reflecting this pressure, in April 2021 Aramco announced a deal for the sale of 49% of its hitherto 100% ownership of the new venture Aramco Pipelines, for US $12,400m., to a consortium led by the US-based EIG Global Energy Partners. One negative consequence was that the Saudi oil major would have to pay leasing fees for the use of Saudi oil pipelines. It was reported in the *Financial Times* at the time of the sell-off that the Abu Dhabi (UAE) Sovereign Wealth Fund, Mubadala Investment Company, was in negotiations to join the EIG-led 49% stake-holding group. In February 2022 it was reported that a deal had been reached on the acquisition of the 49% stake in what was then referred to as Aramco Gas Pipelines (AGP). US company Blackrock would, according to the *Middle East Monitor (MEMO)*, lead a consortium with Keppel Infrastructure Trust, Silk Road Fund, China Merchants Capital and Saudi Arabia's state-owned Hassana Investment Co. In December 2021 a 20-year lease-back arrangement between Aramco itself and AGP had been agreed, whereby the latter would be paid a fee from the mother company for the right to use the pipeline. However, full ownership and operational control of the overall national gas pipeline network would, according to *MEMO*, be retained by Aramco.

In fact, Aramco 'privatizations' were periodically reported as under consideration among various subsidiaries (in addition to the pipeline deals). For instance, in May 2022 Aramco held discussions with US motor oil and lubricants group Valvoline about the latter buying its global products division. A different kind of non-public divestment was reported in February, when a transfer of 4% of Aramco shares to the PIF was announced, meaning that 94% of the shares in the oil company would remain directly held by the state (the original IPO was 1.5%, while a modest second tranche—see *Saudi Vision 2030*—would have represented the balance of 0.5%). In May 2023 it was reported that Aramco, a still essentially state-owned conglomerate, was officially the world's third most valuable company (after the US companies Apple and Microsoft), in part due to the oil price rises related to the war in Ukraine. Its market capitalization at that date stood at US $2,055,2200m.

INDUSTRY, GAS AND MINING

Saudi Arabia has expended substantial oil revenue in financing major industrial projects under successive development plans. The industrialization programme has focused on the construction of refineries and downstream industries to exploit Saudi Arabia's reserves of petroleum and natural gas. According to Aramco, at July 2021 Saudi Arabia had gas reserves of 2,370,400m. cu m—the sixth largest in the world, after Iran, Russia, Qatar, Turkmenistan and the USA.

Saudi Arabia had nine functioning refineries with a total capacity of 2.9m. b/d in 2016, two of which were joint ventures with international oil companies. Major refineries are Ras Tanura (550,000 b/d in 2011—the largest oil refinery in the Middle East), Saudi Aramco/ExxonMobil at Yanbu (400,000 b/d), Petromin/Shell at Jubail (400,000 b/d), Rabigh (400,000 b/d) and Yanbu (240,000 b/d). Aramco revealed plans to upgrade the Ras Tanura refinery, which entailed installing mixed xylene, cumene, isobutane and petroleum coke facilities, together with overhauls at five other refineries. The kingdom was building three grass-roots refineries which were expected to increase distillation capacity by 1.6m. b/d to 3.7m. b/d by the end of 2013. Saudi Aramco and France's Total, and Aramco without a foreign partner (after the withdrawal of the USA's ConocoPhillips), built 400,000 b/d export-oriented refineries at Jubail and Yanbu (each costing about US $10,000m.). The Jubail refinery came on stream in July 2014, and the main unit for making petrol at the new Yanbu refinery—on which Aramco has retained the right to use ConocoPhillips's technology—commenced formal operations in January 2016. Expanded base oil production at Yanbu might have been intended to make up the difference, in preparation for the closure of the Jubail (Jeddah) oil refinery facility that fed Luberef's base oil production there, which took place in November 2017. Aramco announced that it would convert the facility into a hub for the distribution of oil products.

A third planned refinery (and related terminal) at Jazan, in the south-west, was to have a capacity of 400,000 b/d. In October 2017 Aramco announced that refining at Jazan was to be commissioned in mid-2018, with full operations at the refinery to commence by the end of 2019. At the time of the second phase of the Aramco IPO in January 2020, Aramco pushed this refinery target date back to the second half of the year. The refinery was reported to have commenced operations of its primary distillation units by early 2021, but the start-up of full commercial operations was delayed until March 2023. Aramco also plans to build a new facility at Ras Tanura, named the East Coast refinery, capable of processing 400,000 b/d of Arabian heavy crude. The new Saudi refineries will help to ease a global contraction in refining largely responsible for the over-inflated crude oil prices of recent years. Saudi Aramco's expansion plans for the refining sector, which was designed to integrate several new refineries with large petrochemicals complexes, was expected to cost a total of US $70,000m.

An important element of Saudi Arabia's overall product marketing strategy has been the acquisition by Saudi Aramco of refining interests in prime petroleum-importing countries. Aramco owns a 35% equity interest in the Republic of Korea (South Korea)'s largest refining company, Ssangyong Oil, which has a refining capacity of 525,000 b/d, a 25% stake in China's 240,000-b/d Fujian refinery and a 15% interest in Japan's 515,000-b/d Showa Shell refinery. At the end of 2022 Saudi Arabia's domestic refining alone was, according to the *EI Statistical Review of World Energy 2023*, producing an average of 2.9m. b/d, equivalent to 3.6% of the global total.

The exploitation and production of vast natural gas reserves was expected to stimulate the development of energy-intensive industries and provide feedstock for new power and water desalination plants. About 60% of proven reserves (or 172,680m. cu ft) consists of associated gas (found in conjunction with crude petroleum), mainly from the onshore Ghawar oilfield and the offshore Safaniya and Zuluf fields. The Ghawar field alone holds one-third of total gas reserves. The deep Khuff reservoir contains the bulk of non-associated gas deposits. Of the remaining 115,120m. cu ft of non-associated natural gas, 75% has a higher sulphur content (i.e. comprising sour gas), thus leaving only 28,780m. cu ft of conventional gas deposits that are easy to process. The US Geological Survey estimated that Saudi Arabia could possess ultimately recoverable reserves of 19,000,000m. cu ft, while the figure given by Aramco (according to its website, accessed in July 2021) is 2,370,400m. cu ft (3.0% of the world's total).

In November 2006 the Ministry of Petroleum and Mineral Resources and Saudi Aramco announced a US $9,000m. exploration and development strategy to add another 1,416,000m. cu m of non-associated gas resources by 2016. The plan involved drilling 307 new development wells (including over 70 exploration and delineation wells) in the Rub al-Khali, the Nefud basin, north of Riyadh, the Red Sea and the Gulf coast. Only 52 exploratory wells were drilled during 1996–2004, with an exploration success rate of 44%, according to Aramco. Domestic gas demand is projected at 14,500m. cu ft per day by 2030, up from 7,100m. cu ft a day in 2007. However, with annual demand surging by 7%–9%, research and consultancy group Wood Mackenzie expects total consumption to reach 15,000m. cu ft per day by 2025. At present, about 55% of gas output is consumed by the power and desalination sector, with the remaining 45% being used as feedstock for petrochemicals. In July 2019 the EIU reported that Aramco had an annual gas production target of 651,287m. cu m by 2029. Even allowing for an estimated 6% growth in domestic demand annually, this target would far exceed consumption demand, although it also reflects the need for feedstock for new and existing plants. In order to meet its ambitious 2029 target, in July 2019 Aramco signed several contracts, the largest with the US firm McDermott and Italy's Saipem, for the development of the Marjan and the Berri oil and gas facilities. The development of Marjan, based at Tanajib, north of Dammam, included a new gas oil separation facility; 24 oil, gas and water injection platforms; the expansion of existing onshore oil facilities; and the construction of a new gas plant. These were expected to produce 2,500m. cu ft a day of natural gas, 360,000 b/d of natural gas liquids (essential for feedstocks) and 300,000 b/d of crude oil. The new developments at Marjan and Berri were scheduled to become operational in 2023.

Saudi Arabia is the region's third largest natural gas producer, with output of 112,100m. cu m in 2020, after Iran and Qatar, according to the *BP Statistical Review of World Energy 2021*. Several upstream projects are already in place to increase gas production capacity. These included the Karan project, which yielded 1,800m. cu ft per day of natural gas from 2013; and the Wasit project, which began operations in October 2015, supplying 1,700m. cu ft per day to the Master Gas System (MGS). The MGS is the largest integrated gas gathering, processing and distribution system of its kind and is fed entirely by non-associated gas. Associated gas is also produced at the 1m.-b/d Shaybah oilfield. The gas production component came on stream in December 2015, and, according to Saudi Aramco, the facility has been designed to process 2,400m. cu ft of associated gas per day. It also aims to recover 275,000 b/d of 'ethane plus' for eventual export as a petrochemical feedstock. The Fadhili gas plant, 30 km west of Jubail, reached full operational capacity in 2021, processing 2,500m. cu ft of gas per day and supplying 1,700m. cu ft per day of sales gas to the MGS.

In late February 2022 Minister of Energy Prince Abdulaziz bin Salman announced that Aramco had made new gas discoveries. He identified the locations as Shadoon, in the centre of the country, Shehab and Shurfa in the Empty Quarter, Umm Khansar, near the northern border with Iraq, and Samna, in the Eastern Region (Al-Sharqiya), stating that Umm Khansar and Samna were 'unconventional' sources of shale gas, requiring special extraction techniques.

Strong domestic demand also underpinned a US $4,500m. expansion of the MGS, which was completed in 1984. The MGS was delivering 9,300m. cu ft per day of sales gas as of 2015, and Saudi Aramco aimed to increase that total to 12,500m cu ft per day by 2030; reports suggest that by the end of 2021 sales of gas had risen to just under 12,000m cu ft per day. Moreover, the MGS facilitates more than 1m. b/d for export by meeting domestic needs for fuel and feedstock with gas. Three processing plants have been built (at Berri, Shedgum and Uthmaniyah) to separate NGLs from methane, and two fractionation plants, at Ju'aymah on the Gulf coast and at Yanbu on the Red Sea, process the NGLs into ethane, liquefied petroleum gas and condensate.

There are currently seven gas processing plants with a total production capacity of about 10,000m. cu ft per year, plus 1m. b/d of NGLs and about 2,700 metric tons of sulphur at Berri, Shedgum, Uthmaniyah and Hawiyah facilities. Saudi Aramco aims to process 15,500m. cu ft per day through additional plants and capacity expansion. Mega-projects are under way at Ju'aymah, Khurais, Khursaniyah, Hawiya and Yanbu. Gas is carried to Yanbu via the 1,200-km Trans-Arabian pipeline.

The manufacturing sector, which represented a preliminary 15.5% of real GDP in 2022, has received substantial capital investment. Invested capital in non-hydrocarbons sectors totalled SR 343,300m. (US $91,547m.) at the end of 2008, of which chemicals and plastics received almost three-fifths of the aggregate, according to the Saudi Industrial Property Authority. Total capital investment reached 24% of GDP in 2018, almost the global average.

The Saudi Government's net balance of capital investment (i.e. including capital investment outflows) at the end of 2018 was SR 188,000m. (about US $50,000m.), according to IMF figures. Although this is not the totality of Saudi capital investment, it is a useful indicator of it. The figure is given in the Saudi budget—indicative of the role of the state in much capital investment—as the 'net acquisition of Non-Financial Assets' (NFA), and it excludes Aramco's capital investment, as this is deducted before oil revenues are transferred to the Government. The net acquisition of NFAs in 2018 was actually down from the SR 209,000m. registered in 2016, although markedly up from the 2017 total. It was budgeted at SR 248,000m. in 2019. The 2020 out-turn, according to the IMF, was SR 155,000m. This was an unsurprising decline from the 2019, given the economic contraction in 2020, although the 2019 out-turn of SR 169,000m. was markedly under budget. The 2021 out-turn for net acquisition of NFAs, at SR 117,000m., represented an even larger decline than in the previous year, despite the fact the economy and government finances had improved significantly from 2020. The Fund projected that net NFAs would fall even further, to SR 106,000m., in 2022, presumably on the assumption that the Saudi Government's priority in that year would be recurrent spending.

The chemicals/plastics industries generate about 70% of non-oil exports. In August 2023 the business intelligence provider Zawya reported that, according to the Ministry of Industry and Mineral Resources, there were 10,982 'industrial establishments' in operation. These are presumed to be engaged in the manufacture of chemicals, plastics, rubber, wood products, paper and print materials, fertilizers, steel, machine tools, equipment, finished metal goods, cement, building materials, ceramics, glass, textiles and garments, leather, food processing and soft drinks.

The rapid expansion of the state-owned SABIC, founded in 1976, has represented the most successful aspect of Saudi Arabia's diversification drive. SABIC, the Middle East's largest non-oil industrial enterprise, which had total assets of US $83,490m. at the end of 2022, accounts for about 8% and 95%, respectively, of global and total Saudi production of petrochemicals. The company operates 21 major facilities, located at Jubail, Jeddah and Yanbu—15 factories for chemicals, four for fertilizers and two for metals. Twelve of the 21 manufacturing affiliates are joint ventures with foreign companies, three are wholly owned by SABIC, and six are joint venture partnerships with local and regional private investors.

SABIC enjoys a competitive edge over most petrochemicals producers, reflecting its access to subsidized, cheap gas feedstock from Saudi Aramco. The company (which employs more than 31,000 people worldwide) previously announced that it intended to expand annual capacity—both at home and overseas—to an ambitious 130m. metric tons by 2020. An interim target of 100m. tons was supposed to have been reached by 2016; some 93.7m. tons capacity was in fact claimed in 2015. Notably, however, between 2011 and 2015 annual output only rose from 69.0m. tons to 69.7m tons, emphasizing a major disconnect between expanding capacity and actual production. Production in 2019 totalled 72.6m. tons, while net income amounted to SR 5,600m. In 2020, however, amid global recession, total output declined to 60.8m. tons and net income fell sharply to SR 67m. In 2021, due to an ongoing downturn, output fell further to 58.0m. tons, although net income rebounded strongly to reach SR 23,000m. In 2022 there was a slight increase in output, to 61.0m. tons, but net income declined to SR 16,500m.

SABIC is one of the top 10 petrochemical producers globally—in 2014 it described itself as the second largest 'diversified chemical company' worldwide. Its target for overall share of global petrochemical output is 10%. SABIC is among the worldwide market leaders in the production of polyethylene, polypropylene and other advanced thermoplastics, ethyleneglycol, methanol and fertilizers. In 2009 two new facilities—the Eastern Petrochemical Co and the Yanbu National Petrochemical Co (Yansab)—started production. 'Jubail 2' and 'Yanbu 2' remain vital to petrochemicals development.

The petrochemicals sector has attracted private investment in recent years. The Petro Rabigh joint venture between Saudi Aramco (37.5%) and Sumitomo Chemical Co of Japan (37.5%) was forecast to transform Aramco's Rabigh Refinery into a fully integrated petrochemical complex. The first phase of the US $10,000m. project came online in 2009 and was designed to produce 18.4m. metric tons of benzene and high-quality fuels (including gasoline) annually, 2.4m. tons of ethylene derivatives and 1.3m. tons of olefins, as well as a range of plastics, including linear low-density polyethylene and impact copolymer polypropylene. In April 2021 the PIF and SABIC were directed to lead what the Government planned (under its Shareek —'partnership'—programme) would be new investment of SR 12,000,000m. over the following nine years (up to 2030). This was intended to include SR 5,000,000m. ($1,300m.) referred to as SABIC-led 'private investment', along with SR 5,000,000m. state investment and a hoped-for SR 2,000,000m. in foreign investment. Presumably, the barely explained projected investment would include investment promoted by SABIC, which would then include development of the private petrochemicals sector under public-private partnerships and other leveraging arrangements.

Some 70% of SABIC shares were purchased by Aramco from the PIF via the Tadawul in June 2020, in a deal agreed in March 2019. The arrangement, designed to boost the PIF, not least as the relatively high share price arguably did not reflect the shares' true value at a time of falling oil revenues, could tie SABIC to oil industry fortunes. For example, any Aramco bond issuance would now partly relate to its SABIC holding, and much greater transparency would now be required from both SABIC and its new parent company.

In December 2022 Aramco announced plans to develop a new, US $11,000m. petrochemical facility in Jubail on Saudi Arabia's eastern coast, in partnership with TotalEnergies of France. It was reported that the facility, which would be owned and operated by both companies, would become operational in 2027, when it would be integrated into the existing Saudi Arabia Total Refining and Petrochemicals (SATORP) facility in Jubail. Aramco was to provide 62.5% of the funding for the project (and thus presumably hold a commensurate equity proportion) via a planned bond issue; the French firm was to provide 37.5% of the funding. Such projects are always presented as creating a large number of jobs in the kingdom—7,000 were claimed in this case, and it was emphasized that utilizing 'refinery off-gases' and naphtha, as well as Aramco-supplied ethane and gasoline, would be used to produce the chemical products. It was reported in June 2023 that Aramco and TotalEnergies had awarded the engineering, procurement and construction (EPC) contracts for the main processing units and associated utilities. Among the contracted partners were South Korean, Chinese, Saudi and Emirati companies.

Aramco has begun to play a role in Saudi Arabia's attempted political rapprochement with Iraq and more widely (see History). A new joint investment company, the Saudi-Iraqi Investment Company (SIIC), was founded (partly under the authority of the PIF) after high-level bilateral diplomatic engagement. In May 2023 it was reported that the SIIC, which has a US $3,000m. budget, would be involved, via Aramco, in the development of the huge Akkas gasfield in west Iraq, located close to the Syrian border. However, it subsequently appeared that the agreement had not yet been finalized, with Iraq stating that Aramco's 'agreed' investment role was subject to further assessment, including a final decision on the Iraqi side. There were also reports of Aramco investment in the long-delayed development of an Iraqi petrochemicals complex at Nebras.

The Saudi Iron and Steel Co (Hadeed), based in Jubail, is a joint venture of SABIC with Germany's Korf-Stahl. It exports iron products to South-East Asian countries and Japan. According to the World Steel Association's 2023 annual report, steel production in Saudi Arabia increased from 8.7m. metric tons in 2021 to 9.1m. metric tons in 2022 (compared with 4.6m. tons in 2007), resulting in a slight improvement in the kingdom's global ranking, from the 22nd largest producer to the 21st.

The building materials sector, particularly the cement industry, flourished in the early 21st century. The three major producers are Yamama, Saudi Cement Co and Southern Cement. More than 95% of supply is used by the local market. Saudi Arabia's cement output for the year to July 2015 was 59.5m. metric tons (from 14 factories), up from 48.0m. tons in 2011. However, amid a building downturn, total cement output fell to an estimated 50m. tons in 2017. According to the online publication *Global Cement News*, Yamama, the biggest Saudi cement producer, reported total production in 2017 of 47.1m. tons, falling to 42.1m. tons in 2018. The ongoing tightening of the Saudi construction market, owing in part to several unresolved government contracts, was a major contributing factor to the slowdown. While any sustained rise in sales had to contend with the pandemic-related downturn from March 2020, over the year as a whole cement sales totalled about 50.8m. tons, representing a 21% rise compared with the 2019 total. In 2021 and 2022 sales flatlined, at about 51m. tons, despite ongoing housing programmes and an infrastructure boost from PIF plans.

The kingdom boasts substantial mineral deposits, mostly in the north, including copper, zinc, lead, iron ore, gold, silver, magnetite, limestone, colane, gypsum, marble, clay, bauxite, phosphate, tantalum, silica and some uranium. The Government has yet to explore fully the commercial viability of untapped mineral resources.

Ma'aden is the Saudi state-owned mining company. Founded in 1997, it operates under the strategic control of the Director-General of Mining Resources. According to its website (accessed in June 2023), Ma'aden's 'phosphate mine' produces 11.6m. metric tons of ore annually, and its beneficiation plant produces almost 5m. tons per year of concentrated phosphate rock. The phosphate deposits at Al-Jalamid, together with those at Al-Khabra, and given Ma'aden's access to several blocks at Um Wu'al, meant that at the end of 2018 Ma'aden claimed total phosphate ore deposits of just over 700m. tons. Ma'aden's plans for development in the northern region are intended to make it one of the world's largest phosphate reserves and are predicated on tapping foreign investment for further development of phosphate mining and related production. The Ma'aden Wa'ad Al-Shamal Phosphate Company (MWSPC) is a joint venture located in the minerals city of the same name in the Northern Borders region. Ma'aden owns 60% of this fertilizer production centre, which includes seven plants and associated facilities. Ma'aden claims a capacity to produce 3m. tons of fertilizer products annually. Complementary plants to produce ammonia and ammonium phosphate-based fertilizers have been built at Ras al-Khair Resources City in the Eastern region. In December 2018 Ma'aden agreed an EPC deal to build the first of several new plants at Wa'ad Al-Shamal: an ammonia plant with an annual capacity of 1.1m. tons. According to the Ma'aden website (accessed in June 2023), the MWSPC has the capacity to produce 3m. tons of fertilizer products annually. However, in November 2022 Ma'aden told the *Financial Times* that the company would eventually double its productive capacity to 9m. tons of fertilizer products annually.

Ghurayyah in the north-west region of Tabouk holds the world's largest single tantalum deposit, extending over 47 sq km, and gypsum deposits of about 33m. metric tons, graded between 83% and 90%, are found around the Red Sea basin and the Gulf of Aqaba. High-quality gypsum, ideal for manufacturing plaster, has been identified near Yanbu. In the Fursan mountain area (Western region) there are significant marble deposits and silica deposits have been found near al-Jouf, Buraydad, Riyadh and Tabouk. There are about 1.9m. tons of new zinc deposits at Khnaiguiyah. The main open gold mines are situated at al-Amar, al-Duwayhi, al-Hajar, Bulghah and Sukhaybarat in western Saudi Arabia.

Ma'aden is developing a multi-billion dollar aluminium plant, located at Ras al-Khair. The fully integrated scheme (costing some US $10,800m.), based on the 126m.-metric-ton al-Zabirah bauxite mine eventually producing 4m. tons of bauxite ore per year, produced 1.8m. tons of aluminium in 2017. According to the latest available data from Ma'aden, accessed in June 2023, the smelter at al-Zabirah processes 780,000 tons of aluminium a year. In 2014 the Ras al-Khair plant's casthouse began producing primary feedstock billets for the local market. In 2016, according to Ma'aden data, total production of 'low grade bauxite' in the kingdom had fallen to 0.6m. tons, from 0.8m. tons in 2015 and 1.1m. tons in 2014, as supply was still being cut back, having outstripped demand in 2014–15. In 2016 sales of bauxite were 0.6m. tons. Resources of industrial bauxite were estimated at 7m. tons. However, according to a report in June 2023 by industry news site AlCircle, undifferentiated bauxite reserves in 2022 totalled 180m. tons. Total Saudi bauxite sales in that year amounted to 4.8m. tons, making Saudi Arabia the ninth largest bauxite producer globally.

According to SAGIA, Saudi Arabia could produce 6.25m. metric tons per year of aluminium if the 10 planned smelters and alumina refineries were commissioned. However, in 2016 Saudi aluminium production (measured in ingots) was 740,000 tons, according to the US Geological Survey 2017. None the less, this represented a dramatic increase from the 187,000 tons recorded in 2013. The Government opened the minerals sector to foreign mining companies under the 2004 Mining Law, which offered incentives such as 100% foreign ownership, mining leases of 30 years, reduced tax rates of 20% and tax-free importation of machinery and equipment.

According to the Ma'aden website (accessed in June 2023) the 'Ma'aden smelter's' annual production capacity is 780,000 metric tons of 'primary aluminium'. The smelter is fed by the 'Ma'aden refinery', implying refinery singular (as opposed to the grander smelter and production numbers outlined above). Ma'aden also stated that its 'casthouse' is integrated with 'the smelter', resulting in what it calls a 'total design capacity' of 1.2m. tons annually of different aluminium products.

The non-oil industry associated with planned 'economic cities'—each focusing on different sectors—was intended to generate vigorous growth over the medium to long term. Five of the cities were officially launched: the King Abdullah Economic City (KAEC) in Mecca region (light and heavy industry and finance); the Prince Abdulaziz Bin Mousaed Economic City in Ha'il region (transport, logistical services and agribusiness); the Jazan Economic City in the south-west area (energy and labour-intensive industries); the Medina Knowledge Economic City (information technology and communications); and the Sudair Industrial City in Qassim region (telecommunications and electronics). KAEC was the most advanced: situated between Rabigh and Jeddah on the Red Sea, its port facility opened in 2013 and, until the sharp downturn in the international oil price from September 2014 at least, plans for a huge industrial city were advancing. Prince Abd-al Aziz bin Mosaed City changed contractors in 2008, but nothing definite has been reported about it since. Jazan, Medina and Hail were reported to be progressing slowly. Two other schemes were at the planning stage, namely the Tabouk Economic City and the Ras al-Khair Resource City in the Eastern region (near Jubail), with a focus on mining and mineral refining. Ras al-Khair, also now known as Minerals Industrial City, has made some progress, with plans for an alumina smelter, an aluminium refinery and a fertilizer complex. Ras al-Khair is also home to a huge water and power project (see *Electricity and Water*).

In practice, these projects, indelibly associated with King Abdullah, received less attention, while one huge new, state-led project—the establishment of a new economic city known as NEOM on the Red Sea coast, initiated by Crown Prince Mohammed bin Salman in October 2017—has been the focus of mega-development plans. It is likely that the majority of jobs that these statist mega-projects create will continue to be taken up by expatriates. The Saudi British Bank estimated the total cost of building the ambitious economic cities initiated by King Abdullah at US $500,000m. NEOM alone was officially costed at the same amount, without any indication about how much of the overall estimated total international investors would contribute, in addition to the contributions of the Saudi state and the PIF. Under Crown Prince Mohammed bin Salman, the PIF has played an increasingly important role in economic decision-making, to the detriment of bodies such as SAGIA. By early 2020 much of SAGIA's role had been taken over by the newly created investment ministry (see *Saudi Vision 2030*). The Ministry of Investment became the licensing authority for issuing foreign investment permissions. It was reported to have issued a total of 4,358 investment licences in 2022, a 53.9% increase on 2021.

NEOM established a subsidiary company, ENOWA, in March 2022, with a remit to develop what was called 'sustainable energy and water systems' in the new megacity (or gigaproject). The idea was that ENOWA would, according to an *Al-Monitor* report dated 22 March 2022, 'work toward' the NEOM vision of itself as being solely powered by 'renewable energy'. *Al-Monitor* stated that ENOWA was the primary shareholder for a planned green hydrogen plant being built in NEOM. The proposed hydrogen plant is a joint venture between the Saudi company ACWA Power and the US chemical company Air Products. ENOWA is also supposed to be working on 'developing sustainable water' in NEOM via a series of desalination plants. NEOM's external critics have questioned the veracity of the megacity's claimed green credentials. In particular, the proposed desalination plants have been criticized for being environmentally unsound. NEOM argued that the excess of removed salt would be utilized. However, this claimed reutilization process is only at inception stage globally. At mid-2023 progress in building NEOM appeared confined to royal palaces and a designated workers' residential area. A succession of announced new initiatives suggested much greater progress, but in reality these were merely an expansion of ambitious ideas. It was reported that a planned industrial city within NEOM, Oxagon, was being created, while a new living and transportation system, 'The Line', would favour community development as housing and residential facilities were established in close proximity to a network of connecting rail transportation, facilitating ease of movement in an otherwise totally inhospitable environment. Aside from such grandiose ambitions, more tangible, lower-level developments were being reported at NEOM, such as the conclusion of the testing of air taxis in June 2023, following a deal in 2021 with the German aircraft manufacturer Volocopter.

In July 2022 Crown Prince Mohammed told Saudi media that one-half of the US $319,000m. cost of the first phase of NEOM would be funded by the PIF, an unsurprising development that might point to further PIF use of foreign reserves. The other half would come from other regional sovereign wealth funds that were to be 'tapped' by the end of the year, private investors and an IPO that was to be launched on the Tadawul in 2024. The Crown Prince also stated that Saudi Arabia (presumably meaning the PIF) would set up a $80,000m. fund to invest in the companies that were established in NEOM. The Crown Prince also stated that housing for 450,000 people would be provided in NEOM within a timescale of less than three-and-a-half years.

The drive to attract much greater FDI included a further set of decrees issued in 2017 and 2018 which were intended, in part, to increase the involvement of foreign companies in Saudi Arabia. For example, SAGIA announced that more economic sectors would be opened to 100% foreign ownership (subject to certain criteria), including the engineering and retail sectors, making it easier for foreign companies to seek a listing on the Tadawul and to operate in the kingdom.

There was little to indicate, however, that the increased inflow of foreign companies to the kingdom was determining the net FDI figure. By mid-2023 it appeared that the 'Economic City' and SAGIA model had essentially been jettisoned, as the PIF announced in April the creation of four new SEZs, including one based in KAEC, one each in Ras Al-Khair and Jazan, and one dedicated to cloud computing in the King Abdullah City for Science and Technology. The idea was to use loose regulation, low corporate tax and 100% foreign ownership to attract foreign investors and thus increase FDI via the extant Economic City spaces.

Related measures in terms of promoting foreign business activity in Saudi Arabia were those introduced concerning government procurement, for example. In theory, these offered an assurance of greater transparency, which were none the less offset by the 'local value' component and the coercive and highly political nature of so-called anti-corruption measures introduced from November 2017, when several members of the royal family, government ministers, former ministers and senior non-royal businessmen were detained in Riyadh on charges of corruption and embezzlement (see History). The arrests took place on the day after a royal decree was issued establishing a new anti-corruption agency, apparently to replace the National Anti-Corruption Commission (Nazaha). Increased 'Saudization' pressure via what is effectively taxation (see *Population and Labour Force*) is a mixed blessing for foreign companies, which generally prefer the freedom to hire whom they wish at whatever wage they wish. Related to this, the Government approved a plan to increase the industrial sector's share of GDP to 20% by 2020, with the aim of achieving 8% annual growth in non-hydrocarbons industries over the next decade. This ambition needs to be seen in the context of SAMA's breakdown of real GDP data, which showed that in 2019 the non-oil sector expanded by 3.3% in real terms, largely reflecting the 3.8% growth in the private sector. The total contribution of non-hydrocarbons industries to GDP in that year was 14.6%. According to GASTAT, non-oil real GDP grew by 4.8% in 2022, benefiting partly from oil-based growth. The relationship of non-oil private sector activity to public, oil-funded capital and other spending means that non-oil GDP is liable to be inconsistent—a factor compounded by how much non-oil economic activity is state-led in Saudi Arabia.

ELECTRICITY AND WATER

Saudi Arabia's electricity system has to satisfy rapidly growing urban and industrial demand and supply power for small, widely scattered rural settlements. An increasing amount of electricity is produced in association with seawater desalination. In November 1998 10 regional power companies (including the four Saudi Consolidated Electric Cos—East, West, Central and South—which controlled 85% of the kingdom's power supplies) and six smaller regional power generating companies were merged into the Saudi Electricity Co (SEC). A new higher structure of tariffs was introduced prior to the SEC's incorporation as a joint-stock company co-owned by the Government in April 2000 and the new company was mandated to collect tariffs more effectively. The Electricity and Co-generation Regulatory Authority (ECRA) was established in 2001.

The SEC is the largest electricity utility in the Middle East. Some 70% of the kingdom's electricity supply is fuelled by gas, and steam-powered facilities represent 15%. The remainder is accounted for by diesel (10%) and combined-cycle plants (5%). Saudi Arabia uses about 750,000 b/d of heavy crude to fire its power plants. SEC, which accounts for 85% of the kingdom's total capacity, spent US $25,100m. in 2007 on implementing various power generation, transmission and distribution projects. About one-fifth of SEC's 45 power stations are over 25 years old.

According to ECRA, a total power capacity of 120,000 MW is needed by 2030. According to official figures, installed electricity generation capacity had increased steadily over the two decades up to 2018, when, according to revised data obtained by GASTAT from the Water and Electricity Regulatory Authority, the 'available capacity' fell to 76,941 MW (from 80,471 MW in 2017). According to GASTAT, the 'peak load capacity' of electricity increased slightly from 62,076 MW in 2019 to 62,266 MW in 2020. The 'available capacity' in 2021 was given by GASTAT as 83,036 MW. On the basis of an almost 70% increase in 'available capacity' during 2010–21, ECRA's target of 120,000 MW by 2030 appeared just about feasible.

According to GASTAT data, national electricity consumption increased from 289,333 GWh in 2020 to 301,561 GWh in 2021. Anecdotal evidence had suggested that the Government's reduction of subsidization of domestic energy charges (including electricity) and its efforts to promote energy conservation were having some effect. This may still be true, but at the same time greater activity in the wider economy was bound to result in higher energy consumption. In common with other GCC member states, private power developers were expected to provide the bulk of the funding for any new capacity.

In recent years extra capacity has come online, at an estimated cost of US $20,000m. These include the Rabigh-1 plant, Mecca, which produces 1,204 MW and Riyadh PP11, with a capacity of 1,729 MW, both of which commenced commercial operations in 2013, according to the SEC. The SEC also unveiled plans for a further 20,000 MW of capacity by 2018, in addition to 10,000 MW of new capacity from six independent power producer (IPP) projects. They included the 2,400-MW plant in Ras al-Khair; the Riyadh PP11 plant; the 3,927-MW Qurayyah plant (fully operational in 2015); the 2,050-MW Rabigh-2 plant (operational from early 2018); a 1,000-MW plant in Dheba and an 800-MW plant in Shuqaiq.

In 2011 the 'King Abdullah City for Atomic and Renewable Energy' (KA-Care) was established. China, France, South Korea and Argentina subsequently signed separate non-commercially binding bilateral nuclear co-operation agreements with the kingdom, and in 2008 the USA concluded a nuclear agreement with Saudi Arabia.

Under plans issued in 2011 Saudi Arabia intends to commission 16 nuclear power reactors by 2031, at a total cost of US $300,000m. The first two reactors were, in theory, to be built within a decade—with two following every year thereafter. It was originally, and extremely ambitiously, anticipated that nuclear power and renewable energy would provide one-half of the kingdom's power needs by 2030, when peak demand for electricity was projected to reach 120 GW. The kingdom's nuclear ambitions for energy, and conceivably military, purposes, led KA-Care to announce the objective of realizing 17.6 GW of nuclear power by 2032, separate from the kingdom's non-nuclear renewable targets. According to a report published on the British Broadcasting Corporation (BBC) website in February 2022, a recently revised SV 2030 national target for the renewable energy component of domestic electricity generation (possibly including nuclear) was that one-half of Saudi domestically generated electricity should be from renewables by 2030. The report (largely focused on NEOM) pointed out that in 2019 only 0.1% of all Saudi domestic electricity was derived from renewable energy.

In May 2020 the *Middle East Economic Survey (MEES)* reported that Saudi Arabia was holding discussions with five potential foreign partners regarding the establishment of a two-reactor nuclear plant and, separately, for the installation of separate small modular reactors (SMRs) that would be installed off-grid in more remote locations, with a specific purpose. SMRs are simpler and much cheaper than traditional reactors and are primarily used in Russia, where two are in operation. *MEES* reported that KA-Care was in discussions with China National Nuclear Corporation (CNNC) and South Korea's Korea Atomic Energy Research Institute (KAERI) regarding the possibility of utilizing their 'proprietary SMR technologies'. The nuclear plant contract was being discussed with US firm Westinghouse, South Korea's Korea Electric Power Corporation, Russia's Rosatom, France's EdF and the CNNC. The two-reactor plant would reportedly generate some 3 GW–4 GW of nuclear power. Although modest compared with Saudi Arabia's original ambitions, this would be a marked increase on such a facility's normal capacity. Affecting all of this is Saudi Arabia's continued desire to operate the full nuclear fuel cycle. None of the country's claimed uranium has been mined, however, although KA-Care has awarded an exploration contract to the Beijing Research Institute of Uranium Geology—a factor that compounded the complicated politics of the kingdom's nuclear ambitions. In September 2020 the British newspaper *The Guardian* reported that Chinese geologists were in the kingdom 'mapping' Saudi uranium reserves 'at breakneck speed'. A formal agreement was signed with Chinese geologists in the following year. In April 2023 *The New York Times* reported that since around 2020 China had been partnering in the development of an estimated six to eight uranium processing sites in western Saudi Arabia. Uranium enrichment requires the building of milling and processing plants. It seemed probable that these would follow before long, conceivably again in partnership with the Chinese.

In June 2021 the World Nuclear Association reported that Saudi Arabia remained committed to the building of two nuclear plants, and stated that the kingdom was in discussions with US, British and Czech civil nuclear power companies, while noting existing agreements on nuclear technology and reactor construction with Argentina's INVAP, South Korea's KAERI and China's CNNC. In January 2023 the energy minister, Abdulaziz bin Salman (the Crown Prince's half-brother), stated that the in-country development of uranium production and the export of 'nuclear fuel' were more important to the kingdom than building nuclear reactors. The Chinese collaboration on developing Saudi Arabia's uranium mining potential took on an arguably starker meaning in the context of burgeoning Saudi economic and diplomatic relations with China, exemplified by the Chinese-brokered Saudi-Iranian rapprochement in March (see History). The USA's insistence on its '123' standards for civil nuclear partnerships would undermine the Saudis' stated desire not only to mine their own uranium but also to enrich it, including for export. Another Trump (or least a Republican Party) presidency in the USA would possibly enhance prospects for a resumption of US-Saudi bilateral efforts towards a nuclear deal. Otherwise, US congressional opposition seems likely to compound White House reluctance and would probably also limit the prospect of a Saudi-South Korean deal. The extent of France's willingness to rule out Saudi in-country uranium development is harder to predict. The Russian option might be too uncomfortable for Saudi Arabia diplomatically, and in any case Russian capability would probably be affected by US-led sanctions.

The Renewable Energy Project Develop Office (Repdo) was created in February 2017 under the Ministry of Energy, Industry and Mineral Resources. Repdo was intended to be autonomous enough to secure financing for renewable projects under the National Renewable Energy Programme (NREP) set up under SV 2030. In June 2012 the kingdom had announced a US $109,000m. scheme to install 41 GW of solar power capacity over the next two decades. Repdo announced the first phase of one solar and one wind project in the north-west of the kingdom which were intended to generate a combined 0.7 GW. In March 2018 Crown Prince Mohammed bin Salman, as Chairman of the PIF, signed a memorandum of understanding (MOU) for a solar power project with his close business ally, Masayoshi Son of the Japanese conglomerate SoftBank (with which the PIF was already involved as investors in a joint fund). It was unclear if the projects envisaged in the MOU were in addition to, or simply formed part of, the planned NREP. The initiative with SoftBank was for two solar power projects in the kingdom. They came online in 2019, with respective capacity of 3.0 GW and 4.2 GW, which if achieved, and in addition to the earlier initiative, would take the kingdom close to the SV 2030 target for solar power generation. In addition, the MOU with SoftBank, which by definition was not legally binding, stated that solar panels would be manufactured and developed in Saudi Arabia, and that they would have a generating capacity of 150 GW–200 GW by 2030. However, observers question how these ambitious results can be achieved. In January 2019 the official overall Repdo 2030 target was increased from 9.5 GW to 58.7 GW, and an interim target of 27.3 GW by the end of 2024 was announced, comprising 20 GW of photovoltaic (PV) power, 7 GW of wind and 300 MW of concentrated solar power. In July 2019 Repdo announced that a second round of commissions, intended to generate nearly 1.5 GW from six PV plants, was scheduled, prior to issuing a formal request for proposals later that year. In April 2020 Repdo announced a third stage of commissions, beginning with an initial 'request for qualifications'. Four PV projects, to be run on an IPP basis, would reportedly generate a total of 1.2 GW. In April 2021 the *Middle East Economic Digest (MEED)* reported that the PIF had signed a 25-year agreement for a new solar IPP project, which would be based in the planned 'Sudair Industrial City' to be located in central Najd. The project was forecast to have a capacity of 1.5 GW when completed. Of the 12 solar power 'projects' listed on the GASTAT website in June 2021, total capacity amounted to an expected 4.5 GW. In addition to these, in March contracts for the third phase of the NREP were awarded, representing a total prospective 1.2 GW of power. The largest contract, for 0.7 GW, was awarded to a consortium of Saudi Arabia's ACWA Power (40.1%), China's SPIC (39.9%), and the PIF-owned Badeel (Water & Electricity Holding Company) (20%). Meanwhile, the NREP, in partnership with ACWA Power, had apparently revised downwards the official interim target of 27.3 GW by the end of 2024, to 11.8 GW by 2025 (this target was described by the IEA in January 2022 as involving projects 'pending approval by the Ministry of Energy'). In December 2022 an ambitious plan was officially announced for the development of a new 2.6-GW PV facility, based on a Badeel-ACWA 'power purchase' partnership, to be located in Al-Shuaiba in Mecca region. It was asserted that the proposed 'biggest solar facility in the Middle East' would be operating at full capacity by the end of 2025.

About one-fifth of the country remains unconnected to the national power grid, and creating a unified national grid is estimated to require over 30,000 km of new power transmission lines. In 2004 the kingdom had about 250,000 km of transmission lines. According to the GCC Interconnection Authority (GCCIA), a regional inter-exchange electricity grid serving the six GCC states at an estimated cost of US $1,600m. was scheduled to be fully operational in 2011–12. The first phase of the project, linking Saudi Arabia, Kuwait, Bahrain and Qatar, was completed in early 2009, and the second phase, linking the individual grids of the UAE with that of Oman, was completed in July. In October 2013 the GCCIA signed a maintenance contract with a consortium of four Gulf providers for the network's fibre-optic cables and a contract for the leasing of a submarine cable to connect Bahrain to the rest of the grid. According to the GCCIA, by July 2015 the third phase, described as interconnecting Phase 1 and 2 (and therefore presumably interconnecting all six states), had been completed. In 2015 the GCCIA claimed that the net total of 'exchanged energy' between member states had reached 605 GWh, up from 460 GWh in 2014, and in 2016 it gave a sharply increased figure of 1,320 GWh exchanged energy, following what it said were 'agreements signed that year'. The GCCIA's annual report for 2020 indicated that approximately 1,250 GWh had been traded in that year, a marked improvement from the 940 GWh of electricity exchanged in 2019. In 2021 exchanged energy totalled 1,089 GWh and the claimed collective annual saving from the intra-GCC electricity exchange in that was $192.7m. In June 2023 it was reported that 'interconnection stations' were being set up in Iraq that would connect it to the GGCIA, as had been anticipated by the latter in its 2021 *Annual Report*.

Besides power generation demand, Saudi Arabia will require an additional 250m. gallons per day (g/d) of water over the next 20 years, according to local sources. Per capita demand for water is growing by 7% annually. The Saline Water Conversion Corpn (SWCC) projected that total domestic consumption of water would increase from 1,300m. g/d currently to 1,700m. g/d by 2031, 60% of which would be met through desalination. This increase reflects the projected expansion of the industrial and agricultural sectors, as well as burgeoning population growth. The SWCC estimated that funding of SR 160,000m. (US $42,667m.) would be required to meet the rise in demand. In addition, $23,000m. of new investment is needed for building wastewater treatment plants over the next 20 years. The Ras al-Khair power and water desalination plant was reported to have reached its projected water output of 228m. g/d (just under 1.04m. cu m/d) as of July 2016. At June 2020 the plant was reportedly producing water at about the same rate (1.05m. cu m/d).

The SWCC is the world's largest producer of desalinated water, accounting for about 25% of global output. In November 2014 the SWCC issued plans to reach output of 6.5m. cu m/d by 2016, based on its claimed 4m. cu m/d output at that time. In April 2021 CEDA, in its progress review of SV 2030 (see *Saudi Vision 2030*), stated that SWCC's desalinated water output in 2020 was 5.9m. cu m/d. In March 2023 the SWCC claimed that water output had risen to 6.6m. cu m/d. This not only confirmed that the 2016 target had finally been achieved, but also suggested the early attainment of the targets set in 2015 for domestic water consumption and desalination proportion by 2030.

At July 2020 the SWCC website listed 17 plants as fully operational, down from 28 when it published its output ambitions. Under plans drawn up in 2010 the SWCC was expected to invest SR 1,300m. in the renovation of old water desalination plants, in addition to new desalination projects being implemented nationwide. However, the general reduction in public investment in the kingdom from 2015 had compounded the SWCC's obvious difficulty in reaching its planned 2016 target. At 2014 the total length of SWCC's water pipelines amounted to 7,000 km. However, the SWCC's contribution to total desalinated water produced in the kingdom had fallen to under 60% in 2013 (from 84% in 2009), according to ECRA. Based on a statement by the Ministry of Water in September 2022 that Saudi Arabia was producing 9m. cu m/d of desalinated water, the SWCC's contribution (as measured a few months later) had recovered to over 70% of the total.

In 2013 there were 11 Saudi desalinated water producers. Jubail Water and Power Company and Shuaibah Water and Electricity Company accounted for 13.1% and 14.4% of output, respectively, in that year. The SWCC's plans further expansion by privatizing its assets, including the Ras al-Khair power and desalination plant. In June 2020 the SWCC invited bids for the purchase of Ras al-Khair, worth up to US $3,500m., although it was not clear if this would be used for the renovation of old desalination and power facilities or diverted via the Privatisation Supervisory Committee for the Environment, Water and Agriculture into other state investments. In June 2023 SWCC reported that it was overseeing 10 'production systems'.

In June 2022 it was reported that construction of the Jubail 3B independent water plant (IWP) was under way. The Saudi Water Partnership Company had contracted a consortium led by France's energy group Engie, and Saudi Arabian companies Nesma and Ajlan to develop and finance the IWP at Jubail, with construction being carried out by Spanish multinational Acciona and Chinese company SEPCO. It was envisaged that when it became operational, which was scheduled for 2024, Jubail 3B would have the capacity to generate 570,000 cu m of desalinated water daily for 2m. people. Following the completion of Jubail 3B and three other desalination plants, up to 2,360m. cu m of desalinated water would be produced annually.

AGRICULTURE AND FISHING

Agriculture (including forestry and fishing) contributed 2.8% of real GDP in the first quarter of 2023, and employed about 560,000 people in 2019. According to official preliminary figures, agricultural GDP increased by an average of 3.2% per year in 2013–22. Sectoral GDP increased by 3.9% in 2022. Cultivation is confined to oases and to irrigated regions, which as of 2012 comprised only 1.5% of the total land area (according to the World Bank). About 40% of land is used for low-grade grazing. Watermelons, tomatoes, dates and grapes are produced in significant quantities.

In 2009 agricultural projects accounted for nearly one-quarter of the kingdom's expected SR 181,000m. ($48,267m.) private sector investments, enhancing Saudi Arabia's status as a major player in the regional agribusiness. Food (including animal fats and oils) and live animals accounted for 9.3% of total imports in 2022. The kingdom is the GCC's largest agricultural importer. The kingdom consumed an estimated 27.4m. metric tons of food in 2021, of which the maajority was imported, according to Alpen Capital's *GCC Food Report* in September 2021. Assuming the actualization of population and GDP predictions, by 2025 the kingdom's food consumption was forecast to rise to 29.6m. tons—about two-thirds of the estimated GCC total.

Saudi Arabia is subject to important natural limitations on the development of agriculture, principally the scarcity of water. Agriculture accounts for 85%–90% of water demand, which is met mostly by non-renewable groundwater reserves. The Government has initiated an ambitious programme to increase the country's water supply, including surveys for underground water resources, construction of dams, and irrigation and drainage networks, combined with distribution of fallow land, settlement of *bidoun* and the introduction of mechanization. The principal aim of the programme is to raise agricultural production to the level of near self-sufficiency in all foods. Consequently, budgetary allocations for the agricultural sector have increased considerably.

According to data from the Food and Agriculture Organization of the UN (FAO), cereal production totalled around 1.2m. metric tons in both 2020 and 2021, compared with an average of 1.5m. tons per year during 2013–17. Saudi Arabia has diversified to importing more cereal products after its experiment with attempted cereals self-sufficiency, especially wheat, in the 1980s had to be halted.

The National Agricultural Development Co (NADEC), formed in 1981, is a major producer of fruit, open field and greenhouse vegetables. NADEC also specializes in dairy farming and processing and has over 50,000 cattle on six dairy farms and two dairy plants with a total daily production of some 1.5m. litres. The kingdom is 50% self-sufficient in poultry production, with the country ranking among the highest consumers of chicken per capita in the world, according to FAO. A major success has been achieved with dairy farming, using the most modern technical expertise from Sweden, Denmark and Ireland, and Saudi Arabia has some of the world's most efficient dairy farms. Although domestic milk consumption is relatively low, at 60 litres per capita per year, compared with 120 litres in Western Europe, a young and expanding population presents a future growth market for producers. FAO estimated total milk output (from cows, camels, goats and sheep) at some 2.9m. metric tons in 2021, up from 1.9m. tons in 2013.

According to FAO, in 2021 the total national fish catch was 181,949 metric tons (114,490 tons in the aquaculture sector and 67,459 in the traditional marine fisheries sector). New projects launched by the Saudi Fisheries Co in the past decade include a facility to convert fish to fodder, a processing factory and the purchase of shrimping vessels.

TRANSPORT, COMMUNICATIONS AND TOURISM

Until 1964 the only surfaced roads, besides those in the petroleum network, were in the Jeddah-Mecca-Medina area. Since then, roads have been given priority. In late 2020 the Ministry of Education claimed that there was a total of 160,000 km of roads in the kingdom and that just under 30% of these were asphalted. This represented a marked increase from the estimate of 64,000 km for 2015. A causeway links Bahrain with the Saudi mainland. As part of programmes under way since the mid-2010s the Government was committed to spending SR 10,800m. (US $2,880m.) to support the construction of 284 road projects, including highways, secondary roads and branch roads. The greatest regional allocations were for 814 km, 432 km and 428 km of new roads in the Riyadh (see below), Mecca and Asir regions, respectively.

The main seaports are at Jeddah, Yanbu and Jizan on the Red Sea and at Dammam and Jubail on the Gulf. Yanbu and Jubail have both commercial and industrial ports, which function separately, and a new port development at the industrial site of Ras al-Khair (see *Industry, Gas and Mining*) on the north-east coast is expanding. Dhiba is a port facility in the north-west of the kingdom, close to markets in Egypt and Jordan, although it is relatively modest compared with the other Red Sea coast developments. An estimated 12,000 vessels annually use Saudi Arabian ports, which in 2002 had a total of 183 organized and mechanized berths (137 at six commercial ports and 46 at two industrial ports). The volume of cargo (excluding crude oil) handled by Saudi ports in 2020 totalled 299.0m. metric tons (198.3m. tons of goods loaded and 100.7m. tons of goods unloaded), compared with 100.6m. tons in 2001 and 165m. tons in 2011. Containerized traffic through Saudi ports in 2019 amounted to 6.9m. 20-ft equivalent units (TEUs), compared with 3.9m. TEUs in 2006. The Saudi Ports Authority (Mawani) reported that TEUs at all of its hubs reached just over 2m. TEUs in the first quarter of 2023, a 17.6% increase year on year.

Saudi Arabia has upgraded facilities at several major seaports, while developing two new cargo centres along the Red Sea coast. By far the kingdom's largest port, the Jeddah Islamic Port (JIP), which handles more than 70% of total container traffic, or 24% by weight, underwent large-scale expansion in 2009, when its total capacity was doubled through the opening of a third terminal—the Red Sea Gateway (costing US $450m.), with four berths and a 70,000 TEUs stacking area. According to Mawani, in 2019 JIP handled 4.4m TEUs. It also reported that at June 2023 JIP had four terminals (including two container terminals with a combined capacity of 7.5m. TEUs) with a total of 62 berths, some of which host some 7m. head of livestock annually, to cater for burgeoning domestic meat demand, including during the Eid Islamic festivals.

Mawani reported in June 2022 that 13 ports were operating in the kingdom, with a total of 290 platforms handling the cargo of 15,000 ships and 20m. containers. Taking the latter to be an annual figure, this suggested incredible progress, as the figure given two years earlier had been 13m. containers and appeared greatly to exceed the national container target for 2020. The current target is to handle a collective total of 40m. containers by 2030. On past form, doubling handling capacity in a decade could well be attainable, whether demand justifies it or not.

Vela International Marine (Vela), the shipping arm of Saudi Aramco, operates the world's largest fleet of Very Large Crude Carriers (VLCCs); in mid-2020 the fleet comprised 45 vessels. Aramco also owns or leases oil storage facilities around the world, including in the Netherlands (Rotterdam), Sidi Kerir (the Sumed pipeline terminal on Egypt's Mediterranean coast), South Korea, the Philippines and the Caribbean.

The National Shipping Co of Saudi Arabia (Bahri) also operates a fleet of eight VLCCs and through its subsidiaries—National Chemical Carriers and Arabian Chemical Carriers—owns 14 chemical tankers and four container vessels. Bahri is a public company, in which the PIF holds a 28% stake, while the remaining 72% is publicly traded. In June 2012 Saudi Aramco and Bahri signed a US $1,300m. agreement for the sale of Vela International Marine. The merger of the two companies would create the fourth largest fleet of VLCCs in the world. At mid-2023, however, Bahri maintained its separate organization and reported its VLCC stock as numbering 40.

According to a *MEED* press report of 22 December 2021 the General Authority for Civil Aviation (GACA) has stated that there are 35 airports in the kingdom. The principal international airports are at Jeddah (King Abdulaziz), Dhahran (the Eastern Province International Airport and King Fahd International Airport) and Riyadh (King Khalid). There are also more minor, nominally international airports at Medina and Taif, and 13 domestic airports, including locally focused ones such as Arar near the Jordanian border and al-Bahah in the south. More than 68.4m. passengers passed through Saudi Arabian international airports during 2015 (an increase of 9% on the previous year). A new passenger terminal building at King Abdulaziz International airport in Jeddah should have been completed and fully functioning by mid-2016, but opened only (partly) in May 2018. However in November 2019 the new Terminal 1 became operational for the first time to non-Saudi international flights. The terminal was expected to increase annual passenger capacity from 13m. to 30m. in the first phase and 80m. in its 'final phase'. The further and rapid expansion of Jeddah airport, including its dedicated *Hajj* terminal, will be crucial to realizing the pilgrimage targets contained in SV 2030 (see *Saudi Vision 2030*). The capacity of King Khalid International airport is also being expanded from 14m. passengers to 24m. It has five terminals but only three are usually operational. The Government operates the national carrier, Saudi Arabian Airlines (SAUDIA), which links the major Saudi cities and operates regular flights to many foreign countries. SAUDIA controls 90% and 84%, respectively, of domestic and international traffic in the kingdom, according to the Centre of Asia Pacific Aviation. In June 2003 the Council of Ministers approved plans to open up the domestic aviation sector to competition. There are now two privately owned, low-cost carriers (Flynas—formerly known as Nas Air—and Sama Airlines) competing with SAUDIA on international and domestic routes.

In July 2021 the Saudi Government announced a National Transport and Logistics Strategy intended to ensure that the kingdom would become a 'global logistics hub'. Reports suggested that Saudi Arabia was seeking to compete directly with the UAE, a well-established hub responsible for about 10% of goods exported globally. A Saudi Government press release noted that in establishing a second airline and a second Riyadh airport as part of this ambition, the kingdom would become the fifth highest ranked globally in terms of air traffic. Minister of Transport Saleh bin Nasser bin Ali al-Jasser announced in March 2022 that, in collaboration with the PIF, a 'national transport strategy' included plans for a new airport and a new national air carrier in Riyadh. In March 2023 the PIF announced the launch of the country's second air carrier, Riyadh Air. It was envisaged that the transport sector's contribution to GDP would double from 5% to 10% by 2030, while Saudi air transport would increase international flight destinations to 250, and double air cargo capacity to more than 4.5m. metric tons. Although the transport sector's contribution to GDP increased to 5.9% in 2022, the achievement of the 10% target in eight years appeared optimistic without a major and sustained increase in non-oil GDP, including tourism, to convert the establishment of new carriers and airports into real economic growth. The UAE, a key Saudi competitor in the transport arena, seemed unaffected by the Saudi challenge and its recent performance arguably put the Saudi ambitions in perspective—Emirati air travel rose by 56.3% year on year in the first quarter of 2023.

In December 2021 the GACA announced that the 35 airports under its authority would be transferred to the PIF via an initial transfer to Matara, the joint stock company founded by the GACA to oversee privatization of the civil airports. However, while transferring the airports to the PIF may be intended to raise funds for GACA, such a form of intra-governmental monetary circulation did not appear likely to lead to privatization.

Saudi Arabia has the only rail system in the Arabian peninsula, with a total of some 3,650 km of track in 2023, on three lines. The 2,750-km North–South line (completed in 2015) runs from Riyadh to the border with Jordan, and has branch lines to mining operations in the north of the country; the 450-km Riyadh–Dammam line runs from the capital to Dammam on the Gulf coast (with a branch line for freight trains to al-Kharj and Harad); and the 450-km Haramain high-speed electrified line (opened in 2018) connects the west-coast centres of Mecca, Medina and Jeddah, and provides a passenger service for millions of *Umrah* and *Hajj* pilgrims every year, as well as for commuters travelling between the three cities. There are plans to build two new lines (mainly for freight) of 950-km and 115-km in length, connecting Riyadh with Jeddah and Dammam with Jubail, respectively. When completed, the so-called Saudi Landbridge Project, launched in 2006, would provide west–east freight and passenger services, connecting the Red Sea with the Persian (Arabian) Gulf, and would be closely linked with Jeddah Islamic Port and King Abd al-Aziz Port (at Dammam). An 18.1-km elevated metro system linking the holy sites in Mecca opened in 2010; plans are currently under way to build a new 182-km four-line metro system in the city. Plans for the construction of a three-line, 149-km metro system in Jeddah were approved in 2013, while in the same year contracts for construction work on a six-line, 176.5-km metro system in Riyadh (costing some US $22,500m.) were awarded. The Riyadh Metro system was expected to commence operating in late 2023 or early 2024, while the construction of the Jeddah Metro was expected to be completed by 2025.

Work on preparing the new metro and bus service across Greater Riyadh has progressed since 2021, with reports that much of the work on many of the planned stations and related tunnels has been conducted. The Royal Commission for Riyadh City (RCRC, which is itself responsible for the Riyadh Transport Authority—RTA—overseeing the Greater Riyadh area) stated in April that under its plan over 1,000 new buses would eventually operate in the metropolitan area, including on three planned dedicated 'bus and rail' tracks or lines. However, there were indications that overall progress with the RTA network was being hindered by the difficulty of setting up the new bus routes and ensuring that they interconnected with the planned metro lines. Unsurprisingly, the major road works related to the planned new bus routes in metropolitan Riyadh were causing major traffic delays that the lanes themselves were eventually intended to relieve. Financial disputes involving major contractors hired by the RCRC were also an issue, although the threat to suspend work apparently led to the settling of some outstanding bills. In June 2022 the RTA website reported that there would be three 'levels' of bus service—cross city, community, and feeder services—and that there would be a capacity of 1.2m. passengers when the 'trial operation' started. Although parts of the new Riyadh bus service are reportedly already operational, bus lanes and construction work continue to compound the increased traffic problem. However, the fact that part of the new integrated metro and bus system bypass roads should eventually help to ease the congestion.

In the late 1980s Saudi Arabia established satellite transmission and reception stations, facilitating direct telephone dialling to most of the rest of the world. According to the International Telecommunications Union (ITU), in 2016 there were over 50% more mobile telephone accounts in the kingdom than there were residents (adults and children included), with an estimated total of 47.9m. In 2017 this figure fell to 40.2m.— apparently an indication of ongoing rises in living costs (including for the large expatriate population, who were particularly vulnerable to rising charges)—but despite this, the total number gradually rose over the next few years to reach 45.4m in 2021. The number of fixed broadband subscriptions, as the kingdom's fibre-optic expansion took hold, increased from 6.8m. in 2019 to 10.6m. in 2021. According to the ITU, the number of internet users in 2021 was equivalent to 100% of the population (a marked increase from 71% in 2010), reflecting the fact that, for many, the mobile telephone is the principal form of internet access, rather than home broadband. None the less, according to the ITU, the number of fixed-line telephone subscriptions increased from 5.7m. in 2020 to 6.6m. in 2021.

In 2002 the Saudi Communications and Information Technology Commission issued new legislation that provided a comprehensive framework for deregulation of the telecommunications sector. In 2023 there were three mobile telephone providers—Saudi Telecommunications Co (STC—Saudi Telecom), the UAE-based Etihad Etisalat (operating locally under the brand name Mobily) and Kuwait's Zain Group. The STC's monopoly on the fixed-line sector was ended when the authorities awarded three licences to foreign operators—namely Bahrain Telecommunications Corpn (Batelco), Pacific Century CyberWorks of Hong Kong and Verizon Communications of the USA.

The Government views the tourism industry as a source of foreign exchange and job creation and advertises abroad the kingdom's many archaeological and heritage sites. The Saudi Commission for Tourism and National Heritage (SCTH) is keen to promote adventure and sports tourism and has set a target of 6m. international tourist arrivals (excluding pilgrims) annually by 2025. Given the dominance of *Hajj* and *Umrah* in Saudi tourism (see *Saudi Vision 2030*), this appears ambitious. Many facilities are, in fact, designed to encourage Saudi nationals to take a holiday in their own country; an estimated 7.2m. do so.

According to SAMA's figures published up to the end of 2019, citing the SCTH, inbound tourist expenditure in the country totalled US $14,388m. in 2014, rising sharply to $22,275m. in 2015 and climbing to $26,775m. in 2019. Domestic tourist expenditure was more modest, at $16,249m. in 2019, falling to $11,534m. in 2020, owing to the COVID-19 pandemic. GASTAT reported that operating revenues at hotels alone totalled $70,869m. in 2021, but did not publish data for overall tourism revenue. SAMA estimated that Saudization of the 'direct' tourism workforce (excluding taxi drivers) rose from 27.1% in 2020 to 27.4% in 2021. At roughly one-third of employees in the tourism sector, this figure should possibly be viewed with a degree of scepticism, given the number of foreign nationals employed in the Saudi service sectors relevant to (but not exclusively servicing) tourism, including hotels and catering. At the end of 2021 a total of 618,243 individuals were directly employed in the accommodation and catering sectors, out of total tourism-related employment of 767,819. (In practice, a significant amount of these employment totals were not exclusive to tourism and, of the overall total, 206,029— 26.8%—were listed as Saudi nationals.)

From a high of 18.3m. in 2014, the number of tourist arrivals flatlined, before declining to 15.3m. in 2018 and recovering to 17.5m. in 2019. Religious tourism is the main reason for overseas visitors travelling to Saudi Arabia. Some 1.4m. foreign pilgrims arrived in Mecca during 2013 to perform the annual *Hajj*. A disaster at the 2015 *Hajj*, when more than 2,000 people died in a crush (tragically not an especially rare event in Mecca in recent years), did not lead to a significant reduction in the number undertaking *Hajj* or other pilgrimage visits (including *Umrah*) in 2016. The number of foreign pilgrims travelling to Mecca in totalled around 1.8m. in both 2017 and 2018, rising to 1.9m. in 2019.

By mid-2020 the impact of COVID-19 meant that many foreign governments were advising their Muslim citizens against travelling to the kingdom for *Hajj* or *Umrah*, not least on the expectation that Saudi Arabia would massively scale back its plans to receive pilgrims. In the event, the 2020 *Hajj* took place with the participation of as few as 1,000 pilgrims (essentially drawn from among pilgrims already resident in the kingdom).

The SCTH had argued that a focus on Muslim cultural history and business travel would result in a significant increase in tourist visitors (including retaining Saudi nationals who normally went abroad) by the 2020s. Tourism was one of the main sectors targeted for expansion in SV 2030. The hugely ambitious new city of NEOM on the northern Red Sea coast will enhance links, including via a bridge over the Strait of Tiran, to Egypt, while 'Western' entertainment is being promoted by the controversial General Entertainment Authority. Meanwhile, more culturally focused projects have been launched, including at the renowned Nabatean-era site of Mada'in Saleh as part of the focused development of Al-Ula province in the al-Madinah region.

In February 2020 the SCTH evolved into the Ministry of Tourism. The new ministry issued a statement in July claiming that, despite the ongoing economic downturn caused by the pandemic, hotels providing a total of 150,000 rooms would be built over the next three years, mostly through private investment. However, the tourism ministry acknowledged that the COVID-related lockdown had reduced total passenger numbers in and out of the kingdom by 26m. in just four months, and that the number of tourism industry jobs affected by the crisis was some 200,000. Despite this, and in common with the large (and perhaps fanciful) numbers sometimes forecast by the erstwhile SCTH, the ministry predicted that by 2030 some 100m. international and domestic visits would be made annually. In CEDA's account of the impact of SV 2030 five years on from its inception in 2016 (see *Saudi Vision 2030*), it was claimed that the tourism sector had grown by 14% (presumably since 2016), making the Saudi tourism sector 'the fastest growing in the world'. The apparent ease with which the recently introduced electronic visas, including for pilgrimage purposes, could be processed was cited by CEDA as partly explaining what was presented as the tourism sector's good performance (despite the pandemic sharply reducing inbound visitors of any type), and the sector's seemingly favourable prospects. However, *Hajj* numbers in July 2021 totalled only 60,000 Saudi residents (compared with more than 600,000 Saudi residents in 2019), with the continuing restrictions ensuring that there would be no inbound flights by pilgrims for what remained the kingdom's most significant 'tourist' event. The ability to attract non-pilgrimage-oriented visitors remained a necessary component of any prospective boost to tourism. In May 2021 the Royal Commission of the historic Al-Ula province announced a US $15,000m. investment plan for a 'Journey Through Time', supported by $2,000m. state 'seed funding' intended to draw in private investments, including via public-private partnerships.

According to official figures, owing to pandemic-related restrictions, international visitor arrivals declined to 4.1m. in 2020 and further to 3.5m. in 2021. In April 2022 the authorities announced that the number of people permitted to perform *Hajj* in that year would be limited to 1m. (comprising both domestic and foreign pilgrims); in the event, *Hajj* numbers in July 2022 totalled 781,409 pilgrims. However, according to the World Tourism Organization, 16.6m. international visitors arrived in Saudi Arabia in 2022 (comfortably exceeding the Ministry of Tourism's target of 12m.). Furthermore, 7.8m. visitor arrivals were recorded in January–March 2023 alone (which was outside of *Hajj* season, so presumably many were non-pilgrims), making Saudi Arabia the world's second fastest growing tourism destination as well as the most popular travel destination in the Middle East. The number of foreign visitors travelling to Saudi Arabia for *Hajj* in July 2023 was reportedly at least 1.5m., and possibly as many as 1.8m. Total international visitor arrivals looked set to exceed those of

2022, including possibly the largest number of non-pilgrims to date.

FOREIGN TRADE AND INVESTMENT

Driven by the oil-related terms-of-trade gains, the kingdom's external account has improved markedly in recent years, reflected in persistent trade and current account surpluses. The value of Saudi Arabia's exports more than doubled between 2004 (US $125,998m.) and 2008 ($313,333m.). However, it declined to $192,600m. in 2009 in tandem with lower oil prices, before recovering to $251,500m. in 2010, $365,000m. in 2011 and $388,400m. in 2012. However, lower oil prices led to export revenue declining to $375,830m. in 2013 and $342,259m. in 2014. Revenue continued to fall, with oil prices remaining relatively low, registering only $206,095m. in 2015 and $185,874m. in 2016. The value of merchandise exports rose to $294,387m. in 2018 as average oil prices recovered, before dropping again, to $261,617m. in 2019. In 2020 merchandise exports fell even more markedly, to $173,864m., principally reflecting constraints on output amid the COVID-related global recession. Merchandise exports increased sharply in value to $276,198m. in 2021, as the global economy recovered from the disruptions of the pandemic and oil prices rebounded. An upsurge in oil prices following Russia's invasion of Ukraine in February 2022 resulted in an even larger increase in export revenue in that year, to $410,676m.

Exports of petroleum and petroleum products accounted for 77.7% of total exports in 2022. The leading Saudi export markets in that year were China, with 16.2% of the total, India (10.2%), Japan (9.9%) and South Korea (9.2%). Taken together, the European Union (EU) member states represented 11.5% of Saudi Arabia's export market in 2022. Taking 5.6% of the total, the USA was the fifth largest export market for Saudi Arabia in 2022, followed by the UAE with 4.3%.

The value of Saudi Arabia's merchandise imports increased from US $41,050m. in 2004 to $140,281m. in 2019, according to SAMA preliminary figures. In 2020, the first year of the pandemic, it fell to $125,920m., before rebounding to $139,735m. in 2021 and $175,989m. in 2022, as the booming economy and global inflation helped to ramp up import costs. The kingdom's major suppliers in 2022 were China (accounting for 21.0% of total imports by value), the USA (9.1%) and the UAE (6.3%). The EU supplied 19.1% of the total in 2022. Machinery and transport equipment accounted for the largest share of imports in 2022 (33.4%), including road vehicles and parts (10.1%).

The depreciation of the US dollar against other major currencies from 2002 increased the cost of the kingdom's main non-dollar imports, which are priced primarily in Japanese yen, the euro and the British pound sterling. In 2013 surpluses on the merchandise trade and current accounts narrowed as the value of imported goods further increased and oil prices softened, despite continued strong demand in Asia (led by China). A trade surplus of US $222,557m. was recorded in 2013, while the current account surplus reached $132,442m. In 2014 the trade balance fell to $183,862m., while the current account surplus narrowed to $76,916m., again reflecting falling oil revenues. In 2015—a year of sustained low oil prices and slightly higher imports—led to a large fall in the trade balance, to a relatively small surplus of $47,278m. These factors, combined with only a partial easing of a large services deficit, produced a rare overall current account deficit of $56,724m. in 2015. In 2016 a marked slump in imports by value and a firm easing of the services deficit reduced the overall current account deficit to $27,551m. Exports measured by value also fell in 2016, but more modestly than imported goods, resulting in an improvement in the trade balance, to $55,764m. In 2017 Saudi oil production cuts limited the extent of the rise in the kingdom's revenue but contributed to a marked increase in the international price of oil, which increased overall oil income for Saudi Arabia. Combined with a reduction in the cost of imported goods, this contributed to a considerable improvement in the trade balance, to $87,315m. In 2018 a further increase in Saudi oil revenues, owing to a higher average oil price and a relatively stable import bill by value, produced a healthy trade balance, of $168,7490m., while the balance on goods and services was $105,327m. According to SAMA preliminary figures, the trade balance in 2019 fell to $121,336m., reflecting a decline in oil revenues, while the balance on goods and services narrowed to $66,919m. In 2020 the trade balance declined to only $47,944m. and the balance on goods and services to $664m., as oil revenues dropped by 33% overall in that year, in part owing to Saudi compliance with its own production constraint advocacy in OPEC+, while imports fell much more modestly, declining in value by just under 10%. However, in 2021 the trade balance recovered to $136,464m. and the balance on goods and services to $73,486m., exceeding the surpluses in pre-COVID 2019. Owing to booming oil prices and exports in 2022, the surpluses on the trade balance and balance on goods and services rose sharply in that year, to $234,688m. and $183,780m., respectively.

In December 2005, after prolonged negotiations, Saudi Arabia finally joined the World Trade Organization (WTO) as its 149th member, after signing a bilateral trade accord with the USA. The Government was obliged to eliminate (in stages) non-tariff barriers deemed unfair under WTO rules, although it retained the right to block certain imports prohibited under *Shari'a* law, notably pork, alcohol and pornography. It was to phase out all export subsidies on agricultural products; reduce average tariffs on imported goods to 12.4% (agricultural) and 10.5% (industrial) towards the end of a 10-year implementation period; and abolish tariffs on personal computers, semiconductors and other information technology items by January 2008. Saudi Arabia also agreed to allow 'duty free' entry of pharmaceuticals and civil aircraft on accession and to permit majority foreign equity stakes in its telecommunications and financial services industries. The Saudi Government pledged not to participate in the boycott of Israel by the League of Arab States (Arab League, see p. 1146), thus complying with the WTO stipulation of 'freer trade' and 'fairer competition' among the member states. However, in July 2021 Saudi Arabia announced that hitherto tariff-free intra-GCC trade would no longer include goods produced in the UAE's free trade zones, where there is no obligation to have local content in employment or in manufacture. This direct move against the UAE's lucrative trading business was a consequence of a new ruling that, in general, all goods entering Saudi Arabia had to have a minimum of 25% locally employed staff and a minimum of 40% 'local input' in the 'transformation process' (presumably meaning that 40% or more of their manufacture had to take place within the GCC area). In a further potential threat to the UAE's free trade zone operation, it was reported that Saudi Arabia had announced that Israeli-produced goods with at least an Israeli component, and goods produced by companies with at least partial Israeli ownership, would be barred from entering the kingdom, as would goods produced by any company on the Arab League boycott list. While arguably the combined measures were primarily intended to disadvantage and thus compete with a free trade-oriented UAE that was increasingly open to Israeli goods, the announced banning of the latter and of goods exported by other companies on the Arab League boycott list (which in theory could thus be applied to Western companies) meant that Saudi Arabia was, formally at least, recommitted to an Arab boycott that had appeared to be waning, and reversing a rejection of third-party boycotts that had helped the kingdom gain admittance to the WTO.

The principal reason for the Saudi decision was not Israel but competition with the UAE, reflecting the Saudi aspirations to be a rival hub in trade, foreign business and transportation (see *Transport, Communications and Tourism*). In February 2021 relations with the UAE had already become strained when Saudi Arabia announced that in future it would award no government contracts to companies that were not headquartered in the kingdom, and additionally sought to demand that any company operating in the country had to be regionally headquartered there—a move widely regarded as an attempt to usurp the UAE's pivotal position as a regional host to many foreign companies and even perhaps some Saudi ones (such as *Al-Arabiya*, part of the MBC Group, a Dubai-based Saudi media conglomerate). The UAE was also likely to lose some tourism revenues from Saudi Arabia's efforts to promote itself as a tourism hub, and not just as a destination for religious pilgrims, thereby encouraging the many Saudis who take a holiday in the more relaxed atmosphere of the UAE to stay at home, effectively curtailing the amount of business that Saudis conduct in the UAE. Incoming Saudi flight data for 2022 appeared to support the idea of Saudi tourism expanding at the UAE's expense, even if the kingdom's airlines could not compete with the more than 50% year-on-year rise in flight throughput in the UAE in January–March 2023. Saudi Arabia registered almost US $1,000m. of investment in start-ups in 2022, according to data analytics platform MAGNiTT. However, despite this 30% year-on-year rise, the UAE remained the chief regional venture capital market. There was also an undercurrent of political tension between Saudi Arabia and the UAE overlapping with economics, as the two countries held opposing views within OPEC+ and with regard to more political issues in the region, even as rapprochement with Iran appeared to be a shared goal from March 2023.

Since 2000 the kingdom has made advances towards becoming more integrated into the global economy. In marked contrast with the previous three decades, during the early 21st century the country boasted the most open FDI regime in the Gulf region. SAGIA has, since its formation in 2000, acted as a self-styled 'one-stop shop' for global, regional and domestic investors, and for a number of years it enhanced the kingdom's profile within the international investment community. (It now appears to be performing this FDI facilitation role under the aegis of the new investment ministry—see above.) New regulations permitted 100% foreign equity holding (compared with 49% previously) in most industries, including power generation, water desalination and petrochemicals; moreover, wholly foreign-owned businesses qualify for tax breaks and soft loans from the Saudi Industrial Development Fund and can buy properties, except in the holy cities of Mecca and Medina. Furthermore, corporate taxes were reduced from 45% to 20% in most sectors (30% for the gas sector). The Government signed bilateral treaties with several countries to provide relief from double taxation and is a member of the Multilateral Investment Guarantee Agency.

The 'Negative List' (banning FDI on strategic grounds) was cut from 23 to 16. Besides upstream gas exploration and development, non-Saudi investors enjoy access to sectors such as mobile telephones, information and communication technology, extractive mining, transportation, tourism, insurance, education, health care, printing, power transmission and distribution and pipeline services. Furthermore, from the end of 2008 foreigners were allowed to acquire a 75% stake in the insurance, wholesale and retail trade and the aviation and railway sectors (formerly 51%). For fixed-line and mobile telephone companies, the foreign ownership ceiling was raised to 60%.

The Supreme Economic Council was committed under WTO obligations to review those sectors closed to FDI, such as upstream real estate investment, recruitment and fisheries companies. However, several sectors—notably upstream oil exploration, drilling and production, defence and security, and media and publishing—remain closed to foreign investors. In December 2018 the CEDA announced that service providers in the fields of road transportation, recruitment, audiovisual media and real estate brokerage would no longer be excluded from FDI. In June 2019 the Capital Market Authority (CMA) appeared to go much further in terms of permitting foreign ownership, stating that there would no longer be any restriction on ownership for 'foreign strategic investors' who acquired stakes in publicly listed Saudi companies on the Tadawul—a key qualification being that such foreign investors committed to hold any newly acquired shares for a minimum of two years. Notably, however, some sectors, such as banking, insurance and telecommunications, remained subject to the existing 49% foreign ownership share-holding limit. This was unless the specific sector authorities gave explicit permission to foreign strategic investors, thereby enabling the foreign shareholding limit to be exceeded on the Tadawul. However, the Tadawul's listing rules reportedly require a 'free float' of 30% of a Saudi company's shares, so that no single foreign company can in practice take more than a 70% stake in a listed Saudi company. (Shares in real estate companies operating in the holy cities of Mecca and Medina remain subject to their own ownership regulations.)

In 2016 the kingdom was the region's second largest FDI recipient (after Turkey—now known as Türkiye), with net inflows of US $7,453m., according to the UN Conference on Trade and Development (UNCTAD). However, in 2017 the net inward FDI inflow fell dramatically, to $1,419m., before recovering in 2018, to $4,247m. In part, the arrest of Saudi businessmen in November 2017 and their subsequent detention, in some cases for more than a year, played a role in the low level of net inward investment in 2017–18, although in 2017 it was mostly likely to have been caused by Shell selling its joint venture stake in the Saudi Petrochemical Company to SABIC. Notably, the net investment outflow in 2018 more than tripled, to $22,987m., before easing in 2019, to $13,185m. However, net inward FDI in 2019 rose only slightly, to $4,562m. The stock of inward FDI in 2019 was $236,166m.—an only moderate increase from the $227,566m. recorded in 2017. (By contrast, FDI inward stock in 2000 was reported at just $17,600m.) In 2020, according to the IMF net inward FDI increased to $5,399m. (equivalent to 0.8% of GDP), despite the economy contracting in that year. UNCTAD reported that in 2021 the annual inflow of foreign investment soared to $19,286m., a more than threefold increase year on year. However, most of the inflow annual total was due to Aramco selling a $12,400m. stake in an oil pipeline entity to the EIG-led consortium (see *Petroleum*). The SV 2030 target is for an FDI inflow of $100,000m. annually. Furthermore, in 2021, a year of economic recovery, the net outflow foreign investment figure rose strongly, and was in fact higher than that of the FDI inflow. In 2022 net inward FDI was an estimated $7,900m., according to Forbes (cited by *Al-Monitor* in April 2023). This 60% slump from 2021 was more or less as predicted by the IMF, which had forecast a decline to about $8,200m. It was also in line with the typical levels of net FDI inflows over the previous six years, both in terms of the total amount and as a percentage of GDP. Moreover, it made the inward FDI target under the SV 2030 look absurdly disconnected from reality.

The Government also pursued reforms that facilitated the kingdom's accession to the WTO in December 2005, including devising a new 'business-friendly' tax code, revising commercial laws, implementing intellectual property rights, reducing import tariffs, removing non-trade barriers, liberalizing the financial services industry and strengthening insurance and capital market regulations and supervision. WTO membership was expected to improve longer-term growth prospects through increased FDI and non-oil exports. In the World Bank's *Doing Business 2020* report (the final one before the publication was discontinued), Saudi Arabia's ranking jumped by 30 places to 62nd out of 190 economies, owing partly to the simplification of the company incorporation process, the streamlining of electronic trading in imports and exports, and enhanced rights for married women.

FINANCE

SAMA, the central bank, which was established in 1952, is responsible for the formulation of monetary policy, the management of official external assets and the supervision of commercial banks. SAMA is credited with preserving currency and price stability. The riyal has been pegged to the US dollar at $1 = SR 3.745 since June 1986. The current pegged exchange rate regime is expected to remain unchanged in the period leading to the GCC monetary union. Moreover, the main Saudi exports—crude petroleum and gas-based products such as methanol and ammonia-urea—are priced in US dollars.

SAMA boasts an exceptionally solid international liquidity position. Foreign exchange reserves (excluding gold) in June 2015 totalled US $670,298m. (the world's fourth largest), compared with $155,029m. in December 2005. However, as the collapse in oil revenues put pressure on public finances, the Government began to draw relatively heavily on its foreign reserves. By the end of December 2015 they had fallen to $615,985m. As of September 2016 the IMF estimated that Saudi foreign reserves in that year would be equivalent to 27 months of imports—a healthy financial cushion, although lower than the 2014 estimate of 35 months. In May 2017 SAMA gave a figure for its net foreign assets of $497,856m., and reported that they had continued to fall steadily over the preceding 12 months. The Government, despite some curbing of spending and attempts at raising revenues from new taxes and cutting subsidies, was still having to draw on foreign reserves. The Government denied that it was fiscal pressure that was causing the continued drawdowns and claimed that they were due to payments to overseas contractors. It might in fact have been the release of money to the PIF, which, under SV 2030 (see *Saudi Vision 2030*), was tasked with a much more pro-active foreign investment and acquisition programme. Saudi Arabia is also a 'net creditor' to the global banking sector. By 31 March 2023 SAMA's total reserve assets stood at $439,265m., having followed a largely downward trajectory since May 2019, when they stood at $517,778m. Notably, this trend was not particularly affected by higher oil revenues in 2021 and in 2022. As noted above, the PIF had continued to draw on foreign reserves, although their equivalent in import cover exceeded 20 months and thus remained strong.

At the end of 2018 Saudi banks' foreign assets stood at US $61,756m., while foreign liabilities amounted to $29,551m. By the end of 2019 Saudi banks' foreign assets had increased slightly, to $64,898m., while their foreign liabilities had risen to $46,125m. The commercial banks' overall net foreign assets (the balance of assets and liabilities) fluctuated markedly but were on a broadly downward trajectory from the third quarter of 2018. At the end of 2022, according to SAMA, they were equivalent to $22,526m., albeit a marked improvement compared with the $7,950m. recorded at the end of 2021.

As of June 2022 SAMA listed the banking and financial system as having 11 local commercial banks. Alawwal Bank merged with Saudi British Bank in 2019. There are also six specialized credit institutions, namely the Saudi Industrial Development Fund—SIDF (which finances industrial projects); the PIF (which finances large-scale government and private industrial projects, now proposed as a sovereign wealth fund—see *Saudi Vision 2030*); TASNEE—formerly the National Industrialization Co, the Real Estate Development Fund (which finances individuals and corporate residential and commercial real estate); the Saudi Credit & Savings Bank—SCSB (which provides interest-free loans for small and emerging businesses and professions); and the Agricultural Development Fund (which finances farmers and agricultural projects). SAMA also lists 14 foreign banks (JPMorgan Chase & Co, Deutsche Bank, BNP Paribas, National Bank of Kuwait, National Bank of Bahrain, Emirates NBD, Bank Muscat–Oman, Gulf International Bank, EFG Hermes Holdings, Bank Audi, TC Ziraat Bankası, National Bank of Pakistan, State Bank of India and the International Commercial Bank of China) and 92 licensed investment houses, including local firms and joint ventures with foreign banks (notably Barclays Capital, Calyon, Credit Suisse, Goldman Sachs, UBS, Merrill Lynch and Morgan Stanley).

Since the liberalization in 2004 of the insurance sector, 29 insurance companies have received licences to operate in the kingdom. Previously, the only licensed operator was the Riyadh-based National Co for Co-operative Insurance. The kingdom's insurance penetration level as a percentage of GDP (1.5% in 2010) was among the lowest in the world. The life sector is also very small, although it has been growing more rapidly in recent years.

Banking is regulated under the Banking Control Law issued by royal decree in 1966. SAMA's regulatory framework is on a par with the Group of Ten nations' central banks. The IMF commended SAMA for effective supervision of the banking system. SAMA has also introduced global accounting and auditing norms (International Financial Reporting Standards and International Standards on Auditing) for banks and their auditors. Therefore, all banks must now comply with stringent guidelines on provisions against bad debts and with international accounting standards. SAMA reported a non-performing loans ratio of only 3.0% of total loans in 2010. In August 2003 the Council of Ministers approved anti-money laundering legislation designed to bring the kingdom into line with international banking practice.

In March 2021 Saudi Arabia's largest bank in terms of asset size, the NCB, merged with SAMBA and the Saudi National Bank (SNB) was formed. With a market capitalization of SR 171,000m. (US $46,000m.), and assets worth SR 837,000m. ($223,000m.), it was set to be predominant in the sector, reflected in its 25% share of the retail and wholesale banking market. The two former banks' shareholders own the new SNB, and the largest individual shareholder, unsurprisingly, is the PIF. At 31 March 2023 the SNB's total assets were SR 976,053m.

The principal banks, ranked by assets at the end of 2022, were the SNB, Riyad Bank (US $359,653m.) and Al Rajhi Banking and Investment Corpn ($203,000m.). The SNB, Al Rajhi Banking and Riyad Bank announced profits in 2022 of $18,728m., $17,150m. and $7,020m., respectively. At the end of 2019 total banking assets had reached SR 2,631,128m. ($700,887m.)—the second highest in the region after the UAE. The total bank assets figure given by SAMA at 31 March 2023 was SR 3,746,893m., up from SR 3,370,359m. a year previously.

Saudi banks have become more outward-looking, and the most obvious example of this trend is the 55% Saudi-owned Saudi International Bank, which opened as a fully-fledged merchant bank in London, UK, in 1976. SAMA holds 50% of the capital, and the NCB and Riyad Bank have 25% each. The first wholly private Saudi bank abroad—Al-Saudi Banque—opened in Paris, France, also in 1976. Riyad Bank has a share in the Paris-based Union de Banques Arabes et Françaises and in the Gulf Riyad Bank in Bahrain. The NCB has small stakes in European-Arab Holding and the Compagnie Arabe et Internationale d'Investissement, both based in Luxembourg, and in the Amman-based Arab Jordan Investment Bank, which opened in 1978.

Commercial bank credit to the private sector increased by 7.3% in 2019. There continued to be concerns about an asset price bubble, especially in the property market, given ongoing low interest rates, government stimulus measures and related high levels of disposable income and the rapidly rising cost of renting or purchasing real estate. At the end of 2019 'claims on the private sector' represented 59% of total Saudi banks' assets. However, the economic contraction in the first quarter of 2020, induced by the collapse of oil prices, amid a global downturn following the onset of the COVID-19 pandemic, prompted fears that real estate was overvalued, as, in common with the rest of the economy, demand weakened significantly. At 31 March 2023, claims on the private sector were listed by SAMA as a proportion of total banking assets at 63.0%, having rebounded from the 48.6% registered one year previously amid the pandemic weakening.

In 1990 SAMA introduced an electronic trading system that enabled brokers at Saudi banks to trade online. The value of shares traded rose steeply: in 2005 shares were being traded in 79 companies with a market capitalization of US $650,130m. (compared with $40,906m. in 1995). However, only 10 prime stocks, led by SABIC, the STC and the Al Rajhi Banking and Investment Corpn, representing two-thirds of total capitalization and profits of all quoted companies, dominated trading.

By 2018 however the Saudi Stock Exchange (Tadawul) was operating at a different level, as more companies had opted for public share issues and the prospect of further share offerings attracted national and international interest. The benchmark Tadawul All-Share Index (TASI) was also boosted by being upgraded to emerging market status and thus being included in three pre-eminent global index providers: MSCI, FTSE Russell and S&P Dow Jones. The number of qualified foreign investors (QFI) had risen to more than 500 by September 2019 from about 100 in late 2017. The equity market was dominated by financial, petrochemical and telecommunications stocks. Foreign investment on the Saudi bourse, both direct and indirect, remained modest though, at about 5% of the total.

At September 2020 272 companies were listed on the exchange, and market capitalization stood at just over US $2,470,000m. (a sharp increase from about $500,000m. a year earlier)—in part a reflection of the growing interest and a recent series of IPOs, including those of Aramco, Suleiman Al Habib (a health care company) and Amlak International (a real estate financing firm). At 22 June 2023 market capitalization was $2,912,551m., suggesting that the Tadawul was maintaining interest; notably, however, the figure was down on the $2,972,079m. market capitalization registered a year earlier. The rebound after the end of the negative impact of the pandemic on the economy had not been maintained, and market capitalization was down after robust real GDP growth owing to higher oil output in 2022. One explanatory factor was the comparative lack of high-profile IPOs. An IPO was launched by Jamjoom Pharmaceuticals in June 2023, but raised only $336m, which was modest by the standards of some IPOs in recent years, despite the growing interest in health care companies. Mohammed bin Salman's announcement in July 2022 that part of the future financing of NEOM would come from an IPO in 2024 was expected to encourage greater interest in the Tadawul. The Crown Prince himself confidently predicted that the NEOM IPO would add a 'trillion riyals' to the value of the Saudi stock market and add even more value in the future. A total of 227 companies were listed on the Tadawul at June 2023.

The CMA, the sole regulator for the Saudi capital markets, pledged to upgrade trading platforms for the licensing of non-bank mutual funds in order to attract institutional investors and to establish an independent authority that would license financial analysts. The CMA also reduced trading commissions to 0.12% (from 0.15%) and abolished Thursday trading in an effort to curb speculative trading, which was regarded as being largely responsible for the market's recent turbulence. Other measures to instil confidence and improve liquidity included restoring the 10% fluctuation limits, splitting stocks into smaller denominations and permitting foreigners (including expatriates) to invest directly on the Saudi stock exchange by using swap deals or exchange traded funds, which are tradable index-linked financial products (foreign workers were previously restricted to mutual funds). However, at mid-2014 expatriates were still excluded from participating in IPOs, which were reserved for Saudi nationals. The CMA granted foreigners direct access to share trading in June 2015. However, in order for non-resident investors to become QFIs they had to open a special account via existing exchange members. The maximum stake per individual QFI was 20%, and the total foreign ownership portion allowed in a quoted Saudi company was 49%. In May 2016 the maximum foreign stake in a trading Saudi company was increased from 5% to 10%, and the restriction on total foreign ownership (formerly a maximum of 10% of the bourse's market capitalization) was abandoned entirely. These measures no doubt partly reflected the promised IPO of about 5% of Aramco shares, which was expected to prompt a large infusion of foreign capital into the Tadawul. However, in August 2018 the Saudi Government postponed indefinitely the domestic and international IPO of Aramco shares. The IPO was finally conducted in December 2019–January 2020 (see *Saudi Vision 2030*). However, after being reduced to 1.5% of the total Aramco share value and with purchasers being restricted to Gulf nationals, the IPO did not generate the expected level of foreign capital inflows.

In July 2020 the Tadawul announced that at the end of August a futures trading index would be launched on the stock market, to be known as 'Saudi Futures 30', based on the MSCI Tadawul 30 Index created in 2019. Like all major bourses, the Tadawul was affected by the pandemic-related downturn, falling by about 12% by mid-July 2020 since the start of the year. However, at 16 July 2021 the MSCI Tadawul 30 Index had risen by 41% year on year, while the TASI was up by 45%. In July MODON (the Saudi agency responsible for industrial cities and industrial zones) launched an initiative to encourage real estate companies to list on the Tadawul and it was reported that 30 such companies were in discussions with the CMA about doing so, seemingly attracted by the incentive of gaining the automatic right to sell off-plan property. According to the website Trading Economics, at 27 June 2023 the TASI had increased by 981 points (or 9.4%) since the beginning of the year.

In May 2021 the Minister of Finance, al-Jaadan, made the bold commitment that the kingdom would raise US $55,000m. by mid-2025 from privatizations that he predicted would involve 160 projects across 16 sectors, including asset sales and public-private partnerships. More accurately described as opportunities for private companies to operate in what had hitherto been largely a state preserve, his plan seemed to be as much about outsourcing management and investment as actual state asset sales. Also in May 2021, the Minister of Finance told the *Financial Times* about forthcoming opportunities in management and investment, specifically in what he referred to as 'health infrastructure and services to the private sector'. Asset sales—i.e. privatization proper—according to al-Jaadan, would include television broadcasting towers, government-owned hotels and district cooling and desalination plants. The usual mention of wholly privatizing state airline SAUDIA appeared to have finally been abandoned.

BUDGET

The Government's fiscal position improved in the early 21st century, in contrast to the chronic deficits of the 1990s, underpinned by higher-than-budgeted oil receipts and fiscal prudence. The state's huge oil windfalls were used to accumulate official external reserves, reduce public debt and fund extra spending on welfare, education, development projects and national security.

A review of five years of budget plans and out-turns shows that the Saudi Government repeatedly failed to match aspirations with practice. The Government announced in December 2017 that its budget for 2018 was the largest in Saudi history, meaning that the planned outlay of SR 960,000m. would be the biggest budgeted expenditure ever (although two previous out-turns had exceeded this). This seemingly reflected a fiscal confidence born of rising oil prices and, to a lesser extent, an expansion of charges including the newly introduced sales tax and the desire and apparent ability to boost recurrent and capital expenditure, in part to stimulate sluggish recent real GDP growth. The deficit out-turn for the 2018 budget, estimated at SR 135,700m., was actually lower than the SR 195,000m. forecast by the finance ministry, reflecting higher oil revenues than projected and a capital expenditure out-turn that was still below historical trends (as a proportion of the overall total). Total revenue for 2018 was SR 894,000m., largely from oil revenues, which were some SR 17,000m. higher than in 2017. The total expenditure out-turn in 2018 was SR 1,030,000m., and current expenditure was SR 825,000m.—the highest ever recorded.

The 2019 budget projected total revenue of SR 975,000m., some 25% higher than the 2018 out-turn. Notably, oil revenue was projected to rise from SR 492,000m. to SR 662,000m., based on an average oil price of US $80 a barrel. However, oil prices had slumped in late 2018. The expenditure projected by the Government for 2019, of SR 1,110,000m., increased by 13.1% from the 2018 budgeted figure and by 7.2% from the 2018 out-turn. This was due in part to a planned $20,000m. rise in capital expenditure, which for several years had been markedly below trend (itself a drag on growth as well as on much-needed infrastructural development). The budgeted current expenditure assumptions for 2019 suggested that the deficit at the end of the year would be higher than projected. For example, a budgeted 4% cut in the wage bill appeared to be unlikely, and the projected cut of 9% in military outlay was also ambitious. Although military spending fell by 4.3% in 2018 (when it constituted 21.5% of total official public expenditure), a further and larger cut would probably have required an end to Saudi involvement in the Yemen war and/or if threatened Western arms sales freezes became a reality. The overall projected fiscal deficit was a little lower than the 2018 out-turn, at SR 131,000m. (4.2% of projected GDP for 2019). The Government's assumptions for tax revenue were seemingly based on a buoyant expectation of economic performance in 2019; the expatriate levy alone was expected to double in 2019 to SR 56,000m. (owing to the rate of the levy being doubled), comprising some 6% of total projected revenue. The IMF projected a deficit of 7% of GDP. The budget out-turn in 2019 was in line with government projections, as total expenditure was SR 1,059,000m.—modestly below the budgeted sum of government outlays, with the consequent deficit being SR 132,599m., close to the forecast. Based on official data, military expenditure fell by as much as 14%, even though external embargoes failed to materialize, and cuts were made to parts of the wage bill.

The 2020 budget envisaged a firm rise in the deficit, to SR 187,000m. (equivalent to more than 6% of GDP, which was projected then to rise firmly, albeit at a historically modest rate of 2.3%, after the only 0.3% expansion recorded in 2019). Oil revenue in 2020 was expected to fall to SR 513,000m., from an estimated SR 602,000m. in 2019. Total expenditure was projected to amount to SR 1,020,000m.—a modest fall from the previous year's out-turn. However, following the onset of the COVID-19 pandemic and a related decline in oil revenue of around one-third from 2019, and the Government's consequent announcement of US $1,000m. emergency stimulus measures, which were not offset by rises in government taxes and other charges, the budget deficit in 2020, according to SAMA, was SR 293,900m., equivalent to 11.2% of GDP. Despite straitened circumstances, education spending (just under one-fifth of the total and, as is typical, the largest outlay in a Saudi budget) rose by 1.5% in 2020, while defence expenditure, only slightly behind education as a proportion of actual spending, fell by only 1.7%.

In December 2020 Minister of Finance al-Jaadan announced a 2021 budget with a planned outlay of SR 990,000m., some 7% less than the final estimated expenditure for 2020 (which was SR 1,075,734m.). He envisaged a much reduced deficit in 2021 of SR 141,000m., equivalent to 4.9% of a projected improved GDP, stating that real growth of 3.2% was expected in 2021 after a 3.7% contraction in 2020. Part of that reduction would come from a planned further cut in capital expenditure, of 26.3% from the estimated out-turn in 2020, according to an assessment by business management consultant KPMG. Al-Jaadan claimed that the economy had begun to recover in the second half of 2020 from the pandemic-induced recession. The 2021 fiscal out-turn was a deficit rather smaller than the finance minister had projected. The deficit of SR 74,000m., based on IMF data, was equivalent to 2.5% of real GDP (which had risen by 3.2%, as al-Jaadan had accurately forecast). Oil and tax revenues rose markedly in 2021. However, recurrent expenditure rose substantially too, including state sector salaries, which comprised 48% of total spending.

In December 2021 al-Jaadan announced the 2022 budget. He stated that the fiscal deficit at the end of 2021 was equivalent to 2.7% of GDP (higher than the implied percentage based on IMF data), a much healthier out-turn than projected a year earlier, largely due to the boost of the so-called post-pandemic rebound and rising oil prices. Furthermore, the 2022 budget projected a fiscal surplus of SR 90,000m. (US $24,000m.), or 2.5% of GDP, reflecting the same added confidence in the economy, following several months of recovery. After a period of considerable spending restraint and deficits, the projected 2022 surplus was notable, although it was presented by al-Jaadan together with a planned 5.9% cut in fiscal outlay in 2022. Within that spending cut was another reduction in an area of normally large expenditure: the military budget. There was some scepticism about whether this would occur in practice by the end of 2022. Ostensibly, however, a SR 171,000m. ($45,000m.) budget allocation for defence in 2022 represented another cut in military outlay. In theory it reflected the easing of the Saudi military role in the Yemen conflict, but Saudi Arabia's wish to improve its air defence among other things suggested otherwise. Al-Jaadan's budget projections—with revenue forecast to rise by 12.4% from the estimated 2021 out-turn—were also in part based on an assumed boost to non-oil activity compared with 2021. Overall growth was projected at 7.4% in 2022, compared with 2.9% in 2021.

Al-Jaadan's revenue projections for 2022 took account of assumed ongoing rising oil revenues and projected non-oil activity. However he explicitly stated that for 2022, and the future, fiscal expenditure would be 'decoupled' from the health, or otherwise, of the global oil market. In other words, the Minister of Finance was sending out what, in principle, was a new message of prudence. Spending would not simply be allowed to exceed the budgeted amount if oil revenues were bigger than originally projected. However, his prudence would as likely be constrained by other claims on the expected surplus in 2022. Al-Jaadan identified that at least some of the budgeted fiscal surplus would in effect be spent (in addition to adding to foreign reserves) by being transferred to the PIF and to 'development funds'. Among the latter was the newly created National Infrastructure Fund (NIF), which was committed to directing state funds into sectors such as health, energy, transport and water. Al-Jaadan was consciously projecting an image of fiscal rectitude although he had little control over how the PIF and 'development funds' would spend the projected budget surplus. In fact, a few months later, with the war in Ukraine fuelling far faster rises in oil revenues than expected, al-Jaadan stated that all of the expected end-of-year surplus (above the budgeted rise in spending at least) would be transferred to the PIF and, specifically, to the NDF. This appeared to be a fiscal stratagem, as his commitment to tighter spending (and even what appeared to be sizeable cuts in some key areas—see also *Education, Health Care and Housing*) was probably in part because the PIF and other agencies would undertake some spending related to state entities outside of what would otherwise be categorized under fiscal outlay.

In the event, the 2022 fiscal out-turn was a surplus of SR 103,900m. (the first fiscal surplus for nine years), as government revenues rose by 31% owing to soaring oil prices and higher output. Recurrent expenditure still rose despite the fiscal sleight of hand that had been envisaged. The fiscal surplus represented 3.5% of GDP, even as the latter rose by 8.7%, higher than the Government had projected.

For 2023 the Government forecast a much more modest surplus, of just SR 16,000m., representing 0.4% of GDP that was itself envisaged to expand by 3.1%, and the driver of growth was expected to be in the non-oil sector, owing to higher private investment and a consequent expected rise in private sector jobs. Fiscal ceilings were envisaged for the main spending areas as part of the claimed fiscal reform that was supposed to ensure that spending was not shaped by rising (oil) revenue, alongside the afore-mentioned PIF's adoption of some key capital expenditure items. Defence spending—the largest by far of the identified outlays—was allocated 5.8% more than in the 2022 budget. However, as part of an overall planned year-on-year 1.8% reduction in expenditure, the allocation for health care was cut by 4.5%, albeit in a context of envisaged 'private' investment support for a number of health care-related projects. More strikingly, the allocation for infrastructure and transportation was reduced by 26.9%. Again, the assumption behind the projected massive cut (assuming that it happens) was that presumably the PIF and so-called 'private' investors would provide a major amount of funding for related projects.

Gross domestic debt in 2013 constituted just 2.7% of GDP, a steep decline from 119% of GDP in 1999. However, by 2016 it had risen to 13.1% of GDP as local borrowing increased and the overall economy shrank. According to the IMF, gross domestic debt rose to 19.1% of GDP in 2018, amid lower economic growth. Debt-servicing costs are manageable, as four-fifths of aggregate debt comprises medium- or long-term liabilities and is owed to quasi-governmental entities. According to the EIU, external debt represented an estimated 22% of GDP in 2014, or 48% of the value of exports. However, this rose to 26.3% of GDP, or 83% of exports in 2015, and 29.3% of GDP, or 103% of exports in 2016. In 2017 the EIU estimated that Saudi Arabia's 'total debt' represented 29.9% of GDP, although, according to the IMF, external debt was 28.3% of GDP by the end of 2018 (up from 27.7% at the end of 2017). These data represented a marked increase compared with 2010–13, mainly reflecting falling oil revenues and modest growth, amid increased infrastructure and other development projects. In July 2021 the IMF stated that nominal public debt was equivalent to 32.5% of GDP in 2020, after the economy had contracted, and predicted that it would fall to about 30% of GDP by the end of 2021. The Minister of Finance, launching the 2021 budget at the end of 2020, stated that public debt in 2020 was SR 854,000m., and that it would rise to SR 937,000m. in the following year. According to SAMA, total public debt was SR 938,010m. at the end of 2021. At mid-2023 neither SAMA nor GASTAT had yet published data for 2022. However, according to press reports about the debt in US dollars, public debt had risen to the equivalent of SR 968,680m. at the end of 2022. In August the IMF had described Saudi public debt as relatively 'low and sustainable' and noted that it was expected to have fallen from 30% of GDP (at the end of 2021) to 24.3% of (a firmly rising) GDP at the end of 2022.

Saudi Arabia is a major donor to mainly low-income Muslim countries in Asia and Africa; in particular, the kingdom makes significant contributions to the Heavily Indebted Poor Countries Debt Initiative, which was proposed by the World Bank and the IMF in 1996, and to the Exogenous Shocks Facility. Bilateral aid and debt relief have exceeded US $75,000m. over the past three decades. In 2010 net disbursement of official development assistance (ODA) provided by the Saudi Government was $3,480m.—making it the largest donor within the non-Development Assistance Committee (DAC) countries. Saudi Arabia's foreign aid flows averaged 1.0% of GDP in recent years, consistently exceeding the UN target of 0.7% of gross national income. SAMA data (which does not separate concessional loans and aid) for total Saudi aid disbursal reported that net ODA (excluding concessional loans) averaged $7,300m. a year during 2011–18 and was $10,200m. in 2018. According to SAMA's *Annual Report 2021*, in 2020 Saudi bilateral and multilateral aid and loans extended that year totalled SR 17,100m. (approximately $4,600m.), down by nearly 52% on 2019. Hence, Saudi aid disbursal had been fairly constant during 2018–19, before being sharply reduced in 2020.

EDUCATION, HEALTH CARE AND HOUSING

Education spending in Saudi Arabia more than tripled during 2010–20. The ninth Development Plan (2010–14) allocated SR 731,250m. (US $195,000m.) towards increasing the capacity of primary, secondary and tertiary education in order to accommodate an extra 1.7m. students up until 2014. This was to involve—besides building new schools—the construction of 25 technology colleges, 28 technical institutes and 50 industrial training centres. In the 2015 budget, human resource development, which is predominantly education spending, was allocated an increased portion of overall expenditure, rising from 24.5% to 25.1%. Notably, however, in the 2015 budget many universities were scheduled to receive only a modest increase in their allocation of money or a reduction. The overall health care and social development budget was projected to fall in 2016, but in 2017 received a 19% increase in its allocation. The education budget was cut modestly in 2016, although it still comprised the largest single area of expenditure, at about one-quarter of total government outlay. In 2017 the education allocation (under human resource development) was 5% higher than that allocated for 2016, but represented a smaller proportion, at 22.5%, of a projected rising total public expenditure. In the 2019 budget, expenditure on education was projected to remain stable, after falling modestly in 2018 (although the out-turn in 2018 was actually 6.3% higher than the allocated funding). The 2019 education expenditure out-turn was 3% lower than the sum spent in 2018. In the 2020 (pre-COVID-19) budget, education spending rose by 1.5% compared with the 2019 out-turn (representing 19.1% of total expenditure). In 2021 education spending appeared to have fallen significantly, given that the out-turn was officially estimated at SR 191,000m. (after a 2020 out-turn of SR 205,000m.). Another cut was budgeted for 2022: education spending was allocated SR 185,000m. in that year's budget.

The allocation for health care services in the 2017 budget allocation was significantly increased after a planned cutback in 2016, and for 2018 a rise of 10.5% was allocated to the health care and social development budget. In 2019 an 8% rise in the health care out-turn was recorded, following an above-budget rise of 23% in health care spending in 2018. In 2020 expenditure on health and social care recorded an only nominal increase from the 2019 figure of SR 190,325m. In 2021 around SR 191,000m. was spent on health care and social development, according to the official 2022 budget statement—a large overspend on the budgeted total of SR 175,000m. The 2022 budget statement committed the Saudi Government to spending SR 135,000m. on health care and social development. In a budget that projected a relatively modest cut in overall spending (6%), the massive budgeted cut in health care and social development seemed hard to reconcile. The size of the planned reduction may have partly been due to definitional issues in that 'social development' (job-related) sounded very different to the conventional understanding of 'social care'. However, it seemed more likely that the above-mentioned PIF state-related spending (see *Budget*) was part of the explanation.

The 2023 budget stated that there would be a 4.5% cut in what Fitch, an international credit ratings agency, in January 2023 called the 'estimated' health care spending out-turn in 2022. Notably, Fitch indicated that the 2022 out-turn estimate was essentially a flatlining on the 2021 actual figure (despite the huge announced cut in the 2022 budget). Fitch warned that the (rather more modest) planned 4.5% cut in 2023 in what is the second largest area of budget spending, health care, could cause problems in terms of planned health care projects (including new hospitals), given high global inflation and supply-chain problems. In the context of a possible global economic downturn, Fitch argued that the Saudi Government would then utilize oil revenues to ensure that there was no threat to the planned health care projects—an obvious outright transgression of Finance Minister Al-Jaadan's declared new rules on fiscal discipline (see *Budget*).

The demand for new homes is exceptionally high, reflecting rising population growth and economic prosperity; private developers estimate that the kingdom requires investment of US $53,300m. over the next two decades to build 1.5m. new housing units for lower- and medium-income families. A report by Banque Saudi Fransi indicated the need for 1.65m. new residential units by 2015, with the burgeoning middle class fuelling much of that demand. Against this background, King Abdullah in March 2011 announced a programme to build 500,000 low-cost public housing units by 2014 (costing SR 251,250m., or US $67,000m.) in order to tackle the sector's chronic shortfall. It was hoped that this scheme would also create demand for retail and commercial facilities to serve new residential developments. The programme did not have public money allocated to it until the King issued a decree in April 2013 and was reportedly under way in 2014. According to local estimates, however, even with 500,000 extra units, the country's housing stock expansion might not be sufficient to meet growing demand. The Real Estate Development Fund (REDF) was expected to disburse about SR 25,125m. ($6,700m.) for low-cost housing schemes—some SR 5,000m. ($1,333m.) had been disbursed by the REDF by mid-2013—and the Saudi Credit and Saving Bank was to receive SR 10,125m. ($2,700m.) to provide cheap mortgages to poorer households. As of July 2015, according to the EIU, the Government's affordable housing programme had made little progress since being announced. Some SR 22,000m. was kept off-budget in 2015, in part for housing expenditure. Alternatively, such outlays, if desired, could have been met from the budget support provision allocation. However, oil revenues continued to be at a historic low, and consequently liquidity and fiscal constraints negatively affected the Saudi housing sector in 2016. It seems likely that the public housing programme was not immune from this. In 2017 and 2018 the housing sector continued to underperform. The ongoing shortage of affordable accommodation, despite expanded public programmes and some success in putting pressure on landowners to release land for private development, via the so-called White Land Tax, was reflected in high purchase and rental prices in the centre of desirable cities, even though rents were falling elsewhere as demand declined, owing to the higher cost of living. The easing of constraints on existing government infrastructure contracts, and the beginning of new contracts, improved the situation in 2019, combined with higher spending on infrastructure and transportation. At about 4%, real growth in the construction sector greatly exceeded that of the wider economy in 2019, and progress was reportedly made on some existing mixed-use real estate development projects.

Although the 2019 budget projected an increase of SR 20,000m. in funding on housing, the Government's capital spending in this area remained below historic trends, According to media reports, in July 2019 measures to facilitate more lending were undertaken by the Saudi Real Estate Refinance Company (SRC), a subsidiary of the PIF. The SRC claimed that a financing deal with Deutsche Gulf Finance (DGF) of Germany would inject SR 2,250m. of liquidity into the Saudi housing market, as part of a scheme whereby the DGF would buy up existing housing loans and operate them for lower profits. The SRC estimates that the Saudi mortgage market will be worth some SR 213,000m. by 2030. The annual shortfall in meeting housing needs was estimated at approximately

SAUDI ARABIA

100,000 by Saudi officials in July 2021. It was stated that the specific number of people being provided with subsidized housing, including cheaper mortgage options, in the first half of 2021 (under the Sakaani Programme set up under SV 2030) was, at 111,568, significantly down from the 187,000 provided for in the same period of 2020. The main reason given for the fall was a delay in supply due to the pandemic. The 2021 budget envisaged another year of sharply reduced capital expenditure, falling by around 26%, which was likely to have a negative impact on state-led housing provision. In 2022 it seemed that much state-related investment would be directed via the PIF and specifically the new infrastructure fund, the NIF (see *Budget*). The 2022 budget report (issued in December 2021) stated that the PIF's own companies were constructing housing and claimed that one of them, Roshn, was involved in a project to build 395,000 units that would house an estimated 2m. people. It was not stated whether these units would be judged 'affordable' or whether their purchase would be subsidized under the Sakaani scheme or some equivalent form of state support. The number of Saudis helped under the Sakaani scheme at the end of 2021 was 210,000, according to the official budget statement for 2022. Notably, this stated that significantly fewer—130,000 Saudis—would be helped to acquire housing units under the Sakaani Programme during 2022. Further cuts to formal state housing provision were incorporated in the 2023 budget as part of the large reduction in expenditure on infrastructure and transportation. As in 2022, it may have been assumed that the PIF's non-fiscal expenditure—and a hoped-for increase in private investment under PPP and other schemes—would pick up not just the shortfall but the growing housing demand.

Statistical Survey

Source (unless otherwise indicated): General Authority for Statistics, POB 3735, Prince Abdulrahman bin Abdulaziz St, Riyadh 11481; tel. (1) 401-4138; fax (1) 405-9493; e-mail info@stats.gov.sa; internet www.stats.gov.sa.

Area and Population

AREA, POPULATION AND DENSITY

Area (sq km)	2,240,000*
Population (census results)	
28 April 2010	27,136,977
10 May 2022†	
Males	19,678,595
Females	12,496,629
Total	32,175,224
Density (per sq km) at 2022 census	14.4

* 864,869 sq miles.

† Of the total population at the 2022 census, 18,792,262 (males 9,434,131, females 9,358,131) were nationals of Saudi Arabia, while 13,382,962 (males 10,244,464, females 3,138,498) were foreign nationals.

Saudi Arabia-Iraq Neutral Zone: The Najdi (Saudi Arabian) frontier with Iraq was defined in the Treaty of Mohammara in May 1922. Later a Neutral Zone of 7,044 sq km was established adjacent to the western tip of the Kuwait frontier. No military or permanent buildings were to be erected in the zone and the nomads of both countries were to have unimpeded access to its pastures and wells. A further agreement concerning the administration of this zone was signed between Iraq and Saudi Arabia in May 1938. In July 1975 Iraq and Saudi Arabia signed an agreement providing for an equal division of the diamond-shaped zone between the two countries, with the border following a straight line through the zone.

Saudi Arabia-Kuwait Neutral Zone: A Convention signed at Uqair in December 1922 fixed the Najdi (Saudi Arabian) boundary with Kuwait. The Convention also established a Neutral Zone of 5,770 sq km immediately to the south of Kuwait in which Saudi Arabia and Kuwait held equal rights. The final agreement on this matter was signed in 1963. Since 1966 the Neutral Zone, or Partitioned Zone as it is sometimes known, has been divided between the two countries and each administers its own half, in practice as an integral part of the state. However, the petroleum deposits in the Zone remain undivided and production from the onshore oil concessions in the Zone is shared equally between the two states' concessionaires.

POPULATION BY AGE AND SEX
(at 2022 census)

	Males	Females	Total
0–14 years	4,019,178	3,867,712	7,886,890
15–64 years	15,190,066	8,236,419	23,426,485
65 years and over	469,351	392,498	861,849
Total	19,678,595	12,496,629	32,175,224

ADMINISTRATIVE REGIONS
(population at 2022 census)

Aseer	2,024,285	Makkah (Mecca)	8,021,463
Al-Bahah	339,174	Najran	592,300
Eastern	5,125,254	Northern Borders	373,577
Ha'il (Hayil)	746,406	Al-Qassim	1,336,179
Al-Jawf	595,822	Ar-Riyadh	8,591,748
Jazan	1,404,997	Tabouk	886,036
Al-Madinah (Medina)	2,137,983	**Total**	32,175,224

PRINCIPAL TOWNS
(population at 2022 census)

Ar-Riyad (Riyadh, royal capital)	6,924,566	Khamis Mushayt (Khamis Mushait)	535,065
Jiddah (Jeddah, administrative capital)	3,712,917	Ha'il (Hayil)	448,623
Makkah (Mecca)	2,385,506	Al-Hufuf	430,105
Al-Madinah (Medina)	1,411,599	Al-Khubar	409,549
Ad-Dammam (Dammam)	1,386,166	Hafar al-Batin	387,096
Tabouk	594,350	Naijran	381,431
Buraydah (Buraidah)	571,320	Abha	334,290
Al-Ta'if	563,282	Al-Jubayl (Al-Jubail)	302,446

BIRTHS AND DEATHS
(UN estimates)

	2019	2020	2021
Birth rate (per 1,000)	18.5	18.2	17.5
Death rate (per 1,000)	2.7	2.9	2.9

Source: UN, *World Population Prospects: The 2022 Revision*.

2018: Total births 510,679 (birth rate 15.3 per 1,000); Total deaths 80,246 (death rate 2.4 per 1,000).

2020: Total marriages 150,117 (crude marriage rate 4.3 per 1,000).

2022 census (12 months preceding census date): Total births 484,719 (crude birth rate 15.1 per 1,000).

Life expectancy (years at birth, official estimates): 77.9 (males 75.3; females 80.9) at 2022 census.

SAUDI ARABIA

ECONOMICALLY ACTIVE POPULATION
(persons aged 15 years and over, labour force survey, July–September 2016)

	Males	Females	Total
Agriculture, hunting, forestry and fishing	556,585	3,434	560,019
Mining and quarrying	169,237	2,242	171,479
Manufacturing	1,034,584	27,142	1,061,726
Electricity, gas and water	130,350	1,149	131,499
Construction	2,004,992	7,053	2,012,045
Wholesale and retail trade	1,742,082	38,458	1,780,540
Restaurants and hotels	377,589	4,756	382,345
Transport and communications	564,337	6,003	570,340
Financial intermediation	135,677	7,597	143,274
Real estate, renting and business activities	616,186	15,777	631,963
Public administration and defence	1,831,557	42,232	1,873,789
Education	666,843	605,405	1,272,248
Health and social work	363,360	189,443	552,803
Other community and personal services	229,494	20,143	249,637
Private households with employed persons	463,555	510,718	974,273
Extraterritorial organizations	7,987	732	8,719
Total employed	10,894,415	1,482,284	12,376,699
Unemployed	292,966	458,845	751,811
Total labour force	11,187,381	1,941,129	13,128,510

2018 (labour force survey, July–September): Total employed 12,688,042; Unemployed 852,769; Total labour force 13,540,811.

2023 (labour force survey, January–March): Total employed 15,363,372 (Saudi nationals 3,870,481, Non-Saudi nationals 11,492,891).

Health and Welfare

KEY INDICATORS

Total fertility rate (children per woman, 2021)	2.4
Under-5 mortality rate (per 1,000 live births, 2021)	6.7
COVID-19: Cumulative confirmed deaths (per 100,000 persons at 30 June 2023)	26.5
COVID-19: Fully vaccinated population (% of total population at 25 April 2023)	69.9
Physicians (per 1,000 head, 2021)	2.8
Hospital beds (per 1,000 head, 2017)	2.2
Domestic health expenditure (2019): US $ per head (PPP)	1,929.7
Domestic health expenditure (2019): % of GDP	3.9
Domestic health expenditure (2019): public (% of total current health expenditure)	69.2
Total carbon dioxide emissions ('000 metric tons, 2019)	523,780
Carbon dioxide emissions per head (metric tons, 2019)	15.3
Human Development Index (2021): ranking	35
Human Development Index (2021): value	0.875

Note: For data on COVID-19 vaccinations, 'fully vaccinated' denotes receipt of all doses specified by approved vaccination regime (Sources: Johns Hopkins University and Our World in Data). Data on health expenditure refer to current general government expenditure in each case. For more information on sources and further definitions for all indicators, see Health and Welfare Statistics: Sources and Definitions section (europaworld.com/credits).

Agriculture

PRINCIPAL CROPS
('000 metric tons)

	2019	2020	2021
Aubergines (Eggplants)	50.3	109.1	112.0
Barley	616.1	438.1	383.3*
Cantaloupes and other melons	44.9	48.2	55.1
Carrots and turnips	13.4	22.0	24.5
Cucumbers and gherkins	66.4	184.9	188.6
Dates	1,539.8	1,541.8	1,565.8
Grapes	117.6	101.6	106.4

—continued	2019	2020	2021
Maize	47.6	59.2	59.0
Mangoes, mangosteens and guavas	86.5	86.5	88.7
Millet	12.7	11.7	12.2
Okra	22.1	23.3	25.3
Olives	357.8	364.5	382.1
Onions, dry	86.9	259.7	298.0
Potatoes	474.1	562.3	578.1
Pumpkins, squash and gourds	66.4	62.5	64.7
Sorghum	116.6	117.4	119.4
Tomatoes	259.9	598.8	620.9
Watermelons	687.7	522.2	624.1
Wheat	500.2	554.6	612.6

* FAO estimate.

Aggregate production ('000 metric tons, may include official, semi-official or estimated data): Total cereals 1,293.6 in 2019, 1,181.8 in 2020, 1,187.2 in 2021; Total fruit (primary) 2,784.2 in 2019, 3,021.5 in 2020, 3,008.1 in 2021; Total roots and tubers 474.1 in 2019, 562.3 in 2020, 578.1 in 2021; Total vegetables (primary) 702.2 in 2019, 1,618.5 in 2020, 1,596.8 in 2021.

Source: FAO.

LIVESTOCK
('000 head, year ending September)

	2019	2020	2021
Asses*	98.7	98.6	98.5
Camels	492.9	500.0*	498.6*
Cattle	567.0	700.0	700.0*
Chickens*	200,740	204,569	208,398
Goats	3,711.2	6,100.0	6,095.8
Sheep	9,419.7	9,423.7*	9,367.3*

* FAO estimate(s).

Source: FAO.

LIVESTOCK PRODUCTS
('000 metric tons, FAO estimates unless otherwise indicated)

	2019	2020	2021
Camel meat	104.0	100.0	108.3
Camel offals, edible	21.2	20.4	22.1
Camels' milk	133.8	135.5	135.3
Cattle hides, fresh	6.2	6.0	5.8
Cattle meat*	43.0	42.0	40.0
Cows' milk†	2,393.8	2,593.8	2,600.0
Chicken meat*	800.0	900.0	910.0
Goat meat	31.4	52.2	52.9
Goats' milk	69.2	96.0	96.0
Goats' skins, fresh	5.6	9.3	9.4
Sheep meat	91.4	91.3	90.6
Sheep offals, edible	18.3	18.3	18.1
Sheep's (Ewes') milk	85.0	85.1	84.8
Sheepskins, fresh	15.7	15.7	15.6
Hen eggs	348.9	351.0	348.2
Wool, greasy	13.7	14.2	14.4

* Unofficial figures.
† Official figures.

Source: FAO.

Forestry

ROUNDWOOD REMOVALS
('000 cubic metres, excl. bark, FAO estimates)

	2019	2020	2021
Total	307.8	314.6	321.4

Source: FAO.

Fishing

(metric tons, live weight)

	2019	2020	2021
Capture	65,477	57,805	67,459
Pink ear emperors	2,706	2,409	2,428
Blue swimming crab	7,605	1,766	2,826
King soldier bream	1,550	1,001	1,003
Emperors (Scavengers)	3,392	5,447	5,799
Spinefeet (Rabbitfishes)	314	653	1,286
Narrow-barred Spanish mackerel	3,258	3,017	3,657
Indian mackerel	1,004	808	1,039
Green tiger prawns	10,640	2,352	3,051
Aquaculture	75,563*	99,907	114,490
Nile tilapia	9,141	21,168	26,334
Barramundi (Giant seaperch)	3,859	18,303	14,000
Gilthead seabream	1,444	10,984	9,800
Whiteleg shrimp	60,891	46,630	60,712
Total catch	141,040*	157,712	181,949

* FAO estimate.
Source: FAO.

Mining

('000 metric tons unless otherwise indicated)

	2019	2020	2021
Crude petroleum (million barrels)*	3,580	3,372	3,331
Silver (kg)	7,123	6,493	6,818†
Gold (kg)	12,593	11,822	12,413†
Salt (unrefined)	2,778	2,220	2,331†
Gypsum (crude)	3,472	3,803	3,993†
Pozzolan	583	930	977

* Including 50% of the total output of the Neutral (Partitioned) Zone, shared with Kuwait.
† Estimate.
Source: Saudi Central Bank, Riyadh.

Natural gas (excluding flared and recycled, million cu m, estimates): 113,100 in 2020; 114,500 in 2021; 120,400 in 2022 (Source: Energy Institute, *Statistical Review of World Energy*).

Industry

SELECTED PRODUCTS
(including 50% of the total output of the Neutral Zone; '000 barrels unless otherwise indicated)

	2019	2020	2021
Motor spirit (petrol) and naphtha	244,427	211,068	262,221
Jet fuel and kerosene	84,723	53,167	45,990
Gas-diesel (distillate fuel) oils	385,754	360,359	407,034
Residual fuel oils	154,538	126,135	154,063
Petroleum bitumen (asphalt)	14,309	12,733	15,292
Liquefied petroleum gas	14,665	12,914	14,003
Cement ('000 metric tons)	44,341	53,418	n.a.
Electrical energy (million kWh sold)	279,678	289,333	301,564

Sources: Saudi Central Bank, Riyadh.

Crude steel ('000 metric tons): 5,461 in 2016; 4,831 in 2017; 5,240 in 2018 (Source: US Geological Survey).

Finance

CURRENCY AND EXCHANGE RATES

Monetary Units:
100 halalah = 20 qurush = 1 Saudi riyal (SR).

Sterling, Dollar and Euro Equivalents (31 May 2023):
£1 sterling = 4.637 riyals;
US $1 = 3.750 riyals;
€1 = 4.006 riyals;
100 Saudi riyals = £21.57 = $26.67 = €24.96.

Exchange Rate: Since June 1986 the official mid-point rate has been fixed at US $1 = 3.75 riyals.

BUDGET
(million riyals)

Revenue	2020	2021	2022
Petroleum revenues	413,049	562,191	857,272
Other revenues	368,785	403,295	410,891
Total	781,834	965,486	1,268,164

Expenditure	2020	2021	2022
Education	205,029	191,908	201,523
Economic resource development	61,463	71,068	76,519
Health and social development	190,372	197,200	226,637
Infrastructure and transport development	59,685	50,993	41,414
Municipal services	47,347	38,563	75,448
Defence and security	204,125	201,891	228,067
Public administration	36,218	34,165	40,867
Public programme unit	156,439	146,659	159,137
Security and Regional Administration	115,057	106,486	114,696
Total	1,075,734	1,038,933	1,164,309

Source: Saudi Central Bank, Riyadh.

INTERNATIONAL RESERVES
(US $ million in December)

	2020	2021	2022
Gold (national valuation)	433	433	433
IMF special drawing rights	8,392	21,584	20,606
Reserve position in IMF	3,637	3,904	3,921
Foreign exchange	441,178	429,497	434,880
Total	453,640	455,418	459,840

Source: IMF, *International Financial Statistics*.

MONEY SUPPLY
('000 million riyals at 31 December)

	2020	2021	2022
Currency outside banks	206.28	204.37	199.97
Demand deposits at commercial banks	1,282.59	1,360.11	1,328.16
Time and savings deposits	473.97	495.33	654.76
Other deposits	186.43	249.01	312.48
Broad money	2,149.27	2,308.82	2,495.37

Source: Saudi Central Bank, Riyadh.

COST OF LIVING
(Consumer Price Index for all cities; base: 2018 = 100)

	2020	2021	2022
Food and beverages	111.3	117.3	121.6
Clothing and footwear	101.5	103.7	102.4
Housing, fuel and water	90.8	88.6	90.2
All items (incl. others)	101.3	104.4	107.0

SAUDI ARABIA

NATIONAL ACCOUNTS
(million riyals at current prices)

Expenditure on the Gross Domestic Product

	2020	2021*	2022*
Government final consumption expenditure	769,834	780,328	844,957
Private final consumption expenditure	1,218,702	1,382,826	1,483,106
Increase in stocks	98,944	25,913	93,857
Gross fixed capital formation	663,546	792,559	1,039,586
Total domestic expenditure	2,751,026	2,981,625	3,461,505
Exports of goods and services	685,680	1,074,381	1,658,809
Less Imports of goods and services	683,189	798,809	964,757
GDP in purchasers' values	2,753,517	3,257,197	4,155,559
GDP at constant 2010 prices	2,632,363	2,735,597	2,974,802

Gross Domestic Product by Economic Activity

	2020	2021*	2022*
Agriculture, forestry and fishing	81,511	87,840	99,976
Mining and quarrying:			
crude petroleum and natural gas	522,226	787,083	1,357,279
other	13,388	15,317	17,664
Manufacturing:			
petroleum refining	81,974	132,845	251,150
other	266,012	308,167	358,902
Electricity, gas and water	42,779	42,981	44,302
Construction	160,449	169,990	186,791
Trade, restaurants and hotels	277,761	312,899	340,028
Transport, storage and communications	164,223	173,032	197,360
Finance, insurance, real estate and business services:			
ownership of dwellings	206,332	210,911	216,529
other	155,806	160,452	182,690
Government services	576,972	577,633	591,183
Other community, social and personal services	86,815	80,193	101,144
Sub-total	2,636,247	3,059,342	3,944,999
Net taxes on products	117,270	197,855	210,560
GDP in purchasers' values	2,753,517	3,257,197	4,155,559

*Preliminary.

BALANCE OF PAYMENTS
(US $ million, preliminary)

	2020	2021	2022
Exports of goods	173,864	276,198	410,676
Imports of goods	−125,920	−139,735	−175,989
Balance on goods	47,944	136,464	234,688
Exports of services	8,984	10,303	31,893
Imports of services	−56,264	−73,281	−82,801
Balance on goods and services	664	73,486	183,780
Primary income received	21,725	27,671	26,469
Primary income paid	−7,777	−12,462	−15,376
Balance on goods, services and Primary income	14,612	88,695	194,873
Secondary income paid	−37,427	−44,371	−44,120
Current balance	−22,814	44,324	150,753
Capital account (net)	−1,845	−1,318	−2,461
Direct investment assets	−4,911	−23,860	−18,826
Direct investment from liabilities	5,399	19,286	7,886
Portfolio investment assets	−53,552	−55,631	−49,737
Portfolio investment liabilities	29,862	17,097	12,797
Other investment assets	−4,879	−22,276	−77,529
Other investment liabilities	6,211	25,522	−9,698
Net errors and omissions	608	−1,429	−8,706
Reserves and related items	−45,920	1,715	4,480

Source: Saudi Central Bank, Riyadh.

External Trade

PRINCIPAL COMMODITIES
(distribution by SITC, million riyals)

Imports c.i.f.	2020	2021	2022
Food and live animals	76,071	76,281	98,024
Cereals and cereal preparations	20,371	20,087	28,046
Mineral fuels, lubricants and related materials	15,979	27,704	53,540
Chemicals and related products	61,309	69,335	82,937
Medicinal and pharmaceutical products	21,716	24,898	24,966
Basic manufactures	78,716	82,458	103,375
Iron and steel	23,492	25,731	31,757
Non-ferrous metals	11,594	13,552	17,322
Machinery and transport equipment	183,214	193,382	238,036
Power generating machinery and equipment	10,119	10,093	17,643
Machinery specialized for particular industries	10,271	12,116	15,966
General industrial machinery equipment and parts	30,339	28,731	34,180
Telecommunications and sound recording and reproducing apparatus and equipment	28,610	31,030	31,331
Electrical machinery, apparatus, etc.	20,245	21,165	26,247
Road vehicles and parts	53,469	57,526	72,168
Miscellaneous manufactured articles	73,118	82,945	82,484
Total (incl. others)	517,491	573,185	712,038

Exports f.o.b.	2020	2021	2022
Mineral fuels, lubricants, etc.	447,738	758,218	1,226,284
Petroleum, petroleum products and related materials	435,640	740,503	1,198,593
Natural gas, manufactured	12,097	17,713	27,690
Chemicals and related products	117,983	171,477	197,995
Organic chemicals	36,783	53,930	60,962
Plastics in primary form	58,132	84,478	81,867
Basic manufactures	21,704	27,088	28,383
Machinery and transport equipment	30,414	38,379	40,824
Total (incl. others)	651,952	1,035,672	1,541,941

PRINCIPAL TRADING PARTNERS
(million riyals)

Imports c.i.f.	2020	2021	2022
Australia	2,464	5,922	7,202
Bahrain	6,950	9,747	12,141
Belgium	4,971	7,235	6,575
Brazil	8,334	9,224	13,598
Canada	6,952	7,640	4,857
China, People's Republic	101,562	113,381	149,252
Egypt	10,129	15,781	24,827
France (incl. Monaco)	17,371	15,988	16,714
Germany	26,869	28,093	30,000
India	24,530	30,277	39,509
Indonesia	6,810	7,254	11,073
Italy	15,926	17,244	19,431
Japan	21,767	22,732	25,195
Korea, Republic	14,725	12,899	19,767
Netherlands	6,646	7,875	8,589
Oman	6,253	6,708	15,831
Poland	5,241	5,318	5,339
Russian Federation	5,182	5,391	8,141

SAUDI ARABIA

Statistical Survey

Imports c.i.f.—continued	2020	2021	2022
Singapore	5,197	3,558	7,871
Spain	8,152	8,880	10,447
Switzerland (incl. Liechtenstein)	5,645	8,246	17,719
Thailand	8,530	8,756	10,858
Türkiye	9,341	486	2,956
United Arab Emirates	34,287	46,770	45,103
United Kingdom	11,922	13,764	15,570
USA	55,145	60,549	65,002
Viet Nam	4,588	5,446	7,805
Total (incl. others)	517,491	573,185	712,038

Exports (incl. re-exports)	2020	2021	2022
Bahrain	17,417	26,341	37,015
Belgium	11,955	18,371	25,949
Brazil	5,175	11,871	16,709
China, People's Republic	120,016	190,911	249,926
Egypt	18,896	38,710	51,711
France (incl. Monaco)	5,903	14,766	28,397
India	60,208	99,966	157,187
Indonesia	8,721	14,067	19,535
Italy	10,480	19,298	24,284
Japan	62,307	102,598	152,890
Jordan	7,454	11,692	16,212
Korea, Republic	54,379	87,342	142,159
Malaysia	9,549	9,283	31,512
Netherlands	17,183	16,204	24,469
Oman	4,331	4,434	22,621
Pakistan	7,102	13,945	19,507
Poland	5,402	10,297	31,317
Singapore	20,171	26,426	37,337
South Africa	8,192	14,827	16,095
Spain	8,314	11,420	18,576
Taiwan	15,577	26,337	39,126
Thailand	12,299	18,116	26,094
Türkiye	10,124	16,151	19,113
United Arab Emirates	44,349	56,481	66,783
USA	31,024	53,517	87,117
Total (incl. others)	651,950	1,035,672	1,541,941

Transport

RAILWAYS
(traffic)

	2017	2018	2019
Passenger journeys ('000)	1,485	1,577	1,805
Passenger-km (million)	447	465	518
Freight carried ('000 metric tons)	3,690	3,430	3,620
Net freight ton-km (million)	2,074	1,943	2,012

SHIPPING

Flag Registered Fleet
(at 31 December)

	2020	2021	2022
Number of vessels	533	554	596
Total displacement ('000 grt)	7,902.8	8,083.2	7,809.8

Source: Lloyd's List Intelligence (www.bit.ly/LLintelligence).

International Seaborne Freight Traffic
('000 metric tons, excluding crude oil)

	2018	2019	2020
Goods loaded	159,058	156,126	198,327
Goods unloaded	108,038	106,190	100,706

Source: Saudi Ports Authority, Riyadh.

CIVIL AVIATION
(Saudi Arabian airlines)

	2020	2021	2022
Aircraft movements	87,637	138,097	168,143
Domestic	62,451	104,827	102,668
International	25,186	33,270	65,475
Passengers carried (million)	11.1	15.1	24.8
Domestic	7.0	10.6	12.7
International	4.2	4.5	12.1
Cargo carried ('000 metric tons)	450	525	585

Source: Saudi Central Bank, Riyadh.

Tourism

Country of nationality	2019	2020	2021
Algeria	433,350	53,226	2,324
Bahrain	510,900	99,854	239,947
Bangladesh	472,388	81,748	69,203
Egypt	1,099,854	431,790	308,253
India	1,571,070	338,965	316,488
Indonesia	1,428,935	293,291	11,467
Jordan	836,678	242,834	196,898
Kuwait	2,132,114	629,240	623,462
Malaysia	411,971	80,514	19,654
Oman	260,550	100,789	70,146
Pakistan	2,210,877	483,290	257,640
Qatar	46,152	10,372	254,013
Sudan	316,683	87,666	153,844
Syrian Arab Republic	26,573	70,698	160,372
Türkiye	478,615	176,999	2,609
United Arab Emirates	784,305	165,716	94,927
United Kingdom	355,266	78,655	54,125
USA	893,981	121,347	61,084
Total (incl. others)	17,525,620	4,138,178	3,477,216

Tourism receipts (US $ million, excl. passenger transport): 4,036 in 2020; 3,817 in 2021 (provisional); 23,475 in 2022 (provisional).

Source: World Tourism Organization.

PILGRIMS TO MECCA FROM ABROAD

	2019*	2022†	2023‡
Total	1,855,027	781,409	1,660,915

* Figure for Islamic year 1440 (11 September 2018 to 31 August 2019).
† Figure for Islamic year 1443 (10 August 2021 to 30 July 2022).
‡ Figure for Islamic year 1444 (31 July 2022 to 19 July 2023).

Note: Numbers of foreign pilgrims were severely restricted by international travel restrictions imposed as part of efforts to address the global COVID-19 pandemic during Islamic years 1441 and 1442.

SAUDI ARABIA

Communications Media

	2019	2020	2021
Telephones ('000 main lines in use)	5,378.0	5,749.1	6,594.6
Mobile telephone subscriptions ('000)	41,298.6	43,215.4	45,427.3
Broadband subscriptions, fixed ('000)	6,801.9	7,890.3	10,588.2
Broadband subscriptions, mobile ('000)	40,052.3	41,379.6	42,974.7
Internet users (% of population)	95.7	97.9	100.0

Source: International Telecommunication Union.

Education

(2021/22 unless otherwise indicated)

	Institutions	Teachers	Students
Pre-primary*	3,807	25,638	295,285
Primary	13,073	234,751	3,138,791
Intermediate	8,278	120,371	1,483,324
Secondary (general)	5,402	114,615	1,377,784
Special†	2,090	10,402	26,942
Adult education‡	2,132	1,601	58,941
Technical and vocational	283	11,232	262,225
Higher	n.a.	65,531	1,220,686

* 2017/18 figures.
† 2013/14 figures.
‡ 2014/15 figures.

Source: Ministry of Education, Riyadh; Saudi Central Bank, Riyadh.

Pupil-teacher ratio (qualified teaching staff, primary education, UNESCO estimate): 14.8 in 2020/21 (Source: UNESCO Institute for Statistics).

Adult literacy rate (UNESCO estimates): 97.6% (males 98.6%; females 96.1%) in 2020 (Source: UNESCO Institute for Statistics).

Directory

The Constitution

The Basic Law of Government was introduced by royal decree in 1992.

Chapter 1 defines Saudi Arabia as a sovereign Arab, Islamic state. Article 1 defines God's Book and the Sunnah of his prophet as the constitution of Saudi Arabia. The official language is Arabic. The official holidays are Id al-Fitr and Id al-Adha. The calendar is the Hegira calendar.

Chapter 2 concerns the system of government, which is defined as a monarchy, hereditary in the male descendants of Abd al-Aziz bin Abd al-Rahman al-Faisal Al Sa'ud. It outlines the duties of the Heir Apparent. The principles of government are justice, consultation and equality in accordance with Islamic law (*Shari'a*).

Chapter 3 concerns the family. The State is to aspire to strengthen family ties and to maintain its Arab and Islamic values. Article 11 states that 'Saudi society will be based on the principle of adherence to God's command, on mutual co-operation in good deeds and piety and mutual support and inseparability'. Education aims to instil the Islamic faith.

Chapter 4 defines the economic principles of the State. All natural resources are the property of the State. The State protects public money and freedom of property. Taxation is only to be imposed on a just basis.

Chapter 5 concerns rights and duties. The State is to protect Islam and to implement the *Shari'a* law. The State protects human rights in accordance with the *Shari'a*. The State is to provide public services and security for all citizens. Punishment is to be in accordance with the *Shari'a*. The Royal Courts are open to all citizens.

Chapter 6 defines the authorities of the State as the judiciary, the executive and the regulatory authority. The judiciary is independent, and acts in accordance with *Shari'a* law. The King is head of the Council of Ministers and Commander-in-Chief of the Armed Forces. The Prime Minister and other ministers are appointed by the King. It provides for the establishment of a Majlis al-Shura (Consultative Council).

Chapter 7 concerns financial affairs. It provides for the annual presentation of a state budget. Corporate budgets are subject to the same provisions.

Chapter 8 concerns control bodies. Control bodies will be established to ensure good financial and administrative management of state assets.

Chapter 9 defines the general provisions pertaining to the application of the Basic Law of Government.

The Government

HEAD OF STATE

King: HM King SALMAN BIN ABDULAZIZ AL SA'UD (acceded to the throne 23 January 2015).

COUNCIL OF MINISTERS
(September 2023)

Prime Minister: Crown Prince MOHAMMED BIN SALMAN BIN ABDULAZIZ AL SA'UD.

Minister of Defence: Prince KHALID BIN SALMAN BIN ABDULAZIZ AL SA'UD.

Minister of the Interior: Prince ABDULAZIZ BIN SA'UD BIN NAYEF AL SA'UD.

Minister of the National Guard: Prince ABDULLAH BIN BANDAR BIN ABDULAZIZ AL SA'UD.

Minister of Culture: Prince BADR BIN ABDULLAH BIN MOHAMMED BIN FARHAN AL SA'UD.

Minister of Islamic Affairs, Dawa (Call) and Guidance: Dr ABDULLATIF BIN ABDULAZIZ BIN ABDULRAHMAN AL-SHEIKH.

Minister of Justice: Dr WALEED BIN MOHAMMED AL-SAMAANI.

Minister of Foreign Affairs: Prince FAISAL BIN FARHAN AL SA'UD.

Minister of Health: FAHAD AL-JALAJEL.

Minister of Commerce: Dr MAJID BIN ABDULLAH AL-QASABI.

Minister of Media: SALMAN AL-DOSARI.

Minister of Environment, Water and Agriculture: Eng. ABDULRAHMAN AL-FADHLI.

Minister of Energy: Prince ABDULAZIZ BIN SALMAN BIN ABDULAZIZ AL SA'UD.

Minister of Municipal and Rural Affairs, and Housing: MAJID BIN ABDULLAH BIN HAMAD AL-HOGAIL.

Minister of Hajj and Umrah: Dr TAWFIQ BIN FAWZAN BIN MOHAMMED AL-RABEEAH.

Minister of Finance: MOHAMMED BIN ABDULLAH BIN ABDULAZIZ AL-JADAAN.

Minister of Economy and Planning: FAISAL BIN FADEL BIN MOHSEN AL-IBRAHIM.

Minister of Communications and Information Technology: Eng. ABDULLAH BIN AMER AL-SAWAHA.

Minister of Transport: Eng. SALEH BIN NASSER BIN ALI AL-JASSER.

Minister of Human Resources and Social Development: Eng. AHMED BIN SULAIMAN BIN ABDULAZIZ AL-RAJHI.

Minister of Education: YOUSEF BIN ABDULLAH BIN MOHAMMED AL-BENYAN.

Minister of Industry and Mineral Resources: Eng. BANDAR BIN IBRAHIM AL-KHORAYEF.

Minister of Investment: Eng. KHALID BIN ABDULAZIZ AL-FALIH.

Minister of Tourism: AHMAD BIN AQIL AL-KHATIB.

Minister of Sports: Prince ABDULAZIZ BIN TURKI BIN FAISAL AL SA'UD.

Minister of State for Consultative Council Affairs: Dr ISSAM BIN SAAD BIN SAEED.

SAUDI ARABIA

MINISTRIES

Most ministries have regional offices in Jeddah.

Council of Ministers: Murabba, Riyadh 11121; tel. (11) 488-2444.

Ministry of Commerce: Riyadh 11162; tel. (11) 401-2222; fax (11) 403-3481; e-mail CS@mci.gov.sa; internet mci.gov.sa.

Ministry of Communications and Information Technology: Intercontinental Rd, Riyadh 11112; tel. (11) 452-2222; fax (11) 452-2220; e-mail info@mcit.gov.sa; internet www.mcit.gov.sa.

Ministry of Culture: Riyadh.

Ministry of Defence: Riyadh 11165; tel. (11) 478-9000; fax (11) 402-6457; internet www.moda.gov.sa.

Ministry of Economy and Planning: POB 358, University St, al-Malaz, Riyadh 11182; tel. (11) 401-1444; fax (11) 404-9473; e-mail info@mep.gov.sa; internet www.mep.gov.sa.

Ministry of Education: POB 225085, King Abdullah Rd, Riyadh 11153; tel. (11) 475-3000; fax (11) 441-9004; internet www.moe.gov.sa.

Ministry of Energy: POB 247, Riyadh 11191; tel. (11) 478-7777; fax (11) 476-9017; e-mail webmaster@mopm.gov.sa; internet www.mopm.gov.sa.

Ministry of Environment, Water and Agriculture: POB 7878, Riyadh 11195; tel. (11) 401-6666; fax (11) 403-1415; e-mail moait@moa.gov.sa; internet www.mewa.gov.sa.

Ministry of Finance: Airport Rd, Riyadh 11177; tel. (11) 405-0000; fax (11) 403-3130; e-mail ccc@mof.gov.sa; internet www.mof.gov.sa.

Ministry of Foreign Affairs: POB 55937, Riyadh 11544; tel. (11) 4067777; fax (11) 403-0645; e-mail info@mofa.gov.sa; internet www.mofa.gov.sa.

Ministry of Hajj and Umrah: POB 2475, Jeddah 11183; tel. (800) 430-4444; e-mail hajcc@haj.gov.sa; internet www.haj.gov.sa.

Ministry of Health: Abd al-Aziz St, Riyadh 11176; tel. (11) 212-5555; fax (11) 402-9876; e-mail 937@moh.gov.sa; internet www.moh.gov.sa.

Ministry of Human Resources and Social Development: Al Imam Saud bin Abdul Aziz Branch Rd, Exit 9, POB 12484, Riyadh 11157; tel. (11) 200-6666; fax (11) 478-9175; e-mail info@mlsd.gov.sa; internet mlsd.gov.sa.

Ministry of Industry and Mineral Resources: Riyadh.

Ministry of the Interior: POB 1261, Riyadh 11431; tel. (11) 401-1111; fax (11) 403-3125; e-mail info@moi.gov.sa; internet www.moi.gov.sa.

Ministry of Investment: POB 5927, Riyadh 11432; tel. (11) 203-5777; fax (11) 263-2894; e-mail info@sagia.gov.sa; internet www.sagia.gov.sa.

Ministry of Islamic Affairs, Dawa (Call) and Guidance: King Fahd Rd, Riyadh 11232; tel. (11) 223-6222; fax (11)477-2938; e-mail info@moia.gov.sa; internet www.moia.gov.sa.

Ministry of Justice: POB 7775, Riyadh 11137; tel. (11) 405-7777; fax (11) 405-5399; e-mail info@moj.gov.sa; internet www.moj.gov.sa.

Ministry of Media: King Fahad Rd, al-Ageeq District, Riyadh; tel. (11) 297-4700; e-mail info@media.gov.sa; internet www.media.gov.sa.

Ministry of Municipal and Rural Affairs, and Housing: POB 955, Riyadh 11136; tel. (11) 456-9999; fax (11) 456-3196; e-mail minister_office@momra.gov.sa; internet www.momra.gov.sa.

Ministry of the National Guard: Riyadh 11173; tel. (11) 491-2222; fax (11) 499-4457; internet www.sang.gov.sa.

Ministry of Sports: Al Jamiah St, Riyadh 12641; tel. (11) 476-8917; e-mail info@gsa.gov.sa; internet gsa.gov.sa.

Ministry of Tourism and National Heritage: POB 66680, Riyadh 11586; tel. (11) 880-8855; fax (11) 880-8844; e-mail info@scth.gov.sa; internet www.scth.gov.sa.

Ministry of Transport: King Abdulaziz Rd, Riyadh 11178; tel. (11) 874-4444; fax (11) 874-4588; e-mail mot@mot.gov.sa; internet www.mot.gov.sa.

Majlis al-Shura (Consultative Council)

Al-Yamamh Palace, Riyadh 11212; tel. (11) 482-1666; fax (11) 481-6985; e-mail webmaster@shura.gov.sa; internet www.shura.gov.sa.

In March 1992 King Fahd issued a decree to establish a Consultative Council of 60 members, whose powers include the right to summon and question ministers. The Council, whose members are appointed by the King and serve a term of four years, was inaugurated in December 1993. The Council's membership was increased to 90 when its second term began in July 1997; it was expanded further, to 120, in May 2001, and to 150 in April 2005. King Fahd issued a decree extending the legislative powers of the Council in November 2003, including the right to propose new legislation.

Chairman: Dr ABDULLAH BIN MOHAMMED BIN IBRAHIM AL-SHEIKH.

Political Organizations

There are no political organizations in Saudi Arabia.

Diplomatic Representation

EMBASSIES IN SAUDI ARABIA

Afghanistan: POB 93337, Riyadh 11673; tel. (11) 480-3459; fax (11) 480-3451; e-mail afgembriyad@hotmail.com; Ambassador AHMED JAVED MUJADIDI.

Albania: POB 94004, al-Fazari Plaza, Unit No. G16, Diplomatic Quarter, Riyadh 11693; tel. (11) 281-6535; fax (11) 281-6536; e-mail embassy.riyadh@mfa.gov.al; internet www.ambasadat.gov.al/saudi-arabia; Ambassador SAMI SHIBA.

Algeria: POB 94388, Riyadh 11693; tel. (11) 488-7171; fax (11) 482-1703; e-mail Mail@algerianembassy-saudi.com; internet algerianembassy-saudi.com; Ambassador (vacant).

Angola: Riyadh; Ambassador FREDERICO MANUEL DOS SANTOS E SILVA CARDOSO.

Argentina: POB 94369, Villa 4, Habib al-Handali Rd, Olaya District, Riyadh 11693; tel. (11) 465-2600; fax (11) 465-3075; e-mail earab@mrecic.gov.ar; internet earab.mrecic.gov.ar; Ambassador GUILLERMO NIELSEN.

Australia: POB 94400, Abdullah bin Hozafa al-Sahmi Ave, Diplomatic Quarter, Riyadh 11693; tel. (11) 250-0900; fax (11) 250-0902; internet www.saudiarabia.embassy.gov.au; Ambassador MARK DONOVAN.

Austria: POB 94373, Diplomatic Quarter, Riyadh 11693; tel. (11) 480-1217; fax (11) 480-1526; e-mail riyadh-ob@bmeia.gv.at; internet www.bmeia.gv.at/riyadh; Ambassador (vacant).

Azerbaijan: POB 94005, Villa B804, Dareen St, Riyadh 11693; tel. (11) 419-2382; fax (11) 419-2260; e-mail riyadh@mission.mfa.gov.az; internet riyadh.mfa.gov.az; Ambassador SHAHIN ABDULLAYEV.

Bahrain: POB 94371, Riyadh 11693; tel. (11) 488-0044; fax (11) 488-0208; e-mail riyadh.mission@mofa.gov.bh; internet www.mofa.gov.bh/riyadh; Ambassador Sheikh ALI BIN ABDULRAHMAN BIN ALI AL KHALIFA.

Bangladesh: POB 94395, 8039 Dareen St, Riyadh 11693; tel. (11) 419-5300; fax (11) 419-3555; e-mail mission.riyadh@mofa.gov.bd; internet www.bangladeshembassy.org.sa; Ambassador MOHAMMAD JAVED PATWARY.

Belgium: POB 94396, Main Rd 2, House A2, Diplomatic Quarter, Riyadh 11693; tel. (11) 488-2888; fax (11) 488-2033; e-mail riyadh@diplobel.fed.be; internet saudiarabia.diplomatie.belgium.be; Ambassador PASCAL H. GRÉGOIRE.

Benin: POB 94013, Villa 10, Abi Ishaq al-Harbi St, King Fahad District, Riyadh 11693; tel. (11) 2290193; fax (11) 2290148; Ambassador ADAM BAGOUDOU.

Bosnia and Herzegovina: POB 94301, 10 Ghazi bin Qis St, Riyadh 11693; tel. (11) 456-7914; fax (11) 454-4360; e-mail baembsaruh@hotmail.com; Ambassador (vacant).

Brazil: POB 94348, 3 Dareen St, Diplomatic Area, Riyadh 11693; tel. (11) 488-0018; fax (11) 488-1073; e-mail brasemb.riade@itamaraty.gov.br; internet www.gov.br/mre/pt-br/embaixada-riade; Ambassador SERGIO BATH.

Brunei Darussalam: POB 94314, 29 al-Fujairah St, al-Warood Area, Riyadh 11693; tel. (11) 456-0814; fax (11) 456-1594; e-mail riyadh.arabsaudi@mfa.gov.bn; Ambassador Dato' Seri Setia Haji AWANG YUSOFF BIN Haji AWANG ISMAIL.

Bulgaria: 4067 Dareen St, Bldg B-53, Assafarat District (Diplomatic Quarter), Riyadh 12512; tel. (11) 251–1553; e-mail embassy.riyadh@mfa.bg; internet www.mfa.bg/en/embassies/saudiarabia; Ambassador LUBOMIR POPOV.

Burkina Faso: POB 94330, Riyadh 11693; tel. (11) 465-2244; fax (11) 465-3397; e-mail burkinafaso.ksa@arab.net.sa; Ambassador (vacant).

Burundi: POB 94355, 29 Asad al-Kenani St, Ali Mursalat District, Riyadh 11693; tel. (11) 269-4855; e-mail burundi.embassyriyadh@yahoo.com; Ambassador NAHAYO JACQUES YA'COUB.

Cameroon: POB 94336, Riyadh 11693; tel. (11) 488-0022; fax (11) 488-1463; e-mail ambacamriyad@yahoo.fr; internet www.ambacamsaudi.org; Ambassador IYA TIDJANI.

Canada: POB 94321, Riyadh 11693; e-mail ryadh.general@international.gc.ca; internet www.canadainternational.gc.ca/saudi_arabia-arabie_saoudite; Ambassador JEAN-PHILIPPE LINTEAU.

Chad: POB 94374, al-Murabah Area, Riyadh 11693; tel. (11) 405-5999; fax (11) 405-0403; Ambassador HASSAN SALEH ALGADAM ALDJINEDI.

SAUDI ARABIA

China, People's Republic: POB 75231, Riyadh 11578; tel. (11) 483-2126; fax (11) 281-2070; e-mail chinaemb_sa@mfa.gov.cn; internet sa.china-embassy.gov.cn; Ambassador CHEN WEIQING.

Comoros: POB 94379, Villa 11, al-Olaya al-Taghlabi St, Riyadh 11693; tel. (11) 293-6002; fax (11) 293-4797; e-mail ambassadeuniondescomores@yahoo.com; Ambassador HABIB ABBAS ABDULLAH.

Côte d'Ivoire: POB 94303, 10 Abdurahman al-Tubashi, al-Rahmania, Riyadh 11693; tel. (11) 470-8387; fax (11) 470-8507; e-mail acisa@ambaci-riyadh.org; internet arabiesaoudite.diplomatie.gouv.ci; Ambassador DRISSA COULIBALY.

Cuba: POB 52336, al-Souban St, cnr Prince Mansour bin Abd al-Aziz, Olaya District, Riyadh 11563; tel. (11) 464-2492; fax (11) 466-4612; e-mail embacubarabia@nesma.net.sa; internet misiones.minrex.gob.cu/en/saudi-arabia; Ambassador VLADIMIR GONZALEZ QUESADA.

Cyprus: 6345 Prince Faisal bin Saad bin Abd al-Rahman, al-Woroud District, Riyadh 12251-3052; tel. (11) 460-2203; fax (11) 460-2212; e-mail cyprusvisariyadh@gmail.com; internet www.fb.com/cyprusinksa; Ambassador STAVROS AVGOUSTIDES.

Czech Republic: POB 94305, Saad Bin Gharir St, al-Nuzha District, Riyadh 11693; tel. (11) 4503617; fax (11) 5409879; e-mail riyadh@embassy.mzv.cz; internet www.mzv.cz/riyadh; Ambassador PAVEL KAFKA (designate).

Denmark: POB 94398, Main Rd One, Riyadh 11693; tel. (11) 488-0101; fax (11) 488-1366; e-mail ruhamb@um.dk; internet saudiarabien.um.dk; Ambassador LISELOTTE PLESNER.

Djibouti: POB 94340, Riyadh 11693; tel. (11) 454-3182; fax (11) 456-9168; e-mail dya_bamakhrama@hotmail.com; Ambassador DYA-EDDINE SAID BAMAKHRAMA (concurrent ambassador to Yemen).

Egypt: POB 94333, Abdullah bin Sahmi St, Diplomatic Quarter, Riyadh 11693; tel. (11) 481-0464; fax (11) 481-0463; internet www.fb.com/egyptian.consulate.in.riyadh; Ambassador AHMED FAROUK MOHAMED TAWFIQ.

Equatorial Guinea: Riyadh; Ambassador BENIGNO PEDRO MATUTE TANG.

Eritrea: POB 94002, Ummal Hammam Prince Turki bin Abdulaziz Rd, Riyadh 11693; tel. (11) 480-1726; fax (11) 482-7537; e-mail erembassy@erembassy.com; Chargé d'affaires WEINI GEREZGIHER.

Ethiopia: POB 94341, Abu Bakr al-Karkhi, Safarat Diplomatic Quarter, Riyadh 11693; tel. (11) 482-4056; fax (11) 482-3821; e-mail ethiopion@awal.net.sa; internet ethiopianembassyriyadh.org; Ambassador LENCHO AYELE BATI.

Finland: POB 94363, Riyadh 11693; tel. (11) 488-1515; fax (11) 488-2520; e-mail sanomat.ria@formin.fi; internet www.finland.org.sa; Ambassador ANU-EERIKA VILJANEN.

France: POB 94367, Riyadh 11693; tel. (11) 434-4100; fax (11) 434-4179; e-mail admin-francais.riyad-amba@diplomatie.gouv.fr; internet www.ambafrance-sa.org; Ambassador LUDOVIC POUILLE.

Gabon: POB 94325, al-Morsalat Q. bin Tofiel St, Riyadh 11693; tel. (11) 456-7173; fax (11) 453-6121; e-mail ambagabonriyad@yahoo.com; Ambassador GUY IBRAHIM MEMBOUROU.

The Gambia: POB 94322, 88–2 Dareen St, Riyadh 11693; tel. (11) 205-2158; fax (11) 456-2024; e-mail gamextriyadh@yahoo.com; Ambassador OMAR GIBRIL SALLAH.

Georgia: POB 94419, 60 Prince Faisal bin Saad bin Abdulrahman St, al-Woroud District, Riyadh; tel. (11) 400-2841; fax (11) 400-5982; e-mail riyadh.emb@mfa.gov.ge; Ambassador VAKHTANG JAOSHVILI.

Germany: POB 94001, Riyadh 11693; tel. (11) 277-6900; fax (11) 488-0660; e-mail info@riad.diplo.de; internet saudiarabien.diplo.de; Ambassador MICHAEL KINDSGRAB.

Ghana: POB 94339, 7885 Prince Ahmed bin Abdul Rahman bin Faisal St, al-Sulaimanyah, Riyadh 11693; tel. (11) 454-5126; fax (11) 450-9819; e-mail info@ghanaembassyksa.com; internet ghanaembassy-saudiarabia.com; Ambassador Alhaji MOHAMMED HABIB TIJANI.

Greece: POB 94375, Riyadh 11693; tel. (11) 480-1975; fax (11) 480-1969; e-mail gremb.ria@mfa.gr; internet www.mfa.gr/saudi-arabia; Ambassador ALEXIS KONSTANTOPOULOS.

Guinea: POB 94326, Riyadh 11693; tel. (11) 488-1101; fax (11) 482-6757; e-mail riydambagunee@yahoo.fr; Ambassador MAHMOUD NABANIOU CHERIF.

Guinea-Bissau: Riyadh; Ambassador DINO SEIDI.

Hungary: POB 94014, al-Waha District, Ahmad al-Tunisi St 23, Riyadh 11693; tel. (11) 454-6707; fax (11) 456-0834; e-mail mission.ryd@mfa.gov.hu; internet rijad.mfa.gov.hu; Ambassador BALAZS SELMECI.

India: POB 94387, Riyadh 11693; tel. (11) 488-4144; fax (11) 488-4189; e-mail info@indianembassy.org.sa; internet www.eoiriyadh.gov.in; Ambassador SUHEL AJAZ KHAN.

Indonesia: POB 94343, Riyadh 11693; tel. (11) 488-2800; fax (11) 488-2966; e-mail riyadh.kbri@kemlu.go.id; internet www.kemlu.go.id/riyadh; Ambassador ABDUL AZIZ AHMAD.

Iran: Riyadh; Ambassador ALIREZA ENAYATI (designate).

Iraq: POB 94345, Riyadh 11693; tel. (11) 480-6514; fax (11) 481-6671; e-mail rydemt@iraqmfamail.com; internet www.mofa.gov.iq/riyadh; Ambassador SAFIA TALEB AL-SUHAIL.

Ireland: POB 94349, Riyadh 11693; tel. (11) 488-2300; fax (11) 488-0927; e-mail riyadhembassy@dfa.ie; internet www.dfa.ie/irish-embassy/saudi-arabia/; Ambassador GERRY CUNNINGHAM.

Italy: POB 94389, 3639 Amr Aldamri St, Diplomatic Quarter, Riyadh 11693; tel. (11) 488-1212; fax (11) 480-6964; e-mail segreteria.riad@esteri.it; internet www.ambriad.esteri.it; Ambassador ROBERTO CANTONE.

Japan: POB 4095, Riyadh 11491; tel. (11) 488-1100; fax (11) 488-0189; e-mail info@jpn-emb-sa.com; internet www.ksa.emb-japan.go.jp; Ambassador IWAI FUMIO.

Jordan: POB 94316, Riyadh 11693; tel. (11) 488-0051; fax (11) 488-0072; e-mail jordan.embassy@nesma.net.sa; Ambassador ALI HASSAN AL-KAYED.

Kazakhstan: POB 94012, 6691 Amr al-Damri, al-Safarat, Riyadh 11693; tel. (11) 480-6406; fax (11) 480-9106; e-mail riyadh@mfa.kz; internet www.gov.kz/memleket/entities/mfa-riyadh; Ambassador BERIK ARYN.

Kenya: POB 94358, Riyadh 11693; tel. (11) 488-2484; fax (11) 488-2629; e-mail riyadh@mfa.go.ke; internet www.kenyaembassy.org.sa; Ambassador PETER OGEGO.

Korea, Republic: POB 94399, Riyadh 11693; tel. (11) 488-2211; fax (11) 488-1317; e-mail emsau@mofa.go.kr; internet sau.mofa.go.kr; Ambassador PARK JUN-YONG.

Kosovo: 3474 Amr al-Damri St, al-Safarat, Riyadh 12512; tel. (11) 453-5799; e-mail embassy.saudiarabia@rks-gov.net; internet ambasadat.net/arabi-saudite; Ambassador LULZIM MJEKU.

Kuwait: Diplomatic Quarter, Riyadh 00965; tel. (50) 055-4256; e-mail riyadh@mova.gov.kw; Ambassador Sheikh SABAH NASSER SABAH AL-AHMAD AL-SABAH.

Kyrgyzstan: 6575 Amr al-Damri St, Assafarat District, Riyadh 12511-3562; tel. (11) 229-3272; fax (11) 229-3274; e-mail kgembassy.sa@mfa.gov.kg; internet mfa.gov.kg/en/dm/Embassy-of-the-Kyrgyz-Republic-to-the-Kingdom-of-Saudi-Arabia; Ambassador ULUKBEK MARIPOV.

Lebanon: POB 94350, Abu Bakr al-Karkh, Diplomatic Quarter, Riyadh 11693; tel. (11) 480-4060; fax (11) 480-4703; e-mail embassy@lebanon.org.sa; internet www.lebanon.org.sa; Ambassador FAWZI KABBARA.

Liberia: 4059 Ibrahim Ashami St, al-Wurud, Riyadh 12254-7721; tel. (11) 498-3142; fax (11) 498-3142; e-mail libemriyadh@gmail.com; Chargé d'affaires ABU KAMARA.

Libya: POB 94365, Riyadh 11693; tel. (11) 488-9757; fax (11) 488-3252; e-mail libianembassy@yahoo.com; Chargé d'affaires FATEH BASHENA.

Madagascar: Bldg 1, Abdullah bin Hilal St, al-Masif District, Riyadh; tel. (11) 263-1743; e-mail ambamriy@yahoo.fr; Chargé d'affaires a.i. CHAMARLY JONCHELIN ANDRIANJAFIMANANJARA.

Malaysia: POB 94335, Diplomatic Quarter, Riyadh 11693; tel. (11) 488-7100; fax (11) 482-4177; e-mail malriyadh@kln.gov.my; internet kln.gov.my/web/sau_riyadh; Ambassador Datuk WAN ZAIDI WAN ABDULLAH.

Maldives: POB 2228, Abu al-Izz al-Khurasani St, Riyadh 11451; tel. (11) 462-6787; fax (11) 464-3725; e-mail admin@maldivesembassy.org.sa; internet www.maldivesembassy.sa; Ambassador MOHAMED KHALEEL.

Mali: POB 94331, Quartier Rahmaniya, 37 al-Douma St, Riyadh 11693; tel. (11) 464-5640; fax (11) 419-5016; e-mail consulat@sbm.net.sa; Ambassador BOUBACAR GOURO DIALL.

Malta: POB 94361, 7733 Abbas al-Rasheedi St, Suleimaniya, Riyadh 11693; tel. (11) 463-2345; fax (11) 463-3993; e-mail maltaembassy.riyadh@gov.mt; internet foreignandeu.gov.mt/en/embassies/me_riyadh; Ambassador Dr CLIVE AQUILINA SPAGNOL.

Mauritania: POB 4361, 7217 Khallad bin Khalid, Riyadh 12252; tel. (11) 248-8006; fax (11) 248-8009; e-mail mauritaniariyadh@gmail.com; Ambassador ABDALLAH NAJI ABBAH KABD (designate).

Mauritius: POB 94259, 84 al-Fazari Plaza, Abdullah al-Sahmi St, Diplomatic Quarter, Riyadh 11693; tel. (11) 482-9567; fax (11) 482-5725; e-mail emb.riyadh@govmu.org; Ambassador SHOWKUTALLY SOODHUN.

Mexico: Abdullah ibn Hudhafad al-Sahmi Ave, Block 2, Portal 9, Local 42, Entrance C-9, Hai al-Safarat (Diplomatic Quarter), Riyadh 12512–7977; tel. (11) 480-8822; fax (11) 480-8833; e-mail embassyofmexico@embamex.org.sa; internet embamex.sre.gob.mx/arabiasaudita; Ambassador ANIBAL GÓMEZ TOLEDO.

Morocco: POB 94392, Abdullah bin Huthafah al-Sahmi St, Diplomatic Quarter, Riyadh 11693; tel. (11) 481-1858; fax (11) 482-7016; e-mail info@moroccanembassy.sa; internet www.moroccanembassy.sa; Ambassador MUSTAPHA MANSOURI.

Mozambique: Villa 1, Ibn Naim St, Salahedeen District, Riyadh; tel. (11) 269-4209; fax (11) 269-4219; Ambassador FAIZAL CASSAMO.

Myanmar: POB 94490,5 al-Kadi St, King Fahd Area, Riyadh; tel. (11) 229-3525; fax (11) 229-3306; e-mail meriyadh2007@gmail.com; internet www.meriyadh.org; Ambassador U KO KO LATT.

Nepal: POB 94384, al-Urubah St (nr Sulymanieh Hotel, al-Jouf Rd), Riyadh 11693; tel. (11) 461-1108; fax (11) 464-0690; e-mail eonriyadh@mofa.gov.np; internet sa.nepalembassy.gov.np; Ambassador NAWARAJ SUBEDI.

Netherlands: POB 94307, Abdullah Hizaf Asehmi St, Riyadh 11693; tel. (11) 442-2300; fax (11) 488-0544; e-mail riy@minbuza.nl; internet www.netherlandsworldwide.nl/countries/saudi-arabia; Ambassador JANET ALBERDA.

New Zealand: POB 94397, Diplomatic Quarter, Riyadh 11693; tel. (11) 488-7988; fax (11) 488-7911; e-mail nzembassyksa@mfat.govt.nz; Ambassador BARNEY RILEY.

Niger: POB 94334, Abdulla al-Angari St, Riyadh 11693; tel. (11) 470-8698; fax (11) 205-4323; e-mail ambassadeduniger_riyadh@yahoo.com; Ambassador ABUBAKAR HASSAN DAN SOKOTO.

Nigeria: POB 94386, Abubakar al-Razi Sq., Abdullah bin Huzafah al-Sahami Rd, Diplomatic Quarter, Riyadh 11693; tel. (11) 482-3024; fax (11) 482-4134; e-mail nigeria@nigeria.org.sa; internet www.nigeria.org.sa; Ambassador YAHAYA LAWAL.

Norway: POB 94380, Riyadh 11693; tel. (11) 488-1904; fax (11) 488-0854; e-mail emb.riyadh@mfa.no; internet www.norway.no/saudi-arabia; Ambassador THOMAS LID BALL.

Oman: POB 94381, opp. King Saud University, al-Raed Quarter, Riyadh 11693; tel. (11) 482-3120; fax (11) 482-3738; e-mail riyadh@mofa.gov.om; Ambassador FAISAL BIN TURKI AL-SAEED.

Pakistan: POB 94007, Bldg 8224, Diplomatic Quarters, Riyadh 11693; tel. (11) 488-7272; e-mail info.parepriyadh@mofa.gov.pk; internet pakistaninksa.com; Ambassador AHMED FAROOQ.

Peru: POB 94433, Bldg 7393, Ibn Younis al-Sadafi St, Riyadh 11693; tel. (11) 482-2474; fax (11) 483-0474; e-mail peru.riyadh@gmail.com; internet www.gob.pe/en/embajada-del-peru-en-arabia-saudita; Ambassador CARLOS ZAPATA.

Philippines: POB 94366, Site D3, Collector Rd C, Diplomatic Quarter, Riyadh 11693; tel. (11) 482-3559; fax (11) 488-3945; e-mail rype@riyadhpe.com; internet riyadhpe.dfa.gov.ph; Ambassador RENATO VILLA (designate).

Poland: POB 94016, Umar bin Dhafr St, Villa 20, al-Wourood Area, Riyadh 11693; tel. (11) 454-9274; fax (11) 454-9210; e-mail rijad.amb.sekretariat@msz.gov.pl; internet rijad.msz.gov.pl; Ambassador ROBERT ROSTEK.

Portugal: POB 94328, Prince Faisal bin Sa'ad bin Abdulrahman St, Bldg No. 56, al-Wourood Area, Riyadh 11693; tel. (11) 482-6964; fax (11) 482-6981; e-mail portriade@nesma.net.sa; internet www.riade.embaixadaportugal.mne.pt; Ambassador NUNO MATHIAS.

Qatar: POB 94353, Riyadh 11461; tel. (11) 482-5544; fax (11) 482-5694; e-mail riyadh@mofa.gov.qa; Ambassador BANDAR MOHAMED ABDULLAH AL-ATTIYAH.

Romania: POB 94319, Villa 8, Amin al-Rehany St, King Fahad Quarter, Riyadh 11693; tel. (11) 263-0456; fax (11) 456-9985; e-mail riyadh@mae.ro; internet riyadh.mae.ro; Chargé d'affaires a.i. DOAMNA OANA GHICA.

Russian Federation: POB 94308, al-Wasiti St, Bldg 13, Rahmania, Riyadh 11693; tel. (11) 481-1875; fax (11) 481-1890; e-mail rusembass@mail.ru; internet www.riyadh.mid.ru; Ambassador SERGEI KOZLOV.

Senegal: POB 94352, Riyadh 11693; tel. (11) 488-0157; fax (11) 488-3804; Ambassador MAMADOU SALL.

Serbia: Bldg 26, Abd al-Qader Jaza'eri St, al-Olaya District, Riyadh; tel. (11) 4613010; fax (11) 4616696; e-mail embsrb.riyadh@yahoo.com; internet www.mfa.gov.rs/en/foreign-policy/bilateral-cooperation/saudi-arabia/embassies-consulates; Ambassador MUHAMED JUSUFSPAHIĆ.

Sierra Leone: POB 94329, 27 al-Farooqi St, al-Maseef, Riyadh 11693; tel. (11) 494-1303; fax (11) 453-7339; e-mail slembassy.sa@foreignaffairs.gov.sl; Ambassador Dr IBRAHIM JALLOH.

Singapore: POB 94378, Riyadh 11693; tel. (11) 480-3855; fax (11) 483-0632; e-mail singemb_ruh@mfa.sg; internet www.mfa.gov.sg/riyadh; Ambassador S. PREMJITH (designate).

Slovakia: Riyadh; e-mail emb.riyadh@mzv.sk; internet www.mzv.sk/en/web/rijad; Ambassador RUDOLF MICHALKA.

Somalia: POB 94372, Ali bin Farhoon St, al-Wuroud District, Riyadh 11693; tel. (11) 460-6774; fax (11) 460-5705; Ambassador (vacant).

South Africa: POB 94006, 150 King Khalid Rd, Umm al-Hammam District (East), Riyadh 11693; tel. (11) 442-9716; fax (11) 442-9708; e-mail riyadh.info@dirco.gov.za; Ambassador MOGOBO DAVID MAGABE.

South Sudan: Riyadh; Chargé d'affaires KHAMIS HAGAR.

Spain: POB 94347, Riyadh 11693; tel. (11) 488-0606; fax (11) 488-0420; e-mail emb.riad.info@maec.es; internet www.exteriores.gob.es/Embajadas/riad; Ambassador JORGE HEVIA SIERRA.

Sri Lanka: POB 94360, 44 Ahmed Abdul Gaffoor al-Attar St, Olaya District, Riyadh 11693; tel. (11) 460-8235; fax (11) 460-8846; e-mail slemb.riyadh@mfa.gov.lk; internet www.slemb.org.sa; Ambassador PACKEER MOHIDEEN AMZA.

Sudan: POB 94337, 8394 Abdullah bin Hudhafa al-Sahmi, Diplomatic Quarter, Riyadh 11693; tel. (11) 488-7979; fax (11) 488-7729; e-mail info@sudanembassy.org.sa; internet sudanembassy.org.sa; Ambassador ADEL BASHIR.

Sweden: POB 94382, Tayma St, Lenah Residential Area, Diplomatic Quarter, Riyadh 11693; tel. (55) 330-1441; fax (11) 482-7796; e-mail ambassaden.riyadh@gov.se; internet www.swedenabroad.com/riyadh; Ambassador PETRA MENANDER.

Switzerland: POB 94311, Riyadh 11693; tel. (11) 488-1291; fax (11) 488-0632; e-mail rya.vertretung@eda.admin.ch; internet www.eda.admin.ch/riad; Ambassador YASMINE C. ZWAHLEN.

Tajikistan: Yusuf bin al-Hanbali St, al-Worood Quarter, Riyadh 11393; tel. (11) 205-4709; fax (11) 205-4708; e-mail tajembsaudi@gmail.com; internet mfa.tj/en/saudi; Ambassador AKRAM KARIMI.

Tanzania: POB 94320, Bldg 1, Ibn Hibatullah Rd, Riyadh 11693; tel. (11) 454-2833; fax (11) 454-9660; e-mail riyadh@nje.go.tz; internet www.sa.tzembassy.go.tz; Ambassador MOHAMED JUMA ABDALLAH (designate).

Thailand: POB 94359, Riyadh 11693; tel. (11) 488-1174; fax (11) 488-1179; e-mail thairuh@mfa.go.th; internet www.thaiembassy.org/riyadh; Ambassador DARM BOONTHAM.

Tunisia: POB 94368, Riyadh 11693; tel. (11) 488-7900; fax (11) 488-7641; e-mail at.riyadh@diplomatie.gov.tn; Ambassador HICHEM FOURATI.

Türkiye (Turkey): POB 94390, 8604 Abdullah ibn Hudhafah al-Sahmi St, Riyadh 11693; tel. (11) 482-0101; fax (11) 488-7823; e-mail embassy.riyadh@mfa.gov.tr; internet riyadh.emb.mfa.gov.tr; Ambassador FATIH ULUSOY.

Turkmenistan: POB 94019, 4 Ahmed al-Bihki St, al-Wourood District, Riyadh 11693; tel. (11) 205-4898; fax (11) 205-2990; e-mail info@turkmenemb-sa.org; internet saudi.tmembassy.gov.tm; Ambassador ORAZMUHAMMET CHARYYEV.

Uganda: POB 94344, Abi al-Mudhaffar al-Falaki St, Riyadh 11693; tel. (11) 521-1881; e-mail ugariyadh@hotmail.com; internet riyadh.mofa.go.ug; Ambassador ISAAC BIRUMA SEBULIME.

Ukraine: POB 94010, 6 Hassan al-Badr St, Salah al din District, Riyadh 11693; tel. (11) 450-8536; fax (11) 450-8534; e-mail emb_sa@mfa.gov.ua; internet saudiarabia.mfa.gov.ua; Ambassador ANATOLIY PETRENKO.

United Arab Emirates: POB 94385, Abu Bakr al-Karkhi Q. Omer bin Omaeah St, Diplomatic Quarter, Riyadh 11693; tel. (11) 488-1227; fax (11) 482-7504; e-mail riyadhemb@mofaic.gov.ae; internet www.mofaic.gov.ae/en/missions/al-riyadh; Ambassador Sheikh NAHYAN BIN SAIF BIN MOHAMMED AL NAHYAN.

United Kingdom: POB 94351, Riyadh 11693; tel. (11) 481-9100; fax (11) 481-9350; internet www.gov.uk/world/saudi-arabia; Ambassador NEIL CROMPTON.

USA: POB 94309, Riyadh 11693; tel. (11) 488-3800; fax (11) 488-7360; e-mail usembriyadhwebsite@state.gov; internet sa.usembassy.gov; Ambassador MICHAEL A. RATNEY.

Uruguay: POB 94346, C-40 al-Radaef St, Diplomatic Quarter, Riyadh 11693; tel. (11) 462-0739; fax (11) 462-0638; e-mail uruarabia@mrree.gub.uy; Ambassador NELSON YEMIL CHABEN LABADIE.

Uzbekistan: POB 94008, Villa 17, Talha bin al-Barra St, Sulaimania Quarter, Riyadh 11693; tel. (11) 263-5223; fax (11) 263-5105; e-mail uzembriyadh@gmail.com; Ambassador ULUGBEK MAKSUDOV.

Venezuela: POB 94364, Plaza al-Kindi, nr Cultural Palace, Lower Floor, Office 57, Diplomatic Quarter, Riyadh 11693; tel. (11) 480-7141; fax (11) 480-0901; e-mail embvenar@embvenar.org.sa; Ambassador DAVID NIEVES VELÁSQUEZ CARABALLO.

Viet Nam: Villa 11B, al-Safah St, al-Rayyan District, Riyadh; tel. (1) 4547887; fax (11) 454-8844; e-mail vnemb.sa@mofa.gov.vn; internet vnembassy-riyadh.mofa.gov.vn; Ambassador DANG XUAN DUNG.

Yemen: POB 94356, Abu Bakr Karkhi St, al-Safarat, Diplomatic Quarter, Riyadh 11693; tel. (11) 488-1769; fax (11) 488-1562; internet www.yemembassy-sa.org; Ambassador SHAYA'E BIN MOHSEN AL-ZINDANI.

SAUDI ARABIA

Zambia: 22 al-Abass al-Ahnaf, al-Mursalat District, Riyadh; tel. (11) 454-2295; fax (11) 456-6641; e-mail zembassy@yahoo.com; Ambassador DANKEN MULIMA.

Judicial System

Judges are independent and governed by the rules of Islamic (*Shari'a*) law. A new Judicial Law approved in May 2007 provided for a number of significant changes to the courts system. The new legislation called for the establishment of appeal courts, criminal courts and specialized courts. A Supreme Court was to be established in Riyadh, and new appeals courts were planned for each of the kingdom's 13 regions. There were to be general courts to deal with all conflicts except labour, commercial and family disputes, and criminal courts to address crimes. Family and personal conflicts were to be handled by civil courts. The President and judges of the Supreme Court were formally appointed in October 2020.

Supreme Judicial Council: POB 11291, Riyadh; tel. 920002729; fax (11) 4829802; e-mail info@scj.gov.sa; internet www.scj.gov.sa; comprises 11 mems; supervises work of the courts; reviews legal questions referred to it by the Minister of Justice and expresses opinions on judicial questions; reviews sentences of death, cutting and stoning; Chair. Dr WALEED BIN MOHAMMED AL-SAMAANI (Minister of Justice).

Supreme Court: Riyadh; monitors the application of Islamic *Shari'a* and the *Shari'a*-compliant laws issued by the authorities on matters outside the jurisdiction of the general judiciary; Pres. KHALID BIN ABDULLAH AL-LUHAIDAN.

Court of Cassation: consists of Chief Justice and an adequate number of judges; includes department for penal suits, department for personal status and department for other suits.

Courts of First Instance: these are established in all the provinces of the Kingdom and include the general courts, criminal courts, matrimonial courts, business courts and labour courts.

General (Public) Courts: consist of one or more judges; sentences are issued by a single judge, with the exception of death, stoning and cutting, which require the decision of three judges.

Summary Courts: consist of one or more judges; sentences are issued by a single judge.

Specialized Courts: the setting up of specialized courts is permissible by Royal Decree on a proposal from the Supreme Judicial Council.

Attorney-General: Sheikh SA'UD BIN ABDULLAH AL-MUJIB.

Religion

ISLAM

Arabia is the centre of the Islamic faith, and Saudi Arabia includes the holy cities of Mecca and Medina. Except in the Eastern region, where a large number of people follow Shi'a rites, the majority of the population are Sunni Muslims, and most of the indigenous inhabitants belong to the strictly orthodox Wahhabi sect. The Wahhabis originated in the 18th century, but first became unified and influential under Abdulaziz (Ibn Sa'ud), who became the first King of Saudi Arabia. They are now the keepers of the holy places and control the pilgrimage to Mecca. In 1986 King Fahd adopted the title of Custodian of the Two Holy Mosques; the title was retained by his successors. The country's most senior Islamic authority is the Council of Senior Ulama.

Mecca: birthplace of the Prophet Muhammad, seat of the Grand Mosque and Shrine of Ka'ba.

Medina: burial place of Muhammad, second sacred city of Islam.

Presidency of Religious Affairs at the Grand Mosque and the Prophet's Mosque: f. 2023; under direct control of the King; supervises the imams and muezzins of the two holy mosques and their affairs; Pres. Sheikh Dr ABDULRAHMAN AL-SUDAIS.

Grand Mufti and Chairman of Council of Senior Ulama: Sheikh ABDUL AZIZ IBN ABDULLAH AL-SHEIKH.

CHRISTIANITY

The Roman Catholic Church

A small number of adherents, mainly expatriates, form part of the Apostolic Vicariate of Northern Arabia. The Vicar Apostolic is resident in Bahrain.

The Anglican Communion

Within the Episcopal Church in Jerusalem and the Middle East, Saudi Arabia forms part of the diocese of Cyprus and the Gulf. The Anglican congregations in the country are entirely expatriate. The Bishop in Cyprus and the Gulf is resident in Cyprus, while the Archdeacon in the Gulf is resident in Qatar.

Other Denominations

The Greek Orthodox Church is also represented.

The Press

Since 1964 most newspapers and periodicals have been published by press organizations, administered by boards of directors with full autonomous powers, in accordance with the provisions of the Press Law. These organizations, which took over from small private firms, are privately owned by groups of individuals experienced in newspaper publishing and administration (see *Publishers*).

There are also a number of popular periodicals published by the Government and by the Saudi Arabian Oil Co, and distributed free of charge. The press is subject to no legal restriction affecting freedom of expression or the coverage of news.

DAILIES

Arab News: POB 10452, SRP Bldg, Madinah Rd, Jeddah 21433; tel. (12) 639-1888; fax (2) 283-6228; e-mail general@arabnews.com; internet www.arabnews.com; f. 1975; English; publ. by Saudi Research and Publishing Co; Editor-in-Chief FAISAL J. ABBAS.

Al-Bilad (The Country): POB 6340, Jeddah 21442; tel. (2) 275-0020; fax (2) 275-0016; e-mail info@albiladdaily.com; internet www.albiladdaily.com; f. 1934; Arabic; publ. by Al-Bilad Publishing Org; Editor-in-Chief MOHAMED ODEH AL-JUHANI.

Al-Eqtisadiah: POB 478, Riyadh 11411; tel. (1) 212-8000; fax (1) 441-7885; e-mail edit@aleqt.com; internet www.aleqt.com; f. 1992; business and finance; publ. by Saudi Research and Publishing Co; Editor-in-Chief ABDULRAHMAN AL-MANSOUR.

Al-Jazirah (The Peninsula): POB 354, Riyadh 11411; tel. (11) 487-0000; fax (11) 487-1120; e-mail ccs@al-jazirah.com.sa; internet www.al-jazirah.com; f. 1972; Arabic; publ. by Al-Jazirah Corpn for Press, Printing and Publishing; Dir-Gen. ABDUL LATIF BIN SAAD; Editor-in-Chief KHALID BIN HAMAD AL-MALIK.

Al-Madina al-Munawara (Medina—The Enlightened City): POB 807, Makkah Rd, Jeddah 21421; tel. (12) 224-9444; fax (12) 671-1877; e-mail webmaster@al-madina.com; internet al-madina.com; f. 1937; Arabic; publ. by Al-Madina Press Establishment; Chair. HAIDAR BIN LADEN.

Al-Nadwah (The Council): POB 5803, Jarwal Sheikh Sayed Halabi Bldg, Mecca; tel. (12) 520-0111; fax (12) 520-3055; internet www.alnadwah.com.sa; f. 1958; Arabic; publ. by Makkah Printing and Information Establishment; Editor AHMAD BIN SALEH BAYUSUF.

Okaz: POB 9218, Seaport Rd, Jeddah 21413; tel. (2) 676-0000; fax (2) 676-4010; internet www.okaz.com.sa; f. 1948; Arabic; publ. by Okaz Org. for Press and Publication; Chair. ABDULLAH SALEH KAMEL.

Al-Riyadh: POB 2943, Riyadh 11476; tel. (11) 487-1000; fax (11) 441-7417; internet www.alriyadh.com; f. 1965; Arabic; publ. by Al-Yamama Press Establishment; Editor FAHAD RASHID AL-ABDUL KARIM.

Saudi Gazette: Jeddah 23344; tel. (12) 676-0000; fax (12) 672-7621; e-mail webeditors@saudigazette.com.sa; internet www.saudigazette.com.sa; f. 1976; English; publ. by Okaz Org. for Press and Publication; Editor-in-Chief JAMEEL AL-THEYABI.

Al-Watan: POB 15155, Airport Road, Abha; tel. (17) 227-3333; fax (17) 227-3756; e-mail editor@alwatan.com.sa; internet www.alwatan.com.sa; f. 1998; publ. by Assir Establishment for Press and Publishing; Editor Dr OTHMAN BIN MAHMOUD AL-SINI.

Al-Yaum (Today): POB 565, Dammam 31421; tel. (13) 858-0800; fax (13) 858-8777; e-mail mail@alyaum.com; internet www.alyaum.com; f. 1965; publ. by Dar al-Yaum Press, Printing and Publishing Ltd; Editor-in-Chief OMAR ABDEL RAHMAN EL-SHADI.

WEEKLIES

Al-Muslimoon (The Muslims): POB 13195, Jeddah 21493; tel. (12) 669-1888; fax (12) 669-5549; f. 1985; Arabic; cultural and religious affairs; publ. by Saudi Research and Publishing Co; Editor-in-Chief Dr ABDULLAH AL-RIFA'E.

Saudi Economic Survey: POB 1989, Jeddah 21441; tel. (12) 657-8551; fax (12) 657-8553; e-mail info@saudieconomicsurvey.com; internet kawalodesign.com/ses; f. 1967; English; review of Saudi Arabian economic and business activity; Publr SAIFUDDIN A. ASHOOR; Gen. Man. WALID S. ASHOOR.

Sayidaty (My Lady): POB 4556, Madina Rd, Jeddah 21412; tel. (1) 212-8000; fax (12) 212-1748; e-mail contact@sayidaty.net; internet www.sayidaty.net; f. 1981; publ. in Arabic and English edns; women's magazine; publ. by Saudi Research and Publishing Co; Editor-in-Chief LAMA IBRAHIM AL-SHETHRI.

SAUDI ARABIA

Al-Shams (The Sun): Riyadh; internet shms.pressera.com; f. 2005; tabloid format; sports, culture, entertainment; Editor-in-Chief KHALAF AL-HARBI.

Al-Yamama: POB 2110, Dammam 31451; tel. (13) 826-6444; fax (13) 827-0089; f. 1952; literary magazine; Editor-in-Chief ABDULLAH AL-JAHLAN.

OTHER PERIODICALS

Ahlan Wasahlan (Welcome): POB 8013, Jeddah 21482; tel. (12) 686-1676; fax (12) 686-2006; monthly; flight journal of Saudi Arabian Airlines; Gen. Man. and Editor-in-Chief MANSOUR AL-BADAL.

Al-Daragh: POB 2945, Riyadh 11461; tel. (11) 434-8529; fax (11) 401-3597; e-mail magazine@darah.org.sa; internet www.darahjournal.org.sa; history journal; publ. by King Abd al-Aziz Foundation for Research and Archives; Pres. FAHAD BIN ABDULLAH AL-SAMARI.

Majallat al-Iqtisad wal-Idara (Journal of Economics and Administration): King Abd al-Aziz University, POB 9031, Jeddah 21413; 2 a year; Chief Editor Prof. ABD AL-AZIZ A. DIYAB.

Al-Manhal (The Spring): POB 2925, Jeddah; tel. (12) 643-2124; fax (12) 642-8853; e-mail info@al-manhalmagazine.com; f. 1937; monthly; Arabic; cultural, literary, political and scientific; Editor ZUHAIR N. AL-ANSARI.

The MWL Journal: Press and Publications Dept, Rabitat al-Alam al-Islami, POB 537, Mecca; tel. (12) 560-0919; e-mail info@themwl.org; internet www.themwl.org; monthly; English; Chief Editor OSMAN ABU ZEID.

Al-Rabita: POB 537, Mecca; tel. (12) 560-0919; fax (12) 543-1488; e-mail info@themwl.org; internet www.themwl.org; Arabic; Chief Editor Dr OSMAN ABUZAID.

Al-Tijarah (Commerce): POB 1264, Jeddah 21431; tel. (12) 658-1122; fax (12) 651-7373; e-mail info@jcci.org.sa; f. 1960; monthly; publ. by Jeddah Chamber of Commerce and Industry; Chair. MOHAMMED YOUSUF NAGHI.

NEWS AGENCIES

Saudi Press Agency (SPA): POB 7186, King Fahd Rd, Riyadh 11171; tel. (11) 401-9001; fax (11) 401-9046; e-mail info@spa.gov.sa; internet www.spa.gov.sa; f. 1970; Chair. ABDULLAH BIN FAHD AL-HUSSEIN; Dir-Gen. ALI AL-ZAHRANI.

Union of News Agencies of the Organization of Islamic Cooperation (UNA): POB 5054, Jeddah 21422; tel. (12) 665-2056; fax (12) 665-9358; e-mail info@una-oic.org; internet www.una-oic.org; f. 1972; operates under the auspices of the Org. of the Islamic Conference; Dir-Gen. MOHAMED AL-YAMI.

Publishers

Literature, Publishing & Translation Commission: Riyadh; tel. 8001189999; internet lpt.moc.gov.sa; f. 2020; regulates publishing industry; Chair. BADR BIN ABDULLAH BIN MOHAMMED BIN FARHAN AL SA'UD; CEO Dr MOHAMMED HASAN ALWAN.

Assir Establishment for Press and Publishing: POB 15156, Abha; tel. (17) 227-3333; fax (17) 227-3590; f. 1998; publishes Al-Watan; Gen. Man. HATEM HAMID.

Al-Bilad Publishing Organization: POB 6340, al-Sahafa St, Jeddah 21442; tel. (12) 672-3000; fax (12) 671-2545; publishes Al-Bilad; Dir-Gen. AMIN ABDULLAH AL-QARQOURI.

Dar al-Maiman Publishers and Distributors: POB 90020, Riyadh 11613; tel. (11) 462-7336; fax (11) 280-0587.

Dar al-Shareff for Publishing and Distribution: POB 58287, Riyadh 11594; tel. (11) 403-4931; fax (11) 405-2234; f. 1992; fiction, religion, science and social sciences; Pres. IBRAHIM AL-HAZEMI.

Dar al-Yaum Press, Printing and Publishing Ltd: POB 565, Dammam 31421; tel. (13) 858-0800; fax (13) 858-8777; e-mail mail@alyaum.com; internet www.alyaum.com; f. 1964; publishes Al-Yaum; Chair. WALID BIN HAMAD AL-MUBARAK; Gen. Man. HASSAN AL-HUDAIB.

International Publications Agency (IPA): POB 70, Dhahran 31942; tel. and fax (13) 895-4925; publishes material of local interest; Man. SAID SALAH.

Al-Jazirah Corpn for Press, Printing and Publishing: POB 354, Riyadh 11411; tel. (11) 487–0000; fax (11) 487-1120; e-mail ccs@al-jazirah.com; internet www.al-jazirah.com; f. 1964; 42 mems; publishes Al-Jazirah daily newspaper; Chair. ABD AL-RAHMAN BIN IBRAHIM ABU HAMAD; Editor-in-Chief KHALID BIN HAMAD AL-MALIK.

Al-Madina Press Establishment: POB 807, Jeddah 21421; tel. (12) 671-2100; fax (12) 671-1877; f. 1937; publishes Al-Madina al-Munawara; Gen. Man. AHMAD SALAH JAMJOUM.

Makkah Printing and Information Establishment: POB 5803, Jarwal Sheikh Sayed Halabi Bldg, Mecca; tel. (12) 542-7868; publishes Al-Nadwah daily newspaper; Chair. MUHAMMAD ABDOU YAMANI.

Okaz Organization for Press and Publication: POB 1508, Jeddah 21441; tel. (12) 672-2630; fax (12) 672-8150; internet okaz.com.sa; publishes Okaz and Saudi Gazette; Chair. ABDULLAH SALEH KAMEL.

Al-Rushd Publishers: POB 17522, Riyadh 11494; tel. (11) 460-4818; fax (11) 460-2497; e-mail info@rushd.com.sa; internet www.rushd.com.sa; scientific and academic publs.

Saudi Publishing and Distributing House: Umm Aslam District, nr Muslaq, POB 2043, Jeddah 21451; tel. (12) 629-4278; fax (12) 629-4290; e-mail info@spdh-sa.com; internet www.spdh-sa.com; f. 1966; publishers, importers and distributors of English and Arabic books; Chair. MUHAMMAD SALAHUDDIN.

Saudi Research and Publishing Co: POB 478, Riyadh 11411; tel. (11) 212-8000; fax (11) 442-9555; internet www.srpc.com; publs include Arab News, Asharq al-Awsat, Al-Majalla, Al-Muslimoon and Sayidati; Dep. Gen. Man. SALEH AL-DOWAIS.

Al-Yamama Press Establishment: POB 851, Al Sahafa Qtr, Riyadh 11421; tel. (11) 299-6111; fax (11) 441-7580; e-mail info@alriyadh.com; internet www.alyamahpressportal.com; publishes Al-Riyadh and Al-Yamama; Dir-Gen. SAKHAL MAIDAN.

Broadcasting and Communications

TELECOMMUNICATIONS

Etihad Etisalat (Mobily): POB 9979, Riyadh 11423; tel. (56) 031-4099; e-mail ird@mobily.com.sa; internet www.mobily.com.sa; f. 2004; 27.99% stake owned by Etisalat Emirates Gp (Etisalat—United Arab Emirates); awarded the second licence to provide mobile telephone services 2004; Chair. Dr NABEEL M. AL-AMUDI; CEO SALMAN BIN ABDULAZIZ AL-BADRAN.

Saudi Telecommunications Co—Saudi Telecom (STC): POB 87912, Riyadh 11652; e-mail wsmc@stc.com.sa; internet www.stc.com.sa; f. 1998; partially privatized 2002; provides telecommunications services in Saudi Arabia; Chair. Prince MOHAMMED K. AL-FAISAL; CEO OLAYAN MOHAMMED AL-WETAID.

Zain Saudi Arabia: POB 295814, Riyadh 11351; tel. (59) 241-1111; e-mail corporate.communications@sa.zain.com; internet www.sa.zain.com; f. 2007; wholly owned by Mobile Telecommunications Co KSC (Zain Kuwait); awarded the third licence to provide mobile telephone services 2007; Chair. Prince NAIF BIN SULTAN BIN MUHAMMAD BIN SAUD AL-KABEER; CEO Eng. SULTAN BIN ABDULAZIZ AL-DEGHAITHER.

Regulatory Authority

Communications and Information Technology Commission (CITC): POB 75606, Riyadh 11588; tel. (11) 461-8000; fax (11) 461-8120; e-mail info@citc.gov.sa; internet www.citc.gov.sa; f. 2001 under the name Saudi Communications Comm.; present name adopted 2003; regulatory authority; Chair. Eng. ABDULLAH BIN AMER AL-SAWAHA (Minister of Communications and Information Technology); Gov. Dr MOHAMMED BIN SAUD AL-TAMIMI.

BROADCASTING

Saudi Broadcasting Authority (SBA): c/o Ministry of Culture and Information, POB 7971, Riyadh 11472; tel. (11) 442-5999; fax (11) 403-8177; e-mail info@sba.sa; internet www.sba.sa; six television channels and 5 radio channels, broadcasting programmes in Arabic and English; f. 1962; established as Saudi Broadcasting Corpn (SBC); present name adopted in 2018 to prevent confusion with the Saudi Broadcasting Channel (SBC); CEO MOHAMMAD BIN FAHD AL-HARITHI.

Saudi Aramco FM Radio: Bldg 3030 LIP, Dhahran 31311; tel. (13) 876-1845; fax (13) 876-1608; e-mail fmradio@aramco.com; f. 1948; English; private; for employees of Saudi Aramco; Man. ESSAM Z. TAWFIQ.

Finance

BANKING

Central Bank

Saudi Central Bank (SAMA): POB 2992, Riyadh 11169; tel. (11) 463-3000; fax (11) 466-2966; e-mail info@sama.gov.sa; internet www.sama.gov.sa; f. 1952 as Saudi Arabian Monetary Agency; name changed as above in Dec. 2016; functions include stabilization of currency, administration of monetary reserves, regulation of banking and insurance sectors, and issue of notes and coins; Gov. AYMAN AL-SAYARI.

National Banks

Alinma Bank: POB 66674, al-Anoud Tower, King Fahad Rd, Riyadh 11586; tel. (11) 218-5555; fax (11) 218-5000; e-mail info@alinma.com; internet www.alinma.com; f. 2006; Chair. ABDULMALEK BIN ABDULLAH AL-HOGAIL.

Bank Albilad: 8229 al-Mutamarat, Unit 2, Riyadh 12711-3952; tel. (11) 479-8888; fax (11) 479-8898; internet www.bankalbilad.com; f. 2004; Chair. NASSER BIN MOHAMMED AL-SUBAIE; CEO ABDULAZIZ MOHAMMED AL-ONAIZAN.

Al-Rajhi Banking and Investment Corpn (Al-Rajhi Bank): POB 28, al-Akariya Bldg, Oleya St, Riyadh 11411; tel. (11) 460-0423; fax (11) 460-0625; e-mail contactus@alrajhibank.com.sa; internet www.alrajhibank.com.sa; f. 1988; operates according to Islamic financial principles; Chair. ABDULLAH BIN SULAIMAN AL-RAJHI; CEO WALEED A. AL-MOGBEL.

Riyad Bank Ltd: POB 22622, King Abd al-Aziz St, Riyadh 11416; tel. (11) 401-3030; fax (11) 404-1255; internet www.riyadbank.com; f. 1957; Chair. Eng. ABDULLAH MOHAMMED AL-ISSA; CEO TAREQ A. AL-SADHAN.

Saudi National Bank (SNB): The Saudi National Bank Tower, 3208 King Fahd Rd, Al-Aqeeq District, Unit No. 778, Riyadh 13519; tel. 920001000; fax (12) 646-5892; e-mail contactus@alahli.com; internet www.alahli.com; f. 2021 by merger of National Commercial Bank and SAMBA Financial Group; Chair. SAEED MOHAMMED AL-GHAMDI; CEO TALAL AL-KHEREIJI (acting).

Specialist Bank

Arab Investment Co SAA (TAIC): POB 4009, King Abd al-Aziz St, Riyadh 11491; tel. (11) 476-0601; fax (11) 476-0514; e-mail taic@taic.com; internet www.taic.com; f. 1974 by 17 Arab countries for investment and banking; Chair. ABDULAZIZ SALIH O. AL-FURAIH; CEO IBRAHIM MILAD AL-ZLITNI (acting).

Banks with Foreign Interests

Arab National Bank (ANB): POB 56921, Riyadh 11564; tel. (11) 402-9000; fax (11) 402-7747; e-mail info@anb.com.sa; internet www.anb.com.sa; f. 1980; Arab Bank PLC, Jordan, 40%, Saudi shareholders 60%; Chair. SALAH RASHED AL-RASHED; Man. Dir OBAID A. AL-RASHED.

Bank al-Jazira: POB 6277, King Abd al-Aziz St, Jeddah 21442; tel. (12) 6098888; fax (12) 6098881; e-mail info@baj.com.sa; internet www.baj.com.sa; 94.17% Saudi-owned; Chair. Eng. TAREK OTHMAN AL-KASABI; CEO NAIF A. AL-ABDULKAREEM.

Banque Saudi Fransi (Saudi French Bank): POB 56006, Ma'ather Rd, Riyadh 11554; tel. 920000576; fax (11) 408-4631; e-mail communications@alfransi.com.sa; internet www.alfransi.com.sa; f. 1977; present name adopted 2002; Saudi shareholders 68.9%, Calyon, Paris La Défense 31.1%; Chair. MAZIN ABDULRAZZAK AL-ROMAIH; Man. Dir and CEO BADR AL-SALLOUM.

Saudi British Bank (SABB): POB 9084, Riyadh 11413; tel. 920007222; fax 8001248888; e-mail sabb@sabb.com; internet www.sabb.com; f. 1978; 29.2% owned by HSBC Holdings BV, 18.2% by Olayan Saudi Investment Co, 10.8% by Natwest Markets NV; merged with Alawwal Bank in 2019; Chair. LUBNA SULAIMAN OLAYAN; Man. Dir TONY KREBS.

Saudi Investment Bank (SAIB): POB 3533, Riyadh 11481; tel. (11) 418-3100; fax (11) 477-6781; e-mail info@saib.com.sa; internet www.saib.com.sa; f. 1976; provides a comprehensive range of traditional and specialized banking services; Chair. ABDALLAH SALIH JUMAH; CEO FAISAL ABDULLAH AL-OMRAN.

Small & Medium Enterprises Bank (SME Bank): Riyadh; tel. 8003033333; e-mail smebankcare@smebank.gov.sa; internet smebank.gov.sa; f. 2021 to support the goals of Saudi Vision 2030; aims to raise the contribution of small and medium enterprises to gross domestic product (GDP) from 20% to 35%; Chair. YOUSEF BIN ABDULLAH AL-BENYAN; CEO ABDUL RAHMAN MANSOUR (acting).

Government Specialized Credit Institutions

Agricultural Development Fund (ADF): al-Maather St, Riyadh; tel. (11) 211–8888; fax (11) 219–5555; internet adf.gov.sa; f. 2008; replaced the Saudi Arabian Agricultural Bank; provides funding for the development of agricultural sector; Chair. Eng. ABDUL RAHMAN AL-FADHLI; Gen. Man. MUNEER AL-SAHLI.

Real Estate Development Fund (REDF): POB 5591, Riyadh 11139; tel. 920010092; fax (11) 479-0148; f. 1974; provides interest-free loans to Saudi individuals and cos for private or commercial housing projects; Chair. MOHAMMED BIN ABDULLAH BIN ABDULAZIZ AL-JADAAN (Minister of Finance); Dir-Gen. MANSOUR BIN MADI.

Saudi Credit Bank: POB 3401, Riyadh 11471; tel. (11) 402-9128; f. 1973; provides interest-free loans for specific purposes to Saudi citizens of moderate means; Man. IBRAHIM AL-HINAISHIL.

STOCK EXCHANGE

Saudi Stock Exchange (Tadawul): 6897 King Fahd Rd, al-Ulaya, Riyadh 12211-3388; tel. 920001919; fax (11) 218-9133; e-mail csc@saudiexchange.sa; internet www.saudiexchange.sa; f. 2001; restructured as a jt-stock co in 2007; 223 listed cos (2022); Chair. KHALID ABDULLAH AL-HUSSAN; CEO MOHAMMED SULAIMAN AL-RUMAIH.

Regulatory Authority

Capital Market Authority: POB 87171, Riyadh 11642; tel. (11) 245-1111; e-mail info@cma.org.sa; internet www.cma.org.sa; f. 2003 to regulate and develop the Saudi Arabian capital market; Chair. MOHAMMED BIN ABDULLAH AL-KUWAIZ.

INSURANCE

Al-Alamiya Co for Co-operative Insurance: POB 6393, Riyadh 11442; tel. 8002444481; e-mail customer.care@sa.rsagroup.com; internet www.alalamiya.sa; part of the Royal & Sun Alliance (RSA) Group; Chair. ABDULAZIZ BIN HASAN; CEO KAMRAN MAZHAR JAFFERY.

Al-Jazira Takaful: POB 5215, Jeddah 21422; tel. (9) 668–8877; fax (12) 667–7284; e-mail info@ajt.com.sa; internet www.ajt.com.sa; Islamic life insurance; Chair. ABDULMAJEED BIN IBRAHIM AL-SULTAN; CEO and Man. Dir SAQR NADERSHAH.

Allied Cooperative Insurance Group: POB 40523, Riyadh 11511; tel. (12) 225-5444; fax (12) 661-7421; e-mail customercare@acig.com.sa; internet www.acig.com.sa; Chair. YASSER BIN MUHAMMAD AL-JARALLAH; CEO ALI BIN YAHYA AL-JAAFARI.

Bupa Arabia: Prince Saud al-Faisal, al-Khalidiyah District, Jeddah; tel. 920000456; internet bupa.com.sa; f. 1997; Chair. Eng. LOAY HISHAM NAZER; CEO TAL HISHAM NAZER.

Chubb Arabia Cooperative Insurance Co: Southern Tower, 8th Floor, Khobar Business Gate, King Faisal Bin Abd al-Aziz St (Coastal Rd), al-Khobar; tel. (13) 849-3655; fax (13) 849-3660; e-mail customerservice.chubbarabia@chubb.com; internet www.chubb.com/sa/; f. 1974 as Ace Arabia Insurance Co Ltd; present name adopted 2016 following acquisition of Chubb Corpn by ACE Ltd; Chair. Sheikh NABIL YOUSEF JAMIL JOKHDAR; CEO KAMRAN MAZHAR.

Mediterranean and Gulf Cooperative Insurance and Reinsurance Co (MEDGULF): POB 2302, Riyadh 11451; tel. (11) 441-4442; fax (11) 405-5588; e-mail customer-service@medgulf.com.sa; internet www.medgulf.com.sa; Chair. RAKAN ABDULLAH RASHED ABUNAYYAN; CEO Dr GOETZ KORAS.

Al-Rajhi Co for Co-operative Insurance: 3485 al-Thumamah Rd, al-Rabie District, Riyadh 13316–8450; tel. 920004414; internet www.alrajhitakaful.com; f. 1990 as Al-Rajhi Insurance Co; renamed as above 2006; Chair. ABDULLAH SULAIMAN AL-RAJHI; CEO SAUD GHONAIM AL-GHONAIM.

Salama Cooperative Insurance Co (SALAMA): Salama Tower, al-Madina Rd, Jeddah; tel. 920023355; e-mail customer.care@salama.com.sa; internet www.salama.com.sa; Chair. MOUNTASAR MOHAMMED FOUDAH.

Saudi National Insurance Co (E.C.): POB 5832, Jeddah 21432; tel. (12) 660-6200; fax (12) 667-4530; e-mail snic@eajb.com.sa; internet www.snic.com.sa; f. 1974; Chair. Sheikh HATEM ALI JUFFALI; Gen. Man. OMAR S. BILANI.

Tawuniya (NCCI): POB 86959, Riyadh 11632; tel. (11) 252-5800; fax (11) 400-0844; e-mail info@tawuniya.com.sa; internet tawuniya.com.sa; f. 1985 by royal decree as Nat. Co for Co-operative Insurance; name changed as above 2007; owned by 3 govt agencies; proposed privatization approved by the Supreme Economic Council in May 2004; initial public offering of shares in Dec. 2004; Chair. ABDULAZIZ IBRAHIM AL-NOWIASER; CEO ABDULAZIZ HASAN AL-BOUQ.

United Cooperative Assurance Co (UCA): POB 5019, 1st & 4th Floors, al-Mukmal Tower al-Khaledia District, Prince Saud Al Faisal St, Jeddah 21422; tel. (11) 217-5335; fax (11) 464-0329; e-mail uca@uca.com.sa; internet www.uca.com.sa; f. 1974 as United Commercial Agencies Ltd; name changed as above 2007; all classes of insurance; Chair. KHALID HUSSEIN ALI REZA; CEO MOHAMMED BASRAWI.

Wala'a Cooperative Insurance Co: POB 31616, al-Khobar 31952; tel. 8001199222; e-mail walaa@walaa.com; internet www.walaa.com; f. 1976; fmrly Saudi United Insurance; operated by Saudi United Cooperative Insurance Co; acquired SABB Takaful Co in 2022; provides all classes of insurance for businesses and govt agencies; majority shareholding held by Ahmad Hamad al-Gosaibi & Bros; Chair. SULAIMAN ABDULLAH AL-KADI; CEO JOHNSON VARUGHESE.

SAUDI ARABIA

Trade and Industry

GOVERNMENT AGENCIES

Saudi Space Commission (SSC): 8461 Ushba, Al Shohda District, Unit 1, Riyadh 13241–3512; tel. (11) 244-3999; fax (11) 244-3888; e-mail info@ssc.gov.sa; internet saudispace.gov.sa; f. 2018; Chair. ABDULLAH BIN AMER AL-SWAHHA.

DEVELOPMENT ORGANIZATIONS

Arab Petroleum Investments Corpn (APICORP): POB 9599, Dammam 31423; tel. (13) 847-0444; fax (13) 847-0011; internet www.apicorp.org; f. 1975; affiliated to the Org. of Arab Petroleum Exporting Countries; specializes in financing petroleum and petrochemical projects and related industries in the Arab world and in other developing countries; shareholders: Kuwait, Saudi Arabia and the UAE (17% each), Libya (15%), Iraq and Qatar (10% each), Algeria (5%), Bahrain, Egypt and Syria (3% each); Chair. Dr AABED BIN ABDULLAH AL-SAADOUN; CEO KHALID BIN ALI AL-RUWAIGH.

National Agricultural Development Co (NADEC): Nadec Al-Murabba District, south of Riyadh Palace Hotel, POB 2557, Riyadh 11461; tel. (11) 202-7777; e-mail info@nadec.com.sa; internet nadec.com; f. 1981; the Govt has a 20% share; Chair. ABDULAZIZ SALEH AL-REBDI; CEO SOLAIMAN ABDULAZIZ AL-TWAIJRI.

Public Investment Fund (PIF): POB 6847, Riyadh 11452; tel. (11) 405-0000; e-mail info@pif.com; internet www.pif.gov.sa; f. 1971 to facilitate devt of the nat. economy; 100% state-owned; fmrly under the control of the Ministry of Finance; transferred to Council of Development and Economic Affairs 2015; provides the Govt's share of capital to mixed capital cos; has managed Sanabil al-Saudia, a sovereign wealth fund, since 2008; Chair. Crown Prince MOHAMMED BIN SALMAN BIN ABDULAZIZ AL SA'UD; Gov. YASIR BIN OTHMAN AL-RUMAYYAN.

Saudi Fund for Development (SFD): King Fahd Rd, POB 50483, Riyadh 11523; tel. (11) 279-4000; fax (11) 464-7450; e-mail info@sfd.gov.sa; internet www.sfd.gov.sa; f. 1974 to finance projects in developing countries; state-owned; Chair. AHMED BIN AQIL AL-KHATIB (Minister of Tourism); CEO SULTAN BIN ABDULRAHMAN AL-MARSHAD.

Saudi Industrial Development Fund (SIDF): 3015 King Abdullah Financial District, al-Aqeeq, Unit 2, Riyadh 13519-6483; tel. (11) 825-1555; e-mail info@sidf.gov.sa; internet www.sidf.gov.sa; f. 1974; supports and promotes local industrial devt, providing medium-term interest-free loans; also offers marketing, technical, financial and administrative advice; Chair. Eng. BANDAR BIN IBRAHIM AL-KHORAYEF (Minister of Industry and Mineral Resources); CEO Prince SULTAN BIN KHALID BIN FAISAL AL SA'UD.

Small and Medium Enterprises General Authority (Monsha'at): POB 12128, Riyadh; tel. 8003018888; e-mail info@monshaat.gov.sa; internet www.monshaat.gov.sa; f. 2016; aims to regulate and support the development of small and medium enterprises; Gov. SAMI AL-HUSSAINI.

TASNEE: POB 26707, Riyadh 11496; tel. (11) 222-2205; fax (11) 400-2255; e-mail info@taldeen.com.sa; internet www.tasnee.com; f. 1985 as Nat. Industrialization Co to promote and establish industrial projects in Saudi Arabia; 100% owned by Saudi nationals; Chair. Eng. MUBARAK BIN ABDULLAH AL-KHAFRAH; CEO MUTLAQ H. AL-MORISHED.

CHAMBERS OF COMMERCE

Eastern Province Chamber of Commerce and Industry (Asharqia Chamber of Commerce and Industry): POB 719, Dammam 31421; tel. (13) 857-1111; fax (13) 857-0607; e-mail info@chamber.org.sa; internet www.chamber.org.sa; f. 1952; Chair BADER AL-REZIZA.

Federation of Gulf Co-operation Council Chambers (FGCCC): POB 2198, Dammam 31451; tel. (13) 899-3749; fax (13) 899-4668; e-mail info@fgccc.org; internet www.fgccc.org; f. 1979; Pres. AJLAN BIN ABDULAZIZ AL-AJLAN.

Federation of Saudi Chambers (FSC): POB 16683, Riyadh 11474; tel. (11) 218-2222; internet fsc.org.sa; fmrly Council of Saudi Chambers; present name adopted in 2021; Chair. Dr AJLAN BIN ABDULAZIZ AL-AJLAN; Sec.-Gen. HUSSEIN AL-ABDULQADER; fed. of 28 chambers.

Ha'il Chamber of Commerce and Industry: POB 1291, Ha'il; tel. (16) 532-1060; fax (16) 533-1366; e-mail info@hc.org.sa; internet hc.org.sa; Pres. ABDULAZIZ AL-ZAKARIYA.

Jazan Chamber of Commerce and Industry: POB 201, Jazan; tel. (17) 322-4459; fax (17) 322-4231; e-mail info@jazancci.org.sa; internet jazancci.org.sa; Chair. AHMED BIN MOHAMMED ABO HADI; Sec.-Gen. Dr MAJED BIN IBRAHIM AL-GOHARI.

Jeddah Chamber of Commerce and Industry (JCCI): POB 1264, Jeddah 21431; tel. (12) 239-8000; fax (12) 651-2070; e-mail info@jcci.org.sa; internet www.jcci.org.sa; f. 1946; Chair. Sheikh MOHAMMED YOUSUF NAGHI; Sec.-Gen. IMAD M. HASHEM; 26,000 mems.

Makkah Chamber of Commerce and Industry: POB 1086, Mecca 21955; tel. (12) 534-3838; e-mail info@makkahcci.org.sa; internet makkahcci.org.sa; f. 1947; Pres. HISHAM BIN MOHAMMED KAAKI.

Medina Chamber of Commerce and Industry (MCCI): POB 443, King Abdulaziz Rd, Medina; tel. (14) 825-8366; e-mail info@mcci.org.sa; internet www.mcci.org.sa; Pres. MUNEER BIN SAAD; Sec.-Gen. ABDULLAH AHMED ABU AL-NASR.

Riyadh Chamber of Commerce and Industry: POB 596, Riyadh 11421; tel. (11) 404-0044; fax (11) 402-1103; e-mail callcenter@rdcci.org.sa; internet www.chamber.sa; f. 1961; acts as arbitrator in business disputes, information centre; Chair. AJLAN A. AL-AJLAN; Sec.-Gen. NASSER O. ABUHAIMED; 70,000 mems.

Ta'if Chamber of Commerce and Industry: POB 1005, Ta'if; tel. (12) 736-6800; e-mail info@taifcci.org.sa; internet taifchamber.org.sa; Pres. Dr SAMI BIN ABDULLAH AL-ABIDI; Sec.-Gen. Eng. DASMAN BIN HAMDAN AL-FAQIH.

Yanbu Chamber of Commerce and Industry: POB 58, Yanbu; tel. (14) 322-7878; fax (14) 322-6800; e-mail info@ynbcci.org.sa; internet www.ynbcci.org.sa; f. 1979; publishes quarterly magazine; Pres. AHMED BIN SALEM AL-SHAGHDALI.

STATE HYDROCARBONS COMPANIES

Saudi Arabian Oil Co (Saudi Aramco): POB 5000, Dhahran 31311; tel. (13) 872-0115; fax (13) 873-8190; e-mail webmaster2@aramco.com; internet www.aramco.com; f. 1933; previously known as Arabian-American Oil Co (Aramco); in 1993 incorporated the Saudi Arabian Marketing and Refining Co (SAMAREC, f. 1988) by merger of operations; holds the principal working concessions in Saudi Arabia; in 2019 launched an Initial Public Offering (IPO) and started trading on the Tadawul stock exchange in Riyadh; operates 4 wholly owned refineries (at Jeddah, Ras Tanura, Riyadh and Yanbu); Chair. YASIR OTHMAN AL-RUMAYYAN; Pres. and CEO AMIN H. NASSER.

  Aramco Gulf Operations Co (AGOC): POB 688, Khafji City 31971; tel. (13) 765-2000; e-mail info@agoc.com.sa; internet www.agoc.com.sa; f. 2000; wholly owned by Saudi Aramco; holds concession for offshore exploitation of Saudi Arabia's half-interest in the Saudi Arabia-Kuwait Neutral Zone; Chair. KHALED A. AL-BURAIK; Pres. and CEO ALI AL-AJMI.

  Petromin Corpn (Petromin Oils): POB 1432, Jeddah 21431; tel. (12) 215-7000; fax (12) 215-7111; e-mail info@petromin.com; internet petromin.com; f. 1968; owned by al-Dabbagh Group; mfr and marketing of lubricating oils and other related products; Group CEO KALYANA SIVAGNANAM; Man. Dir SAMER NAWAR.

  Rabigh Refining and Petrochemical Co (Petro Rabigh): POB 101, Rabigh 21911; tel. (12) 425-0390; fax (12) 425-8755; e-mail investor.relations@petrorabigh.com; internet www.petrorabigh.com; f. 2005; jt venture between Saudi Aramco and Sumitomo Chemical (Japan); operation of integrated oil refining and petrochemical production facilities at Rabigh; initial public offering of 20% of shares announced 2008; Chair. IBRAHIM BIN QASSIM AL-BUAINAIN; Pres. and CEO Eng. OTHMAN ALI AL-GHAMDI.

  Saudi Aramco Lubricating Oil Refining Co (LUBEREF): POB 5518, Jeddah 22411; tel. (12) 427-5497; fax (12) 636-6933; e-mail webmaster@luberef.com; internet www.luberef.com; f. 1975; owned 70% by Saudi Aramco and 30% by Jadwa Industrial Investment Co; Chair. IBRAHIM Q. AL-BUAINAIN; Pres. and CEO TAREQ AL-NUAIM.

  Saudi Aramco Mobil Refinery Co Ltd (SAMREF): POB 30078, Yanbu; tel. (14) 396-4000; fax (14) 396-0942; e-mail info@samref.com.sa; internet samref.com.sa; f. 1981; operation of oil refining facilities at Yanbu; operated by Saudi Aramco and Mobil, capacity 402,000 b/d; Chair. AHMAD A. AL-SA'ADI; Pres. and CEO IBRAHIM M. AL-NITAIFI.

  Saudi Aramco Shell Refinery Co (SASREF): POB 10088, Jubail Industrial City 31961; tel. (13) 357-2000; fax (13) 357-2525; e-mail info@sasref.com.sa; internet www.sasref.com.sa; f. 1986; operation of oil refining facilities at Jubail; operated by Saudi Aramco and Shell; capacity 305,000 b/d; exports began 1985; Chair. YASSER MUFTI; Pres. and CEO ZIYAD H. JURAIFANI.

Saudi Basic Industries Corpn (SABIC): POB 5101, Riyadh 11422; tel. (11) 225-8000; fax (11) 225-9000; e-mail info@sabic.com; internet www.sabic.com; f. 1976; 70% owned by Saudi Aramco, 30% owned by private investors in Saudi Arabia and other institutions; mfrs of chemicals, fertilizers, plastics and metals; Chair. Eng. KHALID HASHIM AL-DABBAGH; CEO Eng. ABDULRAHMAN AL-FAGEEH.

Projects include:

  Arabian Petrochemical Co (Petrokemya): POB 10002, Jubail 31961; tel. (13) 358-7000; fax (13) 358-4480; f. 1981; wholly owned subsidiary of SABIC; owns 50% interest in ethylene glycol plant; Pres. NAWAF AL-ANAZI.

  Eastern Petrochemical Co (Sharq): POB 10035, Jubail 31961; tel. (13) 357-5000; fax (13) 358-0383; f. 1981 to produce linear low-

SAUDI ARABIA

density polyethylene, ethylene glycol; a SABIC jt venture with Japanese cos led by Mitsubishi Corpn; Chair. ABD AL-AZIZ AL-JARBOOA.

Al-Jubail Petrochemical Co (Kemya): POB 10084, Jubail 35713; tel. (13) 357-6000; fax (13) 358-7858; f. 1980; produces linear low-density polyethylene, high-density polyethylene and high alfa olefins; jt venture with Exxon Corpn (USA) and SABIC; Chair. HOMOOD AL-TUWAIJRI; Pres. ABD AL-AZIZ SULAYMAN AL-HAMAAD.

National Industrial Gases Co (Gas): POB 10110, Jubail 31961; tel. (13) 357-5738; fax (13) 358-8880; 70% SABIC-owned jt venture with Saudi private sector; Pres. ALI AL-GHAMDI.

Saudi-European Petrochemical Co (Ibn Zahr): POB 10330, Jubail 31961; tel. (13) 340-6776; fax (13) 341-6798; e-mail info@ibnzahr.sabic.com; f. 1985; produces methyl-tertiary-butyl-ether (MTBE) and propylene; SABIC has an 80% share, Ecofuel and APICORP each have 10%; Chair. NAWAF AL-ANAZI.

Saudi Kayan Petrochemical Co: POB 110320, Jubail Industrial City 31961; tel. (13) 356-3345; fax (13) 359-3111; e-mail khateebaba@saudikayan.sabic.com; internet www.saudikayan.com; f. 2006; jt venture between SABIC and Al-Kayan Petrochemical Co; initial public offering of 45% of shares in 2008; production of ethylene, propylene, polypropylene, ethylene glycol, butene-1 and specialized products incl. aminomethyls, dimethylformamide and choline chloride; Chair. AHMED AL-SHAIKH; Pres. OMAR A. AL-RUHAILY.

Saudi Methanol Co (ar-Razi): POB 10065, Jubail Industrial City 31961; tel. (13) 357-7800; fax (13) 358-5552; f. 1979; jt venture with a consortium of Japanese cos; Pres. NABIL A. MANSOURI; Exec. Vice-Pres. H. MIZUNO.

Saudi Petrochemical Co (Sadaf): POB 10025, Jubail 31961; tel. (13) 357-3000; fax (13) 357-3343; f. 1980 to produce ethylene, ethylene dichloride, styrene, crude industrial ethanol, caustic soda and methyl-tertiary-butyl-ether (MTBE); Shell Chemicals Arabia has a 50% share; Pres. MOSAED S. AL-OHALI.

Saudi Yanbu Petrochemical Co (Yanpet): POB 30333, Yanbu 21441; tel. (14) 396-5000; fax (14) 396-5006; e-mail info@yanpet.sabic.com; ExxonMobil and SABIC each have a 50% share.

Yanbu National Petrochemical Co (Yansab): POB 31396, Yanbu Industrial City 41912; tel. (14) 325-9000; fax (14) 325-9502; e-mail shares@yansab.sabic.com; internet www.yansab.com.sa; f. 2006; 51% owned by SABIC; Chair. ABDULRAHMAN A. SHAMSADDIN.

Foreign Concessionaire

Saudi Arabian Chevron Inc.: POB 363, Riyadh; tel. (11) 462-7274; fax (11) 464-1992; also office in Kuwait; f. 1928; fmrly Getty Oil Co; renamed Saudi Arabian Texaco Inc. 1993, renamed as above 2007; holds concession (5,200 sq km at Dec. 1987) for exploitation of Saudi Arabia's half-interest in the Saudi Arabia-Kuwait Neutral (Partitioned) Zone; Pres. AHMAD AL-OMAR.

UTILITIES

Power and Water Utility Company for Jubail and Yanbu (MARAFIQ): POB 11133, Jubail Industrial City 31961; tel. 920020081; fax (13) 340-1168; internet www.marafiq.com.sa; f. 2003; equal ownership held by the Royal Comm. for Jubail and Yanbu, Saudi Aramco, Saudi Basic Industries Corpn and the Public Investment Fund; operation and devt of utility services; Chair. KHALID M. AL-SALEM; Pres. and CEO MOHAMMED BERKI AL-ZUABI.

Saudi Water Partnership Co (SWPC): POB 300091, Moon Tower, Floors 18-19, King Fahed Rd, Riyadh 11372; tel. 920002988; e-mail info@swpc.sa; internet www.swpc.sa; f. 2003 as Water and Electricity Co; present name adopted in 2019; wholly owned by Ministry of Finance; responsible for managing supply and demand of electricity and water; Chair. Eng. ABDULRAHMAN AL-FADHLI (Minister of Environment, Water and Agriculture); CEO KHALED BIN ZWAID AL-QURESHI.

Electricity

ACWA Power: POB 22616, Riyadh 11416; tel. (11) 283-5555; fax (11) 283-5500; internet www.acwapower.com; f. 2008; develops privately financed power and water projects; Chair. MOHAMMAD ABUNAYYAN; Vice-Chair. and CEO PADDY PADMANATHAN.

Saudi Electricity Co (SEC): POB 57, Riyadh 11411; tel. 920000222; internet www.se.com.sa; f. 1999 following merger of 10 regional cos, to organize the generation, transmission and distribution of electricity into separate operating cos; jt-stock co; Chair. Dr KHALID BIN SALEH AL-SULTAN; CEO KHALED BIN HAMAD AL-GNOON.

Water and Electricity Regulatory Authority (WERA): POB 4199, Riyadh 12711; tel. (11) 201-9000; fax (11) 201-9044; e-mail info@wera.gov.sa; internet wera.gov.sa; f. 2001 as Electricity & Co-Generation Regulatory Authority to regulate the power industry and to recommend tariffs; Chair. Prince ABDULAZIZ BIN SALMAN BIN ABDULAZIZ AL SA'UD (Minister of Energy); Gov. ABDULRAHMAN BIN MOHAMMED AL-IBRAHIM.

Water

National Water Co (NWC): POB 676, Riyadh 11421; tel. (11) 211-3016; fax (11) 440-9595; e-mail riyadhcontact@nwc.com.sa; internet www.nwc.com.sa; f. 2008 to consolidate all govt-run water and wastewater management services and to facilitate the gradual privatization of the sector; Chair. Eng. ABDULRAHMAN AL-FADHLI (Minister of Environment, Water and Agriculture); CEO Eng. NEMER AL-SHEBEL.

Saline Water Conversion Corpn (SWCC): POB 5968, Riyadh 11432; tel. (11) 463-1111; fax (11) 463-0236; e-mail info@swcc.gov.sa; internet www.swcc.gov.sa; f. 1974; provides desalinated water; Gov. Eng. ABDULLAH BIN IBRAHIM AL-ABDULKAREEM; Chair. Eng. ABDULRAHMAN AL-FADHLI (Minister of Environment, Water and Agriculture); 32 desalination plants (2021).

MAJOR COMPANIES

Abdullah Ibrahim Muhammad Al-Subeaei Co (AIMS): POB 11515, Jeddah 21463; tel. (12) 613-3333; internet aims.com; f. 1933; investment, real estate, construction, hospitality, education, industrial, properties, retail and leasing; Chair. SALEH ABDULLAH IBRAHIM AL-SUBEAEI.

Almarai Co: POB 8524, Riyadh 11492; tel. (11) 470-0005; fax (11) 470-1555; e-mail info@almarai.com; internet www.almarai.com; f. 1977; manufacturer of dairy products, fruit juices, baked goods, poultry and other food products; Chair. Prince NAYEF BIN SULTAN BIN MUHAMMAD BIN SAUD AL-KABIR; CEO ABDULLAH AL-BADR.

Saleh & Abd al-Aziz Abahsain Co Ltd: POB 209, al-Khobar 31952; tel. (13) 898-4045; fax (13) 899-1557; e-mail info@abahsain.net; internet www.abahsain.net; f. 1947; trade in general heavy machinery and machinery for construction and engineering; Man. Dir NAIM ANSARI; Gen. Man. FAISAL MEHTAB.

Alhamrani Group: POB 1229, Jeddah 21431; tel. (12) 606-5555; fax (12) 606-0265; e-mail info@alhamrani.net; internet alhamrani.net; f. 1951; retail and aftersales services for automotive industry; automated banking and security equipment; construction materials and airport and aviation services; Chair. and CEO ABDULAZIZ A. ALHAMRANI.

Alpha Trading and Shipping Agencies Ltd: POB 205, Jeddah 21411; tel. (12) 644-0808; fax (12) 642-1188; e-mail central@alpha-trading.com; internet www.alpha-trading.com; f. 1965; trade in foodstuffs, raw materials and commodities; Chair. Sheikh ABD AL-QADIR MUHAMMAD AL-FADL.

Arab Supply and Trading Co (ASTRA Group): POB 245, Tabouk; tel. (14) 422-0400; fax (14) 423-7649; e-mail astra@astra.com.sa; internet www.astra.group; f. 1976; farming; manufacturing; tourism; telecommunications; banking and investment; wholesale and retail trade; medical and pharmaceutical products and services; Chair. SABIH AL-TAHER AL-MASRI; Pres. KHALID MASRI; 6,000 employees (2023).

Arabian Cement Co Ltd: POB 8605 King Abd al-Aziz Rd, Jeddah 23523; tel. (12) 694-9700; fax (12) 694-9690; e-mail info@arabiacement.com.sa; internet arabiancement.com.sa; f. 1955; produces ordinary Portland cement and sulphate-resistant cement; owns subsidiary Cement Industry Products Co Ltd; Chair. ABDULLAH MUHAMMAD NOOR RAHIMI; CEO Dr BADR OSAMA GOHAR.

Consolidated Contractors Co WLL: POB 234, Bldg 53, 7101 al-Sayf al-Daoula al-Hamdani St, al-Rawbah, Riyadh 12814; tel. (11) 510–3780; fax (11) 464–5963; internet www.ccc.net; general construction and engineering projects, incl. infrastructure and heavy industry; major shareholders are members of Saudi royal family; subsidiary of Consolidated Contractors Co, Athens (Greece); Group Chair. SAMER S. KHOURY.

Dallah al-Baraka Group: Bldg 2860, Saleh Kamel Business Center, Ash Shati District, Jeddah 23612-7246; tel. (12) 592-5999; fax (12) 671-3603; e-mail prd@dallah.com; internet www.dallah.com; f. 1969; divided into business, finance and media divisions; industrial investment; agriculture; trading; real estate; transport; tourism; construction; financial services; communications; satellite broadcasting; Chair. ABDULLAH SALEH KAMEL; CEO ABDULAZIZ YAMANI.

Dar al-Arkan Real Estate Development Co: Makkah Rd, Al Wizarat, Riyadh 12622; tel. (11) 123–3333; e-mail info@alarkan.com; internet www.daralarkan.com; f. 1994; real estate devt; Chair. YOUSUF BIN ABDULLAH AL-SHELASH.

Eastern Province Cement Co: POB 4536, King Fahd Rd, Dammam 31412; tel. (13) 881-2222; fax (13) 881-2000; internet www.epcco.com.sa; f. 1982 as Saudi-Kuwaiti Cement Co; present name adopted 1994; Chair MOHAMMED SAAD AL-FARAJ; CEO Eng. FAHAD RAHED AL-OTAIBI.

Al-Faisaliah Group (AFG): POB 16460, Bldg 19, Qurtubah District, Riyadh 11464; tel. (11) 243-9878; e-mail info@alfaisaliah.com;

internet www.alfaisaliah.com; f. 1971; sale, installation and management of electrical, electronic and telecommunications equipment; computers; health care; petrochemicals; dairy and agricultural products; Chair. ABDULRAHMAN ABDULLAH AL-FAISAL; Pres. MOHAMMED K. A. AL-FAISAL.

Grain Silos and Flour Mills Organization: POB 3402, Riyadh 11471; tel. (11) 247-2220; internet www.sago.gov.sa; f. 1972; autonomous body formally responsible to the Ministry of Environment, Water and Agriculture; production of flour and animal feeds for domestic consumption; Chair. Eng. ABDULRAHMAN BIN ABDULMOHSEN AL-FADHLI (Minister of Environment, Water and Agriculture).

Hoshan Group: King Fahad Rd, Olaya District, Riyadh 11421; tel. (11) 217-0000; fax (11) 465-6248; e-mail info@hoshangroup.com; internet www.hoshangroup.com; f. 1964 as Hoshan Co; office furniture and equipment, telecommunications, engineering, information technology and microfilm products; Chair. and CEO RAKAN AMER EL-HOSHAN; approx. 1,000 employees (2022).

Jabal Omar Development Co: POB 56968, al-Shubaikah District, Mecca 21955; tel. (12) 547-8888; fax (12) 547-9998; e-mail info@jodc.com.sa; internet jabalomar.com.sa; f. 2006; construction and real estate devt; Chair. SAEED MOHAMMED AL-GHAMDI; CEO KHALID AL-AMOUDI.

Jadawel International Co Ltd: POB 61539, Riyadh 11575; tel. (13) 463-1760; fax (13) 465-1013; e-mail info@jadawelinternational.com; internet jadawel.com; f. 1984; real estate devt and sale of building supplies; Chair. and CEO MUHAMMAD BIN ISA AL-JABER.

Abdullatif Mohammed Salah Jamjoom & Bros Co: POB 1247, al-Ammariyah, Jeddah 21437; tel. (12) 645-4172; fax (12) 645-7785; e-mail khaled@jamjoom.com; internet www.jamjoom.com; f. 1971; automotive, pharmaceuticals, manufacturing and transporting metal products, real estate; Chair. and CEO Sheikh ABD AL-QAFAR MUHAMMAD JAMJOON.

Al-Jubail Fertilizer Co (Al Bayroni): POB 10046, Jubail 31961; tel. (13) 341-6488; fax (13) 341-7122; f. 1979; 50% owned by SABIC Agri-Nutrients Co; Chair. Eng. SAMIR ALI AL-ABDRABBUH.

Isam Khairy Kabbani Group: King Abdul Aziz Rd, An Nahdah, Jeddah 23523; tel. (12) 627-8000; e-mail info@ikkgroup.com; internet namat.com/ikktest; f. 1968; oil and gas pipelines; wholesale and retail trade in construction materials, electrical goods, tools, hardware and food products; Chair. Sheikh HASSAN KABBANI; CEO AMR MAMOUN AL-KABBANI; 14,000 employees (2023).

Kingdom Holding Co: POB 1, Riyadh 11321; tel. (11) 211-1111; e-mail media@kingdom.com.sa; internet kingdom.com.sa; f. 1979; est. as Kingdom Establishment for Commerce and Trade; present name adopted in 1996; project financing, contracting and trading; Chair. Prince ALWALEED BIN TALAL; CEO Eng. TALAL IBRAHIM AL-MAIMAN.

Makkah Construction & Development Co: Faqih Commercial Center, 7th Floor, Makkah al-Mukarramah, al-Azizia General St, POB 7134, Mecca 21955; tel. (12) 558-2652; fax (12) 558-3086; e-mail mosahem@mcdc.com.sa; internet www.mcdc.com.sa; f. 1988; Chair. AHMED ABDULAZIZ AL-HAMDAN.

Manufacturing and Building Co Ltd (MABCO): POB 52743, Riyadh 11573; tel. (11) 498-1222; fax (11) 498-4807; f. 1977; manufacture of pre-cast components for construction of buildings; Pres. OMAR ABD AL-FATTAH AGGAD; Gen. Man. WAJIH AL-BAZ; 500 employees.

Marei bin Mahfouz Group & Co Ltd: An Naseem, Mecca 24245-4443; tel. (12) 550-0088; fax (12) 550-0099; e-mail info@mbmgroup.com.sa; internet www.mbmgroup.com.sa; f. 1976; manufacturer; investor in real estate; import and export; wholesale and retail; medical services; Chair. MAREI MUBARAK BIN MAHFOUZ; Exec. Dir Dr MAHFOUZ MAREI BIN MAHFOUZ; 1,150 employees.

Muhammad Abd al-Aziz Al-Rajhi and Sons Investment Co: POB 14665, Riyadh 11434; tel. (11) 243-8000; fax (11) 419-1430; e-mail info@rajhi-invest.com; internet www.rajhi-invest.com/index-en.html; f. 2015; estab. through merger of Manafea Holding Co with Muhammad Abd al-Aziz Al Rajhi & Sons Holding Co to become a closed-joint stock co; investments in finance, real estate, hotels, industry and private equity; Chair. YAZID BIN MOHAMED AL-RAJHI; CEO MOHAMED EL-SAMMAN.

Napco National: POB 538, 1st Industrial City, Dammam 31421; tel. (13) 847-2288; e-mail info@napconational.com; internet www.napconational.com; f. 1956; manufacture and wholesale trade in plastics; CEO MOUNIR FREM; over 5,000 employees (2023).

National Gas and Industrialisation Co (GASCO): Bldg 331, Prince Abdulaziz Ibn Musaid Ibn Jalawi St, Al Olaya, Riyadh 12221; tel. (11) 466-4999; fax (11) 466-4999; e-mail info@gasco.com.sa; internet www.gasco.com.sa; f. 1963; supply and transportation of LPG, LPG tanks and accessories; Chair. ABDULAZIZ FAHAD AL-KHAYAL; CEO ABDULRAHMAN ABDULAZIZ BIN SULAIMAN.

National Glass Industries Co (Zoujaj): POB 41619, Riyadh 11531; tel. (11) 265-2323; e-mail zoujaj@zoujaj-glass.com; internet zoujaj-glass.com; f. 1990; manufacture of glass products; Chair. OMAR RIYADH MUHAMMAD AL-HUMAIDAN.

National Gypsum Co: POB 187, Riyadh 11411; tel. (11) 464-1963; internet www.gypsco.com.sa; f. 1958; Chair. and Man. Dir AHMAD ABDULLAH AL-THUNAYAN.

National Industrialization Co (TASNEE): POB 26707, Riyadh 11496; tel. (11) 222-2205; fax (11) 400-2255; e-mail admin@tasnee.com; internet www.tasnee.com; f. 1985; petrochemicals, chemicals, plastics and metal; industrial services; Chair. Eng. MUBARAK BIN ABDALLAH AL-KHAFRA; CEO MUTLAQ AL-MORISHED.

National Methanol Co (Ibn Sina): POB 10003, Jubail 31961; tel. (13) 340-5500; f. 1981; began commercial production of chemical-grade methanol in 1984; jt venture between SABIC and CTE (the latter being jointly owned by US cos Celanese Corpn and Duke Energy); Chair. ABDULLAH AL-ASSAF; Pres. NABIL MASOURI.

National Pipe Co Ltd: POB 1099, al-Khobar 31952; tel. (13) 868-3298; fax (13) 882-7286; e-mail qc.dept@npc.com.sa; internet www.npc.com.sa; f. 1978; manufacture and marketing of spiral-welded steel pipes for oil and gas transmission; jt venture between Rezayat Group, Nippon Steel Corpn (Japan) and Sumitomo Corpn (Japan); Chair. TEYMOUR ALIREZA; Gen. Man. EIJI MIKAMI.

Olayan Financing Co: POB 8772, Riyadh 11492; tel. (11) 839-2000; internet olayan.com; f. 1947; investment in industrial devt and technology projects; CEO NABEEL AL-AMUDI.

Qassim Cement Co (QCC): POB 4266, Buraidah 52271-6735; tel. (16) 316-5555; fax (16) 381-6041; e-mail qcc@qcc.com.sa; internet www.qcc.com.sa; f. 1976; production of 4m. metric tons annually; Chair. Dr MOHAMMAD BIN NASSER AL-DAWOOD; CEO OMAR BIN ABDULLAH AL-OMAR; 565 employees (2023).

Riyadh Cables Group: POB 26862, Riyadh 11496; tel. (11) 265-0850; e-mail rcgc@riyadh-cables.com; internet riyadh-cables.com; f. 1984; mfr of electrical cables; Chair. KHALED A. AL-GWAIZ; CEO BORJAN SEHOVAC; over 3,000 employees (2023).

Saad Trading and Contracting Co: POB 3250, al-Khobar 31952; tel. (13) 882-2220; fax (13) 882-7989; f. 1986; design; building and construction contracting; engineering; building maintenance; CEO MA'AN ABD AL-WAHID AL-SANEE; Gen. Man. STUART F. SMITH.

SABIC Agri-Nutrients Co: POB 11044, Jubail 31961; tel. (13) 340-6621; fax (13) 341-2367; e-mail investorrelations@safco.sabic.com; internet www.sabic-agrinutrients.com; f. 1965 as Saudi Arabian Fertilizer Co; present named adopted in 2020; owned 50.1% by SABIC, 49.9% being held by the private sector and the public; Chair. ABDULRAHMAN SALEH AL-FAGEEH; CEO Eng. ABDULRAHMAN A. SHAMSADDIN.

Mahmood Saeed Group: al-Mahjar, Jeddah 22423; tel. (12) 636-0020; e-mail info@mscc.com.sa; internet mscc.com.sa; f. 1948; manufacturing, real estate, furniture, trading, food and beverages, and cosmetics; Chair. Sheikh MAHMOOD MUHAMMAD SAEED QASSIM; CEO Dr AYMAN KHALIL.

Al-Safi Danone Ltd: POB 10525, Riyadh 11443; tel. (11) 270-3466; e-mail info@alsafidanone.com; internet alsafiarabia.com; f. 1979; est. as Al-Safi; name changed as above in 2001 when jt venture launched with French food group Danone; dairy products; Chair. MUHAMMAD A. AL-SARHAN; CEO TOLGA SEZER.

Saudi Arabian Amiantit Co (Amiantit): Bldg 101, Industrial Area 1, Dammam 3224-3361; tel. (13) 847-1500; fax (13) 847-1398; e-mail info@amiantit.com; internet www.amiantit.com; f. 1968; production and marketing of pipes, fibreglass and rubber products; Chair. Prince KHALED BIN ABDULLAH BIN ABD AL-RAHMAN AL SA'UD; CEO FERAS BIN GHASSAB AL-HARBI.

Saudi Arabian Military Industries (SAMI): POB 6511, Riyadh Front, Bldg 3706, Unit 2, Airport Rd, Riyadh 13455; tel. 920000977; internet www.sami.com.sa; f. 2017 to build a self-sufficient defence industry in the Kingdom; Chair. AHMED BIN AQEEL AL-KHATEEB; CEO Eng. WALID ABUKHALED.

Saudi Arabian Mining Co (Ma'aden): POB 68861, Riyadh 11537; tel. (11) 874-8000; fax (11) 874-8300; e-mail info@maaden.com.sa; internet www.maaden.com.sa; f. 1997; privatization approved by the Supreme Economic Council 2004; wholly owned by Govt until 2008 when one-half of the company's shares were offered on Tadawul; 67.2% owned by Govt; Chair. YASIR AL-RUMAYYAN; CEO ROBERT WILT.

Saudi Basic Industries Corpn (SABIC): POB 5101, Riyadh 11422; tel. (11) 225-8000; fax (11) 225-9000; e-mail info@sabic.com; internet www.sabic.com; f. 1976; 70% owned by Saudi Aramco, 30% owned by private investors in Saudi Arabia and other institutions; mfrs of chemicals, fertilizers, plastics and metals; Chair. Eng. KHALID HASHIM AL-DABBAGH; CEO Eng. ABDULRAHMAN AL-FAGEEH.

Saudi Binladin Group (SBG): POB 8918, Jeddah 21492; tel. (12) 664-3033; e-mail info@sbg.com.sa; internet www.sbg.com.sa; f. 1931; reorg. and present name adopted 1989; construction and investment holding co; Chair. ABDULAZIZ AL-DUAILEJ; CEO KHALID AL-GWAIZ.

Saudi Cable Co: POB 4403, Jeddah 21491; tel. (12) 608-7666; fax (12) 637-9877; f. 1975; manufacture of building wires, power and telecommunication cables (including fibre optic cables), copper and aluminium rod, PVC compounds, information technology products, power transmission and distribution products, turnkey services; affiliate of Xenel Industries Ltd; Chair. ABDUL RAHMAN IBRAHIM AL-KAYAL; Group CEO NAEL FAYEZ.

Saudi Cement Co: 3964, King Saud, al-Amamrah Area, Unit 1, Dammam 32415–7102; tel. (13) 835-8000; fax (13) 834-3091; e-mail contactus@saudicement.com.sa; internet saudicement.com.sa; f. 1955; Chair. KHALED ABDULRAHMAN AL-RAJHI.

Saudi Ceramic Co: POB 3893, King Fahad Rd, Riyadh 11481; tel. (11) 829-8888; e-mail info@saudiceramics.com; internet www.saudiceramics.com; f. 1977; manufacture and marketing of ceramics, sanitary ware and electric water heaters; Chair. YOUSUF SALEH ABAL KHAIL; CEO MAJED ABDULLAH AL-ISSA.

Saudi Fisheries Co (SFC): POB 8705, Nasr Bin Ghanem, Al Malaz, Riyadh 12641; tel. 920000527; e-mail info@alasmak.com.sa; internet alasmak.com.sa; f. 1980; Chair. ABDULRAHMAN BIN SAUD AL-OWAIS; CEO AWWAD FAROUK AL-DASOUQI.

Saudi Industrial Investment Group: POB 99833, Riyadh 11625; tel. (11) 2192522; fax (11) 2192523; e-mail info@siig.com.sa; internet www.siig.com.sa; f. 1996; Chair. Eng. KHALIL IBRAHIM AL-WATBAN; CEO ABDULRAHMAN SALEH AL-ISMAIL.

Saudi International Petrochemical Co (Sipchem): King Sa'ud Rd, al-Hada District, al Khobar; tel. (13) 801-9392; e-mail marketing@sipchem.com; internet www.sipchem.com; f. 1999 to develop and invest in the petrochemical and chemical industries; produces a range of petrochemical and chemical products through its affiliates: Int. Methanol Co, Int. Diol Co, Int. Acetyl Co, Int. Vinyl Acetate Co, Int. Gases Co, Sipchem Marketing Co and 11 others; Chair. Eng. KHALID A. AL-ZAMIL; CEO ABDULLAH AL-SAADOON.

Saudi Iron and Steel Co (Hadeed): POB 10053, Jubail 35721; tel. (13) 357-6000; fax (13) 358-7858; internet www.sabic.com/en/products/metals; f. 1979; fully owned manufacturing affiliate of SABIC; Exec. Dir ABDULAZIZ AL-AMIR.

Saudi Pharmaceutical Industries and Medical Appliances Corpn (Spimaco): POB 20001, Riyadh 11455; tel. (11) 252-3333; fax (11) 252-3300; e-mail info@spimaco.sa; internet www.spimaco.com.sa; f. 1986; mfr of pharmaceutical products; Chair. MOHAMMED TALAL AL-NAHAS; CEO KHALED SALEH AL-KHATTAF.

Saudi Plastic Products Co Ltd (SAPPCO): POB 4916, Industrial Area 1, 3rd St, Dammam 31412; tel. (11) 847-1703; fax (11) 847-1969; e-mail sales-dammam@sappco.com.sa; internet www.sappco.com.sa/dammam; f. 1970; mfr and supplier of UPVC pipes and fittings; Man. Dir FAISAL AL-SALEH.

Saudi Research and Marketing Group: POB 53108, Makkah Rd, Riyadh 11583; tel. (11) 2128000; e-mail info@srmg.com; internet www.srmg.com; f. 1972; Chair. Eng. ABD AL-RAHMAN BIN IBRAHIM RWAITA; CEO JOMANA RASHED AL-RASHID; over 1,900 employees (2022).

Saudi United Fertilizers Co (Al-Asmida): POB 11682, 2468 al-Murad Bldg, al-Quds St, Al-Hamra District, Jeddah 21463; tel. (12) 665-9448; fax (12) 284-1230; e-mail alasmida@suf-ksa.com; internet www.suf-ksa.com; f. 1976; import and export of agricultural fertilizers, pesticides, forage seeds, field sprayers and agricultural machinery; Gen. Man. MARWAN MURAD.

Saudia Dairy and Foodstuff Co Ltd (SADAFCO): POB 5043, Jeddah 21422; tel. (12) 629–3370; e-mail sadafco@sadafco.com; internet sadafco.com; f. 1976; mfr and distributor of food products and beverages; Chair. Sheikh HAMAD SABAH AL-AHMAD; CEO PATRICK STILLHART.

Savola Group: 2444 Taha Khusaifan-Ashati, Unit 15, Prince Faisal bin Fahd Rd, Ashati District, Jeddah 23511-7333; tel. (12) 268-7700; e-mail info@savola.com; internet www.savola.com; f. 1979; production of food and beverages; Chair. SULAYMAN A. K. AL-MUHAIDIB; CEO WALID KHALED FATANI.

Seera Group: POB 52660, Imam Saud bin Abdulaziz bin Mohammed Rd, Taawun District, Riyadh 11573; e-mail media@seera.sa; internet www.seera.sa; f. 1979; travel and tourism services; Chair. Eng. MUHAMMAD BIN SALEH AL-KHALIL; Man. Dir and CEO ABDULLAH BIN NASSER AL-DAWOOD; over 4,600 employees (2022).

Southern Province Cement Co: POB 548, King Fahd Rd, Abha 62581; tel. (17) 227-1500; fax (17) 227-1003; e-mail ho@spa.com.sa; internet spcc.sa; f. 1978; Chair. Dr HAMAD BIN SULAIMAN AL-BAZAI; CEO AQEEL KADASAH.

Al-Suwaiket Trading and Contracting Co: POB 691, Dhahran Airport 31932; tel. (13) 857-9784; fax (13) 857-2904; e-mail ho@alsuwaiket.com; internet www.alsuwaiket.com; f. 1947; general contracting; electro-mechanical engineering; telecoms and electronics; drilling, wells and pipeline services; Pres. MUBARAK ABDULLAH AL-SUWAIKET.

Tamimi Group: Industrial Area 1, King Fahd Rd, Dammam 32234; tel. (13) 807-5700; e-mail tamimi-ho@al-tamimi.com; internet tamimigroup.com.sa; f. 1942; over 30 cos in more than 9 sectors; includes Tamimi Global, Tamimi Commercial Division, Tamimi Markets, Tamimi Energy Holding Co, Tamimi Real Estate, etc.; Chair. TARIQ AL-TAMIMI.

Xenel Industries Ltd: POB 2824, Jeddah 21461; tel. (12) 604-8000; e-mail communications@xenel.com; internet www.xenel.com; f. 1973; agricultural commodities, industrial services, heavy industries, energy, petrochemicals, construction, infrastructure devt, health care, logistics and real estate.

Yamama Saudi Cement Co: POB 293, Riyadh 11411; tel. (11) 408-5600; fax (11) 403-3292; e-mail headoffice@yamamacement.com; internet www.yamamacement.com; f. 1956; production and marketing of cement and paper products; Chair. Prince TURKI BIN MUHAMMAD BIN ABDUL AZIZ BIN TURKI; CEO JEHAD BIN ABDUL AZIZ AL-RASHED.

Yanbu Cement Co: POB 5330, Jeddah 21422; tel. (12) 653-1555; fax (12) 653-1420; e-mail customercare@yanbucement.com; internet www.yanbucement.com; f. 1977; Chair. FAHAD BIN SULAIMAN AL-RAJHI; CEO ALI BIN ABDULLAH SULEIMAN AL-AYED.

Al-Zamil Group: POB 9, al-Khobar 31952; tel. (13) 882-4888; fax (13) 813-6222; e-mail info@zamil.com; internet zamil.com; f. 1920; involved in real estate and land devt and the marketing of products from numerous subsidiaries, incl. Zamil Marine Services Co, Zamil Industrial, Yamama Factories, Arabian Gulf Construction Co Ltd, Zamil Investment Co, Zamil Coating Co and Zamil Plastic Industries; Pres. KHALID A. AL-ZAMIL; CEO ADIB AL-ZAMIL.

TRADE UNIONS

Trade unions are illegal in Saudi Arabia.

Transport

RAILWAYS

In 2023 the rail network in Saudi Arabia comprised some 3,650 km of track, on three lines. The 2,750-km North–South line (completed in 2015) runs from Riyadh to the border with Jordan, and has branch lines to mining operations in the north of the country; the 450-km Riyadh–Dammam line runs from the capital to Dammam on the Gulf coast (with a branch line for freight trains to al-Kharj and Harad); and the 450–km Haramain high-speed line (opened in 2018) connects the west-coast centres of Mecca, Medina and Jeddah, and provides a passenger service for millions of *Umrah* and *Hajj* pilgrims every year. There are plans to build two new lines (mainly for freight) of 950-km and 115-km in length, connecting Riyadh with Jeddah and Dammam with Jubail, respectively. The so-called Saudi Landbridge Project would connect the Red Sea with the Persian (Arabian) Gulf and would be closely linked with Jeddah Islamic Port and King Abd al-Aziz Port (at Dammam).

An 18.1-km elevated metro system linking the holy sites in Mecca opened in 2010; plans are currently under way to build a new 182-km four-line metro system in the city. Plans for the construction of a three-line, 149-km metro system in Jeddah were approved in 2013, while in the same year contracts for construction work on a six-line, 176.5-km metro system in Riyadh were awarded. The Riyadh Metro system was expected to commence operating in 2024, while the construction of the Jeddah Metro was expected to be completed by 2025.

Saudi Railway Co (SAR): Diplomatic Quarter Bldg S-24, POB 64447, Riyadh 11452; tel. (11) 250-1111; fax (11) 480-7517; e-mail customerservices@sar.com.sa; internet www.sar.com.sa; f. 2006; in 2019, following its merger with the state-owned Saudi Railway Organisation, SAR became the sole national railway agency of Saudi Arabia; Chair. Eng. SALEH BIN NASSER BIN ALI AL-JASSER (Minister of Transport); CEO BASHAR AL-MALIK.

ROADS

Asphalted roads link Jeddah to Mecca, Jeddah to Medina, Medina to Yanbu, al-Ta'if to Mecca, Riyadh to al-Kharj, and Dammam to Hufuf, as well as the principal communities and certain outlying points in Saudi Aramco's area of operations. The east–west 1,395-km trans-Arabian highway (Highway 40) links Dammam, Riyadh, al-Ta'if, Mecca and Jeddah.

Saudi Public Transport Co (SAPTCO): POB 10667, Bldg 7995, al-Takhasusi St, al-Nakhil District, Riyadh 11443; tel. 920026888; fax 920026889; e-mail info@saptco.com.sa; internet www.saptco.com.sa; f. 1979; operates a public bus service throughout Saudi Arabia and to neighbouring countries; the Govt holds a 30% share; Chair. Eng. KHALID BIN SALEH AL-MADEFER; CEO Eng. KHALID BIN ABDULLAH HAMAD AL-HOGAIL.

SAUDI ARABIA

SHIPPING

On average, over 95% of Saudi Arabia's imports and exports pass through the country's sea ports. Responsibility for the management, operation and maintenance of a number of ports began to be transferred to the private sector from 1997, but all ports remain subject to regulation and scrutiny by the Ports Authority.

Jeddah is the principal commercial port and the main point of entry for pilgrims bound for Mecca. Dammam is the second largest commercial port and Saudi Arabia's main port on the Persian (Arabian) Gulf.

There are five other major ports in the country, located at Jubail, Yanbu, Jazan, Dhiba (the closest port to the Suez Canal) and Ras al-Khair. Both Jubail and Yanbu comprise one commercial and one industrial port. Yanbu is the focal point of Saudi Arabia's area of most rapid growth, on the west coast. Jazan is the main port for the southern part of the country, while Ras al-Khair Industrial Port, which is located on the Gulf coast some 60 km north of Jubail, was built primarily to handle mineral exports and was inaugurated in 2016.

The Port of NEOM, which incorporated the existing port of Dhiba, commenced operations in May 2023. The port is located in the NEOM special economic zone and serves as the primary seaport of entry to the north–west of the country.

Port Authorities

Saudi Ports Authority (Mawani): POB 5162, Riyadh 11422; tel. (11) 405-0005; fax (11) 405-3508; e-mail mawanicare@mawani.gov.sa; internet mawani.gov.sa; f. 1976; regulatory authority; Chair. Eng. SALEH BIN NASSER BIN ALI AL-JASSER (Minister of Transport); Pres. OMAR TALAL HARIRI.

Dammam Port (King Abdulaziz Port): POB 28062, Dammam 31437; tel. (13) 858-3199; fax (13) 857-1727; 43 berths for general cargo, container, ro-ro, dangerous cargo and bulk grain shipments; draughts range from 8 m to 13.5 m; the port has a 200-metric-ton floating crane and a fully equipped ship-repair yard.

Dhiba Port: POB 190, Dhiba; tel. (14) 432-1072; fax (14) 432-2679; f. 1994; 10 berths.

Jazan Port: POB 16, Jazan; tel. (17) 322-1389; fax (17) 317-0777; f. 1976; 12 berths.

Jeddah Islamic Port: POB 9285, Jeddah 21188; tel. (12) 627-7777; fax (12) 647-7411; 62 berths for general cargo, container traffic, roll-on roll-off (ro-ro) traffic, livestock and bulk grain shipments, with draughts ranging from 8 m to 16 m; the port also has a 200-metric-ton floating crane, cold storage facilities and a fully equipped ship-repair yard.

Jubail Commercial Port: POB 276, Jubail 31951; tel. (13) 362-0600; fax (13) 362-3340; e-mail jubail@ports.gov.sa; f. 1974; 16 berths.

Jubail Industrial Port (King Fahad Industrial Port): POB 31951, Jubail Industrial City 547; tel. (13) 396-0079; fax (13) 357-8011; f. 1982; 34 berths; largest industrial port in the Middle East.

Ras al-Khair Port: POB 11065, Jubail 31961; tel. (13) 344-8710; fax (13) 13 344-8731; f. 2016; 14 berths.

Yanbu Commercial Port: POB 1019, Yanbu al-Bahar; tel. (14) 398-7000; fax (14) 322-7643; f. 1965; 12 berths.

Yanbu Industrial Port (King Fahad Industrial Port Yanbu): POB 30325, Yanbu Industrial City 41912; tel. (14) 396-7036; fax (14) 396-7009; f. 1980; 34 berths.

Principal Shipping Companies

Arabian Establishment for Trade and Shipping (AET): POB 832, 2nd Floor, Al-Matbouli Plaza, al-Ruwaiz District, Jeddah 21421; tel. (12) 652-5500; fax (12) 657-1104; e-mail aetjed@aetshipping.com; internet www.aetshipping.com; f. 1963; shipping agency; Gen. Man. ANTHONY ROBINSON.

Bihar International Co: POB 14437, Prince Sultan St, Rawda District, Jeddah 21424; tel. (12) 691-2219; fax (12) 691-3882; internet www.biharinternational.co; f. 1973 as Bakri Navigation Co Ltd; owns and operates a fleet of oil tankers, tug boats and utility vessels; Chair. FAHAD GHALEB AL-HUSAINI.

National Shipping Co of Saudi Arabia (Bahri): POB 8931, al-Olaya Towers, Tower B, Floor 12, Riyadh 11492; tel. (11) 478-5454; fax (11) 477-8036; e-mail info@bahri.sa; internet www.bahri.sa; f. 1978; transportation of crude petroleum and petrochemical products; routes through Red Sea and Mediterranean to USA and Canada; operates a fleet of 89 ships; merged with Vela International Marine Ltd 2013; Chair. MOHAMMED ABDULAZIZ AL-SARHAN; CEO Eng. ABDULLAH AL-DUBAIKHI.

Saudi Shipping and Maritime Services Co Ltd (TRANSHIP): POB 7522, Jeddah 21472; tel. (12) 645-0638; e-mail bunker@tranship.com; internet www.ssmsc.com; owns 2 tankers, 2 barges and 1 tugboat; also offers bunkering services; Chair. Prince SA'UD BIN NAYEF BIN ABD AL-AZIZ; CEO STEWART HENDRY.

CIVIL AVIATION

The four main international airports in Saudi Arabia are: King Abdulaziz International Airport (KAIA, in Jeddah), King Khalid International Airport (in Riyadh), King Fahd International Airport (serving Dammam) and Prince Mohammad bin Abdulaziz International Airport (in Medina).

General Authority of Civil Aviation (GACA): POB 47360, Riyadh 11552; tel. (11) 525-3333; fax (11) 525-3222; e-mail gaca-info@gaca.gov.sa; internet gaca.gov.sa; f. 1934 as the Presidency of Civil Aviation; name changed as above 1977; regulatory authority; Pres. ABDUL AZIZ DAHILJ.

Flynas: 8018 Abi Bakr al-Siddiq, al-Rabi, Riyadh 13316-4040; tel. (11) 434-9000; e-mail csu@flynas.com; internet www.flynas.com; f. 2007; founded as Nas Air; present name adopted 2013; low-cost domestic and international services; CEO BANDER AL-MOHANNA.

Nesma Airlines: Jeddah; tel. 920003232; internet www.nesmaairlines.com; f. 2007; owned by Nesma Holding Group; operates flights from Saudia Arabia to Cairo, Egypt; Pres. and Chair. FAISAL BIN SALEH AL-TURKI.

Riyadh Air: Riyadh; internet www.riyadhair.com; f. 2023; the second national flag carrier of Saudi Arabia; owned by the Public Investment Fund (PIF, q.v.); Chair. YASIR AL-RUMAYYAN; CEO TONY DOUGLAS.

Saudi Arabian Airlines (SAUDIA): POB 620, Jeddah 21231; tel. (12) 686-4588; fax (12) 686-4587; e-mail webmaster@saudiairlines.com.sa; internet www.saudiairlines.com; f. 1945; began operations 1947; regular services to 25 domestic and 52 international destinations; Chair. Eng. SALEH BIN NASSER BIN ALI AL-JASSER (Minister of Transport); Dir-Gen. IBRAHIM AL-OMAR.

SaudiGulf Airlines: Dammam 32552; tel. (13) 892–6222; fax (13) 883–0830; e-mail customer.care@saudigulfairlines.com; internet www.saudigulfairlines.com; f. 2013; owned by Abd al-Hadi Abdullah al-Qahtani & Sons Group (AHQ); Chair. Sheikh TARIQ ABDEL HADI AL-QAHTANI; CEO ABDULMOHSEN MAHMOUD JONAID.

Tourism

Dur Hospitality: POB 5500, Abdullah bin Huthafa al-Sahmi St, Diplomatic Quarter, Riyadh 11422; tel. (11) 481-6666; fax (11) 480-1666; e-mail info@dur.sa; internet www.dur.sa; f. 1975; construction and management of hotels, resorts and other tourism facilities; Saudi Govt has a 40% interest; Chair. BADR BIN ABDULLAH AL-ISSA; CEO SULTAN AL-OTAIBI.

Defence

As assessed at November 2022, the strength of the Royal Saudi Arabian Armed Forces totalled 257,000: army 75,000; navy 13,500; air force 20,000; air defence forces 16,000; national guard 130,000; and strategic missile forces 2,500. Paramilitary forces totalled 24,500: 15,000 Border Guard; 9,000 facilities security force; and 500 special security force.

Defence Budget: SR 171,000m. in 2022.

Chief of the General Staff: Gen. FAYYADH BIN HAMID BIN RAGAD AL-RUWAILI.

Commander of the National Guard: Lt-Gen. NAIF BIN MAJID BIN SAUD AL SA'UD.

Director-General of Public Security Forces: Maj.-Gen. MUHAMMAD AL-BASSAMI.

Commander of Joint Forces: Gen. MUTLAQ BIN SALIM BIN MUTLAQ AL-AZIMA.

Commander of Land Forces: Lt-Gen. FAHD BIN ABDULLAH BIN MUHAMMAD AL-MITAIR.

Commander of Air Force: Prince Lt-Gen. TURKI BIN BANDAR BIN ABDULAZIZ AL SA'UD.

Commander of the Navy: Adm. FAHD BIN ABDULLAH AL-GHFAILI.

Commander of Air Defence Forces: Lt-Gen. MAZYAD BIN SULAIMAN BIN MAZYAD AL-AMRO.

Commander of Strategic Missiles Force: JARALLAH BIN MUHAMMAD BIN JARALLAH AL-ELWAIT.

Education

The educational system in Saudi Arabia resembles that of other Arab countries. Educational institutions are administered mainly by the

Government. The private sector plays a significant role at the first and second levels, but its total contribution is relatively small compared with that of the public sector.

Pre-elementary education is provided on a small scale, mainly in urban areas. Elementary or primary education is of six years' duration and the normal entrance age is six. Intermediate education begins at 12 and lasts for three years. Vocational and technical education programmes can be entered after completion of the intermediate stage. Secondary education begins at 15 and extends for three years. After the first year, successful pupils branch into science or arts groups. The proportion of females enrolled in Saudi Arabian schools has increased significantly since 1970, when only about 25% of pupils were female. According to UNESCO estimates, enrolment of children in the primary age-group stood at 99.6% (boys 99.3%; girls 99.5%) in 2020/21. In the same year enrolment at lower secondary schools included 98.6% of children (boys 99.5%; girls 97.6%) in the relevant age-group, while enrolment at upper secondary level was 99.4% (boys 99.5%; girls 99.3%).

Princess Nora bint Abdulrahman University, established as Riyadh University for Women in 1970, moved to a new campus in the capital in 2011. The Imam Mohammad ibn Sa'ud Islamic University comprises 14 colleges and four institutes. It also includes two institutes abroad for teaching Islamic and Arab knowledge, in Djibouti and Indonesia. Since 2006 foreign universities have been permitted to establish campuses in the kingdom. The budget for 2023 envisaged expenditure on education of SR 189,000m., equivalent to 17.0% of total projected spending.

Bibliography

Aarts, Paul, and Nonneman, Gerd (Eds). *Saudi Arabia in the Balance: Political Economy, Society, Foreign Affairs*. London, C. Hurst & Co, 2005/New York, NY, New York University Press, 2006.

Aldukheil, Abdulaziz. *Saudi Government Revenues and Expenditures: A Financial Crisis in the Making*. Basingstoke, Palgrave Macmillan, 2013.

Alshamsi, Mansoor Jassem. *Islam and Political Reform in Saudi Arabia*. Abingdon, Routledge, 2008.

Anderson, Irvine H. *Aramco, the United States, and Saudi Arabia: A study in the Dynamics of Foreign Oil Policy, 1935–50*. Princeton, NJ, Princeton University Press, 1982.

Bronson, Rachel. *Thicker Than Oil: America's Uneasy Partnership with Saudi Arabia*. Oxford, Oxford University Press, 2008.

Cigar, Norman L. *Saudi Arabia and Nuclear Weapons: How Do Countries Think About the Bomb?*. Abingdon, Routledge, 2016.

Commins, David. *The Wahhabi Mission and Saudi Arabia*. London, I. B. Tauris, 2009.

Islam in Saudi Arabia. London, I. B. Tauris, 2014.

Cordesman, Anthony H. *Saudi Arabia Enters the 21st Century: The Military and International Security Dimensions*. Westport, CT, Greenwood Press, 2003.

Saudi Arabia: Guarding the Desert Kingdom. Boulder, CO, Westview Press, 2004.

Cordesman, Anthony H., and Obaid, Nawaf. *National Security in Saudi Arabia*. Westport, CT, Praeger Publishers, 2005.

Crawford, Michael. 'The Da'wa of Muhammad Ibn Abd al-Wahhab before the Al Saud', *Journal of Arabian Studies*. Vol. 1, No. 2, June 2011.

Craze, Joshua (Ed.). *The Kingdom: Saudi Arabia and the Challenge of the 21st Century*. London, C. Hurst & Co, 2009.

Dawisha, Adeed. 'Saudi Arabia and the Arab-Israeli Conflict: The Ups and Downs of Pragmatic Moderation', *International Journal* Vol. 38, no. 4, Dec. 1983.

Al-Enazy, Askar H. *The Creation of Saudi Arabia: Ibn Saud and British Imperial Policy, 1914–1927*. Abingdon, Routledge, 2009.

Espinoza, Raphael A. *The Macroeconomics of the Arab States of the Gulf*. Oxford, Oxford University Press, 2013.

Al-Fahad, Abdulaziz. 'From Exclusivism to Accommodation: Doctrinal and Legal Evolution of Wahhabism', *New York University Law Review* Vol. 79, No. 2, 2004.

Fandy, Mamoun. *Saudi Arabia and the Politics of Dissent*. Basingstoke, Palgrave, 1999.

Firro, Tarik K. *Wahhabism and the Rise of the House of Saud*. Eastbourne, Sussex Academic Press, 2018.

Furtig, Henner. *Iran's Rivalry with Saudi Arabia between the Gulf Wars*. Reading, Ithaca Press, 2000.

Haykel, Bernard, Hegghammer, Thomas, and Lacroix, Stéphane. *Saudi Arabia in Transition: Insights on Social, Political, Economic and Religious Change*. Cambridge, Cambridge University Press, 2015.

Hegghammer, Thomas. *Jihad in Saudi Arabia: Violence and Pan-Islamism since 1979*. Cambridge, Cambridge University Press, 2010.

Hertog, Steffen. *Princes, Brokers, and Bureaucrats: Oil and the State in Saudi Arabia*. Ithaca, NY, Cornell University Press, 2010.

Hill, Ginny, and Nonneman, Gerd. *Yemen, Saudi Arabia and the Gulf States: Elite Politics, Street Protests and Regional Diplomacy*. London, Chatham House, 2011.

Hinds, Matthew Fallon. *The US, the UK and Saudi Arabia in World War II: the Middle East and the Origins of a Special Relationship*. London, I. B. Tauris, 2016.

Hiro, Dilip. *Cold War in the Islamic World: Saudi Arabia, Iran and the Struggle for Supremacy*. London, C. Hurst & Co, 2018.

Holden, David, Johns, Richard, and Buchan, James. *The House of Saud*. London, Sidgwick & Jackson, 1981.

Hope, Bradley, and Scheck, Justin. *Blood and Oil: Mohammed bin Salman's Ruthless Quest for Global Power*. London, John Murray, 2020.

House, Karen Elliott. *On Saudi Arabia: Its People, Past, Religion, Fault Lines—And Future*. New York, Knopf, 2012.

Hubbard, Ben. *MBS: The Rise to Power of Mohammed Bin Salman*. London, William Collins, 2020.

Ibrahim, Fouad N. *The Shi'is of Saudi Arabia*. London, Saqi Books, 2006.

International Crisis Group. 'Can Saudi Arabia Reform Itself?', *ICG Middle East Report* 28, 14 July 2004.

'The Shiite Question in Saudi Arabia', *ICG Middle East Report* 45, 19 September 2005.

Ismail, Raihan. *Saudi Clerics and Shi'a Islam*. New York, NY, Oxford University Press, 2016.

Kéchichian, Joseph. *Legal and Political Reforms in Saudi Arabia*. Abingdon, Routledge, 2012.

Keynoush, Banafsheh. *Saudi Arabia and Iran: Friends or Foes?*. London, Palgrave Macmillan, 2016.

Lacroix, Stéphane. *Les islamistes saoudiens: une insurrection manqué*. Paris, Presses Universitaires de France, 2010.

(trans. Holoch, Georges). *Awakening Islam: Religious Dissent in Contemporary Saudi Arabia*. Cambridge, MA, Harvard University Press, 2011.

Lippman, Thomas W. *Inside the Mirage: America's Fragile Relationship with Saudi Arabia*. New York, Perseus Books, 2003.

Saudi Arabia on the Edge. Dulles, VA, Potomac Books, 2012.

Mabon, Simon. *Saudi Arabia and Iran: Soft Power Rivalry in the Middle East*. London, I. B. Tauris, 2013.

The Struggle for Supremacy in the Middle East: Saudi Arabia and Iran. Cambridge, Cambridge University Press, 2023.

Mandaville, Peter. *Wahhabism and the World: Understanding Saudi Arabia's Global Influence on Islam*. Oxford, Oxford University Press, 2022.

Mason, Robert. *Foreign Policy in Iran and Saudi Arabia: Economics and Diplomacy in the Middle East*. London, I. B. Tauris, 2014.

Al-Mazrouei, Noura Saber. *The UAE and Saudi Arabia: Border Disputes and International Relations in the Gulf*. London, I. B. Tauris, 2016.

McLoughlin, Leslie. *Ibn Saud: Founder of a Kingdom*. London, Palgrave Macmillan, 1993.

Niblock, Tim (Ed.). *State, Society and Economy in Saudi Arabia*. London, Croom Helm, 1981.

Saudi Arabia: Power, Legitimacy and Survival. Abingdon, Routledge, 2006.

The Political Economy of Saudi Arabia (with Monica Malik). Abingdon, Routledge, 2007.

Nonneman, Gerd. 'Saudi-European Relations, 1902–2001: A Pragmatic Quest for Relative Autonomy', *International Affairs*. Vol. 77, No. 3, July 2001.

Obaid, Nawaf E. *The Oil Kingdom at 100: Petroleum Policy-Making in Saudi Arabia*. Washington, DC, Washington Institute for Near East Policy, 2001.

al-Othaimeen, Abdullah. *History of the Kingdom of Saudi Arabia*. Riyadh, Obeikan, 2014, 17th edn.

Partrick, Neil. *Saudi Arabian Foreign Policy: Conflict and Cooperation*. London, I. B. Tauris, 2016.

Philby, H. St. J. B. *Arabia and the Wahhabis*. London, 1928.

Arabia. London, Benn, 1930.

Saudi Arabia. London, 1955.

Quandt, Willam B. *Saudi Arabia in the 1980s: Foreign Policy, Security and Oil*. Oxford, Basil Blackwell, 1982.

Al-Rasheed, Madawi. *Contesting the Saudi State: Islamic Voices from a New Generation*. Cambridge, Cambridge University Press, 2007.

(Ed.). *Kingdom Without Borders: Saudi Arabia's Political, Religious and Media Frontiers*. London, C. Hurst & Co, 2008.

A History of Saudi Arabia, 2nd edn. Cambridge, Cambridge University Press, 2010.

A Most Masculine State: Gender, Politics, and Religion in Saudi Arabia. Cambridge, Cambridge University Press, 2013.

(Ed.) *Salman's Legacy: The Dilemmas of a New Era in Saudi Arabia*. London, C. Hurst & Co, 2018.

The Son King : Reform and Repression in Saudi Arabia. London, C. Hurst & Co, 2020.

Al-Rasheed, Madawi, and Vitalis, Robert (Eds). *Counter Narratives: History, Contemporary Society and Politics in Saudi Arabia*. New York, Palgrave, 2004.

Riedel, Bruce. *Kings and Presidents: Saudi Arabia and the United States since FDR*. Washington, DC, Brookings Institution Press, 2019.

Rieger, René. *Saudi Arabian Foreign Relations: Diplomacy and Mediation in Conflict Resolution*. Abingdon, Routledge, 2016.

Rundell, David. *Vision or Mirage: Saudi Arabia at the Crossroads*. London, I. B. Tauris, 2020.

Shahi, Afshin. *The Politics of Truth Management in Saudi Arabia*. Abingdon, Routledge, 2013.

Silverfarb, Daniel. 'The Anglo-Najd Treaty of December 1915', *Middle Eastern Studies*, Vol. 16, No. 3, 1980, pp. 167–177.

Stenslie, Stig. *Regime Stability in Saudi Arabia: The Challenge of Succession*. Abingdon, Routledge, 2011.

'Power Behind the Veil: Princesses of the House of Saud', *Journal of Arabian Studies*. Vol. 1, No. 1, June 2011.

Alsultan, Fahad M., and Saeid, Pedram. *The Development of Saudi-Iranian Relations since the 1990s: Between Conflict and Accommodation*. Abingdon, Routledge, 2017.

Al-Tamimi, Naser. *China-Saudi Arabia Relations, 1990–2012: Marriage of Convenience Or Strategic Alliance?* Abingdon, Routledge, 2013.

Thompson, Mark. 'Assessing the Impact of Saudi Arabia's National Dialogue', *Journal of Arabian Studies*. Vol. 1, No. 2, June 2012.

Saudi Arabia and the Path to Political Change: National Dialogue and Civil Society. London, I. B. Tauris, 2014.

Trofimov, Yaroslav. *The Siege of Mecca: The Forgotten Uprising in Islam's Holiest Shrine and the Rise of Al Qaeda*. New York, Doubleday, 2007.

Vassiliev, Alexei. *The History of Saudi Arabia*. London, Saqi Books, 1998.

King Faisal: Personality, Faith and Times. Saqi Books, 2013.

Vitalis, Robert. *America's Kingdom: Mythmaking on the Saudi Oil Frontier*. Stanford, CA, Stanford University Press, 2006.

Wald, Ellen R. *Saudi, Inc.: The Arabian Kingdom's Pursuit of Profit and Power*. New York, NY, Pegasus Books, 2018.

Wilson, Rodney, al-Salamah, Abdullah, Malik, Monica, and al-Rajhi, Ahmed. *Economic Development in Saudi Arabia*. London, RoutledgeCurzon, 2003.

Yamani, Mai. *Changed Identities: The Challenge of the New Generation in Saudi Arabia*. London, Royal Institute of International Affairs, 1999.

Cradle of Islam: The Hijaz and the Quest for an Arabian Identity. London, I. B. Tauris, 2004.

SPANISH NORTH AFRICA

The territories of Spanish North Africa comprise mainly Ceuta and Melilla, two enclaves within Moroccan territory on the north African coast. Attached to Melilla, for administrative purposes, are Peñón de Vélez de la Gomera, a small fort on the Mediterranean coast, and two groups of islands, Peñón de Alhucemas and the Chafarinas. Ceuta and Melilla are seen as integral parts of Spain by the Spanish Government and have the status of autonomous cities, although Morocco has put forward a claim to both. Sovereignty over the uninhabited island of Perejil (known as Laila to the Moroccans) is disputed between Spain and Morocco.

CEUTA

Geography

The ancient port and walled city of Ceuta is situated on a rocky promontory on the North African coast overlooking the Strait of Gibraltar, the Strait here being about 25 km wide. Ceuta was retained by Spain as a *plaza de soberanía* (a presidio, or fortified enclave, over which Spain has full sovereign rights) when Morocco became independent from France in 1956, and was administered as part of Cádiz Province until 1995. Ceuta now functions as a bunkering and fishing port, occupying an area of 19.7 sq km. At the census of January 2021, the population was recorded at 84,071. Official estimates put the population at 82,833 at 1 January 2023, with a density of 4,204.7 people per sq km.

History

Ceuta was conquered by Juan I of Portugal in 1415. Following the union of the crowns of Spain and Portugal in 1580, Ceuta passed under Spanish rule and in 1694, when Portugal was formally separated from Spain, the territory requested to remain under Spanish control. During the 16th, 17th and 18th centuries, Ceuta endured a number of sieges by the Muslims. Ahmad Gailan, a chieftain in northern Morocco, blockaded the town in 1648–55. The Sultan of Morocco, Mulai Ismail (1672–1727), attacked Ceuta in 1674, 1680 and 1694, after which he maintained a blockade against the town until 1720. Ahmad Ali al-Rifi, a chieftain from northern Morocco, made yet another unsuccessful assault in 1732. A pact of friendship and commerce was negotiated between Spain and Morocco at Aranjuez, Spain, in 1780, a peaceful agreement following in the next year over the boundaries of the enclave. In 1844–45 there was another dispute about the precise limits of Ceuta. Further disagreement led to the war of 1859–60. Spanish forces, after an engagement at Los Castillejos, seized Tetuán from Morocco. Following another battle at Wadi Ras in March 1860, the conflict came to an end. A settlement was then made, which enlarged the enclave of Ceuta and obliged Morocco to forfeit to Spain 100m. pesetas as war indemnities. In 1974 the town became the seat of the Capitanía General de Africa.

Since 1939 both Ceuta and Melilla, the other Spanish enclave in North Africa, have been ruled as integral parts of Spain, though this arrangement is disputed in the territories. All those born in Ceuta, Melilla and the island dependencies are Spanish citizens and subjects. Both Ceuta and Melilla have local assemblies, and are administered as an integral part of Spain by the Delegado del Gobierno (Government Delegate), who is directly responsible to the Ministry of Home Affairs in Madrid. The Government Delegate is usually assisted by a Sub-Delegate. There is also one delegate from each of the ministries in Madrid. Each enclave elects one deputy and two senators to the Cortes Generales (parliament) in Madrid.

In November 1978 King Hassan of Morocco stated his country's claim to Ceuta and the other main Spanish enclave in North Africa, Melilla, a claim that was reiterated following the opening of the Spanish frontier with Gibraltar in early 1985. In October 1981 Spain declared before the United Nations (UN) that Ceuta and Melilla were integral parts of Spanish territory. Spain rejects any comparison between the two enclaves and Gibraltar. From 1984 there was increasing unease over Spanish North Africa's future, following rioting in Morocco in January and the signing of the treaty of union between Libya and Morocco in August. In July 1985 the joint Libyan-Moroccan assembly passed a resolution calling for the 'liberation' of Ceuta and Melilla.

Details of Ceuta and Melilla's new draft statutes, envisaging the establishment of two local assemblies, with jurisdiction over such matters as public works, agriculture, tourism, culture and internal trade, were approved by the central Government in December 1985. Unlike Spain's other regional assemblies, however, those of Ceuta and Melilla were not to be vested with legislative powers. After negotiations with representatives of the Muslim community, in May 1986 the central Government agreed to grant Spanish nationality to more than 2,400 Muslims resident in the enclaves. At the general election held in June, the ruling Partido Socialista Obrero Español (PSOE) was successful in Ceuta.

In February 1988 it was announced that, in accordance with regulations of the European Community (EC, now European Union—EU, see p. 1140), to which Spain had acceded in 1986, Moroccan citizens would in due course require visas to enter Spain. Entry to Spanish North Africa, however, was to be exempt from the new ruling.

In March 1988 the central Government and principal opposition parties in Madrid reached a broad consensus on draft autonomy statutes for Spanish North Africa. Morocco's Minister of Foreign Affairs formally presented his country's claim to Ceuta and Melilla to the UN General Assembly in October. At the Spanish general election held that month, the ruling PSOE retained its Ceuta seats, despite allegations by the opposition Partido Popular (PP) that many names on the electoral register were duplicated.

In April 1990 the Spanish Government presented the autonomy statutes for discussion in the territories. It was confirmed that the enclaves were to remain an integral part of Spain, and that they were to be granted self-government at municipal, rather than regional, level. The draft autonomy statutes of Ceuta and Melilla were submitted to the lower legislative house of the Cortes Generales, the Congreso de los Diputados (Congress of Deputies), in Madrid for discussion in October 1991. In November thousands of demonstrators, many of whom had travelled from the enclaves, attended a protest march in Madrid (organized by the Governments of Ceuta and Melilla), in support of demands for full autonomy for the territories. In early 1992, however, the central Government confirmed that the assemblies of Ceuta and Melilla were not to be granted full legislative powers. At the general election of June 1993 the PSOE of Ceuta lost its one seat in the Congress of Deputies and its two seats in the Senado (Senate) to the PP.

The final statutes of autonomy were approved by the Spanish Government in September 1994. The statutes provided for 25-member local assemblies, with powers similar to those of the municipal councils of mainland Spain. Each assembly would elect from among its members a Mayor/President, who would head a Council of Government. In October a general strike in Ceuta, in protest against the proposals for limited self-government, received widespread support. Following their approval by the Congress of Deputies in December, the autonomy statutes were ratified by the Senate in February 1995.

Elections for the new local assemblies were held in May 1995. In Ceuta the PP won nine of the 25 seats, Progreso y Futuro de

Ceuta (PFC) six, the nationalist Ceuta Unida (CEU) four and the PSOE three. Basilio Fernández López of the PFC was re-elected Mayor/President, heading a coalition with CEU and the PSOE. Mustafa Mizziam Ammar, leader of the Partido Democrático y Social de Ceuta (PDSC), became the first Muslim candidate ever to be elected in the territory.

At the general election held in March 1996, the three PP delegates to the Cortes Generales in Madrid were re-elected. In July Mayor/President Fernández López resigned after seven months at the head of a minority administration, and was replaced by Jesús Fortes Ramos of the PP.

During 1996 both Ceuta and Melilla appealed to the EU for financial assistance to counter an increase in the number of (mostly African) migrants attempting to cross the border. Negotiations in Madrid in October between the Spanish Minister of the Interior and his Moroccan counterpart resulted in an agreement on the establishment of two joint commissions to address the specific problems of illegal immigration and drug trafficking. In December, for the first time since the signing of a joint accord in 1992, Morocco agreed to the readmission of migrants held in the Spanish enclaves. In September the Secretary-General of the North Atlantic Treaty Organization (NATO) confirmed that Ceuta and Melilla would remain outside the Alliance's sphere of protection if Spain were to be fully integrated into NATO's military structure.

At the elections of June 1999 the most successful party was the Grupo Independiente Liberal (GIL), which secured 12 of the 25 seats in Ceuta's Assembly. Antonio Sampietro Casarramona of the GIL replaced Jesús Fortes Ramos of the PP as Mayor/President in August, following the latter's removal from office by a motion of censure supported by a rebel PSOE deputy, Susana Bermúdez. In March 2000 Sampietro and Bermúdez were charged with bribery, following claims that the latter's allegiance had been illicitly obtained. At the general election held on 12 March, Ceuta's three PP representatives in Madrid, one deputy and two senators, all secured re-election.

In early 1999 it was conceded that the security barrier along Ceuta's border with Morocco was proving inadequate. The EU-funded project had been initiated five years previously but remained unfinished. Between January and July alone a total of 21,411 migrants were apprehended on Ceuta's frontier and returned to Morocco. In November border security was reinforced by the army. Further improvements to the barrier were completed in February 2000. The implementation in that month of new legislation relating to immigrants' rights obliged the border post at Ceuta to provide legal assistance to those being denied entry to Spain by the police. In May it was revealed that during 1999 a total of 700,000 migrants had been refused admission to Spanish North Africa.

In January 2000 Prime Minister José María Aznar visited Ceuta and Melilla (although in his capacity as President of the PP, rather than President of the Government), describing the enclaves as constant parts of Spain's future. Morocco subsequently cancelled a scheduled official visit of the Spanish Minister of Foreign Affairs. In May Aznar declared that the controversial immigration law would need to be reviewed, as, since its entry into force in February, more than 82,000 immigrants had applied for Spanish residency permits. Large numbers of migrants continued to enter the two enclaves illegally throughout 2000, and further clashes between migrants and the security forces were reported. Reforms to the immigration law, which entered into force in January 2001, were intended to benefit those seeking asylum, but offered severe penalties to individuals who entered the enclaves illegally, and to traffickers and employers who assisted them. Protests against the reforms were staged in Spanish North Africa, and mainland Spain.

In January 2001 five Ceuta councillors resigned their posts and announced their departure from the GIL, thus depriving the party of its majority in the Assembly. Former PSOE deputy Bermúdez subsequently withdrew her backing for the GIL, which had previously enabled the party to assume office. A motion of censure against Sampietro, proposed by the PP, the PSOE, the PDSC and one of the former GIL councillors, was carried in February, with the support of 17 of the 25 deputies, and Juan Jesús Vivas Lara of the PP was appointed Mayor/President. A new Council of Government was subsequently announced, including the five 'rebel' councillors (now members of the Grupo Mixto).

In September 2002 Morocco reasserted its claims to Ceuta and Melilla at the UN. This followed a confrontation between Spain and Morocco in July over the occupation of Perejil, a small islet near Ceuta, by 12 Moroccan soldiers. (The islet was subsequently retaken by Spanish soldiers.) In response to several border incidents and in an attempt to halt illegal immigration, Spain ordered the permanent closure of the border with Morocco at Benzu in October.

A bilateral immigration accord signed by Spain and Morocco in February 2003 proposed the repatriation to Morocco of 200 illegal immigrant minors from Ceuta and Melilla in March. In early 2003 measures to strengthen border security were increased. A series of suicide bombings launched against Western targets in Casablanca in May, killing up to 45 people, resulted in a further tightening of border security. It was believed that one of the leaders of the militant Islamist group allegedly responsible for the attacks was a resident of Ceuta, and that others involved in the bombings had subsequently fled to mainland Spain via the territory. In June the Spanish Government's delegate in Ceuta initiated a request to the Ministry of Foreign Affairs in Madrid to withdraw citizenship from any dual nationals in the enclave who were proven criminals, members of fundamentalist groups or pro-Moroccan. At the regional elections held in May 2003, the PP achieved an absolute majority in Ceuta for the first time, winning 19 of the 25 seats, while the Unión Demócrata Ceutí (UDCE), representing the Muslim population, secured three. Vivas remained as Mayor/President.

In 2003 an estimated 3,000 migrants passed through Ceuta, and the enclave received more than 1,400 asylum requests (of which 18% were successful), compared with 372 in 2002 and 82 in 2001. In December 2003 Morocco and Spain made progress towards reaching an accord on the repatriation of illegal immigrant minors; however, a final agreement was not signed. Human rights groups criticized the two centres provided by the Spanish Government for migrants as inadequate.

At the March 2004 general election, the PP retained the deputy and senators elected by Ceuta. In November the central Government announced plans to build reception centres on the mainland, to which illegal immigrants arrested in Ceuta and Melilla would be transported. Following a series of attempts to scale the walls separating the territories from Morocco, security on both sides of the border was increased from September 2005. In October the Spanish Government authorized €3m. to improve facilities for immigrants in the enclaves.

In early 2006 Spanish premier José Luis Rodríguez Zapatero made the first official visit by a Prime Minister to the enclaves in over 25 years. Zapatero's visit was condemned by the Moroccan authorities as a provocation, despite relations between Spain and Morocco having been favourable during the first two years of his administration.

In February 2007 the Spanish Government reached an agreement with the Governments of Ceuta and Melilla to abandon plans to change the cities' status from Ciudades Autónomas (Autonomous Cities) to Comunidades Autónomas (Autonomous Communities). In return, more powers would be devolved to the cities in the areas of employment and social services, and their budgets would be increased. At elections in May, the PP again won 19 of the 25 seats in the Assembly; the UDCE, in alliance with the left-wing Izquierda Unida, secured four seats, while the PSOE won two. Vivas resumed office as Mayor/President. In October ongoing divisions within the local branch of the PSOE led to its dissolution, and the party's national leadership delegated a commission to assume temporary responsibility for PSOE activities in Ceuta. (The local branch of the PSOE resumed activities under a newly elected Secretary-General, José Antonio Carracao Meléndez, in December 2008.)

In November 2007 a two-day visit to Ceuta and Melilla by King Juan Carlos, his first since acceding to the throne in 1975, was warmly welcomed by residents, but prompted Morocco to recall its ambassador from Madrid. The ambassador returned to the Spanish capital in January 2008, following a visit to Rabat by the Spanish Minister of Foreign Affairs and Co-operation, Miguel Ángel Moratinos, who delivered a conciliatory letter from Prime Minister Zapatero to Morocco's King Mohammed VI.

At the March 2008 and November 2011 general elections, the PP retained Ceuta's one seat in the Congress of Deputies and its two seats in the Senate. Meanwhile, at elections to the Assembly held in May 2011, the PP retained the largest representation, with 18 seats. The 'Caballas' coalition, comprising the UDCE and the Parti Socialista del Pueblo del Ceuta (PSPC), won four seats, while the PSOE took three. A new Council of Government, under the continued leadership of Vivas, took office in June.

A minor reorganization of the Government took place in March 2012. The development and environment portfolio was divided, with responsibility for environmental affairs passing to the Councillor for Public Services and Communities. In April Vivas announced a further reorganization; most notably, Francisco Márquez de la Rubia assumed responsibility for a new Council of Planning and Relations with Governmental Organizations, and Guillermo Martínez Arcas became Councillor of Finance, the Economy and Human Resources. In June 2013 Emilio Carreira Ruiz replaced Martínez, following the latter's resignation.

In February 2014 15 people drowned off the beach at Tarajal after some 1,400 would-be migrants were forced back by the Civil Guard while attempting to swim around a breakwater marking the border between Ceuta and Morocco. The incident prompted renewed concerns over illegal migration into Spanish North Africa, and criticism of the Civil Guard. In March the Minister of Home Affairs, Jorge Fernández Díaz, authorized heightened security measures along the territories' borders. The Spanish Government subsequently approved legislation allowing for the immediate expulsion to Morocco of some migrants intercepted at the borders with Ceuta and Melilla without prior identification. Despite claims that this violated international law, the new legislation entered into effect in April. In February 2015 a judge in Ceuta announced that 16 members of the Civil Guard were to be officially investigated over their actions with regard to the fatalities at Tarajal. The Provincial Court of Cádiz eventually ruled, in July 2020, that there was insufficient evidence to warrant their prosecution.

Meanwhile, in June 2014 Premi Mirchandani Tahilram resigned as Councillor of Youth, Sport, Tourism and Festivals, and from the Assembly, amid controversy over the purchase of vehicles by his department. His responsibilities were reallocated among existing members of the Council.

Elections to the Assembly took place in May 2015. The PP remained the largest party, although its representation was reduced to 13 seats. The 'Caballas' coalition and the PSOE each received four seats, the Movimiento por la Dignidad y la Ciudadanía de Ceuta three seats and the Ciudadanos movement took one. Vivas remained at the head of a renewed Council of Government, which took office on July. At the November general election, and again at a further general election held in June 2016, owing to the failure of the political parties to form a government, the PP retained Ceuta's one seat in the Congress of Deputies and its two seats in the Senate.

In August 2017 the Government Delegate ordered the closure of the border between Ceuta and Morocco at Tarajal for one week, following an attempt illegally to enter the territory by almost 300 people, of whom 186 people were reportedly successful. Around 800 people took part in a mass attempt to cross the border fence in July 2018, with 602 succeeding in entering Ceuta. The Government of Ceuta warned the new central Government that illegal migration risked turning the territory into 'a mega encampment'.

In February 2019 the Councillor for Finance, the Economy, Public Administration and Employment, Kissy Chandiramani Ramesh, replaced Juan Bravo Baena as Ceuta's representative in the Congress of Deputies. She was in turn replaced in the Council by Alberto Gaitán Rodríguez. At a general election held in April, the PSOE gained Ceuta's seat in the Congress of Deputies, with the PP placed third behind a new far-right party, VOX Ceuta (commonly referred to as Vox). The PP's share of the vote declined from 51.9% in 2016 to just 21.4%; turnout was recorded at 64.0%. Ceuta's two seats in the Senate also went to the PSOE. At elections to the Assembly on 26 May, the PP's representation declined to just nine seats. The PSOE won seven seats, Vox six, the Movimiento por la Dignidad y la Ciudadanía de Ceuta (MDyC) two and Caballas one. Vivas remained as Mayor/President, albeit at the head of a minority, seven-member PP administration, which took office in June. María Isabel Deu del Olmo became Vice-President and Councillor of the Presidency, Government and Institutional Relations.

Further elections to the Congress of Deputies took place in November 2019, following the failure of coalition talks (see Spain). Vox secured Ceuta's seat in the chamber, while also taking one of the territory's two seats in the Senate; the other seat was regained by the PP.

In March 2020 Vivas effected an extensive reorganization of the Council, most notably appointing two additional Vice-Presidents. Deu became First Vice-President, while the Councillor of Education and Culture, Carlos Rontomé Romero, and the Councillor of Health, Consumption and Governance, Francisco Javier Guerrero Gallego, were appointed as Second and Third Vice-Presidents, respectively. Chandiramani returned as Councillor of Finance, the Economy and Public Administration; Gaitán took the post of Councillor of Development and Tourism. Meanwhile, a Council of Social Services was created, responsibility for which was allocated to Dunia Mohamed Mohand.

In January 2021 Guerrero resigned from both the Council and the Assembly amid controversy over reports that he had received a vaccination against the coronavirus disease (COVID-19) ahead of vaccine supplies being made available to the public. Gaitán was subsequently appointed as Third Vice-President and Councillor of Health, Consumption and Governance, while Alejandro Ramírez Hurtado assumed the development and tourism portfolio.

The issue of illegal migration to Spanish North Africa gained further prominence in mid-2021, with around 8,000 migrants (including 1,500 children) estimated to have arrived in Ceuta, having swum from Morocco, on 17–18 May alone. (By contrast, the number of migrants arriving illegally at Ceuta and Melilla by sea or by land totalled 2,228 in the whole of 2020, and 7,899 in 2019.) The Spanish Prime Minister, Pedro Sánchez Pérez-Castejón, visited Ceuta on 18 May 2021, pledging to restore order amid the unprecedented influx of migrants, and more than 200 Spanish military and police personnel were deployed to the enclave. Sánchez criticized Moroccan border control, amid widespread reports that guards had allowed the migrants to traverse the border unimpeded. The lack of intervention, in contrast to standard practice, was attributed by some to ongoing tensions over Spain's hosting of Brahim Ghali, the leader of Morocco's Polisario Front, which advocates for the independence of Western Sahara (see Morocco).

By 23 May 2021 around 7,000 of the migrants had been returned to Morocco, according to the Spanish Ministry of Home Affairs, with bilateral tensions somewhat ameliorated by expressions of gratitude from the Spanish Government for Morocco's co-operation in readmitting the migrants. The decision to commence the deportation from Ceuta of hundreds of unaccompanied migrant children from August was denounced by human rights groups.

In April 2022 Spain and Morocco signed a joint declaration providing for the full normalization of movement of people and goods at Ceuta and Melilla, including 'appropriate customs control devices' for migrants seeking to enter the enclaves by land and sea. The land borders between Morocco and both enclaves, which had been closed since March 2020 owing to the global COVID-19 pandemic, were duly reopened in May 2022. A new border customs office was inaugurated in Ceuta in February 2023.

Following elections to the Assembly held on 28 May 2023, the PP's representation remained unchanged, at nine seats, while the PSOE and Vox lost one seat apiece, taking six and five seats, respectively. The MDyC won three seats, while Ceuta Ya! (formed in 2021 as a successor to the 'Caballas' coalition) took two. In June Vivas effected a wide-ranging reorganization of the Council, abolishing the vice-presidential roles and consolidating the eight councils into six. Gaitán was appointed as Councillor of Presidency and Governance; Ramírez was designated as Councillor of Development, Environment and Urban Services, as well as Government Spokesperson, while

Chandiramani remained as head of the finance ministry, which was restructured as the Council of Finance, Economic Transition and Digital Transformation. Pilar Orozco was named Councillor of Education, Culture, Youth and Sports; Nabila Benzina as Councillor of Health and Social Services; and Nicola Cecchi as Councillor of Trade, Tourism and Employment.

Economy

Ceuta, like the other Spanish enclave in North Africa—Melilla—is a free port. Both enclaves are in fact of little economic importance, while the other Spanish North African possessions are of negligible significance. The chief reason for Spanish retention of these areas is their predominantly Spanish population, though they also serve a strategic military function. The registered population of Ceuta increased fivefold in the last century, and continued to grow in 2011–20, albeit at an average annual rate of only 0.1%. At the census of 2021 the population was recorded at 84,071. According to official estimates, the population stood at 82,833 in January 2023. There are large numbers of immigrants from Morocco in both enclaves, while in recent years the two territories have received significant numbers of illegal migrants from sub-Saharan Africa.

In 1991 Ceuta's gross domestic product (GDP) was 33.6% below the average for the whole of Spain. In that year the average disposable family income of Ceuta was only 76.9% of that of Spain. Social security benefits accounted for 22.8% of the average family income. By 1996, although family income per capita was 0.8% below the Spanish average, purchasing power was 3.0% higher. In 2021, according to preliminary figures, GDP at current prices totalled €1,760.1m., while real GDP grew by 4.0%. In the same year, according to official estimates, the GDP of Ceuta was equivalent to €21,244 per head, ranking it 13th (in terms of GDP per head) of the 19 Spanish autonomous regions (the 17 Autonomous Communities, together with Ceuta and Melilla).

The hinterland of both cities is small. Development is restricted by the lack of suitable building land. Ceuta, in particular, suffers from intermittent water shortages.

Agriculture, Industry and Tourism

In 2021 agriculture and fishing provided less than 0.1% of GDP (excluding taxes), according to preliminary figures, while manufacturing provided 1.4%, mining and energy 4.6% and construction 4.4%. Far more important was the services sector, which accounted for some 89.4% of GDP. Most of the population's food has to be imported, with the exception of fish, which is obtained locally. Sardines and anchovies are the most important items. In 2004 a total of 237 metric tons of fish were landed in Ceuta. A large proportion of the tinned fish is sold outside Spain. More important to the economies of the cities is the port activity; most of their exports take the form of fuel supplied—at very competitive rates—to ships. Most of the fuel comes from the Spanish refinery in Tenerife. Ceuta's port is busier than Melilla's, receiving a total of 10,116 ships in 2022; 1.3m. metric tons of freight were handled in that year. In 2022 Ceuta's trade deficit was recorded at €342.6m. Mineral fuels and oils (and products thereof) accounted for 61.7% of imports. The leading sources of imports in that year were Poland (30.4%), Italy (13.8%) and Portugal (12.4%); other significant sources were France (7.4%) and the United Kingdom (5.2%). Machinery and equipment (and parts thereof) accounted for 4.0% of Ceuta's exports in 2022. Morocco was the principal destination for Ceuta's exports (28.8%) in that year; other significant sources were Portugal (12.7%), the UK (10.1%), Sri Lanka (8.6%) and Hong Kong (7.2%). Commercial agricultural activity in the territories is negligible, and industry is largely geared to meeting some of the everyday needs of the cities.

Tourism previously made a significant contribution to the territories' economies. Almost 1m. tourists visited Ceuta in 1986, attracted by duty-free goods. However, expensive ferry-boat fares and the opening of the Spanish border with Gibraltar in 1985 had an adverse effect on the enclaves' duty-free trade, and tourist numbers declined to 68,205 in 2004, of whom 50,962 were Spanish. In 2019 77,259 visitors arrived in Ceuta, of whom 58.0% were Spanish. Visitor numbers were negatively affected by the coronavirus disease (COVID-19) outbreak in 2020, when they were recorded at 26,149, 77.3% of whom were from Spain. By 2022 arrivals had recovered to 61,416, of whom 78.0% were from Spain.

In 2022 the total labour force was estimated at 40,500, of whom 11,500 (28.4%) were unemployed.

Finance and Inward Investment

In 1989 a campaign to attract more investment to Ceuta was launched. Tax concessions and other incentives were offered. In the three years to 1990 the Spanish Government's investment in Ceuta totalled 9,000m. pesetas for the purposes of public works, and its health service was allocated 347m. pesetas. Upon the accession of Spain to the European Community (now the European Union—EU) in January 1986, Ceuta and Melilla were considered as Spanish cities and European territory, and joined the Community as part of Spain. They retained their status as free ports. The statutes of autonomy, adopted in early 1995, envisaged the continuation of the territories' fiscal benefits. On 28 February 2002 euro notes and coins entered circulation as sole legal tender in the enclaves. Following the enlargement of the EU in 2004 and corresponding plans to downgrade aid to Spain, in 2005 the Government of Ceuta, together with Melilla and two other Spanish regions, Murcia and Asturias, began a campaign to maintain EU aid at existing levels. However, following a further enlargement of the EU in 2007, Ceuta was no longer eligible for support in the long term; subsidies were to be progressively reduced from 2007, with a view to their eventual withdrawal.

There was a projected balanced budget in 2023, with revenue and expenditure both totalling €345.8m. Ceuta's consolidated budget for that year included current and capital transfers from the Spanish state of €139.7m. and €8.3m., respectively. The annual rate of inflation averaged 0.4% in 2011–20; consumer prices increased by 7.7% in 2022.

Statistical Survey

Sources (unless otherwise stated): Administración General del Estado, Beatriz de Silva 4, 51001 Ceuta; tel. 956512616; fax 956511893; Instituto Nacional de Estadística, Paseo de la Castellana 183, 28071 Madrid; tel. 915839100; fax 915839158; internet www.ine.es; *Memoria Socioeconómico y Laboral de 2004:* Consejo Económico y Social, Edif. La Tahoma, Esquina Salud Tejero y Dueñas, Ceuta; tel. 956519131; fax 956519146; e-mail ces-ceuta@ceuta.es.

AREA AND POPULATION

Area: 19.7 sq km (7.6 sq miles).

Population (census results): 83,517 at 1 November 2011; 84,071 (males 42,536, females 41,535) at 1 January 2021. *2023* (official estimate at 1 January, provisional): 82,833.

Density (at 1 January 2023, provisional): 4,204.7 per sq km.

Population by Age and Sex ('000 persons, official estimates at 1 January 2023, provisional): *0–14 years:* 14.9 (males 7.7, females 7.3); *15–64 years:* 57.2 (males 29.3, females 27.9); *65 years and over:* 10.7 (males 4.8, females 5.8); *Total* 82.8 (males 41.8, females 41.0). Note: Totals may not be equal to the sum of components, owing to rounding.

Births, Marriages and Deaths (2021): Live births 719 (birth rate 8.7 per 1,000); Marriages 424 (5.1 per 1,000); Deaths 681 (death rate 8.2 per 1,000).

Life Expectancy (years at birth, 2021): 78.5 (males 76.0; females 81.2).

Immigration and Emigration (excl. Spanish territory, 2021): Immigrants 771; Emigrants 249.

Economically Active Population ('000 persons aged 16 years and over, 2022): Agriculture 0.0; Mining and utilities 0.3; Manufacturing 0.8; Construction 1.9; Trade, transport and accommodation 7.5; Information and communications 0.4; Finance, insurance, real estate and business services 3.7; Public administration, defence, education,

SPANISH NORTH AFRICA

health and social services 13.6; Other services 0.9; *Total employed* 29.0; Unemployed 11.5; *Total labour force* 40.5 (males 23.4, females 17.1). Note: Totals may not be equal to the sum of components, owing to rounding.

AGRICULTURE, ETC.

Livestock (animals slaughtered, 2004): Goats 108; Sheep 1,025.

Fishing (metric tons, live weight of catch): 304.1 in 2002; 310.8 in 2003; 236.8 in 2004.

FINANCE

Currency and Exchange Rates: 100 cent = 1 euro (€). *Sterling and Dollar Equivalents* (31 May 2023): £1 sterling = 1.1574 euros; US $1 = 0.9361 euros; 10 euros = £8.64 = $10.68. *Average Exchange Rate* (euros per US $): 0.8755 in 2020; 0.8455 in 2021; 0.9496 in 2022. Note: The local currency was formerly the Spanish peseta. From the introduction of the euro, with Spanish participation, on 1 January 1999, a fixed exchange rate of €1 = 166.386 pesetas was in effect. Euro notes and coins were introduced on 1 January 2002. The euro and local currency circulated alongside each other until 28 February, after which the euro became the sole legal tender.

Budget (€ '000, 2023): *Revenue:* Current operations 301,594.3 (Direct taxation 11,835.0, Indirect taxation 139,085.9, Rates and other revenue 9,895.0, Current transfers 139,737.4, Property income 1,041.0); Capital operations 44,209.5 (Capital transfers 8,309.5, Transfers of real investments 3,400.0, Assets 1,500.0, Liabilities 31,000.0); Total 345,803.8. *Expenditure:* Current operations 275,666.7 (Wages and salaries 85,418.0, Goods and services 106,201.0, Financial 2,894.7, Current transfers 80,653.0, Contingency funds 500.0); Capital operations 70,137.1 (Real investments 25,369.5, Capital transfers 14,317.2, Assets 4,600.0, Liabilities 25,850.4); Total 345,803.8.

Cost of Living (Consumer Price Index; base: 2021 = 100): All items 97.8 in 2019; 97.4 in 2020; 107.7 in 2022.

Gross Domestic Product (€ million at current prices): 1,774.9 in 2019; 1,662.1 in 2020 (provisional); 1,760.1 in 2021 (preliminary).

Gross Domestic Product by Economic Activity (€ million at current prices, 2021, preliminary): Agriculture and fishing 1.4; Manufacturing 23.0; Mining and energy 73.2; Construction 70.5; Wholesale and retail trade 298.8; Real estate and housing 158.5; Information and communications 16.0; Finance, insurance, and business services 104.3; Public administration and defence; compulsory social security; education; health and social service activities 792.3; Other services 52.9; *Sub-total* 1,591.0; Net taxes on products 169.1; *GDP at market prices* 1,760.1.

EXTERNAL TRADE

Principal Commodities (€ million, 2022): *Imports:* Milk and dairy products, eggs, honey, etc. 0.4; Fruits and vegetables 0.9; Mineral fuels and oils, and products thereof 237.0; Textile materials and clothing 1.9; Footwear 0.6; Machinery and equipment (incl. electrical), and parts thereof 2.2; Vehicles (excl. rail or tram), and parts thereof 133.3 Total (incl. others) 384.3. *Exports:* Plastics and articles 0.2; Pharmaceutical products 4.2; Machinery and equipment (incl. electrical), and parts thereof 16.6; Vehicles (excl. rail or tram), and parts thereof 2.5; Total (incl. others) 41.7.

Principal Trading Partners (€ million, 2022): *Imports:* Belgium 11.8; China, People's Republic 2.1; Czech Republic 1.2; Denmark 2.8; France 28.3; Germany 2.7; India 0.1; Indonesia 1.2; Italy 53.0; Malaysia 0.3; Morocco 0.1; Norway 0.0; Netherlands 0.5; Poland 116.9; Portugal 47.7; Sweden 0.0; Türkiye 0.6; United Kingdom 20.1; USA 1.2; Viet Nam 0.3; Total (incl. others) 384.8. *Exports:* Algeria 1.8; Belgium 0.7; China, People's Republic 0.0; Czech Republic 0.9; Denmark 0.6; Dominican Republic 0.0; France 1.5; Germany 0.9; Hong Kong 3.0; Ireland 0.7; Italy 1.5; Morocco 12.0; Netherlands 0.5; Portugal 5.3; Sri Lanka 3.6; Switzerland 0.9; United Kingdom 4.2; Total (incl. others) 41.7.

Source: Foreign Trade Database, Agencia Tributaria (Madrid).

TRANSPORT

Road Traffic ('000 motor vehicles in use at 31 December 2022): Vehicles registered 64,032 (Passenger cars 41,468, Buses and coaches 58, Lorries and vans 7,083, Motorcycles 14,450, Tractors and trailers 342, Other 631) (Source: Dirección General de Tráfico, Ministerio del Interior, Madrid).

Shipping (domestic and international, 2022): Vessels entered 10,116; Goods handled ('000 metric tons) 1,258; Passenger movements ('000) 1,820.

Civil Aviation (2022): Flights 7,005; Passengers carried ('000) 80.

TOURISM

Visitor Arrivals (by country of residence, 2002): France 2,653; Germany 700; Italy 1,076; Portugal 1,062; Spain 41,593; United Kingdom 1,430; USA 2,939; Total (incl. others) 61,356. *2022:* Total 61,416 (Spain 47,932).

COMMUNICATIONS MEDIA

Telephones (main lines in use, 2004): 24,849.

EDUCATION

Pre-primary (2005/06): 24 schools; 149 teachers; 2,961 students. *2021/22* (provisional): 3,305 students.

Primary (2005/06): 22 schools; 411 teachers (excl. 42 engaged in both pre-primary and primary teaching); 5,948 students. *2021/22* (provisional): 6,904 students.

Secondary: First Cycle (2005/06): 16 schools (of which 6 schools also provided second-cycle education and 5 provided vocational education, see below); 209 teachers (excl. 34 engaged in both secondary and primary teaching and 234 engaged in more than one cycle of secondary); 3,874 students. *2021/22* (provisional): 4,744 students.

Secondary: Second Cycle (2005/06): 34 teachers; 1,298 students. *2021/22* (provisional): 1,390 students (excl. distance learning).

Secondary: Vocational (2005/06): 83 teachers; 970 students. *2021/22* (provisional): 3,119 students.

Source: Ministry of Education, Culture and Sport, Madrid.

Directory

Government

HEAD OF STATE

King of Spain: HM King Felipe VI (succeeded to the throne 19 June 2014).

Government Delegate in Ceuta: Rafael García Rodríguez.

MEMBERS OF THE SPANISH PARLIAMENT

Deputy elected to the Congress of Deputies in Madrid: Javier Celaya Brey (PP).

Representatives to the Senate in Madrid: Cristina Diaz Moreno (PP), Abdelhakim Abdeselam al-Lal (PP).

COUNCIL OF GOVERNMENT
(September 2023)

The executive is formed by members of the Partido Popular (PP).

Mayor/President: Juan Jesús Vivas Lara.

Councillor of Presidency and Governance: Alberto Gaitán.

Councillor of Education, Culture, Youth and Sports: Pilar Orozco.

Councillor of Health and Social Services: Nabila Benzina.

Councillor of Finance, Economic Transition and Digital Transformation: Kissy Chandiramani Ramesh.

Councillor of Trade, Tourism and Employment: Nicola Cecchi.

Councillor of Development, Environment and Urban Services, and Government Spokesperson: Alejandro Ramirez Hurtado.

GOVERNMENT OFFICES

Delegación del Gobierno: Beatriz de Silva 4, 51001 Ceuta; tel. (956) 984400; fax (956) 984403.

Office of the Mayor/President: Plaza de Africa s/n, Asamblea, 1°, 51001 Ceuta; tel. and fax (956) 528222; e-mail consejeriapresidencia@ceuta.es; internet www.ceuta.es.

Council of Development, Environment and Urban Services: Plaza de Africa s/n, Asamblea, 3°, 51001 Ceuta; tel. and fax (956) 510051; e-mail medioambiente@ceuta.es.

Council of Education, Culture, Youth and Sports: Plaza de Africa s/n, Asamblea, 2°, 51001 Ceuta; tel. and fax (956) 205053; e-mail educacioncultura@ceuta.es.

Council of Finance, Economic Transition and Digital Transformation: Edif. Ceuta Center, 51001 Ceuta; e-mail hacienda@ceuta.es.

Council of Health and Social Services: Carretera San Amaro 12, Ceuta; tel. (856) 200680; fax (856) 200723; e-mail sanidad@ceuta.es; internet www.ceuta.es/sanidad.

Council of Trade, Tourism and Employment: Avda de Africa s/n, Ceuta; tel. (956) 528395; e-mail turismoydeporte@ceuta.es.

Assembly

Election, 28 May 2023

Party/Group	Seats
Partido Popular (PP)	9
Partido Socialista Obrero Español (PSOE)	6
VOX	5
Movimiento por la Dignidad y la Ciudadanía (MDyC)	3
Ceuta Ya!	2
Total	**25**

Election Commission

Junta Electoral de Zona de Ceuta (JEZ): Sede Judicial Banco de España, 51001 Ceuta; tel. (956) 511712.

Political Organizations

Ceuta Ya!: Ceuta; tel. (956) 528157; e-mail comunicacion@ceutaya.es; internet fb.com/ceutaya; f. 2021; left-wing; Leader MOHAMED MUSTAFA.

Izquierda Unida (IU): Teniente Coronel Gautier 51, 1°, 51002 Ceuta; tel. (956) 811941; e-mail info@izquierdaunida.org; internet www.izquierda-unida.es; alliance of left-wing parties; Federal Co-ordinator ALBERTO GARZÓN.

Movimiento por la Dignidad y la Ciudadanía (MDyC): Ceuta; tel. (636) 769020; e-mail mdyc@ceuta.es; internet www.mdycceuta.com; f. 2014 left-wing; Leader FATIMA HAMED HOSSAIN.

Partido Democrático y Social de Ceuta (PDSC): Bolivia 35, 51001 Ceuta; Muslim party; Sec.-Gen. TAREK MIZZIAM.

Partido Popular (PP): Teniente Arrabal 4, Edif. Ainara, Bajo, 51001 Ceuta; tel. (956) 518191; fax (956) 513218; e-mail ceuta@pp.es; internet ppceuta.es; fmrly Alianza Popular; national-level, centre-right party; Pres. JUAN JESÚS VIVAS LARA; Sec.-Gen. YOLANDA BEL BLANCA.

Partido Socialista Obrero Español (PSOE): Daóiz 1, 51001 Ceuta; tel. (956) 515553; internet web.psoe.es/ambito/ceuta/index.do; national-level, centre-left party; Pres. JUAN HERNÁNDEZ LOZANO; Sec.-Gen. JUAN ANTONIO GUTIÉRREZ TORRES.

Partido Socialista del Pueblo de Ceuta (PSPC): Echegarray 1, Local 1D, 51001 Ceuta; tel. and fax (956) 518869; f. 1986 by dissident members of PSOE and others; forms part of 'Caballas' coalition with Unión Demócrata Ceutí.

Unión Demócrata Ceutí (UDCE): Avda Teniente-Coronel Gautier 22, 2° dcha, Ceuta; Muslim party; forms part of 'Caballas' coalition with Partido Socialista del Pueblo de Ceuta; Leader MUHAMMAD ALÍ.

VOX Ceuta (Vox): Ceuta; e-mail info@ceuta.voxespana.es; internet www.voxespana.es/ceuta; far-right; Pres. JUAN SERGIO REDONDO PACHECO.

There are also various civic associations.

Judicial System

Tribunal Superior de Justicia de Andalucía, Ceuta y Melilla: Plaza Nueva, 10, Palacio de la Real Chancillería, 18071 Granada, Spain; tel. (955) 062627; fax (958) 002720; e-mail informacion@juntadeandalucia.es; Pres. LORENZO JESÚS DEL RÍO FERNÁNDEZ.

Religion

CHRISTIANITY

The Roman Catholic Church

Bishop of Cádiz and Ceuta: RAFAEL ZORNOZA BOY (resident in Cádiz), Vicar-Gen. of Ceuta FRANCISCO JESÚS FERNÁNDEZ ALCEDO, Obispado de Ceuta, Plaza de Nuestra Señora de Africa, 51001 Ceuta; tel. (956) 517732; fax (956) 807142; e-mail vicgenceuta@obispadocadizyceuta.es; internet www.obispadodecadizyceuta.org.

OTHER RELIGIONS

Ceuta has a large Muslim population, as well as Jewish and Hindu communities.

The Press

El Faro de Ceuta: Sargento Mena 8, 51001 Ceuta; tel. 956524148; e-mail ceuta@grupofaro.es; internet elfarodeceuta.es; f. 1934; morning; Editor RAFAEL MONTERO PALACIOS.

El Pueblo de Ceuta: Independencia 11, 1°, 51001 Ceuta; tel. 956514367; fax 956517650; e-mail ceuta@elpueblodeceuta.es; internet elpueblodeceuta.es; f. 1995; daily; Man. Dir ÁNGEL MUÑOZ TINOCO.

NEWS AGENCY

Agencia EFE: Milán Astray 1, 1°, Of. 8, 51001 Ceuta; tel. 956517550; fax 956516639; e-mail ceuta@efe.com; Correspondent RAFAEL PEÑA SOLER.

PRESS ASSOCIATION

Asociación de la Prensa: Beatriz de Silva 14, 1° E, 51001 Ceuta; tel. 956403713; fax 956528205; Pres. RAFAEL PEÑA SOLER.

Broadcasting

RADIO

Onda Cero Radio Ceuta: Delgado Serrano 1, 1° dcha, 51001 Ceuta; tel. (856) 200068; e-mail ceuta@ondacero.es; internet www.ondacero.es.

Radio Nacional de España: Real 90, 51001 Ceuta; tel. (956) 524688; fax (956) 519067; e-mail informativos.ceuta@rtve.es; internet www.rtve.es/noticias/ceuta; Dir SANDRA ASWANI ALCAZAR.

Radio Popular de Ceuta/COPE: Sargento Mena 8, 1°, 11701 Ceuta; tel. (956) 524200; fax (956) 524202; internet www.cope.es; Dir JUAN ANTONIO MONTERO ÁVALOS.

Radio Televisión Ceuta: Ceuta; tel. (956) 524417; fax (956) 524420; e-mail admon@rtvce.es; internet www.rtvce.es; f. 2000; owned by Sociedad Española de Radiodifusión; commercial; Dir JOSÉ MANUEL GONZÁLEZ NAVARRO.

TELEVISION

Radio Televisión Ceuta: Ceuta; tel. (956) 524417; e-mail admon@rtvce.es; internet www.rtvce.es; f. 2000; Dir JOSÉ MANUEL GONZÁLEZ NAVARRO.

Trade and Industry

Cámara Oficial de Comercio, Industria y Navegación: Dueñas 2, 51001 Ceuta; tel. (956) 129599; e-mail camerceuta@camaras.org; internet www.camaradeceuta.es; chamber of commerce; Pres. KARIM BULAIX.

Confederación de Empresarios de Ceuta: Paseo de las Palmeras, Edif. Corona 26–28, 51001 Ceuta; tel. (856) 200038; e-mail info@confeceuta.es; internet www.confeceuta.es; employers' confed; Pres. ARANTXA CAMPOS; Sec.-Gen. JOSÉ ALBERTO GONZÁLEZ-RUIZ.

UTILITIES

Aguas de Ceuta Empresa Municipal, SA (ACEMSA): Solis 1, Edif. San Luis, Ceuta; tel. 956524619; e-mail aguasdeceuta@acemsa.es; internet www.acemsa.es; Pres. KISSY CHANDIRAMANI RAMESH.

Empresa de Alumbrado Eléctrico de Ceuta SA: Beatriz de Silva 2, Ceuta 51001; tel. (900) 103306; fax (956) 519534; e-mail info@electricadeceuta.com; internet www.electricadeceuta.com; generates and transmits electricity.

TRADE UNION

Comisiones Obreras de Ceuta: Alcalde Fructuoso Miaja 1, 51001 Ceuta; tel. (956) 516243; fax (956) 517991; e-mail ccoo.ce@ceuta.ccoo.es; internet www.ceuta.ccoo.es; Sec.-Gen. EMILIO POSTIGO.

Transport

Much of the traffic between Spain and Morocco passes through Ceuta; there are ferry services to Algeciras, Almería, Málaga and Melilla. Plans for an airport are under consideration. Aeropuertos Españoles y Navegación Aérea (AENA) operates a heliport at the port of Ceuta, from which helicopter services to Málaga are provided by Helisureste.

Port of Ceuta: Autoridad Portuaria de Ceuta, Muelle de España s/n, 51001 Ceuta; tel. (956) 527000; fax (956) 527001; e-mail calidad@puertodeceuta.com; internet www.puertodeceuta.com; Pres. JUAN MANUEL DONCEL.

Acciona Trasmediterránea: Muelle Cañorero Dato 6, 51001 Ceuta; tel. (956) 522238; e-mail pasajeceu@trasmediterranea.es;

internet www.trasmediterranea.es; f. 1917; services between Algeciras and Ceuta.

Tourism

Servicios Turísticos de Ceuta: Baluarte de los Mallorquines, Edrissis s/n, 51001 Ceuta; tel. (856) 200560; fax (856) 200565; e-mail turismo@ceuta.es; internet www.turismodeceuta.com.

Defence

Military authority is vested in a Commandant-General. The enclaves are attached to the military region of Sevilla. In August 2003 Spain had 8,100 troops deployed in Spanish North Africa, compared with 21,000 in mid-1987. Two-thirds of Ceuta's land area are used exclusively for military purposes.

Commandant-General: Gen. MARCOS LLAGO NAVARRO.

Education

The conventional Spanish facilities are available; however, there are also teachers of the Islamic religion in the city. In higher education, links with the University of Granada are maintained and there is a branch of the Spanish open university (Universidad Nacional de Educación a Distancia).

MELILLA

Geography

Melilla is situated north of the Moroccan town of Nador, on the eastern side of a small peninsula jutting into the Mediterranean Sea. It was retained by Spain as a *plaza de soberanía* (a presidio, or fortified enclave, over which Spain has full sovereign rights) when Morocco became independent in 1956, and was administered as part of Málaga Province until 1995. Melilla is an active port. The territory's area totals 12.5 sq km. At the census of January 2021, the population (including the islets governed with Melilla) was recorded at 86,450. Official estimates put the population at 85,603 at 1 January 2023, giving a density of 6,848.2 people per sq km.

The Peñón de Vélez de la Gomera, Peñón de Alhucemas and Chafarinas Islands

These rocky islets are administered with Melilla. The Peñón de Vélez de la Gomera is situated 117 km south-east of Ceuta, lying less than 85 m from the Moroccan coast, to which it is connected by a narrow strip of sand. This rocky promontory, of 1 ha in area, rises to an altitude of 77 m above sea level, an ancient fortress being situated at its summit. The Peñón de Alhucemas lies 155 km south-east of Ceuta and 100 km west of Melilla, being 300 m from the Moroccan coast and the town of al-Hocima. It occupies an area of 1.5 ha. The uninhabited rocks of Mar and Tierra lie immediately to the east of the Peñón de Alhucemas. The three Chafarinas Islands (from west to east: Isla del Congreso, Isla de Isabel II and Isla del Rey) are situated 48 km east of Melilla and about 3.5 km from the Moroccan fishing port of Ras el-Ma (Cabo de Agua). The islands are of volcanic origin, their combined area being 61 ha. Spain maintains small military bases on some of the islets.

History

Spain secured control of Melilla in 1556, the town having been conquered in 1497 by the ducal house of Medina Sidonia, which had been empowered to appoint the governor and seneschal with the approval of the Spanish Crown. Rif tribesmen attacked Melilla in 1562–64. Later still, the Sultan of Morocco, Mulai Ismail (1672–1727), assaulted the town in 1687, 1696 and 1697. Sultan Muhammad bin Abdallah (1757–90) besieged Melilla in 1771 and 1774. However, an agreement concluded between Spain and Morocco in 1780 at Aranjuez, Spain, led in 1781 to a peaceful delimitation of the Melilla enclave. Under the terms of an agreement signed after Spain's Moroccan campaign of 1860, Melilla's boundaries were extended in 1861. Conflict with the Rif tribesmen gave rise in 1893–94 to the 'War of Melilla', which ended with a settlement negotiated at Marrakesh, Morocco. It was not until 1909 that Spanish forces, after a hard campaign, occupied the mountainous hinterland of Melilla between the Wadi Kert and the Wadi Muluya—a region in which, some 15 km behind Melilla, were situated the rich iron mines of Beni Bu Ifrur. In July 1921 the Rif tribes, under the command of Abd al-Krim, defeated a Spanish force near Annual and threatened Melilla itself. Only in 1926, with the final defeat of the Rif rebellion, was Spanish control restored over the Melilla region.

The Chafarinas Islands came under Spanish control in 1847. The Peñón de Alhucemas was occupied in 1673. The Peñón de Vélez de la Gomera, about 80 km further west, came under Spanish rule in 1508, but was then lost not long afterwards and reoccupied in 1564. All three possessions are, like Melilla, incorporated into the province of Málaga. Spanish sovereignty over the uninhabited island of Perejil (Laila), which lies north-west of Ceuta, is uncertain.

The population of Melilla is mostly Spanish. The proportion of Arab residents, however, has greatly increased, owing to the large number of immigrants from Morocco. Those born in the territory are Spanish citizens and subjects. Melilla was the first Spanish town to rise against the Government of the Popular Front in July 1936, at the beginning of the Spanish Civil War. Like Ceuta, Melilla was retained by Spain when Morocco became independent in 1956. In addition to its function as a port, Melilla now serves as a military base, with more than one-half of the enclave's land area being used solely for military purposes. In October 1978 King Hassan of Morocco attempted to link the question of the sovereignty of Melilla to that of the return of the British dependent territory of Gibraltar to Spain. (See Ceuta for further details on the status of the two enclaves within Spain and on Morocco's relationship with Spain and the North African enclaves.)

In early 1986 the central Government in Madrid agreed to grant Spanish nationality to more than 2,400 Muslims resident in Melilla and Ceuta. At that time only around 7,000 of the estimated 27,000-strong Muslim community in Melilla held Spanish nationality. By mid-1986, however, the number of Muslims applying for Spanish nationality in Melilla had reached several thousand. As a result of delays in the processing of the applications, Aomar Muhammadi Dudú, the leader of the newly founded Partido de los Demócratas de Melilla (PDM), accused the Government of failing to fulfil its pledge to Muslim residents.

At the general election of June 1986, the ruling Partido Socialista Obrero Español (PSOE) was defeated by the centre-right Coalición Popular (CP) in Melilla, the result indicating the strong opposition of the Spanish community to the Government's plan to integrate the Muslim population. Tight security surrounded the election, and 'parallel elections', resulting in a vote of confidence in the PDM leader, were held by the Muslim community. Polling was accompanied by several days of unrest. Talks in Madrid between representatives of the main political parties in Melilla and the Ministry of the Interior resulted in concessions being made to the enclave. In September Dudú agreed to accept a senior post in the Ministry, with responsibility for relations with the Muslim communities of Spain. In November, however, Muslim leaders in Melilla announced that they wished to establish their own administration in the enclave, in view of the Madrid Government's failure to fulfil its promise of Spanish citizenship for Muslim residents. The Spanish Minister of the Interior reiterated assurances of the Government's commitment to integrating the Muslim community. Later in the month thousands of Muslims took part in a peaceful demonstration in support of

Dudú, who had resigned his Madrid post after only two months in office. (He subsequently went into exile in Morocco and lost the support of Melilla's Muslim community.)

In February 1987 police reinforcements were dispatched from Spain, in response to a serious escalation of inter-racial tensions in Melilla. Numerous demonstrators were detained, and several prominent Muslims were charged with sedition and briefly held in custody. King Hassan reaffirmed his support for the Muslims of the Spanish enclaves.

In March 1988 the central Government and main opposition parties in Madrid reached a broad consensus on draft autonomy statutes for the Spanish External Territories. (See Ceuta for details of the statutes.)

The results of the October 1989 general election were declared invalid, following the discovery of serious irregularities. At the repeated ballot in March 1990, both seats in the Senate and the one seat in the Congreso de los Diputados (Congress of Deputies) were won by the Partido Popular (PP), the latter result depriving the PSOE of an overall majority in the Madrid lower chamber.

At elections to the municipal council held in May 1991, the PP secured 12 of the 25 seats, and Ignacio Velázquez Rivera of the right-wing Partido Nacionalista de Melilla (PNM) was elected Mayor/President, replacing the previous PSOE incumbent. At the general election of June 1993 the PSOE candidate defeated the PP member in the Congress of Deputies; the PP also lost one of its two seats in the Senado (Senate).

The final statutes of autonomy for Ceuta and Melilla were approved by the Spanish Government in September 1994 (see Ceuta). At elections for the new local Assembly, held in May 1995, the PP won 14 of the 25 seats, the PSOE five seats, the Coalición por Melilla (CpM), a new Muslim grouping, four seats and the right-wing Unión del Pueblo Melillense (UPM) two seats. Ignacio Velázquez (PP/PNM) was returned as Mayor/President, in which position he now became head of a new Council of Government.

At the general election held in March 1996, the PSOE lost its seat in the lower house to the PP, which also took both seats in the Senate. In the same month thousands of Muslims took part in a demonstration, organized by the CpM, to protest against their position on the margins of society.

In March 1997 a motion of censure against Velázquez resulted in the Mayor/President's defeat. The opposition then declared Enrique Palacios, who had earlier defected from the PP, to be Mayor/President, although the central Government continued to recognize Velázquez as the rightful incumbent. In May, for the first time, the Mayor/Presidents of both Ceuta and Melilla attended a conference of the autonomous regions' presidents, held in Madrid. Despite the attempted 'coup' in Melilla, the territory was represented by Velázquez. In November another defector from the PP, Abdelmalik Tahar, accused Velázquez and five associates of having subjected him to blackmail and threats, as a result of which he had relinquished his seat on the Council of Government, thereby permitting the PP to replace him and regain its majority. Following a judicial ruling leading to the successful revival of the motion of censure against Velázquez in February 1998, Palacios took office as Mayor/President, accusing his predecessor of serious financial mismanagement. A new PP-led motion of censure, urging that (despite the bribery charges against him) Velázquez be restored to office, was deemed to be illegal and therefore rejected in a decree issued by Palacios, who also ordered the temporary closure of the Assembly. In July Palacios accused the PP of having employed public funds, amounting to more than 200m. pesetas, to secure the votes of some 2,500 Muslims at the 1995 local elections. The PP denied the allegations.

During 1997 there was increased concern regarding the numbers of illegal immigrants. In June police reinforcements were drafted into Melilla, following renewed disturbances in which one immigrant died. More than 100 illegal immigrants were immediately returned to Morocco as part of a special security operation, and on the same day a total of 873 Moroccans were denied entry to Melilla. (More than 10,000 Moroccans continued to cross the border each day, to work in the enclave.) In August the Spanish General Prosecutor demanded emergency measures to address the immigration crisis. In the same month various non-governmental organizations condemned the rudimentary conditions in which more than 900 illegal immigrants, mainly from sub-Saharan Africa and Algeria, were being held in Melilla. In December the Spanish Government announced that 1,206 sub-Saharan Africans were to be transferred from Ceuta and Melilla to the mainland.

At the June 1999 local elections the Grupo Independiente Liberal (GIL), recently founded by Jesús Gil, the controversial Mayor of Marbella, secured seven of the 25 seats in the Assembly of Melilla. In July the two newly elected PSOE councillors defied a central directive to vote with the five PP delegates (in order to obstruct the accession of the GIL to the city presidency), and instead gave their support to Mustafa Aberchán Hamed of the CpM, which had won five seats. Aberchán was thus elected to replace Palacios as Mayor/President (becoming the first Muslim to hold this post), and formed a minority Council of Government with the GIL. The two rebel PSOE councillors subsequently relinquished their seats. In October, following a disagreement between the CpM and the GIL, Aberchán reached a broad agreement with members of the PP and UPM, enabling him to remain in office. In November the Melilla branch of the GIL announced that henceforth it was to operate independently of the mainland party, and concluded a new agreement with Aberchán to renew its participation in the Melilla Government. As a result, the socialist councillors withdrew from the administration.

In December 1999 Aberchán announced the composition of a new coalition Government, the post of First Vice-President being allocated to Crispin Lozano of the GIL, while Palacios of the newly founded Partido Independiente de Melilla (PIM) became Second Vice-President. In the same month the PP's Ignacio Velázquez was barred from public office for six years, having been convicted of neglecting his duty during his tenure as Mayor/President; in 1992 Velázquez had convened a session of the Council, which was scheduled to vote on a motion of censure against him, in full knowledge of the fact that at least one member was due to be in Madrid that day, thus rendering any vote invalid. However, he was acquitted of charges of misappropriation of public funds. In May 2000, following the defection to the opposition of two GIL deputies and one UPM deputy, Aberchán refused to resign. Later that month the national leadership of the PP and the PSOE met in Madrid in an attempt to negotiate a solution to the political crisis in Melilla. The two parties agreed that, if Aberchán's Government was removed from office, they would form a coalition government in partnership with the UPM, whose leader, Juan José Imbroda Ortiz, would be nominated Mayor/President. In July the remaining five GIL deputies in the Assembly defected to the opposition, which introduced a motion of censure against Aberchán, who subsequently announced that the CpM was to withdraw from the legislature. Some 2,000 Muslim citizens of Melilla demonstrated in support of Aberchán. At the same time Palacios suspended the motion of censure by decree, reportedly without having consulted Aberchán. (Palacios was subsequently barred from public office for seven years, having been found guilty of perversion of the course of justice.) The opposition successfully overturned the decree in the courts, and at the ensuing vote on the motion of censure against Aberchán in September, the motion was adopted with the support of 16 of the 25 deputies, and Imbroda was elected as Mayor/President. In late 2000 four members of the GIL announced their departure from the party. In January 2002 Velázquez resigned as Councillor of the Presidency, after the Supreme Court upheld his 1999 conviction.

At elections to the Assembly in May 2003, a coalition of the PP and the UPM won 15 seats and the CpM took seven; Imbroda remained as Mayor/President. At the general election held on 14 March 2004, the PP retained Melilla's seats in the Congress of Deputies and the Senate. In September Imbroda met the recently elected Spanish Prime Minister, José Luis Rodríguez Zapatero, to discuss the possibility of Melilla becoming a Comunidad Autónoma (Autonomous Community). The plan was, however, abandoned in February 2007, owing to disagreement over the content of the proposed statute of autonomy; instead, the Spanish Government agreed to devolve more powers to Ceuta and Melilla in the areas of education and social services.

In May 2004, meanwhile, the Government of Melilla announced plans to improve security along the border with Morocco. In August, however, in the first mass entry for three years, some 450 people attempted to enter Melilla illegally by climbing the security fence; as many as 40 people were believed to have succeeded. During August–October 2005 increasing numbers of would-be migrants attempted to scale the security barriers separating Melilla from Morocco. It was subsequently announced that one barrier would be doubled in height (to 6 m), and that border security would be increased. Meanwhile, the Spanish Government announced funding of €17m. for security in Melilla.

At local elections held in May 2007, the PP (which had by then absorbed its coalition partner, the UPM) obtained 15 seats in the Assembly, the same number as previously, thereby retaining its overall majority; the CpM and the PSOE each won five seats. The inauguration of the Assembly was delayed until July owing to an appeal against the election result by the CpM, which alleged that the PP had engaged in acts of electoral fraud. The appeal was rejected by the Supreme Court of Justice of Andalusia, which ruled that the evidence was not sufficient. Imbroda was subsequently re-elected as Mayor/President. A two-day visit to Melilla and Ceuta by Spain's King Juan Carlos and Queen Sofia in November was criticized by the Moroccan authorities and prompted protests on the Moroccan side of the border.

At the March 2008 general election, the PP retained Melilla's one seat in the Congress of Deputies and its two seats in the Senate. Attempts by illegal migrants to cross the border between Melilla and Morocco increased in October, after heavy flooding damaged the recently fortified fence separating the two territories. Although additional security forces were deployed to patrol the damaged areas, it was reported that in one incident almost one-half of a group of some 60 sub-Saharan Africans succeeded in entering Melilla; 17 others were reportedly arrested.

At the May 2011 local elections, the PP again won 15 seats in the Assembly. The CpM took six seats, while the PSOE's representation declined to just two. The Partido Populares en Libertad (PPL), which had been established in March by former PP Mayor/President Ignacio Velázquez, also won two seats. A new Council of Government, under Imbroda, took office in July. At the general election held in November, the PP retained Melillas seat in the Congress of Deputies and its two seats in the Senate. Abdelmalik el-Barkani Abdelkader was sworn in as Government Delegate to Melilla in 2012, becoming the first Muslim to hold that post.

In February 2014 it was reported that a group of 214 migrants had succeeded in entering Melilla following an attempt by up to 300 people to breach the security fence separating Melilla from Morocco. The deaths (through drowning) of 15 migrants at the border between Ceuta and Morocco earlier that month (see Ceuta) prompted protests against the Spanish Government's immigration policy in both territories. The Government announced heightened security measures and in April 2015 the European Union (EU, see p. 1140) agreed to provide €5m. in additional funding towards the immigration processing centres in Ceuta and Melilla.

Elections to the Assembly took place in May 2015. The PP remained the largest party, although it failed narrowly to secure a majority, winning only 12 seats. The CpM took seven seats, the PSOE three, Ciudadanos (Cs) two and the PPL one. A new Council of Government was formed in July, again under Imbroda. The PP was joined in government by the PPL: that party's sole deputy, Paz Velázquez Clavarana, was appointed as Second Vice-President and Councillor of the Presidency. At the general election held in November the PP retained Melilla's one seat in the Congress of Deputies, as well as its two seats in the Senate. A fresh general election was held in June 2016, owing to the failure of the political parties to form a government. The PP again won all three seats representing Melilla. In August and September at least 140 migrants succeeded in entering Melilla during two large-scale attempts to breach the border fence. A further 200 people successfully breached the fence in a similar mass attempt in January 2018.

In June 2018 Sabrina Moh Abdelkader was appointed as Govenment Delegate to Melilla, replacing el-Barkani. At a general election held on 28 April 2019, the PP retained Melilla's seat in the Congress of Deputies, despite its share of the vote decreasing from 49.9% in 2016 to just 23.9%. The PP also retained both seats in the Senate.

Elections to the Assembly took place on 26 May 2019. The PP retained its status as the largest party, although its tally was reduced further, to 10 seats. The CpM took eight seats, the PSOE four and Cs one. The far-right nationalist VOX party (commonly referred to as Vox) secured representation for the first time, with two seats. Although Imbroda was expected to form a new Council of Government, at the new Assembly's inaugural session on 15 June the CpM, the PSOE and Cs' sole deputy, Eduardo de Castro González, collaborated to elect the latter as Mayor/President. De Castro's new Council took office on 4 July. The number of councillors was reduced from 10 to eight, with the CpM gaining three posts and the PSOE and Cs both two. Gloria Rojas Ruiz, the PSOE's local Secretary-General, became Vice-President, Government Spokesperson, and Councillor of Education, Culture, Sports, Festivals and Equality, and Julio Liarte Parres, an independent nominated by Cs, Councillor of Finance, Economy and Employment.

A further general election took place in November 2019, owing to the failure of coalition talks in Spain (see Spain). The PP again retained the territory's seat in the Congress of Deputies, while also securing both seats in the Senate.

In December 2019 de Castro announced a substantial reorganization of the Council of Government, reducing its composition to seven members (four from the CpM, three from the PSOE and de Castro himself). This followed a court ruling in the previous month affirming that only elected members of the Assembly were eligible to be appointed to the Council. Rojas was promoted to First Vice-President, Government Spokesperson and Councillor of the Presidency and Public Administration. Hassan Mohatar Maanan, of the CpM, became Second Vice-President, Deputy Spokesperson, and Councillor of Environment and Sustainability. The PSOE's Elena Fernández Treviño joined the Council as Councillor of Education, Culture, Festivals and Equality.

In April 2021 the national leadership of the Cs announced that it was to expel de Castro from the party, amid allegations that he had sought to conceal investigations into allegations against him of misconduct in the commissioning of city services. De Castro stated that he would resign as Mayor/President in due course. However, following confirmation of his expulsion from the Cs in July, de Castro announced that he would, in fact, remain in office as an independent.

In February 2022 former Mayor/President Imbroda appealed for Melilla to be included within the EU's Schengen Agreement on border controls, in order to protect the enclave from migratory pressures. In the following month more than 2,000 people attempted to traverse the border fence between Morocco and Melilla, with around 500 (mostly originating from sub-Saharan Africa) successfully entering the enclave. Moroccan border police attempting to stop their advance were reportedly pelted with rocks and other makeshift projectiles. In response, the far-right Vox party called for Spanish troops to be deployed to Melilla to protect the enclave's border with Morocco. A joint declaration signed by Spain and Morocco in April provided for the full normalization of movement of people and goods at Melilla and Ceuta, including 'appropriate customs control devices' for migrants seeking to enter the enclaves by land and sea.

On 24 June 2022 at least 23 would-be migrants died and dozens were injured following a mass attempted incursion by some 2,000 people (mostly sub-Saharan African adult males) at the border fence between Morocco and Melilla. (Human rights group Amnesty International reported that at least 37 people had been killed, with at least 76 others remaining missing as of June 2023.) Despite the deployment of large numbers of Moroccan and Spanish security forces, more than 500 individuals managed to enter a border control area by cutting through the fence and around 130 individuals succeeded in entering Melilla. Those who died were reportedly either killed in the crush or succumbed to their injuries, some of which were allegedly incurred from falling from the top of the fence. The Spanish Prime Minister, Pedro Sánchez, asserted that the incursion was a 'violent and organized attack' staged by human traffickers, while human rights organizations demanded an official investigation into the incident, amid claims that the security personnel had used excessive force.

A Moroccan court sentenced 33 asylum seekers to 11 months' imprisonment in connection with the unrest in June 2022, following their conviction in July of illegal entry, disobedience, armed gathering and violence against public officials. A UN working group of experts claimed in October that the deaths at the border demonstrated 'a willingness to sacrifice the lives of African and other migrants and refugees to secure the perimeter of Europe', and in December Amnesty International urged Spain and Morocco to open safe, legal routes for those seeking asylum in Europe.

In June 2023, on the eve of the first anniversary of the unrest, Amnesty International Secretary-General Agnès Callamard issued a statement in which she unequivocally criticized the Spanish and Moroccan authorities' for their failure thus far to conduct full independent investigations. (An investigation by the Spanish authorities was dropped in December 2022 after state prosecutors determined that there was no evidence of any criminal misconduct.) Callamard also alleged that the authorities of both countries continued to impede efforts to ensure accountability for the loss of life, in what appeared increasingly to be 'a deliberate and concerted coverup'.

Meanwhile, at elections to the Assembly held on 28 May 2023, the PP regained a legislative majority, winning 14 of the 25 seats. The CpM and the PSOE both lost ground, taking five and three seats, respectively, while Vox secured two seats. The remaining seat was won by Somos Melilla (founded in 2019 as Adelante Melilla), which had campaigned on a pro-change platform. The PP's outright victory allowed Imbroda to return to his former role of Mayor/President. He was sworn in on 11 July at the head of an eight-member Council.

Economy

Melilla, a free port, is of little economic importance to Spain, while the other possessions governed with Melilla are of negligible significance. The chief reason for Spanish retention of the areas is their predominantly Spanish population, though they also serve a strategic military function. The population of Melilla increased at an annual average rate of 0.6% in 2011–20. The census of January 2021 recorded the population at 86,450. Provisional official estimates put the population at 85,603 at 1 January 2023. There are large numbers of immigrants from Morocco in Melilla.

In 1991 Melilla's gross domestic product (GDP) was 30.5% below the average for the whole of Spain. In that year the average disposable family income was 84.8% that of Spain. Social security benefits accounted for 24.3% of the average family income. By 1996, although family income per capita was 6.0% below the Spanish average, purchasing power was 6.6% higher. However, an unofficial report issued in October 1996 classified Melilla as by far the poorest city in Spain. In 2021, according to preliminary data, GDP at current prices was €1,609.2m., while real GDP grew by 4.1%. In the same year, according to official estimates, the GDP of Melilla was equivalent to €19,266 per head, ranking it 16th (in terms of GDP per head) of the 19 Spanish autonomous regions (the 17 Autonomous Communities, together with Ceuta and Melilla).

Agriculture, Industry and Tourism

In 2021, according to preliminary data, agriculture and fishing contributed less than 0.1% to GDP (excluding taxes), while manufacturing contributed 1.0%, mining and energy 3.7% and construction 4.8%. The services sector was by far the largest, contributing 90.4% in that year. Melilla's hinterland is small, and development is restricted by the lack of suitable building land. Most of the population's food has to be imported, with the exception of fish, which is obtained locally. Sardines and anchovies are the most important items. More important to the economy is the port activity (although Melilla's port is less busy than Ceuta's), most exports taking the form of fuel supplied—at very competitive rates—to ships. Most of the fuel comes from the Spanish refinery in Tenerife. Melilla's port received a total of 1,197 vessels in 2022; in that year 565,000m. metric tons of freight were handled by the port. In 2022 Melilla registered a trade surplus of €3.1m. The principal imports in that year were machinery and equipment (and parts thereof), which accounted for 35.8% of the total value, as well as vehicles (and parts thereof), textile materials and clothing, and footwear. In 2022 the principal sources of imports were Slovakia (accounting for 28.5% of the total value) and Germany (16.2%); other major suppliers were the People's Republic of China, Italy, the USA, Portugal and the Netherlands. The principal export in 2022 was machinery and equipment (and parts thereof), which accounted for 56.1% of the total value. The principal destination for exports was Morocco (accounting for 71.3% of the total, by value). Commercial agricultural activity in the enclave is negligible, and industry is largely geared to meeting some of the everyday needs of the city.

Tourism is a significant contributor to the territory's economy. In 2019 67,179 visitors arrived in Melilla, of whom 66.6% were Spanish. Visitor numbers declined to 33,240 in 2020, amid the coronavirus disease (COVID-19) pandemic, 71.8% of whom were from Spain. By 2022 arrivals had recovered to 50,330, of whom 77.5% were from Spain.

In 2022 the total labour force was estimated at 38,400, of whom 8,300 (21.6%) were unemployed.

Finance and Inward Investment

Upon the accession of Spain to the European Community (now European Union—EU) in January 1986, Ceuta and Melilla were considered as Spanish cities and European territory, and joined the Community as part of Spain. They retained their status as free ports. The statutes of autonomy, adopted in early 1995, envisaged the continuation of the territories' fiscal benefits. On 28 February 2002 euro notes and coins entered circulation as sole legal tender in the enclaves. In June 1994 the EU announced substantial regional aid. With assistance from the European Social Fund, a programme of employment and vocational training for Melilla was announced in 1996. Projected Spanish investment was €16.9m. in 2002 and €45.4m. in 2003, the latter including some €16.7m. for the expansion of the airport. However, the successive enlargements of the EU that took place in 2004 and 2007 limited Spain's access to EU aid, with the result that subsidies for Melilla were to be progressively reduced from 2007, with a view to their eventual withdrawal. In 2006 it was announced that the central Government would invest some €83m. in 2007–13, 47% less than had been invested in 2000–06.

There was a projected balanced budget in 2023, with revenue and expenditure both totalling €355.5m. Melilla's consolidated budget for that year included current and capital transfers from the Spanish state of €192.7m. and €20.5m., respectively. The annual rate of inflation averaged 0.4% in 2011–20; consumer prices increased by 8.6% in 2022.

Statistical Survey

Source (unless otherwise stated): Instituto Nacional de Estadística, Paseo de la Castellana 183, 28071 Madrid; tel. 915839100; fax 915839158; internet www.ine.es.

AREA AND POPULATION

Area: 12.5 sq km (4.8 sq miles).

Population (census results): 81,323 at 1 November 2011; 86,450 (males 43,823, females 42,627) at 1 January 2021. *2023* (official estimate, 1 January, provisional): 85,603.

Density (at 1 January 2023, provisional): 6,848.2 per sq km.

Population by Age and Sex ('000 persons, official estimates at 1 January 2023, provisional): *0–14 years:* 18.0 (males 9.2, females 8.8); *15–64 years:* 57.5 (males 29.4, females 28.2); *65 years and over:* 10.0 (males 4.6, females 5.4); *Total* 85.6 (males 43.2, females 42.4). Note: Totals may not be equal to the sum of components, owing to rounding.

Births, Marriages and Deaths (2021): Live births 930 (birth rate 11.1 per 1,000); Marriages 279 (marriage rate 3.3 per 1,000); Deaths 574 (death rate 6.9 per 1,000).

SPANISH NORTH AFRICA

Melilla

Life Expectancy (years at birth, 2021): 79.8 (males 77.4; females 82.4).

Immigration and Emigration (excl. Spanish territory, 2021): Immigrants 1,178; Emigrants 782.

Economically Active Population ('000 persons aged 16 years and over, 2022): Agriculture 0.0; Mining and utilities 0.9; Manufacturing 0.2; Construction 0.5; Trade, transport and accommodation 5.4; Information and communication 0.1; Finance, insurance, real estate and business services 4.7; Public administration, defence, education, health and social services 15.8; Other services 2.5; *Total employed* 30.1; Unemployed 8.3; *Total labour force* 38.4 (males 20.2, females 18.2).

FINANCE

Currency and Exchange Rates: 100 cent = 1 euro (€). *Sterling and Dollar Equivalents* (31 May 2023): £1 sterling = 1.1574 euros; US $1 = 0.9361 euros; 10 euros = £8.64 = $10.68. *Average Exchange Rate* (euros per US $): 0.8755 in 2020; 0.8455 in 2021; 0.9496 in 2022. Note: The local currency was formerly the Spanish peseta. From the introduction of the euro, with Spanish participation, on 1 January 1999, a fixed exchange rate of €1 = 166.386 pesetas was in effect. Euro notes and coins were introduced on 1 January 2002. The euro and local currency circulated alongside each other until 28 February, after which the euro became the sole legal tender.

Budget (€ '000, 2023): *Revenue:* Current operations 310,634.7 (Direct taxation 12,159.9, Indirect taxation 74,347.2, Rates and other revenue 25,930.3, Current transfers 192,654.1, Property income 5,543.2); Capital operations 44,884.0 (Capital transfers 20,497.0, Transfers of real investments 25.0, Assets 462.0, Liabilities 23,900.0); Total 355,518.8. *Expenditure:* Current operations 286,183.7 (Wages and salaries 98,357.2, Goods and services 136,104.3, Financial 3,142.5, Current transfers 48,279.7, Contingency fund 300.0); Capital operations 69,335.1 (Real investments 39,859.8, Capital transfers 3,967.0, Assets 462.0, Liabilities 25,046.3); Total 355,518.8.

Cost of Living (Consumer Price Index; base: 2021 = 100): All items 96.2 in 2019; 96.3 in 2020; 108.6 in 2022.

Gross Domestic Product (€ million at current prices): 1,625.1 in 2019; 1,522.2 in 2020 (provisional); 1,609.2 in 2021 (preliminary).

Gross Domestic Product by Economic Activity (€ million at current prices, 2021, preliminary): Agriculture and fishing 1.0; Manufacturing 15.1; Mining and energy 53.4; Construction 69.6; Wholesale and retail trade 256.9; Real estate and housing 155.7; Information and communications 10.7; Finance, insurance, and business services 104.9; Public administration and defence; compulsory social security; education; health and social service activities 735.3; Other services 52.1; *Sub-total* 1,454.6; Net taxes on products 154.6; *GDP at market prices* 1,609.2.

EXTERNAL TRADE

Principal Commodities (€ million, 2022): *Imports:* Fruits and vegetables 0.3; Textile materials and clothing 1.0; Footwear 1.0; Machinery and equipment (incl. electrical), and parts thereof 6.4; Vehicles (excl. rail or tram), and parts thereof 4.8; Total (incl. others) 17.9. *Exports:* Fruits and vegetables 0.1; Plastics and articles 3.4; Machinery and equipment (incl. electrical), and parts thereof 8.3; Total (incl. others) 14.8.

Principal Trading Partners (€ million, 2022): *Imports:* Austria 0.3; Brazil 0.2; Belgium 0.0; China, People's Republic 1.7; Denmark 0.2; France 0.1; Germany 2.9; Hungary 0.4; India 0.1; Indonesia 0.1; Italy 1.5; Japan 0.4; Morocco 0.2; Netherlands 0.6; Poland 0.0; Portugal 0.9; Slovakia 5.1; Thailand 0.2; Türkiye 0.3; United Kingdom 0.1; USA 1.0; Viet Nam 0.3; Total (incl. others) 17.9. *Exports:* France 3.0; Mauritania 0.2; Morocco 10.7; Netherlands 0.1; Portugal 0.5; Switzerland 0.0; Total (incl. others) 15.0.

Source: Foreign Trade Database, Agencia Tributaria (Madrid).

TRANSPORT

Road Traffic ('000 motor vehicles in use at 31 December 2022): Vehicles registered 69,575 (Passenger cars 47,401, Buses and coaches 55, Lorries and vans 11,954, Motorcycles 8,776, Tractors and trailers 733, Other 656) (Source: Dirección General de Tráfico, Ministerio del Interior, Madrid).

Shipping (domestic and international, 2022): Vessels entered 1,197; Goods handled ('000 metric tons) 565; Passenger movements ('000) 638.

Civil Aviation (2022): Flights 9,772; Passengers transported ('000) 447; Goods transported 22 metric tons.

TOURISM

Visitor Arrivals (by country of residence, 2002): France 476; Germany 432; Italy 331; Netherlands 425; Spain 23,648; Total (incl. others) 31,812. *2022:* Total 50,330 (Spain 39,001).

EDUCATION

Pre-primary (2005/06): 20 schools; 159 teachers, 3,237 students. *2021/22* (provisional): 4,264 students.

Primary (2005/06): 15 schools; 422 teachers (excl. 20 engaged in both pre-primary and primary teaching); 5,996 students. *2021/22* (provisional): 7,873 students.

Secondary: First Cycle (2005/06): 9 schools (of which 4 schools also provided second-cycle education and 5 provided vocational education); 255 teachers (excl. 10 engaged in both primary and secondary teaching, and 198 engaged in more than one secondary cycle, and excl. 33 specialists); 3,923 students. *2021/22* (provisional): 4,823 students.

Secondary: Second Cycle (2005/06): 53 teachers; 1,339 students. *2021/22* (provisional): 1,441 students (excl. distance learning).

Secondary: Vocational (2005/06): 65 teachers; 703 students. *2021/22* (provisional): 2,273 students.

Source: Ministry of Education, Culture and Sport, Madrid.

Directory

Government

HEAD OF STATE

King of Spain: HM King FELIPE VI (succeeded to the throne 19 June 2014).

Government Delegate in Melilla: SABRINA MOH ABDELKADER.

MEMBERS OF THE SPANISH PARLIAMENT

Deputy elected to the Congress of Deputies in Madrid: SOFIA ACEDO REYES (PP).

Representatives to the Senate in Madrid: FERNANDO ADOLFO GUTIÉRREZ DÍAZ DE OTAZU (PP), ISABEL MARÍA MORENO MOHAMED (PP).

COUNCIL OF GOVERNMENT
(September 2023)

The executive is formed by the Partido Popular (PP).

Mayor/President of Melilla: JUAN JOSÉ IMBRODA.

First Vice-President and Councillor of Economy, Trade, Technological Innovation, Tourism and Development: MIGUEL MARÍN COBOS.

Second Vice-President and Councillor of Environment and Nature: MANUEL ÁNGEL QUEVEDO MATEOS.

Third Vice-President and Councillor of Public Safety: DANIEL VENTURA RIZO.

Councillor of Presidency, Public Administration and Equality: MARTA FERNÁNDEZ DE CASTRO RUÍZ.

Government Spokesperson, and Councillor of Culture, Cultural Heritage and the Mayor: FADELA MOHATAR MAANAN.

Councillor of Social Policy and Public Health: RANDA MOHAMED EL-AOULA.

Councillor of Education, Youth and Sports: MIGUEL ÁNGEL FERNÁNDEZ BONNEMAISÓN.

Councillor of Finance: DANIEL CONESA.

GOVERNMENT OFFICES

Delegación del Gobierno: Avda de la Marina Española 3, 52001 Melilla; tel. (95) 2991000; fax (95) 2991116; e-mail gabinete_prensa.melilla@seap.minhap.es.

Office of the Mayor/President: Palacio de la Asamblea, Plaza de España, 52001 Melilla; tel. (95) 2699100; fax (95) 2699230; e-mail presidencia@melilla.es; internet www.melilla.es.

Council of Culture, Cultural Heritage and the Mayor: Antiguo Edif. Mantelete, Duque de Ahumada s/n, 52071 Melilla.

Council of Economy, Trade, Technological Innovation, Tourism and Development: Palacio de la Asamblea, Plaza de España, 52001 Melilla.

Council of Education, Youth and Sports: Querol 7, 52001 Melilla; tel. (95) 2699214; fax (95) 2699279; e-mail educacion@melilla.es.

SPANISH NORTH AFRICA

Council of Environment and Nature: Palacio de la Asamblea, Plaza de España, 52001 Melilla; tel. (95) 2699157; fax (95) 2699161; e-mail consejeriamedioambiente@melilla.es.

Council of Finance: Avda del Duquesa de la Victoria 21, Melilla.

Council of the Presidency, Public Administration and Equality: Justo Sancho Miñano 2, 52801 Melilla; tel. (95) 2976294; fax (95) 2976275; e-mail consejeriaeconomia@melilla.es.

Council of Public Safety: Palacio de la Asamblea, Plaza de España, 52001 Melilla.

Council of Social Policies and Public Health: Calle, Carlos Ramírez de Arellano 10, Melilla; tel. (95) 2699301; fax (95) 2699302; e-mail consejeriabienestarsocial@melilla.es.

Assembly

Election, 28 May 2023

	Seats
Partido Popular (PP)	14
Coalición por Melilla (CpM)	5
Partido Socialista Obrero Español (PSOE)	3
VOX	2
Somos Melilla	1
Total	**25**

Election Commission

Junta Electoral de Zona de Melilla: Plaza del Mar, s/n Edificio V Centenario, Torre Norte, Planta Primera, Sala de Vistas, 52001 Melilla; tel. (952) 699051; fax (952) 699044.

Political Organizations

Ciudadanos Melilla (Cs) (Citizens): Melilla; e-mail agrupacioncsmelilla@gmail.com; internet melilla.ciudadanos-cs.org.

Coalición por Melilla (CpM): Ejército Español 21, 1° dcha, 52001 Melilla; tel. (600) 344451; e-mail info@coalicionpormelilla.org; internet coalicionpormelilla.org; f. 1995 by merger of Partido del Trabajo y Progreso de Melilla and Partido Hispano Bereber; majority of members are from the Muslim community; mem. of left-wing Izquierda Unida coalition; Pres. MUSTAFA HAMED (MO) ABERCHÁN; Sec.-Gen. HASSAN MOHATAR.

Partido Popular (PP): Roberto Cano 2, 1° izqda, POB 384, 52001 Melilla; tel. (95) 2681095; fax (95) 2684477; e-mail melilla@pp.es; internet www.ppmelilla.es; national-level, centre-right party; absorbed the Unión del Pueblo Melillense in 2007; Pres. JUAN JOSÉ IMBRODA ORTIZ; Sec.-Gen. MIGUEL MARÍN.

Partido Socialista de Melilla-Partido Socialista Obrero Español (PSME-PSOE): Edif. Argo, Doctor García Martínez 3, 52006 Melilla; tel. (95) 2677807; fax (95) 2679857; e-mail psoe@psoemelilla.es; internet web.psoe.es/ambito/melilla/news/index.do; national-level, centre-left party; Sec.-Gen. GLORIA ROJAS.

Somos Melilla: Calle General Aizpuru 9, Bajo, Melilla; tel. (69) 2313371; e-mail info.somosmelilla@gmail.com; internet fb.com/somosmelilla; Pres. AMIN AZMANI.

VOX Melilla (Vox): Calle Pablo Vallescá 19, 52006 Melilla; tel. (95) 1636535; internet twitter.com/Vox_Melilla; far-right; Pres. JOSÉ MIGUEL TASENDE SOUTO.

There are also various civic associations in Melilla.

Religion

As in Ceuta, most Europeans are Roman Catholics. Melilla likewise has a large Muslim community, as well as Hindu and Jewish communities.

ISLAM

Comisión Islámica de Melilla (CIM): 52005 Melilla; e-mail cim.comisionislamicademelilla@gmail.com; internet cimelilla.org; Pres. HASSAN LABOUDI.

CHRISTIANITY

The Roman Catholic Church

Melilla is part of the Spanish diocese of Málaga.

The Press

El Faro de Melilla: Castelar 5, 1°, Melilla; tel. 952690029; fax 952683992; e-mail melilla@grupofaro.es; internet elfarodemelilla.es; Pres. RAFAEL MONTERO PALACIOS; Editor-in-Chief ANGELA M. PERAZZI.

Melilla Hoy: Polígono Industrial SEPES, La Espiga, Naves A-1/A-2, 52006 Melilla; tel. 952690000; fax 952675725; e-mail redaccion@melillahoy.es; internet www.melillahoy.es; f. 1985; Editor ENRIQUE BOHÓRQUEZ LÓPEZ-DÓRIGA.

Sur: Músico Granados 2, 52001 Melilla; tel. 952213438; fax 952673674; internet www.diariosur.es; local edn of Málaga daily; Perm. Rep. AVELINO GUTIÉRREZ PÉREZ.

El Telegrama de Melilla: Polígono La Espiga, Nave A-8, 52006 Melilla; tel. 952691443; fax 952691469; e-mail telegramademelilla@yahoo.es; internet www.eltelegrama.es; Dir MARIA TERESA GALLARDO MONTIEL.

NEWS AGENCY

Agencia EFE: Teniente Aguilar de Mera 1, Edificio Monumental, 1°, Local 9, 52001 Melilla; tel. 952685235; fax 952680043; e-mail melilla@efe.com; Correspondent (vacant).

PRESS ASSOCIATION

Asociación de la Prensa: Apdo de Correos 574, 29880 Melilla; tel. 952-681854; fax 952-675725; Pres. JOSÉ MARÍA NAVARRO GIL.

Broadcasting

RADIO

Cadena Dial Melilla: Cardenal Cisneros 8 Bajo, 52005 Melilla; tel. (97) 1224176; fax (95) 2681573; e-mail radiomelilla@unionradio.es; internet www.cadenadial.com.

Onda Cero Radio Melilla: Músico Granados 2, 52004 Melilla; tel. (95) 2691283; fax (95) 2673764; e-mail info@ondaceromelilla.net; internet www.ondaceromelilla.net/ml.

Radio Melilla: Cardenal Cisneros 8 Bajo, 52001 Melilla; tel. (95) 2681708; e-mail radiomelilla@prisaradio.com; internet www.cadenaser.com; owned by Sociedad Española de Radiodifusión; commercial.

Radio Nacional de España (RNE): Calle Altos de la Vía 3, 52001 Melilla; tel. (95) 2696289; fax (95) 2683108; e-mail informativos.melilla@rtve.es; internet www.rtve.es; state-controlled; Rep. MONTSERRAT COBOS RUANO.

TELEVISION

A fibre-optic cable linking Melilla with Almería was laid in 1990. From March 1991 Melilla residents were able to receive three private TV channels from mainland Spain: Antena 3, Canal+ and Tele 5.

Antena 3: Edif. Melilla, Urbanización Rusadir, 29805 Melilla; tel. (95) 2688840; internet www.antena3.com.

Trade and Industry

Cámara Oficial de Comercio, Industria y Navegación: Cervantes 7, 52001 Melilla; tel. (95) 2684840; fax (95) 2683119; e-mail info@camaramelilla.es; internet www.camaramelilla.es; f. 1906; chamber of commerce; Pres. MARGARITA LÓPEZ ALMENDÁRIZ; Vice-Pres. HAMED MAANAN BENAISA BOUJI.

Confederación de Empresarios de Melilla (CEME-CEOE): Plaza 1 de Mayo, bajo dcha, 52003 Melilla; tel. (95) 2678295; tel. \; e-mail prevención@cemelilla.org; internet www.cemelilla.org; f. 1979; employers' confed; Pres. ENRIQUE ALCOBA.

UTILITIES

The Spanish electricity company Endesa operates an oil-fired power station in Melilla.

TRADE UNION

Confederación Sindical de Comisiones Obreras (CCOO): Calle Primero de Mayo, 1°, 52001 Melilla; tel. (95) 2676535; fax (95) 2672571; e-mail lopd@ccoo.es; internet www.melilla.ccoo.es; Sec.-Gen. FERNANDO LEZCANO.

Transport

There is a daily ferry service to Málaga and a service to Almería. Melilla airport, situated 4 km from the town, is served by daily flights to Almería, Granada, Málaga and Madrid, operated by Iberia Regional/Air Nostrum. Flights to Málaga are also operated by Air Europa.

Port of Melilla: Autoridad Portuaria de Melilla, Avda de la Marina Española 4, 52001 Melilla; tel. (95) 2673600; fax (95) 2674838; e-mail sac@puertodemelilla.es; internet www.puertodemelilla.es; Pres. VÍCTOR GAMERO; Dir LUIS JOSÉ AYALA NAVARRO.

Acciona Trasmediterránea: Estación Marítima s/n, CP 52001 Melilla; tel. (95) 2690985; fax (95) 2682685; e-mail mlnpax@trasmediterranea.es; internet www.trasmediterranea.es; operates ferry service between Melilla and Almería and Málaga, in mainland Spain.

Tourism

Oficina Provincial de Turismo: Pintor Fortuny 21, 52004 Melilla; tel. (95) 2976151; fax (95) 2976153; e-mail info@melillaturismo.com; internet www.melillaturismo.com.

Defence

More than one-half of Melilla's land area is used solely for military purposes. (See also Ceuta.)

Commandant-General: Maj.-Gen. LUIS SÁEZ ROCANDIO.

Education

In addition to the conventional Spanish facilities, the Moroccan Government finances a school for Muslim children in Melilla, the languages of instruction being Arabic and Spanish. The Spanish open university (Universidad Nacional de Educación a Distancia) maintains a branch in Melilla.

Bibliography

Baeza Herrazti, A. (Ed.). *Ceuta hispano-portuguesa*. Ceuta, Instituto de Estudios Ceutíes, 1993.

Ceuta y Melilla en las relaciones de España y Marruecos. Madrid, Instituto Español de Estudios Estratégicos, Centro Superior de Estudios de la Defensa, 1997.

Domínguez Sánchez, C. *Melilla*. Madrid, Editorial Everest, 1978.

Europa Ethnica (Vols 1–2). *Ceuta and Melilla—Spain's Presence on African Soil*. Vienna, Braumüller, 1999.

Gold, P. *Europe or Africa?: A Contemporary Study of the Spanish North African Enclaves of Ceuta and Melilla*. Liverpool, Liverpool University Press, 2000.

Lafond, P. *Melilla*. Barcelona, Lunwerg Editores, 1997.

Mir Berlanga, F. *Melilla en los Siglos Pasados y Otras Historias*. Madrid, Editora Nacional, 1977.

Resumen de la Historia de Melilla. Melilla, 1978.

Vicente, Angéles. *Ceuta, Une Ville Entre Deux Langues: Une Étude Sociolinguistique de sa Communauté Musulmane*. Paris, L'Harmattan, 2005.

Zurlo, Y. *Ceuta et Melilla: Histoire, représentations et devenir de deux enclaves espagnoles*. Paris, L'Harmattan, 2005.

SYRIAN ARAB REPUBLIC

Geography

Before 1918 the term 'Syria' was rather loosely applied to the whole of the territory now forming the modern states of the Syrian Arab Republic, Lebanon, Israel and Jordan, now known as the Levant. To the Ottomans, as to the Romans, Syria stretched from the Euphrates to the Mediterranean, and from the Sinai to the hills of southern Türkiye (known as Turkey prior to June 2022), with Palestine as a smaller province of this wider unit. The present Syria has a much more limited extent, covering 185,180 sq km (71,498 sq miles—including the occupied Golan Heights, Occupied Territories, see p. 374).

The frontiers of the present-day state are largely artificial, and reflect to a considerable extent the interests and prestige of outside powers—the United Kingdom, France and the USA—as these existed in 1918–20. The northern frontier with Türkiye is defined by a single-track railway line running along the southern edge of the foothills—probably the only case of its kind in the world—while eastwards and southwards boundaries are highly arbitrary, being straight lines drawn for convenience between salient points. Westwards, the frontiers are again artificial, although less crudely drawn, leaving the headwaters of the Jordan river outside Syria and following the crest of the Anti-Lebanon hills, to reach the sea north of Tripoli in Lebanon.

PHYSICAL FEATURES

Geographically, Syria consists of two main zones: a fairly narrow western part, made up of a complex of mountain ranges and intervening valleys; and a much larger eastern zone that is essentially a broad and open platform dropping gently towards the east and crossed diagonally by the wide valley of the Euphrates river.

The western zone, which contains over 80% of the population of Syria, can be further subdivided as follows. In the extreme west, fronting the Mediterranean Sea, there lies an imposing ridge rising to 1,500 m above sea level, and known as the Jebel Ansariyeh. Its western flank drops fairly gradually to the sea, giving a narrow coastal plain, but on the east it falls very sharply, almost as a wall, to a flat-bottomed valley occupied by the Orontes river, which meanders sluggishly over the flat floor, often flooding in winter, and leaving a formerly malarial marsh in summer. Further east lie more hill ranges, opening out like a fan from the south-west, where the Anti-Lebanon range, with Mount Hermon (2,814 m), is the highest in Syria. Along the eastern flanks of the various ridges lie a number of shallow basins occupied by small streams that eventually dry up or form closed salt lakes. In one basin lies the city of Aleppo, once the second town of the Ottoman Empire and still the largest city of Syria. In another is situated Damascus, irrigated from five streams and famous for its clear fountains and gardens—now the capital of the country. One remaining sub-region of western Syria is the Jebel Druse, which lies in the extreme south-west, and consists of a vast outpouring of lava, in the form of sheets and cones. Towards the west this region is fertile, and produces good cereal crops, but eastwards the soil cover disappears, leaving a barren countryside of twisted lava and caverns. Owing to its difficulty and isolation, the Jebel Druse has tended socially and politically to act independently, remaining aloof from the rest of the country.

The entire eastern zone is mainly steppe or open desert, except close to the banks of the Euphrates, the Tigris and their larger tributaries, where irrigation projects allow considerable cultivation on an increasing scale. The triangularly shaped region between the Euphrates and Tigris rivers is spoken of as the Jezireh (*jazira*, island), but is in no way different from the remaining parts of the east.

CLIMATE

The presence of ranks of relatively high hills aligned parallel to the coast has important climatic effects. Tempering and humid effects from the Mediterranean are restricted to a narrow western belt, and central and eastern Syria show marked continental tendencies: that is, a very hot summer with temperatures often above 38°C (100°F) or even 43°C, and a moderately cold winter, with frost on many nights. Very close to the Mediterranean, frost is unknown at any season, but on the hills altitude greatly reduces the average temperature, so that snow may lie on the heights from late December to April, or even May. Rainfall is fairly abundant in the west, where the height of the land tends to determine the amount received, but east of the Anti-Lebanon mountains the amount decreases considerably, producing a steppe region that quickly passes into true desert. On the extreme east, as the Zagros ranges of Persia are approached, there is once again a slight increase, but most of Syria has an annual rainfall of less than 250 mm.

POPULATION

At mid-2023 the total Syrian population was 23,227,014, according to United Nations (UN) estimates. The capital of Syria is Damascus, situated in the south of the country. Following the outbreak of civil conflict between government forces and opposition groups opposed to the rule of President Bashar al-Assad in 2011, a significant number of Syrian nationals were displaced by the escalating violence. At 31 August 2023 5,211,718 Syrian refugees were registered with the Office of the UN High Commissioner for Refugees (UNHCR) in countries across the Middle East and North Africa. The largest concentrations of Syrian refugees were found in Türkiye (which hosted 3,298,817 registered refugees in August 2023), Lebanon (795,322 in June 2023) and Jordan (655,283 in August 2023). In July 2023 a further 267,839 refugees were registered in Iraq, predominantly in the north of that country, and 149,454 in Egypt. Another 45,003 Syrians were registered in other North African countries at December 2022. However, the UN estimated the total number of people displaced by the conflict to be around 12m. at the end of 2018. This number included many people who had remained in the region, but were not registered as refugees, those who had travelled to Europe and other countries outside the Middle East and North Africa, as well as around 6.6m. internally displaced persons (IDPs). In December 2022 the number of IDPs amounted to 6.8m., according to UNHCR. According to the UN Relief and Works Agency for Palestine Refugees in the Near East (UNRWA), 575,234 Palestinian refugees were registered in Syria at July 2022.

As a result of Syria's ethnic diversity, there is a surprising variety of language and religion. Arabic, the official language, is spoken over most of the country, but Kurdish (a minority language) is widely used along the northern frontier and Armenian in the cities. Aramaic, the language of Christ, survives in a small number of villages. More than 80% of the population are Muslims (mostly Sunnis), but there is a substantial Christian minority of various sects.

History

EYAL ZISSER

THE SYRIAN ARAB REPUBLIC UNDER HAFIZ AL-ASSAD

The rise to power of Hafiz al-Assad—as the so-called Corrective Movement of 16 November 1970—amounted to a watershed in Syrian history, and opened up a whole new era. Assad was able to bring about domestic stability, which in turn enabled him to turn the Syrian Arab Republic into a regional power.

At the beginning of his rule President Assad worked to conciliate and bring closer various social sectors of Syrian society that in the past had demonstrated reservations about, or even hostility to, the Arab Socialist Renaissance (Baath) Party regime, which had been in power since 1963. In order to reach his goal, Assad was prepared to waive, or even retreat from, certain ideological principles that the regime had insisted upon in the past. He was mainly interested in gaining the support of the Sunni urban sector. To do this, he employed a policy of economic openness that was intended to restore to this sector its high status in the business and economic life of the country. Assad also sought to gain favour with the Islamic circles in Syria by softening the secular, and even atheistic, image of his regime. He began to attend prayer services in Sunni mosques. He also took steps to try to gain religious legitimacy for the members of his own ethnic community, the Alawites. This led, in 1972, to the Lebanese Shi'a cleric Imam Musa al-Sadr issuing a *fatwa* (religious ruling) recognizing members of the Alawite community as Shi'a, and, consequently, as legitimate Muslims.

During the first years of his rule Assad invested special efforts in establishing a system of governmental institutions, including a Constitution, the People's Assembly, the institution of the presidency, and the National Progressive Front, an umbrella organization encompassing all the political parties whose activity was permitted. This system was intended to gain legitimacy for Assad and his regime, and to give the country the perception of stability.

In the regional and inter-Arab arena, Assad worked to moderate the tension and ideological polarization that had characterized the Syrian regime's relations with neighbouring Arab states. Thus, for example, he improved relations with Jordan and Saudi Arabia, rehabilitated ties with Iraq, and began acquiring an influential position for Syria in Lebanon.

Syria participated in the Fourth Arab–Israeli War (the Yom Kippur War) in October 1973. The conflict failed to achieve Syria's goal of regaining control of the Golan Heights from Israel. By the end of the war the attacking Syrian forces even found themselves driven back to the ceasefire lines from which they had begun, and in certain areas they were driven back even beyond these lines. Israel and Syria signed a Disengagement Agreement on 31 May 1974 to end the fighting (see Documents on Palestine). However, unlike Israel's similar agreement with Egypt, this did not eventuate in a political process leading to a peace agreement and the return of the Golan Heights to Syria, although Syria did receive the city of Quneitra.

THE ISLAMIC REVOLT, 1976–82

In 1976 Syria was confronted by social and economic difficulties, precipitated by worldwide fluctuations in the price of oil. The Syrian economy was affected, as it relied upon remittances from Syrian workers in the oil-rich states of the Persian (Arabian) Gulf. The economic crisis contributed to the outbreak of a revolt against the Syrian regime by the Islamic Movement in February 1976. The revolt gained strength at first and enjoyed wide support among the urban population in the cities of northern Syria. Its high point was reached with the rebels' seizure of the city of Hama in February 1982. Only with great effort and the use of military power was the regime able to suppress the revolt and liquidate the Islamic Movement as an organized force.

SYRIAN INVOLVEMENT IN LEBANON

In June 1976, shortly after the outbreak of the Islamic Revolt, at the invitation of the Maronite Christian leadership then heading the Lebanese state, Syrian military forces entered Lebanon. The Syrians' mission was to bring the Lebanese civil war, which had erupted in April 1975, to an end and to help Lebanon to become a stable and economically successful state, although with the proviso that it would remain under Syrian tutelage and hegemony. However, the powerbrokers in Lebanon were not yet prepared to settle the dispute among themselves under these conditions, so Syria was unable to bring the civil war to an end. Somewhat surprisingly, the supporters of the leftist bloc in Lebanon who might have been considered the natural allies of the Syrians—the members of the Sunni community, the Druze under the leadership of Kamal Joumblatt, and the fighters of the Palestine Liberation Organization—rejected the Syrians' compromise proposals for ending the crisis. They even clashed militarily with the invading Syrian forces. Thus, towards the end of the 1970s, instead of bringing Lebanon under its control, Syria found itself mired in the Lebanese 'swamp' without any means or prospect of extricating itself in the foreseeable future.

THE EGYPT-ISRAEL PEACE TREATY

On 19 November 1977 Egyptian President Anwar Sadat made an historic visit to Israel. It led to the signing of the Camp David Accords in September 1978 and the Egypt-Israel Peace Treaty in March 1979 (see Documents on Palestine). These agreements weakened Syria's standing significantly, as they left the country to face Israel alone on the military and political fronts and, of course, reduced its prospects of retrieving the Golan Heights from Israel. In 1978 Syria, together with Iraq, had succeeded in establishing an Arab Rejectionist Front, the aim of which was to serve as a counterbalance to Sadat's peace initiative. However, very quickly an open rupture became evident in Syrian–Iraqi relations. Its source lay in the ideological rivalry between the two factions of the Baath Party ruling in Iraq and Syria, but also, mainly, in the personal rivalry and lack of trust between Iraqi President Saddam Hussain (who took power in July 1979) and Syrian President Assad. The rupture between the two countries developed into an unbridgeable chasm after the outbreak of war between Iraq and Iran in September 1980, as Syria decided to support Iran.

Israel was cognizant of Syria's domestic and foreign difficulties. In 1981 and 1982 in particular it worked to exploit Syria's weaknesses and advance its own political and security interests. On 14 December 1981 the Israeli Knesset (parliament) ratified an act applying Israeli law to the Golan Heights, and on 6 June 1982 Israel invaded Lebanon in what it called 'Operation Peace for Galilee'. This war was intended to push Syria out of Lebanon and establish a new order there. The idea was to place power in the hands of Israel's allies among the Christian community, namely the supporters of the Maronite Phalangist Party led by Bashir Gemayel. He was elected as President of Lebanon in August, but less than a month later was killed in an explosion at his headquarters, for which Syria was widely assumed to be responsible. Bashir's elder brother, Amin, succeeded him as President. Israel compelled Amin's Lebanese regime to sign a peace treaty on 17 May 1983. However, this agreement ultimately proved to be worthless and invalid. Israel thus found its intervention in Lebanon to be fruitless, and its problems deepened as a result of a massacre at the Palestinian refugee camps of Sabra and Chatila, which was carried out by Phalangist forces whom Israel had allowed into the camps.

With Israel's withdrawal from Lebanon, the USA sought to take its place. The country strengthened its ties with Amin Gemayel's administration, sent US troops to Beirut (the Lebanese capital), and towards the end of 1983 even engaged in armed confrontation with the Syrian military. In December

Syrian forces shot down two US fighter planes, and their pilots were briefly held by the Syrian army.

Eventually, over the course of several years, Syria succeeded in restoring its former dominance over Lebanon. Suicide attacks carried out by militant Palestinian groups widely believed to be supported by Syria (and the Shi'a Hezbollah organization established by Iran's Islamic Revolutionary Guard Corps—IRGC) succeeded in pushing Israel and the USA out of Lebanon, leaving Syria as the only powerbroker in the country.

These developments enabled Syria to turn its military failures into an important political victory. The Lebanese civil war was brought to an end by the October 1989 Ta'if Agreement, signed by the various warring factions. This also constituted an important step on Syria's path to imposing its dominance over Lebanon and establishing a 'Pax Syriana' that would ensure the country's rehabilitation process under Syrian hegemony. Other steps in this direction were the October 1990 Syrian takeover of the enclave held by the Commander of the Lebanese army, the Maronite Gen. Michel Aoun, a strong critic of the Ta'if Agreement; the surrounding of the presidential palace in Baabda; and, later, Syria's success in persuading Hezbollah to accept the Ta'if Agreement (which that organization had initially opposed) and to integrate into the Lebanese political system.

RIFTS WITHIN SYRIA

In November 1983 President Hafiz al-Assad suffered a heart attack. This precipitated a power struggle inside the Syrian upper echelon. Hafiz's brother, Rifaat, sought to exploit his brother's ill health in order to advance his own position as the presumed successor to the presidency. Rifaat commanded an elite army unit deployed around the Syrian capital, Damascus. Rifaat's actions, however, prompted others in the upper echelon to challenge his position. President Assad subsequently recovered and managed to bring the struggle over the succession to an end by removing his brother from all of his positions of influence in the Government. Rifaat was appointed Vice-President, a position with no formal powers, and he later went into a lengthy exile in Western Europe.

The decline of the Union of Soviet Socialist Republics (USSR), which ended in its total collapse and dissolution in 1991, was of major importance in setting the tone of events in Syria in the late 1980s, as the USSR had been a key partner of the Baath regime. With the formation of new world and regional orders in the wake of the Soviet collapse, the USA became the leading power. This new situation obliged the Syrian regime to shift its policies.

Thus, from the end of the 1980s Syria attempted to improve its relations with Western states, and the USA in particular. Consequently, Syria joined the anti-Iraq coalition led by the USA during the Gulf crisis of August 1990–March 1991, and in October 1991 even joined the Middle East peace process and for the first time in its history expressed a readiness to sign a peace treaty with Israel. At the same time Syria continued to develop its ties with Iran, and from 1997 it even worked to advance its relations with Saddam Hussain's Iraq.

ISRAELI-SYRIAN PEACE NEGOTIATIONS, 1991–2009

The regional peace conference that opened in Madrid, Spain, in October 1991 in the context of the Middle East peace process marked the beginning of two decades of Israeli-Syrian negotiations. The talks proceeded to the point where both sides almost reached a peace agreement. However, the gulf between the two states was ultimately so wide as to be unbridgeable.

The Israeli leadership, for its part, refused to meet Syria's demand that Israel withdraw completely from the Golan Heights to the 4 June 1967 line. Such a move would have meant retreating to the edge of Lake Tiberias (the Sea of Galilee). This was even beyond the Israeli–Syrian international border agreed upon and marked in 1923 by the British Mandate authorities in Palestine and the French Mandate authorities in the Levant.

Syria, for its part, found it difficult to adopt a policy of public diplomacy and to undertake confidence-building steps that would have helped the Israeli leadership to gain public support for the concessions being demanded from Israel in the framework of the peace agreement.

During Itzhak Rabin's second term as Prime Minister of Israel (1992–95) he granted Syria the so-called 'Rabin Deposit'. This was a promise delivered to the US Secretary of State, Warren Christopher, which stated that Israel would be prepared to withdraw to the June 1967 borders if Syria was prepared to sign a peace treaty. The latter would have to meet Israel's requirements, especially in the realms of security arrangements, sequence of implementation, and normalization of relations between the two states.

Shimon Peres, who replaced Rabin after the latter's assassination, sought to gain Assad's support by proposing broad and deep economic co-operation between Israel and Syria. Benjamin Netanyahu, during his first term as Israeli Prime Minister (1996–99), also conducted indirect talks with Syria via his confidant, the US Jewish businessman Ronald Lauder. During the premiership of Ehud Barak, who followed Netanyahu as Prime Minister (1999–2001), US President Bill Clinton undertook to advance the talks, and in a meeting with the Syrian President in Geneva, Switzerland, in March 2000 Clinton tried unsuccessfully to gain Assad's support for several of Barak's ideas regarding the marking of the Israeli–Syrian border. Ultimately, however, all the efforts at reaching a breakthrough in the talks between the two states failed on account of disagreements over the core issues mentioned above.

THE END OF THE HAFIZ AL-ASSAD ERA: DOMESTIC STAGNATION

In contrast to the changes and dynamics in Syrian foreign policy, on the domestic front the status quo remained in place. The situation was exacerbated by President Assad's deteriorating health, which turned him into an absentee leader during the 1990s, with his public appearances becoming few and far between.

None the less, the regime worked to give its institutions an element of democracy and liberalism. For example, independent candidates who were not members of the Baath Party or its satellite parties were permitted to run in the 1990, 1994 and 1998 elections to the People's Assembly. Assad also showed a willingness to engage in dialogue with the leaders of the Syrian Muslim Brotherhood, who in the past had numbered among his bitterest enemies. In the economic sphere, the Government adopted policies characterized by a greater openness and some degree of liberalization.

However, there is no doubt that the main lesson that President Assad drew from the collapse of the USSR was that any demand for genuine change in Syria's political system must be quashed, for such change could turn out to be disastrous for the stability of his regime, and could even threaten its very existence. It seems that during the last decade of his rule Assad focused his attention on the question of the presidential succession. His aim was to ensure the continuity and stability of his regime after his death.

BASHAR AL-ASSAD IN POWER

On 10 June 2000 President Hafiz al-Assad died, and, as expected, his son, Bashar, took his place. Bashar's passage into the Syrian upper echelon had begun on 21 January 1994, following the death of his older brother, Basil. After Basil's death, Hafiz did everything he could to ensure that Bashar would succeed him. Immediately after the announcement of Hafiz al-Assad's death, the People's Assembly convened in an extraordinary session. Its members approved an amendment to the Constitution reducing the minimum age required to become President from 40 to 34 years, Bashar al-Assad's age when his father died. The Assembly subsequently approved Bashar's candidacy as President for a term of seven years. A referendum on this decision was held on 10 July 2000. A majority of 97.3% voted in favour. Another referendum was held on 27 May 2007, regarding a second term for Bashar, and this time his bid was approved by a majority of 97.6%. On 3 June 2014—following a change in the Constitution introduced in June 2012 in the wake of the outbreak of the Syrian revolution—Bashar was elected President, for the first time directly, for a third term. On this occasion Bashar secured 92.2% of the valid votes cast.

BASHAR AND THE 'OLD GUARD'

Despite his youth and lack of experience, Bashar al-Assad was able within just a few years to impose his authority on the Syrian governmental system, with its whole array of Baath Party apparatuses, governmental institutions, and military and security forces. The heads of these entities were mostly his father's confidants and contemporaries, men of the 'old guard', who were often perceived as obstacles in Bashar's way when he wanted to advance social and economic reforms. As the years passed, however, many of Hafiz al-Assad's former associates died and others retired.

THE 'DAMASCUS SPRING'

When Bashar al-Assad came to power, people were struck by his youth and the fact that he had resided in London, United Kingdom, even if only for a few months. His appointment as President aroused hopes, and even expectations, that he would bring about reforms, and perhaps even permit a greater political openness in Syria.

Indeed, during the first months of his rule President Assad showed a certain tolerance towards the regime's critics and those seeking to reform it, permitting them to form discussion groups. The first such society was the Forum for National Dialogue, which held its inaugural meeting in Damascus in August 2000, chaired by Riad Seif, a businessman and People's Assembly member. Participants in these forums expressed criticism of the Baath regime and its policies, and demanded the advancement of democracy in the country. The regime's manifestations of tolerance at this time were labelled the 'Damascus Spring'.

However, this 'liberalism' quickly came to an end because the regime's senior members were concerned about a loss of control, such as had happened in Eastern Europe towards the end of the 20th century. The regime thus returned to a policy of heavy-handedness against its critics, and many were imprisoned.

ECONOMIC REFORM

During the first decade of his rule Bashar al-Assad managed to advance a series of economic measures, even if these were rather limited in scope. These reforms opened up the Syrian economy to the outside world and encouraged the activity of the private sector at the expense of the public sector, which was controlled by the Government and the Baath Party. These moves helped the new President to gain the support of the middle classes and the Sunni economic elite in the big cities, especially Damascus and Aleppo. However, the new measures also undermined the agricultural sector, which provided employment for residents of rural and peripheral areas.

THE REGIONAL AND INTERNATIONAL ARENAS

Like his father, President Bashar al-Assad registered his greatest successes in the field of foreign policy. He positioned himself as the head of the radical bloc in the Arab world, fostered close relations with Iran, and became a key partner in the anti-Israel and anti-Western 'Axis of Resistance', which included Iran, Hezbollah and the Palestinian Islamic Resistance Movement (Hamas). His anti-Western stance found expression primarily in inflammatory rhetoric, which he used as early as the outbreak of the second Palestinian *intifada* (uprising) in late 2000, then during the US-led invasion of Iraq in early 2003, the war between Israel and Hezbollah in Lebanon during mid-2006, and Israel's offensive against Hamas in Gaza (code-named 'Operation Cast Lead') at the beginning of 2009. Apart from Assad's harsh rhetoric against Israel and the ongoing aid he rendered to Hamas and Hezbollah, Syria was accused of supporting, or at least turning a blind eye to, the activities of the extremist Islamist al-Qa'ida group in Iraq against the US forces stationed there. Al-Qa'ida recruits reached Iraq via Syria and even used Syrian territory for the establishment of training and supply bases.

In response, the US Administration of President George W. Bush sought to isolate Syria internationally. In the wake of the assassination of former Lebanese Prime Minister Rafiq Hariri in February 2005, for which Syria was initially blamed, the Bush Administration, at the end of March, forced Syria to withdraw its troops from Lebanon. The USA also brought about the establishment of a United Nations (UN) commission of inquiry and an international court, which the US Administration hoped would convict Assad of Hariri's murder. In October the intermediate report of the UN International Independent Investigation Commission (the Mehlis Report) was published. It accused Assad of being responsible for Hariri's assassination. However, it later became apparent that Hezbollah, not Syria, had orchestrated the assassination (although doubts continued to be expressed in some quarters).

Assad ultimately emerged as the victor in this confrontation with the USA, which had been ongoing for most of the first decade of his presidency. This was mainly because the USA lacked the necessary determination to act against Syria in such a way as to bring about Assad's downfall. Syria was not viewed as important enough for the US Administration to invest the great effort and resources needed to overthrow Assad's regime, especially after the USA had found itself so deeply involved in the protracted conflicts in Iraq and Afghanistan.

Barack Obama was inaugurated as US President in January 2009. His new Administration sought to improve relations with Syria and to return a US ambassador to Damascus. (The previous ambassador had been recalled to the USA following the assassination of Prime Minister Hariri in Lebanon in February 2005.) Robert Ford was duly appointed as the USA's ambassador to Syria in December 2010.

It should be noted that, although Bashar al-Assad adopted a very sharp tone in his statements, like his father before him, he was politically astute enough to manifest restraint and pragmatism in his actions. In accordance with this approach, the improvement of relations with Turkey (officially known as Türkiye from June 2022) at the beginning of the 2000s should be mentioned. This was achieved, ostensibly, at the cost of abandoning Syria's longstanding ideological commitment to recover the Alexandretta district annexed by Türkiye in 1939. President Assad also refrained from responding to Israel's bombing in September 2007 of the nuclear installation that Syria was reportedly building with assistance from the Democratic People's Republic of Korea (North Korea) in the region of Deir el-Zor, in north-eastern Syria. Nor did the Syrian President respond to the assassination of the Hezbollah military commander Imad Mughniyeh in the centre of Damascus in February 2008, nor to the killing of his confidant, Brig.-Gen. Muhammad Suleiman, in August. Suleiman had served as Assad's Special Presidential Adviser for Arms Procurement and Strategic Weapons. The Arab and foreign media attributed these two killings to Israel.

In early 2008 Syria and Israel began peace negotiations on the basis of a promise that Israeli Prime Minister Ehud Olmert had relayed to President Assad, stating that Israel would withdraw from all of the Golan Heights. However, these negotiations ended with Olmert's resignation from the premiership in July. Under Netanyahu, who became Israeli Prime Minister in March 2009, contacts between Syria and Israel regarding a peace settlement continued, although these ended with the outbreak of the Syrian revolution in March 2011.

SOCIOECONOMIC CRISIS

Despite the impression that Syria gave of political and economic stability, towards the end of Bashar al-Assad's first decade as President the country found itself engulfed in a severe economic and social crisis.

Years of severe drought constituted one of the roots of the crisis. During the second half of the first decade of the 2000s Syria experienced the most severe dry spell in its history. The damage caused by the drought was particularly acute in the country's north-eastern provinces, in the al-Jazira region, which is one of Syria's most important grain producers, and

SYRIAN ARAB REPUBLIC

also in the south-western Hawran region, with the city of Dar'a at its centre.

According to data published by the Ministry of Agriculture and Agrarian Reform, in 2008 Syria's wheat crop declined by 35% compared with the previous year. In 2009 a recovery in wheat production was recorded, although output was still down by 25% compared with the record level registered in 2006. In the wake of the drought, hundreds of villages were abandoned by their inhabitants, and hundreds of thousands of villagers migrated to the cities, where they placed an additional heavy burden on state infrastructure, and relief and welfare resources.

The crisis precipitated by the drought added to another ongoing crisis engendered by the natural increase of the Syrian population, which was among the highest in the world. The country's population had become younger, but, at the same time, was largely unemployed, poor and devoid of hope for the future.

The repercussions of this demographic process were felt mainly in the rural areas and the periphery of the country. As noted above, these areas had also suffered from the policy of economic openness that the Government had adopted soon after Bashar al-Assad had assumed the presidency in June 2000. According to the new economic policy, many of the privileges that had previously been granted to the rural and peripheral areas were cancelled. These areas were thus confronted by numerous major problems, and this situation played an important role in the outbreak of the Syrian revolution at the beginning of 2011.

THE SYRIAN REVOLUTION: PROTESTS, UPRISING, CIVIL WAR AND *JIHAD*

On 18 March 2011 demonstrations broke out in the southern city of Dar'a and in several other cities and villages in the north of Syria, including Hama and Banyas. These protests heralded the arrival in Syria of the 'Arab Spring', which had already reached Tunisia, Egypt, Libya and Yemen.

The demonstrations in Syria were initially confined to the rural and peripheral areas. However, it should be noted that these peripheral areas provided the Baath Party and the Baathist regime established after the revolution of 8 March 1963 with their power base. Over the years the peripheral areas had always given the Baath Party their loyal support; from them, the Government drew its power, and in fact the regime's leadership hailed from these areas. Now, however, this periphery was rejecting the regime.

This development brought to the surface and made clearly visible a lengthy and ongoing process that had unfolded in Syria during the previous several decades, a process in which the popular bases of support for the Baathist regime had narrowed and diminished significantly.

Despite the initially limited nature of the protest movement, it rapidly spread across the country. The brutal means employed by the authorities to repress the demonstrations contributed to this, as did the deployment of the army from late April 2011. Within a few weeks the protests turned into a widespread popular uprising against Bashar al-Assad's regime, and, ultimately, into a bloody and indecisive civil war.

Over time, the violent unrest in Syria took on an ethnic character and, even worse, a religious character as well. It became a holy war for Islamist groups, some native to Syria and others made up of volunteers who had travelled to the country from all over the Arab and Muslim world. In their view, they were fighting against what they perceived as the Alawi 'heretics' who ruled from Damascus and who were allies of the Shi'a bloc in the Middle East, comprising the Iranian state and Hezbollah in Lebanon.

Syria also became an arena of regional and international struggle, primarily involving the USA and the Russian Federation, as well as regional powers such as Saudi Arabia, Qatar, Türkiye and Iran. The involvement of these foreign countries only exacerbated the crisis in Syria and prolonged the fighting. Russia, Iran and Hezbollah joined the conflict on the side of the Syrian regime, while the Sunni and anti-Iranian states of Saudi Arabia, Qatar and Türkiye mobilized to help the rebels, resulting in a proxy war between the Shi'a and Sunni axes being waged on Syrian soil.

By mid-2019, after eight years of civil war, the number of people killed in the fighting amounted to almost 600,000. About 11m. Syrians—approximately one-half of the country's population—had lost their homes, and about 6m. of those had become refugees, fleeing from their homeland across Syria's borders. This was the direct result of the war conducted by both sides, but it was also the result of the regime's deliberate policy of purging areas suspected of supporting the rebels completely of their inhabitants.

Several stages can be discerned in Syria's descent into civil war, which led to the state's collapse and the disintegration of Syrian society into its component parts. This ultimately led to Syrian territory being turned into a battleground for regional and international forces, which thereafter determined the country's fate.

THE FIRST STAGE, THE 'SYRIAN SPRING': PROTEST AND REVOLUTION, MARCH 2011–MARCH 2013

The first stage was characterized by the slow and gradual, yet continuous, loss of the regime's assets, both in terms of manpower and territory in the rural and peripheral areas. The Syrian regime was weakened, but it did not collapse, and it continued to maintain the cohesion of its political and military elites and of its governmental, military and security institutions and apparatuses.

The rebels, on the other hand, failed in their efforts to unite their ranks and establish a political leadership and military command to conduct the war against the regime. The leadership bodies established by the rebels, such as the Syrian National Council (SNC), which was founded in August 2011, and the Syrian National Coalition, formed in November 2012, ultimately had little influence. The same was true for the Free Syrian Army, founded in July 2011 with the aim of uniting under its authority all the rebel groups throughout the country. It failed in this task and became a weak umbrella organization without any practical ability to control the rebels in the field.

Also during this stage, President Assad's allies, especially Iran and Russia, mobilized to help the regime both financially and militarily. Russia, for its part, prevented the adoption of any UN resolution condemning the Syrian regime, placing responsibility for the crisis in the country upon it or calling for action against it. On the other hand, the Western states, led by the USA, demonstrated indecision and a reluctance to become actively involved in the crisis in Syria. They limited themselves to severing ties with the Syrian regime and imposing economic sanctions.

Several landmark events took place during this phase of the crisis. On 15 March 2011 a demonstration, which was quickly dispersed, was held in the al-Hamidiyah Souq, in the centre of Damascus. Then, on 18 March, protests broke out in the city of Dar'a. The regime's use of military force to try to quell the uprising began there on 25 April. On 23 December, in Kafr Sousa, Syria experienced its first terrorist attacks aimed at the headquarters of the General Security Services, which left 44 people dead and 166 injured. The attacks were carried out by the Front for the Support of the People of Syria (the al-Nusra Front, or Jabhat al-Nusra), a branch of the extremist Islamic State in Iraq and the Levant (ISIL, renamed Islamic State in 2014) organization. In mid-July 2012 four of Syria's most senior security officials died as a result of a bombing carried out at the headquarters of the national security service in central Damascus. In the wake of this incident, groups of rebels stormed the centre of the capital, as well as Aleppo, the country's second largest city. Finally, on 5 March 2013, the city of Raqqa fell to the rebels and subsequently became the de facto capital of the territory held by ISIL. This was the first provincial capital to be lost by the regime.

THE SECOND STAGE: STRATEGIC STALEMATE, MARCH 2013–JUNE 2014

The second stage was marked by the Syrian regime's success in recovering from the initial challenges to its authority and remaining in power. This was due in part to aid it received from Hezbollah, and the encouragement and backing of Iran. Another factor was the failure of the rebels to capitalize on their earlier military achievements and to bring their campaign to a victorious conclusion. The rebels counted among their forces hundreds of armed groups operating all over the country. However, they found it difficult to close ranks and unite. They were unable to create agreed-upon military and political leadership apparatuses that could lead them to a final victory. As noted above, the leadership bodies established by the rebels, such as the SNC and the Syrian National Coalition, and even the Free Syrian Army, ultimately had little influence. The process of Islamist radicalization within the rebel movement also seemed to benefit President Assad, insofar as it prompted many of his opponents, both inside Syria and abroad, to return to his side as they recoiled from the rising power of Islamist extremism. These factors resulted in a strategic stalemate, such that none of the contending factions was able to subdue its opponents.

The turning point that marked the beginning of this phase was the success of the pro-regime Hezbollah fighters in retaking the city of Qusayr, south of Homs, on 5 June 2013. This was the first city that the regime had managed to reoccupy. During late 2013 regime forces also reclaimed the ridge of the Qalamun Mountain range overlooking the Syrian–Lebanese border.

No less significant was the agreement signed between the USA and Russia on 14 September 2013 to bring about the elimination of Syria's chemical weapons. This accord was reached after the Syrian regime had allegedly used chemical weapons against its opponents in Ghouta, in the suburbs around Damascus, on 21 August. The chemical attack killed up to 1,429 people, mostly civilians, leading to a threat by the US Administration of military action against President Assad and his regime. However, following a Russian initiative, an agreement was reached on 14 September whereby the USA withdrew its threats of military action in exchange for a pledge from the Syrian regime to discontinue the use of chemical weapons. This agreement reflected the determination of the Obama Administration to do everything in its power to avoid being drawn into direct involvement in the war in Syria, and particularly to avoid sending US troops to fight on Syrian territory.

THE THIRD STAGE: THE RISE OF ISLAMIC STATE, JUNE 2014–MID-2015

During this period the decline of the Syrian state continued, and even accelerated, while the power of the non-state entities active all over the country rose. This stage began with Islamic State's seizure of large parts of northern Iraq and eastern Syria during mid-2014. Parallel to this, other rebel groups active in the more westerly parts of Syria managed to push the regime's forces out of most of their strongholds in the south and north of the country. The al-Nusra Front, led by Abu Muhammad al-Jawlani, was the leading rebel force. Al-Nusra had begun as a Syrian branch of ISIL, but on 24 January 2013 its leader had declared independence from that organization.

The turning point marking the beginning of this third stage was the conquest by Islamic State fighters of the city of Mosul in Iraq on 10 June 2014. Subsequently, Islamic State managed to gain control of Syria's al-Jazira region (mainly in the governorates of Deir el-Zor and Raqqa). In May 2015 Islamic State fighters also captured the historic city of Palmyra.

In March 2015, in the north of Syria, the rebel fighters of the Army of Conquest (Jaysh al-Fath), a force operating jointly with the al-Nusra Front and other rebel groups, managed to seize control of Idlib governorate, including its capital city. In late 2014, on the southern front, al-Nusra and its allies had already taken control of the rural areas of Dar'a and Quneitra governorates, as well as most of the rural areas of Rif Dimashq (Rural Damascus) governorate, including the majority of the Syrian Golan Heights.

Against the background of Islamic State's rise, but also in view of the successes of the other rebel groups, during mid-2014 there were signs of a turning point in the Syrian civil war. The rebels' achievements in the battles against the regime tipped the balance in their favour and raised doubts about President Assad's ability to maintain his rule even in the heart of the Syrian state, i.e. in the narrow strip stretching from Damascus to Aleppo and the Alawi coastal area in the north, and perhaps to Dar'a and the mountainous Jabal al-Druze in the south.

In eastern Syria, Islamic State liquidated all of its rivals and became almost the only force active in the region. Apart from Islamic State, there were Kurdish forces, especially the Kurdish Democratic Union Party and its military arm, the People's Protection Units, which operated mainly in the Kurdish enclaves in the north-east of the country. On 16 March 2016 these Kurdish forces announced the establishment of a federation in the Kurdish areas of northern Syria, the 'Federation of Northern Syria—Rojava' (meaning 'west' in Kurdish). The name alluded to Western Kurdistan, a term that the Kurds had used for Syrian Kurdistan.

In the western parts of Syria, the al-Nusra Front was the leading force. It showed itself to be pragmatic and willing to co-operate with other Salafi Islamist groups, especially the Army of Islam, led by Zahran Alloush, and the Ahrar al-Sham movement, led by Hashim al-Sheikh Abu Jabir.

However, at the critical moment, Iran and Russia came to the aid of President Assad, enabling him to survive.

THE FOURTH STAGE: THE RUSSIAN INTERVENTION, SEPTEMBER 2015

In September 2015 Russian air force fighter squadrons landed in Syria. Several thousand members of the Iranian IRGC arrived at the same time. Their mission was to provide aid to President Assad's regime. Russia's strategy in Syria sought to emulate the model used in its war in Chechnya in the 1990s, i.e. it intended to deploy military force to crush the rebellion and subjugate the rebel movement. This force came in the form of massive bombing from the air and ground attacks aimed at inducing the flight of the civilian population in the areas suspected of supporting the rebels. Some of the cleared areas were retaken by forces of the Syrian regime led by IRGC or Hezbollah fighters.

During the first months of 2016 the Russian and Iranian military intervention enabled the Syrian regime to take the initiative from the insurgents and to regain control of a number of key positions in northern and southern Syria. For example, during this period the Syrian army managed to expel Islamic State fighters from Palmyra and from the outskirts of Homs, and to tighten control over the Damascus–Dar'a axis in the south of the country.

THE FIFTH STAGE: THE END OF THE BATTLE FOR 'VITAL SYRIA' AND THE EFFORT TO REACH A SETTLEMENT AND END THE WAR (DECEMBER 2016–)

On 22 December 2016 the Syrian army, with Russian and Iranian assistance, succeeded in retaking complete control of Aleppo. This military achievement was perceived by many as the end of the battle for the heart of the country, or 'Vital Syria', control over which was regarded as the key to victory.

The capture of Aleppo led to a Russian effort to bring the fighting in Syria to an end, under conditions favourable to Russia and its allies, but with a readiness to accept the division of the country between the areas controlled by the regime in Damascus and the areas in which the various rebel factions would continue to operate, under the auspices of Türkiye, Jordan and the USA. On 20 December 2016 Russia reached agreement with Türkiye and Iran (in the 'Moscow Declaration') regarding the partitioning of Syria into 'protected areas' (spheres of influence). Russia brought the Moscow Declaration before the UN Security Council for approval, and it was adopted as Resolution 2336 on 31 December. On 29 December a ceasefire had been declared, even though it did not include Islamic State and Jabhat Fatah al-Sham. On 23 January 2017 peace talks were held in Astana, Kazakhstan, with the participation of representatives of President Assad and his opponents, and mediated by Russia, Iran and Türkiye, with the aim of diminishing the violence in Syria and stabilizing the ceasefire.

On 5 May 2017, again in Astana, Russia, Türkiye and Iran signed a memorandum of understanding committing themselves to be the guarantors for the establishment of four 'de-escalation' or 'protected' zones: Idlib governorate and parts of neighbouring governorates in the north of the country, near the border with Türkiye; the region between the cities of Hama and Homs; the rural area to the east of Damascus; and parts of the Dar'a and Qunaytra governorates near the border with Israel and Jordan. In these zones, armed military operations were prohibited, including activity by the Syrian air force. The memorandum also stipulated that humanitarian aid would be extended to the four areas and the provision of public services, water and electricity would be restored. Finally, the three guarantor states agreed to deploy their military forces at crossing, inspection and observation points throughout the four areas in order to supervise the implementation of the agreement. However, these agreements were not honoured by the Syrian regime, which refused to accept them. Thus, for example, during the first months of 2018 the Syrian army, aided by Russia, conducted an attack on rebel strongholds in the Ghouta al-Sharqiya region and seized control of the area. From there, the Syrian army moved in the direction of additional de-escalation areas in the north, centre and south of the country.

The Chemical Attacks in Khan Shaykhun and Douma and the US Counter-strike

On the morning of 4 April 2017 reports emerged from the town of Khan Shaykhun in northern Syria that sarin gas had been used during an attack by Syrian military aircraft, killing more than 110 residents, most of whom were women and children, and injuring several hundred others. In response, on 7 April US President Donald Trump ordered a strike of 59 *Tomahawk* missiles against the Shu'ayrat air base east of Homs, from which, according to US intelligence reports, the Syrian aircraft that attacked Khan Shaykhun had taken off. On 7 April 2018, as part of the Syrian regime's efforts to take control of the Ghouta al-Sharqiya region, it once more used chemical weapons—apparently chlorine gas—in the town of Douma. It was reported that 42 people were killed in the attack, most of them women and children, and hundreds more were injured. In response, on 14 April 2018 the USA, together with the UK and France, fired more than 100 missiles from warships and aircraft at a number of different targets, including military bases, research institutes and chemical weapons storage facilities. However, as in Khan Shaykhun, the action did not seem to signify a major shift in the West's policy of avoiding direct involvement in the Syrian conflict, but rather a limited punitive measure.

THE DEFEAT OF ISLAMIC STATE

While President Assad was re-establishing his regime's authority over western Syria, Islamic State was losing control over most of its strongholds in northern Iraq and eastern Syria under pressure of attack by the US-led international coalition. Inside Syria, the Assad regime pushed Islamic State out of its strongholds in the centre of the country, around the cities of Palmyra and Homs, and shortly thereafter Syrian forces moved eastward deep into the Syrian Desert (al-Badiya), in the direction of the Syrian–Iraqi border. In northern Syria, the Kurds, with US assistance and sometimes with the aid of Sunni Arab rebel groups backed by Türkiye, expelled Islamic State from the areas that it had subjugated in the north of Aleppo governorate and in Raqqa governorate.

On 10 July 2017 the Iraqi Government announced the reoccupation of the city of Mosul and the defeat of Islamic State there. On 5 September the Syrian army joined up with its besieged forces in the town of Deir el-Zor. Finally, on 17 October Kurdish fighters—members of the Syrian Democratic Forces, who were operating with the support and assistance of the USA—captured Islamic State's de facto capital of Raqqa.

The decline of Islamic State signified the failure of political Islam and perhaps also of the *salafi-jihadist* movement in Syria. Thus, the Syrian regime, with Russian and Iranian assistance, was soon able to force Islamist rebel groups out of the areas that they had controlled in western Syria. For example, Jaysh al-Islam was forced out of Ghouta al-Sharqiya, and Ahrar al-Sham was expelled from the Aleppo area.

On 28 July 2016, as the war began to turn in favour of the Syrian regime, the al-Nusra Front announced its withdrawal from its parent organization, al-Qa'ida, and the establishment of a new organizational framework, called Jabhat Fatah al-Sham. The group's leader, Abu Mohammad al-Jawlani, explained that this step was taken 'in accord with the guidance and instruction' he had received from 'the blessed leadership [of the al-Qa'ida Organization]', and 'at the request of the people of the Syrian lands (Bilad al-Sham), and in order to serve their needs'. Al-Qa'ida leader Ayman al-Zawahiri gave his approval to the path taken by al-Jawlani.

On 28 January 2017 Jabhat Fatah al-Sham joined Jaysh al-Tahrir—a body established by 16 factions that had seceded from Ahrar al-Sham al-Islamiyya, led by Hashim al-Sheikh Abu Jabir, a former leader of Ahrar al-Sham—following the willingness shown by the leadership of Ahrar al-Sham to participate in the Russian-sponsored peace talks on the future of Syria. Together, they formed Tahrir al-Sham (Liberation Front of the Syrian Lands), and Abu Mohammad al-Jawlani was placed at its head.

Several months later a dispute broke out between al-Zawahiri and al-Jawlani over the question of whether Tahrir al-Sham was authorized to conduct an independent 'Syrian policy' that took into consideration the constraints under which the organization was operating, or whether it was obliged to follow the guidance of al-Zawahiri, whose views and evaluation of the situation were completely different. This dispute led to a rift between the two leaders.

Islamic State leader Abu Bakr al-Baghdadi died in October 2019 after he detonated a suicide bomb during a raid by US special forces on his compound in Barisha, Idlib governorate. A few days later Islamic State announced the appointment of Abu Ibrahim al-Hashimi al-Qurashi as al-Baghdadi's successor. However, al-Qurashi was himself killed during an operation by US special forces in February 2022 in Atme, Idlib governorate. (Like al-Baghdadi, al-Qurashi had reportedly detonated a suicide bomb.) Abu Hassan al-Hashimi al-Qurashi was announced as the new leader of Islamic State in March, although he was killed during combat in Dar'a governorate in November. The fourth leader of Islamic State, Abu al-Hussein al-Husseini al-Qurashi, was allegedly killed in Aleppo governorate in April 2023 as a result of a Turkish military operation. By this time US forces had additionally killed several other senior Islamic State members after conducting air strikes in northern Syria. In August Islamic State announced the appointment of its fifth leader, Abu Hafs al-Hashimi al-Quraishi.

THE RENEWED STRUGGLE FOR SYRIA

By mid-2018 President Assad had over two-thirds of Syria's territory under his control, owing to Russian and Iranian support. In April the Syrian army regained control over Ghouta al-Sharqiya, east of Damascus, and a month later, also in the vicinity of Damascus, government troops reoccupied al-Hajar al-Aswad and Yarmouk Palestinian refugee camp, which had been under the control of Islamic State. In July government forces regained control over southern Syria, including the city of Dar'a, where the protests against Assad had erupted in March 2011.

These military victories removed the existential threat to the Syrian regime, but paradoxically led to an increase in foreign involvement in Syria and an intensification of the struggles between the various regional and international forces operating in the country.

In December 2018 US President Trump declared that he had decided to withdraw US special forces deployed in Syria, which were effectively controlling almost one-quarter of Syria's territory, mainly in the east and north of the country. In January 2019 Trump made a public statement in which he described

Syria as 'nothing but sand and death', indicating his Administration's strategic lack of interest in Syria. Furthermore, in March Trump formally recognized Israel's annexation of the Golan Heights, but probably did so because of domestic political considerations and in an attempt to bolster his base of support rather than with regards to overall US policy in Syria and the wider Middle East. However, following Joe Biden's inauguration as US President in January 2021, senior US officials made it clear that the USA had no intention of withdrawing its forces from Syria or normalizing diplomatic relations with Assad's regime.

The establishment of Kurdish autonomy with US backing was perceived by Türkiye as a threat to its internal stability. Thus, Türkiye launched a series of military operations—Euphrates Shield in August 2016, Olive Branch in January 2018 and Peace Spring in October 2019—which were designed to prevent the Kurds from achieving territorial continuity from the east to the shores of the Mediterranean. Türkiye also established a buffer zone in northern Syria under the control of Syrian rebels aligned with the Turkish Government. In March 2020 Türkiye embarked on Operation Spring Star and confronted Syrian military forces and Hezbollah fighters seeking to seize, with Russian support, the Idlib area. In February 2022 Türkiye launched Operation Winter Eagle against the Kurds in an area north-east of Aleppo.

The foothold that Iran gained in Syria aroused much concern in Israel and led to a series of incidents between the Quds Force of the IRGC, which was deployed in Syria, and the Israeli military. On 10 February 2018 Iran launched an unmanned aerial vehicle (UAV—drone) towards Israel from the Tiyas air base in Syria. Israel shot down the UAV and attacked the Iranian installations at Tiyas. It did so again on 9 April and 29 April. Following an Iranian effort to retaliate, on 9 May Israel attacked Iranian sites at a number of locations within Syria. Tensions between Israel and Iran continued to cast a shadow over the efforts to stabilize the security situation in Syria. Israel continued to conduct air strikes aimed at the Iranian military presence in Syria, as well as at the bases of pro-Iranian Shi'a militias that operated on Syrian territory.

Tension also grew between Russia and Iran over their influence in Syria, as well as their security and military apparatus and economic assets in the country. In January 2017 Russia had signed an agreement with the Syrian Government to lease Humaymim military air base and Tartous military harbour for a period of 49 years. Iran had also signed a series of military, security and energy co-operation agreements with Syria in recent years. Reports from Syria repeatedly pointed to tensions and even clashes between forces loyal to Russia and those loyal to Iran.

Evidence of the close relationship between Syria and Russia was demonstrated in mid-March 2022, when it was reported that 150 Syrian troops had arrived in Ukraine to assist the Russian armed forces, following their full-scale invasion of Ukraine in late February (see Russia and Ukraine). Russian troops were also withdrawn from Syria and redeployed to Ukraine, although Russian air strikes on Islamic State positions continued. During a meeting with Russian President Vladimir Putin in March 2023, Assad reportedly requested that Russia increase the number of troops and military bases that it maintained in Syria.

THE DOMESTIC FRONT: IMPASSE AND STAGNATION

In mid-2022 the struggle for Syria still appeared to be far from over, and the conflict remained at a stalemate. Political isolation and economic stagnation continued, and even intensified, in the wake of the onset of the coronavirus disease (COVID-19) pandemic in early 2020 and the implementation of the Caesar Syria Civilian Protection Act by the US Administration in June. The Caesar Act, named after a Syrian photographer known by the pseudonym 'Caesar', who had documented acts of torture committed by the Syrian regime against civilians, imposed sanctions on entities conducting business with the Syrian Government and its military and intelligence agencies. The Act severely undermined commercial activity in Syria and eventually also exacerbated the economic crisis in Lebanon, which in turn negatively affected the Syrian economy.

As the economic situation continued to deteriorate, large sections of the population were left impoverished, although the focus of the Syrian regime was on investing its resources to restore its military capabilities. One of the manifestations of the economic crisis was the collapse of the local currency, from about £S500 = US $1 in late 2019 to about £S4,000 = US $1 in early 2022, as a result of trade sanctions, the erosion of salaries and the shortage of basic products, all of which were exacerbated by the COVID-19 pandemic. The economic crisis fuelled social tensions and waves of unrest and popular protest, for example in the city of al-Suweida on Mount Druze in June 2020. Further unrest was reported in February 2022, after the Government introduced changes in the subsidy distribution mechanism that denied hundreds of thousands of Syrians the right to purchase food and basic necessities at subsidized prices. Meanwhile, tensions arose within the Assad family, between Bashar al-Assad and his wife Asma on one side and on the other Bashar's cousin, Rami Makhlouf, a prominent businessman, whose property and assets were confiscated by the Syrian authorities in May 2020.

Although the Syrian regime had emerged from the conflict in a stronger position than its opponents, the Government lacked manpower and resources, and had found it difficult to restore stability to the country and to rehabilitate state institutions and the economy.

The demographic reality that emerged in the wake of the war benefited the regime and may have a significant long-term impact on the balance of power between the various religious communities in the country. In the territories controlled by the regime, only about 10m. inhabitants remained. There were another 3m. people in the Kurdish-controlled areas and a further 4m. in Idlib governorate. Since 70% of the refugees who had fled Syria were Sunnis, the demographic weight in government-controlled territories of Alawites and Druze, most of whom had remained in the country, rose significantly. The Office of the UN High Commissioner for Refugees (UNHCR) estimated in mid-2023 that the total Syrian refugee population was more than 5.2m., including almost 3.3m. in Türkiye, 0.8m. in Lebanon, 0.7m. in Jordan, over 0.2m. in Iraq and 0.1m. in Egypt. Meanwhile, UNHCR estimated that there were 6.8m. internally displaced people within Syria as of December 2022, and some 15.3m. people were in need of humanitarian and protection assistance at the end of April 2023. The UN Human Rights Office estimated in June 2022 that 306,887 civilians had been killed in Syria as a result of the civil war since March 2011—approximately 1.5% of the pre-war population.

The Syrian regime's ongoing efforts to regain effective control of the country were slow and gradual. The authorities attempted to restore state institutions and social and economic services, through which the regime sought to spread its patronage over Syrian society. As part of this process, elections to the People's Assembly were held on 19 July 2020. According to the official results, the National Progressive Front—comprising 10 parties led by the ruling Baath Party—secured 177 of the legislature's 250 seats. Voter turnout was officially recorded at only 33.2%. Voting was restricted to government-controlled areas, and opposition figures denounced the elections as illegitimate. On 30 August President Assad appointed a new Government, which took office on 2 September. The former Minister of Water Resources, Hussein Arnous, was appointed as Prime Minister.

President Assad won re-election for a further seven-year term at a presidential election held on 26 May 2021. According to the official results, Assad had secured 95.2% of the valid votes cast. Voter turnout was officially recorded at 78.6%. However, several opposition groups had boycotted the election and accused the authorities of 'showing contempt to the Syrian people'. Nevertheless, despite this opposition and the election being denounced by many Western countries, Assad was sworn in for a fourth consecutive term as President on 17 July. On 10 August Assad issued a decree forming a new, largely unchanged Council of Ministers under the renewed premiership of Arnous.

The regime also abolished the office of Mufti of the Republic in November 2021 and instead established a Council of

Religious Legislation (Majlis al-'Ilm al-Fikhi), composed of clerics from all of the country's Muslim communities under the control of the Minister of Awqaf (Religious Endowments). In April 2022 Lt-Gen. Ali Mahmoud Abbas replaced Gen. Ali Abdullah Ayoub as Minister of Defence, while Maj.-Gen. Abdel Karim Mahmoud Ibrahim was appointed as Chief of the General Staff of the Army and Armed Forces—a post that had been vacant since 2018.

On 6 February 2023 a 7.8-magnitude earthquake struck southern and central Türkiye and northern and western Syria. The confirmed death toll in Syria amounted to 8,476, and many people were displaced. It was the deadliest earthquake in present-day Syria since the 1822 Aleppo earthquake. Damages were estimated at US $14,800m. Owing to the resulting infrastructural damage and the country's pre-existing humanitarian crisis, the Syrian Government had difficulty providing support to the victims in the territories under its control. It also refrained from distributing aid to the victims in the territories controlled by the rebels in northern Syria, where the impact of the earthquake was particularly severe. The USA temporarily relaxed its sanctions against Syria to facilitate the transportation of humanitarian aid supplies to the survivors. A smaller earthquake on 20 February caused further damage in the Syria–Türkiye border region.

Following Assad's re-election, there were signs that Syria's relations with its Arab neighbours were starting to improve, easing the country's isolation in the region. Several Arab states, such as Jordan, Oman and the United Arab Emirates (UAE), restored diplomatic relations with Syria, while others renewed dialogue with the Assad regime, mainly to discuss security issues. The talks initially focused on combating Islamist extremism and terrorism, particularly Islamic State, but the security dialogue was subsequently expanded to include the situation in Iraq, Lebanon and the region in general. The Syrian Government also reconciled with Hamas (which had supported the Syrian opposition forces during the civil war); bilateral relations were restored in September 2022, and high-ranking Hamas members visited Damascus in the following month. In March, moreover, Assad had travelled to the UAE, his first visit to an Arab country since the outbreak of the war, and he also visited Oman in February 2023. In the same month the Egyptian Minister of Foreign Affairs, Sameh Hassan Shoukry, travelled to Damascus for talks with the Assad regime, while his Syrian counterpart, Faysal Mikdad, visited Egypt in April. In May it was announced that Syria's diplomatic relations with Tunisia and Bahrain would be restored. Some Western countries also made contact with Syria, seeking its help in combating radical Islamist terrorism and facilitating the return of Syrian refugees.

Syria's relations with Saudi Arabia also improved. The two countries began a security dialogue on the subjects of countering terrorism and drug trafficking (particularly of fenethylline) from Syria. It was subsequently announced that the two countries' respective embassies would be reopened and civil aviation links would be restored. The Saudi Government declared that the regional policy of isolating Syria had negatively affected the Syrian people.

Against this background, the members of the League of Arab States (the Arab League) decided in May 2023 to reinstate Syria's membership of the organization. (Syria had been suspended from the League in November 2011 in response to the suppression of anti-Government demonstrations by the Assad regime.) The Arab League's efforts to normalize ties with the Assad regime attracted criticism from the USA and the UK, however.

Meanwhile, Turkish forces had begun a new offensive in north-eastern Syria and Iraq in April 2022, targeting Kurdish militias operating in the region. Nevertheless, ongoing Russian-led efforts to facilitate a reconciliation between Syria and Türkiye were reportedly making progress in mid-2023. Assad emphasized that talks with Türkiye should be focused on ending the Turkish occupation of Syrian territory and Turkish support for Syrian militia groups.

However, Syria's relations with other members of the international community remained tense in 2023. The European Union imposed additional sanctions in April against Syrians accused of human rights abuses and drug trafficking. In the same month Israel conducted air strikes against military targets in Syria, after Israel was attacked by rockets allegedly fired by Syrian-based Palestinian militants. Meanwhile, at least 19 people were reportedly killed in March by US air strikes targeting pro-Iranian militias in eastern Syria, following a drone attack on a US-led coalition military base that had resulted in the death of a US contractor.

Economy

OMAR S. DAHI and MOHAMMAD AL-ASADI

INTRODUCTION

March 2023 marked the 12th anniversary of the start of the conflict in the Syrian Arab Republic, which the United Nations (UN) has called one of the biggest humanitarian catastrophes since the Second World War. In this essay we use the term 'Syrian conflict' as the most neutral and simplest description of the nature of the upheaval in the country. Other scholarly descriptions include 'uprising', 'civil war' or 'uprising-cum-civil war' and 'proxy war'. Terms such as revolution, war on Syria, as well as a variety of other descriptors are often used by the different partisans and, as with all conflicts, these are heatedly debated. However, no term can capture fully the complexity of the events since 2011.

Though the years of the conflict left a lasting devastation, the last three years have seen a particularly severe deterioration in living standards across the entire country. In 2023 the UN Office for the Coordination of Humanitarian Affairs estimated that almost 7 out of every 10 people in Syria, or about 15.3m., needed assistance, the largest number of people since the conflict began and an increase from 14.6m. in 2022. Almost one-half (46%) of those in need were children. About one-half of the population had been involuntarily displaced, with about 6.5m. people internally displaced and over 4.8m. refugees outside Syria's borders, primarily in Turkey (officially known as Türkiye from June 2022), Lebanon, Jordan and Europe. More than 470,000 deaths were estimated to have been caused by the conflict and many more tens of thousands injured, leaving many with permanent physical disabilities. On 6 February 2023 two high-magnitude earthquakes struck northern Syria and southern Türkiye, killing more than 50,000 people and causing over US $80,000m. in damage across both countries. The impact of the earthquake on Syria was complex, deepening the humanitarian crisis in affected areas, but also coinciding with regional re-engagement with the Syrian Government by several countries.

Syria is now widely characterized as a 'frozen conflict'. Direct armed conflict has significantly diminished since 2017, but without any short- or medium-term prospect of a comprehensive or even partial political settlement. Rather, there have been various formal and informal truces and ceasefire agreements brokered by the Government of Syria and the various armed groups and, more importantly, under the decisive influence of the Russian Federation, the USA, Türkiye and Iran, which all have a significant presence inside the country. Syrian territory is now de facto divided into several areas of territorial control, characterized by spheres of influence of these foreign countries along with their domestic allies. The largest area is under the control of the Syrian Government and its allies, including Russian and Iranian troops. The north-east is controlled by the Syrian Democratic Forces and their allies, including the USA. Another region, in northern Syria, is controlled by the Turkish Government and its allied forces, and a region in north-west Syria is largely controlled by an armed group called the Liberation Front of the Syrian Lands. There does not seem to be any actionable desire on the part of any of the main actors to change the status quo, and other international events, including the Russian invasion of Ukraine in February 2022, have relegated the 'Syrian file' to minimal importance, both regionally and internationally.

The main operating UN resolution guiding the peacebuilding process is UN Security Council Resolution 2254, although this has existed alongside parallel processes initiated by Russia—sometimes known as the Astana Process. There have also been periodic diplomatic meetings in Geneva, Switzerland, bringing together Syrian Government, opposition and civil society representatives ostensibly to negotiate a new constitution that would shape a subsequent political process. However, there is widespread acknowledgement that these initiatives have stalled indefinitely, pending a significant shift in the positions of the major actors, most notably the USA, Russia and Türkiye.

The humanitarian catastrophe, death and widespread displacement, infrastructural and environmental destruction, geographic partition, a war economy, and various economic sanctions have all fundamentally shaped the Syrian economy and created new drivers of conflict. These, along with regional and international geopolitics, are likely to continue to shape prospects for the Syrian economy in the short- to medium-term.

GROWTH AND STRUCTURAL CHANGE FROM INDEPENDENCE UNTIL 2010

Long part of the socialist bloc during the Cold War, Syria's relative isolation from the West started to change in the 1990s with the collapse of the Union of Soviet Socialist Republics (USSR) and the rise of uncontested US hegemony in the region, a decline in assistance from the oil-rich Arab countries, and dwindling domestic resources. In the 1960s and 1970s Syria had adopted a state socialist economy, with state-led enterprises, agrarian reform and significant expenditure on health and education facilitated by the oil boom of the 1970s. Syria had positioned itself as an anti-Western, anti-imperialist state in alliance with the Soviet bloc, and a leader in the Arab confrontation with Israel to liberate the Occupied Territories and support Palestinian self-determination.

At the domestic level, state socialism was also accompanied by suppression of political dissent and—following a civil war in the late 1970s and early 1980s—any form of independent organization or political life. Economic liberalization in Syria happened in piecemeal fashion in the 1970s, 1980s and 1990s, and was driven by either strategic political considerations, such as rapprochement with the wealthy Gulf states, or in the aftermath of an economic crisis.

In the 2000s, under the current President, Bashar al-Assad, economic liberalization accelerated and Syria tried to shed its state socialist legacy in favour of growth led by the private sector. Economic liberalization was heavily characterized by crony capitalism, an alliance of wealth and power, and a significant rise in inequality. Nevertheless, the economic record of the 2000s included positive developments in reducing overall debt, and a reasonable rate of growth in per capita gross domestic product (GDP). By 2011 Syria was in the lower middle-income category, according to the World Bank. In 2007 it ranked 108th in the UN Development Programme Human Development Index, just behind Indonesia, but ahead of non-oil-rich regional countries such as Egypt (112th) and Morocco (126th). Syria's ranking, however, was weighed down by its relatively low GDP per capita. Life expectancy at birth was estimated at 73.6 years in 2005, which would have placed it among the medium-to-high human development countries. Syria's debt-to-GDP ratio entering 2011 was around 25%, which is very low for a developing country.

The aggregate statistics masked some deep regional inequalities, shaped by growth being significantly concentrated around the major cities of Damascus and Aleppo. This was reflected in large discrepancies in poverty incidence among governorates. While headcount poverty did not exceed 6% in Damascus in 2007, it hovered around 20% in Rural Damascus, Al-Hasakah, Deir el-Zour and Al-Raqqah (Raqqa), despite the latter three areas' location in the oil-rich east. Rural areas suffered, particularly with the declines in agricultural production and investment. Syria's manufacturing sector was never a major driver of economic growth, but it showed some signs of dynamism, particularly in the textile and pharmaceutical industries. Although it was planned to reach 15% by the end of the 10th five-year plan (2006–10), the manufacturing share of GDP in 2010 stood at 8.5%. None the less, the output of pharmaceutical factories in the country expanded at an average annual rate of 6.5% between 2006 and 2010 and textile production increased by an average of 7.3% per year between 2002 and 2007. However, trade liberalization, particularly with Syria's more dynamic neighbour, Türkiye, resulted in significant setbacks for industry.

In short, by 2011 Syria had reasonable macroeconomic indicators, and deprivation and poverty were not major factors. Rather, Syria had witnessed economic liberalization without institutional reform or political liberalization, a huge increase in horizontal and vertical inequality, or the capture of wealth by an unaccountable and highly connected elite.

OVERVIEW OF CONFLICT DYNAMICS

Without attempting a comprehensive account of the conflict, this section will summarize the main conflict dynamics and their impact on the economy in order to contextualize the analysis in the remainder of the essay.

The first phase of the conflict, 2011–13, witnessed a civil uprising in many parts of the country and from mid- to late 2011 the rise of armed groups, which proliferated dramatically in 2012 and 2013 as funding and weapons poured into the country. Syria's borders since then have been routinely penetrated by regional and international powers for humanitarian and military purposes. The Syrian Government's response involved significant and brutal repression, which escalated as the armed conflict increased in intensity, and involved mass sieges and often indiscriminate shelling as well as widespread human rights violations. At this point, internal economic connections started to fragment and internal trade began to stall. Moreover, physical destruction was increasing. Destruction and armed conflict in residential areas, coupled with fears of reprisal, led to accelerated and then massive displacement both internally and externally. State-owned enterprises, factories and other economic infrastructure were also increasingly targeted. Finally, at the external level, economic sanctions imposed by the USA, the European Union (EU) and other Arab states contributed to a steep economic decline. The EU sanctions, which included a boycott of crude petroleum purchases, coupled with gradual economic fragmentation, led to a steep fall in Syrian oil production from around 400,000 barrels per day (b/d) in 2006 (although the figure was lower entering 2011) to less than 50,000 b/d in 2013, representing a massive blow to Syrian public finances.

From late 2013 until 2015 many of the smaller armed groups were defeated or consolidated into larger ones, the militant organization Islamic State in Iraq and the Levant (later known as Islamic State) emerged on the scene, and external powers slowly began to have a more significant footprint in Syria, primarily through interventions by the USA and Russia. This turned what was a fragmentation into a segmentation (UN-ESCWA, 2020), in which distinct areas of control were slowly emerging, and further severing Syria's internal connections, while there was an increase in the tying of some of the segmented areas to neighbouring countries—most prominently the north of Syria with Türkiye. This increasingly gave rise to an illicit economy and war profiteering through smuggling between the various areas of control, as well as with the outside world. All areas, both then and today, have never ceased some form of economic exchange—in agriculture, electricity, crude petroleum, and in other goods and services.

The years 2015–19 saw a period of reconsolidation. The Government of Syria, with Russian and Iranian support, regained control of significant areas of territory, with the USA along with its allies in the Democratic Socialist Unionist Party controlling areas in the north-east, and Türkiye and other armed groups controlling areas in the north-west. This also coincided with a significant decline in direct armed conflict, culminating in the US-led coalition's claim of complete territorial victory over Islamic State in eastern Syria in March 2019. Reduced fighting, coupled with territorial consolidation, implied an improvement in human development indicators.

However, this nascent positive trend failed to take root. First, a regional economic crisis, particularly Lebanon's severe financial woes, has damaged a major trade and financial artery for Syria. Second, economic sanctions, especially the secondary sanctions enforced by the USA (under the Caesar Syria Civilian Protection Act of 2019) have inhibited both third-party investments as well as the ability of humanitarian organizations to work inside the country. Third, there is a general Syria donor 'fatigue' and allocations to the country are dwindling. All three factors, coupled with the coronavirus disease (COVID-19) pandemic and a global cycle of monetary tightening have led to an unprecedented economic freefall in the country.

Despite the continued absence of a comprehensive political settlement, 2023 was significant as several countries normalized ties with the Syrian Government and increased diplomatic engagement. Syria was readmitted to the League of Arab States (Arab League) after being suspended in 2011, and the Syrian President conducted a state visit to the United Arab Emirates (UAE). The Kingdom of Saudi Arabia also decided to resume diplomatic relations with Syria and invited the Syrian President to attend the 2023 Arab League summit in May, and the Jordanian foreign affairs minister visited Syria in February for the highest-ranking visit from that country since the start of the Syrian conflict.

2023 EARTHQUAKE

In February 2023 north-eastern Syria and southern Türkiye were hit by a devastating earthquake that resulted in thousands of casualties, tens of thousands of displaced people, and widespread destruction of infrastructure and physical capital. The event is included here as a separate section due to its uniqueness as well as the multiplicity of outcomes emanating from it across different sectors.

According to a field assessment conducted by the Syrian Center for Policy Research (SCPR), the number of Syrians who lost their lives due to the earthquake totalled 10,695, of whom 6,392 were inside Syria and the remainder in southern Türkiye. It is estimated that around 170,000 Syrians were displaced by the earthquake. Around 12,800 buildings were damaged, of which around 2,700 were completely destroyed. Four governorates were directly affected by the earthquake. Idlib, controlled by the Salvation Government, suffered the largest share of destroyed buildings, at 46.6% of the total. Some 34% of the total number of damaged buildings were in the countryside around Aleppo, controlled by the Interim Government, while around 1,000 buildings were destroyed in the city of Aleppo, controlled by the Government of Syria. Idlib and Aleppo were also among the governorates most severely affected by the conflict. The earthquake was less severe in the governorates of Latakia and Hama, both controlled by the Government of Syria, with fewer than 1,000 buildings being damaged in each.

The earthquake had various economic, social and political repercussions. On the socioeconomic side, the SCPR estimates that the capital stock and household wealth loss of the earthquake reached US $2,230m. In addition, the earthquake is estimated to have resulted in a decrease in Syria's GDP for 2023 of 2.2 percentage points. The total economic loss—combining the loss of physical capital and the impact on GDP—is estimated at US $5,850m. Around 90,000 workers lost their jobs, raising the unemployment rate by 1.8 percentage points nationally. Additionally, abject poverty is expected to increase by 10.5 and 3.8 percentage points in Idlib and Aleppo, respectively.

Given the multiplicity of actors (both state and non-state) and overlapping sovereignty, mobilization both by the Governments of Syria and Türkiye as well as international organizations, particularly various UN agencies, was widely reported to be far slower than it should have been. This failure was widely condemned as resulting in unnecessary deaths. On the other hand, humanitarian mobilization by Syrian civil society, both inside and outside the country and across the political divide, was remarkable. On a political and diplomatic level, the tragedy spurred several governments in the region, notably those of Jordan and the UAE, to provide humanitarian support. This also factored into the ongoing regional political rehabilitation of Syria's Government.

STATE, INSTITUTIONS AND WAR ECONOMY

In 2023 Syria remained among the five lowest ranked countries on the Fragile States Index, which is prepared by the Fund for Peace and measures risk and vulnerability in 179 countries. State fragility can be easily identified in almost all aspects of Syria's sovereignty, governance and socioeconomic conditions. In particular, three main sources of fragility continue to play a major role in shaping the political and socioeconomic landscape of the country: the absence of government control in major parts of the country; weak institutions; and the prevalence of war economy structures.

State

One of the major legacies of the conflict in Syria is the loss of the state's monopoly on the use of force. This has resulted in the emergence of three main areas of control, each of which is ruled by a major entity that is supported by one or more external actors. The relative stability of the territories' frontlines since early 2020 has generated what appears to be a new reality in the Syrian conflict that is likely to persist in the short- to medium-term. However, maintaining the status quo threatens to exacerbate economic decline, as none of the three main territories can survive by drawing solely on its own resources (The Carter Center, 2021). Furthermore, the loss of the monopoly on the use of force is observed on an intra-territorial level, as the power is now shared by several actors, creating an overlapping structure of sub-control areas within the major territories. This situation has resulted in the majority of Syria's borders being out of the Government's control, in a clear sign of its weakening sovereignty. On the sub-territorial level, a number of internal armed groups continue to challenge the Syrian Government's claim to a continued monopoly on the use of force, particularly in the southern governorates of Dar'a and al-Suweida. Tension between these groups and the government-backed forces increased during 2021 and early 2022. This can largely be attributed to worsening socioeconomic conditions, and the spread of kidnapping and other criminal activities committed by gangs linked to government-backed armed groups (The Carter Center, 2022).

Institutions

Despite experiencing one of the most brutal armed conflicts over the past 12 years, the institutional capacity of the state, in the government-controlled territories at least, had remained relatively resilient until recently, particularly when compared to other fragile or conflict-affected countries. Theoretical and empirical evidence from economic development literature shows that conflict results in the breakdown of formal institutions and the rise of informal structures that organize the activities in society during the conflict (Aron, 2003). Consistent with this line of evidence-based argument, the early years of conflict in Syria witnessed several elements of institutional informalization. This structural change in institutions was intensified as the loss of public revenue, human resources and territorial control accelerated after 2013. However, part of this process was in response to evolving conditions, in a strategy to shift certain state functions and obligations to informal structures (Hallaj, 2021). This strategy, although it strengthened the extractive nature of economic institutions, succeeded in maintaining a minimum level of institutional functionality and prevented a full collapse of state institutions.

However, a recent trend of re-institutionalization has emerged, in an attempt to restore a significant share of state control over pivotal socioeconomic aspects. This trend comes as an inevitable response to the widening imbalance between public revenue and revenue generated by war profiteers, the emergence of potentially threatening pockets of power, and shortages in basic goods and services and the associated resentment among loyal communities (Dahi, 2022). The recent re-formalization trend is particularly evident in the trade sector and in the public finance domain.

Yet this attempt to upgrade the capacity of economic institutions has not been part of a wider political, governance and security structural transformation. Hence, to date, it has only generated a limited rather than a meaningful transformation in the institutional capacity of the country. Consequently, economic institutions in Syria, similar to political ones, remain highly extractive. Syria ranked 136th out of 137 countries in the BTI Economic Transformation Index of 2021, which assesses the transformation towards a market economy and covers the period from 1 February 2019 to 31 January 2021 (Bertelsmann Stiftung, 2022). Furthermore, the quality of government services deteriorated substantially during 2020–22. This is evident in the Government's failure to provide some basic administrative services, such as the issuance of travel documents and the management of fuel derivatives distribution.

War Economy Structures

The 12 years of conflict in Syria have drastically altered the pre-conflict economic landscape of the country and created parallel economic structures to the formal economy, which is typical in a war-torn economy. In such an environment, organized economic activities that are conducted outside the control of the state and used to support military activities constitute a considerable share of the economy. The expansion of these activities is proportional to the level of state fragility and institutional weakness. The more fragile the state and the weaker the institutions, the larger the share of the war economy held by such activities.

Although the emergence of war economy structures is perceived as a direct outcome of the armed conflict, the expansion of such structures creates a self-reinforcing mechanism that exacerbates fragility, perpetuates the conflict and impedes the restoration of a normally functioning economy. As economic conditions in Syria have worsened in recent years, activities associated with the war economy have expanded, deepened and become more organized. In addition, the relative prevalence of some activities (such as looting and kidnapping) has declined in favour of other more lucrative and foreign currency generating activities, particularly those exploiting natural resources, controlling trade routes (including informal ones), and in the drug industry.

In areas that fall outside the control of the Government, exploiting crude petroleum and controlling trade routes dominate the economic activities fuelling the conflict. Areas controlled by the Democratic Federation of Northern Syria and the Kurdish-led Syrian Democratic Forces rely primarily on extracting crude oil and selling it to the central Government in Damascus or smuggling it to the Kurdish Autonomous Region in Iraq. In addition, collecting tariffs on the goods imported from the Kurdish Autonomous Region constitutes a significant source of finance for the ruling authorities, which control two major newly established border crossings. The tariffs are usually collected through a network of patronage on both sides of the border (Hasan and Khaddour, 2021). In the northern and north-western areas under opposition influence, controlling trade routes constitutes the major aspect of the war economy. Primarily, collecting tariffs on goods crossing from Türkiye or to government-controlled areas is a key source of finance for armed opposition forces and groups. Despite the high costs and the relative complexity of these routes, they are often used to convey some goods from the opposition-held territories, the Turkish market, or even international markets to government-controlled areas. This indicates the high level of economic interconnectivity between the territories, despite their political division (Tokmajyan and Khaddour, 2022).

Three main factors have forced influential economic actors in government-controlled territories to engage in more unconventional finance-generating activities compared to those prevailing in areas outside the Government's control. First, the scarcity of oil resources, relative to areas to the east of the Euphrates river, has deprived patronage networks of their monopoly on the extraction, distribution and smuggling of crude oil. Second, neighbouring the stressed small economies of Lebanon and Jordan has made controlling international trade routes less lucrative, compared with the oil-rich Kurdish Autonomous Region and Türkiye. Third, the escalating financial needs of state entities, including formal and semi-formal military forces, has placed additional pressure on the state budget and forced the Government and its business allies to rely on unconventional methods of economic support, particularly in light of the tightened sanctions and the deteriorating value of the national currency, the Syrian pound.

Consequently, two major activities have dominated the war economy structure in government-controlled areas during the past few years: smuggling and the drug industry. According to some estimates, there are 120–150 illegal crossing points along the Syrian–Lebanese border. Oil derivatives, poultry and flour are among the most smuggled goods from Lebanon into Syria. It is estimated that 100 tankers of fuel entered Syria on a daily basis during 2020–21, yielding illegal trade revenue of US $235m. annually (Daher, Ahmad and Taha, 2022). On the other hand, research by the Center for Operational Analysis and Research (COAR) suggests that drug production and exports, particularly of Captagon (fenethylline), has become a significant source of foreign currency in Syria (COAR, 2021). According to some estimates, the volume of interdicted Syrian narcotics abroad more than tripled between 2018 and 2020; the amount of Captagon and hashish intercepted exceeded 46 metric tons in 2020 (COAR, 2021). The second quarter of 2022 witnessed a notable expansion of drug trafficking through Jordan to Gulf Cooperation Council countries, as the economic situation in Syria deteriorated further following the Russian invasion of Ukraine. Jordanian officials have accused Syria and Iran of sponsoring organized drug gangs on the Syrian–Jordanian border, where the Jordanian army has become increasingly engaged in fighting hundreds of armed drug traffickers (Middle East Eye, 2022).

MACROECONOMIC SITUATION

Despite the relative improvement in security and stability since 2020, the macroeconomic landscape in Syria has been deteriorating steadily. Four key external factors have induced this deterioration: economic sanctions and their financial and commercial implications; the COVID-19 pandemic and the resulting turbulence in trade with partner countries; the political and financial unrest in neighbouring Lebanon; and the Russian invasion of Ukraine and the associated rise in global food and oil prices. However, one of the most significant determinants of Syria's economic degradation is the structural imbalances that have accumulated in the economy over the past 12 years. As explained earlier, state fragility and institutional weakness have eroded the Government's control over significant natural and financial resources and weakened its fiscal position in favour of associated patronage networks or non-government armed forces. This has had a considerable impact on the state's capacity to use fiscal and monetary policies effectively and hence has exacerbated demand and output imbalances.

Output and Growth

The economic losses arising from the conflict are large and growing. By 2022 GDP had decreased by around 68% compared with its pre-conflict level. (This figure is based on the authors' calculations, using data from the SCPR, the World Bank and the authors' own estimates). Syria has been reclassified by the World Bank as a low-income country, a downgrade from its status as a lower middle-income country prior to the conflict (World Bank, 2022). Energy, mining, manufacturing and construction are among the sectors worst affected by the conflict.

The fragmentation of fiscal policy, a continued decline of the Syrian pound and the impact of the earthquake all point to a further contraction in GDP in 2023. Although it has played a role in filling some of the gaps caused by state failure during the conflict, the private sector remains largely underproductive. Private investment as a percentage of GDP declined from 12.3% in 2010 to 4.4% in 2019 (Zhao et al., 2022). Even following the enactment in 2021 of new legislation aimed at attracting potential investors, the investment environment in Syria remains highly challenging. In addition to the political, institutional and war economy-related factors mentioned earlier (including sanctions), the energy and fuel shortages, skilled labour emigration and devastated infrastructure all hinder the effective participation of private sector entities in economic activity (Sukkar, 2022).

Public Finances

The fiscal situation in Syria continued its dramatic deterioration in 2023. Despite the projected 27% nominal increase in public revenue in the 2023 budget (Ministry of Finance 2022), the exchange rate adjusted value was estimated to be around 32% lower than that of 2022 (The Central Bank of Syria devalued the official value of the Syrian pound several times in 2023). Although the Government ostensibly continues to broaden tax collection, tax evasion prevails, particularly among warlords and the new business elite that has emerged during the conflict. Consequently, the tax burden remains regressively distributed among taxpayers.

By the same token, the nominal value of public expenditure was forecast to increase year on year by 24.2% in 2023. In real terms, this would be equivalent to a contraction in expenditure of 32.6% (based on the parallel market's exchange rate). Despite an expansion of the Syrian Government's restructuring of subsidies—in August 2023 the Government decided to cut fuel subsidies, raising fuel derivative prices by between 130% and 220%—these subsidies continued to constitute a considerable share of planned public expenditure, at more than 30% of the total. Notably, around 82% of forecast total public expenditure in the 2023 budget was dedicated to current expenditure. It is also worth noting that the largest share of expenditure, that dedicated to defence, is routinely undisclosed by the budget.

Although the planned fiscal deficit has stabilized at around 30% of total public expenditure in the past three years, the SCPR estimated that the real fiscal deficit (constituting off-budget expenditure, including military expenditure and some types of subsidies) would equate to 50% of GDP in 2023. Only a small share of the announced budget deficit, namely 16.5%, was planned to be covered by government bonds, while the rest of it was expected to be financed through seigniorage. This raises inflationary expectations yet further. In addition, interdependence between fiscal and current account balances induces a twin deficit situation, where fiscal and trade deficits reinforce each other. (The interdependence between trade and fiscal deficits can be shown through the following equation: $CA \equiv (S-I) + (T-G)$, where CA refers to current account balance; S to private savings; I to private investment; T to tax; and G to government purchases.) This is a typical and chronic problem in several conflict-affected countries.

Furthermore, an inappropriately financed and persistent fiscal deficit raises fiscal sustainability concerns. Despite the absence of official debt figures for Syria, the SCPR estimates that the debt-to-GDP ratio reached 250% in 2022. Based on these figures, it can be projected that the country will not be able to restore a sustainable fiscal position (i.e. a debt-to-GDP ratio below 100%) within 20 years, even if an inclusive, internationally-backed political settlement were reached today.

Monetary Policy

The Central Bank of Syria has exhausted the vast majority of its pre-conflict foreign currency reserves during the 12 years of conflict. As a result, monetary policy has lost a primary tool for controlling the exchange rate. With the substantial deterioration in the country's exporting ability and the heavy reliance on food and fuel imports since 2020, the value of the national currency has continued to depreciate significantly.

In an attempt to control the surging inflation rate and currency depreciation, the Government and the Central Bank began to implement a series of contractionary measures in early 2021. On the one hand, the Government restricted cash payments in real estate deals and required the buyer to deposit 15% of the estimated value of the property in a bank account (Syria Report, 2022). The deposit share was increased to 50% of the estimated property's value in February 2023. On the other hand, the Central Bank tightened its control over daily bank withdrawals and curbed cash transfers between governorates. Such procedures aimed to drain liquidity in the money market and to reduce speculation against the Syrian pound. Although they were successful in moderating the downward trend of the national currency in the few months following their enforcement, the measures contributed to stifling economic activity and discouraged the expansion of businesses. In April 2022 the Central Bank raised the minimum interest rate on bank deposits from 7% to 11%, in a further attempt to absorb increasing inflationary pressures. In February 2023 the Central Bank started implementing a new strategy in the currency market, adjusting the official exchange rate when the differential with the parallel market expanded significantly.

Despite these measures, between January 2020 and July 2023 the Syrian pound depreciated by more than 1,250% against the US dollar on the black market. In addition, the inflation rate has surged dramatically since 2019, registering rises of 113%, 110% and 85% in 2020, 2021 and 2022 respectively, according to the SCPR. There was expected to be a resurgence in inflation in 2023, due to the sharp decline in the value of the Syrian pound, the lifting of fuel subsidies and substantial further monetization of the fiscal deficit.

PHYSICAL CAPITAL AND INFRASTRUCTURE

Demolished infrastructure and destroyed production assets are among the most visually shocking aspects of armed conflict. Economically, they constitute a considerable share of total economic loss in severely conflict-affected countries. In addition, reconstructing destroyed physical assets and infrastructure is one of the most costly activities of the post-conflict economic recovery process.

Considered one of the most violent internal conflicts since the Cold War, the Syrian conflict has generated massive losses in the country's production base and the enabling infrastructure. Three main types of losses can be directly linked to the conflict in this regard—destroyed capital, flight capital and inoperative capital. The first category constitutes physical assets and infrastructure destroyed by armed clashes. Calculations by the authors of this essay based on UN-ESCWA estimates indicate that the accumulated loss of physical capital and infrastructure in Syria reached US $143,200m. in 2021. According to the ESCWA report, more than 50% of physical losses up until 2019 had been incurred by highly productive sectors, mainly mining, manufacturing, transport and energy. In addition, the most affected governorates were Aleppo and Rural Damascus, where most of the productive industries are concentrated (UN-ESCWA, 2020).

The second type of capital losses is associated with the capital that left the country in the early years of the conflict, either in cash or in the form of productive assets. As the conflict spread throughout the country in 2012–13, many business people transferred their liquid assets to other countries, mainly Lebanon and Egypt. Some experts estimate that US $10,000m.–$15,000m. were transferred to Lebanon alone during the conflict (Kanaan, 2020). Furthermore, some manufacturers dismantled their factories and transferred them to neighbouring countries, particularly to Türkiye and Jordan. One assessment indicates that up to $35,000m. fled the country in different forms due to the conflict (Sirop, 2019).

The third type of capital loss associated with the conflict constitutes the inoperative productive assets that had to be suspended due to the need for modernization, repair or lack of input materials or energy. This type of loss is most common in the manufacturing and agriculture sectors. A prominent example of this type of loss can be observed in the agro-food industry, which was one of the leading sectors in pre-conflict Syria. A recent study shows that more than one-half of the private sector establishments in the agro-food industry are now inoperative (Halali, 2021). The study indicates that among the most pressing obstacles facing this industry are the difficulties in obtaining input materials, the high cost of energy, the lack of skilled labour due to migration, and damaged infrastructure. Public sector entities working in this field face deeper challenges. In addition, outdated production lines represent a major barrier to efficient production. Some public sector factories are operating at only 10%–20% of their full production capacity. This results in the draining of the public budget, with tens of billions of dollars annually being provided in the form of financial subsidies.

A major implication of the accumulated losses incurred in physical capital and infrastructure is the disruption in the provision of basic services. This is particularly evident in power generation and distribution, health services and housing.

According to official estimates, the country's power generation contracted by more than 55% between 2010 and 2022 (Aida, 2022). Since 2011, three major power plants, accounting for 18.3% of the total pre-conflict power generation capacity, have been completely destroyed. Additionally, the generation capacity of the remaining power plants has deteriorated significantly due to lack of maintenance. Moreover, the transmission grid was frequently targeted during armed clashes and hence suffered significant damage. However, the lack of fuel has been the main determinant causing power generation shortages in recent years (Hatahet and Shaar, 2021). The use of renewable energy remains negligible in Syria.

The deliberate destruction of health facilities was a distinctive feature of the Syrian conflict. Estimates by the World Health Organization show that only 56% of the country's public hospitals and 50% of public health centres were fully functioning in April 2022, while 23% and 30% of them, respectively, were completely out of service. This has had severe implications for the health status of the population, as one-half of the Syrian population became unable to access appropriate health services. In addition, the vast destruction of the local pharmaceutical industries and supporting infrastructure was one of the main factors leading to the declining availability of medicines, particularly for people with chronic diseases (Nasser and Dukmak, 2022).

Another key implication of the physical losses sustained during the conflict is the severe shortage of housing. The housing sector is estimated to have incurred the largest share of physical destruction among all sectors, with around 17.5% of total capital loss up to 2018 (UN-ESCWA, 2020). Some scholars estimate that Syria suffers from a housing gap of more than 2m. housing units. This includes an estimated 1m. housing units that were totally or partially destroyed during the conflict (Ezzi and Haddad, 2021). As a result, a significant share of internally displaced persons live in temporary houses made of mud bricks and corrugated iron, or in more substantive houses that do not meet basic building standards. This is especially the case in the governorates of Idlib and Aleppo, contributing to the large number of casualties in these areas caused by the February 2023 earthquake.

LABOUR AND HUMAN CAPITAL

In contrast to physical capital, labour and human capital loss belong to the hidden costs of the conflict. None the less, the long-term effects of this type of loss surpass those of the physical losses. In addition, the level of depreciation of the human capital base during war has proved to be a determinant factor for post-war growth (Smolny, 2000).

Between 2011 and 2018, labour and human capital losses in Syria accounted for 22% of lost economic output on average. During the same period, around 64% of the average negative growth could be attributed to physical capital destruction, while the remainder was associated with total factor productivity deterioration (Devadas, Elbadawi and Loayza, 2019). This situation has changed dramatically since 2019. Although destruction of physical capital has almost halted since 2020, estimates indicate that the economy shrank by around 7.7% between 2020 and 2022. (This projection is based on calculations by the authors, using World Bank estimates and data from the Syrian Central Bureau of Statistics.) Around 40% of this contraction is estimated to have occurred in 2020, amid the COVID-19 pandemic. However, the majority of this lost output is due to the deterioration in human capital and in total factor productivity.

The Syrian labour market suffers from a twofold problem: lack of skilled labour and low wages. During the past three years the shortage of skilled workers has increased as a result of two main factors. First, the consequences of the deterioration in the country's educational system during the war have started to materialize in the form of poor educational and training output. The UN Children's Fund (UNICEF) estimates that 2.4m. school-age Syrian children did not attend school in 2021. Damaged school buildings, overcrowded classrooms, unaffordable transportation and a lack of teachers were among the main factors behind this large number of absentee pupils. Additionally, planned public expenditure on education fell by more than 80% in real terms between 2010 and 2021. The vast majority of the planned expenditure (88%) was dedicated to salaries and other current expenditure categories (UNICEF-Syria, 2022). This has had a substantial impact on vocational education institutions in particular, where the provision of necessary materials and equipment has become increasingly challenging. Covering this gap is beyond the capacity of local and international non-governmental organizations, owing to funding and sanctions-related constraints (Qaddour and Husain, 2022). The education situation in the north-western territories looks even more difficult in the absence of a unified organizational authority. Unpaid teachers, recruitment of children for combat and attacks on educational facilities place extra pressures on the incentives for education.

Second, the conflict-induced flight of skilled human capital has caused a chronic drain in the knowledge and skills base of the country and generated a wide human capital gap in several sectors. Among the worst affected sectors are higher education, medicine and vocational work. The number of academic staff in Syrian universities declined by around 19% between 2011 and 2020. Accordingly, the student-faculty ratio in Syrian universities deteriorated from 35:1 to 155:1 during the same period (Central Bureau of Statistics, 2022). Some faculties performed worse relative to others in this regard. For instance, the Faculty of Information Technology, the Faculty of Economics and the Faculty of Applied Science at Damascus University witnessed very poor student-faculty ratios of 107:1 (30:1 in 2011), 138:1 (53:1 in 2011) and 249:1 (31:1 in 2011), respectively. Comparing these ratios with those in some developing countries, such as Brazil (19:1) and India (24:1) (Indo-Asian News Service, 2019), reflects a grim reality. In a similar manner, the ratio of physicians to population in Syria deteriorated from 1:636 in 2011 to 1:713 in 2020. In contrast, the share of Syrian physicians out of all foreign physicians in Germany increased sixfold between 2010 and 2021, constituting the largest group of foreign physicians in the country (Dernbach, 2022). In the north-western governorate of Idlib, the lack of vocational skills constitutes a key challenge for employers. A recent field study found a clear gap between supply and demand of knowledge and practical competences for several occupations, including carpentry, plumbing, and electrical and wiring work (REACH, 2022).

Combined with several other factors, the shortage of skilled labour has had negative consequences for labour productivity, and hence for workers' income. Based on data from the Central Bureau of Statistics, average annual worker productivity and hence remuneration declined sharply between 2010 and 2021, losing around 98% of its pre-conflict level in real terms. Accordingly, real wages experienced a dramatic contraction during the same period, despite the multiple increases in nominal wages. The Syrian Government increased public sector pay on seven occasions between 2010 and 2021. Three of the increases occurred between 2019 and 2021, as the Government intensified efforts to counter the chronic reduction in purchasing power. More recently, the Government announced a 100% increase in public sector wages that was to take effect in September 2023. The downward trend of real wages has accelerated during the past few years. Although the average monthly wage of a public sector employee holding a PhD more than tripled between 2016 and 2021, according to the public sector pay scale, the foreign-exchange-adjusted wage decreased by around 57% (COAR, 2020; Syrian Arab News Agency, 2021). In a similar manner, the average nominal daily wage for unskilled labour increased more than fivefold between April 2019 and April 2022. In real terms, the average daily wage could be traded for 3.3 kg of wheat flour in April 2022, compared with 8.0 kg in April 2019 (World Food Programme, 2022). Furthermore, real wages are estimated to have declined by around 33% during the first half of 2023 (Kassioun 2023). Considering the most recent cut in fuel subsidies, implemented in August, and the accompanying surge in inflation, real wages are expected to witness a further sharp contraction, despite the announced increase in nominal wages.

The chronic deterioration in labour productivity and hence in real wages has trapped the economy in a vicious cycle of low productivity, low output and low incomes. Conflict dynamics and economic sanctions play a key role in sustaining this cycle. This, in turn, has pushed many Syrians well below the poverty line. Ultimately, the vast majority of Syrian households have become dependent on external sources for securing their basic needs, namely humanitarian aid and remittances.

ECONOMIC RECONSTRUCTION

Economic reconstruction is a key component in the multi-pronged transition to peace in conflict-affected countries. Despite the significant reduction in major military operations in Syria since 2020, the prospects for a sound economic reconstruction process in the foreseeable future remain grim. The main factors are: the massive drain on government resources, the lack of an inclusive political settlement, primary and secondary economic sanctions imposed by the USA and EU, and a continued retreat of the rule of law.

In addition to political factors, the availability of adequate economic resources in the aftermath of conflict is a key determinant of the magnitude and duration of the economic recovery and reconstruction phase. Economic reconstruction in this context refers to development policies and interventions aimed at countering the socioeconomic repercussions of the conflict and restoring a 'normal' development path, through rehabilitating basic services and rebuilding physical and human infrastructure, stabilizing the macroeconomic environment, and laying the ground for market-led inclusive economic growth (del Castillo, 2008). Based on the aforementioned estimations of human and physical capital losses during the conflict, the reconstruction needs in Syria are expected to be massive.

From an economic perspective, the primary restrictions on an effective economic reconstruction process in Syria can be described using a three-gap model. In such a model, economic growth is assumed to be constrained by the savings gap, the foreign exchange gap and the fiscal gap.

The savings gap reflects the shortage of domestic savings to match domestic investment opportunities, causing investments to be restricted by the availability of foreign capital inflows (Todaro and Smith, 2015). This gap originated in the Syrian context during the early years of the conflict and was exacerbated as the conflict deepened. Shortly after the outbreak of hostilities, national savings received a deep shock, as large capital outflows headed to neighbouring countries. By the end of 2011 bank deposits were 19.3% below the 2010 level in nominal terms. The decline in real terms was even more severe. With the successive contractions in real output and constant currency depreciation, the remaining savings have gradually lost their value. Although bank deposits in 2021 were 3.5 times their nominal value in 2010, the US dollar value of the deposits in the same year, totalling approximately US $2,000m., was equivalent to only 7% of that in 2010. Moreover, demand deposits in 2021 constituted 71% of total deposits, compared with less than 45% in 2010 (Central Bank of Syria, 2022). Comparing these figures with the massive capital investments required for initiating a broad-based reconstruction and recovery process reveals the huge savings gap in the country. Such a gap would have to be bridged by encouraging foreign savings, including flight capital, to be involved in financing reconstruction projects. Optimizing the utilization of the available national savings could reduce the reliance on foreign ones to some extent. The foreign component remains essential, however.

The foreign exchange gap represents the case that results when the trade deficit exceeds the value of capital inflows, causing investments, and hence output growth, to be constrained by the availability of foreign currency required for importing capital goods. The chronic deficit in the Syrian trade balance, unmatched by foreign currency inflows, has drained most of the Central Bank's foreign currency reserves. Accordingly, the Central Bank has repeatedly reduced the number of imported items that can be financed through its import financing list. The most recent version of the list, issued in August 2023, includes 69 items of basic foods and agricultural and medical products, in addition to supplies required for basic manufacturing. This has forced most producers to rely on other foreign currency sources, including their own reserves, for importing their production inputs and supplies. With a high marginal import share for post-conflict reconstruction investments in Syria expected—primarily due to the high level of productive capital destruction in the country—the demand for foreign currency is expected to increase significantly during any potential reconstruction process. This is expected to be particularly true in the initial reconstruction phase. During this period, exports, as a major source of foreign currency, are most likely to recover only gradually. Hence, external support, in the form of grants, loans or foreign currency term deposits at the Central Bank, would be essential.

The fiscal gap addresses the shortages in public investments, both in physical infrastructure and in human capital, required for raising the rate of return of private investments. At the official launch of a post-conflict reconstruction process (the National Development Program for Post-Crisis Syria) in Syria in August 2017, the funds allocated for investments under the reconstruction category in the public budget were, given the severity of the situation, trivial—ranging between US $100m. and $300m. annually. Much more public investment is needed to jump-start a stagnant war-torn economy. Even with the restoration of central government control over oil and gas resources in the north-eastern territories of the country, public funds are expected to remain significantly below the minimum basic requirements for initiating a broad-based reconstruction process. Syria's oil production in 2010, estimated at around 385,000 b/d, was hardly sufficient to cover the country's own consumption. Second, bridging the fiscal gap and channelling a considerable share of reconstruction funds via the public budget is essential for the success of reconstruction efforts in Syria, for a number of reasons. Among the most important ones are enhancing the national ownership of the reconstruction programme; promoting the post-conflict legitimacy of the central Government against non-state actors; and widening the absorptive capacity of the economy by expanding the formal institutional capacities and improving physical infrastructure.

The above analysis shows that there are several major economic deficiencies hindering economic reconstruction in post-crisis Syria. Without external assistance, overcoming these constraints looks unattainable, particularly in the absence of inclusive political and economic institutions, and under the current economic and financial sanctions. This is a typical situation in countries affected by severe conflicts. As theoretical and empirical evidence shows, countries seriously affected by armed conflict rely more heavily on external financing resources in the post-conflict phase, compared with countries moderately affected by conflict. In particular, foreign aid, foreign investments and external debt were found to be significantly higher in the severely affected countries relative to the moderately affected ones (Al-Asadi, 2021).

In addition to the purely economic aspects, socioeconomic factors will play a significant complementary role in any successful post-conflict economic reconstruction effort in Syria. Among these factors are promoting reconciliation and strengthening social cohesion; the disarmament, demobilization and reintegration of former combatants as part of wider security sector reform; and restoring a considerable part of the human capital that left the country during the conflict.

Bibliography and Sources

Aida, Najwa. 'No improvement is expected on electricity as power generation remains low.' *Al-Baath*, Damascus, 9 March 2022, p. 6.

Al-Asadi, Mohammad. 'Financing Resources for Reconstruction in Severely Conflict-affected Countries'. *Review of Middle East Economics and Finance*, Vol. 17, No. 1, February 2021, pp. 1–25. doi.org/10.1515/rmeef-2020-0025.

Aron, Janine. 'Building Institutions in Post-Conflict African Economies'. *Journal of International Development*, Vol. 15, No. 4, 2003, pp. 471–485.

Bertelsmann Stiftung. *BTI 2022 Country Report—Syria*. 2022. bti-project.org/fileadmin/api/content/en/downloads/reports/country_report_2022_SYR.pdf.

The Carter Center. *A Path to Conflict Transformation in Syria: A Framework for a Phased Approach*. 2021. www.cartercenter.org/resources/pdfs/peace/conflict_resolution/syria-conflict/path-to-conflict-transformation-in-syria-jan-2021.pdf.

The Carter Center. *The Quarterly Review on Syrian Military and Security Dynamics*. January–March 2022. www.cartercenter.org/resources/pdfs/peace/conflict_resolution/syria-conflict/2022/quarterly-conflict-summary-january-march-2022.pdf.

Central Bank of Syria. *Annual Banking and Monetary Bulletin 2021*. Damascus, 2022.

Central Bureau of Statistics. *The Annual Statistical Abstract* [Arabic]. 2022. cbssyr.sy/index-EN.htm.

Center for Operational Analysis and Research. *The Syrian Economy at War: Labor Pains Amid the Blurring of the Public and Private Sectors*. 2020. coar-global.org/2020/11/20/the-syrian-economy-at-war-labor-pains-amid-the-blurring-of-the-public-and-private-sectors.

Center for Operational Analysis and Research. *The Syrian Economy at War: Captagon, Hashish, and the Syrian Narco-State*. 2021. coar-global.org/2021/04/27/the-syrian-economy-at-war-captagon-hashish-and-the-syrian-narco-state.

Daher, Joseph. *State institutions and regime networks as service providers in Syria*. CADMUS, European University Institute Research Repository, 2020. hdl.handle.net/1814/67553.

Daher, Joseph, Ahmad, Nizar, and Taha, Salwan. 'Smuggling between Syria and Lebanon, and from Syria to Jordan: the evolution and delegation of a practice'. *Policy Briefs*, No. 32/2022, 2022. middleeastdirections.eu, cadmus.eui.eu/handle/1814/74453.

Dahi, Omar S. 'Informalization and re-formalization of trade institutions in Syria during the war (2011–2021)', in *Syrian Trade, Health and Industry in Conflict Time (2011–2021): A study on the impact of war, public policies and sanctions*, Konrad-Adenauer-Stiftung and Syrian Center for Policy Research, 2022, pp. 24–43. www.kas.de/en/web/syrien-irak/single-title/-/content/syrian-trade-health-and-industry-in-conflict-time-2011-2021.

Del Castillo, Graciana. *Rebuilding War-Torn States: The Challenge of Post-Conflict Economic Reconstruction*. New York, Oxford University Press, 2008.

Dernbach, Andrea. 'Einwanderungsgesellschaft: Deutschlands Gesundheitssystem hängt von Migration ab – Politik'. *Der Tagesspiegel*, 10 May 2022. www.tagesspiegel.de/politik/einwanderungsgesellschaft-deutschlands-gesundheitssystem-haengt-von-migration-ab/28320164.html.

Devadas, Sharmila, Elbadawi, Ibrahim, and Loayza, Norman. *Growth after War in Syria*. Policy Research Working Paper No. 8967, World Bank, 2019.

Erkmen, Serhat, Heras, Nicholas A., and Semenov, Kirill. *Security Scenarios for Syria in 2021–2022*. Discussion Paper 34, Geneva Centre for Security Policy, 2021. www.gcsp.ch/publications/security-scenarios-syria-2021-2022.

Ezzi, Mazen, and Haddad, Wajih. 'The Housing Crisis in Syria: Do Social Housing and Housing Cooperatives Still Have a Role?' *The Syria Report*, 2021. syria-report.com/hlp/the-housing-crisis-in-syria-do-social-housing-and-housing-cooperatives-still-have-a-role.

Halali, Reem. *Food Industry in Syria: Current Status and Prospects* [Arabic]. Damascus, Syrian Economic Sciences Society, 2021.

Hallaj, Omar A. *Formality, Informality, and the Resilience of the Syrian Political Economy*. Geneva Centre for Security Policy, 2021. www.gcsp.ch/publications/formality-informality-and-resilience-syrian-political-economy.

Hasan, Harith, and Khaddour, Kheder. *The Making of the Kurdish Frontier: Power, Conflict, and Governance in the Iraqi-Syrian Borderlands*. Carnegie Endowment, 2021. carnegieendowment.org/files/Hasan_Khaddour_XBORDER_Kurdish_Frontier.pdf.

Hatahet, Sinan, and Shaar, Karam. 'Syria's Electricity Sector After a Decade of War: A Comprehensive Assessment'. *Wartime and Post-Conflict in Syria*, Issue 13/2021, European University Institute, 2021. cadmus.eui.eu/bitstream/handle/1814/72182/QM-02-21-984-EN-N.pdf?sequence=8.

Hejazi, Jomaa, and Ghosn, Ziad. *A Developmental Perspective Review of the Syrian Public Budget for the year 2022*. [Arabic]. General Federation of Trade Unions, Labor Observatory for Research & Studies, Damascus, 2022.

Indo-Asian News Service. 'India's student-teacher ratio lowest among compared countries, lags behind Brazil and China'. *India Today*, 14 July 2019. www.indiatoday.in/education-today/news/story/india-s-student-teacher-ratio-lowest-lags-behind-brazil-and-china-1568695-2019-07-14.

Kanaan, Ali. *Lebanon in the Face of a Potential Financial Crisis: The Repercussions on the Syrian Economy* [Arabic]. General Federation of Trade Unions, Labor Observatory for Research & Studies, Damascus, 2022.

Middle East Eye. 'Jordan accuses Syria and Iran of orchestrating "drugs war" along border'. 2022. www.middleeasteye.net/news/jordan-accuses-syria-iran-drugs-war-orchestrating-along-border.

Nasser, Rabie, and Dukmak, Amr. 'Syrian Conflict and Health Capabilities', in *Syrian Trade, Health and Industry in Conflict Time (2011–2021): A study on the impact of war, public policies and sanctions*, Konrad-Adenauer-Stiftung and Syrian Center for Policy Research, 2022, pp. 44–64. www.kas.de/en/web/syrien-irak/single-title/-/content/syrian-trade-health-and-industry-in-conflict-time-2011-2021.

Qaddour, Kinana, and Husain, Salman. *Syria's Education Crisis: A Sustainable Approach after 11 Years of Conflict*. The Middle East Institute, Washington, DC, 2022. www.mei.edu/sites/default/files/2022-03/Syria%E2%80%99s%20Education%20crisis%20-%0A%20Sustainable%20Approach%20After%2011%20years%20of%20Conflict_1.pdf.

REACH. 'Labour Market Profile: Dana City'. March 2022. www.impact-repository.org/document/reach/d74166be/REACH_SYR_Profile_Labour-Market-Assessment-Dana_-March-2022.pdf.

Sirop, Rasha. 'How Syrians' Money Was Smuggled Abroad?' *Tishreen* [Arabic], 17 August 2019.

Smolny, Werner. 'Post-war Growth, Productivity Convergence and Reconstruction'. *Oxford Bulletin of Economics and Statistics*, Vol. 62, No. 5, 2000, pp. 589–606.

Sukkar, Nabil. 'A plan of 15 proposals directed to the government to abandon the austerity policy and contraction'. *Al Watan* [Arabic], 8 February 2022.

Syrian Arab News Agency. 'The Assistant Minister of Finance explains how to calculate compensation according to the new decree' [Arabic]. 2021. sana.sy/?p=1541774.

Syrian Center for Policy Research. *Syria: Justice to Transcend Conflict*. 2020. www.scpr-syria.org/justice-to-transcend-conflict.

The Syria Report. 'Government Raises Mandatory Bank Deposit Rate for Real Estate Sales'. 2022. syria-report.com/hlp/government-raises-mandatory-bank-deposit-rate-for-real-estate-sales/.

Todaro, Michael P., and Smith, Stephen. *Economic Development*. Harlow, Pearson, 2015.

Tokmajyan, Armenak, and Khaddour, Kheder. *Border Nation: The Reshaping of the Syrian-Turkish Borderlands*. Carnegie Endowment, 2022. carnegieendowment.org/files/Tokmajyan_Khaddour_Syria_Turkey_final.pdf.

United Nations Economic and Social Commission for Western Asia. *Syria at War: Eight Years On*. Beirut, 2020. www.unescwa.org/sites/default/files/pubs/pdf/syria-at-war-report-en.pdf.

UNICEF. *Every Day Counts: An outlook on education for the most vulnerable children in Syria*. Damascus, 2022. www.unicef.org/syria/media/10116/file/Education%20Strategic%20Shift%20Think%20Piece.pdf.

World Food Programme. *Market Price Watch Bulletin*, Vol. 89, April 2022.

World Bank. *Syria's Economic Update*. 2022. thedocs.worldbank.org/en/doc/529543cc65226921d485b7491c310fab-0280012022/original/mpo-sm22-syria-syr-kcm2.pdf.

World Health Organization. 'Summary of key performance indicators-Whole of Syria'. April 2022. reliefweb.int/report/syrian-arab-republic/summary-key-performance-indicators-whole-syria-april-2022.

Zhao, Luan R., et al. *Syria Economic Monitor: Lost Generation of Syrians*. World Bank, Washington, DC, 2022. documents.worldbank.org/en/publication/documents-reports/documentdetail/099335506102250271/idu06190a00a0d128048450a4660ae3b937ae4bd.

Statistical Survey

Sources (unless otherwise stated): Central Bureau of Statistics, rue Nezar Kabany, Abou Roumaneh, Damascus; tel. (11) 3335830; fax (11) 3322292; e-mail infocbs@cbssyr.sy; internet cbssyr.sy/index.htm; Central Bank of Syria, al-Jerida square, POB 2254, Damascus; e-mail info@cb.gov.sy; internet www.cb.gov.sy.

Area and Population

AREA, POPULATION AND DENSITY

Area (sq km)	
Land	184,050
Inland water	1,130
Total	185,180*
Population (census results)	
3 September 1994	13,782,315
22 September 2004	
Males	9,196,878
Females	8,723,966
Total	17,920,844
Population (UN estimates at mid-year)†	
2021	21,324,367
2022‡	22,125,249
2023‡	23,227,014
Density (per sq km) at mid-2023‡	126.2

* 71,498 sq miles; including the Israeli-occupied Golan region (1,154 sq km).
† Source: UN, *World Population Prospects: The 2022 Revision*.
‡ Projection.

Note: According to the UN Relief and Works Agency for Palestine Refugees in the Near East, 575,234 Palestinian refugees were registered in Syria at July 2022. Following the outbreak of civil conflict during 2011, large numbers of Syrian nationals fled here fierce fighting in the country. At mid-2023 the number of Syrian refugees registered with the UN High Commissioner for Refugees totalled 5.2m., including some 3.3m. in Türkiye, 795,000 in Lebanon and 655,000 in Jordan.

POPULATION BY AGE AND SEX
('000, UN projections at mid-2023)

	Males	Females	Total
0–14 years	3,527.2	3,364.6	6,891.8
15–64 years	7,624.3	7,614.8	15,239.0
65 years and over	473.9	622.3	1,096.2
Total	11,625.4	11,601.6	23,227.0

Note: Totals may not be equal to the sum of components, owing to rounding.

Source: UN, *World Population Prospects: The 2022 Revision*.

GOVERNORATES
(official estimates at mid-2019)

	Area (sq km)	Population ('000)	Density (per sq km)
Dar'a	3,730	925	248.0
Deir el-Zor	33,060	1,206	36.5
Dimashq (Damascus, capital)	—	2,079	—
Halab (Aleppo)	18,500	3,964	214.3
Hamah (Hama)	10,160	2,082	204.9
Al-Hasakah	23,330	1,803	77.3
Hims (Homs)	40,940	1,734	42.4
Idlib	6,100	1,130	185.2
Al-Ladhiqiyah (Latakia)	2,300	1,319	573.5
Quneitra	1,860	117	62.9
Al-Raqqah (Raqqa)	19,620	905	46.1
Rif Dimashq (Rural Damascus)	18,140*	3,200	176.4
Al-Suweida	5,550	530	95.5
Tartous	1,890	1,152	609.5
Total	185,180	22,146	119.6

* Includes area for Dimashq (Damascus, capital).

BIRTHS, MARRIAGES AND DEATHS
(excl. nomad population and Palestinian refugees, estimates)

	Live births	Marriages	Deaths
2009	721,587	241,422	86,642
2010	870,100	227,808	91,981

Source: UN, *Demographic Yearbook*.

Crude birth rate (per 1,000): 18.9 in 2019; 19.7 in 2020; 20.1 in 2021 (Source: UN, *World Population Prospects: The 2022 Revision*).

Crude death rate (per 1,000): 5.0 in 2019; 5.0 in 2020; 5.1 in 2021 (Source: UN, *World Population Prospects: The 2022 Revision*).

Life expectancy (years at birth, estimates): 72.1 (males 69.1; females 75.2) in 2021 (Source: World Bank, World Development Indicators database).

SYRIAN ARAB REPUBLIC

ECONOMICALLY ACTIVE POPULATION
(labour force sample survey, persons aged 15 years and over, 2021)*

	Males	Females	Total
Agriculture, hunting, forestry and fishing	482,607	181,908	664,515
Mining and quarrying } Manufacturing } Electricity, gas and water }	450,145	87,800	537,945
Construction	491,901	6,025	497,926
Wholesale and retail trade } Restaurants and hotels }	774,364	112,004	886,368
Transport, storage and communications	295,379	19,248	314,627
Financing, insurance, real estate	48,859	12,393	61,252
Public administration and defence } Community, social and personal services }	1,167,172	743,110	1,910,282
Total employed	**3,710,427**	**1,162,488**	**4,872,915**
Unemployed	692,057	670,626	1,362,683
Total labour force	**4,402,484**	**1,833,114**	**6,235,598**

* Figures refer to Syrians only, excluding armed forces.

Health and Welfare

KEY INDICATORS

Total fertility rate (children per woman, 2021)	2.7
Under-5 mortality rate (per 1,000 live births, 2021)	22.3
HIV/AIDS (% of persons aged 15–49, 2021)	<0.1
COVID-19: Cumulative confirmed deaths (per 100,000 persons at 30 June 2023)	14.3
COVID-19: Fully vaccinated population (% of total population at 18 April 2023)	10.7
Physicians (per 1,000 head, 2016)	1.2
Hospital beds (per 1,000 head, 2017)	1.4
Domestic health expenditure (2012): US $ per head (PPP)	72.3
Domestic health expenditure (2012): % of GDP	1.6
Domestic health expenditure (2012): public (% of total current health expenditure)	45.3
Access to improved water resources (% of persons, 2020)	94
Access to improved sanitation facilities (% of persons, 2020)	90
Total carbon dioxide emissions ('000 metric tons, 2019)	25,714
Carbon dioxide emissions per head (metric tons, 2019)	1.3
Human Development Index (2021): ranking	150
Human Development Index (2021): value	0.577

Note: For data on COVID-19 vaccinations, 'fully vaccinated' denotes receipt of all doses specified by approved vaccination regime (Sources: Johns Hopkins University and Our World in Data). Data on health expenditure refer to current general government expenditure in each case. For sources and further definitions, see Health and Welfare Statistics: Sources and Definitions section (europaworld.com/credits).

Agriculture

PRINCIPAL CROPS
('000 metric tons)

	2019	2020	2021
Almonds, with shell	80.3	123.0	87.8
Anise, badian, fennel, coriander	54.7	79.6	68.1
Apples	286.6	267.8	301.6
Apricots	39.4	35.0	33.6
Aubergines (Eggplants)	188.3	227.4	253.0
Barley	3,053.1	2,245.8	252.3
Cabbages and other brassicas	61.9	58.5	64.4
Cantaloupes and other melons	93.1	139.1	123.3
Cherries, sweet	66.0	42.2	44.3
Chick peas	52.4	63.6	36.2
Chillies and peppers, green	96.2	95.9	119.0
Cucumbers and gherkins	182.7	224.6	186.4
Figs	43.0	46.5	41.0
Garlic	49.1	53.7	59.8
Grapefruits (incl. pomelos)	44.5	42.1	47.3*
Grapes	252.0	243.3	212.5
—continued	2019	2020	2021
Lemons and limes	152.8	105.6	114.1
Lentils	100.7	200.2	93.6
Lettuce and chicory	49.3	56.5	56.6
Maize	215.3	227.0	309.8
Olives	844.3	781.2	566.0
Onions and shallots, green	32.1	41.4	37.2
Onions, dry	78.3	76.7	84.2
Oranges	706.3	503.0	527.4
Peaches and nectarines	48.0	53.7	49.7
Pistachios	31.8	69.4	43.1
Potatoes	635.5	647.3	594.6
Pumpkins, squash and gourds	111.7	128.3	120.8
Seed cotton	114.7	97.5	66.5
Sugar beet	18.5	0.0	0.0
Tomatoes	1,345.5	1,268.4	1,259.3*
Watermelons	216.5	328.3	436.9
Wheat	3,085.1	2,848.5	1,951.8

* FAO estimate.

Aggregate production ('000 metric tons, may include official, semi-official or estimated data): Total cereals 6,356.6 in 2019, 5,322.6 in 2020, 2,514.8 in 2021; Total fruit (primary) 2,312.9 in 2019, 2,158.2 in 2020, 2,257.8 in 2021; Total oilcrops 989.5 in 2019, 926.1 in 2020, 689.9 in 2021; Total roots and tubers 635.5 in 2019, 647.3 in 2020, 594.6 in 2021; Total treenuts 133.2 in 2019, 214.6 in 2020, 155.1 in 2021; Total vegetables (primary) 2,537.1 in 2019, 2,614.1 in 2020, 2,626.7 in 2021.

Source: FAO.

LIVESTOCK
('000 head, year ending September)

	2019	2020	2021
Asses	69.4	61.3	56.8
Buffaloes	7.1	7.2	6.4
Camels	39.7	39.7	35.9
Cattle	788.3	884.6	872.3
Chickens	18,498	18,741	16,686
Goats	1,844.2	1,995.9	1,906.5
Horses	12.8	10.3	9.5
Sheep	14,557.7	16,073.1	16,783.2

Source: FAO.

LIVESTOCK PRODUCTS
('000 metric tons)

	2019	2020	2021
Buffaloes' milk	6.4	6.9	6.7
Cattle hides, fresh*	8.0	9.9	9.7
Cattle meat	51.9	64.4	63.0
Cows' milk	1,081.0	1,309.9	1,236.0
Chicken meat	122.0	124.8	112.4
Goat meat	11.0	12.0	10.5
Goats' milk	123.4	131.4	104.6
Sheep meat	116.2	148.4	160.4
Sheep offals, edible*	25.6	32.6	35.3
Sheep's (Ewes') milk	574.4	705.6	703.4
Sheepskins, fresh*	19.3	24.6	26.6
Hen eggs	122.9†	121.5†	n.a.
Honey (natural)	2.6	2.9	3.3
Wool, greasy*	15.7	14.1	12.0

* FAO estimate(s).
† Unofficial figure.

Source: FAO.

SYRIAN ARAB REPUBLIC

Forestry

ROUNDWOOD REMOVALS
('000 cubic metres, excl. bark, FAO estimates)

	2019	2020	2021
Sawlogs, veneer logs and logs for sleepers	16.0	16.0	16.0
Other industrial wood	23.8	23.8	23.8
Fuel wood	35.6	36.3	36.5
Total	75.4	76.1	76.3

Sawnwood production ('000 cubic metres): *1980:* Coniferous (softwood) 6.6; Broadleaved (hardwood) 2.4; Total 9.0. *1981–2021:* Production as in 1980 (FAO estimates).

Source: FAO.

Fishing

(metric tons, live weight, FAO estimates)

	2019	2020	2021
Capture	4,080	3,845	4,310
Freshwater fishes	2,500	2,300	2,530
Sardinellas	220	220	245
Atlantic mackerel	140	140	155
Aquaculture	2,250	2,300	2,350
Common carp	945	950	1,000
North African catfish	500	500	500
Blue tilapias	600	600	600
Other tilapias	200	245	245
Total catch	6,330	6,145	6,660

Source: FAO.

Mining

('000 metric tons unless otherwise indicated)

	2017	2018	2019
Phosphate rock*	100	2,000	2,000
Salt (unrefined)*	25	25	40
Gypsum*	150	150	150
Natural gas (million cu m)	3,487	3,468	3,327
Crude petroleum	1,079	1,051	1,511

* Estimates.

2020: Crude petroleum ('000 metric tons) 1,964; Natural gas (million cu m) 2,922.

2021: Crude petroleum ('000 metric tons) 4,598; Natural gas (million cu m) 3,075.

2022: Crude petroleum ('000 metric tons) 4,564; Natural gas (million cu m) 3,068.

Sources: US Geological Survey; Energy Institute, *Statistical Review of World Energy*.

Industry

SELECTED PRODUCTS
('000 metric tons unless otherwise indicated)

	2018	2019	2020
Olive oil (virgin)	118.3	153.8	138.2
Soybean oil*	0.7	0.8	1.2
Cottonseed oil*	1.9	2.6	3.1
Plywood (cu m)†	8.0	8.0	8.0
Paper and paperboard†	75	75	75
Cement (hydraulic)‡	1,600	n.a.	n.a.
Motor spirit (gasoline)	672	577	527
Gas-diesel (distillate fuel) oil	2,554	2,193	2,002
Residual fuel oils (Mazout)	3,339	2,868	2,618
Electrical energy (million kWh)	18,286	17,648	16,365

* Unofficial figures.
† FAO estimates.
‡ Estimated production.

2021 (FAO estimates): Plywood (cu m) 8.0; Paper and paperboard ('000 metric tons) 75.

Sources: FAO; US Geological Survey; UN Energy Statistics Database.

Finance

CURRENCY AND EXCHANGE RATES

Monetary Units
  100 piastres = 1 Syrian pound (£S).

Sterling, Dollar and Euro Equivalents (31 May 2023)
  £1 sterling = £S8,036.600;
  US $1 = £S6,500.000;
  €1 = £S6,943.950;
  £S10,000 = £1.24 sterling = $1.54 = €1.44.

Exchange Rate Between April 1976 and December 1987 the official mid-point rate was fixed at US $1 = £S3.925. On 1 January 1988 a new rate of $1 = £S11.225 was introduced. Prior to the outbreak of civil conflict in 2011, in addition to an official exchange rate, there was a promotion rate (applicable to most travel and tourism transactions) and a flexible rate. By mid-2018 it was estimated that the value of the Syrian currency, in relation to the US dollar, had depreciated by around 100% since 2011. The official exchange rate was reported at 434 pounds per US dollar at the end of 2019, but this rate, together with the unofficial exchange rate, continued to deteriorate during 2021–22. In July 2023 the central bank reduced the official exchange rate from 6,500 to 9,900 pounds per US dollar; the unofficial rate, meanwhile, was more than 11,000 pounds per US dollar at that time, representing a new record low.

BUDGET
(£S '000 million)

Revenue	2019	2020	2021
Tax revenues and duties	563.1	812.0	2,540.0
Salaries and wages	40.0	50.0	75.0
Income, profits and capital earnings	117.0	175.0	609.0
International trade	122.0	123.0	535.0
Excises	133.9	210.0	514.5
Property	51.5	76.0	290.5
Other	98.7	178.1	516.0
Proceeds of public services and properties	14.4	17.9	27.8
Miscellaneous revenues	1,304.1	601.0	939.2
Available surplus	1,054.8	1,113.7	2,509.3
Exceptional proceeds	945.6	1,455.4	2,483.8
Total	3,882.0	4,000.0	8,500.0

SYRIAN ARAB REPUBLIC

Statistical Survey

Expenditure	2019	2020	2021
Community, social and personal Services	1,973.9	2,308.4	3,463.4
Agriculture, forestry and fishing	91.6	90.5	156.6
Extractive industries	38.6	29.2	37.7
Manufacturing industries	36.1	30.9	56.0
Utilities	123.1	81.7	187.6
Construction	20.1	9.6	15.0
Trade	14.6	12.4	28.8
Transport and communications	54.5	51.9	83.9
Finance	39.3	33.3	38.3
Other	1,490.1	1,352.1	4,432.7
Total	**3,882.0**	**4,000.0**	**8,500.0**

INTERNATIONAL RESERVES
(excluding foreign exchange, US $ million at 31 December)

	2008	2009	2010
Gold (national valuation)	38	38	54
IMF special drawing rights	56	438	430
Total	**94**	**476**	**484**

IMF special drawing rights: 407 in 2020; 789 in 2021; 750 in 2022.

Source: IMF, *International Financial Statistics*.

MONEY SUPPLY
(£S million at 31 December)

	2009	2010	2011
Currency outside depository corporations	480,952	540,246	626,292
Transferable deposits	507,088	610,145	495,450
Other deposits	810,695	890,649	759,896
Broad money	**1,798,734**	**2,041,040**	**1,881,637**

Source: IMF, *International Financial Statistics*.

COST OF LIVING
(Consumer Price Index; base: 2010 = 100)

	2018	2019	2020
Food and non alcoholic beverages	947.7	1,089.0	2,538.7
Clothing and footwear	916.8	1,014.1	1,673.5
Housing, electricity, gas and other fuels (incl. water)	464.8	490.8	614.9
All items (incl. others)	**790.1**	**896.2**	**1,919.7**

NATIONAL ACCOUNTS
(£S million at current prices)

Expenditure on the Gross Domestic Product

	2019	2020	2021
Government final consumption expenditure	1,435,781	2,784,252	5,202,545
Private final consumption expenditure	7,108,455	13,786,087	25,758,216
Gross fixed capital formation	2,279,322	4,417,786	8,257,377
Changes in stocks	1,115,095	2,169,310	4,044,380
Total domestic expenditure	**11,938,652**	**23,157,434**	**43,262,518**
Exports of goods and services	3,843,762	7,452,147	13,920,838
Less Imports of goods and services	3,878,096	7,520,719	14,048,277
GDP in market prices	**11,904,318**	**23,088,862**	**43,135,079**
GDP at constant 2015 prices	**4,667,742**	**4,177,629**	**4,056,478**

Gross Domestic Product by Economic Activity

	2019	2020	2021
Agriculture, hunting, forestry and fishing	2,450,514	4,755,656	8,883,777
Mining and utilities	2,628,233	5,095,503	9,517,669
Manufacturing	557,004	1,080,204	2,018,539
Construction	403,674	782,246	1,462,120
Retail trade and hotel and restaurants	2,675,893	5,190,739	9,697,838
Transport, storage and communications	1,127,985	2,187,672	4,087,293
Other services	2,061,015	3,996,839	7,467,838
Sub-total	**11,904,316**	**23,088,859**	**43,135,074**
Taxes on products (net)*	2	3	6
GDP in market prices	**11,904,318**	**23,088,862**	**43,135,079**

* Figures obtained as residual.

Source: UN National Accounts Main Aggregates Database.

BALANCE OF PAYMENTS
(US $ million)

	2008	2009	2010
Exports of goods	15,334	10,883	12,273
Imports of goods	−16,107	−13,933	−15,876
Balance on goods	**−773**	**−3,049**	**−3,603**
Exports of services	4,415	4,798	7,333
Imports of services	−3,171	−2,734	−3,533
Balance on goods and services	**471**	**−985**	**197**
Primary income received	540	344	313
Primary income paid	−1,689	−1,451	−1,827
Balance on goods, services and primary income	**−678**	**−2,092**	**−1,317**
Secondary income received	1,335	1,247	1,450
Secondary income paid	−185	−185	−500
Current balance	**472**	**−1,030**	**−367**
Capital account (net)	0	13	50
Direct investment from abroad	1,466	2,570	1,469
Portfolio investment assets	−55	−241	−193
Other investment assets	−631	−626	61
Other investment liabilities	−42	212	−85
Net errors and omissions	−1,159	−550	1,142
Reserves and related items	**50**	**348**	**2,076**

Source: IMF, *International Financial Statistics*.

External Trade

PRINCIPAL COMMODITIES
(distribution by SITC, £S million)

Imports	2019	2020	2021
Food and live animals	440,872	921,545	2,053,234
Sugar and sugar confectionery	93,387	185,434	380,904
Cereals and cereal preparations	132,999	338,981	845,753
Crude materials (inedible) except fuels	106,005	161,600	329,412
Oil seeds	49,522	83,020	173,323
Mineral fuels, lubricants, etc.	1,192,141	1,785,903	6,471,721
Petroleum and petroleum products	1,125,597	1,655,348	6,168,683
Chemicals and related products	317,798	601,476	1,242,300
Medicinal and pharmaceutical products	82,541	177,515	241,945
Plastics in primary forms	88,683	159,269	413,261

SYRIAN ARAB REPUBLIC

Imports—continued	2019	2020	2021
Basic manufactures	398,244	596,567	1,671,985
Textile yarns and fabrics	94,779	148,267	597,564
Iron and steel	110,391	151,214	423,376
Machinery and transport equipment	425,936	398,343	928,288
Electrical machinery apparatus and appliances	75,211	65,161	331,666
Total (incl. others)	2,982,669	4,622,918	13,153,168

Exports	2019	2020	2021
Live animals and animal products	399,116	926,245	1,510,845
Vegetables and fruit	183,194	494,710	1,042,541
Coffee, tea, cocoa and spices	145,673	229,980	216,571
Crude materials (inedible) except fuels	216,287	237,832	379,804
Mineral fuels, lubricants, etc.	52,268	75,497	68,101
Petroleum and petroleum products	46,303	75,497	68,101
Electrical energy	5,965	—	—
Animal and vegetable oils, fats and waxes	38,730	70,211	125,340
Chemicals and related products	84,352	168,397	377,732
Essential oils and perfume materials	69,535	154,406	265,505
Basic manufactures	236,578	587,511	895,748
Non-metallic mineral manufactures	126,466	225,496	414,801
Miscellaneous manufactured articles	108,800	221,961	426,076
Articles of apparel and clothing accessories	70,063	138,552	260,048
Total (incl. others)	1,138,890	2,308,106	3,822,093

PRINCIPAL TRADING PARTNERS
(£S million)

Imports c.i.f.	2019	2020	2021
Argentina	45,061	75,102	169,860
Belgium	34,783	37,390	88,181
Brazil	32,246	62,369	224,142
China, People's Republic	329,964	506,295	1,158,525
Egypt	135,721	285,567	701,893
France	18,039	22,007	n.a.
Germany	27,306	59,335	94,966
India	86,178	191,417	423,723
Italy	120,474	44,428	110,240
Iran	76,055	127,658	233,274
Jordan	33,665	41,535	217,912
Korea, Republic	52,548	69,669	n.a.
Lebanon	90,184	101,302	307,957
Malaysia	20,615	33,452	94,962
Romania	46,080	110,400	159,594
Russian Federation	82,222	203,188	436,912
Spain	21,002	35,519	70,852
Ukraine	81,699	162,411	479,815
United Arab Emirates	110,254	171,685	493,885
Total (incl. others)	2,982,669	4,622,918	13,153,168

Exports f.o.b.	2019	2020	2021
Algeria	26,378	29,697	n.a.
Croatia	38,401	67,146	30,996
Egypt	133,294	204,355	185,377
Germany	17,656	29,667	40,488
India	15,719	21,803	24,622
Iraq	86,873	536,906	780,678
Jordan	36,918	115,591	182,198
Kuwait	40,087	67,104	n.a.
Lebanon	140,738	300,308	544,938
Netherlands	13,848	22,326	31,335
Qatar	35,152	36,058	n.a.
Saudi Arabia	189,300	359,151	651,467
Spain	8,642	14,623	23,189
Türkiye	57,668	82,402	254,083
United Arab Emirates	121,217	115,557	276,181
Yemen	43,827	60,855	n.a.
Total (incl. others)	1,138,890	2,308,106	3,822,093

Transport

RAILWAYS
(traffic)

	2019	2020	2021
Passengers carried ('000)	730	264	466
Passenger-km ('000)	30,396	17,000	30,000
Freight ('000 metric tons)	784	714	969
Freight ton-km (million)	100	87	180

ROAD TRAFFIC
(motor vehicles in use)

	2019	2020	2021
Passenger cars	829,529	880,125	844,113
Buses	8,417	10,323	4,645
Lorries, trucks, etc.	661,120	656,902	673,135
Motorcycles	489,261	521,289	542,004

SHIPPING
Flag Registered Fleet
(at 31 December)

	2020	2021	2022
Number of vessels	54	51	51
Total displacement ('000 grt)	71.3	59.3	131.5

Source: Lloyd's List Intelligence (www.bit.ly/LLintelligence).

CIVIL AVIATION
(traffic on scheduled services)

	2013	2014
Kilometres flown (million)	7	7
Passengers carried ('000)	476	476
Passenger-km (million)	533	533
Total ton-km (million)	2	2

Source: UN, *Statistical Yearbook*.

2021 (domestic and international): Departures 5,705; Passengers carried 672,219 (Source: World Bank, World Development Indicators database).

Tourism

FOREIGN VISITOR ARRIVALS
(incl. excursionists)*

Country of nationality	2019	2020	2021
Iran	19,439	3,824	4,836
Iraq	257,527	52,414	177,149
Jordan	356,940	46,324	69,958
Kuwait	7,081	1,200	2,684
Lebanon	1,549,207	294,962	262,432
Russian federation	50,711	41,351	36,568
Saudi Arabia	8,016	1,031	690
Türkiye	2,068	552	1,759
USA	18,590	3,152	15,444
Total (incl. others)	2,424,285	479,364	660,956

* Figures exclude Syrian nationals resident abroad.

Tourism receipts (US $ million, excl. passenger transport): 3,757 in 2009; 6,190 in 2010; 1,753 in 2011.

Source: World Tourism Organization.

Communications Media

	2019	2020	2021
Telephones ('000 main lines in use)	2,843	2,857	2,821
Mobile telephone subscriptions ('000)	17,734	16,660	16,991
Broadband subscriptions, fixed ('000)	1,493.2	1,548.1	1,575.8
Broadband subscriptions, mobile ('000)	1,653.6	2,724.1	3,714.6
Internet users (% of population, estimate)	34.7	35.8	n.a.

Source: International Telecommunication Union.

Education

(2020/21 unless otherwise indicated)

	Institutions	Teachers	Males	Females	Total
Pre-primary	1,950	6,954	58,933	55,346	114,279
Primary	9,038*	230,630†	1,084,056	1,034,993	2,119,049
Secondary: general	1,575	59,674†	636,047‡	685,044‡	1,321,091‡
Secondary: vocational*	656	13,062	65,902	41,186	107,088
Higher§	7*	8,446	205,773	273,395	479,168

* 2018/19.
† 2013/14.
‡ 2021/22.
§ Including parallel education.

Source: partly UNESCO Institute for Statistics.

Pupil-teacher ratio (primary education, UNESCO estimate): 23.8 in 2021/22 (Source: UNESCO Institute for Statistics).

Adult literacy rate (UNESCO estimates): 86.3% (males 91.8%; females 80.7%) in 2015 (Source: UNESCO Institute for Statistics).

Directory

The Constitution

A new and permanent Constitution was endorsed by 97.6% of voters in a national referendum held on 12 March 1973. The 157-article Constitution defines Syria as a 'Socialist popular democracy' with a 'pre-planned Socialist economy'. Under the new Constitution, Lt-Gen. Hafiz al-Assad remained President, with the power to appoint and dismiss his Vice-President, Premier and government ministers, and also became Commander-in-Chief of the Armed Forces, Secretary-General of the Baath Socialist Party and President of the National Progressive Front. According to the Constitution, the President is elected by direct popular vote for a seven-year term. Legislative power is vested in the People's Assembly, with 250 members elected for a four-year term by universal adult suffrage.

Following the death of President Hafiz al-Assad on 10 June 2000, the Constitution was amended to allow his son, Bashar al-Assad, to accede to the presidency. Bashar al-Assad also became Commander-in-Chief of the armed forces, Secretary-General of the Baath Socialist Party and President of the National Progressive Front.

At a national referendum, held on 26 February 2012, a new Constitution was approved by 89.4% of participating voters. Turnout was officially reported at 57.4%, although this figure was disputed by the opponents of President Assad. Among the most significant of its new provisions, the document imposed upon the President a limit of two seven-year terms (although this was not retroactive) and removed reference to the 'leading role' of the ruling Baath Arab Socialist Party. The Constitution entered into effect on 27 February.

The Government

HEAD OF STATE

President: Lt-Gen. Dr Bashar al-Assad (assumed office 17 July 2000; confirmed by referendum 27 May 2007; elected 3 June 2014; re-elected 26 May 2021).

Vice-Presidents: Dr Najah al-Attar, Maj.-Gen. Ali Mamlouk.

COUNCIL OF MINISTERS
(September 2023)

Prime Minister: Hussein Arnous.
Minister of Defence: Lt-Gen. Ali Mahmoud Abbas.
Minister of Foreign Affairs and Expatriates: Dr Faysal Mikdad.
Minister of Awqaf (Religious Endowments): Dr Mohammad Abdelsattar al-Sayyed.
Minister of Presidential Affairs: Mansour Fadlallah Azzam.
Minister of Local Administration and Minister of Environment: Hussein Makhlouf.
Minister of Administrative Development: Salam Mohammad al-Saffaf.
Minister of Economy and Foreign Trade: Mohammad Samer Abdelrahman al-Khalil.
Minister of the Interior: Maj.-Gen. Mohammed Khaled al-Rahmoun.
Minister of Tourism: Mohammad Rami Radwan Martini.
Minister of Higher Education and Scientific Research: Dr Bassam Bashir Ibrahim.
Minister of Public Works and Housing: Suhail Mohammad Abdullatif.
Minister of Communications and Technology: Iyad Mohammad al-Khatib.
Minister of Culture: Lubana Mshaweh.
Minister of Education: Dr Muhammad Amer Mardini.
Minister of Justice: Ahmad al-Sayyed.
Minister of Water Resources: Tammam Ra'ad.
Minister of Finance: Dr Kinan Yaghi.
Minister of Transport: Eng. Zuheir Khazim.

Minister of Petroleum and Mineral Resources: Dr FIRAS HASSAN QADDOUR.
Minister of Health: Dr HASSAN AL-GHABASH.
Minister of Industry: Dr ABDEL QADER JOKHADAR.
Minister of Agriculture and Agrarian Reform: MOHAMMAD HASSAN QATANA.
Minister of Electricity: GHASSAN AL-ZAMIL.
Minister of Internal Trade and Consumer Protection: MOHSEN ABDUL KARIM ALI.
Minister of Social Affairs and of Labour: LOUAI EMAD EL-DIN AL-MUNAJJID.
Minister of Information: BOUTROS AL-HALLAQ.
Ministers of State: AHMED BUSTAJI, ABDULLAH ABDULLAH, Dr DIALA BARAKAT.

MINISTRIES

Office of the President: Damascus.
Office of the Prime Minister: rue Chahbandar, Damascus; tel. (11) 2226000; fax (11) 2237842.
Ministry of Administrative Development: Damascus.
Ministry of Agriculture and Agrarian Reform: Baramkeh, Damascus; tel. (11) 23497533; fax (11) 23497534; e-mail info@moaar.gov.sy; internet moaar.gov.sy.
Ministry of Awqaf (Religious Endowments): place al-Misat, Damascus; tel. (11) 4419080; fax (11) 4419969; e-mail mow.gov@gmail.com; internet mow.gov.sy.
Ministry of Communications and Technology: rue Abed, Damascus; tel. (11) 2261550; fax (11) 2323273; e-mail info@moct.gov.sy; internet www.moct.gov.sy.
Ministry of Culture: rue George Haddad, Rawda, Damascus; tel. (11) 2222000; fax (11) 22226000; e-mail info@moc.gov.sy; internet www.moc.gov.sy.
Ministry of Defence: place Omayad, Damascus; tel. (11) 2131702; fax (11) 2125280; e-mail info@mod.gov.sy; internet www.mod.gov.sy.
Ministry of Economy and Foreign Trade: rue Maysaloun, Damascus; tel. (11) 2256700; fax (11) 2225695; e-mail econ-min@net.sy; internet www.syrecon.org.
Ministry of Education: rue Shahbander, al-Masraa, Damascus; tel. (11) 3313205; fax (11) 4420435; e-mail itwebdevel@moed.gov.sy; internet moed.gov.sy.
Ministry of Electricity: BP 4900, rue al-Kouatly, Damascus; tel. (11) 2133972; fax (11) 5811689; e-mail shakwa@moe.gov.sy; internet moe.gov.sy.
Ministry of Environment: Damascus.
Ministry of Finance: Al-Sabaa Baharat Sq., rue Zaki Al-Arsozi, Damascus; tel. (11) 2211300; fax (11) 2224701; internet www.syrianfinance.gov.sy.
Ministry of Foreign Affairs and Expatriates: Kafarsouseh, Damascus; tel. (11) 2181000; fax (11) 2146252; e-mail info@mofaex.gov.sy; internet www.mofaex.gov.sy.
Ministry of Health: rue Majlis al-Sha'ab, Damascus; tel. (11) 3311020; fax (11) 3311114; e-mail info@moh.gov.sy; internet www.moh.gov.sy.
Ministry of Higher Education and Scientific Research: BP 9251, place Mezzeh Gamarik, Damascus; tel. (11) 2129867; fax (11) 2134074; e-mail public@mohe.gov.sy; internet www.mohe.gov.sy.
Ministry of Industry: BP 12835, rue Maysaloun, Damascus; tel. (11) 2256700; fax (11) 2231096; e-mail info@moid.gov.sy; internet www.moid.gov.sy.
Ministry of Information: Immeuble Dar al-Baath, Autostrade Mezzeh, Damascus; tel. and fax (11) 6664681; e-mail info@moi.gov.sy; internet www.moi.gov.sy.
Ministry of the Interior: rue al-Bahsah, al-Marjeh, Damascus; tel. (11) 2219400; fax (11) 2324835; internet syriamoi.gov.sy.
Ministry of Internal Trade and Consumer Protection: Damascus.
Ministry of Justice: rue al-Nasr, Damascus; tel. (11) 2214105; fax (11) 2246250; internet www.moj.gov.sy.
Ministry of Labour: place Yousuf al-Azmeh, al-Salheyeh, Damascus; tel. (11) 2325387; fax (11) 2255143.
Ministry of Local Administration: rue 17 Nissan, Damascus; tel. (11) 2145700; fax (11) 2145731; e-mail info@mola.gov.sy; internet www.mola.gov.sy.
Ministry of Petroleum and Mineral Resources: BP 40, al-Adawi, Insha'at, Damascus; tel. (11) 3137930; fax (11) 4463942; e-mail it@mopmr.gov.sy; internet mopmr.gov.sy.
Ministry of Public Works and Housing: Saadallah al-Jabri St, Hijaz, Damascus; tel. (11) 2211494; fax (11) 2259400; internet mopwh.gov.sy.
Ministry of Social Affairs: Damascus.
Ministry of Tourism: BP 6642, rue Barada, Damascus; tel. (11) 2334050; fax (11) 2262678; e-mail g.services@syriatourism.org; internet www.syriatourism.org.
Ministry of Transport: BP 33999, rue al-Jala'a, Damascus; tel. (11) 3336801; fax (11) 3323317; e-mail min-trans@net.sy; internet www.mot.gov.sy.
Ministry of Water Resources: Damascus.

President

Presidential Election, 26 May 2021

Candidate	Votes	%
Bashar Hafiz al-Assad	13,540,860	95.2
Mahmoud Ahmad Marei	470,276	3.3
Abdallah Salloum Abdallah	213,968	1.5
Total*	**14,225,104**	**100.0**

* Excluding 14,000 invalid votes (0.1% of the total votes cast).

Legislature

People's Assembly: People's Assembly, Damascus; tel. (11) 3224046; fax (11) 3712532; e-mail info@parliament.gov.sy; internet www.parliament.gov.sy.
Speaker: HAMOUDEH SABBAGH.

Election, 19 July 2020

Party	Seats
National Progressive Front*	177
Others	73
Total	**250**

* The National Progressive Front (NPF) is headed by the Baath Arab Socialist Party, which accounted for a majority of the seats won by NPF, and comprises nine other organizations.

Political Organizations

National Progressive Front (NPF—Al-Jabha al-Wataniyah al-Taqadumiyah), headed by the late President Hafiz al-Assad, was formed in March 1972 as a coalition of five political parties. At the time of the legislative elections in May 2012, the NPF consisted of 10 parties:

Arab Democratic Unionist Party (Hizb al-Ittihad al-'Arabi al-Dimuqrati): f. 1981, following split from the Arab Socialist Union; considers the concerns of the Arab world in general as secondary to those of Syria itself in the pursuit of pan-Arab goals; Chair. GHASSAN AHMAD OSMAN.

Arab Socialist Movement (Harakat al-Ishtiraki al-'Arabi): Damascus; f. 1963, following split from Arab Socialist Union; contested the 2007 election to the People's Assembly as two factions (see also National Vow Movement); Leader OMAR ADNAN AL-ALAWI.

Arab Socialist Union (al-Ittihad al-Ishtiraki al-'Arabi): Damascus; f. 1973, following the separation of the Syrian branch from the international Arab Socialist Union; Nasserite; supportive of the policies of the Baath Arab Socialist Party; Leader SAFWAN AL-QUDSI.

Baath Arab Socialist Party (al-Hizb al-Ba'th al-'Arabi al-Ishtiraki): National Command, BP 9389, Autostrade Mezzeh, Damascus; tel. (11) 6622142; fax (11) 6622099; e-mail baath@baath-party.org; internet www.baath-party.org; Arab nationalist socialist party; f. 1947, as a result of merger between the Arab Revival (Baath) Movement (f. 1940) and the Arab Socialist Party (f. 1940); in power since 1963; supports creation of a unified Arab socialist society; approx. 1m. mems in Syria; brs in most Arab countries; Pres. Lt-Gen. Dr BASHAR AL-ASSAD.

Democratic Socialist Unionist Party (al-Hizb al-Wahdawi al-Ishtiraki al-Dimuqrati): f. 1974, following split from the Arab Socialist Union; Chair. FADLALLAH NASR AL-DIN.

National Vow Movement (Harakat al-'ahd al-Watani): a breakaway party from the Arab Socialist Union; a faction of the Arab Socialist Movement; awarded three seats in 2007 election to the People's Assembly; Leader GHASSAN ABD AL-AZIZ OSMAN.

Socialist Unionists (Al-Wahdawiyyun al-Ishtirakiyyun): e-mail alwahdawin@gmail.com; internet www.alwahdawi.net; f. 1961, through split from the Baath Arab Socialist Party following that organization's acceptance of Syria's decision to secede from the United Arab Republic; Nasserite; aims for Arab unity, particularly a new union with Egypt; produces weekly periodical *Al-Wehdawi*; Chair. FAYEZ ISMAIL.

Syrian Arab Socialist Union Party: Damascus; tel. (11) 239305; Nasserite; Sec.-Gen. SAFWAN KOUDSI.

Syrian Communist Party (Bakdash) (al-Hizb al-Shuyu'i al-Suri): BP 7837, Damascus; tel. (11) 4455048; fax (11) 4446390; internet www.syriancp.org; f. 1924 by Fouad Shamal in Lebanon and Khalid Bakdash (died 1995); until 1943 part of joint Communist Party of Syria and Lebanon; party split into two factions under separate leaders, Bakdash and Faisal (q.v.), in 1986; Marxist-Leninist; publishes fortnightly periodical *Sawt al-Shaab*.

Syrian Communist Party (Faisal) (al-Hizb al-Shuyu'i al-Suri): Damascus; f. 1986, following split of Syrian Communist Party into two factions under separate leaders, Faisal and Bakdash (q.v.); aims to end domination of Baath Arab Socialist Party and the advantages given to mems of that party at all levels; advocates the lifting of the state of emergency and the release of all political prisoners; publishes weekly periodical *An-Nour*; Sec.-Gen. HANIN NIMR.

Syrian Social Nationalist Party (Centralist Wing) (al-Hizb al-Suri al-Qawmi al-Ijtima'i): e-mail ssnpsocialmedia@gmail.com; internet www.ssnp.com; f. 1932 in Beirut, Lebanon; fmrly mem. of NPF, but withdrew prior to 2012 legislative elections; also known as Parti Populaire Syrien; seeks creation of a 'Greater Syrian' state, incl. the Syrian Arab Republic, Lebanon, Jordan, the Palestinian territories, Iraq, Kuwait, Cyprus and parts of Egypt, Iran and Türkiye (Turkey); advocates separation of church and state, the redistribution of wealth, and a strong military; supports Syrian involvement in Lebanese affairs; has brs worldwide, and approx. 90,000 mems in Syria; Leader RABI BANAT.

There are numerous opposition parties, within Syria or in exile, which are forced to operate on a clandestine basis. Formed in 1980, the **National Democratic Rally** (NDR—Tajammu' al-Watani al-Dimuqrati) is an alliance of banned, secularist opposition parties, several of which are opposition wings of parties that joined the ruling NPF.

A current member of the NDR, the **Syrian Democratic People's Party** (al-Hizb al-Sha'ab al-Suri al-Dimuqrati—leader ABULLAH HOSHA) was founded in 1973 as the Syrian Communist Party (Political Bureau), following the decision by founder Riad at-Turk to split from that party after its leader, Khalid Bakdash, decided to allow the organization to join the NPF. The party adopted its current name in 2005. The party publishes an online newsletter (www.arraee.com).

There is also a **Marxist-Leninist Communist Action Party**, which regards itself as independent of all Arab regimes.

An illegal Syrian-based organization, the **Islamic Movement for Change**, claimed responsibility for a bomb attack in Damascus in December 1996.

Diplomatic Representation

EMBASSIES IN SYRIA

Algeria: Immeuble al-Noss, Abu Rumaneh St, Rawda, Damascus; tel. (11) 3334548; e-mail ambaldam@mail.sy; Ambassador KAMEL BOUCHAMA.

Argentina: BP 116, Ziad Ibn Soufian, Rawda, Damascus; tel. (11) 3334167; fax (11) 3327326; e-mail easir2015@gmail.com; internet easir.cancilleria.gob.ar; Ambassador SEBASTIAN ZAVALA.

Armenia: 2 Saad Ben Abi Uakksi, Immeuble 2, Mezzeh Ouest, Damascus; tel. (11) 6133617; fax (11) 6133618; e-mail armsyriaembassy@mfa.am; internet syria.mfa.am/hy; Ambassador TIGRAN GEVORGYAN.

Austria: 7 rue Farabi, Mezzeh Est, Damascus; tel. (11) 6132504; fax (11) 6132507; e-mail damaskus-ob@bmeia.gv.at; internet www.bmeia.gv.at/damaskus; Ambassador PETER KROIS.

Bahrain: BP 36225, Damascus; tel. (11) 6132314; fax (11) 6130502; e-mail damascus.mission@mofa.gov.bh; Ambassador WAHEED MUBARAK SAYYAR.

Belarus: BP 1623, 13 rue Qurtaja, Mezzeh Est, Damascus; tel. (11) 6118097; fax (11) 6631143; e-mail syria@mfa.gov.by; internet syria.mfa.gov.by; Ambassador YURI SLUKA.

Brazil: 10 rue Ahmad al-Abed, Shaban Bldg, Mezzeh Villas, Damascus; tel. (11) 6124551; fax (11) 6124553; e-mail brasemb.damasco@itamaraty.gov.br; internet www.gov.br/mre/pt-br/embaixada-damasco; Ambassador ANDRE SANTOS.

Bulgaria: BP 2732, 8 rue Pakistan, place Arnous, Damascus; tel. (11) 4454039; fax (11) 4419854; e-mail embassy.damascus@mfa.bg; internet www.mfa.bg/en/embassies/syria; Chargé d'affaires PLAMEN HRISTOV.

Chile: BP 3561, Immeuble 68, rue Arwa Ibn al-Ward, West Malki, Damascus; tel. (11) 3712257; fax (11) 3712247; e-mail echile.siria@minrel.gob.cl; internet chile.gob.cl/siria; Chargé d'affaires JOSÉ PATRICIO BRICKLE.

China, People's Republic: BP 2455, 83 rue Ata Ayoubi, Damascus; tel. (11) 3316688; fax (11) 3338067; internet sy.chineseembassy.org; Ambassador SHI HONGWEI.

Cuba: BP 3055, Immeuble Istouani et Charbati, 40 rue al-Rachid, Damascus; tel. (11) 3339624; fax (11) 3333802; e-mail embajador@sy.embacuba.cu; internet www.cubadiplomatica.cu/siria; Ambassador LUIS MARIANO FERNANDEZ RODRIGUEZ.

Cyprus: BP 9269, 278G rue Malek bin Rabia, Mezzeh Ouest, Damascus; tel. (11) 6130812; fax (11) 6130814; e-mail cyembdam@scs-net.org; Chargé d'affaires SEVAG AVEDISSIAN.

Czech Republic: BP 2249, 51 rue Misr, Abou Roummaneh, Damascus; tel. (11) 3331383; fax (11) 3338268; e-mail damascus@embassy.mzv.cz; internet www.mzv.cz/damascus; Ambassador EVA FILIPI.

Denmark: BP 2244, Fatmeh Idriss 6, rue al-Ghazzawi, Mezzeh Ouest, Damascus; tel. (11) 61909000; fax (11) 61909033; e-mail beyamb@um.dk; internet syrien.um.dk; staff resident in Beirut, Lebanon.

Egypt: 17 rue Nissan, Kafarsouseh, Damascus; tel. (11) 2144885; e-mail egypt@tvcabo.co.mz; Chargé d'affaires MAHMOUD OMAR.

Eritrea: BP 12846, Autostrade al-Mazen West, 82 rue Akram Mosque, Damascus; tel. (11) 6112357; fax (11) 6112358; Chargé d'affaires a.i. HUMMED MOHAMED SAEED KULU.

Greece: BP 30319, Immeuble Pharaon, 11 rue Farabi, Mezzeh Est, Damascus; tel. (11) 6113035; fax (11) 6114920; e-mail gremb.dam@mfa.gr; internet www.mfa.gr/damascus; Chargé d'affaires NIKOLAOS PROTONOTARIOS.

Holy See: BP 2271, place Ma'raket Ajnadin, Damascus (Apostolic Nunciature); tel. (11) 3332601; fax (11) 3327550; e-mail noncesy@mail.sy; Apostolic Nuncio Most Rev. MARIO ZENARI (Titular Archbishop of Iulium Carnicum).

Hungary: BP 2607, 12 rue al-Salam, Mezzeh Est, Damascus; tel. (11) 6110787; fax (11) 6117917; internet www.mfa.gov.hu/kulkepviselet/sy; Chargé d'affaires JÁNOS BUDAI.

India: BP 685, 3455 rue ibn al-Haitham, Abou Roumaneh, Damascus; tel. (11) 3347351; e-mail hoc.damascusmea.gov.in; internet eoi.gov.in/damascus; Ambassador Dr IRSHAD AHMAD (designate).

Indonesia: BP 3530, Immeuble 26, Bloc 270A, 132 rue al-Madina al-Munawar, Mezzeh Est, Damascus; tel. (11) 6119630; fax (11) 6119632; e-mail kbridamaskus@kemlu.go; internet kemlu.go.id/damascus; Ambassador WAJID FAUZI.

Iran: BP 2691, Autostrade Mezzeh, nr al-Razi Hospital, Damascus; tel. (11) 6117675; internet damascus.mfa.gov.ir; Ambassador HOSSEIN AKBARI.

Iraq: BP 3874, al-Mahdi bin Barkah St, Abu Rumaneh, Damascus; tel. (11) 3341290; fax (11) 3341291; e-mail dmkemb@mofa.gov.iq; internet www.mofa.gov.iq/damascus; Chargé d'affaires a.i. Dr YASSIN SHARIF AL-HUJAIMI.

Jordan: rue Immeuble 27, Tarablous, Damascus; tel. (11) 6136260; fax (11) 6136263; e-mail embjor@yahoo.com; Chargé d'affaires BASEL AL-KAYED.

Korea, Democratic People's Republic: Immeuble Jasr Toura 52, rue Fares al-Khouri-Jisr Tora, Damascus; tel. (11) 4411335; fax (11) 4424735; e-mail koreaembasyria@yahoo.com; Chargé d'affaires a.i. KIM HEE-RYONG.

Kuwait: rue Ghazawi, Mazzeh, Damascus; tel. (11) 6118853; fax (11) 6117647; e-mail damascus@mofa.gov.kw; Ambassador AZIZ RAHIM AL-DIHANI.

Lebanon: rue el-Mekdad Ben Amro, Immeuble B2, Mezzeh Est, Damascus; tel. (11) 2146338; fax (11) 6116394; e-mail lebembassysyria@hotmail.com; Ambassador SAAD ZAKHIA.

Mauritania: ave al-Jala'a, rue Karameh, Abou Roumaneh, Damascus; tel. (11) 3339317; fax (11) 3330552; Ambassador AHMEDOU ADI MUHAMMAD AL-RAZI.

Morocco: 35 rue Abu Bakr al-Karkhi Villas, Mezzeh Est, Damascus; tel. (11) 6110451; fax (11) 6117885; e-mail sifmar@scs-net.org; Ambassador (vacant).

Nigeria: 4717 rue Ben Alkattab St, Mezzeh-West Villas, Damascus; tel. (11) 6128923; fax (11) 6128925; e-mail nigeria.damascus@foreignaffairs.gov.ng; Chargé d'affaires IBRAHIM YUNUSA MUHAMMAD.

Oman: BP 9635, rue al-Farabi, Mezzeh Ouest, Damascus; tel. (11) 6133385; e-mail oman-em@scs-net.org; Ambassador Sayyid TURKI BIN MAHMOUD AL-BUSAIDI.

SYRIAN ARAB REPUBLIC

Pakistan: BP 9284, rue al-Farabi, Mezzeh Est, Damascus; tel. (11) 6132694; fax (11) 6132662; e-mail parepdam@scs-net.org; Ambassador Air Marshal (retd) SHAHID AKHTAR.

Panama: Immeuble 10, Office 4, rue al-Bizm, Malki St, Damascus; tel. (11) 3739001; fax (11) 3738801; e-mail consuladodepanama damasco@gmail.com; Chargé d'affaires HAISAM CHEHABI.

Philippines: BP 36849, 56 rue Hamzeh bin al-Mutaleb, Mezzeh, Damascus; tel. (11) 6132626; fax (11) 6110152; e-mail damascus.pe@dfa.gov.ph; internet damascuspe.dfa.gov.ph; Chargé d'affaires JOHN G. REYES.

Poland: BP 501, rue Baha Eddin Aita, Abou Roumaneh, Damascus; tel. (11) 3333010; fax (11) 3315318; e-mail damaszek.amb.sekretariat@msz.gov.pl; internet www.damaszek.msz.gov.pl; Chargé d'affaires ROBERT ROKICKI.

Romania: BP 4454, 8 rue Ibrahim Hanano, Damascus; tel. (11) 3327572; fax (11) 3327571; e-mail damascamb@gmail.com; internet damasc.mae.ro; Ambassador DANUT FLORIN SANDOVICI.

Russian Federation: BP 3153, rue Umar bin al-Khattab, al-Dawi, Damascus; tel. (11) 4423155; fax (11) 4423182; e-mail ruembsyria@mail.ru; internet www.syria.mid.ru; Ambassador ALEKSANDR YEFIMOV.

Saudi Arabia: BP 3858, rue al-Jala'a, Abou Roumaneh, Damascus; tel. (11) 3334914; fax (11) 3337383; e-mail syemb@mofa.gov.sa; Chargé d'affaires a.i. FALEH AL-REHAILI.

Serbia: BP 739, 18 rue al-Jala'a, Abou Roumaneh, Damascus; tel. (11) 3336222; fax (11) 3333690; e-mail ambasada@srbija-damask.org; Ambassador RADOVAN STOJANOVIĆ.

Somalia: 7 rue Abu Bakr al-Karkhi Villas, Mezzeh Est, Damascus; tel. and fax (11) 6111220; e-mail webmaster@somaligov.net; internet www.syria.somaligov.net; Chargé d'affaires FARHAN GURHAN.

South Africa: BP 9141, rue al-Ghazaoui, 7 Jadet Kouraish, Mezzeh Ouest, Damascus; tel. (11) 61351520; fax (11) 6111714; e-mail admin.damascus@foreign.gov.za; Ambassador BARRY PHILIP GILDER.

Sudan: rue al-Farabi, Est Villah, Mezzeh, Damascus; tel. (11) 6112905; fax (11) 6112904; e-mail sud-emb@net.sy; Ambassador Dr TARIQ AL-TOM.

Sweden: BP 4266, Immeuble du Patriarcat Catholique, rue Chakib Arslan, Abou Roumaneh, Damascus; tel. (11) 6190900; e-mail ambassaden.damaskus@gov.se; internet www.swedenabroad.se/en/embassies/syria-damaskus; Chargé d'affaires ANN DISMORR.

Tunisia: Damascus; Ambassador MOHAMED MHADHBI.

United Arab Emirates: BP 33787, Abou Roumaneh, Damascus; tel. (11) 3330308; fax (11) 3327961; e-mail damascusemb@mofaic.gov.ae; Chargé d'affaires ABDUL HAKIM IBRAHIM AL-NUAIMI.

Venezuela: BP 2403, Immeuble al-Tabbah, 5 rue Lisaneddin bin al-Khateb, place Rauda, Damascus; tel. (11) 6124835; fax (11) 6124833; e-mail embavenez@tarassul.sy; Ambassador JOSÉ GREGORIO BIOMORGI MUZZATIZ.

Yemen: Immeuble 176, rue Shafai, Est Villas, Mezzeh, Damascus; tel. (11) 6133890; fax (11) 6133893; e-mail yemenemb.dam@mail.sy; Ambassador ABDULLAH ALI SABRI (appointed by the al-Houthi government in San'a).

Judicial System

The Courts of Law in Syria are principally divided into two juridical court systems: Courts of General Jurisdiction and Administrative Courts. Since 1973 the Supreme Constitutional Court has been established as the paramount body of the Syrian judicial structure.

The Supreme Constitutional Court: Damascus; tel. (11) 3331902; This is the highest court in Syria. It has specific jurisdiction over: (i) judicial review of the constitutionality of laws and legislative decrees; (ii) investigation of charges relating to the legality of the election of members of the Majlis al-Sha'ab (People's Assembly); (iii) trial of infractions committed by the President of the Republic in the exercise of his functions; (iv) resolution of positive and negative jurisdictional conflicts and determination of the competent court between the different juridical court systems, as well as other bodies exercising judicial competence. The Supreme Constitutional Court is composed of a Chief Justice and six Justices. They are appointed by decree of the President of the Republic for a renewable period of four years; Chief Justice MOHAMMAD JIHAD AL-LAHAM.

Courts of General Jurisdiction: The Courts of General Jurisdiction in Syria are divided into six categories: (i) The Court of Cassation; (ii) The Courts of Appeal; (iii) The Tribunals of First Instance; (iv) The Tribunals of Peace; (v) The Personal Status Courts; (vi) The Courts for Minors. Each of the above categories (except the Personal Status Courts) is divided into Civil, Penal and Criminal Chambers; (i) The Court of Cassation: This is the highest court of general jurisdiction. Final judgments rendered by Courts of Appeal in penal and civil litigations may be petitioned to the Court of Cassation by the Defendant or the Public Prosecutor in penal and criminal litigations, and by any of the parties in interest in civil litigations, on grounds of defective application or interpretation of the law as stated in the challenged judgment, on grounds of irregularity of form or procedure, or violation of due process, and on grounds of defective reasoning of judgment rendered. The Court of Cassation is composed of a President, seven Vice-Presidents and 31 other Justices (Councillors); (ii) The Courts of Appeal: Each court has geographical jurisdiction over one governorate (*mohafazat*). Each court is divided into Penal and Civil Chambers. There are Criminal Chambers, which try felonies only. The Civil Chambers hear appeals filed against judgments rendered by the Tribunals of First Instance and the Tribunals of Peace. Each Court of Appeal is composed of a President and sufficient numbers of Vice-Presidents (Presidents of Chambers) and Superior Judges (Councillors). There are 54 Courts of Appeal; (iii) The Tribunals of First Instance: In each governorate there are one or more Tribunals of First Instance, each of which is divided into several Chambers for penal and civil litigations. Each Chamber is composed of one judge. There are 72 Tribunals of First Instance; (iv) The Tribunals of Peace: In the administrative centre of each governorate, and in each district, there are one or more Tribunals of Peace, which have jurisdiction over minor civil and penal litigations. There are 227 Tribunals of Peace; (v) Personal Status Courts: These courts deal with marriage, divorce, etc. For Muslims, each court consists of one judge, the 'Qadi Shari'i'. For Druzes, there is one court consisting of one judge, the 'Qadi Mazhabi'. For non-Muslim communities, there are courts for Roman Catholics, Orthodox believers, Protestants and Jews; (vi) Courts for Minors: The constitution, officers, sessions, jurisdiction and competence of these courts are determined by a special law.

Public Prosecution: Public prosecution is headed by the Attorney-General, assisted by a number of Senior Deputy and Deputy Attorneys-General, and a sufficient number of chief prosecutors, prosecutors and assistant prosecutors. Public prosecution is represented at all levels of the Courts of General Jurisdiction in all criminal and penal litigations and also in certain civil litigations as required by the law. Public prosecution controls and supervises enforcement of penal judgments.

Administrative Courts System: The Administrative Courts have jurisdiction over litigations involving the state or any of its governmental agencies. The Administrative Courts system is divided into two courts: the Administrative Courts and the Judicial Administrative Courts, of which the paramount body is the High Administrative Court.

Military Courts: The Military Courts deal with criminal litigations against military personnel of all ranks and penal litigations against officers only. There are two military courts: one in Damascus, the other in Aleppo. Each court is composed of three military judges. There are other military courts, consisting of one judge, in every governorate, which deal with penal litigations against military personnel below the rank of officer. The different military judgments can be petitioned to the Court of Cassation.

Religion

The majority of Syrians follow a form of Islamic Sunni orthodoxy. There are also a considerable number of religious minorities: Shi'a Muslims; Isma'ili Muslims; the Isma'ili of the Salamiya district, whose spiritual head is the Aga Khan; a large number of Druzes, the Nusairis or Alawites of the Jebel Ansariyeh (a schism of the Shi'a branch of Islam, to which about 11% of the population, including President Assad, belong) and the Yezidis of the Jebel Sinjar; and a minority of Christians.

The Constitution states that 'Islam shall be the religion of the President', but does not enshrine Islam as the religion of the state itself.

CHRISTIANITY

Orthodox Churches

Greek Orthodox Patriarchate of Antioch and all the East: BP 9, Damascus; tel. (11) 5424400; fax (11) 5424404; e-mail info@antiochpat.org; internet antiochpatriarchate.org; Patriarch of Antioch and all the East His Beatitude JOHN X; has jurisdiction over Syria, Lebanon, Iran and Iraq.

Syrian Orthodox Patriarchate of Antioch and all the East: BP 22260, Bab Touma, Damascus; tel. (11) 5438383; e-mail secretary@syriacpatriarchate.org; internet syriacpatriarchate.org; Patriarch of Antioch and all the East His Holiness IGNATIUS APHREM, II; the Syrian Orthodox Church includes one Catholicose (of India), 37 Metropolitans and one Bishop, and has an estimated 4m. adherents throughout the world.

The Armenian Apostolic Church is also represented in Syria.

The Roman Catholic Church

Armenian Rite

Patriarchal Exarchate of Syria: Exarchat Patriarcal Arménien Catholique, BP 22281, Bab Touma, Damascus; tel. (11) 5413820; fax (11) 5419431; f. 1985; represents the Patriarch of Cilicia (resident in Beirut, Lebanon); Exarch Patriarchal Bishop JOSEPH ARNAOUTIAN; 4,500 adherents (2020).

Archdiocese of Aleppo: Archevêché Arménien Catholique, BP 97, 33 al-Tilal, Aleppo; tel. (21) 2123946; fax (21) 2116637; e-mail armen.cath@mail.sy; Archbishop BOUTROS MARAYATI; 5,000 adherents (2019).

Chaldean Rite

Diocese of Aleppo: Evêché Chaldéen Catholique, BP 4643, 1 rue Patriarche Elias IV Mouawwad, Soulémaniyé, Aleppo; tel. (21) 4441660; fax (21) 4600800; e-mail audoa@scs-net.org; Bishop ANTOINE AUDO; 5,000 adherents (2021).

Latin Rite

Apostolic Vicariate of Aleppo: BP 327, 14 rue al-Fourat, Aleppo; tel. (21) 2682399; fax (21) 2689413; e-mail vicariatlatin@mail.sy; f. 1762; Vicar Apostolic (vacant); Apostolic Administrator Rev. Fr RAIMONDO GIRGIS; 12,500 adherents (2020).

Maronite Rite

Archdiocese of Aleppo: Archevêché Maronite, BP 203, 57 rue Fares el-Khoury, Aleppo; tel. (21) 2118048; fax (21) 2123048; e-mail maronite@scs-net.org; Archbishop JOSEPH TOBJI.

Archdiocese of Damascus: Archevêché Maronite, BP 2179, 6 rue al-Deir, Bab Touma, Damascus; tel. (11) 5412888; fax (11) 5436002; e-mail mgrsamirnassar@gmail.com; f. 1527; Archbishop SAMIR NASSAR; 6,000 adherents (2020).

Melkite Rite

Melkite Greek Catholic Patriarchate of Antioch: Patriarcat Grec-Melkite Catholique, BP 22249, 12 ave al-Zeitoun, Bab Charki, Damascus; tel. (11) 5441030; fax (11) 5417900; e-mail info@pgc-lb.org; internet www.pgc-lb.org; or BP 70071, Antélias, Lebanon; tel. (4) 413111; fax (4) 418113; f. 1724; jurisdiction over 1.5m. Melkites throughout the world (incl. 234,000 in Syria); Patriarch of Antioch and all the East, of Alexandria and of Jerusalem His Beatitude JOSEPH ABSI; the Melkite Church includes the patriarchal sees of Damascus, Cairo and Jerusalem and four other archdioceses in Syria; seven archdioceses in Lebanon; one in Jordan; one in Israel; and seven eparchies (in the USA, Brazil, Canada, Australia, Venezuela, Argentina and Mexico).

Archdiocese of Aleppo: Archevêché Grec-Catholique, BP 146, 9 place Farhat, Aleppo; tel. (21) 2119304; fax (21) 2119308; Archbishop GEORGES MASRI; 18,000 adherents (31 Dec. 2020).

Archdiocese of Busra and Hauran: Archevêché Grec-Melkite-Catholique, Khabab, Hauran; tel. (15) 855012; fax (15) 855394; Archbishop ELIAS AL-DEBEI; 19,125 adherents (2020).

Archdiocese of Homs: Archevêché Grec-Catholique, BP 1525, rue el-Mo'tazila, Boustan al-Diwan, Homs; tel. (11) 7810114; fax (11) 7821943; e-mail isidore_battikha@yahoo.fr; Archbishop JEAN-ABDO ARBACH; 26,000 adherents (2021).

Archdiocese of Latakia: Archevêché Grec-Catholique, BP 151, rue al-Moutannabi, Latakia; tel. (41) 460777; fax (41) 476002; e-mail saouafnicolas@yahoo.fr; Archbishop GEORGES KHAWAM.

Syrian Rite

Archdiocese of Aleppo: Archevêché Syrien Catholique, place Mère Teresa de Calcutta, Azizié, Aleppo; tel. (21) 2126750; fax (21) 2126752; e-mail a_chahda@hotmail.com; Archbishop DENYS ANTOINE CHAHDA; 8,500 adherents (2019).

Archdiocese of Damascus: Archevêché Syrien Catholique, BP 2129, 157 rue Al-Mustaqeem, Bab Charki, Damascus; tel. and fax (11) 5445344; Archbishop YOUHANNA JIHAD MTANOS BATTAH; 7,000 adherents (2021).

Archdiocese of Hassaké-Nisibi: Archevêché Syrien Catholique, BP 6, Hassaké; tel. (52) 320812; fax (52) 316340; Archbishop Most Rev. JOSEPH CHAMIL; 35,000 adherents (31 Dec. 2011).

Archdiocese of Homs: Archevêché Syrien Catholique, BP 368, rue Hamidieh, Homs; tel. and fax (31) 2628608; Archbishop YACOUB MOURAD; 12,000 adherents (2021).

The Anglican Communion

Within the Episcopal Church in Jerusalem and the Middle East, Syria forms part of the diocese of Jerusalem (see Israel).

Other Christian Groups

Protestants in Syria are largely adherents of either the National Evangelical Synod of Syria and Lebanon or the Union of Armenian Evangelical Churches in the Near East (for details of both organizations, see Lebanon).

The Press

Since the Baath Arab Socialist Party came to power, the structure of the press has been modified according to socialist patterns. Most publications are issued by political, religious or professional associations (such as trade unions), and several are published by government ministries. However, two privately owned daily newspapers have been launched in recent years. Anyone wishing to establish a new newspaper or periodical must apply for a licence.

The major dailies are *Al-Baath* (the organ of the party), *Tishreen*, *Al-Thawra* and the *Syria Times*, all published in Damascus.

DAILY NEWSPAPERS (PRINT AND ONLINE)

Al-Baath (Renaissance): BP 9389, Autostrade Mezzeh, Damascus; tel. (11) 6622141; fax (11) 6622140; e-mail info@albaath.news.sy; internet www.albaath.news.sy; f. 1946; morning; Arabic; organ of the Baath Arab Socialist Party; Editor ILYAS MURAD.

Baladna: BP 2000, al-Huda Bldg, al-Eskandaria St, Damascus; tel. (11) 6122515; fax (11) 6122514; internet www.baladnaonline.net; Arabic; privately owned; publ. by United Group for Publishing, Advertising and Marketing; Chief Editor SAMIR AL-SHIBANI.

Champress: Immeuble Arnos, place Arnos, Damascus; tel. (11) 44681199; fax (11) 44681190; e-mail mail@champress.com; internet www.champress.com; privately owned; political; online only; Arabic; Dir ALI JAMALO.

Al-Fida' (Redemption): Hama; Al-Wahda Foundation for Press, Printing and Publishing, BP 2448, Dawar Kafr Soussat, Damascus; tel. (33) 2760555; fax (11) 2216851; e-mail fedaa@alwehda.gov.sy; internet fedaa.alwehda.gov.sy; morning; Arabic; political; Editor A. AULWANI.

Al-Furat: Al-Wahda Foundation for Press, Printing and Publishing, BP 2448, Dawar Kafr Soussat, Damascus; tel. (11) 2224324; fax (51) 218418; e-mail furat@alwehda.gov.sy; internet furat.alwehda.gov.sy; Editor OSMAN KHALAF.

Al-Horubat: Homs; Al-Wahda Foundation for Press, Printing and Publishing, BP 2448, Dawar Kafr Soussat, Damascus; tel. (31) 2134859; fax (11) 2216851; e-mail oruba@alwehda.gov.sy; internet ouruba.alwehda.gov.sy; morning; Arabic; political.

Al-Jamahir (The People): Aleppo; Al-Wahda Foundation for Press, Printing and Publishing, BP 2448, Dawar Kafr Soussat, Damascus; tel. (21) 2129335; fax (21) 214308; e-mail jamahir@alwehda.gov.sy; internet jamahir.alwehda.gov.sy; Arabic; political; Editor JIHAD ATEF.

Syria Times: BP 5452, Medan, Damascus; tel. (11) 2260845; fax (11) 2260513; e-mail editor-in-chief@syriatimes.sy; internet syriatimes.sy; English; publ. by Al-Wahda Foundation for Press, Printing and Publishing; Editor-in-Chief REEM HADDAD.

Al-Thawra (Revolution): Al-Wahda Foundation for Press, Printing and Publishing, BP 2448, Dawar Kafr Soussat, Damascus; tel. (11) 2138534; fax (11) 2150428; e-mail admin@thawra.sy; internet thawra.sy; f. 1963; morning; Arabic; political; Editor-in-Chief BASHAR MUHAMMAD.

Tishreen (October): BP 5452, Medan, Damascus; tel. (11) 2131100; fax (11) 2246860; e-mail tnp@mail.sy; internet www.tishreen.news.sy; Arabic; publ. by Tishreen Foundation for Press and Publishing; Editor-in-Chief MOHAMMED AL-BAYRAQ.

Al-Wahda (Unity): Latakia; Al-Wahda Foundation for Press, Printing and Publishing, BP 2448, Dawar Kafr Soussat, Damascus; tel. (41) 552559; fax (11) 2216851; e-mail wehda@alwehda.gov.sy; internet wehda.alwehda.gov.sy; Arabic; political.

Al-Watan: Duty Free Zone, Damascus; tel. (11) 2137400; fax (11) 2139928; e-mail info@alwatan.sy; internet www.alwatan.sy; f. 2006; Arabic; political; privately owned; Chief Editor WADDAH ABD AL-RABBO.

OTHER NEWSPAPERS (PRINT AND ONLINE)

Abyad wa Aswad (White and Black): 8 rue Hekmat Alasale, Almastaba 4, Muhajirin; tel. (11) 3739968; fax (11) 3739949; e-mail a-and-a@scs-net.org; internet www.awaonline.net; f. 2002; weekly; Arabic; privately owned; Editor AYMAN AL-DAQUQ.

Al-Iqtisadiya: rue Abd al-Munim Riyad 13, Damascus; tel. (11) 3737344; fax (11) 3737348; internet iqtissadiya.com; f. 2001; weekly; Arabic; economic; privately owned; Man. Dir NABIL ZUREIK; Editor WADDAH ABD AL-RABBO.

SYRIAN ARAB REPUBLIC

Directory

Kantsasar: BP 133, Aleppo; tel. and fax (21) 2246753; e-mail info@kantsasar.com; internet www.kantsasar.com; weekly; Armenian; publ. by Armenian Prelacy of Aleppo; Editor MARY MERDKHANIAN.

Kassioun: BP 35033, Damascus; tel. (11) 3120598; e-mail general@kassioun.org; internet www.kassioun.org; weekly; publ. by the Syrian Communist Party (Bakdash).

Kifah al-Oummal al-Ishtiraki (The Socialist Workers' Struggle): Fédération Générale des Syndicats des Ouvriers, rue Qanawat, Damascus; weekly; Arabic; labour; publ. by Gen. Fed. of Labour Unions; Editor SAEED AL-HAMAMI.

Al-Maukef al-Riadi (Sport Stance): Al-Wahda Foundation for Press, Printing and Publishing, BP 2448, Dawar Kafr Soussat, Damascus; tel. (11) 225219; e-mail riadi@thawra.com; internet riadi.alwehda.gov.sy; weekly; Arabic; sports.

An-Nour (Light): BP 7394, Damascus; tel. (11) 3324914; fax (11) 3342571; internet www.an-nour.com; f. 2001; weekly; Arabic; political and cultural; organ of the Syrian Communist Party (Faisal); Gen. Man. HABIB OSTA.

Sawt al-Shaab (Voice of the People): Damascus; f. 1937, but publ. suspended in 1939, 1941, 1947 and 1958; relaunched in 2001; fortnightly; Arabic; organ of the Syrian Communist Party (Bakdash).

PERIODICALS

Al-Arabieh (The Arab Lady): Syrian Women's Asscn, BP 3207, Damascus; tel. (11) 3313275; fax (11) 3311078; monthly; Editor MAJEDA KUTEIT.

Al-Fikr al-Askari (The Military Idea): BP 4259, blvd Palestine, Damascus; fax (11) 2125280; f. 1950; 6 a year; Arabic; official military review publ. by the Political Administration Press.

Al-Ghad (Tomorrow): Association of Red Cross and Crescent, BP 6095, rue Maysat, Damascus; tel. (11) 2242552; fax (11) 7777040; monthly; environmental health; Editor K. ABED-RABOU.

Al-Irshad al-Zirai (Agricultural Information): Ministry of Agriculture and Agrarian Reform, rue Jabri, Damascus; tel. (11) 2213613; fax (11) 2216627; 6 a year; Arabic; agriculture.

Jaysh al-Sha'ab (The People's Army): Ministry of Defence, BP 3320, blvd Palestine, Damascus; fax (11) 2125280; f. 1946; monthly; Arabic; army magazine; publ. by the Political Dept of the Syrian Army.

Al-Kalima (The Word): Al-Kalima Association, Aleppo; e-mail contact@al-kalima.com; monthly; Arabic; religious; Publr and Editor FATHALLA SAKAL.

Al-Kanoun (The Law): Ministry of Justice, rue al-Nasr, Damascus; tel. (11) 2214105; fax (11) 2246250; monthly; Arabic; juridical.

Layalina: Damascus; tel. (11) 6122515; fax (11) 6122514; internet layalina.sy.pressera.com; monthly; Arabic; social and lifestyle; publ. by United Group for Publishing, Advertising and Marketing; Chair. MAJD SULEIMAN.

Al-Maaloumatieh (Information): National Information Centre, BP 11323, Damascus; tel. (11) 2127551; fax (11) 2127648; e-mail nice@net.sy; f. 1994; quarterly; computer magazine; Editor ABD AL-MAJID AL-RIFAI.

Al-Ma'arifa (Knowledge): Ministry of Culture, rue al-Rouda, Damascus; tel. (11) 3336963; f. 1962; monthly; Arabic; literary; Editor ABD AL-KARIM NASIF.

Al-Majalla al-Batriarquia (The Magazine of the Patriarchate): Syrian Orthodox Patriarchate, BP 914, Damascus; tel. (11) 4447036; f. 1962; monthly; Arabic; religious; Editor SAMIR ABDOH.

Al-Majalla al-Tibbiya al-Arabiyya (Arab Medical Magazine): rue al-Jala'a, Damascus; tel. (11) 3331890; internet www.arabmedmag.com; monthly; Arabic and English; publ. by Arab Medical Comm; Dir KHALID KALLAS; Editor Dr AL-LOUJAMI MAZEN.

Majallat Majma' al-Lughat al-Arabiyya bi-Dimashq (Magazine of the Arab Language Academy of Damascus): Arab Academy of Damascus, BP 327, Damascus; tel. (11) 3713145; fax (11) 3733363; e-mail mla@net.sy; f. 1921; quarterly; Arabic; Islamic culture and Arabic literature, Arabic scientific and cultural terminology; Chief Editor Dr SHAKER FAHAM.

Al-Mouallem al-Arabi (The Arab Teacher): National Union of Teachers, BP 2842-3034, Damascus; tel. (11) 225219; f. 1948; monthly; Arabic; educational and cultural.

Al-Mouhandis al-Arabi (The Arab Engineer): Order of Syrian Engineers and Architects, BP 2336, Immeuble Dar al-Mouhandisen, place Azme, Damascus; tel. (11) 2214916; fax (11) 2216948; f. 1961; four a year; Arabic; scientific and cultural; Dir Eng. M. FAYEZ MAHFOUZ; Chief Editor Dr Eng. AHMAD AL-GHAFARI.

Al-Munadel (The Militant): c/o BP 11512, Damascus; fax (11) 2126935; f. 1965; monthly; Arabic; magazine of Baath Arab Socialist Party; Dir Dr FAWWAZ SAYYAGH.

Al-Nashra al-Iktissad (Economic Bulletin): Damascus Chamber of Commerce; tel. (11) 2218339; fax (11) 2225874; e-mail dcc@net.sy; f. 1922; quarterly; finance and investment; Editor GHASSAN KALLA.

Al-Sinaa (Industry): Damascus Chamber of Commerce, BP 1305, rue Mou'awiah, Harika, Damascus; tel. (11) 2222205; fax (11) 2225874; e-mail dcc@net.sy; monthly; commerce, industry and management; Editor Y. HINDI.

Souriya al-Arabiyya (Arab Syria): Ministry of Information, Immeuble Dar al-Baath, Autostrade Mezzeh, Damascus; tel. (11) 6622141; fax (11) 6617665; monthly; publicity; in four languages.

Syria Today: Baramkeh, Free Zone, Damascus; tel. (11) 88270310; fax (11) 2137343; internet www.syria-today.com; monthly; English; economic and social development; Chair. LOUMA TARABINE; Man. Editor FRANCESCA DE CHÂTEL.

Al-Tamaddon al-Islami (Islamic Civilization Society): Darwichiyah, Damascus; tel. (11) 2240562; fax (11) 3733563; e-mail isltmddn@hotmail.com; f. 1932; monthly; Arabic; religious; published by Al-Tamaddon al-Islami Assn; Pres. of Assn AHMAD MOUAZ AL-KHATIB.

Al-Yakza (The Awakening): Al-Yakza Association, BP 6677, rue Sisi, Aleppo; tel. (11) 1935; monthly; Arabic; literary social review of charitable institution; Dir HUSNI ABD AL-MASSIH.

Al-Zira'a (Agriculture): Ministry of Agriculture and Agrarian Reform, rue Jabri, Damascus; tel. (11) 2213613; fax (11) 2244023; f. 1985; monthly; Arabic; agriculture.

NEWS AGENCY

Syrian Arab News Agency (SANA): BP 2661, Baramka, Damascus; tel. (11) 2129702; fax (11) 2228265; e-mail sanagm@sana.sy; internet www.sana.sy; f. 1966; supplies bulletins on Syrian news to foreign news agencies; 9 offices abroad; 43 foreign correspondents; Dir-Gen. ABDUL RAHIM AHMED.

Publishers

Arab Advertising Organization: BP 2842-3034, 28 rue Moutanabbi, Damascus; tel. (11) 2225219; fax (11) 2220754; e-mail sy-adv@net.sy; internet www.elan-sy.com; f. 1963; exclusive govt establishment responsible for advertising; publishes *Directory of Commerce and Industry*, *Damascus International Fair Guide*, *Daily Bulletin of Official Tenders*; Dir-Gen. MONA F. FABAH.

Damascus University Press: Baramkeh, Damascus; tel. (11) 2119890; fax (11) 2235779; e-mail intrelation@damascusuniversity.edu.sy; internet www.damascusuniversity.edu.sy; f. 1923; medicine, engineering, social sciences, law, agriculture, arts, etc.; Dir HIBA AL-AWAD.

Dar al-Awael: BP 10181, Damascus; tel. (11) 44676270; fax (11) 44676273; e-mail alawael@scs-net.org; internet www.daralawael.com; f. 1999; academic publr; Dir-Gen. ISMAIL ABDULLAH.

Dar al-Fikr: BP 962, Damascus; tel. (11) 2211166; fax (11) 2239716; e-mail mailus@darfikr.com; internet darfikr.com; f. 1957; Islamic studies, academic and gen. non-fiction; Dir-Gen. MUHAMMAD ADNAN SALIM.

Institut Français du Proche-Orient: BP 344, Damascus; tel. (11) 3330214; fax (11) 3327887; e-mail secretariat@ifporient.org; internet www.ifporient.org; f. 1922; sociology, anthropology, Islamic studies, archaeology, history, language and literature, arts, philosophy, geography, religion; publs include *Syria* (biannual journal), *Bulletin d'Etudes Orientales* (annual journal), *Bibliothèque Archéologique et Historique* (series), *Publications de l'Institut Français de Damas* (series); Dir MICHEL MOUTON.

OFA-Business Consulting Center—Documents Service: BP 3550, 3 place Chahbandar, Damascus; tel. (11) 3318237; fax (11) 4426021; f. 1964; numerous periodicals, monographs and surveys on political and economic affairs; Dir-Gen. SAMIR A. DARWICH; one affiliated br., OFA-Business Consulting Centre (foreign co representation and services).

The Political Administration Press: BP 3320, blvd Palestine, Damascus; fax (11) 2125280; publishes *Al-Fikr al-Askari* (six a year) and *Jaysh al-Sha'ab* (monthly).

Syrian Documentation Papers: BP 2712, Damascus; f. 1968; publishers of *Bibliography of the Middle East* (annual), *General Directory of the Press and Periodicals in the Arab World* (annual), and numerous publications on political, economic, literary and social affairs, as well as legislative texts concerning Syria and the Arab world; Dir-Gen. LOUIS FARÈS.

Tishreen Foundation for Press and Publishing: BP 5452, Medan, Damascus; tel. (11) 2131100; fax (11) 2246860; publishes *Syria Times* and *Tishreen* (dailies).

United Group for Publishing, Advertising and Marketing: Immeuble al-Huda, rue al-Eskandaria, Mazzeh, Damascus; tel. (11) 6122515; fax (11) 6122514; internet www.ug.com.sy; publs *Baladna* newspaper, *Layalina* magazine, *What's On* magazine; Chair. MAJD SULEIMAN.

SYRIAN ARAB REPUBLIC

Al-Wahda Foundation for Press, Printing and Publishing (Institut al-Ouedha pour l'impression, édition et distribution): BP 2448, Dawar Kafr Soussat, Damascus; tel. (11) 225219; internet www.alwehda.gov.sy; publs *Al-Fida'*, *Al-Horubat*, *Al-Jamahir*, *Al-Thawra* and *Al-Wahda* (dailies), *Al-Maukef al-Riadi* (weekly) and other commercial publs; Dir-Gen. ZIAD GHOSN.

Broadcasting and Communications

TELECOMMUNICATIONS

Syrian Telecom: BP 11774, Autostrade Mezzeh, Damascus; tel. (11) 2240300; fax (11) 6110000; e-mail ste-gm@net.sy; internet www.syriantelecom.com.sy; f. 1975; Gen. Dir SAIF AL-DIN AL-HASSAN.

MTN Syria: BP 34474, Immeuble al-Mohandis al-Arabi, Autostrade Mezzeh, Damascus; tel. (944) 222-222; fax (11) 6666094; e-mail customercare@mtn.com.sy; internet www.mtn.com.sy; f. 2001 as Spacetel Syria; name changed to Areeba Syria in 2004; present name adopted in 2007 following the acquisition of a 75% stake by MTN Group (South Africa); provider of mobile telephone services; Chair. JAMAL RAMADAN; CEO ZIAD SABAH.

Syriatel: Immeuble STE, 6e étage, rue Thawra, Damascus; tel. (11) 23730000; fax (11) 6723006; e-mail info@syriatel.com.sy; internet syriatel.sy; f. 2000; provider of mobile telephone services; Chair. AHMED AL-ALI; CEO MOURID SAKHR AL-ATASSI.

BROADCASTING

Radio

General Organization of Radio and Television (ORTAS—Organisme de la Radio-Télévision Arabe Syrienne): place Omayyad, Damascus; tel. (11) 720700; fax (11) 2234930; e-mail ortas@ortas.gov.sy; internet ortas.online; radio broadcasts started in 1945, television broadcasts in 1960; radio directorate consists of four departments: Radi, Shaab, Shabab FM, and a multi-lingual news service; television directorate operates one satellite and two terrestrial channels, broadcasting in Arabic, English and French.

Syriana FM Radio: Damascus; f. 2012.

Television

General Organization of Radio and Television: see Radio.

Addounia TV: Damascus; tel. (11) 5667272; fax (11) 5667271; internet www.addounia.tv; privately owned news channel; awarded broadcasting licence mid-2007; began broadcasting Oct. 2008.

Talaqi TV: Damascus; f. 2012; Head MAHER AL-KHOULI.

Finance

BANKING

Central Bank

Central Bank of Syria (Banque Centrale de Syrie): POB 2254, Damascus; tel. (11) 9985; fax (11) 2223262; e-mail info@cb.gov.sy; internet cb.gov.sy; f. 1956; Gov. MUHAMMAD ISSAM HAZIMA.

Other Banks

Agricultural Co-operative Bank: BP 4325, rue al-Tajehiz, Damascus; tel. (11) 2213462; fax (11) 2221393; e-mail agrobank@mail.sy; internet agrobank.gov.sy; f. 1888; Chair. Dr ABDUL RAZZAQ QASIM.

Ahli Trust Bank: BP 6228, Damascus; tel. (11) 3346408; fax (11) 3346410; internet www.bankatb.com; f. 2005; 47% owned by Banque BEMO Saudi Fransi; private commercial bank; Chair. BASSAM MAMARI.

Arab Bank Syria SA (ABS): BP 38, rue al-Mahdi bin Barakeh, Abou Roumaneh, Damascus; tel. 963119421; fax (11) 3349844; internet arabbank-syria.sy; f. 2005; jt venture between Syrian investors (51%) and Arab Bank (Jordan—49%); private commercial bank; Chair. Dr KHALID WASSIF AL-WAZANI.

Bank of Syria and Overseas: BP 3103, Harika-Bab Barid, Lawyers' Syndicate Bldg, nr Chamber of Commerce, Damascus; tel. (11) 2260560; fax (11) 2260555; e-mail bsomail@bso.com.sy; internet www.bso.com.sy; f. 2004; jt venture between Banque du Liban et d'Outre Mer (BLOM, Lebanon—39%), the World Bank's Int. Finance Corpn (10%) and Syrian investors (51%); private commercial bank; Chair. Dr RATEB AL-SHALLAH; CEO MICHEL AZZAM.

Banque BEMO Saudi Fransi SA (BBSF): 39 rue Ayyar, Salhiah, Damascus; tel. (11) 3113020; fax (11) 3119499; e-mail info@bbsfbank.com; internet www.bbsfbank.com; f. 2004; jt venture between Syrian investors (51%), Banque Saudi Fransi (Saudi Arabia—27%) and Banque Européenne pour le Moyen-Orient (Lebanon—22%); private commercial bank; Chair. RIAD OBEGI; CEO OMAR AL-GHARAWI.

Byblos Bank Syria: BP 5424, al-Chaalan, rue Amine Loutfi Hafez, Damascus; tel. (11) 3348240; fax (11) 3348205; e-mail byblosbanksyria@byblosbank.com; internet www.bbs.sy; f. 2005; 41.5% owned by Byblos Bank SAL (Lebanon), 51% by Syrian investors and 7.5% by the Org. of Petroleum Exporting Countries' Fund for Int. Devt; private commercial bank.

CHAM Bank: BP 33979, place al-Najmeh, Damascus; tel. (11) 33919; fax (11) 3348731; e-mail info@chambank.com; internet www.chambank.com; f. 2006; jt venture between Dar Investment Co (Kuwait—12.5%), Commercial Bank of Kuwait (10%), Islamic Devt Bank (Kuwait—9%) and several Syrian and other Gulf investors; private commercial bank run on Islamic principles; Chair. ALI YOUSEF AL-AWADHI.

Commercial Bank of Syria (Banque Commerciale de Syrie): BP 933, place Yousuf al-Azmeh, Damascus; tel. (11) 2381400; e-mail info@cbs-bank.sy; internet www.cbs-bank.sy; f. 1967; govt-owned bank; Chair. Dr ESSAM QUREIT; Gen. Man. Dr ALI YOUSSEF.

Industrial Bank: BP 7578, Immeuble Dar al-Mohandessin, rue Maysaloon, Damascus; tel. (11) 2245514; fax (11) 2228412; e-mail ind-bank@mail.sy; internet www.industrialbank.gov.sy; f. 1959; nationalized bank providing finance for industry; Gen. Man. WAJIH BITAR.

International Bank for Trade and Finance: place Hejazz, Damascus; tel. (11) 2388000; fax (11) 2325789; e-mail info@ibtf.com.sy; internet www.ibtf.com.sy; f. 2004; 49% owned by Housing Bank for Trade and Finance (Jordan), 51% by Syrian investors; private commercial bank; CEO FADI AL-JALILATI.

Popular Credit Bank: BP 2841, 6e étage, Immeuble Dar al-Mohandessin, rue Maysaloon, Damascus; tel. (11) 2215752; fax (11) 2230624; internet www.pcb-bank.sy; f. 1967; govt-owned bank; provides loans to the services sector and is sole authorized issuer of savings certificates; Chair. Dr MUNTHER AL-AWWAD; Dir-Gen. Dr NIDAL AL-ARBEED.

Real Estate Bank: BP 2337, place Yousuf al-Azmeh, Damascus; tel. (11) 2218602; fax (11) 2233107; e-mail support@reb.sy; internet www.reb.sy; f. 1966; govt-owned bank; provides loans and grants for housing, schools, hospitals and hotel construction; Chair. Dr BASIL ASSAAD; Gen. Man. Dr MADIN ALI.

Syria International Islamic Bank: BP 35494, Damascus; tel. (11) 2053; e-mail info@siib.sy; internet www.siib.sy; f. 2006; 49% Qatari-owned (incl. Qatar Int. Islamic Bank—30%); private commercial bank run on Islamic principles; Chair. TAYSEER AL-ZOUBI; CEO BASHAR AL-SITT.

Syrian Lebanese Commercial Bank SAL (SLCB): c/o Commercial Bank of Syria, BP 933, Immeuble G.M., 6e étage, place Yousuf Azmeh, Damascus; tel. (11) 2225206; fax (11) 2243224; e-mail info@slcb.com.lb; internet www.slcb.com.lb; f. 1974; 84.2% owned by Commercial Bank of Syria, 10% by Banque du Crédit Populaire SAL, 5% by Syrian Insurance Co; head office in Beirut, Lebanon; Gen. Man. ALI MOHAMED YOUSSEF.

STOCK EXCHANGE

Damascus Securities Exchange: BP 6564, Damascus; tel. (11) 5190000; fax (11) 5190099; e-mail info@dse.sy; internet www.dse.sy; f. 2009; 27 listed cos (Jan. 2023); Chair. FADI AL-JALILATI.

Supervisory Body

Syrian Commission on Financial Markets and Securities: BP 31845, Damascus; tel. (11) 3310950; fax (11) 3310722; e-mail info@scfms.sy; internet www.scfms.sy; f. 2005; Chair. Dr ABDUL RAZZAQ QASIM.

INSURANCE

Arabia Insurance Co—Syria (AICS): POB 34801, Damascus; tel. (11) 9405; e-mail arabia-insurance@arabiasyria.com; internet www.arabiasyria.com; f. 2006; Gen. Man. BASSEL ABBOUD.

General Social Security Organization: BP 2684, rue Port Said, Damascus; tel. (11) 2323116; e-mail info@taminat.gov.sy; internet www.taminat.gov.sy; Dir-Gen. KHALAF AL-ABDULLAH.

Syria International Insurance (Arobe Syria): BP 33015, Hosari Bldg, 1st Floor, al-Brazil St, Tajheez, Damascus; tel. (11) 9279; fax (11) 3348144; e-mail info@aropesyria.com; internet www.aropesyria.com; f. 2006; owned by Arope Insurance (Lebanon); all classes of insurance; Gen. Man. Dr MAHER AMARI.

Syrian General Organization for Insurance (Syrian Insurance Co): BP 2279, 29 rue Ayyar, Damascus; tel. (11) 2218430; fax (11) 2220494; e-mail syrinsur@syrian-insurance.com; f. 1953; nationalized co; operates throughout Syria; Chair. ADEL AL-KADAMANI; Dir-Gen. SULAYMAN AL-HASSAN.

SYRIAN ARAB REPUBLIC

Syrian Kuwaiti Insurance Co: BP 5778, 7 April St, Mazzeh, Damascus; tel. (11) 9276; fax (11) 6645130; internet www.skicins.com; f. 2006; owned by Gulf Insurance Co of Kuwait; all classes of insurance; Chair. KHALID SAUD AL-HASSAN; Gen. Man. SAMER FOUAD BAKDASH.

Trust Syria Insurance Co: BP 30578, Immeuble Trust, rue Murshid Khatir, Damascus; tel. (11) 4472650; fax (11) 4472652; e-mail mail@trustsyria.com; internet www.trustsyria.com; f. 2006; all classes of insurance; CEO GHAZI ABU NAHEL.

United Insurance Co: Abo Rummaneh, Damascus; tel. (11) 3330241; fax (11) 3341933; e-mail info@uic.com.sy; internet www.uic.com.sy; f. 2006; awarded Syria's first private insurance co licence in 2006; Chair. MARAWAN AFFAKI; Gen. Man. MALEK AL-BUTROS.

Supervisory Body

Syrian Insurance Supervisory Commission (SISC): POB 5648, 29 Ayar St, Insurance Bldg, Damascus; tel. (11) 3061; fax (11) 2226224; e-mail sisc.sy@mail.sy; internet www.sisc.sy; f. 2004; Gen. Man. RAAFID MOHAMMAD.

Trade and Industry

STATE ENTERPRISES

Syrian industry is almost entirely under state control. There are national organizations responsible to the appropriate ministry for the operation of all sectors of industry, of which the following are examples:

Cotton Marketing Organization: BP 729, rue Bab al-Faraj, Aleppo; tel. (21) 2238486; fax (21) 2218617; e-mail cmo-aleppo@mail.sy; internet www.cmo.gov.sy; f. 1965; governmental authority for purchase of seed cotton, ginning and sales of cotton lint; Pres. and Dir-Gen. Dr AHMAD SOUHAD GEBBARA.

General Company for Phosphate and Mines (GECOPHAM): BP 288, Homs; tel. (31) 2751122; fax (31) 2751123; e-mail info@gecopham.sy; internet gecopham.sy; f. 1970; production and export of phosphate rock; Gen. Man. YOUNES RAMADAN.

General Organization for Engineering Industries: BP 3120, Damascus; tel. (11) 2121824; fax (11) 2116201; e-mail goengind@net.sy; internet www.handasieh.sy; 14 subsidiary cos.

General Organization for the Exploitation and Development of the Euphrates Basin (GOEDEB): Raqqa; Dir-Gen. Dr Eng. AHMAD SOUHAD GEBBARA.

General Organization for Food Industry (GOFI): BP 105, rue al-Fardous, Damascus; tel. (11) 2457008; fax (11) 2457021; e-mail foodindustry@mail.sy; internet www.syriafoods.net; f. 1975; food processing and marketing; Chair. and Gen. Dir KHALIL JAWAD.

General Organization for the Textile Industries: BP 620, rue al-Fardoss, Bawabet al-Salhieh, Damascus; tel. (11) 2216200; fax (11) 2216201; e-mail syr-textile@mail.sy; internet textile.org.sy; f. 1975; control and planning of the textile industry and supervision of textile manufacture; 27 subsidiary cos; Dir-Gen. Dr JAMAL AL-OMAR.

Syrian Petroleum Company (SPC): BP 2849, Damascus; tel. (11) 9247; fax (11) 3137979; e-mail spccom1@scs-net.org; internet www.spc.com.sy; f. 1958; state agency; holds the oil and gas concession for all Syria; exploits the Al-Suweida, Karatchouk, Rumelan and Jbeisseh oilfields; also organizes exploration, production and marketing of oil and gas nationally; Man. Dir Dr Eng. FIRAS KADDOUR.

Al-Furat Petroleum Co: BP 7660, Damascus; tel. (11) 6183333; fax (11) 6184444; e-mail afpc@fpc.net.sy; internet afpc.sy; f. 1985; 50% owned by SPC and 50% by a foreign consortium of Syria Shell Petroleum Devt B.V. and Deminex Syria GmbH; exploits oilfields in the Euphrates river area; Chair. SAID HUNEDI; Gen. Man. OLE MYKLESTAD.

DEVELOPMENT ORGANIZATIONS

State Planning Commission: Rukeneddin, Damascus; tel. (11) 5161015; fax (11) 5161010; internet www.planning.gov.sy; Head AMER HOSNI LUTFI.

Syrian Consulting Bureau for Development and Investment: BP 12574, Bldg 1, Abu Roummaneh, Jadet bin al-Haytham, Damascus; tel. (11) 3340710; fax (11) 3340711; e-mail scb@scbdi.com; internet www.scbdi.com; f. 1991; ind; Man. Dir NABIL SUKKAR.

CHAMBERS OF COMMERCE AND INDUSTRY

Federation of Syrian Chambers of Commerce: BP 5909, rue Mousa Ben Nousair, Damascus; tel. (11) 3337344; fax (11) 3331127; e-mail syr-trade@mail.sy; internet www.fedcommsyr.org; f. 1975; Pres. MUHAMMAD GHASSAN AL-QALLA'A; Sec.-Gen. MUHAMMAD HAMSHO.

Aleppo Chamber of Commerce: BP 1261, Aleppo; tel. (21) 2238236; fax (21) 2214096; e-mail info@aleppochamber.sy; internet www.aleppochamber.sy; f. 1885; Pres. MUHAMMAD AMER HAMWI; Gen. Sec. MOHAMMED FADEL KATERJI.

Aleppo Chamber of Industry: Abd al-Rahman al-Kawakbi St, Aleppo; tel. (21) 2033; fax (21) 2116385; e-mail info@aci.org.sy; internet www.aci.org.sy; f. 1935; Pres. FARES SHEHABI; Gen. Man. MUHAMMAD GHREWATI.

Damascus Chamber of Commerce: BP 1040, rue Mou'awiah, Damascus; tel. (11) 2245475; fax (11) 2225874; e-mail dcc@net.sy; internet www.dcc-sy.com; f. 1890; Pres. MUHAMMAD ABU AL-HODA AL-LAHHAM.

Damascus Chamber of Industry: BP 1305, rue Harika Mou'awiah, Damascus; tel. (11) 2215042; fax (11) 2245981; e-mail dci@mail.sy; internet www.dci-syria.org; Pres. SAMER AL-DEBS; Sec. MOHAMED AKRAM HALLAQ.

Hama Chamber of Commerce: BP 147, rue al-Kouatly, Hama; tel. (33) 2525203; fax (33) 2517701; e-mail hamacham@scs-net.org; internet www.hamachamber.com; f. 1934; Pres. ABDEL LATEEF SHAKER; Man. Dir FIRAS KAZKAZ.

Homs Chamber of Commerce: BP 440, rue Abou al-Of, Homs; tel. (31) 2471000; fax (31) 2464247; e-mail hcc@homschamber.com; internet homschamber.com; f. 1928; Pres. IYAD DRACK SIBAI; Gen. Man. M. FARES HUSSAMI.

Latakia Chamber of Commerce and Industry: 8 rue Attar, Latakia; tel. (41) 479531; fax (41) 478526; e-mail lattakia@chamberlattakia.com; internet www.chamberlattakia.com; Pres. KAMAL ISMAIL AL-ASSAD.

Tartous Chamber of Commerce and Industry: POB 403, Tartous; tel. (43) 329852; fax (43) 329728; internet tcci-sy.net; Pres. WAHIB KAMEL MERI; Sec.-Gen. KIFAH QADDOUR.

UTILITIES

Electricity

Public Establishment for Electricity Generation and Transmission (PEEGT): BP 3386, 17 rue Nessan, Damascus; tel. (11) 2229654; fax (11) 2229062; e-mail peegt@net.sy; f. 1965; present name adopted 1994; state-owned; operates 11 power stations through subsidiary cos; Dir-Gen. Dr AHMAD AL-ALI; Gen. Man. HISHAM MASIAJ.

Gas

Syrian Gas Company: BP 4499, Homs; tel. (31) 2496101; fax (31) 2496640; e-mail info@sgc.gov.sy; internet www.sgc.gov.sy; f. 2003; state-owned; responsible for production, processing and distribution of gas supplies; Dir-Gen. Eng. AMIN AL-DAGHRI.

Water

The Ministry of Water Resources is responsible for planning and regulation in the Syrian water sector; it oversees the operations of 14 regional water establishments that manage the provision of drinking water and sewerage facilities. The Ministry of Water Resources is responsible for the management of water resources and the provision of irrigation water. An Integrated Water Resource Management Project, co-ordinated by the State Planning Commission, was initiated in 2006 with the aim of modernizing and integrating the various authorities responsible for the sector.

MAJOR INVESTMENT HOLDING COMPANIES

CHAM Holding: Sahnaya–Dar'a Highway, Damascus; tel. (11) 9962; fax (11) 6731274; e-mail info@chamholding.sy; internet www.chamholding.sy; f. 2007; investment holding; real estate, utilities, transport, tourism, financial services; Chair. TARIQ KREISHATI.

Nahas Enterprises Group: BP 3050, Damascus; tel. (11) 2234000; fax (11) 222 88 61; e-mail info@nahas.sy; internet www.nahas-group.com; f. 1900; transport, tourism, hospitality, chemicals and infrastructure; Chair., Pres. and CEO SAEB NAHAS.

Souria Holding: BP 3852, Immeuble 3, rue Misr, Abou Roummaneh, Damascus; tel. (11) 3329100; fax (11) 3316065; e-mail info@souriaholding.com; internet www.souriaholding.com; f. 2007; real estate, hospitality, retail, health care and infrastructure; Chair. HAYTHAM SOUBHI JOUD.

MAJOR COMPANIES

Fouad Takla Co: BP 2785, Immeuble Takla 15, place Arnos, Damascus; tel. (11) 4416761; fax (11) 4421910; e-mail contact@fouadtakla.com; internet www.fouadtakla.com; f. 1964; construction and devt.

Al-Matin Group: BP 1191, Homs; tel. (31) 5360586; fax (31) 5360585; e-mail info@almatin.com; internet almatin.com; f. 1976; mfrs of polypropylene bags, packaging materials and plastic pipes.

NASCO Group: BP 3993, Damascus; tel. (11) 3319200; fax (11) 3319220; e-mail nasco@net.sy; internet www.thenascogroup.com; f. 1988; oilfield contracting and services; five affiliate cos; Chair. ATTIA NASREDDIN.

National Co for Pharmaceutical Industry (NCPI): BP 13020, Aleppo; tel. (21) 2251310; fax (21) 2120504; e-mail info@ncpipharma.com; f. 1989; drugs mfrs; Chair. and Man. Dir HAYSSAM AL-KAMAL.

TRADE UNIONS

General Federation of Labour Unions (Ittihad Naqabat al-Ummal al-Am fi Suriya): BP 2351, rue Qanawat, Damascus; f. 1948; Chair. MUHAMMAD SHAABAN AZZOUZ; Sec. MAHMOUD FAHURI.

Order of Syrian Engineers and Architects: BP 2336, Immeuble al-Mohandessin, place Azmeh, Damascus; tel. (11) 2214916; fax (11) 2216948; e-mail osea.sy@hotmail.com; f. 1950; Pres. Dr GHYATH KATINI.

Transport

RAILWAYS

A new railway line linking Aleppo with Mersin in southern Turkey (now known as Türkiye) began operating in March 2009. Another new line connecting Aleppo with Gaziantep, also in southern Turkey, was inaugurated in December; services commenced in late 2010. Meanwhile, by 2011 plans were under way for a mixed underground/elevated metro system in Damascus. Construction work on the 16.5-km Green Line, comprising 17 stations, was initially scheduled to commence in 2012, with completion anticipated by 2016. However, the project was halted by the country's descent into civil conflict.

General Establishment of Syrian Railways: Al Razi St, Aleppo; tel. (21) 2213900; e-mail mailoffice@cfssyria.sy; internet www.cfssyria.sy; f. 1897; Dir-Gen. NAJIB AL-FARES.

General Organization of the Hedjaz-Syrian Railway: BP 2978, rue Hedjaz, Damascus; tel. (11) 3331625; internet hijazerail.com; f. 1908; the Hedjaz Railway has 347 km of track (gauge 1,050 mm) in Syria; services operate between Damascus and Amman, Jordan, on a branch line of about 24 km from Damascus to Katana, and there is a further line of 64 km from Damascus to Serghaya; Dir-Gen. MAHMOUD SAQBANI.

ROADS

In mid-2009 the Government announced plans for the construction of two major new highways: a north–south highway linking Bab al-Hawha, near the Turkish border, with Nasib, on the border with Jordan; and an east–west highway linking the Mediterranean port of Tartous with the Iraqi border. However, progress on these projects came to a halt as Syria descended into civil conflict from 2011.

Public Establishment for Road Communications: rue Hamra, Damascus; tel. (11) 2221133; fax (11) 3319199; e-mail it@perc.gov.sy; internet www.perc.gov.sy; f. 2003; Dir-Gen. Eng. YASSER HAIDER.

SHIPPING

Latakia is Syria's principal port; it has a 972-m quay with draughts ranging from 11.8 m–13.3 m. A concession to manage and operate the container terminal at Latakia was awarded to a consortium led by the French CMA CGM Group in 2009. Syria's other major ports are at Banias and Tartous.

Regulatory and Port Authorities

General Directorate of Syrian Ports: BP 505, rue Algerie, Latakia; tel. (41) 2573333; fax (41) 2575805; e-mail info@gdp.gov.sy; internet www.gdp.gov.sy; Dir-Gen. Rear-Adm. SAMER KOBRUSLY.

Latakia Port Authority: BP 220, rue Baghdad, Latakia; tel. (41) 476452; fax (41) 475760; e-mail info@lattakiaport.gov.sy; internet www.lattakiaport.gov.sy; Gen. Man. HATEM AMJAD SAREE SULAIMAN.

Syrian General Authorities for Maritime Transport (SYRIA-MAR): BP 314, place Zat al-Sawary, Latakia; tel. (41) 370681; fax (41) 371013.

Tartous Port Authority: El Mina St, BP 86, Tartous; tel. (43) 313752; fax (43) 315602; e-mail info@tartousport.gov.sy; internet www.tartousport.gov.sy.

Principal Shipping Companies

Ismail, A. M., Shipping Agency Ltd: BP 74, rue al-Mina, Tartous; tel. (43) 221987; fax (43) 318949; operates eight general cargo vessels; Man. Dir MAHMOUD ISMAIL.

Muhieddine Shipping Co: BP 1099, rue al-Chourinish, Tartous; tel. (43) 323090; fax (43) 317139; internet www.muhieddineshipping.net; operates seven general cargo ships.

Riamar Shipping Co Ltd: BP 284, Immeuble Tarwin, rue du Port, Tartous; tel. (43) 314999; fax (43) 212616; operates six general cargo vessels; Chair. and Man. Dir ABD AL-KADER SABRA.

Al-Sham Shipping Co: BP 33436, Damascus; tel. (11) 3311960; fax (11) 3311961; e-mail al-sham@al-sham.com; internet www.al-sham.com; f. 1994; operates two general cargo vessels; Chair. MUHAMMAD A. HAYKAL.

Syro-Jordanian Shipping Co: BP 148, rue Port Said, Latakia; tel. (41) 471635; fax (41) 470250; e-mail syjomar@net.sy; f. 1976; operates two general cargo ships; Chair. OSMAN LEBBADY; Tech. Man. M. CHOUMAN.

Tartous International Container Terminal JSC: BP 870, Tartous; tel. (43) 328882; fax (43) 328831; e-mail info@ictsi.sy; internet www.ictsi-sy.com; f. 2006; owned by; in 2006 Philippines-base International Container Terminal Services, Inc was awarded a 10-year concession to operate a container terminal at Tartous; the concession was terminated in Jan. 2013; CEO and Gen. Man. ROMEO A. SALVADOR.

CIVIL AVIATION

There are international airports at Damascus and Aleppo. Syrianair also operates domestic flights from airports in Qamishli and Deir el-Zor. However, following the outbreak of civil conflict in 2011 the number of flights operated from and to Syrian airports seriously declined.

Syrian Civil Aviation Authority (SCAA): BP 6257, place Nejmeh, Damascus; tel. (11) 3333815; fax (11) 2232201; e-mail info@scaa.sy; internet scaa.sy; Chair. Maj.-Gen. OMAR RIDA; Dir-Gen. Eng. BASEM MANSOUR.

Cham Wings Airlines: rue al-Fardous, Damascus; tel. (11) 2158111; e-mail cs@chamwings.com; internet chamwings.com; f. 2007; first private int. airline in Syria; flights from Damascus serving destinations in the Middle East and Europe; Chair. ISSAM SHAMMOUT.

Syrian Arab Airlines (Syrianair): BP 417, Social Insurance Bldg, 5th Floor, Youssef al-Azmeh Sq., Damascus; tel. (11) 2450098; fax (11) 22492323498132; e-mail feedback@syriaair.com; internet www.syriaair.com; f. 1946; refounded 1961 to succeed Syrian Airways, after revocation of merger with Misrair (Egypt); domestic passenger and cargo services (from Damascus, Aleppo, Latakia and Deir el-Zor) and routes to Europe, the Middle East, North Africa and the Far East; Chair. and Man. Dir NACHAAT NUMIR; Dir-Gen. TALAL ABDEL KARIM.

Tourism

Middle East Tourism: BP 201, Malki St, Shawki Ave, Damascus; tel. (11) 3325655; fax (11) 3326266; e-mail daadouche@net.sy; internet www.daadouche.com; f. 1952; Pres. MAHER DAADOUCHE.

Syrian Arab Co for Hotels and Tourism (SACHA): BP 5549, Mezzeh, Damascus; tel. (11) 2223286; fax (11) 2219415; f. 1977; Chair. DIRAR JUMA'A; Gen. Man. ELIAS ABOUTARA.

Defence

As assessed at November 2022, the total strength of the Syrian armed forces was 169,000: army est. 130,000—including conscripts; air defence command—an army command—est. 20,000; navy est. 4,000; air force est. 15,000. Paramilitary forces were estimated to number 100,000, with the National Defence Force, an umbrella of disparate regime militias, accounting for some 50,000. Military service is officially compulsory for a duration of 30 months.

The total strength of anti-Government forces was estimated at 132,500 at November 2022: Syrian Democratic Forces (a coalition of rebel forces led by Kurdish groups, based in north-east Syria) c. 50,000; Syrian National Army (SNA—comprising predominantly Syrian Arab and Turkmen rebels operating under Turkish command in the Aleppo governorate and north-west Syria; also includes National Front for Liberation, which began to merge with SNA in late 2019) c. 70,000; Hayat Tahrir al-Sham (formerly known as Jabhat al-Nusra) c. 10,000; Huras al-Din (an al-Qa'ida affiliate) c. 2,500.

Defence Budget: £S243,000m. (est.) in 2012.

Commander-in-Chief of the Army and Armed Forces: Lt-Gen. BASHAR AL-ASSAD.

Minister of Defence and Deputy Commander-in-Chief of the Army and Armed Forces: Lt-Gen. ALI MAHMOUD ABBAS.

Chief of the General Staff of the Army and Armed Forces: Maj.-Gen. ABDEL KARIM MAHMOUD IBRAHIM.

Navy Commander: Maj.-Gen. MOHSEN ISSA.

Republican Guard Commander: Brig.-Gen. MALIK ALIAA.

Education

Primary education, which begins at six years of age and lasts for six years, is officially compulsory. In 2014 primary enrolment included 83% of children in the relevant age-group. Secondary education, beginning at 12 years of age, lasts for a further six years, comprising two cycles of three years each. In 2014 enrolment at secondary schools included 48% of children in the appropriate age-group.

There are agricultural and technical schools for vocational training. The main language of instruction in schools is Arabic, but English and French are widely taught as second languages. The combined budgetary expenditure of the Ministries of Education and of Higher Education in 2008 was estimated at £S63,286m., equivalent to some 10.5% of total government spending.

The United Nations Relief and Works Agency for Palestine Refugees in the Near East (UNRWA) provides education for Palestinian refugees in Syria. At January 2022 UNRWA operated 102 schools in Syria, with an estimated total enrolment of 49,500 pupils.

Bibliography

Abboud, Samer, and Arslanian, Ferdinand. *Syria's Economy and the Transition Paradigm*. St Andrews Papers on Contemporary Syria, Boulder, CO, Lynne Rienner Publishers, 2008.

Abboud, Samer, and Said, Salam. *Syrian Foreign Trade and Economic Reform*. Boulder, CO, Lynne Rienner Publishers, 2009.

Alhouis, Ahed. *U.S. Foreign Policy Towards Syria: Perceiving Syria*. Abingdon, Routledge, 2015.

Allsopp, Harriet. *The Kurds of Syria: Political Parties and Identity in the Middle East*. London, I. B. Tauris, 2014.

Allsopp, Harriet, and van Wilgenburg, Wladimir. *The Kurds of Northern Syria: Governance, Diversity and Conflicts*. London, I. B. Tauris, 2019.

Beck, Martin, Jung, Dietrich, and Seeberg, Peter. *The Levant in Turmoil: Syria, Palestine, and the Transformation of Middle Eastern Politics*. London, Palgrave Macmillan, 2016.

Belcastro, Francesco. *Syrian Foreign Policy: The Alliances of a Regional Power*. London, Routledge, 2019.

Bentley, Michelle. *Syria and the Chemical Weapons Taboo: Exploiting the Forbidden*. Manchester, Manchester University Press, 2016.

Beshara, Adel (Ed.). *The Origins of Syrian Nationhood: Histories, Pioneers and Identity*. Abingdon, Routledge, 2011.

Bseiso, Jehan, Hofman, Michiel, and Whittall, Jonathan (Eds). *Everybody's War: The Politics of Aid in the Syria Crisis*. Oxford, Oxford University Press, 2022.

Çakmak, Cenap. *Post-Conflict Syrian State and Nation Building: Economic and Political Development*. New York, Palgrave Macmillan, 2015.

Chaitani, Youssef. *Post-colonial Syria and Lebanon: The Decline of Arab Nationalism and the Triumph of the State*. London, I. B. Tauris, 2007.

Chatty, Dawn. *Syria; the Making and Unmaking of a Refuge State*. London, C. Hurst & Co, 2017.

Chen, Zhao, Jizhou, Zhao, and Mengmeng, Huang. *Syrian Civil War and Europe*. Abingdon, Routledge, 2022.

Çiçek, M. Talha. *War and State Formation in Syria: Cemal Pasha's Governorate during World War I, 1914–1917*. Abingdon, Routledge, 2014.

Commins, David. *Historical Dictionary of Syria* (3rd edn). Lanham, MD, Scarecrow Press, 2014.

Cordesman, Anthony H. *Israel and Syria: The Military Balance and Prospects of War*. Westport, CT, Praeger Security International, 2008.

Dagher, Sam. *Assad or We Burn the Country: How One Family's Lust for Power Destroyed Syria*. New York, Little, Brown, 2020.

Donati, Caroline. *L'exception syrienne: entre modernisation et résistance*. Paris, Editions La Découverte, 2009.

Fedden, Robin. *Syria: an Historical Appreciation*. London, 1946.

Firro, Kais M. *Metamorphosis of the Nation (al-Umma): The Rise of Arabism and Minorities in Syria and Lebanon, 1850–1940*. Eastbourne, Sussex Academic Press, 2009.

Gani, Jasmine K. *The Role of Ideology in Syrian-US Relations: Conflict and Cooperation*. Basingstoke, Palgrave Macmillan, 2014.

Gani, Jasmine K., and Hinnebusch, Raymond (Eds). *Actors and Dynamics in the Syrian Conflict's Middle Phase: Between Contentious Politics, Militarization and Regime Resilience*. Abingdon, Routledge, 2022.

Ghrawi, Amer Nizar. *An Elusive Hope: State Reform in Syria, 2000–2007*. Berlin, Klaus Schwarz Verlag, 2015.

Goodarzi, Jubin. *Syria and Iran: Diplomatic Alliance and Power Politics in the Middle East*. London, I. B. Tauris, 2009.

Greenhalgh, Michael. *Syria's Monuments: Their Survival and Destruction*. Leiden, Brill, 2017.

Gunter, Michael M. *Out of Nowhere: The Kurds of Syria in Peace and War*. London, Hurst & Co, 2014.

Haddad, Bassam. *Business Networks in Syria: The Political Economy of Authoritarian Resilience*. Palo Alto, CA, Stanford University Press, 2011.

Haddad, J. *Fifty Years of Modern Syria and Lebanon*. Beirut, 1950.

Hetou, Ghaidaa. *The Syrian Conflict: The Role of Russia, Iran and the US in a Global Crisis*. New Delhi, Routledge India, 2018.

Heydemann, Steven. *Authoritarianism in Syria: Institutions and Social Conflict, 1946–1970*. Ithaca, NY, Cornell University Press, 1998.

Heydemann, Steven, and Leenders, Reinoud (Eds). *Middle East Authoritarianisms: Governance, Contestation, and Regime Resilience in Syria and Iran*. Redwood City, CA, Stanford University Press, 2013.

Hinnebusch, Raymond E. *Authoritarian Power and State Formation in Ba'thist Syria: Army, Party and Peasant*. Oxford, Westview Press, 1990.

Hinnebusch, Raymond E. et al. *Syrian Foreign Policy and the United States: From Bush to Obama*. St Andrews Papers on Contemporary Syria, Boulder, CO, Lynne Rienner Publishers, 2009.

Hinnebusch, Raymond E., and Schmidt, Søren. *The State and the Political Economy of Reform in Syria*. St Andrews Papers on Contemporary Syria, Boulder, CO, Lynne Rienner Publishers, 2008.

Hinnebusch, Raymond E., and Tür, Özlem (Eds). *Turkey-Syria Relations: Between Enmity and Amity*. Farnham, Ashgate, 2013.

Hokayem, Emile. *Syria's Uprising and the Fracturing of the Levant*. London, International Institute for Strategic Studies, 2013.

Homet, M. *L'Histoire secrète du traité franco-syrien*. New edn, Paris, 1951.

Hopwood, Derek. *Syria 1945–1986*. Abingdon, Routledge, 2013.

Kedar, Mordechai. *Asad in Search of Legitimacy: Messages and Rhetoric in the Syrian Press, 1970–2000*. Brighton, Sussex Academic Press, 2004.

Khatib, Line. *Islamic Revivalism in Syria: The Rise and Fall of Ba'thist Secularism*. Abingdon, Routledge, 2011.

Khoury, Philip Shukry. *Syria and the French Mandate: The Politics of Arab Nationalism, 1920–1945*. Princeton, NJ, Princeton University Press, 2014.

Kienle, Eberhard (Ed.). *Contemporary Syria: Liberalization between Cold War and Cold Peace*. London, I. B. Tauris, 1994.

Lawson, Fred H. *Why Syria Goes to War: Thirty Years of Confrontation*. Cornell University Press, 1996.

(Ed.). *Demystifying Syria*. London, Saqi Books, 2009.

Lefèvre, Raphaël. *Ashes of Hama: The Muslim Brotherhood in Syria*. London, C. Hurst & Co, 2013.

Lesch, David W. *The New Lion of Damascus: Bashar al-Asad and Modern Syria*. Yale University Press, 2005.

Syria: The Fall of the House of Assad. New Haven, CT, Yale University Press, 2013.

Syria. Cambridge, Polity Press, 2019.

Leverett, Flynt L. *Inheriting Syria: Bashar's Trial by Fire*. Washington, DC, Brookings Institution Press, 2005.

Lister, Charles R. *The Syrian Jihad: Al-Qaeda, the Islamic State and the Evolution of an Insurgency*. London, Hurst & Co, 2017.

Lobmeyer, Hans Gunther. *Opposition and Resistance in Syria*. London, I. B. Tauris, 2004.

Matar, Linda, and Kadri, Ali (Eds). *Syria: From National Independence to Proxy War*. Cham, Palgrave Macmillan, 2019.

Mazur, Kevin. *Revolution in Syria: Identity, Networks, and Repression*. Cambridge, Cambridge University Press, 2021.

McHugo, John. *Syria: From the Great War to Civil War*. London, Saqi Books, 2014.

Perthes, Volker. *The Political Economy of Syria Under Asad*. London, I. B. Tauris, 1995.

Syria under Bashar al-Asad: Modernisation and the Limits of Change. Abingdon, Routledge, 2005.

Phillips, Christopher. *The Battle for Syria: International Rivalry in the New Middle East*. New Haven, CT, Yale University Press, 2016.

Pierret, Thomas. *Religion and State in Syria: The Sunni Ulama from Coup to Revolution*. Cambridge, Cambridge University Press, 2013.

Pipes, Daniel. *Greater Syria: the History of an Ambition*. New York, Oxford University Press, 1990.

Provence, Michael. *The Great Syrian Revolt and the Rise of Arab Nationalism*. Austin, TX, University of Texas Press, 2005.

Rabil, Robert G. *Syria, the United States, and the War on Terror in the Middle East*. Westport, CT, and London, Praeger Security International, 2006.

Rabinovich, Itamar. *The Brink of Peace. The Israeli-Syrian Negotiations*. Princeton, NJ, Princeton University Press, 1999.

The View from Damascus: State, Political Community and Foreign Relations in Twentieth-Century Syria. London, Vallentine Mitchell & Co Ltd, 2008.

Rabinovich, Itamar, and Valensi, Carmit. *Syrian Requiem: The Civil War and Its Aftermath*. Princeton, NJ, Princeton University Press, 2021.

Ramírez Díaz, Naomí. *The Muslim Brotherhood in Syria: the Democratic Option of Islamism*. Abingdon, Routledge, 2017.

Rathmell, Andrew. *Secret War in the Middle East: The Covert Struggle for Syria, 1949–1961*. London, I. B. Tauris, 1995.

Roberts, David. *The Ba'th and the Creation of Modern Syria*. Abingdon, Routledge, 1987.

Rubin, Barry. *The Truth About Syria*. London, Palgrave Macmillan, 2007.

Saleh, Yassin al-Haj. *The Impossible Revolution: Making Sense of the Syrian Tragedy*. London, C. Hurst & Co, 2017.

Scheller, Bente. *The Wisdom of Syria's Waiting Game: Syrian Foreign Policy Under the Assads*. London, Hurst, 2013.

Schmidinger, Thomas. *Rojava: Revolution, War and the Future of Syria's Kurds*, (trans. by Schiffmann, Michael). London, Pluto Press, 2018

Silander, Daniel, and Wallace, Don. *International Organizations and the Implementation of the Responsibility to Protect: the Humanitarian Crisis in Syria*. Abingdon, Routledge, 2015.

Smith, Lee. *The Consequences of Syria*. Stanford, CA, Hoover Institution Press, 2014.

Sottimano, Aurora, and Selvik, Kjetil. *Changing Regime Discourse and Reform in Syria*. St Andrews, University of St Andrews Centre for Syrian Studies, 2008.

Sunayama, Sonoko. *Syria and Saudi Arabia: Collaboration and Conflicts in the Oil Era*. London, I. B. Tauris, 2007.

Tejel, Jordi. *Syria's Kurds: History, Politics and Society*. Abingdon, Routledge, 2008.

Tibawi, A. L. *Syria*. London, 1962.

Torrey, Gordon H. *Syrian Politics and the Military*. Ohio State University, 1964.

Van Dam, Nikolaos. *The Struggle for Power in Syria*. London, Croom Helm, 1979.

Destroying a Nation: the Civil War in Syria. London, I. B. Tauris, 2017.

von Maltzahn, Nadia. *The Syria-Iran Axis: Cultural Diplomacy and International Relations in the Middle East*. London, I. B. Tauris, 2013.

Yildiz, Kerim. *The Kurds in Syria: The Forgotten People*. London, Pluto Press, 2005.

Zachs, Fruma. *Making of a Syrian Identity: Intellectuals and Merchants in Nineteenth-Century Beirut*. Leiden, Brill, 2005.

Zisser, Eyal. *Asad's Legacy: Syria in Transition*. London, C. Hurst & Co, 2000.

Commanding Syria; Bashar al-Asad and the First Years in Power. London, I. B. Tauris, 2006.

Ziter, Edward. *Political Performance in Syria: From the Six-Day War to the Syrian Uprising*. Basingstoke, Palgrave Macmillan, 2015.

Zwier, Paul J. *Peacemaking, Religious Belief, and the Rule of Law: the Struggle Between Dictatorship and Democracy in Syria and Beyond*. Abingdon, Routledge, 2018.

TUNISIA
Geography

Tunisia is the smallest of the countries that comprise the 'Maghreb' of North Africa, but it is more cosmopolitan than Algeria or Morocco. It forms a wedge of territory, 163,610 sq km (63,170 sq miles) in extent, between Algeria and Libya. It includes the easternmost ridges of the Atlas Mountains, but most of the country is low-lying and bordered by a long and sinuous Mediterranean coastline that faces both north and east. Ease of access by sea and by land from the east has favoured the penetration of foreign influences, and Tunisia owes its distinct national identity and its varied cultural traditions to a succession of invading peoples: Phoenicians, Romans, Arabs, Turks and French. It was more effectively Arabized than either Algeria or Morocco and remnants of the original Berber (Amazigh) population are confined to a few isolated localities in the south.

PHYSICAL FEATURES

The principal contrasts in the physical geography of Tunisia are between a humid and relatively mountainous northern region, a semi-arid central expanse of low plateaux and plains, and a dry Saharan region in the south. The northern region is dominated by the easternmost folds of the Atlas mountain system that form two separate chains, the Northern and High Tell, separated by the valley of the River Medjerda, the only perennially flowing river in the country. The Northern Tell, which is a continuation of the Algerian Tell Atlas, extends along the north coast at heights of between 300 m and 600 m. South of the Medjerda valley lies the broader Tell Atlas, which is a continuation of the Saharan Atlas of Algeria, and comprises a succession of rugged sandstone and limestone ridges. Near the Algerian frontier these reach a maximum height of 1,544 m at Djebel Chambi, the highest point in Tunisia, but die away eastward towards the Cap Bon peninsula, which extends north-east to within 145 km of Sicily.

South of the High Tell or Dorsale ('backbone') central Tunisia consists of an extensive platform sloping gently towards the east coast. Its western half, known as the High Steppe, comprises alluvial basins rimmed by low, barren mountains, but eastward the mountains give way first to the Low Steppe, a gravel-covered plateau, and ultimately to the flat coastal plain of the Sahel. Occasional watercourses cross the Steppes, but they flow only after heavy rain and usually fan out and evaporate in salt flats, or sebkhas, before reaching the sea.

The central Steppes give way southward to a broad depression occupied by two great seasonal salt lakes or shotts. The larger of these, the Shott Djerid, lies at 16 m below sea level and is normally covered by a salt crust. It extends from close to the Mediterranean coast near Gabès almost to the Algerian frontier and is adjoined on the north-west by the Shott al-Rharsa, which lies at 21 m below sea level. South of the shotts Tunisia extends for over 320 km into the Sahara. Rocky, flat-topped mountains, the Monts des Ksour, separate a flat plain known as the Djeffara, which borders the coast south of Gabès, from a sandy lowland partly covered by the dunes of the Great Eastern Erg.

CLIMATE

The climate of northern Tunisia is Mediterranean in type, with hot, dry summers followed by warm, wet winters. Average annual rainfall reaches 1,500 mm in the Kroumirie Mountains, the wettest area in north Africa, but over most of the northern region it varies from 400 mm to 1,000 mm. The wetter and least accessible mountains are covered with forests in which cork oak and evergreen oak predominate, but elsewhere lower rainfall and overgrazing combine to replace forest with meagre scrub growth. South of the High Tell rainfall is reduced to between 200 mm and 400 mm annually, which is insufficient for the regular cultivation of cereal crops without irrigation, and there is no continuous cover of vegetation. Large areas of the Steppes support only clumps of wiry esparto grass, which is collected and exported for paper manufacture. Southern Tunisia experiences full desert conditions. Rainfall is reduced to below 200 mm annually and occurs only at rare intervals. Extremes of temperature and wind are characteristic, and vegetation is completely absent over extensive tracts. The country supports only a sparse nomadic population except where supplies of underground water make cultivation possible.

POPULATION

At the April 2004 census the population was 9,910,872 and the overall density was 64.1 per sq km. By the April 2014 census, the population had reached 10,982,754, and the overall density was 71.1 per sq km. By mid-2023 official projections put the total population at 12,224,364.

Most of the people live in the more humid, northern part of the country, including in the capital, Tunis, which is situated close to the site of ancient Carthage, At the April 2014 census the population of Tunis was recorded at 638,845. However, the capital's population can sometimes be cited as much higher, owing to the designation of other large settlements, including Ariana (114,486 in April 2014) and Ettadhamen (142,953 in April 2014), as suburbs. Indeed, United Nations estimates put the population of Tunis and its suburbs at 2,475,446 at mid-2023. No other town approaches Tunis in importance, but on the east coast both Sfax (population 650,405 at mid-2023) and Sousse (221,530 in April 2014) provide modern port facilities, as does Bizerta (136,917 in April 2014) on the north coast, while some distance inland the old Arab capital and holy city of Qairawan, now known as Kairouan (139,070 in April 2014), serves as a regional centre.

History

NEIL PARTRICK

Based on an original essay by RICHARD I. LAWLESS

PRE-COLONIAL AND COLONIAL PERIODS

In antiquity Tunisia enjoyed great prosperity under the Carthaginians and then the Romans. In the seventh century CE Arab invasions from the east destroyed Byzantine rule, and for a short time the newly established Arab city of Kairouan in central Tunisia became the centre of Arab rule in the Maghreb. Over the following centuries, despite numerous revolts by the local Berber (often referred to in contemporary parlance as Amazigh) inhabitants against successive Arab dynasties, the region was progressively Islamized and Arabized. By the end of the 15th century Tunisia became involved in the struggle between the rival Spanish and Ottoman Empires for control of the Mediterranean, and in the late 16th century Ottoman forces captured Tunis.

The Ottomans established the 'regency' of Tunis, but direct Ottoman rule was brief, with authority passing to a military caste who administered the country enjoying a large measure of autonomy. At the beginning of the 18th century one of these Turkish officers of Cretan origin established the Husainid dynasty, which reigned until 1957. Husainid rule brought some semblance of order, but was threatened by the growing strength of the European powers. In the early 19th century the European powers forced the *Bey* (ruler) to suppress the activities of the corsairs (pirates operating along the Barbary Coast), which had provided a considerable part of state revenues.

As France, Britain and Italy competed for influence, Tunisia tried to modernize its society and institutions, but quickly fell into debt, and in 1869 the *Bey* was obliged to accept financial control by the European powers. In order to secure its own position, particularly in the face of Italian imperial expansion, France decided on military intervention in April 1881. The French encountered no serious resistance, and the Marsa Convention of 1883 formally established a French protectorate over Tunisia. The *Bey* remained the nominal ruler but, although Tunisian traditional institutions were retained, effective power passed to the French resident-general and the French administration. There was an influx of European settlers—French, Italian and Maltese—but it was not until 1931 that the French outnumbered the Italians. None the less, by the last decade of French rule Europeans represented only 7% of the total population, and much of Tunisian society remained intact.

INDEPENDENCE

Inspired by the nationalist movement in Egypt, the Destour (Constitution) movement was founded in 1920, calling for a self-governing constitutional regime with a Legislative Assembly. French attempts to conciliate opinion by administrative reforms failed to satisfy the more radical elements, and in 1925 the movement was dissolved. The movement was revived in the 1930s, but split when younger members formed the Néo-Destour in 1934. Under the leadership of Habib Bourguiba, a French-trained lawyer, the Néo-Destour became a mass party and later established an important alliance with the labour movement, the Union Générale des Travailleurs Tunisiens (UGTT, now the Union Générale Tunisienne du Travail), led by Farhat Hached. After the Second World War (1939–45) peaceful progress towards autonomy came to a halt owing to growing settler opposition, procrastination on the part of the French Government, and the consequent alienation of the nationalists. Tunisian resentment erupted in strikes and demonstrations in early 1952, and a wave of violence spread throughout the country. Lengthy negotiations eventually led to an accord in June 1955 granting internal autonomy to Tunisia, which was accepted by Bourguiba and a majority of the Néo-Destour, although the party reaffirmed that it would be satisfied only with complete independence. Negotiations led by Bourguiba resulted in an agreement in March 1956 under which France formally recognized the independence of Tunisia. In July 1957 the Constituent Assembly, elected immediately after the declaration of independence, voted to abolish the monarchy, proclaimed Tunisia a republic and designated Bourguiba President. Tunisian demands for the evacuation of French forces from the French base at Bizerta were rejected by the French Government, preoccupied as it was with the deteriorating situation in neighbouring Algeria. Periodic clashes, anti-French rioting and diplomatic skirmishes occurred sporadically for several years over the presence of French troops in Tunisia. However, following clashes between Tunisian and French forces in June 1961 around the French base at Bizerta, during which over 1,000 Tunisians were killed, new negotiations resulted in the evacuation of the base in October 1963.

BOURGUIBA ESTABLISHES HIS SUPREMACY

After independence Bourguiba set about constructing a political system that devolved from and depended on him. The authority that he was able to command derived from his successful leadership of the independence movement and his ability to manipulate and control the political system that he created, thereby preventing the emergence of anyone who could pose a challenge to him. He quickly strengthened his control over the Néo-Destour party (renamed the Parti Socialiste Destourien—PSD—in 1964) and, by exploiting rivalries within the UGTT, brought the powerful trade union movement within the Bourguiba system. A new Constitution, promulgated in June 1959, confirmed the authority of the President, who was empowered to formulate general policy, choose the members of the Government, hold supreme command of the armed forces, and make all appointments to civil and military posts. In contrast, the National Assembly, elected for five years, met for only six months of the year, and its role was largely limited to the ratification of policy decisions taken by the President. There was no effective cabinet and no parliamentary control. The system was in many respects a presidential monarchy, and indeed Bourguiba saw himself as assuming the position of the former *Bey*, even continuing some of the ceremonial practices of the monarchy. In presidential elections in November Bourguiba was elected unopposed, and in elections to the National Assembly all 90 seats were won by the Néo-Destour party. The Communists were unable to compete with the nationalism of the Néo-Destour and from 1963 were suppressed. Later, a new left wing emerged, comprising mainly intellectuals and lacking support among the working class. Bourguiba's attempt to give a liberal interpretation to Islam led to some resistance from conservative religious forces, but Bourguiba could count on the influential writings of Islamic reformer Tahar al-Haddad, who, prior to independence, had advocated the emancipation of women. Although not implementing a wholly secular political system, in 1956 Bourguiba instituted a secular-style personal status law (in contrast to the presumed civil status of Muslims under *Shari'a*—Islamic law) and abolished *Shari'a* courts.

In 1961 Bourguiba appointed Ahmed Ben Salah as Secretary of State for Planning and Finance and quickly added agriculture and education to his minister's responsibilities. Ben Salah embarked on an ambitious programme of reform centred on the introduction of the co-operative system in former French agricultural estates. However, the co-operatives operated at a loss, owing largely to poor management, and were opposed by the peasantry and the bourgeoisie. By 1968 resistance to the new system began to increase. Ben Salah's response was to extend the agricultural co-operative system across the whole country, even though there were no funds or trained personnel to support this. By mid-1969, after the army fired on peasants demonstrating against the co-operatives, Bourguiba withdrew his support from Ben Salah, who was removed from office, arrested, tried and sentenced to 10 years' imprisonment.

After a brief period when the political system was opened to free discussion, Bourguiba quickly reasserted his authority within the PSD and the state. In November 1974 Bourguiba was re-elected President of the Republic, and elections to the National Assembly were uncontested, with the electorate being offered only a single party list. The new Assembly approved amendments to the Constitution, allowing Bourguiba to be appointed President-for-life. As Bourguiba reasserted his authority, the coercive force of the state was increasingly deployed, targeting students and members of left-wing groups. Meanwhile, the UGTT was becoming an increasingly vocal critic of government policy and an outlet for political dissenters. After organizing a general strike in January 1978, the union's leadership was taken into custody and charged with subversion.

The modernization project was stalling, and disaffection with the system increased dramatically. In January 1980 there was an attack on the town of Gafsa in central Tunisia. Responsibility was claimed by a hitherto unknown group, the Tunisian Armed Resistance, which declared that it aimed to free Tunisia from the 'dictatorship' of the PSD. The Tunisian Government claimed that the attackers were Tunisian migrant workers who had been trained in Libya and encouraged to destabilize the Bourguiba regime. In response to the attack, France sent military aircraft to Gafsa and naval vessels to the Tunisian coast.

LIMITED POLITICAL LIBERALIZATION; MOUNTING UNREST

In April 1980 Mohamed Mzali was appointed Prime Minister. His new Government included a member of the opposition Mouvement des Démocrates Socialistes (MDS) and three ministers who had resigned in 1977 in protest against the harsh measures taken against strikers. In February 1981 an amnesty was granted to all members of the radical Mouvement de l'Unité Populaire (MUP) except its leader-in-exile, Ben Salah. In April Bourguiba declared that he saw no objection to the operation of political parties, provided that they rejected violence and religious fanaticism and were not dependent 'ideologically or materially' on any foreign group. In July the one-party system ended with the official recognition of the Parti Communiste Tunisien (PCT), which had been banned since 1963. Bourguiba now perceived the rise of political Islam as the greatest threat to his rule and decided that co-opting his former enemies on the left would increase the stability of the regime. At parliamentary elections in November 1981 the Front National—a joint electoral pact formed by the PSD and the UGTT—won all the National Assembly seats on 94.6% of the votes; the MUP and the MDS failed to reach the required threshold for seats of 5% of the vote, but were accorded official status in 1983.

These limited moves towards political liberalization did not stop mounting domestic unrest. In January 1984 widespread rioting and looting broke out in the south and quickly spread to the north, including Tunis. After a week of disturbances Bourguiba intervened to reverse the increases in the price of bread and other staples that had prompted the unrest, and order was re-established.

Throughout 1984 and 1985 there were public sector strikes, and the confrontation between the Government and the UGTT intensified. The appointment in April 1986 of a senior military officer and former head of military security, Gen. Zine al-Abidine Ben Ali, as Minister of the Interior, suggested a change in domestic policy. Bourguiba had always been suspicious of the armed forces and ensured that they were kept out of politics. In July Mzali was replaced as premier by Rachid Sfar (previously Minister of Finance) and dismissed as PSD Secretary-General. Mzali subsequently fled the country but was sentenced *in absentia* to four years' imprisonment and 15 years' hard labour. Parliamentary elections in November were boycotted by all the opposition parties, and once again the PSD won all the seats in the Assembly.

SUPPRESSION OF ISLAMIST ACTIVISTS

By 1987 the Government had consolidated its control over the UGTT, and left-wing militancy was no longer perceived as a threat. Islamist fundamentalism, however, posed the greatest threat to the regime. Political Islamism in Tunisia was dominated by the Mouvement de la Tendance Islamique (MTI), but there were smaller, more radical groups; the precise relationship of which to the MTI was unclear. Scores of Islamists were detained in early 1987, among them the Secretary-General of the MTI, Rachid Ghannouchi, who was arrested on charges of violence and collusion with foreign powers to overthrow the Government. Relations with Iran soured; Iranian diplomats in Tunis were accused of inciting terrorism and helping to plan the overthrow of Bourguiba. In May the Government approved the creation of the Association for the Defence of Human Rights and Public Liberty, as a rival to the independent Ligue Tunisienne des Droits de l'Homme (LTDH), which the Government accused of favouring the MTI. The Government insisted that the MTI was responsible for bomb explosions in Sousse and Monastir in August, in which 13 foreign tourists were injured, even though the radical group Islamic Jihad had claimed responsibility. Six young Tunisians later confessed to planting the bombs and stated that they were members of the MTI. In September the trial opened of 90 Islamists accused of threatening state security and plotting against the Government. Ghannouchi was among 69 people who received custodial sentences, with seven others being sentenced to death.

FOREIGN RELATIONS UNDER BOURGUIBA

Although relations with France were strained during the first decade of independence, by the early 1970s France had become a major source of financial assistance to Tunisia, and on his first official visit to the country, in July 1972, Bourguiba paid eloquent tribute to the former colonial power. Links with the USA—established before independence when the Tunisian nationalists enjoyed the support of the US labour movement—were strengthened, and the USA became another major source of financial aid. In the Arab world Bourguiba was critical of the leadership of President Nasser of Egypt, and Nasserist policies were described by his Minister of Foreign Affairs as 'micro-imperialism'. After a visit to Palestinian refugee camps in Jordan in 1965, Bourguiba expressed strong support for the Palestinian cause, but controversially also called for direct negotiations with Israel on the basis of the United Nations (UN) partition plan for Palestine of 1947. Tunisia refused to participate in meetings of the League of Arab States (the Arab League, see p. 1146) and severed diplomatic relations with Egypt.

However, the war between Israel and the Arab states in June 1967 led to immediate Tunisian reconciliation with the rest of the Arab world. The Arab states' humiliating defeat led to a wave of demonstrations in Tunisia in support of Nasser and pan-Arabism, and there were several hostile actions against Tunisia's small Jewish community. Diplomatic relations with Egypt were restored, and Bourguiba reaffirmed Tunisia's support for the Palestine Liberation Organization (PLO). Tunisia sent a small military force to Egypt during the October War of 1973 and gave active diplomatic support to the Arab cause. However, after Egypt signed a peace treaty with Israel in 1979, Tunisia severed diplomatic relations with Egypt. The Arab League imposed a political and economic boycott on Egypt and transferred its headquarters from Cairo to Tunis. When Israel invaded Lebanon in 1982, Tunisia allowed the PLO to transfer its base to Tunis. In 1985 the Israeli air force attacked the PLO headquarters in Tunis.

Relations between Tunisia and its wealthy eastern neighbour, Libya, became strained after President Bourguiba swiftly reversed an agreement in 1974 to establish a union of the two. One source of tension was the delimitation of their respective sectors of the continental shelf in the Gulf of Gabès, in which were located important petroleum deposits. In 1977 both sides agreed to submit to arbitration by the International Court of Justice (ICJ), and agreement was finally reached in 1982. Relations deteriorated further in 1985, following Libya's expulsion of some 30,000 Tunisian migrant workers. Tunisia announced in 1987 that the dispute with Libya was over;

consular links were resumed, and the border between the two countries was reopened.

BEN ALI TAKES POWER

During the second half of 1987 Bourguiba's behaviour became increasingly erratic. Reports emerged of a disagreement between Bourguiba and Ben Ali, newly appointed as Prime Minister, about the fate of the Islamists tried in September, with the President apparently demanding a retrial and the death penalty for all 90 accused. In November seven doctors declared that Bourguiba was unfit to govern, on grounds of senility and ill health, and, in accordance with the Constitution, Ben Ali was sworn in as President. There was no evident opposition to Ben Ali's takeover, which had been approved in advance by the majority of ministers and senior military officers.

On assuming power President Ben Ali immediately began a policy of national reconciliation, ordering the release of a large number of political and non-political prisoners, including Ghannouchi and other leading members of the MTI, and the MDS leader, Ahmad Mestiri; Ben Salah was pardoned, and he subsequently returned to Tunisia from exile. Ben Ali undertook to introduce a more democratic system of government. Under amendments to the Constitution, the post of President-for-life was abolished; the President was to be elected every five years and limited to two consecutive terms in office. In April 1988 the National Assembly approved a multi-party system. In order to gain legal recognition, political parties were required to uphold the aims of, and work within, the Constitution, and were not permitted to pursue purely religious, racial, regional or linguistic policies. In July the National Assembly modified the Press Code, relaxing some of its repressive clauses. Ben Ali began consultations with opposition parties, the UGTT, employers' organizations and youth and women's groups, which led to the announcement of a National Pact, purporting to guarantee basic freedoms, in September. The leftist Rassemblement Socialiste Progressiste and the liberal Parti Social pour le Progrès, together with the newly formed Union Démocratique Unioniste (UDU), were all granted legal recognition. The new administration emphasized Tunisia's Arab and Islamic identity, and government relations with the Islamists generally improved. However, the MTI, now transformed into a political party, Ennahdha—or Parti de la Renaissance—was denied official status.

The ruling party was renamed the Rassemblement Constitutionnel Démocratique (RCD); at its first congress Ben Ali was re-elected party Chairman, and Prime Minister Hedi Baccouche was appointed Vice-Chairman. In parliamentary elections in April 1989, the first multi-party elections for almost a decade, the RCD won all 141 seats, with 80% of the votes cast. Ennahdha, forbidden from campaigning as a party, presented 'independent' candidates in 19 of the 25 constituencies, taking 13% of the total vote and 25% of the vote in many constituencies (30% in Tunis) and replacing the MDS as the main opposition force. Ben Ali was confirmed as President by 99% of voters. Ghannouchi subsequently went into voluntary exile in Paris, and Abdelfattah Mourou assumed the leadership of Ennahdha within Tunisia.

SUPPRESSION OF THE ISLAMIST MOVEMENT

Following their failure to secure legal recognition, the Islamists increased their political agitation, particularly in universities. In February 1990 protests in Sfax culminated in clashes between police and students belonging to the Union Générale des Etudiants de Tunisie (UGET), an organization considered close to Ennahdha. About 600 student activists were detained. The Government accused Ennahdha of exploiting the students and of inciting unrest among the workforce, including a strike by 10,000 municipal workers. Ennahdha, together with the six legal opposition groups, boycotted municipal elections in June, stating that they were neither free nor fair. In November several members of Ennahdha were arrested, following the discovery of explosives that were allegedly to have been used for terrorist activities. Ennahdha's senior officials denied that the movement was involved in terrorism, although some independent reports claimed that the party had a military wing. In December senior officials of Ennahdha were arrested and accused of attempting to establish an Islamic state. In February 1991 an armed attack took place on RCD offices in Tunis. The authorities stated that Ennahdha had planned the attack, and Ghannouchi appeared to condone it by stating that the violence was in response to state violence.

The crackdown on the Islamist movement intensified. The UGET was disbanded after the police claimed to have found weapons and subversive material linked to Ennahdha. In May 1991 some 300 people, including about 100 members of the security forces, were arrested in connection with an alleged Islamist plot. In July 1992 almost 200 purported Ennahdha members were put on trial for allegedly plotting to take power by force. It was claimed that Ghannouchi had received funds from Iran, Sudan and Saudi Arabia to overthrow the Tunisian regime. These mass trials were seen as the culmination of the Tunisian Government's long campaign against Ennahdha, whose organizational structures within the country were largely destroyed and its leaders imprisoned or forced into exile, mainly in Europe. Ghannouchi was given a life sentence.

THE 1994 ELECTIONS: BEN ALI RE-ELECTED FOR A SECOND TERM

In March 1994 President Ben Ali was elected for a second term, winning 99.9% of the vote, according to official sources, which also reported that 94.9% of eligible voters had participated in the presidential election. Two viable alternative candidates, including Moncef Marzouki, the former President of the LTDH, had been arrested after announcing their intention to contest the presidency. At the parliamentary elections the RCD swept to victory, winning 97.7% of the vote and taking all of the 144 seats allocated under the majority list system.

BEN ALI'S THIRD PRESIDENTIAL TERM

At Tunisia's first contested presidential election since independence, held in October 1999, Ben Ali secured 99.4% of the vote. In parliamentary elections held concurrently, the RCD took 91.6% of the votes cast and all 148 of the contested seats in the National Assembly.

Ben Ali appointed Mohamed Ghannouchi as Prime Minister in place of Hamed Karoui, who had held the premiership for a decade. Mohammad Ghannouchi, who had been the Minister of International Co-operation and Foreign Investment since 1992, was an economist with wide experience in planning, finance and investment.

In November 1999 Ben Ali released 600, mostly Ennahdha, political prisoners. In April 2000 Taoufik Ben Brik, a Tunisian national and correspondent for the Swiss daily La Croix, began a 42-day hunger strike in protest against police harassment. The repercussions of the Ben Brik affair led to some superficial government changes, including to the human rights portfolio, and the President replaced some senior military officers, including Gen. Salah Laouani, head of the Brigades d'Ordre Publique, and Gen. Mokhtar Gmati, Commander of the National Guard, who had both been closely involved in Ben Ali's takeover in 1987.

During a visit to the United Kingdom in June 2000, Marzouki announced that a national democratic conference was planned for December supposedly to lay the foundations for a democratic state in Tunisia within a decade. Marzouki, now the spokesman for the Conseil National des Libertés en Tunisie, an officially banned dissident grouping, expressed the hope that Ennahdha members would participate in the proposed conference, thus bringing together the divided secular and Islamist opponents of the regime. In July 2000 Marzouki was dismissed from his university post after publicly criticizing the Tunisian authorities during a visit to Europe and later received a 12-month prison sentence.

In June 2001 the President of the LTDH, Mokhtar Trifi, launched a campaign calling for a general amnesty law, an initiative that was supported by Marzouki and a former Minister of Education, Mohamed Charfi, and later by the Secretary-General of the UGTT, Abdessalem Jerad. In July Judge Mokhtar Yahyaoui addressed an open letter to President Ben

Ali condemning the pressure exerted by the regime on judges, forcing them to give judgments 'dictated in advance, to which there was no appeal and which were not in accordance with the law'. This was the first time that a senior member of the judiciary had spoken out publicly in this way. In December Yahyaoui was dismissed from his post. The Association des Magistrats Tunisiens, which in May had adopted a resolution calling for the independence of the judiciary, issued a communiqué expressing support for Judge Yahyaoui.

Shortly before President Jacques Chirac of France visited Tunis in December 2001, the Tunisian authorities revoked the travel restrictions imposed on Marzouki, enabling him to leave the country to take up a university post in France.

In mid-April 2002 a tanker lorry exploded outside the Ghriba synagogue on the island of Djerba in south-eastern Tunisia, killing 21 people, most of them German tourists, and injuring 20 others. The Tunisian Government initially insisted that the explosion was an accident. However, in June the Qatari-based television station Al Jazeera broadcast a statement by Sulayman Abu Ghaith, spokesman for al-Qa'ida, confirming that the attack had been carried out by his organization.

FURTHER CONSTITUTIONAL CHANGES

In November 2001 Ben Ali announced what he termed a 'fundamental reform' of the Constitution, although he gave few details of the proposed changes. The Parti Démocrate Progressiste—the dissident faction of the MDS not represented in parliament—together with the unrecognized Forum Démocratique pour le Travail et les Libertés (FDTL, also known as Ettakatol), led by Dr Mustapha Ben Jafaâr, and the Congrès pour la République (CPR), founded by Marzouki, set up a 'democratic co-ordination committee' to campaign against a fourth mandate for Ben Ali, and to press for an amnesty for political prisoners, freedom of expression and the independence of the judiciary. In April 2002 the Chamber of Deputies raised the maximum age for presidential candidates from 70 to 75 years, giving Ben Ali (who would be 68 years of age at the 2004 election) the opportunity to seek two additional mandates and fuelling speculation that he intended to make himself 'President for life'. A total of 99.52% of voters approved the changes at a national referendum held in May 2002, according to official figures, with voter participation put at 95%.

The President finally legalized the FDTL in October 2002. The party had tried to obtain legal status for eight years. The LTDH President, Trifi, declared that these presidential gestures were wholly insufficient and that what was needed was the liberalization of political life, a general amnesty and an independent judiciary.

In July 2003, despite persistent speculation regarding his health, Ben Ali confirmed that he would seek a fourth term as President. Ben Ali made several changes to the composition of the Council of Ministers in August. At the end of that month the UDU stated that the party's leader, Abderrahmane Tlili, had been attacked in the street and seriously injured, and that documents had been stolen from his car. In September Tlili was arrested in connection with alleged financial irregularities arising from his tenure as head of the country's Office de l'Aviation Civile et des Aéroports. In June 2004 he was sentenced to nine years' imprisonment and fined heavily, having been found guilty of corruption in awarding contracts. Many suspected a political motive behind the charges.

In January 2004 Mohamed Daouas was replaced as Governor of the Banque Centrale de Tunisie by the former Minister of Finance, Taoufik Baccar, and assigned to 'other functions'. Daouas, a vociferous supporter of economic reform, had urged greater transparency in private sector companies, and there was speculation that this had alarmed many wealthy business executives, some of whom had close links with Ben Ali and his entourage, and might have precipitated his replacement.

THE PRESIDENTIAL AND LEGISLATIVE ELECTIONS OF OCTOBER 2004

At the October 2004 presidential election, which was contested by four candidates, Ben Ali was re-elected for a fourth mandate with 94.5% of the vote, according to official sources. Mohamed Bouchiha, leader of the Parti de l'Unité Populaire (PUP) was second-placed, winning 3.8% of the vote. In the concurrent legislative elections, the RCD, with its powerful party machine, won all 152 contested seats in the Chamber of Deputies (out of a total of 189). The MDS took 14 of the 37 seats reserved for opposition parties. Turnout in the elections was officially put at 91%, but independent sources claimed that the real figure was much lower, especially in Tunis.

BEN ALI'S FOURTH TERM

Addressing the nation in November 2004, after being sworn in for a fourth term, President Ben Ali pledged to adopt an approach that would balance the need for stability, continued progress and comprehensive and sustained development with 'the irreversible process of democratic pluralism'.

Indirect elections (by an electoral college composed of deputies, mayors and municipal councillors) to the newly created and Chamber of Deputies-approved upper house, the Chamber of Advisers, took place in July 2005, at which the RCD secured 71 of the 85 elected seats. All 43 of its 'regional' seats were taken by the RCD, and those allocated to farmers (14) and employers (14) also went to RCD loyalists. However, the 14 seats reserved for the trade unions remained vacant, as the UGTT declined to participate. The remaining seats in the Chamber of Advisers were filled by presidential appointees in August.

In February 2006 Ben Ali pardoned 1,298 prisoners and granted conditional release to a further 359 detainees, including more than 70 members of Ennahdha and eight men sentenced in 2004 for engaging in subversive activities on the internet. Among those released was Hamadi Jebali, a former member of Ennahdha's political bureau, who had spent more than 15 years in gaol.

In June 2006 the Tunisian press reported that 10 university students had been arrested in Gafsa, on suspicion of links with al-Qa'ida; the police later detained another group of 10 youths, whom, it was claimed, had planned to join the Base of Holy War in the Land of the Two Rivers (Tanzim Qa'idat al-Jihad fi Bilad al-Rifidain) organization, also known as al-Qa'ida in Iraq. The Government's concerns about the operations of terrorist groups linked to al-Qa'ida appeared to be validated in January 2007, when the police shot dead 14 members of a suspected militant Islamist organization and arrested several others in Soliman, near Tunis. Belhaj Kacem stated that the group—which had been assembled by six militants who had entered the country from Algeria, and which was suspected of having links to al-Qa'ida Organization in the Land of the Islamic Maghreb (AQIM)—had been in possession of explosives and of details of foreign embassies and diplomatic staff in Tunis. It appeared that the crackdown on Ennahdha, which had always advocated peaceful means to conduct politics, was driving some militants towards more extremist groups linked to international terrorist networks.

In a speech to commemorate the 50th anniversary of the Republic in July 2007, Ben Ali focused on Tunisia's improved access to education, social security, health care and services, such as safe drinking water. Such relative socioeconomic successes also masked the harsher realities and tensions within the country.

During early 2008 riots erupted in the mining town of Redeyef, near Gafsa, in one of the country's most underdeveloped regions. Rising prices and growing unemployment prompted peaceful demonstrations that escalated into violence as protesters clashed with police. Residents were reportedly angered by the recruitment policies implemented by the state-owned Compagnie des Phosphates de Gafsa, one of the few sources of employment in the area. In June one man was killed and 22 others injured when security forces opened fire on protesters in the town.

Meanwhile, the Government intensified its campaign against radical Islamists, but scaled back its restrictions on Ennahdha. Following the imprisonment in August 2008 of 13 Islamists convicted of instituting a terrorist cell, 14 other militants were arrested in October on suspicion of planning terrorist attacks. The arrests raised the number of detentions on terrorism charges in the country to more than 160 within a year. In November, however, President Ben Ali authorized the release of 21 prisoners, most of whom were Ennahdha members.

President Ben Ali announced his presidential candidacy for a fifth term in August 2009 and received the endorsement of several political and social organizations, including the UGTT.

With five of the eight officially sanctioned opposition parties publicly declaring their support for President Ben Ali, the outcome of the presidential election, which was contested by four candidates on 25 October 2009, was in little doubt. According to official figures, Ben Ali won 89.6% of the 4.7m. votes cast. At the concurrent legislative elections, the RCD took all 161 directly elected seats in the Chamber of Deputies. The remaining 53 seats were divided among the opposition parties in proportion to their share of the vote.

UPRISING AND THE DEPARTURE OF BEN ALI

Universal and long-latent public disaffection with the repressive nature of the Ben Ali regime finally culminated into mass mobilization against it in December 2010, following the widely reported self-immolation of a fruit seller in the small town of Sidi Bouzid.

Mohamed Bouazizi, who has since become a symbol of the unrest that spread throughout the Middle East and North Africa region in 2011 (and became known as the 'Arab spring'), set himself alight in the main square of Sidi Bouzid on 17 December 2010, after police arrested him for selling fruit and vegetables without a permit. His apparent plight—lack of economic opportunity, compounded by official interference and corruption—reflected that of many other young Tunisians, who quickly took up his cause. Riots ensued in Sidi Bouzid, and soon after in neighbouring towns; as reports of fatalities, allegedly perpetrated by the security services, began to emerge, the protests spread throughout the country, overwhelming the Government's capacity to contain them. At the end of December demonstrations erupted in Tunis, by which time the concessions offered by the Government and Ben Ali himself to appease the protesters merely galvanized them further. Ben Ali adopted increasingly drastic measures, such as the removal of key ministers, but serious protests in early January 2011 signalled that the regime's ability to retain control was rapidly disintegrating. On 14 January Ben Ali fled the country for Saudi Arabia, bringing his 23-year rule to an abrupt end.

Violence and protests continued after Ben Ali's departure, as the remnants of the ruling RCD attempted to restore political control in the face of widespread opposition. Prime Minister Mohamed Ghannouchi assumed the presidency when Ben Ali left the country, but was forced to resign after a Constitutional Court ruling that the parliamentary Speaker, Fouad Mebazaa, was the legitimate interim President. Mebazaa formed a new coalition Government, comprising some former RCD figures, as well as opposition politicians, on 17 January 2011. However, the involvement of former government officials angered the public, and further protests ensued. Mebazaa announced the establishment of a new and enlarged administration, which excluded RCD members. Soon afterwards, the National Assembly conferred on Mebazaa the power to rule by decree in order to seek to contain the protests, which continued to focus on the presence of former regime officials within the state apparatus. However, it became apparent that the public would settle for nothing less than wholesale change, and finally, on 7 March, a third interim Government was installed, under a new Prime Minister, Béji Caïd Essebsi, who had served as a Minister of Foreign Affairs under President Bourguiba. The new Government appeared to meet with public approval, and the unrest began to subside. Its first act was to dissolve the hated state security administration (also known as 'National Security' or, commonly, the *Mukhabarat*), although the Ministry of the Interior would continue in the years ahead to contain old regime security apparatchiks—see below). The new Government also confirmed its commitment to free and fair elections and the suspension of the 1959 Constitution.

A High Authority for the Achievement of the Objectives of the Revolution, Political Reform and Democratic Transition was established by the new Government with a remit to implement a 'roadmap to democracy', and plans were initiated for the organization of elections to a constituent assembly on 24 July 2011. However, these plans advanced haltingly; the High Authority's meetings failed to make any progress, and the interim Government inexplicably disbanded a second commission set up to investigate official corruption and embezzlement. However, efforts to remove all remaining vestiges of the Ben Ali regime continued; officials were barred from office, and on 9 March the RCD itself was dissolved. Officials who had served in the Ben Ali Government in the previous 10 years, including those who had held senior posts within the regime, were banned from contesting the forthcoming elections. Meanwhile, a wide range of charges against Ben Ali and his family were gradually drawn up, and by June, when he was tried for the first time, *in absentia*, he was subject to at least 18 civil lawsuits and some 182 military charges. By August he and his wife had been convicted of embezzling state funds and sentenced (in their absence) to 35 years' imprisonment, with an additional 15 years each for the illegal possession of weapons and illicit drugs.

The High Authority continued to experience difficulty in gaining consensus over the elections and proposed 'transition to democracy', suffering a major reverse when Ennahdha withdrew its participation on two occasions, owing to disagreements. Eventually, the High Authority admitted that the organization of elections in July 2011 was too great a political and logistical challenge, and the poll was postponed until 23 October. Meanwhile, public wariness about the intentions of the interim Government persisted throughout much of the transitional period, with various opposition groups continuing to hold demonstrations and strikes.

ELECTIONS TO THE NATIONAL CONSTITUENT ASSEMBLY

The elections to the National Constituent Assembly (NCA) took place on 23 October 2011. It had been agreed that a majority in the new Assembly should determine who held power in the new government, but that the body should also draft a new constitution determining the details of the new political system. At an election involving 81 parties and associations, Ennahdha emerged with the largest representation in the NCA, winning 89 of the 217 seats contested, although it needed to form a coalition with two secular parties—the liberal CPR (29 seats), led by Moncef Marzouki, and the left-leaning Ettakatol (20 seats)—in order to command a working majority. It is arguable that participation in the coalition helped to strengthen the dominant moderate Islamist trend in Ennahdha represented by its leader, Rachid Ghannouchi. In June 2012 the al-Qa'ida leader, Ayman al-Zawahiri, condemned Ennahdha for not imposing *Shari'a* law in Tunisia, terming the group's Islamism 'US-approved'. As an indicator of the dramatic shift in Tunisian politics, in December 2011 the NCA approved Marzouki as an interim (and symbolic) President. He, in turn, appointed Jebali, a senior member of Ennahdha and a longstanding opponent of the former regime, as Prime Minister.

Among the challenges that the NCA had to resolve was the role of religion in public life. In order to counter the potential exploitation by political Salafists of the greater space afforded by the dramatic changes, the Assembly's members considered measures to prevent the country's mosques from being used for partisan political activities. However, the Constitution was expected to seek to uphold the legal independence of the mosques. The Government was aware of the ideological challenge from Tunisia's Salafists and the willingness of some of these to support or engage in new external struggles. In July 2014, amid increasing security concerns, the Government announced that it would shut down some of the many mosques that had been established without legal authorization during and after the uprising. The authorities linked these unauthorized mosques to Salafi violence in the country.

A seemingly genuine move towards a pluralist political system resulted from the upheaval in Tunisia (unlike the more limited, leadership-orientated changes in Egypt and Yemen, for instance). However, aspects of the old state apparatus remained, such as the powers of the largely unreconstructed Ministry of the Interior. This was the focus of political complaints in April 2012, for example, after the heavy-handed policing of an opposition protest in Tunis.

In July 2012 Rachid Ghannouchi, who early that month had been re-elected by more than 70% of Ennahdha party members (defeating challengers committed to the imposition of *Shari'a* law) commented that the Government was interested in broadening its base. His announcement, which was received with guarded enthusiasm by some secular parties, was regarded by certain observers as an indication that Ennahdha was seeking to restructure the Government.

The assassination of a leading secular opposition politician, Chokri Belaïd, in February 2013 fuelled a political crisis. The NCA, largely divided on Islamist–secular lines, had failed to agree on a new constitution. Salafists associated with the banned Ansar al-Sharia, which had refused to recognize the legitimacy of the new political process, were accused of responsibility for the murder. Critics of Ennahdha claimed that it was inhibited within its own Government from taking action against Salafists allegedly involved in illegal activity. Jebali resigned as Prime Minister, and President Marzouki appointed the Minister of the Interior, Ali Laârayedh, to replace him. A new Council of Ministers was appointed in March, including Lotfi Ben Jeddou as Minister of the Interior. The overthrow of the elected Muslim Brotherhood administration of Mohamed Mursi in Egypt in June increased tensions in Tunisia still further, especially when young secular activists formed a group modelled on one in Egypt, known as Tamarrud ('resistance'), in opposition to the Tunisian Islamist-led Government. The murder of another secular leftist figure, Mohamed Brahimi, outside his home near Tunis in July caused further dissent and subsequently prompted some 60–70 defections from the NCA, as well as confrontations in Tunis and in Brahimi's hometown, Sidi Bouzid, where the revolt against Ben Ali had first erupted in December 2010. Ben Jeddou accused a fugitive militant, Boubaker Hakim, of carrying out the murders of Belaïd and Brahimi. Hakim was associated with Ansar al-Sharia, which denied involvement in either attack. Speculation that underlying the murders was an intention to provoke clashes in order to justify a state crackdown highlighted the power and influence of the Ministry of the Interior, although the military's limited history of political intervention made coup scenarios unlikely. In August 2013 the Tunisian authorities formally designated Ansar al-Sharia a terrorist group. The Ennahdha administration also sought to control the Ministry of the Interior, the National Guard and the army by removing elements affiliated with the old regime and replacing them with government loyalists.

In late July 2013 Ettakatol announced that it would withdraw from the coalition administration unless a new government of national unity was formed. The independent Minister of Education, Salem Labyadh, also resigned. A grouping of opposition parties—the Front de Salut National—was formed to co-ordinate pressure for dissolution of the governing institutions. The largest and most powerful union, the UGTT, began to organize strike action in support of demands for the Government's resignation. The Front Populaire (FP) opposition grouping, of which Belaïd and Brahimi had been leading figures, also urged the dissolution of the Government and the organization of fresh elections, and there were widespread demands for urgent political agreement on the constitution. However, the 'legitimate' Salafists—i.e. those committed to peaceful political engagement—continued to argue that even majority backing for a secular constitution in a referendum would be illegitimate. Rachid Ghannouchi emphasized that the NCA was legitimately elected and should not have to suspend itself. Although Ennahdha indicated that it was open to the formation of a new governing coalition, in January 2014 the party relinquished the office of Prime Minister, and, largely speaking, a role in the Government, pending elections scheduled for later in the year. The terms of the new Constitution were agreed shortly afterwards, and the draft document was approved by an overwhelming majority of NCA members in late January. A new interim Prime Minister, Mehdi Jomaâ, was then formally appointed by President Marzouki (having been designated premier under a cross-party agreement reached in the previous month). The new Council of Ministers comprised largely independents, although Ennahdha's Ben Jeddou remained as Minister of the Interior. Following the entry into effect of the Constitution in February, the state of emergency was removed in the following month.

Differences persisted within Ennahdha, however: Jebali tendered his resignation as Secretary-General in March 2014 and reportedly promoted the idea of a new party of supposedly more moderate Islamists. In May Sahbi Atik resigned as leader of Ennahdha's grouping within the NCA. Several NCA members had already resigned from the party, in part over disputes about the constitution and specifically the role of the state in protecting Islam. Atik subsequently formed a rival party to Ennahdha. However, a major political crisis was seemingly averted as Tunisia proceeded towards legislative and presidential elections respectively scheduled for 26 October and 23 November. Meanwhile, there were several legal judgments allowing the return to Tunisia of some senior RCD officials from the Ben Ali era. In November 2013 two NCA members resigned from the opposition Nidaa Tounes (NT—Tunisia's Call) bloc, in protest against the alleged entry into the party of former officials associated with the previous regime.

Violence associated with Islamist extremism, both within Tunisia and abroad, continued to trouble the Government. In July 2014 the Ministry of the Interior issued a draft 'anti-terrorism law', comparable with the loose and unaccountable powers that had facilitated the state security apparatus under anti-terrorism measures during the Ben Ali era. In May a legal judgment outlawed the National League for the Protection of the Revolution, which had campaigned to protect what the organization held to be the gains of the uprising against Ben Ali.

The domestic and regional security repercussions of the regional uprisings that had begun in 2011 were exemplified in July 2014, when 14 Tunisian border police were killed in an attack by Ansar al-Sharia militants in Jebel Chaambi, near Kasserine (close to the Algerian border); the area had also been the site of an ambush on Tunisian troops in April 2013, in which at least eight soldiers were killed. The Tunisian military had begun a major offensive around Jebel Chaambi in April 2014, involving air strikes and the deployment of heavy weapons. In July it was reported that some 6,000 members of the Tunisian military would take part in cross-border security operations with 8,000 Algerian counterparts. In addition, five Tunisian military 'counter-terror' operations were due to take place within Tunisia, including in the south-west close to the border with Libya. At the end of July Tunisian forces began a major bombardment of alleged terrorist targets in Jebel Samama.

THE ELECTION OF PRESIDENT ESSEBSI AND THE NIDAA TOUNES-LED GOVERNMENT

In the legislative elections, held on 26 October 2014, the essentially secular NT bloc secured 86 of the 217 NCA seats. Ennahdha's representation declined to 69 seats, the Union Patriotique Libre (UPL) won 16 seats, the FP 15 and Afek Tounes eight; the remaining 23 seats were distributed among smaller political groupings.

The presidential election, in which Ennahdha declined to participate, seemingly calculating that it could not win and that this would suit the party's longer-term interests, took place in two rounds: on 23 November and 21 December 2014. The poll was essentially a contest between Marzouki, who lacked party support but had a significant youth following, owing to his perceived integrity, and the 88-year-old Béji Caïd Essebsi, who had served as interim Prime Minister after Ben Ali had been deposed and who had garnered the backing of the NT and 11 smaller parties. After the second round of voting, Essebsi was declared the new President, completing the NT's assumption of power, although some cabinet positions were awarded to members of other parties, and the NT lacked a parliamentary majority. The integrity of the electoral process was largely endorsed by international observers. However, following Essebsi's election as President, demonstrators in Souk Lahad (in a part-Amazigh region of Kébili) set fire to the local National Guard and NT buildings in protest against an incoming administration that they perceived as connected to the Ben Ali regime.

In early January 2015 Habib Essid, who had served as Minister of the Interior under Ben Ali and Essebsi, was appointed as Prime Minister. Essid's proposed Council of Ministers, which excluded Ennahdha, was blocked by the opposition in the Assembly. A month later, however, Essid successfully formed a coalition administration. Despite his past associations, Essid's appointment as premier had been formally welcomed by Ennahdha, which agreed to join the new NT-led Government. However, the FP condemned the return to power of another figure from the Ben Ali era. (The group had also opposed the re-election of Marzouki.) Ennahdha's backing gave the Essid administration a parliamentary majority, and the coalition was also supported by the UPL and the pro-Essebsi Afek Tounes. The cabinet included Farhat Horchani, a supposed political independent, as Minister of National Defence and Taieb Baccouche, the Secretary-General of the NT, as Minister of Foreign Affairs.

The inclusion of Ennahdha in the new Government caused ructions within the NT. However, the matter was largely resolved following internal NT elections in March 2015 and a party conference in June. Elections had been called because of various disputes between reformers and conservatives. In addition to the dispute over the coalition with Ennahdha, proposals for the upcoming conference—such as that Nabil Karoui, the President of the private Nessma TV corporation, be included on the party's constituent board, the executive body within the NT, in appreciation for the network's support during the parliamentary elections—had threatened to split the party in two. Moreover, there were also differences over the role of Essebsi's son, Hafedh, the head of the constituent board. In early June, following the internal party election, Al Jazeera reported that Boujemâa Rmili had been appointed as the new head of the 'executive board' of the NT—a role pivotal to the co-ordination of policy within the four-party ruling coalition. Hafedh Essebsi remained powerful, however, and later in June he became one of three party Vice-Presidents.

More so than his immediate predecessor, Essebsi was administering the presidency as an executive office, a capability made possible by his party's plurality in parliament. At 88 years of age, however, there were practical constraints on his ability to wield executive authority by himself, and, despite his recent leadership of NT, other figures (aside from his son) had influence within the party. On becoming President, however, Essebsi had resigned his party leadership role out of constitutional propriety. This did not weaken him significantly within the NT, however, because of his son's power.

Anti-corruption protests under the banner 'Winou el petrole?' ('Where is our oil?'), organized by the political opposition, were conducted from early 2015. Demonstrators blamed the NT administration for alleged abuses in the energy sector and urged the full nationalization of the oil sector. In June Prime Minister Essid rebuffed the allegations in a combative interview on Tunisian television. In late July a leading Ettakatol figure, Mohamed Bennour, criticized the NT for allegedly attempting to establish a monopoly of power and claimed that its national (economic) reconciliation bill undermined the established transitional justice system founded after the collapse of the Ben Ali regime. The bill, if adopted, could enable corruption charges against former regime figures to be withdrawn, and, for some critics of the NT, it confirmed their view that the party was tantamount to the RCD. Others argued that many of Ben Ali's business allies had never relinquished their economic power, including in relation to the state.

MILITANT ISLAMIST TERRORIST ATTACKS

Militant attacks in 2015 led to the restoration of the state of emergency by the Government. A planned attack on parliament in mid-March, while 'anti-terror' legislation was being debated, resulted in the murder of 21 Western tourists by militants in the adjacent Bardo National Museum. The massacre prompted a further government clampdown, the introduction of new anti-terrorism proposals (which were criticized by opposition and international human rights groups, owing to concerns that political dissent and freedom of speech could be constrained) and a tougher approach to alleged Salafi mosques and preachers. The attack was blamed by the authorities on the Okba Ibn Nafaa Brigade, which had recently declared itself an AQIM affiliate, and in particular on an Algerian national, Lokmane Abou Sakhr. Notably, the Bardo murders followed the killing of Ansar al-Sharia operatives by the Tunisian authorities. Abou Sakhr and eight others were killed by the Tunisian security forces shortly after the incident. The Sunni militant organization Islamic State claimed responsibility for the Bardo attack. In December 2014, in its first overt message addressed to Tunisians, the organization had also claimed responsibility for the deaths of Belaïd and Brahimi. In early April 2015 Abu Yahya al-Tunisi of Islamic State's self-declared 'Wilayat Tarabulus' ('Tripoli Province') urged Tunisians to travel to Libya for training to help the group to establish an Islamic State entity in Tunisia.

The Bardo killings precipitated a marked downward trend in the country's key source of revenue—tourism—amid heightened security concerns. This trend was magnified in late June 2015, when militants killed 38 people (including 37 Western tourists) in the north-eastern resort city of Sousse. The massacre was apparently conducted by an Islamic State sympathizer, Saifeddine Rezgui, a Tunisian national. Media reports suggested that the dismissal of some Ministry of the Interior personnel after the overthrow of Ben Ali had removed experienced personnel who might have been able to prevent such attacks. It subsequently emerged that Rezgui had been trained by Islamic State in Libya. The security forces conducted numerous counter-terrorism operations following these attacks. For example, 92 raids were conducted in mid-July, resulting in the arrests of 322 people. In a contentious move, 28 out of 80 mosques accused of operating without a licence were closed.

The Okba Ibn Nafaa Brigade claimed responsibility for an attack on a customs post in Kasserine near the Algerian border in late August 2015 that left one customs officer dead and two injured. In late September the Government lifted the state of emergency in response to an apparent improvement in the security situation. However, at the beginning of October the authorities reported that they had foiled a major terrorist plot in Tataouine. Militants in vehicles had been intercepted in late September while allegedly attempting to cross into Tunisia. It was believed that the plot had been orchestrated by Islamic State.

In mid-September 2015 opposition parties protested against the coalition's national (economic) reconciliation bill, repeating the accusation that it had been designed to exonerate former members of the Ben Ali regime. In support of the bill, the NT contended that it would enable the state to recover lost money efficiently. The bill would allow the return of those accused of corruption if they repaid monies allegedly misappropriated from the state.

In October 2015 Rachid Ghannouchi appealed to the West for a Tunisian version of the 'Marshall Plan'—a US programme of financial support that had been introduced to bolster the European democracies following the end of the Second World War. At the same time, civil rights groups and opposition factions continued to criticize the performance of the coalition. This also had risks. Notably, the Tunisian National Dialogue Quartet, a grouping of four influential civil bodies of long standing: UGTT, the Union Tunisienne de l'Industrie, du Commerce et de l'Artisanat (UTICA—the employers' trade union), the LTDH and the Ordre National des Avocats de Tunisie (the Tunisian Bar Association) had been awarded the Nobel Peace Prize in the same month. This reflected the important role that the Quartet, representing different interests, had played during a period of often violent instability in upholding the political principles of the 2011 uprising. (Since 2011 the UGTT had been able to resume its historically autonomous role after the increasingly coercive Ben Ali had largely succeeded in co-opting it.) The process of National Dialogue that the four Quartet members led had enabled mediation between the interests of the authorities and opposing groups.

That a political amalgam like the FP would argue that the coalition was in crisis was not surprising, but Ana Yakiz, a civil rights group founded after Ben Ali's downfall to monitor the progress of the revolution, was also strongly critical of what it called the slow pace of change. In a more politicized contribution, Tarek Kahlaoui, a leading CPR figure, denounced the NT as a 'Trojan horse' of the former regime and criticized the party's support for Syrian President Bashar al-Assad (see *Relations with the Wider Middle East*).

In late November 2015 an assault, claimed by Islamic State, on a contingent of presidential guards travelling by bus in Tunis resulted in the deaths of 13 people. A series of measures was announced in an attempt to tighten security, including a 15-day closure of the border with Libya and the establishment of a youth employment programme in areas where militants were present. President Essebsi urged those in his party, including his son Hafedh, still pursuing their factional interests to show some 'patriotism' and 'self-restraint' in these circumstances, and thanked the UGTT for postponing a strike over wages.

In December 2015, in response to growing concerns about Islamist extremism, President Essebsi reinstated Abderrahmen Haj Ali, the veteran commander of the presidential guard under Ben Ali, as head of national security—a change supported by Ennahdha.

DIVISIONS WITHIN NIDAA TOUNES

The crisis within the NT over the influence of Hafedh Essebsi, whose allies sought the abolition of the party's political bureau so that he could take power, continued. Intra-party tensions had also been raised by President Essebsi's pursuit of increasingly close relations with Ennahdha. In December 2015 Mohsen Marzouk, who had already stepped down as the NT's Secretary-General, and who led the faction opposed to Hafedh Essebsi, threatened to form a breakaway bloc. Twenty-two deputies eventually resigned from the NT bloc to form a separate Marzouk-led grouping. They claimed a more leftist affiliation than their parent party.

In mid-January 2016, at this time of crisis for the four-party coalition Government, Ghannouchi, the leader of Ennahdha, spoke at the NT's annual conference, together with President Essebsi. This apparent expression of solidarity reflected the reality of the two parties' increasingly close ties and reflected Ennahdha's increasing embrace of a politics that, if not entirely secular, was largely prepared to accept the separation of religion and state. The two leaders' joint message was that there should be no politics of exclusion, in order to avoid Tunisia's transformation deteriorating into the type of civil conflict seen in some other Arab states.

In an echo of the initial spark that had precipitated the 2010–11 revolt and Ben Ali's downfall, from January 2016 riots occurred in Kasserine following the suicide of a young man who had apparently failed to find a job. Protest action continued in several cities within Kasserine governorate, particularly in Kasserine City, before spreading to two neighbouring governorates: Sidi Bouzid and Siliana. The protests continued to escalate: throughout January and February hundreds of young Tunisians demonstrated against unemployment by conducting sit-ins outside government buildings in most Tunisian governorates. Although the Government accused 'extremists' of exploiting the anger and in late January prematurely declared that the protests were over, it took the issue of unemployment seriously, while declaring a curfew as a precaution. Compounding the sense of crisis, police and other security personnel had begun conducting sit-ins over pay from early January, which continued through the first week or more of the civilian demonstrations. With the number of people out of work officially standing at about 700,000, including some 250,000 graduates, who were disproportionately represented among the demonstrators, unemployment was a serious issue.

The leftist label that had been applied to the breakaway Marzouk faction of the NT prompted suggestions by some observers that Marzouk's grouping had supported the protests in Kasserine. Even more controversial was the allegation that Marzouk's bloc had received funding from the United Arab Emirates (UAE)—a claim reported by, among other sources, Lebanese newspaper *Al-Akhbar* (a newspaper that is sympathetic to Hezbollah—a militant Lebanese Shi'a organization—and broadly opposed to the UAE). The supposed logic of such a move was that the UAE would be keen to have an anti-Muslim Brotherhood party under its influence. However, Marzouk's withdrawal from the NT had given Ennahdha a parliamentary majority, and it was possible that it would use this majority to install its own premier again. Mohamed Ben Salem, a leading Ennahdha deputy, claimed in December 2015 that the UAE had been supporting the NT because of its opposition to Ennahdha. It was therefore conceivable that the UAE had redirected its funding to the more firmly anti-Ennahdha faction of the NT led by Marzouk.

The split within the NT left Ennahdha as the largest party in parliament, with 69 deputies, while the NT was reduced to 64. The 22 defecting deputies, including two government ministers, led by Marzouk formed a new bloc initially referred to as al-Hurra (The Free), which was subsequently formalized into a new party, the Mouvement Machrouu Tounes (MMT—the Movement of Tunisia's Project). Marzouk claimed that his party was the legitimate heir to Bourguiba's modernist tradition. The NT had portrayed itself as the sole keeper of this tradition, with its rigid separation of religion and state, yet it claimed to be somehow distinct from the RCD, the former ruling party of Bourguiba and Ben Ali.

The more fundamental political reality of the new situation, however, was that, as their political opponents in the broad leftist FP alliance had claimed, only two pre-eminent 'sheikhs'—Rachid Ghannouchi and President Essebsi—would decide whether Prime Minister Essid or a replacement would lead the Government. Compounding the fraught political atmosphere were suggestions that these two leading political players were attempting to secure the support of Ben Ali loyalists. Arguably, the presence of Afek Tounes in the ruling coalition was already evidence of this.

In January 2016 Essid responded to the increasing political uncertainty by effecting a minor cabinet reorganization, reflecting the slightly altered balance of power within the existing four-party coalition. Frustrating for some observers, given the country's precarious security situation, a new Minister of the Interior was appointed—the sixth since 2011. On this occasion, Mohamed Najem Gharsalli was replaced by Hédi Majdoub. Youssef Chahed, the new local affairs minister, was given responsibility for the upcoming municipal elections. His affiliation to the NT raised suspicions that he might try to manipulate the process to the advantage of his party. Minister of Foreign Affairs Baccouche (a member of the NT) was replaced by an independent, Khmaïyes Jhinaoui, although he was believed to be close to the NT.

On balance, however, the new cabinet seemed to advantage Ennahdha. The replacement of the Minister of Religious Affairs removed a figure who had dismissed several imams associated with the party. The appointment of Omar Mansour, who was regarded as close to Ennahdha, as Minister of Justice frustrated opposition activists who had been seeking redress over the assassination of Belaïd. The latter's lawyer had accused Ennahdha and the NT of a conspiracy to cover up responsibility for the killing.

In March 2016 several deaths were reported near the border with Libya following clashes between the security forces and militants believed to be affiliated to Islamic State. On 7 March some 50 people were killed near the border town of Ben Guerdane. They were reportedly mostly militants who had died during skirmishes with the security forces. Three days later up to 10 more people were killed, including at least two suspected Islamic State militants. Islamic State did not claim responsibility for the 7 March clashes. It was alleged in semi-official reports that some of the attackers were Algerians, although there seemed little doubt that many were Tunisian nationals (Tunisians were disproportionately represented among Islamic State fighters). Later in that month a security expert and former Ministry of National Defence spokesman, Brig.-Gen. Mokhtar bin Nasser, commented that 'sleeper cells' might have been established throughout the country. Experts conjectured that Islamic State's objective was to establish a bridgehead in the strategic border areas in preparation for further attacks in Tunisian territory. In response, Libya closed two crossing points. Meanwhile, the Tunisian Ministry of National Defence announced plans to recruit thousands of unemployed youths into the military specifically to increase the state's capacity to respond to increasing security threats and possibly to prevent alienated youths from joining Islamic State.

In May 2016 Ennahdha held its 10th party congress, which was attended by President Essebsi. As with Ghannouchi's participation in the NT's conference earlier in the year, this symbolized some coalescence in the two parties' policies, as well as their cohabitation at the highest level of Tunisian politics. Ghannouchi was re-elected as party leader by an overwhelming majority of delegates and introduced a new party platform that reflected the increasing convergence of Ennahdha's policy outlook with that of the political descendants of former President Bourguiba. Part conviction, part political convenience, the specifics of Ghannouchi's modernist Islamist platform confirmed an already apparent trend in Ennahdha—that politics and Islam should be kept largely (although not entirely) separate. More precisely, the party agreed that *da'wah* (carrying out Islamic precepts in the social or cultural sphere) would no longer be a party responsibility but that of individual Muslims. However, Ennahdha would continue to maintain an Islamic identity in the party political sphere. In essence, this was very similar to the separation of religion and state and to the practical meaning of secular politics. Ghannouchi, however, demurred from accepting that Ennahdha was therefore officially no longer Islamist, as some in the leadership would accept, and, unsurprisingly, nobody in the party was willing formally to adopt the 'secularist' tag embraced by followers of Bourguiba such as the NT.

In what seemed like a highly symbolic political act, a few days after the historic Ennahdha congress that had resulted in the party reaching an accommodation with secularism, former President Bourguiba returned to Tunis. In June 2016 a statue of the country's independence leader, which Ben Ali had removed 28 years earlier as part of an effort to foster his own cult of personality, was restored to its original location in the centre of the capital in a ceremony overseen by President Essebsi.

Meanwhile, speculation continued about the circumstances under which Ben Ali might return to Tunisia (alive), in part because of the coalition Government's commitment to the national (economic) reconciliation bill and also because some of his senior associates had already conducted talks in Tunis in April 2016. Ben Ali's lawyers had declared that the former President would not return without an explicit guarantee that any proffered official pardon would be upheld in law and in practice—an arguably difficult guarantee to maintain in perpetuity. The NT's detractors argued that talks with Ben Ali's senior associates were intended to increase the party's support at the municipal elections due in late 2016. Jilani Hammami, a leading FP figure, claimed in May that Ennahdha was also attempting to reach a deal with the former President's ruling party. Hammami noted that Ghannouchi had proposed his own version of the economic reconciliation law that the NT had sponsored. Youth activists challenging the reconciliation bill launched a campaign under the slogan 'I will not forgive'.

In July 2016 the authorities arrested members of an alleged Islamic State cell in Sousse, claiming that they were preparing another major terrorist attack in the city. In August the Okba Ibn Nafaa Brigade claimed responsibility for an attack on a military unit in Semama (a mountainous area in Kasserine), which left three soldiers dead. In early October the Government announced that it had thwarted a terrorist attack on a National Guard facility in Khamada, a town in Kasserine. In mid-October the state of emergency was renewed for another three months, and 19 members of a militant Islamist cell were imprisoned. Shortly afterwards the Government announced that it had thwarted a planned attack on a cabinet member, presumed to be the Minister of the Interior. A weapons cache was discovered in Ben Guerdane in November. In March major clashes had taken place between Tunisian forces and Islamist militants who were attempting to seize control of border posts near the town. The Government touted the apparent success of the security forces in routing the militants as a turning point in its counter-terrorism campaign.

THE APPOINTMENT OF A NEW GOVERNMENT UNDER YOUSSEF CHAHED

On 30 July 2016 parliament approved a motion of no confidence in Prime Minister Essid, prompting his resignation. On 3 August Chahed was appointed by President Essebsi to form a new Government. Chahed's administration was approved by the legislature on 27 August. The Ministers of Foreign Affairs, the Interior and National Defence retained their posts, while the independents Ghazi Jeribi and Lamia Zribi joined the Government as the Ministers of Justice and of Finance, respectively. Among others, Ennahdha was allocated the key post of Minister of Industry and Commerce. Eight members of the new Government were women, and five were under 35 years of age. Three relatively minor parties, which had previously participated in nine-party national unity talks, resigned from the process, and some critics accused the President of nepotism, as Chahed was a (very distant) relative. Chahed emphasized that the focus of his Government would be on combating terrorism and corruption and revitalizing the economy, potentially by reducing government spending. This message was echoed by Ghannouchi, who, at a meeting of Ennahdha party activists in September, conceded that public sector job cuts might have to be cut if economic problems, including a large fiscal deficit and substantial government debt, continued.

The budget, which was released in October 2016 and included a proposed public sector pay freeze and increases in taxes and utility rates, was condemned by the FP, which organized a protest rally and accused the Government of being beholden to the International Monetary Fund (IMF). The UGTT joined the FP in criticizing the Government's austerity plan. A public sector strike was called for early December. In November President Essebsi asserted that his party, the NT, had been a force for stability in Tunisia at a time when Ennahdha was promoting Islamism, and claimed that during the uprising he had helped to prevent a 'bloodbath' in a country 'without much experience of democracy'. However, popular discontent remained rife, with youth activists arguing that the state had not fundamentally changed, but that it was under a new leadership unable or unwilling to implement structural changes to address the original economic and political causes of the revolt. In December a youth dialogue conference, supported by the Government and involving some 40,000 young people, was held in Monastir to discuss strategies to influence the Government's decision-making process.

President Essebsi was criticized by some sections of the media and political opinion after a lethal terrorist attack in Berlin, Germany, in December 2016, which was linked to a Tunisian national, Anis Amri, who subsequently pledged allegiance to Islamic State before being shot dead by the police in Italy. The incident seemingly raised greater domestic security concerns rather than worries about Tunisia's relations with Europe. Essebsi initially defended the Government's security strategy by declaring that Tunisians returning from armed conflict in other parts of the region could not all be jailed. (Amri had been living in Europe, where he was imprisoned, but the Tunisian authorities had resisted attempts to have him returned to Tunisia—see below). The President attempted to quell the consequent outrage caused by this seemingly dismissive comment by arguing that all precautions were taken to prevent militants from influencing other Tunisians. The authorities linked Amri to a three-person cell in Kairouan governorate, which had reportedly declared its loyalty to him and to Islamic State.

The assassination of a Tunisian expert on unmanned aerial vehicles (drones), Mohamed Zouari, outside his home in Sfax in mid-December 2016 raised concerns about national security vulnerabilities of a more traditional kind. The fact that Zouari had links to the Islamic Resistance Movement (Hamas—a Palestinian militant Islamist group) and potentially to the development of its military capabilities raised the possibility of Israel's involvement in the killing. It was reported that a new national intelligence co-ordination body had been founded to share intelligence among the different security departments. The ability of the killer and, after the murder, according to Al Jazeera, the Israeli media to travel freely to Zouari's house raised genuine concerns about Tunisia's intelligence and domestic security capabilities. The issue was politically precarious, reflecting the ongoing domestic sensitivity of the Palestinian question and the difficulty for the Tunisian Government in confronting Israel, a regional military power, while attempting to maintain cordial relations with the West. Ghannouchi, on behalf of Ennahdha, had no hesitation in condemning Israel for the killing, however. Five Tunisians were arrested in connection with the murder.

At the end of December 2016 the authorities intercepted an alleged nine-man Ansar al-Sharia cell in the north-eastern governorate of Manouba. Separately, the threat of Tunisian militants returning from combat in Libya was underlined in early January 2017 when Wannas Ben Hassine Ben Mohamed Fekih, a militant with links to AQIM and Islamic State, was intercepted by the Tunisian authorities. In December 2016 the ousting of Islamic State from the Libyan province of Sirte had raised fears in Tunisia—the largest exporter (proportionately speaking at least) of Islamist militants in the region—of an influx of Tunisian fighters returning home and engaging in violence. The Chahed administration had made it clear that it did not want other countries to return Tunisians who were believed to have been engaged in fighting abroad. President Essebsi had announced that they could, and should, return if they stood trial under anti-terrorism laws.

Majdoub, the Minister of the Interior, declared in January 2017 that the number of Tunisians who had fought abroad as Islamist militants was exaggerated. He claimed that the total was 2,929 and that of those, 800 had already returned, of whom 127 had been placed under house arrest. However, this suggested that 673 militants had returned unhindered.

Periodic arrests and related interceptions of terrorist plots continued in Tunisia in early 2018. In April Okba Ibn Nafaa issued a statement inciting Tunisians to attack 'French interests' in Tunisia. (This had followed the stabbing of two tourists in the Roman ruins at El-Kif, although the attack was not believed to have been terrorism-related.) In June Islamic State claimed that it had carried out the attack that had taken place on part of an oil pipeline at Sfax. Shortly before this, the authorities announced they had arrested members of two Islamist militant cells in Sousse and Manouba. In an attack claimed by the Okba Ibn Nafaa group, six Tunisian guards were killed at a border post in July, and the group issued a threat to any Western tourists intent on visiting Tunisia.

Major unrest in the cities of Meknassi and Manzel Bouziane in Sidi Bouzid governorate, where the 2011 uprising had begun, and in Ben Guerdane in January 2017 raised concerns about the possibility of a comparable revolt. Disgruntled leftist politicians saw an opportunity to exploit rising popular disillusionment for political gain. Members of the NT, the MMT, the FP and the socialist al-Ichtiraki formed a national salvation front in that month and invited other parties to join them.

Education continued to be a source of political discontent, owing to a dispute over changes mooted during the Essid administration. Teachers' unions criticized the Minister of Education, Néji Jalloul, and what they considered to be his, and the Government's, insufficient commitment to state education amid the expansion of private education in the country. Jalloul argued that the reforms were intended to offer more choice to pupils throughout the state sector. Any closure of schools was, according to the Government, a necessary exercise in reducing costs, not an attempt to limit public education. Further social cuts in the 2018 budget, announced at the end of 2017, increased the education protesters' accusations of underfunding. In March former education minister under Ben Ali, Hatem Ben Salem, had become a particular target of hostility from the teachers' unions, which accused him of presiding over the 'blocking' of pupils from disadvantaged backgrounds from receiving a full education.

The Chahed administration had assumed office promising to prioritize combating corruption. The National Anti-Corruption Commission (NACC) was to be given more impetus. A youth non-governmental organization, I-Watch, was encouraged to mobilize Tunisians to monitor any signs of corrupt activity, and in December 2016 it appealed to religious leaders to support this effort in their sermons. Encouraged by the NACC, the Prosecutor-General announced action against 12 senior state officials in February 2017.

ECONOMIC AND LABOUR PROTESTS

In March–April 2017 youths protesting against unemployment blocked a road that linked the predominantly Amazigh and relatively deprived city of Tataouine to the desert of the central western territory of Kamour. The objective was to obstruct what they regarded as 'corporate plunder' surrounding foreign-linked oil development work. The Tataouine protests developed into a general strike, prompting Chahed to visit the city at the end of April in an attempt to quell the unrest. Protesters demanded that the oil companies operating in Tataouine employ some of the province's jobless youths and fund local development. The apparent failure of talks with the Prime Minister prompted the protesters to demand Chahed's resignation.

President Essebsi responded to the protests in Tataouine and the wider discontent in the country in a speech on 10 May 2017. He controversially urged an amnesty for returning members of the Ben Ali regime—a bitterly disputed government policy. His declaration that the army would ensure that key economic resources, such as hydrocarbons and phosphates, would be developed unhindered was seen as a warning to protesters and an attempt to reassure foreign business partners and investors. Essebsi also announced that he was in discussion with the Minister of the Interior about reforming the 'exhausted' security services. His comments were criticized by former President Marzouki, who maintained that the army should protect the country's borders, not intervene in labour disputes. However, the Minister of National Defence, Horchani, readily endorsed the deployment of military forces to protect the country's key industrial infrastructure. Essebsi's comments exacerbated the tensions in Tataouine. Protesters stormed the municipal buildings in Tataouine and burned down a vacated National Guard base; the Guard had earlier been deployed by Chahed to support the army. In response, some of the protesters' tents were burned down. A solidarity demonstration, also appealing for 'the right to development', was held in El Fouar in the south-western governorate of Kébili. After just a month in office, the governor of Tataouine, Mohamed Ali el-Barhoumi, resigned in late May after the protests had become more violent. In June clashes between the security forces and civilians in Sidi Bouzid erupted again, following a dispute between market traders that had left one person dead and led to violent reprisals before the intervention of the authorities. In July security officers, concerned about the number of attacks on their colleagues nationwide, staged a protest outside the Assembly, urging the rapid approval of an Armed Forces Protection Bill.

In September 2017 President Essebsi secured approval in the Assembly for an amnesty for former members of the Ben Ali administration in exchange for the return of funds obtained by allegedly corrupt means. Earlier in that month Essebsi had discreetly overseen a major reshuffle of Chahed's Government affecting 13 ministries and notable for the return of several former regime figures, including to the key interior, defence and finance portfolios.

Unrest in Tataouine and other areas nursing economic grievances persisted, and was exacerbated by the inclusion of increased taxes and prices, alongside further cuts to services, in the 2018 budget. In January 2018 unrest had erupted again among workers in the Gafsa region who had not been hired by the Gafsa Phosphate Company, and in February workers at Tatouine's Kamour oil facility protested about the failure to implement an agreement reached between workers and employers following a major dispute in 2017. General protests broke out in April 2018 in Tataouine and Kasserine governorates.

MUNICIPAL ELECTIONS OF MAY 2018

After a delay of nearly a year following disputes about electoral law, municipal elections took place on 6 May 2018. Voter registration had been low, and only about 40% of registered voters participated in the poll. Of security service personnel (who voted separately from the rest of the population) only 12%

who had registered to vote actually participated. Independent candidates together won the most votes, while Ennahdha and the NT came in second and third, respectively. The outcome was arguably a vote of no confidence in what had become the new political establishment. Nor did it seem to be an endorsement of the new regime's proposals to concede meaningful power to elected politicians outside of Tunis. Nearly five years later, and just a few months before the next round of municipal elections were due, the councils were abolished by presidential fiat (see *Saïed Dissolves Local Councils*).

Tunisia's image as relatively progressive (among Arab states) in terms of the position of women, was enhanced in late July 2018 when its legally based amnesty for rapists who married their victims was repealed, following Jordan, which had just taken the same action. President Essebsi caused controversy in August by appealing for equal inheritance rights for women and urging a further advance of women's rights by putting inter-religious marriage on an equal legal footing with Islamic marriage by removing the ban on Tunisian women marrying non-Muslims. (The law, as it stands, assumes that a female Tunisian from a mainstream Sunni Islam background is more likely to adopt her husband's tradition, than vice versa). Essebsi was attacked for political opportunism, including by his predecessor, Marzouki.

Internal divisions in the NT, and wider discontent with its direction at the head of the coalition government continued in 2018 and were exacerbated by the party's poor performance in the local elections. President Essebsi urged in July that Chahed either resign or 'regain parliamentary confidence' in the face of divisions within the party and the coalition and wider popular dissent relating to austerity and seemingly widespread corruption (an issue that had played its part in the 2011 uprising). The trade union movement was also angry, as were other social groups and political critics of the Government, about ongoing and, in their view, unnecessary, austerity measures.

Chief among the dissenters in the Government was the President's son, Hafedh Essebsi, the executive director of the NT, who appeared determined to use the mounting dissatisfaction to oust Chahed. In May 2018 a breakaway faction of NT parliamentary members expressed support for a major reorganization of cabinet positions to try to address the crisis, as did the wider party (although members were divided over the issue of whether Chahed should remain in office), while Ennahdha, the National Destourian Initiative party (al-Moubadra) and UTICA were opposed. The UGTT, however, expressed support for a reshuffle. There had also been much discussion of the so-called 'Carthage 2'—the proposed new political accord—intended by its proponents as a possible way through the governing impasse that enabled Chahed to remain as premier.

In late May 2018 Chahed dismissed interior minister Lotfi Brahem following an incident in which more than 100 migrants had died off the Tunisian coast (see *Foreign Relations*). It was alleged that the ship in which the migrants had been travelling had been sunk by the Tunisian authorities. A total of 10 Tunisian security employees were dismissed following the incident. The affair was presented by some as a consequence of a hard-line Tunisian external security policy, enforced by a minister from the old regime at the head of an essentially unreformed ministry. There had been a similar tragedy in October 2017 when 45 migrants had died. For many observers, Brahem appeared to be a useful scapegoat at a time of increasing political crisis for Chahed. Brahem was replaced on a permanent basis in late July 2018 by Hichem Fourati, who Chahed claimed was not involved in any of the political wranglings currently causing difficulties for the Government.

In an attempt to address ongoing concerns relating to alleged widespread corruption, in June 2018 the official anti-corruption body (Instance Nationale de Lutte Contre la Corruption—INLUCC), introduced a new system for handling complaints of corruption in the public and private sector. The INLUCC claimed that over 245 cases had been referred to the courts during the previous 12 months.

In July 2018 al-Massar, a self-styled 'Social Democratic Path' party, withdrew from the four-party governing coalition of which it was a minor member, although its Secretary-General, Samir Taieb, defied his party to remain in the Government as agriculture minister. Moreover, the Minister for Constitutional Affairs had resigned from the Government a few days earlier. Chahed remained in office, however, owing partly to the lack of a clear successor from within the NT.

END TO POWER-SHARING BETWEEN ISLAMISTS AND SECULARISTS

In early September 2018 President Essebsi and Rachid Ghannouchi reportedly failed to secure support for a parliamentary vote of no confidence in Chahed. By that time an informal alliance between Ennahdha (with 68 deputies) and a new pro-Chahed bloc, Coalition Nationale (CN—with 43 deputies, most of whom had left the NT) now held a parliamentary majority. On 14 September the NT suspended Chahed. In late September Essebsi decided that the Government, in part divided by the rivalry and differing agenda of Chahed and Hafedh Essebsi, the head of the NT, should rule without Ennahdha, and the Islamist party was dismissed from the coalition.

Ennahdha had good reason to be angry at the conduct of the NT-led Government and had long been frustrated by its representation in cabinet. However, the President's past role in the cabinet's formation, behind the scenes, to the benefit of his party, the NT, and his desire, as far as possible to favour his son, Hafedh, might have made the dismissal of Ennahdha from the coalition a blessing in disguise for the Islamist party. This was emphasized by the Government's evident unpopularity, exemplified by regular public protests about economic conditions. President Essebsi's formal expression of continued support for Chahed's premiership (irrespective of the latter's ongoing rivalry with Hafedh Essebsi within the NT) underlined the continued polarization and dysfunctionality in Tunisian politics.

President Essebsi's actions in September 2018 also sought to address the inherent practical problem of a system that promoted power-sharing between a directly elected president and an indirectly elected premier, whose authority is supposed in part to stem from the President's continued support and from holding a majority, however tacit, in the Assembly. When both presidential and Assembly support for the premier was clearly limited or even non-existent, as was the case with Chahed, there was a major impasse or simply an inevitable collapse of authority. The President suggested that a constitutional change was needed for his successor to prevent this awkward form of power-sharing. It was unclear what the precise nature of the change that President Essebsi had in mind might be. In theory, enhanced executive powers would be one way for the next president to more easily jettison a prime minister. Some observers argued that behind the scenes, President Essebsi, for all his willingness as head of state to manage relations with the Islamists on an arguably democratic basis, encouraged the exit of Ennahdha. That party, after all, is a rival to the NT. The exit of Ennahdha would perhaps enable the strife-riven NT to more clearly identify itself, while, more prosaically, President Essebsi might have calculated that the interests of the Ben Ali-era elite (of which he was a leading member) were better served by weakening an anti-corruption effort that Chahed was enabling, with Ennahdha's support. Weakening the Islamists could weaken their de facto ally, Prime Minister Chahed.

President Essebsi also announced in late September 2018 that presidential and parliamentary elections would be conducted simultaneously in December 2019. In April 2018 he had confirmed to his party's national conference that he would not be standing for re-election as head of state.

After several months of deliberation and weeks of tension, involving President Essebsi rejecting the proposed formation of a new Government, a new cabinet was appointed in mid-November 2018—the 10th administration since the 2011 uprising. Chahed remained as Prime Minister, and his new Government retained nine NT members and several members from the MMT and al-Moubadra; the latter party held five portfolios, including one held by Kamel Morjane, who had served as foreign minister under Ben Ali. He was put in charge of the Ministry of Public Service and Governance.

Although the agreement on a new cabinet was a step forward, the Government had arguably become more unstable than when Ennahdha was a formal part of it. As the second largest party in the Assembly in late 2018, Ennahdha could easily unsettle a government that would otherwise need to rely in parliament on the support of several small parties. Furthermore, the divisions within the NT inevitably became unsustainable, given the clash of personalities and the Chahed-led Government's economic failings and ongoing austerity measures, and the ensuing popular challenges to its authority.

In an indication of the state of flux in Tunisian politics, especially within the NT, in October 2018 the UPL, under its leader Slim Riahi, merged with the NT after Riahi switched his allegiance from Chahed to Essebsi. For his part, Jomaâ suggested that such a union might also appeal to his own party, al-Badil Ettounsi (Tunisian Alternative). However, Riahi's political career ended in February 2019, when he was imprisoned for five years on corruption charges (see below).

In November 2018 the UGTT announced a general strike for January 2019 in opposition to government economic policy, including a recent increase in the price of petrol and rising unemployment that disproportionately affected Tunisians aged under 25, and demanded a rise in public sector pay. Social unrest continued to be related to these factors, as well as regionally specific issues in more deprived parts of the country.

In January 2019, while the strike was taking place, large demonstrations were conducted in Tunis and other major cities over several days. These included violent clashes between some protesters and members of the security forces. Nearly 800 people were arrested, and several civilians and police officers were injured. President Emmanuel Macron of France was visiting the country at that time (see *Relations with the West*); the upheaval compounded a sense of unease and vulnerability in Tunisia's internal political and social relations. During their joint press conference, President Essebsi took a tough line against the disturbances and said that the judicial authorities, although not perfect, were doing a good job in dealing with those whose protests were not, in his view, democratically or economically motivated.

Perhaps taking his cue from President Essebsi, interior minister Fourati used the example of the very small number of Tunisians protesting as a proportion of the total, who, he claimed, had carried out attacks on police stations and banks and conducted other forms of criminality, to imply that many of the protests 'had nothing to do with democracy' or rising prices (which the protesters had claimed as a motivating factor). In the end, however, the finance minister Ridha Chalghoum, a figure loathed by some of the protesters, responded to aspects of their grievances by announcing improved welfare benefits aimed at the poorest 250,000 Tunisian families, including a large increase in the supplement paid to the poorest, equivalent to about TD 150 a month at that time, to TD 210. However, the total package of approximately TD 170m. would need the approval of the outgoing parliament. Many protesters remained angry about the direction of government fiscal and spending policy, including Chalghoum's budget bill (presented in October 2018), which, although attempting to tackle unemployment, they considered as too business-friendly, given, for example, its proposed corporate tax cuts (see *Economy*).

In February 2019 several unemployed university graduates from the central-west part of the country staged a symbolic march toward the border with Algeria symbolically 'demanding' asylum, owing to their lack of work. In October 2018 a similar protest had been conducted by unemployed graduates from the same region at their local authority headquarters. Disaffection seemed to be growing, including with the inertia and deeply partisan rivalry afflicting the Government and several of its most senior members. A US think tank, the International Republican Institute, conducted a poll in early 2019 that reported that 87% of Tunisians thought that their country was heading 'in the wrong direction'.

Meanwhile, former President Marzouki claimed in January 2019 that the UAE (see *Relations with Other Maghreb States*) was seeking to bring down the Government and that it had been undermining the democratic changes brought about in Tunisia since 2011; he also claimed that the UAE was using 'terrorism' and 'corrupt media' to do this. Critics had claimed that the UAE had allegedly been interfering in Tunisia's domestic politics in order to weaken the Islamist party, Ennahdha. Marzouki appeared to be implying that, rather than him being the beneficiary of the Gulf state's alleged machinations, as had been claimed by his critics, it was Hafedh's wing of the NT that had benefited and that through them the UAE wanted to bring down Prime Minister Chahed, who had the support of Ennahdha.

In late January 2019 the unsurprising (and second) break-up of the internally riven NT finally occurred after many months of internecine party struggle. The founding of Tahia Tounes (TT—Long Live Tunisia), with its breakaway ministers and other deputies totalling nearly one-half of NT's former tally), fundamentally weakened the NT within the Assembly (following Marzouki's breakaway in 2016 (see above). Ennahdha's position was consequently further enhanced, becoming the largest party in the Assembly (although it still lacked an overall majority). Despite the Hafedh wing's opposition to Chahed being supported by Ennahdha, the Prime Minister was now even more reliant on Ennahdha in order to stay in office and on President Essebsi's lack of power to engender either an alternative premier or a different way for Chahed to remain in power. The Prime Minister held a tentative majority of Ennahdha's bloc of deputies, and those of the CN bloc were counted on his side. The TT was founded with the express aim of being unlike the established parties, and it claimed that its structure would be horizontal. However, the appointment of a former minister, Selim Azzabi, as the party's Secretary-General in April 2019 belied this claim.

The NT needed to attract more support from among the many smaller parties in the Assembly. It has already gained those of the UPL. However, its leader, Riahi, who had become Secretary-General of the NT following the latter's internal split, was imprisoned in February 2019 for five years, having been found guilty of corruption. The Prime Minister's anti-corruption campaign, unsurprisingly perhaps, seemed to be hurting those who were not aligned with either him or Ennahdha.

In February 2019 the leftist FP bloc criticized Chahed for depending on Ennahdha. Its leader Hamma Hammami called on Chahed to resign as premier, focusing on the irony, especially from this faction's perspective, of this secular politician's reliance on Ennahdha, formally speaking sitting outside of the Government, to continue to govern. The vitriol against Ennahdha was partly explained by the fact that leftists continued to hold it responsible for the killing in 2013 of Belaïd (see above). In late May 2019 nine of the FP's 14-member parliamentary bloc quit the FP group in a dispute over whether the FP should work with liberal deputies against Ennahdha.

In late May 2019 the TT merged with al-Moubadra, a faction with an association, not least via its leader Morjane, with the Ben Ali era (but, unlike the Parti Destourien Libre—PDL—which had been founded in 2013 by Hamed Karoui, it was not a slavish devotee of that period). With an expanded TT, Chahed and his supporters could now hope to inflict more damage on his former party, the NT.

In May 2019 the scheduled dates for the polls were amended: parliamentary elections were brought forward to 6 October, and presidential elections to 17 November (with a second round on 24 November if a run-off was required). However, President Essebsi died following a long illness on 25 July, and the presidential election was brought forward again—this time in order that the constitutionally mandated maximum of 90 days (before a new elected President is installed) was observed. The presidential poll was now scheduled for 15 September (and a potential second round would take place on 22 September); the parliamentary poll was still scheduled for 17 November.

President Essebsi's funeral provided an important moment of unity among the increasingly fractious Tunisian political elite, and provoked genuine grief among some of the wider population. Mohamed Ennaceur, the Speaker of the Assembly, was appointed to serve as interim President, in accordance with the Constitution, until presidential elections were held in September 2019. There was no instability arising from this transition, nor was any necessarily expected. The greater worry, more perhaps for those outside of the country, was whether the new or, more accurately, the reformed regime instituted from 2011 was stable enough to outlast Béji Caïd Essebsi. After all, he had been instrumental, first as Prime Minister after the uprising of 2011, then as President, in facilitating power-sharing between those, like himself, from the old guard, and the 'next generation' organized in several 'post-Ben Ali' secular parties, as well as with the pre-eminent Tunisian Islamist grouping in the form of Ennahdha. This pivotal aspect to political peace and the ability to face down an incipient radical, unconstitutional Islamist threat, had been aided by Essebsi, for all his politicking and manipulation, including since the NT took a lead role in government, at the expense of both Ennahdha and even Prime Minister Chahed himself. Essebsi had embodied the commitment of a section of the old guard to some form of democracy and had arguably encouraged Ennahdha's relatively successful transition to vaunted 'Muslim Democrats'. Set against this was the responsibility of the members of the Assembly, including Essebsi's NT, to ensure the promised establishment of a functioning Constitutional Court. In 2022 the Court existed but was not yet functional, with deputies having succeeded in agreeing on appointees as judges to sit in it.

TUNISIA'S POLITICAL ORDER CHALLENGED AGAIN

By early 2019 the ongoing discontent within and with the Tunisian party political system had spurred the growth in the North African republic of a global phenomenon: populist politics. The appeal of two new self-styled outsider (would-be) politicians (and their leader-orientated parties) played a decisive role in prompting the Assembly to pass electoral legislation in mid-June outlawing the participation in the election of candidates with media companies or who have run charities for more than the 12 months prior to an election in which they wished to stand; it also prevented candidates from standing who had a criminal record. Specifically, the bill targeted what it called 'political advertising' and appeared to target directly Nabil Karoui, the owner of the Nessma television channel, a leading businessman and a former leading figure in the NT (see above). Reports on Nessma TV (which could perhaps be likened to adverts) had been critical of established politicians and their agenda. This benefited Karoui, who was clearly the greatest threat to the bill's proposers, Ennahdha and Prime Minister Chahed's TT. In late June Karoui became leader of the party Qalb Tounes (QT—Heart of Tunisia). The proposed legislation also attracted some support from a very small number of secularist deputies. On 25 June deputies from the NT and the FP filed a motion in the Assembly, calling the move unconstitutional.

By mid-2019 Nabil Karoui was registering more support for himself and his—non-existent in formal terms—'Karoui party' than any would-be rival, including Ennahdha, at least as measured by one public opinion poll and in Ennahdha's private polling. Both the TT and the NT were losing support to the benefit of the two main populist leaders and to a third, more conventional but also relatively new and secular grouping, the PDL, a neo-Destourian bloc claiming, in effect, a mantle from former presidents Bourguiba and Ben Ali). The appeal of this party and its female leader, Abir Moussi, was their support for judicial measures to exclude all Islamists from the formal political process and, in a related way, to oppose the modified political order following Ben Ali's removal as a 'conspiracy'. Other populist newcomers included al-Badil Ettounsi, led by former premier Jomaâ. Many deputies, including several of the established left-wing factions, but clearly not the majority of deputies, opposed the new electoral bill, seeing it as a stitch-up between Islamists and Chahed designed only to benefit themselves at the expense of the prized democratic transformation of the Republic. Its chief target, Karoui, took to social media to denounce moves that, so he claimed, revealed the falsehood of Ennahdha's own claim to have undergone a democratic transformation. Karoui, together with other opponents of the bill, appeared likely to gain from measures that had in any case been held up by President Essebsi, who had refused to give the legislation his assent. Essebsi had presumably believed that the legislation benefited only the opponents of his party and his son and no doubt offended the principles that he needed to associate himself with, as he was the country's first freely elected President, who consequently claimed to govern for the whole nation, despite his profound political allegiance to the NT and his own son. Unless abandoned, the legislation would become the concern of Ennaceur as interim head of state.

PRESIDENTIAL HOPEFULS (OR NOT)

Chahed, despite attracting much criticism for the Government's economic policy while Prime Minister and performing very poorly in recent opinion polls, decided to contest the presidency as the TT's nominee. It was unclear if Ennahdha would present its own candidate or, as had been the party's practice since 2011, lend their support to an allied or sympathetic candidate, who in theory could be Chahed. At the beginning of August 2019 Rachid Ghannouchi announced that he and his party were willing to do a deal with Chahed, whereby one of them could become president and the other prime minister. The Ennahdha leader was understandably focused on the TT founder and leader and not the more established NT—a more avowedly anti-Islamist grouping. In the following week it was reported that the party had chosen its vice-president, Abdelfattah Morrou, as its candidate.

Former President Marzouki, who had determinedly been promoting himself in the form of several highly provocative comments about the UAE (see above and below) put himself forward as a candidate again, this time representing his al-Hirak Tounes al-Irada (Tunisian Movement–The Will, which he had founded in December 2015). Jomaâ, who had flirted with joining the NT (see above), put himself forward as a presidential candidate but seemingly on behalf of al-Badil Ettounsi. It was not clear who the NT's nominee would be. Hafedh Essebsi did not put himself forward as a candidate.

In early August 2019 the NT named the Minister of National Defence, Abdelkarim Zbidi, as its candidate for the presidential election, although formally he was to stand as an independent. Following the 2011 uprising Zbidi was appointed defence minister and held on to the position under two Presidents and many different administrations. His evident appeal to the defence ministry and the military top brass, as well as to politicians of different stripes including the NT (and its breakaway factions) and Ennahdha, had lain in his apparent neutrality and efficiency. Critics suggested that he would be the USA's preferred choice as Tunisian head of state, especially after alleged Tunisian security establishment tensions with France (see *Relations with the West after 11 September 2001*), which Zbidi attempted to play down. Traditionally, the defence ministry and the interests of the military that it tends to represent, have been less important in Tunisia's discreet political order (unlike almost all other Arab states and Tunisia's neighbouring non-Arab African states) than the interior ministry and its domestic security apparatus. It is within the Tunisian Ministry of the Interior that a continuity of operations and personnel from before the uprising of 2011 and in the period ever since that belie the language and practice of a claimed 'revolution'.

Meanwhile, in early July 2019 Nabil Karoui and his brother Ghazi were charged with money laundering relating to a business deal in 2016. Their assets were frozen, and both men were forbidden from leaving the country. Nabil Karoui was arrested on 23 August 2019 and detained in Mornaguia prison in Manouba governorate.

A record 26 candidates were approved to contest the presidential election. Notably, they included Chahed of the TT, Hamma Hammami of the FP, Jomaâ of al-Badil Ettounsi, Mourou of Ennahdha, Marzouki of al-Hirak Tounes al-Irada, Nabil Karoui (despite being in prison) and Riahi (who was also in gaol) of the Nouvelle Union Internationale. Among the notable independent candidates were Zbidi and Kaïs Saïed, a professor of law, who campaigned on a programme of social conservatism, while pledging to introduce legislation to allow the electorate to recall politicians if they were suspected or charged with corruption. After the first round of voting on 15 September 2019 Saïed caused an upset by leading the field, with 18.4% of the total votes cast, followed by Karoui with 15.6%. The results were widely considered as a blow to the political establishment, with Chahed finishing in fifth place with only 7.8% of the vote and Marzouki taking just 3.0%. The turnout was recorded at 49.0% of registered voters. Saïed and Karoui thus proceeded to a run-off round.

Former President Ben Ali died in Jeddah, Saudi Arabia on 19 September 2019 and was buried in Medina, where he was laid to rest in a cemetery beside the Prophet Mohamed Mosque.

PRESIDENTIAL AND PARLIAMENTARY TUSSLES

Parliamentary elections took place on 6 October 2019. Ennahdha secured 52 seats out of a possible 217 (down from 69 in 2014) with 19.6% of the vote and held the plurality in the new chamber, as the NT had split since the previous poll. Ennahdha's success, such as it was, was in part due to it successfully presenting themselves as the party most willing to work with the likely winner of the presidential poll, the independent, Saïed. He had not expressed any party preference, and thus his supporters' votes were, in a sense, up for grabs. Another aspect of Ennahdha's relative success seems to have been its conscious choice to return to the rhetoric of Islam and of 'revolution'. Nabil Karoui's QT secured 38 seats with 14.6% of the votes cast. As a new party this was arguably impressive, especially as it left him, and the party essentially created in his image, as the main standard-bearer for the secularist trend in Tunisia. The Courant Démocratique (Democratic Current), a self-styled social democratic trend, won 22 seats (up from three in 2014), and the Coalition de la Dignité/Al Karama (Dignity Coalition), a new grouping of Islamically conservative figures who none the less supported the uprising of 2011, won 21 seats. The PDL won 17 seats and made it clear that it would not be joining a coalition that would inevitably be led by Ennahdha. The TT, the party of Prime Minister Chahed, took just 14 seats, while the NT secured only three seats and Afek Tounes two. The divided secular trend had assembled enough seats to form a potential blocking majority. However, the party with the plurality, Ennahdha, would, in accord with established practice, be given the opportunity to try to form a majority. As striking as the relative weakness of the secular trend was the low turnout—just 41.7%, compared with 67.7% in the legislative election of 2014. Perhaps there was some voter disaffection when faced with a choice between a mass of parties and independent candidates who were themselves associated with electoral (multi-candidate) lists in the legislative poll: 222 parties were involved in the contest, although only 20 were reportedly able to field candidates in every part of the country.

On 13 October 2019 Saïed won a convincing victory in the second round of the presidential election, taking more than 70% of the votes cast. Although only 49% of registered Tunisian voters took part in the second round run-off, his resounding defeat of his only rival, Nabil Karoui, arguably gave President Saïed, who was inaugurated on 23 October, the authority to range beyond the head of state's allotted responsibilities. While the latter are conventionally confined to a role in (but by no means total control of) external affairs (including defence and security), his post-uprising predecessors had already played a significant role in domestic politics. In the case of Saïed's immediate predecessor, Essebsi, this was in part because he was committed to the NT stream and then to the component of it upheld by his son.

The assumed need for President Saïed's involvement in domestic politics also reflected the ongoing reality of a legislature that lacked a clear majority among disparate parties that could provide a sound and durable basis for governmental survival. However, the legislature's incapacity arguably also compounded Saïed's problems. His popularity, relatively speaking, was precisely because he was not perceived as a creature of the post-2011 political system, but neither was he able to rely on any part of what emerged in its wake. The main parties and smaller factions had, since 2011, presented themselves largely in terms of being an Islamist or secularist variant of parliamentary clientelism, seeking, in Ennahdha's case, a guaranteed place for themselves in the system or, in the case of many of the secularists, promoting some version of the old Bourguiba-led state. This common interest between two supposedly different trends—and their attempted co-operation—led to the post-2011 system being described by some academics as a 'pacted transition'. Frustration with the relatively ineffectual politicking that this had engendered led to the main parties (and their fissiparous breakaway factions in the case of the NT) performing badly in the legislative polls, and new trends such as Nabil Karoui and his QT party performing strongly in the disadvantaged north-west, although not sufficiently strongly to stabilize a new political dispensation. Karoui and others had promoted a discussion about sovereignty amid popular concerns about perceived external pressure, such as over the economy and legalizing homosexuality (an issue that benefited both Saïed and the Dignity Coalition, which were opposed). By September 2020, however, Karoui had lost about one-quarter of his deputies—a reflection of the naked opportunism that had brought candidates to join his apparent rising tide at the time of the election. Another key new party, the PDL, in effect promoted going 'back to the future' with its unashamed support for Ben Ali's state model and argument that the 2011 uprising was a conspiracy. Perhaps the clearest break was the success of the Dignity Coalition, disparagingly referred to in some quarters as the *takfiri* coalition'. It was unambiguously conservatively Islamist, even Salafist, and thus did not seek to position itself in the modernist Islamic and politically flexible way that Ennahdha had.

The messy parliamentary political situation had helped President Saïed. However, his lack of any party political base in parliament was also a handicap for him and made it very difficult to play a significant domestic political role. Perhaps his anti-corruption focus, which benefited the Democratic Current in legislative elections, would help at least to engender some traction on this touchstone issue of the 2011 uprising. However, the political outsider did not have a wider institutional base to draw on either. The man who was dubbed the 'boomerang of the revolution', as he represented a supposed return to first principles, had his electoral support to bolster him, but little else.

Saïed had for many years advocated a political model based on a decentralized but more indirect practice of democracy. This would involve empowered and elected regional governorates that themselves would choose national legislative representatives in order, supposedly, that they could be withdrawn from office much more easily by, in this case, their regional appointees, if they failed to meet expectation. Upon Saïed's election as President, some observers suggested that an elected assembly was unlikely to vote to disband itself in favour of a weaker body. However, Saïed's popularity seemed to reflect his independence and respected academic authority and, at that time at least, willingness to listen, and whose solidity led to him being dubbed 'Robocop'. His maintenance of consistent positions, whether practical or not, seemed to equate with integrity for many Tunisians.

In November 2019 Ennahdha's leader, Rachid Ghannouchi, was elected Speaker of parliament, following his election as a deputy in September—the first time that he had sought elected office. Having attracted the support of the QT, this development augured well for the formation of a new coalition Government, and in the following week Habib Jemli of Ennahdha was appointed as Prime Minister.

After nearly two months of negotiations, on 10 January 2020 Jemli presented to parliament a proposed government comprising independents. This was roundly rejected in the Assembly. Ennahdha's sworn opponent, the PDL, claimed that, despite appearances, this was essentially a 'Muslim Brotherhood' administration. Nabil Karoui and his QT rejected the proposed administration for not being sufficiently independent and for what he considered as inadequacies in its programme. Under the Constitution, the failure of the party with a plurality of seats in the Assembly to facilitate a new government gave the initiative to President Saïed to nominate a presumptive prime minister. He chose a former finance minister, Elyes Fakhfakh, to put together an administration. Fakhfakh was not a creature of Ennahdha. His preferment by the popular new President, who seemed to be behind Fakhfakh's assertion in late January that his Government would consist only of 'pro-revolution' parties, thereby ruling out the QT and the PDL among others, was not welcomed by Ennahdha. The latter argued that the new Government should be as broad-based as possible to ensure that the necessary and painful economic reforms could be agreed. In part this was a genuine belief of

Ennahdha, whose own period leading a Government had suffered from division from within its ranks and from without. At the same time, Ennahdha was also engaged in a power struggle with a President who was not only far more popular that it, but who was, from Ennahdha's perspective, seeking to usurp the role of parliament in favour of a more presidential system of governance. Given Saïed's own idea for reforming the role of parliament (arguably weakening it) and his predecessor's public musing on whether there needed to be a more presidential model, Ennahdha's concerns appeared to have been fairly well founded.

Ennahdha made clear that it was prepared to accept fresh elections rather than what it regarded as a narrow political basis for the Fakhfakh Government. In the event, although disinclined to support his party-based Government, once he had allocated ministerial portfolios, Ennahdha, finally accepted it. The Assembly approved the new Government in late February 2020. Its formation was announced by the UGTT and not, as had been expected, by Speaker Ghannouchi. Arguably this was testament to the importance of Tunisia's main trade union federation to any hopes for political progress.

Strikingly, although Ennahdha had finally backed Fakhfakh, he gave the party only six portfolios out of 33 cabinet seats—markedly below the proportion of seats that it held in parliament and, as proposed, did not include Nabil Karoui or the QT. However, whether ostensibly 'pro-revolution' or not, there were deep differences among the Government's constituent parts over aspects of economic policy. A Government led by a former finance minister mindful of the need to reduce public debt and intent on trying to tackle such issues was likely to cause difficulties and attract opposition. In fact the threat of fresh elections hung in the air, despite the formation of a new administration. Following the outbreak of the coronavirus disease (COVID-19) pandemic in March 2020, the Fakhfakh Government was granted decree powers by parliament for strictly defined circumstances. Using these powers to deal with an obvious national and global crisis helped to stabilize the Government, at least for a while.

However, substantive political tensions continued to affect relations among the parliamentary deputies and political life in general. Emblematic of this was Ennahdha's decision to respond to the efforts of Fathi Laayouni, a lawyer and mayor of El-Krim, a district of Tunis, to set up a *zakat* fund to raise money from private, Islamically prescribed donations, for public services. Ennahdha had tabled a motion in parliament in November 2019 for this initiative to become a national policy and a part of the state budget. This was rejected as many secular deputies—chief among them the PDL bloc—who feared that this was an attempt to Islamicize Tunisia through the back door. When Laayouni formally set up the *zakat* fund in El-Krim in May 2020, the Government responded by stating that a public fund (not using the word *zakat*) was legal as a way of raising finance from private donations, but made clear that this did not mean that a *zakat* fund specifically would be legal. PDL leader Mousi said that Ennahdha was attempting to create a 'parallel state', and there was much public debate about the supposed subversion of the civic state. In the same month relations between Ennahdha and the PDL in particular fell to a new low when the former sought the expulsion of the latter's deputies from the legislature on the basis that Mousi had brought into the Assembly an image of Bourguiba—a powerful symbol of secularism that was intended to antagonize Ennahdha and other Islamist deputies. In early July the controversy over the proposed *zakat* fund continued when the head of the judiciary rejected a request by the Governor of Tunis that Laayouni should be prevented from introducing his fund.

In June 2020 Mustafa bin Jaafar, the President of the Assembly, who had overseen the writing of the new Constitution in 2011–14, gave an interview to the British-Qatari news website *Arabi21*. He claimed that such was the depth of current political divisions between the Islamist and secular blocs that there needed to be another formal and urgent national political dialogue to try to resolve it, and that it should be overseen by President Saïed. A call of this kind from such a figure carried weight, but it would have antagonized Ennahdha (and some other parties) on the basis that it would have only increased the interference of the President in legislative and domestic governance.

In July 2020 Mousi and her PDL colleagues accused Ennahdha of facilitating the entry of terrorists to parliament. The leader of the Dignity Coalition, Seifeddine Makhlouf, had reportedly sought to bring in as a guest a man to whom parliamentary security had refused entry. However, the director of Ghannouchi's office allegedly overrode their objections. This incident and the suggestion that Ennahdha was in contact with 'terrorists' in gaol was part of the PDL's attempt to force a vote on Ghannouchi's removal as Speaker.

Although on previous occasions the stasis in Tunisian politics was in part related to external factors, this appeared to be becoming a more dominant element. Ghannouchi's perceived strong association with Turkey (and, by extension, Qatar) included a private visit to Turkey (officially known as Türkiye from June 2022) in January 2020, where he held talks with President Recep Tayyip Erdoğan. The visit was used as fuel by Ghannouchi's opponents to accuse the Speaker of trying to identify Tunisia with the Muslim Brotherhood camp. In the ensuing months the relationship between Ennahdha and Turkey became yet more controversial as Turkey playing an increasingly direct military role in Libya, whose internal collapse was obviously a matter of Tunisian national security. Some secular politicians outside of Ennahdha, such as Najib Chebbi of the Parti Démocrate Progressiste, supported its line that established Tunisian foreign policy was to support the internationally recognized Government of National Accord in Tripoli (the GNA, a relatively Islamist administration backed by Turkey—see *Relations with the West after 11 September*). Others, such as the Democratic Current and the PDL, were so motivated by their anti-Islamist agenda that they perceived the Speaker and Ennahdha to be associating Tunisia with Islamists throughout the region, including in Libya, in an irresponsible manner. Ennahdha was therefore in effect presented as a national security problem. In early June a total of 94 deputies backed a PDL motion criticizing Turkey's role in Libya, in part to undermine Ennahdha and Ghannouchi. The latter had responded by demanding a re-founding of the coalition to include the QT and the Dignity Coalition.

In turn, the argument that domestic politicians were in so many words tools of external actors was also used by Ennahdha against its detractors. The UAE continued to be accused by Ennahdha and others of pursuing its regional 'counter-revolutionary' agenda in both Tunisia and Libya, and thus the effort to unseat Ghannouchi was presented by the Speaker himself as a 'coup' attempt funded in Abu Dhabi. Specific evidence of some secularist deputies being on the UAE's payroll could not be presented, but it was, for example, plain that UAE and other sympathetic Gulf media focussed on an alleged Muslim Brotherhood regional conspiracy involving Ghannouchi, Turkey and Qatar and on attempts to vote him out as being part of a Tunisian struggle against such an axis. Included in this media war were Emirati, Saudi and Egyptian allegations, asserted at the time of attempted in the Tunisian parliament to remove him as Speaker, that Ghannouchi had immense personal wealth (later apparently wholly disproven). Furthermore, Ennahdha's competition with President Saïed, whose popularity and motivations Ennahdha was suspicious of, was further fuelled by and expressed in the issue of Libya. On the one hand, for example, in May 2020 President Saïed bemoaned what he considered Ghannouchi's inappropriate meddling in Tunisian foreign policy. It was arguably Saïed's role, as President, to embody this abroad even if the Government formed by parliament had its own foreign affairs minister. Ghannouchi's stances had brought criticism of the Speaker from some quarters in Libya and elsewhere. On the other hand, in the same month Ghannouchi reacted strongly to what he argued was Saïed's 'ignorance' of foreign affairs in suggesting that the solution to the Libyan conflict was a kind of national convention to bring the country together (as had notably been used in Afghanistan, in a gathering of its tribal components). While Ghannouchi also faced some internal party dissent as a result of becoming embroiled in these external conflicts, he mostly maintained the support of Ennahdha in the face of efforts to remove him.

The attempt to unseat Ghannouchi overlapped with efforts to force Prime Minister Fakhfakh to stand down over allegations of personal corruption via shares that he held in companies that were alleged to have unfairly benefited from state contracts, combined with his unpopular economic policies (see Economy). While Ennahdha had the backing of the secular QT, and more predictably perhaps from the Dignity Coalition, as well as the Future Bloc and some independents, in its attempt to unseat the premier, the drive to unseat the Speaker was solely a secular political initiative, led by the LDP and the Democratic Current, among others. In an environment in which the COVID-19 pandemic and lockdown measures had increased joblessness and reduced incomes, combined with a proposal to freeze public sector wages, Fakhfakh was never going to be popular, however justified fiscally his measures were. For the QT there was the additional issue of Fakhfakh having set out his political stall by saying he only wanting the support of 'pro-revolution' parties and thus rejecting the QT and in particular Nabil Keroui, who had allowed praise of Ben Ali on Nessma TV while he was President. In mid-July 2020 Fakhfakh resigned, after a petition calling for him to stand down had already been signed by 109 of the 217 deputies, and without the support of Ennahdha, whom he had earlier dismissed from his Government, his position had become untenable.

On 25 July 2020 Hichem Mechichi, the interior minister and a former legal adviser to President Saïed, was designated by the latter to try to form a new government; he had a month to propose one to the legislature. In the same week, Ghannouchi survived a vote of confidence as Speaker. Politically damaged but unbowed, Ghannouchi made it clear that he believed that he had been the victim of a 'coup attempt' orchestrated from outside of the country (principally meaning the UAE but also including Saudi Arabia and Egypt). This left Mechichi to continue his efforts to form what he declared on 10 August would be a technocratic administration. Unsurprisingly, this echoed the nature of the Government that Fakhfakh had sought to maintain in power. However, Mechichi avoided the partisan-sounding demand that it be 'pro-revolution'—a statement of Fakhfakh's that had alienated Ennahdha. Mechichi succeeded in forming his Government, taking office on 2 September. Ennahdha lent the prospective Government what Ghannouchi called its 'begrudging' support and would, by definition, have only a limited, if any, role in it. At the same time, Ennahdha maintained its own form of coalition, one that had helped it to keep Ghannouchi in his Speaker's chair—a role that linked the roles of parliament and the executive, in the sense that the survival of the Government, formally at least, depended on the support of parliament, while legislation required majority approval too. Weighted down by growing popular discontent, not least over the impact of the pandemic in economic as well as health terms, Mechichi's position did not look secure, not least as he, like the President, lacked a significant political base in the Assembly. Relations with Ghannouchi were becoming increasingly difficult.

PROTESTS RESUME ABOUT REGIONAL FAULT LINES

In a measure of how much Tunisia's parliamentary and governmental theatrics were not able to resolve fundamental economic problems, in June 2020 protests broke out once again in Tataouine, accompanied by protests in Kébili. The discontent that had driven the oil industry-focused protests of 2017 in Tataouine and Kébili (see above) had bubbled up periodically ever since, although at their height, these protests had been partly assuaged by the Government's promises that more would be done to provide jobs, as these partly foreign-owned economic projects were not resolving local unemployment problems. However, in mid-2020 as the economy struggled, particularly in the south of the country, and now made worse by the impact of the COVID-19 lockdown, protests erupted again.

Especially problematic for the Government, the UGTT urged a general strike in protest against the harsh suppression of the protests at a time when the measures taken to combat the pandemic were also dividing the Government. In July 2020 protests spread to Remada, about 80 km from Tataouine. Demands were made for President Saïed to visit these areas. The protests were exacerbated by the security forces killing a young man near the Libyan border, who, according to the authorities, was involved in smuggling. However, the incident was seen differently on the streets, where anger about perceived discrimination by the Government against an Amazigh-dominated south ran high—a tension not reduced by the high level of southerners among security forces attracted by reliable employment. International human rights groups condemned the harsh suppression of the protests, and President Saïed stated that Tunisians had a right to protest peacefully and that the economic situation in the disadvantaged south was 'unacceptable'. The demonstrations and the authorities' response to them served further to exacerbate Tunisia's politically divided leadership.

By January 2021—the 10th anniversary of the uprising that led to the fall of the Ben Ali regime—popular protests had become a major and widespread source of instability, giving rise to increased speculation that drastic political measures might be taken, whether sanctioned by the formal leadership or not. Eight Tunisian cities were affected by protests, and demonstrators' longstanding complaints about the economy were compounded by growing deterioration wrought by the pandemic-related shutdown and weakened economic activity and anger about perceived corruption among the political class amid widespread popular misery, as well as perceived police brutality in dealing with the protesters. President Saïed's professed anger about corruption was a source of tension between him and his Prime Minister, Mechichi, as well as with the Speaker, Ghannouchi, and this enabled President Saïed to maintain the popular wave of support on which he had been elected in 2019.

Meanwhile, in early January 2021 Prime Minister Mechichi had dismissed his Minister of the Interior, Taoufik Charfeddine, appointing Walid Dhahbi to the position later in that month. Charfeddine was known to be politically close to the President, and so his dismissal suggested that the Prime Minister was trying to assert himself in an increasing power struggle in which Ghannouchi represented the third element, in his capacity as Speaker, and in view of wider support for Ennahdha, which retained a plurality of seats in the Assembly.

In mid-February 2021 Mechichi dismissed a further five cabinet ministers, including the Minister of Justice, in a sign that popular discontent and the political impasse was finding expression in a rather desperate attempt to put the blame on relatively powerless middle-ranking political figures. In response to the moves that apparently did not meet President Saïed's approval, the latter sent a handwritten letter to Mechichi, suggesting that the changes were not in accord with the Constitution and including, according to the Tunis Afrique Presse (TAP—the state press agency), 'a reminder of a set of principles relating to the need for the political authority in Tunisia to express the true will of the people'. Such a political criticism of what was supposed to be the premier's domain did not augur well, and Saïed's implication that he, unlike the Prime Minister, understood 'the true will of the people', suggested an arrogance at odds with democratic principles, at least according to the part-parliamentary, part-presidential model under which Tunisia was operating, as sanctioned by the 2014 Constitution. Saïed was evidently becoming increasingly impatient with that model.

The appointment of Kamel Ben Younes as the chief executive officer of TAP in April 2021 prompted anger from journalists as well as from liberal critics of the Tunisian authorities. While TAP had been associated with propaganda during the era of Ben Ali, following the uprising that overthrew him it had become associated with relatively free speech. Critics of Ben Younes' appointment claimed that this stance would change, as he was close to Ennahdha, although Prime Minister Mechichi said that Younes was principally an administrator; for his part, Ben Younes asserted that, as a journalist, he had worked for a wide variety of media outlets, including the British Broadcasting Corporation. Angry Tunisian journalists and members of the media trade union affiliated to the UGTT none the less tried to prevent him from entering the TAP building in Tunis and threatened strike action.

As the Government maintained its day-to-day operations largely by continuing the duplication of some roles and in some case by appointing interim office holders, a more pronounced initiative to break the impasse became increasingly necessary. Consultations between two political rivals—Ennahdha and the QT—encouraged discussions of a process of national dialogue that would, it was envisaged, include the President as well as, necessarily, the Prime Minister. In June 2021 media reports outside the country gave increased expression to the idea, and in that month Araby Al-Jadid (a Qatari-owned Arabic language site based in the UK) reported that the President was holding consultations with former senior government figures including former Prime Minister and current deputy leader of Ennahdha, Laârayedh. The site also reported that the UGTT had proposed a national dialogue initiative.

In June 2021 Moussi, the leader of the PDL, was physically assaulted in the Assembly while filming proceedings on her mobile telephone. Known for her determination to confront Islamists in the Assembly, she had already become a lightning rod for that group's disdain for those seen as old regime sympathizers. The assault was brutal; she was slapped and kicked by two male deputies reportedly belonging to the Salafist Dignity Coalition, in full view of the Assembly and the cameras. Some observers suggested that it symbolized an attack on Tunisia's already faltering democracy or at the very least on freedom of speech and representation. It was not clear that Moussi had committed even a technical offence by using her telephone in this way. In a gesture that secured even more coverage, the outspoken deputy consequently wore a crash helmet and a bullet-proof vest in the chamber, in order to make a statement about the apparent danger posed to deputies like her—and to all women—by the Dignity Coalition and, as she presented it, by Islamists opposed to secularism, including equal rights.

An (Un)Constitutional Coup?

Political tensions were reaching crisis point by mid-2021. The economy had continued to falter amid an ongoing pandemic and a political impasse, exacerbated by Prime Minister Mechichi's inability to lead, in view of the unfavourable parliamentary arithmetic, which showed no sign of easing. The ongoing inability of Assembly members to agree on the membership of the Constitutional Court, the key role of which was written into the Constitution of 2014, symbolized both the desperate impasse and prevented a way out of it—rival ideas for a resolution necessitated a change to the agreed part-presidential, part-parliamentary form of governance. After what are presumed to have been conversations with Mechichi and, more importantly, the security services and the military, as well as regional and international allies, on 25 July 2021 President Saïed surprised many in Tunisia by assuming full political control of the country. Using the questionable legitimacy of the emergency provisions laid out in Article 80 of the Constitution in the face of 'imminent danger' to Tunisia to justify his actions, Saïed issued and enforced a decree suspending the Assembly—and specifically the powerful office of the Speaker of Parliament, Ennahdha leader Rachid Ghannouchi—and dismissed the Prime Minister, as well the Ministers of Defence, Interior and Justice.

The absence of a functioning Constitutional Court made any deliberation about the legitimacy of President Saïed's measures academic, even if, under the Constitution, the Court was allowed to rule that any such action had been taken legitimately, only 30 days after the action in question. The inherent politicization of the appointment of the Constitutional Court and the risk, for President Saïed, including prior to this action, that it might under certain circumstances be used to impeach a non-party-aligned head of state lacking, by definition, the guaranteed protection of parliamentary-appointed members, helped to explain why he had played his part in preventing its establishment prior to 25 July 2021.

Following President Saïed's assumption of emergency powers, a night-time curfew was declared, and public gatherings of more than three individuals were outlawed. Troops surrounded the Assembly building, barring Ghannouchi and other parliamentarians from entering. Saïed asserted that his intervention in the political order—and his creation of a presidential executive—was a temporary measure, and that he would rule in partnership with a new Prime Minister. He stated that the Assembly, like many of the components of normal political life, would resume its functions after one month. However, he did not make clear where the balance of authority would lie under the suggested dispensation. Predictably, the President's detractors and the great majority of deputies opposed his actions, which were branded as a 'coup' by many, including by Ennahdha deputies and other party figures, whose use of such language was arguably provocative in such circumstances. One senior Ennahdha official went so far as to suggest that the US Administration should pass emergency legislation to suspend its donations of COVID-19 vaccines.

Immediately after Saïed assumed emergency powers, Ennahdha supporters took to the streets angrily to denounce the President's 'anti-democratic' actions, judging them illegal and therefore not even the 'constitutional coup' that some observers had labelled his intervention. Clashes between protesters and security forces were reported in Tunis and other large cities. At the same time, plenty of other Tunisians willingly took to the streets but in a more celebratory mood, including those whose placards presented the President's actions in simply and implacably anti-Ennahdha terms, considering his assumption of sole authority as the end for the Muslim Brotherhood and its influence in Tunisian politics. It was these deeply politically polarizing stances that soon made the debate about the need, under Article 80, for the President's rule by decree to be co-ordinated with both the Prime Minister and Speaker to be almost irrelevant. Whether the action was politically the right one or not was essentially all that counted, and it appeared that, for all the increased political inertia and popular disaffection, especially with the Assembly (not just with the party with the most seats, Ennahdha), Tunisians were either on one side of that argument or the other. Popular frustration with party politics gave President Saïed greater support regarding the affair than his detractors.

In some ways it appeared that the supposedly apolitical President had acted in an archly political manner, reminiscent of dictatorial figures in 19th- and 20th-century European history, who exploited popular disdain for squabbling politicians to present themselves as above the factional fray and as enforcing the popular will for decisive decision-making. There were some in Tunisia and certainly among supportive foreign Arab states (see *Relations with the Wider Middle East*) who favoured this approach. They did not see the danger (at least for Tunisians, if not for authoritarian Arab rulers) of revisiting the mode of governance that preceded 2011. So much would inevitably depend on for how long and to what extent President Saïed would exercise his greatly enhanced executive powers.

In a suggestion both of institutional resistance to an excessively flagrant breach of the extant mode of government, and of President Saïed's need to accommodate himself to such resistance, senior figures from the Supreme Judicial Council publicly met the President in late July 2021 and stated that they would not accept his adoption of quasi-judicial powers. Having already lifted the constitutionally based immunity from prosecution of suspended deputies, the President hoped that at least some of them could be gaoled, perhaps by a cowed judiciary, for alleged infractions of the law. Two days later he announced his intention to ensure that those politicians and officials allegedly guilty of misappropriation of public funds—totalling US $4,500m. according to Saïed—would be prosecuted. It appeared that he was not only seeking to achieve control over the legislative branch of government, but was also willing to assume quasi-judicial powers. In any case, judges were normally appointed by the President, according to the 2014 Constitution, but such appointments had to be made in consultation with both a Prime Minister (when in office) and the Supreme Judicial Council (itself seemingly appointed by the executive). As the Prosecutor-General was a presidential appointee (and potentially a presidential dismissal), then it seemed likely that Saïed could 'legally' prosecute perceptibly errant legislators using hand-picked judges with or without any such consultation.

If nothing else, these developments suggested that, even if only within the apparently limited time frame of his assumption of exclusive executive authority, President Saïed was determined to reformulate the political system. Having established himself previously as an advocate of a change to a political system that had inherently sought to straddle both a parliamentary and a presidential model, while proposing a more executive presidency, Saïed now seemed to be determined to secure the latter for himself—and by fiat, not consensual political agreement. The President's contravening of conventional notions of democracy by assuming judicial authority as well as executive and, by default, legislative authority, arguably made a simple resumption of an already frail if not flawed democratic system difficult. His moves, although in part responding to popular exasperation with parliamentary stasis amid economic and health crises, risked damaging parliamentary authority beyond the stated temporary suspension. Saïed's assumed right to pursue elected representatives, even if they were allegedly corrupt, did not bode well for Tunisia's fledgling democracy or its stability, however popular his moves initially appeared to be. Notably, the Association des Magistrats Tunisiens made a statement on 27 July 2021 that appeared to back the President's pursuit of corruption by public officials by calling on the Office of the Prosecutor-General to 'fulfil its role' and to prosecute those individuals suspected of corruption.

Ennahdha's call for a national dialogue, made in immediate response to the exceptional powers acquired by President Saïed, but stating that it was also done in response to the social, economic and health crises, made sense and arguably captured the mood of the clear majority of deputies, albeit perhaps not most Tunisians. Saïed had already shown himself resistant to that call when it had been made by the President of the Assembly a year earlier (see above), reflecting his disdain for moves that sought to put all political actors on an equal footing. Apparently stiffened in his resolve by international and regional support or at least tacit sympathy (see *Relations with the West* and *Relations with the Wider Middle East*), it seemed unlikely that he was going to extend a helping hand to Ennahdha or any other opposition party. Notably, only two out of the 12 parties represented in the Assembly had backed his intervention—the Mouvement Echaâb/Mouvement du Peuple (People's Movement), which had 15 seats, and the Parti Patriotique Démocratique Socialiste, which held only one—while three parties (Afek Tounes, the TT and Ettakatol) in effect abstained. Ennahdha had the support of its erstwhile rival, the QT, in addition to the Salafist Dignity Coalition, the Al Massar (as the Mouvement Ettajdid—the successor to the PCT—had become), the Hizb al-Amal (Hope Party), al-Tiyar al-Democratiya (Democratic Renewal) and Parti Républicain (al-Joumhouri). It was not clear what the position of the PDL and its 17 deputies was.

Importantly, the UGTT expressed reservations about President Saïed's moves but did not strongly criticize him. Soon after Saïed's assumption of autocratic powers, he met the UGTT leadership in a show of inclusion that seemed to encourage the powerful union's relative acquiescence. However, Noureddine Taboubi, the Secretary-General of the UGTT, stated in early August 2021 that the union's acceptance of the President taking 'exceptional measures' (the supposed constitutional characterization of Saïed's intervention) in order to prevent the country 'slipping' (i.e. into chaos) did 'not mean that it will accept any domination or injustice against anyone'. Taboubi urged that early elections be held, leading to the formation of a new government under a new Prime Minister. Taboubi also emphasized that the UGTT could help steer Tunisia to what he called 'the shores of safety'. This attempted leverage was indicative of the significance of the UGTT as a leading component of civil society, which could support and lend some moral authority to Saïed's measures, or indeed choose not to do so. Taboubi also demanded a 'roadmap' laying out the path to what would be a kind of political normalization, as opposed to the dramatic change that the events of late July had seemed to presage.

It remained to be seen whether the moves that continued to be described as temporary could be accompanied by such a roadmap, as demanded by critics and as presumably desired by at least some of President Saïed's Western backers. Notably, just a few days after introducing them, the President said that the 30-day emergency measures could be extended. Free speech palpably tightened, while the Tunis office of Al Jazeera, long associated with a sympathetic disposition towards the Muslim Brotherhood, was shuttered. Yassine Ayari, an independent parliamentary deputy and a prominent, long-time critic of Saïed and of the wider state apparatus, including the military, was arrested on the day after Saïed's assumption of emergency powers and sentenced to two months in prison, on charges of insulting the military on social media in 2018. Notably, in a political system that, even after Tunisia's claimed 'revolution' in 2011, continued to criminalize insulting the military, the deputy had already been imprisoned in 2015 on a similar charge.

President Saïed, after all, could not have acted without obtaining the approval of the (arguably unreconstructed, post-Ben Ali) security services and of the military. His justification, following his imposition of purely executive rule on 25 July 2021, for wanting many Tunisian deputies to be prosecuted was their alleged corruption. However, Ayari's incarceration suggested a more autocratic tendency than the President sought to present to Western media. It was also suggested that the Tunisian armed forces were mediating behind the scenes as tensions rose. Tunisian and other academics addressing developments in an online forum of the renowned UK think tank Chatham House (the Royal Institute of International Affairs) in early August did not think that it was worth discussing Tunisia's possible road to an Egyptian-style full revolution, i.e. restoring the status quo ante, or the role of the Tunisian military in Saïed's peremptory assumption of sole executive authority or in imminent political developments. However, at the online forum, Tunisian academic Dr Aymen Bessalah commented that part of the 'unfinished business' of 2011 was tackling the continued existence of military courts, which continued to suppress criticism of the armed forces. Bessalah noted that the proposed reform of these courts had not led to the tabling of specific legislation in parliament. After his arrest in July 2021, Ayari asserted that the President's actions on 25 July represented 'a reversal of the constitution [...] with the use of the army'.

The Tunisian armed forces do not have a formally established role, as observed by a Tunisian analyst to the *Financial Times*, David Gardner, on 2 August 2021. Rather than directly oppressing the other organs of state, as might be said to describe how the Egyptian military operates, Gardner claimed that the Tunisian army has played 'a mediating role in a country of strong democratic institutions'. None the less, President Saïed warned that the army would respond to any armed revolt with a hail of bullets.

The Tunisian military's role in the body politic is not like in Egypt's post-Second World War history, which is characterized by repeated, if sometimes discrete, military intervention and by the armed forces' archly political role, contrary to superficial notions of 'revolution'. However, as part of the security apparatus, Tunisia's armed forces have undoubtedly proven to be important to Tunisian politics. The Chatham House forum noted that security sector reform has not been undertaken in Tunisia since Ben Ali's overthrow in 2011. More specifically, Bessalah remarked that the military's most recent operation was the implementation of the urgently needed rollout of the COVID-19 vaccine. It is especially noteworthy in this respect that just 24 hours before President Saïed presumably notified or sought approval from both the military and the security/police forces for his assumption of autocratic powers, he put the military in charge of what was becoming a highly politicized but conventionally civil function: distributing vaccines and controlling social and economic activity to counter the pandemic. Perhaps to ensure military loyalty, among the many senior officials whom he dismissed upon assuming emergency powers was the Prosecutor of the First Military Court.

In sympathetic foreign Arab media (see *Relations with the Wider Middle East*) everything that President Saïed did after assuming emergency powers was welcomed. Hashemi Nuwayra, a Tunisian columnist, writing in Dubai's state-owned daily newspaper *Al-Bayan* in late July 2021, presented Saïed's moves as a 'correction' of Tunisia's political system. His terminology echoed a long history of Arab political interventions, conducted almost exclusively in tandem with the military and often, but not exclusively, by military men. Hafiz al-Assad's self-styled 'correctionist movement' in the Syrian Arab Republic in 1970 presented itself as putting the country on a new and necessary political path, and in the process al-Assad ruled autocratically as President for the next three decades.

A Restored Dictatorship?

President Saïed sought to address Western concerns in a meeting with reporters from the liberal US newspaper *The New York Times*. Saïed stated to Vivian Yee and her colleagues that as a law professor he understood how democratic constitutions worked and was not, at his age, about to turn into a dictator. Fundamentally, he appeared to be keen to exercise emergency powers in order to reform and 'clean up' the political order in a way that enhanced his executive power and that of a successor.

It was not clear if his apparent death blow to Ennahdha—as seen in parts of the Gulf, for example—was what the normally astute President Saïed was also seeking to carry out. He must surely have known that, unless he went as far as the leader of the Egyptian coup of 2013, Gen. Abd al-Fatah al-Sisi, as some of his most implacable critics suggested he was doing, he would still have to work in some form with Ennahdha, or any Islamist successor, even if some of the Islamist party's lieutenants were arrested. The latter were wise enough to issue an order for their supporters to get off the streets in order to see what transpired in the days ahead—something that in any case was required under the emergency decrees. The fact that the President had seemingly succeeded in uniting disparate parliamentary and popular forces in opposition to him did not augur well for the stability of his 'exceptional' measures.

Speaking to *The New York Times* at the end of July 2021, Rachid Ghannouchi claimed that the measures taken by the President were undemocratic and indicative of a probable exercise of dictatorship. He also contended that the 'turmoil' was due not to a 'search for freedom' but to widespread 'resentment over the course of economic progress'; in other words, the popular anger about corruption amid inequality and economic recession, owing to the COVID-19 pandemic, was fuelling the desire for political change, which the President had exploited. Ennahdha itself showed signs of imploding; cynics might say that this too could have fitted Saïed's game plan, along with the impact on the party of possible corruption trials. A week later Ghannouchi addressed a party summit; his tone had begun to soften, and he framed the President's intervention as an opportunity to correct past mistakes and, as before, recommended a national dialogue led by the President as the holder of 'legitimacy' as the elected head of state. Ghannouchi and his ageing male colleagues in Ennahdha had been the focus of much criticism from the youth wing over their stewardship of the party, and this stance did nothing to assuage that criticism. In September 113 prominent party members, including a number of former ministers, tendered their resignations, publishing a joint statement criticizing the party leadership and specifically Ghannouchi's failure to form a common front to oppose Saïed's political manoeuvrings.

However, the results of a poll conducted a few days after President Saïed's intervention suggested that 84% of Tunisians backed the head of state's actions. In remarks to local media, ordinary Tunisians did not sound fearful about the future of democracy but, rather, angry about widespread economic and health crises. Increased economic pressure was in part due to government policies characterizable as eight years of austerity in light of an IMF-recommended reduction in state provision, for example, in terms of subsidized staple foods and other items. This, together with Tunisia being hit particularly hard by the COVID-19 pandemic (the country had the highest per capita infection rate in Africa, for example), had reduced popular enthusiasm for Tunisia's perceptible parliamentary theatre.

In August 2021 Saïed's Minister of Interior in his 'interim' Government appointed nine new senior security officials, having alleged that his ministry had been infiltrated by opponents (itself a telling indication of the mindset of the Saïed regime and a likely indication of how the interregnum would develop). Notably in January 2022, amid popular discontent in Tunis manifesting in violent clashes (see below), the Ministry of the Interior, at Saïed's encouragement, purged itself of some of these alleged infiltrators. However, as with almost all measures adopted since July 2021, the apparent aim of this move was to shore up a nascent security-focused autocracy under Saïed himself.

By September 2021 speculation was rife about who President Saïed would appoint as his new Prime Minister for the remainder of the interregnum. On 23 August Saïed had renewed the emergency measures indefinitely. However, on 29 September he announced that he had designated Najla Bouden Romdhane as Prime Minister. The appointment of the first female Prime Minister of an Arab-majority country, at the helm of a cabinet that included eight female ministers (one-third of its total composition), seemed calculated to offset potential Western disquiet. Critics contested that Bouden, a geologist and former senior education official, lacked the political acumen for the premiership at such a challenging time in Tunisian politics.

Saïed's 25-member Government was ostensibly modern and technocratic, in contrast to the image of his Islamist critics. These technocrats included the economist Samir Saïed as Minister of Economy and Planning and Ali Mrabet, an academic and head of the COVID-19 vaccine campaign, as Minister of Health. A former banker, Sihem Boughdiri Nemsia, was appointed Minister of Finance; notably, she did not wear *hijab* during the inauguration ceremony, which was held in mid-October 2021. The incoming ministers swore their allegiance to the Republic, and thus to the President as its head of state.

Only four members of the outgoing cabinet were reappointed to the new Government. Notably returning to office was Taoufik Charfeddine, reappointed as Minister of the Interior, having been dismissed in January 2021 by Mechichi, who was said to have opposed Charfeddine's reported plans to dismiss a large number of security officials, presumably in response to social unrest over challenging socioeconomic conditions (see below). Among the other three retained cabinet members was the Minister of Foreign Affairs, Migration and Tunisians Abroad, Othman Jerandi.

There was little pretence that Prime Minister Bouden was in charge of the Council of Ministers, with Saïed regularly chairing cabinet sessions. This appeared less like the French Fifth Republic (in which Presidents allow governments to operate relatively independently) than a classic Middle Eastern or North African autocracy in which the President or monarch is usually the head of government.

In late December 2021 a Tunisian court (operating in the context of Saïed's use of emergency powers to rein in the judiciary) imposed a four-year prison sentence *in absentia* on former President Marzouki. Saïed himself a few days later made reference to pursuing 'traitors' who were 'seeking refuge overseas'. Marzouki had earlier responded to the autocratic powers being exercised by the incumbent by vowing to return to the country to overturn the 'coup' that he alleged had taken place in Tunisia.

A poll conducted in December 2021 suggested that, were a presidential election to be held at that time, Saïed would secure 82% of the vote (roughly on a par with polling at the time of his July intervention). The December poll put the leader of the PDL, Abir Moussi, on just 6% of the vote. However, the same poll indicated that in the event of parliamentary elections the PDL would come first, with 36% of the votes, followed by the pollsters' hypothetical pro-Saïed party with 21%, while Ennahdha would garner just over 20%. In late December clashes erupted between protesters in Kasserine City and security forces who deployed significant force to disperse those gathered.

In January 2022 there were a series of clashes in Tunis between those opposed to the repressive emergency powers that continued to be employed by the security forces under Saïed. No doubt economic factors also played a part in the anger, with unemployment remaining high, amid deep-seated socioeconomic inequalities in the region, despite improvements in the national economy (see Economy). After the crackdown on protests in the capital, three political parties—Ettakatol, al-Joumhouri and the Dignity Coalition—

together with a reported 'representative' of 'national figures', filed a complaint with the Public Prosecutor's Office against the Minister of Interior and the Director-General of Public Security.

In February 2022 Saïed dissolved the Supreme Judicial Council—which, while state-appointed, had been established in 2016 to guarantee the independence of the judiciary—accusing its members of accepting bribes and delaying investigations, and denouncing it as a 'thing of the past'. The head of the Council, Youssef Bouzakher, strenuously denied Saïed's claims and deplored the latter's actions as 'a dangerous indication of the failure to abide by the country's Constitution, voicing concern that Tunisia was 'returning to the rule of Ben Ali, and perhaps even worse'. Following widespread international censure, the Minister of Justice announced that Saïed intended to reform, rather than abolish, the Council, with a Provisional Judicial Council to be appointed in the interim.

Ennahdha Squeezed

On 31 December 2021 President Saïed ordered the house arrest of Ennahdha deputy leader and former Minister of Justice Noureddine Bhiri, together with Fathi al-Baladi, a former security official. They were both arrested on suspicion of terrorism allegedly linked to the improper issuance of Tunisian citizenship and travel documents to foreign nationals. The accusations were strenuously denied by both men. Bhiri, who was reported to have been 'near death' in January 2022, after going on hunger strike, and al-Baladi were released from house arrest in March. Ennahdha presented Bhiri's hunger strike as a rejection of the alleged campaign to smear him and, ironically perhaps, as an expression of the 'independence' of the judiciary, something that the party was keen to assert in the midst of Saïed's interference in the judicial branch of government. In keeping with the latter, the authorities stated that Bhiri had been released pending the appointment of a new Supreme Judicial Council, which would investigate his case.

At the end of March 2022 President Saïed formally dissolved the already suspended parliament during, strikingly, a meeting of the National Security Council. The apparent prompt for Saïed's action was a virtual parliamentary session, held under the *de facto* but *sotto voce* direction of Speaker Ghannouchi, which, the President would argue, was illegal since it contravened his suspension of the Assembly's activities. The virtual session, which involved the participation of 116 deputies (out of 217 originally elected in 2019), declared all the President's decisions since the July 2021 intervention to be illegal. As such, it was perhaps unsurprising that Saïed responded by crushing what remained of the Assembly.

Ghannouchi had prudently avoided chairing the virtual session (despite his absence arguably weakening its claimed legitimacy). However, the Second Deputy Speaker, Tarek Ftiti, was present, along with other elected Ennahdha deputies and a number of QT, Dignity Coalition, TT and independent deputies, and Saïed decreed that the Ministry of Justice was to investigate their participation in the 'illegal' gathering.

In early May 2022 Saïed announced that all existing political parties would be excluded from a planned committee that was be charged with overseeing a 'national dialogue'.

Given the mass resignations, state pressure and ongoing internal differences over how to respond to Saïed's autocratic rule, it was, if anything, a surprise that Ennahdha did not totally implode. Other potential dissidents seemed to want to bide their time. This caution and the fact that more members did not leave the party, despite discontent with Ghannouchi and, presumably, covert offers of incentives to abandon him, was perhaps a reflection of a fear shared among remaining Ennahdha members that the President might exploit a major fissure in Ennahdha—the epitome of the Islamism targeted by Saïed—further to repress it and them, and, by extension, to clamp down on opposition in general. Ironically, that same caution was, of course, a contributory factor preventing Ghannouchi from doing what these dissidents had criticized him for failing to do.

In mid-July 2022 Imad Hammami, a former cabinet minister during Chahed's premiership and a prominent member of Ennahdha prior to his suspension from the party in September 2021 owing to 'repeated transgressions' of party policy, stated in a media interview that Ghannouchi's decades of party rule had contributed to its disastrous political standing, and predicted that Ennahdha would end up as a rump unit. In the interview, aired by the Dubai-based Al-Arabiya News Channel, Hammami stressed the need for President Saïed to be supported to help extricate Tunisia from the 'corrupt' party system that had existed prior to July 2021, and argued that 'political Islam' was finished in the region.

Meanwhile, in late June 2022 a judicial order was issued preventing Ghannouchi from leaving Tunisia, and in mid-July the Ennahdha leader was summoned to court in connection with allegations of money laundering and foreign financing, potentially in connection with terrorism. After an all-day hearing, the judge ordered that Ghannouchi be released pending further investigations, despite suggestions that he might be subject to pre-trial detention, an outcome that the veteran Ennahdha leader pointed to as an indication that Saïed had failed to eradicate completely the independence of the judiciary.

CONSTITUTIONAL FIAT?

In May 2022 President Saïed appointed constitutional law expert Sadeq Belaid to head a committee to redraft the 2014 Constitution. There was suspicion among Tunisians that, having effectively staged a coup, and with his autocratic rule having proven far from temporary, Saïed was now bent on a formal legal gloss being applied to the mechanisms for a semi-permanent dictatorship. Notably, the UGTT, which had initially sought to engage with Saïed and influence events but which had subsequently become increasingly critical in response to successive allegedly illegal acts, refused to engage with Belaid's constitutional redrafting.

In June 2022 Belaid commented to the media that he envisaged the adoption of a presidential political model (as opposed to the part-parliamentary part-presidential system enshrined in the 2014 Constitution seemingly in reaction to the authoritarian and one-man-rule model since independence), and urged the media to 'get on board the moving train'. Belaid bemoaned that under the 2014 charter the elected head of state and commander-in-chief could only, as he put it, exercise blocking powers and propose the removal of Article 1—which proclaimed that the Tunisian state was free, independent and sovereign, with Islam as its religion, Arabic as its language and republicanism as its system of governance—arguing that the religious aspect was something that could be exploited for extremist purposes. Belaid appeared to be taking his cue from Saïed, who had used a Ramadan address in 2021 to state that the practice of Islam was not a matter for the Tunisian state, and that the state itself could not have a religion but could instead have a moral dimension. Utilizing his understanding of constitutional and, less obviously, philosophical matters, Saïed also argued that the state did not have the right to position itself as the exclusive entity for the worship of Allah and that Muslims primarily had a relationship with Allah, not with anybody claiming Islamic authority. Such views were likely to have elicited considerable sympathy among Tunisians, regardless of how individuals might have viewed the President's monopoly on power.

Belaid drew criticism from the Dignity Coalition, which argued that Belaid and Saïed were playing to a Western gallery, over an issue that was supposedly settled under the 2014 Constitution. In June 2022 a member of the so-called Citizens Against The Coup online activist group reportedly claimed that Belaid and his committee were being influenced (as former President Bourguiba had been) by a 'radical left' with a 'secular neurosis'.

At the beginning of June 2022 Saïed issued a decree granting himself the power to appoint and dismiss judges, prosecutors and other state legal officials, with dismissal automatically leading to criminal prosecution. He promptly dismissed 57 judges, who he alleged were corrupt and had been defending terrorists and compromising the independence of the judiciary. In other words, upholding judicial independence required him to act contrarily to judicial independence. The Association des Magistrats Tunisiens criticized the move and adamantly rejected the President's accusations against its members.

Meanwhile, the Constitutional Court remained dysfunctional, and therefore unable to challenge the President's rule by decree, or indeed any draft constitution, since its membership had still not been appointed. Given Saïed's evident desire to extinguish any independent legal expression that might run counter to his political priorities, this would presumably have pleased him greatly.

On 30 June 2022 the President's office published the draft Constitution, which proved to be less the work of Belaid than had been expected. The reworking of Articles 1 and 2, for instance, was more secular and inclusive than the 2014 Constitution, as Belaid had envisaged; there was no longer any explicit reference to the Tunisian state in terms of Islam, nor to its civilian nature, with Tunisia now simply described as a 'free, independent and sovereign state'. However, elsewhere the draft charter stated that Tunisia 'belongs to the Islamic Ummah' (the worldwide Muslim community), which it could be argued was still exclusivist. Furthermore, a new article proclaimed that Tunisia would work to 'achieve the objectives of Islam in preserving [people's] souls, money, religion, and liberty'.

The draft charter clearly and squarely placed political authority for both domestic and foreign affairs principally in the hands of the office of the presidency. While this had been recommended by some prior to Saïed's assumption of direct rule in July 2021 as a way out of the undoubted political impasse, critics of the proposed amendments decried the proposed shift in the balance of power towards an executive presidency. While the proposed Constitution provided for a bicameral parliament as well as a President, sovereignty unambiguously lay with the President, who was still defined (among other things) as head of the armed forces and who would appoint the government (instead of it being appointed by parliament, which had been the case between 2011 and July 2021). Parliament could in theory remove a government that it deemed unsatisfactory, but this would require a two-thirds' majority, which would inevitably prove challenging to secure given the likely exigencies of Tunisian politics in what had all the appearances of an authoritarian order. In addition, the proposed parliament would not be majorly empowered in legislative terms. The President would initiate major domestic and foreign affairs decisions and introduce legislation, while legislative deputies were defined as part of an assembly of the country's regions and provinces and were to be elected on that basis. Arguably this was the kind of parochial political chamber that Saïed, as an established constitutional reform advocate, had proposed for some time.

The President could unilaterally suspend parliament in the event of a national security emergency (which had been the claimed basis for his July 2021 intervention). Furthermore, the draft charter sought to enshrine in law Saïed's recent efforts to render the judiciary beholden to the presidency (including on questions of constitutionality) with its proposal that the President have exclusive responsibility for the appointment (and presumably dismissal) of judges, thereby rendering it highly unlikely that any judicial body might move to suspend or remove a sitting President. In any case, the draft Constitution did not provide for any constitutional basis for legislative, judicial or other state bodies to suspend or remove a sitting President, even in the case of proven infirmity, criminality or unconstitutionality. The absence of such a safeguard was in line with the expressed fears of many of the Tunisian political parties since Saïed's power grab.

On 3 July 2022 Belaid issued a statement declaring that the published draft differed from the document submitted by his committee and professing that he did not support the President's proposals, which he argued would facilitate a potential dictatorship. Belaid effectively urged the public to reject the charter at a plebiscite, which was held as scheduled on 25 July. While the UGTT once again adopted its well-practised equivocation in the face of state power when it said in early July that it would not encourage its large membership to boycott the referendum, a number of political parties did call for a boycott, including the PDL, as well as the so-called National Salvation Front—which had been founded in opposition to Saïed in May and which included, inter alia, Ennahdha, the Dignity Coalition and the Hope Party. Arguably, this was largely an Ennahdha-front body set up to try and take the heat off its leading member amid an increasingly tough political environment. However, it also included some NT remnants, among whom Ennahdha had for a period in government found collaborators (see above).

In the event, the draft charter was overwhelmingly endorsed at the referendum, securing the approval of 94.6% of those who cast their ballots, according to the final results released by the official election commission in mid-August 2022. Turnout was low, at 30.5% of the registered electorate. The National Salvation Front, chaired by Ahmed Najib Chebbi, vehemently denounced the plebiscite as 'illegal and unconstitutional', and appealed for Saïed's resignation, citing the low turnout. There was widespread disapproval from the international community, including from the UN, which in late July had announced that it was to review the new charter.

Nevertheless, the new Constitution entered into force on 17 August 2022. Its adoption was met with widespread expressions of concern from domestic and international human rights organizations, including Amnesty International, which warned that the new charter 'could lead to the weakening of human rights safeguards and the rule of law ... [following] a year marked by a regression on human rights protections in Tunisia'. Amnesty also noted the 'lack of transparency' in the drafting of the new Constitution, its divergence from the draft prepared by the committee headed by Belaid and the removal from its preamble of any reference to universal human rights principles.

Following the adoption of the new Constitution, parliamentary elections were scheduled to be held in December 2022. However, it seemed unlikely that these would be conducted in a free and fair manner. Even if electoral participation was not constrained, the powers of the planned elected assembly would be significantly less under the terms of the new Constitution than under the 2014 charter.

Meanwhile, it appeared as if President Saïed was facing a growing political challenge from the opposition of Tunisia's trade unions to the socioeconomic pressures that continued periodically to motivate protests and strikes. In mid-June 2022 mass participation in a general strike organized by the UGTT, in protest against deteriorating economic conditions, brought the public transport system to a standstill and forced state-owned companies across many sectors to grind to a halt. In mid-July the UGTT was reported to be planning a second round of major industrial action in protest against steep rises in food and oil prices, and IMF-prescribed cuts in social provision and a freeze on public wages.

Conditional IMF financial support had been an ongoing thorn of political and economic contention in the side of Tunisia for some time, irrespective of the nature and holder of political authority. However, this contention had arguably grown under Saïed's rule, with his actions alienating a broad swathe of organized political and (despite the UGTT's relative equivocation) trade union opinion. Following initial caution and an apparent desire to maintain engagement with the regime, the UGTT had for several months been making strongly critical statements regarding Saïed's management of the economy. Further multifaceted criticism of the authorities, including an allegation made by UGTT Secretary-General Noureddine Taboubi in June 2022 that the Saïed leadership had adopted a secret agenda for the normalization of Tunisia's relations with Israel (see Foreign Relations) appeared to indicate a firmly entrenched domestic conflict that was unlikely to be resolved easily. The allegation seemed to have little substance behind it; in fact, Saïed himself periodically made what were considered by some to be anti-Semitic as well as anti-Israeli comments, to the extent of appearing insensitive to the killings at the Djerba synagogue in May 2023 (see Heightened Terrorist Threat to Domestic Security).

However, Saïed was not above using his political office to seek to regain the populist upper hand. In March 2022, for example, he went on the rhetorical offensive, declaring a 'relentless war' on food 'speculators and criminals' for what he called their avaricious desire for profit while 'the people' went hungry amid rising global food and energy prices following the full-scale Russian invasion of Ukraine in late February. Facing nationalist, Islamist and leftist opposition aggrieved at socioeconomic hardship exacerbated by the Russo–Ukrainian war, and arguably by the IMF, it seemed that the Tunisian President stood to gain from his own populist discourse, regardless of the possible negative economic reality of the adoption of any extra-legal measures.

Compounding the depth of the semi-permanent 'state of exception' (the claimed legal legitimacy for the original intervention, according to a clause of the since scrapped Constitution), President Saïed had decreed at the end of July 2021 the stripping of immunity from prosecution of deputies. Through such a measure the arrest of former deputies seen as representing a security—or as likely a political—risk would be more easily carried out. Ironically, this move had arguably indicated that Tunisia was still a state of law, even if the presidential ruling was seemingly arbitrarily drawn up and introduced, and it lacked meaningful means of challenge.

In September 2022 a new presidential decree entitled Law 54 introduced in Tunisia what was a common technique across Arab-majority states, that of handing down a prison sentence (up to five years in this case) and a fine of up to TD 50,000 for spreading 'false information and rumours'. If the alleged offence targeted a state official, the punishment was doubled.

In late November 2022 Rachid Ghannouchi appeared before a regional Tunisian anti-terrorism court accused of facilitating the movement of jihadists to Syria and Iraq during his time in government. This accusation had long been made against him, whether his party controlled the Ministry of the Interior or not, and in fact this particular case stemmed from a nearly one-year-old legal complaint brought by a deputy of the rival NT (an apparent opponent of Saïed's so-called 'coup') who, significantly, lodged his complaint with the military judiciary. Ironically, due to civilians (including Ghannouchi) being involved, the military court referred the case to the anti-terrorism court. These proceedings, however, failed to progress.

Ghannouchi was again ordered to appear before an anti-terrorism court in February 2023—at a time when several other leading Islamist personalities were also being arraigned. On this occasion the alleged connivance in foreign militancy by Tunisian Islamists involved a misplaced police officer's recording of an alleged conversation between Ghannouchi and a member of Ansar al-Sharia, even though, according to the Ghannouchi-sympathetic *MEMO* (*Middle East Monitor*), the police leadership had denied ever having been presented with such a recording. The conversation was supposedly about conducting militant attacks abroad. The upper echelon of the police had allegedly deleted the recording to protect Ghannouchi. This alleged interaction between the then Minister of the Interior and a member of Ansar al-Sharia continued to be a feature of court proceedings against Ghannouchi in April, but were superseded by perceptibly more substantive allegations. In that month Ali Laârayedh, a former premier and minister in governments including that of Ennahdha, was investigated under the same court proceedings regarding Ennahdha's alleged encouragement of Tunisians fighting in Iraq and Syria. Laârayedh's lawyers alleged that the charges brought against him were based on 'falsified data' and that he was only being detained due to a political agenda.

LEGISLATIVE ELECTIONS FAIL TO INTEREST TUNISIANS

Little more than 10% of registered Tunisian voters took part in elections to the new, post-'coup' Assembly in mid-December 2022. Saïed's self-styled 'corrective' intervention had arguably been able to exploit a populist wellspring of Tunisian discontent with party politics, whoever was in government. However, the embarrassingly low turnout, following modest participation in the overwhelming vote of approval for the President's new and self-serving Constitution, suggested that all was not well with this seeming autocrat's bid to build a populist basis for what looked like anti-democratic moves. It could be argued that the so-called (new) legislature—in terms of the formal powers ascribed to its elected component—was weak compared with its predecessor, and that therefore it would inevitably fail to elicit mass enthusiasm. On the other hand, the whole point of President Saïed's intervention was to reduce the power of the plethora of competing political parties whose numbers in parliament had determined the government of the day, and for the President to thus be above such a small political 'fray' by embodying a sovereignty separate from the elected chamber and based wholly on a direct mandate. To have effectively rejected this political model by not voting in significant numbers for the kind of assembly that Saïed had long advocated, was arguably a rejection of his overall project. The President's authority, however, was still embodied in his direct election—even if that was under a different political system (and arguably regime), to the one that Saïed was now exclusively creating. His assumed re-election—under the rules of the old order at least—was not due until October 2024. In theory, the President could relax the political atmosphere ahead of that poll in order to make the campaign a more open one than was anticipated as of mid-2023, when a climate of political fear persisted. To do so would fit with the still publicly expressed hopes of Tunisia's Western allies. If Saïed did this, he would arguably be proving that his authoritarian measures were genuinely a relatively short-term interregnum. To do this, Saïed would need to release those political opponents whose detention or imprisonment had been legally contested, and therefore re-enable an autonomous judiciary and even allow the formation of the promised, but never delivered, post-2011 constitutional court. Otherwise, the so-called 'state of exceptions', based on Saïed's claimed 'exceptional' measures, would simply become a permanent state of affairs.

MILITARY COURTS/MILITARY COMPLICITY?

In January 2023 a military court gave gaol terms to six people, including four politicians associated with the Islamist grouping Al-Karama, following an incident at Tunis airport in March 2021 when they objected to a police officer trying to prevent a woman from travelling. Perceiving the police officer's actions to be arbitrary, the six individuals had objected and had been arrested in the ensuing fracas. Since the onset of the supposed political interregnum under President Saïed, the use of military courts had become more widespread. They had been utilized to prosecute civilians prior to 2021, usually in cases where alleged civilian behaviour had in some way directly impugned the reputation or morale of the armed forces. The use of military courts, however, increased substantially after 2021 and involved a wide variety of 'offences', often related to members of the opposition, even if it was still suggested that the armed forces' morale or standing had been impugned. Saïed of course was, as President, also Commander-in-Chief of the Armed Forces. Notably, however, there was some opposition from the military to its own justice system being used for a political clampdown. In a meeting of the Brookings Institute on 26 July 2023, Tunisian expert and fellow of the North Atlantic Treaty Organization (NATO) Defense College, Eya Jrad, said that the Tunisian military justices had in March issued a statement specifically asking not to be obliged to adjudicate on matters affecting domestic politics.

The Tunisian military's relationship to Saïed's intervention from 2021—and to his continued amassing of authority by curtailing the powers of other centres of authority—became increasingly significant. Following a seeming regime change in 2011 facilitated by the military's important but passive role of non-objection, Saïed had used the military literally to shut down the parliament in July 2021, appointed four former senior serving officers as ministers, deployed the military rather than the more traditional interior ministry officers to arrest political opponents, and had senior military officers standing with him when he made official pronouncements. It is arguable that Saïed's 2022 Constitution made official the politicization of Tunisia's nascent military in that the Constitution no longer prescribed it a neutral role. Sharan Grewall, a Brookings Institute fellow, interviewed retired senior Tunisian military officers and senior politicians for his 2023 book '*Soldiers of Democracy? Military Legacies and the Arab Spring*'. He told the meeting of the Brookings Institute in July that Saïed had been able to exploit a military that had long been treated by governments as 'apolitical' and that the military had viewed this as not questioning orders. Compounding the situation, Grewall argued, was that fact that since 2021 Saïed had increased funding for the military, as well as his utilization of high-ranking military officials as political advisers. At the same time, Tunisia's rumbunctious party politics (pre-2021) was, Grewall argued, seen within the armed forces as unfamiliar and synonymous with chaos. He went on to contend that all of this made the 2021 'coup' feasible as an intervention, and may also sustain the military's support for Saïed going forward. The military's 'incomplete professionalism', as Grewall put it, means that it can be manipulated, as it does not have an institutional sense of what is politically or legally 'right' and 'wrong'. He asserted that without developing their own 'Office of General Counsel' as a military institution able to provide legal, including constitutional, guidance, then the armed forces will continue to be manipulated. Drawing on his interviews with military men, the academic also said that another civil-led but military-backed political intervention could occur in Tunisia in the medium term, but the armed forces themselves are unlikely to take the initiative unless *in extremis*—for example, if Saïed ordered them to quash potential demonstrations against economic hardship.

This latter observation notably contrasts with Saïed's hitherto cautious allowance of UGTT-encouraged popular protest. A different view was expressed in the Brookings seminar by a Tunisian academic, Mohammed Dhia Hammami, who noted that the armed forces have crossed into civil life or asserted themselves politically before, such as undertaking road building under Bourguiba; resisting being arraigned before a truth and reconciliation process after 2011; and, admittedly under Saïed but pre-2021, by being placed on the frontline in the state's battle against COVID-19.

ARRESTING DEVELOPMENTS

A series of high-profile arrests of senior Ennahdha leaders, judges and at least one leading business figure began in February 2023. A senior Islamist figure from Ennahdha, Said Ferijani, was arrested in late February. His arrest was followed by that of another senior Islamist figure (and relative), Rachid Ferijani. Other party officials, as well as some former state administrators described as having worked with Ennahdha in government, were also detained and/or charged. In mid-February two senior judges were arrested by the state authorities—the former Republic's Representative at the Court of First Instance in Tunis, Judge Bashir al-Akrami, and the former First President of the Court of Cassation, Judge Al-Taib al-Rashed, on charges of having conspired against 'state security'. However, it is more likely that the two judges—and other judicial figures who had come under pressure—were unwilling to follow the directives of the Ministry of Justice under President Saïed's control, or perhaps more direct 'messaging' from the President. A businessman, described on UK-based Arabic news-site *Al-Arab* as a 'shadow prime minister', Kamal Latif, was also arrested. The Emirati-linked news-site stated that Latif had been given this label because he had been closely connected to every government since 2011 (the period in which Ennahdha had been a lead actor in government, or when secular forces mostly now associated with the opposition had been leading actors in government). The dragnet extended beyond Ennahdha and those sympathetic to it, however.

The detractors of the opposition group the National Salvation Front (NSF) saw it as effectively serving an Ennahdha agenda, while allowing the latter to try to avoid overt confrontation with the state. In practice, both Ennahdha and the NSF's non-Islamists were being put under pressure. For instance, Jaouhar ben Mubarak, a leading NSF figure and secularist who had been a Saïed supporter but was now a critic, was arrested in late February 2023. At the same time, as part of the wave of arrests, a brother of the formal head of the NSF, Ahmed Chebbi, was held, along with another senior NSF figure, Chaima Issa. They and another nine known opponents of Saïed's 'intervention' were accused by the President of being engaged in 'terrorism'. Chillingly, he warned the judges who were to try their case that any leniency would mean that they were fellow-travelling with terrorism.

In late April 2023 the Speaker of the former Tunisian legislature, and leader of Ennahdha, Rachid Ghannouchi, was arrested. In mid-May he was sentenced to one year's imprisonment, having been found guilty of charges of incitement to violence against Tunisian state security and of plotting such acts. He did not appear in court, having refused to do so on the basis that this would grant legitimacy to what he argued was a political trial. Ghannouchi had indeed warned that a political clampdown against his party and other opposition groupings could lead to civil conflict in Tunisia. It seemed, however, that this warning was used to support the authorities' allegation against him of incitement. It was also reported in Emirati-linked publications that Ghannouchi's son-in-law, Rafic 'Abdelsalam' (born Bouchlaka), had also been arrested. Abdelsalam is married to one of Ghannouchi's daughters, Soumaya Ghannouchi, herself a de facto spokeswoman for Ennahdha in the West. Abdelsalam served as Minister of Foreign Affairs in an Ennahdha-led Government in 2012–14. His detractors, including specifically *Al-Ain* in an online piece published on 9 May 2023 (accessed via *Middle East Wire*), accused him of being a corrupt financier for the Ennahdha of which he is, stated the article, a 'politbureau (sic)' member. In late April Mondher Ounissi, the Vice-President of Ennahdha, was appointed acting party President in Ghannouchi's stead by the party's Executive Committee.

At the end of February 2023 Saïed caused anger among neighbouring Maghreb countries and wider African states, the domestic Tunisian opposition, the leaders of some Western European states, including France, and, perhaps most significantly, the World Bank (see Economy) when he stated that Tunisia was awash with 'African' migrants who wanted to turn it into 'only' an 'African country', to the exclusion of its Arab identity. Given the relatively small number of Tunisian residents of sub-Saharan heritage, this seemed like a calculated statement for populist appeal at home and in certain right-wing European circles, including that of his ally, Prime Minister Giorgia Meloni of Italy, who continued to defend the Tunisian President against IMF and other financing pressure. Notably, the EU subsequently proposed a Meloni-encouraged financing package that included €100m. for additional border control measures (see Economy).

In July 2023 the second anniversary of the Saïed intervention led to different opposition attempts to mark the event. Notably the NSF, although itself broadbased, failed to gain co-operation in this outside of its own supporters, largely because it was seen as aiding Ennahdha, even though it included secularist elements who had been opposed to that party. Relatedly, in January a former leader of Courant Démocratique had tried to build on the perceptible setback for Saïed of the low December 2022 poll turnout by promoting what he had called an 'inclusive' dialogue of Tunisian political and economic stakeholders and the Government, but he made it clear that he did not seek the NSF's or specifically Ennahdha's participation. In any case, it would have been very hard to imagine Ennahdha sitting down with the Government while several of its leading figures were in gaol, even though rumours periodically circulated that such a bilateral dialogue was precisely what was happening in private. It would be odd, however, if there were no exchanges at all, even if only completely discreet ones of the 'Track Two' variety.

Other opposition platforms being formed included an attempted alliance of the UGTT, the Tunisian League for the Defence of Human Rights and the Tunisian Order of Lawyers. The UGTT was increasingly siding with the opposition, something that arguably the leading opposition force, Ennahdha, found useful. While their relations had never been good, given the trade union federation's long secular and (pre-2011) regime-aligned position, it was advantageous to the Islamists for this legal and still powerful body to take the lead in holding protests and calling for change. Although the UGTT's continued demands for higher state salaries and its opposition to privatization effectively placed it in a de facto alignment with President Saïed in his opposition to the IMF's perceptibly austerity package (see Economy), this was arguably merely a tactical stance by Saïed and simply a defence of vested interests on the part of the UGTT.

In March 2023 the UGTT urged its members and others to back a nationwide demonstration against the 'state of exceptions' under Saïed. Notably, the President responded to the UGTT-organized protests quite calmly, encouraging a relatively cautious response from police and security forces. It seemed a tactically clever way to emphasize that his was not a brutal autocracy, especially if a powerful civil societal organization such as the UGTT could not only organize and strike, but could protest politically too. That said, in February Saïed expelled the UGTT's guest, the head of the European Confederation of Trade Unions, amid an increasingly fractious relationship between the state and the UGTT. It remained to be seen whether Saïed or the UGTT would seek to be more ameliorative towards each other. The union bloc had long proven useful to incumbent Tunisian leaders, and its support would arguably be needed by Saïed on the assumption that he would adhere to the presidential election timetable and go to the polls in 2024.

In January, February and March 2023, President Saïed made several cabinet changes. The first followed the setback of the December 2022 legislative poll, and sought to offset the contentions concerning education and agriculture by appointing new ministers to these portfolios (a plain-clothes military man to the latter), in addition to dismissing the Minister of Trade and Export Development. The IMF talks delayed further cabinet changes that rumours suggested would include the replacement of Prime Minister Najla Bouden herself, but, in the event, she survived presumably because disagreeing with her about IMF demands for cuts was a useful domestic political ploy for the President. In early February 2023 Saïed replaced the Minister of Foreign Affairs, Migration and Tunisians Abroad, Othman Jerrandi, with Nabil Ammar, a veteran Tunisian representative in the EU. No official reason was given, although it followed Tunisian tensions with France over the 'escape' of a leading Algerian opposition figure who had travelled to France via Tunisia and whose 'secret' journey Algeria accused the French Government of having been responsible for and having pressured Tunisia into allowing. In March interior minister Taoufik Charfeddine resigned, stating that he wanted to spend more time with his children—a classic diplomatic cover, which, in Charfeddine's case, was probably true as his wife had been killed in an accident the previous year. Kamel Feki was appointed to this key regime portfolio in his stead.

SAÏED DISSOLVES LOCAL COUNCILS

On 9 March 2023 President Saïed decreed the abolition of municipal councils. Elected a year prior to his own victory, the local councils were due for re-election in October. Saïed argued that they were not 'neutral.' As they were usually elected from candidates standing on a party ticket, this was an odd complaint but one wholly in keeping with the President's justification for events since July 2021. It was noted in press reports that one-third of the councils had been run by Ennahdha administrations. New electoral rules for the successor bodies were promised, but, as of September 2023, had not been published. Assuming that fresh municipal elections would take place by the end of the year, it seemed likely that they would take the same form as those for the new Assembly in December 2022 (i.e. largely devoid of a genuine ideological or factional competition genuinely representative of Tunisian opinion). Also in March 2023 the new Assembly (partly made up of provincial representatives) sat for the first time, four months since its election. Seven seats remained vacant, but 25 women were elected. More relevantly, there were, not surprisingly, no real opposition members in a body that now arguably only had nominally legislative authority.

HEIGHTENED TERRORIST THREAT TO DOMESTIC SECURITY

In October 2018 Tunisians were shocked to witness a resumption of terrorist attacks after more than three years in which the authorities had been successful in preventing ongoing threats from actually being realized, even if the state of emergency remained in place since the 2015 attacks. In the centre of Tunis on 29 October 2018 an apparently lone suicide bomber exploded a device, injuring 15 people, the majority of whom were police officers. The assailant, who died, was a woman who had reportedly been educated to degree level, and was apparently not affiliated to any particular group. In June 2019 two further suicide attacks were carried out simultaneously in central Tunis, killing two people, including a police officer, and injuring eight others. Islamic State was quick to claim these apparently co-ordinated attacks. Although foreigners were not, apparently, being targeted, the focus on the symbols of the state's security capability compounded the sense of renewed threat and of political crisis. Prime Minister Chahed announced in July that, as part of the enhancement of security measures in light of the recent terrorist attacks, that the wearing of the *niqab* (the full face veil) would be banned from all public and government offices. Interestingly, what ostensibly was no more than a practical security measure, put Tunisia—an overwhelmingly Muslim country with an Islamist party holding a plurality of seats in parliament—in a comparable situation to France, which had banned the full face veil in April 2011, although there was a wider ban in that country, covering anywhere defined as public.

In July 2019 Minister of National Defence Zbidi emphasized what he described as an ongoing threat to Tunisian security. This was despite what security forces had achieved in arresting senior figures from Islamic State and related *jihadist* groups in March and April in the west and centre of the country. It was clear that the rising confrontation in neighbouring Libya in May had affected Tunisians' already heightened sense of insecurity (see *Relations with Other Maghreb States*). Tunisia had recently included expanded defence and security co-operation with the USA (see *Relations with the West*) and the security budget was taking up some 15% of the official budget, according to a statement by Chahed in early 2019, which, he admitted, undermined the Government's ability to fund projects that tackled the high rate of unemployment.

Efforts were made further to tighten internal security, and the number of actual terrorist incidents appeared to fall in mid-2019. In mid-October a lone individual fatally stabbed a French national and injured a soldier in northern Tunisia, and later that month the Tunisian military and National Guard killed a man described as a 'senior leader' of Okba Ibn Nafaa Brigade and injured another in clashes in Kasserine. Arguably, this suggested that the Tunisian authorities were having some success, including in gathering the intelligence that made such operations possible. This did not eliminate the threat, however. A suicide attack on a police patrol near the US embassy in Tunis in March 2020 killed one Tunisian police officer and injured four others.

It remained the case that Tunisia's long border with Libya was highly vulnerable to penetration in either direction by Libyan and Tunisian-based Islamist militants alike, as was its long western border with Algeria, including Kasserine and the relatively lawless Chaambi mountains national park, where Okba ibn Nafaa Brigade is based. A US travel advisory issued on 6 August 2020 warned its nationals inside Tunisia not to travel within 30 km of the Libyan border. Both inside Libya and across its borders, fighters, whether Libyan or foreign, remained a security threat, including those associated with transnational groups such as AQIM (including the Okba Ibn Nafaa Brigade) and Libyans sympathetic to Islamic State.

It could be, however, that increasing instability in the Sahel region (encompassing Mauritania, Mali, Burkina Faso, Niger and Chad) reflected the focus of AQIM-related groups there rather than in North Africa and in turn further encouraged the migration of fighters from countries like Tunisia. It is not clear if this necessarily included the migration of many Tunisians themselves, but for many years they had been the largest national group, proportionately speaking, in AQIM. In 2017 a refocus on the Sahel in AQIM ranks had led to the founding of a new group, the Jamaat Nusrat al-Islam wal Muslimeen (Group for Support of Islam and Muslims). According to analysis in June 2019 by the US Jamestown Foundation, a definite decrease in AQIM's organizational capacity in North African countries such as Tunisia did not mean that it did not have the capacity to act there. This would seem to be confirmed by such attacks as that in Tunis in March 2020 and periodic incidents in fellow Maghreb countries. Although the Okba Ibn Nafaa Brigade by necessity was confined to remote areas in the Kasserine region, it could still draw on wider recruits from the south of the country. These areas consider themselves to be systematically disadvantaged by the Government (hence the

Amazigh-dominated protests about economic conditions—see *Protests Resume on Regional Fault Lines*) and are also areas that disproportionately provide recruits for the security forces, usually through economic necessity and, likewise, a disproportionate number of deaths in clashes with militants. Events further afield, such as a coup in Mali in August (eight years after a previous abrupt change of regime) greatly advantaged AQIM in that country and beyond and emphasized how domestic security problems can threaten—or even provide the pretext for overthrowing—Governments, and how the resultant instability can further benefit groups such as AQIM. Just as AQIM professed itself in favour of the popular anti-regime revolt in Algeria from early 2019, so militant Islamists welcomed the apparent weakening of Ennahdha in Tunisia from July 2021, following President Saïed's assumption of emergency powers. The repression of Tunisia's nascent democracy signalled a setback for gradualist Islamism and was thus viewed favourably by forces such as AQIM.

In mid-March 2022 an attack on a National Guard facility in Kairouan governorate was attributed by Tunisian media to an unspecified 'terrorist cell', although no claims of responsibility were issued. The attack highlighted Tunisia's continued vulnerability to those seeking to foment instability and, conceivably, to exploit extant political insecurity. Ten days later the authorities stated that its security forces had dismantled and arrested members of 150 militant cells in the previous six months, some of whom, it was alleged, were intent on joining the Algerian branch of Islamic State (formerly Jund al-Khilafah), which was based in the mountainous areas between Tunisia and Algeria. The Tunisian authorities claimed that these cells were intent on attacking neighbouring countries, as well as planning an attack on Tunisia's Minister of the Interior. While hard to ascertain the veracity of these official statements, they served as something of a propaganda tool for the Saïed regime in the context of his targeting of Tunisia's parliamentary Islamists, Ennahdha, with the proclaimed arrest of Islamist militants highlighting to Tunisians and neighbours alike the ongoing threat posed to regional security by militant Islamist extremists.

On 9 May 2023 another seemingly militant-inspired attack, but carried out by a Tunisian national security officer, was conducted on El Ghriba synagogue in Djerba. Five people, including two worshippers (one of Franco-Tunisian identity), the gunman and two other national security officers, were killed. In April Tunisian and French counter-terrorism officers had reportedly held a meeting to discuss deeper co-operation against such threats (see *Foreign Relations*). In general, however, Tunisians no longer perceived terrorism as a major national concern, at least not compared with the wave of assaults and the related vulnerability proximate to the Libyan border that had been such a feature a few years earlier.

FOREIGN RELATIONS

Relations with the West

Former President Ben Ali had pursued a moderate, pro-Western foreign policy. However, relations with the USA and its European allies became strained after Iraq invaded Kuwait in August 1990. Ben Ali condemned the deployment of a US-led multinational force in the Gulf region, clearly in order to appeal to his domestic audience, arguing that it was not in the interests of either the Arabs or world peace. For a brief period in the aftermath of the Gulf War, Tunisia's stance damaged relations with those countries that had participated in military operations to liberate Kuwait.

In February 1991 the USA reduced economic aid, and ended military assistance, although subsequent investment agreements with the USA indicated a rapid improvement in relations. Robert Pelletreau, the US Assistant Secretary of State, visited Tunis in December 1995 for talks with President Ben Ali and leading ministers. He praised the country's economic reforms and stated that military co-operation between the two countries would continue. In a report to the US Senate Committee on Foreign Relations in February 2001 the US State Department reiterated its strong criticism of Tunisia's human rights record, but the new US Administration of George W. Bush continued to regard Tunisia as an important strategic ally, and, as in the case of previous presidencies, conveniently disregarded these criticisms.

Relations with Tunisia's key European allies also quickly recovered after the Gulf War, but, although relations remained close, especially with France, they were strained by Tunisian disquiet at the activities of its Islamist opponents who had been granted asylum in Europe, and continuing concern in Europe over human rights abuses in Tunisia. Jacques Chirac's election to the French presidency in May 1995 was welcomed by the Tunisian authorities, and it was hoped that the new French administration would support Tunisia in its negotiations with the European Union (EU) over the association agreement and maintain an unyielding policy towards Islamist militants in France. In June French police arrested several Tunisians and Algerians living in France who were alleged to be part of a network providing arms to Islamist groups in Algeria and to the Front Islamiste Tunisien (which appeared to have close links with the radical Algerian Groupe Islamique Armée—GIA—although Rachid Ghannouchi, the leader of Ennahdha, denied any contacts between his party and this group). In October President Chirac made a state visit to Tunis, where he praised Ben Ali for promoting modernization, democracy and social harmony, and promised an increase in aid to Tunisia.

Ben Ali visited France in October 1997. During the visit two economic agreements were signed, providing additional French financial support for Tunisia. The longstanding dispute over French-owned property in Tunisia was also resolved. However, while economic co-operation continued to develop, relations at the political level were soured by highly critical reports about the Ben Ali regime in the French media during the Tunisian presidential and parliamentary elections in October 1999.

Italy was Tunisia's second largest trading partner after France and the third biggest source of foreign investment, but relations between the two countries were strained during the 1990s, owing to the problem of illegal immigration from Tunisia into Italy and disputes over fishing rights. In August 1998 the two countries signed an accord under which Tunisia agreed to do more to prevent Tunisians from entering Italy illegally and to take back illegal immigrants apprehended by the Italian authorities in exchange for a substantial aid agreement. Later in the year the two countries agreed to promote greater maritime co-operation. None the less, disputes over fishing rights continued to cause friction. During the second half of 2000 new agreements were signed with Italy on defence co-operation and the employment of Tunisian workers.

In December 1993 the EU's Council of Ministers mandated the European Commission to begin talks with Tunisia on a new partnership agreement to replace the co-operation agreement signed in 1976. The Tunisian Ministry of Foreign Affairs welcomed the talks, which it described as 'a political signal' marking European approval of Tunisia's progress towards political pluralism and its respect for human rights. Talks with the EU began in Brussels, Belgium in March 1994, and negotiations were completed in July 1995 when Tunisia became the first southern Mediterranean country to sign a new economic association agreement as part of the EU's plan for a Euro-Mediterranean Partnership. The agreement involved the gradual removal of tariffs on industrial imports from the EU, a high-risk strategy for the country's vulnerable manufacturing sector. The European Commission insisted that such partnership agreements with the Maghreb states were essential and, by strengthening the economies of those countries, would reduce Islamist violence and stem the flow of migrants to Europe.

The President of the European Commission, Romano Prodi, visited Tunis in January 2001 as part of a tour of the Maghreb aimed at reviving the Euro-Mediterranean Partnership. It was reported that Tunisia had become increasingly disillusioned with the EU accord, arguing that European financial support had not been sufficient to offset the losses resulting from the progressive reduction of tariffs on European imports and the costs of preparing the economy for free trade.

Relations with the West after 11 September 2001

Following the September 2001 suicide attacks on New York and Washington, DC, USA, President Ben Ali vehemently denounced the perpetrators and reiterated Tunisia's 'principled and deeply anchored stand against terrorism in all its forms and manifestations'. In contrast to the 1991 Gulf War, there were no popular demonstrations against the US offensive in Afghanistan, but some observers believed that Tunisian popular opinion was in favour of Osama bin Laden. In April 2001 Italian police had arrested several Tunisians who were accused of belonging to the Milan cell of the Algerian-based Groupe Salafist pour la Prédication et le Combat (GSPC—the forerunner of AQIM), which was providing logistical support for, and planning terrorist attacks in Europe on behalf of, al-Qa'ida. The Italian police believed that more Tunisians were members of the GSPC network, which had cells in several European countries. Following the attacks the Tunisian press accused the banned Islamist party, Ennahdha, whose leadership was based in Europe, of having links with al-Qa'ida, allegations that were strongly denied by Ennahdha representatives.

Anti-war demonstrations were held in Tunisia after the US-led military intervention in Iraq that commenced in March 2003. On a visit to Austria, the Tunisian Minister of Foreign Affairs stated that the military campaign in Iraq represented a failure for all those who had been working for a peaceful solution to the crisis. In December US Secretary of State Colin Powell began a brief tour of the Maghreb states in Tunisia, regarded by the USA as a staunch ally in the 'war on terror'. Ben Ali visited Washington, DC, in February 2004. He was the first Arab leader to visit the US capital after President Bush presented his initiative on democracy in the Middle East, and at the end of 2003 the US Assistant Secretary of State William Burns announced that the USA had chosen Tunisia as the regional centre for its Middle East Partnership Initiative to promote democracy and political reform.

In March 2006 US Secretary of Defense Donald Rumsfeld visited Tunis for talks with President Ben Ali and Minister of National Defence Morjane, as part of a tour of Maghreb countries; the discussions covered issues including military co-operation and counter-terrorism. In a further visit in May US Under-Secretary of State Robert Zoellick acknowledged the positive role that Tunisia had played in the normalization of relations between the USA and Libya. In June 2007 the Minister of Foreign Affairs, Abdelwahab Abdallah, met Vice-President Cheney and Secretary of State Condoleezza Rice during an official visit to Washington, DC. The meetings were described as friendly and positive. The two parties discussed the deterioration of the situation in the Palestinian territories and other recent developments in the Middle East. Bilateral relations were strengthened in September 2008, when Rice visited Tunisia during a brief tour of Maghreb states.

Following the September 2001 attacks on the USA, the French authorities quickly reassessed their attitude to the Ben Ali regime. After Tunisia had been diplomatically ostracized by senior French politicians, the French Minister of Foreign Affairs, Hubert Védrine, visited Tunis in October, followed by President Chirac, who held talks with Ben Ali in December. Chirac shocked and angered the Tunisian opposition by praising Ben Ali for his 'exemplary policy of combating terrorism'. Following the suicide bomb attack in Djerba in April 2002, French police arrested several alleged accomplices of the Tunisian perpetrator. French Minister of Foreign Affairs, Dominique de Villepin, praised Ben Ali during a visit to Tunis in November, stating that 'an open and dynamic Tunisia' under his leadership 'deserved the full support of France'. In December French police arrested Khemais Toumi, a prosperous businessman living in Marseilles, who provided financial backing for the secular opposition in Tunisia, after the Tunisian authorities requested his extradition. In 1997 Toumi had been sentenced *in absentia* by a Tunis court to five years' imprisonment on fraud charges, but no request had been made at that time for his extradition. Lawyers for Toumi expressed concern that, with the marked improvement in relations between Paris and Tunis, their client would be handed over to the Tunisian authorities, and fears were expressed for his physical safety.

President Chirac angered dissidents and human rights activists during a three-day state visit to Tunis in December 2003 by declaring that Tunisia had made great advances in 'the first human right which is the right to eat, receive health care and an education and have a place to live'. Members of his entourage had no illusions about the absence of democracy under the Ben Ali regime, but insisted that discreet diplomacy was more effective than grand declarations. In July 2004 the French Minister of Foreign Affairs, Michel Barnier, emphasized the Euro-Mediterranean dimension of Franco-Tunisian relations and urged the two countries to bring about a new momentum in relations between the EU and the Maghreb through the so-called Barcelona Process (the co-operation and dialogue instituted by the Euro-Mediterranean Partnership).

Shortly after being elected, French President Nicolas Sarkozy made an official visit to Tunisia in July 2007. Although Sarkozy raised the issue of human rights, he declared that he was not in Tunisia to lecture the regime but to praise its efforts in moving towards democracy. The main items discussed with Ben Ali were security issues, and Sarkozy called for closer co-operation between Tunisian and French counter-terrorism security services. He also launched the idea of a Mediterranean Union that he hoped would build upon the Barcelona Process to foster closer economic, political and cultural ties between all countries bordering the Mediterranean Sea. In April 2008 President Sarkozy met Ben Ali again during a state visit to Tunisia, where the two leaders supervised the signing of several agreements designed to increase nuclear and aviation co-operation. Ben Ali also expressed his support for Sarkozy's recently renamed Union for the Mediterranean (UfM), which had been modified in early 2008 to encompass not just those nations bordering the Mediterranean Sea, but all EU member states. When the UfM was inaugurated in Paris in July, Ben Ali was among the many leaders of the 43 member nations to be in attendance.

Relations with France became strained in March 2009, when the French Minister of Foreign and European Affairs, Bernard Kouchner, accused the Tunisian Government of 'attacks on human rights [and] the harassment and sometimes jailing of journalists'. However, French Prime Minister, François Fillon, subsequently praised the democratization process under Ben Ali. France initially misjudged the determination of sections of the Tunisian public to overthrow the regime illustrated by a wave of protests that began in late 2010. Three days before Ben Ali fled Tunisia in January 2011, France's Minister of Foreign and European Affairs, Michèle Alliot-Marie, offered to send French security forces to help his regime to tackle the burgeoning protests.

Following the change of regime, efforts were made by the Governments of Tunisia and France to improve bilateral relations. In July 2012 Tunisia's interim President, Moncef Marzouki, met the new French President, François Hollande, in Paris, for discussions. France backed the EU's granting of advanced partner status to Tunisia in late 2012 (see below). In July 2013 Hollande made an official visit to Tunis, accompanied by, *inter alia*, a human rights activist and a liberal film director of Tunisian origin. The political message, following his Government's strong condemnation of the murder of Belaïd earlier in the year, seemed clear. The removal of the state of emergency in Tunisia in March 2014, following the introduction of the new Constitution under the caretaker administration, helped to strengthen Tunisia's ties with France and with other EU states.

The issue of terrorism was discussed during visits to Tunis by Italian President Carlo Azeglio Ciampi and Minister of Foreign Affairs Renato Ruggiero in October 2001 and by Italian Prime Minister Silvio Berlusconi in November. Several Tunisians had been arrested in Italy on terrorism charges both before and after the September 2001 attacks in the USA. Some progress in handling questions of illegal immigration and fishing rights resulted in an improvement in bilateral relations. In July 2003, after a sharp increase in the number of illegal immigrants trying to reach Italy by sea from Tunisia, the Tunisian Minister of the Interior promised new legislation aimed at both migrants seeking illegally to enter Italy and traffickers. The Government of Prodi, in power from May 2006, made the Mediterranean and the wider Middle East a foreign policy priority. The Minister of Foreign Affairs, Massimo D'Alema, visited Tunisia in April 2007 and stated that both countries were committed to achieving peace and security in the area. Human rights issues were not mentioned, as the meeting between D'Alema and Ben Ali focused almost exclusively on the Arab–Israeli conflict. Following the change of regime in Tunisia in January 2012, Italy sought to improve bilateral relations, and in May, during an official visit to Tunis by Italian President Giorgio Napolitano, the two countries signed a strategic agreement that included Italy's commitment to Tunisia obtaining EU advanced partner status. Relations deepened following the granting of that status. However, Italy remained concerned about the extent of illegal immigration coming from North Africa, including that of Tunisians who (directly and indirectly) migrated from Tunisia during the political upheaval, and who continued to try to enter Italy and other southern European countries.

Prodi, by now the President of the European Commission, visited Tunis in April 2003 to discuss bilateral relations between Tunisia and the EU. Prodi called for the strengthening of economic and political relations between the EU and all the southern Mediterranean countries. In December Tunis hosted the first '5+5 Dialogue Summit' of the heads of state and government of the Union of the Arab Maghreb (UMA, see p. 1169) and of France, Italy, Malta, Portugal and Spain. The meeting, organized on the initiative of President Ben Ali, was intended in part to act as a forum to express concerns about the impending enlargement of the EU, amid fears that this would be at the expense of the Maghreb countries, and also as a further attempt to revive the UMA. Prodi stated that the enlarged EU must give priority to strengthening co-operation with Algeria, Morocco and Tunisia, but pointed out that this would prove less difficult if the Maghreb countries resolved their own internal disputes and accelerated 'the continuous progress towards democracy'. However, the meeting appeared to have done little to alleviate issues of contention between the Maghreb states, notably the Western Sahara issue. In November 2005 Gijs de Vries, the EU Co-ordinator for Counter-Terrorism, called for even closer ties between European intelligence services and their North African counterparts. Despite some criticism of its approach to Tunisian media support, the EU contributed €2m. in 2004/05 to a journalist training programme in Tunisia. While the European Parliament has often been critical of the Tunisian regime and its human rights record, the EC has been on friendlier terms with Tunisia and has financed several projects aimed at strengthening the Tunisian economy.

Following the commencement of negotiations in June 2009 between Tunisia and the EU over Tunisia's application for advanced partner status in its partnership with the EU, the mixed opinions among EU members were revealed in a debate on the issue in the European Parliament in January 2010. Some EU members expressed concerns about Tunisia's democratic and human rights failings—concerns that were reiterated by a European Commission report, published in May, on Tunisia's progress in implementing a five-year Action Plan it had agreed with the EU in 2005. The report praised Tunisia's progress in economic reform, but highlighted 'persistent shortcomings' in democratic advancement, the rule of law and human rights.

Tunisia remained keen to gain advanced partner status, which would confer additional benefits such as preferential trade terms, membership of various European agencies and observer status at the Council of Europe. In June 2010, demonstrating Tunisian sensitivity on the subject, the legislature approved amendments to the penal code outlawing any action that 'incites foreigners to take action that harms the country's economic interests'. The amendments were reportedly aimed at Tunisian opposition figures who had been lobbying against the granting by the EU of advanced partner status until Tunisia improved its record on human rights. With the political transformation in Tunisia in 2011, its prospects for securing EU advanced partner status were greatly improved. Indicative of the improved relationship, in 2012 the EU committed itself to more than doubling its planned aid disbursements to the Tunisian Government. In November Tunisia was granted advanced status as a privileged partner of the EU. A four-year economic action (or reform) plan was instituted at the beginning of 2013, setting out the practical basis of Tunisia's new advanced status. Under the plan, the EU was to give financial, technical and advisory support to Tunisia in the implementation of essentially free market reforms. The EU emphasized, however, that Tunisia must strengthen the rule of law, protect human rights and basic freedoms, and deepen civil society, as the basis for a healthy and functioning democracy.

The Tunisian Government considered that its advanced partner status would, by definition, give the country preferential access to the EU market, as well as to low-cost EU loans. The EU, for its part, expressed the hope that the closer association would encourage the opening of talks on agricultural trade liberalization and negotiations for the opening up of the Tunisian air transport sector with a view to boosting tourism.

Franco-Tunisian relations were strained in 2014, when Hollande's hope that Marzouki would be re-elected as Tunisian President was expressed publicly. In general, the Tunisian Government felt that the Hollande administration had not provided enough financial and political support for its transition. The shared Franco-Tunisian vulnerability to terrorism resulted in mutual support during solidarity demonstrations. President Hollande was one of only three senior Western figures present in Tunis after the Bardo attack in March 2015. Tunisian Prime Minister Jomaâ had attended the demonstration that followed the attack on the offices of satirical newspaper *Charlie Hebdo* in Paris in January. Furthermore, the exigencies of the domestic Tunisian situation made the Government's resumption of the state of emergency less of a hindrance to normal bilateral relations than it had been up to 2014. President Essebsi's official visit to France a month after the Bardo attack helped to improve matters further.

Notably, former French President Sarkozy sought to exploit residual Franco-Tunisian sensitivities when in July 2015 he spoke in Tunis as the guest of the Tunisian Government. His main public focus, however, appeared to be the exploitation of intra-Maghreb tensions. Sarkozy criticized Algeria for, in his view, failing to counter growing militancy in North Africa and the Sahel. Although causing official embarrassment, this stance connected with some of the political elite in Tunisia, where concerns were quietly expressed about Algeria's inability to contain militancy in its border regions.

Relations with France continued to focus on counter-terrorism. On the eve of a visit to Tunisia by French President Macron in February 2018, President Essebsi gave an interview on French television in which he emphasized Tunisia's co-operation with France, Germany and the USA in matters of counter-terrorism, noting that Tunisia had made an agreement with the Macron administration for a conversion of some of Tunisia's debt. However, during his visit Macron offered only a relatively modest financial package of US $338m.

In January 2019 President Macron visited President Essebsi in Tunis. The French head of state announced an aid and soft loan package worth €272m. (see Economy), which he said was as much about political solidarity with Tunisia's democratic transformation since 2011 as it was aid *per se*. The civil war in Libya was also a primary concern for both countries' representatives in their talks. A complicating factor was that France was reportedly (according to certain French media sources and some Qatari news sites) the pre-eminent Western country backing a Libyan military leader, Gen. Khalifa Haftar (who had served as Qaddafi's former military chief), while also engaging with the internationally recognized Government of National Accord (GNA) in Tripoli, the Libyan capital.

In May 2019 Rachid Ghannouchi led a visit by a delegation from his party to France, where they met several senior French government officials. Although not doing so in any kind of official Tunisian capacity, they declared their support for President Essebsi. It was notable that the delegation was visiting at a time of particular tumult in Tunisian politics, and even greater upheaval in neighbouring Libya. With Ennahdha, an ostensibly opposition party holding a plurality in the Tunisian parliament, and Islamism generally still a potent force throughout North Africa and the wider Arab world, the visit underscored Ennahdha's undoubted if latent power ahead of the presidential and parliamentary elections to be held in Tunisia later in the year.

President Macron attended President Essebsi's funeral in July 2019, and, during his brief visit to Tunis, he expressed strong admiration for Essebsi's democratic legacy for Tunisia.

In June 2020 President Saïed visited Paris for his first official visit as head of state. He and President Macron were reported to have discussed the conflict in Libya, which Saïed feared could threaten national security, should the Libyan civil war intensify. It was also an issue that divided Tunisia and France, because the official position of Tunisia was one of engagement with the GNA Government in Tripoli (see *Relations with Other Maghreb States*) as the internationally recognized authority in the capital, but also support for national dialogue and neutrality in terms of the competing claims and interventions of various external actors. Notably, Tunisian state representatives have previously met players in the Libyan equation other than in the Tripoli Government, even as they have avoided Tripoli's arch-enemy, Gen. Haftar.

For its part, France under Macron has shared Tunisian concerns about the original intervention by the North Atlantic Treaty Organization (NATO) in Libya and associated itself with Gen. Haftar, who has reportedly received French military aid. France also seemed to have an understanding with Haftar's Gulf Arab allies and with Egypt over Libya. Before his departure for Paris, President Saïed faced domestic pressure to demand an apology for colonial 'crimes' in a debate in parliament led by the head of the Islamist Dignity Coalition group. However, the National Assembly vote on this matter failed. In the event, the meeting of the two Presidents proved successful and apparently avoided much reflection on the issue. Notably, the two men differed publicly in one key aspect of their public statements: France, unsurprisingly, attacked Turkish intervention in Libya but not that of other countries, while President Saïed asserted Tunisia's neutrality in North African regional matters while emphasizing that the GNA was the recognized Libyan Government, although he added that it was a temporary administration that needed to be replaced 'by the will of the people'. (See *Relations with Other Maghreb States*).

In common with the other main European players and with the USA, France offered a measured observation following Saïed's intervention in July 2021. It noted the suspension of parliament, but appeared to accept the need for 'emergency' and 'temporary' measures' to address Tunisia's problems. However, Saïed's formal dissolution of parliament in March 2022 elicited a statement from the French Ministry for Europe and Foreign Affairs expressing the French Government's desire for the 'rule of law' and the 'independence of the judiciary' to be maintained. The official French position on the Tunisian judiciary appeared to represent a clear division between Paris and Tunis following the series of moves by the Tunisian President over several months that were directly in contravention of the judiciary's independence and thus the rule of law. However, the still relatively cautious French response was unacceptable to some Tunisians, many of whom had for some time perceived Saïed to be conducting a permanent political coup, in a process that had destroyed an agreed, albeit precarious, political system.

Relations with the French Government became more fractious as what Paris had hoped would be a temporary intervention began to look more and more like a long-term affair. Several events in February 2023 set back bilateral relations, even as the two states maintained their overall defence, security and economic relationship. President Saïed's outburst against 'African migrants' and the consequent use of the military to transfer black migrants to isolated desert encampments was strongly criticized by the French Government, in contrast to that of Italy, even though France, of course, continued to hope that Tunisia would remain vigilant against unofficial migration from Tunisian shores to Europe. Earlier that month the transit of the Algerian opposition figure Amira Bouraoui from Algeria via Tunisia to France appeared to involve the exertion of French pressure on Tunisia at the expense of the latter's normally carefully managed relations with Algeria (see *Relations with other Maghreb States*). In addition, the wave of Tunisian arrests of opposition figures attracted criticism from France. Although the role of the Tunisian military in the harsh policing of migration would not have been welcomed by France, nor would Saïed's utilization of them in other 'political' modes (see above), the discreet military to military and security to security relations of the two countries continued unabated.

In the wake of the December 2016 Berlin terrorist attack, which involved a young Tunisian national, Anis Amri (see *The Appointment of a New Government under Youssef Chahed*), who was shot dead in Milan later in that month after opening fire on two Italian police officers, Tunisia and Italy pledged to work more closely together in sharing intelligence in an effort to prevent such outrages. Amri had previously been imprisoned in Italy for violent behaviour, following a failed asylum bid, but the Italian authorities had been unable to deport him. The Italian Minister of Foreign Affairs and International Co-operation, Angelino Alfano, met his Tunisian counterpart, Jhinaoui, and President Essebsi in Tunis in January 2017 to discuss the issue. A framework accord was signed by Essebsi and Italian President Sergio Mattarella in February pledging co-operation in combating illegal migration and human trafficking and enforcing border controls within the Maghreb.

The deaths of (mainly Tunisian) migrants in two accidents in May and June 2018 after the boats on which they had been travelling out of Tunisian waters sank in controversial circumstances, had implications for relations with Italy regarding immigration to Europe. In November 2017 the Italian Prime Minister Paolo Gentiloni had met his Tunisian counterpart to discuss mounting tensions caused by increasing numbers of migrants seeking to enter Italy by sea from Tunisia. Fears that Islamist terrorists might be attempting to enter Europe in this way, owing to several recent incidents in the continent involving Maghrebis, contributed to these popular and political concerns. The election of new coalition Government in Italy in March 2018 brought a harder line on immigration. The new Italian interior minister, Matteo Salvini, caused outrage across the political spectrum in Tunisia when, in June, he accused Tunisia of deliberately sending its criminals to Italy. Following the second of the two maritime accidents, in which 68 people drowned, Salvini commented that the 'party was over' for illegal migrants coming to Europe. Subsequent mutual efforts were made to restore bilateral relations. Later in June the Italian authorities announced that they had arrested several alleged Tunisian jihadists.

The number of Tunisians seeking to enter Europe, primarily via Italy, and the role of Tunisia in the maritime migrant route from North Africa to Europe was brought into focus by two more maritime accidents in May and July 2019, and relations with Italy remained tense. In May in broadly the same location (off the coast near Sfax) as the disaster of June 2018, a migrant boat carrying mostly Libyans sank, killing some 70 people. In July another boat sank, this time off the Tunisian city of Zarsis, killing 86 people, almost all of whom had escaped the fighting in Libya. At the end of 2019 the numbers of Tunisian migrants trying to reach Europe had reportedly risen significantly since the previous year.

Relations continued to be affected by Italian concerns about ongoing immigration from Tunisia, especially following the outbreak of the COVID-19 pandemic in early 2020. Although the number of migrants arriving on Italian shores was markedly down compared with the high levels seen in 2016–17, the Italian Government, under pressure from popular opinion and from right-wing nationalist critics, raised the issue with the President Saïed during his visit in July 2020. A bilateral agreement had been in place allowing Italy to repatriate a large number of Tunisians, but owing to COVID-19 this was reduced to a relatively small number. Part of the Italian concern was the difficulty in enforcing quarantine regulations in places like the island of Lampedusa, where many migrants arrive from Tunisia. Another factor irritating some Italians was the fact that Tunisian migrants are essentially economically motivated, unlike Libyans who are escaping a war zone. Furthermore, the ongoing problems in the Tunisian economy suggested that the outflow would only increase. The number of migrants arriving in Italy by sea in 2019 was a relatively low, at 11,471, many of whom had departed from Tunisia. The Italian interior minister noted in a meeting with President Saïed in July 2020 that as many as 11,191 migrants had arrived by sea since the start of that year; 5,237 came via Tunisia, of whom some 4,000 were Tunisian nationals. Furthermore, seaborne migrant numbers appeared to be increasing significantly. According to the website Politico, nearly 6,000 migrants arrived in Italy by sea in the course of a single week in early August, 1,851 of them from Tunisia. The Italian Government was under pressure from right-wing parties to arrest migrants upon arrival. President Saïed emphasized the need for internal Tunisian measures to prevent smugglers putting Tunisian lives at risk; on his visit to Italy he called it a 'democratic failure' that joblessness and poverty were not sufficiently addressed in Tunisia to prevent migration. It seemed unlikely, however, that enough would be done domestically, given the fact that the COVID-19 pandemic and subsequently the Russian invasion of Ukraine from February 2022 were aggravating the country's inherent economic problems, to prevent migrant outflows negatively affecting Tunisian relations with Italy. Giorgia Meloni, Italy's right-wing Prime Minister, proved a de facto cheerleader for Saïed in the EU and other international circles in 2023 (see above and below).

The assumption of autocratic powers by President Saïed in July 2021 was received cautiously by European powers, including France. In essence, as in the case of the USA (see below), there was not outright opposition to a man who was already seen as a welcome focus of popular support in contrast to Ennahdha; nor were their demands wholly at variance with how Saïed apparently wanted to proceed. Arguably, this fitted in with the priorities of the USA whose National Security Advisor, Jake Sullivan, met Saïed a week after his assumption of emergency powers. After that meeting, the message communicated by US Secretary of State Antony Blinken was that Tunisia needed to 'get back on track', including the restoration of the office of the Prime Minister. Notably, French foreign minister Jean-Yves Le Drian told his Tunisian counterpart that the authorities needed to 'allow a rapid return to a normal functioning of Tunisia's democratic institutions'. The reported specifics of the French demand were that there be a 'rapid appointment of a prime minister and the formation of a government'. This appeared to give the Tunisian President room for manoeuvre, especially as he had made it clear that he intended to rule in conjunction with a new Prime Minister, in an apparent unification (under Saïed) of the dual executive nature of Tunisian government before 25 July.

Following the popular protests of early 2011, US President Barack Obama indicated his Administration's support for the aims of the protesters, while calling for all parties to avoid violence. Obama also urged the Tunisian Government to demonstrate respect for human rights and to commit to holding elections. In February US Secretary of State Hillary Clinton made an official visit to Tunisia, during which she met interim President Mebazaa and Prime Minister Essebsi, pledging US assistance in Tunisia's efforts to institute political and social reforms. In April 2012 the USA committed to a sovereign loan guarantee of nearly US $500m. for a Tunisian bond issue and to the payment of Tunisia's relatively modest debts to the World Bank and African Development Bank. Bilateral 'anti-terrorism training' was resumed after a seven-year hiatus, reflecting the US Administration's desire to ensure that the Government in Tunisia supported US interests, and that a worsening security situation in Libya threatening to weaken border security in Tunisia and Algeria, and already affecting some neighbouring Sahel states, did not aid al-Qa'ida or related groups in North and West Africa. In June the Tunisian Minister of National Defence, Zbidi, signalled the Government's desire to enhance its defence relations with the USA when he emphasized to the US ambassador to Tunisia the need for the logistical capabilities of the country's armed forces to be improved. Relations were adversely affected in September, however, when the angry reaction in much of the Muslim world to a US-made film denigrating the Prophet Mohamed prompted—or provided a pretext for—an attack on the US embassy, in which several Tunisians were killed. Tunisian Salafists, possibly connected to the banned Ansar al-Sharia, were suspected of involvement. In the context of a larger-scale attack, linked to al-Qa'ida, on a US consulate in neighbouring Libya earlier in September, the US Administration was all the more perturbed by the incident in Tunisia, and by what it perceived as the Ennahdha-led Government's leniency towards the country's Salafists. Tunisian-US relations became strained again in May 2013, when 20 Tunisians were found guilty of involvement in the attack on the US embassy but received only suspended sentences. The USA strongly condemned the murder of two leading secular opposition politicians in February and July, which precipitated a political crisis in Tunisia.

Ennahdha's leader, Rachid Ghannouchi, visited Washington, DC, in February 2014, where he met senior US officials, seemingly keen to highlight his party's apparent commitment to democracy, including its agreement to leave office in a peaceful transition. Later in that month US Secretary of State John Kerry visited Tunisia, meeting both President Marzouki and the new Prime Minister, Jomaâ; and the US travel advisory, in place since September 2013, warning US citizens that it was too dangerous to visit Tunisia was revoked at the end of March 2014.

In November 2014, shortly before the NT assumed governance of the country, the Ministry of National Defence denied reports that the USA had requested that its air force be granted overflight rights and other privileges to assist it in launching possible air strikes against Islamic State targets in neighbouring Libya. The Ministry claimed that the USA did not need access to its airspace to attack such targets, although some analysts disputed this assertion. However, since the overthrow of Libyan leader Muammar al-Qaddafi in late 2011, the USA had refrained from such attacks, allowing Egypt and the UAE to take the lead in aerial operations over Libya.

In light of the Bardo National Museum and Sousse attacks in 2015 and the USA's ongoing efforts to combat Islamist militancy in Iraq, Syria and Yemen, bilateral relations improved, even though in July the USA (in common with the UK) once again warned its citizens not to travel to Tunisia. In May President Essebsi visited the USA for talks with President Obama, and the two heads of state signed a security agreement. In July Tunisia was granted 'Major non-NATO ally' status by the USA, a designation conferred on only five other Arab countries and only one other in the Maghreb (Morocco). These bilateral defence and security understandings reportedly caused disquiet in Algeria, which was concerned about being surrounded by US allies. This added to the existing difficulties in Tunisian-Algerian relations. Improving Tunisian-US relations, together with the West's increased interest in targeting Islamic State in Libya after the formation of a new national unity Government in that country, encouraged NATO to declare publicly its desire to establish an intelligence-gathering base inside Tunisia as part of the campaign against regional Islamist militancy. Jens Stoltenberg, the NATO Secretary-General, confirmed this in July 2016. However, the establishment of any kind of 'foreign base' was ruled out by the Tunisian Minister of Foreign Affairs, Jhinaoui, who was mindful of the likely Algerian, and domestic, reaction. However, there was little that Tunisia could do to prevent NATO military action against Islamic State in Libya, whether President Essebsi was in favour (see below) or Rachid Ghannouchi was opposed (as he and Algerian President Abdelaziz Bouteflika had agreed in March). In October reports emerged of an alleged US military base in Tunisia, although the Tunisian authorities claimed that any US personnel in the country were there solely in a training capacity. In November 2017 President Essebsi stated that there were 70 US military personnel operating US drones near the Libyan border, in concert with Tunisians learning how to operate the drones themselves, and that the US presence was known to the Algerian authorities. He noted that their purpose was purely to support counter-terrorism operations in Libya.

Tunisian relations with the US Administration of President Donald Trump, which took office in January 2017, were complicated by the latter's overt bias towards Israel, most obviously with regard to the status of Jerusalem and the US President's decision in December to upgrade the US diplomatic mission in Jerusalem to that of an embassy. Demonstrations took place throughout Tunisia, and the Government issued a statement emphasizing the international legal status of the city. In practice, political leaders in Tunisia had long avoided taking a strongly anti-Israeli stance. However, popular anger, reflected in demonstrations, trade union agitation and media comment made it difficult for the Tunisian Government to be detached. In February 2020 the UGTT organized a protest in Tunis in opposition to the so-called 'Deal of the Century' (the Trump Administration's proposal for, what many observers considered, a truncated and not wholly sovereign Palestinian state alongside Israel). In August a protest was held outside the UAE embassy in Tunis against that country's normalization of diplomatic relations with Israel, which had been facilitated by the USA.

Although it had not been denied that there were US military personnel operating on Tunisian territory, this had been presented, including by President Essebsi (see above), as in an area proximate to Libya and focused entirely on that country's ongoing conflict. However, it appeared as if the US presence on the ground in Tunisia had been gradually expanding, and that the counter-terrorism training mission for Tunisian security forces was not just focused on events to Tunisia's east. *The New York Times* reported in March 2019 that the US mission was at that time comprised some 150 troops and that it ranged widely in terms of its role and presence inside Tunisia and in the purpose of its advice to the Tunisian armed forces. The newspaper reported that the US military presence in Tunisia constituted one of the largest such US operations in Africa. Notably, the US forces reportedly had permission to fly from several air bases inside Tunisia, although the Government intended that this activity should remain secret.

In July 2019 the USA and Tunisia conducted their third Strategic Dialogue, on this occasion led by US Secretary of State Mike Pompeo and Minister of Foreign Affairs Jhinaoui. This had followed fast on the heels of a meeting of the two countries' Joint Economic Commission. These meetings took place at a time when the US Congress had been resisting the Trump Administration's attempts to cut aid to Tunisia, despite the USA's apparent appreciation of Tunisian security forces' role in intercepting AQIM and other militants. The Strategic Dialogue was expected to focus on domestic and cross-border security. An 'Arab Barometer' survey found that only 45% of Tunisians wanted stronger ties with the USA, compared with 63% wanting closer relations with the People's Republic of China, 57% with Turkey and 50% with the Russian Federation.

Regular US-Tunisian diplomatic contact continued at a very senior level. In July 2020 the new foreign minister Noureddine Erray conducted extensive discussions with Pompeo, and in August President Saïed and Pompeo discussed a range of issues including co-operation on tackling COVID-19 and regional security. Inevitably, security remained a crucially important area of these conversations and of ongoing bilateral co-operation, regardless of generally anti-US popular opinion in Tunisia. The Government benefited from the fact that the USA and many European states emphasized the importance of Tunisia's relatively unusual (by regional standards) democratic credentials, which could encourage greater financial support.

In an extraordinary development, US National Security Advisor Sullivan met President Saïed in person for an hour one week after the latter's suspension of the political process on 25 July 2021. Sullivan's mission to Tunis, at the behest of US President Joe Biden, suggested that the Biden Administration, with its projected renewed interest in democracy and human rights after the Trump presidency, was keen to assert such values. However, the fact that the US emissary should be the US President's top security official also suggested that traditional US security concerns would also be at the forefront of the discussions. In line with the carefully worded comments of senior European politicians, Sullivan was described in the official National Security Council gazette as having emphasized the need for a 'rapid formation' of a new Government under a new Prime Minister and 'ensuring the timely return of the elected parliament'. The use of the word 'timely' suggested that a reopened parliament was not the USA's priority any more than that of European or Arab supporters (see below) of the Tunisian President.

A few days before Sullivan's visit to Tunis, Blinken had spoken to President Saïed by telephone and, according to the official report, had issued carefully chosen words, urging that Saïed 'maintain open dialogue with all political actors and the Tunisian people' and that Tunisia must 'not squander its democratic gains'. In an acknowledgement of Saïed's own professed motivations for taking the exclusive reins of executive power, Blinken referred to the USA's willingness to help Tunisia address the economic and pandemic-related challenges that it faced. The USA was obviously keenly aware that these were reasons cited by Saïed for his assumption of unalloyed power.

In a press briefing in February 2022, a US Department of State spokesperson stated that the Biden Administration was 'deeply concerned' by Saïed's decision to dissolve the Supreme Judicial Council (see *A Restored Dictatorship*). Price also spoke of the need for a 'political reform process' that was compatible with the 'aspiration of the Tunisian people'. Following the endorsement by popular referendum, in July, of Saïed's draft charter, which afforded the President near-absolute power, the US Department of State expressed concern that 'weakened checks and balances in Tunisia's new constitution could compromise the protection of human rights and fundamental freedoms' and appealed for respect for the constitutional principle of the separation of powers.

The USA continued what some US analysts likened to a 'milk toast' (i.e. weak) criticism of repressive measures by Saïed, which, on the face of it, the US Administration should be vehemently opposed to. It seems that fear of a security vacuum if it were to encourage criticism of measures that were effectively licensed by the Tunisian military is partly behind this US caution. Yet, it is understood that the USA did not in fact adjudge the Tunisian military as having been instrumental in the so-called 'coup', so US caution in its criticism appears a little odd. Furthermore, the USA significantly reduced its military aid to Tunisia in 2022 (by 50%), which sent a message to the authorities, but arguably not to Saïed himself. It was also a possibly confusing message, as it was offset by ongoing US arms sales to Tunisia, including of fighter jets as well as more basic armaments. The Tunisian military's involvement in the US-led 'African Lion' military exercise in mid-2023 also suggested business as usual on both sides, with Tunisia's participation in this large-scale training exercise emphasizing a Tunisian-Western military orientation that stretches back to Bourguiba's rule.

The UK was particularly affected by the 2015 Sousse attack, in which 30 Britons were killed, and its decision to discourage its nationals from travelling to Tunisia, and then to warn that further such attacks in the country were 'highly likely', caused major damage to the bilateral relationship. In April 2016 the British and Japanese Governments pledged to fund a UN initiative to enhance Tunisian border security. When a British court stated in March 2017 that the response of the Tunisian security forces to the Sousse attack had been inadequate, Tunisia's General Directorate for National Security accused the British judge of 'cowardice' and of insulting the memory of those Tunisian security personnel who had lost their lives. The British Foreign and Commonwealth Office announced in July that it was suspending its general warning against travel to Tunisia and instead advised British nationals to avoid specific parts of the country, none of which were the popular coastal areas. In September-October 2019 a series of bilateral trade events were held with relatively senior governmental and business participation, and in October the UK and Tunisia signed a bilateral Association Agreement to replacement the UK's former commitment to the EU-Tunisia Association Agreement (as the UK finally left the bloc on 31 December 2020). In June 2022 President Saïed hosted a visit from a state minister attached to the British Foreign, Commonwealth and Development Office, during which both sides expressed their desire to enhance Tunisian-UK relations and to broaden the areas of bilateral co-operation, particularly within the fields of culture, the economy, energy and tourism.

The opinion of European states was divided largely, but not wholly, between those of a more right-wing hue and more liberal administrations when it came to the seeming semi-permanency of the Saïed autocratic leadership. The French and German Governments, for example, expressed their opprobrium about the atmosphere that President Saïed was stoking inside Tunisia, whereas the Italian Government of Giorgia Meloni was publicly understanding, and former Eastern Bloc countries such as Hungary and Poland (both led by right-wing governments) largely kept their counsel. Italy's right-wing Prime Minister, Meloni, visited Tunisia with her then Dutch counterpart, the relatively moderate Mark Rutte, and Ursula von der Leyen, the President of the European Commission, in mid-June 2023. The offer of an EU aid package worth more than US $900m. (see Economy) then followed, as both the Italian and Dutch premiers were seemingly concerned about immigration sensitivities in their own countries and the proposed package included additional money for the Tunisian authorities to extend their migration control measures. Saïed was arguably able to utilize Tunisian political actors like the PDL to his advantage, despite their professed opposition to the President's domestic political clampdown, as they held protests—for example, in Sfax in June—in opposition to what they assumed would be EU pressure (following the above deal) to resettle a large number of immigrants (as opposed to allowing them to cross the Mediterranean). Tunisian relations with Spain seemed largely to focus on trade and mutual security and migration concerns. In May Spain's trade minister Xiana Mendez visited Tunisia with a large business delegation and noted the exponential year-on-year rise in the value of bilateral trade in 2022.

Relations with other Maghreb States

After Ben Ali came to power, relations with Libya improved substantially. Qaddafi visited Tunis in February 1988, when it was agreed to abolish entry visas for Tunisians and Libyans crossing the Tunisian–Libyan border, and that both countries would abide by the judgment of the ICJ concerning the delineation of their respective sectors of the continental shelf in the Gulf of Gabès. In May Ben Ali and Qaddafi held an unscheduled summit on the island of Djerba. The two leaders signed an agreement providing for a social and economic union of the two countries, the free movement of people and goods across their common frontier, the establishment of a common identity card system and the freedom to live, work and own property. Several joint industrial, economic and cultural projects were initiated immediately after the summit. In August Ben Ali visited Libya, where he and Qaddafi signed a series of agreements including one concerning the settlement of the dispute over the continental shelf in the Gulf of Gabès. During the visit a technical commission was established to examine means of accelerating co-operation and some degree of unification between Tunisia and Libya. In September an agreement was signed establishing a joint Tunisian-Libyan company, which would exploit the offshore '7 November' oilfield in the Gulf of Gabès. An agreement to link the two countries' electricity grids was signed. During a visit to Tunis in December Qaddafi addressed the National Assembly, stating that he favoured 'constitutional unity' between the two countries but would not try to impose it. However, despite a great deal of rhetoric, Qaddafi appeared reluctant actually to implement co-operation agreements such as the joint exploration of the Gulf of Gabès and the financing of infrastructure projects in Tunisia. Tunisia and Libya, with Algeria, Mauritania and Morocco, were founder members of the UMA in February 1989. However, the UMA never developed into a coherent and functioning union.

The decision by the UN Security Council in April 1992 to impose sanctions against Libya over the Lockerbie affair (see *Libya*) was reluctantly accepted by Tunisia. Although flights to and from Libya were suspended, Tunisia insisted that land and sea links would remain open. Tunisia was Libya's principal trading partner in the Arab world. Sanctions against Libya created a mini-boom in southern Tunisia, amid a sharp increase in cross-border trade and in transit traffic. The Tunisian Government made efforts to negotiate a solution to the Lockerbie affair; Ben Ali visited Libya and consulted with President Muhammad Hosni Mubarak of Egypt in an attempt to resolve the deadlock between Libya and the West in the approach to the UN Security Council's sanctions review. Failure to resolve the Lockerbie affair also frustrated Ben Ali's efforts to forge closer relations between the UMA and the EU. On a visit to Tunis in December 1993, the French Minister of Defence suggested that Libya's membership of the UMA was a serious impediment to closer relations between the UMA and EU. As a result of UN sanctions, Tunisia became the main point of entry for international companies working in Libya. Tunisia continued to appeal for the lifting of UN sanctions against Libya. A series of economic agreements were signed in 1995, and following regular bilateral visits and discussions, several similar agreements were signed during 1997–98.

The Libyan Secretary for Foreign Liaison and International Co-operation, Omar al-Muntasir, visited Tunis in February 1999 at the same time as the US Secretary of Defense, William Cohen, who asked Ben Ali to show more support for UN sanctions against Libya and to use his influence with Qaddafi to persuade Libya to surrender the two suspects in the Lockerbie affair. In January, however, Ben Ali had repeated an appeal for the lifting of sanctions against Libya 'to end the suffering of the Libyan people', arguing that sanctions had also aggravated regional tensions and undermined Tunisia's own economic development plans. None the less, Tunisia did not follow some sub-Saharan African states in openly flouting the air embargo. President Ben Ali held talks with Qaddafi at the summit meeting of the Organization of African Unity (OAU, now the African Union—AU, see p. 1119) in the Algerian capital, Algiers, in July, and the Libyan leader visited Tunis on his return from the meeting. Ben Ali attended the special OAU summit meeting in Libya in September, which coincided with extensive celebrations to mark the 30th anniversary of Qaddafi's regime. While hosting a visit by the Libyan leader in May 2003, Tunisia declared that it would continue its efforts to achieve the final lifting of UN sanctions against Libya, and the two countries reiterated their solidarity with the Iraqi people and their commitment to Iraq's independence and territorial integrity. The UN voted to lift sanctions against Libya in September.

In 2004 Ben Ali held talks with senior members of the Libyan Government to discuss reinforcing bilateral relations and reviving the UMA (which was at that time under Libyan presidency). The lifting of sanctions on Libya and the re-admission of the Libyan leadership to the international system meant closer co-operation with Tunisia. Trade between the two countries increased as Libya began to catch up after years of isolation. In April 2007 it was announced by the two Governments that Tunisian building firms would help Libya to build over 40,000 homes by 2010. Libya's Secretary for the Economy, Trade and Investment spoke of the necessity to increase exchanges, which at that time stood at around US $2,000m. per year.

Regime change in Libya was welcomed by 'post-revolution' Tunisia. In April 2012 Libya's transitional Government and Tunisia signed a land border agreement to combat organized crime, terrorism and trafficking and in July agreed to increase co-operation in information technology. Their greatly improved relationship also gave impetus to renewed talk in the Maghreb of reviving the almost defunct UMA. Any significant progress would, however, require improved Moroccan–Algerian relations and a more stable Libya. Following the near collapse of the Libyan state and the rise of armed militias, a west Libyan Amazigh (Berber) tribe reportedly engaged in confrontation with local Arabs. From early 2013 there were widespread reports that AQIM forces were seeking to enter Algeria via Tunisia. Jebel Chaambi, a mountainous area west of Kasserine and close to the Algerian border, was the scene of repeated fighting involving jihadist militia and both Tunisian and Algerian security forces from April, when mines killed security personnel. In July at least eight Tunisian security personnel were killed in an apparent ambush by jihadist militia. The Tunisian military renewed its activities in Jebel Chaambi in April 2014, and in July 14 more soldiers were killed in an ambush by Islamist militants. The border area with Algeria, like that with Libya, continued to be the focus of intense activity by the Tunisian security forces, which carried out a series of raids and arrests throughout 2014 and 2015. Two deadly attacks in the Jebel Chaambi region, involving many casualties, were conducted by armed groups in July 2014. Ansar al-Sharia was known to be active in the area.

Tunisia's relations with Algeria continued to be dominated by the Islamist threat. In December 1991 Rachid Ghannouchi and other senior Ennahdha members were reportedly expelled from Algeria to Sudan. Relations with Algeria improved appreciably after the second round of Algeria's legislative elections were cancelled in January 1992 following the military takeover depriving the Front Islamique du Salut (FIS) of victory in the polls. The situation in Algeria was a constant factor in Tunisian decision-making with respect to domestic opposition and the choices made to counter political Islamism. Tunisia welcomed the appointment of Mohamed Boudiaf as Chairman of the High Council of State, and the military junta's campaign to suppress the FIS. In February 1993 Boudiaf's successor, Ali Kafi, visited Tunis, and during his stay letters were exchanged with President Ben Ali to ratify the official demarcation of the 1,000-km border between the two countries. Ben Ali and Kafi also expressed their determination to work together to counter the threat of terrorism (assumed by many commentators more accurately to mean the threat of militant Islamism) in the region. In December the Algerian and Tunisian foreign affairs ministers met at Tabarka to celebrate the final demarcation of the frontier between the two countries, the precise line of which had been disputed after independence. Following a UMA summit meeting in Tunis in April 1994, the new Algerian head of state, Liamine Zéroual, held talks with Ben Ali and the two leaders issued a statement expressing their commitment to democracy, pluralism and the promotion of human rights, and condemning fanaticism and extremism. However, Zéroual's appeals for dialogue with Algeria's banned Islamist party appeared to alarm Ben Ali, who had rejected any negotiations with the Tunisian Islamist opposition. After an attack by Algerian Islamist militants against a Tunisian frontier post near Tozeur in February 1995, in which six Tunisian soldiers were reportedly killed, security along the border was strengthened. Ben Ali held talks with Algeria's new President, Bouteflika, at the OAU summit meeting in Algiers in July 1999 and again in September, during which they discussed improving bilateral co-operation and the revival of the UMA. In May 2000 the Tunisian authorities announced that their security forces had repulsed a cross-border attack by a group of Algerian Islamist guerrillas linked to the Da'wa wal Djihad organization, during which three militants were killed and two Tunisian soldiers injured. The incident, the most serious since 1995, occurred shortly after Tunisia signed a customs agreement with Algeria aimed at combating smuggling which, Algeria insisted, helped to finance its radical Islamist opponents.

During 2001 the Algerian army Chief of Staff, Gen. Mohamed Lamari, held talks with Ben Ali and his military and security officials about intensifying the battle against Islamist militants, better surveillance of their borders to prevent Tunisian and Algerian members of al-Qa'ida from returning to their country of origin from Afghanistan, and dismantling North African Islamist networks in Europe. It was reported that numerous Islamist activists from Tunisia, who had taken refuge in Algeria and joined local GIA groups, had been arrested and handed over to the Tunisian authorities. In June 2006 the Tunisian press reported that a group of 10 Tunisians, who had participated in training at a GSPC camp in eastern Algeria, had been arrested by the Tunisian security forces as they crossed the border between the two countries. It was believed that the Tunisians had planned to travel to Iraq in order to join the insurgency against US and allied forces. Local sources suggested that young Tunisian Islamists who wanted to join al-Qa'ida in Iraq now transited via the GSPC network in Algeria rather than through networks in Libya. In December 2008 Prime Minister Ghannouchi and his Algerian counterpart, Ahmed Ouyahia, signed a preferential trade agreement. The need for mutual co-operation between Tunisia and Algeria was emphasized by the collapse of the Qaddafi regime in Libya. This resulted in instability at their borders with Libya and an exodus of regime figures, as well as migrants from sub-Saharan Africa. However, the Islamist Ennahdha Government in Tunisia, despite conducting pragmatic foreign relations, was viewed with some suspicion in Algeria. The installation of a secular administration in Tunisia in early 2015 was undoubtedly preferred by the Algerian regime while border security remained a source of tension. In light of the increased militant Islamist attacks in Tunisia in 2015, which the Tunisian authorities associated predominantly with Libya, Algeria announced plans in September to build an earth berm wall along its entire land borders with Tunisia and Libya.

The NT Government, like the Ennahdha-led administration, was keen to emphasize practical bilateral co-operation with Algeria, despite concerns about threats seemingly emanating from inside that country. However, claims were reported in the Moroccan press in January 2015 of an Algerian plan to exploit Tunisian–Moroccan differences (particularly during Ennahdha's rule in 2011–14) by, *inter alia*, encouraging Sahrawi militants, already based in Algeria, to operate out of Tunisia. President Bouteflika received Ennahdha's leader, Rachid Ghannouchi, in July 2015 apparently to facilitate improved bilateral relations after Tunisia and the USA had concluded a new security deal. Despite, or perhaps because of, improved Tunisian-Algerian relations, Algeria expedited the construction of a security barrier on its border with Tunisia. In January 2017 it was reported that Algeria had established 20 security centres along its side of the 300-km perimeter, as well as a National Gendarmerie air base, which controlled a squadron of aircraft to monitor the border. In February 2017 Ghannouchi met Bouteflika and openly praised him for his role in 'achieving national consensus in Tunisia between Ennahdha and Nidaa Tounes'.

Tunisia's normally good relations with Morocco were strained in May 1994, after Tunisia expelled some 600 Moroccans who the authorities claimed were living there without permission or had broken Tunisian laws. Later in that year the Tunisian authorities expelled several hundred more Moroccans on the grounds that they were trying to enter Italy as illegal immigrants. The route through Tunisia was used by many of the Moroccans who enter Italy illegally every year. In early 1996 Tunisia condemned Morocco for trying to block UMA activities in retaliation for alleged Algerian interference in the Western Sahara dispute. In November both countries appealed for the revival of the UMA. This message was repeated in March 1999, when President Ben Ali made a state visit to the Moroccan capital, Rabat, during which a bilateral free trade agreement was signed. Morocco's new ruler, King Mohammed VI, visited Tunis in May and Ben Ali made an official visit to Morocco in July 2001. In June 2017 Prime Minister Chahed led a Tunisian delegation to Rabat, where he met his Moroccan counterpart, Saâdeddine el-Othmani, for diplomatic and economic discussions. In a gesture of support for the Moroccan authorities, Tunisia deported a pro-democracy dissident Moroccan prince, Moulay Hisham Al-Alawi, who had been a critic of King Mohamed VI, to France (from where he had travelled to Tunisia).

Ben Ali was closely involved in the movement towards Maghreb unity, and in February 1989 Tunisia signed the treaty creating the UMA with Algeria, Morocco, Libya and Mauritania. Tunisia was chosen as the site of the new Maghreb Investment and Foreign Trade Bank, and a Tunisian diplomat, Mohamed Amamou, was appointed UMA Secretary-General. In January 1993 Tunisia assumed the annual presidency of the organization. Tunisian officials emphasized that Ben Ali's presidency had been a success and that 11 co-operation agreements had been signed during his one-year term of office, including plans for a Maghreb free trade zone. However, in reality, he failed to give new impetus to the organization, largely because two of its members, Algeria and Libya, remained preoccupied with their own problems: Algeria plunged into civil war by escalating Islamist violence and Libya subjected to even tighter UN sanctions. Algeria and Morocco's rivalry over the issue of Western Sahara also undermined the workings of the UMA. Neither King Hassan of Morocco nor Qaddafi attended the summit in April 1994 when Ben Ali handed over the presidency to the new Algerian head of state, Liamine Zéroual. Although at least 40 accords had been adopted by the UMA, only five had been ratified by all five member states. Following the suspension of UN sanctions against Libya in April 1999, some tentative moves were made to revive the organization; however, plans for a heads of state summit meeting in Algiers in November—the first for five years—were cancelled, owing to renewed tensions between Algeria and Morocco. In January 2002 former Tunisian Minister of Foreign Affairs, Habib Boularès, was appointed UMA Secretary-General, however, subsequent attempts to convene a summit meeting of UMA heads of state failed, often because of the decision of King Mohamed of Morocco not to attend.

In February 2006 former Tunisian Minister of Foreign Affairs, Habib Ben Yahia, replaced Boularès as Secretary-

General of the UMA. Prospects for greater regional collaboration and a galvanized UMA were to some extent enhanced by the series of regime or government changes in the Maghreb in the context of the 'Arab Spring'. However, instability was also a deterrent to a deepening of the union, even though it had enhanced security co-operation, most obviously between Tunisia and Algeria—a factor that Ennahdha's (possibly temporary) departure from the Tunisian Government might have encouraged. In July 2014 the foreign affairs ministers of Tunisia, Algeria, Egypt, Sudan, Chad and Niger—all states that neighbour the increasingly unstable Libya—met in Hammamet, in Tunisia's Nabeul province. It was agreed that a security committee would be established to co-ordinate measures to protect their borders. At the end of July Tunisia increased security at the Libyan border, closing a border crossing in response to what one Tunisian official described in the regional press as the 'state of anarchy' on the Libyan side of the border.

Tunisian-Libyan relations during 2015 were increasingly captive to the sensitivity that Tunisia felt about Libya's failure to prevent militants from entering Tunisia via its western and south-western borders, and were complicated by the fact that Libya was governed by two rival administrations. The Tunisian Government largely held Libya responsible for the terrorist threat to Tunisia. Given the Islamist nature of that threat, Tunisia was in theory more sympathetic to the vehemently anti-Islamist leadership in the eastern Libyan coastal city of Tobruk, where Gen. Haftar, an ally of the UAE, and by extension Saudi Arabia and Egypt, was based. (The UAE and Egypt launched air strikes against Islamist targets in Libya in 2015.) However, the geographical practicalities of the Islamist Libyan leadership based in Tripoli being physically closer to Tunisia and the latter's need to secure some co-operation in securing their mutual border led to engagement.

Representatives of the Tripoli administration reportedly held a meeting with President Essebsi in May 2015, prompting criticism from the anti-Islamist Tobruk authorities, which threatened to expel the Tripoli official based in the city, and from Tunisia's Arab allies outside of the Maghreb. In the same month there were reports that the Tunisian Government had agreed to an exchange of consular-level officials with the Tripoli regime. Notably, Libya Dawn, a political group and militia associated with the Muslim Brotherhood, maintained a presence in this part of Libya. In mid-December 2014 Libya Dawn had claimed to be in control of the border with Tunisia following fighting with Tripoli government forces earlier in that month. Libya Dawn had also threatened to seize UAE-owned oil facilities in retaliation for the Gulf state's support for the Tobruk administration. Relations between Tunisia and the Tobruk authorities were maintained, notwithstanding a reported assassination attempt on the Libyan Minister of the Interior in Tunisia in July 2015. In February, meanwhile, Tunisia played host to tribal reconciliation talks between rival Libyan groupings from the west of the country.

Tunisia continued to try to present itself as neutral but supportive with regard to the internal problems in Libya. In July 2018 Jhinaoui congratulated Gen. Haftar on his success in regaining control of territory from Islamic State and other militants in eastern Libya.

Tunisian diplomatic efforts included attempts not to alienate Gen. Haftar's strong Emirati and Egyptian supporters, which were complicated by Tunisia's deteriorating relations with the UAE. Rumours of an Emirati-sponsored coup attempt in Tunisia began to circulate in late 2017, and in January 2018 the Emiratis were seen by some in Tunisia as fomenting the public protests over the 2018 budget. At the end of 2017 Tunisia had cancelled Emirates Airline flights into Tunisia, and the UAE responded similarly to flights from Tunisia's state airline. However, in January 2018 the UAE allowed Emirates to resume its flights to Tunisia. Accusations of Emirati interference in Tunisian politics, primarily in order to weaken Ennahdha, none the less continued to be made, including by former President Marzouki (see above). Furthermore, Tunisia's desire to stay out of the ongoing intra-Gulf conflict did not make for smooth Tunisian relations with the UAE. That the UAE would be the first Gulf Arab state to normalize relations with Israel (see Relations with the West) in August 2020 compounded the difficult relations between Tunisia and the UAE. Pro-Palestinian sympathy had continued to be expressed across the Tunisian political divide, and this issue made it difficult for Tunisia to continue to steer a relatively neutral path in the intra-Gulf dispute (see Relations with the Wider Middle East). The apparent end to the intra-Gulf divide and the end of the blockade on Qatar in January 2021 helped to de-conflict Tunisia's management of these relationships, although Tunisian events from 25 July served to reopen the divide in Tunisia's relations with Gulf states, not least as it appeared that President Saïed had seized power unilaterally with the approval of the UAE and Saudi Arabia (see below).

The Tunisian Government's attempt to improve relations with the Tripoli administration was not welcomed by some Tunisian opposition figures. It did, however, occur in the context of what had been a more pragmatic international stance towards the Muslim Brotherhood by Saudi Arabia since as far back as the death of King Abdullah in January 2015. Saudi Arabia had been suspicious of the former Islamist Government in Tunisia, although it had maintained cordial relations at the foreign ministry level (Saudi Arabia had differentiated between Ennahdha and some of its harder-line, non-Tunisian, compatriots). Tunisia welcomed the formation of a new Libyan national unity Government in January 2016, as this incorporated Tripoli Islamists and some of their opponents, although Gen. Haftar and those allied with him continued to oppose the new administration and refused to reconcile fully. Tunisia hoped that a more inclusive Libyan Government would be able to control its borders, although it was far from clear that all of Tunisia's Islamic State problems originated in other countries. Indeed, in August 2015 the previous Libyan administration had accused Tunisia of 'exporting terrorism' to its country on the basis that Tunisians were disproportionately represented among Islamic State militants and that there had been several attacks in Tunisia supposedly reflecting this. Between July and August 2015, following the Bardo National Museum and Sousse attacks, Tunisia had taken measures to create a supposedly defensible land border with Libya. However, Tunisia opposed military action against Islamic State, which Western allies claimed would be conducted in support of the new Libyan Government. In an effort to reconcile the new Libyan administration and the forces of Gen. Haftar, Tunisia hosted Libyan unity talks in July 2016.

In March 2016 Jhinaoui met his Maghreb counterparts in Rabat to discuss regional security matters. Jhinaoui declared that Tunisia was opposed to Western air strikes against Islamic State in Libya, arguing that this would push the problem further in Tunisia's direction. He noted that the militants were especially well placed in the western Libyan city of Sabratha, which was situated about 70 km from the nearest Tunisian town. Ben Guerdane, a Tunisian border town, was regarded as a possible focus for an Islamic State attack. The border crossing nearby was reportedly facilitating a steady flow of Libyans into Tunisia. Fayez al-Sarraj, the Prime Minister of the new Libyan Government, declared that there was strategic co-operation between Libya and Tunisia, although this was evidently insufficient to ensure the security of their joint border. In April Jhinaoui was directly contradicted by President Essebsi, who declared that, as long as military action was confined to Islamic State targets in Libya, then he would support it. In late 2016 the USA established a drone base in Tunisia near to the border with Libya.

Tunisia continued to play a role in mediating an end to the Libyan conflict. In November 2016 Tunis hosted the AU's ad hoc Libya committee, comprising foreign ministers from various African states, including, most notably, Egypt. In February 2017 Rachid Ghannouchi met al-Sarraj and Gen. Haftar. Ghannouchi also brokered a meeting between a Libyan Islamist politician, Ali Sallabi, and a senior Algerian official, Ouyahia. Later in that month the Egyptian Minister of Foreign Affairs, Sameh Shokri, travelled to Tunisia to meet the Tunisian and Algerian foreign ministers to discuss joint efforts to resolve the Libyan conflict. By late 2019 events had clearly moved into a more unstable mode, heightening Tunisian concerns and apparently suggesting that countries such as Egypt has opted for a more overtly partisan approach to a country in which they had already been meddling.

In April 2019 an attempted coup in Libya led by Gen. Haftar, who had attempted to seize Tripoli with his Libyan National Army, was semi-openly backed by Arab states with which Tunisia had sometimes had difficult relations since 2011, namely the UAE, Saudi Arabia and Egypt, which privately granted Gen. Haftar funding, weapons and associated military support. France also apparently supported Gen. Haftar, even more discreetly. All of his backers had, none the less, publicly professed their support for the formal GNA in Tripoli. In March 2019 it had come to public attention that the Tunisian authorities had arrested a UN expert on illicit weapons, Moncef Kartas (a German-Tunisian national), compounding the sense that the Tunisian Government and Tunisia itself was not immune from the upheaval that external Arab actors were promoting in Libya. Some observers claimed that Kartas had been detained partly to appease the UAE in its capacity as a promoter of armed revolt in Libya. In May it was confirmed that Kartas had been released and returned to Germany.

Tunisia hosted UN-led talks aimed at ending the conflict in Libya in November 2020, following a ceasefire the previous month. The fighting within Libya was not confined to Gen. Haftar's attempt at toppling his own Government, however, and involved instability much closer to Tunisia. The threat arising from Gen. Haftar's actions was that more Libyans might seek to enter Tunisia by land, when Tunisia was already reportedly hosting more than half a million Libyan refugees from the civil war. The spillover into Tunisia itself of Tunisian jihadists who had fought or trained in Libya remained a major and proven threat (see *Heightened Terrorist Threat to Domestic Security*). More speculatively, the possibility of a vehemently anti-Islamist Libyan government of the kind sought by Gen. Haftar, augured badly for Libyan-Tunisian relations. After all, what had been Tunisia's relatively democratic political processes had given Ennahdha influence over decision-making and Ennahdha could present an image of Tunisia as being sympathetic to a Muslim Brotherhood-inclined Islamist dimension. In his capacity as Speaker of the Tunisian parliament, Ghannouchi had, controversially, congratulated the Tripoli-based Government for its apparent defeat of Haftar in May 2020, while the Turkish Government had strongly intervened in support of the GNA (see *Presidential and Parliamentary Tussles*).

Under President Saïed, the official Tunisian foreign policy towards Libya was firmly asserted as neutrality in terms of regional intervention and the need for an internal Libyan resolution (albeit perhaps aided by outside parties in a diplomatic arena) that would include fresh elections to replace the GNA, which the Tunisian President had described as 'temporary' (see *Relations with the West*). Tunisian-Libyan relations had thus become caught up in the intra-Tunisian political divide. Following Saïed's successful weakening of Ennahdha from late July 2021, it seemed that Tunisia's relations with Libya might be set back. The Libyan administration in Tripoli comprised elements of the Muslim Brotherhood and was supported by Turkey, including militarily.

Libya's contested polity was reflected by its Turkish-backed, but West-courting premier replacing the head of Libya's all-important state oil company in mid-July 2022 with an individual favoured by Gen. Haftar who was on good terms with Saïed's Saudi and Emirati backers. This appeared to suggest that Tunisian-Libyan relations would remain pragmatic and not prone to the relative strength (or otherwise) of Libyan or Tunisian Islamists. That said, even after a decisive legal judgment being made in Libya in January 2023, the national unity Government in Tripoli continued to uphold a highly controversial energy and related maritime sovereignty agreement with Türkiye that was denounced by many of Libya's eastern Mediterranean neighbours (some of whom had sovereignty claims contradicted by it), as well as being opposed by some leading eastern Libyan politicians. With Tunisia seeking to maintain good relations with the EU amid its own political clampdown, and to preserve the co-operation of affected and key Arab neighbours such as Egypt, Tunisian-Libyan relations were likely to proceed cautiously even as Türkiye had for some time being sending out signals regionally that it was generally less wedded to Islamist movements.

Algeria's own 'Arab Spring'-style protests came very belatedly, from February 2019, and longstanding President Bouteflika resigned in March; as in Tunisia in 2011, the protests were handled relatively peacefully by the regime in Algiers. Given the sometimes difficult border issues that Tunisia has with Algeria—both countries have previously argued that the other was contributing to their own domestic security problems via their country's jihadists and their policies toward them—the protest movement in Algeria in 2019 unsurprisingly made these factors more sensitive. For Tunisia and Morocco, the shared fear was of their neighbour, Algeria, degenerating into a failed state like Libya, although in their public comments President Essebsi and other Tunisian leaders took a very careful line emphasizing non-interference in what was, by definition, an Algerian matter. By late 2023 the prospect of Algeria collapsing in the manner of Libya, which Tunisia and Morocco both feared, had not materialized, even though many of the issues that contributed to the Algerian upheaval remained unresolved, and large public protests continued.

In December 2018 Tunisian Minister of Foreign Affairs Jhinaoui stated that Tunisia was ready to do what it could to ease ongoing Algerian–Moroccan tensions, arguing that any success in this arena could assist the resumption of desired intra-Maghreb co-operation. However, apart from some assumed intelligence-sharing concerning cross border jihadists, such co-operation remained limited at late 2023.

Tunisia and Algeria continued to engage regularly, and President Saïed visited his recently elected Algerian counterpart Abdelmadjid Tebboune in February 2020. The Libyan conflict was the pre-eminent issue on their agenda, and the two men agreed that its resolution required an end to foreign military intervention. This was consistent with the established foreign policies of both countries, including since the beginning of the Libyan uprising in 2011. Algeria had also considered changing its constitutionally underwritten non-interventionist position in favour of what were dubbed 'peace-keeping operations'. Algeria has armed forces comprising nearly half a million soldiers and a powerful armed capability. Such a development would be closely observed in Tunis, and with some trepidation.

On the face of it, President Saïed's assumption of autocratic powers in July 2021 should have been welcomed by Algeria, given the obvious anti-Islamist political undertow to the President's actions, and to a lesser extent conceivably welcomed for the same reason by Morocco. What transpired, however, was careful Algerian consultation with senior Tunisian officials to try to discern the likely political direction of the country. Morocco, until September partly governed by the Parti de la Justice et du Développement (Party of Justice and Development), an affiliate of the Muslim Brotherhood, but, under King Mohammed VI, steering a foreign policy that included establishing formal diplomatic ties with Israel in late 2020, was likewise in practice cautious. Security was the obvious priority for Algeria, which had suffered profound civil fracture in the 1990s, but appeared now to be in a more plural and consensual era of politics. Morocco too prioritized security, although its primary concerns in this respect focused on Western Sahara. In February 2022 the head of Morocco's lower house of parliament met with the Tunisian ambassador in Rabat, Mohamed Ben Abbad, with the latter describing Tunisian-Moroccan relations as an 'indefectible fraternal'. In theory, bilateral relations might have suffered amid worsening Moroccan-Algerian relations (see below), which led to Algeria applying pressure on Tunisia. However, Tunis managed relatively successfully to maintain diplomatic equidistance between Algiers and Rabat, despite Tunisia's regional relations tending to reflect a more Western orientation than that of Algeria.

Given the potential for greater Tunisian instability, including a Tunisian and regional boost to militant Salafist opinion, Algeria (like all of Tunisia's North African neighbours) was wary of anything that might compound the Islamist militant threat in the Maghreb and Sahel. Furthermore, it appeared that Algiers, where the *pouvoir* still retained significant control, despite the country's political arrangements shifting after the so-called second wave of Arab uprisings from 2019, was wary about domestic Tunisian political developments supported by Western-aligned and ambitious Gulf states such as Saudi Arabia and the UAE (see *Relations with the Wider Middle East*).

In mid-December 2021 Algerian President Tebboune visited Saïed in Tunis for a two-day engagement that involved the signing of a number of economic agreements, as well as an Algerian loan to Tunisia reportedly worth some US $300m. However, Tebboune was more interested in trying to persuade the Tunisian leader to join Algeria's proposed new regional bloc, which excluded Morocco, given these two countries' worsening relations, but potentially included some sub-Saharan states. However, Saïed appeared to be of the view that being drawn into an Algerian-led bloc would be a repetition of Tunisia's past error, following the overthrow of the Ben Ali regime, when it was perceived by key Arab states (including Algeria) to be aligned in one perceptible, largely Islamist Arab bloc. Saïed was also aware of how Tunisia had been at the forefront of Arab politics during Bourguiba's presidency, when the Palestinian question was more of a rhetorically unifying intra-Arab and intra-Tunisian subject (see below). The Ennahdha-CPR-Ettakatol coalition that came to power following the ousting of Ben Ali in 2011 was often seen by incumbent foreign regimes as encouraging regime change elsewhere in the region, including in Syria, whose leader had been strongly criticized by Ghannouchi, and which Algeria was now seeking, with Egyptian support, to readmit to the Arab League. Under Saïed's leadership, this perceived divisive Arab alignment would not be tolerated (especially as his claim to legitimacy was rooted in the purported need to expunge Islamist policy from Tunisia's governance).

Former President Marzouki stated in November 2021 that Tunisia should seek to pursue a resolution between Morocco and Algeria via the UMA, and 'autonomy' for Western Sahara. However, Saïed showed little interest. During Saïed and Tebboune's meeting in December, the two leaders agreed that Libya should arrange its own political affairs via domestic processes—a position that Tunisia had asserted before and one that was in line with Tunisia and Algeria's shared rejection of foreign intervention (which was obviously rife on both sides in Libya).

A meeting of the Arab League heads of state scheduled to be hosted by Algeria in early 2022 was postponed due to the failure of Egyptian efforts to persuade Saudi Arabia (which presumably was subject to some US persuasion) to agree to Syria's return to the group. The next Arab League summit was held in Algeria in early November (without Syrian representation), at which Saïed had a platform to promote the Republic of Tunisia and his stewardship of its foreign relations.

Tunisian-Algerian relations became strained in late May 2022 when Tebboune, himself enjoying a questionable 'democratic' mandate, spoke publicly in the Italian capital, Rome, alongside Italian President Sergio Mattarella of the political 'impasse' in Tunisia, declaring that Algeria stood ready to help its neighbour 'return to the democratic path'. This display of foreign interference was not appreciated in Tunis, where it was seen at least in part as an attempt by Tebboune to leverage Algerian acceptance for Saïed's actions as a means of pressing the Tunisian President to align himself more closely with Algeria's position regarding the latter's dispute with Morocco. Saïed's not doing so may have heightened Algerian concerns that Tunisia moving closer to Saudi Arabia, Egypt and the UAE, the political and financial support of which Saïed needed, might lead Tunisia to follow Morocco in normalizing relations with Israel.

The potential prospect of Algeria raising the price of its natural gas that is, lucratively for Tunisia, delivered to Italy via Tunisia appeared to constitute an additional form of political leverage, and a concerning one given Tunisia's constrained economic and fiscal circumstances. As noted, Algeria had clear concerns about Saïed's July 2021 political intervention, even though it was useful to Algeria to a degree. The fact that Algeria extended a loan to, and thus implicit backing of, Saïed just six months later suggested that relations had been managed quite well. However, Algerian sensitivities were apparent in late June 2022, when the Algerian delegation walked out of an Arab League meeting of social security ministers hosted by Tunisia, after the Tunisian hosts displayed a map of the Arab states that depicted the disputed Western Sahara as a part of Morocco, in line with an instruction issued by the Arab League to its member states and partners in December 2021.

Nevertheless, in early July 2022 Saïed visited Algiers to attend celebrations held to commemorate the 60th anniversary of Algeria's independence. During a meeting between Saïed and Tebboune, the two discussed mutual concerns about Libya while Tebboune committed to reopening the bilateral border, which Algeria had closed two years previously as part of restrictive measures introduced to counter the transmission of COVID-19. However, the duration of the border closure was interpreted by some observers as part of Algerian efforts to pressure Tunisia into adopting a less neutral position on the Western Sahara question, although Saïed did not show any public sign at least of being swayed. On 15 July Algeria duly opened the border in an apparent victory for Saïed's diplomacy. As of the end of August, Tunisia's fears of an increase in the price of Algerian gas had not materialized.

President Saïed's hosting of a Japanese-African event (the Eighth Tokyo International Conference on African Development) in Tunis in August 2022 upset Tunisia's otherwise carefully crafted equidistance between Morocco and Algeria over the Western Sahara question. While Morocco had long appreciated Tunisia's mediatory stance on the Libyan conflict, including under Saïed, when the Tunisian President decided to have a one-on-one meeting with the leader of the Western Saharan political movement (see Morocco) on the sidelines of the Japanese-organized event, this seemingly unnecessarily alienated Morocco. It may have been, however, that Saïed was building on the understandings that in July 2022 had, as noted above, seen the Tunisian–Algerian border opened and no increase in the price of Algerian gas. This had followed Algeria's provision to Tunisia of a loan and aid package in December 2021. From Morocco's perspective, however, the Saïed's meeting in August 2022 smacked of an unwarranted interference that represented a significant shift by Tunisia, which had observed Arab diplomatic conventions hitherto. Saïed excused his action by claiming that the AU, for example, always invited the Sahrawi leader to meetings and that Tunisia was merely seeking to promote reconciliation. In early December Algeria extended a fresh loan of US $200m. to Tunisia and a grant of $100m., continuing a pattern of financial support that seemed likely to maintain Saïed's tilt towards what was, after all, a major regional actor, including in the energy sector. The two countries' shared 1,000-km border, and residual mutual threats from terrorist groups operating across it, continued to encourage the strength of their bilateral co-operation.

Relations with the Wider Middle East

After Ben Ali came to power in 1987 his Prime Minister, Baccouche, toured the Arab Gulf states, which ranked among Tunisia's major sources of economic aid, to explain to Arab leaders the new administration's domestic and foreign policies. In 1988 the Tunisian Government announced that it would be resuming diplomatic relations with Egypt, severed in 1979 after Egypt signed a peace agreement with Israel. In 1989 Dr Boutros Boutros-Ghali, then Minister of State for Foreign Affairs, became the first Egyptian minister to visit Tunisia for a decade, and in the following year Ben Ali made the first visit to Cairo by a Tunisian President since 1965, signing several bilateral co-operation agreements. Relations with Saudi Arabia also remained cordial, although the Tunisian Government was concerned about the extent of Saudi support for Tunisian Islamists.

President Ben Ali's decision to condemn the deployment of a UN-authorized, US-led multinational force in the Gulf region following Iraq's invasion of Kuwait in August 1990, and the expression of strong pro-Iraqi sentiments among Tunisians during the crisis, seriously strained Tunisia's previously close relations with Saudi Arabia and the Gulf Arab states, notably Kuwait, which withdrew its ambassador from Tunis. After the ceasefire in the Gulf conflict in February 1991, Tunisia quickly sought to restore links that had been cut as a result of its support for Iraq. Ben Ali sent a cordial message to the Amir of Kuwait, congratulating him on regaining his sovereignty. However, it was not until 1994—when the Kuwaiti Minister of Foreign Affairs and First Deputy Prime Minister, Sheikh Sabah al-Ahmad al-Jaber, visited Tunis—that it was reported that normal diplomatic relations would be restored. Bilateral co-operation finally resumed in 1996. In 2001 Tunisia recalled its ambassador from Qatar after the Qatari-based satellite television channel Al Jazeera broadcast live interviews with several leading Tunisian human rights activists, and with exiled Ennahdha leader Rachid Ghannouchi. Following the overthrow of the Ben Ali regime, Qatar's Crown Prince Sheikh Tamim bin Hamad bin Khalifa Al Thani visited Tunisia in July 2012, where he signed several agreements intended to facilitate increased Qatari investment in the country's energy and power sectors. Tunisia's relations with Saudi Arabia were complicated by the ousted Ben Ali's presence there (allegedly in possession of appropriated Tunisian state funds). However, there were periodic negotiations on the matter, and Saudi Arabia conducted high-level meetings with senior Tunisian officials following the change of regime. Although Saudi Arabia appeared to have encouraged the Egyptian military's overthrow of President Mohamed Mursi in mid-2013, it seemed to have less obvious interest in trying to influence events in Tunisia, despite alleged connections with some local Salafists.

In March 2014, following Ennahdha's departure from power, President Marzouki visited Saudi Arabia and other member states of the Gulf Cooperation Council (GCC), in an effort to secure higher levels of aid and investment. Even when Saudi Arabia had been officially hostile to the Muslim Brotherhood, it had been cautious not to rule out engagement with every form of Islamist leader. Following the accession of King Salman in Saudi Arabia in January 2015, the NT's assumption of power and the establishment of a Tunisian Government arguably more akin to that of former Saudi ally, Ben Ali, bilateral relations improved further.

In December 2015 President Essebsi visited Saudi Arabia to meet King Salman to discuss economic and regional security issues. Bilateral agreements on civil defence, energy and transportation were signed. Saudi Arabia supported the continued leading role of Essebsi's NT in Tunisia's ruling coalition, although under King Salman more pragmatic relations had been fostered with parties connected to the Muslim Brotherhood, such as Ennahdha. In January 2016 the Tunisian Minister of Foreign Affairs, Baccouche, met his Saudi counterpart, Prince Adel al-Jubeir, who was on a tour of the region. However, in March the Tunisian Government, despite hosting a summit of Arab foreign ministers, refused to back a Saudi-led effort, which had received significant inter-Arab support, to label Hezbollah as a terrorist group.

Tunisia's stance towards the Saudi-led Arab military intervention in Yemen that began in March 2015 was more cautious than that of Morocco and Jordan (fellow monarchies close to Saudi Arabia), Egypt, which became closer to Saudi Arabia after the 2013 Egyptian coup, and other Arab members of the military coalition. This echoed a caution also found in, for example, Algeria. Historically, Tunisia had been wary of coalitions associated with Western powers, such as that formed during the 1990–91 Gulf crisis, in part reflecting its residual Arab nationalism.

Al Jazeera adopted a critical tone towards the NT, the leading party within Tunisia's ruling coalition until January 2016, accusing it of being anti-Islamist and repressive in the Ben Ali tradition. However, in May, in a reflection of the tiny emirate's increasing regional importance, President Essebsi visited Doha, the Qatari capital, on an official visit and was effusive with his praise for Qatar, which was one of the largest investors in Tunisia, second only to France. Essebsi also thanked Qatar for hosting a comparatively large Tunisian expatriate population of some 20,000 nationals.

In the same way that it tried to avoid the regional confrontation over the war in Yemen, so Tunisia tried not to become embroiled in the dispute between Qatar and neighbouring Gulf states that began in June 2017. However, the continued presence of Ennahdha in its coalition Government led Saudi Arabia and other anti-Qatar Arab countries to voice suspicion that Tunisia's sympathies lay with Doha. Moreover, a report in a UAE newspaper in June 2018 that a senior Iranian official had sought Tunisian mediation in the Saudi–Iranian regional conflict was firmly denied by the Tunisian authorities. Tunisia continued to navigate the intra-GCC divide cautiously. In theory, following President Essebsi's announcement in September that Ennahdha (which is affiliated to the Muslim Brotherhood), would be leaving the Government (see above), relations with Qatar would be weakened, and concomitantly, relations with Qatar's Gulf opponents would become more cordial. However, in practice premier Chahed enthusiastically hosted a visiting Qatari delegation in Tunis in March 2019, as part of the two countries' ongoing bilateral strategic dialogue. Later in that month Tunisia hosted an Arab League summit that was a victim of precisely the same intra-Gulf divide, as Qatar's Amir Sheikh Tamim and Saudi Arabia's Crown Prince Mohammed bin Salman left early, and some other Arab states were represented at only a junior level.

Baccouche attracted national, regional and international controversy by adopting stances on Syria and Libya that were out of step with Arab and international opinion. He committed his country to restoring relations with Syria in an announcement seemingly antithetical to the preference of President Essebsi, who wished to adhere to a discernible inter-Arab consensus, although it was debatable whether Baccouche would have issued this statement if Essebsi had been vehemently opposed. Baccouche, a relative leftist, might have judged that establishing limited Tunisian relations with a perceptibly secular regime in Syria, itself opposed by an armed opposition dominated by militant Islamists, including Tunisian Islamic State fighters, would be a wise move. Ultimately, however, his removal in January 2016 did not precipitate the suspension of Tunisia's relations with Syria. Tunisia continued to adopt controversial foreign policy stances. In May, for example, Essebsi declared during his visit to Qatar, a country sympathetic to the Muslim Brotherhood, that 'political Islam has no future in Tunisia'.

The Tunisian and Egyptian administrations under Presidents Ben Ali and Mubarak found common cause in their efforts against Islamist militancy. In 1997 the Egyptian Prime Minister, Kamal al-Ganzouri, visited Tunis, where he signed several economic and cultural co-operation agreements. Both countries pledged to increase bilateral trade, and agreement was reached in principle on the creation of a free trade zone. In 1998 the two countries agreed to dismantle customs duties over the next 10 years. Following the change of regime in both countries in 2011, Tunisia sought further to improve its most important African and Arab relationship. In July 2012 President Marzouki visited the new Egyptian President, Mursi, in Cairo, where the latter strongly praised the role of Tunisia in beginning the 'Arab Spring' protests that led to uprisings in the Middle East and North Africa. The forced removal of Mursi from office in July 2013 was strongly condemned by Tunisia, with the resultant deterioration in relations exacerbated by Tunisia's own political crisis. However, the installation of a new, apparently secular Government in Tunisia, similar to the regime that had taken power in Egypt, precipitated an improvement in bilateral relations. In September 2015 President Essebsi and Prime Minister Essid met Ibrahim Mehleb, the Egyptian premier, in Tunis. As well as agreements on economic, tourism and cultural projects, both sides expressed a desire for the new unity Government in Libya to succeed. The unrest in Tunisia in early 2016 prompted Egyptian President Abd al-Fatah al-Sisi to urge Tunisians 'not to ruin their country', presumably reflecting his fear of popular revolt at home and regionally. Although it had aided his accession, it had also brought Islamists to power and weakened his regime. In February 2017 Tunisia publicly supported Egypt's approach to resolving the Libyan conflict, having involved Egypt in Tunisian-Algerian talks on the subject (see above).

The assertion of a sole executive in Tunisia, following President Saïed's intervention on 25 July 2021, seemed to have occurred in close consultation between Saïed and his Egyptian counterpart, al-Sisi, as well as between Tunis and Abu Dhabi and, perhaps to a lesser but none the less important extent, between Tunis and Riyadh. In a post on social media in early August, amid the ongoing domestic and international furore over his recent measures, the Tunisian President talked of the economic 'support' of 'sisterly' countries and said that the time would come when it would be appropriate to reveal these states' names. The clandestine tone implied direct economic and political backing for Tunisia's new political direction, at a time when it was wrestling with enormous economic and health challenges and seeking to reassure foreign investors. Egyptian support was likely to be solely political, but Cairo's close alignment with Abu Dhabi and Riyadh emphasized the convergence of interests (see below).

Tunisia maintained good relations with Iraq following the first Gulf War; the Ben Ali administration regularly urged the UN to revoke sanctions against Iraq and broadly condemned US and British air strikes against Iraq in late 1999. In that year Tunisia signed a trade agreement with Iraq, and Tunisia's Minister of Trade and Handicrafts, Mondher Zenaïdi, made several visits to the Iraqi capital, Baghdad, to discuss bilateral trade under the UN's 'oil-for-food' programme for Iraq. By the end of the year Tunisia was reported to have won contracts worth US $200m. to supply goods to Iraq since the 'oil-for-food' programme began. Responding to pressure from public opinion, in 2000 Tunisia defied the air embargo against Iraq and sent two aircraft to Baghdad carrying humanitarian and medical aid. Tunisia expressed 'deep regret' at US and British air strikes against targets near Baghdad in February 2001. A free trade agreement was signed during a visit to Tunis by the Iraqi Vice-President, Taha Yassin Ramadan, in that year. In March 2003 as the Iraq crisis deepened, the Tunisian Minister of Foreign Affairs visited Baghdad for talks with Iraqi leader Saddam Hussain. Ben Ali again expressed 'deep regret' at the US-led military intervention in Iraq. Relations with the subsequently installed Shi'a-led Government in Iraq were, for the most part, cordial, but, given Tunisia's wariness of Shi'a-led Iran, which became a close ally of Iraq, and Tunisia's relatively good relations with Sunni-led Gulf Arab states, there were limits to the extent of its engagement with Iraq.

Tunisia claimed to have played a leading role, together with Norway, in the secret talks between the PLO and Israel that led to the signing of the Declaration of Principles on Palestinian Self-Rule (Documents on Palestine, see p. 1220) in September 1993. Tunisia welcomed the breakthrough in PLO-Israeli relations, and shortly afterwards an Israeli delegation arrived in Tunis for talks with Tunisian and PLO officials. Salah Masawi, the Director-General of the Tunisian Ministry of Foreign Affairs, declared that there was no obstacle to Tunisia establishing diplomatic relations with Israel. The Ministry welcomed the PLO-Israel Cairo Agreement of May 1994 on implementing Palestinian self-rule in Gaza and Jericho. The PLO offices in Tunis were closed in the following month, as Yasser Arafat, the Chairman of the PLO, and the rest of the Palestinian leadership prepared to move to Gaza, where the Palestinian (National) Authority (PA) was to be established.

As the PLO departed, Tunisia made new moves towards the normalization of relations with Israel. The first party of Israeli tourists to visit Tunisia since independence arrived in June 1994, following an agreement made in October 1993 with Israel's Deputy Minister of Foreign Affairs, Yossi Beilin (the first senior Israeli minister to visit Tunisia), and direct telephone links were established with Israel in July. In October the Tunisian and Israeli foreign affairs ministers met at the UN General Assembly in New York and agreed in principle to open interests sections (which Tunisia referred to as 'economic channels') in the Belgian embassies in Tunis and Tel Aviv, Israel. At a subsequent meeting at the US State Department in Washington, DC, with Warren Christopher and the Israeli Minister of Foreign Affairs, Shimon Peres, the Tunisian Minister of Foreign Affairs, Ben Yahia, stated that this was the first step towards full diplomatic relations. After the Palestinian elections in January 1996, an agreement was reached between Tunisia and Israel to proceed with low-level diplomatic relations from April. Tunisia thus became the fourth Arab state to establish diplomatic ties with Israel, after Egypt, Jordan and Morocco. At the same time, Tunisia agreed to recognize PA passports. In April 1996 Israel opened an interests office in the Belgian embassy in Tunis; however, Tunisia delayed sending its own representative to Israel in response to Israeli attacks on southern Lebanon. None the less, some contacts between the two countries were made, but the victory of Binyamin Netanyahu in the Israeli elections in May and the formation of a right-wing Government quickly brought the process of normalization to a halt. President Ben Ali defended the actions of those countries that had taken steps to normalize relations with Israel, stating that they were intended 'to push the peace process forward'. In November, however, the Tunisian leadership condemned Israeli intransigence towards the peace process and criticized Israel's building of settlements in the Occupied Territories. The normalization of relations was suspended, the head of the Tunisian interests office in Tel Aviv departed in August 1997, and the only remaining Tunisian diplomat returned to Tunis early in 1998. However, after the appointment of a new Government in Israel led by the Labour leader, Ehud Barak and a revival of the Middle East peace process, Tunisia's relations with Israel improved, and the Israeli interests office in Tunis reopened in October 1999. In October 2000, in response to violent clashes between Israel and the Palestinians, Tunisia again closed its interests office in Tel Aviv and imposed a freeze on the normalization of relations with Israel.

In March 2004 President Ben Ali caused a diplomatic storm when, at just two days' notice, he postponed indefinitely the annual summit-level meeting of the Arab League Council, due to be held in Tunis. Plans to relaunch the Saudi-sponsored Arab peace plan had been dealt a serious blow by Israel's 'targeted killing' of Sheikh Ahmad Yassin, the founder and spiritual leader of Hamas, and Saudi Arabia, Bahrain, Oman and the UAE had already declared that they would not attend the summit. However, the Arab League's Secretary-General, Amr Moussa, stated that Tunisia's decision would have dangerous consequences for joint Arab action and accepted an offer by Egypt to host the summit. In response, Tunisia insisted that, as it held the rotating chairmanship of the League, it retained the right to host the meeting at a date to be arranged. In April Moussa announced that a consensus had been reached on rescheduling the summit, and it was later announced that it would be held in Tunis in May. The eventual summit called for a revival of the Middle East peace process, condemned spiralling violence in the Israeli–Palestinian conflict and appealed for the UN to assume a stronger role in Iraq. The Libyan leader, Qaddafi, walked out of the opening session; four other Arab leaders departed before the closing session, and eight did not attend the meeting at all.

In July 2004 Ben Yahia chaired the first meeting of the so-called Arab 'troika' on Iraq, comprising Tunisia, Algeria and Bahrain, established at the recent Arab League summit. The Secretary-General of the Arab League and Iraq's Minister of Foreign Affairs, Hoshiyar al-Zibari, also attended the session, at which Iraq's request for Arab troops to be sent to Baghdad to protect the UN mission and for Arab participation in the reconstruction of Iraq were discussed.

In February 2005, after Israeli Prime Minister Ariel Sharon accepted an invitation from Ben Ali to attend the second WSIS, to be hosted by Tunisia in November, Tunisian opposition parties and human rights groups condemned the proposed visit, which would be the first by an Israeli Prime Minister. The PA urged Ben Ali to cancel the invitation to Sharon. Tunisian officials played down the significance of the invitation, stating that the summit was an international event to which every country in the world was invited. In the event, Israel was represented by the Deputy Prime Minister and Minister of Foreign Affairs, Silvan Shalom. Protesters chanting anti-Israeli slogans denounced the visit as a move to normalize relations between the two countries.

Under Tunisia's Ennahdha-led Government, there was no noticeable tilt towards Hamas, although it did take a more hostile position with regard to Israel. A measure of the change in tone when Ennahdha left office was the new Government's decision, in April 2014, to allow a group of uninvited Israeli tourists to enter the country in order to join an annual pilgrimage to Djerba. The justification was made on economic grounds, and in effect returned the Government's stance on relations with Israel to that of the Ben Ali era.

Shortly before Essebsi's election as President in late 2014, NT Secretary-General Baccouche, who in February 2015 became the Minister of Foreign Affairs, stated that 'resistance' to Israel was important at the 'public' and 'diplomatic' levels, and that the Palestinian cause had been undermined by intra-Palestinian divisions. This implied that the fairly consistent Tunisian Government's stance towards Israel, from Ben Ali onwards, would be upheld by what became the new leadership (i.e. critical engagement with Israel and support for the Palestinians). In the previous month President Essebsi had received PA President Mahmoud Abbas in Tunis.

Residual Tunisian–Israeli tension was exemplified in June 2015 by the attempted visit of former President Marzouki, a non-Islamist and relative moderate, to Gaza, together with professed international human rights activists, to express political solidarity with the Palestinian people. Marzouki's attempted visit, which led to him being detained by the Israeli Navy, was emblematic of a widespread Tunisian Arab nationalist fealty with the Palestinian cause. Tunisia's belief that Israel was involved in the assassination of a Tunisian drone expert in December 2016 exacerbated bilateral tensions. Furthermore, President Essebsi's praise of Iran in April 2017 (see below) included the largely rhetorical comment that Iran was the 'best hope' against Israel. Widespread outrage in Tunisia following the announcement by the US Government that it was to relocate its embassy in Israel to Jerusalem led to demonstrations and demands by some for a new 'anti-normalization' law, reflecting growing popular anger at nascent signs of the perceived normalization of Tunisia's relations with Israel.

Demonstrations took place in Tunis (and in most Arab capitals) in May 2018, when the USA formally opened its embassy in Jerusalem, in support of the Palestinian cause. In June 2019 Tunisians protesters staged a demonstration outside the Bahraini embassy in Tunis in protest at a conference organized by the USA in the Bahraini capital, Manama, to promote the economic component of the US Administration's so-called 'Deal of the Century' to resolve the Israeli–Palestinian conflict. In July pro-Palestinian demonstrations were organized by the UGTT in several Tunisian cities, overlapping in Hammamet with the campaign for an 'anti-normalization' law by a teachers' organization.

The Palestinian issue continued to affect Tunisian attitudes to Israel and also to those Arab states, encouraged by the USA, that were seen as far more interested in relations with the Jewish state than in resolving the historical Palestinian question. A Tunisian 'anti-normalization' committee organized a protest outside the UAE embassy in Tunis in August 2020 following that country's normalization of relations with Israel, which had been overseen by the USA. Although not a mass demonstration, the participants were allowed to display banners that used strong language, including a statement that the only means of achieving justice for Palestinians was 'the gun'. The head of the Tunisian National Syndicate of Journalists, Najib al-Bghouri, stridently attacked the Emirati-Israeli agreement, indicative of the fact that unions representing the opinion of professional workers (as well as supporters of many Tunisian political parties) did not favour normalization with Israel.

Saïed's political opponents perceived him, to varying degrees, to be discreetly encouraging relations with Israel and consequently soft-pedalling the Palestinian issue. Small issues were seemingly blown out of proportion. Al-Joumhouri claimed in May 2022 that the resumption of Israeli tourists visiting Tunisia, following the cessation of travel owing to COVID-19 restrictions, and Saïed allegedly encouraging Israelis to compete in a sports tournament held in Hammamet were a front for a normalization of relations with Israel, with the Israeli delegation described as being 'received' by the authorities in Hammamet. The Tunisian Minister of Religious Affairs, Brahim Chaïbi, adamantly denied the claim and asserted that his Government was firmly opposed to the normalization of relations with Israel. As noted above, Saïed actually invoked what were described as anti-Semitic tropes to deflect blame for economic problems and proved insensitive when the world-renowned Tunisian synagogue in Djerba was attacked by a member of his own national security forces in May 2023, seemingly oblivious not just to the diplomatic niceties expected but to the economic consequences for his country's tourism sector. Saïed could, of course, yet see an attraction in opening up Tunisian relations with Israel that otherwise seem to have little substance, even privately. However, Saïed, like any Tunisian leader, would be mindful of Algerian opposition to such an opening to Israel, given how much such an action would likely damage Algerian-Moroccan relations.

In 2001 Mohamed Ghannouchi became the first Tunisian Prime Minister to visit Iran since the Islamic Revolution in 1979. Tunisia had severed diplomatic relations with Iran in 1987, after accusing it of supporting Islamist militancy in Tunisia, but relations had been restored in 1990. In February 2006, following talks in Tunis, eight co-operation agreements were signed during a visit to the Iranian capital, Tehran, by Tunisia's Minister of Foreign Affairs, Abdelwahab Abdallah. During the visit Iran's President Mahmoud Ahmadinejad expressed his gratitude for Tunisia's support for Iran's right to access nuclear technology for peaceful purposes. In the wake of the political upheaval in Tunisia in 2010–11, Iran was keen to present itself as the ally of revolt in the Arab world against countries that it viewed as being under US influence. However, following its change of leadership, Tunisia indicated that its moderate Islamist direction did not make it an automatic ally of Shi'a Islamist-led Iran. Relations did become more cordial—increasingly so following the election in June 2013 of Hassan Rouhani as Iranian President—but were still not substantive. In September 2015 the Iranian Minister of Foreign Affairs, Mohammad Javad Zarif, visited Tunis to discuss future co-operation with newly elected President Essebsi and Ghannouchi. Further talks took place in 2016.

Under the NT-led Government, Tunisia's relations with Iran improved significantly. Notably, in June 2017 Zarif visited Tunis and met his Tunisian counterpart and President Essebsi. The sympathy of FP politicians for Iranian-backed Syria might also have played a small part, in that their visit to Syria to meet President Assad in March had encouraged much mutually reinforcing rhetoric about the importance of upholding 'Arabism' against sectarian militants. More significantly, however, President Essebsi singled out Iran for praise in April when he received in Tunis the Iranian Minister of Culture and Islamic Guidance. The fact that a head of state would receive such a relatively minor Iranian figure itself was notable, but Essebsi argued that Iran should be praised for its actions against 'terrorists' in Syria and Iraq. Shortly thereafter, President Essebsi made a public case for Tunisia resuming full diplomatic relations with Syria, which prompted reports of disquiet among the leadership of Saudi Arabia and the other Gulf states. The assumption of the presidency by Saïed in October 2019 was not expected significantly to alter this relationship. Notably, Rachid Ghannouchi visited Iran in June 2020, ostensibly to emphasize inter-parliamentary relations, but also no doubt keen to signal that Tunisia's foreign policy was not overtly aligned against Iran's interests.

Tunisian relations with Saudi Arabia have been affected by several of the factors that complicate Tunisia's relations with the UAE (see above). In the Saudi Arabian case, these have included Tunisian political disquiet (not publicly expressed by the Government but inevitable, given widespread political and popular opinion on the subject) of the Saudi Arabian regime's increasingly close (if still relatively discreet) relationship to Israel. For Tunisia, however, any form of diplomatic normalization with Israel, let alone full diplomatic engagement, remained a non-starter for the Tunisian Government, unlike, seemingly, for Saudi Arabia and for several other Gulf states. The UAE's normalization of ties with Israel in August 2020 and those of Bahrain (a particularly close Saudi ally) in September increased Tunisia's difficulties in keeping relations with Riyadh on an even keel. It also offered Qatar the opportunity to exploit this situation to move closer to an increasingly economically desperate Tunisia.

However, President Saïed's assumption of sole executive authority from 25 July 2021 helped to smooth Tunisia's relations with the UAE and Saudi Arabia in particular, to Qatar's relative disadvantage, after hitherto poisonous intra-Gulf relations had improved in January of that year, following a formal rapprochement, under the aegis of the GCC, that normalized Saudi-Qatari relations. The statement by Rachid Ghannouchi, the dismissed Speaker of parliament and still leader of Ennahdha, that the UAE was behind what he described as the 'coup' in Tunisia, was par for the course in terms of a constant Ennahdha refrain that the Emiratis were chief among those who had been intervening in Tunisia's post-2011 political arena, to the Islamists' disadvantage. For its part, the UAE, in common with Egypt and Saudi Arabia, kept its counsel over the events that ensued from 25 July 2021. Alongside the predictable lack of criticism of Saïed, the semi-official media in Saudi Arabia and the UAE especially trumpeted the events as the end of the Muslim Brotherhood not only in Tunisia, but also in the wider region.

In August 2021 Saudi Arabia announced that it would provide financial support to Tunisia. In the same month the UAE dispatched pandemic-related medical supplies to Tunisia. In January 2022 a US $200m. allocation to aid Tunisia's importation of Saudi oil products was announced by the Saudi Export-Import Bank. In March Saïed met with the Saudi Minister of the Interior who was in Tunis to attend an Arab League meeting of interior affairs ministers; during their meeting Saïed was reported to have expressed a wish to develop 'security and military co-operation' with Saudi Arabia to 'counter terrorism, extremism and organized crime'. In the same month Tunisian-Emirati relations received a fillip with a UAE-based company's revival of a $5,000m. real estate investment in Tunis. This is the kind of project that Emirati 'soft' diplomacy prefers: sound business in support of those that it wishes to support and/or influence. Also in March Prime Minister Bouden telephoned Abu Dhabi Crown Prince Sheikh Mohammed bin Zayed Al Nahyan, at that time the de facto ruler of the UAE, and discussed their mutual desire to consolidate the bilateral relationship further. Meanwhile, during a meeting with Bouden in the same month, the Qatari ambassador in Tunis emphasized Qatar's desire to support specific Tunisian sectors such as small and medium-sized enterprises and social housing.

While it seemed wise for both Saïed and Ghannouchi to refrain from explicitly mentioning near neighbour and still-powerful Egypt directly, there was little doubt that Cairo had been kept in the loop by the Tunisian President while he assumed emergency powers. For Saudi Arabia, despite its historically flexible approach to differing branches of the Muslim Brotherhood in the region, the assertion by Saïed of executive authority was undoubtedly welcome. It did not appear likely, however, that the controversial domestic political realignment in Tunisia would necessarily improve the prospects for any kind of Tunisian engagement with Israel. The more pressing issue was whether Saudi Arabia, along with the UAE, might come under US pressure to soften the perceived bankrolling of Tunisia following the controversial adoption of the new Tunisian Constitution in August 2022 that granted near-absolute power to the President. However, owing to the USA's increased desire to maintain and deepen relations with its Arab allies in the context of the Russian invasion of Ukraine, the Biden Administration was less likely to apply significant pressure on the Gulf states, and in particular oil-rich Saudi Arabia and the UAE, for supporting Saïed. In any case, given the Saudi and Emirati support of the Tunisian President's domestic and foreign policies, their compliance with any potential US coercion was by no means guaranteed. Confirmation of the ongoing good Tunisian-Saudi relations was the announcement by Saudi Arabia in late July 2023 of a total of US $500m. in aid to ease Tunisian fiscal pressure, with $400m. of this in the form of a soft loan and the balance as a grant.

Tunisian relations with Syria had partly been coloured by the Islamists' leading role in the post-2011 Tunisian governments and, at the extremes, by the disproportionate numbers of Tunisian jihadists who had fought for Islamic State in Syria and Iraq, as well as for similar groups in Libya. Some critics of Ennahdha specifically considered that, while in power (albeit never its exclusive preserve), the group had not done enough to stop the movement of such jihadists. Ghannouchi was arraigned in court in November 2022 on precisely this charge (see above).

Critics of this argument would, of course, emphasize that the so-called 'export' of Tunisian jihadists did not begin after 2011, given their earlier role in Afghanistan and other 'theatres'. President Saïed's assumption of autocratic powers from 2021 had created the possibility of fellow secular-style Arab authoritarians improving their countries' relations, as had been the case for some time with regard to Egyptian President al-Sisi and Syria's Assad. Assad's rehabilitation, in formal intra-Arab terms, at the Saudi-hosted Arab League summit in mid-May 2023 included a meeting with Saïed on the summit's sidelines. While this meeting was seen by some Maghrebi pundits as a sign that Tunisia was moving its foreign alignment in a non-Western direction, it was notable that less than two months later the Tunisian armed forces participated in 'African Lion', the largely US-organized, month-long, military exercise involving African states and the USA, held in Morocco, Senegal and Ghana. (This itself arguably confirmed the more forward role of the Tunisian armed forces in the state and its leadership's greater projection of its identity than previously, including during the 2011 overthrow of Ben Ali.)

Relations with Syria were in any case now an Arab norm and had been prefigured by pro-Western Arab allies of President Saïed such as the UAE. After the Jeddah Summit in May 2023, the Syrian Minister of Foreign Affairs and Expatriates, Dr Faysal Mikdad, visited Saïed in Tunis and preparations were made for the reopening of the Syrian embassy there. Reflecting this flexibility in Tunisian foreign policy was an improvement in the country's relations with a Türkiye that prior to and after Erdoğan's re-election in May 2023 had, in any case, sought more amicable relations with former Arab foes. The new Speaker of the newly formed Tunisian Assembly conducted a visit to Türkiye in early April 2023, meeting with President Erdoğan. There seemed every prospect following Erdoğan's successful re-election that Turkish relations with Tunisia would be strengthened further.

Economy

NEIL PARTRICK

Based on an original essay by the editorial staff

INTRODUCTION

In 2002 fiscal policy was tightened in response to excessive demand, and the economy was affected by a series of shocks, including a terrorist attack, a slowdown in export markets and another drought. This led to a correction in the external balance of payments, despite a decline in tourism, and a sharp deceleration in gross domestic product (GDP) growth. The economy returned to a higher growth rate of 5.6% in 2003, driven by a recovery in agricultural output, and inflation was stable at 2.7%. The Government, meanwhile, continued its tight budgetary policy. In 2005, although the tourism and energy sectors performed well and the textile industry survived the challenge from Asian competition, there was again a slowdown in agriculture, and growth slipped to an estimated 4.2%. As international petroleum prices continued to rise sharply, the cost of fuel subsidies increased, leading the Government to raise retail oil prices and launch an energy-saving strategy.

GDP growth accelerated to 5.6% in 2006, owing to an agricultural recovery, the expansion of non-textile manufacturing and the strength of the services sector. However, inflation increased to 4.5%, leading to a tightening of monetary policy in the second half of the year. Macroeconomic results were strong in 2007: growth accelerated to 6.3% and inflation averaged 3.1%. Although the current account deficit widened (largely owing to worsening terms of trade) and the dinar (TD) recorded a depreciation of about 3%, both were comfortably financed by higher foreign direct investment (FDI), as reflected by an increase in international reserves. Inflation rose to 4.9% in 2008, fuelled by rapidly increasing import costs, which in turn precipitated a widening of the trade deficit. Real GDP growth slowed slightly, but remained robust at 4.6%. The global economic downturn, which particularly affected European Union (EU) countries (Tunisia's main export destination), had taken full effect by early 2009. As a result, exports declined in that year by 18%, although the trade deficit narrowed slightly, as imports also fell markedly. Owing to falling demand for Tunisia's manufactured goods, industrial production declined by 7%. Overall growth was supported by expansion in both agriculture and services; however, the pace of real GDP growth slowed to 3.1%, thus reducing inflation, to 3.5%. Although domestic demand remained at a low level, and the real value of agriculture and fisheries output contracted in 2010, exports rebounded strongly, by 21%, as the eurozone started to recover. As a result, overall growth showed a slight rise in 2010, to 3.7%.

In 2011, according to the Institut National de la Statistique (INS), real GDP contracted by 1.9%. This poor performance largely reflected the impact of the political upheaval (see History), which contributed to a reduction in manufacturing and other (non-agricultural) business activities, softened domestic consumption, reduced FDI, as well as a decline in foreign remittances when members of Tunisia's large workforce in Libya were obliged by the conflict there to return home. In August 2013 the INS stated that average inflation in 2011 was 4.3%, following a 5.2% rise in 2010.

The INS reports that real GDP rose by 4.1% in 2012, a reflection of heightened economic activity in the context of relative political stabilization. In 2013 real GDP growth was 2.8%, according to INS data, with the services sector the main driver of expansion. Offsetting growth in 2013 was the deterioration in agriculture and manufacturing (owing partly to strikes in the latter), and only modest European demand as the eurozone emerged from a financial crisis. In 2014 real GDP growth remained fairly constant, at 2.9%. However, in 2015 real growth fell to just 1.2% after terrorist attacks had a negative impact on tourism and investment. In 2016 real growth once again increased at the same modest rate of 1.2%. In the context of ongoing security concerns, the economy was still relatively subdued, although the value of both exports and imports rose after contracting in 2015.

The Governor of the Banque Centrale de Tunisie (BCT), Mustapha Kamel Nabli, was replaced by Chédli Ayari, formerly of the World Bank, in July 2012. It was feared that Ayari would simply follow the Government's prioritization of growth. Indeed, average monthly inflation rose by 7% in 2012, compared with 2011. The six-month inflation average to the end of June 2013 was 8.25%, compared with the same period in the previous year. Imported inflation in turn followed government-encouraged growth. According to the International Monetary Fund (IMF), however, smaller rates of increase in food prices meant that by the end of 2013 inflation was down to 6%, and at the end of 2014 it was 4.8%, according to the Economist Intelligence Unit (EIU).

The Government's supplementary budget in February 2015 contained oil price reductions, helping to explain why inflation at the end of 2015 was 4%. By June 2016 the annual rate had eased further, to 3.9%, according to the INS. However, by June 2017 it had reached 4.8%, year on year, partly reflecting a rise in oil prices. The BCT reported in 2018 that inflation was 7.3%, suggesting that ongoing rises in oil revenue were continuing to stimulate price increases. According to the IMF (in its Rapid Financing Instrument—RFI—assessment of April 2020), inflation was 6.7% in 2018. In July 2020, however, the INS stated that year on year inflation was running lower, at 5.7%. It seemed likely since the outbreak of the coronavirus (COVID-19) pandemic early in the year that lower demand for some of the items that made up the basket of goods of the official retail inflation index explained the relative softening of inflationary pressures. The IMF estimated that inflation stood at 5.7% year on year at the end of 2020.

In May 2022 the BCT stated that inflation had risen to 7.5% in the year to the end of April. The full-scale Russian invasion of Ukraine from February 2022 had, in part, been driving global inflation, which fed into Tunisia's rising imported costs including on fuel and foodstuffs. The BCT raised interest rates by 75 basis points in response to sharply rising inflation. The annual inflation rate at June 2023 was 9.3%, according to the INS—a figure partly reflecting ongoing imported price rises in food and energy, among other key items.

Despite pressure from the World Bank, the IMF and Tunisia's own central bank, until the late 1990s the Government moved relatively slowly to privatize public companies, fearing that this would aggravate unemployment. In 2006, however, recognizing Tunisia's relatively high level of external debt compared with other emerging market economies with similar ratings, the Government, consistent with IMF advice, allocated two-thirds of the proceeds from the partial privatization of Tunisie Télécom (see *Transport and Communications*) to reduce external debt. By 2008, in relative terms, Tunisia's external debt stock had declined considerably, to 38.6% of GDP, compared with 54% in 2005. By the end of 2013, however, the external debt stock was rising strongly, reaching US $26,000m. The debt service ratio was 10.8% at the end of 2013, and was expected to exceed 11% in 2014—a still-manageable figure. The EIU stated that external debt remained at about $26,000m. at the end of 2014, rising to $27,000m. at the end of 2015 (some 63.4% of nominal GDP), and reached $29,000m. at the end of 2016 (equivalent to almost 70% of GDP). Further external debt was created by successive bond issues; this led to the level rising to more than 97% of GDP by the end 2018, although this fell slightly in 2019 (see *Foreign Aid*). At 31 March 2023, according to the BCT, gross external debt amounted to $41,833m. This was 3% higher than the figure at the end of 2021, when it was equivalent to 95% of GDP (at current prices).

A new investment law was introduced in September 2016, although ambiguity surrounded the assumption that 'prior approval' had been eliminated, as the new law claimed that 'investment is free'. It appeared that some sectors would still be less free than others. Other aspects of the law included allowing 30% of a new company's management to comprise foreigners during the first three years of its operation, up from a total of four foreigners previously. A Higher Council for Investments, consisting of ministers connected to particular economic sectors, was to be created to attract FDI.

Despite marked improvements in the standard of living in Tunisia during the 1990s, both the IMF and the World Bank identified unemployment as the country's greatest problem and stated that annual growth of 6%–7% would be required via increased levels of domestic and foreign investment, faster export growth and further structural reforms. However, some analysts argued that many foreign investors were deterred by the repressive policies of the regime of President Zine al-Abidine Ben Ali, and evidence of widespread corruption and nepotism. Unemployment remained high, at 15.3%, in 2002, and declined only marginally, to 14.2%, in 2004. Unemployment increased to 14.7% in that year, as industrial output contracted. In March 2010 the Government announced that it was to allocate TD 187m. to support job creation, with a focus on helping graduates into work. A World Bank study indicated that 38% of Tunisian graduates had never been in employment, and that 66% remained unemployed 18 months after graduation. Following Ben Ali's downfall in early 2011, amid popular, youth-orientated revolt, the interim Government announced an emergency economic stimulus plan of US $1,500m., with the aim of tackling unemployment and regional disparities (unemployment and related underdevelopment being far worse in the central-western part of the country). Overall unemployment was 18.9% at the end of 2011, falling slightly by the end of 2012, to 16.7%. Upheaval in Libya had, meanwhile, caused many Tunisian migrants to return home, where the domestic economy was foundering. In 2012 youth unemployment remained very high, at 33%, despite increased public spending and improved political conditions.

At the end of March 2014 the INS stated that the overall unemployment rate was 15.2%, although the real rate was likely to be double this (see below). The official unemployment rate has hardly changed since, reaching 15.4% in March 2018, although unofficially it was likely to have remained at about 30%. The INS reported that by the end of 2019 the official rate had fallen slightly, to 14.9%. At the end of the first quarter of 2020 the INS put the figure at 15.1% (although unofficial assumptions of unemployment continued to be about double this level). In its most recent Article IV review, conducted in February 2021, the IMF estimated that unemployment had risen to 16.2% in September 2020, owing mainly to the effects of the COVID-19 pandemic, although, again, this is likely to have been a significant underestimate of the true figure. In May 2023 unemployment was being referred to by the main trade union federation, the Union Générale Tunisienne du Travail (UGTT), as standing at 'more than 15%'—a figure that continued to seem like an understatement, in part because the main trade unions were seeking to side with President Kaïs Saïed in his opposition to the economic strictures that the IMF was looking to impose.

The Fund agreed a two-year stand-by agreement (SBA) with the Tunisian Government in June 2013, making US $1,750m. available upon request to support the economy in the event of financing problems. In its assessment of the economy in May 2014, the IMF stated that, although much of the performance criteria had not been met under the SBA arrangement up to the end of 2013, the change of government and the approval of a new Constitution in January 2014 suggested that things could be 'broadly on track'. Some $1,100m. had been disbursed by April 2015. At that point the IMF declared that foreign reserves were above what it deemed to be a 'critical' threshold because of donor support, FDI and 'market access'. However, the Fund warned that action was needed to ensure higher government receipts (subsidized oil prices had been reduced in February) and better fiscal management and banking supervision. Real growth in 2016 was 1.2%, according to the INS—the same rate recorded in the previous year. Tourism and investment had remained below historic trends. Real growth rose by 1.9% in 2017, owing to stronger growth in agriculture and some tourism-related sectors. Offsetting this was the performance of the mining sector, which recorded a contraction of almost 16%, largely owing to the negative impact of regular industrial disputes. A contraction of almost 40% (compared with the same period in 2017) in the mining sector was recorded in the first quarter of 2018, and the economy as a whole registered growth of 2.6%.

In June 2016 the IMF approved a new, four-year tranche of US $2,900m. so that Tunisia could pursue 'inclusive growth' that would boost employment and ensure that the most vulnerable were protected. Commenting on the very difficult political environment in which the SBA had operated, the IMF stated that, despite pressures from Salafists and terrorism, and the related tourism downturn, the Tunisian Government had pursued a reform programme as agreed and, therefore, that the new IMF agreement was a reflection of this commitment. Following a staff visit in February 2017, the IMF projected that the economy would expand by 2.5% in 2017. This would be supported, according to the Fund, by the adoption of legislation to encourage private sector activity, and by the increased economic activity resulting from the successful Tunisia 2020 conference held in November 2016. However, this growth figure began to look optimistic by mid-2017, with the trade deficit rising rapidly and tourism receipts lower than expected, and in the event real GDP rose by only 1.9% in 2017. Notably, the IMF delayed issuing the second tranche of the new funding framework, amounting to $314m. and due by the end of 2016, until June 2017, arguing that progress on implementing promised government reforms, such as wage bill and subsidy controls, had been slower than anticipated. The third tranche was disbursed at the end of 2017, and the fourth tranche in July 2018. Following a staff visit in June 2019, the IMF stated that a further tranche of approximately $245m. would be made available, bringing total disbursements under the funding framework to $1,600m. The Fund noted that growth had accelerated in 2018 to 2.6% (similar to the INS's figure of 2.7%). The IMF projected a modest rise in GDP in 2019 of 2.7%, based partly on the assumption of a mixed adherence in the second half of the year to agreed fiscal and financial targets (in line with Tunisia's performance in the first half of 2019). If true, and official Tunisian trade data from the first quarter of 2019 supported the IMF's assumptions, then Tunisia was once again heading for large fiscal and current account deficits by the end of 2019. Financing would, the IMF argued, be derived from a mix of pledged assistance from the Fund and other soft lenders, and commercial borrowing. In issuing its policy advice, the IMF noted that the fiscal and current account deficits would, however, make such commercial borrowing more expensive. In the event, annual real growth in 2019 was only 1.0%, significantly below expectations, owing in part to sluggish agricultural expansion (registered at only 0.5%, compared with 9.5% in 2018). Furthermore, the IMF's forecast for real growth in 2019 had been based partly on the hope that both the run-up to the elections for the presidency and parliament, which took place during September–October 2019, and their political consequences, would not undermine fiscal discipline. In the event, the political parties' acute awareness of the unpopularity of fiscal constraints created difficulties in cutting spending ahead of the polls, and the lack of a clear majority for the incoming administration compounded the difficulty of governing without accommodating widespread spending demands. In the first quarter of 2020 (most of which was unaffected by the COVID-19 epidemic), growth had already contracted, by 0.7% year on year.

Following the deleterious impact of the COVID-19 pandemic from late March 2020 and the efforts to contain it, both within Tunisia and in the wider global economy, the Government, in co-ordination with the IMF, issued a 'request for purchase' under the existing RFI available to Tunisia that totalled US $745m., which constituted 100% of its quota under the arrangement. The Fund claimed that the RFI 'purchase' would enable the Government to meet emergency health care and social welfare needs, to support companies that would otherwise go bankrupt and to maintain an adequate level of foreign reserves relative to imports (see *Finance and Budget*), that would cover about three months of import purchases. According to preliminary IMF data published in February 2021 after its Article IV review, real GDP contracted by 8.2% in 2020. The IMF noted that this was the largest contraction since the country's independence and urged measures be taken to address a sharp rise in unemployment, especially among the young and/or the low-skilled, which had been caused by restrictions on trade and international travel. By mid-2021 it was assumed that Tunisia would become more reliant on domestic financing, owing in part to bodies such as the international credit ratings agency Fitch considering that the Fund's recommendation of fiscal retrenchment and revenue-boosting policies had become even more politically untenable (see *Finance and Budget*).

Almost inevitably, in 2021 Tunisia experienced a recovery from the COVID-19-driven GDP contraction of 2020. According to IMF data, real growth in 2021 was 3.1%. In the first quarter of 2022, according to the INS, real GDP year on year—i.e. compared with the first quarter of 2021—was up by 2.4%. The strong recovery in real growth registered in the second quarter of 2021 (15.7% year on year), as economic demand strongly recovered from its low base when COVID-19 economic constraints were eased locally and globally, was followed by only modest growth in the third and fourth quarters of the year. The INS stated that year-on-year growth in the first quarter of 2022 reflected a recovery in the tourism and agriculture sectors, in particular. The 2.4% overall GDP rise was, however, in line with the gradual upward trend in annual growth seen after the second quarter of 2021.

At May 2022 the Government was projecting a 2.6% rise in GDP over the year as a whole; the IMF was projecting a more modest 2.2%. In fact the IMF's 'Staff Statement on Tunisia', released on 30 March, had said that real growth remained weak in relation to the economy's 'strong potential' and related this to 'macroeconomic disequilibria', as Tunisia was still recovering economically from the impact of COVID-19. It warned, too, that Tunisian structural problems would be compounded, as in many other countries, in light of the impact of the conflict in Ukraine (for example, in fuelling inflation of the price of imported foodstuffs, including grain). In the event, GDP grew by only 1.7% in 2022, according to the INS, given the ongoing supply-chain issues caused by the pandemic and high inflation driven by soaring energy costs, as well as the ongoing effects of the drought on domestic agriculture.

As of 31 March 2023 real GDP growth was given by the INS as 2.1% year on year—a figure that reflected the continued drag on the economy, owing to limited investment amid uncertainty about future IMF assistance. President Saïed continued to hold out against the terms of a proposed US $1,900m. new loan package. The Fund, which had not visited Tunisia for more than a year was, as of July, assuming that real growth in 2023 as a whole would be only 1.3%, perhaps reflecting these differing priorities. Saïed continued to position himself in populist (and UGTT-supported) fashion, against his own Prime Minister Najla Bouden, who was in favour of accepting the package. Some observers suggested that Tunisia might have to default on its debt repayments, unless a compromise was reached.

Internationally, President Saïed enjoyed the public sympathy of Premier Giorgia Meloni of Italy during a meeting of the Group of Seven (G7) industrialized nations in May 2023, at which she argued for giving him more time. Political factors, not least her Government's concerns about illicit migration from North Africa and Saïed's professed opposition to African migration (see History and below), played a part in this support. More independent analysts sympathized with Tunisia's rejection of an IMF package that arguably risked undermining the growth that it was supposed to encourage by cutting jobs and income via privatization of state-owned enterprises and reducing food and fuel subsidies. It had been argued that Tunisia should seek less risky aid via other channels that should include longer-term agricultural reform (the rural areas of Tunisia stood to lose the most from cutting subsidies). In October 2022 Tunisia had actually accepted the US $1,900m. IMF loan package that *The Financial Times* described as including new targeted and expanded existing aid to those liable to suffer the most from the proposed subsidy cuts. The newspaper noted that the Fund had presented the further cuts to the civil service salary bill in the context of progress having already been made by the Government in this respect. In June 2023 the EU, seemingly at Meloni's behest, announced, after a visit to Tunis by a delegation of the European Commission, that it was 'willing to offer' an equivalent aid package worth $967m. that appeared to be related to the stalled IMF deal, although Meloni continued to urge the Fund to show flexibility. The proposed EU aid deal would obviously constitute financing for a struggling fiscal and current account, although notably it reportedly included $100m. for 'border control' measures that would be additional costs.

AGRICULTURE

The 2002–06 Development Plan endorsed food self-sufficiency as a national objective, but Tunisia has generally had a negative food trade balance since the 1980s: the deficit reached TD 1,300m. by 2011, and fell only slightly, to TD 1,200m., in 2012. In the first half of 2013 the deficit was narrowing again, at TD 349m., as exports rose substantially in the early months of the year compared with recent trends. At the end of 2014, however, the food deficit stood at TD 1,572m. The deficit declined to TD 522m. in 2015, before rising sharply again, to TD 1,672m., at the end of 2016. The deficit narrowed to TD 1,064m. in 2017. Relatedly, the World Bank reported that real agricultural growth of 2.5% was achieved in 2017—a little higher than overall GDP growth in that year and a marked improvement compared with the 8.5% contraction in agricultural GDP in 2016. In 2018 real agricultural growth of 10.2% was attained, which was significantly above trend. However, in 2019 growth in the agricultural sector fell sharply, to less than 1%, although its contribution to overall GDP remained at about the same level. Reflecting these developments, the agricultural trade deficit remained essentially unchanged between 2017 and 2018, but in 2019 it worsened markedly, registering a negative balance of TD 2,102m. Counterintuitively, perhaps, in 2020, when the COVID-19 pandemic spread globally, Tunisia's agricultural trade deficit eased, to TD 1,564m., according to the INS, as lower economic activity and incomes led to weaker demand for imported goods. By the end of 2022 the deficit had risen firmly again, to TD 2,337m., as a recovering economy led to more imported inflation, while drought hit the domestic agricultural sector.

After independence, agriculture's contribution to GDP declined steadily, from 22% in 1965 to 8.9% in 2019, according to the INS. In 2020, according to preliminary IMF data, the agricultural (and fisheries and food) sector contracted by 0.7%, markedly below the estimated overall GDP contraction of 8.2% in that year. At the end of 2021 INS data showed that agriculture was, at 10.1%. actually constituting an enlarged proportion of GDP. Furthermore, at the end of 2021 real growth in the sector was 6.5% year on year. However, according to revised data from the INS, real growth in the agriculture, fisheries and food sector for the year to the end of the first quarter of 2022 was only 1.2%. This had followed the onset of drought conditions. At the end of March 2023 the sector had contracted by 3.1% year on year, after year-on-year growth in the second, third and fourth quarters of 2022, albeit of less than 1%.

The agricultural sector's share of national employment has also fallen significantly, from 46% in 1960 to 14.5% in the third quarter of 2021, according to the INS, albeit a small increase from 11.1% in the first quarter of 2019. Agricultural output had been steadily increasing since the 2010 drought. Measured from a base of 100 in 2000, the INS agricultural production index reached a monthly average of 127.7 in 2011 (after falling to 121.9 in 2010). It rose to 132.7 in 2012, and averaged 136 per month in the first half of 2013. The INS subsequently started a new agricultural production index, measured from a base of 100 in 2010. This showed a steady rise to 113.3 in 2014 and 119.3 in 2015, before weakening slightly in 2016, when it averaged 116.7. During January–April 2017 the index averaged 109.2. It ended 2017 much higher, at 127.4, and rose to 138.7 in January 2018, although it had fallen to 108.7 by March of that year.

The fragmentation of landholdings and the need to consolidate them into larger, more efficient units has remained not only an obstacle to increasing the profitability of the agricultural sector, but also a highly sensitive issue for the Government. According to the INS, the total area that was used for agriculture had grown to 10.45m. ha by the end of 2014, up from 9.28m. ha in 2010, and the number of farms had risen to 509,810 by the end of 2014, up from 507,287 in 2010.

Wheat, grown in a belt across the northern part of the country, is the main cereal crop. The Government guarantees the price to the grower. Cereal production has continued to fluctuate markedly from year to year. There was a dramatic decline in 1987–88 as a result of drought and the worst plague of locusts for 30 years, and particularly good harvests were recorded in 1992 (2.6m. metric tons) and 1996 (2.8m. tons). Then, in 2001–02 Tunisia experienced one of the worst droughts in more than 50 years. The Government estimated output at only 0.6m. tons for 2002, with demand projected at 2.5m. tons. In 2003 production recovered to reach 2.9m. tons, and the 2004 crop, following plentiful rainfall, was estimated at 2.5m. tons. In 2005 production declined to 2.1m. tons, despite favourable weather conditions; the wheat crop was down by 5%, and the barley crop fell by 24% owing to a decrease in the areas under cultivation. In 2006 the wheat and barley crops were estimated at 1.2m. tons and 395,000 tons, respectively, and imports of cereals increased by 8.2%. The 2007 harvest was the worst in almost a decade, falling to 1.19m. tons in total, on account of poor rains. Wheat production fell by 37% to 918,999 tons, and barley output dropped by more than 50%, to 269,100 tons. In response to this decline in production, the Government intervened in support of cereal farmers, offering them fixed prices for their produce, freezing the price of seeds and improving the availability of credit and grants.

A 2007 World Bank study of Tunisia's agricultural sector stated that cereal production was inefficient, uncompetitive and used up precious water resources. However, the Government prefers to reduce reliance on food imports. Cereal output showed no improvement in 2008, reaching just 1.1m. metric tons, although after a significantly improved harvest it reached 2.5m. tons in 2009. An extremely poor harvest in 2010 reduced yields significantly, and, according to the INS, cereal production fell to just 1.1m. tons. Improved harvests helped to push up total cereal production to 2.3m. tons in 2011 and 2012. A marked reduction in grain output was expected in 2015 as the cereal harvest contracted owing to drought. Consequently, production declined to 1.4m. tons, according to the US Department of Agriculture (USDA), down from 2.3m. tons in 2014. According to data from the Food and Agriculture Organization of the United Nations (FAO), cereal production showed a further, if slight, decline on 2015, to 1.3m. tons in 2016, before recovering to 1.6m. tons in 2017. In 2018 wheat production was 1.5m. tons, and barley production was 700,000 tons. In March 2019 the USDA forecast production of 1.3m. tons of wheat and 600,000 tons of barley in 2019/20, based on what it claimed was an extension of seeding that was being conducted at an earlier point in the crop cycle, owing to very good weather in last few months of 2018. By the end of 2020, however, wheat production had fallen to just over 1m. tons, although in 2021, according to the FAO, it recovered to 1.2m. Meanwhile, barley production fell to 466,000 tons in 2020 and 430,100 tons in 2021.

FAO figures (accessed in May 2022), which revised those it had published for Tunisia a year earlier, suggested that the USDA's assumptions had underplayed the probable performance for 2019/20. The FAO's Gross Production Index Number (GPIN) system, using a base figure of 100 for the period 2004–06, shows that in 2019 Tunisia registered 186.9 for barley production. This was up significantly from the 64.7 GPIN seen in 2018, and markedly higher than the average for the five years including 2019. However, at 95.5 the GPIN for 2020 reflected a major downturn in barley production that year from 2019. In 2021 lower rainfall was reflected in a GPIN for barley of 88.1. Similar to the barley trend pre-2020, the GPIN of wheat was 130.2 in 2019, having been 96.2 in 2018 and averaging under 100 over 2015–17. In 2020 wheat output, like barley, was down on 2019: registering a GPIN of 93.2. However, unlike barley, and somewhat counter-intuitively, wheat's GPIN in 2021 rose, to 106.8. Data for 2022 was not available at July 2023. By then the onset of drought conditions seemed set to be reflected in much lower GPINs for barley, wheat and other crops.

FAO's *GIEWS Country Brief: Tunisia* published in July 2021 reported 'above average' cereal production in 2021 as collection of the winter harvest began. It forecast total cereal output of 1.8m. metric tons—some 20% higher than in 2020. FAO suggested that this reflected comparatively good conditions for sowing in late 2020 and, after a shortage of rain at the beginning of 2021, relatively high levels of rain in spring in the more productive north of the country, coinciding with the 'grain filling' period. FAO also suggested a good performance, despite a domestic shortage of fertilizer (see *Minerals*). In the central and southern areas, where cereal production is less prevalent, poor rainfall in the first half of 2021 negatively affected pastoral land for livestock (see historical data below), necessitating the purchase of costlier alternative feedstock. However, by mid-2023 low or absent rainfall over many months had led to a period of extended drought. Reporting from Tunisia in late May, *The Arab Weekly*, a British-based online publication, stated that the Tunisian Ministry of Agriculture expected that the grain harvest in 2023 would be about 250,000 tons, compared with a harvest of 750,000 tons in 2022. The latter would itself have been produced in adverse conditions. The concern of local farmers was that, for all that the Government perhaps could, and should, do more to assist farmers, these fundamentally poor conditions were likely to become a regular feature, owing to the effects of anthropogenic climate change.

Grapes are grown around Tunis and Bizerte, with additional production in the south-west of the country, including the Tozeur region. Wine production reached a peak of almost 2.0m. hl in 1963. However, annual output had declined to about 340,000 hl by the early 1990s. Following new investment in vineyards, production then increased to 469,000 hl in 1999, but declined to 325,000 hl in 2002 as a result of the drought. Output recovered to 402,000 hl in 2006, but contracted again in 2008, to 300,000 hl. The INS reported that wine production stood at 284,000 hl in 2012, declining to 215,000 hl in 2014, before rising again to 244,000 hl in 2015, then falling to 177,000 hl in 2017.

Stimulated by rising domestic demand and favourable prices, production of table grapes has increased significantly over the last two decades; by 2002 it had reached 75,000 metric tons, and by 2008 output had risen to 122,000 tons. According to FAO, production declined to 97,000 tons in both 2009 and 2010, but rose steadily in subsequent years, reaching 150,000 tons in 2015, before declining to 134,000 tons in 2016. FAO reports that in 2017 output increased to 152,000 tons, before falling slightly, to 146,860 tons, in 2018. The FAO stated that in both 2020 and 2021 output flatlined at exactly 150,000 tons. Likewise, FAO data, using the above GPIN production indices, show that grape production remained relatively constant in the four years up to and including 2020, when it stood at 106.6 (contrasted with 105.4 in 2019, 109.7 in 2018 and 104.4 in 2017). In 2016 it was 95.4.

That said, Tunisia's grape production continues to be volatile and in some parts of the country can struggle. The south-west of the country, close to the Sahara desert, has continued to see a decline in grape production. According to an online report on 19 May 2022 in *Al-Araby*, the Tozeur Farmers Union stated that the grape production industry had declined each year since the 2016 drought. The website reported that in 2021 nearly one-half of the Tozeur region's farmers were unable to sell their overly dry grape harvest. In line with this, according to significantly revised figures from the International Trade Centre, the value of Tunisia's overall grape exports fell by 58% in 2020 from their 2019 value, having risen by 27.7% in 2019 from their 2018 value.

In 2019/20 Tunisia was the world's third largest producer of olive oil (after Spain and Italy). In the 2000/01 agricultural year a national programme was initiated to safeguard olive groves from the adverse effects of drought, but there was still a fall in production, to 30,000 metric tons—the lowest for 10 years. Olive oil production increased to 72,000 tons in the 2002/03 season, and to 280,000 tons in 2003/04, but fell to 130,000 tons in the following year (lower output typically following an exceptionally good year). In 2005/06 production increased to 220,000 tons, but then fell in 2006/07 to 170,000 tons, with exports (mainly to Italy and Spain) set at 120,000 tons. A return to growth was experienced once again in 2007/08, when production reached 200,000 tons, with exports of 169,000 tons. A similar level of production was recorded in the following year, with 180,000 tons produced in 2011/12. Virgin olive oil production totalled 174,600 tons in 2010, 112,400 tons in 2011, 192,600 tons in 2012 and 191,800 tons in 2013, according to FAO estimates. However, the USDA estimated that it fell to 80,000 tons during the 2013/14 agricultural year, owing to poor weather, including heavy rain.

Production of oil olives (i.e. olives cultivated for olive oil) reached 1m. tons in 2008, but output subsequently declined. According to FAO, olive production increased to 1.7m. tons in 2015 (from 376,000 tons in the previous year), but declined to 700,000 tons in 2016. However, according to revised FAO data (for the period 2016–20, accessed in May 2022), olive production fell sharply in 2017 to 500,000 tons; production more than tripled in 2018, to 1.6m. tons, fell sharply again in 2019, to 1.2m. tons, and then nearly doubled in 2020, to 2.0m. tons. In 2021, according to FAO, output collapsed to 700,000 tons following what overall was a difficult harvest, given low rainfall in the first six months of the year.

In the 2015 agricultural year, according to the INS, olive oil production continued to decline, totalling just 140,000 metric tons, reflecting the poor weather conditions of the previous years. From the uprising of 2010–11 until early 2016, the olive oil production sector lost 300 firms and 40,000–50,000 jobs. According to Statista.com, olive oil production for the agricultural year 2019/20 was 350,000 metric tons, up sharply from 140,000 tons in the previous year, owing to favourable climatic conditions. Olive oil exports grew by 66% year on year in 2020, according to INS data. Olive oil export values varied significantly year by year during 2017–21, owing partly to variable harvests: according to the INS, they fell by 26.8% in 2021, having risen by 74.3% in 2020, fallen by 40.5% in 2019, and risen by 92.9% in 2018.

The 2021/22 crop year, according to projections by *Olive Oil Times* in November 2021 (in part sourcing Ministry of Agriculture projections), was expected to see Tunisian output of olive oil fall to about 240,000 metric tons, of which at least 180,000 tons were to be exported. However, the publication argued that the sector has seen an overall upward trend over two decades (something that, despite output being erratic, is not contradicted by production data).

Citrus fruits are grown mainly in the Cap Bon peninsula. In 2000/01 production totalled 271,000 metric tons, but output decreased in subsequent years, owing to the effects of drought and then heavy rainfall; it increased to 243,000 tons in 2004/05 (from 209,000 tons in the previous year) and to 262,000 tons in 2005/06. In the 2007/08 season output increased significantly, to 300,000 tons, with 27,400 tons designated for export. By the 2010/11 season, output had risen further, to 352,000 tons. According to FAO data, output of citrus fruit was 448,863 tons in 2011 and 454,900 tons in 2012, falling slightly in 2013, to 436,429 tons. The USDA reported that in 2015/16 citrus fruit production declined to 380,000 tons, and FAO estimated production in 2016 at 342,000 tons. However, in 2016/17 there was a bumper citrus fruit harvest, and three months before the end of that marketing year the USDA estimated that total production had reached a record 560,000 tons. According to FAO data, the combined output of grapefruit, lemons and limes, melons, cantaloupes and related fruits, and oranges totalled 391,000 tons in 2017, up from 373,000 tons in 2016. In 2018 the combined total production of these fruits was, according to FAO, 530,233 tons—a bumper harvest in line with the USDA's assumptions for the previous year. The combined total production of these fruits was, at 401,562 tons, significantly down in 2019. Using a derived total for citrus fruit production from FAO data, output amounted to 712,527 tons in 2021, up by 7% from 2020.

Dates are exported mainly to the EU, principally France, although new markets include Asia and North America. Date production declined in 2007/08, to 124,000 metric tons, although in subsequent seasons, production rose significantly. By 2010 Tunisia produced 174,000 tons, and in 2011 and 2012 production rose, respectively, to 180,000 tons and 193,000 tons, according to FAO data. Output increased to 241,000 tons in 2016 and to 260,000 tons in 2017, before slipping to 241,333 tons in 2018, then picking up again in 2019, to 288,700 tons. Based on FAO's GPIN data, Tunisia's date output in 2020 was up sharply on 2019 (150.2 compared with 130.8). This fitted with a total output of 332,000 tons in 2020. According to FAO, 345,000 tons of dates were produced in 2021.

Sfax is the main centre of the fishing industry. The industry has received substantial state investment for fleet modernization, for the upgrading of fishing ports and for research. The majority of fishing vessels are concentrated in the south, along the Gulf of Gabès (although pollution and overfishing have reduced this region's contribution to the country's total annual catch) and around the ports of Sousse, Mahdia and Monastir in the central region. The Government has sought to offset overfishing in the Gulf of Gabès by offering incentives for the development of fishing grounds along the northern coastline. The total catch has been relatively steady in recent years. According to FAO estimates, it stood at 153,700 metric tons in 2019, 145,200 tons in 2020 and 150,200 tons in 2021. In 2022 it was 149,300 tons, according to *Tunis Afrique Press* in March 2023, citing the National Observatory of Agriculture. In December 2020 it published a report about fisheries stocks in the Mediterranean, in which it claimed that there was overfishing in 75% of the Mediterranean area, although it stated that this high figure actually represented a modestly declining trend. According to the INS, the export value of fish (including crustaceans and molluscs) in 2020 was TD 405.7m., down 16% on 2019. *Tunis Afrique Press* reported the 2022 export value total to be TD 871m., compared with TD 708m. in 2021.

MINERALS

Oil was first discovered in 1964 at al-Borma, in the south of the country near the Algerian border, and important finds were subsequently made off shore at Ashtart, east of Sfax in the Gulf of Gabès (these deposits accounting for a substantial proportion of Tunisia's total output by the mid-1980s). The *BP Statistical Review of World Energy 2021* estimated that Tunisia's petroleum reserves were about 400m. barrels.

Production has come principally from al-Borma, Ashtart and four other concessions—Adam, Didon, Miskar and Oued Zar. In 2005 the Adam field, located in the Borj el-Khadra concession, became Tunisia's largest producing oilfield, at 18,000 barrels per day (b/d), with the al-Borma and Ashtart fields producing about 12,000 b/d and 11,500 b/d, respectively. Although annual oil production declined progressively from the 1980s, falling to 3.3m. metric tons by 2006, it was estimated to have increased to 4.6m. tons in 2007, following new discoveries and the development of the Oudna field. However, production declined slightly, to 4.2m. tons, in 2008, and then further still, to 4.0m. tons in 2009 and to 3.8m. tons in 2010. Oil production fell further in 2011, to a reported 3.3m. tons (of which 2.7m. tons were exported). According to revised historic data published in the *BP Statistical Review of World Energy 2021*, oil output averaged 82,000 b/d in 2012, 76,000 b/d in 2013 and approximately 71,000 b/d in 2014, and continued to fall gradually, averaging 64,000 b/d in 2015, 60,000 b/d in 2016 and declining more sharply in 2017, to 48,000 b/d.

Problems at some oilfields in early 2015 undermined oil production. Overall, the oil and natural gas (see below) production slump was precipitated by industrial action, parliamentary obstruction and a decline in foreign investment that hindered the development of new hydrocarbons fields. These issues continued throughout 2016. In May 2017 the Minister of Energy, Mining and Renewable Energy, Hela Chikhrouhou, confirmed that overall national output had been negatively affected by the unrest, with production declining to just 44,000 b/d.

The Trading Economics website (citing data from the US Energy Information Agency) stated that output averaged 31,000 b/d each month from January to April 2018. However, according to BP data, overall average daily oil production actually rose slightly in 2018, to 52,000 b/d. None the less, production resumed its declining trajectory subsequently, falling to 42,000 b/d in 2019 and 36,000 b/d in 2020.

The *Middle East Economic Survey (MEES)* website (accessed in May 2022), put oil output at a lower level in 2020, i.e. 32,000 b/d. However, *MEES* reported that in 2021 total oil and condensate output had risen to 40,100 b/d, the first such rise in 14 years. A key factor in this, according to *MEES*, was the offshore Halk El-Menzel oilfield, operated by Topic. This came on stream at the beginning of 2021, and as of May 2022 was producing 5,800 b/d. The 2022 *Statistical Review of World Energy* (the longstanding BP report now published by Energy Intelligence) put the 2021 output a little higher, but at a still modest 43,000 b/d, up from an average of 34,000 b/d in 2020. According to *Tunis Afrique Press* in April 2023, oil output in February of that year averaged 33,200 b/d, down from 37,800 b/d one year earlier. This suggested that Tunisian oil production struggled to be sustainable at 40,000 b/d, let alone in excess of that.

Tunisia's petroleum refinery, at Bizerte, has a capacity of about 34,000 b/d. Plans to increase output there have long been abandoned, and in 2005 the Government announced that it would build a new refinery at La Skhirra. In 2007 it was revealed that Qatar Petroleum International was to invest US $2,500m. in the new facility. In July 2012 a visit by Qatar's Heir Apparent (now Amir), Sheikh Tamim bin Hamad Al Thani, revived the state's commitment, and a new build-own-operate arrangement by Qatar Petroleum was announced. It was envisaged that this would eventually enable total refined oil production to reach 154,000 b/d, providing for a theoretical surplus of 60,000 b/d for export above projected domestic demand. However, by July 2023 it appeared that Bizerte was still the only functioning oil refinery in Tunisia. In any case, output at a second refinery would have been limited by oil production projections. Notably, Eni, an Italian oil major, withdrew from Tunisia in 2021, citing a desire to invest in cleaner technology. However, it also stated that it was focusing on 'more profitable' oilfields (presumably itself a reflection of assumed modest potential oil output volumes in Tunisia).

There are five oil export terminals on the Mediterranean coast, the largest of which is at La Skhirra, which also handles about 22% of Algeria's oil exports. The others are at Gabès,

Zarzis, Bizerte and the Ashtart offshore terminal. In 2001 a 126-km pipeline with a capacity of 22,000 b/d was completed to link the Sidi al-Kilani oilfield to the petroleum storage facilities at La Skhirra. Tunisia became a member of the Organization of Arab Petroleum Exporting Countries in 1982, but in effect withdrew from the organization in 1986 in view of the decline in its oil output.

Tunisian reserves of natural gas were estimated at about 2,300,000m. cu ft at the end of 2014. The INS reported that natural gas output rose from 26,900 metric tons in 2012 to 31,500 tons in 2013, before declining to 29,700 tons in 2014 and 24,300 tons in 2015. In August 2020 the INS reported that the production of gas was 4.9m. tons of oil equivalent (toe). According to INS data accessed in July 2023, gas output in 2018 (the most recent year for which INS data was available) was 5.1m. toe. *Tunis Afrique Press* reported in April 2023 that the national 'supply' of gas (measured in toe) had, as of February, dropped by 8% compared with one year earlier.

Almost all of Tunisia's gas production came from the al-Borma field until 1995, when the offshore Miskar field was brought on stream by BGIT, which invested US $600m. to develop the field (the biggest foreign investment ever made in the country at that time). The Miskar project, completed in 1997, has since supplied about 90% of total national production. BGIT has a long-term contract to deliver gas to the Société Tunisienne de l'Electricité et du Gaz (STEG). In 2007 BGIT stated that it would invest a further $500m. to extend the life of the Miskar field, and would cover $800m. of the $1,200m. cost of developing the offshore Hasdrubal gas field, located just south of Miskar; L'Entreprise Tunisienne d'Activités Pétrolières (ETAP) would contribute the remainder. In November 2006 Petrofac LTD was awarded a $400m. contract to build new Hasdrubal onshore gas storage and liquefied petroleum gas (LPG) production facilities. Natural gas provides 98% of Tunisia's domestic energy sources.

The Government approved an LPG project for the impoverished southern governorate of Tataouine in April 2012. The project included the Nawara gas field in Tataouine, itself a 50:50 joint venture between ETAP and OMV, an Austrian energy company. This was to connect, via a 370-km pipeline, to a gas treatment plant at Gabès, which would enable gas distribution within Tunisia. Although the project had been due to start producing LPG in 2016, it was delayed, owing to popular unrest relating to land acquisition and employment issues. Production at Nawara finally commenced in August 2019, but only in the 'start-up' phase, where it remained as at February 2020. By that time it had been expected that Nawara would increase national gas production by 50%—and reach about 85m. cu ft, or just over 2.4m. cu m per day of gas, 7,000 b/d of oil and 3,200 barrels of oil equivalent per day of LPG. In April 2021 it was reported that output from Nawara had begun at about 2.2m. cu m per day, and output was gradually rising. However, according to *MEES*, Tunisia's total gas output in 2020 was equivalent to nearly 510m. cu m per day (1,860m. cu m annually). Even when operating at full capacity, it did not appear as if Nawara's contribution to Tunisia's overall and increasingly insufficient gas capacity was that significant. *MEES* stated in July 2023 that Tunisia's gas exports for the year to June, stood at 1,760m. cu m, down by 5%, compared with the same period in 2022. This export total implied that only limited gas was available for domestic use. A Tunisian government spokesperson stated in November 2022 that Tunisia would be given 'priority' in accessing Algerian gas (at a time when Algeria was being sought increasingly as an alternative supply source, owing to constraints on supply and sales of Russian gas). It seemed as if the Tunisian President's conduct of foreign policy in the Maghreb was increasingly reflecting Algeria's importance as a producer of hydrocarbons (see History).

The Transmed gas pipeline, constructed to supply Algerian natural gas to Italy, crosses Tunisia and became operational in 1983. Liftings from the pipeline became a new source of natural gas for STEG. Work to expand its annual capacity from 16,000m. cu m to 24,000m. cu m was completed during 1997. In 2003 Tunisia and Libya established a joint venture gas company, Jointgas, to manage the construction of a gas pipeline from Libya in order to provide a new source of supply in addition to the gas that Tunisia receives from the Transmed pipeline in the form of dues. In 2013 the two countries signed a deal obliging Libya to supply Tunisia with 650,000 barrels per month (equivalent) of oil and gas, beginning in 2014. However, the civil war in Libya resulted in the suspension of this agreement, although illicit energy supplies regularly cross the border into Tunisia in relatively modest but still-significant quantities.

In 2008 Tunisia was the world's fifth largest producer of phosphate rock, which is chiefly mined in the central area of the country, accounting for about 5% of world supply. The Compagnie des Phosphates de Gafsa (CPG) is responsible for production, about 80% of which is processed locally into fertilizers and phosphoric acid in plants belonging to Groupe Chimique, the state processing company. From the early 1990s until 2010 annual production of raw phosphates ranged from about 6m. to 8m. metric tons. According to INS data, output reached 8.2m. tons in 2010, compared with 7.2m. tons in the previous year. The political upheaval delayed production for much of 2011, as strikes and protests interrupted the flow of materials to and from mines. Only 2.5m. tons of phosphates were mined in that year. Export revenues for mining products and phosphates declined by more than 40% between 2010 and 2011. Overall phosphate production rose again in 2012, albeit from a very low base. In January 2015 Agence Ecofin reported that CPG's output in 2014 of just under 4m. tons was significantly below its 5.5m. ton target, owing to the discontinuation of some production units. CPG stated in March 2016 that total phosphate output in 2015 had fallen to 3.2m. tons. Output in 2016 was negatively affected by industrial action, among other constraining factors, and this continued throughout 2017 and 2018. None the less, in 2017 total output reached approximately 4.2m. tons—by far the strongest performance since 2010, albeit still modest compared with that year's total of 8.2m tons. Total output declined again in 2018 to just over 3m. tons. In 2019 output was 3.7m. tons, according to CPG. The EIU reported in July 2021 that Tunisia's phosphate industry had been subdued since 2011 but that Tunisia was still one of the largest producers of the commodity in the world, and it remained the country's largest source of export revenue. In April 2022 CPG told Reuters news agency that in 2021 its total phosphate output was 3.7m. tons, and that its output in the first quarter of 2022 had 'doubled' compared with the same period in 2021, to 1.3m. tons. If sustained, this implied a potential annual output in 2022 of over 5m. tons (the CPG target for 2022 was 5.5m. tons). This would far exceed the recovery in phosphate production levels witnessed in 2017, itself the best year since 2010. It was not clear from CPG data if the target was realized. Notably, CPG claimed on its website (accessed in July 2023) that 'the annual production of marketable ore exceeds 8 million tons', yet the most up-to-date published figure on the CPG website was the 2019 total of just over 3.7m. tons. The 8m. figure remained, it seemed, a capacity figure, not an actual output, and one that has not been reached since 2010. According to the BCT, phosphate production in 2022 amounted to just under 3.6m. tons.

The EIU reported that the Gafsa chemical fertilizer plant had suffered strike action that contributed to the closing of the plant in November 2020–May 2021 and that in late 2020 only about one-quarter of domestic fertilizer demand was being satisfied.

Tunisia took advantage of the suspension of much of Russian energy and related petrochemicals exports following Russia's invasion of Ukraine in February 2022 by raising its naphtha exports to the Republic of Korea (South Korea), hitherto a major importer of Russian naphtha. The port of La Skhirra (and the site of an oil refinery and liquids storage) was the dispatch point for 82,000 metric tons of naphtha (some 740,000 barrels) in 2022, after no such exports to South Korea in 2021 and only about 192,000 barrels in 2020.

Production of iron ore declined after independence in 1956, when it was more than 1m. metric tons per year. By 1995 output was down to 225,000 tons. The Jerissa mine has contributed about 70% of total production, with the remainder extracted from the Tamera-Douaria mine. According to INS data, total production was 214,300 tons in 2006, 180,400 tons in 2007 and 206,500 tons in 2008. After a pronounced decline in

2009, to 151,300 tons, when demand slumped, output rebounded to reach 180,500 tons in 2010, before decreasing to 171,100 tons in 2011. From 2011 iron ore output was on a marked upward trajectory, reaching 307,600 tons in 2014. According to a US Government report, iron ore production amounted to about 300,000 tons in 2018, up from some 240,000 tons in 2017. The iron minerals production index published by the INS showed the same trend, reaching 171.6 in 2014, from a base of 100 in 2010. However, the index declined to 159.5 in 2015, owing to interruptions to production.

In 2011 Tunisian mining in general went into decline, principally as a result of the political upheaval and related strike action and migration. INS data indicated that average monthly mining production (base 2000 = 100) fell from 97.2 in 2010 to 41.6 during 2011. By 2013 average monthly output had recovered to 50.5, and the index averaged 56 during the first four months of 2014. By the end of 2017 the index had fallen to 43.5 and was subsequently highly erratic, apparently owing to disruptions in the industry; it decreased to a low of 7.4 in February 2018, but rose to 59.5 in April. After declining to 27.7 in December, the index largely stabilized at a higher level, reaching 46.9 in April 2019. At January 2020 the index stood at 66.1, although by May it had fallen to 48.3, as a result of sharply lower production since the onset of the COVID-19 pandemic. One year later, Tunisia's index score was little better, registering 48.8 in May 2021 (albeit a recovery on the 40.4 seen in April). However, as Tunisia and the world began to stage a modest recovery from the contraction of a year earlier, the mining sector then began a largely upward trend through to and including December, when the index stood at 64.5. In fact, in real GDP growth terms, the 'extraction of mining products' was listed by INS as having risen progressively more strongly in each quarter from the second quarter of 2021 onwards (after the major contraction seen throughout much of 2020 and into 2021). In the first quarter of 2022 real GDP in the mining sector rose by 75.1% year on year, having risen by 59.1% in the fourth quarter of 2021, by 31.4% in the third quarter of 2021 and by 23.8% in the second quarter of 2021. In 2021 mining represented 4.2% of overall real GDP, up from 3.5% in 2020.

Lead output fell steadily until the early 1990s, but recovered to 5,000 metric tons in 2003, 5,470 tons in 2004 and 8,708 tons in 2005. Lead ore output was given by the INS as 13,600 tons in 2005. The INS has not published any subsequent output data for lead ore. According to INS trade data, in 2018 exports of lead product (lead and lead articles) rose in value by 43% compared with 2017. However, their value fell by 103% in 2019 and by a further 72% in 2020.

Annual zinc production was about 36,000 tons in 2001–03, but fell to 29,011 tons in 2004 and to 15,889 tons in 2005. This decline reflected the closure between May 2004 and September 2005 of three lead-zinc mines (Fej Lahdoum, Boujabeur and Bougrine), owing to the depletion of reserves. Similarly, there has since been a lack of production data on zinc. However, the INS stated that the volume of zinc exports in 2019 was 1.28m. kg, a fall of 186% on 2018 when 3.66m. kg was exported, more or less unchanged from the 2017 export volume total. The INS had published no zinc export data by volume, historical or contemporary, by July 2023. However, the INS stated that the value of zinc exports in 2021 was TD 23.4m., up by 73.4% from 2020.

The export value of mining products and phosphates rose by more than 25% between 2011 and 2012 and then stabilized at about TD 1,600m. per year until 2015, before increasing again in 2016, by almost 30%, despite constraints on output. In 2017 it stood at TD 1,412m., declining slightly in 2018, to TD 1,374m., but rising in 2019, to TD 1,667m. According to the latest INS data (not updated by the INS since January 2021 and apparently based on different data composition), the value of all 'mines, phosphates and derivatives' exports in 2020 was TD 867m., down sharply from TD 1,246m. in 2019.

INDUSTRY

Tunisia's industrial sector ranges from traditional activities, such as textiles and leather, to 'downstream' industries based on the country's phosphate reserves. The greater part of Tunisia's industry is located in Tunis. Other industrial centres are Sousse, Sfax, Gabès, Bizerte, Gafsa, Béja and Kasserine. There are free trade zones, termed Parcs d'Activités Economiques, at Bizerte and Zarzis, which opened in the 1990s. Companies established in the zones receive tax concessions and are exempt from most customs duties.

By 2001 industry was reported to be generating 18.5% of GDP and more than 80% of exports, despite growing competition from the EU. The EIU estimated that industry's share of GDP stood at 24.5% in 2016, having accounted for a comparable share of the economy over the previous decade. After three years of sustained growth, manufacturing slowed in 2002, owing largely to reduced activity in the textile and mechanical/electrical industries, affected by weak demand from abroad. In that year the sector's contribution to GDP stood at 18.6%. In subsequent years textiles suffered from overseas competition. The decline in export demand, and consequently in output, had a marked effect on the manufacturing sector, with its share of GDP falling to 16.3% in 2012, to 15.9% in 2013 and 15.5% in 2015; in 2016 the sector's share rose to 16.1% of GDP, but fell to 15.2% in 2017. The IMF estimated that in 2020 the output of the sector contracted by 1.1% (compared with an overall contraction of real GDP of 8.2% in that year). In 2021, according to the INS, manufacturing represented 14.4% of GDP.

According to the INS, real growth in the different components of the manufacturing sector rose strongly in the year ending March 2021 (as would be expected after a major contraction). Typically, the various manufacturing components showed modest but steady growth for each quarter from the second quarter of 2020 to the first quarter of 2022—mechanical and electrical industries rose by 4.1%, chemical industries were up by 2.1%, and the combined 'various industries' category rose by 2.5%. From calendar year 2020 to calendar year 2021, chemical industries rose by 28.9% in real terms, according to the INS, and textiles rose by 12.9% over the same period.

The textiles sector remains an important contributor in manufacturing and exports. In 2021 textiles contributed 2.6% to GDP. Following the expiry of the World Trade Organization Agreement on Textiles and Clothing in January 2005 and the abolition of trade quotas, Tunisian producers were exposed to increased competition from Asian companies and the sector contracted in that year. Textiles made up 37.7% of overall exports in 2005, and 33.6% in 2006, with respective values of TD 5,133.1m. and TD 5,150.6m. Tunisia was the fourth largest supplier to the EU, after the People's Republic of China, India and Turkey (now Türkiye). The value of textiles exports increased to TD 5,189.7m. in 2007, and was broadly maintained in 2008, before declining in 2009 to TD 4,728.5m. as European demand slumped. There was some recovery in 2010, when exports reached TD 5,048.5m. In 2015 their value fell a little, to TD 4,991.5m. Textiles, clothing and leather goods represented just 2.7% of GDP in 2015 (compared with 3.6% in 2010), accounting for 18.1% of total Tunisian exports.

The INS production index (with 2000 as its base year) showed that this sector had recovered in 2013 (91.7) after a slump in 2012 (88.9). At the end of 2015 it stood at 98.0, rising to 100 by April 2016. A revised INS series, with 2010 as the base year (100), showed a further weakening, to 89.7 in April 2017, from 91.8 in December 2016, although the index had fluctuated during the intervening months. From December 2018 the index often exceeded 100, registering 106.4 in April 2019. However, the index fell from early 2020 as a result of the COVID-19 pandemic. In January it stood at 96.1, but it dropped steadily, falling to 71.9 by May. By April 2021, however, it had recovered to 89.0 as the economy began to rebound from the worst effects of the pandemic, and the index followed a broadly upward trend through to September 2021, when it stood at 99.4, before declining to 78.7 in November and then recovering to 89.1 by the end of the year. At February 2023 the index stood at 109.7, having been at above 100 since July 2022 (with the sole exception of a sharp slump in August, when it atypically registered 70.5). In keeping with the index's expected poor performance in 2020, the total value of textiles, clothing and leather goods exports in that year fell by 16% to TD 7,700m., having risen by 4% to reach TD 8,900m. in 2019. A derived total obtained from the summation of the value of exports of cotton and cotton products, raw fibres, leather and leather products and different clothing items represented only

4.1% of the export total in 2020, presumably reflecting the omission of certain items otherwise captured by the 'textiles, leather and clothing' category. According to BCT data, in April 2023 (the most recent month for which trade data was available), the export value of textiles, leather and clothing was 19.6% of that month's overall export total. In 2021 and the first quarter of 2022, based on the previous year's prices, the sector saw strong real growth. In the first quarter of 2022 it expanded by 10.8% year on year. In the first quarter of 2023, based on the previous year's prices, real growth was 13.8% year on year.

Tunisian steel production has declined, owing to technical difficulties at the al-Fouladh complex at Menzel Bourguiba, where production was suspended indefinitely in 2007 following a fire. Another steel mill, with a capacity of 100,000 metric tons per year, is sited at Bizerte. At September 2009 annual steel output was estimated at 150,000 tons, a figure that, according to the World Steel Association (WSA), remained constant up to 2014. However, the WSA estimated that it declined to approximately 50,000 tons annually during 2015–17. According to INS data (the most recent available data being for 2017), raw steel billet production had been in decline since 2010, when it stood at 115,100 tons, until 2017, when it registered 77,500 tons. Rolled metal products generally averaged about 465,000 tons annually over the same timeframe, and output stood at 463,600 tons in 2017.

Overseas motor companies operating in Tunisia include Isuzu, Pirelli, Fiat, GM and Ford. In 2007 the Government sold the Société Tunisienne des Industries Automobiles (involved in vehicle assembly and coach-building) to the local Groupe Mabrouk. By the end of 2015 the mechanical and electrical products sector represented just over 31% of exports by value, which itself represented TD 8,592.7m. In April 2023 (the most recent month for which data was available) exports of mechanical and electrical products represented an estimated 47% of that month's export total by value, up from 45% of the total in the previous month. In 2019 the automotive sector constituted a much smaller proportion of the overall export total, at 11.7%, although in that year the value of motor vehicle exports rose by just under 11%, to TD 20,428m.

The automotive production index stood at 99 at April 2016, falling from 104.5 at the end of 2015. By the end of 2016 mechanical and electrical products represented 45.5% of exports by value, a rise of nearly 16% since the end of 2015. In April 2017 the sector stood at 102 in the production index, having ended 2016 at 105.9. It stood at 102.2 in April 2018, having risen to 112.8 at the end of 2017. The index reached 115.0 in December 2018, before declining to 101.3 in April 2019. In May 2020 it stood at just 67.1, owing to the economic shock of the COVID-19 pandemic, having fallen from 111.1 at the beginning of the year, following strong exports in 2019. By April 2021 it had recovered to 101.1.

Cement production during the late 1990s averaged about 4.7m. metric tons. Privatization of the cement companies began in 1998, when two state-owned cement plants were sold. Overall cement production rose to 6.4m. tons in both 2004 and 2005, and increased gradually in subsequent years to reach 8.1m. tons by 2010. Meanwhile, a group of investors from Europe and Saudi Arabia announced plans to build a TD 175m. cement plant, with a capacity of 1.5m. tons per year, at Al-Akarit. In the first half of 2015 grey cement production stood at 4.75m. tons, similar to the figure for 2014. White cement output in the first half of 2015 was just 222,408 tons, down from 250,096 tons in the same period of 2014. According to the INS industrial production index, 2010 (139.6) was the best year for cement output since 2000 (100). The upheaval in 2011 resulted in a decline in the index to 115.2, although cement production improved slightly in 2012 (118.7) and 2013 (123.7). However, the monthly index only averaged 115.9 during 2015 and in March 2016 it was 119.8. The more general 'construction materials' index (with ceramics and glass also included) stood at 105.8 in April 2019, up from 94.4 in December 2018. In May 2020 the index had fallen to 67.1 as a result of the COVID-19 pandemic, having started the year at 91.5. It had recovered significantly, to 106.6, by April 2021, but by the end of that year it had fallen slightly, to 97.9. The index for 'building materials, ceramics and glass' stood at 84.3 in February 2023, having been on a broadly downward trend since October 2022, when it was 102.1. Real GDP growth in the overall economy for 2022 as a whole was 2.4%.

The chemicals sector, comprising the state-owned Industries Chimiques Maghrébines at Gabès and 'mixed' (partly state-owned) companies at Sfax, processes phosphate rock into phosphatic fertilizers and phosphoric acid. Since 1995 production of the latter has ranged between about 1.0m. and 1.4m. metric tons. In 2000 the state-owned Chemical Products and Detergents Co and the Cosmetics, Detergents and Perfumes Co were sold to a Dutch multinational company. In 2013 a US $498m. phosphoric acid plant, owned in a joint venture by CPG, Groupe Chimique, and the Indian fertilizer company Coromandel International, commenced operations. Press reports stated that the plant would use 1.4m. tons of Tunisian phosphate rock annually to produce 360,000 tons of phosphoric acid. However, fertilizer output has been depressed since the index of production (from a base of 100 in 2000) reached its highest point, 108.4, in 2010. The index declined to 46 in 2011, before rising to 61.6 in 2012 and 62.4 in 2013. At the end of 2015 the chemicals industrial production index (2010:100), a sector dominated by fertilizers, was registering 84.8, and in April 2016 it was 89.0. The index declined to 63.6 at the end of 2018, although it recovered to 75.0 in April 2019. By May 2020 the index had fallen to 66.3 as a result of the COVID-19 pandemic, having begun the year at 93.0. However, as of February 2023 it had risen, to 88.0, having been on a broad upward trend since July 2022, when it stood at 66.3.

In 2015 total phosphoric acid (fertilizer) production reached 1.4m. metric tons, up from 1.1m. tons in 2011. In 2015 total fertilizer production stood at just over 3m. tons, only slightly down on 2014. In May 2017 President Béji Caïd Essebsi claimed that phosphate production had increased by 50% since 2011 and was approaching output levels last achieved in 2010 before the uprising. However, in 2017 total fertilizer output fell to 2.7m. tons, according to the INS. From late 2020 until May 2021 domestic fertilizer production was affected significantly by strike action at the major facility at Gafsa (see *Minerals*).

Under the terms of the association agreement with the EU in the mid-1990s, Tunisia dismantled trade barriers to EU industrial goods in stages over a 12-year period. In advance of the implementation of the agreement, the Government started an industrial modernization programme to improve the competitiveness of Tunisian industry, with financial support from the EU, the World Bank and two Tunisian state funds (the Fonds de Promotion et de Maîtrise de Technologie and the Fonds pour le Développement de la Compétitivité Industrielle).

STEG is responsible for the transmission and distribution of electricity, but lost its monopoly on generation in 1996 as the Government sought to open up the construction, operation and ownership of power facilities to private investors. None the less, STEG still handles about 80% of production. Tunisia is linked to Algeria and Morocco through a 220-kV grid.

In 2009 the Government published plans for the development of renewable energy sources, with the aim of deriving more than 4% of the country's energy from renewables by 2014. Research suggested that Tunisia was capable of producing up to 1,000 MW of wind power; by 2009 the country's installed capacity from this source was only 55 MW, although this had risen to 240 MW by the end of 2018. Tunisia's wind energy target for 2030 was to achieve capacity of 1,755 MW. In line with this goal, STEG signed a deal in May 2023 with Saudi investment firm SWICORP and Spain's infrastructure company Acciona to build a 75-MW wind farm with 14 wind turbines intended to generate up to 6 MW each, in what will be a first in Tataouine governorate. Construction of the farm was, according to *Construction News*, not scheduled to start until 2025.

Tunisia's existing solar power capacity of 11 MW (largely at the Tozeur I facility) was, according to *MEES*, boosted in March 2022 by the start-up of the Tozeur II 10-MW facility, increasing the country's total installed solar capacity to 21 MW. Also announced in March 2022, according to *Construction News*, was the ratification of a deal under which AMEA Power of the United Arab Emirates (UAE) would operate a concession agreement and a power purchase agreement (PPA) for a 100-MW solar project in Kairouan. The development of the plant was originally awarded in principle as a concession to AMEA and its Chinese partner, TBEA Xinjiang New Energy Co Ltd, by Tunisia in 2019 as part of its 2030 New Energy Vision plan. The AMEA project aimed to generate 25.5 MWh. In December 2022 *Tunis Afrique Press* reported that the African Development Bank (AfDB) was to be the chief lender among a range of international finance that had been raised to fund the design, construction and operation of AMEA's photovoltaic plant at Kairouan.

In December 2021 the Government announced the approval of a total of five Independent Power and Water Producers (IPWPs), after bids were originally submitted in 2019; if fully realized, these would have a total installed capacity of 500 MW—i.e. 0.5 GWh. In addition to the AMEA contract, Norway's Scatec Solar won a contract for 300 MW of capacity, including a 200-MW photovoltaic project in Tataouine and two 50-MW photovoltaic solar plants in Tozeur and Sidi Bouzid. A consortium of France's Engie and Nareva Renouvelables of Morocco was awarded a contract to develop a 100-MW solar power project at Gafsa. The PPA 20-year concessions were signed with state energy company STEG under a build-own-operate model. Under its official plans, the Tunisian Government is seeking to expand the country's installed solar power capacity by 2030 to three times the total capacity that the IPWP contracts awarded at the end of 2021 would generate. The Government's solar power capacity target is 3.8 GW. However, a report by the website *Energy & Utilities* in March 2022 stated that government concessions awarded up to that date would generate 1.1 GW, and existing capacity at the end of 2020 was, according to the report, only 95 MW, i.e. less than 0.1 GW.

The Government signed a nuclear co-operation agreement with France in 2008. A planned nuclear power station, which could produce up to 1,000 MW of energy, was at that time expected to be operational in 2023. In 2015 Tunisia also signed a Memorandum of Understanding with the Russian state which was supposed to lead to co-operation in clean nuclear energy use. However, in March 2021 the World Nuclear Association described Tunisia as a country whose prospective nuclear power programme was only at the stage of 'discussion as a policy option'—a categorization clearly distinguishable from those states having official 'plans'. A Stanford University scholar, Khalil Mirri, observed in his self-published research in March 2022 that no civil nuclear plants had begun to be constructed in Tunisia at that point. This was a situation that seemed unlikely to change in the near future.

By the end of 2007 total electricity production in Tunisia had reached 13,960m. kWh, with total national consumption standing at 12,085m. kWh. However, the economic downturn brought about a decline in demand towards the end of 2008, resulting in a fall in output, to 11,078m. kWh, in that year. Output rose subsequently, to reach an estimated 14,850m. kWh in 2015. In 2016 the INS estimated that electricity production fell slightly, to 14,806 kWh, before rising to 15,430 kWh in 2017.

In 2018 the INS stated that electricity consumption amounted to 15,548m. kWh—a figure derived from data for low-, medium- and high-voltage electricity usage. As might be expected given demographic trends, consumption has been on a steadily rising trajectory; having been 15,490m. kWh in 2017, 15,037m. kWh in 2016, 14,991m. kWh in 2015, and 14,768m. kWh in 2014. However, according to the website of the Ministry of Energy, Mining and Renewable Energy, in 2020 electricity 'demand' (taken to be the same as consumption) was 15,353m. kWh, up from 13,015m. kWh in 2010. This suggests that consumption declined during 2018–20, a trend possibly related to economic retrenchment in 2020.

According to government data, at the end of 2014 total installed electricity capacity in Tunisia was 4,321 MW. At the end of 2015 installed capacity was 4,753 MW, up markedly on 2014. Total electricity capacity reached 5,547 MW in 2018, generated by 25 plants, producing 19,252m. kWh. In 2020 output rose to 19,578m, kWh. In that year the Government stated that only 3% of the country's electricity generation came from renewables, and the rest from natural gas. The target of renewables producing 30% of the country's electricity needs by 2030 therefore seemed increasingly unlikely to be fulfilled. By mid-2023, when some new power projects utilizing solar and wind power were supposed to have been under way, none had yet actually broken ground.

TRANSPORT AND COMMUNICATIONS

Tunisia has some 20,000 km of primary and secondary roads, most of which are surfaced and relatively well maintained. Construction began in 2000 on the Tunis–Bizerte motorway, a US $120m. project funded in part by a loan from the Arab Fund for Economic and Social Development. By the mid-2000s work was also under way on the construction of a motorway from M'Saken to Sfax, part of the eventual M'Saken–Sfax–Gabès motorway. In 2007 Tunisia and Libya announced plans to build a toll highway between Sfax and Tripoli, the Libyan capital. Even more ambitiously, the 'Maghreb Motorways Project' has been proposed, stretching from Mauritania, via Morocco (and the disputed territory of Western Sahara), Algeria, Tunisia to Libya. According to the website WorldHighways.com, a budget of US $1,800m. for the project was suggested at the end of 2017, but no progress had been reported by mid-2023, in view of regional diplomatic disputes, security issues and conflict, in the case of Libya.

Severe flooding in 2015 damaged roads and precipitated demands—in the region of Jendouba, for example, where crops had been ruined—for the Government to construct a promised canal system to alleviate flooding in the future. In October 2015 the AfDB granted Tunisia over US $210m. for a 719-km road renovation programme predominantly targeting the country's less developed interior (the west, centre-west and north-west regions), and for a maintenance programme for a further 2,500 km of roads. Carriageways were to be widened and repaired to improve transport links between underdeveloped parts of Tunisia.

The funding of Tunisia's ongoing project to rehabilitate its rural roads seemed to have been facilitated in December 2018 when the Kuwait Fund for Arab Economic Development announced that it would lend Tunisia US $102m. to rehabilitate 148 such roads in 22 governorates, totalling 912 km. Previously, in 2015, the Kuwait Fund had funded the construction of a 15-km two-lane ring road around the Greater Tunis region. In May 2022 the AfDB lent Tunisia $107m. to rehabilitate 230 km of roads in the governorates of Gafsa, Kairouan, Kasserine, Sidi Bouzid and Siliana. In May 2023 the Arab Fund for Social & Economic Development granted Tunisia $52m. for new road building in Beja, Jendouba, Le Kef and Nabeul.

Tunisia's rail network is operated by the state-owned Société Nationale des Chemins de Fer Tunisiens (SNCFT), and consists of a north–south coastal line and four east–west branch lines to Jendouba, Le Kef, Kasserine and Tozeur. According to the SNCFT website (accessed in July 2023), the national network transports about 1.5m. metric tons of freight per year, and it reported that in 2017 some 1.4m. tons were moved on the rail system. Capacity was given by SNCFT in July 2023 as 4.38m. tons per year (a derived total based on its published figure of 12,000 tons per day). Much of the intra-Tunisian cargo is normally transported by road, emphasizing how crucial the ongoing maintenance, as well as the planned renovation and expansion, was of the country's road system.

SNCFT carried some 41m. passengers (on suburban and mainline services) in 2017. SNCFT states that it runs 23 rail lines covering a distance of 2,165 km. Urban railway transport is handled by the Société des Transports de Tunis. There are international airports at Tunis-Carthage, Enfidha-Hammamet, Djerba-Zarzis, Monastir-Skanès, Sfax-Thyna, Tabarka-7 Novembre, Tozeur-Nefta and Gafsa-Ksar. Construction of the new international airport at Enfidha, some 60 km south of Tunis, was completed in late 2009. Initial annual passenger-handling capacity at Enfidha-Hammamet (called Zine al-Abidine Ben Ali at that time) was 7m.; after further expansion schemes, it was scheduled to become Tunisia's largest airport, with a capacity of 30m. passengers. In 1995 the state's 85% shareholding in TunisAir, the national airline, was reduced to 45.2% as part of the Government's privatization programme. Tunisian charter airlines include Carthage Airlines and Nouvel Air. In 2011, when the tourism industry was in decline, owing to the political upheaval, incoming air passenger numbers fell significantly, to 3.8m., from 5.6m. in 2010. TunisAir transported 3.8m. passengers in 2018 and 3.4m. passengers in 2019. The number of passengers carried by TunisAir fell drastically in 2020, to just under 1m., as a result of the COVID-19 pandemic. According to TunisAir, cargo air transportation dropped by 130%, from 7,316.7 metric tons in 2019 to 3,135.5 tons in 2020. In the first two months of 2023 passenger numbers reached nearly 300,000, according to *AfricanManager*, citing TunisAir itself; this was over 36% higher than in the same period of 2022. If maintained for the remainder of 2023—and a rise over the summer period is normally assumed—then this would mean that annual numbers would have recovered markedly, even if they were still less than the pre-pandemic level. According to an article in *Tunis-Numerique* in April 2023, air passenger numbers amounted to about 509,000 in the first quarter of 2023, up by 24% (from about 412,000) in the same period in 2022. The state airline company's revenues rose by nearly 30% year on year in the first quarter of 2023. It seemed that international tourism was recovering in Tunisia, although it was still probably negatively affected by the rising cost of living globally and its effect on airfares and other costs.

There are ports at Tunis-La Goulette, Sousse, Sfax, Gabès, Skhirra, Bizerte, Radès and Zarzis. The country's main shipping company is the state-owned Compagnie Tunisienne de Navigation. The Office de la Marine Marchande et des Ports is responsible for the management of ports.

In 2005 a feasibility study was launched into the possibility of building a deep-water port at Enfidha, capable of accommodating large ships up to a capacity of 80,000 metric tons; bids were invited for the construction of the port from early 2009. In 2007 the Government announced that it would privatize port management and cargo handling. The Enfidha port project was formally submitted in 2010, but progress remained slow. At the end of 2017 the Minister of Transport and Logistics, Radhouane Ayara, promised measures to speed up its completion, but by 2021 Tunisia's port infrastructure remained in need of significant refurbishment and modernization. According to the Oxford Business Group, work was 'estimated' to begin in 2022 on constructing a new deep-water port in Enfidha. The Enfidha port project was projected to cost €1,000m. and the port would cover 3,000 ha: 1,000 ha for the port facility and 2,000 ha for the logistics area.

A new direct sea link between Tunisia and Morocco was inaugurated in 2008, with the aim of accelerating shipments between the two countries and reducing the costs of using indirect routes via Europe.

TELECOMMUNICATIONS

In 1998 the country's first global system for mobile communications (GSM) service began operations under the then wholly state-owned Tunisie Telecom (TT) with 30,000 subscribers in the Tunis-Nabeul-Hammamet region. Orascom Telecom of Egypt was awarded the country's second GSM licence in 2002; Orascom signed an agreement with Kuwait's Wataniya Telecom to operate the licence jointly under the name Tunisiana. In 2004 China's ZTE was awarded the contract to supply and install a third generation (3G) mobile telecommunications network in Tunisia. TECOM Investments and Dubai Investment Group of the UAE purchased a 35% stake in TT in 2006.

In 2009 a combined fixed-line and mobile (2G—second generation—and 3G) telephone licence was awarded to a consortium of France Télécom and a Tunisian company, Divona Télécom. The licence was also to encompass high-speed broadband internet access, and represented part of the Government's plan to develop the most advanced telecommunications network in the region. Tunisiana purchased licences from the Government in 2012 for mobile and fixed-line services. In July of that year the Government announced that it planned to sell its 25% stake in Tunisiana by auction. It was reported in mid-2013 that the Dubai authorities had offered to put up for sale their 35% share in TT (in which the Tunisian Government retained its own holding). TT secured a €100m. loan commitment from the European Investment Bank (EIB) in December 2016 to help the company to expand its national infrastructure. TT planned to establish 1,500 fourth generation (4G) stations across Tunisia and to lay 2,000 km of fibre optic cable. In May 2023 the Government claimed that plans commercially to launch the 5G network would be successfully realized in 2024. TT claimed in November 2022 that it had successfully tested this capacity, and Ooredoo made the same claim to a successful test.

According to the International Telecommunication Union (ITU), in 2021 there were 1.66m. fixed-line subscribers. In contrast, in the same year there were some 15.6m. mobile telephone subscribers, a figure that had been on an upward trajectory from the 12.4m. recorded in 2010. Mobile telephone ownership in 2020 covered 127% of the population. The ITU stated that in 2021 79% of the population used the internet from either mobile or fixed sources (defined as use within the previous three months).

In 2021 fixed-line internet subscriptions stood at just 1.46m. (12% of the population), having increased only slightly in two years. The most significant growth in internet access, however, was via mobile broadband subscriptions, which in 2021 totalled just under 10m. (83% of the population) and liable to have been a very large proportion of how Tunisians were accessing the internet.

FINANCE AND BUDGET

The BCT is the sole bank of issue of Tunisia's national currency, the dinar. It performs all the normal central banking functions, although in 1994 a new foreign exchange market opened in Tunis, ending the BCT monopoly on quoting prices for the dinar against hard currencies. In 1994 the Government introduced legislation to tighten banking regulation, and ordered Tunisian banks to set aside 50% of their profits to cover bad debts, meet a capital adequacy requirement of 5%, cease making unsecured loans and reduce their exposure to any single sector to no more than 25%. By the late 1990s a restructuring of the banking system was under way, with financial assistance from the World Bank, the AfDB and the EU.

The global financial crisis forced the Government to delay its plans for full convertibility of the currency, although in September 2009 the Prime Minister reiterated the administration's commitment to enabling this. Various capital reforms, such as a floating exchange rate, needed to be put in place before full convertibility could be achieved. In November 2010 Ben Ali confirmed 2014 as the new target date for full convertibility of the dinar. The interim Government that was installed following Ben Ali's departure from office in January 2011 was expected to pursue the plan for currency convertibility, and for the development of Tunis as a regional financial centre. Subsequent events, however, knocked these aspirations off course.

The Tunis stock exchange, the Bourse des Valeurs Mobilières de Tunis (Bourse de Tunis or BVM(T)), was established as a state-run institution in 1969; it was converted in 1994 into a private company, regulated by an independent monitoring body. Regulations were introduced in 1995 to make it easier for foreign investors to do business on the exchange. In March 2010 the Government announced plans to develop the bourse by offering a reduction in corporation tax to 20% for five years to companies that offered at least 30% of their capital to the public before the end of 2014. This was countered with separate plans to introduce a 10% capital gains tax on profits above TD 10,000 and on shares bought on or after 1 January 2011 and held for less than one year. The plans adversely affected investor confidence and the bourse fell, prompting the Government to reconsider its proposal. The measure was not introduced at the beginning of the year, by which time political turmoil had erupted throughout the country. At the end of 2012 market capitalization had fallen from the 2010 figure of TD 15,282m. and stood at TD 13,780m. However, by the end of 2014 it had recovered and risen to TD 17,324m., with 77 companies being traded, compared with just 59 in 2012. A total of 78 companies were listed by the BCT as being traded at the end of 2015, but market capitalization, measured as a percentage of GDP, was, at 20.9%, below that registered in 2010, when it was 24.1%. At the end of 2020 there were 80 listed companies, with market capitalization at TD 23,092m. Despite the pandemic-related downturn, the bourse's market capitalization fell by only 2.7% in 2020. In 2021 market capitalization was, at TD 23,262m., up by only a modest 0.7%; 80 companies' shares were being traded. According to the BCT, market capitalization as a percentage of GDP was 16.6% in 2022, down from 17.8% in 2021, after an only modest rise in nominal growth during that time. However, the number of companies whose shares were traded on the bourse in 2022 rose to 82.

The 2008 budget was set at TD 15,342m., assuming real GDP growth of 6.1% and a projected deficit of 3% of GDP, based on an average oil price of US $75 per barrel. Current spending was forecast to rise to over TD 8,000m. The Government announced significant increases in public sector pay, while maintaining subsidies on fuel and food to offset the continuing rise in oil and food prices on world markets. Taxation revenue (accounting for 85% of government income) was forecast to reach TD 10,000m., and total investment was expected to rise by 15%, with 60% coming from the private sector. The 2009 budget, drafted just as the global financial system was heading towards recession, attempted to stabilize the Tunisian economy. It was predicated on a slight decline in growth, to 5%, owing to an expected weakening of the export market and a decline in tourism receipts. The Government increased spending by 12.5% to TD 17.200m. and observed that reduced revenues were likely to result in a deficit of 3% of GDP.

However, in July 2009 the Government was forced to issue a supplementary budget, as slower than expected growth resulted in much poorer tax receipts than had been anticipated. In order to compensate for reduced revenues, the supplementary budget announced higher spending, which the Government predicted would push the deficit up to 3.8% of GDP. The 2010 budget set an increase in expenditure of 5.4%, to TD 18,300m., with capital spending rising by 18% to TD 4,600m. and wages rising by 8%, to TD 6,800m. The 2011 budget projected real GDP growth of 5.4% in that year, on the basis of a 6.1% increase in revenues to TD 15,400m. and a 4.9% rise in spending to TD 19,200m. However, the political turmoil and widespread unrest forced the interim Government, which assumed power after the overthrow of Ben Ali, to introduce a supplementary budget. It raised spending by 11%, to TD 21,300m., in order to boost subsidies and salaries to meet the immediate demands of the protesters, and growth fell significantly, to just 1%. The incoming Government in November 2011 introduced a budget for 2012 that projected a rise in spending by 7.5% over 2011, and committed 37% of total expenditure to wages and 40% to the impoverished interior regions. Earlier projected cost savings by cutting fuel subsidies were abandoned and food subsidies were increased. The budget deficit was projected at 6% of GDP by the end of 2012. In presenting its budget, the Government assumed that it could contain the deficit on the basis of real economic growth of 4.5% and a strong rise in foreign investment, after the contraction experienced in 2011. The actual out-turn in 2012, according to the BCT, was a budget deficit that was a little under the projection, at 5.1% of GDP, or TD 3,600m. (excluding, according to BCT estimates, privatization receipts or grants). BCT public finance data state that this was partly offset by a total of TD 1,700m. in 'privatization and grants' in 2012. Inward investment did indeed rise sharply in 2012, by as much as 40% from the low base of the previous year.

The IMF reported in May 2014 that, largely reflecting a rising wage bill, the overall fiscal deficit rose in 2013 to the equivalent of 6.1% of GDP, from 5.7% in 2012. However, the Fund noted that the underlying fiscal position had actually improved in 2013, taking account of exceptional expenditure in that year, with a structural deficit equivalent to 4.6%, down from a similarly adjusted deficit figure of 5% of GDP in 2012. According to INS data, real growth in 2013 was 2.3%, down from 4.7% in 2012.

In 2014 the government budget projected that real GDP in that year would grow by 4%. However, in March, two months after the new Government had taken office, this forecast was revised down to 2.8% to reflect the problems in the energy and mineral sectors. These factors contributed to what proved to be a poorer actual out-turn than envisaged. According to the BCT, the fiscal deficit in 2014 was TD 4,403m., representing a 12.7% increase on the end of 2013. At the end of 2014, including grants and (limited) privatization receipts, the fiscal deficit was the equivalent of 4.5% of GDP, according to the EIU.

In mid-2015 the EIU estimated that the fiscal deficit would decline only slightly as a percentage of GDP by the end of 2015, to 4.3%. In part, this was due to modest growth, forecast by the EIU at 1.8%, as tourism activity declined and the agricultural sector was undermined by poor harvests. These factors prompted the Government to revise its growth projection of 3% for 2015 to just 1% in a supplementary budget issued in July 2015. The original budget had been predicated on an oil price of US $95 per barrel, but the ongoing slump in global oil prices had negatively affected state energy revenues (although it had made the Government's fuel bill cheaper).

Amid only modest growth, tax receipts were expected inevitably to decline markedly, yet the new budget proposals included a small reduction in petrol duty, a tax exemption for those earning under TD 5,000 (US $2,534) a year and subsidies for low-cost housing. Moreover, as TD 1,000m. was allocated for bank recapitalization, if the Government were to meet its budget deficit target of 5% of GDP, it would probably require another reduction in its investment budget for infrastructural development, even though GDP by value was projected to increase more slowly than previously expected. The reductions in public subsidies and expected wage rises that the previous Government had envisaged for 2015 in order to fund bank recapitalization and higher investment were seemingly assigned lower priority as the new Government sought to maintain its unity and popular support.

The actual budget deficit out-turn in 2015 was about 5% of GDP, according to the EIU's analysis in December of that year; the Government forecast was that it would be 4.4% of GDP. Real growth slumped in 2015 to a modest 1% and oil revenues were below the forecast level, as global prices remained relatively low. Public debt was 54.9% of GDP in that year. Minister of Finance Slim Chaker said that public debt was expected to rise to 59% of GDP in 2018–19. (This was also well above the Government's targets, as stated to the IMF in May 2016 (see *Planning*), even though his calculations were based on an optimistic average GDP growth rate of 3.9%.) Public debt rose to 62.4% of GDP at the end of 2016.

The Government stated in its December 2015 budget statement that in 2016 tax revenues would rise by 11% to TD 20,600m. (US $10,200m.). Income tax revenue would, it said, be boosted by a rise in local wages and more efficient tax collection, and an extra TD 500m. would come from a value-added tax increase on most products, from 12% or 18% to 20%, and from some new taxes, including on gambling. Offsetting the likelihood of these projected revenue rises, however, was the possibility that GDP growth would not increase to the 2.5% expected by the Government, especially as labour disputes were an ongoing feature of the Tunisian economy. If growth was more modest than officially expected, then this would lower the amount of tax collected (and thus make debt a larger proportion of GDP than forecast). Furthermore, the Government also announced a reduction in customs duties on equipment and raw materials for small and medium-sized enterprises (SMEs) to try to boost investment in the small business sector. In the short term, this would of course cut government income, not raise it as it might do indirectly over the longer term. The actual revenue out-turn in 2016 was TD 21,246m., 5.6% up on 2015. In terms of planned expenditure, current expenditure of TD 18,700m. was budgeted for, most of which would be public sector wages, which were due to rise by 12% to TD 13,000m., or 13.8% of GDP. The IMF stated in June 2017 that the 2016 public sector wage bill probably reached 14.5% of GDP, whereas overall expenditure (including net lending) was estimated to have remained fairly stable, at 28.7% of GDP, compared with 28.8% of GDP in 2015. In the event, the actual expenditure out-turn in 2016 was TD 26,081m., up by 9.2% on the 2015 out-turn and representing 29.1% of GDP.

However, in its Memorandum to the IMF (see *Planning*), the Government had said that wages would be no more than 12.7% of GDP in 2016, owing to inflation-linked limits and regional redeployments, thereby supposedly releasing money for investment to the equivalent of 7% of GDP, it was claimed. In the Government's IMF Memorandum it was also noted that the 2016 budget would be subject to one-off costs associated with the increased security outlay following the recent terrorist attacks in Tunisia. Softening the budgeted outlay slightly, however, was a planned reduction in food and fuel subsidies, which declined to TD 2,600m., owing to lower global oil and food prices. Given ongoing capital expenditure costs and the officially admitted one-off security costs, then a sizeable deficit still seemed likely, even if some increases in revenues could see it record a deficit figure lower than 2015. The Government's 2016 budget, based on an assumed deficit of 4.4% of GDP in 2015, projected that the deficit would be cut to 3.9% of GDP. Notably, the Government's Memorandum sent to the IMF in May 2016 (see *Planning*) set a deficit target of 2.4% by 2019, and assumed a structurally adjusted deficit of 3.6%. However, the Memorandum noted that the extant commitment of US $1,050m. in soft loans would help to offset the budgetary shortfall (see *Foreign Aid*). The IMF's assessment in February 2017 was that the fiscal deficit for that year would only improve modestly, from 6% of GDP in 2016, to 5.6%, some way off the 2019 target. It noted that the huge public sector wage bill and the impact of low growth on revenues were still major contributory factors. In the event, the actual 2016 deficit out-turn was 5.4% of GDP. In June 2017 the IMF forecast that the deficit would remain static as a percentage of GDP in that year.

The 2017 budget, agreed in November 2016, was ambitious in that it was predicated on growth of 2.5%, up from 1% in 2016. Although the Government's 2017 fiscal deficit target of 5.4% of GDP was the same as the actual 2016 deficit out-turn, this seemed very optimistic because the Government's own estimate of the 2016 shortfall at the time was 5.8%, and because the 2017 deficit target was based on an overestimated 2016 GDP figure. Overall spending was set to grow by 12%, to TD 32,700m., although a large part of the increase was projected to be driven by a 23% rise in investment spending, which could have a welcome stimulatory effect on the economy. The Government optimistically stated that the wage bill (typically more than one-half of the overall expenditure total) would rise by only 4.2% (i.e., less than inflation), owing in part to planned two-year pay settlements and a recruitment freeze. It was also optimistic because the Government planned to limit food and fuel subsidy growth to just 3.4%. The Government's revenue projections also optimistically assumed that proposed new tax rises could be successfully agreed upon and, based on unrealistic expectations concerning GDP growth and the efficiency of the tax collection system, assumed an implausibly high overall tax take. The resultant deficit was likely to be a higher proportion of GDP than the Government's official 5.4% forecast. Financing the deficit was partly allowed for in that the Government also projected a doubling of foreign borrowing in 2017. However, indicative of the probable failure of the Government to meet the budget's spending, revenue and deficit targets was the fact that in December 2016 parliament approved a supplementary financing law, permitting a further TD 1,200m. in borrowing, on the assumption that the deficit would actually be 6% of GDP at the end of 2017. With overall public debt expected to exceed 65% of GDP by the end of 2017, the Government was likely to require external financial support. At the end of 2017 the budget out-turn was, indeed, worse than officially forecast. According to the EIU, the official deficit in 2017 was TD 5,700m. (5.9% of GDP), up from TD 4,900m. (5.4% of GDP) in 2016. Real GDP growth in 2017 remained at the relatively low level of 1.9%, compounding the Government's difficulty in achieving fiscal revenue (as a proportion of GDP) close to that originally forecast, and probably increasing the deficit to more than the predicted 5% of GDP. However, both revenue and expenditure rose more sharply in 2017 than in 2016. Revenue increased by 12.5% in 2017, compared with 5.2% in 2016, and expenditure rose by 9.2% in 2016 and then by 13.2% in 2017. The EIU noted that the large 2017 fiscal deficit contributed to public debt reaching about 70% of GDP in that year.

The 2018 budget was contested by trade unions seeking to negotiate higher public wages. An agreement in July 2018 between the Government and the main trade union federation to keep increases to the minimum wage below the rate of inflation, if adhered to, would have eased some of the fiscal pressures, but other proposed revenue-raising measures, including new taxes, were difficult to enforce and made further cuts even more unpalatable, given the rising cost of living.

In the event, the out-turn in 2018 was an improvement over that of the previous year. The budget deficit, at TD 4,700m. (4.4% of GDP), was below the official target range, owing in part to stronger real GDP growth of 2.5% in 2018. Revenue rose more sharply in 2018 than the previous two years, helping to offset a rise in expenditure. The fiscal deficit in 2018 was 4.6% of GDP, according to the IMF, reflecting the rise in real GDP growth. Public debt was 72% of GDP in 2018, according to the EIU.

The 2019 budget assumed that there would be a reduction in spending as a result of promised (but controversial) cuts to subsidies, although, with no new taxes expected in advance of the 2019 elections, this seemed unlikely. The Government committed itself to reducing the fiscal deficit at the end of 2019 to 3.9% of GDP. This was ambitious, given the hitherto challenging 5% target, particularly as real GDP growth was not guaranteed to be any higher than in 2018. The Government's budget was based on a projected 3.1% rise in GDP. However, neither the IMF (see above) nor the EIU expected GDP growth to reach this level; indeed, when the budget was issued, the EIU assumed that there would be a reduction in the rate of GDP growth. Consequently, it appeared as if a fiscal deficit of at least 5% of GDP was more probable by the end of 2019, and that Tunisia would therefore face a financial shortfall. Since 2011 concessional loans had helped to stabilize the fiscal position. However, it seemed that the Government might need to increase its commercial borrowing to meet its rising financing requirements, although, given the country's large debt-to-GDP ratio, it would probably incur higher rates of interest.

In the event, the 2019 budget out-turn recorded a deficit equivalent to 3.4% of GDP—below what the Government had been projecting, even as a proportion of an over-optimistic growth forecast, and what some analysts had feared. However, the Government still required significant financing, including foreign loans and debt issuance, with as much as US $2,960m. expected to come from foreign sources, including the assumed transfer of the final tranche of an Extended Funds Facility (EFF) from the IMF (totalling $450m.) to help to meet the deficit, according to a Reuters report in October 2019, which cited a senior government official.

Also in October 2019, the Government presented its budget for 2020, which projected a further reduction in the size of the fiscal deficit, to 3% of GDP. This was a difficult objective to achieve, in view of the fact that budget outlays were projected to rise to TD 47,000m.—an increase of nearly 16% and the largest expenditure in the country's history—and that overall economic growth was unlikely to be strong (the Government projected only a 2% rise in real GDP). Wages were expected to constitute about 40% of overall spending (some US $7,000m.)—a factor compounded by an agreement that had just been reached with the UGTT, no doubt with the upcoming elections in mind. Ostensibly the Government also viewed the 2020 budget as targeting the very real problem of mounting public debt, which reached 73% of GDP at the end of 2019 (and the level was more than double this, if the losses of state-owned enterprises and the state pension system's deficit—contingent liabilities—were included). The budget allocated 20% of expenditure to servicing the Government's component of total debt. It was expected that a Eurobond issue would provide some of the financing of the forecast 2020 deficit; in October 2019 it was reported that the Government planned to issue bonds worth nearly $900m. (a significant contribution to the envisaged nearly $3,000m. shortfall). In the event, many of these assumptions were either rendered irrelevant, or made far worse, by the onset of the COVID-19 crisis from March 2020, which put even greater pressure on public finances as state relief had to be provided to both business and the public, and the lockdown greatly reduced the Government's revenue from taxation and other sources.

The Government's RFI 'purchase' agreement with the IMF in April 2020 (see *Introduction*) was intended to bring emergency relief to the Government's finances and the wider economy. The agreed Tunisian 'purchase' provided the desired scope for the Government to provide emergency support for some companies, as well as for the wider public. The agreement was also intended to provide a basis for what the IMF envisaged as regional and international financial support from other sources.

The 2020 fiscal out-turn resulted, as expected, in a large deficit, estimated by the IMF in its Article IV report of February 2021 to be equivalent to 11.3% of GDP. Unsurprisingly, in the context of the COVID-19 pandemic, in 2020 tax revenue fell from 25.1% of GDP in 2019 to 23.6% of (sharply lower) GDP; in nominal terms, revenue was 9% lower. Wage and salary costs in 2020, typically the largest components of Tunisian state expenditure, comprised 17.6% of GDP in 2020 (up from 14.6% of GDP in 2019).

The Government's total package of emergency economic relief for 2020–21, according to the IMF's Article IV report, was equivalent to 4.3% of GDP. The Fund estimated that the direct fiscal cost (excluding grants and loans), drawn from the 2020 and 2021 budgets, was some TD 2,600m., or 2.3% of GDP. Spending on health care and aid payments to the poorest families and to the long-term unemployed comprised the largest share of the outlay.

In December 2020 parliament approved the budget for 2021. It projected that by the end of that year the fiscal deficit would fall to 6.6% of GDP (which was expected to increase in 2021). The Government assumed it would be able to control expenditure in light of an expected winding-down of the emergency coronavirus-related measures, a lower wage bill and reduced spending on energy. Moreover, the Government also expected a significant boost in revenue, owing to an expanding economy and higher exports. However, although some of the emergency fiscal measures were expected to ease, in February 2021 the IMF reported that the Government was considering the recruitment of some 10,000 long-term unemployed into the public sector, as well as the first phase of hiring 30,000 construction workers. The Government also forecast stronger real GDP growth (4%) for 2021 than the IMF's projected 3.8%. The Tunisian authorities projected that the financing of the expected 2021 deficit would mostly (about 70%) come from external borrowing, including bond issues, which the Fund described as potentially fiscally 'risky'.

By November 2021, however, the Government was expecting that the fiscal deficit would, at a projected TD 9,800m. at that year's end, be higher than that originally budgeted for (38% more than at the end of 2020), owing to the steeply rising cost of fuel imports throughout 2021. The Government had issued a Supplementary Finance Act in September 2021 to extend spending on what was reportedly being estimated as a further TD 3,200m. in fuel subsidies than had been budgeted for in December 2020. The end-year deficit in 2021 was 7.8% of GDP, according to Fitch in its March 2022 analysis.

The IMF had expected a higher financing requirement for Tunisia in 2021 (18.3% of GDP) than in 2020 (17.2% of GDP) and had also expected that the domestic component would be higher than officially envisaged, including via a higher share of loans from the CBT and what the Fund called a probable need for 'contingent measures'. The higher financing requirement was expected partly because of what the IMF had identified in 2021 as rising debt and arrears on the part of state-owned enterprises, as well as cumulative costs incurred as a result of the pandemic that had been partly cushioned by the CBT's emergency measures in 2020.

On 28 December 2021 Minister of Finance Sihem Boughdiri gave details of the 2022 budget (as included in a new finance law). It included a commitment to increase public spending by 3% year on year to US $19,800m. (TD 56,864m.), according to Agence France-Presse (AFP). She said that the finance law would lay out budgetary plans for 2022 that, on the basis of anticipated government revenues, assumed a budget deficit of TD 9,300m., or what the minister said would be 6.7% of GDP. Boughdiri argued that, on that basis, the total financing requirement would be TD 18,673m. (Presumably taking into account ongoing financing costs separate from the budget deficit, such as those the IMF had expected in 2021: debt arrears, state-owned enterprise costs and 'cumulative costs'.) In March 2022 Fitch estimated that Tunisia's 'deficit and debt maturities' at the end of the year would be 9.2% of GDP. The 2022 budget assumed that an IMF deal would be agreed by the end of June, and that, as part of a related $4,000m. that Tunisia expected in external financing, a US-supported bond issue would occur, fresh support would follow from external creditors, and a sizeable loan not reliant on an IMF deal would be agreed. Taking her financing figure into account, Boughdiri said that the overall government debt at the end of 2022 would be equivalent to 82.6% of GDP. The same AFP press report stated that at the end of 2021 external debt was equivalent to 100% of GDP.

In May 2022 BCT Governor Marouane el-Abassi stated that that year's fiscal deficit would in fact be 9.7% of GDP, as opposed to the 6.7% that had been forecast in December 2021. Abassi said that this would require the Government to find an extra TD 5,000m., resulting in a total of TD 25,000m. in financing being needed at the end of 2022. (This was likely to be at or higher than the IMF's financing projection—see above—for 2021). He noted that the war in Ukraine had greatly compounded import, and therefore fiscal, costs.

In March 2022 Fitch projected that the year-end 2022 deficit would be 8.5% of GDP. This was lower than the figure the BCT projected two months later; however, the economic prognosis for Tunisia (and for many other countries that largely import their food and energy) was worsening all the time. Although in the first quarter of 2022 Tunisia's fiscal revenues had seemed to be rising following the scrapping of emergency tax holidays and as the economy was performing more strongly than under the COVID-19 constraints of 2020 and part of 2021, inflationary pressures caused by food and energy price rises were an increasing burden through the second quarter of the year and were not expected to ease much in the third quarter.

In the event, the fiscal out-turn for 2022 was below Fitch's expectations, but a still sizeable deficit equivalent to 7.7% of GDP. The 2023 budget, presented in December 2022, claimed that the deficit could be brought down to 5.2% of GDP. The finance minister announced major cuts to commodities and food subsidies, but did so on the assumption that the initialled IMF loan deal of US $1,900m. would soon be finalized. The budget, at the IMF's behest, but also out of simple fiscal practicality, proposed a series of graduated real estate tax levies intended to offset the still-assumed rises in a wage bill that represented a projected 55% of the overall outlay for 2023. (The Fund has also urged much greater tax collection per se—in practice more a problem of administration and, arguably, political will, than of the potential revenue actually being available.) Following the initialled IMF arrangement, Tunisia reached agreements with the French Government and the EU for deficit financing, albeit relatively modest, worth about $200m. and $100m., respectively. A larger EU aid deal, worth $967m., was announced in principle in June 2023. The IMF had all but insisted in the run-up to its provisionally agreed loan package being announced that such international support should be forthcoming rapidly.

At the time of the BCT Governor's comments in May 2022, it was reported by Reuters that the Government intended to respond to the increased fiscal deficit and to cover larger 'Treasury charges' (i.e. the cost of borrowing from the BCT) by borrowing TD 12,150m. from abroad, raising TD 8,120m. from 'internal borrowing resources' and by using what the authorities described as 'Treasury resources' of TD 801m. Put differently, this BCT 'support', while potentially including BCT debt issuance (which would require relatively high and rising interest repayments, given that Tunisian debt would be comparatively expensive to fund), would probably also include quantitative easing—the BCT, in effect, printing money. Notably, an IMF deal on which at least some external financing would rely, had still not been forthcoming. In March 2022 Fitch's assessment of Tunisia's deteriorating access to external financing was that the country would therefore borrow heavily from 'domestic sources'; in other words, from the BCT.

The IMF argued in 2021 that Tunisia's overall stock of debt could become unsustainable without a major reform programme enjoying broad political support for reining in spending and significantly increasing revenue. Without a more optimistic fiscal prognosis, the Fund argued that issuing, in effect, fresh external debt through planned further bond issues, would be untenable. This assessment was shared by Fitch, which in late July 2021 assessed Tunisia's fiscal predicament in light of the suspension of parliament earlier in that month (see History). Fitch argued that the temporary emergency powers assumed by the President precluded any prospect of his forging a political consensus behind unpopular cuts and/or a firm rise in the tax take. A more positive prospect for Tunisia that could arguably offset some of the state's health care-related expenditure costs and indirectly aid fiscal revenue streams in 2021 was the large provision of free vaccines against COVID-19 by Saudi Arabia, the UAE, USA and France, most of which arrived in July, providing the potential for full vaccination of about one-quarter of the population.

In June 2023 Fitch further downgraded Tunisia's credit rating to CCC− from CCC+, stating that the absence of the implementation of the formally agreed IMF financing deal was raising questions about further external financing, with the ratings agency envisaging that the 2023 requirement would be the equivalent of 16% GDP. A lack of existing external financing had already meant that the Government had been reliant on short-term domestic financing to meet fiscal deficits and large debt maturities, according to Fitch. The latter included Eurobond repayments that would amount to €500m. in 2023 and €850m. in 2024. Fitch assumed that the IMF financing deal would eventually be fully agreed and drawn on, but noted that the Government's own financing plan for 2023 relied on this source of funding, even though it might not in practice be useable until 2024, given the ongoing political disputes about its implementation. In that environment, and without many of the other sources of external financing that normally follow an IMF arrangement, the BCT would in effect have to print money in order to relieve a liquidity-starved monetary environment, as the domestic debt market would be too stretched to meet financing needs. As mentioned, agreements to support the Government fiscally by France and the EU were made in principle in late 2022 in the context of an assumed IMF deal being actualized. A seemingly separate EU aid package worth US $967m., announced in principle in June 2023, also seemed to be conditional on the IMF deal going through. More positively, Fitch assumed that the current account deficit would narrow in 2023 as tourism revenues recovered, compounding a developing trend (see *Tourism*).

In June 2012 the USA committed itself to a US $30m. sovereign loan guarantee for a planned Tunisian government bond issue worth at least $450m., intended to ease the growing public debt burden. There were also discussions with Islamic financial institutions in the Gulf for a *sukuk* (Islamic bond) to assist in easing the debt burden. In July 2013 the legislature approved the issue of a $700m. *sukuk*, although this was subsequently reduced to $625m. A Samurai bond, equivalent to $400m., was also reportedly issued in 2013. In March 2014 the Governor of the BCT stated that a $2,000m. foreign bond issue programme was being planned, half of it to be underwritten by the Japanese Government. In October an $825m. Tunisian bond was issued on the Japanese market, backed by the Japan Bank for International Cooperation. The Government issued a $1,000m. Eurobond in February 2017, followed by a €500m. Eurobond in October 2018 and a €700m. Eurobond in July 2019. In 2021 the Government committed officially to seek external budget support equivalent to 4.7% of GDP and specifically to access the Eurobond market for funds equivalent to about 2.2% of projected GDP. In view of the fiscal pressure that the Government was under, and, as already mentioned, the improbability of it being able to make fiscal retrenchments in the manner desired by the IMF, such projected external financing seemed unlikely to be achieved. A continued use of central bank liquidity injections and an eventual full agreement and utilization of IMF-related external financing seemed to be inevitable.

A loan of US $200m. was ratified by the Turkish parliament in June 2013, to be used over a six-year period for Tunisian public infrastructure projects. An additional $200m. was to be lent by Turkey's Eximbank to support Tunisia's imports of goods from Turkey, including for public projects. The final tranche, of some $200m., of a $500m. Turkish loan reportedly agreed in 2013 was paid to Tunisia in February 2014. In late 2013 Qatar gave $500m. to Tunisia to bolster its foreign reserves. In November 2016 Qatar pledged to provide Tunisia with a further $1,250m. in assistance, although it was unclear how much of this was subsequently disbursed. Despite intra-Gulf divisions between Qatar and a bloc led by Saudi Arabia, the Tunisian Government continued to engage actively with Qatar, in part to secure more aid. Qatar also remained a major investor in Tunisia; for example, in May 2019 the Qatari state, through a publicly owned energy company and its sovereign wealth fund, acquired a 60% stake in the Carthage Power Company. At the time of the Qatari Amir's visit to Tunisia in February 2020, Tunisia's ambassador to Qatar, Sami Saidi, stated that $250m. of the $1,250m. that Qatar had committed had already been invested by the Qatar Fund for Development (QFfD) in what he described as 'several development projects'. The Tunisian ambassador also stated that the Qatari-Tunisian Friendship Fund (under the aegis of the QFfD) was setting up a scheme to create 50,000–100,000 Tunisian jobs either directly or indirectly under a scheme costed at $97m. Addressing rising unemployment (see *Planning* and *Tourism*) was a key economic and political priority for the Government, although the funding for this particular Qatari initiative arguably sounded both very low, and the terms were very vague. Qatar, none the less, planned to open a branch of the QFfD in Tunisia, which could help to deliver such objectives, provided that the staff have the authority and capacity to achieve them. Qatar has a significant banking presence in Tunisia via the 35 branches of the Qatar National Bank, and the Qatari state has stakes in two Tunisian banks. This could facilitate the proposed development projects.

After President Saïed's assumption of autocratic powers in 2021, Tunisia's prognosis in terms of external financial support changed. Political moves that had significantly disadvantaged the Muslim Brotherhood (Ennahdha) would, in theory, encourage Gulf states that are perceptibly unfriendly to the Muslim Brotherhood to proffer more assistance to Tunisia, and countries such as Türkiye and Qatar markedly less. In July it was reported by the respected website Africa Intelligence that the BCT's hopes, at a time of intense budget pressure and 'fraught' talks with the IMF, for an additional US $2,000m. from Qatar or, it was reported, an additional $1,000m. from Libya, looked increasingly forlorn.

In October 2021, however, Tunisia conducted talks with both Saudi Arabia and the UAE over external financing, in light of the expected major fiscal deficit (see above). However, despite the BCT's Director-General of Financing and External Payments, Abdelkarim Lassoued, telling Bloomberg that 'very advanced' discussions were being held with its two Gulf partners about budget support, no specific information on any Saudi or Emirati transfers to the BCT had been announced as at September 2022. A relatively small sign that Saudi Arabia and the UAE might eventually step into the breach in a more major way occurred in January 2022, when the Saudi Export-Import Bank signed a loan agreement with the Tunisian Company of the Refining Industries (STIR) for US $200m. to finance imports of Saudi oil derivatives. This was at a time when oil imports were an increasingly heavy burden on the Tunisian state.

Bank refinancing, mostly to large state and private banks, was recorded as having risen by TD 500m. to reach TD 5,000m. by January 2014, despite lower reserve requirements. The IMF stated in May that the declining performance of the banks as measured in terms of overall capital adequacy ratio, and, for six of them, the minimum capital requirement, was due largely to the Government's attempt to realign the banking sector with international standards, hence the poorer performance as measured by higher standards. The IMF warned that tougher standards of refinancing could also impact on what had been rising profits, and that assets remained weak. None the less, bank refinancing continued to grow, accelerating from TD 12,200m. in March 2018 to TD 16,750m. in March 2019. In its July 2019 report (issued under the EFF), the IMF reported that refinancing had 'broadly stabilized' at about TD 16,000m.

In late 2013 the World Bank held back a promised US $500m. concessionary loan owing to what had, in its assessment, been insufficient progress in economic reform. With the change of government in January 2014, a planned tax rise in the budget for 2014 (involving new taxes on private, transport and farming vehicles) was abandoned by the outgoing administration led by Ali Laârayedh, as this had been a contributory factor provoking riots in some parts of the country. A week after a meeting between Tunisian Prime Minister Mehdi Jomaâ and World Bank President Jim Yong Kim in Washington, DC, USA, in April 2014, Kim announced that Tunisia would receive $1,200m. in assistance during that year. The flow of inward investment into Tunisia contracted sharply again in 2013, decreasing by 30% to US $1,100m., and declined by another 5% in 2014, to a little over $1,000m. At the end of 2017 the BCT announced that Tunisia's foreign investment 'liabilities' totalled TD 2,100m., equivalent to 2.2% of GDP (compared with 2.1% in 2016); at the end of 2018 liabilities had reached TD 2,742m. (2.6% of GDP). Measured as a stock, FDI rose from $11,500m. at the end of 2000 to, according to the EIU, an estimated $35,300m. at the end of 2014. FDI inflows declined sharply in 2011, but they recovered somewhat in 2012, before decreasing again during 2013–14, owing in part to renewed political instability. In 2015 the stock of FDI was estimated by the EIU to have increased a little, to reach $36,000m. The EIU estimated that at the end of 2018 the stock of FDI had reached about $39,000m. (up from approximately $38,000m. in 2017). In 2018 the estimated inward investment stock was equivalent to more than 97% of GDP. Despite agreement on a new foreign investment law, issues surrounding its interpretation, as well as wider security concerns, domestic disputes over the alleged corruption issue (see History), and the complex number of companies still tied to the family of former President Ben Ali, had prevented any significant rise in investment by mid-2020. According to BCT data, FDI in 2019 was $1,090m., or 2.2% of GDP. FDI fell to $680.2m. in 2020, or 1.7% of GDP—a sharp decline that presumably reflected increased investment outflows and lower investment inflows as the COVID-19 pandemic spread. In 2021, still affected by the COVID-19-related downturn, FDI fell further, to $641.5m., according to the BCT.

PLANNING

With help from the IMF, from the latter 1980s the Government adopted a radical four-year programme designed to provide a secure basis for the economy for the next decade. The strategy depended on an increase in exports of agricultural and manufactured goods, a rise in revenues from tourism, and severe reductions in the Government's investment budget. Meanwhile, trade was to be liberalized and the Tunisian dinar was to be devalued, in an attempt to maintain export competitiveness. The economy broadly recovered over the period of the programme, but fluctuations in performance reflected movements in the international price of oil and the susceptibility of the harvest to recurring droughts. The 1992–96 Plan envisaged reductions in subsidies on consumer and other products, the disposal of state assets except in strategic sectors, the elimination of price controls on manufactured goods, and the introduction of selective charges for health, education and other services.

The 1997–2001 Plan envisaged total spending of TD 42,000m. over the five-year period, of which the government budget would provide TD 33,775m. with the remainder funded by external financing. The Plan targeted an average rate of real GDP growth of 6% per year. Meanwhile, the Government had announced new measures in 1996 to encourage foreign investment during the 1997–2001 period, including allowing investors to buy up to 49% of any local company without prior authorization.

The 2002–06 Plan set a per capita growth rate target of 4.8% and a 5.4% annual economic growth rate by 2006, with increasing emphasis on private sector involvement in the transport, telecommunications and banking sectors. The Plan for 2007–11 sought to accelerate economic growth to 6.1% per year and to reduce unemployment. The Government intended to continue the gradual liberalization of the economy, increasing the role of private sector activity to 75% and the proportion of private investment to 63%, and cutting external financing. The principal sectors targeted for development were information technology, the engineering and electrical industries, and chemicals.

The 12th Development Plan, covering the years 2010–14, incorporated revisions forced by the economic downturn. The new Plan sought to attain an average annual growth rate of 5.5% and to raise income per head to more than TD 8,300 by 2014. It aimed to create 415,000 jobs, and to reduce the unemployment rate to 11.6%—targets that were missed by a substantial margin—and to increase the level of investment to the equivalent of 26% of GDP. (The unemployment rate at the end of 2014 was 17.6%, according to the INS.) The target of attracting an average of TD 3,250m. annually over the plan period proved too optimistic, especially as inflows fell sharply in 2011 in response to the political upheaval. A budget deficit target of below 2.7% of GDP was set, as well as a reduction in the level of public debt to 40.4% of GDP. In practice (see *Finance and Budget*), the deficit was 4.5% of GDP in 2014. Public debt rose from 40.4% of GDP in 2010 to 46.8% in 2012, but it declined to 44.6% in 2013. According to the EIU, at June 2015 public debt totalled TD 17,229m., close to the above target, although the EIU expected debt as a portion of GDP to rise further during the second half of the year.

Few details were available of the 13th Plan (2015–19) However interim Prime Minister Mehdi Jomaâ said in March 2014 that measures to reduce the burgeoning cost of consumer subsidies were under consideration.

In May 2016 Prime Minister Habib Essid issued a 'Letter of Intent' including the Government's request to the IMF for a new tranche of funding that was formally agreed in June 2016. The framework to the economic restructuring plan was outlined to the IMF in an official 'Memorandum on Economic and Financial Measures' (MEFM). This accompanied Essid's Letter of Intent and was tantamount to the Government's conventional five-year plan, albeit missing some of the traditional targets but containing fiscal ones. The latter included the proposal that the public deficit (excluding grants) would not exceed 2.4% of GDP by 2019, although the 'structural deficit' allowing for variations in the economic cycle might rise to 3.6%, and that debt to GDP would be stabilized at 51% (even though, at the end of 2015, it was 54.6% of GDP and was likely to rise further by the end of 2016; it stood at an estimated 70% of GDP at the end of 2017). A more flexible exchange rate system was proposed, using the foreign-exchange auction system, which was introduced in February 2016. Reductions in energy subsidies were planned, according to the MEFM, as was an overhaul of the tax system to raise revenues.

In the event, however, further details on the Government's plan were not released to the legislature as had been planned for June 2016, as the Government faced a variety of political crises. The new Government, led by Youssef Chahed, also encountered difficulties in implementing its economic plans because of popular resistance to IMF-endorsed efforts to rein in spending and to increase fiscal revenue streams. For example, a US $70m. emergency budget line for low-income families was introduced in January 2018, in an attempt to ease revolt against the government budgetary law, which proposed tax increases together with further cuts. Chahed admitted that the high unemployment rate was the main challenge. He also claimed that plans to stimulate exports, thereby narrowing the increasingly large trade deficit, would result in much stronger growth by 2020. However, divisions within the Government, in part encouraged by Chahed's rivals for the premiership and disputant party coalition members leveraging union and other discontent, meant that agreement on more specific and workable economic plans was difficult to achieve. In response to unrest in January 2019 (see History), a further anti-poverty initiative was announced, with a comparatively large increase in welfare benefits proposed, pending legislative approval.

Few details were available about the 14th Plan, covering the 2020–24 period, other than the principal (and optimistic, with the benefit of hindsight) objective of achieving annual real GDP growth of 5% through the improvement of the business environment, progress in the implementation of tax reforms, the modernization of public administration and reduction in the unemployment rate.

At the onset of the COVID-19 crisis, in March 2020 the Government announced a TD 2,500m. emergency economic plan to meet immediate health care and social needs and to protect jobs and businesses. It announced its plan with the IMF's subsequent support package in mind (see *Finance and Budget*). In fact, the IMF's assistance covered almost all of the

Government's projected additional expenditure, although a potentially widening fiscal deficit would also need to be covered (possibly by a further provision of—as yet unscheduled—IMF support). Inherent in the Government's proposals and in the IMF's pledged support was that the desired emergency spending measures would need to be followed by fiscal restraint in some areas, such as wages. It is significant in this respect that the Government's tax revenues fell by 12.6% in the first four months of 2020 (although the majority of this period took place before a lockdown of the economy was imposed in mid-March). It was therefore almost certain that the fall in tax revenue as a whole would be even greater than this.

In June 2020 Prime Minister Elyes Fakhfakh proposed a public sector wage freeze. However, this was immediately followed by a day of comprehensive industrial action organized by the UGTT. It subsequently became doubtful that, in the context of a struggling economy and amid relatively high inflation, the Government would persist with a measure that would only compound already weak consumer demand. Fakhfakh's resignation as premier in July, owing in part to the unpopularity of his proposals, compounded the remote possibility of the wage freeze being implemented. However, the Government found scope to adjust the fuel subsidy via the introduction of an automatic fuel price adjustment mechanism to reduce the subsidy in a period of low international prices for oil and thus enhance fiscal revenue. This saved as much as TD 2,000m. in 2020, although in theory it would necessitate a rise in government expenditure if and when oil prices rose again.

One of the Government's most notable responses to the COVID-19 crisis was to adjust the projected deficit for 2020 to 7% of GDP (from its 3.4% target at the time of the original budget for 2020—see *Finance and Budget*). Some observers suggested that this was too alarmist a prognosis for the fiscal deficit, in view of the Government's probable access to further financing as a result of support from the IMF and other international bodies (although setting a proportion of GDP as a fiscal target meant that much depended on the even less predictable issue of how much the economy shrank by as a result of the pandemic). In April the World Bank contributed US $35m. to Tunisia's expanding health care costs as a result of the crisis (although $15m. of this was a redirection of monies from an existing fund for Tunisia). It has been argued that the relatively modest resources (up to an estimated TD 170m. in revenue in 2020) of the National Solidarity Fund could also be considered as financing of the expected wider budget deficit. However, to emphasize that this is partly only an accounting issue, it should be noted that the Fund's aid to the needy is financed partly by state grants in the first place.

Part of the 'understanding' for receiving IMF fiscal support in 2020–21 was that the Government would reduce fuel subsidies, cut state wages and abandon what the IMF described as 'lower priority public investment'. In the event, in 2021 the Government cut fuel subsidies on three occasions by April, and the price of a litre of petrol rose to TD 2.095 (about 75 US cents)—not a modest amount, in view of the weakening value of the dinar and a rising rate of joblessness. State wages and salaries were to be frozen in 2021, according to an official plan submitted by Tunisia to the IMF in May, and the Government was reported to be considering promoting early retirement and part-time working by state officials. Such IMF-encouraged austerity measures had played their part in the popular discontent that facilitated President Saïed's assumption of autocratic powers in July 2021 (see History). As wages for public sector workers had been increased in 2020, it seemed unlikely that pay could be frozen in 2021 without popular opposition. Furthermore, Saïed's assumption of autocratic powers had relied in part on populist measures to satisfy the electorate.

At the same time that BCT Governor Abassi had commented (in December 2021) positively about Tunisia securing external financing and not, as he put it, 'resorting to the Paris Club', the Tunisian authorities were negotiating with the IMF for a hoped for TD 4,000m. (equivalent) in financing to bridge partly the fiscal gap. The Government would have been obliged under any fresh IMF deal to adhere to additional IMF-requested fiscal constraints, including further reducing subsidies on essentials. In other words, the tough economic and political conditions under which the IMF had already encouraged Tunisia to operate, would prospectively be further compounded by fresh government cuts. These, in turn, would conceivably reduce economic demand and increase social, and even political, instability. At the end of the first quarter of 2022 the total of Tunisia's outstanding purchase and loans from the IMF was TD 1,600m.

In December 2021 Abassi had suggested that a new IMF deal might be concluded by the end of the first quarter of 2022. An IMF team did visit Tunis in late March, giving rise to the 'IMF Staff Statement on Tunisia', published on 30 March. Abassi had claimed in December 2021 that Tunisia's burgeoning financing needs (including external needs) would be realized and its extant financing debts would be met without seeking debt restructuring. He also said that a fresh IMF special drawing rights arrangement might be negotiated (Tunisia had already used up its extant allocation; see *Introduction*) and suggested that other financial 'funds' (i.e. borrowing) might be obtained too. In the absence of a wider set of agreements including further fiscal retrenchment, this seemed unlikely, leading to increased fears that Tunisia might not be able to service its external debts (see below). However, in July 2022 an IMF team arrived in Tunisia to begin a two-week period of negotiations with the BCT and the Ministry of Finance over a bail-out package, which was thought to be worth up to €2,000m. The Fund issued a summary statement in the same month. However, by mid-2023 no full report had been issued, owing apparently to the absence of the President's agreement to implement the fiscal terms of the IMF's proposed financing arrangements.

The Government continued to adopt the somewhat antiquated approach of releasing national 'plans' for the economy, even though in recent years, as shown above, the details of Government objectives had become decidedly sketchier and the relevance of each plan itself more questionable. The 2023–25 plan had sought to put emphasis on the regional features of development, and in light of this, non-coastal areas such as the central and eastern governorates were, apparently, to be targeted for greater support. The Minister of Economy and Planning, Samir Saïed, addressed meetings in these areas in the first half of 2023 and in other less developed parts of the country too, in order to promote the proposals. However, their implementation, amid relative economic austerity, would be difficult. Arguably related to this was the still-ongoing dissatisfaction of grassroots representatives of Tunisia's large number of so-called 'site workers', traditionally casualized labour that the UGTT represents only partly. Under a revised agreement reached in 2021, they are all supposed to be absorbed eventually into local and national arms of the public sector, as long as they are of working age. Until that time, they will continue to be a discontented and otherwise low-waged cohort of 'the hidden unemployed'.

TRADE

Tunisia's trade growth in recent years has centred principally on the expansion of its links with the EU since the signing of the association agreement in 1995. The country's major exports include textiles, agricultural products, leather goods and phosphates. The main imports are consumer goods, machinery, raw and processed materials, and agricultural and industrial equipment. Tunisia's balance of trade deficit has been traditionally offset by earnings from tourism and remittances from Tunisians working abroad.

In 2011 an already significant trade deficit widened further, from TD 8,298m. in 2010 to TD 8,610m., as import costs continued to rise and exports increased only modestly. Generally, the size of Tunisia's non-merchandise surplus offsets a large portion of the deficit, but the decline in tourism revenues (as Tunisia was undergoing an uprising and an eventual change of leadership) and in foreign remittances (due principally to instability in Libya), minimized this and resulted in a current account deficit of TD 4,500m. Owing to the decline in net FDI, the Government drew down some of its foreign exchange reserves to finance partly the shortfall on the current account. Foreign exchange fell by TD 2,400m. from the end of 2010 to the end of 2011. In 2011 declining tourism revenue and falling foreign remittances helped the current account deficit to rise to TD 4,766m., or 9% of real GDP.

An only modest economic recovery for much of 2012 meant that the trade deficit widened further, to TD 11,630m., with a higher volume, and rising international prices, of imports, and a relatively small increase in exports. According to BCT data, a marked recovery in tourism receipts and a more modest, but still strong, rise in foreign remittances helped to ease the services deficit. However, the rising trade imbalance caused the overall current account deficit to increase still further, to TD 5,765m., or the equivalent of 10.9% of real GDP. In 2013 there was a further slight rise in the trade deficit, to TD 11,808.3m. The current account deficit for 2013 was TD 6,437m., chiefly the result of the ongoing and widening merchandise deficit, and services revenue, despite the recovery in tourism income, remained virtually unchanged from the previous year. According to preliminary IMF data, the 2013 current account deficit was equivalent to 8.4% of GDP, slightly up from 8.2% in 2012.

In mid-2014 the IMF expected that the current account deficit would narrow to 7.2% of GDP in that year, and would fall still further in 2015, reflecting improving economic conditions among Tunisia's trading partners, higher revenues from phosphate sales and tourism, and a lowering in the costs of imported commodities. According to the INS, however, the trade deficit for the first half of 2014 was TD 6,727m., firmly up on the equivalent period in 2013. This trend led to a rise in the overall 2014 trade shortfall on 2013, although the non-merchandise balance, recorded at over TD 2,500m., helped to mitigate the extent of the goods and services deficit, which totalled TD 7,369m. at the end of 2014 according to the BCT. At the end of 2015, according to the BCT, the goods and services deficit had expanded further, to TD 9,153.4m. The non-merchandise balance in 2015 offset this to some extent, with the overall current account deficit standing at TD 7,601m. The balance of goods traded in 2016 produced a deficit of TD 12,621m., according to the BCT, moderately up on the 2015 goods balance of TD 12,005m. According to the EIU, the estimated overall goods and services deficit in 2016 was TD 9,437m. However, only a small services balance of TD 687m. was recorded in that year, according to the BCT. If the surpluses on additional non-merchandise items were included, this produced a derived current account deficit figure of TD 7,737m., in line with the 2015 figure. Trade data released by the BCT for the first half of 2017 showed that the goods deficit had reached TD 7,535m., with the value of both exports and imports in the second quarter of 2017 up markedly on the same period in 2016, suggesting that the increase in the goods deficit at the end of 2017 would be larger than the previous year. In the event it reached TD 15,595m. Although the value of Tunisian exports in 2017 had risen strongly, the weakness of the national currency had helped to increase the import bill to more than TD 50,000m., a rise of nearly 20% on 2016, compared with an average annual increase in 2011–16 of less than 5%. A small services balance in 2017 of TD 869m., albeit some TD 200m. higher than the 2016 total, could not wholly offset this.

INS data for 2018 show a markedly increased trade deficit in that year of TD 19,049m., 22% higher than the shortfall in the previous year. Another major rise in imports (by value) had occurred as a result of increasing oil export revenues following a further upturn in the average oil price. According to the BCT, the positive services balance rose significantly in 2018, to TD 1,897m., partly offsetting the trade deficit. According to the BCT, the decline in the average international price of oil in 2019 helped significantly to reduce the total value of imports, and an increase of 6.5% in the value of exports (mainly reflecting the higher value of exports of mechanical and electrical industries products, despite a decline in agricultural exports) helped to bring down the trade deficit to TD 15,929m. in that year. (However, the INS reported a small increase in the size of the trade deficit, claiming that the value of imports had actually risen.) Once again, a healthy surplus on the services balance, which rose to TD 3,470m. in 2019, helped to offset the ongoing trade deficit. In 2020 the goods deficit eased by more than TD 6,000m., owing to a contraction of real GDP and falling living standards, and the erstwhile services surplus tipped into a small deficit.

In 2018 the current account deficit, including services and other items, was TD 11,722m., according to BCT data. This represented, as the IMF showed in its June 2019 staff assessment, a further and marked deterioration in the current account deficit which had been widening since 2011. In November 2018 the EIU estimated that the financing requirement for the 2018 current account deficit would be equivalent to approximately 11% of GDP, creating a borrowing need beyond the offsetting impact of inward investment and concessional loans. According to the BCT, in 2019 the deficit balance on the current account was in line with what the BCT had reported as the decline in the trade deficit, and was markedly down, standing at TD 9,686m. In terms of financing the current account deficit in 2019, a number of inflows, including a strong balance listed under 'other investments' (where IMF and aid inflows are captured), meant that there was more than enough funding to meet the shortfall, even as the BCT indicated that direct investment assets had risen by less than TD 100m. The half-yearly current account balance at mid-2020 was a deficit of TD 4,524m., equivalent to 4% of GDP.

The BCT stated that, at the end of 2020, the deficit on the current account had narrowed to TD 7,125m. Funding the 2020 current account shortfall would rely on the continued, if reduced inflows described as 'capital and financial operations'. Among the financing items listed under this heading, according to the BCT, was a healthy balance listed as 'other investments' at a time when the value of 'direct investments' in the Tunisian economy had fallen markedly.

In 2021 the increase in value of Tunisian exported goods—up by 20.5% on 2020—could not compensate for a 22.7% rise in Tunisia's already large imported goods bill. This resulted in a more than TD 3,000m. increase in the goods deficit. The value of exported services rose by 33% in 2021, greater than the increase in the value of imported services, which rose by 26.5%. However, this only produced a modest services surplus of TD 500m. The rise in 'factor income' in 2021—the net balance rose by 75% to TD 3,900m.—helped to offset the increase in the current account deficit—which in 2021 was TD 8,000m., up from TD 7,100m. in 2020.

The IMF estimated that Tunisian overseas workers' remittances rose from just over US $2,000m. in 2019 to $2,250m. in 2020. Preliminary figures indicated that workers' remittances rose far more strongly in 2021. Although workers' remittances of a country's own nationals are conventionally listed under that country's 'current transfers', the BCT lists 'labour income' under 'factor income', of which labour income constitutes the lion's share of factor income inflows. The labour component of the latter rose by 29% in 2021. At nearly TD 2,000m., this significantly helped to offset the impact of Tunisia's trade deficit on its widening current account deficit.

As ever, in funding this deficit, the Tunisian exchequer continued to rely on a healthy net balance of 'capital and financial operations', which the BCT reported at TD 8,351m. at the end of 2021. Of these, the net balance on the 'other investments' category nearly doubled, to represent over three-quarters of the total net balance of 'capital and financial transactions' in 2021. Put another way, the gross inflow described as 'other investments' had gone up more than threefold on 2020. There was also a nearly fourfold increase in the net balance of 'direct investments' (due largely to a strong gross inflow), compared with the unsurprisingly low level seen in 2020.

The trade deficit in 2022 rose by nearly TD 9,000m. to about TD 25,200m., according to the INS, owing mainly to a rise of nearly TD 20,000m. in imported goods by value, albeit offset by an increase of nearly TD 11,000m. in exports by value. The ongoing inflation in the costs of imported goods, including energy and food items, was a factor in the rising import bill, and Tunisia's chief exports—mechanical and electrical goods, textiles and agricultural produce—rose firmly over the course of 2022, partly reflecting the increased costs involved. The overall current account deficit given by the BCT for 2022 was TD 12,400m. The balance of services in that year was markedly higher than that of 2021, reaching about TD 4,300m. according to the BCT's *Financial Statistics* report of April 2023 (albeit as part of data at slight variance with those of the INS, even though reporting largely the same broad trends). A large rise in tourism revenue played its part (it rose by TD 1,200m., according to the BCT) in a strong services surplus. A high level of workers' remittances was likely to have helped to offset the size of the trade deficit in 2022. However, the bulk of the financing of the current account deficit was met, according to the BCT, by another strong rise in 'financial operations'; in 2022 they increased by more than TD 4,300m.

INS data at the end of April 2023 showed a cumulative trade deficit for the first four months of the year of TD 7,100m., loosely on trend with the position at the end of 2022 and confirming the continued, if easing (in terms of energy prices), high cost of imports.

The association agreement with the EU entered into effect in 1998. Its main provisions were as follows. EU capital goods and semi-finished goods that were not also manufactured in Tunisia (accounting for 12% of Tunisia's imports from the EU at that time) would be exempt from import duty from the date the agreement entered into force. EU exports of specified goods that were also manufactured in Tunisia (28% of Tunisian imports from the EU) would be subject to the progressive elimination of import duties over a period of five years after entry into force. Duties on EU exports of goods that were deemed to be 'more sensitive' in the Tunisian economic context (30% of Tunisian imports from the EU) would be phased out over a period of 12 years. Duties on EU exports of goods that were deemed to be 'most sensitive' (29.5% of Tunisian imports from the EU at that time) would be maintained for the first five years of the agreement before being phased out over a seven-year period. Tunisia (which already had duty-free access to the EU market for industrial goods) would benefit from a limited relaxation of EU quota and tariff restrictions on some agricultural exports, although olive oil exports to the EU remained subject to existing restrictions. In January 2000 negotiations began with the EU on the extension of free trade to agricultural products, and an agreement came into effect from January 2001. This raised the annual quota of duty-free olive oil exports entering the EU from 46,000 metric tons to 50,000 tons, with further annual increases to a maximum of 56,000 tons by 2005. It also fixed the quantities of other agricultural exports permitted to enter the EU duty-free. The EU's quota for soft wheat exports to Tunisia was raised to 460,000 tons, and a quota for 100,000 tons of vegetable oil exports was also introduced.

The Tunisian Government expected that investment of about TD 2,200m. (60% for the modernization of businesses and 40% for infrastructural development and other initiatives to improve the business environment) would be required during the first five years of exposure to increased EU competition. Preparatory studies had indicated that about one-third of Tunisian industrial companies were likely to be put out of business by the new trade measures, and a further third would find the transition difficult. Under the association agreement, the EU pledged to provide financial assistance to help the Tunisian economy to adjust, including support for industrial restructuring, training and promotion of the private sector. Although the agreement did not come into force formally until March 1998, Tunisia began implementing its provisions from January 1996, when import duties on EU capital goods were abolished. In November 2012 Tunisia was finally accorded privileged, or advanced, status as an EU trading partner. This status should bring preferential access to the EU market (and also brought a related increase in EU aid), but it will also subject Tunisia's domestic economy to greater competition—and oblige it to introduce a range of more rigorous market reforms. Macrofinancial arrangements (MFA) were agreed between Tunisia and the EU in response to the negative economic impact of the terrorist attacks of 2014. A second, 'MFA-II', worth US $500m., was agreed in October 2017; with an initial $200m. disbursement to be paid by the end of 2017, followed by two loans of some $150m. in 2018.

In July 2018 Tunisia joined the Common Market for Eastern and Southern Africa (COMESA), despite being a north-west African Saharan country. None the less, Tunisia appeared to be encouraged by the lack of a developed manufacturing base in sub-Saharan Africa, which it could potentially develop thereby boosting its own export earnings. For similar reasons Tunisia has sought to join the Economic Community of West African States and the Economic Community of Central African States.

At late 2022 Tunisia had free trade access to 20 other African countries as a member of COMESA. In June of that year the German Ministry of Trade had launched a scheme to boost Tunisia's trade with sub-Saharan Africa, which at that time comprised only about 3% of Tunisia's overall export market.

TOURISM

Tourism is a major source of foreign currency earnings for Tunisia, accounting for about 6% of GDP in 2010, and the hotels and restaurants sector (including resident and non-resident spending) represented 4.8% of GDP in 2013. The tourism sector was estimated to comprise 14.5% of GDP in 2014; tourism's contribution to GDP was projected to decline from 2015, principally owing to attacks against Western tourists by Islamist militants in that year (see History).

The main centres for tourists are Hammamet, Sousse, Djerba, Monastir and Tunis. Since the 1960s the country has been a popular destination for Western European visitors. However, it has had to compete with many other Mediterranean holiday destinations, and foreign tourists have sometimes been deterred by fear of terrorist incidents. More recently, Tunisia has been looking to attract new visitors from Eastern Europe, China, Japan and Australia, and to diversify its range of tourist attractions.

The number of foreign tourist arrivals grew to 5.2m. in 2000, representing a rise of about 7% on the previous year, and tourism revenues increased to TD 2,100m. Receipts increased to TD 2,400m. in 2001, with 5.4m. tourist arrivals. In 2002, however, tourist arrivals decreased to 5.1m., reflecting a 19% drop in European visitors, in part as the result of a tanker bomb attack on Djerba. Tourism earnings declined to TD 2,024m., but still contributed more than 6% of GDP and 17% of external receipts, and the sector employed 13.5% of the labour force in that year. Tourism receipts were down by 4.6%, to TD 1,929m., in 2003, although the number of tourist arrivals remained the same, at 5.1m., reflecting an increase in the number of visitors from Arab countries. The number of European tourists decreased by 2.7%. In 2004 arrivals totalled some 6.0m. and receipts rose to TD 2,290m. The number of tourists from other Maghreb countries reached 2.3m. In the same year the Government established the National Tourism Commission, chaired by the Minister of Tourism and Handicrafts. There were 6.4m. tourist arrivals in 2005 and receipts reached TD 2,587m. Arrivals from European countries increased by 11.1%. In 2006 arrivals reached 6.5m., and receipts totalled TD 2,751m., and in 2007 a further rise in the sector, to 6.8m. arrivals with receipts of TD 3,045m., was recorded. Despite the rise in arrivals, the tourism sector's dependence on the mass low-cost market has been highlighted in a report by the EIB. It noted that numbers of tourists from Europe (with the exception of France) had fallen, and that the sector had failed to respond to the needs of independent and other higher-spending visitors. In April 2009 the Government launched a new strategy for tourism, designed specifically to attract higher-spending visitors and to increase the number of visitors from the Gulf states and China. After an increase in arrivals to 7.1m. in 2008, tourism showed signs of being affected by the economic downturn in Europe. Arrivals for 2009 totalled 6.9m., and remained at that level in 2010. The political upheaval in 2011 resulted in a decline in tourist arrivals, to a reported 4.8m. In January 2012 the Government launched a new tourism promotion initiative. However, the combination of social unrest in Tunisia and the ongoing debt crisis in the eurozone did not help to ease the decline in Tunisian tourism. Data published by the INS in July 2013 revised the tourist arrivals figure for 2011 downward to 3.1m. In 2012, however, non-resident tourist numbers rebounded to 6.0m.

According to the INS, the total number of incoming visitors to Tunisia in 2015 was 4.2m., compared with 6.1m. in 2014 and 6.3m. in 2013. The most obvious contribution to this decline was the Bardo National Museum attack in Tunis in March 2015. The number of tourist nights (resident in-country) during the first half of 2015 contracted by 18% compared with the first half of 2014. These trends were exaggerated following the Sousse attack in June, which occurred just before Tunisia's peak tourist season in the second half of the year (see History).

The BCT reported that the decline in incoming visitors in July 2015 (the tourism high season and most recent month on which it has data) was 26% compared with July 2014. However, at 743,300, the number of monthly visitors in July 2016 was on a firm upward trajectory, aided by the lack of terrorist attacks on Western targets in Tunisia since June 2015. According to government estimates, the number of visitors in 2016 totalled 6.5m., representing an increase of 23% on 2015, and, reportedly reached 7m. in 2017. In contrast, the INS reported that the number of incoming foreign tourists in 2016 was just over 4.5m., which was in line with its figure for 2015. The authorities, apparently believing that the tourism industry was in a stronger position than this, and encouraged by developments such as the restoration of direct flights from the United Kingdom in January 2018, announced a target of 8m. visitors in 2018, a significant increase on even the pre-terrorist attack figures.

According to the BCT, tourism earnings declined from TD 3,523m. in 2010 to TD 2,433m. in 2011, but recovered to TD 3,175m. in 2012; its figure for the sum of 2013 quarterly data, TD 3,889m., suggested that tourism revenue subsequently returned to trend growth. In the first half of 2015 tourism receipts declined by 17%, to TD 1,130m., compared with the same period in 2014. The still-negative impact of the 2015 attacks on the Tunisian tourism industry meant that by the end of 2016 tourism receipts had declined further to reach their lowest level since 2005, according to the BCT, even though overall visitor numbers had increased. Receipts totalled just TD 2,373m., although this was only a modest decline of 1.7% on 2015. According to the EIU, in 2018 tourism, although beginning to recover, accounted for just 6% of Tunisia's foreign currency earnings, compared with 16% in 2010. The EIU also reported that the tourism sector lost about one-quarter of its workforce in the eight years from 2010. However, visitor numbers had, the EIU indicated, begun to recover in 2016, and in 2018 stood at 8.3m., surpassing comfortably the annual total achieved in 2010.

The Government estimated that tourist arrivals amounted to 9.5m. in 2019—a sharp rise from the previous year. However, tourist visits were drastically curtailed following the onset of the COVID-19 pandemic in early March 2020 and the subsequent lockdown and suspension of most international flights, amid restrictions on non-essential travel. Arrivals fell to 2.0m. for the year as a whole. Some 400,000 Tunisian workers in the tourism sector were at risk of losing their jobs in 2020, and revenue from the sector was expected to fall by some US $1,400m. (total revenue in 2018 was $1,713m., in an indication of the drastic fall in receipts), according to government estimates in April of that year. According to the IMF, the tourism sector's contribution to GDP fell from 5.1% in the third quarter of 2019 to just 2.2% in the third quarter of 2020. In December 2021 the tourism minister, Mohamed Moez Belhassine, stated that in the year to 20 November 2021 tourism revenues rose by 6.2%, year on year, to TD 1,900m. Given that in 2020 tourism revenues were expected to be approximately TD 900m., it seems that in that year—'the COVID year'—tourism revenue was not quite as devastated as had been projected. That said, the BCT stated that in 2020 FDI in what it termed 'tourism and real estate' totalled only TD 17m., compared with TD 202m. in 2019 and TD 134m. in 2018. What was not in doubt was that economic recovery in the tourism sector in 2021 was slow. Arrivals in 2021 rose to just 2.5m. According to the BCT's *Financial Statistics* report published in April 2023, there were some 5.2m. foreign visitors to Tunisia in 2022, confirming a strong recovery in the tourism sector, as indicated by a significant rebound in tourism receipts (see *Trade*).

UNEMPLOYMENT

In July 2020 Fitch forecast that unemployment in Tunisia would rise from just under 15% at the end of 2019 to 21% by the end of 2020, and some observers expected it to increase even more drastically. Official data, however, seemed to tell a different story. The INS stated that unemployment in the third quarter of 2020 was only marginally higher, at 16.2%—a figure that is likely to be markedly below the actual proportion of the workforce that was unemployed at that time. When the AFP reported details of the 2022 budget in late December 2021 (see above), at the same time it also stated that the official unemployment rate was 18%. As of 31 March 2023 official unemployment stood at 16.1%, according to the INS.

FOREIGN AID

The principal sources of economic aid for Tunisia continue to be Western countries and international institutions. The World Bank group has been the most important multilateral donor, providing loans and credits for investment in a variety of projects. The AfDB is another large multilateral donor. Important bilateral donors have included France, the USA and Gulf Arab states (although in 1991 the US Government reduced its aid owing to Tunisia's muted support for Iraq during the Gulf crisis). Japan has also extended substantial credit to Tunisia for the purchase of Japanese goods and services. Tunisia's receipts of official development aid had risen from US $178m. in 1984 to $393m. by 1990, and during the 1990s it continued to obtain substantial external funds, principally from the World Bank, the EU and members of the Organisation for Economic Co-operation and Development. By March 2003 the World Bank portfolio in Tunisia comprised 21 active projects, amounting to a total net commitment of $1,200m. In June 2004 the World Bank approved a new country assistance strategy to be implemented over a four-year period starting in 2005, including a lending programme in the range of $200m.–$300m. a year to achieve key development objectives: the first and most urgent objective was to reduce unemployment, which remained high at 15%; the second was to improve the education system; and the third was to boost the performance of social programmes while maintaining budget balances. In July 2004 the World Bank approved a $130m. loan for the second phase of an education programme and a $13m. loan to develop the information and communication technologies sector. The Bank also approved a $36m. loan for export development projects. In 2005–06 the World Bank approved further loans to support water supply and sewerage projects. In May 2009 the AfDB signed a $250m. loan agreement to support Tunisia's efforts towards integration into the global economy. The agreement was approved by the Chamber of Deputies in July, together with further loans from the International Bank for Reconstruction and Development (IBRD) and the EIB.

Following the outbreak of political unrest in December 2010 and the overthrow of Ben Ali's regime a month later, Tunisia's need for financial support rose dramatically, not least to support the additional promises made by the interim Government to address the protesters' grievances over salaries and prices. The AfDB and the World Bank provided US $1,500m. in emergency funding almost immediately, and subsequently the Group of Eight (G8) leading industrialized nations pledged an additional $25,000m. in loans over the next five years. A new loan tranche, of $500m., was agreed by the World Bank and the AfDB from October 2015, partly in response to the recent terrorist attacks but also as the third part of a series of economic development and job development loans since 2010. At the time of this announcement, the World Bank confirmed that it had 22 different investment and assistance operations in Tunisia, with loans totalling $1,000m. and small grants totalling $51m., including water and wastewater projects and assistance for small businesses. The Tunisian Government claimed to the IMF in May 2016 that the budget for that year would be aided by $550m. from the World Bank and, separately, $500m. from the AfDB. Also in that month, the World Bank announced that it would provide up to $5,000m. worth of loans over a five-year period to support economic development projects focused on young people and poorer regions in Tunisia. In mid-2019 the World Bank had 11 programmes operating in Tunisia via the IBRD, which were valued at $2,210m. For the 2019 financial year, the World Bank stated that it had four specific projects planned, valued at $650m.

In accordance with its economic development goals in Tunisia, in May 2018 the World Bank announced that it was to provide an investment loan of some US $100m. to assist with the Tunisian Government's efforts to improve primary and pre-primary education in disadvantaged regions. In September the World Bank disbursed a loan of some $500m. to support government spending, crucially raising Tunisia's foreign reserves from the equivalent of 68 days of import cover, to 78 days. Following a visit to Tunisia in February 2022, the World Bank announced that it would provide Tunisia with $400m. to support what it called 'social reforms'. It was also announced that additional World Bank monies would be forthcoming to Tunisia to support the SME sector and to help the Government 'acquire vaccines' and provide the 'necessary health support' needed.

In May 2019 the AfDB announced a $120m. loan to support Tunisian financial sector reform—a second tranche for this purpose, making a total of $348m. since 2016.

In July 2017 Prime Minister Chahed visited Washington, DC, in a bid to persuade the US Administration of President Donald Trump not to lower its aid budget to Tunisia as part of a planned overall reduction in international aid. Official US data indicated that in 2019 a commitment of US $1,100m. in direct assistance was made to Tunisia. Separately, as of August 2019 the US Agency for International Development reported that it was funding $48m. worth of projects in Tunisia. It seemed that as long as the latest IMF deal (originally proposed in late 2022) remained politically unconfirmed, then a lot of prospective external financing continued to be in doubt. Notably, the Fund's preliminary report (published July 2022 in advance of what 12 months later was a still unpublished full report) claimed that it was vital for ongoing government efforts to rein in aspects of recurrent public spending to be supported by the 'rapid release of financing'. The commitment of the French Government and the EU were tied to the IMF deal proposed in late 2022. Tunisia's financing problems were related not only to the seemingly stalled IMF agreement, but also to another aspect of the President Saïed's combative approach to foreign and domestic relations. In March 2023 the World Bank announced that it was suspending co-operation with the Tunisian Government in light of Saïed's racist comments about African migrants (see History). Minister of Trade and Export Development Kalthoum Ben Rejeb noted that this was a 'postponement' of the current dialogue, not a termination of relations, and pointed to the World Bank's ongoing intention, so he claimed, to provide financing for the project to connect Tunisia's and Italy's electricity grids.

Tunisia's total foreign debt had increased from US $3,526m. in 1980 to $8,475m. by 1992 and to $11,379m. by 1996. After a decline in 1998, to $10,850m., debt rose to $11,872m. in 1999, of which $9,487m. was long-term public debt. The debt-servicing ratio was 15.9% in 1999, up from 15.4% in 1998. Under the terms of the 2000 budget, external borrowing was set at TD 1,500m., compared with TD 1,117m. in 1999 and TD 977m. in 1998. In 2000 total foreign debt was $11,500m. and the debt-servicing ratio was 22.6%. According to the IMF, total external debt that year rose to 60.2% of GDP from 59.6% of GDP in 1999. Foreign exchange reserves stood at TD 2,810m. at the end of 2001. In 2002 external debt was 61% of GDP and the debt-servicing ratio was 17.2%. Foreign exchange reserves totalled $2,437m. at June 2003.

The outstanding balance of medium- and long-term external debt, measured in TD, amounted to 17,357m. at the end of 2003, compared with TD 16,115m. at the end of 2002. The debt service ratio was down to 13.1% and reserves increased to TD 3,645m. At the end of 2004 external debt had increased to TD 19,238m., and reserves rose to TD 4,733m., and by the end of 2005 the debt balance amounted to TD 20,435m., with reserves standing at TD 5,872m. In 2006, according to the latest and revised data from the BCT, external debt eased to TD 19,728m. as a result of some early repayments, with the ratio to GDP standing at 43%. However, it rose again slightly, in absolute terms, in 2008 to TD 21,301m., but fell as a proportion of GDP, to 38.6%. By the end of 2010 external debt was a slightly lower proportion of strongly rising GDP, at 37.2%, and totalled TD 23,582m. According to the BCT, the debt service ratio was a manageable 9.3%. At the end of 2011 the BCT stated external debt had risen to TD 25,391m., which, in a poor economic year, represented about 39% of GDP. At mid-2012 BCT data indicated that external debt had risen sharply, to TD 34,636.9m., equivalent to approximately 50% of GDP. At late 2013 external debt remained at about 49% of GDP, although the World Bank noted that this was not yet at an alarming level. At the end of 2015 external debt was given as TD 42,068m., which represented fractionally more than 50% of GDP. However, according to the BCT, gross external debt, including both government and private sector debt, at the end of 2016 had reached TD 67,513.4m., representing 76% of GDP. The EIU estimated that the total external debt at the end of 2018 was US $35,000m. (approximately TD 103,600m.), equivalent to 87.9% of GDP. According to the IMF, Tunisia's external debt stood at 90.3% of GDP at the end of 2019, and in April 2020, when the IMF granted Tunisia's request for funding under the RFI, it projected that external debt would reach about 110% of GDP by the end of the year. According to BCT data, Tunisia's gross external debt position at December 2021 was TD 56,800m., up by just over TD 1,500m. year on year, indicating that, as expected, external debt continued to rise up to the end of 2021. (Presumably, this BCT figure excludes some parts of Tunisia's external debt stock that are captured in IMF data; however, the trend remains consistent.) According to ceicdata.com, Tunisia's external debt stock at the end of September 2021 was US $39,600m., down slightly from $39,900m. at the end of June. Revised BCT data (published in its April 2023 *Financial Statistics* report) gave the external debt stock as TD 76,324m. at the end of 2021, which, at the equivalent of $26,538m., or just 58% of nominal GDP, suggested that it continued to exclude some of the external debt included in IMF and EIU data. However, it still captured the overall trend.

Foreign currency reserves totalled TD 8,756m. at the end of 2006, increasing to TD 9,638m. at the end of 2007; by the end of 2008 they had risen further, to TD 11,742m. The level of reserves rose to TD 14,932m. in 2009, and then again, to TD 17,978m., in 2010. In 2011 reserves were estimated by the EIU to have dropped by as much as TD 1,500m., as export earnings declined and the economy contracted amid the political upheaval; however, in the first half of 2012 reserves were anticipated to have recovered fairly strongly. In June 2013 an EIU report estimated that foreign reserves had fallen to under US $7,000m. (about TD 11,475m.), less than 100 days of import cover, but considered that the intended *sukuk* should ensure sufficient cover. The IMF noted in its May 2014 assessment that this and other credit lines had kept BCT reserves above three months' import cover. The BCT reported that Tunisia's total international reserves were TD 14,255m. in June 2015, down slightly on the previous reporting period but markedly up on two years earlier. By January 2016 the figure for gross international reserves was TD 14,256m. However, by June 2016 international reserves had declined more markedly, to TD 13,046m., although they had picked up slightly from the April total of TD 13,012m. International reserves totalled TD 13,117m. at the end of 2016. The country's gross international reserves represented over 100 days of import cover. In May 2019 the BCT reported that Tunisia's foreign currency assets totalled TD 13,551m., representing just over two months of import cover. Foreign assets (international reserves, consisting of central bank assets only) at the end of 2019 had risen markedly, to TD 20,830m., partly as a result of the securing of foreign financing, including under the IMF's SBA. In its Article IV report of February 2021, the IMF estimated that at the end of 2020 Tunisia's foreign assets stood at TD 24,561m., equivalent to six months of import cover (although this was based only on the estimated import bill for 2020). This increase followed the acquisition of foreign loans and aid as a result of the COVID-19 crisis (see *Introduction*).

According to Fitch's credit rating assessment in July 2021, Tunisia's foreign exchange reserves amounted to TD 24,500m. in June, representing a sharp fall from the agency's estimate of TD 26,118m. at the end of 2020 (both figures were presumably based on total external currency holdings and not just the majority that are held in the BCT). This marked decline in foreign assets, owing to liquidity pressures without external funding, compounded a sense that Tunisia would have no choice but to rely on an already large and relatively squeezed level of domestic debt financing (in turn further squeezing out private borrowing), unless a major overhaul of economic policy that enjoyed broad political support was forthcoming. In February 2022 the BCT stated that foreign assets totalled

TD 25,248m., a modest increase from TD 25,041m. at the end of 2021; however, the latter was strongly up on TD 22,206m. at the end of November 2021. This suggested that foreign reserves had continued to fluctuate, but from the end of December 2021 through to the end of February 2022 they appeared to have been on an upward trajectory. Reflecting a slight easing of fiscal pressure, at the end of 2021 foreign reserves had fallen to TD 23,633m., according to the BCT. However, ongoing financing issues reflected by current account and fiscal deficits, even if they ease as expected in 2023–24, prompted Fitch to warn in June 2023 that the Government drawing on foreign reserves to plug the financing gap was a distinct possibility.

The political upheaval from mid-2021, when President Saïed dismissed Prime Minister Hichem Mechichi, suspended parliament and assumed extraordinary powers (see History), cast Tunisia's ability to attract fresh aid from Western countries in some doubt. In June the USA had pledged nearly US $500m. for infrastructure projects (an area in which the IMF had urged the Tunisian Government to rein in spending). It was reported in the British magazine *The Economist* in August that since Tunisia's uprising in 2011, the USA and EU together had provided over $3,000m. in grants, putting Tunisia ahead of other Arab countries in terms of the disbursement of Western aid. This figure was equivalent to about 3% of Tunisian GDP in 2020, compared with about 1% in the case of Egypt and Morocco. It was not clear whether this level of Western support would continue, although Saudi Arabia and the UAE, which both backed President Saïed's assumption of autocratic powers (as this reduced the influence of moderately Islamist forces in Tunisia), were discussing with Tunisia how they might help to offset budgetary and debt pressures.

Statistical Survey

Source (unless otherwise stated): Institut National de la Statistique, 70 rue al-Cham, BP 265, 1002 Tunis; tel. (71) 891-002; fax (71) 792-559; e-mail ins@ins.tn; internet www.ins.tn.

Area and Population

AREA, POPULATION AND DENSITY

Area (sq km)	
Land	154,530
Inland waters	9,080
Total	163,610*
Population (census results)	
28 April 2004	9,910,872
23 April 2014	
Males	5,472,249
Females	5,510,227
Total	10,982,476
Population (official projections at 1 July)	
2021	11,981,822
2022	12,106,152
2023	12,224,364
Density (per sq km) at 1 July 2023	79.1†

* 63,170 sq miles.
† Land area only.

POPULATION BY AGE AND SEX
('000 persons, official projections at 1 July 2023)

	Males	Females	Total
0–14 years	1,630.4	1,505.3	3,135.7
15–64 years	3,819.1	4,037.9	7,857.0
65 years and over	590.3	641.3	1,231.7
Total	6,039.9	6,184.5	12,224.4

Note: Totals may not be equal to the sum of components, owing to rounding.

GOVERNORATES
(official estimates at 1 January 2022)

	Area (sq km)*	Population ('000)	Density (per sq km)
Ariana	498	669.4	1,344.2
Béja	3,558	308.3	86.6
Ben Arous	761	717.5	942.8
Bizerte	3,685	598.2	162.3
Gabès	7,175	405.5	56.5
Gafsa	8,990	354.6	39.4
Jendouba	3,102	404.9	130.5
Kairouan	6,712	600.3	89.4
Kasserine	8,066	464.1	57.5
Kébili	22,084	170.8	7.7
Le Kef	4,965	247.4	49.8
Mahdia	2,966	446.5	150.5
Manouba	1,060	424.1	400.1
Médenine	8,588	520.1	60.6
Monastir	1,019	607.8	596.5
—continued			
Nabeul	2,788	868.8	311.6
Sidi Bouzid	6,994	458.2	65.5
Siliana	4,631	228.8	49.4
Sousse	2,621	749.7	286.0
Sfax	7,545	1,024.6	135.8
Tataouine	38,889	151.8	3.9
Tozeur	4,719	115.9	24.6
Tunis	346	1,075.8	3,109.2
Zaghouan	2,768	190.4	68.8
Total	154,530	11,803.6	76.4

* Land area only.

PRINCIPAL TOWNS
(population at 2014 census)

Tunis (capital)	638,845	Gabès	130,984
Sfax (Safaqis)	272,801	Soukra	129,693
Sousse	221,530	Ariana	114,486
Ettadhamen	142,953	El Mourouj	104,586
Kairouan (Qairawan)	139,070	Gafsa	95,242
Bizerta (Bizerte)	136,917		

Mid-2023 (incl. suburbs, UN projections): Tunis (capital) 2,475,446; Sfax (Safaqis) 650,405 (Source: UN, *World Urbanization Prospects: The 2018 Revision*.

BIRTHS, MARRIAGES AND DEATHS

	Registered live births		Registered marriages		Registered deaths	
	Number	Rate (per 1,000)	Number	Rate (per 1,000)	Number	Rate (per 1,000)
2017	208,000	18.2	95,336	16.7	68,846	6.0
2018	202,694	17.5	92,861	16.1	67,464	5.9
2019	195,345	16.7	82,944	14.2	71,533	6.1
2020	172,794	14.6	65,198	n.a.	75,058	6.3
2021	159,884	13.5	76,871	n.a.	100,227	8.5

Life expectancy (years at birth): 73.8 (males 70.7; females 77.1) in 2021 (Source: World Bank, World Development Indicators database).

TUNISIA

ECONOMICALLY ACTIVE POPULATION
(labour force survey, '000 persons aged 15 years and over, July–September)

	2018	2019	2020
Agriculture, forestry and fishing	497.5	483.2	510.4
Manufacturing	654.9	644.9	638.8
Electricity, gas and water*	38.4	43.3	35.3
Construction	494.0	510.3	492.3
Trade	456.9	441.3	448.1
Hotels and restaurants	145.5	158.9	128.0
Transport and communications	193.0	197.8	184.5
Financial intermediation	29.9	36.7	36.8
Real estate, renting and business activities	182.0	190.9	190.3
Public administration, education and health	660.4	664.8	670.8
Other community, social and personal services	148.2	157.9	155.7
Sub-total	3,500.7	3,530.1	3,490.9
Activities not adequately defined	2.0	13.5	20.7
Total employed	3,502.7	3,543.6	3,511.6
Unemployed	642.8	628.3	676.6
Total labour force	4,145.5	4,171.9	4,188.2
Males	2,949.2	2,965.7	2,984.0
Females	1,196.3	1,206.2	1,204.2

* Including mining and quarrying.

Note: Totals may not be equal to the sum of components, owing to rounding.

Health and Welfare

KEY INDICATORS

Total fertility rate (children per woman, 2021)	2.1
Under-5 mortality rate (per 1,000 live births, 2021)	16.3
HIV/AIDS (% of persons aged 15–49, 2021)	<0.1
COVID-19: Cumulative confirmed deaths (per 100,000 persons at 30 June 2023)	238.1
COVID-19: Fully vaccinated population (% of total population at 20 June 2023)	51.8
Physicians (per 1,000 head, 2017)	1.3
Hospital beds (per 1,000 head, 2017)	2.2
Domestic heath expenditure (2020): US $ per head (PPP)	399.9
Domestic heath expenditure (2020): % of GDP	3.7
Domestic heath expenditure (2020): public (% of total current health expenditure)	58.7
Access to improved water resources (% of persons, 2020)	98
Access to improved sanitation facilities (% of persons, 2020)	97
Total carbon dioxide emissions ('000 metric tons, 2019)	29,908
Carbon dioxide emissions per head (metric tons, 2019)	2.5
Human Development Index (2021): ranking	97
Human Development Index (2021): value	0.731

Note: For data on COVID-19 vaccinations, 'fully vaccinated' denotes receipt of all doses specified by approved vaccination regime (Sources: Johns Hopkins University and Our World in Data). Data on health expenditure refer to current general government expenditure in each case. For more information on sources and further definitions for all indicators, see Health and Welfare Statistics: Sources and Definitions section (europaworld.com/credits).

Agriculture

PRINCIPAL CROPS
('000 metric tons)

	2019	2020	2021
Almonds, with shell	75.0	62.0	75.0
Anise, badian, fennel, coriander*	11.1	11.1	11.2
Apples	116.0	153.0	155.0
Apricots	36.0	38.0	38.0
Artichokes	21.0	31.0	28.0
Barley	912.0	466.0	430.1
Broad beans, dry	88.0	58.0	76.0
Cabbages and other brassicas*	30.1	30.2	30.2
Cantaloupes and other melons*	105.5	106.3	105.8
Carrots and turnips*	212.5	212.2	212.9
Chillies and peppers, green	435.0	420.0	430.0
Cucumbers and gherkins*	70.0	70.3	70.1
Dates	289.0	332.0	345.0
Figs	27.0	19.6	20.0
Garlic*	24.8	24.8	24.9
Grapefruit and pomelos*	102.0	102.9	102.3
Grapes	148.0	150.0	150.0
Lemons and limes	54.3	55.0	55.0
Lettuce and chicory*	74.8	75.0	75.2
Olives	700.0	2,000.0	700.0
Onions, dry*	190.5	193.1	196.5
Onions and shallots, green*	287.1	293.9	299.5
Oranges	440.0	366.0	410.0
Peaches and nectarines	140.0	147.0	150.0
Peas, green*	52.9	53.7	53.5
Potatoes	435.0	450.0	450.0
Pumpkins, squash and gourds*	85.9	85.9	86.3
Sugar beet*	87.4	86.6	86.0
Tangerines, mandarins, etc.	84.7	66.8	79.3
Tomatoes	1,534.0	1,423.0	1,416.0
Watermelons	491.0	450.0	475.0
Wheat	1,455.0	1,042.0	1,193.0

* FAO estimates.

Aggregate production ('000 metric tons, may include official, semi-official or estimated data): Total cereals 2,426.9 in 2019, 1,564.9 in 2020, 1,679.3 in 2021; Total fruit (primary) 2,424.2 in 2019, 2,373.9 in 2020, 2,478.6 in 2021; Total oilcrops 715.4 in 2019, 2,015.3 in 2020, 715.3 in 2021; Total pulses 133.0 in 2019, 100.5 in 2020, 120.4 in 2021; Total roots and tubers 435.0 in 2019, 450.0 in 2020, 450.0 in 2021; Total treenuts 78.2 in 2019, 65.1 in 2020, 78.2 in 2021; Total vegetables (primary) 3,235.1 in 2019, 3,128.0 in 2020, 3,137.9 in 2021.

Source: FAO.

LIVESTOCK
('000 head, year ending September, FAO estimates)

	2019	2020	2021
Asses	242.7	242.9	243.1
Camels	237.7	237.9	238.0
Cattle	639.9	634.5	630.4
Chickens	96,087	97,648	99,209
Goats	1,144.9	1,121.3	1,097.9
Sheep	6,397.0	6,320.1	6,243.2
Turkeys	12,198	12,717	13,225

Source: FAO.

TUNISIA

LIVESTOCK PRODUCTS
('000 metric tons)

	2019	2020	2021
Cattle hides, fresh*	4.9	5.4	5.9
Cattle meat	44.7	49.4	53.5
Cattle offals, edible*	6.7	7.4	8.0
Cows' milk*	1,348.0	1,379.0	1,405.0
Chicken meat	144.8	144.0	150.3
Goat meat	9.6	10.2	10.8
Goats' milk*	11.2	11.1	11.0
Sheep meat	54.9	55.7	56.4
Sheep offals, edible*	8.3	8.4	8.5
Sheep's (Ewes') milk*	22.0	21.0	25.0
Sheepskins, fresh*	10.1	10.2	10.4
Turkey meat*	82.4	85.5	88.7
Hen eggs	102.0	103.8	n.a.
Honey (natural)*	3.7	3.6	3.7
Wool, greasy*	9.7	9.7	9.8

*FAO estimates.
Source: FAO.

Forestry

ROUNDWOOD REMOVALS
('000 cu m, excl. bark, FAO estimates)

	2011	2012	2013
Sawlogs, veneer logs and logs for sleepers	25	41	86
Pulpwood	75	55	100
Other industrial wood	118	118	118
Fuel wood	2,188	3,569	3,610
Total	2,406	3,783	3,914

2014–21: Production assumed to be unchanged from 2013.
Source: FAO.

SAWNWOOD PRODUCTION
('000 cu m, incl. sleepers, FAO estimates)

	2019	2020	2021
Coniferous (softwood)	24.6	24.3	24.3
Broadleaved (hardwood)	2.0	—	—
Total	26.6	24.3	24.3

Source: FAO.

Fishing

('000 metric tons, live weight)

	2019	2020	2021
Capture*	131.0	121.8	124.2
Mullets*	13.0	12.4	12.8
Common pandora*	5.2	5.0	5.1
Jack and horse mackerels*	6.2	5.9	6.1
Sardinellas*	14.7	14.0	14.4
European pilchard*	18.8	17.9	18.4
European anchovy*	2.6	2.5	2.6
Little tunny	6.2	4.0	2.9
Atlantic mackerel*	3.4	3.3	3.4
Common cuttlefish*	5.6	5.3	5.4
Aquaculture	22.7	23.4	26.0
Gilthead seabream	18.0	15.6	17.8
Total catch (incl. others)*	153.7	145.2	150.2

*FAO estimates.
Source: FAO.

Mining

('000 metric tons unless otherwise indicated)

	2016	2017	2018
Crude petroleum*†	2,506	2,117	2,048
Natural gas (million cu m)†	2,400	2,200	2,200
Iron ore: gross weight	285	240	300†
Iron ore: metal content	178	150	188†
Phosphate rock‡	3,664	4,422	3,341
Salt (marine)†	1,600	1,600	1,580
Gypsum (crude)	850	850†	900†

* Source: Energy Institute, *Statistical Review of World Energy*.
† Estimate(s).
‡ Figures refer to gross weight. The estimated phosphoric acid content (in '000 metric tons) was: 1,060 in 2016 (estimate); 1,282 in 2017; 1,000 in 2018 (estimate).

Crude petroleum: 1,737 in 2020; 2,121 in 2021; 1,842 in 2022 (Source: Energy Institute, *Statistical Review of World Energy*).

Source (unless otherwise indicated): US Geological Survey.

Industry

SELECTED PRODUCTS
('000 metric tons)

	2016	2017	2018
Superphosphates	385	301	246
Cement	9,000	8,000	7,800
Crude steel	92	50	83
Quicklime	206	189	149
Motor spirit (gasoline)	29	21	23
Gas-diesel (distillate fuel) oils	439	314	407
Residual fuel oils (mazout)	409	327	338
Electrical energy (million kWh)	19,808	20,589	21,012

Electrical energy (million kWh): 22,140 in 2019, 21,633 in 2020.
Gas-diesel (distillate fuel) oils: 41 in 2019, 421 in 2020.
Residual fuel oils (mazout): 52 in 2019, 394 in 2020.
Motor spirit (gasoline): 49 in 2020.

Sources: US Geological Survey; UN Energy Statistics Database.

Finance

CURRENCY AND EXCHANGE RATES

Monetary Units
1,000 millimes = 1 Tunisian dinar (TD).

Sterling, Dollar and Euro Equivalents (31 May 2023)
£1 sterling = 3.857 dinars;
US $1 = 3.120 dinars;
€1 = 3.333 dinars;
100 Tunisian dinars = £25.92 = $32.05 = €30.00.

Average Exchange Rate (dinars per US $)
2020   2.8124
2021   2.7945
2022   3.1036

TUNISIA

Statistical Survey

CENTRAL GOVERNMENT BUDGET
(million dinars)*

Revenue†	2020	2021	2022
Tax revenue	27,147.0	30,404.8	35,449.4
Direct taxes	12,608.6	12,665.6	14,359.2
Trade taxes	2,254.4	2,460.4	2,971.4
Value added tax	513.2	641.7	809.3
Excise	11,044.0	13,071.9	15,043.0
Other taxes	726.8	1,565.2	2,266.5
Non-tax revenue	2,567.9	3,098.2	4,165.5
Total	29,714.9	33,503.0	39,614.9

Expenditure‡	2020	2021	2022
Current expenditure	33,686.9	34,761.1	42,353.9
Wages and salaries	19,200.0	20,175.4	21,123.5
Goods and services	2,262.0	1,995.7	1,932.3
Interest payments	3,736.2	3,701.3	4,661.8
Transfers and subsidies	8,488.0	8,888.7	14,636.3
Non-allocated	0.7	0.0	0.0
Capital expenditure	7,207.3	8,680.1	8,194.2
Total	40,894.2	43,441.2	50,548.1

* Figures include special funds, but exclude the social security system.
† Excluding grants from abroad and receipts from privatization (million dinars): 779.2 in 2020; 44.3 in 2021; 1,378.0 in 2022.
‡ Excluding net lending (million dinars): 386.2 in 2020; 276.5 in 2021; −38.2 in 2022.

Source: Ministry of Finance, Tunis.

CENTRAL BANK RESERVES
(US $ million at 31 December)

	2020	2021	2022
Gold (national valuation)	252.1	242.6	241.6
IMF special drawing rights	15.5	55.8	48.4
Reserve position in IMF	175.4	170.4	162.1
Foreign exchange	9,203.7	8,218.9	7,485.2
Total	9,646.7	8,687.7	7,937.3

Source: IMF, *International Financial Statistics*.

MONEY SUPPLY
(million dinars at 31 December)

	2020	2021	2022
Currency outside depository corporations	15,159	16,588	18,176
Transferable deposits	23,240	25,612	27,030
Other deposits	38,651	42,223	46,170
Securities other than shares	6,815	7,098	8,558
Broad money	83,865	91,521	99,934

Source: IMF, *International Financial Statistics*.

COST OF LIVING
(Consumer Price Index; base: 2015 = 100)

	2020	2021	2022
Food	130.2	138.4	153.5
Housing, water, gas, electricity and other fuels	127.1	133.5	141.6
Clothing	143.9	154.7	169.6
All items (incl. others)	132.0	139.6	151.1

NATIONAL ACCOUNTS
(million dinars at current prices)

Expenditure on the Gross Domestic Product

	2019	2020	2021
Government final consumption expenditure	23,138.5	25,854.7	27,369.6
Private final consumption expenditure	88,306.7	88,526.9	96,360.5
Gross fixed capital formation	23,898.7	18,953.5	20,838.8
Change in inventories	453.4	−3,723.4	−924.5
Total domestic expenditure	135,797.3	129,611.7	143,644.4
Exports of goods and services	56,504.8	45,401.0	54,959.6
Less Imports of goods and services	69,332.9	55,379.1	68,138.0
GDP in purchasers' values	122,969.2	119,633.6	130,466.1
GDP at constant 2015 prices	96,787.5	88,252.9	92,140.8

2022: GDP at constant 2015 prices 94,387.1.

Gross Domestic Product by Economic Activity

	2020	2021	2022
Agriculture and fishing	12,418.3	13,227.4	14,148.5
Mining (excluding hydrocarbons)	416.9	549.2	716.4
Manufacturing (excluding hydrocarbons)	16,382.4	18,809.7	21,678.8
Hydrocarbons, electricity and water	4,287.8	5,557.7	6,066.7
Construction and public works	4,678.9	5,243.7	5,042.7
Transport and telecommunications	8,275.5	9,211.0	10,651.4
Hotels and restaurants	3,053.2	3,716.3	4,912.1
Trade	14,004.4	15,395.7	17,028.7
Other market services	11,544.6	12,261.9	13,619.7
Non-market services	35,123.1	37,875.1	40,615.6
Gross value added at factor cost	110,185.2	121,847.4	134,480.5
Indirect taxes, *less* subsidies	9,448.5	8,618.4	9,413.0
GDP in purchasers' values	119,633.6	130,466.1	143,893.5

Source: Central Bank of Tunisia, Tunis.

BALANCE OF PAYMENTS
(US $ million)

	2019	2020	2021
Exports of goods	15,001	13,834	16,810
Imports of goods	−20,499	−17,370	−21,476
Balance on goods	−5,498	−3,535	−4,665
Exports of services	4,174	2,183	2,933
Imports of services	−3,047	−2,234	−2,793
Balance on goods and services	−4,372	−3,586	−4,526
Primary income received	547	595	686
Primary income paid	−1,463	−1,670	−1,780
Balance on goods, services and primary income	−5,288	−4,661	−5,620
Secondary income received	1,935	2,150	2,872
Secondary income paid	−38	−23	−33
Current balance	−3,391	−2,533	−2,781
Capital account (net)	137	365	221
Direct investment liabilities	810	592	533
Portfolio investment liabilities	13	−31	−33
Other investment assets	−162	188	−179
Other investment liabilities	3,970	1,604	1,954
Net errors and omissions	533	610	489
Reserves and related items	1,910	795	204

Source: IMF, *International Financial Statistics*.

External Trade

PRINCIPAL COMMODITIES
(million dinars)

Imports c.i.f.	2020	2021	2022
Agricultural products	7,006.6	7,777.5	10,803.2
Energy, fuels and lubricants	6,391.8	8,266.0	15,134.9
Textiles	6,165.9	7,141.0	9,072.3
Mechanical and electrical machinery and equipment	21,022.8	26,161.4	30,047.4
Miscellaneous manufacturing products	10,253.0	12,057.7	15,375.2
Total (incl. others)	51,536.2	62,864.9	82,789.2

Exports f.o.b.	2020	2021	2022
Agricultural products	5,275.0	5,069.4	6,799.7
Energy, fuels and lubricants	3,450.8	5,354.3	8,169.1
Textiles	8,061.6	9,226.4	11,167.6
Mechanical and electrical machinery and equipment	17,563.1	21,407.7	24,509.7
Miscellaneous manufacturing products	4,355.4	5,596.2	6,927.1
Total (incl. others)	38,705.9	46,654.0	57,573.2

PRINCIPAL TRADING PARTNERS
(million dinars)

Imports c.i.f.	2020	2021	2022
Algeria	2,548.5	2,215.5	4,929.5
Belgium	852.7	980.8	970.5
Brazil	785.9	843.1	1,159.3
China, People's Republic	5,516.9	6,535.4	8,665.5
Egypt	703.0	754.1	977.8
France (incl. Monaco)	6,589.1	7,181.5	8,320.1
Germany	3,562.5	4,109.8	4,492.8
India	801.4	1,181.0	1,651.0
Italy	7,319.5	8,477.4	1,981.2
Japan	475.1	507.8	570.6
Korea, Republic	420.0	894.1	632.8
Netherlands	580.7	706.7	692.0
Russian Federation	1,066.2	1,498.3	2,810.4
Saudi Arabia	581.6	1,309.7	2,034.1
Spain	2,160.6	2,638.6	3,353.5
Türkiye	2,588.2	3,396.4	5,071.1
United Kingdom	600.0	660.7	682.0
USA	1,489.6	1,575.0	2,396.4
Total (incl. others)	51,536.2	62,864.9	82,789.2

Exports f.o.b.	2020	2021	2022
Algeria	829.0	661.2	1,021.1
Belgium	779.5	870.4	1,055.7
France (incl. Monaco)	10,105.0	11,182.7	12,752.8
Germany	4,779.5	5,969.8	7,436.8
Italy	6,521.1	8,570.7	9,679.1
Libya	1,257.8	1,804.3	2,463.0
Morocco	568.8	708.3	850.6
Netherlands	880.6	1,208.3	1,276.4
Poland	428.8	445.8	597.4
Spain	2,268.8	1,897.2	2,581.2
Switzerland (incl. Liechtenstein)	348.3	565.1	760.4
Türkiye	447.6	740.5	1,112.2
United Kingdom	774.0	760.6	1,422.8
USA	823.6	1,065.4	1,352.5
Total (incl. others)	38,705.9	46,654.2	57,573.2

Transport

RAILWAYS
(traffic)

	2020	2021	2022
Passengers carried ('000)	20,672	22,037	33,098
Passenger-km (million)	581	633	754
Freight carried ('000 metric tons)	21,570	25,077	24,316
Freight net ton-km (million)	335	412	407

SHIPPING

Flag Registered Fleet
(at 31 December)

	2020	2021	2022
Number of vessels	86	86	89
Total displacement ('000 grt)	336.6	336.6	339.2

Source: Lloyd's List Intelligence (www.bit.ly/LLintelligence).

International Seaborne Freight Traffic
('000 metric tons)

	2018	2019	2020
Goods loaded*	8,400	7,306	7,148
Goods unloaded	16,587	15,261	15,815

* Excluding Algerian crude petroleum loaded at La Skhirra.

CIVIL AVIATION
(traffic on scheduled services)

	2013	2014	2015
Kilometres flown (million)	59	45	47
Passengers carried ('000)	4,649	4,629	3,496
Passenger-km (million)	5,960	6,055	4,869
Total ton-km (million)	15	13	10

Source: UN, *Statistical Yearbook*.

2021 (domestic and international): Departures 17,557; Passengers carried 1.7m.; Freight carried 6m. ton-km (Source: World Bank, World Development Indicators database).

Tourism

FOREIGN TOURIST ARRIVALS BY NATIONALITY
('000)

	2019	2020	2021
Algeria	2,935.0	401.3	30.4
China, People's Republic	29.0	4.3	1.2
Czech Republic	107.6	19.0	12.7
France	890.5	261.5	302.5
Germany	275.9	29.0	39.9
Italy	124.1	26.9	29.1
Libya	1,956.1	533.8	868.2
Morocco	65.7	15.5	11.2
Poland	106.8	16.5	35.4
Russian Federation	633.3	2.3	85.0
United Kingdom	204.1	11.6	7.9
Total (incl. others)	9,429.0	2,012.4	2,475.4

Receipts from tourism (US $ million, excl. passenger transport): 852 in 2020; 1,025 in 2021 (provisional); 1,657 in 2022 (provisional).

Source: World Tourism Organization.

TUNISIA

Communications Media

	2019	2020	2021
Telephones ('000 main lines in use)	1,454.2	1,533.3	1,659.1
Mobile telephone subscriptions ('000)	14,771.0	14,852.9	15,644.7
Broadband subscriptions, fixed ('000)	1,193.9	1,334.7	1,496.9
Broadband subscriptions, mobile ('000)	9,097.5	8,988.0	9,965.4
Internet users (% of population)	66.7	72.8	79.0

Source: International Telecommunication Union.

Education

(2020/21 unless otherwise indicated)

	Institutions	Teachers	Students
Primary (public)			
1st cycle	4,582	68,871	1,303,758
2nd cycle	1,448	73,474	1,072,483
Secondary (public)			
Higher	198*	22,086	232,614

* 2012/13 figure.

Pupil-teacher ratio (qualified teaching staff, primary education, UNESCO estimate): 16.8 in 2019/20 (Source: UNESCO Institute for Statistics).

Adult literacy rate (UNESCO estimates): 82.7% (males 89.1%; females 76.5%) in 2021 (Source: UNESCO Institute for Statistics).

Directory

The Constitution

Having dismissed the Prime Minister and his Government and suspended the Assembly of the Representatives of the People (ARP) on 25 July 2021, on 22 September President Kaïs Saïed partially suspended the 2014 Constitution, granting himself almost unlimited power to rule by decree. On 13 December 2021 he announced a roadmap to normal governance, which included a national referendum on a revised constitution in July 2022 and parliamentary elections in December 2022. On 5 February 2022 Saïed dissolved the Supreme Judicial Council (Conseil Supérieur de la Magistrature—CSM), the highest judicial body, which was responsible for the independence of the judiciary. On 13 February he established by decree a new Provisional Supreme Judicial Council (Conseil Supérieur Provisoire de la Magistrature—CSPM). The CSPM, the decisions of which he was empowered to veto or overturn, was sworn in on 7 March. The CSM asserted that the President's action was unconstitutional. On 30 March Saïed formally dissolved the ARP.

In May 2022 President Saïed appointed a committee, headed by Sadeq Belaid, to draw up proposals for a redrafting of the 2014 Constitution. On 30 June 2022 the office of the President published the text of the draft charter, which provided for near-absolute power to be accorded to the President. Belaid publicly distanced himself from the draft charter on 3 July, stating that its provisions differed substantively from those submitted by his committee.

Nevertheless, at the referendum, held as scheduled on 25 July 2022, the draft Constitution was overwhelmingly endorsed by the electorate, with some 94.6% of participants voting affirmatively, according to results released by the Independent High Authority for Elections (Instance Supérieure Indépendante pour les Elections) in mid-August. Turnout was low, at just 30.5% of the registered electorate. Despite widespread international criticism levelled at the purportedly undemocratic nature of the process of drafting the new charter, as well as of the provisions of the charter itself, the Constitution was formally promulgated on 17 August 2022, with Saïed to continue to rule by decree pending the staging of parliamentary elections in December.

The new Constitution provided for a formalized shift from the presidential-parliamentary shared system of governance in place prior to July 2021, to an executive presidency in which the head of state held near-absolute power. The President was to be responsible for appointing government ministers, initiating major domestic and foreign affairs policy, drafting the annual state budget and introducing draft legislation. An elected bicameral parliament was to serve alongside the President, comprising a newly reconstituted ARP (reduced from 217 to 161 members) and a new upper chamber, the National Council of Regions and Districts, whose members would be appointed by directly elected regional councils—providing for an effective decentralization of power. However, parliament was to be accorded limited legislative powers. The President would have the right to dissolve parliament, while parliament would have no constitutional basis for removing the President. Parliamentary deputies were to hold office for a five-year term.

The President, who would also be head of the armed forces, would be eligible to serve two five-year terms; however, this could be extended if it was felt there was 'imminent danger to the state'. Moreover, the President could unilaterally suspend parliament in the event of a national security emergency. Parliament could in theory remove a government that it deemed to be unfit for office; however, this would require a two-thirds' majority, which, given the concentration of power around the office of the President, was likely to prove extremely difficult to secure.

Judges were to be appointed (and could be dismissed) by direct presidential order. The Supreme Judicial Council was to continue to oversee the judiciary; however, no provisions were included to guarantee the Council's independence, nor were details regarding its composition made clear. A constitutional court, provided for under the terms of the 2014 charter but not yet established owing to protracted disagreement over the appointment of the court's members, was to comprise nine judges, to be nominated by direct presidential order. A provision in the 2014 charter that had proscribed the trial of civilians before military courts was removed.

Articles 1 and 2 of the new Constitution were more secular than in the 2014 charter, with previous explicit references to Tunisia as an Islamic and civilian state removed and Tunisia now simply described as a 'free, independent and sovereign state'. However, Article 5 of the new charter stated that Tunisia 'belongs to the Islamic Ummah' (the worldwide Muslim community), and that Tunisia was required to seek to 'achieve the objectives of Islam in preserving [people's] souls, money, religion, and liberty', which critics contended could be used as a constitutional mandate to undermine human rights or to discriminate against members of other religious groups.

As with the 2014 charter, the new Constitution guaranteed freedom of speech and belief, and of peaceful assembly and demonstration, as well as of the right to form trade unions, including the right to strike (although members of the military, judiciary, internal security forces and customs were excluded from this). The state was to promote gender equality and to seek to eliminate violence against women. Persons with disabilities were to be protected from discrimination and the state was to take measures to ensure their full integration into society. However, references to the principle of universal human rights were removed, while the freedom to perform religious rites would be protected 'unless they disturb public security'. In addition, international rights groups noted with concern the sweeping emergency powers granted to the President, and the lack of any oversight mechanism to ensure that human rights and the rule of law were preserved during a state of emergency.

The Government

HEAD OF STATE

President: Kaïs Saïed (took office 23 October 2019).

COUNCIL OF MINISTERS
(September 2023)

Prime Minister: Ahmed Hachani.
Minister of Defence: Imed Memmiche.
Minister of Justice: Leila Jaffel.
Minister of the Interior: Kamal Feki.
Minister of Foreign Affairs, Migration and Tunisians Abroad: Nabil Ammar.
Minister of Religious Affairs: Brahim Chaïbi.
Minister of Finance: Sihem Boughdiri Nemsia.

Minister of Economy and Planning: SAMIR SAÏED.
Minister of Communication Technologies: NIZAR BEN NEJI.
Minister of Transport: RABII MAJIDI.
Minister of the Environment: LEÏLA CHIKHAOUI.
Minister of Public Works and Housing: SARRA ZAAFRANI ZENZERI.
Minister of Industry, Mines and Energy: NEILA NOUIRA GONJI.
Minister of Trade and Export Development: KALTHOUM BEN REJEB.
Minister of Culture: HAYET KETAT GUERMAZI.
Minister of Tourism: MOHAMED MOEZ BELHASSINE.
Minister of Education: MOHAMED ALI BOUGHDIRI.
Minister of Higher Education and Scientific Research: MONCEF BOUKTHIR.
Minister of Social Affairs: MALEK EZZAHI.
Minister of Family, Women, Children and the Elderly: AMEL BELHAJ MOUSSA.
Minister of Employment and Vocational Training: (vacant).
Minister of Agriculture, Water Resources and Fisheries: ABDELMONEM BELATI.
Minister of Youth and Sports: KAMEL DEGUICHE.
Minister of Health: ALI MRABET.
Minister of State Properties and Real Estate Affairs: MOHAMED REKIK.

There was also one Secretary of State.

MINISTRIES

Office of the President: Palais de Carthage, 2016 Carthage; tel. (71) 242-038; e-mail contact@carthage.tn; internet www.carthage.tn.

Office of the Prime Minister: pl. du Gouvernement, La Kasbah, 1030 Tunis; tel. (71) 565-400; e-mail boc@pm.gov.tn; internet www.pm.gov.tn.

Ministry of Agriculture, Water Resources and Fisheries: 30 rue Alain Savary, 1002 Tunis; tel. (71) 786-833; fax (71) 780-391; e-mail mag@ministeres.tn; internet www.agriculture.tn.

Ministry of Communication Technologies: 88 Ave Mohamed V, 3 bis rue d'Angleterre, Belvedere, 1002 Tunis; tel. (70) 244-688; fax (70) 244-699; internet www.mtcen.gov.tn.

Ministry of Culture: 8 rue du 2 Mars 1934, La Kasbah, 1002 Tunis; tel. (71) 563-006; fax (71) 563-816; internet www.culture.gov.tn.

Ministry of Economy and Planning: Tunis.

Ministry of Education: blvd Bab Benet, 1030 Tunis; tel. (71) 568-768; e-mail ministere@minedu.edunet.tn; internet www.education.gov.tn.

Ministry of Employment and Vocational Training: Ouled Hafouz St, 1002 Tunis; tel. (71) 798–196; fax (71) 794–615; e-mail webmaster@mfpe.gov.tn; internet www.mfpe.gov.tn.

Ministry of the Environment: rue de développement, Cité El Khadra, 1003 Tunis; tel. (71) 243-800; fax (71) 955-360; e-mail boc@mineat.gov.tn; internet www.environnement.gov.tn.

Ministry of Family, Women, Children and the Elderly: 2 rue d'Alger, 1001 Tunis; tel. (71) 252-514; fax (71) 349-900; e-mail boc@maffepa.gov.tn; internet www.femmes.gov.tn.

Ministry of Finance: pl. du Gouvernement, La Kasbah, 1008 Tunis; tel. (71) 561-782; fax (71) 573-527; e-mail communication@finances.tn; internet www.finances.gov.tn.

Ministry of Foreign Affairs, Migration and Tunisians Abroad: ave de la Ligue des états arabes, 1030 Tunis; tel. (71) 847-500; fax (71) 785-025; e-mail email.dct@diplomatie.gov.tn; internet www.diplomatie.gov.tn.

Ministry of Health: Bab Saâdoun, 1006 Tunis; tel. (71) 577-000; fax (71) 567-100; e-mail msp@rns.tn; internet www.santetunisie.rns.tn.

Ministry of Higher Education and Scientific Research: ave Ouled Haffouz, 1030 Tunis; tel. (71) 786-300; fax (71) 801-701; e-mail mes@mes.rnu.tn; internet www.mes.tn.

Ministry of Industry, Energy and Mines: Immeuble Beya, 40 rue 8011, Montplaisir, 1002 Tunis; tel. (71) 905-132; fax (71) 902-742; e-mail mind@ministeres.tn; internet www.tunisieindustrie.gov.tn.

Ministry of the Interior: ave Habib Bourguiba, 1000 Tunis; tel. (71) 333-000; fax (71) 340-888; internet www.interieur.gov.tn.

Ministry of Justice: 31 blvd Bab Benet, 1019 Tunis; tel. (71) 561-444; fax (71) 586-106; e-mail info@e-justice.tn; internet www.e-justice.tn.

Ministry of National Defence: blvd Bab Menara, 1008 Tunis; tel. (71) 560-244; fax (71) 561-804; e-mail defcab@defense.tn; internet www.defense.tn.

Ministry of Public Works and Housing: Ave Habib Chrita, Cité Jardins, Belvédère, 1002 Tunis; tel. (71) 842-244; fax (71) 840-495; e-mail brc@mehat.gov.tn; internet www.equipement.tn.

Ministry of Religious Affairs: 76 blvd Bab Benet, 1019 Tunis; tel. (71) 570-147; fax (71) 572-296; e-mail mar@ministeres.tn; internet www.affaires-religieuses.tn.

Ministry of Social Affairs: 27 blvd Bab Benet, 1006 Tunis; tel. (71) 150-000; e-mail mas@social.gov.tn; internet www.social.tn.

Ministry of State Properties and Real Estate Affairs: ave Mohamed V (en face de la Banque Centrale), Tunis 1000; tel. (70) 131-400; fax (71) 342-552; e-mail ministere.mdeaf@mdeaf.gov.tn; internet www.mdeaf.gov.tn.

Ministry of Tourism: 1 ave Muhammad V, 1001 Tunis; tel. (71) 341-077; fax (71) 354-223; e-mail boc@tourisme.gov.tn; internet www.tourisme.gov.tn.

Ministry of Trade and Export Development: angle ave du Ghana, rue Pierre de Coubertin et rue Hédi Nouira, Tunis 1001; tel. (71) 240-155; fax (71) 354-435; e-mail mcmr@ministeres.tn; internet www.commerce.gov.tn.

Ministry of Transport: 13 rue Borjine, Montplaisir, 1073 Tunis; tel. (71) 905-026; fax (71) 901-559; e-mail boc@mt.gov.tn; internet www.transport.tn.

Ministry of Youth and Sports: ave Med Ali Akid, Cité El Khadhra, 1003 Tunis; tel. (71) 841-433; fax (71) 800-267; e-mail mjsep@jeunesse-sport.tn; internet www.sport.tn.

President

Presidential Election, First Ballot, 15 September 2019

Candidate	Votes	%
Kaïs Saïed	620,711	18.40
Nabil Karoui	525,517	15.58
Abdelfattah Mourou	434,530	12.88
Abdelkrim Zbidi	361,864	10.73
Youssef Chahed	249,049	7.38
Ahmed Safi Saïd	239,951	7.11
Lotfi M'raihi	221,190	6.56
Seifeddine Makhlouf	147,351	4.37
Abir Moussi	135,461	4.02
Mohamed Abbou	122,287	3.63
Mohamed Moncef Marzouki	100,338	2.97
Mehdi Jomaa	61,371	1.82
Others	153,353	4.54
Total*	**3,372,973**	**100.00**

* Excluding 92,211 invalid or blank votes.

Presidential Election, Second Ballot, 13 October 2019

Candidate	Votes	%
Kaïs Saïed	2,777,931	72.71
Nabil Karoui	1,042,894	27.29
Total*	**3,820,825**	**100.00**

* Excludes 71,260 invalid or blank votes.

Legislature

On 25 July 2021 President Kaïs Saïed suspended the Assembly of the Representatives of the People (ARP) for a period of 30 days, having concurrently removed the Prime Minister and his Government from office. The Speaker of the ARP, Rachid Ghannouchi, denounced the President's actions as unconstitutional and accused him of carrying out a coup. On 26 July Ghannouchi and other deputies were prevented from entering the parliament building by the armed forces. On 13 December the President announced that the Assembly would remain suspended until 17 December 2022, when fresh legislative elections would be held. On 30 March 2022 the President dissolved the Assembly after it defied him by voting (via an online plenary session) to repeal the decrees that he had used to assume near total power.

A new Constitution was promulgated on 17 August 2022, providing for a formalized shift from the presidential-parliamentary shared system of governance in place prior to July 2021, to an executive presidency in which the head of state would hold near-absolute power. An elected bicameral parliament was to serve alongside the President, comprising a newly reconstituted ARP (reduced from 217 to 161 members) and a new upper chamber, the National Council of Regions and Districts (NCRD), whose members would be appointed by directly elected regional councils. However, parliament was to be accorded only very limited legislative powers.

At elections to the ARP held on 17 December 2022 (in which, according to new electoral legislation introduced in mid-September, candidates were elected directly rather than via party lists for a term of five years), only 21 candidates secured victory—including 10 unopposed. The official turnout was just 11.2% of the electorate, with the poll being boycotted by the majority of political parties, which denounced the vote as a sham and challenged the legitimacy of the new parliamentary lower chamber. Amid growing calls for the election process to be abandoned, a second round of voting took place on 29 January 2023 to fill a further 131 seats in the ARP; there were no candidates for the remaining nine seats. As in the first round, the turnout for the run-off poll was extremely low, again at around an estimated 11%. Although all candidates had to contest the polls as independents, a majority were affiliated to the pro-Saïed Mouvement du 25 juillet. By the time of the new ARP's official inauguration on 13 March 2023, a total of 154 seats had been filled, with only 25 female representatives among them. Indirect elections to the NCRD were to be held at a later date.

Assembly of the Representatives of the People: Palais du Bardo, 2000 Tunis; tel. (71) 510-200; fax (71) 514-608; e-mail anc@anc.tn; internet www.arp.tn.

President (Speaker): IBRAHIM BOUDERBALA.

Election Commission

Independent High Authority for Elections (Instance Supérieure Indépendante pour les Elections) (ISIE): 5 rue l'Île de Sardaigne, Les Jardins du Lac, 1053 Tunis; tel. (70) 018-555; fax (71) 190-916; e-mail contact@isie.tn; internet www.isie.tn; f. 2011; Pres. FAROUK BOUASKER.

Political Organizations

Afek Tounes: 37 rue Charles Nicole, Hay el Mahragane, 1002 Tunis; tel. (31) 400-493; e-mail contact@afektounes.tn; internet afektounes.tn; f. 2011; liberal; formed the Coordination des Forces Démocratiques coalition with Courant Démocratique, Parti Républicain and Forum Démocratique pour le Travail et les Libertés in Sept. 2021; Pres. of the Political Bureau FADHEL ABDELKEFI.

Coalition de la Dignité (Al Karama): Tunis; a coalition of Front de la Réforme, Parti de la Justice et du Développement, and Congrès pour la République; f. 2019; Pres. SEIFEDDINE MAKHLOUF.

Coalition Nationale: Tunis; f. 2018; a parliamentary bloc comprising former members of Nidaa Tounes, Machrou Tounes, Union Patriotique Libre (UPL) and independents.

Congrès pour la République (CPR): 45 rue Ali Dargouth, 1001 Tunis; tel. (71) 346-001; fax (71) 346-002; e-mail cprtunisie@yahoo.fr; internet www.cprtunisie.net; f. 2001.

Courant de l'Amour (al-Mahabab): Tunis; f. 2013; Leader MUHAMMAD HECHMI HAMDI.

Courant Démocratique: 25 rue de Marseille, Tunis; tel. (71) 255-555; fax (71) 255-552; internet attayar.tn; f. 2013; formed the Coordination des Forces Démocratiques coalition with Afek Tounes, Parti Républicain and Forum Démocratique pour le Travail et les Libertés in Sept. 2021; Sec.-Gen. NABIL HAJJI.

Ennahdha (Parti de la Renaissance): rue Elless, ave Mohamed V, Montplaisir, 1073 Tunis; tel. (71) 900-907; fax (71) 901-679; e-mail webmaster@nahdha.tn; internet www.ennahdha.tn; fmrly Mouvement de la Tendance Islamique (banned in 1981); awarded legal status in 2011; Islamist-orientated; Pres. RACHID GHANNOUCHI.

Forum Démocratique pour le Travail et les Libertés (Ettakatol—FDTL): Résidence Omar, Bloc B, 1er étage, Montplaisir, 1001 Tunis; tel. (71) 903-036; fax (71) 903-067; e-mail communication@ettakatol.org; internet www.ettakatol.org; f. 1994; formed the Coordination des Forces Démocratiques coalition with Afek Tounes, Parti Républicain and Courant Démocratique in Sept. 2021; Pres. KHELIL EZZAOUIA.

Front de Salut National (FSN): Tunis; f. 2022; an alliance of political parties opposed to President Kaïs Saïed's political reforms; mems include, inter alia, Ennahdha, Al Karama and various civil society groups; Leader AHMED NÉJIB CHEBBI.

Al Massar (Voie Démocratique et Social): 7 ave de la Liberté, Tunis; tel. (71) 349-307; e-mail secretariat.almassar@gmail.com; internet www.fb.com/AlMassar.Page.Officielle; f. 2012 by merger of Mouvement Ettajdid and Parti du Travail Tunisien; Sec.-Gen. FAOUZI CHARFI.

Mouvement Echaâb (Mouvement du Peuple): Tunis; tel. (71) 321-932; e-mail infoechaab@gmail.com; internet fb.com/echaab.tunisie; f. 2011; Sec.-Gen. ZOUHAIR MAGHZAOUI.

Nidaa Tounes (NT) (Call for Tunisia): rue du Lac de Constance, Les Berges du Lac, 1053 Tunis; tel. (71) 283-110; fax (71) 283-122; e-mail contact@nidaatounes.org; internet www.nidaatounes.org/site; f. 2012; merged with Union Patriotique Libre in Oct. 2018; Pres. SALEH AL-MUBARAKI.

Parti Destourien Libre (PDL): Tunis; tel. (71) 909-145; e-mail contact@pdl-tunisie.com; internet pdl-tunisie.com; f. 2013; Pres. ABIR MOUSSI.

Parti Républicain (al-Joumhouri): Tunis; tel. (36) 314-767; e-mail contact@aljoumhouri.org; internet fb.com/AljoumhouriOfficiel; f. 2012 by merger of fmr Parti Démocrate Progressiste, Afek Tounes and 7 others; Afek Tounes and others subsequently withdrew their participation; centrist; promotes freedom of expression and seeks to uphold democratic process; formed the Coordination des Forces Démocratiques coalition with Afek Tounes, Forum Démocratique pour le Travail et les Libertés and Courant Démocratique in Sept. 2021; Sec.-Gen. ISSAM CHEBBI.

Parti des Travailleurs Tunisiens (POT): Tunis; e-mail pcot@albadil.org; f. 1986 as Parti Communiste des Ouvriers Tunisiens; legalized 2011; name changed as above 2012; mem. of Front Populaire; Sec.-Gen. HAMMA HAMMAMI.

Qalb Tounes (QT) (Au Coeur de la Tunisie): Immeuble Chammam, 2e étage, ru du Lac d'Annecy, Tunis 1053; tel. (46) 309-409; e-mail contact@9albtounes.com; f. 2019; Leader NABIL KAROUI.

Tahia Tounes (TT) (Long Live Tunisia): Tunis; f. 2019; created by fmr mems of Nidaa Tounes to contest the 2019 elections; secular; Pres. YOUSSEF CHAHED; Sec.-Gen. SONIA BEN CHEIKH.

Diplomatic Representation

EMBASSIES IN TUNISIA

Algeria: rue du Lac d'Annecy, Les Berges du Lac, BP 75, 1053 Tunis; tel. (71) 964-682; fax (71) 961-929; e-mail ambdztn@yahoo.fr; internet www.ambdz.tn; Ambassador AZZOUZ BAALLAL.

Argentina: rue du Lac Victoria, Les Berges du Lac, BP 12, 1053 Tunis; tel. (71) 964-871; fax (71) 963-006; e-mail etune@mrecic.gov.ar; internet etune.cancilleria.gob.ar; Ambassador JOSÉ MARIA ARBILLA.

Austria: 16 rue ibn Hamdiss, BP 23, al-Menzah, 1004 Tunis; tel. (71) 239-038; fax (71) 755-427; e-mail tunis-ob@bmeia.gv.at; internet www.bmeia.gv.at/botschaft/tunis.html; Ambassador ULLA KRAUSS-NUSSBAUMER.

Bahrain: 14 ave Dinars, Les Berges du Lac 2, Almanzah Althamen, Tunis; tel. (71) 966-301; fax (71) 860-355; e-mail tunis.mission@mofa.gov.bh; internet www.mofa.gov.bh/tunis; Ambassador EBRAHIM MAHMOOD AHMED ABDULLA.

Belgium: 47 rue du 1er juin, BP 24, 1002 Tunis; tel. (71) 781-655; fax (71) 792-797; e-mail tunis@diplobel.fed.be; internet tunisia.diplomatie.belgium.be; Ambassador FRANÇOIS DUMONT.

Brazil: rue du Lac Léman, Les Berges du Lac, BP 93, 1053 Tunis; tel. (71) 965-455; fax (71) 862-462; e-mail brasemb.tunis@itamaraty.gov.br; internet www.gov.br/mre/pt-br/embaixada-tunis; Ambassador FERNANDO JOSÉ DE ABREU.

Bulgaria: 5 rue Ryhane, BP 6, Cité Mahrajène, 1082 Tunis; tel. (71) 798-962; fax (71) 791-667; e-mail embassy.tunis@mfa.bg; internet www.mfa.bg/embassies/tunisia; Ambassador VESELIN DYANKOV.

Burkina Faso: 58 ave Habib Achour, Les Berges du Lac 1, 1053 Tunis; tel. (71) 963-363; fax (71) 234-944; e-mail amba.bf.tunis@planet.tn; internet fb.com/ambassadebftunis; Chargé d'affaires a.i. SEYDOU KI.

Cameroon: 24 angle rue Hédi Chaker et Habib Thameur, Carthage Byrsa, 2016 Tunis; tel. (71) 275-752; e-mail ambacamtunis@ambacam.tn; Ambassador SAMUEL DJOBO.

Canada: rue de la Feuille d'Erable, Les Berges du Lac II, BP 48, 1053 Tunis; tel. (71) 010-200; fax (71) 010-393; e-mail tunis@international.gc.ca; internet www.canadainternational.gc.ca/tunisia-tunisie; Ambassador LORRAINE DIGUER.

China, People's Republic: 22 rue Dr Burnet, Mutuelleville, 1002 Tunis; tel. (71) 780-064; fax (71) 792-631; e-mail chinaemb_tn@mfa.gov.cn; internet tn.china-embassy.org; Ambassador WAN LI.

Congo, Democratic Republic: 3 rue d'El Menzah 1, 2037 Tunis; tel. (71) 741-725; internet ambardcongo-tunisie.com; Chargé d'affaires a.i. FRANÇOIS MANDUAKILA.

Côte d'Ivoire: 17 rue el-Mansoura, BP 21, Belvédère, 1002 Tunis; tel. (71) 755-911; fax (71) 755-901; internet www.tunisie.diplomatie.gouv.ci; Ambassador IBRAHIM SY SAVANÉ.

Cuba: 3 rue Ile de Créte, Les Jardins du Lac, 1053 Tunis; tel. (71) 197-332; fax (71) 197-333; e-mail secretunez@topnet.tn; internet misiones.minrex.gob.cu/es/tunez; Ambassador Mariem Martinez Laurel.

Czech Republic: 98 rue de Palestine, BP 53, Belvédère, 1002 Tunis; tel. (71) 781-916; fax (71) 793-228; e-mail tunis@embassy.mzv.cz; internet www.mzv.cz/tunis; Ambassador Jan Vyčítal.

Egypt: ave Mohamed V, Quartier Montplaisir, rue el-Ferdaouss, BP 191, 1002 Tunis; tel. (71) 903-223; fax (71) 904-389; e-mail egyptembassytunis@gmail.com; Ambassador Ihab Fahmy.

Equatorial Guinea: 3 rue Tertullien, Notre Dame, Tunis; tel. (71) 794-105; e-mail ambaguineetunisie@gmail.com; Ambassador Gertrudis Nsang Ndong.

Finland: Dar Nordique, rue du Lac Neuchâtel, Les Berges du Lac, BP 239, 1053 Tunis; tel. (71) 861-777; fax (71) 961-080; e-mail sanomat.tun@formin.fi; internet finlandabroad.fi/web/tun; Chargé d'affaires Teemu Sepponen.

France: 2 pl. de l'Indépendance, 1000 Tunis; tel. (31) 315-111; fax (71) 105-100; internet tn.ambafrance.org; Ambassador Anne Guéguin.

Gabon: 7 rue de l'Ile de Rhodes, Les Berges du Lac II, 1053 Tunis; tel. (71) 197-216; fax (71) 197-217; e-mail ambassadedugabonentunisie@gmail.com; internet fb.com/AmbassadeDuGabonEnTunisie; Chargé d'affaires a.i. Franck Aubame Ondzagha.

Germany: 1 impasse du Lac Windermere, Les Berges du Lac I, BP 222, 1053 Tunis; tel. (71) 143-200; fax (71) 143-299; e-mail passtermin@tuni.diplo.de; internet tunis.diplo.de; Ambassador Peter Prügel.

Greece: 6 rue Saint Fulgence, Notre Dame, 1082 Tunis; tel. (71) 288-411; fax (71) 789-518; internet www.mfa.gr/tunis; Ambassador Evangelos Tsaoussis.

Hungary: 12 rue Achtart, BP 572, Nord Hilton, 1082 Tunis; tel. (71) 780-544; fax (71) 781-264; e-mail mission.tun@mfa.gov.hu; internet tunisz.mfa.gov.hu; Ambassador Lajos Mile.

India: 4 pl. Didon, Notre Dame, 1002 Tunis; tel. (71) 787-819; fax (71) 783-394; e-mail hoc.tunis@mea.gov.in; internet embassyofindiatunis.gov.in; Ambassador Ngulkham Jathom Gangte.

Indonesia: 15 rue du Lac Malaren, BP 58, 1053 Tunis; tel. (71) 860-377; fax (71) 861-758; e-mail kbritun@gnet.tn; internet www.kemlu.go.id/tunis; Ambassador Zuhairi Misrawi.

Iran: 10 rue Dr Burnet, Belvédère, 1002 Tunis; tel. (71) 790-084; fax (71) 793-177; Ambassador Mohammad Reza Raouf Shibani.

Iraq: route Principale, Les Berges du Lac, 2045 Tunis; tel. (71) 965-824; fax (71) 964-750; e-mail tunemb@mofa.gov.iq; Chargé d'affaires Abdul Hakim al-Qassab.

Italy: 1 rue de l'Alhambra, Mutuelleville, 1002 Tunis; tel. (71) 321-811; fax (71) 892-150; e-mail ambitalia.tunisi@esteri.it; internet www.ambtunisi.esteri.it; Ambassador Fabrizio Saggio.

Japan: 9 rue Apollo XI, BP 163, Cité Mahrajène, 1082 Tunis; tel. (71) 791-251; fax (71) 786-625; e-mail eoj.tunis@tn.mofa.go.jp; internet www.tn.emb-japan.go.jp; Ambassador Takeshi Osuga.

Jordan: 95 ave Jugurtha, Mutuelleville, 1002 Tunis; tel. (71) 785-829; fax (71) 786-461; e-mail tunis@fm.gov.jo; Ambassador (vacant).

Korea, Republic: Immeuble Blue Sq, ave de la Bourse, Les Berges du Lac 2, 1053 Tunis; tel. (71) 198-597; fax (71) 198-598; e-mail tunisie@mofa.go.kr; internet overseas.mofa.go.kr/tn-fr/index.do; Ambassador Sun Nahm-Kook.

Kuwait: 32 rue al-Mansoura, El Menzah IV, 1004 Tunis; tel. (71) 754-556; fax (71) 767-659; e-mail kuwait.embassy.tunis@gmail.com; Ambassador Mansur Khaled al-Omar.

Lebanon: rue d'Ormia, Les Berges du Lac, 1053 Tunis; tel. and fax (71) 960-001; e-mail ambassade.liban@planet.tn; Ambassador Toni Franjieh.

Libya: 74 ave Mohamed V, 1002 Tunis; tel. (71) 780-866; fax (71) 795-338; Chargé d'affaires Mustafa Qadara.

Mali: BP 109, Cité Mahrajène, 1082 Tunis; tel. (71) 792-589; fax (71) 791-453; Ambassador Moussa Sy.

Malta: ave de la Bourse, Les Berges du Lac, BP 71, 1053 Tunis; tel. (71) 965-811; fax (71) 965-977; e-mail maltaembassy.tunis@gov.mt; Ambassador Simon Pullicino.

Mauritania: 17 rue Fatma Ennechi, BP 62, al-Menzah, Tunis; tel. (71) 233-634; fax (71) 233-804; Ambassador (vacant).

Morocco: 14 impasse Azzouz Rebai, Centre INES Manar 2, 2092 Tunis; tel. (71) 241-391; e-mail ambassadedumaroc.tn@gmail.com; Chargé d'affaires a.i. Mohamed Ibomraten.

Netherlands: 6–8 rue Meycen, Cité Mahrajène, 1082 Tunis; tel. (71) 155-300; fax (71) 155-335; e-mail tun@minbuza.nl; internet www.paysbasetvous.nl/votre-pays-et-les-pays-bas/tunisie; Ambassador Josephine Frantzen.

Nigeria: 3 rue Abdelhamid Mamlouk, el-Manar II, BP 272, Belvédère, 1002 Tunis; tel. (71) 882-291; e-mail nigeria.tunis@foreignaffairs.gov.ng; internet tunis.foreignaffairs.gov.ng; Ambassador Asari Edem Allotey.

Oman: 129 ave Jugurtha, BP 39, Mutuelleville, 1002 Tunis; tel. (71) 790-808; e-mail tunis@mofa.gov.om; Ambassador Hilal bin Abdullah bin Ali al-Sinani.

Pakistan: BP 56, ave Habib Achour, pl. Tahar Hadded, Les Berges du Lac 1, Tunis; tel. (71) 860-404; e-mail pareptunis1@gmail.com; internet mofa.gov.pk/tunis-tunisia-our-team; Ambassador Javed Ahmed Umrani.

Poland: Le Grand Blvd de la Corniche, Les Berges du Lac II, 2045 Tunis; tel. (71) 196-193; fax (71) 196-203; e-mail tunis.amb.sekretariat@msz.gov.pl; internet tunis.msz.gov.pl; Ambassador Justyna Porazińska.

Portugal: 2 rue Sufétula, Belvédère, 1002 Tunis; tel. (71) 893-981; fax (71) 791-008; e-mail ambport@hexabyte.tn; internet www.tunes.embaixadaportugal.mne.pt; Ambassador Nuno de Melo Belo.

Qatar: ave Hédi Karray, ave Urbain Nord, Cité Mahrajène, 1080 Tunis; tel. (71) 231-600; fax (71) 749-073; e-mail tunis@mofa.gov.qa; internet tunis.embassy.qa; internet www.qatarembassy.tn; Ambassador Saad bin Nasser al-Humaidi.

Romania: 108 ave Taieb Mehiri, La Marsa, BP 57, Gammarth, 1004 Tunis; tel. (71) 749-986; fax (71) 749-903; e-mail tunis@mae.ro; internet tunis.mae.ro; Chargé d'affaires a.i. Constantin Tudor.

Russian Federation: 4 rue Bergamotes, BP 48, el-Manar I, 2092 Tunis; tel. (71) 882-446; fax (71) 882-478; e-mail ambrustn@mail.ru; internet www.tunisie.mid.ru; Ambassador Alexander Y. Zolotov.

Saudi Arabia: ave Mohamed Bouazizi, Centre Urbain Nord C, Cité Mahrajène, 1080 Tunis; tel. (71) 232-449; fax (71) 751-441; Ambassador Abdulaziz al-Saqr.

Senegal: 122 ave de la Liberté, BP 22, Belvédère, 1002 Tunis; tel. (71) 860-387; internet fb.com/AmbassadeSenegalTunisie; Ambassador Ramatoulaye Ba Faye.

Serbia: 4 rue de Majeur, Les Berges du Lac, 1053 Tunis; tel. (71) 966-088; fax (71) 658-475; e-mail amb.serbia@gnet.tn; internet tunis.mfa.gov.rs; Chargé d'affaires a.i. Savo Đurica.

South Africa: 7 rue Achtart, Nord Hilton, BP 251, 1082 Tunis; tel. (71) 800-311; fax (71) 796-742; internet www.dirco.gov.za/tunis; Ambassador Moses Siphosezwe Amos Mazango.

Spain: 24 ave Dr Ernest Conseil, Cité Jardin, 1002 Tunis; tel. (71) 782-217; fax (71) 786-267; e-mail emb.tunez@maec.es; internet www.exteriores.gob.es/embajadas/tunez; Ambassador (vacant).

Sudan: Les Berges du Lac II, 1053 Tunis; tel. (71) 197-155; fax (71) 197-050; e-mail sudanitunis@gmail.com; Ambassador Ahmed Abdelwahid Ahmed Mohamed.

Sweden: rue du Lac Neuchâtel, Les Berges du Lac, 1053 Tunis; tel. (71) 121-300; e-mail ambassaden.tunis@gov.se; internet swedenabroad.se/fr/ambassade/tunisie-tunis; Ambassador Anna Block Mazoyer.

Switzerland: 22 rue Platon Z. A. Kheireddine, BP 73, Le Kram, 2015 Tunis; tel. (71) 191-997; fax (71) 180-234; e-mail tun.vertretung@eda.admin.ch; internet www.eda.admin.ch/tunis; Ambassador Josef Philipp Renggli.

Türkiye (Turkey): 4 ave Hédi Karay, Centre Urbain Nord, BP 134, 1082 Tunis; tel. (71) 132-300; fax (71) 767-045; e-mail ambassade.tunis@mfa.gov.tr; internet tunis.emb.mfa.gov.tr; Ambassador Çağlar Fahri Çakiralp.

Ukraine: 7 rue Saint Fulgence, Notre Dame, 1002 Tunis; tel. (71) 845-861; fax (71) 840-866; e-mail emb_tn@mfa.gov.ua; internet tunis.mfa.gov.ua; Ambassador Volodymyr Khomanets.

United Arab Emirates: 9 rue Achtart, Nord Hilton, Belvédère, 1002 Tunis; tel. (71) 788-888; fax (71) 788-777; e-mail tunisemb@mofaic.gov.ae; internet www.mofaic.gov.ae/en/missions/tunis; Ambassador Dr Iman Ahmed al-Salami.

United Kingdom: rue du Lac Windermere, Les Berges du Lac, 1053 Tunis; tel. (71) 108-700; fax (71) 108-749; e-mail britishembassytunis@fcdo.gov.uk; internet www.gov.uk/world/tunisia; Ambassador Helen Winterton.

USA: Les Berges du Lac, 1053 Tunis; tel. (71) 107-000; fax (71) 107-090; e-mail tuniswebsitecontact@state.gov; internet tn.usembassy.gov; Ambassador Joey R. Hood.

Venezuela: 4 blvd Principal, Les Berges du Lac, 1053 Tunis; tel. (71) 861-844; fax (71) 860-896; e-mail ambassade.venezuela@yahoo.es; Ambassador Carlos Federico Feo Acevedo.

Yemen: 9 rue Ibn Abi Taleb, 2091 el-Menzah VI, BP 47, 1004 Tunis; tel. (71) 237-933; Ambassador Abdunasser Hussein Ba-Habib.

Judicial System

The Court of Cassation (Cour de Cassation) in Tunis has three civil sections and one criminal section. There are three Courts of Appeal (Cours d'Appel) in Tunis, Sousse and Sfax, and 13 Courts of First Instance (Cours de Première Instance), each having three chambers, except the Court of First Instance in Tunis, which has eight chambers.

A Supreme Judicial Council (Conseil Supérieur de la Magistrature—CSM) was established, under the terms of the 2014 Constitution, in 2016. The independent body oversaw the proper functioning of the judicial system in Tunisia and had the right to appoint judges of various courts. The CSM comprised 45 magistrates, 30 of whom were elected by the Assembly of the Representatives of the People; these 30 members then appointed the 15 other members.

On 5 February 2022 President Kaïs Saïed ordered the dissolution of the CSM and on 13 February he established by decree a new Provisional Supreme Judicial Council (Conseil Supérieur Provisoire de la Magistrature—CSPM). The CSPM, the decisions of which President Saïed was empowered to veto or overturn, was sworn in on 7 March. The First President of the Court of Cassation was appointed to act as the President of the new body, while the respective First Presidents of the Administrative Tribunal (Tribunal Administratif) and the Court of Auditors (Cour des Comptes) were appointed as its Vice-Presidents.

Conseil Supérieur Provisoire de la Magistrature (Provisional Supreme Judicial Council—CSPM): Tunis; f. 2022; est. to replace the independent Conseil Supérieur de la Magistrature (f. 2016); all mems appointed by the Pres. of the Republic; Pres. MONCEF KCHAOU.

Religion

An estimated 99% of the population are Muslims. Minority religions include Judaism and Christianity. The Christian population comprises Roman Catholics, Greek Orthodox, and French and English Protestants.

ISLAM

Grand Mufti of Tunisia: HICHEM BEN MAHMOUD.

CHRISTIANITY

The Roman Catholic Church

Archbishop of Tunis: Most Rev. ILARIO ANTONIAZZI, Evêché, 4 rue d'Alger, 1000 Tunis; tel. (71) 335-831; fax (71) 335-832; e-mail eveche.tunisie@evechetunisie.org; internet www.eglisecatholiquetunisie.com.

The Protestant Church

Reformed Church of Tunisia: 36 rue Charles de Gaulle, 1000 Tunis; tel. (71) 327-886; e-mail eglisereformee@yahoo.fr; internet www.ertunis.com; f. 1880; c. 220 mems; Pastor WILLIAM BROWN.

The Press

DAILY NEWSPAPERS (PRINT AND ONLINE)

Al-Chourouk (Sunrise): 25 rue Jean Jaurès, BP 36619, Tunis; tel. (71) 331-000; fax (70) 014-167; e-mail contact@alchourouk.com; internet www.alchourouk.com; Arabic; Dir SAIDA AL-AMRI; Editors-in-Chief ABD AL-HAMID RIAHI, FATIMA BIN ABDULLAH AL-KARAY.

Essahafa: 6 rue Ali Bach-Hamba, 1000 Tunis; tel. (71) 341-066; fax (71) 349-720; e-mail contact@essahafa.info.tn; internet www.essahafa.tn; f. 1936; Arabic; Editor-in-Chief LOTFI ELARABY EL-SENOUSY.

La Presse de Tunisie: 17 rue Garibaldi, 1000 Tunis; tel. (71) 341-066; fax (71) 349-720; e-mail redaction@lapresse.tn; internet www.lapresse.tn; f. 1936; French; Editors-in-Chief JALEL MESTIRI.

Le Quotidien: 25 rue Jean Jaurès, 1000 Tunis; tel. (71) 331-000; fax (71) 253-02; internet www.lequotidien.tn; f. 2001; French; Dir SLAHEDDINE AL-AMRI; Editor-in-Chief CHOUKRY BAKOUCHE.

As-Sabah (The Morning): ave Muhammad Bouazizi, BP 441, al-Menzah, 1004 Tunis; tel. (71) 238-222; fax (71) 752-527; e-mail contact@assabahnews.tn; internet www.assabahnews.tn; f. 1951; Arabic; Dir MOHAMED WAHADA; Editor-in-Chief SUFIAN RAGAB.

Le Temps: ave Muhammad Bouazizi, al-Menzah, 1004 Tunis; tel. (71) 238-222; fax (71) 752-527; internet www.letemps.com.tn; f. 1975; French; Dir MUSTAPHA AL-JABER; Editor-in-Chief RAOUF KHALSI.

Tunisia Live: 17 rue Charles de Gaulle, Tunis; tel. (71) 324-702; fax (71) 324-703; internet www.tunisia-live.net; f. 2011; English; online only; Man. Editor SIMON SPEAKMAN CORDALL.

PERIODICALS

Afrique Economie: 16 rue de Rome, BP 61, 1015 Tunis; tel. (71) 348-074; fax (71) 353-172; e-mail iea@planet.tn; f. 1970; monthly; Dir RIADH ZERZERI.

Al-Akhbar (The News): 1 passage d'al-Houdaybiyah, 1000 Tunis; tel. (71) 344-100; fax (71) 355-079; internet www.akhbar.tn; f. 1984; weekly; Arabic; general; Dir MUHAMMAD BEN YOUSUF.

Al-Anouar al-Tounissia (Tunisian Lights): 25 rue al-Cham, 5000 Tunis; tel. (71) 331-000; fax (71) 253-024; internet www.alanouar.com; Arabic; Dir SLAHEDDINE AL-AMRI.

Al-Bayan (The Manifesto): 61 rue Abderrazek, Chraîbi, 1001 Tunis; tel. (71) 339-633; fax (71) 338-533; f. 1976; weekly; general; organ of the Union Tunisienne de l'Industrie, du Commerce et de l'Artisanat; Dir HÉDI DJILANI.

Bulletin Mensuel de Statistiques: Institut National de la Statistique, 70 rue al-Cham, BP 265, 1080 Tunis; tel. (71) 891-002; fax (71) 792-559; e-mail ins@ins.tn; internet www.ins.tn; monthly.

Echaâb: 41 ave Ali Dargouth, 1001 Tunis; tel. (71) 255-020; fax (71) 355-139; internet www.echaab.info.tn; weekly; Dirs HUSSAIN ABBASI, SAMI TAHIRI.

L'Economiste Maghrébin: 3 rue el-Kewekibi, 1002 Tunis; tel. (71) 790-773; fax (71) 793-707; e-mail contact@promedia.tn; internet www.leconomistemaghrebin.com; f. 1990; bi-monthly; French; Dir HÉDI MÉCHRI.

L'Expert: 58 rue Echam, 1002 Tunis; tel. (31) 401-714; e-mail lexpert.tn@gmail.com; internet www.lexpertjournal.net; CEO ABDELLATIF BEN HEDDIA.

L'Hebdo Touristique: rue 8601, 40, Zone Industrielle, La Charguia 2, 2035 Tunis; tel. (71) 786-866; fax (71) 794-891; e-mail haddad.tijani@planet.tn; f. 1971; weekly; French; tourism; Dir TIJANI HADDAD.

IBLA: Institut des Belles Lettres Arabes, 12 rue Jemaâ el-Haoua, 1008 Tunis; tel. (71) 560-133; fax (71) 572-683; e-mail ibla@gnet.tn; internet www.iblatunis.org.tn; f. 1937; 2 a year; French, Arabic and English; social and cultural review on Maghreb and Muslim-Arab affairs; Dir JOHN MACWILLIAMS.

Journal Les Annonces: 6 rue de Sparte, BP 1343, Tunis; tel. (71) 350-177; fax (71) 347-184; e-mail nejib.azouz@planet.tn; f. 1978; 2 a week; French and Arabic; Dir (vacant).

Journal Officiel de la République Tunisienne: ave Farhat Hached, 2040 Radès; tel. (71) 299-914; fax (71) 297-234; f. 1860; official gazette; Arabic and French; online only; publ. by Imprimerie Officielle (State Press); Pres. and Dir-Gen. ROMDHANE BEN MIMOUN.

Al-Mawkif: 10 rue Eve Nohelle, 1001 Tunis; tel. (71) 332-271; fax (71) 332-194; e-mail mawkef_21@yahoo.fr; f. 1984; weekly; organ of the Parti Démocrate Progressiste (which merged into Parti Républicain in 2012); Man. Dir AHMED NÉJIB CHEBBI.

Al-Moussawar: 10 rue al-Cham, Tunis; tel. (71) 289-000; fax (71) 289-357; internet www.almoussawar.com; weekly.

Mouwatinoun (Citizens): Tunis; tel. (71) 903-036; e-mail communication@ettakatol.tn; internet ettakatol.org; f. 2007; monthly; Arabic; organ of the Forum démocratique pour le travail et les libertés (FDTL).

Réalités: 2 rue de Cameroun, 1002 Tunis; tel. (71) 795-140; fax (71) 893-489; e-mail redaction@realites.com.tn; internet www.realites.com.tn; f. 1979; weekly; Arabic and French; Dir TAÏEB ZAHAR; Editor-in-Chief ZYED KRICHEN.

Tounes el Khadra: 8451 rue Alain Savary, al-Khadra, 1003 Tunis; tel. (71) 291-016; fax (71) 291-121; e-mail elamri.onss@gmail.com; internet www.touneselkhadra.com; f. 1976; bi-monthly; agricultural, scientific and technical; organ of the UTAP; Dir MABROUK BAHRI; Editor GHARBI HAMOUDA.

Tunis Hebdo: 1 passage d'al-Houdaybiyah, 1000 Tunis; tel. (71) 344-100; fax (71) 355-079; f. 1973; weekly; French; general and sport; Dir and Editor-in-Chief MUHAMMAD BEN YOUSUF.

NEWS AGENCY

Tunis Afrique Presse (TAP): 7 ave Slimane Ben Slimane, al-Manar, 2092 Tunis; tel. (71) 889-000; fax (71) 883-500; e-mail tap@tap.info.tn; internet www.tap.info.tn; f. 1961; Arabic, French and English; offices in Algiers (Algeria), Rabat (Morocco), Paris (France) and New York (USA); daily news services; Pres. and Man. Dir KAMEL BEN YOUNES.

Publishers

Al-Dar al-Arabia Lil Kitab: 4 ave Mohieddine el-Klibi, BP 32, al-Manar 2, 2092 Tunis; tel. (71) 888-255; fax (71) 888-365; f. 1975; general literature, children's books, non-fiction; Chief Officer LOTFI BEN MBAREK.

TUNISIA

Directory

Centre de Publications Universitaires: Campus Universitaire, BP 255, 1080 Tunis; tel. (71) 600-025; fax (71) 601-266; internet www.cpu.rnu.tn; educational books, journals.

Cérès Editions: 6 rue Alain Savary, Belvédère, 1002 Tunis; tel. (71) 280-505; fax (71) 287-216; e-mail info@ceres-editions.com; internet www.ceres-editions.com; f. 1964; social sciences, art books, literature, novels; Man. Editor Karim Ben Smaïl.

Dar Cheraït: Centre Culturel et Touristique Dar Cheraït, Route Touristique, 2200 Tozeur; tel. (76) 452-100; fax (76) 452-329; internet www.darcherait.com.tn.

Dar al-Kitab: 5 ave Bourguiba, 4000 Sousse; tel. (73) 25097; f. 1950; literature, children's books, legal studies, foreign books; Pres. Taïeb Kacem; Dir Fayçal Kacem.

Dar as-Sabah: ave Mohamed Bouazizi, BP 441, al-Menzah, 1004 Tunis; tel. (71) 238-222; fax (71) 657-693; e-mail redaction@assabah.com.tn; internet www.assabah.com.tn; f. 1951; 200 mems; publishes daily and weekly papers, including the dailies *As-Sabah* and *Le Temps*, which circulate throughout Tunisia, North Africa, France, Belgium, Luxembourg and Germany; Chair. Muhammad Sakher el Materi; Dir-Gen. Mustapha al-Jaber.

Editions Apollonia: 4 rue Claude Bernard, 1002 Tunis; tel. (52) 704-467; fax (71) 799-190; art, literature, essays, poetry.

Editions Bouslama: 15 ave de France, 1000 Tunis; tel. (71) 240-056; fax (71) 381-100; f. 1960; history, children's books; Man. Dir Ali Bouslama.

Institut National de la Statistique: 70 rue al-Cham, BP 265, 1080 Tunis; tel. (71) 891-002; fax (71) 792-559; e-mail ins@ins.tn; internet www.ins.nat.tn; publishes a variety of annuals, periodicals and papers concerned with the economic policy and devt of Tunisia.

Librairie al-Manar: 60 ave Bab Djedid, BP 179, 1008 Tunis; tel. (71) 253-224; fax (71) 336-565; e-mail librairie.almanar@planet.tn; f. 1938; general, educational, Islam; Man. Dir Habib M'Hamdi.

Société d'Arts Graphiques, d'Edition et de Presse (SAGEP): 15 rue du 2 mars 1934, La Kasbah, 1000 Tunis; tel. (71) 564-988; fax (71) 569-736; f. 1974; prints and publishes daily papers, magazines, books, etc.; Dir-Gen. Mahmoud Meftah.

Sud Editions: 7 ave Khaireddine Pacha, 1073 Tunis; tel. (71) 903-850; fax (71) 903-857; e-mail contact@sudeditions.com; internet www.sudeditions.com; f. 1976; Arab literature, art and art history, history, sociology, religion; Man. Dir Youssef Asswad.

GOVERNMENT PUBLISHING HOUSE

Imprimerie Officielle de la République Tunisienne: 40 ave Farhat Hached, 2098 Radès; tel. (71) 434-211; fax (71) 434-234; e-mail iort@iort.gov.tn; internet www.iort.gov.tn; f. 1860; Pres. and Dir-Gen. Moncef Aouadi.

Broadcasting and Communications

TELECOMMUNICATIONS

Ooredoo: Immeuble Zénith, Les Jardins du Lac, 1053 Tunis; tel. (22) 111-111; e-mail supportlink@ooredoo.tn; internet www.ooredoo.tn; f. 2002 as Orascom Telecom Tunisia (Tunisiana); name changed 2014; subsidiary of Ooredoo QSC (Qatar); CEO Mansoor Rashid al-Khater.

Orange Tunisie: Immeuble Orange, Centre Urbain Nord, 1003 Tunis; tel. (30) 013-001; internet www.orange.tn; f. 2010; launched mobile telephone network in May 2010; 49% stake owned by France Télécom; Chair. Marwan Mabrouk.

Société Tunisienne d'Entreprises de Télécommunications (SOTETEL): rue des Entrepreneurs, Zone Industrielle, BP 640, La Charguia 2, 1080 Tunis; tel. (71) 135-100; fax (71) 940-584; e-mail contact@sotetel.tn; internet www.sotetel.tn; f. 1981; privatized in 1998; CEO Karim Laabidi.

Tunisie Télécom: Jardins du Lac II, 1053 Tunis; tel. (71) 901-717; fax (71) 900-777; internet www.tunisietelecom.tn; 65% state-owned, 35% owned by Abraaj Group (UAE); CEO Lassâad Ben Dhiab.

Regulatory Authority

Instance Nationale des Télécommunications (INT): rue Echabia, Montplaisir, 1073 Tunis; tel. (70) 608-440; fax (71) 909-435; e-mail contact@intt.tn; internet www.intt.tn; f. 2001; Pres. Mohamed Taher Missaoui.

BROADCASTING

Office National de la Télédiffusion (ONT) (National Broadcasting Corporation of Tunisia): Cité Ennassim 1, Montplaisir, BP 399, 1080 Tunis; tel. (71) 188-000; fax (71) 904-923; e-mail ont@telediffusion.net.tn; internet www.telediffusion.net.tn; f. 1993; supervision and management of the radio and television broadcasting networks; Pres. and Dir-Gen. Dhaker Baccouch.

Radio

Etablissement de la Radiodiffusion Tunisienne: 71 ave de la Liberté, 1002 Tunis; tel. (71) 782-700; fax (71) 780-993; internet www.radiotunisienne.tn; govt service; originally merged with Télévision Tunisienne; became independent 2006; broadcasts in Arabic, French, German, Italian, Spanish and English; radio stations at Gafsa, El-Kef, Monastir, Sfax, Tataouine and Tunis (3); television stations Tunis 7 and Canal 21; Pres. and Man. Dir Sofiane Ben Aïssa (acting).

Express FM: 1 rue Monastir 2045, l'Aouina Tunis; tel. (71) 760-769; e-mail contact@expressfm.tn; internet www.radioexpressfm.com; f. 2010; Gen. Man. Mourad Guediche.

Jawhara FM: blvd 14 Jan 2011, Khzema Est, 4000 Sousse; tel. (73) 300-000; fax (73) 275-810; e-mail direction@jawharafm.net; internet www.jawharafm.net; f. 2005; owned by Jawhara des médias et des télécommunications.

Mosaïque FM: rue Chebbia Montplaisir, 1073 Tunis; tel. (71) 113-000; fax (71) 905-316; e-mail contact@mosaiquefm.net; internet www.mosaiquefm.net; f. 2003; first privately owned radio station when launched in 2003; broadcasts in Arabic and French to Tunis and the north-east of the country; Gen. Man. Noureddine Boutar.

Shems FM: 5 rue du Lac d'Annecy, Les Berges du Lac, 1053 Tunis; tel. (31) 367-000; e-mail contact@shemsfm.net; internet www.shemsfm.net; f. 2010.

Zitouna FM: 61 ave Habib Bourguiba, 2016 Carthage; tel. (71) 136-000; fax (71) 195-174; e-mail contact@zitounafm.net; internet www.zitounafm.net; f. 2007.

Television

Etablissement de la Télévision Tunisienne: ave de la Ligue des Etats Arabes, Notre Dame, 1030 Tunis; internet www.tunisiatv.tn; formerly merged with Radiodiffusion Tunisienne; became independent 2006; Pres. and Dir-Gen. Awatef Dali.

  Al-Wataniya 1: rue du Ligue Arabe, Tunis 1002; tel. (71) 143-300; fax (71) 781-058; e-mail web@tunisiatv.tn; internet www.watania1.tn; operated by Etablissement de la Télévision Tunisienne.

  Al-Wataniya 2: rue 13, 2 Haut Chotrana, Soukra, 2036 Tunis; tel. (70) 944–944; fax (70) 944–935; e-mail web@tunisiatv.tn; internet www.watania2.tn; operated by Etablissement de la Télévision Tunisienne.

Hannibal TV: 85 ave du 13 Août, Choutrana II, Soukra, 2036 Tunis; tel. (70) 944-944; fax (70) 944-935; internet www.hannibaltv.com.tn; f. 2005; privately owned channel; Proprietor Larbi Nasra.

Nessma TV: 75 ave Mohamed V, Cité Jardins, 1002 Tunis; tel. (71) 465-647; e-mail communication@nessmatv.tv; internet www.nessma.tv; f. 2009; covers Maghreb region; 50% owned by Karoui Group and rest by Quinta Communication and Mediaset Group.

Finance

BANKING

Central Bank

Banque Centrale de Tunisie (BCT): 25 rue Hédi Nouira, BP 777, 1080 Tunis; tel. (71) 122-000; fax (71) 340-615; e-mail boc@bct.gov.tn; internet www.bct.gov.tn; f. 1958; Gov. Marouane el-Abassi.

Commercial Banks

Amen Bank: ave Mohamed V, 1002 Tunis; tel. (71) 148-000; e-mail crc@amenbank.com.tn; internet www.amenbank.com.tn; f. 1967 as Crédit Foncier et Commercial de Tunisie; name changed as above in 1995; Chair. Rached Fourati; Gen. Mans Karim Ben Yedder, Néji Ghandri.

Arab Banking Corpn Tunisie (ABC Tunisie): Immeuble ABC, rue du Lac d'Annecy, Les Berges du Lac, 1053 Tunis; tel. (71) 861-861; fax (71) 860-921; e-mail abc.tunis@bank-abc.com; internet www.bank-abc.com/world/tunis/en/Pages/default.aspx; f. 2000; Chair. Muzaffer Aksoy; CEO Saber Ayadi.

Arab Tunisian Bank: 9 rue Hédi Nouira, 1001 Tunis; tel. (71) 351-155; e-mail contact@atb.com.tn; internet www.atb.tn; f. 1982; 64.2% owned by Arab Bank PLC (Jordan); Dir-Gen. Riadh Hajjej.

Attijari Bank: 24 rue Hédi Karray, Centre Urbain Nord, 1080 Tunis; tel. (70) 012-000; fax (70) 022-100; e-mail courrier@attijaribank.com.tn; internet www.attijaribank.com.tn; f. 1968 as Banque du Sud; present name adopted 2006; 37.11% owned by

TUNISIA

Attijariwafa Bank (Morocco), 17.46% by Banco Santander (Spain); Pres. MONCEF CHAFFAR; Dir-Gen. SAÏD SEBTI.

Banque Internationale Arabe de Tunisie (BIAT): 70–72 ave Habib Bourguiba, BP 520, 1080 Tunis; tel. (71) 131-000; e-mail correspondent.banking@biat.com.tn; internet www.biat.com.tn; f. 1976; Chair. ISMAIL MABROUK; Gen. Man. MOEZ HADJ SLIMEN.

Banque Nationale Agricole (BNA): rue Hédi Nouira, 1001 Tunis; tel. (71) 831-000; e-mail bna@bna.tn; internet www.bna.com.tn; f. 1989 by merger of Banque Nationale du Développement Agricole and Banque Nationale de Tunisie; Chair. GHARBI NAJIA; CEO MONDHER LAKHAL.

Banque de Tunisie SA: 2 rue de Turquie, BP 289, 1001 Tunis; tel. (71) 125-500; fax (71) 125-410; e-mail finance@bt.com.tn; internet www.bt.com.tn; f. 1884; Chair. ERIC CHARPENTIER; Gen. Man. HICHEM REBAI.

Banque Tuniso-Koweïtienne (BTK Bank): 10 bis ave Muhammad V, BP 49, 1001 Tunis; tel. (80) 101-652; e-mail satisfaction.client@btknet.com; internet www.btknet.com; Chair. FAOUZI ELLOUMI; Man. Dir LASSAAD BEN ROMDHANE.

BH Bank: 18 ave Mohamed V, Tunis; tel. (71) 126-000; fax (71) 337-957; e-mail contact@bhbank.tn; internet www.bh.com.tn; f. 1984; 32.62% govt-owned; CEO WAJDI KOUBAÂ.

Société Tunisienne de Banque (STB): rue Hédi Nouira, BP 638, 1001 Tunis; tel. (70) 140-000; fax (70) 143-333; e-mail stb@stb.com.tn; internet www.stb.com.tn; f. 1957; 24.81% govt-owned; merged with Banque Nationale de Développement Touristique and Banque de Développement Economique de Tunisie in 2000; Chair. AMEL MDINI; Man. Dir LASSAAD ZNATI JOUINI (acting).

Union Bancaire pour le Commerce et l'Industrie (UBCI): 1008 Tunis; tel. (70) 000-050; fax (71) 849-338; e-mail chokri.chrouda@bnpparibas.com; internet www.ubci.tn; f. 1961; affiliated with, and 50% owned by, BNP Paribas (France); Chair. HASSINE DOGHRI; Gen. Man. MOHAMED KOUBAA.

Union Internationale de Banques SA: 65 ave Habib Bourguiba, BP 109, 1000 Tunis; tel. (81) 102-525; e-mail uibcontact@uib.com.tn; internet www.uib.com.tn; f. 1963 as a merging of Tunisian interests by the Société Franco-Tunisienne de Banque et de Crédit with Crédit Lyonnais (France) and other foreign banks, incl. Banca Commerciale Italiana; 52.3% owned by Société Générale (France); Chair. KAMEL NEJI; Dir-Gen. RAOUL LABBE DE LA GENARDIERE.

Merchant Banks

Capital African Partners Bank (CAP Bank): 10 bis rue Mahmoud El Matri, Mutuelleville, 1002 Tunis; tel. (71) 143-800; e-mail info@cap-bank.com; internet www.cap-bank.com; f. 1997 as Banque d'Affaires de Tunisie (BAT); Pres. and CEO HABIB KARAOULI.

International Maghreb Merchant Bank (IM Bank): Immeuble Maghrebia, Bloc B, 3ème étage, Les Berges du Lac, 2045 Tunis; tel. (71) 800-266; fax (71) 800-410; internet www.imbank.com.tn; f. 1995; Pres. OLIVIER PASTRÉ; Exec. Dir AHMED BESBES.

Development Banks

Banque de Tunisie et des Emirats (BTE): blvd Beji Caid Essebsi, 1082 Tunis; tel. (71) 112-000; fax (71) 287 409; e-mail dg@bte.com.tn; internet www.bte.com.tn; f. 1982 as Banque de Tunisie et des Emirats d'Investissement; name changed as above in 2005; owned by the Govt of Tunisia and Abu Dhabi Investment Authority; Chair. KHALIFA ALI AL-KAMEZI; Gen. Man. FERIEL CHABRAK.

Banque Tunisienne de Solidarité (BTS): 56 ave Muhammad V, 1002 Tunis; tel. (70) 018-424; e-mail bts@bts.com.tn; internet www.bts.com.tn; f. 1997; provides short- and medium-term finance for small-scale projects; Pres. and Dir-Gen. KHALIFA SBOUI.

Banque Tuniso-Libyenne (BTL): Immeuble BTL, Blvd Maître Mohamed Beji Caïd Essebsi, Centre Urbain Nord, 1082 Tunis; tel. (70) 131-700; fax (70) 131-900; e-mail banque.tuniso-libyenne@btl.tn; internet www.btl.tn; f. 1983 as Banque Arabe Tuniso-Libyenne de Développement et de Commerce; present name adopted 2005; owned 50% by the Tunisian Govt and 50% by the Libyan Foreign Bank; promotes trade and devt projects between Tunisia and Libya, and provides funds for investment in poorer areas; Chair. MOHAMED SAID FTIRA; CEO HATEM ZAARA.

Tunisian Saudi Bank: 32 rue Hédi Karray, BP 20, 1082 Tunis; tel. (70) 243-000; fax (71) 753-233; e-mail contact@tsb.com.tn; internet www.tsb.com.tn; f. 1981 as Société Tuniso-Saoudienne d'Investissement et de Développement; present name adopted in 2017; provides long-term finance for devt projects; Chair. ABDULRAHMEN MOHAMED RAMZI ADDES; Pres. and Dir-Gen. NABIL CHAHDOURA.

Offshore Banks

Albaraka Bank Tunisia: 88 ave Hédi Chaker, 1002 Tunis; tel. (71) 186-500; fax (71) 780-235; e-mail contact@albarakabank.com.tn; internet www.albarakabank.com.tn; f. 1983 as Beit Ettamouil Saoudi Tounsi; name changed to above 2009; Islamic bank; Chair. ABDUL ELAH SABBAHI; Man. Dir MOHAMED EL-MONCER.

Alubaf International Bank: ave de la Bourse, Les Jardins du Lac II, 1053 Tunis; tel. (70) 015-600; fax (71) 198-000; e-mail alub@alubaf.com.tn; internet www.alubaf.com.tn; f. 1985; 100% owned by Libyan Arab Foreign Bank; Chair. (vacant); Gen. Man. ALTAHER M. AL-SHAMES.

North Africa International Bank (NAIB): ave Kheireddine Pacha, BP 485, 1002 Tunis; tel. (71) 950-800; fax (71) 950-840; e-mail naib@naibank.com; internet www.naibbank.com; f. 1984; Chair. and Gen. Man. ABUAJILA HARAKAT ABULJAM.

Tunis International Bank: 18 ave des Etats-Unis d'Amérique, BP 81, 1002 Tunis; tel. (71) 782-411; fax (71) 782-479; e-mail tibtunis@tib.com.tn; internet www.tib.com.tn; f. 1982; 86.6% owned by United Gulf Bank (Bahrain); Man. Dir MOHAMED AQRABI.

STOCK EXCHANGE

Bourse des Valeurs Mobilières de Tunis (Bourse de Tunis): 34 ave de la Bourse, Les Berges du Lac II, 1053 Tunis; tel. (71) 197-910; fax (71) 197-903; e-mail info@bvmt.com.tn; internet www.bvmt.com.tn; f. 1969; Chair. MOURAD BEN CHAABANE; Dir-Gen. BILEL SAHNOUN.

INSURANCE

Caisse Tunisienne d'Assurances Mutuelles Agricoles (CTAMA—MGA): 100 ave de la Liberté, 1002 Tunis; tel. (70) 556-800; fax (71) 784-149; e-mail ctama@planet.tn; internet ctama.com.tn; f. 1912; Pres. NEJI HANNACHI; Dir-Gen. LAMJED BOUKHRIS.

Cie d'Assurances Tous Risques et de Réassurance (ASTREE): 45 ave Kheireddine Pacha, BP 780, 1002 Tunis; tel. (71) 904-211; fax (71) 794-723; e-mail mail@astree.com.tn; internet www.astree.com.tn; f. 1949; Pres. HABIB BEN SAAD; Dir-Gen. ABDEL MONEM KOLSI.

Cie Méditerranéenne d'Assurances et de Réassurance (COMAR): Immeuble COMAR, ave Habib Bourguiba, 1001 Tunis; tel. (71) 340-899; fax (71) 344-778; e-mail contact@comar.tn; internet www.comar.tn; f. 1969 as Cie Maghrébine d'Assurances Réunies; Chair. SALAHEDDINE LADJIMI.

Cie Tunisienne pour l'Assurance du Commerce Extérieur (COTUNACE): 14, rue Borjine, Montplaisir, 1073 Tunis; tel. (71) 908-600; fax (71) 909-439; e-mail benmaiz@cotunace.com.tn; internet www.cotunace.com.tn; f. 1984; Pres. and Dir-Gen. NEBGHA DRISS.

Société Tunisienne d'Assurance et de Réassurance (STAR): ave de Paris, 1000 Tunis; tel. (70) 255-000; fax (71) 132-332; e-mail contact@star.com.tn; internet www.star.com.tn; f. 1958; Pres. SAMIR MLAOUHIA; Dir-Gen. HASSENE FEKI.

Tunis Re (Société Tunisienne de Réassurance): 12 ave du Japon, BP 29, 1073 Tunis; tel. (71) 904-911; fax (71) 904-930; e-mail tunisre@tunisre.com.tn; internet www.tunisre.com.tn; f. 1981; various kinds of reinsurance; Chair. SLAH KANOUN; Gen. Man. LAMIA BEN MAHMOUD.

Insurance Organization

Fédération Tunisienne des Sociétés d'Assurances (FTUSA): 9 bis rue de la Nouvelle Delhi, 1002 Tunis; tel. (71) 148-820; fax (71) 908-422; e-mail contact@ftusa.tn; internet www.ftusanet.org; Pres. HASSENE FEKI.

Trade and Industry

GOVERNMENT AGENCIES

Centre de Promotion des Exportations (CEPEX): Centre Urbain, BP 225, 1080 Tunis; tel. (71) 130-320; fax (71) 237-325; e-mail rapidcontact@tunisiaexport.tn; internet www.cepex.nat.tn; f. 1973; state export promotion org.; Pres. and Dir-Gen. MOURAD BEN HASSINE.

Foreign Investment Promotion Agency (FIPA): rue Slaheddine al-Ammami, Centre Urbain Nord, 1004 Tunis; tel. (70) 241-500; fax (71) 231-400; e-mail fipa.tunisia@fipa.tn; internet www.investintunisia.tn; f. 1995; Dir-Gen. JALEL TEBIB.

Office du Commerce de la Tunisie (OCT): 65 rue de Syrie, 1002 Tunis; tel. (71) 800-040; fax (71) 788-974; e-mail octmail@gnet.tn; f. 1962; Pres. and Dir-Gen. ELYES BEN AMEUR.

CHAMBERS OF COMMERCE AND INDUSTRY

Chambre de Commerce et d'Industrie du Centre: rue Chadly Khaznadar, 4000 Sousse; tel. (73) 225-044; fax (73) 224-227; e-mail contact@ccicentre.org.tn; internet www.ccicentre.org.tn; f. 1892; Pres. NÉJIB MELLOULI; Sec.-Gen. MOHAMED EZZEDINE ABELKEFI.

Chambre de Commerce et d'Industrie du Nord-Est: Tom Bereaux Bizerte Center, angle rues 1er mai, Med Ali, 7000 Bizerte;

tel. (72) 431-044; fax (72) 431-922; e-mail ccine.biz@gnet.tn; internet www.ccibizerte.org; f. 1902; 30 mems; Pres. FAOUZI BEN AISSA; Sec.-Gen. SAMI BEN HAJ.

Chambre de Commerce et d'Industrie de Sfax: rue du Lieutenant Hammadi Tej, BP 794, 3000 Sfax; tel. (74) 296-120; fax (74) 296-121; e-mail ccis@ccis.org.tn; internet www.ccis.org.tn; f. 1895; 35,000 mems; Pres. RIDHA FOURATI; Sec.-Gen. TAOUFIK HACHICHA.

Chambre de Commerce et d'Industrie de Tunis: 31 ave de Paris, 1000 Tunis; tel. (71) 247-322; fax (71) 354-744; e-mail www.ccitunis.org.tn; internet www.ccitunis.org.tn; f. 1885; Pres. MOUNIR MOUAKHAR; Sec.-Gen. ABDERRAZAK SANHAJI.

INDUSTRIAL AND TRADE ASSOCIATIONS

Agence des Ports et des Installations de Pêches (APIP): Port de Pêche de La Goulette, BP 64, 2060 Tunis; tel. (71) 738-300; fax (71) 735-396; e-mail apip@apip.com.tn; internet www.apip.nat.tn; fishing ports authority; Pres. and Dir-Gen. FAOUZI BEN HAMIDA.

Agence de Promotion de l'Industrie et de l'Innovation (APII): 63 rue de Syrie, 1002 Tunis; tel. (71) 792-144; fax (71) 782-482; e-mail apii@apii.tn; internet www.tunisieindustrie.nat.tn; f. 1987 by merger; co-ordinates industrial policy, undertakes feasibility studies, organizes industrial training and establishes industrial zones; overseas offices in Belgium, France, Germany, Italy, Sweden, the UK and the USA; 24 regional offices; Dir-Gen. OMAR BOUZOUADA.

Centre Technique du Textile (CETTEX): rue des Industries, Zone Industrielle, Bir el-Kassaâ, BP 279, Ben Arous, 2013 Tunis; tel. (71) 381-133; fax (71) 382-558; e-mail cettex@cettex.com.tn; internet www.cettex.com.tn; f. 1992; responsible for the textile industry.

Cie des Phosphates de Gafsa (CPG): Cité Bayech, 2100 Gafsa; tel. (76) 226-022; fax (76) 224-132; e-mail cpg.gafsa@cpg.com.tn; internet www.cpg.com.tn; f. 1897; production and marketing of phosphates; Pres. and Dir-Gen. RIDHA CHALGHOUM.

Entreprise Tunisienne d'Activités Pétrolières (ETAP): 54 ave Mohamed V, 1002 Tunis; tel. (71) 285-300; fax (71) 285-280; e-mail contact@etap.com.tn; internet www.etap.com.tn; f. 1974; state-owned; responsible for exploration, production, trade and investment in hydrocarbons; Pres. and CEO (vacant).

Office des Céréales: 30 rue Alain Savary, 1080 Tunis; tel. (70) 557-300; fax (70) 557-400; internet www.oc.com.tn; f. 1962; responsible for the cereals industry; Chair. and Dir-Gen. BASHIR AL-KATHIRI.

Office National des Mines: 24 rue de l'Energie, BP 215, 1080 Tunis; tel. (71) 808-013; fax (71) 808-098; e-mail contact@onm.nat.tn; internet www.onm.nat.tn; f. 1963; geology and mining research; research and study of mineral wealth; Dir-Gen. MOHAMED BEN SALEM.

Office des Terres Domaniales (OTD): 60 rue Alain Savary, 1003 Tunis; tel. (71) 771-086; fax (71) 808-454; e-mail boc@otd.nat.tn; internet www.otd.nat.tn; f. 1961; responsible for agricultural production and the management of state-owned lands; Pres. and Dir-Gen. MOHAMED ALI JENDOUBI.

UTILITIES

Electricity and Gas

Société Tunisienne de l'Electricité et du Gaz (STEG): 38 rue Kemal Atatürk, BP 190, 1080 Tunis; tel. (71) 341-311; fax (71) 349-981; e-mail dpsc@steg.com.tn; internet www.steg.com.tn; f. 1962; responsible for generation and distribution of electricity and for production of natural gas; Pres. and Dir-Gen. HICHEM ANENE.

Water

Société Nationale d'Exploitation et de Distribution des Eaux (SONEDE): 2 ave Slimane Ben Slimane, el-Manar 2, 2092 Tunis; tel. (71) 887-000; fax (71) 871-000; e-mail sonede@sonede.com.tn; internet www.sonede.com.tn; f. 1968; production and supply of drinking water; Pres. and Dir-Gen. AHMED SOULA.

MAJOR COMPANIES

Groupe Chimique Tunisien: 7 rue du Royaume d'Arabie Saoudite, 1002 Tunis; tel. (71) 783-822; fax (71) 783-495; e-mail gct.reclamation@gct.com.tn; internet www.gct.com.tn; f. 1947; production of phosphoric acid and fertilizers; Pres. and Dir-Gen. ABDELWAHEB AJROUD.

Industries Maghrébines de l'Aluminium (IMAL): 14 rue 8612, Zone Industrielle, La Charguia 1, 2035 Tunis; tel. (71) 206-750; fax (71) 206-752; f. 1964; manufacture and distribution of aluminium products; Chair. MONCEF EL-HORRY; 50 employees.

Industries Mécaniques Maghrébines (IMM): Zone Industrielle, BP 189, Carthage, 1080 Tunis; tel. (71) 941-411; fax (71) 941-393; e-mail latrous.tahar@gnet.tn; f. 1982; production suspended 1988, recommenced 1991; production of light commercial vehicles; Man. Dir TAHAR LATROUS.

Mont Blanc: ave Abderrahmmen el-Bahri, 2097 Boumhal el-Bassatine; tel. (70) 020-720; e-mail contact@montblanc.com.tn; internet www.montblanc-electromenager.com; f. 1988; manufacturer of electrical home appliances; Dir-Gen. KAYS ELLAFI.

Société Industrielle de Conserves Alimentaires et de Pêches SA: lot 36, rte de Boumerdes, Zone Industrielle, Mahdia; tel. (73) 670-111; fax (73) 670-115; e-mail capafrica.sicap@topnet.tn; internet www.capafrica-sicap.com; fish, fruit and vegetable processing and canning.

Société Tunisienne Automobile, Financière, Immobilière et Maritime (STAFIM): rue du Lac Léman, Les Berges du Lac, 1053 Tunis; tel. 70019800; internet www.peugeottunisie.com; f. 1930; distribution and sales of cars, spare parts, engines and mechanical machinery.

Tunisienne de Conserves Alimentaires (TUCAL): route de Mateur, Km 8.5, 2010 La Manouba; tel. (71) 601-611; fax (71) 601-251; e-mail info.tucal@tucal.com.tn; internet www.tucal.tn; manufacture and distribution of canned food products.

TRADE UNIONS

Union Générale des Etudiants de Tunisie (UGET): 11 rue d'Espagne, Tunis; f. 1953; Sec.-Gen. HOUSSEM BOUJARRA.

Union Générale Tunisienne du Travail (UGTT): 29 pl. Mohamed Ali, 1000 Tunis; tel. (71) 259-621; fax (71) 354-114; e-mail secretariat.general@ugtt.org.tn; internet www.ugtt.org.tn; f. 1946 by Farhat Hached; affiliated to ITUC; 700,000 mems in 24 affiliated unions (2020); 13-mem. exec. bureau; Gen. Sec. NOUREDDINE TABBOUBI.

Union Nationale de la Femme Tunisienne (UNFT): 56 blvd Bab Benet, 1006 Tunis; tel. (71) 560-801; e-mail unft@email.ati.tn; internet www.unft.org.tn; f. 1956; promotes the rights of women; 30,000 mems; 28 regional delegations, 199 professional training centres, 18 professional alliances; Pres. RADHIA JERBI.

Union des Travailleurs de Tunisie (UTT): 12 rue de Athenes, 1001 Tunis; tel. (71) 247-626; fax (71) 247-616; e-mail contact@utt.tn; internet www.utt.tn; Sec.-Gen. ISMAIL SAHBANI.

Union Tunisienne de l'Agriculture et de la Pêche (UTAP): ave Alain Savary, 1003 Tunis; tel. (71) 806-800; fax (71) 809-181; e-mail contact@utap.org.tn; internet www.utap.org.tn; f. 1955 as Union Nationale des Agriculteurs Tunisiens (which supplanted the Union Générale des Agriculteurs Tunisiens, f. 1950); name changed as above in 1995; Pres. ABDEL MAJID ZAR.

Union Tunisienne de l'Industrie, du Commerce et de l'Artisanat (UTICA): rue Ferjani Bel Haj Ammar, Cité el-Khadhra, 1003 Tunis; tel. (71) 142-000; fax (71) 142-100; e-mail contact@utica.org.tn; internet www.utica.org.tn; f. 1946; mems: 17 national federations and 370 syndical chambers at national level; Pres. SAMIR MAJOUL.

Transport

RAILWAYS

Société Nationale des Chemins de Fer Tunisiens (SNCFT): 67 ave Farhat Hached, BP 693, 1001 Tunis; tel. (71) 345-511; fax (71) 345-378; e-mail brc@sncft.com.tn; internet www.sncft.com.tn; f. 1956; state org. controlling all Tunisian railways; Pres. and Dir-Gen. TAOUFIK BOUFAYED.

Société des Transports de Tunis (TRANSTU): 33 ave du Japon, Montplaisir, 1073 Tunis; tel. (71) 904-932; fax (71) 904-883; internet www.transtu.tn; f. 2003 following merger of the Société Nationale des Transports and the Société du Métro Léger de Tunis; operates 6 light rail routes (totalling 61.3 km in length) with 189 trains, and 232 local bus routes (totalling 7,284 km in length) with 1,439 buses; also operates an 18-km railway line in the suburbs of Tunis-Goulette-Marsa, with 18 trains; Pres. and Dir-Gen. MOEZ SALEM.

ROADS

Société Nationale de Transport Interurbain (SNTRI): ave Muhammad V, BP 40, Belvédère, 1002 Tunis; tel. (71) 905-433; fax (71) 791-621; e-mail marketing@sntri.com.tn; internet www.sntri.com.tn; f. 1981; state-owned bus company; Dir-Gen. KARIM DAOUES.

Société des Transports de Tunis (TRANSTU): see Railways.

There are 12 **Sociétés Régionales des Transports**, responsible for road transport, operating in different regions in Tunisia.

SHIPPING

Tunisia has seven major ports: Tunis-La Goulette, Radès, Bizerta, Sousse, Sfax, Gabès and Zarzis. There is a special petroleum port at La Skhirra. In 2009 the Government invited bids for the construction of a new deep-water port at Enfidha. The project was subsequently

Port Authority

Office de la Marine Marchande et des Ports (OMMP): Bâtiment Administratif, Port de la Goulette, 2060 La Goulette; tel. (71) 240-000; fax (71) 735-812; e-mail ommp@ommp.nat.tn; internet www.ommp.nat.tn; maritime port administration; Pres. and Dir-Gen. FOUED OTHMEN.

Principal Shipping Companies

Cie Générale Maritime: Bloc D7, Apt 74, 1003 Tunis; tel. and fax (71) 860-430; Chair. ELIAS MAHERZI.

Cie Tunisienne de Navigation SA (CTN): 5 ave Dag Hammarskjöld, BP 40, 1001 Tunis; tel. (71) 322-755; fax (71) 345-736; e-mail cotunav@ctn.com.tn; internet www.ctn.com.tn; f. 1959; state-owned; brs at Bizerta, La Goulette, Sfax and Sousse; Pres. and Dir-Gen. IMED ZAMMIT.

Gabès Marine Tankers (GMT): Immeuble SETCAR, route de Sousse, Km 13, 2034 Tunis; tel. (71) 454-644; fax (71) 450-350; e-mail gabesmarine@gmt.com.tn; internet www.setcar-group.com; f. 1994; part of the Setcar Group; Chair. FÉRID ABBÈS.

Gas Marine: Immeuble SETCAR, route de Sousse, Km 13, 2034 el-Zahra; tel. (71) 454-644; fax (71) 454-650; Chair. HAMMADI ABBÈS.

Hannibal Marine Tankers: 2ème Etage, Residence Lakeo, rue du Lac Michigan, Les Berges du Lac, 1053 Tunis; tel. (71) 960-037; fax (71) 960-243; e-mail hannibal.tankers@gnet.tn; Gen. Man. AMEUR MAHJOUB.

Société Nouvelle de Transport Kerkennah (SONOTRAK): 179 ave Muhammad Hédi Khefacha, 3000 Sfax; tel. (74) 212-220; internet www.sonotrak.tn; f. 1976; Pres. and Dir-Gen. FARHAT ZOUAGHI.

Tunisian Shipping Agency: Zone Industrielle, Radès 2040, BP 166, Tunis; tel. (71) 448-379; fax (71) 448-410; Chair. MOHAMED BEN SEDRINE.

CIVIL AVIATION

There are international airports at Enfidha-Hammamet, Tunis-Carthage, Sfax, Djerba, Monastir, Tabarka, Gafsa and Tozeur.

Office de l'Aviation Civile et des Aéroports: BP 137 and 147, Aéroport International de Tunis-Carthage, 1080 Tunis; tel. (70) 149-009; fax (71) 781-460; e-mail farah.boughzala@oaca.nat.tn; internet www.oaca.nat.tn; f. 1970; civil aviation and airport authority; Pres. and Gen. Dir MOHAMED REJEB.

Nouvelair Tunisie: Zone Touristique Dkhila, 5065 Monastir; tel. (70) 020-920; e-mail call.center@nouvelair.com.tn; internet www.nouvelair.com; f. 1989 as Air Liberté Tunisie; name changed as above in 1996; Tunisian charter co; flights from Tunis, Djerba and Monastir airports to Scandinavia and other European countries; Pres. and Dir-Gen. CHOKRI ZARRAD.

TunisAir (Société Tunisienne de l'Air): Charguia II, Carthage, 2035 Tunis; tel. (71) 942-322; fax (70) 836-900; e-mail resaonline@tunisair.com.tn; internet www.tunisair.com; f. 1948; 74% govt-owned; 75% of assets owned by Tunisian Govt, 20% by private investors and 5% by Air France; flights to Africa, Europe and the Middle East; Pres. and Dir-Gen. KHALED CHELLI.

Tunisair Express: 10 rue de l'Artisanat, La Charguia 11, 2035 Tunis; tel. (70) 101-300; e-mail info@tunisairexpress.com.tn; internet www.tunisairexpress.net; f. 1992 as Tuninter; Tunisian charter co; Dir-Gen. YOSR CHOUARI.

Tunisavia (Société de Transports, Services et Travaux Aériens): blvd du leader Yasser Arafat, Tunis-Carthage International Airport, 2035 Tunis; tel. (71) 280-555; fax (71) 281-333; e-mail info@tunisavia.com.tn; internet www.tunisavia.com.tn; f. 1974; helicopter and charter operator; CEO KARIM MILAD; Gen. Man. MOHSEN NASRA.

Tourism

Office National du Tourisme Tunisien: 1 ave Mohamed V, 1001 Tunis; tel. (71) 341-077; fax (71) 341-145; e-mail ontt@ontt.tourism.tn; internet www.discovertunisia.com; f. 1958; Dir-Gen. JAMEL BOUZID (acting).

Defence

As assessed at November 2022, the total strength of the Tunisian armed forces was 35,800: army 27,000 (incl. 22,000 conscripts); navy est. 4,800; air force 4,000. There was also a 12,000-strong National Guard under the authority of the Ministry of the Interior. Military service is selective and lasts for one year.

Defence Budget: TD 4,000m. in 2022.

Chief of Staff of the Army: Brig.-Gen. MOHAMED EL-GHOUL.

Chief of Staff of the Navy: Rear-Adm. ADEL JEHANE.

Chief of Staff of the Air Force: Gen. MOHAMED EL-HAJJEM.

Education

Education is compulsory in Tunisia for a period of 10 years between the ages of six and 16. Primary education begins at six years of age and normally lasts for six years. Secondary education begins at 12 years of age and lasts for seven years, comprising a first cycle of three years and a second cycle of four years. In 2020/21, according to UNESCO estimates, the total enrolment at primary schools included 99.2% of children in the relevant age-group. Secondary school enrolment in 2015/16 was equivalent to 92.9% of children in the relevant age-group. According to UNESCO, in 2018 expenditure on education was equivalent to 12.4% of total budgeted government spending.

Arabic is the first language of instruction in primary and secondary schools, but French is also used. French is used almost exclusively in higher education. The University of Tunis was opened in 1959. In 1988 the university was divided into two separate institutions: one for science, the other for arts. In 1986 two new universities were opened, at Monastir and Sfax.

Bibliography

Abadi, Jacob. *Tunisia Since the Arab Conquest: The Saga of a Westernized Muslim State*. Reading, Ithaca Press, 2012.

Abderrahim, Tasnim, Krüger, Laura-Theresa, Besbes, Salma, and McLarren, Katharina (Eds). *Tunisia's International Relations Since the 'Arab Spring': Transition Inside and Out*. Abingdon, Routledge, 2018.

Alexander, Christopher. *Tunisia: Stability and Reform in the Modern Maghreb*. Abingdon, Routledge, 2010.

Tunisia: from Stability to Revolution in the Maghreb. Abingdon, Routledge, 2016.

Alvi, Hayat. *The Political Economy and Islam of the Middle East: The Case of Tunisia*. Cham, Palgrave Macmillan, 2019.

Amami, Mohamed. *Tunisie: La Révolution Face à la Mondialisation des Fondamentalismes Contemporain*. Velle le Chatel, France, Sefraber, 2015.

Anderson, Lisa. *The State and Social Transformation in Tunisia and Libya: 1830-1980*. Princeton, NJ, Princeton University Press, 2014.

Assaad, Ragui, and Boughzala, Mongi (Eds). *The Tunisian Labor Market in an Era of Transition*. Oxford, Oxford University Press, 2018.

Ayari, Michaël. Le Prix de l'Engagement: Politique dans la Tunisie Autoritaire, Gauchistes et Islamistes sous Bourguiba et Ben Ali (1957-2011). Paris, Karthala, 2017.

Baduel, Pierre Robert. *Un temps insurrectionnel pas comme les autres: La chute de Ben Ali et les printemps arabes*. Paris, Éditions Non Lieu, 2018.

Quand la Tunisie ouvrait la voie... Combats et débats d'une année révolutionaire. Paris, Éditions Non Lieu, 2020.

Ben Achour, Yadh. *Tunisie: une révolution en pays d'islam*. Geneva, Labor et Fides, 2018.

Ben Romdhane, Mahmoud. *Tunisie: État, économie et société*. Paris, Éditions Publisud, 2011.

Bourguiba, Habib. *Hadith al-Jamaa*. (Collected Broadcasts) Tunis, 1957.

Bousnina, Adel. *Population et Développement en Tunisie*. Paris, L'Harmattan, 2015.

Dawood Sofi, Mohammad. *The Tunisian Revolution and Democratic Transition: the Role of al-Nahda*. Abingdon, Routledge, 2022.

Erdle, Steffen. *Ben Ali's 'New Tunisia' (1987–2009): A Case Study of Authoritarian Modernization in the Arab World*. Berlin, Klaus Schwarz Verlag, 2010.

Fortier, Edwige. *Contested Politics in Tunisia: Civil Society in a Post-Authoritarian State*. Cambridge, Cambridge University Press, 2018.

Gana, Nouri. *The Making of the Tunisian Revolution: Contexts, Architects, Prospects*. Edinburgh, Edinburgh University Press, 2013.

Gbe, Eric, and Chouikha, Larbi. *Histoire de la Tunisie depuis l'Indépendance*. Paris, La découverte, 2015.

Guen, Moncef. *La Tunisie indépendante face à son économie*. Paris, 1961.

Kasmi, Mohamed Salah. *Tunisie: L'Islam Local Face à l'Islam Importé*. Paris, L'Harmattan, 2014.

Martin, Alexander P. *Tunisian Civil Society: Political Culture and Democratic Function Since 2011*. London, Routledge, 2021.

Masri, Safwan M. *Tunisia: An Arab Anomaly*. New York, Columbia University Press, 2017.

McCarthy, Rory. *Inside Tunisia's al-Nahda: Between Politics and Preaching*. Cambridge, Cambridge University Press, 2018.

Murphy, Emma C. *Economic and Political Change in Tunisia: From Bourguiba to Ben Ali*. London, St. Martin's Press, 2000.

Nabi, Mahmoud Sami. *Making the Tunisian Resurgence*. Singapore, Palgrave Macmillan, 2019.

Perkins, Kenneth J. *Historical Dictionary of Tunisia* (African Historical Dictionaries, No. 45). Metuchen, NJ, and London, Scarecrow Press, 1989.

A History of Modern Tunisia (2nd edn). Cambridge, Cambridge University Press, 2014.

Powel, Brieg, and Sadiki, Larbi. *Europe and Tunisia: Democratization via Association*. Abingdon, Routledge, 2010.

Resta, V. *Tunisia and Egypt after the Arab Spring: Party Politics in Transitions from Authoritarian Rule*. London, Routledge, 2023.

Rudebeck, Lars. *Party and People: A Study of Political Change in Tunisia*. London, C. Hurst, 1969.

Saidi, Heidi. *Histoire Tunisienne Modernites Elites et Finance dans la Tunisie*. Paris, L'Harmattan, 2014.

Salehi, Mariam. *Transitional Justice in Process: Plans and Politics in Tunisia*. Manchester, Manchester University Press, 2022.

Salem, Norma. *Habib Bourguiba, Islam and the Creation of Tunisia*. London, Croom Helm, 1984.

Sarihan, A. *The Role of the Military in the Arab Uprisings: The Cases of Tunisia and Libya*. London, Routledge, 2023.

Seddik, Youssef, and Vanderpooten, Gilles. *La Révolution Inachevée: Tunisie, Trois Ans Après*. La Tour d'Aigues, France, L'Aube, 2014.

Webb, Edward. *Media in Egypt and Tunisia: From Control to Transition?*. New York, NY, Palgrave Macmillan, 2014.

Wolf, Anne. *Political Islam in Tunisia: the History of Ennahda*. London, Hurst & Co, 2017.

Yousfi, Hèla. *Trade Unions and Arab Revolutions: the Tunisian Case of UGTT*. Abingdon, Routledge, 2018.

Zayani, Mohamed (Ed.). *A Fledgling Democracy: Tunisia in the Aftermath of the Arab Uprisings*. Oxford, Oxford University Press, 2023.

TÜRKIYE (TURKEY)

Geography

The Republic of Türkiye (known as the Republic of Turkey prior to June 2022) consists essentially of the large peninsula of Asia Minor, which is bounded by the sea on three sides (the Black Sea to the north, the Aegean to the west and the Mediterranean to the south) and high mountain ranges on the fourth (eastern) side. The small region of European Türkiye, containing the cities of İstanbul (Constantinople) and Edirne (Adrianople), is, by contrast, defined by a purely artificial frontier, the exact position of which has varied considerably since the 19th century, according to the fluctuating fortunes and prestige of Türkiye itself. Another small territory, the Hatay, in southern Türkiye and centred on İskenderun (Alexandretta), is bordered to the west by the Mediterranean sea and to the east by the Syrian Arab Republic, from which it was acquired as part of a diplomatic bargain in 1939. The total area of Türkiye is estimated at 783,562 sq km (302,535 sq miles), of which 769,604 sq km is land and 13,958 sq km is inland waterways.

PHYSICAL FEATURES

The geological structure of Türkiye is extremely complicated, and rocks of almost all ages occur, from the most ancient to most recent. Broadly speaking, Türkiye consists of a number of old plateau blocks, against which masses of younger rock series have been squeezed to form fold mountain ranges of varying size. As there were several of these plateau blocks, rather than just one, the fold mountains run in many different directions, with considerable irregularity, and hence no simple pattern can be discerned—instead, one mountain range gives place to another abruptly, and can pass suddenly from highland to plain or plateau.

In general outline, Türkiye consists of a ring of mountains enclosing a series of inland plateaux, with the highest mountains to the east, close to Armenia and Iran. Mount Ararat is the highest peak in Türkiye, reaching 5,165 m, and there are neighbouring peaks almost as high. In the west the average altitude of the hills is distinctly lower, though the highest peak (Mount Erciyas, or Argaeus) is over 3,900 m. The irregular topography of Türkiye has given rise to many lakes, some salt and some fresh, and generally more numerous than elsewhere in the Middle East. The largest, Lake Van, covers nearly 4,000 sq km.

Two other features may be mentioned. Large areas of the east and some parts of the centre of Asia Minor have been covered in sheets of lava, which are often of such recent occurrence that soil has not yet been formed—consequently, wide expanses are sterile and uninhabited. Second, in the north and west, cracking and disturbance of the rocks has taken place on an enormous scale. The long, indented coast of the Aegean Sea, with its numerous oddly shaped islands and estuaries, is due to cracking in two directions, which has split the land into detached blocks of roughly rectangular shape. Often the lower parts have sunk and been drowned by the sea. The Bosphorus and Dardanelles owe their origin to this faulting action, and the whole of the Black Sea coast is due to subsidence along a great series of fissures. Movement and adjustment along these cracks has by no means ceased, so that at the present day earthquakes are frequent in the north and west of Türkiye.

Owing to the presence of mountain ranges close to the coast, and the great height of the interior plateaux (varying from 800 m to 2,000 m), Türkiye has special climatic conditions, characterized by great extremes of temperature and rainfall, with wide variation from one district to another. In winter, conditions are severe in most areas, except for those lying close to sea level. Temperatures of −30°C to −40°C can occur in the east, and snow lies there for as many as 120 days each year. The west has frost on most nights of December and January, and (again apart from the coastal zone) has an average winter temperature below 1°C. In summer, however, temperatures over most of Türkiye exceed 30°C, with 43°C in the south-east. There can hence be enormous seasonal variations of temperature—sometimes over 50°C, among the widest in the world.

Rainfall, too, is remarkably variable. Along the eastern Black Sea coast, towards the Georgian frontier, over 2,500 mm fall annually; elsewhere, amounts are very much smaller. Parts of the central plateau, being shut off by mountains from the influence of sea winds, are arid, with annual totals of under 250 mm, and expanses of salt steppe and desert are frequent. The main towns of Anatolia, including Ankara, the capital, are placed away from the centre and close to the hills, where rainfall tends to be greater and water supplies better.

It is necessary to emphasize the contrast that exists between the Aegean coastlands, which, climatically, are by far the most favoured regions of Türkiye, and the rest of the country. Round the Aegean, winters are mild and fairly rainy, and the summers hot, but tempered by a persistent northerly wind, the Meltemi, or Etesian wind, which is of great value in ripening fruit, especially figs and sultana grapes.

POPULATION

According to the results of the census conducted in October 2000, the country's population numbered 67,803,927. At the time of the most recent periodic census, in October 2011, this figure had risen to 74,525,696. By 31 December 2022, according to official figures, the population had increased further to 85,279,553, giving an average population density of 110.8 inhabitants per sq km (land area only). Ankara is the administrative capital, although the commercial and financial centre of the country is İstanbul, which had a population of 15.9m. in 2022, according to official figures. Ankara was the second largest city, with a population of 5.8m.

The Turkish language, which is of central Asiatic origin, is spoken over most, but by no means all, of the country. This was introduced into Türkiye in Seljuq times, and was originally written in Arabic characters. Roman (i.e. European) script has been compulsory since 1928. In addition, there are a number of non-Turkish languages. Kurdish is widely spoken in the south-east, along the Syrian and Iraqi frontiers; and Caucasian dialects, distinct from either Turkish or Kurdish, occur in the north-east. Greek and Armenian were once widespread but, since the 1920s, have been current only in the city of İstanbul.

History

Revised by GARETH JENKINS

ANCIENT HISTORY

The history of Türkiye (known as Turkey prior to June 2022) stretches back to the very beginnings of human civilization. Excavations at Çatal Höyük, in central Anatolia south of Konya, show that agriculture, urban settlement and trade were flourishing more than 6,000 years ago in what is now Türkiye. Written history begins much later, with colonies of merchants from Assyria at Kültepe, near present-day Kayseri, just after 2000 BCE. Around 1700 BCE the Hittites established an empire which lasted until around 1200 BCE and was one of the dominant states of the eastern Mediterranean, having diplomatic and military relations with Egypt. The Hittite Empire collapsed soon after 1200 BCE, as a result of a wave of immigrants—the Phrygians, Cimmerians, Lydians and others whose archaeological remains are often impressive but who left virtually no written records. Among these invaders were Greek-speakers who established towns along Turkey's western coast on the Aegean, in the region known as Ionia, and later expanded along the Mediterranean and Black Sea coasts.

In 546 BCE Persia conquered the whole of Anatolia. However, this and the subsequent conquest by Alexander the Great in 334 BCE and the establishment of the Roman province of Asia in 133 BCE did not impede the steady spread of Greek language and culture in the cities.

In 330 CE the Emperor Constantine founded a new capital at Byzantium, until then a trading settlement and relatively minor city, and renamed it Constantinople. The city quickly became one of the world's major urban centres. It was the Roman/Byzantine capital until 1453 and the Ottoman capital up to the proclamation of the Republic in 1923. It was officially renamed Istanbul in 1930.

SELJUQS AND OTTOMANS

The disappearance of the Byzantine Empire was the outcome of a process that began at the Battle of Manzikert in August 1071, when Byzantine armies were defeated by the Seljuq Turks and central and eastern Anatolia passed under Turkish and Islamic rule. The following 400 years saw the loss of the remaining Byzantine possessions and the expansion of Ottoman power northwards into the Balkans. Though the Byzantines had been fighting their Muslim Arab neighbours for several hundred years, the Turks were newcomers. Their conquests were made easier by the Fourth Crusade, which conquered Constantinople from the Byzantines in 1204 and effectively fragmented Byzantine territory. The Seljuqs swiftly established a new Islamic empire in Anatolia after 1071, based at Konya, and the Turkish language quickly began to supplant Greek for official purposes, while a Persian court culture and Arabic religious culture replaced Roman and Greek traditions. Turkmen and other nomads moved into Anatolia, changing both its demographics and the pattern of agriculture. Substantial numbers of Greeks and other non-Muslims remained part of Anatolian society until the early 20th century. Within a few centuries of Manzikert, and even before the fall of Constantinople in 1453, Anatolia was widely known as 'Turkey' in many European countries.

Seljuq ascendancy was short-lived, its power broken by the Mongol invasions of the 13th century and its territory fragmented into local emirates across Anatolia. The emirate closest to the Byzantine heartlands was established at Söğüt by Osman Gazi, founder of the Ottoman dynasty, in northwestern Anatolia around 1290. His armies conquered the important city of Bursa in 1324, and the second Ottoman ruler proclaimed himself 'Sultan', although several decades would pass before this title was widely recognized. Ottoman armies first crossed the Dardanelles in 1348, immediately after the Black Death. Adrianople, the capital of Thrace, was taken in 1365 and became the new Ottoman capital. The invasion of Timur resulted in a major military reverse at the Battle of Ankara in 1402, but the Ottoman conquests were resumed less than a generation later. The conquest of Constantinople completed the transformation of a frontier-warrior emirate into a new regional empire and was followed by further expansion into the Balkans and also into the Middle East. By 1530 the Ottoman Empire extended from Hungary to Egypt.

After Süleyman I ('the Magnificent'), the Ottoman Empire began losing ground to the West. The Battle of Lepanto (in Turkish İnebahtı) in 1579 meant the end of Ottoman sea domination and the abandonment of hopes of expansion into Italy. A generation ago scholars spoke confidently of an 'Ottoman' decline, but this word is out of vogue with many 21st-century historians. None the less, it is clear first that, with some exceptions (military technology being the main one), the Ottomans did not experience the set of dynamic changes and innovations that were taking place in Europe. Most importantly, the printing press was not allowed to operate until the early 18th century. Nevertheless, Turkish military power was still capable of staging major incursions into Central Europe: for instance, the famous but unsuccessful siege of Vienna in 1689.

Ottoman attempts at reform were made in the 1730s, with the recruiting of officers from France, but the Janissary armies, hereditary warrior guilds, were strongly resistant to change. The rise of Russian power was witnessed under Peter the Great (1672–1725) and Catherine I (1684–1727). Military reverses culminated in the loss of the Crimea, and the important commercial routes it controlled, to the Russians at the Treaty of Küçük Kaynarca in 1774. The Empire was now so weak that its survival was in doubt. It was not until the reign of Selim III during 1787–1807 that the Ottoman Government began to respond to the challenge to its survival by promoting not only military reforms but a wide range of other changes, and systematically exploiting international alliances and diplomacy. Napoleon's invasion of Egypt in 1798 was the final wake-up call for the Empire.

However, the immediate and most serious danger to the Ottomans was from Russia, which fought a total of eight wars with the Empire between 1774 and 1918. The threat of Russian expansion enabled the Turks to obtain diplomatic and practical support from the British and the French, but in the Balkans the Christian nationalities of the Empire began to struggle for independence, beginning with the Serbs in 1804 and the Greek War of Independence (1821–30). At the outset of this period the Ottomans had no army in the modern sense and no civil service—only 2,000 scribes. By the end of the 19th century Turkey had a modern army and an imperial civil service of about 100,000 officials. A second major thread in 19th-century Ottoman history is the arrival of several million Muslim migrants from Circassia, the Caucasus and the Balkans, as a result of Christian conquests in those areas. These migrations tipped the balance in Anatolia in favour of Muslims even before the First World War (1914–18), and without them much of present-day Türkiye might not have remained either Turkish or Muslim. At least one-half of the Turkish population today is believed to be descended from these immigrants.

In 1839 the Ottoman Government embarked on a period of educational, legal and administrative reform known as the *Tanzimat* (reordering). This process accelerated in the wake of the Crimean War (1853–56) after the United Kingdom and France rejected Russian proposals for a joint partition of the Ottoman Empire and instead fought a war to protect it. However, the reforms had only a limited impact and in the 1870s, after the deaths of the *Tanzimat* reformers, the Empire slid rapidly into financial bankruptcy. Christian uprisings began in Bulgaria and the western Balkans, and harsh reprisals (known as the Bulgarian Atrocities) ended the friendship between the UK and Turkey for the next half a century and created an image problem for Turkey that has persisted to this day.

In 1876 a new pro-Islamic and anti-British Sultan, Abdülhamit II, acceded to the throne. After initially allowing the promulgation of a Constitution and the opening of Turkey's first ever parliament, in 1878 Abdülhamit II suspended the former and closed the latter. He then ruled as an autocrat until 1908. During this period Turkey was effectively a collective protectorate of the European 'Great Powers' with only limited freedom of action, and its final disappearance was widely supposed to be only a matter of time. None the less, technological and economic modernization continued, and the late 19th century was a period of relative prosperity.

In 1908 Abdülhamit was forced to reintroduce the Constitution and parliament by the Committee of Union and Progress (CUP), an underground political party formed of army officers and officials, bent on modernization and 'Turkification'. It took the CUP several years to consolidate its hold on power. During this period attacks first by Italy (1911) and then by an alliance of Greece, Bulgaria and Serbia (1912–13) resulted in the loss of nearly all of the empire's remaining territories in the Balkans and the Aegean Sea.

By early 1914 the Government was dominated by a triumvirate of leading members of the CUP, Enver Pasha, Ahmed Cemal Pasha and Talat Pasha (the only civilian member of the junta). Although civilian public opinion seems to have expected Turkey to stay neutral in the First World War, Enver Pasha was staunchly pro-German and struck at Russian targets in the Black Sea in the hope that what he regarded as a likely German victory in the war would enable the Ottoman Empire to recapture some of the territory it had lost over the previous centuries. His actions were followed by a Russian invasion and occupation of eastern Turkey for several years. The Russian incursion raised the question of the loyalty of the Christian Armenian population, some of whom had previously staged armed revolts against Ottoman rule. In what appeared to have been a combination of prejudice and a pre-emptive move to guard against further Armenian rebellions, in 1915, with the exception of the Armenians in İstanbul, which was also home to the foreign diplomatic community, virtually the entire Armenian population of Anatolia was dispatched on forced marches to what is now the Syrian Arab Republic. The vast majority of those deported were believed either to have been killed or to have died of hunger and disease during the journey.

The acrimonious historical debate that followed now revolves less around whether such things happened than whether or not the deaths constituted a 'genocide' and what the exact numbers were. In what are purported to be his personal notes, Minister of the Interior Talat Pasha, who oversaw the deportations, put the number of Armenians who were forcibly displaced at 924,158. Armenian historians claim that some 1.5m. Armenians were killed. Demographers of the Ottoman Empire estimate that in all about 3.3m. Ottomans of all faiths died as a result of the wars between 1911 and 1923, out of a population of about 17m. A large number of the dead, perhaps as many as 2m., were Muslims, mainly as the result of disease and famine. Whatever the exact number of fatalities, the legacy of 'the Armenian massacres' remains a very strong influence on Western perceptions of the Turks, while Turkish families with their own direct memories of suffering in the First World War are often equally uncompromising. Some European politicians would like to see acknowledgement of guilt for the events of 1915 made a condition for Turkish admission to the European Union (EU), although this is not part of the Union's formal position.

Despite Turkey's defeats by Russia, the Ottoman armies scored some important successes. An invading British army suffered a humiliating defeat at Kut al-Amara, on the Euphrates river, and a bold but mismanaged Allied landing on the Dardanelles Straits intended to force open the routes to Russia via İstanbul led to an equally great military disaster at Gallipoli in 1915 and an estimated 500,000 deaths. Two years later, however, the Ottoman Arab lands fell quickly to a British army entering from Egypt, and soon afterwards Bulgaria surrendered, severing Turkish links with Germany. On 30 October 1918 an armistice was signed at Mudros, and French, Italian and British occupation forces moved into Turkey.

Preliminary discussions about the post-war partitioning of the Ottoman lands had been taking place between the British and French since 1915; areas of influence in the Arab world were defined in the 1916 Sykes–Picot Agreement. It was taken for granted that the Arab territories would be permanently removed from Ottoman control. Yet Greece, the Armenians and some of the Western powers also eyed the Empire's Turkish heartlands. A partition treaty signed at Sèvres in August 1920 reduced Turkey to a small rump state, and gave areas of Anatolia to Greece, France, Italy and new Kurdish and Armenian states, while the UK would effectively have İstanbul and its free zone. The treaty was signed by four representatives of the Sultan but never ratified by Turkey. It was the lowest point in Turkey's fortunes as a nation and has remained something of an obsession with Turkish public opinion ever since.

The agreement signed at Sèvres was the logical outcome of numerous discussions of partition over the previous century. The difficulty had always been how to implement them. By the time the Treaty of Sèvres was signed, Greek armies had been in possession of İzmir for over a year and were advancing eastwards along the Menderes valley. The Greeks had hoped to use *force majeure* to seize most of western Turkey and make it part of a Greater Greece. However, a resistance movement had been established in Ankara with its own National Assembly.

THE RISE OF ATATÜRK

The 'Young Turk' Government had collapsed with the armistice of 1918; its leaders fled abroad, and the CUP dispersed. Although there continued to be an Ottoman legislative assembly in İstanbul, power had effectively returned to the Sultan, who was now propped up by the forces of the occupying powers.

Meanwhile, the Allied powers were at last completing arrangements for the partition of the Ottoman Empire. After a series of conferences, a treaty was drawn up and signed by the Allied representatives and those of the Sultan's Government at Sèvres on 10 August 1920. The Treaty of Sèvres was very harsh—far more so than that imposed on Germany. However, it was never implemented. While the Allies were imposing their terms on the Sultan and his Government in İstanbul, a resistance movement arose in the interior of Anatolia, based on the rejection of the treaty and the principles on which it was founded.

The leader of the movement was a general, Mustafa Kemal, who was born in 1880 in Salonika, then an Ottoman city. A career army officer by education, Kemal was sidelined during the 'Young Turk' revolution but made his name within the Ottoman military when he served with distinction as commander of a division during the Allied invasion at Gallipoli in 1915.

However, he remained unknown to the public at large and was not regarded as a potential threat by the Allies that occupied İstanbul. Kemal also appeared to enjoy the confidence of the Sultan and was given the task of disbanding the Ottoman army in Anatolia. On 19 May 1919—four days after the Greek landing in İzmir—he arrived at Samsun, on the Black Sea coast. After meeting with British officials, he continued his journey into Anatolia, where, instead of disbanding the Ottoman army, he set about organizing a resistance movement against foreign occupation.

Leading figures moved to Ankara, the base of the resistance, from İstanbul to take part in the struggle. On 23 July 1919 Mustafa Kemal and his associates convened the first National Congress in Erzurum and drew up a national programme. Delegates from all over the country attended a second congress, held in September. An Executive Committee, presided over by Kemal, was formed, and chose Ankara, then a minor provincial town, as its headquarters. Ankara soon became the effective capital of the resistance movement and forces. On 28 January 1920 the last Ottoman parliament, which was dominated by supporters of the Resistance, approved the National Pact, which decisively rejected the occupation of territories inhabited by a Muslim—i.e. Turkish or Kurdish—majority. In April a new Grand National Assembly of 350 deputies met in Ankara, proclaiming sovereignty in the name of the nation and adopting the National Pact.

There remained the military task of expelling the invaders. The Greco–Turkish war fell into three stages, covering roughly the campaigns of 1920, 1921 and 1922. In the first campaign, the Resistance, hopelessly outmatched in numbers and material, was badly defeated and the Greeks advanced far into Anatolia. Greek gunfire was even heard in Ankara. The second campaign began with Greek successes, but the Turks rallied and defeated the invaders first at İnönü—from which İsmet Pasha, who commanded the Turkish forces there, later took his surname—and then, on 24 August 1921, in a major battle on the Sakarya river, where the Turkish forces were under the personal command of Mustafa Kemal. This victory considerably strengthened the Resistance, which was henceforth generally perceived as the effective Government of Turkey. The French and Italians withdrew from the areas of Anatolia assigned to them under the Treaty of Sèvres and negotiated separate terms with the new Government. The Soviets, now established on Turkey's eastern frontier, had already done so at the beginning of the year.

In August 1922 the third and final phase of the war began. The Turkish army drove the Greeks back to the Aegean and reoccupied İzmir on 9 September. Mustafa Kemal now prepared to cross to Thrace. To do so he had to cross the Straits, still under Allied occupation. The French and Italian contingents withdrew, and the British followed. On 11 October an armistice was signed at Mudanya, whereby the Allied Governments agreed to the restoration of Turkish sovereignty in Eastern Thrace. In November the last Sultan, Vahdettin (Mehmet VI), was deposed and went into exile. A peace conference opened at Lausanne, Switzerland, in November. The Treaty of Lausanne, a landmark in the history of the region, was eventually signed on 24 July 1923. It recognized Turkish sovereignty over virtually all of Turkey's present territories, defining relations between Greece and Turkey and abolishing privileges for foreigners in the country. The only reservations related to the status of Mosul in northern Iraq, which was not settled until 1926, and the demilitarization of the Straits, which were not to be fortified without the consent of the powers. This consent, given at the Montreux Conference in 1936, continues to define international rights over the Turkish waterways of the Dardanelles and the Bosphorus.

THE TURKISH REPUBLIC

Once peace was established, Mustafa Kemal (who was to assume the name of Atatürk—'Father of the Turks'—in 1934) embarked on a process of Westernization and the integration of Turkey, on a basis of equality, into the modern Western world. Between 1922 and 1938, the year of his death, Kemal carried through a series of far-reaching reforms intended to create a strong nation-state.

The first changes were constitutional. On 29 October 1923 Turkey was declared a Republic, with Kemal as President. After the deposition of Sultan Vahdettin in November 1922, a brief experiment was made with a purely religious sovereignty and Abdülmecit II was proclaimed as Caliph but not Sultan. The experiment was not successful. Abdülmecit II followed his predecessor into exile in 1924 and the Caliphate was abolished. The Kemalist regime was effectively a single-party dictatorship, with the Cumhuriyet Halk Partisi (CHP—Republican People's Party) forming the main instrument for the enforcement of government policy. The Constitution of 20 April 1924 made the elected parliament the sole repository of sovereign power. Executive power was to be exercised by the President and a cabinet chosen by him.

The next object of attack was the religious system, already weakened by the removal of the Sultan-Caliph, which Kemal saw as the source of Turkey's backwardness. In 1924 the office of the Sheikh ul-Islam (Şeyhülislam—the head of the Sunni Muslim religious establishment in the Ottoman Empire) was replaced by a state-controlled Directorate of Religious Affairs. The separate Islamic schools (*medreses*) were simultaneously closed down. Symbolically, the most striking reform was the abolition of the fez in 1925. However, this was probably less important in the long run than the abrogation of the old legal system in 1926 and the introduction of new civil, criminal and commercial codes of law adapted from Europe. These meant that Turkey had finally broken completely with *Shari'a* (Islamic) law. In 1928 the Arabic script, which had previously been used to write Turkish, was replaced with a version of the Latin alphabet. When combined with an overhaul of the Turkish language itself, including removing many loan words and grammatical constructions, the effect was to cut off younger generations from the Ottoman past.

National policymaking in the new republic had as its principal goal the defence of national sovereignty, but the pursuit of economic development came a close second. During the mid-1920s economic policy was generally conceived of along free market lines, although it was assumed that there should be 'national' ownership of business and that foreign nationals were unwelcome. As a result, from 1928 the 'colonies' of foreign business people in İstanbul were encouraged to leave. By 1932 restrictions were in place on the currency that remained in force until the late 1980s. Many Turkish indigenous businesses set up in the early Republic proved unviable and the state became regarded as the main locomotive of economic development. Industrial enterprises were set up by the state along lines loosely copied from the Union of Soviet Socialist Republics (USSR). Factories for staple commodities, including textiles, paper, chemicals, glass, and iron and steel, were established. By the beginning of the Second World War (1939–45) the Turkish economy was still overwhelmingly agricultural and traditional, but the foundations of a new order had been laid.

The foreign policy of the Republic was, for a long time, one of strict non-involvement in foreign disputes, and the maintenance of friendly relations with as many powers as possible. By the late 1930s, however, the growing threat of German, and especially Italian, expansionism prompted Turkey to strengthen its links with the UK, culminating in a mutual defence pact in May 1939 between Turkey, France and the UK.

In 1925 there was a major Kurdish revolt in the south-eastern provinces. It was defeated and its leader, Şeyh Sait, was hanged. Kurdish leaders were exiled, but further revolts followed. One of the most serious was the Dersim Uprising of 1937, which briefly challenged the central Government, before being defeated. Public use of Kurdish was discouraged (although it only became illegal in 1982) and manifestations of Kurdish ethnic identity were prohibited. However, provided that they did not advertise their ethnic origins, Kurds were able to serve at all levels in the civilian Government and the army.

The death of Mustafa Kemal Atatürk in November 1938 was a great shock to Turkey. He was succeeded as President by İsmet İnönü, a less charismatic but more socially orthodox figure than Atatürk. İnönü ruled Turkey until May 1950.

TURKEY DURING THE SECOND WORLD WAR

Despite the May 1939 Pact with the French and the British, the Turkish Government decided to remain neutral at the outbreak of the Second World War. In June 1941, when German expansion in the Balkans had brought the German armies to within 161 km of İstanbul, the Turkish Government further protected itself by signing a friendship and trade agreement with Germany.

One main consideration holding Turkey back from active participation in the war was mistrust of the USSR, and the widespread feeling that Nazi conquest and Soviet 'liberation' were equally to be feared. Hence, it was not until August 1944, when they were confident that it would lose the war, that the Turks broke off diplomatic relations with Germany. On 23 February 1945 Turkey declared war on Germany in order to comply with the formalities of entry to the UN Conference.

The war years subjected Turkey to severe economic strains, which made the İnönü Government deeply unpopular. Between 1945 and 1950 Turkish opposition politicians began to press for the right to set up their own parties and to contest free elections. When the Charter of the United Nations (UN) was introduced for ratification in the Turkish parliament in 1945, a group of members, led by Celâl Bayar, Adnan Menderes, Fuad Köprülü and Refik Koraltan, used the occasion to press for democratic freedoms in Turkey and were expelled from the ruling party. In November President İnönü announced the end of the single-party system. In January 1946 the opposition leaders registered the new Demokrat Parti (DP—Democrat Party).

TURKEY UNDER THE DP

In the general election of 21 July 1946 the DP opposition won 70 out of 416 parliamentary seats, but there can be little doubt that completely free elections would have given them many more. During the years that followed, a series of changes in both law and practice ensured the growth of democratic liberties. Freedom of the press and of association were extended and on 15 February 1950 a new electoral law was approved, guaranteeing free and fair elections. On 28 May a new general election was held, in which the DP won an overwhelming victory. İnönü resigned, and Celâl Bayar replaced him as President. A new cabinet was formed, with Adnan Menderes as Prime Minister. The new regime adopted an economic policy friendlier to private enterprise, both Turkish and foreign, but its policies were erratic and its control over the economy weakened as time passed. The primary determinant of the DP's political success was its ability to satisfy rural voter aspirations. This included removing some of the restrictions that Atatürk had placed on the role of Islam in public life. During the first half of the 1950s the Turkish economy grew rapidly, with the result that the DP won a resounding victory in the general election of May 1954.

By the second half of the 1950s the economy was in serious trouble, with lower growth, a spiralling trade deficit and a sharp increase in inflation. Hence, in the 1957 general election the DP's share of the vote fell to less than 50%, although it retained power.

FOREIGN AFFAIRS, 1945–60

In foreign affairs, both the CHP and the DP Governments followed a firm policy of unreserved identification with the West in the Cold War. From May 1947 the USA extended economic and military aid to Turkey on an increasing scale. In 1950 Turkey dispatched troops to fight in Korea. In August 1949 Turkey became a member of the Council of Europe, and early in 1952 acceded to full membership of the North Atlantic Treaty Organization (NATO).

In January 1957 the USA announced a new programme of economic and military assistance for those countries in the region that were willing to accept it. From the mid-1950s relations with Greece steadily deteriorated, not least over the campaign by Greek Cypriots to unite Cyprus (which at the time was a British colony and was home to a large number of Turkish Cypriots), with mainland Greece. A compromise was reached in the form of Cyprus's independence from Britain in 1960, with Turkey, Greece and the UK as guarantor powers and a Constitution that was designed to ensure power-sharing between the two communities on the island.

Adherence to NATO and the Central Treaty Organization remained the basis of Turkey's foreign policy during the late 1950s. By the beginning of 1960, however, the Menderes Government was beginning to explore the possibilities of an improved bilateral relationship with the USSR. This was the start of a general multilateralization of Turkish foreign policy that would expose conflicts between Turkey's regional interests and its commitment to an alliance with the USA.

THE 1960 COUP

Heavy trade deficits and inflation continued to create severe political difficulties for the DP Government. Hostility between the DP and the opposition CHP grew steadily more marked, and was sharpened towards the end of 1959 by suspicions that the DP was planning to hold elections in the near future, ahead of schedule.

In May 1959 political tension between the two main parties had resulted in violence during a political tour of Anatolia conducted by the opposition leader, İsmet İnönü. The Government banned all political meetings, tightened censorship and increasingly suppressed opposition activities. At the end of April 1960 student unrest led to the imposition of martial law. As martial law administrator, the Turkish army found itself, for the first time in half a century, sucked into politics. In the early hours of 27 May, with civilian politics on the point of collapse, the military seized power. President Bayar, Prime Minister Menderes, most DP deputies, and a number of officials and senior officers were arrested. The Government was replaced by a junta of military officers, 'the Committee of National Unity', headed by Gen. Cemal Gürsel.

The coup was successful and initially almost bloodless. The Menderes regime was accused of violating the Constitution and moving towards dictatorship. However, the officers insisted that they were temporary custodians of authority and would hand over to the duly constituted civilian authorities.

THE RETURN TO CIVILIAN GOVERNMENT

The Committee of National Unity, which had originally comprised 37 members, was reduced to 23 on 13 November 1960 following a purge of hardliners as preparations for a return to civilian rule continued. A new Constituent Assembly, to act as a temporary parliament, was convened at the beginning of January 1961. It comprised the 23 members of the Committee of National Unity, acting jointly with a House of Representatives of 271 members, both elected and nominated. In this the CHP predominated. At the same time, party politics were again legalized, and a number of new parties emerged. Some of them proved short-lived, but one, the Adalet Partisi (AP—Justice Party), founded by Gen. Ragip Gümüşpala, who had been Commander of the Third Army at the time of the coup, attracted the support of many former adherents of the DP, which was now illegal.

A special committee of the Assembly framed a new Constitution, which included significant departures from the 1924 version. It provided for a court to determine the constitutionality of laws, a bicameral legislature (comprising a National Assembly and a Senate), and a commitment to 'social justice' as one of the aims of the state. However, in September 1961 the former Prime Minister, Adnan Menderes, and two of his former ministers were hanged, following an 11-month trial. In September 1990, following a prolonged campaign by right-wing factions, their bodies were exhumed and re-buried in İstanbul with state honours.

On 15 October 1961 the CHP won 173 seats and the AP 158 seats in the election to the National Assembly, and 36 and 70 seats, respectively, in the Senate. As support for the DP was still strong, and the CHP had failed to achieve an overall majority, a coalition became necessary. On 10 November İnönü, the leader of the CHP, was asked to form a government and, after much hesitation and strong pressure from the army, the AP agreed to join forces with its rival. A new administration was formed, with İnönü as Prime Minister, Akıf İyidoğan of the AP as Deputy Prime Minister and 10 other ministers from each of the two coalition parties.

DEMIREL GOVERNMENT

In the Senate elections in June 1964 the AP won 31 out of the 51 seats contested, thus increasing its already large majority in the house. Its success was clouded by the death of the party's leader, Gen. Gümüşpala. In November Süleyman Demirel was elected leader in his place, although he was without a seat in parliament. İnönü survived more than one narrow vote of confidence but was finally defeated on 13 February 1965 during voting on the budget in the National Assembly.

In the general election of 11 October 1965, the AP under Demirel won an overall majority. The Demirel Government proved only marginally more successful than its predecessor in achieving its objectives. However, elections in June 1966 for one-third of the seats in the Senate showed that the AP was not losing popularity. Meanwhile, in March President Gürsel was succeeded by Senator Cevdet Sunay, also a former army Chief of Staff.

Bülent Ecevit, Minister of Labour in 1961–65, was elected Secretary-General of the CHP and announced his intention to turn it into a social democratic party. However, six months later 48 senators and members of the National Assembly resigned from the party, on the grounds that it was becoming overly radical.

MILITARY INTERVENTION

Demirel's AP Government was faced by growing political violence from early 1968 onwards. Tension in the universities, emanating from non-political educational grievances and from clashes between political extremists of the right and the left, took an increasingly violent form. Parliamentary politics also became deeply confused, with divisions on all sides. Elections in October 1969 produced an enlarged majority for the AP, but the party soon split, with a number of Demirel's right-wing opponents forming a new DP. A new party, the Milli Nizam Partisi (MNP—National Order Party), with right-wing policies and theocratic tendencies, was formed in January 1970 by Prof. Necmettin Erbakan. It was the first sign of the Islamist revival in Turkey.

Disorder increased, but it was still a considerable surprise when, on 12 March 1971, the Chief of the General Staff and the army, navy and air force commanders delivered a memorandum to the President, demanding the cabinet's resignation. Later that day Demirel resigned. It subsequently emerged that the commanders had intervened ahead of a more radical coup by less senior officers.

MILITARY DOMINATION OF POLITICS

A new army-backed Government was formed by a former Prime Minister, Dr Nihat Erim, with the support of both the AP and the CHP. Bülent Ecevit, the CHP Secretary-General, resigned from office and refused to co-operate with the new administration. Erim's programme promised sweeping reforms in taxation, land ownership, education, power and industry, but the Government's attention was first directed to the suppression of political violence. The military ultimatum was followed by further bombings, kidnappings and clashes between right- and left-wing students and between students and police. On 28 April 1971 martial law was proclaimed, initially for one month, in 11 provinces, including Ankara and İstanbul. Newspapers were suppressed, strikes were banned and large numbers of left-wing supporters were arrested.

In May 1972 a Council of Ministers drawn from the AP, the National Reliance Party and the CHP, headed by Ferit Melen, was approved. There was a shift to the left within the CHP in May. İnönü resigned after 34 years as Chairman and was replaced by Ecevit. Meanwhile, martial law was renewed at two-month intervals. President Sunay's term of office expired in March 1973. Gen. Faruk Gürler, who had been army commander during the 1971 coup, resigned from his post as Chief of Staff in order to stand for the presidency, his candidacy receiving the strong support of the armed forces. Despite obvious military support for Gen. Gürler, 14 ballots failed to produce a result, and eventually the AP, CHP and Cumhuriyetci Güven Partisi (CGP—Republican Reliance Party) agreed on a compromise candidate, Senator Fahri Korutürk, a former head of the navy, with no party political affiliation. He was elected President on 6 April 1973. The following day Melen resigned, and was succeeded as Prime Minister by Naim Talu, an independent senator, who formed a Government with AP and CGP participation. Gradually, the armed forces withdrew from political affairs, and in September martial law was lifted.

FOREIGN POLICY DEVELOPMENTS

The 1960 constitutional arrangement on Cyprus broke down in December 1962. Tensions remained high through the mid-1960s and Turkish military intervention on the island was avoided only by international pressure, mainly from the USA, after attacks on Turkish enclaves by Greek Cypriots in November 1967. In February 1974 Greece announced that petroleum had been found in Greek territorial waters in the Aegean. This led to a dispute over the extent of national jurisdiction over the continental shelf and territorial waters, with both sides making aggressive moves in Thrace and the Aegean. The already tense situation in the Aegean was followed by a coup in Cyprus in July.

This coup was carried out by the Cypriot National Guard, led by officers from Greece, apparently with the support of the military regime in power in Athens at the time. Declaring its intention of protecting the Turkish community in Cyprus and preventing the union of Cyprus with mainland Greece, Turkey proclaimed its right to intervene as a guarantor state under the Zürich agreement of 1959. On 20 July 1974 Turkish troops landed in Cyprus and took control of the northern areas of the island. Negotiations were under way in August when Turkey launched a second offensive that gave it about one-third of the total area of Cyprus, but this came at a very high cost in terms of its standing in the world.

The flight of Greek Cypriot refugees from the north early in 1975 effectively left the Turks free to take over the administration and economy, and to establish a de facto partition of the island. The Turkish Cypriots unilaterally declared a 'Turkish Federated State' in northern Cyprus on 13 February, and continued pressing for the establishment of a bi-regional federal state system on the island. Subsequent rounds of negotiations between Greece and Turkey failed to achieve results. The US Congress imposed an embargo on military aid and the supply of arms to Turkey in February, on the grounds that US military equipment had been used in the Turkish invasion of Cyprus in July 1974 and that Turkey had failed to make substantial progress towards resolving the Cyprus crisis. After lengthy negotiations, a new bilateral defence agreement was reached between the two countries in March 1976, but the agreement was not immediately ratified, owing to the strength of the Greek lobby in the US Congress.

Finally, after lengthy negotiations, a five-year defence and economic co-operation agreement between Turkey and the USA was signed on 29 March 1980. In return for economic aid to help Turkey modernize its army and fulfil its NATO obligations, the USA obtained access to more than 25 military establishments, allowing expanded surveillance of the USSR. The USA's readiness to come to an agreement increased after the Soviet invasion of Afghanistan in December 1979, which heightened Turkey's strategic importance.

ECEVIT GOVERNMENT

Elections to the National Assembly and for 52 Senate seats were held on 14 October 1973. In the National Assembly, the CHP, with 185 seats, replaced the AP as the largest party but failed to win an overall majority. The CHP was believed to have won many votes from former supporters of the banned Türkiye İşçi Partisi (Workers' Party of Turkey), while the AP lost support to the DP and a new organization, the Milli Selamet Partisi (MSP—National Salvation Party). Led by Erbakan, the MSP had been founded in 1972 to replace the banned MNP, sharing its fundamentalist Islamist policies, and became the third largest party in the new National Assembly. Prime Minister Talu resigned, but then remained in office for a further three months while negotiations on the formation of a coalition government continued. On 25 January 1974 a Government was formed by the CHP and the MSP, with Bülent Ecevit as Prime Minister and Erbakan as his deputy. The Council of Ministers was composed of 18 CHP members and seven from the MSP.

The new Government, an apparently unlikely coalition of the left-of-centre CHP and the reactionary MSP, proclaimed its reforming intentions, but made significant concessions to the demands of its Muslim supporters. In February 1974 Turkey was for the first time represented at a summit meeting of the Organization of the Islamic Conference (OIC, now Organization of Islamic Cooperation).

The differences between the MSP and the CHP had been submerged during the Cyprus crisis, but once more became apparent in September 1974 as the MSP wanted a hard line taken on Cyprus, while Ecevit favoured early elections, which he seemed likely to win. On 16 September Ecevit resigned. He had miscalculated about being able to force early elections. Turkey remained without a government with a parliamentary majority for more than six months. In November Prof. Sadi Irmak attempted unsuccessfully to form a coalition to prepare for new elections in 1975 but remained in office in an interim capacity.

DEMIREL RETURNS TO POWER

In March 1975 Süleyman Demirel returned to power, leading a hard-line right-wing coalition, the Nationalist Front, consisting of four parties: Demirel's AP, the MSP, the CGP and the neo-fascist Milliyetçi Hareket Partisi (MHP—Nationalist Action Party) founded by Col (retd) Alparslan Türkeş, who became Deputy Prime Minister. The precarious nature of this coalition prevented the Government from taking radical measures lest they upset co-operation between the four parties. This prevented Demirel's Government from addressing the pressing problems of a deteriorating economy and increasing political violence. Erbakan refused to countenance the austerity measures demanded by the International Monetary Fund (IMF), while Türkeş stood in the way of a crackdown on political violence, some of which the 'Grey Wolves' of the MHP were thought to have instigated.

Increasing political violence throughout Turkey between left- and right-wing groups, especially in the universities, and growing economic paralysis persuaded the authorities to bring forward the general election, which was officially scheduled for October 1977, to June of that year.

However, the election failed to produce a decisive majority. While the CHP increased its share of seats in the National Assembly to 213 out of 450, the AP also increased its representation from 149 to 189 seats. Ecevit, the leader of the CHP, formed a Council of Ministers, but failed to agree a coalition with the smaller parties. A week later he was defeated in a vote of confidence. Demirel, the leader of the AP, was subsequently invited to form a new administration, and on 1 August members of the MSP and the MHP were awarded key portfolios in a coalition Government. There was a flare-up of violence on campuses. By mid-December one-third of the universities were shut, and 250 people had died in political violence. After losing a no-confidence vote in the legislature, the Demirel Government resigned on 31 December. On 2 January 1978 Ecevit returned to power with a new coalition.

ECEVIT RETURNS TO POWER

After the chaos of Demirel's administration, the appointment of Ecevit as Prime Minister was widely welcomed; however, his popular support was not reflected in the National Assembly. His majority was dependent upon the support of a small group of defectors from the AP, 10 of whom became ministers, while the number of deputies who had changed allegiance had resulted in a 'pool' of about 20 independents. Radical reforms were urged on Ecevit, but the insecure parliamentary majority, the country's economic weakness and the unwanted reputation of the CHP in conservative rural areas as a radical party made him cautious. The Government adopted an economic stabilization programme, signed a stand-by arrangement with the IMF and began work on restructuring the severe short-term debt burden. However, it was unable to secure the huge amounts of international financial assistance necessary to make the stabilization programme work and few of the economic targets were reached. Ecevit was unwilling to take further austerity measures demanded by the IMF as a condition for further aid. Moreover, political violence continued to escalate.

By December 1978 more than 800 people had been killed, particularly in the eastern provinces. These new areas of violence reflected a change of tactics by the MHP, which during 1978 campaigned in central and eastern Anatolia. Türkeş's appeal to nationalism gained him supporters, particularly in areas where Turks lived with other ethnic groups, notably the Kurds. The violence culminated in December at the south-eastern town of Kahramanmaraş in the most serious outbreak of ethnic fighting since the 1920s. There the historic enmity between the orthodox Sunni majority and the heterodox Alevi minority had been exacerbated by the activities of right- and left-wing agitators. On 21 December 1978 the Alevis turned the funeral of two members of the left-wing teachers' association, murdered the day before, into a large-scale demonstration. The mourners were fired on by Sunni supporters of Türkeş and indiscriminate rioting erupted. After three days, more than 100 people had been killed, at least 1,000 had been injured and large parts of the Alevi quarters had been reduced to ruins. Order was not restored until the army intervened on 24 December.

MARTIAL LAW

The violence led to the imposition of martial law on 26 December 1978. Martial law was imposed for two months (renewed subsequently at two-monthly intervals) in 13 provinces, all, except İstanbul and Ankara, in the east, although the mainly Kurdish areas of the south-east were excluded to prevent friction. Ecevit announced that it was to be 'martial law with a human face', and instituted a co-ordination committee for its implementation, comprising himself, Gen. Kenan Evren, the Chief of the General Staff, and Lt-Gen. Şahap Yardımoğlu, the Chief Martial Law Administrator.

In April 1979 six ministers, defectors from the AP, issued a public memorandum criticizing Ecevit for taking insufficient account of their views and demanding tougher measures to combat political violence, particularly by left-wing groups, and Kurdish separatism. They also demanded a redirection of economic policies to allow more Western investment and greater freedom for private enterprise. The gulf between their views and those of Ecevit's left-wing supporters in the CHP became more and more pronounced, and the impossibility of reconciling the left- and right-wing elements in the coalition became clear. In response to the growth of Kurdish separatism, and alarmed by Kurdish violence in Iran, Ecevit agreed to extend martial law into six more provinces, all in the Kurdish south-east. Three CHP deputies promptly resigned, reducing the party's minority representation in the National Assembly to 211 of 450.

During the next few months, further resignations by CHP deputies reduced Ecevit's parliamentary majority still further, and in October 1979 by-elections the AP achieved substantial additional gains. Ecevit resigned on 16 October. Eight days later Demirel formed a new Government with the backing of the right-wing MHP and the MSP, affording the Government a majority of four.

Disorder grew steadily, as did the warning signs of military involvement in politics. On 2 January 1980 the generals publicly urged all the political parties to reach a consensus on anti-terrorist measures. The weakness of the Government was illustrated by parliament's inability to choose a new head of state when President Korutürk's term expired in April. As neither the right nor the left was prepared to compromise on the choice of candidate, the President of the National Assembly, Ihsan Sabri Çağlayangil, took office as acting President. By August political violence had almost reached the level of a civil war. Although martial law continued to be extended every two months in 20 of the 67 provinces, clashes between rightists and leftists had caused some 2,000 deaths since the beginning of the year, and there was a growing trend towards the assassination of national figures.

THE 1980 COUP AND ITS AFTERMATH

On 12 September 1980 the armed forces, led by Gen. Evren, seized power in a bloodless coup, the third in 20 years. The main reasons for their intervention were the failure of the Government to deal with the country's political and economic chaos or to combat left- and right-wing terrorism. The leaders of the coup formed a five-member National Security Council (NSC), sworn in on 18 September. The Chairman of the NSC, Gen. Evren, became head of state. Martial law was extended to the whole country and the legislature was dissolved. On 21 September the NSC appointed a mainly civilian Council of Ministers, with a retired naval commander, Bülent Ulusu, as Prime Minister and Turgut Özal as Deputy Prime Minister and Minister for Economic Affairs. Former political leaders, suspected terrorists and political extremists were detained, while all political activity was banned, and trade union activities were restricted.

Although its rule was harsh, the military Government was committed to the eventual return of civilian rule within a framework that would prevent disorder. In October 1981 a Consultative Assembly was formed to draft a new constitution and to prepare the way for a return to parliamentary rule.

A new, extremely restrictive and authoritarian Constitution was approved by referendum on 7 November 1982, with a 91% majority, largely because to refuse it would have meant continued military rule. An appended 'temporary article' automatically installed Gen. Evren as President for a seven-year term. The opposition was not allowed to canvass openly against the new Constitution.

During its period in power the military regime purged several hundred left-wing university professors, closed newspapers, tightened press censorship and held mass trials of labour leaders and others. Torture and ill-treatment appeared to be routine during interrogation and just under 50 convicted terrorists were executed. In May 1983 the President revoked the 30-month ban on political activity and allowed political parties to be formed under strict rules. All the former political parties, which had been dissolved in October 1981, were to remain proscribed, along with 723 former members of the legislature and leading party officials who were banned from active politics for 10 years. Despite its excessive harshness, the military achieved its twin aims of restoring political stability and ushering in economic growth. Turkey after 1982 was a very different country from what it had been in the 1970s.

CIVILIAN RULE RETURNS UNDER ÖZAL

A general election was held on 6 November 1983, and parliamentary rule was restored, with a 400-seat unicameral Türkiye Büyük Millet Meclisi (TGNA—Turkish Grand National Assembly). Election was on the basis of proportional representation (with a minimum requirement of 10% of the total votes to discourage small parties), voting was compulsory, and every candidate had to be approved by the NSC.

The President banned a total of 11 parties from participating in the general election. The conservative Anavatan Partisi (ANAP—Motherland Party), led by Turgut Özal, won 211 of the 400 seats in the TGNA and the armed forces' preferred party, the centre-right Milliyetçi Demokratik Partisi (MDP—Nationalist Democracy Party), was beaten into third place, with the centre-left Halkçı Parti (HP—Populist Party) coming second. The result reflected the great popularity of Özal as the architect of economic recovery after 1980. He was appointed Prime Minister and named his Council of Ministers in December 1983. The MDP voted to disband itself in May 1986. Many of its members joined the new right-wing Hür Demokrat Partisi (Free Democratic Party), which was formed by Mehmet Yazar. By the end of 1986 there were four recognized parliamentary groups in the TGNA—ANAP, the Sosyal Demokrat Halkçı Parti (SHP—Social Democratic Populist Party), the Demokratik Sol Parti (DSP—Democratic Left Party) and the Doğru Yol Partisi (DYP—True Path Party).

Concern continued throughout the 1980s and the early 1990s regarding the persistent and widespread use of torture against political prisoners. In December 1985 a case brought before the Human Rights Commission of the Council of Europe by five European countries, alleging that Turkey had violated the European Convention for the Protection of Human Rights and Fundamental Freedoms, was settled out of court. Turkey agreed to rescind all martial law decrees within 18 months, to introduce an amnesty for political prisoners and to allow independent observers from the Council of Europe to monitor progress. In July 1987 all martial law decrees in Turkey were repealed.

FURTHER STEPS TOWARDS DEMOCRACY

In a national referendum, held in September 1987, a narrow majority approved the repeal of the restrictions imposed on over 200 politicians in 1981, banning them from taking an active part in public life for a period of 10 years. This enabled Bülent Ecevit to take over the leadership of the DSP (he never returned to the CHP), while Süleyman Demirel was elected as leader of the DYP.

As the polls for the referendum closed, Prime Minister Özal, who had campaigned against the repeal of the ban, immediately announced that a general election would be held on 1 November 1987 (a year earlier than required). Seven parties contested the general election, which was the first free election in Turkey since the 1980 military coup. ANAP obtained 36.3% of the votes cast (which, because of the 'weighted' electoral system, meant that it was allotted 292 of the seats in the TGNA, now enlarged from 400 to 450 seats), while the SHP (24.7% of the votes) won 99 seats, and the DYP (19.1% of the votes) took 59 seats. Özal formed an expanded Council of Ministers in December.

ÖZAL BECOMES PRESIDENT

In mid-October 1989 Özal declared his candidacy for the presidential election to be conducted in the TGNA on 31 October. On 9 November Özal succeeded Gen. Evren as President, and unexpectedly appointed Yıldırım Akbulut, the Speaker of the TGNA and a former Minister of the Interior, to succeed him as Prime Minister. Akbulut was subsequently elected as ANAP party leader.

At an ANAP party congress, convened on 15 June 1991, former Minister of Foreign Affairs Mesut Yılmaz defeated Akbulut in a contest for the party leadership. On the following day Akbulut resigned as Prime Minister, and on 17 June, in accordance with the Constitution, President Özal invited Yılmaz to head a new administration.

THE 1991 GENERAL ELECTION

At the general election on 20 October 1991, the DYP, under the leadership of Demirel, received an estimated 27.3% of the votes cast, narrowly defeating ANAP (with 23.9%) and the SHP (with 20.6%). Demirel assumed the premiership at the head of a coalition, comprising members of the DYP and the SHP: one effect of military rule had been to end the feud between politicians of the centre-left and centre-right. On 25 November the coalition partners announced a programme for political and economic reform that included the drafting of a new constitution, improvements in anti-terrorist legislation and human rights, and increased levels of cultural recognition and of autonomy in local government for Kurds in Turkey.

FOREIGN AFFAIRS, 1980–93

Relations between Turkey and the European Community (EC, now the EU) were poor in the 1970s. In January 1982, as a result of the human rights situation in Turkey and particularly the imprisonment of Bülent Ecevit by the military, the European Parliament voted to suspend relations with Turkey, and in March aid to Turkey was frozen.

In 1981 Greece joined the EC, adding a new dimension to Turkish–EC difficulties and the normalization of relations. In September 1986 the Turkish–EC Association Council (which was established in 1963 but had been suspended since the military coup in 1980) met for talks in Brussels, Belgium. Turkey, however, failed to gain access to the suspended EC aid because of Greek vetoes. In April 1987 Turgut Özal, ignoring the advice of EC ambassadors in Ankara, made a formal application to become a full member of the EC. Yet, in December 1989 the EC rejected Turkey's application to start negotiations until at least 1993.

Meanwhile, Özal moved to boost Turkish-US relations. Following the annexation of Kuwait by Iraq in August 1990, he broke with Turkish diplomatic tradition and allowed US troops logistical support in the coming Gulf War. In mid-January 1991 parliament approved a resolution that effectively endorsed the unrestricted use of Turkish airbases by coalition forces. On the following day US aircraft began bombing missions into north-east Iraq from NATO bases inside south-east Turkey. In February and March, the USA announced substantial increases in military and economic aid to Turkey for 1991 and 1992.

Turkish-Greek relations became further strained when the Turkish-backed 'Turkish Federated State of Cyprus' unilaterally declared independence, as the 'Turkish Republic of Northern Cyprus' ('TRNC'), in November 1983. It is still only recognized by Turkey. In March 1987 a disagreement between Greece and Turkey over petroleum-prospecting rights in the Aegean Sea almost resulted in military conflict. However, relations improved considerably in 1988: in February the Turkish Government officially annulled a decree, issued in 1964, that curbed the property rights of Turkey's ethnic Greek population. In return, the Greek Prime Minister, Andreas Papandreou, officially accepted Turkey's status as an associate member of the EC by signing the Protocol of Adaptation (consequent on Greece's accession to the EC) to the EC-Turkey

Association Agreement in April 1988, which the Greek Government had hitherto refused to do. However, the situation deteriorated later in the same month, when Greece insisted on linking the possibility of Turkey's entry into the EC with the ending of the Turkish presence in Cyprus.

Following the dissolution of the USSR in December 1991, the Turkish Government sought to further its political, economic and cultural influence in the Central Asian region, and in particular to forge strong links with the six Muslim states of the former USSR. In June 1992 leaders of 11 countries, including both Turkey and Greece and six former Soviet republics, established a Black Sea economic alliance (now the Organization of the Black Sea Economic Cooperation, based in İstanbul), and expressed their commitment to promoting greater co-operation with regard to transport, energy, information, communications and ecology.

POLICY TOWARDS THE TURKISH KURDS, 1980–93

During the 1980s Kurdish-nationalist terrorism became a serious problem for Turkey in its south-eastern provinces. In 1984 the outlawed Marxist Partiya Karkeren Kurdistan (PKK—Kurdistan Workers' Party), led by Abdullah Öcalan, which demanded the creation of revolutionary Kurdish and Turkish national homelands in Turkey and its neighbours, launched a violent guerrilla campaign, concentrating its attacks against local pro-Government militia and civilians. However, by July 1987, as a result of international pressure to return to democracy, martial law was replaced by a state of emergency under a district governor in all of the south-eastern provinces. Nevertheless, the violence in the south-east grew.

In late 1992 Turkish air and ground forces (in excess of 20,000 troops) struck at PKK bases inside northern Iraq, hoping to take advantage of losses inflicted upon the Kurdish rebels by a simultaneous offensive, initiated by Iraqi Kurdish *peshmerga* (militia) forces in October, with the aim of forcing the PKK out of Iraq. By December most Turkish ground forces had been withdrawn from Iraqi territory.

ÇILLER BECOMES PRIME MINISTER

In April 1993 President Özal died. He was succeeded by Süleyman Demirel on 16 May. In June Minister of State Tansu Çiller was elected to replace Demirel as DYP leader, thus becoming Turkey's first female Prime Minister.

On taking office, Çiller was immediately confronted with a dramatic increase in separatist violence. The PKK's announcement of the end of a unilateral ceasefire that it had declared in March 1993 was followed by a wave of bomb explosions in Turkish tourist resorts and abductions of foreign nationals by the PKK, as well as a series of attacks against Turkish diplomatic missions and business interests in Europe. This triggered increased military action and a political crackdown on Kurdish activities.

The pro-Kurdish Halkın Emek Partisi (HEP—People's Labour Party) was outlawed in July 1993. In March 1994 parliament voted to strip seven members of the Demokrasi Partisi (DEP—Democracy Party, the successor to HEP) and one independent Kurdish deputy of their parliamentary immunity from prosecution, and six deputies were subsequently detained. On 16 June Turkey's Constitutional Court banned the DEP and ruled that its 13 deputies should be expelled from the TGNA, owing to their alleged associations with the PKK. In December the six deputies detained since March, along with two DEP deputies arrested in July, were convicted on charges of supporting separatist movements and, despite international protests, received prison sentences of between three-and-a-half and 15 years. In October 1995 the Supreme Court released two of the deputies but upheld the sentences on the others.

In early 1994 the Turkish economy had suffered its biggest collapse since 1979. The main beneficiary was the Islamist movement. In the March 1994 nationwide local elections the Islamist Refah Partisi (RP—Welfare Party) won 19% of the votes cast and took control of both Ankara and İstanbul. These elections marked a decisive shift in the country's political life.

Despite continuing dissension within the Government, Çiller's coalition held together throughout the remainder of 1994, sustained, not least, by a shared fear of the RP. The Government's main priorities now related to passing democratic reforms so as to enable the customs union with the EU, planned since the 1960s and prepared for in a series of reductions in tariffs over 25 years. Turkey and the EU agreed on the customs union in March 1995. Turkey pledged not to block the accession of the Republic of Cyprus to the EU. For the customs union to come into force on 1 January 1996, the European Parliament had to ratify the change, and there was no prospect of this without significant progress on human rights in Turkey. In July Çiller secured approval from the TGNA for several democratization measures, including the lowering of the minimum voting age and the removal of certain restrictions on trade unions and political participation. In addition, the number of parliamentary seats was to be increased by 100, to 550.

Turkey's still strained relationship with Greece deteriorated in 1994 after Greece signed the UN Convention on the Law of the Sea, permitting the extension of its territorial waters in the Aegean Sea from six to 12 nautical miles. The Turkish Government, fearing the loss of shipping access to international seas, declared that any expansion of Greek territorial waters would be considered an act of aggression, to which Turkey would respond. As the Convention entered into force in November, both sides conducted military exercises in the Aegean. Tensions between the two countries overshadowed the negotiations in early 1995 to conclude the customs union between the EU and Turkey. Greece finally withdrew its opposition to the agreement in March, following the adoption of a formal timetable for accession negotiations with Cyprus. In Cyprus, President Glavkos Klerides had signed a bilateral defence agreement with Greece that, in Turkish eyes, upset the strategic balance between the two countries. In June 1994, in response to the ratification of the Law of the Sea Convention by the Greek Parliament, the TGNA granted the Government powers to defend the country's interests militarily in the Aegean.

In September 1995 Deniz Baykal was elected as the new leader of the CHP. Negotiations subsequently failed to secure agreement on the continuation of the ruling coalition. In October Çiller formed a caretaker Government to take the country to an early general election.

THE ISLAMISTS ENTER GOVERNMENT

The overriding objective of Tansu Çiller's caretaker administration prior to the general election, scheduled for 24 December 1995, was to secure endorsement by the EU of the long-proposed customs union. In October the Supreme Court had cancelled the charges against four Kurdish former deputies, while the TGNA voted to amend the 'anti-terror' laws, one of the outstanding concerns of the European Parliament, in order to permit greater freedom of expression. The customs union was finally approved by the European Parliament on 13 December and entered into force on 1 January 1996.

The election campaign was dominated by domestic issues, such as the high rate of inflation. The outcome of the election failed to resolve the country's political uncertainties: the RP won 158 of the 550 seats in the enlarged TGNA, having obtained 21.4% of the votes cast, while the DYP secured 135 seats (19.2%), ANAP 132 seats (19.7%), the DSP 76 seats (14.6%) and the CHP 49 seats (10.7%). The remaining votes were shared among smaller parties, which gained no representation.

After prolonged negotiations, on 28 February 1996 the two main secular right-wing parties, ANAP and the DYP, concluded an agreement, including a rotating premiership, with ANAP leader Mesut Yılmaz occupying the office in the first year. The new coalition still needed the support of the DSP if it was to control an absolute majority in the TGNA, but a formal arrangement proved impossible to secure.

Within weeks it was evident that the DYP-ANAP coalition would not last long, not least because of the intense personal animosity between Yılmaz and Çiller. By the end of May 1996 Çiller was publicly urging Yılmaz to resign. In early June the TGNA, with the support of DYP deputies, voted to debate a censure motion against the Government. However, on 6 June Yılmaz resigned.

On 7 June 1996 Erbakan was invited to form a government, and negotiations to establish a new coalition began. On 28 June the RP and DYP reached agreement, and their coalition won a confidence vote in the TGNA on 8 July. Erbakan, as leader of the RP, became Prime Minister, while Çiller assumed the deputy premiership and foreign affairs portfolio. The new Government announced that its objective was to secure political and economic stability; it promised to pursue further European integration and undertook to honour existing international and strategic agreements, providing they did not threaten the national interest. Almost immediately Erbakan embarked on a tour of Middle East and Asian Muslim countries.

YILMAZ REPLACES ERBAKAN

A meeting of the military-dominated NSC on 28 February 1997 led to the publication of an 18-point memorandum setting out recommendations to ensure the protection of secularism in Turkey. On 5 March, under intense pressure, Erbakan reluctantly signed the memorandum, which committed the Government to: increasing the length of compulsory state education from five to eight years; closing unauthorized Islamist schools and acting against Muslim brotherhoods (*tarikatlar*); blocking the employment of soldiers expelled from the army for fundamentalist activities; and reducing co-operation with Iran.

Although the immediate political crisis had apparently been resolved, DYP dissidents began to call for the dissolution of the Government and the organization of early elections. In June 1997, following the loss of his parliamentary majority, Erbakan resigned. He expected to become the junior partner in a new coalition with Çiller. However, President Demirel selected not Çiller but ANAP leader Mesut Yılmaz to form a new coalition. On 30 June Yılmaz was appointed Prime Minister, having successfully gained the support of the DSP and the newly founded Demokrat Türkiye Partisi (Democratic Turkey Party), along with that of several DYP defectors, to form a coalition with a 12-seat majority. The new Government's programme, announced on 7 July, stressed its commitment to secularism and echoed many of the recommendations of the 18-point memorandum drawn up by the NSC (including the controversial education reforms). The Government received a vote of confidence on 12 July. Legislation promulgating the education reforms secured parliamentary approval in August.

Meanwhile, in May 1997 the armed forces launched their most ambitious military incursion into northern Iraq to date, in pursuit of PKK activists, in an operation entailing the mobilization of some 50,000 troops. A further offensive against PKK positions in northern Iraq in October was accompanied by the lifting of the 10-year-old state of emergency in three of the nine south-eastern provinces (Bitlis, Batman and Bingöl).

DOMESTIC DIFFICULTIES PERSIST

On 16 January 1998 the Constitutional Court banned the RP on the grounds that it had conspired against the secular order. In addition, former Prime Minister Erbakan and six other RP officials were barred from holding political office for five years. A month later some 100 former RP deputies joined the new Fazilet Partisi (FP—Virtue Party), which had been founded in December 1997 under the leadership of İsmail Alptekin, and by early March 1998 the FP had become the largest party in the TGNA.

At the end of the month the NSC criticized the Government for advocating a relaxation of the enforcement of anti-Islamic legislation. The Government subsequently proposed further measures to curb Islamist radicalism, and the universities announced their decision to enforce a dress code that prevented female students wearing the *hijab* (an Islamic headscarf) from attending classes.

Also in March 1998 the Court of Appeals ruled that former Prime Minister Çiller could not be prosecuted over allegations that she had misused government funds during her premiership. While admitting that she had withdrawn substantial sums from a secret government 'slush fund', Çiller had claimed that she could not disclose the destination of the money for reasons of national security. In May the TGNA confirmed that an inquiry would be conducted into corruption allegations against Prime Minister Yılmaz in connection with tenders for government contracts. In early June Yılmaz announced that he would resign at the end of the year to make way for a broadly based interim Government that would oversee the holding of early legislative elections in April 1999. In August 1998 12 former RP politicians, including Erbakan and the FP leader, Recai Kutan, were charged with illegally diverting funds from the party prior to its dissolution.

Following corruption allegations against Prime Minister Yılmaz connected with the privatization of a bank, the Türk Ticaret Bankası, on 25 November 1998 the TGNA approved a motion of no confidence in the Government, which subsequently resigned. Protracted political manoeuvring resulted in the formation, in January 1999, of an interim administration headed by Ecevit, comprising members of the DSP and independents.

ÖCALAN CAPTURED

Ecevit thus happened to be in power when the Turkish Government scored one of its most striking successes. Relations with Syria, which had already deteriorated in July 1998 (owing to Syria's long-running support for the PKK), worsened in early October after Turkey threatened the use of force if Syria did not expel PKK leader Abdullah Öcalan (known to be residing in that country) and close down its training camps in Syria and the Beqa'a valley in Lebanon. Following a meeting of Turkish and Syrian officials in late October, an agreement was signed under which Syria pledged not to allow the PKK to operate on its territory. Öcalan was also forced to leave the country.

Turkey recalled temporarily its ambassador to Italy in October 1998, after that country hosted a meeting of the Kurdish parliament-in-exile. Relations deteriorated further when Öcalan arrived in Italy and the Italian Government refused to extradite him to Turkey. However, Öcalan's request for asylum was denied and in January 1999 he left Italy. On 15 February Öcalan, who had been using a Greek Cypriot passport, was captured at the Greek embassy in Kenya and returned to Turkey. Widespread protests by PKK supporters were held throughout Europe.

Öcalan was charged with treason on 23 February 1999 and held personally responsible for the deaths of some 30,000 people during the 15-year Kurdish struggle for autonomy. In April a further operation was launched against the PKK, involving the deployment of some 15,000 Turkish troops in northern Iraq. On 29 June, however, Öcalan was found guilty and sentenced to death, and on 2 August he issued a statement from his prison cell announcing that the PKK would cease all offensive operations and pursue its goals by peaceful means.

1999 GENERAL ELECTION

On 18 April 1999 elections took place to the 550-seat TGNA. Ecevit's DSP became the largest party in the TGNA with 136 seats, followed by the MHP (129 seats) and the FP (111 seats). ANAP and the DYP obtained 86 seats and 85 seats, respectively; three seats were won by independents. The Halkın Demokrasi Partisi (HADEP—People's Democracy Party) performed strongly in the south-east but failed to secure the 10% of the national vote necessary for representation in the TGNA. On 3 May President Demirel invited Bülent Ecevit to form a new administration, and on 28 May a three-party coalition Government, comprising the DSP, the MHP and ANAP, was announced. The new Government had 351 seats in the TGNA, and was thus the first since 1995 to command an overall parliamentary majority. Also in May 1999 the Chief Public Prosecutor instituted a court case against the FP, with the aim of dissolving the party.

There was a marked improvement in Turkish-Greek relations, which in turn contributed to Greek acceptance of the decision of the EU summit meeting in Helsinki, Finland, in December 1999 to grant Turkey the status of a candidate for EU membership. Ankara responded by encouraging the Turkish Cypriots to participate in UN-sponsored negotiations on the Cyprus problem. An exchange of visits by the Greek and Turkish Ministers of Foreign Affairs in January and February

2000, the first for nearly 40 years, confirmed the improvement in relations; during these visits several bilateral agreements were signed and a joint working group on the reduction of military tensions in the Aegean region was established.

Although the judiciary rejected Öcalan's appeal against his death sentence, the Government on 12 January 2000 granted a stay of execution until such time as the European Court of Human Rights had considered the PKK leader's case.

SEZER ELECTED PRESIDENT

On 29 March 2000 the TGNA rejected constitutional amendments proposed by the Government, including measures that sought to reduce the presidential term of office from seven to five years, to introduce a system of direct presidential elections and to allow an incumbent head of state to seek re-election—the specific aim of this last provision being to enable President Demirel to serve a second term. Following a second rejection of the amendments on 5 April, on 5 May the TGNA elected Ahmet Necdet Sezer, hitherto President of the Constitutional Court and the Government's nominee, as Turkey's 10th President, with 330 votes out of 533 in a third round of voting.

FEBRUARY 2001 FINANCIAL CRISIS AND AFTERMATH

Turkey experienced its worst financial crisis for many years in late February 2001, when the Government was forced to float the lira. The crisis followed months of increasing pressure on the currency and was finally triggered by a clash between President Sezer and Prime Minister Ecevit at a meeting of the NSC on 19 February. Ecevit walked out when the President accused him of protecting ministers suspected of corruption. The immediate reaction of the markets was a massive flight of capital and a collapse in share prices. On 22 February the Government released the lira from its 'peg' with the US dollar, thereby effectively devaluing the currency by about one-third. Ecevit resisted opposition calls for his resignation, instead appointing Kemal Derviş, a senior World Bank official, as Minister of State responsible for economic policy with extensive new powers.

Derviş quickly drew up a recovery plan, envisaging the implementation of long-delayed privatization and liberalization measures, and applied to the IMF for emergency support. Protracted negotiations ensued, during which the IMF insisted on key steps being taken before it would agree to new loans, including the closure of loss-making state-owned banks and the privatization of the telecommunications industry. After the Government had secured parliamentary approval for these and other measures in early May 2001, the IMF on 15 May approved additional stand-by credit of US $8,000m., bringing total IMF resources available to Turkey to a record $19,000m.

BANNING OF THE FP—OTHER PARTY DEVELOPMENTS, 2001–02

The FP was banned by the Constitutional Court on 22 June 2001 on the grounds that the party had become the focus of anti-secular activities in breach of the Constitution. The Court also ordered the expulsion from the TGNA of two FP deputies for anti-secular offences, the remaining FP deputies being required to become independents.

In July 2001, with the support of about one-half of the former FP deputies, Kutan announced the formation of a new Islamist party, to be called Saadet Partisi (Felicity Party). Most of the remaining FP deputies declared their support for an ostensibly more reformist Islamist party, the Adalet ve Kalkınma Partisi (AKP—Justice and Development Party), founded in August by the former mayor of İstanbul, Recep Tayyip Erdoğan. The AKP quickly emerged as the stronger of the two successor Islamist parties. However, the Constitutional Court ruled in January 2002 that Erdoğan's conviction on a sedition charge in 1999 had disqualified him from politics and banned him from standing in the next general election.

EXTERNAL RELATIONS, 2001–02

The TGNA in October 2001 gave the Government authority to send Turkish troops abroad to participate in the US-led military operation against the militant Islamist al-Qa'ida network and Taliban forces in Afghanistan and also to allow more foreign troops to be stationed in Turkey. In January 2002, Turkey supplied a contingent to the multinational International Security Assistance Force being deployed in Afghanistan. Turkey's backing of a Turkish Cypriot decision to resume the UN-sponsored negotiations in Cyprus in January helped to reactivate the process of rapprochement between Turkey and Greece, as required by the EU as a precondition for the opening of formal accession negotiations with Turkey. Senior Turkish and Greek officials met in Ankara in March to discuss the Aegean Sea delimitation and related issues, and agreed to submit intractable differences to the International Court of Justice, based in The Hague, Netherlands. The two sides also signed an agreement for the construction of a natural gas pipeline from Turkey to Greece.

2002 GOVERNMENT CRISIS

Early in October 2001 the Government secured the TGNA's approval of several amendments to the Constitution intended to facilitate Turkey's accession to the EU, including an easing of the ban on the Kurdish language. In the following month the legislature approved revisions to the Civil Code under which women obtained equal status with men in family affairs. However, there remained strong parliamentary opposition, particularly from the MHP, to abolishing the death penalty—a key EU requirement—and to introducing other human rights reforms.

Amid further signs of political deadlock, in July 2002 Derviş announced his resignation from the Government, but was persuaded by the President to remain in office until 10 August to reassure the financial markets and the IMF. Derviş was, nevertheless, present when Deputy Prime Minister Hüsamettin Özkan and Minister of Foreign Affairs İsmail Cem launched a new pro-EU organization, the Yeni Türkiye Partisi (New Turkey Party). The new party joined the widespread demands for an early poll. When the MHP also voiced its support, the increasingly isolated Ecevit was forced to submit and call a general election for 3 November, nearly 18 months ahead of schedule. This decision cleared the way for the TGNA's formal approval in early August of the delayed human rights and other reforms, including: the abolition of the death penalty except in time of war; the ending of the ban on broadcasting in languages other than Turkish; allowing the teaching of Kurdish in regulated private schools; the lifting of penalties for criticism of the armed forces and other state institutions; the easing of restrictions on public demonstrations and association; greater freedom for non-Muslim religions; the redefinition of police duties and powers; and the revision of press laws and regulations.

2002 PARLIAMENTARY ELECTIONS—ERDOĞAN BECOMES PRIME MINISTER

On 20 September 2002 Turkey's High Electoral Board concurred in the Constitutional Court's decision to prohibit Erdoğan and Erbakan from participating in the forthcoming elections. Nevertheless, in the polling on 3 November the AKP achieved a decisive victory, securing 363 of the 550 TGNA seats, with 34.3% of the votes. None of the parties that had been represented in the outgoing parliament won seats in the new Assembly. The CHP was the only other party to achieve representation in the TGNA, winning 178 seats with 19.4% of the vote, while nine seats were secured by independent candidates (to whom the minimum national threshold did not apply). In view of Erdoğan's exclusion, the AKP deputy leader, Abdullah Gül, became Prime Minister and Minister of Foreign Affairs, heading a Council of Ministers that had been reduced from 38 to 25 members. However, Erdoğan was recognized as the real leader of the new Government and immediately undertook a tour of EU capitals. Following the rapid adoption of constitutional amendments lifting the prohibition on him holding political office, Erdoğan was elected to the

TGNA in a by-election on 9 March 2003 and was installed as Prime Minister two days later. He subsequently formed a new 23-member Council of Ministers, which included Gül as Minister of Foreign Affairs.

The commutation of Öcalan's death sentence to life imprisonment in October 2002 was followed in January 2003 by Turkey's signature of the protocol of the European Convention on Human Rights. In June the TGNA adopted more human rights reforms, including further legislation to permit education and broadcasting in Kurdish and other minority languages. In July the TGNA also passed a law downgrading the army-dominated NSC to an entirely advisory body.

In November 2003 there were four massive suicide bombings in İstanbul within five days. The first two truck bombs exploded outside two synagogues on the Jewish Sabbath on 15 November. Five days later two truck bombs were detonated outside the Turkish headquarters of the Hong Kong and Shanghai Banking Corporation (HSBC) and the British consulate general. In total, the attacks killed 63 people, including the drivers of the vehicles, and injured over 700 more. The dead included three Britons, among them the Consul General, Roger Short, and six members of Turkey's Jewish community. Investigations by the security authorities concluded that the bombings had been perpetrated by Turkish nationals connected to the al-Qa'ida network, all of whom had been trained outside Turkey.

VOTE AGAINST US TROOP DEPLOYMENT—DEVELOPMENTS FOLLOWING THE US-LED CAMPAIGN IN IRAQ

The major foreign policy dilemma facing the new AKP Government in early 2003 was whether to accede to a US request for permission to deploy US troops in the south-east of Turkey in the event of an invasion of Iraq. After protracted negotiations concluded with an offer by the USA to provide US $30,000m. in aid and loans, the Government agreed in late February to submit a resolution on US troop deployment to a parliamentary vote. However, amid overwhelming popular opposition to a US-led campaign in Iraq, the TGNA on 1 March failed to provide the required two-thirds' majority for the deployment of the US troops. Nevertheless, later in March, after the invasion of Iraq had begun, the TGNA approved the opening of Turkish airspace to US military aircraft for a six-month period, in return for US aid and loans of up to $9,400m. In early April US Secretary of State Colin Powell pledged that northern Iraq would not come under the control of Kurdish separatists. However, Iraqi Kurdish forces entered the northern Iraqi city of Kirkuk in mid-April, prompting Turkish fears that the area's petroleum reserves could provide the economic foundations for an independent Kurdish state. In July, while Turkish-US relations were still at a low ebb, 11 Turkish soldiers were detained by US forces in Sulaimaniya, Iraq, over an alleged assassination plot against local Kurdish leaders. The soldiers were hooded and handcuffed in an incident that was perceived by the Turkish public as a national insult.

DOMESTIC POLITICS, 2004–06

Buoyed by what was widely regarded as its success in overseeing a strong economic recovery, the AKP secured 41.6% of the votes in the local government elections of 28 March 2004, while the CHP won only 18.2%. In May, in the latest of the series of reforms intended to make Turkey compliant with EU human rights and democratic standards, the TGNA adopted draft constitutional amendments to confirm the abolition of the death penalty and dissolve anti-terrorist state security courts, to guarantee full equality for women and to establish full parliamentary control over the budget of the armed forces. However, tensions between the AKP and the staunchly secularist state establishment, notably the army and the judiciary, continued, particularly over the ban on the *hijab* in universities.

PKK VIOLENCE AND OFFICIAL RETALIATION

In June 2004 the PKK abandoned the ceasefire it had declared after Öcalan's capture in 1999. Although its attacks were on a far lower scale than in the 1990s, its return to violence opened up a serious breach between the Turkish and US administrations, since about 5,000 PKK militants continued to enjoy a safe haven in northern Iraq, in territory ostensibly controlled by the Kurdistan Regional Government, which was closely allied with the USA. Although the US Government officially classified the PKK as a terrorist organization, the US authorities in Iraq refused to take military action against it, leading to Turkish accusations that they were applying double standards.

In August 2005 Erdoğan travelled to Diyarbakır, the largest city in the predominantly Kurdish south-east of Turkey, and promised that 'we will resolve all problems with more democracy, more civil rights and more prosperity'. However, in the following month the Demokratik Halk Partisi (Democratic People's Party), the successor to HADEP, was banned by the Turkish courts. It was replaced by another pro-Kurdish party, the Demokratik Toplum Partisi (DTP—Democratic Society Party). The DTP called on the PKK to restore its ceasefire, but its appeal went unheeded.

THE TURKEY-EU RELATIONSHIP, 2004–07

Turkey's hopes of joining the EU increased in 2004 and 2005, but during 2006 and 2007 negotiations became steadily more deadlocked, while opinion in some EU countries hardened against Turkey and Turkish popular support for membership of the Union markedly waned. In February 2004 the AKP Government had dramatically reversed previous Turkish policies on Cyprus by supporting a settlement of the Cyprus issue based on proposals by UN Secretary-General Kofi Annan, which provided for a bi-communal federal state, thereby shifting from its previous stance of support for a sovereign Turkish Cypriot state. However, the Greek Cypriots rejected the deal by a ratio of three to one and went on to join the Union. Although the Greek Cypriot Government declared that it would not veto Turkey's membership application, Turkey did not recognize the Republic of Cyprus, creating a serious new obstacle for its membership prospects.

An EU summit meeting held in Brussels in December 2004 announced that, providing Turkey complied with a series of requirements, formal accession negotiations would commence on 3 October 2005. These requirements included the Turkish signature of an additional protocol extending its customs union with the EU to the 10 new member states, including the Republic of Cyprus. In July 2005 Turkey signed the additional protocol. However, the protocol could not come into effect until it was ratified by the Turkish parliament. Since implementation would require Turkey to open its harbours and airports to Greek Cypriot ships and aircraft, the AKP Government refused to submit the protocol for parliamentary ratification until the EU lifted its embargo on direct trade and flights to the 'TRNC'.

At an emergency meeting of EU foreign ministers on 2 October 2005 it was agreed that Turkey would eventually have to recognize the Republic of Cyprus, but that this would not be a pre-condition for the start of accession negotiations. Similarly, Turkey was not required to implement the additional protocol immediately. On 3 October the EU formally opened accession negotiations with Turkey. By June 2006 sufficient progress had been made to allow Turkey to close its first chapter in the process, on science and research.

THE EU AND FREEDOM OF EXPRESSION ISSUES

The EU continued to press Turkey for further human rights improvements, notably: the reduction of the political role of the military; the removal of legal restrictions affecting Turkey's non-Muslim communities; and wider freedom of expression.

A critical case arose in December 2005, when Orhan Pamuk, Turkey's best-known novelist, was charged under Article 301 of the Penal Code for having 'denigrated Turkey and the Turkish people' in comments made to a Swiss radio station about the Armenian massacres of 1915. Faced with an international outcry, the courts retreated and in January 2006 the charges against Pamuk were dropped. In contrast, the Turkish Armenian newspaper editor Hrant Dink was convicted under Article 301.

TÜRKIYE (TURKEY)

Dink was shot dead outside his office in İstanbul in January 2007 by a 17-year-old boy from Trabzon with apparent links to the religious nationalist far right. Dink's murder exposed sharp divisions in Turkish society. Several thousand Turkish demonstrators marched under the slogan 'We are all Armenians', but the murderer was treated as a hero by some of the police officers holding him.

On 18 April 2007 there was further violence when three Protestant Christian missionaries, two foreign nationals and one Turkish Christian convert were repeatedly stabbed and had their throats cut by a group of youths at a missionary publishing house in the central Anatolian town of Malatya. Five individuals subsequently received life sentences for the killings.

Concerns about freedom of expression further strained Turkey's already deteriorating relations with the EU. With Greek Cypriot vessels still denied access to Turkish airports and harbours, EU leaders met in December 2006 to consider retaliatory measures. On 15 December they agreed that eight of the 35 chapters of the *acquis communautaire* would be blocked, and negotiations could not be closed on any chapter, until Turkey opened its ports.

THE 2007 PRESIDENTIAL AND PARLIAMENTARY ELECTIONS

The seven-year term of office of President Ahmet Necdet Sezer was due to end in May 2007. Sezer had been a major stumbling block for the AKP Government, making frequent use of his veto, not only for legislation but also for civil service appointments. He was also widely regarded, along with the military, as the main barrier preventing the AKP Government from introducing Islamist legislation.

Initially, Prime Minister Erdoğan planned to stand for the presidency himself. However, after repeated warnings from the military that it would not tolerate a First Lady who, like Erdoğan's wife, wore the *hijab*, he decided to nominate the Minister of National Defence, Mehmet Vecdi Gönül, whose wife did not cover her head. However, the Speaker of the TGNA, Bülent Arınç (leader of the more strongly Islamist faction in the AKP), insisted that the party's candidate should be the Deputy Prime Minister and Minister of Foreign Affairs, Abdullah Gül, whose wife wore the *hijab*.

The first round of the vote in parliament was held on 27 April 2007 but was boycotted by the CHP. The AKP failed to obtain the requisite 367 votes but could have expected to win the necessary straight majority in the later rounds. However, later that day the military posted a statement on its website implicitly threatening to stage a coup if the AKP persevered with Gül's candidacy. On 1 May the Constitutional Court upheld an application by the CHP to annul the vote on the grounds that the TGNA had been inquorate. The AKP responded by announcing that early parliamentary elections would be held on 22 July.

The AKP secured a resounding victory in the general election held on 22 July 2007 with 46.7% of the popular vote, taking 341 seats in the TGNA. The CHP received 20.9% and 112 seats. The MHP became the third largest party in parliament, winning 14.3% of the votes and 71 seats. Pro-Kurdish deputies contested the elections as independents, winning 23 seats and promptly forming a group for the DTP. It was the first time for 13 years that openly pro-Kurdish representatives had held seats in the TGNA.

On 28 August 2007 Gül was duly elected President, securing the support of 339 deputies in the fourth round of voting. On 21 October a public referendum approved the introduction of popular elections for the presidency, with effect from August 2014, and the reduction of the presidential term from seven to five years.

POST-ELECTION POLITICS—BID TO CLOSE THE AKP

Hopes that a new and more liberal era was about to open in Turkish politics proved misplaced. Throughout early 2008 the Government focused on ending the ban on the *hijab* in universities. The necessary two-thirds' majority in the TGNA was secured after the MHP decided to support the change. However, the amendments were annulled by the Constitutional Court on 5 June, although by then the Government was facing a much more serious challenge. On 16 March the chief public prosecutor had applied to the Constitutional Court for the AKP to be outlawed on the grounds that it was attempting to eradicate secularism. He also called for 70 of its leading figures, including Prime Minister Erdoğan, to be expelled from the TGNA and banned from holding political office for five years. The Constitutional Court announced its verdict on 30 July, finding the AKP guilty of attempting to undermine secularism, but narrowly voting to impose a US $20m. fine rather than closing the party down.

ERGENEKON TRIAL AND ARRESTS OF AKP OPPONENTS

On 20 October 2008 the trial began of 86 people charged with belonging to an organization known as 'Ergenekon', a reference to a mythical valley in Central Asia where the early Turks were said to have taken refuge from their enemies. Prosecutors alleged that the suspects—many of whom were rivals or bitter enemies—were members of a vast clandestine network committed to staging a campaign of violence to undermine the AKP and precipitate a military coup. The case polarized opinion in Turkey. Newspapers supporting the Government presented allegations against those accused as if they were fact, and there were attempts to widen the accusations to include serving army officers and even some opposition leaders. Sceptics pointed to legal flaws in the process and to the unlikelihood of such a wide and disparate band of people being linked in a single conspiracy. Their only shared characteristic was that they were all outspoken critics of the Government.

EFFORTS TO IMPROVE RELATIONS WITH ARMENIA

Meanwhile, in August 2008 Armenia's President Serzh Sargsyan invited President Gül to attend a football match between Armenia and Turkey. Gül accepted and travelled to the Armenian capital, Yerevan, on 6 September. However, hopes of a breakthrough in bilateral relations were dashed when it became clear that Armenia's neighbour and Turkey's close partner, Azerbaijan, would not agree to Turkey lifting its sanctions against Armenia. These had been introduced in the early 1990s after Armenia seized 17% of Azerbaijan's territories, including Muslim majority districts around the disputed enclave of Nagornyi Karabakh, driving about 1m. people to seek refuge in Azerbaijan.

Nevertheless, in October 2009 Turkey and Armenia signed a protocol in Geneva, Switzerland, outlining the steps that they would take to restore full diplomatic and political ties. The agreement prompted a furious reaction from Azerbaijan. Fearful of losing one of its closest allies, the Turkish Government rapidly backed down, assuring Azerbaijan that any normalization of ties with Armenia would be dependent on the latter relinquishing its control over Nagornyi Karabakh. The parliaments in both Turkey and Armenia refused to ratify the protocol and hopes of a rapprochement evaporated.

PROGRESS ON THE KURDISH ISSUE STALLED

In July 2009 the Government launched a series of meetings and consultations in order to identify Kurdish grievances and formulate ways to address them. In October the Government announced that a group of PKK militants would soon arrive at Turkey's Habur border crossing with Iraq to commence what it described as a process by which the entire organization would eventually lay down its arms. However, the Government had neither sufficiently prepared the Turkish public nor established the necessary legal framework. When eight militants duly crossed the border on 19 October, they were greeted as conquering heroes by thousands of PKK supporters, prompting a Turkish nationalist backlash, including attacks on ethnic Kurds living in western Turkey. Alarmed, the Government cancelled plans for the return of another group of PKK militants and instead launched a crackdown on the Kurdish nationalist movement. On 11 December the Constitutional

Court formally outlawed the DTP, dissolving the party and confiscating its assets. In the following months hundreds of Kurdish nationalists were imprisoned on charges of belonging to a PKK 'umbrella' organization, the Koma Civakên Kurdistan (KCK—Union of Communities of Kurdistan).

Although most of the DTP's parliamentary deputies transferred to another pro-Kurdish party, the Barış ve Demokrasi Partisi (BDP—Peace and Democracy Party), the dissolution of the DTP and the KCK arrests strengthened those who argued that the only way to extract concessions from the Turkish state was through violence. In June 2010 the PKK announced that it was intensifying its insurgency.

TENSION OVER CONSTITUTIONAL REFORM

In March 2010 the Government announced a package of proposed constitutional reforms, which it claimed would expedite Turkey's accession to the EU and resolve persistent constitutional disputes between the executive, legislative, judicial and military branches of the Turkish state. The amendments included: a restructuring of the Supreme Council of Judges and Public Prosecutors, the Constitutional Court, and the Council of State, which would result in greater government control over their composition and activities; revised criteria for the dissolution of political parties and the establishment of a parliamentary commission to oversee closure cases; measures to allow the trial of military personnel in civilian courts and to limit the jurisdiction of military courts over civilians; the removal of immunity from prosecution for the instigators of the 1980 military coup; allowing collective bargaining for civil servants; the establishment of the office of Ombudsman; and the removal of barriers to the introduction of positive gender discrimination. On 12 September 2010 the changes were put to a public referendum. The Government's refusal to include any measures to address the grievances of Turkey's Kurdish minority resulted in the pro-Kurdish BDP organizing a largely successful boycott of the referendum in predominantly Kurdish areas of the country. Nevertheless, in Turkey as a whole, 57.9% of voters approved the reforms.

A NEW ERA IN THE CHP

In May 2010 Deniz Baykal was forced to resign as leader of the CHP, following allegations published in the media regarding his private life. At a party conference held in Ankara later that month, Kemal Kılıçdaroğlu was elected unopposed as leader. Although it was ostensibly a social-democratic party, under Baykal the CHP had become characterized by strident Turkish nationalist rhetoric and its relentless criticism of the AKP's policies rather than an ability to offer solutions. Despite his failure to inspire the Turkish electorate, Baykal had proved highly adept at consolidating his power base within the party. As a result, before he could return it to its social-democratic roots, Kılıçdaroğlu had first to purge the CHP of Baykal loyalists. During late 2010 and early 2011 Kılıçdaroğlu gradually succeeded in removing nationalist Baykal loyalists from positions of power in the CHP, replacing them with liberals and social democrats and moving the party's policy platform towards the centre-left. However, in a country with a traditionally strong electoral bias towards parties of the centre-right, this appeared likely to reduce rather than enhance the CHP's prospects of eventually assuming power. A further disadvantage was that Kılıçdaroğlu was a member of the Alevi religious community, at a time when there had been a marked increase in the Sunni majority's sense of Islamic identity.

DETERIORATION IN RELATIONS WITH ISRAEL

Since early 2009, following a public disagreement in January between Prime Minister Erdoğan and Israeli President Shimon Peres regarding the conflict in the Gaza Strip, the previously cordial relations between Turkey and Israel had deteriorated significantly. In October Turkey announced the cancellation of Israel's involvement in a major military exercise.

In May 2010 a total of 10 Turks were killed during a raid by Israeli marine commandos on a ship, the MV *Mavi Marmara*. The ship had been chartered by a Turkish charitable organization, İnsan Hak ve Hürriyetleri ve İnsani Yardım Vakfı (the Foundation for Human Rights and Freedoms and Humanitarian Relief), as part of a flotilla of vessels attempting to break the Israeli blockade of Gaza. Erdoğan responded by recalling the Turkish ambassador to Israel, while also accusing Israel of carrying out an act of 'state terror'. Israeli Prime Minister Benjamin Netanyahu insisted that Israeli troops had acted in self-defence after being attacked by pro-Palestinian activists on board the ship. Erdoğan responded by declaring that the re-establishment of normal ties between the two countries was impossible unless Israel issued a formal apology, paid compensation to the families of those killed and lifted its blockade of Gaza. In September 2011, following the publication of the findings of a UN inquiry into the incident, Minister of Foreign Affairs Ahmet Davutoğlu announced that Turkey would, with immediate effect, downgrade its relations with Israel to second secretary level and suspend military co-operation between the two countries, citing the Israeli Government's refusal to apologize for the deaths.

RENEWED CONCERNS OVER FREEDOM OF EXPRESSION

The Ergenekon investigation was expanded from late 2008, and many more government opponents were arrested and imprisoned on charges of belonging to an alleged clandestine organization dedicated to conspiring to overthrow the AKP administration. Several other cases followed, most notably the 'Sledgehammer' investigation into an alleged coup plot. A detailed plan of the alleged coup was given anonymously to a pro-AKP journalist in January 2010. During the months that followed, more than 200 serving and retired members of the Turkish military, including over 10% of the country's serving generals and admirals, were arrested and imprisoned on charges of complicity in the alleged coup plot. Initially, many people had been prepared to accept the main allegations in the cases. However, as the absurdities and contradictions of the cases began to emerge, those who questioned the conduct of the investigations became targets themselves.

In March 2011 nine left-wing journalists, who had initially welcomed the Ergenekon investigation but had recently begun to express concerns that the police were fabricating evidence, were arrested and imprisoned on charges of being members of Ergenekon. Afraid of meeting a similar fate, most independent journalists began to exercise self-censorship.

THE 2011 GENERAL ELECTION

In the run-up to the general election of 12 June 2011, opinion polls indicated that popular support was running at 26%–28% for the CHP and 11%–12% for the ultra-nationalist MHP. As a result, the AKP sought to attract Turkish ultra-nationalist voters to push the MHP under the 10% threshold for representation in the TGNA and to increase the number of AKP seats. During the election campaign AKP officials adopted fierce Turkish nationalist, and often anti-Kurdish, rhetoric in an attempt to undermine the MHP. More disturbing was the posting on the internet of a series of covertly recorded videos of leading members of the MHP apparently engaged in sexual relations. A total of 10 leading members of the MHP, including nine of the 17 members of the party's National Executive, subsequently stood down as parliamentary candidates in the election. However, the perception that the MHP was the victim of a government-backed defamation campaign boosted its popular support, and the party won 13.0% of the votes in the general election and 53 seats in the TGNA. Candidates supported by the BDP, who were running as independents in order to circumvent the 10% threshold for political parties, won another 36 seats. Nevertheless, the AKP still won 49.8% of the vote and 327 seats, well ahead of the CHP with 26.0% and 135 seats.

KURDISH DECLARATION OF DEMOCRATIC AUTONOMY

On 28 February 2011, shortly before the spring thaw began to open the mountain passes in the PKK's main battlegrounds in south-eastern Turkey, the organization announced another period of intensified violence. Previously, the PKK leadership in the Qandil mountains of northern Iraq had consulted with Öcalan before making any important strategic decisions, communicating with him by means of his weekly meetings with his lawyers. However, when the Turkish authorities repeatedly prevented Öcalan's lawyers from meeting with him, the PKK leadership announced the intensification in violence itself, leaving Öcalan with little option other than to endorse a *fait accompli*.

Another shift in the focus of Kurdish nationalism occurred during early 2011, when a coalition of groups and organizations led by the BDP and known collectively as the Demokratik Toplum Kongresi (DTK—Democratic Society Congress) launched a campaign of civil disobedience in protest against the continuing arrests of Kurdish nationalists. The DTK warned that, unless the AKP started to address Kurdish grievances, it would push for what it termed 'democratic autonomy' and the devolution of some of the powers of the central Government to the regions. In July, frustrated by the Government's continued refusal to make concessions, the DTK issued a proclamation of democratic autonomy. In the short term, the announcement had little practical effect. Nevertheless, it did effectively set a new minimum level for the concessions that the Kurdish nationalists would accept.

ADJUSTING TO THE ARAB UPRISINGS

The appointment of Ahmet Davutoğlu as Minister of Foreign Affairs in May 2009 was followed by an intensification of Turkey's efforts to form closer political and economic ties with the other Muslim countries of the Middle East. Bilateral trade boomed, and Turkey established what it termed 'High-Level Strategic Co-operation Councils', in which ministers from Iraq, Syria, Jordan and Lebanon held regular joint meetings with their Turkish counterparts. In addition, the AKP abolished visa requirements for almost all of the Muslim countries in the Middle East.

To the concern of its Western allies, particularly the USA, the AKP also cultivated closer ties with Iran. During early 2010 Davutoğlu travelled several times to Tehran, the Iranian capital, to try to broker an agreement that would prevent additional international sanctions. In June Turkey, then a non-permanent member of the UN Security Council, voted against the imposition of further UN sanctions on Iran, although its opposition was not enough to prevent the approval of the measures.

Rather than a strategic shift from West to East, Turkey's eagerness to foster closer ties with other Muslim countries was based more on a desire to create a zone of Turkish influence by forming close links with the ruling elites in the region. The main exception was Egypt, where the ruling AKP had always aligned itself more closely with the opposition Muslim Brotherhood than the regime of President Hosni Mubarak. As a result, after cautiously endorsing the popular protest movement in Tunisia, the AKP administration vigorously welcomed the uprising in Egypt.

However, the situation changed when the unrest in the Arab world spread to Libya. Initially, Turkey was outspoken in its support for the regime of Libyan leader Muammar al-Qaddafi, with whom the Turkish Government had enjoyed a warm relationship, but amid growing concerns that Turkey risked supporting the losing side, its position began to shift. In May Turkey joined other NATO members in approving a plan under which the Alliance would assume command of all air operations in Libya.

The Turkish Government had also formed close political and personal ties with the regime of Syrian President Bashar al-Assad. Initially, the AKP administration refused to condemn Syria's brutal suppression of pro-reform protests. However, as the death toll began to mount, and thousands of Syrian refugees fled into Turkey, the Government's policy started to change. On 22 November 2011 Erdoğan publicly urged Assad to resign. Over the following months Turkey became one of the most outspoken supporters of the rebel Free Syrian Army, which was fighting to overthrow Assad, allowing its members to operate in Turkey and facilitating its purchases of arms and equipment.

The Arab uprisings also had a negative effect on Turkey's relations with Iran. The Turkish Government suspected that Iran had been instrumental in fomenting Bahrain's Shi'a Muslim majority against the ruling Sunni elite in February 2011, while the deployment in eastern Anatolia of an early warning radar as part of NATO's proposed missile shield was heavily criticized by Iran. Tehran was unconvinced by Turkish denials that the radar was aimed at Iran and threatened to target Turkey if Iran ever came under attack from the USA or Israel.

CONSERVATIVE AUTHORITARIANISM AND THE GEZI PARK PROTESTS

During late 2012 and early 2013 Erdoğan sought to concentrate ever more de facto political power in his own hands and became more assertive in seeking to implement measures that reflected his own conservative Sunni Muslim beliefs. He had also long sought to make his mark on İstanbul by redeveloping the Taksim Square area, the symbolic centre of the modern city, including constructing a shopping mall and mosque complex in Gezi Park, adjacent to the square. Despite the lack of necessary permits, preliminary work on the project had started in late 2012. In May 2013 a small number of environmentalists began a peaceful protest in the park in an attempt to prevent workers uprooting trees. Security forces removed the demonstrators, only for them to return to the park to resume their protests. On 31 May, after a video of an assault on protesters by the police was widely circulated on the internet, the number of protesters grew significantly, and on 1 June the police were forced to withdraw from Taksim Square and Gezi Park.

On 15 June 2013 the police took back control of Taksim Square, demolished the makeshift camp that had been constructed in Gezi Park and forcibly expelled the protesters. However, protests continued in central İstanbul and elsewhere in the country. By the time the protests had abated in September, the Ministry of the Interior estimated that more than 3m. citizens had taken to the streets in the first spontaneous instance of mass anti-Government protest in modern Turkish history. During the demonstrations, eight protesters were killed and more than 7,000 were injured. Although the protesters succeeded in forcing the AKP to abandon its plans to redevelop Gezi Park, they were too diverse to coalesce into a cohesive political movement.

REGIONAL ISOLATION

When Erdoğan publicly urged President Assad to resign in November 2011, he had calculated that the conflict in Syria would be short and that Assad's Alawite regime would be replaced by a predominantly Sunni government that would look to Turkey for leadership. However, the conflict increasingly exposed the limitations of Turkey's foreign ambitions. On 22 June 2012 Syria's air defences shot down a Turkish reconnaissance aircraft after it allegedly crossed into Syrian airspace. The Turkish Government threatened retribution but amid overwhelming public opposition to active involvement in the conflict in Syria, it refrained from retaliating.

From early 2013, under pressure from the USA, the Turkish Government had begun to prevent Islamist extremists from travelling through Turkey to join the campaign in Syria to overthrow Assad. The result was tension and occasional clashes. On 11 February a car bomb at the Cilvegözü border crossing killed 17 people. On 11 May two car bombings in the Turkish border town of Reyhanlı killed 52 people. The Turkish Government publicly accused Assad of responsibility, although Turkish security officials privately admitted that they suspected the attacks to have been carried out by Islamist extremists, such as the Islamic State in Iraq and the Levant (ISIL—renamed Islamic State in June 2014) in retaliation for Turkey preventing the movement of militants across the Turkish–Syrian border.

Meanwhile, in July 2013 the Egyptian military dealt another blow to the AKP's hopes of creating a sphere of Turkish influence in the Middle East when it removed President Muhammad Mursi and his Muslim Brotherhood Government, in a military coup. Erdoğan made repeated calls for Mursi to be reinstated, which not only brought Turkey into conflict with Saudi Arabia and the United Arab Emirates (UAE)—both of which had welcomed Mursi's ouster—but also led to the new Egyptian military regime expelling the Turkish ambassador in November.

DIALOGUE WITH ÖCALAN

Even though his isolation in prison on the island of İmralı meant that he could no longer influence the organization's tactics and strategies, Öcalan remained a revered figure, both to the PKK and to the broader Kurdish nationalist movement. From December 2012 Turkish officials held discussions with Öcalan about a negotiated end to the PKK insurgency. They also began to moderate the terms of his confinement, allowing him to receive occasional visits from representatives of the BDP.

Öcalan was confident that he could persuade the AKP to introduce reforms to address Kurdish demands, including greater cultural rights and a measure of autonomy for south-eastern Turkey. In March Öcalan urged the PKK to announce a unilateral ceasefire. The PKK complied, and in May it began to withdraw its fighting units from Turkey pending a comprehensive peace agreement.

However, the AKP refused either to commence negotiations or to provide any details of what concessions it might be prepared to make to Kurdish nationalist demands. In September 2013 the PKK announced a cessation of the withdrawal of its units from Turkey and in March 2014 those units that had withdrawn from Turkey during 2013 began to re-infiltrate the country. However, the territorial gains made by Islamic State in June 2014 forced the PKK to readjust its focus, particularly after Islamist extremists attacked the de facto autonomous Kurdish enclave of Rojava in Syria, which was controlled by the Partiya Yekîtiya Demokrat (PYD—Democratic Union Party), an affiliate of the PKK. The PKK subsequently refrained from relaunching its insurgency in Turkey and despatched units to support the PYD.

A NEW DOMESTIC POWER STRUGGLE

In the run-up to the June 2011 election, Erdoğan had announced that it would be the last time that he would stand for parliament. It was an open secret that Erdoğan planned to contest the Turkish presidency and then push through a new constitution, replacing Turkey's parliamentary system with a presidential one.

Initially, the scale of the AKP's electoral victory boosted Erdoğan's presidential ambitions. However, it also galvanized dissident elements within the Turkish Islamist movement, particularly followers of the Islamic preacher Fethullah Gülen, who had gone into exile in the USA in 1999. Since the 1980s Gülen's followers had gradually built up a vast network of schools, non-governmental organizations (NGOs), businesses and media organizations in Turkey, which had been allied with the AKP against secularists.

Gülen's supporters feared that Erdoğan would turn against them once he had concentrated all political power in his own hands. On 8 February 2012 public prosecutors affiliated with the Gülen Movement issued a summons to Hakan Fidan, the head of the Milli İstihbarat Teşkilatı (MİT—National Intelligence Organization) and a known Erdoğan loyalist, accusing him of collaborating with the PKK. Erdoğan responded by reassigning the public prosecutors who had issued the summons and initiating a purge of suspected Gülen sympathizers from the police and judiciary.

The relationship between the AKP and the Gülen Movement reached a new low in November 2013, when Erdoğan announced a proposal to close down the *dershane* system of privately owned schools, which prepared students for the nationwide university entrance examination. Gülen's followers controlled about 40% of the *dershane* schools, which served both as a source of income and as a recruiting tool for the movement. On 17 December pro-Gülen prosecutors in İstanbul ordered the detention of 52 pro-AKP business people on suspicion of involvement in corruption. On 24 December pro-Gülen prosecutors in Ankara ordered the detention of 41 more suspects with close ties to the AKP leadership and issued a summons for Bilal Erdoğan, the Prime Minister's son. Erdoğan hit back by dismissing the prosecutors who had launched the corruption investigations, which were then suspended.

In January 2014 the first of what were to become dozens of audio recordings of telephone conversations apparently showing Erdoğan and his close associates fixing government contracts and manipulating judicial process were posted on the internet. Erdoğan accused Gülen's followers of trying to defame the AKP in the run-up to the local elections in March. In February the AKP introduced new laws tightening political control over the judiciary and transferring responsibility for regulating the internet from the civilian courts to the Telecommunications Directorate, which was staffed by political appointees. The AKP effected a further purge of suspected Gülen sympathizers. By July over 7,000 police officers and more than 500 judicial officials had been removed from their positions.

However, the revelations and controversies appeared to have little impact on the AKP's grassroots support. In local elections on 30 March 2014 the AKP won 43.1% of the total votes, ahead of the CHP with 26.5% and the MHP with 17.8%.

ERDOĞAN ELECTED AS PRESIDENT

Erdoğan made it clear that he regarded the AKP's local election victory as giving him a mandate to stand in the presidential election in August 2014 and introduce a presidential system. In an attempt to attract Erdoğan's conservative Sunni Muslim voter base, the CHP and MHP announced Ekmeleddin Ihsanoğlu, a former Secretary-General of the OIC, as their joint candidate. The other candidate was Selahattin Demirtaş, head of the pro-Kurdish BDP. Erdoğan won the election, held on 10 August, in the first round of voting, securing 51.8% of the valid votes cast, ahead of Ihsanoğlu with 38.4%, and Demirtaş with 9.8%. Prior to taking office on 28 August, Erdoğan arranged for Minister of Foreign Affairs Davutoğlu to succeed him as party Chairman and Prime Minister. Davutoğlu was duly confirmed in the post of AKP Chairman at a party conference on 27 August and was formally appointed at the head of a largely unchanged Government on 29 August.

RISING KURDISH HOPES

In 2014, in order to reinforce its calls for democratic autonomy for the predominantly Kurdish south-east of Turkey, the BDP split into two parties: the Halkların Demokratik Partisi (HDP—Peoples' Democratic Party) to compete at national level and the Demokratik Bölgeler Partisi (DBP—Democratic Regions Party) to contest local elections. However, Kurdish nationalist hopes of creating a network of autonomous regions in the Middle East suffered a setback in mid-2014 as Islamic State made deep inroads into Rojava.

By September 2014 Islamic State had advanced to the outskirts of the Syrian town of Kobane, close to the Turkish border, and its capture from the PYD's military wing, the Yekîneyên Parastina Gel (YPG—People's Protection Units), appeared imminent. The Turkish Government refused to allow either supplies of food, water and medicine or Kurdish volunteers to cross from Turkey into Kobane. On 7 October Erdoğan dismissively referred to the town as having effectively already fallen to Islamic State. In response, the HDP called for Kurds to take to the streets in protest. The demonstrations quickly spiralled out of control: over a period of three days more than 50 people were killed in the worst incident of civil unrest in Turkey for over 20 years. However, supported by air strikes by a US-led coalition and by units of the PKK, the YPG gradually gained the upper hand. By 27 January 2015 the last Islamic State militants had been driven out of Kobane.

THE AKP LOSES AND REGAINS ITS PARLIAMENTARY MAJORITY

In September 2014, a little over a month after Erdoğan had been elected President, his aides announced that he had designated a 1,150-room complex in Beştepe, on the outskirts of Ankara, as his presidential palace. Originally intended as the Office of the Prime Minister, and funded by the prime ministerial budget, the recently completed palace cost around US $615m. to build and was constructed, in violation of two court orders, on environmentally protected land. In January 2015 Erdoğan began to chair meetings of the cabinet once a month. He also started regularly issuing orders to, and receiving briefings from, individual ministers, bypassing Prime Minister Davutoğlu, the ostensible head of the executive.

In the run-up to the general election of 7 June 2015 Erdoğan campaigned openly for the AKP, calling for it to be given a large majority so that it could amend the Constitution and replace Turkey's parliamentary system with a presidential model. However, the outcome of the election dealt a severe blow to Erdoğan's plan. The AKP won only 40.9% of the vote, giving it just 258 of the 550 seats in the TGNA, compared with 327 in 2011. The CHP finished in second place with 25.0% of the vote and 132 seats, ahead of the MHP with 16.3% and 80 seats, while the HDP entered parliament for the first time as a party with 13.1% and 80 seats. On 9 June 2015 Davutoğlu submitted the resignation of his cabinet and began talks with the opposition in an attempt to form a coalition government. However, Erdoğan used his influence in the AKP to push for a new election, supported by the MHP, which was confident of increasing its vote if a new election were held and rebuffed offers from Davutoğlu to form a coalition. On 25 August the Yüksek Seçim Kurumu (YSK—Supreme Electoral Board) announced that a fresh election would take place on 1 November.

The campaign for the November 2015 election was overshadowed by increasing government control over the media and a deteriorating security situation, as a string of suicide attacks on Kurdish nationalist rallies by Islamic State sympathizers led to the HDP cancelling all public meetings. However, this time Erdoğan remained out of the public eye, leaving Davutoğlu to lead the AKP's election campaign. On 1 November the AKP increased its share of the vote to 49.5%, regaining a majority by taking 317 seats in parliament. The CHP finished second with 25.3% and 134 seats, ahead of the MHP with 11.9% and 40 seats. The HDP was fourth with 10.8%, but its strong performance in the predominantly Kurdish south-east of the country meant that it won 59 seats.

Following the election, Erdoğan began to pressurize the new AKP Government to use its renewed parliamentary majority to introduce a presidential system. However, Davutoğlu was less enthusiastic about seeing executive power officially transferred from the Prime Minister to the President. Gradually, he started to distance himself from Erdoğan and to try to establish his own political power base. However, the AKP National Executive was still controlled by Erdoğan loyalists. On 29 April 2016 these loyalists changed the AKP's internal regulations to strip Davutoğlu of any control over the party. In early May Davutoğlu announced that he would resign. On 22 May he was replaced as AKP Chairman and Prime Minister by Binali Yıldırım, a staunch Erdoğan loyalist who immediately announced that his priority would be the official introduction of a presidential system of government.

FADING KURDISH HOPES, RISING TENSIONS

On 28 February 2015 a delegation from the HDP held a press conference at which they read out a statement by PKK founder Öcalan outlining a roadmap for negotiations to resolve the Kurdish issue. However, on 22 March Erdoğan publicly distanced himself from Öcalan's plans, insisting that there could be no negotiations unless the PKK first laid down its arms.

On 20 July 2015 an Islamic State sympathizer killed 32 Kurdish nationalist sympathizers in a suicide bombing in the town of Suruç, close to the Syrian border. The PKK accused the Turkish security forces of complicity in the attack. On 22 July two police officers were killed, allegedly by PKK supporters, in the south-eastern town of Ceylanpınar. On 24 July the Turkish Government launched the first of hundreds of air strikes against PKK assets in northern Iraq. On 25 July the PKK announced an end to its ceasefire and resumed attacks inside Turkish territory. Most attacks occurred in the south-east but, starting in January 2016, the PKK also deployed suicide bombers in the west of the country, including staging mass casualty attacks in Ankara and İstanbul. In addition, the PKK urged its supporters to launch a series of urban insurrections in the south-east. By May the security forces had largely succeeded in suppressing these uprisings, but at the cost of hundreds of civilian lives, widespread destruction of property and infrastructure, and the displacement of over 350,000 people. On 22 May, under pressure from Erdoğan, parliament passed a motion lifting the legal immunity of all current members of the TGNA. By July 2018 a total of 12 HDP parliamentary deputies had been arrested and imprisoned on terrorism charges, including the party's co-chairs, Selahattin Demirtaş and Figen Yüksekdag. The authorities had also detained hundreds of lower-ranking officials from the HDP and the DBP and seized 94 of the 102 DBP-controlled local authorities, replacing the elected officials with state-appointed trustees. Although the PKK remained primarily focused on supporting the PYD in northern Syria, it continued to attack the security forces, mainly through the use of roadside improvised explosive devices (IEDs) in south-eastern Turkey. However, with the exception of a double bombing in İstanbul in December 2016 that killed 38 police officers, the PKK appeared wary of risking adverse publicity by staging more mass casualty attacks in the west of the country. None the less, by July 2018 at least 3,500 people, including more than 1,200 members of the security forces, were believed to have been killed since the upsurge in violence in mid-2015.

THE LENGTHENING SHADOW OF THE SYRIAN CIVIL WAR

Following the attack in Suruç on 20 July 2015 and a double suicide bombing by Islamic State sympathizers in Ankara on 10 October, which killed 105 Kurdish nationalist sympathizers, the Turkish authorities began to tighten restrictions on the organization's activities in Turkey. The result was a shift in the focus of Islamic State attacks as it began to target Turkey directly for the first time. On 12 January 2016 an Islamic State sympathizer killed 13 foreign tourists in a suicide bombing in central İstanbul. Another four foreign tourists were killed in a similar attack in İstanbul on 19 March. On 1 May three police officers were killed in an Islamic State suicide car bomb attack in the south-eastern city of Gaziantep—the first time that the organization had directly targeted the Turkish state. On 28 June a total of 45 people were killed, most of them Turkish citizens, in a triple Islamic State suicide attack at İstanbul's Atatürk Airport. On 20 August a total of 57 people were killed in an Islamic State suicide bombing at a wedding organized by the local branch of the HDP in Gaziantep. In the early hours of 1 January 2017 a lone Islamic State gunman killed 39 people celebrating the new year at a nightclub in İstanbul.

The attacks came at a time when the tourism industry was already struggling after the Russian Federation imposed economic sanctions on Turkey, including effectively banning its citizens from visiting the country. On 24 November 2015 Turkey had shot down a Russian SU-24 warplane that had strayed into Turkish airspace while conducting air strikes against rebel forces in Syria.

On 28 June 2016 Turkey formally ended six years of tensions with Israel, signing an agreement in which Turkey recognized the Israeli blockade of Gaza and Israel agreed to pay compensation to the families of those killed in the MV *Mavi Marmara* incident. On 29 June Erdoğan apologized to Russia for the downing of the SU-24, prompting Moscow to promise to ease the tourism ban. However, security concerns resulted in a sharp drop in the number of foreign visitors to Turkey in 2016, which fell by some 30% to about 25.4m., compared with 36.2m. in 2015. The easing of the Russian travel ban helped support a resurgence in tourist numbers. With no major terrorist attacks occurring in 2017, by mid-2018 tourist arrivals had returned to 2015 levels.

During late 2015 and early 2016 the potential for cooperation to stem the flow of Syrian refugees through Turkey to Europe resulted in increased engagement with the EU. In March 2016 the two sides signed an agreement under which Turkey agreed to prevent undocumented refugees from crossing the Aegean Sea to Greece in return for up to €6,000m. in aid. Although the agreement reduced the flow of refugees to the EU, it did little to address the situation of the 3m. Syrians registered in Turkey. Starting in late 2016, rising social tensions led to numerous violent clashes, resulting in several deaths, between the refugees and local communities.

THE FAILED MILITARY COUP OF JULY 2016

Late on 15 July 2016 a cabal of officers in the Turkish army, air force and gendarmerie staged a coup in an apparent attempt to overthrow the Government, seizing key sites in İstanbul and Ankara, and bombing parliament and the headquarters of the national police. The coup was carried out in the name of hardline secularists, although it was unclear whether they were the main driving force. The Turkish Government blamed members of the Gülen Movement who had infiltrated the armed forces. The attempt attracted little support from either the military, the overwhelming majority of whom remained loyal to the Government, or the general public. The total number of participants in the attempted coup was estimated at about 8,500, or approximately 1.5% of the total strength of the armed forces. None the less, rather than wait for forces loyal to the regime to suppress the uprising, President Erdoğan appeared on national television to call on his supporters to take to the streets; tens of thousands responded. Confrontations and clashes continued through the night, resulting in around 300 deaths, including an estimated 250 civilians. By early morning on 16 July, the coup had been suppressed.

THE STATE OF EMERGENCY AND ERDOĞAN'S PURGES

Following the failed coup, a state of emergency was declared, initially for three months from 20 July 2016, although it was subsequently renewed seven times before finally being lifted on 18 July 2018. The state of emergency suspended some of the provisions of the Constitution and effectively allowed Erdoğan to bypass the TGNA and govern by decree. Although the state of emergency was ostensibly designed to allow the authorities greater freedom to pursue those members of the Gülen Movement who were suspected of complicity in the coup, in practice it was used by Erdoğan to target all of his perceived rivals, opponents and critics—including many, such as secularists and leftists, who had no connection with the Gülen Movement. During the two years that the state of emergency was in force, more than 130,000 state employees were dismissed and over 100,000 people were arrested on charges of involvement in the coup, amid widespread allegations of torture and physical abuse. In addition, nearly 2,900 private schools, universities and NGOs and 110 media outlets were closed down.

In the aftermath of the coup attempt, the Turkish Government repeatedly pressurized the USA to extradite Gülen. The USA refused, arguing that Turkey had failed to provide any evidence of his involvement. The resultant stand-off severely strained bilateral ties.

OPERATION EUPHRATES SHIELD

The tensions between Turkey and the USA were exacerbated by Washington's close military co-operation with the YPG in the war against Islamic State in northern Syria. In October 2015 the YPG became the dominant element in a coalition of anti-Islamic State organizations, known collectively as the Syrian Democratic Forces (SDF). In August 2016 Turkish troops and tanks, together with Syrian rebel militias allied with Turkey, crossed into northern Syria in Operation Euphrates Shield. Officially, the incursion was designed to drive Islamic State from a pocket of land to the west of the Euphrates river, between two areas controlled by the PYD. However, the Turkish operation also appears to have been an effort to pre-empt the Syrian Kurds and occupy the territory before the SDF could drive out Islamic State, link up with the PYD enclave of Afrin farther west, and establish a continuous strip of PYD territory along most of the Turkish–Syrian border. By October Turkey and its allied militias had driven 30 km south from the border and laid siege to the town of al-Bab. The town eventually fell in February 2017. However, Turkish hopes of continuing the advance into PYD-controlled territory were thwarted when the SDF, the USA, Russia and the Syrian regime came together to block the troops' progress, leaving Turkey in control of a pocket of territory just across the border in Syria, unable to move west, south or east.

THE 2017 CONSTITUTIONAL REFERENDUM

Before the failed coup of July 2016, opinion polls suggested that the majority of the Turkish public were opposed to Erdoğan's aspirations to establish a presidential system of government. However, his perceived steadfastness in the face of the attempted putsch boosted Erdoğan's popular support. He also formed an alliance with MHP Chairman Devlet Bahçeli, who had come to rely on Erdoğan's control over the country's highly politicized judicial system to prevent a challenge to his leadership of the MHP. Bahçeli's support gave Erdoğan enough seats in the TGNA to gain approval for a constitutional referendum on 16 April 2017 on the introduction of an executive presidency. The weeks leading up to the vote were marred by numerous restrictions on the 'No' campaign. There were also numerous reports of voting irregularities on the day of the referendum itself. None the less, the proposed constitutional changes were only narrowly approved, by 51.4% to 48.6%. The new system was scheduled to be formally introduced after simultaneous parliamentary and presidential elections in November 2019.

OPERATION OLIVE BRANCH

On 20 January 2018 the Turkish military and members of Syrian rebel militias, which Turkey had trained and rebadged as the Syrian National Army (SNA), launched an incursion, codenamed Operation Olive Branch, into the SDF-held enclave of Afrin in north-western Syria. Unlike during Operation Euphrates Shield in 2016–17, Russia allowed Turkish warplanes and unmanned aerial vehicles (drones) to operate in Syrian airspace over Afrin, in an attempt to pressurize the SDF into abandoning its alliance with the USA in north-eastern Syria and working more closely with the Syrian regime instead. By early March 2018 Turkey and the SNA had conquered most of northern Afrin, linking it with the territory seized during Operation Euphrates Shield and driving the SDF back to the outskirts of Afrin city in the east of the enclave. Afrin city finally fell on 18 March. Over the weeks that followed, Turkey transformed the territory seized by Euphrates Shield and Olive Branch into a de facto Turkish protectorate, into which it began to relocate some of the Syrian refugees who had fled to Turkey during the early years of the Syrian civil war.

THE 2018 PRESIDENTIAL AND PARLIAMENTARY ELECTIONS

On 18 April 2018, amid growing expectations that Turkey was heading for a severe economic downturn in late 2018 and 2019, Erdoğan abruptly called presidential and parliamentary elections for 24 June, more than 16 months ahead of schedule. The elections were held under the continuing state of emergency, allowing government officials to impose restrictions on the campaigns by the opposition parties, while Erdoğan was able to use his now almost complete control over the country's mainstream media to limit coverage of his rivals. In the cities in western Turkey the voting process itself appeared to be relatively free and fair. However, outside urban areas, there were numerous reports of irregularities and the results contained a number of statistical anomalies, all of them in favour of the AKP and its electoral ally, the MHP. In the presidential election, Erdoğan secured a second term with 52.6% of the vote, ahead of Muharrem İnce of the CHP with 30.6% and the HDP's Demirtaş, who campaigned from prison, with 8.4%. In the parliamentary election, the AKP won 42.6% of the vote and 295 seats, leaving it short of a majority in the expanded 600-member TGNA and resulting in it forming an informal coalition with the MHP, which had won 11.1% and 49 seats. The CHP finished second with 22.7% and 146 seats, ahead of the HDP with 11.7% and 67 seats. The remaining 43 seats were won by the newly established İyi Partisi (İP—Good Party), which had been founded in October 2017 by former dissident members of the MHP and which took 10.0% of the vote.

THE NEW PRESIDENTIAL SYSTEM

On the afternoon of 9 July 2018 as Erdoğan was sworn in for a second term, Turkey officially transitioned from a parliamentary system to one in which almost all political power was concentrated in the presidency. The post of Prime Minister was abolished and the President became the head of the executive. Although parliament retained some of its legislative functions, the President was also able to promulgate laws in the form of decrees. On the evening of 9 July Erdoğan issued such a decree merging a number of ministries and reducing their total number from 22 to 16. Only four members of the previous Government were included in his new cabinet, with the remaining positions being filled by bureaucrats and members of the business community close to the AKP. Erdoğan's son-in-law, Berat Albayrak, was given overall control of the economy. On 18 July, two years after it was first introduced, Erdoğan allowed the state of emergency to expire.

THE 2019 LOCAL ELECTIONS

The nationwide local elections on 31 March 2019 took place amid growing popular disenchantment with the Erdoğan Government, particularly as a result of a sustained economic downturn and the continued presence in Turkey of an estimated 3m. Syrian refugees. The local elections were also the first in which electoral alliances were permitted, allowing the main opposition CHP to form partnerships with other parties, particularly the İP, while the AKP co-operated with the MHP. The HDP focused on predominantly Kurdish areas and did not field candidates in the metropolises of western Turkey, such as İstanbul and Ankara. Given Kurdish voters' antagonism towards the AKP-MHP, this indirectly helped the other opposition parties. Nevertheless, backed by an aggressive campaign in the now largely government-controlled Turkish media, the AKP-MHP alliance still won 51.6% of the popular vote, only two percentage points down on their combined vote in the June 2018 general election. However, boosted by its electoral alliance and tactical voting by Kurds, the CHP candidates defeated the incumbent AKP mayors in the metropolitan municipality elections in İstanbul, Ankara and Antalya and the MHP mayor in Adana, while also retaining control of İzmir. It was the first time in 25 years that the AKP or one of its predecessor parties had lost in İstanbul and Ankara and meant that the CHP now controlled five of the six largest cities in Turkey. The AKP retained control of the sixth, Bursa, by a narrow margin. In İstanbul, the provisional results suggested that the CHP's Ekrem İmamoğlu had defeated Binali Yıldırım of the AKP by 13,000 votes. Under pressure from Erdoğan, the YSK ordered a rerun on 23 June 2019. The result was the worst electoral setback for Erdoğan since the AKP first took office in 2002 as İmamoğlu won by a margin of 800,000 votes.

DISSENT WITHIN THE AKP

Many in the AKP had long been uneasy at what they regarded as Erdoğan's use of the party as a vehicle for his own ambitions and at the allegations of corruption and extravagance that had become associated with his regime, but they had largely remained silent for fear of incurring Erdoğan's wrath. However, with opinion polls suggesting that popular support for the AKP was in decline, some began to make preparations to form breakaway parties. On 12 December 2019 former Prime Minister Ahmet Davutoğlu, who had resigned from the AKP three months earlier, founded a party known as the Gelecek Partisi (GP—Future Party). On 9 March 2020 former Deputy Prime Minister Ali Babacan, who had resigned from the AKP in July 2019, established the Demokrasi ve Atilim Partisi (DEVA—Democracy and Progress Party). Babacan had the backing of former President Abdullah Gül, although Gül did not assume an active role in DEVA.

THE S-400S AND TENSIONS WITH THE USA

In July 2019 Turkey began to take delivery of the first of two S-400 air defence systems that it had purchased from Russia, despite warnings from Washington that they could potentially compromise the security of NATO and be used to identify vulnerabilities in the F-35 stealth aircraft, which were expected to form the core of the alliance's air power for the next 20 years. After the S-400s started to arrive in Turkey, the USA cancelled the planned sale of 100 F-35s to Turkey and began to discuss applying sanctions against Ankara under the Countering America's Adversaries Through Sanctions Act. Turkey had originally stated that the S-400s would become operational in April 2020, but as of July 2023 they had yet to be activated.

INCREASED REGIONAL ASSERTIVENESS AND TENSIONS WITH RUSSIA

Under pressure from the Turkish Government, on 6 October 2019 US President Donald Trump announced that US troops who had been fighting alongside the SDF against Islamic State in north-eastern Syria would be withdrawn. The announcement left the SDF unprotected. On 9 October Turkey launched a cross-border military offensive into north-eastern Syria. Erdoğan claimed the objective of what was codenamed Operation Peace Spring was to push the SDF back 32 km from all along the Turkish border, creating a 'safe zone' into which some of the Syrian refugees in Turkey would be resettled. Although it suffered initial territorial losses, the SDF was able to halt the Turkish advance by reaching an agreement with the Syrian and Russian Governments that resulted in Syrian and Russian forces being deployed to SDF-held areas. On 17 October Erdoğan agreed, under US pressure, to a ceasefire that left Turkey and the SNA in control of a new thin strip of territory along part of the border to add to the areas captured in Operation Euphrates Shield and Operation Olive Branch. The gains fell well short of the operation's original objectives.

As the northern front stabilized, attention shifted to western Syria and the governorate of Idlib. Although most of Idlib was controlled by hard-line Islamist rebel factions, Turkey had maintained 12 military outposts in the governorate since October 2017, ostensibly to monitor a ceasefire agreement. Throughout late 2019 and early 2020, Turkey deployed thousands of troops, backed by armour and artillery, to support these outposts and to try to block an offensive by Syrian regime forces and Russian aircraft. The result was a series of direct clashes as Turkish forces came under regime artillery fire. On 27 February at least 34 Turkish soldiers were killed in an air strike by Syrian and Russian aircraft on the village of Balyun. As Turkey sent in large numbers of reinforcements, a flurry of high-level contacts between the Russian and Turkish Governments produced a de facto ceasefire.

Meanwhile, Turkey's relations with Russia were further strained by Ankara's increasing involvement in the Libyan Civil War in support of the Tripoli-based Government of National Accord (GNA) and the Tobruk-based Libyan National Army (LNA), which was supported by Russia, Egypt, Saudi Arabia and the UAE. In November 2019, in return for the promise of Turkish military support, the GNA agreed to a demarcation line dividing a large swathe of the eastern Mediterranean between Turkey and Libya in defiance of rival claims from Greece, Egypt and Cyprus. Following the agreement, Turkey began to send military advisers and large shipments of weapons and equipment to the GNA, including drones. In early 2020 it also began dispatching thousands of Syrian mercenaries, many of them affiliated with the SNA, to fight alongside the GNA's forces. By April Turkish military support, particularly its supplies of drones, had enabled the GNA to halt and then reverse an offensive launched by the LNA one year earlier, which had reached the outskirts of Tripoli. Yet the GNA's battlefield successes also galvanized the LNA's backers, with both the UAE and Russia stepping up their military support to Tobruk. A temporary ceasefire was announced in August (subsequently made permanent in October), which stated that all foreign forces would be withdrawn from Libya. As efforts for a permanent political resolution of the Libyan civil war continued, military personnel from Turkey and its Syrian proxies remained in the country, but Turkish influence in Libya was clearly in decline. After the failure of attempts to hold legislative and presidential elections in December 2021, Turkey began to try to reposition itself as a neutral intermediary between the rival factions for power in Libya, not least in the hope of preserving Libyan recognition of Turkish claims to a large part of the Mediterranean. In July 2023 it remained unclear whether these efforts would be successful.

THE COVID-19 CRISIS

When Turkey announced its first confirmed case of the novel coronavirus disease (COVID-19) on 10 March 2020, there were already signs that the Turkish economy was heading for a downturn. Although Erdoğan introduced a series of measures to try to contain the spread of the virus, he was reluctant to impose a full lockdown for fear of exacerbating the economic situation. Instead, he opted for weekend curfews and the indefinite closure of cafés, restaurants, educational establishments and other public meeting places. By mid-April Turkey was recording about 5,000 new COVID-19 cases and nearly 100 associated deaths each day. The daily number of new cases and fatalities began to decline from late April, but it was not until early June that the Government gradually began to lift restrictions in the hope of stimulating the economy and saving the summer tourism season.

However, the daily official number of new confirmed cases had risen again to over 1,000 by mid-June 2020, with medical personnel reporting that the true figures were considerably higher. Similarly, there was a growing discrepancy between the official COVID-19 death rate and the excess mortality rate in the municipal death registers, with the latter suggesting that between three and four times more people were dying from the disease than was indicated by the official figures. On 30 September the Minister of Health, Fahrettin Koca, publicly admitted that the Government had been knowingly publishing erroneous COVID-19 statistics, misrepresenting the number of people recorded as being seriously ill with the disease as the number having merely tested positive for the virus. It was not until late November that the Government began publishing separate figures for those who had tested positive and those who were seriously ill with the disease.

On 30 November 2020 a series of new restrictions was introduced, although again they stopped short of a full lockdown. The official daily number of new cases reached a peak of 33,198 on 9 December, before gradually declining to 5,277 by 25 January 2021. Meanwhile, on 13 January Turkey launched its national vaccination programme, using the Chinese Sinovac vaccine. Use of the US/German Pfizer-BioNTech vaccine was introduced in Turkey from early April.

Nevertheless, the daily number of new cases increased rapidly from March 2021, as the more highly transmissible Delta variant of the virus took hold, reaching a peak of 63,082 on 17 April. On 19 April the Government introduced an almost complete lockdown. As the daily number of new infections started to fall, the Government implemented a gradual easing of the lockdown from 1 June, not least in the hope of attracting foreign tourists for the summer season. However, the reopening of the economy was followed by a steady rise in the daily number of new cases, which amounted to 40,786 on 31 December. The rate of increase accelerated in early 2022 as a result of the spread of the Omicron variant, and the daily number of new cases peaked at 111,157 on 4 February. However, despite calls from medical professionals, the Government refused to reintroduce more stringent restrictions, for fear of exacerbating the parlous state of the economy. The daily number of new cases fell, from 59,885 on 28 February to 14,336 on 31 March, 1,772 on 30 April and just 971 on 31 May, when the Government stopped publishing daily statistics. On 9 June all of the remaining COVID-19 restrictions were lifted, ahead of the summer tourist season.

THE 2020 NAGORNYI KARABAKH WAR

With resistance from its rivals limiting its room for manoeuvre in Syria, Libya and the eastern Mediterranean, Turkey turned its attention to the Caucasus. During July–August 2020 Turkey and Azerbaijan staged joint military exercises, and Turkish military advisers were reported to have helped Azerbaijan to finalize plans to retake the enclave of Nagornyi Karabakh, control of which Azerbaijan had ceded to Armenia in 1994. Turkey also played a key role in the resultant war, which broke out on 27 September 2020, supplying Azerbaijan with Turkish-made drones, which were largely operated by Turkish technicians and against which Armenia had no effective defence, while Turkish military advisers helped Azerbaijan to co-ordinate the conduct of its military campaign. In addition, Turkey despatched several thousand Syrian mercenaries, recruited from Turkish-occupied areas of Syria, to support Azeri ground troops.

Although Armenia was closely allied with Russia, Turkey correctly calculated that, unlike in Syria and Libya, Moscow was unlikely to intervene extensively on the ground in Nagornyi Karabakh. By the time Russia had pressured Azerbaijan into accepting a ceasefire, which was signed on 9 November 2020 and came into effect on the following day, Azerbaijan had made significant territorial gains. Azerbaijan's unequivocal military victory provided a major boost for Erdoğan, enabling him to present himself as a regional gamechanger.

A NEW ERA IN US-TURKISH RELATIONS

Joe Biden's victory in the US presidential election on 3 November 2020 was greeted with dismay in Ankara, as he was widely expected to adopt a more hard-line approach to Turkey than outgoing President Trump, who had generally been prepared to accommodate Erdoğan's regional ambitions. However, it was Trump who, on 14 December, finally ratified sanctions against Ankara over its purchase of the S-400s from Russia, including the imposition of a ban on new US military sales to Turkey.

President Biden did not engage with Erdoğan at all until 23 April 2021, when he notified him that, on the following day, the USA would for the first time formally recognize the Armenian Genocide of 1915.

REGIONAL OUTREACH

Saudi Arabia and the UAE had long regarded the Muslim Brotherhood as a threat to their national security. After the military coup in Egypt in 2013, İstanbul had become the Brotherhood's main organizational hub as the Turkish Government sought to instrumentalize its support for the group to further its own regional ambitions. However, faced with a rapidly deteriorating economic situation at home and an increasingly desperate need for an influx of foreign funds, throughout 2020 and 2021 President Erdoğan quietly scaled back Turkey's support for the Brotherhood and discreetly reached out to Saudi Arabia and the UAE, which had hitherto been Turkey's main rivals for influence in the Middle East region. In the first public confirmation of the thaw in relations, in November 2021 Abu Dhabi's Crown Prince Mohammed bin Zayed Al Nahyan made an official visit to Ankara, during which he promised to invest US $10,000m. in the Turkish economy. In February 2022 Erdoğan made a reciprocal visit to the UAE, during which he and his counterpart signed 12 agreements pledging increased bilateral economic co-operation. In April Erdoğan visited Saudi Arabia for the first time since 2017 to hold talks about possible Saudi investments in Turkey. In June 2022 Saudi Arabia's de facto ruler, Crown Prince Mohammed bin Salman bin Abdelaziz Al Sa'ud, made a reciprocal visit to Ankara to discuss closer co-operation between the two countries in trade, defence, energy and tourism, with Turkish officials vigorously calling for Saudi funds to invest in Türkiye (as the country was now officially known).

Since late 2021 Türkiye has also sought to repair ties with Egypt, which is the major ally of Saudi Arabia and the UAE in North Africa. In April 2022 Turkey announced that it would appoint an ambassador to the Egyptian capital, Cairo, for the first time since the coup of 2013.

THE WAR IN UKRAINE

The Russian invasion of Ukraine on 24 February 2022 took Ankara by surprise, forcing President Erdoğan to cut short an official visit to Africa and scramble to try to preserve Turkey's hitherto close ties with both Moscow and Kyiv. Although the Turkish Government condemned the invasion and continued to supply Ukraine with weapons, especially the highly effective Bayraktar drones, it refused to join its NATO allies in imposing sanctions on Russia or closing its airspace to Russian aircraft. By April Russians had become the leading foreign buyers of real estate in Turkey, and Turkish officials publicly encouraged Russian businesses and individuals sanctioned elsewhere to invest in Turkey instead.

Ankara's ambivalent policy towards the conflict in Ukraine strained its relations with both Kyiv and Türkiye's NATO allies. Ankara threatened in early June 2022 to block the applications for NATO membership of Sweden and Finland as they sought protection from possible future Russian aggression. President Erdoğan insisted that the two countries must lift their arms embargoes on Türkiye, cease support of the YPG and extradite nearly 100 of his predominantly Kurdish critics and opponents who were wanted in Türkiye on terrorism charges. The impasse appeared to have been resolved at the NATO summit in Madrid, Spain, on 28–30 June, when Ankara withheld its veto of Sweden's and Finland's applications, in return for a commitment by both countries to address Türkiye's concerns. However, Erdoğan subsequently repeatedly warned that the Turkish parliament would refuse to ratify Swedish and Finnish membership of NATO, unless they delivered on Ankara's demands.

President Erdoğan's determination to try to maintain his ties with Russia frequently strained his relations with Ukraine, no more so than when Türkiye failed to intercept Russian ships carrying stolen Ukrainian grain from transiting Turkish waters—and, in several well-documented cases, selling some of the grain to Turkish companies at below market rates. Nevertheless, Türkiye once again demonstrated the importance of its geostrategic location when, together with the UN, it played a critical role in an agreement reached by Ukraine and Russia on 22 July to establish a 'grain corridor' to enable grain stored in Ukrainian ports to be shipped through the Bosphorus strait to be sold on the global market. The first shipment left the Ukrainian port of Odesa on 1 August.

NEW TENSIONS WITH THE USA OVER SYRIA AND GREECE

The war in Ukraine, and Ankara's subsequent refusal to sever its ties with Russia reinforced the perception in Washington that Türkiye was a difficult but necessary ally. In October 2021 Ankara made a request to the US Government to buy 40 new F-16 fighter jets and modernization kits for 80 of its existing F-16 fleet, in an attempt to upgrade the ageing Turkish air force and partly to compensate for Türkiye's expulsion from the F-35 programme. However, although the White House responded positively to the request, it came as President Erdoğan threatened to stage a new military operation into northern Syria against the SDF—a move that would antagonize the US Administration and further harden already strong resistance in the US Congress to new defence and armament sales to Türkiye. Reluctant to risk a new crisis with the USA, in early 2022 Erdoğan sought to appeal to hard-line nationalists among his domestic support base by stoking long-running tensions with Greece over the boundaries of the two countries' airspaces and territorial waters, including by questioning the sovereignty of a number of Greek islands close to the Turkish coast. In May, during an official visit to Washington, Greek Prime Minister Kyriakos Mitsotakis publicly called on the USA not to sell any F-16 planes or modernization kits to Türkiye. Although his speech triggered outrage in Ankara, it bore results in Washington. In June the US House of Representatives approved an amendment to the National Defense Authorization Act that barred the sale of warplanes to Türkiye, unless the US Government could guarantee that they would not be used for repeated unauthorized overflights of Greek territory. Although Erdoğan continued to threaten to defy the USA over Syria and Greece, he was aware that following his words with action would risk a major confrontation with Washington.

THE FEBRUARY 2023 EARTHQUAKES

On 6 February 2023 southern and central Türkiye was struck by an earthquake with a magnitude of 7.8. A separate earthquake, measuring 7.7, followed later that day. The two earthquakes were 95 km (59 miles) apart and caused unprecedented destruction and loss of life across a broad swathe of south and south-eastern Türkiye, affecting 14m. people—around 16% of the country's population. There were more than 30,000 aftershocks. More than 50,000 people are believed to have been killed and 1.5m. left homeless. In March the UN estimated the cost of repairing the damage at more than US $100,000m. The scale of the disaster was a national trauma, and the Government initially came under severe criticism from survivors and opposition parties for its perceived slow rescue and relief efforts.

MAY 2023: ERDOĞAN RETAINS POWER DESPITE A FALL IN SUPPORT

With opinion polls suggesting that popular support for Erdoğan—and even more so for the AKP—was in long-term decline, questions proliferated about the prospects for simultaneous parliamentary and presidential elections, due to be held by June 2023. Although Erdoğan's authoritarianism, and an accompanying rise in corruption and nepotism played a part, the main reason for his fading popularity appeared to be the increasingly desperate state of the economy, as inflation soared and the currency depreciated.

Although a Turkish nationalist himself, Erdoğan had previously displayed a willingness to court support from other segments of society. However, his need for the MHP's support effectively locked him into pursuing hard-line Turkish nationalist policies, making it impossible for him to resume talks to try to resolve the long-running Kurdish issue. In June 2021 the country's Constitutional Court, which was dominated by Erdoğan loyalists, accepted an indictment to outlaw the pro-Kurdish HDP and ban 451 of its leading members from holding political office for a period of five years. The decision was greeted with dismay by the party's Kurdish supporters. However, the memory of the brutal suppression of the 2015–16 urban uprisings meant that there was little desire for a return to violence or mass public protests. The case was still ongoing in July 2023.

In March 2023 Erdoğan called simultaneous parliamentary and presidential elections for 14 May. Opinion polls suggested that the six-party opposition alliance, led by the CHP and the İP, was set to overturn the parliamentary majority of the AKP-MHP alliance. However, despite soaring inflation that had reached more than 85% in October 2022, falling living standards and widespread criticism of the Government's response to the February 2023 earthquakes, the AKP received 35.3% of the vote and 268 seats in parliament, and the MHP 10.0% and 50 seats. The result gave the AKP-MHP alliance 318 seats in the 600-member assembly—323 seats if the five won by the Yeniden Refah Partisi (YRP—New Welfare Party), which had formed an election alliance with the AKP-MHP and received 2.9% of the vote, are taken into account. The CHP took 25.4% of the vote and 169 seats and the İP 9.9% and 43 seats. To guard against its possible outlawing by the Constitutional Court, the HDP fielded candidates on the ticket of the Yeşil Sol Parti (YSP—Green Left Party), winning 8.8% of the vote and 61 seats. The YSP had formed an electoral alliance with the Türkiye İşçi Partisi (TİP—Workers' Party of Turkey), which took 1.7% of the vote and four seats.

In the run-up to the presidential election, most opinion polls suggested that it would be won by Kemal Kılıçdaroğlu, the CHP leader and the candidate of the six-party opposition alliance, who also received informal support from the YSP. However, on 14 May 2023 Kılıçdaroğlu received only 44.9% of the vote, behind Erdoğan with 49.5%. With neither candidate receiving more than one-half of the vote, there was a second-round run-off ballot on 28 May, which Erdoğan won with 52.2% of the votes cast, against 47.8% for Kılıçdaroğlu.

FOREIGN RELATIONS 2022–23: ECONOMIC WOES FUEL RAPPROCHEMENT

The economic downturn in Türkiye resulted in Erdoğan continuing to pursue a more conciliatory foreign policy through late 2022 and into 2023, in the hope of attracting an inflow of much-needed foreign capital.

Türkiye continued to try to maintain cordial relations with both sides in the war in Ukraine. Russia remained Türkiye's largest supplier of energy, one of its largest markets for tourists and an increasingly lucrative market for Turkish exports.

TÜRKIYE (TURKEY)

While Türkiye was also useful to Russia, not least as a means of circumventing Western flight restrictions and sanctions, including serving as a conduit for black market and grey market trade.

Erdoğan also sought to retain trade and defence ties with Ukraine, not least to preserve Türkiye's often troubled relations with the West. At the end of March 2023 the Turkish parliament finally ratified Finland's membership of NATO. In early July the President announced that Türkiye would do the same for Sweden, later adding that he expected ratification to take place in October. However, he made it clear that, in return, he expected the USA to approve the F-16 sale.

In addition, Türkiye avoided renewing natural gas exploration activities in the eastern Mediterranean in waters claimed by Greece and Cyprus, for fear that the resultant tensions could sour still further relations with the EU, its main trading partner.

The ongoing crisis in the Turkish economy also meant that, from late 2022 and into 2023, Erdoğan continued to court former regional rivals such as Saudi Arabia and the UAE, in the hope that they would pump more money into Türkiye. In July 2023 the President concluded a tour of three Gulf states by signing deals worth US $50,700m. with the UAE.

Economy

Revised by GARETH JENKINS

INTRODUCTION

Türkiye (as Turkey was officially redesignated in June 2022) is about 1,450 km (900 miles) long and some 500 km (300 miles) wide, covering an area of 783,562 sq km (302,535 sq miles). The population of Türkiye stood at 64,729,501 at the end of 2000, rising to 85,279,553 by the end of 2022. These totals exclude Turkish citizens working abroad, the majority of whom are in Germany. However, there were also an estimated 5m. migrants inside Türkiye at the end of 2022, of whom approximately 3.6m. were Syrian refugees. Türkiye's population density increased from 82.6 per sq km at the end of 2000 to 110.8 per sq km at the end of 2022. İstanbul, the country's largest city, had an estimated population of 15.9m. in December 2022 (compared with 8.8m. in 2000). It is followed by Ankara (the capital) and İzmir, with estimated populations of 5.8m. and 4.5m., respectively

The country possesses significant natural advantages: fertile land yielding a wide variety of grains, fruit and vegetables, and other products; an extensive range of minerals; and a number of natural ports. The climate is varied and, on the whole, favourable. Türkiye's gross domestic product (GDP) per head on a purchasing-power parity (PPP) basis was US $37,301 in 2022, well below the average for Organisation for Economic Co-operation and Development (OECD) member states. Starting in the 1960s millions of Turks began to go abroad to seek employment, mainly in blue-collar jobs in Western Europe, but also in Middle Eastern countries such as Libya, Saudi Arabia and the other states of the Persian (Arabian) Gulf. However, blue-collar out-migration subsequently decreased due to stricter visa regimes in Europe and falling demand for Turkish labour in the Middle East, although in recent years there has been an increase in white-collar out-migration, especially among young people.

Severe economic, political and social volatility in the late 1970s led to a recession in 1980 (when a military coup took place), when gross national income (GNI) contracted by 1.1%. In 1980–90 GNI, at constant 1987 prices, increased at an average annual rate of 5.5%, with a growth rate of 9.2% in 1990. In 1991 the adverse effects of the Gulf War led to growth of just 0.9%. GNI growth improved in 1992 and 1993, but, after a severe financial crisis early in 1994 and an austerity programme in April, GNI contracted by 6.1% in that year. None the less, GNI growth resumed quickly, increasing by 8.0% in 1995 and 7.9% in 1996. The strongest sectoral growth in both years was recorded in trade and industry.

Figures published by the OECD revealed that, although income per head rose by 6.1% in 1995, to US $2,928, the wealthiest 20% of the population had an income of $8,037 per head, while the poorest had only $717, giving Türkiye the worst income distribution of all OECD countries, except Mexico. According to World Bank estimates, GNI rose by 8.6% in 1997, yielding a GNI per head of $3,130 on a conventional exchange-rate basis and $6,470 on a PPP basis. In 1998, as a result of adverse external factors, GNI growth decelerated to 3.9%, yielding GNI of $3,160 per head on a conventional exchange-rate basis and $6,594 on a PPP basis.

A sharp decline in economic growth had already been predicted for 1999 before two major earthquakes in north-western Türkiye in August and November inflicted huge damage on industry and infrastructure. Consequently, GNI contracted by 6.4%, resulting in per-head income decreasing to US $2,878 and GDP declining by 5.0%. By mid-2000 a recovery appeared to be under way, as reflected in the 5.6% GDP growth in the first quarter. In November, however, the fragility of the recovery was exposed by a major banking and stock market crisis, in which the Central Bank of the Republic of Türkiye expended some US $7,000m. to support the lira, before the Government secured an additional stand-by facility of $7,000m. from the International Monetary Fund (IMF) in December. In 2000 overall GDP growth stood at 3.5%; total GDP amounted to $198,800m., (or $455,500m. on a PPP basis), producing GDP per head of $3,000 ($6,800 at PPP).

The respite proved to be only temporary. After a public clash between the President and the Prime Minister in February 2001 over the latter's alleged failure to combat corruption, the financial system neared collapse in Türkiye's worst economic crisis in living memory. A massive flight of capital forced the Government to float the lira and to accept an immediate devaluation of over one-third (see *Budget, Investment and Finance*). Difficult negotiations with the IMF resulted in the approval in May of a further stand-by credit equivalent to US $8,000m. (bringing the total granted to Türkiye since December 1999 to a record $19,000m.), but only on even stricter conditions that long-promised economic restructuring and counter-inflationary measures would be implemented, including reductions in subsidies, reform of the banking sector and privatization of state-owned enterprises. Following the crisis, which was aggravated by the economic effects of the September 2001 attacks on the USA, expected GDP growth of 4.5% in 2001 turned into a contraction of 7.4%, and inflation rose to 68.5%. Total GDP in that year declined to $148,166m. (or $427,000m. at PPP), giving a figure for GDP per capita of $2,226 (or $6,419 at PPP).

The economic crisis necessitated the conclusion in February 2002 of a new agreement with the IMF for a stand-by credit of SDR 12,800m., with renewed pledges of structural reform. Although the political crisis that developed in mid-2002 and a general election in November created new uncertainties for the economy, a growth rate of 7.8% was recorded in 2002, with total GDP rising to US $182,848m. (or $453,300m. at PPP). According to the World Bank, total GNI was $173,300m. ($438,000m. at PPP) in 2002 and GNI per head was $2,500 ($6,300 at PPP). The official rate of unemployment rose to 10.3% in 2002 (from 8.4% in 2001), while the inflation rate fell to 29.7%.

The US-led military campaign in Iraq during March–April 2003 posed further difficulties for the Turkish economy. Türkiye also encountered new difficulties with the IMF, which in May withheld a US $476m. tranche of the latest stand-by credit, owing to slow progress in the Government's economic reform programme. However, an extended review of Türkiye's compliance resulted in the IMF Executive Board deciding in August to release the stand-by tranche and to extend the repayment period into 2006. Further releases of $502m. in December 2003, $495m. in April 2004 and $661m. in July of that year brought total disbursements under the 2002 stand-by arrangement to about $17,000m. of the $19,000m. available.

Strong economic growth of 5.9% in 2003 produced a GDP of US $492,900m. and per capita income of $7,216 (both on a PPP basis). The official rate of unemployment increased slightly to 10.5% of a total labour force of 23.6m., while the inflation rate declined to 18.4%. Vigorous growth continued in 2004, at a rate of 9.9%, and inflation was halved to 9.5%, while official unemployment declined to 9.3%, its lowest level for 30 years. On a PPP basis, total GDP in 2004 was $551,900m., while GDP per head stood at $8,015. In May 2005 the IMF approved a further stand-by arrangement of SDR 6,660m. (about $10,000m.) to support Türkiye's economic and financial programme until May 2008 (see *Budget, Investment and Finance*).

Economic recovery and more solid financial foundations were symbolized by the introduction on 1 January 2005 of the new Turkish lira (YTL), equivalent to 1m. old lira and subdivided into 100 kuruş. (The name of the currency reverted to Turkish lira on 1 January 2009.) The GDP growth rate remained high in 2005, at 7.7%, but it subsequently began to slow down towards the 5% long-run growth rate projected by the OECD. Even before the global financial crisis affected the country, GDP growth rates were in decline, decreasing to 5.0% in 2007 and 1.1% in 2008. In 2009 GDP contracted by some 4.8% as the effects of the financial crisis took hold. Growth resumed in 2010, with GDP expanding by 8.2% and continued in 2011, when growth was recorded at 8.5% and GDP per head rose to US $19,799 on a PPP basis. However, lower GDP growth rates were recorded in the following years due to tighter monetary policies to deal with inflationary pressures and reduce the current account deficit.

In December 2016 the Turkish Statistical Institute (Turkstat) announced that it was changing the methods by which it calculated GDP. The resultant revised headline figures were questioned by economists because they not only added some US $140,000m., or around 20%, to the country's GDP, but were not consistent with the changes recorded in the components used to calculate GDP, such as industrial output. Nonetheless, the result was an official figure for GDP growth of 3.5% in 2016, rising to 7.3% in 2017, before declining sharply to 2.6% in 2018 and to 0.9% in 2019.

The impact of the coronavirus disease (COVID-19) pandemic resulted in a GDP contraction of 10.3% on an annual basis in the second quarter of 2020. Although economic activity picked up through the second half of the year, GDP growth for 2020 as a whole was still only 1.8%. However, GDP rebounded strongly in 2021, growing by 11.0% before slowing to 5.6% in 2022. On a PPP basis, GDP per head increased to US $27,318 in 2019, $28,119 in 2020, $30,472 in 2021 and $37,301 in 2022. Despite the impact of the devastating February 2023 earthquakes, government measures to boost economic activity in the run-up to the May elections produced GDP growth of 4.0% on an annual basis in the first quarter of that year. However, there was considerable scepticism about the accuracy of the data provided by Turkstat, which had become increasingly politicized as President Tayyip Erdoğan tightened his grip on power. Nevertheless, in June the OECD forecast that GDP would grow by 3.6% in 2023 as a whole and by 3.7% in 2024.

AGRICULTURE AND FISHING

Türkiye relies substantially on agriculture. It is the largest producer and exporter of agricultural products in the Middle East and North Africa, although the sector's overall role has shrunk considerably over recent decades and Türkiye is no longer self-sufficient in food production. In 2022 the agricultural sector accounted for 16.0% of total employment but only 6.5% of GDP. The sector has been constrained by high rates of interest and inflation, structural deficiencies such as fragmented and small land holdings, a lack of grassroots farmers' organizations and poor marketing facilities. Efforts to remedy such deficiencies formed part of the Government's structural reform programme that followed the financial crises of November 2000 and February 2001 and was shaped by Türkiye's aspiration to join the European Union (EU) and its commitments under IMF conditionality. Although the slow pace of eliminating subsidies came under repeated IMF and World Bank criticism in 2002–03, the producer support estimate (PSE) of 26.5% in 2004 (as a percentage of the value of gross farm receipts) was lower than the OECD average of 29.9%. However, by 2005 the PSE in Türkiye had increased to 32.1%, overtaking the OECD average, which declined to 27.8% in that year. Türkiye's PSE fell to 20.2% in 2011 and 19.8% in 2015, before rising to 27.7% in 2016 and then declining again to 22.8% in 2017 and 13.5% in 2019. It then rose again to 19.6% in 2020 and fell back to 15.1% in 2021, compared with an EU average of around 17.6%.

In 2022 some 23.1m. ha, or about 29% of the total land area, were in some sort of agricultural use. However, the area devoted to permanent crops decreased from 4.1% in 1980 to 3.2% in 1996, while irrigated land rose from 9.6% to 15.4% of cropland over the same period. The irrigated area rose from 4.3m. ha in 1996 to 4.9m. ha in 2003 and 6.2m. ha in 2022. Of Türkiye's 3m. agricultural units, about 60% are small, the average size of a family farm being only 6 ha. The principal agricultural exports by value are hazelnuts, wheat, cotton, grapes and citrus fruits. Other important crops are barley, sunflower and other oilseeds, maize, sugar beet, potatoes, tea and olives.

Following the introduction of land reforms and the improved utilization of land, machinery and farmer education resources, agricultural output increased by some 30% in 1971, but in subsequent years the expansion targets set in successive five-year plans were not met. In 1980–90 the rate of increase continued to fluctuate, leading to an average annual growth rate of 1.3%. In 1990–96 an average annual increase of 1.2% was recorded. By 2000–04 the average annual growth rate had declined to 0.8%. Agriculture provided 59.4% of total export revenue in 1979, but the proportion declined to about 20% in the late 1980s and to 13.6% in 1994, increasing to 15.8% in 1999. The sector's share of export revenue then contracted to 13.9% in 2000 and 5.0% in 2011, before rising to 14.2% in 2015 and slipping back to 9.5% in 2017, 3.5% in 2020 and 3.1% in 2022. The agricultural sector, including forestry and fishing, contributed 14.9% of GDP in 1999. Thereafter, agriculture's share of GDP declined, from around 12% in 2000–04 to 7.7% in 2008. The sector's share increased to 9.1% during the recession in 2009, before declining again. Agriculture's share of GDP was 5.6% in 2021 and 6.5% in 2022.

In an attempt to alleviate the poverty of the south-eastern provinces of Türkiye, the Government drew up the South-East Anatolia Project (Güneydoğu Anadolu Projesi—GAP) in the early 1980s, covering a total area of 74,000 sq km. Some 495 projects were integrated into GAP, which envisaged the construction of 22 dams on the Tigris and Euphrates rivers and their tributaries, 19 power plants, and an irrigation network with the potential to cover 8.5m. ha. GAP has been affected by delays resulting from attacks by Kurdish separatists and disputes over financing. In March 2015 the Government announced an investment of another US $10,000m. in the project. The project is scheduled to be completed by the end of 2023.

About one-half of the cultivated area is devoted to cereals, of which the most important is wheat. The principal wheat-growing area is the central Anatolian plateau, but the uncertain climate causes wide fluctuations in production. Barley, rye and oats are other important crops grown on the central plateau. Maize is grown along the Black Sea coastal regions, and leguminous crops in the İzmir hinterland. Rice is also grown in various parts of the country. In the 1990s the annual wheat harvest usually stayed above 18m. metric tons per year, owing to good weather, improved cultivation methods and increased levels of irrigation. Between 2005 and 2009 annual wheat production rose to approximately 21m. tons, declining to 17.7m. tons in 2008, before recovering to 20.6m. tons in 2009. Wheat production remained relatively consistent at 20.0m. tons in 2018, 19.0m. tons in 2019 and 20.5m. tons in 2020. However, a severe drought resulted in a drop in production in 2021 to 17.7m. tons before rising again to 19.8m. tons in 2022.

Production of tuber crops (mainly potatoes and onions) averaged around 6.0m. metric tons in 2006–10. Production of potatoes stood at 5.1m. tons in 2021 and 5.2m. tons in 2022. Production of onions was 2.5m. tons in 2021 and 2.4m. tons in 2022. Output of pulses totalled 1.1m. tons in 2021, increasing to 1.2m. tons in 2022. Total vegetable production increased from 18.3m. tons in 1995 to 31.8m. tons in 2021, falling slightly to 31.6m. tons in 2022.

Cotton, grown mainly in the İzmir and Adana regions, was once an important export earner. In recent years it has lost some of its importance, although the irrigation of agricultural land in the eastern Haran region has partly revived its fortunes. In 2021 production of cotton lint stood at 832,500 metric tons, rising to 1.1m. tons in 2022. Türkiye is the seventh largest producer of cotton seed. Output remained at 1.3m.–1.5m. tons through the 1990s and early 2000s. However, in recent years it has grown, reaching 2.3m. tons in 2021 and 2.6m. tons in 2022. Sugar beet production rose from 17.8m. tons in 2021 to 19.0m. tons in 2022.

Türkiye produces what is regarded as a particularly fine type of tobacco. The three principal producing regions are the Aegean hinterland, the Black Sea coast and the Marmara-Thrace region. The bulk of the crop is produced in the Aegean region, where the tobacco is notable for its light golden colour and mild taste. The finest tobacco is grown on the Black Sea coast, around Samsun. Although a traditional Turkish export, its relative position as an export staple has declined in recent years. Most of Türkiye's tobacco exports go to the USA and Eastern European countries. Over the past few decades tobacco production has followed a generally downward trajectory (having reached a record 324,000 metric tons in 1976). Output totalled 71,500 tons in 2021 and 82,250 tons in 2022. In 1999 260,000 ha were devoted to the crop, but by 2022 the area had declined to 95,000 ha.

The coastal area of the Aegean, with mild winters and hot, dry summers, produces grapes, citrus fruits, figs and olives. Production of figs increased from 320,000 metric tons in 2021 to 350,000 tons in 2022. The outstanding product, however, is the sultana type of raisin. Türkiye normally ranks second worldwide as a sultana producer, but in years of good yields becomes the largest producer in the world. Sultana production increased from 290,000 tons in 2021 to 370,000 tons in 2022. Production of all varieties of grapes amounted to 4.2m. tons in 2020, 3.9m. tons in 2021 and 4.2m. tons in 2022.

The citrus fruit sector has expanded steadily over the past few decades. In 2003 citrus fruit production included 1.25m. metric tons of oranges, 550,000 tons of mandarins and 135,000 tons of grapefruit. Total production of oranges (which amounted to 842,000 tons in 1995) decreased from 1.7m. tons in 2021 to 1,3m. tons in 2022. Total production of mandarins and tangerines increased from 1.8m. tons in 2021 to 1.9m. tons in 2022. Total production of grapefruit and pomelos stood at 249,000 tons in 2021 before falling to 198,000 tons in 2022. For lemons, total production was 1.6m. tons in 2021 and 1.3m. tons in 2022. Other significant fruit production in 2022 included 4.8m. tons of apples, 803,000 tons of apricots, 656,000 tons of sweet cherries, 1.0m. tons of peaches and nectarines, 551,000 tons of pears, and 349,000 tons of plums and sloes.

The Black Sea area, notably around Giresun and Trabzon, produces the greatest quantity of hazelnuts (filberts) of any region in the world. Hazelnuts have been grown there since 300 BCE. A harvest of 684,000 metric tons was recorded in 2021, increasing to 765,000 tons in 2022. Türkiye is the world's leading exporter of hazelnuts, accounting for more than 50% of global output and trade. Significant quantities of walnuts, almonds and pistachios are also grown, with an output of 335,000 tons of walnuts, 190,000 tons of almonds and 39,000 tons of pistachios in 2022.

Türkiye is also an important producer of oilseeds, principally sunflower, groundnut, soybean and sesame. Total sunflower production was 2.4m. metric tons in 2021, rising to 2.6m. tons in 2022. Moreover, the country remains a major producer of olives. Olive production totalled 1.7m. tons in 2021 and 3.0m. tons in 2022.

Until 1972 Türkiye was one of the seven countries with the right to export opium under the United Nations Commission on Narcotic Drugs. Much opium, however, was exported illegally, particularly to the USA and Iran. Partly as a result of pressure from the US Government, the Turkish Government made the cultivation of opium poppies illegal in 1972, but the ban was lifted in July 1974 and the flowers are grown in certain provinces under strict controls. Opium gum is no longer tapped from the living plant. The poppy pods (opium straw) are sold to the Government, which processes them into concentrate for export as the basis for morphine and other drugs.

Sheep and cattle are raised on the grazing lands of the Anatolian plateau. Stock-raising forms an important branch of the agricultural sector. The sheep population is mainly of the Karaman type and is used primarily as a source of meat and milk. The bulk of the clip comprises coarse wool suitable only for carpets, blankets and poorer grades of clothing fabric. However, efforts have been made to encourage breeding of Merino sheep for wool. In 2022 total production of Merino wool was 12,240 metric tons. The Angora (Ankara) goat produces the fine, soft wool known as mohair. Türkiye used to be one of the world's largest producers of mohair, with an average output of about 9,000 tons per year. However, production has fallen considerably in recent years and in 2022 total mohair production was just 417 tons. Poultry meat has largely displaced traditional meats such as lamb, mutton and goat in domestic consumption. In 2022 the numbers of heads of cattle, sheep and goats were 17.0m., 44.7m. and 11.6m., respectively. In that year Türkiye produced 2.4m. tons of poultry meat, up from 2.2m. tons in 2021, and 19,809m. eggs, up from 19,298m. in 2021. Although several government projects have been introduced to increase productivity, the ratio of meat output to heads of livestock animals has remained largely stable.

Türkiye has 8,333 km of coastline and some 1,200 inland water resources, but fishing potential has been reduced by over-fishing, pollution and ecological changes. The development of aquaculture in inland waters has been one of the aims of the GAP, while the Black Sea Fishery Improvement Project aims to increase catches within a sustainable framework. In 2022 around 200,000 people were directly employed in the fishing industry and 2m. indirectly. The total catch increased from 799,844 metric tons in 2021 to 849,808 tons in 2022. These figures include a significant increase in aquaculture production, which rose from 471,686 tons in 2021 to 514,805 tons in 2022.

MINERALS AND MINING

Türkiye has a diversity of rich mineral resources, including significant quantities of bauxite, borax, coal and lignite, chromium, copper, iron ore, manganese and sulphur. The mining and quarrying sector employed some 145,000 workers in 2022. However, in that year the sector's share of GDP remained very small, at around 1.0%, and it engaged less than 0.5% of the employed population. Similarly, the share of mining and quarrying exports, including oil and natural gas, in total export earnings also remained low, at approximately 1.8% in 2021 and 2022. In 2022 imports of mining and quarrying products, including oil and natural gas, accounted for 20.7% of the total cost of imports, up from 14.7% in 2021. Imports of oil and raw materials are major contributors to Türkiye's persistently high current account deficit.

The most important state-owned enterprise in the mining sector used to be Etibank, established in 1935, which worked through its subsidiaries, Ereğli Coal Mines, East Chromium Mines, Turkish Copper, Keban Lead Mines and Keçiborlu Sulphur Mines. During the early 1960s state-owned enterprises increased their predominance over the private sector, with an investment programme that was supported by the Mining Investment Bank, established in 1962. But the policy of encouraging the private sector to play a greater part in the mining industry failed to overcome the general reluctance of private investors to view mining as a worthwhile area for long-term investment, with the result that the private sector remains under-capitalized. An additional factor mitigating against the development of mining has been the long-held suspicion of foreign investment. A law enacted in 1973 restricted foreign participation in mining development projects. However, this restriction was relaxed in January 1980, allowing up to 49% foreign participation in mining ventures. In response, the publicly owned Etibank entered into a joint-venture agreement with a US company (Phelps Dodge) in 1983 for copper mining. Etibank was privatized in 2001. Eti Holding AŞ disposed of most of its mining subsidiaries and in 2004 was renamed Eti Mine Works. It is still publicly owned, but its mining operations are limited mainly to boron production.

Bituminous and anthracite coal is found at and around Zonguldak on the Black Sea coast. Most of the seams are of good coking quality, the coke being used in the steel mills in nearby Karabük. In 2022 coke production was 4.8m. metric tons, up from 4.6m. tons in 2021. Lignite is found in many parts of central and western Anatolia, and total reserves are estimated at up to 8,000m. tons. Production of lignite amounted to 80.9m. tons in 2022, up from 80.1m. tons in 2020. Seams located in western Türkiye are operated by the West Lignite Mines. The other main mines are at Soma, Degirmisaz, Tunçbilek and Afsin Elbistan. The latter was developed with extensive German and international financial assistance, as part of an ambitious integrated energy project.

Practically all of Türkiye's iron ore comes from the Divriği mine, situated between Sivas and Erzurum, in the north-east of the country, and operated by the Turkish Iron and Steel Corpn (Ereğli Demir ve Çelik Fabrikalari TAŞ—Erdemir). The average grade of ore is 60%–66%, and reserves are estimated at 149.9m. metric tons. Output of gross iron ore increased from 21.5m. metric tons in 2020 (compared with just 1.7m. tons in 1979) before declining to 16.1m. tons in 2021.

Türkiye is one of the world's largest producers of chromite (chromium ore). The richest deposits are in Güleman, south-eastern Türkiye, in the vicinity of İskenderun; in the area around Eskişehir, north-western Anatolia; and between Fethiye and Antalya on the Mediterranean coast. The Güleman mines, producing nearly 50% of the country's total, are operated by Eti Krom. Little chromium is used domestically, but the mineral is a major earner of foreign exchange. Output of chromite decreased from 3.1m. metric tons in 2020 to 2.8m. tons in 2021.

Copper has been mined in Türkiye since ancient times. Current production comes from the Black Sea region, particularly the far east, and south-eastern Türkiye, with mines in the provinces of Elazığ and Siirt. Annual production of copper stood at 107,000 metric tons in 2020 and 108,100 tons in 2021. Production of bauxite increased substantially from 678,000 tons in 2018 to 2.8m. tons in 2021. Most of the output is exported to Germany, the United Kingdom and the USA. Known reserves of copper ore are estimated at 90m. tons.

Eskişehir, in north-western Anatolia, is the world's leading centre for the mining of meerschaum, a soft white mineral that hardens on exposure to the sun and looks like ivory. Meerschaum has long been used by Turkish craftsmen for pipes and cigarette holders.

Manganese, magnesite, lead, sulphur, salt, asbestos, antimony, zinc and mercury are important mineral resources. Of these, manganese ranks first in importance. Deposits, worked by private enterprise, are found in many parts of the country, but principally near Eskişehir and in the Ereğli district. In 2020 manganese production stood at 101,766 metric tons, before falling back to 86,654 tons in 2021. Lead is mined at Keban, west of Elazığ. Production was 81,500 tons of metal content in 2020 and 93,700 tons in 2021. Antimony is mined near Balıkesir and Niğde. In 2021 antimony production was 4,210 tons of metal content. Antimony reserves in Türkiye represent around 2.7% of world reserves. Large uranium deposits have been discovered in the Black Sea, between 1 km and 2 km below sea level. Türkiye's first commercially viable silver mine was opened in January 1988. Silver production rose from 98.3 tons in 2020 to 162.7 tons in 2021. In April 1996 a project to develop Türkiye's first gold mine (reserves were discovered in 1990) near Bergama, in İzmir province, was finally approved. In 2002 potential gold reserves were officially estimated at 440 tons. Despite public opposition, successive governments have encouraged gold mining. Gold production decreased from 42.1 tons in 2020 to 39.3 tons in 2021.

The Uludağ (Bursa) tungsten deposits are among the richest in the world. However, Türkiye is not a major producer of tungsten. Other minerals are barytes, perlite, phosphate rock, boron minerals, cinnabar and emery. Türkiye supplies more than 80% of the world market for emery.

PETROLEUM AND NATURAL GAS

Petroleum was first discovered in Türkiye in 1950 and all large discoveries have been in the Hakkari basin, in the south-east of the country. In 2021 Türkiye reported the discovery of an additional 60m. barrels of oil in 26 different locations, taking its estimated reserves to 312m. barrels. It is mostly heavy-grade petroleum with a fairly high sulphur content. Production of crude petroleum fluctuated after reaching 3.5m. metric tons in 1973. Owing to the small size of Türkiye's main oilfields in the fractured terrain of the south-eastern Hakkari basin, petroleum production declined steadily from 1980 to 1985. Production increased in the early 1990s and reached 3.9m. tons in 1993; it then declined gradually to 3.4m. tons in 1997, 2.9m. tons in 1999 and 2.6m. tons in 2001. In 2003 petroleum production rose to 2.8m. tons, at an average of 59,000 barrels per day (b/d), but output decreased to 2.1m. tons (43,000 b/d) in 2004 and remained at approximately the same level for the next decade. New discoveries of oil enabled production to reach 70,000 b/d in June 2023, compared with average consumption of around 1m. b/d.

Türkiye also produces natural gas. Prior to new discoveries in the Black Sea in the 2020s, the country's largest non-associated field was the offshore Marmara Kuzey field in the Thrace-Gallipoli basin of the Sea of Marmara. In July 2001 it was announced that gas had been discovered in the Mersin and İskenderun bays in south-western Türkiye, while in March 2002 the new Gocerler gas field in the Thrace basin began production, 16 months after its discovery. In October 2017 Türkiye announced that it had purchased its first deep-sea drill ship to explore for hydrocarbons in the Mediterranean and Black Sea. Three more purchases of drill ships followed over the next four years. In 2020 Türkiye's deployment of one of its drill ships to explore for natural gas off the Cypriot coast triggered heightened tensions with Greece and Cyprus—and resulted in Turkish energy officials being sanctioned by the EU. Türkiye subsequently withdrew the vessel from the Mediterranean and focused on exploration activities in the Black Sea. On 9 August 2022 Türkiye deployed its latest drill ship, the Abdulhamid Han, to conduct exploration activities in the eastern Mediterranean, although it avoided another confrontation with the EU by drilling in Turkish waters. In August 2020 President Erdoğan announced the discovery of 405,000m. cu m of gas in Turkish waters in the Black Sea. In June 2021 he announced the discovery of a further 135,000m. cu m in the Black Sea. The first Black Sea gas began to come onshore in April 2023, although it was expected to be 2028 until the field was operating at full capacity, by which time it was expected to meet 30% of Türkiye's annual needs. Annual gas production stood at about 800m. cu m during 2005–07, but fell to 650m. cu m during 2008–11. Gas production was 441m. cu m in 2020, but decreased to 394m. cu m in 2021 and 360m. cu m in 2022. However, domestic production has never exceeded 5% of domestic consumption. In 2022 domestic gas consumption fell by 10.5% year on year to 53,521m. cu m, of which local production accounted for only 0.7%. In 2022 some 32.5% of the gas consumed was utilized by households, 27.1% was used for electricity generation and 25.0% by industry.

Imports of mineral fuels and oils stood at US $28,931m. in 2020, $50,692m. in 2021 and $96,549m. in 2022. Türkiye's dependence on imported petroleum and gas has increased as domestic growth rates have risen. Petroleum and gas imports accounted for 19.3% of the total value of imports in 2019, falling to 13.2% in 2020 and rising again to 18.7% in 2021 and 26.5% in 2022. The Russian Federation was Türkiye's main supplier of petroleum and petroleum products in 2022, accounting for 40.8% of the total, followed by Iraq (26.4%), Kazakhstan (9.0%), India (4.7%) and Saudi Arabia (4.0%). In 2022 Russia supplied 39.4% of Türkiye's gas imports, followed by Iran (17.2%), Azerbaijan (15.9%), the USA (10.3%) and Algeria (9.6%), in the form of liquefied natural gas (LNG).

As of July 2023 17 domestic and foreign companies had exploration and processing licences, but the Turkish Petroleum Corpn (TPAO), a 99% state-owned Turkish company, accounted for about 75% of total oil output. In 1983 the Government introduced a new law intended to liberalize conditions for foreign companies, enabling them to export as much as 35% of any onshore petroleum that they discovered, and up to 45% of any offshore output, prompting several joint venture exploration agreements between major foreign oil companies and TPAO.

Refining and other downstream operations are dominated by the Turkish Petroleum Refineries Corpn (TÜPRAŞ), which has four refining complexes: Batman in the south-east, Aliağa near İzmir, İzmit near İstanbul and the Central Anatolian Refinery at Kırıkkale near Ankara. The Star Refinery outside İzmir, which is operated by Socar of Azerbaijan and has a capacity of 214,000 b/d, began operating in 2019. In July 2023 work was continuing on the construction of the Doğu Akdeniz refinery at Ceyhan on Türkiye's eastern Mediterranean coast, which was to be operated by Çalık Holding and have a capacity of 212,000 b/d. In 2017 Ersan Petrol received a licence to operate a refinery with a capacity of 30,000 b/d in the province of Kahramanmaraş. The refinery was originally scheduled to begin operations in 2022. However, financing difficulties meant that it was still inoperative as of July 2023. Doubts about the refinery's viability were exacerbated by Kahramanmaraş being badly affected by the devastating February 2023 earthquakes.

Having privatized a 31.5% stake in TÜPRAŞ (for US $2,300m.) in 2000, the Government confirmed in July 2001 that its holding would be reduced to under 50% by a further offering. In 2000 the Government had also privatized a majority stake in Petrol Ofisi AŞ (POAŞ), the dominant petroleum distributor, while plans were drawn up for partially privatizing the state oil and gas pipeline authority, BOTAŞ. In May 2001 new legislation liberalized Türkiye's gas market, ended BOTAŞ's monopoly in gas importation, and separated the company into units for gas importation, transport, storage and distribution by 2009, in preparation for their privatization (except for the transport unit). The Government sold its remaining shares in POAŞ through a public tender in 2002 and a deal with the controlling group in August. Responding to IMF pressure, the Government confirmed in the same month that it intended to privatize most of the rest of the country's energy sector. A major petroleum market reform bill, proposed in March 2003, provided for the liberalization of the pricing of oil and oil products, as well as the integration of pipeline, refining and distribution functions. Further legislation approved in December aimed to remove remaining state controls in the sector, to liberalize pricing of petroleum and petroleum products, to end restrictions on merging procedures, and to integrate pipeline, refining and distribution functions. In early 2005 some 14.8% of government-owned shares in TÜPRAŞ were sold to institutional investors based abroad. In a privatization tender process in September, a consortium comprising Koç Holding AŞ and Royal Dutch Shell, acquired a 51% share in TÜPRAŞ for $4,140m. However, in February 2017 BOTAŞ and the TPAO were both transferred to Türkiye's sovereign wealth fund (SWF), which had been formally established in August 2016. In July 2023 the Government was using the assets in the SWF as collateral against foreign loans, which effectively ruled out the privatization of BOTAŞ and TPAO for the foreseeable future.

TPAO operates a 500-km pipeline running from the oilfields around Batman to Dörtyol on the Gulf of İskenderun. A 986-km pipeline from Kirkuk, in northern Iraq, to Türkiye has a capacity of 1.5m. b/d. Completion and full commissioning of a second pipeline, alongside the first, took place in July 1987. Following the imposition of economic sanctions on Iraq by the UN in August 1990, the twin pipeline from Kirkuk to Türkiye's Mediterranean terminal at Ceyhan remained closed until December 1996, costing BOTAŞ an estimated US $400m. per year in lost revenues. However, the reopening of the pipeline did little to curb the large-scale smuggling of Iraqi oil into Türkiye, estimated at up to 100,000 b/d and costing the Turkish treasury large sums in lost tax revenue.

Starting in the early 1990s, Türkiye began looking to the Caspian Sea and Central Asia to provide most of its future oil and gas needs, and became involved in several projects to develop supplies there. In 1994 TPAO became part of the Azerbaijan International Operating Company, a consortium of foreign petroleum companies in a production-sharing agreement with Azeri state oil company SOCAR, to develop offshore oilfields in the Caspian Sea. TPAO also became a partner in the Azeri Shah Deniz field in 1996 and has established a petroleum exploration company with the Government of Kazakhstan.

Oil and gas transportation was a controversial issue in the Caspian Sea and Central Asia regions. Türkiye, Russia and Iran competed to route the rich energy resources of Azerbaijan, Kazakhstan, Turkmenistan and Uzbekistan through their territories en route to Western markets. Türkiye's main priority was a 1,760-km oil pipeline to transport 1m. b/d of Azeri and Kazakh Caspian Sea petroleum from Baku in Azerbaijan through Georgia and then across Türkiye to the Mediterranean port of Ceyhan. The Governments of Türkiye, the USA and Azerbaijan all declared their support for the Baku–Ceyhan route, which would reduce the dependence of Caspian Sea energy exports on Russia and bypass Iran. In November 1999 Türkiye, Azerbaijan, Georgia and Kazakhstan signed a legal framework agreement to enable what was renamed the Baku–Tbilisi–Ceyhan (BTC) pipeline to proceed. In February 2001 ChevronTexaco of the USA, which had previously opposed the pipeline, announced its willingness to join the Main Export Pipeline Company, while the following month a memorandum of understanding on the pipeline was signed in Astana, the Kazakh capital, by the Governments of Türkiye, Azerbaijan, Georgia and Kazakhstan. Construction of the Turkish section of the pipeline began in September 2002, and the pipeline was finally opened in May 2005, at a ceremony in Baku. The BTC pipeline has a projected lifespan of 40 years. In 2009 it transported 782,000 b/d (160,000 cu m) of oil. The volume of oil transported through BTC averaged 569,900 b/d in 2020, 549,200 b/d in 2021 and 617,658 b/d in 2022.

Türkiye's enthusiasm for the BTC pipeline had been due to its concerns about the use of the crowded Bosphorus to export petroleum. In July 1994 Türkiye imposed stricter controls for ships transporting hazardous goods through the Bosphorus, following a collision in March. Russia, which exports a large proportion of its petroleum by way of the Bosphorus, protested against the measure. In 2011 the Turkish Government announced a plan to build a 45-km-long canal, to be known as Kanal İstanbul, linking the Black Sea to the Sea of Marmara through the European part of İstanbul, in an attempt to alleviate congestion in the Bosphorus. The project is highly controversial, with environmentalists warning that it could severely damage the ecosystems in the two seas. Opinion polls suggested that more than 80% of residents of İstanbul were opposed to the scheme. Feasibility studies for the project commenced in early 2012. On 26 June 2021 President Erdoğan oversaw what he described as the ground-breaking ceremony for Kanal İstanbul, when he formally inaugurated the construction of a bridge over a reservoir that lies along the canal's proposed route. He predicted that the canal would be completed by 2027. However, by July 2023 it was still unclear how Kanal İstanbul would be financed or whether it would ever be built.

In November 2013 Türkiye signed a number of energy agreements with the Kurdistan Regional Government (KRG) in Iraq, including an agreement to build a new pipeline to carry oil from northern Iraq to Ceyhan on the Turkish Mediterranean coast. The agreements were criticized by the federal Iraqi Government in Baghdad, which claimed that they violated its exclusive right to enter into agreements related to Iraq's natural resources. None the less, in 2013 the KRG completed a pipeline from the Taq Taq region in Iraqi Kurdistan to the Kirkuk–Ceyhan pipeline, bypassing territory under the direct control of the federal government in Iraq. Despite some continuing tensions, relations between the KRG and Baghdad improved after the failed independence referendum of September 2017. However, shipments were halted in March 2023 after an arbitration ruling in favour of the Iraqi Government over oil exports from the KRG. In May the Iraqi Government notified Türkiye to resume flows from Iraq. However, they remained suspended as of July 2023. The volume of oil transported through the Kirkuk–Ceyhan pipeline stood at 532,000 b/d in 2019, 526,000 b/d in 2020 and 513,000 b/d in 2021.

Demand for natural gas is projected to rise in Türkiye over the coming years, although an increasing government focus on renewables means that the expansion is likely to be less than was forecast in the early 2000s. The main consumers are still expected to be industry and power plants.

In December 1997 Türkiye and Russia signed a 25-year contract (the so-called 'Blue Stream' agreement) for a large increase in Russian natural gas supplies, mostly to be delivered via a 1,210-km dual pipeline, linking Isobilnoye in southern Russia to Dzhugba on the Black Sea coast, under the sea to the Turkish port of Samsun and on to Ankara. The agreement envisaged the import of an additional 3,000m. cu m of gas per year through the pipeline, with an increase to 16,000m. cu m by 2010. Russian supplies received through the Black Sea pipeline would supplement those received by Türkiye through the existing pipeline route (crossing Ukraine, Moldova, Romania and Bulgaria), so that Russia would continue to provide at least one-half of Türkiye's total annual demand for imported gas well into the 21st century. Work on what would become the world's deepest underwater gas pipeline was finally completed, one year behind schedule, in October 2002, at a cost of US $3,200m., with gas flows commencing in March 2003.

Another source of natural gas supply to Türkiye is via a pipeline from Iran, for which a US $20,000m. agreement was concluded in August 1996, for the construction of a 1,400-km pipeline from Tabriz, in Iran, to Ankara. Despite US disapproval, Türkiye proceeded with the project and awarded the contract for the construction of the first section of the pipeline, from the Iranian border to Erzurum, in early 1997; the second section, from Erzurum to Ankara, was built at a later date. Each country was responsible for financing the section of the pipeline in its own territory. Following delays in completion, for which each side blamed the other, an agreement was reached in January 2000 that deliveries would commence in mid-2001. However, in July inauguration of the pipeline was postponed, owing to what Türkiye described as technical difficulties on the Iranian side, although Iran denied that it was to blame for the further delay. The pipeline was eventually inaugurated in January 2002. The agreement concluded in 1996 committed Türkiye to paying for a minimum of 10,000m. cu m per year. In 2007–16 Iranian supplies averaged around 7,500m. cu m per year. Iranian supplies totalled 5,321m. cu m in 2020, 9,434m. cu m in 2021 and 9,405m. cu m in 2022.

A separate scheme for the shipment of gas from Turkmenistan to Türkiye was the Trans-Caspian Gas Pipeline (TCGP), for which BOTAŞ signed an agreement with Turkmenistan in May 1999, envisaging the construction of a 1,690-km pipeline running under the Caspian and via Azerbaijan and Georgia, which would transport up to 30,000m. cu m of gas per year to Türkiye, with additional gas possibly being sent onwards to Europe. However, although Turkish officials argued that Türkiye's anticipated future gas needs would support more than one new pipeline, some observers regarded the TCGP proposal as a direct competitor to the 'Blue Stream' and other pipeline projects and pointed out that major gas reserves in Azerbaijan's Shah Deniz field were much closer to Türkiye. Pending further progress on the TCGP project, in March 2001 Türkiye signed a bilateral agreement with Azerbaijan providing for the supply of gas, mainly from the Shah Deniz field over 15 years, starting in 2005 with imports of 2,000m. cu m, which were expected to rise to 6,500m. cu m by 2008. In late 2001 the Azeri and Georgian parliaments ratified the necessary transit agreements for a 1,000-km pipeline linking Baku to Erzurum via Georgia, which would have an initial capacity of 22,000m. cu m a year, rising to 30,000m. cu m, and so would be able to pipe gas from Turkmenistan, when, and if, the TCGP was constructed, to Baku. The South Caucasus pipeline came on stream in December 2006, and supplies to Türkiye began early the following year.

In December 2003 Türkiye signed an agreement with Greece, providing for the construction of a 300-km pipeline through which, commencing in 2006, up to 11,000m. cu m per year of gas would be pumped from Bursa in Türkiye to Komotini in northern Greece, for onward diversion to Western European markets. Work on the pipeline officially began in July 2005 with a ceremony, attended by the Turkish and Greek Prime Ministers, on the River Meric/Evros border between the two countries. It was stated that the longer-term aim was to extend the pipeline to Italy as part of the Southern Europe Gas Ring Project.

In May 2012 the Shah Deniz consortium accepted a bid from Türkiye's Trans-Anatolia Gas Pipeline (TANAP), a project based on an agreement between Türkiye and Azerbaijan, which would link the Southern Caucasus pipeline corridor through Georgia to a number of proposed links in EU countries. TANAP was officially inaugurated in June 2018 and became operational in July 2019. TANAP was expected eventually to transport 16,000m. cu m per annum, of which 6,000m. cu m was to be used for Türkiye's domestic consumption and the remainder exported to Europe.

In October 2016 Russia and Türkiye signed an intergovernmental agreement for the construction of a new natural gas pipeline under the Black Sea, to be called TurkStream. The pipeline starts at the Russkaya compressor station near Anapa on the Russian Black Sea coast and runs 910 km under the sea to Kiyikoy, a village on the Turkish Black Sea coast in the north-western province of Kırklareli. From Kiyikoy, an overland pipeline runs 180 km to link with the existing gas network near the town of Lüleburgaz. Construction of the pipeline, which has an annual capacity of 31,500m. cu m, was completed in November 2018 at an estimated cost of US $12,000m. The first gas flowed through the pipeline to Türkiye in January 2020. In 2022 17,100m. cu m of gas was transported through TANAP to Türkiye and Europe.

The energy market is regulated by the Energy Market Regulatory Authority (EMRA), which was established in 2001 with an initial remit to regulate the electricity market. In 2002–05 EMRA's remit was broadened to include the natural gas, petroleum and liquefied petroleum gas (LPG) markets. Its role is to ensure a 'financially viable, stable and transparent energy market', which will function within a 'competitive environment' in order to provide 'sufficient electricity, natural gas, petroleum and LPG of good quality to consumers, at low cost, in a reliable and environment friendly manner'. EMRA is a public corporation linked to the Ministry of Energy and Natural Resources, with some administrative and financial autonomy, and focuses particularly upon privatization and market liberalization.

MANUFACTURING AND INDUSTRY

State Economic Enterprises (SEEs) played a leading role in Türkiye's industrialization process from the 1930s. However, from the 1960s the private sector generated nearly one-half of industrial output and invested at rates similar to the public sector. The symbiotic relationship between the private and public sectors began to break down in the second half of the 1970s. After a long period of economic and political uncertainty, the Government announced its long-awaited plans for privatization of the SEEs in May 1987. Initially, the Government's share in 22 private companies would be sold, followed by the denationalization of the more efficient and profitable SEEs.

As a first measure, one-half of the Government's shareholding of 40% in Teletas, a telecommunications company, was sold to the private sector in early 1988. A sharp reduction in share prices on the İstanbul Stock Exchange (ISE) then slowed the privatization programme. Five state-owned cement works were sold directly to a French company (although the completion of this sale was suspended in 1991). Similarly, USAS, an aircraft services firm, was sold directly to a Scandinavian airline in early 1989. The fact that these were sold directly to foreign companies, rather than to the public on the ISE, attracted widespread criticism. As the ISE recovered at the end of 1989, the Government proceeded with the sale of its minority shareholdings in private sector companies. Such holdings in six companies were sold in early 1990. Subsequent privatizations enjoyed varying degrees of success. Small portions of state-owned shareholdings were sold in a number of major companies, such as Petkim Petrokimya Holding AŞ, the petrochemicals giant, and Erdemir, the iron and steel complex. In the first half of 1992 the Government of Süleyman Demirel undertook five such sales, with estimated total revenue of TL 552,000m. In July the Government announced the sale of 11 state cement companies, which together accounted for 18% of total cement production in Türkiye. In late 1992 and 1993 the privatization programme continued at a steady rate, but, under the Government of Tansu Çiller, few sales were completed. In July 1994 legislation to accelerate privatization was declared to be unconstitutional by the Constitutional Court, although new legislation was approved in November. None the less, the programme generated only US $354m. in 1994 and $576m. in 1995; the target revenue was $5,000m.

Although every Government from the mid-1980s claimed that privatization was a key part of economic policy, only US $3,500m. had been raised from the sale of state enterprises by 1997. In May 1998 the Privatization Administration (ÖİB) sold a 12.2% stake in Türkiye İş Bankası (one of the country's leading commercial banks) for $651m., while in July it accepted a bid of $1,160m. for a 51% holding in the petrol distributor POAŞ. However, this bid effectively lapsed some weeks later, when the prospective buyer (a consortium of four local firms) failed to secure the necessary finance. In April 1999 the ÖİB suspended the privatization of POAŞ in view of adverse market trends and pre-election political uncertainties. In July, however, following a change of government, the ÖİB relaunched the privatization programme—a key element of the economic restructuring programme agreed with the IMF in December 1998 (see *Budget, Investment and Finance*). The sale of a 51% share in POAŞ was finally completed in March 2000 (for $1,260m.), while a 31.5% holding in TÜPRAŞ was sold in April (for $2,300m.). Other enterprises designated for early complete or partial privatization included Türk Telekomünikayson, Erdemir, the İskenderun Iron and Steel Works (İSDEMIR), and Petkim, as well as the national carrier Turkish Airlines (Türk Hava Yolları) and parts of the power generation industry. Privatizing a strategic share in Türk Telekomünikayson proved to be especially controversial. A first offer of a 33.5% stake was abandoned after no bids had been received by the 15 September 2000 deadline, whereupon the proposal was restructured so that the purchaser would obtain majority management rights. Following the massive financial crisis of February 2001, privatization of a 51% stake in Türk Telekomünikayson (then valued at $10,000m.) was a condition of further IMF assistance. The disposal of a 45% share received reluctant parliamentary approval in May, on the basis that the Government would retain a 'golden share', giving it the power to block any onward disposal thought to be undesirable.

The privatization programme was further delayed by the effect of the crisis in 2001, in which industrial output declined by 9% and the contribution of the industrial sector to GDP contracted by 7%. In a letter of intent to the IMF in July 2002, the Government stated that the ÖİB had adopted a new strategy for reducing the state's holding in TÜPRAŞ to under 50%, through a tender for a strategic partner and/or the placement of exchangeable bonds, since a public offering was not feasible in current market conditions. The Government continued by stating that it had reduced its stake in Erdemir to below 50% by means of a sale to an investment fund, that its remaining 25.8% stake in POAŞ would shortly be sold to the existing strategic investor, and that at least 51% of the shares in Petkim would be offered by October. The letter expressed confidence that these and other sales would meet the indicative target of US $700m. in privatization proceeds in 2002. As regards other plans, the letter recorded that 'roadmaps' had been drawn up for the privatization of Türk Telekomünikayson, the TEKEL tobacco and alcohol monopoly, and the Türkiye Şeker Fabrikaları sugar company, that all state-owned thermal generation and electricity distribution assets would be offered in February 2003 (with the exception of projects eligible for Treasury guarantee), and that two distribution subsidiaries of the BOTAŞ pipeline authority would be privatized by the end of that year. Few of these targets were achieved, however, and the Government was obliged in April 2004 to submit a new timetable to the IMF, under which the sale of the remaining 55% state-owned share of Türk Telekomünikayson (now Telekomünikayson Kurumu) to the Saudi-led Oger Telecoms Joint Venture Group for $6,550m. was approved in mid-2005, while a tender was launched for a block sale of 49.5% of Erdemir.

Overall, the value of privatized assets remained low, at an annual average of US $546m. from 1989 to 2003. This was mainly due to uncertainty about successive governments' privatization policies and the recurrent economic crises of the 1990s. However, the value of privatized assets increased significantly, to $1,266m. in 2004 and $8,209m. in 2005. Following the re-election of the Adalet ve Kalkınma Partisi (AKP—Justice and Development Party) in 2007, privatization proceeds increased from $4,259m. in that year to $6,300m. in 2008, with the sale of Petkim generating $2,000m. Privatization revenues decreased significantly, to $2,300m., in 2009 due to the global financial crisis, but increased again, to $3,100m., in 2010.

Türkiye's growth rates were industry-led until the mid-1990s. As a result, the share of industry (including manufacturing industry, mining and utilities) in the economy increased from 12% of GDP in 1952 to 26% in 1995. The sector's share was 27.8% in 2020, 26.0% in 2021 and 27.1% in 2022.

A 5% reduction in industrial output in 1999 was followed by a 5.6% expansion in 2000, during which lower interest rates helped to boost consumer demand, especially for motorcars and household appliances. A sharp contraction of industrial output in 2001 was followed by renewed growth of 9.2% in 2002 and 9.1% in 2003. Overall, the average annual growth rate of industrial GDP was 7.8% in 1980–90, slowing to 2.8% in 1990–2002. The growth rate picked up again after the 2001 crisis and remained at 6%–10%. Between 1980 and 1998 the share of industrial products in total exports increased from 36% to 77.4%, with the share increasing further, to 93.2%, in 2003. The share averaged around 85% in 2004–08. In 2020 industrial products accounted for 94.3% of total exports, rising slightly to 94.5% in 2021 and 2022.

In 2002 the textiles and clothing sector accounted for 21.5% of total industrial output (at a value of US $27,700m.) and 33.8% of export revenue (at a value of $12,200m.). From 2003 onwards the share of textiles and clothing in export revenue began to decline as exports of other industrial products such as motor vehicles began to increase. Textiles and clothing accounted for 10.1% of total exports in 2020, 9.0% in 2021 and 7.7% in 2022.

Inaugurated in the late 1930s, the iron and steel industry in Türkiye has been one of the fastest growing in the world. Total output of crude steel reached 14.3m. metric tons in 2000, increasing to 18.3m. tons in 2003. In 1996 an agreement with the EU provided for the elimination of duties by both sides. The value of iron and steel exports totalled US $12,600m. in 2020 (compared with $1,600m. in 1998), $22,400m. in 2021 and $14,600m. in 2022

Cement production, on the strength of the expansion in the construction industry, rose to a then record 20.0m. metric tons in 1986. The industry is now almost entirely privately owned as a result of the privatization programme of the 1990s. Following privatization, production has continued to increase, with occasional declines in years when the economy as a whole has done badly. Output stood at 78.9m. tons in 2021 before falling back to 73.7m. tons in 2022.

Among food industries, the state-controlled sugar industry is the most important. In 2019 total production of raw sugar was 2.5m. metric tons, rising to 2.6m. tons in both 2020 and 2021. There have been plans to privatize the sugar industry since 2001; in November 2016 the Government announced plans to complete the sale of all of the state-owned refineries by the end of 2018. However, the sales proved politically controversial. At mid-2023 they were not expected to be completed before the end of the year.

Although the majority of motor vehicles sold in Türkiye are imported, production in the country's automotive industry has increased considerably since the early 2000s. In 2020 production stood at a total of 1,335,981 vehicles (855,043 passenger cars), declining to 1,331,643 (782,835 passenger cars) in 2021, before rising again to 1,402,189 vehicles (810,889 passenger cars) in 2022.

From 2005 the value of exported motor vehicles (including passenger cars, tractors, trucks and buses) exceeded the value of imports, leading to an increase in the trade surplus from US $1,200m. in 2005 to $7,900m. in 2008. The trade balance was still positive in 2009, but declined to $4,600m. owing to lower export demand during the global economic downturn. In 2011 imports of motor vehicles and trailers began to exceed exports, resulting in a trade deficit of $1,333m. However, by 2016 the deficit had returned to surplus and remained in surplus thereafter, amounting to $9,126m. in 2022.

Durable consumer goods is another manufacturing industry in which Türkiye's output and export performance have made significant progress. In 2022 production of selected durable goods was as follows: 9.6m. refrigerators and freezers, 7.7m. washing machines and 6.9m. dishwashers, compared with 9.7m. refrigerators and freezers, 7.7m. washing machines and 6.9m. dishwashers in 2021. White goods accounted for 2.0% of total exports in 2021, falling to 1.0% in 2022.

In 1970 Türkiye's first petrochemicals complex, situated at İzmit, began production of ethylene, polythene, polyvinyl chloride, chlorine and caustic soda. Two other petrochemicals plants were established at Aliaga, near İzmir, and at Yumurtalık, near Adana. They are operated by Petkim, which was originally state-owned but was largely privatized in 2005 and 2008. Similarly, the privatizations have meant that the once state-dominated fertilizer sector is now entirely in private sector hands and consists of around 1,200 companies of various sizes. Türkiye produces approximately 80% of its requirements of fertilizers, although it is heavily dependent on imported inputs. Production of solid fertilizer was 6.0m. metric tons in 2022, down from 8.6m. tons in 2021. Other manufacturing industries include tobacco, chemicals, pharmaceuticals, metal working, engineering, leather goods, glassware and ferrochrome.

The power sector, along with the transport, communications and tourism sector, has continued to hold priority in the Government's development programmes for every year since 1989. Despite the progress made in power plant construction in recent years, many more units will have to be built to meet increased domestic and industrial demand, although official projections in the late 1980s that demand would increase fivefold to 100,000 MW by 2020 were revised downwards in 2003. Despite growing investment in renewables, fossil fuels continue to account for the majority of production. In 2022 coal accounted for 34.6% of total electricity generated, ahead of natural gas (22.2%), hydroelectric plants (20.6%) and renewables (18.8%).

Total electricity generation increased from 305,595m. kWh in 2020 (compared with 124,922m. kWh in 2000) to 331,492m. kWh in 2021 and 326,015m. kWh in 2022.

In mid-1995 construction of a gas-fuelled generating station in Marmara was initiated by a consortium of one Turkish and three foreign companies. The power plant, which was estimated to cost US $540m., had a potential capacity of 3,600m. kWh. In November an agreement was signed with foreign creditors and contractors for the construction of the 672-MW Birecik hydroelectric plant on the Euphrates river. The agreement was the first of many build-operate-transfer schemes, under which the ownership of the plant is transferred to the Turkish Government once it becomes fully operational and profitable, or after a period of 15 years.

More controversial among recent hydroelectric power projects has been the 1,200-MW Ilisu dam on the Tigris river in south-eastern Türkiye, the construction of which was strongly opposed on environmental and social grounds as its reservoir displaced 30,000 people and submerged most of the ancient Kurdish town of Hasankeyf. The dam was also opposed by Syria and Iraq, on the grounds that the Tigris water flow would be reduced, although Türkiye denied that this would be the case. The first of the plant's six generators was commissioned in April 2020. Another similarly controversial dam has been built on the Coruh river at Yusufeli in north-eastern Türkiye. Around 15,000 people, mostly from Türkiye's Georgian minority, are believed to have lost their homes by the time the project was completed in late 2021. The dam began test production in August 2023.

From mid-1996 preparations were undertaken for the construction of the country's first nuclear generator, at Akkuyu on the southern Mediterranean coast. The US $4,000m. plant was put out to tender in December and construction was to have been completed in 2005. The 1,300-MW plant was originally planned to supply some 2% of Türkiye's energy needs. In July 2000, however, the Government announced that the project had been suspended indefinitely on cost grounds, although it might be reconsidered in the future. In May 2010 the Government announced that Rosatom of Russia would build the country's first nuclear power plant, comprising four 1,200-MW units, at Akkuyu. In April 2023 Rosatom announced that the first unit had entered production and the other three would be operational by the end of 2026. When completed, Akkuyu is now forecast to supply around 10% of Türkiye's consumption of electricity. In May 2014 the Government announced that a consortium headed by Mitsubishi Heavy Industries of Japan and Areva of France would build another nuclear power plant, comprising four 1,200-MW units, at Sinop on the Black Sea coast. The first reactor at the plant was expected to enter service in 2023, with all four reactors becoming operational by 2026. However, in December 2018 the Japanese consortium that had been planning to build the plant withdrew from the project after failing to agree financing terms with the Turkish Government. At August 2023 there appeared little prospect of work beginning on the Sinop plant in the near future.

TOURISM

Tourism is one of Türkiye's fastest-growing industries and is an important source of foreign currency. In the 1990s Kurdish nationalist activity and its associated violence affected tourist centres but posed less of a threat to the prospects of the tourism industry, which were more governed by international factors such as the economic fortunes of the European countries from where most tourists to Türkiye originated. Following a 20.6% year-on-year decline in tourist arrivals in 1999, and a concomitant decline in tourist revenue to US $5,203m. (from $7,177m. in 1998), owing to political unrest and earthquake-related disruption, arrivals recovered to 10.4m. in 2000, while revenue increased to $7,636m. The tourism sector performed well in 2001, despite the country's economic and financial crisis, the number of arrivals totalling 10.8m. and revenue increasing to $10,067m. In 2002 tourist arrivals increased to 12.8m., and tourism revenue rose to $11,901m. In the first half of 2003 the war in neighbouring Iraq resulted in tourist arrivals decreasing by about 11%, compared with the same period in 2002, but a strong recovery in the second half of the year produced a total of 13.3m. arrivals in 2003, generating increased tourism revenue of $13,203m. Despite concern that the bomb attacks in İstanbul in late 2003 and in 2004 (see History) would have a negative effect, tourist arrivals rose by some 26% in 2004, to 16.8m., and tourism revenue increased to $15,888m. The increase in tourist arrivals and revenue continued in 2005–06, with an average number of arrivals of 20.0m. and average revenue of $17,500m. per year. In 2007 and 2008 the number of tourist arrivals stood at 23.3m. and 26.3m., respectively, while revenue was reported at $18,487m. and $21,951m., respectively. Between 2000 and 2008 tourism revenue had experienced an average annual growth rate of 11.7%. Between 2009 and 2012 the average number of foreign visitors was approximately 30.0m., and average tourism revenue was $22,000m.

In October 1999 the ÖİB invited bids for various state-owned tourist assets, including hotels and land, as part of the Government's strategy of promoting private sector development of the tourism sector. Plans were also drafted in 2000–01 for the diversification of tourism away from coastal resorts, to inland attractions such as hot springs and to winter sports, with the aim of bringing tourists to Türkiye throughout the year rather than mainly in the summer season. The Government's longer-term objective was to achieve a total of 60m. tourist arrivals per year by 2020, generating annual revenue of US $50,000m. Nevertheless, this target seemed over-ambitious even before a series of terrorist attacks in the first half of 2016, including three that targeted tourists in İstanbul, triggered a sharp downturn in arrivals. In 2015 the total number of tourist arrivals was 36.2m. and receipts amounted to $31,465m., falling to 25.4m. and $22,107m., respectively, in 2016. However, the tourism sector rebounded in following years as the total number of tourists rose to 32.4m. in 2017, 39.5m. in 2018 and 45.1m. in 2019, while revenue increased to $26,284m. in 2017, $29,513m. in 2018 and $34,520.3m. in 2019. However, the COVID-19 pandemic resulted in a sharp decline in arrivals and revenue. In 2020 the number of arrivals fell to 16.0m. and revenue to $12,059m. The partial easing of restrictions in 2021 resulted in arrivals rebounding to 30.0m. and revenue to $24,484m., before growing still further in 2022 to 51.4m. and $46,285m. respectively. In 2022 the major countries of origin were Germany (5.7m.), Russia (5.2m.), the UK (3.4m.), Bulgaria (2.9m.) and Iran (2.3m.).

BUDGET, INVESTMENT AND FINANCE

In the 1960s and 1970s Five-Year Economic Development Plans aimed to achieve self-sustained economic growth through import-substituting industrialization. In the 1980s import substitution was replaced with emphasis on export-led growth and liberalization, even though the Government continued to play a significant role as producer and employer. In May 1989 the Government published the sixth Five-Year Plan (1990–94), which envisaged an average annual growth rate of 7%, reaching 8.3% in 1994. However, actual growth in this period remained low, at an average of 2.2% per year. In May 1995 the Government published the seventh Plan (postponed by one year owing to an economic crisis), for the period 1996–2000, which envisaged economic growth increasing to an annual 7.1%, but actual growth remained at 3.2%. The eighth Five-Year Plan, for 2001–05, was approved by the Grand National Assembly in June 2000. This was followed by a new planning framework that was linked to Türkiye's third Pre-Accession Economic Programme, agreed with the EU in August 2003. The first National Development Plan under the new framework covered the 2004–06 period and set the following objectives: achieving high and sustainable growth; creating a high-technology-oriented economy that could compete in international markets; developing human resources and increasing employment; improving infrastructure services and environmental protection; and reducing the developmental differences among the regions, ensuring rural development and reducing social imbalances. Growth rates after the 2001 crises remained high, ranging between 7.6% and 9.9% during 2002–05, before slowing down to 5.9% in 2006 and 5.0% in 2007. As a result of the global financial crisis, the GDP growth rate declined to 1.1% in 2008, and recorded a contraction of 4.8% in 2009. Growth resumed in 2010 and 2011, with impressive rates of over 8% in each year. Following changes to the method by which the Turkish Statistical Institute calculates GDP (see *Introduction*), growth of 3.5% was recorded for 2016, representing a decrease from 6.1% (4.0% before the revision) in 2015. GDP growth was 3.0% in 2018, 0.9% in 2019, 1.8% in 2020 and 11.0% in 2021, as the economy rebounded strongly from the COVID-19 pandemic. In 2022 GDP growth was 5.6%.

The Central Bank (Merkez Bankası) started operations on 3 October 1931. Historically, the Central Bank controlled exchange operations and extended credits to state-owned enterprises by discounting the treasury-backed bonds issued by these institutions. Legislation adopted in 1987 granted the Government wide-ranging powers over the Central Bank. Following the stand-by agreement with the IMF in April 1994, however, the ability of the Government to draw on central bank credits was curtailed. Although the Government reneged on its commitment during the elections of 1995, the IMF was instrumental in the signing of a protocol between the Central Bank and the Treasury, leading to significant limitations to central bank credits to the Government. In addition, the protocol, for the first time in the history of the country, transferred the power of setting short-term interest rates to the Central Bank.

The independence of the Central Bank acquired a new impetus after the 2001 financial crisis and the stand-by agreement with the IMF. Until 1997 its monetary policy was geared towards controlling public and private expenditures through money supply as an intermediate target. From 1997 onwards, however, there was a gradual shift towards inflation targeting, which was implicit until 2005 and became explicit in 2006. The Central Bank was relatively more successful in achieving the implicit target during 2003–05, but it failed to hit the explicit target during 2006–08. For 2009 the Central Bank upwardly revised the target to 7.5%, which helped it to meet its goal for the first time since the transition to explicit inflation targeting, with inflation standing at 6.3% in that year. However, inflation increased to 8.6% in 2010. The inflation rate fell to 6.5% in 2011, increasing to 8.9% in 2012. It declined to 7.4% in 2013 but rose again to 8.2% in 2014 and 8.8% in 2015, before slipping back to 8.5% in 2016 and then climbing rapidly through 2017 and the first part of 2018. At year-end 2017, annual inflation stood at 11.9%, rising to 15.9% in July 2018. In August 2018, a rise in tensions between Ankara and Washington resulted in the USA doubling its tariffs on imports of iron and steel from Türkiye. The crisis triggered a run on the Turkish lira and annual inflation rose to 25.2% in October 2018, before declining to 20.3% in December 2018 and 11.8% in December 2019. Inflation climbed steadily throughout 2020 and 2021, driven by a weak Turkish lira. After closing 2021 at 36.1%, inflation continued to climb in 2022, reaching 61.1% at the end of March, 78.6% at the end of June, 83.5% at the end of September and peaking at 85.5% at the end of October, before falling back to 64.3% at the end of December. Inflation continued to fall throughout early 2023 to 50.5% at the end of March and 38.2% at the end of June. However, it then resurged to 47.8% at the end of July as a result of an increase of two percentage points in value-added tax and a sharp rise in food prices. None the less, there continued to be scepticism about the accuracy of the official inflation data and a widespread belief that the real figures were much higher. A group of academics and economists, known collectively as ENAG, estimated that annual inflation was 122.9% in the year to the end of July 2023.

In June 1999 a law was approved providing for the reform of the financial sector. The legislation, which came into effect in early 2000, incorporated core principles of the Basel Committee on Banking Supervision relating to risk-based capital requirements, loan administration procedures, auditing practices and credit risk issues, and envisaged the establishment of an independent Regulatory and Supervisory Board for Banking, the members of which (appointed for six-year terms) were to be nominated by the Treasury, the Ministry of Finance, the Central Bank, the State Planning Organization, the Capital Markets Board and the Banks' Association of Türkiye. This body monitors the observance of financial regulations and is empowered to order the merger or acquisition of institutions experiencing financial difficulty.

The principal sources of budgetary revenue in Türkiye are income tax, import taxes and duties, value-added tax on the sale of goods, and revenues from state monopolies.

The 1994 Currency Crisis

From 1989 onwards political instability affected the Government's ability to implement its economic plans. In 1993 the budget deficit was three times that of the previous year and reached 9.2% of GNI. In early 1994 two US credit rating agencies downgraded Türkiye's credit rating, which resulted in a 'run' on foreign currencies. The value of the lira was officially devalued by 12% against the US dollar. However, the currency continued to decline. Interest rates rose to 150%–200% as the Government of Tansu Çiller and the Central Bank desperately tried to bring the financial markets under control. In April the Government announced a programme of austerity measures to reduce the budget deficit, lower inflation, and restore domestic and international confidence in the economy. By May the lira stabilized at around TL 30,000 to the dollar, having stood at some TL 16,000 at the beginning of the year. As the austerity measures began to have a degree of success, the markets stabilized and the lira stayed below 40,000 to the dollar until the end of the year. The measures also helped to restore a degree of international confidence in the Turkish economy and to secure an IMF stand-by loan, approved in July, of Special Drawing Rights (SDR) 610m. (approximately US $873m.). The budget deficit for 1994 was substantially reduced in real terms, accounting for 3.7% of GNI. None the less, the budget deficit continued to exert serious inflationary pressure on the economy and to attract much domestic and international criticism. The Government continued to borrow heavily on the domestic market, although foreign borrowing became prohibitively expensive because of the crisis and was thus reduced. Inflation increased dramatically to 106.3% in 1994, from 66.1% in 1993.

Inflation remained high at 93.6% in 1995 and the actual budget deficit increased to TL 320,000,000m. Çiller abandoned the 14-month IMF stand-by agreement in September, after the collapse of her Government. By October widespread strike action was costing the country an estimated US $500m. in lost export revenue and production, and threatened to undermine attempts to control inflation and restore economic stability. Prior to the general election in December, Çiller was able to settle the public sector wage dispute and, more importantly, to secure ratification of the EU customs union, which entered into force on 1 January 1996 (see Foreign Trade and Balance of Payments).

In July 1996 a new Government, established the previous month, approved an increase in the minimum wage and salary increases of 50% for state workers and pensioners. Despite efforts by Prime Minister Necmettin Erbakan to limit the budget deficit, it remained high, at 8.2% of GNI, and the annual rate of inflation fell only slightly, to 82.4%.

Agreement with the IMF

The coalition Government of Prime Minister Mesut Yılmaz, which took office in mid-1997, made a determined effort in its first year to stem the rise in inflation and improve economic management, notably by accelerating privatization. GNI expanded by an impressive 8.6% in 1997, whereas inflation worsened to 99%. By July 1998 year-on-year inflation had declined to 72% from 101% in January. The reduction was achieved largely through a freeze in public sector prices. In June the Government signed an accord with the IMF under which the Fund would monitor the Turkish economy for 18 months. The agreement, which committed the Government to keeping a tight rein on public expenditure and boosting privatization and tax receipts, set targets for wholesale inflation of 50% by the end of 1998 and 20% by the end of 1999. Tax reform legislation, adopted in July, reduced the tax burden for most people and aimed to encourage full declaration of earnings. However, in the same month the Government was forced to compromise on its pledge to keep down public sector pay increases when it agreed to an immediate 20% rise, with a further 10% for the three months from October. In 1998 the Government recorded an actual budget deficit of TL 3,697,824,000m., equivalent to 6.7% of GNI. This was in spite of a primary surplus (excluding expenditure on servicing the debt) of TL 2,479,000,000m., equivalent to 4.3% of GNI. The inflation reduction target was not met, with the consumer price index rising by 70% in 1998.

The increasing need for social security reform, and the importance attached to it by the IMF, led the new Government, elected in April 1999, to publish a draft bill proposing an increase in the pensionable retirement age, from 38 to 58 for women and from 43 to 60 for men, over a 10-year period. Legislation to reform the financial sector was enacted in June, and in the same month the Government imposed a 20% ceiling on public sector pay increases, despite trade union demands that increases be linked to the prevailing inflation rate of more than 60%. On 13 August constitutional amendments were approved, permitting international arbitration in disputes between state bodies and foreign investors and allowing the privatization of state-owned utilities.

State finances were severely disrupted by the earthquakes of August and November 1999, which contributed to a primary budget deficit equivalent to 2.7% of GNI, while consumer price inflation during the year was recorded at 68.8%. In November the Grand National Assembly approved a new 'national solidarity' tax law, intended to raise in excess of TL 700,000,000m. (about US $1,360m.) to finance post-earthquake reconstruction. A new tax on government bonds resulted in a 6% decline in share values on the ISE, with particularly heavy losses being sustained by banks as major holders of such bonds.

The 2000 budget was a key component of the Government's economic restructuring programme for the period 2000–02; the first tranche of a SDR 2,892m. (about US $3,800m.) IMF stand-by credit was released, following the Fund's approval of the programme in December 1999. With the ambitious goal of increasing the rate of GNI growth to 5.8% in 2002, its key elements were 'up-front' fiscal adjustment to achieve a stable primary budget surplus of around 4% of GNI; a more diversified debt management policy and increased privatization to contain the burden of interest payments; reduction of consumer and wholesale price inflation to 25% and 20%, respectively, in 2000, and to 7% and 5%, respectively, in 2002; a firm exchange-rate commitment supported by consistent incomes policies; and structural reform to strengthen public finances, reduce inequalities in the tax burden and curb waste in public expenditure. As part of the anti-inflation programme, a new 'exchange rate substitution' policy took effect on 1 January 2000, under which the managed peg used since 1994 was abandoned in favour of a peg set according to a predetermined devaluation rate (20% in 2000), itself set against a 'basket' of the US dollar and the euro. The IMF arrangement was supplemented in May 2000 by a World Bank 'economic reform loan' of $750m., with a maturity of 15 years, including a five-year grace period.

The Government's sale of a 51% stake in POAŞ in March 2000 (for US $1,260m.) and of a 31.5% stake in TÜPRAŞ in April (for $2,300m.) were the main components of first-half proceeds from privatization of some $5,000m., so that the full-year target of $7,600m. was likely to be exceeded in the second half, during which the sale of a 20% stake in Türk Telekomünikayson was scheduled. The Government also raised $2,500m. from the sale to a Turkish-Italian consortium of a third global system for mobile telephones. GDP growth in the first half of 2000 of more than 5%, compared with the same period in 1999, suggested that the economy was recovering from the 1999 reverse, although consumer price inflation remained well above the Government's 25% target for 2000. However, the Government's intentions were again frustrated by a major banking liquidity crisis and flight of capital in November, during which the Central Bank expended $7,000m. of its reserves in supporting the lira before the IMF eased the situation in December by granting a supplemental reserve facility of SDR 5,800m. (about $7,000m.). Another package of reforms agreed with the IMF included the familiar objectives of curbing inflation, reducing the budget deficit and expediting privatization.

The 2001 Banking Crisis

No sooner had the new programme been introduced than Türkiye's gravest economic crisis in three decades struck in February 2001, triggered by a public clash between President Ahmet Necdet Sezer and Prime Minister Bülent Ecevit over the latter's alleged inaction against ministers and officials suspected of corruption. The immediate reaction of the markets was a decline in the share price index to over 60% below its 2000 high, capital flight involving the movement of some US $5,000m. out of Türkiye on 19 February 2001 alone and a rise in overnight interest rates to the equivalent of 4,000% annually, as the Central Bank mounted an abortive effort to defend the lira. Ceding to market forces, the Government ended the 'crawling peg' with the US dollar on 22 February and allowed the lira to float freely, with the result that its value decreased by 36% over two days. Ecevit responded by appointing a new Central Bank governor and installing Kemal Derviş, hitherto a senior World Bank official, as Minister of State responsible for economic policy, charged in particular with securing yet another IMF disbursement of funds. Derviş quickly drew up a 'recovery' plan for a radical restructuring of the banking sector, including the placing of the three main state-owned banks under a joint administration headed by technocrats, the liquidation of other insolvent banks and full independence for the Central Bank. Also envisaged was swift action to privatize debt-laden, state-owned enterprises long allocated for divestment, beginning with a 51% share in Türk Telekomünikayson and including major stakes in Turkish Airlines and the state sugar, alcohol and tobacco monopolies.

Protracted negotiations with the IMF resulted in approval being given on 15 May 2001 to an additional stand-by facility of SDR 6,000m. (about US $8,000m.), bringing the total made available to Türkiye since December 1999 to SDR 15,100m. Of this amount, Türkiye had drawn SDR 8,100m. (about $10,000m.) by mid-May. In addition, the World Bank undertook to provide further loans of up to $2,500m. The IMF approved the latest facility only after the Turkish Government had secured parliamentary approval of its 'recovery' plan, in the face of strong opposition on the grounds that Türkiye was surrendering its national economic sovereignty. However, the strength of such opposition, not least within the ruling coalition, raised immediate doubts about the Government's commitment to reform, with the result that the IMF suspended disbursements in late June, thus provoking a further sharp depreciation of the lira (to just over 50% of its pre-February value) and a further slump in share prices. The disbursements were resumed on 12 July, after the Government had given new assurances, in particular on its commitment to reform the banking sector and privatize Türk Telekomünikayson. In August the IMF Executive Board 'commended the Turkish authorities on the strong implementation of their ambitious economic reform programme'. However, the Government's hopes that GDP contraction could be contained to 3% in 2001 were shattered by the negative effects on the already beleaguered Turkish economy of the global economic slowdown, aggravated by the effects of the September suicide attacks on the USA. The outcome was that Türkiye's GDP declined by 7.4% (and GNI by 9.4%) in that year, while year-on-year inflation almost doubled to 68.5% and the budget deficit reached the equivalent of 17.2% of GNI.

A restatement of economic reform objectives accompanying the 2002 budget included the completion of the restructuring of the banking sector by the end of 2002, improved transparency in the use of public funds, the enhancement of the private sector through a revitalized privatization programme, and the removal of obstacles to foreign and domestic investment. The budget package and associated measures secured the endorsement of the IMF, which, on 4 February, approved a new three-year stand-by credit of SDR 12,800m. (about US $17,500m.) for Türkiye, enabling the Government to draw SDR 7,300m. immediately. The new arrangement replaced the December 1999 stand-by credit as expanded in May 2001, the remaining undisbursed element of which (SDR 3,300m.) was included in the new credit. By August 2002 Türkiye had drawn SDR 9,000m., although in approving the release of a third tranche on 7 August the IMF warned that the country's latest political crisis had unsettled domestic financial markets and revealed 'vulnerabilities'. In 2002 a budget deficit equivalent to 14% of GDP was recorded, and the Government failed to achieve the IMF-supported target of a public sector primary surplus of 6.5% of GNI. However, the net public debt to GNI ratio declined to less than 80% at the end of 2002, compared with more than 90% at the end of 2001.

Austerity Budget of 2003
The finalization of the budget for 2003 by the new AKP Government was delayed until March, owing to uncertainties about the economic effect on Türkiye of hostilities in neighbouring Iraq. Türkiye suffered a loss of some US $30,000m. in US grants and loans, following the Grand National Assembly's rejection of US troop deployment through Türkiye. Although the USA subsequently pledged $9,400m. in return for full access to Turkish airspace, the $20,000m. shortfall necessitated the presentation of an austerity budget in 2003, which provided for higher tobacco and excise duties, new vehicle and property taxes, and reductions in spending totalling more than TL 3,000,000,000m. The IMF welcomed the austerity budget and also the Government's renewed commitment to the structural reform programme and the achievement of a public sector primary surplus of 6.5% of GNI in 2003. By May, however, familiar slippages were already apparent in meeting reform objectives, with the result that the IMF suspended the transfer of the latest stand-by tranche of $476m., citing in particular the Government's failure to address obstacles to foreign investment, to simplify the social security system and to expedite the privatization of Türk Telekomünikasyon. The Fund eventually agreed in August to release the withheld tranche. The outcome for 2003 was economic growth of 5.9% and an inflation rate reduced to 18.4%, although the public sector primary surplus was just below target, at 6.2% of GNI.

As the result of a sizeable fiscal differential of about 1.8% of GNI, mainly owing to above-inflation increases in minimum wages and 20% rises in pensions, in March 2004 the Government obtained parliamentary approval for a supplementary budget reducing discretionary spending for all ministries by 13%, and increasing excise duties on petroleum, alcohol, tobacco and gas. This corrective action, together with continuing economic growth of more than 5% and a further reduction of inflation to under 10% year-on-year by mid-2004, enabled the IMF in July to release the latest US $661m. tranche of the 2002 stand-by arrangement. Meanwhile, an Investment Advisory Council, established in March, was charged in particular with improving Türkiye's low level of foreign direct investment (FDI), which had averaged only about $800m. per year in the previous decade, well below FDI received by comparable emerging economies.

The Government's budget for 2005 was based on an expectation of GDP growth of 5%, providing for a shift in expenditure towards public investment and scientific research, and reductions in corporation tax and the top rate of personal income tax. In approving a further three-year US $10,000m. stand-by arrangement for Türkiye in May 2005, the IMF commended the authorities' recent economic achievements, adding that they would 'reduce Türkiye's remaining vulnerabilities'. Capital outflows and pressure on the currency in 2006 demonstrated that Türkiye remained vulnerable to global liquidity conditions, but the fiscal consolidation process continued. For example, in 2005 the primary balance recorded a surplus of 6.2% of gross national product (GNP, quite close to the IMF requirement of 6.5%), whereas the overall budget deficit remained relatively low, at 1.4% of GNP. This trend continued in 2006, when the primary surplus and the overall budget deficit were estimated at 6.7% and 0.7% of GNP, respectively.

Encouraged by Türkiye's growth performance in 2003 and 2004, the AKP Government requested a new stand-by agreement from the IMF in April 2005, proposing a three-year economic policy programme of its own. The programme stated that the economic policies of the preceding two years had led to sustainable improvement in economic performance, which the Government wanted to consolidate, and that strengthening the convergence towards EU norms was an essential target for the next three years. Given these aims, the Government introduced explicit inflation targeting in 2006 and indicated that reliance on ad hoc revenue measures would be reduced, that the tax base would be widened and that the social security system would be reformed.

However, progress was mixed. The IMF was impressed by Türkiye's continued success in meeting the primary surplus target of 6.5% of GDP, but stressed its concerns about the heavy reliance on ad hoc revenue measures in order to achieve its targets. The IMF recommended a move away from the primary surplus rule towards an expenditure ceiling rule, with a view to encouraging fiscal reform aimed at widening the tax base and reducing excessive reliance on employment-and income-related tax rates. Similarly, there were some attempts to reform the social security system (for example, extension of the retirement age, amalgamation of public insurance schemes, and some reforms aimed at rationalizing health care expenditures), but these did not have a significant effect on the level of expenditures.

Effects of the Global Financial Crisis
These mixed results, combined with an unplanned fiscal stimulus in 2007, led to friction between the IMF and the Turkish Government. The IMF review published in August 2008 drew attention to both supply-side shocks that slowed growth and led to increased inflationary pressure, and to policy changes and wider political developments that distracted attention from the economic policy reform agenda. Around the time of the IMF review, Türkiye first began to feel the effect of the global financial crisis. Although the financial sector was not as exposed to pre-crisis vulnerabilities as Europe and the USA, Türkiye entered into recession in the final quarter of 2008. GDP contracted by 4.8% in 2009, and the primary balance target of 6.5% of GDP was abandoned in favour of a counter-cyclical deficit target for 2010–12. This counter-cyclical policy amendment contributed to the resumption of growth in 2010, but ambiguity surrounded the Government's exit strategy and concerns remained regarding the expenditure-dependent nature of Türkiye's growth performance.

Such concerns were underpinned by two perennial issues: high real interest rates and persistent current account deficits.

The current account deficit peaked at 6.1% of GDP in 2006 and remained well above the critical 5% level in subsequent years. Due to economic contraction in 2009, the current account deficit narrowed to 1.9% of GDP. However, it subsequently started to deteriorate again, reaching 5.8% of GDP in 2010 and 8.9% in 2012, before falling to 4.7% in 2014 and 3.8% in 2016 and then rising again to 5.5% in 2017. But the combination of a decline in demand for imports as a result of the economic slowdown in the second half of 2018 and the boost to exports as the result of the depreciation in the value of the Turkish lira in August 2018 meant that the current account deficit began to narrow, reaching 1.5% of GDP at the end of 2018. In 2019 Türkiye recorded a current account surplus for the first time since 2001, at 0.9% of GDP. However, the current account deficit started to widen again during 2020, reaching 4.9% of GDP by the end of the year, before narrowing to 1.7% in 2021 and expanding again to 5.4% in 2022. The devastating earthquakes of February 2023 were expected to ensure that the current account deficit expanded still further by the end of the year.

FOREIGN AND DOMESTIC DEBT

A heavy burden of foreign debt, contracted in the late 1970s and extended through subsequent rescheduling, has long severely hampered the Government's structural adjustment efforts, which have also been complicated by rising domestic debt. At the end of 1998 foreign debt stock totalled US $101,000m., while domestic debt totalled $44,500m. During 1998 the Government borrowed a total of $2,400m. on international capital markets (later raised to $2,600m. through the issue of additional bonds). In 1999 its international borrowing target (as formulated prior to the August earthquake) was about $3,000m., with an additional estimated $1,000m. for project financing. At the end of 1999 the outstanding external debt stock totalled $111,215m., while domestic debt totalled TL 26,679,144,000m. in March 2000, the corresponding figures rising to $119,600m. at the end of 2000, and TL 90,332,000,000m. by June 2001, respectively. By the end of 2001 domestic debt had risen to TL 122,157,260,000m., while external debt had fallen to $113,901m. By the end of 2002 domestic debt had risen further to TL 149,869,691,000m., while total external debt had increased to $131,058m. The corresponding figures at the end of 2003 were TL 194,386,700,000m. and $147,035m., after which external debt increased to $160,000m. by January 2005 and domestic debt to YTL 234,800m. by June. The ratio of net public debt (the combined total of foreign and domestic currency-denominated debt) to GNP declined from 90.5% in the crisis year of 2001 to 44.8% in 2006.

During 2007–11 Türkiye's government debt-to-GDP ratio fluctuated between 39% and 46%, and remained far below the 60% level prescribed in the convergence criteria for EU membership. It fell to 31.3% in 2013, 28.6% in 2014 and 27.5% in 2015, before rising to 28.3% in 2017 and 30.4% in 2018. In addition, the Turkish Government repaid all outstanding IMF loans in 2013. None the less, the reduction in public debt has been accompanied by increased private sector borrowing from abroad. In early 2017, in an apparent effort to win favour from the electorate, government spending rose sharply, prior to the constitutional referendum that was scheduled for April (see History). Government spending was also increased in the run-up to the presidential and parliamentary elections of June 2018 (see History) and the local elections of March 2019 as the Government sought to alleviate the impact of the economic downturn. The Government's financial assistance measures during the COVID-19 crisis from early 2020 were relatively limited by OECD standards. However, when combined with the decrease in tax revenue as a result of the pandemic, they helped to fuel an increase in government debt, which rose to 42.0% of GDP in 2021, up from 39.5% in 2020 and 32.6% in 2019. However, the post-pandemic economic recovery helped reduce government debt to 31.1% of GDP by the end of 2022, although it was forecast to rise again during 2023—not least as a result of spending related to the February earthquakes and May elections.

FOREIGN TRADE AND BALANCE OF PAYMENTS

Türkiye has had a persistent foreign trade deficit since 1947. Following the economic reforms of 1980 and the introduction of export-led policies, however, the deficit decreased in the early 1980s. In the early 1990s Türkiye's trade deficit began to increase again and it has become a constraint on the country's economic performance. Annual trade deficits in the 1990s and 2000s became closely associated with the growth rate in each year and with the manufacturing industry's dependence on imported investment and intermediate goods, which constituted around 90% of total imports throughout the period. In 1990 exports and imports stood at US $13,000m. and $22,300m., respectively, generating an export/import ratio of 58%. In 1995 the corresponding figures were: $21,600m. of exports, $35,700m. of imports and an export/import ratio of 60%. The value of both exports and imports continued to record high growth rates each year, but the trade balance continued to be negative. For example, in 2000 the value of exports and imports increased to $27,700m. and $54,500m., respectively, generating an export/import ratio of 51%. Between 2005 and 2008 export and import growth continued and the export/import ratio improved. In 2008 there were $132,027m. of exports and $201,964m. of imports, with an export/import ratio of 65.4%. During the recession of 2009 imports declined more rapidly than exports, leading to an improved export/import ratio of 72.5%. However, as growth resumed, the export/import ratio deteriorated to 56% in 2011, recovering to 64.4% in 2012, deteriorating again to 60.3% in 2013 and then improving to 65.1% in 2014. It grew further, to 71.8% in 2016, before slipping again to 66.7% in 2017 and then rising again on the weak Turkish lira to 75.3% in 2018 and 84.6% in 2019, before falling to 77.2% in 2020, rising again to 83.0% in 2021 and falling to 70.3% in 2022.

Türkiye's trade deficit used to be partly offset by a net surplus on invisible earnings (services and transfers), particularly helped by expatriate workers' remittances. A major contributor to the invisibles balance from the early 1980s onwards was the contribution from Turkish contractors working in the Middle East and Central Asia. Workers' remittances were for a long time an important source of foreign exchange. They totalled US $5,356m. in 1998, but decreased to $4,572m. in 1999 and $4,560m., in 2000. In 2001 they decreased sharply, to $2,786m., and further to $1,936m. and $729m. in 2002 and 2003, respectively. In 2008 total workers' remittances amounted to $1,324m, since when they have remained low, amounting to just $169m. in 2020; however, they totalled $517m. in 2021 and $443m. in 2022. Receipts from tourism represent another important source of foreign exchange. In 2022 Turks living abroad who returned to Türkiye for holidays were estimated to account for around 20% of total tourism revenue.

A current account deficit of US $2,437m. was recorded in 1996, increasing to an unprecedented level of $9,821m. in 2000, as a result of an overvalued lira, rising oil prices and strong domestic demand. Owing to a major financial and economic crisis, the current account showed a surplus of $3,392m. in 2001, but reverted to rising deficit positions of $1,523m. in 2002, $8,036m. in 2003 and $15,604m. in 2004. In 2005 and 2006 the current account deficit stood at $22,603m. and $31,764m., amounting to 6.4% and 6.5% of GDP, respectively. The current account deficit remained high, at around 10% of GDP in 2011, leading to renewed concerns about its sustainability and its implications for the Turkish economy's external vulnerabilities. The current account deficit stood at 4.9% of GDP in 2020, before falling to 1.7% of GDP in 2021 and rising again to 5.4% in 2022. The main determinant of the current account deficit in Türkiye has been the high level of dependence on the import of energy and intermediate goods. Raw materials and intermediate goods accounted for 83.4% of total imports in 2022, up from 75.7% in 2021.

The overall balance of payments recorded a small surplus of US $441m. in 1998 that increased significantly, to $5,354m., in 1999. In 2000 Treasury borrowing on the international capital markets and a doubling of net capital inflow to $9,400m. financed most of the record current account deficit, but an overall balance of payments deficit of $3,934m. was recorded. In the crisis year of 2001 the deficit rose sharply, to $12,888m., but in 2002 the overall deficit was reduced to $214m., while in 2003 an overall surplus of $4,087m. was recorded, rising slightly, to $4,307m., in 2004. In 2005 the overall surplus on the balance of payments increased substantially, to $23,176m., but it declined to $10,621m. in 2006—mainly owing to capital outflows that tested the credibility of the new Central Bank Governor during the global liquidity squeeze. In 2008 the balance of payments recorded a deficit of $2,800m., primarily owing to a large current account deficit and substantial capital outflows. However, as growth resumed, Türkiye became a preferred destination for international investors again, and increased portfolio investment inflows led to a balance of payments surplus of $14,968m. in 2010. A modest surplus of $1,0148m. was recorded in 2011, rising to $22,821m. in 2012, which declined to $10,763m. in 2013, before rising again to $11,831m. in 2015. The balance of payments recorded a deficit of $813m. in 2016 rising to $27,633m. in 2018. The Central Bank's foreign exchange reserves (excluding gold) rose from $17,755m. at the end of 2001 to $25,527m. at the end of 2002, $32,058m. at the end of 2003 and $34,374m. at the end of 2004. The bank foreign currency reserves (excluding gold) rose still further to $70,000m. in 2008 and $109,280m. in 2013, before falling to $90,604m. in 2016 and declining in subsequent years to reach $78,609m. in 2019.

In July 2018 President Erdoğan had entrusted overall management of the economy to his son-in-law Berat Albayrak, who was appointed Minister of Treasury and Finance. Under Albayrak's direction, in 2020 the Government allegedly spent US $128,000m. of the Central Bank's reserves in efforts to support the Turkish lira. A large proportion of the spending was financed by currency swap agreements with state-owned Turkish banks. On 9 November 2020 Albayrak resigned after Erdoğan abruptly dismissed Central Bank Governor Murat Uysal, an Albayrak loyalist, and replaced him with Naci Ağbal. Albayrak was replaced by Lütfi Elvan, a former AKP Deputy Prime Minister. Without the reserves needed to launch a sustained intervention, Ağbal raised interest rates to try to protect the currency. In March 2021 he defied Erdoğan, who was anxious to cut rates to try to stimulate growth, by raising them again. Erdoğan dismissed Ağbal and replaced him with the more pliant Şahap Kavcıoğlu. Kavcıoğlu kept interest rates unchanged, but he had little room for manoeuvre if the currency came under renewed pressure. Frustrated by Erdoğan's refusal to allow Kavcıoğlu to raise interest rates, Elvan resigned on 2 December. He was succeeded by Nureddin Nebati, an associate of Albayrak, with whom he frequently consulted. Backed by Nebati, Kavcıoğlu oversaw an aggressive campaign of interest rate cuts, reducing the Central Bank's benchmark one-week repo rate to 8.5% in February 2023, compared with 19% in March 2021, and then holding it unchanged through the elections of May 2023 and fuelling pressure on the Turkish lira, which—despite currency interventions by the banks—fell to record lows. Although he had promised during the election campaign to continue cutting interest rates—in line with his unorthodox belief that high interest rates cause high inflation—Erdoğan dismissed Nebati in June and replaced him as Minister of Treasury and Finance with Mehmet Şimşek, who was known to hold more orthodox beliefs. The President also dismissed Kavcıoğlu and appointed Hafize Gaye Erkan to head the Central Bank as its first ever female Governor. On 22 June Erkan raised interest rates by 650 basis points to 15%, the first increase for 27 months. However, neither this increase nor another one of 250 basis points on 20 July stemmed the fall in the Turkish lira and interest rates were still far below the rate of inflation—increasing speculation that Erdoğan had set limits for the increases and was likely to push for cuts again to try to stimulate growth in the run-up to the March 2024 local elections. Meanwhile, Erkan put a stop to large-scale currency intervention, with the result that the Central Bank's net official foreign currency reserves had risen to $59,600m. by 28 July. However, the swap transactions meant that the Bank's real net foreign assets remained negative.

Türkiye's principal imports in 2022 by value were mineral fuels (26.5%), machinery and mechanical appliances (21.5%), chemicals (13.5%), and iron and steel (5.6%). The principal exports in 2022 by value were machinery and mechanical appliances (25.6%), road vehicles (10.1%), live animals and foodstuffs (9.5%), iron and steel (6.7%), chemicals (8.0%), textiles (7.8%), and electrical machinery and equipment (5.3%).

The EU is Türkiye's principal trading partner, taking about 55% of its exports and supplying 44% of its imports until 2007. From 2008 onwards the EU's share in Türkiye's foreign trade declined gradually to 44.5% of exports and 38.0% of imports in 2015, rising to 50.0% of exports and 36.0% of imports in 2018 and then falling to 41.3% of exports and 31.5% of imports in 2021. In 2022 the EU accounted for 40.5% of exports and 28.5% of imports. In terms of individual countries, Germany was Türkiye's main trading partner until 2005. In that year Germany received 12.8% of Turkish exports and supplied 11.6% of its imports. During 2006–21 Germany continued to be the largest market for Turkish exports, but its share has declined, amounting to 8.6% in 2021 and 8.3% in 2022. The second largest market for Turkish exports in 2022 was the USA (6.6%), followed by Iraq (5.4%), the UK (5.1%) and Italy (4.9%). Historically, European countries, particularly Germany, constituted the main sources of Turkish imports. However, the shares of Russia and the People's Republic of China increased rapidly from 2005 onwards. In 2022 Russia was the largest supplier of imports, accounting for 16.2% of the total, followed by China (11.4%), Germany (6.6%), Switzerland (4.2%) and the USA (4.2%). Foreign trade figures also indicate that in recent years Türkiye has diversified the sources of its imports and destinations for its exports, with its traditional markets in the EU being supplemented by new partners in Africa, Asia and the Middle East.

In 1963 the Government signed an association agreement with the European Community (EC, now the EU), under which Türkiye was granted financial aid and preferential tariff quotas. A package of minor improvements was introduced at the end of 1976 and the association agreement was revised in July 1980, offering Türkiye a five-year financial aid package. After the military coup of September 1980, NATO members became divided over support for the Turkish regime: in December 1981 the USA promised to accelerate aid to Türkiye, but in March 1982 EC aid worth US $586m. was frozen. This aid remained blocked, despite the reconvening of the Türkiye-EC Association Council in September 1986. In 1987 Türkiye submitted an application for full EC membership. The frozen aid was partly released in early 1988. At the end of 1989 the European Commission published its report in response to Türkiye's application for full membership. The report drew attention to both economic and political problems in Türkiye, as well as the country's unsatisfactory human rights record, and proposed that negotiations should not start until after 1992. Although an agreement to construct a customs union as of 1 January 1995 was secured in 1993, its establishment was postponed in late 1994, owing to persistent concerns regarding the Turkish Government's record on human rights, democracy and the rule of law. Negotiations in early 1995 finally led to an agreement providing for the removal of barriers to non-agricultural trade, which was signed at a meeting of the EU-Türkiye Association Council in March. The accord was formally ratified by the European Parliament in December, and came into effect on 1 January 1996. The EU agreed to provide ECU 1,800m. over a five-year period, in order to assist the implementation of the new trade regime and to alleviate any initial hardships resulting from the agreement. However, some $470m. in EU adjustment funds to support the customs union was blocked in September 1996 by Greece, and by the European Parliament as a result of concern over Türkiye's human rights record.

Türkiye's relations with the EU suffered a further setback in December 1997, when the EU decided to exclude Türkiye from the list of countries eligible to join the organization in the near future. Although the European Commission subsequently published a strategy in March 1998 for enhancing co-operation by building on the customs union that came into force in 1996, EU financial assistance to Türkiye remained blocked at the insistence of Greece. However, the improvement in Greek-Turkish relations in the wake of the August 1999 earthquake resulted in Greece ending its veto on EU aid to Türkiye and also backing the decision of the EU summit in Helsinki, Finland, in

December, to grant Türkiye candidate status. In December 2000 the EU and Türkiye concluded an accession partnership agreement, which provided a framework for EU support in return for legal and administrative reforms aimed at satisfying the EU's Copenhagen criteria for accession. In March 2001 the Government published a detailed programme for meeting the requirements of EU membership, setting out plans for the harmonization of economic, social and administrative structures with the EU's *acquis communautaire*. In December 2002 an EU summit in Copenhagen, Denmark, decided that Türkiye's progress towards compliance with EU democratic and human rights criteria would be reviewed in December 2004 and that accession negotiations would begin 'without delay' if the review were positive. The Government thereafter pursued a programme of enacting the constitutional, legal and human rights reforms required by the EU. However, further difficulties with the EU arose over Türkiye's signature in August 2003 of a customs union with the 'Turkish Republic of Northern Cyprus' without consulting the European Commission.

In December 2004 an EU summit meeting finally set 3 October 2005 as the date for the opening of accession negotiations with Türkiye, subject to strict conditions being met. These included the Turkish signature of an additional protocol extending its customs union with the EU to the 10 new member states, including the Republic of Cyprus. After some hesitation, Türkiye signed the additional protocol in late July, but issued a declaration emphasizing that this did not imply recognition of the Greek Cypriot Government. Accession negotiations began, as scheduled, in October, and the science and technology chapter of the *acquis communautaire* was completed in 2006. However, the extension of the additional protocol to Cyprus remained unresolved.

In December 2006 the EU Council suspended the opening of eight chapters of the *acquis communautaire* in response to Türkiye's failure to extend the additional protocol to Cyprus, allowing free access of Cypriot vessels to Turkish ports and airports. In addition, the Council decided that Türkiye could open accession talks in other policy areas, but that no chapters could be closed, unless the Commission confirmed that Türkiye had implemented its commitments with respect to the additional protocol.

Developments between 2007 and 2011 were characterized by a further decline in Türkiye's reform implementation and in the EU's commitment to Turkish membership. During this period nine chapters that were not subject to suspension under the Council Decision of 2006 were opened for negotiations. However, progress was slow. In addition, France blocked the opening of five more chapters in 2008, as these were considered to be directly linked to accession—a prospect that France and Germany would prefer to substitute with a special partnership that falls short of membership. Although the European Commission announced in May 2012 that the EU would seek to revive the accession negotiations with the Turkish Government, the process remained stalled. In June 2013 the EU eventually agreed to resume the accession negotiations with Türkiye by opening the regional policy chapter. However, excessive use of police force against demonstrators protesting against increasing authoritarianism, insensitivity towards environmental issues and religiously motivated interventions in citizens' lifestyles resulted in a further postponement. The regional policy chapter was eventually opened in November 2013. However, after subsequent limited progress in the years that followed, no more chapters were opened. EU concerns about the deterioration in human rights and the rule of law in Türkiye and Ankara's aggressive policies towards Greece and the Republic of Cyprus over drilling for natural gas in the eastern Mediterranean meant that as of September 2023 Türkiye's accession process was effectively frozen.

Under a Free Zones Law of 1985, Türkiye has established 18 special sites within the country deemed to be outside the customs border. Consequently, they are exempt from foreign trade and other regulations, providing Turkish and foreign companies operating within them with special incentives. The free zones operating in August 2023 were Mersin (1987), Antalya (1987), Aegean (1990), İstanbul Atatürk Airport (1990), Trabzon (1992), İstanbul-Leather (1995), İzmir Menemen-Leather (1998), Rize (1998), Samsun (1998), İstanbul Thrace (1998), Kayseri (1998), Europa (1999), Gaziantep (1999), Adana Yumurtalık (1999), Bursa (2001), Denizli (2001), Kocaeli (2001), Tubitak-Marmara Research Technology Centre (2002) and West Anatolia (2021).

ECONOMIC PROSPECTS

Reports by the OECD and the IMF have consistently indicated two principal sources of vulnerability in Türkiye: high inflation rates and large current account deficits as a percentage of GDP. The election of the AKP in November 2002 as the first single-party Government in more than a decade resulted in a period of sustained political and economic stability in Türkiye. Interest rates, which had previously often exceeded 30% in real terms, declined, and both corporate investment and consumer spending grew rapidly. The high economic growth rates achieved during the first years of the AKP administration in office were driven mainly by domestic demand, which was financed in large part by borrowing, as a strong Turkish lira enabled banks and companies to secure financing at relatively low cost. In addition, the introduction of a mortgage system and a series of legal amendments to help construction companies led to a rapid rise in construction and real estate prices.

Nevertheless, although Türkiye's rate of household debt to GDP is relatively low by the standards of industrialized nations, most is in credit cards and personal loans rather than longer-term credits such as mortgages. In addition, Türkiye has one of the lowest personal savings rates in the world, making sustained economic growth largely dependent on continued access to low-cost loans from foreign creditors. Moreover, the AKP has failed to introduce much-needed structural reforms, not least a comprehensive overhaul of the country's judicial system. After its collapse in August 2018, the Turkish lira was relatively stable throughout 2019. But despite direct and indirect interventions by the Central Bank, it lost 24% of its value against the US dollar in 2020 and a further 44% in 2021. The Turkish lira depreciated by another 22% in 2022 and a further 27% in the first seven months of 2023, amid concerns about President Erdoğan's idiosyncratic policy prescriptions. Although in June 2023 he had appointed an economic team with more orthodox views, there was widespread scepticism about how much room for manoeuvre he would allow them, particularly in the run-up to the March 2024 local elections, when he was expected to push for increased government spending and lower interest rates in order to create the impression of economic well-being amongst voters.

During 2020 and 2021 the economic situation was exacerbated by the economic repercussions of the COVID-19 pandemic. Meanwhile, Turkstat's credibility had been further damaged by its alleged manipulation of its published data, most strikingly its employment and inflation figures. For the former, it has repeatedly lowered the official unemployment rate by artificially reducing the size of the labour force. There has also been a large gap between Turkstat's inflation figures and calculations by independent researchers, as well as a large, and growing, gap between its consumer and producer inflation rates—with the latter running at more than twice the size of the former in July 2023. Although the inflow of foreign exchange during the 2023 tourism season eased some of the pressure on the Turkish lira, the respite was expected to be only temporary and the currency was expected to depreciate further during the latter part of 2023.

TÜRKIYE (TURKEY)

Statistical Survey

Source (unless otherwise stated): T. C. Başbakanlık Türkiye İstatistik Kurumu (Turkish Statistical Institute), Devlet Mah. Necatibey Cad. 114, 06420-Yücetepe/Ankara; tel. (312) 4547000; e-mail info@tuik.gov.tr; internet www.turkstat.gov.tr.

Area and Population

AREA, POPULATION AND DENSITY

Area (sq km)	
Land	769,604
Inland water	13,958
Total	783,562*
Population (periodic census results)	
22 October 2000	67,803,927
2 October 2011	
Males	37,431,004
Females	37,094,692
Total	74,525,696
Population (annual census results at 31 December)†	
2020	83,614,362
2021	84,680,273
2022	85,279,553
Density (per sq km) at 31 December 2022	110.8‡

* 302,535 sq miles.
† In accordance with new methodology employing Address Based Population Registration System introduced in 2007.
‡ Land area only.

POPULATION BY AGE AND SEX
(annual population census at 31 December 2022)

	Males	Females	Total
0–14 years	9,612,722	9,122,389	18,735,111
15–64 years	29,341,142	28,751,631	58,092,773
65 years and over	3,750,248	4,701,421	8,451,669
Total	42,704,112	42,575,441	85,279,553

PROVINCES AND METROPOLITAN MUNICIPALITIES
(annual population census at 31 December 2022)

	Area (sq km)	Population	Density (per sq km)
Adana*	14,046	2,274,106	161.9
Adıyaman	7,606	635,169	83.5
Afyon	14,719	747,555	50.8
Ağrı	11,499	510,626	44.4
Aksaray	7,966	433,055	54.4
Amasya	5,704	338,267	59.3
Ankara*	25,402	5,782,285	227.6
Antalya*	20,791	2,688,004	129.3
Ardahan	4,968	92,481	18.6
Artvin	7,367	169,403	23.0
Aydın*	7,904	1,148,241	145.3
Balıkesir*	14,473	1,257,590	86.9
Bartın	2,080	203,351	97.8
Batman	4,659	634,491	136.2
Bayburt	3,739	84,241	22.5
Bilecik	4,307	228,673	53.1
Bingöl	8,254	282,556	34.2
Bitlis	7,095	353,988	49.9
Bolu	8,323	320,824	38.5
Burdur	7,135	273,799	38.4
Bursa*	10,886	3,194,720	293.5
Çanakkale	9,950	559,383	56.2
Çankırı	7,492	195,766	26.1
Çorum	12,796	524,130	41.0
Denizli*	11,804	1,056,332	89.5
Diyarbakır*	15,204	1,804,880	118.7
Düzce	2,593	405,131	156.2
Edirne	6,098	414,714	68.0
Elazığ	9,281	591,497	63.7
Erzincan	11,728	239,223	20.4
Erzurum*	25,331	749,754	29.6
Eskişehir*	13,902	906,617	65.2
Gaziantep*	6,845	2,154,051	314.7
Giresun	6,832	450,862	66.0
Gümüşhane	6,437	144,544	22.5
Hakkari	7,179	275,333	38.4

—continued	Area (sq km)	Population	Density (per sq km)
Hatay*	5,831	1,686,043	289.2
Iğdir	3,588	203,594	56.7
Isparta	8,871	445,325	50.2
İstanbul*	5,315	15,907,951	2,993.0
İzmir*	12,016	4,462,056	371.3
Kahramanmaraş*	14,457	1,177,436	81.4
Karabük	4,109	252,058	61.3
Karaman	8,869	260,838	29.4
Kars	10,139	274,829	27.1
Kastamonu	13,158	378,115	28.7
Kayseri*	17,109	1,441,523	84.3
Kırıkkale	4,570	277,046	60.6
Kırklareli	6,300	369,347	58.6
Kırşehir	6,530	244,519	37.4
Kilis	1,428	147,919	103.6
Kocaeli*	3,625	2,079,072	573.5
Konya*	40,814	2,296,347	56.3
Kütahya	12,014	580,701	48.3
Malatya*	12,103	812,580	67.1
Manisa	13,229	1,468,279	111.0
Mardin*	8,806	870,374	98.8
Mersin*	15,512	1,916,432	123.5
Muğla*	12,949	1,048,185	80.9
Muş	8,067	399,202	49.5
Nevşehir	5,392	310,011	57.5
Niğde	7,365	365,419	49.6
Ordu*	5,952	763,190	128.2
Osmaniye	3,196	559,405	175.0
Rize	3,922	344,016	87.7
Sakarya*	4,880	1,080,080	221.3
Samsun*	9,364	1,368,488	146.1
Siirt	5,473	331,311	60.5
Sinop	5,817	220,799	38.0
Sivas	28,567	634,924	22.2
Şanlıurfa*	19,336	2,170,110	112.2
Şırnak	7,152	557,605	78.0
Tekirdağ*	6,342	1,142,451	180.1
Tokat	10,073	596,454	59.2
Trabzon*	4,664	818,023	175.4
Tunceli	7,686	84,366	11.0
Uşak	5,363	375,454	70.0
Van*	22,983	1,128,749	49.1
Yalova	850	296,333	348.6
Yozgat	14,074	418,442	29.7
Zonguldak	3,310	588,510	177.8
Total	783,562	85,279,553	108.8

* Metropolitan municipalities, representing the country's largest urban agglomerations.

BIRTHS, MARRIAGES AND DEATHS

	Live births		Marriages		Deaths	
	Number	Rate (per 1,000)	Number	Rate (per 1,000)	Number	Rate (per 1,000)
2018	1,256,282	15.4	554,389	6.8	426,785	5.2
2019	1,189,939	14.4	542,314	6.6	436,624	5.3
2020	1,117,942	13.4	488,335	5.9	509,048	6.1
2021	1,083,336	12.9	563,140	6.7	566,485	6.7
2022	1,035,795	12.2	574,358	6.8	504,839	5.9

Life expectancy (estimates, years at birth): 76.0 (males 73.0; females 79.1) in 2021 (Source: World Bank, World Development Indicators database).

TÜRKIYE (TURKEY)

ECONOMICALLY ACTIVE POPULATION
(sample surveys, '000 persons aged 15 years and over)

	2020	2021	2022
Agriculture, hunting, forestry and fishing	4,737	4,948	4,866
Mining and quarrying	132	147	157
Manufacturing	5,059	5,662	6,158
Electricity, gas and water	291	334	348
Construction	1,546	1,777	1,846
Wholesale and retail trade; repair of motor vehicles, motorcycles and personal and household goods	3,714	4,052	4,363
Hotels and restaurants	1,371	1,413	1,699
Transport, storage and communications	1,448	1,585	1,775
Financial intermediation	313	299	315
Real estate, renting and business activities	2,026	2,215	2,371
Public administration and defence; compulsory social security	1,921	1,995	2,022
Education	1,763	1,805	1,893
Health and social work	1,462	1,614	1,836
Other community, social and personal service activities	912	950	1,104
Total employed	26,695	28,797	30,752
Unemployed	4,040	3,919	3,582
Total labour force	30,735	32,716	34,334
Males	20,990	22,156	22,862
Females	9,746	10,560	11,473

Note: Totals may not be equal to the sum of components, owing to rounding.

Health and Welfare

KEY INDICATORS

Total fertility rate (children per woman, 2021)	1.9
Under-5 mortality rate (per 1,000 live births, 2021)	9.0
HIV/AIDS (% of persons aged 15–49, 2011)	<0.1
COVID-19: Cumulative confirmed deaths (per 100,000 persons at 30 June 2023)	118.8
COVID-19: Fully vaccinated population (% of total population at 22 November 2022)	62.3
Physicians (per 1,000 head, 2020)	2.0
Hospital beds (per 1,000 head, 2018)	2.9
Domestic health expenditure (2020): US $ per head (PPP)	994.1
Domestic health expenditure (2020): % of GDP	3.6
Domestic health expenditure (2020): public (% of total current health expenditure)	78.8
Access to improved water resources (% of persons, 2020)	97
Total carbon dioxide emissions ('000 metric tons, 2019)	396,843
Carbon dioxide emissions per head (metric tons, 2019)	4.8
Human Development Index (2021): ranking	48
Human Development Index (2021): value	0.838

Note: For data on COVID-19 vaccinations, 'fully vaccinated' denotes receipt of all doses specified by approved vaccination regime (Sources: Johns Hopkins University and Our World in Data). Data on health expenditure refer to current general government expenditure in each case. For more information on sources and further definitions for all indicators, see Health and Welfare Statistics: Sources and Definitions section (europaworld.com/credits).

Agriculture

PRINCIPAL CROPS
('000 metric tons)

	2019	2020	2021
Almonds, with shell	150	159	178
Anise, badian, fennel and coriander	307	315	332
Apples	3,619	4,300	4,493
Apricots	847	833	800
Aubergines (Eggplants)	823	835	833
Bananas	548	728	883
Barley	7,600	8,300	5,750
Beans, dry	225	280	305
Beans, green	596	547	510
Cabbages and other brassicas	820	852	860
Cantaloupes and other melons	1,777	1,725	1,639
Carrots and turnips	666	591	593
Cauliflowers and broccoli	315	311	339
Cherries, sour (Morello)	182	189	184
Cherries, sweet	664	725	690
Chick peas	630	630	475
Chillies and peppers, green	2,626	2,637	3,091
Cotton lint	814	n.a.	n.a.
Cucumbers and gherkins	1,917	1,886	1,890
Figs	310	320	320
Grapefruit and pomelos	249	238	249
Grapes	4,100	4,209	3,670
Groundnuts, with shell	169	216	234
Hazelnuts, with shell	776	665	684
Leeks and other alliaceous vegetables	234	225	213
Lemons and limes	950	1,189	1,550
Lentils	354	371	263
Lettuce and chicory	500	520	541
Maize	6,000	6,500	6,750
Mushrooms and truffles	49	55	61
Oats	265	315	276
Olives	1,525	1,317	1,739
Onions and shallots, green	142	129	126
Onions, dry	2,200	2,280	2,500
Oranges	1,700	1,334	1,742
Other spices	261	273	290
Peaches and nectarines	831	892	892
Pears	531	546	530
Peas, green	98	108	112
Pistachios	85	296	119
Plums and sloes	318	329	333
Potatoes	4,980	5,200	5,100
Pumpkins, squash and gourds	590	698	772
Quinces	181	189	192
Rice, paddy	1,000	980	1,000
Rye	310	296	200
Seed cotton	2,200	1,774	2,250
Soybeans (Soya beans)	150	155	182
Spinach	230	232	218
Strawberries	487	547	669
Sugar beet	18,086	23,026	18,250
Sunflower seed	2,100	2,067	2,415
Tangerines, mandarins, etc.	1,400	1,586	1,819
Tea leaves	1,407	1,418	1,450
Tobacco, unmanufactured	70	77	73
Tomatoes	12,842	13,204	13,095
Walnuts	225	287	325
Watermelons	3,871	3,492	3,469
Wheat	19,000	20,500	17,650

Aggregate production ('000 metric tons, may include official, semi-official or estimated data): Total cereals 34,399 in 2019, 37,185 in 2020, 31,864 in 2021; Total fruit (primary) 23,321 in 2019, 24,151 in 2020, 25,043 in 2021; Total oilcrops 6,390 in 2019, 5,710 in 2020, 7,015 in 2021; Total pulses 1,230 in 2019, 1,297 in 2020, 1,057 in 2021; Total roots and tubers 4,980 in 2019, 5,200 in 2020, 5,100 in 2021; Total vegetables (primary) 25,382 in 2019, 25,961 in 2020, 26,646 in 2021.

Source: FAO.

TÜRKIYE (TURKEY)

Statistical Survey

LIVESTOCK
('000 head, year ending September)

	2019	2020	2021
Asses	126.9	108.3	95.8
Buffaloes	184.2	192.5	185.6
Cattle	17,688.1	17,965.5	17,850.5
Chickens	342,567	379,349	391,394
Ducks	520	560	540
Geese and guinea fowls	1,157	1,374	1,478
Goats	11,205.4	11,985.8	12,341.5
Horses	102.5	90.0	83.7
Mules	29.4	25.1	22.2
Sheep	37,276.0	42,126.8	45,177.7
Turkeys	4,541	4,798	4,704

Source: FAO.

LIVESTOCK PRODUCTS
('000 metric tons)

	2019	2020	2021
Buffaloes' milk	79.3	63.8	63.6
Cattle hides, fresh*	149.0	150.2	163.6
Cattle meat	1,330.2	1,341.4	1,460.7
Cattle offals, edible*	114.4	115.4	125.6
Cows' milk	20,782.4	21,749.3	21,370.1
Chicken meat	2,138.5	2,138.5	2,245.8
Goat meat	87.1	90.4	94.6
Goats' milk	577.2	589.6	622.8
Sheep meat	316.2	345.6	385.9
Sheep offals, edible*	41.0	44.8	50.0
Sheep's (Ewes') milk	1,521.5*	1,101.1	1,143.8
Sheepskins, fresh*	57.5	62.8	70.2
Turkey meat	59.6	58.2	51.3
Hen eggs	1,243.6	1,236.7	1,206.1
Honey (natural)	109.3	104.1	96.3
Wool, greasy	70.6	79.8	85.9

* FAO estimate(s).

Source: FAO.

Forestry

ROUNDWOOD REMOVALS
('000 cubic metres, excl. bark, FAO estimates)

	2019	2020	2021
Sawlogs, veneer logs and logs for sleepers	10,400	9,791	11,000
Pulpwood	11,500	12,715	12,650
Other industrial wood	800	800	1,140
Fuel wood	5,750	5,397	5,856
Total	28,450	28,703	30,646

Source: FAO.

SAWNWOOD PRODUCTION
('000 cubic metres, incl. railway sleepers)

	2019	2020	2021
Coniferous (softwood)	5,915.0	6,975.0	6,150.0
Broadleaved (hardwood)	2,290.0	2,400.0	2,800.0
Total	8,205.0	9,375.0	8,950.0

Source: FAO.

Fishing
('000 metric tons, live weight)

	2019	2020	2021
Capture	463.2	364.4	328.2
European pilchard	19.1	21.3	15.8
European sprat	38.1	26.8	28.0
European anchovy	262.5	171.3	151.6
Atlantic bonito	1.6	22.7	2.6
Striped venus	36.6	21.8	16.8
Aquaculture	373.4	421.4	471.7
Trout	125.7	146.6	165.7
Gilthead seabream	99.7	109.8	133.5
Seabasses	137.4	148.9	155.2
Total catch	836.6	785.8	799.8

Source: FAO.

Mining
('000 metric tons unless otherwise indicated)

	2017	2018	2019
Hard coal	1,764	1,621	1,207
Lignite	84,303	99,207	80,820
Crude petroleum ('000 barrels)	17,950	20,805	21,900
Natural gas (marketed, million cu m)	354	436	483
Iron ore: gross weight	9,992	9,550	16,382
Iron ore: metal content	6,050	5,777	9,110
Copper[1]	83	80	74
Bauxite	940.7	1,000.0[2]	818.6
Lead: mine output[1]	68	76	71
Lead: concentrates[1]	93	76[2]	71[2]
Chromium[3]	7,849.5	10,757.2	8,666.1
Silver (kilograms)	151,490	197,320	242,000
Gold (kilograms)[1,4]	23,090	27,100	38,000
Marble	13,567	13,939	10,493
Limestone[5]	478,730	557,029	342,112
Dolomite	19,816.9	26,197.9	13,593.3
Bentonite	1,481.6	1,332.0	1,533.6
Kaolin	1,362.8	1,515.6	1,283.6
Gypsum	10,223.1	10,896.5	7,489.1
Magnesite: mine output	1,694.1	1,958.9	1,496.1
Feldspar: mine output	7,153.9	5,540.0	5,068.0
Borate minerals: mine output	5,801.5	6,000.0[2]	5,500.0[2]
Borate minerals: concentrates	1,640.0	2,200.0	2,000.0
Nitrogen[6]	302.0	550.0	390.0
Perlite: mine output	1,116.6	1,089.0	1,174.5
Pumice	7,774.0	7,259.4	5,392.1
Pyrites[2,7]	40.0	40.0	40.0
Sodium sulphate: concentrates	268.8	275.0	212.1

[1] Figures refer to metal content of ores and concentrates.
[2] Estimated production.
[3] Figures refer to gross weight of ores.
[4] Figures include estimated output from the by-products of refining other base metals.
[5] Excluding production used for making cement.
[6] Nitrogen content of ammonia.
[7] Figures refer to gross weight of minerals.

Quartzite ('000 metric tons) 2,521.1 in 2014; 2,839.4 in 2015.

Silica sand ('000 metric tons) 2,521.1 in 2014; 2,839.4 in 2015.

Source: US Geological Survey.

Hard coal ('000 metric tons): 1,616.3 in 2020; 1,718.2 in 2021; 1,789.2 in 2022.

Lignite (incl. asphaltite, '000 metric tons): 71,239.4 in 2020; 80,157.5 in 2021; 86,485.1 in 2022.

TÜRKIYE (TURKEY)

Industry

SELECTED PRODUCTS
('000 metric tons unless otherwise indicated)

	2020	2021	2022
Flour	10,066.7	9,996.3	n.a.
Sugar	2,815.7	2,663.4	2,636.3
Tea (made)	341.9	348.9	307.0
Cigarettes (million)	152,577	163,721	170,865
Nuts, processed (bleached, without shell)	160.1	199.5	202.0
Apricots, dried	105.6	117.0	104.9
Oil (crude) of sunflower seeds	729.5	682.2	719.2
Cotton yarn	1,575.4	1,994.1	1,790.4
Wool yarn	30.7	33.2	34.6
Footwear with leather uppers ('000 pairs)	82,631.0	94,534.7	106,970.5
Carpets and rugs ('000 sq m)	599,389	696,901	616,613
Cement	80,912.2	84,684.4	81,323.6
Ready-mixed concrete	207,738.4	245,721.1	254,120.1
Non alloy steel in ingots	13,168.6	14,292.4	12,219.0
Cologne ('000 litres)	106,808.9	79,902.6	93,014.8
Detergents and washing preparations	3,279.2	3,290.9	4,718.8
Domestic refrigerators and freezers ('000)	9,712.3	12,080.5	10,003.7
Domestic dishwashing machines ('000)	5,635.0	6,879.0	6,921.6
Domestic washing machines ('000)	10,692.9	11,584.7	n.a.
Ovens ('000)	12,169.6	13,727.7	28,641.0
Vacuum cleaners ('000)	4,187.5	4,134.4	3,376.9
Gas boilers (hermetic) ('000)	1,347.7	1,378.1	1,409.8
Tyres for automobiles ('000 units)	28,086.5	34,556.5	35,190.6
Automobiles ('000)	1,065.4	1,064.2	1,119.6
Electrical energy (million kWh)	306,703.1	334,723.1	326,200.0*

* Preliminary figure, rounded.

Finance

CURRENCY AND EXCHANGE RATES

Monetary Units
100 kuruş = 1 Turkish lira.

Sterling, Dollar and Euro Equivalents (28 April 2023)
£1 sterling = 24.234 liras;
US $1 = 19.444 liras;
€1 = 21.352 liras;
1000 Turkish liras = £41.26 = US $51.43 = €46.83.

Average Exchange Rate (Turkish liras per US $)
2020 7.0086
2021 8.8504
2022 16.548

Note: A new currency, the new Turkish lira, equivalent to 1,000,000 of the former units, was introduced on 1 January 2005. Figures in this survey have been converted retrospectively to reflect this development. (The name of the currency reverted to Turkish lira on 1 January 2009, although new Turkish lira banknotes and coins remained in circulation for a further year.)

CENTRAL GOVERNMENT BUDGET
(million Turkish liras)

Revenue	2020	2021	2022*
Tax revenue	833,251	1,164,988	2,353,286
Taxes on income	263,898	397,629	863,906
Taxes on property	17,281	21,092	26,512
Taxes on goods and services	314,910	377,377	678,638
Taxes on international trade	185,452	297,477	658,042
Stamp duties and fees	51,705	70,288	118,589
Other tax revenues	4	1,103	7,558
Non-tax revenues	165,896	199,119	387,287
Revenues from special budget institutions	21,536	28,958	48,936
Revenues from regularity and supervisory institutions	7,762	8,972	12,847
Total	1,028,446	1,402,038	2,802,355

Expenditure	2020	2021	2022*
Current expenditure	433,050	537,114	969,196
Compensation of employees	287,785	346,279	615,278
Social security contributions	48,294	57,380	96,842
Good and service purchase	96,971	133,455	257,076
Capital expenditures	93,742	131,282	276,403
Transfers	513,233	652,320	1,174,974
Current transfers	498,063	626,828	1,126,152
Capital transfers	15,171	25,492	48,822
Lending	29,750	101,978	209,944
Interest payments	133,962	180,852	310,903
Total	1,203,737	1,603,545	2,941,420

* Provisional.

Source: Ministry of Treasury and Finance, Ankara.

General Government Budget (incl. central and local government accounts and social welfare funds, '000 million Turkish liras): *Total revenue*: 2,240.2 in 2021; 3,967.8 in 2022 (provisional); 5,748.3 in 2023 (budget figure). *Total expenditure*: 2,430.8 in 2021; 4,399.7 in 2022 (provisional); 6,399.2 in 2023 (budget figure) (Source: Ministry of Treasury and Finance, Ankara).

INTERNATIONAL RESERVES
(US $ million at 31 December)

	2020	2021	2022
Gold (national valuation)	43,241	38,489	45,846
IMF special drawing rights	1,407	7,709	7,331
Reserve position in IMF	162	158	150
Foreign exchange	48,389	63,179	70,408
Total	93,199	109,535	123,735

Source: IMF, *International Financial Statistics*.

MONEY SUPPLY
(million Turkish liras at 31 December)

	2020	2021	2022
Currency outside depository corporations	170,154	215,507	307,261
Transferable deposits	1,072,136	1,934,179	2,804,269
Other deposits	2,114,880	3,008,780	5,148,777
Securities other than shares	45,936	48,446	31,327
Broad money	3,403,106	5,206,912	8,291,633

Source: IMF, *International Financial Statistics*.

COST OF LIVING
(Consumer Price Index; base: 2003 = 100)

	2020	2021	2022
Food and non-alcoholic beverages	560.5	696.6	1,293.2
Clothing and footwear	255.6	277.0	364.2
Housing, water, electricity, gas and other fuels	508.2	598.3	1,013.6
All items (incl. others)	469.6	561.6	967.7

NATIONAL ACCOUNTS
(million Turkish liras at current prices)

Expenditure on the Gross Domestic Product

	2020	2021	2022
Government final consumption expenditure	766,000.1	946,644.2	1,778,066.1
Private final consumption expenditure	2,865,751.8	4,008,034.9	8,674,877.0
Increase in stocks	209,140.4	270,749.4	816,637.7
Gross fixed capital formation	1,383,494.4	2,039,952.6	4,443,791.8
Total domestic expenditure	5,224,386.6	7,265,381.1	15,713,372.7
Exports of goods and services	1,450,511.5	2,559,041.0	5,686,593.4
Less Imports of goods and services	1,626,678.1	2,575,633.1	6,393,391.9
GDP in purchasers' values	5,048,220.1	7,248,789.0	15,006,574.2

TÜRKIYE (TURKEY)

Statistical Survey

Gross Domestic Product by Economic Activity

	2019	2020	2021
Agriculture, forestry and fishing	276,325.5	336,623.1	401,806.0
Mining and quarrying	48,154.6	59,220.3	96,725.3
Manufacturing	788,787.5	965,941.6	1,609,778.7
Electricity, gas and water supply	105,106.1	124,677.9	181,644.6
Construction	233,279.1	264,934.0	367,218.8
Wholesale and retail trade; repair of motor vehicles and motorcycles	536,733.4	625,252.8	944,434.3
Transport, storage and communication	479,439.1	537,626.9	837,280.5
Hotels and restaurants	145,475.5	104,631.5	190,531.9
Financial and insurance activities	134,289.3	187,692.3	211,640.6
Real estate, renting and business activities	511,715.9	557,404.7	704,150.7
Public administration and defence; compulsory social security	227,136.6	265,019.0	324,100.5
Education	189,283.2	206,343.0	252,861.9
Health and social work	113,764.3	143,200.7	192,038.4
Private households with employed persons	2,088.8	1,668.0	1,717.8
Other services	90,294.2	107,433.7	165,262.0
Sub-total	3,881,873.3	4,487,669.6	6,481,192.0
Taxes, *less* subsidies	429,859.5	560,550.4	767,597.0
GDP in purchasers' values	4,311,732.8	5,048,220.1	7,248,789.0

2022: Agriculture, forestry and fishing 969,494.4; Mining and quarrying; electricity, gas and water supply 750,887.4; Manufacturing 3,310,952.4; Construction 721,247.5; Services 3,975,855.6; Information and communication 351,166.9; Financial and insurance activities 503,118.5; Real estate activities 507,072.1; Professional, administrative and support service activities 681,784.3; Public administration, education, human health and social work activities 1,377,893.8; Other service activities 286,042.9; *Sub-total* 13,435,515.9; Taxes less subsidies 1,571,058.2; *GDP in purchasers' values* 15,006,574.2.

BALANCE OF PAYMENTS
(US $ million)

	2020	2021	2022
Exports of goods	168,378	224,686	253,403
Imports of goods	−206,252	−253,999	−343,087
Balance on goods	−37,874	−29,313	−89,684
Exports of services	38,243	61,408	90,285
Imports of services	−23,884	−29,596	−40,413
Balance on goods and services	−23,515	2,499	−39,812
Primary income received	6,221	6,724	8,429
Primary income paid	−14,789	−17,403	−16,994
Balance on goods, services and primary income	−32,083	−8,180	−48,377
Secondary income received	4,141	4,135	3,550
Secondary income paid	−3,946	−3,187	−3,924
Current balance	−31,888	−7,232	−48,751
Capital account (net)	−36	−64	−35
Direct investment assets	−3,246	−6,451	−4,928
Direct investment liabilities	7,700	13,325	13,094
Portfolio investment assets	−2,894	−2,260	−4,495
Portfolio investment liabilities	−6,662	3,011	−9,033
Other investment assets	1,876	−13,409	−4,064
Other investment liabilities	10,794	34,776	43,074
Net errors and omissions	−7,490	1,739	27,449
Reserves and related items	−31,846	23,435	12,311

Source: IMF, *International Financial Statistics*.

External Trade

PRINCIPAL COMMODITIES
(distribution by SITC, US $ million, excl. military goods)

Imports c.i.f.	2020	2021	2022
Food and live animals	9,916.6	11,378.2	14,038.2
Crude materials (inedible) except fuels	15,571.4	24,456.2	25,859.5
Metalliferous ores and metal scrap	7,939.1	14,403.3	12,513.6
Mineral fuels, lubricants, etc.	10,897.4	17,410.0	96,548.0
Petroleum, petroleum products, etc.	6,780.4	10,744.4	19,991.9
Chemicals and related products	30,848.7	44,424.8	49,109.3
Plastics in primary forms	8,892.2	14,217.7	15,099.3
Basic manufactures	32,127.8	47,771.7	58,219.0
Textile yarn, fabrics, etc.	5,265.5	6,448.5	8,078.0
Iron and steel	9,558.9	17,410.4	20,083.7
Non-ferrous metals	7,556.3	12,905.4	15,800.2
Machinery and transport equipment	62,685.9	70,865.2	78,191.1
Power generating machinery and equipment	7,655.5	8,629.5	8,732.4
Machinery specialized for particular industries	5,392.3	7,433.1	8,277.0
General industrial machinery, equipment and parts	9,504.1	11,338.9	12,960.7
Telecommunications and sound recording equipment	5,846.2	5,932.7	5,353.9
Electric machinery and parts	9,658.3	12,399.2	14,178.7
Road vehicles	15,062.7	15,242.0	17,298.7
Miscellaneous manufactured articles	10,991.6	12,124.0	15,146.6
Goods not classified elsewhere	43,962.2	39,546.8	21,167.0
Non-monetary gold	25,184.2	5,499.3	20,440.7
Total (incl. others)	219,516.8	271,425.6	363,710.1

Exports f.o.b.	2020	2021	2022
Food and live animals	17,460.5	20,957.0	24,084.0
Vegetables and fruit	8,679.2	9,886.8	10,201.7
Crude materials (inedible) except fuels	4,640.9	6,661.2	7,347.8
Mineral fuels, lubricants, etc.	4,567.8	8,310.4	16,410.3
Petroleum, petroleum products, etc.	4,369.6	7,813.1	15,060.0
Chemicals and related products	12,527.2	16,107.1	20,386.1
Basic manufactures	43,248.1	63,702.5	67,351.1
Textile yarn, fabrics, etc.	11,710.2	15,176.8	14,606.4
Iron and steel	10,113.9	18,940.6	17,108.1
Manufactures of metals	7,174.3	9,605.4	11,276.8
Machinery and transport equipment	49,825.0	60,562.0	65,018.8
Electric machinery and parts	10,425.4	13,399.3	14,473.4
Road vehicles	21,308.9	24,266.9	25,698.4
Miscellaneous manufactured articles	29,847.4	39,457.2	43,131.6
Clothing and accessories (excl. footwear)	15,355.1	18,744.4	19,914.9
Goods not classified elsewhere	4,998.2	6,365.5	5,782.9
Non-monetary gold	2,780.0	3,482.7	1,051.3
Total (incl. others)	169,637.8	225,214.5	254,170.9

TÜRKIYE (TURKEY)

PRINCIPAL TRADING PARTNERS
(US $ million, excl. military goods*)

Imports c.i.f. (excl. grants)	2020	2021	2022
Belgium	3,716.1	5,628.4	4,420.6
Brazil	3,228.3	3,827.1	4,830.9
China, People's Republic	23,041.4	32,238.1	41,354.6
Czech Republic	2,746.3	2,713.6	2,895.4
France	6,988.1	7,931.5	9,429.7
Germany	21,732.8	21,726.3	24,033.0
India	4,830.1	7,936.1	10,697.1
Iran	1,192.7	2,823.7	3,353.7
Iraq	8,201.7	1,664.1	1,419.2
Italy	9,199.6	11,562.7	14,082.3
Japan	3,743.4	4,389.3	4,640.8
Korea, Republic	5,734.3	7,597.0	9,004.4
Malaysia	1,990.0	3,098.1	4,288.7
Netherlands	3,628.6	4,508.6	4,497.1
Poland	3,005.1	3,635.8	4,294.4
Romania	2,769.3	3,434.4	3,335.6
Russian Federation	17,829.3	28,959.4	58,848.9
Saudi Arabia	1,719.7	3,456.3	4,152.1
Spain	5,039.4	6,311.6	7,004.0
Switzerland	7,770.8	3,054.9	15,335.9
Ukraine	2,590.4	4,524.7	4,455.4
United Arab Emirates	5,603.8	2,442.7	4,471.0
United Kingdom	5,582.7	5,558.2	5,904.6
USA	11,525.0	13,147.6	15,228.1
Total (incl. others)	219,516.8	271,425.6	363,710.1

Exports f.o.b.	2020	2021	2022
Azerbaijan	2,085.3	2,342.8	2,504.4
Belgium	3,634.7	4,899.3	4,778.5
Bulgaria	2,634.4	3,953.4	4,721.6
China, People's Republic	2,865.9	3,662.7	3,281.3
Egypt	3,136.2	4,513.7	4,556.7
France	7,195.2	9,111.1	9,534.6
Germany	15,978.7	19,311.0	21,141.8
Greece	1,799.8	3,118.9	3,302.7
Iran	2,253.1	2,770.7	3,067.2
Iraq	9,142.0	11,125.6	13,750.3
Iran	2,253.1	2,770.7	3,067.2
Israel	4,704.1	6,355.8	7,032.3
Italy	8,082.6	11,473.0	12,386.0
Lebanon	930.7	1,694.5	2,678.0
Libya	1,653.1	2,771.3	2,840.8
Morocco	2,057.2	2,976.9	3,094.1
Netherlands	5,195.1	6,764.8	8,026.2
Poland	3,474.7	4,673.8	5,417.6
Romania	3,894.0	5,175.0	6,947.3
Russian Federation	4,506.7	5,774.4	9,343.0
Saudi Arabia	2,505.0	265.4	1,046.5
Spain	6,683.5	9,619.6	9,654.4
Ukraine	2,090.3	2,900.5	3,059.4
United Arab Emirates	2,828.0	5,493.4	5,252.7
United Kingdom	11,235.6	13,703.7	13,004.8
USA	10,183.0	14,720.4	16,885.3
Total (incl. others)	169,637.8	225,214.5	254,170.9

*Imports by country of origin, exports by country of last consignment.

Transport

RAILWAYS
(traffic)

	2020	2021	2022
Passengers carried ('000)	148,314	191,600	318,114
Passenger-km (million)	8,297	10,666	19,669
Freight carried ('000 metric tons)*	34,552	38,157	38,897
Freight ton-km (million)	15,428	14,433	16,551

*Excluding parcels and departmental traffic.

ROAD TRAFFIC
(motor vehicles by use)

	2020	2021	2022
Passenger cars	13,099,041	13,706,065	14,269,352
Minibuses	493,395	484,806	487,381
Buses and coaches	212,407	208,882	208,442
Small trucks	3,938,732	4,115,205	4,277,424
Trucks	859,670	886,303	919,125
Motorcycles and mopeds	3,512,576	3,744,370	4,141,914
Special purpose vehicles	70,309	78,482	85,276

SHIPPING

Flag Registered Fleet
(at 31 December)

	2020	2021	2022
Number of vessels	1,350	1,353	1,401
Total displacement ('000 grt)	5,141.2	5,067.6	5,469.4

Source: Lloyd's List Intelligence (www.bit.ly/LLintelligence).

International Seaborne Traffic
(freight handled at port authorities, '000 metric tons)

	2019	2020	2021
Goods unloaded	221,404.8	226,539.5	232,633.1
Goods loaded	131,676.6	138,902.8	153,763.7

CIVIL AVIATION
(scheduled services)

	2020	2021	2022
Domestic services:			
Kilometres flown ('000)	572,994	738,352	786,150
Number of passengers	49,740,303	68,466,177	78,323,824
Freight handled (metric tons)	500,551	698,344	784,022
International services:			
Kilometres flown ('000)	280,756	466,266	702,476
Number of passengers	31,875,837	59,689,585	103,465,515
Freight handled (metric tons)	1,989,970	2,734,174	3,379,120

Source: General Directorate of State Airports Authority, Ankara.

Tourism

VISITOR ARRIVALS BY NATIONALITY

Country	2020	2021	2022
Bulgaria	1,242,961	1,402,795	2,882,512
France	311,708	621,493	986,090
Georgia	410,501	291,852	1,514,813
Germany	1,118,932	3,085,215	5,679,194
Iran	385,762	1,153,092	2,331,076
Iraq	387,587	836,624	1,208,895
Netherlands	271,526	645,601	1,244,756
Poland	145,908	585,076	1,135,903
Romania	269,076	496,178	886,555
Russian Federation	2,128,758	4,694,422	5,232,611
Ukraine	997,652	2,060,008	675,467
United Kingdom	820,709	392,746	3,370,739
USA	148,937	371,759	1,013,478
Total (incl. others)	12,734,213	24,712,266	44,564,395

Tourism receipts (million US $, excl. passenger transport, incl. expenditure of Turkish nationals residing abroad): 14,817.3 in 2020; 30,173.6 in 2021; 46,284.9 in 2022.

TÜRKIYE (TURKEY)

Communications Media

	2019	2020	2021
Telephones ('000 main lines in use)	11,532.9	11,448.6	12,310.0
Mobile telephones ('000 subscribers)	80,790.9	82,128.1	86,288.8
Broadband subscriptions, fixed ('000) *	14,232.0	16,734.8	18,135.7
Broadband subscriptions, mobile ('000)*	62,407.7	65,629.7	70,029.0
Internet subscribers ('000)	76,639.7	82,364.6	88,164.7

* Source: International Telecommunication Union.

Education
(2021/22)

	Institutions	Teachers	Students
Pre-primary	36,644	107,171	1,885,004
Primary	43,455	687,224	10,726,968
Secondary	12,804	389,307	6,543,599
Higher	3,925	185,384	7,829,148

Secondary (General): 6,242 institutions, 175,275 teachers and 3,250,334 students in 2018/19.

Secondary (Vocational and technical training): 6,264 institutions, 195,959 teachers and 2,399,260 students in 2018/19.

Pupil-teacher ratio (primary education, UNESCO estimate): 17.0 in 2016/17 (Source: UNESCO Institute for Statistics).

Adult literacy rate (UNESCO estimates): 96.7% (males 99.1%; females 94.4%) in 2019 (Source: UNESCO Institute for Statistics).

Directory

The Constitution

In October 1981 the National Security Council (NSC), which took power in September 1980, announced the formation of a Consultative Assembly to draft a new constitution, replacing that of 1961. The Assembly consisted of 40 members appointed directly by the NSC and 120 members chosen by the NSC from candidates put forward by the governors of the 67 provinces; all former politicians were excluded. The draft Constitution was approved by the Assembly in September 1982 and by a national referendum in November. Its main provisions (including subsequent amendments) are summarized below:

Legislative power is vested in the unicameral Turkish Grand National Assembly (TGNA), which comprises 600 deputies. The election of deputies is by universal adult suffrage for a four-year term (reduced from five years, following an amendment in May 2007). Executive power is vested in the President of the Republic, who is elected by universal suffrage for a five-year term. The President may not serve for more than two terms of office. The President is empowered to: appoint a Prime Minister and senior members of the judiciary, the Central Bank and broadcasting organizations; dissolve the Assembly; and declare a state of emergency entailing rule by decree.

In July 2003 the TGNA approved an amendment reducing the number of NSC members from 13 to six. The NSC was henceforth to be a predominantly civilian advisory body, comprising the President, Prime Minister, Chief of General Staff, and Ministers of Foreign Affairs, National Defence and Internal Affairs. Amendments approved by the Assembly in May 2004 included guarantees of equal rights between men and women, the removal of references to capital punishment and the abolition of State Security Courts. At a national referendum held in September 2010, a package of amendments to the Constitution, including a restructuring of the Supreme Council of Judges and Public Prosecutors, limitations on the judicial powers of the Constitutional Court and the Council of State, and restrictions on the jurisdiction of military tribunals, were approved by 57.9% of participating voters. Further changes to the Constitution were approved at a national referendum in April 2017, including, most notably, the abolition of the post of Prime Minister. Under these reforms, the President was to become head of government and to accrue extensive powers of appointment over government bodies. These reforms were initially expected to be implemented after the legislative and presidential elections scheduled for November 2019; however, those elections were subsequently brought forward to June 2018 and the reforms entered into effect on 9 July. (For details about constitutional amendments, see History.)

The Government

HEAD OF STATE

President: RECEP TAYYIP ERDOĞAN (took office 28 August 2014; re-elected 24 June 2018 and 28 May 2023).

Vice-President: CEVDET YILMAZ.

COUNCIL OF MINISTERS
(September 2023)

The executive is formed by the Adalet ve Kalkınma Partisi (AKP).

Minister of Justice: YILMAZ TUNÇ.
Minister of Family and Social Services: MAHINUR ÖZDEMIR.
Minister of Labour and Social Security: Prof. Dr VEDAT IŞIKHAN.
Minister of Environment, Urbanization and Climate Change: MEHMET ÖZHASEKI.
Minister of Foreign Affairs: HAKAN FIDAN.
Minister of Energy and Natural Resources: ALPARSLAN BAYRAKTAR.
Minister of Youth and Sports: OSMAN AŞKIN BAK.
Minister of Treasury and Finance: MEHMET ŞIMŞEK.
Minister of the Interior: ALI YERLIKAYA.
Minister of Culture and Tourism: MEHMET ERSOY.
Minister of National Education: YUSUF TEKIN.
Minister of National Defence: Gen. YAŞAR GÜLER.
Minister of Health: FAHRETTIN KOCA.
Minister of Industry and Technology: MEHMET FATIH KACIR.
Minister of Agriculture and Forestry: IBRAHIM YUMAKLI.
Minister of Trade: ÖMER BOLAT.
Minister of Transport and Infrastructure: ABDULKADIR URALOĞLU.

MINISTRIES

President's Office: Cumhurbaşkanlığı Külliyesi, 06560 Beştepe, Ankara; tel. (312) 5255555; fax (312) 5255831; e-mail contact@tccb.gov.tr; internet www.tccb.gov.tr.

Ministry of Agriculture and Forestry: Üniversiteler Mah., Dumlupınar Bul. 161, 06800, Çankaya, Ankara; tel. (312) 2873360; fax (312) 2877266; e-mail tarimbilgi@tarim.gov.tr; internet www.tarimorman.gov.tr.

Ministry of Culture and Tourism: İsmet İnönü Bul. 32, Emek, 06100 Emek, Ankara; tel. (312) 4708000; fax (312) 3124359; internet www.kultur.gov.tr.

Ministry of Energy and Natural Resources: Enerji ve Tabii Kaynaklar Bakanlığı, Türk Ocağı Cad. 2, 06520 Ankara; tel. (312) 2126420; fax (312) 2225760; e-mail ozelkalem@enerji.gov.tr; internet www.enerji.gov.tr.

Ministry of Environment, Urbanization and Climate Change: Mustafa Kemal Mah., 278 Eskişehir Devlet Yolu (Dumlupınar Bul.) Km 9, Çankaya, Ankara; tel. (312) 4101000; e-mail cevrevesehircilikbakanligi@hs01.kep.tr; internet csb.gov.tr.

Ministry of Family and Social Services: Eskişehir Yolu, Söğütözü Mah. 2177, Cad. 10A, 06510 Çankaya, Ankara; tel. (312) 7054000; internet www.aile.gov.tr.

Ministry of Foreign Affairs: Dr Sadık Ahmet Cad. 8, 06100 Balgat, Ankara; tel. (312) 2921000; internet www.mfa.gov.tr.

Ministry of Health: Üniversiteler Mah., Dumlupınar Bul. 6001, Cad. 9, 06800 Bilkent-Çankaya, Ankara; tel. (312) 5851000; internet www.saglik.gov.tr.

TÜRKIYE (TURKEY)

Ministry of Industry and Technology: Mustafa Kemal Mah., Dumlupınar Bul. 2151, Cad. 154/A, 06510 Çankaya, Ankara; tel. 4446100; fax (312) 2196738; e-mail info@sanayi.gov.tr; internet www.sanayi.gov.tr.

Ministry of the Interior: İçişleri Bakanlığı, Bakanlıklar, Ankara; tel. (312) 4224000; fax (312) 4181795; internet www.icisleri.gov.tr.

Ministry of Justice: Adalet Bakanlığı, 06659 Kizilay, Ankara; tel. (312) 4177770; fax (312) 4193370; e-mail info@adalet.gov.tr; internet www.adalet.gov.tr.

Ministry of Labour and Social Security: Emek Mah. 17, Sok. 13, 06520 Çankaya, Ankara; tel. (312) 2966000; fax (312) 2961860; internet www.csgb.gov.tr.

Ministry of National Defence: Milli Savunma Bakanlığı, 06100 Ankara; tel. (312) 4026100; internet www.msb.gov.tr.

Ministry of National Education: Milli Eğitim Bakanlığı, Atatürk Bul., Bakanlıklar,06648, Ankara; tel. (312) 4191410; fax (312) 4177027; e-mail meb@meb.gov.tr; internet www.meb.gov.tr.

Ministry of Trade: Söğütözü Mah. 2176, 06530 Çankaya, Ankara; tel. (312) 2047500; e-mail basingtb@gmail.com; internet www.trade.gov.tr.

Ministry of Transport and Infrastructure: Hakkı Turayliç Cad. 5, 06338 Emek, Ankara; tel. (312) 2031000; e-mail uab@hs01.kep.tr; internet www.uab.gov.tr.

Ministry of Treasury and Finance: Maliye Bakanlığı,İnönü Bul. 36, 06510 Emek, Ankara; tel. (312) 4152900; e-mail bilgi@sgb.gov.tr; internet www.hmb.gov.tr.

Ministry of Youth and Sports: Örnek Mah., Oruç Reis Cad. 13, Altındağ, Ankara; tel. (312) 5966000; fax (312) 5966010; e-mail genclikvesporbakanligi@hs01.kep.tr; internet www.gsb.gov.tr.

President

Presidential Election, 14 May 2023, First Round

Candidate	Votes	%
Recep Tayyip Erdoğan	27,133,849	49.5
Kemal Kılıçdaroğlu	24,595,178	44.9
Sinan Oğan	2,831,239	5.2
Muharrem İnce*	235,783	0.4
Total†	54,796,049	100.0

* Despite Muharrem İnce, the leader of the recently formed Memleket Partisi, having withdrawn from the contest on 11 May, his name appeared on the ballot papers.
† Excluding 1,037,101 invalid votes (1.9% of total votes cast).

Presidential Election, 28 May 2023, Second Round

Candidate	Votes	%
Recep Tayyip Erdoğan	27,834,589	52.2
Kemal Kılıçdaroğlu	25,504,704	47.8
Total*	53,339,293	100.0

* Excluding 684,288 invalid votes (1.3% of total votes cast).

Legislature

Grand National Assembly: TBMM 06543, Bakanlıklar, Ankara; tel. (312) 4205000; e-mail baskanlik@tbmm.gov.tr; internet www.tbmm.gov.tr.

Speaker: NUMAN KURTULMUŞ.

General Election, 14 May 2023

Party	Votes	%	Seats
Adalet ve Kalkınma Partisi (AKP)	18,586,137	35.32	268
Cumhuriyet Halk Partisi (CHP)	13,374,463	25.41	169
Yeşil Sol Parti (YSP)	4,624,094	8.79	61
Milliyetçi Hareket Partisi (MHP)	5,283,345	10.04	50
İyi Parti (İP)	5,211,632	9.90	43
Yeniden Refah Partisi (YRP)	1,505,736	2.86	5
Türkiye İşçi Partisi (TİP)	903,742	1.72	4
Total (incl. others)	52,628,182*	100.00	600

* Excluding 1,365,867 invalid votes (representing 2.5% of the total votes cast).

Election Commission

Yüksek Seçim Kurulu (YSK) (High Electoral Board): Kızılay Mah., Ihlamur Sok. 4, 06420 Sıhhıye, Ankara; tel. (312) 4191039; fax (312) 4195308; internet www.ysk.gov.tr; independent; Chair. AHMET YENER.

Political Organizations

Legislation enacted in March 1986 stipulated that a party must have organizations in at least 45 provinces, and in two-thirds of the districts in each of these provinces, in order to take part in an election. A political party is recognized by the Government as a legitimate parliamentary group only if it has at least 20 deputies in the Grand National Assembly.

Adalet ve Kalkınma Partisi (AKP) (Justice and Development Party): Söğütözü Cad. 6, Çankaya, Ankara; tel. (312) 2045000; fax (312) 2045044; internet www.akparti.org.tr; f. 2001; Islamist-orientated; Chair. RECEP TAYYIP ERDOĞAN; Sec.-Gen. FATIH ŞAHIN.

Bağımsız Türkiye Partisi (BTP) (Independent Türkiye Party): E Cad. 11, Çankaya, Ankara; tel. (312) 2122212; fax (312) 3092003; e-mail btp@btp.org.tr; internet www.btp.org.tr; f. 2001; Chair. HÜSEYIN BAŞ.

Büyük Birlik Partisi (BBP) (Great Unity Party): Gazi Mah., Silahtar Cad. 90, Yenimahalle, Ankara; tel. (312) 4340920; e-mail bilgi@bbp.org.tr; internet www.bbp.org.tr; f. 1993; Pres. MUSTAFA DESTICI; Sec.-Gen. ÜZEYIR TUNÇ.

Cumhuriyet Halk Partisi (CHP) (Republican People's Party): Anadolu Bul. 12, Söğütözü, Ankara; tel. (312) 2074000; fax (312) 2074039; e-mail chp@chp.org.tr; internet www.chp.org.tr; f. 1923 by Mustafa Kemal (Atatürk); dissolved 1981 and reactivated 1992; merged with Sosyal Demokrat Halkçı Parti (Social Democratic Populist Party) 1995 and with the Yeni Türkiye Partisi 2004; left-wing; Chair. KEMAL KILIÇDAROĞLU; Sec.-Gen. NESLIHAN HANCIOĞLU.

Demokrasi ve Atılım Partisi (DEVA Partisi): Mustafa Kemal Mah. 2158, Sok. 9, 06510 Çankaya, Ankara; tel. (850) 2556565; internet devapartisi.org; f. 2020; Pres. ALI BABACAN.

Demokrat Parti (DP) (Democratic Party): Sadık Ahmet Cad. 3, 06520 Balgat, Ankara; tel. (312) 2488600; e-mail dp@dp.org.tr; internet www.dp.org.tr; f. 1983 as Doğru Yol Partisi (True Path Party); renamed as above 2007; merged with Anavatan Partisi (Motherland Party) 2009; centre-right; Chair. GÜLTEKIN UYSAL.

Demokratik Sol Parti (DSP) (Democratic Left Party): Mareşal Fevzi Çakmak Cad. 17, Beşevler, Ankara; tel. (312) 2124950; fax (312) 2124188; e-mail dsp@dsp.org.tr; internet www.dsp.org.tr; f. 1985, drawing support from mems of the fmr Republican People's Party; centre-left; Chair. ÖNDER AKSAKAL; Gen. Sec. MÜZEYYEN OKUR.

Emek Partisi (EMEP) (Labour Party of Türkiye): Fevzi Çakmak 1 Sok. 15/5, Kızılay, Ankara; tel. (312) 2324197; fax (212) 5880300; e-mail emekpartisi@emep.org; internet www.emep.org; f. 1996; advocates scientific socialism; Chair. SELMA GÜRKAN.

Genç Parti (GP) (Youth Party): İller Sok. 7, Mebusevleri, 06580 Tandoğan, Ankara; fax (312) 2969757; e-mail info@gencparti.org; internet www.gencparti.org; f. 2002; populist, nationalist; Chair. CEM UZAN.

Halkların Demokratik Partisi (HDP) (People's Democratic Party): Barbaros Mah., Büklüm Cad., Büklüm Sok. 117, 06680 Çankaya, Ankara; tel. (312) 4271780; fax (312) 4288957; e-mail bilgi@hdp.org.tr; internet www.hdp.org.tr; f. 2012 by mems of the Halkların Demokratik Kongresi (a coalition of 33 left-wing groups formed 2008); democratic socialist; Co-Chairs MITHAT SANCAR, PERVIN BULDAN.

İyi Partisi (İP) (Good Party): Mustafa Kemal Mah., Şehit Öğretmen Şenay Aybüke Yalçın Cad. No. 9, Çankaya, Ankara; tel. (312) 4080808; fax (312) 4080809; e-mail bilgi@iyiparti.org.tr; internet iyiparti.org.tr; f. 2017; Chair. MERAL AKŞENER.

Liberal Demokrat Parti (LDP) (Liberal Democrat Party): 100 Yıl Mah., Hülya Sok. 35/1, Çankaya, Ankara; tel. and fax (532) 3941188; e-mail info@ldp.org.tr; internet www.ldp.org.tr; f. 1994; Chair. GÜLTEKIN TIRPANCI.

Memleket Partisi: Yukarı Öveçler Mah. 1290, Sok. 4, Çankaya, Ankara; tel. (312) 8880888; fax (312) 4721212; e-mail info@memleketpartisi.org.tr; internet www.memleketpartisi.org.tr; f. 2021; Leader MUHARREM İNCE.

Millet Partisi (MP) (Nation Party): Oğuzlar Mah. 1397, Cad. 14, Çankaya, Ankara; tel. and fax (312) 4194060; e-mail iletisim@milletpartisi.org.tr; internet www.milletpartisi.org.tr; f. 1992; Chair. CUMA NACAR.

Milliyetçi Hareket Partisi (MHP) (Nationalist Movement Party): Ceyhun Atıf Kansu Cad. 128, Balgat, Ankara; tel. (312) 4725555; fax (312) 4731544; e-mail bilgi@mhp.org.tr; internet www.mhp.org.tr;

TÜRKIYE (TURKEY)

f. 1983; fmrly the Democratic and Conservative Party; Chair. DEVLET BAHÇELI; Sec.-Gen. İSMET BÜYÜKATAMAN.

Saadet Partisi (SP) (Felicity Party): Balgat Mah., 141 Cad., Çankaya, Ankara; tel. (312) 2848800; fax (312) 2856246; e-mail bilgi@saadet.org.tr; internet www.saadet.org.tr; f. 2001; replaced conservative wing of Islamist fundamentalist and free-market advocating Fazilet Partisi (Virtue Party), which was banned in that year; Chair. TEMEL KARAMOLLAOĞLU; Sec.-Gen. MESUT DOĞAN.

Sol Parti (Left Party): Mithatpaşa Cad. 58/12, Kızılay, Ankara; tel. (312) 4197318; fax 2320347; internet solparti.org; f. 1996 as Özgürlük ve Dayanisma Partisi; present name adopted 2019; Chair. ÖNDER İŞLEYEN.

Türkiye İşçi Partisi (TİP) (Workers' Party of Turkey): Bayraktar Mah., Vedat Dalokay Cad. 100/1 2, Çankaya, Ankara; tel. (312) 4179370; e-mail tip@tip.org.tr; internet tip.org.tr; f. 2017; Chair. ERKAN BAŞ.

Türkiye Komünist Partisi (TKP) (Communist Party of Türkiye): Kızılırmak Cad. 13/4, Ankara; tel. (312) 4172968; fax (312) 4172534; e-mail iletisim@tkp.org.tr; internet www.tkp.org.tr; f. 2014; Sec.-Gen. KEMAL OKUYAN.

Vatan Partisi (VP) (Patriotic Party): Toros Sok. 9, Sihhiye, Ankara; tel. (312) 2318111; fax (312) 2292994; e-mail international@vatanpartisi.org.tr; internet www.vatanpartisi.org.tr; f. 1992; fmrly İşçi Partisi; Chair. DOĞU PERINÇEK.

Yeniden Refah Partisi (New Welfare Party): Balgat Mah. 1421, Cad. 15, Çankaya, Ankara; tel. (312) 287 0010; e-mail bilgi@yenidenrefahpartisi.org.tr; internet yenidenrefahpartisi.org.tr; f. 2018; Islamist; Pres. FATIH ERBAKAN.

Yeşil Sol Parti (YSP) (Green Left Party): Atatürk Bul. 88, Daire 16, Çankaya, Ankara; tel. (546) 2443374; e-mail iletisim@yesilsolparti.com; internet yesilsolparti.org; f. 2012; full name Yeşiller ve Sol Gelecek Partisi (Party of Greens and the Left Future); Co-spokespersons ÇIĞDEM KILIÇGÜN UÇAR, İBRAHIM AKIN.

Yurt Partisi (Homeland Party): Meşrutiyet Cad. Bayındır 2, Sok. 59/5, Kızılay, Ankara; tel. (312) 4189034; e-mail iletisim@yurtpartisi.org.tr; internet www.yurtpartisi.org.tr; f. 2002; nationalist and conservative party; Leader SAADETTIN TANTAN.

The following proscribed organizations have been engaged in an armed struggle against the Government:

Devrimci Halk Kurtuluş Partisi—Cephesi (DHKP—C) (Revolutionary People's Liberation Party—Front): faction of Dev-Sol; subsumed parent org. in 1996; Leader GÜLTEN MATUR (arrested Nov. 2022).

Partiya Karkeren Kurdistan (PKK) (Kurdistan Workers' Party): internet pkk-online.com; f. 1978; 57-mem. directorate; launched struggle for an independent Kurdistan in 1984; declared ceasefire 2000; renamed Congress for Freedom and Democracy in Kurdistan (KADEK) 2002 and KONGRA-GEL 2003; return to fmr name, PKK, announced April 2005, following resumption of armed struggle; name KONGRA-GEL continued to be used by some elements; military wing, Hezên Parastina Gel (HPG—People's Defence Forces), re-emerged 2004; Chair. MURAT KARAYILAN; Leader ABDULLAH ÖCALAN.

Diplomatic Representation

EMBASSIES IN TÜRKIYE

Afghanistan: Cinnah Cad. 88, 06550 Çankaya, Ankara; tel. (312) 4422523; fax (312) 4426256; e-mail info@afghanembassy.org.tr; internet afghanembassy.org.tr; Ambassador AMIR MOHAMMAD RAMIN.

Albania: İlkbahar Mah., Medeni Müdafi Sok. 35, Çankaya, Ankara; tel. (312) 4416103; fax (312) 4416109; e-mail embassy.ankara@mfa.gov.al; internet www.ambasadat.gov.al/turkey; Ambassador BLERTA KADZADEJ (designate).

Algeria: Şehit Ersan Cad. 42, 06680 Çankaya, Ankara; tel. (312) 4687719; fax (312) 4687593; e-mail cezayirbe@algerianembassy.com.tr; internet algerianembassy.com.tr; Ambassador AMAR BELANI.

Angola: İlkbahar Mah., Galip Erdem Cad. 616, Sok. 16, Çankaya, Ankara; tel. (312) 4282770; fax (312) 4282772; e-mail info@embassyangolatr.org; internet www.embassyangolatr.org; Ambassador JOSÉ GONÇALVES MARTINS PATRÍCIO.

Argentina: Karaca Sok. 19, 06700 Ankara; tel. (312) 4462061; fax (312) 4462063; e-mail eturq@mrecic.gov.ar; internet eturq.cancilleria.gob.ar; Ambassador PATRICIA BEATRIZ SALAS.

Australia: Kat 7, Uğur Mumcu Cad. 88, 06700 Gaziosmanpaşa, Ankara; tel. (312) 4599500; fax (312) 4464827; e-mail ankara.embassy@dfat.gov.au; internet turkey.embassy.gov.au; Ambassador MILES ROBERT ARMITAGE.

Austria: Atatürk Bul. 189, 06680 Kavaklıdere, Ankara; tel. (312) 4055190; fax (312) 4254226; e-mail ankara-ob@bmeia.gv.at; internet www.bmeia.gv.at/oeb-ankara/die-botschaft; Ambassador Dr JOHANNES WIMMER.

Azerbaijan: Diplomatik Site, Bakü Sok. 1, 06450 Oran, Ankara; tel. (312) 4911681; fax (312) 4920430; e-mail ankara@mission.mfa.gov.az; internet ankara.mfa.gov.az; Ambassador RASHAD EYNADDIN MAMMADOV.

Bahrain: İlkbahar Mah. 19, Sok. 606, Oran, Çankaya, Ankara; tel. (312) 4912655; e-mail ankara.mission@mofa.gov.bh; internet www.mofa.gov.bh/ankara; Ambassador IBRAHIM YOUSUF AL-ABDULLAH.

Bangladesh: Oran Mah., Cad. 14, Çankaya, Ankara; tel. (312) 4952719; fax (312) 4952744; e-mail mission.ankara@mofa.gov.bd; internet ankara.mofa.gov.bd; Ambassador AMANUL HAQ.

Belarus: Abidin Daver Sok. 17, 06550 Çankaya, Ankara; tel. (312) 4416769; fax (312) 4416674; e-mail turkey@mfa.gov.by; internet turkey.mfa.gov.by; Ambassador VIKTOR RYBAK.

Belgium: Eskişehir Yolu 2176, Cad. 9, Kat 10–11, Söğütözü, 06530 Çankaya, Ankara; tel. (312) 4056166; fax (312) 4468251; e-mail ankara@diplobel.fed.be; internet turkey.diplomatie.belgium.be; Ambassador PAUL HUYNEN.

Bolivia: Ankara; tel. 3123940; e-mail emboliviaturquia@gmail.com; Ambassador EDGAR ADOLFO SEJAS VERA.

Bosnia and Herzegovina: Paris Cad. 47, 06680 Çankaya, Ankara; tel. (312) 4273602; fax (312) 4273604; e-mail bh_emba@ttmail.com; Ambassador ADIS ALAGIC.

Brazil: Reşit Galip Cad., İlkadım Sok. 1, 06700 Gaziosmanpaşa, Ankara; tel. (312) 4481840; fax (312) 4482972; e-mail brasemb.ancara@itamaraty.gov.br; internet www.gov.br/mre/pt-br/embaixada-ancara; Ambassador CARLOS MARTINS CEGLIA.

Brunei Darussalam: Rafet Canıtez Cad., Arif Nihat Asya Sok. 33, Oran, 06450 Çankaya, Ankara; tel. (312) 4904460; fax (312) 4904462; e-mail info@brunei.org.tr; Ambassador MUHAMMAD SHAFIEE BIN Haji KASSIM.

Bulgaria: Atatürk Bul. 124, 06680 Kavaklıdere, Ankara; tel. (312) 4672071; fax (312) 4686956; e-mail embassy.ankara@mfa.bg; internet www.mfa.bg/embassies/turkey; Ambassador ANGUEL HRISTOV TCHOLAKOV.

Burkina Faso: İlkbahar Mah., Galip Erdem Cad. 618, Sok. 23, Çankaya, Ankara; tel. (312) 4907151; fax (312) 4907153; e-mail abfank14@outlook.com; Ambassador VINTA SOMÉ.

Burundi: Rafet Canıtez Cad., Arif Nihat Asya Sok. 2, Oran, Çankaya, Ankara; tel. (312) 4426142; fax (312) 4426145; e-mail ankaradiplobdi@outlook.com; Ambassador GERARD NTAHORWAROYE BIKEBAKO.

Cambodia: Kazım Özalp Mah., Koza Sok. 24, 06680 Çankaya, Ankara; tel. (312) 4391078; fax (312) 4391071; e-mail camemb.tur@mfaic.gov.kh; internet www.cambodiaembassytr.com; Ambassador SOK CHEA (designate).

Cameroon: Büyükesat Mah., Koza Cad. 45, 06700 Çankaya, Ankara; tel. (312) 4460111; fax (312) 4460222; e-mail info@ambacamturquie.com; internet ambacamturquie.com; Ambassador VICTOR TCHATCHOUO.

Canada: Cinnah Cad. 58, 06690 Çankaya, Ankara; tel. (312) 4092700; fax (312) 4092712; e-mail ankra@international.gc.ca; internet www.canadainternational.gc.ca/turkey-turquie; Ambassador KEVIN HAMILTON (designate).

Chad: İlkadım Sok. 18, Ankara; tel. (312) 4901940; fax (312) 4901927; e-mail amb.tchadankara@gmail.com; Ambassador ADOUM DANGAI NOKOUR GUET.

Chile: Reşit Galip Cad., İrfanli Sok. 14/1–3, 06700 Gaziosmanpaşa, Ankara; tel. (312) 4473418; fax (312) 4474725; e-mail embassy@chile.org.tr; internet chileabroad.gov.cl/turquia; Ambassador RODRIGO ARCOS.

China, People's Republic: Ferit Recai Ertuğrul Cad. 18, Oran, Ankara; tel. (312) 4900660; fax (312) 4464248; e-mail chinaemb_tr@mfa.gov.cn; internet tr.china-embassy.org; Ambassador LIU SHAOBIN.

Colombia: Abdullah Cevdet Sok. 4, 06680 Çankaya, Ankara; tel. (312) 4464388; fax (312) 4464399; e-mail eturquia@cancilleria.gov.co; internet turquia.embajada.gov.co; Ambassador JULIO ANÍBAL RIAÑO VELANDIA.

Congo, Democratic Republic: İlkbahar Mah. 606, Sok. 12, Çankaya, Ankara; tel. (312) 4660916; fax (312) 4660918; e-mail missionrdcankara@gmail.com; Ambassador DJUMA KAUZENI RASHIDI.

Congo, Republic: Reşit Galip Cad. 98, Gaziosmanpaşa, Ankara; tel. (312) 4465469; fax (312) 4467085; e-mail ambacoturc@yahoo.fr; Ambassador JEAN-JAURES ONDELE.

TÜRKIYE (TURKEY)

Costa Rica: Kazim Özalp Mah., Karaca Sok. 24/8, Çankaya, Ankara; tel. (312) 4392332; fax (312) 4392372; e-mail embcr-tk@rree.go.cr; Ambassador Gustavo Alonso Campos Fallas.
Côte d'Ivoire: Reşit Galip Cad., İlkadım Sok. 3, 06700 Gaziosmanpaşa, Ankara; tel. (312) 4460115; fax (312) 4460116; e-mail ambaci.tq@gmail.com; Ambassador Khadidjata Toure.
Croatia: Aziziye Mah., Kırkpınar Sok. 18/5, 06690 Çankaya, Ankara; tel. (312) 4469460; fax (312) 4464700; e-mail ankara@mvep.hr; internet tr.mvp.hr; Ambassador Hrvoje Cvitanović.
Cuba: Pak Sok. 1/28, 06550 Çankaya, Ankara; tel. (312) 4428970; fax (312) 4426115; e-mail secretary@embacubatr.net; internet misiones.minrex.gob.cu/en/turkey; Ambassador Alejandro Francisco Diaz Palacios.
Czech Republic: Kaptanpaşa Sok. 15, 06700 Gaziosmanpaşa, Ankara; tel. (312) 4056139; fax (312) 4463084; e-mail ankara@embassy.mzv.cz; internet www.mzv.cz/ankara; Ambassador Pavel Vacek.
Denmark: Yildiz Kule, Kat 22, Yukarı Dikmen Mah., Turan Güneş Bul. 106, Cankaya, Ankara; tel. (312) 4083300; fax (312) 4472498; e-mail ankamb@um.dk; internet tyrkiet.um.dk; Ambassador Danny Annan.
Djibouti: İlkbahar Mah., Galip Erdem Cad. 21, Yıldız-Çankaya, Ankara; tel. (312) 4919513; fax (312) 4919510; e-mail info@djiboutiembassy.com.tr; internet www.djiboutiembassy.com.tr; Ambassador Aden Houssein Abdillahi.
Dominican Republic: Ankara; Ambassador Elvis Antonio Alam Lora.
Ecuador: Kazim Ozalp Mah., Kelebek Sok. 21/1, 06700 Gaziosmanpaşa, Ankara; tel. (312) 4460160; fax (312) 4460173; e-mail eecuturquia@cancilleria.gob.ec; Ambassador Fanny de Lourdes Puma.
Egypt: Atatürk Bul. 126, 06680 Kavaklıdere, Ankara; tel. (312) 4261026; fax (312) 4270099; e-mail embassy_egypt@yahoo.com; internet www.misirbuyukelciligi.com/misir-buyukelciligi-ankara; Ambassador Amr El Hamamy (designate).
El Salvador: Aziziye Mah., Pak Sok. 1/57, Portakal Çiçegi Rezidans, 06690 Çankaya, Ankara; tel. (312) 5441117; e-mail embajadasv-tur@rree.gob.sv; internet fb.com/EmbajadaTurquiaSV; Ambassador Hector Jaime.
Equatorial Guinea: İlkbahar Mah., Cad. 608, Turan Güneş Bul. 612, Sok. 12, Çankaya, Ankara; tel. (312) 4903124; fax (312) 4901647; e-mail embaregeturk@gmail.com; Ambassador José Esono Micha Akeng.
Estonia: Yıl Mah. 100, Gölgeli Sok. 16, 06700 Gaziosmanpaşa, Ankara; tel. (312) 4056970; fax (312) 4056976; e-mail embassy.ankara@mfa.ee; internet ankara.mfa.ee; Ambassador Väino Reinart.
Ethiopia: Oran Mah., Mühittin Çöteli Sok. 6, Çankaya, Ankara; tel. (312) 4360400; fax (312) 4481938; e-mail ethembank@ttnet.net.tr; internet www.ankara.mfa.gov.et; Ambassador Adem Mohammed.
Finland: Kader Sok. 44, 06700 Gaziosmanpaşa, Ankara; tel. (312) 4574400; fax (312) 4680072; e-mail sanomat.ank@formin.fi; internet finlandabroad.fi/turkey; Ambassador Ari Mäki.
France: Paris Cad. 70, 06540 Kavaklıdere, Ankara; tel. (312) 4554545; fax (312) 4554527; e-mail amba.ankara@diplomatie.gouv.fr; internet tr.ambafrance.org; Ambassador Isabelle Dumont.
Gabon: İlkbahar Mah. 609, Sok. 35, Oran, Çankaya, Ankara; tel. (312) 4920569; fax (312) 4913516; e-mail embagabonturkey@gmail.com; Ambassador Jean Bernard Avouma.
The Gambia: Hilal Mah., Hollanda Cad. 31, Çankaya, Ankara; tel. (312) 4425771; fax (312) 4425707; e-mail gamembank@gmail.com; Ambassador Alkali F. Conteh.
Georgia: Kılıç Ali Sok. 12, Oran, Ankara; tel. (312) 4918030; fax (312) 4918032; e-mail ankara.emb@mfa.gov.ge; internet www.turkey.mfa.gov.ge; Ambassador George Janjgava.
Germany: Atatürk Bul. 114, 06680 Kavaklıdere, Ankara; tel. (532) 7874096; fax (312) 4555337; e-mail info@ankara.diplo.de; internet www.ankara.diplo.de; Ambassador Jürgen Schulz.
Ghana: İlkbahar Mah. 606, Sok. 10, Oran, Çankaya, Ankara; tel. (312) 4425479; fax (312) 4418569; e-mail ankara@mfa.gov.gh; internet ghanaembassy-turkey.com; Ambassador Francisca Ashietey-Odunton.
Greece: Zia ür-Rahman Cad. 9–11, 06670 Gaziosmanpaşa, Ankara; tel. (312) 4480873; fax (312) 4463191; e-mail gremb.ank@mfa.gr; internet www.mfa.gr/turkey; Ambassador Lazaris Christodoulos.
Guatemala: Beyaz Zambaklar Sok. 42/2, Gaziosmanpaşa, Ankara; tel. (312) 4262036; fax (312) 4262037; e-mail embturquia@minex.gob.gt; Ambassador Jairo David Estrada Barrios.
Guinea: Büyükesat Mah., Uğur Mumcu Sok. 76, 06700 Gaziosmanpaşa, Ankara; tel. (312) 4368620; fax (312) 4368677; e-mail ambaguiankara@maege.gov.gn; Ambassador Oumar Kallé.
Guinea-Bissau: Ankara; e-mail djamancabdu@gmail.com; Ambassador Malam Mane.
Holy See: Apostolic Nunciature, Birlik Mah. 3, Cad. 37, PK 33, 06610 Çankaya, Ankara; tel. (312) 4953514; fax (312) 4953540; Apostolic Nuncio Most Rev. Marek Solczyński (Titular Archbishop of Caesarea).
Hungary: Sancak Mah. Layoş, Koşut Cad. 2, 06550 Yıldız, 06550 Çankaya, Ankara; tel. (312) 4422273; fax (312) 4415049; e-mail mission.ank@mfa.gov.hu; internet ankara.mfa.gov.hu; Ambassador Viktor Matis.
India: Cinnah Cad. 77A, 06680 Çankaya, Ankara; tel. (312) 4382195; fax (312) 4403429; internet www.indembassyankara.gov.in; Ambassador Virander Kumar Paul.
Indonesia: Hilal Mah., Sukarno Cad. 24/1, Çankaya, Ankara; tel. (312) 9697354; fax (312) 9697336; e-mail ankara.kbri@kemlu.go.id; internet www.kemlu.go.id/ankara; Ambassador Achmad Rizal Purnama.
Iran: Tahran Cad. 10, 06700 Kavaklıdere, Ankara; tel. (312) 4574100; fax (312) 4682823; internet turkey.mfa.gov.ir; Ambassador Mohammad Hassan Habibollahzadeh.
Iraq: Turan Emeksiz Sok. 11, 06700 Gaziosmanpaşa, Ankara; tel. (312) 4687421; fax (312) 4684832; e-mail ankemb@mofa.gov.iq; Ambassador Majid al-Lacmavi.
Ireland: Uğur Mumcu Cad. 88, MNG Binası B Blok Kat 3, 06700 Gaziosmanpaşa, Ankara; tel. (312) 4591000; fax (312) 4468061; e-mail ankaraembassy@dfa.ie; internet www.dfa.ie/irish-embassy/turkey/; Ambassador Sonya McGuinness.
Israel: Mahatma Gandhi Cad. 85, 06700 Gaziosmanpaşa, Ankara; tel. (312) 4597500; fax (312) 4597555; e-mail info@ankara.mfa.gov.il; internet embassies.gov.il/ankara; Ambassador Irit Lillian.
Italy: Atatürk Bul. 118, 06680 Kavaklıdere, Ankara; tel. (312) 4574200; e-mail ambasciata.ankara@esteri.it; internet ambankara.esteri.it; Ambassador Giorgio Marrapodi.
Japan: Reşit Galip Cad. 81, 06692 Gaziosmanpaşa, Ankara; tel. (312) 4460500; fax (312) 4371812; e-mail politika@an.mofa.go.jp; internet www.tr.emb-japan.go.jp; Ambassador Takahiko Katsumata.
Jordan: Dede Korkut Sok. 18 Mesnevi, 06690 Çankaya, Ankara; tel. (312) 5011111; fax (312) 4404327; e-mail ankara@fm.gov.jo; Ambassador Hazem al-Khatib.
Kazakhstan: Kiliç Ali Sok. 6, Diplomatik Site, 06450 Oran, Ankara; tel. (312) 4919100; fax (312) 4904455; e-mail ankara@mfa.kz; Ambassador Yerkebulan Sapiyev.
Kenya: İlkbahar Mah. Galip Erdem Cad. 613, Sok. 11/1, Yıldız Çankaya, Ankara; tel. (312) 4914508; e-mail kembankara@gmail.com; internet www.kenyaembassy.org.tr; Ambassador Leonard Boiyo.
Korea, Republic: Cinnah Cad., Alaçam Sok. 5, 06690 Çankaya, Ankara; tel. (312) 4684820; e-mail turkey@mofa.go.kr; internet overseas.mofa.go.kr/tr-ko; Ambassador Lee Won-Ik.
Kosovo: Hirfanli Sok. 14/2, Gaziosmanpaşa, Ankara; tel. (312) 4467054; fax (312) 4467055; e-mail embassy.turkey@ks-gov.net; internet www.ambasada-ks.net/tr; Ambassador Agon Vrenezi.
Kuwait: Reşit Galip Cad. 110, Gaziosmanpaşa, Ankara; tel. (312) 4450576; fax (312) 4462826; e-mail info@kuwaitembassy.org.tr; Ambassador Wael al-Enezi.
Kyrgyzstan: Galip Erdem Cad. 25, Turan Gunes Bul., 06550 Çankaya, Ankara; tel. (312) 4913506; fax (312) 4913513; e-mail kgembassy.tr@mfa.gov.kg; Ambassador Ruslan Kazakbaev.
Latvia: Reşit Galip Cad. 95, Çankaya, Ankara; tel. (312) 4056136; fax (312) 4056137; e-mail embassy.turkey@mfa.gov.lv; internet www.mfa.gov.lv/turkey; Ambassador Pēteris Vaivars.
Lebanon: Kızkulesi Sok. 44, Gaziosmanpaşa, 06700 Ankara; tel. (312) 4467485; fax (312) 4461023; e-mail lebembas@ttmail.com; Ambassador Ghassan Moallem.
Libya: Cinnah Cad. 60, Çankaya, Ankara; tel. (312) 4381110; fax (312) 4429130; e-mail info@libembtr.ly; Ambassador Mustafa El-Gelaib.
Lithuania: Mahatma Gandhi Cad. 38, 06700 Gaziosmanpaşa, Ankara; tel. (312) 4470766; fax (312) 4470663; e-mail amb.tr@urm.lt; internet tr.mfa.lt; Ambassador Ričardas Degutis.
Luxembourg: Reşit Galip Cad. 70/2, 2 Gaziosmanpaşa, Ankara; tel. (312) 4591400; fax (312) 4365055; e-mail ankara.amb@mae.etat.lu; internet ankara.mae.lu; Ambassador Angèle Da Cruz.
Malaysia: Koza Sok. 56, 06700 Gaziosmanpaşa, Ankara; tel. (312) 4463547; fax (312) 4464130; e-mail mwankara@kln.gov.my; internet www.kln.gov.my/web/tur_ankara; Ambassador Sazali Mustafa Kamal.
Mali: İlkbahar Mah. 606, Sok. 24, Çankaya, Ankara; tel. (312) 4911193; fax (312) 4911106; e-mail ambaduml.ank@gmail.com; Ambassador Issa Ousmane Coulibaly.

TÜRKIYE (TURKEY)

Malta: Kazım Özalp Mah., Reşit Galip Cad. 70/1, Gaziosmanpaşa, Ankara; tel. (312) 4478051; fax (312) 4378270; e-mail maltaembassy.ankara@gov.mt; internet foreignaffairs.gov.mt/en/Embassies/ME_Ankara; Ambassador THERESA CUTAJAR.

Mauritania: Oran Mah., Şemsettin Bayramoğlu Sok. 7, Çankaya, Ankara; tel. (312) 4917063; fax (312) 4917064; e-mail embassyofmauritania.ankara@gmail.com; Ambassador Cheikh SID AHMED EL BEKAYE OULD HAMADY.

Mexico: Pak Sok. 1/110, 06690 Çankaya, Ankara; tel. (312) 4423033; fax (312) 4420221; internet embamex.sre.gob.mx/turquia; Ambassador JOSÉ LUIS MARTÍNEZ Y HERNANDEZ.

Moldova: Ehlibeyt Mah., Ceyhun Atıf Kansu Cad. 106, Başkent Plaza, Balgat, Çankaya, Ankara; tel. (312) 4465527; fax (312) 4465816; e-mail ankara@mfa.gov.md; internet turcia.mfa.gov.md; Ambassador DMITRI CROITOR.

Mongolia: A. Fethi Okyar Sok. 4, Oran Diplomatik Sitesi, 06450 Oran, Ankara; tel. (312) 4921028; fax (312) 4921064; e-mail ankara@mfa.gov.mn; internet www.mongolianembassy.com.tr; Ambassador MUNKHBAYAR GOMBOSUREN.

Montenegro: Büyükesat, Gökçek Sok. 11, 06700 Ankara; tel. (312) 4364698; fax (312) 4361546; e-mail turkey@mfa.gov.me; Ambassador PERIŠA KASTRATOVIĆ.

Morocco: Reşit Galip Cad., Rabat Sok. 11, 06700 Gaziosmanpaşa, Ankara; tel. (312) 4376020; fax (312) 4468430; e-mail amb.ankara@maec.gov.ma; Ambassador MOHAMED ALI LAZRAK.

Netherlands: Yıldırım Kule 221, Mevlana Bul., 06520 Çankaya, Ankara; tel. (312) 4091800; fax (312) 4091898; e-mail ank@minbuza.nl; internet www.netherlandsworldwide.nl/countries/turkey; Ambassador JOEP WIJNANDS.

New Zealand: Kizkulesi Sok. 11, Gaziosmanpaşa, Ankara; tel. (312) 4463333; fax (312) 4463317; e-mail newzealandembassyankara@gmail.com; Ambassador ZOE COULSON-SINCLAIR.

Nicaragua: Ankara; Ambassador MARIO ANTONIO BARQUERO BALTODANO.

Niger: Mahatma Gandhi Cad. 40, Gaziosmanpaşa, Ankara; tel. (312) 4361013; fax (312) 4361017; internet www.ambaniger-tr.org; Ambassador SALOU ADAMA GAZIBO.

Nigeria: Uğur Mumcu Sok. 56, 06700 Gaziosmanpaşa, Ankara; tel. (312) 4481076; fax (312) 4481082; e-mail embassynigeriaturkey@gmail.com; internet www.embassynigeriaturkey.com; Ambassador ISMAIL ABBA YUSUF.

North Macedonia: Karaca Sok. 24/5–6, 06700 Gaziosmanpaşa, Ankara; tel. (312) 4399204; fax (312) 4399206; e-mail ankara@mfa.gov.mk; Ambassador JOVAN MANASIJEVSKI.

Norway: Yukarı Dikmen Mah., Turan Güneş Bul. 106, 12 Yıldız Kule İş Merkezi, 06540 Çankaya, Ankara; tel. (312) 4084800; fax (312) 4084899; e-mail emb.ankara@mfa.no; internet www.norway.no/turkey; Ambassador ERLING SKJONSBERG.

Oman: Diplomatik Alan, Besim Atalay Sok. 7, Oran, Ankara; tel. (312) 4910940; fax (312) 4900682; e-mail ankara@mofa.gov.om; Ambassador Dr QASSIM BIN MUHAMMAD BIN SALIM AL-SALHI.

Pakistan: Gaziosmanpaşa Mah., İran Cad. 37, 06700 Çankaya, Ankara; tel. (312) 4271410; fax (312) 4671023; e-mail info@pakembassyankara.com; internet www.pakembassyankara.com; Ambassador Dr YOUSAF JUNAID.

Panama: Portakal Çiçeği Residence, Aziziye Mah., 1/23 Pak Sok., 06540 Çankaya, Ankara; tel. (312) 4390220; fax (312) 4390221; e-mail embpanamaturquia@mire.gob.pa; Ambassador MARIELA SAGEL ROSAS.

Paraguay: Aziziye Mah., Pak Sok., Portakal Çiçegi Rezidans, No. 1 D:62, Çankaya, Ankara; tel. (312) 4386463; e-mail embaparturquia@mre.gov.py; Ambassador CEFERINO ADRIAN VALDEZ PERALTA.

Peru: Reşit Galip Cad. 70/1, 06700 Ankara; tel. (312) 4469039; fax (312) 4474076; e-mail peruankara@gmail.com; Ambassador CESAR AUGUSTO DE LAS CASAS DIAZ.

Philippines: Kazim Özalp Mah., Kumkapi Sok. 36, 06700 Gaziosmanpaşa, Ankara; tel. (312) 4423824; fax (312) 4423856; e-mail ankara.pe@dfa.gov.ph; internet ankarape.dfa.gov.ph; Chargé d'affaires a.i. JUAN E. DAYANG, Jr.

Poland: Atatürk Bul. 241, 06650 Kavaklıdere, Ankara; tel. (312) 4572000; fax (312) 4678963; e-mail ankara.wk.dyzurny@msz.gov.pl; internet ankara.msz.gov.pl; Ambassador MACIEJ LANG.

Portugal: Kirlangiç Sok. 39, Gaziosmanpaşa, Ankara; tel. (312) 4054109; fax (312) 4463670; e-mail ankara@mne.pt; internet www.ancara.embaixadaportugal.mne.pt; Ambassador JAIME VAN ZELLER LEITAO.

Qatar: Bakü Sok. 6, Diplomatik Site, Oran, Ankara; tel. (312) 4907274; fax (312) 4906757; e-mail qeank@yahoo.com; internet ankara.embassy.qa; Ambassador Sheikh MOHAMMED BIN NASSER BIN JASSIM AL THANI.

Romania: Bükreş Sok. 4, 06680 Çankaya, Ankara; tel. (312) 4663706; fax (312) 4271530; e-mail ankara@mae.ro; internet ankara.mae.ro; Ambassador STEFAN-ALEXANDRU TINCA.

Russian Federation: Karyağdı Sok. 5, 06692 Çankaya, Ankara; tel. (312) 4392183; fax (312) 4383952; e-mail rus-ankara@yandex.ru; internet www.turkey.mid.ru; Ambassador ALEKSEI YERKHOV.

Rwanda: Aşağı Dikmen Mah., Galip Erdem Cad. 62, Çankaya, Ankara; tel. (312) 4918434; fax (312) 4918490; e-mail ambankara@minaffet.gov.rw; Ambassador FIDELIS MIRONKO.

Saudi Arabia: Turan Emeksiz Sok. 6, 06700 Gaziosmanpaşa, Ankara; tel. (312) 4685540; fax (312) 4274886; e-mail tremb@mofa.gov.sa; Ambassador FAHAD BIN ASAAD ABU AL-NASR.

Senegal: Oran Mah., Ferit Recai Ertuğrul Cad. 33, Çankaya, Ankara; tel. (312) 4420046; fax (312) 4420056; e-mail senegalbuyukelciligi@gmail.com; Ambassador CHEIKH GUEYE.

Serbia: Remzi Oguz Arik Mah., Yazanlar Sok. 1, 06691 Kavaklıdere, Ankara; tel. (312) 4260236; fax (312) 4278345; e-mail embserank@gmail.com; internet www.ankara.mfa.gov.rs; Ambassador ZORAN V. MARKOVIĆ.

Sierra Leone: İlkbahar Mah., Medine Müdafii Cad. 608, Sok. 14, Ankara; tel. (312) 4906843; fax (312) 4913904; e-mail info@tr.slembassy.gov.sl; internet www.sierraleoneembassy.org.tr; Ambassador MOHAMED HASSAN KAISAMBA.

Singapore: Yıldızevler Mah. 719, Sok. 5, 06550 Çankaya, Ankara; tel. (312) 4424330; fax (312) 4426144; e-mail singemb_ank@mfa.sg; internet www.mfa.gov.sg/ankara; Ambassador KOK LI PENG (designate).

Slovakia: Atatürk Bul. 245, 06692 Kavaklıdere, Ankara; tel. (312) 4675075; fax (312) 4682689; e-mail emb.ankara@mzv.sk; internet www.mzv.sk/web/ankara; Ambassador JAN PSENICA.

Slovenia: Kırlangıç Sok. 36, 06700 Gaziosmanpaşa, Ankara; tel. (312) 4054221; e-mail sloembassy.ankara@gov.si; internet www.ankara.veleposlanistvo.si; Ambassador GORAZD RENČELJ (designate).

Somalia: Reşit Galip Cad. 100, 06700 Gaziosmanpaşa, Ankara; tel. (312) 4364028; fax (312) 4364029; e-mail ankaraembassy@mfa.gov.so; internet ankara.mfa.gov.so; Ambassador JAMA ABDULLAHI.

South Africa: Filistin Sok. 27, 06700 Gaziosmanpaşa, Ankara; tel. (312) 4056861; fax (312) 4466434; e-mail general.ankara@dirco.gov.za; internet www.southafrica.org.tr; Ambassador DIPUO LETSATSI-DUBA.

South Sudan: Kız Kulesi Sok. 1, Gaziosmanpaşa, Ankara; tel. (312) 4360285; fax (312) 4360284; e-mail info@southsudanankara.org; internet www.southsudanankara.org; Ambassador MAJOK GUANDONG THIEP.

Spain: Prof. Dr Aziz Sancar Cad. 8, 06690 Çankaya, Ankara; tel. (312) 4401796; fax (312) 4426991; e-mail emb.ankara@maec.es; internet www.exteriores.gob.es/embajadas/ankara; Ambassador FRANCISCO JAVIER HERGUETA GARNICA.

Sri Lanka: Kırlangıç Sok. 41, 06700 Gaziosmanpaşa, Ankara; tel. (312) 4271021; fax (312) 4271026; e-mail slemb.ankara@mfa.gov.lk; internet www.srilanka.org.tr; Ambassador S. H. U. DISSANAYAKE.

Sudan: Hilal Mah. 676, Turan Güneş Bul. Sok. 6, Çankaya, Ankara; tel. (312) 4466327; fax (312) 4468506; Ambassador NADIR YOUSIF EL-TAYEB.

Sweden: Katip Çelebi Sok. 7, 06692 Kavaklıdere, Ankara; tel. (312) 4554100; fax (312) 4554120; e-mail ambassaden.ankara@gov.se; internet www.swedenabroad.com/ankara; Ambassador STAFFAN HERRSTROM.

Switzerland: Atatürk Bul. 247, 06680 Kavaklıdere, Ankara; tel. (312) 4573100; fax (312) 4671199; e-mail ankara@eda.admin.ch; internet www.eda.admin.ch/ankara; Ambassador JEAN-DANIEL RUCH.

Tajikistan: Ferit Recai Ertuğrul Cad. 20, 25009 Oran, Ankara; tel. (312) 4911607; fax (312) 4911603; e-mail tajemb_turkey@yahoo.com; Ambassador ASHRAFJON GULOV.

Tanzania: İlkbahar Mah., Medine Müdafii Cad. 16, Çankaya, Ankara; tel. (312) 4901061; fax (312) 4901063; e-mail ankara@nje.go.tz; internet www.tr.tzembassy.go.tz; Ambassador IDDI SEIF BAKARI (designate).

Thailand: Koza Sok. 87, 06700 Gaziosmanpaşa, Ankara; tel. (312) 4374318; fax (312) 4378495; e-mail thiank@ttmail.com; internet www.thaiembassy.org/ankara; Ambassador APIRAT SUGONDHABHIROM.

Tunisia: Ferit Recai Ertuğrul Cad. 19, Oran Diplomatic Site, Ankara; tel. (312) 4919635; fax (312) 4919634; e-mail at.ankara@superonline.com; Ambassador AHMED BEN SGHAÏER (designate).

'Turkish Republic of Northern Cyprus': Rabat Sok. 20, 06700 Gaziosmanpaşa, Ankara; tel. (312) 4462920; fax (312) 4465238; e-mail ankara@mfa.gov.ct.tr; internet ankara.mfa.gov.ct.tr; Ambassador ISMET KORUKOĞLU.

TÜRKIYE (TURKEY)

Turkmenistan: Koza Sok. 28, 06700 Çankaya, Ankara; tel. (312) 4417122; fax (312) 4417125; e-mail tmankara@ttnet.net.tr; internet turkey.tmembassy.gov.tm; Ambassador MEKAN ISHANGULIYEV.

Uganda: Büyükesat Mah., Mahatma Gandi Cad. 55, Çankaya, Ankara; tel. (312) 4370195; fax (312) 4370178; e-mail ugandaembassyturkey@gmail.com; internet ugandaembassyankara.org; Ambassador NUSURA TIPERU.

Ukraine: Sancak Mah. 512, Sok. 17, 06550 Çankaya, Ankara; tel. (312) 4421593; fax (312) 4406815; e-mail emb_tr@mfa.gov.ua; internet turkey.mfa.gov.ua; Ambassador VASYL BODNAR.

United Arab Emirates: Sancak Mah., Doğu Kent Bul. 596, Sok. 5, Çankaya, Ankara; tel. (312) 4901414; fax (312) 4912333; e-mail ankara@mofa.gov.ae; internet www.mofaic.gov.ae/en/missions/ankara; Ambassador SAEED THANI HAREB AL-DHAHERI.

United Kingdom: Şehit Ersan Cad. 46/A, 06680 Çankaya, Ankara; tel. (312) 4553344; fax (312) 4553352; internet www.gov.uk/world/turkey; Ambassador JILL MORRIS.

USA: Atatürk Bul. 110, 06100 Kavaklıdere, Ankara; tel. (312) 4555555; fax (312) 4670019; e-mail webmasterankara@state.gov; internet tr.usembassy.gov; Ambassador JEFFRY LANE FLAKE.

Uzbekistan: Sancak Mah. 549, Sok. 3, Yıldız, 06550 Çankaya, Ankara; tel. (312) 4413871; fax (312) 4427058; e-mail uzemb_ankara@yahoo.com; internet www.uzembassy.org.tr; Ambassador ALISHER AGHZAMHODZHAYEV.

Venezuela: İlkbahar Mah., Gallip Erdem Cad. 608, Sok. 24, Çankaya, Ankara; tel. (312) 4412145; fax (312) 4406755; e-mail embve.tuank@mppre.gob.ve; internet turquia.embajada.gob.ve; Ambassador FREDDY MOLINA (designate).

Viet Nam: Birlik Mah. 14, Sok. 414, 06610 Çankaya, Ankara; tel. (312) 4468049; fax (312) 4465623; e-mail dsqvnturkey@yahoo.com; internet www.vietnamembassy-turkey.org; Ambassador DO SON HAI.

Yemen: Fethiye Sok. 2, 06700 Gaziosmanpaşa, Ankara; tel. (312) 4462637; fax (312) 4461778; e-mail yemenemb@superonline.com; Ambassador MUHAMMAD SALIH AHMED TARIQ.

Zambia: Mahatma Gandi Cad. 58, Gaziosmanpaşa, Çankaya, Ankara; tel. (312) 4909086; fax (312) 4909173; e-mail zambiaturkey@gmail.com; internet www.zambiaembassy.org.tr; Ambassador WILLIAM SIKAZWE.

Zimbabwe: Filistin Cad. 39, 06700 Ankara; tel. (312) 4467803; e-mail zimankara@zimfa.gov.zw; internet www.zimankara.org.tr; Ambassador ALFRED MUTIWAZUKA.

Judicial System

Until the foundation of the Republic of Turkey (now Türkiye), a large part of the Turkish civil law—the laws affecting the family, inheritance, property, obligations, etc.—was based on the Koran, and this holy law was administered by special religious (Shari'a) courts. The legal reform of 1926 was not only a process of secularization, but also a radical change of the legal system. The Swiss Civil Code and the Code of Obligation, the Italian Penal Code and the Neuchâtel (Cantonal) Code of Civil Procedure were adopted and modified to fit Turkish customs and traditions.

According to current Turkish law, the power of the judiciary is exercised by judicial (criminal), military and administrative courts. These courts render their verdicts in the first instance, while superior courts examine the verdict for subsequent rulings.

Constitutional Court: Ahlatlıbel Mah., İncek Şehit Savcı, Mehmet Selim Kiraz Bul. 4, 06805 Çankaya, Ankara; tel. (312) 4637300; fax (312) 4637400; e-mail bilgi@anayasa.gov.tr; internet constitutionalcourt.gov.tr. Consists of 17 members, appointed by the President. Reviews the constitutionality of laws, at the request of the President of the Republic, parliamentary groups of the governing party or of the main opposition party, or of one-fifth of the members of the National Assembly, and sits as a high council empowered to try senior members of state. The rulings of the Constitutional Court are final. Decisions of the Court are published immediately in the Official Gazette, and shall be binding on the legislative, executive and judicial organs of the state; Chief Justice ZÜHTÜ ARSLAN.

Court of Cassation: Atatürk Bul. 100, 06658 Bakanlıklar, Ankara; tel. (312) 4161000; e-mail iletisim@yargitay.gov.tr; internet www.yargitay.gov.tr. Court of the last instance for reviewing the decisions and verdicts rendered by judicial courts. It has original and final jurisdiction in specific cases defined by law. Members are elected by the Supreme Council of Judges and Public Prosecutors; Chief Justice MEHMET AKARCA.

Council of State: Üniversiteler Mah., Dumlupınar Bul. 149, Eskişehir Yolu 10, Çankaya, Ankara; tel. (312) 2531000; fax (312) 2531001; internet danistay.gov.tr. An administrative court of the first and last instance in matters not referred by law to other administrative courts, and an administrative court of the last instance in general. Hears and settles administrative disputes and expresses opinions on draft laws submitted by the Council of Ministers. Three-quarters of the members are appointed by the Supreme Council of Judges and Public Prosecutors; the remaining quarter is selected by the President of the Republic; Pres. ZEKI YIĞIT.

Military Court of Appeals: A court of the last instance to review decisions and verdicts rendered by military courts, and a court of first and last instance with jurisdiction over certain military persons, stipulated by law, with responsibility for the specific trials of these persons. Members are selected by the President of the Republic from nominations made by the Military Court of Appeals.

Supreme Military Administrative Court: A military court for the judicial control of administrative acts concerning military personnel. Members are selected by the President of the Republic from nominations made by the Court.

Court of Jurisdictional Disputes: Settles disputes among judicial, administrative and military courts arising from disagreements on jurisdictional matters and verdicts.

Court of Accounts: A court charged with the auditing of all accounts of revenue, expenditure and government property, which renders rulings related to transactions and accounts of authorized bodies on behalf of the National Assembly.

Council of Judges and Prosecutors (CJP): 06330 Yenimahalle, Ankara; tel. (312) 2041000; fax (312) 2227145; e-mail proje@hsk.gov.tr; internet www.cjp.gov.tr. The Minister of Justice serves as the President of the Supreme Council, while the Under-Secretary to the Minister of Justice is an ex officio member. The remaining 20 members of the Council comprise four appointed directly by the President of the Republic, three nominated by the Court of Appeals, two by the Council of State, one by the Justice Academy and 10 elected by judges and prosecutors; each of these members is appointed for a four-year term. Decides all personnel matters relating to judges and public prosecutors; Pres. YILMAZ TUNÇ (Minister of Justice).

Public Prosecutor: The law shall make provision for the tenure of public prosecutors and attorneys of the Council of State and their functions. The Chief Prosecutor of the Republic, the Chief Attorney of the Council of State and the Chief Prosecutor of the Military Court of Appeals are subject to the provisions applicable to judges of higher courts.

Office of the General Prosecutor of the Supreme Court of Appeals: Ehlibeyt Mah. 1242, Cad. 34, Balgat, Ankara; tel. (312) 5733500; Gen. Prosecutor BEKIR ŞAHIN.

Military Trial: Military trials are conducted by military and disciplinary courts. These courts are entitled to try the military offences of military personnel and those offences committed against military personnel or in military areas, or offences connected with military service and duties. Military courts may try non-military persons only for military offences prescribed by special laws.

Religion

ISLAM

Turkish children are officially designated Muslim at birth unless their parents are adherents of another state-recognized religion; this means that some 99% of the population are officially Muslim. However, Türkiye is a secular state. Although Islam was specified as the official religion in the Constitution of 1924, an amendment in 1928 removed this privilege. Since 1950 a number of Governments have tried to re-establish links between religion and state affairs, but secularity was protected by the revolution of 1960, the 1980 military takeover and the 1982 Constitution.

Diyanet İşleri Başkanlığı (Presidency of Religious Affairs): Üniversiteler Mah., Dumlupınar Bul. No. 147/A, 06800 Çankaya, Ankara; tel. (312) 2957000; e-mail basin@diyanet.gov.tr; internet www.diyanet.gov.tr; Pres. Prof. Dr ALI ERBAŞ.

CHRISTIANITY

The town of Antioch (now Antakya) was one of the earliest strongholds of Christianity, and by the 4th century CE had become a patriarchal see. Formerly in Syria, the town was incorporated into Turkey (now Türkiye) in 1939. Constantinople (now İstanbul) was also a patriarchal see, and by the 6th century the Patriarch of Constantinople was recognized as the Ecumenical Patriarch in the East. Gradual estrangement from Rome developed, leading to the final breach between the Catholic West and the Orthodox East, usually assigned to the year 1054.

There are estimated to be about 100,000 Christians in Türkiye.

The Orthodox Churches

Armenian Patriarchate: Ermeni Patrikliği, Sevgi Sok. 6, 34130 Kumkapı, İstanbul; tel. (212) 5170970; fax (212) 5164833; e-mail

TÜRKIYE (TURKEY)

haybadtivan@gmail.com; internet www.turkiyeermenileripatrikligi.com; f. 1461; 100,000 adherents (incl. workers from Armenia—2007); Patriarch Archbishop SAHAK MASHALIAN; Deputy Patriarch Fr KRIKOR DAMADIAN.

Bulgarian Orthodox Church: Bulgar Ortodoks Kilisesi, Halâskâr Gazi Cad. 319, Şişli, İstanbul; Rev. Archimandrite GANCO ÇOBANOF.

Greek Orthodox Church: The Ecumenical Patriarchate (Rum Ortodoks Patrikhanesi), Sadrazam Ali Paşa Cad. 35, 34220 Fener-Haliç, İstanbul; tel. (212) 5255416; e-mail ecpatr.pressoffice@gmail.com; internet www.ec-patr.org; Archbishop of Constantinople (New Rome) and Ecumenical Patriarch BARTHOLOMEW I.

The Roman Catholic Church

Türkiye Catholic Bishops' Conference: Conferenza Episcopale Cattolica di Turchia, Satırcı Sok. 2, Şişli, 34373 İstanbul; tel. (212) 2307312; fax (212) 2303195; e-mail cet@katolik-kilisesi.org; internet www.katolik-kilisesi.org; f. 1976; Pres. Most Rev. MARTIN KMETEC (Archbishop of İzmir).

Armenian Rite

Patriarchate of Cilicia: f. 1742; RAPHAËL BEDROS XXI MINASSIAN (resident in Beirut, Lebanon).

Archdiocese of İstanbul: Sakızağacı Cad. 31, PK 183, 80072 Beyoğlu, İstanbul; tel. (212) 2441258; fax (212) 2432364; f. 1928; Archbishop LÉVON BOGHOS ZÉKIYAN.

Latin Rite

Metropolitan Archdiocese of İzmir: Church of St Polycarp, Necatibey Bul. 2, PK 267, 35210 İzmir; tel. (232) 4840531; fax (232) 4845358; e-mail curiaves@yahoo.it; f. 1818; Archbishop of İzmir Most Rev. MARTIN KMETEC.

Apostolic Vicariate of Anatolia: Mithat Paša Cad. 5, PK 75, 31201 İskenderun; tel. (535) 9272823; fax (326) 6139291; f. 1990; Vicar Apostolic PAOLO BIZZETI.

Apostolic Vicariate of İstanbul: Papa Roncalli Sok. 65A, 34373 İnönü Mah., Şişli, İstanbul; tel. (212) 2480775; fax (212) 2411543; e-mail vapostolique@yahoo.fr; f. 1742; Vicar Apostolic MASSIMILIANO PALINURO.

Maronite Rite

The Maronite Patriarch of Antioch, Cardinal Nasrallah Pierre Sfeir, is resident in Bkerké, Lebanon.

Melkite Rite

The Greek Melkite Patriarch of Antioch, Grégoire III Laham, is resident in Damascus, Syria.

Syrian Rite

The Syrian Catholic Patriarch of Antioch, Ignace Pierre VIII Abdel Ahad, is resident in Beirut, Lebanon.

Patriarchal Exarchate of Türkiye: Sarayarkası Sok. 15, PK 84, 34437 Ayazpaşa, İstanbul; tel. (212) 2432521; fax (212) 2490261; e-mail info@suryanikatolikkilisesi.com; f. 1908; Patriarchal Exarch Fr ORHAN ÇANLI.

The Anglican Communion

Within the Church of England, Türkiye forms part of the diocese of Gibraltar in Europe. The Bishop is resident in the United Kingdom.

Anglican Chaplaincy in İstanbul: Christ Church, Serdar Ekram Sok. 82, Karaköy, İstanbul; tel. (212) 2515616; fax (212) 2435702; e-mail anglicanistanbul1@gmail.com; Chaplain Rev. Canon IAN SHERWOOD.

JUDAISM

There are estimated to be about 23,000 Jews in Türkiye.

Jewish Community of Türkiye: Türkiye Hahambaşılığı, Yemenici Sok. 23, Beyoğlu, 34430 Tünel, İstanbul; tel. (212) 2938794; fax (212) 2441980; e-mail info@musevicemaati.com; internet www.musevicemaati.com; Chief Rabbi ISAK HALEVA.

The Press

PRINCIPAL DAILIES

Akşam (Evening): Davutpaşa Cad. 31, Küçükçekmece, İstanbul; tel. (212) 4493000; fax (212) 4819561; e-mail editor@aksam.com.tr; internet www.aksam.com.tr; publ. by Türkmedya AŞ; Chief Editor MURAT KELKITLIOĞLU.

Bugün (Today): Meliha Avni Sozen Cad. 17, Mecidiyeköy, Sisli, İstanbul; tel. and fax (212) 3558500; internet www.bugun.com.tr; f. 2003; publ. by Koza Davetiye; News Dir MURAT TAŞKIN.

Cumhuriyet (Republic): Prof. Nurettin Mazhar Öktel Sok. 2, 34381 Şişli, İstanbul; tel. (212) 3437274; fax (212) 3437264; e-mail webeditor@cumhuriyet.com.tr; internet www.cumhuriyet.com.tr; f. 1924; morning; left-wing, nationalist; Editor-in-Chief AYKUT KÜÇÜKKAYA.

Fotomaç: Barbaros Bul. 153, Cam Han, Beşiktaş, İstanbul; tel. (212) 3543368; fax (212) 3543557; e-mail spor@fotomac.com.tr; internet www.fotomac.com.tr; f. 1991; sport; publ. by Turkuvaz Radyo Televizyon Gazetecilik ve Yayıncılık AŞ (a subsidiary of Çalık Holding); Editor-in-Chief ZEKI UZUNDURUKAN.

Gazete Haberturk: Abdülhakhamit Cad. 25, Beyoğlu, İstanbul; tel. (212) 3136000; fax (212) 3136590; e-mail internet@haberturk.com; internet www.haberturk.com; f. March 2009; publ. by Ciner Yayın Holding; Editor-in-Chief GÜLIN ÇELIKLER.

Günes (Sun): İkitelli, Atatürk Mah., Bahariye Cad. 31, Küçükçekmece, İstanbul; tel. (212) 4493010; fax (212) 4819924; internet www.gunes.com; f. 1997; publ. by Türkmedya AŞ; Editor-in-Chief TURGAY GÜLER.

Hürriyet (Freedom): Hürriyet Dünyası, 100. Yıl Mah., 78 Matbaacılar Cad., 34204 Bağcılar, İstanbul; tel. (212) 6770000; e-mail interneteditor@hurriyet.com.tr; internet www.hurriyet.com.tr; f. 1948; morning; political; independent; publ. by Demirören Media Group; Man. Dir DENIZ AYAS.

Hürriyet Daily News: Hürriyet Dünyası, 100. Yıl Mah., 2264 Sok., 34204 Bağcılar, İstanbul; tel. (212) 6770000; fax (212) 4496014; e-mail hdnmail@hurriyet.com.tr; internet www.hurriyetdailynews.com; f. 1961 as Daily News; later renamed Turkish Daily News; renamed as above 2000; English language; publ. by Hürriyet Gazetecilik ve Matbaacılık AŞ; Editor-in-Chief GÖKÇE AYTULU.

Milliyet: Demirören Medya Center 1/51, 100. Yıl Mah, 2264 Sok., Bağcılar, İstanbul; tel. (212) 3379999; e-mail milliyetdijital@milliyet.com.tr; internet www.milliyet.com.tr; f. 1950; morning; political; publ. by Demirören Media Group; Man. Dir SULEYMAN KAYA.

Posta (Post): Kuştepe Mah., Mecidiyeköy Yolu Cad., Trump Towers Kule, 34387 Şişli, İstanbul; tel. (212) 5056111; fax (212) 5056520; e-mail internetreklam@posta.com.tr; internet www.posta.com.tr; f. 1995; publ. by Demirören Gazetecilik AŞ (Demirören Group); Chair. YILDIRIM DEMIRÖREN.

Radikal: 100 Yıl Mah., 78 Matbaacılar Cad., 34204 Bağcılar, İstanbul; tel. (212) 6770000; fax (212) 4496209; internet www.radikal.com.tr; f. 1996; liberal; merged with economics and business daily Referans 2010; publ. by Hürriyet Gazetecilik ve Matbaacılık A.Ş; Editor-in-Chief CEM ERCIYES.

Sabah (Morning): Barbaros Bul. 153, Cam Han, Beşiktaş, İstanbul; tel. (212) 3543000; e-mail editor@sabah.com.tr; internet www.sabah.com.tr; publ. by Turkuvaz Radyo Televizyon ve Gazetecilik AŞ (a subsidiary of Çalık Holding); Exec. Editor ERDAL ŞAFAK.

Star: Atatürk Mah., 31 Bahariye Cad., İkitelli, 34679 Küçükçekmece, İstanbul; tel. (212) 4732000; fax (212) 4732094; e-mail editor@stargazete.com; internet www.stargazete.com; f. 1999; Man. Editor NUH ALBAYRAK.

Takvim (Calendar): Barbaros Bul. 153, Cam Han 5, Beşiktaş, İstanbul; tel. (212) 3543000; fax (212) 3543769; e-mail takvim@takvim.com.tr; internet www.takvim.com.tr; lifestyle, entertainment and sport; publ. by Turkuvaz Radyo Televizyon ve Gazetecilik AŞ (a subsidiary of Çalık Holding); Man. Editor ERGÜN DILER.

Türkiye: 29 Merkez Mah., Ekim Cad., 34197 Yenibosna, İstanbul; tel. (212) 4543000; fax (212) 4543100; e-mail info@turkiyegazetesi.com.tr; internet www.turkiyegazetesi.com.tr; f. 1970; nationalist, pro-Islamic; Editor-in-Chief ISMAIL KAPAN.

Vakit (Time): Evren Mah., Bahar Cad., 24 Şehit Doğan Öztürk Sok., Bağcılar, İstanbul; tel. (212) 5509004; fax (212) 5507099; e-mail haber@vakit.com.tr; internet www.vakit.com.tr; f. 1978; Editor-in-Chief MUZAFFER ARAN.

Yeni Asır (New Century): İsmet Kaptan Mah., Gaziosmanpaşa Bul. 5, 35260 Çankaya, İzmir; tel. (232) 4883480; fax (232) 4464222; e-mail yasir@yeniasir.com.tr; internet www.yeniasir.com; f. 1895; political; publ. by Turkuvaz Haberleşme ve Yayıncılık AŞ (subsidiary of Çalik Holding); Editorial Dir ERCAN DEMIR.

Yeni Çağ (New Age): Çobançeşme Mah., Kalender Sok. 12, 34196 Yenibosna, İstanbul; tel. (212) 4524040; fax (212) 4524058; e-mail irtibat@yenicaggazetesi.com.tr; internet www.yenicaggazetesi.com.tr; f. 2002; nationalist; Editor-in-Chief HAYRI KÖKLÜ.

Yeni Şafak (New Dawn): Maltepe Mah. 6, Fetih Cad. 4, Topkapı, İstanbul; tel. (212) 6122930; fax (212) 6121903; e-mail iletişim@yenisafak.com; internet yenisafak.com; f. 1995; Editor-in-Chief ERSIN ÇELIK.

TÜRKIYE (TURKEY)

WEEKLIES

BusinessWeek Türkiye: Ebulula Mardin Cad. 83, İstanbul; tel. (212) 3245515; fax (212) 3245505; e-mail destek@infomag.com.tr; internet www.businessweek.com.tr; business and economics; publ. by Infomag Publishing Ltd and Bloomberg LP (USA); Man. Editor SERDAR TURAN.

Ekonomist: Hürriyet Medya Towers, 34212 Güneşli, İstanbul; tel. (212) 4103200; fax (212) 41032554103581; e-mail ekonomist@doganburda.com; internet www.ekonomist.com.tr; f. 1991; business and economics; publ. by Doğan Burda Dergi Yayıncılık ve Pazarlama AŞ; Man. Editor Dr ORHAN KARACA.

Newsweek Türkiye: Abdülhakhamit Cad. 25, Beyoğlu, İstanbul; tel. (212) 3136000; fax (212) 3137455; internet www.newsweek.com.tr; news, business, economics; publ. by Ciner Gazete Dergi Basım Yayıncılık Sanayi ve Ticaret AŞ; Man. Editor SELÇUK TEPELI.

Para: Para Dergisi, Barbaros Bul. 153, Cam Han, Beşiktaş, İstanbul; tel. (212) 3543000; fax (212) 3543792; e-mail para@paradergi.com.tr; internet www.paradergi.com.tr; business and economics; publ. by Turkuvaz Gazete Dergi Basım AŞ; Man. Editor OĞUZ DEMIR.

Tempo: Trump Towers Kule 2, Şişli, İstanbul; tel. (212) 4103200; fax (212) 4103311; e-mail tempo@doganburda.com; internet www.tempomag.com.tr; f. 1987; celebrity gossip, lifestyle; publ. by Doğan Burda Dergi Yayıncılık ve Pazarlama AŞ; Editor-in-Chief AYŞEGÜL SAVUR ÖZGEN.

Vatan (Homeland): Demirören Medya Center 1/51, 100 Yıl Mah, 2264 Sok., Bağcılar, İstanbul; tel. (212) 3042100; e-mail gazetevatandijital@gazetevatan.com; internet www.gazetevatan.com; f. 2002; publ. by Demirören Media Group; Man. Dir ERKAN MENGI.

Yeni Aktüel: Barbaros Bul. 153, Cam Han, Beşiktaş, İstanbul; tel. (212) 3543000; fax (212) 3543792; internet www.sabah.com.tr/aktuel; culture; publ. by Turkuvaz Gazete Dergi Basım AŞ; Man. Editor DEFNE ASAL ER.

PERIODICALS

Atlas: Trump Towers, Kule 2, 34387 Şişli, İstanbul; tel. (212) 4103200; fax (212) 4103564; e-mail atlas@doganburda.com; internet www.atlasdergisi.com; f. 1993; monthly; archaeology, geography; publ. by Doğan Burda Dergi Yayıncılık ve Pazarlama AŞ; Publ. Dir MURAT KÖKSAL.

Capital: Trump Towers, Kule 2, 34387 Şişli, İstanbul; tel. (212) 4103228; fax (212) 4103227; e-mail capital@doganburda.com; internet www.capital.com.tr; f. 1993; monthly; business, economics; publ. by Doğan Burda Dergi Yayıncılık ve Pazarlama AŞ; Man. Editor SEDEF SEÇKIN BÜYÜK.

Chip: Kuştepe Mah., 12 Mecidiyeköy Yolu Cad., Trump Towers Kule 2, 34387 Şişli, İstanbul; tel. (212) 4103152; fax (212) 4103216; internet www.chip.com.tr; f. 1996; monthly; computing; publ. by Doğan Burda Dergi Yayıncılık ve Pazarlama AŞ; Publ. Dir CENK TARHAN.

Global: Büyükdere Cad. 65, Saadet Apt 8/15, Mecidiyeköy, İstanbul; tel. (212) 2133736; fax (212) 2133735; internet www.globaldergisi.com; business, economics; Man. Editor MÜGE MEŞE.

Güncel Hukuk: Trump Towers Kule 2, 34387 Şişli, İstanbul; tel. (212) 4103200; fax (212) 4103581; e-mail guncelhukuk@doganburda.com; internet www.guncelhukuk.com.tr; monthly; law; publ. by Doğan Burda Dergi Yayıncılık ve Pazarlama AŞ; Editor-in-Chief Prof. Dr KÖKSAL BAYRAKTAR.

Infomag: Ebulula Mardin Cad. 83, Beşiktaş, İstanbul; tel. (212) 3245515; fax (212) 3245505; e-mail info@infomag.com.tr; internet www.infomag.com.tr; monthly; business; Man. Editor SERDAR TURAN.

Platin: Akpınar Mah., Hasan Basri Cad. 4, İstanbul; tel. (212) 4493050; e-mail info@platinonline.com; internet www.platinonline.com; monthly; business, economics; publ. by Türkmedya AŞ; Man. Editor BAHAR AKGÜN.

NEWS AGENCIES

Anadolu Ajansı: GMK Bul. 132, 06430 Maltepe, Ankara; tel. (312) 9992420; fax (312) 2318446; e-mail kurumsaliletisim@aa.com.tr; internet www.aa.com.tr; f. 1920; Chair. and Dir-Gen. ŞENOL KAZANCI.

ANKA Haber Ajansı: Atatürk Bul. 154B, Çankaya, Ankara; tel. (312) 5144140; e-mail haber@ankahaber.net; internet ankahaber.net; Dir-Gen. GOKSEL BOZKURT.

Bagımsız Basın Ajansı (BBA): Değirmenler Çıkmazı 6, Mahmut Şevket Paşa Köyü, 34829 Beykoz, İstanbul; tel. (216) 3194804; fax (216) 3194921; e-mail bba@bba.tv; internet www.bba.tv; f. 1971; provides camera crew, editing and satellite services in Türkiye, the Balkans, the Middle East and the former Soviet republics to broadcasters worldwide; Co-Pres FERIT KAYABAL, KADRI KAYABAL.

Doğan Haber Ajansı (Doğan News Agency): Doğan TV Center, 34204 Bağcılar, İstanbul; tel. (212) 4135555; fax (212) 4135598; e-mail ajans@dha.com.tr; internet www.dha.com.tr; f. 1999 by merger of Hürriyet Haber Ajansı and Milliyet Haber Ajansı; subsidiary of Doğan Yayın Holding (Doğan Media Group); 34 bureaux worldwide; Dir-Gen. KUBILAY GÜLBEK.

İKA Haber Ajansı (Economic and Commercial News Agency): Atatürk Bul. 199/A-45, Kavaklıdere, Ankara; f. 1954; Dir ZIYA TANSU.

TEBA—Türk Ekonomik Basın Ajansı (Turkish Economic Press Agency): Süleyman Hacı Abdullahoğlu Cad. 5, D3 Balgat, Ankara; tel. (312) 2842006; fax (312) 2840638; e-mail teba@tebahaber.com.tr; internet www.tebahaber.com.tr; f. 1981; private economic news service; Propr YELDA CALTAS; Editor AKIN TOKATLI.

Ulusal Basın Ajansı (UBA): Meşrutiyet Cad. 5/10, Ankara; Man. Editor OĞUZ SEREN.

JOURNALISTS' ASSOCIATION

Türkiye Gazeteciler Cemiyeti: Türkocağı Cad. 1, Cağaloğlu, İstanbul; tel. (212) 5138300; fax (212) 5268046; e-mail cemiyet@tgc.org.tr; internet www.tgc.org.tr; f. 1946; Pres. TURGAY OLCAYTO; Sec.-Gen. SIBEL GÜNEŞ.

Publishers

Altın Kitaplar Yayınevi Anonim ŞTİ: Gülbahar Mah. Altan Erbulak Cad. 3, Sok. 14, İstanbul; tel. (212) 4463888; e-mail iletisim@altinkitaplar.com.tr; internet www.altinkitaplar.com.tr; f. 1959; fiction, non-fiction, biography, children's books, encyclopedias, dictionaries; Publrs FETHI UL, TURHAN BOZKURT; Chief Editor MÜRSIT UL.

Arkadas Co Ltd: Yuva Mah. 3702, Sok. 4, 06105 Yenimahalle, Ankara; tel. (312) 3960111; fax (312) 3960141; e-mail info@arkadas.com.tr; internet www.arkadas.com.tr; f. 1980; fiction, educational and reference books; Gen. Man. CUMHUR ÖZDEMIR.

Arkeoloji ve Sanat Yayınları (Archaeology and Art Publications): Hayriye Cad. 5/2 Mateo Mratoviç Apt., 34425 Beyoğlu, İstanbul; tel. (212) 2930378; fax (212) 2456877; e-mail info@arkeolojisanat.com; internet www.arkeolojisanat.com; f. 1978; classical, Byzantine and Turkish studies, art and archaeology, numismatics and ethnography books; Publr NEZIH BASGELEN; Senior Editor AHMET BAŞGELEN.

Bilgi Yayınevi: Meşrutiyet Cad. 46/A, Yenişehir, 06420 Ankara; tel. (312) 4318122; fax (312) 4317758; e-mail info@bilgiyayinevi.com.tr; internet www.bilgiyayinevi.com.tr.

Doğan Burda Dergi Yayıncılık ve Pazarlama AŞ: Trump Towers, 34387 Şişli, İstanbul; tel. (212) 4780300; fax (212) 4103581; e-mail dalan@doganburda.com; internet www.doganburda.com; jt venture between Doğan Yayın Holding (Doğan Media Group) and Hubert Burda Media Holding GmbH & Co KG (Germany); publishes 27 magazines and periodicals; Chair. Dr BEGÜMHAN DOĞAN FARALYALI; CEO MELIH CEM BASAR.

Iletisim Yayınları: Binbirdirek Meydanı Sok., Iletisim Han 3, 34122 Cağaloğlu, İstanbul; tel. (212) 5162260; fax (212) 5161258; e-mail iletisim@iletisim.com.tr; internet www.iletisim.com.tr; f. 1984; fiction, non-fiction, encyclopedias, reference.

Inkilap Kitabevi: Çobançeşme Mah. Altay Sok. 8 Yenibosna, İstanbul; tel. (212) 4961111; fax (212) 4961112; e-mail siparis@inkilap.com; internet www.inkilap.com; f. 1935; general reference and fiction; Man. Dir A. FIKRI; Dir of Foreign Rights S. DIKER.

Kabalci Yayınevi: Abbasağa Mah. Yıldız Cad. 51/1, Beşiktaş, İstanbul; tel. (212) 5226305; fax (212) 5268495; e-mail support@kabalci.com.tr; internet www.kabalci.com.tr; art, history, literature, social sciences; Pres. SABRI KABALCI.

Metis Yayınları: Ipek Sok. 5, 34433 Beyoğlu, İstanbul; tel. (212) 2454696; fax (212) 2454519; e-mail bilgi@metiskitap.com; internet www.metiskitap.com; f. 1982; fiction, literature, non-fiction, social sciences; Dir SEMIH SÖKMEN.

Nobel Medical Publishing: Millet Cad. 111 Çapa, İstanbul; tel. (212) 6328333; fax (212) 5870217; e-mail destek@nobeltip.com; internet www.nobeltip.com; f. 1974; medical books and journals; CEO ERSAL BINGÖL.

Nurdan Yayınları Sanayi ve Ticaret Ltd Sti: Saray Mah., Ahmet Tevfik İleri 17, Ümraniye, İstanbul; tel. (212) 6321123; fax (212) 6324224; e-mail iletisim@nurdanyayinlari.com; internet www.nurdanyayinlari.com; f. 1980; children's and educational; Dir NURDAN TÜZÜNER; Editor ÇIĞDEM TÜZÜNER.

Parantez Yayınları AŞ: Asmalı Mescid Mah. Tünel Meydanı, Tünel Geçidi İşhanı C Blok, D 424 Beyoğlu, İstanbul; tel. and fax (212) 2526516; e-mail parantez@yahoo.com; internet www.parantez.net; f. 1991; Publr METIN ZEYNIOĞLU.

TÜRKIYE (TURKEY) — Directory

Payel Yayınevi: Cağaloğlu Yokusu Evren han Kat 3/51, 34400 Cağaloğlu, İstanbul; tel. (212) 5284409; fax (212) 5124353; f. 1966; science, history, literature; Editor AHMET ÖZTÜRK.

Remzi Kitabevi AŞ: Akmerkez E3 Blok Kat. 14, Etiler, İstanbul; tel. (212) 2822080; fax (212) 2822090; e-mail post@remzi.com.tr; internet www.remzi.com.tr; f. 1927; general and educational; Dirs EROL ERDURAN, ÖMER ERDURAN, AHMET ERDURAN.

Seckin Yayınevi, Inc.: Eskişehir Yolu, Mustafa Kemal Mah. 2158, Sok. 13, Çankaya, Ankara; tel. (312) 4353030; fax (312) 4352472; e-mail seckin@seckin.com.tr; internet www.seckin.com.tr; f. 1959; accounting, computer science, economics, law, engineering; CEO KORAY SEÇKIN.

Türk Dil Kurumu (Turkish Language Institute): Atatürk Bul. 217, 06680 Kavaklıdere, Ankara; tel. (312) 4575200; fax (312) 4680783; e-mail bilgi@tdk.gov.tr; internet tdk.gov.tr; f. 1932; non-fiction, research, language; Pres. Prof. Dr GÜRER GÜLSEVIN.

Varlık Yayınları AŞ: Perpa Ticaret Merkezi, B Blok, Şişli, 34384 İstanbul; tel. (212) 2213171; fax (212) 3200646; e-mail varlik@varlik.com.tr; internet www.varlik.com.tr; f. 1933; fiction and non-fiction books, and cultural monthly review; Dirs FILIZ NAYIR DENIZTEKIN, METE TIL.

GOVERNMENT PUBLISHING HOUSE

Ministry of Culture and Tourism: İsmet İnönü Bul. 32, 06100 Ankara; tel. (312) 4708000; fax (312) 2315036; e-mail yayimlar@kutuphanelergm.gov.tr; internet www.kultur.gov.tr; f. 1973; Dir ALI OSMAN GÜZEL.

PUBLISHERS' ASSOCIATION

Türkiye Yayıncılar Birliği Derneği (Turkish Publishers' Association): İnönü Cad., Opera Apt. 43, D.4 34437 Gümüşsuyu, İstanbul; tel. (212) 5125602; fax (212) 5117794; e-mail info@turkyaybir.org.tr; internet www.turkyaybir.org.tr; f. 1985; Pres. KENAN KOCATÜRK; Gen. Sec. NAZLI BERIVAN AK; 416 mems (2022).

Broadcasting and Communications

TELECOMMUNICATIONS

TT Mobil İletişim Hizmetleri AŞ: Abdi İpekçi Cad. 75, 34367 Maçka, İstanbul; tel. (212) 4441444; fax (312) 3060732; internet www.ttmobil.com.tr; f. Feb. 2004 as TT&TIM İletişim Hizmetleri AŞ; present name adopted Jan. 2016; provides mobile telecommunications services; Chair. Dr ÖMER FATIH SAYAN; CEO ÜMIT ÖNAL.

Türk Telekomünikasyon AŞ (Türk Telekom): Turgut Özal Bul., 06103 Aydınlıkevler, Ankara; tel. (312) 4441444; fax (312) 3060732; internet www.turktelekom.com.tr; 55% owned by Oger Telecoms Joint Venture Group, 25% by Turkish Govt, 5% by Türkiye Wealth Fund and 15% is publicly traded; Chair. Dr ÖMER FATIH SAYAN; CEO ÜMIT ÖNAL.

Turkcell İletişim Hizmetleri AŞ: Turkcell Küçükyalı Plaza, Aydınevler Mah., İnönü Cad. 20, Küçükyalı Ofispark, B Blok, Maltepe, İstanbul; tel. (212) 3131000; fax (212) 5044058; e-mail musteri.hizmetleri@turkcell.com.tr; internet www.turkcell.com.tr; f. 1994; provides mobile telecommunications services; Chair. BÜLENT AKSU; CEO MURAT ERKAN.

Türksat AŞ: Yağlıpınar Mah., Türksat (Küme Evler), İdari Bina Apt 1, Gölbaşı, Ankara; tel. (312) 9253000; fax (850) 8044444; e-mail info@turksat.com.tr; internet www.turksat.com.tr; satellite and cable telecommunications services; Chair. Prof. KEMAL YÜKSEK; Gen. Man. HASAN HÜSEYIN ERTOK.

Vodafone Telekomünikasyon AŞ (Vodafone Türkiye): İdealtepe Mah., Denizciler Cad., Dik Sok. 12-10, 34841 Küçükyalı Maltepe, İstanbul; tel. (212) 5420000; fax (212) 5425000; internet www.vodafone.com.tr; f. 1994 as Telsim; name changed 2006, following acquisition by Vodafone Group PLC (UK); offers mobile telecommunications services; CEO ENGIN AKSOY.

Regulatory Authorities

Bilgi Teknolojileri ve İletişim Kurumu (Information and Communication Technologies Authority): 276 Eskişehir Yolu Km 10, 06530 Çankaya, Ankara; tel. (312) 2947200; fax (312) 2947145; e-mail info@btk.gov.tr; internet www.btk.gov.tr; f. 2000; Chair. Dr ÖMER ABDULLAH KARAGÖZOĞLU.

Directorate of Communications: 144 Mevlana Bul., Çankaya, Ankara; tel. (312) 5902000; e-mail webinfo@iletisim.gov.tr; internet www.iletisim.gov.tr; Dir FAHRETTIN ALTUN.

BROADCASTING

Regulatory Authority

Radyo ve Televizyon Üst Kurulu (RTÜK) (Radio and Television Supreme Council): Üniversiteler Mah. 1597, Cad. No. 13 Bilkent, 06800 Ankara; tel. (312) 2975000; e-mail rtuk@rtuk.gov.tr; internet www.rtuk.org.tr; f. 1994; responsible for assignment of channels, frequencies and bands, controls transmitting facilities of radio stations and TV networks, draws up regulations on related matters, monitors broadcasting and issues warnings in case of violation of the broadcasting law; Pres. EBUBEKIR ŞAHIN.

Radio

Türkiye Radyo ve Televizyon Kurumu (TRT) (Turkish Radio and Television Corpn): Turan Güneş Bul., 06550 Oran, Ankara; tel. (312) 4634343; fax (312) 4633177; e-mail tsr@trt.net.tr; internet www.trt.net.tr; f. 1964; controls Turkish radio and television services, incl. 4 national radio channels; Dir-Gen. Prof. Dr MEHMET ZAHID SOBACI.

There are also more than 50 local radio stations, an educational radio service for schools and a station run by the Turkish State Meteorological Service. The US forces have their own radio and television service.

Television

Digitürk: Cihannüma Mah., 34363 İstanbul; tel. (212) 4737373; fax (212) 3260099; e-mail pr@digiturk.com.tr; internet www.digiturk.com.tr; f. 1999; subscription-based satellite television service offering 170 channels; also internet service provider; owned by beIN Media Group (Qatar); CEO YOUSUF AL-OBAIDLY.

Türkiye Radyo ve Televizyon Kurumu (TRT) (Turkish Radio and Television Corpn): Turan Güneş Bul., 06550 Oran, Ankara; tel. (312) 4634343; e-mail trtgenelmudurlugu@hs01.kep.tr; internet www.trt.net.tr; f. 1964; four national, one regional and two international channels in 2008; Kurdish-language channel (TRT 6) launched 2009; Arabic-language service (TRT 7) launched 2010; Dir-Gen. Prof. Dr MEHMET ZAHID SOBACI.

Finance

BANKING

Regulatory Authority

Bancacılık Düzenleme ve Denetleme Kurumu (BDDK) (Banking Regulation and Supervisory Agency): Buyukdere Cad. 106, Esentepe Şişli, İstanbul; tel. (212) 2145000; internet www.bddk.org.tr; f. 1999; Chair. Prof. ŞAHAP KAVCIOĞLU.

Central Bank

Türkiye Cumhuriyet Merkez Bankası AŞ (Central Bank of the Republic of Türkiye): Hacı Bayram Mah., İstiklal Cad. 10, 06050 Ankara; tel. (312) 5075000; fax (312) 5075640; internet www.tcmb.gov.tr; f. 1931; bank of issue; bank was granted policy independence in 2001; Gov. HAFIZE GAYE ERKAN.

State Banks

Türkiye Cumhuriyeti Ziraat Bankası (Agricultural Bank of the Republic of Türkiye): Doğanbey Mah., Atatürk Bul. 8, 06107 Ulus, Ankara; tel. (312) 5842000; fax (312) 5844053; e-mail zbmail@ziraatbank.com.tr; internet www.ziraat.com.tr; f. 1863; absorbed Türkiye Emlâk Bankası AŞ (Real Estate Bank of Turkey) in 2001; Chair. BURHANEDDIN TANYERI; Gen. Man. ALPASLAN ÇAKAR.

Türkiye Halk Bankası AŞ: Barbaros Mah., Şebboy Sok 4/1, 34746 Ataşehir, İstanbul; tel. (216) 5037070; fax (216) 3409399; e-mail dialog@halkbank.com.tr; internet www.halkbank.com.tr; f. 1938; absorbed Türkiye Öğretmenler Bankası TAŞ 1992; acquired 96 brs of Türkiye Emlak Bankası 2001; merged with Pamukbank TAŞ 2004; Chair. RECEP SÜLEYMAN ÖZDIL; Gen. Man. OSMAN ARSLAN.

Türkiye Vakıflar Bankası TAO (Vakifbank) (Foundation Bank of Türkiye): Saray Mah., Dr Adnan Büyükdeniz Cad. 7/A-B, 34768 Ümraniye, İstanbul; fax (212) 3167126; e-mail vakifbank@hs01.kep.tr; internet www.vakifbank.com.tr; f. 1954; Chair. MUSTAFA SAYDAM; Gen. Man. ABDI SERDAR ÜSTÜNSALIH.

Principal Commercial Banks

Akbank TAŞ: Sabancı Center, 34330 4 Levent, 80745 İstanbul; tel. (212) 4442525; fax (212) 2697787; e-mail bizeulasin@akbank.com; internet www.akbank.com; f. 1948; absorbed Ak Uluslararası Bankası AŞ Sept. 2005; 20% owned by Citigroup; Chair. SUZAN SABANCI DINÇER; CEO EYÜP ENGIN.

TÜRKIYE (TURKEY)

Alternatifbank AŞ: Cumhuriyet Cad. 22–24, Elmadağ, 34367 İstanbul; tel. (212) 3156500; fax (212) 2331500; e-mail kalite@abank.com.tr; internet www.alternatifbank.com.tr; f. 1991; 95.6% owned by Anadolu Group; Chair. OMER HUSSAIN AL-FARDAN; CEO KAAN GÜR.

ICBC Turkey Bank AŞ: Maslak Mah. Dereboyu Cad. 2, 34398 Maslak, İstanbul; tel. (212) 3355335; fax (212) 3281328; e-mail ir@icbc.com.tr; internet www.icbc.com.tr; f. 1986; 92.8% owned by Industrial and Commercial Bank of China (ICBC); Chair. and Gen. Man. GAO XIANGYANG.

ING Bank AS: Eski Büyükdere Cad., Ayazaga Köyyolu 6, Maslak, 34398 İstanbul; tel. and fax (212) 3351000; e-mail disyazisma@ing.com.tr; internet www.ingbank.com.tr; f. 1990; fmrly Oyak Bank; owned by ING Groep NV (Netherlands); name changed as above 2008; Chair. JOHN T. MCCARTHY; CEO ALPER GÖKGÖZ.

Şekerbank TAŞ: Büyükdere Cad. 171, Metrocity İş Merkezi, A Blok 34330 1 Levent, İstanbul; tel. (212) 3197000; e-mail sekerbank.haberlesme@sekerbank.hs03.kep.tr; internet www.sekerbank.com.tr; f. 1953; 33.98% owned by TuranAlem Securities (Kazakhstan); Chair. HASAN BASRI GÖKTAN; Gen. Man. ORHAN KARAKAŞ.

Türk Ekonomi Bankası AŞ (TEB): Meclısı Mebusan Cad. 57, 34427 Fındıklı, İstanbul; tel. (216) 6353535; fax (212) 2525058; e-mail info@teb.com.tr; internet www.teb.com.tr; f. 1927; fmrly Kocaeli Bankası TAŞ; jt venture between Colakoğlu Group and BNP Paribas SA (France); Fortis Bank AS merged into TEB2011; Chair. AKIN AKBAYGIL; Exec. Dir and Gen. Man. ÜMIT LEBLEBICI.

Türkiye Garanti Bankası AŞ (Garanti BBVA): Nispetiye Mah., Aytar Cad. 2, 34340 Levent Beşiktaş, İstanbul; tel. (212) 4440333; e-mail garantibankasi@hs02.kep.tr; internet www.garantibbva.com.tr; f. 1946; 86% owned by BBVA Group (Spain); Chair. SÜLEYMAN SÖZEN; Pres. and CEO RECEP BAŞTUĞ.

Türkiye İş Bankası AŞ (İşbank): İş Kuleleri, 34330 Levent, İstanbul; tel. 7240724; fax (212) 3160900; internet www.isbank.com.tr; f. 1924; Chair. ADNAN BALI; Gen Man. HAKAN ARAN.

Yapı ve Kredi Bankası AŞ: Yapı Kredi Plaza, Blok D, Büyükdere Cad., 34330 Levent Beşiktaş, İstanbul; tel. (212) 3397000; fax (212) 3396000; internet www.ykb.com.tr; f. 1944; merged with Koçbank AŞ 2006; Chair. ALI Y. KOÇ; CEO GÖKHAN ERÜN.

Development and Investment Banks

İller Bankasi Genel Müdürülüğü: Emniyet Mah., Hipodrom Cad. 9/21, Yenimahalle, Ankara; tel. (312) 5087000; e-mail bilgiedinme@ilbank.gov.tr; internet www.ilbank.gov.tr; Chair. and Gen. Man. ERTAN YETIM; Gen. Man. YUSUF BÜYÜK.

Türkiye Kalkınma Bankası (Development Bank of Türkiye): Saray Mah., Dr Adnan Büyükdeniz Cad. 10, 34768 Ümraniye, İstanbul; tel. (216) 6368700; e-mail haberlesme@kalkinma.com.tr; internet www.kalkinma.com.tr; Chair. RACI KAYA; Gen. Man. İBRAHIM H. ÖZTOP.

Türkiye Sınai Kalkınma Bankası AŞ (Industrial Development Bank of Türkiye): Meclisi Mebusan Cad. 81, Findikli, 34427 İstanbul; tel. (212) 3345050; e-mail info@tskb.com.tr; internet www.tskb.com; f. 1950; Chair. H. ADNAN BALI; CEO MURAT BILGIÇ.

Savings Deposit Insurance Fund Bank

Birleşik Fon Bankasi AŞ: Büyükdere Cad. 143, 34394 Esentepe, İstanbul; tel. (212) 3401000; fax (212) 3473217; e-mail info@fonbank.com.tr; internet www.fonbank.com.tr; fmrly Bayindirbank; name changed as above 2005; control passed to Savings Deposit Insurance Fund 2001; Chair. İSMAIL GÜLER; Gen. Man. CEMAL OKUMUŞ.

Banking Organization

Banks' Association of Türkiye: Nıspetıye Cad. Akmerkez B3 Blok. Kat 13–14, 34340 Etiler, İstanbul; tel. (212) 2820973; fax (212) 2820946; e-mail tbb@tbb.org.tr; internet www.tbb.org.tr; f. 1958; Chair. ALPASLAN CAKAR.

SOVEREIGN WEALTH FUND

Türkiye Varlık Fonu Yönetimi A.Ş. (Türkiye Wealth Fund Management Co): Muallim Naci Cad. 22, Ortaköy, İstanbul; tel. (212) 3712200; e-mail info@turkiyevarlikfonu.com.tr; internet turkiyevarlikfonu.com.tr; f. 2016 to develop, invest and manage state reserves and strategic assets; Chair. RECEP TAYYIP ERDOĞAN (President); Gen. Man. Prof. ERIŞAH ARICAN.

STOCK EXCHANGE

Borsa İstanbul AŞ: Resitpaşa Mah., Tuncay Artun Cad., 34467 Emirgan, İstanbul; tel. (212) 2982100; fax (212) 2982500; e-mail international@borsaistanbul.com; internet borsaistanbul.com; f. 2013 by merger of İstanbul Menkul Kıymetler Borsası and İstanbul Gold Exchange; 599 cos traded on equity market; Chair. Prof. Dr ERIŞAH ARICAN; CEO KORKMAZ ERGUN.

INSURANCE

Principal Companies

AgeSA Hayat ve Emeklilik AŞ (AgeSA): İçerenköy Mah., Umut Sok, Quick Tower Sitesi 10-12/9, Ataşehir, İstanbul; tel. (216) 6333333; fax (216) 6343888; e-mail musteri@agesa.com.tr; internet www.agesa.com.tr; f. 2007 by merger of Aviva Hayat ve Emeklilik and AK Emeklilik as AvivaSA Hayat ve Emeklilik AŞ; present name adopted in 2021; life; 40% stakes owned by Ageas Insurance International NV (Belgium), and 40% by Sabancı Holding; Chair. HALUK DINÇER; Gen. Man. MUSTAFA FIRAT KURUCA.

AKSigorta AŞ: Fatih Sultan Mehmet Mah., Poligon Cad., Buyaka 2 Sitesi, Blok 8A, 34771 Ümraniye, İstanbul; tel. (216) 2808888; fax (216) 2808800; e-mail bilgi@aksigorta.com.tr; internet www.aksigorta.com.tr; f. 1960; life and non-life; Chair. HALUK DINÇER; Gen. Man. UĞUR GÜLEN.

Allianz Sigorta AŞ: Küçükbakkalköy Mah. Kayisdağı Cad. 1, 34750 Ataşehir, İstanbul; tel. (850) 3999999; fax (216) 5566777; e-mail info@allianz.com.tr; internet www.allianz.com.tr; f. 1923; general, non-life; also offers life insurance through its subsidiary, Allianz Hayat ve Emeklilik AŞ; fmrly Koç Allianz Sigorta AŞ; 64.4% owned by Allianz AG (Germany); Chair. CANSEN BAŞARAN-SYMES; CEO TOLGA GÜRKAN.

Anadolu Sigorta TAŞ (Anadolu Insurance Co): Rüzgarlıbahçe Mah., Çam Pınarı Sok 6, 34805 Beykoz, İstanbul; tel. (850) 7240850; fax (850) 7440745; e-mail bilgi@anadolusigorta.com.tr; internet www.anadolusigorta.com.tr; f. 1925; life and non-life; 35.53% owned by Türkiye İş Bankası AŞ; Chair. FÜSUN TÜMSAVAŞ; CEO MEHMET ŞENCAN.

AXA Sigorta AŞ: Kılıç Ali Paşa Mah., Meclis-i Mebusan Cad. 15, 34427 Salıpazarı, İstanbul; tel. (212) 3342424; fax (212) 2521515; e-mail axasigorta@hs02.kep.tr; internet www.axasigorta.com.tr; life and non-life; Chair. CHRISTOPHE KNAUB; CEO YAVUZ ÖLKEN.

Eureko Sigorta: Altunizade Mah., Prof. Fahrettin Kerim Gökay Cad. 20, 34662 Üsküdar, İstanbul; tel. (216) 4001188; fax (216) 4742290; e-mail esmusterihizmetleri@eurekosigorta.com.tr; internet www.eurekosigorta.com.tr; f. 1989 as Garanti Sigorta; renamed as above Oct. 2007; 80% owned by Eureko BV (Netherlands) and 20% by Türkiye Garanti Bankası AŞ; non-life; Chair. ROBERT OTTO; Gen. Man. UCO PIETER VEGTER.

Groupama Sigorta AŞ: Groupama Plaza, Eski Büyükdere Cad. 2, 34398 Maslak, İstanbul; tel. (212) 3676767; fax (212) 3676868; e-mail groupamasigorta@hs02.kep.tr; internet www.groupama.com.tr; f. 1959 as Başak Sigorta; 99% stake owned by Groupama Investment Bosphorus Holding AŞ; present name adopted 2009, following merger with Güven Sigorta TAŞ; life and non-life; Gen. Man. PHILIPPE-HENRI BURLISSON.

Türkiye Sigorta AŞ: Büyükdere Cad. 110, Esentepe, Şişli, 34394 İstanbul; tel. (212) 3556565; fax (212) 3556464; e-mail bilgi@turkiyesigorta.com.tr; internet turkiyesigorta.com.tr; f. 2020 after the sovereign wealth fund, Türkiye Varlık Fonu Yönetimi (q.v.) bought and merged several public insurance cos; Chair. AZIZ MURAT ULUĞ; Gen. Man. ATILLA BENLI.

Insurance Organization

Türkiye Sigorta ve Reasürans Şirketleri Birliği (Asscn of the Insurance and Reinsurance Companies of Türkiye—TSB): Büyükdere Cad., Büyükdere Plaza 195, 1-2, 34394 Levent, İstanbul; tel. (850) 5029600; fax (850) 5225041; e-mail genel@tsb.org.tr; internet www.tsb.org.tr; f. 1954 by merger of the Association of the Insurance Companies of Turkey and the Central Office of Insurers; present name adopted 1975; Pres. ATTILA BENLI.

Trade and Industry

GOVERNMENT AGENCIES

Özelleştirme İdaresi Başkanlığı (ÖİB) (Privatization Administration): Ziya Gökalp Cad. 80, Kurtuluş, 06600 Ankara; tel. (312) 5858000; fax (312) 5858051; e-mail info@oib.gov.tr; internet www.oib.gov.tr; co-ordinates privatization programme; Pres. BEKIR EMRE HAYKIR.

Rekabet Kurumu (Turkish Competition Authority): Üniversiteler Mah. 1597, Cad. 9, 06800 Bilkent, Ankara; tel. (312) 2914444; fax (312) 2667920; e-mail rekabetkurumu@hs01.kep.tr; internet www.rekabet.gov.tr; f. 1997; prevents restriction of competition, oversees mergers and monitors state aid; Pres. BIROL KÜLE.

Türkiye Atom Enerjisi Kurumu (Turkish Atomic Energy Authority): Mustafa Kemal Mah., Dumlupınar Bul. 192, Çankaya, Ankara; tel. (312) 2958700; fax (312) 2878761; e-mail tenmak@tenmak.gov.tr; internet www.taek.gov.tr; f. 1956; controls the development of peaceful uses of atomic energy; 7 mems; Pres. ZAFER DEMIRCAN.

TÜRKIYE (TURKEY)

CHAMBERS OF COMMERCE AND INDUSTRY

Türkiye Odalar ve Borsalar Birliği (TOBB) (Union of Chambers and Commodity Exchanges of Türkiye): Dumlupınar Bul. 252, Eskişehir Yolu 9 Km, 06530 Ankara; tel. (312) 2182000; fax (312) 2194090; e-mail info@tobb.org.tr; internet www.tobb.org.tr; f. 1950; Pres. Rıfat Hısarcıklıoğlu.

Ankara Sanayi Odası (ASO) (Ankara Chamber of Industry): Atatürk Bul. 193, Kavaklıdere, Ankara; tel. (312) 4171200; fax (312) 4175205; e-mail aso@hs02.kep.tr; internet www.aso.org.tr; f. 1963; Pres. M. Nurettin Özdebir.

Ankara Tabip Odası (ATO) (Ankara Chamber of Commerce): Mithatpaşa Cad. 62/18 Kızılay, 06420 Ankara; tel. (312) 4188700; fax (312) 4187794; e-mail ato@ato.org.tr; internet www.ato.org.tr; Chair. Dr Muharrem Baytemür.

İstanbul Sanayi Odası (İSO) (İstanbul Chamber of Industry): Meşrutiyet Cad. 63, Tepebaşı, 34430 İstanbul; tel. (212) 2522900; fax (212) 2495084; e-mail info@iso.org.tr; internet www.iso.org.tr; f. 1952; Chair. Erdal Bahçıvan.

İstanbul Ticaret Odası (İTO) (İstanbul Chamber of Commerce): Reşadiye Cad. 34112 Eminönü, İstanbul; tel. (212) 4440486; fax (212) 5131565; e-mail ito@ito.org.tr; internet www.ito.org.tr; f. 1882; more than 300,000 mems; Pres. Şekib Avdagıç.

EMPLOYERS' ASSOCIATIONS

Türk Sanayicileri ve İşadamları Derneği (TÜSİAD) (Turkish Industrialists' and Businessmen's Association): Meşrutiyet Cad. 74, 34420 Tepebaşı, İstanbul; tel. (212) 2491929; fax (212) 2490913; e-mail tusiad@tusiad.org; internet www.tusiad.org; f. 1971; c. 600 mems; Chair. Orhan Turan; Sec.-Gen. Ebru Dicle.

Türkiye İşveren Sendikaları Konfederasyonu (TİSK) (Turkish Confederation of Employer Associations): Koç Kuleleri, Söğütözü Mah., Söğütözü Cad. 2, 06510 Çankaya, Ankara; tel. (312) 4397717; fax (312) 4397592; e-mail tisk@tisk.org.tr; internet tisk.org.tr; f. 1962; represents (on national level) 23 employers' asscns; official representative in labour relations; Pres. Özgür Burak Akkol; Sec.-Gen. Akansel Koç.

UTILITIES

Electricity

Elektrik Üretim Anonim Şirketi (EÜAŞ) (Electricity Generation Co Inc): Mustafa Kemal Mah., Dumlupınar Bul. 7, km 166, 06520 Çankaya, Ankara; tel. (312) 2955000; e-mail basinhalk@euas.gov.tr; internet www.euas.gov.tr; f. 2001, following devolution of responsibilities of fmr Elektrik Üretim-İletim AŞ into separate entities for generation, transmission and wholesale activities; responsible for electricity generation; Chair. and Gen. Man. İzzet Alagöz.

Enerji Piyasası Düzenleme Kurulu (EPDK) (Energy Market Regulatory Authority): Mustafa Kemal Mah. 2078, Sok. 4, 06510 Çankaya, Ankara; tel. (312) 2014001; fax (312) 2014050; internet www.epdk.gov.tr; f. 2001; regulation and supervision of energy market; Pres. Mustafa Yılmaz.

Türkiye Elektrik Dağıtım AŞ (TEDAŞ): Nasuh Akar Mah., Türk Ocağı Cad. 2, Balgat, 06520 Çankaya, Ankara; tel. (312) 4495000; fax (312) 2138873; e-mail bilgi@tedas.gov.tr; internet www.tedas.gov.tr; responsible for distribution and sale of electricity; owns 21 regional distribution cos; Pres. and Man. Dir Ömer Sami Yapıcı.

Türkiye Elektrik İletim Anonim Şirketi (TEİAŞ) (Turkish Electricity Transmission Company): Nasuh Akar Mah., Türkocağı Cad. 12, Balgat, 06100 Çankaya, Ankara; tel. (312) 2038061; e-mail teias@hs01.kep.tr; internet www.teias.gov.tr; f. 2001 (see EÜAŞ); responsible for electricity transmission; Chair. and Gen. Man. Orhan Kaldırım.

Water

Devlet Su İşleri Genel Müdürlüğü (DSİ) (General Directorate of State Hydraulic Works): Mustafa Kemal Mah., Anadolu Bul. 9, 06530 Çankaya, Ankara; tel. (312) 4545454; e-mail dsi.gnlmud@hs01.kep.tr; internet www.dsi.gov.tr; f. 1954; controlled by the Ministry of Energy and Natural Resources; responsible for the planning and devt of water resources; Dir-Gen. Lütfi Akca.

MAJOR INVESTMENT HOLDING COMPANIES

Alarko Şirketler Topluluğu: Muallim Naci Cad. 69, 34347 Ortaköy, İstanbul; tel. (212) 2275200; fax (212) 2270427; e-mail info@alarko.com.tr; internet www.alarko.com.tr; f. 1954; interests in industry, tourism, real estate, energy and food processing sectors; Chair. İzzat Garih; CEO Ümit Nuri Yıldız.

Anadolu Endüstri Holding AŞ: Fatih Sultan Mehmet Mah., Balkan Cad. 58, Buyaka E Blok Tepeüstü, 34771 Ümraniye, İstanbul; tel. (216) 5788500; internet www.anadolugrubu.com.tr; f. 1950; approx. 80 subsidiary cos in automotive, agriculture, food and beverages, health and manufacturing sectors; Chair. Tuncay Özilhan; CEO Hurşıt Zorlu.

Çalık Holding AŞ: Büyükdere Cad. 163, 34394 Zincirlikuyu, İstanbul; tel. (212) 3065000; fax (212) 3065600; e-mail info@calik.com; internet www.calik.com; f. 1981; subsidiary cos active in energy, construction, textiles, finance, media and telecommunications sectors; Chair. Ahmet Çalık; approx. 16,000 employees (2023).

Çukurova Holding: Kat 16, Levent Mah., Cömert Sok., Yapı Kredi Plaza A-Blok, 34330 Beşiktaş, İstanbul; tel. (212) 3701200; fax (212) 3701235; e-mail cukurovaholding@cukurovaholding.com.tr; internet www.cukurovaholding.com.tr; f. 1923; industrial and commercial conglomerate; stakes in several companies in industry, manufacturing, construction, telecommunications, media, transport, energy and financial services; Chair. Mehmet Emin Karamehmet.

Doğan Şirketler Grubu Holding AŞ: Burhaniye Mah., Kisikli Cad. 65, 34676 Üsküdar, İstanbul; tel. (216) 5569000; fax (216) 5569200; e-mail press@doganholding.com.tr; internet www.doganholding.com.tr; f. 1980; investment holding; interests in energy, media, industrial, trade, financial services and tourism sectors; owns and operates several of Türkiye's largest-selling national newspapers, as well as holding interests in radio and television broadcasting, and publishing; Chair. Begümhan Doğan Faralyalı; CEO Çağlar Göğüş.

Doğuş Grubu Binaları (Doğuş Group): Büyükdere Cad. 249, 34398 Maslak, İstanbul; tel. (212) 3353232; fax (212) 3353090; e-mail diletisim@dogusgrubu.com.tr; internet www.dogusgrubu.com.tr; f. 1951; interests in financial services, automotive and construction industries, tourism, energy, real estate and media; subsidiary cos incl. Doğuş İnşaat and Doğuş Otomotiv; Chair. and CEO Ferit F. Şahenk; over 21,000 employees (2023).

Eczacıbaşı Holding AŞ: Kanyon Ofis, Büyükdere Cad. 185, 34394 Levent, İstanbul; tel. (212) 3717000; fax (212) 3717110; internet www.eczacibasi.com.tr; f. 1942; production of pharmaceuticals, health and beauty products, and building products; Chair. Bülent Eczacıbaşı; Group CEO Atalay M. Gümrah; over 13,500 employees (2023).

Hacı Ömer Sabancı Holding AŞ: Sabancı Centre, 34330 4 Levent, İstanbul; tel. (212) 3858080; fax (212) 3858888; e-mail info@sabanci.com; internet www.sabanci.com; f. 1967; owns subsidiaries and jt-venture cos in financial services, automotive, tire manufacturing and repair, retail, cement and energy sectors; Chair. Güler Sabancı; CEO Cenk Alper.

İhlas Holding AŞ: İhlas Plaza 11 B/21, Merkez Mah 29, Ekim Cad., 34197 Yenibosna, İstanbul; tel. (212) 4542000; fax (212) 4542136; e-mail iletisim@ihlas.com.tr; internet www.ihlas.com.tr; f. 1993; media and publishing, broadcasting, manufacturing, construction, mining and energy; Chair. and CEO Ahmet Mücahid Ören; 2,702 employees (2021).

Koç Holding AŞ: Nakkaştepe Azizbey Sok. 1, 34674 Kuzguncuk, İstanbul; tel. (216) 5310000; fax (216) 5310099; e-mail iletisim@koc.com.tr; internet www.koc.com.tr; f. 1926; subsidiary cos incl. Arçelik, Ford Otomotiv and Tüpraş; Chair. Ömer M. Koç; CEO Levent Çakıroğlu.

Ordu Yardımlaşma Kurumu (OYAK) (Armed Forces' Pension Fund): Ön Cebeci Mah., Ziya Gökalp Cad. 64, 06600 Kurtuluş, Ankara; tel. (312) 4156100; fax (312) 4341250; internet www.oyak.com.tr; f. 1961; holds investments in 26 cos in manufacturing, finance and services sectors, incl. ERDEMİR and Oyak-Renault; Chair. Mehmet Taş; CEO Süleyman Savaş Erdem.

Tekfen Holding AŞ: Kültür Mah., Tekfen Sitesi, Budak Sok., A Blok 7, 34340 Beşiktaş, İstanbul; tel. (212) 3593300; fax (212) 3593305; e-mail tekfen@tekfen.com.tr; internet www.tekfen.com.tr; f. 1956; comprises 38 cos dealing in construction, engineering and manufacturing, agriculture and industry, banking, real estate and investment; Chair. Zekeriya Yıldırım; Pres. Hakan Göral; 11,950 employees (2022).

Zorlu Holding AŞ: Büyükdere Cad. 199, 34394 199 Levent, Şişli, İstanbul; tel. (212) 4562000; e-mail kurumsaliletisimvesurdurulebilirlik@zorlu.com; internet www.zorlu.com.tr; f. 1953; manufacture of textiles and consumer goods, energy generation, tourism, property management; subsidiary cos incl. Vestel; Chair. Ahmet N. Zorlu; CEO Ömer Yüngül.

MAJOR COMPANIES

Akçansa Çimento Sanayi ve Ticaret AŞ: Palladium Tower, Barbaros Mah., Kardelen Sok. 2 D:124–125, 34746, Ataşehir, İstanbul; tel. (216) 5713000; fax (216) 5713111; internet www.akcansa.com.tr; f. 1996; jt venture between Hacı Ömer Sabancı Holding AŞ and HeidelbergCement Group (Germany); production of cement; Pres. Burak Orhun; Gen. Man. Vecih Yılmaz.

Aksa (Akrilik Kimya San. AŞ): Merkez Mah., Ali Raif Dinçkök Cad. 2, Taşköprü, 77602 Çiftlikköy, Yalova; tel. (226) 3532545; fax (226)

TÜRKIYE (TURKEY)

3533307; e-mail aksa@aksa.com; internet www.aksa.com; f. 1968; produces acrylic fibres and general chemical products; Chair. RAIF ALI DINÇKÖK; Gen. Man. CENGIZ TAŞ.

Alliance Healthcare AŞ: Basın Ekspres Yolu, Kavak Sok., Ser Plaza 3, A Blok Kat. 3, 34197 Yenibosna, İstanbul; tel. (212) 4527200; fax (212) 4527222; e-mail iletisim@alliance-healthcare.com.tr; internet www.alliance-healthcare.com.tr; f. 1987; fmrly Hedef Alliance; distribution of pharmaceutical and cosmetic products; Chair. AXEL VIAENE; Gen. Man. SELIM TAŞO.

Anadolu Efes Biracılık ve Malt Sanayii AŞ (Anadolu Efes): Fatih Sultan Mehmet Mah., Balkan Cad., E Blok 58/24, 34771 Ümraniye İstanbul; tel. (216) 5868000; e-mail iletisim@tr.anadoluefes.com; internet www.anadoluefes.com.tr; f. 1969; subsidiary of Anadolu Endüstri Holding AŞ; production of beverages; Gen. Man. ONUR ALTÜRK.

Arçelik AŞ: Karaağaç Cad. 2–6, 34445 Sütlüce, İstanbul; tel. (212) 3143434; fax (212) 3143482; e-mail kurumsal@arcelik.com; internet www.arcelikglobal.com; f. 1955; 57.2% owned by Koç Holding; produces domestic appliances; subsidiary: Grundig Elektronik AŞ; Chair. RAHMI M. KOÇ; CEO HAKAN HAMDI BULGURLU.

Aygaz AŞ: Büyükdere Cad. 145, 34394 Zincirikuyu, İstanbul; tel. (212) 3541515; fax (212) 2883963; e-mail aygazhizmethatti@aygaz.com.tr; internet www.aygaz.com.tr; f. 1961; 51.2% stake owned by Koç Holding AŞ (2022); supply and distribution of liquefied petroleum gas; Chair. RAHMI M. KOÇ; Gen. Man. MELIH POYRAZ.

BİM Birleşik Mağazalar AŞ: Abdurrahmangazi Mah., Ebubekir Cad. 73, 34887 Sancaktepe, İstanbul; tel. (216) 5640303; fax (216) 3117978; e-mail iletisim@bim.com.tr; internet www.bim.com.tr; f. 1995; retailer of food and basic consumer goods; Chair. and CEO MUSTAFA LATIF TOPBAŞ.

Çolakoğlu Metalurji AŞ: Rüzgarlıbahçe Mah., Çam Pınarı Sok. 1, Kat. 16, 34805 Beykoz, İstanbul; tel. (216) 4442627; fax (216) 5371401; e-mail colakoglu@colakoglu.com.tr; internet www.colakoglu.com.tr; f. 1969; manufactures steel wire rod in coils, reinforcing bars, billets and slabs; Gen. Man. UĞUR DALBELER.

Ereğli Demir ve Çelik Fabrikaları TAŞ (Erdemir): Barbaros Mah., Ardıç Sok. 6, 34746 Ataşehir, İstanbul; tel. (216) 5788000; fax (216) 4694810; e-mail grupiletisim@erdemir.com.tr; internet www.erdemir.com.tr; f. 1960; fmr state-owned enterprise; majority owned by Oyak Group since 2006; manufactures steel and iron products; Chair. SÜLEYMAN SAVAŞ ERDEM; Gen. Man. NIYAZI ASKIN PEKER.

Ford Otosan AŞ: Akpınar Mah., Hasan Basri Cad. 2, 34885 Sancaktepe, İstanbul; tel. (216) 5647100; internet www.fordotosan.com.tr; f. 1959; jt venture between Koç Holding and Ford Motor Co (USA); manufactures passenger cars, trucks and engines; Chair. ALI YILDIRIM KOÇ; Gen. Man. GÜVEN ÖZYURT.

Habaş (Habaş Sınai ve Tibbi Gazlar İstihsal Endüstrisi AŞ): Fuat Paşa Sok. 1, 34880 Soğanlık, İstanbul; tel. (216) 4536400; fax (216) 4522570; internet www.habas.com.tr; f. 1956; production of medical and industrial gases, electricity, steel, machinery; distribution of natural gas; also owns Anadolubank.

İÇDAŞ: Mahmutbey Mah., Dilmenler Cad. 20, 34218 Bağcılar, İstanbul; tel. (212) 6040404; fax (212) 6519789; e-mail icdas@icdas.com.tr; internet www.icdas.com.tr; f. 1970; produces steel bars and high alloy steels; Gen. Man. TARIK YEGÜL.

Kordsa Global AŞ: Alikahya Fatih Mah., Sanayici Cad. 90, 41310 İzmit; tel. (262) 3167000; fax (212) 3167070; e-mail info@kordsa.com; internet www.kordsa.com; f. 1973; manufactures nylon and polyester yarn, industrial and cord fabrics; subsidiary of Hacı Ömer Sabancı Holding AŞ; Chair. CEVDET ALEMDAR; CEO İBRAHIM ÖZGÜR YILDIRIM.

Mercedes-Benz Türk AŞ: Akçaburgaz Mah., Süleyman Şah Cad. 6/1, 34522 Esenyurt, İstanbul; tel. (212) 8673000; fax (212) 8674477; internet www.mercedesbenzturk.com.tr; f. 1967; manufactures civil and military vehicles; CEO SÜER SÜLÜN.

Migros Ticaret AŞ: Atatürk Mah., Turgut Özal Bul. 7, 34758 Ataşehir, İstanbul; tel. (216) 5793000; fax (216) 5793500; e-mail iletisim@migros.com.tr; internet www.migroskurumsal.com; f. 1954; retail, marketing and distribution; in 2005 took over Tansaş retail chain; Chair. TUNCAY ÖZILHAN; Gen. Man. Dr Ö. ÖZGÜR TORT.

Oyak-Renault Otomobil Fabrikaları AŞ: Fatih Sultan Mehmet Mah., Balkan Cad. 47, 34770 Ümraniye, İstanbul; tel. (224) 2194500; fax (224) 2194641; internet www.oyak-renault.com; f. 1969; 51% owned by Renault (France), 49% owned by Oyak Group; manufactures automobiles; Gen. Man. KAAN ÖZKAN.

Petkim Petrokimya Holding AŞ: Siteler Mah., Necmettin Giritlioğlu Cad. 6, 35800 Aliağa, İzmir; tel. (212) 3050000; fax (212) 3050100; e-mail musterisikayetleri@petkim.com.tr; internet www.petkim.com.tr; f. 1965; 51% owned by SOCAR Turkey Petrokimya AŞ; produces petrochemicals; Chair. SÜLEYMAN GASIMOV; Gen. Man. ANAR MAMMADOV.

Petrol Ofisi AŞ (POAŞ): Libadiye Cad. 82F, 34700 Üsküdar, İstanbul; tel. (216) 2753000; e-mail info@poas.com.tr; internet www.petrolofisi.com.tr; f. 1941; fmr State Economic Enterprise, privatized in 2000; 100% stake owned by VIP Turkey Enerji AŞ; distribution of petroleum and petroleum products; Chair. JAVED AHMED; CEO MEHMET ABBASOĞLU.

Philip Morris Tütün Mamulleri Sanayi ve Ticaret AŞ: Küçükçamlıca Mah., Ord. Prof. Fahrettin Kerim Gökay Cad. 58–58/1, 34696 Üsküdar, İstanbul; tel. (216) 5443000; fax (216) 5443040; f. 1991; 100% owned by Philip Morris Int. (USA); manufactures cigarettes.

Sanko Textile and Trading Co: Sani Konukoğlu Bul. 1, Başpınar, Gaziantep; tel. (342) 2116000; e-mail marketing@sanko.com.tr; internet www.sankotextile.com; f. 1943; manufacturers and exporters of yarns and knitted fabrics.

Sarkuysan Elektrolitik Bakır Sanayii ve Ticaret AŞ: Emek Mah., Asiroglu Cad. 147, 41700 Darcia-Kocaeli; tel. (262) 6766600; fax (262) 6766680; e-mail info@sarkuysan.com; internet www.sarkuysan.com; f. 1972; produces copper products, cast iron parts for the manufacture of automobiles and machinery; Chair. HAYRETTIN ÇAYCI; Gen. Man. SEVGÜR ARSLANPAY.

Tofaş (Türk Otomobil Fabrikası AŞ): Büyükdere Cad. 145, 34394 Zincirlikuyu, İstanbul; tel. (212) 2753390; fax (212) 2753988; internet www.tofas.com.tr; f. 1968; jt venture between Koç Holding AŞ and Stellantis NV; manufactures automobiles and automobile parts; Chair. ÖMER M. KOÇ; CEO CENGIZ EROLDU.

Toyota Otomotiv Sanayi Türkiye AŞ: Toyota Cad. 2, Arifiye, 54580 Sakarya; tel. (264) 2950295; fax (264) 2951295; e-mail iletisim@toyotatr.com; internet www.toyotatr.com; f. 1990; 90% owned by Toyota Motor Europe NV/SA, 10% by Mitsui & Co Ltd; Gen. Man. ERDOĞAN ŞAHIN.

Türkiye Kömür İşletmeleri Kurumu (TKI) (General Directorate of Turkish Coal Enterprises): Hipodrom Cad. 12, 06560 Yenimahalle, Ankara; tel. (312) 5401000; fax (312) 3841635; e-mail sosyalmedya@tki.gov.tr; internet www.tki.gov.tr; f. 1957; coal mining; Gen. Man. Dr HASAN HÜSEYIN ERDOĞAN.

Türkiye Petrol Rafinerileri AŞ (TÜPRAŞ): Gülbahar Mah. Büyükdere Cad. 101A, 34394 Şişli, İstanbul; tel. (212) 8789000; fax (212) 2113081; e-mail info@tupras.com.tr; internet www.tupras.com.tr; f. 1983; privatization completed 2006; 77% owned by Koç Holding AŞ, 20% by Aygaz AŞ, 3% by OPET Petrolcülük AŞ; refining of crude oil; Chair. ÖMER M. KOÇ; Gen. Man. İBRAHIM YELMENOĞLU.

Türkiye Petrolleri Anonim Ortaklığı (TPAO) (Turkish Petroleum Corpn): Söğütözü Mah., Nizami Gencevi Cad. 10, 06530 Çankaya, Ankara; tel. (312) 2072000; fax (312) 2869000; e-mail tpao@tpao.gov.tr; internet www.tpao.gov.tr; f. 1954; State Economic Enterprise; explores for, drills and produces crude petroleum and natural gas; Chair. and Gen. Man. MELIH HAN BILGIN.

Türkiye Şeker Fabrikaları AŞ: Mithatpaşa Cad. 14, 06100 Yenişehir, Ankara; tel. (312) 4585500; internet www.turkseker.gov.tr; produces sugar and manufactures machinery used in sugar production; Chair. and Gen. Dir Dr MUHIDDIN ŞAHIN.

Ülker: Kısıklı Mah. 1, Ferah Cad., 34692 İstanbul; tel. (216) 5242900; internet www.ulker.com.tr; f. 1944; manufacture and distribution of food products and beverages; Chair. AHMET BAL; CEO METE BUYURGAN.

Vestel AŞ: Levent 199, Büyükdere Cad. 199, 34394 Şişli, İstanbul; tel. (212) 4562000; internet www.vestel.com.tr; subsidiary of Zorlu Holding; manufacture and distribution of domestic appliances and other electronic goods; group comprises 28 cos worldwide (2021); Group Chair. AHMET NAZIF ZORLU.

TRADE UNIONS

Confederations

DİSK (Türkiye Devrimci İşçi Sendikaları Konfederasyonu) (Confederation of Progressive Trade Unions of Türkiye): Dikilitaş Mah., Eren Sok. 4, Beşiktaş, İstanbul; tel. (212) 2910505; fax (212) 2404209; e-mail disk@disk.org.tr; internet disk.org.tr; f. 1967; member of ITUC and European Trade Union Confed.; Pres. ARZU ÇERKEZOĞLU; Sec.-Gen. ADNAN SERDAROĞLU; 22 affiliated unions (2023).

Hak-İş (Hak İşçi Sendikaları Konfederasyonu) (Confederation of Turkish Real Trade Unions): Tunus Cad. 37, Çankaya, Ankara; tel. (312) 4177900; fax (312) 4250552; e-mail hakis@hakis.org.tr; internet hakis.org.tr; f. 1976; mem. of ITUC, European Trade Union Confed. and TUAC; Pres. MAHMUT ARSLAN; 21 affiliated unions (2023).

KESK (Kamu Emekçileri Sendikaları Konfederasyonu) (Confederation of Public Employees' Trade Unions): 44/1 Selanik Cad. Kat 1, Kızılay, Ankara; tel. (312) 4367111; fax (312) 4367470; e-mail kesk@kesk.org.tr; internet kesk.org.tr; f. 1995; mem. of ITUC and European Trade Union Confed.; Co-Chair. MEHMET BOZGEYIK, ŞÜKRAN KABLAN YEŞIL; Gen. Sec. ŞENOL KÖKSAL; 11 affiliated unions (2023).

TÜRKIYE (TURKEY)

Memur-Sen (Memur Sendikaları Konfederasyonu) (Confederation of Public Servants' Trade Unions): Zübeyde Hanım Mah., Sebze Bahçeleri Cad. 86, 06400 Altındağ, Ankara; tel. (312) 2300972; fax (312) 2303989; e-mail info@memursen.org.tr; internet www.memursen.org.tr; f. 1995; Pres. ALI YALÇIN; Sec.-Gen. MAHMUT FARUK DOĞAN; 11 affiliated unions (2023).

Türk-İş (Türkiye İşçi Sendikaları Konfederasyonu) (Confederation of Turkish Trade Unions): Bayındır Sok. 10, 06410 Kizilay, Ankara; tel. (312) 4333125; fax (312) 4336809; e-mail turkis@turkis.org.tr; internet www.turkis.org.tr; f. 1952; mem. of ITUC, European Trade Union Confed. and OECD/Trade Union Advisory Cttee; Pres. ERGÜN ATALAY; Gen. Sec. PEVRUL KAVLAK; 34 affiliated unions (2023).

Türkiye Kamu-Sen (Türkiye Kamu Çalışanları Sendikaları Konfederasyonu) (Confederation of Turkish Public Employees' Unions): Kat 7, Erzurum Mah., Talatpaşa Bul. 160, Ankara; tel. (312) 4242200; fax (312) 4242208; e-mail haber@kamusen.org.tr; internet www.kamusen.org.tr; f. 1992; Pres. ÖNDER KAHVECI; Gen. Sec. TALIP GEYLAN; 11 affiliated unions (2023).

Principal Affiliated Trade Unions

Belediye-İş (Türkiye Belediyeler ve Genel Hizmetler İşçiler Sendikası) (Municipal and Public Services Workers): Necatibey Cad. 59, Kızılay, Ankara; tel. (312) 2318343; fax (312) 2320874; e-mail belediyeis@belediyeis.org.tr; internet belediyeis.org.tr; f. 1983; affiliated to Türk-İş; Pres. NIHAT YURDAKUL; Gen. Sec. İSMAIL DUMAN.

Genel-İş (Türkiye Genel Hizmetler İşçileri Sendikası) (Municipal Workers): Çankırı Cad. 28, Kat 4–9, 06030 Ulus, Ankara; tel. (312) 3091547; fax (312) 3091046; e-mail bilgi@genel-is.org.tr; internet www.genel-is.org.tr; f. 1962; affiliated to DİSK; Pres. REMZI ÇALIŞKAN; Gen. Sec. ŞÜKRET SEVGENER.

Hizmet-İş Sendikası (Municipal and Public Service Workers): Gazi Mustafa Kemal Bul. 86, Maltepe, 06570 Çankaya, Ankara; tel. (312) 2318710; fax (312) 2319889; e-mail hizmet-is@hizmet-is.org.tr; internet hizmet-is.org.tr; f. 1979; affiliated to Hak-İş; Pres. MAHMUT ARSLAN; Gen. Sec. OĞUZ AKSOY.

Petrol-İş (Türkiye Petrol, Kimya ve Lastik İşçileri Sendikası) (Petroleum, Chemicals and Rubber Industry): Altunizade Mah., Kuşbakışı Cad. 23, 34662, Üsküdar, İstanbul; tel. (212) 4749870; fax (212) 4749867; e-mail headoffice@petrol-is.org.tr; internet www.petrol-is.org.tr; f. 1954; affiliated to Türk-İş; Pres. SÜLEYMAN AKYÜZ; Gen. Sec. SALIH AKDUMAN.

Sağlık-Sen (Sağlık ve Sosyal Hizmet Çalışanları Sendikası) (Health and Social Workers): Zübeyde Hanım Mah., Sebze Bahçeleri Cad. 86, Altındağ, Ankara; tel. (312) 4441995; fax (312) 2308365; e-mail info@sagliksen.org.tr; internet www.sagliksen.org.tr; f. 1995; affiliated to Memur-Sen; Pres. MAHMUT FARUK DOGAN; Gen. Sec. DURALI BAKI.

Tarım-İş (Türkiye Orman, Topraksu, Tarım ve Tarım Sanayii İşçileri Sendikası) (Forestry, Agriculture and Agricultural Industry Workers): Bankacı Sok. 10, 06700 Kocatepe, Ankara; tel. (312) 4190456; fax (312) 4193113; e-mail info@tarimis.org.tr; internet www.tarimis.org.tr; f. 1961; affiliated to Türk-İş; Pres. IHLAMI POLAT; Gen. Sec. RECEB KOCAPIÇAK.

Tekgıda-İş (Türkiye Tütün, Müskirat Gıda ve Yardımcı İşçileri Sendikası) (Tobacco, Drink, Food and Allied Workers): Konaklar Mah., Faruk Nafiz Çamlıbel Sok. 5, Levent 4, İstanbul; tel. (535) 9736317; fax (212) 2789534; e-mail bilgi@tekgida.org.tr; internet www.tekgida.org.tr; f. 1952; affiliated to Türk-İş; Pres. MUSTAFA TÜRKEL; Gen. Sec. IBRAHIM ÖREN.

Teksif (Türkiye Tekstil, Örme, Giyim ve Deri Sanayii İşçileri Sendikası) (Textile, Knitting and Clothing Workers): Ön Cebeci Mah., Ziya Gökalp Cad., Aydımuş Sok. 1, 06600 Kurtuluş, Ankara; tel. (312) 4312170; fax (312) 4357826; e-mail teksif@teksif.org.tr; internet www.teksif.org.tr; f. 1951; affiliated to Türk-İş; Pres. NAZMI IRGAT; Gen. Sec. MEHMET KAFA.

Tes-İş (Türkiye Enerji, Su ve Gaz İşçileri Sendikası) (Electricity, Water and Gas Workers): Beştepe Mah., Meriç Cad. 23, 06510 Yenimahalle, Ankara; tel. (312) 2126510; fax (312) 2126552; e-mail info@tes-is.org.tr; internet www.tes-is.org.tr; f. 1963; affiliated to Türk-İş; Pres. IRFAN KABALOGLU.

Türk Eğitim-Sen (Türkiye Eğitim ve Öğretim Bilim Hizmetleri Kolu Kamu Çalışanları Sendikası) (Teachers and University Lecturers): Kat 6, Erzurum Mah., Talatpaşa Bul. 160, Cebeci, Ankara; tel. (312) 4240960; fax (312) 4240968; e-mail iletisim@turkegitimsen.org.tr; internet turkegitimsen.org.tr; f. 1992; affiliated to Türkiye Kamu-Sen; Pres. TALIP GEYLAN; Gen. Sec. HAYDAR URFALI.

Türk Maden-İş (Türkiye Maden İşçileri Sendikası) (Mining): Strazburg Cad. 7, Sıhhiye, Ankara; tel. (312) 2317355; fax (312) 2298931; e-mail bilgi@madenis.org.tr; internet www.madenis.org.tr; affiliated to Türk-İş; Pres. NURETTIN AKÇUL; Gen. Sec. MEHMET ALI ÇAKIR.

Türk-Metal (Türkiye Metal, Çelik, Mühimmat, Makina ve Metalden Mamul, Eşya ve Oto, Montaj ve Yardımcı İşçileri Sendikası) (Auto, Metal and Allied Workers): Beştepe Mah. 4, Sok. 3, Söğütözü, Yenimahalle, Ankara; tel. (312) 2926400; fax (312) 2844018; e-mail bilgiislem@turkmetal.org.tr; internet www.turkmetal.org.tr; f. 1963; affiliated to Türk-İş; Pres. PEVRUL KAVLAK; Gen. Sec. TALIPHAN KIYMAZ.

Türkiye Çimse-İş (Türkiye Çimento, Seramik, Toprak ve Cam Sanayii İşçileri Sendikası) (Cement, Ceramics, Clay and Glass Industries): Esat Cad. 43, Küçükesat, Çankaya, Ankara; tel. (312) 4195830; fax (312) 4251335; e-mail bilgi@cimse-is.org.tr; internet www.cimse-is.org.tr; f. 1963; affiliated to Türk-İş; Pres. ZEKERIYE NAZLIM; Gen. Sec. HASAN EMER.

Yol-İş (Türkiye Yol, Yapı ve İnşaat İşçileri Sendikası) (Road, Construction and Building Workers): Sümer 1, Sok. 18, Kızılay, Ankara; tel. (312) 2324687; fax (312) 2324810; e-mail yol-is@yolis.org.tr; internet yol-is.org.tr; f. 1963; affiliated to Türk-İş; Pres. RAMAZAN AĞAR; Gen. Sec. GÖKHAN GEDIKLI.

Transport

RAILWAYS

A 533-km high-speed rail link between Ankara and İstanbul was inaugurated in 2014. The Marmaray Project, a 76-km suburban line between the European and Asian sections of İstanbul, incorporating a 13.6-km tunnel under the Bosphorus Strait, was completed in 2019. Construction commenced in 2022 of a 503-km high-speed rail link between Ankara and İzmir; the line was expected to be operational in 2027.

İstanbul operates a three-line, 41.6-km light railway system; the third line began operating in January 2021. İstanbul also has eight metro lines totalling 136.6 km in length and serving 107 stations. A further five metro lines (with 104 stations) are currently under construction. Ankara, Adana, Bursa and İzmir also operate metro and light railway systems.

TCDD Taşımacılık AŞ (Turkish State Railways—Transportation): Anafartalar Mah., Hipodrom Cad. 3, Altındağ, Ankara; tel. (312) 3090515; e-mail byhim@tcdd.gov.tr; internet www.tcddtasimacilik.gov.tr; f. 1924 as Türkiye Cumhuriyeti Devlet Demiryolları (TCDD); present name adopted in 2013 after TCDD was defined as the infrastructure operator and TCDD Taşımacılık AŞ as the railway operator; operates all railways and connecting ports of the State Railway Admin., which acquired the status of a state economic enterprise in 1953, and a state economic establishment in 1984; Dir-Gen. METIN AKBAŞ.

Metro İstanbul: Yavuz Selim Mah., Metro Sok. 3, 34220 Esenler, İstanbul; e-mail info@metro.istanbul; internet www.metro.istanbul; f. 1988; est. as İstanbul Ulasim; present name adopted 2016; operates light rail, metro, tram and funicular and aerial cable car lines in İstanbul as an affiliate co of İstanbul Metropolitan Municipality (İstanbul Büyükşehir Belediyesi); Gen. Man. ÖZGÜR SOY.

ROADS

Karayolları Genel Müdürlüğü (KGM) (General Directorate of Highways): İnönü Bul. 14, 06100 Yücetepe, Ankara; tel. (312) 4499000; fax (312) 4497155; e-mail info@kgm.gov.tr; internet www.kgm.gov.tr; f. 1950; Gen. Man. ABDULAKADIR URALOĞLU.

SHIPPING

The ports of Bandırma, Derince, Haydarpaşa (İstanbul), İskenderun and İzmir, all of which are connected to the railway network, are operated by Turkish State Railways (Türkiye Cumhuriyeti Devlet Demiryolları—TCDD), while the port of İstanbul and five smaller ports are operated by the Turkish Maritime Organization. Responsibility for some 13 ports, including those of Antalya and Trabzon, was transferred from the Turkish Maritime Organization to private companies under separate 30-year agreements in 1997–2003. In 2007 control of the port of Mersin was transferred from the TCDD to the private sector under a 36-year concession agreement. A similar arrangement involving the port of Samsun commenced in 2010. In 2011 the Government announced plans to construct a 45-km canal through the European portion of the country (East Thrace), connecting the Black Sea to the Sea of Marmara (and thence to the Aegean and Mediterranean Seas). The Kanal İstanbul project was intended to relieve congestion in the Bosphorus Strait. The project finally received government approval in early 2020 and the tendering process for contracts commenced in 2021. The project was estimated to cost at least US $15,000m. and to take around seven years to complete.

TÜRKIYE (TURKEY)

Regulatory and Port Authorities

Turkish Maritime Organization (Türkiye Denizcilik İşletmeleri—TDI): Genel Müdürlüğü, Rıhtım Cad. Merkez Han 32, 34425 Karaköy, İstanbul; tel. (212) 2515000; fax (212) 2495391; e-mail tdibasin@tdi.com.tr; internet www.tdi.com.tr; Chair. FAHRETTIN SORAN; Gen. Man. MEHMET ALI YIĞZI.

Ambarlı Port Authority: Asma Kat İç Kapı 38, Marmara Mah., Liman Cad. 49, Beylikdüzü, İstanbul; tel. (212) 8756848; fax (212) 8756849; e-mail ambarli.liman@uab.gov.tr; internet ambarliliman.uab.gov.tr; Pres. ENGIN ERAT.

Bandırma Port Authority: Paşabayır Mah., Cumhuriyet Cad., 10200 Bandırma, Balkesir; tel. (266) 7149450; fax (266) 7149451; e-mail bandirma.liman@uab.gov.tr; internet bandirmaliman.uab.gov.tr; Pres. KÜRŞAT AYYILDIZ.

İskenderun Port Authority: Çay Mah. 5, Temmuz Cad. 43, İskenderun; tel. (326) 6141192; fax (326) 6140226; e-mail iskenderun.liman@uab.gov.tr; internet iskenderunliman.uab.gov.tr; Pres. HÜSEYIN DEMIR.

İstanbul Port Authority: Kemenkeş Mah., Rıhtım Cad. 33, 34225 Karaköy, İstanbul; tel. (212) 2492197; fax (212) 2524969; e-mail istanbul.liman@uab.gov.tr; internet istanbulliman.uab.gov.tr; Pres. MUSTAFA KIRAN.

İzmir Port Authority: Atatürk Cad. 178, 35210 İzmir; tel. (232) 4637320; fax (232) 4636663; e-mail izmir.liman@uab.gov.tr; internet izmirliman.uab.gov.tr; Pres. UNAL HAKAN ATALAN.

Mersin Port Authority: Yeni Mah., Cad. 5307, İsmet İnönü Bul. 101, Sok. 4, Akdeniz, Mersin; tel. (324) 2377462; fax (324) 3415877; e-mail mersin.liman@uab.gov.tr; internet mersinliman.uab.gov.tr; Pres. HARUN BAŞTÜRK.

Port of Derince: TCDD Liman İşletme Müdürlüğü, Derince; tel. (262) 2397300; fax (262) 2234278; e-mail derinceliman@tcdd.gov.tr.

Samsun Port Authority: Kale Mah., Sahil Cad. 9, 55030 Samsun; tel. (362) 4359013; fax (362) 4322744; e-mail samsun.liman@uab.gov.tr; internet samsunliman.uab.gov.tr; Pres. HASAN ÖZER.

Principal Shipping Companies

Akmar Shipping Group: Küçükbakkalköy Mah. Cicek Sok. 4, Aksoy Plaza, 34750 Kadıköy, İstanbul; tel. (216) 5762666; fax (216) 5727195; e-mail operations@akmar.com.tr; internet www.akmar.com.tr; f. 1987; Chair. NECDET AKSOY.

Deniz Nakliyatı TAŞ (Turkish Cargo Lines): Fahrettin Kerim Gökay Cad. Denizciler İş Merkezi No. 18, 1A Blok Kat. 1, Altunizade/Üsküdar, İstanbul; tel. (216) 4747400; fax (216) 4747430; e-mail tcl@tcl.com.tr; internet www.tcl.com.tr; f. 1955; bulk carriers; Chair. M. GÜNDÜZ KAPTANOĞLU; Gen. Man. (vacant); 2 large and 2 small handy bulk/ore carriers.

İstanbul Deniz Otobusleri Sanayi ve Ticaret AŞ: Kennedy Cad., Hizli Feribot Iskelesi Yenikapi, İstanbul; tel. (212) 4556900; fax (212) 5173958; e-mail info@ido.com.tr; internet www.ido.com.tr; f. 1987; ferry co; privatized in 2011; Gen. Man. MURAT ORHAN.

Kiran Group of Shipping Companies: Prof. Fahrettin Kerim Gökay Cad. 18/2, Altunizade, Üsküdar, İstanbul; tel. (216) 5541400; e-mail kiran@kiran.com.tr; internet www.kiran.com.tr; f. 1959; Chair. TAHIR KIRAN; Man. Dir GOKHAN KIRAN; 16 vessels.

Ozsay Deniz Elektroniği AŞ: Esentepe Mah., İnönü Cad. 147, 34870 Kartal, İstanbul; tel. (216) 4933610; e-mail info@ozsay.com; internet www.ozsay.com; f. 1976; mfr of maritime navigation and communication equipment; Pres. RECEP KALKAVAN; Man. Dir OMER KALKAVAN.

Türkiye Denizcilik İşletmeleri Denizyolları İşletmesi Müdürlüğü (TDI): Kemenkeş Karamustafapaşa Mah., Kemenkeş Cad. 47, 34425 Karaköy Beyoğlu, İstanbul; tel. (212) 2515000; fax (212) 2495391; e-mail tdibilgiedinme@tdi.gov.tr; internet www.tdi.com.tr; ferry co; Chair. FAHRETTIN SORAN; Man. Dir MEHTAP YÜKSEL.

Yardimci Shipping Group of Cos: Evliya Celebi Mah., Tersaneler Cad. 18, 34944 Tuzla, İstanbul; tel. (216) 3956383; fax (216) 3951278; e-mail info@yardimci.gen.tr; internet www.yardimci.gen.tr; f. 1974; Shipyard Man. ADEM KARADENIZ.

CIVIL AVIATION

In 2023 there were 58 airports in Türkiye; 35 of these airports provided domestic and international flights, while 23 provided solely domestic services. The largest of the airports providing both services are İstanbul and Sabiha Gökçen (both serving İstanbul, with the former located in the European part of the city and the latter in the Asian part), Esenboğa (Ankara), Adnan Menderes (İzmir), Antalya, Dalaman, Milas–Bodrum, Adana, Trabzon, Isparta Süleyman Demirel and Nevşehir–Kapadokya.

Devlet Hava Meydanları İşletmesi Genel Müdürlüğü (General Directorate of State Airports Authority): Emniyet Mah. Mevlana Bul. 32, 06560 Etiler, Ankara; tel. (312) 2042000; fax (312) 2123917; e-mail iletisimmerkezi@dhmi.gov.tr; internet www.dhmi.gov.tr; f. 1984; responsible for air traffic control in Turkish airspace; Chair. of Bd and Gen. Man. HÜSEYIN KESKIN.

Sivil Havacılık Genel Müdürlüğü (Directorate General of Civil Aviation): Gazi Mustafa Kemal Bul. 128A, 06570 Maltepe, Ankara; tel. (312) 2036140; fax (312) 2124684; e-mail bilgi@shgm.gov.tr; internet web.shgm.gov.tr; Dir-Gen. Prof. Dr KEMAL YÜKSEK.

Onur Air Taşımacılık AŞ: Atatürk Havalimanı B Kapısı, Teknik Hangar Yanı 34149, Yeşilköy, İstanbul; tel. (212) 4686687; fax (212) 4686615; e-mail pr@onurair.com; internet www.onurair.com.tr; f. 1992; international and domestic passenger and cargo charter services; 28 aircrafts; Gen. Man. TEOMAN TOSUN.

Pegasus Hava Taşımacılığı AŞ (Pegasus Airlines): Aeropark Yenişehir Mah., Osmanlı Bul. 11, 34912 Kurtköy, İstanbul; tel. (216) 5607000; fax (216) 5607093; e-mail info@flypgs.com; internet www.flypgs.com; f. 1990; domestic and international scheduled and charter services; 69 aircraft; Chair. ALI ISMAIL SABANCI; Gen. Man. MEHMET NANE.

SunExpress (Güneş Ekspres Havacilik AŞ): Yenigöl Mah. Nergiz Sok. 84, 07230 Antalya; tel. (242) 3102626; fax (242) 3102650; e-mail travelcenter@sunexpress.com; internet www.sunexpress.com; f. 1989; 50% owned by Deutsche Lufthansa AG (Germany) and 50% by Turkish Airlines; charter and scheduled passenger and freight; serves European destinations; 83 aircraft; 10m. passengers; Man. Dir Dr MAX KOWNATZKI.

TAV Havalimanları Holding AŞ: İstanbul Atatürk Havalimanı, Dış Hatlar Terminali, 34149 Yeşilköy, İstanbul; tel. (212) 4633000; fax (212) 4653100; e-mail info@tav.aero; internet www.tavairports.com; f. 1997; construction and management of airport facilities; manages Esenboğa (Ankara), Adnan Menderes (İzmir), Milas-Bodrum (Muğla), Gazipaşa–Alanya (Antalya) and Antalya airports, as well as airports in Georgia, North Macedonia, Saudi Arabia, Latvia, Croatia, Kazakhstan and Tunisia; Chair. EDWARD ARKWRIGHT; Pres. and CEO Dr MUSTAFA SANI ŞENER.

Türkiye Hava Yolları AO (THY) (Turkey Airlines Inc): Türkiye Hava Yolları Genel Yönetim Binası, Atatürk Havalimanı, 34149 Yeşilköy, İstanbul; tel. (212) 4636363; fax (212) 4652121; e-mail customer@thy.com; internet www.thy.com.tr; f. 1933; established as Türk Hava Yolları AO (Turkish Airlines Inc); current name adopted 2022; 49.12% state-owned; extensive internal network and scheduled and charter flights to destinations in the Middle East, Africa, the Far East, Central Asia, the USA and Europe; 133 aircraft; Chair. AHMET BOLAT; Gen. Man. BILAL EKŞI.

Tourism

Ministry of Culture and Tourism: see Ministries.

Defence

As assessed at November 2022, the total strength of the Turkish Armed Forces was 355,200 (including conscripts): army est. 260,200; navy est. 45,000; air force est. 50,000. There were also 378,700 reserves and a Paramilitary Force of 156,800 (gendarmerie 152,100 and coastguard 4,700). Military service of 12 months is compulsory for men aged between 20 and 41 years.

Defence Expenditure: TL 138,000m. in 2022.

Chief of the General Staff: Gen. METIN GÜRAK.

Commander of the Turkish Land Forces: Gen. SELÇUK BAYRAKTAROĞLU.

Commander of the Turkish Naval Forces: Adm. ERCÜMENT TATLIOĞLU.

Commander of the Turkish Air Force: Gen. ZIYA CEMAL KADIOĞLU.

Commander of the Turkish Gendarmerie: Gen. ARIF ÇETIN.

Education

An education reform bill approved in 2012 extended the duration of compulsory education from eight to 12 years. It includes four years of elementary school, four years of middle school and four years of high school. For 2023 government expenditure on education was budgeted at about TL 650,000m. (equivalent to 14.5% of total projected spending)

Elementary school starts from six years of age. This may be preceded by an optional pre-school education for children aged between three and five years. In 2019/20, according to UNESCO estimates, total enrolment at pre-primary level was equivalent to 39.8% of children (boys 40.4%; girls 39.1%) in the relevant age-group. Primary education is now entirely free, and co-education is the accepted basis for universal education. In 2019/20, according to UNESCO estimates, 95.1% of children (boys 95.3%; girls 94.9%) in the relevant age-group were enrolled in primary education.

The secondary education system encompasses general high schools, and vocational and technical high schools. In addition, 'open' high schools provide secondary education opportunities to young working people through the media and other new technologies. Those students who wish to proceed to an institute of higher education must pass the state matriculation examination. The study of a modern language (English, French or German) is compulsory. In 2019/20, according to UNESCO estimates, 97.9% of children (boys 98.4%; girls 97.5%) in the relevant age-group were enrolled in lower secondary education, while the comparable ratio for upper secondary enrolment was 82.0% (boys 82.8%; girls 81.2%).

Since 1984, higher educational institutions in Türkiye have been administered by an autonomous state institution, the Council of Higher Education. Almost all institutions were designated as universities. The sector has expanded rapidly in recent years, with more than 100 new universities having been established since 2006. The system also includes institutes of high technology, post-secondary vocational schools and academies for police and military training.

Bibliography

General and Historical Context

Adly, Amr. *State Reform and Development in the Middle East: Turkey and Egypt in the Post-Liberalization Era*. Abingdon, Routledge, 2013.

Ahmad, Feroz. *The Young Turks*. Oxford, Oxford University Press, 1969.

The Turkish Experiment in Democracy 1950–1975. London, Hurst, for Royal Institute of International Affairs, 1977.

Akçam, Taner. *From Empire to Republic: Turkish Nationalism and the Armenian Genocide*. London, Zed Books, 2004.

Aksin, Sina. *Turkey from Empire to Revolutionary Republic: The Emergence of the Turkish Nation from 1789 to the Present*. New York, New York University Press, 2006.

Al, Serhan. *Patterns of Nationhood and Saving the State in Turkey: Ottomanism, Nationalism and Multiculturalism*. Abingdon, Routledge, 2019.

Alderson, A. D. *The Structure of the Ottoman Dynasty*. Oxford, 1956.

Allen, W. E. D., and Muratoff, P. *Caucasian Battlefields: A History of the Wars on the Turco-Caucasian Border, 1828–1921*. Cambridge, 1953.

Ateş, B. (Ed.). *Military Innovation in Türkiye: An Overview of the Post-Cold War Era*. London, Routledge, 2023.

Athanassopoulou, Ekavi. *Strategic Relations between the US and Turkey 1979–2000: Sleeping with a Tiger*. London, Routledge, 2014.

Aymes, Marc, Gourisse, Benjamin, and Massicard, Élise. *Order and Compromise: Government Practices in Turkey from the Late Ottoman Empire to the Early 21st Century*. Leiden, Brill, 2015.

Bean, G. E. *Aegean Turkey*. London, Benn, 1966.

Turkey's Southern Shore. London, Benn, 1968.

Besleney, Zeynel Abidin. *The Circassian Diaspora in Turkey: A Political History*. London, Routledge, 2014.

Bisbee, Eleanor. *The New Turks*. London, Greenwood Press.

Boghossian, Roupen. *Le conflit turco-arménien*. Beirut, Altapress, 1987.

Cahen, Claude. *Pre-Ottoman Turkey*. London, Sidgwick and Jackson, 1968.

Cassels, Lavender. *The Struggle for the Ottoman Empire, 1717–1740*. London, John Murray, 1967.

Coles, Paul. *The Ottoman Impact on Europe*. London, Thames and Hudson, 1968; New York, Brace and World, 1968.

Davison, Roderic H. (updated by Dodd, Clement H.). *Turkey. A Short History*. Huntingdon, Eothen Press, 3rd edn, 1998.

De Bellaigue, Christopher. *Rebel Land: Among Turkey's Forgotten People*. London, Bloomsbury, 2009.

Goodwin, Jason. *Lords of the Horizons: A History of the Ottoman Empire*. New York, Henry Holt, 1999.

Gül, Murat. *The Emergence of Modern Istanbul: Transformation and Modernisation of a City*. London, I. B. Tauris, 2009.

Hale, William. *The Political and Economic Development of Modern Turkey*. London, Croom Helm, 1981.

Turkish Foreign Policy, 1774–2000. London, Frank Cass, 2002.

Hanioğlu, Şükrü. *A Brief History of the Late Ottoman Empire*. Princeton, NJ, Princeton University Press, 2008.

Atatürk: An Intellectual Biography. Princeton, NJ, Princeton University Press, 2011.

Heper, Metin, and Sayari, Sabri (Eds). *The Routledge Handbook of Modern Turkey*. Abingdon, Routledge, 2012.

Heyd, Uriel. *Foundations of Turkish Nationalism: The Life and Teachings of Ziya Gökalp*. London, Luzac and Harvill Press, 1950.

Jacoby, Tim, and Mann, Michael. *Social Power and the Turkish State*. London, Taylor and Francis, 2004.

Kasaba, Resat. *The Ottoman Empire and the World Economy: The Nineteenth Century*. Albany, NY, State University of New York Press, 1989.

Kazamias, A. M. *Education and the Quest for Modernity in Turkey*. London, Allen and Unwin, 1967.

Kazancigil, Ali, and Ozbudun, Ergun (Eds). *Atatürk: Founder of a Modern State*. London, Hurst, 1981.

Kedourie, Elie. *England and the Middle East: The Destruction of the Ottoman Empire, 1914–1921*. Cambridge, 1956.

Ker-Lindsay, James. *Crisis and Conciliation: A Year of Rapprochement Between Greece and Turkey*. London, I. B. Tauris, 2007.

Kerslake, Celia, Öktem, Keren, and Robins, Philip (Eds). *Turkey's Engagement with Modernity: Conflict and Change in the Twentieth Century*. Basingtoke, Palgrave Macmillan, 2010.

Kinnane, Dirk. *The Kurds and Kurdistan*. Oxford, 1965.

Kinross, Lord. *Within the Taurus*. London, 1954.

Turkey. London, 1960.

Kinross, Patrick. *Atatürk: The Rebirth of a Nation* (New edn). London, Phoenix, 2001.

Kinzer, Stephen. *Crescent and Star: Turkey between Two Worlds*. New York, Farar, Straus and Giroux, 2001.

Koray, Enver. *Türkiye Tarih Yayınları Bibliografyası 1729–1950; A Bibliography of Historical Works on Turkey*. Ankara, 1952.

Kushner, David. *The Rise of Turkish Nationalism*. London, Frank Cass, 1980.

Lamb, Harold. *Suleiman the Magnificent: Sultan of the East*. New York, 1951.

Landau, Jacob M. *Pan-Turkism: A Study in Irredentism*. London, Hurst, 1981.

(Ed.). *Atatürk And The Modernization Of Turkey*. Abingdon, Routledge, 2019.

Lewis, Bernard. *Istanbul and the Civilization of the Ottoman Empire*. Norman, OK, University of Oklahoma Press, 1963.

The Emergence of Modern Turkey (3rd edn). New York, NY, Oxford University Press, 2001.

Lewis, G. L. *Turkey* ('Nations of the Modern World' series). London, 1955; 3rd edn, New York, Praeger, 1965.

Lewy, Günter. *The Armenian Massacres in Ottoman Turkey: A Disputed Genocide*. Salt Lake City, UT, University of Utah Press, 2005.

Liddell, Robert. *Byzantium and Istanbul*. London, 1956.

Linke, L. *Allah Dethroned*. London, 1937.

Çatal Hüyük. London, Thames and Hudson, 1967.

Lloyd, Seton. *Early Anatolia*. London, 1956.

Mango, Andrew. *Atatürk*. London, John Murray, 1999.

Turkey and the War on Terror: For Thirty Years We Fought Alone. Abingdon, Routledge, 2005.

Mantran, Robert. *Histoire de la Turquie*. Paris, 1952.

McDowall, David. *A Modern History of the Kurds*. London, I. B. Tauris, 1996.

Mellaart, James. *Earliest Civilizations of the Near East*. London, Thames and Hudson, 1965.

Moorehead, A. *Gallipoli*. London, Wordsworth Editions, 1997.

Newman, Bernard. *Turkish Crossroads*. London, 1951.

Turkey and the Turks. London, Herbert Jenkins, 1968.

Nezir-Akmese, H. *The Birth of Modern Turkey: The Ottoman Military and the March to WWI* (International Library of Twentieth Century History). London, I. B. Tauris, 2005.

TÜRKIYE (TURKEY)

Olsson, Tord, Ozdalga, Elisabeth, and Raudvere, Catharina (Eds). *Alevi Identity*. London, RoutledgeCurzon, 1998.

Ostrogorsky, G. *History of the Byzantine State*. Oxford, 1956.

Özbudun, Ergun. *Party Politics and Social Cleavages in Turkey*. Boulder, CO, Lynne Rienner Publishers, 2013.

Pelt, Mogens. *Military Intervention and a Crisis of Democracy in Turkey: The Menderes Era and its Demise*. London, I. B. Tauris, 2014.

Pope, Hugh. *Sons of the Conquerors: The Rise of the Turkic World*. New York, Overlook Press, 2005.

Price, M. Philips. *A History of Turkey: From Empire to Republic*. London, 1956.

Quataert, Donald. *The Ottoman Empire, 1700–1922*. Cambridge, Cambridge University Press, 2000.

Ramsaur, E. E. *The Young Turks and the Revolution of 1908*. Princeton, NJ, Princeton University Press, 1957.

Reisman, Arnold. *Turkey's Modernization: Refugees from Nazism and Atatürk's Vision*. Washington, DC, New Academia Publishing, 2006.

Rice, Tamara Talbot. *The Seljuks*. London, 1962.

Robinson, Richard D. *The First Turkish Republic*. Cambridge, MA, Harvard University Press, 1963.

Rogan, Eugene. *The Fall of the Ottomans: The Great War in the Middle East, 1914-1920*. London, Allen Lane, 2015.

Rugman, Jonathan, and Hutchings, Roger. *Atatürk's Children: Turkey and the Kurds*. London, Cassell, 1996.

Runciman, Sir Steven. *The Fall of Constantinople, 1453*. Cambridge, Cambridge University Press, 1965.

Salter, Cedric. *Introducing Turkey*. London, Methuen, 1961.

Seal, Jeremy. *A Coup in Turkey: A Tale of Democracy, Despotism and Vengeance in a Divided Land*. London, Chatto & Windus, 2021.

Shankland, David. *Islam and Society in Turkey*. Huntingdon, Eothen Press, 1999.

The Alevis in Turkey: The Emergence of a Secular Islamic Tradition. London, RoutledgeCurzon, 2003.

Shaw, Stanford. *History of the Ottoman Empire*. Cambridge, Cambridge University Press, 1976.

Stark, Freya. *Ionia*. London, 1954.

Lycian Shore. London, 1951.

Riding to the Tigris. London, 1956.

Steinhaus, Kurt. *Soziologie der turkischen Revolution*. Frankfurt, 1969.

Stone, Norman. *Turkey: A Short History*. London, Thames and Hudson, 2011.

Sumner, B. H. *Peter the Great and the Ottoman Empire*. Oxford, 1949.

Toynbee, A. J., and Kirkwood, D. P. *Turkey*. London, 1926.

Tunaya, T. Z. *Atatürk, the Revolutionary Movement and Atatürkism*. İstanbul, Baha, 1964.

Üngör, Uğur Ümit. *The Making of Modern Turkey: Nation and State in Eastern Anatolia, 1913-1950*. Oxford, Oxford University Press, 2012.

Vaughan, Dorothy. *Europe and the Turk: A Pattern of Alliances, 1350–1700*. Liverpool, 1954.

Vere-Hodge, Edward Reginald. *Turkish Foreign Policy, 1918–1948*. London, 2nd revised edn, 1950.

Vertigans, S. *Islamic Roots and Resurgence in Turkey: Understanding and Explaining the Muslim Resurgence*. New York, Praeger, 2003.

Volkan, Vamik D., and Itzkowitz, Norman. *Turks and Greeks, Neighbours in Conflict*. Huntingdon, Eothen Press, 1994.

Webster, D. E. *The Turkey of Atatürk: Social Progress in the Turkish Reformation*. Philadelphia, PA, 1939.

Wittek, P., and Heywood, C. (Ed.). *The Rise of the Ottoman Empire: Studies on the History of Turkey, 13th–15th Centuries*. London, Curzon Press, 2002.

Yılmaz, Bahri. *Challenges to Turkey: The New Role of Turkey in International Politics since the Dissolution of the Soviet Union*. New York, St Martin's Press, 2004 and 2005.

Contemporary Political History

Abbas, Tahir. *Contemporary Turkey in Conflict: Ethnicity, Islam and Politics*. Edinburgh, Edinburgh University Press, 2017.

Akçapar, Burak. *Turkey's New European Era: Foreign Policy on the Road to EU Membership*. Lanham, MD, Rowman & Littlefield Publishers, 2006.

Aktar, Ayhan, Kızılyürek, Niyazi, and Özkırımlı, Umut (Eds). *Nationalism in the Troubled Triangle: Cyprus, Greece and Turkey*. Basingstoke, Palgrave Macmillan, 2010.

Alexander, Yonah, Brenner, Edgar H., and Krause, Serhat Tutuncuoglu (Eds). *Turkey: Terrorism, Civil Rights, and the European Union*. Abingdon, Routledge, 2008.

Alisa, Marcus. *Blood and Belief: The PKK and the Kurdish Fight for Independence*. New York, New York University Press, 2007.

Altunisik, Meliha Benli, and Kavli, Özlem Tur. *Turkey: Challenges of Continuity and Change (The Contemporary Middle East)* (2nd edn). London, Routledge, 2014.

Aras, Bülent, and Keyman, E. Fuat (Eds). *Turkey, the Arab Spring and Beyond*. Abingdon, Routledge, 2019.

Aras, Ramazan. *The Formation of Kurdishness in Turkey: Political Violence, Fear and Pain*. London, Routledge, 2014.

Armstrong, H. C. *Grey Wolf: Mustafa Kemal, an Intimate Study of a Dictator*. London, 1937.

Atasoy, Yildiz. *Turkey, Islamists and Democracy: Transition and Globalization in a Muslim State*. London, I. B. Tauris, 2005.

Ayata, B., and Harders, C. (Eds). *The Affective Dynamics of Mass Protests: Midān Moments and Political Transformation in Egypt and Turkey*. London, Routledge, 2023.

Aydın-Düzgit, Senem, and Tocci, Nathalie. *Turkey and the European Union*. London, Palgrave Macmillan, 2015.

Azak, Umut. *Islam and Secularism in Turkey: Kemalism, Religion and the Nation State*. London, I. B. Tauris, 2010.

Babacan, Errol, Kutun, Melahat, Pinar, Ezgi, and Yılmaz, Zafer (Eds). *Regime Change in Turkey: Neoliberal Authoritarianism, Islamism and Hegemony*. London, Routledge, 2021.

Bahrampour, Firouz. *Turkey, Political and Social Transformation*. New York, Gaus, 1967.

Bengio, Ofra. *The Turkish-Israeli Relationship: Changing Ties of Middle Eastern Outsiders*. Basingstoke, Palgrave Macmillan, 2010.

Berkes, Niyazi. *The Development of Secularism in Turkey*. London, C. Hurst and Co, 1999 (2nd edn; first published 1964).

Bermek, Sevinç. *The Rise of Hybrid Political Islam in Turkey: Origins and Consolidation of the JDP*. London, Palgrave Macmillan, 2019.

Birand, Mehmet Ali. *The Generals' Coup in Turkey: An Inside Story of September 12, 1980*. Oxford, Brassey's, 1987.

Bozdaglioglu, Y. *Turkish Foreign Policy and Turkish Identity: A Constructivist Approach (International Relations Series)*. London, Routledge, 2003.

Brennan, Shane. *Turkey and the Politics of National Identity: Social, Economic and Cultural Transformation*. London, I. B. Tauris, 2013.

Buğra, Ayşe. *New Capitalism in Turkey: The Relationship between Politics, Religion and Business*. Cheltenham, Edward Elgar, 2014.

Bürger, Christian. *Türkei ante portas—Der Beitritt der Türkei zur Europäischen Union*. Frankfürt am Main, Peter Lang, 2009.

Çağaptay, Soner. *The Rise of Turkey: The Twenty-First Century's First Muslim Power*. Lincoln, NE, Potomac Books, 2014.

The New Sultan: Erdogan and the Crisis of Modern Turkey. London, I. B. Tauris, 2017.

Erdogan's Empire: Turkey and the Politics of the Middle East. London, I. B. Tauris, 2020.

Canan-Sokullu, Ebru (Ed.). *Debating Security in Turkey: Challenges and Changes in the Twenty-First Century*. Lanham, MD, Lexington Books, 2013.

Çarkoğlu, A., and Kalaycıoğlu, M. E. *The Rising Tide of Conservatism in Turkey*. Basingstoke, Palgrave Macmillan, 2009.

Çarkoğlu, A., and Rubin, B. M. (Eds). *Turkey and the European Union: Domestic Politics, European Integration, and International Dynamics*. London, Frank Cass, 2003.

Greek-Turkish Relations in an Era of Detente. London, Frank Cass, 2004.

Religion and Politics in Turkey. Abingdon, Routledge, 2005.

Casier, Marlies, and Jongerden, Joost (Eds). *Nationalisms and Politics in Turkey: Political Islam, Kemalism and the Kurdish Issue*. Abingdon, Routledge, 2010.

Cengiz, Fatih Çağatay. *Turkey: The Pendulum between Military Rule and Civilian Authoritarianism*. Leiden and Boston, MA, Brill, 2020.

Cengiz, Firat, and Hoffmann, Lars (Eds). *Turkey and the European Union: Facing New Challenges and Opportunities*. Abingdon, Routledge, 2013.

Christofis, Nikos (Ed.). *Erdoğan's 'New' Turkey: Attempted Coup d'état and the Acceleration of Political Crisis*. Abingdon, Routledge, 2019.

The Kurds in Erdogan's 'New' Turkey: Domestic and International Implications. Abingdon, Routledge, 2021.

Ciddi, Sinan. *Kemalism in Turkish Politics: The Republican People's Party, Secularism and Nationalism*. Abingdon, Routledge, 2010.

Çifçi, Denız. *The Kurds and the Politics of Turkey: Agency, Territory and Religion*. London, I. B. Tauris, 2019.

Çinar, Kürşat. *The Decline of Democracy in Turkey: A Comparative Study of Hegemonic Party Rule*. Abingdon, Routledge, 2019.

Cizre, Ümit. *Secular and Islamic Politics in Turkey: The Making of the Justice and Development Party*. Abingdon, Routledge, 2007.

The Turkish AK Party and its Leader: Criticism, Opposition and Dissent. Abingdon, Routledge, 2016.

Cohn, Edwin J. *Turkish Economic, Social and Political Change*. New York, Praeger, 1970.

Davutoğlu, Ahmet. *Stratejik derinlik: Türkiye'nin uluslararası konumu (Strategic Depth: Turkey's International Position)*. İstanbul, Küre Yayıları, 2001.

Delibas, Kayhan. *The Rise of Political Islam in Turkey: Urban Poverty, Grassroots Activism and Islamic Fundamentalism*. London, I. B. Tauris, 2013.

Demir, Mustafa. *The Geopolitics of Turkey-Kurdistan Relations: Cooperation, Security Dilemmas, and Economies*. Lanham, MD, Lexington Books, 2019.

Dismorr, Ann. *Turkey Decoded*. London, Saqi Books, 2008.

Dodd, Clement H. *Politics and Government in Turkey*. Manchester, Manchester University Press, 1969.

Dönmez, Rasim Özgür, and Yaman, Ali (Eds). *Nation-Building and Turkish Modernization: Islam, Islamism, and Nationalism in Turkey*. London, Lexington Books, 2019.

Dursun-Özkanca, Oya. *Turkey-West Relations: The Politics of Intra-alliance Opposition*. Cambridge, Cambridge University Press, 2019.

Eligür, Banu. *The Mobilization of Political Islam in Turkey*. Cambridge, Cambridge University Press, 2010.

Eralp, Doğa Ulas (Ed.). *Turkey as a Mediator: Stories of Success and Failure*. Lanham, MD, Lexington Books, 2016.

Erşen, Emre, and Köstem, Seçkin (Eds). *Turkey's Pivot to Eurasia: Geopolitics and Foreign Policy in a Changing World Order*. London, Routledge, 2019.

Fuller, Graham. *The New Turkish Republic: Turkey as a Pivotal State in the Muslim World*. Washington, DC, US Institute of Peace Press, 2007.

Gokay, Bulent. *Soviet Eastern Policy and Turkey, 1920–1991 (Routledge Studies in the History of Russia and Eastern Europe)*. Abingdon, Routledge, 2006.

Gourlay, William. *The Kurds in Erdoğan's Turkey: Balancing Identity, Resistance and Citizenship*. Edinburgh, Edinburgh University Press, 2021.

Güneş, Cengiz. *The Kurdish National Movement in Turkey: From Protest to Resistance*. Abingdon, Routledge, 2011.

Gürcan, Efe Can. *Challenging Neoliberalism at Turkey's Gezi Park: From Private Discontent to Collective Class Action*. Basingstoke, Palgrave Macmillan, 2015.

Hale, William. *Turkey, the US and Iraq*. London, Saqi Books, 2007.

Politics of Modern Turkey. Abingdon, Routledge, 2008.

Hale, William, and Özbudun, Ergun. *Islamism, Democracy and Liberalism in Turkey*. Abingdon, Routledge, 2009.

Houston, Christopher. *Islam, Kurds and the Turkish Nation State*. Oxford, Berg, 2001.

Howe, Marvine. *Turkey Today: A Nation Divided over Islam's Revival*. Boulder, CO, Westview Press, 2000.

Ibrahim, Ferhad, and Gurbey, Gulistan (Eds). *The Kurdish Conflict in Turkey: Obstacles and Chances for Peace and Democracy*. New York, Palgrave Macmillan, 2001.

Ifantis, Kostas, and Verney, Susannah. *Turkey's Road to European Union Membership: National Identity and Political Change*. Abingdon, Routledge, 2008.

Jabar, Faleh A. (Ed.). *The Kurds: Nationalism and Politics*. London, Saqi Books, 2006.

Jenkins, Gareth. *Context and Circumstance: The Turkish Military and Politics*. Oxford, Oxford University Press, 2001.

Political Islam in Turkey. New York, Palgrave Macmillan, 2006.

Jonasson, Ann-Kristin. *The EU's Democracy Promotion and the Mediterranean Neighbours: Orientation, Ownership and Dialogue in Jordan and Turkey*. Abingdon, Routledge, 2013.

Joppien, Charlotte. *Municipal Politics in Turkey: Local Government and Party Organisation*. Abingdon, Routledge, 2017.

Joseph, Joseph S. *Turkey and the European Union*. New York, Palgrave Macmillan, 2006.

Karasipahi, Sena. *Muslims in Modern Turkey: Kemalism, Modernism and the Revolt of the Islamic Intellectuals*. London, I. B. Tauris, 2008.

Kastoryano, Riva (Ed.). *Turkey Between Nationalism and Globalization*. Abingdon, Routledge, 2013.

Kavakli Birdal, Nur Banu. *Confronting Honour Killings in Turkey: The Interaction of State and Civil Society*. London, I. B. Tauris, 2015.

Kayaalp, Ebru. *Remaking Politics, Markets and Citizens in Turkey: Governing through Smoke*. London, Bloomsbury, 2014.

Kaylan, M. *The Kemalists: Islamic Revival And The Fate Of Secular Turkey*. New York, Prometheus Books, 2005.

Kirişci, Kemal. *Turkey and the West: Fault Lines in a Troubled Alliance*. Washington, DC, Brookings Institution Press, 2017.

Kumbaracıbaşı, Arda Can. *Turkish Politics and the Rise of the AKP: Dilemmas of Institutionalization and Leadership Strategy*. Abingdon, Routledge, 2009.

Liel, Alon. *Turkey in the Middle East: Oil, Islam and Politics*. Boulder, CO, Lynne Rienner Publishers, 2001.

Linden, Ronald Haly, et al. *Turkey and its Neighbors: Foreign Relations in Transition*. Boulder, CO, Lynne Rienner Publishers, 2012.

Lord, Ceren. *Religious Politics in Turkey: From the Birth of the Republic to the AKP*. Cambridge, Cambridge University Press, 2018.

Martin, Natalie. *Security and the Turkey—EU Accession Process: Norms, Reforms and the Cyprus Issue*. Basingstoke, Palgrave Macmillan, 2015.

Massicard, Elise, and Watts, Nicole (Eds). *Negotiating Political Power in Turkey: Breaking up the Party*. Abingdon, Routledge, 2012.

Murat Tezcür, Güneş (Ed.). *The Oxford Handbook of Turkish Politics*. Oxford, Oxford University Press, 2022.

Öcalan, Abdullah (trans. Klaus Happel). *Prison Writings: The Roots of Civilisation*. London, Pluto Press, 2007.

Öney, Berna. *Ethnicity and Party Politics in Turkey: The Rise of the Kurdish Party during the Kurdish Opening Process*. London, Routledge, 2019.

Özcan, Ali Kemal. *A Theoretical Analysis of the PKK and Abdullah Öcalan*. Abingdon, Routledge, 2005.

Özerdem, Alpaslan, and Özerdem, Füsun (Eds). *Human Security in Turkey: Challenges for the 21st Century*. Abingdon, Routledge, 2013.

Özerdem, Alpaslan, and Whiting, Matthew (Eds). *The Routledge Handbook of Turkish Politics*. Abingdon, Routledge, 2019.

Özkırımlı, Umut. *The Making of a Protest Movement in Turkey: #occupygezi*. Basingstoke, Palgrave Macmillan, 2014.

Özyürek, Esra, Özpınar, Gaye, and Altındiş, Emrah (Eds). *Authoritarianism and Resistance in Turkey: Conversations on Democratic and Social Challenges*. Cham, Springer, 2019.

Park, Bill. *Modern Turkey: People, State and Foreign Policy in a Globalised World*. Abingdon, Routledge, 2011.

Polat, Necati. *Regime Change in Contemporary Turkey: Politics, Rights, Mimesis*. Edinburgh, Edinburgh University Press, 2017.

Poulton, Hugh. *Top Hat, Grey Wolf and Crescent: Turkish Nationalism and the Turkish Republic*. London, Hurst and Co, 1997.

Rabasa, Angel. *The Rise of Political Islam in Turkey*. Santa Monica, CA, RAND Corporation, 2008.

Robins, Philip. *Turkish Foreign Policy since the Cold War*. London, C. Hurst, 2002.

Rodriguez, Carmen, et al (Eds). *Turkey's Democratization Process*. Abingdon, Routledge, 2013.

Roy, O. *Turkey Today: A European Nation?* London, Anthem Press, 2005.

Rubin, Aviad, and Sarfati, Yusuf. *The Jarring Road to Democratic Inclusion: a Comparative Assessment of State-Society Engagements in Israel and Turkey*. Lanham, MD, Lexington Books, 2016.

Rubin, Barry, and Çarkoğlu, Ali. (Eds). *Religion and Politics in Turkey*. Abingdon, Routledge, 2009.

Salapatas, Dimitris. *The Aegean Sea Dispute between Greece and Turkey: The Consequences for NATO and the EU*. London, Akakia Publications, 2014.

Sarfati, Yusuf. *Mobilizing Religion in Middle East Politics: A Comparative Study of Israel and Turkey*. Abingdon, Routledge, 2013.

Sayarı, Sabri, Musil, Pelin Ayan, and Demirkol, Özhan (Eds). *Party Politics in Turkey: A Comparative Perspective*. Abingdon, Routledge, 2018.

Sirkeci, İbrahim, Elçin, Doğa, and Şeker, Güven. *Politics and Law in Turkish Migration*. London, Transnational Press London, 2015.

Stone, Norman. *Turkey: A Short History*. London, Thames & Hudson, 2011.

Süsler, Buğra. *Turkey, the EU and the Middle East: Foreign Policy Cooperation and the Arab Uprisings.* Abingdon, Routledge, 2022.

Tabak, Husrev, Tüfekçi, Özgür, and Chiriatti, Alessia. *Domestic and Regional Uncertainties in the New Turkey.* Newcastle-upon-Tyne, Cambridge Scholars Publishing, 2017.

Taspinar, Omar. *Kurdish Nationalism and Political Islam in Turkey: Kemalist Identity in Transition.* London, Routledge, 2011.

Tokdoğan, Nagehan. *Yeni Osmanlıcılık: Hınç, Nostalji, Narsisizm (New Ottomanism: Resentment, Nostalgia, Narcissism).* İstanbul, İletişim Yayınları, 2018.

Tol, Gönül. *Erdoğan's War: A Strongman's Struggle at Home and in Syria.* Oxford, Oxford University Press, 2023.

Tuğal, Cihan. *The Fall of the Turkish Model: How the Arab Uprisings Brought Down Islamic Liberalism.* New York, NY, Verso, 2016.

Turam, Berna (Ed.). *Secular State and Religious Society: Two Forces in Play in Turkey.* New York, Palgrave Macmillan, 2012.

Turan, Ilter. *Turkey's Difficult Journey to Democracy: Two Steps Forward, One Step Back.* Oxford, Oxford University Press, 2015.

Uğur, Mehmet, and Canefe, Nergis. *Turkey and European Integration: Accession Prospects and Issues (Europe and the Nation State).* London, Routledge, 2004.

Ünal, Mustafa. *Counterterrorism in Turkey: Policy Choices and Policy Effects Toward the Kurdistan Workers' Party (PKK).* Abingdon, Routledge, 2011.

Uslu, Nasuh. *Turkish Foreign Policy in the Post-Cold War Period.* Hauppauge, NY, Nova Publishers, 2007.

Vali, Ferenc A. *Bridge Across the Bosphorus: The Foreign Policy of Turkey.* Baltimore, MD, Johns Hopkins University Press, 1970.

Verney, Susannah, Bosco, Anna, and Aydın-Düzgit, Senem (Eds). *The AKP Since Gezi Park: Moving to Regime Change in Turkey.* Abingdon, Routledge, 2019.

Waldman, Simon A., and Caliskan, Emre. *The New Turkey and its Discontents.* London, Hurst & Co, 2016.

Yadirgi, Veli. *The Political Economy of the Kurds of Turkey: From the Ottoman Empire to the Turkish Republic.* Cambridge, Cambridge University Press, 2017.

Yavuz, M. Hakan, and Öztürk, Ahmet Erdi. *Islam, Populism and Regime Change in Turkey: Making and Re-making the AKP.* London, Routledge, 2019.

Yavuz, M. H. *Secularism and Muslim Democracy in Turkey.* Cambridge, Cambridge University Press, 2009.

Yesilada, Birol. *EU-Turkey Relations in the 21st Century.* Abingdon, Routledge, 2012.

Yesilada, Birol, and Rubin, Barry (Eds). *Islamization of Turkey under the AKP Rule.* Abingdon, Routledge, 2012.

Yıldız, K. *The Kurds in Turkey: EU Accession and Human Rights.* London, Pluto Press, 2005.

Yıldız, Kerim, and Breau, Susan. *The Kurdish Conflict: International Humanitarian Law and Post-Conflict Mechanisms.* Abingdon, Routledge, 2010.

Yılmaz, Bahri. *Challenges to Turkey: The New Role of Turkey in International Politics Since the Dissolution of the Soviet Union.* New York, St Martin's Press, 2006.

Zihnioğlu, Özge. *EU–Turkey Relations: Civil Society and Depoliticization.* Abingdon, Routledge, 2019.

Zurcher, Erik J. *Turkey: A Modern History.* London, I. B. Tauris, 2017, revised edn.

Economy

Aydin, Z. *The Political Economy of Turkey.* London, Pluto Press, 2005.

Insel, Ahmet. *La Turquie entre l'ordre et le développement.* Paris, L'Harmattan, 1984.

Issawi, Charles. *The Economic History of Turkey.* Chicago, IL, University of Chicago Press, 1980.

Kara, Alper, and Altunbas, Yener. *Banking under Political Instability and Chronic High Inflation: The Case of Turkey.* New York, Palgrave Macmillan, 2007.

Nas, Tevfik. *Tracing the Economic Transformation of Turkey from the 1920s to EU Accession.* Leiden, Martinus Nijhoff Publishers, 2008.

Odekon, M. *The Costs of Economic Liberalization in Turkey.* Bethlehem, PA, Lehigh University Press, 2005.

Onis, Z., and Rubin, B. M. (Eds). *The Turkish Economy in Crisis.* London, Frank Cass, 2003.

Onis, Ziya, and Senses, Fikret (Eds). *Turkey and the Global Economy: Neo-Liberal Restructuring and Integration in the Post-Crisis Era.* Abingdon, Routledge, 2013.

Rittenberg, Libby (Ed.). *The Political Economy of Turkey in the Post-Soviet Era.* Westport, CT, Praeger Publishing, 1998.

Togan, Sübidey. *Economic Liberalization and Turkey.* Abingdon, Routledge, 2010.

Yalman, Galip L., Marois, Thomas, and Güngen, Ali Riza (Eds). *The Political Economy of Financial Transformation in Turkey.* Abingdon, Routledge, 2018.

THE UNITED ARAB EMIRATES

ABU DHABI   AJMAN   DUBAI   FUJAIRAH   RAS AL-KHAIMAH   SHARJAH   UMM AL-QAIWAIN

Geography

The coastline of the United Arab Emirates (UAE) extends for nearly 650 km (400 miles) from the frontier of the Sultanate of Oman to Khor al-Udaid, on the Qatari peninsula, in the Persian (Arabian) Gulf, interrupted only by an isolated outcrop of the Sultanate of Oman, which lies on the coast of the Persian Gulf to the west and the Gulf of Oman to the east at the Strait of Hormuz. Six of the seven emirates lie on the coast of the Persian Gulf, while the seventh, Fujairah, is situated on the eastern coast of the peninsula, and has direct access to the Gulf of Oman. The area is one of extremely shallow seas, with offshore islands and coral reefs, and often an intricate pattern of sand-banks and small gulfs as a coastline. There is a considerable tide. The waters of the Gulf contain abundant quantities of fish, hence the important role of fishing in local life.

The climate is arid, with very high summer temperatures; except for a few weeks in winter, air humidity is also very high. The total area of the UAE has been estimated at 77,700 sq km (30,000 sq miles), relatively small compared with neighbouring Oman and Saudi Arabia, and it has a rapidly growing population. At the most recent national census, in 2005, the population was enumerated at 4,106,427, giving a population density of 119.5 people per km. By mid-2023 the United Nations estimated that it had reached 9,516,871. Non-nationals made up some 88.5% of the UAE's population in 2022. Most of the population is concentrated in the emirates of Abu Dhabi and Dubai, the principal commercial regions of the country. Abu Dhabi is the largest emirate, with an area of about 67,340 sq km and a population of an estimated 2,908,173 in 2016, according to the Statistics Centre of Abu Dhabi. The city of Abu Dhabi is also the capital of the UAE. The most important port is Dubai, the capital of the UAE's second largest emirate, which had an estimated population of 3,549,900 (including 3,265,250 non-nationals) in 2022, according to the Dubai Statistics Centre. Dubai's significance originally derived from its position on one of the rare deep creeks of the area, and it now has a large transit trade. However, in recent years it has become a centre for international commerce and tourism.

Many inhabitants are still nomadic Arabs, and the official language is Arabic, which is spoken by almost all of the native population. Arabs are outnumbered, however, by non-Arab immigrant workers, mainly from India, Bangladesh, Pakistan and the Philippines. Most UAE nationals are Muslims, mainly of the Sunni sect.

History

KRISTIAN COATES ULRICHSEN

On 16 January 1968 British Prime Minister Harold Wilson announced that the United Kingdom intended to withdraw from all positions east of the Suez Canal, Egypt, by the end of 1971. The UK was under growing economic pressure from a serious financial crisis that had started in 1966 and a balance of payments crisis that had resulted in a currency devaluation in November 1967. With economic problems and an ideological distaste for colonialism, Wilson's Government had already expressed in 1966 its intent to withdraw from Aden by the end of 1968 and, in 1967, had also formulated plans for the UK's departure from Malaysia and Singapore. The announcement of the UK's impending withdrawal from all positions east of Suez nevertheless took the sheikhs in the Persian (Arabian) Gulf (and British officials) completely by surprise, particularly since the Minister of State at the Foreign Office, Goronwy Roberts, had, in November 1967, reaffirmed Wilson's pledge, made just seven months earlier, that 'the Gulf is an area of such vital importance not only to the economy of Western Europe but also to world peace that it would be totally irresponsible of us to withdraw our forces from the area'.

On 18 February 1968 the Rulers of Abu Dhabi and Dubai met at Al-Sameeh, a location close to their mutual border, and agreed to create a two-emirate union as the basis for a larger federal entity and to invite the other five sheikhdoms—Ajman, Fujairah, Ras al-Khaimah, Sharjah and Umm al-Qaiwain—(as well as Bahrain and Qatar) to join. The agreement reached between Sheikh Zayed bin Sultan Al Nahyan of Abu Dhabi and Sheikh Rashid bin Said Al Maktoum of Dubai also resolved a number of outstanding issues relating to their emirates' respective onshore and offshore boundaries. The first meeting of all nine rulers (from the seven so-called Trucial States that now comprise the United Arab Emirates—UAE, plus Bahrain and Qatar) took place in Dubai on 25 February 1968, and two days later the Dubai Agreement was signed, providing for the creation of a Union of Arab Emirates to take effect on 30 March. Sheikh Zayed would become the President of the union, while the Deputy Ruler of Qatar, Sheikh Khalifa bin Hamad Al Thani, would become its Prime Minister. Further progress was, however, complicated by underlying tensions, particularly between the Rulers of Bahrain and Qatar and the two dominant Trucial States (Abu Dhabi and Dubai) over how such a union should be realized. Moreover, Sheikh Mohammed bin Hamad Al Sharqi, the Ruler of Fujairah, expressed his unease about the dominance of the 'big four' at the Dubai meeting and suggested that the Rulers of the five smaller sheikhdoms had only been given an hour to study the Dubai Agreement before signing it.

Although a further meeting of the Supreme Council of Rulers (comprising the rulers of the seven emirates) in October 1968 resulted in an agreement on the creation of an external defence force (while recognizing the right of each sheikhdom to maintain its own army), two subsequent gatherings in Doha, Qatar, in May 1969 and Abu Dhabi in October ended in failure. Strong support for the nine-member Union of Arab Emirates came from Kuwait, with its Minister of Foreign Affairs, Sheikh Sabah al-Ahmad al-Jaber al-Sabah, being a particularly forceful advocate for the concept. However, persistent disagreements between Qatar and Bahrain over the location of a permanent capital overshadowed the Doha meeting in May, while at the October meeting in Abu Dhabi Qatar and Dubai (which had been linked through dynastic intermarriage and, since 1966, a currency union) attempted to force Bahrain out of the union. Sheikh Saqr bin Muhammad of Ras al-Khaimah also walked out of the Abu Dhabi summit after demanding control of the Ministry of Defence, which had been granted to Abu Dhabi. While the October gathering concluded without agreement, it nevertheless revealed the closer alignment between the four other northern sheikhdoms (Ajman, Fujairah, Sharjah and Umm al-Qaiwain) and Abu Dhabi as the basis for a union of the Trucial States minus Bahrain and Qatar.

In the event, the dismissal of Iran's longstanding territorial claim to Bahrain by a United Nations (UN) mission that visited the archipelago in 1970 prompted Bahrain to declare its independence as a sovereign state on 15 August 1971, while Qatar followed suit on 3 September. Sheikh Rashid bin Said Al Maktoum of Dubai also briefly considered independence, but he ultimately reached agreement with the other Trucial leaders in July 1971. A meeting of the Trucial States Council in Dubai on 10 July was followed eight days later by the announcement that the UAE would come into effect before the end of the year. Only six of the Rulers opted to join at this stage, with Sheikh Saqr of Ras al-Khaimah refusing to commit, while not ruling out joining the federation at an unspecified later date. Although Sheikh Saqr justified his decision not to participate in the formation of the UAE on the grounds of the inequality of representation in federal organizations, a group of Ras al-Khaimah notables formed a committee and submitted a petition to the Ruler urging him to change his mind and join the federation.

CREATION OF FEDERAL INSTITUTIONS

The six-member federation that was established on 2 December 1971 faced a challenging domestic and regional environment as well as a protracted struggle over the balance of power between the federal and emirate levels. Even as a collective entity, the UAE was tiny in terms of population, if not territorially as small as Bahrain and Qatar: the first formal census taken in 1968 revealed the population of Dubai to be approximately 59,000, compared with 46,000 in Abu Dhabi and just 3,744 in Umm al-Qaiwain out of a total population of 180,000. The fact that federal arrangements had been formulated in haste as a series of compromises meant that in the early years of the federation a number of issues remained as sources of political tension among the emirates. Another challenge was ensuring that pre-existing historical links between individual amirs and neighbouring countries would eventually be incorporated into a new set of bilateral relationships as foreign policy developed at the federal level.

Far from being a 'core-periphery' issue as in many of the postcolonial states that had come into existence during the decolonization period in the 1950s and 1960s, the splits in the UAE resembled more of a struggle between its two most powerful constituent territories, with associated 'coalitions' of supporting emirates on either side. This was most evident in the persistent tension over constitutional arrangements, the integration of local security forces, and the conduct of regional and foreign policy in the 1970s and 1980s, when, in all three cases, sharp divisions occurred. Moreover, the 'founding fathers' of the UAE had to forge a working relationship with each other, and balance both individual emirate and collective federal interests in policymaking. This was not always an easy task for Rulers who had been used to wielding sole executive authority and had, in two cases, been in power since 1928 (Ajman) and 1929 (Umm al-Qaiwain), respectively.

From the beginning, the new federal institutions were confronted with the challenge of formalizing and institutionalizing the mechanisms for inter-emirate co-operation and the upward transfer of authority (and legitimacy) in specific areas to the federal level. Federal Law No. 1/1972 established the structure of governance in the UAE and defined the jurisdiction of the ministries and the authority vested in the ministers. The principle of power-sharing (albeit in a federation dominated by Abu Dhabi and Dubai) was enshrined in the first cabinet announced by Sheikh Zayed, who had been elected as President of the UAE, alongside Sheikh Rashid of Dubai as Vice-President and Sheikh Rashid's eldest son, Sheikh Maktoum bin Rashid Al Maktoum, as Prime Minister. Six cabinet posts were allocated to representatives of Abu Dhabi, including the key Ministries of the Interior, Foreign Affairs and Information, while Dubai received the defence, finance, and economy and industry portfolios. Three cabinet posts were also apportioned to Sharjah, while Ajman and Umm al-Qaiwain received two each and Fujairah one.

Institutional capacity-building took time to develop and proceeded from a very low starting point in 1971. The Gulf political analyst and historian J. E. Peterson (see Bibliography) observed that the federal civil service numbered just 4,000 in 1971 (but rose rapidly to 24,000 by 1977 and 38,000 by 1983), that all federal ministries 'had to be built entirely from scratch', and, most remarkably, that the Ministry of Foreign Affairs 'began with only the Minister and a staff of three'. In addition to integrating senior members of the seven ruling families into positions of leadership, other key posts were filled by their senior technocratic advisers such as Ahmad Khalifa al-Suwaidi and Mani bin Said al-Otaiba, who became, respectively, the UAE's first Minister of Foreign Affairs and first Minister of Petroleum, and Mehdi al-Tajir, one of the Ruler of Dubai's closest advisers, who was named as the UAE's first ambassador to the UK in 1971. All three were scions of leading tribal families and among the first generation of Emiratis to acquire a formal education and professional training. Their appointments reflected in part the fact that, as Andrea Rugh (see Bibliography) observed in her study of the political culture of leadership, after the creation of the UAE:

'another way that rulers cemented their relationships was through appointments to advisory councils, federal cabinet positions, heads of organizations, and other highly visible positions. Barring other circumstances, these positions were assigned in recognition of family or tribal loyalties. The position in effect co-opted future commitment and provided access to influence for the group's members—a patronage system of sorts.'

Other mechanisms for distributing power among the seven emirates were the Federal Supreme Council (FSC—which consists of the seven Rulers and acts as the source of executive and legislative authority) and the Federal National Council (FNC—which consists of 40 members apportioned among the emirates by size). The FNC came into existence with the adoption of a provisional Constitution and convened for the first time in February 1972. Until 2006 the membership of the FNC was entirely appointed by the ruler of each emirate and the seats apportioned according to the emirates' relative size. Thus, Abu Dhabi and Dubai were assigned eight members, while Ras al-Khaimah and Sharjah appointed six representatives, and Ajman, Fujairah and Umm al-Qaiwain each selected four. The FNC views all federal legislation and can vote to approve, amend or reject draft bills, although Article 110 of the Constitution gave the FSC the power to approve a bill over the objections of the FNC. Membership of the FNC, particularly when it was an all-appointed body, tended to be drawn from the business community and prominent local merchant families.

EVOLUTION OF REPRESENTATIVE INSTITUTIONS

While the FNC never threatened to shift the focus of decision-making away from the FSC or the Council of Ministers, there were occasions when it achieved success in raising and channelling broader concerns over sensitive issues. A prominent example occurred in 1986 when the FNC succeeded in amending a law on state security that had prompted widespread public debate. The FNC also played a prominent role in attempts to resolve a constitutional impasse in the late 1970s (see below), holding a joint session with the Council of Ministers in February 1979 that resulted in a memorandum to the FSC that recommended measures to strengthen the federation.

Together, the creation of the FNC and the FSC in the 1970s were instrumental in the development of a hybrid system of governance aptly described by Sheikh Fahim bin Sultan Al Qasimi, the Minister of Economy and Commerce in the 1990s, as one in which:

'we have developed without undermining the social, cultural and political fabric of our society. This has been due in large part to leadership [of Sheikh Zayed] ... Our system combines the best of the old with the best of the new. We have retained democratic Islamic traditions, foremost among which is the *majlis*, the open council in which national and local leaders meet regularly with citizens to discuss issues of concern' (see Bibliography).

While the FNC remained an appointed and strictly consultative body for the first 34 years of its existence, a cautious and initially very limited exercise in political participation began shortly after Sheikh Zayed's death in November 2004. In early 2006 the formal position of Minister of State for Federal National Council Affairs was created, and Anwar bin Mohammed Gargash, the Minister of State for Foreign Affairs, was appointed to oversee the first election in the UAE's history for one-half of the 40 seats on the FNC (the remaining 20 council members were appointees). A National Election Committee was formed under Gargash. The first election took place in December with a small electoral college that was chosen by each of the seven emirate leaderships. A total of 6,595 people were eventually included in the electoral college that was eligible to vote for the 456 candidates (391 men and 65 women)—a figure equivalent to just 0.08% of the population. The final voting pool was composed predominantly of university graduates and people aged between 21 and 40, who were forbidden to form political parties and alliances, or campaign on 'national' issues.

One woman, Dr Amal al-Qubaisi, was elected in Abu Dhabi in the 2006 election, and eight others were nominated subsequently for the 20 appointed members of the FNC, giving a total female representation of nine out of 40. However, the greater visibility of women in public and political life, while positively encouraged at the federal level, did not always proceed as smoothly in some of the more conservative emirates. In a study of the 2006 election compiled by researchers at the Dubai School of Government, one female candidate stated that: 'In Ras al-Khaimah, we found many obstacles since the nature of our society there is a tribal one, which prevents women from playing a leadership role.' Another interviewee added that 'Even if the trend is generally positive in the UAE, based on what I witnessed in Umm al-Qaiwain, there was no female participation'.

Several of the 20 elected members did use the subsequent FNC term (2006–11) to request that the Government submit draft laws to the FNC for debate prior to their approval, but these efforts were unsuccessful. Ahead of the September 2011 election, the electoral register was expanded 20-fold to 129,274, but turnout declined sharply to 27.8% and voting largely followed tribal lines, particularly in the northern emirates. Once again, one woman, Sheikha Issa bint Ghanem al-Arrai, was elected, this time in Umm al-Qaiwain. However, some FNC members expressed their disappointment at what they considered the 'slow pace' of FNC sessions and, in particular, persistent ministerial absences from the Council. In an interview with *The National* daily newspaper, one member from Dubai, Hamad al-Rahoomi, summarized in 2015 the challenges that he felt were undermining the performance of the FNC:

'How can we tell people, "Come and vote, the council is important, we monitor the Government?" How can we give ourselves to the people when it is no secret that we are struggling now to meet with the Government? This is unacceptable. We have a problem with low turnout during the elections and want to give the council value. One of the reasons why people are not getting involved in the elections is because no minister is available to attend the sessions. This affects the reputation of the FNC'.

Ahead of the October 2015 elections to the FNC, the franchise was extended yet again, with the size of the electoral college rising substantially to 224,279—a figure 34 times higher than the initial 2006 list and a 65% increase on the 2011 figure.

Following the 2015 poll, held on 3 October, the UAE made regional history as Amal al-Qubaisi was elected as the first female Speaker of an Arab parliamentary chamber. In December 2018 the Government Communication Office in Abu Dhabi announced 50% of the members of the new FNC due to be elected in October 2019 would be women. At the election, held on 5 October 2019, seven of the 20 elected seats were won by female candidates, and an additional thirteen women were duly appointed to the FNC to meet the 50% target. The size of the electoral college increased significantly once more, to 337,738 members—an increase of 51% compared with 2015, attributable principally to the allocations to Sharjah, Ras al-Khaimah and Fujairah, which more than doubled compared with 2015. The emirate-level allocations in the 2019 electoral college were: 101,549 members from Abu Dhabi, 60,772 from Dubai, 64,293 from Sharjah, 55,289 from Ras al-Khaimah, 39,017 from Fujairah, 10,165 from Ajman and 6,653 from Umm al-Qaiwain. Saqr Ghobash was elected Speaker of the FNC in mid-November.

CONSTITUTIONAL GRIDLOCK

The growth and expansion of the FNC was not inevitable. Three major challenges—two domestic and one regional—dominated the opening two decades of the federal experiment in the UAE between 1971 and the Gulf crisis of 1990. As such, it was by no means certain that the federal arrangement put in place in 1971 would thrive, or even survive, as many other such experiments in the previous decade had failed. British officials, in particular, viewed the early development of the UAE with a cautiously optimistic yet still ambivalent attitude. One such assessment prepared in June 1973 by Anthony Harris, an official at the UK's Foreign and Commonwealth Office, cautioned that 'in forming our policy towards the UAE we must bear in mind the chances of it falling apart' and added that:

'We still believe that the arrangement which we helped to establish in the Gulf in 1971 is a suitable basis for its development and stability. The UAE however is the most vulnerable of the new states. It is bedevilled by a lack of co-operation between the rulers of the constituent states, which is a continuation of their traditional distrust and tribal rivalries . . . Although other rulers are not so important, they have considerable nuisance value, notably Sharjah and Ras al-Khaimah'.

Although the provisional Constitution carefully delineated the separation of powers between the federal and emirate levels, throughout the 1970s arguments continued over the balance of power between the two. Malcolm Peck (see Bibliography) described the key fault line as being:

'whether the union would take the form of a centralized state, with the seven emirates closely integrated under the Federal Government, or would pursue a gradualist approach towards greater federal power, with each emirate retaining its essential autonomy'.

Sheikh Zayed was the leading proponent of a stronger 'presidential' system, and during the decade he redistributed the oil wealth that had accrued to Abu Dhabi in an effort to build stronger federal institutions. In February 1972 the federal Government intervened in the succession process in Sharjah after the assassination of the incumbent Ruler, Sheikh Khalid bin Mohammed Al Qasimi, by his predecessor, whom the UK had ousted seven years earlier to ensure that Sheikh Sultan bin Mohammed Al Qasimi became ruler. Later that year the federal Government intervened again to end a brief yet violent territorial clash between Sharjah and Fujairah that left four people dead, while another, more serious, incident between Fujairah and Ras al-Khaimah culminated in the accidental shooting down of a helicopter that was carrying one of the sons of the Ruler of Dubai over the disputed Masafi zone. In his history of UAE foreign policy (see Bibliography), Emirati scholar Hassan Hamdan al-Alkim suggested that the helicopter that was shot down was carrying the present Ruler of Dubai, Sheikh Mohammed bin Rashid Al Maktoum, and that the incident actually related to another long-running frontier dispute involving an area of land astride the Dubai–Sharjah boundary, which was only resolved by a demarcation agreement in 1985 after an earlier attempt at international mediation had failed. In his 1979 history of the UAE, revealingly subtitled *Unity in Fragmentation* (see Bibliography), Saudi academic Ali Mohammed Khalifa recorded Sheikh Zayed expressing his frustration over the persistence of inter-emirate conflicts in 1976:

'I spent nearly a week in the northern emirates in an attempt to settle some border disputes of minor consequence . . . I can say, with both bitterness and sorrow, that their disputes often involve a few tens of meters, and do you believe that we have not been able to build a hospital on a piece of real estate because two emirates claim sovereignty over it?'

Sheikh Rashid of Dubai led the alternative group that fiercely resisted the centralization of authority and advocated instead the preservation of strong emirate-level power. Dubai's more advanced economic development and bureaucratic and physical infrastructure meant that it was far less reliant upon support from the federal (or Abu Dhabi) level than the northern emirates. With the UAE's budget being funded almost entirely by Abu Dhabi, the leadership in Dubai was less directly vested in the federal level than its larger neighbour, at least initially. Moreover, the spirit of compromise between Sheikh Rashid and Sheikh Zayed that had made possible the union of 1971 was not unshakable, and on several occasions during the mid- to late 1970s policy disagreements between Dubai and Abu Dhabi threatened to tear apart the fledgling federation.

One example occurred in May 1976 during a tumultuous debate in the FNC as recorded by al-Alkim:

'a disagreement arose in the FNC over the question of contributions by individual emirates to the federal budget. Abu Dhabi's representatives in the FNC urged other members not to pass the budget until the Finance Minister had made public the contribution of each emirate. Although Dubai was not mentioned in what was reported to be a "heated debate", some members demanded that all emirates should contribute in accordance with their national resources. Dubai's members responded to the "unspoken attack" by demanding information about the alleged deposits of the UAE Development Bank in foreign banks'.

Amid such tensions, the debates over constitutional arrangements escalated in 1976 when a 28-strong committee of ministers and FNC members was appointed to draft a permanent constitution. The committee reflected the broader schism within the UAE as its members diverged over the degree of centralization that would (or would not) limit the powers of the individual emirates. Particular controversy centred on Article 23 of the provisional Constitution, which granted the individual emirates control over all natural resources (and the resulting revenue from them). At issue was the question of whether resource revenues should be considered the property of the emirate or the nation as a whole. Supported by Sheikh Zayed, the proponents of greater federalization argued that Article 23 was impeding the redistribution of wealth across the UAE and urged the other emirates, particularly Dubai, to increase their contributions to the federal budget. As a result, the constitutional committee recommended that each emirate should transfer 75% of its income to the federal treasury, while it also suggested that Abu Dhabi and Dubai should lose their veto in the Supreme Council of Rulers.

The staunch opposition of the leaders of Dubai and Ras al-Khaimah to any modification of Article 23 and strengthening of the federal layer of authority precipitated a three-year constitutional impasse between 1976 and 1979. Abdullah Omran Taryam served in the Council of Ministers as Minister of Education and then Minister of Justice between 1973 and 1979, when he resigned, in part because of concerted opposition to his educational reforms from Islamists and members of Muslim Brotherhood-affiliated groups in the UAE. He subsequently recounted how Mehdi al-Tajir, the Ruler of Dubai's key adviser, 'was of the opinion that the new constitution should not be adopted as a whole, but rather a step-by-step gradual process should be sought'. As a result, 'the committee's activity became largely ceremonial' and 'reminiscent of those pre-union meetings which had been characterized by lobbying'. Frustration over the deadlock led Sheikh Zayed to declare that he would not accept a further term as President after his five-year mandate expired at the end of 1976. The draft Constitution was presented to the Supreme Council of Rulers in July 1976, but a failure to reach consensus meant that the provisional Constitution was extended for a further five-year period. This was a pragmatic outcome that reflected the deadlock between the two camps, which were 'mindful that such a fundamental revision could jeopardize many of the compromises on which the federation was based'. Although the compromise meant that a crisis was averted and Sheikh Zayed continued as President, the failure to resolve the contested issues meant that the matter resurfaced three years later.

An increase in regional volatility in early 1979 led to a renewed attempt to strengthen the federal powers of the union to better equip the UAE to confront the turbulent aftermath of the Islamic Revolution in Iran. The FNC and the Council of Ministers, which had developed a close working relationship, had initially held a joint meeting on 27 June 1978, just as the series of protests that ultimately led to the overthrow of the Shah of Iran, Muhammad Reza Pahlavi, were gaining in momentum, and had started a debate on how to strengthen the national Government. The FNC and the Council of Ministers met again on 3 February 1979, 18 days after the Shah had fled Iran, and submitted an 11-point memorandum to the Supreme Council of Rulers that appealed for a significant increase in the powers of the federal Government, including the abolition of internal borders, the unification of all armed forces and the federal management of oil revenues. Indeed, the memorandum stated explicitly that 'It is not acceptable that the state relies, in organizing its finances, on what one emirate might give it, and what another emirate does not'. The measures to create a stronger and more cohesive federal government were supported by the Rulers of Abu Dhabi, Ajman, Fujairah and Sharjah, and were discussed by the Supreme Council of Rulers on 19 March.

Concurrent with the submission of the memorandum, a series of demonstrations in support of greater federal power were held across the UAE amid an outpouring of public support for Sheikh Zayed. In his 1987 account of the formation of the UAE and its early years, Taryam described what happened on 19 March 1979 when the Supreme Council of Rulers met in Abu Dhabi to 'discuss the federal issue and study the joint committee's memorandum':

'Thousands of citizens from various walks of life, students, government officials, and tribesmen, assembled in process from various emirates and marched towards the palace where the meeting was in progress. There they shouted slogans, calling upon the rulers to collaborate, demanding consolidation of the union, more powers for the federal institutions, support for the President of the state, and approval of the memorandum. They were not against their rulers, on the contrary they were supporting them, but they wanted them to come closer together for the sake of the future of the region'.

Taryam further described how:

'The rulers interrupted their meeting and Sheikh Zayid came out and, deeply moved, made a speech before the crowds thanking them for their sentiments and their united stand and telling them it was his desires and that of the other rulers to try to realize what they were demanding. He then asked them to return to their work and leave their demands in his good care'.

The unprecedented public protests in support of the federation were not sufficient to break the deadlock as the Rulers of Dubai and Ras al-Khaimah withdrew from the meeting of the Supreme Council of Rulers, and Abu Dhabi and Dubai subsequently exchanged criticism. For the second time in a decade, the Kuwaiti Minister of Foreign Affairs, Sheikh Sabah al-Ahmad al-Jaber al-Sabah, was called in to mediate after an appeal by Sheikh Rashid of Dubai. As a result of Sheikh Sabah's mediation, and also that of King Khalid bin Abdulaziz Al Sa'ud of Saudi Arabia, Dubai agreed to contribute to the federal budget and, crucially, Sheikh Rashid himself was named Prime Minister of the UAE on 30 April 1979, replacing his son, Sheikh Maktoum bin Rashid Al Maktoum. Since 1979 the Ruler of Dubai has continued to hold the premiership, first through Sheikh Rashid (1979–1990), then Sheikh Maktoum again (1990–2006) and subsequently Sheikh Mohammed bin Rashid Al Maktoum (2006–).

In his comparative study of development trajectories in the UAE and Kuwait, Michael Herb (see Bibliography) suggested that 'From 1976 to 1979, a space opened in Emirati politics as a result of the dispute between Abu Dhabi and Dubai.' Moreover, Herb noted that 'Citizens used this political space to press for reforms that would create a UAE with a stronger federal government' and 'a political system that would give citizens a stronger voice. In short, they wanted the UAE to be more like Kuwait' with its active and vocal parliamentary life. Certainly, the eyewitness account provided by Taryam of the events of 1979 suggested a groundswell of support not for any Western-centric notion of 'democracy' but rather for a stronger and more functional federation that blended the 'traditional' exercise of power and authority with modern bureaucratic forms of governance.

THE 1980s CONSOLIDATION

While the integration of defence forces remained a contentious issue throughout the 1980s, the decade did not witness a repeat of the constitutional crisis that had marked the period between 1976 and 1979. There were several reasons for this 'rapprochement' among the emirates, one of which was the worsening regional situation. Another was that, over time, the 'founding fathers'—those Rulers who had participated in the fraught negotiations to create the federation between 1968 and 1971—gradually left the stage and a new generation of rulers came to power in a series of orderly transitions that contrasted markedly with some of the violent contestations of power that had characterized previous eras of change. In 1981 Sheikh Ahmed bin Humaid Al Nuaimi of Ajman and Sheikh Ahmed bin Rashid Al Mu'alla of Umm al-Qaiwain, who had been in power since 1928 and 1929, respectively, both died, while in May Sheikh Rashid of Dubai suffered a severe stroke. Although Sheikh Rashid made a partial recovery and remained the Ruler of Dubai until his death in October 1990, progressively more power and responsibility was devolved to his sons, particularly his designated successor, Sheikh Maktoum, and his third son, Sheikh Mohammed.

For Emirati historian Fatma al-Sayegh (see Bibliography), the period between 1979 and 1986 was one of 'accepting the federation'. During this period Dubai began to contribute systematically to the federal budget, and by 1986 all seven emirates were doing so in accordance with their respective economic size. In December 1980 the UAE Currency Board was upgraded into a Central Bank seven years after its establishment in May 1973, although the new entity initially struggled to gain credibility across the federation. In particular, the Central Bank was unable to assist the Ras al-Khaimah National Bank when it collapsed in 1985 or prevent the dissolution of Sharjah's four commercial banks after that emirate defaulted on a loan in 1989. Moreover, in 1991 the Central Bank 'was relegated to being little more than a bystander' during the collapse of the Bank of Credit and Commerce International (BCCI), despite the fact that many of BCCI's 'majority shareholders were resident in Abu Dhabi and included some of the greatest champions of federal integration'.

With domestic political issues becoming less controversial as the 1980s progressed and the federation matured (with the attempted coup in 1987 in Sharjah a notable exception—see below), the primary focus of inter-emirate divergence shifted towards the Iran–Iraq War. Although the outbreak of the conflict in September 1980 was partly responsible for the creation of the Cooperation Council for the Arab States of the Gulf (Gulf Cooperation Council—GCC, see p. 1131) in May 1981, the eight-year war left the UAE divided as four emirates (Abu Dhabi, Ajman, Fujairah and Ras al-Khaimah) supported Saddam Hussain's Iraq while the other three (Dubai, Sharjah and Umm al-Qaiwain) leaned towards Ayatollah Ruhollah Khomeini's Iran, 'their primary trading partner and the home of many of their merchant expatriates'. During this period 'Abu Dhabi, along with other Gulf Cooperation Council and Arab nations, bankrolled Saddam's war against Tehran; Dubai served as a key transit point for war material destined for Iran.' The closer ties with the Khomeini regime favoured by Dubai and Sharjah exposed the federal UAE Government 'to embarrassment and pressure from Saudi Arabia and other neighbors', which provided staunch political and financial support to Iraq throughout the war.

In spite of the aforementioned obstacles to formalizing the closer integration of the seven emirates and the temporary increases in tension, the general direction throughout the 1980s and into the 1990s was towards gradual and incremental co-operation as the very idea of the UAE became more deeply embedded in everyday life. The very survival of the federation distinguished the UAE from almost every other attempt to create federal entities in the Arab world between the 1950s and the 1970s. High-profile failures during this period included the political union of Egypt and Syria between 1958 and 1961 (the United Arab Republic), as well as the short-lived Arab Federation, which had joined together the Hashemite kingdoms of Iraq and Jordan for five months prior to a bloody coup that toppled the Iraqi monarchy in July 1958. Moreover, a British attempt in 1962 to unify a collection of British-protected emirates and sultanates in southern Yemen into the Federation of South Arabia also ended in ignominy five years later with the full withdrawal of British forces from Aden amid a violent anti-colonial insurgency.

No one factor in itself led to the widespread acceptance of the federation; rather, it was a combination of the passage of time and generational change among the ruling élites and general population alike, the steady leadership and adherence to the spirit of political compromise and consensus provided by Sheikh Zayed, the utilization of Abu Dhabi's oil reserves for the federation, and the external legacy of the 1990 Iraqi invasion of Kuwait, which illustrated the dangers confronting the smaller Gulf States in a volatile region, as well as the 1991 Gulf War, in which forces from the UAE participated as part of a multinational coalition formed by the George H. W. Bush Administration in the USA.

Speaking in 1996, on the 25th anniversary of the creation of the UAE, Sheikh Zayed offered his own perspective on the formation and durability of the union:

'We believe that wealth in itself is of no value unless it is dedicated to the prosperity and welfare of the people. States cannot be built upon wishes, nor can hopes be achieved by dreams. Our federation has stood firm in the face of crisis. It has prospered through hard work, perseverance and sacrifice and by placing the interests of the nation above any other'.

Fittingly, in 1996 the long-running constitutional issue was resolved with the removal of the 'provisional' designation from the 1971 document, while the reference to Abu Dhabi as the 'temporary' capital pending the construction of the new Al Karama city was also removed. The decision to make permanent the two most visible symbols of statehood—the Constitution and the capital—signified the durability of a federation that had, at times in its first two decades, appeared to be destined for fragmentation and even failure.

MANAGING POLITICAL TRANSITIONS

When Sheikh Zayed died aged 86 years on 2 November 2004 after a period of declining health, the presidency of the UAE and rulership of Abu Dhabi passed smoothly to his eldest son and designated successor, Sheikh Khalifa bin Zayed Al Nahyan. While Sheikh Khalifa had been heir apparent for more than three decades since his appointment as Heir Apparent of Abu Dhabi in 1966, his uncontested assumption of power in 2004 took some external observers by surprise. The prima[ry] reason for such uncertainty over the management of [the] leadership transition lay in a misreading of the fami[ly] dynamics among the many sons of Sheikh Zayed. In partic[ular] it had been assumed that, since he had no full brothers, Sh[eikh] Khalifa's influence was weak compared with that of po[werful] factions of brothers such as the six 'Bani Fatima' sons of S[heikh] Zayed's favoured wife, Sheikha Fatima bint Mubarak a[nd] Sheikh Zayed's decision in December 2003 to bring his [increas]ingly powerful third son (and elder Bani Fatima) [Sheikh] Mohamed bin Zayed, formally into the line of succ[ession as] Deputy Heir Apparent of Abu Dhabi) further encou[raged] speculation.

The first presidential succession in the history of [the UAE as] a federation began on 1 November 2004 with th[e announce]ment of a cabinet reorganization. Reported to hav[e had Sheikh] Zayed's approval, the reorganization included [the appoint]ment of the first female cabinet member in U[AE history]. Sheikha Lubna bint Khalid Al Qasimi beca[me Minister of] Economics and Planning. Sheikh Zaye[d's death was] announced the following evening, ending [a period of] uncertainty, during which the UAE had [postponed] hosting the annual GCC Summit schedu[led for December] and had reportedly blocked 'websites rel[ating to Zayed's] cancer'. A 40-day period of mourning was d[eclared in Novem]ber, although, as a British academic [later] observed:

THE UNITED ARAB EMIRATES

'It is worth noting how differently this period of mourning was interpreted by the different emirates... in Fujairah, Umm al-Qaiwain, and Ajman... the interpretation was very strict: in exactly the same way as Abu Dhabi, posters of Zayed were mounted everywhere ... In stark contrast, apart from a few large-scale mourning posters hung off the sides of (mainly non-governmental) buildings dotted around the city, in Dubai it was really "business as usual"'.

Sheikh Khalifa's decades-long service as his father's deputy and his chairmanship of the Supreme Petroleum Council and the Abu Dhabi Investment Authority meant that even prior to 2004 he had for a significant role in the day-to-day running of governmental affairs, particularly in the key areas of overseeing energy and investment policy. Sheikh Khalifa wielded great influence over economic policymaking, in part through the work of the Research and Studies Department, as well as through a sophisticated public relations unit in his Crown Prince's Court, which was itself closely linked to the *Akhbar al-Arab* newspaper, and he buttressed his social support by reaching out to influential tribal groups across Emirati society.

However, after becoming President, power and influence—both at the federal level and in Abu Dhabi—began to ebb away from Sheikh Khalifa towards the bloc of Bani Fatima princes led by Heir Apparent Sheikh Mohamed bin Zayed. Meanwhile, after the January 2006 accession of Sheikh Mohammed bin Rashid Al Maktoum as Ruler of Dubai (and as Prime Minister of the UAE), the federal structure of the UAE came under growing strain as Dubai began to follow increasingly autonomous positions on a number of key domestic and external issues. The empowerment of the Bani Fatima and the rise of Dubai converged in one of Sheikh Mohammed bin Rashid's first acts as federal Prime Minister in February when he undertook a sweeping government reorganization that reshaped the contours of the political landscape within the UAE in the new 'post-Zayed' era. The two features that stood out in the reorganization were the further empowerment of key Bani Fatima figures, most notably through the appointment of Sheikh Abdullah bin Zayed Al Nahyan as Minister of Foreign Affairs and International Co-operation and Sheikh Hamdan bin Zayed Al Nahyan as Deputy Prime Minister, and the promotion to formal cabinet posts of several of Sheikh Mohammed bin Rashid's most important Dubai-based advisers, including them Dr Anwar bin Mohammed Gargash (who became Minister of State for Federal National Council Affairs) and Mohammed bin Abdullah al-Gargawi (who was named as Minister of State for Cabinet Affairs).

Abu Dhabi and was, on the following day, duly elected President of the UAE at a meeting of the Supreme Council of Rulers. As Mohammed bin Zayed had been de facto ruler for the past decade, there was no major shift in domestic policy in Abu Dhabi or the UAE, and the biggest question was the identity of the new Crown Prince and specifically whether Mohammed bin Zayed would appoint one of his brothers or sons. The issue was settled in March 2023 when Mohammed bin Zayed named his eldest son, Khalid, as his heir apparent in Abu Dhabi, and placated two of his most powerful brothers, Sheikh Mansour bin Zayed and Sheikh Tahnoon bin Zayed, with additional economic responsibilities—the former being appointed as Chairman of Mubadala and the latter as Chairman of the Abu Dhabi Investment Authority.

March 2023 also saw the appointment by Mohammed bin Zayed of Sheikh Mansour as Vice-President of the UAE alongside the incumbent Vice-President, the Ruler of Dubai, Sheikh Mohammed bin Rashid. The move was notable because the post of Vice-President had been held by the Dubai ruling family since the creation of the UAE in 1971 and was seen as a political counterbalance to Abu Dhabi. Given that Sheikh Mansour is more than 20 years younger than Mohammed bin Rashid, it remains to be seen whether the position of Vice-President will remain in Dubai's hands once Mohammed bin Rashid dies, or whether Sheikh Mansour's appointment is the first step in the concentration of all presidential authority in Abu Dhabi, consistent with the centralization of power in the UAE since 2011.

Meanwhile, a dispute that began in Ras al-Khaimah in 2003 illustrated how a badly managed or contested transition could potentially cause internal rifts and damage the UAE's carefully constructed international image. In 1999 the ageing Sheikh Saqr bin Mohammed al-Qasimi devolved most of his powers to his eldest son and longstanding Heir Apparent, Sheikh Khalid bin Mohammed al-Qasimi, only to replace Sheikh Khalid as Heir Apparent with his much younger half-brother, Sheikh Saud bin Mohammed al-Qasimi, in June 2003. The precise reasons for the sudden switch from Sheikh Khalid—who had been Heir Apparent since 1961—to Sheikh Saud were unknown, although Sheikh Khalid's well-publicized opposition to the 2003 US-led invasion of Iraq and his publicly stated support for an elected FNC and women's suffrage may have played a role. The new Heir Apparent, Sheikh Saud, was, moreover, linked by blood and marriage to two of Dubai's most important merchant families, and may also have been seen as a more 'business-friendly' leader-in-waiting than his half-brother.

Sheikh Khalid and his supporters did not accept Sheikh Saud's elevation to Heir Apparent, and a sizeable crowd threatened briefly to besiege the palaces belonging to Sheikh Saqr and Sheikh Saud before federal UAE forces intervened to maintain order. Sheikh Khalid himself vowed 'to oppose this decision for as long as I live'. In 2008, moreover, Sheikh Khalid established an international lobbying network in the USA and the UK as part of a high-profile public relations campaign intended to secure his reinstatement as Heir Apparent. In 2009 and 2010, as Sheikh Saqr weakened, Sheikh Khalid mounted a lobbying operation in Washington, DC, USA, which included meetings with members of the US Congress. Rather more negatively, Sheikh Khalid also initiated a media campaign designed to portray Ras al-Khaimah as the weak point in the US-led 'war on terror' and to link it to international criminal and smuggling groups, the militant Islamist al-Qa'ida organization, and Iran.

Even more damaging to the UAE's international profile, US public relations firm California Strategies, in an attempt to undermine Sheikh Saud, commissioned a private security expert in the USA to compile a report on the security of Ras al-Khaimah, which highlighted putative links to global terror networks. The report suggested that Ras al-Khaimah had become 'a thoroughfare for smuggling drugs, weapons, explosives and personnel from Iran, Afghanistan and specific African countries', as well as 'a point of entry for terrorists' and 'a base of operation allowing Iranian personnel to operate within the confines of the UAE'. The report additionally alleged that Ras al-Khaimah's 'open and loosely controlled ports provide supply lines to counter any Iranian sanctions imposed by the international community' and sought to associate Sheikh Saud with the discovery of an al-Qa'ida-linked cell in 2009 that had allegedly planned an attack in Dubai.

After Sheikh Saqr died on 27 October 2010, Sheikh Khalid made an abortive attempt to seize power as he entered Ras al-Khaimah and proclaimed himself ruler. However, federal security forces surrounded Sheikh Khalid's compound and placed him under 'palace arrest' as the Federal Supreme Council acknowledged Sheikh Saud's accession. As in 2003, the intervention of federal forces was instrumental in determining the pathway of succession and ending the attempted contestation of power.

THE ISLAMIST CHALLENGE

The rapid economic development that took place in the UAE during the first two decades of the federation did not occur entirely within a political vacuum. Arab nationalism had grown in Dubai, while the rise of educated urban élites in Sharjah and other emirates magnified broader awareness of political issues and ideologies. As in other Gulf States that had experienced an oil-fuelled socioeconomic transformation, education emerged as a critical battleground between Islamists and the ruling families. This was, in part, due to the influential early role of teachers and other professionals from areas such as Egypt, the Palestinian Territories and Jordan, who had settled in the Gulf and exercised a formative role in the development of educational (and legal) institutions. Similarly, the introduction of the first 'modern' schools in the 1950s and 1960s and the return home of the first generation of students who had travelled abroad for their studies provided a boost to local and nationalist presses and the first cultural clubs that began to appear in the years immediately prior to 1971.

Many of the incoming professionals were either members of the Muslim Brotherhood who had fled the crackdown on the organization in Egypt in the 1960s or were sympathetic to the Muslim Brotherhood's ideals, which they had been exposed to as students in major Arab capitals. This included a cadre of Emirati students and activists who had studied in Egypt and Kuwait and who formed, in 1974, Jamiat al-Islah wa Tawjih (the Association for Reform and Guidance) in Dubai. Inspired by the ideals of the Muslim Brotherhood but claiming to be operationally and ideologically autonomous, initially al-Islah was not only tolerated but cautiously welcomed by several of the rulers in the UAE. Mansour al-Noqaidan (see Bibliography), the Chief Editor of the Dubai-based Al Mesbar Center for Studies and Research, noted that:

'Sheikh Mohammed bin Khalifa Al Maktoum was the first Chairman of the Board of Directors of the Society. Meanwhile, Sheikh Rashid bin Said Al Maktoum volunteered to build the Society's headquarters in Dubai at his own expense, which he followed by establishing two more branches of the Society in the emirates of Ras al-Khaimah and Fujairah. It was also said that the then head of state, late Sheikh Zayed bin Sultan Al Nahyan, donated a plot of land for establishing a branch of the Society in Abu Dhabi in the late 1970s, but the decision to establish such a branch was put off later'.

Important assistance to al-Islah during this formative period was also extended by the Kuwaiti branch of the Muslim Brotherhood, which helped both administratively and through the organization of a series of exchanges, meetings and summer camps in Kuwait. Within the UAE, an important patron was the Ruler of Ras al-Khaimah, Sheikh Saqr bin Mohammed al-Qasimi, who was purported to have been a member of al-Islah and whose cousin, Sheikh Sultan bin Kayed al-Qasimi, reportedly served as Chairman of the organization.

The initial policy of acquiescence towards al-Islah by the UAE authorities manifested itself in the appointment of two members of the organization to cabinet positions in the 1970s. A founding member of al-Islah, Said Abdullah Salman, became Minister of Housing in the very first federal cabinet established in 1971, and eight years later he was named as Minister of Education, while in 1977 Mohammed Abdulrahman al-Bakr was appointed as Minister of Justice and of Islamic Affairs and Awqaf (Religious Endowments). One prominent member of al-Islah noted retrospectively that, in the early years, 'the Government was happy with us, they trusted us at that time'. As Courtney Freer observed in her study of al-Islah (see Bibliography), by allocating cabinet positions to members of the group 'the state allowed them a platform through which they could enact policies that remained in place for decades—particularly in the education sector'. Thus, by the end of the 1970s the education and justice portfolios had enabled al-Islah 'to establish a firm foothold in the religious and educational institutions of the UAE'.

Owing largely to its prominence and influence within the education sector, relations between al-Islah and the federal Government began to cool during the 1980s in a process that accelerated in the 1990s as members of the group drifted into what the UAE authorities perceived as overt political activism. The federal Government's concerns about the potential extension of al-Islah's influence throughout Emirati society were well-merited as members of the group had by the start of the 1980s occupied key positions within the UAE's educational establishment. When Said Abdullah Salman was appointed as Minister of Education in 1979, he also became the Chancellor of the newly created UAE University, which developed into a centre of al-Islah-inspired student activism. Indeed, Sheikh Sultan bin Kayed al-Qasimi, the cousin of the Ruler of Ras al-Khaimah, directed the Curriculum Division within the Ministry of Education between 1977 and 1983, the year that both al-Islah cabinet members (Salman and al-Bakr) were dismissed.

Al-Islah influence survived the loss of these ministerial posts in 1983 and continued to percolate through Emirati society for another decade until the start of the first concerted government crackdown on the group in 1994. The group's control of student unions and the organization of summer camps and other activities, such as Scout groups, for Emirati youth were one source of unease for the authorities, as was the influence of al-Islah preachers at increasingly politicized Friday prayers.

During the 1980s al-Islah published an eponymous magazine that portrayed the organization as a defender of traditional social values against the perceived encroachment of 'Western' values such as the sale of alcohol in the UAE. By the late 1980s a number of articles that had appeared in *Al-Islah* magazine indicated that the organization was moving beyond social criticism into outright opposition to government education policy. In 1987 *Al-Islah* campaigned aggressively against the acting Minister of Education, Ahmed Humaid al-Tayer, while a year later the magazine virulently opposed the introduction of a Basic Education Project, a pre-university course in Arabic, English and Mathematics for incoming students at UAE University.

The first overt clash between *Al-Islah* and the political authorities occurred in October 1988, when the magazine ceased publication for six months. It subsequently adopted 'a more subdued tone' when it reappeared in April 1989. Over the next five years the magazine abandoned much of its political edge and focused instead on less sensitive topics such as 'the risk posed by foreigners against the culture and identity of the country'. Also in 1988, Dubai's Ministry of Awqaf (Religious Endowments) ordered preachers to submit in advance written copies of their Friday sermons and to avoid all areas of potential controversy. However, al-Islah's influence within the education sector continued to grow throughout the early 1990s, with an additional area of government concern emerging over the group's control of the allocation of student scholarships, which were granted almost exclusively to sympathizers and members.

Mounting concern about al-Islah's status as a potentially powerful alternative focus of loyalty prompted a systematic federal government crackdown on its activities in 1994, when the group's headquarters in Dubai was closed down and transferred to Ras al-Khaimah. This shift in government attitude was partly in response to a visit in 1994 to several Gulf states, including the UAE, by Egyptian President Hosni Mubarak, during the course of which he had warned Gulf rulers of the growing threat from militant Islamist groups, which were waging a low-intensity insurgency in Egypt at the time. Mubarak also increased Egyptian support for security agencies in the UAE and other GCC states. An (unnamed) member of al-Islah claimed in 2012 that 'After Mubarak's visit to the UAE, Sheikh Zayed gave the file to state security for them to investigate and because state security's survival is based on presenting threats they made the case against us'.

Also in 1994, the federal Government replaced the hitherto independent Board of Directors of al-Islah with government appointees and began to make it progressively more difficult for the society to function autonomously from government control. The years after 1994 were a period of 'silent tension' and 'soft pressure' as al-Islah retreated to its stronghold in Ras al-Khaimah, where the apparent protection of Sheikh Saqr bin Mohammed caused periodic tension between the emirate and Abu Dhabi. In the late 1990s and early 2000s many members of al-Islah who had worked, some for many years, in the Ministry of Education began to be transferred to jobs elsewhere in the public sector. Among those affected was Mohammed al-Roken, a lawyer and human rights activist, who was banned from writing his regular newspaper column in 2000 and removed from his position as Vice-Dean of *Shari'a* (Islamic law) and Law at UAE University two years later. After the 11 September 2001 attacks against the USA, moreover, the authorities' disquiet about Islamist activities within the UAE increased further with the discovery that two of the 19 people involved in those attacks had been Emirati citizens. As a result, more than 250 people, mainly Islamists, were arrested between 2001 and 2003 as officials, particularly in Abu Dhabi, increasingly came to view such groups as a threat to state security.

In August 2003 a series of meetings were held between three senior members of al-Islah and the Deputy Heir Apparent of Abu Dhabi, Sheikh Mohamed bin Zayed Al Nahyan, during which the latter reportedly asked the delegation from al-Islah 'to choose between renouncing their Islamist ideology, ceasing the public propagation of their ideas, or remaining affiliated with the Brotherhood but transferring out of the education sector'. However, the meetings ended without agreement from al-Islah, and, in the years that followed, the political authorities in the UAE continued to transfer members of al-Islah from educational positions to less sensitive areas of employment. In the mid-2000s government policy in the UAE towards al-Islah still resembled the earlier pattern of quiet harassment rather than the major effort to suppress the organization that commenced in 2011.

During the 2000s al-Islah was shielded from the full force of a security crackdown by the protection offered by the ageing ruler of Ras al-Khaimah, who was, after Sheikh Zayed's death in 2004, the last surviving member of the seven original founders of the UAE and thus regarded as an elder statesman of considerable prestige. Sheikh Saqr bin Mohammed's death in October 2010 removed this protection less than three months before the 'Arab spring' uprisings in other parts of the Middle East and North Africa provided state security 'hawks' with the opportunity to dismantle the group and to eliminate its perceived 'threat' once and for all. The political upheaval caused by the 'Arab Spring' in early 2011 revealed a sense of unease among officials in Abu Dhabi at the rise of the Muslim Brotherhood and its affiliates to power in Egypt and Tunisia, and prompted a security crackdown that targeted that movement's Emirati branch. The UAE subsequently developed an assertive approach to foreign and security policy that combined sophisticated local security capabilities with a far more expansive policy scope and that sought overtly to influence the pace and direction of change in states undergoing political transition after 2011.

REGIONAL POWER PLAYS

In Yemen, the UAE was from March 2015 to July 2019 involved in the heaviest and longest military operations in its history. Together with Saudi Arabia, the UAE led the coalition of primarily Gulf and Arab states that intervened to restore the Government of President Abd al-Rabbuh Mansour Hadi, which had been overthrown by rebels working in collaboration with deposed former Yemeni President Ali Abdullah Saleh (see Yemen). Saudi and Emirati political and military officials effectively carved Yemen into distinct operational spheres of influence that correspond roughly to the old division between North and South Yemen prior to Yemeni unification in 1990. Whereas Saudi forces faced a direct physical threat to border security from Yemeni rebel incursions and incoming missile fire that has killed hundreds of Saudi civilians inside the kingdom, Emirati threat perceptions were more indirect and consistent with the desire to suppress militant Islamist groups across the Arab world.

Whether in Yemen, Sudan, where UAE support for the military coup that ousted long-time President Omar al-Bashir in April 2019, and Libya, where the UAE emerged as one of the primary backers of Field Marshal Khalifa Haftar, Emirati leaders cast aside the cautious approach and emphasis on mediation that characterized foreign policymaking during Sheikh Zayed's long rule. In its place, Mohammed bin Zayed promoted an interventionist approach that repositioned the UAE as an assertive actor in regional affairs. Meanwhile, they also faced international criticism for their support of military strongmen in Libya and Sudan. In addition, in June 2017 the UAE formed part of a so-called 'Anti-Terror Quartet' with Saudi Arabia, Bahrain, and Egypt, and engaged in a political and economic boycott of neighbouring Qatar that lasted until January 2021. Senior Emirati leaders began to re-engage with their Qatari counterparts in the months after the signing of the Al-Ula Declaration which settled the Gulf dispute, with Sheikh Tahnoon bin Zayed, the National Security Adviser, visiting Doha in August 2021 and the Amir of Qatar travelling to Abu Dhabi in May 2022 to offer his condolences after the death of President Khalifa. Mohammed bin Zayed subsequently visited Doha in December, during the Fédération Internationale de Football Association (FIFA) 2022 World Cup in Qatar, and Qatar's Amir travelled again to Abu Dhabi in January 2023 to participate in a six-country leaders' summit convened by Mohammed bin Zayed that was notable for the absence of any Saudi participation.

This new approach to regional and foreign policy was not without cost, which included a series of three missile and drone (unmanned aerial vehicle) attacks launched from Yemen against Abu Dhabi in January 2022. Emirati forces in Yemen suffered unexpectedly heavy casualties in 2015 and 2016, including 52 deaths in a single missile attack on their base at Safer in September 2015. For a nation that had not experienced a single operational fatality until 2014 (when an Emirati police officer was killed on duty in Bahrain), the death toll was shocking, and gave rise to a 'cult of martyrdom' as officials attempted to portray their sacrifice as part of a 'nation-building' myth comparable to that experienced by European nations in the 19th century. Moreover, the political sensitivity of the death toll became clear when Emirati authorities sought to criminalize the spreading of casualty lists, partially out of concern that the heavy concentration of casualties in the comparatively poorer northern emirates might trigger a domestic backlash against a war associated heavily with Abu Dhabi and Mohammed bin Zayed. In Libya, the support for Haftar undermined the internationally-recognized UN-backed political process opposed by Haftar's forces while the standoff with Qatar angered US officials, owing to the strategic value of the Qatari relationship for the USA and the impediments arising from the intra-Gulf feud to the US-led efforts to rally Sunni Arab states against Iran and international terrorism during the Donald Trump presidency (2017–21).

The UAE departed decisively from the traditions of Arab diplomacy in August 2020 when it announced that it had agreed to normalize its relations with Israel, following direct talks brokered by the Trump Administration. The Abraham Accords peace agreements (in which the UAE was joined by Bahrain) were signed at a ceremony in Washington, DC, on 15 September. Israel's Prime Minister, Naftali Bennett, and President, Isaac Herzog, both visited the UAE, in December 2021 and January 2022, respectively, and the UAE and Israel signed a free trade agreement in May 2022 as bilateral ties expanded rapidly. As of September 2023 the UAE had yet to receive Israeli Prime Minister Benjamin Netanyahu, however, despite Netanyahu suggesting that Abu Dhabi would be his first foreign visit after he returned to power in December 2022 as head of a hard-line coalition Government that has drawn sustained international criticism. Elsewhere, in 2021 the UAE moderated the hawkish approach to regional affairs that had characterized its post-2011 policies and made efforts to repair relations with Qatar and Turkey (officially redesignated as Türkiye in June 2022), even as points of friction with Saudi

Arabia began to emerge. Mohammed bin Zayed and Turkish President, Recep Tayyip Erdoğan, exchanged visits in November 2021 and February 2022 as relations thawed after years of tension. More controversially, the UAE also took the lead in 'normalizing' ties with the regime of Bashir al-Assad in the Syrian Arab Republic, with the UAE foreign affairs minister visiting the Syrian capital, Damascus, in November 2021 and President Assad travelling to Abu Dhabi and Dubai in March 2022 to meet senior Emirati leaders, including Mohammed bin Zayed and Mohammed bin Rashid.

Economy

ROBERT E. LOONEY

INTRODUCTION

The United Arab Emirates (UAE) dates from 2 December 1971. The country comprises seven emirates, with Ras al-Khaimah the last to join in early 1972. Initially, the federation faced slim odds of survival because of animosity between the various emirates. However, the leadership of Sheikh Zayed bin Sultan Al Nahyan, the first President of the UAE, made the idea of a sustainable nation a reality. He served from 1971 until his death in 2004. The UAE remains the only successful federal experiment in the Arab world.

Before the discovery of petroleum, the economy of the Trucial States involved pearling, fishing, trade and some agriculture. Piracy was also a significant source of income in the 19th century. However, an economic transformation began after the discovery of petroleum off the coast of Abu Dhabi in 1958, the beginning of petroleum exports in June 1962, and later the OPEC price increases of 1973–74. The economy grew at an average annual rate of 14.3% during 1976–81.

With the collapse of oil prices in the early 1980s, economic growth slowed to an average annual rate of 2.3% during 1982–99. However, with the start of the commodity super cycle, growth recovered to 6.0% from 2000 until the global financial crisis of 2007–08. During the post-financial period from 2009 to 2015 and the oil price collapse in 2014–15, average annual growth slowed to 3.4%. Average annual growth declined to 2.2% in 2016–22, despite the oil price increases stemming from the invasion of Ukraine by the Russian Federation in February 2022.

During the past three decades there has been a general slowing of growth, with the country's gross domestic product (GDP) declining from an average annual rate of 6.1% in the 1990s to 5.0% in the 2000s and 3.4% in 2010–22. However, per capita income fell from US $40,015 in 1980 to $26,622 in 1990, before increasing to $34,689 in 2000 and $51,306 in 2022. With a GDP of $507,500m. in 2022, the UAE was the second largest economy in the Middle East and North Africa region (MENA), following Saudi Arabia ($1,108,000m.), but ahead of Egypt ($475,000m.), Iran ($352,000m.), Iraq ($270,000m.) and Qatar ($225,000m.).

The UAE had a population of about 10m. in 2022. Considerable structural change has occurred since 1980, with the country's gradual diversification away from oil. Industry (including oil) dropped from 72.7% of GDP in 1980 to 47.5% in 2022, while the share of services increased from 26.9% to 51.6% during this period. Agriculture, never extensive, accounted for 0.5% of GDP in 1980 and 0.9% in 2022. Declining oil rents show the country's transition from a complete dependence on hydrocarbons. These fell from 49.1% of GDP in 1980, to 20.8% in 2000 and to 15.7% by 2021. By comparison, Kuwait's oil rents fell from 67.0% (1980) to 50.3% (2000) and were 27.5% in 2020. During this period, those in Qatar fell from 67.7% in 1980 to 40.8% (2000) and 15.3% in 2021.

The UAE is by far the most open economy to international trade and finance in the Middle East, with global trade (imports plus exports) as a share of GDP increasing from 78.4% in 1980 to 87.3% in 2000 and 166.4% in 2022.

The UAE has contrasting economic trends among its member emirates. Despite political integration, each emirate has substantial authority over economic policymaking, resulting in little co-ordination in economic affairs. Abu Dhabi dominates the UAE economy because of its wealth from petroleum resources. Dubai has diversified and become an entrepôt for regional trade, moving away from its reliance on the oil industry. The northern emirates are comparatively underdeveloped, but there are hubs of economic activity. Sharjah, the third largest economy, has bustling real estate and business services, manufacturing, mining, and wholesale and retail trading industries.

The UAE has made remarkable progress both economically and in human development. It stands out from most of its neighbours for achieving political stability and a successful transition to a modern, dynamic market economy. This success is impressive given the volatile environment caused by changing US involvement in the Middle East, the 'Arab Spring', and conflicts with Iran, Yemen, the Syrian Arab Republic, Iraq and Libya. Despite these challenges, the UAE has emerged as a dominant force in the Organization of the Petroleum Exporting Countries (OPEC) and the MENA region.

EVOLUTION OF THE ECONOMY

In the 1980s the economy of the UAE contracted at an average annual rate of 0.5%. Inflation averaged 5.1%, and exports grew by an average of 0.1% yearly. However, the situation improved in the 1990s: petroleum exports generated stable revenue; exports increased by 5.1% in 1992 and 16.8% in 2002. This export surge supported the Government's plans for industrial expansion and diversification.

However, the country's economic growth was unstable. It rose to 8.6% in 1997 but dropped to 0.8% in 1998 when international oil prices fell. Growth then increased to 3.7% in 1999 and 12.3% in 2000. However, it declined again to 1.3% in 2001 and 2.5% in 2002, following the 11 September 2001 attacks against the USA. In 2003 and 2004 growth improved to 8.8% and 9.6%, respectively, because of higher oil prices. GDP growth fluctuated, however, falling to 4.9% in 2005, rising to 9.8% in 2006, and then falling again, to 3.2% in 2007.

Rents increased because of housing shortages and high demand. Developments in the real estate market, along with a weak US dollar, lower interest rates and higher commodity prices, led to inflation. Consumer price inflation reached 11.1% in 2007, and GDP growth was 3.2% in 2008. However, the global financial crisis and falling oil prices caused the economy to slow down later in the year. Dubai's property market suffered, as the emirate had borrowed heavily to fund growth in property and infrastructure. Excessive borrowing resulted in negative credit assessments from the major international rating agencies.

In 2009 GDP fell by 5.2%, due to decreased petroleum output, lower non-oil growth caused by OPEC-agreed production cuts, a property market correction in Dubai, and tight credit conditions. The hydrocarbons sector declined by 6.3%. Non-hydrocarbons growth slowed from an average annual rate of 8% in 2006–08 to 1% in 2009.

In November 2009 Dubai World, the state-owned investment corporation, postponed repayments on debts of around US $59,000m. for six months. This development supported fears of a significant default on the emirate's sovereign debt, and international share prices declined sharply.

In December 2009 Abu Dhabi advanced Dubai US $10,000m. to prevent it from defaulting on a $4,100m. bond repayment, which was owed by government-owned property developer Nakheel. The Dubai authorities responded to maintain confidence in the banking system and reduce the impact of financial turmoil on economic activity. In May 2010 Dubai World restructured some $23,500m. of its debt with creditors.

The economy bounced back in 2010, due to better global conditions and higher oil prices. However, the effects of the global financial crisis continued to affect the property market and associated sectors. GDP grew by 1.6%, and the average inflation rate was 0.9%. In 2011 the Arab Spring revolts and demonstrations caused social and political unrest in some Arab countries. The northern emirates saw increased infrastructure spending and subsidized basic food prices by the UAE. The Government also introduced employment sponsorship system reforms to improve the labour market and prevent abuses, and the UAE was not significantly affected by the Arab Spring.

Despite global uncertainty and regional political unrest, the economy recovered in 2011. GDP increased by 6.9% because of increased oil production and higher oil prices. However, the International Monetary Fund (IMF) cautioned that even though Dubai World had completed its debt restructuring, other government-related entities (GREs) still needed to refinance their debt with external funding.

The UAE's economic growth rate was 4.8% in 2012 and rose slightly to 5.1% in 2013. The property sector stabilized in Abu Dhabi and started to recover in Dubai. Non-oil growth increased, supported by tourism, transport and the recovering property sector, particularly in Dubai. GREs made progress in restructuring and financing their debts. However, the UAE's GDP growth rate slipped to 4.2% in 2014 because of the rapid fall in the international oil price, resulting in lower export revenues.

The IMF advised the UAE Government to focus on gradual fiscal consolidation while maintaining investment spending, controlling public wages, phasing out subsidies, reducing GREs transfers and generating more revenue from non-hydrocarbon economic activity. By 2015 the growth rate was 6.8% and average inflation was 4.1%. To avoid an unsustainable rise in the fiscal deficit, the Government sought additional revenue sources and reduced capital spending. It also reformed energy subsidies and introduced a value-added tax (VAT) in January 2018.

There were spending cuts in state-linked firms in Abu Dhabi, particularly in the energy industries. This action resulted in thousands of job losses. Foreign companies that provided business and financial services also reduced their presence in the country. However, Dubai implemented an expansionary fiscal policy by continuing to invest in more transport infrastructure projects. In November 2015 the Government enacted a new public-private partnership law, enabling the emirate to secure private-sector funding for significant projects, such as extending the Dubai Metro Red Line to the 2020 World Expo exhibition site.

In March 2015 the UAE joined a coalition of member states of the League of Arab States (Arab League) led by Saudi Arabia to fight al-Houthi militants in Yemen. In June 2017 the UAE, Saudi Arabia, Bahrain and Egypt cut diplomatic ties with Qatar and imposed an economic blockade. They accused Qatar of supporting terrorism and aligning with Iran, which they believed was backing the al-Houthi rebels. However, despite the diplomatic tensions, the Dolphin Gas Project pipeline continued to supply Qatari gas to the UAE, via its route from Qatar to Oman through the UAE. In January 2021 the states lifted the blockade against Qatar and normalized their relations after a summit meeting in Al-Ula, Saudi Arabia of the Cooperation Council of the Arab States of the Gulf (Gulf Cooperation Council—GCC), where they signed a formal declaration.

The UAE's GDP growth decreased to 5.6% in 2016 because of the weakened oil market, and in 2017 the economy only grew by 0.7%. Oil-related GDP declined by 3.0% because the UAE cut production by 2% as part of an OPEC agreement in November 2016 (see *Oil, Gas and Renewables*). This agreement aimed to control supply and increase petroleum prices. However, the non-oil sector grew by 2.5%, partly offsetting the decline. The non-oil sector grew thanks to increased employment, higher government spending and better growth among the UAE's principal trading partners.

In 2017 inflation increased to 2.0%. GDP growth rose only slightly to 1.3% in 2018 (following the extension of OPEC restrictions on oil production), while the inflation rate increased to 3.1%. Oil-related GDP growth resumed, although non-oil growth slowed to 1.3% in 2018. Property prices in Dubai had fallen even further since 2014. In addition, its GDP growth rate slowed to only 1.9%—the lowest level since 2010. However, many observers predicted that Dubai would gain advantages from the completion of infrastructure projects and an increase in tourism from the hosting of Expo 2020.

In September 2018 the federal Government adopted a new law to improve the commercial climate. The UAE's military involvement in Yemen concerned businesses, particularly potential foreign investors. The new law allowed 100% foreign ownership of companies outside existing business parks, subject to the decision of the respective emirates and possibly exempting the need for a local partner.

In July 2019 the Government further relaxed foreign ownership restrictions for 122 business activities, particularly in the manufacturing, agricultural and services sectors. The economy grew by 1.1% in 2019, but prices for fuel and housing decreased, causing deflation of 1.9%.

In early 2020 the coronavirus disease (COVID-19) pandemic began to have a severe impact on the economy. The country recorded its first cases at the end of January. The outbreak rapidly spread in March, leading the individual emirates and federal Government to implement tight measures to curb the spread of the virus. These measures included suspending public transport, closing hospitality venues in Dubai from early April, and restricting travel both between emirates and internationally. These measures were impactful because, at the time, the travel and tourism sector contributed 20% of Dubai's GDP. The health crisis caused the postponement of the Dubai Expo 2020 until October 2021. The collapse of global oil demand and prices also affected the economy, along with supply chain disruptions. GDP contracted by 5.0% in 2020, with non-oil GDP declining by 5.4% and oil GDP dropping by 3.8%. Consumer prices fell by 2.1% in 2020.

The UAE gradually eased restrictions from April 2020 onwards and began issuing visas to foreign visitors in September. However, in January 2021, as COVID-19 cases surged, the Government introduced additional measures, including mandatory testing and restrictions on large gatherings. In December 2020 the Government started a vaccination programme with the Sinopharm vaccine, and by June 2022 it had fully inoculated 98% of the population.

The pandemic cast doubt on the divergent development strategies of Abu Dhabi and Dubai, the UAE's two most prosperous and powerful emirates. Abu Dhabi faced lower oil prices, well below the UAE's fiscal break-even price of US $69 per barrel. This development prompted it to increase diversification efforts from its hydrocarbons-based economic development model, already threatened by renewable energy technology and the oil price collapse in 2014–15. Meanwhile, Dubai's key sectors, including tourism, construction and real estate, were at risk because of the halt in global travel caused by the pandemic.

The Abu Dhabi Economic Vision 2030 (released in 2008) had ambitious diversification plans, but the economy remained primarily focused on the hydrocarbons sector. Oil and gas made up most exports and government revenues. The diversification occurred in the downstream industry by adding value to the hydrocarbons output.

In 2019 Abu Dhabi launched a three-year US $13,600m. economic stimulus plan called Ghadan 21 to achieve broader diversification. The plan aimed to support small and medium-sized enterprises (SMEs) and partner with the private sector on infrastructure projects. Originally designed as a start-up accelerator programme, it became a pandemic stimulus package in 2020. Abu Dhabi's two key diversification strategies involve the development of world-class transport, tourism and digital infrastructure; and foreign acquisitions by sovereign wealth funds to provide non-oil investment income, as well as cushioning future liquidity risks.

In 2022 there was strong economic growth in the UAE because of recovering energy demand, high international oil prices and the reopening of economies after the COVID-19 pandemic. The country's GDP increased by 7.4%, and Abu Dhabi's expanded by 9.3%, driven by hydrocarbons and the non-oil industrial, construction and service sectors. Although the oil sector faced OPEC production restraints, the non-oil private sector continued to perform strongly, supported by consistent efforts at both emirate and federal levels to provide a supportive environment for businesses and bolster economic diversification. The authorities also directed oil revenue to local companies through schemes and government capital investment.

Dubai's economy grew by 4.2% in 2022 due to the UAE's initiatives to attract foreign residents and investments. This action led to a construction, tourism, retail and leisure boom. However, the recent increase in policy interest rates by the Central Bank of the United Arab Emirates (CBUAE), starting in 2022, and lower oil prices may slow down this growth, especially in construction and retail. Despite this, the Government's investment in non-oil sectors will probably continue, ensuring progress. Abu Dhabi's Government is also supporting the growth of the financial industry and renewable energy domestically and internationally.

ECONOMIC PLANNING

Economic planning in the UAE does not follow the usual five-year plans that are standard in much of the developing world. Instead, a series of strategy or vision documents attempt to articulate the Government's priorities and set targets for achieving various goals, thus focusing decision-making in the various ministries. These documents also give the private sector a sense of where the economy is likely to be headed, thus reducing risk to potential investments.

In 2007 the UAE Prime Minister announced the country's first national strategy. This strategy covered economic, infrastructure, social, governmental, justice and rural development. The goal was to achieve greater federal co-operation in policy-making and administration. The strategy set targets for all the federation's ministries to accomplish over three years. In 2010 the federal Government released its plan for 2011–13. The key priorities of this strategy included upgrading education and health care systems, social development, and improving government services.

In January 2012 the Abu Dhabi Government approved new projects in various sectors, such as infrastructure, social services, housing, health and education. The authorities also announced US $90,000m. spending on capital projects for 2013–17, including infrastructure development and diversification ventures. These mainly focused on projects outside the centre of the capital. Next, Abu Dhabi announced Ghadan 21 in June 2018, a three-year investment and reform programme worth AED 50,000m. It aimed to boost growth and employment, and reduce business costs. The first phase began in September with 50 initiatives, including a loan scheme for small enterprises.

The federal Government launched the Strategy for the Fourth Industrial Revolution in September 2017 to develop new technologies and innovation for economic diversification. Then, in September 2021, the 'Projects of the 50' scheme was announced, intended to boost the country's development over the next 50 years through increased foreign investment and exports, as well as technology programmes.

The Government wants to reduce its economic involvement with the Projects of the 50 growth strategy. There is a focus on expanding the role of the private sector, particularly in high-technology industries. The plan also includes improving business regulations, diversifying from hydrocarbon revenues and reducing reliance on expatriate labour. The Government aims to upskill Emiratis to create a more self-sufficient workforce.

The Projects of the 50 is the latest in a long series of policies aiming to create long-term sustainable economic growth independent of hydrocarbon revenues. On balance, the plan seems more realistic in scale than its predecessors, such as 'Vision 2021' (launched in 2010) or the 30 national pillars announced in September 2017.

The UAE private sector has, to a large extent, depended on government support for contracts, subsidies and friendly regulations. The Projects of the 50 is to allocate US $2,700m. over five years through the state-owned Emirates Development Bank to support projects by Emiratis in 'new and crucial' sectors. This programme aims to build the digital economy, adding $6,800m. to GDP (equating to 1.9% growth) and increasing industrial output by 30% over five years to September 2026.

There are financial incentives for public sector employees to start up private companies. The Government will also boost the salaries of university graduates entering the private sector by up to AED 5,000 (US $1,360) per month for five years after recruitment. This action seeks to address the problem that private sector wages and conditions are less favourable than in the public sector, but it also helps entrench reliance on government action, curtailing the development of a fully fledged entrepreneurial private sector.

A vital target of the Projects of the 50 is to attract US $150,000m. in foreign direct investment (FDI) over the next nine years. That sounds difficult, but it amounts to an average of $16,700m. per year—lower than the annual average of $18,900m. in 2019 and 2020.

The Projects of the 50 initiative promotes industrial sectors associated with the 'fourth industrial revolution', including the digital, space, advanced and circular economies, and emphasizing green energy. The Government has also launched 'golden' and 'green' visas (see *Demographics/Labour*) to encourage investors and expatriates with skills in these fields to live and work in the country.

Finally, in early July 2023 the Government approved plans to set up a Ministry of Investment. The ministry is to promote the investment environment: recent changes have helped boost net FDI inflows to US $20,700m. in 2021, from $1,100m. in 2009. The ministry approved an updated National Energy Strategy 2050 to make the UAE a net-zero emissions economy by 2050. Interim targets include raising the share of clean energy in the total energy mix to 30% by 2031, tripling the contribution of renewable energy and increasing national energy investments of up to AED 200,000m. ($54,500m.) by 2030. It also approved a National Hydrogen Strategy to ensure the UAE is among the largest producers of low-carbon hydrogen by 2031, by developing supply chains and creating hydrogen hubs.

These initiatives should contribute to the UAE's strategy to move away from its dependency on hydrocarbons, boosting foreign and domestic investment in the non-oil sector, including renewables, and meeting global decarbonization targets. However, the strategy could face difficulties if the oil price collapses, which would curtail the UAE's ability to maintain capital expenditure at levels that support the overall strategy.

SOCIOECONOMIC DEVELOPMENT

Unlike many oil-producing developing countries, the UAE's economic expansion has significantly improved the quality of life of its population. The UAE's economic growth since the early 1990s propelled the country to 26th place (out of 191) in the United Nations (UN) Development Programme's Human Development Index (HDI) for 2021/22. This places the UAE as the highest ranked country in the MENA region, above Saudi Arabia (35th), Qatar (42nd), and Kuwait (50th). In 2021 life expectancy in the UAE was 78.7 years, and the mean years of schooling was 12.7. The UAE's gross national income (GNI) per capita in 2021 (2017 purchasing power parity—PPP—$) was US $62,574, ranking 15 places lower than its HDI score, suggesting broad-based participation in the country's prosperity. During 2015–21 the UAE's HDI ranking rose nine places, and improvement accelerated, with the country's HDI score growing by 0.48% during the 2000s and 0.80% in 2010–21.

With a Gini coefficient of 26.0, the UAE's income distribution was relatively equal during 2010–21. The share of income of the poorest 40% was 23.0, while that of the richest 10% was 20%, and that of the wealthiest 1% was 15.8%. However, there are significant gender differences, with GNI per capita (2017 PPP $) at US $77,318 for males and $28,921 for females. However, the mean years of schooling for males was 12.8 years, only slightly higher than 12.5 for females. In 2021 the labour participation rate was 88% for males but only 46.5% for females. However, women held 50% of the seats in parliament in 2022.

The Legatum Institute's 2023 Prosperity Index presents a broader picture of the country's socioeconomic progress. The index has three comprehensive measures of prosperity: (a) 'inclusive societies' (safety and security, personal freedom, governance, and social capital, 12 reflections of wealth); (b) 'open economies' (investment environment, enterprise conditions, infrastructure and market access, and economic quality); and (c) 'empowered people' (living conditions, health, education, and natural environment). The UAE ranked 44th out of 167 countries on the 2023 Index, the same ranking as in 2011. The UAE ranked highest in enterprise conditions (22nd), infrastructure and market access (22nd), and economic quality (26th), with economic quality defined as how well an economy can generate wealth sustainably and with the full engagement of the workforce. The country was also highly ranked, at 32nd, for investment environment and 33rd for health. The UAE ranked lowest in personal freedom (146th), natural environment (119th), and social capital (78th).

The three broad categories show the UAE's strength is in 'open economies', where the country ranked 26th, three places higher than in 2011. The country's chief weakness is in 'inclusive societies', where it ranked 79th, 12 places lower than in 2011, with the most significant drop in safety and security (a decline of 23 places) and social capital (a decrease of 20 places). Legatum defines social capital as the strength of personal and social relationships, institutional trust, social norms and civic participation in a country. The country had an intermediate ranking of 45 for the 'empowered people category', with the most significant gain, of 22 places, for the natural environment. However, living conditions declined by nine places.

The country's governance is another area where significant gains have occurred in recent years. The World Bank's Governance Indicators show the UAE with one of the highest levels of governance in the MENA region. The UAE's overall governance (a composite of voice and accountability, political stability, absence of violence, government effectiveness, regulatory quality, the rule of law and control of corruption) has hovered around the 70th percentile since 2002.

The country ranks the lowest in voice and accountability (a rough measure of democracy). The country's ranking fell from the 37th percentile in 1996 (when the data began) to the 17th percentile in 2021. Political stability and the absence of violence also declined from the 80th percentile in 2000 to the 67th in 2021. However, those areas directly affecting the economy improved. Government effectiveness improved from the 68th percentile in 2003 to the 90th by 2021. Regulatory quality (a rough measure of the business climate) improved from the 68th percentile in 2003 to the 82nd in 2021. Similarly, the rule of law increased from the 58th percentile in 2007 to the 77th in 2021. Finally, control of corruption improved from the 55th percentile in 1998 to the 84th in 2021.

DEMOGRAPHICS/LABOUR

At the start of 2023 the UAE's population was 9,441,129. However, the UN estimates that in 2020 88.1% of the population were immigrants. The pattern of population growth reflects periods of high emigrant worker arrivals coinciding with the general growth of the economy, with the population increasing at an average annual rate of 11.8% during the oil boom years of 1976–81, dropping to 5.8% during the period of lower oil prices, 1982–99. However, with the commodity super cycle starting in the early 2000s, population growth increased to an average of 9.0% during 2000–08, dropping to 3.5% during the post-financial crisis period of 2009–15. With the effects of the 1994–95 oil price drops present, combined with the effects of the COVID-19 pandemic, average annual population growth declined to 0.8% in 2016–22.

With a large emigrant workforce, the country's population has proportionately more individuals in the working-age years of 15–64 than is usually the case for a nation at this stage of its development. In 1976–81 71.5% of the population were in this age group, falling to 70.8% in 1982–99. However, with the commodity super cycle, those in the working-age group increased to 80.2% in 2000–08. During the post-financial crisis years of 2009–15, those in this group increased to 85.5%, dipping to 83.8% during the slow-growth period of 2016–22.

The influx of migrant workers has given the UAE an automatic demographic dividend, with few young and old people to support. Those under 14 years of age were 27.0% of the population in 1976–81, but by 2016–22 this group had dropped to 14.8%. Those aged over 65 were 1.4% of the population in 1976–81 and 2016–22.

The average unemployment rate during the 1990s was 1.9%, which increased to 2.7% in the 2000s. Unemployment dropped to 2.1% in 2010–15, but with the effects of the 1994–95 fall in oil prices and the 2020 pandemic, it increased to 2.7% in 2016–22. Unemployment rose to 4.3% in 2020 but fell to 3.1% in 2021 and 2.8% in 2022. However, youth unemployment (those aged 15–24) is relatively high, especially during the COVID-19 pandemic. Youth unemployment decreased from 7.3% in 2005 to 4.8% in 2016. However, it increased to 7.2% in 2017 and 7.4% in 2019, before reaching 14.1% in 2020. Unemployment subsequently dropped, to 10.5% in 2021 and 9.3% in 2022.

In 2019 the federal Government approved a plan to offer five- or 10-year residence permits to investors and entrepreneurs, as well as permanent residency investors in medicine, engineering and science. The federal Government in the following year also introduced 'golden visas', designed to enable expatriates with exceptional skills to live, work and study in the country. The Government implemented further visa initiatives in 2022 intended to increase the appeal of the UAE as a place to live, work and invest. Visitors would be allowed to stay for double the length of time, to 60 days, and local sponsorship regulations were eliminated.

A vital component of the Government's Projects of the 50 programme is to 'emiratize' the UAE's workforce. All firms must have Emiratis as one-10th of their workforce by 2026. Every private sector company is to increase the number of Emiratis employed by at least two percentage points per year to reach at least 10% of its workforce within five years. The jobs should be in 'knowledge and skilled' roles, ensuring firms cannot pack Emiratis into low-skilled, low-earning jobs—presumably regardless of their employment profile.

Previous attempts at 'emiratization' have been unsuccessful because of a shortage of the necessary skills in the workforce and the cost of employing Emiratis, who most often demand higher pay than expatriates. If the Government enforces the new policy strictly, costs will rise for private sector companies, putting pressure on prices, cash flows and balance sheets.

OIL, GAS AND RENEWABLES

According to the *Statistical Review of World Energy 2023*, the UAE had 97,800m. barrels of oil and 5,900,000m. cu m of natural gas reserves. Abu Dhabi has the majority of reserves, with over 90% of the total, and Dubai, Sharjah and Ras al-Khaimah follow. The UAE is the holder of the world's seventh largest proven oil reserves and the 10th largest proven gas reserves globally.

Most of the acreage, onshore and off shore, has undergone exploration, and recent drilling has not yielded significant discoveries. Instead, the continued increase in proven reserves has mainly focused on appraisal activities at existing fields and deploying enhanced oil recovery techniques. Still, several successful licensing rounds launched in recent years promise future discoveries.

The UAE's average annual crude petroleum output has fluctuated since the late 1980s, due to OPEC production quotas and market conditions. In 2016 the output reached 4.0m. barrels per day (b/d) before falling to 3.9m. b/d in 2017. This decline resulted from the OPEC agreement in November 2016 to cut crude production from January 2017 for at least six months. OPEC extended the agreement to December 2018, and crude oil production remained at around 3.9m. b/d in 2018. OPEC then extended the restrictions on output until March 2020, with a six-month extension in January 2019 and another in July.

In May 2020, in response to the COVID-19-related collapse in global oil demand, the OPEC+ group, which includes the Russian Federation, enacted an overall reduction of 9.7m. b/d, which held in place until the end of July. OPEC+ reduced the cut to 7.7m. b/d from August and planned for a further decrease to 5.8m. b/d in January 2021. The cut would have expired in

April 2022. However, the group has since abandoned its pre-agreed production cut schedule. Instead, the group makes a series of monthly adjustments, not exceeding around 500,000 b/d in any month. This formula has allowed it to react rapidly to changes in underlying oil market fundamentals, thus mirroring shifts in global demand with commensurate shifts in supply.

For January 2021 OPEC+ agreed to reduce the cut from 7.7m. b/d to 7.2m. b/d and to return another 1.5m. b/d of supply over the rest of the year. It held output steady from February to April before opting to raise supplies by 350,000 b/d in May and June, and by 441,000 b/d in July. As of July, the official reduction stood at 5.8m. b/d.

At its July 2021 meeting OPEC+ disagreed on the next steps for its production-cut deal and faced vehement opposition from the UAE. The proposal was for a 400,000 b/d monthly increase in output from August to December, coupled with an extension of the deal from April 2022 until the end of that year. The UAE favoured production increases from August, but refused to extend the agreement unless the production baseline against which OPEC+ measured its cuts was altered. Talks continued after the meeting, and the group subsequently reached a compromise. It committed to the 400,000 b/d monthly output hikes and the extension of the deal to the end of 2022. Several producers, including the UAE, received higher production baselines because of the agreement. For the UAE, the baseline has been increased from 3.2m. b/d to 3.5m. b/d. The UAE has somewhat been disadvantaged by the terms of the deal, given that its reference production level is far below its current 4m. b/d capacity. The Abu Dhabi National Oil Company (ADNOC) aims to raise production to capacity once the OPEC+ restraints are lifted and has ample scope to do so. However, the group seems determined to limit its output growth until 2024, since the deal has been extended until the end of that year. Moreover, OPEC+ enacted an additional 2m. b/d cut in November 2022, which has since been extended until December 2024. Also, OPEC enacted an additional 1.16m. b/d cut in May 2023 that was remain in place until the end of the year.

The UAE's shift in strategy goes beyond oil production increases. It is also expanding its presence in other sector segments beyond upstream oil, including trading. In March 2021 it launched its own Murban crude oil futures contract. On top of its rising long-run production targets, the demands of launching the contract and building sufficient liquidity around it inherently conflict with the country's OPEC membership.

The UAE, a member of the Gas Exporting Countries Forum, pioneered exporting liquefied natural gas (LNG) among Middle Eastern nations. The UAE's proven reserves of natural gas totalled 5,938,725m. cu m (3.2% of global reserves) at the end of 2020. Gas production stood at 58,000m. cu m in 2022. To help meet the growing domestic demand for natural gas, in November 2021 the UAE announced plans to invest US $20,000m. to become self-sufficient in natural gas by 2030 (the UAE currently imports some natural gas from Qatar).

The UAE has excellent potential for renewable energy. Supportive mechanisms are in place to help encourage investment (loans, energy production payments, utility quota obligations and capacity targets). High solar irradiation levels and rising gas feedstock import reliance should ensure that renewable energy will be crucial to diversification efforts. Abu Dhabi and Dubai have aggressive long-term sustainability goals, with the renewable energy share of the two emirates' power mixes rising rapidly over the coming decades.

Growth will likely be driven by solar power. In 2022 solar power increased to 14% of Dubai's total 14,517 MW production capacity. The increase in solar power in Dubai is part of the UAE's transition towards renewable energy. A significant source of solar PV will be the 5-GW Mohammed bin Rashid Al Maktoum (MBM) Solar Park, of which phase four is under construction, while the tender process for phases five and six is under way.

POWER

The UAE's power market generated 149 TWh of electricity in 2022, ranking among the biggest in the MENA region. The power market can fulfil domestic consumption requirements, and the Government aims to export power to neighbouring markets. During 2013–21 the sector expanded at an average annual rate of 3.0%. In 2021 the industry contributed 4.4% to GDP.

The UAE generates most of its electricity through thermal-fired power plants, with gas being the primary source and oil playing a secondary role. The country has abundant reserves of oil and gas, which have given it a competitive edge in terms of energy costs and funding. Therefore, gas- and oil-fired power plants dominate the power market. The Government plans to release stocks for export instead of using them for power generation. This approach seeks to benefit from the rising oil and gas prices, while reducing greenhouse gas emissions in the power sector.

The UAE has set targets for its energy mix in the National Energy Strategy 2050. By 2030 it aims to have 30% of electricity coming from carbon-free sources, and by 2050 that target will increase to 50%. It plans to have 44% of the energy mix coming from renewables, 38% from gas, 12% from clean coal and 6% from nuclear sources by 2050. Solar power through the Mohammed bin Rashid al Maktoum Solar Park and nuclear energy from the Barakah plant will drive the growth of carbon-free sources over the next 10 years.

This strategy is the first of its kind for the market. It focuses on balancing energy supply and demand. The plan is to increase renewable and nuclear power capacity. It also aims to improve energy efficiency in the most energy-intensive sectors. By 2030 the target is to improve efficiency by 24%, with a goal to improve it by 40% by 2050.

The state has a significant role in the power market, but private companies are joining in on non-hydropower renewables. The Government wants foreign investors to join, which would provide opportunities for renewable energy growth.

AGRICULTURE

The Food and Agriculture Organization of the UN (FAO) established an agricultural experimental station at Digdagga (Ras al-Khaimah) in 1955, causing a transformation in the UAE's agricultural sector. Traditionally, agriculture consisted of nomadic pastoralism and oasis cultivation. Dates were the principal crop. Today, while dates are still the primary crop, the production of vegetables has increased sharply. However, this increase and an extensive forestry programme have significantly lowered the country's water tables. To solve this issue, the Government has constructed desalination plants.

Agriculture remains a small sector in the UAE, averaging 0.9% of GDP in the 1980s, 1.7% in the 1990s, 1.6% in the 2000s, and 0.7% in 2010–22. Growth averaged 9.2% in the 1980s, increasing to 13.0% in the 1990s, but contracting by 1.5% annually in the 2000s and expanding by 1.1% in 2010–22.

The UAE uses about two-thirds of its agricultural land for the cultivation of date palms. Dates make up around 60% of the country's agricultural produce. There are approximately 40m. date palm trees. However, most date farms are small, family-run operations established decades ago to settle the Bedouin. Date production was 8,000 metric tons in 1970, increasing to 141,463 tons in 1988. Production expanded rapidly, reaching 757,601 tons by 2000. However, after rising to 825,300 tons in 2010, production declined rapidly, falling to 221,529 tons in 2012. Production increased to 344,713 tons in 2017 and remained around that level until 2021, when production reached 351,077 tons (according to UN estimates). In 2020 the UAE exported about US $235m. worth of dates, accounting for approximately 60% of agricultural output.

The other primary agricultural product in the UAE is vegetables: mainly tomatoes, cabbage, eggplants, squash and cauliflower. As with dates, vegetable production increased rapidly but declined quickly thereafter to a lower production level. In 1970 the UAE produced 5,497 metric tons of vegetables, rising to 191,574 tons in 1983. Production then increased rapidly, reaching 2,124,839 tons in 2000. However, after 2000 production declined rapidly, falling to 176,684 tons in 2007. Production then gradually increased to 331,659 tons in 2017.

The National Dialogue for Food Security, which was launched by the Ministry of Climate Change and the Environment in March 2022, focuses on local farms to reduce import dependence. The project aims to promote innovation in food production using hydroponic, aeroponic and aquaponic farming to increase yields, while saving resources. This initiative will lead to more domestic production and better income for UAE farms, without affecting the food trade. The project will focus on producing red meat, poultry, eggs, dairy products, dates, leafy vegetables, tomatoes, cucumbers, peppers and eggplants.

MANUFACTURING

The UAE's manufacturing sector grew at an average annual rate of 5.9% in 2002–08, dropping to 4.6% in 2009–21. In 2021 the manufacturing sector accounted for 10.4% of GDP and 3.7% of non-oil GDP, making it the second largest non-hydrocarbon sector, after wholesale and retail trade.

In June 2004 Abu Dhabi's Government created the Higher Corporation for Specialized Economic Zones. These zones aimed to develop strategic industry clusters and attract investment by creating dedicated areas with modern infrastructure and services. The Industrial City of Abu Dhabi (ICAD), established in Mussafah, was the first of many specialized zones. By late 2005 45 factories were operating in ICAD.

In December 2005 ICAD 2 was launched. The Government adopted a law to attract foreign investment into the emirate by allowing 100% ownership by foreign investors in specialized zones. In late 2010 the Abu Dhabi Ports Co launched the first phase of the Khalifa Industrial Zone Abu Dhabi (KIZAD) project. The formation of this venture would result in one of the largest integrated industrial zones in the world. Investors would be allowed complete foreign ownership. New industrial development projects were given the go-ahead by the Government in January 2012. Among the proposals were the creation of two new industrial areas, in Ruwais and Medinat Zayed, as well as a major investment in automobile manufacturing.

In 2007 Emirates Aluminium began building an aluminium smelter plant at Taweelah. The project cost US $5,700m. It was a joint venture between Abu Dhabi's Mubadala Development Co and Dubai Aluminium (DUBAL). The smelter became operational in December 2009. At the start of 2011 it reached its full first-phase capacity of 750,000 metric tons annually.

In 2011 an investment of US $4,500m. was announced to increase the capacity of the smelter to 1.3m. metric tons per year by 2014. Then, in 2013, Emirates Global Aluminium was created by Mubadala Development Co and the Investment Corporation of Dubai. They integrated the businesses of DUBAL and Emirates Aluminium. Later, in 2017, Emirates Global Aluminium opened an office in the People's Republic of China, to source raw materials and supplies.

The UAE is in an excellent competitive position to take advantage of increased production when the various plans reach fruition. The World Economic Forum's (WEF) Global Competitiveness Report for 2019 (the latest available) ranks the UAE 25th out of 141 countries. The UAE ranks exceptionally highly in several of the Index's 12 building blocks (pillars), including institutions (15th), infrastructure (12th), ICT adoption (2nd), skills (39th), labour market (34th), financial system (31st), business dynamism (31st) and innovation capability (33rd).

The UAE's market economy stands out in the Middle East, with the 2023 Index of Economic Freedom, published by the Heritage Foundation ranking the country the 24th freest globally and 1st out of 14 countries in the MENA region. The Heritage Foundation notes: 'Economic restructuring has been underpinned by efforts to strengthen the business climate, boost investment, and foster the emergence of a more vibrant private sector.'

TOURISM

The UAE has several advantages in competing as a tourist destination. Dubai's airport is one of the busiest in the world and continues to grow. The UAE has a reputation for being one of the safest destinations in the Middle East. Many see Dubai as a year-round short-break destination for European and Middle Eastern tourists. Hotel construction is proliferating. However, the sector faces some difficulties. The Russia–Ukraine conflict severely limits Central and Eastern European arrivals, primarily from these markets. The focus of development in the tourism sector has been on Dubai and Abu Dhabi. Other emirates have yet to benefit from this growth, although this is starting to change.

The UAE's tourism industry has rapidly expanded, with 19.3m. arrivals in 2015, increasing to 21.8m. in 2017 and 25.3m. in 2019. However, with the onset of the COVID-19 pandemic, arrivals dropped to 8.1m. in 2020. Recovery is under way, but arrivals may not return to 2019 levels until 2024. The sector has a large impact on the economy.

In 2019 tourism accounted for 11.6% of the UAE's GDP, but by 2022 its share had dropped to 9.0%. The sector employed 11.6% of the workforce in 2022. In 2019 visitor spending was US $39,500m., accounting for 9.5% of total exports. However, in 2022 tourist spending fell to $32,000m.

In Dubai, the principal tourist destination, the main emphasis has been on diversification into luxury beach and resort developments catering predominantly to holidaymakers—rather than the business travellers who constitute the core clientele of many of Dubai's longer-established hotels. Promoting the UAE as a year-round destination for 'sunshine tourism' has been aimed principally at the upper end of the European, Asian and US markets. In November 2013 Dubai won the right to host the 2020 World Expo—the first time that the exhibition was staged in the Middle East, although the COVID-19 pandemic led to its postponement until October 2021.

Construction of the Saadiyat Island project in Abu Dhabi was ongoing in 2023. This was a tourist resort 500 m off shore from Abu Dhabi City which was to cost US $27,000m. A project to develop nearby Jubail Island was announced in 2019. The number of visitors to Dubai reached 16.7m. in 2019. Following the pandemic, Dubai received more than 14.3m. international visitors in 2022.

Although the sector is rebounding strongly from the COVID-19 pandemic and its after-effects, a new threat may derail the recovery. In July 2023 the first known case of the potentially fatal Middle East Respiratory Syndrome coronavirus (MERS-CoV) in 20 months was detected in the UAE. The World Health Organization expects further cases. Since 2012 2,605 cases of MERS-CoV and 936 associated deaths have been recorded in 27 countries. The UAE has reported 94 cases (including the current case) and 12 related deaths since July 2013.

Although the number of cases worldwide has been small, the fatality rate, at 36%, is high. The UAE will seek to understand how the patient became infected, as it prioritizes stopping the spread of the disease. Any broader outbreak would damage the tourism sector (which has just recovered from the impact of COVID-19) and complicate the country's high-profile hosting of the UN Climate Change Conference (COP 28), which is due to take place in Dubai in late November 2023.

REAL ESTATE

The construction and real estate sector is the largest single borrowing sector in the UAE, aside from personal loans, representing 19% of total lending as of mid-2022 and accounting for about 13% of the UAE's GDP in 2021. Real estate is the sixth most important non-hydrocarbon sector, accounting for 8.2% of non-oil GDP. Its performance is, therefore, critical to financial health and non-oil economic performance. Despite the global economic slowdown, rising interest rates, and ongoing real estate oversupply, the sector is seeing marked growth in prices and transaction volumes. Demand for residential property is rising strongly at the higher end of the market, owing to regional oil wealth and investment from traditional expatriate sources such as South Asia, and boosted by the liberalization of residency and foreign investment laws, by growing demand for expatriate labour and by demand from wealthy Russians in search for a safe haven from Western sanctions.

In 2023 Dubai is experiencing a real estate boom. This is Dubai's third boom in real estate prices since 2008, and it is occurring when many of the world's leading housing markets face a downturn caused by the sharp increase in interest rates. In May 2023 residential values in Dubai surged by 12.8% year on year, marking the 27th consecutive month of expansion. This upswing follows a decline that lasted almost six years. The average price of apartments reached AED 1,294 (US $352) per sq ft in June, while prices of villas hit AED 1,525 ($415)—increases of 30% and 22%, respectively, since January 2022.

In the luxury market, Dubai is even more of an outlier. In the first quarter of 2023 prices rose at an annualized pace of 44%—the sharpest rise among 46 leading markets. Indeed, between the first quarter of 2020 and the first quarter of 2023, prime residential prices in Dubai soared by almost 150%. This was two-and-a-half times the increase seen in Miami, Florida, the second strongest market.

The price gains at the top end of the property market are partly because of the increasing numbers of ultra-high-net-worth foreign nationals purchasing property in Dubai. The city was the world's fourth most active market for luxury home sales in 2022, with 219 transactions. The total value of 'ultra-prime' transactions—homes priced above US $10m.—was $3,800m., which was topped only by New York ($4,400m.), Los Angeles ($4,300m.), and London ($4,300m.).

Three key factors differentiate the current boom from earlier real estate cycles. First, among ultra-high-net-worth individuals the UAE has strengthened its reputation as a safe haven since the February 2022 invasion of Ukraine. The Government has managed to maintain close ties with both Russia and the USA, despite the increase in geopolitical tensions. According to unofficial estimates, the Russian population in the UAE has risen fivefold, to 500,000, since the war began. Chinese, Indian, Russian and Iranian investors were among the top 10 buyers of luxury homes in Dubai in 2022.

Second, in contrast to previous property cycles, developers are more cautious. They demand upfront payments covering most of the value of a property before construction begins. A well-regulated pre-sales model exists, whereby developers pay the full land cost before marketing the apartments to buyers. After that, developers deposit the money collected from buyers into government escrow accounts, with funds only disbursed for construction costs. Developers, therefore, cannot use the money to pay down debt or abscond with the funds, as they did during the 2008 financial crash. This model has limited the accumulation of leverage previously associated with real estate and, crucially, curbed the supply of prime stock. Luxury prices are set to grow by around 10%–15% in 2023—probably the fastest rate globally—supported by a clear supply–demand imbalance.

Third, and most importantly, Dubai remains relatively affordable, in stark contrast to many other leading property markets, where values have risen sharply in recent years. Despite the recent rises in value, the average price of secondary apartments at the end of the first quarter of 2023 was 18% below the 2014 peak. Furthermore, in the luxury market buyers can get better value. A budget of US $1m. buys 1,130 sq ft of prime space in Dubai, compared with 230 sq ft in Hong Kong, 350 sq ft in New York, and 365 sq ft in London.

BANKING AND FINANCE

Between 2013 and 2021 banking and finance grew at an average annual rate of 4.6%. In 2021 the sector accounted for 7.3% of non-oil GDP. Today the UAE is home to the Middle East's leading financial centre. However, four decades ago the country lacked its own currency and had a simple financial regulatory framework. After oil prices quadrupled in 1974, the number of banks operating in the state increased, both domestic and international. This development led to the establishing of the CBUAE and the use of more complex financial products such as derivatives. The banking sector in the UAE is the largest in terms of asset volume in the GCC area. By the end of 2022 the industry's total asset value exceeded US $996,600m., higher than its closest rivals, Saudi Arabia and Qatar.

The banking sector has continued to top other GCC counterparts regarding asset value. Non-performing loans rose to 7.6% of total gross loans during the 2020 COVID-19 pandemic, but declined to 7.3% in 2021 and 6.4% in 2022. However, the industry faces market fragmentation. The UAE's banking sector is widely considered to be overcrowded, with over 50 banks operating in the country (23 local and 28 foreign).

On 1 April 2017 the National Bank of Abu Dhabi and First Gulf Bank merged to create a new bank named First Abu Dhabi Bank. Smaller banks are likely to merge to stay competitive because of consolidation. First Abu Dhabi Bank has assets worth AED 1,180m., making it the largest bank in the UAE. The merger made it one of the largest banks in the region, behind Qatar National Bank and surpassing Emirates NBD. The National Bank of Abu Dhabi had a considerable asset value but was a second-tier consumer bank. First Gulf Bank's business model was based on the retail business. Therefore, the banks' pairing was complementary.

In July 2023 the UAE became an observer at the Asia/Pacific Group on Money Laundering, a regional body of the Financial Action Task Force (FATF). The UAE was already a member of the FATF's Middle East and North Africa Financial Action Task Force. The FATF sets and monitors international standards in anti-money laundering and countering the financing of terrorism. In February 2022 the UAE was added to the FATF's 'grey list' of non-compliant countries, due to deficiencies in its money laundering and illicit financing legislation and implementation. In early July 2023 the FATF acknowledged that the UAE had made progress in addressing its non-compliance, but the grey listing was maintained.

The UAE's application for observer status was part of its attempts to remove its grey listing. The listing raises the costs for cross-border business with the country, while adding to reputational risks. However, the UAE is only fully compliant with 13 of the FATF's 40 Recommendations, while the effectiveness of its anti-money laundering and countering the financing of terrorism regime is 'substantial' in only one of the 13 measures. As a result, delisting is unlikely to happen soon.

The WEF's 2019 Global Competitiveness Report ranks the UAE's financial system 31st out of 141 countries. In domestic credit to the private sector it ranks 39th, but in the financing of SMEs it ranks ninth. Venture capital availability ranks fourth, while market capitalization ranks 39th. The sector ranks lower in stability, with the soundness of banks ranking 46th and non-performing loans 83rd.

TRANSPORT

The UAE has a road network of 4,080 km, and road transport is the primary mode of freight. However, the country has a limited road network compared to others in the region. Roads are crucial for transporting goods and connecting businesses in the supply chain. Unfortunately, high levels of congestion and traffic incidents result in significant supply chain disruptions and delays, especially in urban areas like Dubai and Abu Dhabi. This is a significant issue for project cargoes, consumer demand and connecting airports with customers, since the country has no developed rail network. The sector contracted at an average annual rate of 0.1% in 2013–21, primarily because of a 33% fall in 2020. The industry accounted for 4.5% of GDP in 2021.

Future projects focus on urban road improvements and surrounding ports and airports. Dubai has set a goal of making 25% of all road trips in the emirate smart and driverless by 2030, as part of its Autonomous Transportation Strategy, released in 2016. Dubai's Roads and Transport Authority announced plans in 2022 to build 37 km of dedicated bus and taxi lanes in the emirate. The project should reduce bus travel times by more than 40% during peak hours, owing to which an increase of 30% in public transport riders is projected by 2030.

Railway projects account for a significant component of the UAE's transport infrastructure project pipeline, with the Abu Dhabi and Dubai Governments pursuing a long list of urban transit initiatives to improve mobility and reduce traffic congestion. The federal Government also has long-term plans for a high-speed and freight railways network throughout the UAE.

The US $11,000m., 1,200-km Etihad Rail Project, the UAE's masterplan for a national freight and passenger rail network, remains the primary growth driver for rail infrastructure. The first phase involves connections between the Shah oil- and gasfield with the port of Ruwais. Later stages include lines connecting Ruwais to the border with Saudi Arabia; Habshan with the ports of Khalifa and Jebel Ali; and the northern emirates of Fujairah, Ras al-Khaimah, and Sharjah to the rest of the network. Although the entire project was initially scheduled for completion in 2018, the tender for the second phase was suspended in 2016. Etihad Rail announced a revised plan in March 2017 that reduced the number of parallel routes in the second and third phases. Freight operations were inaugurated in the second quarter of 2023, and overall completion is now anticipated in 2024, as passenger operations have yet to commence.

The UAE has excellent port facilities that take advantage of its location on a major trade route between Europe and Asia. It is also a crucial hub for exporting hydrocarbons from the Persian Gulf. Most international shipping firms use the UAE's ports as calling points, making it a dominant regional transshipment hub and a crucial link in global supply chains. This international trade connectivity results in efficient export and import lead times, making the country attractive to investors. The main container ports are Mina Jebel Ali and Port Rashid (both in Dubai), Khorfakkan (Sharjah), Khalifa (Abu Dhabi), Port of Fujairah, and Port Khalid (Sharjah).

More than 60% of cargo destined for GCC states arrives via UAE seaports, with Mina Jebel Ali accounting for over 63.2% of container throughput. Mina Jebel Ali, operated by DP World, is the UAE's largest container port and one of the 10 largest container ports globally. The port has enjoyed relatively strong growth over the past decade, but is susceptible to downturns. The port can handle six mega ships simultaneously.

Aviation is crucial to the UAE economy. The advanced sector helps export to foreign markets, reduces transport costs and improves the flexibility of freight transportation. This has a significant impact on the tourism, hospitality, trade and finance sectors. The UAE's strategic location at the centre of several land masses has made it a global hub for air travel. It facilitates flights to various destinations around the world.

Air travel is widely used in the UAE for domestic passenger and freight transport. The two major airports, Dubai International Airport and Abu Dhabi International Airport, invest heavily in development to maintain their global significance. The country's five national airlines, which include Emirates and Etihad Airways, are expansive and appealing, leading to an increase in passenger numbers across the UAE's seven international airports.

The WEF's 2019 Global Competitiveness Index ranks the country's transport sector eighth out of 141 countries, with road connectivity ranking 23rd and the quality of road infrastructure seventh. The UAE's airport connectivity ranks 19th, while the efficiency of air transport services ranks seventh. Finally, liner shipping connectivity ranks 12th, with the efficiency of seaport services 12th.

TRADE

The UAE is heavily reliant on international trade. Both the export and import of goods and services volumes amount to a significant percentage of the UAE's total GDP, at 98.9% and 67.4%, respectively, in 2022. The UAE's economic diversification efforts and aggressive transport infrastructure drive are paying off significantly in terms of export revenue from services. In the 2000s growth in exports of goods and services both averaged 12.0%. However, in 2010–22 growth in exports of goods and services averaged 5.1% yearly, while growth in exports of goods averaged 3.5%. The UAE's most prominent services exports are currently commercial and financial services, tourism, and transport.

The UAE's diversification programme has also been achieved by developing its emirates into major transshipment and re-export hubs for the MENA region. In 2021 the UAE ranked second highest in re-export value, behind only the USA. The UAE has minimal local manufacturing capacity. Therefore, the country has small domestic steel and aluminium manufacturing capacity, and all exports of commercial vehicles, industrial equipment, gold and diamonds are re-exports from other destinations. The emergence of the UAE as a regional transshipment hub has been chiefly due to the open trade regime available to exporters and importers. For example, as a general rule, imports into the UAE due to be re-exported within six months are exempt from customs duty.

In 2021 the UAE's primary exports were crude petroleum (US $58,500m.), refined oil ($42,500m.), gold ($32,800m.), broadcasting equipment ($16,500m.) and diamonds ($13,600m.). Principle imports included gold ($46,000m.), broadcasting equipment ($18,500m.), refined petroleum ($16,700m.), diamonds ($13,600m.) and cars ($9,300m.).

With exports consistently outpacing imports, the UAE consistently runs current account surpluses. In the 1980s these averaged 15.5% of GDP, dipping to 5.7% in the 1990s but increasing to 9.9% in the 2000s and 10.0% in 2010–22. Even in the COVID-19 pandemic year of 2020, the UAE ran a current account surplus of 6.0% of GDP.

The country's trade diversification is evident because the top five export markets accounted for only 18.1% of exported products from the UAE in 2021 (according to the latest available data). In 2021 the UAE's principal export partner was China, accounting for 10.3% of total exports. Saudi Arabia was second, accounting for 6.2% of export activity. India and Iraq are also important export partners. The well-diversified nature of the UAE's export markets will limit its external demand shocks.

Owing to the vast number of free trade zones (FTZs) in the UAE, it is estimated that more than three-quarters of goods enter the country duty free. In addition, the country is highly reliant on imports, meaning that the UAE is a highly attractive import market for many countries. In 2021 China was the UAE's largest import partner, accounting for 19.2% of total product imports. The majority of the products imported from China are electrical and machinery goods. India is the country's second largest import partner, accounting for 7.7% of total product imports in 2021. The USA (6.2% of total product imports), Japan (4.0%), and Germany (3.1%) make up the remainder of the UAE's top five import partners.

In addition to the WTO, the UAE is a member of the GCC, along with Saudi Arabia, Bahrain, Oman, Kuwait and Qatar. The GCC is a political and economic organization created in the 1980s, and since 2015 a customs union and free trade agreement (FTA) have also been launched between the six members. The UAE's GCC membership means it is part of a single market and customs union with a common external tariff. The UAE also has free trade access to many countries in the region under the Greater Arab Free Trade Area Agreement. The UAE-India Comprehensive Economic Partnership Agreement came into effect on 1 May 2022. The UAE also has FTAs with Israel and Indonesia and is pursuing bilateral trade agreements with several other countries.

MONETARY POLICY

The CBUAE conducts monetary policy in the UAE. The CBUAE tends to mirror the monetary policy of the US Federal Reserve to maintain its currency peg against the US dollar (sometimes with a slight lag). Like most central banks, the CBUAE's main priority is inflation. Inflation in the UAE has been subdued in recent years. After increasing from 2.0% in 2017 to 3.1% in 2018, inflation decreased by 1.9% in 2019, 2.1% in 2020 and 0.1% in 2021, primarily due to the declining rents that had resulted in deflation in the housing component (by 35.1%) of the consumer price index (CPI). This trend has more than offset the more robust pass-through of oil prices to the domestic economy, increasing transport prices, which weigh 12.7% of the CPI basket. With global inflation affecting most of the CPI components and elevated energy costs putting further pressure on transport prices, inflation rose to 4.8% in 2022, with the IMF expecting inflation to dip slightly, to 3.4%, in 2023.

The UAE's fixed exchange rate regime limits the independence of monetary policy and its ability to respond to inflationary evolutions. Monetary policy beyond the policy rate has traditionally centred around mopping up excess liquidity, since a substantial share of the UAE's enormous oil revenues tends to end up in the banking system via government and government-related entities deposits.

The CBUAE imposes a 7.0% reserve ratio on demand deposits and 1.0% on time deposits. The CBUAE also plays a crucial role in maintaining financial stability and is the single integrated regulator of the UAE's financial services industry, except for capital markets, which are regulated and supervised by the Securities and Commodities Authority. Other objectives include encouraging credit growth to SMEs and promoting saving among the population.

FISCAL POLICY

The UAE runs consistent budget surpluses with an occasional deficit. In the 1990s government revenues averaged 28.7% of GDP, increasing to 30.0% in the 2000s and 31.7% in 2010–22. Government expenditures were consistently lower, at 28.3% of GDP in the 1990s, dropping to 21.2% in the 2000s and increasing to 29.3% in 2010–22. As a result, the surplus averaged 1.8% of GDP (1990s), 8.4% (2000s) and 2.5% (2010–22). The Government registered a budget deficit of 2.5% of GDP in 2020, 6.6% in 2015, 3.1% in 2016 and 0.2% in 2017, following the 2014–15 oil price drop.

The UAE continues to boast a solid fiscal profile underpinned by large financial buffers and modest debt levels. Government debt relative to GDP increased from 13.8% in 2014, to fund the country's budgetary shortfall, to 26.8% at the end of 2019. It then surged to 40.1% of GDP in 2020 on the back of the dual shock from the outbreak of COVID-19 and the collapse in global oil prices. That said, the shift to a fiscal surplus of 4.0% of GDP in 2021 and 9.0% in 2022 reduced the debt-to-GDP ratio to 30.0% in 2022.

Authorities at the local and federal levels continue to introduce revenue-raising measures. The Government has already introduced excise taxes on alcohol, tobacco and sugary drinks, and VAT at a standard initial rate of 5.0%. In addition, the different emirates have introduced some specific fees at the local level (such as the Abu Dhabi road tolls). In June 2023 the UAE introduced a 9.0% tax on corporate income, further boosting non-hydrocarbon revenues.

On the expenditure side, the Government has already moved forward with reductions in fuel subsidies, with diesel prices now linked to global benchmarks. There has also been a reduction in capital transfers to government-related entities, and increases in water and electricity tariffs. Most of these measures were rolled back to provide short-term relief for COVID-affected businesses. However, fiscal discipline has resumed, with spending directed toward productive areas and industrial developments, especially in Abu Dhabi.

PROSPECTS

Business-friendly reforms to attract foreign investment and talent, and plans to increase hydrocarbon production should support the UAE's long-term growth trajectory. This is especially the case if oil prices remain relatively elevated. The COVID-19 shock and the associated collapse in global oil prices have encouraged the authorities to accelerate their reform drive to improve the business environment, diversify the economy and keep the population rising. These measures will support the UAE's long-term growth and make it likely to be the fastest expanding economy of the GCC countries over the next eight to 10 years. Reinforcing the positive momentum currently propelling the economy was the announcement in August 2023 that the UAE (together with five other countries) had been invited to join the BRICS (Brazil, Russia, India, China and South Africa) grouping, with effect from January 2024.

Statistical Survey

Sources (unless otherwise stated): Central Bank of the UAE, POB 854, Abu Dhabi; tel. (2) 6652220; fax (2) 6652504; e-mail admin@cbuae.gov.ae; internet www.centralbank.ae; Federal Competitiveness and Statistics Authority, Festival Offices Tower, 9th Floor, Festival City, Dubai; tel. (4) 6080000; fax (4) 3273535; e-mail info@fcsa.gov.ae; internet fcsc.gov.ae.

Area and Population

AREA, POPULATION AND DENSITY

Area (sq km)	77,700*
Population (census results)	
17 December 1995	2,411,041
5 December 2005	
UAE nationals	825,495
Males	417,917
Females	407,578
Non-UAE nationals	3,280,932
Total	4,106,427
Population (official estimates at 31 December)	
2018	9,366,829
2019	9,503,738
2020	9,282,410
Density (per sq km) at 31 December 2020	119.5

* 30,000 sq miles.

Mid-2023 (UN projection): Total population 9,516,871 (Source: UN, *World Population Prospects: The 2022 Revision*).

POPULATION BY AGE AND SEX
('000, UN projections at mid-2023)

	Males	Females	Total
0–14 years	748.9	699.2	1,448.1
15–64 years	5,739.4	2,151.8	7,891.2
65 years and over	95.3	82.3	177.5
Total	**6,583.6**	**2,933.3**	**9,516.9**

Note: Totals may not be equal to the sum of components, owing to rounding.

Source: UN, *World Population Prospects: The 2022 Revision*.

Population by Sex (official estimates at 31 December 2020): Total 9,282,410 (males 6,468,460, females 2,813,950).

POPULATION BY EMIRATE
(official estimates at mid-2010, UAE nationals only)

	Area (sq km)	Population	Density (per sq km)
Abu Dhabi	67,340	404,546	6.0
Ajman	259	42,186	162.9
Dubai	3,885	168,029	43.3
Fujairah	1,166	64,860	55.6
Ras al-Khaimah	1,684	97,529	57.9
Sharjah	2,590	153,365	59.2
Umm al-Qaiwain	777	17,482	22.5
Total	**77,700**	**947,997**	**12.2**

Note: Figures for non-nationals, totalling 7,316,073, were not available.

THE UNITED ARAB EMIRATES

PRINCIPAL LOCALITIES
(estimated population at mid-2003)

Dubai	1,171,000	Ras al-Khaimah	102,000
Abu Dhabi (capital)	552,000	Fujairah	54,000
Sharjah City	519,000	Umm al-Qaiwain	38,000
Al-Ain	348,000	Khor Fakkan	32,000
Ajman	225,000		

Mid-2023 (urban agglomerations, UN estimates): Dubai 3,007,583; Sharjah City 1,830,858; Abu Dhabi (capital) 1,566,999; Al-Ain 645,203; Ajman 411,397 (Source: UN, *World Urbanization Prospects: The 2018 Revision*).

Dubai (official estimate at 31 December 2022): 3,549,900 (Source: Statistics Centre, Municipality of Dubai).

Fujairah (official estimate at mid–2022): 316,790 (Source: Fujairah Statistics Centre, Fujairah City, Emirate of Fujairah).

Sharjah (2022 census, preliminary): Sharjah City 1,600,000; Khor Fakkan 53,000; Kalba 51,000 (Source: Department of Statistics and Community Development, Sharjah).

Ajman (population at 2017 census): 504,846 (Source: Ajman Statistics Centre, Ajman).

Abu Dhabi (2016): 2,908,173 (Source: Statistics Centre Abu Dhabi, Al Maryah Island, Abu Dhabi).

BIRTHS, MARRIAGES AND DEATHS

	Live births	Marriages*	Deaths
2016	98,299	15,778	8,988
2017	97,733	15,146	8,829
2018	95,313	14,804	8,784
2019	94,697	14,909	9,006
2020	97,572	17,653	10,357

* Muslim marriages only.

2021: Marriages 18,380.

Life expectancy (years at birth, estimates): 78.7 (males 77.2; females 80.9) in 2021 (Source: World Bank, World Development Indicators database).

EMPLOYMENT
(persons aged 15 years and over)

	2005	2006*	2007†
Agriculture, hunting, forestry and fishing	193,044	209,066	225,499
Mining and quarrying	38,694	41,906	45,199
Oil and gas	33,200	35,956	38,783
Manufacturing	336,585	364,521	393,173
Electricity, gas and water supply	34,207	37,046	39,958
Construction	534,398	578,753	624,242
Wholesale and retail trade; repair of motor vehicles, motorcycles and personal and household goods	502,427	544,129	586,897
Hotels and restaurants	116,615	126,294	136,220
Transport, storage and communications	162,768	176,278	190,133
Financial intermediation	31,015	33,589	36,229
Real estate, renting and business activities	77,858	84,320	90,947
Public administration and defence; compulsory social security	286,105	309,851	334,207
Community, social and personal service activities	114,736	124,259	134,026
Private households with employed persons	222,506	240,975	259,916
Total employed	**2,650,958**	**2,870,987**	**3,096,646**

* Preliminary figures.
† Estimates.

2013 ('000 persons aged 15 years and over, estimates): Agriculture, hunting, forestry and fishing 251.8; Mining and quarrying 80.2 (Oil and gas 66.9); Manufacturing 679.6; Electricity, gas and water 66.3; Construction 1,145.9; Wholesale and retail trade; repair of motor vehicles, motorcycles and personal and household goods 1,121.2; Hotels and restaurants 293.3; Transport, storage and communications 439.9; Financial intermediation 94.7; Real estate, renting and business activities 225.9; Public administration and defence; compulsory social security 674.8; Community, social and personal service activities 233.6; Private households with employed persons 554.6; *Total employed* 5,861.8.

Health and Welfare

KEY INDICATORS

Total fertility rate (children per woman, 2021)	1.5
Under-5 mortality rate (per 1,000 live births, 2021)	6.4
HIV/AIDS (% of persons aged 15–49, 2020)	0.1
COVID-19: Cumulative confirmed deaths (per 100,000 persons at 30 June 2023)	24.9
COVID-19: Fully vaccinated population (% of total population at 20 June 2022)	103.7
Physicians (per 1,000 head, 2020)	2.9
Hospital beds (per 1,000 head, 2017)	1.4
Domestic health expenditure (2020): US $ per head (PPP)	2,459.8
Domestic health expenditure (2020): % of GDP	3.5
Domestic health expenditure (2020): public (% of total current health expenditure)	61.0
Total carbon dioxide emissions ('000 metric tons, 2019)	188,859
Carbon dioxide emissions per head (metric tons, 2019)	20.5
Human Development Index (2021): ranking	26
Human Development Index (2021): value	0.911

Note: For data on COVID-19 vaccinations, 'fully vaccinated' denotes receipt of all doses specified by approved vaccination regime (Sources: Johns Hopkins University and Our World in Data). Data on health expenditure refer to current general government expenditure in each case. For more information on sources and further definitions for all indicators, see Health and Welfare Statistics: Sources and Definitions section (europaworld.com/credits).

Agriculture

PRINCIPAL CROPS
('000 metric tons)

	2019	2020	2021*
Almonds, with shell	1.3	0.4	0.9
Aubergines (Eggplants)	27.0	27.4	14.9
Cabbages	25.4	35.5	35.8
Cantaloupes and other melons	4.1	4.4	3.7
Cauliflowers and broccoli	18.6	18.2	14.6
Chillies and peppers, green	5.2	6.4	4.8
Cucumbers and gherkins	91.9	105.8	114.1
Dates	341.2	351.5	351.1
Figs	1.5	1.6	1.3
Lemons and limes	7.6	8.0	9.0
Maize	26.1	26.4	23.6
Mangoes, mangosteens and guavas	8.2	10.2	10.4
Onions and shallots, green*	26.7	26.9	27.1
Pumpkins, squash and gourds	21.4	21.3	19.2
Spinach*	2.5	2.5	2.5
Tobacco, unmanufactured*	0.3	0.3	0.3
Tomatoes	60.1	80.1	75.5

* FAO estimates.

Aggregate production ('000 metric tons, may include official, semi-official or estimated data): Total cereals 26.1 in 2019, 26.4 in 2020, 23.6 in 2021; Total fruit (primary) 371.2 in 2019, 390.5 in 2020, 388.3 in 2021; Total vegetables (primary) 310.9 in 2019, 349.4 in 2020, 331.7 in 2021.

Source: FAO.

LIVESTOCK
('000 head, year ending September)

	2019	2020	2021*
Camels	494.5	497.5	511.2
Cattle	100.9	103.1	104.6
Chickens*	24,872	25,401	25,930
Goats	2,350.1	2,399.3	2,381.5
Sheep	2,044.0	2,054.6	2,082.1

* FAO estimates.

Source: FAO.

THE UNITED ARAB EMIRATES

LIVESTOCK PRODUCTS
('000 metric tons, FAO estimates)

	2019	2020	2021
Camel meat	36.9	37.6	39.1
Camel offals, edible	6.2	6.3	6.6
Camels' milk	74.6	85.4	78.3
Cattle meat	18.0	18.7	19.2
Cows' milk	50.9	55.9	52.6
Chicken meat	44.9	54.1	56.0
Goat meat	58.3	60.1	63.2
Goat offals, edible	11.7	12.0	12.6
Goats' milk	73.2	81.6	75.9
Goats' skins, fresh	7.3	7.6	8.0
Sheep meat	4.9	4.9	4.1
Sheep's (Ewes') milk	31.4	34.2	31.9
Hen eggs	56.6	53.7	56.0

Source: FAO.

Forestry

ROUNDWOOD REMOVALS
('000 cu m, excl. bark, FAO estimates)

	2019	2020	2021
Total (all broadleaved)	18.9	18.9	19.0

Source: FAO.

Fishing

('000 metric tons, live weight)

	2019	2020	2021
Capture	62.6	58.9	61.2
Orange-spotted grouper	0.2*	0.2	0.1
Spangled emperor	7.9	7.3	7.9
Pink ear emperor	7.7	6.4	7.8
Grunts and sweetlips	2.0	1.3	1.3
King soldier bream	1.4	1.4	1.3
Sardinellas	3.8	3.4	2.1
Narrow-barred Spanish mackerel	5.4	5.0	5.0
Orangespotted trevally	2.1	1.6	2.0
Longnose trevally	1.8	2.3	2.2
Aquaculture	3.2*	3.0	2.7
Total catch	65.9*	62.0	63.9

* FAO estimate.
Source: FAO.

Mining

	2020	2021	2022
Crude petroleum (million metric tons)	165.9	163.4	181.1
Natural gas ('000 million cu m)*	50.6	58.3	58.0

* Excluding gas flared or recycled.
Source: Energy Institute, *Statistical Review of World Energy*.

Industry

SELECTED PRODUCTS
('000 barrels unless otherwise indicated)

	2017	2018	2019
Cement ('000 metric tons)*	17,400	16,300	16,400
Aluminium ('000 metric tons)	2,611	2,640	2,570
Iron ('000 metric tons, direct reduced)	3,608	3,784	3,667
Raw steel ('000 metric tons)	3,309	3,247	3,327
Motor spirit (petrol)	35,770	35,770	35,040
Kerosene and jet fuel	104,775	105,485	103,295
Gas-diesel (distillate fuel) oil	83,585	83,585	82,855
Residual fuel oils	17,885	17,155	16,425

* Estimates.

Liquefied petroleum gas: 14,053 in 2016.

Source: partly US Geological Survey.

Electrical energy (million kWh): 138,454 in 2019; 137,310 in 2020; 149,053 in 2022.

Finance

CURRENCY AND EXCHANGE RATES

Monetary Units
  100 fils = 1 UAE dirham (AED).

Sterling, Dollar and Euro Equivalents (31 May 2023)
  £1 sterling = 4.541 dirhams;
  US $1 = 3.673 dirhams;
  €1 = 3.923 dirhams;
  100 UAE dirhams = £22.02 = $27.23 = €25.49.

Exchange Rate: The Central Bank's official rate was set at US $1 = 3.671 dirhams in November 1980. This remained in force until December 1997, when the rate was adjusted to $1 = 3.6725 dirhams.

BUDGET OF THE CONSOLIDATED GOVERNMENTS
(million UAE dirhams)

Revenue	2018	2019	2020*
Tax revenues	15,472	15,489	12,016
Customs	7,996	8,005	6,210
Others	7,476	7,485	5,806
Non-tax revenues	462,267	462,764	357,607
Petroleum and gas	196,826	197,037	152,852
Enterprise profits	149,647	149,808	116,214
Other	115,794	115,919	88,542
Total	477,740	478,253	369,623

Expenditure	2018	2019	2020*
Current	325,798	388,716	323,916
Wages and salaries	82,840	107,722	108,976
Goods and services	86,608	119,428	85,781
Subsidies and transfers	46,233	43,213	41,151
Others	110,116	118,354	88,007
Development	62,412	53,669	48,745
Total	388,209	442,386	372,661

* Preliminary.

2020 ('000 million UAE dirhams, revised figures): Total revenue 367,865.5; Total expenditure 399,544.5.

2021 ('000 million UAE dirhams, preliminary figures): Total revenue 463,869.3; Total expenditure 402,381.9.

2022 ('000 million UAE dirhams, preliminary figures): Total revenue 596,774.7; Total expenditure 401,056.8.

THE UNITED ARAB EMIRATES

Statistical Survey

INTERNATIONAL RESERVES
(excluding gold, US $ million at 31 December)

	2020	2021	2022
IMF special drawing rights	220.5	3,314.7	3,153.7
Reserve position in IMF	814.7	791.7	800.0
Foreign exchange*	102,164.0	123,766.5	130,110.8
Total	103,199.2	127,873.0	134,064.5

*Figures exclude the Central Bank's foreign assets and accrued interest attributable to the governments of individual emirates.

Source: IMF, *International Financial Statistics*.

MONEY SUPPLY
(million UAE dirhams at 31 December)

	2020	2021	2022
Currency outside depository corporations	94,724	94,082	101,936
Transferable deposits	664,534	814,175	864,731
Other deposits	719,349	654,768	736,367
Broad money	1,478,607	1,563,025	1,703,034

Source: IMF, *International Financial Statistics*.

COST OF LIVING
(Consumer Price Index; base: 2014 = 100)

	2019	2020	2021
Food and non-alcoholic beverages	105.7	109.6	109.5
Clothing and footwear	114.2	119.6	115.6
Housing (incl. rent) and utilities	104.5	100.6	97.1
All items (incl. others)	109.0	106.7	106.9

All items (Consumer Price Index; base: 2010 = 100): 112.1 in 2020; 112.1 in 2021; 117.5 in 2022 (Source: IMF, *International Financial Statistics*).

NATIONAL ACCOUNTS
(million UAE dirhams at current prices)

Expenditure on the Gross Domestic Product

	2019	2020	2021
Government final consumption expenditure	188,124.7	194,820.5	224,366.8
Private final consumption expenditure	601,625.3	515,566.6	606,950.4
Increase in stocks	75,467.0	48,004.9	56,506.9
Gross fixed capital formation	268,737.4	268,629.8	316,206.3
Total domestic expenditure	1,133,954.4	1,027,021.8	1,204,030.5
Exports of goods and services	1,483,643.9	1,289,993.6	1,561,359.5
Less Imports of goods and services	1,085,603.1	1,005,130.5	1,276,310.1
Statistical discrepancy	228.9	—	—
GDP in market prices	1,532,224.1	1,311,884.9	1,489,079.9
GDP at constant 2015 prices	1,451,018.4	1,380,783.7	1,432,813.3

Gross Domestic Product by Economic Activity

	2019	2020	2021
Agriculture, livestock and fishing	11,448.4	12,106.8	13,063.0
Mining, quarrying and utilities	409,190.9	278,837.9	424,066.1
Manufacturing	134,639.0	136,221.6	151,035.7
Construction	137,391.8	131,861.0	118,977.1
Wholesale and retail trade, and repairs; restaurants and hotels	234,957.2	202,322.5	223,233.6
Transport, storage and communications	135,791.9	106,541.7	109,444.1
Other activities	468,804.9	443,993.4	449,260.2
GDP in market prices	1,532,224.1	1,311,884.9	1,489,079.9

Source: UN National Accounts Main Aggregates Database.

Gross Domestic Product by Emirate

	2007	2008	2009
Abu Dhabi	545,368	705,159	596,434
Dubai	310,056	342,900	294,158
Sharjah	54,002	65,026	60,946
Ajman	12,633	14,441	13,885
Ras al-Khaimah	14,580	16,413	15,738
Fujairah	9,172	9,904	9,330
Umm al-Qaiwain	2,246	2,424	2,314
Total	948,056	1,156,267	992,805

2020: Abu Dhabi 678,841; Dubai 382,405 (preliminary); Ajman 29,592; Fujairah 20,001.
2021: Abu Dhabi 840,513 (preliminary); Dubai 419,116 (preliminary); Ajman 31,362 (preliminary); Fujairah 22,336.
2022: Dubai 463,794 (preliminary); Fujairah 25,247 (estimate).

BALANCE OF PAYMENTS
('000 million UAE dirhams)

	2019	2020	2021
Exports of goods f.o.b.	1,152.4	999.5	1,187.4
Imports of goods f.o.b.	−856.9	−778.0	−897.1
Trade balance	295.5	221.6	290.3
Services (net)	7.6	59.7	94.5
Income (net)	7.6	−6.9	−2.7
Balance on goods, services and income	310.7	274.3	382.1
Current transfers (net)	−173.6	−196.9	−205.8
Current balance	137.1	77.5	176.2
Capital and financial accounts (net)	−90.4	−97.1	−96.8
Net errors and omissions	−11.3	6.0	5.3
Overall balance	−35.7	13.1	−85.0

External Trade

PRINCIPAL COMMODITIES
(distribution by HS, million UAE dirhams)

Imports c.i.f.	2019	2020	2021
Vegetables and vegetable products	23,301.9	23,178.4	25,445.0
Mineral products	65,946.2	44,265.5	52,990.3
Chemical products, etc.	57,491.5	49,730.0	64,471.3
Plastics, rubber and articles thereof	24,107.6	21,345.8	29,479.1
Textiles and textile articles	25,995.8	21,705.9	28,621.0
Pearls, precious or semi-precious stones, precious metals, etc.	215,131.5	192,698.5	271,481.5
Base metals and articles of base metal	55,291.9	47,614.9	60,163.3
Machinery and electrical equipment	238,194.4	221,368.0	258,723.3
Vehicles and other transport equipment	90,218.7	64,335.3	82,134.2
Total (incl. others)	914,851.5	785,112.1	991,633.5

Exports f.o.b.*	2019	2020	2021
Prepared foodstuffs, beverages, spirits and tobacco	21,791.9	22,559.7	25,519.3
Mineral products (excl. petroleum)	21,544.0	13,103.5	19,783.6
Chemical products, etc.	11,057.5	10,716.8	12,994.2
Plastics, rubber and articles thereof	17,297.6	20,817.4	25,866.0
Pulp of wood, waste, scrap and articles of paper	4,344.4	5,061.4	5,660.7
Pearls, precious or semi-precious stones, precious metals, etc.	76,073.1	111,833.5	133,311.9
Base metals and articles of base metal	48,523.3	42,392.8	70,512.3
Machinery and electrical equipment	12,317.2	10,691.6	15,278.9
Total (incl. others)†	231,236.7	254,641.6	331,628.8

*Excluding petroleum exports and excluding re-exports; re-exports amounted to (million dirhams): 457,410.3 in 2019; 363,413.1 in 2020; 463,263.4 in 2021.
†Excluding free zone exports.

THE UNITED ARAB EMIRATES

Statistical Survey

SELECTED MAJOR TRADING PARTNERS
(million UAE dirhams)

Imports	2019	2020	2021
Australia	12,192.1	6,281.4	9,131.2
Bahrain	15,739.8	9,074.6	10,124.5
Belgium	9,877.2	8,388.5	11,369.2
Brazil	9,918.1	8,425.8	9,870.0
Canada	6,589.4	6,684.7	10,213.9
China, People's Republic	149,755.9	144,429.6	190,219.2
Egypt	8,606.2	11,780.1	6,200.5
France (incl. Monaco)	24,832.2	17,483.8	22,354.4
Germany	36,997.6	26,711.1	30,479.1
Guinea	8,744.5	25,093.4	9,477.9
Hong Kong	9,981.9	4,692.7	4,678.9
India	98,185.4	60,486.1	76,667.8
Italy (incl. San Marino)	24,087.5	20,348.1	29,303.8
Japan	46,324.7	34,728.8	39,881.6
Korea, Republic	14,101.1	14,905.7	13,209.6
Malaysia	10,207.4	7,857.4	9,773.9
Mali	11,821.2	10,832.5	26,909.2
Russian Federation	10,262.5	7,134.7	13,623.8
Saudi Arabia	25,139.7	23,782.4	27,096.7
South Africa	10,204.1	13,559.7	16,360.1
Sudan	4,519.3	6,824.5	10,653.6
Switzerland	15,076.3	11,104.1	19,633.7
Thailand	12,559.1	11,059.3	14,179.6
Türkiye	12,985.3	11,167.4	35,185.8
United Kingdom	26,765.9	21,491.3	19,716.7
USA	73,115.4	60,551.5	61,856.2
Viet Nam	26,420.4	21,492.0	27,915.6
Total (incl. others)	914,851.5	785,112.1	991,633.5

Exports*	2019	2020	2021
Bahrain	5,007.4	3,588.1	4,924.8
Bangladesh	3,237.1	2,911.1	3,571.3
China, People's Republic	8,273.4	9,793.4	12,265.0
Egypt	3,787.6	4,071.1	9,157.1
Hong Kong	3,244.7	17,120.0	25,778.5
India	23,956.7	19,737.0	45,715.9
Iraq	9,187.5	7,538.9	7,932.5
Italy (incl. San Marino)	1,674.8	18,229.4	7,021.8
Japan	4,434.3	3,341.2	6,344.7
Jordan	2,361.0	2,075.0	4,336.3
Kenya	2,939.1	2,284.9	3,176.0
Korea, Republic	2,628.6	1,859.4	2,493.1
Kuwait	9,927.1	7,359.1	12,657.7
Malaysia	2,460.1	3,918.5	4,988.9
Netherlands	2,582.4	1,724.1	3,753.2
Oman	16,221.3	12,286.7	15,794.7
Pakistan	3,537.1	5,502.5	5,654.5
Saudi Arabia	30,925.1	25,568.2	37,828.2
Singapore	5,239.0	3,132.7	4,150.1
Somalia	2,493.7	2,962.4	3,048.3
Sri Lanka	3,110.1	1,752.1	1,248.9
Switzerland	20,914.0	29,228.7	27,329.7
Thailand	2,876.1	1,443.4	2,282.1
Türkiye	8,746.2	18,429.2	9,901.9
United Kingdom	2,054.9	2,805.2	3,630.8
USA	7,337.7	6,244.2	10,615.6
Total (incl. others)	231,236.7	254,641.6	331,628.8

*Data for non-petroleum exports and excluding re-exports (million dirhams): 457,410.3 in 2019; 363,413.1 in 2020; 463,263.4 in 2021.

Transport

SHIPPING

Flag Registered Fleet
(at 31 December)

	2020	2021	2022
Number of vessels	950	970	1,013
Total displacement ('000 grt)	1,462.9	1,538.4	1,524.6

Source: Lloyd's List Intelligence (www.bit.ly/LLintelligence).

CIVIL AVIATION
(traffic at major airports)

	2019	2020	2021
Aircraft arrivals*	308,799	146,148	192,122
Aircraft departures*	308,668	145,607	192,140
Passenger arrivals ('000)	32,405.6	11,076.8	16,913.6
Passenger departures ('000)	32,655.9	11,778.2	15,824.7
Passengers in transit ('000)	62,894.9	15,536.2	13,176.9

*Excluding aircraft movements at local airports: 48,892 in 2019; 39,818 in 2020; 43,882 in 2021.

Tourism

VISITOR ARRIVALS BY NATIONALITY

	2018	2019	2020
Bangladesh	138,470	164,696	66,327
Canada	197,828	208,668	68,753
China, People's Republic	879,172	1,039,873	182,601
Egypt	341,718	371,962	248,152
France	420,776	463,184	196,329
Germany	825,316	862,330	264,555
India	2,893,917	2,974,058	1,275,364
Iran	331,217	307,245	53,981
Iraq	108,270	124,417	60,706
Italy	304,108	325,514	110,508
Jordan	172,730	172,762	64,695
Kazakhstan	146,668	171,016	81,325
Korea, Republic	157,494	167,111	39,287
Kuwait	412,160	389,803	101,625
Lebanon	134,974	128,126	52,729
Netherlands	177,102	177,587	63,992
Nigeria	179,663	261,008	82,948
Oman	4,526,895	5,862,816	1,322,664
Pakistan	853,836	875,231	436,430
Philippines	391,602	394,191	108,790
Russian Federation	833,597	902,976	348,975
Saudi Arabia	2,055,305	1,956,156	528,737
Spain	123,406	145,117	55,003
Switzerland	126,745	125,649	35,532
Ukraine	128,355	160,418	76,895
United Kingdom	1,422,042	1,424,997	435,818
USA	778,845	788,909	217,500
Total (incl. others)	23,092,384	25,281,572	8,084,236

*Figures refer to international arrivals at hotels and similar establishments.
†Total includes domestic tourists.

Receipts from tourism (US $ million, excl. passenger transport): 38,398 in 2019; 24,615 in 2020; 34,445 in 2021 (provisional).

Source: World Tourism Organization.

Arrivals in Dubai (visitors spending at least one night, '000): 5,510 (India 865; Saudi Arabia 400; United Kingdom 392; Russian Federation 296) in 2020; 7,280 (India 910; Saudi Arabia 491; Russian Federation 444; United Kingdom 420) in 2021; 14,360 (India 1,842; Oman 1,311; Saudi Arabia 1,216; United Kingdom 1,043) in 2022 (Source: Statistics Centre, Municipality of Dubai).

Communications Media

	2019	2020	2021
Telephones ('000 main lines in use)	2,362.6	2,380.9	2,243.0
Mobile telephone subscriptions ('000)	19,602.8	18,374.3	18,237.1
Broadband subscriptions, fixed ('000)	3,046.0	3,245.1	3,573.1
Broadband subscriptions, mobile ('000)	23,438.6	22,178.6	22,586.4
Internet users (% of population)*	99.1	100.0	100.0

* Persons aged 15–74 years.

Source: International Telecommunication Union.

Education

(2021/22 unless otherwise indicated, government schools only)

	Institutions	Teachers	Students
Pre-primary	191	10,178*	38,424
Primary	449	23,471*	174,903
Secondary	233	14,261*	242,056
Higher	68	8,861	47,586†

* 2020/21.
† Figure excludes 91,570 students in non-federal institutions.

Private schools (2021/22 unless otherwise indicated): *Institutions:* Pre-primary 455; Primary 657; Secondary 745. *Teachers* (2020/21): Pre-primary 17,413; Primary 41,793; Secondary 21,773. *Students:* Pre-primary 114,411; Primary 410,209; Secondary 250,647.

Source: Ministry of Education, Abu Dhabi.

Pupil-teacher ratio (qualified teaching staff, primary education, UNESCO estimate): 19.2 in 2021/22 (Source: UNESCO Institute for Statistics).

Adult literacy rate (UNESCO estimates): 98.1% (males 98.8%; females 97.2%) in 2021 (Source: UNESCO Institute for Statistics).

Directory

The Constitution

A provisional Constitution for the UAE took effect in December 1971. This laid the foundation for the federal structure of the Union of the seven emirates, previously known as the Trucial States.

The highest federal authority is the Supreme Council of Rulers, which comprises the Rulers of the seven emirates. It elects the President and Vice-President from among its members. The President appoints a Prime Minister and a Council of Ministers. Proposals submitted to the Council require the approval of at least five of the Rulers, including those of Abu Dhabi and Dubai. The legislature is the Federal National Council (FNC), a consultative assembly comprising 40 members, of whom one-half are appointed by the emirates and the remainder are chosen by electoral colleges for a two-year term. A constitutional amendment extending the FNC's term to four years was endorsed by the Supreme Council of Rulers in December 2008 and approved by the FNC in January 2009.

In July 1975 a committee was appointed to draft a permanent federal constitution, but the FNC decided in 1976 to extend the provisional document for five years. The provisional Constitution was extended for another five years in December 1981, and for further periods of five years in 1986 and 1991. In November 1976, however, the Supreme Council amended Article 142 of the provisional Constitution so that the authority to levy armed forces was placed exclusively under the control of the federal Government. Legislation designed to make the provisional Constitution permanent was endorsed by the FNC in June 1996, after it had been approved by the Supreme Council of Rulers.

The Government

HEAD OF STATE

President: Sheikh MOHAMMED BIN ZAYED AL NAHYAN (Ruler of Abu Dhabi; elected by the Supreme Council of Rulers as President of the UAE on 14 May 2022).

Vice-President: Sheikh MOHAMMED BIN RASHID AL MAKTOUM (Ruler of Dubai).

Vice-President: Sheikh MANSOUR BIN ZAYED AL NAHYAN.

SUPREME COUNCIL OF RULERS
(with each Ruler's date of accession)

Ruler of Abu Dhabi: Sheikh MOHAMMED BIN ZAYED AL NAHYAN (2022).
Ruler of Ajman: Sheikh HUMAID BIN RASHID AL-NUAIMI (1981).
Ruler of Dubai: Sheikh MOHAMMED BIN RASHID AL MAKTOUM (2006).
Ruler of Fujairah: Sheikh HAMAD BIN MOHAMMED AL-SHARQI (1974).
Ruler of Ras al-Khaimah: Sheikh SAUD BIN SAQR AL-QASIMI (2010).
Ruler of Sharjah: Sheikh SULTAN BIN MOHAMMED AL-QASIMI (1972).
Ruler of Umm al-Qaiwain: Sheikh SAUD BIN RASHID AL-MU'ALLA (2009).

COUNCIL OF MINISTERS
(September 2023)

Prime Minister and Minister of Defence: Sheikh MOHAMMED BIN RASHID AL MAKTOUM.
Deputy Prime Minister and Minister of the Interior: Lt-Gen. Sheikh SAIF BIN ZAYED AL NAHYAN.
Deputy Prime Minister and Minister of the Presidential Court: Sheikh MANSOUR BIN ZAYED AL NAHYAN.
Deputy Prime Minister and Minister of Finance: Sheikh MAKTOUM BIN MOHAMMED BIN RASHID AL MAKTOUM.
Minister of Foreign Affairs and International Co-operation: Sheikh ABDULLAH BIN ZAYED AL NAHYAN.
Minister of Tolerance and Coexistence: Sheikh NAHYAN BIN MABARAK AL NAHYAN.
Minister of Cabinet Affairs and the Future: MOHAMMED BIN ABDULLAH AL-GERGAWI.
Minister of Federal Supreme Council Affairs: ABDULLAH MUHAIR AL-KETBI.
Minister of Health and Prevention and Minister of State for Federal National Council Affairs: ABDULRAHMAN BIN MOHAMED AL-OWAIS.
Minister of Energy and Infrastructure: SUHAIL BIN MOHAMMED FARAJ FARIS AL-MAZROUEI.
Minister of Industry and Advanced Technology: Dr SULTAN BIN AHMED AL-JABER.
Minister of Justice: ABDULLAH BIN SULTAN BIN AWAD AL-NUAIMI.
Minister of Education: Dr AHMAD BELHOUL AL-FALASI.
Minister of Culture and Youth: SALEM BIN KHALID AL-QASSIMI.
Minister of Human Resources and Emiratisation: Dr ABDULRAHMAN AL-AWAR.
Minister of Community Development: SHAMMA AL-MAZRUI.
Minister of Economy: ABDULLAH BIN TOUQ AL-MARI.
Minister of Investment: MOHAMMED HASSAN AL-SUWAIDI.
Minister of Climate Change and Environment: MARIAM BINT MOHAMMED SAEED HAREB AL-MEHAIRI.
Minister of State for Financial Affairs: MOHAMED HADI AL-HUSSAINI.
Minister of State for Defence Affairs: MOHAMMED BIN AHMAD AL-BOWARDI.
Minister of State for Early Education: SARA MUSALLAM.
Minister of State for Foreign Trade: Dr THANI BIN AHMED AL-ZEYOUDI.
Minister of State for Government Development and the Future: OHOOD BINT KHALFAN AL-ROUMI.

THE UNITED ARAB EMIRATES

Minister of State for Public Education and Advanced Technology: SARAH BINT YOUSEF AL-AMIRI.
Minister of State for Artificial Intelligence, Digital Economy, and Remote Work Applications: OMAR BIN SULTAN AL-OLAMA.
Minister of State for International Co-operation: REEM BINT EBRAHIM AL-HASHIMY.
Minister of State and Secretary-General of the Cabinet: MARYAM AL-HAMMADI.
Ministers of State: Dr MAITHA BINT SALEM AL-SHAMSI, Sheikh SHAKHBUT BIN NAHYAN BIN MUBARAK AL NAHYAN, AHMED ALI AL-SAYEGH, KHALIFA SHAHEEN AL-MARAR, HAMAD BIN MUBARAK AL-SHAMSI, JABR GHANEM AL-SUWAIDI, NOURA BINT MOHAMMED AL-KAABI.

FEDERAL MINISTRIES

Office of the Prime Minister: POB 212000, Dubai; tel. (4) 3304433; fax (4) 4404433; e-mail info@pmo.gov.ae; internet uaecabinet.ae.
Office of the Deputy Prime Minister: POB 831, Abu Dhabi; tel. (2) 4451000; fax (2) 4450066.
Ministry of Cabinet Affairs and the Future: POB 899, Abu Dhabi; tel. (2) 4039999; fax (2) 6777399; e-mail contactus@moca.gov.ae; internet www.mocaf.gov.ae.
Ministry of Climate Change and the Environment: POB 213, Old Airport Rd, Abu Dhabi; tel. and fax (2) 4444747; e-mail info@moccae.gov.ae; internet www.moccae.gov.ae.
Ministry of Community Development: POB 281, Sheikh Rashid bin Saeed St, al-Muntazah, Abu Dhabi; fax (2) 6429131; e-mail sugg.comp@mocd.gov.ae; internet www.mocd.gov.ae.
Ministry of Culture and Youth: POB 17, Abu Dhabi; tel. 800552255; fax (2) 4452504; e-mail info@mcy.gov.ae; internet mcy.gov.ae.
Ministry of Defence: POB 111330, Abu Dhabi; tel. (2) 4444448; fax (2) 4414460; e-mail info@mod.gov.ae; internet www.mod.gov.ae.
Ministry of Economy: POB 901, Abu Dhabi; tel. (2) 6131111; fax (2) 6260000; e-mail info@economy.ae; internet www.economy.ae.
Ministry of Education: POB 45253, Abu Dhabi; tel. (2) 4089999; fax (4) 2176006; e-mail emc@moe.gov.ae; internet www.moe.gov.ae.
Ministry of Energy and Infrastructure: POB 59, Al Fallah St, Abu Dhabi; tel. 80066367; fax (2) 6190001; e-mail info@moei.gov.ae; internet www.moei.gov.ae.
Ministry of Finance: POB 433, Abu Dhabi; tel. (2) 6987200; fax (2) 6768414; e-mail info@mof.gov.ae; internet www.mof.gov.ae.
Ministry of Foreign Affairs and International Co-operation: King Abdullah bin Abd al-Aziz Al Saud St, al-Bateen, Abu Dhabi; tel. (2) 2222000; fax (2) 4931970; e-mail mofa@mofa.gov.ae; internet www.mofa.gov.ae.
Ministry of Health and Prevention: 11th Floor, Dusit Thani Hotel, al-Muroor Rd, Abu Dhabi; tel. (2) 6520530; fax (2) 6317644; e-mail info@moh.gov.ae; internet www.moh.gov.ae.
Ministry of Human Resources and Emiratisation: POB 809, Sultan bin Zayed I St, Abu Dhabi; tel. (4) 7023333; fax (4) 4494293; e-mail ask@mohre.gov.ae; internet www.mohre.gov.ae.
Ministry of Industry and Advanced Technology: Abu Dhabi.
Ministry of the Interior: POB 398, Zayed Sport City, Arab Gulf St, Abu Dhabi; tel. (2) 4414666; fax (2) 4022776; e-mail moi@moi.gov.ae; internet www.moi.gov.ae.
Ministry of Investment: Abu Dhabi.
Ministry of Justice: POB 260, Khalifa City (A), Sector 133, St 12, Abu Dhabi; tel. (2) 6921000; fax (2) 6810680; e-mail customer.s.ad@moj.gov.ae; internet ejustice.gov.ae.
Ministry of the Presidential Court: POB 280, Abu Dhabi; tel. (2) 6222221; fax (2) 6222228; e-mail ihtimam@mopa.ae; internet www.mopa.ae.
Ministry of State for Federal National Council Affairs: POB 130000, Saif Ghubash St, Abu Dhabi; tel. (2) 4041000; fax (2) 4041155; e-mail mfnca@mfnca.gov.ae; internet www.mfnca.gov.ae.
Ministry of State for Financial Affairs: POB 433, Abu Dhabi; tel. (2) 771133; fax (2) 793255.
Ministry of State for Foreign Affairs: POB 1, Abu Dhabi; tel. (2) 6660888; fax (2) 6652883.

Legislature

Formed under the provisional Constitution, the Federal National Council (FNC) is composed of 40 members from the various emirates (eight each from Abu Dhabi and Dubai, six each from Sharjah and Ras al-Khaimah, and four each from Ajman, Fujairah and Umm al-Qaiwain). Each emirate appoints its own representatives separately. The FNC studies laws proposed by the Council of Ministers and can reject them or suggest amendments. In December 2005 Sheikh Khalifa announced that elections would be introduced to choose one-half of the members of the FNC, which would also be expanded and granted enhanced powers. In August 2006 a National Electoral Committee was established to preside over the elections, which were held during 16–20 December. A constitutional amendment extending the FNC's term from two to four years was endorsed by the Supreme Council of Rulers in December 2008 and approved by the FNC in January 2009. Further partial elections were held on 24 September 2011, 3 October 2015 and 5 October 2019.

Federal National Council (FNC): POB 836, Abu Dhabi; tel. (2) 6199500; fax (2) 6812846; e-mail info@almajles.gov.ae; internet www.almajles.gov.ae.

Speaker: SAQR GHOBASH.

Political Organizations

There are no political organizations in the UAE.

Diplomatic Representation

EMBASSIES IN THE UNITED ARAB EMIRATES

Afghanistan: POB 5687, Embassies Area, Airport Rd, Abu Dhabi; tel. (2) 4472666; e-mail abudhabi@mfa.af; internet fb.com/afghanistaninae; Chargé d'affaires AHMAD SAYER DAUDZAI.
Albania: POB 62069, Villa 75, al-Ma'ani St, al-Mushrif Area, Abu Dhabi; tel. (2) 6582505; fax (2) 6582705; e-mail embassy.uae@mfa.gov.al; internet www.ambasadat.gov.al/united-arab-emirates/en; Ambassador RIDI KURTEZI (designate).
Algeria: POB 3070, Embassies Area, Airport Rd, Abu Dhabi; tel. (2) 4448949; fax (2) 4447068; e-mail ambalg@embassy-algeria-uae.com; internet www.embassy-algeria-uae.com; Ambassador AMOR FRITAH.
Angola: POB 36532, Villa 176, Salama Bint Butti St, al-Mushrif Area, Abu Dhabi; tel. (2) 4477042; fax (2) 4477043; e-mail info@adangola.ae; internet angolaembassy.ae; Ambassador JÚLIO BELARMINO GOMES MAIATO.
Argentina: POB 3325, Villa 196, 11th St, al Karamah, Abu Dhabi; tel. (2) 4436838; fax (2) 4431392; e-mail eearb@mrecic.gov.ar; internet eearb.cancilleria.gob.ar; Ambassador JORGE AGUSTIN MOLINA ARAMBARRI.
Armenia: POB 6358, 24 al-Karamah St, Zone 2, Embassies District, Abu Dhabi; tel. (2) 4444196; fax (2) 4444197; e-mail armemiratesembassy@mfa.am; internet uae.mfa.am; Ambassador KAREN GRIGORYAN.
Australia: POB 32711, al-Muhairy Centre, 16th Floor, Sheikh Zayed I St, Abu Dhabi; tel. (2) 4017500; fax (2) 4017501; e-mail abudhabi.embassy@dfat.gov.au; internet www.uae.embassy.gov.au; Ambassador HEIDI VENAMORE.
Austria: POB 35539, Sky Tower, 5th Floor, Office 504, Reem Island, Abu Dhabi; tel. (2) 6944999; fax (2) 6944988; e-mail abu-dhabi-ob@bmeia.gv.at; internet www.bmeia.gv.at/oeb-abu-dhabi; Ambassador ETIENNE BERCHTOLD.
Azerbaijan: POB 45766, al-Bateen Area, Abu Dhabi; tel. (2) 6662848; fax (2) 6663150; e-mail azembuae@emirates.net.ae; internet abudhabi.mfa.gov.az; Ambassador ELCHIN BAGIROV.
Bahrain: POB 3367, Abu Dhabi; tel. (2) 6657500; fax (2) 6674141; e-mail abudhabi.mission@mofa.gov.bh; internet www.mofa.gov.bh/AbuDhabi/Home.aspx; Ambassador Sheikh KHALID BIN ABDULLAH BIN ALI AL KHALIFA.
Bangladesh: POB 2504, Villas 46 & 48, Sector 19, Zone W31, al-Jawwalah St, al-Saadah Area, Abu Dhabi; tel. (2) 4465100; fax (2) 4464733; e-mail mission.abudhabi@mofa.gov.bd; internet abudhabi.mofa.gov.bd; Ambassador MD. ABU ZAFAR.
Barbados: Abu Dhabi; e-mail abudhabi@foreign.gov.bb; Ambassador GABRIEL ABED.
Belarus: Villa 434, 26th St, al-Rowdha, Abu Dhabi; tel. (2) 4453399; fax (2) 4451131; e-mail uae@mfa.gov.by; internet uae.mfa.gov.by; Ambassador ANDREI LUCHENOK.
Belgium: POB 3686, Capital Plaza, Office Tower, 8th Floor, Corniche, Abu Dhabi; tel. (2) 4100200; e-mail abudhabi@diplobel.fed.be; internet unitedarabemirates.diplomatie.belgium.be; Ambassador ANTOINE DELCOURT.
Bosnia and Herzegovina: POB 43714, Villa 31, al-Walidain St, Abu Dhabi; tel. (2) 6313088; e-mail abudhabi@nje.go.tz; internet www.bhmc.ae; Ambassador BOJAN DOKIĆ.
Brazil: POB 3027, Abu Dhabi; tel. (2) 6320606; fax (2) 6327727; e-mail brasemb.abudhabi@itamaraty.gov.br; internet www.gov.br/

mre/pt-br/embaixada-abu-dhabi; Ambassador SIDNEY LEON ROMEIRO.

Brunei Darussalam: POB 5836, Villa 11, W-48, New Mushrif Area, Abu Dhabi; tel. (2) 4486999; fax (2) 4486333; e-mail abudhabi.uae@mfa.gov.bn; internet mfa.gov.bn/uae-abudhabi; Ambassador Haji HARUN BIN Haji JUNID.

Bulgaria: POB 73541, Villa 6, al-Nahyan Camp, Jafn St, Abu Dhabi; tel. (2) 6443381; e-mail embassy.abu.dhabi@mfa.bg; internet www.mfa.bg/embassies/uae; Ambassador IVAN JORDANOV.

Canada: POB 6970, Abu Dhabi Trade Towers, West Tower, 9th and 10th Floors, Abu Dhabi; tel. (2) 6940300; fax (2) 6940399; e-mail abdbi@international.gc.ca; internet www.canadainternational.gc.ca/uae-eau; Ambassador RADHA KRISHNA PANDAY.

Chad: POB 2859, Villa 27, Khallab St, Muroor Area, Abu Dhabi; tel. (2) 6442744; fax (2) 6442724; e-mail chad—embassy@ambatchad-eau.ae; internet fb.com/www.ambachadeau.td/; Ambassador KEDALLAH YOUNOUS HAMIDI ELHADJ MAMADI.

Chile: POB 129949, St 4, Sector 22, al-Mushrif, Abu Dhabi; tel. (2) 4472022; fax (2) 4472023; e-mail info@chile-uae.com; internet chile.gob.cl/emiratos-arabes-unidos; Ambassador PATRICIO DIAZ BROUGHTON.

China, People's Republic: POB 2741, Plot 26, W-22, Abu Dhabi; tel. (2) 4434276; fax (2) 4436835; e-mail chinaemb_ae@mfa.gov.cn; internet ae.chineseembassy.org; Ambassador ZHANG YIMING.

Colombia: POB 60376, Villa 1, Plot 5, al-Bateen Area, West 39, Abu Dhabi; tel. (2) 6505756; e-mail cabudhabi@cancilleria.gov.co; internet emiratosarabesunidos.embajada.gov.co; Ambassador LUIS MIGUEL MERLANO HOYO.

Comoros: S 17 10A, Bain al-Gesrain Area, Abu Dhabi; tel. (2) 5583765; fax (2) 5584298; e-mail ambcomad@eim.ae; Ambassador SAID NASSUR SAID TOIHIR.

Congo, Democratic Republic: Abu Dhabi; Ambassador MARIE NDJEKA OPOMBO.

Costa Rica: POB 92244, Villa 136, al-Dheed St, al-Maqta, Abu Dhabi; tel. (2) 5547458; e-mail embcr-ae@rree.go.cr; internet www.embcr-uae.org; Ambassador FRANCISCO JOSÉ CHACÓN HERNÁNDEZ.

Cuba: Villa 23, al-Azbaj St, al-Mushrif, Abu Dhabi; tel. (2) 4430327; e-mail embajador@embacubaemiratos.ae; internet misiones.minrex.gob.cu/en/united-arab-emirates; Ambassador NORBERTO ESCALONA CARRILLO.

Cyprus: POB 63013, Villa No. 32, Al Nahyan Camp, Nashash St, Abu Dhabi; tel. (2) 6654480; fax (2) 6657870; e-mail cyembadb@eim.ae; Ambassador MEROPI CHRISTOFI.

Czech Republic: POB 27009, Villa A09, Marina Village, Breakwater, Abu Dhabi; tel. (2) 6782800; fax (2) 6795716; e-mail commerce_abudhabi@mzv.cz; internet www.mzv.cz/abudhabi; Ambassador JOSEF KOUTSKY (designate).

Denmark: POB 105415, Abu Dhabi; tel. (2) 4410104; fax (2) 4410021; e-mail auhamb@um.dk; internet fae.um.dk; Ambassador ANDERS BJORN HANSEN.

Djibouti: Villa 29/2, 13 al-Najdah St, Abu Dhabi; tel. (2) 6330160; fax (2) 6330167; e-mail ambadjib@emirates.net.ae; Ambassador MOUSSA MOHAMED AHMED.

Dominica: POB 4438, Bldg 100, Plaza 30, al-Ladeem St, al-Nahyan Area, Abu Dhabi; tel. (2) 6442163; e-mail embassyuae@dominica.gov.dm; internet www.dominicaembassyuae.com; Ambassador PAUL AVONDALE.

Dominican Republic: Abu Dhabi; tel. (2) 6580788; fax (2) 6580747; e-mail uaedominicanembassy@gmail.com; Ambassador JULIO CASTAÑOS ZOUAIN.

Egypt: POB 4026, Sheikh Rashid bin Saeed al-Maktoum St (Old Airport Rd), Abu Dhabi; tel. (2) 8137000; fax (2) 4449878; e-mail egemb_abudhabi@mfa.gov.eg; internet fb.com/profile.php?id=100068796596741; Ambassador SHARIF MAHMOUD SAID.

Equatorial Guinea: 4th Floor, 404 al-Safa Bldg, al-Najda St, Abu Dhabi; Ambassador HASSANE SOUARE.

Eritrea: POB 2597, Villa 7, Zayed First St, Madinat Zayed Area, Abu Dhabi; tel. (2) 6331838; fax (2) 6346451; e-mail erimb75@emirates.net.ae; Ambassador OSMAN MUHAMMAD OMAR.

Estonia: Office Tower 3, Level 2, Etihad Towers, Abu Dhabi; tel. (2) 4083777; e-mail embassy.abudhabi@mfa.ee; internet abudhabi.mfa.ee; Ambassador JAAN REINHOLD.

Eswatini: POB 109337, Al Zaab Area, 13th St, Villa 3, between 28th and 30th St, Khalidiya, Abu Dhabi; tel. (2) 6669637; fax (2) 6669630; e-mail swazuae@eim.ae; Ambassador SIFISO MLANDVO DLAMINI.

Ethiopia: Villa 19, Ahl al-Ma'arifa St, Al Nahyan, Abu Dhabi; tel. (2) 6655111; fax (2) 6660096; e-mail abudhabi.embassy@mfa.gov.et; internet fb.com/ethiopianembassyabudhabi; Ambassador OUMER HUSSEIN OBA.

Fiji: Etihad Towers, 13th Floor, Corniche Rd, Abu Dhabi; tel. (2) 6813002; fax (2) 6813006; e-mail info@fijiemb.ae; internet www.fijiembassyuae.com; Ambassador NAIPOTE TAKO KATONITABUA.

Finland: POB 3634, al-Masood Tower, Hamdan St, Abu Dhabi; tel. (2) 8853666; fax (2) 6325063; e-mail sanomat.abo@formin.fi; internet www.finland.ae; Ambassador MARIANNE NISSILA.

France: POB 4014, Etihad Tower 3, 22nd Floor, Corniche W, Abu Dhabi; tel. (2) 7131000; fax (2) 4434158; e-mail contact@ambafrance.ae; internet ae.ambafrance.org; Ambassador NICOLAS NIEMTCHINOW.

The Gambia: POB 3675, 7 Salalah St, al-Nahyan St, Abu Dhabi; tel. (2) 6668585; e-mail info@embgambia.ae; internet embgambia.ae; Ambassador FAFA SANYANG.

Georgia: POB 107886, 20 al-Udhouq St, Nahayan Stadium Area, Abu Dhabi; tel. (2) 5533683; e-mail abudhabi.emb@mfa.gov.ge; internet uae.mfa.gov.ge; Ambassador PAATA KALANDADZE.

Germany: POB 2591, Abu Dhabi Mall, West Tower, 14th Floor, Abu Dhabi; tel. (2) 5967700; fax (2) 6446942; e-mail info@abu-dhabi.diplo.de; internet uae.diplo.de; Ambassador ALEXANDER SCHONFELDER.

Ghana: Villa 39, al-Nawal St, al-Rowdha, Abu Dhabi; tel. 24412159; e-mail abudhabi.mission@mfa.gov.gh; internet abudhabi.mfa.gov.gh; Chargé d'affaires a.i. AKWASI ADOMAKO.

Greece: POB 5483, Villa 1, 6–14 Ghbaynah St, al-Bateen, Abu Dhabi; tel. (2) 4492550; fax (2) 4492455; e-mail gremb.abd@mfa.gr; internet www.mfa.gr/abu; Ambassador ANTONIS ALEXANDRIDIS.

Guatemala: 61 al-Asrab St, Abu Dhabi; tel. (2) 5825357; e-mail embemiratosau@minex.gob.gt; Ambassador WILLY GOMEZ.

Holy See: Abu Dhabi; Apostolic Nuncio Most Rev. CHRISTOPHE ZAKHIA EL-KASSIS.

Hungary: POB 44450, Al Khazna Tower, Abu Dhabi; tel. (2) 6766190; fax (2) 6766215; e-mail mission.abu@mfa.gov.hu; internet abudhabi.mfa.gov.hu; Ambassador OSAMA IBRAHIM NAFFA.

India: POB 4090, Plot No. 10, Sector W-59/02, off Airport Rd, Diplomatic Area, Abu Dhabi; tel. (2) 4492700; fax (2) 4444685; e-mail amb.abudhabi@mea.gov.in; internet www.indembassyuae.gov.in; Ambassador SUNJAY SUDHIR.

Indonesia: POB 7256, Villa 474, Zone 2, Sector 79, Sultan bin Zayed St, al-Bateen Area, Abu Dhabi; tel. (2) 4454448; fax (2) 4455453; e-mail indoemb@emirates.net.ae; internet www.kemlu.go.id/abudhabi; Ambassador HUSIN BAGIS.

Iran: POB 4080, Diplomatic Area, next to Abu Dhabi International Exhibition Centre, Abu Dhabi; tel. (2) 4447618; fax (2) 4448714; e-mail publicdiplomacy.abu@mfa.gov.ir; internet unitedarabemirates.mfa.gov.ir; Ambassador REZA AMERI.

Iraq: POB 6389, Embassies Area, 41 West 59/2, Abu Dhabi; tel. (2) 4418022; fax (2) 4418155; e-mail adbemb@mofa.gov.iq; internet mofamission.gov.iq/en/Emirates; Ambassador MUDHAFAR MUSTAFA AL-JUBOURI.

Ireland: POB 61581, al-Yasat St, al-Bateen, Abu Dhabi; tel. (2) 4958200; fax (2) 6819233; e-mail irishvisaofficedubai@gmail.com; internet www.embassyofireland.ae; Ambassador ALISON MILTON.

Israel: Abu Dhabi; tel. (2) 2455811; e-mail info@abudhabi.mfa.gov.il; Ambassador AMIR HAYEK.

Italy: POB 46752, Villa 438–439, St 26, al-Manaseer Area, Abu Dhabi; tel. (2) 4435622; e-mail italianembassy.abudhabi@esteri.it; internet www.ambabudhabi.esteri.it; Ambassador LORENZO FANARA.

Japan: POB 2430, Mubarak bin Muhammed St, Abu Dhabi; tel. (2) 4435696; fax (2) 4434219; e-mail embjpn@ab.mofa.go.jp; internet www.uae.emb-japan.go.jp; Ambassador AKIO ISOMATA.

Jordan: POB 4024, Rashid bin Saeed al-Maktoum St, Diplomatic Area, Abu Dhabi; tel. (2) 5099000; fax (2) 4449157; e-mail abudhabi@fm.gov.jo; internet www.jordanembassy.ae; Ambassador NASSAR HABASHNEH.

Kazakhstan: 44 Rashid bin Saeed al-Maktoum St, al-Safarat District, Abu Dhabi; tel. (2) 4498778; fax (2) 4498775; e-mail abudhabi@mfa.kz; Ambassador MADIYAR MENILBEKOV.

Kenya: POB 3854, Dalma al-Kharama St, Abu Dhabi; tel. (2) 6666300; fax (2) 6652827; e-mail abu_dhabi@mfa.go.ke; Ambassador KARIUKI MUGWE.

Korea, Republic: POB 3270, 33 Airport Rd, Embassies District, Abu Dhabi; tel. (2) 6439122; fax (2) 6439130; e-mail uae@mofa.go.kr; internet are.mofa.go.kr; Ambassador YOO JEH-SEUNG.

Kosovo: Hamdan bin Mohammad St, al-Masood Tower, 9th Floor, Abu Dhabi; tel. (2) 5555112; e-mail embassy.uae@rks-gov.net; Ambassador XHABIR HAMITI.

Kuwait: POB 926, al-Maqtaa District, Rabdan, Abu Dhabi; tel. (2) 4477146; fax (2) 4477675; e-mail q8embassy@gmail.com; Ambassador JAMAL AL-GHUNAIM.

Kyrgyzstan: Villa 5, Bayn al-Jesrain, Qaryat al-Beri, Abu Dhabi; tel. (2) 5584955; e-mail kgembassy.uae@gmail.com; internet mfa.gov.kg/en/dm/abu-dabi-en; Ambassador ABDILATIF JUMABAEV.

Latvia: Villa 24, Sector W 36, Plot N–84A, al-Bateen, Abu Dhabi; tel. (2) 4473267; e-mail embassy.uae@mfa.gov.lv; internet www2.mfa.gov.lv/en/uae/embassy; Ambassador Dana Goldfinca.

Lebanon: POB 4023, Old Airport Rd, Abu Dhabi; tel. (2) 4492100; fax (2) 4493500; e-mail lebanon3@eim.ae; internet www.abudhabi.mfa.gov.lb; Ambassador Fouad Shahab Dandan.

Libya: POB 5739, al-Khaleej al-Arabi St, St 6, al-Bateen Area, Abu Dhabi; tel. (2) 4418222; fax (2) 4418233; e-mail libya_emb_ae@foreign.gov.ly; Ambassador Sofian Shibani.

Lithuania: POB 59431, Villa 173, Hameem St, al-Nahyan Camp, Abu Dhabi; tel. (2) 3090447; e-mail amb.ae@mfa.lt; Ambassador Ramunas Davidonis.

Luxembourg: POB 44909, Nation Towers, Apartment 6201, 62nd Floor, Corniche Rd, Abu Dhabi; tel. (2) 2079999; e-mail abudhabi.amb@mae.etat.lu; internet abudhabi.mae.lu; Ambassador Robert Michel Lauer.

Malaysia: POB 3887, Tamouh Tower, 12 Marina Sq., Reem Island, Abu Dhabi; tel. (2) 4482775; fax (2) 4482779; e-mail mwabudhabi@kln.gov.my; internet www.kln.gov.my/web/are_abu-dhabi; Ambassador Ahmad Fadil Bin Haji Shamsuddin.

Maldives: POB 114690, Villa 54, Jdeerah St, Abu Dhabi; tel. (2) 6740200; e-mail admin@maldivesembassy.ae; internet maldivesembassy.ae; Ambassador Aminath Shabeena.

Mali: POB 25828, Villa 59, Sector West 48, Plot 36, Mushrif, Abu Dhabi; tel. 503780061; e-mail ambamaliabudhabi@yahoo.com; internet www.fb.com/lemaliauxemirats; Ambassador Mamary Camara.

Malta: POB 30501, Villa 31, 10 St, al-Maqtaa Area, Abu Dhabi; tel. 24448646; e-mail maltaembassy.abudhabi@gov.mt; internet fb.com/MaltaintheUAE; Ambassador Maria Camilleri Calleja.

Mauritania: POB 2714, Villa 726, Shakhbout bin Sultan St, Abu Dhabi; tel. (2) 4462724; fax (2) 4462772; e-mail amba.rim.abudhabi@hotmail.com; Ambassador Mohamed Mohamed Rara.

Mexico: POB 108543, 16 al-Bidyah St, Bain al-Jessrain, Abu Dhabi; tel. (2) 25119900; fax (2) 5580077; e-mail informacioneau@sre.gob.mx; internet embamex.sre.gob.mx/emiratosarabesunidos; Ambassador Luis Alfonso de Alba Gongora.

Moldova: POB 31705, 20 al-Thikra St, al-Mushrif Area, Abu Dhabi; tel. (2) 4440505; fax (2) 4440506; e-mail abudhabi@mfa.gov.md; internet uae.mfa.gov.md; Chargé d'affaires a.i. Dana Paiu.

Mongolia: Abu Dhabi; Ambassador Odonbaatar Shijeekhuu.

Montenegro: POB 95083, Villa 1, Bldg 69, 29 Rabdan St, al-Mushrif, Abu Dhabi; tel. (2) 4418901; fax (2) 4418900; e-mail montenegro.embassy@yahoo.com; Chargé d'affaires Isidora Dabović.

Morocco: POB 4066, Ave 26 (al-Nahyan St), al-Manaseren Area, Abu Dhabi; tel. (2) 4443973; fax (2) 4433917; e-mail sifmabo@yahoo.com; Ambassador Mohamed Ait Ouali.

Mozambique: Khalifa Bin Shakbout St, al-Falah St, Khalidiyah, Abu Dhabi; tel. (2) 4477724; fax (2) 4477798; e-mail embamocuae@gmail.com; Ambassador Tiago Recibo Castigo.

Nepal: POB 38282, Villa 5, al-Aradah St, al-Nahyan Area, Abu Dhabi; tel. (2) 6344767; fax (2) 6344469; e-mail eonabudhabi@mofa.gov.np; internet ae.nepalembassy.gov.np; Ambassador Tej Bahadur Chhetri (designate).

Netherlands: POB 46560, Centro Capital Centre, Office Tower, Bldg 11, 14th Floor, al-Khaleej al-Arabi St, Abu Dhabi; tel. (2) 6958000; e-mail abu@minbuza.nl; internet www.netherlandsworldwide.nl/countries/united-arab-emirates; Ambassador Gerard Paul Marie-Hubert Steggs.

New Zealand: POB 62292, Level 25, Suite 2503, International Tower Capital Centre, Abu Dhabi; tel. (2) 4963333; fax (2) 4963300; e-mail nzembassy.abu.dhabi@mfat.govt.nz; Ambassador Richard G. Kay.

Niger: Villa 85, Alasrab St, al-Rawdah, al-Mushrif Area, Abu Dhabi; tel. (2) 3092882; fax (2) 3090520; e-mail ambanigeruae@gmail.com; Ambassador (vacant).

Nigeria: POB 110171, Villa 642/3, off Arab Gulf Rd, Third St, nr Singapore embassy, Abu Dhabi; tel. (2) 4431503; fax (2) 4431792; e-mail nigerabudhabi@yahoo.co.uk; Ambassador Muhammad Dansanta Rimi.

North Macedonia: POB 108225, Villa 10, Dyeenah St, Abu Dhabi; tel. (2) 6505130; fax (2) 6359744; e-mail abudabi@mfa.gov.mk; internet abudabi.mfa.gov.mk/mk; Ambassador Abdulkadar Memedi.

Norway: POB 47270, Etihad Tower 3, Level 11, W Corniche, Abu Dhabi; tel. (2) 4038400; e-mail emb.abudhabi@mfa.no; internet www.norway.no/united-arab-emirates; Ambassador Olav Myklebust.

Oman: 19 al-Saada St, al-Mushrif, Abu Dhabi; tel. (2) 4463333; fax (2) 4464633; e-mail abudhabi@fm.gov.om; Ambassador Dr Ahmed Bin Hilal al-Busaidi.

Pakistan: Plot 2, Sector W59, Diplomatic Area, Abu Dhabi; tel. (2) 4447800; fax (2) 4447172; e-mail parepabudhabi@pakistanembassyuae.org; internet www.pakistanembassyuae.org; Ambassador Faisal Tirmzi.

Panama: POB 4372, Villa E-05, Hill Abu Dhabi, Abu Dhabi; tel. (4) 3372538; fax (4) 3372539; e-mail embpanamaeau@mire.gob.pa; Ambassador Rebecca Sharona Pérez Cervantes.

Paraguay: Abu Dhabi; Ambassador Jose Aguero Avila.

Philippines: POB 3215, W-48, St No. 8, Sector 2–23, Plot 51, al-Qubaisat, Abu Dhabi; tel. (2) 6390006; fax (2) 6390002; e-mail auhpe@philembassy.ae; internet abudhabipe.dfa.gov.ph; Ambassador Alfonso F. A. Ver.

Poland: POB 2334, cnr Delma and Karama Sts (13th and 14th Sts), Abu Dhabi; tel. (2) 4465200; fax (2) 4462967; e-mail abuzabi.amb.rk@msz.gov.pl; internet abuzabi.msz.gov.pl; Ambassador Jakub Sławek.

Portugal: POB 114587, Villa A42, Marina Park Office, Abu Dhabi; tel. (2) 6505541; fax (2) 6505532; e-mail abudhabi@mne.pt; Ambassador Fernando d'Orey de Brito e Cunha Figueirinhas.

Qatar: POB 3503, W 59/2, Diplomatic Area, Sec 30, Abu Dhabi; tel. (2) 8855886; fax (2) 4493311; e-mail abudhabi@mofa.gov.qa; Ambassador Dr Sultan Salmeen Saeed al-Mansouri.

Romania: POB 70416, 9 al-Zakharia St, al-Rowdha, Abu Dhabi; tel. (2) 4459919; fax (2) 4461143; e-mail abudhabi@mae.ro; internet abudhabi.mae.ro; Ambassador Bogdan Octavian Badica.

Russian Federation: POB 8211, Khalifa St, East Plots 65/67, Abu Dhabi; tel. (2) 4635480; fax (2) 6788731; e-mail rusembuae@mail.ru; internet www.uae.mid.ru; Ambassador Timur Zabirov.

Rwanda: Abu Dhabi; tel. (56) 4153903; internet www.fb.com/rwandauae; Ambassador John Mirenge.

Saint Kitts and Nevis: Office 1–A, 1st Floor, Bldg No. 3, Plaza 30, Mireekh St, al-Nahyan, Abu Dhabi; tel. 524097066; e-mail info@uaeembassy@gov.kn; Ambassador Justin Hawley.

Saudi Arabia: POB 4057, Embassies Area, al-Karama St, Abu Dhabi; tel. (2) 4445700; fax (2) 4448491; e-mail aeemb@mofa.gov.sa; internet embassies.mofa.gov.sa/sites/uae; Ambassador Turki Bin Abdullah al-Dakheel.

Serbia: Villa 19, Sector 22, St 4, Mushraf West 47, Abu Dhabi; tel. (2) 4476444; fax (2) 4474411; e-mail embsruae@gmail.com; internet www.abudhabi.mfa.gov.rs; Chargé d'affaires a.i. Danica Savović.

Seychelles: POB 43107, Villa No. 6/1, Murror Area, 23rd St, Abu Dhabi; tel. (2) 4917755; fax (2) 4917714; e-mail seychellesembuae@gmail.com; Ambassador Gervais Moumou.

Sierra Leone: POB 41586, Villa 65, 6th St, al-Mushrif, Abu Dhabi; tel. (2) 4471222; fax (2) 4471250; e-mail embassy@slembassyuae.com; internet www.slembassyuae.com; Ambassador Rashid Sesay.

Singapore: 11 al-Nawal St, al-Manhal, Abu Dhabi; tel. (2) 2222083; fax (2) 6819666; e-mail singemb_auh@mfa.sg; internet www.mfa.gov.sg/abu-dhabi; Ambassador Kamal R. Vaswani.

Slovenia: 12-01 Office Tower, Capital Plaza, Khalifa St, Corniche, Abu Dhabi; tel. (2) 6727062; e-mail sloembassy.abudhabi@gov.si; internet www.abudabi.veleposlanistvo.si; Ambassador Natalia al-Mansour.

Somalia: POB 4155, Plot 31, al-Karama St, Abu Dhabi; tel. (2) 6669700; fax (2) 6651580; e-mail somaliem@emirates.net.ae; internet somaliembassyuae.com; Chargé d'affaires Ahmed Daahir Mohamed.

South Africa: POB 29446, Abu Dhabi; tel. (2) 4176400; e-mail abudhabi.dha@dirco.gov.za; internet www.dirco.gov.za/abudhabi; Ambassador Saa'd Cachalia.

South Sudan: Abu Dhabi; Ambassador Garang Garang Diing.

Spain: POB 46474, 96 al-Ladeem St, Al Nahyan Commercial Bldgs, Abu Dhabi; tel. (2) 4079000; fax (2) 6274978; e-mail emb.abudhabi@maec.es; internet exteriores.gob.es/embajadas/abudhabi; Ambassador Íñigo de Palacio España.

Sri Lanka: POB 46534, Villa 18A, Sector E 18/3, Salam St, Abu Dhabi; tel. (2) 6316444; fax (2) 6331661; e-mail slemb.abudhabi@mfa.gov.lk; internet www.embassyofsrilankauae.com; Ambassador Udaya Indrarathna.

Sudan: POB 4027, Rabdan St, Abu Dhabi; tel. (2) 4446699; fax (2) 4490530; e-mail sudembii@emirates.net.ae; Ambassador Abdelrahman Ahmed Khalid Sharfi.

Sweden: POB 31867, al-Otaiba Tower, 12th Floor, Zayed 1st St (Electra St), junction with 4th St, Abu Dhabi; tel. (2) 4178800; fax (2) 4178850; e-mail ambassaden.abu-dhabi@gov.se; internet swedenabroad.se/abu-dhabi; Ambassador Liselott Andersson.

Switzerland: POB 46116, al-Khaleej al-Arabi St, Centro Capital Center Bldg, 17th Floor, Office Bldg adjacent to Rotana Centro Hotel, Abu Dhabi; tel. (2) 6274636; fax (2) 6269627; e-mail adh.vertretung@eda.admin.ch; internet www.eda.admin.ch/uae; Ambassador Arthur Mattli.

THE UNITED ARAB EMIRATES

Syrian Arab Republic: POB 4011, Airport Rd, Diplomatic Area, Abu Dhabi; tel. (2) 4448768; fax (2) 4449387; e-mail info@syrianembassy.ae; internet www.syrianembassy.ae; Ambassador Dr GHASSAN ABBAS.

Tajikistan: POB 75213, Diplomatic Area, Abu Dhabi; tel. (2) 4417950; fax (2) 4417951; e-mail tajikemb.uae@gmail.com; internet tajikembassy.ae/uae; Ambassador SHARIFI BAHODUR MAHMUDZODA.

Tanzania: POB 43714, Villa 144, 14th Madinat Zayed St, Abu Dhabi; tel. (2) 6313088; e-mail abudhabi@nje.go.tz; internet www.ae.tzembassy.go.tz; Ambassador Lt-Gen. (retd) YACOUB MOHAMED.

Thailand: POB 47466, Villa 137, al-Ma'mourah Alley, al-Nahyan District, Abu Dhabi; tel. (2) 5576551; fax (2) 5576552; e-mail thaiauh@emirates.net.ae; internet www.thaiembassy.org/abudhabi; Ambassador SORAYUT CHASOMBAT.

Tonga: Office 3601, Etihad Towers, Corniche West St, Abu Dhabi; tel. (2) 5586664; Ambassador AKAU'OLA.

Tunisia: POB 4166, Villa A11, Ave Corniche, al-Khalidia, Abu Dhabi; tel. (2) 6811331; fax (2) 6812707; e-mail at.abou@diplomatie.gov.tn; Ambassador MOEZ BENAMIM.

Türkiye (Turkey): POB 3204, Villa 440, 26th St, Embassies Area, Abu Dhabi; tel. (2) 4109999; fax (2) 4109905; e-mail embassy.abudhabi@mfa.gov.tr; internet abudhabi.be.mfa.gov.tr; Ambassador TUGAY TUNÇER.

Turkmenistan: POB 43422, Embassies Area, Plot No. 87, al-Safarat St, next to Egyptian Embassy, Abu Dhabi; tel. (2) 4491088; fax (2) 4492961; e-mail tkmemb_abudhabi@sanly.tm; internet uae.tmembassy.gov.tm; Ambassador MURAT KELDY SIDMAMEDOV.

Tuvalu: Abu Dhabi; Ambassador AUNESE MAKOI SIMATI.

Uganda: Villa 17, West 17/02, al-Falah St 9, al-Bateen, Abu Dhabi; tel. (2) 6659931; fax (2) 6659934; e-mail info@ugandaembassyuae.com; internet abudhabi.mofa.go.ug; Ambassador ZAAKE WANUME KIBEDI.

Ukraine: POB 35572, Villa 13, Jdeerah St, Abu Dhabi; tel. (2) 6327586; fax (2) 6327506; e-mail embua@embukr.ae; internet uae.mfa.gov.ua; Ambassador DMYTRO SENIK.

United Kingdom: POB 248, al-Hisn St, al-Markaziyah W, Abu Dhabi; tel. (2) 6101100; fax (2) 6101586; internet www.gov.uk/world/united-arab-emirates; Ambassador EDWARD HOBART.

Uruguay: Villa 8–1/20, al-Mushref Area, Abu Dhabi; tel. (2) 6418860; fax (2) 6418864; e-mail uruemirates@mrree.gub.uy; Ambassador ALVARO CERIANI.

USA: POB 4009, Plot 38, Sector W59–02, St No. 4, Abu Dhabi; tel. (2) 4142200; e-mail webmasterabudhabi@state.gov; internet ae.usembassy.gov; Chargé d'affaires a.i. ERIC GAUDIOSI.

Uzbekistan: POB 111446, Villa 2, Plot No. 10, Zone East 38/1, Plot 10/B, Muroor, Abu Dhabi; tel. (2) 4422215; fax (2) 4488216; e-mail uzbekembassy@uzbekembassy.ae; internet www.uzembassy.ae; Ambassador ABDULAZIZ AKKULOV.

Venezuela: POB 60925, Villa 32, al-Kharama St, Abu Dhabi; tel. (2) 4452240; fax (2) 4436621; e-mail secretaria@embavenez-uae.org; internet www.embavenezabudhabi.ae; Chargé d'affaires ROBERT NORIEGA.

Viet Nam: Villa 147, Salama bint Butti St, Sector 20, al-Mushrif, Abu Dhabi; tel. (2) 4496710; fax (2) 4496730; e-mail vnemb1@emirates.net.ae; internet vnembassy-abudhabi.mofa.gov.vn; Ambassador NGUYEN MANH TUAN.

Yemen: POB 2095, al-Rashid Rd, Diplomatic Area, Abu Dhabi; tel. (4) 3970131; fax (4) 3972901; e-mail yemenemb@eim.ae; Ambassador FAHAD SAEED AL-MSHY;AL-MENHALI.

Zimbabwe: 651 Mubarak bin Mohammed St, al-Manhal, Abu Dhabi; tel. (2) 6222088; e-mail info@zimembassyuae.com; internet www.zimembassyuae.com; Ambassador LOVEMORE MAZEMO.

Judicial System

The 95th article of the Constitution of 1971 provided for the establishment of the Union Supreme Court and Union Primary Tribunals as the judicial organs of state.

The Union has exclusive legislative and executive jurisdiction over all matters that are concerned with the strengthening of the federation, such as foreign affairs, defence and Union armed forces, security, finance, communications, traffic control, education, currency, measures, standards and weights, matters relating to nationality and emigration, Union information, etc.

The late President Sheikh Zayed signed the law establishing the new federal courts on 9 June 1978. The new law effectively transferred local judicial authorities into the jurisdiction of the federal system.

Primary tribunals in Abu Dhabi, Sharjah, Ajman and Fujairah are now primary federal tribunals, and primary tribunals in other towns in those emirates have become circuits of the primary federal tribunals.

The primary federal tribunals may sit in any of the capitals of the four emirates and have jurisdiction on all administrative disputes between the Union and individuals, whether the Union is plaintiff or defendant. Civil disputes between Union and individuals will be heard by primary federal tribunals in the defendant's place of normal residence.

The law requires that all judges take a constitutional oath before the Minister of Justice and that the courts apply the rules of *Shari'a* (Islamic religious law) and that no judgment contradicts the *Shari'a*. All employees of the old judiciaries will be transferred to the federal authority without loss of salary or seniority.

Shari'a Court: Shari'a courts have exclusive jurisdiction to hear family disputes, including matters of divorce, inheritance and child custody.

Federal Supreme Court: Pres. and Chief Justice MOHAMMED BIN HAMAD AL-BADI.

Attorney-General: Dr HAMAD SAIF MOHAMMED BIN MUSALLAM AL-SHAMSI.

Religion

ISLAM

Most of the inhabitants are Sunni Muslims, while about 16% of Muslims are Shi'a.

CHRISTIANITY

Roman Catholic Church

Apostolic Vicariate of Southern Arabia: POB 54, Abu Dhabi; tel. (2) 4461895; fax (2) 4465177; e-mail info@avosa.org; internet www.avosa.org; f. 1889; fmrly Apostolic Vicariate of Arabia; renamed as above, following reorg. in 2011; responsible for most of the Arabian peninsula (incl. the UAE, Oman and Yemen), containing an estimated 998,500 Catholics (Jan. 2020); Vicar Apostolic Most Rev. PAOLO MARTINELLI (Titular Bishop of Musti in Numidia).

The Anglican Communion

Within the Episcopal Church in Jerusalem and the Middle East, the UAE forms part of the diocese of Cyprus and the Gulf. The Anglican congregations in the UAE are entirely expatriate. The Bishop in Cyprus and the Gulf resides in Cyprus, while the Archdeacon in the Gulf is resident in Qatar.

The Press

ABU DHABI

Abu Dhabi Magazine: POB 662, Abu Dhabi; tel. (2) 6214000; fax (2) 6348954; internet abudhabimag.com; f. 1969; Arabic, some articles in English; monthly; Editor ZUHAIR AL-QADI.

Abu Dhabi Official Gazette: POB 19, Abu Dhabi; tel. (2) 6688413; fax (2) 6669981; e-mail gazette@ecouncil.ae; f. 1965; Arabic; daily; official reports and papers.

Abu Dhabi Tempo: POB 33760, Abu Dhabi; tel. (2) 6673349; fax (2) 6673389; f. 2009; monthly; local community news; distributed free of charge; publ. by BrandMoxie; Editor SANA BAGERSH.

Al-Ain Times: POB 15229, Al-Ain; tel. (3) 7358854; fax (3) 7671997; e-mail alaintimes@gmail.com; internet www.alaintimesuae.com; f. 2006; English and Arabic; weekly; publ. by Alpha Beta Publrs and Media Consultants; Chief Editor FADWA M. B. AL-MUGHARIBI.

Akhbar al-Arab: POB 54040, Abu Dhabi; tel. (2) 4486000; f. 1999; daily; political.

Alrroya Aleqtisadiya (Economic Vision): POB 112494, Abu Dhabi; tel. (2) 6517777; fax (2) 6517772; internet www.alrroya.com; f. 2009; Arabic; business daily; publ. by Imedia LLC; Man. Editor REFAAT JAAFAR.

Al-Ittihad (Unity): POB 63, Al Ittihad Bldg, Mohammed Bin Khalifa St, Abu Dhabi; tel. (2) 4455555; internet www.alittihad.ae; f. 1969; Arabic; daily and weekly; publ. by Abu Dhabi Media Co; Editor-in-Chief HAMAD AL-KAABI.

Majid: POB 63, Abu Dhabi; tel. (2) 6121111; e-mail info@majid.ae; internet www.majid.ae; f. 1979; Arabic; weekly; children's magazine; publ. by Abu Dhabi Media Co; Man. Editor AHMAD OMAR.

The National: POB 769555, Abu Dhabi; tel. (2) 4145000; internet www.thenational.ae; f. 2008; English; daily; publ. by International Media Investments; Editor-in-Chief MINA AL-ORAIBI.

THE UNITED ARAB EMIRATES

Zahrat al-Khaleej (Splendour of the Gulf): POB 63, Abu Dhabi; tel. (2) 4144144; fax (2) 4144145; e-mail communications@admedia.ae; internet www.zahratalkhaleej.ae; f. 1979; Arabic; weekly; publ. by Abu Dhabi Media Co; Editor-in-Chief TALAL TOHME.

DUBAI

Al-Bayan (The Official Report): POB 2710, Dubai; tel. (4) 3444400; fax (4) 3447846; e-mail albayanonline@albayan.ae; internet www.albayan.ae; f. 1980; Arabic; daily; publ. by Awraq Publishing, a subsidiary of Arab Media Group; CEO SAMI AL-QAMZI; Editor-in-Chief MONA ABU SAMRA.

Emarat Al-Youm: POB 191919, Dubai; tel. (4) 3062240; e-mail 1971ey@gmail.com; internet www.emaratalyoum.com; Arabic; business daily; publ. by Awraq Publishing, a subsidiary of Arab Media Group; Editor SAMI AL-RIYAMI.

Emirates 24/7: POB 191919, Dubai; tel. (4) 3062222; fax (4) 3407698; e-mail news@emirates247.com; internet www.emirates247.com; f. 2005; English; online; Editor-in-Chief KHADEEJA AL-MARZOOQI.

Emirates Woman: POB 2331, Dubai; tel. (4) 4273000; fax (4) 4282274; e-mail motivate@motivate.ae; internet emirateswoman.com; f. 1981; English; monthly; fashion, health and beauty; publ. by Motivate Publishing; Editor AMY SESSIONS.

Gulf News: Sheikh Zayed Rd, POB 6519, Dubai; tel. (4) 4067666; fax (4) 3441627; e-mail feedback@gulfnews.com; internet www.gulfnews.com; f. 1978; English; daily; 2 weekly supplements, *Junior News* (Wed.), *Gulf Weekly* (Thur.); publ. by Al-Nisr Publishing; Editor-in-Chief ABDUL HAMID AHMAD.

Al-Jundi (The Soldier): POB 123888, Dubai; tel. (4) 3532222; fax (4) 3267070; e-mail info@aljundi.ae; internet www.aljundi.ae; f. 1973; Arabic; monthly; military and cultural; Editor-in-Chief Maj. MOHAMED ALI AL-KETBI.

Khaleej Times: POB 11243, Dubai; tel. (4) 3383535; fax (4) 3383345; e-mail editor@khaleejtimes.com; internet www.khaleejtimes.com; f. 1978; a Galadari enterprise; English; daily; distributed throughout the region and in India, Pakistan and the UK; free weekly supplement, *Weekend* (Fri.); Editor-in-Chief MUSTAFA AL-ZAROUNI.

Al-Manara: Office 129, Bldg 10, Dubai Media City; tel. (4) 3901777; fax (4) 3904554; Arabic; lifestyle; Editor-in-Chief WALID AL-SAADI.

Trade and Industry: POB 1457, Dubai; tel. (4) 2280000; fax (4) 2028888; e-mail customercare@dubaichamber.com; internet www.dubaichamber.com; f. 1975; Arabic and English; monthly; publ. by Dubai Chamber of Commerce and Industry.

UAE Digest: POB 500595, Dubai; tel. (4) 3672245; fax (4) 3678613; internet www.sterlingp.ae; English; monthly; publ. by Sterling Publications; current affairs; Man. Editor K. RAVEENDRAN.

What's On: POB 2331, Dubai; tel. (4) 4273000; fax (4) 2822274; e-mail whatson@motivate.ae; internet whatson.ae; f. 1979; English; monthly; publ. by Motivate Publishing; Group Editor and Man. Partner IAN FAIRSERVICE.

Xpress: POB 6519, Dubai; tel. (4) 3447100; fax (4) 3441627; e-mail editor@alnisrmedia.com; internet gulfnews.com/xpress; f. 2007; English; weekly; publ. by Al-Nisr Publishing; Editor NIRMALA JANSSEN.

RAS AL-KHAIMAH

Akhbar Ras al-Khaimah (Ras al-Khaimah News): POB 87, Ras al-Khaimah; Arabic; monthly; local news.

Al-Ghorfa: POB 87, Ras al-Khaimah; tel. (7) 2333511; fax (7) 2330233; f. 1970; Arabic and English; free monthly; publ. by Ras al-Khaimah Chamber of Commerce and Industry; Editor-in-Chief SAID BIN SALEH AL-KIYUMI.

Ras al-Khaimah Magazine: POB 200, Ras al-Khaimah; tel. (7) 2466666; fax (7) 2333355; e-mail ae.rak.mun@m; Arabic; monthly; commerce and trade; Chief Editor AHMAD ABDUL HADI AL-AHMAD.

SHARJAH

Al-Azman al-Arabia (Times of Arabia): POB 5823, Sharjah; tel. (6) 5356034.

The Gulf Today: POB 30, Sharjah; tel. (6) 5777999; fax (6) 5777737; internet gulftoday.ae; f. 1996; English; daily; Editor-in-Chief AYSHA ABDULLAH OMRAN TARYAM.

Al-Khaleej (The Gulf Today): POB 30, Sharjah; tel. (6) 5777888; fax (6) 5775057; e-mail akadv@alkhaleej.ae; internet www.alkhaleej.ae; f. 1970; Arabic; daily; political; independent; Exec. Editor RAED BERQAWI.

Al-Tijarah (Commerce): Sharjah Chamber of Commerce and Industry, POB 580, Sharjah; tel. (6) 5302222; fax (6) 5302226; e-mail altijarah@sharjah.gov.ae; internet www.altijarahmag.com; f. 1970; Arabic/English; monthly magazine; circ. 50,000; annual trade directory; Editor-in-Chief ABDULLAH BIN SULTAN MUHAMMAD AL-OWAIS.

NEWS AGENCY

Emirates News Agency (WAM): POB 3790, Abu Dhabi; tel. (2) 4044333; fax (2) 4454695; e-mail feedback@wam.ae; internet wam.ae; f. 1977; operated by the Govt; Exec. Dir MOHAMMED JALAL AL RAISI.

Publishers

All Prints: POB 857, Abu Dhabi; tel. (2) 6336999; fax (2) 6320844; e-mail allprints@allprints.ae; internet www.allprints.ae; f. 1968; publishing and distribution; Partners BUSHRA KHAYAT, TAHSEEN S. KHAYAT.

ITP: POB 769377, Dubai; tel. (2) 2450085; fax (4) 4443030; e-mail info@itp.com; internet www.itp.com; f. 1987; publishes more than 60 magazines, incl. *Ahlan!*, *Arabian Business*, *Time Out Dubai*, *Viva*; CEO ALI AKAWI.

Kalimat Publishing and Distribution: POB 21969, Sharjah; tel. (6) 5566696; fax (6) 5566691; e-mail info@kalimat.ae; internet kalimat.ae; f. 2007; children's books; CEO Sheikha BODOUR AL-QASIMI.

Motivate Publishing: POB 2331, Dubai; tel. (4) 4273000; fax (4) 4282274; e-mail motivate@motivate.ae; internet motivatepublishing.com; f. 1979; books and magazines; Man. Partner and Group Editor IAN FAIRSERVICE.

Sterling Publications: POB 500595, Dubai; tel. (4) 3672245; fax (4) 3678613; publs include *UAE Digest*, *Banking*, *Business Review* and *Ajman Today*; Man. Dir SANKARA NARAYANAN; Man. Editor K. RAVEENDRAN.

PUBLISHERS' ASSOCIATION

Emirates Publishers Association (EPA): 1st Floor, E Entrance, Sharjah Publishing City, Sharjah; tel. (6) 5069000; fax (6) 5535787; e-mail info@epa.org.ae; internet www.epa.org.ae; f. 2009; Pres. ALI OBAID BIN HATEM; Exec. Dir RASHID AL-KOUS.

Broadcasting and Communications

TELECOMMUNICATIONS

Emirates Integrated Telecommunications Co (du): POB 502666, al-Salam Tower, Dubai Media City, Dubai; tel. (155) 800155; fax (4) 3604440; e-mail talk-to-us@du.ae; internet www.du.ae; f. 2006; commenced operations under the brand name du in Feb. 2007; 50% owned by the federal Govt, 20% by Emirates Communications and Technology LLC, 10% by Mubadala Investment Co and 20% by public shareholders; provides fixed line and mobile telephone services, broadband and television throughout the UAE; Man. Dir AHMAD ABDULKARIM JULFAR; CEO FAHAD AL-HASSAWI.

Emirates Telecommunications Corpn (Etisalat): POB 3838, Abu Dhabi; tel. (2) 6283333; fax (2) 6317000; e-mail customercare@etisalat.ae; internet www.etisalat.com; f. 1976; provides telecommunications services throughout the UAE; Chair. JASSEM MOHAMED BU ATABA AL-ZAABI; CEO Eng. HATEM DOWIDAR.

Thuraya Telecommunications Co: POB 283333, Dubai; tel. (4) 4488888; fax (4) 4488999; e-mail customer.care@thuraya.com; internet www.thuraya.com; f. 1997; mobile satellite technology and services for maritime and land-based use; Chair. RASHED AL-GHAFRI; CEO SULAIMAN AL-ALI.

Regulatory Authority

Telecommunications and Digital Government Regulatory Authority (TDRA): POB 26662, Abu Dhabi; tel. (4) 7774444; fax (2) 7772229; e-mail info@tdra.gov.ae; internet www.tdra.gov.ae; f. 2004 as Telecommunications Regulatory Authority; present name adopted in 2020; Chair. TALAL HUMAID BELHOUL; Dir-Gen. MAJED SULTAN AL-MESMAR.

BROADCASTING

Radio

Abu Dhabi Radio: POB 63, Abu Dhabi; tel. (2) 4455555; e-mail commercial@admedia.ae; internet www.admedia.ae; f. 1969; broadcasts in Arabic over a wide area; also broadcasts in French, Bengali, Filipino and Urdu; affiliated channels include Emarat FM, Quran Kareem Radio, Sawt Al Musiqa; owned and operated by Abu Dhabi Media Co; Chair. ANAS BARGHOUTI; Gen. Man. ABDUL RAHIM AL-BATEEH AL-NUAIMI (acting).

Arabian Radio Network: POB 502012, Zone C, 2nd Floor, Dubai Properties HQ Bldg, Knowledge Village, Dubai; tel. (4) 4555888; e-mail info@arn.ae; internet arn.ae; f. 2001; owned by Arab Media Group; operates 9 stations; Gen. Man. MAHMOUD AL-RASHEED.

Capital Radio: POB 769312, Abu Dhabi; tel. (50) 8270333; e-mail info@cruae.ae; internet www.cruae.ae; f. 1979; govt-operated; English-language FM music and news station.

Channel 4 Radio Network: POB 442, Ajman; tel. (4) 5670444; e-mail info@channel4fm.com; internet www.channel4fm.com; f. 1997; operates 89.1 Radio 4, 104.8 Channel 4, 103.2 Coast, 101.3 Gold and 107.8 Radio Al Rabia stations; owned by Ajman Independent Studios LLC.

Umm al-Qaiwain Broadcasting Network: POB 444, Umm al-Qaiwain; tel. (6) 7666044; e-mail admin@ubn.ae; internet www.ubn.ae; f. 1978; broadcasts music and news in Arabic, Malayalam, Sinhala and Urdu; Gen. Man. ALI JASSEM AHMAD.

Television

Abu Dhabi TV: POB 63, Abu Dhabi; tel. (2) 4455555; e-mail sales@admedia.ae; internet www.adtv.ae; f. 1969; reorg. 2008; broadcasts entertainment and news programmes; affiliated channels include Emirates Channel, Abu Dhabi Sports; owned by Abu Dhabi Media Co; Exec. Dir HAITHAM AL-KATHIRI.

Ajman Television Network: POB 442, Ajman; tel. (6) 7038000; e-mail program@ajmantv.com; internet www.ajmantv.com; f. 1996; broadcasts in Arabic and English; Chair. ABDULLAH MUHAMMAD.

Dubai Media Inc: POB 835, Dubai; tel. (4) 3077000; fax (4) 3360060; e-mail mailus@dmi.ae; internet www.dmi.gov.ae; f. 2004; channels include Dubai Television, Dubai One, Sama Dubai, Dubai Sports; state-owned; Chair. Sheikh MAKTOUM BIN MOHAMMED BIN RASHID AL MAKTOUM.

Middle East Broadcasting Center (MBC): POB 76267, Dubai; tel. (4) 3919999; fax (4) 3919900; e-mail callcenter@mbc.net; internet www.mbc.net; f. 1991; broadcasts throughout region via satellite; channels include Al-Arabiya News Channel, MBC Persia (Farsi service), MBC 1, 2, 3 and 4 (entertainment); Chair. Sheikh WALID AL-IBRAHIM.

Sharjah Media Corpn: see Radio.

Regulatory Authority

Media Regulatory Office (MRO): Abu Dhabi; internet mcy.gov.ae; f. 2021; replaced National Media Council (f. 2006); under Ministry of Culture and Youth; Exec. Dir Dr RASHID KHALFAN AL NUAIMI.

Finance

BANKING

Central Bank

Central Bank of the United Arab Emirates: POB 854, Abu Dhabi; tel. (2) 6915555; fax (2) 5572111; e-mail contactus@cbuae.gov.ae; internet www.centralbank.ae; f. 1973; acts as issuing authority for local currency; superseded UAE Currency Bd in Dec. 1980; Chair. Sheikh MANSOUR BIN ZAYED AL NAHYAN; Gov. KHALED MOHAMED BALAMA.

Principal Banks

Abu Dhabi Commercial Bank (ADCB): POB 939, Abu Dhabi; tel. (2) 6962222; fax (2) 6109753; e-mail info@adcb.com; internet www.adcb.com; f. 1985 by merger; 60% govt-owned, 40% owned by private investors; merged with Union National Bank and acquired Al Hilal Bank in 2019; Chair. KHALDOON AL-MUBARAK; Group CEO ALA'A MUHAMMAD KHALIL ERAIQAT.

Abu Dhabi Islamic Bank: Sheikh Rashid Bin Saeed St, Abu Dhabi; tel. 600543216; e-mail customerservice@adib.ae; internet www.adib.ae; f. 1997; Chair. JAWAN AWAIDHA SUHAIL AL-KHAILI; Group CEO NASSER AL-AWADHI.

Ajman Bank PJSC: POB 7770, Block C, 13th Floor, al-Mina Rd, Ajman Free Zone, Ajman; tel. (6) 7018111; fax (6) 7479999; e-mail info@ajmanbank.ae; internet www.ajmanbank.ae; f. 2008; 25% owned by Govt of Ajman; *Shari'a*-compliant services; Chair. Sheikh AMMAR BIN HUMAID AL-NUAIMI; CEO MUHAMMAD AMIRI.

Bank of Sharjah: POB 1394, Sharjah; tel. (6) 5694411; fax (6) 5694422; e-mail enquire@bankofsharjah.com; internet www.bankofsharjah.com; f. 1973; Chair. Sheikh MOHAMMED BIN SAUD AL-QASIMI; Exec. Dir and Gen. Man. VAROUJAN NERGUIZIAN.

Commercial Bank of Dubai PSC: POB 2668, Mankhool St, Dubai; tel. (4) 2112848; e-mail cbd-ho@cbd.ae; internet www.cbd.ae; f. 1969; 20% owned by Govt of Dubai; Chair. HUMAID MOHAMMAD OBAID YOUSUF AL-QUTAMI; CEO Dr BERND VAN LINDER.

Commercial Bank International PSC: POB 4449, al-Riqah St, Deira, Dubai; tel. (4) 5039000; fax (4) 2279038; e-mail ccc@cbi.ae; internet www.cbiuae.com; f. 1991; Chair. SAIF ALI AL-SHEHHI; CEO ALI SULTAN RAKKAD AL-AMRI.

Dubai Bank PJSC: POB 65555, Sheikh Zayed Rd, Dubai; e-mail info@dubaibank.ae; tel. (4) 3328989; fax (4) 3290071; f. 2002 by Emaar Properties, a real estate developer; Chair. HESHAM ABDULLAH AL-QASSIM.

Dubai Islamic Bank PJSC: POB 1080, Airport Rd, Deira, Dubai; tel. (4) 6092222; e-mail contactus@dib.ae; internet www.dib.ae; f. 1975; acquired Noor Bank in 2020; Chair. Dr MUHAMMAD EBRAHIM AL-SHAIBANI; CEO ADNAN CHILWAN.

Emirates Investment Bank PJSC: POB 5503, Level 15, Festival Tower, Dubai Festival City, Dubai; tel. (4) 2317777; fax (4) 2317788; internet www.eibank.com; f. 1976 as Arab Emirate Investment Bank Ltd; name changed as above in 2010; Chair. OMAR ABDULLAH AL-FUTTAIM; CEO GAURAV SHAH.

Emirates Islamic Bank PJSC: POB 6564, Dubai; tel. (4) 599995; fax (4) 3582659; e-mail info@emiratesislamicbank.ae; internet www.emiratesislamic.ae; f. 1976 as Middle East Bank; became a Public Joint Stock Co (PJSC) in 1995; present name adopted 2004; subsidiary (99.8% owned) of Emirates Bank Int; Chair. HESHAM ABDULLA AL-QASSIM; CEO SALAH AMIN.

Emirates NBD PJSC: POB 2923, Baniyas Rd, Deira, Dubai; tel. (4) 2256256; fax (4) 2227662; e-mail ibrahims@emiratesbank.com; internet www.emiratesnbd.com; f. 2007 by merger of Emirates Bank Int. PJSC with Nat. Bank of Dubai PJSC; 56% owned by Govt of Dubai; Chair. Sheikh AHMAD BIN SAID AL MAKTOUM; CEO SHAYNE NELSON.

First Abu Dhabi Bank (FAB): POB 6316, Al Qurm, Business Park, Abu Dhabi; tel. (2) 6811511; e-mail atyourservice@bankfab.com; internet www.bankfab.com; f. 1979; Chair. Sheikh TAHNOON BIN ZAYED AL NAHYAN; Group CEO HANA AL-ROSTAMANI.

HSBC Bank Middle East Ltd: POB 66, Dubai; tel. 554722; e-mail customerexperienceuae@hsbc.com; internet www.hsbc.ae; Chair. SAMIR ASSAF.

Investbank PSC: POB 1885, Sharjah; tel. (6) 5980555; fax (6) 5693807; e-mail sharjah@investbank.ae; internet www.investbank.ae; f. 1975; Chair. Sheikh SULTAN BIN AHMED AL QASIMI; CEO AHMAD MOHAMED FAWZI ABU EIDEH.

Mashreqbank PSC: POB 1250, Omer bin al-Khattab St, Deira, Dubai; tel. (4) 4244444; e-mail media@mashreq.com; internet www.mashreqbank.com; f. 1967 as Bank of Oman; present name adopted 1993; Chair. and Pres. ABDUL AZIZ ABDULLA AL-GHURAIR; CEO AHMED ABDELAAL.

Al-Masraf: POB 46733, al-Masraf Tower, Hamdan St, Abu Dhabi; tel. (2) 0529999; e-mail info@almasraf.ae; internet www.almasraf.ae; f. 1976 as Arab Bank for Investment and Foreign Trade; renamed as above 2007; jtly owned by the UAE Federal Govt, the Libyan Arab Foreign Bank and the Banque Extérieure d'Algérie; Chair. FARHAT OMAR BEN GDARA; CEO CHARLES DOGHLASS (acting).

National Bank of Fujairah PSC: POB 2979, Dubai; tel. (600) 565551; fax (4) 3979100; e-mail nbfho@nbf.ae; internet www.nbf.ae; f. 1982; owned by Govt of Fujairah (40.13%), Investment Corpn of Dubai (9.78%), Easa Saleh al-Gurg LLC (21.66%), Fujairah Investment Co (45.22%) and UAE citizens (23.21%); Chair. Sheikh SALEH BIN MUHAMMAD AL-SHARQI; CEO VINCE COOK.

National Bank of Ras al-Khaimah PSC (RAKBANK): POB 5300, Rakbank Bldg, Oman St, al-Nakheel, Ras al-Khaimah; tel. (4) 2130000; fax (4) 3263640; e-mail contactus@rakbank.ae; internet rakbank.ae; f. 1976; 52.75% owned by Govt of Ras al-Khaimah; Chair. Sheikh MUHAMMAD OMRAN AL-SHAMSI; CEO RAHEEL AHMED.

National Bank of Umm al-Qaiwain PSC: POB 800, Umm al-Qaiwain Private Properties Dept Bldg, King Faisal St, Umm al-Qaiwain; tel. (6) 7066857; fax (6) 7655440; e-mail nbuq@nbq.ae; internet www.nbq.ae; f. 1982; Chair. Sheikh RASHID BIN SAUD AL-MU'ALLA; CEO ADNAN EDRIS MOHAMED SHARIF AL-AWADHI.

Sharjah Islamic Bank: Sharjah Islamic Bank Tower, Sharjah; tel. (6) 5999999; e-mail contact.center@sib.ae; internet www.sib.ae; f. 1976 as Nat. Bank of Sharjah; present name adopted 2005, reflecting the bank's conversion to *Shari'a*-compliant operations; commercial bank; Chair. ABDULRAHMAN MOHAMED AL-OWAIS; CEO MUHAMMAD AHMAD ABDULLAH.

United Arab Bank: POB 25022, Al Majaz 1, UAB Tower, Sharjah; tel. (6) 5075222; fax (6) 5733907; e-mail info@uab.ae; internet www.uab.ae; f. 1975; affiliated to Société Générale, France; 40% owned by Commercial Bank of Qatar; Chair. Sheikh FAISAL BIN SULTAN BIN SALEM AL-QASSIMI; CEO SHIRISH BHIDE.

Development Bank

Emirates Development Bank: Mubadala Tower, Abu Dhabi; tel. 80027274; internet www.edb.gov.ae; f. 2015; created through a

THE UNITED ARAB EMIRATES

merger of the Emirates Industrial Bank and the Real Estate Bank; Chair. Dr SULTAN BIN AHMED AL-JABER (Minister of Industry and Advanced Technology); CEO AHMED MOHAMED AL-NAQBI.

Bankers' Association

United Arab Emirates Banks Federation: POB 44307, Abu Dhabi; tel. (2) 4467706; fax (2) 4463718; e-mail info@uaebf.ae; internet www.uaebf.ae; f. 1983; Chair. ABDUL AZIZ ABDULLA AL-GHURAIR (Chair., Mashreqbank PSC); Dir-Gen. JAMAL SALEH.

SOVEREIGN WEALTH FUNDS

Abu Dhabi Investment Authority (ADIA): POB 3600, 211 Corniche, Abu Dhabi; tel. (2) 4150000; fax (2) 4151000; internet www.adia.ae; f. 1976; manages Govt of Abu Dhabi's investment portfolio; Chair. Sheikh TAHNOON BIN ZAYED AL NAHYAN; Man. Dir Sheikh HAMED BIN ZAYED AL NAHYAN.

Abu Dhabi Investment Co (Invest AD): POB 46309, Abu Dhabi; tel. (2) 6658100; fax (2) 6650575; e-mail clientservices@investad.com; internet www.investad.com; f. 1977; investment of govt funds, and advisory activities in the UAE and the Middle East; 98% owned by Abu Dhabi Investment Council and 2% by Nat. Bank of Abu Dhabi; Chair. MOHAMED ALI AL-DHAHERI; CEO MOHAMMAD BEHZAD SALEEMI.

Emirates Investment Authority: POB 3235, Abu Dhabi; tel. (2) 4190000; e-mail careers@eia.gov.ae; internet www.eia.gov.ae; f. 2007; federal sovereign wealth fund; Chair. Sheikh MANSOUR BIN ZAYED AL NAHYAN (Deputy Prime Minister and Minister of the Presidential Court); CEO MUBARAK RASHID AL-MANSOURI.

Investment Corpn of Dubai: POB 333888, Dubai International Financial Center, 6th Floor, DIFC Gate Village, Dubai; tel. (4) 7071333; fax (4) 7071444; e-mail info@icd.gov.ae; internet www.icd.gov.ae; f. 2006; manages Govt of Dubai's investment portfolio; Chair. Sheikh HAMDAN BIN MOHAMMED BIN RASHID AL MAKTOUM (Vice-Pres. of UAE and Ruler of Dubai); Exec. Dir and CEO MOHAMMED I. AL-SHAIBANI.

Mubadala Investment Co: Al Mamoura A Bldg, Abu Dhabi; tel. (2) 4130000; fax (2) 4130001; e-mail contact@mubadala.com; internet www.mubadala.com; f. 2017; established through merger of Mubadala Development Co and International Petroleum Investment Co; Chair. Sheikh MANSOUR BIN ZAYED AL NAHYAN; Man. Dir and Group CEO KHALDOON KHALIFA AL MUBARAK.

STOCK EXCHANGES

Abu Dhabi Securities Exchange (ADX): POB 54500, Abu Dhabi; tel. (2) 6277777; e-mail info@adx.ae; internet www.adx.ae; f. 2000 as Abu Dhabi Securities Market, renamed as above 2008; 49 listed cos (Feb. 2023); Chair. HISHAM KHALID MALAK; CEO ABDULLA SALEM AL-NUAIMI.

Dubai Financial Market (DFM): POB 9700, Sheikh Zayed Rd, Dubai; tel. (4) 3055555; fax (4) 3055191; e-mail customerservice@dfm.ae; internet www.dfm.ae; f. 2000; restructured to comply with Shari'a principles in 2006; 65 listed cos (2020); Chair. HELAL SAEED AL-MARRI; CEO HAMED AHMED ALI.

NASDAQ Dubai: POB 53536, The Exchange Bldg, Level 8, Gate Village, Dubai International Financial Centre, Dubai; tel. (4) 3055455; e-mail info@nasdaqdubai.com; internet www.nasdaqdubai.com; f. 2005 as Dubai Int. Financial Exchange; renamed as above 2008; Chair. ABDUL WAHED AL-FAHIM; CEO HAMED ALI.

Regulatory Authority

Securities and Commodities Authority: POB 33733, Abu Dhabi; tel. 800722823; fax (2) 6274600; e-mail contactus@sca.ae; internet www.sca.gov.ae; f. 2000; Chair. MOHAMED ALI AL-SHORAFA AL-HAMMADI; CEO MARYAM BUTI AL-SUWAIDI.

INSURANCE

Abu Dhabi National Insurance Co (ADNIC): POB 839, Abu Dhabi; tel. 8008040; e-mail info@adnic.ae; internet www.adnic.ae; f. 1972; subscribed 24% by the Govt of Abu Dhabi and 76% by UAE nationals; all classes of insurance; Chair. MUHAMMAD BIN SAIF AL NAHYAN; CEO AHMAD IDRISS.

Al-Ain Ahlia Insurance Co: POB 3077, Abu Dhabi; tel. and fax (2) 6119999; e-mail info@alaininsurance.com; internet www.alaininsurance.com; f. 1975; Chair. MUHAMMAD BIN J. R. AL-BADIE AL-DHAHIRI; Gen. Man. MUHAMMAD MAZHAR HAMADEH.

Dubai Insurance Co PSC: POB 3027, Dubai; tel. (4) 2693030; fax (4) 2693727; e-mail info@dubins.ae; internet www.dubins.ae; f. 1970; Chair. BUTI OBAID AL-MULLA; CEO ABDELLATIF ABUQURAH.

Al-Fujairah National Insurance Co PSC: Insurance Bldg, Ground Floor, Hamad bin Abdullah St, Fujairah; tel. (9) 2233355; e-mail fuj@fujinsco.ae; internet www.afnic.ae; f. 1976; 84.75% owned by Govt of Fujairah; Chair. ABDUL GHAFFOUR BAHROUZIAN; CEO ANTOINE MAALOULI.

Sharjah Insurance Co: Al Raha Tower, Corniche Al Mamzar, al-Khan, Sharjah; tel. (6) 5195666; e-mail sico@shjins.ae; internet www.shjins.com; f. 1970; Chair. AHMED MOHAMED HAMAD AL-MIDFA; Gen. Man. SOUHIL GAROUGE.

Union Insurance Co PSC: POB 119227, Single Business Tower, Sheikh Zayed Rd, Dubai; tel. (4) 3787777; fax (4) 3787778; e-mail unins@emirates.net.ae; internet www.unioninsurance.ae; national insurance co of Ajman emirate; Chair. Sheikh NASSER BIN RASHID BIN ABDULAZIZ AL-MOALLA; Man. Dir and CEO ABDUL MUTTALEB AL-JAEDI.

Trade and Industry

GOVERNMENT AGENCIES

Emirates Nuclear Energy Corpn (ENEC): Masdar City, Abu Dhabi; tel. (2) 3130555; e-mail info@enec.gov.ae; internet www.enec.gov.ae; f. 2009; focuses on the regulation and development of UAE's nuclear energy sector; Chair. KHALDOON KHALIFA AL-MUBARAK; CEO MOHAMED AL-HAMMADI.

Federal Authority for Nuclear Regulation (FANR): Landmark Tower, First Floor, al-Markaziyah W, Abu Dhabi Corniche, Abu Dhabi; tel. (2) 6516666; fax (2) 6516661; e-mail info@fanr.gov.ae; internet www.fanr.gov.ae; f. 2009; regulatory body for nuclear sector; Chair. ABDULLA NASSER AL-SUWAIDI; Dir-Gen. CHRISTER VIKTORSSON.

Ras al-Khaimah Economic Zone (RAKEZ): POB 10055, al Nakheel, Ras al-Khaimah; tel. (7) 2041111; fax (7) 2077120; e-mail info@rakez.com; internet www.rakez.com; Man. Dir Sheikh MOHAMMED BIN HUMAID AL-QASIMI; Group CEO RAMY JALLAD.

UAE Space Agency: POB 7133, Abu Dhabi; tel. (2) 2022222; fax (2) 2022000; e-mail info@space.gov.ae; internet www.space.gov.ae; f. 2014; Chair. ALI SARAH BINT YOUSEF AL-AMIRI (Minister of State for Advanced Technology); Dir-Gen. Dr SALEM BUTTI SALEM AL-QUBAISI.

DEVELOPMENT ORGANIZATIONS

Abu Dhabi Fund for Development (ADFD): POB 814, King Abdullah bin Abdulaziz Al Sa'ud St, al-Bateen Area, Abu Dhabi; tel. (2) 6677100; fax (2) 6677070; e-mail info@adfd.ae; internet www.adfd.ae; f. 1971; offers economic aid to other Arab states and developing countries in support of their devt; Chair. Sheikh MANSOUR BIN ZAYED AL NAHYAN (Deputy Prime Minister and Minister of the Presidential Court).

Department of Economic Development Abu Dhabi: al-Falah St, Abu Dhabi; tel. (2) 8158888; fax (2) 6727749; e-mail contact@abudhabi.ae; internet added.gov.ae; f. 1974; supervises Abu Dhabi's Economic Vision 2030 programme; Chair. MOHAMMED ALI AL-SHORAFA AL-HAMMADI; Under-Sec. RASHED ABDULKARIM AL-BALOOSHI.

General Holding Corpn (Senaat): POB 4499, Abu Dhabi; tel. (2) 6144444; fax (2) 6144445; e-mail info@senaat.co; internet www.senaat.co; f. 1979 as Gen. Industry Corpn; merged with its subsidiary Abu Dhabi Basic Industries Corporation PJSC (ADBIC, f. 2007) and rebranded as Senaat in 2012; Chair. and Man. Dir TAHNOON BIN ZAYED AL NAHYAN.

Mubadala Investment Co: Al Mamoura A Bldg, POB 45005, Abu Dhabi; tel. (2) 4130000; fax (2) 4130001; e-mail contact@mubadala.com; internet www.mubadala.com; f. 2017; est. through merger of International Petroleum Investment Co (f. 1984) and Mubadala Development Co (f. 2002); absorbed Abu Dhabi Investment Council (f. 2007) in 2018; manages govt investments abroad; wholly owned by Govt of the Emirate of Abu Dhabi; Chair. Sheikh MANSOUR BIN ZAYED AL NAHYAN; CEO and Man. Dir KHALDOON KHALIFA AL-MUBARAK.

Supreme Council for Financial and Economic Affairs: Abu Dhabi; f. 2020; Chair. Sheikh MOHAMMED BIN ZAYED AL NAHYAN (Pres. of the UAE and Ruler of Abu Dhabi).

CHAMBERS OF COMMERCE

Federation of UAE Chambers of Commerce and Industry: POB 3014, Abu Dhabi; tel. (2) 6214144; fax (2) 6339210; POB 8886, Dubai; tel. (4) 2387774; fax (4) 2208842; e-mail info@fcciuae.ae; internet www.fcciuae.ae; f. 1976; seven mem. chambers; Chair. ABDULLA MOHAMED AL-MAZROUI; Sec.-Gen. HUMAID MOHAMMED BIN SALEM.

Abu Dhabi Chamber of Commerce and Industry: POB 662, Abu Dhabi; tel. (2) 6214000; fax (2) 6215867; e-mail contact.us@adcci.gov.ae; internet www.abudhabichamber.ae; f. 1969; 45,000 mems; Chair. ABDULLA MOHAMED AL-MAZROUI; Dir-Gen. MUHAMMAD HELAL AL-MUHAIRI.

Ajman Chamber of Commerce and Industry: POB 662, Ajman; tel. 80070; e-mail info@ajmanchamber.ae; internet www

.ajmanchamber.ae; f. 1977; Chair. ABDULLAH MUHAMMAD AL-MUWAJA; Dir-Gen. SALEM AL-SUWAIDI.

Dubai Chambers: POB 1457, Dubai; tel. (4) 2280000; fax (4) 2028888; e-mail customercare@dubaichamber.com; internet www.dubaichamber.com; f. 1965 as Dubai Chamber of Commerce and Industry; reorganized as Dubai Chambers in 2022; Chair. ABDUL AZIZ AL-GHURAIR; Pres. and CEO HASSAN AL-HASHEMI (acting).

Fujairah Chamber of Commerce and Industry: POB 738, Fujairah; tel. (9) 2230000; fax (9) 2221464; e-mail chamber@fujcci.ae; internet www.fujcci.ae; Chair. Sheikh SAEED SOROUR SAIF AL-SHARQI; Dir-Gen. SULTAN JAMEA AL-HANDASI.

Ras al-Khaimah Chamber of Commerce and Industry: al-Jaz'ah St, Ras al-Khaimah; tel. (7) 2260000; fax (7) 2260112; e-mail info@rakchamber.ae; internet www.rakchamber.ae; f. 1967; Chair. MOHAMED ALI MUSABBEH AL-NUAIMI; Dir-Gen. MOHAMED HASSAN AL-SABAB.

Sharjah Chamber of Commerce and Industry: POB 580, Sharjah; tel. (6) 5302222; fax (6) 5302226; e-mail scci@sharjah.gov.ae; internet www.sharjah.gov.ae; f. 1970; 33,500 mems; Chair. ABDALLAH SULTAN AL-OWAIS; Dir-Gen. MOHAMED AHMED AMIN.

Umm al-Qaiwain Chamber of Commerce and Industry: POB 436, Umm al-Qaiwain; tel. (6) 7651111; fax (6) 7657055; e-mail info@uaqchamber.ae; internet www.uaqchamber.ae; Chair. and CEO KHALFAN AHMED MESFER.

STATE HYDROCARBONS COMPANIES
Abu Dhabi

Abu Dhabi National Oil Co (ADNOC): POB 898, Abu Dhabi; tel. (2) 7070000; fax (2) 6023389; internet www.adnoc.ae; f. 1971; state co; deals in all phases of oil industry; owns two refineries: one on Umm al-Nar island and one at Ruwais; Habshan Gas Treatment Plant (scheduled for partial privatization); gas pipeline distribution network; a salt and chlorine plant; holds 60% participation in operations of ADMA-OPCO and ADCO, and 88% of ZADCO; has 100% control of Abu Dhabi Nat. Oil Co for Oil Distribution (ADNOC-FOD), Abu Dhabi Nat. Tanker Co (ADNATCO), Nat. Drilling Co (NDC) and interests in numerous other cos, both in the UAE and overseas; ADNOC is operated by Supreme Petroleum Council; Chair. Sheikh MOHAMMED BIN ZAYED AL NAHYAN (Pres. of the UAE and Ruler of Abu Dhabi); Man. Dir and CEO Dr SULTAN BIN AHMED AL-JABER (Minister of Industry and Advanced Technology).

Subsidiaries include:

ADNOC Distribution: POB 4188, Abu Dhabi; tel. (2) 6771300; fax (2) 6722322; internet adnocdistribution.ae; f. 1973; 100% owned by ADNOC; distributes petroleum products in the UAE and worldwide; CEO BADER SAEED AL-LAMKI.

ADNOC Drilling: POB 4017, SKEC 2, Zone 1, E-17, Abu Dhabi; tel. (2) 6776100; fax (2) 6779937; internet adnocdrilling.ae; f. 1972; drilling operations; Chair. Dr SULTAN AHMED AL-JABER; CEO ABDULRAHMAN ABDULLA AL-SEIARI.

ADNOC Gas Processing: POB 665, Sheikh Khalifa Energy Complex, Khalifa St, Abu Dhabi; tel. (2) 6030000; fax (2) 6037414; internet adnoc.ae/adnoc-gas-processing; f. 1978; started production in 1981; recovers condensate and LPG from Asab, Bab and Bu Hasa fields for delivery to Ruwais natural gas liquids fractionation plant; capacity of 22,000 metric tons per day; 68% owned by ADNOC; Total and Shell own 15% each, and Partex has a minority interest of 2%; CEO Dr AHMED MOHAMED AL-ABRI.

ADNOC LNG: POB 3500, Fatima bint Mubarak St, Abu Dhabi; tel. (2) 6061111; fax (2) 6065500; internet www.adnoc.ae/en/adnoc-lng; f. 1973; 70% owned by ADNOC, 15% by Mitsui and Co, 10% by BP, 5% by Total; operates LGSC and the LNG plant on Das Island, which uses natural gas produced in association with oil from offshore fields and has a design capacity of approx. 2.3m. metric tons of LNG per year and 1.29m. tons of LPG per year; the liquefied gas is sold to the Tokyo Electric Power Co, Japan; CEO FATIMA AL-NUAIMI.

ADNOC Offshore: POB 303, World Trade Center, Hamdan bin Mohammed St, Abu Dhabi; tel. (2) 6040000; fax (2) 6669785; internet www.adnoc.ae/adnoc-offshore; formed through the merger of ADNOC's upstream oil and gas cos: Abu Dhabi Marine Operating Co (ADMA-OPCO) and Zakum Devt Co (ZADCO); 60% owned by ADNOC; CEO AHMED AL-SUWAIDI.

ADNOC Onshore: POB 270, Corniche Rd West, Abu Dhabi; tel. (2) 6040000; fax (2) 6669785; internet adnoc.ae/adnoc-onshore; f. 1978; shareholders are ADNOC (60%), BP and Total (each 10%), CNPC (8%), JODCO (5%), CEFC (4%), and GS Energy (3%); oil exploration, production and export operations from onshore oilfields; average production (2017): 1.6m. b/d; CEO OMAR OBAID AL-NASRI.

ADNOC Refining: Al Mu'aziz St, Sas al-Nakhl, Abu Dhabi; tel. (2) 6027000; fax (2) 6027001; internet adnoc.ae/adnoc-refining; f. 1999; refining of crude petroleum; production of chlorine and related chemicals; CEO ABDULLA ATEYA AL-MESSABI.

National Petroleum Construction Co (NPCC): POB 2058, Abu Dhabi; tel. (2) 5549000; fax (2) 5549111; e-mail marketing@npcc.ae; internet www.npcc.ae; f. 1973; 'turnkey' construction and maintenance of offshore facilities for the petroleum and gas industries; Chair. Dr MOHAMED RASHED AL-HAMELI; CEO AHMED AL-DHAHERI.

Ajman

National Ajman Petroleum Co (NAPCO): Ajman Port, Ajman; tel. (6) 7445344; fax (6) 7441434; e-mail info@napco.ae; internet www.napco.ae; Chair. Sheikh AHMED BIN HUMAID AL-NOAIMI; Man. Dir KAMAL MISHRA.

Dubai

Dubai Petroleum Establishment: Sheikh Zayed Rd, al-Safa St, Dubai; tel. (4) 3432222; fax (4) 3012200; internet www.dubaipetroleum.ae; f. 1963 as Dubai Petroleum Co; reorg. and renamed as above 2007; wholly owned by Dubai authorities; responsible for managing Dubai's offshore petroleum assets; Chair. Sheikh AHMED BIN SAEED AL-MAKTOUM.

DUGAS (Dubai Natural Gas Co Ltd): POB 4311, Dubai (Location: Jebel Ali); tel. (4) 8812121; fax (4) 8812221; internet dugas.ae; wholly owned by Dubai authorities; Dep. Chair. and Dir SULTAN AHMAD BIN SULAYEM.

Emarat: POB 9400, Dubai; tel. (4) 3434444; fax (4) 3433393; e-mail info@emarat.ae; internet www.emarat.ae; f. 1981 as Emirates General Petroleum Corpn, renamed as above 1996; wholly owned by Ministry of Finance; marketing and distribution of petroleum; Chair. SUHAIL BIN MOHAMMED FARAJ FARIS AL-MAZROUEI (Minister of Energy and Infrastructure); Gen. Man. Eng. ALI KHALIFA AL-SHAMSI.

Emirates National Oil Co (ENOC): POB 6442, ENOC Complex, Sheikh Rashid Rd, Dubai; tel. (4) 3374400; e-mail info@enoc.com; internet www.enoc.com; f. 1993; responsible for management of Dubai-owned cos in petroleum-marketing sector; Chair. Sheikh SAEED MOHAMMED AHMAD AL-TAYER; Chief Exec. SAIF HUMAID AL-FALASI.

Emirates Petroleum Products Co Pvt. Ltd (EPPCO): POB 5589, Dubai; tel. (4) 372131; fax (4) 3031605; internet www.eppcouae.com; f. 1980; jt venture between Govt of Dubai and Caltex Alkhaleej Marketing; sales of petroleum products, bunkering fuel and bitumen; Chair. Sheikh HAMDAN BIN RASHID AL MAKTOUM.

Ras al-Khaimah

RAKGAS LLC: POB 434, Ras al-Khaimah; tel. (7) 2277555; fax (7) 2287333; e-mail info@rakgas.ae; internet rakgas.ae; f. 1984 as Ras al-Khaimah Gas Commission; present name adopted 2007; owned by Ras al-Khaimah Govt; principal activities include gas exploration and production; operates processing facilities at Khor Khwair; holds interests in exploration blocks offshore in Ras al-Khaimah and in Africa; Chair. Sheikh SAUD BIN SAQR AL-QASIMI (Ruler of Ras al-Khaimah); CEO CHRIS WOOD.

Sharjah

Sharjah Liquefied Petroleum Gas Co (SHALCO): POB 787, Sharjah; tel. (6) 5286333; fax (6) 5286111; e-mail shalco@shalco.ae; f. 1984; 100% owned by Sharjah authorities; gas processing; producer of liquefied commercial propane and commercial butane; Dir-Gen. SALEH AL-ALI.

Sharjah National Oil Corpn (SNOC): POB 787, al-Layyah, Sharjah; tel. (6) 5199700; fax (6) 5199777; e-mail info@snoc.ae; tel. www.snoc.ae; f. 1999; Pres. Sheikh SULTAN BIN AHMED AL-QASIMI (Deputy Ruler of Sharjah); CEO HATEM AL-MOSA.

Umm al-Qaiwain

Petroleum and Mineral Affairs Department: POB 9, Umm al-Qaiwain; tel. (6) 7666034; Chair. Sheikh SULTAN BIN AHMAD AL-MU'ALLA.

UTILITIES
Abu Dhabi

Dept of Energy (DoE): al-Maqam Tower, Bldg 99, 32nd Floor, 33 St, Hamouda bin Ali al-Dhaheri, Abu Dhabi; tel. (2) 2070777; e-mail info@doe.gov.ae; internet www.doe.gov.ae; f. 2018 to manage the energy sector of Abu Dhabi; Chair. Eng. AWAIDHA MURSHED AL-MARAR.

Abu Dhabi Distribution Co: POB 219, Abu Dhabi; tel. (2) 4166000; fax (2) 4160444; e-mail contactcentre@addc.ae; internet www.addc.ae; f. 1998; distribution of water and electricity; Chair. MUBARAK OBAID AL-DHAHERI.

Abu Dhabi National Energy Co (TAQA): POB 55224, Abu Dhabi; tel. (2) 6914900; fax (2) 6914666; e-mail info@taqa.com; internet www.taqa.com; f. 2005; 74.1% owned by Abu Dhabi

THE UNITED ARAB EMIRATES

Government; owns assets in power, water, petroleum and mineral sectors in the UAE and abroad; provides more than 85% of the water and electricity produced in Abu Dhabi; Chair. MOHAMMED HASSAN AL-SUWAIDI; CEO JASIM HUSAIN THABET.

Abu Dhabi Transmission and Despatch Co: POB 173, Abu Dhabi; tel. (2) 4164000; e-mail info@transco.ae; internet www.transco.ae; f. 1999; operation and devt of the transmission network for water and electricity; Man. Dir AFIF SAIF AL-YAFEI.

Al-Ain Distribution Co: 25 Bunat al-Watan St, Al-Ain; tel. (3) 7636000; fax (3) 8117000; internet www.aadc.ae; f. 1999; distribution of water and electricity; Chair. Eng. MUHAMMAD SALEM AL-DAHERI.

Bayounah Power Co: POB 33477, Abu Dhabi; tel. (2) 6333757; fax (2) 6730403; e-mail info@bpc.ae; internet www.bpc.ae; f. 1999; operates two power stations at Abu Dhabi (also water desalination) and Al-Ain; Chair. AHMAD HILAL AL-KUWAITI; Man. Dir ABDULLAH AL-MERAIKHI.

Emirates Water and Electricity Co PJSC (EWEC): POB 51111, Abu Dhabi; e-mail info@ewec.ae; internet ewec.ae; f. 2018; replaced Abu Dhabi Water and Electricity Co (ADWEC); responsible for forecasting and managing the supply and demand of electricity and water; Chair. MOHAMMED HASSAN AL-SUWAIDI; CEO OTHMAN JUMA HAMAID AL-ALI.

Al-Mirfa Power Co: POB 18626, Abu Dhabi; tel. (3) 7080700; fax (3) 7632026; e-mail info@ampc.ae; internet www.ampc.ae; f. 1999 to control Mirfa and Madinat Zayed plants; capacity 300 MW electricity per day, 37m. gallons water per day; Gen. Man. AREF AL-ALI.

As part of the privatization programme, several independent power and water projects (IWPPs) have been established, including Arabian Power Co, Emirates CMS Power Co, Gulf Total Tractebel Power Co, Shuweihat CMS International Power Co, and Taweelah Asia Power Co (TAPCO). In each IWPP, ADWEA retains a 60% shareholding while the remaining 40% is owned by private investors.

Dubai

Dubai Electricity and Water Authority (DEWA): POB 564, Dubai; tel. (4) 6019999; e-mail customercare@dewa.gov.ae; internet www.dewa.gov.ae; f. 1992 following merger of Dubai Electricity Co and Dubai Water Dept; management and devt of the water and electricity sectors; Chair. MATAR HUMAID AL-TAYER; CEO and Man. Dir SAID MUHAMMAD AHMAD AL-TAYER.

Northern Emirates (Ajman, Fujairah, Ras al-Khaimah and Umm al-Qaiwain)

Etihad Water and Electricity: POB 1672, Dubai; tel. 8003392; fax (4) 2576070; e-mail cs@fewa.gov.ae; internet etihadwe.ae; f. 2020 to replace the Federal Electricity and Water Authority; generation and distribution of electricity and water in the northern emirates; operates six power-generating plants and three water desalination plants; scheduled for part-privatization; Chair. SUHAIL BIN MOHAMMED FARAJ FARIS AL-MAZROUEI (Minister of Energy and Infrastructure); Dir-Gen. MUHAMMAD MUHAMMAD SALEH.

Sharjah

Dana Gas: POB 2011, Sharjah; tel. (6) 5194444; fax (6) 5566522; e-mail mail@danagas.com; internet www.danagas.com; f. 2005; Chair. HAMID JAFAR; CEO PATRICK ALLMAN-WARD.

Sharjah Electricity and Water Authority (SEWA): Sharjah; tel. 600566665; e-mail contactus@sewa.gov.ae; internet www.sewa.gov.ae; Chair. SAEED SULTAN AL-SUWAIDI.

MAJOR COMPANIES

Abu Dhabi

Abu Dhabi Media Co (ADMC): POB 63, Abu Dhabi; tel. (2) 4455555; e-mail commercial@admedia.ae; internet www.admedia.ae; f. 2007; fmrly Emirates Media, Inc; owns Abu Dhabi Television, 6 radio stations (Abu Dhabi FM, Abu Dhabi Classic FM, Emarat FM, Quran Kareem FM, Star FM and Kadak FM) and 2 newspapers (*Al-Ittihad* and *Majid*); CEO ABDUL RAHEEM AL-BATEEH AL-NUAIMI (acting).

Abu Dhabi National Chemicals Co (Chemaweyaat): POB 43237, IPIC Sq., Muroor Rd, Abu Dhabi; tel. (2) 4110000; fax (2) 6359259; e-mail khalifaalsuwaidi@chemaweyaat.com; internet www.chemaweyaat.com; f. 2008; jt venture between Abu Dhabi Investment Council (40%), Int. Petroleum Investment Co (40%), Abu Dhabi Nat. Oil Co (ADNOC) (20%); jt venture agreement with Indorama Ventures in 2013 for the devt of major petrochemicals complex at Chemaweyaat Industrial City, Taweelah; CEO KHALIFA S. AL-SUWAIDI (acting).

Abu Dhabi Polymers (Borouge): POB 6925, Borouge Tower, Shaikh Khalifa Energy Complex, Corniche Rd, Abu Dhabi; tel. (2) 7080000; fax (2) 7080999; e-mail info@borouge.com; internet www.borouge.com; f. 1998; initial public offering (IPO) listed in 2022; production and marketing of polyethylene and polypropylene products; CEO HAZEEM SULTAN AL-SUWAIDI; over 3,000 employees (2022).

Admak General Contracting Co: POB 650, Abu Dhabi; tel. (2) 6264626; fax (2) 6264636; e-mail admak@emirates.net.ae; f. 1968 as M. A. Kharafi; present name adopted 1981; general civil engineering and road contractors; part of the M. A. Kharafi Group of Kuwait; Man. Dir MOHSEN KAMEL MOSTAFA; Exec. Dir SAID A. FOTOUH; 2,600 employees.

ALDAR Properties PJSC: POB 51133, Abu Dhabi; tel. 80025327; e-mail customermanagement@aldar.com; internet www.aldar.com; f. 2005; real estate development, management and investment; Chair. MUHAMMAD KHALIFA AL-MUBARAK; CEO TALAL AL-DHIYEBI.

Emirates Global Aluminium (EGA): POB 11023, Abu Dhabi; tel. (2) 5094444; e-mail info@emal.ae; internet www.ega.ae; f. 2007; jt-owned by Mubadala Investment Co of Abu Dhabi and Investment Corpn of Dubai; consists of Dubai Aluminium (DUBAL) and Emirates Aluminium (EMAL); Chair. KHALDOON KHALIFA AL-MUBARAK; Man. Dir ABDULLA JASSEM KALBAN; CEO ABDULNASSER BIN KALBAN.

Emirates Steel Arkan: POB 9022, Abu Dhabi Industrial City; tel. (2) 5511187; e-mail contactus@emiratessteel.com; internet www.emiratessteelarkan.com; f. 2001 as Emirates Iron and Steel Factory; present name adopted in 2021 after merger with Arkan Group; 87.5% owned by ADQ; production capacity 3.5m. metric tons per year; Chair. HAMAD ABDULLA MOHAMED AL-SHORAFA AL-HAMMADI; CEO Eng. SAEED GHUMRAN AL-REMEITHI.

Hafilat Industries LLC: POB 91207, Abu Dhabi; tel. (2) 5507472; fax (2) 5502155; e-mail info@hafilat.ae; internet www.hafilat.ae; jt venture between Specialised Investment Group, Emirates Link Group and Volgren (Australia); bus and coach manufacturing; Chair. KHALAF SAGHIR AL-QUBAISI; CEO IYAD AL-ANSARI.

Mechanical and Civil Engineering Contractors (MACE) Ltd: POB 2307, Khalidiya St, Abu Dhabi; tel. (2) 6666462; fax (2) 6662616; e-mail mace@emirates.net.ae; internet www.macecontractors.com; f. 1968; Chair. and Man. Dir WILLIAM A. T. HADDAD.

National Central Cooling Co PJSC (Tabreed): POB 29478, Abu Dhabi; tel. 8227333; fax (2) 6455008; e-mail info@tabreed.ae; internet www.tabreed.com; f. 1998; manufacture of air conditioning and district cooling systems; Chair. KHALID ABDULLAH AL-QUBAISI; CEO KHALID AL-MARZOOQI.

Pilco (Pipeline Construction Co): POB 2021, Plot 104, Mussafah Industrial Area M17, Abu Dhabi; tel. (2) 5550902; e-mail pilcoad@pilcoad.ae; internet www.pilcoad.com; f. 1968; fabrication of steel, piping, tanks, pressure vessels and machine components; general services to the oil industry.

Dubai

Al-Ahmadiah Contracting and Trading: POB 2596, Dubai; tel. (4) 3981999; fax (4) 3983327; e-mail admin@alahmadiah.ae; internet www.alahmadiah.com; f. 1970; building and civil engineering contractors; part of the Al-Fajer Group; Man. Dir SERGE MASSOUDI; CEO S. K. JOSHI.

Arab International Logistics (Aramex): POB 3841, Dubai; tel. 544000; e-mail uaecare@aramex.com; internet www.aramex.com; f. 1982; private ownership; listed on Dubai Financial Market in 2005; int. and domestic deliveries, freight forwarding, logistics and warehousing, management solutions, e-business solutions and online shopping; Chair. Capt. MOHAMED JUMA AL-SHAMSI; CEO OTHMAN AL-JADA.

Damac Properties Dubai PJSC: POB 2195, Dubai; internet www.damacproperties.com; f. 2002; Chair. HUSSAIN SAJWANI; Man. Dirs ALI SAJWANI, AMIRA SAJWANI.

Dubai Holding: POB 66000, Umm Suqeim Rd, Dubai; tel. (4) 3622000; fax (4) 3622091; internet dubaiholding.com; f. 2004; supervises major industrial and infrastructure projects in Dubai; oversees activities of seven mem. cos including Dubai Properties Group, Jumeirah Group and Arab Media Group, as well as numerous subsidiaries; Chair. Sheikh AHMED BIN SAEED AL MAKTOUM; Group CEO AMIT KAUSHAL.

Dubai Investments: POB 28171, Dubai; tel. (4) 8122400; e-mail info@dubaiinvestments.com; internet www.dubaiinvestments.com; f. 1995; investments in real estate development, manufacturing industries, health care and education; Chair. ABDULRAHMAN GHANEM A. AL-MUTAIWEE; Man. Dir and CEO KHALID BIN KALBAN.

Emaar Properties PJSC: POB 9440, Dubai; tel. (4) 3661688; e-mail customercare@emaar.ae; internet www.emaar.com; f. 1997; real estate development; Man. Dir MUHAMMAD ALI RASHID AL-ABBAR.

Al-Futtaim Engineering: POB 159, Dubai; tel. (4) 7063111; e-mail info@afet.com; internet afet.com; f. 1974; Man. Dir MURALI S.

Galadari Brothers Group: POB 138, Dubai; tel. (4) 3388800; fax (4) 3381918; e-mail info@galadarigroup.com; internet www.galadarigroup.com; automobiles, engineering, industrial equipment, information technology, media, real estate, retail; Group CEO MOHAMMED ABDULLATIF IBRAHIM GALADARI.

General Enterprises Co (GECO): POB 363, Dubai; tel. (4) 2500993; fax (4) 2364350; e-mail gecobusiness@gecouae.ae; internet www.gecouae.com; general trading and contracting.

Al-Ghurair Group: POB 1, Salahuddin Rd, Hor al-Anz, Dubai; tel. (4) 6037777; fax (4) 2623388; e-mail hr@alghurair.com; internet www.alghurair.com; f. 1960/61; general contracting, banking, import and export, aluminium extrusion and manufacture of aluminium doors, windows, etc., PVC pipes, tiles and marbles, cement and mineral waters; gold and exchange dealers, owners of grain silos and flour mills, printing press, packaging factory, real estate dealers; Chair. Dr NASSER SAIDI; CEO IYAD MALAS.

Gulf Eternit Trading: POB 19690, Dubai; tel. (4) 5124600; fax (4) 5124850; e-mail trading@gulf-eternit.com; internet gulf-eternit.com; f. 1971; design, manufacture and installation of piping systems for industrial, petrochemical, municipal, civil and irrigation applications; part of the Future Pipe Group.

Gulf Extrusions Co LLC: POB 5598, Jebel Ali Industrial Area, Dubai; tel. (4) 8846146; fax (4) 8846830; e-mail mail@gulfex.com; internet www.gulfex.com; f. 1975; member of the Al-Ghurair Group; over 10,000 aluminium product profiles for domestic construction projects and export to other Gulf, European, South East Asian and Canadian markets; CEO OMAR SHEGEM.

Al-Habtoor Group LLC: POB 25444, al-Wasl Rd, al-Safa 2, Dubai; tel. (4) 3941444; fax (4) 3949990; e-mail contacts@habtoor.com; internet www.habtoor.com; f. 1970; civil and building contracting; engineering; hotels and catering; insurance; leasing; transport services; Chair. KHALAF AHMAD AL-HABTOOR.

National Cement Co PSC: POB 4041, Dubai; tel. (4) 3388885; fax (4) 3388886; e-mail cement@nationalcement.ae; internet www.nationalcement.ae; production and sale of cement.

Al-Shirawi Group of Companies: POB 93, Dubai; tel. (4) 2821000; e-mail info@alshirawi.ae; internet www.alshirawi.com; f. 1971; over 30 subsidiary cos active in construction, manufacturing, industrial equipment, logistics, electronics and printing; Chair. MOHAMED AL-SHIRAWI; Man. Dir NAVIN VALRANI.

United Foods Co PSC: POB 5836, al-Quoz, Dubai; tel. (4) 5063800; fax (4) 3381987; e-mail info@unitedfoods.ae; internet www.unitedfoods.ae; f. 1976; manufacture and trading of hydrogenated vegetable oil and edible oils; Chair. ALI BIN HUMAID AL-OWAIS; CEO FETHI MUHAMMAD KHIARI.

Fujairah

Fujairah Building Industries PSC: POB 383, Al Hayl Industrial Area, Fujairah; tel. (9) 2222051; e-mail office@fujfbi.ae; internet www.fujfbi.ae; govt-owned; subsidiaries include Emirates Ceramic Factory, Fujairah Concrete Products, Fujairah Marble and Tiles Factory; Chair. AHMAD SAID MUHAMMAD AL-RAQBANI; Group CEO AHMAD NAIM AL-KHAYYAT.

Fujairah Cement Industries (FCI): Umm al-Qaiwain Bank Bldg, Mezzanine 2nd Floor, Office 203, Hamad bin Abdulla Rd, Fujairah; tel. (9) 2223111; fax (9) 2227718; e-mail info@fujairahcement.com; internet www.fujairahcement.com; f. 1979; cement manufacture and supply; Chair. Sheikh MOHAMMED BIN HAMAD BIN SAIF AL-SHARQI; Gen. Man. SAEED AHMED GHAREIB HOWAISHIL AL-SEREIDI.

Ras al-Khaimah

Julphar Gulf Pharmaceutical Industries: POB 997, Airport Rd, Digdaga, Ras al-Khaimah; internet www.julphar.net; f. 1980; Chair. Sheikh SAQER HUMAID AL-QASIMI; CEO BASEL ZIYADEH.

RAK Ceramics: POB 4714, Ras al-Khaimah; tel. 1025829; internet www.rakceramics.com; f. 1989; manufacture of ceramic tiles and sanitary ware; Chair. Sheikh SAQR BIN SAUD AL-QASIMI; CEO ABDULLAH MASSAAD.

Raknor (PVT) Ltd: POB 883, Ras al-Khaimah; tel. (7) 2668351; e-mail info@raknor.com; internet www.raknor.com; f. 1976; manufacture of concrete blocks; Gen. Man. NASER BUSTAMI.

Sharjah

BuildMart Gulf Building Materials LLC (BMG): POB 150796, Sharjah; tel. (6) 5343811; fax (6) 5343817; internet buildmartgulf.com; production and supply of building materials, steel and aluminium.

CIMCO Trading Co Ltd: POB 21409, Sharjah; tel. (6) 5673013; e-mail sales@cimcotrading.com; internet www.cimcotrading.com; f. 1993; distributor of electrical, mechanical, marine, instrumentation and hardware products.

Dafco Trading and Industrial Co WLL: POB 515, Sharjah; tel. (6) 5621333; fax (6) 5620999; f. 1969; general contracting trading co; operates factories producing bricks and concrete; Man. M. AL-FARHAN.

Hempel Paints (Emirates) LLC: Mussafah 15, Industrial Area, Sharjah; tel. (2) 5552279; fax (6) 5310141; e-mail hempelae@eim.ae; internet www.hempeldecorative.me; f. 1976; manufacture and sale of paints for offshore marine, domestic and industrial use; Chair. RICHARD SAND; Group Pres. and CEO LARS PETERSSON.

SBK Real Estate: Mezzanine 2, Buhaira Tower, Buhaira Corniche St, al-Majaz 3, Sharjah; tel. (6) 5303030; internet www.sbkrealestate.com; f. 1995; Exec. Dir SHAHID HASSAN.

Umm al-Qaiwain

Emirates Panel Manufacture LLC: POB 3998, Industrial Area 1, Umm al-Qaiwain; tel. (6) 7529999; e-mail info@epm.biz; internet www.epm-uae.com; manufacturer of aluminium composite panels and coated coils.

Royal Arabian Foods LLC: POB 2219, Umm al-Qaiwain; tel. (2) 7855333; e-mail sales@rafgroups.com; internet rafgroups.com; f. 2010; importer and exporter of foods, beverages, agro-commodities, etc.

Umm al-Qaiwain Rubber Industries Ltd: POB 79, Umm al-Qaiwain; tel. (6) 7671320; fax (6) 7671221; e-mail info@uril.ae; internet uril.ae; mfr of pipe seals, industrial products and automotive components; CEO AJAY KUMAR GHUWALEWALA.

Transport

REGULATORY AUTHORITY

Ministry of Energy and Infrastructure: see Ministries; Under-Sec. for Infrastructure and Transportation HASSAN MOHAMED JUMA AL-MANSOURI.

RAILWAYS

The Dubai Metro, an urban light-railway system, has a total length of 90 km and 56 stations. In 2006 the Abu Dhabi authorities announced plans for the construction of a 131-km metro system, comprising four lines; as of early 2023, however, the project had not yet been commenced. Plans for the construction of a 1,200-km federal railway network for passengers and freight, linking the seven emirates, gained final government approval in 2009. The first phase of the Etihad Rail network—a 264-km line between Shah and Ruwais—began full commercial operations in 2016. The 605-km second phase of the network, connecting Fujairah and Khorfakkan on the east coast with the town of Ghuweifat on the UAE-Saudi Arabia border, commenced commercial operations in February 2023. In the same month Etihad Rail signed an agreement with Oman Rail to build a 303-km rail line connecting Sohar Port in Oman to the UAE's federal rail network.

Etihad Rail: POB 989, Capital Gate, 6th Floor, Khaleej Al Arabi St, Abu Dhabi; tel. (2) 4999999; e-mail contacts@etihadrail.ae; internet www.etihadrail.ae; f. 2009 as Union Railway Co; current name adopted 2011; charged with construction of, and eventual operations of, a federal railway network for both passengers and freight, to extend throughout the UAE; wholly state-owned; Chair. Sheikh THEYAB BIN MOHAMED BIN ZAYED AL NAHYAN; CEO SHADI MALAK.

ROADS

The road network in the UAE has undergone rapid and extensive development in recent years. Abu Dhabi and Dubai are linked by a good road that is dual carriageway for most of its length. This road forms part of a west coast route from Shaam, at the UAE border with the northern enclave of Oman, through Dubai and Abu Dhabi to Tarif. An east coast route links Dibba with Muscat, Oman. Other roads include the Abu Dhabi–Al-Ain highway and roads linking Sharjah and Ras al-Khaimah, and Sharjah and Dhaid. An underwater tunnel links Dubai Town and Deira by dual carriageway and pedestrian subway.

SHIPPING

Dubai has been the main commercial centre in the Gulf for many years. Following recent expansion, the total capacity of Dubai's Mina Jebel Ali port (the largest man-made harbour in the world) now stands at 22.4m. 20-ft equivalent units (TEUs) per year. Abu Dhabi has also become an important port since the opening in 1972 of the first section of its artificial harbour, Port Zayed. The Khalifa Port Container Terminal in Abu Dhabi, with an initial annual capacity of 2.5m. TEUs, was inaugurated in 2012. A second, 2.5m.-TEU container terminal at Khalifa Port was opened in December 2018. The port of Fujairah is the largest port on the eastern coast of the UAE; the port incorporates two oil terminals and an expanded container terminal was inaugurated in June 2021. There are also smaller container ports in Ras al-Khaimah, Sharjah and Umm al-Qaiwain. In December 2021, following expansion, Abu Dhabi's Mugharraq Port was officially certified as an international port facility.

Abu Dhabi

Abu Dhabi Ports Co (ADPC): POB 54477, Mina Zayed, Abu Dhabi; tel. (2) 6952000; fax (2) 6952177; e-mail customerservice@adports.ae; internet www.adports.ae; f. 2006; responsible for the devt and regulation of Abu Dhabi's ports and related industrial zones; operates 11 ports and terminals in the UAE and Guinea; Chair. Dr FALAH MOHAMMAD AL-AHBABI; CEO Capt. MUHAMMAD JUMA AL-SHAMISI.

Abu Dhabi Terminals PJSC (ADT): POB 136687, Khalifa Port, Bldg 70, Taweelah, Abu Dhabi; tel. (2) 4925000; fax (2) 4925160; e-mail kp.customer@adterminals.ae; internet www.adterminals.ae; f. 2006; replaced Abu Dhabi Seaports Authority (f. 1972); administers Khalifa Port Container Terminal (KPCT); capacity of 5m. TEUs container traffic; jt venture between ADPC and Mubadala; CEO AHMED AL-MUTAWA (acting).

Dubai

Dubai Ports World (DP World): POB 17000, JAFZA 17, 5th Floor, Dubai; tel. (4) 8815555; e-mail info@dpworld.com; internet www.dpworld.ae; f. 2005 by merger of Dubai Ports Authority (f. 1991 by merger of Mina Jebel Ali and Mina Rashid) and Dubai Ports Int. (f. 1999); subsidiary of state-controlled Dubai World; 23% sold via initial public offering 2007; storage areas and facilities for loading and discharge of vessels; operates ports of Mina Jebel Ali and Mina Rashid in Dubai, Port Zayed in Abu Dhabi, Fujairah Port and numerous other international facilities; Group Chair. and CEO SULTAN AHMAD BIN SULAYEM; CEO and Man. Dir, UAE Region ABDULLA BIN DAMITHAN.

Drydocks World—Dubai: POB 8988, Dubai; tel. (4) 3450626; fax (4) 3450116; e-mail drydocks@drydocks.gov.ae; internet www.drydocks.gov.ae; f. 1983; state-owned; dry-docking and repairs, tank-cleaning, construction of vessels and floating docks, conversions, galvanizing, dredging, etc.; CEO and Man. Dir Capt. RADO ANTOLOVIĆ.

Fujairah

Port of Fujairah: POB 787, Fujairah; tel. (9) 2228800; fax (9) 2228811; e-mail mkt_pof@fujairahport.ae; internet www.fujairahport.ae; f. 1983; operated by Dubai Ports World; offers facilities for handling container, general cargo and ro-ro traffic; Chair. Sheikh SALEH BIN MUHAMMAD AL-SHARQI; Gen. Man. Capt. MOUSA MURAD.

Ras al-Khaimah

Saqr Port Authority: POB 5130, Ras al-Khaimah; tel. (7) 2056000; e-mail info@rakports.ae; internet www.rakports.ae; govt-owned; port operators handling bulk cargoes, containers, general cargo and ro-ro traffic; CEO ROGER CLASQUIN.

Sharjah

Sharjah Ports Authority: POB 510, Sharjah; tel. (6) 5281666; fax (6) 5281425; e-mail shjports@eim.ae; internet www.sharjahports.ae; the authority administers Port Khalid, Hamriyah Port and Port Khor Fakkan and offers specialized facilities for container and ro-ro traffic, reefer cargo and project and general cargo; combined annual capacity of 5m. TEUs of containerized cargo; Chair. (Ports and Customs) Sheikh KHALID BIN ABDULLAH AL-QASIMI; Dir-Gen. MOHAMMED MEER AL-SARRAH.

Umm al-Qaiwain

Ahmed bin Rashid Port and Free Zone Authority: POB 279, Umm al-Qaiwain; tel. (6) 7655882; fax (6) 7651552; e-mail abrpaftz@emirates.net.ae; f. 1998; Pres. KHALID BIN RASHID AL-MU'ALLA; Gen. Man. MURTAZA K. MOOSAJEE.

CIVIL AVIATION

There are seven international airports, two in Dubai, and one in each of Abu Dhabi, Al-Ain, Fujairah and Ras al-Khaimah, as well as a smaller one at Sharjah, which forms part of Sharjah port, linking air, sea and overland transportation services.

General Civil Aviation Authority: POB 6558, Abu Dhabi; tel. (2) 4447666; fax (2) 4054535; e-mail info@gcaa.gov.ae; internet www.gcaa.ae; f. 1996; responsible for all aspects of civil aviation; Chair. ABDULLAH BIN TOUQ AL-MARI (Minister of Economy); Dir-Gen. SAIF MUHAMMAD AL-SUWAIDI.

Abu Dhabi Aviation: POB 2723, Abu Dhabi; tel. (2) 5758000; fax (2) 5757775; e-mail adava@abudhabiaviation.com; internet www.abudhabiaviation.com; f. 1976; domestic charter flights; Chair. NADER AHMAD MUHAMMAD AL-HAMADI; Gen. Man. MUHAMMAD IBRAHIM AL-MAZROUI.

Air Arabia: Bldg A1, POB 132, Sharjah; tel. (6) 5088977; fax (6) 5580011; e-mail contactus@airarabia.com; internet www.airarabia.com; f. 2003; 55% owned by private investors, 45% by the Sharjah Govt; low-fare airline; operates scheduled services across the Middle East, N. Africa, South and Central Asia, and Europe; Chair. Sheikh ABDULLAH BIN MUHAMMAD AL THANI; CEO ADIL AL-ALI.

Emirates Airline: POB 686, Dubai; tel. (4) 7003333; internet www.emirates.com; f. 1985; owned by the Dubai Govt; operates services to more than 120 destinations throughout the world; Chair. and Chief Exec. Sheikh AHMAD BIN SAID AL MAKTOUM; Pres. TIM CLARK.

Etihad Airways: POB 35566, Khalifa City A, Abu Dhabi; tel. (2) 5110000; fax (2) 5058111; internet www.etihadairways.com; f. 2003; owned by the Abu Dhabi Govt; Chair. MOHAMMED ALI MOHAMMED AL-SHORAFA; CEO TONY DOUGLAS.

Tourism

Abu Dhabi Department of Culture and Tourism: POB 94000, Abu Dhabi; tel. (2) 4440444; fax (2) 4440400; e-mail info@dctabudhabi.ae; internet tcaabudhabi.ae; f. 2004; Chair. MOHAMED KHALIFA AL-MUBARAK.

Tourism Development and Investment Co (TDIC): POB 126888, Abu Dhabi; tel. (2) 4061400; e-mail info@tdic.ae; internet www.tdic.ae; f. 2006; 100% owned by TCA Abu Dhabi; responsible for the devt of a range of major projects incl. Saadiyat Island; Chair. Sheikh SULTAN BIN TAHNOON AL-NAHYAN; CEO SUFIAN HASAN AL-MARZOOQI.

Dubai Department of Economy and Tourism: POB 594, Dubai; tel. (4) 2821111; e-mail info@visitdubai.com; internet www.visitdubai.com; f. 1997; Chair. Sheikh MOHAMMED BIN RASHID AL MAKTOUM (Vice-Pres. of the UAE and Ruler of Dubai); Dir-Gen. HILAL AL-MARRI.

Fujairah Tourism and Antiquities Authority: POB 500, Fujairah; tel. (9) 2231554; fax (9) 2231006; e-mail info@tourism.fujairah.ae; internet www.fujairahtourism.ae; f. 1995; Chair. Dr AHMED AL-SHAMSI; Gen. Man. SAEED AL-SAMAHI.

National Corporation for Tourism and Hotels (NCTH): POB 6942, Abu Dhabi; tel. (2) 4099999; fax (2) 4099990; e-mail ncth@emirates.net.ae; internet www.ncth.com; f. 1996; 20% owned by Govt of Abu Dhabi; Chair. Sheikh HAMDAN BIN MUBARAK AL-NAYHAN; CEO HANY FARAG.

Ras al-Khaimah Tourism Development Authority: POB 29798, Ras al-Khaimah; tel. (7) 2338998; fax (7) 2338118; e-mail info@raktda.com; internet visitrasalkhaimah.com; f. 2011; CEO RAKI PHILLIPS.

Sharjah Commerce and Tourism Development Authority: POB 26661, Crescent Tower, Sharjah; tel. (6) 5566777; fax (6) 5563000; e-mail info@sharjahtourism.ae; internet www.sharjahtourism.ae; f. 1996; Chair. KHALID JASIM AL-MIDFA; Dir Sheikh SULTAN BIN ABDULLAH BIN SALEM AL-QASIMI.

Defence

The Union Defence Force and the armed forces of the various emirates were formally merged in May 1976. Abu Dhabi and Dubai retain a degree of independence. As assessed at November 2022, the total strength of the Union Defence Force was 63,000: army 44,000; navy 2,500; air force 4,500, presidential guard 12,000. Compulsory military service of 16 months or two years (depending on the level of education attained) for men aged between 18 and 30 years was introduced in 2014.

Defence Budget: an estimated AED 74,800m. in 2022; federal expenditure on defence has been substantially reduced since the early 1980s, but procurement and project costs are not affected, as individual emirates finance these separately.

Chief of Staff of the Federal Armed Forces: Lt-Gen. Eng. ISSA SAIF MOHAMMED AL-MAZROUEI.

Commander of Land Forces: Maj.-Gen. SAEED AL-SHEHHI.

Commander of the Air Forces and Air Defence: Maj.-Gen. IBRAHIM NASSER AL-ALAWI.

Commander of the Naval Forces: Rear Adm. Sheikh SAEED BIN HAMDAN BIN MOHAMMED AL NAHYAN.

Education

Primary education is compulsory, beginning at six years of age and lasting for six years. Secondary education, starting at the age of 12, lasts for three years. After one year, students can choose between science- or arts-based streams. According to UNESCO estimates, total enrolment at pre-primary level in 2019/20 included 94.2% of children (boys 94.2%; girls 94.3%) in the relevant age-group, while enrolment at primary schools included 99.8% of children in the relevant age-group. The enrolment ratio for lower secondary schools was 99.3% in 2019/20, while the ratio for upper secondary enrolment was 97.8% (boys 97.5%; girls 98.2%). There are primary and secondary schools in all the emirates, and further education in technical fields is available in the more advanced areas.

A branch of the Université Paris-Sorbonne opened in Abu Dhabi in 2006, and a branch of New York University in 2009. Dubai hosts branches of universities from Australia, the United Kingdom, Canada and the USA. A US university is also in operation in Sharjah. Four higher colleges of technology (two for male students and two for female students) opened in Abu Dhabi in 1988.

Budgeted federal government expenditure by the Ministry of Education on public education programmes (including universities) in 2023 totalled an estimated AED 9,800m., equivalent to 15.5% of total projected general budgetary expenditure.

Bibliography

Abdullah, M. Morsy. *The Modern History of the United Arab Emirates*. London, Croom Helm, 1978.

Ahmed, Allam, and Alfaki, Ibrahim. *From Oil to Knowledge: Transforming the United Arab Emirates into a Knowledge-based Economy*. Sheffield, Greenleaf, 2016.

Ali, Syed. *Dubai: Gilded Cage*. New Haven, CT, Yale University Press, 2010.

al-Alkim, Hassan Hamdan. *The Foreign Policy of the United Arab Emirates*. London, Saqi Books, 1989.

Almezaini, Khalid A. *The UAE and Foreign Policy: Foreign Aid, Identities and Interests*. Abingdon, Routledge, 2011.

Ansari, Shahid Jamal. *Political Modernization in the Gulf*. Delhi, Northern Book Center, 1998.

Anthony, John Duke. *Arab States of the Lower Gulf: People, Power, Politics*. Washington, DC, Middle East Institute, 1975.

Baskan, Birol. 'The Police Chief and the Sheikh', *The Washington Review of Middle Eastern & Eurasian Affairs*, April 2012.

Bradshaw, Tancred. *The End of Empire in the Gulf: From Trucial States to United Arab Emirates*. London, I. B. Tauris, 2020.

Coates Ulrichsen, Kristian. *The United Arab Emirates: Power, Politics and Policy-Making*. Abingdon, Routledge, 2015.

Insecure Gulf: The End of Certainty and the Transition to the Post-Oil Era. Oxford, Oxford University Press, 2015.

al-Dabbagh, May, and Nusseibeh, Lana. 'Women in Parliament and Politics in the UAE: A Study of the First Federal National Council Elections', *Dubai School of Government/Ministry of Federal National Council Affairs*, Feb. 2009.

Davidson, Christopher. *The United Arab Emirates: A Study in Survival*. Boulder, CO, Lynne Rienner Publishers, 2005.

'After Sheikh Zayed: the Politics of Succession in Abu Dhabi and the UAE', *Middle East Policy*. Vol. 13, Issue 1, 2006.

Dubai: The Vulnerability of Success. London, Hurst & Co, 2008.

Abu Dhabi: Oil and Beyond. London, Hurst & Co, 2009.

From Sheikhs to Sultanism: Statecraft and Authority in Saudi Arabia and the UAE. Oxford, Oxford University Press, 2021.

Davies, Charles. *The Blood Red Arab Flag: An Investigation into Qasimi Piracy*. Exeter, University of Exeter Press, 1997.

Elsheshtawy, Yasser. *Dubai: Behind an Urban Spectacle*. Abingdon, Routledge, 2009.

Fain, W. Taylor. *American Ascendance and British Retreat in the Persian Gulf Region*. Basingstoke, Palgrave Macmillan, 2008.

Al Faris, Abdulrazak, and Soto, Raimundo. *The Economy of Dubai*. Oxford, Oxford University Press, 2016.

Fenelon, K. G. *The United Arab Emirates: An Economic and Social Survey*. London, Longman, 1973.

Freer, Courtney. 'Rentier Islamism: the Role of the Muslim Brotherhood in the Gulf', *LSE Middle East Centre PaperSeries*, 2015. eprints.lse.ac.uk/64446/1/RentierIslamism.pdf.

'The Muslim Brotherhood in the United Arab Emirates: Anatomy of a Crackdown', *Middle East Eye*, 17 Dec. 2014, www.middleeasteye.net/essays/muslim-brotherhood-emirates-anatomy-crackdown-1009823835.

Ghareeb, Edmund, and al-Abed, Ibrahim (Eds). *Perspectives on the United Arab Emirates*. London, Trident Press, 1997.

Guéraiche, William, and Alexander, Kristian (Eds). *Facets of Security in the United Arab Emirates*. Abingdon, Routledge, 2022.

Halliday, Fred. *Arabia without Sultans*. London, Saqi Books, 2002.

Heard-Bey, Frauke. *From Trucial States to United Arab Emirates* (3rd edn). Dubai, Motivate Publishing, 2004.

'The United Arab Emirates: Statehood and Nation-Building in a Traditional Society', *Middle East Journal*. Volume 59, Issue 3, 2005.

Hedges, Matthew. *Reinventing the Sheikhdom: Clan, Power and Patronage in Mohammed bin Zayed's UAE*. Oxford, Oxford University Press, 2022.

Henderson, Simon. 'Succession Politics in the Conservative Gulf Arab States: the Weekend's Events in Ras al-Khaimah', *The Washington Institute Policy Watch*. No. 769, 17 June 2003.

'The Iran Angle of Ras al-Khaimah's Succession Struggle', *The Washington Institute Policy Watch*. No. 1714, 29 Oct. 2010.

Heard, David. *Oil Men, Territorial Ambitions and Political Agents: From Pearls to Oil in the Trucial States of the Gulf*. Berlin, Gerlach Press, 2019.

Herb, Michael. *The Wages of Oil: Parliaments and Economic Development in Kuwait and the UAE*. Ithaca, NY, Cornell University Press, 2014.

Khalifa, Ali Mohammad. *The United Arab Emirates: Unity in Fragmentation*. London, Croom Helm, 1979.

Kumetat, Dennis. *Managing the Transition: Renewable Energy and Innovation Policies in the UAE and Algeria*. Abingdon, Routledge, 2015.

Lienhardt, Peter, and al-Shahi, Ahmed (Ed.). *Shaikhdoms of Eastern Arabia*. New York, St. Martin's Press, 2001.

Luomi, Mari. *The International Relations of the Green Economy in the Gulf: Lessons from the UAE's State-Led Energy Transition*. Oxford, Oxford Institute for Energy Studies, 2015.

Mahdavi, Parvis. *Gridlock: Labor, Migration, and Human Trafficking in Dubai*. Palo Alto, CA, Stanford University Press, 2011.

Mattair, Thomas. *The Three Occupied UAE Islands: The Tunbs and Abu Musa*. Abu Dhabi, Emirates Center for Strategic Studies and Research, 2005.

Al-Mazrouei, Noura Saber. *The UAE and Saudi Arabia: Border Disputes and International Relations in the Gulf*. London, I. B. Tauris, 2016.

Ministry of Information and Culture. *United Arab Emirates: A Record of Achievement, 1971–1996; 25 Years of Development*. Abu Dhabi, 1996.

al-Noqaidan, Mansour. *Muslim Brotherhood in UAE: Expansion and Decline*. Dubai, Al Mesbar Center for Studies and Research, 2012, almesbar.net/4/Muslim%20Brotherhood%20in%20UAE(1).pdf.

Peterson, J. E. 'The Future of Federalism in the United Arab Emirates', in Sindelar, III, H. Richard, and Peterson, J. E. (Eds). *Crosscurrents in the Gulf: Arab Regional and Global Interests*. London, Routledge, 1988.

Plotkin Boghardt, Lori. 'The Muslim Brotherhood on Trial in the UAE', *The Washington Institute Policy Watch*. No. 2064, 12 April 2013.

Al Qassemi, Sultan. 'The Brothers and the Gulf', *Foreign Policy*, 14 Dec. 2012. foreignpolicy.com/2012/12/14/the-brothers-and-the-gulf.

al-Qasimi, Fahim bin Sultan. 'A Century in Thirty Years: Sheikh Zayed and the United Arab Emirates', *Middle East Policy*, Vol. 6, Issue 4, 1999.

Rugh, Andrea B. *The Political Culture of Leadership in the United Arab Emirates*. New York, Palgrave Macmillan, 2007.

Sadjadpour, Karim. 'The Battle of Dubai: The United Arab Emirates and the U.S.-Iran Cold War', *Carnegie Papers Middle East*, July 2011.

Sato, Shohei. 'Britain's Decision to Withdraw from the Persian Gulf, 1964-68: A Pattern and a Puzzle', *Journal of Imperial and Commonwealth History*. Vol. 37, Issue 1, 2009.

Schofield, Richard. *Unfinished Business: Iran, the UAE, Abu Musa and the Tunbs*. London, Royal Institute of International Affairs, 2003.

Spraggon, Martin. *Managing Organizations in the United Arab Emirates: Dynamic Characteristics and Key Economic Developments*. New York, Palgrave Macmillan, 2014.

Taryam, Abdullah Omran. *The Establishment of the UAE, 1950–85*. London, Croom Helm, 1987.

Warren, David H. *Rivals in the Gulf: Yusuf al-Qaradawi, Abdullah Bin Bayyah, and the Qatar-UAE Contest Over the Arab Spring and the Gulf Crisis*. Abingdon, Routledge, 2022.

Wilkinson, John. *Arabia's Frontiers: The Story of Britain's Boundary Drawing in the Desert*. London, I. B. Tauris, 1987.

Yanai, Shaul. *The Political Transformation of Gulf Tribal States: Elitism and the Social Contract in Kuwait, Bahrain and Dubai, 1918–1970s*. Eastbourne, Sussex Academic Press, 2015.

Yates, Athol. *The Evolution of the Armed Forces of the United Arab Emirates by Athol Yates*. Warwick, Helion & Co Ltd, 2020.

Young, Karen E. *The Political Economy of Energy, Finance and Security in the United Arab Emirates: Between the Majilis and the Market*. New York, Palgrave Macmillan, 2014.

Zahlan, Rosemarie Said. *The Origins of the United Arab Emirates: A Political and Social History of the Trucial States*. Abingdon, Routledge, 2016.

YEMEN

Geography

On 22 May 1990 the Yemen Arab Republic (YAR) and the People's Democratic Republic of Yemen (PDRY) merged to form the Republic of Yemen. Yemen consists of the southwestern corner of the Arabian peninsula—the highlands inland and the coastal strip along the Red Sea; and the former British colony of Aden (195 sq km or 75.3 sq miles) and the Protectorate of South Arabia (about 333,000 sq km), together with the islands of Perim (13 sq km) and Kamaran (57 sq km). The Republic of Yemen lies at the southern end of the Arabian peninsula, approximately between longitude 43°E and 56°E, with Perim Island a few kilometres due west, in the strait marking the southern extremity of the Red Sea, and Socotra in the extreme east. Yemen has frontiers with Saudi Arabia and Oman, although atlases have shown considerable variation in the precise boundaries of the three countries, or sometimes have not indicated them at all. (A final agreement on delineation of the border with Saudi Arabia, with the exception of some eastern sections, was signed in 2000, while the border with Oman was officially demarcated in 1995.)

PHYSICAL FEATURES

Physically, Yemen comprises the dislocated southern edge of the great plateau of Arabia. This is an immense mass of ancient granites, once forming part of Africa, and covered in many places by shallow, mainly horizontal, layers of younger sedimentary rocks. The whole plateau has undergone downwarping in the east and elevation in the west, so that the highest land (over 3,000 m) occurs in the extreme west, near the Red Sea, with a gradual decline to the lowest parts (under 300 m) in the extreme east. The whole of the southern and western coasts of Yemen were formed by a series of enormous fractures, which produced a flat but very narrow coastal plain, rising steeply to the hill country a short distance inland. Percolation of molten magma along the fracture-lines gave rise to a number of volcanic craters, now extinct, and one of these, partly eroded and occupied by the sea, forms the site of Aden port.

An important topographical feature is the Wadi Hadramout, an imposing valley running parallel to the coast at 160 km–240 km distance inland. In its upper and middle parts this valley is broad, and occupied by a seasonal torrent; in its lower (eastern) part it narrows considerably, making a sudden turn south-eastwards and reaching the sea. This lower part is largely uninhabited, but the upper parts, where alluvial soil and intermittent flood water are available, support a farming population.

CLIMATE

Rainfall is generally scarce, but relatively more abundant on the highlands and in the west. The climate of the highlands is considered to be the best in all Arabia since it experiences a regime rather like that of East Africa: a warm, temperate and rainy summer, and a cool, moderately dry winter with occasional frost and some snow. Aden receives 125 mm of rain annually, all of it during winter (December–March), while in the lowlands of the extreme east it may rain only once in five or 10 years. In the highlands a few miles north of Aden, falls of up to 760 mm occur, for the most part during summer, and this rainfall also gradually declines eastwards, giving 380 mm–500 mm in the highlands of Dhofar. As much as 890 mm of rain may fall annually on the higher parts of the interior, off the Red Sea coast, with 400 mm–500 mm over much of the plateau, but the coast receives less than 130 mm generally, often in the form of irregular downpours. There is, therefore, the phenomenon of streams and even rivers flowing perennially in the western highlands but failing to reach the coast.

Ultimately, to the north and east, rainfall becomes almost negligible, as the edges of the Arabian Desert are reached. This unusual situation of a reversal in climatic conditions over a few miles is thought to be the result of two streams of air: an upper one, damp and unstable in summer, and originating in the equatorial regions of East Africa; and a lower current, generally drier and related to conditions prevailing over the rest of the Middle East. In this way the low-lying coastal areas have a maximum of rainfall in winter, and the hills of Yemen a maximum in summer. Temperatures are high everywhere, particularly on the coastal plain, which has a southern aspect: mean figures of 25°C (January) to 32°C (June) occur at Aden town, although temperatures of more than 38°C are common. Owing to this climate gradation from desert to temperate conditions, Yemen has a similar gradation of crops and vegetation. In the interior, off the Red Sea coast, the highest parts appear as 'African', with scattered trees and grassland. Crops of coffee, qat, cereals and vegetables are grown, while, lower down, 'Mediterranean' fruits appear, with millet and, where irrigation water is available, bananas. The date palm is the only tree to grow successfully in the coastal region.

To the east, except on the higher parts, which have a light covering of thorn scrub (including dwarf trees that exude a sap from which incense and myrrh are derived), and the restricted patches of cultivated land, the territory is devoid of vegetation. Cultivation is limited to small level patches of good soil on flat terraces alongside the river beds, on the floor and sides of the Wadi Hadramout, or where irrigation from wells and occasionally from cisterns can be practised. The most productive areas are: Lahej, close to Aden town; two districts near Mukalla (about 480 km east of Aden); and parts of the middle Hadramout. Irrigation from cisterns hollowed out of the rock has long been practised, and Aden town has a famous system of this kind, dating back many centuries. Today, however, the main system of irrigation is provided by floodwater.

POPULATION

The area of Yemen is approximately 536,869 sq km (207,286 sq miles). The population was recorded as 19,685,161 at the census of 16 December 2004, giving a population density of 36.7 persons per sq km. According to United Nations (UN) estimates, the population had reached 34,449,825 by mid-2023, resulting in a population density of 64.2 persons per sq km.

The capital of the Republic of Yemen is San'a, which lies on the al-Jehal plateau (2,175 m above sea level) in the north-west of the country. The city had a population of 3,292,497 at mid-2023, according to UN estimates. Other major cities included Aden (1,079,670) and Taiz (940,600).

Since the outbreak of conflict between the Government of President Abd al-Rabbuh Mansour Hadi, supported by a coalition of regional forces led by Saudi Arabia, and an alliance between the al-Houthi movement and the forces of deceased former President Ali Abdullah Saleh in 2014, a significant number of Yemenis have been killed or displaced. According to the Office of the UN High Commissioner for Refugees (UNHCR), as of December 2022 some 4.5m. Yemenis were internally displaced, while the country hosted around 99,900 refugees and asylum seekers (mainly from Somalia and Ethiopia).

History

VINCENT DURAC

INTRODUCTION: THE TWO YEMENS

Although Yemen has a recorded history that dates back several millennia, the Republic of Yemen is the youngest state in the Middle East, dating back to the unification in 1990 of the former Yemen Arab Republic (YAR) in the north and the People's Democratic Republic of Yemen (PDRY) in the south. The YAR came into existence in November 1962 following the overthrow of the Zaidi Shi'a Imamate, which had ruled the north since the 10th century. (Zaidism is a Shi'a sect which emerged in the ninth century after the death of the fourth Shi'a Imam, 'Ali Zain al-'Abidin. Unlike mainstream Shi'as, Zaidis believe that any descendant of Ali can be Imam). Decades of instability and political violence followed. By the time that Lt-Col Ali Abdullah Saleh became President of the YAR in 1978, two of his predecessors had been deposed in military coups and two had been assassinated.

Saleh rose steadily through the ranks as a close associate of Ahmad al-Ghashmi. Al-Ghashmi was a key element in the 1974 coup that brought Ibrahim al-Hamdi to power. Following the coup, Saleh became the military commander of Taiz province. When al-Hamdi was assassinated in October 1977, al-Ghashmi succeeded him as President. However, in June 1978 al-Ghashmi was also assassinated when a suitcase carried by an emissary of the head of state of the PDRY exploded. Al-Ghashmi's death led to the formation of a four-man Presidential Council from which Saleh emerged as President.

Few expected Saleh, a young army officer, to survive in office for any length of time. However, the new President defied the odds by setting out to broaden his support base as much as possible. In 1980, within two years of taking office, Saleh published a National Charter as a guide to national life to which all sectors of the population might subscribe. In August 1982 a General People's Congress (GPC) was established, to which 1,000 members were elected. The Congress then met to amend and adopt the Charter. The GPC held further meetings in 1984 and 1986. The GPC was established as a 'political organization' rather than a political party and contained within it individuals who espoused a wide range of ideological positions. It became the vehicle through which President Saleh would dominate political life in Yemen until the popular uprising of 2011. In 1988—a decade after Saleh first assumed power—parliamentary elections took place in which, as political parties were banned, some 1,300 unaligned candidates competed for 128 seats in a 159-member Consultative Council.

Pre-unification, the YAR was heavily dependent on external aid. The Imamate that had governed the North for much of the 20th century had maintained only the most minimal civil service and public works. As a result, it was international donors who helped to build state institutions and infrastructure. The World Bank, together with the United Nations (UN) Development Programme and the Kuwait Fund for Arab Economic Development, were involved in the establishment of a central planning organization to manage hundreds of externally funded projects. The Bank, together with other donors, also provided support for the drafting of an ambitious five-year plan for the period 1976–81. The plan set out objectives in areas such as power, water, education and health that would require management by a significantly expanded bureaucracy. This led to the emergence of a new technocratic elite to manage the institutions charged with oversight of development projects and initiatives. New ministries of planning, public works and education were established, together with a national grid, all of which were planned and funded by foreign donors and staffed by a new class of foreign-educated technocrats.

In the South, the United Kingdom had played a key role after it took control of the port of Aden in 1839. By the early 1960s anti-British agitation was increasingly widespread. In 1963 the National Front for the Liberation of Occupied South Yemen (NLF) was formed. Within four years the NLF was negotiating the terms of independence from the UK. Following independence in November 1967, the NLF united with two smaller parties to constitute the Unified Political Organization of the National Front, which became the Yemen Socialist Party (YSP) in 1978. The party established a centralized one-party system based on Marxist ideology but with some significant electoral features. The political system included a parliament of 101 members, which was initially elected every three years, and formally issued legislation, established policy guidelines and ratified foreign treaties. In practice, power lay with a Presidential Council, which usually included the President, the Prime Minister and the Secretary-General of the ruling party.

As in the North, political life in the PDRY was characterized by persistent political instability. This peaked in 1986, when violence broke out between different factions of the YSP. In January security forces loyal to President Ali Nasser Muhammad launched an attack inside a meeting of the YSP politburo, assassinating four of its members. This was reportedly a pre-emptive strike in anticipation of a similar move by the President's rivals. Civil war ensued in which at least 2,000 people were killed, and tens of thousands of people left the country, including Ali Nasser and his associates; many fled to the North. In February a new Government was formed under the leadership of Ali Salim al-Baid. By the late 1980s the political system of the PDRY was beginning to undergo major change. A communiqué issued in May 1989 emphasized the need for comprehensive political and economic reform, and the President called for reforms that would reflect the country's commitment to democracy. These initiatives were linked to changes at the broader geopolitical level, in particular the process of reform then taking place in the Union of Soviet Socialist Republics (USSR), the most significant international supporter of the PDRY.

Unification, when it came about, was a rapid and transformative process for both parts of Yemen. The rhetoric of unification had long been used by leaders in the YAR and the PDRY alike. Yet when, in November 1989, following a visit by Saleh to the PDRY, al-Baid consented to the unification of the two countries, the announcement came as a surprise to many. The two Yemens appeared on the face of it to be very different. However, they shared some key characteristics. Both were significantly dependent on outside support. For the YAR, this came principally from neighbouring Saudi Arabia and the USA. With the demise of the USSR, meanwhile, the PDRY lost its most important external ally. The discovery of oil in a border region made unification a plausible strategy for both, given the economic challenges that they faced. Furthermore, each leader almost certainly calculated that he could manipulate the process in order to expand his own power in a unified state.

THE POLITICAL SYSTEM AFTER UNIFICATION

The arrangements agreed for unification provided that the YSP would enjoy an equal share in a transitional government with the GPC, despite the much smaller population of the South. Saleh became President, and al-Baid became the first Prime Minister of the new state. However, the speed with which the unification process took place meant that there was limited time to agree on the measures necessary to harmonize the laws, political systems and security apparatus of what were two very different states. As an interim measure, it was agreed that the legal systems of the two parts of Yemen would remain in force in the territory of each. As a result, from the point of unification onwards Yemen had two sets of laws, two currencies and, crucially, two armies.

The requirement to forge a political system that could accommodate not one but two formerly ruling parties, characterized by highly divergent ideological orientations, led to the drafting of a constitution for the post-unification state that featured provision for political liberties on a scale previously unknown in the peninsula. The 1991 Constitution of the newly unified Republic of Yemen established a participatory parliamentary democracy in which the rights of all adult citizens were guaranteed. It enshrined the legal equality of all citizens and the independence of the judiciary, and enumerated fundamental rights and freedoms. The new Constitution provided for the establishment of a presidential republic with a unicameral parliament and regular elections. In the post-unification period there was a flourishing of political freedoms. A new press law of 1990 guaranteed the right to freedom of expression, of the press and access to information, which led to a huge increase in the number of publications. Following the promulgation of the Constitution, a law on civil society was also enacted, which led to an expansion in the number of civil society organizations from about 300 in the 1990s to more than 5,000 in the early part of the 21st century.

The political system put in place by the new Constitution vested considerable and wide-ranging powers in the office of the President. None the less, presidential prerogative was subject, at least in principle, to parliamentary oversight. Under the terms of the Constitution, the President is Supreme Commander of the Armed Forces, and appoints all members of the Consultative Council (see below), the Supreme Commission for Elections and Referendums, the Supreme Judicial Council, senior government officials, and military and police officers. The President promulgates laws passed by the House of Representatives, issues presidential decrees, proclaims states of emergency, can request amendments to the Constitution and can dissolve parliament. He also appoints the Prime Minister, who forms the Council of Ministers in consultation with the President. However, the Constitution also provides for the election of a 301-member House of Representatives, which is the legislative authority with the power to enact, amend or reject laws, sanction general state policies and the general plan for social and economic development, and approve the state budget. Members of parliament can propose legislation, grant or withdraw confidence from the Government or initiate the process of impeachment of the President. However, in reality these powers exist in principle only. Since the promulgation of the Constitution, parliament has been a weak institution that has rarely exercised its prerogatives in relation to the executive branch of government.

The new political and electoral laws led to the establishment of a range of political parties (some 45 in all). However, most of these were insignificant and only three parties emerged to dominate the political landscape after 1990. Two of these were the former ruling parties of the YAR and the PDRY; the third was a newcomer established prior to the holding of parliamentary elections in 1993. The GPC was established in 1982 in the YAR to consolidate the position of President Ali Abdullah Saleh and to undermine the secret organizations that had emerged in response to the ban on political parties in that country, as well as the local development organizations that predated Saleh's rule. Most of the country's religious, traditional and tribal forces were represented in the party, as well as business leaders and intellectuals. However, the most powerful figures were those with personal, family or tribal ties to the President. Thus, from the outset the party comprised a diversity of political orientations and interests, and lacked a clear guiding ideology; its members included Islamists, former socialists, tribal leaders, moderates and hard-line religious conservatives. The stated goals of the party were those of state-building, democracy, constitutional rule, modernization and the establishment of military and security institutions. However, in effect, the GPC functioned as a source of political patronage to be distributed by the President.

The YSP was the most ideologically cohesive of the large parties in the country, although it too comprised a diversity of political positions within its membership, which led to schismatic cleavages and the transformation of an originally Marxist party into one which espoused social democratic ideals. The party emerged from the communist movement that developed in the course of the struggle against British colonial control in the South in the late 1960s. Following the British withdrawal and the establishment of the PDRY, all political parties were amalgamated into the YSP, which became the only legal party. The YSP adopted socialist policies of nationalization and land redistribution. Internal divisions led to a two-week civil war in 1986, from which al-Baid emerged as leader. From this point on the party moved towards positions in favour of more pluralistic politics, as well as unification.

The third party, the Yemeni Congregation for Reform (generally known as al-Islah), is a creation of the post-unification period. It was established in September 1990, largely by former GPC members, as a vehicle for the interests of more religiously orientated members of the ruling party and also to combat the YSP. Like the GPC, al-Islah comprised a range of ideological orientations. Three tendencies were at play within the party in its early days: tribal forces, Muslim Brotherhood elements, and those of a more radical Islamist orientation. The radical tendency has often been identified with Abdulmajid al-Zindani, a controversial figure who maintained close relations with President Saleh, while in 2004 being designated as a global terrorist by the US Treasury. The diversity that characterizes al-Islah led to the emergence of divergent party positions on democracy and other sensitive political issues, such as the application of *Shari'a* (Islamic law) and the role of women in public life. The radical wing of the party, under al-Zindani, opposed unification in the first place because it provided for a democratic system of governance and for co-operation with the secular, leftist regime of the South. The Muslim Brotherhood component of the party, by contrast, supported democratic participation. However, in the post-unification period, this tended to be expressed in terms of support for pluralism, freedom, justice, and law and order, rather than democracy. Others seemed to adopt democratic practices for purely instrumental reasons.

POLITICAL DEVELOPMENT IN POST-UNIFICATION YEMEN

The first parliamentary elections in the new republic took place in April 1993, after several postponements. The elections were preceded by a period of widespread political participation, in the course of which several mass conferences took place. A nine-day conference was held in December 1991 under the banner of the Bakil tribal confederation; it resulted in a 33-point resolution that called for judicial independence, the strengthening of representative parliamentary and local bodies, and free elections, among other demands. Seven other tribe-based mass conferences took place in 1992, making similar demands for the rule of law, political pluralism, economic development and local autonomy, and al-Islah organized a conference under the slogan 'The Quran and the Sunna Supersede the Constitution and the Law'.

The period preceding the elections was also characterized by increasing levels of tension between the GPC and the YSP, intensified by a series of bombings and political killings that began in mid-1992. This was followed by a brief reconciliation between Saleh and al-Baid, and agreement on the holding of elections. However, the election results merely deepened the political crisis. Prior to the election 2.7m. adults, including 77% of eligible males and 15% of eligible females, registered to vote, and more than 3,600 candidates, including 50 women, contested the poll, the vast majority of them running as independents. According to official figures, the turnout was 84%; however, only 43% of those eligible to vote in fact did so. The results proved to be a major disappointment for the YSP, which had overestimated its capacity to make inroads in the north, where more than 80% of the population lived. The GPC and the newcomer al-Islah emerged as the parties with the largest representation in parliament. The GPC won 123 of the 301 seats in the House of Representatives; al-Islah took 62, and the YSP won just 56 seats. Forty-eight of the remaining seats went to independents, and the rest to candidates from the smaller parties. Only two female candidates were successful, both of them supported by the YSP. The YSP was dominant in most constituencies in the south, whereas the GPC did not exert the same level of dominance in the north. Al-Islah was the only party to field candidates across the entire country, but it failed to win a single seat in the south.

In the aftermath of the elections, relations between the GPC and the YSP deteriorated. The YSP leadership feared that the logic of the electoral system doomed the party to permanent minority status, given the much smaller population of the south and its inability to win support in the north. The GPC, in turn, feared the grassroots organization of the YSP and suspected it of involvement in a series of strikes and outbreaks of rioting that took place during the transitional period. The socialists increasingly sought a greater decentralization of power, reform of the rule of law and the maintenance of some degree of autonomy for the south in the face of increasing northern domination. The northern leadership interpreted these demands as an attempt to secure control over oil reserves that had recently been discovered in the southern province of Hadramout. Political tensions were deepened by the emergent hostility between the YSP and al-Islah, which in turn reflected cultural and ideological differences between the north and south of the country. The YSP leadership was ambivalent about religion and promoted secularism, even if this secularism was largely superficial and secularization in the south limited beyond Aden. Nonetheless, the Islamists portrayed the YSP as a secular, even atheistic party which posed a threat to traditional values, while the YSP presented itself as the party of democracy and order in contrast to the backwardness of al-Islah.

After the vote, some YSP politicians suggested that the party's success in the south entitled it to regional self-rule; in September 1993 the YSP presented an 18-point plan for reform of government. This was rejected by President Saleh, and further attempts at dialogue failed. On 21 May 1994 southern leaders declared secession and the establishment of a new 'Democratic Republic of Yemen'. A short civil war ensued, with the reported loss of between 5,000 and 7,000 lives. In July 1994 northern troops entered Aden, bringing the conflict to a close. The victorious GPC clamped down on southern 'secessionists' and opposition figures, especially in the south, were arrested, often on the basis of little or no evidence. The northern regime confiscated lands, private homes and wealth from leading supporters of the YSP in the south and distributed these to GPC loyalists. Northern elites began to exploit the resources of the south, including the oilfields of Hadramout and Aden port, as hundreds of socialists, dissidents and government critics left the country. None the less, although Saleh and the GPC leadership took advantage of the outcome of the conflict to consolidate their position across Yemen, there was recognition that some degree of power-sharing with the south was necessary in order to avoid the permanent alienation of its population. Although the level of southern representation in government fell, southern politicians were appointed to cabinet positions that had been held by the YSP. These included Faisal bin Shamlan, who contested the presidential election in September 2006, and Abd al-Rabbuh Mansour Hadi, who became Vice-President in October 2004 and in February 2012 succeeded Saleh as President (see below).

That the outcome of the civil war was disastrous for Yemen's experiment with democracy became clear when, in September 1994, a series of constitutional amendments was adopted without being put to a referendum. The Presidential Council that had been elected by parliament under the 1991 Constitution was replaced by a Majlis al-Shura (Consultative Council), which was appointed by the President. The President was given the power to appoint the Prime Minister and the Vice-President, to pass laws when parliament was not in session, to dissolve parliament and to declare a state of emergency. Furthermore, the southern legal code was nullified. In October 1994 Saleh agreed to enter into a coalition with al-Islah. This coalition lasted until further parliamentary elections were held in April 1997.

The GPC won a landslide 226 seats in parliament in the elections of April 1997, albeit with 43% of the vote. Al-Islah came a distant second, with 63 seats from 23% of the vote. (Both seat totals included independents who joined the GPC and al-Islah after the elections.) No other party won more than three seats. The YSP boycotted the poll. The dominance of the GPC was expressed in the fact that it won a higher number of seats in 1997 with fewer candidates than in 1993. The scale of the party's victory meant that it no longer required the support of al-Islah to form a government. Following the elections, the Islamist party entered into opposition, notwithstanding persistent links between its leadership and the GPC. From the 1997 elections until the uprising of 2011, the GPC was the dominant party in Yemeni parliamentary politics, ending the brief period in which it shared power with others. This dominant position underpinned other shifts in the political landscape, paving the way for the development of an unlikely coalition between the YSP and al-Islah almost a decade after the civil war.

The dominance of the GPC was underscored in Yemen's first direct presidential election, held in September 1999, in which Saleh ran against a virtually unknown member of his own party. The law provided that two candidates should run in order to ensure a genuinely competitive election. However, the Constitution also required that prospective candidates should secure the support of at least 10% of members of parliament. Only the GPC and al-Islah were in a position to do this. Al-Islah opted not to contest the elections and to support President Saleh, and the opposition parties selected the Secretary-General of the YSP, Ali Saleh Obad, a southerner, as their preferred candidate. However, although he was generally acknowledged as having little chance of success, the regime refused to approve his candidacy. Instead, Najib Qahtan al-Sha'abi was chosen to contest the election against Saleh. Al-Sha'abi was a southern member of the ruling party and son of a former President of South Yemen. Saleh won the elections by a landslide. Official figures gave him 96.3% of the vote, with turnout reported to be 66%. However, unofficial estimates suggest that the vote for al-Sha'abi reached up to 40% in some areas outside the north of Yemen, and that the real turnout might have been closer to one-half of the official figure.

President Saleh's overwhelming victory in the presidential election was followed in 2001 by another set of constitutional amendments that entrenched his grip on power. These eased restrictions on the President and his ability to dissolve parliament. The amendments also increased the presidential term from five to seven years. As Saleh had been elected only in 1999, this meant that, under the terms of the Constitution, he could serve until 2013. There was widespread speculation in the press that this was intended to enable Saleh's son, Ahmad, to succeed him, as Ahmad would by then have reached the minimum age of 40 years required for eligibility for presidential office.

THE EMERGENCE OF THE JOINT MEETING PARTIES

The increasing dominance of Saleh and the GPC of political life in Yemen led to a realignment among opposition forces. This ultimately led to the formation in 2002 of the Joint Meeting Parties (JMP), a loose alliance of opposition parties in which al-Islah and the YSP were the dominant players. Such an alliance was, on the face of it, extremely unlikely. The two parties had been in violent conflict with one another just eight years earlier, when some leaders of al-Islah had been at the forefront of fomenting anti-socialist feeling, decrying the 'atheism' of the YSP. Meanwhile, socialist leaders regarded al-Islah as a reactionary force doing the bidding of Saudi Arabia. The transformation in their relationship was due in large part to two factors. First, despite the civil conflict of 1994, Saleh sought in its aftermath to reincorporate what remained of the YSP leadership in the country into the political system. He declared an amnesty for most of the southern leaders, and the party was permitted to resume political activity. As a result, although weakened, the YSP was able to reclaim a place in Yemeni political life in spite of its defeat in the civil war. Second, the resounding victory of the GPC in the 1997 parliamentary elections ended its dependence on al-Islah. As a consequence, al-Islah began to move closer to other opposition parties and increasingly to espouse commitment to democratic ideals.

The change in orientation within al-Islah was matched by developments within the YSP, which had begun to restructure around reformist figures like Jarallah Omar, who argued in favour of re-engagement with President Saleh and the GPC and a return to electoral politics following the boycott of the 1997 parliamentary elections. These developments ultimately led to the formation of the JMP, which—together with the two larger parties—also included the Popular Nasserist Unity Party, the Union of Popular Forces (a small Zaidi party), the conservative Zaidi Hizb al-Haqq and the Baath National Party.

The JMP was formed just before the parliamentary elections of April 2003. One of its first initiatives was agreement on a memorandum of understanding which committed the member parties not to compete against other JMP members, either directly or indirectly. However, in practice, opposition party candidates lost to each other in a number of constituencies. The elections were contested by 19 parties, who put forward more than 900 candidates, together with over 400 independents, contesting 301 seats. More than 8m. people registered to vote, and the number of women who registered rose to 1.8m. According to official figures, turnout was 76%. Despite the increased level of co-operation between the opposition parties, the GPC won another landslide victory, taking 238 seats in the House of Representatives, although with just 58% of the popular vote. Al-Islah's share declined from 63 to 46 seats, and the YSP won eight seats. The electoral system disproportionately favoured the ruling party—under a more proportional system, the opposition parties would have won almost one-third of the seats.

Despite the disappointing outcome of the parliamentary elections, there were further steps towards co-operation within the JMP with the publication in 2005 of a programme for comprehensive national and political reform, agreed by the founding parties of the alliance. This called for the replacement of the political system, which concentrated power in the President, with a parliamentary system, the separation of powers, an independent judiciary and administrative decentralization. Co-operation among opposition forces reached a high point with agreement by the JMP on a single candidate to oppose Saleh in the second presidential election, which was held in September 2006. Faisal bin Shamlan was a former Minister for Oil and Mineral Resources who had indirect links both to the PDRY and to the Muslim Brotherhood. Bin Shamlan was generally seen as an honest, if uncharismatic, figure. According to official results, he won 21.8% of the vote to Saleh's 77.2%, although there were allegations of electoral malpractice.

The presidential election of 2006 was the last to be held before the Yemeni uprising of 2011. During the intervening period President Saleh attempted to consolidate his grip on power and to ensure the appointment of close allies and family members to key positions in the political and economic arenas. In February 2009 Saleh postponed parliamentary elections that were due to be held later that year, in the face of the threat of an opposition boycott. The decision to postpone the elections came in spite of the fact that the regime appeared to be stronger than ever. However, by the late 2000s it was also confronted with regional challenges that threatened national unity.

THE AL-HIRAK AND AL-HOUTHI MOVEMENTS

The al-Houthi movement developed in Saada province in the north of Yemen, near the Saudi Arabian border, in the early years of the 20th century. From June 2004 Saada was the site of a conflict between members of a Zaidi revivalist group, al-Shabab al-Mo'men (the Believing Youth), and the regime, which resulted in thousands of casualties and significant destruction. The group was established in the 1990s and quickly became associated with Hussain al-Houthi, a charismatic figure whose rhetoric drew support while antagonizing the Government. Members of the al-Houthi family claim descent from the Prophet Muhammad, and the family purports to defend Zaidi identity from dilution in a wider Sunni Islamic environment. The movement was motivated in part by what was seen as economic discrimination against the province of Saada, as well as the regime's tolerance of Saudi-inspired anti-Shi'a agitation in the north of the country. This included the expression, by Saudi-trained clerics, of the view that Zaidis and other Shi'as are heretics and apostates from true Islam.

Direct conflict with the regime was triggered when militants belonging to the group shouted anti-US and anti-Israeli chants in a Saada mosque in the presence of the President. Attempts at reconciliation between Saleh and al-Houthi failed and in June 2004 the regime sought to arrest him. Fighting broke out and lasted until al-Houthi was killed by the security forces in September 2004. However, this did not end the conflict, as members of al-Houthi's family assumed prominent roles in the organization. His brother, Abd al-Malik al-Houthi, took over the leadership, denouncing the regime's relationship with the USA, while the Government claimed that the rebels sought to establish a theocratic Zaidi state in Yemen with the support of Iran. The latter claim was much disputed in the early years of the conflict, which was largely fuelled by local grievances over economic marginalization, market access and the lack of infrastructure in the region. There were a further five rounds of fighting between 2004 and 2010, with the loss of several thousand lives and the displacement of hundreds of thousands of people. Although a number of ceasefires were implemented, the regime did little to address the underlying causes of conflict, which were transformed from local grievances into deep-seated resentment of the regime in San'a.

The second regional challenge to the regime came from the south. Al-Hirak had its origins in the 1994 civil war, after which Aden was sacked by the northern army, private homes and land were confiscated, southern military commanders were dismissed by the regime in San'a, and many southerners in the army and civil service were retired. Officials from the north came to dominate the leading provincial offices and other key posts, while the southern economy deteriorated. In late 2006 a group of military pensioners began to organize protests and sit-ins demanding higher pensions and/or reinstatement in the army. Their specific demands were quickly overtaken by the more broadly based grievances of the population as civil servants, lawyers, teachers and the unemployed joined what became known as the Southern Movement (Al-Hirak al-Janoubi). In December 2007 the funerals of four men killed by the security forces in suspicious circumstances drew hundreds of thousands of mourners. The protests in the south initially revolved around four sets of demands: equal access to government jobs, benefits and services; genuine economic and political decentralization; the establishment of the rule of law; and better stewardship of the economy. However, the regime responded to peaceful protests with 'a combination of targeted repression, limited concessions and attempted co-option', according to the International Crisis Group. Any concessions made were not part of any concerted vision for development of the south or for broader political inclusion. By 2009 al-Hirak had been transformed from a rights-based movement drawing on the principle of equality under the law to one which increasingly advocated independence for the south.

THE POLITICAL ECONOMY OF YEMEN

The regional challenges to the regime in the form of the al-Houthi and al-Hirak movements had their origins, at least in part, in economic marginalization and distress. This reflected the broader socioeconomic crisis that characterized the country by the end of the first decade of the 21st century. Yemen has a young and rapidly growing population, high levels of poverty, rising unemployment, a poorly performing economy, and diminishing oil and water reserves. Its total population was 30.5m. in mid-2021, according to UN estimates. Its birth rate is the highest in the Arab world and one of the highest globally. Life expectancy is 66.1 years, the lowest in the region. The adult literacy rate is 70.0% (54.9% for women), the second lowest in the Arab world after Morocco. It is also one of the poorest countries in the region. At least 54% of the population lives below the poverty line, although some estimate the figure to be as high as 80%; the rate of unemployment stands at 40%, and youth unemployment is closer to 80%. Yemen occupied 183rd place out of 191 countries and territories on the 2021 UN Human Development Index.

Indeed, from its creation in 1990, the new Republic of Yemen was beset by economic problems. The first of these followed the 1990–91 Gulf War. By the time of the war's outbreak the newly united country occupied a seat on the UN Security Council. Yemen, under President Saleh, opted not to support the US-led coalition in its efforts to expel Iraqi forces from Kuwait. The consequences were catastrophic for Yemen, as it found itself on the wrong side not only of the USA but also of the other Gulf states, on which it depended for aid, and in which hundreds of thousands of Yemenis had found work. After the war some 800,000 Yemeni migrants in Saudi Arabia were expelled to their home country, together with 45,000 from Kuwait and

Iraq, and several thousand more from Qatar, Bahrain and the United Arab Emirates (UAE). The Gulf states cut aid to Yemen, which had amounted to US $200m. per annum, and annual US aid was reduced from $20.5m. to $2.9m. The impact on the economy was immediate. Yemen went from running a balance of payments surplus to running an increasing deficit, and the rate of inflation rose from 33% in 1991 to 120% in 1994. Foreign debt grew to approximately $8,900m. by the end of September 1994, and debt as a percentage of gross domestic product (GDP) increased from 100.1% in 1990 to 189% in 1994.

By 1995 the regime had little alternative but to turn to international financial institutions for assistance in reducing its debt burden and carrying out economic reforms. These included subsidy cuts, price and trade liberalization, and the privatization of state enterprises. The first phase of structural adjustment was implemented in March 1995. To begin with, this was focused on restoring monetary stability. The prices of oil products were increased by 80% and the electricity tariff by 60%, the government budget was reduced, the official exchange rate was lowered, interest rates were increased, and treasury bills were issued. There was no reform of fuel subsidies, which were—and continue to be—a key source of patronage and corruption. In the second phase the state budget again decreased but government revenues increased, inflation came under control, the budget deficit was eliminated and the hard currency reserves of the central bank increased. However, this was achieved with significant social and economic costs to a society ill-equipped to sustain economic stagnation. Despite, or because of, the reforms, poverty and unemployment continued to rise. GDP growth decelerated from 4.6% to 2% in 2004, an insufficient rate to offset the rate of population growth—one of the highest in the Arab world.

Although inflation decreased in the decade up to 2007, for many of the poorest Yemenis this brought no benefit as the cost of essential foodstuffs increased amid rising international prices and the reduction in subsidies. By 2010 the unemployment rate was reported to be as high as 40%, and 43% of the population (some 10.3m. people) were living on US $2 or less a day. In 2010, as part of a further set of negotiations with the International Monetary Fund (IMF), some subsidies on fuel and essential food supplies were removed; this had a significant impact on the poor. The problem was exacerbated by the fact that Yemen is overwhelmingly dependent on imported food: 90% of wheat and 100% of rice is imported. In addition, the reforms were accompanied by a reduction in public sector employment, which had the effect of further limiting work opportunities and reducing incomes for many households. Although between 2000 and 2005 overall poverty levels fell by more than five percentage points to 35%, the gains were largely confined to Yemen's cities. Urban poverty levels fell by over one-tenth, but in rural areas poverty levels remained static, at about 40%, and even increased by 10–15 percentage points in the most deprived areas. From 2007 the impact of the global financial crisis led to even higher poverty levels. By 2010 some 47.6% of rural Yemenis were living below the poverty line, compared with 29.9% in the cities.

Despite the adoption of reforms, Yemen continued to face serious economic problems. This was due partly to the level of reliance on the country's diminishing oil reserves. Between 2000 and 2009 the hydrocarbons sector accounted for 20%–30% of the country's GDP, 80%–90% of exports and 70%–80% of government revenues. However, oil output peaked in 2002 and thereafter entered a steady decline. None the less, the regime ran up successive budget deficits and continued to increase spending on military wages and fuel subsidies.

As was the case elsewhere in the region, the implementation of market-orientated reforms had profound political, as well as socioeconomic, consequences: it was accompanied by the emergence of a crony capitalist class allied to the regime, and dependent on it for favour. Regime control over the process of economic liberalization increased the resources available to it and served to entrench its grip on power until this was challenged in early 2011. In the Yemeni case, the regime ensured that the distribution of the new economic opportunities that flowed from reform remained under its control and became a tool that could be used to strengthen the position of key members of the elite and to co-opt opposition forces. Legal and illegal stratagems, which included access to subsidized fuel and 'sweetheart' deals on state contracts, were used as incentives for politicians and tribal leaders to co-operate with the regime. Favoured actors were allowed access to key sectors of the economy. These included import and export licences, control of oil concessions, oil distribution rights and lucrative contracts to provide mobile phone and online services. Several military personnel controlled the state-subsidized Yemen Economic Corporation, and some members of the military were widely believed to be implicated in diesel and arms smuggling. Members of tribal groups, such as the key al-Ahmar family, exploited their positions to gain valuable import licences, work as partners with international firms, win government contracts and enter the formal economy through control of banks and telecommunications. Members of the President's family also benefited directly through appointment to important posts in state enterprises. According to one report, by the time of the 2011 uprising ownership of the 'commanding heights' of the Yemeni economy was concentrated in the hands of a tiny elite: just 10 families controlled more than 80% of imports, manufacturing, processing, banking, and the telecommunications and transport sectors.

THE YEMENI UPRISING OF 2011

Given the closed nature of the political system, the increasing immiseration of much of the country's population, and the entrenched corruption and nepotism that characterized the economic and political spheres, Yemen was ripe for instability when the wave of uprisings swept the Arab world in 2011. On 15 January, a day after President Zine al-Abidine Ben Ali was forced from power in Tunisia, several dozen student, civil society and opposition activists attended a rally in San'a. Hundreds of activists gathered in front of San'a University, while thousands of protesters gathered elsewhere calling for change.

At first the protests were directed at economic grievances, corruption and widespread concern that President Saleh was grooming his son, Ahmad Ali Abdullah, to succeed him as leader. However, following the President's announcement on 2 February 2011 that he would not seek an additional term in office and that his son would not take over, there were more protests in San'a and Aden. In mid-February tens of thousands of protesters gathered in San'a, Aden and Taiz. As elsewhere in the 2011 uprisings, young people were at the forefront of the movement in Yemen. Some of these belonged to the youth organizations of established political parties, but many had little or no previous political experience. For the most part, the legal opposition parties and established civil society organizations kept their distance from the protests in the early weeks. However, by February the JMP threw its support behind the opposition to Saleh. As the protest movement gained momentum, the demands of the protesters became more explicit. They demanded: the immediate dismantling of the regime; the arrest of those involved in fraud or corruption; the drafting of a new constitution to transform the political system from presidential to parliamentary; a decentralized government; and full transparency.

The regime responded in a number of ways. As well as filling Tahrir Square in San'a with loyal supporters and mounting attacks on the anti-regime protesters, there were also attempts to address economic demands. The President announced pay rises and free food and gas for the military and security services, salary increases for low-paid civil servants and a reduction in income tax, as well as the introduction of new subsidies and price controls and the extension of social welfare assistance to 500,000 families. However, the announcement of concessions did little to dampen the protest movement. A key moment came on 18 March 2011 when the security forces attacked protesters in San'a during morning prayers, killing 52 people. This was the point at which key allies of the regime defected and what had begun as a popular uprising, with strong roots in economic grievance, was transformed into a conflict among elites. The opposition parties declared that dialogue with the Government was now impossible. Furthermore, there were defections from President Saleh's GPC, as about 20 members of parliament and approximately one-half of the country's ambassadors overseas resigned.

The most significant development was the defection of Maj.-Gen. Ali Mohsen al-Ahmar, a distant relative of the President and commander of the First Armoured Division. He was a significant player in the military campaign against the al-Houthi movement in Saada and was often described as the second most powerful man in Yemen. However, in the years before the uprising Ali Mohsen had fallen out with Saleh. It was long suspected that the two had agreed a deal in which the former would support the latter on the basis that Ali Mohsen would succeed Saleh in the presidential office. Saleh's increasing reliance on family members at the centre of the political, security and military apparatus and, in particular, the grooming of his son for the succession, alienated Ali Mohsen. When the opportunity arose in March 2011 directly to challenge the President, Ali Mohsen seized it by announcing that his troops would protect the protesters gathered in San'a. Further challenges to the regime came when members of the family of the late Sheikh Abdullah al-Ahmar also withdrew their support. Sadeq al-Ahmar, the eldest son, succeeded his father as paramount chief of the Hashid tribal confederation. In May there were violent clashes between Saleh's Republican Guards and Sadeq's forces, in which at least 100 people were killed. The direction that the uprising was now taking added to the increasing perception in Yemen that a largely peaceful youth-led revolutionary movement had been hijacked by elite actors, to whom the concerns of the protesters were of marginal significance.

The growing instability and violence in Yemen alarmed key external actors, in particular Saudi Arabia and the USA, each of which had persistent, sometimes overlapping but essentially different interests in the country. Saudi Arabia has long been Yemen's most important and influential neighbour. The two countries share a 1,800 km-long border, the exact line of which was long a source of dispute. It was not until the signing of the Treaty of Jeddah in 2000 that this was resolved.

Saudi Arabia was also concerned about the democratic experiment that was undertaken in Yemen after unification—a form of governance clearly at odds with the Saudi system and anathema to many. The development of the al-Houthi movement was also viewed with considerable suspicion and alarm, with frequently voiced concern that it was part of a broader Iranian strategy to challenge the Saudi position in the region, notwithstanding widespread scepticism regarding the suggestion of close links between the al-Houthis and Tehran. Whatever the basis of Saudi concerns regarding Yemeni political dynamics, the result has been a longstanding pattern of Saudi involvement in the domestic affairs of the country.

The USA's interest in Yemen is of more recent provenance. Prior to 2000 the USA had little interest in the country, not least because Yemen had failed to support the US-led campaign to dislodge Saddam Hussein's forces from Kuwait a decade earlier. However, the attack by al-Qa'ida in the Arabian Peninsula (AQAP) on the USS Cole in Aden harbour in October of that year, in which 17 US naval personnel died, changed that dynamic. The subsequent US-led 'war on terror' brought the two countries together as President Saleh, like other authoritarian rulers in the region, sought to portray himself as a necessary bulwark against Islamist terrorism. The USA began to co-operate with Yemeni security services, which were established, funded and trained with Western assistance after the attack on the USS Cole, and which were under the control of Saleh's son and nephews. None the less, the regime's apparent unwillingness to act decisively against AQAP frustrated the US Administration. An assassination attempt on the Saudi Deputy Minister of the Interior for Security Affairs in August 2009, followed in December by an attempt to bring down a US airliner over Detroit, Michigan, led to a review of US strategy in relation to Yemen, which concluded on the need to address the threat from AQAP in the short term while also working on long-term developmental challenges and securing international support to stabilize the country. None the less, US intervention remained focused on the security sphere. Since the attack on the USS Cole, the USA has provided more than US $850m. in military aid to Yemen.

External actors' concern regarding Yemen's political stability, as the events of early 2011 unfolded, prompted an early international intervention. With the support of the five permanent members of the UN Security Council as well as the European Union (EU), the Cooperation Council for the Arab States of the Gulf (Gulf Cooperation Council—GCC) devised a plan for the transfer of power from President Saleh to his Vice-President, Maj.-Gen. (later Field Marshal) Hadi. Under the plan, on which the youth protesters who had initiated the uprising were not consulted, Saleh and his family would be granted immunity from prosecution and he would retain his position as head of the GPC, while the party would enter into coalition with the JMP. The extent to which the GCC Initiative consolidated the position of established political actors in Yemen disappointed the hopes of many protesters for a more substantive democratic transition. After some delay, during which time the presidential palace was bombed (in June) and Saleh was badly injured, necessitating his departure to Saudi Arabia for medical treatment, in November he signed the agreement and Vice-President Hadi assumed power. However, he did not formally replace Saleh in the role of President until 27 February 2012.

YEMEN AFTER THE GCC INITIATIVE

The agreement, under which Saleh finally stepped down from the presidency, if not from involvement in Yemeni political life, comprised two elements. The first was the GCC Initiative; the second was an agreement on the implementation of the transitional process. The GPC and the JMP were signatories to the agreement. It is notable that under the terms of the deal the opposition parties did not replace the GPC in government. Rather, the JMP entered into coalition with the party that had dominated political life in Yemen since unification and which continued to be led by Saleh. For many in the protest movement, this represented a betrayal of their aspirations for genuine democratic reform. The agreement envisaged a two-phase transitional period. The first phase covered the period up to the holding of a presidential election in February 2012 and came to an end when the new President was inaugurated. The second phase covered the period until 2014 and was to include: consideration of constitutional change; a referendum on the Constitution; reform of electoral laws; and parliamentary and local elections, as well as a presidential election, if required.

In January 2012 parliament approved a controversial law granting immunity from prosecution to Saleh and his family. His close aides were given limited protection from prosecution for 'politically motivated' crimes other than terrorist offences. The concession of immunity to Saleh and his associates led protesters to target members of the JMP for its complicity in the deal. Members of the al-Houthi movement, who had co-operated with other elements in the protest movement, including al-Islah, began to bring weapons to protest meetings as the collaborative relationships that had formed during the uprising began to disintegrate. The first phase of the transition process ended when Hadi was inaugurated as President. As had been agreed, both the GPC and JMP agreed to endorse Hadi as the sole candidate for the office. Despite problems with the register of electors, the poll took place as scheduled on 21 February; Hadi was confirmed as President with 99.8% of the votes cast. A total of 64.8% of eligible voters turned out, which compared well with the 2006 election (when turnout was 58.1%). The level of voter participation was very low in Saada (13.3%) and some southern governorates (e.g. Lahj, 29.3%; Hadramout, 16.1%), but in others the rate was surprisingly high (e.g. Aden, 45.2%,; Abyan, 59.9%,).

The second phase of the transitional process was dominated by the establishment of a National Dialogue Conference (NDC). Its remit extended to the process of formulating a new constitution; constitutional reform; the southern issue; the situation in Saada; steps towards building a democratic system; and sustainable economic and social development. The agreement envisaged that the NDC would cover a wide range of complex, if not intractable, issues involving a diverse set of participants, yet it specified that the work of the Conference should be completed within six months. The NDC was allocated an extraordinary level of responsibility for resolving the very many difficulties that faced Yemen. It was charged not merely with overseeing the post-Saleh transition, but also with the reconfiguration of the political system in order to: satisfy the aspirations of the many groups and sectors of the population that opposed the former regime; overhaul and restore Yemen's democratic system; provide the basis for sustainable economic development; maintain the territorial integrity of the country; and eliminate the threat of radical Islamist violence. Its work was undermined, however, when youth and civil society representatives on the preparatory committee resigned and removed their representation from the NDC. The main factions of the southern movement also withdrew from the NDC, to be replaced by representatives of other southern factions, which enjoyed little support on the ground.

Despite the enormous energy invested in the dialogue process, the NDC failed to gain the support, or even the attention, of much of the population. Indeed, outside the capital, many people were unaware that it was taking place, while, over the course of its deliberations, basic security conditions deteriorated: service delivery worsened, food insecurity increased and more people died during the transition process than had been the case during the 2011 uprising.

CIVIL WAR AND THE SAUDI-LED INTERVENTION

On 21 January 2014 the final NDC document with almost 1,800 recommendations was accepted in a plenary session. Agreement was also reached on extending the transitional phase for another year. Under the terms of this agreement, Hadi would remain in office until a new President was elected, while the deadlines for drafting a new constitution and holding a referendum and fresh elections were extended. In February Hadi announced that a special committee had agreed on a six-region federal structure for Yemen—four in the north, and two in the south. Such a proposal had previously been rejected by the major political parties, and Hadi's announcement was similarly rejected almost immediately by some southern representatives. It was also rejected by the al-Houthis, who argued that the plan distributed natural resources unevenly. They claimed that it deprived the region in which their Saada homeland was located of significant resources and access to the sea. Throughout this period, while al-Houthi political representatives took part in the transitional process, their fighters continued to expand their territorial control. Having secured control of the province of Saada during the course of the 2011 uprising, they moved south. The short-lived alliance with their old adversaries, al-Islah, Ali Mohsen and the al-Ahmar family, began to fray. Tensions within the NDC between the al-Houthis and al-Islah manifested themselves in the outbreak of armed conflict between militias allied to each group. By January 2014 battles raged across the north of the country, from the border with Saudi Arabia to the gates of the city of San'a. As the economy entered rapid decline Hadi introduced a cut in fuel subsidies in order to secure financial aid from the IMF and the World Bank. The protests that ensued gave the al-Houthis the excuse to enter and take control of San'a by September.

The al-Houthi seizure of San'a was made possible in part by a dramatic shift in political dynamics. In its initial phases, former President Saleh and his supporters accepted the transitional process, on the assumption that his continued leadership of the GPC would allow him to maintain influence in public life. However, as Hadi, under pressure from the international community, gradually moved to exclude Saleh and his family from positions of influence, this position changed. By 2014 an utterly unexpected reconfiguration of forces had developed as Saleh and the al-Houthis entered into an alliance of convenience based on their newly shared opponents: Hadi, al-Islah and Ali Mohsen. The al-Houthi expansion was greatly aided by the co-operation, or at least non-resistance, of forces loyal to former President Saleh. By February 2015 Hadi had fled to Aden, where he sought to re-establish his government.

In March 2015 the situation in Yemen was transformed once more as Saudi Arabia led a military intervention that dramatically escalated the conflict. The coalition included Egypt, Morocco, Jordan, Sudan, Kuwait, Oman and the UAE, the last of which played the most significant role after Saudi Arabia. The USA, the UK and France also supported the Saudi-led intervention, which had as its core objectives the defeat of the al-Houthi movement and the restoration of Hadi to power.

In the early phase of the conflict, the al-Houthis and their allies expanded from their northern stronghold into southern territory, forcing Hadi to flee into exile in Saudi Arabia. Despite facing resistance in places, the combination of al-Houthi militias and elements of the army loyal to former President Saleh proved too strong for their adversaries. The Saudi-led aerial campaign had some effect, but largely served to terrorize civilians and contribute to a worsening humanitarian situation. However, the al-Houthi forces and their allies were repelled from Aden and large parts of the surrounding governorates by southern militias supported by the UAE. The second year of the conflict was marked largely by stalemate. However, by the end of the third year a split in the al-Houthi-Saleh alliance had led to the murder of the former President by his erstwhile allies. This was followed by the assertion of al-Houthi control over the northern highlands and the Red Sea coast. By late 2017 the country had effectively become fragmented into a number of zones of control. The al-Houthi forces controlled the north west of the country; Emirati-supported forces became the most important security actors in the southern governorates; and in the northern-central governorates and in the northern parts of Hadramout governorate, in the east, military and security actors associated with al-Islah performed most security and military functions.

Meanwhile, in April 2016 indirect peace negotiations began in Kuwait. These made little progress; a ceasefire was repeatedly breached, and the negotiations were suspended in early August, when the al-Houthis and the GPC announced the formation of a 'Supreme Political Council' to run the country. This was rejected by the government delegation as tantamount to a new 'coup'. By this point, the Saudi-led coalition together with forces loyal to President Hadi had reconquered large parts of Yemen. However, the al-Houthi forces and their allies retained control of San'a and significant territory elsewhere. In September 2018 the newly appointed UN Special Envoy for Yemen, Martin Griffiths, tried to revive diplomacy by attempting to set up 'pre-talks' in order to persuade Hadi's Government and the al-Houthis to sign up to a formal negotiation process. The UN conceded that the gap between the two sides was too great to allow for direct talks to begin without prior agreement on a framework for negotiations. Fundamental difficulties persisted. From the perspective of Hadi's Government, no concession needed to be made as UN Security Council Resolution 2216 of April 2015 had appealed to the al-Houthis to lay down their arms so that Hadi, 'the legitimate president', could return to San'a and oversee the completion of the transitional process. On the other hand, the al-Houthis claimed that their assumption of power in 2015 was a 'popular revolution' and that they were fighting not against the Hadi Government but against the combined threats of Saudi Arabia, the UAE, AQAP and Islamic State. The UN initiative stalled when the al-Houthi delegation failed to attend preliminary discussions in Geneva, Switzerland, in September 2018. The al-Houthis rejected a ceasefire offer from Saudi Arabia in March 2021 and refused to engage with an attempt by the Omani Government to launch a peace process later that year.

Since early February 2021 the conflict has centred on the al-Houthi offensive on the city of Marib, about 170 km east of San'a. The assault began in early 2020 but intensified in early 2021. Saudi airstrikes have prevented the al-Houthis from making further progress towards the city. Marib is of particular significance for a number of reasons, most notably as it is the only major city in northern Yemen that is under the control of the internationally recognized Government. If the al-Houthis succeeded in taking the city, they would remove not only the presence of Hadi's Government from the north, but could also create conditions leading to direct negotiations with the Saudis. This is the reason why the al-Houthis did not respond when the UN Special Envoy called for dialogue to be held in Oman.

Despite the failure of negotiations on a political solution to the conflict, all sides agreed on a two-month ceasefire in April 2022. The ceasefire was sponsored by the UN Special Envoy for Yemen, Hans Grundberg (who had been appointed in

September 2021 to succeed Griffiths), supported by Saudi Arabia and the UAE, and welcomed by Iran. The ceasefire held, being renewed for two months in June and again in August, but while it paved the way for a number of confidence-building measures, including the release of 163 al-Houthi prisoners by the Saudis, there was considerable scepticism regarding the likelihood that it would lead to the conclusion of a political settlement. In June 2022 Abd al-Malik al-Houthi delivered a virtual speech to rallies in Taiz in which he declared that he would keep moving forward until a decisive triumph had been secured. In the same month, the US Special Envoy for Yemen, Timothy Lenderking, stated that the war was not over, describing the situation as a 'lull' and a 'truce'.

The ceasefire was supported by both Saudi Arabia and the UAE, but for very different reasons. For Saudi Arabia, it represented an opportunity to reduce the direct threat to the kingdom from al-Houthi attacks while bringing anti-al-Houthi forces closer together. In supporting the new Presidential Leadership Council (PLC, which was formed in Yemen shortly after the ceasefire was agreed—see below), the Saudi leadership was seeking to strengthen its position in the country, which had been weakened by its failure to achieve its objectives in entering the conflict in the first instance. For the UAE, meanwhile, the opposite was the case—its leverage in Yemen had been greatly increased, as reflected in the number of UAE-backed figures in the PLC.

The divisions within the anti-al-Houthi camp led to a dramatic re-ordering of government in Yemen in April 2022. Days after the UN-sponsored ceasefire took effect, Hadi resigned the presidency, dismissed divisive Vice-President Ali Mohsen al-Ahmar, and handed power to the newly formed PLC. The move was prompted to a significant extent by Saudi Arabia, which responded to the leadership changes with a pledge of US $3,000m. in aid, supported by the UAE. Leadership of the PLC was entrusted to Rashad al-Alimi, formerly one of Hadi's closest advisers. Al-Alimi had held a number of positions in the security and intelligence sectors between 2000 and 2011 and had continued to be active in the GPC in the years that followed the uprising. He also had close ties to both Saudi Arabia and the USA—just hours before his appointment he met with Lenderking. The composition of the eight-member PLC represented an attempt to integrate a diverse array of anti-al-Houthi forces into a single organizational framework. To that end, its membership included Tariq Saleh, a nephew of the former President, as well as four members from the south with close links to the UAE. However, while the establishment of the PLC was welcomed by those who saw it as removing obstacles to co-operation among anti-al-Houthi forces, with the potential to lead to negotiations on a political settlement to the conflict, it was also criticized for failing adequately to represent Yemen's political and regional diversity.

The 2022 ceasefire led to a marked decline in the scale of the conflict, while hopes for a longer-term political solution received a boost when talks brokered by the People's Republic of China in March 2023 led to a restoration of diplomatic relations between Saudi Arabia and Iran, which had been suspended since 2016. The breakthrough had its origins in the Saudi acceptance of the 2022 truce in Yemen and the period of calm that followed on its border with al-Houthi-controlled territory.

However, the conflict has deepened an already serious humanitarian crisis in the country. In November 2021 the UN estimated that the death toll from the war would exceed 370,000 by the end of that year. According to the UN High Commissioner for Human Rights, airstrikes by the Saudi-led coalition were responsible for over two-thirds of civilian deaths. Al-Houthi forces were also accused of responsibility for mass civilian casualties, particularly during the siege of Taiz, the country's third largest city. By the end of 2022 some 4.5m. people were internally displaced, and approximately 316,000 more were seeking asylum in neighbouring countries. In addition, Yemen is host to almost 100,000 refugees and asylum seekers, many from the Horn of Africa. According to UN figures for 2022, about four out of every five Yemenis (some 21.6m. people) needed emergency aid, while 17m. people were food insecure. This included more than 2m. children suffering from acute malnutrition, while some 400,00 children were facing starvation. At least 24.3m. people were in urgent need of water, sanitation and hygiene assistance, and 19.7m. lacked access to adequate health care. Furthermore, Yemen has faced challenges relating to infectious diseases. The largest outbreak of cholera in the country in modern times began in late 2016. Since then, over 1m. cases have been recorded, and several thousand people, mostly children, have died from the disease.

In April 2020 the first recorded case of the novel coronavirus disease COVID-19 in Yemen was detected, in Hadramout. According to Our World in Data, as of 1 September 2023 11,945 confirmed cases of COVID-19 had been recorded in Yemen, including 2,159 related deaths. At that time only 2.4% of the population had been fully vaccinated against the virus; this was one of the lowest rates worldwide. Most of the victims were aged between 40 and 60 years old—significantly younger than the average age of those who had died in Europe and the USA. It is highly likely that many more Yemenis than officially recorded have died of COVID-19 without having sought formal medical treatment; many more sudden deaths were recorded in southern Yemen from May 2020 onwards than would normally be expected. The impact of the pandemic exacerbated the economic crisis facing the country. Yemeni economists forecast a dramatic drop in migrant remittances, which in recent years had been the country's largest source of foreign currency earnings, owing to the economic contraction in Saudi Arabia and elsewhere in the region as a result of the COVID-19 pandemic. In addition, international aid agencies reduced their operations in Yemen in response to funding shortfalls, and the drop in international oil prices significantly reduced the value of Yemen's only significant export in 2020 (see Economy); by late 2021, however, prices had recovered to pre-pandemic levels and following Russia's invasion of Ukraine in February 2022 they rose even further.

The humanitarian crisis in Yemen has been exacerbated by the outbreak of hostilities in Ukraine following Russia's invasion of that country in February 2022. Over one-third of Yemen's wheat imports usually come from Russia and Ukraine. Between February and September the price of wheat rose by 50%, contributing to a 97% rise since September 2021. In addition, donor funding has declined as the international focus on Yemen has weakened. At an international pledging conference in February 2023, some US $1,200m. was pledged, although the sum required to meet the country's humanitarian needs was estimated at $4,300m.

The conflict in Yemen has also led to a significant deterioration in the human rights situation in the country. The environment in areas under al-Houthi control has been likened to that of a 'police state'. Repression, including human rights abuses, of members of the opposition and civil rights activists has become commonplace. In areas under their control, al-Houthi forces arbitrarily detain critics and opponents, as well as journalists, human rights defenders and members of the Baha'i community, subjecting them to detention without access to legal representation, unfair trials and even enforced 'disappearance'. Human rights work in particular has been a target of repression. Working in the sphere of human rights has exposed activists to criticism, accusations of treachery and the possibility of physical harm. In July 2019 the al-Houthi-operated 'Specialized Criminal Court in San'a' sentenced 30 academics and political figures to death on charges including espionage on behalf of the Saudi-led coalition.

However, such practices are not confined to just one side in the conflict. Forces associated with the Southern Transitional Council (STC, a secessionist group that has enjoyed Emirati support) have committed human rights violations and are thus also viewed critically by many in southern Yemen, while the STC treats peacebuilding as threatening and a front for its rivals. In particular, the existence of a network of secret prisons was revealed, and several dozen people have been 'disappeared'. In 2018 Amnesty International reported on the creation by the UAE in southern Yemen of a parallel security structure, which was outside the law and where serious violations apparently went unchecked. Furthermore, local human rights organizations have reported arbitrary detentions being carried out by government forces, as well as by STC forces in the governorates that are partly under their control (chiefly Lahj, Abyan and Shabwah).

Over the course of the conflict, the al-Houthis and their opponents have engaged in the surveillance of political opposition and human rights activists, arbitrary detention, torture and the use of the death penalty. Furthermore, external actors have introduced new forms of combat, notably the use of drone (unmanned aerial vehicle) technology to target prominent al-Houthi leaders and a growing reliance on foreign mercenaries. In February 2020 the UN Panel of Experts on Yemen concluded that Iran was supplying the al-Houthis with advanced weaponry and high-technology components for the production of weaponry, including missiles and drones. The al-Houthis' opponents in the Saudi-led coalition rely on larger, Chinese-made drones to target al-Houthi leaders. In addition, the anti-al-Houthi coalition has relied on foreign mercenaries from a variety of countries in the course of the conflict. These include Eritrean and Sudanese fighters, as well as combatants from Colombia, Panama, Chile and El Salvador. All these developments have led to a deepening of the political crisis and made its resolution even more intractable.

The conflict has also had a chilling effect on civil society in Yemen. The areas under al-Houthi control have witnessed the most severe restrictions on the civil society space, including repression of civil society activity and the closure of organizations affiliated to political opponents or in receipt of Western funding. Civil society activists have been threatened with abduction, arrest and other forms of harassment. Meanwhile, in areas outside al-Houthi control, civil society activists have been threatened by religious groups, militias and newly established security forces. Some 70% of Yemeni civil society organizations have closed, and most have faced violence, looting, provocations, harassment or the freezing of assets, such that it is now difficult for such organizations in Yemen to operate, owing to threats from state and non-state actors alike. In response, some groups have moved to online activism, which is viewed as lower risk than 'street politics'. That said, activists who operate online for political ends also run the risk of arrest, kidnapping or murder, especially in al-Houthi-controlled areas

However, the conflict has not ended popular mobilization in Yemen, particularly in the southern governorates, which have witnessed an increase in protests driven by deteriorating economic conditions. This has been the case both in areas controlled by the internationally recognized Government and in areas controlled by the STC. In September 2021 there were 54 demonstrations, in Aden, Shabwah, Abyan, Socotra, Lahj and Hadramout. By contrast, there were no reports of significant protest in al-Houthi-controlled areas.

The conflict in Yemen has been understood as an expression of domestic and regional political cleavages. For some observers, it has been seen as representing a marriage of convenience between the al-Houthis—marginalized in the negotiations on the GCC settlement after the uprising and further marginalized in the era of President Hadi's administration—and forces loyal to former President Saleh, who sought to capitalize on al-Houthi grievance as well as the movement's fighting prowess in order to reclaim the position of influence that they had enjoyed before the handover of power to Hadi. The conflict has also been read in terms of the broader rivalry between Saudi Arabia and Iran for influence in the region. While there is a great deal of substance underpinning both of these approaches, each simplifies the intrinsic complexity of the situation in Yemen. First, almost as much divides as unites the warring blocs. Second, at the regional level, the essentially sectarian framing of the conflict that underpins its analysis as a 'proxy war' between Sunni Saudi Arabia and Shi'a Iran occludes more than it reveals.

At the domestic level, the al-Houthis and Saleh loyalists joined forces on the basis of a shared enemy in the Hadi Government and the new political order that ensued from the GCC agreement. In the early stages of the 2011 uprising, the al-Houthis decided to join the broad coalition of forces opposed to Saleh's regime. This included al-Islah, the al-Ahmar clan and Ali Mohsen, who was appointed as Hadi's Vice-President in April 2016. However, the al-Houthi movement had its origins in attempts to protect Shi'a Zaidi culture and traditions from encroachment by Wahhabi and Salafi teachings of a kind promoted by elements in al-Islah, as well as Ali Mohsen, and, at times, Saleh. The al-Houthis thus rejected the GCC deal, favoured a complete reform of Yemen's political system and a rejection of the entrenched position of old elites such as the established political parties (al-Islah and the GPC), as well as the al-Ahmars and Ali Mohsen.

Saleh and his supporters initially accepted the GCC Initiative in the expectation that it would allow for his continued role in political life, a view sustained by the fact that he retained leadership of the GPC, even as he handed the presidency to his deputy. However, as President Hadi gradually moved, with the support of the USA, the UK and the EU, to exclude him and his family from positions of influence, resentment of the new political order grew. By 2014 an utterly unexpected reconfiguration of relationships had developed, as former President Saleh and the al-Houthis began to co-operate in opposition to Hadi's Government. The expansion of the al-Houthi militia was greatly assisted by the co-operation of forces affiliated to Saleh. Nonetheless, important tensions persisted between the two sides. Many in the GPC who assisted the initial al-Houthi advance were alarmed by their seizure of San'a, and the party opposed the al-Houthis' announcement in February 2015 that they had created a revolutionary committee to oversee state operations. Longer-standing differences between the two sides also exist. The al-Houthis have been viewed as religious radicals by many in the GPC, a largely centrist, non-religious party, and the al-Houthis held Saleh responsible for the death in 2004 of their leader, Hussain al-Houthi.

The underlying tensions received their clearest expression when Saleh was murdered in early December 2017 by al-Houthi forces who had accused him of collaboration with their enemies. In the weeks prior to his death Saleh had signalled that he intended to change sides and was seeking to negotiate with Saudi Arabia. Since the death of Saleh, the al-Houthis have faced challenges within the territory that they control, particularly from tribal actors. In March 2019 the al-Houthis quashed a rebellion by tribal forces in Hajjah governorate that had reportedly been triggered following an invasion of tribal territory by the al-Houthis. In response, the al-Houthis carried out a series of executions of tribal leaders who had opposed them, as well as collective punishment of their families, notably the destruction of their houses. In the same period there were a number of clashes in Amran governorate, which culminated in the killing of a tribal leader whom the al-Houthis had accused of defecting from the group, as well as significant infighting in Ibb between opposing al-Houthi factions and their local allies. In all cases, the al-Houthis suppressed the challenge that was posed to them, and many tribal leaders bemoaned the lack of support in the fight against the al-Houthis from the anti-al-Houthi coalition and forces loyal to the Hadi Government.

The coalition of domestic forces opposed to the expansion of al-Houthi control is also marked by diversity and internal divisions, comprising as it does the internationally recognized Government, GPC defectors, al-Islah, southern activists and separatists, as well as violent, jihadist groups. Restoring the internationally recognized Government forms the core justification for the Saudi-led intervention. The most important Sunni Islamist group supporting the Government is al-Islah, most of the leadership of which fled to Riyadh, Saudi Arabia, in March 2015. Al-Islah and the GPC are mutually opposed. The GPC sees al-Islah and Ali Mohsen as largely responsible for the unrest that brought down President Saleh's regime in 2011, while Saleh was seen by al-Islah as having hijacked and obstructed the transitional process. Moreover, there are also significant tensions between the Government and al-Islah, which is motivated by hostility to the al-Houthis more than by loyalty to the Government. Similarly, there are deep divisions between the Islamists and the southern separatists. The southern movement is also internally divided. Before the conflict, al-Hirak was highly decentralized, and is now even more so.

Since early 2015 the conflict in Yemen has also been marked by the renewed involvement of external actors. The intervention of Saudi Arabia was motivated by a combination of regional concerns and domestic political developments. Prior to 2015 the Saudis repeatedly suggested that close links existed between the al-Houthis and Iran, notwithstanding the profound differences between Zaidism and the

Ithna'ashara (Twelver) Shi'ism of most of Iran's population. When the al-Houthis seized power in 2015, this was seen as an expansion of Iranian influence through their Yemeni proxies.

However, any reading of the conflict as a proxy sectarian war between Saudi Arabia and Iran is simplistic. Saudi Arabia has long had an interest in its populous neighbour to the south, regarding it as a potential source of instability and challenge. Yet, although it has a history of intervention in various forms in Yemeni political life, Saudi strategy has not followed an unvarying sectarian logic. Saudi Arabia has persistently involved itself in Yemeni affairs by backing certain local actors against others, using Yemeni guest workers as leverage, buying off tribal and other leaders and conducting limited military operations. In large part, Saudi Arabia has followed what has been characterized as a policy of 'containment and maintenance', where enough support is given to whichever regime is in power to prevent state collapse, while a certain level of state dysfunction is desirable.

Iranian involvement in Yemen is less significant and even less driven by sectarian motivations. As with Saudi Arabia, historically Iran has pursued an instrumental foreign policy in Yemen, tied not to religion but to perceptions of where Iranian interests lay. Before the 2011 uprising, Saleh accused Iran of providing the al-Houthis with support, but never supplied definitive proof of this. Cables revealed by the WikiLeaks organization, which publishes secret and classified information on a range of international actors, suggest that the US embassy in San'a was unconvinced of the merit of the claims. There is little doubt that in the post-2011 period, and especially since the al-Houthi takeover of San'a, Iranian support for the al-Houthis has increased. However, it does not match the scale of Iranian commitments in the Syrian Arab Republic, Lebanon and Iraq. In January 2018 the UN Panel of Experts on Yemen concluded that Iran was in non-compliance with UN Security Council Resolution 2216 for failing to prevent the transfer of Iranian-made short-range ballistic missiles to the al-Houthis. Later in 2018 the Panel of Experts reported that Iran might have continued to violate the international arms embargo by supplying the al-Houthis with advanced weaponry. However, the significance of Iranian support might be overstated and, in any case, has been dwarfed by Saudi and Emirati expenditure on the conflict.

Whatever the role of Iran, the Saudi-led military intervention in Yemen was also linked to the succession that took place in Saudi Arabia following the death of King Abdullah bin Abd al-Aziz Al Sa'ud in January 2015. The new monarch, King Salman bin Abd al-Aziz Al Sa'ud, appointed his 29-year-old son, Mohammed bin Salman, as Deputy Crown Prince and Minister of Defence and he has since then pursued an aggressive foreign policy. The elevation of Mohammed bin Salman to Crown Prince in June 2017 tightened his control over the direction of Saudi foreign policy, and thus the outcome of the Yemeni war is linked not only to the assertion of Saudi influence in the face of what is perceived to be Iranian expansionism in the region, but also to the fortunes of the Saudi ruling family.

The view of the conflict as a proxy war between Saudi Arabia and Iran has been placed in critical perspective by the 2023 rapprochement between the two countries. Despite some expectations that this would improve prospects for a lasting peace settlement, no such result has ensued. For this to happen would require direct negotiations between Saudi Arabia and the al-Houthis. However, any agreement between the two would not necessarily include other actors, notably in the south. These include the STC, which has emerged as the strongest southern group, largely due to the support of the UAE, but also other groups in the south who do not feel represented by the separatists. In addition, the conflict has generated a war economy at elite and local levels that has benefited most of the warring parties. Many of those whose participation would be essential to negotiations on a wider political settlement have grown dependent on collecting taxes and levies in the territories they control while providing little by way of services. Any deal that restored the control of the state over those territories would threaten this. In addition, at the local level, faced with economic collapse, inflation and the absence of employment opportunities, large numbers of men, and, increasingly, children have joined armed groups as a source of income.

By late 2021 Saudi Arabia and Iran were the only key external parties to the conflict. The role of the UAE in the conflict had become increasingly significant, but in February 2020 it completed its phased military withdrawal from Yemen, although it remained involved indirectly by means of its support for proxies on the ground (see below). Southern forces supported by the UAE have made some of the few territorial gains that have occurred since the conflict began. They were central to efforts to repel forces aligned with the al-Houthi-Saleh alliance from their territories. Emirati-supported southern forces also played a crucial role in ousting AQAP from the port city of Mukalla. The UAE initially entered the conflict in Yemen in part in the hope of strengthening its alliance with Saudi Arabia. However, while its activities notionally fall under the broad umbrella of the Saudi-led coalition, they are largely planned and executed independently of Saudi oversight. Moreover, the UAE treats al-Islah—a key component of Yemen's Government—with suspicion and associates it with political radicalism and violence. Furthermore, since the outbreak of the conflict the UAE has developed a set of economic and geopolitical interests arising out of its presence in southern Yemen and its patronage of local actors. The effective division of labour which sees the Saudis operate primarily in the northern part of Yemen has given the UAE greater leverage in the south through its direct military presence and support of proxy militias. As a result, it enjoys effective control of energy infrastructure, oilfields and commercial ports, while maintaining selective patronage networks with local Salafi communities and secessionist groups. Increasingly, UAE strategy is directed to three objectives: first, the encouragement of alternative and complementary shipping routes to its main ones out of Dubai; second, the need to prevent jihadist networks from threatening the military bases that the UAE has built in the Horn of Africa—notably in Eritrea and the secessionist 'Republic of Somaliland'—since 2016, which, in turn constitute an effort to contain Iranian influence in Eastern Africa and the Indian Ocean; third, southern Yemeni regions function as a platform for the UAE's 'pivot to the East' policy, which sees it developing closer links with Asian powers such as India and China. In July 2019 the UAE announced the withdrawal and redeployment of its forces from Hodeida, ostensibly as a result of a UN-brokered ceasefire in December 2018 between pro-Government forces and the al-Houthi rebels (but in practice in response to the stalemate that characterized the conflict locally), but confirmed that it would continue its operations against militant Islamists and its support for the southern secessionists. In August 2019 the Yemeni Government criticized the UAE for carrying out airstrikes in the south of the country, ostensibly to prevent pro-Government forces from retaking Aden from fighters associated with the STC, who had seized the city in that month. The STC claimed that Saudi Arabia and Hadi's Government had emboldened Islamists (in effect al-Islah) whom they feared could seize the whole of southern Yemen. The Saudi-led coalition launched airstrikes against the STC on the following day. In November the Saudis and Emiratis negotiated a ceasefire between Hadi's Government and the STC. However, this collapsed in April 2020 when the STC regained control of Aden, which had functioned as the nominal capital of the Saudi-backed Hadi Government since the beginning of the war.

Critical divergences in the objectives of Saudi Arabia and the UAE persist and complicate efforts towards a lasting resolution of the conflict. While Saudi Arabia appears increasingly willing to accept al-Houthi rule in the northern part of Yemen in return for peace on its borders, it is not willing to accept a south that is completely controlled by the STC, which would marginalize key Saudi allies. The UAE, by contrast, backs the STC and opposes al-Islah, which holds a seat on the PLC, but which is viewed by the UAE as a terrorist organization. The UAE supports an independent state in the south, which is at odds with the stated objectives of the PLC.

The Saudi-led intervention in Yemen has been supported by key Western states, which have provided Saudi Arabia and the UAE with critical military and political support. In April 2015 the UN Security Council adopted a resolution that in effect called for an al-Houthi surrender; this development has made the task of securing a peace agreement that is acceptable to all sides even more difficult. Military support from Western powers has contributed to the persistence of the conflict. In May 2017 the USA signed a US $110,000m. contract to supply armaments to Saudi Arabia over the next decade, in an effort to deter the threat from Iran (and tIranian-supported allies, such as the al-Houthis, in the region). However, what appeared to be a significant shift was signalled in early 2021 when newly elected US President Joe Biden identified ending the war in Yemen as a key element of his Administration's foreign policy. He appointed Timothy Lenderking as Special Envoy to Yemen and reversed the USA's designation of the al-Houthis as a foreign terrorist organization—one of the final measures undertaken by the Administration of outgoing US President Donald Trump. In addition, Biden ended support for 'offensive' operations in Yemen and suspended arms sales to Saudi Arabia. The developments raised hopes that the USA would put pressure on the Saudi-led coalition to bring about a swift end to the conflict. However, Saudi Arabia's bombardment and blockade of Yemen continued, and the Biden Administration has not taken any meaningful steps to bring about an end to the Saudi blockade of the country.

The UK has also played a major role in supplying arms to the Saudi-led coalition. Since the start of war in 2014 the UK is on record as having licensed at least £6,300m. worth of arms sales to Saudi Arabia, although the actual figure could be three times as much. The UK has not followed the US lead in ending arms exports to Saudi Arabia. However, in June 2019 the Court of Appeal ruled that the Government had acted unlawfully in licensing arms sales to Saudi Arabia without an assessment of whether past incidents of the Saudi bombardment of civilians in Yemen constituted a breach of international humanitarian law. In June 2020, having concluded that this was not the case, the British Government resumed its sales of weaponry to the kingdom.

The March 2023 breakthrough in Saudi-Iranian relations reflected significant change in the role of international powers in Yemen and the region more broadly. In May the USA announced that it was sending Lenderking to the region to assist efforts to secure a comprehensive peace. This masked the reality of declining US influence and an increase in the importance of China's role. China has no significant ties with any of the local parties to the conflict in Yemen. However, before 2014, it was Yemen's second largest trading partner, after Saudi Arabia. In addition, it has maintained diplomatic and economic ties with all of the major regional players—Saudi Arabia, the UAE and Iran. By contrast, US relations with Saudi Arabia have cooled, while it has not had diplomatic relations with Iran since 1980, following the seizure of the US embassy in Tehran.

Since early 2011 the Republic of Yemen, already beset by an array of deep-seated social, economic and political challenges, has endured constant political instability and violence. With the Saudi-led intervention from 2015, this situation was transformed into an apparently intractable civil war between coalitions of forces that are themselves deeply internally divided, and the costs of which are being borne largely by the country's civilian population. However, the recent persistence of a ceasefire between the warring parties has dramatically reduced the scale of the conflict, while the improved tone of Saudi-Iranian relations gives rise to hopes for an environment more conducive to a lasting political settlement. None the less, the diversity of actors, motivations and agendas, at both regional and local level, suggests that the path forward for Yemen is strewn with substantial obstacles to peace.

Economy

CHARLES SCHMITZ

OVERVIEW

Even before the outbreak of civil conflict in Yemen in 2015, security concerns had taken priority over economic challenges, with the economy being used as a tool to exert political power. Rather than fostering economic growth and long-term development, Yemen's rulers used the economy to consolidate their power. Informal and formal means of coercion allowed Yemen's rulers to forge alliances with the economic elite, while state expenditures were used to build patronage networks, state revenues were diverted to enrich political supporters, and contracts and licences were awarded to political supporters as well (World Bank, 2015). Since the outbreak of the conflict, Yemen's warring factions and their foreign backers have taken economic warfare to new heights. Yemen's currency, petroleum resources, infrastructure, basic commodities and relief supplies have been manipulated to bolster supporters or harm opponents. Since the ceasefire began in April 2022, the al-Houthi have focused their efforts on crippling the economy of the Yemeni Government and solidifying their control over the main levers of Yemen's economy.

The al-Houthis used their control of the domestic market to refashion the economy to their advantage. The al-Houthis control only about one-quarter of the territory of Yemen, but their area is the most vital for Yemen's population, comprising about three-quarters of the population and the lion's share of Yemen's domestic market. Under the United Nations (UN) Verification and Inspection Mechanism for Yemen (UNVIM), implemented to prevent weapons transfers to the al-Houthi, only essential commodities of food and fuel were allowed to enter al-Houthi-controlled Hodeida port on the Red Sea. Goods travelling overland from ports in the south or from Oman supplied the remainder of the needs of those living in al-Houthi territory. At the beginning of 2023 the Saudi-backed coalition relaxed restrictions on commodities entering Hodeida, which enabled the al-Houthis to redirect trade away from Aden and towards Hodeida. The al-Houthis used some economic incentives, such as reducing tariffs and taxes on imported goods, but their main tool was threats. They blocked the transport of goods overland from the ports in the south and east of Yemen, and banned merchants from al-Houthi-controlled markets if they did not use Hodeida port. As a result, UNVIM reports indicated the number of vessels entering Hodeida doubled between January and April, and the amount of non-essential goods increased from zero to over 250,000 metric tons. Most of the redirected maritime traffic came from Aden, reducing tariff and tax revenue to the Yemeni Government.

The al-Houthis have also intervened in the domestic cooking gas market and crude petroleum exports. Yemen's cooking gas was supplied by the government-owned Safer refinery in Marib and transported across the battle lines to al-Houthi-controlled markets, but the al-Houthis blocked the gas coming from Marib and began importing gas through Hodeida port to supply the domestic market and, again, to redirect profits into al-Houthi hands. Some of the al-Houthi-imported gas even reached Aden, outside of al-Houthi territory.

The al-Houthis also prevented oil tankers from loading crude petroleum exports on Yemen's southern coast. In late 2022 al-Houthi drones (unmanned aerial vehicles) exploded just ahead of tankers approaching crude petroleum ports, halting Yemen's main export. The al-Houthis claimed that the Government was stealing Yemen's natural resources that belong to the Yemeni people, whose only government is the al-Houthi authorities. In the talks with Saudi officials that took place in San'a in April 2023, the al-Houthis demanded that Yemeni oil revenues be used to pay public sector salaries in al-Houthi-controlled Yemen. The collapse of oil exports has deprived the Yemeni Government of its main source of income, but Yemen continues to produce small amounts of crude petroleum that are processed in local refineries to supply some of the local market. The combination of halting oil exports, re-routing trade, and halting gas sales has deprived the Yemeni Government of its main revenue streams, which, in turn, has exacerbated Yemen's fiscal and currency crises.

Saudi Arabia and the United Arab Emirates (UAE) pledged a US $3,000m. aid programme when the ceasefire began in April 2022, and in February 2023 it was reported that the Saudis had deposited $1,000m. in the Central Bank of Yemen (CBY) in Aden. However, the aid has failed to stabilize the deteriorating fiscal or currency crises in both al-Houthi- and government-controlled territories. In al-Houthi territory, the exchange rate of the Yemeni riyal (YR) appreciated to around YR 540 = US $1, but the lack of cash has severely restricted liquidity. Al-Houthi authorities responded by effectively freezing bank accounts, allowing only digital withdrawals in an economy that is entirely cash. In the Government's territory, Saudi financial support failed to stem the depreciation of the riyal, which fell to YR 1,400 = US $1 in 2023 (see *Government Finance*). The deposits of Saudi funds in Aden's central bank are used to finance importers of basic commodities, since Yemen has very few exports that earn foreign currency. Without a comprehensive political settlement, which is considered unlikely in the near future, Yemen's financial and fiscal situation will deteriorate further.

International efforts also fell short of announced goals. The UN Donors' Conference held in Stockholm, Sweden in February 2023 garnered US $1,200m. of pledges, but fell far short of the estimated needs of Yemen, of $4,300m.

THE LACK OF LONG-TERM INVESTMENT

Leaders worldwide shape their economies for social and political purposes, but the nature of the political interventions in Yemen's economy inhibited long-term investment and growth. Investors who do not have the favour of the powerful are vulnerable and thus prefer to invest in safer markets outside Yemen. The flight of Yemeni capital not only robs the economy of potential investment, but it also inhibits long-term investments that have the potential to transform the economy by establishing a more productive base and moving away from the traditional sectors. Yemeni investors, even those favoured by the political leadership, prefer more liquid assets and short-term investments, which can be quickly withdrawn in times of trouble.

Investment is important not only because it raises the productivity of labour and the income of the average Yemeni, but also because investment allows the economy to move beyond its dependence on hydrocarbons exports (World Bank, 2015). Like those of its wealthier neighbours, Yemen's economy has traditionally relied heavily upon hydrocarbons exports (which have been severely curtailed by the war since early 2015), although Yemeni leaders have long been aware that their country's hydrocarbons resources are limited. Rather than use the revenues generated from hydrocarbons to foster investment in sustainable, non-oil ventures, Yemeni leaders have tended to use them for current consumption to maintain their regimes. The war revealed Yemen's stark dependence upon hydrocarbons—the collapse of the Yemeni economy is due not only to the war directly, but also to the conflict's impact on the hydrocarbons sector, which has practically ceased production, although by 2019 small quantities were being exported from Mukalla and Shabwa. Though these are often disrupted by acts of sabotage, they still offer some limited revenue for the Saudi-backed Yemeni Government.

Of course, Yemeni leaders are a product of an environment that rewards security over all else, and while there are some successful economic reform programmes supported by Yemen's international partners, such as the Social Welfare Fund, security concerns dominate the economic agenda. Economists acknowledge that poverty contributes to insecurity, and, as a result, that poverty reduction needs to be targeted to limit the potential for social unrest, but security concerns still take priority over economic issues, even among regional and international actors. Thus, Yemeni leaders' focus on political survival in a dangerous environment, although detrimental to long-term economic growth, is not only perversely rational, but also implicitly supported by international leaders.

ECONOMIC PERFORMANCE

The Yemeni population is, on average, poor. Even before the war began in 2015, Yemen was the poorest Arab nation, and the country is particularly poor when compared with its oil-rich neighbours on the Arabian Peninsula. However, when compared with countries across the Red Sea in Africa, Yemen's position improves. The World Bank estimated Yemen's per capita gross national income (GNI) in 2014 at US $1,460, close to the average GNI per capita of countries in sub-Saharan Africa; Yemen is poor, but it is far from the poorest country in the world. Yemen might be considered the richest of the world's poorest countries and the poorest of the world's medium-income countries. However, the war has set Yemen back substantially. Using 2010 as a base, the World Bank estimated that by 2022 the Yemeni economy had contracted by almost 50%, most of which had occurred since the start of the war. The economy was expected to shrink further due to the country's worsening terms of trade and the large import bill.

Standards of living improved significantly over the 50 years following the republican revolution. Life expectancy rose from about 40 years in the 1960s to 63.81 years in 2021, according to the World Bank. World Bank data show that the economy grew at an average of around 5% per year between 1990 and 2010 and that GDP per capita, on a purchasing-power parity basis, doubled in that period. In 2014 gross primary school enrolment was over 95%. Literacy rates for women aged 15–24 had reached 83% in 2015, compared with a rate among this cohort of only 35% two decades earlier. Furthermore, Yemen achieved these improvements during a period of population growth that was among the fastest in the world. In the mid-1980s Yemen's total fertility rate reached approximately nine births per woman. In the 1960s Yemen's population was estimated at just under 6m., compared with an estimated 34.4m. in mid-2023. The fertility rate decreased dramatically in the 2000s, however, and by 2022 it had fallen to 3.6 births per woman—a steep decline from earlier rates. Despite the fall in the fertility rate, Yemen's tremendous population momentum over recent decades means that its population will continue to grow for some time. The rate of population growth was projected at 2.3% in 2022. Population growth is usually a welcome sign for economists as it increases the size of the working population, and results in greater consumption, but rapid population growth also requires the provision of education and employment for a large cohort of young people. If the economy is struggling to grow, population growth can become an additional strain.

The presence or lack of natural resources is not correlated with economic prosperity, but sometimes natural resource scarcity can present challenges. Yemen faces a severe lack of water and a corresponding lack of arable land. Yemen is relatively green compared with its neighbours on the Arabian Peninsula, but that is a very low bar—Yemen's neighbours are located on some of the most arid territory in the world. The greenest areas of Yemen are the southern highlands around Ibb and Taiz, which receive somewhere between 600 mm and 1,000 mm of rain annually, but the rest of Yemen receives much less rainfall. As a result, Yemen has one of the lowest rates per capita of water resources in the world. Yemen's neighbours also lack water resources, but Saudi Arabia and the other Gulf States augment their very scarce fresh water with expensive desalinated water resources. Yemen cannot afford energy-intensive conventional desalination, but developments in alternative technology may allow Yemen to augment its supplies of water from desalinated sources in the future. The use of solar panels is already adversely affecting levels of groundwater by allowing high levels of pumping, unconstrained by the cost of fuel (or any regulation of withdrawals by the state).

The water crisis is exacerbated by the concentration of Yemen's population in the western highlands. The capital, San'a, depends upon water pumped from underground aquifers, but water levels in the aquifers have been declining at a rapid rate in recent years because unregulated withdrawals from modern bore wells draw down water at a much faster rate than rainfall can replenish. This means that San'a's water supplies are becoming scarcer and water must be transported by lorry from areas further away, raising the price of water significantly. The high elevation of the western highlands means that pumping water from further away is uneconomical because large amounts of energy are needed to pump water up the high mountains. Thus, scarce water in the western highlands creates an economic burden. The increase in fuel prices has compounded the cost of transporting water. Some 90% of Yemen's water is used in agriculture, so diverting water from agriculture for urban household needs would impose a cost to the economy, though greater efficiency in irrigation would reduce the burden. Water is the main limiting factor in Yemen's agriculture. In 2018 the World Bank reported that only 2.1% of Yemen was arable, compared with the global average of 10.8%, and on average only about 1.5% of land is under cultivation in Yemen.

Since 2018 rainfall has increased significantly in Yemen. However, the intensity of storms has also increased, such that much of the water flows into the sea rather than being captured for human use, and there has also been widespread storm damage to crops and infrastructure. Ironically, the collapse of the national electrical grid (see Electrical Power) and the widespread adoption of solar panels have also compounded water problems because solar panels have significantly reduced the cost of pumping underground water, which remains unregulated.

Outside the agricultural sector, Yemen's pre-war economy expanded not by increasing productivity, but through population growth and an increase in capital investment. Oil revenue supported consumption and stimulated growth in government employment, trade, transportation, commerce and construction. Except for construction and some light manufacturing, growth in the Yemeni economy was focused on short-term, liquid investments that could be withdrawn quickly without much loss to the investor, such as investments in trade and commerce. Investors in Yemen tend to be risk averse. Long-term investors avoid committing themselves unless they receive political guarantees that their funds will be protected. The lack of investment means that Yemeni labour is unproductive and wages per unit of output are uncompetitive (World Bank, 2015). Productivity-raising investment is almost completely absent, even before the war, especially in manufacturing, which is still dominated by tiny fabrication shops for water tanks and metal doors. Other than its hydrocarbons and natural beauty, Yemen's comparative advantage is its plentiful and hard-working labour force, but tourists and labour-intensive investment alike have shunned Yemen's unpredictable and dangerous political and security environment, especially since the onset of instability and war in recent years.

The war has exacerbated Yemen's economic challenges substantially. The suspension of oil and gas exports has led to a dramatic decrease in per capita income, which has been exacerbated by the destruction of infrastructure and by difficulties in transporting goods. World Bank estimates suggest that by 2022 GDP had fallen by almost 50% since the war began. By comparison, the Great Depression of the late 1920s and early 1930s in the USA witnessed only a 25% reduction in GDP. Much of Yemen's physical infrastructure has been substantially damaged, including roads and bridges, ports and airports, health and sanitation facilities, and communications and energy infrastructure. Several urban, economically important areas, such as Taiz, have been severely damaged. The lack of basic infrastructure has allowed treatable diseases such as cholera to spread. Meanwhile, the collapse of the central Government in San'a has left the large public sector labour force without employment or wages.

Furthermore, the economy has moved to a war footing since 2015. Commanders, militias and traffickers supplying rebel groups have profited from the conflict, and, as a result, the war economy created perverse incentives to continue fighting. For the leadership of all sides in the war, generating revenue to pay soldiers' salaries and keep them supplied with munitions and food is a critical part of the war effort. The Saudi-backed coalition has the resources of Saudi Arabia and the Gulf monarchies to support the war effort, but the al-Houthi rebels in the north (see History) do not have significant external financial backing, beyond the little support that Iran may supply. The al-Houthis operate under what the World Bank has called a 'cash constrained' budget, so they rebuilt the economy to the north to redirect what little wealth remained there into the hands of the al-Houthi leadership. In the far north, the al-Houthis have instituted agricultural taxes based on the old system of the Imamate, which existed from the ninth century CE until the Yemeni revolution in 1962, and under which taxes on farmers and agricultural produce provided the mainstay of revenues, to squeeze what little profit exists in agriculture into al-Houthi hands. Al-Houthi leaders have redirected liquefied petroleum gas (LPG), which is used locally for domestic cooking, and petrol for transportation into the black market, which they control, to profit from high prices caused by scarcities. This became clear when the al-Houthis accused Saudi Arabia of blocking fuel imports into Hodeida in early 2021. State petrol stations closed, but the black market for fuel flourished, and al-Houthi checkpoints prevented oil from entering al-Houthi-controlled areas overland from the south and east, while al-Houthi forces advancing on Marib did not experience a shortage of fuel. The al-Houthis clearly exploited the reduction in fuel imports for their own benefit. In 2023 the al-Houthis blocked the entry of LPG from Marib and imported LPG to supply the al-Houthi-controlled market, thus depriving the Yemeni Government of a source of revenue. In San'a the al-Houthis impose taxes and fees on struggling commercial establishments. The al-Houthis have intervened in currency markets by fixing exchange rates, and then trading on the black market, in effect taxing currency markets and drawing a profit from the differential rates. The al-Houthis are reportedly exploiting the desperation of the local population to pass ownership of urban property, particularly in San'a, to their supporters, as the group attempts to consolidate its presence in the capital. Al-Houthi courts continue to confiscate the assets of people deemed to be enemies, primarily leaders of the Yemeni Government and the military. Al-Houthi efforts to manage the war economy are intended permanently to establish their control over the new economy of the north. The al-Houthis recently dismissed the San'a Chamber of Commerce and replaced it with al-Houthi supporters, after members complained of al-Houthi economic policies squeezing the private sector.

HISTORICAL BACKGROUND

Yemen's economy as it exists today took shape in the 20th century. Largely an agricultural economy until the republican coup in 1962, the economy of the Mutawakkilite Kingdom of Yemen already exhibited some of the challenging characteristics that the economy faces today: it depended upon imports to meet food needs, and upon foreign benefactors for development investment, as its tax revenues failed to cover state expenditures. Nonetheless, the engine of the economy was the domestic agricultural sector, which provided the principal component of GDP and the main source of tax revenue. In southern Yemen, economic activity focused almost entirely on British Aden and largely ignored the rest of southern Yemen. Aden's economy was built on the port's entrepôt trade and support of the British military and bureaucracy, and thus its benefits were largely restricted to the city. Nonetheless, Aden attracted both Yemeni labour and capital, which led to the development of a modern economy under the protection of the British Empire until British rule ended in 1967.

Following the republican coup and the war between the Yemen Arab Republic (YAR—North Yemen) and the socialist People's Democratic Republic of Yemen (PDRY—South Yemen) in 1972, the economy of the YAR was transformed by the exodus of Yemeni labour to Saudi Arabia and the decline in the role of Aden after the closure of the Suez Canal and the rise of a socialist Government. In this period Yemeni labour produced wealth, but in Saudi Arabia not Yemen, and Hodeida, San'a and Taiz were the focus of the new economy. Wealth was transferred to Yemen through worker remittances, which in turn transformed the domestic Yemeni economy into a machine for the import and distribution of consumer durables. Foreign development assistance helped to develop transportation and communications infrastructure, and Yemenis moved out of agriculture into trade and commerce to import and distribute consumer goods. By the early 1990s remittances to Yemen fell as the Saudi economy reached maturity and Saudi Arabia expelled Yemeni workers in September 1990 as punishment for Yemeni support of Iraqi President Saddam Hussain, following Yemen's refusal to condemn Hussain's invasion and occupation of Kuwait in August.

Following the brief civil war of 1994, the Yemeni economy faced the challenge of promoting domestic sources of growth. The International Monetary Fund (IMF) and the World Bank began working with the Yemeni Government in 1995 to institute reforms to stabilize the currency, lower inflation, balance the state budget, reduce subsidies and promote investment. These goals were reached not as a result of fundamental reforms in the economy, but because oil revenues increased dramatically, owing to new finds in the Masila Block in the Hadramout region. Oil production peaked in 2002, but elevated international prices in the 2000s meant that oil revenue remained high throughout the decade. Oil revenue allowed the state to balance its budget and GDP to grow, but without transforming the productive basis of the economy. Oil exports drove economic expansion through 2012, but oil-driven growth was limited by the relative scarcity of Yemen's reserves. Steady declines in production made clear the need to diversify the economy away from the oil sector. With instability arising from the al-Houthi rebellion, which began in 2004 and escalated over the next decade, pressing political and military concerns dominated the state's agenda, not the economy. Thus, when the war halted oil production, it only hastened an already impending economic crisis.

THE HYDROCARBONS SECTOR

Although international oil companies have long been interested in Yemen, oil has only relatively recently been found in exploitable quantities. Imam Yayha allowed the Iraqi Oil Company to explore for oil in the Marib desert in the 1930s, concessions were granted by his son Ahmad for exploration on the Tihama coast in the 1950s, and the Kathiri and Quayti Sultanates in what is now Hadramout also negotiated deals for exploration in the 1960s. However, it was only in the mid-1980s that oil was actually located, and the hydrocarbons industry developed.

Yemen's oil and gas reserves are located in two main fields: the Marib Shabwa stream, which straddles the former border between Marib governorate in the YAR and Shabwa governorate in the PDRY; and the Masila stream farther east in Hadramout governorate, which lies entirely in the former PDRY. The US firm Hunt Oil first developed oil in Marib on the YAR side of the border in 1986, and by 1989 it produced 178,000 barrels per day (b/d), according to the *BP Statistical Review of World Energy*. Geographically, the easiest route to the sea from Marib was south through the PDRY to the Gulf of Aden, but the political division of Yemen meant that the YAR's oil resources were directed by pipeline westward from the desert of Marib over the mountains of the western highlands to the Red Sea port of Ras Issa near Hodeida.

In the mid-1980s oil was also discovered in the Marib Shabwa field in the PDRY's Shabwa governorate by engineers from the Union of Soviet Socialist Republics (USSR). However, Soviet development of oil resources was slow. The PDRY's desire to access Western oil companies was one of the leading motivations for the unification of Yemen in 1990. Following unification, Western oil companies quickly developed the oil of the former PDRY both on the former PDRY's side of the Marib Shabwa stream and at the much larger Masila stream further east in Hadramout. Oil from these fields was shipped south to the coast at Hisn al-Nushaymah, in Shabwa, and al-Dhaba Port in Hadramout. Production at Hunt Oil's field in Marib declined in the 1990s, but the development of the fields in the south after unification kept Yemen's total output rising until 2002, when production peaked at 457,000 b/d, according to BP figures. Thereafter, production declined steadily in the absence of further finds and development. By 2014, the last full year before conflict took hold of the country, average daily production was 147,000 b/d. This dwindled to just 44,000 b/d in 2015 and 16,000 b/d in both 2016 and 2017, but rose to almost 50,000 b/d in 2018 and remained at that level in 2019 and 2020.

Production of oil declined partly because there were no new discoveries—a result of both the absence of new investment in exploration and the relative lack of oil in Yemen. The country is unattractive to investors both because of political instability and violence, and because the Government has not offered favourable terms for exploration and production. Unlike most other oil-producing Middle Eastern countries, Yemen's oil was developed and maintained primarily by foreign private companies, the largest of which today are TotalEnergies of France, Occidental Petroleum of the USA, and Nexen, a subsidiary of the China National Offshore Oil Company. Three Yemeni state firms—the Safer Exploration and Production Operations Company, the Yemeni Company for Investment in Oil and Minerals, and PetroMasila—are also active and have recently expanded their operations at the expense of the private sector. Yemen's contracts with oil companies are based upon production-sharing agreements rather than royalties. Leases are granted for exploration, and, if discoveries are made, the crude petroleum is divided according to an agreement between the Government and the foreign company. In effect, foreign oil companies act as sharecroppers in Yemen. The production-sharing agreements split the risk between the producing firm and the Government. However, amid the onset of instability and then conflict, oil firms became reluctant to share Yemen's risks on the terms offered by the Government.

Opacity in the administration of hydrocarbons exploration, production, export and domestic distribution allows local political leaders to siphon off oil wealth or direct it to favoured supporters. The UN Security Council's investigatory committee on Yemen reported in February 2015 that former President Ali Abdullah Saleh had received significant commissions on all oil contracts, through which he personally enriched himself while head of state in 1978–2012. The Saleh family's assets were reportedly estimated at US $26,000m., almost equal to Yemen's total GDP in 2015. The source for the estimate was a former senior member of the regime who had since become opposed to Saleh, but it was clear that the oil industry was being used in various ways to channel wealth to Saleh's family and to supporters of the regime. The ability to channel oil (and other) revenues to regime supporters depends upon opacity, which in turn tends to deter foreign investors.

In the future, oil will likely not play the dominant role in Yemen's economy that it has in recent decades. During the 2000s and the first part of the 2010s oil constituted about one-third of total economic output and provided about three-quarters of government revenues. Oil revenues passed through the state in the form of employee salaries and state-owned enterprises, and contracts to supply the state provided the economy with a large source of demand. Foreign currency from export sales financed the importation of consumer goods from abroad. The fiscal and external payments balances were healthy over this period, but by 2007 the value of imports had surpassed exports and the current account began to register a deficit and has not since recovered (except for in 2011, when the instability arising from the protests of the so-called 'Arab Spring' led to an extraordinary collapse of consumption).

The significance of oil will not disappear from the Yemeni economy entirely, but production has declined significantly since the onset of the war and there have not been any new discoveries for several years. If the war ends unexpectedly soon and the Government can create a stable investment environment, new funding for the oil sector could possibly slow the rate of decline in oil production, but the era of oil-driven growth appears to be at its end, reminiscent of the era of worker remittance-supported growth ending in the 1990s. Since the onset of the war Yemen's oil revenue does not cover even the cost of importing refined petroleum products for the domestic market, much less the large bill for importing basic food staples.

The war disrupted oil production as firms withdrew their personnel and combatants targeted pipelines. When the Saudi-backed coalition gained control of the east and south of the country, where all the productive oilfields are located, production slowly resumed. Reportedly, about 39,000 b/d were being shipped out of al-Dhaba port from the Masila field in the first half of 2017, and the Saudi-backed Government has offered tenders on oil from the Marib Shabwa field. In 2018 negotiations with the Austrian oil firm OMV concluded with an agreement to restart production in the Marib Shabwa field, and a small amount of oil began to flow from the field from July;

exports reached 50,000 b/d by the end of 2018 and remained at around that level in 2022. In 2023 al-Houthi threats against oil tankers on the southern coast halted oil exports entirely, but some crude petroleum was being processed at the refineries in Aden and Marib for the domestic market.

In the Red Sea, the threat of environmental disaster from the export holding tank at Ras Issa finally appeared to be close to resolution. The *FSO Safer*, the ageing tanker that served as a storage facility and an offshore export platform for oil piped from Marib, had not been maintained, and officials feared that the vessel would spill its 1m. barrels of oil into the sea, creating a massive environmental disaster. However, the warring parties in Yemen used the threat of potential environmental damage for their own purposes. The al-Houthis prevented maintenance because they insisted that they should receive one-half of the revenue from the oil, while the Yemeni Government refused to grant any such demand. In early 2022 the UN managed to broker a deal to repair or replace the tanker; funding was secured in 2023 and in late May work began first to stabilize the tanker, then transfer its contents.

Oil imports have also been affected by the war. In 2021 Saudi Arabia prevented oil tankers from entering Hodeida, citing the al-Houthis' alleged withdrawal of monies from an account established by the UN-brokered Stockholm Agreement to hold oil tax revenue to pay government salaries. Meanwhile, tanker trucks were allowed overland from Aden into al-Houthi-held territory, guaranteeing taxes and protection money for forces nominally allied with the Yemeni Government. In the southern regions, allegations of corruption related to oil deals involving former President Hadi's son and a key presidential adviser, Ahmed al-Essi, continued to surface, while efforts to begin operations at the LNG facility at Balhaf were stalled owing to disputes between Saudi Arabia and the UAE, whose forces occupied the facility, though the private owners of the LNG facility are likely not willing to return to Yemen yet.

OWNERSHIP STRUCTURE

In contrast to the rest of the Middle East, where state-owned companies control oil, Yemen's oil and gas industries were developed and owned by foreign private companies, but the Yemeni Government has expanded its role substantially by taking over expired leases. Before the war, some 60% of oil was produced by private firms and about 40% by the Government. The entire oil industry is overseen by the Ministry of Oil and Minerals. Under the aegis of the Ministry, the Petroleum Exploration and Production Authority is responsible for managing bids and contracts for private concessions. Terms of concessions with foreign firms must be ratified by parliament. The state-owned Safer Exploration and Production Operations Company exploits the Marib section of the Marib Shabwa field, while PetroMasila exploits the most productive fields in the eastern Masila region. Meanwhile the Yemen Company for Investment in Oil and Minerals holds a percentage of shares in private oil consortiums working in the country—another means that the Government uses to profit from privately funded oil production. In 2014 Safer's Block 18 produced 38,000 b/d, while Block 14 in the Masila field produced 35,000 b/d, accounting for the greater part of the state's 40% of oil production. In addition, the Yemen Oil and Gas Corporation operates the country's two refineries, sells the Government's portion of crude petroleum production, and distributes cooking and transportation fuel in the domestic market.

OIL REFINERIES

Yemen has two refineries—in Aden and in Marib. Aden's capacity is far larger at 150,000 b/d; capacity at the Marib facility is only about 10,000 b/d. However, the Aden refinery, built in 1958 by Bechtel Power for British Petroleum (later known as BP), operates at only half capacity. Total demand for refined fuels in Yemen before the war was about 150,000 b/d, so Yemen was forced to import around one-half of its refined fuel needs. The lack of domestic refining capacity means that fulfilling domestic refined fuel needs puts great strain on Yemen's already precarious balance of payments.

One of the ways that Saudi Arabia supports the Yemeni Government is by making occasional deliveries of crude petroleum to the Aden refinery. In 2012 Saudi Arabia made a delivery of some 3m. barrels of crude petroleum to support the transitional Government, which was struggling to supply the domestic market with refined products. In the first half of 2017 Saudi Arabia delivered substantial amounts of LPG to relieve cooking gas shortages in the areas under the control of the Saudi-backed coalition in the south of Yemen. In March 2021 Saudi Arabia made a commitment to supply US $422m. in refined petroleum products to the southern governorates, and in April 2022 Saudi Arabia made another contribution of $600m.-worth of refined petroleum products.

GAS

Yemen's gas reserves are relatively small at 17,000,000m. cubic feet (cu ft), the 31st largest in the world. Initially, Yemen's gas derived from oil production was reinjected into the oilfields to facilitate the further extraction of oil. In the 2000s Yemen began development of its gas resources both for export and as a source of power generation. Exports are processed at the LNG plant at Balhaf, operated by a consortium headed by the French firm TotalEnergies. Completed in 2009, the LNG facility was a US $4,500m. project that represented the largest single investment in Yemen's modern history. Gas exports are handled by the Yemen LNG Company, a consortium led by TotalEnergies, which owns 39% of the company, followed by Hunt Oil (17%), the state-owned Yemen Gas Company (16%), and the Yemeni Social Security and Pension Fund (5%). Gas is piped from Marib through the Shabwa fields to the LNG facility at Balhaf. The consortium signed long-term contracts to supply Korean markets and short-term contracts for operators in the US market. The first shipment of Yemen's LNG arrived in the USA in 2009. TotalEnergies withdrew its employees from Yemen at the onset of major hostilities in 2015, and gas production and exports have yet to resume.

Before the war started in 2015, estimates of Yemen's proven gas reserves and exports suggested that the country could maintain exports at current levels for about 25 years and that annual revenues would reach about US $500m. during that period. Data from the CBY show that revenue from export sales of the government portion of oil production averaged about $2,700m. in 2000–12, so, although gas exports will be important for state revenues, gas will not play the dominant role that oil played in the economy and the Government's finances during the first decade of the 21st century.

The Government controls the distribution of LPG, and its price and availability are key political levers. During the period of the transitional Government between 2012 and 2014 cooking fuel periodically disappeared from markets and prices escalated dramatically, in order to demonstrate the inability of the transitional Government to administer domestic affairs. Government control of cooking gas was also one of the many measures that political leaders took to create networks of patronage. During the war the availability of cooking gas was again used to manipulate the public. Shortages enabled opponents to accuse the Government of negligence. Shortages also enabled illicit operators to profit from black markets in Aden and San'a. The al-Houthi made a dramatic intervention in the cooking gas market in May 2023, preventing gas from the Safer Company in Marib from reaching San'a and forcing those in al-Houthi-controlled territory to use imported gas at much higher prices.

ELECTRICAL POWER

Gas could have a major effect on Yemen's power generation by replacing expensive diesel plants with gas-fired plants. The World Bank reported that at the beginning of the war in early 2015 some 70% of Yemen's electricity was generated in diesel-powered plants, fuel for which was either imported or supplied by Yemen's main refinery in Aden. Small fuel ports along the Red Sea and Gulf of Aden supply fuel shipped from the Aden refinery or purchased on international markets to power plants on the coast or located further inland in the main cities. Use of expensive diesel for power generation represents a loss of economic opportunity for Yemen. Fuel costs the Government about 10% of GDP, but power generation is grossly insufficient.

Even the main cities experienced daily outages of several hours per day before the war. The deficiency of the national grid led many businesses, institutions and households to purchase small generators for backup use, and Yemenis have been forced to privatize power generation in diffuse, small-scale local operations throughout the country, undermining efficiency and raising costs.

In Yemen, gas-fired power generation is a more economical option for large-scale power plants. Most of Yemen's gas is allocated to the LNG plant in Balhaf, but chronic electricity shortages led the Government to consider gas-fired plants and the conversion of older diesel plants to gas. By mid-2019 the Government had only built one gas-fired plant, in Marib, testing of which began in December of that year; additional plants, to be constructed by the People's Republic of China, were planned for the San'a basin, but the war disrupted those efforts.

The World Bank reported in 2017 that the war had significantly damaged the national power grid. By the middle of that year only regional grids in Aden and Mukalla were functioning with any regularity, and they were heavily subsidized by Saudi Arabia and other Gulf states. The lack of electricity undermined critical health infrastructure, including hospitals and public sanitation facilities such as sewage treatment plants, and contributed to the outbreak of cholera among the local population. In July 2018 President Hadi announced an agreement with General Electric of the USA to build more power generation capacity in Aden and Mukalla. The agreement provided for the construction of a 264-MW generator in Aden and a 100-MW generator in Mukalla. The new generators will use gas and heavy oil, in order to conserve Yemen's precious exports of oil. The Government of the UAE signed an agreement with the Yemeni Ministry of Electricity and Energy in June 2019 to construct a new electrical power plant with a capacity of 120 MW in Aden at a cost of US $100m. However, the electrical grid has been politicized by the war. Electricity powers much-needed air conditioning units in the hot temperatures of the south, and reliable provision of electricity demonstrates political capability. The political contests in the south are therefore echoed in the electrical grid, as one side reduces power to the other to undermine its popular support. Demonstrations over the lack of electricity erupt regularly in all parts of the south.

A rare upside to the war has been the widespread adoption of renewable solar power for household consumption, amid the destruction of the national electrical grid and the high cost of diesel fuel. The falling price of solar panels has enabled Yemeni households to switch to solar power for lighting and other domestic electrical needs. The World Bank has estimated that up to 50% of rural households and 75% of urban households are using solar power and that about US $1,000m. has been invested in the sector since 2015. However, solar energy use is having a negative impact on groundwater in the western highlands, as the lower cost of solar energy incentivizes more pumping.

AGRICULTURE

Agriculture was the mainstay of the Yemeni economy until the republican revolution of 1962, after which many Yemenis abandoned agriculture to work in construction and commerce in Saudi Arabia. Remittances enabled Yemeni households to purchase consumer goods that were imported, transported, distributed and sold by the rapidly growing service sector in Yemen. The decline of the remittance economy and the rise of the oil economy in the 2000s further developed the service sector, which continued to facilitate the import of consumer goods, but the source of demand shifted away from remittances towards government employment. Construction also grew rapidly owing to rising incomes, the rapid expansion of the population and increasing urbanization, although Yemen was still only about 39% urbanized by 2021. Meanwhile, agriculture stagnated.

Yemen's agricultural base is limited. Whereas the agricultural sector might have been expected to expand to feed the growing population, the lack of arable land has severely restricted agricultural development. As a result, Yemen imports its staple grains of wheat and rice; all of Yemen's rice and some 90% of its wheat are imported. Given the severely restricted supply of land, Yemeni farmers have quite rationally shifted, wherever possible, from basic grain production to higher value-added products, the most extensive of which is fodder and the most lucrative of which is qat.

Just 2.4% of Yemen's land is arable and only about 1.5% is under cultivation; however, the limiting factor is not land but water. Far more of Yemen's land would be arable and cultivated if water was available. The alluvial coasts of Yemen along the Red Sea and the Gulf of Aden are particularly fertile if watered adequately, and much of the highlands consist of basins that would bloom if water was available.

Just under one-half of the cultivated area of Yemen is fed by rain. Yemen's highlands are well-known for their terraced fields, which have been built up over centuries. The successive series of fields descending the mountainside ingeniously recycles rainwater from one field to the next lower field to maximize the uptake of water. In 2011, according to the Ministry of Agriculture's *Yearbook*, 664,000 ha were fed by rain out of a total 1.4m. ha cultivated that year. Sorghum and corn dominate the rain-fed pastures. In agricultural statistics terminology, the two crops are called cereals, but the reality is that the stalk of the cereal is also fodder for animals, a much higher value-added product. Livestock and livestock products produced about 50% of the value that field crops, including qat, contributed. In 2011 about 55% of land was cultivated for cereals, but these produced only about 12% of agricultural value.

In valleys and lower elevations, wells are an effective means of obtaining water, enabling farmers to provide a more continuous supply of water. Until the 1970s most wells were dug by hand and lined with rocks. Many of the hand-dug wells are still in use, but the introduction of bore wells and diesel pumps dramatically expanded the scope of well use in Yemen. In 2011 a total of 29% of cultivated land was irrigated using wells. The cultivation of qat requires irrigation, and 11% of the cultivated area of Yemen is designated for this stimulant plant, all of which is irrigated by wells or by transporting in water by lorry, although only 1% of Yemen's total agricultural land is fed by water transported in this manner. Transported water is usually reserved for urban areas.

Rain in Yemen derives from moist tropical air driven over the high mountains by the monsoonal winds in the summer. As a result, the rain often comes in torrents that cause rapid overground flow. Traditionally built networks of channels capture these rapid overground flows and direct them to small fields that are surrounded by mud dykes. Water is allowed to fill and percolate through the small fields one after another. This form of agriculture is deployed in highland basins and dominates the alluvial plains along the coasts, where the *wadis* (valleys that have rivers that are usually dry except when heavy rainfall occurs) bring huge flows of water from the highlands over a period of days. A total of 17% of cultivated land in 2011 was irrigated by this form of spate irrigation.

Landholding is fragmented and land markets undeveloped. Agricultural land is such a precious commodity that families are extremely reticent to sell land. In fact, the sale of land carries a social stigma. Land is most often cultivated as part of a multipronged strategy for household survival, and, as a result, most Yemeni farmers are small-scale part-time farmers. Larger landholdings do exist, but these are usually in new agricultural investment projects in the coastal areas, mostly in Tihama on the Red Sea coast. The Ministry of Agriculture's 2011 *Yearbook* indicates that Hodeida governorate produced around one-quarter of Yemen's agricultural output on about 20% of its cultivated land. Significantly, Hodeida's average landholding was 3.8 ha, while the nationwide average was only 1.2 ha per farmer. The densely populated governorates of Ibb and Taiz have average landholdings of only 0.5 ha.

Although a land registry does exist in Yemen, it is ineffective. Rights to property, both agricultural and urban, are maintained largely through the continual maintenance of customary rights. If property rights are not continually reaffirmed, property will be redistributed to those who can maintain claims. In rural villages, tribal or clan elders will reassign rights to land that has been abandoned. In areas of new development, such as in Tihama, connections to the politically powerful enable some individuals to acquire relatively large landholdings.

More Yemenis are involved in agriculture than any other sector of the economy, although the proportion of the workforce in agriculture has declined considerably since the 1990s. World Bank figures show that in 1994 about one-half of workers were employed in agriculture, but in 2015 this had fallen to about one-third of workers. The reduction in the proportion of the labour force working in agriculture is not due to rising productivity, but is a result of a rapidly growing workforce and limited opportunities in agriculture. If there was more land in Yemen, the proportion of workers in agriculture would not have fallen as rapidly. Agriculture's contribution to GDP remains at around 10%, with qat alone accounting for a further 3%. These figures relate to agricultural output alone. Goods and services such as irrigation pumps and pipes, fertilizers, seeds, and the storage, transportation and distribution of agricultural products add to the indirect contribution of agriculture. The market networks for qat, for example, contribute significantly to urban employment.

Qat is a mild stimulant (not a narcotic in medical terms), which about 90% of Yemeni men and 70% of women chew in the afternoon. Qat, like coffee, requires a tropical mountain climate in order to grow, and will not thrive at lower elevations. Qat is chewed fresh: harvested leaves must reach market within a matter of hours and qat leaves older than a day are shunned. Qat cultivation by current methods uses a lot of water. Farmers heavily irrigate plants a few days before harvest to force sprouting of the tender leaves that are most sought by consumers. Most often, farmers flood large basins containing qat plants and allow the water to percolate into the ground. More efficient and targeted means of irrigation are available, but there is apparently little incentive to implement water conservation measures in the qat fields. Due to its geographic characteristics, the San'a governorate is ideally situated to cultivate the plant. San'a is located in a basin high in the western highlands. At a latitude of 15 degrees north and 2,200 m above sea level, its climate is ideal for cultivation of the plant. Its basin contains large aquifers, and its sizeable population (estimated at 3.2m. in mid-2023) lives close to the fields. In 2011 San'a was the largest producer of qat, followed by al-Baidah, Hajjah and Ibb.

Qat production is lucrative. It occupies only about 10% of Yemen's productive land but produces 3% of total GDP. Fresh fruit and vegetables are almost equally lucrative in terms of cultivated area, while livestock is the third lucrative pillar of the agricultural sector. Qat production is still expanding and is an important source of income for rural areas.

Coffee was once among Yemen's most valuable export crops, along with tobacco and tea, and it has made a modest recovery recently. Coffee and qat compete for the same land, so the area under coffee cultivation fell dramatically over the last half century as qat became a more lucrative cash crop. Coffee is not widely consumed in Yemen. The local population tends to prefer tea or *kishr*—a drink made with the husk of the coffee bean. Coffee is exported and contributes in a very small way to ameliorating Yemen's balance of payments deficit. In 2011 about 34,000 ha of Yemen's cultivated land was dedicated to coffee, or about 2.5% of total arable land, although the area under coffee cultivation had increased substantially from 23,000 ha only two years earlier. Coffee exports could expand if greater efforts were made to promote Yemeni coffee in global markets. Several companies marketing Yemeni coffee have appeared in US markets in recent years—a positive sign for future export potential. According to the Food and Agriculture Organization (FAO) of the UN, coffee production rose from 19,000 metric tons in 2018, to 21,000 tons in 2019 and to an estimated 22,000 tons in 2020, before declining to 21,000 tons in 2021.

WATER

Agriculture consumes 90% of Yemen's water and qat takes 40% of the water devoted to agriculture. However, the water allocated to the cultivation of qat is mostly well water, which is responsible for the fall in Yemen's aquifers. In the mid-20th century rising income, the advent of drilling technology and the installation of diesel pumps enabled Yemenis to exploit water at far greater depths than had previously been possible. However, unregulated drilling and the failure of the private markets led to unsustainable withdrawals. FAO estimates that Yemenis have been drawing water at about 160% of the rate of replenishment.

The problem is most acute in the western highlands, where most of the population resides. Withdrawals there occur at four to five times the rate of replenishment. On the Red Sea coast, Hodeida contains one-quarter of all Yemen's well irrigated land, but Hodeida's population density is relatively low and withdrawals are not as large. The problem is more acute in the third major aquifer on the southern coast near Aden, where seawater intrusion destroyed Aden's water sources and the city was forced to divert agricultural water from nearby Lahj. The eastern Hadramout has a vast reservoir of water that supplies the relatively sparse population, but Hadramout is distant from the main population centre in the western highlands. The cost of pumping Hadramout's water up into the highlands is prohibitive, even if the political challenges were not already formidable.

Yemen's water crisis is really a crisis of management rather than a lack of water. If borewells were regulated and withdrawals limited to sustainable levels, Yemen's aquifers would be replenished by the rains. However, the capacity of the state to manage water resources is extremely limited, and the war has largely destroyed what little capacity remained after the overthrow of the Saleh regime in 2011.

The Yemeni Government, in conjunction with international development agencies, has developed strategies to lessen the effects of the crisis. Foremost in its plans is reducing withdrawals to sustainable levels. Given the state's lack of capacity, the best solution appears to be the co-ordination of self-regulating bodies of users in local areas. Suggested policies also focus on building economic incentives that discourage water withdrawals for agriculture by increasing the costs of pumping supplies and eliminating tariffs on the importation of water-intensive crops, particularly qat. Ethiopia has ideal conditions for qat cultivation if Yemeni investors were allowed to take up the opportunity. Other areas for development include managing wastewater that pollutes groundwater in urban areas and increasing the catchment of rainwater. Small-scale, low-cost rain capture systems for urban households could contribute significantly to supplying household needs if the research and development of local capabilities were supported. The widespread adoption of solar panels since 2015 is a good example of Yemen's capacity rapidly to adopt local small-scale technology when incentives support it.

REMITTANCES

Remittances from workers abroad remain an important part of the Yemeni economy. Since the onset of war in 2015, many households have been able to survive only because of remittances from relatives outside the country. World Bank figures showed that remittances to the Yemeni economy remained flat at about US $1,200m. for most of the 1990s and 2000s, but, with the onset of the Arab Spring, remittances rose sharply to an average annual rate of about $3,300m. during 2011–18. In 2021 the Assessment Capacities Project estimated that remittances were almost double the World Bank figures.

A better measure of the significance of remittances to the Yemeni economy is their relative contribution to GDP. In the 1970s and 1980s remittances contributed a substantial proportion of national domestic income (NDI) in the YAR and allowed the economy to run large trade deficits while maintaining current account surpluses. From about 20% of NDI in the early 1970s, remittances increased rapidly to contribute 45% of NDI in the late 1970s and then declined to about 25% of NDI in the mid-1980s. In the late 1980s the absolute value of remittances declined, owing to reduced demand for Yemeni labour in the oil-exporting countries, and the relative proportion of remittances in the overall economy declined even faster because the economy was growing as well. The value of remittances reached over US $1,000m. per year in the early 1980s, but declined in the late 1980s to only $250m. After Yemen was reunified in 1990, remittances remained low during the period leading up to the civil war of 1994, but then recovered to $1,000m. per year in the late 1990s, the same level as the early 1980s. Remittances remained at this level in the first decade of the 2000s, but the Yemeni economy grew significantly, so remittances only contributed about 2% of NDI in the 2000s.

The war since 2015 has revived the importance of the remittance economy. Relatives are sending money to their desperate families inside the war-torn country. The Ministry of Planning and International Co-operation indicated that remittances reached US $3,300m. in 2015, but the overall economy shrank considerably to $27,000m. in 2016 (from $43,000m. in 2014). Thus, remittances took on a relatively greater significance in the war-time economy.

Many observers have indicated that allowing Yemeni workers into Saudi Arabia and other Gulf states would give a significant boost to the Yemeni economy (World Bank, 2017), but the issue of Yemeni workers in the Gulf is fraught with seemingly unresolvable tensions. Yemen would clearly benefit tremendously from reduced unemployment and increased income through remittances. However, Saudi Arabia and the Gulf states view Yemen primarily as a security threat. Saudi Arabia is concerned about masses of poor Yemenis crossing the border in search of work, and the inability of the Yemeni state to control security threats such as the militant Islamist al-Qa'ida organization. Furthermore, Saudi Arabia and the Gulf monarchies argue that Yemeni workers are unskilled and that unskilled labour is not needed in the mature economies of the Gulf. In addition, Saudi Arabia and the Gulf states are facing their own unemployment problems. All the Gulf states are planning for a future non-hydrocarbons economy based upon a highly skilled national workforce and are trying to train their own citizens to take skilled jobs that have long been performed by foreign workers.

However, even allowing for attempts by Saudi Arabia and other Gulf states to encourage employment of Gulf nationals, there remain large low-skilled sectors of those economies that are occupied by non-national labour. In the UAE, almost 90% of the population is non-national, and in Saudi Arabia there were 13.4m. non-national workers, according to the 2022 census. There is clearly still a need in those countries for relatively low-skilled labour, despite recent efforts in Saudi Arabia and Kuwait, in particular, to give preference to their citizens in the area of employment. The World Bank compared the characteristics of registered Yemeni labourers in Saudi Arabia with those from Asia and found that, except for female domestic workers (predominantly Asian), the characteristics of Yemeni workers were no different from their Asian counterparts (World Bank, 2015). The reality is that the Gulf states prefer Asian workers to Yemenis because members of the expatriate Asian labour force very rarely make any political or economic demands upon Gulf societies. Yemenis, in contrast, are culturally close and may make demands for improved conditions or, even more threatening from a Saudi perspective, political change.

To overcome some of the Gulf states' reservations about Yemeni labour, a pilot programme supported by Qatar offered courses in construction for Yemenis. Yemenis were trained to become electricians, plumbers and carpenters. Those who successfully completed the training were offered jobs in Qatar. Such programmes could alleviate the concern that Yemeni workers were not suited for the Gulf job market and act as a vetting process for security concerns.

Saudi official figures from early 2017 reported that around 750,000 Yemenis were working in the kingdom, but there are reportedly many more undocumented workers there. Prior to the war in 2015, the Saudi Government began enforcing more strictly regulations for work permits and forcing undocumented labourers either to acquire regularization documents or leave. Once the war began, the Saudi Government allowed undocumented Yemeni labourers to stay in the country on a temporary basis. A more serious engagement with this issue would be the best way for Saudi Arabia to support Yemen's economy and help to stabilize Yemeni politics on a basis favourable to Saudi interests.

The global economic slowdown caused by the COVID-19 pandemic reduced the flow of remittances to Yemen. Expatriate Yemenis in the Gulf states and elsewhere are vulnerable to economic downturns, and anecdotal evidence from money changers in Yemen indicated that remittances had declined dramatically. However, remittances remained an important source of income and foreign exchange, although precise data do not exist. The dramatic recovery of oil prices in 2022 was expected to bolster the Gulf economies and, in turn, Yemen's remittance inflows.

FOREIGN TRADE

The structure of Yemen's trade shows clearly its dependence upon hydrocarbons exports. The Central Statistical Organization's (CSO) *Yearbook* for 2012 indicated that 67% of the value of Yemen's exports comprised crude petroleum, while gas accounted for 20% and fish just 3%. Yemen's imports were much more diversified than its exports. The primary import items by value were refined petroleum products, which comprised about 30% of the value of imports, followed by wheat, sugar, motor vehicles, medicine, machine parts and construction materials.

The rapid increase in oil exports in the late 1990s and then sustained high prices for oil in the first decade of the 2000s enabled Yemen to maintain a healthy trade balance and a current account surplus. The CBY accumulated a substantial cushion of foreign reserves equal to 6% of GDP in 2001. However, in 2007, even before significant declines in oil export revenue, rising imports—particularly imports of refined petroleum products—forced the trade balance into deficit for the first time since the late 1990s. The current account balance also became negative in that year, as Yemen was consuming more than it was producing. The global financial crisis in 2008–09 and the collapse in oil prices from 2014 severely depressed revenue from Yemen's oil exports, and pushed the trade balance into a large deficit. During the Arab Spring in 2011, imports and consumption fell, providing a brief respite from the deteriorating trade balance, but the recovery during the transitional Government under Hadi led to sizeable trade and current account deficits, despite large grants from Saudi Arabia.

The war all but completely halted the export of Yemen's oil and gas. In August 2016 the Hadi Government began exporting small amounts of oil from Hadramout, but estimates from the Ministry of Planning showed that Yemen's export revenues decreased by 80% in 2015 and that imports declined by 50%, owing to the blockade imposed by the Saudi-backed coalition and the collapse of domestic demand. The war exposed Yemen's heavy dependence upon oil exports. If and when a political settlement is reached, oil and gas exports will resume, but dwindling reserves will prevent Yemen from relying on oil for the same level of export revenues as it did in the past. Yemen will therefore be forced to find new exports to pay for essential imports such as food and fuel.

GOVERNMENT FINANCE

Government finances since the establishment of the two republics in the 1960s have always been precarious. The Imam's finances were based upon taxation of agriculture, but the republican Governments have depended upon tariffs on remittances and, since the 1990s, oil revenues. Oil revenues provided three-quarters or more of government revenues in the 1990s, the 2000s and the 2010s. Oil enabled the Yemeni Government to maintain low levels of debt until very recently, when it began borrowing heavily from domestic banks. Yemen's foreign debt was recorded at 45.7% of GDP in 2014, representing a relatively small debt-to-GDP ratio by international standards. However, the ratio increased significantly following the outbreak of the war, reaching 85.4% in 2016. During the height of the oil-producing era the Government spent most of its revenues on current expenses rather than investment. Its two largest expenses were public sector salaries and fuel subsidies. Government salaries constituted about 10% of GDP and provided a major source of income for about 1m. Yemeni families, and subsidies accounted for a huge proportion of government expenditure. Oil and gas will remain important to government revenues in the future, but will not likely provide the mainstay of revenue as in the past. The

Government will be forced to increase its capacity to tax the local economy if it is to raise revenues—a task that it has conspicuously failed to accomplish in the past.

In the 1970s and 1980s the YAR taxed the booming import trade to finance its current expenditure. Development aid financed capital projects almost entirely. In the early days of the reunified Yemen, the build-up to the war in 1994 prevented reorganization and rationalization of public revenues—with the competing factions putting almost all funds into the war effort. Following the civil war in 1994, the Yemeni Government began a structural adjustment programme negotiated with the IMF, which included measures to increase domestic taxation and eliminate costly subsidies. However, oil revenues increased dramatically in the late 1990s and relieved the pressure on the Government to carry out reforms. Government revenues from oil were less than US $500m. and contributed only about one-quarter of government revenues in the early 1990s, but increased to $1,000m., about two-thirds of government revenues, in the mid-1990s. Following a brief decline in 1998, owing to a global recession, Yemeni production increased dramatically as the Masila stream came online and government revenues rose rapidly to $2,000m., representing about 80% of total revenues. In the 2000s the Government appeared to be reliant on oil. While Yemeni production peaked in 2001, international oil prices rose dramatically, swelling government revenues to $4,500m. in 2008, despite the declines in production. The IMF, the World Bank and foreign governments continually reiterated recommended reforms, including increasing the efficiency and capacity of the state bureaucracy, reducing subsidies, and investing in the future productive capacity of the economy, but oil revenues and the importance of Yemen for international security allowed the Government to resist pressure to implement effective reforms.

In the early days of the republic, subsidies were designed to alleviate poverty, raise the standard of living, and fulfil promises of populist politicians to improve the lives of ordinary Yemeni people. In the 1990s the Government stopped subsidizing most commodities except fuel, although fuel constituted the major share of subsidies. In the 1990s and 2000s subsidies accounted for about one-quarter of government expenditure. As revenues declined and domestic fuel consumption increased, the toll of subsidies on government expenditure increased. Domestic fuel subsidies not only made fuel relatively cheap, but they were also one of the means for the Saleh regime to transfer wealth to its supporters. Meanwhile, the trafficking of subsidized fuel over the borders to foreign markets made fortunes for well-connected regime supporters.

Subsidies were a major issue in the political disputes that led to war breaking out in 2015. The transitional Government of Hadi faced declining oil revenues, owing in part to attacks on oil pipelines by its opponents. Funds for subsidies dried up and the Hadi Government was forced to withdraw subsidies. In early 2014 the Government agreed to a partial and gradual lifting of fuel subsidies over the next year paired with targeted transfers to the poor to offset the hardship of increased fuel prices. However, in a display of political ineptness, Hadi's office suddenly announced the complete withdrawal of subsidies in the middle of that year, without even consulting with the Government. The withdrawal of state support for fuel was used by the al-Houthis to garner popular support for their takeover of San'a in September. The technocratic administration installed by the al-Houthis towards the end of the year partially repealed the measure to end fuel subsidies, but, with the onset of war, the halting of oil production and the blockade of the country, the al-Houthis in effect withdrew subsidies as well. In fact, not only did the al-Houthis end subsidies, but they also began in effect taxing fuel by controlling the supply and manipulating markets. The al-Houthi war economy has completed Yemen's withdrawal from its apparent addiction to oil, but at an extremely high cost to the country.

The republican Governments of Yemen after 1962 enjoyed reliable sources of revenue. In the 1970s and 1980s the Government relied upon tariffs collected at seaports and airports, and in the 1990s, 2000s and 2010s the Government relied upon oil revenues. Other than importers in the earlier period, Yemenis were not taxed. However, the Government was aware that oil would eventually run out and that it would need to implement domestic taxes. As part of agreed economic reforms, a general sales tax was imposed in the 1990s and business income taxes were implemented in the 2000s, but the effective rate of taxation remained low. Only about one-quarter of the Government's revenue in the last decade has come from taxes. About one-half of taxes have come from sales taxes, and the remainder from business income taxes. Business income taxes were contested in the 2000s, as the private sector complained that the state tax agency was corrupt and that taxes benefited only the collectors. For their part, government tax collectors complained that the private sector refused to pay its fair share of taxes. Both assertions were largely true.

The al-Houthi administration in the western highlands does not have access to easy sources of revenue. The al-Houthis have imposed taxes on agriculture, businesses and various other assets to raise money. The dire circumstances of the war have lessened the political cost of imposing heavy taxes, and the effective rate of taxation is now no doubt much higher than during previous regimes.

On the expenditure side, subsidies and salaries have dominated in recent years. Subsidies have consumed one-quarter of government expenditure, and salaries were between one-third and one-half of current expenditure from the mid-1990s. About 1.2m. employees were officially on the public payroll, but the actual number of recipients was undoubtedly lower. Among the reforms constantly reiterated by international development agencies and domestic reformers alike was streamlining government employment. Payrolls were notoriously padded with non-existent or deceased individuals whose salaries were actually paid to military commanders or heads of government offices, for redistribution to regime supporters. Various schemes were proposed for eliminating so-called 'phantom' employees, such as biometric identification of employees, and grants for implementation of such programmes were regularly dispersed, but little progress was ever made. President Hadi raised the issue of 'phantom' soldiers inflating the payroll in mid-2018, after foreign news reporters had revealed widespread corruption in the Saudi-backed Yemeni armed forces. Under the current Government, there are no subsidies and salaries have been paid only sporadically to some employees in the southern and eastern areas controlled by the regime.

The CBY functions not only as the provider of currency and supervisor of monetary policy, but also as the Government's official lender, and the lender of last resort for all other banks in Yemen. During the 2000s the Government borrowed little and balance of payments surpluses allowed the central bank to acquire a significant buffer of foreign reserves. However, persistent trade deficits since 2007 and falling government revenue have depleted foreign reserves and increased public debt. Foreign currency assets of the CBY reached over US $8,000m. in 2008, but then declined steadily to about $4,000m. at the start of the conflict in March 2015. In short, Yemen imported and consumed significantly more than it exported and produced.

The Government relied upon domestic borrowing to cover deficits in the years immediately before the war. Since 2008 World Bank data have shown that the Government faced annual deficits amounting to about 7% of GDP. Rather than borrowing abroad—Yemen has never accrued much foreign debt—the Government borrowed from domestic banks. Total public domestic debt increased, according to IMF figures, from around 12% of GDP in 2007 to 35% of GDP in 2014. State-owned banks and private banks alike lent to the Government.

During the first year of the conflict, the CBY remained neutral. Both sides in the conflict appeared to respect the CBY's independence and the importance of maintaining the integrity of the national currency. The central bank paid salaries on both sides, and revenues from both sides went to the bank. However, in August 2016 the Hadi Government moved the headquarters of the central bank to Aden, after President Hadi accused the al-Houthis of depleting the CBY's foreign reserves to fund their war efforts. From US $4,000m. in March 2015, reserves had fallen to less than $1,000m. by August 2017—much of that sum being frozen in accounts in the USA. However, whether the al-Houthis used these funds for the war or simply paid the import bill without any exports to replenish foreign reserves was not clear. In any case, salaries in the al-Houthi-controlled areas have not been paid since the bank's move to Aden. The Hadi Government introduced new currency in larger denominations in late 2017, and the Yemeni riyal fell in relation to foreign currencies, amid fears that the Government was devaluing the currency. In January 2018 Saudi Arabia pledged to pay $2,000m. into the CBY to save the currency from collapse, but by July the Yemeni riyal had weakened to YR 515 = US $1, prompting the Yemeni Government in Aden to suspend foreign currency sales temporarily. By summer 2023 the Yemeni riyal in Government territory had fallen further, to YR 1,400 = US $1, a new low. Humanitarian organizations feared that the effect of the falling value of the currency on the prices of essential imported goods would lead to further suffering among the civilian population.

In San'a in mid-2018 the al-Houthi authorities began the confiscation of the new currency bills that had been introduced by the Hadi Government in late 2017. Al-Houthi militias confiscated the bills from currency traders who, in turn, refused to deal in the new bills. The al-Houthis created a second currency zone in Yemen, in which the new bills traded in 2023 in government territory at a rate of YR 1,400 = US $1, while in al-Houthi territory the old currency traded at YR 540 = US $1. The issue in al-Houthi-controlled territory is liquidity—the old bills are wearing out. In early 2023 the al-Houthis ordered banks not to allow withdrawals in cash, only in digital currency, which is largely useless in Yemen's cash economy.

While Saudi largesse has kept the government-run CBY in Aden afloat but struggling, the Yemeni riyal has continued to lose value in government-controlled territories.

BANKING

Access to credit is limited in Yemen. An IMF study on the Middle East and North Africa reported that the ratio of loans to the private sector to total GDP is lowest in Yemen. Loans to the private sector represent less than 10% of GDP, whereas in Jordan, Tunisia and Morocco loans to the private sector are close to 80% of GDP on average. Yemen is largely a cash economy and credit is informal. According to the CSO in 2012, there were 12 commercial banks, four Islamic banks and three speciality banks. Most of the assets of the public and private banks were government securities, and the assets of the Islamic banks were foreign. Very little credit was available for private investment in Yemen.

In the late 2000s microfinance organizations grew rapidly in Yemen. The World Bank reported in 2012 that 13 microfinance institutions were registered with the Ministry of Planning and International Co-operation, which were mostly supported by donor organizations. Most microfinance loans were to individuals for consumption needs rather than productive investment.

The war since 2015 has caused considerable disruption to the banking sector, in effect eliminating what little credit was available for the private sector. A survey of Yemen's private sector by the World Bank in 2018 indicated that most businesses paid employees and suppliers in cash, as they did not trust the banking sector to handle such transactions.

THE NON-OIL ECONOMY

Since the mid-2000s the contribution of the hydrocarbons sector to GDP has fallen, while wholesale and retail trade, transport and storage, construction, and communications have grown. In 2021, according to the UN's National Accounts Main Aggregates Database, wholesale and retail trade accounted for 20% of GDP, while transport, storage and communications contributed 16%, manufacturing 10% and construction 5%. The structure of employment has also changed: agriculture declined from about one-half of employment in 1995 to around one-third in 2015, according to FAO, while the number of those employed in trade, government and construction expanded. Yemen's economy is still largely based upon the import, transportation and sale of consumer goods, as it was in the 1970s and 1980s, with the addition of the growth of the public sector during the oil boom years of the 2000s, and construction, which served Yemen's growing cities.

However, as the World Bank has noted, the rising population and the addition of capital have accounted for the growth in Yemen's economy in recent decades, rather than an increase in labour productivity. There is little manufacturing in Yemen. The manufacturing sector is dominated by very small firms, mostly self-employed or employing only one worker. While there are many small workshops producing metal items such as doors or water tanks, wood products such as doors and window sashes, and garments in the apparel and leather industry, a small number of larger firms employ more than one-half of the total workforce. Large-scale manufacturing is concentrated in food processing such as biscuits and milk products. The tobacco sector is important, while cement factories supply the construction industry with approximately one-half of its concrete needs.

PORTS AND THE ADEN FREE TRADE ZONE

Yemen has two major ports—at Hodeida and Aden; there are small ports at Mokha, Mukalla and Nishtun, as well as several special purpose port facilities elsewhere in the country. Under British rule, Aden was the main port for British trade in the southern Arabian Peninsula and the Mutawakkilite Kingdom of Yemen. During the rule of the Imam the USSR developed a deepwater cargo facility at Hodeida that became the main port of the YAR after the British evacuation of Aden, the closure of the Suez Canal (following the Six-Day Arab–Israeli War) and the establishment of the socialist regime in South Yemen in 1967. Before the war that began in 2015, Hodeida still handled the largest volume of trade of any Yemeni port, despite the development of the Aden container facility in the 1990s.

There are three ports near Hodeida: the main port for deepwater cargo ships at Hodeida; the al-Salif port about 80 km (50 miles) north of Hodeida, which is principally used for offloading grain; and the nearby Ras Issa oil terminal, which comprises a floating storage tank and mooring for oil tankers at the termination of the pipeline from Marib to the Red Sea. A lack of maintenance of the storage tank, the *FSO Safer*, created the risk of an oil spill, which would cause a major environmental disaster; the al-Houthis were attempting to use this threat as leverage to attract international aid funding to repair the facility. In May 2023, following lengthy negotiations, work finally got under way to make the tanker stable and transfer the oil to another vessel.

The port of Aden consists of three facilities: the Aden Container Terminal, which was completed in 1999; the older Mukalla cargo facility, which was developed by the USSR; and the oil terminal for Aden refinery at al-Burayqa.

There are smaller ports that can handle mid-sized vessels at Mukalla in eastern Yemen, at Nishtun in the far-eastern governorate of Mahra, and at Mokha on the Red Sea. Yemen has two other ports that host offshore moorings for oil tankers—one at Husn al-Nushayma, which services the Shabwa oilfields, and the other at al-Shihr near Mukalla, which services the Masila oilfields in Hadramout province. The LNG terminal at Bilhaf on the Gulf of Aden has a facility for LNG tankers.

The Aden Free Zone and the Aden Container Terminal in Aden exemplify the challenges of investing and raising labour productivity in Yemen. Aden is a spectacular natural harbour formed from a collapsed volcano that created a sheltered deepwater port. In the late 1950s Aden was one of the busiest ports in the world. The Suez Crisis of 1956, and the British withdrawal and the establishment of the PDRY in 1967, in effect closed the port. The Imamate used the port of Aden during most of its reign, but in the late 1950s the USSR modernized the port at Hodeida, and it became the main port for importing goods into the Kingdom and the YAR after 1962, further depriving Aden of business.

The declaration of Yemeni unification in 1990 opened the doors to substantial development of the port of Aden. So promising was the prospect of reinvigorating the port that the reunified Republic of Yemen declared Aden its economic capital. The possibility of reviving the port with a modern container facility and creating a free trade zone to attract industrial investment from foreigners and Yemenis living overseas ignited the imagination of Yemenis and foreigners alike. The promise was great, but the results have been dismal. The Aden Container Terminal was built and administered by the Singapore Port Authority, until a terrorist attack perpetrated by al-Qa'ida on the *Limburg* oil tanker in the Gulf of Aden in October 2002 and the rise of piracy off the Somali coast reduced greatly the number of ships calling at Aden. The Singapore Port Authority ended its contract, and the Yemeni Government negotiated with the UAE's DP World for the expansion (which never occurred) and administration of the container facility. In 2012 the transitional administration of President Hadi took control of the terminal. The port was closed while conflict raged in Aden in early 2015, but reopened later that year when local forces backed by the Saudi and Emirati armed forces cleared the city of al-Houthi fighters. The port has since revived, and in July 2018 the Port Authority announced that the number of containers offloaded in Aden had reached a level not witnessed since 2012. Furthermore, the battle for Hodeida in late 2018 forced humanitarian agencies to use Aden rather than Hodeida (which handled the largest portion, 70%, of Yemen's foreign trade), which added to Aden's already high level of commercial activity. However, all of Yemen remained a designated war zone with high insurance costs. As a result, transporting cargo by ship to Salalah in Oman then via an overland route was much cheaper (and safer) than landing directly in Aden. The development of trade from Salalah through eastern Yemen led to increased Saudi attention on Mahrah, the easternmost governorate of Yemen. Saudi Arabia accused Oman of facilitating the flow of weapons to the al-Houthis through Mahrah governorate and occupied air, sea and land entrances to the governorate, leading to armed clashes with local tribesmen and officials.

The promise of the Aden port centred on its deep water, which enabled it to service the new generation of large post-Panamax and 'new' Panamax container ships (these descriptions refer to the dimensions of the original and new channels of the Panama Canal). Aden held the very real hope of becoming a major transshipment centre for larger ships. Security difficulties were certainly part of the problem that the project faced, but the larger issue that challenged the port and the associated Aden Free Zone was the insecurity of investment, and, in Aden in particular, the insecurity of property rights.

The Aden Free Zone is outside the traditionally developed areas of Aden, but the problems of the city illuminate the challenges of the Free Zone. Property in Aden and in the south of Yemen is not considered secure. Multiple rounds of property confiscations have legitimized the use of force to acquire assets. The British used military force against the city to establish their domain in the mid-19th century, but the long rule of the British Empire secured the general expectation of stable property rights. Following the British withdrawal in 1967, however, successive waves of confiscation campaigns by socialist rulers destabilized property rights, but the end of socialism in 1990 did not lead to renewed security for property rights; in fact, property became even less secure, as it was now subject to the whims of those in power.

After the fall of socialism, the Yemeni Socialist Party, which was still in power in the south, began the process of returning land and property to its former owners, but little progress had been made when the civil war broke out in 1994. In that conflict, the northern forces deployed against the socialists in Aden were supported not only by southern landowners who had lost their land in the early days of the PDRY, but also by the forces of Ali Nasser Muhammad (led by Hadi), who had been ousted from Aden in internal warfare in 1986. Ali Nasser's troops were socialists who wanted to recover the property taken from them in 1986, but which in turn had been taken from southern property owners a decade earlier, so two groups were competing over the same property. Moreover, the advancing armies of the north included many additional individuals who considered the south as ripe for pillage. Northerners accompanied by well-armed militias carried out a further round of confiscations. The depredations of these northerners caused such turmoil that the Saleh regime was unable completely to subdue the south. Beginning in 2007, the southern movement, or Hirak, agitated for independence from the north (see History). The rise of Hirak was one of several factors that led to the downfall of the Saleh regime in 2011.

However, President Hadi's transitional administration was also unable to gain legitimacy among southerners, even though Hadi is a southerner himself. In an effort to entice southerners to participate in the National Dialogue Conference in San'a in 2013, the President issued a number of decrees that sought to resolve the issue of confiscation of southern land after the war of 1994, supported by a fund created by the UAE, but again without much effect.

Insecurity of property and land deters investment in the Yemeni economy. Only those protected by the regime will invest in Yemen, and even those people place most of their assets outside of the country. For example, Shaher Abdulhak Bishr—who died in 2020 and was a former close associate of Saleh—was known locally as the 'King of Sugar', and owned the Coca-Cola and Mercedes-Benz distribution networks in Yemen, the Taj Sheba Hotel, and one of four local telecommunications companies, MTN. He was widely considered to act as a private envoy for Saleh during his presidency, but a series of leaked documents detailing assets held by international corporations and wealthy individuals in offshore tax havens (the so-called Panama Papers), published in May 2016, revealed that Bishr and his brother had placed most of their significant assets outside Yemen, just as the UN sanctions committee had revealed to be the case with Saleh. The al-Houthis in San'a have confiscated assets and redirected control of the economy to the al-Houthi leadership. If political and security concerns continue to pre-empt economic matters and if capital continues to flee Yemen, the economy cannot move beyond its limited natural resource base to develop the country's real resources, namely its people.

Statistical Survey

Sources (unless otherwise indicated): Republic of Yemen Central Statistical Organization, POB 13434, San'a; tel. (1) 250619; fax (1) 250664; internet www.cso-yemen.com; Central Bank of Yemen, POB 59, Ali Abd al-Mughni St, San'a; tel. (1) 274314; fax (1) 274360; internet cby-ye.com.

Area and Population

AREA, POPULATION AND DENSITY

Area (sq km)	536,869*
Population (census results)	
16 December 1994†	14,587,807
16 December 2004‡	
Males	10,036,953
Females	9,648,208
Total	19,685,161
Population (UN estimates at mid-year)§	
2021	32,981,642
2022¶	33,696,614
2023¶	34,449,825
Density (per sq km) at mid-2023¶	64.2

* 207,286 sq miles.
† Excluding adjustment for underenumeration.
‡ Population is *de jure*.
§ Source: UN, *World Population Prospects: The 2022 Revision*.
¶ Projection.

Note: At December 2022 UNHCR estimated an internally displaced population of some 4.5m. in Yemen, following almost two decades of internal conflict.

POPULATION BY AGE AND SEX
('000, UN projections at mid-2023)

	Males	Females	Total
0–14 years	6,889.8	6,570.0	13,459.8
15–64 years	10,116.5	9,960.8	20,077.3
65 years and over	390.1	522.6	912.7
Total	17,396.5	17,053.4	34,449.8

Source: UN, *World Population Prospects: The 2022 Revision*.

PRINCIPAL TOWNS
(incl. suburbs, UN population projections at mid-2023)

San'a (capital)	3,292,497	Hodeida	734,699
Aden	1,079,670	Al-Mukalla	594,951
Taiz	940,600	Dhamar	404,901
Ibb	771,514		

Source: UN, *World Urbanization Prospects: The 2018 Revision*.

BIRTHS, MARRIAGES AND DEATHS
(UN estimates)

	2019	2020	2021
Birth rate (per 1,000)	31.8	31.3	30.5
Death rate (per 1,000)	6.4	6.5	6.8

Source: UN, *World Population Prospects: The 2022 Revision*.

Registered births: 575,556 in 2016; 645,833 in 2017.
Registered deaths: 25,927 in 2016; 31,999 in 2017.
Marriages (2002, estimate): 10,934 (Source: UN, *Demographic Yearbook*).
Life expectancy (years at birth, estimates): 63.8 (males 60.6; females 67.1) in 2021 (Source: World Bank, World Development Indicators database).

Employment
(labour force survey, '000 persons aged 15 years and over, 2014)

	Males	Females	Total
Agriculture, hunting and forestry	1,048	151	1,199
Fishing	28	0	28
Mining and quarrying	7	0	7
Manufacturing	195	36	231
Electricity, gas and water	7	0	7
Construction	361	0	361
Trade, restaurants and hotels	935	18	953
Transport, storage and communications	361	1	362
Hotels and restaurants	91	2	93
Finance, insurance and real estate	36	0	36
Education	184	47	231
Health and social welfare	41	12	53
Personal and social services	52	6	58
Public administration and defence	518	15	533
Private households with employed persons	14	2	16
Extraterritorial organizations and bodies	23	3	26
Sub-total	3,901	293	4,194
Unspecified	3	0	3
Total	3,904	293	4,197

Source: ILO.

Mid-2015 (estimates in '000): Agriculture, etc. 2,213; Total labour force 6,569 (Source: FAO).

Health and Welfare

KEY INDICATORS

Total fertility rate (children per woman, 2021)	3.8
Under-5 mortality rate (per 1,000 live births, 2021)	61.9
HIV/AIDS (% of persons aged 15–49, 2021)	<0.1
COVID-19: Cumulative confirmed deaths (per 100,000 persons at 30 June 2023)	6.4
COVID-19: Fully vaccinated population (% of total population at 20 June 2023)	2.4
Physicians (per 1,000 head, 2014)	0.3
Hospital beds (per 1,000 head, 2017)	0.7
Domestic health expenditure (2015): US $ per head (PPP)	10.4
Domestic health expenditure (2015): % of GDP	0.4
Domestic health expenditure (2015): public (% of total current health expenditure)	10.2
Access to improved water resources (% of persons, 2020)	61
Access to improved sanitation facilities (% of persons, 2020)	54
Total carbon dioxide emissions ('000 metric tons, 2019)	11,095
Carbon dioxide emissions per head (metric tons, 2019)	0.4
Human Development Index (2021): ranking	183
Human Development Index (2021): value	0.455

Note: For data on COVID-19 vaccinations, 'fully vaccinated' denotes receipt of all doses specified by approved vaccination regime (Sources: Johns Hopkins University and Our World in Data). Data on health expenditure refer to current general government expenditure in each case. For more information on sources and further definitions for all indicators, see Health and Welfare Statistics: Sources and Definitions section (europaworld.com/credits).

Agriculture

PRINCIPAL CROPS
('000 metric tons)

	2019	2020	2021
Bananas	116	119*	115*
Barley	27	21†	20†
Beans, green	3	3*	3*
Cantaloupes and other melons	37	36*	29*
Carrots and turnips	15	16*	15*
Chick peas	39	41*	40*
Chillies and peppers, green	15	16*	15*
Coffee, green	21	22*	21*
Cucumbers and gherkins*	15	15	15
Dates	64	68*	60*
Garlic*	3	3	3
Grapes	134	137	137*
Lemons and limes	26	26*	25*
Maize	48	40†	35†
Mangoes, mangosteens and guavas	362	373*	336*
Millet	50	40†	30†
Okra	23	22*	19*
Onions, dry	223	241*	215*
Oranges	119	124*	115*
Papayas	25	25*	21*
Potatoes	233	234*	228*
Seed cotton	16	10*	11*
Sesame seed	22	23*	21*
Sorghum	231	160†	180†
Tangerines, mandarins, etc.	20	22*	22*
Tobacco, unmanufactured	29	30*	26*
Tomatoes	105	96*	90*
Watermelons	141	142*	149*
Wheat	100	130†	125†

* FAO estimate(s).
† Unofficial figure.

Aggregate production ('000 metric tons, may include official, semi-official or estimated data): Total cereals 457 in 2019, 391 in 2020, 390 in 2021; Total fruit (primary) 1,159 in 2019, 1,201 in 2020, 1,113 in 2021; Total oilcrops 40 in 2019, 34 in 2020, 33 in 2021; Total roots and tubers 233 in 2019, 235 in 2020, 229 in 2021; Total vegetables (primary) 460 in 2019, 468 in 2020, 433 in 2021.

Source: FAO.

LIVESTOCK
('000 head, year ending September)

	2019	2020*	2021*
Asses	713*	712	711
Camels	448	458	453
Cattle	1,818	1,664	1,662
Chickens	69,601*	70,480	71,621
Goats	9,486	9,611	9,344
Horses	2*	2	2
Sheep	9,718	9,239	9,257

* FAO estimate(s).

Source: FAO.

LIVESTOCK PRODUCTS
('000 metric tons)

	2019	2020*	2021*
Cattle hides, fresh	14.1*	17.9	18.0
Cattle meat	75.6	95.6	96.4
Cattle offals, edible	14.3*	18.0	18.2
Cows' milk	234.5	224.6	224.5
Chicken meat	195.9*	200.5	205.9
Goat meat	73.3	80.6	84.5
Sheep meat	57.9	56.7	45.2
Goat offals, edible	14.7*	16.1	16.9
Goats' milk	73.1	68.1	68.9
Goats' skins, fresh	14.7*	16.1	16.9
Sheep offals, edible	11.5*	11.2	8.9
Sheep's (Ewes') milk	59.1	49.7	51.3
Sheepskins, fresh	11.5*	11.2	8.9
Hen eggs	70.4*	70.4	n.a.
Wool, greasy	8.7*	8.8	9.1

* FAO estimate(s).

Source: FAO.

Forestry

ROUNDWOOD REMOVALS
('000 cu m, excl. bark, FAO estimates)

	2019	2020	2021
Pulpwood	2	2	2
Other industrial wood	1	1	1
Fuel wood	592	611	630
Total	595	614	633

Source: FAO.

Fishing

('000 metric tons, live weight of capture)

	2015	2016	2017
Indian mackerel*	10.3	8.7	7.4
Indian oil sardine*	38.9	33.0	28.1
Yellowfin tuna	24.4	21.1	18.1
Pelagic percomorphs*	32.2	28.0	23.8
Sharks, rays and skates, etc.	9.1	7.8	6.6
Cuttlefish and bobtail squids*	12.2	10.5	8.9
Total catch (incl. others)*	176.8	152.1	131.3

* FAO estimates.

2018–21: Figures are assumed to be unchanged from 2017 (FAO estimates).

Source: FAO.

Mining

('000 metric tons unless otherwise indicated)

	2019	2020	2021
Crude petroleum	4,075	3,767	3,501
Natural gas (million cu m)	100	130	130
Salt*	100	n.a.	n.a.
Gypsum (crude)*	100	n.a.	n.a.

* Estimated production.

2022: Crude petroleum ('000 metric tons) 3,405; Natural gas (million cu m) 130.

Sources: Energy Institute, *Statistical Review of World Energy*; US Geological Survey.

Industry

SELECTED PRODUCTS
('000 barrels unless otherwise indicated)

	2017	2018	2019
Liquefied petroleum gas ('000 metric tons)	256	338	443
Motor spirit	1,387	1,387	1,390*
Kerosene	2,920	2,920	2,920*
Distillate fuel oils	5,694	5,694	5,690*
Residual fuel oils	4,052	4,052	4,050*
Cement ('000 metric tons)	1,920	1,880*	1,900*
Electrical energy (million kWh)	4,050	3,487	3,277

* Estimate.

2020: Liquefied petroleum gas 409,000 metric tons; Electrical energy 2,939m. kWh.

Sources: US Geological Survey; UN Energy Statistics Database.

Finance

CURRENCY AND EXCHANGE RATES

Monetary Units
100 fils = 1 Yemeni riyal (YR).

Sterling, Dollar and Euro Equivalents (30 December 2022)
£1 sterling = YR 1,498.85;
US $1 = YR 1,242.00;
€1 = YR 1,324.72;
YR 1,000 = £0.67 = 0.81 = €0.75.

Average Exchange Rate (YR per US $)
2020 743.006
2021 1,035.467
2022 1,110.203

Note: Following the merger of the two Yemens in May 1990, the Yemen Arab Republic's currency was adopted as the currency of the unified country. From the mid-1990s the exchange rate for private transactions was allowed to be freely determined by prevailing markets, but significant regional disparities with the official exchange rate (maintained at YR 250.250 per US dollar for many years) were subsequently reported, and from the early 2000s growing hostilities and political instability contributed to a significant deterioration in the exchange rate in all parts of the country, with prevailing rates of 1,500 riyals per US dollar reported in Aden and some other cities in July 2023.

CENTRAL GOVERNMENT BUDGET
(YR '000 million)

Revenue and grants	2015	2016	2017
Current revenue	1,042.5	898.6	864.4
Tax revenue	474.0	527.8	413.2
Direct taxes	259.3	274.7	235.1
Indirect taxes	214.6	253.0	178.1
Non-tax revenue	568.5	370.9	451.2
Capital revenue	0	—	—
Grants	10.6	—	—
Total	1,053.1	898.6	864.4

Expenditure	2015	2016	2017
Current expenditure	1,839.0	1,645.2	1,273.9
Civil wages and salaries	915.0	648.8	206.4
Materials and services	149.8	106.7	105.8
Interest	605.5	774.2	885.0
Domestic	590.3	768.9	885.0
Foreign	15.2	5.3	—
Transfers and subsidies	117.4	76.3	57.2
Current transfers	96.6	69.7	57.2
Subsidies	20.7	6.7	—
Other current expenditure	51.4	39.2	19.4
Capital development expenditure	44.9	22.5	0.2
Net lending	25.1	—	—
Total	1,909.0	1,667.8	1,274.0

INTERNATIONAL RESERVES
(US $ million at 31 December)

	2011	2012	2013
Gold (national valuation)	82.4	90.0	65.3
IMF special drawing rights	253.9	253.8	251.4
Foreign exchange	4,195.0	5,813.8	5,032.7
Total	4,531.3	6,157.6	5,349.4

IMF special drawing rights: 9.1 in 2020; 663.1 in 2021; 303.5 in 2022.

Source: IMF, *International Financial Statistics*.

MONEY SUPPLY
(YR million at 31 December)

	2011	2012	2013
Currency outside banks	777,407	803,407	784,768
Demand deposits at commercial banks	162,300	231,544	261,599
Total money (incl. others)	993,031	1,104,891	1,116,583

Source: IMF, *International Financial Statistics*.

COST OF LIVING
(Consumer Price Index; base: 2008 = 100)

	2012	2013	2014
Food and non-alcoholic beverages	147.5	164.1	170.8
Clothing and footwear	133.4	155.8	222.2
Housing and related items	157.4	162.1	165.6
All items (incl. others)	153.0	169.8	183.6

NATIONAL ACCOUNTS
(YR million at current prices)

Expenditure on the Gross Domestic Product

	2019	2020	2021
Government final consumption expenditure	735,169	794,751	1,213,746
Private final consumption expenditure	6,451,738	7,252,398	10,618,693
Changes in stocks	103,825	−25,898	−37,876
Gross fixed capital formation	1,095,290	1,141,564	1,669,546
Total domestic expenditure	8,386,022	9,162,814	13,464,109
Exports of goods and services	621,100	636,628	1,225,101
Less Imports of goods and services	2,689,250	2,802,866	4,287,737
Statistical discrepancy	—	—	−101,872
GDP in purchasers' values	6,317,871	6,996,576	10,299,601
GDP at constant 2015 prices	4,379,537	4,432,246	4,387,923

Gross Domestic Product by Economic Activity

	2019	2020	2021
Agriculture, hunting, forestry and fishing	1,224,400	1,348,642	1,978,934
Mining and utilities	363,660	407,537	564,687
Manufacturing	626,307	677,100	1,041,715
Construction	320,519	358,320	509,354
Trade, restaurants and hotels	1,258,753	1,401,202	2,068,043
Transport, storage and communications	963,215	1,101,388	1,581,684
Other services	1,469,177	1,601,079	2,405,543
Sub-total	6,226,031	6,895,267	10,149,959
Indirect taxes (net)*	91,840	101,309	149,642
GDP in purchasers' values	6,317,871	6,996,576	10,299,601

* Figures obtained as residuals.

Source: UN National Accounts Main Aggregates Database.

YEMEN

BALANCE OF PAYMENTS
(US $ million)

	2015	2016	2017
Exports of goods	1,444.2	431.4	1,301.2
Imports of goods	−6,309.2	−6,798.3	−6,515.5
Balance on goods	**−4,865.0**	**−6,366.9**	**−5,214.3**
Exports of services	428.4	465.6	565.3
Imports of services	−1,318.6	−1,107.4	−1,244.6
Balance on goods and services	**−5,755.1**	**−7,008.7**	**−5,893.6**
Primary income received	22.7	18.3	12.9
Primary income paid	−569.4	−381.4	−379.7
Balance on goods, services and primary income	**−6,301.8**	**−7,371.8**	**−6,260.4**
Secondary income received	3,693.2	5,557.6	5,118.4
Secondary income paid	−46.8	−45.9	−67.6
Current balance	**−2,655.5**	**−1,860.1**	**−1,209.7**
Direct investment liabilities	−15.4	280.0	245.0
Other investment assets	−205.6	−275.9	−295.6
Net errors and omissions	278.4	498.5	589.2
Reserves and related items	**−2,598.1**	**−1,357.4**	**−671.1**

External Trade

PRINCIPAL COMMODITIES
(distribution by SITC, YR million)

Imports c.i.f.	2015	2016	2017
Food and live animals	577,628.9	651,270.1	383,954.1
Beverages and tobacco	24,633.4	22,505.8	7,605.9
Mineral fuels, lubricants, etc.	258,628.1	298,510.5	268,884.9
Chemicals and related products	109,756.2	170,304.7	53,300.7
Basic manufactures	173,926.3	300,121.5	88,378.3
Machinery and transport equipment	228,771.1	237,652.0	122,470.5
Miscellaneous manufactured goods	58,176.9	76,695.4	33,074.2
Total (incl. others)	1,526,767.3	1,824,895.7	986,340.1

Exports f.o.b.	2015	2016	2017
Food and live animals	56,957.1	73,816.6	21,252.2
Beverages and tobacco	1,988.9	2,143.9	517.9
Mineral fuels, lubricants, etc.	108,430.6	307.1	0.0
Chemicals and related products	13,462.5	1,998.0	391.4
Basic manufactures	4,401.3	3,552.4	1,405.5
Machinery and transport equipment	32,774.9	9,101.8	2,075.4
Miscellaneous manufactured goods	611.5	1,662.7	39.9
Total (incl. others)	222,303.3	98,308.9	27,303.6

PRINCIPAL TRADING PARTNERS
(YR million)

Imports c.i.f.	2015	2016	2017
Argentina	44,045.2	44,816.7	56,235.5
Australia	66,543.6	50,877.2	49,135.0
Brazil	47,606.9	86,491.2	61,126.5
China, People's Republic	103,770.6	122,283.5	32,958.5
Djibouti	103,466.0	120,932.7	32,902.8
Egypt	24,757.9	43,373.5	18,207.2
France (incl. Monaco)	23,055.8	20,446.6	8,317.3
Germany	35,069.2	22,884.0	3,932.6
India	55,058.6	69,182.3	13,312.5
Indonesia	14,167.8	12,982.0	6,006.4
Italy	7,358.4	13,793.9	8,683.4
Korea, Republic	16,421.0	19,743.8	9,777.5
Malaysia	35,484.0	49,881.3	17,101.9
Oman	114,693.5	165,377.8	175,440.5
Russian Federation	34,723.8	43,949.6	55,432.0
Saudi Arabia	246,778.1	246,395.4	94,545.5
Thailand	25,680.3	20,586.0	12,664.2
Türkiye	66,693.0	110,562.5	50,535.7
United Arab Emirates	163,072.3	330,755.1	161,126.4
USA	49,866.4	40,384.7	22,252.6
Total (incl. others)	1,526,767.3	1,824,895.7	986,340.1

Exports f.o.b.	2015	2016	2017
China, People's Republic	12,977.9	468.8	280.1
Djibouti	2,655.3	3,383.5	287.3
Egypt	3,366.5	3,418.0	1,943.9
France	2,076.3	191.0	25.2
Germany	1,204.8	333.7	652.4
India	13,390.4	208.3	68.9
Italy	821.1	416.2	443.8
Japan	13,560.2	391.7	34.8
Jordan	264.5	1,450.2	38.5
Korea, Republic	57,622.7	142.1	623.4
Malaysia	14,185.9	1,716.4	435.7
Oman	13,928.2	33,146.4	14,979.3
Saudi Arabia	46,945.0	38,407.7	3,529.4
Somalia	7,334.1	6,486.1	1,230.5
United Arab Emirates	1,012.5	2,807.8	758.6
USA	3,039.5	352.3	30.6
Viet Nam	1,466.5	1,811.2	406.6
Total (incl. others)	222,303.3	98,308.9	27,303.6

Transport

SHIPPING

Flag Registered Fleet
(at 31 December)

	2020	2021	2022
Number of vessels	40	40	42
Total displacement ('000 grt)	222.0	220.1	220.1

Source: Lloyd's List Intelligence (www.bit.ly/LLintelligence).

International Seaborne Freight Traffic
('000 metric tons unless otherwise indicated, excluding dhows)

	2015	2016	2017
Vessels entered (number)	383	346	240
Dry cargo:*			
goods loaded	89	113	200
goods unloaded	5,523	6,933	5,577
Petroleum products:			
goods unloaded	1,416	1,515	1,672

* Excluding livestock and vehicles.

Petroleum products (goods loaded): 3,832 in 2011; 4,329 in 2012; 4,329 in 2013.

YEMEN

CIVIL AVIATION
(traffic on scheduled services)

	2013	2014	2015
Kilometres flown (million)	16	16	12
Passengers carried ('000)	1,664	1,666	1,388
Passenger-km (million)	2,120	2,116	1,801

Source: UN, *Statistical Yearbook*.

2021 (domestic and international): Departures 560; Passengers carried 52,035; Freight carried 2.5m. ton-km (Source: World Bank, World Development Indicators database).

Tourism

TOURIST ARRIVALS

	2013	2014	2015
Bahrain	9,039	—	1,401
Egypt	11,155	10,880	3,837
Eritrea	5,777	6,226	2,010
Ethiopia	11,463	4,734	1,858
India	19,896	20,429	20,429
Indonesia	5,391	4,260	1,261
Jordan	6,549	5,364	1,814
Oman	55,431	53,895	22,046
Pakistan	10,289	9,182	3,664
Qatar	3,937	3,178	1,365
Saudi Arabia	237,361	238,820	89,822
Syrian Arab Republic	4,170	—	6,647
Türkiye	7,972	6,268	2,501
United Arab Emirates	17,071	11,496	3,520
United Kingdom	5,501	7,432	2,049
USA	22,657	21,343	7,369
Total (incl. others)	989,566	1,017,491	366,692

Tourism receipts (US $ million, excl. passenger transport): 940 in 2013; 1,026 in 2014; 100 in 2015.

Source: World Tourism Organization.

Communications Media

	2019	2020	2021
Telephones ('000 main lines in use)	1,240	1,240	1,240
Mobile telephone subscriptions ('000)	15,238	15,178	15,178
Broadband subscriptions, fixed ('000)	382	391	391
Broadband subscriptions, mobile ('000)	1,654	1,648	1,648

2017: Internet users (% of population) 26.7.

Source: International Telecommunication Union.

Education

(2015/16 unless otherwise indicated)

	Schools	Teachers	Students Males	Females	Total
Pre-primary	544	1,375	19,507	16,813	36,320
Primary*	12,386	115,101	2,924,778	2,299,540	5,224,318
Secondary	370*	72,701	1,127,277	788,594	1,915,871
Higher†	37	10,261	208,994	101,351	310,345

* 2016/17.
† 2013/14.

Source: partly UNESCO Institute for Statistics.

Pupil-teacher ratio (qualified teaching staff, primary education, UNESCO estimates): 45.3 in 2015/16 (Source: UNESCO Institute for Statistics).

Adult literacy rate (UNESCO estimates): 70.0% (males 85.0%; females 54.9%) in 2015 (Source: UNESCO Institute for Statistics).

Directory

The Constitution

A draft Constitution for the united Republic of Yemen was published in December 1989; it was approved by a popular referendum on 15–16 May 1991.

On 29 September 1994 a total of 52 articles were amended, 29 added and one cancelled, leaving a total of 159 articles in the Constitution. Further amendments to the Constitution were adopted by the House of Representatives in late November 2000 and approved in a national referendum on 20 February 2001.

The Constitution defines the Yemeni Republic as an independent and sovereign Arab and Islamic country. The document states that the Republic 'is an indivisible whole, and it is impermissible to concede any part of it. The Yemeni people are part of the Arab and Islamic nation'. The Islamic *Shari'a* is identified as the basis of all laws.

The revised Constitution provides for the election, by direct universal suffrage, of the President of the Republic; the President is elected for a seven-year term (increased from five years by the amendments approved in 2001). The President is empowered to appoint a Vice-President. The President of the Republic is, ex officio, Supreme Commander of the Armed Forces. The Constitution as amended in 2001 requires presidential candidates to obtain the endorsement of 5% of a combined vote of the appointed Consultative Council and the elected House of Representatives (in place of 10% of the latter chamber alone).

Legislative authority is vested in the 301-member House of Representatives, which is elected, by universal suffrage, for a six-year term (increased from four years by amendment in 2001). The role of the House of Representatives is defined as to 'monitor' the executive. The President is empowered to dissolve the legislature and call new elections within a period of 60 days.

The upper house of the legislature, the Consultative Council, has 111 members (increased from 59 by amendment in 2001), nominated by the President.

The President of the Republic appoints the Prime Minister and other members of the Government on the advice of the Prime Minister.

The Constitution delineates the separation of the powers of the organs of State, and guarantees the independence of the judiciary. The existence of a multi-party political system is confirmed. Serving members of the police and armed forces are banned from political activity.

The Government

HEAD OF STATE

In a bid to support the ongoing peace negotiations and the United Nations-brokered truce between pro-Government troops and the al-Houthi insurgents, on 7 April 2022 President Abd al-Rabbuh Mansour Hadi dismissed Vice-President Ali Mohsen al-Ahmar from his post and delegated his own powers and those of his former deputy to a newly established eight-member Presidential Leadership Council which would be dissolved upon the election of a new President.

Presidential Leadership Council:

Chairman: Maj.-Gen. Dr RASHAD AL-ALIMI.

Deputy Chairmen: SULTAN ALI AL-ARADA, TARIQ MUHAMMAD SALEH, ABDULRAHMAN AL-MAHRAMI, ABDULLAH AL-ALIMI, OTHMAN HUSSEIN MEGALI, AIDAROUS QASSEM AL-ZUBAIDI, FARAJ SALMIN AL-BAHSANI.

YEMEN   Directory

COUNCIL OF MINISTERS
(September 2023)

Prime Minister: Maeen Abdulmalik Saeed.
Minister of Foreign Affairs and Minister of Expatriate Affairs: Dr Ahmed Awadh bin Mubarak.
Minister of Defence: Lt-Gen. Mohsen Mohammed al-Daeri.
Minister of Information, Culture and Tourism: Muammar al-Eryani.
Minister of Planning and International Co-operation: Dr Wa'ed Abdullah Bathib.
Minister of Youth and Sports: Nayef Saleh al-Bakri.
Minister of Finance: Salem Saleh bin Braik.
Minister of Telecommunications and Information Technology: Dr Najeeb Mansour al-Aweg.
Minister of Agriculture, Irrigation and Fisheries: Salim Abdullah Assoqatri.
Minister of Oil and Minerals: Saeed al-Shamsi.
Minister of Higher Education, Scientific Research and Vocational Training: Dr Khaled Ahmed al-Wosabi.
Minister of the Interior: Maj.-Gen. Ebrahim Ali Haidan.
Minister of Legal Affairs and Human Rights: Ahmed Omer Arman.
Minister of Water and the Environment: Eng. Tawfiq al-Sharjabi.
Minister of Industry and Trade: Mohammed Hezam al-Ashwal.
Minister of Transport: Dr Abdulsalam Saleh Humaid.
Minister of Religious Endowments and Guidance: Mohammed Aidha Shabebah.
Minister of the Civil Service and Insurance: Dr Abdunasser Ahmed al-Wali.
Minister of Public Health and Population: Dr Qasem Mohammed Bahibeh.
Minister of Local Administration: Hussein Abdurahman al-Aghbari.
Minister of Justice: Badr Abdo al-Aredha.
Minister of Education: Tareq Salim al-Akbari.
Minister of Electricity and Energy: Eng. Manea Yaslam bin Yamin al-Nahdi.
Minister of Social Affairs and Labour: Dr Mohammed Sa'ed Aza'rori.
Minister of Public Works and Highways: Eng. Salem Muhammad al-Aboudi al-Huraizi.
Minister of State: Ahmed Hamed Lamlas.

MINISTRIES

Owing to the ongoing civil conflict and occupation of the capital, San'a, by the forces aligned with the al-Houthi movement, President Abd al-Rabbuh Mansour Hadi and his internationally recognized Government are based in Aden.

Ministry of Agriculture, Irrigation and Fisheries: POB 2805, San'a; tel. (1) 296456; fax (1) 277177; e-mail alahmadi@hotmail.com; internet www.agricultureyemen.com.
Ministry of Civil Service and Insurance: POB 1992, San'a; tel. (1) 282404; fax (1) 283592; internet www.mocsi.gov.ye.
Ministry of Defence: POB 1399, San'a; tel. (1) 252374; fax (1) 252378.
Ministry of Education: San'a; tel. (1) 252726; fax (1) 274555; e-mail moe@yemen.net.ye; internet www.yemenmoe.net.
Ministry of Electricity and Energy: POB 11422, San'a; tel. (1) 326191; fax (1) 326214; e-mail yempec@y.net.ye.
Ministry of Expatriate Affairs: San'a; tel. (1) 402643; fax (1) 400710; internet www.iayemen.org.
Ministry of Finance: POB 190, San'a; tel. (1) 260370; fax (1) 263040; e-mail support@mof.gov.ye; internet www.mof.gov.ye.
Ministry of Foreign Affairs: POB 1994, San'a; tel. (1) 485500; fax (1) 536986; e-mail media@mofa.gov.ye; internet www.mofa.gov.ye.
Ministry of Higher Education, Scientific Research and Vocational Training: Baghdad St, POB 25235, San'a; tel. (1) 202414; fax (1) 469043; internet moheye.net.
Ministry of Industry and Trade: POB 22210, San'a; tel. (1) 252344; fax (1) 238042; e-mail info@moit.gov.ye; internet www.moit.gov.ye.
Ministry of Information, Culture and Tourism: POB 3040, San'a; tel. (1) 274011; fax (1) 282004.
Ministry of the Interior: POB 4991, San'a; tel. (1) 274147; fax (1) 332511; e-mail moi@yemen.net.ye; internet www.moi.gov.ye.
Ministry of Justice: San'a.
Ministry of Legal Affairs and Human Rights: POB 1192, San'a; tel. (1) 402213; fax (1) 402162; e-mail legal@y.net.ye; internet www.legalaffairs.gov.ye.
Ministry of Local Administration: POB 2198, San'a; tel. (1) 252532; fax (1) 251513; internet www.molayemen.gov.ye.
Ministry of Oil and Minerals: POB 81, San'a; tel. (1) 202306; fax (1) 202314; e-mail mom@y.net.ye; internet www.mom.gov.ye.
Ministry of Planning and International Co-operation: POB 175, San'a; tel. (1) 250713; fax (1) 250662; e-mail kamalmasoud@hotmail.com; internet www.mpic-yemen.org.
Ministry of Public Health and Population: POB 274160, San'a; tel. (1) 252193; fax (1) 252247; e-mail his@moh.gov.ye; internet www.mophp-ye.org.
Ministry of Public Works and Highways: San'a; tel. (1) 262602; fax (1) 262609; internet www.mpwh-ye.net.
Ministry of Religious Endowments and Guidance: San'a.
Ministry of Social Affairs and Labour: San'a; tel. (1) 274921; fax (1) 262806.
Ministry of Telecommunications and Information Technology: San'a; tel. (1) 331469; e-mail mtit@mtit.gov.ye; internet mtit.gov.ye.
Ministry of Transport: POB 2781, San'a; tel. (1) 260903; fax (1) 260901; e-mail info@mot.gov.ye; internet www.mot.gov.ye.
Ministry of Water and the Environment: San'a; tel. (1) 418290; fax (1) 418282; internet www.mweye.org.
Ministry of Youth and Sports: POB 2414, San'a; tel. (1) 472901; fax (1) 472900; e-mail hamod.obad@yahoo.com.

Legislature

House of Representatives: POB 4646, Aden; e-mail info@parliament-ye.com; internet parliament-ye.com.
Speaker: Sultan al-Borkani.

General Election, 27 April 2003

Party	Seats*
General People's Congress (GPC)	238
Yemeni Congregation for Reform (al-Islah)	46
Yemen Socialist Party (YSP)	8
Nasserite Unionist Popular Organization	3
Arab Socialist Baath Party	2
Independents	4
Total	**301**

* Includes the results of three by-elections held in July 2003.

Election Commission

Supreme Commission for Elections and Referendums (SCER): POB 15491, San'a; tel. (1) 202345; fax (1) 402685; e-mail scer@y.net.ye; internet www.scer.gov.ye; f. 1992; under al-Houthi control.

Political Organizations

General People's Congress (GPC): San'a; internet www.almotamar.net; f. 1982; a broad grouping of supporters of fmr President Ali Abdullah Saleh; Chair. Sadeq Ameen Abu Rass.
Al-Haq: San'a; f. 1995; conservative Islamic party; operates within the JMP opposition coalition; Sec.-Gen. Ibrahim Muhammad al-Mansour.
Joint Meeting Parties (JMP): San'a; f. 2006 as a coalition of five parties incl. al-Haq, al-Islah and the YSP; a sixth party, the Arab Socialist Baath Party, joined in 2008; Leader Muhammad al-Zubayri.
League of the Sons of Yemen (Rabitat Abna' al-Yemen—RAY): Aden; tel. (1) 400532; fax (1) 400533; internet www.ray-party.org; f. 1951; represents interests of southern tribes; Leader Abd al-Rahman al-Jifri; Sec.-Gen. Mohsin Muhammad bin Fareed.
Nasserite Unionist Popular Organization: Aden; tel. (1) 536497; internet www.alwahdawi.net; f. 1989 as a legal party; operates within the JMP opposition coalition; Sec.-Gen. Abdullah Noman Muhammad.
National Opposition Council: San'a; a coalition of eight small opposition parties.

YEMEN

Yemen Socialist Party (YSP): San'a; f. 1978 to succeed the United Political Organization—National Front (UPO—NF); fmrly Marxist-Leninist 'vanguard' party based on 'scientific socialism'; has Political Bureau and Cen. Cttee; mem. of the JMP opposition coalition; Sec.-Gen. ABDUL RAHMAN OMAR AL-SAQQAF.

Yemeni Congregation for Reform (al-Islah): POB 23090, San'a; tel. (3) 410730; fax (1) 383879; internet alislah-ye.net; f. 1990 by mems of the legislature, other political figures and tribal leaders; seeks constitutional reform based on Islamic law; a leading mem. of the JMP opposition coalition; Pres. MUHAMMAD AL-YADOUMI.

Other parties in Yemen include the **Arab Socialist Baath Party**; the **Federation of Popular Forces**; the **Liberation Front Party**; the **Nasserite Democratic Party**; the **National Democratic Front**; the **National Social Party**; the **Popular Nasserite Reformation Party**; the **Social Green Party**; the **Yemen League**; the **Yemeni Unionist Congregation Party**; and the **Yemeni Unionist Rally Party**.

Diplomatic Representation

EMBASSIES IN YEMEN

Owing to the political instability and the onset of conflict, from early 2015 many countries moved their operations from San'a to Aden or otherwise withdrew their diplomatic staff from Yemen. Other countries chose to operate their embassies from neighbouring countries.

Algeria: POB 509, 67 Amman St, San'a; tel. (1) 206350; fax (1) 209688; Ambassador KAMAL ABD AL-KADER HEJAZI.

Bulgaria: POB 1518, Asr, St 4, Residence 5, San'a; tel. (1) 208469; fax (1) 207924; e-mail embassy.sanaa@mfa.bg; internet www.mfa.bg/embassies/yemen; Chargé d'affaires HRISTO KULINSKI.

China, People's Republic: POB 482, al-Zubairy St, San'a; tel. (1) 498460; fax (1) 275341; internet ye.chineseembassy.org; Chargé d'affaires SHAO ZHENG.

Djibouti: POB 3322, 6 Amman St, San'a; tel. (1) 445236; fax (1) 445237; e-mail djiembassye@yahoo.com; currently operating from Riyadh, Saudi Arabia; Ambassador DYA-EDDINE SAID BAMAKHRAMA (concurrent ambassador to Saudi Arabia).

Eritrea: POB 11040, Western Safia Bldg, San'a; tel. (1) 209422; fax (1) 214088; Ambassador MUHAMMAD SHEIKH ABD AL-JALIL.

Ethiopia: POB 234, al-Hamadani St, San'a; tel. (1) 208833; fax (1) 213780; e-mail ethoembs@y.net.ye; Ambassador ATO FAISAL ALI.

France: POB 1286, cnr Sts 2 and 21, San'a; tel. (1) 268888; fax (1) 269160; internet www.ambafrance-ye.org; Ambassador JEAN-MARIE SAFA.

Germany: POB 2562, Hadda, San'a; tel. (6) 5901170; e-mail info@sanaa.diplo.de; internet www.sanaa.diplo.de; temporarily operating from Amman, Jordan; Ambassador HUBERT JOSEF JÄGER.

India: POB 1154, San'a; Lotissement Salines Ouest Theatre, Djibouti; tel. (1) 433632; fax (1) 433630; e-mail admin@eoisanaa.org; internet eoiyemen.gov.in; embassy staff based in Djibouti; Chargé d'affaires RAM PRASAD.

Indonesia: POB 19873, Bldg 16, Beirut St, Haddah, San'a; tel. (1) 427210; fax (1) 427212; e-mail sanaa.kbri@kemlu.go.id; internet www.kemlu.go.id/sanaa; currently based in Salalah, Oman; Chargé d'affaires ARDIAN AZLI.

Iran: POB 1437, Haddah St, San'a; tel. (1) 413552; fax (1) 414139; e-mail iranemb.sah@mfa.gov.ir; internet sanaa.mfa.ir; Ambassador (vacant).

Iraq: POB 498, South Airport Rd, San'a; tel. (1) 440184; fax (1) 440187; internet www.mofamission.gov.iq/yem; Ambassador ASAAD ALI YASEEN.

Italy: POB 1152, Haddah St No. 131, San'a; tel. (1) 432587; fax (1) 432590; e-mail ambasciata.sanaa@esteri.it; internet www.ambsanaa.esteri.it; Ambassador LUCIANO GALLI.

Japan: POB 817, Haddah Area, San'a; tel. (1) 423700; fax (1) 417850; e-mail eoj.yemen@sa.mofa.go.jp; internet www.ye.emb-japan.go.jp; operating from Riyadh, Saudi Arabia since 2015; Chargé d'affaires a.i. KAZUHIRO HIGASHI.

Jordan: POB 2152, Hadat Damascus St, San'a; tel. (1) 413276; fax (1) 414516; e-mail sanaa@fm.gov.jo; Ambassador SULEIMAN GHWEIRI.

Korea, Democratic People's Republic: POB 1209, al-Hasaba, Mazda Rd, San'a; tel. (1) 232340; Ambassador CHANG MYONG SON.

Korea, Republic: POB 5005, San'a; tel. (1) 431001; fax (1) 431805; e-mail yemen@mofa.go.kr; internet overseas.mofa.go.kr/ye-ko/index.do; temporarily operating from Riyadh (Saudi Arabia); Ambassador DO BONG-KAE.

Kuwait: POB 3746, South Ring Rd, San'a; tel. (1) 268876; fax (1) 268875; e-mail sanaa@mofa.gov.kw; Ambassador FALAH AL-HAJRAF.

Lebanon: POB 38, St 12, San'a; tel. (1) 203959; fax (1) 201120; e-mail lebem@y.net.ye; Ambassador HADI JABER.

Libya: POB 1506, Ring Rd, St 8, House 145, San'a; tel. (1) 508157; fax (1) 260602; Ambassador IDRIS ABU BAKR.

Malaysia: POB 16157, San'a; tel. (1) 429781; fax (1) 429783; internet www.kln.gov.my/perwakilan/yemen; Ambassador (vacant).

Mauritania: POB 19383, No. 6, Algeria St, San'a; tel. (1) 264188; fax (1) 215926; Ambassador ZEIN EL ABIDINE MOHAMED OULD TALEB.

Morocco: POB 3181, Faj Attan, Hay Assormi, ave Beyrouth, San'a; tel. (1) 426628; fax (1) 426627; e-mail sifama_sanaa@hotmail.com; Chargé d'affaires MOHAMMED AL-CHARIKI.

Netherlands: POB 463, off 14th October St, San'a; tel. (1) 421814; fax (1) 417280; e-mail saa@minbuza.nl; internet www.netherlandsworldwide.nl/countries/yemen; currently operating from Amman, Jordan; Ambassador PETER-DERREK HOF.

Oman: POB 6163, 14th October St, al-Gala Quarter, Bldg 2, Khormaskar, San'a; tel. (1) 208874; fax (1) 204586; e-mail sanaa@mofa.gov.om; Ambassador (vacant).

Pakistan: POB 2848, Ring Rd, off Haddah St, San'a; tel. (1) 434044; fax (1) 434046; internet www.pakistanembassyyemen.com; currently operating from Riyadh, Saudi Arabia; Ambassador Lt-Gen. BILAL AKBAR.

Qatar: POB 19717, San'a; tel. (1) 304640; fax (1) 304645; e-mail sanaa@mofa.gov.qa; Ambassador (vacant).

Russian Federation: POB 1087, 26 September St, San'a; tel. (1) 278719; fax (1) 283142; e-mail embsanaa@mid.ru; internet yemen.mid.ru; Chargé d'affaires EVGENY A. KUDROV.

Saudi Arabia: intersection of Haddah St with Southern Ring Rd, 1 al-Quds St, San'a; tel. (1) 240856; fax (1) 240859; e-mail yeemb@mofa.gov.sa; internet embassies.mofa.gov.sa/sites/yemen; Ambassador MUHAMMAD SAID AL-JABER.

Somalia: POB 101, San'a; tel. (1) 208864; e-mail webmaster@somaligov.net; internet www.yemen.somaligov.net; Ambassador ABDULLAHI HASHI SHURIYE.

Spain: POB 7108, San'a; tel. (1) 429899; fax (1) 429893; e-mail emb.sanaa@maec.es; Ambassador (vacant).

Sudan: POB 2561, 82 Abou al-Hassan al-Hamadani St, San'a; tel. (1) 265231; fax (1) 265234; e-mail mail@esudany.com; Ambassador MUHAMMAD AL-DABI.

Syrian Arab Republic: POB 494, Hadda Rd, Damascus St 1, San'a; tel. (1) 414891; Ambassador (vacant).

Tunisia: POB 2561, Diplomatic Area, St 22, San'a; tel. (1) 471845; fax (1) 471840; e-mail at.sanaa@y.net.ye; Ambassador ALI BEN ARAFA.

Türkiye (Turkey): POB 18371, San'a; tel. (1) 432890; fax (1) 434828; e-mail embassy.sanaa@mfa.gov.tr; internet sanaa.emb.mfa.gov.tr; Ambassador MUSTAFA PULAT.

United Arab Emirates: POB 2250, Ring Rd, San'a; tel. (1) 248777; fax (1) 248779; e-mail sanaa@mofa.gov.ae; Ambassador MOHAMMED HAMAD AL-ZAABI.

United Kingdom: POB 1287, 938 Thaher Himiyar St, East Ring Rd, San'a; internet www.gov.uk/world/yemen; all embassy personnel were withdrawn from Yemen in Feb. 2015; Ambassador ABDA SHARIF (designate); operating from Riyadh (Saudi Arabia).

USA: POB 22347, Sa'awan St, San'a; tel. (1) 7552000; fax (1) 303182; e-mail passanaa@state.gov; internet ye.usembassy.gov; all embassy staff were withdrawn from Yemen in Feb. 2015; now resident in Saudi Arabia; Ambassador STEPHEN H. FAGIN.

Judicial System

Yemen's Constitution guarantees the independence of the judiciary and identifies Islamic law (*Shari'a*) as the basis of all laws.

Yemen is divided into 21 governorates in addition to the Capital Secretariat of San'a (a municipality), each of which is further divided into districts. Each district has a Court of First Instance in which all cases are heard by a single magistrate. Appeals against decisions of the Courts of First Instance are referred to a Court of Appeal. Each governorate has a Court of Appeal with four divisions: Civil, Criminal, Matrimonial and Commercial, each of which consists of three judges.

The Supreme Court of the Republic, which sits in San'a, rules on matters concerning the Constitution, appeals against decisions of the Courts of Appeal and cases brought against members of the legislature. The Supreme Court has eight divisions, each of which consists of five judges.

Supreme Judicial Council: The Supreme Judicial Council supervises the proper function of the courts, and its Chairman is the President of the Republic; Chief of Supreme Judicial Council MOHSEN YAHYA TALEB ABU BAKR.

Supreme Court: Aden; Pres. ALI AHMAD NASSER AL-AWASH.
Attorney-General: QAHER MUSTAFA ALI EBRAHIM.

Religion

ISLAM

The majority of the population are Muslims. Most are Sunni Muslims of the Shafi'a sect, except in the north-west of the country, where Zaidism (a moderate sect of the Shi'a order) is the dominant persuasion.

CHRISTIANITY

The Roman Catholic Church

Apostolic Vicariate of Southern Arabia: POB 54, Abu Dhabi, United Arab Emirates; tel. (2) 4461895; fax (2) 4465177; e-mail info@avosa.org; internet www.avosa.org; f. 1889 as Apostolic Vicariate of Arabia; renamed as above, following reorganization in 2011; responsible for a territory comprising the UAE, Oman and Yemen, with an estimated 998,500 Roman Catholics (Jan. 2020); Vicar Apostolic Most Rev. PAOLO MARTINELLI (Titular Bishop of Musti in Numidia, resident in the UAE).

The Anglican Communion

Within the Episcopal Church in Jerusalem and the Middle East, Yemen forms part of the diocese of Cyprus and the Gulf. The Anglican congregations in San'a and Aden are entirely expatriate; the Bishop in Cyprus and the Gulf is resident in Cyprus, while the Archdeacon in the Gulf is resident in Bahrain.

HINDUISM

There is a small Hindu community.

The Press

DAILIES

Al-Ayyam: POB 648, al-Khalij al-Imami, Crater, Aden; tel. (2) 255170; fax (2) 255692; e-mail editor@al-ayyam.info; internet www.alayyam.info; f. 1958; Editor HISHAM BASHRAHEEL.

Al-Jumhuriya: Taiz Information Office, Taiz; tel. (4) 216748; Arabic; Deputy Editor ZAID MUHAMMAD AL-GHABIRI.

Al-Rabi' 'Ashar Min Uktubar (14 October): POB 4227, Crater, Aden; f. 1968; not publ. on Sat; Arabic; Editorial Dir FAROUQ MUSTAFA RIFAT; Chief Editor MUHAMMAD HUSSAIN MUHAMMAD.

Al-Thawra (The Revolution): POB 2195, San'a; tel. (1) 321532; fax (1) 274035; e-mail althawrah99@gmail.com; internet www.althawranews.net; Arabic; govt-owned; Chair. and Editor-in-Chief ABD AL-RAHMAN AL-HANNOUMI.

PERIODICALS

Almotamar Net: San'a; tel. (1) 208934; fax (1) 402983; e-mail info@almotamar.net; internet www.almotamar.net; online news organ of the General People's Congress; Editor-in-Chief ABD AL-MALIK AL-FUAIDI.

Attijarah (Trade): POB 3370, Hodeida; tel. (3) 213784; fax (3) 211528; monthly; Arabic; publ. by Hodeida Chamber of Commerce.

Al-Balagh: San'a; tel. (1) 280581; fax (1) 280584; internet www.al-balagh.net; Arabic; weekly; Editor ABDULLAH IBRAHIM.

Al-Bilad (The Country): POB 1438, Aden; weekly; centre-right; Editor-in-Chief ABD AL-MALIK AL-FAISHANI.

Dar al-Salam (Peace): POB 1790, San'a; tel. (1) 272946; f. 1948; weekly; Arabic; political, economic and general essays; Editor ABDULLAH MUKBOOL AL-SICGUL.

Al-Hares: Aden; fortnightly; Arabic; publ. by Ministry of the Interior.

Al-Hikma (Wisdom): POB 4227, Crater, Aden; monthly; Arabic; publ. by the Writers' Union.

Al-Mithaq (The Charter): San'a; weekly; organ of the Gen. People's Congress.

Al-Ra'i al-'Am (Public Opinion): POB 293, San'a; tel. (1) 253785; fax (1) 223378; e-mail alraialaam2002@yahoo.com; internet www.alraialaam.com.ye; weekly; independent; Editor KAMAL ALUFI.

Ray: Aden; tel. (1) 400532; Arabic; organ of League of the Sons of Yemen.

Al-Risalah: POB 55777, 26 September St, Taiz; tel. (4) 214215; fax (4) 221164; e-mail alaws@y.net.ye; f. 1968; weekly; Arabic; publ. by Assalam Trading Houses.

Al-Sahwa (Awakening): POB 11126, Hadda Rd, San'a; tel. (1) 230317; fax (1) 251508; e-mail admin@alsahwa-yemen.net; internet www.alsahwa-yemen.net; weekly; publ. by Yemeni Congregation for Reform (al-Islah); Editor-in-Chief MUHAMMAD AL-YOUSUFI.

Sawt al-Yemen (Voice of Yemen): POB 302, San'a; weekly; Arabic.

Al-Shoura: POB 15114, San'a; tel. (1) 277049; fax (1) 251104; internet www.y.net.ye/shoura.

Al-Thawry (The Revolutionary): POB 4227, Crater, Aden; internet www.althawry.org; weekly, on Sat.; Arabic; organ of Cen. Cttee of Yemen Socialist Party.

Al-Wahda al-Watani (National Unity): Al-Baath Printing House, POB 193, San'a; tel. (1) 77511; f. 1982; fmrly Al-Omal; monthly; Editor MUHAMMAD SALEM ALI.

Al-Wahdawi: POB 13010, San'a; tel. (1) 292383; e-mail alwahdawin@gmail.com; internet www.alwahdawi.net; weekly; organ of Nasserite Unionist Popular Org.

Yemen Observer: POB 19183, San'a; tel. (1) 505466; fax (1) 260504; e-mail webmaster@yemenobserver.com; internet www.yemenobserver.com; f. 1996; tri-weekly; English; publ. by Yemen Observer Publishing House; Editor-in-Chief ABD AL-AZIZ OUDAH.

Yemen Post: POB 15531, San'a; tel. (1) 000202; fax (1) 539268; e-mail editor@yemenpost.net; internet www.yemenpost.net; f. 2007; English; weekly; Editor-in-Chief HAKIM AL-MASMARI.

The Yemen Times: POB 2579, Hadda St, San'a; tel. (1) 268661; fax (1) 268276; e-mail yementimes@yementimes.com; internet www.yementimes.com; f. 1990; Mon. and Thur.; English; privately owned.

Yemen Today: POB 19183, San'a; tel. (1) 248444; fax (1) 260504; e-mail info@yemen-today.com; internet www.yemen-today.com; f. 2007; monthly; English; politics and current affairs; publ. by Yemen Observer Publishing House; Editor RYAN SANABANI.

26 September: POB 17, San'a; tel. (1) 262626; fax (1) 274139; e-mail info@26sep.net; internet www.26sep.net; armed forces weekly; Editor-in-Chief ALI AL-SHATIR.

PRESS ASSOCIATION

Yemeni Journalists Syndicate: San'a; tel. (1) 471072; fax (1) 537101; e-mail info@yemenjs.net; internet www.yemenjs.net; f. 1976; Chair. YASSIN AL-MASOUDI; Sec.-Gen. MARWAN AL-DAMMAJ.

NEWS AGENCY

Yemen News Agency (SABA): Five Story Office Bldg and Printing Plant, al-Jama'ah al-Arabia St, al-Hasaba, San'a; tel. (1) 566666; fax (1) 252944; e-mail info@sabanews.net; internet www.sabanews.net; f. 1990 by merger of Saba News Agency and Aden News Agency following reunification of Yemen; mem. of the Fed. of Arab News Agencies and of the Non-Aligned News Agencies; Chair. and Editor-in-Chief TAREQ AHMED MOHAMMED AL-SHAMY.

Publishers

Armed Forces Printing Press: POB 17, San'a; tel. (1) 274240; publishes *26 September*.

Al-Thawrah Corpn: POB 2195, San'a; fax (1) 251505; Chair. M. R. AL-ZURKAH.

Yemen Observer Publishing House: POB 19183, San'a; tel. (1) 248444; fax (1) 260504; internet www.yobserver.com; f. 1996; publs include *Yemen Observer* and *Yemen Today*; Publr FARIS ABDULLAH SANABANI.

14 October Corpn for Printing, Publishing, Distribution and Advertising: POB 4227, Crater, Aden; under control of the Ministry of Information; publs include *Al-Rabi' 'Ashar Min Uktubar*; Chair. AHMAD AL-HUBAISHI.

PUBLISHERS' ASSOCIATION

Yemeni Publishers' Association: f. 2008; Man. Dr NABIL ABADI.

Broadcasting and Communications

TELECOMMUNICATIONS

Public Telecommunications Corpn: POB 17045, Airport Rd, al-Jiraf, San'a; tel. and fax (1) 331140; e-mail info@ptc.gov.ye; internet www.ptc.gov.ye; state-owned; Dir-Gen. Eng. SADIQ MOHAMMED MUSLEH.

Yemen International Telecommunications Co (TeleYemen): POB 168, al-Tahreer Area, San'a; tel. (1) 280000; e-mail info@teleyemen.com.ye; internet www.teleyemen.com.ye; f. 1990 as a jt venture with Cable and Wireless PLC (United Kingdom); wholly owned by Public Telecommunications Corpn since 2003; provides fixed-line, mobile and internet services; CEO Dr ALI NAJI NASRI.

Yemen Mobile Co: San'a; e-mail info@yemenmobile.com.ye; internet www.yemenmobile.com.ye; f. 2004 as a subsidiary of Yemen Int. Telecommunications Co (TeleYemen); initial public offering of 45% of shares in 2006; provides mobile services; Chair. ESAM ALI AHMED AL-HAMLI; Exec. Man. AMER MUHAMMAD HAZA'A.

Y Telecom: San'a; tel. 7654321; e-mail info@ytelecom.com; internet ytelecom.com; provides mobile telephone services; CEO Eng. ALI AIDAROUS.

Yemen Co for Mobile Telephony (SabaFon): POB 4455, Aden; tel. (2) 248370; e-mail customer.service@sabafon.com; internet www.sabafon.com; f. 2001; shareholders include Al-Ahmar Group for Trade, the Iran Foreign Investment Co and Batelco (Bahrain); Chair. HAMDAN ABDULLAH HUSSAIN AL-AHMAR; CEO Eng. FAHED AL-ARIQY.

Yemen Oman United (YOU): San'a; tel. 733111111; internet www.you.com.ye; f. 2000 as Spacetel Yemen; renamed as MTN Yemen in 2006, following merger of MTN Group Ltd with Investcom LLC; renamed as above in 2022 after the sale of MTN Yemen to Emerald International Investment LCC; provides mobile services; CEO RAED AHMAD.

BROADCASTING

Yemen Radio and Television Corpn: POB 2182, San'a; tel. (1) 230654; fax (1) 230761; e-mail info@yemen-tv.net; internet www.yemenrtv.net; state-controlled; operates two television channels and eight regional radio stations for San'a, Taiz, Mukalla, Aden, Lahj, Sayoun, Hodeida and Abyan; Chair. ABDULLAH AL-ZALAB; Gen. Man. ESKANDAR MUHAMMAD AL-ASBAH.

Finance

BANKING

Central Bank

Central Bank of Yemen: POB 452, Aden; tel. (2) 256518; fax (1) 274360; internet cby-ye.com; f. 1971; merged with Bank of Yemen in 1990; Gov./Chair. AHMED BIN AHMED GHALEB AL-MAABQI; Dep. Gov./Vice-Chair. MUHAMMAD OMAR BANAJA.

Principal Banks

Co-operative and Agricultural Credit Bank (CACBANK): POB 2015, Banks Complex, al-Zubairy St, San'a; tel. and fax (1) 250009; e-mail cac.info@cacbank.com.ye; internet www.cacbank.com.ye; f. 1976; Chair. IBRAHIM AHMED HASHEM.

International Bank of Yemen YSC: POB 4444, 106 al-Zubairy St, San'a; tel. (1) 407000; e-mail info@ibyemen.com; internet www.ibyemen.com; f. 1980; commercial bank; 75% private Yemeni interests; 25% foreign shareholders; Chair. KAMAL HUSSAIN AL-JEBRY; Gen. Man. OMAR RASHED.

Islamic Bank of Yemen for Finance and Investment: POB 18452, Mareb Yemen Insurance Co Bldg, al-Zubairy St, San'a; tel. (1) 206117; fax (1) 206116; f. 1996; savings, commercial, investment and retail banking; Chair. ABD AL-KAREM AL-ASWADI; Man. Dir MAHMOUD QAID.

National Bank of Yemen: POB 5, Arwa Rd, Crater, Aden; tel. (2) 252403; e-mail nby.ho@y.net.ye; internet www.nbyemen.com; f. 1970 as Nat. Bank of South Yemen; reorg. 1971; 100% state-owned; Chair. Dr MOHAMED HUSSEIN SAID HALBOUB; Gen. Man. Dr AHMED ALI OMAR BIN SANKAR.

Shamil Bank of Yemen and Bahrain: POB 19382, Haddah St, San'a; tel. (1) 538383; e-mail info@sbyb.net; internet www.sbyb.net; f. 2002; Chair. AHMAD ABUBAKER OMER BAZARA; Gen. Man. SAEED MUHAMMAD BAZARA.

Tadhamon International Islamic Bank: POB 2411, al-Saeed Commercial Bldg, al-Zubairy St, San'a; tel. 8001010; fax (1) 203271; e-mail info@tadhamonbank.com; internet www.tadhamonbank.com; f. 1995 as Yemen Bank for Investment and Devt; became Tadhamon Islamic Bank in 1996; name changed as above in 2002; Chair. SHAWKI AHMED HAYEL SAID; Man. Dir MAHMOUD ATA HASSAN AL-REFAI.

Yemen Bank for Reconstruction and Development (YBRD): POB 541, 26 September St, San'a; tel. (1) 288880; e-mail info@ybrdye.com; internet www.ybrdye.com; f. 1962; 51% state-owned; 49% owned by public shareholders; Chair. HUSSAIN FADHL MUHAMMAD HARHARA; Gen. Man. ABD AL-NASER NOMAN AL-HAJ.

Yemen Commercial Bank (YCB): POB 19845, al-Rowaishan Bldg, al-Zubairy St, San'a; tel. 8008000; internet www.ycb.bank; f. 1993; Board Dir Sheikh MUHAMMAD BIN YAHYA AL-ROWAISHAN; Exec. Pres. and Gen. Man. RABIH AL-HAMIDI.

INSURANCE

Aman Insurance Co (YSC): POB 1133, al-Zubairy St, San'a; tel. (1) 202022; e-mail amaninsco@amaninsco.com; internet www.amaninsco.com; all classes of insurance; Chair. MUHAMMAD ABDULLAH AL-SUNIDAR.

Mareb Yemen Insurance Co: POB 2284, al-Zubairy St, San'a; tel. (1) 402048; e-mail maryinsco74@y.net.ye; internet www.marebyins.com; f. 1974; all classes of insurance; Chair. and CEO KASEM MUHAMMAD ASSABRI.

Saba Yemen Insurance Co: POB 19214, Ishaq Bldg, al-Zubairy St, San'a; tel. (1) 240908; fax (1) 240943; internet www.saba-ins.net; f. 1990; all classes of insurance; Chair. Sheikh MUHAMMAD BIN YAHIAH AL-ROWAISHAN; Man. Dir MUHAMMAD HUSSEIN ZAWIYAH.

Trust Yemen Insurance and Reinsurance Co: POB 18392, Villa 14, Haddah St, San'a; tel. (1) 425007; fax (1) 412570; e-mail info@trust-yemen.com; internet www.trust-yemen.com; f. 1995; all classes of insurance; Chair. GHAZI ABU NAHL.

United Insurance Co: POB 1883, al-Saeed Commercial Bldg, 2nd Floor, al-Zubairy St, San'a; tel. (1) 555555; fax (1) 214012; e-mail uuicyemen@uicyemen.com; internet www.uicyemen.com; f. 1981; general and life insurance; Gen. Man. MOHAMED ABDEL SALAM AL-YOUSIFI.

Al-Watania Insurance Co (YSC): POB 15497, al-Kasr St, San'a; tel. (1) 538888; fax (1) 539950; internet www.alwataniains.com; f. 1993; all classes of insurance.

Yemen General Insurance Co (SYC): POB 2709, YGI Bldg, 25 Algiers St, San'a; tel. (1) 442489; fax (1) 442492; e-mail ygi@yginsurance.com; internet www.yginsurance.com; f. 1977; all classes of insurance; Chair. ABDULJABBAR THABET; Gen. Man. KAIS THABET.

Yemen Insurance Co: POB 8437, San'a; tel. (1) 272806; internet yemenins.com; f. 1990; all classes of insurance; Chair. MUHAMMAD MUBARAK ADHBAN; Gen. Man. KHALID BASHIR TAHIR.

Trade and Industry

GOVERNMENT AGENCIES

General Investment Authority (GIAY): POB 19022, Hadda St, San'a; tel. (1) 434312; fax (1) 434314; e-mail info@giay.org; internet www.investinyemen.org; f. 1992; promotes and facilitates strategic investment in Yemen; Chair. Dr MUSTAFA HUSSEIN AL-MOUTAWAKEL.

Yemen Economic Corpn: POB 1207, San'a; tel. (1) 262501; fax (1) 262508; e-mail yeco@yeco.biz; internet www.yeco.biz; f. 1973; promotes and facilitates investment and development across various sectors of the economy; Gen. Man. ALI MUHAMMAD AL-KUHLANI.

DEVELOPMENT ORGANIZATIONS

Agricultural Research and Extension Authority: POB 87148, Dhamar; tel. (6) 423913; fax (6) 423914; e-mail area@yemen.net.ye; internet www.area.gov.ye; Chair. ABDULLAH M. AL-OLOFI.

Social Fund for Development (SFD): POB 15485, Fij Attan, San'a; tel. (1) 449669; fax (1) 449670; e-mail sfd@sfd-yemen.org; internet www.sfd-yemen.org; f. 1997; autonomous devt agency, governed by a bd of dirs representing the Govt, non-governmental orgs and the private sector, chaired by the Prime Minister.

Yemen Free Zone Public Authority: POB 5842, Aden; tel. (2) 241210; fax (2) 221237; internet www.yemenfreezone.com; f. 1991; supervises creation of a free zone for industrial investment; Vice-Chair. ABD AL-GALIL SHAIF AL-SHAIBI.

CHAMBERS OF COMMERCE

Chamber of Commerce and Industry—Aden: POB 473, Crater 101, Aden; tel. (2) 251104; fax (2) 255660; e-mail cciaden@yemen.net.ye; internet adenchamber.org; f. 1886; Chair. ABUBAKR SALEM AHMED BAOBAID; Dir-Gen. IQBAL MOHAMED MUNIR.

Federation of Chambers of Commerce: POB 16992, San'a; tel. (1) 514127; fax (1) 261269; e-mail info@fycci-ye.org; internet www.fycci-ye.org; Chair. MUHAMMAD ABDO SAID AN'AM; Dir-Gen. MUHAMMAD ABU SAEED.

Hadramout Chamber of Commerce and Industry: POB 8302, Main St, Mukalla City, Hadramout; tel. (5) 353258; fax (5) 303437; Chair. OMER A. R. BAJARASH.

Hodeida Chamber of Commerce: POB 3370, 20 al-Zubairy St, Hodeida; tel. (3) 217401; fax (3) 211528; e-mail hodcci@y.net.ye; f. 1960; 6,500 mems; Chair. ABDEL JALEEL ABDU THABET MUHAMMAD; Gen. Man. MUHAMMAD ABDEL WAHED AL-HUTAMI.

Ibb Chamber of Commerce and Industry: POB 70004, Ibb; tel. (4) 404686; fax (4) 416780; Chair. QASEM MUHAMMAD SAEED AL-MANSOUB; Gen. Man. MUHAMMAD AL-GHORBANI.

YEMEN

Saadah Chamber of Commerce and Industry: POB 3754-2566, Saadah; tel. (7) 513671; fax (7) 521524; Chair. MUHAMMAD R. JARMAN; Gen. Man. ABD AL-BARI TALHAN.

San'a Chamber of Commerce and Industry: San'a; tel. (1) 401206; e-mail info@scciye.org; internet www.scciye.org; f. 1959; Chair. ALI AL-HADI.

Taiz Chamber of Commerce and Industry: POB 5029, Chamber St, Taiz; tel. (4) 210580; e-mail taizchamber@y.net.ye; internet www.taizchamber.com; f. 1962; 10,000 mems; Chair. SHAWQI AHMED HAIL; Gen. Man. MOFID A. SAIF.

Thamar Chamber of Commerce and Industry: POB 87010, Thamar; tel. (5) 501191; fax (6) 509282; Chair. MUHAMMAD DADIYA; Gen. Man. AHMAD AL-HAFAFI.

STATE ENTERPRISES

While the Government is committed to privatization in all areas of trade and industry, there are still numerous state-owned enterprises:

General Corpn for Foreign Trade and Grains: POB 710, San'a; tel. (1) 202361; fax (1) 209511; f. 1976; Dir-Gen. ABD AL-RAHMAN AL-MADWAHI.

General Corpn for Manufacturing and Marketing of Cement: POB 1920, San'a; tel. (1) 215691; fax (1) 263168; Chair. AMIN ABD AL-WAHID AHMAD.

National Co for Foreign Trade: POB 90, Crater, Aden; tel. (2) 42793; fax (2) 42631; f. 1969; incorporates main foreign trading businesses (nationalized in 1970) and arranges their supply to the National Co for Home Trade; Gen. Man. AHMAD MUHAMMAD SALEH (acting).

National Co for Home Trade: POB 90, Crater, Aden; tel. (2) 41483; fax (2) 41226; f. 1969; marketing of general consumer goods, building materials, electrical goods, motor cars and spare parts, agricultural machinery, etc.; Man. Dir ABD AL-RAHMAN AL-SAILANI.

National Dockyards Co: POB 1244, Hedjuff, Aden; tel. (2) 244503; fax (2) 241681; f. 1969; maintenance and repair of ships and vessels; marine engineering; Man. Dir ABDULLAH ALI MUHAMMAD.

Yemen Drug Co for Industry and Commerce (YEDCO): POB 40, San'a; tel. (1) 370210; fax (1) 370209; import, manufacture and distribution of pharmaceutical products, chemicals, medical supplies, baby foods and scientific instruments; Chair. MUHAMMAD AL-KOHLANI; Gen. Man. MUHAMMAD ALI AL-KADIR.

Yemen Trading and Construction Co: POB 1092, 2–4 al-Zubairy St, San'a; tel. (1) 264005; fax (1) 240624; e-mail ytcc@y.net.ye; internet ytcc.com.ye; f. 1979; Gen. Man. AMIN A. KASSIM.

STATE HYDROCARBONS COMPANIES

General Corpn for Oil and Mineral Resources: San'a; f. 1990; state petroleum co; Pres. AHMAD BARAKAT.

Ministry of Oil and Minerals: Aden; e-mail info@mom-ye.com; internet mom-ye.com; responsible for the refining and marketing of petroleum products, and for prospecting and exploitation of indigenous hydrocarbons and other minerals; subsidiaries include:

Aden Refinery Co: POB 3003, Aden 110; tel. (2) 376234; fax (2) 376600; e-mail aden-refinery@arc-ye.com; internet www.arc-ye.com; f. 1952; operates petroleum refinery; capacity 8.6m. metric tons per year; operates two general tankers and one chemical tanker; Exec. Dir MOHAMMED ABUBAKER AL-BAKRY.

Masila Petroleum Exploration and Production Co (Petro-Masila): POB 52137, Ash-Shahir Terminal, Aden; tel. (5) 332168; e-mail info@petromasila.com; internet petromasila.com; f. 2011; Exec. Gen. Man. MOHAMMED BIN SUMAIT.

Petroleum Exploration and Production Authority (PEPA): Aden; tel. (1) 242609; fax (2) 442632; e-mail pepa-chr@pepaye.com; internet pepaye.com; f. 1990; manages petroleum concessions; Chair. Eng. KHALID AHMED MUBARAK BAHAMISH.

Safer Exploration and Production Operations Co: POB 481, Mareb; tel. (1) 6330210; e-mail sseedan@sepocye.com; internet www.sepocye.com; f. 1997; operation of Marib/al-Jawf Blk 18 since 2005; Exec. Man. SALEM KAITI.

Yemen Co for Investment in Oil and Minerals: POB 11993, San'a; tel. (1) 236669; fax (1) 236670; internet www.yicom-ye.com; promotes investment in new exploration areas; supervises operators in several exploration blocks; Exec. Gen. Man. Dr ABDULLAH M. OMAIR.

Yemen Gas Co: al-Raqas St, San'a; internet www.yemengasco.com; f. 1993 as Gen. Gas Corpn; renamed as above 1996; 100% govt-owned; production and distribution of LPG; Deputy Dir NAJEEB AL-OUD.

Yemen General Oil and Gas Corpn: POB 19137, San'a; tel. (1) 446413; fax (1) 446417; e-mail info@yogc.com.ye; internet www.yogc.com.ye; f. 1996; Gen. Man. MAHMOUD SALEM.

Yemen National Oil Co: POB 5050, Ma'alla, Aden; importer and distributor of petroleum products; Gen. Man. MUHAMMAD ABD HUSSEIN.

Yemen Oil Refinery Co: POB 15203, San'a; tel. (1) 218962; fax (1) 218960; e-mail refinery.manager@yorcye.com; internet www.yorcye.com; f. 1996; operates petroleum refinery at Marib; CEO SALEM MUHAMMED KAATI (acting).

Yemen Petroleum Co: San'a; tel. (2) 235120; fax (1) 447691; e-mail info@ypc-ye.com; internet ypc-ye.com; f. 1961; responsible for marketing of oil in domestic market; Exec. Dir GHALEB MABKHOOT BIN MA'ALI (acting).

Yemen LNG Co Ltd: Balhaf; tel. (5) 376093; e-mail pr@yemenlng.com; internet www.yemenlng.com; f. 2005; shareholders include Total SA (France—39.62%), Hunt Oil (USA—17.22%), Yemen Gas Co (16.73%), SK Corpn (Repub. of Korea—9.55%); operates a two-train LNG plant in Marib region; Chair. SAEED AL-SHAMSI (Minister of Oil and Minerals).

UTILITIES

Electricity

Public Electricity Corpn: POB 178, Airport Rd, San'a; tel. (1) 328141; fax (1) 328150; e-mail ypecnt@y.net.ye; internet www.pec.com.ye; Gen. Man. Eng. KHALED RASHID ABDEL MAWLA.

Water

General Authority for Rural Water Supply Projects (GARWSP): San'a; govt agency responsible for water supply in rural areas.

National Water Resources Authority (NWRA): POB 8944, Amran St, al-Hassaba, San'a; tel. (1) 314022; fax (1) 314023; e-mail NWRA-HQ@y.net.ye; internet www.nwrayemen.org; govt agency responsible for management of water resources; Chair. Eng. SALEM HASSAN BASHAIB.

National Water and Sanitation Authority (NWSA): POB 104, San'a; tel. (1) 250158; fax (1) 251536; e-mail NWSAHQ@yemen.net.ye; govt agency responsible for water supply in urban areas; Chair. FOUD ABD AL-ATIF DAIF ALLAH.

MAJOR COMPANIES

Al-Ahwal Holding Group: Djibouti St, San'a; tel. (1) 447573; fax (1) 442058; internet al-ahwal.tripod.com; f. 1961; import and distribution of products in sectors incl. agricultural and industrial machinery, automotive, water treatment and aviation; subsidiaries include Al-Ahwal Gen. Trading Co, ATMA Trading Co and Four Stars Co.

Al-Gharasi International Trading Co: POB 1270, al-Gharasi Bldg, Zubeiry St, San'a; tel. (1) 683179; fax (1) 683173; e-mail info@algharasi.com; internet www.algharasi.com; f. 1972; 8 cos; general trading, distribution of medical supplies and mfrs of food products, plastics and tissue papers.

Al-Hadha Group: al-Hadha Bldg, al-Zubairy St, San'a; internet alhadha.group; 14 cos in Yemen, three abroad; general trading, distribution of LPG, currency exchange, construction, shipping; Chair. ABDULLAH H. AL-HADHA.

Hayel Saeed Anam Group: POB 5302, Taiz; tel. (4) 212334; fax (4) 215171; e-mail info@hsagroup.com; internet www.hsagroup.com; 45 cos in Yemen incl. Yemen Co for Industry and Commerce, Yemen Co for Ghee and Soap Industry, National Dairy and Food Co, National Co for Cement; trading, manufacturing, services and agricultural and marine resources sectors; Group Chair. and CEO ABDUL GABBAR HAYEL SAEED.

Tihama Tractors and Engineering Co Ltd: POB 49, al-Jazaer St, San'a; tel. (1) 219553; e-mail info@tihama-group.com; internet www.tihama-group.com; f. 1963 as Yemen Trading and Shipping Co; present name adopted 1967; originally est. for sale and distribution of agricultural machinery and industrial products; has diversified into management of major telecommunications and infrastructure projects; Chair. AMIN DIRHEM; Gen. Man. MOHAMED AMIN DIRHEM.

Yemen Co for Industry and Commerce (YCIC): POB 5423, Taiz; tel. (4) 218060; fax (4) 218054; e-mail crm@ycic.com; internet ycic.com; f. 1970; producer of baked goods, confectionaries and sweets.

TRADE UNIONS

Agricultural Co-operatives Union: POB 649, San'a; tel. (1) 270685; fax (1) 274125.

General Confederation of Workers: POB 1162, Ma'alla, Aden; f. 1956; affiliated to WFTU; 35,000 mems; Pres. RAJEH SALEH NAJI; Gen. Sec. ABD AL-RAZAK SHAIF.

Trade Union Federation: San'a; Pres. ALI SAIF MUQBIL.

Transport

RAILWAYS
There are no railways in Yemen.

ROADS
General Corpn for Roads and Bridges: POB 1185, al-Zubairy St, Asir Rd, San'a; tel. (1) 202278; fax (1) 209571; responsible for maintenance and construction.

Yemen Land Transport Co: POB 279, Taiz St, San'a; tel. (1) 262108; fax (1) 263117; f. 1961; incorporates fmr Yemen Bus Co and all other public transport of the fmr People's Democratic Repub. of Yemen; oversees provision of public transport; scheduled for privatization; Chair. YAHYA AHMED AL-KOHLANI; Gen. Man. SALEH ABDULLAH ABD AL-WALI.

SHIPPING
Aden is the main port, comprising Aden Main Harbour, Aden Oil Harbour and Aden Container Terminal. Dubai Ports World (DP World), of the UAE, was granted a long-term concession to operate Aden Container Terminal and nearby Ma'alla Container Terminal, in partnership with the Gulf of Aden Port Corporation, from 2008. Aden Container Terminal is the largest such terminal in Yemen, with an annual capacity of more than 1m. 20-ft equivalent units (TEUs). Hodeida port, on the Red Sea, also handles a considerable amount of traffic. The port of Balhaf has been developed to accommodate natural gas liquefaction and export facilities. Al-Mukalla port, in Hadramout governorate, is an important regional centre for trade, fishing and shipbuilding. The port at Dhabah, also in Hadramout, incorporates an oil terminal.

Regulatory and Port Authorities

Maritime Affairs Authority: POB 1443, Hajeef, Maalla, Aden; tel. (2) 221581; fax (2) 221448; internet www.maa-yemen.com; f. 1990 as Public Corpn for Maritime Affairs; renamed as above 2001; protection of the marine environment; registration of ships; implementation of international maritime conventions; Exec. Chair. MURAD ALI MUHAMMAD (acting).

Yemen Arabian Sea Ports Corpn: POB 50793, al-Mukalla, Hadramout; tel. (5) 320633; fax (5) 303508; e-mail info@portofmukalla.com; internet yaspc.co; management and supervision of ports at al-Mukalla and Socotra.

Yemen Gulf of Aden Ports Corpn: POB 1316, Tawahi, Aden; tel. (2) 202666; fax (2) 203521; e-mail info@portofaden.net; internet www.portofaden.net; f. 1888; management and supervision of Port of Aden and other ports in the western Gulf of Aden; Chair. MUHAMMAD ALAWI AMZARBA; Port Officer Capt. SHAKEEB M. ABD AL-WAHED.

Yemen Red Sea Ports Corpn: POB 3183, Almina St, Hodeida; tel. (3) 211561; fax (3) 211561; e-mail info@yrspc.net; internet yrspc.net; management and supervision of the Port of Hodeida as the main port and ports of Mocha and Salif as secondary ports; Chair. Capt. MOHAMMED ABU BAKR ISHAQ.

Principal Shipping Companies

Al-Bukari Shipping Co Ltd: POB 3358, Tahrir Sq, Hodeida; tel. (3) 222888; fax (3) 211741; e-mail bukari@y.net.ye; internet www.bukarishipping.com; f. 1978; shipping agents, stevedoring, cargo, bunkering; Man. Dir SULEIMAN H. AL-BUKARI.

Gulf of Aden Shipping Co: POB 1439, Tawahi, Aden; tel. (2) 201989; fax (2) 202559; e-mail almansoob@y.net.ye; internet www.almansoob.com.ye; f. 1990; cargo operations, arranges crew changes, bunkers and repairs; Operations Man. MUHAMMAD ADAM.

Hodeida Shipping and Transport Co Ltd: POB 3337, San'a St, Hodeida; tel. (3) 228543; fax (3) 228533; e-mail agency@hodship.net; internet www.hodshipyemen.com; f. 1969; shipping agents, stevedoring, Lloyd's agents; clearance, haulage, land transportation, cargo and vessel surveys; Gen. Man. HASSAN A. KASSIM.

Middle East Shipping Co Ltd (Mideast): POB 3700, Hayel Saeed Bldg, al-Tahreer St, Hodeida; tel. (3) 203977; fax (3) 203910; e-mail mideast@mideastshipping.com; internet www.mideastshipping.com; f. 1962; Chair. RASHAD HAYEL SAID ANAM; Gen. Man. AHMAD GAZEM SAID ANAM; brs in Mocha, Aden, Taiz, Mukalla, San'a, Salif, Ras Isa, al-Shihr.

CIVIL AVIATION
There are eight international airports—San'a International (13 km from the city), Aden International Airport (at Khormaksar, 11 km from the port of Aden), Mukalla (Riyan), Taiz, Socotra, al-Ghaydah, Seiyun and Hodeida.

Civil Aviation and Meteorology Authority: POB 1042, Zubairi St, San'a; tel. (1) 274972; fax (1) 274718; e-mail web@cama.gov.ye; internet www.cama.gov.ye; supervisory body for civil aviation and meteorology affairs; Chair. MOHAMMED ABDUL QADIR.

Felix Airways: Al-Hasaba St, Airport Rd, San'a; tel. (1) 565656; fax (1) 252989; e-mail callcenter@felixairways.com; internet www.felixairways.com; f. 2008; 45% owned by Islamic Corpn for the Devt of the Private Sector (Saudi Arabia), 25% by Yemen Airways, 20% by Al-Tayyar Travel Group (Saudi Arabia); low-cost carrier providing domestic services from San'a and Aden and regional services to the UAE, Oman, Saudi Arabia and Djibouti; Chair. Eng. ABDULLAH REHAIMI; CEO Eng. ABDULLAH M. SHAABAN BIN SILM.

Yemen Airways (Yemenia): POB 1183, Alhasabah St, San'a; tel. (1) 232380; e-mail info@yemenia.com; internet www.yemenia.com; f. 1961 as Yemen Airlines; nationalized as Yemen Airways Corpn 1972; present name adopted 1978; merged with airlines of fmr People's Democratic Repub. of Yemen in 1996; owned 51% by Yemeni Govt and 49% by Govt of Saudi Arabia; scheduled for privatization; supervised by a ministerial cttee under the Ministry of Transport; internal services and external services to more than 35 destinations in the Middle East, Asia, Africa, Europe and the USA; Chair. and CEO Capt. AHMAD MASOUD AL-WANI; Man. Dir OMAR BIN ABDULLAH JEFRI.

Tourism

Association of Yemen Tourism and Travel Agencies: San'a; internet www.aytta.org.ye; f. 1996; Chair. YAHYA M. A. SALEH.

General Authority of Tourism: POB 129, San'a; tel. (1) 252319; fax (1) 252317; e-mail gtda@gtda.gov.ye; internet www.gtda.gov.ye; Chair. MUTAHAR TAQI.

Yemen Tourism Promotion Board: PHadda St, San'a; tel. (1) 417893; e-mail director@yementourism.com; internet www.yementourism.com; f. 1999; Exec. Dir MUHAMMAD AL-MANSOUR.

Defence

As assessed at November 2022, Yemen's armed forces comprised 40,000 personnel active in government-controlled areas, incl. militia (both the navy and air force had lost operational capacity). Non-government forces comprised 20,000 members of various groups, incl. al-Houthi rebel forces and Republican Guards loyal to former President Ali Abdullah Saleh. There were also 3,150 troops from Saudi Arabia and Sudan active in Yemen as part of 'Operation Restoring Hope'.

Defence Budget: YR 405,000m. in 2014.

Supreme Commander of the Armed Forces: Maj.-Gen. Dr RASHAD AL-ALIMI.

Chief of the General Staff: Lt-Gen. SAGHEER BIN AZIZ.

Education

Primary education in Yemen is compulsory from the age of six and lasts for six years. Secondary education, beginning at 13, lasts for a further six years. In the 2015/16 academic year enrolment at primary schools included 84.4% of children (boys 89.7%; girls 78.9%) in the relevant age-group. In 2015/16 enrolment at lower secondary schools included 71.6% of students (boys 77.4%; girls 65.5%) in the appropriate age-group, while the comparable rate at upper secondary schools was 43.6% of students (boys 54.4%; girls 32.3%). In 2012 public expenditure on education was equivalent to 15.1% of total government spending, according to UNESCO.

Bibliography

Badeeb, Said M. *The Saudi–Egyptian Conflict over North Yemen 1962–70*. Boulder, CO, Westview Press, 1986.

Blumi, Isa. *Chaos in Yemen: Societal Collapse and the New Authoritarianism*. Abingdon, Routledge, 2010.

Bonnefoy, Laurent (trans. Schoch, Cynthia). *Yemen and the World: Beyond Insecurity*. London, C. Hurst & Co, 2018.

Boucek, Christopher. 'War in Saada: From Local Insurrection to National Challenge', in *Carnegie Endowment for International Peace Middle East Program Paper No. 110*, 2010. carnegieendowment.org/files/war_in_saada.pdf.

Brandt, Marieke. *Tribes and Politics in Yemen: A History of the Houthi Conflict*. London, C. Hurst & Co, 2016.

Brehony, Noel. *Yemen Divided: The Story of a Failed State in South Arabia*. London, I. B. Tauris, 2011.

— *Hadhramaut and its Diaspora: Yemeni Politics, Identity and Migration*. London, I. B. Tauris, 2017.

Burrowes, Robert D. *The Yemen Arab Republic: The Politics of Development 1962–1986*. London, Croom Helm, 1987.

Carapico, Sheila. *Civil Society in Yemen: The Political Economy of Activism in Modern Arabia*. Cambridge University Press, 1998.

— 'No Quick Fix: Foreign Aid and State Performance in Yemen', in Nancy Birdsall, Milan Vaishnav and Robert A. Ayres (Eds). *Short of the Goal: US Policy and Poorly Performing States*. Washington, DC, Centre for Global Development, 2006.

Central Bank of Yemen. *Monetary and Banking Developments*. Monthly (last published Jan. 2015). www.centralbank.gov.ye/newsletter.aspx?keyid=48&pid=46&lang=1&cattype=6.

Central Statistical Organization of Yemen. *Yearbook*, annual.

Colburn, Marta. *The Republic of Yemen: Development Challenges in the 21st Century*. London, Catholic Institute for International Relations, 2004.

Colonial Office. *Accession of Aden to the Federation of South Arabia*. London, HMSO, 1962.

Colton, Nora Ann. 'Yemen: A Collapsed Economy', in *The Middle East Journal*. Vol. 64, No. 3, 2010.

Day, Stephen W. *Regionalism and Rebellion in Yemen: A Troubled National Union*. Cambridge and New York, Cambridge University Press, 2012.

Day, Stephen, and Brehony, Noel (Eds). *Global, Regional, and Local Dynamics in the Yemen Crisis*. Cham, Palgrave Macmillan, 2020.

Detalle, Renaud. *Tensions in Arabia: The Saudi–Yemeni Fault Line*. Baden-Baden, Nomos Verlagsgesellschaft, 2000.

DiRosilia, Benyamin (Ed.). *Yemen: Foreign Relations and Challenges*. New York, Nova Science Publishers, 2012.

Dresch, Paul. *Tribes, Government and History in Yemen*. New York, Oxford University Press, 1994.

— *A History of Modern Yemen*. Cambridge, Cambridge University Press, 2001.

Durac, Vincent. 'The Joint Meetings Party and the Politics of Opposition in Yemen', in *British Journal of Middle Eastern Studies*. Vol. 38, No. 3, 2011.

— 'Civil Society in Contemporary Yemen' in Cavatorta, Francesco (Ed.). *Civil Society Activism Under Authoritarian Rule: A Comparative Perspective*. Abingdon, Routledge, 2012.

— 'Islamism in Yemen: From Ansar Allah to Al-Qaeda in the Arabian Peninsula' in Kraetzschmar, Hendrik, and Rivetti, Paola (Eds). *Islamists and the Politics of the Arab Uprisings: Governance, Pluralisation and Contention*. Edinburgh, Edinburgh University Press, 2017.

Enders, Klaus, Williams, Sherwyn E., Choueiri, Nada G., Sobolev, Yuri V., and Walliser, Jan. *Yemen in the 1990s: From Unification to Economic Reform* (IMF Occasional Paper). Washington, DC, IMF Publication Services, 2002.

Gavin, R. J. *Aden 1839–1967*. London, Hurst, 1973.

Halliday, Fred. *Revolution and Foreign Policy: The Case of South Yemen, 1967–1987*. Cambridge, Cambridge University Press, 2002.

Heyworth-Dunne, G. E. *Al-Yemen: Social, Political and Economic Survey*. Cairo, 1952.

Hill, Ginny. *Yemen Endures: Civil War, Saudi Adventurism and the Future of Arabia*. London, C. Hurst & Co, 2017.

Hill, Ginny, Salisbury, Peter, Northedge, Léonie, and Kinnimont, Jane. *Yemen: Corruption, Capital Flight and Global Drivers of Conflict*. London, Royal Institute of International Affairs (Chatham House), 2013.

Hull, Edmund J. *High Value Target: Countering Al-Qaeda in Yemen*. Dulles, VA, Potomac Books, 2011.

Ingrams, Doreen, and Ingrams, Leila (Eds). *The Records of Yemen 1798–1960*. London, Archive Editions, 1995.

Ingrams, Harold. *The Yemen: Imams, Rulers and Revolutions*. London, 1963.

International Crisis Group (ICG). 'Yemen: Is Peace Possible' in *ICG Middle East Report No. 167*, 9 Feb. 2016. www.crisisgroup.org/middle-east-north-africa/gulf-and-arabian-peninsula/yemen/yemen-peace-possible.

Ismail, Tareq Y., and Jacqueline S. *The People's Democratic Republic of Yemen. Politics, Economics and Society*. London, Pinter, 1986.

Kaussler, B., and Grant, K. A. *Proxy War in Yemen*. London, Routledge, 2022.

Klorman, Bat-Zion Eraqi. *Traditional Society in Transition: The Yemeni Jewish Experience*. Leiden, Brill, 2014.

Kostiner, Joseph. *Yemen: The Tortuous Quest for Unity 1990–94*. London, Chatham House, 1996.

Lackner, Helen. *Why Yemen Matters: A Society in Transition*. London, Saqi, 2014.

— *Yemen in Crisis: Autocracy, Neo-Liberalism and the Disintegration of a State*. London, Saqi Books, 2017.

— *Yemen: Poverty and Conflict*. Abingdon, Routledge, 2022.

Lackner, Helen, and Varisco, Daniel Martin (Eds). *Yemen and the Gulf States: the Making of a Crisis*. Berlin, Gerlach Press, 2018.

Macro, Eric. *Yemen and the Western World since 1571*. London, C. Hurst, and New York, Praeger, 1968.

Mahdi, K. A., Würth, A., and Lackner, H. *Yemen into the Twenty-First Century: Continuity and Change*. Reading, Ithaca Press, 2007.

Manea, Elham. *Regional Politics in the Gulf: Saudi Arabia, Oman and Yemen*. London, Saqi Books, 2005.

Naumkin, Vitaly. *Red Wolves of Yemen: The Struggle for Independence*. Cambridge, Oleander Press, 2004.

Orkaby, Asher. *Beyond the Arab Cold War: the International History of the Yemen Civil War, 1962-68*. New York, Oxford University Press, 2017.

Page, Stephen. *The Soviet Union and the Yemens: Influence in Asymmetrical Relationships*. New York, Praeger, 1985.

Peterson, J. E. *Yemen, the Search for a Modern State*. London, Croom Helm, 1981.

Phillips, Sarah. *Yemen's Democracy Experiment in Regional Perspective: Patronage and Pluralized Authoritarianism*. London, Palgrave Macmillan, 2008.

— *Yemen and the Politics of Permanent Crisis*. Abingdon, Routledge, 2011.

Pridham, B. R. (Ed.). *Economy, Society & Culture in Contemporary Yemen*. Abingdon, Routledge, 2021.

Rabi, Uzi. *Yemen: Revolution, Civil War and Unification*. London, I. B. Tauris, 2015.

Saif, Ahmad A. *A Legislature in Transition: The Yemeni Parliament*. Aldershot, Ashgate Publishing, 2001.

Salisbury, Peter. 'Yemen's Economy: Oil, Imports and Élites', in *Middle East and North Africa Programme Paper*. London, Chatham House, 2011. www.chathamhouse.org/publications/papers/view/179191.

Schmidt, Dana Adams. *Yemen, the Unknown War*. London, Bodley Head, 1968.

Schmitz, Charles, and Burrowes, Robert D. *Historical Dictionary of Yemen*. Lanham, MD, Rowman & Littlefield, 3rd edn, 2018.

Schwedler, Jillian. *Faith in Moderation: Islamist Parties in Jordan and Yemen*. Cambridge, Cambridge University Press, 2007.

Stookey, Robert W. *Yemen: The Politics of the Yemen Arab Republic*. Boulder, CO, Westview Press, 1978.

al-Suwaidi, Jamal S. (Ed.). *The Yemeni War of 1994: Causes and Consequences*. London, Saqi Books, 1995.

vom Bruck, Gabriele. *Islam, Memory and Morality in Yemen: Ruling Families in Transition*. London, Palgrave Macmillan, 2005.

Walker, Jonathan. *Aden Insurgency: The Savage War in South Arabia, 1962–67*. Staplehurst, Spellmount Publrs, 2004.

Ward, Christopher. *The Water Crisis in Yemen: Managing Extreme Water Scarcity in the Middle East*. London, I. B. Tauris, 2014.

Wedeen, Lisa. *Peripheral Visions: Publics, Power, and Performance in Yemen*. Chicago, IL, University of Chicago Press, 2008.

Weir, Shelagh. *A Tribal Order: Politics and Law in the Mountains of Yemen*. London, British Museum Press, 2007.

Willis, John. *Unmaking North and South: Cartographies of the Yemeni Past*. Oxford, Oxford University Press, 2014.

World Bank. *Economic Growth in the Republic of Yemen: Sources, Constraints and Potentials*. Washington, DC, World Bank Publications, 2002.

The Republic of Yemen: Unlocking the Potential for Economic Growth. Washington, DC, World Bank Publications, 2015, documents.worldbank.org/curated/en/673781467997642839/Yemen-Republic-of-Unlocking-the-potential-for-economic-growth.

World Bank, United Nations, European Union and Islamic Development Bank. *Joint Social and Economic Assessment for the Republic of Yemen*. Washington, DC, World Bank Publications, 2012, openknowledge.worldbank.org/handle/10986/11920.

Yadav, Stacey Philbrick. 'Understanding "What Islamists Want": Public Debate and Contestation in Lebanon and Yemen', in *Middle East Journal*. Vol. 64, Issue 2, 2010.

Islamists and the State: Legitimacy and Institutions in Yemen and Lebanon. London, I. B. Tauris, 2013.

PART THREE
Regional Information

REGIONAL ORGANIZATIONS

UNITED NATIONS

Address: 405 East 42nd St, New York, NY 10017, USA.
Telephone: (212) 963-1234; **fax:** (212) 963-4879; **internet:** www.un.org.

The United Nations (UN) was founded in 1945 to maintain international peace and security and to develop global co-operation in addressing economic, social, cultural and humanitarian problems. Its principal organs are the General Assembly, the Security Council, the Economic and Social Council, the International Court of Justice and the Secretariat.

The UN's chief administrative officer is the Secretary-General, elected for a five-year term. The General Assembly comprises representatives of all 193 UN member states. The Security Council investigates disputes between member countries, and may recommend ways and means of peaceful settlement. The Economic and Social Council comprises representatives of 54 member states, elected by the General Assembly for a three-year period: it promotes co-operation on economic, social, cultural and humanitarian matters, acting as a central policy-making body and co-ordinating the activities of the UN's specialized agencies. The International Court of Justice, mandated to adjudicate in legal disputes between UN member states, comprises 15 judges of different nationalities, elected for nine-year terms by the General Assembly and the Security Council.

Secretary-General: ANTÓNIO MANUEL DE OLIVEIRA GUTERRES (Portugal) (2017–26).

MEMBER STATES IN THE MIDDLE EAST AND NORTH AFRICA
(with assessments for percentage contributions to UN budget in 2023, and year of admission)

Country	%	Year
Algeria	0.109	1962
Bahrain	0.054	1971
Cyprus	0.036	1960
Egypt	0.139	1945
Iran	0.371	1945
Iraq	0.128	1945
Israel	0.561	1949
Jordan	0.022	1955
Kuwait	0.234	1963
Lebanon	0.036	1945
Libya	0.018	1955
Morocco	0.055	1956
Oman	0.111	1971
Qatar	0.269	1971
Saudi Arabia	1.184	1945
Syrian Arab Republic	0.009	1945
Tunisia	0.019	1956
Türkiye (Turkey)*	0.845	1945
United Arab Emirates	0.635	1971
Yemen	0.008	1947/67†

* Türkiye was known as Turkey until 1 June 2022.
† The Yemen Arab Republic became a member of the UN in 1947, and the People's Democratic Republic of Yemen was admitted in 1967. The two countries formed the Republic of Yemen in 1990.

SOVEREIGN STATE NOT IN THE UNITED NATIONS
Palestine

Note: Palestine was granted non-member observer state status at the UN in November 2012.

Diplomatic Representation

PERMANENT MISSIONS TO THE UNITED NATIONS
(September 2023)

Algeria: 326 East 48th St, New York, NY 10017; tel. (212) 750-1960; fax (212) 759-5274; e-mail algeria@un.int; internet www.un.int/algeria; Permanent Representative AMAR BENDJAMA.

Bahrain: 866 Second Ave, 14th/15th Floors, New York, NY 10017; tel. (212) 223-6200; fax (212) 223-6206; e-mail bahrain1@un.int; internet www.un.int/bahrain; Permanent Representative JAMAL FARES ALROWAIEI.

Cyprus: 15 East 38th St, 11th Floor, New York, NY 10018; tel. (212) 481-6023; e-mail unmission@mfa.gov.cy; internet www.cyprusun.org; Permanent Representative ANDREAS HADJICHRYSANTHOU.

Egypt: 304 East 44th St, New York, NY 10017; tel. (212) 503-0300; fax (212) 949-5999; e-mail mission.egypt@un.int; Permanent Representative OSAMA MAHMOUD ABDEL KHALEK MAHMOUD.

Iran: 622 Third Ave, 34th Floor, New York, NY 10017; tel. (212) 687-2020; fax (212) 867-7086; e-mail iran@un.int; internet ny.mfa.gov.ir; Permanent Representative Amir SAEED JALIL IRAVANI.

Iraq: 14 East 79th St, New York, NY 10075; tel. (212) 737-4433; e-mail iraq.mission@un.int; Permanent Representative (vacant).

Israel: 800 Second Ave, New York, NY 10017; tel. (212) 499-5344; fax (212) 499-5515; e-mail UNInfo@newyork.mfa.gov.il; internet embassies.gov.il/un; Permanent Representative GILAD ERDAN.

Jordan: 866 Second Ave, 4th Floor, New York, NY 10017; tel. (212) 832-9553; fax (212) 832-5346; e-mail missionun@jordanmissionun.com; Permanent Representative MAHMOUD DAIFALLAH HMOUD.

Kuwait: 321 East 44th St, New York, NY 10017; tel. (212) 973-4300; fax (212) 370-1733; e-mail kuwait@kuwaitmissionun.org; internet www.kuwaitmissionun.org; Permanent Representative TAREQ M. A. M. ALBANAI.

Lebanon: 866 UN Plaza, Rm 531–533, New York, NY 10017; tel. (212) 355-5460; fax (212) 838-2819; e-mail contact@lebanonun.org; internet lebanonun.com; Permanent Representative (vacant).

Libya: 309–315 East 48th St, New York, NY 10017; tel. (212) 752-5775; fax (212) 593-4787; e-mail mission@libya-un.gov.ly; internet www.libyanmission-un.org; see note below on the UN General Assembly's Credentials Committee; Permanent Representative TAHER M. EL-SONNI.

Morocco: 866 Second Ave, 6th and 7th Floors, New York, NY 10017; tel. (212) 421-1580; fax (212) 980-1512; e-mail morocco.un@maec.gov.ma; internet www.un.int/morocco; Permanent Representative OMAR HILALE.

Oman: 3 Dag Hammarskjöld Plaza, 305 East 47th St, 12th Floor, New York, NY 10017; tel. (212) 355-3505; fax (212) 644-0070; e-mail oman@un.int; internet www.un.int/oman; Permanent Representative MOHAMED AL HASSAN.

Qatar: 809 UN Plaza, 4th Floor, New York, NY 10017; tel. (212) 486-9335; fax (212) 758-4952; e-mail pmun@mofa.gov.qa; Permanent Representative ALYA AHMED SEIF AL-THANI.

Saudi Arabia: 809 UN Plaza, 10th and 11th Floors, New York, NY 10017; tel. (212) 557-1525; fax (212) 983-4895; e-mail saudi-mission@un.int; Permanent Representative ABDULAZIZ ALWASIL.

Syrian Arab Republic: 820 Second Ave, 15th Floor, New York, NY 10017; tel. (212) 661-1313; fax (212) 983-4439; e-mail exesec.syria@gmail.com; internet www.un.int/syria; Permanent Representative BASSAM SABBAGH.

Tunisia: 801 Second Ave, 9th Floor, New York, NY 10017; tel. (212) 751-7503; fax (212) 986-1620; e-mail tunisiamission@usa.com; Permanent Representative TAREK LADEB.

Türkiye (Turkey): 821 UN Plaza, 10th Floor, New York, NY 10017; tel. (212) 949-0150; fax (212) 949-0086; e-mail tr-delegation.newyork@mfa.gov.tr; internet www.turkuno.dt.mfa.gov.tr; Permanent Representative SEDAT ÖNAL.

United Arab Emirates: 315 East 46th St, New York, NY 10017; tel. (212) 371-0480; fax (212) 371-4923; e-mail nyunprm@mofaic.gov.ae; internet www.un.int/uae; Permanent Representative LANA ZAKI NUSSEIBEH.

Yemen: 413 East 51st St, New York, NY 10022; tel. (212) 355-1730; e-mail yemenmissionny@gmail.com; internet www.un.int/yemen; Permanent Representative ABDULLAH ALI FADHEL AL-SAADI.

REGIONAL ORGANIZATIONS

OBSERVERS

African Union: 305 East 47th St, 5th Floor, 3 Dag Hammarskjöld Plaza, New York, NY 10017; tel. (212) 319-5490; fax (212) 319-7135; e-mail au-newyork@africa-union.org; internet www.africanunion-un.org; Permanent Observer FATIMA KYARI MOHAMMED.

Asian-African Legal Consultative Organization: 275 West 10th St, New York, NY 10014; tel. (917) 623-2861; fax (206) 426-5442; e-mail aalco@un.int; internet www.aalco.int; Permanent Observer ROY S. LEE.

Cooperation Council for the Arab States of the Gulf: 600 Third Ave, Offices 224/225, New York, NY 10016; tel. (646) 571-2581; fax (212) 319-3434; e-mail gccny@un.int; Permanent Observer SULAIMAN MOHAMMED S. ALANBAR (Saudi Arabia).

International Committee of the Red Cross: 801 Second Ave, 18th Floor, New York, NY 10017; tel. (212) 599-6021; fax (212) 599-6009; e-mail newyork@icrc.org; Head of Delegation LAETITIA COURTOIS.

International Institute for Democracy and Electoral Assistance: 305 East 47th St, 10th Floor, New York, NY 10017; e-mail unobserver@idea.int; Permanent Observer ANNIKA SILVIA-LEANDER.

International Olympic Committee: 708 Third Ave, 6th Floor, New York, NY 10017; tel. (212) 209-3952; fax (212) 209-7100; e-mail IOC-UNObserver@olympic.org; Permanent Observer (vacant).

Inter-Parliamentary Union: 336 East 45th St, 10th Floor, New York, NY 10017; tel. (212) 557-5880; e-mail ny-office@mail.ipu.org; internet www.ipu.org/Un-e/un-opo.htm; Permanent Observer PATRICIA TORSNEY (Canada).

League of Arab States: 733 Third Ave, 22nd Floor, New York, NY 10017; tel. (212) 838-8700; fax (212) 355-8001; e-mail las.mail@un.int; Permanent Observer MAGED ABDELFATTAH ABDELAZIZ.

Organization of Islamic Cooperation: 320 East 51st St, New York, NY 10022; tel. (212) 883-0140; fax (212) 883-0143; e-mail oicny@un.int; internet www.oicun.org; Permanent Observer HAMEED AJIBAIYE OPELOYERU (Nigeria).

Palestine: 115 East 65th St, New York, NY 10021; tel. (212) 288-8500; fax (212) 517-2377; e-mail palestine@un.int; internet palestineun.org; Permanent Observer Dr RIYAD H. MANSOUR.

Parliamentary Assembly of the Mediterranean: 336 East 45th St, New York, NY 10017; tel. (212) 557-5880; fax (212) 251-1014; e-mail pam.unny@pam.int; Permanent Observer QAZI SHAUKAT FAREED.

The following are among a number of intergovernmental organizations that have a standing invitation to participate as Observers in the sessions and work of the General Assembly, but do not maintain permanent offices at the UN: African Development Bank, Asian Infrastructure Investment Bank, Developing Eight, Economic Cooperation Organization, Global Dryland Alliance, Islamic Development Bank, OPEC Fund for International Development, Organization of the Black Sea Economic Cooperation, Union for the Mediterranean.

United Nations Information Centres/Services

Algeria: 41 rue Mohamed Khoudi, 16030 El Biar, Algiers; tel. and fax (21) 92-54-42; e-mail unic.algiers@unic.org; internet algeria.un.org.

Bahrain: POB 26004, UN House, Bldg 69, Rd 1901, Manama 319; tel. 17311676; fax 17311692; e-mail unic.manama@unic.org; internet manama.sites.unicnetwork.org; also covers Qatar and the United Arab Emirates.

Egypt: 1 Osiris St, Garden City, Cairo; tel. (2) 7940412; fax (2) 7953705; e-mail info@unic-eg.org; internet www.unic-eg.org; also covers Saudi Arabia.

Iran: POB 15875-4557; 8 Shahrzad Blvd, Darrous, Tehran; tel. (21) 22873837; fax (21) 22873395; e-mail unic.tehran@unic.org; internet iran.un.org.

Lebanon: UN House, Riad el-Solh Sq., POB 11-8575-4656, Beirut; tel. (1) 981301; fax (1) 970424; e-mail unic-beirut@un.org; internet www.unicbeirut.org; also covers Jordan, Kuwait and Syria.

Morocco: BP 601; ave Ahmed Balafrej Souissi 13, Rabat; tel. (53) 7750393; fax (53) 7750382; e-mail cinu.rabat@unic.org; internet morocco.un.org.

Tunisia: BP 863, Immeuble le Prestige Business Center, rue du Lac Windermere, Tour A, Les Berges du Lac 1053, Tunis; tel. (36) 011-680; fax (71) 900-668; e-mail unic.tunis@unic.org; internet unictunis.org.tn.

Türkiye (Turkey): Yildiz Kule, Turan Güneş Bul. 106, 06550 Cankaya, Ankara; tel. (312) 4541052; fax (312) 4961499; e-mail unic.ankara@unic.org; internet turkiye.un.org.

Yemen: POB 237; Hadda Post Office Area, Sana'a; tel. (1) 410568; fax (1) 412251; e-mail unic.yemen@unic.org; internet yemen.un.org.

Economic Commission for Africa—ECA

Address: Menelik II Ave, POB 3001, Addis Ababa, Ethiopia.
Telephone: (11) 5445000; **fax:** (11) 5514416; **e-mail:** ecainfo@uneca.org; **internet:** www.uneca.org.

ECA, established in 1958, promotes sustainable socioeconomic development in Africa and aims to advance economic integration among African countries. It provides a forum for international co-operation in support of these aims.

MEMBERS

Algeria	Eritrea	Namibia
Angola	Eswatini	Niger
Benin	Ethiopia	Nigeria
Botswana	Gabon	Rwanda
Burkina Faso	The Gambia	São Tomé and
Burundi	Ghana	Príncipe
Cabo Verde	Guinea	Senegal
Cameroon	Guinea-Bissau	Seychelles
Central African	Kenya	Sierra Leone
Republic	Lesotho	Somalia
Chad	Liberia	South Africa
Comoros	Libya	South Sudan
Congo, Democratic	Madagascar	Sudan
Republic	Malawi	Tanzania
Congo, Republic	Mali	Togo
Côte d'Ivoire	Mauritania	Tunisia
Djibouti	Mauritius	Uganda
Egypt	Morocco	Zambia
Equatorial Guinea	Mozambique	Zimbabwe

Organization
(September 2023)

CONFERENCE OF AFRICAN MINISTERS

A Conference of African Ministers of Finance, Planning and Economic Development meets every year and is the main deliberative body of the Commission. It addresses matters of general policy, considers inter-African and international economic policy, and makes recommendations to member states in connection with such matters. The 55th session was held in March 2023, in Addis Ababa, on the theme 'Fostering recovery and transformation in Africa to reduce inequalities and vulnerabilities'.

SECRETARIAT

The secretariat implements the resolutions and programmes adopted by the Conference and the meetings of the Commission's subsidiary bodies. It is headed by an Executive Secretary, who is supported by two Deputy Executive Secretaries.

Executive Secretary: ANTONIO PEDRO (acting).

AFRICAN POLICY CENTRES

The following are focal points for continental policymaking and programming:

  African Centre for Statistics;
  African Climate Policy Centre;
  African Institute for Economic Development and Planning;
  African Land Policy Centre;

African Minerals Development Centre;
African Trade Policy Centre.

SUBREGIONAL OFFICE

North Africa: BP 2062 Rabat Ryad, Morocco; tel. (53) 7717829; fax (53) 7712702; internet www.uneca.org/north-africa; specialization: employment skills and balanced devt; Dir ZUZANA BRIXIOVA SCHWIDROWSKI.

Activities

The Commission's activities are focused on two 'pillars': promoting regional integration in support of the visions and priorities of the African Union (AU), through research and policy analysis, capacity building, and the provision of technical assistance to relevant institutions; and meeting emerging global challenges and the special needs of Africa, with particular emphasis on achieving the Sustainable Development Goals (SDGs) that were adopted in September 2015 by UN heads of state and government. The secretariat's work is guided by major regional strategies, including the Abuja Treaty on the establishment of an African Economic Community, Agenda 2063 (the AU's long-term framework for economic and social transformation of the continent), the AU Development Agency (AUDA-NEPAD), the UN's 2030 Agenda for Sustainable Development, and the Agreement Establishing the AfCFTA, adopted by an extraordinary summit of AU heads of state and of government in March 2018. In early March 2021 the inaugural meeting took place of a new Regional Collaborative Platform: Africa (RCP: Africa), which aimed to enhance the effectiveness and co-ordination of UN development entities. The Platform is chaired by the UN Deputy Secretary-General, with ECA's Executive Secretary and the Director of the UNDP Regional Bureau for Africa acting as Vice-Chairs.

ECA helps organize the annual Africa Regional Forum on Sustainable Development (ARFSD), which reviews progress being made towards achieving the SDGs. The ninth ARFSD, held in Niamey, Niger, in late February–early March 2023, addressed the theme 'Accelerating the inclusive and green recovery from multiple crises and the integrated and full implementation of the 2030 Agenda for Sustainable Development and Agenda 2063'.

During 2023 ECA's work programme focused on the following five strategic directions: Build ECA analytical capabilities; Formulate macroeconomic and structural policy; Design innovative financing models; Integrate regional and subregional transboundary initiatives; and Advocate continental ideas at the global level.

MACROECONOMIC POLICY AND GOVERNANCE

ECA advocates for a sound regional macroeconomic policy framework, with the aim of promoting inclusive growth. Member states are supported in forecasting and analysing macroeconomic indicators, in designing, implementing and evaluating development strategies, in mobilizing financing, and in following up global and regional development frameworks. ECA assists with the collection of data; the preparation of annual economic surveys; the compilation of reports on regional economic conditions, governance and development management; the production of regional and national policy studies covering economic reforms, international and illicit financial flows, domestic resource mobilization, external debt, and exchange rate management; and the dissemination of best practices relating to specific aspects of economic management.

In March 2021 ECA initiated a Liquidity and Sustainability Facility (LSF) to support the issuance by member state governments of sovereign bonds. An ECA policy brief on sovereign debt restructuring in Africa was issued in late 2022. The Commission organized a workshop on debt management in October. In February 2023, noting that—against a background of raised energy and food prices, mounting borrowing costs, and depressed external demand—GDP growth across Africa was estimated at 3.8% in 2022 (underperforming against previous forecasts), the ECA recommended increasing public investment to boost economic growth.

ECA aims to improve member states' capacity for good governance and development management. The Commission provides support for the African Peer Review Mechanism, an AUDA-NEPAD initiative whereby participating member governments mutually assess compliance with a number of codes, standards and commitments that uphold good governance and sustainable development. In January 2017 ECA and the Mechanism signed a Memorandum of Understanding (MOU) establishing a continuous partnership in support of the goals of the AU and the UN. ECA assists civil society organizations to participate in governance; supports the development of private sector enterprises; and helps to improve public administration in member states. To achieve these aims the Commission provides technical assistance and advisory services, conducts studies, and organizes training workshops, seminars and conferences at national, subregional and regional level for ministers, public administrators and senior policymakers, as well as for private and non-governmental organizations (NGOs).

The sixth edition of the *African Governance Report*, on the theme 'African Governance Futures to 2063', was finalized in 2021.

ECONOMIC DEVELOPMENT AND PLANNING

Joint meetings of ECA ministers responsible for economic affairs, planning and economic development and AU ministers responsible for the economy and finance are convened annually. In January 2018 the UN Secretary-General and AU Chairperson signed an AU-UN Framework for the Implementation of Agenda 2063 and the 2030 Agenda for Sustainable Development. ECA's African Institute for Economic Development and Planning (IDEP), founded in 1962, undertakes pan-African capacity development and training programmes, and also conducts policy research and dialogue initiatives.

Since 2006 ECA, with the AfDB and UNDP, has organized an annual African Economic Conference (AEC) to promote an exchange of ideas among economists and policymakers on development policy. The 2022 AEC was held in Balaclava, Mauritius, in December, focusing on the theme 'Supporting climate-smart development in Africa'. In July 2016 the UN designated 2016–25 as the Third Industrial Development Decade for Africa.

In April 2020 ECA established a multi-agency Africa Knowledge Hub for COVID-19, which aimed to collate regional and country health and economic data, analysis of sectoral impacts of the pandemic, and other ongoing research and resources. In mid-2020 ECA and partner agencies initiated an Africa Communication and Information Platform, which aimed to provide national and regional COVID-19 governmental task forces with data on survey responses, and actionable economic and health findings. At that time ECA became part of the Access to COVID-19 Tools (ACT) Accelerator partnership, focused on expediting the development and production of, and promoting equitable global access to, new health diagnostics, therapeutics and vaccines, to combat the pandemic and its onwards economic and social impacts. In August ECA joined the African Vaccine Acquisition Task Team. In 2023 ECA was implementing (in eight member states) a pilot AfCFTA-anchored Pharmaceutical Initiative, which aimed to scale up the expansion of local pharmaceutical production, and to promote continental pooled procurement and harmonized regulatory standards.

ECA hosts the secretariat of an independent Coalition for Dialogue on Africa (CoDA), which was founded in 2009, with the support of ECA, the AU and the African Development Bank (AfDB), and evolved from the other high-level consultative processes, including an African Development Forum. CoDA acts as secretariat for a High-Level Panel on Illicit Financial Flows. In November 2022 CoDA participated in a high-level technical meeting on the legal frameworks for the implementation of the Common African Position on Asset Recovery.

REGIONAL INTEGRATION AND TRADE

ECA supports the implementation of the AU's regional integration agenda, through research; policy analysis; strengthening capacity and the provision of technical assistance to the regional economic communities; and through working on transboundary initiatives and undertaking activities across a variety of sectors. ECA promotes best practice in trade policy development, and undertakes research and dissemination activities on bilateral and international trade negotiations, with a view to helping African countries to benefit from globalization through trade. Projects are undertaken to support governments' strategies on implementing the AfCFTA. The African Trade Policy Centre (ATPC), established in 2003, aims to strengthen the capacities of African governments to formulate and implement sound trade policies and to participate more effectively in international trade negotiations.

In December 2021 ECA, the AU, the AfDB and the UN Conference on Trade and Development issued their 10th joint *Assessing Regional Integration in Africa* report (*ARIA X*); this addressed the liberalization and integration of continental trade in services under the AfCFTA.

In April 2016 an ECA-AU-AfDB Africa Regional Integration Index (ARII) was launched. Using 16 indicators, the Index systematically measured progress in regional integration across areas including governance; investment; trade; infrastructure; industry; the free movement of persons; energy; culture; and macroeconomic policy convergence. An updated version of ARII was released in 2019. In February 2022 ECA issued an AfCFTA Country Business Index (ACBI) Report aimed at linking businesses and policymakers.

ECA organized the sixth African Business Forum in February 2023, in Addis Ababa, on the theme 'Making carbon markets work for Africa'.

ECA acts as the secretariat for the AUDA-NEPAD-co-ordinated (2021–30) Programme for Infrastructure Development in Africa Priority Action Plan (PIDA-PAP II), which covers infrastructure development in transport, energy, ICT, and transboundary water resources. In February 2023 ECA co-organized, in Senegal, a Second Dakar Financing Summit for Africa's Infrastructure, at which AUDA-NEPAD and Afreximbank agreed to establish a facility for financing the preparation of PIDA-PAP II initiatives.

A third Japan-Africa Business Forum was organized in July 2021. The eighth Tokyo International Conference on African Development (TICAD-8) was held in August 2022.

TECHNOLOGY

ECA supports member states in drafting and implementing national policies on innovation and technology, and undertakes relevant research, for example on emerging technologies that might facilitate economic development, and on technology transfer. It also has a focus on measuring the social, economic and other outcomes of policies on innovation and technology. ECA helps to organize the African Science, Technology and Innovation Forum, held regularly since 2018 as a multi-stakeholder event to promote debate and the exchange of knowledge in all aspects of science, technology and innovation, and in particular their contribution to the pursuit of the SDGs.

ECA hosts the secretariat of the African Internet Governance Forum (AfIGF), which it established in 2011, jointly with the AU. The 11th Forum was convened in July 2022 in Lilongwe, Malawi, on the theme 'Digital inclusion and trust in Africa'.

TECHNOLOGY, CLIMATE CHANGE AND NATURAL RESOURCE MANAGEMENT

ECA conducts research in support of policy, legal and regulatory frameworks underpinning the management of natural resources in Africa. It works to strengthen regional and national human and institutional capacities and to widen stakeholder participation in the protection of Africa's environment and in the management of the continent's mineral resources. It promotes research aimed at advancing policy makers' capacities to analyse and address issues related to natural resource management, climate change, and the transition to an inclusive low-carbon blue (ocean-focused) and green (land-based) economy.

The African Climate Policy Centre (ACPC), launched by the ECA in December 2007, helps member states to incorporate climate-related concerns in their development policies. In 2006, with the AU and the AfDB, the Commission initiated a Climate for Development in Africa Programme (ClimDev-Africa) to improve the collection of climate-related data and assist in forecasting and risk management. ECA provides the technical secretariat for ClimDev-Africa. Since 2011 ClimDev-Africa has organized annual Climate Change and Development in Africa Conferences (CCDAs). CCDA-X was held in Windhoek, Namibia, in October 2022, and prepared an African contribution concerning a 'just transition' for the 27th conference of the parties of the UN Framework Convention on Climate Change. In June 2021 ECA and the AU jointly organized the fifth Africa Climate Resilient Investment Summit (ACRIS-5). The first session of the fourth edition of a series of Africa Climate Talks ('ACTs!-4'), co-hosted by the ACPC in July 2022, addressed the theme 'Ensuring a just and equitable transition and human security in Africa: Building resilience'.

ECA assists member states in the assessment and use of water resources and the development of river and lake basins common to more than one country. ECA encourages co-operation between countries with regard to water issues and collaborates with other UN agencies and regional organizations to promote technical and economic co-operation in this area.

ECA aims to advance the development of Africa's extensive mineral and energy resources, focusing on promoting co-operation, integration and public-private sector partnerships; facilitating policy and dissemination of best practices; and supporting capacity building. A joint ECA-AU-AfDB multilateral Working Group on Infrastructure and Energy was established in November 2019. In November 2022 ECA and the UN University jointly launched the JUSTIS internet portal, which aimed to support Africa's large informal employment sector in transitioning to clean energy sources.

GENDER, POVERTY AND SOCIAL POLICY

ECA aims to improve the socioeconomic prospects of women through the promotion of equal access to resources and opportunities, and equal participation in decision making. An African Centre for Gender and Development was established in 1975 to service all national, subregional and regional bodies involved in development issues relating to gender and the advancement of women. The Centre manages the African Women's Development Fund, which was established in June 2000. An African Gender and Development Index, measuring the extent to which member states meet their commitments towards international agreements on gender equality and women's advancement, was inaugurated in January 2005; the fifth phase of the Index was initiated in 2019. In April 2019 ECA launched an African Women Leadership Fund, focused on the provision of sustainable investment capital to businesses owned and led by African women.

The Commission provides information on global processes on social policy, including on the International Conference on Population and Development and the UN's 2030 Agenda for Sustainable Development. ECA maintains an African Social Development Index, which measures degrees of social exclusion. In June 2023 ECA and the AU launched a joint initiative to promote a positive narrative to regional migration, to enhance migration governance and to remove barriers to labour mobility.

DATA AND STATISTICS

The African Centre for Statistics was established in 2006 to enhance the compilation, analysis and dissemination of reliable and comparable statistics. The four main sections of the Centre cover economic, infrastructure and agriculture statistics; demographic and social statistics; statistical development, data innovation and outreach; and geospatial information management systems. ECA assists its member states in population data collection and data processing; analysis of demographic data obtained from censuses or surveys; formulation of population policies; and integrating population variables in development planning. In October 2022 the sixth conference of African ministers responsible for civil registration was convened, in Addis Ababa. (The first was held in August 2010, also in Addis Ababa.)

In September 2021 an online Africa UN Data for Development portal was launched as a collaborative initiative of some 17 UN agencies to make available reliable and comparable socioeconomic data. An Africa SDGs Progress Dashboard was incorporated into the portal in July 2022.

Finance

ECA's regular budget for 2023, an appropriation from the UN budget, was US $88.1m.

Publications

Africa Statistical Flash (monthly).
Africa Sustainable Development Report (every 2 years).
African Governance Report.
African Statistical Yearbook.
Assessing Regional Integration in Africa (with the AU and the AfDB).
Country Profiles.
Economic Performance and Outlook (quarterly).
Economic Report on Africa (annually).
Subregional reports, policy and discussion papers, reports of conferences and meetings, training series, working paper series.

Economic and Social Commission for Western Asia—ESCWA

Address: Riad el-Solh Sq., POB 11-8575, Beirut, Lebanon.
Telephone: (1) 981301; **fax:** (1) 981510; **e-mail:** escwa-ciu@un.org; **internet:** www.unescwa.org.

The UN Economic Commission for Western Asia was established in 1974, to provide facilities of a wider scope for those countries previously served by the UN Economic and Social Office in Beirut. The membership has since expanded, and the present name was adopted in 1985.

MEMBERS

Algeria	Oman
Bahrain	Palestine
Egypt	Qatar
Iraq	Saudi Arabia
Jordan	Somalia
Kuwait	Sudan
Lebanon	Syrian Arab Republic
Libya	Tunisia
Mauritania	United Arab Emirates
Morocco	Yemen

Note: Djibouti submitted a membership application in July 2022.

Organization
(September 2023)

COMMISSION
The Commission normally meets every two years in ministerial session to determine policy and establish work directives. The 30th ordinary ministerial session of the Commission was convened in June 2018, in Beirut. A special session (the seventh), held in December 2022, discussed an application by Djibouti for membership of the organization.

EXECUTIVE COMMITTEE
The Executive Committee, composed of senior officials from member countries, convenes every six months, with a mandate to advise and assist the secretariat in formulating strategy and future priorities, and to support the implementation of the secretariat's programme of work.

SUBSIDIARY COMMITTEES
Specialized intergovernmental committees—on Statistics, Social Development, Energy, Water Resources, Transport and Logistics, Trade Policies, Women, Trade Policies, Financing for Development, and Technology for Development—assist the Commission to formulate medium-term work programmes.

SECRETARIAT
The secretariat comprises an Executive Secretary; two Deputy Executive Secretaries; a Strategy, Planning, Accountability, Results, Knowledge (SPARK) team; an External Relations and Communications Section; a Resources Management and Service Development Division; and the following multidisciplinary thematic clusters: Climate change and natural resource sustainability; Gender justice, population and inclusive development; Shared economic prosperity; Statistics, information society and technology; 2030 Sustainable Development Agenda and Sustainable Development Goals (SDGs) co-ordination; and Governance and conflict prevention.

Executive Secretary: ROLA DASHTI (Kuwait).
Deputy Executive Secretary, Programme: MOUNIR TABET (Canada).

Activities

ESCWA aims to support development and to further economic co-operation and integration in western Asia. It undertakes or sponsors studies of economic, social and development issues of the region, collects and disseminates information, and provides relevant advisory services. The Commission also organizes conferences and intergovernmental and expert group meetings and sponsors training workshops and seminars. In March 2021 the inaugural annual meeting took place of a new Regional Collaborative Platform for the Arab States (RCP: Arab States), with participation by UN development entities active in the region. RCP: Arab States is chaired by the UN Deputy Secretary-General, with ESCWA's Executive Secretary and the Director of the UN Development Programme (UNDP) Regional Bureau for Arab States acting as Vice-Chairs.

A Memorandum of Understanding (MOU) concluded in June 2013 between ESCWA and the League of Arab States (Arab League) provided for participation by ESCWA in ministerial sessions and meetings of the League's Economic and Social Council.

An initiative to draft a common long-term socioeconomic and institutional vision for Arab countries—Arab Vision 2045—is being developed by ESCWA, with support from the Arab League.

UN 2030 AGENDA AND SDG CO-ORDINATION
Since 2016 ESCWA and the Arab League have organized an annual Arab Forum for Sustainable Development (AFSD), with participation by government officials, regional organizations, and representatives of civil society and the private sector, to consider the co-ordinated implementation and follow-up in the Arab region of the UN SDGs. AFSD-2023, convened under the chairmanship of Yemen in March, in Beirut, reviewed the regional progress of SDGs 6 (on clean water and sanitation), 7 (affordable and clean energy), 9 (industry, innovation and infrastructure), 11 (sustainable cities and communities), and 17 (on partnerships). The event included sessions that addressed food systems transformation for food security; the intergenerational effects of violence; the role of renewable energy in accelerating recovery in fragile and crisis-affected countries; sustainable reconstruction; and enabling the circular carbon economy.

The second edition of a five-yearly *Arab Sustainable Development Report (ASDR)*, issued by ESCWA and partner agencies in June 2020, forecast that the Arab region would not achieve the UN SDGs by 2030, and noted that, even prior to the COVID-19 crisis, a rising trend in extreme poverty had been reported there (mainly attributable to conflict).

CLIMATE CHANGE AND NATURAL RESOURCE SUSTAINABILITY
ESCWA's promotes regional and subregional co-operation that advances water, energy and food security in the region. Its Climate Change and Natural Resource Sustainability Cluster co-ordinates the Regional Initiative for the Assessment of Climate Change Impacts on Water Resources and Socio-Economic Vulnerability in the Arab Region (RICCAR), launched in 2009 by ESCWA and the Arab League. Three regional climate research centres have been established within the RICCAR framework. The Cluster also directs the Arab Centre for Climate Change Policies (established in June 2018). In December 2020 ESCWA initiated a regional Climate-SDG Debt Swap Mechanism (DSM), and urged the international donor community to use it to increase funding for climate-resilient initiatives. ESCWA extends technical support to Arab negotiators on climate change. An Arab Regional Parliamentary Forum on the 2030 Agenda: Strengthening Parliamentary Engagement in Climate Action in the Arab Region was convened in November 2022, in Beirut, by ESCWA and partners. ESCWA conducts climate change impact and vulnerability assessments, and analyses environmental and related socioeconomic issues to inform policymaking.

The inaugural Arab Environmental Forum, convened in October 2022, in Cairo, by ESCWA, the Arab League and the UN Environment Programme, discussed a common Arab vision on environmental issues to inform forthcoming global policy meetings.

In March 2018 ESCWA and the Arab League adopted a harmonized regional outlook on energy policy, identifying the following priorities: transitioning towards sustainable energy systems; enhancing resource management; and reducing dependency on fossil fuels. In September ESCWA, the Arab League and the Swedish International Development Agency convened the first co-ordination meeting of a new Regional Initiative for Promoting Small-scale Renewable Energy Applications in Rural Areas of the Arab Region (REGEND), which aimed to enhance social inclusion, livelihoods and gender equality through investment in renewable energy technologies.

ESCWA promotes greater co-operation in the management and use of shared water resources. In November 2021 ESCWA convened a high-level meeting titled 'Water scarcity: a challenge to sustainable development in the Arab region', which drew attention to adverse economic impacts of water shortages, such as increased household expenditure, water delivery and public health costs, and depressed agricultural output. An ESCWA report titled *Groundwater in the Arab Region*, issued in September 2022, noted that two-thirds of the region's (scarce) water resources crossed at least one national boundary. Pollution, high population growth, inefficient management of water resources, conflict, and climate change and extreme weather events were reported to be impediments to access to water resources.

In September 2022 ESCWA issued a report titled *Arab Food Security Vulnerabilities and Pathways,* which considered the state of food supply and security in the region and detailed means of enhancing resilience to future external shocks. The Commission convened a meeting of experts in December, in a virtual format, to discuss means of addressing gaps in the region's food systems. Later in that month ESCWA, the Arab League and partners organized an Arab Forum for Agriculture, in Amman, which addressed, *inter alia*, the role of the private sector in sustainable agriculture development. A Strategy for Sustainable Arab Agricultural Development was being implemented during 2020–30, alongside an Arab Program for Sustaining Food Security that aimed to expand output of basic food commodities by a minimum of 30% by 2030.

GENDER JUSTICE, POPULATION AND INCLUSIVE DEVELOPMENT

ESCWA aims to advance gender equality through the promotion of gender justice and the law; women, peace and security; women's economic empowerment; and the elimination of violence against women. The Commission supports member states in translating global normative frameworks into regional programmes, promotes ratification and implementation of relevant international instruments, compiles gender status indicators, develops training packages, raises awareness by publishing reports and studies, and organizes conferences. In January 2016 ESCWA's Committee on Women adopted the Muscat Declaration: Towards the Achievement of Gender Justice in the Arab Region, which was envisaged as a broad framework within which to pursue gender equality. In November 2019 ESCWA's Committee on Women issued a series of recommendations to advance the regional implementation of the objectives defined in the 1995 Beijing Declaration and Platform for Action (BPfA), including: developing national legislation to mainstream gender equality, enhancing data collection on indicators monitoring violence against women, making use of relevant knowledge and training guidance produced by ESCWA, and promoting private sector engagement in advancing women's role in society. A high-level meeting convened soon afterwards, in Amman, Jordan, to consider implementation of the BPfA, issued an Arab Declaration that restated commitment to the Beijing Declaration. The *Arab Gender Gap Report 2020: Gender Equality and the Sustainable Development Goals,* issued in May 2021, analysed more than 200 regional gender equality indicators relating to the status of women, men, girls and boys at national and regional level. The 10th session of the Committee on Women, convened in November, addressed progress on women-related recovery plans and issues in the context of building back better from the COVID-19 pandemic; it emphasized the need for development models that take into account gender inequality and social justice.

In May 2022 ESCWA helped to organize the inaugural Arab Forum for Equality, in Amman, on the theme 'Towards inclusive youth employment in the Arab region'. The second Arab Forum on Equality was hosted by ESCWA in Beirut, in June 2023, with a focus on food security. The Fourth Arab review of the 2002 Madrid International Plan of Action on Ageing was organized in June 2022 by ESCWA and the UN Population Fund.

ESCWA assists member states with drafting inclusive rights-based social protection, social justice and development policies that take into consideration the needs of diverse social groups, with a particular focus on marginalized and vulnerable people, with a view to alleviating inequalities and eliminating poverty. A revised *Arab Multidimensional Poverty Index,* compiled jointly by ESCWA, the Arab League and other partners, was issued in April 2021. The Index focused on both income and deprivations such as lack of access to education, public infrastructure and health services—with the aim of providing poverty eradication recommendations for the region, in the context of the UN's 2030 Agenda. (The first Index was released in 2017.) A High-level Ministerial Forum on the Future of Social Protection in the Arab Region, organized by ESCWA and partners in November 2021, gave consideration to social protection governance, coverage, responsiveness, and resilience to shocks, in the context of securing a strong regional recovery from the COVID-19 pandemic. In April 2022 ESCWA and partners issued *The COVID-19 Pandemic in the Arab Region: An opportunity to reform social protection systems,* which emphasized the need to address the requirements of vulnerable populations and to ensure social protection benefits for 'invisible' informal workers in the region. A report published in November by ESCWA, UNDP and partners, titled *Social Expenditure Monitor for Arab Countries: Towards Making Budgets More Equitable, Efficient, and Effective to Achieve the Sustainable Development Goals,* found that, measured as a share of GDP, public spending in the Arab region had remained constant over the past decade, at around 34%, of which no more than 8% reached health, social protection and education programmes. Recommendations included enhancing investment in public services through improving tax collection systems and curbing illegal financial flows; and making use of innovative debt relief mechanisms.

In 2020 ESCWA initiated an Arab Digital Inclusion Platform to support digital participation by people with disabilities. An ESCWA Disability Inclusion Policy was initiated in December. In January 2022, with participation by ESCWA, the Arab League and other partners, an EU-Arab Cooperation Forum on the Rights of Persons with Disabilities was established; this in turn created an Arab-EU Research Network on Disability. ESCWA hosted the Network's first event, held in February 2023, concerned with independent living within the community.

In December 2022 ESCWA and the International Telecommunication Union convened, online, the second Accessible Arab Region: ICT for All conference, focused on advancing digital accessibility. (The first conference had been held in December 2021.)

SHARED ECONOMIC PROSPERITY

ESCWA supports member countries in the areas of financing for development; promoting domestic, intraregional and foreign investment; facilitating transboundary flows of goods, services, people and capital, by integrating regional markets; and through the provision of debt management assistance. Continuous assessments are made of the region's macroeconomic performances, and economic research is undertaken. A Developing Debt Optimization Strategies to Enhance Fiscal Space in Arab States initiative was developed by the Commission in 2022. A *Survey of Economic and Social Developments in the Arab Region* is published annually. The 2021–22 edition, issued in December 2022, forecast that the overall GDP of the Arab region would expand by 4.5% in 2023 and by 3.4% in 2024, decelerating from growth of 5.2% in 2022. The average rate of inflation across the region, which had risen to an estimated 14% in 2022, was expected to fall back to 8% in 2023. It was envisaged that Gulf Cooperation Council (GCC) member states and other petroleum-exporting countries would continue to benefit from elevated energy prices in 2023, while oil-importing countries would be beset by challenges that included high energy costs, food supply shortages, and a decline in tourism and in inflows of international aid. Excluding the GCC countries and Libya, more than one-third of the population of the Arab region were reported to be living in poverty in 2022, and the unemployment rate across the region in that year was estimated at 12%.

ESCWA supports member states in creating decent work opportunities and in addressing changes to jobs and skills that arise from technological transformations. At the end of May 2022 ESCWA and partners launched a new initiative, 'Joseur', which aimed to provide skills training for young people in the region, to enhance their employability.

An internet-based platform (the 'SMEs Enablers Portal') was initiated in September 2019 to provide assistance to small- and medium-sized enterprises (SMEs). In October 2020 ESCWA and the International Chamber of Commerce (ICC) launched a Beirut-based ICC-ESCWA Centre of Entrepreneurship (CoE), which aimed to promote entrepreneurial innovation and improve the business operating environment for SMEs in Arab countries. The inaugural ICC-ESCWA Regional Economic Forum, convened in December 2021, noted that only 8% of the overall digital potential of Arab economies had been harnessed (against a measure by which the USA had reached 18% of its digital potential). In April 2022 the ICC-ESCWA CoE supported the launch a new eCommerce Acceleration Programme (eCAP), which aimed to build SMEs' online selling capacities; a second phase of eCAP was initiated in January 2023. At the first Arab SMEs Summit, held under ESCWA auspices in November 2022, in Amman, funding commitments to SMEs amounting to US $130m. were announced.

In May 2023 ESCWA helped to organize, in Riyadh, Saudi Arabia, the fourth annual Competition Forum for the Arab region, which addressed mergers and acquisitions, and means of enhancing the effectiveness of competition authorities in developing member countries.

In April 2013 ESCWA launched a regional Infrastructure Investments and Public-Private Partnerships (PPP) Initiative, in co-operation with the Geneva, Switzerland-based UNECE International Centre of Excellence on PPPs, providing for the establishment of a regional PPP network and of PPP specialist centres (including on Islamic finance, renewable energy and infrastructure).

A COVID-19 Stimulus Tracker, developed by ESCWA, was launched in August 2021. In March 2022, as part of a series of COVID-19 impact assessments that was initiated in 2020, ESCWA released *Rising wealth inequality in the Arab region amid COVID-19,* which reported that since the onset of the COVID-19 pandemic wealth inequality had markedly deepened in the region: while, in early 2022, 10% of the Arab population were reported to control more than 80% of total regional wealth, the wealth of the poorest half had since 2019 diminished by one-third. Bahrain, Kuwait, Oman, Saudi

Arabia, the UAE and Yemen were reportedly among the 20 most unequal countries globally. The need for inclusive growth strategies and social protection was emphasized.

ESCWA has focused on the development of an integrated transport system in the Arab Mashreq region; on the establishment of a transport information system; on the formation of national and regional transport and trade committees, representing both the private and public sectors; on the simplification of cross-border trading procedures; and on the use of electronic data exchange for more efficient transport and trade. A Convention on International Multi-modal Transport of Goods in the Arab Mashreq was adopted in May 2008 by the 25th ministerial session of the Commission. In June 2016 an MOU on future co-operation in transport and trade facilitation was concluded between ESCWA and the International Road Union. In December 2021 the 22nd session of ESCWA's Committee on Transport and Logistics gave consideration to the impact of the COVID-19 pandemic on the Belt and Road Initiative (that was launched by China in 2013, with the aim of developing infrastructure and trade along traditional routes between Asia, Europe and Africa), and implications thereof for the Arab region. ESCWA assists member states with developing sustainable strategies and initiatives to improve road safety.

ESCWA compiles an annual report that addresses the economic and social impacts of Israeli policies on Palestine. The 2022 edition, issued in July, restated that development was being prevented, the Palestinian economy fragmented, and humanitarian crises caused by Israeli actions that included repression against individuals and organizations, settlement expansion in the West Bank, and the blockade of Gaza. The unemployment rate in Gaza was reported to be 47%; average GDP per capita there was reportedly 52% lower than in 2005; and 62% of residents there were reported to be food-insecure.

STATISTICS, INFORMATION SOCIETY AND TECHNOLOGY

ESCWA helps to develop the statistical systems of member states in accordance with the UN Fundamental Principles of Official Statistics, in order to improve the accuracy and comparability of economic and social data, and to make the information more accessible to planners and researchers. Member states are assisted in preparing for population and housing censuses. ESCWA also compiles, processes and disseminates statistics on international trade and transport within the region, and assists member countries to develop relevant statistical capacity. ESCWA's Arab Region Data Portal, initiated in January 2019, provides social and economics statistics on member states.

ESCWA works to increase the capabilities of its member countries in harnessing information and communications technology (ICT) in support of sustainable development and regional integration. It aims to narrow the digital gap between Arab countries and other regions, and, consequently, to improve the competitiveness of local industries and the effectiveness of local services. An ESCWA Technology Centre was inaugurated, in El Hassan Science City, Jordan, in November 2011. (During 2021 this implemented a Women Empowerment for Technology and Entrepreneurship initiative.) A series of Policy Recommendations on Cybersafety and Combating Cybercrime in the Arab Region was issued in April 2015. A second High-level Forum on the World Summit on the Information Society (WSIS) and on the 2030 Agenda for Sustainable Development, convened under ESCWA auspices in March 2019, considered the use of digital technologies as a means of accelerating sustainable development. (The first Forum had been organized in May 2017; the WSIS had been held in two phases, in 2003 and 2005.) An ESCWA Academy of ICT Essentials for Government Leaders in the ESCWA Region initiative was launched in 2020 to assist policymakers. In December 2021 ESCWA, with the Arab League and other partners, organized the inaugural Arab International Digital Cooperation and Development Forum. ESCWA initiated a Digital Arabic Content Award in that year. In January 2023 regional ministers responsible for telecommunications and information technology adopted an Arab Digital Agenda to cover the period 2023–33, which had been jointly prepared by ESCWA and the Arab League. This was focused on five pillars: digital infrastructure, governance, economy, society, and culture, and aimed to mobilize related investment and partnerships.

ESCWA has supported member states' compilation of National Digital Development Reviews (NDDRs).

An Arab Internet Governance Forum (AIGF) process—established under the auspices of ESCWA and the Arab League—was initiated in 2012.

ESCWA's 30th session, convened in Beirut, Lebanon, in June 2018 adopted the Beirut Consensus on Technology for Sustainable Development in the Arab Region, with a focus on using technology and innovation to advance prosperity and peace, as well as the objectives of the 2030 Agenda.

GOVERNANCE AND CONFLICT PREVENTION

ESCWA supports the development of institution-building, open government strategies, and integrated national development planning in member states. It also promotes partnerships aimed at supporting the sustainable development of its least developed members—Mauritania, Somalia, Sudan and Yemen.

A project aimed at mitigating transboundary risks that might derail national development strategies was introduced in 2019. ESCWA, with IOM and the Arab League, co-ordinated the region's first review process of the Global Compact for Safe, Orderly and Regular Migration (that was adopted in December 2018, in Marrakesh, Morocco); a high-level Review Conference was convened, in a virtual format, in February 2021. The 2021 edition of a joint ESCWA-International Organization for Migration (IOM) *Situation Report on International Migration in the Arab Region*, issued in July 2022, noted that in 2020 the region hosted 14% of the global migrant population.

The Commission develops activities in conflict and post-conflict countries and areas, including Iraq, the Palestinian territories, Lebanon, the Syrian Arab Republic and Yemen. Its priorities include analysis and policy formulation for reducing the causes of conflict; capacity building to improve the effectiveness of public administration and the rule of law; forging partnerships among civic entities at local and regional level; and addressing the special needs of countries affected by conflicts.

ESCWA's National Agenda for the Future of Syria (NAFS) initiative, launched in 2012 and ongoing, represents a technical dialogue platform preparing for the challenges of the eventual post-conflict transition in that country. Other projects include the provision of regional and local 'networking academies' in Iraq, to give training in information technology; the Smart Communities Project, providing modern technology for villages in Iraq; the improvement of statistics related to gender in Iraq; and the support of the Coalition of Arab-Palestinian Civil Society Organizations. In 2022 ESCWA introduced a Yemen Vision for Recovery and Development initiative.

In September 2021 ESCWA, the Arab League and other partners released *Attainment of the SDGs in Conflict-Affected Countries in the Arab Region*, which urged an integrated framework to advance implementation of the SDGs in countries that were confronting complex (and frequently recurring) challenges, such as Iraq, Jordan, Lebanon, Libya, Somalia, Sudan, Syria and Yemen.

Finance

ESCWA's proposed regular budget allocation from the UN budget for 2023 was US $48.9m.

Publications

ESCWA Annual Report.
Arab Economic Integration Report.
Arab Gender Gap Report.
Arab Multidimensional Poverty Report.
Arab Society: a Compendium of Social Statistics (every 2 years).
Bulletin of Industrial Statistics for Arab Countries.
ESCWA Centre for Women Newsletter (monthly).
External Trade Bulletin of the ESCWA Region (annually).
National Accounts Studies of the Arab Region.
Situation Report on International Migration in the Arab Region.
Status of Arab Women Report.
Survey of Economic and Social Developments in the Arab Region (annually).
Other reports, case studies, assessments, guides and manuals.

… REGIONAL ORGANIZATIONS

United Nations Children's Fund—UNICEF

Address: 3 United Nations Plaza, New York, NY 10017, USA.
Telephone: (212) 326-7000; **fax:** (212) 326-7096; **internet:** www.unicef.org.

UNICEF was established in 1946 as the UN International Children's Emergency Fund, with an initial focus on post-war Europe. In 1953 the General Assembly extended indefinitely UNICEF's mandate, which had expanded to cover children in developing countries, and revised its name (retaining the same acronym). UNICEF works to promote the rights and wellbeing of all children, adolescents and women, and places particular emphasis on assisting the most vulnerable and disadvantaged.

Organization
(September 2023)

EXECUTIVE BOARD

UNICEF reports on its activities to UN member states meeting in the General Assembly through its Executive Board, which is accountable to the UN Economic and Social Council (ECOSOC).

The Executive Board comprises 36 member governments from all regions, elected in rotation for a three-year term by ECOSOC. As UNICEF's governing body, the Board establishes policy, reviews programmes and approves expenditure. A Bureau is elected by the Board each year, comprising a President and four Vice-Presidents, representing five regional groupings. The Office of the Secretary of the Executive Board services the Board's work and liaises with the Secretariat.

SECRETARIAT

UNICEF's Executive Director is appointed by the UN Secretary-General in consultation with the Executive Board. She is assisted by Deputy Executive Directors for Humanitarian Action and Supply Operations, Management, and Programmes.

Around 85% of UNICEF staff positions are based in field offices. Divisions and programme groups cover child protection; education and adolescent development; nutrition and child development; maternal and newborn child health; immunization; HIV/AIDS; public health emergencies; water, sanitation and hygiene, and climate, energy, environment and disaster risk reduction; social policy and social protection; emergency programmes; supplies; global innovation (see also the UNICEF Global Office of Innovation); private fundraising and partnerships; public partnerships; ethics; data analytics, planning and monitoring; gender equality; human resources; global communication and advocacy; information; research (see UNICEF Innocenti—Global Office of Research and Foresight); programmes; internal audit and investigations; legal affairs; and financial and administrative management. A dedicated UNICEF Office on Global Insight and Policy had seven priority policy areas in 2023: digital technology; environment; finance; governance; human capital; markets; and society.

Executive Director: CATHERINE M. RUSSELL (USA).

UNICEF REGIONAL AND OTHER OFFICES

The UNICEF Office of Emergency Programmes co-ordinates support for humanitarian action, and has a subsidiary Operations Centre.

Regional Office for the Middle East and North Africa: POB 1551, 11821 Amman, Jordan; tel. (6) 5502400; fax (6) 5538880; e-mail menaro@unicef.org; internet www.unicef.org/mena; Dir ADELE KHODR (Lebanon).

UNICEF Global Office of Innovation: Box 8161, 104 20 Stockholm, Sweden; internet www.unicef.org/innovation; f. 2021; implements a UNICEF Global Innovation Strategy, focused on scaling up digital, physical product and programme innovations, and means of innovative financing; manages a network of 9 innovation hubs; Dir THOMAS DAVIN (France).

UNICEF Innocenti—Global Office of Research and Foresight: Via degli Alfani 58, 50121 Florence, Italy; tel. (055) 20330; fax (055) 2033220; e-mail florence@unicef.org; internet www.unicef-irc.org; f. 1988, as the UNICEF International Child Development Centre; undertakes focused research to support UNICEF and other orgs to deliver results to children; works closely with all Fund offices as well as external academic and research institutions; the following research projects were ongoing in 2023: child rights in the digital age, COVID-19 and children, education and learning, and child rights and protection; in 2012 initiated a Multiple Overlapping Deprivation Analysis (MODA) tool to measure and define multidimensional child poverty; maintains a regularly updated Evidence for Action Blog; issued in Jan. 2023 *Prospects for Children in the Polycrisis: A 2023 Global Outlook*; Dir BO VIKTOR NYLUND (Finland).

Activities

UNICEF is dedicated to the wellbeing of children, adolescents and women. It aims to ensure that children worldwide are given the best possible start in life and the opportunity to attain a good level of basic education, and that adolescents are enabled to develop their capabilities and to participate successfully in society. The Fund also provides relief and rehabilitation assistance in emergencies. Through its extensive field network UNICEF undertakes, in co-ordination with governments, local communities and other aid organizations, programmes (that are preferably community-based and low-cost) in health, nutrition, education, the environment, gender issues, development, and water and sanitation.

Child rights and global goals: UNICEF helped to draft the Convention on the Rights of the Child, which was adopted by the UN General Assembly in 1989, and works to realize its guarantees and minimum standards for protecting the rights of children in all capacities. Two optional protocols to the Convention were adopted in 2000, relating to the prevention of child combatants in armed conflict and the ending of the sale, sexual exploitation or abuse of children. A 2011 optional protocol permits the UN Committee on the Rights of the Child to undertake investigations of reported violations of child rights.

UNICEF was a lead organization in the formulation of the Sustainable Development Goals (SDGs), adopted in September 2015 by UN heads of state and of government, as part of the UN's 2030 Agenda for Sustainable Development. The SDGs included new goals and targets aimed at improving the lives of children by 2030, such as: ending all forms of malnutrition, including achieving (by 2025) internationally agreed targets on stunting and wasting in children under five years of age, and addressing the nutritional needs of adolescent girls, pregnant and lactating women and older persons (SDG 2, Target 2.2); ending preventable deaths of newborn babies and children under five years of age, with all countries to reduce neonatal mortality to at least as low as 12 per 1,000 live births, and the under-five mortality rate to at least as low as 25 per 1,000 live births (SDG 3, Target 3.2); ensuring that all girls and boys have access to quality early childhood development, care and pre-primary education (SDG 4, Target 4.2); eliminating gender disparities in, and inequities in access to, education (Target 4.5); eliminating harmful practices, such as child, early and forced marriage, and female genital mutilation (SDG 5, Target 5.3); ending, by 2025, child labour in all its forms, including securing the prohibition and elimination of its worst forms, such as the military recruitment and use of children (SDG 8, Target 8.7); and ending the abuse, exploitation, trafficking, and all forms of violence against and torture of children (SDG 16, Target 16.2).

Strategic plan: UNICEF's strategic plan for 2022–25 (endorsed by the Executive Board in September 2021) aimed to guide action for an inclusive recovery from the COVID-19 crisis and to renew the ambition of achieving the SDGs by 2030. The plan's interconnected goals were that every child (1) survives and thrives, (2) learns, (3) is protected from violence and exploitation, (4) lives in a safe and clean environment, and (5) has an equitable chance in life. Cross-cutting themes concerned gender equality; disability inclusion; peacebuilding; building resilience; and climate action and environmental sustainability.

CHILD SURVIVAL

SDG Target 3.2 requires a reduction by 2030 in the neonatal mortality rate to at least as low as 12 per 1,000 live births, globally, and of the under-five mortality to at least as low as 25 per 1,000 live births. Updated child mortality data is provided on an annual basis by the Inter-agency Group for Child Mortality Estimation, established in 2004 by UNICEF, the World Health Organization (WHO), the World Bank and the UN Population Division. The 2022 edition of the Group's *Levels and Trends in Child Mortality*, released in January 2023, estimated the global under-five mortality rate in 2021 at 38 deaths per 1,000 live births; sub-Saharan Africa had the highest regional rate in that year, at 74 deaths per 1,000 live births. The global neonatal mortality rate was 18 deaths per 1,000 live births (sub-Saharan Africa: 27). In total more than 5m. children under the age of five died in 2021, largely of preventable or treatable causes. By comparison, some 12.5m. children under the age of five died in 1990. It reported that, by 2021, 54 countries (three-quarters of which were in sub-Saharan Africa) were at risk of missing the under-five mortality target set for 2030, and 63 states were deemed to be at risk of missing the 2030 neonatal mortality rate target. The global mortality rate in 2021 for children, adolescents and young people aged from five to 24 was estimated at 17 deaths per 1,000 live births (sub-Saharan Africa: 38). Around 44% of low and middle income countries were reported to have no reliable mortality data over the past five years.

Under the global Partnership for Maternal, Newborn and Child Health (PMNCH), established in 2005, UNICEF works with WHO, the UN Population Fund (UNFPA) and more than 1,300 other partners in countries with high maternal mortality to improve maternal health and prevent maternal and newborn deaths through the integration of a continuum of home, community, outreach and facility-based care, emsbracing every stage of maternal, newborn and child health. In August 2020 UNICEF and WHO jointly launched an updated Every Newborn Action Plan (ENAP), covering five strategic objectives to be pursued during 2020–25: (i) Strengthen and invest in care during labour, birth and the first day and week of life; (ii) Improve the quality of maternal and newborn care; (iii) Reach every woman and newborn to reduce inequities; (iv) Harness the power of parents, families and communities; and (v) Count every newborn: through measurement, programme-tracking and accountability.

UNICEF is a founding partner of Gavi, the Vaccine Alliance, which works to protect all children against vaccine-preventable diseases. UNICEF is a key implementing partner of the COVID-19 Vaccines Global Access (COVAX) Facility, one of four pillars of the Access to COVID-19 Tools Accelerator, which was launched in April 2020 by WHO, the European Commission and France, to generate equitable access to COVID-19 diagnostics, therapeutics and vaccines. On behalf of the COVAX Facility UNICEF co-ordinated the procurement and supply of COVID-19 vaccines, testing kits, personal protective equipment and treatments.

In July 2022 UNICEF and WHO released data that indicated that the annual coverage of children who had received three doses of the anti-diptheria, tetanus and pertussis (DTP3) vaccine had declined from 85% in 2019 to 81% in 2021.

UNICEF works to improve safe water supply, sanitation and hygiene ('WASH') and thereby reduce the risk of diarrhoea and other waterborne diseases, such as cholera, dysentery, Hepatitis A, and typhoid. It places great emphasis on increasing the testing and protection of drinking water, and on promoting the practice of thoroughly washing hands with soap. In March 2021 UNICEF estimated that 3,000m. people worldwide lacked basic hand washing facilities, such as soap and clean water, at home. UNICEF-assisted programmes for the control of diarrhoeal diseases promote the low-cost manufacture and distribution of prepackaged salts. In July 2022 UNICEF reported that each year the deaths of around 484,000 children under five years of age (primarily in sub-Saharan Africa and South Asia) were caused by diarrhoea attributed to poor sanitation and to contaminated drinking water. UNICEF hosts the secretariat of a multi-stakeholder partnership, Sanitation and Water for All, which promotes, co-ordinates and monitors efforts to achieve SDG targets relating to WASH.

UNICEF participates in the Steering Committee of UN-Nutrition, which was initiated in early 2021—uniting the 65-member UN Network for the Scaling up Nutrition (SUN) Movement and UN System Standing Committee on Nutrition—to co-ordinate UN agencies in advancing nutrition and eliminating hunger, malnutrition and obesity. UNICEF's Executive Director acts as Chair. of the SUN Movement Lead Group. According to UNICEF estimates, one-quarter of children under five years of age are underweight, while each year malnutrition contributes to more than one-third of child deaths in that age group and leaves millions of others with physical and mental disabilities. UNICEF supports national efforts to reduce malnutrition, for example, fortifying staple foods with micronutrients, widening women's access to education, improving the nutritional status of pregnant women, strengthening household food security and basic health services, providing food supplies in emergencies, and promoting sound childcare and feeding practices. In April 2015 UNICEF, the World Bank and other partners launched the Power of Nutrition, an independent fund that aimed to raise US $200m., initially, towards ending child undernutrition. By 2023 more than 20,000 hospitals and birthing centres globally had been designated as 'baby-friendly' and were promoting a set of UNICEF-WHO recommendations, the 'Ten Steps to Successful Breastfeeding'.

In 2021 it was estimated that, worldwide, 1.7m. children aged under 15 were living with HIV/AIDS (around 90% of whom were in Africa). Some 160,000 children were estimated to have been newly infected with HIV during that year. Only 52% of children who were living with HIV in 2021 had access to life-saving treatments. In 2020 an estimated 99,000 children died of AIDS-related causes.

In August 2022 UNICEF, UNAIDS, WHO and other partners established a Global Alliance for Ending AIDS in Children by 2030.

CHILD PROTECTION AND INCLUSION

UNICEF affirms that every child has a right to grow up in a safe and inclusive environment, free from violence, exploitation and abuse.

The Fund is actively involved in several global child protection partnerships, including the Inter-Agency Working Group on Unaccompanied and Separated Children; the Inter-Agency Co-ordination Panel on Juvenile Justice; the Donors' Working Group on Female Genital Mutilation/Cutting; and the Better Care Network (aiming to facilitate support for children without adequate family care). UNICEF works with the International Labour Organization and other partners to promote an end to exploitative and hazardous child labour, and supports special projects to provide education, counselling and care in developing countries.

UNICEF has issued programme guidance related to social and behaviour change, and maintains a virtual Behavioural Insights Research and Design laboratory (BIRDLAB), which focuses on innovatively using social and behavioural sciences insights to improve outcomes for children.

With a view to incorporating provisions for the protection of migrant children, UNICEF actively participated in the intergovernmental discussions to formulate a Global Compact on Safe, Orderly and Regular Migration, which was adopted in December 2018. In May 2022 UNICEF and the International Organization on Migration agreed a Strategic Collaboration Framework aimed at protecting the rights of migrant children.

In June 2023 UNICEF reported that 43.3m. children worldwide were living in forced displacement: 25.8m. internally, and 17.5m. as refugees and asylum seekers. The Fund helps to supply humanitarian assistance to displaced children, works to promote their rights, and often establishes child-friendly spaces within refugee camps. UNICEF estimates that some 1.2m. children worldwide are trafficked each year. It promotes ratification of the Optional Protocol to the Convention on the Rights of the Child on the sale of children, child prostitution and child pornography. In June 2016 a Global Inter-agency Working Group issued a set of Terminology Guidelines for the Protection of Children from Sexual Exploitation and Sexual Abuse (the 'Luxembourg Guidelines').

More generally, the Fund supports initiatives to promote the rights of adolescents and their healthy development and social participation.

UNICEF and the Special Representative of the Secretary-General (SRSG) for Children and Armed Conflict co-chair the Global Coalition for Reintegration of Child Soldiers, established in 2018, with broad UN and civil society participation. In this framework former child combatants and other stakeholders have contributed to the development of recommendations aimed at supporting programming on reintegration into peaceful society. In 2021 UNICEF and the SRSG initiated the related Nairobi Process, focused on the effective reintegration of former child fighters. During 2022 UNICEF extended reintegration or other protection support to nearly 12,500 children who had left armed forces and groups. During the period 2005–22 the UN verified 315,000 incidents of grave violations perpetrated against children in conflict situations—including killing and maiming, and also more than 16,000 attacks against schools and hospitals.

It is estimated that landmines kill and maim between 8,000 and 10,000 children every year. UNICEF supports mine awareness campaigns, and promotes the full ratification of the Convention on the Prohibition of the Use, Stockpiling, Production and Transfer of Anti-Personnel Mines and on their Destruction, which was adopted in December 1997 and entered into force in March 1999.

In March 2016 UNICEF and UNFPA jointly initiated a Global Programme to Accelerate Action to End Child Marriage, with a focus on providing education, intervention and health services to adolescent girls and their wider communities in 12 countries in the Middle East, Africa and South Asia; the Programme was renewed for a further four years in March 2020. In March 2018 UNICEF reported that around one-fifth of women globally had become married during childhood, compared with one-quarter a decade earlier.

An UNFPA-UNICEF Joint Programme on Female Genital Mutilation aims to eliminate that practice, with a focus on 17 countries in Africa and the Middle East.

UNICEF works to ensure that children live in a safe and clean environment, in particular advocating for improved air quality, and supports the active involvement of youth in the implementation of climate adaptation strategies and response plans.

The right to a name and nationality is enshrined in the Convention on the Rights of the Child. UNICEF promotes universal registration of births in order to prevent the abuse of children without proof of age and nationality, for example through trafficking, forced labour, early marriage and military recruitment. The Fund provides support for the enactment of legislation, and policies and standards that advance free and universal birth registration. It has facilitated the organization of birth registration data in rural areas of developing countries through text messaging. In mid-2022 UNICEF estimated that, globally, 75% of children below the age of five were registered (compared with 63% in 2009). UNICEF has stated concern that significant numbers of registered children nevertheless lack a certificate or formal proof of registration.

EDUCATION

UNICEF works to ensure that all children receive equal access to quality education, which it identifies as a fundamental human right. UNICEF is the agency assigned formal responsibility within the initiative for education in emergencies, early childhood care and technical and policy support. UNICEF advocates the implementation of the Child Friendly School model, designed to facilitate the delivery of safe, quality education. In September 2019 UNICEF and the International Telecommunication Union launched a Giga initiative, which aimed to ensure internet connectivity for every school. In March 2020 UNICEF, with WHO and the International Committee of the Red Cross, issued guidance to support schools in dealing with the COVID-19 pandemic, including on the implementation of educational strategies to maintain learning in the event of school closures. *The State of Global Learning Poverty: 2022 Update*, released in June of that year by UNICEF, the World Bank and other partners, warned that disruptions arising from the COVID-19 pandemic—which had caused an average global loss of 141 in-person schooling days during February 2020–February 2022—had significantly worsened (already widespread) learning poverty (measured as the number of children who have not acquired a minimal level of proficiency in literacy by age 10). The report observed that in 2019 the average global learning poverty rate in low- and middle-income countries had been 57% (with a peak of 86% in sub-Saharan Africa). Lack of internet access and connectivity were reported to have widely increased reliance on television and radio as learning sources during school closures. The report recommended a RAPID framework of policy interventions, devised with input from UNICEF, to accelerate learning: Reach every child and keep them in school; Assess learning levels regularly; Prioritize teaching the fundamentals; Increase the efficiency of instruction, including through catch-up learning; Develop psychosocial health and wellbeing.

In May 2016 UNICEF released a report which found that—although one-quarter of school-age children globally (some 462m. children) were living in humanitarian emergency-affected countries—education accounted for a negligible proportion (2%) of funds requested under humanitarian appeals. A fund, Education Cannot Wait (ECW), was launched at the inaugural World Humanitarian Summit, held later in May, in Istanbul, Türkiye, with a view to increasing access to learning opportunities for children living through emergencies. The fund, which aimed to support 75m. children by 2030, has a First Emergency-Response Window, a Multi-Year Resilience Window, and an Acceleration Facility (which supports activities and research to improve crisis preparedness and response). In February 2023 donors committed more than US $826m. to ECW for the period 2023–26.

UNICEF also advocates Life Skills-Based Education as a means of empowering young people to cope with challenging situations and to adopt healthy patterns of behaviour.

UNICEF leads and acts as the secretariat of the UN Girls' Education Initiative (UNGEI), which aims to increase the enrolment of girls in primary schools in more than 100 countries. In May 2010 UNGEI participants unanimously adopted the Dakar Declaration on Accelerating Girls' Education and Gender Equality.

SOCIAL POLICY

UNICEF seeks to work with governments and other external partners to strengthen capacities to design and implement cross-sectoral social and economic policies, child-focused legislative measures and increased focus on children in national budgets. UNICEF has identified the following priority areas of support to 'upstream' policy work: child poverty and disparities; social budgeting; decentralization; social security and social protection; and the impact of migration on children. It supports cash transfer programmes to help to address child poverty, and works to identify the impact of social and economic vulnerabilities on children.

UNICEF works with other agencies to advance universal social protection by 2030 (USP2030), with guaranteed equitable access for all to social mechanisms to counter poverty. UNICEF, UNDP, ILO and WHO co-chair the UN Issue-Based Coalition on Social Protection, which serves as a platform for advocacy, policy advice and exchange of information on the creation of sustainable, holistic and integrated social protection systems.

EMERGENCIES AND HUMANITARIAN RESPONSE

UNICEF's activities aimed at providing emergency relief assistance to children and young people affected by conflict, natural disasters and food crises are co-ordinated through its Office of Emergency Programmes and subsidiary Operations Centre (OPSCEN). In situations of violence and social disintegration the Fund provides support in the areas of education, health, mine-awareness and psychosocial assistance, and helps to demobilize and rehabilitate child soldiers.

In December 2022 UNICEF launched a humanitarian appeal for US $10,263m. to meet the urgent requirements during 2023 of 173m. people, including 110m. children, in 155 countries and territories. Since 1998 UNICEF's humanitarian response has been structured within a framework of identified Core Commitments for Children in Humanitarian Action (CCCs), which reflect optimum humanitarian structures, principles and best practices to ensure that every child is protected, their dignity respected and that no child is left behind during humanitarian crises. Revised CCCs were issued in October 2020 to incorporate best practices in providing quality, prompt humanitarian support during fast-moving emergency situations. Within the UN system's 'Cluster Approach', developed to co-ordinate the international response to humanitarian disasters, UNICEF is the lead agency for Education (jointly with Save The Children); Nutrition; and WASH.

UNICEF aims to ensure the uninterrupted provision of education in emergencies. The Fund works to secure (and where necessary to reconstruct) safe learning spaces that are equipped with WASH facilities, to procure learning materials, to train teachers, and to support governments in the use of disaster risk reduction strategies. Emergency education assistance extended by UNICEF includes the provision of 'school-in-a-box' kits in refugee camps, the supply of flashlights to protect girls and women at night, and the organization, in co-operation with WHO, of outreach campaigns to enable the immunization of children in conflict zones. Through the Giga initiative (q.v.) the Office supports distance learning during emergencies. Psychosocial assistance activities include special programmes to support traumatized children, and the provision of 'child-friendly spaces'. UNICEF helps unaccompanied children to reunite with parents or extended families.

Middle East and North Africa: UNICEF, with other partners, implements a 'No Lost Generation' strategy, funded by voluntary donations, which since 2014 has aimed to offer safe, uninterrupted education; protection from exploitation, abuse and violence; social cohesion opportunities; and psychological and psychosocial support to children affected by the protracted conflict in Syria. In 2023 UNICEF appealed for US $329m. under the UN's 2023 Syria Humanitarian Response Plan and $870m. under the Regional Refugee and Resilience Plan (covering neighbouring countries, where around 3m. Syrian children were residing as refugees). UNICEF's activities during 2023 in Syria included providing education services in a formal setting for 2.3m. children and access to safe water for 3.6m. people, and facilitating access to health care for 1.8m. women and children.

In 2023, at a projected cost of US $484m., UNICEF aimed, *inter alia*, to provide 3.6m. people in Yemen with critical WASH supplies, to facilitate access to primary health care for 2.5m. women and children, to treat around 484,600 children for severe acute malnutrition, and to assist 6m. women and children with accessing gender-based violence mitigation, prevention and response services.

In February 2023 UNICEF issued emergency appeals to fund the provision of emergency support to children and caregivers who had survived the earthquakes that in that month had devastated parts of southern Türkiye (requiring US $196m.) and northern Syria ($173m.).

UNICEF and UNRWA co-ordinate in the Palestinian territories to support refugee children, adolescents and women with respect to advocacy, social protection, education, emergency preparedness, facilitating access to primary health care, and ensuring access to sufficient water.

RESEARCH AND ANALYSIS

The Fund promotes the collection and analysis of statistical data relating to the wellbeing of children and women. UNICEF's Multiple Indicator Cluster Survey (MICS) method of household data collection, initiated in 1995, analyses data on child protection, education (including remote learning), health (including HIV/AIDS and COVID-19), nutrition, and water and sanitation. By September 2023 356 MICS surveys had been completed in 120 countries. The seventh MICS round was initiated in March of that year. A MICS Plus initiative, which uses mobile phones to supplement existing household data, was launched in October 2018. UNICEF Innocenti's Multiple Overlapping Deprivation Analysis tool assesses poverty and inequalities within countries. Blogs, reports, articles and datasets are communicated through a UNICEF Blog portal.

The theme in 2023 of UNICEF's flagship *The State of the World's Children* report was 'For every child, vaccination'.

Finance

UNICEF is funded by voluntary contributions from governments and non-governmental and private sector sources. UNICEF's income is divided into contributions for 'regular resources' and for 'other resources' (for special purposes, including expanding the outreach of country programmes of co-operation, and ensuring capacity to deliver urgent critical assistance to women and children). UNICEF's integrated budget for the period 2022–25 amounted to US $26,942m., and included proposed expenditure of $23,259m. for programme activities.

Publications

Humanitarian Action for Children.
Progress for Every Child in the SDG Era.
The State of Food Security and Nutrition in the World (with FAO, WFP, IFAD and WHO).
The State of Global Learning Poverty.
The State of the World's Children (annually).
UNICEF Annual Report.
UNICEF Humanitarian Action for Children Report (annually).
Reports and studies; analyses of the situation of children and women by country or region.

United Nations Development Coordination Office

Address: 405 East 42nd St, 25th Floor, New York, NY 10017, USA.
Telephone: (212) 906-5500; **e-mail:** dcocommunications@un.org; **internet:** un-dco.org.

The Office was established in 1997, as the UN Development Operations Coordination Office (UN DOCO), along with a UN Development Group to enhance the UN's co-ordinated delivery of development assistance. In 2018, as part of extensive reforms to the UN development system, UN DOCO became a subsidiary office of the UN Secretariat, and was renamed the UN Development Coordination Office (DCO), assuming an enhanced role within the system. In particular, the DCO assumed managerial and supervisory functions in respect of the UN Resident Coordinator system.

Organization
(September 2023)

The DCO serves as the secretariat of the UN Sustainable Development Group, at the regional and global levels. At the regional level five DCO Regional Directors provide region-specific support to Resident Coordinators from offices based in Addis Ababa, Ethiopia; Amman, Jordan; Bangkok, Thailand; Panama City, Panama; and Istanbul, Türkiye.

Assistant Secretary-General: OSCAR FERNÁNDEZ-TARANCO (Argentina).

UN Development System

The UN Sustainable Development Group (UNSDG), established as the UN Development Group in 2007 and renamed in 2018, provides strategic direction for the UN development system. Chaired by the UN's Deputy Secretary-General, the UNSDG serves as a high-level forum for inter-agency policy formation, operating through a Core Group and four Strategic Results Groups.

In accordance with the 2018 reforms of the UN development system, the DCO was repositioned as a stand-alone office within the UN Secretariat, and assumed managerial and oversight functions of the Resident Coordinator (RC) system, under UNSDG supervision. The office reports directly to the UNSDG's Chair, and services and facilitates its work, providing technical and advisory support to its members. The DCO's critical functions for the UNSDG and the RC system are defined as: providing focused policy co-ordination and technical support to the Group's global work; supporting the UNSDG regional teams, the RCs and UN Country Teams; and gathering evidence and data on activities in programme countries to inform the UNSDG's analytical work and decision making.

From 2020, with a view to streamlining co-ordination, five Regional Collaborative Platforms (RCPs) were initiated, with participation by all development-focused UN agencies working within each region. Each RCP is chaired by the UN Deputy Secretary-General. The heads of the relevant UNDP Regional Bureau and UN Regional Economic Commission act as Vice-Chairs.

2030 Agenda for Sustainable Development

In September 2015 UN heads of state and government, gathered in New York, USA, at a high-level plenary meeting of the UN General Assembly, adopted an outcome document known as the '2030 Agenda for Sustainable Development'. This had been drafted during an intensive, inclusive three-year collaborative process aimed at designing a new forward-looking global framework for the pursuit of sustainable development and the eradication of extreme poverty. It had five thematic pillars: people, planet, prosperity, peace and partnership, and incorporated the following 17 Sustainable Development Goals (SDGs)—reinforced by 169 specific targets—which were to be pursued during the period 2016–30:

1. End poverty in all its forms everywhere;
2. End hunger, achieve food security and improved nutrition and promote sustainable agriculture;
3. Ensure healthy lives and promote well-being for all at all ages;
4. Ensure inclusive and equitable quality education and promote lifelong learning opportunities for all;
5. Achieve gender equality and empower all women and girls;
6. Ensure availability and sustainable management of water and sanitation for all;
7. Ensure access to affordable, reliable, sustainable and modern energy for all;
8. Promote sustained, inclusive and sustainable economic growth, full and productive employment and decent work for all;
9. Build resilient infrastructure, promote inclusive and sustainable industrialization and foster innovation;
10. Reduce inequality within and among countries;
11. Make cities and human settlements inclusive, safe, resilient and sustainable;
12. Ensure sustainable consumption and production patterns;
13. Take urgent action to combat climate change and its impacts;
14. Conserve and sustainably use the oceans, seas and marine resources for sustainable development;
15. Protect, restore and promote sustainable use of terrestrial ecosystems, sustainably manage forests, combat desertification, and halt and reverse land degradation and halt biodiversity loss;
16. Promote peaceful and inclusive societies for sustainable development, provide access to justice for all and build effective, accountable and inclusive institutions at all levels;
17. Strengthen the means of implementation and revitalize the Global Partnership for Sustainable Development.

The regular UN High-Level Political Forum (HLPF) on Sustainable Development, convened annually in July under the auspices of ECOSOC, is the focus for the system-wide follow up and review of the 2030 Agenda and the SDGs. As the principal UN intergovernmental platform on sustainable development, the Forum adopts negotiated political declarations. An independently produced annual *Sustainable Development Report,* incorporating an SDG Index and Dashboards, is presented to the HLPF. The report is compiled with data from national statistical offices, from international organizations, and from non-official sources, including research centres. The UN Office of Intergovernmental Support and Coordination for Sustainable Development, part of the UN Department of Economic and Social Affairs, supports the HLPF and relevant work of the UN General Assembly and ECOSOC. A voluntary national review (VNR) mechanism is used to report on countries' progress in implementing the 2030 Agenda.

In February 2023 the UN Secretary-General introduced an SDG Stimulus initiative, proposing three deliverable actions that were aimed at advancing the implementation of the SDGs: (i) Tackle the high cost of national debt (including by converting short-term high interest borrowing into long-term debt at lower interest rates); (ii) Massively scale up affordable long-term financing for development, especially through public development banks, and by aligning all financing flows with the SDGs; and (iii) Expand contingency financing to countries in need. The Secretary-General also urged that member states each make National and Global Commitments to SDG

REGIONAL ORGANIZATIONS

Transformation. In April he released a special report titled *Progress towards the Sustainable Development Goals: towards a rescue plan for people and planet*. The 2023 regular HLPF, held in mid-July, focused on progress achieved in the pursuit of SDGs 6 (on clean water and sanitation), 7 (affordable and clean energy), 9 (industry, innovation and infrastructure), 11 (sustainable cities and communities), and 17 (partnerships). On the sidelines of the 2023 regular HLPF a series of 16 VNR Labs was convened to share country-level information and experiences in implementing the 2030 Agenda. The 2023 *Sustainable Development Report*, issued in advance of the Forum, was subtitled *Implementing the SDG Stimulus*, and addressed the need to scale up development finance and to reform the global financial architecture to support the SDGs. At that time only 12% of measurable SDG targets were reported to be on track, while 30% had either stalled or regressed since 2015. The second quadrennial SDG Summit—an HLPF held at the level of heads of state and government—was to be organized in late September 2023, under the auspices of the General Assembly (the first having been held in September 2019). The focus of its agenda was 'rescuing' the SDGs, against the background of a confluence of globally cascading and interlinked crises—including impacts posed by the COVID-19 pandemic, conflicts and climate change on the global economy, poverty levels, food and nutrition, education, health, the environment, social cohesion, and peace and security. Six themed Leaders' Dialogues were to be convened during the summit, to promote pledges for National and Global Commitments to SDG Transformation (these commitments were to be formally registered on a SDG Summit Acceleration and Accountability Platform). The 2023 edition of a quadrennial *Global Sustainable Development Report*, prepared by an independent group of scientists, was to be released prior to the SDG Summit to inform its discussions and decision making. A Summit of the Future was to be organized in 2024 to maintain momentum on pursuing the SDGs.

UN Resident Coordinators

Resident Coordinators have an independent, sustainable development-focused co-ordination function, and act as the designated representative of the UN Secretary-General in a country, with respect to its development operations. They lead the UN Country Team to support co-ordinated, inter-agency activities, as well as other national strategies and development priorities. RCs report both to the UN Secretary-General (through the Chair of the UNSDG) and to the host government on the implementation of a country's UN Sustainable Development Coordination Framework. In 2023 UN Country Teams—including UN agencies, funds and specialized programmes—were based in 132 countries, covering the 162 states and territories in which UN development activities were being undertaken.

OFFICES OF UN RESIDENT COORDINATORS IN THE MIDDLE EAST AND NORTH AFRICA

Algeria: 41 rue Mohamed Khoudi, El Biar, Algiers; tel. (21) 92-01-01; fax (21) 92-54-51; internet algeria.un.org; Resident Coordinator ALEJANDRO ALVAREZ.

Bahrain: UN House 69, Rd 1901, Hoora 319, POB 26814, Manama; tel. 17311600; fax 17311500; e-mail registry.bh@undp.org; internet bahrain.un.org; Resident Coordinator KHALED EL MEKWAD.

The United Nations in the Middle East and North Africa

Egypt: World Trade Center, 1191 Corniche el-Nil St, Boulaq, Cairo; tel. (2) 24564811; fax (2) 25742620; e-mail unrco.eg@un.org; internet egypt.un.org; Resident Coordinator ELENA PANOVA.

Iran: 8 Shahrzad Blvd, POB 15875-4557, Darrous 1948773911, Tehran; tel. (21) 22860691; fax (21) 22868123; e-mail rcs-iranregistry@un.org; internet iran.un.org; Resident Coordinator STEFAN PRIESNER.

Iraq: 22/217 Diwan (UN Compound), Green Zone, Karada Maryam District, Baghdad; e-mail unctiraq@un.org; internet iraq.un.org; Resident Coordinator GHULAM MOHAMMAD ISACZAI.

Jordan: 16 Majed Al Edwan St, Amman 11194; tel. (6) 5100420; e-mail rchc.jo@one.un.org; internet jordan.un.org; Resident Coordinator SHERI RITSEMA-ANDERSON.

Kuwait: UN House, Block 7A, Mishref; tel. 25308000; internet kuwait.un.org; Resident Coordinator GHADA HATIM ELTAHIR MUDAWI.

Lebanon: Arab African International Bank Bldg, Riad el-Solh St, Nejmeh, Beirut; tel. (1) 978405; e-mail unrco.lebanon@un.org; internet lebanon.un.org; Resident Coordinator IMRAN RIZA.

Libya: c/o Immeuble le Prestige Business Center, Tour E et D, 2nd Floor, rue du Lac Windermere, Les Berges du Lac, Tunis 1053; e-mail georgette.gagnon1@un.org; Resident Coordinator GEORGETTE GAGNON.

Morocco: 13 ave Ahmed Balafrej Souissi, 10000 Rabat; tel. (53) 7633090; fax (53) 7633089; e-mail unrc.ma@one.un.org; internet morocco.un.org; Resident Coordinator NATHALIE FUSTIER.

Palestinian Territories: 4A Alar 1 St, POB 490, Jerusalem 91004; tel. (2) 5687260; e-mail unsco-rcop@un.org; internet palestine.un.org; Resident Coordinator LYNN HASTINGS.

Syrian Arab Republic: Mazzah, 8 West Villas Gazawi St, Damascus; tel. (11) 6129811; fax (11) 6114541; e-mail abdelmoula@un.org; internet syria.un.org; Resident Coordinator ADAM ABDELMOULA.

Tunisia: Immeuble le Prestige Business Center, Tour A, rue du Lac Windermere, Les Berges du Lac, Tunis 1053; tel. (36) 011-680; e-mail arnaud.peral@un.org; internet tunisia.un.org; Resident Coordinator ARNAUD PERAL.

Türkiye: Yıldız Kule, Yukarı Dikmen Mahallesi, Turan Güneş Bulvarı, No. 106, Çankaya, Ankara 06550; tel. (312) 4541100; fax (312) 4961463; internet turkiye.un.org; Resident Coordinator ALVARO RODRIGUEZ.

United Arab Emirates: POB 3490, Abu Dhabi; tel. (2) 6961999; fax (2) 4467050; e-mail dena.assaf@un.org; internet unitedarabemirates@un.org; Resident Coordinator DENA ASSAF.

Yemen: POB 551, Sana'a; tel. (1) 448605; fax (1) 448841; e-mail unrc.ye@one.un.org; internet yemen.un.org; Resident Coordinator WILLIAM DAVID GRESSLY.

Finance

With a view to securing consistent funding for the RC system, from 1 January 2019 member states' contributions under the UNSDG's existing cost-sharing mechanism were doubled. Furthermore, in July 2018 a dedicated Special Purpose Trust Fund was established. Its requirements in 2023 totalled US $281m. UN member states were invited to support the inter-agency Joint SDG Fund, a pooled mechanism for integrated policy support and strategic financing.

United Nations Development Programme—UNDP

Address: One United Nations Plaza, New York, NY 10017, USA.
Telephone: (212) 906-5300; **fax:** (212) 906-5364; **e-mail:** hq@undp.org; **internet:** www.undp.org.

UNDP was established in 1965 by the UN General Assembly. Its central mission is to help countries to eradicate poverty and achieve a sustainable level of human development, an approach to economic growth that encompasses individual wellbeing and choice, equitable distribution of the benefits of development, and conservation of the environment.

Organization
(September 2023)

UNDP is responsible to the UN General Assembly, to which it reports through the Economic and Social Council (ECOSOC).

EXECUTIVE BOARD

The Executive Board is responsible for providing intergovernmental support to, and supervising the activities of UNDP, the UN Population Fund (UNFPA) and the UN Office for Project Services. It comprises 36 members, elected by ECOSOC for a three-year term: eight from Africa, seven from Asia and the Pacific, four from Eastern Europe, five from Latin America and the Caribbean and 12 from Western Europe and other countries.

SECRETARIAT

The Administrator is supported by one Associate Administrator and nine Assistant Secretaries-General. Offices and divisions at the secretariat include Offices of the Human Development Report, Audit and Investigations, Ethics, and Independent Evaluation; Global Services Solution and Global Policy Centres; and a Crisis Bureau and Bureaux for Policy and Programme Support, External Relations and Advocacy, and Management Services. Five Regional Bureaux cover Africa; Asia and the Pacific; the Arab states; Europe and the Commonwealth of Independent States; and Latin America and the Caribbean.

Administrator: ACHIM STEINER (Brazil/Germany).

Associate Administrator: HAOLIANG XU (People's Republic of China).

Director, Regional Bureau for Arab States: ABDALLAH AL-DARDARI (Syria).

With a view to streamlining co-ordination, five Regional Collaborative Platforms (RCPs) were initiated from 2020, with participation by all development-focused UN agencies working within each region. Each RCP is chaired by the UN Deputy Secretary-General. The head of the relevant UNDP Regional Bureau and UN Regional Economic Commission act as Vice-Chairs.

COUNTRY OFFICES

In almost every country receiving UN assistance there is an office, headed by a UNDP Resident Representative. UNDP maintains a regional hub for the Arab states in Amman, Jordan.

GLOBAL CENTRES

UNDP supports a network of global centres that undertake specialized research and advance sustainable development-related solutions and policy design.

Global Centre for Technology, Innovation and Sustainable Development: Block A, 29 Heng Mui Keng Terrace, Singapore 119620; tel. 69081063; fax 67744571; e-mail registry.SG@undp.org; internet sgtechcentre.undp.org; f. 2019; administered jtly by UNDP and the Singapore Govt, the Centre aims to identify and promote innovative and technological solutions to sustainable devt challenges; the Centre's focal areas in 2023 included digital solutions for COVID-19, digitalization, sustainable and digital agriculture, smart cities, and sustainable finance.

Global Policy Centre for Resilient Ecosystems and Desertification (GC-RED): UN Gigiri Compound, Block M, Middle Level, United Nations Ave, POB 30218, 00100 Nairobi, Kenya; tel. (20) 7624640; e-mail gc-red@undp.org; f. 2015; aims to promote knowledge sharing on and solutions for inclusive sustainable devt in drylands and other fragile ecosystems; focuses on building ecological and social resistance and on the sustainable management of renewable natural capital to improve livelihoods. The Centre is the managing agent for a jt UNDP-UNEP project, Poverty-Environment Action for the SDGs, which aims to integrate programmes that mainstream poverty-environment linkages into national devt planning processes; Dir ANNE JUEPNER (Germany).

Istanbul International Centre for Private Sector in Development (IICPSD): İstiklal Sk, 34381 İstanbul, Türkiye; tel. (850) 288-2534; e-mail iicpsd@undp.org; internet www.iicpsd.undp.org; f. 2011; managed jtly by UNDP and the Turkish Govt, the Centre supports the devt of inclusive and competitive markets and aims to promote economic devt by engaging people in value chains in production and entrepreneurial roles; Dir SAHBA SOBHANI.

Oslo Governance Centre (OGC): Kongens Gate 12, 0153 Oslo, Norway; tel. (2) 212-1600; e-mail oslo.governance.centre@undp.org; internet www.undp.org/oslocentre; f. 2002, relaunched in June 2015, at the same time as the inaugural edition of a series of Oslo Governance and Peacebuilding Dialogues; the Centre aims to support the devt of more effective and inclusive forms of governance, and to prevent violent extremism; Dir ARVINN GADGIL.

Activities

UNDP works as the UN's global development network, advocating for change and connecting countries to knowledge, experience and resources to help people to build a better life. UNDP's Administrator serves as the Vice-Chair of the UN Sustainable Development Group, which aims to co-ordinate and enhance the efforts of some 36 UN offices and programmes to deliver the UN's 2030 Agenda for Sustainable Development.

UNDP's Strategic Plan for 2022–25 was focused on supporting countries to work towards building resilience, structural transformation and 'leaving no one behind' in order to help achieve the UN Sustainable Development Goals (SDGs) by 2030. Within this framework, UNDP identified the following six 'signature solutions': tackling poverty and inequality; future-proofing governance systems; building resilience; putting the natural environment at the heart of economies and planning; increasing access to energy and accelerating the transition to renewable sources of energy; and combating structural challenges to gender equality. In order to maximize its impact and enhance the development activities of recipient countries, UNDP aimed to promote digitalization, strategic innovation and development financing.

In 2023 UNDP was implementing development activities in 170 countries and territories. It provides advisory and support services to governments and UN teams with the aim of advancing sustainable human development and building national development capabilities. Assistance is mostly non-monetary, comprising the provision of experts' services, consultancies, equipment and training for local workers. Developing countries themselves contribute significantly to the total project costs in terms of personnel, facilities, equipment and supplies. UNDP also supports programme countries in attracting aid and utilizing it efficiently. UNDP's development activities place particular emphasis on people living in poverty—as defined by the US $2.15 per day international poverty line (in purchasing power parity), national poverty lines, and by UNDP's *Global Multidimensional Poverty Index*, which includes indicators such as access to education, food, safe water and electricity. Groups experiencing the greatest social inequalities and exclusion, especially women, female-headed households and youth, are a particular focus of attention.

In 2022 UNDP implemented 674 projects in the Arab states, of which 530 were focused on strengthening effective, inclusive and accountable governance.

HUMAN DEVELOPMENT REPORTS

UNDP's annually updated global *Human Development Report* ranks countries in accordance with three key indicators: life expectancy; adult literacy; and basic income required for a decent standard of living. The 2022 edition was subtitled *Uncertain Times, Unsettled Lives: Shaping our Future in a World in Transformation*. A special human development study titled *New Threats to Human Security in the Anthropocene* was published in February of that year. UNDP country offices support the formulation of national human development reports, which aim to facilitate policymaking, guide the allocation of resources, and monitor progress towards poverty eradication and sustainable development. In addition, UNDP prepares Advisory Notes and bespoke Cooperation Frameworks to highlight country-specific priorities. Regional human development reports are also prepared intermittently.

An Arab Human Development Report, subtitled 'Expanding Opportunities for an Inclusive and Resilient Recovery in the Post-Covid Era', was issued in June 2022.

UNDP's Human Development Report Office also releases annually five updated composite indices: the *Global Multidimensional Poverty Index* (produced jointly with the United Kingdom-based Oxford Poverty and Human Development Initiative), a *Human Development Index*, an *Inequality-Adjusted Human Development Index*, *Gender Inequality Index*, and a *Gender Development Index*.

POVERTY

UNDP's 2022 *Global Multidimensional Poverty (MPI) Index*, issued in October, and using data from 1,200m. people across 111 countries, focused on incorporating into policymaking an understanding of deprivation 'bundles'—i.e. recurring patterns of deprivation. Some 19.1% of people surveyed (one-half of them under the age of 18) were reported to be living in acute MPI, primarily in sub-Saharan Africa, followed by South Asia. More than one-half of people living in MPI were reported to be deprived of both cooking fuel and electricity, and nearly one-half to be deprived of both nutrition and sanitation, rendering them more vulnerable to infectious diseases. The COVID-19 pandemic was observed to have significantly reversed progress in reducing MPI. The report included a particular focus on the MPI situation in India.

UNDP assists member countries to maximize the use of domestic capabilities and institutional and policy mechanisms for the elimination of poverty and the realization of national development goals. Through its support for the multi-stakeholder Global Partnership for Effective Development Cooperation (established in 2011), and by means of Development Finance Assessments, UNDP aims to maximize the development impact of collaboration. It is also the custodian agency of SDG 17 (Strengthen the means of implementation and revitalize the global partnership for sustainable development). In January 2017 the Cape Town Global Action Plan (CTGAP) for Sustainable Development Data was launched at the inaugural UN World Data Forum. The fourth UN World Data Forum—held in April 2023, in Hangzhou, People's Republic of China—issued the Hangzhou Declaration on accelerating progress in the implementation of the CTGAP. In July 2019 UNDP, with the Governments of Germany and Qatar, launched a series of Accelerator Labs, tasked with identifying and analysing specific local development challenges, and pursuing solutions for these. As at mid-2023 there were 91 Labs that were supporting 115 countries. The Accelerator Labs represent a key component of an evolving Global Policy Network, which aims to enhance policy and knowledge capabilities and to connect experts across the organization, in collective pursuit of integrated development solutions. UNDP hosts Global Dev Hub, an online network of international development practitioners and professionals.

UNDP's Administrator co-chairs a global Task Force on Digital Financing that was launched in November 2018 by the UN Secretary-General to support the implementation of the SDGs. In November 2020 UNDP and the Organisation for Economic Co-operation and Development (OECD) jointly launched a UNDP-OECD Framework for SDG Aligned Finance, with the aim of promoting investment in developing countries that would support the pursuit of the SDGs. The UN Secretary-General issued a report in August of that year that addressed the empowerment potential arising from transformative advances in financial technologies ('fintech'), such as mobile payment technologies, crowdfunding platforms, peer-to-peer lending, online marketplaces, and cryptocurrencies and assets. A Tech Access Partnership was initiated in May of that year by UNDP, the UN Conference on Trade and Development (UNCTAD) and partners. UNDP, UNICEF and other partners co-host the Digital Public Goods Alliance, which facilitates investment in digital public goods to accelerate the attainment of the SDGs in low- and middle-income countries. UNDP's Digital Strategy (2022–25), launched in February 2022, aimed to embed a digital focus into all dimensions of the Programme's work; to support governments to establish more inclusive and resilient digital ecosystems; and to continue to upgrade and transform the scope of digital skills to meet present and future technological challenges.

In May 2022—within the framework of the Essential Digital Infrastructure and Services Network (EDISON) Alliance that was initiated by the World Economic Forum in February 2021—UNDP launched a Lighthouse Countries Network aimed at accelerating digital inclusion in the education, health and finance sectors.

UNDP is committed to ensuring that the process of economic and financial globalization, including national and global trade, debt and capital flow policies, incorporates human development concerns. UNDP is a partner—with the IMF, the International Trade Centre, UNCTAD, the World Bank and the World Trade Organization (WTO)—in the Enhanced Integrated Framework (EIF) for trade-related assistance to least developed countries (LDCs), a multi-donor programme which aims to support greater participation by LDCs in the global trading system. EIF funds are channelled through a dedicated EIF Trust Fund that was initiated in 2009.

In April 2016 a Global Platform on Inclusive Business was launched, as an initiative of the G20 to be implemented by UNDP and the World Bank, with a mandate to support policymakers and to promote inclusive business practices and policies. UNDP hosts the secretariat of the Business Call to Action multilateral grouping, which assists private organizations to promote the SDGs and inclusive development. UNDP supports a regular Responsible Business Forum.

GOVERNANCE

Around one-third of UNDP's expenditure is focused on SDG 16: Promote peaceful and inclusive societies for sustainable development, provide access to justice for all and build effective, accountable and inclusive institutions at all levels. UNDP supports national efforts to ensure efficient and accountable governance, to improve the quality of institutions and democratic processes, to foster the rights of Indigenous peoples and other marginalized communities, and to build effective relations between the state, the private sector and civil society, in order to underpin sustainable development.

UNDP is mandated to assist developing countries to fight corruption and improve accountability, transparency and integrity. It has helped to establish national and international partnerships in support of its anti-corruption efforts, and assists governments to conduct self-assessments of their public financial management systems. UNDP co-ordinates the secretariat of the International Aid Transparency Initiative, which was inaugurated in September 2008.

UNDP works to strengthen parliaments and other legislative bodies as institutions of democratic participation. The Programme assists with constitutional reviews and reform, training of parliamentary staff, and capacity building of political parties and civil organizations. It also supports the establishment of electoral commissions, as well as voter registration and education, undertakes missions to help to prepare for and ensure the conduct of free and fair elections, and provides training to journalists to provide impartial election coverage.

UNDP supports projects to improve access to justice, in particular for marginalized populations, and to promote judicial independence, legal reform and understanding of the legal system. UNDP also promotes support for the international human rights system and advocates for the integration of human rights issues into activities concerned with sustainable human development.

Within the context of the Plan of Action to Prevent Violent Extremism launched in 2015 by the UN Secretary-General, and of SDG 16, UNDP has developed a strategic framework: Preventing Violent Extremism through Inclusive Development and the Promotion of Tolerance and Respect for Diversity. In March 2018 UNDP, with International Alert, issued a 'toolkit' to help to improve the design, implementation and monitoring of Prevention of Violent Extremism (PVE) programmes. In May UNDP signed an MOU with the UN Office of Counter-Terrorism to strengthen collaborative PVE efforts. UNDP's Oslo Governance Centre focuses on fostering more effective and inclusive forms of governance and on PVE.

UNDP collaborates with other UN agencies to promote relief and development efforts in countries in crisis, in order to secure reconciliation, reconstruction and the foundations for sustainable human development, and to increase national capabilities to prevent or mitigate future crises.

Special development initiatives undertaken by UNDP in post-conflict countries include the demobilization of former combatants and destruction of illicit small armaments, the rehabilitation of communities for the sustainable reintegration of returning populations, and the restoration and strengthening of democratic institutions and rule of law. The latter is achieved through UNDP's Global Programme on Strengthening the Rule of Law and Human Rights for Sustaining Peace and Fostering Development. UNDP assists the establishment of regulatory frameworks and mechanisms aimed at conflict prevention and consensus building, and promotes conflict analysis and assessments. It supports the UN Global Focal Point (GFP) arrangement for Police, Justice and Corrections Areas in the Rule of Law in Post-Conflict and other Crisis Situations, which co-ordinates and represents a single entry point for UN system-wide rule of law assistance.

A Peace Support Facility—managed by UNDP, the Office of the Special Envoy of the Secretary-General for Yemen, and the UN Resident Coordinator's Office in Yemen—was launched in April 2019 to assist UN peacemaking activities in that country. In August 2020 UNDP and the EU agreed a US $82.4m. three-year Strengthening Institutional and Economic Resilience in Yemen (SIERY) initiative, which aimed to strengthen local authorities, ensure citizens' access to basic services and foster social cohesion.

UNDP was implementing an Iraq-focused Funding Facility for Stabilization (FFS) during the period 1 May 2015–31 December 2023. By 30 June 2023 the Facility had supported the return to their home communities of more than 4.9m. Iraqis who had been displaced by Islamic State, mobilized US $1,550m., and had completed 3,617 projects. Some 49,778 cash-for-work opportunities had been generated through the FFS by that time, 6,618 cash grants provided to women-led households, and 4,153 small business grants distributed. Furthermore, 167 healthcare facilities, 630 schools, six universities, 124 water treatment plants, and 142 electricity substations had been rehabilitated, as well as 36,913 houses, in Anbar, Ninewa and Salah al-Din. An Iraq Social Cohesion Programme was being implemented by UNDP during 2020–24.

Through a Stabilization Facility for Libya that was implemented by UNDP, with support from the international community, during the period April 2016–August 2022, some US $95m. was channelled towards the rehabilitation of key Libyan infrastructure and to support local communities.

UNDP produced three editions of an *Arab Knowledge Report*, in 2009, 2012, and (themed 'Youth and Localization of Knowledge') in 2014. An *Arab Knowledge Index* was first issued in 2015, and updated in 2016. In 2017 this was developed, jointly with the UAE-based Mohammed Bin Rashid Al Maktoum Knowledge Foundation, into a *Global Knowledge Index,* comprising sectoral indices on pre-university education; technical vocational education and training; higher education; research development and innovation; information and communications technology; the economy; and the enabling environment. UNDP and the Foundation jointly maintain an internet-based Arab Knowledge Portal.

UNDP helps to organize an annual Africa Regional Judges Forum.

RESILIENCE

UNDP supports countries and communities in building resilience to potential crises and shocks (such as natural disasters, conflict, impacts of climate change, and public health epidemics and pandemics). It is the focal point within the UN system for strengthening national capacities for natural disaster reduction. UNDP's Crisis Bureau, in conjunction with the Office for the Coordination of Humanitarian Affairs and UN Office for Disaster Risk Reduction, oversees the system-wide Capacity for Disaster Reduction Initiative (inaugurated in 2007). In March 2015, at the Third UN World Conference on Disaster Risk Reduction, UNDP initiated '5-10-50', a global programme to support, over a 10-year period, the disaster reduction efforts of some 50 member states, with a focus on the following five areas: preparedness; risk awareness and early warning; risk governance and mainstreaming; resilient recovery; and local and urban risk reduction.

UNDP co-leads the Regional Refugee and Resilience Plan (3RP) that assists host communities and Syrian refugees in countries neighbouring the Syrian Arab Republic. In June 2023 the Brussels VII Conference on Syria generated US $5,600m. in onwards funding for the 3RP.

UNDP's 3RP regional operations have focused on fostering development and social stability in host communities, expanding access to critical infrastructure, and promoting livelihoods. UNDP's activities within Syria itself have included improving food security; promoting grassroots economic activity and supporting small businesses; expanding ongoing programmes aimed at assisting vulnerable communities; strengthening service delivery; and removing solid waste and debris. Under an inter-agency Lebanon Crisis Response Plan (LCRP) that was launched in February 2022 as part of the ongoing 3RP, some US $3,200m. was requested to fund support activities there during that year.

UNDP established a mine action unit within its Crisis Bureau in order to strengthen national and local demining capabilities including surveying, mapping and clearance of anti-personnel landmines. UNDP works closely with UNICEF to raise awareness and implement risk reduction education programmes, and manages global partnership projects concerned with training, legislation and the socioeconomic impact of anti-personnel devices. In July 2016 UNDP initiated a Development and Mine Action Support Framework.

ENVIRONMENT

UNDP aims to strengthen national capacities to carry out effective and sustainable environmental management policies and practices, including addressing the challenges of climate change. Together with the UN Environment Programme (UNEP) and the World Bank, UNDP is an implementing agency of the Global Environment Facility (GEF), which was established in 1991 to finance international co-operation in projects to benefit the environment.

Community-based initiatives worldwide concerned with climate change mitigation and adaptation, reversal of land degradation, biodiversity conservation, sustainable forestry and water management, and chemicals management including the elimination of persistent organic pollutants, are supported through a Small Grants Programme, administered by UNDP and funded by the GEF. In July 2023 the GEF Council pledged US $500m. to its partnership with UNDP, to be deployed to 88 countries, in particular to address biodiversity loss, to support forest conservation and to help to restore ecosystems.

UNDP recognizes that in parts of the world land degradation, desertification and drought are major causes of rural poverty, and promotes sustainable land management, reform of land tenure, drought preparedness, and the implementation of conventions that aim to protect the environment. UNDP is a partner agency of the Climate and Clean Air Coalition to Reduce Short Lived Climate Pollutants (SLCPs), which was launched in February 2012 with the aim of combating SLCPs, including methane, black carbon and certain hydrofluorocarbons. UNDP also implements projects funded by the International Climate Initiative (launched in 2008 by the German Government). In March 2015 the Green Climate Fund, established by the UNFCCC to support developing countries with implementing emissions mitigation and climate change adaptation policies, approved UNDP as an implementing agency. In October 2021 UNDP and partners launched the online UN Biodiversity Lab, as a resource for governments, policymakers and other stakeholders.

UNDP works to ensure the effective governance of freshwater and aquatic resources, and promotes co-operation in transboundary water management, ocean and coastal management, and efforts to promote safe sanitation and community water supplies. UNDP is the lead agency for the GEF's Blue and Green Islands Integrated Program, and supports a range of projects that incorporate development and ecological requirements in the sustainable management of international waters, within the following framework: global programmes; large marine ecosystems; transboundary lakes, rivers and aquifers; and integrated water resources and coastal area management.

In December 2016 UNDP established an Ocean Action Hub, which acts as a focal point of information resources concerning SDG 14 (on oceans). In June 2022, at the Second UN Oceans Conference, co-hosted by Portugal and Kenya in the Portuguese capital Lisbon, UNDP launched an Ocean Promise initiative, through which it pledged to support 100 coastal countries to develop, by 2030, sustainable, low-emission, climate-resilient blue economies.

During 2023—with a view to preventing a catastrophic oil spill—UNDP was co-ordinating a planned operation to transfer to a secure vessel some 1.14m. barrels of light crude oil that was being stored on a dangerously dilapidated ship (the 'FSO Safer'), moored off the coast of Yemen, and to then scrap the FSO Safer at a green salvage facility. In June the planned operation was insured through UNDP's Insurance and Risk Finance Facility. The transfer operation was undertaken over a 13 week period and completed in late August; by that time donors had pledged US $121m. towards the initiative (a further $22m. was required to complete the project).

ENERGY

In September 2021 the UN Secretary-General convened a landmark High-level Dialogue on Energy (the first UN summit-level meeting on energy in four decades) to address means of achieving the goals of the 2015 Paris Agreement on climate change, and, simultaneously, of attaining SDG 7. The meeting adopted a roadmap to support the achievement of clean energy access for all by 2030 and net-zero emissions by 2050, and resulted in the conclusion by stakeholders of more than 150 'Energy Compacts' reflecting actions and financial commitments to be achieved by 2030. In this context, a UNDP Energy Compact was pledged, in accordance with which the Programme was to mobilize partners to facilitate the supply of clean and affordable energy to 500m. people by 2030, with a focus on very vulnerable communities.

GENDER

UNDP's annual *Gender Inequality Index* and *Gender Development Index* assess gender equality on the basis of life expectancy, education and income. In June 2023 UNDP issued a Gender Social Norms Index and related report, which addressed entrenched biases that sustain gender discrimination.

In March 2021 UNDP established a Gender and Crisis Engagement Facility, which aimed to strengthen women's leadership and participation in crisis contexts, and to target response initiatives specifically to the needs of women and girls. A UNDP report issued in that month called for the implementation of a temporary basic income to support women in crisis-affected developing countries, noting that during the COVID-19 emergency women were more likely to lose paid work and assume caring duties. In September 2020 UNDP and UN Women introduced a COVID-19 Global Gender Response Tracker, to monitor the inclusion of gender-sensitive measures in social protection and labour policy responses to the pandemic crisis.

In March 2022 UNDP and UN Women jointly launched a Gender Justice Platform, which was to support transformational change to ensure the empowerment of women in justice and transitional justice frameworks.

CRISIS RESPONSE

UNDP's 'SURGE' Immediate Crisis Response programme aims to strengthen the agency's capacity to respond quickly and effectively in the recovery phase following a conflict or natural disaster. Under the programme advisers—UNDP staff with special expertise in at least one of 14 identified areas, including early recovery, operational support and resource mobilization—are swiftly deployed to UNDP country offices dealing with crises. UNDP is the lead agency for the Early Recovery cluster response to a humanitarian disaster, linking the immediate needs with medium- and long-term recovery efforts. UNDP 'crisis response packages' aim to restore core government functions; to stabilize livelihoods; to manage debris and the rehabilitation of core infrastructure; and to plan for crisis recovery.

Following the chemical explosion that devastated part of the port of Beirut and nearby areas in August 2020, UNDP prioritized the restoration of livelihoods and small businesses; debris management; and facilitating access to justice for vulnerable groups affected by the disaster. UNDP has supported the implementation of socioeconomic protection measures to assist affected local people. In March 2023, following a devastating earthquake, UNDP deployed recovery workers and SURGE advisors to areas in the north of the Syrian Arab Republic, already severely affected by the ongoing civil conflict in that country.

Finance

UNDP's Integrated Budget for 2022–25, underpinning its Strategic Plan covering that period, projected resources amounting to US $28,265m.; 91% of the total resources were to be allocated to development activities.

Publications

Annual Report of the Administrator.
Human Development Report (annually).
Impact Series.
South-South Quarterly.
Other reports, strategy papers, policy briefings, factsheets.

Funds and Programmes

A number of associated funds and programmes, financed separately by means of voluntary contributions, provide specific services through the UNDP network.

REGIONAL ORGANIZATIONS

GEF Small Grants Programme (SGP): 304 East 45th St, 9th Floor, New York, NY 10017, USA; tel. (646) 781-4385; fax (646) 781-4075; e-mail sgp.info@undp.org; internet sgp.undp.org; f. 1992, becoming operational in 1996; UNDP (also responsible for the capacity building, targeted research, pre-investment activities and technical assistance areas of GEF activity, and for managing the GEF Country Dialogue Workshop Programme) administers the SGP, which provides grants of up to US $50,000; by 30 June 2022 the SGP had, since its inception, supported (at a cost of $752.9m.) 27,348 community-based projects in 136 countries, implemented by local NGOs, addressing biodiversity, climate change mitigation and adaptation, land degradation and sustainable forest management, international waters, and chemicals; initial funding of $128m. had been pledged for the SGP's 7th operational phase covering 2020–24; maintains an innovation library; SGP Global Man. YOKO WATANABE.

Joint SDG Fund: SDG-F Secretariat, c/o UNDP, One United Nations Plaza, New York, NY 10017, USA; tel. (646) 781-4255; e-mail admin@sdgfund.org; internet jointsdgfund.org; f. 2017, superseding a previous SDG Achievement Fund (f. 2014); the Joint SDG Fund is a pooled inter-agency mechanism that provides integrated policy support and strategic financing to assist the design and implementation of joint programmes—under the co-ordination of UN Resident Coordinators and Country Teams—that aim to accelerate progress towards achieving the UN's 2030 Agenda and SDGs; by June 2023 the Fund had mobilized funding amounting to US $1,500m.; leadership and strategic guidance is provided by a Strategic Advisory Group that is co-chaired by the UN Deputy Sec.-Gen. and the UNSDG Chair., and comprises (on a rotational basis) representatives of 15 UN mem. states; UNDP chairs an Operational Steering Cttee.

Multi-Partner Trust Fund Office: 304 East 45th St, 11th Floor, New York, NY 10017, USA; tel. (212) 906-6355; fax (212) 906-6705; e-mail executivecoordinator.mptfo@undp.org; internet mptf.undp.org; f. 2003, initially as the International Reconstruction Fund Facility for Iraq, later the Iraq Trust Fund Office, then, in 2006, the Multi-Donor Trust Fund Office; present name adopted in 2011; engages in collaborative activities to address pandemics, climate change and the conservation of biodiversity, and facilitates UN coherence and devt effectiveness in addressing complex challenges, such as humanitarian crises and peacebuilding; assists the UN system and national govts in managing pooled financing mechanisms: mainly UN Multi-Donor Trust Funds (MDTFs—which are often thematic, and can be established at global, regional or national level), National MDTFs (at times complementing a UN MDTF), and stand-alone Joint Programmes (established by UN agencies in support of a strategic vision); Exec. Co-ordinator JENNIFER TOPPING (Canada).

Programme of Assistance to the Palestinian People (PAPP): POB 51359, Jerusalem; tel. (2) 6268200; fax (2) 6268222; e-mail registry.papp@undp.org; internet www.ps.undp.org; f. 1978; committed to strengthening institutions in the Israeli-occupied territories and emerging Palestinian autonomous areas, to creating employment opportunities and to stimulating private and public investment in the area to enhance trade and export potential; examples of PAPP activities include the construction of sewage collection systems in the northern Gaza Strip; provision of water to both the West Bank and Gaza; construction of schools, youth and health centres; support to vegetable and fish traders through the construction of cold storage and packing facilities; and provision of loans to strengthen industry and commerce; organized in Nov. 2016 the inaugural Palestine Resilience Conference, in Amman; supports a Palestinian Accelerator Lab, which was initiated in Dec. 2019; in Feb. 2020 PAPP, UNRWA and the Saudi Arabian Government signed a US $10m. agreement aimed at rehabilitating 272 damaged houses in the Gaza Strip, under a broader Saudi Arabia-funded programme that hitherto had rehabilitated 13,194 homes there; a $1,300m. UN Sustainable Development Cooperation Framework was implemented by UN agencies in Palestine during 2018–22; UNDP Special Representative of the Administrator in the Occupied Palestinian Territories YVONNE HELLE (Netherlands).

UNDP Montreal Protocol/Chemicals Unit: through its Montreal Protocol/Chemicals Unit UNDP collaborates with public and private partners in developing countries to assist them in eliminating the use of ozone-depleting substances (ODS), in accordance with the Montreal Protocol to the Vienna Convention for the Protection of the Ozone Layer, through the design, monitoring and evaluation of ODS phase-out projects and progs; in particular, UNDP provides technical assistance and training, national capacity building and demonstration projects and technology transfer investment initiatives.

United Nations Capital Development Fund (UNCDF): Two United Nations Plaza, 26th Floor, New York, NY 10017, USA; tel. (212) 906-6565; fax (212) 906-6479; e-mail info@uncdf.org; internet www.uncdf.org; f. 1966; UNCDF facilitates the use of public and private finance to support the poor in LDCs; offers 'last mile' finance models aimed at unlocking public and private resources, in particular at the domestic level, with the goal of reducing poverty and supporting local economic devt; promotes the expansion of inclusive digital local economies, with participation by individuals, households and small businesses; in May 2020 UNCDF and UNDP announced jt support for a new mem. state-led initiative, Remittances in Crisis, that aimed to ensure migrants' means of sending and receiving remittances, and to reduce relevant costs, in view of the widespread restrictions imposed to contain the COVID-19 pandemic; in Jan. 2021 co-launched a Women Enterprise Recovery Fund; UNDP's Administrator serves as the Man. Dir of UNCDF; Exec. Sec. PREETI SINHA.

United Nations Volunteers (UNV): POB 260111, 53153 Bonn, Germany; tel. (228) 8152000; fax (228) 8152001; e-mail unv.media@unv.org; internet www.unv.org; f. 1970; supports sustainable devt, and in particular the attainment of the SDGs; works to mobilize volunteers to serve UNDP initiatives and also to support the activities of other partner UN agencies and bodies; advocates the use of volunteers and the integration of volunteerism and civic engagement into sustainable devt, humanitarian and peace projects worldwide; UNV focuses participation on the following areas: peacebuilding; community resilience for environment and disaster risk reduction; securing access to basic social services; youth; and national capacity devt; a Plan of Action to Integrate Volunteering into the 2030 Agenda was being implemented during 2016–30; in July 2020 UNV hosted a global meeting on Re-imagining Volunteering for the 2030 Agenda; during 2022 12,408 UNVs were deployed in 166 countries, working with some 55 UN entities; an additional 8,747 people volunteered online; some 10,370 UNVs (84% of the total) were from the Global South in 2022; by 2023 the number of people who had served on the ground as UNVs exceeded 70,000; Exec. Co-ordinator TOILY KURBANOV (Russia); publ. *State of the World's Volunteerism Report* (every 3–4 years).

United Nations Environment Programme—UNEP

Address: POB 30552, Nairobi 00100, Kenya.
Telephone: (20) 7621234; **e-mail:** unepinfo@unep.org; **internet:** www.unenvironment.org.

UNEP (commonly referred to as UN Environment) was established in 1972, following recommendations of the 1972 UN Conference on the Human Environment, in Stockholm, Sweden, to facilitate international co-operation on the environment. It has become the lead UN agency for formulating the global environment agenda and promoting sound environmental management in support of sustainable development.

Organization
(September 2023)

UN ENVIRONMENT ASSEMBLY

The Assembly—at which all UN member states are represented—was established in accordance with a resolution adopted in December 2012 by the UN General Assembly; its inaugural meeting was convened in June 2014. The sixth meeting (UNEA-6) was to be convened in late February–early March 2024, in Nairobi, on the theme 'Effective, inclusive and sustainable multilateral actions to tackle climate change, biodiversity loss and pollution'.

COMMITTEE OF PERMANENT REPRESENTATIVES

The Committee, comprising all accredited permanent representatives of member states to UNEP, meets at least four times each year. It prepares the meetings of the Assembly and helps to oversee implementation of Assembly decisions. It is led by a five-member Bureau, elected for a two-year period.

EXECUTIVE OFFICE

UNEP headquarters includes the offices of the Executive Director and Deputy Executive Director; the Governance Affairs Office (which also serves as the Secretariat of Governing Bodies); units serving the Chief Scientist and Chief Digital Officer; and Divisions of

Communications, Early Warning and Assessment, Ecosystems, Industry and Economy, Law, Corporate Services, and Policy and Programmes.

Executive Director: INGER ANDERSEN (Denmark).
Deputy Executive Director: ELIZABETH MARUMA MREMA (Tanzania).

REGIONAL OFFICES

UNEP's regional offices provide a focal point for building national, subregional and regional partnerships and enhancing local participation in UNEP initiatives. A co-ordination office has been established at headquarters to promote regional policy integration, to co-ordinate programme planning, and to provide necessary services to the regional offices.

Africa: NOF Block 2, Level 1, South-Wing POB 30552, Nairobi, Kenya; tel. (20) 7624235; e-mail communication.roa@unep.org; internet www.unenvironment.org/regions/africa; hosts the Secretariat of the African Ministerial Conference on the Environment and the Secretariat of the Bamako Convention on hazardous waste; subsidiary entities incl. an Abidjan, Côte d'Ivoire-based Sub-Regional Office for West Africa, an Addis-Ababa, Ethiopia-based liaison office, and country offices in South Africa and Tanzania; Dir a.i. FRANK TURYATUNGA.

West Asia: POB 10880, Manama, Bahrain; tel. 1978 636; e-mail unepwestasiacommunication@un.org; internet www.unep.org/regions/west-asia; subsidiary offices are located in Baghdad (Iraq), and Jeddah (Saudi Arabia); Dir SAMI DIMASSI.

OTHER OFFICES AND RELATED SECRETARIATS

UNEP administers, or provides secretarial functions for, several multilateral environmental agreements.

Basel, Rotterdam and Stockholm Conventions, Secretariat: 11–13 chemin des Anémones, 1219 Châtelaine, Geneva, Switzerland; tel. 229178271; fax 229178098; e-mail brs@un.org; internet www.basel.int; internet www.pic.int; internet chm.pops.int; Exec. Sec. Dr ROLPH PAYET (Seychelles).

Green Climate Fund, Secretariat: 175 Art Center-Daero, Yeonsu-gu, Incheon 22004, Seoul, Republic of Korea; tel. (2) 458-6059; e-mail info@gcfund.org; internet www.greenclimate.fund/home; f. 2010; acts as the financial mechanism under the UNFCCC and the 2015 Paris Agreement; supports projects investing in low emission and climate resilient devt; offers a wide range of financial products tailored to specific project needs; states may access the Fund through multiple entities simultaneously; a replenishment process was ongoing in 2023; a pledging conf. was to be convened in early Oct., in Bonn, Germany; Exec. Dir MAFALDA DUARTE (Portugal).

Mediterranean Action Plan on the Implementation of the Barcelona Convention, Secretariat: Leoforos Vassileos Konstantinou 48, POB 18019, 11635 Athens, Greece; tel. (210) 7273100; e-mail unepmap@un.org; internet web.unep.org/unepmap; supports the 1995 Convention for the Protection of the Marine Environment and the Coastal Region of the Mediterranean (Barcelona Convention), which has 22 parties (21 Mediterranean countries and the EU); Coordinator TATJANA HEMA.

Minamata Convention on Mercury, Secretariat: 11–13 chemin des Anémones, 1219 Châtelaine, Geneva, Switzerland; fax 227973460; e-mail mea-minamatasecretariat@un.org; internet mercuryconvention.org; Exec. Sec. MONIKA STANKIEWICZ (Poland).

Multilateral Fund for the Implementation of the Montreal Protocol, Secretariat: 1000 De La Gauchetière St West, Suite 4100, Montréal, QC H3B 4W5, Canada; tel. (514) 282-1122; fax (514) 282-0068; e-mail mlf-secretariat@un.org; internet www.multilateralfund.org.

UNEP International Environmental Technology Centre (IETC): 2–110 Ryokuchi koen, Tsurumi-ku, Osaka 538-0036, Japan; tel. (6) 6915-4581; e-mail ietc@un.org; internet www.unep.org/ietc; Dir KEITH ALVERSON.

UNEP Ozone Secretariat: POB 30552, Nairobi, Kenya; tel. (20) 7623851; e-mail mea-ozoneinfo@un.org; internet ozone.unep.org; services both the 1985 Vienna Convention for the Protection of the Ozone Layer and its 1987 Montreal Protocol; Exec. Sec. MEGUMI SEKI (Japan).

United Nations Convention on the Law of the Sea (UNCLOS), Secretariat: Division for Ocean Affairs and the Law of the Sea, Office of Legal Affairs, Rm DC2-0450, United Nations, New York, NY 10017, USA; tel. (212) 963-3962; e-mail doalos@un.org; internet www.un.org/Depts/los/index.htm; the UN Division for Ocean Affairs serves as the secretariat of UNCLOS (1982), and is a focal point for information and assistance to states and intergovernmental orgs, and research, regarding UNCLOS and the related 1994 Agreement Relating to the Implementation of Part XI of the Convention, and 1995 UN Fish Stocks Agreement; the main provisions of UNCLOS were to define sovereignty for coastal states of up to 12 nautical miles over territorial waters, and up to 200 nautical miles over the continental shelf for exploring and exploiting natural resources; states may declare an Exclusive Economic Zone, extending up to 200 nautical miles, to gain further sovereign rights with respect to natural resources or jurisdiction over certain activities; in March 2023 the draft of a further related agreement was finalized, on conserving and sustainably using the marine biodiversity of areas beyond national jurisdiction (see under *Nature Action*); it was formally adopted in June; the following bodies have been est. under UNCLOS: the International Seabed Authority, the Commission on the Limits of the Continental Shelf, and the International Tribunal for the Law of the Sea.

United Nations Scientific Committee on the Effects of Atomic Radiation (UNSCEAR): Vienna International Centre, Wagramerstr. 5, POB 500, 1400 Vienna, Austria; tel. (1) 26060-4360; fax (1) 26060-5902; internet www.unscear.org; f. 1955; secretariat provided by UNEP; convenes annually (70th session: June 2023); Sec. BORISLAVA BATANDJIEVA-METCALF (Slovakia).

Activities

UNEP aims to maintain a constant watch on the changing state of the environment; to analyse trends; to assess problems using a wide range of data and techniques; and to undertake or support projects leading to environmentally sound development. UNEP helps to define and oversee the global environmental agenda, sponsoring international conferences, programmes, plans and agreements regarding all aspects of the environment. It aims to promote its mission through active engagement with the private sector, civil society and other stakeholders.

In June 2022 an international conference titled 'Stockholm+50' was co-hosted by Kenya and Sweden in Stockholm, Sweden, to commemorate the 1972 UN Conference on the Human Environment; this urged genuine commitment to realizing a just transition to sustainable economies. The fourth global session of the UN Science-Policy-Business Forum on the Environment (a biennial series) was convened on the sidelines of Stockholm+50.

In July 2022 the UN General Assembly adopted a landmark resolution that declared the human right to a clean, healthy and sustainable environment. Eight states abstained: Belarus, Cambodia, Ethiopia, the People's Republic of China, Iran, Kyrgyzstan, the Russian Federation and the Syrian Arab Republic.

Medium-Term Strategy: UNEP's Medium-Term Strategy for the period 2022–25, approved by the Assembly in February 2021, aimed to strengthen the Programme's contribution to addressing global environmental and societal challenges and to achieving the UN's 2030 Agenda for Sustainable Development, and its related Sustainable Development Goals (SDGs). It identified climate action, natural action, and chemicals and pollution waste as the key thematic sub-programmes. The Strategy also recognized the need for robust economic governance and innovative science policy, and incorporated these as foundational sub-programmes. In order to deliver on the actions required, the Strategy identified two enabling sub-programmes: finance and economic transformation, and digital transformation. The following were identified as key targets: supporting countries to pursue decarbonization processes, to implement dematerialization practices (limiting the environmental impact of products or services), and to strengthen resilience to climate change; ensuring that states and other stakeholders have increased capacity, finance and access to sustainable technologies to deliver on the adaptation and mitigation commitments of the Paris Agreement; and supporting countries to meet their reporting obligations and implement required transparency framework arrangements.

CLIMATE ACTION

UNEP worked in collaboration with the World Meteorological Organization (WMO) to formulate the 1992 UN Framework Convention on Climate Change (UNFCCC), with the aim of reducing the emission of gases that have a warming effect on the atmosphere (known as greenhouse gases). In 1998 UNEP and WMO established the Intergovernmental Panel on Climate Change (IPCC), as an objective source of scientific information about the warming of the earth's atmosphere.

UNEP's climate action sub-programme aims to achieve long-term climate stability, working in alignment with the emissions reduction targets and climate resilience goals of the Paris Agreement, adopted at the 21st UNFCCC Conference of the Parties (COP) in November 2015.

UNEP, with the UN Industrial Development Organization (UNIDO), hosts a Climate Technology Centre and Network (CTCN) which operates as a part of UNFCCC's Technology Mechanism to accelerate the transfer of climate-related technology and expertise to developing nations. The CTCN's third programme cycle, with a particular focus on Africa, was ongoing during 2023–27. UNEP's Technology Needs Assessment Project aims to support the formulation and implementation of national Technology Needs Assessments (TNAs), within the framework of the UNFCCC, involving, inter alia, detailed analysis of mitigation and adaptation technologies. A Facilitating Implementation and Readiness for Mitigation (FIRM) project works at a national level to develop low carbon strategies, and contributes to the formulation and implementation of National Adaptation Programmes of Action (NAPAs) for addressing climate change.

UNEP's climate change-related activities have a particular focus on strengthening the capabilities of countries to integrate climate change responses into their national development processes, including through adaptation and mitigation initiatives. The latter include a collaborative programme, the UN Reduced Emissions from Deforestation and Forest Degradation (UN-REDD), which was launched in September 2008 by UNEP, the UN Development Programme (UNDP) and the Food and Agriculture Organization of the UN (FAO) to promote a transformation of forest and land use patterns through the implementation at national level of so-called REDD+ strategies.

UNEP encourages the development of and investment in alternative and renewable sources of energy. By August 2023 the UNEP-supported Powering Past Coal Alliance, which had been established in November 2017 to promote renewable energies, comprised 48 national governments, 47 subnational regions, and 71 private corporations. UNEP also supports REN21, a global community representing governments, academia, industry and non-governmental organizations that aims to promote the use of renewable energy sources. UNEP is a member of the Global Bioenergy Partnership to support the sustainable use of biofuels.

Through its Transport Programme UNEP promotes the use of renewable fuels. It also supports the integration of environmental factors into transport planning, leading a worldwide Partnership for Clean Fuels and Vehicles, a Global Fuel Economy Initiative, and a Non-Motorized Transport 'Share the Road' scheme.

UNEP is a founding member of the Climate and Clean Air Coalition (CCAC) to Reduce Short Lived Climate Pollutants (SLCPs), which was launched in February 2012 as an international partnership, with the aim of reducing SLCPs, including methane and black carbon, to counter their negative impact on human health, crop yields and global warming. By August 2023 the partnership comprised 80 governments and 80 non-state partners, and was supporting 75 countries. In October 2021 UNEP launched, with EU support, an International Methane Emissions Observatory to enhance global monitoring and reporting of methane emissions.

NATURE ACTION

UNEP recognizes the urgent need to conserve healthy ecosystems and to prevent further biodiversity loss in order to meet future ecological needs, to enhance human wellbeing and to advance climate change resilience. It supports integrated ecosystem management and the mainstreaming of biodiversity for sustainable development.

UNEP was instrumental in the drafting of the Convention on Biological Diversity (CBD). In June 2018 UNEP, UNDP and the CBD Secretariat collectively initiated the UN Biodiversity Lab, an open source interactive mapping platform which was designed to support policymakers in addressing conservation and development challenges. A Global Biodiversity Information Facility (GBIF) was established in 2001, to provide open and free access to data on biodiversity. By August 2023 this comprised 89,110 data sets, and more than 2,345 records. The GBIF has also contributed to the development of a Biodiversity Habitat Index. A new Kunming-Montreal Global Biodiversity Framework was adopted at the second part of the 15th Conference of the Parties (COP) of the CBD, which was hosted by the People's Republic of China in Montreal, Canada in December 2022 (q.v.).

In December 2017 the UN General Assembly established an Intergovernmental Conference on Marine Biodiversity of Areas Beyond National Jurisdiction (BBNJ), tasked with drafting a legally binding instrument, under UNCLOS, aimed at conserving and sustainably using the marine biological diversity in such areas. The inaugural session of the Intergovernmental Conference was convened in September 2018. The fifth was initiated in August 2022 and resumed in late February–early March 2023, and concluded a final draft of an agreement on BBNJ. This noted the need for international co-operation to protect the high seas on behalf of present and future generations, and to address coherently ongoing biodiversity loss and degradation of oceanic ecosystems—attributed to impacts of climate change such as ocean deoxygenation and warming; to plastic and other marine pollution; acidification; and to the unsustainable use of oceanic resources. An international access and benefit-sharing committee was to be established, to guide the fair and equitable sharing of monetary and non-monetary benefits arising from the use of marine genetic resources. The agreement also provided for the development of marine protected areas and environmental impact assessments, and for a mechanism to resolve disputes. A scientific and technical body, comprising elected marine experts, was also to be established, as well as a capacity-building and transfer of marine technology committee, a clearing house, an implementation and compliance committee, and a secretariat. The Treaty on BBNJ was formally adopted by consensus at a further resumed session of the Intergovernmental Conference, held in June; it was to enter into force 120 days after the 60th ratification.

In January 2020 UNEP and the IUCN initiated a €20m. Global Fund for Ecosystem-based Adaptation, to provide seed capital for rapid targeted support mechanisms promoting innovative approaches to ecosystem-based adaptation strategies. In March 2019 the UN General Assembly designated UNEP and FAO as the lead agencies of the UN Decade on Ecosystem Restoration (2021–30). At the launch of the Decade, in June 2021, UNEP published a synthesis report, *Ecosystem Restoration for People, Nature and Climate*, to demonstrate the urgent need for active engagement in re-establishing healthy ecosystems.

In accordance with its medium-term strategy, from 2022 UNEP was committed to increasing its collaboration with international partners to strengthen the linkages between biodiversity and health and to implement biosecurity measures. In April 2022 UNEP, the World Health Organization (WHO), FAO and the World Organisation for Animal Health concluded a Memorandum of Understanding that provided for the establishment of a Quadripartite Collaboration for One Health, which was collectively to address challenges at the human-animal-plant-ecosystem interface.

UNEP promotes international co-operation in the management of river basins and coastal areas and the development of tools and guidelines to achieve the sustainable management of freshwater and coastal resources. UNEP's Regional Seas Programme, incorporating relevant conventions and action plans, promotes the sustainable management and use of marine and coastal ecosystems.

RESOURCE EFFICIENCY

UNEP encourages governments and the private sector to develop and adopt policies and practices that are cleaner and safer, make efficient use of natural resources, ensure the environmentally sound management of chemicals, and reduce pollution and risks to human health and the environment. UNEP also promotes the transfer of appropriate technologies, and organizes conferences and training workshops to support sustainable production and consumption practices.

In November 2011, under the auspices of UNEP and UNIDO, the global network for Resource Efficient and Cleaner Production (RECPnet) was launched, with a focus on developing and transition countries (by 2023 it was active in more than 70 states). In February 2021 UNEP, with UNIDO and the European Commission, initiated a Global Alliance on Circular Economy and Resource Efficiency to promote broad collaboration on initiatives relating to the circular economy and sustainable consumption and production.

The International Resource Panel (q.v.) works, under UNEP auspices, to address over-consumption, wastage and ecological harm. A 10-Year Framework of Programmes (10YFP) on Sustainable Consumption and Production Patterns was initiated in 2012, hosted by UNEP. A progress report on 10YFP, released in July 2022, emphasized the programme's contribution to global sustainability and to recovery from the COVID-19 pandemic.

Prior to UNEA-5 (initiated in February 2021, with a concluding session held in February–March 2022) UNEP published *Making Peace with Nature*, drawing together findings of its recent major studies and presenting a transformative approach to addressing biodiversity loss, waste and pollution, and climate change—described as the interconnected planetary crises. The Assembly called for greater multilateral co-operation and the urgent adoption of sustainable consumption and production patterns. In March UNEP published its first *Food Waste Index*, which reported that 931m. metric tons of food waste had been generated in 2019, some 17% of total global food production. With FAO, UNEP sponsors the International Day of Awareness of Food Loss and Waste, held on 29 September since 2020.

CHEMICALS AND POLLUTION ACTION

UNEP aims to provide leadership in the sound management of chemicals and waste, in order to address the wide-ranging related human health and environmental concerns. It supports the objectives of various multilateral environmental agreements, and prioritizes the implementation of strong regulatory frameworks.

UNEP administers the Basel Convention on the Control of Transboundary Movements of Hazardous Wastes and their Disposal, which entered into force in 1992 with the aim of preventing the uncontrolled movement and disposal of toxic and other hazardous wastes, particularly the illegal dumping of waste in developing countries by companies from industrialized countries. At August 2023 there were 191 parties to the Convention. In August 2016 the inaugural meeting of an Informal Group on Household Waste was held, in Montevideo, Uruguay, under the auspices of the Convention.

In February 2004 the Rotterdam Convention on the Prior Informed Consent Procedure for Certain Hazardous Chemicals and Pesticides in International Trade entered into force, having been formulated and promoted by UNEP, in collaboration with FAO. The Convention (which had 165 parties by August 2023) aims to reduce risks to human health and the environment by restricting the production, export and use of hazardous substances and by enhancing information exchange procedures. UNEP played a leading role in formulating, and provides technical support to, the 2004 Stockholm Convention on Persistent Organic Pollutants (POPs), addressing particularly hazardous pollutants: pesticides, industrial chemicals and harmful substances that are not produced intentionally. At August 2023 the Stockholm Convention had 186 parties. By that time some 26 POPs were listed under Annex A of the Convention, which requires their elimination; two were listed under Annex B (requiring restrictions on their production and use); and seven unintentionally produced substances were listed under Annex C (they were to be minimized).

UNEP promotes environmentally sustainable water management, regards the unsustainable use of water as one of the most urgent environmental issues, and places a particular focus on shared transboundary waters. The Global Programme of Action for the Protection of the Marine Environment from Land-based Activities (the GPA, adopted in November 1995) focuses on the effects of pollution on freshwater resources, marine biodiversity and the coastal ecosystems of small island developing states (SIDS). A Global Wastewater Initiative (GW2I) was established in 2013 within the framework of the GPA. The third target of SDG 6: Ensure access to water and sanitation for all includes 'halving the proportion of untreated wastewater by 2030 and substantially increasing recycling and safe reuse globally'. A Global Partnership on Marine Litter was established in 2012. In early 2017 UNEP launched a UN Clean Seas campaign to address the issue that 80% of all marine litter, some 8m. metric tons collected each year, consists of single-use or non-recoverable plastic; this generally has a slow rate of degradation, and has been identified as entering the human food chain, and killing marine life. By August 2023 69 countries had joined the Clean Seas campaign.

A joint meeting of the COPs of the Basel, Rotterdam and Stockholm (BRS) Conventions that was held in late April–early May 2019 agreed to put in place a legally binding global framework on monitoring, tracking and managing plastic waste, with a view to restricting dumping in developing nations (countries proposing to export plastic waste were to be required to receive explicit prior consent from the governments of receiving states) and to prompting countries to manage their own plastic waste at the point of generation. In mid-May, accordingly, the parties to the Basel Convention determined to categorize plastic waste of a mixed, contaminated, non-hazardous, non-recyclable, or difficult-to-recycle nature under that Convention's Annex II, i.e. as waste that requires special consideration and transboundary movement restrictions. The parties to the Basel Convention also established a Plastic Waste Partnership, tasked with collecting information and undertaking analysis of the environmental, economic and social impacts of plastics-related policies.

In March 2022 the second session of the fifth UNEA (UNEA-5.2) resolved to establish an intergovernmental negotiating committee to draft a legally-binding multilateral instrument to address plastic pollution, including production, design and disposal.

UNEP was the principal agency in formulating the 1987 Montreal Protocol to the Vienna Convention for the Protection of the Ozone Layer (1985), which provided for a 50% reduction by 2000 in the production of chlorofluorocarbons (CFCs). An amendment to the Protocol was adopted in 1990, which required complete cessation of the production of CFCs by 2000 in industrialized countries and by 2010 in developing countries. The Copenhagen Amendment, adopted in 1992, stipulated the phasing out of production of hydrochlorofluorocarbons (HCFCs) by 2030 in developed countries and by 2040 in developing nations. Subsequent amendments aimed to introduce a licensing system for all controlled substances, and imposed stricter controls on the import and export of HCFCs, and on the production and consumption of bromochloromethane (Halon-1011, an industrial solvent and fire extinguisher). In September 2007 the states parties to the Vienna Convention agreed to advance the deadline for the elimination of HCFCs to 2020 in developed countries and to 2030 in developing countries. In September 2009 the Vienna Convention and Montreal Protocol became the first agreements on the global environment to attain universal ratification; universal ratification of amendments to the Montreal Protocol was achieved in December 2014. UNEP is the implementing agency of the Multilateral Fund for the Implementation of the Montreal Protocol. The Fund, supported by UNEP's OzonAction unit within its Law Division, strengthens the capacity of developing states parties, through their National Ozone Units, to comply with the obligations of the Protocol. (By August 2023 147 of the 197 Parties to the Protocol—known as Article 5 countries—were in compliance.) UNEP, UNDP, the World Bank and UNIDO are the sponsors of the Fund. In November 2019 the states parties to the Montreal Protocol agreed terms of reference for negotiations on an 11th replenishment of the Fund, to cover 2021–23. The process of replenishment was delayed, however, by the onset of the COVID-19 pandemic crisis. In October 2016 the states parties, gathered in Kigali, Rwanda, adopted the Kigali Amendment to the Montreal Protocol, in accordance with which a phased reduction by more than 80% in the production and consumption of hydrofluorocarbon (HFC) gases—substances used increasingly in air conditioners and refrigerators—was to be implemented over 30 years. (HFC consumption levels were to be frozen from 2024 in most developing countries or, exceptionally, from 2028.) The Kigali Amendment entered into force on 1 January 2019; it had received 152 by August 2023.

In February 2006 an International Conference on Chemicals Management (ICCM) adopted a Strategic Approach to International Chemicals Management (SAICM), which aimed to minimize significant adverse impacts of chemicals on the environment and human health. The fourth ICCM session, convened in September–October 2015, addressed issues relating to environmentally persistent pharmaceutical pollutants and highly hazardous pesticides, and agreed a process aimed at ensuring the sound management of chemicals beyond 2020. Deliberations on a new chemicals and waste management framework commenced in 2022; the framework was to be finalized at ICCM5, scheduled to be held in late September 2023, in Bonn, Germany, having been postponed twice as a result of the COVID-19 pandemic.

In October 2013 an intergovernmental meeting in Minamata, Japan, adopted the Minamata Convention on Mercury, which provides for controls relating to the usage, release, mining, import and export, and safe storage of mercury (which acts in humans as a neurotoxin), and for the phasing-out of the production of several mercury-containing products. The Convention entered into force on 16 August 2017, and by August 2023 had been ratified by 144 states and the EU. The fourth Minamata COP—convened in two segments, in November 2021 (virtually) and in late March 2022 (in Bali, Indonesia)—extended the list of mercury-containing products that were to be phased out. It was envisaged that a deadline of 2025 set by the meeting for the phasing-out of compact fluorescent lamps (in favour of non-toxic and more energy-efficient and cost-effective Light Emitting Diode—LED—lighting) would save 26.2m. metric tons of mercury pollution by 2050. The phasing-out of linear fluorescent lamps (fluorescent tube lighting commonly used in shops and offices) was to be addressed by COP5, to be held in October–November 2023, in Geneva, Switzerland.

SCIENCE POLICY

UNEP is mandated to analyse the world environment, to provide early warning information, to assess global and regional trends, and to equip policymakers with data to underpin planning. It is determined to make that data widely available, in order both to broaden societal engagement with environmental challenges and to place science at the centre of transformative decision making. Annual flagship reports produced by UNEP include the *Emissions Gap Report* (assessing progress made to meet commitments under the Paris Agreement on climate change); the *Adaptation Gap Report* (the 2022 edition, released in November of that year, noted that while at least 84% of the parties to the UNFCCC had established adaptation plans, strategies, policies and legislation, sufficient funding to support their implementation was not forthcoming); the *Production Gap Report*; and the biennial *Inclusive Wealth Report*, which evaluates the sustainability of economies and wellbeing of citizens (with inclusive wealth defined as the social value of all a country's assets, including natural resources, production, and human capital). UNEP's *Frontiers* report series identifies emerging issues of environmental concern. Furthermore, with UNEP support, the Intergovernmental Panel on Climate Change and Intergovernmental Science-Policy Platform on Biodiversity and Ecosystem Services issue systematic assessments in their respective areas of interest.

UNEP's Global Environment Outlook (GEO) process of environmental analysis and assessment, launched in 1995, is supported by an extensive network of collaborating centres. The sixth 'umbrella' report on the GEO process (*GEO-6*) was endorsed by UNEA-4 in March 2019. It emphasized that technology and finance should be mobilized to support environmental protections, sustainable development, and a near zero-waste economy—warning that, otherwise, progressive damage to the Earth would have dire impacts on human health and lead to numerous premature deaths, particularly in Africa, Asia and the Middle East. The report also warned, *inter alia*, that children's neurodevelopment and adult fertility were being put at risk by endocrine disruptors (found in many products, such as some plastic containers, detergents and cosmetics), and that pollutants in freshwater systems risked accelerating antimicrobial resistance (AMR). A GEO-7 process was initiated in 2022.

During 2020 UNEP developed a World Environment Situation Room, which was to serve as its online platform for sharing data, information and knowledge. It aimed to use geospatial technologies and other real-time monitoring to highlight environmental threats, health risks, and policy priorities.

UNEP is a sponsoring agency of the Joint Group of Experts on the Scientific Aspects of Marine Environmental Pollution (GESAMP) and contributes to the preparation of reports on the state of the marine environment and on the impact on it of land-based activities. In March 2019 GESAMP issued *Guidelines for the Monitoring and Assessment of Plastic Litter in the Ocean*. In 2020 UNEP established an International Seagrass Experts Network to support research and the exchange of knowledge.

ENVIRONMENTAL GOVERNANCE

UNEP promotes international environmental legislation and the development of policy tools and guidelines aimed at achieving the sustainable management of the world environment and the objectives of the Paris Agreement and the 2030 Agenda. Through its regional offices, and working with other UN agencies, UNEP helps governments to implement multilateral environmental agreements, and to report on their results. At national level it assists governments to develop and implement appropriate environmental instruments, in particular through its so-called Montevideo Programme for the Development and Periodic Review of Environmental Law. UNEP also aims to co-ordinate policy initiatives, and provides training in various aspects of environmental law and its applications.

UNEP hosts the secretariats of a number of global and regional environmental conventions. It also works closely with other mechanisms, such as the Global Environment Facility and the Green Climate Fund, to support countries to meet their environmental obligations. UNEP co-Chairs (with CITES) the InforMEA initiative, which collates comprehensive information on multilateral global and regional, and bilateral environmental instruments. Additionally, InforMEA provides relevant introductory courses and case studies, and information on environmental events. Jointly with FAO and the International Union for the Conservation of Nature (IUCN), UNEP maintains ECOLEX, an internet-based resource for biodiversity-related international and national legislation and policy.

UNEP endorsed the decision of the UN General Assembly in May 2018 to open negotiations on the development of a Global Pact for the Environment, that was to harmonize existing environmental legislation into one document with the aim of assisting governments to formulate and implement localized environmental rules.

UNEP supports member states in combating environmental degradation and natural resources mismanagement, and promotes the integration of environmental concerns into risk reduction policy and practices. A UNEP-UN Office for the Coordination of Humanitarian Affairs Joint Environment Unit identifies acute environmental risks, and co-ordinates and mobilizes appropriate emergency responses to emergencies (including natural disasters, industrial accidents and conflicts). It uses a Flash Environmental Assessment Tool (FEAT) to assess risks from such sites. The Unit hosts an Environmental Emergencies Centre. Impact assessments have been conducted in recent years in Afghanistan, Colombia, the DRC, Iraq, Kosovo, Lebanon, the Palestinian territories, Somalia, South Sudan, Sudan, Ukraine and the Western Balkans. UNEP evaluates the risks posed by environmental impacts on human health, security and livelihoods, and provides field-based capacity building and technical support, in affected countries. It collaborates with the World Bank, UN agencies and other partners to compile Post-Disaster Needs Assessments.

FINANCIAL AND ECONOMIC TRANSFORMATIONS

UNEP recognizes that a transformation of financial and business practices, while promoting more sustainable patterns of consumption or production, is required to achieve the 2030 Agenda and long-term environmental stability. Its activities include promoting environmentally sound technologies; 'green' subsidies; more efficient or circular global value chains; and reducing the environmental footprint of trade.

UNEP is a founding member of the Partnership for Action on Green Economy (PAGE), initiated in February 2013 collectively with the ILO, UNIDO and the UN Institute for Training and Research. During 2021–30 PAGE aimed to support 30 countries in developing green economy strategies in order to generate employment, promote social equity, strengthen livelihoods, enhance environmental stewardship, and ensure sustained growth aligned with the SDGs, the Paris Agreement and the Kunming-Montreal Global Biodiversity Framework. The Green Growth Knowledge Platform, launched in January 2012 by UNEP, the World Bank and other partners, aims to advance efforts to identify and address major knowledge gaps in green growth theory and practice, and to support countries in formulating and implementing policies aimed at developing a green economy. It comprises a Green Policy Platform, Green Industry Platform, and Green Finance Platform. The Economics of Ecosystems and Biodiversity global initiative aims, under the auspices of UNEP, to highlight the values of biodiversity and ecosystem services in economic terms and translate these into decision making.

The UNEP Finance Initiative (UNEP FI), established in 1992 as a partnership between UNEP and the global financial sector, encourages banks, insurance companies and other financial institutions to invest in an environmentally responsible way. A biennial UNEP FI Global Roundtable meeting is held (the 17th took place in October 2022, as a virtual event). UNEP FI regional roundtables are also convened.

DIGITAL TRANSFORMATION

In March 2019 UNEA-4 mandated UNEP with an institutional responsibility to integrate environmental and sustainability values and goals into the global digital economy, as well as to support the harmonization and greater accessibility of relevant data.

In March 2021 UNEP, UNDP and partners established the global Coalition for Digital Environmental Sustainability (CODES), which aimed to anchor environmental sustainability concerns in the Roadmap for Digital Cooperation—an initiative of the UN Secretary-General that was launched in June 2020.

Finance

UNEP's budget for 2022–23 totalled US $200m. UNEP is allocated a contribution from the UN regular budget, and derives most of its finances from voluntary contributions to the Environment Fund and to trust funds.

Publications

Annual Report.
Adaptation Gap Report.
Emissions Gap Report (annually).
Frontiers (normally annually, addresses emerging environmental issues).
Global Chemicals Outlook.
Green Economy Report.
Inclusive Wealth Report.
Our Planet (quarterly).
Ozonaction Newsletter (quarterly).
Planet in Peril: Atlas of Current Threats to People and the Environment.
Production Gap Report (every 2 years).
Sustainable Finance Progress Report.
UNEP Year Book (annually).

Studies, reports (including the *Global Environment Outlook* series), regional and thematic updates, atlases, legal texts, technical guidelines.

Associated Bodies

Global Environment Facility (GEF): c/o United Nations Development Programme, 304 East 45th St, 9th Floor, New York, NY 10017, USA; e-mail gefinfo@undp.org; internet www.thegef.org; f. 1991, by UNEP, the World Bank and UNDP; aims to support the implementation in developing countries of projects in the six thematic areas of climate change; the conservation of biological diversity; the protection of international waters; forests; arresting land degradation; and addressing harmful chemicals and waste. Capacity building to allow countries to meet their obligations under international environmental agreements, and adaptation to climate change, are priority cross-cutting components of these projects. UNEP services the Scientific and Technical Advisory Panel, which provides expert advice on GEF programmes and operational strategies. Funding is channelled through a GEF Trust Fund, a GEF Least Developed Countries Fund (LDC-F—established to address the special needs of the LDCs in relation to the UN Framework Convention on Climate Change, with a particular emphasis on financing the preparation and implementation of NAPAs), and a Special Climate Change Fund (SCCF, established in 2001). In June 2022 29 donor countries pledged US $5,330m. for the 8th periodic replenishment of GEF funds (GEF-8), covering the period July 2022–June 2026; the 7th GEF Assembly was convened in Vancouver, Canada, in Aug. 2023; the GEF acts as the financial mechanism for the following major international environmental conventions: the Minamata Convention on Mercury, Stockholm Convention on Persistent Organic Pollutants, UN Convention on Biological Diversity, UN Convention to Combat Desertification, and the UN Framework Convention on Climate Change; the GEF has 18 partner agencies; Chair. and CEO Dr CARLOS MANUEL RODRIGUEZ (Costa Rica).

Intergovernmental Panel on Climate Change (IPCC): c/o WMO, 7 bis, ave de la Paix, 1211 Geneva 2, Switzerland; tel. 227308208; fax 227308025; e-mail ipcc-sec@wmo.int; internet www.ipcc.ch; f. 1988 by UNEP and the World Meteorological Organization (WMO); comprises some 3,000 scientists as well as other experts and representatives of all UN mem. govts. Approximately every 5 years the IPCC assesses all available scientific, technical and socio-economic information on anthropogenic climate change. The IPCC provides, on request, scientific, technical and socioeconomic advice to the COP to the UN Framework Convention on Climate Change and to its subsidiary bodies, and compiles reports on specialized topics, such as *Aviation and the Global Atmosphere*, *Regional Impacts of Climate Change*, and *Managing the Risks of Extreme Events and Disasters to Advance Climate Change Adaptation*. The IPCC informs and guides, but does not prescribe, policy. On 1 Nov. 2014 the IPCC released a *Synthesis Report*, concluding its Fifth Assessment process; it emphasized that the immediate introduction of new policies and forms of international co-operation was required to achieve necessary reductions in greenhouse gas emissions (of some 40%–70% globally by 2050) at a manageable cost. The 47th session of the IPCC, convened in March 2018, established new task groups on gender, and on the implications for the Panel's future work of the 2015 Paris Agreement on climate change. In April 2016 the IPCC agreed—at the request of the UNFCCC—to produce a special report on the impact of global warming at 1.5°C above pre-industrial levels, and on related global greenhouse gas emission pathways: this was issued in Oct. 2018, and concluded that global warming of even 0.5°C in excess of 1.5°C would expose a significantly higher proportion of the global population to water stress and food scarcity, would increase the incidence and severity of extremely hot weather, would exacerbate sea level rises and almost eradicate ocean corals, and would render insects more than two times as likely to lose one-half of their habitat (with an onwards impact on crop pollination); an IPCC special report on *Climate change, desertification, land degradation, sustainable land management, food security, and greenhouse gas fluxes in terrestrial ecosystems* was considered by the 50th IPCC session in Aug. 2019; in Sept. a further special report, *Ocean and Cryosphere in a Changing Climate*, was presented to the 51st session; a second *Synthesis Report* was released in March 2023 (concluding the Sixth Assessment—'AR6' process, which was initiated in Oct. 2015); 3 instalments, each compiled by a dedicated working group, were published in advance of the full AR6 *Synthesis Report*: the first instalment, *AR6 Climate Change 2021: The Physical Science Basis*, released in Aug. 2021, emphasized that it was unequivocal that the warming consequences of human influence had caused rapid and unprecedented changes to the Earth's atmosphere, oceans, cryosphere and biosphere, and noted that evidence of changes in extremes—e.g. in relation to heavy precipitation, tropical cyclones, heatwaves and droughts—had strengthened since AR5; and now envisaged global warming in excess of 2°C during the 21st century, unless 'deep reductions' in CO_2 were implemented (it was noted that many changes attributed to greenhouse gas emissions, particularly concerning the ocean, global sea level and ice sheets, were irreversible over a very long term); *AR6 Climate Change 2022: Impacts, Adaptation and Vulnerability*, released in Feb. 2022, placed an increased focus on the integration of natural, social and economic sciences—acknowledging the interdependence of humans, biodiversity and climate, and the interaction between climate change and global trends such as mounting (particularly poorly planned) urbanization, the unsustainable use of natural resources, and damage caused by extreme events; it emphasized the need to restore degraded ecosystems and to conserve up to one-half of the Earth's land, freshwater and ocean habitats, and called for urgent, ambitious, accelerated action on climate change adaptation, combined with simultaneous rapid, deep reductions in greenhouse gas emissions; finally, *AR6 Climate Change 2022: Mitigation of Climate Change*, which was issued in April, emphasized that developing appropriate policy measures, technologies and infrastructures to bring about major energy sector and lifestyle transitions could lead by 2050 to a 40%–70% reduction in global greenhouse gas emissions: fossil fuel use would need to be replaced by alternatives such as hydrogen and by widespread electrification, while more effective energy efficiency would be required, involving, *inter alia*, lower consumption, a more efficient use of materials, advancing carbon capture and storage policies on land use, and measures such as promoting 'walkable' cities and zero carbon buildings; the report emphasized the need to address continuing investment gaps. The *AR6 Synthesis Report*, published on 20 March 2023, integrated the findings of its working groups and the special reports commissioned since the process began in 2016; it modelled a range of scenarios given the observed warmings, changes and impacts of future and implemented policies, but reaffirmed that widespread adverse effects of climate change caused by human activity were likely to continue to intensify; Chair. Prof. Dr JAMES (JIM) FERGUSON SKEA (UK); Sec. ABDALAH MOKSSIT (Morocco).

Intergovernmental Science-Policy Platform on Biodiversity and Ecosystem Services (IPBES): UN Campus, Platz der Vereinten Nationen 1, 53113 Bonn, Germany; e-mail secretariat@ipbes.net; internet www.ipbes.net; f. 2012; administered by UNEP; undertakes, periodically, scientific assessments of biodiversity and ecosystems, with a focus on outputs beneficial to humans, including timber, fresh water, fish and climatic stability. IPBES issued a *Thematic Assessment of Pollinators, Pollination and Food Production* in Feb. 2016, and an *Assessment Report on Land Degradation and Restoration* as well as related regional assessment reports (covering Africa, the Americas, Asia and the Pacific, and Europe and Central Asia) in March 2018; the final draft of an *IPBES Global Assessment Report on Biodiversity and Ecosystem Services*—the culmination of a scientific assessment process formally launched in Feb. 2016—was released in May 2019. With a view to enhancing policymaking, the *Global Assessment Report* aimed to provide an overview of the state of global nature and ecosystems, evaluating changes undergone during the previous 5 decades, and including a systematic examination of local and indigenous knowledge; it also considered progress achieved in implementing relevant SDGs, targets, and the Paris Agreement on climate change, and implications for economies, food security, livelihoods, and quality of life of the unprecedented rate of erosion of biodiversity; it noted that up to 1m. species were threatened with extinction and that populations of mammals, fish, birds, reptiles and amphibians had decreased by 60% in the preceding 40 years; the report strongly emphasized the interrelationship between climate change, biodiversity loss and human wellbeing and stated that urgent global action, such as a redirection of government subsidies towards regenerative agriculture, was required to maintain sustainable natural support systems for humanity; mems: 139 states; Chair. ANA MARÍA HERNANDEZ SALGAR (Colombia); Exec. Sec. ANNA LARIGAUDERIE (France).

International Resource Panel (IRP): c/o UNEP Division of Technology, Industry and Economics, 15 rue de Milan, 75441 Paris, Cedex 09, France; tel. 1-44-37-14-50; fax 1-44-37-14-74; e-mail unep-irpsecretariat@un.org; internet resourcepanel.org; f. 2007; aims to build knowledge with a view to improving the local/global use of resources and thus reduce over-consumption, wastage and ecological harm; participating scientists report on technical, scientific and socioeconomic findings relating to resources use; the IRP provides advice to, and fosters linkages between, policymakers, industry stakeholders, and communities; issues assessment reports on, *inter alia,* urbanization, decoupling economic growth from adverse environmental impacts, resource efficiency and governance, pollution reduction, water, land and soils, metals, and food. The IRP's *Global Resources Outlook 2019*, published during UNEA-4 in March of that year, observed that rapid growth in the extraction of minerals represented the principal cause of biodiversity loss and climate change; the report noted that since 1970 resource extraction had increased from 27,000m. metric tons to 92,000m. metric tons in 1997, and stated that the extraction and processing of materials, food and fuels accounted for more than 90% of biodiversity loss and water stress, and for one-half of total global greenhouse gas emissions; meanwhile, the global population had doubled over that period; the report called for urgent systemic reform of resource use. Steering Cttee comprises representatives of UNEP, the European Commission and 27 govts; Co-Chair. IZABELLA MÔNICA VIEIRA TEIXEIRA (Brazil), JANEZ POTOČNIK (Slovenia); Head of Secretariat MERLYN VAN VOORE (South Africa).

The Rio Conventions

Three conventions arose from the UN Conference on Environment and Development (known as the Earth Summit), that was convened in Rio de Janeiro, Brazil, in June 1992: the Convention on Biological Diversity, the UN Framework Convention on Climate Change, and the UN Convention to Combat Desertification in Those Countries Experiencing Serious Drought and/or Desertification, Particularly in Africa (which entered into force in December 1966).

Convention on Biological Diversity: 413 St Jacques St, Suite 800, Montréal, QC H2Y 1N9, Canada; tel. (514) 288-2220; fax (514) 288-6588; e-mail secretariat@cbd.int; internet www.cbd.int; the CBD entered into force at the end of 1993, and is focused on the preservation of the Earth's immense variety of plant and animal species, in particular those threatened with extinction; a Cartagena Protocol on Biosafety regulates the transboundary movement and use of living modified organisms (LMOs) resulting from biotechnology: it entered into force in Sept. 2003, and had been ratified by 173 states parties by Aug. 2023. An Advanced Informed Agreement procedure to govern the import of LMOs and a Biosafety Clearing-House mechanism to facilitate information sharing on LMOs have been established under the Cartagena Protocol. In Oct. 2010 the 10th Conf. of the Parties (COP) to the CBD, meeting in Nagoya, Japan, approved the Nagoya Protocol to the CBD, focused on establishing an international regime on access to and benefit sharing of genetic resources; this entered into force in Oct. 2014 and had 140 ratifications at Aug. 2023. The meeting also adopted a supplementary agreement to the Cartagena Protocol (the so-called Nagoya-Kuala Lumpur Supplementary Protocol) concerned with liability and redress; it entered into force in March 2018, and had received 54 notifications by Aug. 2023. The 12th COP to the CBD, convened in Oct. 2012, in Hyderabad, India, determined formally to classify marine areas of ecological or biological significance. In July 2018 an MOU was concluded between the CBD and FAO's International Treaty on Plant Genetic Resources for Food and Agriculture. The 5th edition of the CBD's *Global Biodiversity Outlook*, issued in Sept. 2020, recommended 8 transformative actions for reversing the degradation of the natural world: conserving land and forest ecosystems; designing sustainable agriculture systems; enabling sustainable (and more plant-based) food systems; ensuring sustainable fisheries and oceans; creating green cities and infrastructure; ensuring sustainable freshwater systems; undertaking sustainable climate action; and implementing an integrated 'One Health' approach to promote healthy ecosystems and healthy people. The first phase of the 15th CBD COP, held in Oct. 2021, in a hybrid in-person and virtual format hosted from Kunming, People's Rep. of China, adopted the Kunming Declaration (themed 'Ecological Civilization: Building a Shared Future for All Life on Earth'), in which more than 100 states committed to mainstreaming biodiversity in decision making and to adopting an effective post-2020 Global Biodiversity Framework (GBF); the meeting also established a US $223.4m. Kunming Biodiversity Fund, which was to support biodiversity conservation in developing states; the second phase of the COP, was hosted by China from Montréal, Canada in Dec. 2022; the meeting endorsed the Kunming-Montreal GBF, which incorporated 23 new environmental targets to counter the loss of biodiversity including the so-called 30x30 aim (Target 3) to protect 30% of land, inland waters and oceans by 2030 and to restore 30% of degraded terrestrial and marine environments; other targets included reducing by half the risk from pesticides, nutrients lost to the environment and the rate of introduction of invasive alien species; govts agreed that by 2030 biodiversity-related funding should reach $200,000m. and subsidies that harm biodiversity should be phased out; the meeting approved the establishment of a Global Biodiversity Framework Fund, to help implement the Kunming-Montreal GBF; this was launched in Aug. 2023 at the 7th GEF Assembly meeting, held in Vancouver, Canada; by Aug. 2023 195 states and the EU were parties to the CBD (the USA and Holy See were not signatories); Exec. Sec. DAVID COOPER (acting).

United Nations Framework Convention on Climate Change (UNFCCC): UN Campus, Platz der Vereinten Nationen 1, 53113 Bonn, Germany; tel. (228) 8151000; fax (228) 815-1999; e-mail secretariat@unfccc.int; internet unfccc.int; WMO and UNEP worked together to formulate the UNFCCC, in response to the first report of the IPCC, issued in Aug. 1990, which predicted an increase in the concentration of greenhouse gases (i.e. carbon dioxide and other gases that have a warming effect on the atmosphere) owing to human activity. The Convention was signed in May 1992 and entered into force in March 1994, committing countries to submitting reports on measures being taken to reduce the emission of greenhouse gases and recommending the stabilization of these emissions at 1990 levels by 2000; however, this was not legally binding. Following the 2nd session of the COP of the Convention, held in July 1996, multilateral negotiations ensued to formulate legally binding objectives for emission limitations. At the 3rd COP, held in Kyoto, Japan, in Dec. 1997, 38 industrial nations endorsed mandatory reductions of combined emissions of the 6 major gases by an average of 5.2% during the period 2008–12, to pre-1990 levels. The so-called Kyoto Protocol was to enter into force once ratified by at least 55 countries party to the UNFCCC, including industrialized countries with combined emissions of carbon dioxide in 1990 accounting for at least 55% of the total global greenhouse gas emissions by developed nations. The 4th COP, convened in Buenos Aires, Argentina, in Nov. 1998, adopted a plan of action to promote implementation of the UNFCCC and to finalize the operational details of the Kyoto Protocol. These included the Clean Development Mechanism, by which industrialized countries may obtain credits towards achieving their reduction targets by assisting developing countries to implement emission-reducing measures, and a system of trading emission quotas. In March 2002 the USA announced that it would not ratify the Kyoto Protocol. The Protocol eventually entered into force on 16 Feb. 2005. The UN Climate Change Conference (COP14), convened in Poznań, Poland, in Dec. 2008, finalized the Kyoto Protocol's Adaptation Fund, which was to finance projects and programmes in developing signatory states that were particularly vulnerable to the adverse effects of climate change. The Copenhagen Accord, agreed at COP15, held in Dec. 2009, determined that international cooperative action should be taken to reduce global greenhouse gas emissions so as to hold the ongoing increase in global temperature below 2°C; it was agreed that enhanced efforts should be undertaken to reduce vulnerability to climate change in developing countries, with special reference to LDCs, SIDS and Africa; developed countries agreed to pursue strengthened carbon emissions targets, while developing nations were to implement actions to slow down growth in emissions. A Green Climate Fund was to be established to support climate change mitigation actions in developing countries, and a Technology Mechanism was also to be established, with the aim of accelerating technology devt and transfer in support of climate change adaptation and mitigation activities. COP16, convened in Cancún, Mexico, in Nov.–Dec. 2010, approved the establishment of a Cancún Adaptation Framework and associated Adaptation Committee. COP17, held in Durban, South Africa, in Nov.–Dec. 2011 concluded with an agreement on a Durban Platform for Enhanced Action. The Platform incorporated agreements to extend the Kyoto provisions regarding emissions reductions by industrialized nations beyond the expiry at the end of 2012 of the initial commitment phase, and to commence negotiations on a new, inclusive global emissions arrangement (to be concluded by 2015). During the conference sufficient funds were committed to enable the inauguration of the Green Climate Fund. In Dec. 2012 COP18, convened in Doha, Qatar, approved an amendment of the Kyoto Protocol to initiate a 2nd commitment period of 8 years. States parties committed to reducing greenhouse gas emissions by at least 18% below 1990 levels during 2013–20. COP18 also secured a commitment by developed nations to mobilize US $100,000m. to support climate change adaptation and mitigation initiatives in affected developing countries. A pledging conference for the (Sondgo, South Korea-based) Green Climate Fund was convened in Berlin, Germany, in Nov. 2014. In July 2015 the Green Climate Fund accredited UNEP as one of the entities through which it was to channel funding; by Aug. 2023 the Fund had committed $12,800m. towards 228 projects. In Dec. 2015 a plenary meeting of COP21, convened in Paris, France, established the Comité de Paris (superseding the Durban Platform) to facilitate and co-ordinate negotiations in order to secure a new climate agreement. The so-called Paris Agreement was adopted on 12 Dec. and incorporated commitments to reduce emissions and to strengthen, through increased financing, the ability of developing countries to adapt to climate change and to recover from the impact of climate-related shocks; a multilateral stocktaking review was to be convened every 5 years, while national action plans, in the form of voluntary national determined contributions (NDCs), were to be submitted for review and updated every 5 years; significantly, states parties agreed to include in the agreement a declared aim to pursue efforts to limit the rise in global temperatures by 2100 to 1.5°C (over pre-industrial levels), alongside the main objective of limiting the rise to 2°C. At a ceremony held in April 2016 175 states parties signed the Paris Agreement and 15 also deposited their instruments of ratification; the accord was to enter into effect 30 days following ratification by at least 55 nations responsible for 55% of man-made greenhouse gas emissions. In early Sept. the People's Republic of China and the USA (together responsible for some 38% of global carbon emissions) both ratified the Convention during the summit of G20 states; the required ratification thresholds were achieved on 5 Oct., enabling the Agreement to enter into force on 4 Nov. COP22 and the first meeting of the parties to the Paris Agreement were convened in Marrakesh, Morocco, in Nov.; COP22 adopted the Marrakech Action Proclamation, which called for the highest level of political commitment to combat climate change, as a matter of urgent priority. In Jan. 2017 the outgoing US Pres. Barack Obama authorized a second payment of $500m. to the Green Climate Fund (a first $500m. instalment by the USA having been paid in March 2016); the incoming US Administration of Pres. Donald Trump had declared that it would not pursue a commitment previously made by the USA to transfer in total $3,000m. to the Fund; COP23 was organized by Fiji and convened in Bonn, in Nov. 2017; it initiated a facilitative process, the 'Talanoa dialogue', to reflect upon and discuss climate action during 2018. A Netherlands-based Global Centre of Excellence on Climate Adaptation—a collaboration between UNEP, the Netherlands and Japan—was established in late 2017. COP24, held in Katowice, Poland, in Dec. 2018, secured an initial agreement on a so-called rulebook on implementation of the Paris Agreement, which was to address the measurement and reporting of emission-reducing efforts; signatory countries also agreed in principle on the need for more ambitious limitations of greenhouse gas emissions, in accordance with the most recent IPCC special report. At COP25, convened in Madrid, Spain, in Dec. 2019, no consensus was reached on the substantial issues of carbon trading, or on addressing effectively the climate change-derived so-called 'loss and damage' increasingly borne by some poorer countries (i.e. irreversible harm caused by extreme weather events); a technical assistance initiative, the Santiago Network, was established in 2019 to support the minimization of loss and damage; COP26, held in Glasgow, Scotland, UK, in Nov. 2021, adopted the Glasgow Climate Pact, which, for the first time, called for the 'phase-down of unabated coal power and inefficient fossil fuel subsidies'. (India had declined to accept a proposed text that alluded to ending their use.) Under the Pact the developed parties to the UNFCCC were urged at least to double by 2025, over 2019 levels, the collective provision of climate finance to support developing members' adaptation activities, and multilateral development banks, etc., were also encouraged to scale up climate finance provision; a new Climate Finance Delivery Plan: Meeting the $100 Billion Goal (focused on the annual mobilization of $100,000m. in climate finance during 2021–25) was welcomed. While the UNFCCC's developed states parties were urged to provide financial support for the Santiago Network, and a Glasgow Dialogue was initiated, wherein, until mid-2024, states parties and other stakeholders were to discuss arrangements for the funding of activities aimed at countering loss and damage. 'Climate justice' was acknowledged by the Pact—i.e. consideration of social equality and human rights in tandem with action on climate change. During COP26 technical negotiations on the rulebook for Article 6 of the Paris Agreement were finalized, establishing detailed reporting requirements (to be obligatory by 2024) on emissions targets, and mechanisms governing the functioning of international carbon markets (for example on the taxation of bilateral trades). Declarations and agreements reached on the sidelines of COP26 included a Global Methane Pledge, according to which more than 100 states resolved to lower global methane emissions by 30% by 2030; the Glasgow Leaders' Declaration on Forests and Land Use (a collective commitment to reverse forest loss and land degradation by 2030); a US-China Joint Glasgow Declaration on Enhancing Climate Action in the 2020s; and the establishment of a Champions Group on Adaptation Finance, of an Infrastructure for Resilient Island States funding mechanism, and of a Just Energy Transition Partnership to support South Africa's decarbonization activities; COP27, convened in Sharm el-Sheikh, Egypt, in Nov. 2022, concluded an agreement to establish a loss and damage fund; no definitive action was agreed, however, on the reduction of carbon emissions; at COP28, to be held in Dubai, UAE, in Nov. 2023, the inaugural review of global progress towards meeting the goals of the 2015 Paris Agreement—'global stocktake'—was to be conducted; a preparatory Bonn Climate Change Conference was convened in June 2023; UNFCCC's Global Climate Action portal had 32,517 stakeholders at Aug. 2023; at Aug. 2023 the UNFCCC had been ratified by 198 parties (197 countries and the EU); the Kyoto Protocol had 192 states parties (191 countries and the EU); and the Paris Agreement had 195 states parties (194 countries and the EU); during the period 4 Nov. 2020–18 Feb. 2021 the USA temporarily withdrew from the Paris Agreement; Exec. Sec. SIMON STIELL (Grenada).

Other Biodiversity-related Conventions

In addition to the CBD, several other global conventions have been negotiated on biodiversity-related issues, of which UNEP hosts the secretariats of the Convention on International Trade in Endangered Species of Wild Flora and Fauna (CITES) and the Convention on the Conservation of Migratory Species of Wild Animals (CMS). A Liaison Group of Biodiversity-related Conventions (BLG) was established by the states parties to the CBD to enhance synergies and collaborative action between its secretariat and related conventions and bodies. The BLG comprises the heads of the secretariats of the CBD, CITES, the CMS, the International Treaty on Plant Genetic Resources for Food and Agriculture, the Ramsar Convention on Wetlands, the World Heritage Convention, the International Plant Protection Convention, and the International Whaling Commission.

Convention on International Trade in Endangered Species of Wild Flora and Fauna (CITES): Palais des Nations, 8-14 ave de la Paix, 1211 Geneva 10, Switzerland; tel. 229178139; fax 227973417; e-mail info@cites.org; internet cites.org; entered into force in 1975; regulates international trade in more than 35,000 species of plants and animals, as well as products and derivatives therefrom; species addressed by the Convention are listed in three appendices: Appendix I, which covers 1,082 species and 36 sub-species that are critically threatened with extinction, in which (except in exceptional circumstances) trade is prohibited; Appendix II, covering 37,420 universally vulnerable species (and 15 sub-species), in which trade is permitted, conditionally; and Appendix III, comprising 211 species and 14 sub-species that are protected in at least one mem. country; CITES has special programmes on the protection of, inter alia, elephants (including an African Elephant Action Plan and, jtly with the CMS, Monitoring the Illegal Killing of Elephants—MIKE), falcons, great apes, hawksbill turtles, sturgeons, tropical timber (jtly with the International Tropical Timber Organization), shark and manta ray, and big leaf mahogany; states parties meet in conference every 3 years; in Aug. 2019 the 18th CITES COP (also referred to as the World Wildlife Conference), held in Geneva, Switzerland, mandated the establishment of a CITES Big Cat Task Force, which was to promote the conservation of and combat illegal trade in cheetahs, jaguars, leopards, lions and tigers; a CITES Strategic Vision Post-2020 was endorsed, with a focus on strengthening environmental, economic and social sustainability and on promoting the achievement of the SDGs; the 19th CITES COP, hosted by Panama, in Nov. 2022, adopted 46 proposals that amended rules and quotas governing trade in further species placed at risk by overhunting, overfishing or overharvesting (including of birds, fish, frogs, lizards, sharks and turtles). The CITES Secretariat contributes to the World Wildlife Seizure ('World WISE') database, which is maintained by the UN Office on Drugs and Crime (UNODC); it supports the International Consortium on Combating Wildlife Crime (ICCWC), which aims to end the poaching of wild animals and illegal trade in wild animals and wild animal products, and in 2014, with UNEP, UNDP and UNODC, launched a #WildforLife campaign against illegal trade in wildlife; the CITES Secretariat is the facilitating body for observance of World Wildlife Day, held annually on 3 March; 184 states and the EU (at Jan. 2023); Sec.-Gen. IVONNE HIGUERO (Panama).

Convention on the Conservation of Migratory Species of Wild Animals (CMS): UN Campus, Platz der Vereinten Nationen 1, 53113 Bonn, Germany; tel. (228) 8152401; fax (228) 8152449; e-mail cms.secretariat@cms.int; internet www.cms.int; concluded under UNEP auspices in 1979, aims to conserve avian, marine and terrestrial species throughout the range of their migration. Memorandums of Understanding concluded under the CMS include conservation measures for the West African Elephant (2005), the Saiga Antelope (2006), Atlantic Populations of the Mediterranean Monk Seal (2007), Dugongs (2007), Migratory Birds of Prey in Africa and Eurasia (2008), High Andean Flamingos and their Habitats (2008) and Migratory Sharks (2010). Other multilateral agreements negotiated under CMS auspices include: the Agreement on the Conservation of Populations of European Bats (adopted in 1991 and entered into force in 1994); the Agreement on Cetaceans of the Black Seas, Mediterranean, and Contiguous Atlantic Area (ACCOBAMS—adopted in 1996, entered into force in 2001); the African-Eurasian Migratory Waterbird Agreement (AEWA—entered into force in Nov. 1999) which focuses on the conservation of waterbirds that migrate along the so-called 'African Eurasian Flyway'; the Agreement on the Conservation of Albatrosses and Petrels (ACAP—signed in 2001, entered into force in 2004); and the Agreement on the Conservation of Gorillas and Their Habitats (concluded in 2007, covering 10 range states, and entered into force in 2008). In Nov. 2014 the COP to the CMS adopted a strategic plan to guide the Convention during the period 2015–23, which was, inter alia, to address underlying causes of the decline of migratory species; to reduce direct pressures on migratory species and their habitats; and to enhance the conservation status of migratory species and the resilience of their habitats. A Multi-Stakeholder Energy Task Force, established in 2016, is tasked with reconciling renewable energy developments with the conservation of migratory species. In Feb. 2020 the 13th CMS COP, held in Gandhinagar, India, assigned the strictest level of protection to 7 further species: the Asian elephant, jaguar, great Indian bustard, little bustard, Bengal florican, Oceanic white-tip shark, and Antipodean albatross. The meeting adopted the Gandhinagar Declaration, which advocated for the concept of 'ecological connectivity' to be prioritized in the Kunming-Montreal Global Biodiversity Framework (q.v.); COP14 was to be convened in Samarkand, Uzbekistan, in Oct. 2023; 133 states parties (as at Jan. 2023); Exec. Sec. AMY FRAENKEL.

United Nations High Commissioner for Refugees—UNHCR

Address: CP 2500, 1211 Geneva 2 dépôt, Switzerland.
Telephone: 227398111; **fax:** 227397377; **e-mail:** unhcr@unhcr.org; **internet:** www.unhcr.org.

The Office of the High Commissioner, established by the UN General Assembly in December 1950 (initially with a three-year mandate to address the needs of refugees in Europe displaced by the Second World War), provides assistance and international protection to refugees and to internally displaced persons, and seeks durable solutions to their problems.

Organization
(September 2023)

The High Commissioner is elected by the UN General Assembly, and is responsible to the General Assembly and to the UN Economic and Social Council (ECOSOC). The High Commissioner is supported by a Deputy High Commissioner; an Assistant High Commissioner for Protection (who manages the division on International Protection, and a co-ordination team and a multi-stakeholder engagement team supporting the Global Compact on Refugees); and an Assistant High Commissioner for Operations (who oversees divisions of Emergency, Security and Supply; and Resilience and Solutions; the seven Regional Bureaux; the Principal Adviser on Internal Displacement, and the Special Adviser on Climate Action).

High Commissioner: FILIPPO GRANDI (Italy).
Deputy High Commissioner: KELLY T. CLEMENTS (USA).

EXECUTIVE COMMITTEE

The Executive Committee of the High Commissioner's Programme (ExCom), established by ECOSOC, meets once a year, and during the period October 2022–October 2023 comprised representatives of 107 states. ExCom gives the High Commissioner policy directives regarding material assistance programmes and advice on international protection. In addition, it oversees UNHCR's general policies and use of funds. A Standing Committee meets throughout the year to support ExCom's activities.

ADMINISTRATION

In 2023 UNHCR was active in 135 countries, and employed 20,739 staff, of whom nearly 90% were field-based. UNHCR Global Service Centres, based in Budapest (Hungary), Copenhagen (Denmark), and Amman (Jordan), provide administrative support to the headquarters.

Activities

The competence of the High Commissioner extends to any person who, owing to well-founded fear of war, violence or persecution, is outside the country of his or her nationality; to stateless people; and to internally displaced persons (IDPs—with similar needs to those of refugees but who have not crossed an international border) or those who are threatened with displacement. IDPs include—in addition to conflict-affected populations—people displaced by situations of general violence, human rights violations, natural or human-made disasters or environmental degradation. UNHCR aims to address the fundamental causes of refugee flows, and has urged recognition and comprehension of the broad patterns of global displacement and migration, and of the mixed nature of many 21st century population flows, which often comprise economic migrants, refugees, asylum seekers and victims of trafficking requiring detection and support.

In the UN system UNHCR is lead co-ordinator in refugee emergencies. Within the UN's overall Cluster Approach to co-ordinate an international response to humanitarian disasters, UNHCR is the lead agency for Protection, and in conflict situations the Office leads the clusters on Camp Co-ordination and Camp Management (CCCM) (the International Organization for Migration—IOM—leads that cluster in natural disaster situations), and on Shelter (with the International Federation of Red Cross and Red Crescent Societies leading in natural disaster situations).

At 31 December 2022 the total population of concern to UNHCR, based on provisional figures, amounted to 112.6m., compared with 94.7m. in the previous year, and with 33.9m. in 2010. The total number of people forcibly displaced as a result of persecution, conflict or other violence amounted to 108.4m. by the end of 2022, including 35.3m. refugees and people in refugee-like situations (of whom 29.4m. came under UNHCR's mandate, and 5.9m. Palestinians under the mandate of the UN Relief and Works Agency—UNRWA), 62.5m. IDPs, and 5.4m. asylum seekers. UNHCR was also concerned with 6m. recently returned refugees and IDPs, 4.4m. stateless persons, and 5.2m. others deemed to require the Office's protection or assistance.

The states hosting the most refugees at end-2022 were Türkiye (3.6m.), Iran (3.4m.), Colombia (2.5m.—including others in need of international protection), Germany (2.1m.), and Pakistan (1.7m.). As at 31 December 2022 Aruba was hosting the largest number of refugees relative to its national population (one in six), owing to an influx of people fleeing socioeconomic turmoil in Venezuela, followed by Lebanon (one in seven, mainly Syrian, refugees), Curaçao (one in 14, mainly Venezuelans), Jordan (one in 16), and Montenegro (1 in 19).

The Office noted that 76% of refugees and other people in need of international protection in 2022 were hosted by low- and middle-income countries that were already under severe economic pressure, and that least developed countries were hosting one-fifth of the global total of refugees.

As at the end of 2022 more than one-half (52%) of all refugees and other people in need of international protection originated from only three countries: Syria, Ukraine and Afghanistan.

In September 2016 a UN high-level Summit on Addressing Large Movements of Refugees and Migrants adopted the New York Declaration for Refugees and Migrants. Several commitments were made therein that aimed to ensure the rights and safety of refugees, acknowledging in particular the vulnerability of women and children, and the risks posed by trafficking and forced labour. The Office was tasked with leading a broad consultative process to formulate a Global Compact on Refugees. This was eventually adopted by the UN General Assembly in December 2018, and had four principal objectives: to relieve the pressure on refugee hosting countries; to enhance refugee self-reliance; to expand access to third-country solutions; and to support conditions in refugees' countries of origin to enable safe, dignified returns. It incorporated a Comprehensive Refugee Response Framework, already approved as an annex to the New York Declaration, which aimed to strengthen the resilience of host communities. It also defined a Programme of Action to support host countries and refugees, determined that a ministerial Global Refugee Forum (GRF) would be convened periodically, and proposed the establishment of multi-stakeholder Support Platforms to address specific refugee situations.

The second GRF was to be convened in December 2023, in Geneva (the first having been held in December 2019).

The Office maintains an online population statistics database. World Refugee Day, sponsored by UNHCR, is held annually on 20 June.

INTERNATIONAL PROTECTION

In the exercise of its mandate UNHCR seeks to ensure that refugees and asylum seekers are protected against *refoulement* (forcible return); that they receive asylum; and that they are treated according to internationally recognized standards. The Office discourages the detention and encampment of refugees and asylum seekers, as this restricts their freedom of movement and opportunities to become self-reliant. UNHCR supervises the application of, and actively encourages states to accede to, the 1951 UN Convention relating to the Status of Refugees (with 146 parties at July 2023) and its 1967 Protocol (which had 147 parties at that time). These define the rights as well as the duties of refugees and contain provisions that address a variety of matters that affect their day-to-day lives. The treatment of refugees is also guided by a number of instruments adopted at regional level. UNHCR works in countries of origin and of asylum to ensure that policies, laws and practices comply with international commitments, and seeks to facilitate swift, just asylum procedure systems.

UNHCR prioritizes the specific needs of refugee women, children, and elderly refugees in its programme planning and implementation. The Office actively seeks solutions to support refugees residing in urban areas (who by 2023 represented more than three-fifths of all refugees). In June 2011 UNHCR issued an updated strategy on Action against Sexual and Gender-Based Violence. A UNHCR Framework for the Protection of Children was adopted in 2012. Since 2017 UNHCR has reported on the number of unaccompanied and separated children in refugee populations, and from 2018 the Office urged national governments to follow suit. In 2022 there were 51,700 new asylum applications from unaccompanied or separated children (compared with 21,000 in the previous year).

UNHCR has attempted to address the issue of military attacks on refugee camps through the promotion of a set of principles aimed at ensuring refugee safety.

In November 2014 UNHCR initiated a global action plan aimed at ending statelessness (lack of legal nationality) by 2024. The Office promotes new accessions to the 1951 Convention Relating to the Status of Stateless Persons (which had 96 states parties at July 2023) and to the 1961 Convention on the Reduction of Statelessness (with 78 states parties at that time).

ASSISTANCE ACTIVITIES

In the early stages of a crisis UNHCR conducts an initial assessment to ascertain the scale of response required and immediate critical requirements. Rapid assessments are undertaken next to identify key priorities for intervention and to estimate total resource requirements. UNHCR uses existing data to accelerate its crisis assessments. The subsequent pattern of operations is as follows: emergency planning (in complex emergencies a UNHCR-led inter-agency Refugee Response Plan is organized); implementation; monitoring; reporting; and evaluation. The Office's assistance can take various forms, including the provision of shelter/non-food items (NFIs—for example household goods, jerry cans, sleeping mats and blankets; also referred to as core relief items—CRIs), clean water, sanitation, medical care, education, and counselling; supporting asylum applications; and facilitating refugee registration. UNHCR has developed a Biometric Identity Management System (BIMS), which swiftly registers and verifies refugees' identities, using iris scans, fingerprints and digital photographs, and gathers detailed social background information on education, skills, etc.

As far as possible, assistance is geared towards the identification and implementation of durable solutions to refugee problems. These generally take one of three forms: voluntary repatriation; local integration; or resettlement onwards to a third country. Where voluntary repatriation, generally the preferred solution, is feasible, the Office assists refugees to overcome obstacles preventing their return to their country of origin. This may be done through negotiations with governments involved, and by arranging transport for and providing basic assistance packages to repatriating refugees, and also by implementing or supporting local integration or reintegration programmes in their home countries, including Quick Impact Projects (QIPs) aimed at income generation and at the restoration of local infrastructures. Similarly, the Office works to enable local communities to support returned IDPs. Some 339,300 refugees repatriated voluntarily to their home countries (numbering 38) in 2022. When voluntary repatriation is not an option, efforts are made to assist refugees to integrate locally and to become self-supporting in their countries of asylum. Assistance in procuring accommodation may be offered, as well as the provision of skills training, or of loans. In cases where resettlement through emigration is the only viable solution to a refugee problem, UNHCR negotiates with governments to obtain suitable resettlement opportunities, to encourage liberalization of admission criteria, and to draft special immigration schemes. Some 114,300 refugees were resettled to third countries in 2022, representing a significant increase over the total in 2021 (57,500).

MIDDLE EAST AND NORTH AFRICA

In 2023 the Syrian refugee population was the largest under UNHCR's mandate. A Regional Refugee and Resilience Plan ('3RP') for 2023, requiring some US $5,696m. in total funding, was being co-ordinated and implemented by UNHCR, UNDP and other humanitarian agencies, and aimed to assist Syrians who had fled to neighbouring countries (at 24 August 2023 a total of 5,216,568 were registered with UNHCR), as well as stateless persons, and members of host communities. Of the total number of Syrian refugees, 301,862 were encamped, and the remainder in urban, peri-urban or rural situations. The 3RP is aligned with national emergency response plans. Some 3,303,034 Syrian refugees were registered in Türkiye (the highest number of refugees being hosted by any single country), while 795,322 were registered (as at 30 June) in Lebanon, 656,762 in Jordan (at 31 July), 267,839 in Iraq (also at 31 July), and (31 July) 148,608 in Egypt. Around 45,003 further exiled Syrians in North Africa were of concern to UNHCR at 31 December 2022. UNHCR's activities in the host countries have included providing refugees with shelter, cash grants and access to health and education; protection monitoring and outreach; field assessments; exploring resettlement opportunities, especially for the most vulnerable people of concern; and supporting the authorities and host communities with a view to mitigating the impact of refugee influxes. In May 2023 UNHCR, UNICEF and the WFP issued the results of a 10th annual joint *Vulnerability Assessment of Syrian Refugees in Lebanon survey (VASyr)*, which, based on an analysis of more than 5,000 refugee households in mid-2022, reported that 93% of Syrian refugee families in Lebanon were borrowing to cover the costs of essential food (which had risen by 332% since mid-2021) and non-food items; 46% were borrowing to pay for accommodation; and 35% to cover medication costs. Only 17% of Syrian refugees in Lebanon held legal residency; and 22% of refugee girls aged 15–19 were married (68% of these were not attending schools). The UNHCR presence in Jordan supports the management of the overcrowded Za'atri refugee camp, in the north of the country. At 31 July 2023 Za'atri and the nearby town of Mafraq were accommodating 169,043 registered Syrian refugees. The majority of Syrian refugees in Jordan were, however, mainly based outside camps. UNHCR has targeted protection and support interventions at Syrian refugees living, often in substandard conditions, outside camps in Iraq (accounting for around three-fifths of all Syrian refugees in that country), and at their host communities; has provided outreach support to Syrian refugees in urban situations; and has monitored the provision of essential assistance and services in refugee camps (the largest of which, a complex near Dahuk, Kurdistan, was accommodating 69,864 Syrian refugees at 31 July 2023). From January 2016 the Turkish authorities permitted many Syrian refugees registered in that country to apply for work permits. Increasing numbers of Afghans, Iranians and Iraqis were also reported to have applied for asylum in Türkiye in recent years. UNHCR's activities in Türkiye have focused on enhancing the protection environment; registration and profiling; status determination; facilitating resettlement to third countries; community support; and livelihoods assistance and activities to enable self-reliance. Health, education, socioeconomic and municipal infrastructure support for host communities and refugees in Türkiye is assisted by a joint World Bank-EU Syrians Under Temporary Protection initiative, financed by a €6,000m. Facility for Refugees in Türkiye, which was established in 2015. During the period 2016–May 2023 37,560 Syrians were resettled to the European Union, and during 2014–May 2023 some 21,568 Syrians were transferred from Türkiye to third countries (predominantly to Canada, the USA, the UK and Norway).

Within Syria UNHCR is responsible for the provision of support to IDPs (numbering more than 6.8m. at mid-2023) in its leadership areas of CCCM and Shelter, as well as providing NFIs, protection, financial assistance, health, community services, and registration and counselling services. UNHCR has also assisted Syrian IDPs through cash-for-shelter activities. From 2019, in response to the increased flow of arrivals from Islamic State's former 'caliphate' to al-Hol camp, in al-Hasakah Governorate, eastern Syria, UNHCR and partners established 24-hour response teams to identify and provide urgent assistance to the most vulnerable cases (in particular to unaccompanied children and people requiring immediate medical assistance). They also provided additional large reception tents, more than 8,000 smaller tents, core relief and winter assistance items, cooking areas, and child friendly spaces and schools. In 2023 al-Hol camp was accommodating—in excess of its capacity—around 50,000 people (of whom the majority were children). Syria also accommodates a significant population of stateless people, totalling 160,000 at 31 December 2022.

UNHCR provided emergency assistance to Syria and Türkiye—including through the provision of shelter items and delivery of NFIs and winterization assistance—following the earthquakes that devastated parts of those countries in February 2023. Under broader inter-agency appeals, UNHCR requested US $150m. for Türkiye, and $52m. for Syria.

UNHCR appealed for US $320.5m. to support its operations in conflict-affected Yemen during 2023, where 21.6m. people were reported to require humanitarian assistance, of whom more than 4.5m. were internally displaced. Yemen was also (as at 1 May 2023) hosting 71,546 refugees, of whom 46,750 were Somalis. Refugees and asylum seekers were mainly accommodated in Aden and in Sana'a (Amanat al-Asimah Governorate). The Office has continued to advocate for resettlement opportunities for the most vulnerable refugees; to extend cash-based interventions; to undertake shelter programmes; extend legal help to asylum seekers, IDPs, returnees and refugees; strengthen community resilience; facilitate durable solutions for IDP returnees; support the implementation of Yemen's national displacement policy; and address continuing incoming migrant flows from the Horn of Africa. Some 38,627 Yemenis were sheltering abroad at 31 December 2022.

UNHCR requested some US $340m. to fund its operations in Iraq during 2023. At that time there were around 1.5m. Iraqi IDPs (in protracted displacement following the 2014–17 Islamic State uprising), of whom around 180,000 were being assisted by UNHCR in 26 formal camps (25 of the camps were in Kurdistan, and one in Ninewa). A process of camp closures had been initiated in August 2019. UNHCR has supported voluntary returns, and advocated with authorities to resolve cases of barred returns and to prevent coerced returns to areas that remain unsafe (owing to the presence of militias, or to contamination by explosive remnants of war and improvised explosive devices, or to the absence of critical infrastructure and destruction of property). There were 5m. Iraqi returnees in 2023. Iraq was also hosting 267,839 Syrian refugees (at 31 July, mainly Syrian Kurds), and more than 38,000 refugees of Palestinian, Iranian, Turkish and other nationalities. Some 97% of the Syrian refugees are located in Kurdistan, in nine camps and in urban and peri-urban areas. UNHCR also remained concerned in that year for (enumerated as at 31 December 2021) 47,093 *bidoun,* Faili Kurd, and other stateless people in Iraq. The Office promotes their applications for Iraqi nationality. Meanwhile, at 31 December 2022 288,261 refugees of Iraqi origin were residing in other countries.

UNHCR has monitored the Iraqi refugee population in Jordan (which numbered 61,081 at 31 March 2023), to ensure that their protection needs are met, given that recent large inflows of Syrian refugees have placed additional strain on local infrastructures and services.

At the end of 2022 Kuwait was hosting 92,000 people of concern to UNHCR, mainly (stateless) *bidoun*, as well as Iraqis and Palestinians. Some 70,000 people were registered as stateless in Saudi Arabia at that time.

In May 2012 a regional stakeholders' conference on Afghanistan endorsed a 'Solutions Strategy for Afghan Refugees' (SSAR), negotiated during 2011 by UNHCR, Afghanistan, Iran and Pakistan, and based on the 'pillars' of voluntary repatriation, sustainable reintegration in Afghanistan, and support for refugee hosting communities On 16 August 2021, in view of the Taliban takeover of Afghanistan, UNHCR issued a formal non-return advisory, aimed at preventing forced returns (including of failed asylum seekers) to that country. Nevertheless, Iran reportedly deported more than 1m. undocumented Afghans throughout that year. At 31 December 2022 750,000 Afghan refugees and asylum seekers abroad were formally registered by UNHCR in Iran; by mid-2023 1m. Afghan asylum seekers were reported to have fled to Iran since August 2021. Most UNHCR-assisted Afghan refugees in Iran had been issued with official 'Amayesh' identification cards. In 2023 UNHCR was leading an inter-agency response plan, launched in March, that required funding of US $613m. to support Afghan refugees and 2.7m. members of host communities in Iran, Pakistan and Central Asia, aligned with the Global Compact and the SSAR. UNHCR was to work with the governments of refugee-receiving countries to include Afghan refugees in national health and education services, and to promote their economic inclusion and access to social safety nets, while pursuing durable solutions. Local activities were to include the extension of protection assistance, the provision of shelter and NFIs, food and cash assistance, health and nutrition support, education, livelihoods and resilience assistance.

Libya is both a destination country for economic migrants (who may find informal employment there), and also a principal country of transit for mixed migration flows of refugees and economic migrants attempting to travel to European destinations (the 'Central Mediterranean Route'). Libya, in return for financial support from Italy and the EU, agreed in 2017 to intercept vessels carrying migrants and to transfer the passengers to Libyan detention centres. UNHCR maintains a monitoring presence at 12 Mediterranean embarkation points in Libya. At 31 August 2023 there were 125,802 IDPs in that country; as well as 705,426 IDP returnees, 47,214 registered refugees, and (as at 30 April) 705,746 migrants (of at least 44 nationalities). As at March there were, according to UNHCR, an estimated 4,265 migrants who were being held in detention centres across Libya (to whom the Office was delivering NFIs and hygiene kits). The Office extends international protection services there to unaccompanied and separated children, sick or elderly people, women at risk of trafficking, and to other vulnerable individuals. It works within Libya as well as in neighbouring countries to provide durable solutions and find credible alternatives for refugees and asylum seekers, including resettlement to third countries. UNHCR and IOM jointly lead the UN component of an AU-EU-UN Tripartite Taskforce on the Situation of Migrants and Refugees in Libya (operational since early 2022). Meeting in March 2023 the Taskforce determined to strengthen efforts to support the development of non-discriminatory legal and policy frameworks for migrants and refugees in that country, and urged the Libyan authorities to end arbitrary detention of migrants and refugees. The Taskforce agreed to enhance support for voluntary humanitarian returns from Libya.

In March 2016 an EU-Turkey accord entered into effect that provided for failed asylum seekers, and migrants arriving post-20 March in the EU via Greece, who did not apply for asylum in Greece, to be returned to Turkey. Among concessions offered to Turkey in return, EU member states were to resettle one Turkey-based Syrian refugee for every migrant returned to that country from Greece. In accordance with the new agreement (to which UNHCR was not a party) former refugee reception centres were reclassified as detention facilities. In view of UNHCR's opposition to mandatory detention, it suspended certain of its activities at the former centres, including the provision of transport. UNHCR personnel continued, however, to provide life-saving assistance at coastal locations, to undertake protection monitoring duties, to identify incomers with specific assistance needs, to offer counselling to new arrivals, and to provide information on rights and procedures. During the period 2016–May 2023 37,560 Syrians were resettled to the EU from Türkiye. It was reported in 2023 that Türkiye was no longer readmitting migrants returned from Greece. Of processed first-instance asylum applications made in the EU in 2022, claims by Syrians and Yemenis were reportedly among those most likely to be accepted.

Given the lack of progress in achieving a settlement agreement for Western Sahara, UNHCR co-ordinates humanitarian assistance for around 90,000 Sahrawi refugees accommodated, in a protracted situation ongoing since 1975, in five camps in the Tindouf area of Algeria. The refugees are heavily dependent on external assistance as there are few opportunities for income generation in the remote camps. UNHCR provides them with protection and basic relief items.

Finance

The regular budget of the UN provides limited finance for UNHCR's administrative expenditure. The majority of UNHCR's programme expenditure is funded by voluntary contributions; around 87% of this is from governments and the EU, 9% from private sector sources, and 3% from other intergovernmental organizations as well as from pooled funding mechanisms. UNHCR also accepts in-kind contributions, such as medicines, tents and vehicles. UNHCR's initial projected funding requirements for 2023 totalled US $10,211m. The proposed budget for the Middle East and North Africa in that year was $2,470m.

Publications

Global Appeal (annually).
Global Report (annually).
Global Trends (annually).
Refworld.
The State of the World's Refugees (every 2 years).
UNHCR Statistical Yearbook (annually).
UNHCR Handbook for Emergencies.
Country reports, analyses, handbooks.

Statistics

PERSONS OF CONCERN TO UNHCR IN THE MIDDLE EAST AND NORTH AFRICA*
('000 persons, at 31 December 2022, provisional figures)

Host Country	Refugees	Asylum seekers	Recently returned refugees and IDPs	IDPs	Stateless persons	Other persons of concern
Algeria	99.1	3.6	—	—	—	—
Cyprus	29.3	36.5	—	—	0.1	—
Egypt	294.6	63.9	—	—	0.0	—
Iran	3,425.1	0.0	—	—	0.0	—
Iraq	273.7	10.6	30.5	1,168.6	47.1	2.0
Israel	1.2	25.2	—	—	0.0	41.6
Jordan	697.8	45.2	—	—	0.1	1.4
Kuwait	0.7	1.0	—	—	92.0	0.0
Lebanon	818.9	8.0	—	—	—	23.6
Libya	2.2	42.5	22.4	161.6	—	—
Saudi Arabia	0.5	3.9	—	—	70.0	—
Syrian Arab Republic	13.1	5.5	306.4	6,781.0	160.0	27.0
Türkiye (Turkey)	3,568.3	272.3	—	—	0.4	—
Yemen	77.5	13.2	0.0	4,523.0	—	0.0

* The table shows only those countries where the total number of persons of concern to UNHCR amounted to more than 10,000. The figures are provided mostly by governments, based on their own methods of estimation. The data do not include 5.8m. Palestinian refugees who came under the care of UNRWA.
Source: UNHCR, *Global Trends, Forced Displacement in 2022.*

United Nations Peacekeeping

Address: Department of Peace Operations, Room S-3727B, United Nations, New York, NY 10017, USA.
Telephone: (212) 963-8077; **fax:** (212) 963-9222; **internet:** peacekeeping.un.org.

The UN undertakes impartial peacekeeping operations (deploying either peacekeeping forces or observer missions), with the consent of the principal parties involved, and without prejudice to their positions or claims, in order to maintain international peace and security and to facilitate the search for political settlements through peaceful means. Each peacekeeping operation is established with a specific mandate, which requires periodic review by the UN Security Council.

Peacekeeping forces—composed of contingents of military personnel, experts and other civilian staff, made available by member states—assist in preventing the recurrence of fighting, restoring and maintaining peace, and promoting a return to normal conditions. To this end, they are authorized, as necessary, to undertake negotiations, persuasion, observation and fact-finding. They conduct patrols and interpose physically between the opposing parties. Peacekeeping forces are permitted to use their weapons only in self-defence. Military observer missions—comprising officers who are made available by member states—monitor and report to the UN Secretary-General on the maintenance of a ceasefire.

The Department of Peace Operations, which replaced the Department of Peacekeeping Operations on 1 January 2019, provides political support and executive direction. It incorporates an Office for the Rule of Law and Security Institutions, an Office of Military Affairs, and a Policy, Evaluation and Training Division. A regional structure of oversight is shared with the Department of Political and Peacebuilding Affairs.

The UN's peacekeeping forces and observer missions are financed, in most cases, by assessed contributions from member states. The approved budget for peacekeeping operations during 1 July 2023–30 June 2024 totalled US $6,053m. At 30 April 2023 outstanding assessed contributions to the peacekeeping budget were reported to amount to $2,800m. Many countries also voluntarily, on a non-reimbursable basis, offer additional resources to operations, such as material items and transportation.

By September 2023 the UN had deployed a total of 71 peacekeeping operations, of which 13 were authorized during the period 1948–88 and 58 since 1988. As at 30 June 2023 121 countries were contributing 75,384 uniformed personnel to the ongoing 12 UN operations. Of these, 64,495 were troops, 2,105 were staff officers, 7,728 police officers, and 1,056 were military observers. By that time 1,632 people had died while serving in the ongoing UN peacekeeping and political missions.

United Nations Disengagement Observer Force—UNDOF

Address: Camp Faouar, Syrian Arab Republic (headquarters); Camp Ziouani, Israel (operational base).
Head of Mission and Force Commander: Maj.-Gen. николай Kumar Thapa (Nepal).

Establishment and Mandate: UNDOF was established by UN Security Council Resolution 350 in May 1974, following the signature of an Agreement on Disengagement of Forces between Israel and the Syrian Arab Republic. The initial task of the mission was to take over territory evacuated in stages by the Israeli troops, in accordance with the disengagement agreement, to hand over territory to Syrian troops, and to establish an area of separation on the Golan Heights. Indirect peace talks between Israel and Syria on reaching a comprehensive peace agreement providing for the withdrawal of the Israeli presence from the Golan Heights were initiated in May 2008, but were discontinued in December, owing to the Israeli military offensive initiated against the Gaza strip at that time; by 2023 the ongoing civil war in Syria rendered their prompt resumption unlikely. Through fixed positions and patrols UNDOF monitors the 'area of separation', which stretches for more than 75 km in length and in breadth measures from around 10 km at its widest (in the centre) to just 200 m (in the extreme south). On either side of the area of separation there is an area of limitation, divided into three zones. UNDOF undertakes inspections of the areas of limited armaments and forces; uses its best efforts to maintain the ceasefire; conducts demining activities; and implements humanitarian activities (including facilitating the transfer of prisoners and war dead).

UNDOF reports on and protests to all parties against all violations of the Agreement on Disengagement of Forces—such as firing across ceasefire lines and into the area of separation, and crossings over the ceasefire lines made by drones, aircraft, military vehicles, individuals, and including all incidents of conflict spillover and retaliatory fire. The mission constantly urges the exercise of restraint and caution against miscalculations that might escalate the situation on the ground. The Israeli and Syrian sides of UNDOF's area of operations are referred to, respectively, as the 'Alpha' and 'Bravo' sides. UNDOF is supported by military observers of the UN Truce Supervision Organization (UNTSO) Observer Group Golan (OGG), which is deployed, under the operational control of UNDOF, in two divisions to two areas: OGG-Damascus and OGG-Tiberias. It focuses on continuous static observation from nine fixed observation points in the area of separation, and on investigations and situational analysis.

Activities: From 2011, as Syria descended into civil war, UNDOF enhanced measures to fortify its positions and to protect its area of operations. In June 2013 the UN Security Council expressed concern that military activities impinging upon the area of separation had the potential to escalate tensions between Israel and Syria, and requested the UN Secretary-General to ensure that UNDOF was sufficiently equipped to fulfil its mandate safely. From July the OGG set up several temporary observation posts along the ceasefire line with a view to enhancing the Force's situational awareness of the area of separation.

In mid-September 2014, in response to the occupation by al-Qa'ida-linked militants of a broad area of the Syrian (so-called Bravo) side of the area of operations, UNDOF's headquarters and the majority of mission personnel and equipment were, on a temporary basis, relocated from Camp Faouar on the Bravo side to Camp Ziouani on the Israeli (Alpha) side. Although most fixed UN positions and observation posts on the Bravo side were vacated, smaller numbers of UNDOF peacekeepers remained at Mount Hermon (Syria, near the border with Lebanon), and a very limited presence remained elsewhere on the Bravo side within easy access to the Alpha line. In December the UN Security Council called on all warring parties to co-operate with UNDOF, and all groups other than UNDOF to abandon UN positions and to return all weaponry and other equipment belonging to the mission. In June 2015 the UN Secretary-General urged the Syrian authorities to halt air strikes in UNDOF's area of operations, and noted with concern the increasing deployment in the area of separation of heavy weaponry and armed vehicles by the Syrian forces and armed groups. During late 2015 Syrian forces were reported to have recaptured several positions from militant groups operating in the Golan Heights area, relieving tensions there. However, air strikes were reported to have intensified in the southern area of UNDOF's operations.

In mid-November 2016 UNDOF deployed a limited resumed presence at Camp Faouar. It was envisaged that a gradual return of UNDOF personnel to the area of separation would be implemented, pending improvements in the overall security situation. In the following month, however, the Secretary-General observed that exchanges of heavy artillery fire between the Syrian military and armed opposition groups were continuing to spill over into the areas of separation and of limitation, and that the militant Islamic Jabhat Fateh al-Sham and the Yarmouk Martyrs Brigade were continuing to clash in the UNDOF area of operations. The UN Secretary-General also demanded that the Israel Defense Forces (IDF) refrain from firing across the ceasefire line, and reiterated that the presence in the area of separation of Syrian armed forces and military equipment violated the Agreement on Disengagement of Forces. He noted that the construction of an earthwork of more than 2 km in length ongoing in the area of separation was of considerable concern to UNDOF as it was being used logistically by armed groups, rendering it a target for Syrian military action. In early May 2018 the Secretary-General expressed utmost concern at missile launches by Syria-based pro-Iranian forces that had targeted positions in Israel, and retaliatory strikes by the Israeli military. He urged the immediate cessation of all provocative and hostile acts. He observed in June that, in defiance of relevant UN Security Council resolutions, terrorist groups were continuing to exchange fire in UNDOF's area of operations. As a consequence of an offensive initiated in July by the Syrian armed forces and allies to oust militants from southwestern areas of Syria, significant numbers of people fled to the area of separation for security.

In mid-October 2018, following agreement between the UN, Syria and Israel, the Qunaytirah border crossing in the Golan Heights was reopened, for the first time since 2014, enabling UNDOF to facilitate humanitarian focused crossings. In December 2018 the UN Secretary-General reported that by August, as Syrian Government forces had increasingly regained territorial control, conflict had largely abated across previously militant-held areas. In December 2019 he stated that, despite a definite improvement in the security situation, UNDOF was reporting the continued presence of armed groups, and attacks against detachments of the Syrian armed forces in the area of limitation on the Bravo side and nearby. Attempted and achieved assassinations of former opposition leaders that had reconciled with the national authorities were also reported. From March 2020, as a COVID-19 containment measure, the gate at the Qunaytirah crossing to the Alpha (Israeli) side was closed, adversely impacting UNDOF and OGG movements between the Alpha and Bravo (Syrian) sides. Also, mounting public unrest in Lebanon since late 2019 was reported to be negatively affecting the mission's primary supply route (for example for fuel, rations and personnel) between Beirut and Damascus. In December 2020 the UN Secretary-General observed that the situation in the southern zone of the area of limitation on the Bravo side was particularly unstable. Meanwhile, movements of UNDOF and OGG personnel through the Qunaytirah crossing were only being permitted on a case-by-case basis, impeding their efficiency. Constant COVID-19 screening, and restrictions on movements between positions were in place. In June 2021 the Secretary-General reported that frequent attacks had continued in the southern part of the area of UNDOF's operations, and in Jasim, Muzayrib, Nawa and Tafas. The Syrian armed forces had reportedly reinforced their presence around Umm Batinah (in the central zone). UNDOF completed its return to the Bravo (Syrian) side in the second half of 2021. In March 2022 the UN Secretary-General called on the IDF to desist from firing into the area of separation and across the ceasefire line, and from physically crossing the latter, and also noted with concern an incident in early December 2021 of firing across the line from the Syrian side. In September 2022 the Secretary-General reported that drones were being flown across the ceasefire line, and unauthorized weapons and equipment had been observed in the area of limitation on sides. He reiterated calls that the IDF should cease firing into the area of separation, and stated concern at the persisting presence there of Syrian armed forces. Reports emerged in November that the IDF had initiated the construction of a paved road close to the Alpha line. In June 2023 the Secretary-General reported that while the ceasefire between Israel and Syria had recently generally been upheld, violations were persisting in the areas of limitation and separation, and he observed that the situation in UNDOF's area of operations remained volatile. In March Syria had informed the President of the UN Security Council that Israel had conducted an air raid (from Ladhiqivih) against Syria's Aleppo International Airport. Three rockets had reportedly been launched from Syrian territory towards the Alpha (Israeli) side on 8 April; in retaliation rocket launchers in Syria were attacked by an Israeli drone. On 18 April a rocket was reportedly fired from the Alpha side towards Tall al-Gharbi in the southern part of the area of limitation on the Bravo side. UNDOF continued to protest to the parties with respect to all observed violations of the Disengagement of Forces Agreement. As at mid-2023 movement by UNDOF and the OGG through the Alpha gate at the Qunaytirah crossing remained restricted by the Israeli forces (which were demanding advance notification), and the mission's movements were also restricted by Lebanese administrative requirements. UNDOF was continuing to conduct fortnightly inspections of the military positions of the Israeli and Syrian armed forces in parts of their respective areas of limitation.

Operational Strength: At 30 June 2023 the mission comprised 1,065 troops and 59 staff officers. Assistance is provided by military observers of the UNTSO's OGG. International and local civilian support staff totalled 125 personnel.

Finance: The General Assembly appropriation for the operation over the period 1 July 2023–30 June 2024 amounted to US $69.3m.

United Nations Interim Force in Lebanon—UNIFIL

Address: Naqoura, Lebanon.

Force Commander and Chief of Mission: Maj.-Gen. AROLDO LÁZARO SÁENZ (Spain).

Maritime Task Force Commander: Rear Admiral AXEL SCHULZ (Germany).

Establishment and Mandate: UNIFIL was established by UN Security Council Resolution 425 in March 1978, following an invasion of Lebanon by Israeli forces. The mission was mandated to confirm the withdrawal of Israeli forces, to restore international peace and security, and to assist the Government of Lebanon in ensuring the return of its effective authority in southern Lebanon. UNIFIL also extended humanitarian assistance to the population of the area, particularly following the second Israeli invasion of Lebanon in 1982. UN Security Council Resolution 1701, approved in August 2006, increased UNIFIL's authorized troop strength to 15,000 and expanded the mission's mandate to include monitoring the ceasefire between the two sides, ensuring that its area of operations is not used for any hostile activity, supporting the deployment of Lebanese troops in southern Lebanon, facilitating humanitarian access to civilian communities, and assisting voluntary and safe returns of internally displaced persons (IDPs). A tripartite forum provides the framework for regular meetings between the UNIFIL Force Commander and senior officials from the Lebanese and Israeli security forces. The UNIFIL Liaison Branch, formed in 2006, tracks and promotes regular three-way communication, and provides rapid responses aimed at anticipating and de-escalating tensions along the Blue Line. Observers from UNTSO's Observer Group Lebanon provide support to UNIFIL in the performance of its tasks, as required. From 2017 UNIFIL was tasked with developing a more comprehensive mechanism for reporting violations of Resolution 1701, and with focusing in more detail on the military presence of Hezbollah. In August 2020 the UN Security Council reduced UNIFIL's maximum authorized troop ceiling from 15,000 to 13,000, and mandated the mission to undertake temporary special measures to assist with the recovery of Lebanon and the Lebanese people in the aftermath of the Beirut port explosion catastrophe. UNIFIL maintains 55 positions in its area of operations (border wall constuction by the Israel Defense Forces—IDF has, however, reportedly limited some visibility).

2006–18: In July 2006 a full-scale conflict erupted between the Israeli armed forces and Hezbollah, prompted by the capture of two Israeli soldiers, and the killing of three others. An estimated 1,000 Lebanese civilians were killed and 900,000 displaced from their homes during the unrest. A ceasefire entered into effect in mid-August, following the adoption by the UN Security Council of Resolution 1701 (q.v.). At the request of the Lebanese Government, Resolution 1701 also established the Maritime Task Force (MTF)—the first naval task force to participate in a UN peacekeeping mission—which was deployed from October to support the Lebanese Navy in monitoring and securing Lebanon's territorial waters and coastline, and preventing the unauthorized entry of arms by sea into Lebanon. In September a Strategic Military Cell was formed to provide guidance to UNIFIL. A UN Mine Action Co-ordination Centre of South Lebanon was also established to co-ordinate efforts to locate and destroy unexploded munitions.

In July–August 2014 stability along the Blue Line was jeopardized by the outbreak of intense conflict in Gaza; several rockets were fired from Lebanon towards Israel at that time, while UNIFIL investigated all incidents and liaised with all parties to diffuse the situation. In March 2015 the President of the UN Security Council expressed deep concern over recent levels of violence in UNIFIL's area of operations. In August 2016 the Lebanese authorities announced that they would file a complaint to the UN Security Council protesting Israeli incursions into the Ghajar and the Sheba'a Farms border settlement area. A meeting between the Lebanese and Israeli militaries that was convened by UNIFIL in February 2018 discussed Israeli plans to construct a security wall at the Israel–Lebanon border, aimed at preventing incursions and attacks by Hezbollah: the Lebanese contingent claimed that the project violated Lebanese sovereignty.

2019–23: The UNIFIL Force Commander urged maximum restraint and stated serious concern over a Hezbollah precision missile attack that was conducted across the Blue Line on 1 September 2019 against Israeli military positions. Israel had reportedly fired back 100 shells in retaliation. At the beginning of October the inaugural meeting was convened of a joint UNIFIL-Office of the UN Special Coordinator for Lebanon (UNSCOL) strategic forum, with a view to enhancing efficiencies between the two entities. From October Lebanese troops were deployed to control mounting national anti-government protests. With the country mired in a deepening economic crisis, domestic budgetary constraints were reported to be undermining the Lebanese military's resources. UNIFIL and UNSCOL, meanwhile, jointly worked to de-escalate local tensions. Despite social lockdown measures that were enacted in March 2020, in response to the COVID-19 pandemic, public unrest re-emerged in Beirut and other areas in late April. In June the UN Secretary-General recommended joint UNIFIL-UNSCOL participation in donor consultations, as a means of strengthening mutual co-ordination. In August UNIFIL troops assisted the Lebanese authorities following the explosion that devastated large parts of Beirut's port and surrounding residential areas. An MTF vessel that had been docked in the port was damaged in the disaster, and 36 naval peacekeepers injured. (The vessel was replaced in September.) UNIFIL deployed an engineering unit temporarily to Beirut to clear debris, to undertake construction work, and to assist with the restoration of damaged heritage sites. The Secretary-General noted in November several ceasefire violations in recent months, and counter efforts by UNIFIL to de-escalate and investigate such situations; almost daily incursions into Lebanese airspace by the IDF were reported. In late August 2021 the UN Security Council tasked the mission with taking 'temporary and special measures' (initially for six months, but subsequently extended) to assist the Lebanese military with logistical and 'non-lethal material' (e.g. food and fuel) support. Against the background of the escalation in May 2021 of conflict between Israel and the Palestinian territories, rockets were fired towards Israel from southern Lebanon on several occasions, with retaliatory artillery fire from the IDF ensuing. UNIFIL conducted technical investigations into the ceasefire violations. In November the Secretary-General condemned a marked escalation of IDF air strikes that were perpetrated in early August against targets in Lebanon, and the subsequent deployment by Hezbollah of a multi-barrel rocket launcher. In July 2022 he reported that UNIFIL's radar capabilities had detected a rocket launch in late April from Qulaylah, on the Lebanese side, that had landed near an Israeli village (Shlomi). In retaliation the IDF had fired around 50 artillery shells towards Wadi Humul (Lebanon). In December 2022 a UNIFIL convoy was attacked, resulting in the death of a peacekeeper; in March 2023 the Secretary-General noted that acts of intimidation against UNIFIL peacekeepers were continuing. At that time the Secretary-General reiterated that the continued maintenance of unauthorized weapons by Hezbollah and other militant groupings represented a grave violation of Resolution 1701, and called for an end to persistent Israeli violations of Lebanese airspace. In July the Secretary-General reported that, on 6 April, UNIFIL had detected 24 rockets fired to the south of the Blue Line, from Sma'iyah, Malkiyah, and Zibqin; six rockets that had failed to launch were also found. On 7 April the IDF had conducted retaliatory air strikes against three targets (deemed by Israel to be Hamas-related terrorist infrastructures) close to Rashidiyah Palestinian refugee camp, south of Tyre. UNIFIL remained in constant contact with both sides, attempting to de-escalate tensions. The mission observed the presence of two tents near Bastrah (south of the Blue Line) in May and June, and requested the Lebanese forces to ensure their removal. Several incidents were observed in the Shab'a Farms area, including weapons pointing by both the Lebanese and Israeli forces; UNIFIL liaised with both sides and interposed between them to defuse tensions. The IDF was reported to be continuing to construct a wall south of the Blue Line. UNIFIL launched seven technical investigations into border incidents that occurred during the period 21 February to 20 June. The Secretary-General stated in July that the mission had not been granted full access to a number of sites of interest (including unauthorized firing ranges that had been observed during air reconnaissance patrols near Dayr Amis, Frun, Qantarah and Zibqin, on the Lebanese side, several sites near the Blue Line associated with Green without Borders—a Lebanese environmental agency, and tunnels under the Blue Line). He reiterated condemnation of persistent incursions into Lebanese airspace by Israeli aircraft and drones. In August the UN Security Council renewed UNIFIL's mandate until 31 August 2024.

UNIFIL works to mark visibly the Blue Line, involving the clearance of minefields, measuring co-ordinates, and the placement of Blue Line markers. As at mid-2023 one-half of the length of the Blue Line remained unmarked, with the potential to intensify border tensions. The UNIFIL MTF works closely with the Lebanese Navy in training, capacity-building and search and rescue activities, and conducts maritime surveillance operations. Vessels hailed by the Task Force are referred to the Lebanese authorities for further inspections. In late October UNIFIL welcomed a landmark agreement between Lebanon and Israel defining a maritime border between the two countries (thus enabling the economic exploitation of natural gas fields). A partial transfer of MTF responsibilities to the Lebanese Navy was ongoing in 2023.

UNIFIL's Force Commander has participated in meetings of the International Support Group (ISG) for Lebanon which was established by the UN Secretary-General in September 2013 to address means of supporting stability in Lebanon, in view of the impact on the country's security and resources of the ongoing civil war in neighbouring Syria.

Operational Strength: At 30 June 2023 the Force comprised 9,304 troops and 202 staff officers. Support is provided by military observers of UNTSO's Observer Group Golan. International and local civilian support staff totalled 809, in 2021.

Finance: The General Assembly appropriation for the operation for the period 1 July 2023–30 June 2024 amounted to US $69.3m.

United Nations Mission for the Referendum in Western Sahara—MINURSO

Address: El-Aaiún, Western Sahara.

Special Representative of the UN Secretary-General and Chief of Mission: ALEXANDER IVANKO (Russia).

Personal Envoy of the UN Secretary-General for Western Sahara: STAFFAN DE MISTURA (Italy/Sweden).

Force Commander: Maj.-Gen. MD FAKHRUL AHSAN (Bangladesh).

Establishment and Mandate: In April 1991 the UN Security Council endorsed the establishment of MINURSO to verify a ceasefire in the disputed territory of Western Sahara, to promote security and stability, and to support the implementation of an agreed settlement plan, involving the repatriation (in co-ordination with the UN High Commissioner for Refugees—UNHCR) of around 90,000 Western Saharan refugees, the release of all Sahrawi political detainees, the exchange of prisoners of war, and the organization of a referendum on the future of the territory. Western Sahara (which has rich phosphate and off-coast fisheries resources) is claimed by Morocco, the administering power since 1975, and by the Algerian-supported (and based) Frente Popular para la Liberación de Saguia el Hamra y Río de Oro—Frente Polisario. Although the referendum, originally envisaged for January 1992, was postponed indefinitely and remained so in 2023, MINURSO has continued to monitor the ceasefire and to work to reduce the threat of mines and unexploded ordnances. MINURSO provided logistical support to a UNHCR-managed Confidence Building Measures initiative—covering, for example, family visits—that was suspended in 2014, owing to local level disagreements. The mission has, on an exceptional basis, also assisted irregular migrants. A Group of Friends of Western Sahara—France, the Russian Federation, Spain (the former colonial power), the United Kingdom and the USA—has a special focus within the UN Security Council on the Western Saharan situation and on preparing resolutions concerning the mandate of MINURSO.

Activities, 1997–2014: In June 1997 direct talks were initiated, under UN auspices, between Morocco and the Frente Polisario, with attendance by Algeria and Mauritania in an observer capacity. In

September the two sides concluded an agreement which aimed to resolve the outstanding issues of contention, including a commitment by both parties to identify, for the purposes of the proposed referendum, eligible Sahrawi voters on an individual basis, in accordance with the results of the last official census in 1974. The process of voter identification resumed in December 1997, and was completed by early 2000. However, all parties continued to dispute the voting lists. In January 2003 the Personal Envoy of the UN Secretary-General elaborated a new arrangement for a political settlement, which was accepted by the Frente Polisario in July, but rejected by the Moroccan Government in April 2004. By August 2005 the Frente Polisario had released all its Moroccan detainees; Morocco, however, reportedly continued to hold around 150 Western Saharan prisoners.

During 2007–12, under the auspices of the Personal Envoy, nine rounds of negotiations were held between representatives of the Moroccan Government and the Frente Polisario, but without significant progression. In January 2014 the Personal Envoy, during a visit to the region affirmed a postponement of bilateral talks pending improved prospects of progress. He continued thereafter to hold confidential consultations with working parties from each side.

2015–18: In early March 2016, during a visit to the region, the UN Secretary-General—while in Frente Polisario-occupied Bir Lehlu—referred to Morocco's presence in Western Sahara as an 'occupation'. In response, the Moroccan authorities declared that he had abandoned neutrality, and in mid-March an estimated 1m. demonstrators marched in Rabat, the Moroccan capital, to protest against the Secretary-General's statement. Soon afterwards, the Moroccan authorities expelled 83 MINURSO civilian staff members and closed a mission liaison office in the coastal city of Dakhla. (It was reported in April 2017 that Morocco had agreed to readmit MINURSO's El-Aaiún-based civilian staff members.)

In August 2016 the UN Secretary-General expressed deep concern over mounting tensions in the Guerguerat area of south-western Western Sahara—at the buffer strip between the Berm (the 2,700 km-long Moroccan-built wall separating the Moroccan- and Frente Polisario-controlled areas) and the Mauritanian border—attributed to the close proximity of armed Moroccan and Frente Polisario units (Morocco having first deployed its military to the area purportedly as part of an anti-trafficking operation). Both sides were urged to avoid an escalation of the situation by withdrawing all armed elements, and to desist from undertaking any action likely to alter the status quo. MINURSO, meanwhile, was tasked with maintaining a presence in Guerguerat and with undertaking mediation. Nevertheless, the unrest continued, escalating in mid-February 2017, when the Frente Polisario began to obstruct the passage through Guerguerat of civilian and commercial vehicles displaying Moroccan insignia, citing this as a deliberate provocation. In late February the Secretary-General strongly urged both the Frente Polisario and Moroccan armed elements to withdraw unconditionally from the Guerguerat area, to avoid restricting traffic, and to adhere fully to their ceasefire obligations. Shortly afterwards Morocco initiated a unilateral withdrawal from the buffer strip, and at the end of April it was confirmed that Frente Polisario forces had redeployed away from the sensitive area. From June the MINURSO presence in Guerguerat reportedly implemented strengthened security measures, owing to terrorist threats made against it. A renewed Frente Polisario presence was reported in the Guerguerat buffer zone from December. In August 2017 the Secretary-General appointed Horst Köhler, former President of Germany, to the role of Personal Envoy.

In January 2018, in view of continuing obstructions of traffic reportedly conducted by the Frente Polisario in Guerguerat, the UN Secretary-General sent a letter to the grouping that urged it to comply with international law. In April the Frente Polisario withdrew its 'policing' presence from Guerguerat, and, consequently, in July MINURSO started to draw down its temporary monitoring post in the area, while maintaining regular ground and air patrols. Visiting the region in late June–early July, the Secretary-General's Personal Envoy met with representatives of local authorities, civil society and the business community. At that time the Frente Polisario stated that increased human rights monitoring and interaction with the Sahrawi people would enhance MINURSO's capacity to fulfil its mandate, noted its objection to the use of Moroccan licence plates on UN vehicles in Western Sahara, and reiterated demands (objected to by Morocco as constituting recognition of the Frente Polisario's claims) that its representatives should be permitted to meet with MINURSO inside Western Sahara and thus be treated on identical terms to Morocco. In July the AU decided to decelerate its own peace activities in Western Sahara (which had been deemed by Morocco as 'biased'), and to place increased focus on supporting—through the establishment of a Troika of AU heads of state—the UN-led political process. In September the UN Secretary-General and his Personal Envoy issued invitations to all parties to initiate new negotiations for a peaceful settlement of the dispute. In October, the UN Security Council urged all parties to engage constructively in the process. An initial roundtable meeting—with participation by representatives from Algeria, Morocco, the Frente Polisario and Mauritania—was convened, under the auspices of the Personal Envoy, in Geneva, in December, to discuss restarting the direct talks process. It was, however, reported that the Frente Polisario and Morocco were continuing to pursue very distinct agendas of, respectively, self-determination for Western Sahara and Morocco's plan (first proposed in 2007) for Western Saharan administrative autonomy within a framework of Moroccan sovereignty.

2019–23: A second roundtable meeting on the future of Western Sahara took place, again under UN auspices, in March 2019. In May Köhler resigned from the role of Personal Envoy. Brahim Ghali, the Secretary-General of the Frente Polisario, wrote formally to the President of the Security Council in October requesting that the UN expedite the appointment of a new Personal Envoy, and accusing Morocco of intransigence, provocations (including continuing to breach the buffer zone at Guerguerat), of committing destabilizing actions, and of attempting to dictate the UN-led peace process with a view to entrenching its presence in Western Sahara. In December Morocco drew the attention of the Council to the Frente Polisario's decision to organize its 15th congress in that month in the Tifariti area east of the Berm—regarded as a neutral buffer by Morocco and as 'liberated' by the Frente Polisario. Meanwhile, in December, Ghali sent another letter to the Security Council, in which he urged the Council and the UN Secretariat to restore the confidence of the Sahrawi people in the UN peace process, including by ensuring the impartiality of MINURSO, and by enabling meetings between the Frente Polisario and mission personnel to take place in the so-called 'liberated' territories. In September 2020 Ghali, in a formal letter to the UN Secretary-General, emphasized that the original Western Sahara settlement plan had been accepted by both the Frente Polisario and Morocco, reiterated the Frente Polisario's position that a referendum on the self-determination of Western Sahara was urgently required and an 'inalienable right', called on the UN General Assembly to schedule such a poll, and—alleging that Sahrawis continued to be subjected to arbitrary arrests, illegal detentions, enforced disappearances, and extrajudicial executions—urged that a human rights monitoring dimension should be incorporated into MINURSO. He also noted that the Frente Polisario's adherence to the ceasefire in Western Sahara was contingent upon the terms of the original settlement plan. In mid-November the Moroccan authorities dispatched military personnel into the buffer zone in order to secure the Guerguerat border crossing into Mauritania, Morocco's principal road trade link with sub-Saharan Africa, which had been obstructed by Saharawi protesters; the Frente Polisario interpreted this as a provocation and declared the ceasefire observed since 1991 to be annulled. Furthermore, the Frente Polisario restricted MINURSO's movements, and both sides limited their engagement with the mission's leadership. Intermittent firing across the Berm subsequently persisted.

In December 2020 outgoing US President Trump recognized Moroccan sovereignty over Western Sahara. The Frente Polisario wrote to the UN in late February 2021 requesting the resumption of the UN-sponsored negotiations process. At the end of March the Frente Polisario welcomed a statement by the new US Secretary of State, Antony Blinken, that urged the acceleration of the appointment of a replacement Personal Envoy of the UN Secretary-General for Western Sahara. A new Special Representative was named in August, and—after the role had been unfilled for nearly 29 months—a new Personal Envoy, Staffan de Mistura, was designated in October. In that month Ghali defended the decision to end the ceasefire, and warned that should the territorial dispute not be resolved under UN auspices the conflict might expand and destabilize the wider region. De Mistura undertook his first visit to the region in January 2022, in an attempt to revive political dialogue. In March the Frente Polisario strongly protested an announcement by the Spanish Government (one of the Friends of Western Sahara, and hitherto an advocate for a referendum on the issue of Sahrawi independence) that—representing a full reversal of policy—it would henceforth support, as 'realistic', Morocco's autonomy plan for Western Sahara. In October 2022 the Security Council extended MINURSO's mandate until 31 October 2023. In March 2023 Spain and Morocco initiated negotiations over the future of Western Sahara's airspace. A letter written in June by the Frente Polisario's co-ordinator with MINURSO, Dr Sidi Mohamed Omar, to the UN Security Council emphasized that the people of Western Sahara would never relinquish the right to self-determination and independence. It was reported in early September that a Frente Polisario commander and other combatants had been killed by a drone near the Dakhla refugee camp in Tindouf, Algeria.

MINURSO has headquarters in the north and south of the disputed territory. There is a liaison office in Tindouf (Algeria) which was established in order to maintain contact with the Frente Polisario and the Algerian Government. The mission's military component is deployed at nine team sites—at Smara, Mahbas, Oum Dreyga, Awsard (all east of the Moroccan-built Berm) and

Bir Lahlou, Tifariti, Mehaires, Mijek, Awsard (to the west of the Berm). The mission uses geospatial imagery to supplement its local observations. In October 2022 the UN Secretary-General reported that lack of access to areas near the Berm was significantly hindering MINURSO's observation activities. By 2023 (despite a verbal promise made in 2014) Morocco had not ended a requirement that MINURSO vehicles should display Moroccan number plates in the area west of the Berm, which has reportedly impacted wider perceptions of the mission's impartiality.

Operational Strength: At 30 June 2023 MINURSO comprised 197 experts on mission, 20 troops, two police officers and seven staff officers. International and local civilian support staff totalled 230, in 2018.

Finance: The General Assembly appropriation to cover the cost of the mission for the period 1 July 2023–30 June 2024 amounted to US $65.1m.

United Nations Peacekeeping Force in Cyprus—UNFICYP

Address: Nicosia, Cyprus.

Special Representative of the UN Secretary-General and Chief of Mission: COLIN STEWART (Canada).

Force Commander: Maj.-Gen. INGRID GJERDE (Norway).

Establishment and Mandate: UNFICYP was established in March 1964 by a UN Security Council resolution to prevent a recurrence of fighting between the Greek and Turkish Cypriot communities, and to contribute to the maintenance of law and order. The Force controls a 180 km buffer zone, established (following the Turkish intervention in 1974) between the ceasefire lines of the Turkish forces and the Cyprus National Guard. It is mandated to investigate and act upon all violations of the ceasefire and buffer zone, as well as to perform humanitarian functions, such as facilitating the supply of electricity and water across the ceasefire lines, and to promote a stable and calm environment. The UN Secretary-General's good offices have supported the conduct of negotiations between the Greek and Turkish Cypriot leaders. In reports to the Security Council the UN Secretary-General has consistently recognized UNFICYP as being indispensable to maintaining calm on the island and to creating the best conditions for his good offices. The mission has sections: military; UN Police; civil affairs; and administration. Its mandate was extended in January 2023 for a 12-month period until 31 January 2024 (hitherto six-monthly extensions had been effected).

Activities, 2002–08: In January 2002 a new series of direct talks between the Greek Cypriot and Turkish Cypriot leaders commenced, under the auspices of the UN Secretary-General's Special Adviser. In November the UN Secretary-General submitted for consideration a document providing the basis for a comprehensive settlement agreement. A revised version was presented to the leaders of the two communities in February 2003. Negotiations on settling outstanding differences were chaired by the Secretary-General's Special Adviser for Cyprus throughout March and a finalized text was presented at the end of that month. The proposed Foundation Agreement was subsequently approved by two-thirds of Turkish Cypriot voters in a referendum held in April, but rejected by some 75% of Greek Cypriot voters. In June the Secretary-General determined to undertake a comprehensive review of UNFICYP's mandate and force levels, in view of the political developments on the island. In October the Security Council endorsed the recommendations of the Secretary-General's review team, which included a reduction in the mission's authorized strength from 1,230 to 860 military personnel and an increase in the deployment of civilian police officers from 44 to 69.

In July 2006 the Turkish Cypriot leader and the Greek Cypriot President, meeting under the auspices of the UN Secretary-General, agreed on a set of principles and decisions aimed at reinstating the negotiating process. UNFICYP hosted a second meeting of the leaders of the two communities in September 2007. They agreed on a need to initiate a settlement process and confirmed that they would continue a bicommunal dialogue under UN auspices. In March 2008 the Special Representative of the UN Secretary-General (SRSG) convened a meeting of the two leaders, who approved the establishment of technical committees and working groups in preparation for detailed political negotiations. The leaders also agreed to the reopening, in the following month, of a crossing between the two communities at Ledra Street, Nicosia. Full negotiations on a political settlement for the island were inaugurated in September.

2009–13: By August 2009 the two leaders had met 40 times in the preceding 12-month period. The second round of full negotiations commenced in September, and by September 2010 a further 44 meetings had been conducted. In October the Limnitis/Yesilirmak crossing point was reopened. In November the UN Secretary-General met directly with the two leaders in order to reinvigorate the settlement discussions. A further meeting between the Secretary-General and the leaders of the two communities was held in January 2011, at which both sides agreed to intensify efforts to reach substantive agreement on outstanding core issues of contention. In October 2011 and January 2012 further tripartite meetings were held, in Greentree, New York, USA, aimed at assessing progress made in the ongoing negotiations, and at addressing unresolved issues, especially related to powersharing, contentious property ownership issues, territory and citizenship. Bilateral meetings continued, in Nicosia, in February–March 2012, but were reported at that time by the UN Secretary-General to be almost deadlocked on outstanding core issues. In April the Special Adviser of the Secretary-General indicated that the UN's participation in negotiations would be reduced to the level of technical discussions and confidence-building measures, pending significant progress in bilateral discussions between the Greek and Turkish Cypriot leaders.

In May 2013 the Special Adviser of the UN Secretary-General hosted a meeting between the new Greek Cypriot leader, Nicos Anastasiades, and his Turkish counterpart, Derviş Eroğlu. Thereafter the Special Adviser met both leaders several times with a view to overcoming the impasse reached in the negotiations process.

2014–16: In early February 2014 the two leaderships finally agreed a Joint Declaration and a roadmap to guide the negotiations, and, consequently, UN-mediated formal talks recommenced soon afterwards, in Nicosia. The Greek Cypriot and Turkish Cypriot leaders met in March and June. Meeting in September, with a new Special Adviser on Cyprus, Espen Barth Eide, the two leaders agreed henceforth to hold at least two meetings each month. In early October, however, accusing the Turkish Government of violating its maritime exclusive economic zone, the Greek Cypriot administration suspended its participation in the process, pending the removal of a Turkish research vessel that had been sent to explore for gas there. A new Turkish Cypriot President, Mustafa Akıncı, took office in April 2015, and soon afterwards, in mid-May, the negotiations process—facilitated by Eide—was resumed. In January 2016 the UN Security Council determined to increase UNFICYP's capacity to a ceiling of 888 troops. At the beginning of 2016 the Greek Cypriot and Turkish Cypriot leaders made an unprecedented joint New Year's television address. In June the two leaders agreed to intensify their engagement to address outstanding issues. In early November they conducted substantial negotiations in Mont Pèlerin, Switzerland, under the auspices of the UN Special Adviser, where, for the first time, they addressed territorial issues. The UN Secretary-General reported that by the end of 2016 significant progress had been made in four thematic areas of the negotiations: the economy; governance and powersharing; property; and matters pertaining to the European Union (EU).

2017–19: A Conference on Cyprus—with participation by the Greek Cypriot and Turkish leaders and also (as guarantor powers) by senior representatives of Greece, Turkey (now known as Türkiye), the United Kingdom, as well as of the EU—was held under UN auspices in Geneva, Switzerland, in January 2017. In June the UN Secretary-General met with the Greek Cypriot and Turkish Cypriot leaders. The Switzerland-based Conference on Cyprus was reconvened in late June–early July (in Crans-Montana); however, the talks broke down over issues including the continued deployment to the island post-reunification of some 1,000 Greek and 30,000 Turkish troops, and the return of property to Greek Cypriot former residents of the north of the island. Nicos Anastasiades was re-elected as Greek Cypriot President in January–February 2018. Anastasiades and Mustafa Akıncı met informally, under UN auspices, in April; both leaders, however, emphasized that the meeting did not represent the resumption of the negotiations process. In July the UN Secretary-General requested the then UN Special Adviser on Cyprus, Jane Holl Lute, to initiate a series of consultations with the parties to the Conference on Cyprus, and in October he instructed her to pursue efforts to finalize terms of reference that would constitute a consensus starting point for the resumption of meaningful negotiations. During the latter month, under the auspices of the SRSG, President Akıncı and President Anastasiades met for the first time since April. In November two new border crossing points were opened, fulfilling a commitment that had been agreed, in May 2015, and bringing to nine the total number of crossing points on the island. Further meetings between Anastasiades and Akıncı were convened during February–August 2019 under the auspices of the SRSG. A trilateral meeting, of the two leaders and the UN Secretary-General, was held in late November.

2020–23: Ersin Tatar succeeded Akıncı as the Turkish Cypriot President in October 2020. In that month, controversially, he partially reopened the Varosha (Maraş) beach quarter of the abandoned town of Famagusta, which had been fenced off as part of the buffer zone since 1974; this was denounced by the Greek Cypriot authorities. UNFICYP's freedom of movement in the vicinity of Varosha was impeded. Following Tatar's election, he and Anastasiades, meeting informally under UN auspices, agreed to participate in an informal meeting to be organized by the UN Secretary-General in a

'5+1' format—i.e. with participation by Anastasiades, Tatar, the guarantor countries Greece, Turkey and the UK, and the UN. In mid-February 2021 President Tatar criticized as 'unacceptable' conditions that had been imposed by his Greek Cypriot counterpart in advance of the pending 5+1 meeting—including a demand that the reopening of Varosha should be ended. The 5+1 meeting took place in Geneva at the end of April, but did not achieve sufficient process to enable the resumption of formal negotiations. In June, however, agreement was reached, facilitated by the SRSG, on harmonizing COVID-19 measures and requirements, enabling the reopening of crossing points that had been closed since early 2020. (The epidemiological situation has been regularly assessed by the bicommunal Technical Committee on Health.) In July 2021 the UN Secretary-General protested a Turkish decision to lift 'military status' from 3.5% of the Varosha area. Jane Holl Lute resigned in August as UN Special Adviser on Cyprus. In December a new SRSG, Colin Stewart, took office. In January 2022 the UN Security Council expressed serious concern at ongoing violations of the ceasefire line, and stated regret over the lack of progress towards establishing an effective mechanism for direct bilateral military contacts. The UN Secretary-General stated concern in July that Türkiye was persistently undertaking provocative activities in territorial waters around Cyprus, in the fenced area of Varosha, and elsewhere in the border zone. In July 2023 the UN Secretary-General reported that thus far no action had been taken to end the reopening of Varosha. At that time the Secretary-General observed that a new Greek Cypriot leader, Nikos Christodoulides, elected in February, had asserted that resolving outstanding Cyprus-related issues was a priority. An in-person meeting had taken place in late February between Presidents Christodoulides and Tatar.

UNFICYP has continued to patrol and to maintain security in the buffer zone, and to liaise with the opposing forces. In January 2023 the UN Secretary-General stated concern at continuing unauthorized construction in the buffer zone. He noted that the Greek National Guard was deploying approximately 290 prefabricated concrete firing positions at the southern ceasefire line; meanwhile, positions along the northern ceasefire line had been enhanced in recent years, including the construction by the Turkish Cypriot military of watchtowers and prefabricated firing positions, and the addition of new surveillance equipment. In July the Secretary-General noted that, since January, five additional prefabricated firing positions had been deployed by the Greek National Guard, and two additional Turkish Cypriot positions had been constructed. UNFICYP stated concern in the following month over ongoing plans for unauthorized Turkish Cypriot construction activities within the buffer zone, in the Pyla/Pile area. Shortly afterwards the mission condemned assaults against UNFICYP personnel and vehicles that were attempting to block construction in that area, and called on the Turkish Cypriot side to respect UNFICYP's mandated authority. In July the Secretary-General also protested the trafficking of irregular migrants through the buffer zone.

UNFICYP has supported demining programmes near the ceasefire line; remained in contact with local authorities to ensure access for Turkish Cypriots to health, educational and social welfare support; and promoted intercommunal civil society events, in support of bicommunal co-operation. The mission is tasked with assisting the work of six of 12 bicommunal technical committees that were established in 2008 to develop confidence building measures. In January 2023 the UN Secretary-General reported that the Technical Committee on Crossings had recently been revitalized.

UNFICYP has also assisted with the implementation of the long-term Nicosia Master Plan—initiated in 1979 to enable both communities in Nicosia to co-operate in improving the city.

Operational Strength: At 30 June 2023 UNFICYP had an operational strength of 749 troops, 52 staff officers and 67 police officers. International and local civilian support staff totalled 151, in 2018.

Finance: The General Assembly appropriated US $56.4m. to the Special Account for UNFICYP to supplement voluntary donations in financing for the period 1 July 2023–30 June 2024.

United Nations Truce Supervision Organization—UNTSO

Address: Government House, Jerusalem.

Head of Mission: Patrick Gauchat (Switzerland).

Establishment and Mandate: UNTSO was established initially to supervise the truce called by the UN Security Council in Palestine in May 1948 and has assisted in the application of the 1949 Armistice Agreements. Its activities have evolved over the years, in response to developments in the Middle East and in accordance with the relevant resolutions of the Security Council. There is no periodic renewal procedure for UNTSO's mandate. UNTSO maintains liaison offices in Beirut, Lebanon; Ismailia, Egypt; and Damascus, Syria. Liaison with Tel Aviv (Israel) and Amman (Jordan) is conducted from the mission's Jerusalem headquarters.

Activities: UNTSO observers attach to and assist UN peacekeeping forces in the Middle East. The mission's Observer Group Golan is currently active in supporting UNDOF (under that mission's operational control) and its Observer Group Lebanon supports UNIFIL. In addition, the mission operates a number of outposts in the Sinai region of Egypt to maintain a UN presence there. UNTSO observers have been available at short notice to deploy to and form the nucleus of newly authorized peacekeeping operations.

Operational Strength: At 30 June 2023 UNTSO had an operational strength of 149 military observers. International and local civilian support staff (in 2021) totalled 232.

Finance: UNTSO expenditure is covered by the regular budget of the UN.

United Nations Political Missions and Peacebuilding

Address: Department of Political and Peacebuilding Affairs, United Nations, New York, NY 10017, USA.

Telephone: (212) 963-1234; **fax:** (212) 963-4879; **internet:** www.un.org/Depts/dpa.

UN political missions and peacebuilding operations work in the field to prevent and resolve conflicts or to promote enduring peace in post-conflict societies. They are supported by the Department of Political and Peacebuilding Affairs (DPPA), which was established on 1 January 2019. The Department assists envoys and advisers bearing the UN Secretary-General's 'good offices' for the resolution of conflicts or implementation of other UN mandates.

Office of the Special Envoy of the United Nations Secretary-General for Syria

Special Envoy of the UN Secretary-General for Syria: Geir Pedersen (Norway).

Establishment and Mandate: In December 2015 the UN Security Council unanimously adopted Resolution 2254, which endorsed a roadmap for peace in Syria (which had been engulfed since 2012 in civil conflict), and called for a formal UN-facilitated, Syrian-led political process—to be organized by the UN Special Envoy—and the establishment of a 'credible, inclusive and non-sectarian' governance structure. The UN Special Envoy is authorized to provide good offices aimed at bringing an end to all violence and human rights violations, and promoting a peaceful solution to the Syrian crisis.

Activities: In November 2015 representatives of the UN, the Arab League, the European Union, and ministers responsible for foreign affairs of the USA, Russian Federation (which in September had decided to intervene militarily in Syria, in support of the al-Assad regime), and 15 other states—meeting in Vienna, Austria, as the 'International Syria Support Group' (ISSG)—determined that political talks between the Syrian Government and opposition factions should commence in early 2016, with a view to expediting an end to the Syrian conflict and to accelerating agreement on a new Syrian constitution, governance structure and elections schedule. The ISSG established a Humanitarian Task Force (HTF), which has met regularly in Geneva, Switzerland, under the chairmanship of the Office of the Special Envoy for Syria. The Group also formed a Ceasefire Task Force (CTF), for which the Office provides secretariat services. The ISSG-sponsored peace talks (referred to as 'Geneva III') commenced at the beginning of February 2016, but were suspended shortly afterwards, reportedly owing to opposition concern over mounting air attacks on rebel areas by Russian and Syrian government forces. In late February the UN Security Council unanimously endorsed a temporary ceasefire deal reached by the USA and Russia; this enabled the delivery of humanitarian aid to challenging areas. The Geneva III series of negotiations was reconvened in March 2016, at which time the UN Special Envoy released a statement of shared goals and principles; a further session of the talks was convened in April. In late April the Special Envoy reported that the cessation of hostilities was barely in force, and that the humanitarian situation had deteriorated severely during that month. By September some 250,000 people were reported to be under siege in eastern Aleppo as

Russian and Syrian government forces attempted to recapture the city from militants. In that month the Special Envoy condemned the destruction in an air strike of part of a convoy of trucks near Aleppo that had been transporting humanitarian aid to civilians. In late October the Security Council strongly condemned attacks on a school complex in Idlib, northwestern Syria, in which at least 22 children and teachers were killed. Following a resumption in mid-November of intense air strikes against eastern Aleppo, by December most of the area was under the control of Syrian government forces. In December the Security Council adopted a resolution that expressed alarm at the 'continued deterioration of the devastating humanitarian situation in Aleppo', and requested the UN and other relevant agencies to monitor evacuations of civilians from the city.

In December 2016 the UN Security Council unanimously adopted a resolution that welcomed efforts by Russia and Turkey (known since June 2022 as Türkiye) to end the conflict in Syria and move peace negotiations forwards. Turkey was a backer of the Syrian opposition, and accommodating a large number of Syrian refugees. (A parallel, complementary negotiations process was initiated by those countries in early 2017 in the Kazakh capital Astana.) A ceasefire entered into effect on 30 December 2016, and held until February 2017. In January 2017 the Security Council expressed alarm at reports of the destruction of cultural heritage in Palmyra, Syria, and of executions by Islamic State being conducted in the theatre there. Two further rounds of ISSG negotiations (referred to as Geneva IV and V) were held during February–March, in Geneva. In early April the Security Council convened to discuss an alleged recent sarin gas attack against the rebel-occupied northwestern Syrian settlement of Khan Sheikhoun that was estimated to have killed nearly 90 people, and was reportedly perpetrated by the Syrian military. The representatives of the UK and USA criticized Russia's backing of the Syrian Government—rejecting Russia's alternative assertion that the chemical weapons had been in the possession of rebels—and affirmed support for a retaliatory US air strike against the Syrian airbase from where the chemical attack had allegedly been launched. In early May, during a session of the Astana negotiations process, an agreement was reached on the establishment of a series of de-escalation zones in Syria. Further rounds of ISSG-sponsored negotiations (Geneva VI, VII, VIII and IX) were held in mid-May, July, December and in January 2018. At the end of January 2018 the UN Special Envoy attended a peace conference for Syria organized in Sochi, Russia, by Russian President Vladimir Putin. The conference issued the Sochi Final Statement, in which it determined that a new committee—comprising diverse Syrian stakeholders—would be tasked, under UN auspices, with drafting a new Syrian Constitution.

A significant military escalation throughout Syria and at its borders occurred in early 2018. In February the UN Secretary-General urged an immediate unconditional de-escalation of tensions, following targeted air strikes by Israel against alleged Iranian positions inside Syria—apparently mandated in retaliation for an Iranian drone launch into Israeli territory from Syria, as well as for the destruction by the Syrian military of an Israeli fighter jet. Later in that month, after a protracted debate, and against a backdrop of intensive warfare and numerous civilian casualties in the rebel-held eastern Ghouta area, which was under bombardment by Syrian government forces, the Council unanimously approved a resolution that demanded a 30-day ceasefire in Syria in order to facilitate the delivery of humanitarian aid as well as to enable medical and other civilian evacuations. Some Islamist groupings, however, were not covered by the UN truce, and it was not fully upheld by the Syrian Government.

In April 2018 the USA, France and the UK conducted air strikes against suspected chemical weapons manufacturing facilities and capabilities in Syria, undertaken, without a UN Security Council mandate, in response to recent chemical attacks allegedly perpetrated by the Syrian regime against civilian sites. The UN Secretary-General subsequently emphasized UN member states' obligation to act in matters of peace and security in accordance with the UN Charter and urged the Security Council to unite over demanding accountability for the use of chemical weapons in Syria. The Special Envoy participated as an observer in a meeting held by Iran, Russia and Turkey in mid-May, in Astana, with attendance by the Syrian Government and by representatives of armed militia active in Syria. At that time the UN Secretary-General noted that Syrian military offensives, supported by Syria's allies, had targeted two of the 'De-escalation Areas' designated under the Astana negotiations process (eastern Ghouta and northern Homs). In June, ahead of further talks on the implementation of the Sochi Final Statement, the UN Envoy reiterated that the process of drafting the proposed new Syrian Constitution should be inclusive, and thus should comprise independent delegates, experts, and representatives of civil society, and should have at least 30% female participation. By July the Syrian armed forces had regained nearly all territory in southern areas of the country. At the end of August the UN Secretary-General appealed urgently to all parties to exercise military restraint and to prioritize the protection of civilians in the northwestern rebel-dominated Idlib area, and urged the leaders of the ongoing Astana negotiations process (the 'Astana guarantors') to intensify efforts to resolve peacefully the situation in Idlib (which was the last remaining De-escalation Area—but had recently been targeted by Russian and Syrian air strikes). In early September the UN Security Council met both formally and informally to address the political and humanitarian dimensions of the situation in Idlib. The UN Secretary-General welcomed the conclusion by Russia and Turkey later in that month of a formal Memorandum on Stabilization of the Situation in the Idlib De-escalation Area, which included the establishment, from mid-October, of a 15 km–25 km demilitarized buffer zone. In February 2019 Russia, Iran and Turkey convened, in Sochi, the fourth trilateral summit of the Astana process.

In September 2019 the UN Secretary-General announced that agreement had been reached on the composition of the proposed Constitutional Committee, to comprise equal representation of Syrian President Assad's Government, civil society and opposition delegates (grouped as the Syrian Negotiations Commission). The principal Kurdish militia engaged in the Syrian conflict (which were regarded by the Turkish authorities as terrorist entities) complained that the Kurdish people did not have sufficient representation on the committee. Following the unexpected initiation in mid-October of the withdrawal of US troops from northern Turkey—where, jointly with Kurdish militia, they had been acting to remove the Islamic State threat—a long-threatened Turkish military offensive into that area ensued, resulting in the swift displacement of up to 160,000 people and numerous civilian casualties. The UN Secretary-General urged an immediate de-escalation of the fighting and emphasized the need to maintain safe humanitarian access to the area. It was reported later in October that Kurdish militia and the Syrian Government had agreed that national forces should enter the area vacated by the US military. The inaugural meeting of the new Constitutional Committee was convened on 30 October. In March 2020 Russia and Turkey agreed a ceasefire and concluded an Additional Protocol to the 2018 Memorandum on Stabilization of the Situation in the Idlib De-escalation Area, which provided for the creation of a jointly patrolled security corridor. In July, in an address to the UN Security Council, the Special Envoy appealed to all Syrian parties to release conflict-related detainees and abductees.

In January 2021 the so-called 'Small Body' of the Constitutional Committee, comprising 45 delegates, met for its fifth session, facilitated by the UN Special Envoy. The Special Envoy subsequently criticized the lack of progress made—notably, while the Syrian regime favoured amending the existing national Constitution, opposition delegates were demanding a new one—and emphasized that there would need to be willingness to compromise in order to further the peace process. Following a trilateral meeting on the sidelines of the Constitutional Committee's session, Iran, Russia and Turkey issued a joint statement, in which they reaffirmed their readiness to support the Committee's work, by means of continuous interaction with the Syrian stakeholders and with the Special Envoy. They also urged a spirit of compromise and constructive engagement. Addressing the Security Council in late May, the Special Envoy noted that an ongoing presidential election in Syria was not being conducted within the framework of Resolution 2254 (which provided for UN-administered inclusive elections to follow the adoption of a new Constitution). At that time he stated concern that, without active efforts by each side to advance the implementation of Resolution 2254, the Syrian conflict might become protracted down generations. In mid-June the Special Envoy condemned the shelling of the al-Shifaa Hospital in Afrin, northern Syria. At the end of July the Special Envoy called for the de-escalation of an upsurge of violent conflict in southwestern Syria. In mid-August he reiterated concern over the deteriorating situation in southern areas of the country, which were causing civilian casualties and displacement, damage to infrastructure, and shortages of critical supplies, including of medicines and fuel. Hostilities and massive displacement continued into early 2022 in northwestern Syria, as in January Russian shelling and air strikes intensified against civilian infrastructure and settlements in and around the rebel-occupied Idlib De-escalation Area; the Russian offensive was supported by Turkish military reinforcements. In early February 2022 a US special operation in Idlib led to the death of the Islamic State leader Abu Ibrahim al-Hashimi al-Qurayshi, as well as reportedly also causing, collaterally, 13 civilian fatalities. Continuing Israeli air strikes against Syrian military and Iran-associated militia targets were also reported. The Special Envoy supported the eighth round of Small Body constitutional negotiations in June, in Geneva; a planned ninth instalment, initially scheduled to have been held in July, was postponed, reportedly in view of an objection by Russia to Geneva as the continuing location of the talks. The 19th round of Astana negotiations was held in November.

Following the earthquakes that devastated parts of Syria and Türkiye in February 2023 the ISSG's HTF met to identify local humanitarian needs in Syria, where up to 8.8m. survivors were thought to require urgent assistance. The opening of additional border crossings to facilitate the ongoing massive relief effort was welcomed. Donors were urged to support a UN flash appeal for

US $398m. In March, as the conflict in Syria entered its 13th year, the Special Envoy called for a comprehensive political resolution to the protracted crisis, noting that the momentum of the ongoing constructive humanitarian co-operation should be translated also to the political process. A session of the Syrian Women's Advisory Board was organized in that month. In early April high-level talks were convened between Syria, Russia, Iran and Türkiye, in Moscow, Russia, under a Russian initiative focused on improving relations between the Syrian administration and Türkiye. The 20th round of the Astana talks on Syria, held in June, emphasized the importance for combating terrorism and enabling the safe return of Türkiye-based Syrian refugees, of normalizing Türkiye-Syria relations. Addressing the Seventh Conference on Supporting the Future of Syria and the Region ('Brussels VII'), chaired by the EU in Belgium in that month, the Special Envoy took note of the recent tragic earthquakes and related constructive humanitarian co-operation, that had been followed by new diplomatic overtures between Arab states and the Syrian Government (in May Syria had been readmitted to the Arab League). He urged the development of confidence measures and the renewal of the intra-Syrian political process, with co-ordinated co-operation by the parties to the conflict, Arab actors, Astana actors, Western actors, and by the UN Security Council membership. He reiterated that no one group of players alone would be able to dictate the outcome of the conflict. He welcomed calls to reconvene the stalled Constitutional Committee meetings process. The Special Envoy continued in 2023 to maintain communication with Syrian civil society and women's representatives, and with regional and international stakeholders.

Office of the Special Envoy of the United Nations Secretary-General for Yemen—OSESGY

Internet: osesgy.unmissions.org.

Special Envoy of the UN Secretary-General for Yemen: HANS GRUNDBERG (Sweden).

Establishment and Mandate: In February 2015 the Shi'a Houthi (Ansar Allah) secessionist rebel grouping, based in northern Yemen, announced that a transitional five-member presidential council would take over from the legitimately elected Yemeni President, prompting the UN Security Council to adopt Resolution 2201, which deplored the dissolution of parliament and overthrow of government institutions by the Houthi militants, demanded that they 'immediately and unconditionally' cede power and urged the pursuit of a consensus solution to the Yemeni political crisis. By late March the then Special Adviser to the UN Secretary-General warned that the country was on the brink of civil war, with violence on both sides escalating. A Special Envoy for Yemen was appointed by the Secretary-General in April, with a mandate to co-operate closely with the UN Security Council, the Gulf Co-operation Council (GCC—in support of its ongoing peace initiative for Yemen), the parties to the ongoing conflict in that country, and other stakeholders.

Activities: In July 2015 the worsening security situation in Yemen was declared a UN system-wide 'Level 3' (severe) humanitarian emergency. In September Yemeni President Abd al-Rabbuh Mansur Hadi returned to Aden (taken over earlier in the year by the Houthi secessionist grouping), following its recapture by Saudi-backed government forces. In October the UN Special Envoy and head of the sanctions committee on Yemen informed the Security Council that both sides to the conflict had agreed to engage in direct negotiations; talks between representatives of the Yemeni Government and a delegation comprising Houthi and other opposition representatives were initiated in late 2015, and resumed thereafter intermittently, with ongoing mediation by the Special Envoy. A ceasefire agreement was concluded in that month, but was subsequently frequently broken. In May 2016 a Djibouti-based UN Verification and Inspection Mechanism was inaugurated to facilitate the unbroken transportation of commercial goods and services, and humanitarian assistance, to Yemen, while simultaneously ensuring compliance with the ongoing sanctions regime. A gathering in November 2017 of the so-called 'Quint' on Yemen (comprising the foreign ministers of Oman, Saudi Arabia, the United Arab Emirates—UAE, the UK and the USA) condemned a recent Houthi missile attack on a civilian area of Riyadh, and urged the Houthis and their allies to engage with the UN Special Envoy (the Houthis had suspended their co-operation, accusing the Envoy of bias against them). Addressing the UN Security Council in early December, the Special Envoy reported on the recent assassination of former President Ali Abdullah Saleh and leaders of Saleh's General People's Congress, and on an intense escalation of the conflict, noting the devastating impact of the heightened conflict on civilians. In mid-December the Special Envoy condemned a further Houthi missile launch against Riyadh.

In February 2018 a newly-appointed Special Envoy, Martin Griffiths, declared that he would prioritize facilitating an inclusive political process based on the GCC initiative and on the outcome document (agreed in January 2014) of a National Dialogue process on Yemen's future, and stressed that achieving this would require significant compromises from all parties to the conflict. In mid-2018 the Special Envoy attempted without success to negotiate an agreement to secure the Houthis' withdrawal from the Red Sea port of Hodeidah (Hudaydah; through which around 70% of Yemen's imports of food, medical supplies and fuel passed), with a view to deterring military action in that area by the Saudi-led coalition (which alleged that the Houthis were smuggling weapons through the port) and to facilitating operations by humanitarian agencies. (The UN Verification and Inspection Mechanism, however, had not hitherto reported the discovery of weaponry on ships screened at Hodeidah and no such discoveries had been reported to the UN's sanctions committee on Yemen. The UN Panel of Experts on Yemen, which supports the sanctions committee, noted that the Houthis had usurped control of national arms stockpiles in 2014, and that external arms supplies were likely to be transported by land.) In August 2018 the Special Envoy called for the organization of Intra-Yemeni consultations to prompt a resumption of the political process (by then suspended for two years). The Intra-Yemeni consultations, held in Geneva in early September, were deemed formally to have relaunched the process, although there was no participation by Houthi representatives. In early November the Special Envoy held a consultative meeting with a number of independent representatives of Yemeni society, and shortly afterwards he met with civil society workers and tribal leaders, and with international and local stakeholders engaged with informal so-called 'Track II' peacemaking initiatives. In mid-November the Special Envoy chaired a meeting of a Yemeni women's technical advisory group, which had been established by his Office to incorporate women's perspectives into his overall strategy. In early December, for the first time in two years, representatives of the Yemeni Government and the Houthi militia held talks—mediated by the Special Envoy, in Stockholm, Sweden. These culminated, in mid-December, in the conclusion of the Stockholm Accords, comprising the Agreement on the City of Hodeidah and Ports of Hodeidah, Salif, and Ras Isa—providing for an immediate ceasefire arrangement and for the phased redeployment of armed forces away from that area; for an executive mechanism to facilitate the exchange of prisoners; and a statement regarding the fiercely contested city of Taïz. (No agreement was then reached, however, on reopening the international airport at Sana'a or on reunifying the Central Bank of Yemen, divided into two entities in September 2016.) A UN Verification and Inspection Mechanism for Yemen (UNVIM) became operational on 5 May 2016 to facilitate the unhindered flow of commercial vessels using Yemen's ports. A Redeployment Coordination Commission was to supervise the ceasefire and the redeployment of forces, and also to oversee mine action operations. The Special Envoy subsequently liaised with both sides on progress achieved in implementing the agreements. A Supervisory Committee overseeing implementation of the prisoner exchange accord convened from January 2019. In January the UN Security Council established the UN Mission in Support of the Hudaydah Agreement (q.v.).

In mid-February 2019 the Yemeni Government and Houthi rebels, under the auspices of the Chairman of the Redeployment Coordination Commission, reached agreement on the first phase of the redeployment of their forces from Hodeidah, Salif and Ras Isa ports and from areas around humanitarian facilities in Hodeidah. At that time they also agreed in principle the second phase of the troop withdrawal. In February the Special Envoy urged combatants to permit humanitarian access to World Food Programme (WFP) grain stores held in the Red Sea Mills facility at Hodeidah. (WFP reported subsequently, however, that its operations in Yemen continued to be severely impeded.) A Peace Support Facility—managed by the OSESGY, UNDP and UN Resident Coordinator's Office in Yemen—was launched in April. An initial redeployment of Houthi forces from Hodeidah, Salif and Ras Isa—monitored by UNMHA—was implemented from 11–14 May. The Special Envoy continued to engage with Yemeni stakeholders, although the resumption of formal Intra-Yemeni consultations stalled. In late July the Special Envoy observed that implementation of the Stockholm Accords was slow. At that time he welcomed a decision by the Saudi-led Coalition to redeploy forces outside Yemen. In early August forces affiliated with the UAE-supported separatist Southern Transitional Council (STC) took control of military camps and state institutions in the southern Yemeni port city of Aden and nearby Abyan, causing numerous civilian casualties. Saudi Arabia undertook air strikes against the STC, which, in turn, prompted fighting between the STC and forces loyal to (Saudi-backed) President Hadi. Meanwhile, Hadi urged the UAE's removal from the Saudi-led military coalition. The Special Envoy condemned the STC's actions and deplored the related harassment and attacks against Yemeni civilians of northern origin. He also condemned continuing Houthi attacks against Saudi civilian infrastructure. During August, despite their divergent policies on Yemen, Saudi Arabia and the UAE agreed to establish a joint committee with the aim of stabilizing the situation in Yemen, and invited participation by the internationally recognized Yemeni Government and the STC in a new Jeddah Dialogue initiative. In mid-September the Special Envoy stated deep concern over Houthi drone attacks that struck two major oil facilities in Saudi Arabia causing significant temporary disruption to production. He called on all parties to exercise restraint and to avoid any further military escalation. In late September the UN Security Council welcomed a proposal by the OSESGY to establish an advisory group to prepare for the resumption of formal consultations. On 5 November the Jeddah Dialogue culminated in the signature of the Riyadh Agreement, with provisions covering security, military and political issues. These included, *inter alia,* the establishment of a national unity government to represent, on an equal basis, southern and northern Yemen, with the STC to be allocated two ministerial positions, and ministerial representation to be given also to other southern Yemeni groupings, such as the Hadhramout Inclusive Conference, National Alliance, and Revolutionary Movement. The accord also provided for the national Government to return to Aden without obstructions. In early February 2020 the Special Envoy welcomed the establishment of a medical air bridge operation conducted by the World Health Organization to transport groups of Yemeni patients to secure medical treatment in Amman, Jordan. Later in that month he condemned a prolonged escalation since January of air strikes and ground attacks in northern Yemen, and called for an immediate freeze on all military activity there. In early April the Special Envoy liaised with the parties to the conflict to reach agreement on implementing a national ceasefire, in view of the COVID-19 emergency. The Saudi-led coalition declared a two-week ceasefire on 8 April; a nationwide cessation of hostilities was not, however, forthcoming.

In June 2020 Saudi Arabia initiated a mechanism to accelerate the implementation of security dimensions of the November 2019 Riyadh Agreement. During June 2020 the OSESGY concluded an online mass consultation on the future of Yemen. At that time the Special Envoy denounced an ongoing military escalation, including intensifying conflict in the Ma'rib and Al-Jawf governorates, where Houthi forces were maintaining a relentless offensive. In late August the Special Envoy, who was working to facilitate the continued flow of commercial fuel imports into Yemen via Hodeidah, stated deep concern at major fuel shortages in Houthi-controlled areas, and called on all parties to work with the Office to resolve the situation. The Special Envoy participated in a high-level ministerial conference on Yemen in mid-September, which released a joint communiqué that addressed the urgent need for military de-escalation. He welcomed a decision reached late in that month by the Yemeni Government and Houthis to free an initial group of conflict-related detainees, representing progress towards fulfilling the 2018 Stockholm commitment to releasing prisoners. (In total 1,056 detainees were freed in October.) The UN Security Council condemned a Houthi attack that was perpetrated in late November against Saudi Arabian oil facilities in Jeddah.

The OSESGY welcomed the installation on 18 December 2020, in accordance with the provisions of the Riyadh Agreement, of a new power-sharing 'unity' Government—with Dr Maeen Abdulmalik Saeed as Prime Minister, and 24 ministerial portfolios divided between the north and the south. He observed that more progress was required on incorporating Yemeni women into the top tiers of government. At the end of December the OSESGY condemned an attack against the airport in Aden that had been timed for the arrival (collectively in one plane) of the new Cabinet, and had caused at least 28 civilian fatalities and many injuries. (The new Cabinet was unharmed.) A subsequent Yemeni Government investigation held the Houthis responsible for the atrocity. In early January 2021 the Special Envoy held discussions with President Hadi, in Riyadh, and then visited the new Yemeni Cabinet in Aden. At that time, as part of an ongoing campaign to exert 'maximum pressure' against Iran, the outgoing US Administration of President Trump designated Ansar Allah (the Houthis) as a foreign terrorist organization. The decision was welcomed by the Yemeni Government. The Special Envoy warned, however, that the designation might further complicate the process of bringing together the opposing sides in the Yemeni conflict.

In March 2021, addressing the UN Security Council, the Special Envoy stated that the civil war was once again in 'full force'. He reported on the extreme risk to around 1m. displaced people and other civilians caused by the continuing Houthi offensive against Ma'rib, and also stated concern over military escalations in Hajjah (in northeastern Yemen) and Taïz, persistent violence in Hodeidah, and over a recent increase in strikes by missiles and drones, including against Saudi Arabian civilian and commercial infrastructure. The Security Council subsequently issued a resolution that emphasized the need for a comprehensive military de-escalation, including an immediate end to the Houthi offensive on Ma'rib, and to the use of child soldiers there. The Council also noted with concern that the lack of progress in the peace process might be exploited by terrorist groupings. In mid-April the Council welcomed a Yemen Government-supported announcement by Saudi Arabia, made on 22 March, that it would work to achieve a comprehensive political solution to the conflict. All parties were urged to engage constructively with the OSESGY, and to negotiate a nationwide ceasefire. Meanwhile, the Special Envoy conducted a series of meetings with stakeholders aimed at bringing about a ceasefire. In mid-May, however, he reported to the Security Council that the Houthi military escalation against Ma'rib was continuing relentlessly, that restrictions on imports through Hodeidah were causing price increases and severe fuel shortages, that the airport at Sana'a was closed and movements restricted, and that the political process was fully stalled. In mid-2021 Griffiths advocated strongly for consensus in implementing a four-point plan for Yemen, which would provide for a nationwide ceasefire, restarting a constructive political process, opening Sana'a airport, and ending restrictions on shipping through Hodeidah. However, despite a round of intense diplomacy by the Special Envoy, no progress was reached on securing a ceasefire. In mid-June Griffiths informed the Security Council that the Houthis were insisting on the conclusion of separate discrete agreements regarding Hodeidah and Sana'a airport before negotiating a ceasefire—i.e. would not agree to the four-point plan in its entirety as a package accord, as was being advocated for by the Yemeni Government. A new Special Envoy, Hans Grundberg, assumed the role in early September. In mid-September Grundberg visited Riyadh, to hold discussions with Yemeni President Hadi and members of his government, as well as with senior Saudi officials. Visiting Aden in early October, Grundberg held discussions with the Yemeni Prime Minister and the Chairman of the STC. In mid-October the UN Security Council condemned recent Houthi attacks against Saudi airports, and deepening maritime insecurity in the Gulf of Aden and Red Sea off the Yemeni coast. The Council again stressed the need for an immediate end to the Houthi escalation in Ma'rib. In mid-November the Houthi forces took control of a significant area of Hodeidah.

In mid-December 2021 Grundberg, addressing the Security Council, stated deep alarm at a considerable escalation of the conflict, and reiterated calls for restraint and dialogue. At the end of the month he again urged a de-escalation, noting that recent Saudi-led coalition air strikes against Sana'a had caused civilian deaths and had damaged civilian residential areas and infrastructure, while the ongoing Houthi offensive against Ma'rib was also causing fatalities, damage, and prompting mass displacement. In mid-January 2022 (for the first time since 2018) the Houthis conducted missile and drone attacks—denounced as 'heinous' by the UN Security Council—against civilian targets in the UAE, including against the international airport serving its capital, Abu Dhabi, and oil installations. The UN Secretary-General deplored air strikes by the Saudi-led coalition in that month against a detention centre in Yemen's Sa'da Governorate, that resulted in the deaths of 91 inmates. In mid-February, reporting to the Security Council, Grundberg emphasized that the war was also being fought on economic fronts, including over trade flows and resources. At that time the Council strongly condemned the ongoing military escalation, reiterating the need for full implementation of the 2019 Riyadh Agreement. For the first time, notably, the Council referred to the 'Houthi terrorist group', emphasizing that the Houthis had attacked civilian sites, recruited children, conducted a policy of sexual violence and repression against professional and politically active women, incited violence against groups on the basis of nationality or religious affiliation, impeded the delivery of humanitarian assistance, perpetrated cross-border terrorist assaults against civilians and civilian infrastructure in Saudi Arabia and the UAE, used waterborne improvised explosive devices (IEDs) to attack shipping, and had also laid IEDs on land.

In early March 2022 Grundberg met with Yemeni President Hadi, as part of a new OSESGY initiative to advance structured bilateral consultations with multiple stakeholders (including women, youth, and other representatives of broad civil society), with a view to developing a multi-track framework for ending the conflict. Urgent requirements and long-term priorities were to be identified along three parallel tracks: security, political and economic. During late March–early April the GCC hosted UN-mediated Yemeni-Yemeni consultations on the conflict, in Riyadh (the Saudi-led coalition called a ceasefire just prior to the talks); on 1 April the UN Special Envoy announced that an initially two-month, potentially renewable, nationwide truce—the first since 2016—had been agreed, to start on 2 April 2022: the first day of the religious holy month of Ramadan. Under the terms of the truce, military offensives and cross-border attacks were to be suspended, fuel vessels were to be permitted access to Houthi-held Hodeidah, and restrictions on roads and commercial flights lifted. The UN Secretary-General urged all stakeholders promptly to implement the agreement. It was reported at that time that since 2016 nearly 400,000 people had been killed by impacts of the conflict, including lack of safe water and healthcare, and starvation.

In mid-April 2022 the Special Envoy reported to the UN Security Council that thus far the truce was largely being respected, and that the OSESGY had created co-ordination mechanisms to support it, and was liaising between the parties with a view to reopening roads to Taïz and other governorates. The OSESGY initiated a Military Coordination Committee in May, with participation by military representatives of the Yemeni Government, Houthis and Coalition Joint Forces Command. On 2 June Grundberg announced that the parties to the conflict had agreed to extend the truce by two months. In-person meetings between the parties to the conflict, organized under UN auspices, had restarted. In early July the OSESGY issued an updated proposal on phased road reopening (with an initial focus on four roads in Taïz). In mid-July the Special Envoy reported to the UN Security Council that, while the truce was holding, allegations were continuing of military reconnaissance overflights, direct and indirect firing, drone attacks, trench and fortification construction, and of the reinforcement of principal front lines (including at Hodeidah, Ma'rib and Taïz). The OSESGY was supporting the implementation of communication channels to address such challenges. The Special Envoy stated deep concern over the need to secure adequate funding for UNVIM's activities (that included facilitating the passage of commercial fuel ships into Hodeidah). Shortly afterwards the OSESGY reported a significant decrease in civilian casualties and displacement since the start of the truce. However, in that month the Special Envoy condemned an attack against a residential neighbourhood in Taïz; a further attack on Taïz in August was also condemned.

On 2 August 2022 the UN-mediated truce in place since 2 April was extended for a further two months, until 2 October. Meanwhile, the Special Envoy pursued discussions aimed at achieving an expanded truce, that would provide, *inter alia,* for an effective disbursement mechanism that would enable the regular issuance of civilian pensions and of civil servant salaries; the successful opening of roads in Taïz and elsewhere; and the addition of more routes to and from Sana'a International Airport; and that would ultimately set a path towards securing a negotiated resolution of the conflict. A fourth extension of the truce was not, however, achieved by the deadline of 2 October; in mid-October, addressing the Security Council, the Special Envoy attributed this to additional demands that had been submitted by the Houthis. He urged all parties to continue to exercise maximum restraint. In late November the Special Envoy reported that, while there had been no major military escalation since the end of the truce, the Houthis had recently conducted attacks against oil terminals and ports in Hadramawt and Shabwa, with the objective of depriving the Government of its principal source of export revenue. In January 2023 the Special Envoy reported that overall the military situation continued to be stable, although limited military activity was occurring along frontlines, in particular in Ma'rib, Dali, Taïz, Hodeidah, and Lahj governorates, and in the Yemen–Saudi Arabia border area. A UN-supported High-level Pledging Event on the Humanitarian Crisis in Yemen, held in February, in Geneva, raised US $1,160m. In March discussions mediated by the Special Envoy and by the International Committee of the Red Cross culminated in an agreement on an implementation plan that provided for the release (effected in mid-April) of 887 conflict-related detainees. On 2 April, marking the first anniversary of the commencement of the 2022 formal six-month truce, the Special Envoy reported that elements of the truce were still largely holding, but that the gains achieved needed to be anchored in political progress towards a comprehensive peaceful resolution of the conflict, and were put at risk by a recent escalation in military activity and divisive rhetoric. He emphasized the interconnectivity of the three parallel tracks of the Office's work programme—security (managed through the Military Coordination Committee), political (through continuous engagement with national actors and regional and international stakeholders), and economic (engagement with relevant experts, civil society representatives, the Yemeni private sector, and international financial institutions). By that time fuel and other commodities were continuing to enter Hodeidah, and commercial flights were operating three times a week between Sana'a and Amman. In mid-April the Special Envoy noted with concern recent military activity in Ma'rib, Shabwa, Taïz and other governorates, and reiterated calls to the conflicting parties to exercise maximum restraint. He subsequently embarked on a series of diplomatic visits, including to the USA, the People's Republic of China, and Japan. Reporting to the Security Council in July, he noted that, after a seven-year hiatus, commercial flights had resumed between Sana'a and Saudi Arabia. Broad consultations aimed at engaging diverse Yemeni stakeholders were convened in August by the Special Envoy.

In 2023 the mission of the OSESGY was based in Amman, Jordan and in Aden and Sana'a, Yemen.

United Nations Mission to Support the Hudaydah Agreement—UNMHA

Head of Mission and Chair of the Redeployment Coordination Commission: Maj-Gen. (retd) MICHAEL BEARY (Ireland).

Establishment and Mandate: On 16 January 2019 UN Security Council Resolution 2452 established UNMHA to support the implementation of a ceasefire accord concluded on 13 December, in Stockholm, Sweden, between the Yemeni Government and Houthi rebel grouping, with respect to Hodeidah (Hudaydah, city and Red Sea port), and also the Red Sea ports of Salif and Ras Isa. UNMHA was tasked with leading and supporting a Redeployment Coordination Commission that was mandated to supervise the ceasefire and the redeployment of forces, as well as mine action operations. The mission was to monitor compliance with the ceasefire, to ensure that security was guaranteed by local security forces (in accordance with Yemeni law), and to co-ordinate UN efforts to support stakeholders in fully implementing the Agreement. The Head of Mission was to report to the UN Secretary-General through the Special Envoy of the Secretary-General for Yemen and also through the Under-Secretary-General for Political and Peacebuilding Affairs. The mission had an authorized strength of 75 observers.

Activities: During early 2019 the mission worked to negotiate a redeployment of forces between the two sides. In May the mission monitored the withdrawal of Houthi forces from the three main port areas and the transfer of responsibility for port security to the national coast guard. It subsequently continued actively to verify the sustained demilitarization of the port area, and to follow up matters related to explosive remnants of war and military activities. In September a joint operations centre was established at the mission to embed Houthi and Yemeni military officers with UNMHA personnel, as a confidence-building measure. Under the UN-mediated truce that entered into effect on 1 April 2022 fuel ships were permitted access to Hodeidah port; UNMHA was able to strengthen routine patrols of Hodeidah, Salif and Ras Isa, and verify damage caused to Hodeidah by the conflict. The Head of Mission conducted regional visits to Jordan, Saudi Arabia and the UAE in February and September 2022, to discuss means of advancing the implementation of UNMHA's mandate. The mission recorded 289 incidents in Hodeidah in 2022 of civilian deaths or injuries caused by landmines or explosive remnants of war, and has placed a focus on intensifying its mine clearance activities. In July 2023 the UN Security Council extended UNMHA's mandate 14 July 2024.

Office of the United Nations Special Coordinator for Lebanon—UNSCOL

Address: UN House, Riad el-Solh Sq., POB 11, 8577 Beirut, Lebanon.

E-mail: unscolwebsite@un.org; **internet:** unscol.unmissions.org.

Special Coordinator for Lebanon: JOANNA WRONECKA (Poland).

Establishment and Mandate: UNSCOL was established in February 2007. The mission is the focal point for the core group of donor countries supporting Lebanon (through an annually updated Lebanon Crisis Response Plan), and co-ordinates the UN presence within Lebanon. It works closely with the UN peacekeeping mission in Lebanon, UNIFIL. The Special Coordinator is responsible for supervising the implementation of Security Council Resolution 1701, which was adopted in August 2006, and called for a cessation of hostilities in Lebanon. UNSCOL comprises divisions of administration, political, co-ordination, public information, and security.

The Special Coordinator works closely with the International Support Group (ISG) for Lebanon, which addresses means of supporting Lebanon in view of the impact on the country's resources of the crisis in neighbouring Syria. The inaugural meeting was convened in October 2019 of a joint UNSCOL-UN Interim Force in Lebanon strategic forum, with a view to enhancing efficiencies between the two entities. In December, following the resignation of the Lebanese Prime Minister, Saad Hariri, on 29 October (prompted by a wave of national anti-Government protests), the ISG urged the prompt formation of a credible government, and the adoption by the administration of a credible and comprehensive set of policy reforms aimed at restoring economic and financial stability. The ISG welcomed the eventual formation of a new Lebanese Government in January 2020, under the premiership of Hassan Diab.

In August 2020 the Special Coordinator expressed solidarity and condolences for the victims of the major chemical explosion that had recently devastated the vicinity of the port of Beirut. Widespread demonstrations after the explosion prompted the resignation on 10 August of Prime Minister Diab. Saad Hariri was reappointed as Prime Minister in October; he did not, however, name a new government, and Diab remained in the role of caretaker Prime Minister. In November the Special Coordinator reported to the UN Security Council that the continuing extreme economic crisis was causing deep poverty and food insecurity for increasing numbers of citizens and refugees, in a situation where there was no adequate social protection system. Meanwhile, the pandemic crisis was further stressing already strained health and educational services. In March 2021, as protests intensified across Lebanon, the ISG, meeting in Beirut, noted the impacts of the COVID-19 pandemic and accelerating socioeconomic deterioration, and called for demonstrations to stay peaceful, as well as for human rights to be upheld. The Group urged prompt transparent investigations into the Beirut port explosion, and into the murder (in February) of a prominent political activist, Lokman Mohsen Slim. Soon afterwards UNSCOL urged the prompt formation of an empowered government. The inaugural meeting was convened in March of a Consultative Group of the Reform, Recovery and Reconstruction Framework (3RF), comprising representatives of the Lebanese Government and civil society, UN, EU, World Bank, and international donors. The French Government organized a virtual conference in June to raise assistance to meet the emergency needs of the underfunded Lebanese military. In mid-July Hariri withdrew from the process of forming a new administration; in response, President Michel Aoun convened binding consultations, which led to the appointment of Najib Mikati to the premiership (Mikati was a former incumbent of the role). In August the ISG stated regret over fatalities and injuries caused by the recent explosion of a fuel tanker in northern Lebanon; the incident also aggravated ongoing acute fuel shortages, which were causing disruptions to essential services. The Special Coordinator welcomed the formation of a new administration in September, under Prime Minister Mikati, and reaffirmed the UN's support for strengthening Lebanese sovereignty, stability and political independence. UNSCOL hosted a digital dialogue in April, with participation by Lebanese youth. The Special Coordinator welcomed the conduct of a general election that was held in May. In late October she commended a landmark agreement concluded between Lebanon and Israel defining a maritime border between the two countries (thus enabling the economic exploitation of natural gas fields). In early November the ISG noted with concern the lack of co-operation among Lebanese political actors who had failed to elect a new President to replace Aoun, whose term of office had ended on 31 October. The Special Coordinator convened a series of consultations with stakeholders, including youth and women's representatives, political and religious figures, and economic experts who addressed the urgent domestic reforms required as a prerequisite to realizing a provisional staff agreement with the International Monetary Fund that had been reached in April. In March 2023, reiterating statements made by the UN Secretary-General and the ISG, the Special Coordinator expressed grave concern over the failure thus far to elect a new Lebanese President and resolve the political vacuum that had prevailed since the end of October 2022. She emphasized that the delay was contributing to the paralysis of state institutions and to the extreme and deepening national socioeconomic crisis. During mid-2023 she engaged in several rounds of meetings with Lebanese stakeholders, including members of parliament, the commander of the national armed forces, and religious leaders. As at early September the presidential vacuum remained.

Office of the United Nations Special Coordinator for the Middle East Peace Process—UNSCO

Address: Gaza; Jerusalem; Ramallah.
Internet: unsco.unmissions.org.

Special Coordinator for the Middle East Peace Process, Personal Representative to the Palestine Liberation Organization and the Palestinian Authority, and the Secretary-General's Envoy to the Quartet: TOR WENNESLAND (Norway).

Establishment and Mandate: UNSCO was established in June 1994 after the conclusion of the Declaration of Principles on Interim (Palestinian) Self-Government Arrangements—the Oslo Accord. UNSCO was to seek, during the transition process envisaged by the Declaration, to ensure 'an adequate response to the needs of the Palestinian people and to mobilize financial, technical, economic and other assistance'. In 1995 UNSCO's mandate was reconfigured as the Office of the Special Coordinator for the Middle East Peace Process and Personal Representative of the Secretary-General to the Palestine Liberation Organization (PLO) and the Palestine (National) Authority (PA).

Activities: UNSCO has been mandated to assist in all aspects of the humanitarian situation confronting the Palestinian people, and supports negotiations and the implementation of political agreements. A Regional Affairs Unit (RAU) assists in the fulfilment of that part of UNSCO's mandate that requires it to co-ordinate its work and to co-operate closely with all of the parties to the Middle East peace process. The Special Coordinator also collaborates closely with key international actors, in particular those that, together with the UN, constitute the Middle East Quartet, i.e. the European Union, the Russian Federation and the USA, and serves as the Envoy of the UN Secretary-General to the Quartet. Furthermore, the RAU provides technical support for the organization of free, fair and transparent Palestinian elections. UNSCO prepares reports for the Ad Hoc Liaison Committee, which is the main policy-level development assistance co-ordination mechanism for the Palestinian Territories.

In May 2021 the Special Coordinator expressed deep concern at an intensification of violent clashes in East Jerusalem, particularly in the Sheikh Jarrah district, where several Palestinian families had been threatened with eviction by Israeli settler groups. The Special Coordinator urged maximum restraint by the Israeli security forces, and UNSCO attempted to work with community and political leaders to de-escalate tensions amid mounting violence and numbers of casualties. In late May, addressing the UN Security Council, the Special Coordinator welcomed a ceasefire that had taken effect on 21 May, following 11 days of severe hostilities—during which intensive Israeli air strikes were directed against densely populated Gaza in retaliation for the firing by Hamas of rockets towards Jerusalem—and emphasized that all perpetrators of violence must be brought to account. In July UNSCO reported that a Rapid Damage and Needs Assessment, conducted during late May–late June, had determined that the May hostilities had caused up to US $190m. in Palestinian economic losses and $380m. in physical damage; recovery requirements were estimated at $485m. In October the Special Coordinator stated deep concern over the extension by the Israeli authorities of tenders for the construction of 1,300 new settler housing units in the West Bank. In early 2022 the Special Coordinator repeatedly stated concern at daily violence occurring in the Palestinian Territories and Israel, and at the advancement of (under international law) illegal Israeli planning processes, evictions of Palestinians and demolition of Palestinian structures, for the purpose of constructing illegal settlements. In May UNSCO released a report that urged the adoption of a more strategic approach to addressing the PA's fiscal and economic crisis. In early August the Special Coordinator expressed deep concern at a 'very dangerous' intensification of violence, following the initiation of an Israeli military aerial offensive (reportedly involving 147 air strikes) aimed at targets in Gaza associated with the Palestinian Islamic Jihad militant grouping; the latter had retaliated with, reportedly, 1,100 rocket and mortar attacks against Israel. After three days a ceasefire, mediated by Egypt, entered into effect. The Special Coordinator subsequently repeatedly reiterated alarm at an intensifying cycle of armed clashes between Palestinians and Israeli security forces in the West Bank, noting a significant increase in lethal Israeli military operations against Palestinians, and lethal terrorist attacks by Palestinians and Israeli Arabs against Israelis. In December a hardline Israeli administration took office, further entrenching political polarization. In late February 2023 the Special Coordinator again urged all sides to refrain from aggravating tensions, following an Israel Defense Forces raid that, while targeting three Palestinian militants in Nablus (West Bank), had killed in total 11 Palestinians, and injured many more. However, further armed clashes followed. The Special Coordinator condemned Israeli settler violence against Palestinians and Palestinian attacks against Israelis, and continued to engage with all stakeholders in an attempt to de-escalate the situation. In early April he called on political, religious and community leaders on all sides to reject inflammatory rhetoric and provocative actions. On 9 May the Special Coordinator stated deep alarmed at Israeli air strikes on Gaza that had killed several Palestinian civilians.

Addressing the UN Security Council in August 2023 the Special Coordinator noted that in recent months Palestinians and Israelis had been suffering near daily violence, and that this trend was exacerbated by a sense of despair over the future. He noted that more than 200 Palestinian and nearly 30 Israeli conflict-related fatalities had occurred thus far in 2023, representing the highest total since 2005. (In early July Israeli forces had launched a massive aerial raid against the West Bank's Jenin camp, that involved at least 10 drone strikes and an estimated 2,000 troops; at least 12 Palestinians, including four children, had been killed, and more than 4,000 people displaced). Meanwhile, the expansion of illegal Israeli settlements was continuing, and the PA's fiscal situation was precarious—exacerbated by external humanitarian funding shortages. He urged a focus on de-escalating tensions and working towards a two-state solution.

United Nations Assistance Mission for Iraq—UNAMI

Address: Amman, Jordan.
Telephone: (6) 5504700; **fax:** (6) 5504705; **e-mail:** unami-information@un.org; **internet:** www.uniraq.com.

Special Representative of the UN Secretary-General for Iraq: JEANINE HENNIS-PLASSCHAERT (Netherlands).

Deputy Special Representative of the UN Secretary-General for Political, Electoral and Constitutional Support: CLAUDIO CORDONE (Italy).

Deputy Special Representative of the UN Secretary-General for Development and Humanitarian Support: GHULAM MOHAMMAD ISACZAI (Afghanistan).

Establishment and Mandate: UNAMI was founded by Security Council Resolution 1500 (14 August 2003), expanded on 10 August 2007 by Resolution 1770, to support post-conflict Iraq. On 19 August 2003, just after the mission's inception, terrorist attacks on the UNAMI headquarters in the Iraqi capital, Baghdad, killed the first Special Representative of the UN Secretary-General (SRSG) for Iraq, Sergio Vieira de Mello, and 21 other UN personnel. UN international staff were subsequently withdrawn from Iraq, and, until the formation of the Iraqi Interim Government at the end of June 2004.

Resolution 2631, approved in May 2022, tasked the mission with supporting the advancement of inclusive political dialogue and reconciliation; efforts to strengthen electoral preparation and processes; security sector reform; regional dialogue and co-operation; co-ordination and delivery of humanitarian and medical assistance; dignified returns or local integration of refugees and displaced persons; the strengthening of essential services; efforts to advance human rights and judicial and legal reforms; gender mainstreaming; the strengthening of child protection; and structured dialogue between the Iraqi Government and the Kurdistan Regional Government. In May 2023 the UN Security Council extended the mission's mandate until 31 May 2024, its core tasks unaltered. The SRSG was requested to prioritize the extension of assistance to the Iraqi authorities and people with regard to advancing inclusive political dialogue and national reconciliation. The SRSG and UNAMI were to assist the authorities in strengthening electoral processes, implementing constitutional provisions, developing processes for resolving disputed internal boundaries, and implementing security sector reforms. UNAMI comprises an Office of Political Affairs and Analysis, an Office of Electoral Assistance, a Development Support Office, a Human Rights Office (HRO), a Public Information Office, and a Gender Unit.

In early 2007 UNAMI facilitated and observed the process of establishing Iraq's Independent High Electoral Commission (IHEC), and subsequently the mission has supported the IHEC in capacity and institution building. UNAMI participates in meetings of the IHEC Board of Commissioners, and has served in an impartial advisory capacity in the process of selecting commissioners.

Activities: With regard to reconstruction and development, UNAMI aims to address the long-term challenge of achieving sustainable food security; to strengthen the overall quality of education and service delivery at all levels; to support policy development, and preserve and conserve the tangible and intangible Iraqi cultural heritage; to improve the human development situation in Iraq and promote good governance; to support the national health strategy of the Iraqi Ministry of Health in meeting basic health needs; to formulate and implement programmes on institutional/policy reform, capacity building, and service provision necessary to rehabilitate and develop the infrastructure of human settlements; and to support the Iraqi authorities in providing adequate assistance and effective protection to, and durable solutions for, uprooted populations in Iraq.

In September 2017 the UN Secretary-General described as 'destabilizing' a referendum on possible independence organized unilaterally in that month by the Kurdistan Regional Government, including in areas—such as Kirkuk—that were not recognized by the Iraqi federal authorities as belonging to Kurdistan. In mid-November UNAMI urged the Kurdistan authorities to acknowledge a decision by the Iraq federal Supreme Court which confirmed that the September referendum in Kurdistan violated the provisions of the national Constitution and that therefore its results and effects should be annulled. In December UNAMI expressed deep concern over reports of violent unrest during demonstrations in the Sulaymaniyah area, urged restraint both by protesters and by the local authorities, and dispatched a fact-finding team. UNAMI subsequently undertook a series of meetings with Kurdistan youth that were aimed at fostering mutual understanding.

UNAMI helped to organize a series of roundtable discussions in late 2017, with the aim of facilitating national reconciliation. In December the Iraqi authorities declared victory over Islamic State. In total, more than 4.5m. Iraqis had been liberated from the terrorist occupation. In mid-February 2018, at an International Conference for the Reconstruction of Iraq, convened in Kuwait, the UN Secretary-General launched an Iraq Recovery and Resilience Programme that had nine components, of which six were national in scope, and three were focused on building trust and economic opportunities in high-risk communities to prevent the emergence of violent extremism. UNAMI assisted the IHEC with the preparations for national and provincial elections that were held on 12 May—including by facilitating the participation of displaced persons in the elections, and with the utilization of new technology for managing election results.

In early January 2020 the UN Secretary-General cautioned maximum restraint in response to the assassination on 2 January, on Iraqi soil, by a US air strike, of General Qassem Soleimani, commander of the elite Quds Force unit of the Iranian Revolutionary Guards Corps. The global coalition against Islamic State immediately suspended its combat operations in Iraq to focus on protecting its bases. On 6 January the Iraqi legislature passed a non-binding resolution demanding that foreign military forces withdraw from Iraq and cease using its land, waters and airspace. In December the SRSG met with senior political figures from Kurdistan in Erbil and Sulaymaniyah, where she emphasized that maintaining constructive relations between the regional and federal governments was critical to national stability. The UN Secretary-General stated in February 2021 that the mission was continuing to report killings, other violence, abductions, disappearances and torture of participants arising from a wave of anti-Government protests that was initiated in central and southern areas of Iraq in October 2019 and was still ongoing. UNAMI extended enhanced technical support to the IHEC in advance of legislative elections that were held in October 2021 (postponed from June). In November the UN Secretary-General reported that the elections had been peaceful and well-managed. At that time the SRSG, participating in a conference that took place in Erbil to address gender equality and women's empowerment strategies, welcomed the increased participation of women in the recent election, both as candidates and as voters. In March 2022 UNAMI issued a gender analysis of the October 2021 polls, which found that, of the 95 female candidates, 57 women (from 16 governorates) had won seats independently of the quota framework that had been in place. At the end of August—in response to an outbreak of violent protests in Iraq that had been prompted by the resignation of a key political actor, in the context of continued failure to achieve agreement on the composition of a new government—UNAMI urged a de-escalation of tensions, and respect for dialogue and for constitutional order. In October 2022 UNAMI welcomed the composition of a new government, under the premiership of Mohammed S. al-Sudani.

The SRSG has repeatedly strongly condemned terrorist atrocities perpetrated in Iraq.

UNAMI's HRO has prepared a series of reports addressing the human rights situation in Iraq, and has documented systematic and widespread severe violations of rights and of international humanitarian law perpetrated by Islamic State and affiliated armed groups, including murders, abductions and rape of civilians, looting, the trafficking and enslavement of women and children, the forced recruitment of children, and wanton destruction of places of religious or cultural significance.

In March 2021 the UN Under-Secretary-General and SRSG on Sexual Violence in Conflict welcomed the recent adoption by the Iraqi Council of Representatives of a Yazidi Survivors' Law, encompassing reparations, rehabilitation, and reintegration support (including through pensions, education, land, and public sector employment quota allocations) for members of the Yazidi, Christian, Shabak and Turkmen communities who had been subjected by Islamic State to crimes such as abductions and sexual violence.

In September 2017 the UN Security Council requested the Secretary-General to establish an independent investigative team, to be headed by a Special Adviser, to support Iraq's efforts in holding Islamic State accountable for its actions. The ensuing UN Investigative Team to Promote Accountability for Crimes Committed by Da'esh/ISIL (UNITAD) was tasked with collecting and preserving evidence of acts committed by Islamic State that might amount to war crimes, crimes against humanity and genocide. The Special Adviser was appointed in May 2018. In May 2021 the Head of UNITAD announced the completion of initial investigations into Islamic State attacks that had been perpetrated against the Yazidi community in Sinjar (northern Iraq), and into the mass killing of unarmed military cadets and personnel at the Tikrit Air Academy in June 2014, and reported that 'clear and convincing evidence' had been established that genocide had been perpetrated against the Yazidis. In September 2022 the UN Security Council effected the fourth extension of UNITAD's mandate (until 17 September 2023). In January 2023 the SRSG welcomed a decree by the Iraqi Council of Ministers that granted Yazidis ownership of residential lands and houses in Sinjar.

In December 2021 UNAMI and OHCHR issued a joint report on *Human rights and freedom of expression: trials in the Kurdistan Region of Iraq.*

United Nations Support Mission in Libya—UNSMIL

Address: Tripoli, Libya.
Internet: unsmil.unmissions.org.
Special Representative of the UN Secretary-General for Libya: ABDOULAYE BATHILY (Senegal).
Establishment and Mandate: Following the outbreak of conflict in Libya in February 2011, UNSMIL was established in September with a mandate to support Libya's transitional authorities in restoring public security and the rule of law; promoting inclusive political dialogue and national reconciliation; and embarking upon the process of drafting a new constitution and preparing for democratic elections. The UN Security Council subsequently modified the

mission's mandate: in accordance with Resolution 2376, adopted in September 2017, the mission was tasked with continuing to undertake mediation and 'good offices' in the framework of the December 2015 Libyan Political Agreement and to support the governance, security and economic arrangements of the Government of National Accord (GNA, q.v.). Furthermore, UNSMIL was to provide support to key Libyan institutions, to undertake human rights monitoring and reporting, to assist with securing and countering the spread of uncontrolled arms and related materiel, to co-ordinate international assistance, and to assist GNA-led efforts to stabilize post-conflict zones. Through its Security Institutions Division the mission mediates between state and non-state actors, encourages armed groupings to support the political process, and works to bring about ceasefires and humanitarian corridors. With the UN Mine Action Service, UNSMIL has helped to reduce the risks posed by improvised explosive devices.

Activities: From July 2014, against a rapidly deteriorating security situation, and discord between rival administrations—i.e. a recently elected House of Representatives which had moved from the Libyan capital Tripoli to the eastern city of Tobruk, and a Tripoli-based pro-Islamist unofficial General National Congress—the Special Representative of the UN Secretary-General (SRSG) for Libya mediated intensively with the parties to the conflict. An UNSMIL-facilitated Libyan Political Dialogue was initiated in Geneva, Switzerland, in January 2015. In mid-October, following the finalization by participants in the Dialogue of a political agreement on establishing the GNA, UNSMIL and the United Kingdom authorities jointly convened discussions in London on finding optimum means of supporting the proposed administration. In mid-December representatives of the Tobruk and Tripoli legislatures, meeting in Skhirat, formally adopted the Libyan Political Agreement. The SRSG has co-operated with neighbouring countries (which hold regular collective consultations on the Libyan crisis at ministerial level) and regional and international organizations in support of the implementation of the Agreement.

The 32-member GNA was appointed in mid-January 2016. Later in that month, however, the composition was rejected by the Tobruk legislature. A revised formation, announced in February, was also not formally approved, and on 12 March it was announced that the GNA would take office without formal endorsement. At the end of March the SRSG welcomed the arrival in Tripoli of a nine-member Libyan Presidential Council—provided for under the Agreement—to assume the function of head of state in the transitional regime. UNSMIL thereafter maintained a constant presence in Libya, but in a partial capacity. In July a session of the Libyan Political Dialogue was held to enable consultations between UNSMIL, the Presidential Council, and other stakeholders over means of implementing the Libyan Political Agreement. The July Dialogue determined to convene regular meetings to follow up measures that were being implemented by the Presidential Council to address several crises, including urgent action required to safeguard oil production and exports, and to resolve disruptions to basic services. In August the House of Representatives rejected a proposal by the Prime Minister, Faiez Serraj, on the proposed formation of a new GNA; consequently, the Presidential Council instructed ministers to continue to perform their functions in a caretaker capacity, pending formal approval. In October the SRSG condemned an attempt by opposition elements to take control by force of the headquarters of the High Council of State (a governmental advisory body provided for under the Libya Political Agreement). At the request of the Presidential Council, UNSMIL convened meetings of the Libyan Political Dialogue in September, in Tunis, and in November, in Malta. In December the UN Security Council urged the mission to re-establish in phases—security conditions permitting—a full permanent presence in Libya. In March 2017 an AU-UN-Arab League-EU 'Libya Quartet' formation was established as a collective framework for co-ordinating efforts to address the Libyan crisis. UNSMIL repeatedly urged all armed groups to desist from undermining the formal political process and has expressed strong condemnation of violations of peace and security in Libya.

In December 2016 the UN Secretary-General reported that a military operation undertaken in Libya against Islamic State during May–November, supported by US air strikes, had retaken nearly the whole of a 300 km stretch of territory around Sirte, and had reduced the militants' presence in Sirte. Islamic State continued to mount terrorist attacks during 2017–23. Violent conflict escalated in 2017 in southern areas of Libya between the Libyan National Army and the Third Force militant grouping (which originated in the northern city of Misratah). Meanwhile, forces loyal to the Presidential Council extended control of key sites in Tripoli, including the international airport. Together with local authorities UNSMIL worked to develop a security structure for Tripoli. Violent clashes occurred frequently between the Benghazi Defence Brigades rebel militia and the Libyan National Army over control of strategic oil facilities in al-Sidra and Ra's Lanuf. Meanwhile, intercommunal conflict persisted in southern Libya. In mid-May 2018 UNSMIL organized a liaison meeting with armed groups in Misratah, aimed at reducing tensions there and promoting dialogue. In September the UN Envoy to Libya secured a ceasefire between warring militias in Tripoli, following a recent escalation of violent clashes there (as a result of which the Libyan capital had been placed under a state of emergency).

In February 2018 Libya's Supreme Court dismissed legal challenges to the content of the long-awaited Libyan Draft Constitution (which had been finalized in July 2017), thus enabling the document to be submitted to a future referendum. In February 2019 the SRSG met with Prime Minister Serraj and the Commander of the Libyan National Army, Gen. Khalifa Haftar, to discuss the holding of a general election and measures to maintain stability in the country and to unify its institutions. At the beginning of April the UN Secretary-General expressed deep concern over an ongoing intensification of military activities. On 4 April Gen. Haftar launched an Libyan National Army offensive aimed at seizing Tripoli. Shortly afterwards the SRSG condemned an aerial attack by the Libyan National Army against Tripoli's only functioning civilian airport (Meitiga Airport), urged the immediate halt to aerial operations, expressed deep concern for the welfare of civilians in the capital, and announced the postponement of a planned Libyan National Conference. From that month Tripoli effectively remained under siege by the Libyan National Army. In early May Premier Serraj declared that he no longer regarded Haftar or Ageela Saleh—the eastern Libyan leader of the House of Representatives, who had sanctioned Haftar's offensive—as political dialogue partners. At that time 41 members of the legislature declared allegiance to a pro-Serraj manifestation of the House of Representatives. In July the SRSG welcomed successful country-wide elections to the membership of Libya's Supreme Judicial Council. In the same month, however, he deplored an attack against a migrant detention compound in the coastal city of Tajoura that had resulted in at least 53 fatalities and severe injuries, stating that this might constitute a war crime. He noted that UNSMIL was monitoring with great concern various ongoing allegations of extrajudicial killings. Reporting to the UN Security Council at the end of July the SRSG emphasized that the geographical scope of the ongoing violence had expanded, and that parties to the conflict had ignored calls for de-escalation and had intensified air strikes, including by armed drones. He also noted a trend towards increased recruitment of foreign mercenaries, the impact of aggressive invective spread by social media and satellite television stations, and that both sides had failed to honour their obligations under international law. On 6 January 2020 the Turkish legislature formally authorized the deployment of Turkish troops to defend the GNA.

In early January 2020 the first of a planned series of meetings of Libyan economic experts was convened, representing the initiation of the economic track of a peace proposal (comprising parallel economic, military and political tracks) that had been issued in mid-2019 by the SRSG; a Libyan Expert Economic Commission was formally convened, for this purpose, in February. At an international conference on Libya held (in accordance with the SRSG's peace plan) in Berlin, Germany, in mid-January 2020—with participation by the UN Secretary-General, the heads of state or of government of Germany, France, Russia, Turkey and the UK, and also by the opposing sides in the Libyan conflict—the foreign leaders pledged not to interfere in Libya's civil war, and adopted a roadmap for future UN-sponsored negotiations aimed at achieving a ceasefire between the opposing militaries. The first round of the UN-mediated talks, held in February, in Geneva, in the format of a 5+5 Libyan Joint Military Commission (JMC)—comprising five senior military officers representing the GNA and five appointed by the Commander of the Libyan National Army, embodying the first stage of the military track of the SRSG's peace plan—reportedly reached some consensus on principles to underpin a ceasefire, but did not result in full agreement. In mid-February the UN Security Council adopted a resolution (with Russia abstaining) that restated strong support for UNSMIL, supported the outcome of the recent Berlin conference and recognized the significant role of the AU and Arab League in working to resolve the conflict. The resolution emphasized deep concern at the activities of terrorist groups and mercenaries in Libya. It also demanded a ceasefire and an immediate end to the supply of arms to both sides in the conflict. At that time representatives of the Libya Quartet and the foreign ministers of Algeria, China, Egypt, France, Germany, Italy, Russia, Turkey, Tunisia, the Republic of the Congo, the United Arab Emirates, the United Kingdom and the USA launched an International Follow-Up Committee on Libya (IFCL). Regular IFCL meetings were subsequently held, under UN auspices, at senior official and technical working group levels. A draft ceasefire agreement was produced by a second round of 5+5 Libyan JMC negotiations that were facilitated by the SRSG in late February. Negotiations under the political track of the SRSG's peace plan also commenced in February, in Geneva.

During April and May 2020 the mission condemned the continuing escalation of conflict, including indiscriminate bombardment of areas of Tripoli, and acts of retribution in western coastal cities.

Opposing parties were urged to refrain from making any provocative statements or actions that might further destabilize Libya; UN member states that were continuing to fuel the conflict by supplying weapons and mercenary fighters were urged to desist; and the whole international community was asked to enforce the Libyan arms embargo. At the beginning of June UNSMIL welcomed a decision by both sides to resume the 5+5 talks. Reports emerged in May that the Wagner Group, a Russian private paramilitary and security contractor, was assisting Gen. Haftar's military campaign. From early June Haftar's forces retreated from Tripoli, and GNA forces regained full control of the city. On 20 July the Egyptian legislature authorized the deployment of troops to support Haftar; it was envisaged that this development risked escalating the conflict. However, on 21 August both sides announced a ceasefire.

In late August 2020 UNSMIL noted an increase in reports of human rights violations across Libya, including arbitrary detentions and restrictions on freedom of movement and assembly. In early September the acting SRSG, Stephanie Williams, welcomed the outcome of recent consultations among Libyan stakeholders, that were held in Montreux, Switzerland, in the presence of representatives of the mission, and provided intra-Libyan proposals to be addressed by a resumed UN-facilitated inclusive Libyan Political Dialogue. On 23 October the acting SRSG welcomed the adoption by the 5+5 JMC delegations—representing the GNA Libyan Army and the Libyan National Army command—of a UN facilitated full, nationwide, permanent and comprehensive ceasefire accord. This also required all foreign troops and mercenaries (including those of the pro-Libyan National Army Russian Wagner Group) to leave Libya before the end of January 2021. On 26 October 2020 the inaugural virtual session was convened of an inclusive Libyan Political Dialogue Forum (LPDF), aimed at achieving consensus on governance arrangements that were to lead to national elections. UNSMIL initiated a website (titled 'Al-Hiwar', i.e. 'Dialogue') to act as an interactive national platform during the LPDF process. The first in-person meeting of the LPDF, organized by UNSMIL (with assistance from UNDP) in mid-November, in Tunis, adopted a political roadmap towards holding presidential and legislative elections on 24 December 2021. In January 2021, following a two-month deadlock, the LPDF eventually agreed a process under which an interim consensual unified executive would be nominated to manage the country pending the scheduled presidential and parliamentary elections. At that time the outgoing acting SRSG alleged that the advancement towards national elections risked being stalled and undermined by a small political class on both sides of Libya's east–west conflict lines that preferred to preserve a system of patronage that guaranteed its own privilege. In mid-March a newly-appointed Special Envoy, Ján Kubiš, welcomed the inauguration of an interim Government of National Unity (GNU), which had been approved by the House of Representatives earlier in the month, and was led by Abdul Hamid Dbeibah, a businessman. At that time the UN Security Council unanimously called for the withdrawal from Libya without further delay of the continuing presence of foreign forces and mercenaries. The deployment of 60 UN ceasefire monitors to Libya was approved by the Council in April. Addressing the Second Berlin Conference on Libya ('Berlin II'), hosted by the German Government and UN on 23 June, the UN Secretary-General noted that an initial unit of the ceasefire monitors was soon to be deployed to Tripoli, and welcomed a decision by the GNU to create a High National Reconciliation Commission.

Addressing a reportedly challenging session of the LPDF that took place in Geneva in late June–early July 2021, the Special Envoy and international partners called on all stakeholders to comply with their responsibilities to facilitate the elections as scheduled by the political roadmap (the 1 July deadline for preparing the constitutional and legislative backing for the polls having been overshot). The Special Envoy welcomed a recent decision by the EU Council to clarify the criteria for imposing sanctions against individuals and entities that were undermining or obstructing the planned Libyan elections. The LPDF session considered a pre-prepared formal bridging proposal aimed at securing the constitutional basis for the planned national elections; meanwhile, three other proposals—not all compliant with the agreed political roadmap—were also submitted by Forum members. A Proposals Bridging Committee was established to seek common ground between the proposals. Following the LPDF session, UNSMIL announced that it would continue to work with the Committee, but that it would not entertain proposals that were not focused on holding the planned elections on 24 December. On 5 July UNSMIL welcomed the launch of an updated national voter registration list, and strongly urged the LPDF to accelerate its deliberations. In late August UNSMIL welcomed the creation of a new joint force that had been tasked with securing Libya's Great Man-Made River fresh water distribution project; the force was deemed to represent significant progress in achieving military unification. In early September UNSMIL demanded an immediate cessation of armed clashes in the Salaheddine area of Tripoli. The mission stated concern in mid-September at the passing by the House of Representatives of a motion of no-confidence motion against the GNU. In November the Special Envoy announced his resignation. The previous acting SRSG was appointed, in December, as the UN Secretary-General's Special Adviser on Libya; she determined to pursue implementation of the three intra-Libyan dialogue tracks and to support the holding of presidential and parliamentary elections (which, in the absence of an agreed legal framework, were postponed from December). In February 2022 the House of Representatives adopted a constitutional amendment that provided for the establishment of an inclusive constitutional review committee. Deeming the mandate of the GNU and term of Dbeibah's premiership to have expired, the House of Representatives appointed a rival Prime Minister—Fathi Bashagha—in that month.

During April–June 2022 three rounds of Libyan constitutional track meetings were held, under UNSMIL auspices, in the Egyptian capital, Cairo. Meetings in the JMC 5+5 format, sponsored by UNSMIL and the UN Secretary-General's Special Adviser, took place in Cairo in June. In late June the Special Adviser (prior to the termination of her mission on 31 July) mediated a High-Level Meeting, in Geneva, between the Speaker of the House of Representatives and the President of the High State Council, at which some consensus was achieved with respect to outstanding contentious provisions of the 2017 Libyan Draft Constitution, and a roadmap was adopted on transitional measures that would lead to the holding of national elections. However, differences that remained over the eligibility requirements for presidential candidates were not resolved during further discussions between the heads of the two Libyan chambers that were held in Türkiye at the beginning of August and in Cairo in mid-August. At the beginning of July 2022 the UN Secretary-General stated concern that a series of protests that had erupted across Libya—including in Tripoli, al-Bayda, Benghazi and Tobruk (where the House of Representatives had been stormed)—should be conducted without violence and policed with restraint. An increase in military activity in Tripoli, Misratah and the Sirte area was reported in that month. On 9 August UNSMIL and the JMC met to strengthen the Libyan ceasefire monitoring mechanism, and to finalize modalities for the withdrawal of foreign fighters from the country. Later in that month UNSMIL stated concern over an ongoing mobilization of forces and increase in threats to use military might to secure political gains. The UN Secretary-General expressed concern shortly afterwards over violent clashes that had erupted in Tripoli between armed supporters of Dbeibah and Bashaga, causing 42 fatalities, of whom four were civilians. At the end of August UNSMIL—which has documented disappearances of human rights defenders, elected politicians and political activists, judges, lawyers, migrants and asylum-seekers—urged Libya to adopt the 2010 International Convention for the Protection of all Persons from Enforced Disappearances, and called for the issue to be addressed through a rights-based national reconciliation process. Addressing the UN Security Council on 31 August the UN Under-Secretary-General for Political and Peacebuilding Affairs, Rosemary DiCarlo, stated deep concern at the security threat posed by continuing delays in implementing the electoral process. She called for an end to hate speech and to incitements to violence, and for the immediate release by the Libyan authorities of all arbitrarily detained migrants. A new SRSG for Libya, Abdoulaye Bathily, was appointed at the beginning of September 2022. In December he supported the initiation of a Sustainable Development Cooperation Framework for Libya, which aimed to boost economic growth during 2023–25, and to contribute to an environment conducive to the advancement of human rights and national wellbeing.

In January 2023 UNSMIL urged the prompt adoption of time-bound arrangements to enable free and fair national elections to be organized during the year ahead. UNSMIL hosted a meeting in March of the 5+5 JMC, with military commanders of security units in the east and west of the country, which aimed to foster national reconciliation and enhance the electoral preparations. In May–June UNSMIL participated in a series of meetings with political organizations and other stakeholders to review new draft election legislation, and extended advice on electoral, constitutional and gender dimensions. The mission urged greater engagement with the elections preparations process from a broad range of Libyan stakeholders and institutions. UNSMIL issued a statement in July that stated great concern over continued abductions, forced disappearances and arbitrary arrests perpetrated by various security actors in Libya against citizens and public figures (including the brief detention in mid-July of a Libyan former minister of finance). The SRSG continued in 2023 to engage with relevant regional and international actors, to mobilize support for the Libyan political process.

REGIONAL ORGANIZATIONS

Special Appointments of the UN Secretary-General Concerned with His Good Offices and with Peacebuilding

SPECIAL ADVISERS

Special Adviser on Africa: CRISTINA DUARTE (Cabo Verde).

Special Adviser and Head of the Investigative Team established pursuant to Security Council Resolution 2379 (on holding Islamic State accountable for atrocities perpetrated in Iraq): CHRISTIAN RITSCHER (Germany).

Special Adviser on the Prevention of Genocide: ALICE WAIRIMU NDERITU (Kenya).

Special Adviser on the Responsibility to Protect: GEORGE OKOTH-OBBO (Uganda).

SPECIAL REPRESENTATIVES

Special Representative on Sexual Violence in Conflict: PRAMILA PATTEN (Mauritius).

Special Representative on Violence against Children: Dr NAJAT MAALLA M'JID (Morocco).

OTHER SPECIAL HIGH-LEVEL APPOINTMENTS

Head of International, Impartial and Independent Mechanism to Assist in the Investigation and Prosecution of Persons Responsible for the Most Serious Crimes under International Law Committed in the Syrian Arab Republic since March 2011 (the Mechanism): CATHERINE MARCHI-UHEL (France).

Humanitarian Envoy: AHMED AL MERAIKHI (Qatar).

Further high-level appointees of the UN Secretary-General are listed under Peacekeeping and Other UN Organizations Active in the Region.

United Nations Relief and Works Agency for Palestine Refugees in the Near East—UNRWA

Address: Gamal Abd al-Nasser St, Gaza City.
Telephone: (8) 2887701; **fax:** (8) 2887699.
Address: Bayader Wadi Seer, POB 140157, Amman 11814, Jordan.
Telephone: (6) 5808100; **fax:** (6) 5808335; **e-mail:** gazapio@unrwa.org; **internet:** www.unrwa.org.

UNRWA was established by the UN General Assembly to provide relief, health, education and welfare services for Palestinian refugees in the Near East, initially on a short-term basis. UNRWA began operations in May 1950 and, in the absence of a solution to the refugee problem, its mandate has subsequently been extended by the General Assembly.

Organization

(September 2023)

The Commissioner-General is the head of UNRWA operations and reports directly to the UN General Assembly. UNRWA has no governing body, but its activities are reviewed and guided by a 27-member Advisory Commission—AdCom—which meets twice a year. The Palestinian (National) Authority, the European Community and the League of Arab States (Arab League) participate in the Commission as observers. UNRWA employs some 120 international staff and more than 30,000 local staff, mainly Palestinian refugees.

Commissioner-General: PHILIPPE LAZZARINI (Switzerland).
Deputy Commissioner-General: LENI STENSETH (Norway).

FIELD OFFICES

Each field office is headed by a director and has departments responsible for education, health and relief and social services programmes, finance, administration, supply and transport, legal affairs and public information. Operational support officers work in Gaza and the West Bank to monitor and report on the humanitarian situation and facilitate UNRWA field activities.

Gaza: Rimal Quarter, al-Azhar Rd, Gaza City; tel. (8) 2887457; Dir MATTHIAS SCHMALE.

Jordan: POB 143464, 11814 Amman; tel. (6) 5809100; fax (6) 5809134; Dir MOHAMMED ADAR.

Lebanon: Bir Hassan, Ghobeiri, Beirut 1107 2060; tel. (1) 840490; fax (1) 840466; e-mail h.samra@unrwa.org; Dir CLAUDIO CORDONE.

Syrian Arab Republic: Mezzeh Highway/Beirut Rd intersection, Damascus; tel. (11) 6133035; fax (11) 6133047; e-mail h.mukhles@unrwa.org; Dir AMANYA MICHAEL EBYE.

West Bank: Sheikh Jarrah, East Jerusalem; tel. (2) 5890400; fax (2) 5322714; Dir GWYN LEWIS.

There are UNRWA liaison offices in Brussels, Belgium; Cairo, Egypt; Geneva, Switzerland; and New York and Washington, DC, USA.

Activities

ROUTINE ASSISTANCE ACTIVITIES

UNRWA's humanitarian support activities for Palestinian refugees in Lebanon, Syria, Jordan, the West Bank and the Gaza Strip include the provision of basic food and medical supplies; activities aimed at generating employment and income for labourers with dependants, while improving the local infrastructure; the provision of extra schooling days to make up for those missed because of the conflict, trauma counselling for children, protection activities, and post-injury rehabilitation; and the reconstruction of shelters. The Agency's delivery of services is guided by its Medium-Term Strategy, covering 2023–28, which works towards seven strategic outcomes: protecting refugees through the realization of their rights under international law; enabling them to lead healthy lives; providing inclusive, equitable quality education for refugee children; enhancing livelihood opportunities; ensuring that the most vulnerable refugees have access to effective social assistance; ensuring that basic needs for shelter, water and sanitation are met; and effectively and responsibly implementing UNRWA's mandate.

Since 2007, following the election in early 2006 in the Palestinian Autonomous Territories of a militant Islamic Resistance Movement (Hamas) administration, both Israel and Egypt have imposed a land, air and sea blockade against Gaza (described by UNRWA as a collective punishment, illegal under international law), with consequent severe socioeconomic and humanitarian impacts. Hamas is opposed to any accommodation with Israel. UNRWA reported in early 2023 that 71% of Palestinian refugees in Gaza were existing below the abject poverty line, 80% were dependent on emergency food assistance, and almost 47% were unemployed.

In 2022 UNRWA was providing essential services to 5.9m. registered refugees, and 762,962 other registered persons. Nearly one-third of refugees were living in 58 official camps serviced by the Agency (19 were in the West Bank; 12 in Lebanon; 10 in Jordan; nine in Syria; and eight in Gaza), while the remaining refugees had settled in local towns and villages and host communities, as well as in 10 further (unofficial) camps.

Health Care: In 2022 there were 140 UNRWA-run primary health care units providing outpatient medical care, disease prevention and control, maternal and child health care and family planning services. (Also, 124 of the health care units offered dental services.) The number of health staff totalled 3,050. UNRWA also operates a hospital in the West Bank and offers assistance towards emergency and other secondary treatment, mainly through contractual agreements with non-governmental and private hospitals. Technical assistance for the health programme is provided by the World Health Organization (WHO). The Agency extended antenatal services to 67,070 women in 2022. As a core element of its operations UNRWA offers mental health and psychosocial care to refugees (in particular children) who are experiencing psychological stress. In 2021

UNRWA integrated a mental health and psychosocial support element into all of its health centres. UNRWA maintains mobile phone applications on non-communicable diseases and on maternal and child health.

Education: In the 2022/23 school year 543,080 pupils were enrolled in 706 UNRWA schools, and there were 19,730 UNRWA educational staff. At that time some 7,810 students were enrolled under UNRWA's Technical Vocational Education and Training (TVET) Programme at eight specialized TVET centres. A further 2,051 students were enrolled at two teacher training colleges. The Agency also manages an online Education in Emergencies (EiE) programme, which uses an UNRWA Digital Learning Platform that was inaugurated in April 2021. Technical co-operation for the Agency's education programme is provided by the UN Educational, Scientific and Cultural Organization. An annual meeting is convened between UNRWA and the Arab League's Council of Educational Affairs. An UNRWA Education Expert Advisory Group was established in June 2022. In the following month an UNRWA Information and Communication Technology for Education (ICT4E) Strategy was launched. In June 2023 the fifth workshop was held of an elected UNRWA student parliament, which had been established in 2017, and has representation from the West Bank, Gaza, Jordan, Lebanon and Syria.

Relief and Social Services: 'Decent standard of living' services include the distribution of food rations, the provision of emergency shelter and the organization of welfare programmes for the poorest refugees. In 2022 special social safety net assistance was being extended to 5.5% of the total registered refugee population (of whom one-quarter were residing in Syria). Furthermore, UNRWA was providing food and emergency cash assistance to 1.8m. beneficiaries at that time. UNRWA rehabilitated 551 camps in 2022, of which 440 were in Lebanon and 89 in Jordan.

Microfinance support: In order to encourage self-reliance the Agency issues grants to ailing businesses and loans to families who qualify as special hardship cases. UNRWA's microfinance programme, launched in 1991, promotes income generating opportunities for Palestinian refugees as well as for low-income communities living near refugee populations. Under the programme (available to refugees in the Occupied Territories, Jordan and Syria) credit and complimentary financial services are extended to small and micro business owners, and to households, with the objective of creating sustainable employment, and with a particular focus on empowering women and children. By 2022 some 632,630 loans, with a total estimated value of US $672.9m., had been awarded under the programme.

UNRWA Microfinance Department Headquarters: POB 19149, Jerusalem; 21 Zalman Sharagi St, Sheikh Jarrah Qtr, East Jerusalem; tel. (2) 5890221; the microfinance programme also operates through national field offices and several local branch offices; launched in Feb. 2012 a 'Mubadarati' initiative that was to provide loans to young entrepreneurs in the West Bank and Gaza.

RECENT EMERGENCIES

In late March 2018, at the start of a series of 'Great March of Return' demonstrations aimed at highlighting the plight of exiled Palestinian refugees, at least 16 Palestinians were reportedly killed by the Israeli military and more than 1,000 injured, while Palestinian militants reportedly fired at an Israeli soldier and Palestinian protesters were reported to have thrown rocks and launched cans of flaming petrol, attached to balloons and kites, over the border fence. In May the UN Secretary-General expressed profound concern and urged maximum restraint by the Israeli security forces and by Hamas in view of a sharp escalation of violence in Gaza, arising from Palestinian demonstrations against the repositioning in that month of the US embassy in Israel to Jerusalem. Some 61 Palestinian protesters were reportedly killed by Israeli troops at that time. Great March of Return protests continued throughout 2019. In February of that year a report into the 2018 border violence issued by a UN Independent Commission of Inquiry accused Israeli soldiers of having intentionally fired at civilians; Hamas and other organizers of the protests were also criticized for allowing the cans of burning petrol to be launched. In late January 2020 mass demonstrations, termed 'A Day of Rage', were organized in Gaza and the West Bank in opposition to a proposed Israel–Palestine peace deal that had recently been announced by US President Trump (and which sanctioned the large-scale annexation of West Bank territory by Israel). In the following month Palestine severed relations with Israel and the USA. In August UNRWA's Commissioner-General, noting the background of the long-term blockade on Gaza, stated extreme concern at the recent closure of Gaza's only power plant—owing to the suspension by Israel of fuel shipments to the territory, in retaliation at the hostile launching of incendiary balloons across the Gaza–Israel border. He called for the unimpeded passage into Gaza of all vital goods, including fuel.

In May 2021, against the background of an intensification of clashes at Jerusalem's al-Aqsa Mosque compound and a severe escalation of Hamas–Israeli conflict, UNRWA stated its opposition to the pending forced eviction of several Palestinian families from their long-term homes in the Sheikh Jarrah neighbourhood of East Jerusalem. The Agency also condemned the killing, as a result of Israeli air strikes, of four Palestinian refugee schoolchildren near the Beit Hanoun refugee camp in Gaza, and emphasized profound concern over the impact on children of the recent extreme military escalation. At that time the UN Secretary-General stated his deep concern over mounting numbers of casualties caused by the intensive Israeli air strikes against densely populated Gaza and by rockets and mortars fired from Gaza to target Israeli population centres. However, the Israeli bombardment of Gaza continued relentlessly (severely damaging local civilian infrastructure, including civilian and UN buildings), Palestinian militant groups continued to launch rockets into Israel, and violent unrest also engulfed East Jerusalem and the West Bank. Terming the pending forced evictions from Sheikh Jarrah and the devastation caused by the intensive Israeli bombardment of civilians in Gaza as part of the ongoing Palestinian 'Nakba'—'catastrophe'—UNRWA repeatedly urged all parties to exercise maximum restraint and to comply strictly with their obligations under international law, including with the duty to protect children. On 19 May UNRWA issued a flash appeal for US $38m. to support the provision of immediate food, non-food, health, WASH, psychosocial and other emergency response activities over the following 30 days. A ceasefire between Hamas and Israel, mediated by Egypt, entered into effect on 21 May. By that time, according to OCHA, 242 Palestinians, of whom 65 were children, had been killed during the intensive bombardment of the strip. According to the Gaza health authorities, a further 1,948 Palestinians, including 610 children, had been injured, and around 2,500 Gaza-based Palestinians had been made homeless. At least 40 UNRWA education facilities were reported to have been damaged by the Israeli bombardment, and Gaza's power supply had been significantly reduced. Meanwhile, 12 people, including two children, had reportedly been killed and around 710 injured by Hamas-associated militant attacks against Israel.

A further escalation of Israeli–Palestinian violence erupted on 5 August 2022, following the sudden initiation of an Israeli military aerial offensive (reportedly involving 147 air strikes) aimed at targets in Gaza associated with the Palestinian Islamic Jihad militant grouping; the latter retaliated with, reportedly, 1,100 rocket and mortar attacks against Israel. Some 48 Palestinians were reportedly killed, including 17 children; 450 Palestinians were internally displaced (some sought shelter in UNRWA schools); and 1,761 housing units in Gaza were damaged. On 7 August an Egypt-mediated truce entered into effect.

In January 2023 UNRWA appealed for US $344.9m. to support humanitarian activities during the coming year in Gaza (to which $311.4m. was allocated) and the West Bank, including East Jerusalem (allocated $32.9m.). The appeal was underpinned by three strategic priorities: facilitating increased access to food for crisis-affected Palestinian refugees (including through the provision of food assistance, cash-for-work, and cash vouchers); maintaining refugees' access to health, education, shelter, shelter repairs, and other critical services; and the effective management and co-ordination of the emergency response processes. In a renewed intensification of Israeli–Palestinian tensions in May of that year at least 15 Palestinian refugees were reported by UNRWA to have been killed. Meanwhile, all UNRWA schools were temporarily closed, and the online EiE programme was activated. In mid-June UNRWA deplored the killing of two Palestinian secondary school children during an Israeli military operation at the Jenin refugee camp that had escalated into a wider violent confrontation between the Israeli security forces and Palestinian armed actors (in total at least seven Palestinian and four Israeli deaths were reported); all parties were called on to refrain from using violence. In early July the Agency's Commissioner-General stated deep concern at the impacts of a new major Israeli operation in the West Bank (reportedly the largest there for two decades)—Israeli forces having launched a massive aerial raid against the Jenin camp, that involved at least 10 drone strikes and an estimated 2,000 troops. Israeli special forces were reported to have searched properties in the camp and to have made numerous arrests of alleged terrorists; at least 12 Palestinian fatalities, reportedly including four children, occurred at that time, and more than 4,000 people were displaced from their homes. UNRWA subsequently appealed for $23.8m. to fund a multisectoral emergency response, focused on restoring basic services and rebuilding homes and livelihoods.

UNRWA also issued an emergency appeal for US $436.7m. to fund its assistance operations for Palestinian refugees in Syria, Lebanon and Jordan during 2023. Of the total, some $247.2m. was to support the requirements of vulnerable Palestinian refugees remaining in Syria (where 57% of the refugees were reported to have borderline to poor food consumption), $160m. to assist Palestinian refugees sheltering in Lebanon (where 93% were living below the poverty line and 86% were relying on UNRWA cash assistance as their primary income source), and $28.8m. to those in Jordan (where there was reported to be an 89% unemployment rate among Palestinian refugee youth). Refugees in need within Syria were to receive UNRWA cash and food assistance, non-food items, and winterization support. Cash assistance was to amount to $23 per person per month, or $33 for those in most acute circumstances. Following the onset in 2011 of the Syrian civil war the capability of that country's national authorities to provide health services to resident Palestinian refugees diminished, resulting in strong reliance on UNRWA's healthcare provision. In 2023 the Agency maintained a total of 23 health centres or 'health points' within Palestinian refugee camps in Syria, and two mobile clinics there (deployed on a flexible basis, when and where needed). These all provided, inter alia, outpatient consultations, immunization, and medicine dispensaries. The Agency also subsidized access to further care via a series of partnerships with external hospitals and laboratories. In Lebanon and Jordan UNRWA subsidized some hospitalization costs for Palestinian refugees. In March UNRWA issued a $16.2m. six-month Syria-Lebanon Flash Appeal to support Palestinian refugees impacted by the devastating earthquakes that had struck northern Syria and southern Türkiye in early February (also causing damage to refugee shelters and UNRWA infrastructure in Lebanon). Within Syria, Palestinian refugees based in Aleppo city and in the Latakia, Neirab, Ein el-Tal and Hama camps were reported to have been particularly badly affected. At mid-May UNRWA reported that 1,076 Palestinian shelters had been damaged (166 severely), and 2,355 Palestine refugees remained displaced by the natural disaster.

In August 2023 UNRWA appealed for US $15.5m. to fund a multisectoral emergency response following lethal armed clashes that occurred during late July–early August in the Ein el-Hilweh Palestinian refugee camp, located in southern Lebanon, causing 13 fatalities, massive displacement, and the occupation by armed militants of the agency's eight local schools. UNRWA was preparing alternative schooling locations, organizing repair and relief interventions, and raising awareness locally of unexploded ordnances. The armed combatants were urged to leave the schools (two of which had been transformed into militant bases).

During 2008–23 UNRWA oversaw the rehabilitation of the Nahr el-Bared camp in Lebanon, which had been extensively damaged from May 2007 by fighting between Lebanese government and rebel forces; the reconstruction of the camp (hindered by budgetary restrictions) aimed to provide 5,000 houses, 1,500 shops, six school complexes and sufficient public space, in order to accommodate more than 27,000 Palestinian refugees.

Statistics

REFUGEES REGISTERED WITH UNRWA*
(31 December 2021)

Country	Number	% of total
Jordan	2,334,789	40.3
Gaza Strip	1,516,258	26.2
West Bank	883,950	15.3
Syria	575,234	9.9
Lebanon	482,676	8.3
Total	5,792,907	100.0

* Additionally, UNRWA was providing assistance to 727,876 eligible other registered persons.

Finance

UNRWA is financed almost entirely by voluntary contributions from governments and the European Union (EU), the remainder being provided by UN bodies, non-governmental organizations, business corporations and private sources, which also contribute to extra-budgetary activities. The protracted crises in Gaza and Syria, as well as the COVID-19 pandemic, and (February) 2023 earthquake that struck northern Syria, have placed extreme pressure on the Agency's resources, and reduced funding for priority initiatives (for example rehabilitation projects resulting from conflict).

In January 2023 UNRWA appealed for US $1,630m. in order to implement its mandate during that year. The total amount included $848m. for its regular programme, $436.7m. for its emergency response in Syria, Lebanon and Jordan, and $344.9m. for emergency humanitarian activities in Gaza and the West Bank. Following a Pledging Conference for UNRWA that was convened in June by the President of the UN General Assembly, at which $828.3m. was pledged, the Agency's Commissioner-General warned that the funding thus far received was insufficient to sustain organizational activities beyond September.

In March 2019 the UNRWA Commissioner-General welcomed a decision by the Organization of Islamic Cooperation to establish a new Waqf (endowment) Fund to Support Palestine Refugees.

Publications

Annual Report of the Commissioner-General of UNRWA.
Gender Bulletin.
Reports on labour markets, microfinance, youth outreach, etc.

World Food Programme—WFP

Address: Via Cesare Giulio Viola 68, Parco dei Medici, 00148 Rome, Italy.
Telephone: (06) 65131; **fax:** (06) 6590632; **e-mail:** wfpinfo@wfp.org; **internet:** www.wfp.org.

WFP became operational in 1962 as the UN's principal food assistance agency. It aims to alleviate acute hunger by providing emergency relief in humanitarian disaster situations. It also assists vulnerable populations in developing countries to improve nutrition, to eradicate chronic undernourishment, and to further social advancement by developing assets and promoting self-reliance. WFP was awarded the 2020 Nobel Peace Prize.

Organization
(September 2023)

The governing body of WFP is the Executive Board. An Executive Director is appointed jointly by the UN Secretary-General and the Director-General of FAO and is responsible for the management and administration of the Programme.

EXECUTIVE BOARD

The Board comprises 36 members, 18 of whom are elected by the UN Economic and Social Council and 18 by the Council of the Food and Agriculture Organization (FAO). The Board meets four times a year.

SECRETARIAT

Around 90% of WFP staff members work in the field. WFP administers some 88 country offices, and maintains six regional bureaux, located in Bangkok, Thailand (for Asia); Cairo, Egypt (for the Middle East, Central Asia and Eastern Europe); Panama City, Panama (for Latin America and the Caribbean); Johannesburg, South Africa (for southern Africa); Kampala, Uganda (for Central and Eastern Africa); and Dakar, Senegal (for West Africa).

Executive Director: CINDY MCCAIN (USA).

Activities

WFP is the frontline UN agency in combating hunger. It focuses its efforts on the world's poorest countries, and aims to provide at least 90% of its total assistance to those designated as 'low-income food-deficit'. WFP has a particular focus on UN Sustainable Development Goal (SDG) 2 (Zero Hunger), to which in 2023 around 78% of the Programme's operational requirements were directed; and SDG 17 (on achieving the Goals through strategic partnerships). A Country Strategic Plan (CSP) framework initiated by WFP in 2016 introduced a system of (standard) CSPs and (interim) ICSPs that were to be aligned flexibly to national priorities. WFP's Strategic Plan for 2022–26 focused on achieving the following five outcomes: People are better able to meet their urgent food and nutrition needs; People have better nutrition, health and education outcomes; People have improved and sustainable livelihoods; National programmes and systems are strengthened; and Humanitarian and development actors are more efficient and effective. A WFP management plan for 2023–25, approved by the Executive Board in November 2022, envisaged that in 2023 78% of resources would be allocated to crisis response operations, 19% to resilience-building activities, and 3% to addressing the root causes of food insecurity. In-kind food transfers were to account for 49% of WFP assistance in 2023, and cash-based transfers for 34%. Although commodity vouchers (redeemable against fixed quantities of specific foods) represented less than 2% of assistance in 2022, it was envisaged that they would be used more in 2023. During 2023 WFP aimed to extend support to 149.6m. people.

WFP manages active trust funds for special purposes outside its regular operational programmes, with a view to supporting CSPs, in areas such as enhancing food security and nutrition, the development of supply chains, innovation acceleration, strengthening government capacities, and improving climate change and disaster risk resilience.

WFP aims to combat poverty in developing countries by promoting self-reliant families and communities. It emphasizes training and capacity-building elements within relief operations, such as income-generating activities and environmental protection measures; and seeks to integrate elements that strengthen disaster mitigation into development projects, including soil conservation, reafforestation, irrigation infrastructure, and transport construction and rehabilitation. No individual country is permitted to receive more than 10% of the Programme's available development resources.

Emergency Preparedness and Response: WFP uses geographic information systems to manage and visualize incoming data on crisis situations. Through its Vulnerability Analysis and Mapping (VAM) initiative the agency aims to identify potentially vulnerable groups of people, and efficiently to focus emergency contingency-planning and long-term assistance activities.

The UN Humanitarian Response Depot—a network of depots, based in Accra, Ghana; Dubai, United Arab Emirates; Subang, Malaysia; Panama City, Panama; Las Palmas, Spain; and Brindisi, Italy—stores essential rapid response equipment. Within the UN's 'Cluster Approach' to co-ordinating the international response to humanitarian disasters, WFP is a joint lead agency for the clusters on Emergency Telecommunications, and Logistics and Food Security, and is also actively involved in the Nutrition Cluster. WFP also manages the UN Humanitarian Air Service (UNHAS). When engaging in a crisis WFP dispatches an emergency preparedness team to quantify the amount and type of food assistance required, and to identify the beneficiaries, timescale and logistics underpinning the ensuing assistance programme. Emergency Food Security Assessments, either prompt or in-depth, analyse the impact of a crisis on households and community food security.

The inaugural meeting was convened in April 2021 of a High-Level Task Force on Preventing Famine, created in March by the UN Secretary-General. In February 2022 WFP's Executive Director warned that the interaction of climate shocks and conflict, compounded by the COVID-19 pandemic and rising prices for food and essential supplies, was causing mounting starvation, mass migration, and destabilization. In March WFP emphasized the need to find solutions to the further shock to global food and energy prices prompted by the Russian Federation's invasion of Ukraine. (Russia and Ukraine were major exporters of cereals to the global markets, Ukraine also of sunflower oil, and Russia of crude and processed petroleum and of fertilizers.) WFP was invited to engage with a joint G7-World Bank Global Alliance for Food Security that was launched in May at a meeting of G7 ministers responsible for development. In July negotiations held in Istanbul, Türkiye, under the auspices of the UN and Türkiye, culminated in the conclusion by Russia and Ukraine, in the presence of the UN Secretary-General and the President of Türkiye, of the UN-backed Black Sea Grain Initiative (BSGI), aimed at alleviating global food insecurity by enabling the resumption of exports of grain, sunflower oil and other essential goods from Odesa and two other Ukrainian Black Sea ports (that had hitherto been blockaded by Russia), and at facilitating fertilizer and grain exports from Russia (which had been subjected to punitive sanctions). Extensions to the BSGI were subsequently agreed; however, on 17 July 2023 the initiative lapsed, the Russian authorities having refused to renew it, claiming that commitments made to Russia had not been fulfilled. During July 2022–15 June 2023 shipments of 31.8m. metric tons of food commodities were facilitated through the BSGI.

In early 2023, noting the continuing global economic slowdown, war in Ukraine, supply chain disruptions, and high cost of food, energy and fuel, WFP reported that annual food price inflation was in excess of 15% in 68 countries, and that in 13 of these it exceeded 50%—significantly shrinking vulnerable households' access to food and nutrition (and increasing WFP's operating costs).

Strengthening Food Systems: WFP has warned that disruption to food systems through conflict drives many of the world's food crises—displacing farmers, devastating food stocks and agricultural assets, disrupting supply chains and markets, driving up prices, and harming livelihoods; and that abrupt disruptions to food systems can also arise from shocks related to climate change and to reliance on global supply chains. Furthermore, systematically poor transportation networks and storage facilities, and unpredictable commercial markets can disrupt access to food. WFP interventions that strengthen local food systems include the establishment and rehabilitation of relevant infrastructure in exchange for cash assistance or food; and supporting and engaging local smallholder farmers (for example through a Home Grown School Meals initiative and locally sourced nutrition fortification programmes).

WFP, FAO, IFAD and the UN Secretary-General collectively undertook preparations for a Food Systems Summit (FSS) that was held in September 2021, with a view to raising global awareness of challenges related to the production, processing and consumption of food, and to improving the output of safe, nutritious food. In January 2022, to support the follow-up to the FSS, a co-ordination hub was launched, under the joint leadership of WFP, FAO and IFAD. The inaugural global FSS+2 Stocktaking Moment (post-FSS review meeting) was convened in July 2023, in Rome, Italy.

Food Security and Nutrition: WFP is a participant in the long-standing intergovernmental Committee on World Food Security (CFS), which develops and endorses policy guidance and recommendations that are based on work undertaken by WFP, IFAD and FAO, and also on scientific evidence-based reports produced regularly by a UN High Level Panel of Experts (HLPE) on Food Security and Nutrition (established in 2009). An HLPE report titled *Food Security and Nutrition: Building a Global Narrative towards 2030* was published in July 2020.

Jointly with 12 other partners WFP participates in the Integrated Food Security Phase Classification (IPC) partnership, which aims to analyse and address the multidimensional characteristics of food security issues. The IPC classifies crises under the following categories: acute food security, chronic food security, or acute malnutrition. The severity of acute food insecurity is categorized in accordance with the following scale: minimal (Phase 1), stressed (Phase 2), crisis (Phase 3), emergency (Phase 4), famine (catastrophe: Phase 5).

WFP co-sponsors, with FAO and the International Food Policy Research Institute, the Food Security Information Network, which compiles a *Global Report on Food Crises*. The 2023 edition of the report, published in May, found that in 2022 258m. people in 58 countries and territories had been acutely food-insecure, and forecast that in 2023 some 310,000 people—of whom three-quarters were in Somalia and the remainder in Burkina Faso, Haiti, Mali, parts of Nigeria, and South Sudan—were at risk of (IPC Phase 5) famine.

WFP recognizes that undernutrition—the insufficient intake of nutrients—undermines energy and health, that poor nutrition can also lead to obesity and be a contributory factor in a variety of non-communicable diseases, and that extreme malnutrition can, as well as being potentially fatal, cause stunting and impaired development in children. The impacts of malnutrition can also have the onwards consequences of undermining economies and impeding sustainable development. WFP implements targeted programmes that prevent and treat malnutrition in high-risk groups such as young children, pregnant and breastfeeding women, and people who are living with HIV or tuberculosis. WFP contributes to the implementation of the Decade of Action on Nutrition (2016–25), declared in April 2016 by the UN General Assembly.

Where used, full WFP rations comprise essential food items (staple foods such as wheat flour or rice; pulses such as lentils and chickpeas; vegetable oil fortified with vitamins A and D; sugar; and iodized salt). Supplementary rations (such as fortified blended foods) are designed to improve the nutritional intake of beneficiaries who have access to some food supplies.

Climate Action: WFP aims to enable farmers to protect their enterprises from the impacts of climatic shocks—such as droughts, floods and tropical storms—noting that, after conflict situations, climate extremes represent the next major threat to food security and livelihoods, having the capacity to destroy crop production and local infrastructures, and to disrupt markets. WFP (including through the Weather Risk Management Facility, a joint initiative with IFAD) promotes access to climate information services and forecast-based financing systems, and also facilitates access to agriculture output index-based macro- and microinsurance schemes. Such activities are increasingly supported by funding mechanisms such as the Green Climate Fund (see UNEP). WFP also supports governments with incorporating climate risk assessments into their planning, and with accessing funding for priority climate risk management activities.

Food for Assets (FFA): WFP's FFA projects focus on enhancing long-term food security by meeting the immediate nourishment requirements of food-insecure people (through food rations or cash-based transfers), thereby providing them with more energy and time to work on building lasting sustainable community assets, and to undertake livelihood and self sufficiency enhancing activities. FFA projects include, for example, building new irrigation or terracing infrastructures; soil and water conservation activities; and constructing schools and health clinics. The implementation, where possible, of targeted cash assistance (including mobile and e-money, physical cash, debit cards, and e- or else card vouchers) to buy food, including fresh produce, boosts local output as well as retail activities, and simultaneously reduces the Programme's food transportation and storage costs. The value of virtual money and vouchers can be increased or reduced depending upon the severity of an emergency situation. WFP's SCOPE digital platform stores data on individual and household beneficiaries and facilitates the management of WFP transfers. WFP continues to provide basic rations in emergency situations, and special nutrition support where needed. It is WFP policy to buy food as near as possible to the communities that require it. In more than 40 developing countries WFP works to build the capacity of smallholder and low-income farmers to compete competitively in the market place.

RECENT OPERATIONS

Middle East and North Africa: During January 2020–December 2024 WFP was implementing a CSP in Iraq, at a cost of US $473m., with the aim of providing immediate humanitarian support, where required, and also supporting resilient food systems and livelihoods, for 1.1m. beneficiaries. An ICSP costing $8,558m. was being undertaken during January 2023–31 December 2025 in Yemen, where protracted conflict and population displacement have severely destabilized the food security situation. In February 2023 WFP warned that 17m. Yemenis were suffering extreme food insecurity. In conflict-affected Syrian Arab Republic—where, in 2023 12.1m. people were reported by WFP to be food-insecure—a $2,866m. ICSP was being implemented during 1 January 2022–31 December 2023. Following the devastating earthquakes that struck northern Syria and southern Türkiye in February 2023, WFP supplied emergency hot meals, ready-to-eat rations, and family food packages to survivors.

A State of Palestine CSP, being implemented during March 2023–February 2028 with a budget of US $534m., aimed to enhance local capacities to enable vulnerable Palestinians consistently to meet their food and nutrition needs, and to have increased access to livelihood opportunities and enhanced resilience to shocks; and to strengthen the capacities of Palestinian national institutions to provide sustainable, inclusive and integrated services, including social protection.

Finance

The Programme is funded by voluntary contributions from donor countries, intergovernmental bodies such as the European Commission, and the private sector. Contributions are made in the form of commodities, finance and services (particularly shipping). Commitments to the International Emergency Food Reserve (IEFR), from which WFP provides the majority of its food supplies, and to the Immediate Response Account (IRA) of the IEFR, are also made on a voluntary basis by donors. (In 2022 some US $385m. was channelled from the IRA to 36 country operations.) WFP's estimated operational requirements for 2023 totalled some $23,100m.

Publications

Food and Nutrition Handbook.
State of Food Security and Nutrition in the World (annually, with FAO, IFAD, UNICEF and WHO).
World Hunger (series).

Food and Agriculture Organization of the United Nations—FAO

Address: Viale delle Terme di Caracalla, 00153 Rome, Italy.
Telephone: (06) 57051; **e-mail:** fao-hq@fao.org; **internet:** www.fao.org.

FAO, the first specialized agency of the UN to be founded after the Second World War, aims to eradicate hunger and malnutrition and achieve food security for all; to eliminate poverty and facilitate economic and social progress for all; and to promote the sustainable management and utilization of natural resources (land, water, air, climate and genetic) for the benefit of present and future generations. FAO serves as a co-ordinating agency for development programmes in the whole range of food and agriculture, including forestry and fisheries.

Organization
(September 2023)

CONFERENCE
The governing body is the FAO Conference of member nations. It meets every two years, formulates policy, determines the organization's programme and budget on a biennial basis, and elects new members. It also elects the Director-General and the Independent Chairman of the Council.

COUNCIL
The FAO Council is composed of representatives of 49 member nations, elected by the Conference for rotating three-year terms. It is the interim governing body of FAO between sessions of the Conference, and normally holds at least five sessions in each biennium. The main Governing Committees of the Council are: the Finance, Programme, and Constitutional and Legal Matters Committees, and the Technical Committees on Agriculture, Commodity Problems, Fisheries and Forestry.

SECRETARIAT
The Director-General is supported by three Deputy Directors-General, a Chief Scientist, a Chief Economist and two Assistant Directors-General. Principal divisions, each headed by a Director, align under Partnership and Outreach; Natural Resources and Sustainable Production; and Economic and Social Development.
Director-General: Qu Dongyu (People's Republic of China).

REGIONAL OFFICES
FAO maintains five regional offices, 11 subregional offices, five liaison offices (in Yokohama, Japan; Washington, DC, USA; Geneva, Switzerland, and New York, USA: liaison with the UN; and Brussels, Belgium: liaison with the EU), and more than 130 country offices.
Near East and North Africa: 11 El-Eslah el-Zerai St, Dokki, POB 2223, Cairo, Egypt; tel. (2) 3316000; e-mail fao-rne@fao.org; internet www.fao.org/neareast; a Regional Conference for the Near East is convened every 2 years (36th session: Feb. 2022, a hybrid virtual and in-person event that was hosted from Baghdad, Iraq); Regional Rep. Abdulhakakim Rajab Elwaer (Libya).
Subregional Office for Central Asia: Ivedik Cad. 55, 06170 Yenimahalle, Ankara, Türkiye; tel. (312) 307-9500; fax (312) 307-1705; e-mail fao-sec@fao.org; Coordinator Viorel Gutu.
Subregional Office for North Africa: rue du Lac Winnipeg, Les Berges du Lac 1, Tunis, Tunisia; tel. (71) 145-700; fax (71) 861-960; e-mail fao-snea@fao.org; internet www.fao.org/neareast/regional-office/north-africa; Subregional Coordinator Philippe Ankers (Switzerland).
Subregional Office for the Gulf Cooperation Council States and Yemen: c/o Ministry of Climate Change and Environment, Airport Rd, Abu Dhabi, United Arab Emirates; e-mail fao-sng@fao.org.

Activities

FAO's Strategic Framework for 2022–31, endorsed by the Conference in June 2021, aimed to support the UN's 2030 Agenda for Sustainable Development by guiding a global transformation to more resilient, inclusive, efficient and sustainable agrifood systems, characterized by four guiding aspirations: Better Production, Better Nutrition, Better Environment, and Better Life, with a strong focus on leaving no one behind. The Framework placed a particular focus on the achievement of Sustainable Development Goal (SDG) 1: End poverty in all its forms everywhere; SDG 2: End hunger, to achieve food security and improved nutrition, and to promote sustainable agriculture; and SDG 10: Reduce inequalities in and among countries. It included four cross-cutting 'accelerators'—innovation, technology, data, and 'complements' (i.e. human capital, governance and institutions)—to be prioritized in all of its programme interventions. The Framework had 20 inter-disciplinary programme priority areas (PPAs), grouped under each of the four aspirations. The PPAs for Better Production were: green innovation, blue (i.e. marine) transformation, one health, small-scale producers' equitable access to resources, and digital agriculture; for Better Nutrition: healthy diets for all, nutrition for the most vulnerable, safe food for everyone, reducing food loss and waste, and transparent markets and trade; for Better Environment: climate change mitigating and adapted agrifood systems, bioeconomy for sustainable food and agriculture, and biodiversity and ecosystem services for food and agriculture; and for Better Life: gender equality and rural women's empowerment, inclusive rural transformation, achieving sustainable urban food systems, agriculture and food emergencies, resilient agrifood systems, FAO's Hand-in-Hand initiative (q.v.), and scaling up investment. A Medium-Term Plan aligned with the 2022–31 Strategic Framework, was being implemented during 2022–25.

FAO aims to serve as a knowledge network in support of development, as well as to provide a neutral forum to enhance public-private collaboration and to bring knowledge directly to the field. In February 2020 FAO was a founding signatory of the Rome Call for Artificial Intelligence Ethics, which outlined fundamental principles to ensure that technological advances serve all of humanity and contribute to protection of the global environment. FAO has aimed to lead efforts to transform food systems on the basis of a digital, data and scientific approach. In December 2020 the FAO Council approved a new Strategy for Private Sector Engagement.

The FAO Director-General assists the UN Secretary-General's chairmanship of a High-Level Task Force (HLTF) on Global Food and Nutrition Security that was established in 2008 and has 22 member (mainly UN) agencies. FAO hosts at its headquarters the intergovernmental Committee on World Food Security (CFS: established in 1974 and reformed in 2009), which is tasked with influencing hunger elimination programmes at global, regional and national level, taking into account that food security relates not just to agriculture but also to economic access to food, adequate nutrition, social safety nets and human rights. FAO, the World Food Programme (WFP) and the International Fund for Agricultural Development (IFAD), and science-based reports produced regularly by a UN High Level Panel of Experts (HLPE) on Food Security and Nutrition (established in 2009), support the policy work of the CFS.

In March 2022, in an address to an extraordinary meeting of the ministers responsible for agriculture of the Group of Seven (G7) advanced economies, the FAO Director-General stated great concern at the outlook for food prices (already at a record high) in the context of the Russian Federation's military invasion of Ukraine—given that Russia and Ukraine had accounted for around 30% of wheat exports and 55% of sunflower oil to global markets in 2021, and were also major exporters of barley, maize and rapeseed oil; in addition, Russia was a significant exporter of fertilizers. FAO was invited to engage with a G7-World Bank Global Alliance for Food Security that was launched in May at a meeting of G7 ministers responsible for development. In July negotiations held in Istanbul, Türkiye, under the auspices of the UN and Türkiye, culminated in the conclusion by Russia and Ukraine of the UN-backed Black Sea Grain Initiative (BSGI), aimed at alleviating global food insecurity by enabling the resumption of exports of grain, sunflower oil and other essential goods from Odesa and two other Ukrainian Black Sea ports (that had hitherto been blockaded by Russia), and at facilitating fertilizer and grain exports from Russia (which had been subjected to punitive sanctions). Extensions to the BSGI were subsequently agreed; however, on 17 July 2023 the initiative lapsed, the Russian authorities having refused to renew it, claiming that commitments made to Russia had not been fulfilled.

In February 2023 FAO's Director-General and the heads of the World Bank Group, WFP, International Monetary Fund and World Trade Organization (WTO) issued a joint statement in which they called for further urgent collective actions (i) to rescue hunger hotspots: through supporting country-level efforts to strengthen crisis preparedness, share information, and address local needs; (ii) to facilitate trade (including supporting measures aimed at increasing the availability of food and fertilizers and strengthening the provision of public goods), to improve the functioning of markets, and to strengthen the role of the private sector; and (iii) to reform harmful subsidies and repurpose them towards initiatives promoting global food security and sustainable food systems.

World Food Day, commemorating the foundation of FAO, is held annually on 16 October.

In 2023, in the Middle East and North Africa, FAO was implementing the following regional initiatives: Water scarcity; Green development of special agricultural products; Gender equality and women's empowerment for inclusive food systems transformation; Addressing climate change in agrifood systems; Rural advisory services for inclusive transformation; Strengthening producers' organizations; and a Red Palm Weevil eradication programme.

Food Systems Summit (FSS): In September 2021, at the start of the 76th UN General Assembly, FAO, WFP, IFAD and the UN Secretary-General collectively hosted the FSS (from New York, USA, in a virtual format), with a view to raising global awareness of challenges related to the production, processing, distribution and consumption of food, and to improving the output of safe, nutritious food. The FSS focused on the following five 'Action Tracks': (1) Ensure access to safe and nutritious food for all (1.1: Promote food security and reduce hunger; 1.2: Improve access to nutritious foods; and 1.3: Make food safer); (2) Shift to sustainable consumption patterns (2.1: Enable, inspire and motivate people to enjoy healthy and sustainable options; and 2.2: Slash food loss and waste and transition to a circular economy); (3) Boost nature-positive production (3.1: Protect natural ecosystems from new deforestation and from being converted into sources of food and feed production; 3.2: Manage, sustainably, existing food production systems; and 3.3: Restore degraded ecosystems and rehabilitate soil function for sustainable food production); (4) Advance equitable livelihoods (4.1: Rebalance agency within food systems—including a greater focus on the rights of and participation by often excluded groups; 4.2: Eliminate worker exploitation and ensure decent work in food systems; and 4.3: Localize food systems—including prioritizing short food chains and local markets); and (5) Build resilience to vulnerabilities, shocks and stress (5.1: Build food systems resilience; 5.2: Ensure universal food access to build resilience—i.e. reframe food as a public common good and human right, rather than as a commodity; and 5.3: Develop climate-resilient development pathways for the transformation of food systems and achievement of the UN SDGs). Governance—i.e. both FSS governance and broader food systems governance—was identified as a cross-cutting action area. A co-ordination hub, jointly led by FAO, WFP and IFAD, was established in January 2022 to support the follow-up to the summit, by collaborating with the intergovernmental CFS and the UN High Level Panel of Experts on Food Security and Nutrition (q.v.), and by strengthening synergies with the UN High-Level Political Forum (HLPF) on Sustainable Development, financing for development, and other intergovernmental processes relating to the environment, biodiversity, climate, food security, health and nutrition. The hub was to be assisted by a Champions Advisory Group comprising strong stakeholder representation by, *inter alia*, producers, the private sector, Indigenous peoples, youth and women. Until 2030 the UN Secretary-General was to submit an annual report to the HLPF on progress in following up the FSS, and was to convene a biennial global post-FSS stocktaking meeting.

In May 2022 FAO helped to launch, as a core group member, a Coalition of Action for Healthy Diets from Sustainable Food Systems. From November FAO and IFAD assumed joint leadership of the Global Environment Facility's new Food Systems Integrated Program: this aimed to channel some US $230m. (to be amplified by co-financing) in grants towards country projects focused on sustainably transforming agrifood systems. In March 2023 FAO and the UN Industrial Development Organization launched the Agrifood Systems Transformation Accelerator, which aimed to foster partnerships and boost private-sector investment in LDCs' food systems.

The inaugural post-FSS global food systems meeting, the UN FSS+2 Stocktaking Moment, was convened in July 2023, in Rome, attended by senior representatives of 182 countries, as well as of UN entities and other stakeholder organizations. The meeting served to strengthen collaboration in support of new sustainable food system strategies; it concluded with the launch of the UN Secretary-General's *Call to Action for Accelerated Food Systems Transformation*.

BETTER PRODUCTION

FAO promotes innovation, technologies and policies to promote green business opportunities across sustainable crop, livestock and forestry production systems, as well as a transformation to efficient, resilient 'blue' food systems.

FAO promotes an integrated One Health approach to the pursuit of safe and resilient agrifood systems and the protection of the environment and biodiversity, working closely with the World Health Organization (WHO), UN Environment Programme and the World Organisation for Animal Health (WOAH). In April 2022 the four organizations concluded a Memorandum of Understanding that provided for the establishment of a Quadripartite Collaboration for One Health, which was collectively to address challenges at the human-animal-plant-ecosystem interface. In October the Quadripartite launched a One Health Joint Plan of Action (OH-JPA), which was aimed at collectively integrating systems and capacities to enhance the prevention, detection and response to threats posed to the health of humans, animals, plants and the environment, while also contributing to sustainable development. In March 2023 the Quadripartite heads jointly issued a call to global action, urging that the concept of One Health should be prioritized in the international political agenda; that One Health policies, strategies and plans should be strengthened and accelerated; that intersectoral One Health-focused workforces should be established; that the prevention of pandemics and health threats should be addressed at source, with focus on activities and locations that present a significant risk of zoonotic spillover from animals to humans; that One Health-related scientific knowledge sharing should be strengthened; and that investment in One Health strategies and plans should be increased.

FAO promotes equitable access to land and water resources and supports integrated land and water management, including river basin management and improved irrigation systems. In May 2012 the CFS endorsed a set of landmark Voluntary Guidelines on the Responsible Governance of Tenure of Land, Fisheries and Forests in the Context of National Food Security, with the aim of supporting governments in safeguarding the rights of citizens to own or have access to natural resources.

FAO's Agro-Ecological Zoning (AEZ) methodology, developed jointly with the International Institute for Applied Systems Analysis, is used for land resources assessment, identifying homogenous and contiguous areas possessing similar soil, land and climate characteristics. FAO's database of Global Agro-Ecological Zones (GAEZ) is updated periodically. FAO has developed AQUASTAT as a global information system concerned with global water issues, and comprising databases, country and regional profiles, surveys and maps. AquaCrop, CropWat and ClimWat are further productivity models and databases which have been developed to help to assess crop requirements and potential yields.

FAO promotes the equitable access of small-scale producers and family farmers to economic and natural resources, markets, services, education, information and technologies. Accessible digital technologies are also promoted, in agrifood systems, to enhance resilience, productivity and market opportunities. A 1,000 Digital Village Initiative was being piloted in 2023 to advance the digitalization of rural areas.

The 2022 edition of FAO's flagship *State of Food and Agriculture* report, issued in November, focused on the contribution of agricultural automation to resilient, sustainable agrifood systems.

Through its Progressive Management Pathway for Antimicrobial Resistance (FAO-PMP-AMR) FAO supports countries to develop national action plans to guide the prudent use of antimicrobials in agriculture and food production and the prevention and control of antimicrobial resistance (AMR) in food systems. In June 2019 FAO, WOAH and WHO collectively established an AMR Multi Partner Trust Fund, with initial funding of US $5m. FAO, WOAH and WHO maintain an online Global Database for Antimicrobial Resistance Country Self Assessment. FAO also helped to formulate a Progressive Control Pathway for Foot and Mouth Disease (PCP-FMD).

FAO works with regional and international associations to develop seed networks, to encourage the use of improved seed production systems, to elaborate quality control and certification mechanisms and to co-ordinate seed security activities, in particular in areas prone to natural or man-made disasters. In November 2011 the FAO Council adopted the Second Global Plan of Action for Plant Genetic Resources for Food and Agriculture (updating the first, 1996 Global Plan). The International Treaty on Plant Genetic Resources for Food and Agriculture, which was adopted by the FAO Conference in 2001 and entered into force in June 2004, provides a framework to ensure access to plant genetic resources and to related knowledge and technologies. The Treaty's Benefit-sharing Fund (BSF) provides finance to enable small-scale farmers in developing countries to conserve principal food crops and build resilience to impacts of climate change. By 2023 around 1,750 gene banks had been established worldwide, storing more than 7m. plant samples, covering both food crops and related wild variants.

FAO hosts the secretariat of the International Plant Protection Convention. Other Regional Plant Protection Organizations (RPPOs) and National Plant Protection Organizations (NPPOs) work to promote harmonized phytosanitary standards and measures in the context of the IPPC. Common global challenges and collective strategies are discussed at an annual RPPO Technical Consultation.

Through the Food Chain Crisis (FCC) Management Framework FAO addresses, by means of a comprehensive, multidisciplinary approach, risks posed to the human food chain, human health, food security, local livelihoods and national economies by threats such as food-borne pathogens, mycotoxins, locust and other insect infestations, avian influenza, peste des petits ruminants (PPR), fall armyworm (FAW), and wheat rust and banana diseases. The Framework integrates prevention, early warning, preparedness, and response to food chain emergencies, from food production to food consumption. The FCC operates through an Intelligence and Coordination Unit, an Emergency and Resilience Division, and the Emergency Prevention Systems (EMPRES)—which has three thematic divisions: EMPRES Plant Protection, EMPRES Animal Health, and EMPRES Food Safety. In November 2021 FAO established a global information system, EMPRES-i+.

In October 2016 FAO and WOAH launched a PPR Global Control and Eradication Strategy, aimed at achieving the eradication by 2030 of PPR, a highly contagious viral disease affecting goats and sheep in around 66 countries in Africa, the Middle East and Asia. In November 2022, while launching the second stage of the eradication initiative, covering the period 2022–26, FAO and WOAH estimated that PPR caused annual economic losses in excess of US $2,100m., globally, and that, in developing and emerging economies, small ruminants represented the principal livestock resource of around 300m. poor rural families. By that time, within the framework of the eradication programme, 68 countries had developed PPR National Strategic Plans aimed at the eradication of the disease.

FAO was implementing a Global Action for Fall Armyworm Control initiative during 2020–23, which aimed to mobilize some US $500m. to co-ordinate global and regional monitoring and control of FAW (a pest that has spread rapidly in recent years and increasingly poses a threat to smallholders' crops in Africa, the Middle East and Asia and the Pacific; in November 2021 FAO reported that more than 70 countries in those regions were combating FAW).

FAO's global Desert Locust Information Service (DLIS) monitors and issues early warning alerts on invasions of desert locusts, swarms of which have the capacity to breed and migrate rapidly, posing a significant threat to food security. FAO also undertakes national capacity-building activities and training on locust control, carries out field assessment missions, co-ordinates locust control operations, and extends emergency assistance during upsurges in locust populations (i.e. when uncontrolled breeding occurs for successive seasons, leading to the formation of 'hopper bands' of flightless juveniles and to adult swarms; in the most extreme scenario widespread intense infestations are referred to as a 'plague'). Three specialized FAO locust commissions cover arid and semi-arid areas of Africa and Asia where desert locusts are particularly prevalent. (In times of plague the scope of desert locusts can spread from their usual habitat, covering around 16m. square km and including around 30 countries, to an area of up to 29m. square km, affecting twice as many countries.) Main responsibility for local survey and control activities lies with national ministries responsible for agriculture. Control methods include aerial, vehicle-mounted or manual spraying of affected areas with conventional chemical pesticides (of which 10 have been approved by an advisory body of experts: the Pesticide Referee Group); biopesticides (promoted by FAO); or insect control regulators. During 2020–21 FAO supported a series of emergency locust control operations in East Africa, Yemen, Iran and Pakistan (see under *Emergency Preparedness and Response*).

The Joint FAO/International Atomic Energy Agency Division maintains a network of agriculture and biotechnology laboratories. Through its Animal Production and Health Laboratory, a WOAH collaborating centre, the Division works to detect and control transboundary animal and zoonotic diseases. It manages a veterinary diagnostic laboratory network (VETLAB) and an iVetNet Information Platform. In 2020 the Division formulated standard operating procedures to detect and monitor the SARS-CoV-2 virus that causes COVID-19, and provided technical guidance on COVID-19 at the animal-human interface to veterinary diagnostic laboratories in more than 100 FAO member states.

FAO hosts the secretariat of the Global Forum on Agricultural Research, which was established in 1996 as a collaboration of research centres, non-governmental and private sector organizations and development agencies. The Forum aims to strengthen research and promote knowledge partnerships concerned with the alleviation of poverty, the enhancement of food security and the sustainable use of natural resources. Furthermore, FAO hosts the secretariat of the Science Council of the Consultative Group on International Agricultural Research (CGIAR), which aims to mobilize global scientific expertise.

FAO aims to facilitate and secure the long-term sustainable development of capture fisheries and aquaculture, in both inland and marine waters, and to promote their contribution to world food security. It plays a leading role in working towards attainment of SDG 14: Conserve and sustainably use the oceans, seas and marine resources for sustainable development. In February 2021 FAO's Committee on Fisheries acknowledged the role of sustainable managed aquatic food systems in combating poverty and malnutrition, leading to the incorporation of a Blue Transformation concept as a priority area in FAO's new Strategic Framework.

FAO collates statistics on global capture and aquaculture production, publishing *The State of World Fisheries and Aquaculture* every two years, while a GLOBEFISH network focuses on market trends, tariffs and other industry issues. FAO extends technical support to improve the management and conservation of aquatic resources, trade of products, preservation, marketing and quality assurance. FAO works to ensure that small-scale fishing communities (accounting for around 90% of the sector's work force) reap equitable benefits from the international trade in fish (including crustaceans and molluscs), fish products and fish by-products (such as fish heads, backbones and viscera). The agency led an initiative in 1999 to establish the Regional Fishery Body Secretariat Network (RSN) as a mechanism to facilitate the exchange of information, data and best practices among FAO and non-FAO regional fishery bodies or arrangements. FAO hosted the eighth meeting of the RSN, as a virtual event, in February 2021.

In February 1999 the FAO Committee on Fisheries adopted voluntary international measures, within the framework of a 1995 Code of Conduct for Responsible Fishing (CCRF), in order to reduce overexploitation of the world's fish resources. Voluntary guidelines concerning the so-called eco-labelling and certification of fish and fish products were adopted in March 2005. FAO's FishCode programme supports developing countries in implementing the CCRF. Several international plans of action (IPOA) have been elaborated within the context of the Code, including the IPOA to Prevent, Deter and Eliminate Illegal, Unreported and Unregulated Fishing (IPOA-IUU, 2001). In June 2014 FAO endorsed a series of Voluntary Guidelines for Securing Sustainable Small-Scale Fisheries (SSF).

In 2017 FAO initiated a Global Programme to Support the Implementation of the 2009 Agreement on Port State Measures to Prevent, Deter and Eliminate Illegal, Unreported and Unregulated Fishing (which had been endorsed by the FAO Conference in November 2009 and entered into force in June 2016), and complementary international instruments. The Global Programme had a particular focus on assisting developing states to formulate related national strategies, policy and legislation.

FAO promotes preventive measures to reduce marine litter and microplastics, including the development of biodegradable materials for fishing gear. In July 2018 the Committee on Fisheries endorsed a series of FAO Voluntary Guidelines for the Marking of Fishing Gear, with a view to reducing the level of discarded so-called 'ghost gear' that represents a significant proportion of marine plastic pollution, putting marine species at risk.

More than 600 fish species are produced in aquaculture, with a particular focus on salmonids, carps, tilapias and shrimps. The establishment of a Global Aquaculture Advancement Partnership (GAAP), conceptualized by FAO, and comprising governments, UN agencies, non-governmental organizations and private sector interests, was approved by more than 50 states in October 2013; GAAP was tasked with pursuing sustainable solutions to meeting the growing global demand for fish products, over a 10–15-year time period. In December 2021 the FAO Council adopted a Global Action Plan on Aquatic Genetic Resources (AqGR), and, with a view to promoting the sustainable conservation of genetic diversity in aquaculture production, FAO has developed an AqGR Monitoring System.

BETTER NUTRITION

FAO participates in the Steering Committee of UN-Nutrition, which was initiated in early 2021—uniting the UN Network for the Scaling up Nutrition (SUN) Movement and UN System Standing Committee on Nutrition—to co-ordinate UN agencies in advancing nutrition and eliminating hunger, malnutrition and obesity.

In November 2014 FAO, WFP and WHO, in co-operation with the HLTF, and other partners, organized the Second International Conference on Nutrition (ICN2, ICN1 having been convened in December 1992). ICN2 reviewed progress achieved since 1992 towards improving nutrition, and—taking into account subsequent advances in science and technology and changes to food systems—endorsed the Rome Declaration on Nutrition and Framework for Action, aimed at eradicating malnutrition and ensuring that nutritious diets become available for all. In April 2016 FAO welcomed the designation by the UN General Assembly of 2016–25 as the UN Decade of Action on Nutrition; implementation of the Decade was led by FAO and WHO, in co-ordination with WFP, IFAD and the UN Children's Fund (UNICEF). A new Framework for the Urban Food Agenda, which aimed to promote issues of nutrition and food systems in urban planning and policymaking, was launched in March 2019.

In the UN's flagship annual *State of Food Security and Nutrition in the World* report, jointly prepared by FAO, IFAD, WFP, UNICEF and WHO, food security is defined as adequate access to food in both quality and quantity. The principal indicator used for ascertaining progress towards the eradication of hunger is SDG 2, Indicator 2.1.1: 'Prevalence of Undernourishment' (PoU—i.e. the estimated proportion of people with habitual food consumption that is insufficient to provide sufficient dietary energy levels to maintain a normal active and healthy life). In 2017 estimates derived from FAO's Food Insecurity Experience Scale (FIES) that related to the prevalence of severe food insecurity were incorporated for the first time into the *State of Food Security and Nutrition in the World*, to supplement the metrics on PoU. (The FIES—initiated by FAO during 2014—provides internationally comparable measurements of the difficulty of accessing food, using data gathered in response to direct interviews with households or individuals.) Severe food insecurity refers to the exhaustion of food supplies, and to resulting hunger and grave impacts on health, wellbeing and ability to function. In 2019 the *State of Food Security and Nutrition in the World* included, for the first time, FIES estimates of the prevalence of moderate as well as severe food insecurity, to address progress made towards achieving SDG 2, Indicator 2.1.2, relating to the ability to access nutritious and sufficient food, beyond the more extreme focus of 2.1.1 on the elimination of hunger. Moderate food insecurity is defined as a lack of assured, consistent access to food, involving the need at certain times to reduce the quality and/or the quantity of food intake.

The 2022 edition of *State of Food Security and Nutrition in the World,* issued in July, reported that the rate of PoU globally had risen significantly during 2019–21, and that, in 2021, some 702m.–828m. people had suffered hunger and around 2,300m. had been moderately or severely food-insecure. Nearly 30% of women of childbearing age were reported to have suffered from anaemia in 2019, an upwards trend in levels of adult obesity was observed, and (in 2020) 5.7% of children worldwide were reportedly clinically overweight, 22% were suffering from stunting, and 6.7% were acutely affected by wasting. Some 43.8% of infants aged under six months were reported to have been exclusively breast-fed in 2020, respresenting an advancement over 37.1% in 2012. In 2020 almost 3,100m. people worldwide reportedly were unable to afford a healthy diet (with a deterioration of conditions particularly notable in Asia, followed by Africa). The report emphasized the role of government policies—such as trade and market interventions, fiscal subsidies, and general services support—in influencing the food availability environment, and recommended means of repurposing existing support to enhance the availability to consumers of nutritious foods.

The Codex Alimentarius Commission sets standards for food products and issues guidelines and codes of practice on food safety and quality and on trade in food. The FAO Organic Agriculture Programme helps to build the capacities of member states in the areas of organic food production, processing, certification and marketing. In February 2019 FAO organized, with the African Union and WHO, in Addis Ababa, Ethiopia, the inaugural International Food Safety Conference, addressing the human health and economic challenges posed by unsafe food. An International Forum on Food Safety and Trade, following on from the Conference, was organized by FAO, WHO and the WTO in April.

In 2011 an Agricultural Market Information System (AMIS) was established under FAO auspices, with a view to improving market transparency and stabilizing food price volatility. The Group on Earth Observations Global Agricultural Monitoring (GEOGLAM) initiative was launched at that time, to strengthen international capacity to produce and disseminate efficient forecasts of agricultural production. The monthly *AMIS Market Monitor* collates data on crop growing conditions recorded in GEOGLAM's regularly updated *Crop Monitor*. GEOGLAM became a full member of the AMIS Secretariat in June 2016.

The FAO Food Price Monitoring and Analysis mechanism issues warnings for countries where the cost of one or more basic food commodity is trending towards an abnormally high level. In March 2022 FAO's Food Price Index recorded the highest levels of global food prices since 1990, reaching 159.3 points. The Index had averaged 97.9 points in 2020, rising to an average of 143.7 points in 2022. In May 2023 the Index stood at 124.3 points. In addition to the Food Price Index, FAO maintains price indices for cereal, dairy, oils and fats, meat, and sugar.

BETTER ENVIRONMENT

FAO hosts the Facilitation Unit of the multi-stakeholder Global Alliance for Climate-Smart Agriculture (GACSA), initiated in September 2014. GACSA develops policy briefs and fosters partnerships to promote climate-smart agricultural practices. FAO's multi-partner Energy-Smart Food Programme promotes energy efficiency and renewable energy in agrifood systems. A Globally Important Agricultural Heritage programme aims to identify and protect traditional agricultural systems that represent models of sustainable agricultural production.

FAO offers policy guidance and technical support to policymakers regarding the development of a sustainable, circular bioeconomy, i.e. harnessing bioscience and biotechnology to provide food, animal feed, paper, bio-based textiles, wood products, bioplastics, biochemicals, biopharmaceuticals and bioenergy.

FAO hosts the Global Soil Partnership, an alliance that promotes sustainable soil management (SSM), with a view to fostering productive, healthy soils and maintaining essential ecoystems. In June 2019 the FAO Conference mandated the development of an FAO Strategy on Mainstreaming Biodiversity across Agricultural Sectors. FAO's inaugural *The State of the World's Biodiversity for Food and Agriculture,* issued in February of that year, emphasized that biodiversity losses are unrecoverable, and that numerous species underpinning food systems are under threat—including plants, animals, insects and micro-organisms ('associated biodiversity') that support food production through ecosystem services, such as maintaining soil fertility, purifying air and water, pollinating plants, and countering livestock and crop diseases and pests. Changes in land and water use and management, overexploitation, overharvesting, pollution, climate change, deforestation, population growth and urbanization were reported to be key drivers of biodiversity loss. The report urged governments and other stakeholders to strengthen frameworks and incentives aimed at reversing the biodiversity crisis.

In December 2021 FAO and the International Fertilizer Association concluded a Memorandum of Understanding (MOU) on future co-operation in promoting sustainable fertilizer use and healthy soils. In January 2022 the FAO Executive Director called for a reversal of soil degradation, caused by unsustainable agricultural practices. In December FAO issued *The Global Status of Black Soils*, and a *Soil Atlas of Asia*.

FAO aims to ensure the conservation of forests and forestry resources while maximizing their potential to contribute to food security and to social and economic development. It assists member countries to formulate, implement and monitor national forestry programmes, and encourages the participation of all stakeholders in developing plans for the sustainable management of tree and forest resources. FAO voluntary guidelines aimed at supporting states to develop mechanisms for monitoring national forest resources were issued in July 2017. FAO's Forest Resources Long-Term Strategy, supporting sustainable forest management over the period 2012–30, aimed to strengthen the quality, harmonizing and sharing of multi-country forest resource information used in policy reviews. A Global Plan of Action for the Conservation, Sustainable Use and Development of Forest Genetic Resources, adopted by the FAO Conference in June 2013, detailed 27 strategic priorities for action. FAO maintains an online Forestry Information System (FORIS).

FAO's first UN Strategic Plan for Forestry, covering the period 2017–30, aimed to reverse the trend of deforestation and to expand global forest coverage by 120m. ha by 2030. At global level FAO undertakes surveillance of forestry related issues; the 2020 edition of a *Forest Resources Assessment* (issued every five years) was published in May 2020. At that time FAO estimated that 420m. ha of forest had been lost as a result of deforestation during the period 1990–2020. It was noted that, globally, forests provide habitat for 68% of terrestrial mammals, 75% of bird species, and 80% of species of amphibians. The 2022 edition of FAO's biennial report *The State of the World's Forests* focused on the potential contribution of three interrelated forestry pathways to the broader goals of a green recovery and more efficient, resilient and sustainable agrifood systems. FAO aimed to support member states to implement the pathways: Halting deforestation and maintaining forests; Restoring degraded lands and expanding agroforesty; and Sustainably using forests and building green value chains.

In September 2008 FAO, with UNEP and the UN Development Programme, launched the UN Collaborative Programme on Reducing Emissions from Deforestation and Forest Degradation in Developing Countries (UN-REDD), with the aim of enabling donors to pool resources (through a trust fund established for that purpose) to promote a transformation of forest resource use patterns.

FAO is a member of the Collaborative Partnership on Forests, an informal voluntary arrangement among 14 agencies with significant forestry programmes, which was established in April 2004. FAO organizes a World Forestry Congress, generally held every six years. World Forestry Congress XV, co-organized by FAO and South Korea in that country's capital, Seoul, in May 2022, adopted the Seoul Forest Declaration, which addressed the role of forests in combating global challenges including land degradation, biodiversity loss, climate change, hunger, and poverty.

World Forest Day, sponsored by FAO and the UN Forum on Forests, is observed on 21 March.

BETTER LIFE

FAO promotes women's equal rights and control over decision making, resources, technologies, services, economic opportunities and institutions, and works to ensure the inclusive transformation and revitalization of rural areas to ensure equal participation by, and benefits to marginalized groups.

During 2020 FAO undertook to roll out a new flagship initiative, Hand-in-Hand, to support the efforts of member countries to eradicate poverty and end hunger (SDGs 1 and 2). With a focus on data and evidence and the use of new technologies, the initiative aimed to accelerate agricultural transformations and sustainable rural development in countries with limited national capacities or with the greatest operational challenges. As part of the approach countries were to be matched to work in close partnership with other organizations, financial institutions, research bodies and donors. In July FAO launched a Hand-in-Hand Geospatial Platform, comprising data on food, agriculture, fisheries, forestry, markets, animal health, natural resources and socioeconomics, to support evidence-based decision making within the scheme. The initiative aimed to facilitate partnerships and donor 'matchmaking', in particular in countries facing challenges to sustainable development.

As a means of addressing urban poverty, malnutrition and food security, FAO works towards transforming urban and peri-urban agrifood systems, through the adoption of supportive policies and initiatives, and by scaling up investments.

FAO and IFAD were mandated to support the UN Decade of Family Farming (2019–28), which aimed to position small-scale family farming at the centre of national agricultural, environmental and social policies. FAO welcomed the adoption by the UN General Assembly in December 2018 of a landmark Declaration on the Rights of Peasants and Other People Working in Rural Areas; this aimed to protect the rights of rural workers and Indigenous peoples and also to recognize their contribution to sustainable development and to preserving biodiversity. In April 2023 FAO estimated that in 2019 857m. people globally were directly employed in primary agricultural production and 375m. in off-farm agrifood system occupations.

In October 2015 the CFS adopted a Framework for Action on Food Security and Nutrition in Protracted Crises, which took into account the disruptive impact of long-term crises on food production systems and livelihoods, on illness and mortality rates, and in relation to the incidence of hunger and severe undernutrition in affected communities. The Framework placed a particular focus on the need for strengthening resilience, on integrating efforts to address both immediate and longer-term challenges, and on promoting the empowerment of women and the productivity of smallholders. A *Global Report on Food Crises*, issued annually (2023: in May) by the Global Network Against Food Crises, comprising FAO, WFP, the EU and other partners, addresses hunger prompted by conflict, insecurity, economic turbulence and climate shocks.

FAO and WFP co-lead the inter-agency Food Security and Livelihoods Cluster during humanitarian crises.

TECHNICAL CO-OPERATION

FAO provides policy advice to support the formulation, implementation and evaluation of agriculture, rural development and food security strategies in member countries. It supports developing countries to strengthen their agricultural trade technical negotiating skills. FAO also co-ordinates and facilitates the mobilization of extrabudgetary funds from donors. It administers a range of trust funds, including a Trust Fund for Food Security and Food Safety, established in 2002 to generate resources for projects to combat hunger, and the Government Co-operative Programme. FAO's Investment Centre, established in 1964, assists member countries to formulate effective projects and programmes to attract rural development investment. The Centre administers cost-sharing arrangements, with, typically, FAO funding 40% of a project.

FAO assembles, analyses and disseminates statistical data on world food and agriculture. FAOSTAT serves as a core database of statistical information relating to nutrition, fisheries, forestry, food production, land use, population, etc. FAO compiles and co-ordinates an extensive range of international databases on agriculture, fisheries, forestry, food and statistics, the most important of these being AGRIS (the International Information System for the Agricultural Sciences and Technology). FAO's Gender and Land Rights Database breaks down land-related statistics by gender. In June 2015 FAO inaugurated a digital platform on family farming, presenting data, legislation, and other relevant information.

EMERGENCY PREPAREDNESS AND RESPONSE

FAO's emergency operations are concerned with all aspects of disaster and risk prevention, mitigation, reduction and emergency relief and rehabilitation, with a particular emphasis on food security and rural populations. FAO works with governments to develop and implement disaster prevention policies and practices; it disseminates information from the various early warning systems and supports adaptation to climate variability and change, for example through the use of drought-resistant crops or the adoption of conservation agriculture techniques. Following an emergency, FAO works with governments and other development and humanitarian partners to assess the immediate and longer-term agriculture and food security needs of the affected population. It determines the appropriate response to a disaster situation through the Integrated Food Security Phase Classification (IPC) scheme. Emergency co-ordination units may be established to manage the local response to an emergency and to facilitate and co-ordinate the delivery of inter-agency assistance. In order to rehabilitate agricultural production following a natural or man-made disaster FAO provides emergency seeds, tools, other materials and technical and training assistance. FAO aims to strengthen the capacity of local institutions to manage and mitigate risk and provides technical assistance to improve access to land for displaced populations in countries following conflict or a natural disaster. Under the UN's Cluster Approach to co-ordinating the international response to humanitarian disasters, FAO and WFP jointly lead the Food Security Cluster, which aims to combine expertise in agricultural assistance and food aid to improve the resilience of food-insecure disaster-affected communities.

FAO's Global Information and Early Warning System (GIEWS), which become operational in 1975, monitors and maintains a database on the crop and food outlook at global, regional, national and subnational level in order to detect emerging food supply difficulties and disasters, and to ensure rapid intervention in countries experiencing food supply shortages. It publishes regular updates, highlighting countries in crisis requiring external assistance for food; countries with unfavourable prospects for current crops; and domestic price warnings (for countries where abnormally high prices are being reported in main markets for basic food commodities). An appropriate international response is then recommended. FAO's Agricultural Stress Index System (ASIS), initiated in 2015, uses earth observation technologies to identify agricultural areas at risk of 'water stress' (drought).

The monthly *FAO Cereal Supply and Demand Brief* provides a detailed assessment of cereal production and of supply and demand conditions. The quarterly publication *Crop Prospects and Food Situation* reviews the global food production situation, and provides regional updates and a special focus on countries experiencing food crises and requiring external assistance. In July 2023 it reported that 45 countries (of which 33 were in Africa) required external food assistance.

In July 2023 FAO's *Crop Prospects and Food Situation* noted severe localized food insecurity in Libya, and widespread lack of access to food in Lebanon and Yemen.

Food Outlook, issued in June and November, analyses developments in global food and animal feed markets.

FAO-led Food Security Information System (FSIS) projects monitor national and broader food security situations.

FAO's Emergency Management Centre for Animal Health (EMC-AH) extends training in Good Emergency Management Practice (GEMP) to veterinary services, to support the building of national animal health emergency management capabilities. EMC-AH deploys (at the request of governments) rapid reaction missions to support preparedness and response activities to prevent and control outbreaks of animal diseases, including zoonotic diseases. EMC-AH collaborates with EMPRES and with FAO's Emergency Centre for Transboundary Animal Diseases (ECTAD). ECTAD facilitates FAO's Global Health Security Agenda (GHSA) and Emerging Pandemic Threats (EPT) programmes: GHSA aims to strengthen the capacity of states to prevent, and works to control outbreaks of, zoonotic and non-zoonotic diseases, while the EPT enhances national capacity to pre-empt the emergence or re-emergence of zoonotic diseases, with a focus on, *inter alia*, avian influenza and (believed to be transmissible to humans via camels) Middle East Respiratory Syndrome.

An FAO Special Fund for Emergency and Rehabilitation Activities was established in 2004. FAO contributes the agricultural relief and rehabilitation component of joint UN humanitarian appeals, which aim to co-ordinate and enhance the effectiveness of the international community's response to an emergency. In December 2022 FAO appealed for US $1,900m. to assist 48m. people during 2023.

In Syria FAO has worked to promote agricultural production and to safeguard livelihoods affected by the ongoing protracted civil war. Vegetable and poultry family farming have been supported, through the provision of basic inputs, and by ensuring basic water infrastructure and sustainable water management; livestock assets protected through the provision of feed and emergency animal health services, and through an initiative aimed at improving the reproductive performance of sheep and dairy cows; complementary income-generating activities, agroprocessing and cash-based transfers have been organized; and food security co-ordination prioritized, including through data collection and analysis, and the development of early warning systems. FAO requested US $71m. under the UN's Global Humanitarian Appeal for 2023 to support 2.7m. people in Yemen. FAO's activities in that country have aimed to address the immediate food and nutrition security needs of extremely vulnerable households (for example, through the delivery of packages aimed at enabling crop, vegetable, poultry and dairy production); to provide emergency livelihoods support to IDPs; to assist fishing communities to increase productivity and market access (through the supply of fishing tools, net repair kits, cooler boxes, and the rehabilitation of fisheries infrastructure); to implement cash-for-work initiatives focused on rehabilitating community agricultural infrastructure; and to facilitate the delivery of fresh meat, milk and eggs to markets through support for the livestock sector (including restocking; vaccination services and veterinary treatments; and the distribution of fodder and feed packages). Under the Global Humanitarian Appeal for 2023 FAO also requested $40m. to assist 426,500 people in Lebanon, and $13.4m. to support 42,238 beneficiaries in Palestine.

FAO Statutory Bodies and Associated Entities

(based at the Rome headquarters, unless otherwise indicated)

Agriculture, Land and Water Use Commission for the Near East (ALAWUC): c/o FAO Regional Office for the Near East, POB 2223, Cairo, Egypt; e-mail Fawzi.Karajeh@fao.org; internet www.fao.org/neareast/alawuc; f. 2000 by merger of the Near East Regional Commission on Agriculture and the Regional Commission on Land and Water Use in the Near East; 16 mem. states.

Codex Alimentarius Commission (Joint FAO/WHO Food Standards Programme): e-mail codex@fao.org; internet www.fao.org/fao-who-codexalimentarius; f. 1963; supports the co-ordination of all international food standards work and publishes a code of international food standards; a Codex Trust Fund (CTF) was inaugurated in 2003; in June 2016 this was superseded by the CTF2, which aimed to support participation by more than 100 developing countries over a 12-year period; there are numerous specialized Codex committees, on e.g. contaminants in foods, food additives, food hygiene, food import and export inspection and certification systems, food labelling, nutrition and foods for special dietary uses, methods of analysis and sampling, pesticide residues, veterinary drug residues, fresh fruits and vegetables, fish and fishery products, fats and oils, and spices and culinary herbs; intergovernmental task forces may be appointed; FAO/WHO Codex co-ordinating committees cover Africa, Asia, Europe, Latin America and the Caribbean, the Near East, and North America and the South West Pacific; the Commission had established by 2023 377 food standards guidelines, codes of practice, limits and principles relating to food production and processing (including Maximum Residue Limits and Risk Management Recommendations for Residues of Veterinary Drugs in Foods); new standards were introduced in 2022 relating to berry fruits, onions and shallots; 188 mem. states and the EU, 235 observers; Sec. TOM HEILANDT.

Commission for Controlling the Desert Locust in Southwest Asia: internet www.fao.org/ag/locusts/SWAC; f. 1964; undertakes to implement measures to control plagues of the desert locust in the region; 32nd session: Dec. 2020, held in a virtual format; 4 mem. states.

Commission for Controlling the Desert Locust in the Central Region: c/o FAO Regional Office for the Near East, POB 2223, Cairo, Egypt; tel. (2) 33316000; fax (2) 37495981; e-mail Mamoon.AlAlawi@fao.org; internet desertlocust-crc.org; f. 1967; covers the Middle East, Near East and the Horn of Africa; 32nd session: June 2022, in Jeddah, Saudi Arabia; 16 mem. states; Exec. Sec. MAMOON AL SARAI ALALAWI.

Commission for Controlling the Desert Locust in the Western Region: 30 rue Asselah Hocine, BP 270, Algiers, Algeria; tel. (21) 73-33-54; e-mail clcpro@fao.org; internet www.fao.org/clcpro/fr; f. 2002; implements preventive locust surveillance and control measures in mem. countries and conducts training for novice and master locust field 'prospectors'; 10 mem. states; Exec. Sec. Dr MOHAMED LEMINE HAMOUNY.

FAO Desert Locust Control Committee: e-mail NSP-Director@fao.org; f. 1955; serves as a primary forum bringing together locust-affected countries, international donors and other agencies, to advise FAO on the management of desert locusts; 4th session: March 2023, in Nairobi, Kenya.

Fishery Committee for the Eastern Central Atlantic: c/o FAO Regional Office for Africa; tel. (06) 57052019; e-mail Ndiaga.Gueye@fao.org; internet www.fao.org/cecaf/en; f. 1967; promotes improvements in inland fisheries in the Eastern Central Atlantic area between Cape Spartel (Morocco) and the Congo River; 23rd session: July 2023, in Harbel, Liberia; 33 mem. states and the EU; Sec. NDIAGA GUEYE.

General Fisheries Commission for the Mediterranean (GFCM): Palazzo Blumenstihl, Via Vittoria Colonna 1, 00193 Rome, Italy; tel. (06) 57056566; fax (06) 57055827; e-mail gfcm-secretariat@fao.org; internet www.fao.org/gfcm; f. 1949 (as the General Fisheries Council for the Mediterranean, present name adopted, as a result of amendments to the GFCM agreement, in 1997); aims to develop aquatic resources, to encourage and co-ordinate research in the fishing and allied industries, to assemble and publish information, and to recommend the standardization of equipment, techniques and nomenclature; covers the Mediterranean, Black Sea and connecting waters; 45th session: Nov. 2022, in Tirana, Albania; 23 mem. states and the EU; Georgia, Russian Fed. and Ukraine have observer status; Exec. Sec. MIGUEL BERNAL.

Near East Forestry and Range Commission: c/o FAO Regional Office for the Near East, 11 El-Eslah el-Zerai St, Dokki, POB 2223, Cairo, Egypt; internet www.fao.org/neareast/nefrc; f. 1953; aims to advise on formulation of forest policy and review and co-ordinate its implementation throughout the region; to exchange information and advise on technical problems; 26th session: Sept. 2023, to be hosted by Jordan; 32 mem. states.

Silva Mediterranea: Rome, Italy; tel. (06) 57054265; e-mail silva.mediterranea@fao.org; internet www.fao.org/forestry/silva-mediterranea; f. 1911, became a statutory body of FAO in 1948; FAO cttee on Mediterranean forestry issues convened under the auspices of the FAO Forestry Commissions for Africa, Europe, and Near East; 24th session: March 2022, in Antalya, Türkiye; 26 mem. states and the EU; Chair. ÜMIT TURHAN (Türkiye).

Finance

FAO's Regular Programme, which is financed by contributions from member governments, covers the cost of FAO's Secretariat, its Technical Co-operation Programme and part of the cost of several special action programmes. In June 2021 the FAO Conference endorsed a budget totalling US $1,005.6m. to fund its activities during 2022–23. Much of FAO's technical assistance programme and emergency relief and rehabilitation activities are funded from extrabudgetary sources, predominantly by trust funds that come mainly from donor countries and international financing institutions. Voluntary contributions of more than $1,600m. were mobilized in 2022.

Publications

Crop Prospects and Food Situation (5/6 a year).
Food Outlook (2 a year).
Global Report on Food Crises (annually, with the EU and WFP).
The State of Agricultural Commodity Markets (every 2 years).
The State of Food and Agriculture (annually).
The State of Food Security and Nutrition in the World (annually, with IFAD, UNICEF, WFP and WHO).
The State of World Fisheries and Aquaculture (every 2 years).
The State of the World's Forests (every 2 years).
Unasylva (2 a year).
Statistical Yearbook.

Other major reports, commodity reviews, regional reviews, statistical pocketbooks, atlases, studies, manuals.

International Atomic Energy Agency—IAEA

Address: POB 100, Wagramerstr. 5, 1400 Vienna, Austria.
Telephone: (1) 26000; **fax:** (1) 26007; **e-mail:** official.mail@iaea.org; **internet:** www.iaea.org.

The IAEA was established in 1957 in accordance with a decision of the UN General Assembly. Although it is an autonomous international organization its statute ensures that the IAEA works within the UN system, in accordance with the purposes, principles and policies of the UN, and reports regularly on its activities to the UN Security Council and General Assembly. Its main objectives are to support peaceful applications of nuclear science and technology and to safeguard against the use of fissionable materials, equipment or facilities to further any military purpose.

Organization
(September 2023)

GENERAL CONFERENCE

The Conference, comprising representatives of all member states, convenes annually for general debate on the Agency's policy, budget and programme. It elects members to the Board of Governors, and approves the appointment of the Director-General; it admits new member states. The 67th regular session of the General Conference was to be held in late September 2023, in Vienna.

BOARD OF GOVERNORS

The Board of Governors consists of 35 member states elected by the General Conference. It is the principal policymaking body of the Agency and is responsible to the General Conference. Under its own authority, the Board approves all safeguards agreements, important projects and safety standards.

SECRETARIAT

The secretariat, comprising some 2,560 staff, is headed by the Director-General, who is assisted by six Deputy Directors-General responsible for the following departments: Technical Co-operation; Nuclear Energy; Nuclear Safety and Security; Nuclear Sciences and Applications; Safeguards; and Management. A Standing Advisory Group on Safeguards Implementation advises the Director-General on technical aspects of safeguards. A Director-General's Office, Secretariat of the Policy-Making Organs, Office of Internal Oversight Services, Office of Legal Affairs, and Office of Public Information and Communication report to the Director-General.

Director-General: Rafael Mariano Grossi (Argentina).

Activities

The Agency's activities focus on three 'pillars': technology (assisting research on, and practical application of, atomic energy for peaceful uses); safety; and verification (ensuring that special fissionable and other materials, services, equipment and information made available by the Agency or at its request or under its supervision are not used for any non-peaceful purpose). The Agency is committed to supporting member states in the use of nuclear science and technology to achieve the Sustainable Development Goals and related targets, adopted by the international community in 2015. The IAEA's medium-term strategy for 2018–23 included the following cross-cutting objectives: Facilitating access to nuclear power and other nuclear technologies; Strengthening the promotion and development of nuclear science, technology and applications; Improving nuclear safety and security; Providing effective technical co-operation; Delivering effective and efficient Agency safeguards; and Providing effective, efficient and innovative management and sound programming and budget planning.

In April 2022 the IAEA convened a First International Conference on Nuclear Law, to address emerging trends in nuclear legal frameworks. In December IAEA legal experts conducted the inaugural IAEA introductory course on nuclear law for university students, at Khalifa University in the United Arab Emirates (UAE).

NUCLEAR ENERGY

The IAEA reported that in June 2023 global operating nuclear power capacity totalled 368.6 GW. At that time the database of IAEA's Power Reactor Information System (PRIS) listed 410 nuclear power reactors in operation worldwide (including 93 in the USA, 56 in France, 55 in the People's Republic of China, 37 in the Russian Federation, 25 in the Republic of Korea—South Korea, 19 in India, and 19 in Canada); meanwhile, 57 reactors were under construction (of which 18 were in China and eight were in India). Some 23 reactors were in a state of suspended operation in Japan, and four in India. The Agency assesses life extension and decommissioning strategies for ageing nuclear power plants. At mid-2023 there were 209 decommissioned reactors in a state of permanent shutdown (including 41 in the USA, 36 in the United Kingdom, 33 in Germany—with that country's last three remaining reactors having been shut down in April, and 27 in Japan). The IAEA helps developing member states to introduce nuclear-powered electricity generating plants through assistance with planning, feasibility studies, surveys of manpower and infrastructure, and safety measures. New facilities are designed with advance decommissioning and waste management plans, with a circular economy focus. The Agency's Site and External Events Design (SEED) review service, launched in 2009, supports member states in the early stages of their nuclear power programme development with establishing suitable regulations to harmonize safety initiatives, and with swiftly identifying potential site hazards. IAEA also undertakes long-term operational SALTO (Safety Aspects of Long Term Operation) review missions. The IAEA issues publications on numerous aspects of nuclear power, and provides training courses on safety in nuclear power plants and other topics. An energy data bank collects and disseminates information on nuclear technology, and the Agency's Power Reactor Information System maintains data on nuclear plants worldwide. The use of nuclear technology in seawater desalination and of radiation hydrology techniques to provide potable water are addressed.

The IAEA has since 1992 been actively engaged in the process to develop an International Thermonuclear Experimental Reactor (ITER), to expand the use of fusion energy. The ITER International Organization—inaugurated in October 2007, and comprising the European Union (EU), China, India, Japan, South Korea, Russia, Switzerland, the UK and the USA—has responsibility for constructing, operating and decommissioning the reactor. The construction phase commenced in 2010, in Saint-Paul-lez-Durance, France, and it was envisaged that the reactor would enter into operation in December 2025. In May 2001 the International Project on Innovative

Nuclear Reactors and Fuel Cycles (INPRO) was inaugurated. INPRO, which in 2023 had 44 members (43 IAEA member states and the European Commission), aims to promote nuclear energy as a means of meeting future sustainable energy requirements and to facilitate the exchange of information by member states to advance innovation in nuclear technology. The IAEA is a permanent observer at the Generation IV International Forum (GIF), which was inaugurated in 2000 to undertake research and development activities aimed at developing the feasibility and performance capabilities of next generation nuclear energy systems, which are expected to become commercially available during 2030–40. GIF member countries adopted the Framework Agreement for International Collaboration on Research and Development of Generation IV Nuclear Energy Systems in 2005, and in February 2015 this was extended for a further 10 years.

NUCLEAR TECHNOLOGY AND APPLICATIONS

In co-operation with the World Health Organization (WHO), the IAEA promotes the use of nuclear techniques in medicine, biology and health-related environmental research, provides training, and conducts research on techniques for improving the accuracy of radiation dosimetry. The IAEA/WHO Network of Secondary Standard Dosimetry Laboratories (SSDLs) comprises 81 laboratories in 62 member states. The Agency's Dosimetry Laboratory in Seibersdorf performs dose inter-comparisons for both SSDLs and radiotherapy centres.

NUCLEAR SAFETY AND SECURITY

The IAEA encourages international co-operation in the exchange of information, promoting implementation of its safety standards and providing advisory safety services. It includes the IAEA International Nuclear and Radiological Event Scale (INES), which measures the severity of nuclear events, incidents and accidents; the Incident Reporting System; an emergency preparedness programme (which maintains an Incident and Emergency Centre, located in Vienna, and a 41-member Response and Assistance Network—RANET); operational safety review teams; the International Nuclear Safety Group (INSAG); the Radiation Protection Advisory Team; and a safety research co-ordination programme.

The nuclear safety programme promotes a global safety regime, which aims to ensure the protection of people and the environment from the effects of ionizing radiation and the minimization of the likelihood of potential nuclear accidents. A Commission on Safety Standards establishes IAEA nuclear, radiation, transport and waste safety standards and provides for their application. In January 2004 the IAEA issued a revised Code of Conduct on the Safety and Security of Radioactive Sources. In September 2006 the IAEA published a primary safety standard, the Fundamental Safety Principles. The Agency established a Global Safety Assessment Network (GSAN) in 2010, facilitating collaboration between experts worldwide with the aim of harmonizing nuclear safety.

Ministers or senior representatives of 140 member states attended the 2020 IAEA International Conference on Nuclear Security, held in February, in Vienna, which concluded with a declaration expressing renewed commitment to enhancing global nuclear security and countering the threat of nuclear terrorism and other malicious acts. A new Nuclear Security Plan, covering the period 2022–25, was formulated on the basis of recommendations concluded at the Conference; it was approved by the Board of Governors in September 2021.

From March 2020 the IAEA offered support to member states in managing nuclear and radiation facilities and activities, and implementing safeguards to prevent the misuse of nuclear material, over the course of the COVID-19 emergency. A COVID-19 Operational Experience (OPEX) Network was launched by the Agency to facilitate the sharing of pandemic-related information by nuclear power plant operators and regulators.

The Agency provides practical help to member states in the management of radioactive waste. The Waste Management Advisory Programme was established in 1987, and undertakes advisory missions in member states. A code of practice to prevent the illegal dumping of radioactive waste was drafted in 1989, and another on the international transboundary movement of waste was drafted in 1990.

In September 1997 the IAEA adopted a Joint Convention on the Safety of Spent Fuel Management and on the Safety of Radioactive Waste Management (the first internationally binding legal device to address such issues). The Convention was to ensure the safe storage and disposal of nuclear and radioactive waste, during both the construction and operation of a nuclear power plant, as well as following its closure. The Convention entered into force in June 2001, and had been ratified by 89 parties at June 2023. An International Conference on Management of Spent Fuel from Nuclear Power Reactors, aimed at reviewing best practices in that area, was held in June 2019, at the IAEA headquarters in Vienna. In January 2022 the IAEA issued a report titled *Status and Trends in Spent Fuel and Radioactive Waste Management*, which noted significant progress in safe management, including through the development of deep geological repositories.

A new database—the Spent Fuel and Radioactive Waste Information System (SRIS)—was launched in June 2020 to provide an integrated overview of national and global spent fuel and radioactive waste inventories and of related policies and regulatory regimes. An International Radiation Monitoring System (IRMIS), with 48 member states at mid-2023, maps real-time information on radiation levels.

Within the framework of the IAEA's Global Nuclear Safety and Security Network expertise and knowledge are shared worldwide.

The Convention on the Physical Protection of Nuclear Material (CPPNM), signed in 1980, commits contracting states to ensuring the protection of nuclear material during transportation within their territory or on board their ships or aircraft. A CPPNM Amendment, aimed at reducing the risk of terrorist attacks against nuclear installations, entered into force on 8 May 2016. IAEA International Physical Protection Advisory Service (IPPAS) teams review national nuclear security practices; by mid-2023 98 IPPAS missions had been undertaken since the Service commenced in 1995. An International Conference on Security of Radioactive Material was held in December 2018, in Vienna.

Following a devastating accident at the Chernobyl nuclear power plant in Ukraine (then part of the Union of Soviet Socialist Republics) in April 1986, two conventions were formulated by the IAEA and entered into force in October. The Convention on Early Notification of a Nuclear Accident commits parties to provide information about nuclear accidents with possible transboundary effects at the earliest opportunity (it had 132 parties by mid-2023); and the Convention on Assistance in the Case of a Nuclear Accident or Radiological Emergency commits parties to endeavour to provide assistance in the event of a nuclear accident or radiological emergency (this had 127 parties by mid-2023).

At the beginning of March 2022, following the initiation of Russia's military invasion of Ukraine, the IAEA Director-General urged restraint, stating concern over the potential threat to the safety of that country's four operational nuclear plants and to other radioactive materials and nuclear facilities, including the closed Chernobyl site. Respect for seven core safety principles ('Seven Pillars') was emphasized by the IAEA as paramount during conflict: (i) maintenance of the physical integrity of all nuclear facilities; (ii) full functioning at all times of all safety and security systems and equipment; (iii) full freedom for operating staff to fulfil their safety and security duties; (iv) maintenance of a continuous secure off-site power supply from the grid for all nuclear sites; (v) uninterrupted logistical supply chains and transportation to and from all sites; (vi) the continuation of effective radiation monitoring systems and emergency preparedness and response measures; and (vii) reliable communications.

In April 2005 the UN General Assembly adopted the International Convention for the Suppression of Acts of Nuclear Terrorism. The Convention, which entered into force in July 2007, urged signatory states to co-operate in the prevention of terrorist attacks by sharing information and providing mutual assistance with criminal investigations and extradition proceedings. Under the provisions of the Convention it was required that any seized nuclear or radiological material should be held in accordance with IAEA safeguards. By the end of 2022 4,075 confirmed incidents had been reported to the IAEA's Incident and Trafficking Database (ITDB, created in 1993 as the Illicit Trafficking Database, and renamed in 2012); of the total, 344 involved confirmed or likely malicious use or trafficking in unauthorized nuclear or other radioactive material. By 31 December 2022 the ITDB had 143 participant states; regular meetings to promote the ITDB system and to co-ordinate activities are convened. In November 2017 the IAEA organized an International Conference on the Physical Protection of Nuclear Material and Nuclear Facilities, in Vienna.

In October 2008 the IAEA inaugurated the International Seismic Safety Centre to serve as a focal point for avoiding and mitigating the consequences of extreme seismic events on nuclear installations worldwide.

SAFEGUARDS AND VERIFICATION

The Treaty on the Non-Proliferation of Nuclear Weapons (known also as the Non-Proliferation Treaty or NPT), which entered into force in 1970, designates five 'nuclear weapon states'—China, France, Russia, the UK and the USA—which have expressed commitment to the ultimate goal of complete nuclear disarmament under effective international controls. At mid-2023 the five nuclear weapon states and 186 non-nuclear weapon states were parties to the NPT. The Treaty requires each member 'non-nuclear weapon state' (one which had not manufactured and exploded a nuclear weapon or other nuclear explosive device prior to 1 January 1967) to conclude a comprehensive safeguards agreement (CSA) with the IAEA. Under a CSA the state undertakes to accept IAEA safeguards on all nuclear material in its peaceful nuclear activities for the purpose of verifying that such material is not diverted to weaponry or other nuclear explosive devices. The five nuclear weapon states have concluded safeguards agreements with the Agency that permit the application of IAEA safeguards to all their nuclear activities, excluding those with 'direct national significance'. NPT review conferences are normally held at five-yearly intervals (2022: in August). A Comprehensive Nuclear-Test-Ban Treaty (CTBT) was opened for signature in September 1996, but is not yet in force. A Treaty on the Prohibition of Nuclear Weapons (TPNW), adopted in September 2017, entered into force on 22 January 2021.

To enable the Agency to conclude that all nuclear material in a state is channelled towards peaceful activities both a CSA and an Additional Protocol to the CSA must be in effect. Additional Protocols, which were introduced from 1997, bind member states to provide inspection teams with improved access to information concerning existing and planned nuclear activities, and to allow access to locations other than known nuclear sites within the country's territory. At mid-2023 IAEA safeguards agreements had been concluded with 178 states and the European Atomic Energy Community (Euratom), while 141 states and Euratom had ratified Additional Protocols to their safeguards agreements. Integrated Safety Assessments of Research Reactors (INSARR) missions are conducted in member states, on the basis of IAEA safety standards, and, during 2012, a programme of complementary Operation and Maintenance Assessment for Research Reactors (OMARR) missions was initiated. In July 2022 the Agency conducted its first Integrated Research Reactor Utilization Review (IRRUR) mission (at La Reina Nuclear Centre, Santiago, Chile), focused on maximizing benefit from the use of research reactors. The IAEA has installed digital surveillance systems at nuclear sites and maintains an imagery database thereof.

India, Pakistan and Israel, which are not parties to the NPT, have concluded item-specific agreements with the IAEA.

In November 2019 the inaugural session was held, at UN headquarters, in New York, of a Conference on the Establishment of a Middle East Zone Free of Nuclear Weapons and Other Weapons of Mass Destruction. The Conference marked a significant step towards implementing a resolution on the establishment of the zone, endorsed by NPT states in 1995.

Under a long-term strategic plan for safeguards, covering the period 2012–23, the IAEA aimed to develop the concept of a safeguards approach that is driven by outcomes and customized to the circumstances of individual states.

Iraq: In June 2007 the UN Security Council, noting testimonials that all of Iraq's known weapons of mass destruction had been deactivated and that the Iraqi Government had declared its support for international non-proliferation regimes, voted to terminate the long-standing mandates of the IAEA weapons inspectors in Iraq and of the UN Monitoring, Inspection and Verification Commission (UNMOVIC, established in March 2002). Under the provisions of Iraq's safeguards agreement the IAEA continued to manage its existing information on Iraq, including satellite images; to update its knowledge of facilities in Iraq; and to undertake a physical inventory verification of the nuclear material present in that country.

In June 2017 the IAEA and Iraq concluded a Country Programme Framework for the period 2018–23, which was to focus on the following priority areas: the industrial application of radiation technologies; nuclear medicine and radiotherapy; the environment; strengthening the regulatory infrastructure; decommissioning and radioactive waste management; nuclear and radiological emergency preparedness; food and agriculture; and water resources management.

Iran: In February 2008 the IAEA Board of Governors reported that Iran was continuing to pursue uranium enrichment activities, and that the Iranian Government needed to continue to build confidence about the scope and purported peaceful nature of its nuclear programme. Consequently, in the following month, the UN Security Council adopted a resolution in which it authorized inspections of any cargo to and from Iran suspected of transporting prohibited equipment and strengthened sanctions against that country. In May the IAEA Director-General, at the request of the UN Security Council, issued a report that concluded there remained several areas of serious concern with regard to Iran, including an ongoing 'green salt' project; high explosives testing; a missile re-entry vehicle project; some procurement activities of military-related institutions; outstanding substantive explanations regarding information with a possible military dimension; and Iran's continuing enrichment-related activities.

In November 2009 the IAEA Board of Governors adopted a resolution urging Iran to suspend immediately construction of a uranium enrichment facility at the Fordow underground site near Qom. An IAEA report issued in February 2010 stated that, while the IAEA continued to verify the non-diversion of declared nuclear material in Iran, the Iranian authorities had not provided the necessary degree of co-operation to enable the Agency to confirm that all nuclear material in Iran was not being diverted for military purposes. In November 2011 the IAEA Board of Governors adopted a resolution expressing 'deep and increasing concern' over the unresolved issues regarding the Iranian nuclear programme and calling upon Iran to engage seriously and without preconditions in discussions aimed at restoring international confidence in the exclusively peaceful nature of its nuclear activities. With a view to intensifying dialogue, senior IAEA experts visited Iran in January–February 2012. The IAEA team was denied access to the military complex at Parchin, southeast of Tehran, the Iranian capital, which was suspected to be the site of an explosives containment vessel, and clarification of unresolved issues relating to possible military dimensions of Iran's nuclear programme was not achieved. In late February IAEA reported that the installation of centrifuges at the Natanz (uranium enrichment) Fuel Plant, in central Iran, had accelerated and more generally that uranium enrichment had increased three-fold since late 2011. (The Iranian authorities, however, insisted that this material was required for a medical research reactor.) Several rounds of talks between representatives of the IAEA and the Iranian authorities on developing a structured approach to communications were convened from May 2012–September 2013, and, in November, the IAEA and Iran agreed a Joint Statement on a Framework for Co-operation. In January 2014 the IAEA Board of Governors endorsed an interim joint plan of action with Iran, that had been concluded later in November 2013 by the Governments of France, Germany and the UK (the 'E3') plus China, Russia and the USA (the E3/EU+3, also known as the P5+1), under which the IAEA—pending the conclusion of a 'long-term comprehensive solution' aimed at ensuring that Iran's nuclear programme remained exclusively peaceful—was to monitor and verify an initial series of voluntary measures that were to be implemented by Iran and reviewed at quarterly intervals. (These measures included the suspension of several nuclear activities, in exchange for an easing of the international sanctions regime.) Iran and the E3/EU+3 subsequently held several rounds of negotiations to determine the text of a final comprehensive accord. In July 2014 the interim joint plan of action, providing for continuing monitoring activities, was extended until November, and in that month it was further extended, until 30 June 2015. In early April the so-called Lausanne Agreement was adopted, providing a political framework for the final stage of negotiations. Under the Agreement it was envisaged, *inter alia*, that Iran would refrain from making nuclear weapons, and that the Fordow facility would be transformed into a centre for nuclear physics. In late June the deadline for the conclusion of negotiations was extended into July, and in mid-July an agreement (the Joint Comprehensive Plan of Action—JCPOA) was finally reached by Iran and the E3/EU+3, under which Iran made a commitment to restrict its nuclear programme (to be monitored by the IAEA) in return for the withdrawal of sanctions; the accord provided, however, for these to be reinstated within 65 days should Iran fail to meet its obligations. At the same time, the IAEA (which was not itself a party to the JCPOA) and the Iranian authorities agreed a roadmap aimed at improving mutual relations. Later in July the UN Security Council adopted Resolution 2231, which endorsed the JCPOA and its provisions. In December the IAEA Board of Governors adopted a 'Final Assessment on Past and Present Outstanding Issues Regarding Iran's Nuclear Programme', summarizing the Agency's relations with Iran, and urged Iran promptly to complete the preparatory process required to enable the implementation of the JCPOA. In mid-January 2016 the IAEA Secretary-General submitted a report simultaneously to the IAEA Board of Governors and to the UN Security Council, in which he confirmed that IAEA inspectors had verified that Iran had undertaken all required initial measures, thereby marking the so-called Implementation Day of the JCPOA. Accordingly, sanctions previously authorized by the Security Council were withdrawn and superseded by the provisions of the JCPOA. Thereafter, Iran was to commence implementation of the Additional Protocol to its Safeguards Agreement with the Agency. At Iran's largest gas centrifuge uranium enrichment facility—the Natanz Fuel Plant—the IAEA was to use an Online Enrichment Monitor to verify that uranium enrichment levels did not (as stipulated under the JCPOA) exceed 3.67%. In August 2017 the IAEA reported that Iran was continuing to implement its nuclear-related commitments under the JCPOA. None the less, in October US President Trump—unilaterally alleging non-compliance by Iran and dissatisfaction with certain provisions of the JCPOA—announced that he would no longer automatically certify the accord every 90 days (a domestic requirement stipulated by the US Congress). In January 2018 President Trump stated that the USA would withdraw its participation from the arrangement following the end of the next 90-day period, if significant amendments were not made. The other signatories, meanwhile, expressed their continuing full commitment to implementing the existing JCPOA, and the IAEA Director-General reiterated that Iran had hitherto been found to be adhering to its related obligations. On 8 May President Trump announced that the USA would terminate its participation in the JCPOA, and initiated the process of reinstating US sanctions against Iran. On the following day the IAEA Director-General once again emphasized that IAEA verifying and monitoring teams had found Iran to be implementing its commitments under the JCPOA, and noted that the agreement represented the world's most robust existing nuclear verification regime. The UN Secretary-General announced deep concern at the US decision, stressing that the JCPOA had contributed to regional and international peace and security, and that concerns relating to the agreement's implementation should be addressed through relevant related mechanisms. In June the IAEA Director-General affirmed that the Agency was continuing to monitor and verify Iran's non-diversion of nuclear material (as requested by the UN Security Council), and subsequently, in his quarterly reports issued through to March 2019, stressed that Iran was continuing to implement its nuclear-related commitments under the JCPOA.

In May 2019, in response to the US sanctions regime and against a background of escalating diplomatic tensions, Iran announced that it was to scale down the implementation of its JCPOA commitments. In the following month the IAEA Director-General noted that Iran's production of low-enriched uranium had increased, although at that time it remained within the (300 kg) limit established by the JCPOA. He urged dialogue to resolve the situation. On 1 July it was reported that the 300 kg cap had been exceeded. In November the acting IAEA Director-General reported to the Board of Governors that Iran had recently initiated uranium enrichment activities at its Pilot Fuel Enrichment Plant in Natanz and at the Fordow facility. By December nine countries (France, Germany and the UK—the founding members, and Belgium, Denmark, Finland, the Netherlands, Norway and Sweden) had joined a so-called Instrument in Support of Trade Exchanges (Instex) clearing house mechanism that aimed to provide an alternative channel to the use of the US currency in trade with Iran, as a means of bypassing the US sanctions against that country (in support of the JCPOA).

In early January 2020, following the assassination in Baghdad, Iraq, by a US air strike, of General Qassem Soleimani, commander of the Quds Force unit of the Iranian Revolutionary Guards Corps, Iran announced that it was to withdraw fully from all commitments under the JCPOA and would henceforth enrich uranium at will, without limitations on levels or on research and development. Consequently, France, Germany and the UK activated the accord's formal dispute resolution mechanism. In June the IAEA expressed serious concern that Iran was blocking inspectors' access to its nuclear sites. Later in the month the IAEA Director-General reported to the Board of Governors that Iran had also not engaged in meaningful discussions relating to possible undeclared nuclear material and nuclear-related activities for more than a year. He urged the Iranian authorities to co-operate with the Agency. In early July the Agency was informed by Iran of a (resolved) fire at the Natanz uranium enrichment facility site. The UN sanctions regime against Iran ended, as scheduled, on 18 October 2020. From September, however, the USA significantly tightened the imposition of punitive sanctions against Iran. The IAEA reported in October that Iran had initiated the construction of an underground advanced centrifuge assembly facility near Natanz, and in the following month the Agency reported evidence of enrichment activities using the sophisticated Natanz centrifuges (in violation of the JCPOA). At the beginning of January 2021 Iran informed the IAEA that, in accordance with national legislation (a so-called Strategic Action Plan to Counter Sanctions) that had been approved in December 2020, the Fordow facility was reinstating production of low enriched uranium up to a purity level of 20%, thereby reverting to the level of output achieved prior to the implementation of the JCPOA. On 11 February IAEA inspectors confirmed that Iran had recently produced uranium metal (a potential component of a nuclear bomb), in Isfahan; the Iranian authorities, however, stated that the metal had been made in the context of a research and development programme. On 21 February, with a view to facilitating constructive dialogue, the IAEA and the Atomic Energy Organization of Iran (AEOI) jointly stated that Iran would continue to implement its CSA with the Agency, and the Agency would continue to conduct basic monitoring activities for up to 3 months. From 23 February, however, Iran ceased to apply the Additional Protocol to its CSA, and barred the Agency from accessing data from surveillance equipment that had been installed at Iranian nuclear facilities to monitor the implementation of the JCPOA. A power cut that occurred at the Natanz complex in mid-April was described by the Iranian authorities as a cyber attack (and 'act of nuclear terrorism'), and was alleged to have been perpetrated by Israel. Soon afterwards technical discussions were initiated between the Agency and Iran to clarify IAEA questions concerning the possible previous presence (reportedly prior to 2003) of nuclear material at undeclared sites. Broader talks aimed at reviving the JCPOA also continued. In May 2021 the temporary arrangement enabling the Agency to continue to monitor Iran's CSA was extended for a further month, until 24 June—at which point the arrangement expired. In early September, during a visit by the IAEA Director-General to Tehran, he and the head of the AEOI determined to maintain contact between the two agencies, and agreed that the IAEA should be given access to install new memory cards and to service surveillance equipment at Iranian nuclear facilities. In mid-December agreement was reached between the Agency and the AEOI that provided for the renewed installation of surveillance cameras at Iran's Karaj centrifuge component manufacturing site. In early March 2022 the IAEA and the AEOI agreed a short-term plan of action aimed at clarifying outstanding issues (relating to the possible previous presence of nuclear material at undeclared sites) that were stalling the restoration of the JCPOA. Reporting to the Board of Governors in June, however, the IAEA Director-General stated that Iran had failed to provide technically credible accounts to resolve these matters, and urged that this should be redressed. In that month, at Iran's request, the IAEA removed 27 cameras, and the other monitoring equipment, that it had previously installed in Iran to verify the implementation of the JCPOA. While the IAEA had been unable to verify Iran's enriched uranium stockpiles since 2021, in February 2023 the Agency's Board of Governors estimated that Iran possessed a total enriched uranium hexafluoride stockpile that amounted to 3,760.8 kg (compared with 1,020.9 kg in February 2020)—including 87.5 kg of uranium enriched up to 60% (approaching weapons grade) that had been generated since February 2021. Particles enriched to 83.7% were also reportedly observed in Iran in January 2023. Following a visit undertaken by the IAEA Director-General to Iran in March, he reported that Iran had stated its readiness to continue to co-operate on addressing outstanding safeguards issues (relating to three locations), and would permit the IAEA to implement further verification and monitoring activities. However, in June he noted to the Board of Governors that progress in this respect had been slow; that Iran's total stockpile of enriched uranium was now more than 21 times the limit specified under the JCPOA; and that since February its stockpile of 60% enriched uranium had expanded significantly, to 114.1 kg. The E3 countries issued a joint statement at that time condemning Iran's 'unabated and dangerous' escalation of its nuclear programme, while the Iranian authorities countered that they would approve further IAEA monitoring if all punitive sanctions against Iran were withdrawn.

Israel: Arab member states have repeatedly called for an IAEA resolution demanding that Israel formally commit to the NPT. The IAEA Conference adopted a resolution in September 2009 that expressed concern about Israel's nuclear capabilities and called upon Israel to accede to the NPT and to place all its nuclear facilities under comprehensive IAEA safeguards. In July 2013 an INSARR mission was sent to Israel to conduct a peer review of the safety of a reactor at the centrally located Soreq Nuclear Research Center. In September 2017 the IAEA and Israel agreed a Country Programme Framework, covering the period 2018–23.

Other States in the Middle East and North Africa: In May 2014 the Agency concluded a 'Practical Arrangements' agreement aimed at strengthening its support for the 22-member Arab Network of Nuclear Regulators (established in 2010 as a subsidiary organization of the League of Arab States).

In September 2019, at the request of the UAE Government, an IAEA team of experts reviewed that country's emergency preparedness and response framework for nuclear and radiological emergencies. Part of the UAE's first nuclear power plant, at Barakah (Barakah-1) became operational in April 2021; a second unit of the plant, Barakah-2. was connected to the national grid in September.

The first nuclear power reactor in Türkiye (formerly known as Turkey) was to be commissioned during 2023, while Egypt was scheduled to commission the construction of its first nuclear power plant by 2026. In February 2023 the IAEA delivered portable medical X-ray equipment to Türkiye, following devastating earthquakes that had struck southern areas of that country, and northern Syria.

In March 2023 the Director-General reported the recent discovery by IAEA inspectors that 10 barrels of natural uranium (i.e. about 2.5 metric tons) were missing from a nuclear site in Libya that was not under state control.

TECHNICAL CO-OPERATION AND OTHER SERVICES

The IAEA provides assistance in the form of experts, training and equipment to technical co-operation projects and applications worldwide, with an emphasis on radiation protection and safety-related activities. In 2020 the IAEA extended technical co-operation assistance to 146 countries and territories (including 35 developed countries), in the principal areas of nuclear knowledge development and management, health and nutrition, food and agriculture, and nuclear safety and security. The IAEA supported the foundation in September 2003 of the World Nuclear University, comprising a global network of institutions that aim to strengthen international co-operation in promoting the safe use of nuclear power in energy production, and in the application of nuclear science and technology in areas including sustainable agriculture and nutrition, medicine, fresh water resources management and environmental protection. An annual IAEA Scientific Forum is held (2023: in September, in Vienna). The IAEA's Marie Sklodowska-Curie Fellowship Programme aims to support women's participation in the nuclear workforce. Through a new IAEA Lise Meitner Programme that was initiated in March 2023, career development for women professionals in the nuclear sector was to be supported.

In October 2014 IAEA launched CONNECT, an internet-based platform for sharing nuclear energy-related information. The International Nuclear Information System (INIS), which was established in 1970, publishes information on the peaceful uses of nuclear science and technology. The IAEA Nuclear Data Section provides cost-free data centre services and co-operates with other national and regional nuclear and atomic data centres in the systematic worldwide collection, compilation, dissemination and exchange of nuclear reaction data, nuclear structure and decay data, and atomic and molecular data for fusion.

The IAEA, World Federation of Nuclear Medicine and Biology, and non-profit Cochrane Collaboration jointly maintain an electronic database of best practice in nuclear medicine.

From early 2020 the IAEA provided real time reverse transcription–polymerase chain reaction (RT-PCR) diagnostic kits, derived from a nuclear technique, to member states (at their request) for use in the fast detection of infection by the severe acute respiratory syndrome coronavirus 2 (SARS-CoV-2) virus that causes COVID-19 (2,036 kits and related items had been delivered to 129 countries by April 2022). An IAEA Zoonotic Disease Integrated Action (ZODIAC) project, launched in June 2020, aimed to establish a global network of national diagnostic laboratories that were to use nuclear and nuclear-derived techniques to conduct co-ordinated surveillance, and prompt detection and control of emerging and re-emerging zoonotic diseases, such as SARS-CoV-2, Middle East respiratory syndrome coronavirus (MERS-CoV), Brucella, dengue fever and Ebola Virus Disease.

Finance

The Agency is financed by regular and voluntary contributions from member states. Expenditure approved under the regular budget for 2023 amounted to some €400m., of which €156.3m. was allocated to nuclear verification activities. The target for voluntary contributions to replenish the IAEA's Technical Co-operation Fund (TCF) in that year was €92.6m. The IAEA Peaceful Uses Initiative, launched in 2010, raises extrabudgetary contributions for Agency activities in the peaceful uses of nuclear technology.

Publications

Annual Report.
IAEA Bulletin (quarterly).
Nuclear Energy e-Newsletter (monthly).
Nuclear Law: The Global Debate.
Nuclear Safety Review (annually).
Nuclear Technology Review (every 2 years, updated annually).
Safeguards Implementation Report (annually).
Technical Cooperation Report (annually).

Series on human health, international law, nuclear security, nuclear energy, safety, safety standards, services, technical reports. In January 2022 an online IAEA Preprint Repository was established, comprising at that time 60 preliminary versions of new technical and scientific texts.

International Bank for Reconstruction and Development—IBRD—World Bank

Address: 1818 H St, NW, Washington, DC 20433, USA.
Telephone: (202) 473-1000; **fax:** (202) 477-6391; **e-mail:** pic@worldbank.org; **internet:** www.worldbank.org.

The IBRD was established in December 1945. Initially, it was concerned with post-Second World War reconstruction in Europe; since then its aim has been to assist the economic development of members by making loans where private capital is not available on reasonable terms to finance productive investments. The World Bank, as it is commonly known, comprises the IBRD and the International Development Association (IDA). The affiliated group of institutions, comprising the IBRD, IDA, the International Finance Corporation (IFC), the Multilateral Investment Guarantee Agency (MIGA) and the International Centre for Settlement of Investment Disputes (ICSID), is referred to as the World Bank Group (WBG), and aims to eradicate extreme poverty, and pursue shared prosperity, while promoting environmentally sustainable development.

Organization
(September 2023)

Officers and staff of the IBRD serve concurrently as officers and staff in IDA. The World Bank has offices in New York, USA; Brussels, Belgium; Paris, France (for Europe); Frankfurt, Germany; London, United Kingdom; Geneva, Switzerland; and Tokyo, Japan; and in some 130 countries of operation. There are also two shared services offices, based in Chennai, India, covering accounting, human resources and information technology support; and in Sofia, Bulgaria, providing corporate and technology support to the WBG's global business operations. The World Bank employed 12,778 staff members and 6,163 consultants at 30 June 2022.

BOARDS OF GOVERNORS AND BOARDS OF DIRECTORS OF THE WBG

The WBG Boards of Governors and WBG Boards of Directors refer to the separate Boards of Governors and Boards of Directors of the IBRD, IDA, IFC and MIGA. When a country is a member of the IBRD and simultaneously of the IDA or IFC, Governors and Alternates, and Executive Directors and Alternates, serve ex officio in those roles on (respectively) the IDA and IFC Boards of Governors and the IDA and IFC Boards of Directors. MIGA Governors and Alternates and Executive Directors and Alternates are appointed separately.

The Development Committee of the WBG and IMF (established in 1974 as the Joint Ministerial Committee of the Boards of Governors of the Bank and the Fund on the Transfer of Real Resources to Developing Countries) reviews development policy issues and financing requirements.

BOARD OF GOVERNORS

The IBRD's Board of Governors consists of one Governor appointed by each member nation. Typically, a Governor is the country's minister responsible for finance, central bank governor, or a minister or an official of comparable rank. The Board normally meets once a year.

EXECUTIVE DIRECTORS

There are 25 Executive Directors and each Director selects an Alternate. Six Directors are appointed by the six members having the largest number of shares of capital stock, and the rest are elected by the Governors representing the other members. The President of the Bank is Chairman of the Board.

PRINCIPAL OFFICERS

The principal officers of the Bank are the President of the Bank, four Managing Directors, three Senior Vice-Presidents (one of whom is the WBG Chief Economist, with responsiblity for Development Economics), and 25 Vice-Presidents (covering seven regions, and responsibilities that include, *inter alia*, Sustainable Development; Human Development; Equitable Growth, Finance, and Institutions; Ethics and Internal Justice; External and Corporate Relations; Infrastructure; Operations Policy and Country Services; and Development Finance).

President and Chairman of Executive Directors: AJAY BANGA (USA).
Vice-President, Middle East and North Africa: FERID BELHAJ (Tunisia).

Activities

The World Bank's primary 'twin objectives' are the achievement of sustainable economic growth and prosperity, and the reduction of extreme poverty in developing countries. Extreme poverty is defined by the Bank through its Multidimensional Poverty Measure (MPM), which takes into account monetary poverty: living on less than US $2.15 per day, and also deprivations in access to basic infrastructure (sanitation, drinking water and electricity) and to education. From 2014/15, in order to support individual countries in pursuing the twin objectives by 2030, the Bank introduced a new country engagement model with a focus on tailoring and targeting support selectively through newly established Country Partnership Frameworks. Jointly with the IMF the Bank undertakes national financial sector assessment reviews, aimed at identifying and rectifying vulnerabilities in financial systems.

In October 2013 the Board of Governors approved the first WBG Strategy to guide and co-ordinate activities across all the member agencies of the Group; the new WBG operating model was inaugurated on 1 July 2014. The Strategy grouped the Bank's technical experts into specialized Global Practices. As at 2023 the Bank's Global Practices were: Agriculture; Education; Energy; Environment and Natural Resources; Extractive Industries; Finance, Competitiveness and Innovation; Governance; Health, Nutrition and Population; Human Development; Jobs and Development; Macroeconomics, Trade and Investment; Poverty; Social Protection; Social Sustainability and Inclusion; Urban, Disaster Risk, Resilience, and Land; Transport; Digital Development; and Water. Cross-cutting global themes in 2023 were: climate change; fragility, conflict and violence; gender; infrastructure; and knowledge management.

DEVELOPMENT

The Bank's Chief Economist leads research, data and analytical activities within the Bank and wider development community. The Development Finance Vice-Presidency manages and monitors policies and procedures relating to the Bank's development financing mechanisms and supports strategic resource mobilization. The Bank establishes and administers trust funds, open to contributions from member countries and multilateral organizations, non-governmental organizations (NGOs), and private sector institutions, in order to support development partnerships. The Bank has consolidated trust funds into a framework of broad 'Umbrella 2.0 Programs', aligned with its priorities. In July 2015 the Third International Conference on Financing for Development (FfD3), convened in Addis Ababa, Ethiopia, approved an Action Agenda in which governments expressed their commitment to strengthen the framework to finance sustainable development activities; to follow up the Agenda, an Inter-Agency Task Force on Financing for Development—with participation by more than 60 UN and other entities—was subsequently established by the UN Secretary-General. It was envisaged that FfD4 would be convened during 2024. In March 2023 the WBG President reported that developing countries would collectively require some US $2,400,000m. annually until 2030 to address ongoing challenges, and that therefore the Bank's delivery of Private Capital Facilitation was to be strengthened. The Bank participated in the Paris Summit for a New Global Financing Pact that was hosted by the French Government, in June 2023.

The Bank's annual *World Development Report* presents policy recommendations on and analysis of various specific aspects of development. The 2023 edition, issued in March, was subtitled 'Migrants, Refugees and Societies', and considered means of managing cross-mobility in a holistic manner that benefits all (i.e. the migrants themselves and their communities of destination and origin). The report addressed three related areas: development and the drivers of cross-border mobility; impacts of mobility, development opportunities, and policy responses; and rethinking the nexus between international protection and development: taking into account that the current distinction between refugees and voluntary economic migrants did not sufficiently reflect the complex reality of many cross-border movements. The report noted ongoing intensive public debate in many destination countries related to the costs and benefits of receiving influxes of migrants and refugees, and sought to identify optimal policy options for all stakeholders, to secure 'better mobility'.

The Bank supports sessions of the Small States Forum (SSF), which represent a platform for high-level dialogue on the particular development needs of 42 micro and small states and eight larger countries that were deemed to be addressing similar challenges (Botswana, Gabon, The Gambia, Jamaica, Guinea-Bissau, Lesotho, Namibia and Qatar). Meeting in October 2022, the SSF emphasized that small economies, already very highly exposed to impacts of climate change, and in a number of cases carrying heavy debt burdens, were—as global repercussions of the war in Ukraine followed on from the COVID-19 pandemic crisis—being confronted by an exceptional convergence of hardships, including inflated food and fuel prices, rising borrowing costs, and outflows of capital. The Forum stressed the need for urgent global action on climate change, and welcomed the ongoing preparation by the World Bank of Country Climate Development Reports for several small states. In January 2023 the Bank reported that small states frequently suffer disaster-related losses equivalent to roughly 5% of GDP.

In October 2016 the Bank, with public and private sector stakeholders, initiated a Digital Development Partnership, tasked with working towards ending the global digital divide, with a view to ensuring that the economic and social benefits of digital connectivity would be universally available. A report titled *People's Money: Harnessing Digitalization to Finance a Sustainable Future* that was issued by the UN Secretary-General in August 2020 addressed the empowerment potential arising from transformative advances in 'fintech' (financial technology), such as mobile payment technologies, crowdfunding platforms, peer-to-peer lending, online marketplaces, and crypto-assets and currencies.

In May 2018 the WBG and the UN Secretary-General (on behalf of the wider UN system) concluded a Strategic Partnership Framework (SPF) governing future co-operation in supporting states to implement the UN's 2030 Agenda for Sustainable Development and set of Sustainable Development Goals (SDGs, adopted by UN heads of state and of government in September 2015). The SPF provided for the following four priority areas of collaboration: finance and implementation support; global action on climate change; activities in humanitarian and post-crisis settings; and harnessing data to enhance development outcomes.

The World Bank hosts the administrative unit of the Global Infrastructure Facility (GIF), which commenced operations in April 2015, tasked with assisting emerging markets and developing economies to generate investment in and to implement infrastructure projects. The GIF partnership included several donor countries, multinational banks and private sector advisers. Eligible projects were to focus on 'climate-smart' investments and those facilitating trade and enhanced interconnectivity. The Bank has participated with other multilateral development banks and partners in the normally annual Global Infrastructure Forum (first convened in April 2016).

CLIMATE AND ENVIRONMENT

Since 2017 all Bank operations have been assessed for climate and disaster risk. In January 2019 the Bank determined promptly to end financial support for oil and gas extraction (other than in exceptional circumstances involving very poor countries). In accordance with the WBG's Climate Change Action Plan for the period 2021–25, climate financing was to represent 35% of its portfolio by 2025. An Environmental and Social Framework (ESF) has been applied since October 2018 to all of the Bank's investment project financing. It supports resilient, inclusive green sustainable development, and includes 10 Environmental and Social Standards (addressing, *inter alia,* labour conditions, resource efficiency and pollution management, biodiversity conservation, land acquisition, and indigenous and traditional communities) that must be adhered to by borrowers.

In June 2023 the WBG and nine other multilateral development banks participating in the Summit for a New Global Financing Pact, held Paris, France, collectively issued Joint MDB Paris Alignment Methodological Principles, to underpin the alignment of new financing with the objectives of the 2015 Paris Agreement on climate change.

As an implementing agency of the GEF the Bank assists countries to prepare and supervise GEF projects relating to biological diversity, climate change and other environmental protection measures. In September 2007 the Bank's Executive Directors approved a Carbon Partnership Facility and a Forest Carbon Partnership Facility to support its climate change activities. The Bank is a partner agency of the Climate and Clean Air Coalition to Reduce Short Lived Climate Pollutants (SLCPs), which was launched in February 2012 with the aim of combating SLCPs, including methane, black carbon and certain hydrofluorocarbons.

Concerned that cities are expanding at an unprecedented rate, the Bank undertakes Urbanization Reviews, providing diagnostic tools and a framework to guide city authorities in decision making. The Bank's urban agenda is aligned to its objectives on poverty reduction and boosting shared prosperity by 2030. The Bank has initiated the following programmes in support of urban development: Low Carbon, Liveable Cities; Resilient Cities; Competitive Cities; and Inclusive Cities. The Bank also convenes periodically a Global Lab on Metropolitan Strategic Planning (MetroLab), to facilitate knowledge sharing on urban development, and co-ordinates the Global Platform for Sustainable Cities, a Global Environment Facility (GEF) initiative that was launched in March 2016 to develop urban sustainability programmes in 11 developing countries.

HUMAN CAPITAL

The Bank's Social Protection Global Practice maintains an *Atlas of Social Protection Indicators of Resilience and Equity* (ASPIRE), which supports analysis of the performance of social assistance, social insurance and labour market programming in 139 countries. During 2012–22 the Bank implemented a long-term Social Protection and Labour Strategy that aimed to assist countries with the development of affordable social protection systems; to enable individuals to manage risk; and to improve resilience through investment in human capital (including in education, health, nutrition and jobs). In April 2014—estimating that 2,500m. adults worldwide were 'unbanked', i.e. excluded from access to formal banking or financial services—the Bank initiated a Financial Inclusion Support Framework. In July 2017 the Bank, ITU and the Committee on Payments and Market Infrastructures jointly launched a Financial Inclusion Global Initiative (FIGI), which aimed to advance research in and to formulate policy recommendations for digital financial inclusion. The third FIGI Symposium was convened in May–June 2021, in a virtual format.

In September 2016 the WBG and the International Labour Organization initiated a Global Partnership for Universal Social Protection to Achieve the SDGs (USP2030). The WBG and the World Health Organization (WHO) issue a biennial *Tracking Universal Health Coverage: Global Monitoring Report*. The WBG co-sponsored the sixth Universal Health Care Financing Forum, which was convened in June 2022, in Washington, DC.

The Bank participates in the multi-stakeholder Partnership for Economic Inclusion (PEI), a platform that aims to establish a global network of formalized partnerships between governments, policymakers, development partners, research organizations and NGOs, with a focus on developing economic inclusion programmes and building a knowledge base of related good practices. In January 2021 the PEI issued *State of Economic Inclusion (SEI) Report 2021: The Potential to Scale*, which reviewed the state of financial inclusion, jobs and social protection, in the context of the pandemic crisis.

The Bank's Women Entrepreneurs Finance Initiative, endorsed by the G20 in July 2017, aimed to support women-led business development by facilitating access to equity and insurance services and mobilizing up to US $1,000m. in institutional financing. The Bank maintains a *Women, Business and the Law* study series, which measures the impacts of legislation in 190 economies worldwide on women's economic opportunities, compared with those of men—focusing on the following eight indicators: mobility, workplace, entrepreneurship, pay, pension, assets, marriage, and parenthood. The 2023 edition of *Women, Business and the Law,* issued in March, included an index in which Afghanistan, Iran, Qatar, Sudan, Yemen and the Palestinian Territories were deemed to have the greatest need for relevant legislative reforms.

PEACE AND STABILITY

In February 2020 the WBG finalized its first strategy to address—through expertise and financing—the underlying causes of Fragility, Conflict and Violence (FCV) during the period 2020–25. The UN-World Bank Fragility and Conflict Partnership Trust Fund, established in 2010, is funded by Switzerland and Norway.

The WBG compiles an annual list of fragile and conflict-affected situations (FCS), which in 2022/23 comprised 37 countries and territories, including Iraq, the Syrian Arab Republic and Yemen (listed as 'conflict states'), and the West Bank and Gaza, Lebanon and Libya (as states experiencing 'institutional and social fragility').

The Bank acts as trustee of the Middle East and North Africa Transition Fund, established by the Deauville Partnership. (The Deauville Partnership was formed in May 2011 by the G8 industrialized nations, in collaboration with regional and international financial institutions and regional governments, to support political and economic reforms being undertaken by several countries in North Africa and the Middle East, notably Egypt, Jordan, Morocco and Tunisia.) The Transition Fund represents a vehicle for supporting those countries in transition to formulate policies and implement reforms.

A regional strategy for the Middle East and North Africa, titled 'Economic and Social Inclusion for Peace and Stability in the Middle East and North Africa', was introduced in 2015/6. This aimed to promote peace and stability by forging a new social contract with a focus on the following four pillars: establishing more accountable and inclusive governance structures and private sector driven economies; increasing regional co-operation; building resilience (including finding solutions to the challenges of forcibly displaced people); and supporting economic recovery and reconstruction.

PANDEMIC RESPONSE

In early March 2020 the Executive Board approved an emergency initial US $12,000m. package comprising fast-track low-cost loans, grants and technical assistance, to support at-risk developing countries with the implementation of COVID-19 prevention, detection and response programmes and to alleviate the impacts of the crisis on businesses and the labour force. On 17 March the IBRD's and IFC's Boards of Directors augmented the total to $14,000m., of which $6,000m. was to be made available in the near term by the IBRD and IDA to support health care activities, and $8,000m. was to be channelled through the IFC to support private businesses (with a view to protecting vulnerable economies and jobs). In April the steering body of the World Bank's then Pandemic Emergency Financing Facility (PEF, an insurance window that was inaugurated in July 2017) allocated $195.8m. to assist 64 developing countries' efforts to combat and contain COVID-19. (The PEF was terminated one year later, on 30 April 2021.) Also in April 2020 the WBG, IMF and the Group of 20 (G20) leading economies agreed a Debt Service Suspension Initiative (DSSI), under which, from 1 May, the debt service payments of up to 73 eligible countries (40 in Africa) were temporarily frozen. Addressing the UN General Assembly in September the Bank's President observed that the DSSI was proving to be inadequate, as the moratorium that was being provided by multilateral lending institutions was not supported by non-participant commercial creditors, or, fully, by some official bilateral creditors. Under a Common Framework for Debt Treatments, endorsed in November by the G20 and by the so-called Paris Club of sovereign creditors (which seeks to find co-ordinated solutions for debtor states), DSSI-eligible countries with particularly challenging debt burdens were, upon their own request, to be given special support. The amount of debt service suspended through the DSSI during May 2020–December 2021 (when it expired, having twice been extended, in November 2020 and in April 2021) totalled $12,900m.; 48 of the 73 eligible countries participated in the initiative. During 1 April 2020–30 June 2022 the WBG mobilized or committed $204,000m. in new financing to counter the economic, health and social impacts of the pandemic.

In January 2023 the Bank's *Global Economic Prospects*—noting the impacts of disruptions caused by the Russian Federation's invasion of Ukraine, elevated inflation and interest rates, and subdued investment—forecast depressed global economic growth during the year ahead of only 1.7%, to be followed by growth of 2.7% in 2024. At the regional level, economic growth of 4.3% was forecast in East Asia and Pacific in 2023 (revised to 5.1% in March); 5.5% in South Asia; 0.1% in Europe and Central Asia; 1.3% in Latin America and the Caribbean; 3.5% in the Middle East and North Africa; and 3.6% in sub-Saharan Africa. In early 2023 the WBG President emphasized that developing and emerging economies were confronting a multi-year period of slow growth, weak investment and heavy debt burdens.

The Bank has collaborated with WHO and other agencies to strengthen health and vaccination systems, to enable the procurement and distribution of vaccines, and advance treatments and tests in low- and middle-income countries. (See WHO for details on the Access to COVID-19 Tools (ACT) Accelerator, which was initiated, with participation by the WBG, in April 2020. From June 2021 the WBG President participated in a Multilateral Leaders Taskforce on vaccines access.) By June 2022 WBG financing totalling US $10,100m. had been approved to support COVID-19 vaccine delivery in 78 countries.

In April 2022 G20 finance ministers reached a provisional consensus on establishing, under World Bank auspices, a new Financial Intermediary Fund for Pandemic Prevention, Preparedness and Response to strengthen investment these areas in low- and middle-income countries. The so-called Pandemic Fund was launched in November, with pledged contributions of US $1,400m. from 24 countries. Its first round of funding was opened in January 2023; by 19 May, when the call for proposals was terminated, more than 175 had been received.

FINANCIAL OPERATIONS

IBRD capital is derived from members' subscriptions to capital shares, the calculation of which is based on their quotas in the IMF. At 30 June 2022 the total subscribed capital of the IBRD was US $307,100m., of which the paid-in portion was $20,500m. (6.5%); the remainder was subject to call if required. In April 2018 the Development Committee endorsed a package of measures that included a series of internal organizational reforms within the WBG, and new policies aimed at strengthening the Group's operational effectiveness (including a shift in the focus of lending to poorer member states). In October the Board of Governors endorsed an increase of $52,600m. in the IBRD's callable capital and of $7,500m. in the paid-in portion. A temporary expansion of IBRD lending at times of global financial crisis was agreed. It was envisaged that the financing capacity of the WBG would increase from around $60,000m. annually to $100,000m. by 2030. Most of the IBRD's lendable funds come from its borrowing, on commercial terms, in world capital markets, and also from its retained earnings and the flow of repayments on its loans. IBRD loans carry a variable interest rate, rather than a rate fixed at the time of borrowing.

IBRD loans usually have a 'grace period' of five years and are repayable over 15 years or fewer. Loans are made to governments, or must be guaranteed by the government concerned, and are normally made for projects likely to offer a commercially viable rate of return. In 1980 the World Bank introduced structural adjustment lending, which (instead of financing specific projects) supports programmes and changes necessary to modify the structure of an economy so that it can restore or maintain its growth and viability in its balance of payments over the medium term.

The IBRD made new lending and investment commitments totalling US $33,072m. during the financial year ending 30 June 2022 (compared with $30,523m. for 125 operations in the previous year). Total disbursements by the IBRD in the year ending 30 June 2022 amounted to $28,168m. Total WBG (i.e. combined IBRD, IDA, IFC, MIGA and recipient-executed trust fund) commitments in 2021/22 amounted to $104,370m., and disbursements to $67,041m.

Of total IBRD lending for 2021/22 US $4,135m. (13%) was allocated to projects in the Middle East and North Africa.

In January 2012 the Bank launched the Program for Results (PforR), a lending instrument that links the disbursement of funds to the delivery of predefined results. By 15 March 2023 146 PforR projects were active, requiring funding of US $47,800m.

A trust fund was established in April 2010 to support a Global Agriculture and Food Security Programme (GAFSP), with total donations amounting to US $900m. In October 2020 the GAFSP Replenishment Period 2020–25 was initiated, during which it was envisaged that $1,500m. would be raised. In May 2022, in response to the wider global impacts of Russia's invasion of Ukraine, the World Bank, IMF and other international financial institutions collectively issued the Joint International Financial Institution Plan to Address Food Insecurity, with a focus on the following six objectives: (i) support vulnerable people; (ii) promote open trade; (iii) mitigate fertilizer shortages; (iv) support food production now; (v) invest in climate-resilient agriculture for the future; and (vi) co-ordinate for maximum impact. At a meeting of G7 ministers responsible for development held in that month a joint G7-World Bank Global Alliance for Food Security was created, with the aim of promptly catalyzing a concerted response to the global hunger crisis. Other international partners were invited to participate. Also in that month the World Bank announced that it would invest up to $30,000m. in new and existing projects in areas that included agriculture, fertilizer production, nutrition, social protection, water and irrigation.

In February 2023 the WBG President and the heads of the IMF, Food and Agriculture Organization of the UN, World Food Programme, and World Trade Organization (WTO) issued a joint statement in which they called for further urgent collective actions (i) to rescue hunger hotspots: through supporting country-level efforts to strengthen crisis preparedness, share information, and address local needs; (ii) to facilitate trade (including supporting measures aimed at increasing the availability of food and fertilizers and strengthening the provision of public goods), to improve the functioning of markets, and to strengthen the role of the private sector; and (iii) to reform harmful subsidies and repurpose them towards initiatives promoting global food security and sustainable food systems.

A joint World Bank/IMF initiative to assist heavily indebted poor countries (HIPCs) to reduce their debt burden to a sustainable level, in order to make more resources available for poverty reduction and economic growth, was established in 1996. An enhanced HIPC scheme was approved in September 1999, incorporating the requirement for applicant countries to formulate, in consultation with external partners and other stakeholders, a results-oriented national strategy to promote growth and reduce poverty, to be presented in the form of a Poverty Reduction Strategy Paper (PRSP). At a pivotal 'decision point' of the process, having developed and successfully applied, for at least one year, a PRSP, applicant countries still deemed to have an unsustainable level of debt qualified for interim debt relief from the IDA and IMF, as well as relief on highly concessional terms from other official bilateral creditors and multilateral institutions. During the ensuing 'interim period' countries were required successfully to implement further economic and social development reforms, as a final demonstration of suitability for securing full debt relief at the 'completion point' of the scheme. In the majority of cases a sustainable level of debt was targeted at 150% of the net present value (NPV) of the debt in relation to total annual exports. Other countries with lower debt-to-export ratios were to be eligible for assistance under the scheme, providing that their export earnings were at least 30% of gross domestic product (GDP), and government revenue at least 15% of GDP. In 2001 the Bank introduced a Poverty Reduction Support Credit to help low-income countries to implement the policy and institutional reforms outlined in their PRSP. In September 2005 the Bank's Development Committee and the International Monetary and Financial Committee of the IMF endorsed a G8 proposal—subsequently referred to as the Multilateral Debt Relief Initiative (MDRI)—to provide additional resources to achieve the cancellation of debts owed by eligible HIPCs; countries that had reached their completion point qualified for immediate assistance.

TECHNICAL ASSISTANCE AND KNOWLEDGE

The Bank's Advisory Services and Analytics (ASA) products include reports, policy notes, workshops, and technical action plans. Highly flexible Reimbursable Advisory Services (RAS)—paid for by clients—represent around 10% of ASA support. The Bank encourages the use of local consultants to assist with projects and to strengthen institutional capability. Annually the Bank issues around 400 working papers, with the aim of catalysing research and stimulating debate. Through its Development Research Group the Bank conducts its own research into a broad range of topics. The Bank supports learning and capacity building, in particular through its Open Learning Campus, established in 2015, and knowledge sharing initiatives. The Bank has supported efforts, such as the Development Gateway, to disseminate information on development issues and programmes, and, since 1988, has organized the Annual Bank Conference on Development Economics (ABCDE) to provide a forum for the exchange and discussion of development-related ideas and research. The 2023 ABCDE was held in June, in Washington, DC, on the theme 'Growth and Resilience'. A Kuala Lumpur, Malaysia-based Global Knowledge and Research Hub was inaugurated by the WBG in 2016.

The Istanbul, Türkiye-based Global Centre for Islamic Finance, inaugurated by the Bank in October 2013, acts as a knowledge hub, to conduct research and training, and to provide technical assistance and advisory services to interested client countries on the development of Islamic financial institutions and markets.

In April 2023 the WBG issued its seventh Logistics Performance Index (LPI 2023) and accompanying report, *Connecting to Compete*, which measured the capacity of 139 states efficiently and swiftly to transport goods across borders, with a focus on the quality of logistics services, trade and transport-related infrastructure, and border controls. The top ranked country was Singapore, followed by Finland, Denmark, Germany, the Netherlands and Switzerland. LPI 2023 noted a significant reduction in port delays achieved through end-to-end supply chain digitalization.

CRISIS SUPPORT

The Bank is a lead organization in providing reconstruction assistance following natural disasters or conflicts, usually in collaboration with other UN agencies or international organizations, and through special trust funds.

The Bank's Global Facility for Disaster Reduction and Recovery—GFDRR focuses on the following thematic areas: risk-informed decision making; reducing risk and mainstreaming disaster risk management; and financial preparedness to manage disaster and climate shocks. Cross-cutting themes in 2023 were: understanding and addressing the disaster risk management-fragility, conflict and violence nexus; inclusive disaster risk management and gender equality; resilience to climate change; resilient recovery; and understanding risk. A Tokyo, Japan-based World Bank-GFDRR Disaster Risk Management Hub was established in 2014. In March 2023 the GFDRR released a 'Global RApid post-disaster Damage Estimation' (GRADE) of the cost (estimated at US $34,200m.) of the physical devastation caused to buildings in Türkiye by the earthquakes that had struck southern areas of that country, and also northern Syria, in the previous month.

From January 2004 the Bank administered the Iraq Trust Fund (ITF), which initially was established as an integral component of the International Reconstruction Fund Facility—approved by an international conference on Iraq held in October 2003 to finance a programme (covering 2004–10) of emergency projects and technical assistance. The Bank was a partner, with the Iraqi Government, the UN Secretariat, the IMF and other financial institutions, in the International Compact with Iraq, a five-year framework for co-operation that was launched in May 2007. In October 2017 the Bank approved a US $400m. package of assistance to support the rehabilitation of key infrastructure to enable the delivery of public services in areas of Iraq that had been liberated from Islamic State.

In May 2020 the Bank's Board of Executive Directors approved a Emergency Locust Response Programme, costing US $500m., which was to provide urgent financing to countries in eastern Africa and the Middle East to eliminate locust swarms that were placing crop production and food security at risk.

A Partnership Framework between the Bank and the UN was signed in April 2017 to provide for greater collaboration in building the resilience of vulnerable communities, in particular in crisis-affected situations.

CO-OPERATION WITH OTHER ORGANIZATIONS

The World Bank co-operates with other international partners with the aim of improving the impact of development efforts. Meetings between the governing bodies of the WBG and IMF are convened annually. WBG-IMF Spring Meetings are held in April, normally in Washington, DC, USA, with participation by ministers of finance, central bankers, business executives, representatives of civil society organizations, and academics. The Bank collaborates with the IMF in implementing the HIPC scheme and the two agencies work closely to achieve a common approach to development initiatives. In May 2000 the Bank signed a joint statement of co-operation with the Organisation for Economic Co-operation and Development. It holds regular consultations with other multilateral development banks and with the European Union with respect to development issues. The Bank is a partner, with the IMF, the UN Conference on Trade and Development, UNDP, the WTO and the International Trade

Commission, in the Enhanced Integrated Framework (EIF) for trade-related assistance to least developed countries (LDCs), which since 2009 has aimed to facilitate greater participation by LDCs in the global trading system; EIF activities are supported by a dedicated EIF Trust Fund. In June 2007 the World Bank and the UN Office on Drugs and Crime launched a joint Stolen Asset Recovery (StAR) initiative, as part of the Bank's Governance and Anti-Corruption strategy. A Global Forum on Asset Recovery (GFAR) was convened in December 2017, in Washington, DC, with assistance from StAR.

In January 2011 the Bank signed a Memorandum of Understanding with the League of Arab States within the framework of the Arab World Initiative, in order to strengthen co-operation in areas of regional economic and social development. In May the Bank inaugurated an Arab Financing Facility for Infrastructure (AFFI), as a partnership between the Bank, IFC and the Islamic Development Bank, in order to improve access to financing for public and private infrastructure projects in the region.

The WBG hosts the Public-Private Infrastructure Advisory Facility (PPIAF), a multi-donor facility that was established in 1999 by Japan and the UK to promote engagement in emerging economies by private sector interests.

Other WBG Institutions

International Centre for Settlement of Investment Disputes (ICSID): f. 1966 under the Convention of the Settlement of Investment Disputes between States and Nationals of Other States; the Convention was designed to encourage the growth of private foreign investment for economic development, by creating the possibility, always subject to the consent of both parties, for a Contracting State and a foreign investor who is a national of another Contracting State to settle any legal dispute that might arise out of such an investment by arbitration and/or conciliation before an impartial, international forum; the governing body of the Centre is its Administrative Council, composed of one representative of each Contracting State, all of whom have equal voting power; the President of the World Bank is (ex officio) the non-voting Chairman of the Administrative Council; at mid-2023 959 cases had been registered with the Centre, of which 675 had been concluded and 284 were pending consideration; mems: 165 (158 Contracting States having signed and ratified the Convention and 7 Signatory States); Sec.-Gen. MEG KINNEAR (Canada); publs *Annual Report*, *ICSID Caseload Statistics* (2 a year), *ICSID Review—Foreign Investment Law Journal* (2 a year).

Multilateral Investment Guarantee Agency (MIGA): f. 1988; mandated to end extreme poverty and promote shared prosperity by encouraging the flow of foreign direct investment to, and among, developing member countries—through the provision of political risk insurance and investment marketing services to foreign investors and host governments, respectively; auth. cap. was initially set at 100,000 shares, equivalent to US $1,082m.; the Convention establishing MIGA provided for an automatic increase of capital stock upon the admission of new mems; by 30 June 2022 MIGA's capital base comprised 186,665 shares, equivalent to $1,919.6m.; total subscriptions to the capital stock amounted to $1,553.3m., of which $366.3m. was paid-in; under MIGA's Strategy and Business Outlook for 2021–23 the Agency aimed to deliver an annual average of $5,500m.–$6,000m. in guarantees, and committed to increasing its share of investments in low-income countries and fragile situations to 30%–33% (from 25%); priority areas of focus were to be clean energy, green finance, green buildings, public transportation, and climate-smart agribusiness; during 2021–25 some 35% of guarantees were to be allocated to climate-related projects; by 2023 MIGA had paid out on 10 claims on its political risk insurance; at that time the amount of insurance available for each project was $220m., and there was a limit of $720m. in guarantees per country; during the year ending 30 June 2022 MIGA issued investment insurance contracts for 54 projects with a value of $4,935m.; during 1988–April 2023 (in which month MIGA's 1,000th project was approved) the total investment guarantees issued by the agency amounted to more than $70,000m., in support of local initiatives in 122 mem. countries, as well as regional, multiregional and global projects; as at 30 June 2022 MIGA's gross guarantee exposure stood at $24,449m., a record high; mems: 182 (of which 25 are industrialized and 157 are developing states); Pres. AJAY BANGA (USA); Executive Vice-Pres. HIROSHI MATANO (Japan); publs *Annual Report*, *MIGA News* (online newsletter, every 2 months), *World Investment and Political Risk*.

Publications

Africa's Pulse (2 a year).
Annual Report.
Commodity Markets Outlook (2 a year).
Digital Development Partnership Annual Interactive Report.
Global Development Finance (annually).
Global Economic Prospects (2 a year).
Global Financial Development Report (annually).
International Debt Report (annually).
Pacific Economic Update.
Poverty and Shared Prosperity (annually).
Results and Performance of the World Bank Group (annually).
State and Trends of Carbon Pricing.
Sustainable Energy for All: Global Tracking Framework (every 2 years).
Women, Business and the Law (annually).
World Bank Economic Review (3 a year).
World Bank Research Observer.
World Development Indicators (annually).
World Development Report (annually).

Technical papers, regional and country reports and strategy documents, sectoral studies.

Statistics

IBRD LENDING COMMITMENTS, BY SECTOR AND REGION
(projects approved, year ending 30 June; US $ million)

	2020	2021	2022
Agriculture, fishing and forestry	1,767	1,260	3,611
Education	1,135	2,017	1,090
Energy and extractives	2,053	2,379	3,069
Financial sector	3,702	3,828	1,877
Health	3,980	2,606	6,252
Industry, trade and services	2,208	3,030	1,916
Information and communication technologies	886	773	509
Public administration	4,301	5,666	6,484
Social protection	4,786	4,800	3,446
Transportation	1,323	2,273	3,036
Water, sanitation and waste management	1,834	1,891	1,782
Total	27,976	30,523	33,072
Africa	1,725	2,025	3,293
East Asia and the Pacific	4,770	6,753	5,482
Europe and Central Asia	5,699	4,559	5,974
Latin America and the Caribbean	6,798	9,464	9,407
Middle East and North Africa	3,419	3,976	4,135
South Asia	5,565	3,746	4,781

Source: World Bank, *Annual Report 2022*.

IBRD AND IDA LENDING IN THE MIDDLE EAST AND NORTH AFRICA, 1 JULY 2021–30 JUNE 2022

Sector	% of total regional commitments*
Agriculture, fishing and forestry	12.0
Education	3.0
Energy and extractives	3.0
Financial sector	3.0
Health	12.0
Industry, trade and services	13.0
Information and communication technologies	3.0
Public administration	16.0
Social protection	27.0
Transportation	7.0
Water, sanitation and waste management	1.0
Total	100.0

* Amounting to US $4,952m. (IBRD: $4,135m.; IDA: $817m.).

Source: World Bank, *Annual Report 2022*.

REGIONAL ORGANIZATIONS

The United Nations in the Middle East and North Africa

International Development Association (IDA)—World Bank

Address: 1818 H St, NW, Washington, DC 20433, USA.
Telephone: (202) 473-1000; **fax:** (202) 477-6391; **internet:** www.worldbank.org/ida.

IDA was established in September 1960 as an affiliate organization to the IBRD, together forming the World Bank. It advances capital to the poorer developing member countries on more flexible terms than those offered by the IBRD. From 2013 IDA participated in the first World Bank Group Strategy aimed at reducing extreme poverty and promoting shared prosperity by 2030.

Organization

(September 2023)

Officers and staff of the IBRD serve concurrently as officers and staff of IDA.

President and Chairman of Executive Directors: AJAY BANGA (USA).

Activities

IDA assistance is aimed at supporting the poverty reduction strategies of the poorer developing countries, i.e. those with an annual gross national income (GNI) per caput of less than US $1,255 in 2022/23. Under IDA lending conditions, credits can be extended to countries whose balance of payments could not sustain the burden of repayment required for IBRD loans. Terms are more favourable than those provided by the IBRD; as at 1 January 2022 the maturity of IDA credits for small economies was 40 years, with a grace period of 10 years; for regular economies 38 years with a grace period of six years; and for so-called blend borrowers (which are entitled to borrow from both IDA and IBRD) 30 years with a five-year grace period.

In 2022/23 75 countries were eligible for IDA assistance, including 16 blend borrowers. Exceptions may be made for countries with GNI greater than US $1,255, but which would otherwise have little or no access to Bank funds.

In 2017 Syria, which had graduated from eligiblity for IDA assistance in 1974, again became a borrowing country.

IDA's development resources are replenished every three years by contributions from the more affluent member countries, which are supplemented by WBG funding and credit repayments. At the same time partner countries review IDA policies and may determine future strategic priorities. In April 2021 the 20th replenishment of IDA funds (IDA20) was launched a year early, with a view to advancing policy and financial support measures for developing nations' COVID-19 pandemic recovery. IDA20, to be implemented during July 2022–June 2025, was finalized in December 2021, at a meeting hosted by Japan in a virtual format. Donor nations pledged US $23,400m., contributing to a replenishment package of $93,000m. The special themes for IDA20—under the broad commitment of 'Building Back Better from the Crisis: Towards a Green, Resilient and Inclusive Future'—were climate change; fragility, conflict and violence; gender and development; human capital; and jobs and economic transformation. Debt, technology, governance and institutions and crisis preparedness were identified as priority cross-cutting issues.

In March 2020 the Boards of Directors of the IBRD and IFC approved an emergency US $14,000m. package comprising fast-track low-cost loans, grants and technical assistance, to support at-risk developing countries in containing and combating the COVID-19 contagion. Some $6,000m. was to be made available in the near term by IDA and the IBRD to support health care activities. In April the WBG, IMF and Group of 20 (G20) leading economies agreed to suspend, for a period of one year from 1 May, the debt service payments of up to 73 eligible developing countries (of which 40 were in Africa); this deadline was subsequently extended to 31 December 2021. On 1 July 2020 the WBG introduced a Sustainable Development Finance Policy for IDA countries, establishing financial incentives for debt and investment transparency.

FINANCIAL OPERATIONS

During the year ending 30 June 2022 new IDA commitments amounted to US $37,727m., compared with $36,028m. in the previous year. In 2021/22 $6,194m. (representing some 16.4% of lending) was for projects in the area of public administration; $5,167m. (13.7%) for transportation sector initiatives; $4,792m. (12.7%) was for social protection; $4,269m. (11.3%) for health initiatives; $4,008m. (10.6%) for agriculture, forestry and fishing; $3,696m. (9.8%) for energy and extractive sector projects; $2,357m. (6.2%) for water, sanitation and waste management projects; $2,335m. (6.2%) for education; $2,317m. (6.1%) for industry, trade and services; $1,346m. (3.6%) for financial sector projects; and $1,245m. (3.3%) for information and communications technology initiatives.

Of total IDA assistance during 2021/22, US $817m. (2.2%) was for the Middle East and North Africa.

In July 2017, under IDA18, an IDA-International Finance Corporation (IFC)-Multilateral Investment Guarantee Agency (MIGA) Private Sector Window (PSW) was established, which aimed to leverage increased private sector investment in IDA-only countries, in particular in fragile and conflict-affected states. The PSW includes a Risk Mitigation Facility, Blended Finance Facility, Local Currency Facility (aimed at reducing currency risk), and a MIGA Guarantee Facility (to expand the coverage of MIGA guarantees); the facilities were to be implemented by IFC on behalf of IDA.

From July 2020 the IDA's Fragility, Conflict and Violence Envelope was assisting fragile states through a Prevention and Resilience Allocation (PRA—targeted at countries deemed to be at risk of descending into large-scale or high-intensity conflict); a Remaining Engaged during Conflict Allocation (RECA); and a Turn Around Allocation (TAA—supporting the implementation of constructive reforms aimed at building resilience in states that were emerging from conflict or from a debilitating social or political crisis).

An IDA Window for Host Communities and Refugees (WHR) supports a UN Comprehensive Refugee Response Framework (CRRF), which aimed to provide long-term development solutions for low-income countries hosting significant influxes of refugees, with a focus on the social and economic inclusion of refugees and on the wellbeing of host communities. Under IDA20 up to US $2,400m. was to be allocated to the WHR.

Through a joint Syrians Under Temporary Protection (SUTP) initiative the World Bank and EU support Türkiye (known until June 2022 as Turkey) in hosting 3.7m. Syrian refugees—representing the highest number of refugees being hosted by any single country globally—through the provision of health, education and socioeconomic assistance for refugees and host communities, and by strengthening municipal infrastructure. The €6,000m. Facility for Refugees in Turkey (FRiT), established in 2015, and jointly led by the World Bank, EU and Turkish Government, had financed more than 80 such initiatives by 2021; a second FRiT project cycle was ongoing during mid-2021–mid-2025. In March 2020 the World Bank Board of Executive Directors approved a US $148.8m. loan to finance a World Bank-EU Turkey Municipal Services Improvement Project in Refugee Affected Areas, which aimed to improve host and refugee communities' access to safe water supplies, sanitation and solid waste services.

In December 2011 the Board of Executive Directors approved the establishment of an Immediate Response Mechanism, enabling countries rapidly to access up to 5% of their undisbursed IDA investment project balances in the event of a crisis. IDA's Crisis Response Window (CRW), established in 2009, aims to strengthen the capacity of IDA-eligible countries to address the impact of exceptionally severe natural and economic shocks in a structured and expedited manner, without damaging their long-term development paths. Under IDA20 some US $3,300m. was to be allocated to the CRW. By February 2023 some $748m. had been made available through an Early Response Financing mechanism of the CRW to support countries severely affected by the global food and nutrition security crisis. In May the Board of Executive Directors approved a new Crisis Facility to supplement CRW financing.

A new IDA Regional Window was initiated under IDA19, in 2020, to support policy reforms and strategic investments aimed at facilitating regional integration, connectivity and development, and the generation of wider public goods, by taking advantage of economies of scale and collective action. The Regional Window was to provide top-up funding to boost projects in areas including critical infrastructure (for example, digital technology, energy and transport); public goods; human capital; the blue economy; and the specific needs of small islands. Some 75% of funding through the new Window was to be allocated to Africa (with a special focus on the fragile Horn of Africa, Lake Chad area, and Sahel), and the remaining 25% distributed to other regions. Under IDA20 US $6,300m. was allocated to the IDA Scale-Up Window (SUW—introduced in 2017 as the IDA18 Scale-up Facility, and renamed in 2020), with a focus on supporting high quality, transformational development projects; additional short maturity loans were also to be made available within the SUW.

REGIONAL ORGANIZATIONS

The WBG's US $500m. Emergency Locust Response Program (ELRP) was approved by the Board of Executive Directors in May 2020 to extend flexible support, in the form of technical assistance, policy advice, and finance, to states in Africa, Middle East and beyond that were affected or at risk from a recent upsurge in locust swarms. The ELRP has a particular focus on monitoring and controlling locust population growth and preventing the spread of swarms, while mitigating control measure-related risks; restoring the livelihoods of affected households; and building capacity to respond swiftly and efficiently to future outbreaks.

Through a WBG multi-donor trust fund on nutrition, IDA supports the Power of Nutrition—an initiative launched in April 2015 by the WBG, UNICEF and partner agencies to finance country-led programmes targeting undernutrition through a combination of public and private contributions.

In April 2015 the WBG and partners made a commitment to achieving universal financial inclusion—access by all adults worldwide to a transaction account. The 2021 edition of the World Bank's Global Findex Database (measuring financial inclusion) found that 76% of the global adult population was 'banked' in 2021, compared with 69% in 2017, 62% in 2014 and with 51% in 2011. The findings of the Database are summarized in the periodic *Little Data Book on Financial Inclusion*.

Publications

ABCs of IDA.
Annual Report.

International Finance Corporation—IFC

Address: 2121 Pennsylvania Ave, NW, Washington, DC 20433, USA.
Telephone: (202) 473-1000; **e-mail:** fjones@ifc.org; **internet:** www.ifc.org.

IFC was founded in 1956 to stimulate economic growth in developing countries through the direct financing of private sector investments. IFC also mobilizes capital in international financial markets, and provides technical assistance and advice to governments and businesses. It is an integral member of the World Bank Group (WBG), although has its own specialized agency status. From 2013 IFC participated in the first WBG Strategy aimed at reducing extreme poverty and promoting shared prosperity by 2030.

Organization
(September 2023)

IFC is a separate legal entity in the WBG. It is guided by a Board of Governors, which meets annually, and a Board of Directors The President of the World Bank is ex officio Chairman of the IFC Board of Directors, which has appointed him President of IFC. Subject to his overall supervision, the day-to-day operations of IFC are conducted by its staff under the direction of the Executive Vice-President.

PRINCIPAL OFFICERS

President: AJAY BANGA (USA).
Managing Director and Executive Vice-President: MAKHTAR DIOP (Senegal).
Vice-President, Africa: SÉRGIO PIMENTA (France/Portugal).
Vice-President, Middle East, Central Asia, Türkiye, Afghanistan and Pakistan: HELA CHEIKHROUHOU (Tunisia).
Director, Central Asia and Türkiye: WIEBKE SCHLOEMER (based in Istanbul, Türkiye).
Director, North Africa: CHEICK-OUMAR SYLLA (based in Cairo, Egypt).
Director, Middle East, Pakistan and Afghanistan: AFTAB AHMED (based in Amman, Jordan).

Activities

IFC aims to advance the economies of developing member countries by lending directly without the need for government guarantees to sustainable private enterprises, and by providing expert advisory services. IFC finances private sector projects either through loans from its own account (known as A-loans); through equity and quasi-equity financing and syndicated loans (B-loans); or through partial credit guarantees and risk management products. IFC also extends funding to financial intermediaries, which then lend onwards to clients. It aims to facilitate the conditions that stimulate the flow of domestic and foreign private investment and generate jobs. IFC may provide finance for a project that is partly state-owned, provided that there is participation by the private sector and that the project is operated on a commercial basis. IFC also mobilizes additional resources from other financial institutions, in particular through syndicated loans, thus providing access to international capital markets. Its range of advisory services aim to improve the investment climate in developing countries. Technical assistance is extended to private enterprises and governments.

To be eligible for financing, projects must be profitable for investors, as well as financially and economically viable; must benefit the economy of the country concerned; and must comply with IFC's environmental and social guidelines. IFC aims to promote best corporate governance and management methods and sustainable business practices, and encourages partnerships between governments, non-governmental organizations and community groups. The longer-term economic, environmental and social impact of projects are assessed in accordance with the IFC's Sustainability Framework.

IFC's authorized share capital is US $2,580m. In July 2010 the Board of Directors recommended a special capital increase of $130m., to raise the authorized capital from $2,450m.; the increase took effect on 27 June 2012, having received the approval of the Board of Governors. A capital increase endorsed by the Board of Governors in October 2018 provided for the conversion of a portion of retained earnings into paid-in capital, and a Selective Capital Increase (SCI) and a General Capital Increase (GCI) that would provide up to $5,500m. in additional paid-in capital; the suspension of IFC grants to the International Development Agency (IDA) after the conclusion of the IDA18 replenishment cycle; and internal reform measures aimed at ensuring increased efficiency. The GCI and SCI took effect on 16 April 2020, followed on 22 April by the initiation of a subscription process. At 30 June 2022 IFC's paid-in capital stood at $21,749m. The World Bank was originally the principal source of borrowed funds, but IFC also borrows from private capital markets. In 2021/22 IFC reported a net income of –$464m.

An IFC 3.0 Strategy, implemented from 2018, aimed to identify market opportunities, generate markets, and boost investment from private sector sources, with a particular focus on designing profitable initiatives with strong development impacts in regions with high rates of poverty and fragility. In April 2019 IFC adopted a series of Operating Principles for Impact Management, which aimed to promote transparency in investments.

In March 2020 the IFC Board of Directors endorsed (as a component of a US $14,000m. WBG package of assistance) $8,000m. in fast track financing that was intended to help protect economies and livelihoods affected by the COVID-19 pandemic. This was extended by $400m. in February 2021 and by $200m. in March 2022, in the framework of IFC's Base of the Pyramid Programme, which focuses on supporting small and informal businesses with small capital bases and low-income households. During the period 1 April 2021–30 June 2022 IFC financing to counter the impacts of the pandemic amounted to $5,300m.

IFC's Global Trade Finance Program (GTFP), founded in 2004, provides guarantees for trade transactions. By September 2022 more than 235 eligible financial institutions in 69 countries were participating in the GTFP, through which IFC had issued more than 68,000 guarantees, totalling US $66,500m.

The Banking on Women Global Trade Finance Programme (BOW-GTFP) supports banks participating in the GTFP network to expand trade finance to women-owned SMEs ('WSMEs').

IFC implements She WINS Arabia and She WINS Africa initiatives (launched, respectively, in 2021 and 2023), which assist local women entrepreneurs through the extension of training, advice, mentorship and enhanced access to finance.

IFC committed US $1,000m. in funds to a Global Trade Liquidity Program (GTLP), which was inaugurated by the WBG in April 2009; by 2021 the GTLP had mobilized support (extended by governments, other development banks and the private sector) of around $53,000m. in an estimated 24,000 trade transactions involving more than 400 financial institutions in 69 emerging markets.

REGIONAL ORGANIZATIONS

IFC's Critical Commodities Programme extends credit to traders to support the movement of food and agricultural products into and out of low-income countries. In 2009 IFC established a Distressed Asset Recovery Programme (DARP).

By 30 June 2022 IFC's Asset Management Company (AMC), comprising 11 active investment funds, had since its inception raised assets totalling US $10,055m. From 1 February 2020 the AMC—hitherto a wholly-owned subsidiary of IFC—was merged fully into the Corporation. AMC investment funds include the Financial Institutions Growth Fund (established in 2015) which by 30 June 2022 had raised funds totalling $505m.; the IFC Sub-Debt Capitalization Fund, which by that time had raised investment commitments totalling $1,725m.; the IFC Equity Capitalization Fund ($1,275m.); the IFC Global Infrastructure Fund ($1,430m.); the IFC Global Emerging Markets Fund of Funds, which invests mainly in private equity funds in emerging and frontier markets ($800m.); and the IFC Catalyst Fund—inaugurated in 2012 to invest in private equity funds providing growth capital for companies addressing resource efficiency in emerging markets—$418m. An IFC Women Entrepreneurs Debt Fund had raised $115m. since 2016 to support female-owned SMEs.

By 30 June 2022 IFC's Middle East and North Africa Fund, which was established in 2015/16, had raised funds totalling US $162m.

IFC was tasked with implementing, on behalf of the IDA, the Risk Mitigation Facility, Blended Finance Facility, Local Currency Facility (aimed at reducing currency risk), and MIGA Guarantee Facility (to expand the coverage of MIGA guarantees) that were included in the US $2,500m. IDA-IFC-MIGA Private Sector Window (PSW), inaugurated in July 2017.

In the year ending 30 June 2022 IFC's long-term investment commitments and core mobilization of funds amounted to US $23,166m. for 296 projects (compared with $23,305m. for 313 projects in the previous year). Of the total approved in 2021/22, $12,569m. was for IFC's own account, while $10,596m. was in the form of loan syndications and parallel loans, underwriting of securities issues and investment funds, public-private partnerships, and funds mobilized by the IFC Asset Management Company. Generally, IFC limits its financing to less than 25% of the total cost of a project, but it may take up to a 35% stake in a venture (although never as a majority shareholder). Disbursements amounted to $15,787m. in 2021/22.

In the financial year 2021/22 some US $252m. in long-term investment commitments from IFC's own account was allocated to Middle East and North Africa (including Afghanistan and Pakistan, but excluding Türkiye which it classifies together with Central Asia). The main areas of IFC activities in the region are financial institutions, infrastructure, manufacturing, renewable energy (for example solar energy projects), and the oil and gas sectors.

IFC's Advisory Services, in the form of advice, dialogue, problem solving and training, aim to promote best practices, improve business standards, increase access to finance, develop a regulatory environment that facilitates entrepreneurship and private sector growth, promote environmental and social sustainability, and enhance infrastructure. Total expenditure on Advisory Services during 2021/22 amounted to US $250.6m. In that financial year 51% of such projects were implemented in IDA countries. IFC manages, jointly financed with the World Bank and MIGA, the Foreign Investment Advisory Service (FIAS), which provides technical assistance and advice on promoting foreign investment and strengthening a country's investment framework, at the request of governments.

Of total expenditure on Advisory Services during 2021/22 US $14.9m. was allocated to the Middle East and $10.9m. to Central Asia and Türkiye.

Publications

Annual Report.
Doing Business (annually).
Other handbooks, discussion papers, technical documents, policy toolkits, public policy journals.

International Fund for Agricultural Development—IFAD

Address: Via Paolo di Dono 44, 00142 Rome, Italy.
Telephone: (06) 54591; **fax:** (06) 5043463; **e-mail:** ifad@ifad.org; **internet:** www.ifad.org.

IFAD was established in 1977 with a mandate to combat hunger and eradicate poverty in the low-income, food-deficit regions of the world. IFAD focuses its activities on the poorest communities in support of inclusive and sustainable rural development.

Organization
(September 2023)

GOVERNING COUNCIL

Each member state is represented in the Governing Council (the Fund's highest authority) by a Governor and an Alternate. Sessions are held annually with special sessions as required. The Governing Council elects the President of the Fund (who also chairs the Executive Board) by a two-thirds' majority for a four-year term. The 46th session of the Council was convened in February 2023.

EXECUTIVE BOARD

The Executive Board is responsible for the conduct and general operation of IFAD and approves project loans and grants; it holds three regular sessions each year. It consists of 18 members and 18 alternates, elected by the Governing Council, who serve for three years. An independent Office of Evaluation reports directly to the Board.

The governance structure of the Fund is based on the classification of members. Membership of the Executive Board is distributed as follows: eight List A countries (i.e. industrialized donor countries), four List B (petroleum-exporting developing donor countries), and six List C (recipient developing countries), divided equally among the Sub-List C categories (i.e. Africa, Europe, Asia and the Pacific, and Latin America and the Caribbean).

President and Chairman of Executive Board: Dr ÁLVARO LARIO (Spain).

Activities

IFAD works to extend financing in support of inclusive rural development and the eradication of rural poverty and hunger. It aims to improve food production systems, to enhance access to agricultural markets and technologies and to strengthen the resilience of rural communities to climate change. IFAD advocates for the world's rural poor, and in particular for the most marginalized groups in developing countries, including small-scale farmers, artisanal fishermen, nomadic pastoralists, rural women, and the landless.

IFAD's Strategic Framework for 2016–25 was devised within the context of the UN's 2030 Agenda for Sustainable Development, with its associated set of Sustainable Development Goals (SDGs). Priority areas of the Strategic Framework include the need to maximize IFAD's strategic positioning, to use its comparative advantage in both a leadership and catalytic role; to forge partnerships with governments, rural communities, farmers' organizations, and other stakeholders; to mobilize increased investment for smallholder agriculture; to improve institutional efficiency; to mobilize resources through innovative means; to innovate in all of IFAD's areas of expertise; to continue to mainstream gender equality and women's empowerment, climate-smart agriculture and the sustainable management of natural resources, the promotion of nutrition-sensitive agriculture, and the development of inclusive financial services and of public-private production partnerships (that promote equal partner status for smallholder food producers in value chain systems); as well as to continue to advance South-South and triangular co-operation (SSTC).

PROJECTS AND PROGRAMMES

IFAD supports rural communities through financing, tools and knowledge, with a focus on specific issues such as climate and the environment, land tenure, water security, and nutrition. It works with rural communities, including women and youth-led organizations, to design inclusive, effective projects, within the framework of a, separately developed, results-based country strategic opportunities programme (COSOP). IFAD supports projects that aim to increase the productive capacity of the poorest communities, to enhance their access to markets, and to strengthen their resilience to the changing climate. IFAD supervises the implementation of the projects it supports and sends monitoring and evaluation missions to all countries of operations. IFAD's development projects usually include several components, such as infrastructure (e.g. improvement of water supplies, small-scale irrigation and road construction); input supply (e.g. improved animal feed, seeds, fertilizers and pesticides); institutional support (e.g. research, training and extension services); and producer incentives (e.g. pricing and marketing improvements).

The Fund supports projects that are concerned with environmental conservation, in an effort to alleviate poverty that results from the deterioration of natural resources. In September 2021 IFAD issued a *Stocktake Report on Agroecology in IFAD Operations: An Integrated Approach to Sustainable Food Systems,* its first comprehensive assessment of agroecological practices—which combine traditional farming knowledge with modern scientific innovation, and aim to integrate ecological, social and economic development. The report addressed the efficient use and natural management of resources; diversification and agrobiodiversity; recycling of nutrients, water, biomass and energy; and innovations that link producers and consumers. The Fund reported at that time that agroecology was a component of three-fifths of the Fund's projects.

At the end of 2022 total IFAD loans approved since 1978 amounted to US $23,241.3m. for 1,181 projects. IFAD approved $880.9m. in loan financing for a total of 14 new projects in 2022 (compared with $1,030.8m. for 27 projects in the previous year). In order to increase the impact of its lending resources on food production, the Fund seeks as much as possible to attract other external donors and beneficiary governments as cofinanciers of its projects. In 2022 external cofinancing amounted to $559.3m., while domestic contributions, i.e. from recipient governments and other local sources, totalled $452.7m.

IFAD has funded efforts to improve the production of durum wheat in the dryland areas of West Asia and North Africa and to support the establishment of a regional animal surveillance and control network to identify and prevent outbreaks of livestock diseases in North Africa, the Middle East and the Arab Peninsula. In 1998 the IFAD Governing Council approved the establishment of a Fund for Gaza and the West Bank as a mechanism of providing financial assistance to those territories.

GRANTS

IFAD extends grants to support research and innovation, both at global or regional level and others with a more country-specific focus. It aims to support the development of pro-poor technologies and approaches, to promote the exchange of knowledge and to facilitate partnerships between other research or development institutions. Technical assistance grants may be extended to support capacity building in the agricultural sector, as well as project preparation and development. By the end of 2022 the Fund had approved 2,918 research, innovation and technical assistance grants, cumulatively amounting to US $1,316.1m. Four grants were approved in 2022, amounting to $1.4m.

INITIATIVES AND FACILITIES

IFAD provides support and technical assistance to numerous initiatives, platforms and facilities with a focus on promoting sustainable rural development.

Adaptation for Smallholder Agriculture Programme: since 2012 promotes financing and new practices and technologies to help small-scale farmers to adapt to and help mitigate the impact of climate change; the third phase of the Programme, effective as ASAP+ since 2021, focuses on addressing food insecurity in the most vulnerable communities.

Agri-Business Capital (ABC) Fund: IFAD was a founder sponsor of the fund in 2019; it is managed as a private investment vehicle to provide capital and technical support to rural small and medium-sized enterprises and local farmer orgs, with a particular focus on generating employment for women and young people.

China/IFAD South-South Triangular Co-operation Facility: established in February 2018 to mobilize knowledge and resources with the aim of accelerating the alleviation of rural poverty, improving the productivity of rural smallholders, advancing rural transformation, and promoting investments between developing countries.

Facility for Refugees, Migrants, Forced Displacement and Rural Stability (FARMS): established in September 2016, with an initial focus on the Near East and North Africa region; aims to enhance social resilience and strengthen the management of natural resources in host rural communities and in communities of origin; committed to implementing small-scale rural infrastructure projects and conducting agricultural training.

Financing Facility for Remittances: established by IFAD in 2006 to support the safe and efficient transfer of migrant remittances to their families and home communities; conducts research on the development impact of remittance flows, and analyses trends, opportunities and regulatory systems; implements a Platform for Remittances, Investments and Migrants' Entrepreneurship in Africa (PRIME Africa) and the Diaspora Investment in Sustainable Rural Youth Entrepreneurship in Mali.

Indigenous Peoples Assistance Facility (IPAF): created in 2007, IPAF funds microprojects that aim to build upon the traditional knowledge and natural resources of Indigenous communities.

Rural Poor Stimulus Facility (RPSF): established in April 2020 by IFAD as a multi-donor initiative to support low-income rural communities to counter the impact of the COVID-19 pandemic, to improve their food security and resilience to market shocks, and to accelerate their recovery from the crisis; during 2022 US $84.7m. was disbursed under the RPSF.

Rural Resilience Programme (2RP): aims to consolidate the financing channels directed to assist small-scale rural producers to adapt to climate change and to contribute to the alleviation of rural poverty and food insecurity.

GLOBAL FORUMS

IFAD convenes and has institutionalized various meetings at regional and international level to stimulate dialogue and to promote effective partnerships. In September 2021 IFAD, with the Food and Agriculture Organization of the UN (FAO), the World Food Programme (WFP) and the UN Secretary-General, organized a Food Systems Summit (FSS), with the aim of raising global awareness of challenges related to the production, processing and consumption of food, and to improving the output of safe, nutritious food. In January 2022, to support the follow-up to the FSS, a co-ordination hub was launched, under the joint leadership of IFAD, FAO and WFP, and assisted by a Champions Advisory Group comprising stakeholder representation by, *inter alia,* producers, the private sector, Indigenous peoples, youth and women.

The seventh meeting of IFAD's Farmers' Forum (established in 2005, to promote dialogue between smallholders and rural producers' associations) was convened in February 2020. Global Forums are convened every four years, with regional events and consultations held in the intervening period. IFAD supported farmer's organizations to hold dialogues on the sidelines of the 2021 FFS. IFAD, with the International Labour Organization, was to lead a new coalition for action, established by the FSS, concerned with decent work and living incomes and wages for all food systems workers.

Since 2009 IFAD has had a formal policy of engagement with Indigenous communities. Subsequently an Indigenous People's Forum has been convened every two years, preceded by a series of regional workshops and consultations. The sixth global Forum was held in February 2023.

A Global Forum on Remittances, Investment and Development has been convened every two years since 2007 to bring together stakeholders in the remittance and migration systems. In 2022 an estimated 200,000 migrant workers transferred US $626,000m. back to family members in low- and middle-income countries (many in rural areas), supporting, *inter alia,* local education, health and housing requirements. IFAD co-ordinates observance of an annual International Day of Family Remittances (on 16 June). In mid-June 2023 IFAD helped host the latest edition of the Forum (GFRID 2023), in Nairobi, Kenya.

EXTERNAL PARTNERS

IFAD works with the private sector and producer organizations, foundations, academic and research institutions, multilateral finance institutions and other organizations and governments to strengthen its impact and accelerate its objectives. IFAD is a long-standing co-sponsor of the Consultative Group on International Agricultural Research. Within the UN, IFAD works closely with FAO and WFP, all of which share the mandate of achieving SDG 2 (End hunger), and provide financial and technical support to the UN's Committee on World Food Security. The three agencies contribute to an Agricultural Market Information System (AMIS), which aims to increase market transparency and to address the stabilization of food price volatility, and with UNICEF and the World Health Organization, compile the annual *State of Food Security and Nutrition in the World* report. In May 2022, in the context of the recent Russian invasion of Ukraine, IFAD, the IMF, World Bank and other international financial institutions collectively issued the Joint International Financial Institution Plan to Address Food Insecurity, with a focus on the following six objectives: (i) support vulnerable people; (ii) promote open trade; (iii) mitigate fertilizer shortages; (iv) support food production now; (v) invest in climate-resilient agriculture for the future; and (vi) co-ordinate for maximum impact.

IFAD participates in the Steering Committee of UN-Nutrition, which was initiated in 2020—merging the UN Network for Scaling up Nutrition (SUN) Movement and UN System Standing Committee on Nutrition—to co-ordinate UN agencies in advancing nutrition and eliminating hunger, malnutrition and obesity.

REGIONAL ORGANIZATIONS

IFAD is an executing agency of the Green Climate Fund, and of the Global Environmental Facility (GEF, which specializes in combating rural poverty and environmental degradation). From November 2022 IFAD and FAO assumed joint leadership of the GEF's new Food Systems Integrated Program: this aimed to channel some US $230m. (to be amplified by co-financing) in grants towards projects focused on sustainably transforming agrifood systems.

Finance

The provisional regular budget for 2023 amounted to US $175.7m. In accordance with the Articles of Agreement establishing IFAD, the Governing Council periodically undertakes a review of the adequacy of resources available to the Fund and may request members to make additional contributions. In February 2021 member countries pledged $3,800m. in contributions to IFAD12, covering 2022–24. The 13th replenishment consultations commenced in February 2023.

Publications

Annual Report.
Journal of Law and Rural Development.
Resilient Food Systems.
Rural Development Report.
State of Food Security and Nutrition in the World (annually, with FAO, WFP, UNICEF and WHO).

Affiliated Bodies

IFAD hosts the secretariat for the following bodies:

Global Donor Platform for Rural Development: internet donorplatform.org; f. 2003; works to co-ordinate and enhance the effectiveness of rural development assistance, and to promote knowledge sharing and other collaborative processes; contributes to the global debate on rural development, alleviating hunger and transforming food systems; holds an annual general meeting; mems: some 40 national devt agencies, multilateral orgs, development banks, research institutions; Co-Chair. CONRAD REIN, TRISTAN ARMSTRONG.

International Land Coalition: e-mail info@landcoalition.org; internet landcoalition.org; f. 1995 as the Popular Coalition to Eradicate Hunger and Poverty, present name adopted in 2003; committed to enhancing equitable and secure access to land, in order to contribute to the empowerment of the rural poor, the devt of their communities and the alleviation of poverty; a full Assembly of Members meets every 3 years as a Global Land Forum (2022: Swemeh, Jordan, in May); mems: more than 300 national, subregional, regional and international agencies; Dir MIKE TAYLOR (Botswana).

Platform for Agricultural Risk Management (PARM): e-mail parm@ifad.org; internet p4arm.org; f. 2014; aims to strengthen agricultural risk management through knowledge sharing, capacity building and collaboration; a steering cttee of 6 devt agencies works closely with other multilateral partners, research institutes, private sector cos and farmers' orgs; Phase II of PARM was ongoing during 2022–26 in Nepal, Niger, the Pacific Islands, Tanzania and Tunisia (Phase I had focused on 8 African countries).

International Monetary Fund—IMF

Address: 700 19th St, NW, Washington, DC 20431, USA.
Telephone: (202) 623-7000; **fax:** (202) 623-4661; **e-mail:** publicaffairs@imf.org; **internet:** www.imf.org.

The IMF was established at the same time as the World Bank in December 1945, to promote international monetary co-operation, global financial stability, and the expansion and balanced growth of international trade.

Organization
(September 2023)

Managing Director: KRISTALINA GEORGIEVA (Bulgaria).
First Deputy Managing Director: GITA GOPINATH (USA).
Director, African Department: ABEBE AEMRO SELASSIE (Ethiopia).
Director, Middle East and Central Asia Department: JIHAD AZOUR (Lebanon).

BOARD OF GOVERNORS

The highest authority of the Fund is exercised by the Board of Governors, on which each member country is represented by a Governor and an Alternate Governor. The Board normally meets once a year. The Board of Governors has delegated many of its powers to the Executive Directors. However, certain important powers including the conditions governing the admission of new members, adjustment of quotas, and the election of Executive Directors remain the sole responsibility of the Board of Governors.

BOARD OF EXECUTIVE DIRECTORS

The 24-member Board of Executive Directors, responsible for the day-to-day operations of the Fund, is in continuous session in Washington, DC, USA. As in the Board of Governors, the voting power of each member is related to its quota in the Fund, but in practice the Executive Directors normally operate by consensus. On 26 January 2016 a reform amendment entered into effect that altered the composition of the Board of Executive Directors in order to increase the representation of emerging dynamic economies and developing countries, as well as determining that the Board be fully elected by member countries or groups of countries.

REGIONAL REPRESENTATION

There is a network of regional offices and Resident Representatives in more than 90 member countries. In addition, special information and liaison offices are located in Tokyo, Japan (for Asia and the Pacific); in New York, USA (for the UN); and in Europe (including in Paris, France; Geneva, Switzerland; and Belgium, Brussels; and—for Central Europe and the Baltic States—in Warsaw, Poland).

Activities

The Fund works to support sustainable growth and to further international monetary co-operation. It extends financial assistance to countries experiencing actual and potential balance of payments difficulties, provides technical assistance and training to strengthen national economic capacities and promotes the dissemination of economic and financial data by its member states. The Fund undertakes regular consultations with its members and monitoring of their economic policies as part of its broader mandate of surveillance and assessment of global macroeconomic and financial stability.

COVID-19 AND THE GLOBAL FOOD AND NUTRITION SECURITY CRISES

In late March 2020 the IMF Managing Director welcomed the efforts of major central banks to ease monetary policy in response to the escalating COVID-19 crisis, and commended fiscal actions implemented by many governments to protect workers and companies in the interim, and to boost health systems. The Managing Director pledged that, under the unprecedented and extraordinary circumstances, the Fund was ready to deploy all its lending capacity and would increase emergency finance massively. At that time the IMF announced US $50,000m. in funding to support poor and middle-income member states with weak health systems to respond to the pandemic; some $10,000m. of this funding was in the form of zero interest rapid emergency loans. Meanwhile, the IMF's Catastrophe Containment and Relief Trust (CCRT), which provides debt relief to countries hit by catastrophic events, was being urgently replenished to enable the poorest economies to maximize and focus all available resources towards combating the pandemic; a first tranche of CCRT grants was extended in mid-April. Also at that time, the Fund, the World Bank Group and the G20 membership agreed a Debt Service Suspension Initiative (DSSI), providing for the temporary suspension of the debt service payments of up to 73 eligible countries (40 of which were in Africa).

In January 2021 the IMF's *World Economic Outlook* estimated that the global economy had contracted by -3.5% in 2020, and noted that women, youth, workers in informal employment, workers in contact-intensive sectors, and people already living in poverty had been particularly adversely affected by the impacts of the pandemic crisis. From June 2021 the IMF Executive Director participated, with the heads of the World Bank, the World Health Organization and the World Trade Organization (WTO), in a Multilateral Leaders Taskforce on vaccines access. They collectively issued a call for action to generate US $50,000m. in new financing to support a comprehensive health, trade and finance roadmap aimed at bringing an end to the COVID-19 crisis, including the implementation of an accelerated co-ordinated strategy to enable the prompt vaccination of people across the whole world against COVID-19. Meanwhile, the IMF was preparing an unprecedented new SDR allocation to assist its member states (see *Special Drawing Rights*). In July the *World Economic Outlook* noted that access to vaccines represented the principal factor underpinning economic normalization, and a major fault line between advanced and developing economies. The amount of debt service suspended through the DSSI during May 2020–December 2021 (when it expired, having twice been extended, in November 2020 and in April 2021) totalled $12,900m.; 48 of the 73 eligible countries participated in the initiative. During April 2020–9 March 2022 some 31 states received SDR 689.6m. (equivalent to $965.3m.) in debt relief through the CCRT (which had been extended through five tranches). By 9 March 2022 (the date of the final published update on such support) the IMF was making available to member states financial assistance and debt service relief totalling around $250,000m.

In early March 2022, in response to the Russian Federation's military invasion of Ukraine, the IMF warned of the severe impact on the global economy of the onwards consequences of the war, with unprecedented economic, financial and communications sanctions having been imposed against Russia, and global energy and grain prices rising significantly. In May the IMF, World Bank and other international financial institutions (IFIs) collectively issued a joint IFI Action Plan to Address Food Insecurity, with a focus on the following six objectives: (i) support vulnerable people; (ii) promote open trade; (iii) mitigate fertilizer shortages; (iv) support food production now; (v) invest in climate-resilient agriculture for the future; and (vi) co-ordinate for maximum impact. The IMF was also to intensify co-operation with other international financial institutions in support of debt restructurings, was to provide emergency assistance where necessary, and was to use a new Resilience and Sustainability Trust (RST) and associated Resilience and Sustainability Facility (RSF) to provide affordable longer term financing for low-income and vulnerable middle-income countries (including small states) that were implementing structural transitions to meet long-term challenges such as pandemic preparedness and climate change adaptation. In January 2023 the IMF's *Global Economic Outlook* estimated global economic growth in 2022 at 3.4%, and the average global rate of inflation in that year at 8.8% (significantly higher than the level of around 3.5% across 2017–19). The continuation into 2023 of Russia's war against Ukraine, and rises in central bank rates aimed at combating inflation were subduing economic expansion. The report recommended that broad-based fiscal relief measures should be removed, with fiscal support more efficiently targeted at the most vulnerable people who were most impacted by elevated food and energy costs. In April the Fund's *World Economic Outlook* forecast that overall global economic growth would decelerate to 2.8% in 2023, with expansion of only 1.3% predicted for advanced economies. The average global inflation rate was forecast to decline to 7% in 2023.

In February 2023 the heads of the IMF, the World Bank Group, the Food and Agriculture Organization of the UN, the World Food Programme and the WTO issued a third joint statement on the global food and nutrition security crisis (further to statements issued in July and September of the previous year). The statement highlighted ongoing initiatives to counter the escalating crisis of rising food and fertilizer prices and falling production, and identified urgent actions to be undertaken.

The Fund's biannual *Global Financial Stability Report* observed in April 2023 the recent sudden failures of two US banks and loss of market confidence in Credit Suisse—a 'global systemically important bank' and thus required to maintain higher levels of capital than other banks. An IMF Conference on Geoeconomic Fragmentation that was convened in the following month, in Washington, DC, gave consideration to a trend of plateauing global flows of goods and capital and parallel surge in trade restrictions, noting the impacts of an uneven recovery from the 2008–09 global financial crisis, of trade tensions between the USA and China, of the United Kingdom's withdrawal from the European Union (EU) and European single market, and of a mounting number of military conflicts, not least Russia's war against Ukraine.

RESOURCES

Members' fully paid quota subscriptions, in the form of currencies and reserve assets, serve as the principal resources of the IMF. The IMF's resources are held in three accounts: a main General Resources Account; a Special Disbursement Account, in which profits from sales of the Fund's gold are invested; and an Investment Account. The IMF's quota resources may be supplemented by borrowing.

Special Drawing Rights (SDRs): The SDR was introduced in 1970 as a substitute for gold in international payments, and was intended eventually to become the principal reserve asset in the international monetary system. SDRs are allocated to members in proportion to their quotas. In September 1997 the Executive Board approved a special allocation of SDR 21,400m., in order to ensure an SDR to quota ratio of 29.32%, for all member countries: the ensuing Fourth Amendment to the Articles of Agreement came into effect on 10 August 2009, following its acceptance by 60% of member countries, having 85% of the total voting power, and the special allocation, equivalent to some US $33,000m., was implemented on 9 September. On the basis of recommendations made in April 2009 by the IMFC and by G20 heads of state and government, in response to the then global financial crisis, the Board of Governors also approved a third general allocation of SDRs, amounting to SDR 161,200m., in August 2009: this became available to all members, in proportion to their existing quotas, effective from 28 August. In April 2021 the IMFC urged the IMF to propose a new SDR general allocation amounting to $650,000m. (some SDR 456,000m.) aimed at boosting member countries' reserves and liquidity in the context of the ongoing recovery from the COVID-19 crisis; this was approved by the Board of Governors on 2 August.

The list of currencies and the weight of each in the SDR valuation basket is revised every five years (ongoing valuation period: 1 August 2022–31 July 2027). In November 2015 the Executive Board resolved to incorporate the Chinese renminbi into the valuation basket, with effect from 1 October 2016, in addition to the currencies of the European Economic and Monetary Union (the euro), Japan (yen), the UK (pound sterling) and the USA (US dollar) (which had made up the basket since 1999). The value of the SDR averaged US $1.33775 in 2022; it stood at $1.33002 on 1 September 2023.

Quotas: Each member is assigned a quota related to its national income, monetary reserves, trade balance and other economic indicators. A member's subscription is equal to its quota and is payable partly in SDRs and partly in its own currency. The quota determines a member's voting power, which is based on one vote for each SDR 100,000 of its quota plus the 250 votes to which each member is entitled. A member's quota also determines its access to the financial resources of the IMF, and its allocation of SDRs.

Quotas are reviewed at five-yearly intervals, to take into account the state of the world economy and members' different rates of development. Special increases, separate from each General Review, may be made in exceptional circumstances.

In February 2020 the Board of Governors adopted a Resolution that concluded, with no increase, the Fifteenth General Review of Quotas, and provided guidance for a forthcoming Sixteenth General Review of Quotas (to be concluded by 15 December 2023). At September 2023 total quotas in the Fund amounted to SDR 476,272.0m.

Borrowing: In May 1996 the participants (11 member states and central banks) in the General Arrangements to Borrow (GAB, established in 1962), concluded an agreement in principle to expand resources available for borrowing from SDR 17,000m. to SDR 34,000m., by securing the support of 25 countries with the financial capacity to assist the international monetary system. Consequently the New Arrangements to Borrow (NAB) was approved by the Executive Board in January 1997 and became effective in November 1998. The GAB ended on 25 December 2018 (the participants having agreed in December 2017 that the initiative had only limited usefulness).

In April 2009 G20 heads of state and of government resolved to expand the NAB facility, to incorporate all G20 economies, in order to increase its resources by up to SDR 367,500m. (US $500,000m.). They also agreed to support a general allocation of SDRs amounting to a further $250,000m., and to use additional resources from sales of IMF gold to provide $6,000m. in concessional financing for the poorest countries over the next two to three years. In April 2010 the IMF Executive Board approved the expansion and enlargement of NAB borrowing arrangements to SDR 369,997m.; this came into effect in March 2011. EU heads of state and of government agreed in December to allocate to the IMF additional resources of up to $270,000m. in the form of bilateral loans. At meetings held in April and June 2012 G20 member states pledged to increase by more than $456,000m. resources to be made available to the IMF as part of a universal protective firewall to serve the Fund's entire membership. In June the Executive Board approved the modalities to enable bilateral borrowing from member countries as a means of supplementing both quota resources and the institution's standing borrowing arrangements; the Board agreed a new framework in August 2016 to maintain temporary access to bilateral borrowing. During 2021–23 some 40 bilateral borrowing agreements were in effect, with a value of around SDR 135,000m. In February 2016 NAB resources were reduced to SDR 182,000m. In January 2020, however, the IMF Executive Board approved an increase in NAB resources to SDR 364,700m. for the period 2021–25.

LENDING

The Fund makes resources available to eligible members on an essentially short-term and revolving basis to provide temporary assistance to contribute to the solution of their payments problems. The IMF holds both usable currencies (where the external payments position of the issuing member is strong) and unusable (weak) currencies. A member obtaining IMF resources 'purchases'—draws—either SDRs, or else the currency of another member in exchange for an equivalent amount (in SDR terms) of its own currency (so-called exchange purchases). The member then later 'repurchases' its own currency—i.e. reverses the transaction.

Before making a purchase, a member must show that its balance of payments or reserve position makes the purchase necessary. Apart from this requirement, reserve tranche purchases (i.e. purchases that do not bring the Fund's holdings of the member's currency to a level above its quota) are permitted unconditionally. With further purchases, however, the Fund's policy of conditionality means that a recipient country must agree to adjust its economic policies, as stipulated by the IMF. All requests other than for use of the reserve tranche are examined by the Executive Board to determine whether the proposed use would be consistent with the Fund's policies, and a member must discuss its proposed adjustment programme (including fiscal, monetary, exchange and trade policies) with IMF staff. In March 2009 the Executive Board approved reforms to modernize the Fund's conditionality policy, including greater use of pre-set qualification criteria and monitoring structural policy implementation by programme review (rather than by structural performance criteria).

Purchases outside the reserve tranche are made in four credit tranches, each equivalent to 25% of the member's quota; a member must then repurchase its own currency within a specified timescale. A credit tranche purchase is usually made under a Stand-by Arrangement (SBA) with the Fund (the core lending instrument, created in 1952 and revised in 2009), or under the Extended Fund Facility (EFF, launched in 1974). An SBA is normally of one to three years' duration, and the amount is made available in instalments, subject to the member's observance of performance criteria; repurchases must be made within three-and-a-quarter to five years. Repurchases under the EFF must be made within four-and-a-half to 10 years.

Members' annual access to IMF resources is reviewed periodically. In February 2016 the Executive Board set the annual access limit under SBAs and EFF credits (q.v.) at up to 145% of a member's quota, with the cumulative access limit set at 435%, with higher access considered in exceptional circumstances. On 6 March 2023 the annual access limit for the EFF was temporarily (for one year) increased to 200%, and the cumulative access limit raised to 600%.

In January 2010 the Fund introduced new concessional facilities for low-income countries as part of broader reforms to enhance flexibility of lending and to focus support closer to specific national requirements. The three new facilities aimed to support country-owned programmes to achieve macroeconomic positions consistent with sustainable poverty reduction and economic growth. They carried a zero interest rate, although this was to be reviewed every two years. An Extended Credit Facility (ECF) succeeded the former Poverty Reduction and Growth Facility (PRGF, used during 1999–2009) to provide medium-term balance of payments assistance to low-income members. ECF loans were repayable over 10 years, with a five-and-a-half-year grace period. A Stand-by Credit Facility (SCF) replaced the high-access component of a former Exogenous Shocks Facility (operational from January 2006–December 2009) in order to provide short-term balance of payments financial assistance in response to the adverse economic impact of events beyond government control, including on a precautionary basis. SCF loans were repayable over eight years, with a grace period of four years. A Rapid Credit Facility (RCF) was to provide financial assistance to PRGF-eligible members requiring urgent balance of payments assistance, under a range of circumstances. Loans were repayable over 10 years, with a five-and-a-half-year grace period. In November 2011 a Rapid Financing Instrument (RFI) was launched, for which all member states were eligible, and which was designed to support urgent balance of payments requirements, including those arising from exogenous shocks such as commodity price changes, natural disasters, and post-conflict and other extreme situations. Low-income member states may also make use of a non-financial Policy Support Instrument (PSI), providing access to IMF monitoring and other support aimed at consolidating economic performance.

In February 2015 the IMF transformed its Post-Catastrophe Debt Relief Trust, established in 2010 following the devastating earthquake in Haiti, into the CCRT. With a similar objective of providing debt relief to low-income member states in order to free up resources to meet exceptional balance of payments needs, the CCRT incorporated a new window to support states affected by public health crises, in addition to a window to respond to natural disasters.

In May 2017 the Executive Board increased the annual access limit under the RCF and the RFI to 60% (from 37.5%) of a member's quota, in circumstances involving large natural disasters. The limits on access to the Fund's concessional facilities for low-income countries were expanded by 50% in 2015, and by a further one-third in May 2019. Following the onset of the COVID-19 pandemic, the Executive Board approved temporary increases in the annual limit on overall access to resources in the General Resources Account and the Poverty Reduction and Growth Facility Trust (PRGT, established in 1999), and increased access to the RCF's Exogenous Shock window and the RFI's regular window; in September 2020 and in March 2021 the exceptional terms were further extended. In June 2021 temporary increases were agreed on access to the RCF's and RFI's Large Natural Disaster (LND) windows. In December the Executive Board endorsed temporary increases until 30 June 2023 on access to the RFI's regular window and to the RCF's Exogenous Shock window, and to both instruments' LND windows. In July 2021 normal access to the PRGT was increased to 145% of a member state's quota. In September 2022 the Executive Board approved a temporary Food Shock Window (FSW) under the RCF, to provide emergency financing for balance of payments assistance relating to the volatility of food supplies and production. Under the FSW, which was to remain open until 29 September 2023, member states were to be permitted to access up to 50% of their quota.

In March 2009 the Executive Board introduced a Flexible Credit Line (FCL) facility, which provided credit to countries with very strong economic foundations, but was also to be primarily considered as precautionary. The FCL had a repayment period of up to five years and no access 'cap'. In August 2010 the duration of the FCL, and credit available through it, were increased. In November 2011 a relatively flexible Precautionary and Liquidity Line (PLL) was initiated, which was to be made available to countries 'with sound economic fundamentals' and 'sound policies' that were encountering broadly challenging circumstances—including as insurance against shocks and as a short-term liquidity window. PLL arrangements may have a duration of either six months or one to two years.

In the year ending 30 April 2022 purchases from the General Resources Account amounted to SDR 8,884m. Outstanding credit from the account as at 31 January 2023 totalled SDR 94,985m. The largest user of credit from the account at that time was Argentina, followed by Egypt, Ukraine, Ecuador and Pakistan.

In 2022/23 a new FCL was approved for Morocco (amounting to SDR 3,726.2m.); and an SDR 2,350.2m. EFF was approved for Egypt.

The Fund's non-financing Policy Coordination Instrument (PCI) enables member states not requiring resources (at the time of approval) to signal commitment to reforms, and also to promote financing from external sources.

SURVEILLANCE

Under its Articles of Agreement, the Fund is mandated to oversee the effective functioning of the international monetary system. The main tools of surveillance are regular, bilateral consultations with member countries conducted in accordance with Article IV of the Articles of Agreement, which cover fiscal and monetary policies, balance of payments and external debt developments, as well as policies that affect the economic performance of a country, such as the labour market, social and environmental issues and good governance, and aspects of the country's capital accounts, and finance and banking sectors. The Executive Board monitors global economic developments and discusses policy implications from a multilateral perspective, based partly on *World Economic Outlook* reports and *Global Financial Stability Reports*. In July 2012 the Executive Board adopted a Decision on Bilateral and Multilateral Surveillance (the so-called Integrated Surveillance Decision), which aimed to strengthen the legal framework underpinning surveillance activities. In September the Board endorsed a Financial Surveillance Strategy detailing steps towards further strengthening the financial surveillance framework.

In the 1990s a two-tier standards framework was initiated: the General Data Dissemination System (GDDS, launched in 1997), applicable to all Fund members, and the Special Data Dissemination Standard (SDDS, established in 1996), designed to provide reliable economic statistical information on member countries engaged in or seeking access to international capital markets. SDDS Plus, introduced in 2012, covers an expanded set of data categories. By mid-2023 78 countries or territories had subscribed to the SDDS, of which 30 had graduated to SDDS Plus. A Dissemination Standards Bulletin Board aims to ensure that information on SDDS subscribing countries is widely available. In July 2015 the Executive Board approved an enhanced GDDS (e-GDDS), which superseded the original GDDS.

The IMF's Financial Sector Assessment Programme (FSAP), initiated in 1999 and strengthened in 2009, aims to promote greater global financial security through the preparation of confidential detailed evaluations of the financial sectors of individual countries.

CAPACITY DEVELOPMENT

Technical assistance is provided by online training courses and engagement, special missions or resident representatives, or through specialized centres.

REGIONAL ORGANIZATIONS

The United Nations in the Middle East and North Africa

A Beirut, Lebanon-based technical assistance centre for the Middle East (METAC) was inaugurated in 2004. In 2011 a IMF-Middle East Center for Economics and Finance was inaugurated in Kuwait.

In May 2009 the IMF launched the first of a series of thematic trust funds: the Trust Fund on Anti-Money Laundering and Combating the Financing of Terrorism (in its third phase of operations during 2020–24). A Managing Natural Resource Wealth Trust Fund was initiated in May 2011; a Revenue Mobilization Trust Fund in August 2016; and a Financial Sector Stability Fund in April 2017.

Publications

Annual Report.
External Sector Report (annually).
F & D—Finance and Development (quarterly).
Fiscal Monitor (2 a year).
Global Financial Stability Report (2 a year).
Handbook on Securities Statistics (published jointly by the IMF, the BIS and the European Central Bank).
Joint BIS-IMF-OECD-World Bank Statistics on External Debt (quarterly).
Regional Economic Outlooks.
World Economic Outlook (2 a year).

Other country reports, staff discussion notes, working papers, economic and financial surveys, occasional papers, pamphlets, books.

Statistics

MEMBERSHIP AND QUOTAS IN THE MIDDLE EAST AND NORTH AFRICA
(million SDR)

Country	September 2023
Algeria	1,959.9
Bahrain	395.0
Cyprus	303.8
Egypt	2,037.1
Iran	3,567.1
Iraq	1,663.8
Israel	1,920.9
Jordan	343.1
Kuwait	1,933.5
Lebanon	633.5
Libya	1,573.2
Morocco	894.4
Oman	544.4
Qatar	735.1
Saudi Arabia	9,992.6
Syrian Arab Republic	293.6
Tunisia	545.2
Türkiye (Turkey)	4,658.6
United Arab Emirates	2,311.2
Yemen	487.0

World Health Organization—WHO

Address: 20 ave Appia, 1202 Geneva 27, Switzerland.
Telephone: 227912111; **fax:** 227913111; **e-mail:** info@who.int; **internet:** www.who.int.

WHO, established in 1948, is the lead agency within the UN system concerned with the protection and improvement of public health. It co-ordinates and undertakes disease control, prevention and surveillance, promotes lifelong good health, and supports the development of equitable, sustainable health systems.

Organization
(September 2023)

WORLD HEALTH ASSEMBLY (WHA)

The Assembly meets once a year (in May) in Geneva, Switzerland, and is responsible for policymaking. It also reviews budgetary contributions; sets the biennial budget; appoints the Director-General; and admits new members. The 76th WHA was held in May 2023.

EXECUTIVE BOARD

The Board is composed of 34 health experts designated by a member state that has been elected by the WHA to serve on the Board; each expert serves for three years. The Board holds a principal annual meeting every January to agree the agenda of the next WHA, and a second meeting in May to follow up the Assembly. The Board is responsible for putting into effect the decisions and policies of the Assembly.

HEADQUARTERS

The Deputy Director-General; Executive Director for Health Emergencies, Preparedness and Response; WHO Chief Scientist (who leads the Science Division); Chef de Cabinet; Head of a WHO liaison office in New York (USA); and Assistant Executive Directors leading divisions of External Relations and Governance; Business Operations (also leading the WHO Academy); and Data, Analytics and Delivery for Impact all report directly to the Director-General. Assistant Executive Directors leading departments of Universal Health Coverage (UHC) and Life Course; UHC and Communicable/Non-Communicable Diseases; UHC/Healthier Populations; Antimicrobial Resistance; and Access to Medicines and Health Products report directly to the Deputy Director-General. The Executive Director for Health Emergencies, Preparedness and Response presides over divisions of Emergency Preparedness; Emergency Response; and Intelligence and Surveillance Systems.

Director-General: Dr TEDROS ADHANOM GHEBREYESUS (Ethiopia).
Deputy Director-General: Dr ZSUZSANNA JAKAB (Hungary).
Chief Scientist: Dr JEREMY FARRAR (UK).
Executive Director, Health Emergencies, Preparedness and Response: Dr MICHAEL RYAN (Ireland).
Special Envoy for Climate Change and Health: VANESSA KERRY (USA).

PRINCIPAL OFFICES

Each of WHO's six geographical regions has its own organization, consisting of a regional committee representing relevant member states and associate members, and a regional office staffed by experts in various fields of health.

Africa Office: Cité du Djoue, BP 06, Brazzaville, Republic of the Congo; tel. 83-94-02; e-mail afrgocom@who.int; internet www.afro.who.int; Dir Dr MATSHIDISO REBECCA MOETI (Botswana).

Eastern Mediterranean Office: POB 7608, Abdul Razzak al Sanhouri St, Cairo (Nasr City) 11371, Egypt; tel. (2) 2765000; fax (2) 6702492; internet www.emro.who.int; Dir Dr AHMED AL-MANDHARI (Oman).

WHO Academy: internet www.who.int/about/who-academy; to be operational from 2024, headquartered at WHO's Lyon Hub (France) (under construction in 2023); aims to offer a single digital learning platform, as well as in-person courses, for WHO internal staff and also for outside learners, supporting lifelong learning on health issues, as well as mid-career training programmes, and health emergency preparedness training and simulations; Head RAUL THOMAS (acting).

WHO Centre for Health Development: I. H. D. Centre Bldg, 9th Floor, 5-1-1 Wakinohama-Kaigandori, Chuo-ku, Kobe, Japan; tel. (78) 230-3100; fax (78) 230-3178; e-mail wkc@who.int; internet extranet.who.int/kobe_centre/en; f. 1995; Dir Dr SARAH LOUISE BARBER (USA).

Activities

WHO is the UN system's co-ordinating authority for health (defined as 'a state of complete physical, mental and social wellbeing and not merely the absence of disease and infirmity'). WHO's objective is stated in its Constitution as 'the attainment by all peoples of the highest possible level of health'. It aims to provide leadership on global public health matters, in partnership, with other agencies, as well as to help to shape the global health research agenda, and to monitor and assess health trends. WHO provides technical and policy support to member countries and extends aid following emergencies and natural disasters.

WHO supports the pursuit of the Sustainable Development Goals (SDGs), which were designed to contribute—either directly or indirectly—to improved global health. SDG 3 explicitly aimed 'to ensure healthy lives and promote wellbeing for all at all ages', and was underpinned by some 13 health targets to be achieved by 2030. These included reducing the maternal mortality ratio to less than 70 per 100,000 live births; ending preventable deaths of newborns, to at least as low as 12 per 1,000 live births, and lowering the under-five mortality rate to at least as low as 25 per 1,000 live births; ending the epidemics of AIDS, tuberculosis (TB), malaria, and neglected tropical diseases, and combating hepatitis, water-borne diseases and other communicable diseases; and reducing by one-third—through prevention and treatment—premature mortality from non-communicable diseases (NCDs); promoting mental health and wellbeing; ensuring universal access to sexual and reproductive health services; strengthening prevention and treatment of substance abuse; enhancing the implementation of the Framework Convention on Tobacco Control; substantially lowering numbers of deaths and illnesses from hazardous chemicals, environmental pollution and contamination; ensuring UHC, including financial risk protection, and access to high-quality essential healthcare services, essential medicines and vaccines for all; advancing research, development and affordability of vaccines and essential medicines for those communicable and NCDs that mainly impact developing countries; significantly increasing health financing and the recruitment, development and training of the health workforce in developing countries; strengthening the capacity of all countries, in particular developing countries, for early warning, risk reduction and management of national and global health risks; and reducing by one-half the number of global deaths and injuries arising from road traffic accidents.

General Programme of Work: WHO's 13th General Programme of Work, adopted by the WHA in May 2018 to guide the organization's activities during 2019–23, had a 'triple billion goal', with the following specific objectives: by 2023 1,000m. more people globally were to benefit from UHC; protection against health emergencies was to be improved for 1,000m. people worldwide; and 1,000m. more people were to enjoy enhanced health and wellbeing. WHO welcomed the establishment in May 2020 of the independent Geneva-based grant-making WHO Foundation, which was to support WHO and its implementing partners in delivering the triple billion objectives.

PANDEMIC PREVENTION, PREPAREDNESS AND RESPONSE

WHO keeps diseases and other health problems under constant surveillance, promotes the exchange of prompt and accurate information and of notification of outbreaks of diseases, and administers the binding 2005 International Health Regulations, which aim to support the international community in preventing and reacting to severe potentially transboundary public health risks. Within the UN system, WHO co-ordinates the international response to emergencies and natural disasters in the health field, in close co-operation with other agencies. In this context, WHO provides expert advice on epidemiological surveillance, control of communicable diseases, public health information, and health emergency training. Its emergency preparedness activities include co-ordination, policymaking and planning, awareness-building, technical advice, training, publication of standards and guidelines, and research. Its emergency relief activities include organizational support, the provision of emergency drugs and supplies, and conducting technical emergency assessment missions. WHO's *R&D Blueprint* is a global preparedness plan focused on the swift activation of research and development activities during epidemics.

Under the International Health Regulations, states parties are required to follow safeguarding procedures including reporting certain critical public health events to WHO, and WHO may declare as a Public Health Emergency of International Concern (PHEIC) any extraordinary event that represents a public health risk to multiple countries, and which requires intensified mobilization of resources, and a co-ordinated global response, under the guidance of a dedicated International Health Regulations Emergency Committee of relevant experts. During the period 2009–mid-2023 seven PHEICs were declared, in respect of outbreaks of H1N1 (swine flu) in 2009, wild poliovirus in 2014 (still in force as at mid-2023), Ebola Virus Disease (EVD) in 2014 and 2019, the Zika virus in 2016, novel coronavirus disease (COVID-19) during the period 30 January 2020–5 May 2023, and mpox (initially referred to as Monkeypox, subsequently renamed) during mid-2022–May 2023.

WHO's Global Alert and Response framework aims to provide an effective international system for co-ordinated response to epidemics and other public health emergencies. The Global Outbreak Alert and Response Network (GOARN), established in 2000 by WHO and several partner institutions in epidemic surveillance, maintains constant vigilance regarding outbreaks of disease, and links worldwide expertise to provide an immediate response capability. WHO assists member states in the development and implementation of domestic capacities for epidemic preparedness and response through strengthening national laboratory capacities and early warning alert and response mechanisms; supporting training programmes; and promoting standardized approaches in relation to biorisk reduction and epidemic-prone infections. In July 2011 WHO launched the Global Infection Prevention and Control (GIPC) Network, which provides technical support to member states, through the dissemination of epidemic-prone infection prevention and control (IPC) policies and guidance; the compilation of relevant indicators; and generic training curricula. In May 2023 the 76th WHA resolved to draft, during 2023–24, the inaugural Global Strategy on IPC.

WHO aims to strengthen the national capacity of member states to reduce the adverse health consequences of disasters, including conflict, natural disasters and food insecurity. WHO has also taken into consideration the potential malevolent use of bacteria, viruses, toxins, or of chemical agents, in acts of biological or chemical terrorism. In responding to emergency situations, WHO works to develop projects and activities that will assist national authorities in rebuilding or strengthening their own capacity to handle the impact of such situations. In April 2015 WHO initiated a global registry of fast-response Emergency Medical Teams (EMTs). In October 2022 the 5th EMT Global Meeting, held in Yerevan, Armenia, launched an EMTs 2030 Strategy, focused on collectively addressing natural disasters and disease outbreaks.

The sudden emergence and global severity of the COVID-19 crisis, from 2020, had a catalytic impact on the development of the global pandemic preparedness and response architecture. A WHO BioHub System for Preparedness and Response to Epidemics and Pandemics, announced in November 2020, aimed to enhance the rapid sharing of viruses and other pathogens between research laboratories worldwide. The first WHO BioHub Facility, based in Switzerland, was initiated in May 2021. A Berlin, Germany-based WHO Hub for Pandemic and Epidemic Intelligence, inaugurated in September, was to support national governments in monitoring emerging variants of concern of COVID-19 and in promptly detecting and responding to pandemic and epidemic risks. In October WHO established a Scientific Advisory Group for the Origins of Novel Pathogens (SAGO), tasked with investigating the origins of the COVID-19 pandemic, and with assessing outbreaks of new diseases with the potential to cause epidemics/pandemics. A special session of the WHA held on 1 December agreed to establish an intergovernmental negotiating body to draft a new global framework instrument on pandemic prevention, preparedness and response (as recommended by an Independent Panel for Pandemic Preparedness and Response—established by the WHA in May 2020 to conduct an independent and comprehensive evaluation of the global response to the COVID-19 pandemic). In March 2022 WHO initiated a Global Genomic Surveillance Strategy for Pathogens with Pandemic and Epidemic Potential, to cover the period 2022–32. In April 2022 a provisional consensus was reached by the ministers responsible for finance of the G20 member states on establishing, under World Bank auspices, a Financial Intermediary Fund for Pandemic Prevention, Preparedness and Response. In May a (second) Global COVID-19 Summit generated pledges of US $712m. towards the new fund, in addition to previous commitments totalling $250m. In April 2023 WHO launched a new Preparedness and Resilience for Emerging Threats (PRET) initiative, which was to have an initial focus on coronaviruses, influenza, respiratory syncytial viruses, and other respiratory pathogens. WHO and partners launched an International Pathogen Surveillance Network (IPSN) in the following month.

WHO CHIEF SCIENTIST AND SCIENCE DIVISION

The WHO Chief Scientist and Science Division covers norms and standards, research and knowledge, and aims to scale up the application of advances in digital health and innovation. The WHO Science Council—comprising nine distinguished scientists—was inaugurated in April 2021, and provides guidance on the organization's science and research strategy. In April 2022 the Science Division issued a policy brief stipulating that all research undertaken by WHO or with WHO's support should be shared equitably, ethically and efficiently.

WHO works to develop national drugs policies and global guidelines, and promotes the rational use of medicines, and compliance with international drug control requirements. It supports national drug-regulatory authorities and drug-procurement agencies and facilitates international pharmaceutical trade through the exchange of technical information and the harmonization of internationally respected norms and standards.

WHO's Family of International Classifications (WHO-FIC) includes the International Classification of Diseases (ICD), providing an etiological framework of health conditions.

An expert WHO Prequalification Team compiles the WHO List of Prequalified Medicinal Products, with the aim of guaranteeing the safety and quality of medicines supplied by procurement agencies.

WHO's Global Strategy on Digital Health, covering 2020–25, prioritizes the development of accessible, appropriate, affordable, sustainable, 'person-centric' digital technologies as a means of promoting UHC and of achieving the SDGs. The Strategy emphasizes that health data must be classified as sensitive personal information that requires a high security standard. WHO released a series of recommendations in April 2019 on means of using digital technology to improve health. Under a partnership on digital health initiated in June 2023 by WHO and the European Commission, WHO was to use the European Union's system of seamless cross-border digital COVID-19 certification (introduced in mid-2021) as the template for developing a new WHO Global Digital Health Certification Network (GDHCN). The GDHCN aimed to facilitate co-ordinated global mobility and protection in the event of future pandemics or other global health threats.

UHC AND THE LIFE COURSE

UHC: In December 2016 WHO launched the UHC Data Portal, which tracks what proportion of national populations have access to 16 essential health services, and provides data on the financial impact on households of private health care. In September 2019 WHO, with 11 other agencies, launched a Global Action Plan for Healthy Lives and Wellbeing for All, under which they pledged to provide more streamlined support to countries' delivery of UHC and of the health-related SDG targets. The first UN High-level Meeting on UHC was convened in that month at the UN General Assembly, in New York, USA, with participation by heads of state and of government, other senior political representatives, health leaders, and policymakers. The meeting adopted a Political Declaration on advancing commitments towards the achievement of UHC. Commitments included the implementation of a recommended additional primary health care investment equivalent to 1% of GDP, the establishment of mechanisms to ensure that no one should suffer financial hardship linked to the cost of health care, and the implementation of interventions to combat diseases, and to protect women's and children's health through accessible essential health services, such as antenatal care, immunization and healthy lifestyle advice. Leaders committed to strengthening their health workforces, health infrastructures, and health governance capacity. They were to present a progress report to the UN General Assembly in 2023.

In November 2020 the 73rd WHA established a Council on the Economics of Health for All, to focus on using investments in health to foster sustainable economic growth; its component 11 leading experts on health and economics were appointed in May 2021.

In June 2023, during the Summit for a New Global Financing Pact, convened in Paris, France, WHO, the African Development Bank, European Investment Bank and Islamic Development Bank collectively launched a Health Impact Investment Platform, focused on strengthening essential, climate and crisis-resilient primary health care services in low and middle income states. Initially some €1,500m. in concessional loans and grants was to be made available through the platform. WHO was to have responsibility for the overall co-ordination of policy, ensuring the alignment of the Platform's financing decisions with national health priorities and strategies.

Access to Medicines and Health Products: WHO promotes access to essential drugs of good quality at low cost, and supports the November 2001 Doha Declaration on the Agreement on Trade Related Aspects of Intellectual Property Rights (TRIPS) and Public Health, which affirms the right of developing countries to protect public health through the full use of flexible TRIPS provisions. The WHO Essential Medicines and Health Products Price and Availability Monitoring application analyses data on the availability and cost of medicines. WHO provides information to health agencies and care providers on the safety and efficacy of drugs, with particular regard to counterfeit and substandard products, and works to keep substandard medicines away from the global supply chain.

WHO Patient Safety facilitates the development of patient safety policy and practice across all WHO member states. WHO promotes worldwide co-operation on blood safety and clinical technology, supporting states in ensuring access (based on Voluntary Non-Remunerated Donation) to safe blood, blood products and transfusions, as well as to healthcare technologies. WHO supported the organization of the fifth Global Ministerial Summit on Patient Safety, which was convened in February 2023, in Geneva.

Life Course and Ageing: WHO supports the Global Strategy for Women's, Children's and Adolescents' Health, which was initiated by the UN Secretary-General in September 2015. The Global Strategy laid out a roadmap that comprised targets aligned with the SDGs—to be achieved by 2030—and was aimed at ending all preventable deaths of women, children and adolescents, and at ensuring that they should thrive and should transform the world. In February 2017 WHO, UNICEF and partners initiated a Network for Improving Quality of Care for Maternal, Newborn and Child Health. In February 2018 WHO released a series of guidelines aimed at establishing global care standards for healthy pregnant women; these aimed to minimize unnecessary medical interventions.

In May 2016 WHO issued guidelines to assist health workers in supporting all girls and women with the physical and mental health consequences of female genital mutilation (FGM)—estimated to number more than 200m. worldwide.

WHO forecasts that by 2050 nearly 2,000m. people globally will be aged over 60 years. Its Global Network of Age-Friendly Cities and Communities aims to support the creation of environments that would enable older people to remain active and healthy. A UN Decade of Healthy Ageing was being observed during 2021–30, with a focus on age-friendly environments; combating ageism; integrated care; and long-term care.

Immunization and Vaccines: WHO, UNICEF and partners collaborated in reducing the global immunization coverage from 20% in the early 1980s to a targeted rate of 80% by the end of 1990. Some 81% of infants had received three doses of a DTP (diphtheria, tetanus and pertussis) vaccine in 2021, the rate having declined—following the onset of the COVID-19 crisis—from 86% at the end of 2019. WHO's guiding Strategic Advisory Group of Experts (SAGE) on Immunization was established in 1999. WHO's Immunization Agenda 2030 (IA2030) aimed to extend vaccines 'to everyone everywhere' by 2030. WHO is a founding partner of Gavi, the Vaccine Alliance, which was established in 2000 to enhance immunization coverage in developing countries through direct funding and new pricing arrangements with manufacturers.

The WHO Vaccine Pipeline Tracker publishes lists of candidate vaccines under development in selected pathogen areas. In 2023 WHO was defining regional priority targets for new vaccine development for non-epidemic pathogens, with a focus on TB, HIV, Klebsiella pneumoniae, Streptococcus pyogenes, Shigella, and respiratory syncytial virus.

WHO's Emergency Use Listing (EUL) procedure reviews the safety, quality and efficacy of as yet unlicensed vaccines, therapeutics and diagnostics.

UHC/COMMUNICABLE AND NONCOMMUNICABLE DISEASES

WHO aims to reduce the burden of infectious and parasitic communicable diseases, identifying these as a major obstacle to social and economic progress, particularly in developing countries. Emerging and re-emerging diseases, those likely to cause epidemics, zoonoses (diseases or infections passed from vertebrate animals to humans by means of parasites, viruses, bacteria or unconventional agents), diseases attributable to factors such as environmental changes and changes in farming practices, outbreaks of unknown etiology, and the undermining of some drug therapies by the spread of antimicrobial resistance, are main areas of concern.

In May 2017 the 70th WHA adopted a Global Vector Control Response programme which, during the period 2017–30, was to support countries and development partners in strengthening vector control as a principal means of preventing and addressing outbreaks of communicable diseases.

WHO works with animal health sector partners at the human–animal interface at national level to identify and reduce animal health and public health risks. In 2019 WHO, FAO and the World Organisation for Animal Health (WOAH) published *A Tripartite Guide to Addressing Zoonotic Diseases in Countries* to support implementation of a multisectoral One Health approach to disease control. In May 2021 WHO, FAO, the UN Environment Programme (UNEP) and WOAH established a One Health High-Level Expert Panel, which was tasked with advancing understanding of the emergence and spread of zoonotic diseases that have the potential to generate human pandemics. In April 2022 the four organizations concluded a Memorandum of Understanding that provided for the establishment of a Quadripartite Collaboration for One Health, which was collectively to address challenges at the human-animal-plant-ecosystem interface. In October 2022 the Quadripartite launched a One Health Joint Plan of Action (OH-JPA), which was aimed at collectively integrating systems and capacities to enhance the prevention, detection and response to threats posed to the health of humans, animals, plants and the environment, while also contributing to sustainable development. In March 2023 the Quadripartite heads jointly issued a call to global action, urging that the concept of One Health should be prioritized in the international political agenda; that One Health policies, strategies and plans should be strengthened and accelerated; that intersectoral One Health-focused workforces should be established; that the prevention of pandemics and health threats should be addressed at source, with focus on activities and locations that present a significant risk of zoonotic spillover from animals to humans; that One Health-related scientific knowledge sharing should be strengthened; and that investment in One Health strategies and plans should be increased.

A Quadripartite Technical Group on the Economics of Antimicrobial Resistance was established in June 2023.

Combating HIV/AIDS, TB and malaria are organization-wide priorities and, as such, are supported not only by their own areas of work but also by activities undertaken in other areas. TB is the principal cause of death for people infected with the HIV virus and an estimated one-third of people living with HIV/AIDS globally are co-infected with TB. In July 2000 a meeting of the G7 and the Russian Federation launched the Global Fund to Fight AIDS, TB and Malaria (as previously proposed by the UN Secretary-General and recommended by the WHA).

COVID-19 Pandemic: On 31 December 2019 WHO's country office in the People's Republic of China reported that a cluster of cases of an apparently zoonotic viral respiratory illness had emerged in Wuhan City, Hubei Province; a week later the Chinese authorities confirmed that a newly identified coronavirus was in circulation. WHO experts were deployed immediately (in January 2020) to address the emerging virus, and technical guidance was issued on relevant clinical management, case definitions, surveillance, infection prevention and control, and on reducing zoonotic transmission; advisory notices for international traffic were also released. On 30 January WHO formally declared the intensifying new coronavirus epidemic to be a PHEIC. In February the highly contagious and rapidly spreading new virus was officially termed severe acute respiratory syndrome coronavirus 2—SARS-CoV-2—and the disease that it was causing in humans was formally named COVID-19. At the beginning of February 2020 WHO launched a preparedness and response plan, with a focus on ending human–human and zoonotic transmission of the virus, protecting frontline health workers, strengthening the capacity of fragile health systems to detect and diagnose the virus and to support patients, and minimizing the social and economic impact of the crisis. A Global Research Roadmap was formulated to effect a co-ordinated scientific response to the epidemic. On 11 March WHO declared the outbreak to be a global pandemic, expressing deep concern at 'the alarming levels of spread and severity'. The declaration was intended to stimulate all governments to adopt emergency protection and social measures to arrest the further spread of COVID-19. During March WHO established, with the UN Foundation and Swiss Philanthropy Foundation, a COVID-19 Solidarity Response Fund. In the following month WHO and partners initiated the Access to COVID-19 Tools (ACT) Accelerator (q.v.), and in early June a US $2,000m. procurement fund was announced to support poorer countries to access COVID-19 vaccines. In May 2021 WHO assigned a new naming system for public discourse of the identified variants of SARS-CoV-2 based on the Greek alphabet, rather than by the country or region where they were first detected. WHO's Director-General participated from mid-2021 in a Multilateral Leaders Taskforce on vaccines access with the WTO Director-General, IMF Executive Director and World Bank President. In August WHO published guidelines on the technical requirements for the issuance of digital certificates demonstrating vaccination against COVID-19. A WHO-WTO-World Intellectual Property Organization Trilateral COVID-19 Technical Assistance Platform was initiated in April 2022. In the following month the second Global COVID-19 Summit raised commitments that were directly in support of COVID-19 and related response activities that totalled nearly $2,500m.

By mid-2023 15 COVID-19 vaccines had been validated for emergency use by WHO's EUL prodecure. According to WHO some 13,461,864,305 COVID-19 vaccine doses had been administered globally by 30 July (including booster doses, i.e. reinforcing a completed primary vaccination schedule). As at 26 May a complete primary vaccination schedule had been completed by more than 70% of the population in 67 of WHO's member states. According to the Global Dashboard for Vaccine Equity—an initiative of WHO, UNDP and the University of Oxford—35.4% of people in low-income countries globally had received at least one dose of a COVID-19 vaccine by 26 July.

The ACT Accelerator, initiated in April 2020 by WHO, the European Commission, the Bill & Melinda Gates Foundation, and the French Government, comprises, *inter alia,* Gavi, the Vaccine Alliance, the Coalition for Epidemic Preparedness Innovations—CEPI, other health organizations, the World Bank Group, scientists, governments, civil society representatives, businesses, and philanthropists. It was tasked with accelerating the development and production of tools to combat the COVID-19 pandemic, and ensuring their equitable distribution. Its work has four pillars: diagnostics, treatment, health system strengthening, and vaccines (known as the COVID-19 Vaccines Global Access—COVAX Facility, and co-led by WHO, Gavi, the Vaccine Alliance, and CEPI). WHO leads the Accelerator's cross-cutting Access and Allocation dimension, which aims to formulate the framework underpinning the fair and equitable allocation of the tools that the Accelerator develops and produces. Gavi manages the COVAX Advance Market Commitment (AMC—the mechanism that supports the participation of low- and middle-income countries in the Facility). COVAX vaccine research and development is led by CEPI. A COVID-19 Vaccine Delivery Partnership (CoVDP), comprising WHO, UNICEF and Gavi was launched in January 2022, with a focus on increasing the COVID-19 vaccination rate (to an aspirational goal of 70% national coverage) in 34 AMC-supported countries where, in January, coverage stood at or at less than 10% of the population. By 26 May 2023 2,200m. people in AMC countries had completed a full primary COVID-19 vaccination schedule, and 642m. had received at least one booster dose.

Notable discrepancies have been reported between countries' COVID-19 data methodologies. Data collection on confirmed COVID-19 case numbers has depended upon the extent of national testing programmes, which by 2022 had largely subsided in states with high COVID-19 vaccination coverage, and was from the start of the pandemic very significantly lower across low-income countries. During the initial stages of data collection inconsistencies were reported relating to the inclusion of deaths that had occurred in care homes for the elderly. As at 2 August 2023 some 6,953,743 COVID-19-related deaths had been formally confirmed worldwide, of which 2,958,858 had been recorded in the Americas, 2,245,851 in Europe, 806,590 in South-East Asia, 415,641 in Western Pacific, 351,372 in Eastern Mediterranean and 175,418 in Africa. At that time Peru had, globally, by far the highest recorded ratio of fatalities attributed to COVID-19 per 100,000 population: 671.4.

Other Communicable Acute Respiratory Diseases: From March 2003 WHO co-ordinated an international investigation into Severe Acute Respiratory Syndrome (SARS), a previously unknown atypical coronavirus, and provided logistical, epidemiological and clinical support to combat its spread.

WHO monitors the spread of the related Middle East respiratory syndrome coronavirus (MERS-CoV); as at 28 February 2023 some 2,604 laboratory-confirmed cases of MERS-CoV had been reported since June 2012, including 936 related deaths. The reported cases had initially arisen in Saudi Arabia (primarily), Iran, Jordan, Kuwait, Qatar, the United Arab Emirates (UAE) and Yemen; by 2023 cases in 20 other countries had been recorded. Evidence of MERS-CoV infection has been found in dromedary camels, representing a direct zoonotic risk to humans.

Cholera: In October 2017 WHO's Global Task Force on Cholera Control (GTFCC—established in 1992, and relaunched in 2014) issued 'Ending Cholera: A Global Roadmap to 2030', in accordance with which best practices—including with regard to the provision of safe water and sanitation, and use of oral vaccines—were to be shared, partnerships strengthened and resources aligned, with a view to reducing deaths from cholera (an acute water-borne bacterial infection) by 90%, and eliminating the disease in up to 20 affected countries by 2030. However, from mid-2021 WHO reported an acute upsurge in cholera outbreaks, with high mortality rates. In 2023 cholera outbreaks were reported to be ongoing in 24 countries (in Africa, the Middle East, South Asia, and Haiti).

Influenza: In March 2014 WHO issued an updated version of a *Global Influenza Preparedness Plan* originally launched in 2005. In May 2011 the 64th WHA adopted a Pandemic Influenza Preparedness (PIP) Framework, which aimed to broaden access to anti-influenza vaccines. In March 2019 WHO initiated a Global Influenza Strategy, covering the period 2019–30, with a focus on preventing seasonal influenza (believed to cause up to 650,000 deaths annually), controlling the spread of influenza from animals to humans, and pandemic preparedness. Updated WHO *Guidelines for the clinical management of severe illness from influenza virus infections* were released in March 2022. In 2023 WHO's Global Influenza Surveillance and Response System (GISRS) comprised 138 national influenza centres, six WHO collaborating centres and four essential regulatory laboratories.

Malaria: In 1998 WHO declared the control of malaria a priority concern, and, with partners, launched a Roll Back Malaria (RBM) initiative. The disease acutely affected 247m. people in 2021, and killed 619,000. (The majority of malaria cases occur in sub-Saharan Africa.) In May 2015 the WHA endorsed a new Global Malaria Strategy, covering the period 2016–30, which—through a continued focus on the promotion of universal access to malaria prevention, diagnosis and treatment; strengthening surveillance; and on the achievement of national malaria-free status—aimed to reduce malaria cases globally by 90% by 2030, as well as to eliminate the disease entirely in at least 35 countries by 2030. In a landmark decision in October 2021 WHO recommended the widespread preventive use of a new vaccine against malaria, RTS,S/AS01 ('Mosquirix'), among children in regions with moderate to high malaria transmission. In early 2023 the vaccine was being delivered in a pilot phase in Ghana, Kenya and Malawi.

By 2023 WHO had certified the following countries, *inter alia,* as malaria-free: UAE (2007), Morocco (2010), and Algeria (in May 2020).

mpox/Monkeypox: From mid-2022 WHO and partners supported surveillance of and analysed a multi-country outbreak of mpox (then known as Monkeypox)—a zoonotic infection originating in areas of Central and West Africa—transmission of which, atypically, had recently spread in non-endemic locations. On 23 July WHO designated the outbreak as a PHEIC. The most significant caseload was reported from WHO's Europe region. Initial evidence had indicated that undetected transmission in the new locations might have been ongoing for some time. Anti-smallpox vaccines were reported to protect against the disease. In late November WHO confirmed that the virus would be named mpox, in order to counter any negative connotations. The PHEIC was terminated on 12 May 2023. By 11 July some 88,288 cases of mpox, and 149 related deaths, had been confirmed in 112 countries and territories worldwide since 1 January 2022.

HIV/Hepatitis: WHO supports governments to develop effective health sector responses to the HIV/AIDS epidemic through enhancing their planning capabilities, implementation capacity, and health systems resources. Guidelines on managing the HIV/AIDS epidemic are regularly revised and updated. WHO and other agencies sponsor the Joint UN Programme on HIV/AIDS (UNAIDS, q.v.); the UNAIDS secretariat is based at WHO headquarters. A WHO-UNAIDS HIV Vaccine Initiative was launched in 2000.

By 2020 eight countries globally had achieved the 90-90-90 'Fast-Track' target on HIV treatment (set by UNAIDS in 2014) of at least 90% of people living with HIV being aware of their serostatus (i.e. presence or not in the blood of detectable antibodies to the virus); 90% of these taking ART; and 90% being virally suppressed: Eswatini (98-98-95); Switzerland (93-98-96); Rwanda (93-98-96); Qatar (93-98-96); Botswana (91-95-98); Slovenia (90-97-96); Uganda (91-98-90); and Malawi (91-94-94). A follow-on 95-95-95 Fast-Track target was to be achieved by 2030, alongside a target of reducing annual new HIV infections by 2030 to (globally) 200,000.

In 2020 some 230,000 people in the Middle East and North Africa were reported to have HIV/AIDS, of whom an estimated 93,000 were receiving ART. Some 16,000 new cases were diagnosed there during 2020, and around 7,900 deaths from AIDS-related illnesses were recorded.

In April 2014 WHO issued its first guidelines on the treatment of chronic Hepatitis C infections, with a view to reducing the number of deaths globally (estimated at up to 500,000 annually) from Hepatitis C-related cirrhosis and cancer of the liver. A *Progress report on HIV, viral hepatitis and sexually transmitted infections*, issued by WHO in July 2019, noted that 257m. people were living with chronic Hepatitis B infection in 2016, and (in 2015) 71m. people had chronic Hepatitis C.

TB: Vaccination with the bacille Calmette–Guérin (BCG) vaccine can confer protection, especially from severe forms of TB in children. At the end of 2021 the global BCG vaccination coverage rate stood at 84%.

In May 2014 the WHA adopted a long-term End TB Strategy, aimed at reducing the global incidence of TB by 90% by 2035. In December 2022 WHO released *Implementing the End TB Strategy: The Essentials 2022*, representing a compendium of policies, guidelines and other resources that support the ongoing strategy. A second UN high-level meeting on TB was to be convened in September 2023 (the first having been held in 2018).

A 'Stop TB' partnership initiative was launched by WHO in 1999 with the World Bank, the US Government and a coalition of NGOs. The Global TB Drug Facility, launched by Stop TB in 2001, aims to increase access to high-quality anti-TB drugs for sufferers in developing countries. Targets (to be attained by 2030) of the Stop TB coalition's Global Plan to End TB during 2023–30 included: all high-risk and vulnerable populations were to have access to periodic screening; 95% of people with TB were to receive a diagnosis; and 50m. people with TB were to have access to appropriate treatments. Furthermore, the plan envisaged that at least one new TB vaccine would be introduced by 2026 for widespread use.

In June 2023 WHO initiated an online TB Research Tracker, focused on new TB treatment regimens, vaccines, and projects related to TB prevention, treatment, and care.

An End TB Strategy was approved by the WHA in May 2014, setting long-term targets for the prevention, care and control of TB (including a 95% reduction in TB deaths and a 90% reduction in TB incidence by 2035). In September 2014 WHO, jointly with the European Respiratory Society, launched a new framework aimed at eliminating TB in countries with low levels of infection.

Polio: In 1988 the WHA launched the Global Polio Eradication Initiative (GPEI), which has most recently set a deadline of 2026 to achieve the elimination of poliomyelitis.

In March 2023 the GPEI reported that remaining un- or under-vaccinated children were to be targeted in the following regions: eastern Afghanistan; the southern area of Khyber Pakhtunkhwa, Pakistan; Tete province, Mozambique; northwestern Nigeria; eastern DRC; south-central Somalia; and northern Yemen.

As at April 2023 Egypt, Israel and Yemen were classified by the GPEI as polio outbreak countries—i.e. having ended indigenous wild poliovirus, but remaining prone to re-infection via the importation of wild or vaccine-derived poliovirus.

Measles: WHO's Measles and Rubella Strategic Framework covering the period 2021–30 aimed to combat, through routine immunization, deaths from measles (which is particularly dangerous for children under the age of five and malnourished children), and also congenital rubella syndrome. WHO, with Gavi, the Vaccine Alliance, UNICEF and other agencies, participates in a wider Measles and Rubella Partnership, which supports the implementation of the Framework. During 2000–18 WHO estimated that effective measles vaccinations had prevented 23m. deaths. By the end of 2018 82 countries were reported to have eliminated measles, and 81 to have eliminated rubella. Some 128,000 fatal cases of measles were reported in 2021 (compared with 761,000 in 2000). At the end of 2021 global coverage with both of two required measles vaccinations together with rubella vaccines stood at 71%. In April 2022 WHO and UNICEF issued a joint warning that COVID-19 pandemic-related disruptions to routine childhood immunisation programmes and increasingly inequitable access to vaccines were undermining worldwide protection from vaccine-preventable diseases. Furthermore, conflict-related population displacement, overcrowding and lack of access to clean water and sanitation risked exacerbating outbreaks of vaccine-preventable diseases.

NCDs: The surveillance, prevention and management of NCDs and mental health are organization-wide priorities. Tobacco use, unhealthy diet, harmful use of alcohol and physical inactivity are regarded as common, preventable risk factors for the four most prominent NCDs, i.e. cardiovascular diseases, cancer, chronic respiratory disease and diabetes. It is estimated that these NCDs are collectively responsible for an estimated 35m. deaths—60% of all deaths—globally each year, and that up to 80% of cases of heart disease, stroke and type 2 diabetes, and more than one-third of cancers, could be prevented by eliminating shared risk factors. WHO aims to monitor the global epidemiological situation of NCDs, to co-ordinate multinational research activities concerned with prevention and care, and to analyse determining factors such as gender and poverty.

In March 2018 a WHO Independent Global High-level Commission was inaugurated, tasked with formulating innovative solutions aimed at advancing the prevention and control of NCDs. A Fourth UN General Assembly High-level Meeting on the Prevention and Control of NCDs was scheduled to be held in 2025.

An International Task Force on Obesity aims to encourage the development of innovative policies for managing obesity. In October 2017 WHO issued guidelines aimed at managing childhood obesity, for use by personnel at primary health care facilities. In May 2018 the WHA endorsed a WHO Global Action Plan on Physical Activity (GAPPA), with a focus on promoting healthy lifestyles and increasing inclusive participation. A WHO Acceleration Plan to Stop Obesity was endorsed by the 75th WHA in May 2022. In May 2023, in the framework of the Acceleration Plan, WHO initiated a Health Service Delivery Framework for Prevention and Management of Obesity.

WHO initiated a Global Diabetes Compact in April 2021, with the aim of supporting effective national diabetes prevention and management programmes. In May the 74th WHA agreed a resolution aimed at enhancing the prevention, diagnosis and control of diabetes and the prevention and management of related risk factors (such as obesity).

WHO's Substance Abuse Programme offers technical support to member countries to address the misuse of all psychoactive substances, irrespective of legal status. In May 2010 WHO endorsed a global strategy to reduce the harmful use of alcohol; this promoted measures including taxation on alcohol, minimizing outlets selling alcohol, raising age limits for those buying alcohol, and the employment of effective measures to deter people from driving while under the influence of alcohol.

In 2012 WHO estimated that tobacco would lead to more than 8m. deaths annually by 2030 (through lung cancer, heart disease, chronic bronchitis and other effects). The Tobacco or Health Programme aims to reduce the use of tobacco, by educating tobacco-users and preventing young people from adopting the habit. In May 1999 the WHA endorsed the formulation of a Framework Convention on Tobacco Control (FCTC) to help to combat the increase in tobacco use; it entered into force in February 2005. A Protocol to Eliminate Illicit Trade in Tobacco Products entered into force on 25 September 2018. The second Meeting of the Parties to the Protocol, held in November 2021, agreed to establish an investment fund to secure financing and strengthen implementation of the Protocol.

WHO monitors and reviews emerging evidence on the health impacts of electronic nicotine delivery systems (ENDS, also known as e-cigarettes) and electronic non-nicotine delivery systems (ENNDS), and offers related guidance to governments.

UHC/HEALTHIER POPULATIONS

In May 2020 the 73rd WHA adopted a resolution on integrated people-centred eye care (referred to as IPEC), aimed at ensuring the widespread use of IPEC. In May 2021 the 74th WHA resolved that by 2030 global coverage of surgery to address refractive errors and cataracts should increase by 40% and 30%, respectively. During the 75th WHA, in May 2022, a WHO *Eye Care in Health Systems—Guide for Action* was issued.

Climate Change, Health and Environment: In January 2018 WHO and UNEP signed an agreement establishing an extensive new programme of WHO-UN Environment collaboration, comprising joint actions aimed at combating environmental health risks, such as antimicrobial resistance, air pollution, and climate change. Furthermore, co-ordination was to be strengthened in the areas of waste and chemicals management, food and nutrition, and water quality. A joint work programme was to be developed, and the two agencies were to convene an annual high-level meeting, to follow up progress and make recommendations for advancing the collaboration. In May 2019 the WHA endorsed a Global Strategy on Health, Environment and Climate Change, which aimed to address environmental health risks and challenges until 2030.

WHO's programme area on environmental health addresses the increasing threats to health and wellbeing from a changing environment, especially in relation to air pollution, water quality, sanitation, protection against UV-radiation, management of hazardous waste, chemical safety and housing hygiene. In October–November 2018 WHO, with UNEP and other partners, organized the inaugural Global Conference on Air Pollution and Health; this committed to a goal of reducing deaths from air pollution by two-thirds by 2030. In April 2022 WHO reported that 99% of the global population was breathing air that did not meet WHO's air quality limits on fine particulate matter and nitrogen dioxide.

In 2022 WHO attributed some 829,000 deaths annually to diarrhoea caused by unsafe drinking water, sanitation systems and hand hygiene. Around 2,000m. people worldwide in 2020 were reported to have no access to clean drinking water. In August 2019 WHO released a report on microplastics in drinking water and urged further assessment of the risks posed to human health by microplastics in the environment.

Nutrition and Food Safety: WHO aims to protect human health against risks associated with biological and chemical contaminants and additives in food. With FAO, WHO establishes food standards (through the work of the Codex Alimentarius Commission and its subsidiary committees) and evaluates food additives, pesticide residues and other contaminants and their implications for health. WHO also addresses the methods of producing, processing and preparing foods that contribute to the incidence of foodborne trematode infections (parasitic infections caused by flatworms). WHO's Global Foodborne Infections Network, established in 2001, promotes integrated laboratory-based surveillance and intersectoral collaboration among human health, veterinary and food-related entities.

ANTIMICROBIAL RESISTANCE

In February 2017 WHO published the first list of antibiotic-resistant 'priority pathogens', posing the most critical risk to human health. In the following month a UN Interagency Coordination Group on Antimicrobial Resistance was established, under the joint chairmanship of the WHO Director-General and the UN Deputy Secretary-General. A series of *WHO Guidelines on Use of Medically Important Antimicrobials in Food-producing Animals* was released in November. In June 2019 WHO, FAO and the World Organisation for Animal Health (the 'Tripartite') collectively established an AMR Multi Partner Trust Fund, with initial funding of US $5m. WHO reported in January 2020 that under investment in the development of new antibiotics was significantly impacting progress in combating drug-resistant infections. In June 2023 WHO published its first global research agenda on AMR in human health, which outlined 40 research topics relating to drug-resistant bacteria, fungi and TB.

EMERGENCY APPEALS

In January 2023 WHO appealed for US $2,540m. to support its emergency operations during 2023, including $772m. for activities related to the COVID-19 pandemic; $253m. for operations in conflict-affected Ukraine; $178m. for drought-affected parts of the Horn of Africa; $165m. for Afghanistan; $134m. for Yemen; and $106m. for Syria. Some $50m. was to be allocated to replenishing WHO's Contingency Fund for Emergencies. In February WHO issued an emergency flash appeal for $42.79m. to provide immediate medical assistance and health services to some 26m. people in Türkiye and Syria affected by recent devastating earthquakes.

WHO has, since 1950, provided technical supervision of UNRWA's programme to provide health care to Palestinians living in the Occupied Territories. A WHO Special Representative is based at UNRWA's headquarters.

Finance

A total programme budget of US $6,834.2m. was approved by the WHA in May 2023 for the two years 2023–24, of which 19.0% was provisionally allocated to the Eastern Mediterranean office (including 33.4% of the total budget for emergency operations and appeals and 49.3% of the budget for polio eradication).

Publications

Bulletin of the World Health Organization (monthly).
Global Status Report on Alcohol and Health.
Global Tuberculosis Report.
International Classification of Diseases.
International Health Regulations.
International Pharmacopoeia.
International Travel and Health.
Levels and Trends in Child Mortality (every 2 years, with the World Bank and UNICEF).
Model List of Essential Medicines (every 2 years).
Public Health Panorama.
Tracking Universal Health Coverage.
Weekly Epidemiological Record.
WHO Drug Information (quarterly).
WHO Report on the Global Tobacco Epidemic.
World Cancer Report (every 5–6 years).
World Health Report (annually).
World Health Statistics.
World Malaria Report (annually, with UNICEF).

WHO also publishes the annual *Eastern Mediterranean Health Journal*.

Technical report series; guidelines; catalogues of specific scientific, technical and medical fields are available.

Associated Agencies

Gavi, the Vaccine Alliance: Global Health Campus, 40 chemin du Pommier, 1218 Grand-Saconnex, Geneva, Switzerland; 2099 Pennsylvania Ave, NW, Suite 200, Washington, DC 20006, USA; tel. 229096500; (202) 478-1050; fax 2229096550; (202) 478-1060; e-mail info@gavi.org; internet gavi.org; f. 2000 by WHO, UNICEF, the World Bank and the Bill & Melinda Gates Foundation as the Global Alliance for Vaccines and Immunization, present name adopted in 2014; aims to improve childhood immunization coverage in developing countries and to accelerate access to new vaccines; promotes specific immunization campaigns and supports the strengthening of health systems and services in low-income countries; works in partnership with govts, international and civil society orgs, research agencies, manufacturers and other private sector bodies; in June 2020 a replenishment meeting, hosted in a virtual format by the UK Government, secured new commitments of US $8,800m. for the period 2021–25; from 2020 Gavi hosted and co-ordinated the COVAX Facility, a mechanism tasked with facilitating rapid, equitable access to COVID-19 vaccines worldwide, and representing the vaccines pillar of the ACT Accelerator (initiated in April, q.v.); Gavi also manages the COVAX Advance Market Commitment, which aims promptly to secure safe, effective doses of COVID-19 vaccines for low- and middle-income countries and economies at the same time as developed states; in Dec. 2021 the Gavi Board agreed to invest $155.7m. during 2022–25 to support the introduction, procurement and delivery of the newly-approved RTS,S vaccine against malaria in endemic African countries; CEO Dr SETH BERKLEY (USA).

Joint UN Programme on HIV/AIDS (UNAIDS): 20 ave Appia, 1211 Geneva 27, Switzerland; tel. 227913666; fax 227914187; e-mail communications@unaids.org; internet www.unaids.org; f. 1996 to lead, strengthen and support an expanded response to the global HIV/AIDS pandemic; guided by UN Security Council Resolution 1308, focusing on the possible impact of AIDS on social instability and emergency situations, and the potential impact of HIV on the health of international peacekeeping personnel; by the Declaration of Commitment on HIV/AIDS agreed in June 2001 by a Special Session of the UN General Assembly on HIV/AIDS, which acknowledged the AIDS epidemic as a 'global emergency'; the Political Declaration on HIV/AIDS, adopted by the June 2006 UN General Assembly High Level Meeting on AIDS; and the June 2016 Political Declaration on HIV and AIDS: On the Fast-Track to Accelerate the Fight Against HIV and to End the AIDS Epidemic by 2030; activities focus on prevention, care and support, reducing vulnerability to infection, and alleviating the socioeconomic and human effects of HIV/AIDS; launched the Global Coalition on Women and AIDS in Feb. 2004; the UNAIDS 2012–26 Strategy was focused on 3 strategic priorities:

Maximize equitable and equal access to HIV services and solutions; Break down barriers to achieving HIV outcomes; and Fully resource and sustain efficient HIV responses and integrate them into health, social protection, humanitarian, and pandemic response situations; in July 2020, jtly with WHO and UNDP, UNAIDS initiated a COVID-19 Law Lab initiative, facilitating the sharing of legal documents from more than 190 states, to support the establishment of robust legal frameworks to manage the pandemic; co-sponsors: WHO, UN Women, UNICEF, UNDP, UNFPA, UNODC, the ILO, UNESCO, the World Bank, WFP, UNHCR; Exec. Dir WINNIE BYANYIMA (Uganda).

International Agency for Research on Cancer: 150 Cours Albert Thomas, 69372 Lyon Cedex 08, France; tel. 4-72-73-84-85; internet www.iarc.fr; f. 1965 as a self-governing body within the framework of WHO; organizes international research on cancer; maintains its own laboratories, an IARC Biobank, a web-based Global Cancer Observatory (GCO), and runs a research programme on the environmental factors causing cancer; issues a series of monographs on the identification of carcinogenic hazards to humans and publishes *The Cancer Atlas*, providing an overview of cancer worldwide; mems: 26 countries; Dir Dr ELISABETE WEIDERPASS.

Other UN and Related Organizations Active in the Region

UN Security Council

The Security Council was established as a principal organ under the UN Charter, tasked with promoting international peace and security and respect for human rights in all parts of the world; its first meeting was held on 17 January 1946. The UN Charter obligates all member states to comply with Council decisions.

The Council's permanent members are the People's Republic of China, France, Russian Federation, United Kingdom and USA, known collectively as the P-5. The remaining 10 members—the Elected 10, or E-10—are normally elected (five each year) by the General Assembly for two-year periods (five countries from Africa and Asia, two from Latin America, one from Eastern Europe, and two from Western Europe and others).

The United Arab Emirates (UAE) was serving as an elected member of the Council during 1 January 2022–31 December 2023, and Algeria was to serve for the period 1 January 2023–31 December 2024. The rotating presidency of the Council was held by the UAE in June 2023.

The UN Security Council may—as provided for under Chapter VII of the UN Charter—take enforcement measures as a means of targeting regimes and entities that are deemed to threaten international peace and security, in situations where diplomatic efforts aimed at achieving a resolution to the situation have failed. The offending entities are expected to comply with a set of objectives issued by the Security Council aimed at restoring order. Such enforcement measures encompass mandatory economic and trade and/or other sanctions (such as financial or diplomatic restrictions, arms embargoes and bans on travel), and also, in certain cases, international military action. Sanctions committees are established to oversee the implementation of economic or political enforcement measures imposed by the Security Council. The Consolidated Sanctions List comprises all individuals and entities on which the Council has imposed sanctions measures, under all punitive regimes. A Focal Point for De-listing, established in December 2006, by Resolution 1730, receives and processes requests from individuals and entities wishing to be removed from sanctions lists, with the exception of the ISIL (Da'esh) and al-Qa'ida Sanctions List. By mid-2023 a total of 119 de-listing requests had been received by the Focal Point; of these, 113 had been fully processed, resulting in the de-listing of 17 individuals and also of 17 entities.

Sanctions Committees that were operational in 2023 included:

Security Council Committee established pursuant to Resolutions 1267 (1999), 1989 (2011) and 2253 (2015) concerning ISIL (Da'esh), al-Qa'ida, and associated individuals, groups, undertakings and entities.

Security Council Committee established pursuant to Resolution 2140 (2014) concerning Yemen.

Security Council Committee established pursuant to Resolution 1970 (2011) concerning the Libyan Arab Jamahiriya.

Security Council Committee established pursuant to Resolution 1636 (2005) concerning events in Lebanon.

Security Council Committee established pursuant to Resolution 1518 (2003) concerning Iraq.

Office of the Ombudsperson of the 1267/1989/2253 ISIL (Da'esh) and al-Qa'ida Sanctions Committee: Rm TB-08041 D, UN Plaza, New York, NY 10017, USA; f. Dec. 2009; reviews requests from individuals, groups, undertakings or entities seeking to be removed from the Islamic State and al-Qa'ida Sanctions List; by mid-2023 100 cases had passed fully through the Ombudsperson process, resulting in the de-listing of 65 individuals and 28 entities; Ombudsperson RICHARD MALANJUM (Malaysia).

International Court of Justice—ICJ

Address: Peace Palace, Carnegieplein 2, 2517 KJ The Hague, Netherlands.
Telephone: (70) 3022323; **fax:** (70) 3649928; **e-mail:** information@icj-cij.org; **internet:** www.icj-cij.org.

Established in 1945, the Court (composed of 15 judges, each of a different nationality) is the principal judicial organ of the UN. All members of the UN are parties to the Statute of the Court. The Jurisdiction of the Court comprises: cases which the parties refer to it jointly by special agreement; matters concerning which a treaty or convention in force provides for reference to the Court through the inclusion of a jurisdictional clause; and legal disputes between states which have recognized the jurisdiction of the Court as compulsory for specified classes of dispute. Judgments are without appeal, but are binding only for the particular case and between the parties. States appearing before the Court undertake to comply with its Judgment. Advisory opinions on legal questions may also be requested by the General Assembly, the Security Council or, if so authorized by the Assembly, other UN organs or specialized agencies.

At July 2023 19 cases were under consideration, or pending before the Court, including further deliberation of a case brought against the USA by Iran concerning alleged violations of the 1955 Treaty of Amity Economic Relations, and Consular Rights which were having an adverse effect on Iranian companies ('certain Iranian assets')—in respect of this case, in October 2018 the Court issued an interim order demanding that the USA remove sanctions against Iran relating to civil aviation and humanitarian goods, and also that the USA cease threatening the imposition of further sanctions against Iran; a case brought by Palestine against the USA relating to the relocation of the US embassy in Israel to Jerusalem; a case brought by Canada and the Netherlands, in June 2023, against the Syrian Arab Republic concerning alleged violations of the Convention against Torture and Other Cruel, Inhuman or Degrading Treatment or Punishment; a case brought by Iran later in that month against Canada that concerns alleged violations of Iran's immunities; and a case brought in July by Canada, Sweden, Ukraine and the UK against Iran alleging that Iran had violated a series of obligations under the 1999 Montreal Convention, in relation to the shooting down by Iranian military personnel on 8 January 2020 of a civil aircraft, Ukraine International Airlines flight PS752 (which had resulted in 176 fatalities). An Advisory Opinion (requested in December 2022 by the UN General Assembly) on the legal status and the consequences of Israel's occupation of Palestinian territory was pending, as was also an Advisory Opinion (requested in March 2023 by the General Assembly) relating to (i) nations' obligations under international law to ensure the protection for present and future generations of the climate system and other parts of the environment from greenhouse gas emissions, and (ii) on the legal consequences for nations that cause significant harm to the climate system and other parts of the environment. In July 2004, at the request of the UN General Assembly, the Court delivered an advisory opinion on: Legal Consequences of the Construction of a Wall by Israel in the Occupied Palestinian Territory. In March 2023 the Court delivered a Judgment on the merits of the case brought by Iran against the USA concerning 'certain Iranian assets'.

President: JOAN E. DONOGHUE (USA).
Registrar: PHILIPPE GAUTIER (Belgium).

Global Crisis Response Group (GCRG) on Food, Energy and Finance

In March 2022 the UN Secretary-General formed the GCRG—guided by a 32-member steering committee comprising leaders of UN agencies and of multilateral development banks—to address the broad global impacts of the ongoing war in Ukraine. A Task Team was established within the GCRG, co-ordinated by the Executive Director of the UN Conference on Trade and Development, to collate and analyse data, and to make policy recommendations along three workstreams, on food, energy and finance.

Office for the Coordination of Humanitarian Affairs—OCHA

Address: United Nations Plaza, New York, NY 10017, USA.
Telephone: (212) 963-1234; **fax:** (212) 963-1312; **e-mail:** unocha@un.org; **internet:** unocha.org.

The Office was established in January 1998 as part of the UN Secretariat, with a mandate to co-ordinate international humanitarian assistance and to provide policy and other advice on humanitarian issues. A complementary service, Reliefweb, provides humanitarian updates on, and analysis of, natural disasters and other crisis situations.

OCHA managed the preparatory process leading to the inaugural World Humanitarian Summit, which was convened in May 2016, in Istanbul, Turkey (Türkiye). Some 55 heads of state and government attending the meeting endorsed a new Agenda for Humanity, incorporating the following five core humanitarian responsibilities: Political leadership to prevent and end conflict; Uphold the norms that safeguard humanity; Leave no one behind; Change people's lives: from delivering aid to ending need; and Invest in humanity.

OCHA facilitates inter-agency appeals, which aim to co-ordinate resource mobilization following humanitarian crises. Since 2013 appeals have been formulated within the framework of a Humanitarian Programme Cycle, comprising the following five elements: needs assessment and analysis; strategic response planning; mobilization of resources; implementation and monitoring; and operational evaluation. In late 2022 OCHA issued its Global Humanitarian Overview (2023), comprising country Humanitarian Needs Overviews, Humanitarian Response Plans (HRPs), and other response initiatives. At that time OCHA appealed for US $51,500m. to respond to the very urgent needs of 203m. people in 69 countries during 2023. Global requirements are adjusted continuously throughout each year as response initiatives are revised to reflect ongoing needs.

The most costly response initiatives for 2023 (as foreseen at November 2022) included the Syria Humanitarian Response Plan (HRP) and Regional Refugee and Resilience Plan (3RP), which required funding of $4,400m. and $5,696m., respectively; and the Yemen HRP (requiring $4,280m.).

In mid-February 2023 OCHA issued two Flash Appeals to provide emergency support for an initial three-month period following the powerful earthquakes that had devastated parts of northern Syria and southern Türkiye. These requested US $1,007m. to meet the immediate needs of some 5.2m. people in the hardest hit provinces in Türkiye, and $398m. to assist 4.9m. people with the most urgent humanitarian needs in Syria (complementary to the 2023 Syrian HRP). It was reported in May 2023 that the ongoing HRP for Sudan—where civil conflict had erupted in April—was only 14% funded.

Under-Secretary-General for Humanitarian Affairs and Emergency Relief Co-ordinator: MARTIN GRIFFITHS (UK).

United Nations Entity for Gender Equality and the Empowerment of Women—UN Women

Address: 405 East 42nd St, New York, NY 10017, USA.
Telephone: (646) 781-4400; **fax:** (646) 781-4444; **internet:** www.unwomen.org.

UN Women was established by the UN General Assembly in July 2010 in order to strengthen the UN's capacity to promote gender equality, the empowerment of women, and the elimination of discrimination against women and girls. It commenced operations on 1 January 2011. In 2021 UN Women helped to stage a Generation Equality Forum which launched a Global Acceleration Plan (GAP) for Gender Equality that was framed around six new multi-stakeholder Action Coalitions, covering: gender-based violence, economic justice and rights, bodily autonomy and sexual and reproductive health rights, technology and innovation, feminist action for climate justice, and feminist movements and leadership. These were to mobilize civil society, governments, private sector interests and international organizations to advance equality during the period 2021–26.

UN Women issued a statement in September 2022 that expressed deep concern over the recent death in state custody in Iran of a young woman, Mahsa Amini, who had reportedly been detained for non-observance of a strict national dress code for women. Shortly afterwards, as related protests mounted in Iran, UN Women issued a further statement that supported demands by women in that country to be free to protest injustice without reprisals and free to exercise bodily autonomy (including with respect to choice of attire).

Executive Director: SIMA SAMI BAHOUS (Jordan).
Regional Director for the Arab States: SUSANNE MIKHAIL ELDHAGEN (Egypt/Sweden).

United Nations Office for Disaster Risk Reduction—UNDRR

Address: 7 bis ave de la Paix, 1211 Geneva 2, Switzerland.
Telephone: 229178907; **e-mail:** undrrcomms@un.org; **internet:** undrr.org.

The Office was established in 1999 as an inter-agency secretariat to implement the International Strategy for Disaster Reduction (ISDR), formally adopted by UN member states in 2000. The ISDR was intended to guide and co-ordinate international efforts towards achieving substantive reduction in disaster losses, and building resilient communities and nations as the foundation for sustainable development activities. The Office (known until 2019 as UNISDR) led efforts to formulate a UN Plan of Action on Disaster Risk Reduction for Resilience, which was adopted in 2013.

In March 2015 the Office organized the Third UN World Conference on Disaster Risk Reduction (WCDRR), held in Sendai City, Japan, which adopted the (non-binding) Sendai Framework for Disaster Risk Reduction, covering the period 2015–30. The Sendai Framework listed seven measurable targets, four priorities, and a set of guiding principles related to disaster risk reduction planning, with the aim of lowering during 2020–30 the global mortality rate from disasters, as well as the numbers of people affected by disasters, compared with the rate in 2005–15; reducing disaster-related economic losses; and preventing disaster-related damage to basic services, infrastructure and livelihoods. Furthermore, public access to disaster risk information and early warning systems was to be enhanced. In view of rapidly advancing urbanization globally, the Sendai Framework placed a focus on building safer cities. In 2018 the ISDR adopted a Sendai Framework Monitor, which aimed to track progress in implementing the Framework in the context of 38 globally agreed indicators.

UNDRR serves as the focal point providing guidance for the implementation of the Sendai Framework. It also organizes the biennial sessions of the Global Platform for Disaster Risk Reduction (seventh session: May 2022, in Bali, Indonesia), and promotes information sharing on disaster risk reduction.

UNDRR has a regional office in Cairo, Egypt, that is the focal point for its activities in the Arab states.

Special Representative of the UN Secretary-General for Disaster Risk Reduction: MAMI MIZUTORI (Japan).

United Nations Office for Disarmament Affairs—UNODA

Address: UN Plaza, Rm S-3024, New York, NY 10017, USA.
Fax: (212) 963-4066; **e-mail:** UNODA-web@un.org; **internet:** www.un.org/disarmament.

UNODA—established in 1982 as the UN Department for Disarmament Affairs, with its present name adopted in 2007—works to promote nuclear disarmament and non-proliferation; to strengthen disarmament regimes with regard to biological and chemical weapons and other weapons of mass destruction; and to support disarmament activities relating to conventional weapons, with a particular focus on landmines and small arms.

Under-Secretary-General and High Representative for Disarmament Affairs: IZUMI NAKAMITSU (Japan).

United Nations Office on Drugs and Crime—UNODC

Address: Vienna International Centre, POB 500, A 1400 Vienna, Austria.
Telephone: (1) 26060-0; **fax:** (1) 263-3389; **e-mail:** unodc@unodc.org; **internet:** www.unodc.org.

The Office was established in November 1997 (as the UN Office of Drug Control and Crime Prevention) to strengthen the UN's integrated approach to issues relating to drug control, crime prevention and international terrorism.

Executive Director: GHADA FATHI WALY (Egypt).

Office of the United Nations High Commissioner for Human Rights—OHCHR

Address: Palais Wilson, 52 rue de Paquis, 1201 Geneva, Switzerland.
Telephone: 229179220; **e-mail:** infodesk@ohchr.org; **internet:** www.ohchr.org.

OHCHR is a body of the UN Secretariat and is the focal point for UN human rights activities. The Office's Geneva headquarters incorporates the following three divisions: Human Rights Council (HRC) and Treaty Mechanisms; Thematic Engagement, Special Procedures and Right to Development; and Field Operations and Technical Co-operation. The High Commissioner is the UN official with principal responsibility for UN human rights activities.

As at 1 June 2023 OHCHR was concerned with 45 thematic mandates (for example addressing the independence of judges and lawyers; rights to freedom of peaceful assembly and of association; arbitrary detention; adequate housing; and obligations relating to the enjoyment of a safe, clean, healthy and sustainable environment).

OHCHR was also concerned as at 1 June 2023 with 14 country mandates, including for Iran (mandate established in 2011), the Palestinian Territories (1993, 'to be maintained pending 'the end of the Israeli occupation'), and Syria (established in 2011). At mid-2023 OHCHR was supporting an International Commission of Inquiry (CoI) that was addressing the situation in Syria, in accordance with a UN Human Rights Council resolution adopted in August 2011; a CoI established in May 2021 to investigate humanitarian and human rights violations that were perpetrated leading up to and since 13 April 2021 in the Palestinian Territories, including East Jerusalem, and in Israel; and an Independent Fact-Finding Mission (FFM) mandated in November 2022 by the HRC's 35th special session to investigate the deteriorating human rights situation in Iran, particularly with respect to women and children. The CoI on Syria's first report was published in November 2011, and regular updates and recommendations have been issued subsequently. In March 2023 the CoI reported that the parties to the conflict in Syria continued to commit widespread human rights violations and abuses prior to the earthquakes that had devastated northern areas of the country in February, and that the emergency response initiative had been hindered by failure (of the parties to the conflict and also of the UN) to secure an immediate pause in hostilities, or to facilitate the delivery of life-saving aid. The adoption by the UN General Assembly in June of a resolution that authorized the establishment of an independent institution to clarify the fate and whereabouts of all missing persons in Syria was welcomed by the CoI. The first report of the CoI on the Palestinian Territories, issued in June 2022, deemed the forced displacement of Palestinians, demolitions of Palestinian homes, expansion of Israeli settlements, settler violence, discrimination against Palestinians, and blockade of Gaza to be factors that were contributing to recurring cycles of violence. The report also noted that the Israeli occupation was used by the Palestinian Authority as a justification for human rights violations and for failing to organize legislative and presidential elections, and that the Hamas leadership in Gaza had shown no commitment to international humanitarian law. In October the CoI notably reported to the UN General Assembly that there were reasonable grounds to conclude that the Israeli occupation of Palestinian territory contravened international law, owing to its permanence and to the Israeli Government's de facto annexation policies. Consequently, in December the UN General Assembly requested the International Court of Justice to issue an Advisory Opinion on the legal status and the consequences of Israel's occupation of Palestinian territory. In May 2023 the CoI on Palestine issued its *Detailed findings on attacks and restrictions on and harassment of civil society actors, by all duty bearers*. In July of that year the FFM on Iran confirmed that its investigations would include the targeting and harassment of journalists connected to Iran, and of their families.

High Commissioner: VOLKER TÜRK (Austria).

United Nations Human Settlements Programme—UN-Habitat

Address: POB 30030, Nairobi, Kenya.
E-mail: unhabitat-info@un.org; **internet:** unhabitat.org.

UN-Habitat was established as the UN Centre for Human Settlements, UNCHS-Habitat, in October 1978, on the recommendation of the First UN Conference on Human Settlements, convened in Vancouver, Canada, in May–June 1976. It led the Habitat Agenda, which was adopted as a Global Plan of Action to achieve 'adequate shelter for all' and 'sustainable human settlements development in an urbanizing world' by the Second UN Conference on Human Settlements (Habitat II), convened in İstanbul, Turkey (Türkiye), in June 1996. In January 2002 it became a full UN programme, serving as a focus for human settlements and sustainable urban development activities in the UN system. UN-Habitat leads the delivery of the New Urban Agenda, adopted in October 2016 by Habitat III, held in Quito, Ecuador. A new UN-Habitat Assembly was inaugurated in May 2019; it convened its second session in June 2023.

In February 2023, following the earthquakes that struck the Syrian Arab Republic and Türkiye, UN-Habitat offered support, and organized an immediate detailed structural assessment of damage caused to buildings in Syria. UN-Habitat provides the secretariat of the World Urban Forum (WUF), which convenes every two years to promote international co-operation in shelter and urban development issues. The 12th WUF (WUF12) was scheduled to be hosted by Egypt, in its capital, Cairo, in November 2024. In November 2021 UN-Habitat supported the inauguration of a new Council on Urban Initiatives, comprising the mayors of Barcelona (Spain), Bogotá (Colombia), Freetown (Sierra Leone), Gaziantep (Türkiye), Mexico City, and New Orleans (USA). The Council aimed to advocate for fairer, healthier and more environmentally responsive urban spaces.

Executive Director: MAIMUNAH MOHD SHARIF (Malaysia).

Regional Office for Arab States: Housing and Building Research Centre, 87 Tahreer St, 9th Floor, Dokki, Giza, Egypt; tel. (2) 37618812; e-mail unhabitat.cairo@unhabitat.org; internet unhabitat.org/roas.

United Nations Conference on Trade and Development—UNCTAD

Address: 8–14 Palais des Nations, 1211 Geneva 10, Switzerland.
Telephone: 229171234; **fax:** 229070057; **e-mail:** unctadinfo@unctad.org; **internet:** unctad.org.

UNCTAD was established in 1964. It is the principal organ of the UN General Assembly concerned with trade and development, and is the focal point within the UN system for integrated activities relating to trade, finance, technology, investment and sustainable development. It aims to maximize the trade and development opportunities of developing countries and to assist them to adapt to the increasing globalization and liberalization of the world economy. UNCTAD undertakes consensus-building activities, research and policy analysis and technical co-operation.

In 2023 Yemen was classified by the UN as one of the world's 46 least developed countries (LDCs). In June 2018 a Gebze, Türkiye-based Technology Bank for LDCs was inaugurated, tasked with broadening the application of innovation, science and technology in, and serving as a knowledge hub for LDCs.

A *Report on UNCTAD Assistance to the Palestinian People*, with a focus on the prospects for economic development in the Palestinian Territories, is published annually.

Secretary-General: REBECA GRYNSPAN (Costa Rica).

United Nations Population Fund—UNFPA

Address: 605 Third Ave, New York, NY 10158, USA.
Telephone: (212) 297-5000; **fax:** (212) 370-0201; **e-mail:** hq@unfpa.org; **internet:** www.unfpa.org.

Created in 1967 as the Trust Fund for Population Activities, the UN Fund for Population Activities (UNFPA) was established as a Fund of the UN General Assembly in 1972 and was made a subsidiary organ of the UN General Assembly in 1979, with the UNDP Governing Council (now the Executive Board) designated as its governing body. In 1987 UNFPA's name was changed to the UN Population Fund (retaining the same acronym). UNFPA works to promote reproductive rights, and universal access to sexual and reproductive health, with a particular focus on women, adolescents and youth.

Executive Director: Dr NATALIA KANEM (Panama).

Regional Office for the Arab States: 70A Nahda St, Sarayat El Maadi, Cairo, Egypt; e-mail info.asro@unfpa.org; internet arabstates.unfpa.org; LAILA BAKER.

REGIONAL ORGANIZATIONS

UN Specialized Agencies and Related Organizations

International Civil Aviation Organization—ICAO

Address: 999 University St, Montréal, QC H3H 5H7, Canada.
Telephone: (514) 954-8219; **fax:** (514) 954-6077; **e-mail:** icaohq@icao.org; **internet:** www.icao.int.

ICAO was founded in 1947, on the basis of the Convention on International Civil Aviation, signed in Chicago, in 1944, to develop the techniques of international air navigation and to help in the planning and improvement of international air transport.

Secretary-General: Juan Carlos Salazar Gómez (Colombia).

Middle East Office: POB 85, Cairo Airport Post Office Terminal One, Cairo 11776, Egypt; tel. (2) 2674840; fax (2) 2674843; e-mail icaomid@icao.int; internet www.icao.int/MID.

International Labour Organization—ILO

Address: 4 route des Morillons, 1211 Geneva 22, Switzerland.
Telephone: 227996111; **fax:** 227988685; **e-mail:** ilo@ilo.org; **internet:** www.ilo.org.

The ILO was founded in 1919 to work for social justice as a basis for lasting peace. It carries out this mandate by promoting decent living standards, satisfactory conditions of work and pay and adequate employment opportunities. Activities include the creation of international labour standards; the provision of technical co-operation services; and training, education, research and publishing activities to advance ILO objectives. ILO flagship programmes include the International Programme on the Elimination of Child Labour and Forced Labour (IPEC+); Global Action for Prevention on Occupational Safety and Health (OSH-GAP); and Social Protection Floors for All.

Director-General: Gilbert F. Houngbo (Togo).

Regional Office for Africa: CCIA Bldg, rue Jean Paul II, 01 BP 3960 Abidjan 01, Côte d'Ivoire; tel. 20-31-89-00; e-mail abidjan@ilo.org; internet www.ilo.org/africa.

Regional Office for Arab States: POB 11-4088, Riad Solh 1107-2150, Beirut, Lebanon; tel. (1) 752400; fax (1) 752405; e-mail beirut@ilo.org; internet www.ilo.org/beirut.

International Maritime Organization—IMO

Address: 4 Albert Embankment, London, SE1 7SR, United Kingdom.
Telephone: (20) 7735-7611; **fax:** (20) 7587-3210; **e-mail:** info@imo.org; **internet:** www.imo.org.

The Inter-Governmental Maritime Consultative Organization (IMCO) began operations in 1959, as a specialized agency of the UN to facilitate co-operation among governments on technical matters affecting international shipping. Its main aims are to improve the safety of international shipping, and to control pollution caused by ships. IMCO became IMO in 1982.

In January 2009 a high level meeting of states from the Western Indian Ocean, the Gulf of Aden and Red Sea areas, held under IMO auspices, adopted the Djibouti Code of Conduct concerning the Repression of Piracy and Armed Robbery. Signatories to the Code agreed to co-operate lawfully in the apprehension, investigation and prosecution of people suspected of committing or facilitating acts of piracy; in the seizure of suspect vessels; in the rescue of ships, persons and property subject to acts of armed robbery; and to collaborate in the conduct of security operations. In January 2017 12 states signed the Jeddah Amendment to the Djibouti Code of Conduct, in accordance with which they were to co-operate—supported by IMO and other stakeholders—in developing national and regional capacity to address wider maritime security issues, with a focus on promoting the 'blue economy' and sustainable development of the maritime sector. By 2023 the Jeddah Amendment had 15 signatories.

Secretary-General: Kitack Lim (Republic of Korea) (outgoing), Arsenio Antonio Dominguez Velasco (Panama) (from 1 Jan. 2024).

Other UN and Related Organizations Active in the Region

International Organization for Migration—IOM

Address: 17 route des Morillons, CP 71, 1211 Geneva 19, Switzerland.
Telephone: 227179111; **fax:** 227986150; **e-mail:** hq@iom.int; **internet:** www.iom.int.

IOM was established in 1951 as the Intergovernmental Committee for Migration (ICM), to address orderly and planned migration meeting the specific needs of emigration and immigration countries; international resettlement; and the voluntary return and reintegration of migrants, refugees and internally displaced persons. ICM's name was changed to IOM in 1989. IOM was admitted as an observer to the UN General Assembly in 1992. In September 2016, at the UN Summit on Addressing Large Movements of Refugees and Migrants, held at the UN General Assembly, in New York, USA, IOM was incorporated into the UN system as a related body. The conference adopted the New York Declaration for Refugees and Migrants, which recognized an unprecedented level of human mobility, and determined to address the root causes of mass migration movements. A commitment was made to negotiate a Global Compact for Safe, Orderly and Regular Migration. The Compact was adopted by an Intergovernmental Conference on International Migration, hosted by Morocco, in December 2018.

IOM's Yemen Crisis Response Plan 2023 required US $183m. to support 4.6m. beneficiaries, through the extension of multisectoral humanitarian assistance, and by addressing drivers of fragility, and assisting the restoration of domestic and public infrastructure. IOM has maintained a mission in Yemen and an office in Sana'a, the Yemeni capital, since 2007. The Lebanon Crisis Response Plan 2023, requiring $35m., aimed to support some 43,000 very vulnerable migrants, refugees and members of local communities, and had a focus on strengthening economic and community resilience and discouraging unsafe migration. IOM was implementing an $307.4m. initiative during 2022–23 to support 1.9m. IDPs, migrants, returnees and host communities in Iraq. Since the start of civil conflict in the Syrian Arab Republic in 2011 IOM has provided emergency relief to migrants and uprooted IDPs within that country (at a projected cost of $98.3m. in 2023) and to displaced persons in neighbouring countries. In February 2023 IOM appealed for $161m. to provide emergency assistance to 800,000 earthquake survivors in southern Türkiye and 630,000 in northwestern Syria.

IOM and UNHCR jointly lead the UN component of an African Union-European Union-UN Tripartite Taskforce on the Situation of Migrants and Refugees in Libya (operational since early 2022). Meeting in March 2023 the Taskforce determined to strengthen efforts to support the development of non-discriminatory legal and policy frameworks for migrants and refugees in that country, and urged the Libyan authorities to end arbitrary detention of migrants and refugees. The Taskforce agreed to enhance support for voluntary humanitarian returns from Libya. IOM was implementing a US $84.7m. Libya Crisis Response Plan during 2023.

Director-General: António Manuel de Carvalho Ferreira Vitorino (Portugal) (outgoing), Amy E. Pope (USA) (from 1 Oct. 2023).

International Telecommunication Union—ITU

Address: Place des Nations, 1211 Geneva 20, Switzerland.
Telephone: 227305111; **fax:** 227337256; **e-mail:** itumail@itu.int; **internet:** www.itu.int.

Founded in 1865, ITU became a specialized agency of the UN in 1947. It aims to encourage world co-operation for the improvement and national use of telecommunications to promote technical development, to harmonize national policies in the field, and to promote the extension of telecommunications throughout the world. ITU helped to organize the World Summit on the Information Society, held, in two phases, in 2003 and 2005, and supports follow-up initiatives. ITU has assumed responsibility for issues relating to cybersecurity. In December 2012 a World Conference on International Communications endorsed new International Telecommunication Regulations (ITRs), updating those previously set down in 1988. World Radiocommunication Conferences, World Telecommunication Standardization Assemblies and World Telecommunication Development Conferences are convened regularly.

Secretary-General: Doreen Bogdan-Martin (USA).

United Nations Educational, Scientific and Cultural Organization—UNESCO

Address: 7 place de Fontenoy, 75352 Paris 07 SP, France.
Telephone: 1-45-68-10-00; **fax:** 1-45-67-16-90; **e-mail:** bpi@unesco.org; **internet:** www.unesco.org.

UNESCO was established in 1946 and aims to contribute, through education, the sciences, culture, communication and information, to the building of peace and the eradication of poverty, and to advancing sustainable development and intercultural dialogue.

UNESCO's World Heritage Programme, inaugurated in 1978, aims to protect historic sites and natural landmarks of outstanding universal significance, in accordance with the 1972 UNESCO Convention Concerning the Protection of the World Cultural and Natural Heritage, by providing financial aid for restoration, technical assistance, training and management planning.

Examples of World Heritage sites include: the ruins of Persepolis (Iran); the ruins of ancient Babylon (Iraq); the archaeological sites of Troy (Türkiye); and the Old City of Sana'a (Yemen).

UNESCO administers the 1954 Hague Convention on the Protection of Cultural Property in the Event of Armed Conflict, and also the 1970 Convention on the Means of Prohibiting and Preventing the Illicit Import, Export and Transfer of Ownership of Cultural Property. In recent years UNESCO has been increasingly concerned about the use of trafficking in looted cultural property as a means of directly financing terrorist activities. In November 2017 UNESCO and the International Criminal Court adopted a Letter of Intent that formalized co-operation between the two organizations in combating the deliberate destruction of cultural heritage.

A UNESCO observatory was established in Beirut, Lebanon, in July 2014 to monitor and assess the state of Syria's cultural heritage. In August 2015 the UNESCO Director-General declared as a war crime the destruction of Baalshamin temple at Palmyra, Syria by Islamic State militants. In April 2016 a team of experts completed a rapid assessment of the state of the museum and archeological site at Palmyra, some of which remained inaccessible. The mission identified a series of emergency measures aimed at securing the museum from the Islamic State insurgency. In January 2017 the UNESCO Director-General condemned the destruction of further parts of the Palmyra site as a war crime. In that month a UNESCO emergency mission was dispatched to Aleppo to undertake a preliminary assessment of conflict-related damage to cultural sites and education institutions there. This found that some 60% of the old city of Aleppo had been severely damaged and that around 30% had been destroyed. In July 2014 the UNESCO Director-General condemned the recent destruction by Islamic State militants of the tomb and mosque of Prophet Jonas in Mosul, Iraq, and demanded that the ongoing intentional destruction of Iraqi religious and cultural heritage should cease. In that month UNESCO approved an Emergency Response Action Plan aimed at safeguarding Iraq's cultural heritage. In August the Director-General demanded the immediate cessation of 'emerging cultural cleansing' in northern Iraq, manifested in attacks against members of religious and ethnic minorities. Following attacks perpetrated in February 2015 by terrorists against Mosul Museum and various archaeological sites in the Nineveh region, as well as book burnings in Mosul, UNESCO welcomed the adoption, in May, of a UN General Resolution on 'Saving the Cultural Heritage of Iraq'. In February 2018 UNESCO initiated the flagship programme 'Revive the Spirit of Mosul', with a particular focus on the human dimension of reconstruction. Under the programme UNESCO was co-ordinating the restoration and rehabilitation of cultural heritage, and of educational and cultural institutions.

UNESCO's Man and the Biosphere Programme supports a world-wide network of biosphere reserves, which aim to promote environmental conservation and research, education and training in biodiversity and problems of land use (including the fertility of tropical soils and the cultivation of sacred sites). As at July 2023 there were 36 biosphere reserves in 14 Arab states, including the Harrat Uwayrid volcanic area in Saudi Arabia, a habitat of critically endangered Arabian leopards and gazelles. The M'Goun massif in the Moroccan High Atlas Mountains, and Iran's Aras mountain range, as well as Qeshm Island (located in the Persian Gulf) the Tabas Geopark, in that country's South Khorasan Province, have been designated as UNESCO Global Geoparks.

Through a variety of projects UNESCO promotes art education, supports the rights of artists, and encourages crafts, design, digital art and performance arts. In October 2004 the UNESCO Creative Cities Network (UCCN) was launched to facilitate public and private sector partnerships, international links, and recognition of a city's unique expertise in seven creative fields: cinema, craft and folk arts, design, gastronomy, literature, media arts, or music. Cities in the Middle East and North Africa participating in the Network in 2023 included Sharjah, Iran, Aswan, Egypt and Tétouan, Morocco (as Cities of Craft and Folk Art); Dubai, UAE, Muharraq, Bahrain and İstanbul, Türkiye (as Cities of Design); Beirut, Lebanon and Baghdad, Iraq (Literature); Essaouira, Morocco (Music); and Buraidah, Saudi Arabia and Zahlé, Lebanon (Gastronomy).

Director-General: AUDREY AZOULAY (France).

UNESCO International Institute for Capacity Building in Africa (UNESCO–IICBA): UNECA Compound, Menilik Ave, POB 2305, Addis Ababa, Ethiopia; tel. (11) 5445284; fax (11) 514936; e-mail info.iicba@unesco.org; internet www.iicba.unesco.org; f. 1999; aims to promote capacity building in the following areas: teacher education; curriculum devt; educational policy, planning and management; and distance education; Dir QUENTIN WODON.

UNESCO Office for the Gulf States and Yemen: 66 Lusail St, West Bay, POB 3945, Doha, Qatar; tel. 4113290; e-mail doha@unesco.org; internet en.unesco.org/fieldoffice/doha; serves as the Cluster Office for Bahrain, Kuwait, Oman, Qatar, Saudi Arabia, United Arab Emirates and Yemen; Dir SALAH KHALED.

UNESCO Office in Beirut: POB 5244, Cité Sportive, Beirut, Lebanon; tel. (1) 850013; e-mail beirut@unesco.org; internet www.unesco.org/en/fieldoffice/beirut; serves as the Regional Bureau for Education in the Arab States, in addition to being the cluster office for Lebanon, Syria, Jordan, Iraq and the Palestinian Territories; Dir COSTANZA FARINA.

UNESCO Office in Cairo: Northern Expansions, Sixth of October City, Giza, GZ 11452, Egypt; e-mail cairo@unesco.org; internet en.unesco.org/fieldoffice/cairo; serves as the Regional Bureau for Science and Technology in the Arab States; Dir a.i. NURIA SANZ.

UNESCO Région du Maghreb: Ave Aïn Khalwiya, Km 5.3, BP 1777RP, Rabat, Morocco; e-mail rabat@unesco.org; internet fr.unesco.org/fieldoffice/rabat; serves Algeria, Libya, Mauritania, Mauritania, Morocco and Tunisia; Dir a.i. KARIM HENDILI.

United Nations Industrial Development Organization—UNIDO

Address: Vienna International Centre, Wagramerstr. 5, POB 300, 1400 Vienna, Austria.

Telephone: (1) 260260; **fax:** (1) 2692669; **e-mail:** unido@unido.org; **internet:** www.unido.org.

UNIDO began operations in 1967 and became a specialized agency in 1985. Its objectives are to promote sustainable and socially equitable industrial development in developing countries and in countries with economies in transition. It aims to assist such countries to integrate fully into global economic system by mobilizing knowledge, skills, information and technology to promote productive employment, competitive economies and sound environment.

Director-General: GERD MÜLLER (Germany).

Universal Postal Union—UPU

Address: POB 312, 3000 Bern 15, Switzerland.

Telephone: 313503111; **fax:** 313503110; **e-mail:** info@upu.int; **internet:** www.upu.int.

The General Postal Union was founded by the Treaty of Bern (1874), beginning operations in July 1875. Three years later its name was changed to the Universal Postal Union. In 1948 UPU became a specialized agency of the UN. It aims to support an efficient, effective and co-ordinated international postal service.

Director-General: MASAHIKO METOKI (Japan).

World Intellectual Property Organization—WIPO

Address: 34 chemin des Colombettes, 1211 Geneva 20, Switzerland.
Telephone: 223389111; **fax:** 227335428; **internet:** www.wipo.int.

WIPO was established in 1970. It became a specialized agency of the UN in 1974 concerned with the protection of intellectual property (e.g. patents, trademarks, industrial designs and literary copyrights) throughout the world. WIPO formulates and administers treaties embodying international norms and standards of intellectual property, establishes model laws, and facilitates applications for the protection of inventions, trademarks etc. WIPO provides legal and technical assistance to developing countries and countries with economies in transition and advises countries on obligations under the World Trade Organization's agreement on Trade-Related Aspects of Intellectual Property Rights.

Director-General: DAREN TANG (Singapore).

World Meteorological Organization—WMO

Address: 7 bis, ave de la Paix, 1211 Geneva 2, Switzerland.
Telephone: 227308111; **fax:** 227308181; **e-mail:** cpa@wmo.int; **internet:** www.wmo.int.

WMO was established in 1950 and was recognized as a specialized agency of the UN in 1951, aiming to improve the exchange of information on meteorology, climatology, operational hydrology and related fields. WMO jointly implements, with UNEP, the UN Framework Convention on Climate Change.

REGIONAL ORGANIZATIONS

In January 2023 WMO estimated the average global temperature in 2022 at 1.15°C higher than pre-industrial levels. The eight years since 2015 were confirmed to be the eight warmest on record. The rate of sea level rise was reported to have reached a record high in 2022, having doubled since 1993. In early July 2023 WMO stated that the preceding month had been the hottest June on record globally—with unprecedented sea surface temperatures and a record minimum extent of Antarctic sea ice.

Secretary-General: PETTERI TAALAS (Finland).

World Tourism Organization—UNWTO

Address: Capitán Haya 42, 28020 Madrid, Spain.
Telephone: (91) 5678100; **fax:** (91) 5713733; **e-mail:** omt@unwto.org; **internet:** www.unwto.org.

The World Tourism Organization was established in 1975 and was recognized as a specialized agency of the UN in December 2003. It works to promote and develop sustainable tourism, in particular in support of socioeconomic growth in developing countries.

In January 2023 the UNWTO World Tourism Barometer reported that during 2022 there had been more than 900m. tourist arrivals globally, more than twice as many as in 2021, and equivalent to 66% of levels in (pre-COVID-19 pandemic) 2019.

The World Tourism Barometer reported in May 2023 that in the first quarter of 2023 tourist arrivals in the Middle East had exceeded pre-pandemic levels; those in southern Mediterranean Europe and North Africa had recovered to 2019 levels; and in the Caribbean, Central America, and Western and Northern Europe tourist arrivals had nearly fully recovered.

Secretary-General: ZURAB POLOLIKASHVILI (Georgia).

World Trade Organization—WTO

Address: Centre William Rappard, 154 rue de Lausanne, 1211 Geneva 21, Switzerland.
Telephone: 227395111; **fax:** 227314206; **e-mail:** enquiries@wto.org; **internet:** www.wto.org.

The World Trade Organization was established in 1995 as the successor to the General Agreement on Tariffs and Trade (GATT), overseeing the multilateral trading system. It facilitates negotiations on global trade agreements, monitors the implementation of trade agreements, undertakes dispute procedures, and promotes development, economic reform, as well as trade capacity among developing nations and countries with economies in transition. The WTO participates in the UN Chief Executives Board for Co-ordination as a related organization.

In November 2001 the fourth WTO Ministerial Conference initiated the Doha Round of negotiations on major reform to the international trading system; progress in implementing the Doha Round was, however, subsequently slow. The 12th WTO Ministerial Conference, held in June 2022, agreed a Geneva Package of measures, that included: a decision relating to e-commerce; an agreement on fisheries subsidies; a ministerial declaration on the WTO Response to the COVID-19 pandemic and preparedness for future pandemics; a ministerial decision on the Agreement on Trade-related Aspects of Intellectual Property Rights (which provided for a partial intellectual property waiver to enable developing countries to manufacture COVID-19 vaccines and export them to other developing countries); and a ministerial declaration on the emergency response to food insecurity.

The WTO has 164 member states, including Bahrain, Cyprus, Egypt, Jordan, Kuwait, Oman, Qatar, the United Arab Emirates and Yemen. Algeria, Iran, Iraq, Lebanon and Libya are observer states.

Director-General: Dr NGOZI OKONJO-IWEALA (Nigeria).

Affiliated Body

SPECIAL TRIBUNAL FOR LEBANON

Address: POB 115, 2260 AC Leidschendam, Netherlands.
Telephone: (70) 800-3400; **e-mail:** stl-pressoffice@un.org; **internet:** www.stl-tsl.org.

In March 2006 the UN Security Council adopted a resolution requesting the UN Secretary-General to negotiate with the Lebanese Government on the establishment of an international tribunal to try those suspected of involvement in a terrorist attack that, in February 2005, had killed 22 people, including the former Prime Minister of Lebanon, Rafik Hariri. The resulting agreement on the Special Tribunal for Lebanon was endorsed by the Security Council in May 2007. The Tribunal, which became operational on 1 March 2009, comprises both international and Lebanese judges and applies Lebanese (not international) law. On its establishment the Tribunal took over the mandate of a terminated UN International Independent Investigation Commission, which had been created by a resolution of the Security Council in April 2005 to gather evidence and assist the Lebanese authorities in their investigation into the February 2005 attacks, and whose mandate had later been expanded to investigate other assassinations that had occurred before and after the attack. A Defence Office has been established within the Tribunal to protect the rights of the suspects, accused and their counsel, providing legal assistance and support where necessary. In January 2011 the Prosecutor submitted to the Pre-Trial Judge an indictment of four suspects—Salim Jamil Ayyash, Mustafa Amine Badreddine, Hussein Hassan Oneissi and Assad Hassan Sabra ('Ayyash et al.')—on charges of conspiracy to commit a terrorist act, in relation to the February 2005 atrocities. The indictment was confirmed in June 2011. In that month the Tribunal passed to the Lebanese authorities arrest warrants for the four suspects. The Tribunal determined in February 2012 to try the four accused in the case *in absentia*, on the grounds that they had apparently absconded. In July 2013 it was confirmed that a sealed indictment had been submitted by the Prosecutor against Hassan Habib Merhi, who was also accused of involvement in the February 2005 attack. In December 2013 the Trial Chamber ruled that Merhi should also be tried *in absentia*. Trial proceedings in the case Ayyash et al. opened in January 2014, without the presence of the defendants, who had continued to evade arrest. In February the Chamber ruled that the Merhi case should be amalgamated into that of Ayyash et al. Hearings were adjourned later in that month, and restarted in late August. In July 2016 the Appeals Chamber found that sufficient evidence had been presented to the Tribunal to assume that the accused Mustafa Amine Badreddine had died, and thus ordered the Trial Chamber to terminate the proceedings against him, without prejudice to resume them should evidence subsequently be presented that he was alive. In August 2017 the presentation of evidence on behalf of 72 victims of the February 2005 terrorist attack commenced in the Ayyash et al. trial. This represented the first ever presentation of evidence by victims of terrorism to an international tribunal. The closing arguments of the prosecution, defence and legal representatives of victims in the Ayyash et al. case were concluded in September 2018. The final judgment was originally scheduled to be delivered in mid-May 2020. In April, however, owing to the COVID-19 pandemic, the date of the public pronouncement of the judgment was postponed until August. On 18 August the Court unanimously pronounced Salim Jamil Ayyash to be guilty beyond all reasonable doubt of being a co-perpetrator of: conspiracy to commit a terrorist act; committing a terrorist act by deploying an explosive device; the intentional premeditated homicide of Rafik Hariri, using explosive materials; the intentional premeditated homicide of an additional 21 people using explosive materials; and the attempted intentional premeditated homicide of 226 others using explosive materials. Hassan Habib Merhi, Hussein Hassan Oneissi and Assad Hassan Sabra were acquitted. In December Ayyash was sentenced to five concurrent terms of life imprisonment. In January 2021 the Defence Counsel for Ayyash filed an appeal against the guilty verdict and sentence. On 29 March the Tribunal's Appeals Chamber ruled that the Ayyash Defence was not entitled to appeal the conviction in the absence of Ayyash himself. In the same month the Prosecutor filed an appeal against the Judgment concerning Hassan Habib Merhi and Hussein Hassan Oneissi. In March 2022 the Appeals Chamber ruled to reverse the 2020 acquittals, convicted them of conspiracy to commit terrorist acts, and issued warrants for their arrest. Both men were sentenced *in absentia* to life imprisonment by the Appeals Chamber in June 2022; the Prosecutor reiterated demands for their surrender, and for support by the international community to secure their arrest.

In August 2011 the Tribunal also established jurisdiction in the cases concerning terrorist attacks perpetrated on 1 October 2004 against Marwan Hamadeh, on 21 June 2005 against George Hawi, and on 12 July 2005 against Elias el-Murr; accordingly the Lebanese authorities were ordered to transfer to the Tribunal all material relevant to these cases. In mid-September 2019 the Tribunal removed confidentiality from a decision that had been made to indict Salim Jamil Ayyash in an additional case on charges (including conspiracy to commit a terrorist act and intentional homicide with premeditation) that related to the three attacks perpetrated during late 2004–mid-2005. Related national and international arrest warrants were issued against Ayyash forthwith. On 24 September the President of the Special Tribunal ordered that the new indictment against Ayyash—who had not been directly contactable—should be publicized in an alternate manner, including through public advertisement. If within 30 days no contact had been made (it was not), the Trial Chamber was to be asked to initiate relevant proceeding *in absentia*. In September 2020 the Trial Chamber confirmed the Special Tribunal's jurisdiction to try Ayyash (the 'Ayyash case') in relation to the three attacks covered by the indictment; in February 2021 it was announced that the trial would, provisionally, commence in June. At the start of June the Trial Chamber cancelled the commencement of the trial and suspended all decisions on filings relating to the case, as a result of the Tribunal's severe financial situation.

On 31 January 2014 the Special Tribunal issued a Contempt Decision (made public in late April), in accordance with which contempt of court proceedings were initiated against two Lebanese journalists and two news corporations in that country, that were accused of having published the names of individuals alleged to be witnesses before the Tribunal. The 2014 Contempt Decision represented the first incidence under international criminal law of corporate entities being charged with contempt of court; the admissibility of proceedings against corporations was upheld by the Appeals Chamber in October, although remained disputed by the Contempt Judge. In September 2015 the Contempt Judge acquitted one journalist of both counts in the case, and the other of one count. In July the Judge found two further accused guilty of knowingly and wilfully interfering with the administration of justice by disseminating information on apparent confidential witnesses in the Ayyash *et al.* case; punitive fines were imposed in August.

The Tribunal entered a non-judicial residual phase on 1 July 2022, during which it was focused on the preservation of records and archives, continuing obligations to victims and witnesses, and meeting information requests from national authorities. In January 2023 the UN Secretary-General agreed to extend the Tribunal's mandate until 31 December, to enable the completion of its residual functions and orderly termination.

President of the Court: IVANA HRDLIČKOVÁ (Czech Republic).
Chief Prosecutor: NORMAN FARELL (Canada).
Registrar: DAVID TOLBERT (USA).
Head of Defence Office: DOROTHÉE LE FRAPER DU HELLEN (France).

AFRICAN DEVELOPMENT BANK—AfDB

Address: Immeuble du Centre de Commerce International d'Abidjan, ave Jean-Paul II, 01 BP 1387, Abidjan 01, Côte d'Ivoire.
Telephone: 20-26-39-00; **e-mail:** afdb@afdb.org; **internet:** www.afdb.org.

Established in 1964, the Bank began operations in July 1966, with the aim of financing economic and social development in African countries. Non-African countries were admitted to the Bank from 1982. The Bank aims to contribute to development and poverty reduction by mobilizing funds for investment and by providing policy and technical assistance. The Bank and two other institutions, the African Development Fund and the Nigeria Trust Fund, constitute the African Development Bank (AfDB) Group.

REGIONAL MEMBERS

Algeria	Eritrea	Namibia
Angola	Eswatini	Niger
Benin	Ethiopia	Nigeria
Botswana	Gabon	Rwanda
Burkina Faso	The Gambia	São Tomé and
Burundi	Ghana	Príncipe
Cabo Verde	Guinea	Senegal
Cameroon	Guinea-Bissau	Seychelles
Central African	Kenya	Sierra Leone
Republic	Lesotho	Somalia
Chad	Liberia	South Africa
Comoros	Libya	South Sudan
Congo,	Madagascar	Sudan
Democratic	Malawi	Tanzania
Republic	Mali	Togo
Congo, Republic	Mauritania	Tunisia
Côte d'Ivoire	Mauritius	Uganda
Djibouti	Morocco	Zambia
Egypt	Mozambique	Zimbabwe
Equatorial Guinea		

The Bank has 27 non-African members.

Organization
(September 2023)

BOARD OF GOVERNORS

The Board of Governors is the highest policymaking body of the Bank, responsible for electing the Board of Directors and the President. Each member country nominates one Governor, usually its Minister of Finance and Economic Affairs, and an alternate Governor or the Governor of its central bank. The Board meets in ordinary session once a year: the 2023 meeting was held in Sharm el-Sheikh, Egypt, in late May.

BOARD OF DIRECTORS

The 20-member Board of Directors, elected by the Board of Governors for a term of three years, is responsible for the general operations of the Bank and meets on a weekly basis.

ADMINISTRATION

The President—who is elected for a five-year term and serves as the Chairperson of the Board of Directors—is responsible for the organization and the day-to-day operations of the Bank, under the guidance of the Board of Directors. The Bank has the following divisions, each headed by a Vice-President: Power, Energy, Climate, and Green Growth; Agriculture, Human and Social Development; Private Sector, Infrastructure and Industrialization; Regional Development, Integration and Business Delivery; Economic Governance and Knowledge Management; Finance; People and Talent Management; and Technology and Corporate Services.

In 2022 Bank field offices were located in 37 member countries. Four regional hubs have been approved: in Nairobi, Kenya (for East Africa), Centurion, South Africa (Southern Africa), Tunis, Tunisia (North Africa), and in Yaoundé, Cameroon (for Central Africa). The Bank's first external representation office (for Asia) was inaugurated in Tokyo, Japan, in October 2012. An African Natural Resources Centre was established in 2013, at the Bank's headquarters.

President and Chairperson of Board of Directors: Dr AKINWUMI A. ADESINA (Nigeria).

FINANCIAL STRUCTURE

The African Development Bank Group of development financing institutions uses a unit of account (UA), which at December 2022 was valued at US $1.33084.

The capital stock of the Bank was at first exclusively open for subscription by African countries, with each member's subscription consisting of an equal number of paid-up and callable shares. In 1978, however, the Governors agreed to open the capital stock of the Bank to subscription by non-regional states on the basis of nine principles aimed at maintaining the African character of the institution. The decision was finally ratified in May 1982, and the participation of non-regional countries became effective on 30 December. It was agreed that African members should still hold two-thirds of the share capital, that all loan operations should be restricted to African members, and that the Bank's President should always be a national of an African state. In May 1998 the Board of Governors resolved that the non-African members' share of the capital be increased from 33.3% to 40%.

In October 2019 an extraordinary meeting of the Board of Governors approved the Bank's seventh general capital increase, of some US $115,000m. At 31 December 2022 the Bank's authorized capital was UA 180,638.83m.; subscribed capital at the end of 2022 was UA 148,768.18m. (of which the paid-up portion was UA 9,974.54m.).

Activities

The Bank's Ten-Year Strategy for 2013–22, adopted in April 2013, focused on achieving inclusive growth and promoting the transition to green growth, with infrastructure development, regional integration, private sector development, governance and accountability, and skills and technology designated as core areas of priority. Further areas of special emphasis included fragile states, gender, agriculture, and food security. The Development and Business Delivery Model that was endorsed by the Board in April 2016 aimed to transform the Bank's internal organization in alignment with its 2013–22 Strategy and the following High 5 priorities: Light up and power Africa, Feed Africa, Industrialize Africa, Integrate Africa, and Improve the quality of life for the people of Africa. It was envisaged that a follow on Ten-Year Strategy, for 2023–32, would be approved in mid-2023.

In March 2009 a Coalition for Dialogue on Africa was inaugurated by the Bank, the United Nations (UN) Economic Commission for Africa (ECA) and the African Union (AU). A joint secretariat supports co-operation activities between the three organizations. The AfDB is actively involved in the AU Development Agency (AUDA-

NEPAD), which aims to promote sustainable development and eradicate poverty throughout the region. The Bank is a strategic partner in AUDA-NEPAD's African Peer Review Mechanism.

In June 2023, during the Summit for a New Global Financing Pact, convened in Paris, France, the AfDB, European Investment Bank, Islamic Development Bank and World Health Organization collectively launched a Health Impact Investment Platform, focused on strengthening essential, climate and crisis-resilient primary health care services in low- and low-and-middle income states.

In May 2023 the Bank reported that GDP growth across Africa had decelerated from 4.8% in 2021 to 3.8% in 2022.

FINANCIAL OPERATIONS

At the end of 2022 the Bank Group had approved total lending of UA 131,617m. for 6,859 operations since the beginning of its activities in 1967. In 2022 the Group approved 284 lending operations amounting to UA 6,155.8m., compared with 196 operations with a value of UA 4,506.3m. in the previous year. Of the total amount approved in 2022, UA 5,327.9m. was for loans and grants, UA 512.7m. for guarantees, and UA 40.1m. for equity participation.

Of the total operations approved in 2022, by High 5 priority sector, UA 1,593.55m. (25.9%) was for Industrialize Africa projects; UA 1,561.36m. (25.4%) was for Improve the quality of life for the people of Africa initiatives; UA 1,341.97m. (21.8%) was for Feed Africa initiatives; UA 1,134.75m. (18.4%) for Integrate Africa; and UA 524.12m. (8.5%) was for Light up and power Africa initiatives. Some 24.2% of expenditure was allocated to agriculture and rural projects; 21.5% to transport; 20.1% to finance; 12.9% to multisector projects; and 10.4% to energy supply initiatives. In terms of geographical distribution, 36.5% of approved Bank Group operations in 2022 were allocated to countries in West Africa, 27.1% to East Africa, 15.5% to Southern Africa, 14.3% to North Africa, and 5.5% to countries in Central Africa; furthermore, around 1% of approvals was for multiregional projects.

African Development Bank: The Bank makes loans at a variable rate of interest, which is adjusted twice a year, plus a commitment fee of 0.75%. Lending approved (including resources allocated under the Post-conflict Country Facility and private and public equity participations) amounted to UA 3,718.8m. for 76 operations in 2022, compared with UA 2,449.1m. for 66 operations in 2021. Since October 1997 fixed and floating rate loans have been made available.

African Development Fund: The Fund commenced operations in 1974. It grants interest-free loans to low-income African countries for projects with repayment over 50 years (including a 10-year grace period) and with a service charge of 0.75% per annum. Grants for project feasibility studies are made to the poorest countries.

In December 2022 a global coalition of donor countries concluded an agreement on ADF-16, replenishing the Fund by a record US $8,900m. for the period 2023–25. A new ADF Climate Action Window was established in 2022, to support climate adaptation in low-income African states.

In 2022 approvals under the ADF amounted to UA 1,817.8m. for 107 projects, compared with UA 1,263.3m. for 66 projects in the previous year.

Nigeria Trust Fund: The AfDB and Nigerian authorities co-manage a Nigeria Technical Cooperation Fund (NTCF), which became operational in 2004 to support regional development initiatives.

REGIONAL DEVELOPMENT, INTEGRATION AND BUSINESS DELIVERY

The Bank, the AU and ECA jointly contribute to Agenda 2063, a long-term vision to guide the economic and social transformation of Africa, within the context of which a series of African Development Goals (ADGs) are to be pursued; Agenda 2063 was adopted by AU heads of state and of government in January 2015. The independent, profit-driven Africa50 Infrastructure Fund—headquartered in Finance City, Casablanca, Morocco—was inaugurated in September 2014, having been endorsed by the Board of Governors in May 2013.

An Africa Growing Together Fund was established in 2014, with the People's Republic of China, to co-finance public and private sector projects in support of regional integration and infrastructure development. In July 2017 the AfDB and the Islamic Development Bank concluded an agreement under which they were to provide some US $2,000m. in support of activities aimed at accelerating economic development in Africa, with a particular emphasis on promoting agriculture and food security, energy, and small and medium-sized enterprises (SMEs). An AfDB Microfinance Capacity Building Fund for Africa was launched in 2011.

An AfDB Regional Integration Strategy was being implemented over the period 2018–28, with a focus on enhancing power and infrastructure connectivity; trade and investment; and financial sector integration. An Africa Regional Integration Index, jointly developed by the AfDB, ECA and the AU, was launched in April 2016. The Index aims to measure, systematically (providing data on member states and regional economic communities), regional integration across areas including governance, investment, trade, infrastructure, industry, the free movement of persons, energy, culture and macroeconomic policy convergence. The second edition of the Index, issued in May 2020, found South Africa to be the most regionally integrated African country. It recommended, *inter alia*, enhancing member states' productive, distributive, and marketing capacities; promoting public-private partnerships to strengthen the continental infrastructure; strengthening regional sectoral value-chain frameworks; fully implementing the African Continental Free Trade Area; enhancing workers' technological and other competencies; and promoting the free movement of people on the continent.

In December 2012 the AfDB Board of Directors approved the Bank's participation as an implementation support agency for the World Bank-administered Middle East and North Africa Transition Fund. The Fund was established by the Deauville Partnership, formed in May 2011 by the (then) Group of Eight (G8) industrialized nations, in collaboration with regional and international financial institutions and regional governments, to support political and economic reforms being undertaken by several countries in North Africa and the Middle East, notably Egypt, Jordan, Morocco and Tunisia.

POWER, ENERGY, CLIMATE AND GREEN GROWTH

In 2012 the Bank initiated, with funding from the Government of Denmark, a Sustainable Energy Fund for Africa (SEFA); in September 2013 the Board approved the conversion of SEFA into a multi-donor trust fund. The Bank's Board of Governors decided in November 2019 to restructure SEFA as a concessional financing facility. Its launch as the SEFA Special Fund was marked by a virtual gathering of donor and development partners, industry representatives and government officials in December 2020. The Bank hosts the secretariats of the African Energy Leaders Group and of the Africa Hub of the UN's Sustainable Energy for All initiative. In December 2016 the Bank's Board of Directors endorsed a trusteeship role for the Bank with respect to the administration and management of the resources of the African Renewable Energy Initiative, which was initiated by the AU in December 2015, with the aim of producing by 2030 some 300 GW of electricity across the continent. The AfDB's New Deal on Energy for Africa and related High 5 priority: Light up and power Africa by 2025 focus on fostering partnerships between governments, the private sector and energy sector initiatives to develop an overarching Transformative Partnership on Energy for Africa, providing innovative financing for the continental energy sector. The AfDB launched an online Africa Energy Portal (AEP) in November 2018. In October 2020 the Bank and AUDA-NEPAD jointly released the recommendations of a baseline study that had examined the planned development of a continental energy transmission grid and market. The fifth round of the AfDB-designed Africa Energy Market Place (AEMP), a collaborative investment platform within the New Deal on Energy framework, was convened online in October 2021.

In April 2014 the Board of Directors endorsed the establishment of an Africa Climate Change Fund, which is hosted by the Bank, and aims to assist the transition of African countries towards climate-resilient and low-carbon development. The AfDB and Green Climate Fund concluded a partnership agreement in November 2017. The Bank announced in March 2019 that it would commit at least US $25,000m. towards climate finance projects during the period 2020–25. In 2022 the AfDB committed 42% of expenditure to climate-sensitive projects, compared with 9% in 2016. The AfDB's Africa Nationally Determined Contributions Hub supports member states in meeting obligations under the 2015 Paris Agreement on climate change. Secretariat services are provided by the Bank to the Africa Financial Alliance on Climate Change (AFAC), which co-ordinates the mobilization of contributions towards climate action and climate-resistant development by, *inter alia*, African central, commercial and development banks, stock exchanges, funds and insurance companies. The 2023 edition of the Bank's *African Economic Outlook*, issued in May 2023, was themed 'Mobilizing Private Sector Financing for Climate and Green Growth in Africa'.

In March 2000 African ministers responsible for water resources endorsed an African Water Vision and a Framework for Action to pursue the equitable and sustainable use and management of water resources in Africa in order to facilitate socioeconomic development, poverty alleviation and environmental protection. An African Ministers' Council on Water (AMCOW) was established in April 2002 to provide the political leadership and focus for implementation of the Vision and the Framework for Action. AMCOW requested the Bank to establish and administer an African Water Facility Special Fund, in order to provide the financial requirements for achieving their objectives; this became operational in December. In November 2021 the Board of Directors approved a revised version of the African Water Facility Strategy (2017–25). A new five-year strategy, titled 'Towards a Water Secure Africa' was also endorsed.

In December 2015 the Bank joined the Inclusive Green Growth Partnership, a collaboration between the Global Green Growth

Institute, UN agencies and multilateral development banks, which aimed to promote social inclusion and green growth at national level. The Bank is also one of 26 partners that support the Africa's Food Systems Forum (formerly the African Green Revolution Forum: renamed in September 2022).

In March 2022 the Board of Directors approved a five-year Africa Circular Economy Facility, which was to focus on institutional capacity building to enhance the regulatory framework for relevant innovations; on a business development programme; and on the provision of technical assistance to the African Circular Economy Alliance (founded in 2017 to minimize waste and damage from economic activities in the region).

PRIVATE SECTOR, INFRASTRUCTURE AND INDUSTRIALIZATION

In 1989 the Bank, in co-ordination with the IFC and UNDP, created the African Management Services Company (AMSCo), which provides management support and training to private companies in Africa. The Bank is one of three multilateral donors, with the World Bank and UNDP, supporting the African Capacity Building Foundation, which was established in 1991 to strengthen and develop institutional and human capacity in support of sustainable development activities. An Enhanced Private Sector Assistance initiative (EPSA) was established, with support from the Japanese Government, in 2005 to support the Bank's strategy for the development of the private sector. The scheme incorporated an Accelerated Cofinancing Facility for Africa and a Fund for African Private Sector Assistance. In October 2010 the Board of Directors agreed to convert the Fund into a multi-donor trust fund. A fifth phase of EPSA, covering the period 2023–25, was announced by the Bank and Japanese Government in August 2022. In 2014 the Bank established a Private Sector Credit Enhancement Facility (PSF), which aimed to increase private sector financing in low-income member countries. No new approvals were made under the PSF in 2022.

The Bank's Africa Trade Fund, launched in 2012, aims to facilitate the integration of member states and of African regional economic communities into multilateral trading systems.

The Africa Investment Forum (AIF) was established by the Executive Board in October 2016, to act as a platform for international investors. In July 2020 the AIF announced that, under its Unified COVID-19 Response, US $3,790m. would be allocated to addressing the impacts of the COVID-19 crisis across the following priority sectors: agriculture and agro-processing, energy, health, telecommunications, and industry and trade. The 2023 edition of the AIF's flagship Market Days event was to be convened in November, in Abidjan.

The AfDB is an executing agency for and, jointly with the AU Commission and AUDA-NEPAD, leads the Programme for Infrastructure Development in Africa (PIDA), which aims to develop the continental energy, transport, transboundary water resources, and information and communications technologies infrastructures. A second PIDA Priority Action Plan (PIDA PAP 2) was being implemented over the period 2011–30. Since 2005 the AfDB has managed the NEPAD-Infrastructure Project Preparation Facility (NEPAD-IPPF), a multi-donor trust fund. The Bank hosts the secretariat of the Infrastructure Consortium for Africa, which was inaugurated in October of that year by several major African institutions and donor countries to accelerate efforts to develop the region's infrastructure. In November 2022, at the 27th Conference of the Parties to the UN Framework Convention on Climate Change, the Bank launched, with the AU, Africa50 and other international partners, a new Alliance for Green Infrastructure in Africa. The Alliance aimed to mobilize US $500m. to accelerate project preparation and financing of green infrastructure schemes.

In July 2016 the AfDB Executive Board approved an Industrialization Strategy for Africa, covering the period 2016–25; this outlined a roadmap for the implementation of priority programmes aimed at advancing the industrial transformation of the continent.

The Bank's Africa SME Programme provides lines of credit and technical assistance to African local financial institutions to support local businesses. The AfDB does not, however, finance SMEs directly.

AGRICULTURE, HUMAN AND SOCIAL DEVELOPMENT

The Bank's Feed Africa strategy aims to transform continental agriculture into a sustainable, business-oriented, globally competitive, inclusive, employment and wealth generating sector, with a focus on ending extreme poverty; eliminating hunger and improving nutrition; making Africa a net exporter of agricultural commodities; and moving to the top (by market share) of agricultural value chains for processed commodities. In October 2015 a conference on Feeding Africa, held in Dakar, under the auspices of the Bank, adopted an action plan, and endorsed several partnerships aimed at developing agribusiness on the continent. The Bank manages a multi-donor Agriculture Fast Track Fund, which was launched in 2013 to boost continental agribusiness and agricultural infrastructure investments. In February 2018 the Board of Directors approved the establishment of a Rockefeller Trust Fund, which was to have a particular focus on supporting the High 5 priorities: Feed Africa and Improve the quality of life for the people of Africa. The AfDB's President participates in the Lead Group of the UN's Scaling Up Nutrition (SUN) Movement.

The Bank hosts the secretariat of an African Fertilizer Financing Mechanism (AFFM), established in 2007 to boost agricultural productivity, food security and the sustainable management of natural resources in Africa. The 11th meeting of the AFFM Governing Council, hosted by the Bank in March 2023, adopted a strategic plan for the period 2022–28, focused on broadening access to finance through policy reforms and capital investments.

The AfDB's operational plan under Strategy 2030 for promoting rural development and food security aimed to transform agriculture and to promote sustainable resilient food supply systems, with a focus on the provision of safe, nutritious food, achieving higher incomes for farmers, and generating economic growth in rural areas. The Bank's support for food systems quadrupled from US $409m. in 2010 to $1,200m. in 2020.

In May 2022, in response to the wider global impacts of the Russian Federation's invasion of Ukraine, the AfDB, IMF, World Bank and other international financial institutions collectively issued a Joint International Financial Institution Plan to Address Food Insecurity. Also in May the Bank approved US $1,500m. for a new African Emergency Food Production Facility to counter the disruption to food and fertilizer supplies resulting from the conflict in Ukraine.

In January 2023 the Bank co-hosted, with the AU, an African Food Summit (so-called Dakar 2—the inaugural meeting having been convened in 2015). The meeting focused on boosting Africa's agricultural productivity and strengthening its food systems.

An AfDB-supported African Leaders for Nutrition (ALN) initiative was launched in January 2018. In February 2019 the AfDB and AU Commission and partners issued a Continental Nutrition Accountability Scorecard, compiled by the ALN to promote commitments towards ending malnutrition. In September 2020 the ALN called for financing for nutrition to be embedded by governments into national COVID-19 response and recovery plans.

The Bank launched an African Gender Equality Index in May 2015. In March 2016 the Bank and UN Women signed a Memorandum of Understanding (MOU) on jointly advancing gender equality in Africa. In May 2016 the AfDB established an Affirmative Finance Action for Women in Africa (AFAWA) initiative, with a view to raising US $3,000m. towards reducing the risks incurred by commercial banks and microfinance institutions in financing businesses owned by women in the region. In April 2020 the AfDB Board of Directors endorsed a Gender Equality Trust Fund dedicated to supporting the AFAWA agenda. The Bank funds a continental 50 Million African Women Speak Project (50MAWSP), which aims to address specific challenges confronting women, including female entrepreneurs, in securing access to financial and non-financial services. A 50 Million Women Digital Platform was launched in November 2019. In December a digital skills training platform for young people, Coding for Employment, was launched. In December 2020 the Bank's Board of Directors initiated a Gender Strategy for 2021–25, based on three pillars: Empowering women through access to finance and markets; Accelerating employability and job creation for women through skills enhancement; and Increasing women's access to social services through infrastructure. An AfDB People Strategy for 2021–26, fostering resilience and diversity, was also introduced in 2020. In 2022 100% of the Bank's sovereign operations were categorized under its Gender Marker System—a tool for systematizing the mainstreaming of gender in its business processes.

In April 2020 the Bank initiated a US $10,000m. COVID-19 Rapid Response Facility, to support the continental recovery from the impacts of the ongoing public health, social and economic emergency. During 2020 the AfDB Group significantly refocused its lending programme to meet the challenges posed by the pandemic crisis, as a result of which loan approvals declined by 43%, compared with 2019, while disbursements increased by 44%. In February 2022 the Bank's Board of Directors approved a new Strategy for Quality Health Infrastructure in Africa 2022–30 to support national health systems, including through strengthening health information systems, promoting regional collaboration and harmonizing health policies and regulation.

ECONOMIC GOVERNANCE AND KNOWLEDGE MANAGEMENT

In April 2022 the AfDB approved a Knowledge Management Strategy, covering the period 2022–31, which aimed to enhance the Bank's provision of knowledge required to optimize the outcomes of development strategies.

The AfDB hosts the African Legal Support Facility, which since 2010 has provided legal advice and technical assistance to African governments negotiating complex commercial transactions.

The Bank Group, with ECA and UNDP, organizes an annual African Economic Conference (AEC), which aims to foster dialogue and the exchange of knowledge on issues affecting the continent. The 17th AEC was held in December 2022, in Balaclava, Mauritius, on the theme 'Supporting climate-smart development in Africa'.

The Bank provides technical assistance to regional member countries in the form of experts' services, pre-investment feasibility studies and staff training. Much of this assistance is financed through bilateral trust funds contributed by non-African member states. The Bank's African Development Institute provides training and seminars for officials of regional member countries in order to enhance the management of Bank-financed projects and, more broadly, to strengthen national capacities for promoting sustainable development. The Institute also manages an AfDB/Japan Fellowship programme that provides scholarships to African students to pursue further education.

FINANCE

The Bank hosts the secretariat of an African Financing Partnership, which was established in 2008 to mobilize private sector resources through collaborations with regional development finance institutions. It also hosts the secretariat of the Making Finance Work for Africa Partnership (MFW4A), which aims to support the development of the financial sector in the sub-Saharan region. Through a Migration and Development Initiative Fund, initiated in 2009, the Bank supports the development of financial services for migrant workers, and facilitates channelling remittances towards productive uses in workers' countries of origin. In 2019 it initiated an Africa Digital Financial Inclusion Facility, which aimed to promote digital financial tools to ensure engagement by a further 332m. Africans (with a particular focus on women) in the formal economy.

In 2008 the AfDB initiated the African Financial Markets Initiative (AFMI), to support the development of bond markets throughout the continent and to stimulate domestic resource mobilization. In February 2015 an AFMI-Bloomberg African Bond Index was launched. A social bond framework was established in 2017. In March 2020 the Bank issued a US $3,000m. Fight COVID-19 social bond in order to mitigate the potential social and economic impact of the global pandemic on member states. By the end of April this had been further subscribed, at $4,500m.

Publications

AfDB Statistics Pocketbook.
Africa Competitiveness Report (every 2 years).
Africa Economic Brief (monthly).
African Development Report (annually).
African Development Review (3 a year).
African Economic Outlook (annually).
African Statistical Yearbook (with the AU and ECA).
Annual Report.

Compendium of Statistics on Bank Group Operations (annually).
Development Effectiveness Review Series.
Other reports, country profiles, working papers, background and Board documents.

Statistics

SUMMARY OF BANK GROUP OPERATIONS
(millions of UA)

	2021	2022	Cumulative total*
AfDB approvals†			
Number	66	76	2,194
Amount	2,449.14	3,718.81	81,045
ADF approvals†			
Number	66	107	3,337
Amount	1,263.25	1,817.81	41,894
NTF approvals			
Number	1	—	105
Amount	3.60	—	491
Special Funds‡			
Number	31	37	696
Amount approved	263.55	275.10	3,948
Group total†			
Number	196	284	6,859
Amount approved	4,506.29	6,155.75	131,617

* Since the initial operations of the three institutions (1967 for the AfDB, 1974 for the ADF and 1976 for the NTF).
† Includes loans and grant operations, private and public equity investments, emergency operations, HIPC debt relief, and loan reallocations and guarantees, and the Post-Conflict Country Facility; Group total approvals include those from the Private Sector Credit Enhancement Facility and the Transition Support Facility.
‡ Includes approvals on the operations of the African Water Facility, the Rural Water Supply and Sanitation Initiative, the Global Environment Facility, the Africa Climate Change Fund, the Climate Investment Funds, the Congo Basin Forest Fund, the Fund for African Private Sector Assistance, the Global Agriculture and Food Security Programme, the Micro Finance Capacity Building Fund, the Migration and Development Initiative Fund, OPEC, the Sustainable Energy Fund for Africa, the Middle East and North Africa Transition Fund, the Trust Fund for Countries in Transition, the Nigeria Technical Cooperation Fund, and the Zimbabwe Multi-Donor Trust Fund.

BANK GROUP APPROVALS BY HIGH 5 PRIORITY, 2022
(millions of UA)

High 5 Priority	AfDB	ADF	Special resources*	Total
Light up and power Africa	248.50	125.33	150.29	524.12
Power generation, transmission and distribution (conventional)	102.01	18.51	66.75	187.27
Power generation (renewable)	139.30	91.60	55.14	286.04
Off-grid solutions	—	7.03	2.86	9.89
Energy sector strengthening and reform	—	0.51	1.99	2.50
Infrastructure for energy sector development	—	—	—	—
Multisector	—	—	—	—
Other	7.19	7.67	23.56	38.42
Feed Africa	737.42	427.09	177.42	1,341.97
National and regional operations in production and value addition	79.50	305.87	145.62	530.99
Investment in infrastructure	2.69	39.30	1.86	43.84
Agriculture finance and agribusiness environment	25.13	20.25	6.23	51.61
Inclusivity and sustainable development	34.69	10.51	14.26	59.46
Multisector	595.41	51.16	9.50	656.07
Industrialize Africa	1,331.22	187.81	74.52	1,593.55
Industrial business environment	76.15	7.80	—	83.95
Financial sector and capital markets development	1,024.43	177.81	47.76	1,250.00
Enterprise development	5.62	2.20	7.45	15.27
Infrastructure for industry	213.29	—	19.31	232.61
Multisector	—	—	—	—
Regional environment improvement	11.72	—	—	11.72
Integrate Africa	325.67	774.75	34.33	1,134.75
Regional infrastructure connectivity	248.28	514.15	18.85	781.29
Trade facilitation and investment	77.39	5.03	0.50	82.91
Support to RECs	—	8.20	4.21	12.41
Regional Operations	—	247.37	10.76	258.13
Improve quality of life for the people of Africa	1,076.00	302.83	182.53	1,561.36
Water supply and sanitation	184.58	114.72	88.8	388.11
Human and social development	7.17	58.33	3.66	69.17
Multisector	671.26	40.53	15.16	726.95
Other	212.98	89.25	74.9	377.14
Total	3,718.81	1,817.81	619.13	6,155.75

* Including the NTF, PSF, TSF and Special Funds (as defined above).
Source: African Development Bank, *Annual Report 2022*.

AFRICAN UNION—AU

Address: Roosevelt St, W21K19, POB 3243, Addis Ababa, Ethiopia.
Telephone: (11) 5517700; **fax:** (11) 5517844; **e-mail:** dic@africa-union.org; **internet:** au.int.

The Constitutive Act of the African Union entered into force in May 2001. In July 2002 the AU became fully operational, replacing the Organization of African Unity (OAU), which had been founded in 1963. The AU aims to support unity, solidarity and peace among African states; to defend African common positions on issues of shared interest; to promote sustainable development and political and socioeconomic integration; and to encourage human rights, democratic principles and good governance in all member states.

MEMBERS

All countries in Africa are members of the AU. The membership is divided into five regions: Central Africa (nine countries); Eastern Africa (14); Northern Africa (seven: including the Sahrawi Arab Democratic Republic—SADR); Southern Africa (10); and Western Africa (15) (totalling 55). The SADR was admitted to the OAU in February 1982, following recognition by more than one-half of the member states, but its membership was disputed by Morocco and other countries which claimed that a two-thirds' majority was needed to admit a state whose existence was in question. Morocco withdrew from the OAU with effect from November 1985 in protest. In July 2016 a Moroccan special envoy met AU leaders to discuss the possibility of Morocco's accession to the AU; it was readmitted at the 28th session of the Assembly in January 2017. The SADR ratified the Constitutive Act in December 2000 and is a full member of the AU. The February 2023 summit meeting confirmed that the following four countries remained suspended from participation in the activities of the AU: Mali (suspended since 1 June 2021, following a military overthrow in late May of the leadership of Mali's transitional administration); Guinea (suspended in September, following the overthrow of President Alpha Condé); Sudan (suspended in the following month, in response to the removal by that country's military of the civilian transitional government); Burkina Faso (suspended in January 2022 pending the restoration of constitutional order following a military coup).

Organization
(September 2023)

ASSEMBLY

The Assembly, comprising heads of state and of government, is the supreme organ of the Union and meets usually twice a year to determine and monitor the organization's priorities and common policies and to adopt its annual work programme. Resolutions are passed by a two-thirds' majority, procedural matters by a simple majority. Extraordinary sessions may be convened at the request of a member state and on approval by a two-thirds' majority. The Assembly ensures compliance by member states with decisions of the Union, appoints judges of the African Court of Human and Peoples' Rights, and hears and settles disputes between member states. It may also appoint individual African heads of state and government to lead the implementation of specific high priority AU initiatives. The 36th ordinary session of the Assembly took place in February 2023, in Addis Ababa, on the theme 'The Year of AfCFTA: Acceleration of the African Continental Free Trade Area Implementation'. The Chairperson of the Assembly is assisted by a four-member Bureau.

Chairperson (2023/24): AZALI ASSOUMANI (President of Comoros).

EXECUTIVE COUNCIL

The Council consists of ministers responsible for foreign affairs and others and meets at least twice a year, with provision for extraordinary sessions. It prepares meetings of, and is responsible to, the Assembly; determines the issues to be submitted to the Assembly for decision; co-ordinates and harmonizes the policies, activities and initiatives of the Union in areas of common interest to member states;

and monitors the implementation of policies and decisions of the Assembly.

PERMANENT REPRESENTATIVES COMMITTEE

The Committee, which comprises ambassadors accredited to the AU, meets at least once a month. It is responsible to the Executive Council, which it advises, and whose meetings, including matters for the agenda and draft decisions, it prepares.

COMMISSION

The Commission is the permanent secretariat of the AU, reporting to the Executive Council. It comprises a Chairperson (elected for a four-year term of office by the Assembly), Deputy Chairperson and six further Commissioners, responsible for: Political Affairs, Peace and Security; Infrastructure and Energy; Health, Humanitarian Affairs and Social Development; Education, Science, Technology and Innovation; Agriculture, Rural Development, Blue Economy and Sustainable Environment; and Economic Development, Trade, Industry and Mining. They are elected on the basis of equal geographical distribution. Members of the Commission serve a term of four years and may stand for re-election for one further term of office. A Panel of Eminent Africans was established to oversee the equitable selection of Commission candidates.

Chairperson (2021–24): MOUSSA FAKI MAHAMAT (Chad).
Director-General: FATHALLAH SIJILMASSI (Morocco).

Commissioners

Economic Development, Trade, Industry and Mining: ALBERT MUCHANGA (Zambia).
Infrastructure and Energy: Dr AMANI ABOU-ZEID (Egypt).
Political Affairs, Peace and Security: BANKOLE ADEOYE (Nigeria).
Agriculture, Rural Development, Blue Economy and Sustainable Environment: JOSEFA LEONEL CORREA SACKO (Angola).
Health, Humanitarian Affairs and Social Development: CESSOUMA MINATA SAMATE (Burkina Faso).
Education, Science, Technology and Innovation: Prof. MOHAMED BELHOCINE (Algeria).

SPECIALIZED TECHNICAL COMMITTEES

There are specialized committees—comprising member states' ministers and senior officials—for agriculture, rural development, water and environment; communication and information communications technology; defence, safety and security; education, science and technology; finance, monetary affairs, economic planning and integration; gender and women's empowerment; health, population and drug control; justice and legal affairs; migration, refugees and internally displaced persons; public service, local government, urban development and decentralization; social development, labour and employment; trade, industry and minerals; transport, transcontinental and inter-regional infrastructure, energy and tourism; and youth, culture and sports. The Nairobi, Kenya-based African Institute for Remittances—supported by the European Commission, the African Development Bank (AfDB), the World Bank, and the International Organization for Migration—is a Specialized Technical Office of the AU Commission.

PAN-AFRICAN PARLIAMENT

The Pan-African Parliament, established in 2004 and located in Midrand, South Africa, comprises five deputies (including at least one woman) from each AU member state, presided over by an elected President. The President and four Vice-Presidents must equitably represent the five African regions. The Parliament convenes at least twice a year; an extraordinary session may be called by a two-thirds' majority of the members. The Parliament has only advisory and consultative powers; its eventual evolution into an institution with full legislative authority is envisaged. A high-level consultation between the Pan-African Parliament and Speakers of Regional and National Parliaments was convened in September 2022. In June 2023 the Parliament organized a workshop focused on enhancing access to African legal information.

JUDICIAL AND HUMAN RIGHTS INSTITUTIONS

African Commission on Human and Peoples' Rights (ACHPR): POB 673, Banjul, The Gambia; tel. 441-05-05; fax 441-05-04; e-mail au-banjul@african-union.org; internet achpr.au.int; f. 1987, in accordance with and a year after the entry into force of the African Charter on Human and Peoples' Rights; tasked with promoting and protecting human rights and basic freedoms, and with interpreting the provisions of the Charter; it comprises 11 Commissioners who are appointed by the AU Assembly for six-year terms in office and meet at least twice a year; a secretariat provides administrative, technical and logistical support. Recommendations of the Commission are not legally-binding; it may use its 'good offices' to support states to abide by the recommendations. Other subsidiary mechanisms to support the Commission's activities include special rapporteurs, working groups and advisory committees, all of which are required to report regularly on their findings. In 2016 the ACHPR issued a set of Principles and Guidelines on Human Rights while Countering Terrorism in Africa; 76th ordinary session: July–Aug. 2023, online; Exec. Sec. LINDIWE KHUMALO (acting).

African Court of Human and Peoples' Rights: POB 6274, Arusha, Tanzania; tel. (27) 2970430; e-mail registrar@african-court.org; internet www.african-court.org; f. Jan. 2004, upon the entry into force in January 2004 of the Protocol to the African Charter on Human and Peoples' Rights (adopted in June 1998); consists of 11 judges, elected by the AU Assembly. Its role is to support the ACHPR and rule on the interpretation and application of the Charter. A Protocol to establish an African Court of Justice was adopted in July 2003 (it entered into effect in February 2009 after receiving the required number of ratifications but has never been operational). In July 2008 the AU summit determined to merge the courts and adopted a Protocol on the Statute of the African Court of Justice and Human Rights; by July 2023 the Protocol had been signed by 33 states and ratified by eight (requiring 15 ratifications to enter into force).

In February 2020 the AU Assembly adopted the following new entities: the Sudan-based Continental Operational Centre for Combating Irregular Migration; the Mali-based African Centre for Study and Research on Migration; the African Migration Observatory (based in Morocco); the Algeria-based AU Mechanism for Police Co-operation (AFRIPOL); the AU Centre for Post-Conflict Reconstruction and Development (Egypt); and the African Observatory of Science, Technology and Innovation (Equatorial Guinea).

PEACE AND SECURITY COUNCIL

The Protocol to the Constitutive Act of the African Union Relating to the Peace and Security Council of the African Union entered into force on 26 December 2003; the 15-member elected Council was formally inaugurated in May 2004 (Northern Africa is represented on the Council by two seats; Central Africa, Eastern Africa, and Southern Africa each by three seats; and Western Africa by four seats). It acts as a decision making body for the prevention, management and resolution of conflicts.

ECONOMIC, SOCIAL AND CULTURAL COUNCIL

The Economic, Social and Cultural Council, inaugurated in March 2005, comprises representatives of civic, professional and cultural bodies at national, regional and diaspora level. Its main statutory organs are an elected General Assembly; a Standing Committee; a Credentials Committee; and Sectoral Cluster Communities, tasked with formulating opinions and advising on AU decision making.

DEVELOPMENT AGENCY

African Union Development Agency (AUDA-NEPAD): 230 15th Rd, Randjespark, Midrand 1685, South Africa; tel. (11) 2563600; e-mail info@nepad.org; internet www.nepad.org; f. 2018; a successor to the New Partnership for Africa's Development (NEPAD) Planning and Co-ordination Agency, the technical body established in 2010 to implement NEPAD projects—NEPAD having been launched in 2001 as a long-term strategy to promote socio-economic devt in Africa. A voluntary African Peer Review Mechanism (APRM), established under NEPAD auspices in accordance with a Declaration on Democracy, Political, Economic and Corporate Governance adopted by AU heads of state and government in June 2002, assesses states' conduct in the areas of democracy and political governance; economic governance and management; corporate governance; and socioeconomic governance; by 2023 the APRM had 41 participants; NEPAD's Programme for Infrastructure Development in Africa (PIDA), of which the AfDB is the executing agency, was initiated in 2010 with the aim of developing the continental energy, information and communications technology, transport and transboundary water resources infrastructures; a second PIDA Priority Action Plan (PIDA PAP 2) was being implemented over the period 2011–30, with NEPAD-AUDA as lead co-ordinating agency; in February 2021 AU leaders approved 69 PIDA PAP 2 projects; NEPAD-AUDA launched in March 2021 a Pandemic Resilience Accelerator for African Health-Related Businesses. A Heads of State and Government Orientation Cttee provides leadership to the NEPAD process, determines policies, priorities and programmes of action and, through its Chair., reports directly to the AU Assembly; the UN allocated US $8.7m. in support of the agency under its 2023 budget; CEO NARDOS BEKELE-THOMAS (Ethiopia).

AFRICAN CONTINENTAL FREE TRADE AREA SECRETARIAT

AfCFTA Secretariat: Africa Trade House, Ambassadorial Enclave, Liberia Rd, Ridge, Accra, Ghana; e-mail info@au-afcfta.org; internet au-afcfta.org; f. 2019 to facilitate the implementation of the AfCFTA (q.v.); Sec.-Gen. WAMKELE KEABETSWE MENE (South Africa).

Activities

In May 1963 30 African heads of state adopted the Charter of the Organization of African Unity (OAU).

In May 1994 the Abuja Treaty Establishing the African Economic Community (AEC, signed in June 1991) entered into force. An extraordinary summit meeting, convened in September 1999, in Sirte, Libya, at the request of the then Libyan leader Col Muammar al-Qaddafi, determined to establish an African Union, based on the principles and objectives of the OAU and the AEC, but furthering African co-operation, development and integration. Heads of state declared their commitment to accelerating the establishment of regional institutions as well as the implementation of economic and monetary union, as provided for by the Abuja Treaty.

In July 2000 at a summit meeting of the OAU held in Lomé, Togo, 27 heads of state and of government signed the draft Constitutive Act of the African Union, which was to enter into force after ratification by two-thirds of member states' legislatures; this was achieved in May 2001. The Union was inaugurated, replacing the OAU, on 9 July 2002, at a summit meeting held in Durban, South Africa. During the transitional year a review of all OAU treaties was undertaken and those deemed relevant were retained by the AU. The AU operates on the basis of both the Constitutive Act and the Abuja Treaty.

AGENDA 2063

The May 2013 session of the Assembly issued a 50th Anniversary Solemn Declaration, which outlined a vision and series of ideals for the economic and social transformation of the continent over the coming 50 years. These were to be translated into concrete actions and objectives by a joint programme with the AfDB and the UN Economic Commission for Africa (ECA) known as Agenda 2063, within the context of which 20 African Development Goals were to be developed. Endorsed by AU heads of state and of government in January 2015, the finalized Agenda 2063 was underpinned by the following so-called African Aspirations: a prosperous Africa, based on inclusive growth and sustainable development; an integrated, politically united continent, based on the ideals of Pan-Africanism and a vision of Africa's Renaissance; an Africa of good governance, democracy, respect for human rights, justice and the rule of law; a peaceful and secure Africa; a strong continental cultural identity, based on common heritage, values and ethics; people-driven continental development (with a particular focus on women and youth); and Africa as a strong, united, influential global player and partner. In June 2015 the AU summit adopted 'The First Ten-Year Implementation Plan of Agenda 2063 and its Financing Mechanism'. The following were designated as Agenda 2063 flagship initiatives: (i) connecting all African capital cities and commercial centres through an African Integrated High Speed Train Network; (ii) formulating an African Commodities Strategy, aimed at transforming the continent from a supplier of raw materials to an active user—for the economic benefit of Africans—of its own resources; (iii) developing the AfCFTA; (iv) promoting free movement of people and an African passport; (v) silencing guns: ending all conflicts, genocides and gender-based violence, and introducing an African Human Security Index; (vi) implementing the proposed 43,200 KW Grand Inga Dam hydropower project on the River Congo, Democratic Republic of the Congo—DRC, which, it was envisaged, would support regional power pools; (vii) establishing a Single African Air Transport Market; (viii) promoting an annual African Economic Forum; (ix) establishing the proposed African continental financial institutions; (x) putting in place a Pan-African E-Network, including a strong intra-African broadband terrestrial infrastructure; (xi) implementing an Africa Outer Space Strategy, to promote climate forecasting, disaster management, remote sensing, defence and security, and agricultural development; (xii) establishing a Pan African E-University; (xiii) advancing continental cyber security, guided by the (2014) AU Convention on Cyber Security and Personal Data Protection; (xiv) establishing a Great African Museum, guided by the (2006) Charter for African Cultural Renaissance; and (xv) compiling an *Encyclopaedia Africana*, to represent an authoritative and authentic resource on African history and life.

In May 2013 the AfDB endorsed an Africa50 Infrastructure Fund, which was to finance, in partnership with regional institutions, transformational projects with a focus on enhancing the transcontinental infrastructure.

An AU Retreat on Institutional Reforms and on preparations for the second decade of Agenda 2063 was organized by the AU Commission in June 2023, in Addis Ababa, with participation by permanent representatives to the AU, and delegates from the AU organs and RECs.

ECONOMIC DEVELOPMENT, TRADE, INDUSTRY AND MINING

The AU recognizes the following regional economic communities, or RECs, in Africa: Common Market for Eastern and Southern Africa (COMESA), the East African Community (EAC), Southern African Development Community (SADC), Communauté Economique des Etats de l'Afrique Centrale (CEEAC), Economic Community of West African States (ECOWAS), IGAD, and the Union of the Arab Maghreb. The inaugural meeting of the AEC took place in June 1997. In July 2007 the ninth AU Assembly adopted a Protocol on Relations between the AU and the RECs, aimed at facilitating the harmonization of policies and ensuring compliance with the schedule of the 1991 Abuja Treaty. Within the framework of the Protocol the AU Commission convenes biannual Joint Coordination Meetings comprising representatives of the AU, RECs, ECA, AfDB, NEPAD and the African Capacity Building Foundation (an AU specialized agency). In July 2023 the fifth annual Mid-Year Coordination Meeting (MYCM) was convened between the AU, African RECs, regional mechanisms, and member states, with a focus on aligning and co-ordinating the implementation of the continental integration agenda.

In June 2022 the AU Commission convened an extraordinary session of the Specialized Technical Committee on Transport, Transcontinental and Interregional Infrastructure, Energy and Tourism to address impacts of the ongoing Russia–Ukraine conflict on the continental energy and infrastructure sectors.

In July 2016 AU heads of state and of government launched an AU Passport policy, with the objective of facilitating the free movement of people on the continent. In late January 2019 the 30th AU Assembly adopted the Protocol to the Treaty Establishing the AEC relating to the Free Movement of Persons, Rights of Residence and Right of Establishment; a draft roadmap to guide the new Protocol's implementation was also adopted at that time. The Protocol was signed by 27 countries at the extraordinary summit held in March; by July 2023 it had been ratified by four states (Mali, Niger, Rwanda, and São Tomé and Príncipe).

The 2023 edition of *Africa's Development Dynamics*, issued in July 2023, jointly by the AU and the OECD Development Centre, on the theme 'Investing in sustainable development', estimated that Africa required US $1,600m. by 2030 to attain the UN Sustainable Development Goals.

African Continental Free Trade Area: In March 2018 the 10th extraordinary summit of AU heads of state and government, convened in the Rwandan capital Kigali, formally initiated the AfCFTA; the Agreement Establishing the AfCFTA was signed by 44 member states. It entered into force on 30 May 2019, and provided for the liberalization of 90% of tariff lines over 10 years for Least Developed Countries (LDCs) and over five years for non-LDCs; trade in sensitive products would be liberalized over 13 years (LDCs) and 10 years (non-LDCs). The AfCFTA was declared operational in early July, at an extraordinary AU summit. At that time it was decided that Ghana would host its secretariat. In early 2020 the Assembly determined that an extraordinary summit should be convened in late May to approve instruments that would enable trading to commence within the AfCFTA on 1 July; the summit and deadline were, however, postponed, in view of the COVID-19 pandemic. In August the AU Commissioner for Trade and Industry emphasized the importance to the continent's recovery from the COVID-19 crisis of implementing the AfCFTA, and the need to boost intra-African trade. In December an extraordinary session of the Assembly confirmed that trading under the AfCFTA would commence on 1 January 2021. By July 2023 the accord had been signed by 54 states, and had been ratified by 44. AfCFTA protocols on e-commerce, competition, investment and intellectual property were under development in 2023.

In support of the implementation of the AfCFTA an online African Trade Observatory (ATO) was launched in July 2019, and a new business-to-business e-commerce platform, the Africa Trade Exchange (ATEX) was initiated in May 2022. The third Intra-African Trade Fair was to be organized jointly by the AU Commission, AfCFTA Secretariat, Afreximbank and Côte d'Ivoire Government in November 2023, in the Ivorian capital, Abidjan.

INFRASTRUCTURE AND ENERGY

An African Energy Commission (AFREC) was inaugurated in February 2008, with the aim of increasing co-operation in energy matters between Africa and other regions. At that time a subsidiary African Electrotechnical Standardization Commission also become operational. In June 2021 the AU initiated an African Single Electricity Market (AfSEM). The AU Commission, NEPAD, the AfDB and other partners jointly lead the Africa Renewable Energy Initiative, which was launched in December 2015 to promote the installation of large-scale renewable energy capacity in Africa, with a medium-term objective of achieving the cross-continent generation of at least 300 GW of energy from renewable sources by 2030. In July 2022 the AU Executive Council adopted an African Common Position on Energy Access and Just Transition.

The Bamako Convention on the Ban of the Import into Africa and the Control of Transboundary Movement and Management of Hazardous Wastes within Africa was adopted by OAU member states in 1991 and entered into force in April 1998. By July 2023 it had been signed by 35 states and ratified by 30.

In January 2012 the Executive Council endorsed an African Civil Aviation Policy. In January 2018 the 30th AU Assembly adopted a Decision on the Establishment of a Single African Air Transport Market (SAATM). By 2023 the SAATM had 34 participating states that accounted for 89% of intra-African air traffic.

A Pan African E-Network Project was initiated in 2009 to advance continental connectivity. In May 2014 heads of African ICT units adopted a comprehensive Continental ICT Strategy for Africa (CISA), covering the period 2014–24, and focusing on the following themes: post and telecommunications infrastructure; capacity development; e-applications and services; enabling environment and governance; mobilization of resources and partnerships; industrialization; and research and development. A joint AU-ECA Digital Identity, Digital Trade and Digital Economy (DITE) initiative was launched in 2019. A Digital Transformation Strategy for Africa, being implemented during 2020–30, aimed to help build by 2030 a secure Digital Single Market in Africa, and to facilitate the full digital empowerment of all people on the continent.

AGRICULTURE, RURAL DEVELOPMENT, BLUE ECONOMY AND SUSTAINABLE ENVIRONMENT

In July 2003 the second Assembly of heads of state and of government adopted the Maputo Declaration on Agriculture and Food Security in Africa, focusing on the need to revitalize the agricultural sector and to combat hunger on the continent by developing food reserves based on African production. The leaders determined to deploy policies and budgetary resources to remove current constraints on agricultural production, trade and rural development; and to implement the Comprehensive Africa Agriculture Development Programme (CAADP), as an integral programme of NEPAD, during the period 2003–14. In June 2014 the 23rd Assembly of heads of state and of government, meeting in Malabo (Equatorial Guinea), extended the CAADP for the period 2014–25. The CAADP has agreed the objective of allocating at least 10% of national budgets to investment in agricultural productivity. It aims to achieve dynamic agricultural markets between African countries and regions; good participation in and access to markets by farmers; a more equitable distribution of wealth for rural populations; more equitable access to land, practical and financial resources, knowledge, information, and technology for sustainable development; development of Africa's role as a strategic player in the area of agricultural science and technology; and environmentally sound agricultural production and a culture of sustainable management of natural resources. By 2023 44 AU member states had signed CAADP compacts. During that year a further 10-year phase of the CAADP was under development, to commence in 2025.

A Revised African Convention on the Conservation of Nature and Natural Resources entered into force in July 2016, and had been ratified by 17 member states at July 2023. In September 2021 the AU Commission, through the Department of Agriculture, Rural Development, Blue Economy and Sustainable Environment and the African Land Policy Centre (managed by the AU, AfDB and ECA), issued a draft continental Land Governance Strategy, which aimed to ensure more equitable land governance with secured land rights and tenure.

In July 2021 the AU Commission initiated a Continental Green Recovery Action Plan, to be implemented during 2021–27, with a focus on strengthening climate finance; assisting the just transition to renewable energy; pursuing nature-based solutions, with a focus on fostering biodiversity; promoting resilient agriculture; and encouraging green and resilient cities. In February 2022 the 35th AU Assembly adopted an AU Climate Change and Resilient Development Strategy and Action Plan to be implemented during the period 2022–32, and an Integrated African Strategy on Meteorology Services (that covered the period 2021–30). An African Green Stimulus Programme and AU Green Recovery Action Plan were also adopted at that time; both were focused on achieving a sustainable continental recovery from the COVID-19 pandemic.

A Pan African Veterinary Vaccine Centre is based at Debre-Zeit, Ethiopia (and includes an AU COVID-19 Diagnostic Laboratory that was inaugurated in May 2020).

An AU Africa Blue Economy Strategy—formulated at the instigation of African leaders who participated in a Sustainable Blue Economy Conference held in November 2018, in Nairobi, Kenya—aims to guide the development and utilization of aquatic resources in Africa, within the Agenda 2063 framework. The Strategy was endorsed in February 2020, at a side event of the AU summit meeting. It has five focal areas: fisheries, aquaculture, conservation and sustainable aquatic ecosystems; shipping and transportation, trade, ports, maritime security, safety and enforcement; coastal and maritime tourism, climate change, resilience, environment, and infrastructure; sustainable energy and mineral resources and innovative industries; and policies, governance, employment, job creation, poverty eradication, and innovative financing.

HEALTH, HUMANITARIAN AFFAIRS AND SOCIAL DEVELOPMENT

On 27 January 2020 the Africa Centres for Disease Control and Prevention (Africa CDC) activated its Incident Management System (IMS)—which is supported by the African Volunteer Health Corps (AVoHC), an entity that facilitates Africa-wide surge staffing during public health crises—to address the viral outbreak that had arisen in the People's Republic of China. On 20 March Africa CDC issued an Africa Joint Continental Strategy for the COVID-19 Outbreak, with the overarching goals of preventing severe illness and death from COVID-19 in member states, and minimizing severe social disruption and economic consequences arising from the pandemic. The Strategy was to be implemented through the Africa CDC IMS and an Africa Task Force for Novel Coronavirus, and to be supported by an AU COVID-19 Response Fund. The Strategy provided, *inter alia*, for collaboration between member states in maintaining supply chains for shared resources, such as personal protective and laboratory equipment; and for support to laboratories to provide, *inter alia*, quality-assured diagnostic testing, specimen referral testing, and next generation sequencing on COVID-19 specimens. In mid-May the inaugural meeting was convened of an AU Taskforce on COVID-19's Impact on Food Security and Nutrition in Africa, with participation by representatives of the AU Commission, AUDA-NEPAD, the AfDB, FAO, the European Commission and the World Bank. An Africa Medical Supplies Platform (AMSP) was launched by the AU in June to facilitate the ordering of essential medical and related inputs. Also in June the AU initiated a Partnership to Accelerate COVID-19 Testing (PACT). Meanwhile, an Africa Vaccine Strategy was launched, which aimed to secure sufficient supplies of COVID-19 vaccines and to ensure their efficient and fair distribution; a high-level Africa Vaccine Acquisition Task Team (AVATT) was established as a component of the Strategy.

In February 2021 the AU Bureau established a new Commission on African COVID-19 Response, under the leadership of South African President Cyril Ramaphosa, who was designated as the AU Champion on COVID-19. In April 2021 the AU and Africa CDC launched a Partnerships for African Vaccine Manufacturing (PAVM) framework, which aimed to enable the sustainable production of vaccines within Africa. In June AU ministers responsible for finance and the World Bank Group agreed to support an AVATT initiative to purchase and deliver vaccines for up to 400m. people across Africa, with a view to protecting 60% of the continent's population. In February 2022 six member states—Egypt, Kenya, Nigeria, Senegal, South Africa and Tunisia—became the first African recipients of mRNA COVID-19 vaccine technology under a global mRNA technology transfer hub initiative that had been launched in June 2021 by the AU, AU CDC, WHO, ACT Accelerator/COVAX and Medicines Patent Pool. In September 2022 the AU Commission and Africa CDC launched a New Public Health Order initiative, which included a roadmap towards continental health security. In May 2023 the AU Commission and Gavi, the Vaccine Alliance concluded a Memorandum of Understanding (MOU) aimed at increasing access to and accelerating the uptake of life-saving vaccines across the continent (building on the Addis Ababa Declaration on Immunization, issued in January 2017 by AU heads of state or government, which comprised commitments to increase political, technical and financial investments in immunization programmes).

The AU promotes the eradication of endemic parasitic and infectious diseases and improving access to medicines. An AU African Health Strategy was being implemented during 2016–30; further long-term strategies included a Sexual and Reproductive Health and Rights Continental Policy Framework (accompanied by a Maputo Plan of Action); the Pharmaceutical Manufacturing Plan for Africa (approved in 2007); the African Regional Nutrition Strategy, covering 2015–25; the Abuja Action Plan towards the Elimination of HIV and AIDS, Malaria and Tuberculosis in Africa by 2030 (approved in 2013); the AIDS Watch Africa Strategic Framework aimed at eliminating AIDS, TB and Malaria by 2030 (endorsed in July 2017); and a Catalytic Framework to End AIDS, TB and Eliminate Malaria in Africa by 2030. A Treaty for the Establishment of the African Medicines Agency was adopted by the Assembly in February 2019. It provided for the establishment of the 'AMA' as a specialized AU body to be tasked with expanding the capacity of AU member states and regional economic commissions to regulate and improve access to safe, high-quality and effective medical products. The treaty entered into effect, having received the required 15 ratifications, in November 2021, although no agreement had been reached regarding the host country for the Agency. The first conference of the parties to the Treaty met in June 2022. An inaugural extraordinary conference session was held in November to discuss the operationalization phase of the AMA.

In August 2010 the AU and the UN Office for the Coordination of Humanitarian Affairs signed an agreement detailing key areas of future co-operation on humanitarian issues, with the aim of strengthening the AU's capacity in the areas of disaster preparedness and response, early warning, co-ordination, and protection of civilians affected by conflict or natural disaster. In January 2016 the AU Assembly endorsed the establishment of an African Humanitarian Agency (AfHA), as well as a Common African Position on achieving effective humanitarian action by 2025. In February 2020 the AU Assembly urged the prompt operationalization of the proposed AfHA. The first biennial *Africa Report on Disaster Risk Reduction* was issued in August 2020. In November 2021 the AU supported the Eighth Africa Regional Platform for Disaster Risk Reduction and Seventh High-Level Meeting on Disaster Risk Reduction, hosted (in a hybrid format) from Nairoibi. The latter meeting adopted a near-term (2021–25) programme of action to guide the continental implementation of the Sendai Framework for Disaster Risk Reduction (which was adopted in March 2015 by the Third UN World Conference on Disaster Risk Reduction, held in Sendai City, Japan, and covers the period 2015–30). In July 2023 the inaugural policy dialogue, addressing Gender, Disaster Risk Reduction, Outbreaks, Epidemics and Food Security, was convened between the AU Commission and the African Risk Capacity.

At the January 2014 Assembly the Chairperson of the AU Commission appointed a Special Envoy for Women, Peace and Security. In June 2015 the 25th AU summit adopted a common position on ending child marriage. The AU's Saleema Initiative on Eliminating Female Genital Mutilation was launched in February 2019.

In June 2020 the AU and UNICEF launched a No Name Campaign, which aimed to promote the registration of births in Africa and to ensure children's right to a legal identity. In November, in the context of the No Name Campaign, the AU convened a videoconferenced High Level Political Dialogue on Birth Registration.

The 13th edition of the African Games, a continental sporting competition, was to be organized in 2024, in Ghana.

EDUCATION, SCIENCE, TECHNOLOGY AND INNOVATION

In January 2016 AU heads of state and of government adopted a Continental Education Strategy for Africa, covering the period 2016–25. An AU Scientific, Technical and Research Commission is based in Abuja, and a virtual AU Network of Sciences connects 54 research institutions in Africa and Europe. In January 2016 AU heads of state and of government adopted the first African Space Policy and Strategy, as an initial step towards establishing an AU outer space programme. A statute establishing an African Space Agency entered into force in January 2019.

POLITICAL AFFAIRS, PEACE AND SECURITY

The African Charter on Human and Peoples' Rights, which was adopted by the OAU in 1981 and entered into force in October 1986, provided for the establishment of the African Commission on Human and Peoples' Rights. A Protocol to the Charter, establishing an African Court of Peoples' and Human Rights, was adopted by the OAU Assembly in June 1998 and entered into force in January 2004. In February 2009 a protocol (adopted in July 2003) establishing an African Court of Justice entered into force. A Protocol on the Statute of the African Court of Justice and Human Rights, aimed at merging the African Court of Human and Peoples' Rights and the African Court of Justice, was opened for signature in July 2008. A further Protocol, relating to the Rights of Women, was adopted by the July 2003 Maputo Assembly. An African Charter on the Rights and Welfare of the Child entered into force in November 1999. The sixth annual African Transitional Justice Forum was convened in September 2022, in Lomé, Togo.

In 1964 the OAU adopted a Declaration on the Denuclearization of Africa, and in April 1996 it adopted the African Nuclear Weapons Free Zone Treaty (also known as the Pelindaba Treaty), which promotes co-operation in the peaceful uses of nuclear energy, and identifies Africa as a nuclear weapons-free zone; the Pelindaba Treaty entered into force in July 2009.

The July 2002 inaugural summit meeting of AU heads of state and of government adopted a Declaration Governing Democratic Elections in Africa, providing guidelines for the conduct of national elections in member states and outlining the AU's electoral observation and monitoring role; an African Charter on Democracy, Elections and Governance entered into force in February 2012.

In 2011 an African Governance Architecture was established by the Assembly, including an African Governance Platform, focused on the promotion of good governance and on strengthening democracy across the continent.

A Convention Governing the Specific Aspects of Refugee Problems in Africa was adopted by OAU member states in 1969. It entered into force in June 1974 and had been ratified by 46 states at July 2023. The Convention promotes close co-operation with the UN High Commissioner for Refugees (UNHCR). The AU Convention for the Protection and Assistance of IDPs in Africa (the 'Kampala Convention')—the first legally binding international treaty providing legal protection and support to people displaced within their own countries by violent conflict and natural disasters—entered into force in December 2012, and had been ratified by 33 countries by July 2023.

A revised AU Migration Policy Framework (MPFA) and accompanying Plan of Action, covering the period 2018–30, were issued in May 2018 (superseding an original MPFA that had been adopted in 2006). The revised MPFA had the following areas of focus: border management; forced displacement; human rights of migrants; internal migration; inter-state co-operation and partnerships; irregular migration; labour migration; migration data management; and migration and development. The seventh Pan African Forum on Migration (PAFoM VII) was hosted by Rwanda, in Kigali, under AU auspices, in October 2022. A Joint Labour Migration Programme for Africa (JLMP), jointly implemented by the AU Commission, International Labour Organization, International Organization for Migration, and ECA, was initiated in January 2015 to improve continental labour migration governance. AU efforts to combat human trafficking are guided by the 2006 Ouagadougou Action Plan to Combat Trafficking in Human Beings.

An AU Convention on Preventing and Combating Corruption entered into force in August 2006, and in May 2009 an associated AU Advisory Board on Corruption was inaugurated. An AU Convention on Cyber Security and Personal Data Protection was adopted in June 2014, and by July 2023 had 14 states parties. In June 2021 the AU Commission, supported by the Council of Europe, organized the second African Cybercrime Forum, in Addis Ababa. (The first had been convened in October 2018.)

The Protocol to the Constitutive Act of the African Union Relating to the Establishment of the Peace and Security Council, adopted by the inaugural AU summit of heads of state and of government in July 2002, entered into force in December 2003, superseding the 1993 Cairo Declaration on the OAU Mechanism for Conflict Prevention, Management and Resolution. The Protocol provides for the development of a collective peace and security framework (known as the African Peace and Security Architecture—APSA). This includes a Peace and Security Council, operational at the levels of heads of state and of government, ministers responsible for foreign affairs, and permanent representatives, to be supported by a five-member advisory Panel of the Wise, a Continental Early Warning System, an African Standby Force (ASF) and a Peace Fund. In February 2004 the Assembly adopted a Common African Defence and Security Policy (CADSP). A Network of African Women in Conflict Prevention and Mediation (FemWise-Africa)—a subsidiary mechanism of the Panel of the Wise—was formally endorsed in July 2017 by AU heads of state and of government. In February 2020 the Assembly requested the AU Commission fully to operationalize FemWise-Africa.

The activities of the AU Peace and Security Council include early warning and preventive diplomacy; peacemaking mediation; peace support operations and intervention; peacebuilding activities and post-conflict reconstruction; and humanitarian action and disaster management. The Council is tasked with implementing the common defence policy of the Union, and ensuring the implementation of the 1999 OAU Convention on the Prevention and Combating of Terrorism (under which signatory states were to exchange information and refrain from granting asylum to terrorists).

The AU Non-Aggression and Common Defence Pact, which entered into force in December 2009, stipulates measures aimed at preventing and at peacefully resolving inter- and intra-state conflicts. The Pact states that an act, or threat, of aggression against an individual member state affects all member states.

The African Centre for the Study and Research on Terrorism (ACSRT) and the Committee of Intelligence and Security Services in Africa (CISSA) were both established in 2004. In 2014 the 23rd Assembly adopted an AU Convention on Cross-Border Cooperation, referred to as the Niamey Convention. An AU Mechanism for Police Cooperation (AFRIPOL), comprising member states' chiefs of police, was launched in May 2017. In December 2019 an AU Ministerial Meeting adopted the Bamako Declaration on Access to Natural Resources and Conflicts between Communities. African Youth Ambassadors for Peace represent five continental regions.

In May 2022 the 16th extraordinary session of the Assembly, convened in Malabo (Equatorial Guinea) issued a Declaration on Terrorism and Unconstitutional Changes of Government, which noted the negative impacts across the continent of a resurgence of unconstitutional changes of government, the expanding threat of terrorism and violent extremism, a proliferation of armed groups, continuing transnational crime, and an influx of foreign terrorist fighters and of private military companies and mercenaries (notably, the Wagner Goup—a Russian private paramilitary and security contractor). It was noted that deficits in governance, and terrorism and violent extremism were being compounded by the impacts of climate change, and that terrorist groupings were self-funding through the exploitation of continental natural resources. The Assembly determined to scale up the implementation of all relevant AU instruments and decisions, and to accelerate the full operationalizion of the ASF. External actors were urged to cease supporting terrorist groups across the continent. The Assembly determined to develop a comprehensive continental strategic plan of action focused on countering terrorism in Africa, and to strengthen the capacity of the AU Commission and of relevant AU agencies.

An AU Policy on Post-Conflict Reconstruction and Development has been pursued since 2006. In December 2021 a Cairo (Egypt)-based AU Centre for Post-conflict Reconstruction and Development (PCRD) was inaugurated.

In January 2018 the 30th AU Assembly requested Morocco to permit the return of an AU Observer Mission to Laayoune (Western Sahara), and to admit independent human rights monitors to the area. The Assembly also called for joint UN-AU facilitated negotiations on the organization of a free and fair referendum to determine the future of Western Sahara. (The Moroccan authorities had expelled the AU Observer Mission in March 2016, with UN international civilian staff, following an incident in which the UN Secretary-General had referred to Morocco's presence in Western Sahara as an 'occupation'.) In July 2018 the 31st AU Assembly, in a change of direction on the matter, decided to decelerate the AU's own peace activities in Western Sahara (which had been deemed by Morocco as 'biased'), and to place increased focus on supporting—through the establishment of a Troika of heads of state—the ongoing UN-led political process there.

AU Peace Fund: In July 2016 the AU Assembly agreed on an initial endowment and subsequent 0.2% import levy to support the activities of the Peace Fund, which included three thematic support windows (on mediation and preventive diplomacy, institutional capacity and peace support operations), as well as a Crisis Reserve Facility. A Board of Trustees was appointed in November 2018, when the Fund was officially inaugurated. It was envisaged that the Fund would become operational in 2023, with a focus on supporting the AU Transition Mission in Somalia; interventions in the political crisis in Sudan; and initiatives in East African Community member states. In May 2023 the Board of Trustees recommended that the endowment of the Crisis Reserve Facility should be doubled from US $5m. to $10m. in 2023/24, to enable effective interventions to secure peace and security across the continent.

African Standby Force (ASF): An extraordinary AU summit meeting, convened in Sirte, in February 2004, adopted a declaration approving the establishment of the multinational ASF, which was to comprise rapidly deployable multidimensional military, police and civilian capabilities, and was to be mandated to undertake observation, monitoring and other peace support missions; to deploy in member states as required to prevent the resurgence or escalation of violence; to intervene as required to restore stability; to conduct post-conflict disarmament and demobilization and other peacebuilding activities; and to provide emergency humanitarian assistance. The Force was to be drawn from five regional brigades: the North African Regional Capability (NARC) Standby Force, the Eastern African Standby Force (EASF), the Force Multinationale de l'Afrique Centrale (FOMAC), the SADC Standby Brigade (SADCBRIG) and ECOWAS Standby Force (ESF). The NARC and the EASF Coordination Mechanism (EASFCOM) maintain liaison offices at the AU's headquarters.

In January 2014 AU leaders endorsed the creation of an interim African Capacity for Immediate Response to Crises (ACIRC), to be deployed as a continental rapid reaction force in emergency situations, pending the ASF's full operationalization (which required substantial additional financing). In July 2016 the 27th AU summit authorized the establishment of a donor-funded AU Special Fund for Prevention and Combating of Terrorism and Violent Extremism. An ASF Continental Logistics Base was inaugurated in Douala, Cameroon, in January 2018.

In May 2022 an extraordinary AU summit was convened to address terrorism and unconstitutional changes of government.

Grand Ethiopian Renaissance Dam (GERD): In mid-2020 the Chairperson of the AU Assembly determined to lead a consultation process aimed at resolving a longstanding dispute concerning Ethiopia's construction of the GERD—on the Blue Nile, the River Nile's main tributary—and its impacts, including potential water losses, on Egypt and Sudan (both downstream Nile countries). The resulting inaugural meeting of the AU Bureau to review progress in Trilateral Negotiations on the GERD was convened in late June. Several meetings were subsequently held, but the negotiations process eventually stalled, with Egypt and Sudan reportedly seeking a legally binding international accord, providing a formal mechanism to resolve future disputes, and Ethiopia unilaterally advocating for a non-binding approach. In September the UN Security Council issued a statement that urged the resumption of constructive negotiations under AU auspices. Electricity production from the GERD commenced in February 2022, and was augmented in August. Intergovernmental talks on the situation were revived in August 2023.

Libya: In May 2014 the AU Peace and Security Council issued a statement expressing deep concern about violent insecurity emerging from the ongoing political transition process in Libya. A Special Envoy was appointed, at the request of the Council, in June. An International Contact Group for Libya, established by the AU, held its inaugural meeting in December. In January 2015 the Chairperson of the AU Commission welcomed the initiation of a UN-mediated national political dialogue in Libya. In October the participants in the dialogue finalized a political agreement on establishing a Government of National Accord. A majority of the participants in the dialogue formally adopted the Libyan Political Agreement at a gathering convened in mid-December, in Skhirat, Morocco. In October the AU High Representative for Libya, the Special Representative of the UN Secretary-General, and the Secretary-General of the League of Arab States (Arab League) announced the formation of a Troika aimed at advancing the ongoing political process. This was superseded in March 2017 by the establishment of an AU-UN-Arab League-EU Quartet formation as a joint framework for co-ordinating efforts to address the Libyan crisis (see under the UN Support Mission in Libya for further details). In November the Chairperson of the AU Commission condemned the reported auctioning of African migrants in Tripoli by international criminal networks, and urged the African Commission on Human and Peoples' Rights to support an investigation that the Libyan authorities had opened into the allegations.

In January 2018 the 30th AU Assembly reiterated deep concern over the continuing political impasse and unstable security situation in Libya. The Assembly requested the AU Commission to re-launch, in close co-operation with the UN, the work of the International Contact Group on Libya. The AU High Representative for Libya and AU High-Level Committee on Libya (established in March 2011) continued to hold regular consultations with Libyan political stakeholders. In July 2018 the AU Chairperson stated concern over a recent escalation of conflict in Libya's 'oil crescent' area. In April 2019 the AU Commission Chairperson, accompanied by several AU Commission officials, held discussions in Tripoli with Libyan stakeholders, including the Chairman of the Presidential Council of Libya, the Prime Minister of the GNA, and the Commander of the Libyan National Army. In the following month the third AU-UN Annual Conference emphasized the need for the UN and regional organizations to support a single roadmap for a political resolution in Libya.

In July 2019 the AU Peace and Security Council stated grave concern over the situation in Libya, and in particular over the plight of African migrants in camps and detention facilities there. It condemned the recent bomb attack against the Tajoura Detention Centre, near Tripoli, that had caused 53 fatalities and severely injured several hundred people, and called for the perpetrators to be held accountable. An extraordinary session of the ACHPR, meanwhile, issued a resolution that condemned lethal fighting and attacks in Libya, including attacks on migrants and refugees; called on the parties to the conflict to cease such attacks; called on the international community to prioritize the protection of the human rights of civilians, migrants and refugees; and urged all parties to focus on dialogue. During July the AU High-Level Committee on Libya proposed the appointment of a joint AU-UN special envoy on Libya, as a means of enhancing co-ordination; in October, however, this was rejected by the UN Security Council. In early September the AU, Rwanda and UNHCR concluded an agreement under which an initial group of 500 detained asylum seekers and refugees in Libya who had originated in the Horn of Africa were to be evacuated (voluntarily) to Rwanda.

The AU participates, with the Arab League, EU, UN and several partner countries, in the International Follow-Up Committee on Libya, which was established to pursue the outcome of the International Conference on Libya that had been held in Berlin, Germany, in February 2020. In August the Chairperson of the AU Assembly welcomed commitments to a ceasefire made by the parties to the Libyan conflict; an agreement on a ceasefire was signed on 23 October. In February 2021 the AU Chairperson commended the election by a UN-facilitated inclusive Libyan Political Dialogue Forum (LPDF, initiated in October 2020) of a unified interim government, to guide Libya towards presidential and legislative elections that were scheduled to be held on 24 December. In mid-March he welcomed the installation of the interim administration. At the end of August the AU Commissioner for Political Affairs, Peace and Security, the Arab League Secretary-General, the UN Special Envoy for Libya, and the foreign ministers of Algeria, Chad, Egypt, Libya, Niger, Nigeria, Sudan and Tunisia, participated in a 'Libya's neighbours' conference, hosted by Algeria. The final communiqué of the conference reaffirmed rejection of all forms of foreign interference in Libya's internal affairs, and called for the withdrawal from Libya's territory of all foreign fighters, mercenaries and troops. The participants decided to send a ministerial delegation to Libya to contact all stakeholders, with a view to pursuing a political resolution of continuing tensions. President Denis Sassou Nguesso of the Republic of the Congo, head of the AU High-Level Committee on Libya, represented the organization at an international conference held in Paris, France, in November, to address the Libyan peace process. The planned elections were postponed in December, in the absence of an agreed legal framework. The Chairman of the AU Commission stated deep concern in late August 2022 over the ongoing build-up of military forces and eruption of violent clashes in Tripoli. In February 2023 the AU Peace and Security Council issued a communiqué that commended the Libyan Authorities for recent positive political developments, including talks that had taken place in January aimed at reaching consensus on an electoral law; and urged the full implementation of the October 2020 ceasefire and of a national action plan (that had been initiated in October 2021) for the withdrawal of mercenaries, foreign fighters and foreign forces from

Libyan territory. In July 2023 the Chair. of the AU High-Level Committee on Libya organized an AU-Libya meeting that gave consideration to establishing a preparatory committee to organize a national conference on reconciliation in Libya.

An AU-EU-UN Tripartite Taskforce on the Situation of Migrants and Refugees in Libya was initiated in early 2022. Meeting in March 2023 the Taskforce determined to strengthen efforts to support the development of non-discriminatory legal and policy frameworks for migrants and refugees in that country, and urged the Libyan authorities to end arbitrary detention of migrants and refugees in that country. The Taskforce agreed to enhance support for voluntary humanitarian returns from Libya.

INTERNATIONAL CO-OPERATION

Forum on China-Africa Cooperation: Co-operation between African states and China is undertaken within the framework of the Forum on China-Africa Cooperation (FOCAC). The first FOCAC ministerial conference was held in October 2000, and subsequently conferences have been held every three years. The eighth FOCAC ministerial meeting, held in late November 2021, in Dakar, Senegal, adopted a China-Africa Cooperation Vision 2035; the Dakar Action Plan covering 2022–24 (the first phase of Vision 2035); the Sino-African Declaration on Climate Change; and a general Declaration. Nine programmes were to be implemented under the Dakar Action Plan. These included a medical and health programme, under which, *inter alia,* China was to donate 600m. further COVID-19 vaccine doses to Africa, and to provide 400m. doses through joint Chinese-African production; poverty reduction, agricultural, and trade and investment programmes; a digital innovation programme; green initiatives; capacity building support; cultural initiatives; and a peace and security programme (which was to include military assistance to the AU). Addressing the conference by videolink, China's President Xi Jinping pledged continued support for expanding Africa's local capacity for COVID-19 vaccine production. A reduced Chinese financial commitment, totalling US $40,000m., was made for 2022–24, compared with $60,000m. in 2019–21. (Concerns over some African nations' debt dependency on China had been raised in recent years.) Themed 'Deepen China-Africa Partnership and Promote Sustainable Development to Build a China-Africa Community with a Shared Future in the New Era', the eighth FOCAC focused on Africa-China co-operation in aligning synergies between the Belt and Road Initiative (launched by China in 2013, with the aim of developing infrastructure and trade along traditional routes between Asia, Europe and Africa), the AU's Agenda 2063, the UN's 2030 Agenda for Sustainable Development, and the national development strategies of African states. The seventh China-Africa Business Forum was staged alongside the conference. From 2014 China superseded the USA as Africa's primary source of foreign direct investment.

Africa-UN Co-operation: In April 2017 the AU Chairperson and UN Secretary-General signed a framework agreement aimed at consolidating co-operation between their respective organizations in the area of peace and security. In this context, in September the AU Commissioner for Peace and Security and the UN Assistant Secretary-General for Peacebuilding Support concluded an MOU on a UN-AU Partnership in Peacebuilding. An AU-UN Joint Declaration on Co-operation for AU Peace Support Operations was signed by the AU Commission Chair and the UN Secretary-General in December 2018; this outlined principles to guide future joint responses to conflicts and political crises in Africa. The Sixth AU-UN Annual Conference was convened in Addis Ababa in December 2022. An inaugural AU-UN Periodic Coordination Meeting was convened (in a virtual format) in June 2022 between AU Commissioners and senior representatives of the UN Secretariat, including from the ECA and UNDP, which aimed to enhance efforts to achieve internationally agreed development goals.

Finance

In mid-2022 the AU Executive Council agreed a budget of US $654.8m. for 2023. Some 33% of expenditure (including the whole operating budget) was to be derived from assessed contributions from member states, and the remaining 67% from partners. The AU Foundation, inaugurated in February 2014, aims to mobilize voluntary contributions towards the financing of development priorities throughout the continent.

Publications

Africa's Development Dynamics (annually, AU/OECD Development Centre).

African Human Rights Yearbook.
AU Echo.
AU Handbook (annually).

Specialized Agencies

Africa Centres for Disease Control and Prevention (Africa CDC): POB 3243, Addis Ababa, Ethiopia; tel. (11) 5517700; e-mail africacdc@africa-union.org; internet africacdc.org; f. 2017; aims to support AU member states in responding to public health emergencies; comprises Regional Collaborating Centres in Libreville, Gabon (for Central Africa), Nairobi, Kenya (East Africa), Cairo, Egypt (North Africa), Lusaka, Zambia (Southern Africa), and Abuja, Nigeria (West Africa); supports region-wide surveillance, public health information activities, and works to strengthen public health institutes and networks of laboratories; in late Jan. 2020 activated its Incident Management System to address the COVID-19 crisis; undertook to support mem. countries to contain the spread of the virus through training in surveillance, detection, laboratory testing and case management; produced a digest of global guidelines and scientific studies relating to the virus; in March adopted an Africa Joint Continental Strategy for the COVID-19 Outbreak; from Sept. worked with WHO to establish a COVID-19 sequencing network of laboratories; during 2021 a digital CDC COVID-19 Travel Pass was developed; in April 2021 launched, with the AU, a Partnerships for African Vaccine Manufacturing (PAVM) framework; organized in Dec. the inaugural International Conference on Public Health in Africa; in July 2022 the AU Exec. Council approved a revised statute of Africa CDC to enable it to become an autonomous public health agency; Dir Dr JEAN KASEYA (DRC).

African Capacity Building Foundation (ACBF): 2 Fairbairn Dr., Mount Pleasant, Harare, Zimbabwe; tel. (4) 304663; e-mail root@acbf-pact.org; internet www.acbf-pact.org; f. 1991 by the World Bank, UNDP, the AfDB, African govts and bilateral donors; designated a specialized agency of the AU in 2017; aims to build sustainable human and institutional capacity for sustainable growth, poverty reduction and good governance in Africa; identifies strategies to support the implementation of the AU's Agenda 2063 strategic framework for the long-term socioeconomic transformation of Africa; hosts the secretariat of an African Think Tank Network, and, since 2014, has organized an annual Africa Think Tank Summit to promote the exchange of innovative solutions and peer learning aimed at advancing Africa's devt agenda; mems: 36 African and 13 non-African govts, the AfDB, World Bank and UNDP; Exec. Sec. Prof. EMMANUEL NNADOZIE (Nigeria).

African Civil Aviation Commission (AFCAC): 1 route de l'Aéroport International LSS, BP 8898, Dakar, Senegal; tel. 33-859-88-00; fax 33-820-70-18; e-mail secretariat@afcac.org; internet www.afcac.org; f. 1969 jtly by the OAU and International Civil Aviation Organization; became an AU specialized agency in 1978; promotes co-ordination and better utilization and devt of African air transport systems and the standardization of aircraft, flight equipment and training progs for pilots and mechanics; organizes working groups and seminars, and compiles statistics; mems: 54 states; Sec.-Gen. ADEFUNKE ADEYEMI.

African Risk Capacity (ARC): Bldg 1, Sunhill Park, 1 Eglin Rd, Sunninghill, 2157 Johannesburg, South Africa; tel. (11) 5171535; e-mail info@arc.int; internet www.africanriskcapacity.org; f. 2012 under the African Risk Capacity Establishment Agreement (which had 36 signatories and had been ratified by 11 states at July 2023); aims to finance risk resistance and contingency measures; uses satellite weather surveillance and World Food Programme-developed software to assess, and disburse immediate funding to, mem. states affected by a natural disaster; in May 2016 the ARC signed MOUs with the AfDB and the Conférence Inter-Africaine des Marchés d'Assurance on future collaboration in planning, preparation and response to extreme weather events and natural disasters; they concluded a further MOU in Aug. 2017 affirming co-operation on strengthening mechanisms to manage weather-related risk; Dir-Gen. IBRAHIMA CHEIKH DIONG (Senegal).

African Telecommunications Union (ATU): ATU Secretariat, POB 35282 Nairobi, 00200 Kenya; tel. (20) 2322120; fax (20) 2322124; e-mail sg@atuuat.africa; internet atuuat.africa; f. 1999 as successor to Pan-African Telecommunications Union (f. 1977); promotes the devt of information communications in Africa, with the aim of making Africa an equal participant in the global information society; works towards universal service and access and full inter-country connectivity; promotes devt and adoption of appropriate policies and regulatory frameworks and the financing of devt; encourages co-operation between mems and the exchange of information; advocates the harmonization of telecommunications policies; mems: 49; 57 assoc. mems comprising fixed and mobile telecoms operators; Sec.-Gen. JOHN OMO (Kenya).

Pan-African Agency of the Great Green Wall (Agence Panafricaine de la Grande Muraille Vert): Lot 414, ilot C, Nouakchott RIM, Mauritania; tel. 45-25-56-88; internet grandemuraillevert.org; f. 2010; co-ordinates implementation of the Great Green Wall initiative; mems: 11 govts; Exec. Sec. Dr IBRAHIM SAID.

Pan African University (PAU) (Université Panafricaine): (Rectorate) BP 5383, Yaoundé, Cameroon; tel. (222) 217090; internet pau-au.africa; f. 2011; Governing Council inaugurated in 2015; aims to develop a network of academic and research centres of excellence across Africa offering postgraduate training in the areas of science, technology, innovation, social sciences and governance; comprises the following specialized institutes: the PAU Institute for Basic Sciences, Technology and Innovation (PAUSTI) (based in Juja, Kenya); PAU Institute for Life and Earth Sciences—including Health and Agriculture (PAULESI) (in Ibadan, Nigeria); PAU Institute for Governance, Humanities and Social Sciences (PAUGHSS) (Yaoundé, Cameroon); the PAU Institute for Water and Energy Sciences—including Climate Change (PAUWES) (Tlemcen, Algeria); and the PAU Virtual and E-University (launched in Dec. 2019) which offers online learning progs; the establishment of a South Africa-based PAU Institute for Space Sciences (PAUSS) was pending.

ARAB FUND FOR ECONOMIC AND SOCIAL DEVELOPMENT—AFESD

Address: POB 21923, Safat, 13080 Kuwait.
Telephone: 24959000; **fax:** 24959390; **e-mail:** hq@arabfund.org; **internet:** www.arabfund.org.

Established in 1968 by the Economic Council of the Arab League, the Fund began its operations in 1974. It participates in the financing of public and private economic and social development projects in the Arab states, and provides grants and expertise to member states.

MEMBERS

All member countries of the League of Arab States.

Organization
(September 2023)

BOARD OF GOVERNORS

The Board of Governors consists of a Governor and an Alternate Governor appointed by each member of the Fund. The Board of Governors is considered as the General Assembly of the Fund, and has all powers.

BOARD OF DIRECTORS

The Board of Directors is composed of eight Directors elected by the Board of Governors for a renewable term of two years. The Board is charged with all the activities of the Fund and exercises the powers delegated to it by the Board of Governors.

Director-General and Chairman of the Board of Directors: BADER M. AL-ASAAD (Kuwait).

FINANCIAL STRUCTURE

In April 2013 the Board of Governors agreed to increase the Fund's subscribed capital to 3,000 Kuwaiti dinars (KD) from KD 2,000m. (effected through a transfer of KD 500m. from the Fund's additional capital reserves to paid-up capital, and through an increase in member states' subscriptions that was paid in instalments over the ensuing five years); the Fund's authorized capital, meanwhile, was increased to KD 4,000m. By 31 March 2023 the Fund's paid-up capital stood at KD 2,903m. At that time shareholders' equity amounted to KD 3,980m.

Activities

The Fund aims to contribute to the financing of economic and social development projects in the Arab states and countries by means of loans granted on concessionary terms to governments and public enterprises and corporations; private sector projects may also be supported through the provision of loans and guarantees, as well as other financial, technical and advisory services. In November 2016 the Board of Directors agreed to reduce the rate of interest on the repayment of loans (over a term of 30 years, increased from 22) from 2.5% to 2% for low-income member states, and from 3% to 2.5% for other beneficiary states. Projects that strengthen the interdependence of Arab countries and enhance social development are prioritized.

In February 2021 the Board of Directors approved a medium-term strategy, covering the period 2021–24, with the following priorities: supporting the development of regional infrastructure, including energy generation, with a particular emphasis on advancing renewable energy sources; expansion of the production sector; provision of technical and institutional assistance to human development initiatives focused on generating employment; preservation of the environment and reduction of carbon emissions; strengthening small and medium-sized enterprises; and supporting joint Arab projects.

During 2022 the Fund approved three loans, totalling KD 52.0m., comprising a KD 10.0m. loan to support the supply of drinking water in Kiffa, Mauritania; a KD 25,0m. loan for a similar drinking water supply initiative in Nouakchott; and also KD 17.0m. loan for an integrated agricultural development project in southern Kasserine Governate, Tunisia. At the end of 2022 total lending since 1974 amounted to KD 11,191.0m. for 709 loans. By the end of 2022 AFESD lending had financed 601 projects in 18 Arab countries (covering around 27.4% of the total cost of those initiatives); during that period some 30.6% of the total value of the loans was allocated to energy and electricity initiatives, 24.8% to transport, 13.6% to water and sewerage, and 13.5% to agriculture and rural development.

In 2022 the Fund extended 11 national grants, amounting to KD 1.1m. Some 94.3% of the finance channelled through national grants in that year supported institutional support and training, 4.7% was for general studies and research, and 1.0% for seminars and conferences. The Fund also approved four inter-Arab grants, at a cost of KD 400,000; in this respect, 46.8% was allocated to institutional support and training, 31.9% for general studies and research, and 21.3% for seminars and conferences. The cumulative total number of grants provided by the end of 2022 was 1,284, with a value of KD 254.9m.

The Fund allocated KD 11.4m. in 2022 (equivalent to 10% of its 2021 net profits) to its Urgent Program to Support the Palestinian People. Cumulative contributions by the end of 2022 since the Program's establishment in 2001 amounted to KD 189.9m. By the end of 2022 the Fund's Programme to Support the Resistance of Jerusalem had received two instalments, in 2010 and 2016, that totalled KD 29.6m.

The Fund administers a Special Account, inaugurated in October 2010, which finances and offers technical and advisory assistance to small and medium-sized private sector commercial and developmental projects. By the end of 2022 49 loans totalling US $1,591m. had been approved through the Special Account.

The Fund acts as the secretariat of the Co-ordination Group of Arab National and Regional Development Financing Institutions. These organizations work together to produce a *Joint Arab Economic Report,* which considers economic and social developments in the Arab states. The Fund co-operates with other organizations in preparing regional studies and conferences, for example in the areas of human resource development, demographic research and private sector financing of infrastructure projects.

AFESD and the World Bank were jointly to support the preparation process to establish an Arab common market for electricity, in accordance with a Memorandum of Understanding approved in September 2016 by Arab League ministers responsible for foreign affairs. In November 2019 AFESD, the Arab League and the World Bank organized the First Pan-Arab Energy Trade Conference, in Cairo, Egypt.

The Fund manages an Arab Fund Fellowships Program, which since its inception in 1997 has awarded scholarship grants (178 by 2022, of which 163 were implemented) to enable Arab citizens with doctorates to conduct advanced research and to lecture at top universities worldwide. A new Abdlatif Y. Al-Hamad Development Award in the Arab World was introduced in 2022.

Publications

Annual Report.
Joint Arab Economic Report (annually).

Statistics

LOANS APPROVED, 2022

	Purpose	Amount (KD million)
Mauritania	Supply of drinking water in Kiffa	10.0
	Supply of drinking water in Nouakchott	25.0
Tunisia	Integrated agricultural development project in southern Kasserine Governate	17.0

Source: AFESD, *Annual Report 2022*.

LOANS BY SECTOR

Sector	2022 Amount (KD million)	2022 %	1974–2022 %
Infrastructure sectors	35.0	67.3	70.2
Transport	—	—	24.8
Telecommunications	—	—	1.3
Energy and electricity	—	—	30.6
Water and sewerage	35.0	67.3	13.6
Productive sectors	17.0	32.7	18.1
Industry and mining	—	—	4.6
Agriculture and rural development	17.0	32.7	13.5
Social services	—	—	8.9
Other	—	—	2.7
Total	**10.4**	**100.0**	**100.0**

Source: AFESD, *Annual Report 2022*.

ARAB MONETARY FUND—AMF

Address: Arab Monetary Fund Bldg, Corniche Rd, POB 2818, Abu Dhabi, United Arab Emirates.
Telephone: (2) 6215000; **fax:** (2) 6326454; **e-mail:** economic@amfad.org.ae; **internet:** www.amf.org.ae.

The Agreement establishing the Arab Monetary Fund (AMF) was approved by the Economic Council of Arab States in Rabat, Morocco, in April 1976 and entered into force on 2 February 1977.

MEMBERS
There are 22 members (see list of subscriptions).

Organization
(September 2023)

BOARD OF GOVERNORS
The Board of Governors is the highest authority of the AMF. It formulates policies on Arab economic integration and the liberalization of trade among member states. The Board of Governors is composed of a governor and a deputy governor appointed by each member state for a term of five years. It meets at least once a year; meetings may also be convened at the request of half of the membership, or of members holding half of the total voting power.

BOARD OF EXECUTIVE DIRECTORS
The Board of Executive Directors exercises all powers vested in it by the Board of Governors and may delegate to the Director-General such powers as it deems fit. It is composed of the Director-General and eight non-resident directors elected by the Board of Governors. Each director holds office for three years and may be re-elected. An Audit and Risk Committee reports directly to the Board.

DIRECTOR-GENERAL
The Director-General of the Fund is appointed by the Board of Governors for a renewable five-year term, and serves as Chairman of the Board of Executive Directors.

The Director-General supervises the Economic Department, Training and Capacity Building Institute, Investment Department, Finance Department, Support Services Department, Legal and Compliance Department, Strategy and Evaluation Unit, and Risk Management Unit; an Internal Audit Office that liaises with the Audit and Risk Committee; and advisory Committees on Loans, Investments, Risk Management, and Administration.

Director-General and Chairman of the Board of Executive Directors: Dr ABDULRAHMAN BIN ABDULLAH AL-HAMIDY.

FINANCE
The Arab Accounting Dinar (AAD) is a unit of account equivalent to three IMF Special Drawing Rights (SDRs). (The average value of the SDR in 2022 was US $1.337750.)

In April 2013 the Board of Governors agreed to increase the AMF's authorized capital from AAD 600m. to AAD 1,200m. Subscribed capital was to increase by AAD 300m. to AAD 900m. At the end of 2022 total paid-up capital was AAD ae.

CAPITAL SUBSCRIPTIONS
(million AAD, 31 December 2022)

Algeria	116.9
Bahrain	13.8
Comoros	0.7
Djibouti	0.7
Egypt	88.2
Iraq	116.9
Jordan	14.9
Kuwait	88.2
Lebanon	13.8
Libya	37.0
Mauritania	13.8
Morocco	41.3
Oman	13.8
Palestine*	5.9
Qatar	27.6
Saudi Arabia	133.4
Somalia	11.0
Sudan	27.6
Syrian Arab Republic	19.9
Tunisia	19.3
United Arab Emirates	53.0
Yemen	42.5

*Palestine's share has been deferred by a Board of Governors' resolution in 1978.

Activities

The establishment of the AMF was seen as a step towards the goal of Arab economic integration. The Articles of Agreement define the Fund's aims as follows:

(*a*) to correct disequilibria in the balance of payments of member states;

(*b*) to promote the stability of exchange rates among Arab currencies, to render them mutually convertible, and to eliminate restrictions on current payments between member states;

(*c*) to establish policies and modes of monetary co-operation to accelerate Arab economic integration and economic development in the member states;

(*d*) to tender advice on the investment of member states' financial resources in foreign markets, whenever called upon to do so;

(*e*) to promote the development of Arab financial markets;

(*f*) to promote the use of the Arab dinar as a unit of account and to pave the way for the creation of a unified Arab currency;

(g) to co-ordinate the positions of member states in dealing with international monetary and economic problems; and

(h) to provide a mechanism for the settlement of current payments between member states in order to promote trade among them.

The AMF functions both as a fund and a bank. It is empowered:

(a) to provide short- and medium-term loans to finance balance of payments deficits of member states;

(b) to issue guarantees to member states to strengthen their borrowing capabilities;

(c) to act as intermediary in the issuance of loans in Arab and international markets for the account of member states and under their guarantees;

(d) to co-ordinate the monetary policies of member states;

(e) to manage any funds placed under its charge by member states;

(f) to hold periodic consultations with member states on their economic conditions; and

(g) to provide technical assistance to banking and monetary institutions in member states.

Strategic Vision 2040: During 2020–40 the AMF was pursuing a Strategic Vision 2040, focused on fulfilling its role as the Arab countries' closest partner in ensuring stability and economic, financial and monetary development, and laying the monetary foundations for Arab economic integration. The Strategic Vision 2040 framework was to be implemented through four five-year medium-term strategic plans. In 2020–25 the AMF was implementing a strategy focused on consolidating its role as the region's single Arab-owned monetary institution and platform for economic, financial and monetary policymaking consultations; enhancing its role as a centre of excellence for knowledge and capacity building; developing lending to support efforts to redress economic and financial imbalances in member states; and strengthening the financial sector (including through the development of bond markets in local currencies, promoting financial inclusion and modern financial technology, assisting the development of the *Shari'a* -compliant finance sector, and promoting financial integration among Arab countries and with other financial blocs).

From early 2020 the AMF supported member states in combating adverse impacts of the COVID-19 pandemic, and in January 2021 initiated a phase aimed at assisting economic recovery, with a focus on supporting economic, monetary, and financial reforms, resolving emergency balance of payments situations, strengthening the enabling environment for small and medium-sized businesses (SMEs), and promoting financial sustainability and economic diversification.

Loans are intended to finance an overall balance of payments deficit and a member may draw up to 75% of its paid-up subscription, in convertible currencies, for this purpose unconditionally (automatic loans). A member may, however, obtain loans in excess of this limit, subject to agreement with the AMF on a programme aimed at reducing its balance of payments deficit (ordinary and extended loans, equivalent to 175% and 250% of its quota, respectively). In addition, a member has the right to borrow up to 100% of paid-up capital under a compensatory loan in order to finance an unexpected deficit in its balance of payments resulting from a decrease in its exports of goods and services or a large increase in its imports of agricultural products following a poor harvest.

Automatic and compensatory loans are repayable within three years, while ordinary and extended loans are repayable within five and seven years, respectively. Loans are granted at concessionary and uniform rates of interest that increase with the length of the period of the loan. In 1996 the AMF established the Structural Adjustment Facility, initially providing up to 75% of a member's paid-up subscription and later increased to 175%. In 2009, in order to enhance the flexibility and effectiveness of its lending to meet the needs of member countries affected by the global financial crisis, the Fund determined to extend an access limit of 175% for lending for both the public finance sector and for the financial and banking sector under the Structural Adjustment Facility. A Short Term Liquidity Facility was approved in that year to provide resources to countries with previously strong track records undergoing financial shortages owing to the sharp contraction in international trade and credit. A Trade Reform Facility was initiated in 2007. An Oil Facility was also introduced in that year, but was deemed by a decision of the Fund's Executive Directors in March 2017 to be no longer in force. In 2016 an SMEs Conducive Environment Support Facility was inaugurated to extend resources of up to 100% of a member's paid-up subscription in convertible currencies to support reforms in the SME sector. The first loans under the new Facility were approved in 2018.

The AMF deploys technical missions to member states to follow up reform programmes supported by the Fund's resources and to assess new requests for loans.

During the period 1978–2022 the AMF extended 199 loans, amounting to AAD 2,851.8m. In 2022 the Fund approved three loans totalling AAD 119.6m. (compared with AAD 147.7m. in 2021), to Egypt, Morocco and Tunisia.

At the end of December 2022 Somalia, Sudan, the Syrian Arab Republic and Yemen were in arrears to the Fund (collectively totalling AAD 243.7m.).

The AMF's technical assistance activities are extended in the form of specialized training of officials or through the deployment of expert support missions. The Fund's Training and Capacity Building Institute (TCBI) offers courses (62, conducted in a virtual format, in 2022) to officials in the financial, monetary, economic, commercial and statistical sectors of Arab countries. The AMF implements an Arab Statistics Initiative (ArabStat).

In February 2023, jointly with the International Monetary Fund (IMF), the AMF organized the Seventh Arab Fiscal Forum, in Dubai, United Arab Emirates (UAE), on the theme 'Fiscal sustainability in the Arab World beyond the COVID-19 pandemic: Challenges and opportunities'. The AMF convened the fifth Annual Arab Regional Tax Forum in March 2023, in Abu Dhabi, UAE.

During 2002–22 the Fund provided AAD 62m. in humanitarian support to the Palestinian people. Some 769 Palestinians were receiving TCBI training at the end of 2022.

The AMF collaborates with Arab Fund for Economic and Social Development (AFESD), the League of Arab States and the Organization of Arab Petroleum Exporting Countries (OAPEC) in writing and publishing a *Joint Arab Economic Report*. The Fund provides the technical secretariat for the Council of Arab Central Banks and Monetary Authorities' Governors, and also serves as the technical secretariat of the Council of Arab Finance Ministers, and for various related task forces and committees.

In 1991 the Council established the Arab Committee on Banking Supervision. In 2005 the Council inaugurated a second technical grouping, the Arab Committee on Payments and Settlements Systems. An Arab Economic Database was initiated December 2014. The AMF actively supports the Financial Inclusion for the Arab Region Initiative (FIARI), which was launched by the Council in September 2017. In February 2020 the AMF launched the Buna Regional Payment Platform, to provide centralized multicurrency clearing and settlement services for financial transactions between Arab states and with their principal external trading partners. It was agreed in April 2021 that the Platform would be hosted by the UAE. A Buna Instant Payment Service was initiated in April 2023.

The AMF participates—with the Islamic Development Bank OPEC Fund, Arab Bank for Economic Development in Africa, and other partners—in the Arab Coordination Group (ACG), a strategic alliance that was established in 1975, and aims collectively to optimize resources to advance sustainable development.

A Memorandum of Understanding (MOU) was concluded between the AMF and the European Stability Mechanism in March 2022 that provided for a general framework on strengthened collaboration. In April an AMF-African Export-Import Bank MOU was signed, with a view to enhancing economic and financial co-operation.

In May 2022 the AMF published *Public Debt in The Arab World: Asymmetric Effects on Economic Growth*, based on data from 10 Arab countries.

In June 2023 the AMF's *Arab Economic Outlook* envisaged that, collectively, Arab economies would demonstrate growth in 2023 of 3.4%, rising to 4% in 2024.

TRADE PROMOTION

Arab Trade Financing Program (ATFP): POB 26799, Arab Monetary Fund Bldg, 7th Floor, Corniche Rd, Abu Dhabi, United Arab Emirates; tel. (2) 6316999; fax (2) 6316793; e-mail finadmin@atfp.ae; internet www.atfp.org.ae; f. 1989 to develop and promote trade between Arab countries and to enhance the competitive ability of Arab exporters; operates by extending lines of credit to Arab exporters and importers through (as at 31 Dec. 2022) 217 national agencies designated by the monetary authorities of 20 Arab and five other countries; participation was also invited from private and official Arab financial institutions and joint Arab/foreign institutions; administers the Inter-Arab Trade Information Network (IATIN), and organizes Buyers-Sellers meetings to promote Arab goods; the total value of lines of credit extended by the Program since its inception amounted to US $19,900m. at 31 Dec. 2022; auth. cap. $1,000m. (at 31 Dec. 2022); 53 national and regional Arab financial institutions and banks are shareholders; Chair. and Chief Exec. ABDULRAHMAN A. AL HAMIDY; publ. *Annual Report* (Arabic and English).

Publications

A Way to Reform.
Annual Report.
Arab Capital Markets (quarterly).
Arab Countries: Economic Indicators (annually).

Arab Economic Outlook (2 a year).
Foreign Trade of the Arab Countries (annually).
Joint Arab Economic Report (annually, jtly with AFESD, the League of Arab States and OAPEC).
National Accounts of the Arab Countries (annually).
Statistical Bulletin of Arab Countries.
Reports on commodity structure (by value and quantity) of member countries' imports from and exports to other Arab countries; other studies on economic, social, management and fiscal issues.

Statistics

LOANS APPROVED, 2022

Borrower	Type of loan	Amount (million AAD)
Egypt	Compensatory	87.7
Morocco	SMEs Conducive Environment Support Facility	12.7
Tunisia	Ordinary	19.2

Source: *Annual Report 2022*.

ASIAN INFRASTRUCTURE INVESTMENT BANK—AIIB

Address: B9 Financial St, Xicheng District, Beijing 100033, People's Republic of China.
Telephone: (10) 83580000; **e-mail:** information@aiib.org; **internet:** www.aiib.org.

MEMBERS
By September 2023 92 (47 regional and 45 non-regional) countries had ratified the Bank's Articles of Agreement to become full members. At that time the Board of Governors had approved a further 14 prospective membership applications (four regional and 10 non-regional).

Organization
(September 2023)

BOARD OF GOVERNORS
All powers of the Bank are vested in the Board. Each member country appoints one Governor and one Alternate Governor to the Board, which meets at least once a year. The Board's first regular Annual Meeting was convened in June 2016, in Beijing. The 2023 (eighth) Annual Meeting was to be held in late September, in Sharm el Sheik, Egypt.

BOARD OF DIRECTORS
The (non-resident) 12-member Board of Directors directs the general operations of the Bank. Powers delegated to it by the Board of Governors include: establishing policy; approving strategy, and an annual plan and budget; overseeing the Bank's management and making decisions with regard to its operations.

ADMINISTRATION
The Bank's President, elected by its shareholders, is supported by a senior management team comprising five Vice Presidents. Administratively, investment operations are divided into two regions and supported by departments for infrastructure investment, banking and social infrastructure. As at 31 December 2021 the Bank had 359 professional staff.

An International Advisory Panel (IAP) of experts, international officials, politicians and academics has been established to provide impartial guidance to the President and to promote the Bank at a global level. In September 2021 the IAP's membership was doubled from six to 12 experts. An agreement to establish an AIIB Interim Operational Hub in Abu Dhabi, United Arab Emirates (UAE), was concluded in April 2023 between the Bank and UAE Government.

President: JIN LIQUN (People's Republic of China).

FINANCIAL STRUCTURE
The Bank's authorized capital stock is US $100,000m., of which 20% is paid-in and the remainder callable. An AIIB Project Preparation Special Fund (PPFS) was established in June 2016, with initial funding of $50m., to support less developed member states to prepare project proposals. In March 2022 the Bank established a Special Fund Window (SFW) with the aim of extending more affordable financing to less developed member states.

The AIIB administers and hosts the secretariat of the Multilateral Cooperation Center for Development Finance (MCDF—created in 2020 to promote investment in cross-border infrastructure and connectivity in developing countries), and manages the Implementing Partner of the Finance Facility of the Multilateral Cooperation Center for Development Finance (MCDF IP) Special Fund. The Bank is also a technical partner of the Global Infrastructure Facility (GIF, an initiative of the G20), and, in that respect, manages a Technical Partner of the GIF (GIF TP) Special Fund.

Activities
The Articles of Agreement establishing the AIIB entered into effect in December 2015, having then been ratified by 17 signatory states with 50.1% of capital subscriptions. The inaugural meeting of the Board of Governors was convened in January 2016.

Since its inception the Bank undertook to engage with stakeholders and prospective clients to formulate its strategic programming and objectives. In April 2021 the Bank initiated a Sustainable Development Bond Framework, clarifying for potential investors the policies and mechanisms governing its commitment to sustainable financing activities; a first Climate Adaptation Bond was issued under the Framework in May 2023. A revised Environmental and Social Framework was issued in May 2021. The following four areas were identified as priority themes in the Bank's corporate strategy for 2021–30: green infrastructure; technology-enabled infrastructure; private capital mobilization; and cross-border connectivity and regional co-operation. The Bank's overall mission was defined as financing the Infrastructure of Tomorrow. By 2025 50% of approvals were to be climate-related, 25%–30% were to relate to cross-border connectivity, and 50% were to be privately financed. In June 2023, during the Summit for a New Global Financing Pact, convened in Paris, France, the AIIB and other multilateral development banks (MDBs) issued Joint MDB Paris Alignment Methodological Principles, to underpin the alignment of new financing with the objectives of the 2015 Paris Agreement on climate change. On 1 July 2023, in accordance with a commitment made by the Bank in October 2021, it confirmed that henceforth every new investment operation was to be consistent with low-carbon and climate-resilient development pathways, in full alignment with the Paris Agreement.

At the June 2023 Paris Summit the AIIB President and World Bank Group President—responding to a series of G20 recommendations made to MDBs that were focused on using financial innovation to expand lending capacity—gave consideration to the establishment of a new guarantee facility that would use the AIIB's capital to issue guarantees against IBRD-approved sovereign-backed loans.

FINANCIAL OPERATIONS
In April 2020 the AIIB established a COVID-19 Crisis Recovery Facility (CRF), making available US $13,000m. to support immediate assistance with regard to healthcare and pandemic preparedness, liquidity support, and fiscal and budgetary support. A Special Fund Window was added in mid-2020 to Facility. The Bank extended the CRF in March 2022, increasing its funding to $20,000m. for the period to 31 December 2023.

In 2021 the AIIB approved US $9,930m. for 51 projects, of which 33 came within the four thematic priorities and 18 were approved under the CRF. Some $1,332.6m. in private capital was mobilized by the Bank in 2021.

During 2016–30 June 2023 the AIIB had approved, cumulatively, US $42,040m. for 221 projects, of which 22% were focused on the energy sector, 17% on the transport sector, 15% were to have a multi-sector impact, 11% were focused on building economic resilience, 9% on public health, 7% on supporting liquidity, 7% were water-related, 6% were urban initiatives, and 4% had a digital infrastructure and technology focus.

The 221 projects that had been approved by the Bank by 30 June 2023 included upgrading and electrifying the Alexandria–Abou Qir metro line in Egypt; climate responsive investments in Jordan; the development of port infrastructure, broadband infrastructure and solar power in Oman; and the expansion of Antalya Airport in Türkiye.

EXTERNAL CO-OPERATION

In April 2016 a co-financing framework agreement was signed with the World Bank, to provide for the joint implementation of projects, and in May Memorandums of Understanding (MOUs) were concluded with the Asian Development Bank (ADB), the European Bank for Reconstruction and Development and the European Investment Bank. An MOU providing for further collaboration with the World Bank was signed in April 2017. In 2022 the Bank signed MOUs with the OPEC Fund for International Development in May and with the CAF Development Bank of Latin America in October. The AIIB was granted observer status at the United Nations in 2018.

Publications

AIIB Sustainable Development Bonds Impact Report.
AIIB Yearbook of International Law.
Annual Report.
Asian Infrastructure Finance Report.

Statistics

SUBSCRIPTIONS AND VOTING POWER
(September 2023)

Country	Subscribed capital (US $ million)	Voting power (% of total)
Regional:		
Afghanistan	86.6	0.18
Australia	3,691.2	3.46
Azerbaijan	254.1	0.41
Bahrain	103.6	0.22
Bangladesh	660.5	0.77
Brunei Darussalam	52.4	0.23
Cambodia	62.3	0.24
China, People's Republic	29,780.4	26.58
Cook Islands	0.5	0.13
Cyprus	20.0	0.15
Fiji	12.5	0.14
Georgia	53.9	0.23
Hong Kong, SAR	765.1	0.81
India	8,367.3	7.60
Indonesia	3,360.7	3.16
Iran	1,580.8	1.02
Iraq	25.0	0.15
Israel	749.9	0.85
Jordan	119.2	0.29
Kazakhstan	729.3	0.83
Korea, Republic	3,738.7	3.50
Kyrgyzstan	26.8	0.20
Lao People's Democratic Republic	43.0	0.22
Malaysia	109.5	0.28
Maldives	7.2	0.19
Mongolia	41.1	0.22
Myanmar	264.5	0.39
Nepal	80.9	0.26
New Zealand	461.5	0.59
Oman	259.2	0.41
Pakistan	1,034.1	1.10
Philippines	979.1	1.05
Qatar	604.4	0.72
Russian Federation	6,536.2	5.98
Samoa	2.1	0.13
Saudi Arabia	2,544.6	2.44
Singapore	250.0	0.41
Sri Lanka	269.0	0.42
Tajikistan	30.9	0.18
Thailand	1,427.5	1.45
Timor-Leste	16.0	0.14
Tonga	1.2	0.13
Türkiye (Turkey)	2,609.9	2.50
United Arab Emirates	1,185.7	1.23
Uzbekistan	219.8	0.38
Vanuatu	0.5	0.13
Viet Nam	663.3	0.77
Sub-total	**73,882.0**	**72.88**
Non-regional:		
Algeria	5.0	0.13
Argentina	5.0	0.13
Austria	500.8	0.63
Belarus	64.1	0.19
Belgium	284.6	0.38
Benin	5.0	0.13
Brazil	5.0	0.19
Canada*	995.4	0.84
Chile	10.0	0.14
Côte d'Ivoire	5.0	0.14
Croatia	5.0	0.14
Denmark	369.5	0.51
Ecuador	5.0	0.13
Egypt	650.5	0.76
Ethiopia	45.8	0.16
Finland	310.3	0.46
France	3,375.6	3.18
Germany	4,484.2	4.16
Ghana	5.0	0.13
Greece	10.0	0.14
Guinea	5.0	0.13
Hungary	100.0	0.22
Iceland	17.6	0.20
Ireland	131.3	0.25
Italy	2,571.8	2.46
Liberia	5.0	0.13
Luxembourg	69.7	0.25
Madagascar	5.0	0.13
Malta	13.6	0.20
Morocco	5.0	0.13
Netherlands	1,031.3	1.10
Norway	550.6	0.67
Peru	154.6	0.27
Poland	831.8	0.92
Portugal	65.0	0.24
Romania	153.0	0.27
Rwanda	5.0	0.13
Serbia	5.0	0.13
Spain	1,761.5	1.74
Sudan	59.0	0.15
Sweden	630.0	0.74
Switzerland	706.4	0.81
Tunisia	5.0	0.13
United Kingdom	3,054.7	2.89
Uruguay	5.0	0.13
Sub-total	**23,082.7**	**27.12**
Total	**96,964.7**	**100.00**

* In June 2023 the Canadian Government suspended co-operation with the AIIB pending an assessment of allegations—that had been made by a Canadian former high-ranking Bank official, and were denied by the AIIB—that the Bank had been infiltrated by the Chinese Communist Party.

As at 4 September 2023 Kuwait and South Africa, both founding signatory countries, had not completed the membership process by ratifying the Bank's Articles of Agreements. Other prospective members at that time were Armenia, Bolivia, Djibouti, Kenya, Lebanon, Libya, Mauritania, Nigeria, Papua New Guinea, Senegal, Togo and Venezuela.

COOPERATION COUNCIL FOR THE ARAB STATES OF THE GULF

Address: POB 7153, Riyadh 11462, Saudi Arabia.
Telephone: (1) 482-7777; **fax:** (1) 482-9089; **e-mail:** site@gccsg.org; **internet:** www.gcc-sg.org.

More generally known as the Gulf Cooperation Council (GCC), the organization was established on 25 May 1981 by six Arab states, all monarchies with petroleum-based economies. Its charter describes the GCC as providing the means for realizing co-ordination, integration and co-operation in all economic, social and cultural affairs.

MEMBERS

Bahrain   Oman   Saudi Arabia
Kuwait   Qatar   United Arab Emirates

In December 2001 the Supreme Council admitted Yemen (which applied to join the organization as a full member in 1996) as a participant in certain ministerial-level meetings and in the biennial Gulf Cup football tournament. In September 2008 Yemen's inclusion in GCC development planning was approved and Yemen was admitted to GCC control and auditing apparatuses. The full or associate accession of Yemen to the GCC has been envisaged, pending the abatement of civil conflict in that country. In May 2011 the GCC invited Jordan and Morocco to submit membership applications. In December 2017 Saudi Arabia and the United Arab Emirates (UAE) formed, outside the scope of the GCC, a 'joint cooperation committee', with a focus on economic, political, military, trade and cultural partnership.

Organization
(September 2023)

SUPREME COUNCIL

The Supreme Council is the highest authority of the GCC. It comprises the heads of member states and holds one regular session annually, and meets in emergency session if demanded by two or more members. The Council also convenes an annual consultative meeting. The Presidency of the Council is undertaken by each state in turn. The Supreme Council draws up the overall policy of the organization and endorses recommendations and laws presented to it by the Ministerial Council and the Secretariat General. The 43rd ordinary annual meeting was held in Riyadh, Saudi Arabia, in December 2022.

CONSULTATIVE COMMISSION

The Consultative Commission, comprising 30 members (five from each member state) nominated for a three-year period, acts as an advisory body, considering matters referred to it by the Supreme Council.

COMMISSION FOR THE SETTLEMENT OF DISPUTES

The Commission for the Settlement of Disputes is convened by the Supreme Council, on an ad hoc basis, as provided for in the GCC charter, to address altercations between member states as they arise.

MINISTERIAL COUNCIL

The Ministerial Council consists of the ministers responsible for foreign affairs of member states (or other ministers acting on their behalf), meeting every three months, and in emergency session if demanded by two or more members. It prepares for the meetings of the Supreme Council, and draws up policies, recommendations, studies and projects aimed at developing co-operation and co-ordination among member states in various spheres. GCC ministerial committees have been established in a number of areas of co-operation; sectoral ministerial meetings are held periodically.

SECRETARIAT

The Secretary-General is appointed by the Supreme Council for a three-year term, renewable once. The position is rotated among member states in order to ensure equal representation. The secretariat assists member states to implement recommendations by the Supreme and Ministerial Councils, and prepares reports and studies, budgets and accounts. Up to eight Assistant Secretaries-General are appointed by the Ministerial Council upon the recommendation of the Secretary-General. There is a Telecommunications Bureau, based in Bahrain, and a GCC delegation office in Brussels, Belgium.

Secretary-General: JASSIM MUHAMMAD AL-BUDAIWI (Kuwait).

Activities

COMPREHENSIVE DEVELOPMENT STRATEGY FOR 2010–25

In December 2010 the 31st summit of GCC heads of state adopted a (revised) comprehensive development strategy for member states, covering 2010–25, with the following strategic goals: pursuing a framework enabling sustainable development; ensuring adequate water for development needs; achieving self-sufficiency in meeting the security and defence needs of the GCC development process; achieving an integrated economic partnership; eliminating sources of vulnerability from the GCC economic environment; deriving maximum benefit from infrastructure facilities; technical and scientific capacity building; enhancing social development in the areas of education and training, health, and intellectual and cultural development; and enhancing the productivity of the GCC labour force.

ECONOMIC CO-OPERATION

In 1985 the Supreme Council endorsed a common industrial strategy for the Gulf states. It approved regulations stipulating that priority should be given to imports of GCC industrial products, and permitting GCC investors to obtain loans from GCC industrial development banks. In November 1986 resolutions were adopted on the protection of industrial products, and on the co-ordination of industrial projects, in order to avoid duplication. In 1989 the Ministerial Council approved the Unified GCC Foreign Capital Investment Regulations, which aimed to attract foreign investment and to co-ordinate investments among GCC countries. Further guidelines to promote foreign investment in the region were formulated during 1997. In December 1999 the Supreme Council amended the conditions determining rules of origin on industrial products in order to promote direct investment and intra-Community trade. In September 2000 GCC ministers responsible for commerce agreed to establish a technical committee to promote the development of electronic commerce and trade among member states. In December 1992 the Supreme Council endorsed Patent Regulations for GCC member states to facilitate regional scientific and technological research. A GCC Patent Office for the protection of intellectual property in the region was established in 1998, in Riyadh, Saudi Arabia. In December 2006 the Supreme Council endorsed a system to unify trademarks in GCC states. An Intellectual Property Training Center is based at the GCC Secretariat.

In December 2001 the Supreme Council, meeting in Muscat, Oman, adopted the 'Economic Agreement Between the Arab GCC States', providing for a future regional economic union. The Agreement set the deadline for a proposed customs union at the start of 2003 and provided for a standard tariff level of 5% for foreign imports (with the exception of 53 essential commodities previously exempted by the Supreme Council). The GCC customs union was inaugurated, as planned, on 1 January 2003, and a GCC Common Market on 1 January 2008. In December 2005 the Supreme Council approved standards for the introduction of a proposed single currency (to be linked to the US dollar). Oman and the UAE withdrew from the single currency process in 2007 and 2009, respectively. An accord on Gulf Monetary Union was signed in June 2009 by Bahrain, Kuwait, Qatar and Saudi Arabia, and was approved in December by the 30th meeting of the Supreme Council. The introduction of the currency was, however, postponed from the planned deadline of January 2010. A GCC unified value added tax framework that was endorsed by the GCC member states in late 2016 became effective in the UAE and Saudi Arabia on 1 January 2018, and in Bahrain on 1 January 2019. Oman published relevant rules in October 2020 that provided for the implementation of the framework from 16 April 2021, and it was envisaged that Kuwait would eventually also follow suit.

In December 2001 the Supreme Council adopted unified procedures and measures for facilitating the intraregional movement of people and commercial traffic. (A simplified passport system had been approved in 1997 to facilitate travel between member countries.) The GCC adopted new measures in August 2003 that permitted nationals of its member states to work in, and to seek loans from, financial institutions in any other member state. In December 2005 the Supreme Council adopted further measures aimed at facilitating the movement of people, goods and services between member countries, and agreed to permit GCC citizens to undertake commercial activities in all member states. In December 2015 the Supreme Council approved mandatory unified legislation for consumer protection in GCC member states. A GCC Labour and Labour Force Strategy, covering the period 2020–30, was approved at the 40th GCC summit in December 2019.

In December 2017 the Supreme Council set a deadline of 2025 for the achievement of full GCC Economic Union. Meeting in December 2019 at the 40th summit GCC heads of state determined that a road map should be developed to guide the completion of studies and projects relating to the finalization of the Economic Union, and, in this respect, designated the following as priority topics: human capital and the promotion of economic sustainability; means of collectively advancing GCC states' global competitiveness; and regional impacts of the People's Republic of China' Belt and Road Initiative. In January 2021 the 41st GCC summit emphasized the need to develop a framework that would enable 'full economic citizenship', facilitating people from GCC member states to work, invest, move and relocate throughout the sub-region.

In December 2021 the 42nd GCC summit emphasized the importance of collective action to advance modern technologies and the digital transformation of the region, including the development of cyber and information security.

A general framework of a Gulf Strategy for Tourism, covering the period 2023–30, was approved by the Supreme Council in December 2022.

It was envisaged that overall the GDP of the GCC countries would expand by 6.3% in 2022 and by 4.6% in 2023. In May 2023 the UN Economic and Social Commission for Western Asia reported that some 3.3m. citizens of GCC member states (particularly concentrated in Saudi Arabia, Oman and Bahrain) were living in poverty.

ENERGY, THE ENVIRONMENT AND TRANSPORTATION

GCC ministers responsible for petroleum hold occasional co-ordination meetings to discuss the agenda and policies of the Organization of the Petroleum Exporting Countries, to which all six member states belong. The GCC member states benefited from rising petroleum prices that were prompted from early 2022 by the imposition of an international sanctions regime against the Russian Federation, a major oil producer, in view of its military invasion of Ukraine. At April 2022 GCC oil production was reported to be 20% higher than one year previously, and to have exceeded pre-COVID-19 pandemic levels.

A Gulf Council Interconnection Authority was established in 1999, with its headquarters in Dammam, Saudi Arabia, to administer a plan to integrate the electricity, transportation and communications infrastructure of the six member states, an objective reiterated in the 2001 Economic Agreement. In July 2023 the Authority signed an agreement with the Iraqi Government to integrate Iraq's electricity grid into those of the GCC. A unified GCC water strategy that was developed in 2013 provided for the establishment of a common water network, including uniform desalination standards and specifications.

In April 2003 a Convention on the Conservation of Wildlife and their Natural Habitats in the Countries of the GCC entered into force. In December 2015 the Supreme Council authorized the preparation of a comprehensive plan for environmental co-operation among GCC member states. A partnership between the GCC and the UN Environment Programme was forged in August 2017. In December 2021 the 42nd GCC summit determined to advance the use of clean technologies as sources of all energy, to combat pollution, to increase vegetation coverage, and to safeguard environmental life.

In December 2012 the 33rd GCC summit approved the creation of a GCC commission for civil aviation. In 2011 a supervisory body was established to advance the development of an interconnected 2,177 km pan-GCC railway; it was envisaged that this would be completed by December 2023.

FOOD SECURITY

The GCC states aim to achieve food security through the best utilization of regional natural resources. A unified agricultural policy for GCC countries, initially endorsed in 1985, was revised in December 1996. Unified agricultural quarantine laws were adopted by the Supreme Council in December 2001. A permanent committee on fisheries aims to co-ordinate national fisheries policies, to establish designated fishing periods and to undertake surveys of the fishing potential in the Arabian (Persian) Gulf. In December 2015 the Supreme Council agreed to strengthen the role of GCC private sector investment in agricultural and livestock projects.

SOCIAL CO-OPERATION

In December 2015 the Supreme Council approved executive regulations concerning the equal rights of GCC citizens to benefit from health services in clinics and hospitals that were affiliated to the ministries of health in each member state. In January 2021 the 41st GCC summit established a new Gulf Center for Disease Prevention and Control, which was to co-ordinate activities aimed at combating the COVID-19 pandemic, and other epidemics. A general framework for a regional plan to standardize preparations for and responses to emergency public health situations was endorsed by the GCC leaders.

In December 2019 the 40th meeting of the Supreme Council endorsed a GCC Cultural Strategy covering the period 2020–30. Periodically, GCC cultural fora and exhibitions are held, on topics such as folklore; poetry; drama; Arabic calligraphy; and intellectual matters.

In December 2022 the 43rd summit endorsed a strategic plan to guide collective media co-operation among member states during 2023–30. A charter to support the preservation of urban heritage in Gulf states was also approved at that time.

COLLECTIVE SECURITY

Although no mention of defence or security was made in the original charter, the summit meeting which ratified the charter also issued a statement rejecting any foreign military presence in the region. The Supreme Council meeting in November 1981 agreed to include defence co-operation in the activities of the organization: as a result, ministers responsible for defence met in January 1982 to discuss a common security policy, including a joint air defence system and standardization of weapons. In November 1984 member states agreed to form the Peninsula ('Al Jazeera') Shield Force for rapid deployment against external aggression, comprising units from the armed forces of each country under a central command to be based in north-eastern Saudi Arabia. In December 1997 the Supreme Council approved plans for linking the region's military telecommunications networks and establishing a common early warning system.

A joint defence pact, to enhance the grouping's defence capability, was adopted by GCC leaders in December 2000. The pact formally committed member states to defending any other member states from external attack, envisaging the expansion of the Peninsula Shield Force from 5,000 to 22,000 troops and the creation of a new rapid deployment function within the Force. In addition, the pact established a Joint Military Committee to promote co-operation in joint military exercises and co-ordination in the field of military industries. In March 2001 the GCC member states initiated a joint air defence system. In December GCC heads of state authorized the establishment of a Joint Defence Council, comprising member states' ministers responsible for defence, to convene annually to address security-related matters and supervise the implementation of the joint defence pact. The Supreme Council determined in December 2006 to establish a specialized security committee to counter terrorism. A Doha-based GCC Criminal Information Center to Combat Drugs (GCC-CICCD) was established in 2007. In December 2009 the 30th Supreme Council meeting ratified a new defence strategy that included upgrading the capabilities of the Peninsula Shield, undertaking joint military projects, and pursuing co-operation in combating the illegal trade of armaments to GCC member states.

In December 2013 the 34th GCC summit mandated the establishment of a unified military command, in order to strengthen the grouping's regional security structures. A joint police force was also endorsed. The meeting announced the establishment of a Gulf Academy for Strategic and Security Studies, in the UAE, to enhance understanding of issues including missile defence, border security and counter terrorism. At the 35th meeting of the Supreme Council, convened in Doha, in December 2014, GCC heads of state confirmed that the GCC police force (GCCPol) was to be established, with headquarters in Abu Dhabi, to focus on organized terrorist and criminal activities throughout the region. A separate joint naval force was to be based in Bahrain.

In December 2017 the Supreme Council resolved to place the Peninsula Shield Force, the GCC Maritime Coordination Centre and GCC air forces under a new Unified Military Command. The mandate of GCCPol was expanded at that time to include combating terrorism and terrorist financing. In December 2018 the 39th GCC summit appointed a commander to lead the new unified military structure. In October 2019 the GCC organized, at its headquarters, a Conference on Counter-Extremism and Terrorism Speech. In December the Supreme Council endorsed a recent study on the proposed establishment of a new Gulf Academy for Strategic and Security Studies; it was envisaged that this would become operational in 2023. A GCC collective military exercise, Arab Gulf Security 2, was conducted in the UAE in February 2020.

GCC member states have promoted co-operation in combating acts of marine piracy in shipping lanes in the Red Sea and Gulf of Aden.

Protection of Kuwait: In August 1990 the Ministerial Council condemned Iraq's invasion of Kuwait, and demanded the full withdrawal of all Iraqi troops from that country; the Peninsula Shield Force was not sufficiently developed to be deployed in defence of Kuwait. During the ensuing war between Iraq and a multinational force which took place in January–February 1991, the GCC co-operated with Egypt and Syria, which, together with Saudi Arabia, played the most active role among the Arab countries in the anti-Iraqi alliance. In March the six GCC nations, Egypt and Syria formulated the Declaration of Damascus, which announced plans to establish a regional peacekeeping force. The Declaration also urged the abolition of all weapons of mass destruction in the area. In June Egypt and Syria, whose troops were to have formed the largest proportion of the proposed peacekeeping force, announced their withdrawal from the project, reportedly as a result of disagreements with the GCC concerning the composition of the force and the remuneration involved.

Meeting in emergency session in early February 2003 GCC ministers for defence and foreign affairs agreed to deploy the Peninsula Field Force in Kuwait, in view of the then impending US military action against neighbouring Iraq (in response to perceived non-compliance with Security Council Resolution 1441, adopted in November 2002, which had demanded that Iraq admit UN weapons inspectors). The full deployment of 3,000 Peninsula Shield troops to Kuwait was completed in early March, and the force was withdrawn two months later. Meanwhile, the GCC Secretary-General urged the resumption of negotiations in place of military conflict. The GCC summit meeting held in Kuwait, in December 2003, issued a statement accepting the USA's policies towards Iraq at that time, emphasizing the importance of UN participation there, condemning ongoing operations by terrorist forces, and denoting the latter as anti-Islamic.

The 2011 Bahrain Dispute: In March 2011, in response to a request from the Bahrain Government following a series of violent clashes between opposition protesters and security forces in that country, the GCC dispatched a contingent of Peninsula Shield Force troops (numbering some 1,000 from Saudi Arabia and 500 from the UAE, with more than 100 armoured vehicles), in order to protect strategic facilities and to help maintain order.

The 2017–21 Qatar Dispute: In mid-2017 Bahrain, Saudi Arabia and the UAE (as well as Egypt) severed diplomatic relations with Qatar (having previously done so in 2014), citing national security considerations in protest at the Qatari regime's ongoing support for the Islamist Muslim Brotherhood movement, and in view of continuing allegations that Qatar was supporting militant extremist Islamist entities. They also closed air, land and sea transport links with Qatar, blocked certain media outlets emanating from there, and announced the expulsion from their territories of Qatari residents and visitors, while recalling their own citizens from Qatar. In June Bahrain, Saudi Arabia, the UAE and four other countries presented Qatar with a list of 13 demands that were to be met by early July. These included severing all ties with Islamist groupings, shutting down the Qatar-based media outlet Al Jazeera, removing Turkish troops from Qatari territory, downgrading diplomatic relations with Iran, and allowing up to 12 years of monitoring aimed at ensuring compliance. In mid-July, in view of Qatar's refusal to accede to the 13 demands, they were withdrawn and replaced by a request to adhere to six broader guiding principles. In late July a list of individuals and entities with alleged terrorist links to Qatar was released (this was later expanded from 18 to 90 names). The heads of state of Bahrain, Saudi Arabia and the UAE declined to attend the annual meeting of the GCC Supreme Council that was held in December, in Kuwait. In September 2018 the Amir of Qatar, Sheikh Tamim bin Hamad Al Thani, addressing the UN General Assembly, stated that his country remained open to unconditional dialogue, and designated the blockade as a violation of international law. Sheikh Tamim failed to attend the GCC summit meeting, convened in Riyadh, in December. In May 2019 Qatar's Prime Minister participated in an emergency GCC meeting on regional security matters, convened by Saudi Arabia, in Makkah. The Qatari Prime Minister also attended the 40th GCC summit, in December 2019, indicating a rapprochement in GCC–Qatar relations. In January 2020, a tentative dialogue between Saudi and Qatari officials was declared by Qatar's minister responsible for foreign affairs to have stalled. Diplomatic relations between Qatar and the other GCC states were eventually resumed in early January 2021 at the 41st summit, where members signed an accord affirming 'Gulf, Arab and Islamic solidarity and stability'. At that time Saudi Arabia announced that it would reopen its airspace, land and sea borders to Qatar. The UAE and Qatar restored full diplomatic relations in June 2023.

EXTERNAL RELATIONS

Yemen: In April 2011, in response to mounting political unrest in Yemen, the GCC proposed a plan to result in the formation of a government of national unity, prior to the holding of new presidential elections. The GCC mediation attempt and Implementation Mechanism were suspended in late May, however, after the refusal of Yemen's serving President, Ali Abdullah Saleh, to sign the plan and resign his position. In October the UN Security Council called on all Yemeni parties to adopt the GCC peace initiative. In late November President Saleh finally signed the GCC-mediated agreement. Accordingly, Saleh relinquished his constitutional powers and, in February 2012, Abd al-Rabbuh Mansur al-Hadi was elected unopposed as the new President. In October of that year the GCC inaugurated a support office in Sana'a, Yemen. In March 2013—in accordance with the provisions of the GCC-mediated agreement—a National Dialogue was initiated on the development of a new Yemeni constitution, and, in January 2014, a conference of the National Dialogue reached agreement on a document which was to form the basis of the constitution.

From mid-2014 Shi'a Ansar Allah ('Houthi') militants instigated protests in Yemen, occupying Sana'a, the capital, and in February 2015 the Houthi rebels took control of the Yemeni parliament and other government institutions. Shortly afterwards, the UN Security Council adopted a resolution demanding that the Houthis relinquish power (although not imposing punitive sanctions on them, as proposed by GCC ministers responsible for foreign affairs), and urging the parties to the conflict to abide by the principles of the GCC-mediated agreement and National Dialogue. (UN sanctions were eventually imposed in April.) During February 2015 the GCC Secretary-General visited Aden, Yemen, for discussions with President Hadi. In late March, at President Hadi's request, the GCC member states (excepting Oman) launched the month-long Saudi-led military operation 'Decisive Storm' to protect the legitimate Yemeni authorities. From late April this was followed by a new operation, 'Restoring Hope', focusing on pursuing a political solution to the Yemeni crisis and on countering terrorism. Egypt, Jordan, Morocco, Pakistan and Sudan also offered their support to the Saudi-led coalition. A conference of Yemeni stakeholders convened in May, with GCC support, adopted the Riyadh Declaration, urging the resumption of the legitimate political process, and referencing the possible framework of a Yemeni 'federal state'. In December the 36th GCC summit welcomed efforts by the envoy of the UN Secretary-General in Yemen, including the initiation of negotiations in that month, in Geneva, Switzerland, aimed at resolving the conflict. A ceasefire agreement was concluded in April 2016, but was subsequently frequently broken. In December the GCC endorsed a roadmap aimed at achieving a comprehensive agreement that had been presented to the parties to the conflict in October by the UN Special Envoy for Yemen. In May 2017 the GCC rejected the recent unilateral formation of a transitional political council in southern Yemen by Maj.-Gen. Aidarous al-Zubaidi (who had recently been dismissed as Governor of Aden by President Hadi). The 38th GCC summit, held in December, condemned the murder by Houthi militants of former Yemeni President Saleh, and urged a political resolution of the crisis—to be mediated by the UN Special Envoy, based on UN Security Council decisions, the GCC peace initiative, and the 2014 outcome document of the Yemeni National Dialogue. From 2016 the GCC consistently condemned missile attacks launched by Houthi fighters against targets in Saudi Arabia.

In mid-2018 the Saudi-led coalition intensified military action around the strategically important Houthi-held port of Hodeidah (Hudaydah)—through which they alleged that the Houthis were smuggling weapons into Yemen. At the beginning of August the UN Special Envoy called for the organization of Intra-Yemeni Consultations to prompt a resumption of the political process (by then suspended for two years). The ensuing Intra-Yemeni Consultations, held in Geneva, in early September, were deemed to have formally relaunched the process, although there was no participation by Houthi representatives. In early December, for the first time in two years, representatives of the Yemeni Government and the Houthi militia held talks, mediated by the UN Special Envoy, in Stockholm, Sweden. On 13 December the Consultations culminated in the conclusion of the Stockholm Agreement, comprising the Agreement on the City of Hodeidah and Ports of Hodeidah, Salif, and Ras Isa, which provided for an immediate ceasefire arrangement and for the phased redeployment of armed forces away from that area; an executive mechanism to facilitate the exchange of prisoners; and a statement regarding the fiercely contested city of Taïz. The two sides determined fully to implement the Agreement, to refrain from taking any action, escalation or decisions that would undermine it, and to continue to engage unconditionally in the consultations process in 2019. A Redeployment Coordination Commission was to supervise the ceasefire (which entered into effect on 18 December 2018) and the redeployment of forces, and also to oversee mine action operations. In January 2019 the UN Security Council established the UN Mission in Support of the Hudaydah Agreement (q.v.). An extraordinary GCC summit that was convened in late May, in Makkah, condemned recent Houthi drone attacks against two oil pumping stations near Riyadh, as well as continuing Houthi missile attacks (including against Makkah) and the recent targeting of commercial ships in the UAE's territorial waters. Division within the GCC with regard to Yemen became apparent in early August when forces affiliated with the UAE-supported separatist Southern Transitional Council (STC) took control of the southern Yemeni port city of Aden and nearby Abyan. Saudi Arabia condemned the STC's action and undertook air strikes against its forces, which, in turn, prompted a wave of combat between the STC and forces loyal to (Saudi-backed) President Hadi. Meanwhile, Hadi urged the UAE's removal from the Saudi-led military coalition. During August, despite their divergent policies on Yemen, Saudi Arabia and the UAE agreed to establish a joint committee with the aim of stabilizing the situation in Yemen, and invited participation by the internationally recognized Yemeni Government and the STC in a new Jeddah Dialogue initiative. Further Houthi attacks aimed at sabotaging the Saudi oil infrastructure occurred in September. On 20 September the Houthis offered to halt attacks against civilian targets in Saudi Arabia and to pursue a peaceful resolution of the conflict.

In mid-October 2019 the Jeddah Dialogue culminated in the signature of the Riyadh Agreement, with provisions covering security, military and political issues. These included, *inter alia*, the establishment of a national unity government be formed, to represent, on an equal basis, southern and northern Yemen, with the STC to be allocated two ministerial positions, ministerial representation to be given also to other southern Yemeni groupings, such as the Hadhramout Inclusive Conference, National Alliance and Revolutionary Movement. The accord also provided for the Government to return to Aden without obstructions. In December the 40th summit of the Supreme Council welcomed the Riyadh Agreement, and determined to continue to support development projects in Yemen. In January 2021 the 41st GCC summit welcomed the arrival (at the end of December 2020) of the Yemeni Government to Aden. It condemned a terrorist attack against the airport in Aden that had been timed to coincide with their arrival (collectively in one plane), and had caused at least 28 civilian fatalities and many injuries. (The new Cabinet was unharmed.) The GCC heads of state condemned Houthi seizures of oil revenues from a special account intended for use in paying the salaries of Yemeni civil servants. It was estimated at that time that the GCC states had channelled more than US $13,000m. in humanitarian and development aid to Yemen since 2015. In mid-January 2022 (for the first time since 2018) the Houthis conducted missile and drone attacks against civilian targets in the UAE, including against the international airport serving its capital, Abu Dhabi, and against oil installations. In late March–early April 2022 the GCC hosted UN-mediated Yemeni-Yemeni consultations on the conflict, in Riyadh; on 1 April the UN Special Envoy to Yemen announced that agreement on a truce had been achieved; this was initiated on 2 April, and was subsequently extended until 2 October. In April 2023 the GCC Secretary-General welcomed the release (mediated in March by the UN Special Envoy and the International Committee of the Red Cross) of nearly 900 detainees by the parties to the Yemeni conflict.

Egypt and Sudan: In September 2021, referencing Ethiopia's controversial Grand Renaissance Dam project, GCC ministers responsible for foreign affairs rejected any action that might negatively impact Egypt and Sudan. The Dam, constructed on the Blue Nile, the River Nile's main tributary, had the potential to cause water losses for downstream Nile countries. GCC ministers stated that the water security of Egypt and Sudan was a part of wider Arab security.

Horn of Africa: In recent years the GCC states have aimed to consolidate influence in the nearby strategically significant states of the Horn of Africa. In April 2015 King Salman ibn Abd al-Aziz Al Sa'ud of Saudi Arabia concluded a military and security agreement with the Eritrean regime, in accordance with which GCC forces established a military presence in Eritrea, from where they conducted operations aimed at suppressing the Houthi rebellion in Yemen. Subsequently the UAE concluded an agreement with the Somaliland authorities enabling a UAE military presence in Berbera, Somaliland (Somalia).

Iran: The GCC has repeatedly condemned Iran's occupation of the island of Abu Musa, as well as military exercises conducted by Iran in the waters around the other disputed Greater and Lesser Tunb islands (located in the Strait of Hormuz, through which petroleum exports are transported), as a threat to regional security. Successive GCC summit meetings have restated support for the UAE's right to regain sovereignty over the islands (and over their territorial waters, airspace, continental shelf and economic zone). In December 2015 the 36th summit meeting emphasized the need to adhere to the Joint Comprehensive Plan of Action (JCPOA) concluded in July between the P5+1 (China, France, the Russian Federation, the UK and the USA) and Iran, that aimed to ensure that Iran's nuclear programme remained exclusively peaceful. The GCC leaders reiterated previous statements that the Arabian Gulf region must be kept free of weapons of mass destruction. In recent years the GCC has consistently accused Iran of providing military and financial support to the Shi'a Houthi militants active in Yemen. In September 2019 Houthi attacks against two major Saudi Arabian oil facilities were attributed by the Saudi authorities to Iran and designated as an 'act of war'. In that month a new US-led Bahrain-based International Maritime Security Construct was established, with the aim of monitoring the safety of, and escorting vulnerable vessels through sea lanes in the Gulf. In October a gathering in Riyadh of GCC ministers responsible for security and defence and their counterparts from Egypt, France, Germany, Greece, Italy, Jordan, the Netherlands, New Zealand, Pakistan, the Republic of Korea (South Korea), the UK and the USA declared a unified position against the recent attacks against the Saudi energy and economic infrastructure, designating the incidents as, furthermore, an assault against the global economy and wider international community. In December the 40th GCC Supreme Council meeting rejected the continuation of Iran's interference in the internal affairs of GCC states, reiterated that Iran had attacked Saudi oil supply facilities in September with a view to sabotaging international energy supplies, and urged worldwide condemnation of such terrorist acts against the global economy. In this respect the Council welcomed efforts by the USA to strengthen its military presence in the Gulf region. The Council also condemned non-compliance by Iran with the JCPOA (uranium enrichment activities by Iran had been confirmed by the International Atomic Energy Agency—IAEA—in November), welcomed efforts by the USA to coerce the Iranian regime into ending regionally destabilizing activities, and also welcomed a recent statement by Saudi Arabia, the UAE, the UK and the USA (the 'Quartet') that stated concern over escalating regional tensions caused by acts of destabilization by Iran and by Houthi militia attacks (reportedly using Iranian-made drones and weaponry) on Saudi Arabia. In January 2021 the 41st GCC summit welcomed a recent decision by the USA to designate the Iranian Revolutionary Guard Corps (a component of the Iranian national military) as a 'terrorist' grouping. In September GCC ministers responsible for foreign affairs denounced continuing Houthi missile and drone strikes against Saudi Arabia. They also condemned continuing Houthi disruption of maritime navigation, including an attack on an oil tanker off the coast of Oman at the end of July. The ministers denounced a recent acceleration in uranium enrichment by Iran, in excess of the level required for peaceful use, and urged the Iranian authorities fully to co-operate with the IAEA. They reiterated their unwavering support for the UAE's sovereignty over the three disputed islands, including over their airspace, territorial waters and continental shelf. In December 2022 the 43rd GCC summit issued a condemnation of continued Iranian support for terrorist groups and sectarian militias in countries including Iraq, Lebanon, Syria, Yemen.

Israel: In May 2002 GCC heads of state declared their support for a Saudi-proposed initiative aimed at achieving a peaceful resolution of the Israel–Palestine crisis. GCC heads of state summits have repeatedly urged the international community to encourage Israel to sign the Nuclear Non-Proliferation Treaty as well as to halt the construction of settlements on occupied Arab territory. In August 2014 GCC ministers responsible for foreign affairs, addressing the impact on Gaza of the military operation 'Protective Edge', profoundly condemned brutal war crimes, aggression against civilians and state-sponsored terrorism by Israel, while absolutely rejecting Israeli justifications given in this regard. In December 2017 the GCC agreed to work towards reversing a decision by the US Administration in that month to recognize Jerusalem as the capital of Israel. In March 2019 the GCC denounced a decision by the USA to accept Israel's 1981 annexation of the Golan Heights (Israeli forces having captured the area from Syria in 1967). In December 2019 the 40th GCC summit condemned the demolition by the Israeli authorities of numerous homes to the east of Jerusalem, and urged the international community to intervene to prevent the forced evictions and displacement of Palestinians and to resist any attempt inconsistent with international law to alter the legal nature or demographic composition of Jerusalem. Under an arrangement concluded in mid-August 2020 by Israel and the UAE—which was aimed at normalizing bilateral diplomatic relations, and had been negotiated under US auspices—Israel agreed temporarily to delay the annexation of West Bank territory from Palestine. Formal agreements on normalizing relations with Israel were signed by both the UAE and Bahrain on 15 September, in Washington, DC, USA. Bahrain and the UAE thus became the first GCC member states to enter into diplomatic relations with Israel. In September 2021 GCC ministers responsible for foreign affairs determined to form an international investigation committee into allegations of violations perpetrated by Israel (which they referred to as 'the Zionist entity') against Palestinians.

USA: The inaugural meeting of a GCC-US Strategic Cooperation Forum (SCF), at the level of ministers responsible for foreign affairs, was convened in March 2012, in Riyadh. In May 2015 a meeting between GCC leaders and then President Obama of the USA determined to organize more frequent ministerial and technical gatherings within the SCF framework; to establish a high-level working group to pursue jointly the development of rapid response capabilities; to strengthen co-operation in military exercises and training activities (with a focus on interoperability against asymmetric threats); and to share expertise on cyber policy and cyber incident response. The fifth SCF, convened in September, condemned activities by al-Qa'ida in the Arabian Peninsula and by affiliates of Islamic State in Yemen. A further GCC-US leaders' meeting was held in April 2016.

In December 2016 the 37th GCC summit condemned as contravening international law the Justice Against Sponsors of Terrorism Act (JASTA) that had recently been passed by the US Congress; JASTA was seen to restrict the scope of foreign sovereign immunity. Meeting in May 2017, in Riyadh, the leaders of the GCC and USA agreed to establish a Riyadh-based Terrorist Financing Targeting Center, and tasked joint working groups with meeting at least twice a year to develop co-operation on issues including combating terrorism, cyber security, and military preparedness. A GCC-US leaders' meeting that was to have been held in October 2018 was postponed by then President Trump of the USA, reportedly owing to slow progress in resolving the ongoing internal GCC dispute over Qatar. The US Administration facilitated the agreements, signed in September 2020, that established formal Bahrain-Israel and UAE-Israel diplomatic relations. In June of that year the first GCC Regional AmCham Summit, with participation by US chambers of commerce, was organized by the Muscat-based Oman American Business Center. In January 2021 the 41st GCC summit welcomed the recent election of Joe Biden to the US presidency.

Joint US-GCC working groups on integrated air and missile defense and maritime security met in March 2022, within the framework of the SCF. In July President Biden met with the GCC leaders and heads of state of Egypt, Iraq and Jordan, in Jeddah, to discuss and strengthen regional security and development. The establishment was commended of a new Combined Task Force 153 (established in April, and focused on the Bab al-Mandeb strait, Red Sea and Gulf of Aden) and Task Force 59 (which became fully operational in January 2023); it was envisaged that these would enhance USA-GCC co-ordination in the defence sphere.

Europe: In January 2003 the GCC established a customs union, which was a precondition of a proposed GCC-European Union (EU) free trade agreement. Negotiations on the agreement, initiated in 2003, were suspended by the GCC in May 2010, owing to a dispute over export duties. An EU-GCC Clean Energy Network project was initiated in 2015. In April 2016 the GCC and the EU agreed to establish an enhanced structured informal dialogue on trade and investment. A fourth GCC-EU Business Forum was convened in December 2019, in Muscat. In February 2022 the 26th regular session of the GCC-EU Joint Council and meeting of ministers responsible for foreign affairs endorsed a Joint Co-operation programme for 2022–27, to strengthen collaboration in areas including regional security, climate, counter terrorism and education. A new EU-GCC strategic partnership was launched in May 2022.

Far East: In December 2008 an agreement establishing a GCC-Singapore Free Trade Area (GSFTA) was signed, in Doha. A gathering of ministers responsible for foreign affairs of the GCC and the Association of Southeast Asian Nations (ASEAN) that was held in September 2019, in New York, USA, agreed to finalize an ASEAN-GCC Framework of Cooperation that was to cover the period 2020–24 and was to address areas including energy; micro, small and medium enterprises; trade and investment; smart cities; Islamic finance; infrastructure and connectivity; agriculture and food security; education; and countering terrorism and violent extremism.

The sixth round of a series of GCC-South Korea negotiations on the development of a free trade agreement (that had been initiated in 2007) was convened in October 2022. An inaugural China-GCC summit was convened in December. The meeting adopted an action plan, for the period 2023–37, to pursue closer bilateral strategic dialogue.

Co-operation with other organizations: The inaugural meeting within a new consultation framework uniting the Secretaries-General of the GCC, the Arab League, the Organization of Islamic Cooperation and the Union of the Arab Maghreb was convened in September 2014.

In March 2016 the Secretaries-General of the GCC and North Atlantic Treaty Organization (NATO) discussed means of deepening co-operation between the two organizations. The NATO summit meeting convened in July in Warsaw, Poland, welcomed the forthcoming establishment of practical co-operation with the GCC.

Finance

All member states contribute equal amounts to the functioning of the GCC.

Publications

GCC News (monthly, available online in Arabic).
GCC: a Statistical Glance (annually).

Associated Bodies

Gulf International Bank (GIB): POB 1017, ad-Dowali Bldg, 3 Palace Ave, Manama 317, Bahrain; tel. 17534000; fax 17522530; internet www.gib.com; f. 1976 by the six GCC states and Iraq; became a wholly owned subsidiary of the Gulf Investment Corporation (without Iraqi shareholdings) in 1991; in April 1999 merged with Saudi Investment Bank; pursues a *Shari'a* governance mechanism; in Jan. 2015 launched Meem by GIB, a *Shari'a*-compliant retail bank, in Saudi Arabia; GIB's total assets US $31,800m. (31 Dec. 2021); CEO ABDULAZIZ A. AL-HELAISSI.

Gulf Investment Corporation (GIC): POB 3402, Safat 13035, Kuwait; tel. 2225000; fax 2225010; e-mail info@gic.com.kw; internet www.gic.com.kw; f. 1983 by the six mem. states of the GCC, each contributing 16.6% of the total capital; investment chiefly in the Gulf region, financing industrial projects; provides merchant banking and financial advisory services; total assets US $3,175m. (31 Dec. 2021); CEO IBRAHIM A. AL-QADHI.

EUROPEAN BANK FOR RECONSTRUCTION AND DEVELOPMENT—EBRD

Address: 5 Bank St, London, E14 4BG, United Kingdom.
Telephone: (20) 7338-6000; **fax:** (20) 7338-6100; **e-mail:** generalenquiries@ebrd.com; **internet:** www.ebrd.com.

MEMBERS

The Bank has 71 country members; the European Union (EU) and the European Investment Bank (EIB) are also shareholder members in their own right. At the end of February 2022 the Board of Directors approved a resolution to suspend the access to EBRD resources and expertise of both the Russian Federation and Belarus, as a consequence of the war against fellow Bank member Ukraine; this decision was endorsed in early April by the Board of Governors. (Belarus remained a Bank shareholder.)

Organization
(September 2023)

BOARD OF GOVERNORS

The Board of Governors, to which each member appoints a Governor (normally the minister responsible for finance of that country) and an alternate, is the highest authority of the EBRD. It elects the President of the Bank. The 2023 meeting was held in Samarkand, Uzbekistan, in May, focusing on 'Investing in resilience', and accompanied by an EBRD Business Forum. The next annual meeting was to be hosted by Armenia, in Yerevan, in May 2024.

BOARD OF DIRECTORS

The Board, comprising 23 Directors elected by the Board of Governors for a three-year term, is responsible for the organization and operations of the EBRD. It is supported by an Independent Project Accountability Mechanism and an Evaluation Department.

ADMINISTRATION

The EBRD's President is supported by a First Vice-President, who also heads the Client Services Group. Five other Vice-Presidents cover Banking; Policy and Partnerships; Finance; Risk and Compliance; and Transformation. The Central Services department includes offices of the General Counsel, Secretary-General, Chief Economist, and corporate strategy and communications sections. A structure of country teams, industry teams and operations support units oversee the implementation of projects. The EBRD has local offices in 35 countries. Resident Offices in Moscow, Russia and Minsk, Belarus were closed in 2022, as a result of the conflict in Ukraine.

President: ODILE RENAUD-BASSO (France).
Managing Director, Türkiye: ARVID TUERKNER (Germany).

FINANCIAL STRUCTURE

In May 2010 EBRD shareholders agreed to increase the Bank's capital from €20,000m. to €30,000m., through the use of a temporary increase in callable capital of €9,000m. and a €1,000m. transfer from reserves to paid-in capital. (A previous capital increase had been implemented in 1996.) At 31 December 2022 subscribed capital was €29,759m., of which paid-in capital amounted to €6,217m. In May 2023 the Board of Governors—recognizing that additional shareholder support would be required to fund the Bank's programme of assistance to Ukraine (which remained under attack from Russia)—agreed to give consideration to a potential third increase in paid-in capital, envisaged at between €3,000m.–€5,000m. A final decision was to be made by the end of the year.

Activities

The EBRD helps its beneficiaries to undertake structural and sectoral reforms to enable their full integration in the international economy. To this end, the Bank promotes the establishment and improvement of activities of a productive, competitive and private nature, particularly small and medium-sized enterprises (SMEs), and works to strengthen financial institutions. It mobilizes national and foreign capital, together with expert management teams, and helps to develop an appropriate legal framework to support a market-orientated economy. The Agreement establishing the EBRD specified that its operations should not displace commercial sources of finance.

The Bank provides extensive financial services, including loans, equity and guarantees, and aims to develop new tailored forms of financing and investment. In accordance with a revised concept introduced in 2017, investment decisions were to be made with regard to six, country-specific 'transition qualities', aimed at achieving more well-governed, competitive, inclusive, green, resilient and integrated sustainable market economies as the planned outcome of the transition process. Bank activities are designed to align with the UN's 2030 Agenda for Sustainable Development and accompanying Sustainable Development Goals. The Bank supports its investments through policy dialogue and technical assistance.

During 2021–25 the Bank was implementing a Strategic and Capital Framework (SCF), which aimed to accelerate transition in countries of operation through the crisis and recovery stages of the COVID-19 pandemic crisis, with a focus on three principal themes: supporting the transition to a 'green', low-carbon economy; accelerating the transition to a digital economy; and promoting equality of opportunity, through enhancing access to skills, employment, finance and entrepreneurship, and strengthening support for women, young people and other vulnerable population groups. By 2025 some 75% of the Bank's lending was to be focused on the private sector. The Bank's Equality of Opportunity Strategy (2021–25) addresses the intersection of characteristics (for example gender, age, level of skills, disability, or displacement) with external stresses and shocks, social biases and legal frameworks.

The EBRD's area of operations has expanded significantly since its inception. The Bank's initial focus was on the transition of countries from Central, Southern and Eastern Europe and the Caucasus, and Central Asia, and on the Russian Federation. New operations were terminated at the end of 2007 in the Czech Republic, which was deemed to have 'graduated' from the Bank. (In March 2021, however, the Bank's Board of Directors approved a request temporarily to resume activities in that country in order to assist its recovery from the COVID-19 pandemic.) Mongolia and Montenegro became new countries of operations in 2006. Türkiye (then known as Turkey), which had been a founding member of the EBRD, became the 30th country of operations in November 2008. Kosovo became a member in December 2012. In March 2011 the Bank signed a Memorandum of Understanding (MOU) with the EIB and the European Commission to enhance co-operation in activities outside of the EU region. In May the then Group of Eight (G8) major industrialized nations declared their support for an expansion of the Bank's geographical mandate to assist transitional economies in the Southern and Eastern Mediterranean (SEMED) region. Several countries in the region have subsequently been granted country of operations status. Meanwhile, India and San Marino became shareholder members of the Bank in July 2018 and in June 2019, respectively. In May 2023 the Board of Governors adopted a resolution that formally endorsed in principle a 'limited and incremental' expansion of the geographical scope of the Bank's activities into Iraq, and also into sub-Saharan Africa—to commence during 2025–30, with an initial focus on six countries (with Benin, Côte d'Ivoire, Ghana, Kenya, Nigeria and Senegal regarded as suitable candidates).

Through a longstanding collaboration with the Food and Agricultural Organization of the UN, and by fostering partnerships with public authorities, agribusinesses, and other international agencies and multilateral banks, the EBRD aims to strengthen regional food security; its Private Sector for Food Security Initiative promotes investment in food production. In May 2022, in response to the wider global impacts of Russia's invasion of Ukraine, the Bank, with the IMF, the World Bank and other international financial institutions collectively issued the Joint International Financial Institution Plan to Address Food Insecurity, with a focus on the following six objectives: (i) support vulnerable people; (ii) promote open trade; (iii) mitigate fertilizer shortages; (iv) support food production now; (v) invest in climate-resilient agriculture for the future; and (vi) co-ordinate for maximum impact.

FINANCIAL OPERATIONS

In the year ending 31 December 2022 the EBRD approved 431 operations, in 35 economies, for which it invested funds of €13,071m. (a significant increase over the €10,446m. invested in 2021). The Bank also directly mobilized external resources in 2022 amounting to an estimated €1,746m. Gross annual disbursements in that year totalled €8,800m. The total project value—including both Bank and non-EBRD finance—was €38,028m. In 2022 18.4% of the Bank's new investment was for Eastern Europe and the Caucasus, 18.4% (also) for Southern and Eastern Mediterranean, 18.0% for Central Europe and the Baltic States, 16.1% for South-Eastern Europe, 12.5% for Türkiye, 11.4% for Central Asia, and 5.3% for Greece. Some 42.7% of project financing in 2022 was allocated to investment in the financial sector. In total 74% of the Bank's investments were focused on the private sector in that year.

High priority is given to attracting external finance for Bank-sponsored projects, in particular in countries at advanced stages of transition, from government agencies, international financial institutions, commercial banks and export credit agencies. The EBRD's Technical Co-operation Funds Programme (TCFP) aims to facilitate access to the Bank's capital resources for countries of operations by providing support for project preparation, project implementation and institutional development. Resources for technical co-operation originate from regular TCFP contributions, specific agreements and contributions to Special Funds (of which the Bank was administering 16 at 31 December 2022). In 2016 the Bank established an Equity Participation Fund (EPF) to attract long-term institutional capital into eligible private sector investments. By the end of 2022 €258m. had been invested under the EPF in 35 schemes.

GREEN FINANCING AND ENERGY SECURITY

The EBRD's founding Agreement specifies that all operations are to be undertaken in the context of promoting environmentally sound and sustainable development. It undertakes environmental audits and impact assessments in areas of particular concern—including assessments of the net carbon footprint resulting from its projects.

In September 2015 the EBRD's Board of Directors endorsed a Green Economy Transition (GET) policy approach, under which financing for sustainable low-carbon projects was to be progressively increased (from 31% of total investments in 2015). In December 2018 the Board of Directors adopted an energy sector strategy for the period 2019–23. It emphasized increased investment in renewable energy and the promotion of cleaner and more resilient sources of energy, and also determined that the Bank should terminate all funding of thermal coal mining or coal-fired electricity generation. In January 2020 the EBRD and International Renewable Energy Agency signed an MOU on future collaboration.

The proportion of EBRD green investment contracted during 2020 (to 19% of total investments, compared with 46% in 2019), owing to the urgency of containing the COVID-19 emergency. In October 2020 the Bank's Board of Governors approved an updated GET 2021–25 strategy, to support inclusive, resilient green recovery from the COVID-19 crisis, and to increase the green proportion of EBRD investment to more than 50% by 2025 (in 2021 and 2022 it accounted for, respectively, 51% and 50% of total investments). Policy engagement on long-term means of achieving decarbonization, resource and energy efficiency, and a reduction in pollution in countries of operation—while leaving no one behind, i.e. promoting a socioeconomically 'just transition'—were to be enhanced over the course of GET 2021–25. Furthermore, from 1 January 2023 the Bank's activities were to be fully aligned with the goals of the 2015 Paris Agreement on climate change. The strategy provided for the extension, initially, of large stimulus packages aimed at boosting economic growth. Principal thematic areas of action included developing green financial systems, climate adaptation, industrial decarbonization, sustainable food systems, support for environmental and urban infrastructure, green buildings, energy systems integration, sustainable connectivity, and safeguarding natural capital. A High-Impact Partnership on Climate Action was launched by the EBRD in November 2021. During that month the Bank issued a joint statement with other major multilateral development banks regarding 'Nature, People and Planet', placing greater emphasis on defining future operations and strategies within a 'nature-positive' framework. From 2022 the disruption to energy supplies and an inflationary impact on energy prices caused by Russia's war against Ukraine heightened focus on energy security, and the need for energy efficiency through a reduction in consumption, and for decarbonization and the diversification of energy sources. The Bank prioritized the further integration of countries of operations in the region into the EU energy grid.

The EBRD's online GET Knowledge Hub covers, *inter alia,* bioenergy, carbon market development, climate change adaptation and climate finance partnerships, carbon pricing and renewable energy. The EBRD issues Environmental Sustainability Bonds (so-called green bonds), and allocates the proceeds from these to its green project portfolio. In November 2020 the Bank doubled (to €1,900m.) funding of its Green Cities programme, promoting urban sustainability and green development. By October 2022, when the annual conference of the programme was held in Vienna, 51 municipal authorities had signed up, requiring commitment to developing and implementing a long-term Green City Action Plan. At January 2023 the Bank's Green Cities portfolio comprised 80 investments. In September 2021 the Bank initiated a new Energy Compact, which was to support the provision of green and reliable energy to the Green Cities.

The EBRD's Green Economy Financing Facilities (GEFF) support investment in green technologies. During 2018–33 the EBRD and the Green Climate Fund (GCF—established under the UN Framework Convention on Climate Change) were implementing a GCF-GEFF partnership that was supporting investments in emissions reduction and climate adaptation technologies. In March 2021 the EBRD and GCF agreed to increase the total value of GCF-GEFF co-operation (by an additional US \$497m.) to \$1,400m. The Bank's Finance and Technology Transfer Centre for Climate Change (FINTECC), engaged in 17 countries of operation in 2023, supports businesses in harnessing innovative technologies to promote renewable energy, energy, water and materials efficiency. A €30m. advisory EBRD Corporate Climate Governance Facility, initiated in late 2022, aims to enhance the capacity of businesses to manage climate-related risks and promote green investment.

In December 2020 the EBRD and the Organisation for Economic Co-operation and Development (OECD) concluded an MOU on enhancing collaboration in areas including the green economy, sustainable and inclusive development, private sector development, and public and corporate governance.

BUSINESS SUPPORT

In 1999 the EBRD established a Trade Facilitation Programme (TFP), which aimed to extend local bank guarantees and trade-related cash advances in order to promote trading capabilities, in particular for SMEs. The Programme became a core element of the Bank's 2020 COVID-19 response, and in July the Bank increased the exposure limit of the TFP to €3,000m. (from €2,000m.). In 2022 the Bank completed 1,768 trade transactions under the Programme.

In December 2013 the EBRD launched a Small Business Initiative (SBI) to promote more efficient management processes, greater accountability within a results-based framework and closer client liaison. During 2022 2,116 advisory projects were initiated under the SBI. Within the SBI a Risk Sharing Facility Framework, approved in April 2015, enables the EBRD to share—through the extension of funded or unfunded risk guarantees—partner banks' risk exposures to local enterprises. The Bank's Star Venture programme and Small Business Impact Fund provide bespoke advice and support to innovative start-up businesses.

TECHNOLOGY AND INNOVATION

An EBRD Knowledge Economy Initiative (introduced in 2014) supports technological advances and innovation. In March 2019 an EBRD Knowledge Economy Index was released, covering 46 economies, including eight external 'comparator' OECD member states. The Index, based on 38 indicators, focused on four pillars: institutions for innovation; skills for innovation; the innovation system; and the ICT infrastructure. The top three ranked EBRD member states were Estonia, Slovenia and Lithuania.

Under its strategy for 2021–25 the Bank is committed to supporting investment in digital projects, in order to promote economic transition and counter digital inequalities. It aims to ensure that technological advances benefit all sectors of society. A Digital Approach was initiated in November 2021, focused on three priority areas: developing enabling legal, regulatory and institutional frameworks, and implementation capacity, as a foundation for digital transformation; promoting adaptation (through investments that enable technology and knowledge transfer, and digitalization); and fostering innovation and new market entrants. A new Digital Hub became operational on 1 January 2022 to support the Digital Approach, and advance cybersecurity. In February the Bank launched the €250m. Venture Capital Investment Programme III facility, focused on supporting new technology companies.

ECONOMIC INCLUSION

The EBRD's Equality of Opportunity Strategy, covering 2021–25, focuses on broadening skills, employment and sustainable livelihoods; fostering inclusive and gender-responsive financial systems and business environments; and creating inclusive and gender-responsive services and public goods.

In February 2021 the EBRD and UN Women launched a partnership aimed at advancing a gender-inclusive recovery from the pandemic crisis. The EBRD's Strategy for the Promotion of Gender Equality, covering 2021–25, supports the mainstreaming of gender considerations in the Bank's projects and policies, and has the following priority areas: Access to Finance and Entrepreneurship; Access to Skills, Employment and Livelihoods; and Access to Services and Public Goods.

The EBRD's Women in Business programme—introduced in 2014, and active in the Western Balkans and SEMED regions (including the West Bank and Gaza, since 2021)—provides advisory and financing services to support SMEs with female management. An EBRD Youth in Business programme supports SMEs managed or owned by young people in the Western Balkans, Egypt and Morocco.

NUCLEAR SAFETY

The Bank administers a number of other funds to support the promotion of nuclear safety, and in particular to decommission potentially harmful Soviet-era facilities and equipment. Funds include the Nuclear Window of the NDEP; the Nuclear Safety Account (NSA), a multilateral programme of action established in 1993; the Chernobyl Shelter Fund (CSF), established in 1997; and International Decommissioning Support Funds, which have enabled the closure of nuclear plants for safety reasons where this would otherwise have been prohibitively costly, in Bulgaria, Lithuania and Slovakia.

SEMED

In September 2011 MOUs on co-operation were concluded between the EBRD and the African Development Bank and the Islamic Development Bank. At that time the EBRD joined other international financial institutions active in the Middle East and North Africa region to endorse the so-called Deauville Partnership, established by the then G8 in May to support political and economic reforms being undertaken by several countries, notably Egypt, Jordan, Morocco and Tunisia. A dedicated SEMED Investment Special Fund (ISF), facilitating investments in the region, was established in February 2012. Jordan and Tunisia were admitted as members of the EBRD in January of that year and, with Morocco (a founding member of the Bank), were granted countries of operations status on 1 November 2013: with immediate effect those countries' assets and capital resources hitherto held in the SEMED ISF were transferred to the balance sheet of the EBRD. In May 2014 the EBRD granted country of operations status to Cyprus on a temporary basis, until the end of 2020. The Board of Governors granted country of operations status to Egypt in October 2015. In July 2017 Lebanon became a shareholder member of the Bank; the Bank's Board of Governors agreed that it become a country of operations in September. In May of that year the Board of Governors determined that the EBRD should also engage in the West Bank and Gaza, for an initial period of five years. The first loans were approved for the West Bank and Gaza in 2018, financed through a separate trust fund. (Investments in the West Bank and Gaza amounted to €22.3m. in 2022.) Libya, accepted as a shareholder member in 2014 pending the conclusion of relevant formalities, formally became the Bank's 71st member in July 2019. Applications by Algeria and by the United Arab Emirates (UAE) to be shareholder members were accepted by the Bank's Board of Governors in, respectively, July 2020 and January 2021. The UAE became the 72nd shareholder in September, and Algeria the 73rd in October. An application by Iraq to be a shareholder member was accepted by the Bank's Board of Governors in October 2020. In May 2023 the Board of Governors agreed in principle to expand lending in future to Iraq, as part of the SEMED group of countries.

The EBRD introduced a financing package in 2016 that aimed to provide up to €900m. towards infrastructure and private sector projects in Jordan and Türkiye, with the aim of building the economic resilience of both countries and assisting them to support large influxes of Syrian refugees. In September 2019 the Bank issued a new strategy for Türkiye, to cover the period 2019–24, with a focus on strengthening financial sector resilience, developing capital markets, expanding the knowledge economy, advancing economic inclusion and gender equality in the private sector, promoting a green economy, and developing regional energy connectivity. In early March 2023 the Bank approved a finance framework for Turkish partner banks of up to €600m. to support relief and reconstruction activities, and livelihoods, jobs and human capital in southeastern areas of Türkiye that had been struck in February by devastating earthquakes. By 31 March cumulative EBRD investment in Türkiye totalled €18,130m. In July 2020 the EBRD undertook its first risk-sharing transaction in the SEMED region, extending an unfunded risk participation guarantee, amounting to US \$5m., to provide a Jordanian Bank with increased working capital to support a major Jordanian manufacturing business during the COVID-19 crisis. In September 2021 the EBRD provided the Bank of Palestine with a \$5m. trade finance line, to enable it to issue guarantees with respect to pre-export and post-import financing. The Bank's trade finance support in 2022 to the food and agribusiness sector in the SEMED region—which was particularly adversely affected by the disruption to imports of Ukrainian grain and wheat—totalled €600m. (of which €297m. was allocated to Morocco and €280m. to Egypt). A €150.5m. loan was extended to Tunisia's state-owned Office des Céréales in that year to fund cereal imports that covered 15% of Tunisia's annual consumption. The Bank invested €75m. in November 2022 to support the construction of Egypt's first green hydrogen facility, and in April 2023 approved a $100m. loan for the development of a new wind farm (projected to be the largest in Africa) to be located in Egypt's Gulf of Suez region.

Publications

Annual Review.
Financial Report (annually).
Law in Transition (annually).
Sustainability Report (annually).
Trade Exchange.
Transition Report (annually).
Working papers, other special reports, fact sheets.

Statistics

BANK COMMITMENTS BY COUNTRY
(in € million)

	2022	Cumulative to 31 Dec. 2022
Central Europe and the Baltic States		
Croatia	297	4,456
Czech Republic	111	1,340
Estonia	74	893
Hungary	215	3,513
Latvia	76	985
Lithuania	208	1,382
Poland	990	12,401
Slovakia	114	2,864
Slovenia	265	1,489
Sub-total	2,350	29,322
South-Eastern Europe		
Albania	154	1,934
Bosnia and Herzegovina	120	2,947
Bulgaria	103	4,401
Kosovo	91	589
Montenegro	23	724
North Macedonia	252	2,492
Romania	709	10,280
Serbia	648	7,927
Sub-total	2,099	31,295
Eastern Europe and the Caucasus		
Armenia	117	2,003
Azerbaijan	86	3,588
Belarus	0	2,858
Georgia	218	4,986
Moldova	525	2,094
Ukraine	1,460	18,096
Sub-total	2,405	33,625
Central Asia		
Kazakhstan	480	9,845
Kyrgyzstan	41	881
Mongolia	108	2,185
Tajikistan	21	908
Turkmenistan	2	334
Uzbekistan	839	3,897
Sub-total	1,490	18,050
Southern and Eastern Mediterranean		
Egypt	1,343	10,144
Jordan	141	1,930
Lebanon	5	859
Morocco	528	3,913
Tunisia	387	1,879
Sub-total	2,404	18,747
Greece	687	6,426
Russian Federation	0	23,355
Türkiye	1,634	16,985

Note: Financing for regional projects is allocated to the relevant countries.

Source: EBRD, *Annual Review 2022*.

ECONOMIC COOPERATION ORGANIZATION—ECO

Address: 1 Golbou Alley, Kamranieh St, POB 14155-6176, Tehran, Iran.
Telephone: (21) 22831733; **fax:** (21) 22831732; **e-mail:** registry@ecosecretariat.org; **internet:** www.eco.int.

ECO was established in 1985 as the successor to the Regional Cooperation for Development, founded in 1964. It aims to advance economic, technical and cultural co-operation among its member states and to promote regional development.

MEMBERS

Afghanistan	Kyrgyzstan	Türkiye (Turkey)
Azerbaijan	Pakistan	Turkmenistan
Iran	Tajikistan	Uzbekistan
Kazakhstan		

The 'Turkish Republic of Northern Cyprus' was granted special guest status in 2012.

Organization
(September 2023)

SUMMIT MEETING

The first summit meeting of heads of state and of government of member countries was held in Tehran, Iran, in February 1992. The 15th summit was held in November 2021, in Aşgabat, Turkmenistan, on the theme 'Into the future together'.

COUNCIL OF MINISTERS

The Council of Ministers, comprising ministers responsible for foreign affairs of member states, is the principal policy and decision-making body of ECO. It meets at least once a year. The Council's chairmanship rotates annually on an alphabetical basis (2023: Azerbaijan).

REGIONAL PLANNING COUNCIL

The Council, comprising senior planning officials or other representatives of member states, meets at least once a year. It is responsible for reviewing programmes of activity and evaluating results achieved, and for proposing future plans of action to the Council of Ministers.

COUNCIL OF PERMANENT REPRESENTATIVES

Permanent representatives or ambassadors of member countries accredited to Iran meet regularly to formulate policy for consideration by the Council of Ministers and to promote implementation of decisions reached at ministerial or summit level.

SECRETARIAT

The secretariat is headed by a Secretary-General, who is supported by four Deputy Secretaries-General. The following Directorates administer and co-ordinate the main areas of ECO activities: Trade and Investment; Transport and Communications; Energy, Minerals and Environment; Agriculture and Industry; Human Resources and Sustainable Development; and Tourism. There are also units covering Project Management; International Relations; Co-ordination and Follow-up; Administration; Legal Affairs; and Judicial and Parliamentary Co-ordination, including the ECO Advocacy Programme for Afghanistan. The secretariat services ECO sectoral ministerial meetings. A High Level Expert Group on Statistics was established in 2006, and an ECO Permanent Steering Committee on Economic Research was created in 2010.

Secretary-General: KHUSRAV NOZIRI (Tajikistan).

Activities

In 1985 ECO replaced the Regional Cooperation for Development (which had been established in 1964 as a tripartite arrangement for economic co-operation between Iran, Pakistan and Turkey—now known as Türkiye). Seven additional members were admitted to ECO in November 1992. The main objectives of co-operation are advancing the sustainable economic development of member states; the development of the regional transport and communications infrastructure; economic liberalization and privatization; the progressive removal of trade barriers and the promotion of intraregional trade; advancing the region's role in global trade, and the gradual integration of member states' economies with the global economy; the mobilization and utilization of the region's material resources; the interconnection of power grids in the region; the effective utilization of the region's agricultural and industrial potential; regional co-operation on narcotics control; ecological and environmental co-operation; strengthening regional cultural ties; and pursuing mutually beneficial co-operation with regional and international organizations. In March 2017 the 13th summit meeting, held in Islamabad, Pakistan, issued the Islamabad Declaration, in which it resolved to implement efficiently an ECO Vision 2025, giving priority to trade; transport and connectivity; energy; tourism; economic growth and productivity; and social welfare and the environment.

Trade and Economic Growth: A regional Chamber of Commerce and Industry (ECO-CCI) was established in 1993. A Transit Trade Agreement and an Agreement on the Simplification of Visa Procedures for Businessmen of ECO Countries came into effect in December 1997 and March 1998, respectively. In April 2008 an ECO Trade Agreement (ECOTA), which envisaged the development of an ECO Free Trade Area, entered into force. An ECOTA Cooperation Council meets regularly; by 2023, however, ECOTA was not yet operational, and in 2022 intra-regional trade was reported to represent only around 8% of member states' total external trade. In July 2020 a virtual meeting on trade facilitation confirmed that a trade specialist had been recruited to identify obstacles to ECOTA's implementation. The Secretary-General noted in September that ECO had initiated studies on the removal of non- and para-tariff barriers to trade. An ECO Regional Network of Special Economic Zones has been proposed.

An ECO Trade and Development Bank (ETDB), headquartered in İstanbul (with its main branches in Tehran, Iran, and Islamabad) commenced operations in 2008.

The first meeting of ECO heads of investment promotion agencies was held in December 2016. In October 2018 ECO heads of privatization administrations issued the Baku Declaration, in which, *inter alia*, they agreed to establish an Investment Forum of the Privatization Organizations of the ECO Member States and International Investors, and to focus on the uses of public-private partnerships. The inaugural Meeting of the Heads of the National Development and Wealth Funds of the ECO member states, convened, in a virtual format, in December 2020, emphasized ECO's strategic focus on attracting investment and expanding intraregional trade as a means of promoting sustainable socioeconomic development. The fourth ECO Business Forum was hosted by Turkmenistan in November 2021, in a hybrid, part virtual, format.

The first meeting of ECO Heads of Tax Administrations was convened in January 2013. In December 2016 an ECO Regional Institute for Standardization, Conformity Assessment, Accreditation and Metrology (RISCAM) was established in Tehran. In February 2018 the inaugural meeting was held of a Karachi, Pakistan-based ECO Reinsurance Company; it was envisaged that this would become fully operational in 2023.

ECO maintains an Ankara, Türkiye-based ECO Coordination Center for Food Security, which co-ordinates the implementation of the ECO/Food and Agriculture Organization of the UN Regional Programme for Food Security. An ECO Veterinary Commission was established, in Tehran, in October 2012. The ECO Seed Association (ECOSA), inaugurated in July 2008, hosts regular international seed trade conferences; the eighth was pending in 2023 (to be held in the Azerbaijani capital, Baku).

Transport and Connectivity: Co-operation in the area of transport and communications is of particular regional importance, given that seven ECO member states are landlocked. Relevant activities are guided by the 1993 Quetta Plan of Action and Istanbul Declaration, and by the Almatı Outline Plan for the Development of Transport Sector in the ECO Region, which was adopted in October 1993 by the first meeting of ECO ministers responsible for transport.

In March 1995 ECO heads of state concluded formal agreements on the establishment of a regional joint shipping company and airline; the latter project was terminated in May 2001 by the Council of Ministers, owing to its unsustainable cost, and replaced by a framework agreement on co-operation in the field of air transport.

A Transit Transport Framework Agreement (TTFA) entered into force in May 2006, and has eight protocols, that cover road, rail and inland water transportation, customs control, motor vehicles (including third-party insurance), and terms of reference for the ECO's Transit Transport Co-ordination Council. In May 2018 ECO transport ministers determined to prioritize complementary networking between dry ports in landlocked member countries and sea ports in coastal member states. ECO specialized and expert working groups manage the development of road and rail corridors under the TTFA, including the Islamabad-Tehran-Istanbul (ITI), Kyrgyzstan-Tajikistan-Afghanistan-Iran (KTAI), Kazakhstan-Turkmenistan-Iran (KTI), Istanbul-Almatı, and Bandar Abbas-Almatı road and rail corridor projects. The ITI road corridor was activated in October 2021. Guidelines on Cross Border Facilitation Measures were endorsed by a Ministerial Meeting on Transport that was held (in a virtual format) in December 2020, with a view to supporting trade flows and the unhindered passage of essential medicines and foods across regional border crossing points. A Ministerial Declaration was adopted at that time which urged member states fully to implement the TTFA; by 2023 the Agreement had been ratified by Azerbaijan, Afghanistan, Iran, Kazakhstan, Kyrgyzstan, Pakistan, Tajikistan and Türkiye. In August 2022, while participating in a Ministerial Transport Conference of Landlocked Developing Countries, hosted (in a hybrid part-virtual format) from Awaza, Turkmenistan, the ECO Secretary-General recommended several actions aimed at facilitating transit to the landlocked ECO member states, including diversifying transit routes, developing border crossing facilities that minimize personal contact, digitizing transit procedures, promoting electronic visas, eliminating costly transshipment measures, and establishing joint border monitoring systems.

In December 2017 the second meeting of ECO ministers responsible for information and communications technologies (ICT) (the first having been held in 2012) adopted the 2025 ECO Regional Strategy for Information Society Development, and an action plan for its implementation. A Ministerial Policy Dialogue on Our Digital Future was organized during the Third ECO Ministerial Meeting on ICT, convened in July 2023, in Tehran.

Energy: An ECO Decade for Enhanced Energy Co-operation was implemented during 2013–22, with the aim of advancing energy sustainability and resilience in the region. In August 2016 the inaugural meeting of ECO public and private sector energy and petroleum consortiums was convened in Tehran. Participants recommended the establishment of an ECO Energy Consortium, to manage the implementation of regional projects in the petroleum, gas, petrochemical, electricity and renewable energy sectors, and an ECO Energy Investment Fund. An ECO experts' group on renewable energy sources meets regularly. A Clean Energy Centre for the ECO region (CECECO) was under development in 2023, as well as a project to establish an integrated ECO Regional Electricity Market.

Tourism: ECO Vision 2025 envisaged the development of a multi-sector regional tourism industry, including, for example, ecological, health and medical, mountain sports, and religious tourism, and a particular focus on the cultural heritage of the ancient Silk Road route. The inaugural meeting of an ECO Tour Operators Network was convened in November 2022, in a virtual format. Ardabil, in northwestern Iran, was being celebrated as the ECO Tourism Capital of 2023 (2024: Shakhrisabz, Uzbekistan).

The fifth ECO Silk Road Food Festival was organized in April 2019, in Zanjan, Iran.

Social Welfare and the Environment: ECO works to combat the cultivation of and trade in illicit drugs in the region. (The ECO region is the source of more than one-half of global seizures of opium; more than 80% of global opium supplies originate in Afghanistan, and many ECO member states are used in transit for its distribution.) In November 2012 the establishment of an ECO Regional Center for Cooperation of Anti-Corruption Agencies and Ombudsmen was agreed, and an accord on establishing an ECO Smuggling and Customs Offences Data Bank entered into force in December 2017.

In October 2012 the Council of Ministers endorsed the Charter of the Parliamentary Assembly of the ECO Countries (PAECO). PAECO's third conference, hosted by Azerbaijan in May 2022, adopted the Baku Declaration, which emphasized the importance of inter-parliamentary co-operation aimed at implementing the UN's 2030 Agenda for Sustainable Development, and of collective targeted actions focused on advancing regional recovery from the impacts of the COVID-19 pandemic.

A Tehran-based ECO Cultural Institute was inaugurated in 2000. In December 2011 the ECO Science Foundation was established in Islamabad. An ECO Educational Institute commenced operations in April 2012, in Ankara. In March 2021 the statute was signed for an ECO Research Centre, to be based in Baku. An ECO Nanotechnology Network and ECO Agricultural Biotechnology Network are under development.

The ECO Regional Center for Risk Management of Natural Disasters, founded in Mashhad, Iran, in 2007, is tasked with promoting interregional co-operation in drought early warning and monitoring activities. The seventh ECO International Conference on Disaster Risk Management was convened in June 2014, in Qabala, Azerbaijan. ECO ministers responsible for ICT finalized an ECO Regional Framework on Disaster Risk Reduction in October of that year. The ECO Secretariat was represented at a high-level regional consultative meeting on risk data governance and disaster information management that was convened in Istanbul, in December 2022. In February 2023 the ECO Secretariat stated solidarity with the people of Türkiye, in view of the devastating earthquakes that had recently struck southern areas of that country and northern Syrian Arab Republic.

The ECO Institute of Environmental Science and Technology (ECO-IEST, established in 2011) is hosted by the Karaj, Iran-based University of the Environment. In December 2014 ECO ministers responsible for the environment issued the Istanbul Declaration on Climate Change and Green Economy, in which they agreed to designate the environment and the impacts of climate change as cross-sectoral organizational priorities. ECO Vision 2025 noted the importance of supporting regional biodiversity and forestry; alleviating the regional impacts of climate change; and combating long-range trans-boundary air pollution.

The fifth ECO Ministerial Meeting on Health, convened in May 2023, gave consideration to the establishment of a regional consultation mechanism to support technical co-operation on communicable diseases.

Finance

Member states contribute to a centralized administrative budget.

Publications

ECO Annual Economic Report.
Drugs Situation in the ECO Region.
Economic Journal.

EUROPEAN UNION—EU

In December 2001 the European Council adopted the Declaration on the Future of the European Union, which aimed to reform EU institutions to ensure the smooth functioning of the Union after enlargement. The full text of the draft constitutional treaty was submitted to the Council of the European Union (often known as the Council) in July 2003. At a summit meeting held in Brussels in June 2004, the heads of state and of government of the then 25 EU member states approved the draft constitutional treaty, which was formally signed in Rome in October by the heads of state or of government of the 25 member states and the three candidate countries of Bulgaria, Romania and Turkey (now known as Türkiye). However, the treaty remained subject to ratification by each member nation (either by a vote in the national legislature or by a popular referendum), and in May and June 2005 it was rejected in national referendums held in France and the Netherlands, respectively.

At an informal summit of the European Council held in Lisbon, Portugal, in mid-October 2007, agreement was reached at an Intergovernmental Conference on the final text of a new reform treaty. The resulting Treaty of Lisbon amending the Treaty on European Union and the Treaty establishing the European Community was signed in Lisbon, on 13 December, by the heads of state or of government of the now 27 member states. The Treaty of Lisbon retained much of the content of the abandoned constitutional treaty. In June 2008 voters in Ireland, which was constitutionally bound to conduct a popular referendum on the issue, rejected ratification of the treaty. Consequently, in December the European Council agreed to a number of concessions, including the removal of a provision in the treaty for a reduction in the number of European Commissioners. A new referendum, held in Ireland in October 2009, approved the treaty. By early November all EU member states had ratified the Treaty of Lisbon, which entered into force on 1 December. The Treaty of Rome was duly renamed the Treaty on the Functioning of the European Union, with references to the European 'Community' changed to the 'Union'. Euratom continued to exist, alongside the EU.

Meetings of the principal organs take place in Brussels, in Luxembourg and in Strasbourg, France. The Treaty of Lisbon created a High Representative of the Union for Foreign Affairs and Security Policy (appointed by the European Council by qualified majority with the agreement of the President of the Commission) to represent the EU internationally, combining the former roles of EU Commissioner responsible for external relations and EU High Representative for the Common Foreign and Security Policy (although foreign policy remains subject to a national veto). The Lisbon Treaty also provided for the creation of a new permanent President of the European Council, elected by the European Council; the creation of this role aimed to promote coherence and continuity in policymaking. The system of a six-month rotating Presidency was retained for the different formations of the Council of the European Union (except for the External Relations Council, chaired by the High Representative). A new system of fixed 18-month troikas (groups of three presidencies) was introduced, sharing the presidencies of most configurations of the Council, to facilitate overall co-ordination and continuity of work.

The Lisbon Treaty provided for a revised system of qualified majority voting in the Council. The European Parliament's legislative powers were consolidated under the Lisbon Treaty, which granted the Parliament the right of co-decision with the Council in an increased number of policy areas, giving it a more prominent role in framing legislation. The maximum number of seats in the European Parliament was raised to 751 from 2014.

The Lisbon Treaty sought to improve democracy and transparency within the Union, introducing the right for EU citizens to petition the Commission to introduce new legislation and enshrining the principles of subsidiarity (that the EU should only act when an objective can be better achieved at supranational level, implying that national powers are the norm) and proportionality (that the action should be proportional to the desired objective). National parliaments are given the opportunity to examine EU legislation to ensure that it rests within the EU's remit, and legislation may be returned to the Commission for reconsideration if one-third of member states find that a proposed law breaches these principles. The Treaty of Lisbon enabled enhanced co-operation for groups numbering at least one-third of the member states. The treaty provided a legal basis for an EU defence force, with a mutual defence clause, and stipulated that the EU has the power to sign treaties and sit on international bodies as a legal entity in its own right. The new framework also provided for the establishment of a European Public Prosecutor's Office to combat EU fraud and cross-border crime and the right to dual citizenship (i.e. of the EU as well as of a member state). Article 50 of the Treaty of Lisbon provides for a member state to withdraw from the Union if it so wishes, 'in accordance with its own constitutional requirements'. Such a member state must notify the European Council of its intention, thereby formally invoking Article 50. If a withdrawing member state later wishes to apply to rejoin the EU, its application will be considered as that of a third country (under Article 49 of the Treaty of Lisbon).

Presidency of the Council of the European Union: Sweden (January–June 2023); Spain (July–December 2023); Belgium (January–June 2024).

President of the European Council: CHARLES MICHEL (Belgium).

High Representative of the Union for Foreign Affairs and Security Policy: JOSEP BORRELL FONTELLES (Spain).

Enlargement

Türkiye (known until June 2022 as Turkey), which had signed an association agreement with the EC in 1963 (which was suspended between 1980 and 1986, following a military coup), applied for membership of the EU in April 1987. In 1999 the European Council granted Türkiye candidate status. In April 2004 a United Nations (UN) plan for the reunification of Cyprus was rejected in a referendum by the Greek Cypriots in the south of the island. Cyprus has been divided since 1974 when Türkiye invaded the northern third of the country in response to a Greek-sponsored coup aiming to unite the island with Greece. Türkiye refuses to recognize the Greek Cypriot Government and is the only country to recognize the Government of the northern section of the country, known as the 'Turkish Republic of Northern Cyprus'. The requirement for the successful resolution of all territorial disputes with members of the EU meant that failure to reach a settlement in Cyprus remained an impediment to Türkiye's accession. The EU agreed to begin accession talks with Türkiye in October 2005, although it warned that membership was not guaranteed. Türkiye had to sign a protocol to update its association agreement with the EU prior to accession negotiations, to cover the 10 new members that had joined the organization in May 2004, including Cyprus. Türkiye, which signed the protocol in July 2005, insisted that the extension of the association agreement did not constitute formal recognition of the Greek Cypriot Government. In November 2006 the Commission demanded that Türkiye open its ports to Cypriot ships, in compliance with its agreement to extend its customs union to the 10 new member states in 2005. Türkiye announced that there could be no progress on this issue until the EU implemented a regulation drafted in 2004 to end the economic isolation of the 'Turkish Republic of Northern Cyprus', which had been blocked by Cyprus. In December 2006, therefore, the Council stipulated that talks would not commence in eight policy areas affected by the restrictions placed on Cypriot traffic by Türkiye. After a period of impasse, negotiations opened in additional policy areas in December 2015 and June 2016, amid increased co-operation between the EU and Türkiye on migration. However, in November 2016 the European Parliament approved a non-binding resolution supporting the temporary suspension of accession negotiations with Türkiye, owing to concerns over human rights and the rule of law following the suppression of an attempted coup in July. In March 2019 Parliament supported a non-binding resolution formally suspending negotiations with Türkiye, owing to continued concerns about human rights and the introduction there of a new Constitution strengthening the powers of President Recep Tayyip Erdoğan.

Bosnia and Herzegovina submitted a formal application for membership of the EU in February 2016; it was granted candidate status in December 2022. Ukraine applied for EU membership at the end of February, and Georgia and Moldova submitted membership applications in early March. In June the European Council awarded candidate status to both Moldova and Ukraine.

The Middle East and the Mediterranean

In November 1995 a conference convened in Barcelona, Spain, issued the Barcelona Declaration, outlining a new EU-Mediterranean partnership. The process of co-operation and dialogue under this agreement became known as the Euro-Mediterranean Partnership, or Barcelona Process. In March 2008 the European Council agreed formally to transform the Barcelona Process into the Union for the Mediterranean (UfM), which was officially launched in July. Members of the UfM comprise the EU member states and 16 Southern Mediterranean countries: Albania, Algeria, Bosnia and Herzegovina, Egypt, Israel, Jordan, Lebanon, Mauritania, Monaco, Montenegro, Morocco, North Macedonia, the Palestinian territories, the Syrian Arab Republic (currently suspended), Tunisia and Türkiye. Libya is an observer. A Secretariat was established in Barcelona in March 2010. A UfM Roadmap for Action was approved by regional ministers of foreign affairs meeting in Barcelona in January 2017. More than 50 regional co-operation projects, with a budget of more than €5,000m., have been approved under the UfM.

In March 2003 the European Commission launched a European Neighbourhood Policy (ENP) with the aim of enhancing co-operation with countries adjacent to the enlarged Union. In 2007 a new European Neighbourhood and Partnership Instrument (ENPI) replaced the existing financial programmes in place. Under the ENP, the EU negotiated bilateral Action Plans with 12 countries, establishing three- to five-year targets for political and economic co-operation. The Action Plans aimed to build on existing contractual relationships between the partner country and the EU (e.g. an Association Agreement or a Partnership and Co-operation Agreement—PCA). From 2014 the ENPI was replaced by the European Neighbourhood Instrument, for which the European Parliament approved funding of more than €15,000m. during 2014–20.

In February 2021 the European Commission and the High Representative of the Union for Foreign Affairs and Security Policy proposed a new Agenda for the Mediterranean to reinforce the strategic partnership between the EU and its Southern Neighbourhood. For 2021–27 the existing funding programmes for the region were absorbed into a new funding instrument, the Neighbourhood, Development and International Cooperation Instrument (NDICI). It was envisaged that up to €7,000m. would be made available under the NDICI for 2021–27 (with total funding of €79,462m.) for the implementation of the Agenda for the Mediterranean.

Turkey (known as Türkiye since June 2022) signed an Association Agreement with the EC in 1963 (suspended between 1980 and 1986 following a military coup), and applied for EU membership in April 1987. Accession talks began in October 2005. In October 2015 a Joint Action Plan was agreed between the European Commission and Turkey in order to ameliorate co-operation in responding to the migration crisis, caused, in particular, by the ongoing civil conflict in Syria. In March 2016 a new agreement was reached, known as the EU-Turkey Statement, providing for the return of migrants crossing into Greek territory and considered not to be in immediate need of international protection. EU-Turkey relations were strained by Turkish President Recep Tayyip Erdoğan's uncompromising stance following a coup attempt in July of that year. Members of the European Parliament (MEPs) adopted non-binding resolutions urging membership negotiations to be suspended in November and, following allegations of human rights abuses surrounding a controversial constitutional referendum held in April 2017, in July 2017 and in March 2019. Relations with the EU were further strained after Turkey suspended application of the 2016 EU-Türkiye agreement in February 2020, announcing that it would open the passage for migrants to cross its borders with Europe (following an upsurge in fighting in Syria, which caused the deaths of more than 30 Turkish soldiers). Given some improvement in relations, in March 2021 the European Council indicated its readiness to re-engage with Turkey on issues including an updated customs union, the resumption of high-level dialogue and increased co-operation in managing migration. In March 2023 the European Commission announced reconstruction aid to Türkiye of €1,000m. and humanitarian aid to Syria of €108m., following devastating earthquakes in those countries in February.

Co-operation agreements concluded in the 1970s with the Maghreb countries (Algeria, Morocco and Tunisia), the Mashreq countries (Egypt, Jordan, Lebanon and Syria) and Israel covered free access to the community market for industrial products, customs preferences for certain agricultural products, and financial aid in the form of grants and loans from the European Investment Bank (EIB). In June 1992 the EC approved a proposal to conclude new bilateral agreements with the Maghreb countries, incorporating: political dialogue; financial, economic, technical and cultural co-operation; and the eventual establishment of a free trade area. An Association Agreement with Tunisia was signed in July 1995 and entered into force in March 1998. A similar agreement with Morocco (concluded in 1996) entered into force in March 2000. In March 1997 negotiations were initiated with Algeria on an Association Agreement that would incorporate political commitments relating to democracy and human rights; this was signed in December 2001 and entered into force in September 2005. An Association Agreement with Jordan was signed in November 1997 and entered into force in May 2002. The so-called Agadir Agreement on the establishment of a Free Trade Zone between the Arabic Mediterranean Nations was signed in February 2004 and came into force in March 2007. An interim EU Association Agreement with Lebanon was signed in June 2002, and entered into force in April 2006. Protracted negotiations on an Association Agreement with Syria were concluded in October 2004. A revised version of the Agreement was initialled in December 2008. In May 2011 the EU announced that co-operation with Syria was to be suspended, owing to the violent suppression of anti-Government protests there from March (and subsequent civil conflict—see below). In December the Council of the EU agreed that negotiations could commence towards Deep and Comprehensive Free Trade Agreements (DCFTAs) with Egypt, Jordan, Morocco and Tunisia. Negotiations with Morocco were initiated in March 2013 but were later suspended; talks with Tunisia commenced in October 2015.

A co-operation agreement between the EC and the countries of the Cooperation Council for the Arab States of the Gulf, which entered into force in January 1990, provided for co-operation in industry, energy, technology and other fields. A customs union was established in January 2003. A co-operation agreement between the EU and Qatar was signed in March 2018. The European Parliament suspended work linked with Qatar in mid-December 2022, following allegations of corruption by Qatar involving MEPs and parliamentary staff.

An Association Agreement with Israel was signed in 1995 and entered into force in June 2000. In late 2004 an ENP Action Plan on further co-operation was agreed by the EU and Israel; it was adopted by the EU in February 2005 and by the Israeli authorities in April.

The EU formed part of the Middle East Quartet (alongside the UN, the USA and the Russian Federation), which was established in July 2002 to mediate between Israel and the Palestinian Territories. An EU Police Mission for the Palestinian Territories commenced operations in January 2006, with an initial three-year mandate, subsequently repeatedly extended, to support the PA in establishing sustainable and effective policing arrangements. In February 2008 the European Commission launched a new mechanism, PEGASE, with a wider remit than the emergency assistance mechanism hitherto in place to provide support to the Palestinian people. PEGASE was established to support activities in four principal areas: governance (including fiscal reform, security and the rule of law); social development (including social protection, health and education); economic and private sector development; and development of public infrastructure (in areas such as water, the environment and energy). In January 2018 the High Representative announced that the EU was pledging an additional €42.5m. in aid to the Palestinian territories, following a decision by US President Donald Trump to reduce US economic support.

During 2002 attempts were made to improve relations with Iran, as negotiations began in preparation for a Trade and Co-operation Agreement. In mid-2003 the EU (in conformity with US policy) warned Iran to accept stringent new nuclear inspections, and threatened the country with economic repercussions unless it restored international trust in its nuclear programme. A comprehensive dialogue between the EU and Iran was suspended by Iran in December 2003. In January 2005 the EU resumed trade talks with Iran after the Iranian authorities agreed to suspend uranium enrichment. However, these talks were halted in August, following Iran's resumption of uranium conversion to gas (the stage preceding enrichment). Following Iran's removal of international seals from a nuclear research facility in January 2006, the EU supported efforts to refer Iran to the UN Security Council. In December the Council criticized the country's failure to implement measures required by both the International Atomic Energy Agency (IAEA) and the UN Security Council in respect of its nuclear programme. EU trade sanctions against Iran were strengthened in August 2008, after Iran failed to halt its uranium enrichment programme. In July 2010 EU ministers responsible for foreign affairs adopted a new set of sanctions, prohibiting investment, technical assistance and technology transfers to Iran's energy sector, and also targeting the country's financial services, insurance and transport sectors. Sanctions were strengthened in 2011 and 2012. In November 2013 negotiations commenced between the E3/EU+3 grouping (comprising the People's Republic of China, France, Germany, Russia, the United Kingdom and the USA, and led by the EU's High Representative) and Iran, with the aim of concluding a comprehensive solution to ensure the long-term safety of Iran's nuclear programme. In July 2015 agreement on a Joint Comprehensive Plan of Action (JCPOA) was reached between Iran and the E3/EU+3, which sought to guarantee the peaceful nature of Iran's nuclear programme. The JCPOA was implemented from January 2016, thereby enabling the EU, the UN and the USA to lift their nuclear-related financial sanctions. However, in May 2018 President Trump announced the USA's withdrawal from the agreement and the reimposition of sanctions. The EU remained committed to the implementation of the JCPOA, but the US sanctions had strained relations with Iran, and Iran had breached the agreement. The election of Joe Biden as US President in November 2020 raised hopes that the USA might return to the JCPOA; negotiations with Iran, with the indirect participation of the USA, resumed in April 2021. In August 2022 the EU presented a new, draft agreement to Iran for consideration. Following the repression by Iranian security forces of widespread protests in Iran after the death of a woman in late 2022 who had been arrested for not wearing a *hijab* (headscarf) in accordance with government rules, in November and December of that year and January 2023 the EU extended sanctions to a number of individuals and entities, including Islamic Republic of Iran Broadcasting.

An Association Agreement with Tunisia entered into force in 1998. The EU and Tunisia established a so-called privileged partnership in 2012. In February 2014 the Council welcomed the adoption, in the previous month, of a new Constitution in Tunisia. An EU-Tunisia agreement was signed in July 2023, which included funding of some €100m. from the EU to help curb migration (Tunisia having become a main departure point for migrants seeking a route to Europe).

An Association Agreement with Egypt (a major beneficiary of EU financial co-operation since the 1970s) was signed in June 2001 and ratified in June 2004. Mass protests took place in Egypt in early 2011, which led to the resignation of President Lt-Gen. Muhammad Hosni Mubarak in February. In August 2013, following the escalation of violence in Egypt in that month, EU ministers responsible for foreign affairs agreed to suspend the sale of armaments to the country. The Association Council of the EU and Egypt met in Luxembourg in June 2022, and new Partnership Priorities were adopted for the period until 2027. The EU and Egypt pledged to enhance dialogue and co-operation in three priority areas: the sustainable modern economy and social development, foreign policy, and stability.

In July 1998 an EU-Yemen co-operation agreement entered into force, focusing on development and economic issues. After the security and humanitarian situation in Yemen deteriorated in 2015, the EU increased its provision of humanitarian aid to the country. The EU delegation to Yemen was evacuated and since 2017 has been based in Amman, Jordan. The EU pledged some €170m. in humanitarian aid to assist the population during the ongoing conflict and famine in 2022.

Formal negotiations on an EU-Libya Framework Agreement were inaugurated in November 2008. Negotiations were suspended in February 2011, when violent clashes broke out in Libya between anti-Government protesters and armed forces loyal to the Libyan leader, Col Muammar al-Qaddafi. Later that month the Council adopted a UN Security Council Resolution prohibiting the sale to Libya of arms and ammunition, and agreed to impose additional sanctions against those responsible for the violent repression of civilian protests. The Council also imposed a visa ban on several people, including al-Qaddafi and members of his family, and froze the assets of al-Qaddafi and 25 other people. After Qaddafi's killing in October, the European Council agreed measures to support the Libyan economy and to assist the UN mission in Libya. A number of frozen assets were released in support of humanitarian and civilian needs, and a ban on the use of European airspace by Libyan aircraft was removed. In November the EU's Tripoli office (opened in August) became the headquarters of a new EU delegation to Libya. In May 2013 a civilian EU Border Assistance Mission (EUBAM) was launched to help to improve border security. By July 2014, however, the security situation in Tripoli had deteriorated and the EU delegation and EUBAM left the country. The EU participated in the Berlin Conference of January 2020, with other representatives of the international community, to support UN efforts seeking a peaceful resolution of the continuing crisis in Libya. In March a new Mediterranean naval mission, EU NAVFOR MED IRINI, was launched to enforce the UN arms embargo on Libya.

In response to the forcible quashing, from March 2011, of anti-Government protests by the Syrian authorities, the EU imposed a number of restrictive measures, including an arms embargo and targeted sanctions, comprising a travel ban and the freezing of assets, against those deemed to be responsible for, or involved with, the repression. By August 2012 the EU had imposed 17 sets of sanctions on the Syrian authorities; sanctions were repeatedly extended. The EU delegation to Syria closed in December, owing to security concerns. In August the High Representative expressed deep concern at reports of the use of chemical weapons in Syria, and in February 2014 the EU pledged €12m. to help to dismantle and destroy stockpiles of chemical weaponry in Syria. By 2014 the EU had identified the Syrian crisis as the largest humanitarian and security crisis worldwide. An EU Strategy for Syria was adopted in April 2017, and in April 2018 the EU co-chaired, with the UN, the second Brussels Conference on Supporting the Future of Syria and the Region (the first having been convened in the previous year); the seventh such conference took place in June 2023. According to an EU report published in September 2019, from the beginning of the Syrian conflict the EU and EU member states had allocated around €17,000m. to the country in humanitarian and development aid, as well as economic and stabilization assistance. The EU, collectively, had been the most significant provider of international aid to Syria throughout the conflict.

The increased tension in the Middle East prior to the military action in Iraq in March 2003 strained relations between member states of the EU. In February 2003 the European Council held an extraordinary meeting to discuss the crisis in Iraq, and issued a statement reiterating its commitment to the central role of the UN in maintaining international order. In April, however, the EU leaders accepted a dominant role for the USA and the UK in post-war Iraq, and Denmark, Spain and the Netherlands announced plans to send peacekeeping troops to Iraq. An EU integrated rule of law mission for Iraq commenced operations in July, with an initial mandate of 12 months. Between 2003 and 2008 the EU provided €933m. in reconstruction and humanitarian assistance to Iraq. In November 2017 a civilian EU advisory mission to Iraq commenced operations in the capital, Baghdad, in order to support the Government in implementing reforms to the security sector.

Meanwhile, in August 2014 the European Council expressed dismay at the worsening security situation in Iraq and Syria, caused by the declaration of an Islamic caliphate over parts of the two countries' territories by Islamic State, and the widespread human rights violations carried out against Christians and other minorities. The European Council noted that the outbreak of civil conflict in Syria had facilitated the emergence of Islamic State in Iraq and the Levant (subsequently renamed Islamic State), which it recognized as a threat to security in Europe, and announced its intention to co-operate with the USA and other countries in order to counter the threat posed by Islamic State and other organizations deemed to pose a terrorist threat. A comprehensive EU regional strategy for Syria, Iraq and the threat from Islamic State was adopted in March 2015, and subsequently reviewed in May 2016.

In January 2018 the EU adopted a new strategy for Iraq, to support the country following the territorial defeat of Islamic State, by supporting the country in the principal areas of territorial integrity, and ethnic and religious diversity; efforts towards the introduction and maintenance of stable and democratic government; humanitarian need; economic growth and job creation; transitional justice; and the introduction of a formal dialogue on migration. A PCA with Iraq, which had been signed in May 2012, entered into force in August 2018. In September 2020 the EU signed a financing agreement with the Government of Iraq, pledging some €90m. in support of stability and the country's socioeconomic recovery and development amid the COVID-19 pandemic.

Aid to Developing and Non-EU Countries

The European Commission's Directorate-General for European Civil Protection and Humanitarian Aid Operations (DG ECHO) was established in 1991 as the Humanitarian Aid and Civil Protection Office, with a mandate to co-ordinate the provision of emergency humanitarian assistance and food aid. ECHO, which became fully operational in 1993 and is based in Brussels, Belgium, finances operations conducted by NGOs and international agencies, with which it works in partnership.

In 2022 ECHO provided aid worth some €150.7m. to those affected by the impact of civil conflict in the Syrian Arab Republic. Funds totalling €219m. were allocated by ECHO to Iraq, Yemen and Palestine. In 2020 €55m. was allocated to North Africa and the European Neighbourhood.

ISLAMIC DEVELOPMENT BANK—IsDB

Address: POB 5925, Jeddah 21432, Saudi Arabia.
Telephone: (12) 636-1400; **fax:** (12) 636-6871; **e-mail:** info@isdb.org; **internet:** www.isdb.org.

The Bank was established following a conference of ministers of finance of member countries of the then Organization of the Islamic Conference (now Organization of Islamic Cooperation), held in Jeddah in December 1973. Its aim is to encourage the economic development and social progress of member states and of Muslim communities in non-member countries, in accordance with the principles of the Islamic *Shari'a* (sacred law). The Bank formally opened in October 1975. The Bank and its associated entities—the Islamic Development Bank Institute, Islamic Corporation for the Development of the Private Sector (ICD), International Islamic Trade Finance Corporation (ITFC), and Islamic Corporation for the Insurance of Investment and Export Credit—constitute the Islamic Development Bank (IsDB) Group.

MEMBERS

There are 57 members (see *Financial Structure*).

Organization

(September 2023)

BOARD OF GOVERNORS

Each member country is represented by a governor, usually its minister of finance, and an alternate. The Board of Governors is the supreme authority of the Bank, and meets annually. The 2023 meeting was held in May, in Jeddah.

BOARD OF EXECUTIVE DIRECTORS

The Board consists of 18 members, one-half of whom are appointed by the nine largest subscribers to the capital stock of the Bank; the remaining nine are elected by Governors representing the other subscribers. Members of the Board of Executive Directors are elected for three-year terms. The Board is responsible for the direction of the general operations of the Bank.

ADMINISTRATION

President of the Bank and Chairman of the Board of Executive Directors: Dr MUHAMMED SULAIMAN AL JASSER (Saudi Arabia).
Vice-President, Country Programmes: Dr MANSUR MUHTAR (Nigeria).
Vice-President, Finance: Dr ZAMIR IQBAL (Pakistan).

REGIONAL HUBS

In accordance with a policy of decentralization introduced in 2017, by 2023 the IsDB had regional hubs based in Dhaka, Bangladesh; Cairo, Egypt; Jakarta, Indonesia; Almatı, Kazakhstan; Rabat, Morocco; Abuja, Nigeria; Dakar, Senegal; İstanbul, Türkiye; and Kampala, Uganda. A further regional hub, for Paramaribo, Suriname, was located in Jeddah. There was also an IsDB Centre of Excellence in Kuala Lumpur, Malaysia.

Morocco: ave Ennakhil/ave al-Haour, Hay Ryad 10104 Rabat; tel. (53) 7548800; fax (53) 7757260; e-mail RORM@isdb.org; internet www.isdb.org/hub/rabat.

FINANCIAL STRUCTURE

The Bank's unit of account is the Islamic Dinar (ID), which is equivalent to the value of one Special Drawing Right (SDR) of the International Monetary Fund. (The average value of the SDR in 2022 was US $1.337750.) In 2016 the Bank introduced the solar year, i.e. corresponding to 1 January–31 December, as the basis of its accounting series; prior to that its reports refer to the lunar year ('Hirja': H).

The Bank's authorized capital is ID 100,000m. In December 2020 the Board of Governors approved a 6th General Capital Increase, raising subscribed capital by ID 5,500m. to ID 55,500m. At 31 December 2022 total committed subscriptions amounted to ID 55,256.7m.

SUBSCRIPTIONS

(million Islamic Dinars, as at 31 December 2022)

Country	Amount	Country	Amount
Afghanistan	9.9	Malaysia	823.1
Albania	9.2	Maldives	25.8
Algeria	1,285.6	Mali	50.9
Azerbaijan	50.9	Mauritania	35.8
Bahrain	72.5	Morocco	256.7
Bangladesh	510.0	Mozambique	25.8
Benin	58.2	Niger	90.2
Brunei Darussalam	128.4	Nigeria	3,874.5
Burkina Faso	90.2	Oman	142.6
Cameroon	128.4	Pakistan	1,285.6
Chad	9.8	Palestine	19.6
Comoros	13.0	Qatar	3,632.4
Côte d'Ivoire	13.0	Saudi Arabia	11,896.8
Djibouti	5.0	Senegal	147.8
Egypt	3,579.7	Sierra Leone	18.2
Gabon	54.6	Somalia	5.0
The Gambia	25.8	Sudan	233.0
Guinea	45.9	Suriname	9.2
Guinea-Bissau	5.0	Syrian Arab Republic	18.5
Guyana	2.5	Tajikistan	18.2
Indonesia	1,138.0	Togo	18.2
Iran	4,174.6	Tunisia	71.6
Iraq	135.1	Türkiye (Turkey)	3,263.8
Jordan	219.8	Turkmenistan	5.0
Kazakhstan	54.0	Uganda	69.0
Kuwait	3,500.0	UAE	3,799.5
Kyrgyzstan	25.8	Uzbekistan	13.4
Lebanon	35.8	Yemen	258.6
Libya	4,771.7		

Activities

The Bank provides interest-free loans—adhering to the Islamic principle that forbids usury. It prioritizes support for infrastructural projects that are expected to have a marked impact on long-term socioeconomic development; provision of technical assistance (e.g. for feasibility studies); equity participation in industrial and agricultural projects; leasing operations, involving the leasing of equipment such as ships, and instalment sale financing; and profit-sharing operations. Funds not immediately needed for projects are used for foreign trade financing.

The IsDB's Member Country Partnership (MCP) Strategy, initiated in 2010, aims to strengthen dialogue with individual member countries and thus to contribute more effectively to their medium- and long-term development plans. In recent years Global Value Chain-driven MCP strategies (GVC-MCPs) have been introduced. Dimensions on women's and youth empowerment were mainstreamed into the MCP Strategy in 2022. A new IsDB business model was introduced in 2020 (with a focus on market efficiency, stimulating local supply chains and job creation). In September 2021 the Bank initiated a Resilience Index to assist economic policymakers. A (digital) e-Disbursement Platform was also initiated in that month to facilitate more efficient tracking of disbursements.

The IsDB participates—with the OPEC Fund, Arab Bank for Economic Development in Africa, Arab Monetary Fund and other partners—in the Arab Coordination Group, a strategic alliance that was established in 1975, and aims collectively to optimize resources to advance sustainable development.

In June 2023, during the Summit for a New Global Financing Pact, convened in Paris, France, the IsDB, African Development Bank, European Investment Bank and World Health Organization collectively launched a Health Impact Investment Platform, focused on strengthening essential, climate and crisis-resilient primary health care services in low- and low-and-middle income states.

COVID-19 Crisis: In April 2020 the IsDB Board of Executive Directors approved a Strategic Preparedness and Response Programme (SPRP) for the COVID-19 Pandemic, with three pillars—Response Track 1 (R1): focused on providing immediate emergency support; Restore Track 2 (R2): medium-term financing for trade and small and medium-sized businesses to promote activities in strategic supply chains; and Restart Track 3 (R3): long-term support to build resilient economies. An IsDB Vaccine Access (IVAC) Facility was established within the SPRP framework, covering vaccine deployment, procurement, and manufacturing support. A COVID-19 Global Coordination Platform was also launched to facilitate the efficiency of health item supply chains; from mid-2020 the UN Office for Project Services joined the Platform. In June 2020 the IsDB issued a $1,500m. International Islamic Sukuk bond (q.v.) to fund part of its COVID-19 response. In February 2021 the Bank and the ITFC signed an accord jointly to facilitate a recently introduced COVID-19 Restore Program (based on R2 of the SPRP). By the completion of the SPRP, in December 2022, the Bank had committed US $4,670m. in pandemic response funding, and had provided for the establishment of 1,522 COVID-19 vaccination centres.

Strategic Realignment: In early 2022, in response to significant rises in the prices of critical food items and fuel that were prompted by the Russian Federation's invasion of Ukraine, the IsDB initiated a new Food Security Response Program (FRSP), which aimed to provide some 700,000 tons of building and food storage capacity and to secure 780,000 metric tons of cereals; some US $10,540m. was approved under the FSRP in 2022. In June the Board of Governors endorsed a Strategic Realignment (2023–2025), to reposition the Bank's programming, taking into account the impacts of the COVID-19 pandemic crisis and conflict in Ukraine. Severe drought in East Africa had further aggravated food security. The Strategic Realignment had three main areas of focus: (i) Boosting recovery; (ii) Tackling poverty and building resilience; and (iii) Driving green economic growth; and two principal pillars. The first pillar, Supporting Green, Resilient and Sustainable Infrastructure, was focused on Clean and renewable energy; Sustainable multi-model transport; Agriculture and rural development; Information and communication technology and digitalization; Social infrastructure; and Urban development, water and sanitation. The second pillar, on Inclusive Human Capital Development, was focused on Universal healthcare/services; Resilient and quality education; Nutrition and food security; Social protection; and Micro, small and medium-sized enterprises and job creation. Islamic finance, climate change, capacity development, and women and youth were cross-cutting themes.

Financial Operations: During 1975–2022 the Bank Group approved a total of ID 119,875.8m. (equivalent to some US $170,492.1m.) for 11,378 operations. In 2022 the Bank approved a net total of ID 7,915.3m., of which ordinary capital resources (OCR) accounted for ID 2,303.2m. ($3,043.4m.). The four principal beneficiaries of Bank approvals in 2022 were Egypt (22.9%), Bangladesh (12.9%), Uzbekistan (8.3%), and Senegal (6.6%). The principal sectoral distribution of OCR approvals in 2022 was as follows: transport 39.4%, agriculture 26.5%, health 15.2%, and energy 12.2%.

Trade Financing: In June 2005 the Board of Governors approved the establishment of the ITFC as an autonomous trade promotion and financing institution within the Bank Group; its inaugural meeting was held in February 2007. Through direct or co-financing the ITFC supports the development of intra-OIC trade. The Bank also finances other trade financing operations, including the Islamic Corporation for the Development of the Private Sector (ICD) and the Awqaf Properties Investment Fund (APIF). In addition, a Trade Cooperation and Promotion Programme supports efforts to enhance trade among member countries of the Organization of Islamic Cooperation (OIC). In 2022 trade financing approved through the ITFC amounted to ID 5,118.9m., and operations approved by the ICD totalled ID 425.2m.

Islamic Financial Markets: The Bank mobilizes resources from the international financial markets through the issuance of the *Shari'a*-compliant International Islamic Sukuk bond (launched in 2003). In November 2019 the Bank introduced a new Sustainable Finance Framework, under which funding raised through the Sukuk bond method was to be directed to green initiatives. The Bank's Kuala Lumpur, Malaysia-based Islamic Financial Services Board (IFSB)—which commenced operations in March 2003—acts as an international standard-setting body for 81 regulatory and supervisory agencies connected to the Islamic financial services industry. The IFSB maintains a database of Prudential and Structural Islamic Financial Indicators, and the IsDB has worked to improve the dissemination of relevant information.

The 16th IsDB Global Forum on Islamic Finance was convened in June 2022, on the theme 'Achieving Shared Prosperity through Social Innovation'.

Technical Assistance: During 1976–2022 the Bank approved 2,361 technical assistance operations, with a cumulative value of ID 1,515.8m. (equivalent to US $2,180.1m.). In 2022 20 new operations were approved through the Bank's Technical Cooperation Programme, amounting to $648,700, and a total of $2m. was approved for 'Reverse Linkage' initiatives, which facilitate the transfer of expertise, knowledge and technology between member states. In March 2018 the Board of Executive Directors approved the establishment of a Public-Private Partnerships (PPP) Advisory Facility, to promote PPP-based infrastructure development in member states.

In February 2021 the IsDB and ICD agreed to enhance the efforts of the IsDB Group Business Forum (known as THIQAH) to attract private sector and market resources.

Seven projects were approved in 2022—in Chad, Djibouti, Jordan, Palestine, Uganda, and Uzbekistan—under the Bank's Strengthening of the Economic Resilience of Vulnerable Enterprises (SERVE) programme. Some US $566m. was mobilized from public and private partners through a Market Access Readiness in Key Economic and Trade Sectors (MARKETS) initiative.

Climate Action: The IsDB's Climate Action Plan (2020–25) aimed to increase the climate action-related proportion of Bank Group investment to 35% by 2025; in 2022 it accounted for 33% of approvals. In November 2022 the ACG committed to issuing US $24,000m. during 2023–30 in investment to combat the climate crisis; this was to include at least $13,000m. in IsDB climate adaptation and mitigation finance.

Food Security: In January 2020 the IsDB and the World Food Programme signed a Memorandum of Understanding (MOU) on co-operation in identifying alternative financing mechanisms and opportunities for collaboration on humanitarian and development projects, with a particular focus on nutrition, food security, agriculture, rural development, and human capital and institutional development. In July the Bank and the Food and Agriculture Organization of the United Nations concluded an MOU on strengthening co-operation.

Human Development: The Bank's Fragility and Resilience Policy focuses on four pillars: investing in crisis prevention; transitioning from relief to development; supporting recovery and resilience; and mobilizing resources for resilience.

An Islamic Solidarity Fund for Development (ISFD), initiated in 2007, promotes human development and pro-poor economic growth; by the end of 2022 the Fund had approved ID 838.2m. (including ID 36.2m. during that year) in concessionary loans and grants for poverty alleviation initiatives.

The IsDB implements scholarship programmes, technical co-operation projects, and a sacrificial meat utilization project (distributing meat sacrificed by pilgrims to needy beneficiaries).

By the end of December 2022 the Bank had, since its inception, offered scholarships to 18,493 students from 122 countries. In 2019 the ISFD initiated a new scholarship programme to advance the educational opportunities of eligible students from least developed countries. An IsDB-International Labour Organization Youth Green Skills Accelerator Challenge was initiated in 2022. The IsDB awards an annual prize for women and girls empowerment in education (previously it had rewarded women's contribution to development).

The Bank supports the implementation of BRAVE Women 2.0, an initiative focused on improving the incomes of women-owned small and medium-sized enterprises (SMEs) in Yemen.

In 2019 the Bank launched, jointly with the International Atomic Energy Agency, a Partnership Initiative for Breast and Cervical Cancer Control in Low-and Middle-Income Countries to improve diagnosis and treatment service in 17 member states.

Science, Technology and Innovation: In September 2017 the IsDB established a US $500m. Transform Fund, which was to provide seed capital to start-up businesses and SMEs for initiatives with a focus on innovation, science and technology, with the wider aim of accelerating progress towards the attainment of the UN Sustainable Development Goals (SDGs, being implemented globally during 2015–30). In April 2020 the Bank announced that, through the Transform Fund, it would provide financial support to innovations with a focus on, *inter alia*, health supply chain management and low cost rapid testing, that would help to control the spread of and reduce the negative socioeconomic impacts of COVID-19. A new digital hub that aimed to link innovators in developing countries with funding and with market opportunities, Engage, was launched by the Bank in February 2018. It was intended also to be a means of promoting the SDGs through science, technology and innovation. The IsDB gives prizes for science and technology to promote excellence in education, research and development.

Other Assistance Activities: The Bank's Communities Outreach Programme (initiated in 1400H as the Special Assistance Programme) supports the economic and social development of minority Muslim communities in non-member countries, in particular in the education and health sectors. It also aims to provide emergency aid in times of natural disasters, and to assist Muslim refugees throughout the world. In 2022 under the programme six projects were approved to support the education sectors in five countries, at a total cost of US $1,255m. A Special Account Resources Waqf Fund finances such operations. By 31 December 2022 the Waqf Fund had resources of some ID 765.6m.

In October 2015 the Bank and the WBG jointly launched a Concessional Financing Facility to support refugees, internally displaced persons and host communities in the Middle East and North Africa region.

A Skills, Training and Education Program (STEP), introduced in 2022, aims to expand access for 600,000 young refugees in 15 member states to in-person and virtual education and entrepreneurship development support. In September 2022 the Bank and the UN High Commissioner for Refugees (UNHCR) agreed to establish a new Global Islamic Fund for Refugees.

The Bank, in co-operation with the UN, established a MENA Concessional Financing Facility in April 2016.

The Bank supports recovery, rehabilitation and reconstruction efforts in member countries affected by natural disasters or conflict. In February 2023 the Bank stated solidarity with the Government of Türkiye and the people of that country and of the Syrian Arab Republic, following devastating earthquakes that had struck southern Türkiye and northern Syria. With a focus on assisting the Turkish authorities and helping Syrian refugees and IDPs, the Bank committed US $3m. to fund immediate humanitarian support, and also determined to pursue a medium- to long-term resilience building approach.

Publications

Annual Report.
IsDB Group Integration Report.
SDG Digest (3–4 a year).
Technical and industry sector reports, investor presentations, guidance notes.

Statistics

CUMULATIVE OPERATIONS APPROVED
(1 January 1976–31 December 2022)

Type of operation	Number of operations	Amount (million Islamic Dinars)
Project financing	3,000	43,961.9
Technical assistance	2,361	1,515.8
Trade financing*	4,156	73,228.9
Special assistance	1,861	1,169.1
Total†	**11,378**	**119,875.8**

* Including operations by the ITFC, the ICD, Treasury operations, and the APIF.
† Excluding cancelled operations.
Source: Islamic Development Bank, *Annual Report 2022*.

Bank Group Entities

International Islamic Trade Finance Corporation (ITFC): POB 55335, Jeddah 21534, Saudi Arabia; tel. (12) 646-8337; fax (12) 637-1064; e-mail itfc@itfc-idb.org; internet www.itfc-idb.org; f. 2007; commenced operations Jan. 2008; aims to promote trade and trade financing in Bank mem. countries, to facilitate access to public and private capital, and to promote investment opportunities; the ITFC's Cooperation and Promotion Program (TCPP) supports the design and implementation of trade-related technical assistance progs; during 2022 the ITFC approved ID 5,118.9m. for trade financing operations; auth. cap. US $3,000m.; CEO HANI SALEM SONBOL.

Islamic Corporation for the Development of the Private Sector (ICD): POB 54069, Jeddah 21514, Saudi Arabia; tel. (12) 644-1644; fax (12) 644-4427; e-mail icd@isdb.org; internet www.icd-ps.org; f. 1999; aims to identify opportunities in the private sector, provide financial products and services compatible with Islamic law, to mobilize additional resources for the private sector in mem. countries, and to encourage the devt of Islamic financing and capital markets; approved projects and capital increases amounting to ID 425.2m. in 2022; the Bank's share of the ICD's capital is 50%, mem. countries' share 30%, and that of public financial institutions of mem. countries 20%; auth. cap. US $4,000m.; mems: 54 countries, the Bank and 5 public financial institutions; CEO and Gen. Man. AYMAN SEJINY.

Islamic Corporation for the Insurance of Investment and Export Credit (ICIEC): POB 15722, Jeddah 21454, Saudi Arabia; tel. (12) 644-5666; fax (12) 637-9755; e-mail ICIEC-Communication@isdb.org; internet iciec.isdb.org; f. 1994; aims to promote trade and promote foreign investment in mem. countries, through the provision of export credit and investment insurance services; has a representative office in Dubai, UAE; new insurance commitments amounted to ID 3,009.5m. in 2022; auth. cap. ID 400m.; mems: 47 countries; CEO OUSSAMA ABDEL RAHMAN KAISSI.

Islamic Development Bank Institute (IsDBI): 8111 King Khalid St, Jeddah 22332–2444, Saudi Arabia; tel. (12) 636-1400; fax (12) 637-8927; e-mail isdbi-info@isdb.org; internet www.isdbinstitute.org; f. 1981 as the Islamic Research and Training Institute, present name adopted in 2021; aims to undertake research enabling economic, financial and banking activities to conform to Islamic law, and to provide training for staff involved in devt activities in the Bank's mem. countries; also organizes seminars and workshops, and holds training courses aimed at furthering the expertise of govt and financial officials in Islamic developing countries; Dir-Gen. Dr SAMI AL-SUWAILEM (acting); publs *Annual Report*, *Islamic Economic Studies Journal* (2 a year), various research studies, monographs, reports.

Islamic Solidarity Fund for Development: 8111 King Khalid St, Jeddah 22332–2444, Saudi Arabia; tel. (12) 636-1400; e-mail isfd@isdb.org; internet isfd.isdb.org; f. 2007; established as a Waqf (trust fund) to reduce poverty in mem. states, meet the basic needs of the poor, improve income generation, and promote human devt, e.g. through education and health care initiatives; approved cap. US $10,000m.; Dir-Gen. Dr HIBA AHMED (Sudan); publ. *Annual Report*.

LEAGUE OF ARAB STATES

Address: POB 11642, Arab League Bldg, Tahrir Sq., Cairo, Egypt.
Telephone: (2) 575-0511; **fax:** (2) 574-0331; **e-mail:** communication.dept@las.int; **internet:** www.lasportal.org.

The League of Arab States (more generally known as the Arab League) was founded in March 1945 with the adoption of the Pact of the League of Arab States, and aims to strengthen mutual ties and to co-ordinate policies and activities to support the common good of all the Arab countries.

MEMBERS

Algeria	Lebanon	Somalia
Bahrain	Libya*	Sudan
Comoros	Mauritania	Syrian Arab
Djibouti	Morocco	Republic*
Egypt	Oman	Tunisia
Iraq	Palestine†	United Arab
Jordan	Qatar	Emirates
Kuwait	Saudi Arabia	Yemen

* Palestine is considered to be an independent state, and therefore a full member of the League.
† Syria was suspended from meetings of the League during November 2011–early May 2023.
Note: Brazil, Eritrea, India and Venezuela have observer status. In March 2018 it was reported that South Sudan had applied for observer status.

Organization
(September 2023)

COUNCIL

The supreme organ of the League of Arab States, the Council consists of representatives of the member states, each of which has one vote, and a representative for Palestine. The Council meets ordinarily every March, normally at the Arab League headquarters, at the level of heads of state ('kings, heads of state and emirs'), and in March and September at the level of ministers responsible for foreign affairs. Meetings of the Council are also convened at the level of delegates. Arab consultative summits may be convoked when deemed necessary to address specific issues. The summit level meeting reviews all issues related to Arab national security strategies, co-ordinates supreme policies of the Arab states towards regional and international issues, reviews recommendations and reports submitted to it by the ministerial meetings, appoints the Secretary-General, and is mandated to amend the League's Pact. Decisions of the Council at the level of heads of state are passed on a consensus basis. Meetings of ministers responsible for foreign affairs assess the implementation of summit resolutions, prepare relevant reports, and make arrangements for subsequent summits. Committees comprising a smaller group of foreign ministers may be appointed to follow up closely summit resolutions. Extraordinary summit meetings may be held at the request of one member state or the Secretary-General, if approved by a two-thirds' majority of member states. Extraordinary sessions of ministers responsible for foreign affairs may be held at the request of two member states or of the Secretary-General. The presidency of ordinary meetings is rotated in accordance with the alphabetical order of the League's member states. Unanimous decisions of the Council are binding upon all member states of the League; majority decisions are binding only on those states that have accepted them.

Specialized ministerial councils are convened to formulate common policies for the regulation and the advancement of co-operation in the following sectors: electricity; environment; health; housing and construction; interior; justice; media; social affairs; telecommunications and information; tourism; transport; water; and youth and sports.

GENERAL SECRETARIAT

The General Secretariat implements the decisions of the Council, and provides financial and administrative services for the personnel of the League. Eight administrative Sectors cover Administrative and financial affairs; Arab national security; Economic affairs; Information and communication; Legal affairs; Palestine and the Occupied Arab Territories; International political affairs; and Social affairs.

The Secretary-General is appointed at summit meetings of the Council by a two-thirds' majority of the member states, for a five-year, renewable term. He appoints the Assistant Secretaries-General and principal officials, with the approval of the Council.

Secretary-General: AHMED ABOUL GHEIT (Egypt).
Deputy Secretary-General: HOSSAM ZAKI (Egypt).

DEFENCE AND ECONOMIC CO-OPERATION

Established under the Treaty of Joint Defence and Economic Co-operation, concluded in 1950 to complement the Pact of the League:

Economic and Social Council: compares and co-ordinates the economic policies of the member states; supervises the activities of the Arab League's specialized agencies. The Council is composed of ministers responsible for economic affairs or their deputies; decisions are taken by majority vote. The first meeting was held in 1953. In February 1997 the Economic and Social Council adopted the Executive Programme of the League's (1981) Agreement to Facilitate and Develop Trade Among Arab Countries, with a view to establishing a Greater Arab Free Trade Area. The Council's 112th session was convened at the League's headquarters in Aug. 2023.

Joint Defence Council: supervises implementation of those aspects of the treaty concerned with common defence. Composed of ministers responsible for foreign affairs and for defence; decisions by a two-thirds' majority vote of members are binding on all.

Permanent Military Commission: composed of representatives of army general staffs; main purpose: to draw up plans of joint defence for submission to the Joint Defence Council.

An Arab Unified Military Command, established in 1964 to co-ordinate military policies for the liberation of Palestine, is inactive.

ARAB PARLIAMENT

Inaugurated in December 2005 (as a transitional institution, with permanent status granted in March 2012), the Arab Parliament is based in Damascus, and comprises 88 members (four delegates from each Arab state, including some representing non-elected bodies).

In June 2022 the Arab Parliament strongly condemned remarks made by senior officials of India's ruling political party that were deemed to be offensive to the Muslim religion.

OTHER INSTITUTIONS OF THE LEAGUE

Other bodies established by resolutions adopted by the Council of the League:

Administrative Tribunal of the Arab League: f. 1964; commenced operations in 1966.

Anti-Human Trafficking Co-ordination Unit: f. 2009.

Arab Fund for Technical Assistance to African Countries: f. 1975 to provide technical assistance for development projects by providing African and Arab experts, grants for scholarships and training, and finance for technical studies.

Central Boycott Office: f. 1951 to prevent trade between Arab countries and Israel, and to enforce a boycott by Arab countries of companies outside the region that conduct trade with Israel.

Higher Auditing Board: comprises representatives of seven member states, elected every three years; undertakes financial and administrative auditing duties.

Activities

The 32nd regular summit of heads of state was hosted by Saudi Arabia, in Jeddah, in mid-May 2023, and included participation by President Bashar al-Assad of Syria (Syria having resumed participation in the League, after a 12-year suspension, earlier in that month). The leaders adopted the Jeddah Declaration, which urged collective Arab action to resolve ongoing regional challenges, including the protracted security crises in Syria, Palestine and Yemen, the recent eruption of civil conflict in Sudan, and the political and economic crisis in Lebanon. The leaders rejected foreign interference in the domestic affairs of Arab countries and all support for non-state militias.

TRADE AND ECONOMIC CO-OPERATION

The first meeting of the Council of Arab Economic Unity, mandated to administer a 1962 Arab Economic Unity Agreement, took place in June 1964. An Arab Common Market Agreement was endorsed by the Council in August. Customs duties and other taxes on trade between the member countries were to be eliminated in stages prior to the adoption of a full customs union, and ultimately all restrictions on trade between the member countries, including quotas, and restrictions on residence, employment and transport, were to be abolished. In practice, however, little progress was achieved in the development of an Arab common market during 1964–2000. In 2001 the Council of Arab Economic Unity's efforts towards liberalizing intra-Arab trade were intensified. A meeting of Council ministers responsible for the economy and trade convened in Baghdad in June, approved an executive programme for developing the proposed common market, determined to establish a compensation fund to support the integration of the least developed Arab states into the regional economy, and agreed to provide technical assistance for Arab states aiming to join the World Trade Organization.

A number of multilateral organizations in industry and agriculture have been formed. Arab Joint Companies have been established for some industries, while others are co-ordinated through Arab Specialized Unions. A Unified Agreement for the Investment of Arab Capital in the Arab States entered into force in September 1981, and the statutes of an Arab Investment Court came into effect in February 1988 (the Court became operational in 2003). Council of Arab Economic Unity agreements aimed at encouraging Arab investment include an accord on Non-Double Taxation and Income Tax Evasion (adopted in December 1998); an accord on Investment Promotion and Protection (June 2000); and an accord on Investment Dispute Settlement in Arab Countries (December 2000).

In February 1997 the Economic and Social Council adopted the Executive Programme of the (1981) Agreement to Facilitate and Develop Trade Among Arab Countries, with a view to creating a Greater Arab Free Trade Area (GAFTA). This aimed to facilitate and develop trade among participating countries through the reduction and eventual elimination of customs duties over a 10-year period, alongside a parallel elimination of trade barriers. In February 2002 the Economic and Social Council agreed to bring forward the inauguration of GAFTA to 1 January 2005. Consequently, customs duties between most member states, which, according to schedule, had been reduced by 50% from January 1998–January 2002, were reduced further by 10% by January 2003, 20% by January 2004, and a final 20% by January 2005; Sudan and Yemen, as less developed economies, were to be subject to a parallel longer schedule of customs reductions. GAFTA (also known as the Pan-Arab Free Trade Area) entered into force, as planned, then with 17 participating countries. In 2009 Algeria became the 18th member of GAFTA, its membership by then accounting for about 96% of the total volume of intra-Arab trade. The Council agreed to supervise the implementation of the free trade agenda and formally to review its progress twice a year. The level of inter-Arab investments subsequently remained lower than anticipated, reportedly owing to restrictive degrees of bureaucracy and regulation.

In September 2018 the Arab League and the International Islamic Trade Finance Corporation (ITFC) signed a formal MOU on co-operation in jointly co-ordinating the 'design, financing and implementation' of technical assistance and capacity building programmes. The MOU designated two ITFC programmes, Arab Africa Trade Bridges and Aid for Trade Initiative for Arab States (Phase 2), as specific formats for collaboration. The two organizations were also jointly to host regional conferences, training courses and workshops in support of trade development and the implementation of GAFTA.

In May 2001 Egypt, Jordan, Morocco and Tunisia issued the Agadir Declaration in which they determined to establish an Arab Mediterranean Free Trade Zone. The so-called Agadir Agreement on the establishment of a Free Trade Zone between the Arabic Mediterranean Nations was signed in February 2004, came into force in July 2006, and entered its implementation phase in March 2007. The signatories to the Agadir Agreement are also members of GAFTA.

The inaugural Arab Economic, Development and Social Summit meeting of Arab leaders, held in January 2009, in Kuwait, under the auspices of the Arab League, considered means of accelerating progress towards the achievement of Arab economic integration; agreed to create a fully functioning Arab Customs Union and Arab Common Market; decided to launch a regional power grid and rail network; and agreed to launch a fund to finance Arab small and medium-sized enterprises (SMEs). Under the Arab Customs Union goods exempt from taxes were to comprise at least 40% of components originating in GAFTA member states. Participants at the third Summit, held in Riyadh, Saudi Arabia, in January 2013, adopted the Riyadh Declaration, in which they determined, inter alia, to strengthen the capacity of joint Arab institutions, including increasing by at least one-half the capital of joint financial institutions; and to implement the ongoing Pan-Arab Strategy for Promoting Renewable Energy. An Arab Customs Cooperation Agreement was approved in September 2015 by the League's Economic and Social Council. In January 2019 the Fourth Arab Economic and Social Development Summit, held in Beirut, Lebanon, agreed a 29-point economic agenda, which included efforts to promote the full implementation of GAFTA and to support countries hosting large numbers of refugees. The Fifth Arab Development Summit was to be hosted by Mauritania, in Nouakchott, in November 2023.

Since 2016 the Arab League and the UN Economic and Social Commission for West Asia (ESCWA) have jointly organized an annual Arab Forum on Sustainable Development, with participation by government officials, regional organizations, and representatives of civil society and of the private sector. The Forum focuses on the co-ordinated implementation and follow-up in the Arab region of the UN's 2030 Agenda for Sustainable Development and Sustainable Development Goals. The sixth session of the Forum, held in mid-March 2023 in Beirut, included sessions that addressed food systems transformation for food security; the inter-generational effects of violence; the role of renewable energy in accelerating recovery in fragile and crisis-affected countries; sustainable reconstruction; and enabling the circular carbon economy.

In December 2019 the 23rd session of the Council of Arab Ministers of Communications and Information Technology initiated an Arab Digital Capital initiative, which aimed to advance digital knowledge in member states. In September 2021 the Arab Federation for Digital Economy (established in April 2018 by the Council of Arab Economic Unity) signed an agreement with a UAE-based company on the establishment of a new Arab digital data hub in Bahrain, to serve the League's member states—with a focus on digital transformation, security, and data protection. The 26th session of the Council of Arab Ministers of Communications and Information Technology, convened in January 2023, adopted an Arab Digital Agenda to cover the period 2023–33, which had been jointly prepared by the Arab League and ESCWA. This was focused on five pillars: digital infrastructure, governance, economy, society, and culture, and aimed to mobilize related investment and partnerships. Al-Quds (Jerusalem) was designated as the Arab Digital Capital lead city for 2023.

In May 2020 the Arab League's Economic Affairs Department issued a report addressing the initial impacts of the COVID-19 crisis on the overall Arab economy, as well as consequences for the health, agriculture, petroleum, aviation and tourism sectors, and for food security and development. The report urged the establishment of a dedicated crisis fund. In March 2021 the 45th meeting of Arab health ministers (held in a virtual format) agreed that an Arab Drug Authority should be established, and launched an Arab platform for the exchange of experiences and expertise in combating the COVID-19 emergency. The platform was to collate the results of national strategies and of clinical trials for COVID vaccines, and was also to be a focus for the channelling of resources to provide health services to refugees in Arab states.

ENVIRONMENT AND WATER RESOURCES

In 2011 the Arab League and ESCWA initiated the Regional Initiative for the Assessment of Climate Change Impacts on Water Resources and Socio-Economic Vulnerability in the Arab Region (RICCAR), a consultative evaluative process. In September 2017 RICCAR issued its first *Arab Climate Change Assessment Report*. In March 2022 the Arab League, ESCWA and partners organized a workshop aimed at developing Arab nations' capacity to participate in climate change negotiations, with a focus on climate adaptation (including smart agriculture), mitigation, technology and finance. The Arabic edition of the UN's 6th *Global Environment Outlook* was launched at a meeting of the Arab League in July.

In June 2022 the international environmental organization Greenpeace urged the Arab League to convene an urgent meeting to address the environmental and humanitarian risks posed by a derelict oil tanker, the Safer, which was situated off the coast of Hodeidah (Yemen).

The inaugural Arab Environmental Forum, convened in October 2022, in Cairo, by the Arab League, ESCWA and the UN Environment Programme, discussed a common Arab vision on environmental issues to inform forthcoming global policy meetings. The second Arab Environmental Forum was to be convened in October 2023, in Muscat (Oman).

The first session of an Arab Ministerial Water Council was convened in June 2009. The Council gave consideration to the development of an Arab Water Strategy; this was launched in March 2011. With support from the Arab League, the Council organized the fifth Arab Water Forum, which took place in September 2021, in Abu Dhabi, UAE, on the theme 'Arab water security for peace and development'. In March–April 2019 the Arab League, ESCWA and other partners organized a Land and Water Days event, at the League's Cairo headquarters, to address the integrated regional management of natural resources as a means of building resilience to the impacts of climate change and land degradation and of ensuring access to water, energy and food. The event culminated in early April in the inaugural joint meeting of Arab ministers responsible for water and for agriculture. The meeting adopted the Cairo Declaration, which urged Arab states and partners to harmonize policies across the water and agriculture sectors and to institutionalize related regional co-ordination mechanisms. In June 2021 the League's foreign ministers issued a resolution that urged the UN Security Council to intervene to help resolve a protracted dispute between Egypt, Sudan and Ethiopia concerning Ethiopia's construction on the Blue Nile (the principal tributary of the River Nile) of the controversial Grand Ethiopian Renaissance Dam, which was deemed by Egypt and Sudan to be a threat to their water security.

The Arab League, the Islamic Development Bank and ESCWA collectively organized an event on the sidelines of the March 2023 World Water Conference that addressed regional efforts to transform the water sector and to develop cross-sectoral partnerships.

In December 2022 the Arab League, ESCWA and partners organized an Arab Forum for Agriculture, in Amman, which addressed, *inter alia,* the role of the private sector in sustainable agriculture development. A Strategy for Sustainable Arab Agricultural Development was being implemented during 2020–30, alongside an Arab Program for Sustaining Food Security that aimed to expand output of basic food commodities by a minimum of 30% by 2030. In March 2023 the League participated in an Arab regional preparatory meeting in advance of the inaugural global Food Systems Stocktaking Moment (the first follow-up conference of the September 2021 Food Systems Summit), which took place in Rome, Italy, in July.

In October 2010 Arab League ministers responsible for electricity adopted a Pan-Arab Strategy for Promoting Renewable Energy, covering the period 2010–30. In September 2016 ministers responsible for foreign affairs approved a Memorandum of Understanding (MOU) on the creation of an Arab Common Market for Electricity; the preparation process was to be supported by the Arab Fund for Economic and Social Development and the World Bank. In April 2017 the ministers responsible for energy of 14 Arab countries concluded an MOU that represented a commitment to the establishment of the proposed Arab Common Market for Electricity (two further Arab countries subsequently signed the MOU). In July 2020 an extraordinary meeting of Arab ministers responsible for energy, held in a virtual format, approved a General Agreement, outlining the planned Market's objectives, and technical guidelines on its development and on the formation of its institutions. The meeting also endorsed an Arab Common Market for Electricity Agreement, defining the legal status of the Market's institutions, and addressing its commercial dimension. A further accord covered operational rules for the Arab electricity networks. The fourth Arab Forum for Renewable Energy and Energy Efficiency was held in Kuwait in May 2018.

HUMAN RIGHTS

A Permanent Arab Commission on Human Rights was established in September 1968, with a primary focus on pursuing a settlement to the Arab-Israeli conflict. The Commission drafted an Arab Charter on Human Rights, which entered into force in January 2008, and provided for the election of a seven-member Arab Human Rights Committee that was inaugurated in March 2009. In February 2013 representatives of the League, jointly with human rights experts from other organizations, convened a conference which approved a set of recommendations aimed at strengthening the regional human rights protection legislative framework. These included amending the Arab Charter on Human Rights to clarify the League's protection mandate and to ensure engagement with NGOs; strengthening the Arab Human Rights Committee; and amending the League's Pact explicitly to mention respect for universal human rights standards. The establishment of an Arab Court on Human Rights was approved in principle by the March 2013 League summit. The Arab Interior Ministers Council (AIMC), initiated in 1982, aims to enhance security co-operation between member states, including by circulating arrest warrants. In June 2023 UN experts warned the Arab League that the AIMC's policy on extradition was failing to assess potential risks of torture or ill-treatment.

In September 2017 the Arab League and the UN High Commissioner for Refugees concluded an MOU on the development of a co-operation framework for providing an effective response to the high number of refugees being hosted in the Arab region.

REGIONAL SECURITY

In 1950 Arab League member states concluded a Joint Defence and Economic Cooperation Treaty. An Arab Deterrent Force was established by the Arab League Council in June 1976 to supervise attempts at that time to cease hostilities in Lebanon; the Force's mandate was terminated in 1983.

The Arab Convention for the Suppression of Terrorism, incorporating security and judicial measures, such as extradition arrangements and the exchange of evidence, entered into effect in May 2000. An Arab Counter-Terrorism Experts Group meets regularly.

The creation of a joint Arab force was agreed upon by the Council in principle, in 2015. The 26th symposium for the heads of Arab armed forces' training bodies was hosted in late November 2022–early December by the League's General Secretariat—with a focus on developing a unified training doctrine for the Arab armed forces. In September of that year the League convened a Youth Online Dialogue on Peace and Security. A first Arab Regional Strategy on Youth, Peace and Security is under development. The third meeting of an Arab Network of Women Peace Mediators was convened in July 2023.

In March 2013 the Arab League, the UN Office for Disaster Risk Reduction (UNDRR), the UN Development Programme and other partners organized the First Arab Conference on Disaster Risk Reduction; the Conference launched an Arab Regional Platform on Disaster Risk Reduction. The Third Arab Preparatory Conference on Disaster Risk Reduction, held in Doha, Qatar, in April–May 2017, addressed regional progress on the implementation of the global Sendai Framework for Disaster Risk Reduction (covering 2015–30). An Arab Strategy for Disaster Risk Reduction up to 2030 was adopted by Arab League heads meeting in April 2018.

In February 2016 the inaugural meeting of an Arab League Committee on Weather, Climate, and Hazards Information Management was organized, in Amman, to address means of combating disaster risks. In April 2018 the second biennial meeting of the Council of Arab Ministers for Meteorology and Climate Affairs addressed, *inter alia,* weather and climate risk management, sand and dust warning systems, aeronautical meteorological services, and the development of a new Arab Climate Outlook Forum (ArabCOF). The 10th session of ArabCOF took place online in December 2022.

Arab–Israeli Affairs: The League regards Palestine as an independent state and therefore as a full League member. In 1951 a Central Boycott Office was established, in Damascus, Syria, to oversee the prevention of trade between Arab countries and Israel, and to enforce a boycott by Arab countries of companies outside the region that conduct trade with Israel.

In 1979 a meeting of the League's Council resolved to suspend Egypt's membership of the League on the date of the signing of its formal peace treaty with Israel (26 March) and to transfer the headquarters of the League to Tunis. In September 1982 the Council adopted a peace plan, which, *inter alia,* demanded Israel's withdrawal from territories occupied in 1967, the right of the Palestinian people to self-determination, under the leadership of the PLO, the creation of an independent Palestinian state, with Jerusalem as its capital, and a guarantee of peace for the states of the region by the UN Security Council. In June 1988 a summit conference agreed to provide finance for the PLO to continue the Palestinian uprising in Israeli-occupied territories. At a summit conference held in May 1989 Egypt was readmitted to the League, and support was expressed for proposals to convene an international conference to discuss the rights of Palestinians: in so doing, the League's Council accepted UN Security Council Resolutions 242 and 338 on a peaceful settlement in the Middle East and thus gave tacit recognition to the State of Israel. In September 1993 the Council, convened in emergency session, approved the recently signed Israeli-PLO Oslo peace accords.

In March 1997 the Council met in emergency session in response to the Israeli Government's decision to proceed with construction of a new settlement at Har Homa (Jabal Abu-Ghunaim) in East Jerusalem. At the end of March ministers responsible for foreign affairs of Arab League states agreed to cease all efforts to secure normal diplomatic relations with Israel and to close diplomatic offices and missions while construction work continued in East Jerusalem. In October 2000 at an emergency summit meeting, convened in response to mounting insecurity in Jerusalem and the Occupied Territories, Israel was accused of inciting the ongoing violent disturbances by stalling the progress of the peace process, and determined to 'freeze' co-operation with Israel. The summit also endorsed the establishment of an 'al-Aqsa Fund', with a value of US $800m., to finance initiatives aimed at promoting the Arab and Islamic identity of Jerusalem, and a smaller 'Jerusalem Intifada Fund' to support the families of Palestinians killed in the unrest. In May 2001 ministers responsible for foreign affairs determined that all political contact with Israel should be suspended in protest against aerial attacks by Israel on Palestinian targets in the West Bank.

In March 2002 a summit-level meeting of the Council of the Arab League unanimously endorsed, as the first (and thereafter enduring) pan-Arab peace initiative, a plan proposed by Crown Prince Abdullah of Saudi Arabia aimed at brokering a peaceful settlement to the Palestinian–Israeli crisis. This entailed the restoration of 'normal' Arab relations with Israel and acceptance of its right to exist in peace and security, in exchange for a full Israeli withdrawal from the Occupied Territories, the establishment of an independent Palestinian state with East Jerusalem as its capital, and the return of refugees. The plan urged compliance with UN Security Council Resolution 194 concerning the return of Palestinian refugees to Israel, or appropriate compensation for their property; however, precise details of eligibility criteria for the proposed return, a contentious issue owing to the potentially huge numbers of refugees and descendants of refugees involved, were not elaborated. In November 2003 the Arab League welcomed a UN Security Council resolution endorsing the adoption in April by the so-called Quartet, comprising envoys from the UN, the European Union, the Russian Federation and the USA, of a 'performance-based roadmap to a permanent two-state solution to the Israeli–Palestinian conflict'.

The March 2009 Arab League summit meeting condemned the intensive military assault on Gaza perpetrated by Israeli forces (with the stated aim of ending rocket attacks launched by Hamas and other militant groups on Israeli targets) during late December 2008–mid-January 2009. In June 2010, in response to an Israeli raid at the end of May on a flotilla of vessels carrying humanitarian aid through international waters towards the Gaza Strip, resulting in nine civilian fatalities, the Arab League Secretary-General demanded the termination of the blockade imposed since 2006 by Israel against Gaza.

The final declaration of the March 2010 summit meeting, held in Sirte, Libya, mandated the formation of an Arab League legal committee to follow up the issue of the 'judaization' of East Jerusalem and the confiscation of Arab property, and to take these issues before national and international courts with appropriate jurisdiction. In March 2013 the meeting of League heads of state, convened in Doha, approved the establishment of an Arab East Jerusalem Fund, to finance projects and programmes that would maintain the Arab and Islamic character of the city.

The Arab League has supported Palestine in its formal application for admission to the UN. The UN General Assembly granted observer status (and consequently recognition of de facto statehood) to Palestine in November 2012. Later in that month, having met with the Palestinian leadership, the League's Secretary-General announced that the Arab League would continue to pursue the objective of full accession by Palestine to the UN.

In July 2013 delegates of the Arab League met with the US Secretary of State to consider a US initiative to restart the Palestinian-Israeli peace talks; subsequently, the Arab League delegation issued a statement endorsing the initiative, and asserting that any future agreement must be based on a two-state solution, through the establishment of an independent Palestinian state in accordance with boundaries as at 4 June 1967, but reiterating the possibility of limited exchanges of territory of equal value and size. In March 2014 Arab League heads of state reiterated that resolving the Palestinian situation remained the core regional challenge for member states, and announced their 'total rejection' of the expectation of the hardline Israeli Prime Minister, Benjamin Netanyahu, that Israel should be considered as a 'Jewish state' and 'Jewish homeland', deeming this potentially to undermine the perceived right of return of Palestinian refugees.

In mid-July 2014 an emergency meeting of Arab League ministers responsible for foreign affairs gathered to address an eruption of intense conflict between the Israeli security forces (which had launched an air, sea and land military bombardment known as Protective Edge) and Hamas militants in Gaza. On 26 August, as a result of Arab League-backed talks, Israel and Hamas concluded an agreement on a truce; the Israeli authorities agreed to ease the Israeli blockade of the territory to permit access for humanitarian assistance and building materials.

In December 2014 the League agreed to provide emergency funds to the Palestinian leadership, following Israel's suspension of customs revenue transfers to the PA. In September 2015 the League's Secretary-General expressed condemnation of a renewed storming by Israeli security forces of the al-Aqsa Mosque compound in Jerusalem. (The al-Aqsa Mosque is known in Judaism as Temple Mount.)

An emergency meeting of Arab League officials was convened in late April 2016 to address a recent declaration by Israel's Prime Minister that Israel would never return annexed Golan to Syria. The Arab League Secretary-General proposed at that time that a special criminal court should be established to charge the Israeli regime with violations of the rights of Palestinians. In September the Arab League condemned a blockade imposed by Israel on 10 villages in the West Bank noting that this was being perpetrated in the context of the Israeli policy of collective punishment. In March 2017 the 28th Arab League summit urged the adoption of a UN resolution drawing attention to illegal Israeli settlements, and stated support for ongoing efforts to relaunch effective Palestinian-Israeli peace negotiations, based on the 2002 Arab peace initiative.

In late July 2017 an extraordinary session of Arab League ministers responsible for foreign affairs addressed a wave of violent unrest that had followed the murder earlier in that month, by armed Palestinians, of two Israeli police officers at the entrance to Jerusalem's al-Aqsa Mosque compound, and a subsequent controversial attempt by the Israeli authorities to install metal detectors there. In December, in a further extraordinary session, Arab League foreign ministers denounced as contrary to international law and potentially inflammatory a recent decision of US President Donald Trump to recognize Jerusalem as the capital of Israel. They demanded that the decision be overturned, and urged the international community to recognize the state of Palestine, and East Jerusalem as its capital. The Arab League Secretary-General condemned the Israeli military's violent suppression at the end of March 2018 of a 'Great March of Return' protest undertaken by Palestinians near the Gaza–Israel border, which had resulted in at least 16 Palestinian fatalities. He urged the International Criminal Court to investigate the killings. An emergency meeting of Arab League foreign ministers was convened in mid-May to address the relocation of the US embassy in Israel from Tel Aviv to Jerusalem, and the recent killing by Israeli security forces of some 61 Palestinians in Gaza who had been protesting the relocation. The meeting determined to take political or economic measures against any country that recognized Jerusalem as the Israeli capital, and demanded an international investigation into crimes committed against the Palestinians in Gaza.

In July 2018 the Arab League condemned legislation recently adopted by the Israeli Knesset that defined Israel as 'the Nation-State of the Jewish People' and revoked the previous status of Arabic as an official language in that country. In September, participating in a meeting of ministers responsible for foreign affairs, convened to address a recent decision by the US Administration to close the Palestinian diplomatic mission in Washington, DC, USA, the Arab League Secretary-General attributed this—as well as the relocation of the US embassy in Israel to Jerusalem, and a recent decision by the US Administration to cease funding of the UN Relief and Works Agency—to clear bias by the USA towards the agenda of the Israeli Government. In March 2019 the 30th summit meeting of Arab League heads of state rejected as invalid under international law a recent US decision to recognize Israeli sovereignty over the Golan Heights. In September Arab League ministers responsible for foreign affairs condemned as 'aggression' a proposal by the Israeli Prime Minister to annex the Jordan Valley and part of the Dead Sea. Meeting again in November, in an emergency session, the Arab League foreign ministers denounced a recent statement by the US Administration that the USA no longer regarded Israel's demolition of Palestinian settlements as a breach of international law. The Secretary-General stated at that time that the USA could not be accepted as a neutral arbiter between Palestinians and Israel. On 1 February 2020 a further emergency session of Arab League foreign ministers, with participation by the PA President, Mahmoud Abbas, dismissed an Israeli-Palestinian peace plan recently proposed by US President Trump, designating it as biased towards Israel and a setback to the peace process. During the gathering Abbas announced that Palestine had severed relations with Israel and the USA. However, Egypt, Saudi Arabia and the UAE urged careful consideration of the plan, and for a resumption of Palestinian-Israeli dialogue, under US auspices. In early June the PA Prime Minister, Mohammad Shtayyeh, announced that Palestine would declare itself a sovereign state, comprising the West Bank and Gaza, with Jerusalem as its capital, should Israel proceed with stated plans to annex land that it had occupied.

In September 2020 the PA relinquished its occupancy of the (rotational) chairmanship of meetings of the League's Council in strong protest at failure by the Council to agree a resolution condemning the formal signature on 15 September by Bahrain and the UAE, in Washington, DC, USA, of agreements (facilitated by the US Administration, and known as the 'Abraham Accords') that established formal relations with Israel. The PA accused the Council of demonstrating a 'regression' of its values and principles. In early 2021 Sudan became the third Arab League member state to sign the Abraham Accords. An emergency meeting of the Council convened in February in Cairo emphasized the need for a two-state solution to the Israel-Palestine situation. At that time the Secretary-General urged the international community to translate support for a two-state solution into practical actions.

In mid-May 2021—against the background of an intensification of clashes at Jerusalem's al-Aqsa Mosque compound and a severe escalation of Hamas–Israeli conflict—Arab League ministers responsible for foreign affairs, meeting in a virtual format, urged the International Criminal Court to mobilize resources to expedite an investigation into crimes allegedly perpetrated by Israel against the Palestinian people. These included the planned eviction of several Palestinian families from East Jerusalem's Sheikh Jarrah neighbourhood, and the alleged use of grenades and tear gas against Muslim worshippers at the al-Aqsa Mosque. The League Council urged the UN Security Council to take action to protect the Palestinian people. A ceasefire between Hamas and Israel, mediated by Egypt, entered into effect on 21 May. In May 2022 the Arab League's Secretary-General rejected, as a violation of international law, controversial comments by the Israeli Prime Minister, Naftali Bennett, that claimed Israeli sovereignty over Jerusalem. In May the UAE and Israel signed a bilateral free-trade deal. Meeting in Cairo, in August, representatives of national boycott offices determined to reinforce efforts to boycott Israel. In November the 31st regular Arab League summit of heads of state and government affirmed the 'centrality' to the organization of the Palestinian cause. In early February 2023—noting a deterioration in the Palestine-Israel situation since the election in December 2022 of a hardline Israeli administration, including numerous deaths of Palestinians caused by the Israeli security forces—the League's Secretary-General condemned ongoing 'open war' and 'organized Israeli crimes' being perpetrated against the Palestinian people. Addressing a meeting of the League's Council held in early March 2023 he reiterated the need for joint Arab action to confront the 'extremist' Israeli Government, in support of Palestine. In mid-March a senior League official condemned the approval by the Israeli Knesset of a proposal to amend national legislation (in contravention of international law) to enable Israelis to return to four settlements in the West Bank that had been evacuated in 2005. Soon afterwards the League's General

Secretariat deplored recent remarks by an Israeli government minister that appeared to deny the existence of the Palestinian people. In July 2023 the League's Secretary-General condemned as 'brutal' and 'criminal', and as 'collective punishment and revenge', a massive Israeli operation against the Jenin Palestinian refugee camp in the West Bank, that involved at least 10 drone strikes and an estimated 2,000 troops.

Iraq: In September 2002 the Arab League's Council, concerned at US threats to attack Iraq in view of its failure to implement UN resolutions, reiterated its complete opposition to the threat of aggression against any Arab country, including Iraq, and demanded the withdrawal of the sanctions against that country. In mid-September, following an ultimatum by the USA that military action against Iraq would ensue were the UN to fail within a short time limit to ensure the elimination of any Iraqi-held weapons of mass destruction, the Arab League urged Iraq to negotiate the return of a UN Monitoring, Verification and Inspection Commission (UNMOVIC). Soon afterwards, following tripartite consultations between the Secretary-General of the League, the UN Secretary-General and the Iraqi foreign minister, Iraq agreed to admit UNMOVIC personnel. An emergency meeting of the Council, convened in early November, reviewed the recent adoption by the UN Security Council of Resolution 1441, establishing a strict time frame for Iraqi compliance with UN demands and authorizing the use of force against Iraq in response to non-compliance. The Council urged Iraq to co-operate with UNMOVIC and IAEA inspection teams, requested the inclusion of Arab weapons inspectors in the teams, and urged that the resolution should not be used as a pretext to launch a war against Iraq, emphasizing the importance of a peaceful resolution of the situation. In March 2003 Arab League heads of state issued a final communiqué rejecting threatened aggression against Iraq and urging that the inspectors be given enough time to complete their work. Later in that month, following the initiation of US-led military action against the Saddam Hussain regime, the Arab League participated in a meeting of Arab organizations convened to consider means of assisting the Iraqi people. In March 2006 the League determined to establish a mission in Iraq to contribute to that country's rehabilitation and national reconciliation.

In early August 2014 the Arab League Secretary-General denounced as crimes against humanity atrocities being committed against Yazidi and Christian minorities in northern Iraq by militants of the terrorist organization Islamic State (known until June of that year as the Islamic State in Iraq and the Levant) and demanded that the perpetrators be brought to international justice. In early September a meeting of the Council, convened at ministerial level, adopted a resolution that called for the implementation of immediate (unspecified) measures to combat Islamic State at the political, defence, security and legal level.

In December 2015 an emergency meeting of Arab League ministers responsible for foreign affairs, convened in Cairo at the request of the Iraqi Government, demanded that Turkey (now known as Türkiye) withdraw its military presence from northern Iraq; this demand was reiterated at the March 2017 summit meeting of heads of state. In September the Arab League rejected a referendum on proposed Kurdish independence that was—in contravention of the federal Iraqi Constitution—organized by the Kurdistan Regional Government. In March 2018, following an announcement by the Iraqi authorities in December 2017 that Islamic State had been defeated in Iraq, the Arab League organized an Iraq reconstruction exhibition and conference, in Cairo.

Lebanon: The Arab League participates in the International Support Group (ISG) for Lebanon (see under UNSCOL) which was established by the UN Secretary-General in September 2013, and also comprises representatives of the UN, EU, People's Republic of China, France, Germany, Italy, Russia, UK and USA.

An Arab League observer mission was deployed to monitor a general election that was held in Lebanon in May 2022. In March 2023 the League's Secretary-General emphasized the need promptly to elect a new Lebanese President, to resolve a political vacuum that had prevailed since the end of the term of office in October 2022 of former President Michel Aoun.

Libya: In May 2014 the Arab League Secretary-General appointed a Special Envoy to Libya, where there had been a significant escalation in political and violent unrest (see under the UN Support Mission in Libya—UNSMIL). A series of consultative regional ministerial meetings on the security situation in Libya took place during that year. An emergency meeting of the Arab League's Council, held in February 2015, following the beheading by Islamic State extremists of 21 Coptic Christians in Libya, sanctioned air strikes that had recently been initiated by Egypt against Islamic State targets in Libya. In May 2016 the Arab League Council, meeting at the level of ministers responsible for foreign affairs, reaffirmed the League's support for the Government of National Accord (GNA) as the legitimate governing body in Libya and agreed that military intervention in Libya could only be authorized at the request of the GNA. In September a new Special Envoy for Libya was appointed.

In March 2017 an Arab League-UN-AU-EU Quartet formation was established as a joint framework for co-ordinating efforts to address the Libyan crisis. In September Arab League foreign ministers urged the UN to release Libya's frozen international assets in order to enable the Presidency Council to fund better national services. In September 2018 the Arab League Secretary-General welcomed efforts by the UN Envoy to Libya to secure a ceasefire between warring militias in the Libyan capital, which had recently been placed under a state of emergency. At a meeting between the Arab League Secretary-General and the UN Envoy held in September 2019 the Arab League Secretary-General emphasized that there should not be foreign intervention in Libya's internal affairs. Meeting in an emergency session in December, the Council addressed efforts (initiated in April) by forces of the eastern Libyan National Army (LNA) military commander Khalifa Haftar to seize control of Tripoli from the GNA. It reaffirmed that both the GNA and LNA had received foreign support, in violation of a UN arms embargo against Libya that had been imposed in 2011. (In late November Türkiye—known as Turkey until June 2022—had agreed to send military support to the GNA, while Egypt and also Jordan, Russia and the UAE, were backing the LNA.) The Arab League participates, with the AU, the EU, the UN and several partner countries, in the International Follow-Up Committee on Libya, established in February 2020, following an international conference on Libya that had been convened in Berlin, Germany, in January. The Arab League, UNSMIL, Algeria and Germany chair the Berlin Process Political Working Group. In March the League Council adopted a resolution condemning 'Turkish interference in the internal affairs of Arab countries'. Following a ceasefire concluded between the Haftar and GNA forces in August, the Arab League urged Libyan stakeholders to engage constructively to achieve a united resolution to the Libyan crisis.

In February 2021 the Arab League's Secretary-General welcomed the election, by a UN-facilitated Libyan Political Dialogue Forum, of a transitional Government of National Unity (GNU), which was to preside pending the outcome of a general election scheduled to be held later in the year. In March, following the formal inauguration of the new interim authority, the Secretary-General and the Libyan Minister of Foreign Affairs discussed means of enhancing Arab support for Libya, and of advancing joint Arab action. Representatives of the Arab League participated in the Second Berlin Conference on Libya ('Berlin II'), hosted by the German Government and UN on 23 June. At the end of August the Arab League's Secretary-General, the AU Commissioner for Political Affairs, Peace and Security, the UN Special Envoy for Libya, and the foreign ministers of Algeria, Chad, Egypt, Libya, Niger, Nigeria, Sudan and Tunisia, participated in a further 'Libya's neighbours' conference, hosted by Algeria. Its final communiqué reaffirmed rejection of all forms of foreign interference in Libya's internal affairs, and called for the withdrawal from Libya's territory of all foreign fighters, mercenaries and troops. The participants decided to send a ministerial delegation to Libya to contact all stakeholders, with a view to pursuing a political resolution of continuing tensions. In early September the Arab Parliament welcomed the outcome of the conference. At that time a Ministerial Council meeting passed a resolution that demanded that Türkiye cease interfering in Libya and undertaking operations in Syria. Later in September the League's Secretary-General stated concern over the recent passing by the House of Representatives of a motion of no-confidence against the GNU, and emphasized that a general election scheduled to be held in Libya on 24 December must proceed; the election was, however, postponed, in the absence of an agreed legal framework. In February 2022 the House of Representatives appointed a rival Prime Minister to the leader (Abdul Hamid Dbeibah) of the GNU, deeming the mandate of the GNU and the term of Dbeibah's premiership to have expired. The Secretary-General subsequently urged all Libyan stakeholders to work responsibly towards establishing political, security and legal conditions that would enable the pending national elections to be held promptly. In September Egypt's minister responsible for foreign affairs withdrew from a League Council session chaired by the GNU's foreign affairs minister, protesting the legitimacy of her role as Libyan national representative. Shortly afterwards the League's Secretary-General welcomed the appointment of a new UN Special Envoy to Libya (that role having been vacant since December 2021). Egypt's minister responsible for foreign affairs, again, and also the League's Secretary-General and, reportedly, the foreign ministers of Saudi Arabia and the UAE refused to participate in a meeting of the Council that was chaired by the GNU's foreign affairs minister in January 2023. The League's General Secretariat stated grave concern over armed clashes that erupted in that month in Tripoli. In August the League's General Secretariat welcomed the completion of a process, initiated in January 2022, to unify the Central Bank of Libya (its institutions having been divided during the period of national civil conflict).

Syrian Arab Republic: A meeting of Arab League ministers responsible for foreign affairs convened in August 2011 to address mounting violent unrest in Syria issued a statement urging the Syrian regime to act reasonably, to stop the ongoing bloodshed, and to respect the 'legitimate demands' of the Syrian people. In mid-November, further to the Syrian Government's failure to implement a peace initiative and ongoing violent repression of political opponents and civilian demonstrators, an emergency ministerial meeting voted to suspend Syria from participation in meetings of the League, and to impose economic and diplomatic sanctions. In March 2012 a newly appointed Joint Special Envoy of the UN and the Arab League on the Syrian Crisis, Kofi Annan (formerly the UN Secretary-General), proposed a six-point plan to achieve a ceasefire and political settlement. Arab League heads of state, gathered later in that month at a summit meeting in Baghdad, endorsed the initiative, and called for its immediate and full implementation. In April the UN Security Council authorized the establishment of a 300-strong UN Supervision Mission in Syria (UNSMIS), to monitor the cessation of violence and to observe and support the full implementation of the six-point peace plan. Repeated violations of the terms of the peace plan, however, continued to be reported. In early June the 'Free Syrian Army' group of anti-Government militants announced that it was no longer committed to the six-point peace plan. On 16 June, in view of the escalating insecurity, UNSMIS suspended its patrols in Syria. In June an extraordinary ministerial-level meeting of the League Council requested the Arab Satellite Communications Organization and the Egyptian company Nilesat to suspend broadcasts via Arab satellites of official and private Syrian television channels. At the end of the month the Secretaries-General of the Arab League and the UN, as well as the ministers responsible for foreign affairs of China, France, Russia, the UK, the USA, Turkey (called Türkiye from mid-2022), Iraq, Kuwait, Qatar, and the High Representative of the EU for Foreign Affairs and Security Policy, gathered in Geneva, Switzerland, as the 'Action Group for Syria', under the chairmanship of the Joint Special Envoy, to address the situation in Syria. The so-called Geneva I conference agreed that a transitional government of national unity should be established in Syria, including members of both the opposition and the present Government, and that this should be tasked with overseeing the drafting of a new constitution and subsequent staging of national elections. On 22 July, by which time the violence in Syria had further intensified, and the situation was deemed to be a civil war, an emergency meeting of Arab ministers responsible for foreign affairs agreed that President Assad should resign and leave the country, and that opposition parties should form a government of national unity. In early August, in view of the failure of the parties to the Syrian conflict to adhere to the six-point peace plan, and of the divisions within the UN Security Council over Syria, Annan announced his resignation as Joint Special Envoy; the Arab League and UN appointed a Joint Special Representative on Syria, Lakhdar Brahimi, who succeeded Annan at the beginning of September. The Security Council determined in mid-August not to extend the mandate of UNSMIS beyond 19 August, and the mission was terminated accordingly.

In November 2012 the Arab League formally recognized the National Coalition for Syrian Revolutionary and Opposition Forces as Syria's 'legitimate representative and main interlocutor with the Arab League'. The National Coalition represented Syria at meetings of the League during 2013–14, but, reportedly owing to divisions amongst League member states over the issue, was not subsequently invited.

A meeting of Arab League ministers responsible for foreign affairs convened in early September 2013, in Cairo—following the alleged use on 21 August of chemical weapons against unarmed civilians in the rebel-held area of Ghouta, Damascus, to lethal effect—urged the UN Security Council and the international community to take 'deterrent' measures against the Syrian regime, which it accused of being responsible for the alleged chemical attack. A meeting held shortly afterwards, in Paris, France, between the US Secretary of State and the leaders of Bahrain, Egypt, Jordan, Kuwait, Morocco, the PA, Qatar and Saudi Arabia, also accused the al-Assad regime of using chemical weapons, and stated that the regime had thereby transgressed an international 'red line'; however, the League member states participating in the meeting did not commit to endorsing a US proposal that punitive military action should be launched against the Syrian regime. In early September the Russian Minister of Foreign Affairs, the US Secretary of State and the Joint Special Representative on Syria gave consideration to a proposal by Russia that Syria should surrender its chemical stockpiles to international control. Soon afterwards, the Syrian regime notified the UN Secretary-General that it was taking measures to accede to the 1992 Convention on the Prohibition of the Development, Production, Stockpiling and Use of Chemical Weapons and on their Destruction, and would observe the obligations imposed by the Convention prior to its national entry into force. In mid-October the UN Security Council authorized the deployment of a joint UN mission with the Organisation for the Prohibition of Chemical Weapons (OPCW), tasked with supervising the destruction by the Syrian authorities, by the end of June 2014, of Syria's chemical weapons stockpiles and production facilities (q.v.). In May Lakhdar Brahimi resigned as the Joint UN-Arab League Special Representative on Syria. From July a Special Envoy of the UN Secretary-General, solely, to Syria was appointed. A meeting of Arab League and EU ministers responsible for foreign affairs, convened in June, agreed to co-operate in addressing issues surrounding the radicalization and recruitment of combatants from EU member states who were participating in, and returning from, the Syrian civil war. The ministers also deemed the presidential election held in Syria earlier in that month—that had returned President Bashar al-Assad to a further seven-year term of office—to have been neither credible nor conducive to resolving the political situation there. At the end of September the UN-OPCW mission was terminated, having completed its mandated tasks. In August 2015 the Security Council established a Joint UN-OPCW Investigative Mechanism, tasked with identifying and holding accountable entities engaged in using chemical weapons in Syria. In November 2017, however, owing to disagreement within the UN Security Council concerning the proposed terms of its renewal, the Mechanism was terminated.

In November 2015 representatives of the Arab League, the UN, the EU and the ministers responsible for foreign affairs of the USA, Russia (which in September had decided to intervene militarily in Syria, in support of the al-Assad regime), and 15 other states—meeting in Vienna, Austria, as the 'International Syria Support Group' (ISSG)—determined that political talks between the Syrian Government and opposition factions should commence in January 2016, in Geneva, with a view to expediting an end to the Syrian conflict and to accelerating agreement on a new Syrian constitution, governance structure and elections schedule. (See under the Office of the Special Envoy of the UN Secretary-General for Syria for fuller details on the UN-sponsored Syrian peace process.) In September the Arab League Secretary-General condemned an intensification of air strikes on eastern districts of Aleppo by Syrian and Russian warplanes (which during that year had increasingly targeted rebel-held areas)—these having caused numerous civilian deaths and injuries. The Secretary-General designated the escalation as 'dangerous' and 'brutal', and as rooted in a false belief that the Syrian civil war might be resolved through military action, and urged the international community to intervene to halt the devastating impact on civilians. He participated in a meeting of the ISSG that was held on the sidelines of the UN General Assembly in that month, at which it was agreed that a recent ceasefire arrangement must be upheld, and that it was of critical importance that the conditions necessary for the resumption of the UN-led political talks on Syria should be fostered. The Secretary-General also discussed the situation with the Russian minister responsible for foreign affairs at that time, as part of an ongoing Arab League-Russia dialogue process. A renewed ceasefire—facilitated by Russia, Türkiye and Iran—entered into effect on 30 December. In April 2017 the Arab League Secretary-General condemned as a 'major crime' a reported recent chemical attack on the northwestern Syrian community of Khan Sheikhoun.

In March 2016 the Arab League formally designated the militant Lebanon-based grouping Hezbollah—which had been providing support to the al-Assad regime—as a terrorist organization. During that month the League refused to recognize the newly unilaterally declared Kurdish Federation in northern Syria, while emphasizing that the reunification of Syria was crucial for the restoration of regional stability.

In February 2018 the Arab Parliament condemned and described as 'brutal' recent Israeli air strikes against alleged Iranian positions in Syria that had apparently been mandated in retaliation for an Iranian drone launch into Israeli territory from Syria, as well as for the downing by the Syrian military of an Israeli fighter jet. In April Arab League heads of state condemned a recent alleged use of chemical weapons against civilians in eastern Ghouta, Syria and requested an independent international investigation into the incident. From September an offensive by US-supported Kurdish-led Syrian defence forces recaptured significant swathes of territory from Islamic State; Raqqa, which had effectively been the capital of Islamic State's self-styled caliphate, was recaptured in October. In March 2019 the Kurdish-led Syrian Democratic Forces took Islamic State's final territorial stronghold, the Syrian town of Baghouz Fawqani, thereby broadly defeating Islamic State's five-year illegal caliphate. In September the League welcomed the formation of a broad-based committee that was to draft a new Constitution for Syria. In February 2021 the Arab Union for Productive Families and Traditional and Developed Industries, a body affiliated to the League's Council of Arab Economic Unity, established a regional office in Damascus, representing the first Arab League active engagement within Syria since 2011. In March 2022 the League Council reiterated its condemnation of Türkiye's operations in Syria as a violation of the UN Charter, and determined to establish a committee on Türkiye's 'intervention' in the internal affairs of other Arab countries. In the same month, addressing the UN Security Council, the Arab League's Secretary-General stated concern over the implications for peace in Syria of Russia's war in Ukraine, and the ongoing confrontation between the USA and Russia (through the former's imposition of severe economic sanctions against the latter). He noted that Russia had provided support to the Syrian regime, and the USA to forces opposed to President al-Assad. On 7 May 2023 the Arab League Council agreed to readmit Syria to participation in the League, following a recent period of increased diplomatic engagement between some member states and the Syrian regime (which by then had regained control of much of the country), including the provision of humanitarian aid to areas devastated by an earthquake that struck parts of northern Syria and southern Türkiye in February. The Council also determined to establish a Ministerial Liaison Committee—comprising Egypt, Iraq, Jordan, Lebanon and Saudi Arabia—to support a full resolution of the 12-year long civil conflict, and to address the consequent massive domestic population displacement and regional refugee crises, and also an expansion of illegal drugs trafficking attributed to deteriorating economic conditions and opportunities caused by the conflict. By that time more than 300,000 civilians were reported to have been killed during the war, and a further 100,000 to have been detained or to have disappeared. In mid-May President al-Assad participated in the 32nd regular summit of Arab League heads of state.

In March 2023, the Syrian government declared that it would not seek any reconciliation with Türkiye, unless Türkiye withdrew all of its proxy forces from Syria.

Yemen: In March 2015 Arab League heads of state expressed support for a military operation, Decisive Storm, led by Saudi Arabia against the Shi'a Houthi insurgency in Yemen. While the operation officially concluded in April, coalition air strikes against rebel positions continued. An extraordinary meeting of Arab League ministers responsible for foreign affairs, convened in Makkah, Saudi Arabia, in May 2020, addressed continuing attacks against oil facilities in Saudi Arabia by Houthi militias. In January 2021 the Secretary-General stated support for the new power-sharing Government installed in Yemen in mid-December 2020, in accordance with the Saudi Arabia-mediated Riyadh Agreement process. The Arab League supported the UN-negotiated ceasefire that was initiated in April 2022.

EXTERNAL RELATIONS

The inaugural meeting within a new consultation framework uniting the Secretaries-General of the Arab League, the Gulf Cooperation Council (GCC), the Organization of Islamic Cooperation (OIC) and the Union of the Arab Maghreb was convened in September 2014.

In March 2022, at Egypt's request, an Arab Ministerial Contact Group was created to promote a resolution to the war in Ukraine (which had significant potential economic repercussions for member states). In the following month the Arab League's Secretary-General and the ministers responsible for foreign affairs from Algeria, Egypt, Iraq, Jordan and Sudan met their Ukrainian and Russian counterparts in Moscow, Russian Federation, to discuss means of achieving a ceasefire in the conflict.

In June 2023 an extraordinary meeting of the League's Council strongly condemned the recent provocative burning of a copy of the Qur'an (Islamic holy book) in Stockholm, Sweden, at the commencement of the Eid al-Adha holiday. The Council called on the international community to criminalize such acts.

The third ministerial session of an Arab-Japanese Political Dialogue was held in September 2023, at the League's headquarters.

Latin America: The first summit of heads of state and of government of the South American-Arab Countries (ASPA) was convened in May 2005, in Brasília, Brazil, and a second ASPA summit was organized in March 2009, in Doha. The third ASPA summit was convened in Lima, Peru, in October 2012, and ASPA IV took place in Riyadh in November 2015. ASPA V, initially scheduled to have been hosted by Venezuela during 2018, was postponed. ASPA also meets at the level of ministers responsible for foreign affairs (every two years, on the sidelines of the UN General Assembly), senior officials (every six months), and in the format of a number of sectoral committees, covering co-operation in the following areas: cultural, economic, environmental, scientific and technological, and social. An Arab-South American Library is being developed in Algiers, Algeria, under the ASPA co-operation initiative. In January 2013 the first ASPA ministerial meeting on energy, held in Abu Dhabi, adopted the Abu Dhabi Declaration on enhanced co-operation. The fourth biennial Brazil-Arab Countries Economic Forum was convened in São Paulo, Brazil, in July 2022.

European Union: A Liaison Office with the European Commission was established in 2009. In January 2015 the Arab League Secretary-General signed an MOU with the High Representative of the EU for Foreign Affairs and Security Policy in order to strengthen relations and enhance co-operation. A Strategic Dialogue was launched in November to facilitate and promote exchanges on political and security issues. The inaugural Arab League-EU leaders' summit, convened in February 2019, in Sharm el-Sheikh, issued a joint declaration on future Euro-Arab co-operation. Regular meetings of ministers responsible for foreign affairs of the Arab League and EU are held.

Sub-Saharan Africa: In October 2010 the Arab League and the AU jointly organized an Africa-Arab summit, held in Sirte, the second such meeting since that convened in 1977. Leaders attending the summit agreed to establish a joint Africa-Arab Fund for Disaster Response. The third summit was held in Kuwait, in November 2013, and the fourth was hosted by Equatorial Guinea, in November 2016, on the theme 'Together for a Sustainable Economic Development'.

In February 2021 the ninth meeting of Arab-African Cooperation—with participation by delegations of senior officials led by the Arab League Secretary-General and the Chairperson of the African Union Commission—agreed to strengthen collaboration on political, social, economic, developmental and cultural matters. The fifth Africa-Arab summit was to be held in November 2023, in Riyadh.

United Nations: In September 2016 the Secretaries-General of the Arab League and the UN signed an agreement governing the development of future co-operation between the two organizations. A UN Liaison Office was opened in Cairo in June 2019. In March 2022 the UAE, in its role as holder of the Presidency of the UN Security Council in that month, convened a meeting attended by the Arab League's Secretary-General that addressed League-UN co-operation.

Finance

The Arab League budgets around US $60m. annually to fund its secretariat, including a small allocation to the Arab Fund for Technical Assistance in African States. Member states' contributions are determined by a scale of assessments, under which Kuwait and Saudi Arabia each contribute 14% to the total budget (the largest national contributions).

Specialized Agencies

All member states of the Arab League are also members of the Specialized Agencies, which constitute an integral part of the Arab League.

Arab Academy for Science, Technology and Maritime Transport (AASTMT): POB 1029, Alexandria, Egypt; tel. (3) 5622366; fax (3) 5610950; internet www.aast.edu; f. 1975 as Arab Maritime Transport Academy; provides specialized training in marine transport, engineering, technology and management; Pres. Prof. Dr ISMAIL ABDEL GHAFAR ISMAIL FARAG; publs *Maritime Technology Bulletin* (6 a year), *Journal of the Arab Academy for Science, Technology and Maritime Transport* (2 a year).

Arab Administrative Development Organization (ARADO): 2A El-Hegaz St, POB 2692 al-Horreia, Heliopolis, Cairo, Egypt; tel. (2) 22581144; fax (2) 22580077; e-mail arado@arado.org; internet www.arado.org; f. 1961 (as the Arab Organization of Administrative Sciences), became operational in 1969; undertakes administration devt, training, consultancy, research and studies, information, documentation; promotes Arab and international co-operation in administrative sciences; incl. the Arab Network of Administrative Information; maintains an extensive digital library; in Sept. 2021 organized the First Arab Forum on Sovereign Sukuk and their Role in the Development of Arab Societies (addressing Shari'a-compliant Islamic financial mechanisms); co-organized in June 2022 the First Arab Conference on Intellectual Property Rights; mems: 22 states; Gen. Dir Prof. NASSER ALI AL-QAHTANI; publs *Arab Journal of Administration* (2 a year), *Arab Administration Newsletter* (quarterly), research series, training manuals.

Arab Atomic Energy Agency (AAEA): 7 rue de l'Assistance, Cité El Khadhra, 1003 Tunis, Tunisia; tel. (71) 808400; fax (71) 808450; e-mail aaea@aaea.org.tn; internet www.aaea.org.tn; f. 1988; Dir-Gen. Prof. SALEM HAMDI (Tunisia); helped to organize the 15th Arab Conf. on the Peaceful Uses of Atomic Energy in Dec. 2021, in Aswan, Egypt; publs *The Atom and Development* (quarterly), other publs in the field of nuclear sciences and their applications in industry, biology, medicine, agriculture, food irradiation and seawater desalination.

Arab Center for the Studies of Arid Zones and Dry Lands (ACSAD): Alsaboura, next to Remote Sensing Bldg, Gate 8, Damascus, Syria; tel. (11) 3944171; fax (11) 3944170; e-mail email@acsad.org; internet www.acsad.org; f. 1968; conducts regional research and devt programmes related to land and water uses, plant and animal resources, agro-meteorology, and socioeconomic studies of arid zones; maintains 13 research stations; holds confs and training courses and encourages the exchange of information by Arab scientists; Dir-Gen. Dr NASER ELDIN OBAID.

Arab Industrial Development, Standardization and Mining Organization (AIDSMO): rue France, Zanagat al-Khatawat, POB 8019, Rabat, Morocco; tel. (37) 274500; fax (37) 772188; e-mail aidsmo@aidsmo.org; internet www.aidsmo.org; f. 1990 by merger of Arab Industrial Development Organization, Arab Organization for Mineral Resources and Arab Organization for Standardization and Metrology; comprises a 13-mem. Executive Council, a High Consultative Committee of Standardization, a High Committee of Mineral Resources and a Co-ordination Committee for Arab Industrial Research Centres; a Council of ministers of mem. states responsible for industry meets every 2 years; in April 2017 AIDSMO convened the inaugural meeting of a working team tasked with linking academia with industry in the Arab region; in April 2021 it established a platform that aimed to support mem. states during the COVID-19 pandemic by facilitating offers of and requests for Arab industrial products, incl. medical and health supplies; promotes investment in green industries in the Arab world; mems: 21 Arab countries; Dir-Gen. ADEL AL-SAQER (Kuwait); publs *Arab Industrial Development* (monthly and quarterly newsletters).

Arab Investment and Export Credit Guarantee Corporation: POB 23568, Safat 13096, Kuwait; tel. 24959555; fax 24959596; e-mail operations@dhaman.net; internet www.dhaman.net; f. 1974; insures Arab investors for non-commercial risks, and export credits for commercial and non-commercial risks; undertakes research and other activities to promote inter-Arab trade and investment; total assets 161.9m. Kuwaiti Dinars (31 Dec. 2021); mems: 21 Arab countries and 4 multilateral Arab financial institutions; Chair. Dr NAIF BIN ABDUL RAHMAN AL-SHAMMARI; Dir-Gen. ABDULLAH A. AL-SABEEH; publs *News Bulletin* (quarterly), *Arab Investment Climate Report* (annually).

Arab Labour Organization: POB 814, Cairo, Egypt; tel. (2) 3362721; fax (2) 3484902; e-mail alo@alolabor.org; internet alolabor.org; f. 1965; promotes co-operation between mem. states in labour issues, including the unification of labour legislation and general conditions of work wherever possible; conducts research, technical assistance and training; the org. has a tripartite structure: govts, employers and workers; 48th Arab Labour Conf.: Sept. 2022 (in Cairo); Dir-Gen. FAYEZ ALI AL-MUTAIRI; publs *ALO Bulletin* (monthly), *Arab Labour Review* (quarterly), *Legislative Bulletin* (annually), series of research reports and studies concerned with economic and social devt issues in the Arab world.

Arab League Educational, Cultural and Scientific Organization (ALECSO): ave Mohamed V, POB 1120, Tunis, Tunisia; tel. (70) 013-900; e-mail alecso@alecso.org.tn; internet www.alecso.org; f. 1970 to promote and co-ordinate educational, cultural and scientific activities in the Arab region; has depts of Education; Culture; Science and Scientific Research Administration; and Information and Communication Management; regional units: Arab Centre for Arabization, Translation, Authorship, and Publication—Damascus, Syria; Institute of Arab Manuscripts—Cairo, Egypt; Institute of Arab Research and Studies—Cairo; Khartoum International Institute for Arabic Language—Khartoum, Sudan; and the Arabization Co-ordination Bureau—Rabat, Morocco; mems: 22 states; Dir-Gen. Prof. Dr MOHAMED OULD AMAR; publs *Arab Journal of Culture* (2 a year), *Arab Journal of Education* (2 a year), *Arab Journal of Science and Information* (2 a year).

Arab Organization for Agricultural Development (AOAD): 7 al-Amarat St, POB 474, Khartoum 11111, Sudan; tel. (1) 83472176; fax (1) 83471050; e-mail info@aoad.org; internet www.aoad.org; f. 1970; began operations in 1972 to contribute to co-operation in agricultural activities, and in the devt of natural and human resources for agriculture; compiles data, conducts studies, training and food security programmes; includes Information and Documentation Centre, Arab Centre for Studies and Projects, and Arab Institute of Forestry and Biodiversity; in Sept. 2017 concluded a co-operation framework with the Islamic Organization for Food Security; in July 2021 signed a co-operation framework agreement with FAO, providing for the implementation of jt projects incl. drafting a roadmap on the devt of sustainable agriculture and food chains, and undertaking a study of the socioeconomic impacts of the red palm weevil (an agricultural pest); a Strategy for Sustainable Arab Agricultural Development was being implemented during 2020–30, alongside an Arab Program for Sustaining Food Security that aimed to expand output of basic food commodities by a minimum of 30% by 2030; Dir-Gen. Prof. IBRAHIM ADAM EL-DUKHIRI (Oman); publs *Agricultural Statistics Yearbook*, *Annual Report on Agricultural Development*, *Report on Agricultural Development*, *the State of Arab Food Security* (annually), *Accession Bulletin* (every 2 months), *AOAD Newsletter* (monthly), *Arab Agricultural Research Journal*, *Agriculture and Development Journal in the Arab Countries* (2 a year).

Arab Satellite Communications Organization (ARABSAT): POB 1038, Diplomatic Quarter, Riyadh 11431, Saudi Arabia; tel. (11) 482-0000; e-mail info@Arabsat.com; internet www.arabsat.com; f. 1976; regional satellite telecommunications org. providing broadcast, telecommunications and broadband services to mems and private users; operates 7 satellites, which cover Arab, European, Central Asian and northern African countries; suspended satellite broadcasts to Syria in June 2012, at the request of the League Council; mems: 21 states; Chair. HAITHAM AL-OHALI; Pres. and CEO BADR BIN NASSER AL-SUWAIDAN.

Arab States Broadcasting Union (ASBU): POB 250, 1080 Tunis Cedex; rue 8840, Centre Urbain Nord, Tunisia; tel. (71) 849000; fax (71) 843054; e-mail asbu@asbu.net; internet www.asbu.net; f. 1969 to promote and study broadcasting, and to exchange expertise and technical co-operation in broadcasting; conducts training and audience research; operates a Multimedia Exchange Network over Satellite (MENOS+) network and digital TV services, backed up by high-security ASBU Cloud servers; established a training academy in 2016, in Tunis; organizes the biennial Arab Festival for Radio and Television, and an Arab Song Festival; 32 active mem. radio and television orgs, 2 participating mem., 12 assoc. mems; publs *Arab Broadcasters* (quarterly), *Arab Radio Review* (quarterly).

Associated Body

Council of Arab Economic Unity: 1113 Corniche el-Nil, 4th Floor, POB 1 Mohammed Fareed, 11518 Cairo, Egypt; tel. (2) 5755321; fax (2) 5754090; f. 1957 by the Economic and Social Council of the Arab League to co-ordinate measures leading to a customs union subject to a unified administration; conduct market and commodity studies; assist with the unification of statistical terminology and methods of data collection; conduct studies for the formation of new joint Arab companies and federations; and to formulate specific programmes for agricultural and industrial co-ordination and for improving road and railway networks; tasked with administering the 1962 Arab Economic Unity Agreement; inaugural meeting held in 1964; representatives of mem. states—usually ministers responsible for economy, finance and trade—meet twice a year; meetings are chaired by the representative of each country for one year on a rotational basis; the Council secretariat is entrusted with the implementation of the Council's decisions and with proposing work plans, including efforts to encourage participation by mem. states parties to the Arab Economic Unity Agreement; the secretariat also compiles statistics, conducts research and publishes studies on Arab economic problems and on the effects of major world economic trends; has permanent committees on Customs issues; Monetary and finance; Economic; Permanent representatives; and Follow-up; affiliated Arab unions have been established under the auspices of the Council; in Nov. 2020 endorsed a Trade Fair for the Arab Countries format, to be implemented as a hybrid of traditional and virtual activities; mems: Egypt, Jordan, Libya, Mauritania, Palestine, Somalia, Sudan, Yemen; Sec.-Gen. MOHAMEDI AHMED AL-NY (Mauritania).

The Arab Bank for Economic Development in Africa, established in 1973 by the Arab League member states, extends loans and grants to sub-Saharan African countries to finance development initiatives.

ORGANIZATION OF ARAB PETROLEUM EXPORTING COUNTRIES—OAPEC

Address: POB 20501, Safat 13066, Kuwait.
Telephone: 24959000; **fax:** 24959755; **e-mail:** oapec@oapecorg.org; **internet:** www.oapecorg.org.

OAPEC was established in 1968 to safeguard the interests of members and to determine ways and means for their co-operation in various forms of economic activity in the petroleum industry. In 2021 OAPEC member states accounted for 54.5% of total proven global crude oil reserves and 26.4% of total global reserves of natural gas. OAPEC member states contributed some 27.5% of total world hydrocarbon liquids production in 2021, and 14.7% of total global marketed natural gas in 2020.

MEMBERS

Algeria	Kuwait	Syrian Arab Republic
Bahrain	Libya	Tunisia*
Egypt	Qatar	United Arab Emirates
Iraq	Saudi Arabia	

* Membership suspended, at Tunisia's request, since 1986.

Organization
(September 2023)

MINISTERIAL COUNCIL

The Council consists normally of the ministers responsible for petroleum of the member states, and forms the supreme authority of OAPEC, responsible for drawing up its general policy, directing its activities and laying down its governing rules. It meets twice yearly, and may hold extraordinary sessions. Chairmanship is on an annual rotating basis (2023: Iraq).

EXECUTIVE BUREAU

The Bureau assists the Council to direct the management of OAPEC, approves staff regulations, reviews the budget, considers matters relating to the organization's agreements and activities and draws up the agenda for the Council. It comprises one senior official from each member state and convenes at least three times a year.

GENERAL SECRETARIAT

The General Secretariat is composed of the Secretary-General's Office; departments of Economics and of Technical Affairs; and the Arab Centre for Energy Studies (established in 1983), which comprises departments of Information and Library, and Finance and Administrative Affairs.
Secretary-General: ALI SABT BEN SABT (Kuwait).

JUDICIAL TRIBUNAL

The Tribunal comprises at any one time not fewer than seven or more than 11 judges from Arab countries (the number of judges in office must always be uneven). Its task is to settle differences in the interpretation and application of the OAPEC Agreement, arising between members and also between OAPEC and its affiliates; disputes among member countries on petroleum activities falling within OAPEC's jurisdiction and not under the sovereignty of member countries; and disputes that the Ministerial Council decides to submit to the Tribunal.

Activities

OAPEC co-ordinates different aspects of the Arab petroleum industry through joint undertakings. It co-operates with the League of Arab States (Arab League) and other organizations, and attempts to link petroleum research institutes in the Arab states. OAPEC collaborates with the Arab League and its subsidiary Arab Fund for Economic and Social Development (AFESD) and Arab Monetary Fund in compiling the normally annual *Joint Arab Economic Report*. OAPEC maintains the OAPEC Energy Data Bank, and an online library, and provides training in technical matters and in documentation and information. The General Secretariat also conducts technical and feasibility studies and carries out market reviews.

In August 2020 OAPEC issued a report on the use of Liquefied Natural Gas as an environmentally preferable marine fuel substitute (in place of high sulphur fuel oil). An OAPEC study titled *Plastic Waste Recycling, Investment Opportunities and Environmental Solutions* was also issued in that month.

In association with AFESD, OAPEC organizes the Arab Energy Conference every four years, attended by OAPEC ministers responsible for petroleum and energy, senior officials from other Arab states, and representatives of invited institutions and organizations concerned with energy issues. The 12th Conference was to be hosted by Qatar in December 2023. OAPEC, with other Arab organizations, participates in the Higher Co-ordination Committee for Higher Arab Action.

An OAPEC Award for Scientific Research is granted every two years. The research topic chosen for 2022 was 'Decarbonization Techniques in the Petroleum Industry and the Circular Carbon Economy'.

In March 2023 the Secretary-General observed that international sanctions imposed from early 2022 against the Russian Federation in response to that country's military invasion of Ukraine had rendered European countries more dependent upon energy imports from OAPEC member states, other Middle Eastern countries, and the USA; and that Russian oil companies had, meanwhile, developed new (Asian) markets for their exports.

Finance

The General Secretariat and Judicial Tribunal have a combined annual budget of around 2.1m. Kuwaiti dinars.

Publications

Annual Statistical Report.
OAPEC Monthly Bulletin.
Oil and Arab Cooperation (quarterly, Arabic).
Secretary-General's Annual Report (Arabic and English editions).
Papers, studies, conference proceedings.

OAPEC-Sponsored Ventures

Arab Maritime Petroleum Transport Company (AMPTC): Head Office, POB 22525, Safat 13086, Kuwait; tel. 24959400; fax 24842996; e-mail amptc.kuwait@amptc.net; internet www.amptc.net; f. 1973; established to undertake transport of crude petroleum, gas, refined products and petro-chemicals, and thus to increase Arab participation in the tanker transport industry; owns and operates a fleet of oil tankers and other carriers; also maintains an operations office in Giza, Egypt; auth. cap. US $500m.

Arab Petroleum Investments Corporation (APICORP): POB 9599, Dammam 31423, Saudi Arabia; tel. (13) 847-0444; fax (13) 847-0022; internet www.apicorp.org; f. 1975; finances investments in petroleum and petrochemicals projects and related industries in the Arab world and in developing countries, with priority being given to Arab jt ventures; projects financed include gas liquefaction plants, petrochemicals, tankers, oil refineries, pipelines, exploration, detergents, fertilizers and process control instrumentation; in Feb. 2013 launched the *Shari'a*-compliant US $150m. APICORP Petroleum Shipping Fund; in July 2016, jtly with the National Shipping Co of Saudi Arabia (Bahri), established the *Shari'a*-compliant $1,500m. APICORP Bahri Oil Shipping Fund; has a banking branch in Bahrain; total assets $8,260m. (30 June 2022); shareholders: Kuwait, Saudi Arabia and United Arab Emirates (17% each), Libya (15%), Iraq and Qatar (10% each), Algeria (5%), Bahrain, Egypt and Syria (3% each); Chair. Dr AABED BIN ABDULLA AL-SAADOUN; CEO KHALID BIN ALI AL-RUWAIGH.

Arab Company for Detergent Chemicals (ARADET): POB 27064, al-Mansour, Baghdad, Iraq; tel. (1) 541-9341; fax (1) 543-0265; e-mail info@aradetco.com; internet www.aradetco.com; f. 1981; produces and markets linear alkyl benzene, heavy alkyl benzene, benzene toluene xylene, normal paraffin, and selected by-products; APICORP holds 32% of shares in the co.

Arab Shipbuilding and Repair Yard Company (ASRY): POB 50110, Hidd, Bahrain; tel. 17671111; fax 17670236; e-mail info@asry.net; internet www.asry.net; f. 1977; operates a 500,000-dwt dry dock in Bahrain; two floating docks operational since 1992, and two slipways became operational in 2008; manages 15 repair berths, and workshops and service centres; has progressively diversified its activities in its target sectors (gas, petroleum, water, chemical, power and industrial), and in 2023 had four operational pillars: ship repair and conversion; rig repair and conversion; naval repair and conversion; and fabrication and engineering; ASRY's infrastructure was undergoing modernization during that year; CEO MAZAN MATAR.

Through an Arab Petroleum Services Company (APSCO), established in 1977, two Tripoli, Libya-based enterprises were established: the Arab Drilling and Workover Company (ADWOC, launched in 1980) and Arab Geophysical Exploration Services Company (AGESCO, founded in 1986)—both 40% owned by APSCO. The Arab Well Logging Company (AWLCO) was established by APSCO in 1983 in the Iraqi capital, Baghdad.

ORGANIZATION OF ISLAMIC COOPERATION—OIC

Address: Medina Rd, Sary St, POB 178, Jeddah 21411, Saudi Arabia.

Telephone: (12) 651-5222; **fax:** (12) 651-2288; **internet:** www.oic-oci.org.

The OIC was formally established, as the Organization of the Islamic Conference, at the first conference of Muslim heads of state convened in Rabat, Morocco, in September 1969. The first conference of Muslim ministers responsible for foreign affairs, held in Jeddah, Saudi Arabia, in March 1970, established the General Secretariat—which became operational in May 1971. In June 2011 the 38th ministerial conference changed the name of the organization to the Organization of Islamic Cooperation (abbreviated, as hitherto, to OIC).

MEMBERS

Afghanistan	Indonesia	Qatar
Albania	Iran	Saudi Arabia
Algeria	Iraq	Senegal
Azerbaijan	Jordan	Sierra Leone
Bahrain	Kazakhstan	Somalia
Bangladesh	Kuwait	Sudan
Benin	Kyrgyzstan	Suriname
Brunei Darussalam	Lebanon	Syrian Arab
Burkina Faso	Libya	Republic*
Cameroon	Malaysia	Tajikistan
Chad	Maldives	Togo
Comoros	Mali	Tunisia
Côte d'Ivoire	Mauritania	Türkiye (Turkey)
Djibouti	Morocco	Turkmenistan
Egypt	Mozambique	Uganda
Gabon	Niger	United Arab
The Gambia	Nigeria	Emirates
Guinea	Oman	Uzbekistan
Guinea-Bissau	Pakistan	Yemen
Guyana	Palestine	

* Suspended from participation in the activities of the OIC and from all its subsidiary organs and specialized and affiliated institutions since August 2012, in view of the Syrian Government's violent suppression of opposition elements and related acts of violence against civilian communities.

Note: Observer status has been granted to Bosnia and Herzegovina, the Central African Republic, the Russian Federation, Thailand, the 'Turkish Republic of Northern Cyprus', the Moro National Liberation Front (MNLF) of the southern Philippines, the United Nations (UN), the African Union (AU), the Non-Aligned Movement, the League of Arab States, the Economic Cooperation Organization and the Parliamentary Union of OIC member states. The revised OIC Charter, endorsed in March 2008, made future applications for OIC membership and observer status conditional upon Muslim demographic majority and membership of the UN.

Organization
(September 2023)

SUMMIT CONFERENCES

The supreme body of the organization is the Conference of Heads of State ('Islamic summit'), which first met in 1969, in Rabat, Morocco. Ordinary summit conferences are normally held every three years, while extraordinary conferences may be convened as necessary. The 15th ordinary summit was to be convened in December 2023, in The Gambia.

CONFERENCE OF MINISTERS OF FOREIGN AFFAIRS

Ordinary conferences take place annually (2023: in Nouakchott, Mauritania, in March), to consider the means of implementing the general policy of the OIC, although they may also be convened for extraordinary sessions.

GENERAL SECRETARIAT

The executive organ of the organization, the General Secretariat is headed by a Secretary-General (who is elected by the Conference of Ministers of Foreign Affairs for a five-year term, renewable only once) and four Assistant Secretaries-General (similarly appointed). The General Secretariat comprises the Cabinet of the Secretary-General, and departments on Palestine and Al-Quds Affairs, Political Affairs, Economic Affairs, Science and Technology (including Environment, Health and Higher Education), Humanitarian Affairs, Dialogue and Outreach Public, Administration and Finance, Legal Affairs, Public Information and Communications, Protocol and Public Relations, Conferences, and Information Technology, as well as a Directorate of Cultural, Social and Family Affairs, Registry Office, Information Resources Center, and Information Department.

Secretary-General: HISSEIN BRAHIM TAHA (Chad).

At the summit conference in January 1981 it was decided that an International Islamic Court of Justice should be established to adjudicate, using Islamic *Shari'a* principles, in disputes between member countries. Experts met in January 1983 to draw up a constitution for the court; however, by 2023 it was not yet in operation.

EXECUTIVE COMMITTEE

The Executive Committee follows up resolutions of OIC conferences. It comprises representatives of the OIC host country, the OIC General Secretariat, and the summit conference and ministerial conference troikas made up of member countries equally representing the OIC's African, Arab and Asian membership.

COMMITTEE OF PERMANENT REPRESENTATIVES

The Committee, comprising member states' accredited Permanent Representatives to the OIC, meets intermittently.

STANDING COMMITTEES

Al-Quds Committee: f. 1975 to implement the resolutions of the Islamic Conference on the status of Jerusalem (Al-Quds Ash-Sharif); meets at the level of ministers responsible for foreign affairs; maintains the Al-Quds Fund; a Bayt Mal Al-Quds Agency was established under the auspices of the Committee; its inaugural meeting was held in Feb. 2000; Chair. King MUHAMMAD VI OF MOROCCO.

Standing Committee for Economic and Commercial Cooperation (COMCEC): f. 1981; Chair. RECEP TAYYIP ERDOĞAN (President of Türkiye).

Standing Committee for Information and Cultural Affairs (COMIAC): f. 1981; Chair. MACKY SALL (President of Senegal).

Standing Committee for Scientific and Technological Cooperation (COMSTECH): f. 1981; Chair. Dr ARIF ALVI (President of Pakistan).

Other committees include the Islamic Peace Committee, the Permanent Finance Committee, the Committee of Islamic Solidarity with the Peoples of the Sahel, the Six-Member Committee on Palestine, and the Committee on UN reform. In addition, there is an Islamic Commission for Economic, Cultural and Social Affairs, and there are several OIC Contact Groups, including on Peace and Dialogue, on the Holy City of Al-Quds, on Iraq, on Muslims in Europe, and on Yemen. A Commission of Eminent Persons was inaugurated in 2005.

INDEPENDENT PERMANENT HUMAN RIGHTS COMMISSION (IPHRC)

Secretariat: 2550 Khalij Al Qamar, al-Hamra District, Jeddah 23212 6885, Saudi Arabia; e-mail info@oic-iphrc.org; internet oic-iphrc.org; f. 2011 to promote the civil, political, social and economic rights enshrined in the covenants and declarations of the OIC, and in universally agreed human rights instruments, in conformity with Islamic values; inaugural session convened in Jakarta, Indonesia, in Feb. 2012; OIC human rights instruments include the Covenant on the Rights of the Child in Islam (2005), and the OIC Declaration on Human Rights (initially adopted in 1990, as the Cairo Declaration on Human Rights in Islam, and amended in 2020 to align with 'universal human rights standards'); 21st regular session: May 2023, themed 'Business and Human Rights: Normative Framework and Implementation Guidelines for OIC Countries'; in that month the IPHRC stated deep concern at the Afghan authorities' discriminatory decision to ban females from participating in secondary and university education; the IPHRC comprises 18 commissioners, equally representing Africa, Asia and the Middle East; Exec. Dir Prof. NOURA BINT ZAID AL-RASHOUD.

Activities

The OIC's aims, as proclaimed in the Charter (adopted in 1972, with revisions endorsed in 1990 and 2008), are:

(i) to promote Islamic solidarity among member states;

(ii) to consolidate co-operation among member states in the economic, social, cultural, scientific and other vital fields, and to arrange consultations among member states belonging to international organizations;

(iii) to endeavour to eliminate racial segregation and discrimination and to eradicate colonialism in all its forms;

(iv) to take necessary measures to support international peace and security founded on justice;

(v) to co-ordinate efforts to safeguard the Holy Places, to support the struggle of the people of Palestine and help them to regain their rights and liberate their land;

(vi) to strengthen the struggle of all Muslim people with a view to safeguarding their dignity, independence and national rights;

(vii) to create a suitable atmosphere for the promotion of co-operation and understanding among member states and other countries.

The first summit conference of Islamic leaders (representing 24 states) took place in 1969 following the burning of the al-Aqsa Mosque in Jerusalem. At this conference it was decided that Islamic governments should 'consult together with a view to promoting close co-operation and mutual assistance in the economic, scientific, cultural and spiritual fields, inspired by the immortal teachings of Islam'. Thereafter the ministers responsible for foreign affairs of the countries concerned met annually, and adopted the Charter of the Organization of the Islamic Conference in 1972.

At the second Islamic summit conference (Lahore, Pakistan, 1974), the Islamic Solidarity Fund was established, together with a committee of representatives that later evolved into the Islamic Commission for Economic, Cultural and Social Affairs. Subsequently, numerous other subsidiary bodies were set up.

In April 2016 the 13th OIC summit adopted OIC-2025, a 10-year plan of joint Islamic action, which included goals for collaboration in the following areas: the environment, climate change and sustainability; combating extremism, sectarianism and Islamophobia; peace and security; poverty alleviation; trade, investment and finance; agriculture and food; employment infrastructure and industrialization; science, technology and innovation; education; health; the advancement and empowerment of women; family welfare and social security; joint Islamic humanitarian action; human rights, good governance and accountability; and developing communications and digital information structures. A successor 2026–35 OIC plan of action was under development in 2023.

An Annual Coordination Meeting of OIC Institutions is convened annually (2022: in December).

ECONOMIC AFFAIRS

In 1991 22 OIC member states signed a Framework Agreement on a Trade Preferential System among the OIC Member States (TPS-OIC); this entered into force in 2003, and was envisaged as representing the first step towards the eventual establishment of an Islamic common market. Rules of origin for the TPS-OIC were adopted in September 2007, and a Protocol on the Preferential Tariff Scheme for TPS-OIC (PRETAS) entered into force in February 2010. In April 2016 the 10th OIC summit endorsed the goal that by 2025 some 25% of member states' trade should be intra-Islamic. OIC has pursued efforts to enhance the role of the private sector through the promotion of intra-OIC small and medium-sized enterprise clusters, in sectors including agrofood processing, and transportation and logistics.

The 18th OIC Trade Fair was to be held during 2023, in Lahore, Pakistan. A World Islamic Economic Forum is convened intermittently. In March 2017 an OIC-People's Republic of China Forum was convened in Beijing, People's Republic of China.

The fourth session of the Islamic Conference of Labour Ministers held in Jeddah, in February 2018, welcomed an OIC Labour Market Strategy 2025. Ministers adopted an OIC Agreement on Mutual Recognition Arrangement of the Skilled Workforce, as well as an OIC Standard Bilateral Agreement on the Exchange of Manpower.

In March 2017 a Memorandum of Understanding was concluded between the OIC and the Dubai, UAE-based International Islamic Centre for Reconciliation and Arbitration, to cover investment and trade conflicts, training programmes and the exchange of expertise.

An inaugural OIC International Forum on Islamic Tourism was convened in June 2014. An Islamic Conference of Tourism Ministers meets regularly (2022: in June, in Baku, Azerbaijan).

CULTURE, SOCIAL AND FAMILY AFFAIRS

OIC's Directorate of Culture, Social and Family Affairs comprises two separate departments, the Cultural Affairs Department, which focuses on Islamic cultural issues, the protection of Islamic sites and interfaith dialogue, and the Social and Family Affairs Department. There is also a Youth Unit. In December 2007 the OIC organized the first International Conference on Islamophobia, aimed at addressing concerns that alleged instances of defamation of Islam appeared to be increasing worldwide (particularly in Europe). OIC leaders denounced stereotyping and discrimination, and urged the promotion of Islam by Islamic states as a 'moderate, peaceful and tolerant religion'. An Islamic Observatory on Islamophobia, established in 2007, has issued regular reports on intolerance against Muslims; the 14th covered the period December 2020–January 2022. In June 2019 the OIC issued the first edition of an *International Islamic Encyclopedia of Tolerance*. In the following month the inaugural meeting of a new OIC Contact Group on Peace and Dialogue agreed a comprehensive Plan of Action on Islamophobia, Religious Discrimination, Intolerance and Hatred Towards Muslims, to cover the period 2020–23. Under the Plan the Islamophobia Observatory and relevant multilateral co-operation were to be strengthened. An open ministerial-level meeting of the OIC Contact Group on Muslims in Europe, convened in September 2022 on the sidelines of the UN General Assembly, urged Muslim community leaders in Europe to intensify efforts to promote peaceful co-existence, tolerance and inclusiveness. In early July 2023 an extraordinary meeting of the OIC Executive Committee was held to address a recent incident in Stockholm, Sweden involving the destruction of an Islamic holy book. During that month the OIC welcomed the adoption by the UN Human Rights Council of a resolution (that had been proposed by OIC member states) titled 'Countering religious hatred constituting incitement to discrimination, hostility or violence'; the resolution condemned religious intolerance and the desecration of holy books. In late July the OIC Secretary-General suspended the status of Sweden's special envoy to the organization, asserting that legislative measures should be taken by that country to criminalize attacks on the Qur'an.

An OIC Plan of Action for the Advancement of Women in Member States was adopted in November 2016 by the sixth session of the Ministerial Conference on Women. The eighth Ministerial Conference, convened in July 2021, in Cairo, Egypt, urged member states to ensure that national social protection programmes were supporting people affected by the COVID-19 pandemic, including those working in the informal sector, and especially women and girls. The ninth Conference of Muslim Women Parliamentarians was organized in January 2020, in Ouagadougou, Burkina Faso.

In December 2012 the statute of a proposed OIC Women Development Organization (WDO) was opened for signature. The inaugural meeting of a OIC Women's Advisory Council was convened in May 2017, in İstanbul (Turkiye). In September the OIC Secretary-General and the Executive Director of UN Women signed a Memorandum of Understanding on Inter-Institutional Co-operation, to cover co-ordination on the advancement of women; the eradication of poverty; sustainable development; and the promotion of good governance and the rule of law.

The inaugural Ministerial Conference on Strengthening Marriage and the Family Institution and Preserving its Values in OIC Member States was convened in Jeddah, in February 2017. This issued the Jeddah Declaration, which emphasized the role of the family—defined as a bond between a man and a woman united through marriage within a *Shari'a* framework—as the grounding of the moral and religious character of individuals.

An OIC Strategy for the Empowerment of the Institution of Marriage and Family was being implemented during 2020–25.

The fourth session of the Islamic Conference of Ministers of Youth and Sports, convened in April 2018, in Baku (Azerbaijan), adopted an OIC Youth Strategy and an OIC Sports Strategy.

In October 2022 the 12th Islamic Conference of Information Ministers was convened, in İstanbul, on the theme 'Combating Disinformation and Islamophobia in the Post-Truth Era'.

HUMANITARIAN ASSISTANCE

OIC's Department of Humanitarian Affairs works to co-ordinate the delivery of emergency relief and rehabilitation assistance to Muslim communities affected by conflict or natural disasters. It also promotes efforts to strengthen disaster risk reduction and response strategies. In May 2016 an agreement was concluded between the

OIC and the Qatari authorities to establish a new OIC Humanitarian Funds secretariat in Doha (Qatar).

In September 2019 the Islamic Development Bank (IsDB) and UN Children's Fund (UNICEF) jointly established a Global Muslim Philanthropy Fund for Children (GMPFC), which was to enable various traditional forms of Muslim philanthropy—such as voluntary 'Sadaqah' donations, Waqf endowments, and obligatory 'Zakat' financing—to support IsDB and UNICEF emergency response and development initiatives in OIC member states. The OIC Secretary-General participated in the third Riyadh International Humanitarian Forum, hosted by Saudi Arabia in February 2023.

In September 2022 the OIC General Secretariat welcomed an agreement by the Islamic Development Bank and the UN High Commissioner for Refugees to establish a new Global Islamic Fund for Refugees.

In early February 2023 the OIC Secretary-General appealed to the organization's member states, institutions and partners to provide humanitarian support in the aftermath of earthquakes that had devastated areas of southern Türkiye and northern Syrian Arab Republic. Later in that month the OIC Secretary-General visited southern Türkiye.

SCIENCE AND TECHNOLOGY

The OIC supports education in Muslim communities, and was instrumental in the establishment of Islamic universities in Niger and Uganda, the American Islamic College of Chicago (USA), and the Islamic Solidarity Centre in Guinea-Bissau. In February 2023 the OIC Secretary-General urged the Islamic universities to develop a digital infrastructure that would modernize their learning environment.

The First Islamic Summit on Science and Technology, hosted by Kazakhstan in September 2017, at the level of heads of state and of government, adopted an OIC Science and Technology Agenda 2026 initiative. A Second Islamic Summit on Science and Technology, hosted by the UAE in a virtual format in June 2021, issued the Abu Dhabi Declaration on Science, Technology and Innovation: Opening New Horizons, which, *inter alia,* supported ongoing research by member states into vaccines, encouraged further innovation, and determined to boost investment in science, technology, engineering and mathematics (STEM) studies (with a particular focus on girls and women).

In March 2012 OIC ministers responsible for water approved the OIC Water Vision 2025, providing a framework for co-operation in maximizing the productive use of members' water resources. The inaugural meeting of an OIC Water Council was held in November 2017. In October 2019 the eighth Islamic Conference of Environment Ministers, convened in Rabat, Morocco, gave consideration to a Draft Strategy for the Activation of the Role of Cultural and Religious Factors in Protecting the Environment and Achieving Sustainable Development in the Islamic World.

In October 2013 Islamic ministers responsible for health, meeting in Jakarta, adopted the OIC Strategic Health Programme of Action, covering the period 2014–23, and also a plan providing a framework for focused national actions to enable the implementation of the Programme. In February 2014 the OIC inaugurated an Islamic International Advisory Group on Polio Eradication (its eighth session was held in December 2021). The First Meeting of OIC National Medication Regulatory Authorities was held in September 2018, in Indonesia. A voluntary civilian OIC humanitarian medical corps and an OIC internet health portal were developed in that year.

POLITICAL AFFAIRS

The OIC's Department of Political Affairs has divisions on African Affairs, Arab Affairs, Asian Affairs, International Organizations and the EU, and Muslim Communities and Minorities. It follows political developments in the Muslim world, oversees relations with non-OIC countries and organizations, promotes good governance, and monitors democratic elections. In the first seven months of 2023 OIC electoral observation teams monitored presidential and legislative elections that were held in Nigeria, and legislative elections in Djibouti (in February); a constitutional referendum in Uzbekistan (in April); and presidential elections in Uzbekistan (in July). Issues that affect Muslim communities in non-OIC member states are addressed. Support is extended to member countries in the areas of crisis management, conflict prevention, mediation and resolution, and peacebuilding, in accordance with resolutions of the Council of Foreign Ministers and Islamic Summit. An OIC Contact Group on Peace and Conflict Resolution was inaugurated by the 13th OIC summit in April 2016 (renamed the Contact Group on Peace and Dialogue in January 2019), and in May 2016 the first consultative session was convened of an OIC Wise Persons Council and group of Special Envoys of the Secretary-General, representing the guiding tier of a new OIC mechanism for conflict resolution and peacebuilding. The inaugural meeting of an OIC Contact Group of Friends of Mediation was held in September 2018. In March 2019 the Council of Foreign Ministers issued a resolution on enhancing the OIC's mediation capabilities. The Fourth OIC Conference on Mediation was convened in June 2022, in Jeddah.

The inaugural meeting within a consultation framework uniting the Secretaries-General of the OIC, the League of Arab States (Arab League), the Cooperation Council for the Arab States of the Gulf (GCC) and the Union of the Arab Maghreb was convened in September 2014. In August 2021 a meeting of the OIC and GCC Secretaries-General emphasized the importance of continuing co-operation between the two organizations.

Iraq: In October 2006, under OIC auspices, Iraqi representatives, meeting in Jeddah, at a conference known as Makkah I, signed the Makkah Agreement, a 10-point plan aimed at ending ongoing sectarian violence. The OIC Secretary-General repeatedly condemned atrocities committed in Iraq from 2014 by the militant organization Islamic State, and emphasized that the practices of the grouping bore no relation to Islamic principles. In September 2016 the OIC Secretary-General, meeting with the Special Representative of the UN Secretary-General on Iraq, addressed efforts by the OIC to convene a second conference in Makkah ('Makkah II'), aimed at facilitating reconciliation in Iraq. In December 2017, following a declaration by the Iraqi authorities that Islamic State had been defeated in Iraq, the OIC helped to organize a meeting tasked with generating ideas and policies that were addressed by a Conference on Reconstruction in Iraq that was convened in February 2018.

In October 2021 the OIC Secretary-General welcomed the organization of orderly legislative elections in Iraq. At the beginning of September 2022, urging restraint, the General Secretariat expressed great concern over an outbreak of violent protests in Baghdad that had been prompted by the resignation of a key political actor, in the context of continued failure to achieve agreement on the composition of a new government. The OIC Office in Iraq co-operates with the UN presence there.

Palestine and Israel: Since its inception the OIC has called for the vacation of Arab territories by Israel, recognition of the rights of Palestinians, and the restoration of Jerusalem to Arab rule.

In January 2009 an expanded extraordinary meeting of the Executive Committee, at ministerial level, convened to address the ongoing intensive bombardment of the Gaza Strip that was initiated by Israeli forces with the stated aim of ending rocket attacks launched by Hamas and other militant groups on Israeli targets. The meeting strongly condemned the Israeli attacks and ensuing destruction and loss of civilian life, and requested the OIC General Secretariat to co-ordinate with member states' civil society organizations to provide urgent humanitarian relief to the Palestinian people. In March, while visiting the affected area, the OIC Secretary-General urged the reconciliation of the different Palestinian political factions. In June 2010 an expanded extraordinary ministerial meeting of the Executive Committee condemned the attack by Israeli security forces, at the end of May, against a flotilla of vessels carrying humanitarian aid to Gaza, which had resulted in nine civilian deaths and caused injuries to at least 40 people. The OIC rejected a UN-commissioned report on the flotilla incident, released in September 2011, which—while concluding that the Israeli army had used 'excessive and unreasonable' force—also found the Israeli naval blockade of Gaza to have been imposed as a 'legitimate security measure' to prevent weapons from reaching Gaza by sea, and found that the flotilla had acted recklessly in attempting to breach the naval blockade. The OIC Secretary-General supported efforts to bring the issue of the blockade of Gaza before competent international legal authorities.

In February 2013 the 12th OIC summit issued a declaration which, *inter alia,* welcomed the decision, in November 2012, of the UN General Assembly to grant Palestine observer status at the UN.

In June 2014 OIC ministers responsible for foreign affairs adopted the Jeddah Declaration, which provided for the establishment of a Ministerial Contact Group on the Holy City of Al-Quds, urged support for a strategic plan to develop the city, and demanded urgent action on the Palestinian issue. The Declaration held Israel to be fully responsible for the impasse in the Middle East peace process, citing Israel's settlements policy, the Judaization of Al-Quds, the blockade, and reluctance to release Palestinian prisoners.

In July 2014 an expanded extraordinary meeting of the Executive Committee was convened, at the level of ministers responsible for foreign affairs, to address ongoing intense insecurity between Gaza and Israel. The OIC ministers urged that emergency sessions of the UN Security Council and UN Human Rights Council be convened to examine the ongoing Israeli actions against Palestine (under an air, sea and land military operation known as Protective Edge), and to provide necessary protection for the Palestinian people. Furthermore, the meeting demanded that the international community designate the leaderships of 'extreme' nationalistic Israeli settler communities as terrorists and criminals wanted for international prosecution. An international legal team was to be constituted within the OIC to pursue the issue of conducting criminal cases against Israeli leaders at the International Criminal Court (ICC). In early August the OIC Secretary-General condemned attacks by the Israeli military against mosques in Gaza. In mid-August a second expanded OIC extraordinary ministerial meeting on the Gaza situation was convened, in Jeddah. The meeting welcomed a recent decision of the UN Human Rights Council to appoint an independent international commission to investigate violations of international humanitarian law in the occupied Palestinian territories, while expressing deep regret at the USA's rejection of this resolution, and the abstention of some European countries. On 26 August, as a result of indirect negotiations between Hamas and Israel, mediated by Egypt, the two sides concluded an agreement on a long-term truce in Gaza. In early September an OIC multi-party delegation undertook a fact-finding field tour of Gaza to assess the extent of the damage sustained under the Israeli bombardment against targets that included residential homes, civilian facilities, farming areas, and local infrastructure. During that month the OIC Secretary-General condemned Israel's confiscation of 400 ha of Palestinian land in the West Bank, near Bethlehem, and emphasized that the Israeli policy of expanding settlements on confiscated land was in violation of relevant international law and resolutions.

The fifth Extraordinary Islamic Summit on Palestine and Al-Quds Al-Sharif, convened under OIC auspices in March 2016, in Jakarta, Indonesia, discussed actions by Israel to alter the demographic profile and eliminate the Islamic identity of areas under its control. An OIC Representative Office in Palestine (Ramallah) was inaugurated in June. In August 2017 an extraordinary meeting of OIC foreign ministers—held in response to violent unrest that had followed the murder, by armed Palestinians, of two Israeli police officers in mid-July, close to the al-Aqsa Mosque in Jerusalem—strongly condemned recent actions by Israel, citing, *inter alia*, an attempt to install metal detectors at the al-Aqsa Mosque compound, its temporary closure, and the development of legislation aimed at effectively altering the demographic composition of Jerusalem. In December the OIC denounced as contrary to international law and as a provocation to Muslim sentiments a recent decision by US President Trump to recognize Jerusalem as the capital of Israel. An extraordinary summit meeting (the OIC's sixth such gathering), convened in Istanbul, declared that the decision lacked any legitimacy and urged the international community to recognize East Jerusalem as the Palestinian capital.

The OIC Secretary-General strongly condemned the Israeli military's suppression at the end of March 2018 of a 'Great March of Return' demonstration by Palestinians, which had resulted in the deaths of at least 16 Palestinian protesters. In mid-May, at the request of Turkey (known as Türkiye from June 2022), the Seventh Extraordinary Islamic Summit Conference in Response to the Grave Developments in the State of Palestine was convened, in İstanbul. The summit condemned in the strongest terms the actions of Israeli troops in Palestine, and held Israel fully accountable for the killing of at least 60 Palestinian civilians attending a protest in Gaza against the relocation in that month of the US embassy from Tel Aviv to Jerusalem (the decision of the US Administration to move its embassy to Jerusalem was deemed to have further emboldened the Israeli Government in its policy towards Palestinian civilians). The summit called on the UN to investigate recent events in Gaza, and called on the OIC General Secretariat promptly to establish an international independent committee of experts to consider the situation, to determine the culpability of Israeli officials, and to report its findings to relevant international bodies. The summit declared the inauguration of the US embassy in Jerusalem to be an act of provocation and hostility against the (Muslim) Ummah, Palestinian national rights and international law.

In July 2018 the OIC Secretary-General condemned legislation recently adopted by the Israeli Knesset that defined Israel as 'the Nation-State of the Jewish People'. He urged the international community to reject the law as discriminatory, noting that it represented disregard for the established historical rights of local Palestinians, Muslims and Christians.

In March 2019 the OIC Council of Foreign Ministers determined to establish a new Waqf (endowment) Fund to Support Palestine Refugees. Later in that month the OIC General Secretariat condemned the recognition by the US Administration of Israeli sovereignty over the occupied Syrian Golan territory, emphasizing that this constituted an explicit violation of relevant international law and UN resolutions. In May the OIC summit meeting urged member states to impose sanctions against countries that join the USA in recognizing Jerusalem as the Israeli capital. In July an extraordinary OIC open-ended ministerial meeting was convened to address an intensification of Israeli actions aimed at the Judaization of Al-Quds—including altering the city's legal status, isolating it from its Palestinian hinterground, and repeated interferences with the al-Aqsa mosque. An extraordinary meeting of the OIC Council was organized in September, at the request of Saudi Arabia, to address and condemn the recently stated intent of the Israeli Prime Minister to impose Israeli sovereignty on the whole of the Jordan Valley, northern Dead Sea area, and on the West Bank, should he be re-elected at ongoing legislative elections. At that time the OIC Secretary-General called for the international community to put in place political and legal mechanisms to hold Israel accountable for its violations of international law and to protect the Palestinian people and their lands. The Secretary-General condemned as biased a proposal made in January 2020 by the US Administration for ending Palestinian–Israeli differences. In February he welcomed the publication of a UN list of businesses engaged in activities relating to illegal Israeli settlements, and strongly condemned the Israeli authorities for approving a scheme to construct thousands of new housing units in Jerusalem. In May the Secretary-General approved a report by the Prosecutor of the ICC which confirmed her position that the Court did have jurisdiction over the Palestinian Territories. An extraordinary (virtual) meeting of OIC ministers responsible for foreign affairs that was held in June, at the request of Palestine, warned against 'dangerous' intentions by Israel to annex parts of Palestine, and emphasized Palestine's continuing right to sovereignty over territory occupied by Israel since 1967. The meeting urged the international community to counter Israel's 'colonial practices' that were contravening the rules-based international order. In late August, reiterating support for the 2002 Arab peace initiative, and affirming the illegality of any unilateral attempt by Israel to annex Palestinian lands, the Secretary-General stated that the situation of Palestine and Al-Quds (Jerusalem) was the OIC's 'pivotal cause', and was at the core of joint Islamic action. Under an arrangement concluded in mid-August 2020 by Israel and the UAE—which was aimed at normalizing bilateral diplomatic relations, and had been negotiated under US auspices—Israel agreed temporarily, but not definitively, to suspend the annexation of West Bank territory from Palestine. Formal agreements on normalizing relations with Israel were signed by both the UAE and Bahrain on 15 September, in Washington, DC, USA.

In February 2021 the OIC General Secretariat welcomed a ruling by a Pre-Trial Chamber of the ICC that the Court's territorial scope extended to Gaza and the West Bank, including East Al-Quds (Jerusalem). In mid-May a virtual open-ended extraordinary meeting of OIC ministers responsible for foreign affairs condemned in the strongest terms ongoing attacks by Israel against the Palestinian people, land and holy sites. The OIC General Secretariat welcomed an Egypt-mediated ceasefire agreement that took effect on 21 May.

In December 2021 an extraordinary meeting of the Council of Foreign Ministers, held in Islamabad (Pakistan), reiterated unequivocal condemnation of all illegal measures taken by Israel to 'colonize' Palestinian territory, including constructing settlement blocks in and around Al-Quds (Jerusalem), and confiscating and demolishing Palestinians' properties, for example in the neighbourhoods of Silwan and Sheikh Jarrah. The Council restated the need to achieve a just, lasting peace rooted in international law, and called on the UN Security Council to bring Israel to account, including through the imposition of sanctions. In February 2022 the OIC General Secretariat condemned 'incessant' attacks perpetrated against Palestinian citizens, as part of a policy of Judaization, by extremist settler groups and Israeli forces, with the aim of seizing Palestinian homes in Sheikh Jarrah. At an emergency meeting of the Council convened in April the OIC Secretary-General condemned all attempts to impose temporal and spatial division on the al-Aqsa Mosque, and called for an unprecedented mobilization of efforts to protect Al-Quds and its holy sites. In October the OIC General Secretariat welcomed the conclusion by Palestinian factions, following an Algeria-sponsored dialogue, of the Algeria Declaration of National Reconciliation. At the end of 2022 the General Secretariat welcomed resolutions recently adopted by the UN General Assembly relating to Palestine, and in particular one that requested the International Court of Justice to issue an Advisory Opinion on the legal status and the consequences of Israel's occupation of Palestinian territory.

In early January 2023 an extraordinary open-ended session of the OIC Executive Committee strongly condemned a provocative visit to the al-Aqsa Mosque undertaken by Itamar Ben-Gvir, the hard-line Israeli Minister of National Security (described by the Committee as a 'minister in the Israeli colonial occupation cabinet'). The Committee demanded that the UN Security Council act urgently to end the all provocative and illegal Israeli measures and policies imposed on the mosque and more broadly on Al-Quds. Meeting in late February a further extraordinary open-ended session of the Executive Committee addressed an ongoing escalation of aggression by Israel against Palestine, including an Israel Defense Forces (IDF) raid on 22 February that, while targeting three Palestinian militants in Nablus, had killed in total 11 Palestinians, and injured many more. The UN Security Council was urged to take all necessary measures to ensure the protection of the Palestinian people, and the ICC was requested to hold Israel to account. The OIC Secretary-General emphasized that Israel's impunity was prolonging its present policies towards Palestine. In early March the General Secretariat condemned the killing by the IDF of at least six Palestinians in a refugee camp at Jenin (West Bank). Continuing acts of violence perpetrated by extremist settlers in the West Bank town of Hawara were also deplored. A further extraordinary meeting of the OIC Executive Committee that was convened in May emphasized the status of the entire area of the al-Aqsa Mosque and al-Haram Al-Sharif (Temple Mount), as a 'pure place of worship for Muslims'. In June the OIC General Secretariat accused Israel of conducting an indiscriminate open war against residential areas of the town of Jenin and its refugee camp, and strongly condemned a recent Israeli decision to shorten settlement construction procedures. In early July the General Secretariat strongly condemned a new major Israeli operation in the West Bank (reportedly the largest there for two decades)—Israeli forces having launched a massive aerial raid against the Jenin camp, that involved at least 10 drone strikes and an estimated 2,000 troops. Every year on 5 June the OIC marks the Naksa Day, the anniversary of Israel's occupation of Palestinian and Arab territory.

Syrian Arab Republic: In December 2011 the OIC Executive Committee convened a ministerial open-ended meeting to address the violent unrest that had prevailed since March in Syria. The OIC Secretary-General strongly condemned the mass killings of civilians perpetrated by Syrian security forces in May–July 2012. An emergency OIC summit, convened in Makkah, Saudi Arabia, in August, determined to suspend Syria from participation in the activities of the organization and from all its subsidiary organs and specialized and affiliated institutions. The meeting demanded the immediate implementation of a UN-Arab League peace plan that had been agreed in March by the Syrian authorities and opposition, but was not being observed, and urged the UN Security Council to take measures to end the ongoing violence and to pursue a peaceful and lasting solution to the Syrian crisis. Syria's suspension from the OIC was opposed by Iran. In February 2013 the 12th OIC summit urged a Syrian-led negotiated solution to the ongoing conflict, and reaffirmed support to the UN-Arab League Joint Special Representative on Syria. In mid-September the OIC Secretary-General welcomed the release of the report by a UN weapons inspection team into the deployment, on 21 August, of chemical weapons against civilians in Damascus, Syria, that had caused an estimated 1,400 fatalities. Condemning the incident as a war crime and crime against humanity, he emphasized the need to hold to account any party involved in the production, transfer, development and use of chemical weapons in Syria. In December an OIC-sponsored Centre for the Treatment of Psychological and Social Shocks was inaugurated in Kayleis, Turkey, to support Syrian refugees in that country. In January 2014 the OIC Secretary-General addressed the Geneva II Syrian peace talks, urging an immediate ceasefire and the creation of a national transitional government. In February 2016 the OIC Secretary-General expressed concern at the stalling of Syrian peace talks in Geneva, Switzerland. In the following month he welcomed a decision by Russia partially to withdraw troops from Syria, and indicated that this would have a positive impact on the negotiations process. In early August the OIC Secretary-General condemned in the strongest terms the high numbers of civilian fatalities and injuries that were occurring as a result of military operations being undertaken in Aleppo by the Syrian Government and allied forces. He stressed that the international community should intervene urgently to halt air raids and the shelling of civilians, and to facilitate the delivery of humanitarian assistance to blockaded areas Syria. He also urged the swift resumption of the UN-guided process to find a political solution in Syria. Shortly afterwards, he issued a message to the Russian minister responsible for foreign affairs, in which he noted that the OIC was following with profound concern the deteriorating situation in Syria, and urged concerted diplomatic efforts towards promptly resolving the crisis in Syria. In late September the OIC Secretary-General again strongly condemned the continued bombing of civilians in Aleppo, and denounced the shelling of humanitarian aid convoys by Syrian Government and allied forces. He stated that these were war crimes for which the Syrian regime ought to be held accountable. Following the entry into effect in December of a ceasefire in Syria, facilitated by Russia, Turkey and Iran, the OIC welcomed several rounds of talks addressing the crisis in Syria that were subsequently organized by those three countries. The OIC also supported the continuation of the UN-supported Geneva-based negotiations process. In early April 2017 the OIC Secretary-General strongly condemned a reported chemical attack against the north-western Syrian settlement of Khan Sheikhoun. In February 2018 he demanded the immediate cessation of raids by the Syrian and allied militaries on civilian residential areas in Idlib and Ghouta. The OIC has participated in meetings of the International Syria Support Group. The OIC Secretary-General repeatedly condemned the destruction by Islamic State of historical monuments in both Syria and Iraq.

Yemen: In March 2015 the OIC Secretary-General expressed support for international efforts to promote constitutional legitimacy in Yemen, in view of ongoing activities being perpetrated by the Shi'a secessionist Ansar Allah ('Houthi') rebel grouping that were aimed at overthrowing government institutions. In May the OIC Secretary-General welcomed the adoption by Yemeni stakeholders of the 'Riyadh Declaration' urging the resumption of the legitimate political process. An OIC Contact Group on Yemen met for the first time in October, in New York. In April 2016 the 13th OIC summit reiterated continued support for the GCC initiative and UN-sponsored peace efforts in Yemen. In August the OIC Secretary-General met the Special Envoy of the UN Secretary-General for Yemen to consider means of strengthening relevant OIC-UN political and humanitarian joint action. Both sides agreed that a special conference should be held to address the provision of humanitarian and development assistance to Yemen. An extraordinary session of OIC foreign ministers was held in November to address the launching by Houthi militia in Yemen of a long-range ballistic missile in the direction of Makkah, Saudi Arabia. In May 2017 the OIC Secretary-General strongly condemned a missile attack against a mosque in Ma'rib, Yemen, which had caused significant fatalities. An emergency meeting of the OIC Council of Foreign Ministers was held in January 2018 to address the Houthi militant campaign against Saudi Arabia. In August the OIC Secretary-General condemned the alleged targeting by Houthi militia of international trade and maritime navigation in the Red Sea's Bab al-Mandab strait; he also deplored recent alleged Houthi attacks on two Saudi Arabian oil tankers. The OIC welcomed advances made during peace talks between the parties to the conflict that were mediated in Sweden by the UN Special Envoy in December, and in which they formally agreed to observe a ceasefire in the port city of Hodeidah (Hudaydah), and for a phased Houthi withdrawal from that area. In early September 2019 the OIC Secretary-General restated the OIC's support for the efforts of the Saudi-led Arab coalition to defeat the Houthi militias and Yemeni terrorist groupings. He welcomed a recent joint Saudi-UAE statement on the promotion of the 'Jeddah Dialogue' between the legitimate Yemeni authorities and the separatist Southern Transitional Council (STC) which had taken control during August of the southern Yemen port city of Aden. On 5 November the Jeddah Dialogue culminated in the signature of the Riyadh Agreement, with provisions covering security, military and political issues. These included the establishment of a national unity government to represent, on an equal basis, southern and northern Yemen and for the national Government to return to Aden without obstructions. In October 2021, when strongly condemning as 'despicable' a terrorist attack in Aden that had targeted a convoy of senior government members, the OIC General Secretariat urged the full implementation of the Riyadh Agreement. During 2017–early 2022 the OIC Secretary-General deplored repeated Houthi long-range ballistic missile launches against Saudi Arabia, and all targeting of civilians and civilian infrastructure. In January 2022 the OIC strongly condemned a Houthi terrorist assault against the airport in Abu Dhabi, UAE. In March the OIC Secretary-General welcomed a decision by the UN Security Council to designate Ansar Allah (the Houthis) as a terrorist group. The OIC Secretary-General attended GCC-hosted UN-mediated Yemeni-Yemeni consultations that were convened in Riyadh in late March–early April, and urged all Yemeni stakeholders to pursue a comprehensive political solution to the conflict; the UN Special Envoy to Yemen announced at the beginning of April that agreement on a truce had been reached, to take effect on 2 April. The OIC General Secretariat welcomed the extension of the truce by two months from 2 June. A further two-month extension was agreed in August, until 2 October.

Combating Terrorism: In December 1994 OIC heads of state adopted a Code of Conduct for Combating International Terrorism, and an OIC Convention on Combating International Terrorism was adopted in 1998. In April 2009 the heads of law enforcement agencies in OIC member states, gathered in Baku, adopted the Baku Declaration on co-operation in combating transnational organized crime, including international terrorism, extremism, aggressive separatism and human trafficking. The OIC has repeatedly urged the worldwide adoption of a clear definition of terrorism. In April 2016 the 13th OIC summit emphasized the need to draft a comprehensive Islamic strategy to combat terrorism and extremism, and for the OIC to play a leading role in global action to avert extremism.

Finance

The OIC's activities are financed by mandatory contributions from member states.

Subsidiary Organs

International Islamic Fiqh Academy: Al Madinah Al Munawarah Rd, Al Faisaliyyah, Jeddah 23442, Saudi Arabia; tel. (12) 690-0347; fax (12) 257-5661; e-mail info@iifa-aifi.org; internet www.iifa-aifi.org; f. 1983; concerned with the study and evolution of Islamic jurisprudence; 57 states; Gen. Sec. Prof. KOUTOUB MOUSTAPHA SANO.

Islamic Centre for Development of Trade: Tour des Habous, ave des FAR, 20000 Casablanca, Morocco; tel. (52) 2314974; fax (52) 2310110; e-mail icdt@icdt-oic.org; internet www.icdt-cidc.org;

f. 1983; supports regular commercial contacts, harmonizes policies and promotes investments among OIC mems; 57 mem. states; Dir-Gen. LATIFA EL BOUADELLAOUI; pubs *Tijaris: International and Inter-Islamic Trade Magazine* (every 2 months), *Inter-Islamic Trade Report* (annually).

Islamic Solidarity Fund: Abbas al-Halawani, AR Rawdah District, Jeddah 23434, Saudi Arabia; tel. (12) 698-1296; fax (12) 256-8185; e-mail mail@isf-fsi.org; internet www.isf-fsi.org; f. 1974; aims to meet the needs of Islamic communities by providing emergency aid and the funds to build mosques, Islamic centres, hospitals, schools and univs; in March 2022 helped to initiate the Global Islamic Fund for Refugees; Exec. Dir Dr HIBA AHMED.

Islamic University of Technology (IUT): Board Bazar, Gazipur 1704, Dhaka, Bangladesh; tel. (2) 9291254; fax (2) 9291260; e-mail vc@iut-dhaka.edu; internet www.iutoic-dhaka.edu; f. 1981 as the Islamic Centre for Technical and Vocational Training and Research, named changed to Islamic Institute of Technology in 1994, present name adopted in 2001; aims to develop human resources in OIC mem. states, with special reference to engineering, technology and technical education; 57 mem. states; Vice-Chancellor Prof. MOHAMMAD RAFIQUL ISLAM (Bangladesh); pubs *Journal of Engineering and Technology* (quarterly), *News Bulletin* (annually), *News Letter* (6 a year), annual calendar and announcement for admission, reports, human resources development series.

Research Centre for Islamic History, Art and Culture (IRCICA): Alemdar Cad. 15, Bâbıâlî Girişi, 34110 Cağaloğlu Fatih, İstanbul, Türkiye; tel. (212) 4020000; e-mail ircica@ircica.org; internet www.ircica.org; f. 1979; organizes regional congresses in Asia, Africa, the Middle East and Europe; Dir-Gen. Prof. Dr MAHMUD EROL KILIÇ; pubs *Newsletter* (3 a year), monographical studies.

Statistical, Economic and Social Research and Training Centre for Islamic Countries (SESRIC): Kudüs Cad. No. 9, Diplomatik Site, 0645 Ankara, Türkiye; tel. (312) 4686172; fax (312) 4673458; e-mail oicankara@sesric.org; internet www.sesric.org; f. 1978; SESRIC's mandate is to collate, process and disseminate socioeconomic statistics and information on, and for the utilization of, its mem. countries; to study and assess economic and social devts in mem. countries with the aim of helping to generate proposals for advancing co-operation; and to organize training activities; the Centre also acts as a focal point for technical co-operation activities between the OIC system and related UN agencies, and prepares economic and social reports and background documentation for OIC meetings; Dir-Gen. ZÜMRÜT ZEHRA (Türkiye); pubs *Statistical Yearbook on OIC Member Countries*, *Journal of Economic Cooperation* (quarterly), *OIC Economic Outlook* (annually).

Specialized Institutions

Islamic Organization for Food Security (IOFS): Astana, Kazakhstan; tel. (72) 999900; fax (72) 999975; e-mail info@iofs.org.kz; internet www.iofs.org.kz; f. 2013; aims to co-ordinate, provide technical advice on, and implement OIC policies on agriculture, rural devt and food security; also tasked with mobilizing financial resources for developing agriculture and enhancing food security in OIC mem. states; in Sept. 2017 concluded a co-operation framework with the Arab Organization for Agricultural Development; in Oct. 2021 the 8th OIC Ministerial Conference on Food Security and Agricultural Development tasked the IOFS with establishing an OIC Food Security Reserve System; Dir-Gen. YERLAN A. BAIDAULET.

Islamic World Educational, Scientific and Cultural Organization (ICESCO): BP 2275, Rabat 10104, Morocco; tel. (5) 37566052; e-mail pcontact@icesco.org; internet icesco.org; f. 1982 as Islamic Educational, Scientific and Cultural Org., present name adopted in 2020; mems: 54 states; Dir-Gen. SALIM BIN MOHAMMED AL-MALIK (Saudi Arabia); pubs *ICESCO Newsletter* (quarterly), *ICESCO Journal of Science and Technology*, *The Societies We Want*.

OIC States Broadcasting Union (OSBU): POB 6351, Jeddah 21442, Saudi Arabia; tel. (12) 672-1121; e-mail osbu@osbu-oic.org; internet www.osbu-oic.org; f. 1975, as the Islamic Broadcasting Union; an OSBU Academy was launched in Feb. 2023; Pres. Dr AMR AL-LAITHI.

OIC Union of News Agencies (OIC-UNA): POB 5054, Jeddah 21422, Saudi Arabia; tel. (12) 665-2056; fax (12) 665-9358; e-mail Info@una-oic.org; internet www.iinanews.org; f. 1972 as the International Islamic News Agency (IINA), present name adopted in 2017; distributes news and reports daily on events, in Arabic, English and French; mems: 57 countries; Dir-Gen. MOHAMMED AL-YAMI (Saudi Arabia).

Science, Technology and Innovation Organization (STIO): c/o COMSTECH Secretariat, 33 Constitution Ave, G-5/2, Islamabad, Pakistan; tel. (51) 9220681; fax (51) 9211115; e-mail comstech@comstech.org; internet www.comstech.org; f. 2010; mandated to implement science, technology and innovation (STI)-related resolutions and decisions, in accordance with the provisions of the OIC Charter; promotes STI activities in mem. states and co-operation and co-ordination between states; maintains an OIC Technology and Innovation Portal; Dir-Gen. (and CEO of COMSTECH) Dr M. IQBAL CHOUDHARY (Pakistan).

The Islamic Development Bank is also an OIC Specialized Institution.

Affiliated Institutions

Islamic Chamber of Commerce, Industry and Agriculture: POB 3831, Clifton, Karachi 75600, Pakistan; tel. (21) 35874910; fax (21) 35870765; e-mail info@iccia.com; internet iccia.com; f. 1979; aims to promote trade and industry among mem. states; comprises national chambers or feds of chambers of commerce and industry; mems: 57; Pres. ABDULLAH SALEH ABDULLAH KAMEL; Sec.-Gen. YOUSEF HASAN KHALAWI.

Islamic Committee of the International Crescent: POB 17434, Benghazi, Libya; tel. (61) 2238080; fax (61) 2220037; e-mail info@icic-oic.org; internet icic-oic.org; f. 1979; aims to attempt to alleviate the suffering caused by natural disasters and war; from 2020 extended humanitarian support to efforts to control the COVID-19 emergency in Libya, Palestine, Syria and Yemen; Pres. ALI MAHMOUD BUHEDMA (Libya); Exec. Dir MOHAMED H. ELASBALI.

Islamic Solidarity Sports Federation: 8535 al Wadi, Ar Rafiah, Riyadh 12752, Saudi Arabia; tel. (11) 480-8986; fax (11) 482-2145; e-mail info@issf.sa; internet issf.sa; f. 1980; organizes the Islamic Solidarity Games (Aug. 2022: Konya, Türkiye); mems: 57 National Olympic Cttees; Pres. Prince ABDULAZIZ BIN TURKI AL-FAISAL (Saudi Arabia); Sec.-Gen. NASSER AYMAN HAZZA MAJALI (Jordan).

OIC Computer Emergency Response Team (OIC-CERT): c/o CyberSecurity Malaysia, Level 7, Tower 1 Cyber Axis Tower Jalan Impact 63000 Cyberjaya Selangor Darul Ehsan, Malaysia; e-mail secretariat@oic-cert.org; internet www.oic-cert.org; f. 2009; aims to promote the exchange of information, to prevent cyberterrorism and computer crimes, and to advance education and technological research and devt; mems: 27.

Organization of Islamic Capitals and Cities (OICC): POB 13621, Jeddah, Saudi Arabia; tel. (12) 698-1953; fax (12) 698-1053; e-mail webmaster@oicc.org; internet oicc.org; f. 1980; aims to preserve the identity and the heritage of Islamic capitals and cities; to achieve and enhance sustainable devt in mem. capitals and cities; to establish and develop comprehensive urban norms, systems and plans to serve the growth and prosperity of Islamic capitals and cities and to enhance their cultural, environmental, urban, economic and social conditions; to advance municipal services and facilities; to support mem. cities' capacity-building progs; and to consolidate fellowship between mems and co-ordinate the scope of co-operation; mems: 141 capitals and cities, 8 observer mems and 14 assoc. mems, in 54 countries across Asia, Africa, Europe and South America; Sec.-Gen. OMAR BIN ABDULLAH KADI.

Other OIC-affiliated institutions are: the Association of Tax Authorities of Islamic Countries; Federation of Consultants from Islamic Countries; General Council for Islamic Banks and Financial Institutions; International Association of Islamic Banks; International Islamic University Malaysia; Islamic Conference Youth Forum for Dialogue and Cooperation; International Union of Muslim Scouts; Islamic World Academy of Sciences; Organisation of Islamic Cooperation Broadcasting Regulatory Authorities Forum; Organization of the Islamic Shipowners' Association; Real Estate Union in Islamic States; Standards and Metrology Institute for Islamic Countries; and the World Federation of Arab-Islamic Schools.

REGIONAL ORGANIZATIONS *Organization of the Petroleum Exporting Countries*

ORGANIZATION OF THE PETROLEUM EXPORTING COUNTRIES—OPEC

Address: Helferstorferstr. 17, 1010 Vienna, Austria.
Telephone: (1) 211-12-3303; **fax:** (1) 216-43-20; **e-mail:** prid@opec.org; **internet:** www.opec.org.

OPEC was established in 1960, by Iran, Iraq, Kuwait, Saudi Arabia and Venezuela. It aims to unify and co-ordinate members' petroleum policies and to safeguard their interests, as well as to stabilize the global petroleum market.

MEMBERS

Algeria	Iran	Nigeria
Angola	Iraq	Saudi Arabia
Congo, Republic	Kuwait	United Arab Emirates
Equatorial Guinea	Libya	Venezuela
Gabon		

Note: Ecuador, having become a member in 1973 withdrew from OPEC in 1992 and Gabon (1975) did so in 1996. Angola became a member in 2007, while Ecuador rejoined in the same year. Indonesia withdrew from OPEC in 2009; having requested, in September 2015, that it rejoin the organization, its membership was reactivated on 1 January 2016. However, following the decision by the Conference in late November to limit production output, Indonesia announced that it was suspending its membership with immediate effect. In June ministers agreed to a request from Gabon that it be readmitted as a full member. Equatorial Guinea was admitted into the organization in May 2017. The Republic of the Congo was admitted as the 15th member in June 2018. Qatar, a member since 1961, withdrew from OPEC in January 2019, reportedly owing to a strategic realignment of its energy policy towards natural gas production, as well as ongoing diplomatic tensions with Saudi Arabia. On 1 January 2020 Ecuador, citing reasons related to the pursuit of fiscal sustainability, left the organization for the second time.

Organization
(September 2023)

CONFERENCE

The Conference is the supreme authority of the organization, responsible for the formulation of its general policy. It consists of representatives of member countries, who examine reports and recommendations submitted by the Board of Governors. It approves the appointment of governors from each country and elects the Chairman of the Board of Governors. It works on the unanimity principle, and normally meets at least twice a year. The Conference Presidency is rotated on an annual basis (2023: Equatorial Guinea).

BOARD OF GOVERNORS

The Board directs the management of OPEC; it implements resolutions of the Conference and draws up an annual budget. It consists of one governor for each member country, and meets at least twice a year.

JOINT MINISTERIAL MONITORING COMMITTEE

Comprising representatives of three OPEC member states (Algeria, Kuwait and Venezuela) and two non-member states (the Russian Federation and Oman), the Committee was established in January 2017 to oversee implementation of the decision on oil production of the 171st (November 2016) OPEC Conference, and the related Declaration of Cooperation made in December by 11 non-member states. (Following the accession of Equatorial Guinea to OPEC in 2017, 10 non-OPEC member states upheld the Declaration.) A subsidiary Joint OPEC-Non-OPEC Technical Committee presents to the JMMC a monthly data report on combined production. The JMMC also facilitates the exchange of joint forecasts and analyses. In October 2022 the Committee agreed to amend the frequency of meetings from monthly to every two months.

SECRETARIAT

Secretary-General: HAITHAM AL-GHAIS (Kuwait).

Office of the Secretary-General: provides the Secretary-General with executive assistance in maintaining contacts with governments, organizations and delegations, in matters of protocol and in the preparation for and co-ordination of meetings; Head SHAKIR MAHMOUD A. AL-RIFAIEY.

Legal Office: provides legal advice, supervises the Secretariat's legal commitments, evaluates legal issues of concern to the organization and member countries, and recommends appropriate action; General Legal Counsel LEONARDO SEMPÉRTEGUI.

Research Division: comprises the Data Services Department (including an Information Centre); the Energy Studies Department; the Petroleum Studies Department; and an Environmental Matters Unit; Dir Dr AYED S. AL-QAHTANI (Saudi Arabia).

Support Services Division: provides the required infrastructure and services to the whole Secretariat, in support of its programmes; comprises departments of: Administration and IT; Finance and Human Resources; and Public Relations and Information.

Activities

OPEC's principal objectives, according to its Statute, are to co-ordinate and unify the petroleum policies of member countries and to determine the best means of safeguarding their individual and collective interests; to devise means of ensuring the stabilization of prices in international oil markets, with a view to eliminating harmful and unnecessary fluctuations; and to provide a steady income to the producing countries, an efficient, economic and regular supply of petroleum to consuming nations, and a fair return on capital to those investing in the petroleum industry. In 2021 OPEC's share of world crude petroleum production was 33.1% (compared with 54.7% in 1974). OPEC members possessed 80.4% of the world's total known crude petroleum reserves at the end of 2021. In 2020 OPEC members also possessed 36% of known reserves of natural gas, and accounted for 16.4% of total production of marketed natural gas.

In November 2016 the Conference adopted its third Long-Term Strategy, setting objectives relating to, *inter alia,* member countries' petroleum revenues, market stability, global demand, share in world oil supply, and future energy demand. (The first such Strategy had been adopted in September 2005.)

PRICES AND PRODUCTION

On 31 August 2023 the OPEC Reference Basket (ORB) price stood at US $88.44, compared with $128.27 on 9 March 2022, $71.67 on 1 December 2021, and $54.38 on 1 January 2021. In 2023 the ORB price was based on the following crude oils: Saharan Blend (Algeria), Girassol (Angola), Djeno (Republic of the Congo), Zafiro (Equatorial Guinea), Rabi Light (Gabon), Iran Heavy (Islamic Republic of Iran), Basra Medium (Iraq), Kuwait Export (Kuwait), Es Sider (Libya), Bonny Light (Nigeria), Arab Light (Saudi Arabia) and Murban (UAE), and Merey (Venezuela).

1980–99: In March 1982 an emergency meeting of ministers responsible for petroleum agreed (for the first time in OPEC's history) to defend the organization's price structure by imposing an overall production 'ceiling' (initially 18m. b/d). Quotas were allocated for each member country except Saudi Arabia, which was to act as a 'swing producer' to supply the balancing quantities to meet market requirements. During 1985, however, most members effectively abandoned the marker price system. In August 1986 all members except Iraq agreed upon a return to production quotas (Iraq declined to co-operate after its request to be allocated the same quota as Iran had been refused). In December members (except Iraq) agreed to return, with effect from 1 February 1987, to a fixed pricing system, at a level of US $18 per barrel as the OPEC Reference Basket (ORB) price (based on a 'basket' of, then, seven crudes, not, as hitherto, on a 'marker' crude, Arab Light). A total production limit of 15.8m. b/d was set. OPEC's role of setting crude oil prices had come to an end, however, and from the late 1980s prices were determined by movements in the international markets, with OPEC's role being to increase or restrain production in order to prevent harmful fluctuations in prices.

In August 1990 Iraq invaded Kuwait (which it had accused, among other grievances, of violating production quotas). Petroleum exports by the two countries were halted by an international embargo, and OPEC ministers promptly allowed an increase in production by other members to stabilize rising prices. In 1993 a Ministerial Monitoring Sub-committee was established to supervise compliance with quotas, owing to members' persistent over production. In July of that year discussions between Iraq and the United Nations (UN) on the possible supervised resumption of Iraqi petroleum exports depressed petroleum prices to below US $16 per barrel, and at the end of the year prices fell below $14, after the Conference rejected any further reduction in the current limit of 24.5m. b/d, which remained in force during 1994 and 1995, although actual output continued to be well in excess of quotas. In May 1996 the UN and Iraq concluded an agreement allowing Iraq to resume exports of petroleum in order to fund humanitarian relief efforts within Iraq, and OPEC's overall production ceiling was raised, accordingly, to 25.0m. b/d from June. Prices declined during the first half of 1997; an escalation in political tension in the Gulf region, however, and in particular Iraq's reluctance to co-operate with UN weapons inspectors, prompted a price increase to about $21.2 per barrel in October. The overall production ceiling was raised to 27.5m. b/d, with effect from the beginning of 1998, but during that year prices declined and OPEC imposed a succession of reductions in output. Non-member countries concluded agreements with OPEC to limit their production, and in March 1999 Mexico, Norway, Oman and Russia agreed to decrease production by a total of 388,000 b/d, while OPEC's own production limit was reduced to 22.97m. b/d. Evidence of almost 90% compliance with the new production quotas contributed to market confidence that stockpiles of petroleum would be reduced, and resulted in sustained price increases during the second half of the year.

2000–15: In September 2000 OPEC heads of state and of government, convened at their first summit meeting since 1975, issued the Caracas Declaration, in which they resolved to promote market stability through their policies on pricing and production, to increase co-operation with other petroleum exporters, and to improve communication with consumer countries. From 2001 overall production was limited to 24.2m. b/d, with a further reduction of 1m. b/d from 1 September. Terrorist attacks in the USA in September gave rise to market uncertainty and a further decline in prices. In December the Conference announced a reduction in output (to 21.7m. b/d) from 1 January 2002, provided that non-OPEC producers also reduced their output, which they agreed to do by 462,500 b/d. From 1 January 2003 the production ceiling was raised to 23m. b/d, but stricter compliance with individual quotas equated to a reduction in actual output, and prices rose above the target range. In January the Conference agreed to raise the production ceiling to 24.5m. b/d from 1 February, and in March (when Venezuelan production resumed after industrial action) members agreed to make up from their available excess capacities any shortfall that might result following US-led military action against Iraq. In the event, the war on Iraq that commenced later in that month led to such a rapid overthrow of Saddam Hussain's regime that there were fears that a petroleum surplus would result, and a production ceiling of 25.4m. b/d was set with effect from the beginning of June: although higher than the previous limit, it represented a 2m. b/d reduction in actual output at that time. The production ceiling of 24.5m. b/d was reinstated from 1 November, in view of the gradual revival of Iraqi exports. In 2004 petroleum prices increased considerably, despite OPEC's raising its production ceiling, in several stages, from the 23.5m. b/d limit imposed from 1 April to 27m. b/d with effect from 1 November. The production ceiling was increased to 27.5m. b/d in March 2005 and to 28m. b/d in June; nevertheless, the ORB price averaged US $50.6 per barrel over the year. The March Conference expressed particular concern that a shortage of effective global refining capacity was also contributing to higher prices, and announced that members had accelerated the implementation of existing capacity expansion plans. During 2006 petroleum prices continued to rise, with the ORB price averaging $61.1 per barrel for the year. In November the production ceiling was lowered to 26.3m. b/d, and a further reduction of 500,000 b/d was announced in December. In November 2007 the third OPEC summit meeting agreed on principles concerning the stability of global energy markets, the role of energy in sustainable development, and the relationship between energy and environmental concerns. At 11 July 2008 the ORB price reached a record high of $147.27 per barrel, although by late October it had decreased to below $60 per barrel. An extraordinary meeting of the Conference, convened in late October, determined to decrease the production ceiling by 1.5m. b/d, with effect from 1 November. A subsequent extraordinary Conference meeting, held in mid-December, agreed to reduce production further, by 4.7m. b/d from the actual total production in September, with effect from 1 January 2009. By 24 December 2008 the ORB price had fallen to $33.36 per barrel.

The ORB price stabilized in early 2009 when a meeting of the Conference determined to maintain current production levels, but urged member states' full compliance with them (this had stood at 79% in February). Meeting in May the Conference noted that the impact of the ongoing global economic crisis had resulted in a reduction in the global demand for petroleum. The Conference welcomed the positive effect of recent production decisions in redressing the balance of supply and demand, and decided to maintain current production levels. By mid-June 2009 the ORB price had risen to US $70.9 per barrel. Reviewing the situation at the next meeting, convened in September, the Conference observed that the global economic situation continued to be very fragile and that the petroleum market remained over supplied, and determined once more to maintain existing production levels. An ordinary meeting of the Conference that was held in June 2011—following, in the first half of that year, the unforeseen eruption of unrest and uncertainty in several Middle Eastern and North African countries and a sharp increase in petroleum prices—failed to reach consensus on a proposed agreement to raise output. In December OPEC ministers agreed to maintain the production ceiling at current actual output levels (some 30m. b/d). This subsequently remained unchanged, and was reaffirmed by the Conference in November 2014.

Extraordinary technical meetings between OPEC officials and experts and counterparts from non-member states were held, for the first time, in May and October 2015, to address declining oil prices. In December OPEC ministers failed to conclude any agreement on production output, and omitted mention of the previous target of 30m. b/d. Factors to which the downward trend in oil prices at that time was attributed included an increase in unconventional energy supplies (shale gas and so-called tight oil—also found in shale and other rock formations with low permeability), in particular from the USA, and weak economic growth in the People's Republic of China and Europe.

2016–19: Meeting in September 2016, in Algiers, Algeria, an extraordinary session of the Conference concluded a preliminary agreement (the 'Algiers Accord') to lower production levels to 32.5m.– 33.0m. b/d. Ministers determined to establish a High Level Committee to analyse and make recommendations on the implementation of OPEC production levels. The Committee was also to be tasked with developing a framework of high-level consultations between OPEC and non-OPEC oil-producing states, to identify risks and recommend proactive measures aimed at balancing the oil market on a sustainable basis. In November the OPEC Conference, having considered the Committee's report, agreed to limit production output to 32.5m. b/d for an initial six-month period from 1 January 2017. Saudi Arabia undertook the largest production cut, of some 486,000 b/d, while Iraq agreed a 210,000 b/d reduction, the UAE 139,000 b/d and Kuwait 131,000 b/d. It was agreed that Iran should freeze its production at the current rate of output; Libya and Nigeria were exempted from the agreement having been affected by conflict and other limitations on production. Indonesia, however, announced that it would suspend its membership of OPEC rather than comply with the new production restrictions.

A meeting held in December 2016 of OPEC and 11 non-OPEC oil producing states (Azerbaijan, Bahrain, Brunei, Equatorial Guinea, Kazakhstan, Malaysia, Mexico, Oman, Russia, South Sudan and Sudan, together styled 'OPEC+') issued a Declaration of Cooperation (DoC) on accelerating the rebalancing of the oil market by achieving—for an initial period of six months starting on 1 January 2017, dependant on the status of supply and demand, global inventories, and OPEC's compliance with the new output limits—a collective adjustment downwards in production by some 600,000 b/d (Russia agreed to a gradual reduction to a total of 300,000 b/d). A Joint Ministerial Monitoring Committee (JMMC), comprising representatives of three OPEC member states (Algeria, Kuwait and Venezuela) and of two non-member states (Russia and Oman) was established in January to oversee the implementation of the DoC. At the 173rd session of the Conference, held on 30 November, ministers agreed to maintain the production limits in a new agreement to cover 1 January–31 December 2018. A new DoC was also signed by non-member states in November 2017. In May 2018 the JMMC reported that OPEC and non-OPEC producers had achieved in February a level of 152% conformity with their production commitments (the highest to date).

In December 2018 OPEC members agreed to reduce production by 800,000 b/d, while non-member co-operating states agreed to a 400,000 b/d reduction over a six-month period commencing on 1 January 2019. Iran was permitted an exemption from the new arrangements; Venezuela and Libya remained exempt from the reduction commitments. The sixth OPEC/non-OPEC Ministerial Meeting (ONOMM), held in July 2019, concluded a Charter of Cooperation. In September attacks against two major Saudi Arabian oil facilities, which temporarily disabled normal production levels, prompted an increase at that time in the oil price. The seventh ONOMM and the 177th meeting of the OPEC Conference were convened in December. An additional reduction in output of 500,000 b/d was agreed, with effect from 1 January 2020.

2020–23: Meeting on 5 March 2020, in Vienna, an extraordinary session of the OPEC Conference noted that the unprecedented ongoing global crisis relating to COVID-19 was adversely impacting demand for petroleum and economic growth forecasts. Accordingly, the Conference recommended that the eighth ONOMM should extend until the end of 2020 the adjustment levels agreed at the previous joint meeting, as well as implementing on a temporary basis until June a further downwards adjustment of 1.5m. b/d, in order to boost oil prices—with OPEC producers' output to be reduced by 1m. b/d and that of the non-OPEC members participating in the DoC by 0.5m. b/d. However, at the ONOMM, held on the following day, Russia refused to implement the recommended cut in production. Saudi Arabia responded immediately by almost halving its official selling prices for April (to US $8, from $14), with a view to boosting its market share and placing pressure on Russia. The failure of the co-operative process prompted an immediate slump in oil prices—the sharpest drop since September 2001. During March 2020, with a view to containing the COVID-19 pandemic, tight restrictions on normal activities were imposed in numerous countries and on international travel and transport, critically reducing oil demand. The ninth ONOMM, held in early April in a virtual format, proposed a series of output reductions. Using crude oil production as at October 2018 as the baseline (except for Russia and Saudi Arabia, which were to use a baseline of 11m. b/d) participating states would be required to reduce overall output by nearly 10m. b/d (about one-tenth of the global supply) during the period 1 May–30 June 2020, by 8m. b/d from 1 July–31 December, and then by 6m. from 1 January 2021–30 April 2022. The level of the reduction in production, however, was contested by Mexico. Following a compromise, under which Mexico would be required, exceptionally, to reduce output at a lower level, full agreement on the collective cuts—which, it was hoped, would stabilize the oil markets—was finalized on 12 April at a 10th ONOMM. In June the OPEC Conference observed that adjustments to petroleum output achieved in May, alongside the gradual loosening of lockdown measures worldwide and accompanying resumption of economic movement, had prompted a tentative recovery and increase in stability in the global oil market. The OPEC member states reconfirmed the arrangements made under the 12 April agreement and designated its full and timely implementation as inviolable; decided that countries that failed to reach full conformity with the agreement during May and June should compensate for their underperformance subsequently; and determined that the first phase of the output adjustments should be extended by a further month, through to 31 July.

The 11th ONOMM, held in June 2020, welcomed Ecuador, Indonesia and Trinidad and Tobago as observers and subscribed to the outcome commitments of the 10th joint ministerial meeting. A planned celebration to mark the 60th anniversary of the foundation of OPEC, to have been hosted by Iraq, was postponed from September in view of the COVID-19 situation. In November the OPEC Secretary-General condemned a recent terrorist attack perpetrated against a petroleum production distribution facility in Jeddah, Saudi Arabia. In early December the 12th ONOMM, held after a brief 180th session of the OPEC Conference, welcomed an overall positive and constructive response in achieving conformity levels. It observed, however, that the widespread re-imposition of strict measures to contain the pandemic crisis would continue to impact adversely the global economy and oil demand recovery. A further voluntary adjustment in production, to 7.2m. b/d, was agreed, to take effect on 1 January 2021. It was also agreed that monthly ONOMMs would be convened from January, in order to review ongoing market conditions and potentially to make gradual monthly adjustments. In March 2021 the 14th ONOMM welcomed a significant voluntary additional reduction in supply effected by Saudi Arabia on 1 February, with the aim of supporting market stability.

The cancellation in early July 2021 of the 18th ONOMM was attributed to rising tensions over the means of calculating individual production targets, and also, reportedly, to the increasing dissatisfaction of some major oil producers (notably the UAE) with continuing restrictions on output, against a background of improving oil demand and rising prices. Eventually the 19th meeting, concluded on 18 July, reached agreement on an upwards monthly production adjustment: an initial increase of 0.4m. b/d was to be introduced in August, and this was to rise steadily each month to 2m. b/d later in the year—pending the planned restoration of pre-COVID-19 levels of production by 31 December 2022.

The 26th ONOMM was held in early March 2022 against the background of Russia's recent military invasion of Ukraine, and the consequent imposition of significant global economic sanctions against Russia. Prior to the meeting Saudi Arabia had reaffirmed commitment to Russia's inclusion in the OPEC+ format. On 1 March the International Energy Agency (IEA) had, in response to the Ukraine crisis, determined to release 60m. barrels of petroleum from its strategic reserves. The ONOMM resolved to maintain the existing monthly production adjustment, asserting that the current price volatility was a result of geopolitical developments and not changes in market fundamentals. An extraordinary meeting of the Conference held on 31 March decided henceforth to use Wood Mackenzie and Rystad Energy (research and business intelligence consultancies) as secondary sources for assessing OPEC member states' crude oil production—replacing the IEA, which, with the USA, had urged the OPEC member states to raise output to calm the increase in prices. The 27th session of the ONOMM, also held at that time, reaffirmed the decision of its 19th meeting (in July 2021) that the baseline for calculating adjustments for several countries would be revised upwards with effect from 1 May 2022, and determined to raise overall monthly production by 0.432 b/d from that time. The ONOMM reiterated that geopolitical developments were the cause of present market volatility. In early June the 29th ONOMM extended the period for compensating for previous underperformance in meeting conformity criteria until 31 December (this having been scheduled to expire on 30 June). An increase in production of 100,000 b/d in September was agreed at the 31st ONOMM in early August. In the following month the 32nd ONOMM noted increased market volatility, and announced that the 100,000 b/d increase would be reversed in October. The 33rd ONOMM, convened in early October, extended the DoC until the end of 2023, and determined to adjust downward overall production by 2m. b/d (from the August 2022 production levels) at the start of November. The decision, which the OPEC Secretary-General stated aimed to sustain oil prices and a secure energy market in the face of a global economic slowdown, was criticized by the US Administration and other governments as inflationary and counter to their efforts to restrict Russian energy revenue. A statement issued at the conclusion of the 34th ONOMM, held in early December, reiterated that the decision had been a proactive one which had stabilized global markets. Meeting at the beginning of April 2023 the JMMC noted ongoing voluntary downwards production adjustments totalling 1.66m. b/d that, against a background of falling prices, were aimed at supporting the stability of the oil market. At the beginning of June the 35th ONOMM agreed a formal downwards adjustment of overall production, by 1.4m. b/d, to be implemented during 1 January 2024–31 December. The 36th ONOMM was to be convened in November 2023, unless market developments required new consideration or additional measures.

ENERGY DIALOGUES AND RESEARCH

In March 2010 OPEC, the IEA and the IEF agreed to greater co-operation and a wider joint programme of work. In February 2023 OPEC, the IEA and the IEF convened the 13th annual Joint Symposium on Energy Outlooks, in Riyadh, Saudi Arabia. The trilateral OPEC-IEA-IEF co-operation also organizes a dialogue on Physical and Financial Energy Market Interactions, comprising a series of high-level joint workshops and technical meetings. With the IEA and other partners OPEC participates in the Joint Oil/Organisations Data Initiative (JODI), which aims to improve the transparency of data on gas and petroleum production. In October 2019 the OPEC Secretary-General and his counterpart from the Gas Exporting Countries Forum (GECF) signed a Memorandum of Understanding on future co-operation between the respective organizations. The third High-Level Meeting of the OPEC-GECF Energy Dialogue was held in October 2022.

A formal Energy Dialogue with Russia was established in December 2005, providing for regular ministerial meetings, together with technical exchanges, seminars and joint research, on such subjects as petroleum market developments and prospects, data flow, investments across the supply chain, and energy policies. The eighth meeting of the Dialogue was held in October 2021. From December 2016 Russia participated in the OPEC+ format (q.v.). A formal OPEC-India Energy Dialogue was inaugurated in December 2015; its fifth meeting was also held in October 2021.

In December 2005 an official dialogue was inaugurated between OPEC and China, with the aim of exchanging views on energy issues, particularly security of supply and demand, through annual ministerial meetings, technical exchanges and energy roundtables. The Second High-level Meeting of the OPEC-China Energy Dialogue, held in December 2017, agreed to hold regular joint gatherings of technical experts. In May 2020 OPEC and China made a commitment to work together to help stabilize the global oil industry in view of the ongoing COVID-19 economic crisis. The sixth meeting of the Dialogue was hosted by China, in its capital Beijing, in May 2023.

The second high-level OPEC-Africa Energy Dialogue was convened in February 2023, with participation by the African Union, African Petroleum Producers' Organization, and African Refiners and Distributors Association. (The first high-level Dialogue had taken place in June 2021.)

Since 2001 OPEC has organized occasional high-level international seminars, with participation by government ministers, oil company executives, academics, representatives of international organizations, and other specialists; the eighth was convened in July 2023, in Vienna.

The OPEC Academy, established in 2018, offers petroleum industry-related courses, training, lectures and fellowship programmes, both online and at OPEC headquarters. In September 2023 the OPEC Academy and City of Vienna organized the third annual edition of a joint Vienna Energy Scholar Programme.

ENVIRONMENTAL CONCERNS

In November 2007 the third meeting of OPEC heads of state and of government acknowledged the challenge of climate change, but emphasized the continuing need for stable petroleum supplies to support global economic growth and development, and urged that policies aimed at combating climate change should be balanced, taking into account their impact on developing countries, including countries heavily dependent on the production and export of fossil fuels. The meeting stressed the importance of cleaner and more efficient petroleum technologies, and the development of technologies such as carbon capture and storage. The OPEC Secretary-General makes an annual statement to the high-level segment of the Conference of the Parties (COP) to the UN Framework Convention on Climate Change (UNFCCC). In June 2016 OPEC ministers declared their support for the Paris Agreement concluded at the 21st COP, held in December 2015.

The 16th edition of OPEC's annual *World Oil Outlook,* issued in October 2022, forecast that demand for global primary energy would increase by 23% by 2045 and envisaged that oil would account for 29% of global energy sources in that year. Addressing the 27th UNFCCC COP, in November 2022, the OPEC Secretary-General noted that petroleum would remain part of the 'global energy mix', and that the oil industry's expertise and resources could support the development of efficient technological means of reducing greenhouse gas emissions.

Finance

OPEC has an annual budget of about €25m.

Publications

Annual Report.
Annual Statistical Bulletin.
Monthly Oil Market Report.
OPEC Bulletin (monthly).
OPEC Energy Review (quarterly).
World Oil Outlook (annually).
Reports, information papers, press releases.

OPEC FUND FOR INTERNATIONAL DEVELOPMENT

Address: POB 995, 1011 Vienna, Austria.
Telephone: (1) 515-64-0; **fax:** (1) 513-92-38; **e-mail:** info@ofid.org; **internet:** www.ofid.org.

The OPEC Fund for International Development (commonly referred to as OFID) was established 1976 by OPEC member countries, in order to assist developing countries and to promote South-South co-operation. A revised agreement to establish the Fund as a permanent international agency was signed in May 1980.

MEMBERS

Algeria	Iran	Nigeria
Ecuador	Iraq	Saudi Arabia
Gabon	Kuwait	United Arab Emirates
Indonesia	Libya	Venezuela

Organization
(September 2023)

ADMINISTRATION

OFID is administered by a Ministerial Council and a Governing Board (serviced by committees for Budget and Strategy, Ethics, Development Effectiveness, and Audit and Risk). Each member country is represented on the Council by its minister responsible for finance. The Board consists of one representative and one alternate for each member country. OFID has departments of Financial Operations, Communication, Risk Management, Corporate Services, Strategic Planning and Economic Services, General Counsel and Legal Services, Public Sector Operations, and Private Sector and Trade Finance Operations.

Chairman, Ministerial Council: Dr KHALID AL-MABROUK ABDALLA AL-MABROUK (Libya).
Director-General of the Fund: Dr ABDULHAMID ALKHALIFA (Saudi Arabia).

FINANCIAL STRUCTURE

The resources of OFID consist of contributions by OPEC member countries, and income received from operations or otherwise accruing to the Fund. Its unit of account is the US dollar.

The initial endowment of OFID amounted to US $800m. Its resources have been replenished four times—the Fourth Replenishment, covering 2013–24 and totalling $1,000m., was approved by the Ministerial Council in June 2011. OFID's resources have also been increased by the profits accruing to several OPEC member countries through the sales of gold held by the International Monetary Fund (IMF). At the end of 2022 the total pledged contributions by member countries amounted to $3,461.5m., and paid-in contributions totalled $2,864.1m. In July 2019 the Ministerial Council approved a new Strategic Framework 2030, with a focus on diversifying the Fund's financial resources; enhancing its development impact, including its contribution to delivering the UN's Sustainable Development Goals (SDGs); fostering partnerships; and improving institutional efficiency. In 2020, under Strategic Framework 2030, OFID established a Special Capital Resources (SCR) fund, through which it extends long-term and low-cost sovereign (i.e. state-guaranteed) loans to support social and economic development in Least Developed Countries. OFID's other capital resources were renamed Ordinary Capital Resources (OCR), and have a focus on operations in medium-income countries.

Activities

OFID aims to reinforce financial co-operation between OPEC member countries and other developing countries ('partner countries', of which there were 125 in 2023) through the provision of financial support to the latter on appropriate terms, to assist them in their economic and social development. Eligible beneficiaries of the Fund's assistance are the governments of developing countries other than OPEC member countries, and international development agencies whose beneficiaries are developing countries. OFID gives priority to the countries with the lowest incomes. It is empowered to provide concessional loans for balance of payments support and for the implementation of development projects and programmes; to contribute to the resources of other international development agencies; to finance technical assistance, research, food aid and humanitarian emergency relief through grants; and to participate in the financing of private sector activities in developing countries. Development projects aim to foster self-reliance.

Since 2006 OFID has presented an Annual Award for Development, to recognize individuals or bodies that had made a significant contribution to enhancing sustainable development.

FINANCIAL OPERATIONS

By the end of 2022 OFID commitments since operations began in 1976 totalled US $24,679m. During that year OFID's total approvals, for 48 transactions, amounted to $1,670m., of which $1,439m. was allocated through the OCR and $225m. through the SCR. Some $469m. was committed to fund initiatives in the Middle East, North Africa, Eastern Europe and Central Asia; $285m. to West and Central Africa; $266m. to Asia and the Pacific; $143m. to Latin America and the Caribbean; and $99m. to Eastern and Southern Africa.

OFID's public sector operations are co-financed, and are aligned with partner countries' development priorities, emphasizing strengthening institutions and capacity building. In 2022 OFID provided US $979m. for 21 public sector projects.

OFID's private sector window fosters productive private enterprise and local capital market development. Loans are extended to businesses to finance initiatives with well defined developmental objectives, such as strengthening infrastructure, enhancing utilities and advancing industrial capacity. Direct equity investments and investments in private equity structures are also made, and loans are extended to financial institutions with the aim of improving the capital base of banks, and for onwards lending to medium-sized and small enterprises (MSMEs). In 2022 OFID provided US $287m. for nine private sector projects. Through its trade finance window OFID extends loans, lines of credit and guarantees to support international trade operations in developing countries. The Fund has assisted more than 7,000 beneficiaries through risk-sharing initiatives.

Private sector approvals in 2022 included (in February) a US $20m. contribution to part-fund an initiative in Egypt that supported import financing for crude oil and other refined products. Public sector approvals included (in August) a $100m. contribution to part-fund an emergency food security project in Jordan.

OFID extends grants to support technical assistance, capacity building, special development and emergency aid initiatives in partner countries, with a view to building public goods and assisting disadvantaged populations. Under OFID's Strategic Framework 2030 all grants were to be directed towards activities that had a measurable development impact. During 1976–2022 OFID approved more than US $644m. in grant funding.

In June 2022 OFID launched a Food Security Action Plan fund, through which it was to channel US $1,000m. over a three-year period to finance the emergency provision of food supplies and also initiatives aimed at fostering longer term resilience. The Plan was part of a broader Arab Coordination Group commitment to extend $10,000m. to enhance food security. Under OFID's inaugural Climate Action Plan, initiated in September, some 25% of all new financing was to be committed to projects with a climate action dimension by 2025, rising to 40% by 2030. From 2023 all new projects were assessed for climate action potential and low carbon options.

In January 2023 OFID launched a 3-year fixed-rate sustainability bond, raising US $1,000m., which was to be used to finance and refinance sustainable development projects that contribute to achieving the UN SDGs.

PARTNERSHIPS

OFID is a lead partner in the global Sustainable Energy for All (SEforALL) initiative that was launched by the United Nations (UN) Secretary-General in September 2011. In June 2012 the Ministerial Council issued a landmark declaration that reaffirmed member states' commitment to eradicating global energy poverty. Consequently, initiatives concerning energy, food security and sustainable water access, as well as enabling investment in transport projects, were given heightened priority. The Fund supports public and private sector projects aimed at accelerating the transition to modern, clean and renewable energy sources, in the context of UN SDG 7 concerning universal access to energy, energy efficiency and increased use of renewable resources, and related targets incorporated into the 2015 Paris Agreement on climate change. In November 2022 OFID, SEforALL and the UN Capital Development Fund jointly launched a Climate Finance and Energy Innovation Hub.

OFID participates—with the Islamic Development Bank, Arab Bank for Economic Development in Africa, Arab Monetary Fund and other partners—in the Arab Coordination Group (ACG), a strategic alliance that was established in 1975, and aims collectively to optimize resources to advance sustainable development. The Arab Development Portal, launched in 2016 by the ACG and the UN Development Programme, provides continually updated data and information online relating to development in the Arab region. In June 2022 OFID hosted its inaugural Development Forum, on the theme 'Driving Resilience & Equity', attended by ministers and senior officials of member states, the ACG and other multilateral development institutions. The 18th annual meeting ACG heads of institutions, hosted by OFID, in Vienna, in June 2023, determined to scale up support to Africa. (A second OFID Development Forum was also held at that time.)

OFID also works closely with other regional development institutions, including the West African Development Bank (BOAD). A new agreement on co-operation was signed with the European Bank for Reconstruction and Development in April 2023. In October 2021 OFID signed a co-operation agreement with the Corporación Andina de Fomento (CAF—Banco de Desarrollo de América Latina), in accordance with which the Fund was to provide up to US $600m. to support public sector projects in Latin America and the Caribbean over the period 2022–24.

In February 2023 OFID channelled emergency grant funding of US $1m. through the International Federation of Red Cross and Red Crescent Societies to support emergency and medium-term relief activities in the Syrian Arab Republic and Türkiye, which had been struck by devastating earthquakes.

Publications

Annual Report (in Arabic, English, French and Spanish).
OFID Quarterly.
Pamphlet series, author papers, books and other documents.

Statistics

SOVEREIGN OPERATIONS BY SECTOR
(US $ million)

	2022	1976–2022
Sector:		
Agriculture	220	2,435
Education	11	1,033
Energy	14	2,672
Health	—	778
Policy-based lending	435	435
Trade finance	283	2,357
Transport and storage	173	4,733
Water and sanitation	15	1,452
Others	111	2,861
Total	1,262	18,755

Source: OFID, *Annual Report 2022*.

OTHER REGIONAL ORGANIZATIONS

Agriculture, Food, Forestry and Fisheries

(For organizations concerned with agricultural commodities, see Commodities)

Arab Authority for Agricultural Investment and Development (AAAID): POB 2102, Khartoum, Sudan; tel. (18) 7096100; fax (18) 3772600; e-mail info@aaaid.org; internet www.aaaid.org; f. 1976; aims to accelerate agricultural devt in the Arab world and to ensure food security; acts principally by equity participation in agricultural projects in mem. countries; AAAID has adopted new progs to help to raise productivity of food agricultural products and introduced zero-tillage farming technology for developing the rainfed sector, which achieved a substantial increase in crop yields, incl. of sorghum, cotton, sesame and sunflowers; mems: 21 countries; Pres. and Chair. MOHAMED BIN OBAID AL-MAZROUEI (UAE); publ. *Annual Report* (Arabic and English).

Association of Agricultural Research Institutions in the Near East and North Africa: POB 950764, 11195 Amman, Jordan; tel. (6) 5818729; fax (6) 5920350; e-mail r.shibli@cgiar.org; internet www.aarinena.org; f. 1985; aims to strengthen co-operation among national, regional and international research institutions; operates the internet-based Near East and North Africa Rural and Agricultural Knowledge and Information Network; Pres. Dr HAMDAN ALWEHAIB (Oman); Exec. Sec. Dr RIDA ABDULLAH URAIK SHIBLI (Jordan).

Consultative Group on International Agricultural Research (CGIAR): CGIAR System Management Office, 1000 ave Agropolis, 34394 Montpellier, France; tel. 4-67-04-78-00; e-mail contact@cgiar.org; internet www.cgiar.org; f. 1971, under the initial sponsorship of the World Bank, FAO and the UN Development Programme; supports international agricultural research aimed at improving crops and animal production in developing countries, and works in partnership with govts, international and regional orgs, private businesses and foundations to support its network of research centres; in 2010 a CGIAR Fund was established to administer donations to the various progs, while a Consortium, governed by a 10-mem. Board, was established to unite the strategic and funding supervision of the research centres; a Science Council was also established to promote the quality, relevance and impact of science in CGIAR and to advise on strategic scientific issues; CGIAR was granted international org. status in 2012; maintains nine gene banks, which conserve (in 2023) some 736,210 accessions of root and tuber crops, cereals, grain legumes, bananas, forages and tree species and co-ordinate distributions of germplasm; in June 2016 CGIAR funders and centres approved a new CGIAR System Framework, under which representatives of funders and of developing countries were to meet in a System Council, comprising up to 20 voting mems; a further reform process, to unify governance, funding and strategic objectives under the brand One CGIAR, was initiated in 2021; an Integrated Framework Agreement, to consolidate the One CGIAR transition, was approved by the Boards of CGIAR's research centres in Feb. 2023; a new portfolio of initiatives was introduced in July 2021, under the theme of 'Transforming Food, Land, and Water Systems in a Climate Crisis'; mems: 15 research centres; 2,273 contributing partners; Chair. of the CGIAR System Board LINDIWE MAJELE SIBANDA (Italy).

International Centre for Agricultural Research in the Dry Areas (ICARDA): Dalia Bldg, 2nd Floor, Bashir El Kassar St, Verdun, 1108–2010 Beirut, Lebanon; tel. (1) 813303; e-mail icarda@cgiar.org; internet www.icarda.org; f. 1975; focuses on the problem-solving needs of resource-poor farmers; supports the improvement of water use efficiency, rangeland and small ruminant production in all dry-area developing countries; promotes within Western and Central Asia and North Africa the improvement of bread, durum wheat and chickpea production, and of farming systems; undertakes research, training and dissemination of information, in co-operation with national, regional and international research institutes, univs and ministries of agriculture, in order to enhance production, alleviate poverty and promote sustainable natural resource management practices; mem. of the network of 15 agricultural research centres supported by the Consultative Group on International Agricultural Research; Dir-Gen. Dr ALY ABOU SABAA; publs *Annual Report*, *Caravan Newsletter* (2 a year).

International Organisation of Vine and Wine (Organisation Internationale de la Vigne et du Vin—OIV): 35 rue de Monceau, 75008 Paris, France; tel. 1-44-94-80-80; fax 1-42-66-90-63; e-mail contact@oiv.int; internet www.oiv.int; f. 2001 (agreement establishing an International Wine Office signed Nov. 1924, name changed to International Vine and Wine Office in 1958); supports research into vine and vine product issues in the scientific, technical, economic and social areas, disseminates knowledge, and facilitates contacts between researchers; organizes annual World Congress; mems: 48 countries; the European Union and 15 other orgs and territories participate as observers; Pres. LUIGI MOIO (Italy); Sec. PAU ROCA (Spain).

International Plant Protection Convention, Secretariat: Vialle delle Terme di Caracalla, 00153 Rome, Italy; tel. (06) 5705-4812; e-mail ippc@fao.org; internet www.ippc.int; f. 1992; provides operational support to the IPPC (adopted first in 1951 and revised in 1997), including the formulation of international standards for phytosanitary measures, exchanging plant health information and providing other policy guidelines; inaugural International Plant Health Conference: Sept. 2022, in London, UK; Sec. OSAMA EL-LISSY (USA).

World Organisation for Animal Health (WOAH) (Organisation mondiale de la santé animale—OIE): 12 rue de Prony, 75017 Paris, France; tel. 1-44-15-18-88; fax 1-42-67-09-87; e-mail woah@woah.org; internet www.woah.org; f. 1924 as Office International des Epizooties, present name adopted in 2003; objectives include promoting international transparency of animal diseases; collecting, analysing and disseminating scientific veterinary information; providing expertise and facilitating international co-operation in the control of animal diseases; promoting veterinary services; providing new scientific guidelines on animal production, food safety and animal welfare; launched in May 2005, jtly with FAO and WHO, a Global Strategy for the Progressive Control of Highly Pathogenic Avian Influenza (H5N1), and, in partnership with other orgs, has convened confs on avian influenza; in May 2017 adopted its first global strategy on animal welfare; maintains the World Animal Health Information System (WAHIS); in April 2022 WOAH, WHO, UNEP and FAO concluded an MOU that provided for the establishment of a Quadripartite Collaboration for One Health, collectively to address challenges at the human-animal-plant-ecosystem interface; a Quadripartite One Health Joint Plan of Action was adopted in Oct., and the first in-person meeting of heads of the Quadripartite was convened in March 2023; WOAH experts work in a network of 51 collaborating centres and 260 reference laboratories (covering 119 diseases); mems: 182 countries; Dir-Gen. Dr MONIQUE ELOIT (France); publs *Disease Information* (weekly), *World Animal Health* (annually), *Scientific and Technical Review* (3 a year), other manuals, codes, etc.

Arts and Culture

Afro-Asian Writers' Association: f. 1958; reactivated in Aug. 2013 when an Exec. Board met in Hanoi, Viet Nam; mems: writers' orgs in 67 countries; publs *Lotus Magazine* (quarterly in English, French and Arabic), *Afro-Asian Literature Series* (in English, French and Arabic).

Organization of World Heritage Cities (OWHC): Maison Chevalier, 5 rue Cul-de-Sac, Québec, G1K 4H6, Canada; tel. (418) 692-0000; e-mail secretariat@ovpm.org; internet www.ovpm.org; f. 1993; assists cities inscribed on the UNESCO World Heritage List to implement the Convention concerning the Protection of the World Cultural and Natural Heritage (1972); promotes co-operation between city authorities, in particular in the management and sustainable devt of historic sites; holds a World Congress every 2 years (2022: Québec, Canada, in Sept.); mems: more than 300 cities worldwide; Pres. BRUNO MARCHAND (Canada); Sec.-Gen. MIKHAËL DE THYSE; publ. *Newsletter* (monthly).

Commodities

African Petroleum Producers' Organization (APPO): 76 ave Amilcar Cabral, Area 3, Poto-Poto, Centre-Ville-Brazzaville, Republic of the Congo; tel. 563-59-27; e-mail info@apposecretariat.org;

internet apposecretariat.org; f. 1987 as the African Petroleum Producers' Assen (APPA), present name adopted in 2017; aims to reinforce co-operation among regional petroleum producing countries and to stabilize prices; Council of Ministers responsible for the hydrocarbons sector meets twice a year; holds regular African Petroleum Congress and Exhibition (CAPE); mems: Algeria, Angola, Benin, Cameroon, Chad, Democratic Rep. of the Congo, Rep. of the Congo, Côte d'Ivoire, Egypt, Equatorial Guinea, Gabon, Ghana, Libya, Namibia, Niger, Nigeria, Senegal, South Africa; Pres. (2023) SAMOU SEÏDOU ADAMBI (Benin); Sec.-Gen. Dr OMAR FAROUK IBRAHIM (Nigeria); publ. *APPA Bulletin* (2 a year).

East Mediterranean Gas Forum (EMGF): 1A Ahmed El Zomor St., Nasr City, Cairo, Egypt; tel. (2) 22766464; internet emgf.org; f. Jan. 2020 as an int. org. at the inaugural formal ministerial meeting of mems of a grouping first established in the previous year; charter signed in Sept. 2020; committed to developing the region's natural gas markets and infrastructure; 8th Ministerial Meeting convened in Dec. 2022, in Cairo; mems: Cyprus, Egypt, France, Greece, Israel, Italy, Jordan, Palestinian Authority; Sec.-Gen. OSAMA MOBAREZ (Egypt).

Gas Exporting Countries Forum (GECF): POB 23753, Tornado Tower, 47th–48th Floors, West Bay, Doha, Qatar; tel. 44048400; fax 44048415; internet www.gecf.org; f. 2001; aims to represent and promote the mutual interests of gas exporting countries, and to promote dialogue between gas producers and consumers; a ministerial meeting is convened annually; the inaugural meeting of heads of state was convened in Doha in 2011; the Forum became a partner in the Joint Oil Data Initiative in April 2014; in Oct. 2019 concluded an accord on future co-operation with OPEC; 7th GECF Summit: Feb. 2024, in the Algerian capital, Algiers; mems: Algeria, Bolivia, Egypt, Equatorial Guinea, Iran, Libya, Nigeria, Qatar, Russian Fed., Trinidad and Tobago, United Arab Emirates, Venezuela; observers: Angola, Azerbaijan, Iraq, Malaysia, Mozambique, Norway, Peru; Sec.-Gen. MOHAMED HAMEL (Algeria); publs *Annual Statistical Bulletin*, *Global Gas Outlook 2050*.

International Grains Council (IGC): 1 Canada Sq., Canary Wharf, London, E14 5AE, United Kingdom; tel. (20) 7513-1122; fax (20) 7513-0630; e-mail igc@igc.int; internet www.igc.int; f. 1949 as International Wheat Council, present name adopted in 1995; responsible for the administration of the International Grains Agreement, 1995, comprising the Grains Trade Convention and the Food Aid Convention (under which donors pledge specified minimum annual amounts of food aid for developing countries in the form of grain and other eligible products); aims to further international co-operation in all aspects of trade in grains, to promote international trade in grains, and to achieve a free flow of this trade, particularly in developing mem. countries; seeks to contribute to the stability of the international grain market; acts as a forum for consultations between mems; provides comprehensive information on the international grain market (with effect from 1 July 2009 the definition of 'grain' was extended to include rice, and from 1 July 2013 it was expanded further, to include oilseeds); contributes, with FAO, WFP and other agencies, to the G20-initiated Agricultural Market Information System, which aims to increase market transparency and to address the stabilization of food price volatility; holds an annual IGC Grains Conference (2023: in June); mems: 30 states parties to the Grains Trade Convention; Chair. ANITA KATIAL (USA); Exec. Dir ARNAUD PETIT (France); publs *World Grain Statistics* (annually), *Grain Shipments* (annually), *Fiscal Year Reports* (annually), *Grain Market Report* (monthly), *IGC Grain Market Indicators* (weekly).

International Olive Council: Príncipe de Vergara 154, 28002 Madrid, Spain; tel. (91) 5903638; fax (91) 5631263; e-mail iooc@internationaloliveoil.org; internet www.internationaloliveoil.org; f. 1959; administers the International Agreement on Olive Oil and Table Olives, which aims to promote international co-operation in connection with problems of the world economy for olive products; most recent (2015) version entered into force on 1 Jan. 2017; works to prevent unfair competition, to encourage the production and consumption of olive products, and their international trade, and to reduce the disadvantages caused by fluctuations of supplies on the market; also takes action to foster a better understanding of the nutritional, therapeutic and other properties of olive products, to foster international co-operation for the integrated, sustainable devt of world olive growing, to encourage research and devt, to foster the transfer of technology and training activities in the olive products sector, and to improve the interaction between olive growing and the environment; mems: 17 countries and the European Union; Exec. Dir ABDELLATIF GHEDIRA (Tunisia); publ. *OLIVAE* (2 a year, in Arabic, English, French, Italian and Spanish).

International Wool Textile Organization: rue de l'Industrie 4, 1000 Brussels, Belgium; tel. (2) 505-40-10; e-mail iwto@iwto.org; internet www.iwto.org; f. 1930; sets global standards in the wool textile industry; has working groups that address wool sustainability; wool for consumer health and wellbeing; sheep welfare (including maintaining a set of Wool Sheep Welfare Specifications); wool trade biosecurity (focused on positive animal health outcomes, incl. combating Foot-and-Mouth disease in flocks); and the use of wool in interior design (promoting the natural flame-resistant and pollutant-absorbing qualities of wool in the manufacture of e.g. carpets and upholstery); holds an annual congress and an annual Wool Round Table; mems: 33 in 22 states; Pres. WOLF EDMAYR (South Africa); Sec.-Gen. DALENA WHITE.

Economic and Sustainable Development Co-operation

African Training and Research Centre in Administration for Development (Centre Africain de Formation et de Recherche Administratives pour le Développement—CAFRAD): Pavillon International, Blvd Mohammed V, POB 1796, 90000 Tangier, Morocco; tel. (539) 322707; e-mail cafrad@cafrad.org; internet cafrad.org; f. 1964, with support from UNESCO; undertakes research into administrative problems in Africa and documents results; provides a consultation service for govts and orgs; holds workshops to train senior civil servants; organizes webinars and seminars; mems: 36 African countries; Dir-Gen. Dr STÉPHANE MONNEY MOUANDJO (Cameroon); publ. *Cahiers Africains d'Administration Publique* (2 a year).

African-Asian Rural Development Organization (AARDO): No. 2, State Guest Houses Complex, Chanakyapuri, New Delhi 110 021, India; tel. (11) 26877783; fax (11) 26115937; e-mail aardohq@aardo.org; internet www.aardo.org; f. 1962; aims to promote social change and develop participative co-operation among its mems; provides assistance in evolving an integrated approach, as the crucial pre-requisite in rural Asia and Africa; facilitates exchange of knowledge, best practices and technical assistance concerning rural and agricultural devt among its mems; provides technical and financial support to its mem. countries to undertake pilot projects; organizes training, study visits, deputation of experts; holds international workshops and seminars; awards more than 389 training fellowships at institutes in Bangladesh, Rep. of China, Egypt, India, Rep. of Korea, Malaysia, Nigeria, Pakistan, Philippines, Thailand and Zambia; mems: 18 African countries, 14 Asian countries, 2 assoc. mems; Sec.-Gen. MANOJ NARDEOSINGH (Mauritius); publs *African-Asian Journal of Rural Development* (2 a year), *Annual Report*, *AARDO Newsletter* (quarterly).

Agadir Agreement: f. 2004, upon the adoption of the Agadir Agreement on the establishment of a Free Trade Zone between the Arabic Mediterranean Nations by the govts of Egypt, Jordan, Morocco and Tunisia (implementing a Declaration made in Agadir, Morocco, in May 2001); the Agreement entered into force in July 2006 and its implementation commenced in March 2007; a Technical Unit to follow up implementation of the Agreement was established in April 2007; a business council was established in Jan. 2016 within the framework of the Agadir Agreement; a Business Forum of the Agadir Agreement and the West African OIC countries was convened in Casablanca, Morocco, in May 2018; mems: Egypt, Jordan, Morocco, Tunisia.

Arab Bank for Economic Development in Africa (Banque Arabe pour le Développement Economique en Afrique—BADEA): Sayed Abdar-Rahman el-Mahdi St, POB 2640, Khartoum 11111, Sudan; tel. (1) 83773646; fax (1) 83770600; e-mail badea@badea.org; internet www.badea.org; f. 1973 by mem. states of the Arab League; provides loans and grants to sub-Saharan African countries to finance devt projects; BADEA participates—with the Islamic Development Bank, OPEC Fund, Arab Monetary Fund and other partners—in the Arab Coordination Group, a strategic alliance that was established in 1975, and aims collectively to optimize resources to advance sustainable devt; in Nov. 2020 BADEA, the African Export-Import Bank and the International Islamic Trade Finance Corporation initiated a US $1,500m. Collaborative COVID-19 Pandemic Response Facility, which aimed to support African countries in addressing the pandemic; during 2020 the Bank approved commitments totalling $780.4m., including $300.0m. for 19 public sector projects, $95.5m. for 4 private sector operations, $375.0m. for 8 trade finance operations, and $9.9m. for 28 technical assistance operations; Chair. Dr FAHAD ALDOSSARI (Saudi Arabia); Dir-Gen. Dr SIDI OULD TAH (Mauritania); publs *Annual Report*, *Co-operation for Development* (quarterly), studies on Afro-Arab co-operation.

Arab Gulf Programme for the United Nations Development Organizations (AGFUND): 8360 Prince Satam ibn Abdul Aziz-Ar rafiah, Riyadh 12751-4694, Saudi Arabia; tel. (11) 441-8888; e-mail info@agfund.org; internet agfund.org; f. 1981; provides grants for projects in mother and child care carried out by UN orgs, Arab non-governmental orgs and other int. bodies, and co-ordinates assistance by the nations of the Gulf; financing comes mainly from mem. states, all of which are mems of OPEC; in Dec. 2017 the AGFUND Board of Dirs approved support for 10 devt projects aimed at pursuing the UN's Sustainable Devt Goals; mems: Bahrain, Kuwait, Oman, Qatar, Saudi Arabia, UAE; Pres. HRH Prince TALAL BIN ABDAL-AZIZ.

Community of Sahel-Saharan States (Communauté des états Sahelo-Sahariens—CEN-SAD): Pl. d'Algeria, POB 4041, Tripoli, Libya (since 2019 operating from interim offices in N'Djamena, Chad); e-mail censad_sg@yahoo.com; f. 1998 (fmrly known as COMESSA); aims to strengthen co-operation between signatory states in order to promote their economic, transportation, communications, social and cultural integration and to facilitate conflict resolution and poverty alleviation; partnership agreements have been concluded with the African Union, the European Union, ECOWAS, FAO, CILSS and BADEA; the 7th meeting of CEN-SAD ministers responsible for defence was convened in Abuja, Nigeria, in June 2018, to discuss, *inter alia,* the risk posed by the deliberate recruitment by Islamic State of insurgents in Nigeria and other mem. states; organized in April 2021 a high-level meeting on counter terrorism; the Sec.-Gen. visited Libya in March 2022 to advance the return of the org. to its Tripoli Headquarters; mems: Benin, Burkina Faso, Cape Verde, Central African Republic, Chad, Comoros, Côte d'Ivoire, Djibouti, Egypt, Eritrea, The Gambia, Ghana, Guinea, Guinea-Bissau, Kenya, Liberia, Libya, Mali, Mauritania, Morocco, Niger, Nigeria, São Tomé and Príncipe, Senegal, Sierra Leone, Somalia, Sudan, Togo, Tunisia; Sec.-Gen. BRIGI RAFINI (Niger).

Council of Arab and African States bordering the Red Sea and Gulf of Aden: a founding charter was signed in Riyadh, Saudi Arabia, in Jan. 2020; aims to promote the sustainable devt and management of shared marine resources, to address security challenges such as piracy and smuggling, and to advance economic co-operation, trade and investment among the mem. littoral states; mems: Djibouti, Egypt, Eritrea, Jordan, Saudi Arabia, Somalia, Sudan and Yemen.

Developing Eight (D-8): Darüşşafaka Cad., Seba Center 45, Istinye, 34460 Istanbul, Türkiye; tel. (212) 3561823; fax (212) 3561829; e-mail secretariat@developing8.org; internet www.developing8.org; f. 1997; aims to foster economic co-operation between mems and to strengthen the role of developing countries in the global economy; project areas include trade; agriculture and food security; transportation; industrial devt; energy and minerals; tourism; and health; granted observer status at the UN in Oct. 2014; in April 2015 announced a partnership with UNIDO that aimed to accelerate inclusive, sustainable industrial devt through the promotion of trade capacity building and entrepreneurship in mem. states; the implementation phase of the D-8 Preferential Trade Agreement (signed in 2006) entered into effect on 1 July 2016; a D-8 Charter entered into force on 1 Sept. 2017; the 9th summit meeting, convened in Oct. in Istanbul, decided to establish a D-8 Project Support Fund, a D-8 Research and Development Centre, and a Hamadan, Iran-based D-8 University; the 10th summit meeting, hosted by Bangladesh in April 2021, adopted a D-8 Decennial Roadmap for 2020–30, which included the goal (to be achieved by 2030) of increasing the volume of intra-D-8 trade to 10% of the organization's total trade; during phase 1 of the Roadmap, covering 2020–22, new projects were to be developed; these were to be implemented during phase 2 (2023–27); and were to be reviewed during phase 3 (2028–30); a single card payment system (the 'DP8') has been envisaged, with the aim of facilitating intra-D-8 commerce; mems: Bangladesh, Egypt, Indonesia, Iran, Malaysia, Nigeria, Pakistan, Türkiye; Sec.-Gen. ISIAKA ABDULQADIR IMAN (Nigeria).

Economic Research Forum: POB 12311, 21 al-Sad al-Aaly St, Dokki, Cairo, Egypt; tel. (2) 33318600; fax (2) 33318604; e-mail erf@erf.org.eg; internet www.erf.org.eg; f. 1993; works to conduct indepth economic research, to compile an economic database for the Arab countries, Iran and Türkiye, and to provide training to contribute to sustainable devt in the region; holds an annual conference; convenes regular workshops and seminars; Man. Dir IBRAHIM AHMED ELBADAWI (Suda); publs *ERF Newsletter* (quarterly), *Middle East Development Journal* (annually), *Annual Report*.

Global Dryland Alliance (GDA): Onaiza, Zone 66, St 826, Villa 50, POB 22043, Doha, Qatar; tel. (974) 4037-7200; e-mail info@globaldrylandalliance.com; f. 2017; aims to reduce hunger and poverty in dryland countries, including through joint research and technological innovation and working with local govts to enhance food security policies and planning; works to identify, disseminate, and implement solutions to counter particular agricultural, water, and energy challenges of dryland countries; awarded observer status at the UN General Assembly in 2020; mems: 13 countries; Exec.-Dir BADER OMAR AL DAFA (Qatar).

Group of 15 (G15): f. 1989 by 15 developing nations during the 9th summit of the Non-Aligned Movement; retains its original name although membership has expanded; promotes co-operation to address the global economic and political situation; liaises with other groupings, incl. G7; mems: Algeria, Argentina, Brazil, Chile, Colombia, Egypt, India, Indonesia, Iran, Jamaica, Kenya, Malaysia, Mexico, Nigeria, Senegal, Sri Lanka, Venezuela, Zimbabwe.

Group of 77 (G77): United Nations Secretariat Bldg, Rm S-0518, New York, NY 10017, USA; tel. (212) 963-4777; fax (212) 963-3515; e-mail secretariat@g77.org; internet www.g77.org; f. 1964 by the 77 signatory states of the Joint Declaration of the Seventy-Seven Countries (the G77 retains its original name, owing to its historic significance, although its membership has expanded); the inaugural ministerial meeting, held in Algiers, Algeria, in Oct. 1967, adopted the Charter of Algiers as a basis for G77 co-operation; subsequently, G77 Chapters were established with liaison offices in Geneva (UNCTAD), Nairobi (UNEP), Paris (UNESCO), Rome (FAO/IFAD), Vienna (UNIDO), and the Group of 24 (G24) in Washington, DC (IMF/World Bank); as the largest intergovernmental org. of developing states in the UN the G77 aims to enable developing nations to articulate and promote their collective economic interests and to improve their negotiating capacity within the UN system; an inaugural South Summit, bringing together all G77 heads of state and govt, was convened in Havana, Cuba, in April 2000; a 2nd Summit was held in Doha, Qatar, in June 2005; in Sept. 2006 G77 ministers responsible for foreign affairs, and the People's Rep. of China, endorsed the establishment of a Consortium on Science, Technology and Innovation for the South; G77 approves funds allocated through the Perez-Guerrero Trust Fund for South-South Cooperation (PGTF, f. 1983); during 1986–2021 some 379 projects, with a cumulative value of US $15.9m., were approved through the PGTF; an annual meeting of G77 foreign ministers is held at the start (in Sept.) of the regular session of the UN General Assembly; an Intergovernmental Follow-up and Coordination Committee on South-South Cooperation meets every 2 years; periodic sectoral ministerial meetings are organized in preparation for UNCTAD sessions and prior to the UNIDO and UNESCO General Conferences, and with the aim of promoting South-South co-operation; other special ministerial meetings are also convened periodically; mems: 134 countries; chairmanship rotates annually on a regional basis (2023: Cuba).

Indian Ocean Rim Association (IORA): Nexteracom Tower 1, 3rd Floor, Ebene, Mauritius; tel. 454-1717; fax 468-1161; e-mail hq@iora.net; internet www.iora.int; f. 1997 as the Indian Ocean Rim Association for Regional Co-operation, present name adopted in 2013; aims to promote the sustained and balanced devt of the region and of its mem. states and to create common ground for regional economic co-operation, *inter alia,* through trade, investment, infrastructure, tourism, and science and technology; the third IORA Ministerial Blue Economy Conference (BEC-3) was held in Sept. 2019; the inaugural Leaders' summit meeting was held in Jakarta, Indonesia, in March 2017; IORA working groups on maritime safety and security and on the blue economy held inaugural meetings in Aug. and Dec. 2019, respectively; the 8th Indian Ocean Dialogue—IOD—was held, in a virtual format, in Dec. 2021, on the theme 'Post Pandemic Indian Ocean: Leveraging Digital Technologies for Health, Education, Development and Trade in IORA Member States' (inaugural IOD convened in 2014); an IORA Action Plan on Maritime Safety and Security was being implemented during 2022–26; mems: Australia, Bangladesh, Comoros, France (representing the French Overseas Department of Réunion), India, Indonesia, Iran, Kenya, Madagascar, Malaysia, Maldives, Mauritius, Mozambique, Oman, Seychelles, Singapore, Somalia, South Africa, Sri Lanka, Tanzania, Thailand, United Arab Emirates, Yemen. Dialogue Partner countries: People's Rep. of China, Egypt, Germany, Italy, Japan, Rep. of Korea, Türkiye, UK, USA. Observers: Indian Ocean Research Group Inc., Western Indian Ocean Marine Science Asscn; Sec.-Gen. SALMAN AL-FARISI (Indonesia).

Nile Basin Initiative (NBI): POB 192, Entebbe, Uganda; tel. (41) 7705000; e-mail nbisec@nilebasin.org; internet www.nilebasin.org; f. 1999; aims to achieve sustainable socioeconomic devt through the equitable use and benefits of the Nile Basin water resources and to create an enabling environment for the implementation of programmes with a shared vision; highest authority is the Nile Basin Council of Ministers (COM); other activities undertaken by a Nile Basin Technical Advisory Committee; in March 2015 Egypt, Ethiopia and Sudan signed a declaration of principles, which provided for priority to be given to downstream Nile countries with regard to power generated by Ethiopia's controversial Grand Renaissance Dam project; an extraordinary COM meeting was held in Entebbe, in March 2017, to facilitate Egypt's full resumption of activities in the org. (it having been suspended in 2010); the inaugural NBI summit of heads of state was convened in June 2017; a Regional HydroMet Project, to facilitate the exchange of data and monitoring information among mems, was launched in Dec. 2019; mems: Burundi, Democratic Rep. of the Congo, Egypt, Ethiopia, Kenya, Rwanda, South Sudan, Sudan, Tanzania, Uganda; observer: Eritrea; Chair. JUMAA H. AWESO (Tanzania); Exec. Dir SYLVESTER ANTHONY MATEMU (Tanzania); publ. *Corporate Report* (annually).

REGIONAL ORGANIZATIONS

Other Regional Organizations

Organisation for Economic Co-operation and Development: 2 rue André-Pascal, 75775 Paris Cedex 16, France; tel. 1-45-24-82-00; fax 1-45-24-85-00; e-mail webmaster@oecd.org; internet www.oecd.org; f. 1961, replacing the Organisation for European Economic Co-operation (f. 1948); serves as a forum for governments to discuss, develop and attempt to co-ordinate their economic and social policies; aims to promote policies designed to achieve the highest level of sustainable economic growth, employment and increase in the standard of living, while maintaining financial stability and democratic government, and the expansion of world trade; in Oct. 2021, in the context of an OECD/G20 Base Erosion and Profit Shifting (BEPS) initiative introduced in 2013, 136 countries and jurisdictions (accounting for more than 90% of global GDP, and including all OECD and G20 member states), formally approved an updated final Statement on the Two-Pillar Solution to Address the Tax Challenges Arising from the Digitalisation of the Economy, providing for multinational enterprises to be subject, from 2023, to a minimum 15% tax rate; a related multilateral convention was to be implemented from 2023; mems: 38 states, incl. Israel and Türkiye; Sec.-Gen. MATHIAS CORMANN (Australia).

Organization of the Black Sea Economic Cooperation (BSEC): Darüşşafaka Cad., Seba Center İş Merkezi, No: 45, Kat 3, Istinye 34460 İstanbul, Türkiye; tel. (212) 2296335; fax (212) 2296336; e-mail info@bsec-organization.org; internet www.bsec-organization.org; f. 1992 as the Black Sea Economic Cooperation (name changed on entry into force of BSEC Charter on 1 May 1999); aims to strengthen regional co-operation, particularly in the field of economic devt; the following institutions have been established within the framework of BSEC: a Parliamentary Assembly (established in 1993), a Business Council (1992), a Black Sea Trade and Development Bank (inaugurated in 1998), a BSEC Co-ordination Centre, and a Black Sea International Studies Centre (opened in 1998); in Jan. 2022 the Moldovan Chair. (for that year) designated the following as its priority sectoral focus areas: environmental protection and blue economy; transport, trade and connectivity; and culture and tourism; regional security was disrupted in the following month by the Russian Fed.'s invasion of Ukraine; in July negotiations held in İstanbul under the auspices of the UN and Türkiye (which had assumed a mediatory role between Russia and Ukraine) culminated in the conclusion by Russia and Ukraine of the UN-backed Black Sea Grain Initiative (BSGI), enabling the resumption of exports of grain, sunflower oil and other essential goods from Odesa and two other Ukrainian Black Sea ports (that had hitherto been blockaded by Russia), and at facilitating fertilizer and grain exports from Russia (which had been subjected to punitive sanctions); under the agreement UN, Turkish and Ukrainian personnel were to monitor the loading of grain at Ukrainian ports, and an İstanbul-based UN-Türkiye-Russia-Ukraine joint co-ordination centre was to supervise the safe navigation of loaded vessels through the Black Sea exportation corridors towards the Bosphorus Strait; the centre was also to inspect ships entering Ukraine, to ensure that they were not carrying military weaponry; Russia and Ukraine agreed to desist from attacking any of the commercial vessels or ports covered by the BSGI; extensions to the BSGI were subsequently agreed; however, on 17 July 2023 the initiative lapsed, the Russian authorities having refused to renew it, claiming that commitments made to Russia had not been fulfilled; mems: Albania, Armenia, Azerbaijan, Bulgaria, Georgia, Greece, Moldova, North Macedonia, Romania, Russian Fed., Serbia, Türkiye, Ukraine; 13 countries incl. Egypt, Israel and Tunisia have been granted observer status; 5 countries incl. Iran have been granted sectoral dialogue partnership status; Sec.-Gen. LAZĂR COMĂNESCU (Romania).

Partners in Population and Development (PPD): PPD Secretariat Bldg Complex, Block-F, Plots-17/ B & C, Agargaon Administrative Zone, Dhaka 1212, Bangladesh; tel. (2) 9117842; fax (2) 9117817; e-mail partners@ppdsec.org; internet www.partners-popdev.org; f. 1994; aims to implement the decisions of the International Conference on Population and Development, held in Cairo, Egypt in 1994, in order to expand and improve South-South collaboration in the fields of family planning and reproductive health; administers a Visionary Leadership Programme, a Global Leadership Programme, a Scholarship Programme and other training and technical advisory services; in April 2018 concluded a Memorandum of Understanding (MOU) with UNFPA to strengthen South-South co-operation in population and devt; an MOU was signed with the League of Arab States in Dec. 2020; mems: 27 developing countries from Asia, Africa, Latin America and the Middle East; Chair. LINDIWE ZULU (South Africa); Exec. Dir ADNENE BEN HAJ AISSA.

Union of the Arab Maghreb (Union du Maghreb arabe—UMA): 73 rue Tensift, Agdal, Rabat, Morocco; tel. (53) 7681371; fax (53) 7681377; e-mail sg.uma@maghrebarabe.org; internet www.maghrebarabe.org; f. 1989; aims to encourage jt ventures and to create a single market; structure comprises a council of heads of state (meeting annually), a council of ministers responsible for foreign affairs, a follow-up committee, a consultative council of 30 delegates from each country, a UMA judicial court, and 4 specialized ministerial commissions; chairmanship rotates annually between heads of state; a Maghreb Investment and Foreign Trade Bank, funding jt agricultural and industrial projects, has been established and a customs union created; mems: Algeria, Libya, Mauritania, Morocco, Tunisia; Sec.-Gen. Dr TAYEB AL-BAKOUSH (Tunisia).

World Economic Forum: 91–93 route de la Capite, 1223 Cologny/ Geneva, Switzerland; tel. 228691212; fax 227862744; internet www.weforum.org; f. 1971; comprises commercial interests gathered on a non-partisan basis, under the stewardship of the Swiss Government, with the aim of improving society through economic devt; convenes an annual meeting in Davos-Klosters, Switzerland; the 2023 meeting took place in Jan., on the theme 'Cooperation in a Fragmented World'; also holds a regular World Economic Forum on the Middle East and North Africa; organizes the following programmes: Technology Pioneers; Women Leaders; a Network of Global Future Councils; New Champions; and Young Global Leaders; and aims to mobilize the resources of the global business community in the implementation of initiatives including the Global Health Initiative, the Disaster Relief Network, and the G20/International Monetary Reform Project; organizes an Annual Meeting on Cybersecurity (2022: in Nov.); compiles a Global Competitiveness Index; in 2018 the Forum opened a Centre for the Fourth Industrial Revolution, in San Francisco, CA, USA, as a focal point for international dialogue regarding the impact of advanced technologies, and a Centre for Cybersecurity, located in Geneva, Switzerland; in Jan. 2019 launched a Global Humanitarian Action Executive Alliance; the Essential Digital Infrastructure and Services Network (EDISON) Alliance was initiated by the Forum in Feb. 2021, to promote cross-sectoral collaboration in advancing equitable global access to the digital economy; the Forum is governed by a guiding Foundation Board, an advisory International Business Council, and an administrative Managing Board; regular mems: reps of 1,000 leading commercial cos in 56 countries worldwide; selected mem. cos taking a leading role in the movement's activities are known as 'partners'; Exec. Chair. KLAUS MARTIN SCHWAB (Switzerland); publ. *The Global Competitiveness Report*.

Economics and Finance

Accounting and Auditing Organization for Islamic Financial Institutions (AAOIFI): Al Nakheel Tower, Office 1001, Bldg 1074, Rd 3622, Seef Area 436, Bahrain; tel. 244496; fax 250194; internet aaoifi.com; f. 1991; aims to develop accounting, auditing and banking practices and to harmonize standards among mem. institutions; Sec.-Gen. Dr OMAR MUSTAFA ANSARI.

Afreximbank: 72B el-Maahad el-Eshteraky St, Heliopolis, Cairo 11341, Egypt; tel. and fax (2) 24564100; e-mail info@afreximbank.com; internet afreximbank.com; f. 1993 as the African Export Import Bank, in accordance with an agreement concluded by multilateral orgs and mem. states; commenced operations 1994; aims to promote and finance trade within and beyond Africa; organized (in Cairo) in Dec. 2018, jtly with the AU Commission, the inaugural Intra-African Trade Fair; the 3rd Fair was to be held in Nov. 2023, in Abidjan, Côte d'Ivoire; in March 2021 operationalized a US $1,000m. AfCFTA Adjustment Facility which was to enable AU mem. states to manage losses in tariff revenues arising from the initiation of trading under the African Continental Free Trade Area; the Bank established, in March 2020, a Pandemic Trade Impact Mitigation Facility, with funds of up to $3,000m., to support mems confronting economic, financial and health crises as a result of the COVID-19 pandemic; later in that year the Bank offered guarantees of up to $2,000m. under a new financing facility to support the procurement of COVID-19 vaccines; in Nov. Afreximbank, BADEA, and the International Islamic Trade Finance Corporation initiated a $1,500m. Collaborative COVID-19 Pandemic Response Facility, which aimed to support African countries in addressing the pandemic; a General Capital Increase of $6,500m. was approved at the Bank's annual meeting in July 2021; in March 2022 Afreximbank launched a $4,000m. Ukraine Crisis Adjustment Trade Financing Programme for Africa (UKAFPA) to support the regional response to impacts of the war in Ukraine, particularly the rising cost of fertilizer, fuel and grain imports; in Feb. 2023 concluded an MOU with AUDA-NEPAD on establishing a facility to fund the preparation of continental infrastructure projects; brs are located in Côte d'Ivoire (Abidjan), Cameroon (Yaoundé), Kenya (Nairobi), Nigeria (Abuja) and Zimbabwe (Harare); mems: 51 participating or shareholder states; Pres. Dr BENEDICT OKEY ORAMAH (Nigeria).

Equator Principles Association: e-mail secretariat@equator-principles.com; internet www.equator-principles.com; f. July 2010; aims to administer and develop further the Equator Principles, first adopted in 2003, with the support of the International Finance Corporation, as a set of industry standards for the management of environmental and social risk in project financing;

4th version of the Equator Principles (EP4) entered fully into effect on 1 Oct. 2020; holds an annual meeting and workshop; mems: 139 signed-up financial institutions from 39 countries; CEO Max Griffin (UK).

Financial Action Task Force (FATF) (Groupe d'action financière—GAFI): 2 rue André-Pascal, 75775 Paris Cedex 16, France; tel. 1-45-24-90-90; fax 1-44-30-61-37; e-mail contact@fatf-gafi.org; internet www.fatf-gafi.org; f. 1989, on the recommendation of the G7; mandated to develop and promote policies to combat money laundering and the financing of terrorism; formulated 40 recommendations for countries worldwide to implement in order to combat money laundering and the financing of terrorism and proliferation; these are periodically revised; established partnerships with regional task forces in the Caribbean, Asia-Pacific, Central Asia, Europe, East and South Africa, and the Middle East, and Central and North Africa; has developed terrorist financing-related risk indicators; mems: 37 state jurisdictions, the European Commission, the Cooperation Council for the Arab States of the Gulf; 1 observer country, 9 regional assoc. mems and 23 observer orgs; Pres. (1 July 2022–30 June 2024) T. Raja Kumar (Singapore); Exec. Sec. Violaine Clerc (France); publ. *Annual Report*.

Group of 20 (G20): internet www.g20.org; f. Sept. 1999; established initially as an informal deliberative forum of ministers responsible for finance and central bank governors representing both industrialized and 'systemically important' emerging market nations; aims to strengthen the international financial architecture and to foster sustainable economic growth and devt; an extraordinary meeting of heads of state and of govt to discuss extreme concerns regarding global financial markets and the world economy was convened in Washington, DC, USA, in Nov. 2008; a further summit meeting, held in London, United Kingdom, in April 2009, issued as its final communiqué a Global Plan for Recovery and Reform; detailed declarations were also issued on measures agreed to deliver substantial resources (of some US $850,000m.) through international financial institutions; as a follow-up to the London meeting, G20 leaders gathered in Pittsburgh, PA, USA, in Sept. 2009; the meeting adopted a Framework for Strong, Sustainable, and Balanced Growth and resolved to expand the role of the G20 to be at the centre of future international economic policymaking; summit meetings were held in June 2010, in Canada, and in Nov., in Seoul, Rep. of Korea; the 6th G20 summit, held in Cannes, France, in Nov. 2011, concluded an Action Plan for Growth and Jobs, and addressed measures to secure financial stability in some countries using the euro; the 7th summit, convened in Los Cabos, Baja California Sur, Mexico, in June 2012, further considered means of stabilizing the eurozone, with a particular focus on reducing the borrowing costs of highly indebted mem. countries; an SME Finance Forum was launched in that year; in Sept. 2013 11 heads of state and govt participating in the summit meeting held in St Petersburg, Russia, issued a statement condemning an alleged chemical attack perpetrated against civilians in Ghouta, Syria, on 21 Aug., and urging a strong international response; the meeting also adopted a new Base Erosion and Profit Shifting Action Plan, developed by the OECD with the aim of combating corporation tax avoidance globally; in Feb. 2016 G20 ministers responsible for finance and central bank governors (FMCBG) met in Shanghai, People's Rep. of China, to discuss policy options to counter a deceleration in global economic growth; the 2016 summit meeting was held in Sept., in Hangzhou; a G20-Africa Partnership conf. was convened in June 2017, in Berlin, Germany; in a communiqué issued by the 2017 summit meeting, held in July, in Hamburg, Germany, 19 of the participating leaders (excluding US Pres. Trump) renewed commitment to implementing the 2015 Paris Agreement on climate change; the communiqué also noted the right of countries to protect their markets with 'legitimate trade-defence instruments'; the 2018 summit, convened in late Nov.–early Dec., in Buenos Aires, Argentina, released a communiqué in which, *inter alia*, participating leaders reaffirmed commitment to improving the rules-based international order and pledged support to 'necessary' reform to the functioning of the WTO; the 2019 G20 summit, convened in June, in Osaka, Japan, noted the recent intensification of geopolitical and trade tensions, reaffirmed support for reform of the WTO, endorsed a series of G20 Principles on Artificial Intelligence (based on principles formulated by the OECD), determined to promote cross-border data exchange, agreed to work towards eliminating marine plastic litter by 2050, and made a collective statement on combating exploitation of the internet for terrorism/ violent extremism; an emergency summit was held in mid-March 2020, in a virtual format, to discuss the COVID-19 pandemic; a further virtual summit, convened subsequently to address the coordination of related medical and economic planning, issued a statement committing to close collaboration in sharing data, research and best practices and to the financing of pandemic response efforts; leaders endorsed measures being taken by central banks to safeguard their economies, and pledged $5,000,000m. in funding to combat the impacts of the coronavirus emergency; in April G20 finance ministers and central bank governors endorsed a G20 Action Plan on supporting the global economy in relation to measures imposed to counter COVID-19; the meeting announced a temporary Debt Service Suspension Initiative (DSSI), providing for the world's poorest countries to freeze repayment of official bilateral credit, with effect from 1 May; in mid-July the (virtual) FMCBG meeting pledged to continue to deploy all possible policy tools to alleviate the impacts of the ongoing global crisis; Saudi Arabia hosted that year's summit, in a virtual format, in Nov.; the meeting endorsed a Common Framework for Debt Treatments beyond the DSSI, to provide structural support, on a case-by-case basis, as requested, to LDCs with unsustainable debt; in May 2021 a G20 Global Health Summit, convened in Rome, Italy, adopted the Rome Declaration, which included commitments to common principles aimed at overcoming the COVID-19 crisis and preparing for and preventing future disease pandemics; in July the FMCBG meeting gave support to a proposal— that had been agreed by the G7 leadership in June and subsequently endorsed by OECD mem. states—to introduce a minimum global corporate tax rate of 15%; in July the G20 finance ministers also notably endorsed for the first time the taxation of carbon dioxide emissions ('carbon pricing'), as a tool for addressing climate change; a G20 summit meeting was held in late Oct., in Rome; leaders agreed to implement the 15% global corporate tax rate by 2023; they also resolved to accelerate efforts to achieve global net zero greenhouse gas emissions, to continue to mobilize climate finance commitments, to increase the provision of and access to COVID-19 vaccines for low- and middle-income countries and to establish a G20 Joint Finance-Health Task Force to formulate a mechanism to fund pandemic prevention, preparedness and response; the amount of debt service suspended through the DSSI during May 2020–Dec. 2021 (when it expired, having been twice extended, in Nov. 2020 and in April 2021) totalled $12,900m.; 48 of the 73 eligible countries participated in the initiative; the April 2022 FMCBG meeting, convened in a hybrid virtual and in-person format hosted from Washington, DC, considered the humanitarian and economic impacts of the Russian invasion of Ukraine; a provisional consensus was reached on establishing, under World Bank auspices, a new Financial Intermediary Fund for Pandemic Prevention, Preparedness and Response; a meeting of G20 foreign ministers, convened in early July, in Bali, Indonesia, considered (without achieving consensus) the impacts on global energy and food security of the Russia–Ukraine war; Russia's foreign minister withdrew from a session in response to criticism of Russia's military and territorial aggression; G20 heads of state and govt met in Bali in Nov., although Russia's Pres. Putin did not attend; a consensus was reached to conclude a joint final declaration which stated that most mems strongly condemned the ongoing war in Ukraine; it also confirmed that the use or threat of nuclear weapons was inadmissible and that adhering to international humanitarian law was essential; other measures were agreed with regard to addressing the 'multidimensional' crises facing the global community, including renewed commitment towards limiting the increase in temperatures to 1.5°C, efforts to enhance food security, a pledge to calibrate monetary measures to counter rising inflation, and a commitment to enhance implementation of the G20 Common Framework for Debt Treatments beyond the DSSI; during 2023 revised G20/OECD Principles of Corporate Governance were to be published (representing the international standard for corporate governance; the Principles had first been issued in 1999, and previously revised in 2015); issued a report in Feb. 2023 on the G20 macrofinancial implications of crypto-assets; the 18th meeting of G20 heads of state and or of govt was held in Sept., hosted by India, in New Delhi; parallel meetings to promote dialogue and engagement with different groups are held concurrently with the summit gatherings, including with representatives of the private sector (Business 20), civil society (Civil 20), labour orgs (Labour 20), women (Women 20), tourism and young people (Youth 20), and think tanks and research institutes (Think 20–T20); the Global Infrastructure Fund (GIF), a G20 initiative, aims to enhance investment in infrastructure projects in developing economies and emerging markets; mems: Argentina, Australia, Brazil, Canada, People's Rep. of China, France, Germany, India, Indonesia, Italy, Japan, Rep. of Korea, Mexico, Russian Fed., Saudi Arabia, South Africa, Türkiye (Turkey), UK, USA, the African Union and the European Union; observers: Netherlands, Spain; the presidency rotates among the participating states on an annual basis (Nov. 2022–Nov. 2023: India).

Intergovernmental Group of 24 (G24) on International Monetary Affairs and Development: 700 19th St, NW, HQ1 Rm 2-588, Washington, DC 20431, USA; tel. (202) 623-6101; fax (202) 623-6000; e-mail g24@g24.org; internet www.g24.org; f. 1971; aims to co-ordinate the position of developing countries on monetary and devt finance issues; operates at the political level of ministers responsible for finance and governors of central banks; in April 2022, in the context of the COVID-19 pandemic, called for more widespread global attention to debt vulnerability, and recommended the creation of an inclusive forum to reconsider the suitability of the global international financial and economic architecture and its ability to respond quickly and fairly to global crises; mems (Africa): Algeria,

REGIONAL ORGANIZATIONS

Côte d'Ivoire, Democratic Rep. of the Congo, Egypt, Ethiopia, Gabon, Ghana, Kenya, Morocco, Nigeria, South Africa; (Latin America and the Caribbean): Argentina, Brazil, Colombia, Guatemala, Ecuador, Haiti, Mexico, Peru, Trinidad and Tobago, Venezuela; (Asia and the Middle East): Egypt, India, Iran, Lebanon, Pakistan, Philippines, Sri Lanka, Syrian Arab Rep.; the People's Rep. of China has the status of special invitee at G24 meetings; G77 participant states may attend G24 meetings as observers, 11 institutional and 5 country observers; Chair. ADAMA COULIBALY (Côte d'Ivoire); Dir Dr IYABO MASHA.

International Arab Society of Certified Accountants (IASCA): POB 921100, Amman 11192, Jordan; tel. (6) 5100900; fax (6) 5100901; e-mail info@iascasociety.org; internet www.iascasociety.org; f. 1984; supervises qualifications for Arab accountants and aims to maintain standards; mems in 21 countries; Chair. TALAL ABU-GHAZALEH (Jordan); Exec. Dir SALEM AL-OURI; publs *Arab Certified Accountant* (monthly), *ASCA Bulletin* (monthly), *IASCA Newsletter* (monthly), *International Audit Standards*, *Abu-Ghazaleh Dictionary of Accountancy*.

Islamic Financial Services Board: Sasana Kijang, Level 5, Bank Negara Malaysia, 2 Jalan Dato Onn, 50840 Kuala Lumpur, Malaysia; tel. (3) 91951400; fax (3) 91951405; e-mail ifsb_sec@ifsb.org; internet www.ifsb.org; f. 2002; aims to formulate standards and guiding principles for regulatory and supervisory agencies working within the Islamic financial services industry; has developed, in co-operation with the Basel Committee on Banking Supervision, Core Principles for Islamic Finance Regulation (CPIFR); Guiding Principles on *Shari'a* Governance Systems for Institutions offering Islamic Financial Services, and Guiding Principles on Governance for *Takâful* Undertakings (Islamic insurance) were adopted in Dec. 2009; Guiding Principles for *Retakâfu* (Islamic reinsurance) adopted in April 2018; mems (full, assoc. and observers): 187, incl. 80 regulatory and supervisory authorities, 10 orgs, 97 financial institutions, professional firms, industry associations and stock exchanges in 57 jurisdictions; Chair. Dr PERRY WARJIYO (Indonesia); Sec.-Gen. Dr BELLO LAWAL DANBATT (Malaysia); publ. *IFSB Bulletin* (3 a year).

Union of Arab Banks (UAB): POB 11-2416, Riad el-Solh 1107 2210, Beirut, Lebanon; tel. (1) 377800; fax (1) 364927; e-mail uab@uabonline.org; internet www.uabonline.org; f. 1974; aims to foster co-operation between Arab banks and to increase their efficiency; prepares feasibility studies for projects; organizes an annual International Arab Banking Summit, with participation by govt ministers, central bank governors, IMF and World Bank Group execs, representatives of the banking sector, and other policymakers; mems: more than 330 Arab banks and financial institutions; Chair. MOHAMED EL-JARRAH EL-SABBAH (Egypt); Sec.-Gen. WISSAM HASSAN FATTOUH (Lebanon).

Union of Arab Securities Authorities: Securities and Commodities Authority Bldg, 1st Floor, POB 117555, Dubai, United Arab Emirates; tel. (4) 2900000; fax (4) 2900059; e-mail info@uasa.ae; internet www.uasa.ae; f. 2007; Chair. ABDULLAH BIN SALEM AL SALMI; Sec.-Gen. JALIL TARIF.

Vulnerable Twenty Group (V20): 2E Maison de la Paix, Chemin Eugène-Rigot, 1202 Geneva, Switzerland; e-mail secretariat@V-20.org; internet www.v-20.org; f. 2015, in accordance with a proposal outlined in the Costa Rica Action Plan of the Climate Vulnerable Forum (CVF); comprises the ministers responsible for finance of mem. states of the CVF, with the following objectives: to promote the mobilization of both public and private climate finance; to exchange and share best practices on the financial and economic aspects of climate action; to develop new approaches to climate finance; and to undertake collective action, including jt advocacy; a Climate Vulnerable Forum-V20 Joint Multi Donor Fund was launched in Dec. 2020; inaugural (virtual) climate vulnerables' finance summit held in July 2021; in June 2022 the V20 reported that during 2000–19 climate change had eradicated one-fifth of vulnerable countries' wealth, and demanded the creation of a dedicated international funding mechanism to support their adaptation to the climate crisis; 9th ministerial dialogue held in Oct. 2022; chair. rotates (mid-2022–mid-2024: Ghana); mems: 48 (Afghanistan, Bangladesh, Barbados, Bhutan, Burkina Faso, Cambodia, Colombia, Comoros, Costa Rica, Democratic Rep. of the Congo, Dominican Rep., Ethiopia, Fiji, The Gambia, Ghana, Grenada, Guatemala, Haiti, Honduras, Kenya, Kiribati, Lebanon, Madagascar, Malawi, Maldives, Marshall Islands, Mongolia, Morocco, Nepal, Niger, Palau, Palestine, Papua New Guinea, Philippines, Rwanda, Saint Lucia, Samoa, Senegal, South Sudan, Sri Lanka, Sudan, Tanzania, Timor-Leste, Tunisia, Tuvalu, Vanuatu, Viet Nam, Yemen).

Education

Alliance israélite universelle: 27 ave de Ségur, 75007 Paris, France; tel. 1-53-32-88-55; fax 1-48-74-51-33; e-mail info@aiu.org; internet www.aiu.org; f. 1860 to work for human rights and the emancipation of the Jewish people; has subsequently focused on education; maintains 40 schools in France, the Mediterranean area and Canada; library of 150,000 vols, 3,000 periodicals and 1,000 manuscripts; also maintains a digital library; mems: 8,000 in 16 countries; Pres. MARC EISENBERG.

Arab Bureau of Education for the Gulf States: Riyadh 12511-3113, Saudi Arabia; tel. (11) 4800555; e-mail abegs@abegs.org; internet www.abegs.org; f. 1975; co-ordinates and promotes co-operation and integration among mem. countries in the fields of education, culture, science, information and documentation; aims to unify the educational systems of all Gulf Arab states; includes the Gulf Arab States' Educational Research Center (POB 25566, Safat, Kuwait), Arab Educational Training Center for Gulf States (Doha), and Arabic Language Educational Center for Gulf States (Sharjah); mems: Bahrain, Kuwait, Oman, Qatar, Saudi Arabia, United Arab Emirates, Yemen; Dir-Gen. Dr ABDULRAHMAN BIN MOHAMMED AL-ASSIMI; publs *Risalat Ul-Khaleej al-Arabi* (quarterly), *Arab Gulf Journal of Scientific Research* (2 a year).

Association of Arab Universities: POB 401, Amman 11941, Jordan; tel. (6) 5062048; e-mail secgen@aaru.edu.jo; internet www.aaru.edu.jo; f. 1964; a scientific conf. is held every 3 years; council meetings held annually; mems: 280 univs; Sec.-Gen. Prof. AMR EZZAT SALAMA; publ. *AARU Journal*.

European Union of Arabic and Islamic Scholars (Union Européenne des Arabisants et Islamisants—UEAI): Institute of Asian and African Studies, Moscow State University, Mokhovaya 11, Moscow 101999, Russian Federation; e-mail dvfrolov@yandex.ru; internet www.ueai.info; f. 1962; organizes congress of Arabic and Islamic Studies every 2 years; mems: more than 200; Pres. LALE BEHZADI; Sec.-Gen. DMITRY R. ZHANTIEV.

Islamic World Academy of Sciences (IAS): Ismail Al-A'asoufi St, Khilda, Amman 11183, Jordan; tel. (6) 5522104; fax (6) 5511803; e-mail ias@go.com.jo; internet www.iasworld.org; f. 1986; serves as a consultative organization of the OIC and developing countries in the field of science and technology; convenes international scientific conferences; organizes and supports capacity building workshops in basic sciences in developing countries; provides experts and consultants in science and technology to developing countries upon request; mems: 106; Dir-Gen. Dr ADNAN BADRAN (Jordan); publ. *The Medical Journal* (quarterly).

Organisation of Southern Cooperation (OSC): Egypt St, House no. 1986, 1165 Addis Ababa, Ethiopia; internet osc-ocs.org; f. 2020, as the Organization of Educational Cooperation, by participants in the International Summit on Balanced and Inclusive Education, convened in Jan., in Djibouti, at which time a Universal Declaration on Balanced and Inclusive Education was signed; at the inaugural regular session of the General Assembly, held in Dec. 2021, in Geneva, Switzerland, an 8-year strategic plan was adopted, titled 'Building the Education we Need—Shaping the Future we Want', focused on enhancing systemic governance and policy frameworks; building capacities in balanced and inclusive education; democratizing knowledge and research; bridging the techno-digital divide; enhancing horizontal and cross-sectoral co-operation; strengthening solidarity-based financing and sustainable debt agreements; and reinforcing South-South co-operation and integration; at an extraordinary session of the General Assembly, convened in late June 2023, in Addis Ababa, the present name was adopted, to reflect the org.'s focus on the Global South; Sec.-Gen. MANSSOUR BIN MUSSALLAM.

Environment and Energy

Arab Union of Electricity (AUE): POB 2310, Amman 11181, Jordan; tel. (6) 5819146; fax (6) 5859403; e-mail contact-us@auptde.org; internet auptde.org; f. 1987; aims to enhance the electricity sector in Arab states; mems: 32 full; 20 assoc., 2 observing mems; Sec.-Gen. NASSER AL-MUHANNAD.

Framework Convention for the Protection of the Marine Environment of the Caspian Sea: Tehran Convention Secretariat, c/o UNEP Regional Office for Europe, 11 chemin des Anémones, 1219 Châtelaine, Geneva, Switzerland; tel. 229178696; e-mail tehranconvention@unep.ch; internet www.tehranconvention.org; the Framework Convention for the Protection of the Marine Environment of the Caspian Sea (Tehran Convention) was adopted in Nov. 2003 by the Governments of Azerbaijan, Iran, Kazakhstan, Russian Fed. and Turkmenistan; the Aktau Protocol Concerning Regional Preparedness, Response and Co-operation in Combating Oil Pollution Incidents was adopted in Aug. 2011; the 5th Conference of the Parties was convened in Aşgabat, Turkmenistan, in May 2014; the Tehran Convention process is funded by the Global Environment Facility, the European Union and UNEP.

REGIONAL ORGANIZATIONS — Other Regional Organizations

International Coral Reef Initiative: e-mail fstaub@icriforum.org; internet www.icriforum.org; f. 1994 at the inaugural Conference of the Parties of the Convention on Biological Diversity; a partnership of govts, international orgs and NGOs; aims to raise awareness at all levels on the degradation of coral reefs around the world; promotes sustainable management practices and supports the conservation of reefs and related marine ecosystems; administers the Global Coral Reef Monitoring Network; the 36th General Meeting, held online in Dec. 2021, adopted a 2021–24 plan of action titled 'Turning the Tide for Coral Reefs'; the 37th General Meeting was scheduled to be held in Sept. 2023; the secretariat is co-chaired by developed and developing countries, on a rotational basis (2021–23: USA); mems: 93 govts, int. and reg. orgs; publ. *Status of Coral Reefs of the World*.

International Energy Agency: 9 rue de la Fédération, 75739 Paris Cedex 15, France; tel. 1-40-57-65-00; fax 1-40-57-65-09; e-mail info@iea.org; internet www.iea.org; f. 1974; serves as an autonomous org. within the framework of the OECD to develop co-operation on energy policy and to co-ordinate response measures during petroleum supply crises; mandate subsequently extended to include environmental protection and economic devt; mems: 30 states, incl. Türkiye; Sec.-Gen. Dr FATIH BIROL (Türkiye).

International Energy Forum (IEF): POB 94736, Diplomatic Quarter, Riyadh 11614, Saudi Arabia; tel. (11) 481-0022; fax (11) 481-0055; e-mail info@ief.org; internet www.ief.org; f. 1991; promotes dialogue on energy matters; ministers responsible for energy affairs from states accounting for about 90% of global oil and gas supply and demand convene, usually, every 2 years; a meeting of the International Business Energy Forum, attended by CEOs of leading energy cos, precedes the gathering; since 2005 the IEF secretariat has co-ordinated the work of the Joint Oil Data Initiative (JODI), formally established as a multi-agency permanent reporting mechanism in 2002; an annual symposium with OPEC and the International Energy Agency has been held since 2011; signed an MOU with IRENA in Jan. 2020 to promote greater collaboration between the orgs; mems: 72 states, including the mems of OPEC and the IEA; Sec.-Gen. JOSEPH McMONIGLE (USA).

International Renewable Energy Agency (IRENA): Masdar City, POB 236, Abu Dhabi, United Arab Emirates; tel. (2) 4179000; e-mail info@irena.org; internet www.irena.org; f. 2009 at a conf. held in Bonn, Germany; aims to promote the devt and application of renewable sources of energy; to act as a forum for the exchange of information and technology transfer; and to organize training seminars and other educational activities; inaugural Assembly convened in April 2011; 12th Assembly held in Jan. 2022, in Abu Dhabi, UAE; hosts SEforALL's Renewable Energy hub; signed an MOU with IEF in Jan. 2020; initiated in Jan. 2021 a Global High-Level Forum on Energy Transition; promotes 3 subregional Clean Energy Corridors; mems: 167 (incl. the European Union); Dir-Gen. FRANCESCO LA CAMERA (Italy); publ. *World Energy Transitions Outlook*.

International Solar Alliance (ISA): Surya Bhawan, National Institute of Solar Energy Campus, Gwal Pahari, Faridabad-Gurugram Rd, Gurugram, 122003 Haryana, India; tel. (124) 2853090; e-mail info@isolaralliance.org; internet isolaralliance.org; f. 2015, as a coalition of solar resource rich countries; aims to increase the use of solar energy to meet energy needs of mem. and prospective mem. countries in an equitable and sustainable manner, and to provide a platform for collaboration; granted observer status at the UN General Assembly in Dec. 2021; mems: 114 signatory countries; Dir-Gen. Dr AJAY MATHUR (India); publs *ISA Programmes*, *ISA Journals*.

IUCN—International Union for Conservation of Nature: 28 rue Mauverney, 1196 Gland, Switzerland; tel. 229990000; e-mail membership@iucn.org; internet www.iucn.org; f. 1948, as the International Union for Conservation of Nature and Natural Resources; supports partnerships and practical field activities to promote the conservation and sustainable use of natural resources, to secure the conservation of biological diversity; develops programmes to protect and sustain the most important and threatened species and ecosystems and assists govts to devise and carry out national conservation strategies; incorporates the Species Survival Commission, a science-based network of volunteer experts aiming to ensure conservation of present levels of biodiversity; compiles the annually updated Red List of Threatened Species; by 30 June 2023 the list had assessed some 150,388 species of animals, plants and fungi, and determined 42,108 to be vulnerable, endangered or close to extinction; from July 2021 an IUCN Green Status of Species standard was used for the first time, to measure how near a species is to being fully ecologically functional across its range, and how successful conservation action has been; at that time Green Status assessments were presented for 181 species; also maintains a Green List of Protected and Conserved Areas and a Red List of Ecosystems; maintains a Restoration Barometer as the standard global tool for monitoring progress in restoring ecosystems (the first *Restoration Barometer* report was issued in Dec. 2022); maintains a conservation library and documentation centre and units for monitoring traffic in wildlife; organizes a World Conservation Congress every 4 years (2025: Abu Dhabi, UAE, in Oct.); the 2021 Congress (held in Marseilles, France, in Sept.) voted decisively in favour of a resolution that called for a global moratorium on deep seabed mining, in view of potential risks posed by such activities to oceanic biodiversity and ecosystems; in June 2023 supported the Govt of the Comoros to host a Blue Future Ministerial Conference, which issued the Moroni Declaration for Ocean and Climate Action in Africa; mems: more than 1,400 mem. orgs, agencies and asscns in some 160 countries; Pres. RAZAN AL MUBARAK (United Arab Emirates); Dir-Gen. Dr BRUNO OBERLE (Switzerland) (until Dec. 2023); publs *Annual Report*, *IUCN Restoration Barometer* (annually), *PARKS-The International Journal of Protected Areas and Conservation* (2 a year), other periodicals, reports and policy briefs.

Sustainable Energy for All (SEforALL): Andromeda Tower, 15th Floor, Donau-City-Str. 6, 1220 Vienna, Austria; e-mail info@seforall.org; internet www.se4all.org; f. 2011, as an initiative of the UN Secretary-General; works towards the attainment of Sustainable Development Goal 7, i.e. to secure by 2030 universal access to modern energy sources, to increase, by 50%, the use of renewable energy, and to enhance energy efficiency worldwide; aims to develop international partnerships and funding arrangements in support of these objectives; in 2016 established a Co-ordination Cttee to maintain a close working relationship with the UN and to co-ordinate activities; in response to the COVID-19 pandemic SEforALL focused work on sustainable cold chain infrastructure (in support of equitable vaccine distribution), the power needs of healthcare facilities, and incorporating sustainable energy into recovery plans; organizes a regular Forum (2022: Kigali, Rwanda, in May); CEO (and Special Rep. of the UN Sec.-Gen. for Sustainable Energy for All) DAMILOLA OGUNBIYI (Nigeria).

WWF International: 28 rue Mauverney, 1196 Gland, Switzerland; tel. 223649111; internet wwf.panda.org; f. 1961 (as World Wildlife Fund), name changed to World Wide Fund for Nature in 1986, present name adopted in 2001; aims to stop the degradation of natural environments, conserve biodiversity, ensure the sustainable use of renewable resources, and promote the reduction of both pollution and wasteful consumption; focuses on the following Global Goals: ensuring that major fisheries and ocean ecosystems remain productive and resilient, and improving livelihoods and biodiversity; securing the future of endangered species; protecting the integrity of forests; protecting freshwater ecosystems and flow regimes; ensuring a global shift towards a low carbon, climate resilient future; and ensuring sustainable food systems that maintain food security while conserving nature; has identified 35 'priority places' worldwide that represent major intact ecosystems or support irreplaceable and threatened biodiversity; major efforts are focused on the following 'ecoregions': Baltic; Barents; Borneo; Caucasus; Danube and Carpathian; European Alps; Greater Annamites (a mountain rainforest area of South-East Asia); Mediterranean; Mekong; North-East Atlantic; Valdivian (a temperate rainforest zone comprising parts of southern Chile and border areas of Argentina); the East and West African marine ecoregions; and the Lower Mekong Dry Forests Ecoregion; also places a strategic focus on priority species that either form a key element of the food chain, support the stability or regeneration of habitats, demonstrate broader conservation needs, are necessary for the health and livelihoods of local communities, are exploited commercially, or are important cultural icons; undertakes activities aimed at reducing the ecological 'footprint' of humanity in the following priority areas: carbon, energy and climate; sustainable cities; farming; fishing; forestry; and water; mems: offices in more than 100 countries, 5 assoc. orgs, c. 5m. individual mems worldwide; Pres. Dr ADIL NAJAM (Pakistan); Dir-Gen. KIRSTEN SCHUIJT (Netherlands); publs *Annual Report*, *Living Planet Report*.

Governance and Security

African Parliamentary Union: BP V314, Abidjan, Côte d'Ivoire; tel. 20-30-39-70; fax 20-30-44-05; e-mail upa1@aviso.ci; internet www.apunion.org; f. 1976 (as Union of African Parliaments); aims to promote democracy and to facilitate interaction between African legislators and parliamentary institutions; mems: 41 parliaments; Sec.-Gen. GADO BOUBACAR IDI.

Afro-Asian Peoples' Solidarity Organization (AAPSO): 89 Abdel Aziz Al-Saoud St, POB 11559-61 Manial El-Roda, Cairo, Egypt; tel. (2) 3636081; fax (2) 3637361; e-mail aapso@idsc.net.eg; internet www.aapsorg.org; f. 1958; acts among and for the peoples of Africa and Asia in support of genuine independence, sovereignty, socioeconomic devt, peace and disarmament; holds General Congress normally every 2 years; mems: nat. cttees and affiliated orgs in 90 countries and territories, assoc. mems in Europe and Latin America;

Pres. HELMY AL-HADIDI; Sec.-Gen. NOURI ABDEL RAZZAK HUSSEIN (Iraq); publs *Solidarity Bulletin* (monthly), *Socio-Economic Development* (3 a year).

Arab Inter-Parliamentary Union (Union Interparlementaire Arabe): Unit 1B, Bldg 201, Maarad St, Marfaa Area, Beirut, Lebanon; tel. (1) 985960; fax (1) 985963; e-mail info@arabipu.org; internet www.arabipu.org; f. 1974; aims to strengthen contacts and promote dialogue between Arab parliamentarians, to co-ordinate activities at international forums, to enhance democratic concepts and values in the Arab countries, to co-ordinate and unify Arab legislation, and to strengthen Arab solidarity; mems from 22 countries; Pres. MOHAMMED RIKAN HADID ALHALBOOSI (Iraq); Sec.-Gen. FAYEZ AL SHAWABKEH.

Caspian Summit: inaugural meeting of heads of state of the 5 littoral Caspian Sea states was held in Aşgabat, Turkmenistan, in April 2002, in order to further discussions on the status and demarcation of the sea; a special working group, at the level of deputy mins responsible for foreign affairs, had been established in 1996 to negotiate a legal framework on the shared use of the Caspian Sea; subsequent summits were convened in Tehran, Iran, in Oct. 2007, Baku, Azerbaijan, in Nov. 2010, and Astrakhan, Russian Fed., in Sept. 2014; in Aug. 2018, at the 5th summit meeting, convened in Aktau, Kazakhstan, heads of state signed the Convention on the Legal Status of the Caspian Sea, as well as protocols to previous intergovernmental agreements; the accords were to govern the shared resources and security of the sea, *inter alia*, through the delineation of territorial and exclusive fishing rights, the prohibition of any foreign military presence, and strengthened co-operation in maritime shipping, transport interconnection and the prevention of incidents; a business forum and a Caspian Youth Summit took place at the sidelines of the summit for the first time in 2010; the First Caspian Economic Forum was convened in Aug. 2019, in Awaza, Turkmenistan; mems: Azerbaijan, Iran, Kazakhstan, Russian Fed., Turkmenistan.

Conference on Interaction and Confidence Building Measures in Asia: 010000 Astana, 55/20 Mangilik Yel. Ave, Kazakhstan; tel. (7172) 57-65-10; e-mail s-cica@s-cica.org; internet www.s-cica.org; f. 1999; aims to provide a structure to enhance co-operation, and to promote peace, security and stability throughout the region; inaugural meeting of heads of state held in June 2002, adopted the Almatı Act; a secretariat was established in June 2006; activities focused on a catalogue of confidence-building measures grouped as: economic dimension; environmental dimension; human dimension; fight against new challenges and threats (such as drug trafficking, terrorism, transborder crime, human trafficking, money laundering, illicit trade in small arms and light weapons); and military-political dimension; supports the Heart of Asia-Istanbul Process; an informal ministerial meeting was held in New York, USA, in Sept. 2017, to mark 25 years since the formation of CICA was proposed in 1992; the 5th summit meeting, held in Dushanbe, Tajikistan, in June 2019, adopted a declaration entitled Shared Vision for a Secure and More Prosperous CICA Region; at the 6th summit meeting, held in Oct. 2022, in Astana, mems resolved to transform the legal status of the grouping into an international org.; the role of Exec. Dir was renamed Sec.-Gen. and a Deputy Sec.-Gen. was to be appointed; mems: 27 states; 9 observer states; 5 observer orgs (UN, OSCE, League of Arab States, IOM, and Parliamentary Assembly of Turkic States); Sec.-Gen. KAIRAT SARYBAY (Kazakhstan).

European Political Community (EPC): f. 2022 (the format having first been proposed in May by Pres. Emmanuel Macron of France); conceived of as a broad platform to promote inter-European exchange of views, political dialogue and co-operation with respect to Europe-wide strategic challenges, with a view to strengthening continental stability, security, peace and prosperity; the format is informal: as such, the participants do not issue collective formal declarations; meetings between European leaders may take place in smaller (e.g. bilateral, trilateral) formats on the sidelines of the EPC's summits; inaugural summit held in Oct. 2022, in Prague, Czech Rep., with participation by the heads of state or govt of the 27 EU mem. states (the European Council of the EU agreed in June 2022 to support the EPC format), the 4 European Free Trade Association countries (i.e. Iceland, Liechtenstein, Norway and Switzerland), the UK, 6 as yet non-EU Western Balkans countries (Albania, Bosnia and Herzegovina, Kosovo, Montenegro, North Macedonia and Serbia), 5 Eastern European countries (Armenia, Azerbaijan, Georgia, Moldova and Ukraine), and Türkiye; subsequent summits were to be convened biannually, hosted alternately by EU and non-EU mems; the 2nd summit was held in June 2023, in Bulboaca, Moldova.

Group of Seven (G7): an informal meeting of major advanced economies, originally comprising France, Germany, Italy, Japan, UK and the USA, first convened in Nov. 1975, at Rambouillet, France, at the level of heads of state and of govt; Canada became a permanent participant in 1976; from 1991 the Russian Fed. was invited to participate in summit meetings outside the formal framework of co-operation and in 1997 Russia became a participant in nearly all meetings, excepting those related to finance and the global economy; from 1998 the name of the co-operation framework was changed to Group of Eight—G8, and during 2003–13 Russia participated fully in the grouping; from March 2014, however, owing to Russia's interference in Ukraine's domestic affairs and its recognition of Crimea (hitherto a Ukrainian autonomous territory) as a sovereign state, and subsequent annexation of Crimea, Russia's participation was suspended, and the group reverted to its former membership and name; an annual meeting is convened, with the Presidents of the European Commission and the European Council, the chairmanship and venue of which are rotated; summit meetings address and seek consensus on social and economic issues confronting the international community; regular discussions at the level of ministers of finance and central bank governors take place to consider devts in the global economy and economic policy; sectoral ministerial meetings are also convened to address areas such as energy, the environment and foreign affairs; an emergency teleconference of G7 finance ministers and central bank governors was held in early March 2020 to discuss policy tools that might protect the global economy from the impacts of the then suddenly expanding and intensifying COVID-19 global public health emergency; at a virtual summit meeting held in mid-April support was expressed by all leaders other than Pres. Trump for the ongoing efforts of the World Health Organization (WHO) and partner agencies to combat the COVID-19 pandemic (Trump, meanwhile, had recently suspended US funding to WHO); at the end of May the USA, scheduled to be hosting the 46th summit meeting in the following month, postponed the gathering until later in the year; in the event, no summit was convened; at a virtual mini-summit gathering hosted by the UK in Feb. 2021 mem. states pledged US $7,500m. in additional funding to redress 'vaccine inequality' (the theme of the meeting) by accelerating the distribution of surplus COVID-19 vaccines to developing countries; in early June, meeting in London, UK, G7 finance ministers jtly agreed support for a global minimum corporate tax rate of 15%; the 2021 summit meeting—hosted by the UK, in Carbis Bay, Cornwall, in mid-June—reaffirmed support for the UN-sponsored ACT-Accelerator and COVAX Facility (see WHO) as the principal means of providing vaccines to the poorest nations, and pledged to secure a further 1,000m. COVID-19 vaccine doses over the next year for low- and middle-income countries; the so-called Carbis Bay Declaration also incl. commitments to continue to invest in research and innovation, with a view to ensuring the efficacy of vaccines against emerging variants of COVID-19; to engage constructively at the WTO on the issue of introducing temporary intellectual property waivers for COVID-19 vaccine patents; to support the strengthening of the global health system, incl. global surveillance for potentially dangerous diseases; to continue to support economies and protect employment, while investing in training, skills, innovation, and the creation of decent jobs and quality infrastructure; to support a new $650,000m. general allocation of IMF special drawing rights; to continue to pursue the goal of phasing out inefficient fossil fuel subsidies by 2025; to ensure that by 2026 40m. more girls are receiving education; and to co-operate with China, in particular on addressing climate change; the communiqué also called on China to respect human rights and fundamental freedoms, especially in relation to Xinjiang and Hong Kong; a virtual meeting of the G7 leaders, with participation by the Secs-Gen. of the UN and of NATO, was held in late Aug. to address the recent takeover of Afghanistan by the militant Taliban org.; at the end of Aug. a virtual meeting on Afghanistan was convened by the ministers responsible for foreign affairs of the G7 states, EU, Turkey (now known as Türkiye) and Qatar (which had assisted with the civilian evacuation process), again with participation by the NATO Sec.-Gen.; in Dec. G7 foreign ministers, convened in Liverpool, UK, condemned the Russian military build-up on its border with Ukraine and urged a de-escalation of tensions; the G7 strongly reaffirmed its commitment to Ukraine's territorial integrity; in mid-Feb. 2022 the G7 stated its continuing grave concern over the 'threatening military build-up' of Russian forces around Ukraine, and called on Russia to resolve tensions through diplomatic channels and substantively to withdraw its military presence; on 24 Feb., in response to Russia's initiation on that day of a full-scale military invasion of Ukraine, the G7 leaders issued a statement that condemned the assault on Ukraine, terming it a serious threat to the UN Charter and rules-based international order; meeting in Brussels, in March, the G7 leaders determined to increase collective contributions to the World Food Programme and to other int. agencies concerned with alleviating food insecurity; a virtual meeting of G7 leaders held in early May, with participation by Pres. Zelensky of Ukraine, pledged to continue to provide Ukraine with military and defence support, to help strengthen the country's energy and economic security, and to expand co-operation, including on information security; firm commitments were made at that time to (i) phase out dependency on Russian energy, including by phasing out or banning imports of Russian oil, through finding alternative suppliers and expediting the transition to clean energy sources; (ii) prohibit or prevent the provision of key services on which Russia depends; and (iii) continue to take action against Russian banks connected to the global economy and of systemically critical importance to the Russian financial system; at the annual summit, convened in late June, in Schloss Elmau, Germany, the leaders issued a communiqué in which they pledged to stand firmly by Ukraine, incl. through the provision of budgetary and humanitarian assistance, military aid, and support for Ukraine's long-term reconstruction; the leaders also agreed to establish a Partnership for Global Infrastructure and Investment (PGII), which aimed to mobilize (by 2027) $600,000m. for projects in developing economies, and a G7 Climate Club, to promote climate actions aligned with the goals of the 2015 Paris Agreement, and committed to achieving a fully decarbonized electricity supply by 2035; some $4,500m. in additional funding was committed to a new G7 Global Alliance for Food Security that had been launched in May by a meeting of G7 ministers responsible for devt; the leaders determined generally to cease direct international public financing of fossil fuels by the end of 2022; in Aug. G7 foreign ministers and the High Representative of the EU called upon Russian forces immediately to give back to Ukraine full control of all of its nuclear facilities, to ensure their safety; meeting in Sept. the G7 finance ministers stated their collective political intention to impose a price cap on Russia's oil exports, with a view to reducing that country's revenues; the 49th G7 leaders' summit was hosted by Japan in Hiroshima, in mid-May 2023, with additional invited participation by the leaders of Australia, Brazil, Comoros, Cook Islands, India, Indonesia, Republic of Korea, Viet Nam, and Ukraine; the ensuing Hiroshima Leaders' Communiqué, emphasizing respect for the UN Charter and international partnership, reaffirmed unwavering support to Ukraine 'for as long as it takes' to counter Russia's war of aggression, and committed (as detailed in a G7 Leaders' Statement on Ukraine) to intensifying diplomatic, financial, humanitarian and military support for Ukraine, to increasing costs for Russia and supporters of its war, and to continuing to work towards mitigating the negative global impacts of the conflict (particularly for the most vulnerable people worldwide); the leaders issued a G7 Clean Energy Economy Action Plan, endorsed a series of Circular Economy and Resource Efficiency Principles, and—in a G7 Leaders' Statement on Economic Resilience and Economic Security—determined to focus on diversifying and deepening partnerships, and on 'de-risking' economic activities (while stressing that sustainable economic relations with China, rather than a 'decoupling', were envisaged); the leaders issued a Hiroshima Action Statement for Resilient Global Food Security, and endorsed a G7 Global Plan for Universal Health Care Action Agenda, as well as an annex on a G7 Vision for Operationalising Data Free Flow with Trust (DEFT—aimed at combining enhanced cross-border data flows with strengthened data privacy and security; a G7 Action Plan for Promoting DEFT had been launched in May 2022); a G7 Leaders' Hiroshima Vision on Nuclear Disarmament was issued by the May 2023 summit, which also emphasized the importance of ensuring a free and open, inclusive, prosperous, secure, rules-based Indo-Pacific; mems: Canada, France, Germany, Italy, Japan (holding the presidency in 2023), UK, USA; European Commission representation.

International Institute for Democracy and Electoral Assistance (International IDEA): Strömsborg, 103 34 Stockholm, Sweden; tel. (8) 698-3700; fax (8) 20-2422; e-mail info@idea.int; internet www.idea.int; f. 1995; aims to promote sustainable democracy in new and established democracies; works with practitioners and institutions promoting democracy in Africa, Asia, Arab states and Latin America; in Nov. 2020 hosted a high-level global conf., in a virtual format, to commemorate its 25th anniversary, on the theme 'Democracy Now and Next'; mems: 31 states, 2 observer; Sec.-Gen. Dr KEVIN CASAS-ZAMORA (Costa Rica).

Inter-Parliamentary Union (IPU): 5 chemin du Pommier, CP 330, 1218 Le Grand-Saconnex/Geneva, Switzerland; tel. 229194150; fax 229194160; e-mail postbox@mail.ipu.org; internet www.ipu.org; f. 1889; aims to promote peace, co-operation and representative democracy by providing a forum for multilateral political debate between representatives of national parliaments; Fifth World Conference of Speakers of Parliament was initiated as a virtual event in Aug. 2020 and was concluded in Vienna, hosted by the Austrian Govt, in Sept. 2021; mems: nat. parliaments of 179 sovereign states; 14 inter-parliamentary asscns as assoc. mems; Pres. DUARTE PACHECO (Portugal); Sec.-Gen. MARTIN CHUNGONG (Cameroon); publs *Annual Report*, *IPU Information Brochure* (annually), *Women in Parliament* (annually), *IPU Strategy*.

Jewish Agency for Israel (JAFI): POB 92, 48 King George St, Jerusalem 91000 Israel; tel. (2) 6202222; e-mail pniyottzibor@jafi.org; internet www.jewishagency.org; f. 1929; reconstituted 1971 as an instrument through which world Jewry can work to develop a national home; constituents are the World Zionist Organization, United Israel Appeal, Inc. (USA), and Keren Hayesod; Dir-Gen. AMIRA AHARONOVICH.

MIKTA: c/o Dept of Foreign Affairs and Trade, R. G. Casey Bldg, John McEwen Crescent, Barton ACT 0221, Australia; tel. (2) 6261-1111; internet www.mikta.org; f. 2013; inaugural meeting of ministers responsible for foreign affairs of the 5 MIKTA countries was held on the sidelines of the UN General Assembly, in New York, USA, in Sept. 2013 in order to establish a cross-regional consultative partnership; 5th ministerial meeting, convened in Seoul, Rep. of Korea, in May 2015, adopted a vision statement reaffirming mems' shared values and determination to promote multilateral co-operation and to strengthen global governance; subsequently the ministers agreed to meet 2–3 times a year; a MIKTA Interfaith and Intercultural Dialogue was initiated in Dec. 2016; the 8th consultation meeting of MIKTA speakers of parliament was held in March 2023, in Istanbul, Türkiye; priority themes in 2023 were: strengthening multilateralism, inclusive recovery and digital transformation; mems: Australia, Indonesia (holding the rotating presidency in 2023), Rep. of Korea, Mexico, Türkiye.

North Atlantic Treaty Organization (NATO): blvd Léopold III, 1110 Brussels, Belgium; tel. (2) 707-41-11; fax (2) 707-45-79; e-mail natodoc@hq.nato.int; internet www.nato.int; NATO implements the objectives of the Atlantic Alliance, which was established on the basis of the 1949 North Atlantic Treaty and aims to provide common security for its mems through co-operation and consultation in political, military and economic fields, as well as scientific, environmental, and other non-military aspects; the highest authority of the Alliance is the North Atlantic Council (NAC), which meets at the level of permanent representatives of mem. countries, ministers of foreign affairs, defence ministers, or heads of state or govt (2023: Vilnius, Lithuania, in July); in March 2011 NATO initiated Operation Unified Protector in order to monitor and enforce a UN-imposed arms embargo against the Libyan authorities; later in that month NATO mems determined to enforce the UN sanctioned no-fly zone over Libya, alongside a military operation to prevent further attacks on civilians and civilian-populated areas, undertaken by a multinational coalition under British, France and US command; on 27 March, NATO mem. states agreed to assume full command of the operation to protect civilians in Libya; the Operation was extended for 90 days from 27 June, and for a further 90 days in late Sept.; in late Oct., following the capture by opposition forces of the last remaining govt-controlled city, Sirte, and the arrest (and subsequent death) of the Libyan leader, Col Muammar al-Qaddafi, the NAC authorized the conclusion of the Operation with effect from the end of that month; leaders attending the Sept. 2014 Newport, UK summit meeting of NATO heads of state and govt expressed willingness to develop a long-term partnership with Libya, possibly leading to that country's membership in the Alliance's so-called Mediterranean Dialogue; Iraq was granted NATO partner status in April 2011; in early 2012 a NATO Transition Cell was established in Iraq to support the devt of the partnership; in June 2012 the NAC met, at the request of Turkey (officially known as Türkiye since 1 June 2022), in accordance with Article 4 of the North Atlantic Treaty—invoked when the territorial integrity, political independence or security of any of the parties is threatened—following the shooting down by Syrian forces of a Turkish military jet; in Dec. NATO ministers of foreign affairs agreed to strengthen Turkey's air defence capabilities along its border with Syria; meeting in late Aug. 2013 the NAC strongly condemned the apparent use on 21 Aug. of chemical weapons against civilians in Ghouta, Damascus, Syria; the NAC determined to continue closely to review the situation in Syria and to continue to support Turkey in protecting the Alliance's south-eastern border; in July 2015 NATO's Secretary-General strongly condemned a bomb attack on the town of Suruç, in southeastern Turkey, near its border with Syria, which had resulted in around 30 fatalities and numerous injuries; at the end of the month, at the request of the Turkish Government, under Article 4 of the North Atlantic Treaty, the NAC gathered again to consider the ongoing threat to peace and security in Turkey; the Council expressed strong solidarity with that country, and determined to observe closely the situation in the southeastern border area; in late Nov. an extraordinary meeting of the NAC emphasized solidarity with Turkey following the shooting down of a Russian plane that had entered its airspace; in May 2017 the NATO Secretary-General stated that the Alliance would participate formally in a non-combat capacity in the global coalition against Islamic State, and noted that a recently established Joint Intelligence and Security Division would place a particular focus on foreign fighters travelling to Iraq and Syria; in Feb. 2017 NATO defence ministers agreed to establish a regional Hub for the South, to address threats arising from North Africa and the Middle East; this—based at Joint Allied Force Command Naples (Italy)—was declared fully operational in July 2018; in July 2018, at the request of the Iraqi Govt—which had declared victory over Islamic State in December 2017—NATO heads of state and government authorized a new NATO Mission Iraq (NMI), with a focus on training; the NMI was established in Oct. 2018; in early Jan. 2020 NATO temporarily suspended the NMI's activities, for safety reasons, following the assassination on 2 Jan., on Iraqi soil, by a US air strike, of Gen. Qassem Soleimani, commander of the elite Quds Force unit of the Iranian Revolutionary Guards Corps; on 6 Jan. the Iraqi legislature passed a non-binding resolution demanding that foreign military forces withdraw from Iraq and cease using its land, waters and airspace; NATO's Sec.-Gen. reiterated that the killing was an act made unilaterally by the US Administration, and noted that there was consensus among the NATO Allies in condemning support by Iran for various terrorist groups, unanimous agreement that Iran should never acquire nuclear weaponry, and concern over a recent escalation of provocations and hostile acts perpetrated by Iran; in Feb. 2021 NATO ministers responsible for defence determined to strengthen and expand the NMI from 500 to 4,000 personnel, on the basis of a request by the Iraqi Govt, with a focus on countering the continuing threat from Islamic State; in June 2022 a trilateral memorandum was concluded between Finland, Sweden and Türkiye which addressed the latter's concerns that, upon the planned admission of those countries into the org., any arms exports should not assist the separatist Kurdistan Workers' Party—Partiya Karkeren Kurdistan; in mid-March 2023, following a meeting with his Finnish counterpart, Türkiye's Pres. Recep Tayyip Erdoğan announced that, as Finland had taken 'authentic and concrete' measures to address Türkiye's security concerns (as agreed in the June 2022 Trilateral Memorandum), ratification of that country's NATO application would proceed through the Turkish legislature; this was effected at the end of March 2023; on 4 April Finland formally deposited its instrument of accession to NATO; in July Pres. Erdoğan gave his approval for Sweden's accession; mems: 31 states, incl. Türkiye; Sec.-Gen. JENS STOLTENBERG (Norway).

Organisation for the Prohibition of Chemical Weapons (OPCW): Johan de Wittlaan 32, 2517 JR The Hague, Netherlands; tel. (70) 4163300; fax (70) 3063535; e-mail public.affairs@opcw.org; internet www.opcw.org; f. April 1997, on the entry into force of the Chemical Weapons Convention (CWC); CWC states parties are obligated to declare any chemical weapons-related activities, to secure and destroy any stockpiles of chemical weapons within the stipulated deadlines, as well as to inactivate and eliminate any chemical weapons production capacity within their jurisdiction; OPCW verifies the irreversible destruction of declared chemical weapons stockpiles, as well as the elimination of all declared chemical weapons production facilities; mem. states undertake to provide protection and assistance if chemical weapons have been used against, or threaten, a state party, and, together with OPCW inspectors, monitor the non-diversion of chemicals for activities prohibited under the CWC and verify the consistency of industrial chemical declarations; the OPCW is a lead partner in the UN Counter-Terrorism Implementation Task Force's working group concerned with preventing and responding to weapons of mass destruction; in March 2013 the UN Secretary-General invited the OPCW to assist a UN fact-finding mission which was appointed at that time to investigate allegations relating to the use of chemical weapons by combatants in the ongoing conflict in Syria (which was not a signatory of the CWC); in Aug. the investigation team refocused its activities on the alleged use of chemical weapons in an attack in the Syrian capital, Damascus; in mid-Sept. the mission's report confirmed that chemical weapons had been used in Syria; at that time the Syrian Govt deposited its instrument of accession to the CWC in accordance with a Russo-US agreement on a framework for the safeguarding and destruction of Syria's chemical weapons stockpiles; in Oct. the UN Security Council authorized the deployment of a jt OPCW-UN mission to supervise the destruction by the Syrian authorities of all chemical weapons stockpiles and production facilities; the mission confirmed all declared materials had been destroyed or removed in Aug. 2014 and the mission was terminated in the following month; a new Joint Investigative Mechanism, comprising experts appointed by the UN and OPCW, was approved by the UN Security Council in Aug. 2015 to investigate the alleged use of toxic chemicals against civilians in Syria, with the aim of bringing perpetrators to account; in Oct. and Nov. 2017 the Russian Fed. vetoed proposed UN Security Council resolutions that were to have extended the mandate of the Joint Investigative Mechanism for a further year; an OPCW Fact-Finding Mission was tasked with investigating the circumstances of the chemical attack reportedly perpetrated in April 2017 at Khan Sheikhoun, Syria; in June the mission confirmed that sarin had been used against civilians during that incident, and in Oct. the mission's 7th report apportioned blame for the attack to the Syrian regime; in April 2018 the OPCW issued the findings of a technical assistance team that, at the request of the UK Govt, had investigated the nature of a nerve agent that had been deployed offensively in Salisbury, UK, in March; also in April, the OPCW mandated a Fact-Finding Mission to investigate the suspected use of chemicals in an attack on Douma, eastern Ghouta, Syria; its final report, issued in March 2019, declared that there were reasonable grounds to believe that a toxic chemical (containing reactive chlorine) had been used as a weapon in the 2018 attack; in June 2019 a new Investigation and Identification Team (IIT) became operational, with the aim of identifying the perpetrators of the use of chemical weapons in Syria where the Joint Investigative Mechanism had not reached a conclusion; initially the IIT focused on incidents that had occurred in Ltamenah, Syria, in March 2017 (a report issued in April 2020 found that sarin had been deployed there); its 2nd report, issued in April 2021, determined that the Syrian air force had used chemical weapons in Saraqib, Syria, in Feb. 2018; in Jan. 2023 a 3rd report addressed the use of chemical weapons in Douma in April 2018; in June 2021 the OPCW issued new non-binding guidelines for chemical safety and security for small- and medium-sized businesses; mems: 193 states parties to the Convention; Dir-Gen. FERNANDO ARIAS (Spain).

Organisation Internationale de la Francophonie (International Organization of La Francophonie—La Francophonie): 19–21 ave Bosquet, 75007 Paris, France; tel. 1-44-37-33-25; internet www.francophonie.org; f. 1970 as l'Agence de coopération culturelle et technique; promotes co-operation among French-speaking countries in the areas of education, culture, peace and democracy, and technology; implements decisions of the Sommet francophone; technical and financial assistance supports projects in every mem. country, mainly to aid rural people; a Parliamentary Assembly of the Francophonie is also based in Paris; in Nov. 2020 Burundi was readmitted after a 4-year suspension; signed a Memorandum of Understanding with the World Health Org. in April 2021; in early June Mali was suspended from participation in the org. following the detention of that country's interim leaders by the military; 18th summit meeting: Djerba, Tunisia, in Nov. 2022; mems: 54 mem. states and regional authorities, 27 countries with observer status and 7 assoc. mems; Sec.-Gen. LOUISE MUSHIKIWABO (Rwanda); publ. *Journal de l'Agence de la Francophonie* (quarterly).

Organization of Turkic States (OTS): Binbirdirek, Piyer Loti Cad. No. 2, 34122 Fatih, İstanbul, Türkiye; tel. (212) 2831644; fax (212) 2831686; e-mail info@turkicstates.org; internet www.turkicstates.org; f. 2009, as the Cooperation Council of Turkic Speaking States (more commonly referred to as the Turkic Council; present name adopted in Nov. 2021); aims to promote stability and co-operation within Central Asia and the Caucasus; an extraordinary summit meeting was held in a virtual format in April 2020 to address the COVID-19 pandemic; condemned as illegitimate elections that were held in March–April in the territory of Nagornyi Karabakh (disputed by Azerbaijan and Armenia); in Sept., in response to an outbreak of conflict between Armenian and Azerbaijani forces in Nagornyi Karabakh, urged the immediate and full withdrawal of all Armenian forces from the territory; an informal summit was held in a virtual format in March 2021; at the 8th summit meeting, held in Nov., in Istanbul, heads of state adopted a new name for the grouping and determined to formulate a new strategic roadmap to strengthen co-operation during the period 2022–26; the 9th summit was convened in Nov. 2022, in Samarkand, Uzbekistan; an extraordinary summit was held in March 2023, in Ankara, with a focus on emergency disaster management and humanitarian assistance, following the massive earthquake that had devastated parts of southern Türkiye and northern Syrian Arab Rep. in the previous month; in May dispatched an OTS election observation mission to monitor the presidential election in Türkiye; affiliated to Parliamentary Assembly of Turkic States (TURKPA), International Org. of Turkic Culture (TURKSOY), Turkic Academy, Turkic Culture and Heritage Foundation and Turkic Business Council; mems: Azerbaijan, Kazakhstan, Kyrgyzstan, Türkiye, Uzbekistan; observers: Hungary, Turkmenistan, Turkish Republic of Northern Cyprus; Sec.-Gen. KUBANYCHBEK OMURALIEV (Kyrgyzstan).

Parliamentary Assembly of Turkic States (TURKPA): 106 S.S. Akhundov str, 7 microdistr., Baku AZ1116, Azerbaijan; tel. (412) 5635835; fax (412) 5635834; e-mail info@turk-pa.org; internet turk-pa.org; f. 2008; aims to promote political dialogue, as well as co-operation with regard to socioeconomic, cultural, humanitarian, legal, and other issues of mutual interest; upholds the principles of parliamentary democracy; in Oct. 2021 a TURKPA mission of observers monitored voting in the presidential election held in Uzbekistan; 11th plenary session held in Cholpon-Ata, Kyrgyzstan, in June 2022; mems: Azerbaijan, Kazakhstan, Kyrgyzstan, Türkiye; Chair. NURLANBEK SHAKIEV (Kyrgyzstan); Sec.-Gen. MEHMET SÜREYYA ER (Türkiye).

Parliamentary Union of the OIC Member States (PUIC): 34 Pesyan St, Zaferanieh, Tehran 1986833553, Iran; tel. (21) 22418860; fax (21) 22418858; e-mail g.s@puic.org; internet www.puic.org; f. 1999; mems: 53 parliaments; Sec.-Gen. MOUHAMED KHOURAICHI NIASSE (Senegal).

Shanghai Cooperation Organisation (SCO): 7 Ritan Rd, Chaoyang District, Beijing, People's Republic of China; tel. (10) 65329807; fax (10) 65329808; e-mail sco@sectsco.org; internet sectsco.org; f. June 2001, replacing the Shanghai Five (f. 1996 to address border disputes); aims to achieve security through mutual co-operation; promotes economic co-operation and measures to eliminate terrorism and drug trafficking; a Convention on the Fight against Terrorism, Separatism and Extremism was signed in June 2002; Treaty on Long-term Good Neighbourliness, Friendship and Co-operation was signed in Aug. 2007; holds annual summit meeting and regular sectoral ministerial meetings; maintains an SCO anti-terrorism centre in Tashkent, Uzbekistan; adopted in July 2017 the

SCO Development Strategy until 2025—focused on advancing regional co-operation in areas incl. regional security; energy; transport and infrastructure; agriculture; finance; innovation; environment; information and communication technology; education; and culture; reconvened in Oct. 2017 (after a 7-year hiatus) its Afghanistan Contact Group; an SCO Interbank Asscn, comprising banks in mem. states, was established in 2005 as a means of financing regional investment projects; in mid-2018 the Chinese Pres. announced the initiation by China through the Bank of a new US $4,700m. loan programme; the summit meeting held in June 2018 approved an SCO Antarctic Strategy and corresponding implementation plan, covering 2018–23; in mid-July 2021 SCO ministers responsible for foreign affairs convened an emergency summit to address the deteriorating security situation in Afghanistan as the long-term presence there of foreign troops was withdrawn; 22nd summit meeting of Council of Heads of State held in Samarkand, Uzbekistan, in Sept. 2022; in March 2023 monitored parliamentary elections held in Turkmenistan; Varanasi, India, was celebrated as the inaugural SCO Cultural and Tourism Capital during 2022–23; India hosted the 2023 summit meeting, held in a virtual format in July, at which Iran was admitted as the 9th mem. of the grouping; mems: People's Rep. of China, India, Iran, Kazakhstan, Kyrgyzstan, Pakistan, Russian Fed., Tajikistan, Uzbekistan; observers: Afghanistan, Belarus, Mongolia; dialogue partners: Azerbaijan, Armenia, Cambodia, Egypt, Kuwait, Nepal, Qatar, Saudi Arabia, Sri Lanka, Türkiye, UAE; Sec.-Gen. ZHANG MING (People's Republic of China).

Union for the Mediterranean (UfM) Secretariat: Palacio de Pedralbes, Pere Duran Farell 11, 08034 Barcelona, Spain; tel. (93) 5214147; fax (93) 5214119; e-mail secretary-general@ufmsecretariat.org; internet www.ufmsecretariat.org; f. 2008 as a continuation of the Euro-Mediterranean Partnership (Barcelona Process), which had been launched in 1995; the statutes of the secretariat were adopted in March 2010; its mandate is defined by the July 2008 Paris Declaration of the Euro-Mediterranean summit, and by the subsequent Marseilles Declaration, adopted in Nov. of that year; the UfM was established as a framework for advancing relations (political, economic and social) between the European Union and countries of the Southern and Eastern Mediterranean, in accordance with the goals detailed in the 1995 Barcelona Declaration: i.e. working to create an area of stability and shared economic prosperity, underpinned by full respect for democratic principles, human rights and fundamental freedoms; in Nov. 2020, commemorating 25 years since the launch of the Barcelona Process, UfM ministers (meeting in a virtual format) declared 28 Nov. as the International Day of the Mediterranean, to be observed annually; mems: 27 European Union states, the European Commission and 15 Mediterranean countries; Sec.-Gen. NASSER KAMEL (Egypt).

Industrial and Professional Relations

African Regional Organization of ITUC (ITUC-Africa): Route Internationale d'Atakpamé, POB 44101, Lomé, Togo; tel. 225-07-10; fax 225-61-13; e-mail info@ituc-africa.org; internet www.ituc-africa.org; f. 2007; mems: 17m. workers and 101 affiliated trade unions in 51 African countries; Pres. MODY GUIRO (Senegal); Gen. Sec. KWASI ADU-AMANKWAH (Ghana).

Arab Trade Union Confederation: Box 578 925, Amman 11190, Jordan; tel. (6) 5824829; e-mail info@ituc-arabtradeunion.org; internet arabtradeunion.org; mems: 15 nat. labour unions from 12 Arab countries; Pres. HUSSEIN ABASSI (Tunisia); Exec. Sec. MUSTAPHA TLILI.

International Confederation of Arab Trade Unions (ICATU): POB 3225, Samat at-Tahir, Damascus, Syria; tel. (11) 4459544; fax (11) 4420323; e-mail icatu-cisa@hotmail.com; f. 1956; mems: trade unions in 18 countries, and 11 affiliate int. feds; publ. *Al-Oummal al-Arab* (every 2 months).

Law

Arab Organization for Human Rights (AOHR): 91 al-Marghany St, Heliopolis, Cairo, Egypt; tel. (2) 4181396; fax (2) 4185346; e-mail info@aohr.net; internet aohr.net; f. 1983; aims to defend fundamental freedoms of citizens of the Arab states; assists political prisoners and their families; has consultative status with UN Economic and Social Council; General Assembly convened every 3 years; mems: 22 institutional branches and affiliated NGOs, 23,000 individual mems in 70 countries; Exec. Dir MOHAMMED RADI SHADY; Sec.-Gen. ALAA SHALABI; publs *Newsletter* (monthly), *Annual Report*, *The State of Human Rights in the Arab World*.

Asian-African Legal Consultative Organization (AALCO): 29–C, Rizal Marg, Diplomatic Enclave, Chanakyapuri, New Delhi 110021, India; tel. (11) 24197000; fax (11) 26117640; e-mail mail@aalco.int; internet www.aalco.int; f. 1956; considers legal problems referred to it by mem. countries and serves as a forum for Afro-Asian co-operation in international law, including international trade law, and economic relations; provides background material for confs, prepares standard/model contract forms suited to the needs of the region; promotes arbitration as a means of settling international commercial disputes; trains officers of mem. states; has permanent UN observer status; has established International Commercial Arbitration Centres in Kuala Lumpur, Malaysia; Cairo, Egypt; Lagos, Nigeria; and Tehran, Iran; mems: 47 countries; Sec.-Gen. Dr KAMALINNE PINITPUVADOL (Thailand).

International Association of Jewish Lawyers and Jurists: 10 Daniel Frisch St, Tel Aviv 6473111, Israel; tel. 3-6910673; fax 3-6953855; e-mail office@ijl.org; internet www.intjewishlawyers.org; f. 1969; promotes human rights and international co-operation based on the rule of law; works to combat anti-Semitism and Holocaust denial; holds international confs; mems: lawyers, judges, judicial officers and academic jurists in more than 50 countries; Pres. MEIR LINZEN (Israel); CEO RONIT GIDRON-ZEMACH (Israel); publ. *Justice*.

International Criminal Court (ICC): Oude Waalsdorperweg 10, 2597 AK The Hague, Netherlands; tel. (70) 5158515; fax (70) 5158555; e-mail otp.informationdesk@icc-cpi.int; internet www.icc-cpi.int; f. 2002, upon the entry into force of the Rome Statute of the ICC, adopted by 120 states participating in a UN Diplomatic Conference in July 1998; by June 2023 31 cases had been brought before the Court; in March 2011 the ICC Prosecutor agreed to open an investigation into the Situation in Libya; in late June the Court issued arrest warrants against the Libyan leader Col Muammar al-Qaddafi, Saif al-Islam (his son), and Abdullah al-Senussi (his former Head of Military Intelligence), regarding crimes against humanity (murder and persecution) committed in Libya—through the state apparatus and security forces—from 15 Feb. until at least 28 Feb.; in Sept. the Prosecutor requested INTERPOL to issue a Red Notice for the arrest of the 3 Libyan indictees; Col Qaddafi was killed during fighting with opposition forces on 20 Oct.; in late Nov. Saif al-Islam was detained in southern Libya; al-Senussi was detained by Mauritanian security forces in mid-March 2012 and in Sept. was extradited to Libya; despite the ICC indictments the Libyan authorities expressed their intention of bringing al-Islam and al-Senussi to trial within Libya on charges relating to their conduct under the al-Qaddafi regime, and in May 2012 the Libyan National Transitional Council presented a formal challenge to the ICC concerning the admissibility of the Court's case against the 2 men, on the grounds that the Libyan national judicial system was itself actively investigating their alleged crimes; in May 2013 an ICC Pre-Trial Chamber rejected Libya's challenge to the admissibility of the case against Saif al-Islam, stressing Libya's obligation to transfer him to the Court; this ruling was upheld in May 2014 by the ICC Appeals Chamber; in Oct. 2013 a Pre-Trial Chamber concluded that the al-Senussi case was inadmissible before the Court and should proceed within Libya (this decision was upheld in July 2014 by the ICC Appeals Chamber); in July 2015 death sentences were passed on al-Islam (and 8 other defendants) in Libya; in April of that year the Court unsealed a pre-existing warrant for the arrest of al-Tuhamy Mohamed Khaled, who had led the Libyan Internal Security Agency under the Muammar al-Qaddafi regime, and was accused of perpetrating crimes against humanity and war crimes including imprisonment, persecution, torture, cruel treatment and outrages against human dignity (Khaled's death was confirmed by the Court in Sept. 2022 and his case terminated); in Aug. 2015 the Court issued a warrant for the arrest of Mahmoud Mustafa Busayf al-Werfalli, with regard to seven incidents, involving 33 persons, that had taken place in or around Benghazi, Libya, during June 2016–July 2017; reports emerged in June 2017 that Saif al-Islam had been released by a militant group that had held him in detention since 2011: the Court demanded that he be immediately arrested and surrendered to its jurisdiction; however, he subsequently declared his intention to contest presidential elections then scheduled to be held in Libya in Dec. 2018; in Jan. 2018 the Prosecutor issued a statement condemning the detonation of car bombs outside the Bi'at al-Radwan Mosque in Benghazi, which had resulted in the deaths of at least 34 people; she also expressed horror at images made public in that month that apparently showed al-Werfalli executing 10 individuals in front of the mosque that had been attacked (in retaliation for the bombings); in July the Court released a second warrant for al-Werfalli, relating to the recent Bi'at al-Radwan Mosque executions; in June 2022 the case against al-Werfalli was terminated upon confirmation of his death; in early Nov. 2018 the Prosecutor ruled as inadmissible a request by Saif al-Islam to have the international arrest warrant against him overturned, and in March 2020 the Appeals Chamber confirmed, unanimously, the admissibility of the case against Saif al-Islam; in Jan. 2013 more than 50 UN member states, led by Switzerland, signed a letter urging the UN Security Council to refer the situation ongoing in Syria to the Court; in May 2014, however, the adoption of a draft UN Security Council resolution that proposed the referral to the Court of the situation in Syria was vetoed by the People's Rep. of China and Russia; in May 2014 the Prosecutor reopened a preliminary examination (previously concluded in 2006) into the situation in Iraq, in view of the submission in January 2014 of further information to her Office that alleged that British armed forces had committed war crimes during the period 2003–08, involving the systematic abuse of detainees in Iraq (although Iraq is not a state party to the Rome Statute, the Court has jurisdiction over alleged crimes committed on its territory by nationals of countries that are states parties); in June 2013, following a referral from the Comoros Government, the Prosecutor agreed to initiate a preliminary examination into a raid undertaken on 31 May 2010 by Israeli forces on a flotilla delivering humanitarian aid to Gaza ('Registered Vessels of Comoros, Greece and Cambodia'); the examination was, however, terminated in 2014; in July 2014 Palestinian officials lodged a complaint with the Court that accused the Israeli Government of perpetrating war crimes during its then ongoing air, sea and land military bombardment of the Gaza Strip; on 1 Jan. 2015 Palestine submitted a document to the Court's Registrar that declared its acceptance of the retrospective jurisdiction of the ICC, and in mid-Jan. 2015 the Chief Prosecutor opened a preliminary investigation into 'alleged crimes committed in the occupied Palestinian territory, including East Jerusalem, since 13 June 2014'; in Dec. 2019 the Prosecutor concluded that there was a reasonable basis to proceed with a full investigation into the situation in Palestine; prior to initiating an investigation, however, she requested a Pre-Trial Chamber to issue a jurisdictional ruling to determine the scope of the precise territorial jurisdiction under the remit of the Court; in Feb. 2021 the Court ruled that it did have jurisdiction over the Palestinian Territories and the investigation was opened in the following month; Prosecutor KARIM A. A. KHAN (UK); Registrar OSVALDO ZAVALA GILER (Ecuador).

International Criminal Police Organization (INTERPOL): 200 quai Charles de Gaulle, 69006 Lyon, France; tel. 4-72-44-70-00; fax 4-72-44-71-63; internet www.interpol.int; f. 1923, reconstituted 1946; promotes co-operation and mutual assistance between police forces in different countries; centralizes records and information on international criminals; operates a global police communications network linking all mem. countries; co-ordinates and supports international law enforcement operations; in June 2021 est. I-Familia—a global dna kinship matching database, aimed at advancing the identification of missing persons; provides targeted training to police around the world, and in 2019 launched a Global Network of authorized law enforcement colleges and training bodies; holds a General Assembly annually (2023: Vienna, Austria, in Nov.), and organizes regular regional meetings; mems: 195 countries; Pres. Maj.-Gen. AHMED NASSER AL-RAISI (United Arab Emirates); Sec.-Gen. JÜRGEN STOCK (Germany); publ. *Annual Report*.

Medicine and Health

Arab Medical Association Against Cancer: Cairo, Egypt; tel. 795547875; e-mail drsamikhatib@gmail.com; internet amaac.org/; f. 2001, successor to Arab Council Against Cancer (f. 1995); aims to raise the awareness of cancer prevention and control, to advance the level of knowledge of cancer professionals, and to improve the efficacy of cancer treatment in Arab countries; 19th Annual Pan Arab Cancer Congress held in Jordan, in Feb. 2019; Sec.-Gen. SAMI KHATIB (Jordan); Dir ATEF BADRAN (Egypt); publ. *Pan Arab Journal of Oncoloy* (quarterly).

Federation of Islamic Medical Associations: 8–2 Gulberg Complex, Jail Rd, Lahore, Pakistan; tel. (42) 35716231; fax (42) 35715855; e-mail tanveer.zubairi@gmail.com; internet fimaweb.net; f. 1981; aims to foster the unity and welfare of Muslim medical and health care professionals, to promote Islamic medical activities including health services, education and research through co-operation and co-ordination among mem. orgs, to promote the understanding and the application of Islamic principles in the field of medicine, to mobilize professional and economic resources in order to provide medical care and relief to affected areas and communities, and to promote the exchange of medical information and technical expertise among mem. orgs; holds annual confs; mems: 29 asscns, 17 assoc. mems; Pres. ABDUL RASHID ABDUL RAHMAN; publs *FIMA Yearbook* (annually), *FIMA Newsletters* (monthly).

World Medical Association (WMA): 13 chemin du Levant, CIB-Bâtiment A, 01210 Ferney-Voltaire, France; tel. 4-50-40-75-75; e-mail wma@wma.net; internet www.wma.net; f. 1947; works to achieve the highest international standards in all aspects of medical education and practice, to promote closer ties among doctors and national medical asscns by personal contact and all other means, to study problems confronting the medical profession, and to present its views to appropriate bodies; holds an annual General Assembly (2022: Berlin, Germany, in Oct.); mems: 115 nat. medical asscns; Pres. Dr OSAHON ENABULELE (Nigeria); Sec.-Gen. Dr OTMAR KLOIBER (Germany); publ. *The World Medical Journal* (quarterly).

Posts and Telecommunications

Arab Permanent Postal Commission: c/o Arab League Bldg, Tahrir Sq., POB 11642, Cairo, Egypt; tel. (2) 5750511; fax (2) 5740331; f. 1952 as Arab Postal Union (APU), present name adopted in 1992; aims to establish stricter postal relations between the Arab countries than those laid down by the Universal Postal Union, and to pursue the devt and modernization of postal services in mem. countries; mems: 22 countries; publs *APU Bulletin* (monthly), *APU Review* (quarterly), *APU News* (annually).

Religion

Middle East Council of Churches: Makhoul St, Deeb Bldg, POB 5376, Beirut, Lebanon; tel. (1) 353938; e-mail info@mecc.org; internet mecc.org; f. 1974; mems: 27 churches; Gen. Sec. Dr MICHEL ABS (Lebanon); publs *MECC News Report* (monthly), *Al Montada Newsletter* (quarterly, in Arabic), *Courrier oecuménique du Moyen-Orient* (quarterly).

Muslim World League (MWL) (Rabitat al-Alam al-Islami): POB 537, Makkah, Saudi Arabia; tel. (12) 5309444; fax (12) 5601319; e-mail info@themwl.org; internet www.themwl.org; f. 1962; aims to advance Islamic unity and solidarity, and to promote world peace and respect for human rights; provides financial assistance for education, medical care and relief work; in April 2020 donated US $1m. to assist the UN Relief and Works Agency for Palestinian Refugees in the Near East's operations to manage local impacts of the COVID-19 pandemic; in Oct. 2022 initiated a campaign to provide relief to people affected by severe flooding in Pakistan; 44 offices worldwide, 3 councils, 3 subsidiary bodies; Sec.-Gen. Dr MOHAMMED BIN ABDULKARIM AL-ESSA; publs *Al-Rabita Arabic*, *Muslim World League Journal* (monthly, English and Arabic).

World Council of Churches (WCC): 150 route de Ferney, Postfach 2100, 1211 Geneva 2, Switzerland; tel. 227916111; fax 227910361; e-mail info@wcc-coe.org; internet www.oikoumene.org; f. 1948 to promote co-operation between Christian Churches and to prepare for a clearer manifestation of the unity of the Church; activities are grouped under the following programmes: Unity, Mission and Ecumenical Relations; Public Witness and *Diakonia*; and Ecumenical Formation; in July 2020 the (acting) Gen. Sec. wrote formally to the Pres. of Türkiye (Turkey), Recep Tayyip Erdogan, stating WCC members' grief and dismay over a decision to reconvert the Hagia Sophia museum in İstanbul into a mosque—following a recent Turkish legal ruling that Hagia Sophia (founded in 537 as a Christian cathedral, converted into a mosque in 1453, designated in 1934 as a secular museum, and also later included as part of the Historic Areas of İstanbul UNESCO World Heritage site) had been unlawfully repurposed in 1934; the Gen. Sec. emphasized the importance of inter-faith dialogue and expressed concern that the recent decision might aggravate divisions between religious communities; mems: 352 Churches in more than 110 countries; Gen. Sec. Rev. Prof. Dr JERRY PILLAY (South Africa); publs *Current Dialogue* (2 a year), *Ecumenical Review* (quarterly), *International Review of Mission* (quarterly).

World Jewish Congress: 501 Madison Ave, New York, NY 10022, USA; tel. (212) 755-5770; e-mail contactus@wjc.org; internet www.worldjewishcongress.org; f. 1936 as a voluntary asscn of representative Jewish communities and orgs throughout the world; aims to foster the unity of the Jewish people and to advocate on their behalf; mems: Jewish communities in over 100 countries; Pres. RONALD S. LAUDER.

Science

CIESM—The Mediterranean Science Commission (Commission internationale pour l'exploration scientifique de la mer Méditerranée): Villa Girasole, 16 blvd de Suisse, 98000 Monaco; tel. 93-30-38-79; fax 92-16-11-95; e-mail contact@ciesm.org; internet www.ciesm.org; f. 1919 for scientific exploration of the Mediterranean Sea; organizes multilateral research investigations, workshops, congresses; includes 6 permanent scientific cttees; mems: 23

countries; Pres. HSH Prince ALBERT II of MONACO; Dir-Gen. Prof. FREDERIC BRIAND; publs Congress reports.

European-Mediterranean Seismological Centre (EMSC): c/o CEA, Bât. BARD 1, Centre DAM, Ile de France, Bruyères le Châtel, 91297 Arpajon Cedex, France; fax 1-69-26-71-47; e-mail contact@emsc-csem.org; internet www.emsc-csem.org; f. 1976; supports rapid determination of seismic hypocentres in the region; maintains database; mems: 5 key nodal mem. institutions, 66 active mem. institutions/observatories/laboratories, 4 mems by right; Pres. FLORIAN HASLINGER (Switzerland); Sec.-Gen. RÉMY BOSSU (France); publ. *Newsletter* (2 a year).

Social Sciences

African Centre for Applied Research and Training in Social Development (ACARTSOD): Africa Centre, Wahda Quarter, Zawia Rd, POB 80606, Tripoli, Libya; tel. (21) 4835103; fax (21) 4835066; e-mail fituri_acartsod@hotmail.com; f. 1977 under the jt auspices of the ECA and OAU (now AU); aims to promote and co-ordinate applied research and training in social devt, and to assist in formulating national devt strategies; Exec. Dir Dr AHMED SAID FITURI.

Arab Towns Organization (ATO): POB 68160, Kaifan 71962, Kuwait; tel. 24849705; fax 24849319; e-mail ato@arabtowns.org; internet www.arabtowns.org; f. 1967; works to preserve the identity and heritage of Arab towns; to support the development and modernization of municipal and local authorities in mem. towns; to improve services and utilities in mem. towns; to support development schemes in mem. towns through the provision of loans and other assistance; to support planning and the co-ordination of development activities and services; to facilitate the exchange of service-related expertise among mem. towns; to co-ordinate efforts to modernize and standardize municipal regulations and codes among mem. towns; to promote co-operation in all matters related to Arab towns; manages the Arab Towns Development Fund, the Arab Institute for Urban Development, the Arab Towns Organization Award, the Arab Urban Environment Centre, the Arab Forum on Information Systems, and the Heritage and Arab Historic City Foundation; mems: more than 400 cities; Sec.-Gen. AHMED HAMAD AL-SABEEH; publ. *Al-Madinah Al-Arabiyah* (every 2 months).

Council for the Development of Social Science Research in Africa (CODESRIA): ave Cheikh, Anta Diop X Canal IV, BP 3304, CP 18524, Dakar, Senegal; tel. 33-825-98-22; internet www.codesria.org; f. 1973; promotes research, organizes confs, working groups and information services; mems: research institutes and univ. faculties and researchers in African countries; Pres. ISABEL CASIMIRO (Mozambique); Exec. Sec. Dr GODWIN MURUNGA (Kenya); publs *Africa Development* (quarterly), *CODESRIA Bulletin* (quarterly), *African Journal of International Affairs* (2 a year), *Journal of African Transformation* (2 a year), *African Sociological Review* (2 a year), *Afrika Zamani* (annually), *Identity, Culture and Politics* (2 a year), *Afro-Arab Selections for Social Sciences* (annually), directories of research.

International African Institute (IAI): School of Oriental and African Studies, Thornhaugh St, Russell Sq., London, WC1H 0XG, United Kingdom; tel. (20) 7898-4420; e-mail iai@soas.ac.uk; internet www.internationalafricaninstitute.org; f. 1926; established to promote the study of African peoples, their languages, cultures and social life in their traditional and modern settings; organizes an international seminar prog. bringing together scholars from Africa and elsewhere; links scholars in order to facilitate research projects, especially in the social sciences; Chair. Prof. ALCINDA HONWANA; publs *Africa* (quarterly), *Journal of African Cultural Studies* (quartely).

Social Welfare and Human Rights

Amnesty International: 1 Easton St, London, WC1X 0DW, United Kingdom; tel. (20) 7413-5500; fax (20) 7956-1157; e-mail contactus@amnesty.org; internet www.amnesty.org; f. 1961; an independent, democratic, self-governing worldwide movement of people who campaign for internationally recognized human rights, such as those enshrined in the Universal Declaration of Human Rights; undertakes research and action focused on preventing and ending grave abuses of the rights to physical and mental integrity, freedom of conscience and expression, and freedom from discrimination, within the context of its work impartially to promote and protect all human rights; major policy decisions are taken by an International Council comprising representatives from all nat. sections; financed by donations; no funds are sought or accepted from govts; mems: more than 10m. individuals; nationally organized sections in more than 70 countries; other groups and networks (e.g. AI's Urgent Action Network); Sec.-Gen. AGNES CALLAMARD (France); publs *Annual Report*, *International Newsletter* (monthly), *The Wire* (quarterly), country reports.

Arab Women's Solidarity Association United: Cairo, Egypt; e-mail awsa_sc@yahoo.com; f. 1982; aims to promote the active participation of Arab women in social, economic, cultural, and political life; works to develop income-generating projects for economically underprivileged women and to raise awareness of the impact of political and social inequality on the lives of Arab women; granted consultative status with the United Nations Economic and Social Council in 1985; Pres. Dr NAWAL EL-SAADAWI.

International Federation of Red Cross and Red Crescent Societies (IFRC): POB 303, 1211 Geneva 19, Switzerland; tel. 227304222; fax 227304200; e-mail secretariat@ifrc.org; internet www.ifrc.org; f. 1919; aims to prevent and alleviate human suffering; conducts relief operations for refugees and victims of disasters, co-ordinates relief supplies and assists in disaster prevention; supports humanitarian activities by national Red Cross and Red Crescent societies; major appeals underway as at June 2023 included 100m. Swiss francs and 350m. Swiss francs to support the survivors of earthquakes that in Feb. had devastated parts of, respectively, Syria and Türkiye; mems: 192 nat. socs; Pres. FRANCESCO ROCCA (Italy) (outgoing); Sec.-Gen. JAGAN CHAPAGAIN (Nepal); publs *Annual Report*, *Red Cross Red Crescent* (quarterly), *Weekly News*, *World Disasters Report*, *Emergency Appeal*.

Médecins Sans Frontières (MSF): 140 route de Ferney, 1202 Geneva 21, Switzerland; tel. 228498484; fax 228498488; e-mail office-gva@geneva.msf.org; internet www.msf.org; f. 1971; independent medical humanitarian org. composed of physicians and other mems of the medical profession; aims to provide medical assistance to victims of war and natural disasters; operates longer-term progs of nutrition, immunization, sanitation, public health, and rehabilitation of hospitals and dispensaries; awarded the Nobel Peace Prize in 1999; in 2020 MSF initiated new projects and adapted existing progs to respond to the COVID-19 pandemic; priority areas of focus included the protection of most at-risk and otherwise vulnerable people, including in countries with systemically fragile health provision, and protecting healthcare workers; mems: 25 asscns in more than 69 countries worldwide; Int. Pres. Dr CHRISTOS CHRISTOU (Greece); publs *International Activity Report* (annually), *Dispatches* (quarterly).

Union Africaine de la Mutualité (African Union of Mutuals): rue Aram, Lot 14, Secteur 7, Hay Riad, Rabat, Morocco; tel. and fax (5) 37570988; internet www.uam.org.ma; f. 2007; promotes co-operation among African companies concerned with health care and social insurance; mems: 40 orgs in 17 African countries; Pres. ABDELMOULA ABDELMOUMNI (Morocco); Sec.-Gen. CLARISSE KAYO MAHI (Côte d'Ivoire).

Sport and Recreations

Confederation of African Football (Confédération africaine de football—CFA): 3 Abdel Khalek Sarwat St, El Hay El Motamayez, POB 23, 6th October City, Egypt; tel. (2) 38247272; fax (2) 38247274; internet www.cafonline.com; f. 1957; promotes football in Africa; organizes inter-club competitions and Cup of Nations (2022: Cameroon, in Jan.–Feb.); General Assembly held every 2 years; mems: nat. asscns in 54 countries; Pres. PATRICE MOTSEPE (South Africa); Sec.-Gen. VERON MOSENGO-OMBA (Democratic Republic of the Congo); publ. *CAF News* (quarterly).

Fédération Internationale de Football Association (FIFA) (International Federation of Association Football): FIFA-Str. 20, POB 8044, Zürich, Switzerland; tel. 432227777; fax 432227878; internet www.fifa.com; f. 1904; aims to promote the game of association football and foster friendly relations among players and national asscns; to control football and uphold the laws of the game as laid down by the International Football Association Board; to prevent discrimination of any kind between players; and to provide arbitration in disputes between national asscns; organizes several major competitions; the FIFA World Cup is held every 4 years (2026: Canada, Mexico and the USA, in June–July); the FIFA Women's World Cup is also organized on a quadrennial basis (2023: Australia and New Zealand, in July–Aug.); the FIFA Congress meets annually; the Fed.'s 37-mem. Council is the main decision making body between meetings of the Congress; in Feb. 2022, in response to the Russian Fed.'s military invasion of Ukraine, FIFA and UEFA jtly suspended Russian national and club teams from participation in international competition football; mems: 211 nat. asscns, 6 continental confeds; Pres. GIANNI INFANTINO (Switzerland); Sec.-Gen. FATMA SAMBA DIOUF SAMOURA (Senegal) (until 31 Dec. 2023); publs *FIFA News* (monthly), *FIFA Magazine* (every 2 months), *FIFA*

Directory (annually), *Laws of the Game* (annually), *Competitions' Regulations*, *Technical Reports* (before and after FIFA competitions).

International Basketball Federation (Fédération Internationale de Basketball—FIBA): 5 route Suisse, POB 29, 1295 Mies, Switzerland; tel. 225450000; fax 225450099; e-mail info@fiba.com; internet www.fiba.com; f. 1932, as International Amateur Basketball Federation; present name adopted in 1989; world governing body for basketball; mems: 212 affiliated nat. feds; Pres. SAUD ALI AL THANI (Qatar); Sec.-Gen. ANDREAS ZAGKLIS (Greece); publ. *FIBA Assist* (monthly).

International Olympic Committee (IOC): Château de Vidy, 1001 Lausanne, Switzerland; tel. 216216111; fax 216216718; internet www.olympic.org; f. 1894 to ensure the regular celebration of the Olympic Games; the IOC is the supreme authority on all questions concerning the Olympic Games and the Olympic movement; established the independent World Anti-Doping Agency (WADA) in 1999; Olympic Games are held every 4 years—summer games 2024: Paris, France; winter games 2026: Milan and Cortina d'Ampezzo, Italy; mems: 206 national Olympic cttees; Pres. THOMAS BACH (Germany); publs *Newsletter* (weekly), *Olympic Review* (quarterly).

Union of Arab Olympic Committees: POB 62997, Riyadh 11595, Saudi Arabia; tel. (1) 482-4927; internet uanoc.org; f. 1976 as Arab Sports Confederation to encourage regional co-operation in sport; mems: 21 Arab nat. Olympic Committees, 10 Arab sports feds; Pres. ABDULAZIZ BIN TURKI AL-FAISAL; Sec.-Gen. ABDULAZIZ AL-ANAZI; publ. *Annual Report*.

Technology

Arab Information and Communication Technology (ICT) Union: Beirut, Lebanon; e-mail info@arabictunion.org; internet arabictunion.org; f. 2018; aims to support the devt of Arab ICT enterprises and promote collaboration within the industry; mems: 8 nat. ICT asscns; Sec.-Gen. AHMED AL-HUJAIRY.

Federation of Arab Engineers: 30 Sharia Ramses, Cairo, Egypt; tel. (2) 27735610; fax (2) 25749404; e-mail arabengs@hotmail.com; internet www.arabfedeng.org; f. 1963 as Arab Engineering Union; a regional body of the World Federation of Engineering Organizations; co-operates with the Arab League, UNESCO and other regional engineering feds; organizes a Pan-Arab conf. on engineering studies every 3 years and annual symposia and seminars in different Arab countries; mems: engineering asscns in 15 Arab countries; Sec.-Gen. Dr ADEL AL-HADITHI.

Trade and Industry

Arab Federation for Oil and Gas Technologies: POB 954183, Amman 11954, Kindi St, Bldg 23, Jordan; tel. (6) 5511170; fax (6) 5541986; e-mail ali@enana.com; internet www.afoget.com; f. 2011; facilitates regional co-operation and provides technical support in the oil and gas sector; works under the auspices of the Council of Arab Economic Unity; Sec.-Gen. Dr RAAD MUSLIH.

Arab Federation for Paper, Printing and Packaging Industries: POB 5456, 13th St, Bldg 31, 901 District, Al Karada Quarter, Abi Nawas St, Baghdad, Iraq; tel. (1) 717-6375; fax (1) 717-6374; e-mail info@afpppi.com; internet www.afpppi.com; f. 1977; mems: in 15 countries; Chair. Dr FADI GEMAYEL.

General Arab Insurance Federation: POB 611, 11511 Cairo, Egypt; tel. (2) 5743177; fax (2) 5762310; e-mail gaif@gaif.org; internet www.gaif.org; f. 1964; mems: 330 cos; Sec.-Gen. CHAKIB ABOUZAID (Morocco).

Gulf Organization for Industrial Consulting (GOIC): POB 5114, Doha, Qatar; tel. 4858888; fax 4831465; e-mail goic@goic.org.qa; internet www.goic.org.qa; f. 1976 by the Gulf Arab states; aims to encourage industrial co-operation among Gulf Arab states, to pool industrial expertise and to encourage jt devt of projects; undertakes feasibility studies, market diagnosis, assistance in policymaking, legal consultancies, project promotion, promotion of small and medium-sized industrial investment profiles and technical training; maintains industrial data bank; mems: mem. states of the Cooperation Council for the Arab States of the Gulf; Sec.-Gen. AHMED BIN MOHAMMED AL MOHAMMED (Oman); publs *GOIC Monthly Bulletin* (in Arabic), *The Industrial Cooperation in the Arabian Gulf Journal* (quarterly).

Union of Arab Chambers (UAC): POB 11-2837, Beirut, Lebanon; tel. (1) 826020; fax (1) 826021; e-mail uac@uac-org.org; internet www.uac-org.org; f. 1951; aims to enhance Arab economic devt, integration and security through the co-ordination of industrial, agricultural and trade policies and legislation; mems: in 21 Arab countries; Pres. SAMEER ABDULLA NASS (UAE); Sec.-Gen. Dr KHALED HANAFI; publs *Arab Economic Report*, *Al-Omran Al-Arabi* (every 2 months), economic papers, proceedings.

Transport

African Airlines Association: POB 20116, Nairobi 00200, Kenya; tel. (20) 2320144; fax (20) 6001173; e-mail afraa@afraa.org; internet www.afraa.org; f. 1968; aims to give African air companies expert advice in technical, financial, juridical and market matters; to improve air transport in Africa through inter-carrier co-operation; and to develop manpower resources; mems: 45 nat. carriers, representing 85% of African airlines; Pres. (2023) JENNIFER BAMUTURAKI (Uganda); Sec.-Gen. ABDERAHMANE BERTHÉ; publs *Newsletter*, *Africa Wings*, reports.

Arab Air Carriers' Organization (AACO): Beirut Harbor, 1504 Bldg, George Haddad St, Saifi, 1107 2020 Beirut, Lebanon; tel. (1) 989250; fax (1) 989253; e-mail info@aaco.org; internet aaco.org; f. 1965; promotes co-operation in the activities of Arab airline cos; mems: 36 Arab air carriers; Chair. IBRAHIM ABDUL RAHMAN AL OMAR; Sec.-Gen. ABDUL WAHAB TEFFAHA; publs bulletins, reports and research documents.

Youth and Students

Pan-African Youth Union (Union pan-africaine de la jeunesse): Khartoum, Sudan; tel. (960) 184-833; fax (183) 526-695; e-mail info@pyu.org; internet pyu.org; f. 1962; encourages the participation of African youth in socioeconomic and political devt and democratization; organizes confs and seminars, youth exchanges and youth festivals; mems: youth groups in 54 African countries and liberation movements; Pres. JULIANA RATOVOSON (acting); publ. *MPJ News* (quarterly).

World Union of Jewish Students (WUJS): Apt 6B, Rabbi Zeira 3, Jerusalem 93182, Israel; e-mail info@wujs.org.il; internet www.wujs.org.il; f. 1924; promotes dialogue and co-operation among Jewish univ. students worldwide; organizes an annual Congress; mems: 32 nat. unions representing nearly 1m. students; Pres. YANA NAFTALIEVA (Switzerland); publs *The Student Activist Yearbook*, *WUJS Report*.

MAJOR COMMODITIES OF THE MIDDLE EAST AND NORTH AFRICA

Note: For each of the commodities in this section, there is a statistical table relating to recent levels of production and another table relating to prices on world markets. Each production table shows estimates of output for the world and for the Middle East and North Africa. In addition, the table lists the main producing countries of the Middle East and North Africa and, for comparison, the leading producers from outside the region.

ALUMINIUM AND BAUXITE (Aluminium or aluminum, Al)

Aluminium (known as aluminum in the USA and, generally, Canada) is the second most abundant metallic element in the earth's crust after silicon, comprising about 8% of the total. However, it is much less widely used than steel, despite having about the same strength and only half the weight. Aluminium has important applications as a metal because of its lightness, ease of fabrication and other desirable properties. Other products of alumina (aluminium oxide trihydrate, into which aluminium ore is refined) are materials in refractories, abrasives, glass manufacture, other ceramic products, catalysts and absorbers. Alumina hydrates are used for the production of aluminium chemicals, fire retardant in carpet backing, and industrial fillers in plastics and related products. Bauxite is the principal aluminium ore. Nepheline syenite, kaolin, shale, anorthosite and alunite are all potential alternative sources of alumina, but these are not currently economic to process. Of all bauxite mined, approximately 85% is converted to alumina (Al_2O_3) for the production of aluminium metal. The developing countries, in which at least 70% of known bauxite reserves are located, supply some 60% of the ore required. According to the US Geological Survey (USGS), in 2022 32% of potential world bauxite resources were located in Africa, 23% in Oceania, 21% in Latin America and the Caribbean, and 18% in Asia.

The industry is structured in three stages: bauxite mining, alumina refining, and smelting. After mining, bauxite is fed direct to process if mine-run material is adequate (as in Jamaica), or else it is crushed and beneficiated. Where the ore 'as mined' presents handling problems, or weight reduction is desirable, it may be dried prior to shipment. The alumina is separated from the ore by the Bayer process, through precipitation from a chemical solution. The ratio of bauxite to alumina is approximately 1.95:1. The smelting of the aluminium from alumina is generally by electrolysis in molten cryolite. Owing to the high consumption of electricity by the smelting process, alumina is usually smelted in areas where low cost electricity is available. However, most of the electricity now used in primary smelting in the Western world is generated by hydroelectricity—a renewable energy source.

Production of Bauxite
(crude ore, '000 metric tons)

	2019	2020	2021	2022*
World total (excl. USA)	387,000	391,000	384,000	380,000
Middle East and North Africa	5,649	6,405	n.a.	n.a.
Regional producers				
Iran†	780*	800*	n.a.	n.a.
Saudi Arabia	4,050*	4,305	4,780	4,800
Türkiye	819	1,300*	n.a.	n.a.
Other leading producers				
Australia	105,544	104,328	103,000	100,000
Brazil†	31,938	31,000*	33,000*	33,000
China, People's Republic*	105,000	92,700	90,000	90,000
Guinea*†	67,000	86,000	86,000	86,000
India	22,321	20,200*	17,400*	17,000
Indonesia	16,593	20,800*	21,000*	21,000
Jamaica†	9,022	7,546	5,950	3,900
Malaysia	901	300*	n.a.	n.a.
Russian Federation	5,574	5,570	5,680	5,000

* Estimated production.
† Dried equivalent of crude ore.
Source: US Geological Survey.

The World Market and the Region The high degree of 'vertical integration' (i.e. the control of successive stages of production) in the industry means that a significant proportion of trade in bauxite and alumina is in the form of intra-company transfers. The increasing tendency to site alumina refineries near to bauxite deposits has also resulted in a shrinking bauxite trade, but there is a growing free market in alumina, serving the needs of the increasing number of independent (i.e. non-integrated) smelters. The major markets for aluminium are in transportation, packaging, building and construction, electrical and other machinery and equipment, and consumer durables. Although the production of aluminium is energy intensive, its light weight results in a net saving, particularly in the transportation industry, where the use of the metal as a substitute for steel, in particular in the manufacture of road motor vehicles and components, is well established. Aluminium is valued by the aerospace industry for its weight saving characteristics and for its low cost relative to alternative materials. Aluminium-lithium alloys command considerable potential for use in this sector, although the traditional dominance of aluminium in the aerospace industry has been challenged since the 1990s by 'composites' such as carbonepoxy, a fusion of carbon fibres and hardened resins, the lightness and durability of which can exceed that of many aluminium alloys. The recycling of aluminium is economically, as well as environmentally, desirable, as the process uses only 5% of the electricity required to produce a similar quantity of primary aluminium. Recycling is of commercial significance in many countries, but the world leaders were Brazil, Japan and Argentina in the late 2010s. In that decade, Saudi Arabia developed a rolling mill that included a recycling unit with the capacity to process 120,000 metric tons of aluminium cans per year.

According to industry sources, in 2020 the largest bauxite-producing companies in the world, based on production volumes, were Rio Tinto Group (Australia/United Kingdom—the aluminium-related business is based in Canada, until 2015 under the name Rio Tinto Alcan), Alcoa (USA), Aluminium Corporation of China Ltd (Chinalco—especially its listed subsidiary, Chalco), United Company RUSAL (Russian Federation) and Hydro (Norway—Norsk Hydro). Many of the other major companies are located in countries boasting the availability of cheap power: Dubai Aluminium Co, China Power Investment Co, BHP Billiton (Australia/UK—in 2015 BHP bauxite and aluminium interests were spun off into a separate company, South32), Shandong Xinfa Aluminum and Electricity Group (People's Republic of China) and Aluminium Bahrain BSC, or Alba. In 2020, according to industry analysts, based on primary aluminium production output, the largest companies were Chalco, Hongqiao (People's Republic of China), United Company RUSAL (Russian Federation), Shandong Xinfa (People's Republic of China) and Rio Tinto.

In 2022, according to USGS estimates, the People's Republic of China alone provided 58% of world smelter production of primary aluminium (40.0m. metric tons of a world total of 69.0m. tons), followed by India (6%), the Russian Federation (5%), Canada and the United Arab Emirates (4%), and Bahrain and Australia (2%). China displaced the USA as the most significant country for the international aluminium industry in the 2000s, accounting for about two-fifths of both consumption and production globally by 2013. By 2018, according to the USGS, the country accounted for 18% of semi-fabricated aluminium material imports (down from 33% in 2017). The USA was for many years the world's principal producing country, but in 2001 US output of primary aluminium was surpassed by that of Russia and of China. By 2022 the USA had fallen to ninth place among world producers (just ahead of Iceland). In the same year, when smelter output was less than one-half that of 2015, production of primary aluminium by China was estimated to be close to 47 times that of the USA.

The Middle East and North Africa produces some bauxite, but mainly features in the aluminium industry worldwide because it provides inexpensive energy. About one-quarter of the cost of alumina production is accounted for by energy, but smelting to obtain the primary aluminium can result in energy requirements absorbing almost one-half of total costs, depending on prices; therefore petroleum-rich countries in the region—notably Bahrain and the UAE—have long been a popular location for smelters. In the 21st century, Türkiye (Turkey before 2022) in particular has developed secondary aluminium production, and in 2015 a rolling mill also began operations in Saudi Arabia. Notwithstanding significant investment in the ready availability of inexpensive energy in the region, the bauxite raw material is often imported from investment projects elsewhere (such as mines in Guinea).

Türkiye is traditionally the region's largest producer of bauxite, but also has flourishing refineries and smelters to furnish its domestic industries. In 2020 the country's estimated production was 0.3m. metric tons of alumina, and 80,000 metric tons of the primary metal were produced in the same year (bauxite output grew to 1.3m. tons in that year). The country's only primary aluminium producer is Eti Alüminyum, which has its smelter in Seydişehir, near Konya, including an integrated refinery with supply from seven bauxite mines within 25 km. Smelter capacity was increased by technical upgrades from about 2015. Two other companies have mines elsewhere in Türkiye, but there are no other refineries or smelters.

In 2009 Saudi Arabia embarked on a joint venture between its main mining company, Saudi Arabian Mining (Ma'aden), and Alcoa to develop the world's most efficient integrated aluminium project, including a bauxite mine, refinery, smelter and rolling mill. Commercial metallurgical bauxite production began at the Al Ba'itha mine in Qassim province in 2013, and by 2016 the country had become the region's largest producer. The mine is connected by a 600-km railway with Ras Al-Khair, to the south-east, where the so-called 'Minerals Industrial City' and alumina refinery, smelter and rolling mill have been built. Aluminium production began in 2013, using imported feedstock at first, and the alumina refinery achieved its first full year of production in 2015 (0.8m. metric tons). This was reported to be the largest-capacity refinery in the Middle East and North Africa, supplying alumina to the smelter and rolling mill, which also upped production from 2015, including flat-rolled aluminium products for the first time.

Iran has native bauxite resources, as well as inexpensive energy. The country has one alumina refinery (Iran Alumina Co), which is supplied from the country's largest mine, Jajarm. There are some other mines, and two smelter companies (four smelters), but prevailing international conditions meant that investment in the industry is lacking. Bauxite production had been 0.9m. metric tons at the beginning of the 2010s, but was some 0.5m. tons in the middle years of the decade. Estimated alumina production was fairly stable at 240,000 metric tons in 2020, with primary metal production estimated at 450,000 metric tons in the same year.

The UAE has plentiful supplies of cheap energy and was therefore favoured by two smelters, at Al Taweelah in Abu Dhabi and at Jebel Ali in Dubai. In 2013 Emirates Aluminium (Emal) and Dubai Aluminium (Dubal) announced their merger into Emirates Global Aluminium, which also had investments in African bauxite mines, notably in Guinea. In 2019 the company's new refinery (only the second in the region) at Al Taweelah produced its first alumina, using ore from Guinea. The UAE and Bahrain are among the world's largest producers of primary aluminium (2.5m. and 1.6m. metric tons, respectively, in 2021). The UAE has a small secondary aluminium industry (rolling mills), while Aluminium Bahrain BSC, or Alba, continues to invest in its smelters, and capacity was expanded in 2019. Oman and Egypt also each have small smelters.

Global Forum The IAI, based in London, UK, is a global forum of producers of aluminium dedicated to the development and wider use of the metal. In 2023 the IAI had 25 member companies, representing every part of the world, including Russia and China, and responsible for more than 60% of global bauxite, alumina and aluminium production.

Aluminium Price on the London Metal Exchange
(average settlement price, US $ per metric ton)

	Average	High	Low
2005	1,898.31	(December) 2,247.45	(June) 1,731.30
2010	2,173.12	(December) 2,350.67	(June) 1,931.39
2015	1,664.68	(April) 1,819.19	(November) 1,467.89
2020	1,703.99	(December) 2,014.67	(April) 1,459.93
2021	2,472.85	(October) 2,934.39	(January) 2,003.98
2022	2,705.02	(March) 3,498.37	(September) 2,224.76

Source: World Bank, *Commodity Price Data* (Pink Sheet).

Prices The international benchmark price for aluminium cited here and by the World Bank is the average settlement price (unalloyed primary ingots, high grade—minimum 99.7% purity) traded on the London Metal Exchange (LME). Aluminium prices were particularly affected by the global recession precipitated by the international financial crisis of 2008, with the average price falling to US $1,664.83 per metric ton for 2009, the lowest level since 2003. Recovery was strong, but average annual prices declined in 2011–13; an improvement in 2014 was not sustained into 2015–16, and in November of the earlier year prices reached the lowest nominal monthly price in six years. Meanwhile, the average annual price in 2016 was its lowest since 2003. A recovery took prices generally upwards over 2017–18 (reaching their highest point since early 2012 in October 2017—$2,131 per ton). However, prices began to fall again in late 2018 and continued to decline throughout 2019 and the first half of 2020. From early 2021 prices had begun to recover, rising throughout the year and into early 2022; by March of the latter year the price was averaging $3,498 per ton (the highest monthly price since June 1988); the high prices were a consequence of higher input costs (specifically fuel, caused by the ongoing Russia–Ukraine conflict) leading to supply disruption in many regions. Prices dropped thereafter (to $2,269 per ton in May 2023) as primary aluminium output in China increased following the cessation of its uncompromising COVID-19 containment policy in December 2022.

CHROMIUM (Cr)

Chromium, historically used as an alloying element, is a hard, lustrous metal, the name of which derives from the Greek *kroma* (colour). It is only obtained from chromite (the name applied both to the metal-bearing mineral and to the ore containing that mineral—the terms chromite ore, chromium ore and chrome ore are used interchangeably). About 91% of total demand for chromite is from the metallurgical industry, some 5% from the chemical industry and about 4% from the refractory and foundry industries. For the metallurgical industry, most chromite ore is smelted in an electric arc furnace to produce ferrochromium or ferrochrome, an alloy with iron. Within this industry the major use of chromium remains as an alloying element—it is essential to the composition of stainless steel, which is valued for its toughness and resistance to most forms of corrosion. Chromium chemicals are also used for wood preservation, dyeing and tanning. Chrome plating is a popular way of enhancing the appearance of motor vehicles, kitchen appliances, etc. Chromite is also used as a refractory mineral.

The US Geological Survey (USGS) estimated world reserves to be at least 560m. metric tons of shipping-grade chromite ore in 2022, including Kazakhstan 230m. tons, South Africa 200m. tons, India 100m. tons, Turkey (Türkiye from 2022) 26m. tons, Finland 8m. tons and the USA 630,000 tons. What the USGS describes as the world's resources of shipping-grade chromite ore (i.e. not only economic reserves) are reckoned to be greater than 12,000m. tons, 95% located in southern Africa and Kazakhstan. South Africa is the leading producer of chromite ore supplies and of ferrochromium. South African charge-grade, high-carbon ferrochromium (which has a chromium content of 52%–55%) has been replacing the more expensive high- and low-carbon ferrochromiums (which have a chromium content of 60%–70%) since the development, during 1965–75, of the argon-oxygen decarbonizing process.

Production of Chromium Ore
('000 metric tons, gross weight)

	2018	2019	2020	2021
World total	47,200	45,000	34,000	42,200
Middle East and North Africa*	11,951	9,656	6,744	7,370
Regional producers				
Iran	119	122	135	47
Oman	885	732	382	340†
Türkiye	10,757	8,666	6,165	6,961
United Arab Emirates	190	136	62	22
Other leading producers				
Albania	1,143	1,288†	627	650
Brazil	450†	199	227	200†
Finland	2,211	2,415	2,293	2,274
India	4,076	4,139	2,402	4,249
Kazakhstan	6,689	7,019	6,326	6,500†
Madagascar	109	76	12	14†
Russian Federation	511	594	608	600†
South Africa	17,850	17,656	13,197	18,550
Sudan	27	13	6†	5†
Zimbabwe	1,756	1,550	1,197	1,325

2022 (gross weight, '000 metric tons, estimates): World 41,000 (Türkiye 6,900; India 4,200, Kazakhstan 6,500, South Africa 18,000).
* Total of the major regional producers only (if figures available): Iran, Oman, Türkiye, UAE.
† Estimated production.

Source: US Geological Survey.

The World Market and the Region From the second half of the 19th century, after the discovery of chromite reserves near Bursa, Turkey (subsequently Türkiye) was a leading producer of the ore. Although that country's pre-eminent position has now long been displaced by South Africa and, more recently, by Kazakhstan and India, it remains important in the ore trade internationally and, to a lesser extent, in the production of ferrochromium. As with the ore, South Africa is the world's dominant ferrochromium producer, second only to the People's Republic of China (see below), accounting for an estimated 3.7m. tons, or 26% of world output, in 2021. Türkiye's failure to maintain investment in the chromite-ferrochromium-stainless steel production chain meant that towards the end of the 2010s the domestic industry was in need of restructuring, while ore production was declining. While South Africa is the world's leading producer of chromite ore, it is not its largest exporter (India, Kazakhstan and Türkiye have all exported more historically) since it processes much of its production. The world's principal importer of chromite ore is the People's Republic of China, which is also the largest producer of ferrochromium (an estimated 41% in 2021). Türkiye also imports some ore, and also exports more high-carbon ferrochromium than it imports. The situation for low-carbon ferrochromium is similar but at lower volumes (Türkiye's only producer is Eti Elektrometalurji, which also has mines and concentration plants). In 2021, according to the USGS, Türkiye produced 100,750 metric tons of ferrochromium (of a world total of 14.5m. tons), down from a 2013 peak of 132,603 tons. The Yıldırım Group company Eti Krom is important in the Turkish chromium industry. It claims to be the world's biggest producer of so-called 'hard lumpy' marketable ore, and is the only chromite supplier in Türkiye that can extract chromium throughout the entire year, as well as the country's only high-carbon ferrochromium producer. The group also owns mines and smelters in other countries. Türkiye's exports of chromium ores and concentrates earned around $340m. in 2022, representing an increase of some 28% compared with the previous year.

Oman's production of chromite ore is not a significant contributor to the world total, but there are few exporters so it accounted for 1.3% of global exports (by value) in 2022. The country has been mining for chromite since the 1980s, and has an estimated 2% of world reserves of the ore, according to the USGS. There were six mining companies at 2019, but only Gulf Mining Group had any downstream processing capacity, with a chromite ore concentration processing plant (most chromite ore internationally is exported as a concentrate) and, since 2013, a ferrochromium smelter in the Sohar free zone. The company put the expanded facility into commission at the beginning of 2015 (Oman's high-carbon ferrochromium production amounted to 72,000 metric tons in that year), planning further expansion of the plant and the award of additional mining licences to provide feedstock.

Iran has a small chromite extractive industry and, historically, has also produced ferrochromium. However, restrictions on ore imports have meant that no significant amounts of ferrochromium were produced during most of the 2010s. The United Arab Emirates has some chromite resources, in Abu Dhabi and Fujairah. Mining has resulted in some output, but there has been little development or investment.

Chromite Ore and Ferrochromium Prices
(US import values, annual averages, US $ per metric ton)

	Chromite ore	Ferrochromium
2005	110	1,300
2010	212	2,564
2015	216	2,593
2020	179	1,878
2021	197	2,837
2022	340	6,800

Source: US Geological Survey.

Prices Chromite and ferrochromium prices tend to be negotiated on a private contract basis, although some publications produce indicator prices. The USGS provides a series of average annual import values that can provide an index for the movement of international prices: gross quantity of chromite ore (44% Cr_2O_3 f.o.b. South Africa) and the chromium content of ferrochromium (high-carbon, containing 49% to 51% chromium).

COTTON (*Gossypium*)

Cotton is the name given to the soft hairs that grow on the epidermis of the seed of the plant genus *Gossypium*. The most important of the four species cultivated for fibre is *G. hirsutum*, upland cotton, which originated in Mexico and now accounts for about 90% of the cotton harvest. *G. barbadense* is the extra long staple cotton, originating in Peru and accounting for a further 5%–8%; it is generally known by a number of names, such as Pima, American or Creole cotton and, with a reputation for quality, Egyptian and Sea Island cotton. The two Old World commercial species are *G. arboreum*, the tree cotton of South Asia, and *G. herbaceum* or Levant cotton.

The initial development of the cotton fibres takes place within a closed pod, called a boll, which, after a period of growth of about 50–75 days (depending upon climatic conditions), opens to reveal white tufts of cotton hair. After the seed cotton has been picked, the cotton fibre, or lint, has to be separated from the seeds by means of a mechanical process, known as ginning. (Cotton has been cultivated since antiquity, but the invention of the cotton gin in the 18th century revolutionized production costs and led to it becoming the natural fibre most widely used in clothing.) Depending upon the variety and growing conditions, it takes about three metric tons of seed cotton to produce one ton of raw cotton fibre. After ginning, a fuzz of very short cotton hairs remains on the seed. These are called linters, and may be removed and used in the manufacture of paper, cellulose-based chemicals, explosives, etc. The remaining cottonseed can have an oil extracted, the residual meal or cake being used for animal feed, etc.

About one-half of the cotton produced in the world is used in the manufacture of clothing, about one-third is used for household textiles and the remainder is used for numerous industrial products (tarpaulins, rubber reinforcement, abrasive backings, filters, high quality papers, etc.). The official cotton 'season' (for trade purposes) runs from 1 August to 31 July of the following year, and quantities are measured in both metric tons and bales; for statistical purposes, one bale of cotton is 226.8 kg (500 lb) gross or 217.7 kg (480 lb) net. The price of a particular type of cotton depends upon its availability relative to demand and upon characteristics related to yarn quality and suitability for processing. These include fibre length, fineness, cleanliness, strength and colour. The most important of these is length. Generally, the length of the fibre determines the quality of the yarn produced from it, with the longer fibres being preferred for the finer, stronger and more expensive yarns.

Production of Cotton
('000 metric tons)

	2019/20	2020/21	2021/22	2022/23*
World total	26,123	24,227	25,208	25,325
Middle East and North Africa	939	808	1,016	1,297
Leading regional producers				
Egypt	66	47	61	93
Iran	71	86	87	87
Syria	30	30	28	28
Türkiye	751	631	827	1,067
Other leading producers				
Australia	136	610	1,197	1,263
Brazil	3,000	2,356	2,552	2,874
China, People's Republic	5,977	6,445	5,835	6,684
India	6,205	6,009	5,313	5,443
Pakistan	1,350	980	1,306	849
USA	4,336	3,181	3,815	3,150
Uzbekistan	531	692	631	740

* Preliminary.

Source: US Department of Agriculture.

The World Market and the Region Cotton is the world's leading textile fibre. However, with the increased use of synthetics, cotton's share in the world's total consumption of fibre declined from 48% in 1988 to about 31% in 2012. About one-third of the decline in its market share was attributed to increases in the real cost of cotton relative to prices of competing fibres, and the remaining two-thirds to other factors, for example greater use of chemical fibre filament yarn (yarn that is not spun but is extruded in a continuous string) in domestic textiles, such as carpeting. In the 21st century, two important factors in the international trade in cotton have been output in the USA, which is among the world's leading producers without the matching levels of consumption, and the Chinese market (although officially enforced limits on the use of cotton in the People's Republic of China had ramifications for the international market). According to data compiled by the US Department of Agriculture (USDA), consumption of cotton worldwide had reached a record peak of 27.0m. metric tons in 2006/07, only for the greatest contraction in cotton consumption since the Second World War (by some 11%) to be precipitated after the world financial crisis in 2008 triggered a crash in commodity prices and a global economic recession. Consumption recovered to 26.2m. tons in 2018/19, but had fallen again to 23.8m. tons by 2022/23. The largest cotton consumers are China (33% of the world total in 2022/23) and India (21%); Pakistan, Bangladesh, Türkiye (Turkey before 2022) and Viet Nam are among other important consumers. China was for a time overwhelmingly the largest importer of cotton, but in 2015/16–2017/18 was displaced by both Bangladesh and Viet Nam. China and Bangladesh took turns as the largest importer of cotton in 2019/20–2022/23; in the latter year Bangladesh bought 18% of global imports. Viet Nam purchased 17% in that year, followed by China (also 17%—down from 54% in 2011/12), Pakistan, Türkiye, India and Indonesia. The world's principal exporters of cotton are the USA (34% in 2022/23), Australia (18%), Brazil (17%), Greece and India (3% each), and Benin (almost 3%);

REGIONAL INFORMATION
Major Commodities of the Middle East and North Africa

Uzbekistan is also traditionally an important exporter, as are Burkina Faso and Mali.

Cotton is a major crop in Türkiye, the leading regional producer. Exports of yarn, fabric and garments are also an important source of income in the country, so it also imports cotton. The Middle East and North Africa imported about 13% of the international trade in cotton in 2022/23; 11% was imported by Türkiye alone. The next largest regional importers were Iran and Egypt. Türkiye and Egypt, the latter famed for the fine quality of its extra long staple cotton, are nevertheless not major contributors to world exports (contributing, respectively, around 2% and 1% of global sales in 2022/23), although they are the region's major exporters. The region accounts for 8% of world consumption of cotton, Türkiye, Egypt and Iran with their large populations being the largest consumers, but 83% of regional consumption goes to Türkiye, to feed its textiles and clothing industries. Elsewhere in the Middle East and North Africa, Iran and Syria grow cotton, mainly for domestic markets, while Israel and Iraq grow smaller amounts (15,241 metric tons and 3,266 metric tons, respectively, in 2022/23).

Global Forum The International Cotton Advisory Committee (ICAC), an intergovernmental body, established in 1939, with its headquarters in Washington, DC, USA, publishes statistical and economic information and provides a forum for consultation and discussion among its members. The ICAC had 26 member governments at July 2023.

Cotton Price (Cotlook 'A')
(US $ per metric ton)

	Average	High	Low
2005	1,217	(October) 1,283	(January) 1,130
2010	2,283	(December) 3,703	(January) 1,706
2015	1,552	(May) 1,606	(January) 1,485
2020	1,586	(December) 1,786	(April) 1,401
2021	2,231	(November) 2,790	(January) 1,923
2022	2,865	(May) 3,610	(October) 2,198

Source: World Bank, *Commodity Price Data* (Pink Sheet).

Prices Although co-operation in cotton affairs has a long history, there have been no international agreements governing the cotton trade. Proposals to link producers and consumers in price stabilization arrangements have been opposed by the USA (the world's largest cotton exporter), and by Japan and the European Union (EU). Liverpool, United Kingdom, is the historic centre of cotton-trading activity, and international cotton prices are still collected by organizations located there. However, almost no US cotton has been imported through Liverpool in the 2000s, and consumption in the textile industry in the United Kingdom has fallen to negligible levels. The Cotton Outlook (Cotlook) 'A' index has long since changed from Liverpool quotations, then in August 2004 from c.i.f. Northern Europe to C/F Far East. The cotton quality base for the index is middling upland cotton, 1–3/32 inch. A decline in world cotton stocks in 2010 limited supplies, not only maintaining prices at high levels, but creating problems for indexing. From 22 June the usual Cotlook 'A' index was suspended, owing to a lack of quotations on offers, and the new 'A' forward index was then relied on. The World Bank cites the Cotlook 'A' figures, which recorded average monthly prices as being weaker in the second half of 2015 through to the end of the first quarter of 2016, strengthening and then stabilizing in the second half of the year, before rising to a peak in May 2017. The second half of 2017 saw a decline in average monthly prices, but prices peaked once more in June 2018. Prices fell again in the second half of 2018, through 2019 and into 2020, before rising from the second half of the year. Prices continued to increase throughout 2021 and the first half of 2022, reaching $3.61 per kg by May, the highest level in 11 years. By mid-2023, however, prices were trending lower, reaching $2.07 per kg ($2,073 per ton) in May, as a result of historically high energy prices and associated challenges in the producing countries, specifically lower profit margins for spinning mills.

GOLD (Au)

Gold minerals commonly occur in quartz, and are also found in alluvial deposits and in rich, thin underground veins. In South Africa gold occurs in sheets of low-grade ore (reefs) which may be at great depths below ground level. Gold is associated with silver, which is the commonest by-product of gold mining. Uranium oxide is another valuable by-product, particularly in the case of South Africa. Depending upon its associations, gold is separated by cyaniding, or else is concentrated and smelted. Gold is a dense, malleable metal, bright yellow in colour, and is one of the least reactive chemical elements.

Gold, silver and platinum are customarily measured in troy weight. A troy pound (now obsolete) contains 12 ounces, each of 480 grains. One troy oz is equal to 31.1 grams (1 kg = 32.15 troy oz), compared with the avoirdupois oz of 28.3 grams. Gold purity is measured in carats, in parts per 24, with 24 carats being pure gold (for gemstones and pearls, a carat is a unit of weight).

In modern times the principal function of gold has been as bullion in reserve for bank notes issued. From the early 1970s, however, the USA actively sought to 'demonetize' gold and so to make it simply another commodity. This objective was later adopted by the International Monetary Fund (IMF), which has attempted to end the position that gold occupied for many years in the international monetary system (see below). Gold remains an important investment commodity.

Production of Gold Ore
(metric tons, gold content)

	2019	2020	2021	2022
World total	3,596.3	3,482.1	3,580.7	3,627.7
Middle East and North Africa*	61.4	60.6	59.4	n.a.
Regional producers				
Egypt	14.9	14.1	12.9	n.a.
Iran	8.5	8.5	8.5	n.a.
Türkiye	37.1	41.5	39.4	30.9
Leading producers				
Australia	325.1	328.0	307.2	313.9
Brazil	100.0	98.9	93.1	86.7
Burkina Faso	82.6	93.4	102.7	96.2
Canada	185.2	173.3	192.9	194.5
China, People's Republic	383.2	368.3	332.0	375.0
Congo, Democratic Republic	60.4	52.4	49.1	44.5
Ghana	142.4	130.1	124.7	127.0
Indonesia	92.3	100.9	116.4	124.9
Kazakhstan	74.6	79.2	76.6	81.9
Mali	96.8	92.4	99.3	101.7
Mexico	109.0	110.4	124.8	124.0
Peru	143.3	101.6	127.3	125.7
Russian Federation	327.2	331.7	330.9	324.7
South Africa	113.2	102.5	113.6	92.6
Sudan	78.0	81.8	85.1	80.1
USA	200.4	193.4	186.8	172.7
Uzbekistan	93.2	100.2	104.9	110.8

* Total for the major reporting regional producers only in 2019, 2020 and 2021: Egypt, Iran and Türkiye.

Sources: Metals Focus; World Gold Council; US Geological Survey.

The World Market and the Region As a portable real asset which is easily convertible into cash, gold is widely esteemed as a store of value. Another distinguishing feature of gold is that new production in any one year is very small in relation to existing stocks. Much of the world's gold is in private bullion stocks, held for investment purposes, or is hoarded as a 'hedge' against inflation. Private investment stocks of gold throughout the world are estimated at 15,000–20,000 metric tons, much of it held in East Asia and India. By the beginning of 2013 the end of the decade-long bull run was apparent, as the gold price faltered. According to the World Gold Council, the first quarter of 2023 saw a 13% drop in demand for gold (excluding the over-the-counter market) compared to the same period of the previous year. The decline was attributed to investors' decreased global holdings of exchange traded products (ETPs). Although modest, the net reduction of 29 tons was in stark contrast to the significant gains experienced in the first quarter of 2022. Meanwhile, a reduction in Indian demand in particular was believed to be the result of record high local prices for gold discouraging jewellery consumers and investors alike. Lower Indian demand was offset somewhat by an improved economic outlook in China following the cessation of its uncompromising COVID-19 containment policy in December 2022—with the associated improvement in local consumption. Global jewellery consumption levels were similar to those of the first quarter of 2022, while gold bar and coin investment grew by 5% over the same period. There was, however, a sharp decline in consumption of gold in the technology sector (principally electronics)—to just 70 tons (the second-lowest quarterly figure since 2000, and a sign of the many prevailing global economic difficulties).

Gold reserves were discovered near Johannesburg, South Africa, in 1884, and their exploitation formed the basis of the country's subsequent economic prosperity. For more than 100 years South Africa was the world's leading gold producer. In 2007, however, the country relinquished primacy to China, where output had been rising steadily since 1999. China's position was confirmed in 2008 (when it accounted for 12% of world production), in which year the USA also exceeded South African production. By 2022 the output of 12 countries exceeded that of South Africa. In the Middle East and North Africa, Turkey (Türkiye from 2022) was the largest mine

REGIONAL INFORMATION

Major Commodities of the Middle East and North Africa

producer, and only 29th in the world. The region was, however, significant in secondary production, investment and jewellery.

Türkiye is the region's main mine producer of gold. At the beginning of the 21st century the country had no gold mines, but by 2023 it had 19 and was firmly established as Europe's largest producer. Output reached 33.5 metric tons in 2013, encouraged by foreign investment attracted by a reformed mining code, but despite some decline, production remained fairly steady in the second half of the 2010s. In July 2019 the industry association predicted mine output increasing to 50 tons per year before the mid-2020s, although other commentators noted investor doubts about political stability and increasing concerns about mine workers' safety. Indeed, following record production in 2020 of 41.5 metric tons, output fell to just 30.9 tons two years later. Türkiye also remains a significant importer of gold, given its position as the world's fourth largest consumer. Egypt, too, is a major consumer of gold and, in the modern world at least, a relatively new mining producer. In 2023 three gold mines were in operation in Egypt—the Sukari open-cast mine began operations in 2010 and produces almost all of the country's output, while the Iqat mine was discovered in 2020 and has thus far begun only experimental production (in late 2022). A third mine, Hammash Misr, is located in the Eastern Desert, 100 km west of the resort town of Marsa Alam. Exports of the precious metal accounted for 3% of the country's total export value in that year. Another country on the gold-rich geological Arabian-Nubian shield, Saudi Arabia is a long-established gold producer, although its mine output dwindled to a low point in 1990, then recovering to significant production in 2003. Only in 2017 and 2018 were those levels of output matched and exceeded, with official sources in 2019 announcing the intention to double production by 2025. Iranian gold production increased steadily from negligible levels at the beginning of the century, to more than triple in the 2010s alone. In 2019 Iran was reported to be using its gold production and reserves to back a digital cryptocurrency to evade US sanctions against it, and certainly domestic output of gold proved a valuable international commodity. The previous year the Government had announced an initiative to encourage small-scale gold mining projects, as well as larger investments. Other countries in the region, such as Yemen and those in North Africa in particular, were considered likely to have gold mineral reserves, but they lacked the political security to exploit them. Many of these countries are large consumers of gold.

The Middle East and North Africa, as measured by key regional bullion markets, alone provided 19% of world scrap supply in 2018. After the People's Republic of China (19%) and India (9%), Turkey (subsequently Türkiye) was the largest individual supplier of fabricated old gold scrap, with 77.4 metric tons, or 7% of the world total, followed, in the region, by Egypt on 45.9 tons, Iran 29.8 tons, the United Arab Emirates 25.1 tons, Saudi Arabia 13.0 tons, Morocco 9.0 tons, Algeria 7.6 tons and Iraq 7.5 tons. The boost in supply in 2018 came from reduced consumer demand in particular, because of weak currencies and rising economic uncertainty, notably in Türkiye and Iran. In the region, Türkiye has the largest gold reserves and the biggest fabrication demand. Jewellery demand in 2021 recovered substantially (by some 31%) following COVID-19-related restraint in 2020, although the fourth quarter saw substantially lower demand for jewellery as well as bar and coin—a result of significant local currency depreciation and surging inflation. Iraq, Egypt, Kuwait and Israel are also large jewellery consumers. Egyptian demand in the first quarter of 2023 grew by 6% year on year (bolstered by jewellery consumption in particular). Meanwhile, the introduction of a sales tax in the UAE had dented jewellery consumption severely in 2018. By the first quarter of 2023 higher prices had curtailed demand in that country (which was approximately 22% lower than one year earlier), with Iranian domestic consumption also down (by some 15%) over the same period. Meanwhile, tax changes in Jordan in 2018 increased local fabrication. In Saudi Arabia, despite increasing mine production, the 'Saudization' policy was affecting ancillary gold trades, notably fabrication, but the country still had the largest gold reserves in the region after Türkiye. There was a more moderate level of fabrication supply and demand in Morocco and Algeria.

International Association The World Gold Council (WGC), founded in 1987, is an international association of gold producing companies which aims to promote gold as a financial asset and to increase demand for the metal. The WGC, based in London, United Kingdom, had 33 corporate members in 2023.

Prices The unit of dealing in international gold markets is the 'good delivery' gold bar, weighing about 400 oz (12.5 kg). The principal centres for gold trading are London, Hong Kong and Zürich, Switzerland. The dominant markets for gold futures (buying and selling for future delivery) are the New York Commodity Exchange (COMEX) in the USA and the Tokyo Commodity Exchange (TOCOM) in Japan. A small group of dealers meets twice on each working day (morning and afternoon) to 'fix' the price of gold in the London Bullion Market (LBM), and the tables above are based on the second of these daily 'fixes'. During any trading day, however, prices may fluctuate above or below these levels. (A new LBM Association gold price was launched on 20 March 2015, to be operated by an independent third-

Gold Prices on the London Bullion Market
(afternoon 'fixes', US $ per troy oz)

	Average	Highest		Lowest	
1990	383.59	n.a.		n.a.	
2000	279.11	(7 February)	313	(27 October)	264
2010	1,224.52	(9 November)	1,421	(5 February)	1,058
2015	1,160.06	(22 January)	1,296	(17 December)	1,049
2020	1,769.59	(6 August)	2,067	(19 March)	1,474
2021	1,798.60	(4 January)	1,943	(30 March)	1,684
2022	1,800.09	(8 March)	2,039	(19 October)	1,632

Gold Prices in Various Currencies
(afternoon 'fixes', annual averages, per troy oz)

	Rand	Yen	Rupees
1990	991	55,448	6,698
2000	1,933	30,075	12,534
2010	8,946	107,090	55,974
2015	14,746	140,384	74,313
2020	29,171	188,771	131,203
2021	26,589	197,452	132,986
2022	29,397	236,044	141,287

Source: World Gold Council.

party provider, ICE Benchmark Administration—IBA.) Prices in other markets and other currencies vary. In real terms, the average annual London gold price reached a record height in 1980. Between 1980 and 2001 the LBM gold price reflected a significant fall in the price of the commodity (from an average of US $615 per troy oz in the earlier year to just $271 per troy oz in the latter). The rise in the average annual price of gold through the 2008 collapse in commodity prices and the onset of global recession was pronounced. During global crises, investors often look to gold as a so-called 'safe haven', which places upward pressure on prices. Indeed, following the twin crises of the early 2020s (the COVID-19 pandemic and Russia's renewed military invasion of Ukraine), gold reached record daily highs (breaching $2,000 per troy oz multiple times during that period). In April 2023 the monthly price averaged more than $2,000 per troy oz for the first time in history. By June 2023 the price had settled a little, to average $1,942.90 per troy oz.

Gold: Monetization and Demonetization During the 19th century gold was increasingly adopted as a monetary standard, with prices set by governments. In 1919 the Bank of England allowed some South African gold to be traded in London 'at the best price obtainable'. The market was suspended in 1925–31, when sterling returned to a limited form of the gold standard, and again in 1939–54. In 1934 the official price of gold was fixed at US $35 per troy oz and, by international agreement, all transactions in gold had to take place within narrow margins around that price. In 1960 the official gold price came under pressure from market demand. As a result, an international gold 'pool' was established in 1961 at the initiative of the USA. Originally a consortium of leading central banks with the object of restraining the London price of gold in case of excessive demand, it later widened into an arrangement by which eight central banks agreed that all purchases and sales of gold should be handled by the Bank of England. However, growing private demand for gold continued to exert pressure on the official price, and the gold 'pool' was ended in 1968, in favour of a two-tier price system. Central banks continued to operate the official price of $35 per oz, but private markets were permitted to deal freely in gold. However, the free market price did not rise significantly above the official price. In August 1971 the USA announced that it would cease dealing freely in gold to maintain exchange rates for the dollar within previously agreed margins. This 'floating' of the dollar against other major currencies continued until December, when it was agreed to raise the official gold price to $38 per oz. Gold prices on the free market rose to $70 per oz in August 1972. In February 1973 the US dollar was devalued by a further 10%, the official gold price rising to $42.22 per oz. Thereafter the free market price rose even higher, reaching $127 per oz in June 1973. In November it was announced that the two-tier system would be terminated, and from 1974 governments were permitted to value their official gold stocks at market prices.

In 1969 the IMF had introduced a new unit for international monetary dealings, the special drawing right (SDR), with a value of US $1.00, and the first allocation of SDRs was made on 1 January 1971. The SDR was linked to gold at an exchange rate of SDR 35 per troy oz, but this came under pressure from the devaluations of the US currency, and in July 1974 the direct link between the SDR and the US dollar was ended. Instead, the SDR was valued in terms of a weighted 'basket' of national currencies. At the same time the official gold price of SDR 35 per troy oz was retained as the IMF's basis for valuing official reserves. In 1976 the membership of the IMF agreed on proposals for far reaching changes in the international monetary system. These reforms, which were implemented on a gradual basis during 1977–81, included a reduction in the role of gold in the international system and the abolition of the official price of gold. A principal objective of the IMF plan was achieved in April 1978, when central banks were able to buy and sell gold at market prices. The physical quantity of reserve gold held by the IMF and member countries' central banks as national reserves has subsequently fallen (see below). The USA still maintains the largest national stock of gold, although the volume of its reserves has been substantially reduced. At the end of 1949 US gold reserves were 701.8m. oz, but since the beginning of the 1980s the level has been in the range of 261.4m.–264.6m. oz. At July 2023 US gold reserves reportedly stood at 8,133 tons, or 261.5m. oz.

During 1996 substantial amounts of gold bullion, jointly exceeding 500 metric tons, were sold by the central banks of Belgium and the Netherlands, and the Swiss National Bank announced its intention to allocate part of its gold reserves to fund a new humanitarian foundation. In the same year the UK first suggested a scheme to use some sales of IMF gold to finance debt relief for the world's poorest countries, principally in Africa. In July 1997 the Reserve Bank of Australia announced that it had disposed of more than two-thirds of its bullion holdings (reducing its reserves from 247 tons to 80 tons) over the previous six months. National sales of gold became far more common and, in response to concerns that the official sector's unco-ordinated gold sales were depressing gold prices, in 1999 the European Central Bank (ECB), in a joint statement with the central banks of Switzerland and 13 members of the European Union (Sweden, the UK and the 11 countries then in the eurozone), announced a five-year moratorium on new sales of gold held in official reserves. Total gold reserves held by the 15 signatory banks totalled 16,336 metric tons, accounting for around 48% of global gold reserves. The agreement—referred to as the Central Bank Gold Agreement (CBGA) and also known as the Washington Agreement on gold—allowed impending sales that had already been decided to proceed, although total sales were not to exceed 400 tons per year over the five-year period. The announcement also stated that gold would remain an important element of global monetary reserves. The European agreement was generally welcomed for removing uncertainty from the gold market, although the permitted rate of sales (400 tons per year) was more than 100% greater than the average net sales by the signatory countries in 1989–98. In March 2004 the renewal of the CBGA was announced, to cover the five-year period from September 2004 to September 2009, without the UK but with Greece as a new signatory. The second CBGA ended the moratorium on sales not already decided, and annual sales quotas were raised to 500 tons in order to take into account the consolidation of the price of gold that had occurred. Slovenia became a signatory of the second CBGA in December 2006, immediately prior to its adoption of the euro as its currency. Cyprus and Malta likewise became CBGA signatories on adopting the euro in January 2008, as did Slovakia in January 2009. The third CBGA entered effect at the end of September 2009, with the same signatories as those to the second agreement. Under the new CBGA, covering the five-year period to 2014, the cap on annual sales was again reduced to 400 tons (with the signatories noting that the intention of the IMF to sell 403 tons of gold could be accommodated within the overall quotas). Despite speculation that the low level of official sales made a fourth CBGA unnecessary, a new five-year agreement was concluded in May 2014 and it took effect on 27 September; the cap on sales was removed, but this marked the end of the era of significant official gold sales. It was reported in mid-2019 that the ECB and 21 other European central banks would not be renewing the CBGA for a fourth time, citing the maturity of the gold market as the reason for its decision.

NATURAL GAS

Natural gas, which is also known as fossil gas, is a naturally occurring hydrocarbon gas mixture consisting primarily of methane. Natural gas is known as 'associated gas' when found with other hydrocarbons such as petroleum or coal, and as 'unassociated gas' when found on its own. 'Associated gas' in an oilfield exists partly as a gas cap above the oil and partly dissolved in oil—it is the presence of gas under pressure in new oilfields which drives the crude petroleum to the surface. 'Associated gas' is unavoidably produced with oil and may be flared, reinjected or used as fuel. Most natural gas is used as fuel, although usually it first has to have impurities removed (ethane, propane, butanes, pentanes and other heavy hydrocarbons, water vapour, hydrogen sulphide, carbon dioxide and sometimes helium and nitrogen). Natural gas should not be confused with gasoline (petrol), which in North America is referred to colloquially as 'gas'.

Natural gas, like petroleum, is extracted both from onshore and offshore wells in many areas of the world. Most natural gas requires some processing to make it suitable as saleable gas for pipelines, etc., the first stage being the removal of water vapour and condensates. Acid gas is then extracted for the production of elemental sulphur—gas containing large quantities of sulphur is known as sour gas, gas without sulphur is sweet gas—tail gas and, ultimately, waste off-gas. Most of the gas is processed to dehydrate further, and to remove mercury and nitrogen-rich gas, before being ready for transportation and sale. Some gas is further fractionated and 'sweetened' to produce ethane, propane, butane, pentane, etc. As natural gas is not a pure product, when the reservoir pressure drops as 'unassociated gas' is extracted from a field under supercritical pressure or temperature conditions, higher molecular weight components may partially condense upon isothermic depressurizing—an effect called retrograde condensation—and the liquid thus formed may get trapped as the pores of the gas reservoir get depleted. This problem can be dealt with by re-injecting dried gas free of condensate to maintain the underground pressure and to allow re-evaporation and extraction of condensates. More frequently, the liquid condenses at the surface, and one of the tasks of the gas plant is to collect such condensate. The resulting liquid is called natural gas liquid (NGL), which has commercial value.

By far the biggest component of all natural gas by volume (at least 75%) is methane, CH_4. Other components are ethane (C_2H_6), propane (C_3H_8) and butane (C_4H_{10}). All those hydrocarbons are gases at normal temperatures and pressures. Suspended in the gas are various heavier hydrocarbons, pentane (C_5H_{12}), octane, etc., which are liquids at normal temperatures and pressures. Gas with a relatively high proportion of propane, butane and the heavier hydrocarbons is known as wet gas. 'Associated' natural gas tends to be wetter than 'unassociated gas'. Methane is the normal pipeline natural gas used for domestic and industrial purposes. It liquefies at very low temperatures (−160°C) and very high pressures, and in this condition is known as liquefied natural gas (LNG). Propane and butane are used as cylinder gases for a large number of industrial and domestic purposes—camping gas and cigarette lighter gas is either propane or butane—and the two gases liquefy at higher temperatures and lower pressures than methane. In their liquid state they are known as liquefied petroleum gases. Pentane and other heavier liquids are used for a variety of purposes, including the spiking of heavy crude oils and as petrochemical feedstocks. Such hydrocarbons, liquid at normal temperatures and pressures, are known as natural gasolines or condensate. Together, liquefied petroleum gases and natural gasolines are referred to as natural gas liquids.

Production of Natural Gas
(exajoules, excluding gas flared or recycled, and including natural gas produced for gas-to-liquids transformation)

	2019	2020	2021	2022
World total	142.9	139.0	145.9	145.6
Middle East and North Africa	30.0	29.9	32.0	32.4
Leading regional producers				
Algeria	3.1	2.9	3.6	3.5
Egypt	2.3	2.1	2.4	2.3
Iran	8.4	9.0	9.2	9.3
Oman	1.3	1.3	1.5	1.5
Qatar	6.4	6.3	6.4	6.4
Saudi Arabia	4.0	4.1	4.1	4.3
United Arab Emirates	2.0	1.8	2.1	2.1
Other leading producers				
Australia	5.3	5.3	5.3	5.5
Canada	6.1	6.0	6.2	6.7
China, People's Republic	6.4	7.0	7.5	8.0
Indonesia	2.4	2.1	2.1	2.1
Malaysia	2.8	2.6	2.8	3.0
Nigeria	1.8	1.8	1.6	1.5
Norway	4.1	4.0	4.1	4.4
Russian Federation	24.4	23.0	25.3	22.3
Turkmenistan	2.3	2.4	2.9	2.8
USA	33.4	33.0	34.0	35.2
Uzbekistan	2.1	1.7	1.8	1.8

Source: Energy Institute, *Statistical Review of World Energy 2023*.

The World Market and the Region According to an annual statistical report by Energy Institute, the Middle East and North Africa contains more than two-fifths of the world's proven reserves of natural gas. At the end of 2020 the Middle East alone boasted 40% of world reserves, with North Africa having a further 3%. The Russian Federation, Turkmenistan and other former Soviet states together constitute the next largest regional reserve, at 30% of the world total, followed by Asia-Pacific (9%—the People's Republic of China alone has 5%) and North America (8%). The individual countries with the largest proven reserves were Russia (20%—the second largest producer), Iran (17%), Qatar (13%) and Turkmenistan (7%). It is widely believed that such figures are conservative estimates. In spite of these huge reserves, natural gas was an under-utilized resource in much of the Middle East and North Africa into the 1980s. In contrast to petroleum, it was difficult to export, requiring either large pipeline systems or very expensive conversion into LNG. Where gas was found with oil—'associated gas'—the oil was taken and the gas 'flared' (ignited and burned). Algeria was the first country of the region to exploit gas reserves, building an LNG plant in 1964 and the first trans-continental pipeline (Transmed) to Europe in 1983. Liquefying natural gas is an expensive process, however, and it was mainly in the 1980s that other countries of the region began to realize the value of what was being 'flared'. Gas came to be substituted for petroleum use where possible, and in an era of high oil prices the increased use of natural gas freed crude petroleum for export. As a result, the flaring of 'associated gas' was gradually reduced in the 1980s and 1990s, and exports also increased. Equally, regional petrochemical and metal industries increasingly utilized gas rather than petroleum. By 1991 the Middle East and North Africa had more gas-fired power stations than Western Europe and North America combined.

The global market for natural gas, in terms of energy equivalence, is now about 70% of the size of that for crude petroleum. With regard to the environment, gas has a number of advantages over oil and coal, compared to both of which it produces less carbon dioxide on combustion and generally contains less sulphur. In addition, the use of gas for generating electricity continues to increase significantly because the fuel can be used in combined-cycle turbines. Such turbines generate power with a 50% rate of efficiency, compared with the 34% generally achieved by standard, single-cycle oil- or coal-fired power stations. Apart from nuclear energy, gas is the fuel best suited to this process. Natural gas is also a major petrochemical feedstock. With environmental awareness growing, the Middle East and North Africa has realized the value of gas for production of methanol and, from it, methyl-tertiary-butyl ether. In the ongoing search for ever cleaner fuels, methanol, dependent on a gas feedstock, may one day become an important vehicle fuel.

By far the largest consumer of natural gas globally is the USA, followed by the Russian Federation. In 2022, according to Energy Institute's annual statistical energy report, the USA's demand reached 31.72 exajoules (22.4% of the global total). In the same year the Russian market consumed 14.69 exajoules (10.4% of the total). Russia is also a significant exporter of natural gas; until recent years it had found an important market in the European Union (EU—itself the fourth largest market globally—12.36 exajoules or 8.7% of the total), and the EU had been, traditionally, the destination for more than one-half of Russia's natural gas exports (with Germany and Italy the largest individual European customers). However, in the aftermath of sanctions imposed on Russia in response to its renewed military invasion of Ukraine in 2022 (and consequent Russian restrictions and then suspension—in September, when the Nord Stream pipelines supplying gas from Russia to Germany were compromised by suspected sabotage—of gas supplies to Europe), it was reported in mid-2023 that the EU had reduced its level of gas imports from Russia to 15% of total gas imports in the first quarter 2023, down from 31% one year earlier. Other important consumers globally include the People's Republic of China (13.53 exajoules in 2022, 9.5% of the total, overtaking the EU as the third largest market globally), Iran (8.24 exajoules, 5.8% of the total) and Canada (4.38 exajoules, 3.1% of the total).

In 2004 Iran overtook Algeria as the leading regional producer of natural gas for the first time. Iran subsequently retained regional primacy in each subsequent year except 2012–13, when its output was surpassed by that of Qatar. Iran's potential as a producer and exporter of natural gas is enhanced by the fact that most of its reserves (as much as 80%, according to some sources), both offshore and onshore, comprise so-called 'unassociated gas' and have not yet been developed. The South Pars field (part of the same geological formation as Qatar's North Field) has been estimated to contain 14,000,000m. cu m in reserves of natural gas—some 40% of the country's total reserves—and 18,000m. barrels of gas condensates. Development began in 2002, and by 2016 production of natural gas from South Pars projects accounted for more than one-half of total Iranian output. A key challenge for Iran, however, is the development of export outlets, possibly including LNG facilities, to allow the realization of its export potential. Originally, several of the South Pars project's phases were to be devoted, in part at least, to the development of LNG production and export facilities requiring international partnerships and access to technology that is effectively controlled by US corporations. In the context of long-standing political tensions between US Administrations and the Iranian regime, and the resulting international sanctions, any LNG projects that had not been abandoned entirely remained a distant prospect at the beginning of the 2020s. Following a further round of indirect talks between the Biden Administration and Iran's regime in mid-2022, no significant progress towards an end to sanctions was reported, and the June 2021 election of conservative Ebrahim Raisi to the presidency of Iran appeared to further undermine any prospects for improved relations in the immediate future. Despite the wealth of its natural gas resources, in 2022 Iran remained an insignificant trader of the commodity in both regional and global terms. A natural gas pipeline between Iran and Turkey (subsequently Türkiye) became operational in 2002, and, according to the Energy Information Administration (EIA) of the USA, in 2021 Türkiye (along with its largest market, Iraq) was the destination for some 97% of Iran's exports of natural gas. Iran also supplies Armenia and Azerbaijan with gas. In 2020 completion of a long-mooted pipeline from Iran to Pakistan remained unlikely, given US hostility to Pakistan constructing its section of the pipeline, thereby violating US sanctions against Iran. In the north of the country, Iran imports some natural gas from Turkmenistan.

Qatar's proven reserves of natural gas are the third largest in the world, after Russia and Iran, and the second largest in the region. The offshore North Field is the largest resource of 'non-associated' natural gas in the world. Qatari production is highly export-orientated (hydrocarbons provided more than three-quarters of government revenue in 2020), and in 2022 mineral fuels provided 87% of total export earnings, and 65% from petroleum gases alone. In 2006 Qatar surpassed Indonesia as the world's leading exporter of LNG and the country retained this position until 2021, when it was overtaken by Australia. In 2022, however, Qatar resumed its position as leading exporter, providing 21% of sales on international markets. Qatar's trade in LNG is conducted by Qatargas. In 2022 Qatargas had 14 operational LNG trains, providing annual liquefaction capacity of 78m. metric tons. The expansion of Qatar's capacity to export natural gas is regarded by the Government as crucial to the country's future economic development. The Dolphin Gas Project, which sought to link the natural gas networks of Oman, the United Arab Emirates and Qatar to the Persian (Arabian) Gulf region's first natural gas pipeline, launched commercial operations in 2007. The Qatari Government has also developed gas-to-liquids capacity totalling, as of 2022, 294,000 barrels per day (b/d) of gas-to-liquids products, condensate and LPG. This capacity is divided between the Oryx and Pearl facilities, the latter—the biggest of its kind—being the world's first integrated gas-to-liquids project, joining upstream output of natural gas with conversion facilities on shore.

Saudi Arabia has the third largest natural gas resource in the region. Moreover, exploration for natural gas has been carried out in less than 20% of Saudi Arabia's territory. More than one-half of the country's reserves are 'associated' with petroleum. Petroleum is overwhelmingly the main export (although natural gas, manufactured, still provided 1.6% of total export revenues in 2022) but natural gas is encouraged for domestic use. Given that a key element of the Saudi Government's economic strategy is to substitute gas for oil domestically (for oil production, power generation, desalination, etc.) to release greater volumes of petroleum for export, in late 2006 the Ministry of Petroleum and Mineral Resources and the Saudi Arabian Oil Co (Saudi Aramco) announced plans to boost reserves by some 1,400,000m. cu m of 'unassociated gas' through discoveries, together, possibly, with an additional 1,400,000m. cu m of 'associated gas'. The most important but frustrated ventures in the search for 'unassociated gas' were pursued in the country's Rub al-Khali (the 'Empty Quarter') desert. However, significant discoveries of 'non-associated' gas were made in the offshore Khuff formation, where the Karan gasfield came on stream in 2012, with daily output of some 50m. cu m. The offshore Dorra gasfield, located in the Saudi Arabian-Kuwaiti Neutral (Partitioned) Zone, began production in 2008, but the plans of the two countries were opposed by Iran, which also claims part of the area. Development of the field was suspended in 2013 pending resolution of issues regarding the transport to facilities onshore of Saudi Arabia and Kuwait's shares of the field's output. In early 2022 Kuwait and Saudi Arabia signed an agreement for joint development, with production shared equally between the two countries.

Algeria was long the region's principal gas producer, pioneering exports of LNG by pipeline. Despite its ageing infrastructure and failure to develop new finds sufficiently quickly, in the 2010s Algeria remained the fourth largest producer in the Middle East and North Africa, and the largest producer on the African continent. It has the fourth largest proven reserves in the region, and the second largest, after Nigeria, in Africa. More than one-half of Algeria's reserves, which consist largely of 'associated gas', lie in the huge Hassi R'Mel field. The country also possesses vast, undeveloped reserves of shale gas. In 2022 Algeria was the ninth largest exporter of LNG in the world, and the third largest in the region after Qatar and Oman. In 2022 44% of total export earnings were from petroleum gases in various forms. The state-owned Société Nationale pour la Recherche, la Production, le Transport, la Transformation et la Commercialisation des Hydrocarbures (Sonatrach) is the Algerian agency responsible for, *inter alia*, the production and wholesale distribution of natural gas. It must hold a stake of at least 51% in any natural gas venture. Algeria exports gas to Europe by the Enrico Mattei (formerly Transmed) pipeline to Italy (via Tunisia), by the Pedro Duran Farell (formerly Maghreb–Europe Gas) pipeline to Spain (via Morocco) and the Medgaz pipeline directly to Spain and, thereafter,

France. Work on a proposed GALSI pipeline to northern Italy (via Sardinia) stalled in 2014. Plans for a trans-Saharan natural gas pipeline project (TSGP) from Warri, Nigeria, to Hassi R'Mel, Algeria, were reported to be close to completion. The pipeline, a formidable undertaking of more than 4,000 km in length and a cost approaching US $12,000m., was to carry Nigerian natural gas to European markets after linking with Medgaz and the Enrico Mattei pipeline. As of mid-2023, however, construction of the pipeline had not yet begun, and the project was likely to have been compromised by the July 2023 coup that ousted Niger's President Bazoum, and the subsequent sanctions imposed on the new regime in that country by the Economic Community of West African States (ECOWAS—as the pipeline was to pass through Niger, with extensive construction work required in that country). Analysts have pointed to the pipeline's potential strategic importance in the context of ongoing discussions among European nations about the need to reduce dramatically reliance on Russian gas.

The UAE's largest reserves are in the emirate of Abu Dhabi, including the Khuff reservoirs (shared with Saudi Arabia) of 'unassociated gas', which contain some of the largest deposits in the world. Domestic consumption has been encouraged, although needs have long been met, in part, by supplies from Qatar, because the development of domestic production focused on NGLs and condensates, and on enhanced oil recovery (EOR—gas reinjection to facilitate production of crude petroleum from mature oilfields). Moreover, much of the UAE's natural gas is difficult to develop and process economically owing to its high sulphur content. Despite the difficulties, sour gas processing facilities have been invested in, and the country also shares in an international natural gas pipeline with Qatar and Oman. In 2022 the UAE was the fifth largest LNG exporter in the region after Qatar, Algeria, Oman and Egypt.

Egypt is the largest natural gas producer in Africa after Algeria. Its reserves have been boosted substantially by the discovery of rich deposits in the Mediterranean, the Nile Delta and the Western Desert. For example, in 2015 the discovery was announced of a so-called super giant field, possibly the largest ever, off the coast of Egypt in the Mediterranean Sea. Soaring production in the first decade of the 21st century prompted Egypt's Ministry of Petroleum to pursue a strategy of expanding natural gas usage for industrial, commercial and domestic purposes. Growth in consumption of natural gas occurred largely as a result of the conversion of Egypt's thermal power plants to the use of gas for generating purposes. However, the failure subsequently to develop new reserves led, after about 2010, to a decline in both production and reserves of natural gas, and the Government was obliged to prioritize usage for power generation. Shortages of natural gas for power generation, notably in 2015, were alleviated through imports of LNG. The development of exports, already constrained by a policy whereby reserves of natural gas were divided equally between domestic consumption, future generation and exports, was likewise inhibited by shortages of supplies for domestic usage. LNG exports, for example, were still 9,000m. cu m in 2009, but fell to nothing in 2015. By 2019 LNG exports had recovered somewhat to 4,700m. cu m. Following a significant fall in exports in the following year, foreign sales recovered substantially in 2021 and 2022, reaching 9,000m. cu m and 8,900 cu m, respectively, following the February 2021 resumption of operations at the Damietta plant, which had been dormant for eight years.

In Oman, natural gas is regarded as a key element of the country's economic diversification strategy, which has included investment in production, processing and pipelines. Although domestic consumption of natural gas has risen rapidly since 2000, Oman continued to export more than one-half of its output (exclusively as LNG) owing to long-term contractual commitments, notably to the Republic of Korea (South Korea). In 2022 Oman was the second largest exporter of LNG in the region, after Qatar, and eighth largest in the world. Plans to import Iranian gas were stalled in 2019, owing to uncertainty surrounding the possible consequences of challenging US sanctions in the region. Natural gas provided 24% of mineral fuel export earnings in 2022, and 18% of total export revenues in the same year.

Elsewhere in the Middle East and North Africa, natural gas is produced in Bahrain (0.6 exajoules in 2022), Kuwait (0.5), Libya (0.5), Iraq (0.3), Syria (0.1) and Yemen. The last five listed countries, however, have had their development of the resource interrupted and damaged by war and civil conflict. War damage and lack of investment meant that Iraq was still flaring almost one-half of its production in 2021, although it resolved to end the practice in the southern fields by 2027. Libya exports natural gas to Europe via the Greenstream pipeline, but instability in the country has meant erratic production, processing and export in the 2010s. Syria has been affected by both civil war and international sanctions, and its 2022 production was less than one-half of the 0.3 exajoules it had reached in 2010, before the internal conflict. The war in Yemen ended its LNG exports in 2015—the LNG liquefaction facilities had been the country's largest industrial initiative ever, spurred by a 2005 export contract with South Korea—and natural gas production became minimal, having reached 0.4 exajoules in 2013, before the advent of rising civil unrest and outright civil war.

Global Forum The Gas Exporting Countries Forum (GECF) was founded in 2001 in Teheran, Iran, and is based in Doha, Qatar. At mid-2023 the GECF's 12 members included Algeria, Egypt, Iran, Libya, Qatar and the UAE. Iraq participates as an observer. Yemen has also expressed interest in joining. Some member countries, notably the Russian Federation and Iran, have expressed ambitions for the GECF to become a 'Gas OPEC' but, unlike crude petroleum, the production of which is controlled to a large extent by the Organization of the Petroleum Exporting Countries (OPEC) and is thus dominated by the politics of oil pricing and the Organization's internal disputes, gas diplomacy, at least prior to Russia's renewed invasion of Ukraine in 2022, had remained largely free of historical East–West recriminations. Gas supply is a central element in the plans of the Cooperation Council for the Arab States of the Gulf (Gulf Cooperation Council) for economic development and, although those plans concentrate on domestic consumption, several countries of the region are members of the GECF.

Natural Gas Prices
(US $ per million BTUs)

	Europe	USA	LNG (Japan)
2012	11.47	2.75	16.55
2013	11.79	3.72	15.96
2014	10.05	4.37	16.04
2015	6.82	2.61	10.93
2016	4.56	2.49	7.37
2017	5.72	2.96	8.61
2018	7.68	3.16	10.67
2019	4.80	2.57	10.56
2020	3.24	2.01	8.31
2021	16.12	3.85	10.76
2022	40.34	6.37	18.43

Source: World Bank, *Commodity Price Data* (Pink Sheet).

Prices The World Bank cites three indicator prices, all measured in US dollars per mmbtu—(metric) million British thermal units. The European price is that at the Netherlands Title Transfer Facility (TTF); the US one the 'spot' price at Henry Hub, Louisiana; and the Japanese price is for liquefied natural gas, c.i.f. import price.

The Europe natural gas price strengthened in the mid-2000s to peak at US $13.41 per mmbtu in 2008, before the international commodity price crash and financial crisis of that year caused its decline. Since recovery to an average price of $11.79 per mmbtu in 2013, the annual price fell each year to 2016. Recovery then continued until September 2018 (a monthly average of $9.52 per mmbtu) but the price declined steadily afterwards, to reach just $1.58 per mmbtu in May 2020. The average monthly price grew substantially thereafter, reaching $70.04 per mmbtu in August 2022, by far its highest level on record (and further evidence of the potential unintended consequences of Russia's political and economic isolation); by May 2023, however, the price had fallen back to just $10.11—this development was attributed to a warmer winter in Europe, efficiency gains caused by the higher prices, LNG imports (especially from the USA) to Europe replacing Russian imports, and resultant higher stocks in Europe.

The US natural gas price reached a record $8.86 per mmbtu in 2008, before the commodity price crash, reaching its lowest point since 1999 in 2016. The annual price increased thereafter, and the average monthly price peaked at $4.12 per mmbtu in November 2018, tending downwards then to reach just $1.72 per mmbtu in July 2020, the lowest monthly price since March 2016. The price had recovered to reach $8.71 per mmbtu by August 2022, its highest level in almost 15 years, before falling back significantly over the course of the next year, to just $2.15 in May 2023. The US natural gas price has performed the worst of the three indicator prices since the 2008 financial crisis, owing largely to the plentiful domestic supplies secured from shale gas during this period.

The LNG (Japan) price peaked at US $12.53 per mmbtu in 2008, before the commodity price crash, but reached a new height of $16.55 per mmbtu in 2012. A price of $16.04 per mmbtu was achieved in 2014, the annual average price declining thereafter until 2016. Average monthly prices reached a low point of $6.27 per mmbtu in May 2016, then tended upwards to reach $12.01 in January 2019. The price fell during most of 2020, but began climbing again towards the end of the year and through 2021 and 2022. Prices reached their highest levels on record in September of the latter year ($23.73 per mmbtu); by May 2023, however, the price had fallen back down to $14.04 per mmbtu.

OLIVES (*Olea europaea*)

The olive tree (*Olea europaea*) appears to have originated in the Middle East, in the Eurasian territories between the southern

REGIONAL INFORMATION

Major Commodities of the Middle East and North Africa

Caucasus, the Iranian plateau and the Levant coast, being spread through the ancient Mediterranean world by the Phoenicians, Greeks and Romans. The Spanish took the olive to the Americas, and it has spread further since. The olive is a small species of evergreen tree related to lilacs, jasmine and the ash tree. It is ubiquitous throughout the Mediterranean basin, its fruit and the oil thereof fundamental to the various cuisines and indeed cultures of the region. The fruit is a drupe or stone fruit, with oil rich flesh surrounding a seed known as a stone or pit. The fruit ripens from green, through reds or browns to purple or black, in the summer and the autumn.

Cultivation of the olive is thought to have originated more than 6,000 years ago in the eastern Mediterranean. The vast bulk of the fruit harvested is used for oil (the very word 'oil' originates from the olive), but it is also eaten as a so-called table olive. Most varieties of olive cannot be eaten from the tree, because the fruit has a bitter component known as oleuropein, which has to be removed before eating (usually by fermentation). The olive has a relatively low sugar content and a high oil content, depending on variety and time of year. Methods for removing oleuropein and other unpalatable phenolic compounds from olives vary considerably, generally by region and custom, but usually involve curing and fermentation and treatment with lye (sodium or potassium hydroxide), brine or successive rinsing in water. The exact fermentation process has a significant impact on the final product, and there are five main types: the Spanish or Sevillian (more than one-half of the world's table olives are prepared in this manner), the Sicilian or Greek, the Picholine or directly brined, the water cured and, with only minor fermentation, the salt cured. The California or artificially ripened process does not involve fermentation. Table olives can be green, semi-ripe or black, depending on when they are harvested and treated, although most black table olives are actually green olives chemically treated to blacken them.

Olive oil is harvested from the ripe olive by grinding the fruit into a paste and putting that paste under pressure ('pressing') to extract the oil. The pomace, or solid remains of the fruit after pressing, can have further oil extracted by chemical means. According to the International Olive Council (IOC), virgin olive oil is 'obtained...solely by mechanical or other physical means under conditions, particularly thermal conditions, that do not lead to alterations in the oil, and which have not undergone any treatment other than washing, decantation, centrifugation and filtration.' Olive oil consists of more than four-fifths oleic acid, and some other fatty acids such as linoleic acid and palmitic acid. Extra virgin olive oil is defined as having a free acidity, expressed as oleic acid, of not more than 0.8g per 100g (0.8%); virgin olive oil not more than 2% free fatty acid; and ordinary olive oil not more than 3.3% free fatty acid. Refined olive oil is obtained from virgin olive oil to be not more than 0.3% free fatty acid. Other categories involve non-consumable lampante oil and olive pomace oils. Modern methods of production use a lot of water, the waste of which poses a disposal problem, not being biodegradable.

Production of Olives
('000 metric tons)

	2018	2019	2020	2021
World total	24,585	21,628	23,729	23,054
Middle East and North Africa*	8,313	8,164	8,741	7,443
Major regional producers				
Algeria	861	869	1,080	705
Egypt	1,084	981	968	976*
Morocco	1,561	1,912	1,409	1,591
Syria	665	844	781	566
Tunisia	1,617	700	2,000	700
Türkiye	1,500	1,525	1,317	1,739
Other major producers				
European Union*	15,355	12,423	14,069	14,595
Greece	2,765	3,240	n.a.	n.a.
Italy	1,954	2,194	2,207	2,271
Portugal	739	939	735	1,376
Spain	9,820	5,965	8,138	8,257

* FAO estimate(s).
Source: FAO.

The World Market and the Region Olives and olive oil are widely used throughout the Mediterranean world, and the highest consumption per head is among the main producers. Spain is the largest grower of olives, but the country with the most consumption per head is, by far, Greece, followed by Spain and Italy, then Tunisia, Portugal, Syria, Jordan and Lebanon. Olive consumption has spread widely around the world, and the olive tree is also grown now in the Americas, China and Australia, for example.

The European Union (EU) dominates world production of olives, in particular the countries of Spain, Italy and Greece. In 2022/23, according to the IOC, the EU not only accounted for 28% of world production of table olives, but for 35% of all exports of olives, amounting to some 271,000 metric tons. The Middle East and North Africa was the next most important olive region, with production put at 605,000 tons in Türkiye (Turkey before 2022), 600,000 tons in Egypt (which had dramatically increased its olive acreage from the 2000s), 298,000 tons in Algeria, 128,000 tons in Morocco and 115,000 tons in Syria. Iran, Jordan and Tunisia also produced significant olive harvests, but many of the region's countries were only satisfying domestic consumption. In the mid-2010s Egypt overtook Morocco as the second largest exporter after the EU, but Morocco soon regained its position until 2022/23 when, according to preliminary figures, Türkiye provided 26% of world exports, Morocco 14% and Egypt 10%.

Production of Olive Oil
('000 metric tons)

	2019/20	2020/21	2021/22*	2022/23†
World total	3,269	3,020	3,398	2,730
Middle East and North Africa	1,235	823	983	1,095
Major regional producers				
Morocco	145	160	200	156
Syria	118	143	106	135
Tunisia	440	140	240	180
Türkiye	230	194	235	380
Other major producer				
European Union	1,920	2,051	2,272	1,505

* Provisional.
† Preliminary.
Source: International Olive Council.

Even more so than with table olives, the production and export of olive oils is dominated by the EU countries, and by Spain in particular. In 2022/23, according to preliminary figures from the IOC, the EU manufactured 55% of world production of olive oil, and provided 59% of all exports, amounting to some 588,500 metric tons. The Middle East and North Africa was the next most important olive oil region, with production put at 380,000 tons in Türkiye, 180,000 in Tunisia, 156,000 tons in Morocco, 134,500 tons in Syria and 81,000 tons in Algeria. Jordan, Lebanon, Egypt, Libya and Israel also produced olive oils, but again many of the region's countries were only satisfying domestic consumption. In 2022/23 the largest exporter of olive oil after the EU was Tunisia, with 15% of the world total, followed by Türkiye with 13% and Morocco with 3%.

The most serious pest for olive groves is the olive fruit fly (*Dacus oleae* or *Bactrocera oleae*), which can ruin the fruit by laying eggs in the flesh just before autumn ripening. More recently, in the 2010s, many producing countries have expressed concern about the threat posed by the spread of olive quick decline syndrome (complesso da disseccamento rapido dell'olivo, CoDiRO or CDRO). CDRO is mainly caused by a strain of *Xylella fastidiosa*, a bacterium spread by plant-sucking insects that restricts the flow of sap in the tree, affecting the extremities and causing dieback. It was first identified in southern Italy in 2013.

International Association The International Olive Council (IOC), with headquarters in Madrid, Spain, was formed in 1959 under the aegis of the United Nations. It was known as the International Olive Oil Council until 2006, changing its name under the 2005 International Agreement on Olive Oil and Table Olives. In 2015 a new Agreement was signed. At August 2023 IOC members numbered 19 countries (including seven non-Mediterranean countries: Argentina, Georgia, Iran, Jordan, Saudi Arabia, Uruguay and Uzbekistan) and the European Union. The USA is not a member of the IOC, but since 2010 has maintained parallel standards. IOC members account for 98% of the world's olive production. The Council provides a forum for the exchange of information among olive and olive oil producers, encourages trade and research, and publishes statistics.

Prices The leading role of the European Union in the production and export of olive oil means that EU prices are now the most accurate and readily available guide to the international market. The price for EU extra virgin olive oil (c.i.f. Italy—until December 2011, less than 1% free fatty acid, ex-tanker prices, UK) is cited in this survey, using data from the IMF. Prices averaged more than US $4,000 per metric ton each month in 2022; by December the price had reached $5,792 per ton, and continued to climb into 2023. In June the price had reached $7,240 per ton, which was by far the highest price on record for olive oil, and was largely attributed to prolonged drought in Spain.

Olive Oil Price
(annual averages, US $ per metric ton)

Year	Price
2005	5,519.2
2010	3,171.3
2015	4,292.8
2020	2,628.3
2021	4,184.8
2022	4,469.9

Source: IMF, Commodity Data Portal.

PETROLEUM

Crude oils, from which petroleum is derived, consist essentially of a wide range of hydrocarbon molecules which are separated by distillation in the refining process. Refined oil is treated in different ways to make the different varieties of fuel. More than four-fifths of total world oil supplies are used as fuel for the production of energy in the form of power or heating.

Petroleum, together with its associated mineral fuel, natural gas, is extracted both from onshore and offshore wells in many areas of the world. It is the leading raw material in international trade. Globally, demand for this commodity totalled an estimated 97.3m. barrels per day (b/d) in 2022, an increase of 3.1% compared with the previous year. The world's 'published proven' reserves of petroleum and natural gas liquids at 31 December 2020 were estimated to total 244,421m. metric tons, equivalent to 1,732,366m. barrels (1 metric ton is equivalent to approximately 7.3 barrels, each of 42 US gallons or 34.97 imperial gallons, i.e. 159 litres). The dominant producing region is the Middle East, whose proven reserves in December 2020 accounted for 48.3% of known world deposits of crude petroleum, gas condensate and natural gas liquids. The Middle East accounted for 36.0% of world output in 2022. Latin America (including Mexico) held 51,694m. tons of proven reserves (19.0% of the world total) at the end of 2020, and accounted for 9.6% of world production in 2022.

From storage tanks at the oilfield wellhead, crude petroleum is conveyed, frequently by pumping for long distances through large pipelines, to coastal depots where it is either treated in a refinery or delivered into bulk storage tanks for subsequent shipment for refining overseas. In addition to pipeline transportation of crude petroleum and refined products, natural (petroleum) gas is, in some areas, also transported through networks of pipelines. The properties of different crude petroleums (e.g. colour, viscosity, etc.) vary considerably, and these variations are a determinant both of price and of end use after refining.

The most important of the petroleum products is fuel oil, composed of heavy distillates and residues, which is used to produce heating and power for industrial purposes. Products in the kerosene group have a wide number of applications, ranging from heating fuels to the powering of aviation gas turbine engines. Gasoline (petrol) products fuel internal combustion engines (principally in road motor vehicles), and naphtha, a gasoline distillate, is a commercial solvent that can also be processed as a feedstock. Propane and butane, the main liquefied petroleum gases, have a wide range of industrial applications and are also used for domestic heating and cooking.

The World Market and the Region Of the 10 countries with the world's largest proven petroleum reserves, six—Saudi Arabia, Iran, Iraq, Kuwait, the UAE and Libya—are located within the Middle East and North Africa, as were five of the 10 leading producers in the world in 2022: Saudi Arabia (second), Iraq (fifth), UAE (seventh), Iran (eighth) and Kuwait (10th). Furthermore, seven of the 13 Organization of the Petroleum Exporting Countries (OPEC) members are to be found in the region. In 2022, according to Energy Institute's *Statistical Review of World Energy 2023*, the countries of the Middle East and North Africa, with estimated output of 1,588m. metric tons (about 34m. barrels daily), accounted for some 36% of world production of crude petroleum totalling an estimated 4,407m. tons. However, while the world is dependent on the region for such a significant proportion of its energy supplies, the region is far more dependent on its hydrocarbons revenues. Macroeconomic data, for instance, indicate that in 2022 foreign sales of petroleum accounted for more than three-quarters of Saudi Arabia's export revenues. Petroleum exports historically accounted for about 80% of Iran's total export earnings, while in 2014 official data estimated hydrocarbons as being responsible for some 15% of the country's nominal gross domestic product (GDP), although US sanctions in the late 2010s were undermining performance in the sector. In 2022 crude petroleum accounted for just 4% of Iran's total export revenue. Between 2018 and 2022 crude petroleum revenues in Iran fell by an average of 68% each year—a result of US sanctions and the COVID-19 pandemic. According to official and IMF data, Iraq's petroleum sector accounted for more than 57% of GDP (for crude) and an estimated 95% of central government revenues in 2022. In the same year sales of crude petroleum accounted for 93% of the total value of Iraq's exports. Exports of crude petroleum were responsible for about 70% of Kuwait's total export revenues in 2022, and in 2017 hydrocarbons accounted for around 50% of Kuwait's GDP. In 2022 export revenues from crude petroleum accounted for 82% of Libya's total receipts. In the same year crude petroleum accounted for about 28% of Algeria's export revenues, while hydrocarbons overall contributed 40% of total government income in 2021.

Saudi Arabia is the largest regional producer and exporter. Its role has been of particular significance within OPEC, which has often been described as a type of cartel that aims to increase petroleum prices above the competitive level by restricting its members' production of petroleum through a system of quotas. Like many cartels, OPEC has been vulnerable to overproduction and to deception regarding pricing by members whose interests, for a variety of reasons, including extent of reserves and demographic factors, often do not coincide. However, OPEC differs from classic cartels in one important aspect, namely that one of its producers, Saudi Arabia, is much larger than all of the others. This status has meant that Saudi Arabia has assumed the role of OPEC 'swing' producer, i.e. the country modifies its output in order to defend the official world price of oil. This is partly explained by the fact that decreases in the world price of petroleum impose greater short-term losses on Saudi Arabia than on other member states. Over the longer term, however, Saudi Arabia has pursued a policy that aligns it with OPEC's so-called price 'doves', i.e. those members who favour relatively high production and low prices in order to safeguard markets for petroleum—Iran, for example, has traditionally been regarded as an OPEC price 'hawk', keen to limit production and increase the petroleum price. The debate over so-called 'peak oil' focused attention on any perceived sign of Saudi Arabia's apparent inability to continue to fulfil that role, and caused some analysts to speculate that the country no longer possessed the spare production capacity necessary to maintain stability, which contributed to the anxiety caused on international markets by the 2019 attack on the Abqaiq processing facility (see below). Historically, the onshore Ghawar field, the world's largest, has accounted for about one-half of the country's output. Saudi Arabia's hydrocarbons industry is the purview of the state-controlled Saudi Arabian Oil Co (Saudi Aramco), one of the largest oil companies in the world measured by reserves and hydrocarbons output. Supervision of Saudi Aramco is undertaken by the Ministry of Energy, Industry and Mineral Resources and by the company's Supreme Council, which determines strategy. That strategy is now focused by the so-called Vision 2030 policy, which aims to reduce the country's dependence on petroleum and to enhance processing and refining capacity in Saudi Arabia.

The proven petroleum reserves of Iran rank as the second largest in the region and the fourth largest in the world. The most important producing oilfield is the Ahvaz field in Khuzestan province, in the south west of the country. All exploration for and production of petroleum is undertaken by the state-owned National Iranian Oil Co (NIOC), under the direction of the Ministry of Petroleum. About 80% of production in the provinces of Khuzestan, Bushehr, Fars and

Production of Crude Petroleum
('000 metric tons, including natural gas liquids)

	1985	1995	2005	2022
World total	2,791,547	3,279,064	3,931,474	4,407,186
Middle East and North Africa	660,051	1,150,097	1,427,460	1,587,993
Leading regional producers				
Algeria	47,061	55,811	86,438	63,649
Iran	110,351	185,457	207,871	176,541
Iraq	69,839	26,026	89,934	221,310
Kuwait	55,489	104,889	130,411	145,715
Libya	48,391	67,893	81,966	51,018
Qatar	15,318	21,831	52,559	74,084
Saudi Arabia	172,072	431,263	516,628	573,092
United Arab Emirates	55,960	114,411	136,553	181,117
Other leading producers				
Angola	11,452	31,173	62,434	57,771
Brazil	29,470	37,504	88,981	163,058
Canada	85,685	111,906	142,679	273,983
China, People's Republic	124,900	149,020	181,353	204,720
Kazakhstan	22,660	20,633	61,486	84,139
Mexico	145,854	150,213	186,491	97,680
Nigeria	73,832	95,061	121,144	69,006
Norway	39,211	138,400	138,434	88,952
Russian Federation	542,306	310,749	474,819	548,517
United Kingdom	127,611	129,894	84,721	36,241
USA	498,705	383,554	308,988	759,460
Venezuela	91,504	155,325	169,409	37,306

Source: Energy Institute, *Statistical Review of World Energy 2023*.

Kohgiluyeh and Boyerahmad is undertaken by a NIOC subsidiary, the National Iranian South Oil Co. Refinery capacity is sufficient to meet all domestic demand for refined petroleum products, including gasoline—the country became a net exporter of gasoline in 2019, after the Persian Gulf Star refinery was commissioned. The ending of some international economic sanctions between 2016 and 2018 gave rise to hopes of renewed foreign investment in Iran, with the Government hoping to boost production back to pre-revolutionary levels (which would require investment in the region of some US $30,000m., according to reports published in 2016), but renewed US sanctions ended such ambitions in the short term. Indeed, in 2018–2021 sales of crude petroleum fell precipitously (but regained some ground in 2022, as post-pandemic demand recovered); the main markets in 2021 were Malaysia, the People's Republic of China and the UAE.

Iraq's petroleum reserves, already ranked third in the region and fifth in the world (though unofficial estimates put them much higher), might well be larger than current official estimates, given speculation about the potential of unexplored areas of the country's western and southern deserts. Most proven reserves and functioning oilfields are in the north and south of the country. Iraq's oil industry was damaged not only by the war with Iran, but also by the imposition of subsequent economic sanctions, and by the wars with multinational forces in 1991 and 2003 and post-war turbulence, which has also discouraged foreign investment (as has the absence of a clear legal participation framework for international oil companies). Production and development of hydrocarbons is currently the nationwide remit of Iraq's Ministry of Oil, except in the Kurdish Autonomous Region (KAR) in the north, where the International Energy Agency (IEA) has indicated proven reserves close to the cities of Kirkuk, Khanaqin and Mosul amounting to 4,000m. barrels. (The Kurdish Regional Government—KRG—has claimed that the area under its control could also contain as much as 45,000m. barrels in unproven reserves.) Conflicting claims by the Government in Baghdad and the KRG to exercise control over petroleum resources remain a fundamental problem (see below), but in 2019 the Energy Information Administration (EIA) of the USA estimated that 88% of Iraqi oil was being produced in the south of the country. Ongoing infrastructure issues also present a significant challenge, although the need for either natural gas- or water-injection programmes in order to maintain oil reservoir pressure resulted in the Common Seawater Supply Project, which, at an estimated cost of US $4,000m.–$6,000m., aims to transport prepared seawater via pipeline for injection at petroleum production locations. In March 2021 France's TotalEnergies took over the project (along with four others), although Iraq's oil ministry did not release details of the value of the deal. Refinery capacity, notably at Baiji, suffered damage during fighting against Islamic State in the 2010s, but was also deteriorating as a result of general neglect and failure to update facilities. Plans to expand refinery capacity continued to stall in the late 2010s, and Iraq continues to satisfy domestic demand for refined products, in particular for gasoline, only through imports. The most important export terminal is at Basra, but Iraq also had a major export pipeline in the Iraq–Turkey (Türkiye from 2022) pipeline to Ceyhan on the Turkish Mediterranean coast. The pipeline's operations were repeatedly disrupted and its infrastructure had deteriorated even before the Iraqi Government closed the pipeline in March 2014 in response to sabotage. With the assistance of international investors, however, the KRG was already constructing and had begun to operate two independent pipelines, both of which connect to the Turkish section of the Iraq–Turkey pipeline. One pipeline runs from Khurmala Dome and the other from the Tawke oilfield, both to Fishkabur (Faysh Khabur) on the border with Türkiye.

The Kurdistan administration has enacted its own hydrocarbons legislation, and concluded exploration, development and production-sharing contracts with international oil companies, but jurisdictional conflict with the federal Government of Iraq has remained an issue. The offensive by fighters belonging to Islamic State of Iraq and the Levant (ISIL—subsequently renamed Islamic State) in mid-2014 aggravated such tensions. Before 2014 the federal Government produced most of the oil in the north, mainly from the Kirkuk and Bai Hassan oilfields. The Kurdish Regional Government (KRG) had insisted that any projected development of output from the Kirkuk field should not proceed without its assent. In June, after Iraqi army units fled under attack by Islamic State fighters, Kurdish forces occupied Kirkuk and pledged to retain control of oilfields and infrastructure close to the city pending the participation of the local population in a referendum to decide whether the city—and other disputed areas—should become part of the Kurdish Autonomous Region (KAR). At the time of the occupation, petroleum production in the KAR was reported at less than 30,000 b/d, compared with 650,000 b/d prior to the closure by the Iraqi Government of the Iraq–Turkey pipeline earlier in the year. In June the closure of the pipeline was compounded by that of the Baiji refinery. The KRG began to export petroleum produced under its control through its independent pipelines to Ceyhan, and oil produced at all northern Iraqi fields was subsequently exported via KRG infrastructure. After a referendum held in the KAR in September 2017 resulted in a vote in favour of independence, Iraqi armed forces launched a successful military operation to regain control of some of the territory, including Kirkuk, that had been under Kurdish control since 2014. In May 2018 Iraq's Federal Supreme Court commenced an investigation to determine the legality of oil exports undertaken by the KRG after the Iraqi Ministry of Oil initiated legal proceedings against the KRG's Ministry of Natural Resources. Federal legislation enacted in 2018 required all foreign sales of oil from the KAR to be made via the State Oil Marketing Organization, a national Iraqi company based in the federal capital, Baghdad. Furthermore, in February 2022 Iraq's Federal Supreme Court ruled that the KRG lacked the authority to produce and market crude petroleum (or natural gas), and that all hydrocarbons assets should be handed to the central government and contracts between international oil companies and the KRG were to be considered void.

Kuwait, too, has reserves in addition to its officially documented allocation, in the 'Neutral/Partitioned Zone', where proven reserves estimated to amount to 5,000m. barrels are shared on an equal basis with Saudi Arabia. Kuwait's reserves are heavily concentrated in mature fields, including the Greater Burgan field, which is believed to be the second largest oilfield in the world. The country's oil policy is determined and the oil industry supervised by the Supreme Petroleum Council (SPC), to which government ministers, including the Prime Minister, and representatives of the private sector are appointed by the Amir of Kuwait. Foreign and domestic investment in the country's oil industry is overseen by the Kuwait Petroleum Corpn (KPC), while KPC subsidiaries are responsible for upstream development (Kuwait Oil Co), the downstream industry (Kuwait National Petroleum Co—KNPC) and the petrochemicals industry (Petrochemicals Industries Co). Foreign trade in petroleum is the remit of KNPC and the Kuwait Oil Tanker Co. Meanwhile, the Kuwait Foreign Petroleum Exploration Co manages the KPC's foreign operations, and Kuwait Petroleum International (KPI) is responsible for international upstream and downstream activities. Separate arrangements govern activities in the 'Neutral/Partitioned Zone', where the Kuwait Gulf Oil Co is active in both onshore and offshore operations. Foreign investment, however, is impeded by a constitutional ban on the ownership of national resources by foreign interests, although joint ventures have been encouraged. The country's refinery capacity is far in excess of domestic demand, and Kuwait is consequently a major exporter of refined petroleum products, in addition to crude.

The petroleum resources of the United Arab Emirates are dominated by the emirate of Abu Dhabi, which has 95% of the country's reserves. However, each of the UAE's seven emirates determines oil industry policy within its own frontiers. In Abu Dhabi, policy and targets are determined by the Supreme Petroleum Council and implemented through the Abu Dhabi National Oil Co and its subsidiaries. Oil production in the UAE is concentrated on the Upper and Lower Zakum oilfields, which together were the source of more than one-third of the country's total output of crude petroleum in 2016. The country has both onshore and offshore fields. The reserves of many mature oilfields have been boosted substantially through extensive use of enhanced oil recovery technology since the early 2000s. Refining capacity is mainly in Abu Dhabi and Dubai, but there is also one refinery in each of the emirates of Ras Al Khaimah and Fujairah. Fujairah has the advantage of a coastline on the Gulf of Oman, beyond the strategically significant and vulnerable Strait of Hormuz, and it is therefore the most significant of the UAE's export terminals. In 2012 the Abu Dhabi Crude Oil Pipeline, which links Habshan with Fujairah, commenced operations. The pipeline substantially boosted the UAE's export capability and, once the annual capacity is increased as planned to some 660m. barrels, most of the UAE's exports of crude petroleum will be able to avoid leaving the Gulf by sea through the narrow strait. The value of crude petroleum exports were estimated at around 43% of the total value of exports in 2022.

Libya's proven reserves of petroleum are the largest in Africa. The Sirte (Surt) basin is the location of about four-fifths of those reserves and is where most of the country's production is concentrated. Before the 2011 civil war, which culminated in the fall of the regime led by Muammar al-Qaddafi, the country's petroleum industry was administered by the National Oil Corpn. Foreign companies were permitted to participate in the industry on the basis of exploration and production-sharing agreements. However, in mid-2023, it remained unlikely that any viable timetable for reform of the legislation governing the country's hydrocarbons sector (under consideration since before 2011) would be determined before the re-establishment of political stability, itself conditional upon the resolution of the various armed conflicts that remained ongoing in Libya at that time. That conflict also damaged refinery, pipeline and export capacity, although, in general, operations have been maintained despite interruptions. In 2022 exports of crude petroleum accounted for 82% of the total value of exports (the main market being Europe)—some 16% higher than the previous year.

REGIONAL INFORMATION — Major Commodities of the Middle East and North Africa

The resources of Qatar's three major oilfields at al-Shaheen (off shore), Dukhan (onshore) and Idd al-Shargi (off shore) together represent more than 85% of the country's total crude petroleum production capacity. Qatar's petroleum industry is administered entirely by state-owned Qatar Petroleum (QP), although some of the country's offshore oilfields are operated by international oil companies on the basis of production-sharing agreements. The al-Shaheen oilfield alone, one of the world's largest, generally accounts for about 40% of Qatari output. However, Qatar's major oilfields are maturing, and production has either stagnated or declined since 2013. Exports of crude petroleum provided 14% of the value of total Qatari exports in 2022 (some 52% higher than the previous year), although this was substantially lower than the value of exports of natural gas. Hydrocarbons as a whole were believed to have provided 85% of government income in 2022.

Algeria's main oilfields are, for the most part, in the eastern regions, the Hassi Messaoud field alone generally accounting for as much as 40% of the country's output of crude petroleum. Sonatrach, a state-owned entity, plays the leading role in the production of crude petroleum in Algeria, although foreign companies have been allowed to enter the hydrocarbons sector via production-sharing agreements in which Sonatrach is the main stakeholder. Refinery capacity has been increased in the 2010s, although in 2018 the country was reported to be considering the construction of additional capacity abroad. Exports depart from seven terminals, at Algiers, Annaba, Arzew, Béjaïa, Oran and Skikda (the site of the largest refinery), and at La Skhirra in Tunisia. The terminals are supplied via a pipeline network totalling more than 3,800 km in length. In 2022 Algeria's exports by value consisted of 42% of petroleum oils, while mineral fuels (i.e. including natural gas) as a whole provided some 89% of the total. Hydrocarbons accounted for more than one-third of government revenue in 2021.

Owing to the dispersed location of most of Oman's petroleum reserves, production costs are high (international oil companies therefore enjoy contractual terms that are among the most generous in the region). The country is the largest non-OPEC petroleum producer in the Middle East and North Africa, although Oman cooperates with OPEC to regulate oil prices. According to Energy Institute, the country produced 51.4m. metric tons of petroleum in 2022. Petroleum Development Oman (PDO), in which the state holds a 60% stake, is responsible for administering hydrocarbons policies that are determined by the country's Ministry of Oil and Gas and subject to the approval of Oman's ruler, Sultan Qaboos bin Said al-Said. PDO accounts for about 70% of Oman's crude petroleum output, which is exported via a single terminal at Mina al-Fahal. PDO operates a national pipeline network totalling some 1,800 km in length. In 2022 Oman's foreign sales of crude petroleum accounted for 46% of the value of all exports. According to provisional figures, in 2021 refined exports increased significantly owing to increased capacity, and there were some natural gas exports, but almost two-thirds of hydrocarbon exports (in 2022) were crude petroleum.

Egypt's mainly small, mature oilfields are located in the Eastern Desert, the Gulf of Suez, the Mediterranean Sea, the Nile Delta and the Western Desert, with most production in the Gulf and the Western Desert. These operations make the country the largest non-OPEC petroleum producer in Africa—Egypt produced 29.9m. metric tons of petroleum in 2022. Coordination of production is undertaken by the state-owned Egyptian General Petroleum Corpn (EGPC), which has also been directly responsible for up to one-fifth of output in the 2010s. International oil companies play a major role in the industry, on the basis of production-sharing agreements with the EGPC. Output has been in decline since the mid-1990s, but this has been mitigated to some extent by enhanced oil recovery techniques at the country's mature oilfields and the discovery of some new, for the most part modest, resources. Political upheaval in Egypt after 2011 reportedly had little impact on petroleum output, owing to the remoteness of the main producing areas from major population centres. In 2022, according to an industry source, Egypt's refinery capacity was the highest in Africa, estimated to total 762,000 b/d and distributed among eight refineries, of which the largest was the facility at El Nasr. One aim of further expansion of the refinery sector was to boost the country's capacity to produce petrochemicals and high-octane gasoline. As refining capacity exceeds domestic output of petroleum, some crudes are imported, processed and re-exported. Egypt derives substantial revenues in the form of transit fees for petroleum (and other goods) exported from the Persian (Arabian) Gulf via the Suez Canal and the Suez–Mediterranean pipeline. The country is not as dependent on hydrocarbon revenues as others in the region; in 2022 crude petroleum was responsible for 6% of Egypt's total export revenues, up 2% on the previous year.

Most of Syria's oilfields are located in central and eastern regions of the country, and along the River Euphrates (the two most important are the Omar and Jbessa fields). They were therefore very vulnerable to the civil war and the struggle against Islamic State in the 2010s. According to Energy Institute, petroleum production had declined to around 1m. metric tons per year in 2016–18, which was far short of the 30m. tons per year of the early 2000s or even the 18.5m. tons in 2010, before the civil war. Production was slightly up in 2018–22, reaching 4.6m. tons in the latter year. Widespread conflict has resulted in damage to infrastructure (notably refineries and pipelines), the absence of foreign investment and the loss of markets abroad (international sanctions barred Syria from its traditional European markets, and the main markets with access to refineries capable of processing Syrian Heavy, one of the two crude blends Syria exports). Syria's Ministry of Petroleum and Mineral Resources administers the country's petroleum sector via the Syrian Petroleum Co (SPC). Revenues from hydrocarbons had contributed more than one-third of total export earnings and up to one-quarter of government revenues in some years before the civil war, but recovery of the industry to provide such support again seemed unlikely even into the late 2020s.

The majority of Yemen's reserves are believed to lie in the Say'un-Masila basin in the south of the country, while the remainder are located in the Marib-Jawf basin, in the north. Petroleum production in 2022 was put at 3.4m. metric tons, up on the 2016 low of 1.6m. tons, although still far from the 6.9m. tons reported in 2014, before the civil war became firmly entrenched, or the peak 21.6m. tons of 2002. Yemen's petroleum sector is administered by several subsidiaries of the General Corpn for Oil, Gas and Mineral Resources. Before the war most of Yemen's foreign sales were shipped to Asian destinations via three (out of a total of five) export terminals, of which Ras Isa was the most important. The terminals were supplied by a pipeline network totalling some 1,065 km in length. The Marib–Ras Isa pipeline, which supplies the main terminal, was repeatedly sabotaged by suspected anti-Government elements from 2011, even provoking a cessation of exports in 2012. Export and refining infrastructure has suffered heavily during the war, and the larger of the country's two refineries, at Aden (the other is at Marib) was forced to cease operations in 2016 (and was reportedly still struggling to resume activities in 2020). Most foreign involvement in the industry has ended, owing to the poor security situation, and production has largely shut down, although some exports continue.

Of the petroleum producing countries of the region, Tunisia has the smallest proven reserves. In 2022 its output was 1.8m. metric tons of petroleum. It has one refinery. Türkiye (Turkey before 2022), by contrast, which is not a major producer of petroleum, has considerable refining presence (six refineries) and vital transport and processing facilities. The country is a crucial hub for the transport of hydrocarbons from the Middle East, the southern Caucasus and Central Asia. Other countries of the region, too, are notable importers.

International Organizations International petroleum prices are strongly influenced by the Organization of the Petroleum Exporting Countries, founded in 1960 in Baghdad, Iraq. Its purpose is to coordinate the production and marketing policies of those countries with substantial net petroleum exports in order to secure stable and fair prices for producing countries, a regular supply of petroleum for consuming countries and a return on capital for countries and corporations that invest in the industry. OPEC came under scrutiny in the 1970s when Arab countries imposed an oil embargo (in 1973), which led to a steep rise in prices on world markets. The embargo—initiated by the Organization of Arab Petroleum Exporting Countries (OAPEC)—was initiated in response to US involvement in the Yom Kippur War. In the meantime, however, the USA had withdrawn from the Bretton Woods Accord, which led to the floating of the US dollar (and other currencies) and an increase in US dollar reserves. The resultant devaluing of that currency meant that petroleum producing countries were receiving less real income from their exports (since petroleum, at this time, was priced and traded in US dollars). OPEC subsequently released a statement confirming that it would henceforth peg the price of a barrel of oil against the price of gold.

OPEC member countries experienced severe economic setbacks in the mid-1980s as prices dropped substantially (by as much as two-thirds). The overall decline in prices was attributed to an oversupply of petroleum and significantly reduced consumer demand. Prices recovered somewhat in the late 1980s, but only to around one-half of the record levels seen at the start of the decade. Recovery was encouraged by the introduction of a production ceiling and the OPEC reference 'basket' (ORB) for pricing. The 1990s was a comparatively stable decade, although Iraq's invasion of Kuwait and the resultant Gulf War created some volatility in world markets. However, the decade was characterized by general weakness in pricing, with particularly mild winters in the northern hemisphere countries in the late 1990s causing prices to drop to 1986 levels. None the less, crude prices strengthened and then stabilized in the early 2000s, before reaching record levels later in the decade (see below). Following historically low prices for crudes in 2015–16, OPEC and non-OPEC producers agreed in late 2016 to reduce output for the first time since the global financial crisis in 2008. Saudi Arabia, which had been most significantly impacted by the low prices, assumed the largest reduction in output, while Russia, the UAE, Kuwait and Qatar also agreed to reduced production quotas. Nigeria and Libya were granted exemptions. The deal (and subsequently the enlarged alliance of countries) is often referred to as 'OPEC+'; the deal itself has since been extended multiple times. (Meanwhile, production in the USA increased significantly during the same period, overtaking that of both Saudi Arabia and the Russian Federation.) Production quotas remained in place as of July 2023. In October 2022 reduced production amounting to some 2m. b/d was agreed among the OPEC+ alliance. In April 2023 a further voluntary reduction was announced, bringing the total agreed reduction in production for 2023 to 3.66m. b/d, equivalent to almost 4% of global demand. At another meeting in mid-2023 no further cuts were agreed (although Saudi Arabia did commit to its own, voluntary one-month reduction in supply of 1m. b/d in July), however OPEC+ announced that it would limit production to 40.46m. b/d in 2024. Iran, Libya and Venezuela continued to be exempt from the production quotas. US President Biden's Administration, meanwhile, continued to disapprove of production cuts in 2023, citing the possible impact on continuing market uncertainty. In June 2020 OPEC production had reached its lowest level in nearly 30 years as members sought to reverse the plummeting prices of crude (a consequence of the global contraction in industrial activity during attempts to contain the COVID-19 pandemic). The strategy of OPEC+ to stockpile supplies during the pandemic, however, resulted in rapid price recovery from May 2021, when their quotas began to increase once again. By May of the following year prices were at an almost 10-year high; indeed the average price of the ORB for 2022 was its highest since 2013.

OPEC distinguishes between founder members and full members. At mid-2023 it had 13 members in total. Qatar terminated its membership in 2019. Iran, a founder member, is among those members that seek to ensure that a greater proportion of oil revenues accrue to national authorities at the expense of that appropriated by international oil companies involved in production activities.

Two OPEC members and two other North African countries are also members of a regional body, while a fifth North African country is an observer. The (then) four African members of OPEC (Algeria, Gabon, Libya and Nigeria) formed the African Petroleum Producers' Association (APPA) in 1987. Angola, Benin, Cameroon, Chad, the Democratic Republic of the Congo (DRC), the Republic of Congo, Côte d'Ivoire, Egypt, Equatorial Guinea, Ghana, Mauritania, South Africa and Sudan subsequently joined the association, in which Tunisia has observer status. Apart from promoting co-operation among regional producers, the APPA, which is based in Brazzaville, Republic of the Congo, co-operates with OPEC in stabilizing oil prices.

Price History of the OPEC 'Basket' of Crude Oils
(US $ per barrel)

	Average	High	Low
2012	109.45	(March) 122.97	(June) 93.98
2013	105.87	(February) 117.75	(May) 100.65
2014	96.29	(June) 107.89	(December) 59.46
2015	49.49	(May) 62.16	(December) 33.64
2016	40.76	(December) 51.67	(January) 26.50
2017	52.43	(December) 62.06	(June) 45.21
2018	69.78	(October) 79.39	(December) 56.94
2019	64.04	(April) 70.78	(January) 58.74
2020	41.47	(January) 65.10	(April) 17.66
2021	69.89	(October) 82.11	(January) 54.38
2022	100.08	(June) 117.50	(December) 79.68

Source: OPEC, *Annual Reports* and *Monthly Oil Market Reports*.

Prices There was international concern over the volatility of prices in the first half of 2012, as the OPEC reference 'basket' (ORB) moved from US $124 per barrel to less than $90 per barrel, in spite of steady supply levels (including a recovery in Libyan production). The average price of the ORB grew by 1.9% compared with the previous year. Global economic growth decelerated to 3.0%, with the People's Republic of China alone contributing around one-third. The moderate growth was attributed to the ending of financial assistance packages in many developed economies, and the resulting decline in petroleum demand among OECD countries. However, demand in non-OECD countries remained robust, growing by 1.2m. b/d. In Japan, however, crude petroleum consumption increased by 36% as nuclear power plants remained closed and the country sought an alternative electricity supply. Price growth over the year was attributed to resurgent turmoil in the Middle East and supply disruptions in the North Sea fields. The price of Brent crude in 2012 was 0.2% higher than in 2011, averaging $111.63 for the year. The world economy demonstrated some growth in the first half of 2013, but gathered momentum in the second half. Global economic growth slowed to 2.9% in the year overall, while the fluctuation in petroleum prices witnessed in 2012—causing a great deal of market volatility—was largely avoided. Overall world demand for crude increased in 2013 (by some 1.3m. b/d), aided in OECD countries by optimism in manufacturing and other industrial sectors. Japanese demand, meanwhile, declined during the year as it relied more heavily on natural gas and coal for its energy needs, although this was partly offset by increased naphtha consumption resulting from growth in the petrochemical industry. In 2013 the average price of the ORB declined by 3.3%. Following strong growth early in the year (supported by healthy demand and ongoing maintenance issues in the North Sea), petroleum prices declined in the third quarter, following the publication of poor economic data from the USA and China, the world's two largest consumers. Ongoing economic problems in the eurozone and record inventories in the USA also exerted downward pressure on prices later in the year. The price of Brent crude averaged $108.62 per barrel in 2013, which represented a fall of 2.7% compared with the previous year. The price of the ORB declined significantly in 2014, by 9.0% compared with 2013. Following minimal movement in the first half of the year, prices declined precipitously from June over concerns of oversupply and subdued growth in demand. Surges in Libyan production appeared to justify such concerns, placing crude stocks at levels higher than they had been for five and a half years, while the drop in demand was also attributed to weaker than expected economic data in China and Europe, and ongoing maintenance to refineries. At the end of the year the ORB price reached its lowest point for more than five years; in fact it lost almost one-half of its value during the course of 2014.

The ORB price continued to fall in early 2015 as a result of oversupply: it reached a six-year low in January of US $44.38 per barrel (the seventh consecutive month of decline), before picking up in February. The price of Brent crude averaged just $52.41 in 2015, which represented a decline of almost 50% compared with the previous year's average. The average price of the ORB, meanwhile, fell to $49.49. Oversupply (which had persisted for some 18 months) and ongoing concerns about a slowing Chinese economy were identified as contributing to the steep decline in prices, as was the strength of the US dollar over the same period. The price of the ORB fell sharply again at the beginning of 2016 (by some 21%), to just $26.50 per barrel. The price represented its lowest value since September 2003. However, it recovered somewhat in the first half of the year. The significant decline in prices in January was again attributed to a weaker Chinese economy, a reduction in demand owing to lower seasonal heating requirements (a consequence of a milder northern-hemisphere winter), and ongoing global oversupply. Prices were steady in the second half of the year, until December, when the average price of the ORB rose by some 20%—the first time in 18 months that the price had averaged more than $50 per barrel. News of cooperation between OPEC and non-OPEC producers to rebalance the market (specifically to remove some 1.8m. b/d from the market) led to the steep rise in prices over the month, though the yearly average for 2016 was still the lowest for 12 years. The global economy was generally strong in 2017, which resulted in higher prices for petroleum; global GDP growth was estimated at 3.7% for the year. Economies in China, the USA and the EU had demonstrated forward momentum and increased demand, however, price growth was slow in the first half of the year, and weakened somewhat in June–July—a temporary trend attributed to oversupply and high inventories among producing countries. Damage sustained in the Gulf of Mexico as a result of Hurricanes Harvey, Irma and Maria in the second half of the year, however, raised supply concerns and caused a sharp rise in prices. By November the price of the ORB had risen more than 35% since June, to over $60 per barrel.

From June 2018 the ORB included Congolese Djeno crude in its pricing for the first time, a result of the Republic of Congo's recent accession to OPEC. The price of the ORB remained historically low in that year, although it grew steadily through most of 2018 (increasing by 33.1% year on year) before recording a sharp drop in the final two months. Global economic growth remained steady at 3.6% (slightly down from 2017), although ongoing trade tensions between the USA and China began to impact the latter country, which witnessed a deceleration in growth to its lowest level since 2008. The price of the ORB reached US $79.39 per barrel in October, an increase attributed to positive market sentiment, which was supported by the voluntary production adjustments by OPEC member countries under the Declaration of Cooperation (global stocks were at their lowest since 2014), and increased global demand—up by some 1.43m. b/d over the year. Prices dropped once more from October, with analysts pointing to the easing of supply disruptions and the expectation of a reduction in demand resulting from weak economic growth forecasts—prompted, in part, by continuing US–China tensions over trade. Moreover, higher-than-expected crude production in the USA in particular led to fears of oversupply, with the average price of the ORB falling to just $56.94 per barrel in December. Global economic growth in 2019 was lower than in the previous two years, which was attributed to a slow-down in global trade—a result of ongoing trade disputes involving the USA—as well as lower growth in emerging markets. India in particular registered GDP growth some 2% lower than a year earlier. Demand for crude petroleum and prices over the year were consequently lower than the previous year. Prices in particular were negatively affected by trade disputes between the USA and China. None the less, price growth in the first half of the year was strong (the ORB reached $70.78 per barrel in April), before concerns over global demand led to considerable declines in the second half of the year (prices reached just $59.62 per barrel in August). As the COVID-19 pandemic took hold in the first half of 2020 crude petroleum prices entered a precipitous decline; the average price of the ORB was just $17.66 per barrel in April, its lowest level in almost two decades. The plummeting prices were the result of historically low demand (as much industrial production ground to a halt), oversupply and dire predictions of global economic performance. (It was reported that the world economy shrank by 3.5% over the year.) However, by the end of 2020 the ORB and Brent crude prices had recovered substantially (as many countries relaxed the 'lockdown' measures introduced earlier in the year in an attempt to halt the spread of the virus, and supply cuts among OPEC members and non-members alike began to have an effect), averaging $49.17 per barrel and $50.22 per barrel, respectively, in December. Notwithstanding these gains, the average price for the ORB for the year was its lowest since 2016.

Prices showed strong growth through most of 2021—with its average year-to-date price in October some 68% higher than one year earlier—on the back of a stronger than expected economic performance by many major economies in the second half of 2020, US supply disruptions resulting from severe winter weather, strong demand in advance of the summer driving season (in the northern hemisphere) and declining stocks in many important consuming countries in 2021. Global economic growth was revised upwards to 5.8%, supporting the price recovery; US, Chinese and Indian growth rates were estimated at 5.7%, 8.1% and 8.3%, respectively. The price of Brent crude increased by some 64% in 2021 to average US $70.95 per barrel for the year, its highest level since 2018. The first half of 2022 was characterized by historically high crude prices, a consequence of the resurgent conflict in Ukraine, and the imposition, in response, by many important consumers (including the USA and the European Union—EU) of sanctions on Russian fuel exports—although this was mitigated to some extent be increased Indian and Chinese imports. By June the average price for the ORB was $117.72 per barrel, its highest level since 2013. The price of Brent crude averaged $117.50 over the same month. The average price of the ORB subsequently fell in each month from July amid geopolitical concerns, renewed COVID-19 impacts in China, a well-supplied market and high inflation. Brent crude averaged $99.04 per barrel, which still represented an increase of almost 40% compared with 2021. The average price of the ORB began to recover in January 2023 as China ended its COVID-19 containment policy (supporting an increase in industrial activity and leading to strong demand from Chinese buyers). However, high supply in the USA and Northwest Europe towards the middle of the year pushed prices lower, causing a further round of OPEC+ production cuts in April (see above). By May the average prices for the ORB and Brent crude were $75.82 per barrel and $75.69 per barrel, respectively. In December 2022 and February 2023, meanwhile, the EU had banned maritime imports of all crude and refined petroleum products, respectively, from Russia in retaliation for its renewed military invasion of Ukraine. Reports of higher prices by July, however, suggested that OPEC+ supply cuts, rather than the EU's ban on Russian imports, were the principal cause of the upward trend. Indeed, according to International Energy Agency (IEA) data, in May 2023 India and China received some 80% of all Russian petroleum exports in that month, with some 90% of Russian seaborne crude petroleum destined for Asia (compared with just 34% before the renewed conflict with Ukraine)—statistics that appeared to suggest that demand in that region had effectively replaced demand in Europe.

PHOSPHATE

Phosphate is the naturally occurring form of the element phosphorus (P), and inorganic phosphates are found in phosphate rock, which is defined as unprocessed ore or concentrates containing some form of apatite (a group of calcium phosphate minerals that are the primary source of phosphorus-based fertilizers). Phosphorus is one of 14 nutrients essential to plant life, being particularly important in the capture and conversion of the sun's energy. It is the 11th most common element in the earth's crust, but is reactive and therefore highly dispersed in compounds. It was the first element to be discovered chemically (isolated by a German alchemist in 1669), and was mainly noted for its chemiluminescence or ability to glow in the dark. The main source was bone ash after calcium phosphate was identified in bones, but in the 1840s Justus von Liebig proved that phosphorus was crucial for plant growth and Sir John Bennet Lawes patented a technique for making fertilizer by treating phosphate rock with sulphuric acid, marking the start of the modern era of phosphate exploitation. The original source of mined phosphate was the organic phosphate associated with bird and bat guano. Mining involved the excessive exploitation of mostly tropical Pacific islands (notably Nauru, and Banaba or Ocean Island in Kiribati), but by the mid-20th century rock phosphate was increasingly mined.

Most phosphate rock is sedimentary, formed from deposits of geologically ancient marine life, and some (about 15% of exploited resources) is magmatic or igneous, but such occurrences are outside the Middle East and North Africa. World sedimentary resources are concentrated in northern Africa, overwhelmingly Morocco, the Middle East, China and North America. Ore grades of phosphate rock are usually defined by a phosphorus pentoxide (P_2O_5) content of between 2% and 35%. Beneficiation can increase content to between 27% and 40%, but the process is expensive. Since 2012 advanced flotation technology has made the exploitation of lower grade sedimentary deposits more economically viable. The direct application of phosphate is not usually helpful, so it is best administered as soluble phosphorus in a fertilizer. Phosphorus-based fertilizers are made by acidification of phosphate rock, still usually involving sulphuric acid (the biggest industrial use of sulphur is for fertilizer manufacture), in the manufacture of wet-process phosphoric acid.

Production of Phosphate Rock
(gross weight, metric tons)

	2019	2020	2021	2022*
World total	224.0	223.0	226.0	220.0
Middle East and North Africa	66.5	66.8	70.2	71.0
Regional producers				
Egypt*	5.0	4.8	5.0	5.0
Israel†	2.8	3.1	2.4	3.0
Jordan	9.2	8.9	10.0	10.0
Morocco	35.2	37.4	38.1	40.0
Saudi Arabia*	9.5	9.0	9.2	9.0
Tunisia	4.1	3.2	3.7	4.0
Other leading producers				
Australia*	2.2	2.5	2.5	2.5
Brazil‡	3.0	5.2	6.0*	5.5
China, People's Republic	93.3	90.9	90.0*	85.0
Peru	4.0	3.3	4.2	4.2
Russian Federation	13.8	13.8	14.0*	13.0
USA	23.3	23.5	21.6	21.0
Viet Nam	4.5	4.4*	4.5*	4.5

* Estimated production.
† Beneficiated ore.
‡ Concentrate.

Source: US Geological Survey.

The World Market and the Region About 85% of rock phosphate production is destined for the manufacture of phosphorus-based fertilizers, the most widely used being di-ammonium phosphate (DAP) and mono-ammonium phosphate (MAP). The rest is used for the extraction of elemental phosphorus (which has a wide range of chemical uses) and the manufacture of animal feed, or for some direct application agriculturally, conditions permitting. World phosphate reserves were put by the US Geological Survey (USGS) at 72,000m. metric tons in 2022, 69% of which were in Morocco. The next most significant reserves were in Egypt (4%), followed by Tunisia and Algeria (3% each), the People's Republic of China (almost 3%), and Brazil and South Africa (both 2%). Overall resources are put at more than 300,000m. tons, with substantial phosphate deposits identified on the continental shelf and in sea mounts in the Atlantic and Pacific Oceans. Morocco is the largest exporter of phosphate, but its output is surpassed by that of China (although several sources considered official Chinese production figures, as used in the table above, to be overstated) and sometimes that of the USA.

Moroccan phosphate figures include the disputed area of Western Sahara. Phosphate exports earned 3% of the total value of Moroccan exports in 2022, according to provisional figures. The country, without the large internal demand of China or the USA, is the world's largest exporter of phosphate rock, supplying 37% of the international market in 2018. Processing capacity also enabled the country to provide 55% of the phosphoric acid on the world market in 2015. Morocco manufactures some phosphorus-based fertilizer, but the output and export of such fertilizer by China is greater; however, Morocco still supplied 23% of world exports in 2018. China supplied 30% and the USA 12% in the previous year. The phosphate mining and fertilizer manufacturing sector accounted for about 5% of Morocco's gross domestic product (GDP) in 2015. All phosphate operations in the country are conducted by the state-owned Office Chérifien des Phosphates (Office of Moroccan Phosphates—OCP), its 27 subsidiaries and joint ventures together known as the OCP Group. The company has stated its intent to increase mining capacity from 30m. to 52m. metric tons per year between 2016 and 2026, and to develop beneficiation infrastructure and fertilizer production during the same period.

Saudi Arabia is the other notable producer of phosphate in the region, developing also its downstream capabilities in the 2010s. The exploitation of new ore deposits in the north of the country in the latter part of the decade involved not only increased mining, but the development of beneficiation plants and other processing capacity, as well as the expansion of fertilizer factories in Ras Al-Khair. The International Fertilizer Association expected Morocco and Saudi Arabia to be the main providers of new capacity in the world phosphate sector up to the early 2020s, but other countries in the Middle East and North Africa were also increasing output, mainly of phosphate ore. Apart from Jordan, Egypt, Israel and Tunisia (see production table above), phosphate rock was also mined in Algeria, Türkiye (Turkey before 2022) and, to a lesser and varying extent, Syria, Iran and Iraq.

Global Forum The International Fertilizer Industry Association is based in Paris, France, and was founded in 1927 as the International Superphosphate Manufacturers' Association. In 2023 it had more than 450 members (including 14 Middle East and North African countries), and it represents the global industry, promoting plant nutrients, improving the operating environment of member companies and keeping industry information.

Phosphate Price
(annual averages, US $ per metric ton)

	Phosphate rock
2005	44.0
2010	105.3
2015	120.3
2020	76.0
2021	123.2
2022	266.1

Source: UNCTAD.

Prices According to the UN Conference on Trade and Development's UNCTADstat database, phosphate rock from Morocco's primary phosphate mining town of Khouribga (70% BPL, bone phosphate of lime or tricalcium phosphate), on a free alongside (f.a.s) contract, Casablanca, reached a peak annual average price of US $242.7 per metric ton in 2008, maintaining a monthly average of $450.0 per ton in October 2008 through to March 2009, fluctuating downwards thereafter. This dramatic historical price 'spike' experienced by phosphate, and indeed fertilizers generally, came about in the context of soaring commodity prices, but was magnified by demand in India, the largest importer of phosphorus-based fertilizers and phosphate rock. Indian import demand in particular soared and domestic subsidy did not encourage farmer caution, while protective measures led to a restriction on exports internationally. Other factors, combining in a 'perfect storm', included increased biofuel and livestock production, the latter needing grain and both needing fertilizers, at a time when grain stocks were low. High prices affected not only grain but also energy (natural gas is used in nitrogen fertilizer production) and sulphur (used in the production of many phosphorus-based fertilizers). The situation was anomalous, and the phosphate price settled into the 2010s. Prices fell substantially in the second half of 2019 but recovered throughout 2020 and grew substantially in 2021–22 and the first half of 2023; in May of the latter year the average phosphate price was $345 per ton, which represented a rise of close to 500% compared with the same month three years earlier. Analysts pointed to the recent rapid rise in the price of phosphates (and fertilizers) as another reason for growing global food insecurity.

SUGAR

Sugar is a sweet crystalline substance which may be derived from the juices of various plants. Chemically, the basis of sugar is sucrose, one of a group of soluble carbohydrates which are important sources of energy in the human diet. It can be obtained from trees, including the maple and certain palms, but virtually all manufactured sugar is derived from two plants, sugar beet (*Beta vulgaris*) and sugar cane, a giant perennial grass of the genus *Saccharum*.

Sugar cane, found in tropical areas, grows to a height of up to 5 m (16 ft). The plant is native to Polynesia, but its distribution is now widespread. It is not necessary to plant cane every season, as if the root of the plant is left in the ground it will grow again in the following year. This practice, known as 'ratooning', may be continued for as long as three years, when yields begin to decline. Cane is ready for cutting 12–24 months after planting, depending on local conditions. More than one-half of the world's sugar cane is still cut by hand, but rising costs are hastening the change to mechanical harvesting. The cane is cut as close as possible to the ground, and the top leaves, which may be used as cattle fodder, are removed.

During factory processing the cane passes first through shredding knives or crushing rollers, which break up the hard rind and expose the inner fibre, and then to squeezing rollers, where the crushed cane is subjected to high pressure and sprayed with water. The resulting juice is heated, and lime is added for clarification and the removal of impurities. The clean juice is then concentrated in evaporators. This thickened juice is next boiled in steam heated vacuum pans until a mixture or 'massecuite' of sugar crystals and 'mother syrup' is produced. The massecuite is then spun in centrifugal machines to separate the sugar crystals (raw cane sugar) from the residual syrup (cane molasses).

After the milling of sugar, the cane has dry fibrous remnants known as bagasse, which is usually burned as fuel in sugar mills. Bagasse can also be pulped and used for making fibreboard, particle board and most grades of paper. As the costs of imported wood pulp have risen, cane growing regions have turned increasingly to the manufacture of paper from bagasse. In view of rising energy costs, some countries (such as Cuba) have encouraged the use of bagasse as fuel for electricity production in order to conserve foreign exchange expended on imports of petroleum. Other by-products can be utilized as an animal feed or distilled into alcoholic beverages (notably in Brazil).

The production of beet sugar follows the same process as sugar from sugar cane, except that the juice is extracted by osmotic diffusion. Its manufacture produces white sugar crystals that do not require further refining. In most producing countries, it is consumed domestically, but any fall in the production of beet sugar by the European Union (EU) can mean that it becomes a net importer of white refined sugar. Beet sugar accounted for about one-fifth of estimated world sugar production (21% in 2022/23), according to the US Department of Agriculture (USDA). The production data in the first table (below), therefore, is for sugar cane, covering all crops harvested, except crops grown explicitly for feed, and in the second table for sugar beet. The third table covers the production of raw sugar by the centrifugal process (including beet sugar). While global output of non-centrifugal sugar (i.e. produced from sugar cane which has not undergone centrifugation) is not insignificant, it tends to be destined for domestic consumption. The main producer of non-centrifugal sugar is India, where it is known as gur, but countries such as Brazil and Colombia are also significant producers.

Most of the raw cane sugar produced in the world is sent to refineries outside the country of origin, unless the sugar is for local consumption. Cuba, Thailand, Brazil and India are among the few cane producers that export part of their output as refined sugar. The refining process further purifies the sugar crystals and eventually results in finished products of various grades, such as granulated, icing or castor sugar. The ratio of refined to raw sugar is usually about 0.9:1.

In the closing decades of the 20th century sugar encountered increased competition from other sweeteners, including maize based products, such as isoglucose (a form of high-fructose corn syrup, or HFCS), and chemical additives, such as saccharine, aspartame (APM) and xylitol. APM was the most widely used high intensity artificial sweetener in the early 1990s, its market dominance then came under challenge from sucralose, which is about 600 times as sweet as sugar (compared with 200–300 times for other intense sweeteners) and is more resistant to chemical deterioration than APM. In 1998 the US Government approved the domestic marketing of sucralose, the only artificial sweetener made from sugar. Sucralose was stated to avoid many of the taste problems associated with other artificial sweeteners. From the late 1980s research was conducted to formulate means of synthesizing thaumatin, a substance derived from the fruit of the West African katemfe plant, *Thaumatococcus*

Production of Sugar Cane
('000 metric tons)

	2018	2019	2020	2021
World total	1,932,562	1,958,234	1,864,663	1,859,390
Middle East and North Africa*	25,541	23,407	18,918	21,234
Leading regional producers				
Egypt	15,823	15,336	10,284	12,361
Iran	9,100	7,550*	7,840	8,258
Morocco	616	519	792	613
Other leading producers				
Brazil	47,557	753,470	757,117	715,659
China, People's Republic	108,097	109,388	108,121	106,664
India	379,905	405,416	370,500	405,399
Mexico	56,842	59,334	53,953	55,485
Pakistan	67,174	66,380	81,009	88,651
Thailand	135,073	131,002	74,968	66,279

* FAO estimate(s).

Source: FAO.

Production of Sugar Beet
('000 metric tons)

	2018	2019	2020	2021
World total	273,417	280,823	255,526	270,156
Middle East and North Africa*	37,945	39,718	47,552	40,921
Leading regional producers				
Egypt	10,377	12,247	15,336	14,827*
Iran	6,291	5,550*	5,435	5,147
Morocco	3,711	3,693	3,632	2,574
Türkiye	17,436	18,086	23,026	18,250
Other leading producers				
France	39,914	38,024	26,195	34,365
Germany	26,191	29,728	28,618	31,945
Poland	14,303	13,837	14,947	15,274
Russian Federation	42,066	54,350	33,915	41,202
USA	30,193	25,991	30,490	33,340

* FAO estimate(s).
Source: FAO.

Production of Centrifugal Sugar
(raw value, '000 metric tons, Oct.–Sept. marketing year)

	2019/20	2020/21	2021/22	2022/23*
World total†	166,559	180,114	180,583	177,279
Middle East and North Africa	7,185	8,040	7,580	7,795
Leading regional producers				
Egypt	2,740	2,780	2,855	2,760
Iran	1,010	1,535	1,600	1,550
Morocco	640	580	430	440
Türkiye	2,750	3,100	2,650	3,000
Other leading producers				
Australia	4,285	4,335	4,120	4,200
Brazil	30,300	42,050	35,450	38,050
China, People's Republic	10,400	10,600	9,600	9,000
European Union (EU)	17,040	15,216	16,497	14,899
Guatemala	2,764	2,565	2,575	2,558
India	28,900	33,760	36,880	32,000
Mexico	5,596	6,058	6,556	5,708
Pakistan	5,340	6,505	7,560	6,860
Russian Federation	7,800	5,625	6,000	7,184
Thailand	8,294	7,587	10,157	11,040
USA	7,392	8,376	8,307	8,420

* Advance estimates.
† Including beet sugar production ('000 metric tons): 40,692 in 2019/20 (Egypt 1,500, Iran 560, Morocco 590, Türkiye 2,750; China, People's Republic 1,400, EU 16,807, Russian Federation 7,800, USA 3,946); 37,291 in 2020/21 (Egypt 1,530, Iran 835, Morocco 535, Türkiye 3,100; China, People's Republic 1,500, EU 14,992, Russian Federation 5,625, USA 4,619); 38,105 in 2021/22 (Egypt 1,580, Iran 850, Morocco 380, Türkiye 2,650; China, People's Republic 900, EU 16,288, Russian Federation 6,000, USA 4,677); 38,007 in 2022/23 (Egypt 1,475, Iran 825, Morocco 390, Türkiye 3,000; China, People's Republic 1,080, EU 14,682, Russian Federation 7,184, USA 4,676).
Source: US Department of Agriculture.

daniellii, which is about 2,500 times as sweet as sugar. As of 2005, the use of thaumatin had been approved in the EU, Israel and Japan, while in the USA its use as a flavouring agent had been endorsed. By 2011 sugar use was resurgent because of health concerns about other sweeteners—for example, sugar producers attempted to preserve this advantage in the US courts by preventing the Corn Refiners Association from renaming HFCS 'corn sugar'.

The World Market and the Region Production of sugar cane is dominated by Latin America and the Caribbean, which usually grows about one-half of the world total: 49% in 2021, according to the Food and Agriculture Organization of the United Nations (FAO). Production of sugar beet is dominated by the European Union, which grew 42% of the world total in 2021, according to FAO. The Middle East and North Africa is not a major grower of sugar cane or of beets, although Türkiye (Turkey before 2022) and Egypt are important individual producers of the latter, and the region accounts for close to 5% of world exports of centrifugal sugar (2022/23 figures of the US Department of Agriculture—USDA). However, in the same year the region bought almost one-quarter of all imports. Algeria, the United Arab Emirates, Morocco and Egypt are the main exporters of the processed product. The UAE is an entrepôt for the region, so also figures as a significant importer. The largest individual importers in 2022/23, according to USDA, were Algeria (15% of the regional total), Saudi Arabia and UAE (13% each), Morocco (11%), and Iraq (10%) and Egypt (6%). Israel and Tunisia were also important importers.

International Associations and Agreements In 1958 the first International Sugar Agreement (ISA) was negotiated. A second ISA, which came into effect in 1969, established the International Sugar Organization (ISO—see below) to administer the agreement. The implementation of a third ISA, which took effect in 1978, was supervised by an International Sugar Council (ISC), which was empowered to establish price ranges for sugar trading and to operate a system of quotas and special sugar stocks. Owing to the reluctance of the USA and of EC countries (which were not party to the agreement) to accept export controls, the ISO ultimately lost most of its power to regulate the market, and since 1984 the activities of the organization have been restricted to recording statistics and providing a forum for discussion between producers and consumers. Subsequent ISAs, without effective regulatory powers, have been in operation since 1985. At the end of 1992 the USA withdrew from the ISO, following a disagreement over the formulation of members' financial contributions. Special arrangements for the sugar trade were incorporated into the successive Lomé Conventions that were in operation from 1975 between the EU and a group of African, Caribbean and Pacific (ACP) countries. A special protocol on sugar, forming part of each Convention, required the EU to import specified quantities of raw sugar annually from ACP countries. In June 1998, however, the EU indicated its intention to phase out preferential sugar prices paid to ACP countries within three years. Under the terms of the Cotonou Agreement, a successor to the fourth Lomé Convention covering the period 2000–2020, the protocol on sugar was to be maintained initially, but would become subject to review within the framework of negotiations for new trading arrangements (negotiations for more WTO-compatible Economic Partnership Agreements—EPAs began in 2002). In 2001 the EU Council adopted the EBA (Everything but Arms) regulation, whereby the least developed countries were granted unlimited duty-free access to the EU for all goods except arms and ammunition. EBA was to apply to sugar from October 2009. Meanwhile, in September 2007 the EU Council of Ministers criticized the protocol on sugar on the grounds that it was not compatible with EU sugar reforms (themselves undertaken in response to upheld complaints before the WTO by Australia, Brazil and Thailand about export subsidies for ACP countries) and did not take into account the specific needs of different ACP regions. The EU offered duty- and quota-free access to the ACP countries after 2015, in compensation for the loss of subsidies and quotas. A transitional period from October 2009 until September 2015 was to effect the progressive removal of reciprocal trade barriers. On the basis of data for 2009, the 86 members of the ISO together contributed 83% of world sugar production and 95% of world exports of sugar; ISO members additionally accounted for 69% of global sugar consumption and 47% of world imports. At July 2023 the ISO had 88 members (Madagascar joined in 2014, the United Kingdom acceded to the ISO independently in 2021 and Saudi Arabia joined in 2022), including both the EU and its 27 member states. The ISO is based in London, United Kingdom.

Sugar Prices
(annual averages, US $ per metric ton)

	ISA (World)	USA	EU
2005	218	469	665
2010	469	792	442
2015	296	547	363
2020	283	595	373
2021	390	740	386
2022	408	788	344

Source: World Bank, *Commodity Price Data* (Pink Sheet).

Prices In tandem with world output of cane and beet sugars, stock levels (of centrifugal sugar) are an important factor in determining the prices at which sugar is traded internationally. These stocks, which were at relatively low levels in the late 1980s, had increased significantly, if not consistently, by the 1990s. Stocks increased fairly steadily after 2000, with a peak at some 49m. metric tons at the end of 2014/15, before decreasing over the next two years. Stocks reached a new peak of 54m. tons by the end of 2018/19.

The World Bank records three sugar prices, to reflect the major markets. The world price that it quotes is the ISA daily price for raw sugar (f.o.b., stowed at greater Caribbean ports); the US price is for sugar under nearby futures contract (c.i.f.); and the increasingly anachronistic EU-negotiated import price for raw, unpackaged sugar from African, Caribbean and Pacific (ACP) countries under the Lomé Conventions (c.i.f., European ports). Following lower production in 2015/16, output rose significantly in 2016/17–2018/19 (on the back of near-record production in India and Thailand), while consumption remained steady over the same period—causing a weakening of world prices. In 2020, average prices trended upwards before steadying. It was reported that recovering oil prices and an expected sugar supply deficit were pushing prices upwards again in 2021, with prices continuing to rise in 2022 and the first half of 2023 (fuelled, in part, by unusual rainfall in India and by a reduction in petroleum production by OPEC countries placing upward pressure on transportation costs). By May 2023 the ISA world price had increased to US $560 per metric ton (its highest level in almost 12 years), while the US price was $938 per ton (its own highest level since the mid-1970s) and the EU price had increased slightly to $355 per ton.

TEA (Camellia sinensis)

Tea is a beverage made by infusing in boiling water the dried young leaves and unopened leaf-buds of the tea plant, an evergreen shrub or small tree. Black (known as red tea in China) and green tea are the most common finished products (white, yellow, oolong and post-fermented tea are also well known). Black tea, which has greater longevity, accounts for the bulk of the world's supply, and is associated with machine manufacture and plantation cultivation, which guarantees an adequate supply of leaf to the factory. Green tea, produced mainly in the People's Republic of China and Japan, is grown mostly on smallholdings, and much of it is consumed locally. There are two main varieties of tea, the China and the Assam, although hybrids may be obtained, such as Darjeeling; leaf size is also important, varying between the large Assam leaf and the small China leaf, with a medium Cambodian leaf. In this survey, wherever possible, data on production and trade relate to tea leaves, i.e. dry, unmanufactured tea (green tea and black tea).

The tea plant can grow up to 16 m, but cultivated ones are usually kept at about waist height, because the leaves and buds harvested every week to a fortnight are the top 3–5 cm of the plant (known as flushes). Once picked, tea leaves are withered, to preserve them, while black tea is oxidized using either what is known as the orthodox treatment, or the CTC (crush, tear, curl) method—the latter means of breaking the leaves also produces the fannings or dust grades that are commonly used in tea bags—before being dried and graded.

The World Market and the Region Of the world crop of tea leaves, according to the Food and Agriculture Organization of the United Nations (FAO), 7% was sold abroad in 2021 (compared with 11% in 2004). Tea production worldwide has increased every year of the 21st century, up to and including 2021, but the growth in exports has been more erratic. Since 2005 China has been the largest producer of tea in the world. Tea exports reached a then record level of 2.05m. metric tons in 2013, although it had declined to only 1.85m. tons in 2015 before recovering in 2016–20, to a new record level of 2.17m. tons in the latter year. Exports were 2.05m. tons in 2021. The major exporting countries, Kenya, China, Sri Lanka and India, have long dominated the market. China and India both have large domestic markets for their tea, but still export substantial amounts. In 2021 Kenya provided 27% of world exports, China 18%, Sri Lanka 14% and India 10% (the next largest exporters were Viet Nam, with 4%, Argentina with 3%, and Indonesia and Rwanda, with some 2% each). Malawi is also an important exporter.

For much of the 20th century India and Sri Lanka were the two leading exporters of tea, with approximately equal sales. During the 1960s India and Sri Lanka together exported more than two-thirds of all the tea sold by producing countries, but their joint foreign sales gradually declined during the 1970s, until they came to constitute less than one-half of world exports (in 2021 some 23%). Over the years Sri Lankan sales came to exceed those of India by a comfortable margin (Indian exports had been exceeded by those of Sri Lanka throughout much of the 2000s—and, indeed, by those of China). Exports by Sri Lanka took primacy in 1997–2004. Kenya was the main tea exporter in 2005–10, but was overtaken by China, India and Sri Lanka the following year. However, in 2013 its foreign sales reached a record high of 448,809 metric tons, which was almost 50% higher than the previous year. Exports by India have been surpassed by those of China (whose sales include a large proportion of green tea) in every year since 1996; in 2011 China resumed its place as Asia's largest tea exporter for the first time in centuries, although Sri Lanka interrupted that order again the following year. A newer challenge to the four principal exporters came from Viet Nam, which became the world's fifth largest seller of tea on the international market from 2000, exporting almost three times as much as the Far East's next largest exporter, Indonesia, in 2020. In 2011 Argentina had exceeded Indonesian sales to become the world's sixth largest exporter for the first time, maintaining that position in 2012–19, before falling to seventh in 2020. In 2016–20 Uganda was estimated to have sold more tea abroad than Indonesia (and more than Argentina in the latter year), but its exports fell fourfold in 2021 following the Government's decision to ban the export of raw materials (in order to encourage the domestic manufacturing sector).

For many years the United Kingdom was the largest single importer of tea. From the late 1980s consumption and imports expanded significantly in developing countries (notably in countries of the Middle East) and, particularly, in the USSR, which in 1989 overtook the United Kingdom as the world's principal tea importer. However, internal factors following the break-up of the USSR in 1991 caused a sharp decline in tea imports by its successor republics; as a result, the United Kingdom regained its position as the leading tea importer in that year. In 1992–99 the United Kingdom remained the principal destination of tea exports. Since 2000, however, imports by the Russian Federation have exceeded those of the United Kingdom by a substantial and, generally, increasing margin (except in 2001, when the United Kingdom briefly regained its position as the principal importer). In 2021 Russia imported 154,983 metric tons of tea, accounting for 8% of the world market, although Pakistan was the largest importer (a position it had maintained since 2016), buying 260,231 tons. Next, in terms of imports, came the USA with 116,230 tons and the United Kingdom with 108,237 tons. Other major importers of tea in 2021 were Egypt, the United Arab Emirates, Morocco and Iraq.

Türkiye (Turkey before 2022) is the largest producer of tea in the world after the four traditionally dominant growers, China, India, Sri Lanka and Kenya, but it has a large internal market. The industry was only established in the 1920s on any scale, after the disintegration of the Ottoman Empire and loss of access to traditional coffee-growing territories. For many years the state held a monopoly in the sector, and the state-owned company still dominates, but the private sector share of output first exceeded the state's in 2014 and then consistently from 2016. In 2018 the private sector accounted for some 58% of tea produced. Most Turkish output is Rize tea from the eponymous province on the eastern Black Sea coast, with neighbouring Trabzon the next largest producer. The bulk of Turkish tea is processed as black tea. Green tea has been produced since 2003, and organic tea from 2009.

Iran is the other notable tea-producing country in the Middle East and North Africa. Although Iran produces far less than Türkiye, it generally exports about two-fifths of its output, so in 2021 it sold 9,807 metric tons abroad, compared with the 5,815 tons exported by Türkiye. Both are small-scale exporters. As a force in international commodity markets for tea, however, the Middle East and North Africa is significant, importing 24% of world imports in 2021. After Pakistan, Russia, the USA and the United Kingdom, most of the world's largest importers of tea were in the Middle East and North Africa: Egypt with 72,771 tons, UAE 68,263 tons, Morocco 66,368 tons, Iraq 59,044 tons, Iran 55,150 tons, Saudi Arabia 31,027 tons and Türkiye 19,871 tons.

Production of Tea Leaves
('000 metric tons, FAO estimates unless otherwise indicated)

	2018	2019	2020	2021
World total	26,086.1	26,660.1	27,197.7	28,191.6
Middle East and North Africa*	1,579.7	1,498.2	1,502.7	1,533.5
Regional producers				
Iran	99.2†	90.8†	85.0	83.5
Türkiye†	1,480.5	1,407.4	1,417.7	1,450.0
Other leading producers				
Argentina	360.0	362.0	321.0	339.3
Bangladesh	340.0	394.0	391.0	393.0
China, People's Republic	11,350.0	12,075.0	12,747.0	13,757.0
India	5,820.0	6,044.0	5,482.0	5,482.2
Indonesia	610.0	560.0	626.0	563.0
Japan†	86.3	81.7	69.8	78.1
Kenya	2,143.0	1,995.0	2,476.0	2,338.0
Sri Lanka	1,321.0	1,305.0	1,211.0	1,302.0
Viet Nam†	1,081.2	1,017.6	1,045.6	1,073.0

* Figures represent the sum of output in listed countries.
† Official figure(s).

Source: FAO.

International Associations An International Tea Agreement (ITA), signed in 1933 by the governments of India, Ceylon (now Sri Lanka) and the Netherlands East Indies (now Indonesia), established the International Tea Committee (ITC), based in London, United Kingdom, as an administrative body. Although ITA operations ceased after 1955, the ITC has continued to function as a statistical and information centre. In 2023 there were eight producer/exporter members (the tea boards or associations of Bangladesh, India, Indonesia, Kenya, Malawi, Sri Lanka and Tanzania, and the China Chamber of Commerce of Import and Export of Foodstuffs,

Native Produce and Animal By-products), four consumer members (the tea associations of Canada, Ireland, Italy and the USA), 20 associate members and 45 corporate members. In 1969 the Food and Agriculture Organization of the United Nations (FAO) formed a Consultative Committee on Tea (renamed Intergovernmental Group on Tea in 1970), and an exporters' group, meeting under this committee's auspices, set voluntary export quotas in an attempt to avert an overall long-term decline in the real price of tea. This succeeded in raising prices for two years, but collapsed subsequently as (mainly) African countries—Kenya in particular—opposed efforts to restrict their rapidly increasing production. The regulation of tea prices is further complicated by the perishability of tea, which impedes the effective operation of a buffer stock.

Tea Prices
(annual averages, US $ per metric ton)

	Three auctions*	Colombo	Kolkata
1990	2,056	1,877	2,809
2000	1,876	1,793	1,806
2005	1,647	1,843	1,621
2010	2,885	3,290	2,805
2015	2,777	2,975	2,392
2020	2,699	3,404	2,686
2021	2,689	3,126	2,831
2022	3,051	3,873	2,835

*Three auction average for Kolkata, Colombo and Mombasa/Nairobi.

Source: World Bank, *Commodity Price Data* (Pink Sheet).

Prices Much of the tea traded internationally is sold by auction, principally in the exporting countries. Until declining volumes brought about their termination in June 1998 (Kenya having withdrawn in 1997, and a number of other exporters, including Sri Lanka and Malawi, having established their own auctions), the weekly London auctions in the United Kingdom had formed the centre of the international tea trade.

The World Bank provides a number of tea price indexes. The first cites a three auction average, based on quotations at Kolkata (India), Colombo (Sri Lanka) and Mombasa/Nairobi (Kenya). As noted above, Colombo is the largest single auction site for tea in Asia, and the price given is another arithmetic average, this time of weekly quotes for all tea (Sri Lanka, all origins). The much smaller Kolkata auctions provide the third price: for leaf tea, including excise duty (weekly quotes average). Kolkata is the largest of the Indian tea auctions, but Guwahati is also important. There are four additional tea auctions in India and one in Bangladesh.

TOBACCO (*Nicotiana tabacum*)

Tobacco originated in South America and was used in rituals and ceremonials or as a medicine; it was smoked and chewed for centuries before its introduction into Europe, the Middle East, Africa and South Asia in the 16th century. The generic name *Nicotiana* denotes the presence of the alkaloid nicotine in its leaves. The most important species in commercial tobacco cultivation is *N. tabacum*. Another species, *N. rustica*, is widely grown, but on a smaller scale, to yield cured leaf for oriental tobacco, snuff or simple cigarettes and cigars.

Commercially grown tobacco (from *N. tabacum*) can be divided into four major types—flue cured (e.g. Virginia, the most grown tobacco variety in the world), air cured (including burley, cigar, light and dark), fire cured and sun cured (including oriental)—depending on the procedures used to dry or 'cure' the leaves. Each system imparts specific chemical and smoking characteristics to the cured leaf, although these may also be affected by other factors, such as the type of soil on which the crop is grown, the type and quantity of fertilizer applied to the crop, the cultivar used, the spacing of the crop in the field and the number of leaves left at topping (the removal of the terminal growing point). Each type is used, separately or in combination, in specific products. All types are grown in Asia.

As in other major producing areas, local research organizations in Asia have developed new cultivars with specific, desirable chemical characteristics, disease resistance properties and improved yields. Almost all tobacco production in South Asia is from smallholdings; there is no cultivation of the crop on estates, as is common with tea. Emphasis has been placed on improving yields by the selection of cultivars, by the increased use of fertilizers and by the elimination or reduction of crop loss (through use of crop chemicals) and on reducing requirements for hand labour through the mechanization of land preparation. Harvesting continues to be entirely a manual operation, as the size of farmers' holdings and the cost of harvesting devices (now commonly used in the USA and Canada) preclude such development in Asia. The flue curing process requires energy in the form of petroleum, gas, coal or wood. To ensure that supplies of wood are continuously renewed, the tobacco industry in, for example, Pakistan and Sri Lanka encourages the planting of trees. Much oriental, or 'Turkish' tobacco, common in places once part of the Ottoman Empire, is sun cured, although some types are fire cured, such as Latakia, which is an aromatic fire-cured tobacco popular in Syria and Cyprus. Turkish tobacco was popular in the manufacture of cigarettes. Dokha tobacco, which originated in Iran and is popular in the region, in the United Arab Emirates in particular, is not cured and cut, but dried in the dry desert environment where it is harvested. It is then finely shredded and blended with herbs, spices, etc., without preservatives, herbicides or other additives common to mass-produced cigarettes. It is commonly smoked with a midwakh pipe. Unlike mu'assel (maassel) or shisha (sheesha) tobacco, dokha is not marinated in flavoured molasses. Shisha is smoked through water with a hookah pipe (qalyân, argileh, nargilah).

Production of Tobacco
(unmanufactured, farm sales weight, '000 metric tons)

	2018	2019	2020	2021
World total	6,053	6,527	5,813	5,889
Middle East and North Africa*	161	167	177	163
Leading regional producers				
Algeria	11	15	11	9
Iran*	22	20	21	21
Lebanon*	11	10	10	10
Syria	14	13	19	14
Türkiye	75	70	77	73
Yemen	19	29	30*	26*
Other leading producers				
Argentina	104	106*	106*	102*
Bangladesh	89	129	86	89
Brazil	756	770	702	744
China, People's Republic	2,241	2,612	2,134	2,128
India*	747	759	766	758
Indonesia	195	270	261*	237
Korea, DPR*	84	85	85	85
Malawi	95	102*	102*	105*
Mozambique	115	142	67	93*
Pakistan	107	104	133	168
Tanzania	50	71	38	59
USA	242	212	169	217
Zambia	25	30*	29*	27*
Zimbabwe	240	185	203	162

* FAO estimate(s).

Source: FAO.

The World Market and the Region Between one-third and two-fifths of world tobacco production are traded internationally. Until 1993, when it was overtaken by Brazil, the USA was the world's principal tobacco exporting country. Since 1993 Brazil has consolidated its position as the world's leading exporter of tobacco, largely at the expense of the USA and Zimbabwe. Brazil's share of global exports of unmanufactured tobacco increased in volume from 13% in 1993 to about one-quarter from the mid-2000s (20% in 2021). The principal type of tobacco cultivated by Middle Eastern farmers is oriental, which is generally sun cured, although some tobacco varieties in the region are fire cured or merely dried. Little tobacco is grown in North Africa. Although Egypt is an important cigarette manufacturer and one of the largest consumers in the region, the state prohibits the growing of tobacco. Several other countries manufacture and export cigarettes, notably Türkiye (Turkey before 2022), the UAE, Jordan and Morocco. Shisha and dokha tobaccos are popular in Iran and the Gulf states in particular.

In 2021, according to FAO, Türkiye earned $439m. from exports of unmanufactured tobacco and of tobacco products, although the country was also a significant importer, as were Algeria, Iran, Egypt and the UAE. Syria was once a significant tobacco grower, producing between 20,000 and 30,000 metric tons per year in the 2000s. Sales abroad collapsed because of civil war in the 2010s, as they did in Yemen, which had become the region's second largest grower after Türkiye. Algeria, Lebanon, Tunisia, Iraq, Oman, Morocco and Libya also grow some tobacco, mainly for domestic consumption.

International Association The International Tobacco Growers' Association (ITGA), with headquarters in Castelo Branco, Portugal, was formed in 1984 by growers' groups in Argentina, Brazil, Canada, Malawi, the USA and Zimbabwe. In 2023 its members numbered 24 countries, including Lebanon. ITGA members account for more than 80% of the world's internationally traded tobacco. The Association provides a forum for the exchange of information among tobacco producers, conducts research and publishes studies on tobacco issues.

REGIONAL INFORMATION

Major Commodities of the Middle East and North Africa

Tobacco Price
(US $ per metric ton)

	Average	High	Low
2005	2,790	(December) 2,946	(January) 2,696
2010	4,333	(January) 4,466	(April) 4,180
2015	4,908	(May) 5,018	(December) 4,790
2020	4,336	(February) 4,442	(December) 4,200
2021	4,155	(October) 4,242	(August) 3,973
2022	4,270	(December) 4,399	(September) 4,147

Source: World Bank, *Commodity Price Data* (Pink Sheet).

Prices According to the World Bank, general US import prices (c.i.f.) for unmanufactured tobacco of any origin soon recovered from the commodity slump of late 2008 and early 2009, and the average annual price continued to rise until 2011. Prices were fairly stable in 2015, but weakened towards the end of the year and into 2016. From mid-2017 prices climbed steadily, reaching their highest level since May 2015 in August 2018 (US $4,978 per ton), before falling through most of 2019. Prices were steady through most of 2020, only falling below $4,200 per ton in the first two months of 2021. Prices fluctuated in the second half of 2021, but stayed above $4,100 per ton throughout 2022; the average monthly price had reached $4,526 per ton by March 2023 (its highest level since 2019), before falling back to $4,142 per ton in May.

WHEAT (*Triticum*)

The most common species of wheat, *Triticum vulgare*, includes hard, semi-hard and soft varieties which have different milling characteristics but which, in general, are suitable for bread making. Another species, *T. durum*, is grown mainly in semi-arid areas, including regions bordering the Mediterranean Sea. This wheat is very hard, and is suitable for the manufacture of semolina, the basic ingredient of pasta and couscous. A third species, spelt (*T. spelta*), is also included in production figures for wheat. It is grown in very small quantities in parts of Europe and is used mainly as animal feed.

Although a most adaptable crop, wheat does not thrive in hot and humid climates, and it requires timely applications of water (either through rainfall or irrigation). Wheat is an important crop in most countries in Asia north of the Tropic of Cancer, wherever the terrain is favourable and sufficient water is available. The most concentrated producing areas in the Middle East and North Africa region are to be found where there is a good river-fed supply of water.

Production of Wheat
('000 metric tons, including spelt)

	2019/20	2020/21	2021/22	2022/23*
World total	759,392	773,450	781,047	790,198
Middle East and North Africa	59,679	57,938	55,695	53,870
Leading regional producers				
Egypt	8,559	9,102	9,842	9,500
Iran	15,550	15,000	12,000	13,200
Morocco	4,025	2,870	7,540	2,700
Türkiye	17,500	18,250	16,000	17,250
Other leading producers				
Australia	14,480	31,923	36,237	39,685
Canada	32,670	35,437	22,422	33,824
China, People's Republic	133,600	134,250	136,946	137,723
European Union	138,799	126,684	138,244	134,341
India	103,600	107,860	109,586	104,000
Pakistan	24,349	25,248	27,464	26,400
Russian Federation	73,610	85,352	75,158	92,000
Ukraine	29,171	25,420	33,007	21,500
USA	52,581	49,751	44,804	44,902

* Preliminary.

Source: US Department of Agriculture.

The World Market and the Region Wheat is the principal cereal in international trade. According to data from the US Department of Agriculture (USDA), in 2022/23 the European Union (EU) and the People's Republic of China each accounted for 17% of world wheat production, with India accounting for 13%. France and Germany were the EU's main producers; according to FAO, in 2021 France accounted for 26% of EU output (5% of the world total), Germany 16% and Poland 9%. The EU was also the leading exporter of wheat for three consecutive production years until 2016/17, when it was third, because the USA, traditionally the world's leading exporter, reclaimed the top position. However, in 2017/18 the Russian Federation became the leading exporter. The EU regained the top position in 2019/20, but was overtaken by Russia once more in 2020/21; Russia remained the largest exporter in 2021/22–2022/23; in the latter year it contributed a 21% share of international trade (with the EU exporting around 16% and the USA 10%). The strength of Russia as an exporter is that it has a relatively small internal market, as do Canada (12%) and Ukraine (8%). Russia and Ukraine alone account for close to one-third of total wheat supplies on the global market. Meanwhile, Australia saw its exports of wheat more than double in 2020/21, and exports increased again in 2021/22 and 2022/23; in the latter year it contributed 15% of the global total. Any significant decline in production in the other major producers, notably China and India, can impact hugely on world trade through their consequent need for greater imports. In 2022/23 USDA estimated the largest importing region, by far, to be the Middle East and North Africa (32% of world imports), followed by East Asia (12%), sub-Saharan Africa (as defined by USDA, all African states except the five Mediterranean littoral countries—also 12%), South-East Asia (almost 12%), South Asia (higher than usual in that year—India replenishing stocks after poor harvests in previous years—just over 6%) and South America (almost 6%). Developed countries were formerly the principal consumers of wheat, but the role of developing countries as importers has been steadily increasing and they now regularly account for approximately two-thirds of world imports.

World consumption, which has, in the long term, been increasing at a similar rate to production, varies much less from year to year than the wheat harvest. Wheat food use has been expanding at the expense of rice: its growth is associated with rising consumer incomes and an increasing number of fast-food outlets. Substantial amounts of wheat are used for animal feed in Europe and, when prices are favourable, in North America. Substantial quantities were also used for feed in the 1980s in what was then the USSR, but this volume decreased sharply in response to the diminution in livestock numbers. Some wheat is used for feed in Japan, while the Republic of Korea (South Korea) imports wheat for feed when prices are low in comparison with those of coarse grains such as sorghum and maize (corn). According to USDA, domestic consumption of wheat was highest in the EU until 2010/11, but is now exceeded by East Asia and, from 2016/17, South Asia. At 2022/23 the largest consuming region was East Asia (20%), followed by South Asia (almost 20%), the Middle East and North Africa (14%) and the EU (almost 14%).

The Middle East and North Africa is the leading wheat importing region of the world, although it is not the primary consumer—because it is not a significant producer. Nevertheless, North African output more than doubled between 2000 and 2015, and by the end of the 2010s Middle Eastern countries too were attempting to increase production of a commodity in such high demand in the region. Saudi Arabia, for example, in 2019 reversed earlier water-conserving policies against growing wheat. Consequently, production increased to some 625,000 tons in 2022/23 (a significant increase from some 12,000–13,000 tons annually in 2015/16–2018/19). Türkiye, Iran, Egypt and Morocco are the region's main producers, but others include Iraq and Algeria (3.7m. tons and 3.0m. tons, respectively, in 2022/23) and Syria (2.1m. tons).

In the last few years of the 2010s, aided by favourable rainfall and some post-conflict recovery in Iraq and Syria in particular, increased Middle East production was offsetting growth in demand, damping imports. Türkiye still had historically high levels of imports, because of its policy to encourage the processing and export of flour (and Türkiye overtook Egypt in 2022/23, according to preliminary figures). Iran, meanwhile, had imposed a wheat import ban in order to encourage domestic production. Egypt, with its large population and many processing industries, continued to be among the world's largest importers of wheat (11.1m. metric tons in 2022/23).

Global Forum The International Grains Council (IGC) is based in London, United Kingdom. It is the successor body of the International Wheat Council (IWC). From 1949 nearly all world trade in wheat was conducted under the auspices of successive international agreements, administered by the IWC. The early agreements involved regulatory price controls and supply and purchase obligations, but such provisions became inoperable in more competitive market conditions, and were abandoned in 1972. The IWC subsequently concentrated on providing detailed market assessments to its members and encouraging them to confer on matters of mutual concern. A new Grains Trade Convention, which entered into force in July 1995, gave the renamed IGC a wider mandate to consider all coarse grains as well as wheat (rice was added to the definition of grains from 1 July 2009 and oilseeds from 1 July 2013). This facilitates the provision of information to member governments, and enhances their opportunities to hold consultations. In addition, links between governments and industry are strengthened at an annual series of grain conferences sponsored by the IGC. In July 2023 the IGC consisted of 29 members, plus the EU.

REGIONAL INFORMATION

Wheat Price
(US $ per metric ton)

	Average	High	Low
2005	152	(October) 168	(April) 141
2010	224	(December) 307	(June) 158
2015	204	(January) 248	(September) 173
2020	232	(November) 273	(June) 198
2021	315	(November) 379	(March) 273
2022	430	(May) 522	(January) 374

Source: World Bank, *Commodity Price Data* (Pink Sheet).

Prices Hard Red Winter is one of the most widely traded wheat varieties. The export price of US No. 1 Hard Red Winter (ordinary protein, delivered at Gulf ports for prompt or 30 days shipment) is cited by the World Bank as an indicator. Average monthly prices ended below US $300 per metric ton for the first time in 18 months at the end of 2013 and remained below that level from July 2014. One year later average monthly prices fell below $200 per ton and stayed below that level for the whole of 2017 (with the exception of July). The price began to recover in early 2018, but by mid-2019 the price had fallen below $200 per ton for the second time that year. It recovered strongly thereafter, reaching its highest level in five years—$225 per ton—in January 2020. Prices continued to increase throughout 2021 and the first half of 2022; in May of the latter year the price soared to its highest level on record—fuelled by Russia's renewed military invasion of Ukraine (and the resultant supply disruptions in the latter country as the ongoing hostilities resulted in an effective blockade of Ukrainian ports, preventing crucial grain exports) and an Indian export ban (intended to regulate inflated domestic prices)—and prompting widespread fears of a developing global humanitarian crisis in those countries where these wheat imports were a critical food staple. Prices only began to decline in July 2022 following a UN-backed agreement, brokered by Türkiye between the Russian Federation and Ukraine, to allow the resumption of grain exports from Ukrainian Black Sea ports. By May 2023 the price had fallen to $368 per ton. However, in July it was reported that Russia had withdrawn from the agreement, prompting renewed fears of dramatic price increases that might jeopardize global food security.

The Food Aid Conventions and the Food Assistance Convention Since 1967 a series of Food Aid Conventions (FACs), linked to the successive Wheat and Grains Trade Conventions, have ensured continuity of supplies of food aid in the form of cereals to countries in need. Under the last FAC, negotiated in 1999, the donor countries (including the member states of the EU) pledged to supply a minimum of some 5m. metric tons of food aid annually to developing countries, with priority given to least developed countries and other low-income food importing nations. Aid was provided mostly in the form of cereals, and all aid given to least developed countries was in the form of grants. The FAC sought to improve the effectiveness, and increase the impact, of food aid by improved monitoring and consultative procedures. In mid-2004 FAC members undertook a renegotiation of the 1999 FAC in order 'to strengthen its capacity to meet identified needs when food aid is the appropriate response'. However, it was decided that this renegotiation should await the conclusion of discussions on trade related food aid issues in agriculture negotiations at the World Trade Organization. Meanwhile, it was agreed to extend the FAC, 1999, for two years from July 2005; further, one-year extensions were agreed subsequently and it only finally expired on 30 June 2012. In December 2010 formal negotiations on the future of the FAC had commenced, so the extensions were to give the discussions a fair chance of fruition. A new Food Assistance Convention was adopted in London on 25 April 2012, and was open for signature from 11 June to the 34 signatories and the EU. It came into force on 1 January 2013 (after ratification by six signatories—Canada, Denmark, the EU, Japan, Switzerland and the USA), and from that date was open to other signatories. Rather than focusing only on certain specified food items (expressed in wheat-equivalent tons), the new instrument focused on 'nutritious food', leaving it up to the parties to express commitments in wheat tons or monetary terms, as part of the mechanisms for information sharing and registration of undertakings.

ACKNOWLEDGEMENTS

We gratefully acknowledge the assistance of the following organizations in the preparation of this section: the Food and Agriculture Organization of the United Nations (FAO); the International Aluminium Institute; the International Monetary Fund; the International Olive Council; the International Sugar Organization; the US Department of Agriculture; the US Department of Energy; the US Geological Survey, US Department of the Interior; the World Gold Council; and the World Bank.

DOCUMENTS ON PALESTINE

Note: The inclusion of a document does not imply the Editor's endorsement of its content.

DECLARATION OF FIRST WORLD ZIONIST CONGRESS

*The Congress, convened in Basle by Dr Theodor Herzl in August 1897, adopted the following programme.**

The aim of Zionism is to create for the Jewish people a home in Palestine secured by public law.

The Congress contemplates the following means to the attainment of this end:

1. The promotion on suitable lines, of the settlement of Palestine by Jewish agriculturists, artisans and tradesmen.

2. The organization and binding together of the whole of Jewry by means of appropriate institutions, local and general, in accordance with the laws of each country.

3. The strengthening of Jewish sentiment and national consciousness.

4. Preparatory steps towards obtaining government consent as are necessary, for the attainment of the aim of Zionism.

* Text supplied by courtesy of Josef Fraenkel.

MCMAHON CORRESPONDENCE*

Ten letters passed between Sir Henry McMahon, British High Commissioner in Cairo, and Sherif Husain of Mecca from July 1915 to March 1916. Husain offered Arab help in the war against the Turks if Britain would support the principle of an independent Arab state. The most important letter is that of 24 October 1915, from McMahon to Husain:

...I regret that you should have received from my last letter the impression that I regarded the question of limits and boundaries with coldness and hesitation; such was not the case, but it appeared to me that the time had not yet come when that question could be discussed in a conclusive manner.

I have realized, however, from your last letter that you regard this question as one of vital and urgent importance. I have, therefore, lost no time in informing the Government of Great Britain of the contents of your letter, and it is with great pleasure that I communicate to you on their behalf the following statement, which I am confident you will receive with satisfaction:

The two districts of Mersina and Alexandretta and portions of Syria lying to the west of the districts of Damascus, Homs, Hama and Aleppo cannot be said to be purely Arab, and should be excluded from the limits demanded.

With the above modification, and without prejudice to our existing treaties with Arab chiefs, we accept those limits.

As for those regions lying within those frontiers wherein Great Britain is free to act without detriment to the interest of her ally, France, I am empowered in the name of the Government of Great Britain to give the following assurances and make the following reply to your letter:

(1) Subject to the above modifications, Great Britain is prepared to recognize and support the independence of the Arabs in all the regions within the limits demanded by the Sherif of Mecca

(2) Great Britain will guarantee the Holy Places against all external aggression and will recognize their inviolability

(3) When the situation admits, Great Britain will give to the Arabs her advice and will assist them to establish what may appear to be the most suitable forms of government in those various territories

(4) On the other hand, it is understood that the Arabs have decided to seek the advice and guidance of Great Britain only, and that such European advisers and officials as may be required for the formation of a sound form of administration will be British

(5) With regard to the *vilayets* of Baghdad and Basra, the Arabs will recognize that the established position and interests of Great Britain necessitate special administrative arrangements in order to secure these territories from foreign aggression, to promote the welfare of the local populations and to safeguard our mutual economic interests

I am convinced that this declaration will assure you beyond all possible doubt of the sympathy of Great Britain towards the aspirations of her friends the Arabs and will result in a firm and lasting alliance, the immediate results of which will be the expulsion of the Turks from the Arab countries and the freeing of the Arab peoples from the Turkish yoke, which for so many years has pressed heavily upon them...

* British White Paper, Cmd. 5957, 1939.

ANGLO-FRANCO-RUSSIAN AGREEMENT (SYKES–PICOT AGREEMENT)
(April–May 1916)

*The allocation of portions of the Ottoman empire by the three powers was decided between them in an exchange of diplomatic notes. The Anglo-French agreement*dealing with Arab territories became known to Sherif Husain only after publication by the new Bolshevik Government of Russia in 1917:*

1. That France and Great Britain are prepared to recognize and protect an independent Arab State or a Confederation of Arab States in the areas (A) and (B) marked on the annexed map (*not reproduced here—Ed.*), under suzerainty of an Arab Chief. That in area (A) France, and in area (B) Great Britain shall have priority of right of enterprises and local loans. France in area (A) and Great Britain in area (B) shall alone supply foreign advisers or officials on the request of the Arab State or the Confederation of Arab States.

2. France in the Blue area and Great Britain in the Red area shall be at liberty to establish direct or indirect administration or control as they may desire or as they may deem fit to establish after agreement with the Arab State or Confederation of Arab States.

3. In the Brown area there shall be established an international administration of which the form will be decided upon after consultation with Russia, and after subsequent agreement with the other Allies and the representatives of the Sherif of Mecca.

4. That Great Britain be accorded

(*a*) The ports of Haifa and Acre

(*b*) Guarantee of a given supply of water from the Tigris and the Euphrates in area (A) for area (B)

His Majesty's Government, on their part, undertake that they will at no time enter into negotiations for the cession of Cyprus to any third Power without the previous consent of the French Government.

5. Alexandretta shall be a free port as regards the trade of the British Empire and there shall be no discrimination in treatment with regard to port dues or the extension of special privileges affecting British shipping and commerce; there shall be freedom of transit for British goods through Alexandretta and over railways through the Blue area, whether such goods are going to or coming from the Red area, area (A) or area (B); and there shall be no differentiation in treatment, direct or indirect, at the expense of British goods on any railway or of British goods and shipping in any port serving the areas in question.

Haifa shall be a free port as regards the trade of France, her colonies and protectorates, and there shall be no differentiation in treatment or privilege with regard to port dues against French shipping and commerce. There shall be freedom of transit through Haifa and over British railways through the Brown area, whether such goods are coming from or going to the Blue area, area (A) or area (B), and there shall be no differentiation in treatment, direct or indirect, at the expense of French goods on any railway or of French goods and shipping in any port serving the areas in question.

6. In area (A), the Baghdad Railway shall not be extended southwards beyond Mosul, and in area (B), it shall not be extended northwards beyond Samarra, until a railway connecting Baghdad with Aleppo along the basin of the Euphrates

will have been completed, and then only with the concurrence of the two Governments.

7. Great Britain shall have the right to build, administer and be the sole owner of the railway connecting Haifa with area (B). She shall have, in addition, the right in perpetuity and at all times of carrying troops on that line. It is understood by both Governments that this railway is intended to facilitate communication between Baghdad and Haifa, and it is further understood that, in the event of technical difficulties and expenditure incurred in the maintenance of this line in the Brown area rendering the execution of the project impracticable, the French Government will be prepared to consider plans for enabling the line in question to traverse the polygon formed by Banias-Umm Qais-Salkhad-Tall 'Osda-Mismieh before reaching area (B).

(*Clause 8 referred to customs tariffs.*)

9. It is understood that the French Government will at no time initiate any negotiations for the cession of their rights and will not cede their prospective rights in the Blue area to any third Power other than the Arab State or Confederation of Arab States, without the previous consent of His Majesty's Government who, on their part, give the French Government a similar undertaking in respect of the Red area.

10. The British and French Governments shall agree to abstain from acquiring and to withhold their consent to a third Power acquiring territorial possessions in the Arabian Peninsula; nor shall they consent to the construction by a third Power of a naval base in the islands on the eastern seaboard of the Red Sea. This, however, will not prevent such rectification of the Aden boundary as might be found necessary in view of the recent Turkish attack.

11. The negotiations with the Arabs concerning the frontiers of the Arab State or Confederation of Arab States shall be pursued through the same channel as heretofore in the name of the two Powers.

12. It is understood, moreover, that measures for controlling the importation of arms into the Arab territory will be considered by the two Governments.

* E. L. Woodward and Rohan Butler (Eds). *Documents on British Foreign Policy 1919–1939*. First Series, Vol. IV, 1919. London, HMSO, 1952.

BALFOUR DECLARATION
(2 November 1917)

Balfour was British Secretary of State for Foreign Affairs, Rothschild the British Zionist leader.

Dear Lord Rothschild,

I have much pleasure in conveying to you on behalf of His Majesty's Government the following declaration of sympathy with Jewish Zionist aspirations, which has been submitted to and approved by the Cabinet.

'His Majesty's Government view with favour the establishment in Palestine of a national home for the Jewish people, and will use their best endeavours to facilitate the achievement of this object, it being clearly understood that nothing shall be done which may prejudice the civil and religious rights of existing non-Jewish communities in Palestine, or the rights and political status enjoyed by Jews in any other country.'

I should be grateful if you would bring this declaration to the knowledge of the Zionist Federation.

Yours sincerely, Arthur James Balfour

HOGARTH MESSAGE*
(4 January 1918)

The following is the text of a message which Commander D. G. Hogarth, CMG, RNVR, of the Arab Bureau in Cairo, was instructed on 4 January 1918 to deliver to King Husain of the Hedjaz at Jeddah:

1. The *Entente* Powers are determined that the Arab race shall be given full opportunity of once again forming a nation in the world. This can only be achieved by the Arabs themselves uniting, and Great Britain and her Allies will pursue a policy with this ultimate unity in view.

2. So far as Palestine is concerned, we are determined that no people shall be subject to another, but—

(*a*) In view of the fact that there are in Palestine shrines, Wakfs and Holy places, sacred in some cases to Moslems alone, to Jews alone, to Christians alone, and in others to two or all three, and inasmuch as these places are of interest to vast masses of people outside Palestine and Arabia, there must be a special régime to deal with these places approved of by the world.

(*b*) As regards the Mosque of Omar, it shall be considered as a Moslem concern alone, and shall not be subjected directly or indirectly to any non-Moslem authority.

3. Since the Jewish opinion of the world is in favour of a return of Jews to Palestine, and inasmuch as this opinion must remain a constant factor, and, further, as His Majesty's Government view with favour the realization of this aspiration, His Majesty's Government are determined that in so far as is compatible with the freedom of the existing population, both economic and political, no obstacle should be put in the way of the realization of this ideal.

In this connection the friendship of world Jewry to the Arab cause is equivalent to support in all States where Jews have political influence. The leaders of the movement are determined to bring about the success of Zionism by friendship and co-operation with the Arabs, and such an offer is not one to be lightly thrown aside.

* British White Paper, Cmd. 5964, 1939.

ANGLO-FRENCH DECLARATION*
(7 November 1918)

The object aimed at by France and Great Britain in prosecuting in the East the war let loose by the ambition of Germany is the complete and definite emancipation of the peoples so long oppressed by the Turks and the establishment of national Governments and Administrations deriving their authority from the initiative and free choice of the indigenous populations.

In order to carry out these intentions France and Great Britain are at one in encouraging and assisting the establishments of indigenous Governments and Administrations in Syria and Mesopotamia, now liberated by the Allies, and in the territories the liberation of which they are engaged in securing and recognizing these as soon as they are actually established.

Far from wishing to impose on the populations of these regions any particular institutions they are only concerned to ensure by their support and by adequate assistance the regular working of Governments and Administrations freely chosen by the populations themselves. To secure impartial and equal justice for all, to facilitate the economic development of the country by inspiring and encouraging local initiative, to favour the diffusion of education, to put an end to dissensions that have too long been taken advantage of by Turkish policy which the two Allied Governments uphold in the liberated territories.

* Report of a Committee set up to consider Certain Correspondence between Sir Henry McMahon and the Sherif of Mecca in 1915 and 1916, 16 March 1939 (British White Paper, Cmd. 5974).

RECOMMENDATIONS OF THE KING-CRANE COMMISSION*
(28 August 1919)

The Commission was set up by President Wilson of the USA to determine which power should receive the Mandate for Palestine. The following are extracts from their recommendations on Syria:

1. We recommend, as most important of all, and in strict harmony with our Instructions, that whatever foreign administration (whether of one or more Powers) is brought into Syria, should come in, not at all as a colonising Power in the old sense of that term, but as a Mandatory under the League of Nations with the clear consciousness that 'the well-being and development' of the Syrian people form for it a 'sacred trust'.

2. We recommend, in the second place, that the unity of Syria be preserved, in accordance with the earnest petition of the great majority of the people of Syria.

3. We recommend, in the third place, that Syria be placed under one mandatory Power, as the natural way to secure real and efficient unity.

4. We recommend, in the fourth place, that Amir Faisal be made the head of the new united Syrian State.

5. We recommend, in the fifth place, serious modification of the extreme Zionist program for Palestine of unlimited immigration of Jews, looking finally to making Palestine distinctly a Jewish State.

(1) The Commissioners began their study of Zionism with minds predisposed in its favor, but the actual facts in Palestine, coupled with the force of the general principles proclaimed by the Allies and accepted by the Syrians have driven them to the recommendation here made.

(2) The Commission was abundantly supplied with literature on the Zionist program by the Zionist Commission to Palestine; heard in conferences much concerning the Zionist colonies and their claims; and personally saw something of what had been accomplished. They found much to approve in the aspirations and plans of the Zionists, and had warm appreciation for the devotion of many of the colonists, and for their success, by modern methods in overcoming great, natural obstacles.

(3) The Commission recognised also that definite encouragement had been given to the Zionists by the Allies in Mr Balfour's often-quoted statement, in its approval by other representatives of the Allies. If, however, the strict terms of the Balfour Statement are adhered to—favoring 'the establishment in Palestine of a national home for the Jewish people', 'it being clearly understood that nothing shall be done which may prejudice the civil and religious rights of existing non-Jewish communities in Palestine'—it can hardly be doubted that the extreme Zionist program must be greatly modified. For 'a national home for the Jewish people' is not equivalent to making Palestine into a Jewish State; nor can the erection of such a Jewish State be accomplished without the gravest trespass upon the 'civil and religious rights of existing non-Jewish communities in Palestine'. The fact came out repeatedly in the Commission's conference with Jewish representatives, that the Zionists looked forward to a practically complete dispossession of the present non-Jewish inhabitants of Palestine, by various forms of purchase.

In his address of 4 July 1918, President Wilson laid down the following principle as one of the four great 'ends for which the associated peoples of the world were fighting': 'The settlement of every question, whether of territory, of sovereignty, of economic arrangement, or of political relationship upon the basis of the free acceptance of that settlement by the people immediately concerned, and not upon the basis of the material interest or advantage of any other nation or people which may desire a different settlement for the sake of its own exterior influence or mastery.' If that principle is to rule, and so the wishes of Palestine's population are to be decisive as to what is to be done with Palestine, then it is to be remembered that the non-Jewish population of Palestine—nearly nine-tenths of the whole—are emphatically against the entire Zionist program. The tables show that there was no one thing upon which the population of Palestine were more agreed than upon this. To subject a people so minded to unlimited Jewish immigration, and to steady financial and social pressure to surrender the land, would be a gross violation of the principle just quoted, and of the people's rights, though it kept within the forms of law.

It is to be noted also that the feeling against the Zionist program is not confined to Palestine, but shared very generally by the people throughout Syria, as our conferences clearly showed. More then 72%—1,350 in all—of all the petitions in the whole of Syria were directed against the Zionist program. Only two requests—those for a united Syria and for independence—had a larger support. This general feeling was duly voiced by the General Syrian Congress in the seventh, eighth and tenth resolutions of their statement.

The Peace Conference should not shut its eyes to the fact that the anti-Zionist feeling in Palestine and Syria is intense and not lightly to be flouted. No British officer, consulted by the Commissioners, believed that the Zionist program could be carried out except by force of arms. The officers generally thought that a force of not less than 50,000 soldiers would be required even to initiate the program. That of itself is evidence of a strong sense of the injustice of the Zionist program, on the part of the non-Jewish populations of Palestine and Syria.

Decisions requiring armies to carry out are sometimes necessary, but they are surely not gratuitously to be taken in the interests of serious injustice. For the initial claim, often submitted by Zionist representatives, that they have a 'right' to Palestine, based on an occupation of 2,000 years ago, can hardly be seriously considered.

There is a further consideration that cannot justly be ignored, if the world is to look forward to Palestine becoming a definitely Jewish State, however gradually that may take place. That consideration grows out of the fact that Palestine is the Holy Land for Jews, Christians, and Moslems alike. Millions of Christians and Moslems all over the world are quite as much concerned as the Jews with conditions in Palestine, especially with those conditions which touch upon religious feelings and rights. The relations in these matters in Palestine are most delicate and difficult. With the best possible intentions, it may be doubted whether the Jews could possibly seem to either Christians or Moslems proper guardians of the holy places, or custodians of the Holy Land as a whole.

The reason is this: The places which are most sacred to Christians—those having to do with Jesus—and which are also sacred to Moslems, are not only not sacred to Jews, but abhorrent to them. It is simply impossible, under those circumstances, for Moslems and Christians to feel satisfied to have these places in Jewish hands, or under the custody of Jews. There are still other places about which Moslems must have the same feeling. In fact, from this point of view, the Moslems, just because the sacred places of all three religions are sacred to them, have made very naturally much more satisfactory custodians of the holy places than the Jews could be. It must be believed that the precise meaning in this respect of the complete Jewish occupation of Palestine has not been fully sensed by those who urge the extreme Zionist program. For it would intensify, with a certainty like fate, the anti-Jewish feeling both in Palestine and in all other portions of the world which look to Palestine as the Holy Land.

In view of all these considerations, and with a deep sense of sympathy for the Jewish cause, the Commissioners feel bound to recommend that only a greatly reduced Zionist program be attempted by the Peace Conference, and even that, only very gradually initiated. This would have to mean that Jewish immigration should be definitely limited, and that the project for making Palestine distinctly a Jewish commonwealth should be given up.

There would then be no reason why Palestine could not be included in a united Syrian State, just as other portions of the country, the holy places being cared for by an international and inter-religious commission, somewhat as at present, under the oversight and approval of the Mandatory and of the League of Nations. The Jews, of course, would have representation upon this commission.

* US Department of State. *Papers Relating to the Foreign Relations of the United States. The Paris Peace Conference 1919.* Vol. XII. Washington, 1947.

ARTICLE 22 OF THE COVENANT OF THE LEAGUE OF NATIONS
(28 April 1919)

To those colonies and territories which as a consequence of the late War have ceased to be under the sovereignty of the States which formerly governed them and which are inhabited by peoples not yet able to stand by themselves under the strenuous conditions of the modern world, there should be applied the principle that the well-being and development of such peoples form a sacred trust of civilization and that securities for the performance of this trust should be embodied in this Covenant.

The best method of giving practical effect to this principle is that the tutelage of such peoples should be entrusted to advanced nations who by reason of their resources, their experience or their geographical position can best undertake this responsibility, and who are willing to accept it, and that this tutelage should be exercised by them as Mandatories on behalf of the League.

The character of the Mandate must differ according to the stage of the development of the people, the geographical situation of the territory, its economic conditions and other similar circumstances.

Certain communities formerly belonging to the Turkish Empire have reached a stage of development where their existence as independent nations can be provisionally recognized subject to the rendering of administrative advice and assistance by a Mandatory until such time as they are able to stand alone. The wishes of these communities must be a principal consideration in the selection of the Mandatory. [...]

In every case of Mandate, the Mandatory shall render to the Council an annual report in reference to the territory committed to its charge.

The degree of authority, control, or administration to be exercised by the Mandatory shall, if not previously agreed upon by the Members of the League, be explicitly defined in each case by the Council.

A permanent Commission shall be constituted to receive and examine the annual reports of the Mandatories and to advise the Council on all matters relating to the observance of the Mandates.

CHURCHILL MEMORANDUM*
(3 June 1922)

The Secretary of State for the Colonies has given renewed consideration to the existing political situation in Palestine, with a very earnest desire to arrive at a settlement of the outstanding questions which have given rise to uncertainty and unrest among certain sections of the population. After consultation with the High Commissioner for Palestine the following statement has been drawn up. It summarizes the essential parts of the correspondence that has already taken place between the Secretary of State and a Delegation from the Moslem Christian Society of Palestine, which has been for some time in England, and it states the further conclusions which have since been reached.

The tension which has prevailed from time to time in Palestine is mainly due to apprehensions, which are entertained both by sections of the Arab and by sections of the Jewish population. These apprehensions, so far as the Arabs are concerned, are partly based upon exaggerated interpretations of the meaning of the Declaration favouring the establishment of a Jewish National Home in Palestine, made on behalf of His Majesty's Government on 2 November 1917. Unauthorized statements have been made to the effect that the purpose in view is to create a wholly Jewish Palestine. Phrases have been used such as that Palestine is to become 'as Jewish as England is English'. His Majesty's Government regard any such expectation as impracticable and have no such aim in view. Nor have they at any time contemplated, as appears to be feared by the Arab Delegation, the disappearance or the subordination of the Arabic population, language or culture in Palestine. They would draw attention to the fact that the terms of the Declaration referred to do not contemplate that Palestine as a whole should be converted into a Jewish National Home, but that such a Home should be founded *in Palestine*. In this connection it has been observed with satisfaction that at the meeting of the Zionist Congress, the supreme governing body of the Zionist Organization, held at Carlsbad in September 1921, a resolution was passed expressing as the official statement of Zionist aims 'the determination of the Jewish people to live with the Arab people on terms of unity and mutual respect, and together with them to make the common home into a flourishing community, the upbuilding of which may assure to each of its peoples an undisturbed national development'.

It is also necessary to point out that the Zionist Commission in Palestine, now termed the Palestine Zionist Executive, has not desired to possess, and does not possess, any share in the general administration of the country. Nor does the special position assigned to the Zionist Organization in Article IV of the Draft Mandate for Palestine imply any such functions. That special position relates to the measures to be taken in Palestine affecting the Jewish population, and contemplates that the Organization may assist in the general development of the country, but does not entitle it to share in any degree in its Government.

Further, it is contemplated that the status of all citizens of Palestine in the eyes of the law shall be Palestinian, and it has never been intended that they, or any section of them, should possess any other juridical status.

So far as the Jewish population of Palestine are concerned, it appears that some among them are apprehensive that His Majesty's Government may depart from the policy embodied in the Declaration of 1917. It is necessary, therefore, once more to affirm that these fears are unfounded, and that the Declaration, re-affirmed by the Conference of the Principal Allied Powers at San Remo and again in the Treaty of Sèvres, is not susceptible of change.

During the last two or three generations the Jews have recreated in Palestine a community, now numbering 80,000, of whom about one-fourth are farmers or workers upon the land. This community has its own political organs; an elected assembly for the direction of its domestic concerns; elected councils in the towns; and an organization for the control of its schools. It has its elected Chief Rabbinate and Rabbinical Council for the direction of its religious affairs. Its business is conducted in Hebrew as a vernacular language, and a Hebrew Press serves its needs. It has its distinctive intellectual life and displays considerable economic activity. This community, then, with its town and country population, its political, religious and social organizations, its own language, its own customs, its own life, has in fact 'national' characteristics. When it is asked what is meant by the development of the Jewish National Home in Palestine, it may be answered that it is not the imposition of a Jewish nationality upon the inhabitants of Palestine as a whole, but the further development of the existing Jewish community, with the assistance of Jews in other parts of the world, in order that it may become a centre in which the Jewish people as a whole may take, on grounds of religion and race, an interest and a pride. But in order that this community should have the best prospect of free development and provide a full opportunity for the Jewish people to display its capacities, it is essential that it should know that it is in Palestine as of right and not on sufferance. That is the reason why it is necessary that the existence of a Jewish National Home in Palestine should be internationally guaranteed, and that it should be formally recognized to rest upon ancient historic connection.

This, then, is the interpretation which His Majesty's Government place upon the Declaration of 1917, and, so understood, the Secretary of State is of opinion that it does not contain or imply anything which need cause either alarm to the Arab population of Palestine or disappointment to the Jews.

For the fulfilment of this policy it is necessary that the Jewish community in Palestine should be able to increase its numbers by immigration. This immigration cannot be so great in volume as to exceed whatever may be the economic capacity of the country at the time to absorb new arrivals. It is essential to ensure that the immigrants should not be a burden upon the people of Palestine as a whole, and that they should not deprive any section of the present population of their employment. Hitherto the immigration has fulfilled these conditions. The number of immigrants since the British occupation has been about 25,000...

* Palestine, Correspondence with the Palestine Arab Delegation and the Zionist Organization (British White Paper, Cmd. 1700), pp. 17–21.

MANDATE FOR PALESTINE*
(24 July 1922)

The Council of the League of Nations:

Whereas the Principal Allied Powers have agreed, for the purpose of giving effect to the provisions of Article 22 of the Covenant of the League of Nations to entrust to a Mandatory selected by the said Powers the administration of the territory of Palestine, which formerly belonged to the Turkish Empire, within such boundaries as may be fixed by them; and

Whereas the Principal Allied Powers have also agreed that the Mandatory should be responsible for putting into effect the declaration originally made on 2 November 1917 by the Government of His Britannic Majesty, and adopted by the said Powers, in favour of the establishment in Palestine of a National Home for the Jewish people, it being clearly understood that nothing should be done which might prejudice the civil and religious rights of existing non-Jewish communities in Palestine, or the rights and political status enjoyed by Jews in any other country; and

Whereas recognition has thereby been given to the historical connection of the Jewish people with Palestine and to the grounds for reconstituting their National Home in that country; and

Whereas the Principal Allied Powers have selected His Britannic Majesty as the Mandatory for Palestine; and

Whereas the Mandate in respect of Palestine has been formulated in the following terms and submitted to the Council of the League for approval; and

Whereas His Britannic Majesty has accepted the Mandate in respect of Palestine and undertaken to exercise it on behalf of the League of Nations in conformity with the following provisions; and

Whereas by the aforementioned Article 22 (paragraph 8), it is provided that the degree of authority, control or administration to be exercised by the Mandatory, not having been previously agreed upon by the Members of the League, shall be explicitly defined by the Council of the League of Nations;

Confirming the said Mandate, defines its terms as follows:

ARTICLE 1. The Mandatory shall have full powers of legislation and of administration, save as they may be limited by the terms of this Mandate.

ARTICLE 2. The Mandatory shall be responsible for placing the country under such political, administrative and economic conditions as will secure the establishment of the Jewish National Home, as laid down in the preamble, and the development of self-governing institutions, and also for safeguarding the civil and religious rights of all the inhabitants of Palestine, irrespective of race and religion.

ARTICLE 3. The Mandatory shall, so far as circumstances permit, encourage local autonomy.

ARTICLE 4. An appropriate Jewish Agency shall be recognized as a public body for the purpose of advising and co-operating with the Administration of Palestine in such economic, social and other matters as may affect the establishment of the Jewish National Home and the interests of the Jewish population in Palestine, and, subject always to the control of the Administration, to assist and take part in the development of the country.

The Zionist organization, so long as its organization and constitution are in the opinion of the Mandatory appropriate, shall be recognized as such agency. It shall take steps in consultation with His Britannic Majesty's Government to secure the co-operation of all Jews who are willing to assist in the establishment of the Jewish National Home.

ARTICLE 5. The Mandatory shall be responsible for seeing that no Palestine territory shall be ceded or leased to, or in any way placed under the control of, the Government of any foreign Power.

ARTICLE 6. The Administration of Palestine, while ensuring that the rights and position of other sections of the population are not prejudiced, shall facilitate Jewish immigration under suitable conditions and shall encourage, in co-operation with the Jewish Agency referred to in Article 4, close settlement by Jews on the land, including State lands and waste lands not required for public purposes.

ARTICLE 7. The Administration of Palestine shall be responsible for enacting a nationality law. There shall be included in this law provisions framed so as to facilitate the acquisition of Palestinian citizenship by Jews who take up their permanent residence in Palestine.

ARTICLE 13. All responsibility in connection with the Holy Places and religious buildings or sites in Palestine, including that of preserving existing rights and of securing free access to the Holy Places, religious buildings and sites and the free exercise of worship, while ensuring the requirements of public order and decorum, is assumed by the Mandatory, who shall be responsible solely to the League of Nations in all matters connected herewith, provided that nothing in this Article shall prevent the Mandatory from entering into such arrangements as he may deem reasonable with the Administration for the purpose of carrying the provisions of this Article into effect; and provided also that nothing in this Mandate shall be construed as conferring upon the Mandatory authority to interfere with the fabric of the management of purely Moslem sacred shrines, the immunities of which are guaranteed.

ARTICLE 14. A special Commission shall be appointed by the Mandatory to study, define and determine the rights and claims in connection with the Holy Places and the rights and claims relating to the different religious communities in Palestine. The method of nomination, the composition and the functions of this Commission shall be submitted to the Council of the League for its approval, and the Commission shall not be appointed or enter upon its functions without the approval of the Council.

ARTICLE 28. In the event of the termination of the Mandate hereby conferred upon the Mandatory, the Council of the League of Nations shall make such arrangements as may be deemed necessary for safe-guarding in perpetuity, under guarantee of the League, the rights secured by Articles 13 and 14, and shall use its influence for securing, under the guarantee of the League, that the Government of Palestine will fully honour the financial obligations legitimately incurred by the Administration of Palestine during the period of the Mandate, including the rights of public servants to pensions or gratuities.

* British White Paper, Cmd. 1785.

REPORT OF PALESTINE ROYAL COMMISSION (PEEL COMMISSION)*
(July 1937)

The Commission under Lord Peel was appointed in 1936. The following are extracts from recommendations made in Ch. XXII:

Having reached the conclusion that there is no possibility of solving the Palestine problem under the existing Mandate (or even under a scheme of cantonization), the Commission recommend the termination of the present Mandate on the basis of Partition and put forward a definite scheme which they consider to be practicable, honourable and just. The scheme is as follows:

The Mandate for Palestine should terminate and be replaced by a Treaty System in accordance with the precedent set in Iraq and Syria.

Under Treaties to be negotiated by the Mandatory with the Government of Transjordan and representatives of the Arabs of Palestine on the one hand, and with the Zionist Organization on the other, it would be declared that two sovereign independent States would shortly be established—(1) an Arab State consisting of Transjordan united with that part of Palestine allotted to the Arabs, (2) a Jewish State consisting of that part of Palestine allotted to the Jews. The Mandatory would undertake to support any requests for admission to the League of Nations made by the Governments of the Arab and Jewish States. The Treaties would include strict guarantees for the protection of minorities. Military Conventions would be attached to the Treaties.

A new Mandate should be instituted to execute the trust of maintaining the sanctity of Jerusalem and Bethlehem and ensuring free and safe access to them for all the world. An enclave should be demarcated to which this Mandate should apply, extending from a point north of Jerusalem to a point south of Bethlehem, and access to the sea should be provided by a corridor extending from Jerusalem to Jaffa. The policy of the Balfour Declaration would not apply to the Mandated Area.

The Jewish State should pay a subvention to the Arab State. A Finance Commission should be appointed to advise as to its amount and as to the division of the public debt of Palestine and other financial questions.

In view of the backwardness of Transjordan, Parliament should be asked to make a grant of £2,000,000 to the Arab State.

*Palestine Royal Commission: Report, 1937 (British Blue Book, Cmd. 5479).

WHITE PAPER*
(May 1939)

The main recommendations are extracted below:

10....His Majesty's Government make the following declaration of their intentions regarding the future government of Palestine:

(i) The objective of His Majesty's Government is the establishment within ten years of an independent Palestine State in such treaty relations with the United Kingdom as will provide satisfactorily for the commercial and strategic requirements of both countries in the future. This proposal for the establishment of the independent State would involve consultation with the Council of the League of Nations with a view to the termination of the Mandate.

(ii) The independent State should be one in which Arabs and Jews share in government in such a way as to ensure that the essential interests of each community are safeguarded.

(iii) The establishment of the independent State will be preceded by a transitional period throughout which His Majesty's Government will retain responsibility for the government of the country. During the transitional period the people of Palestine will be given an increasing part in the government of their country. Both sections of the population will have an opportunity to participate in the machinery of government, and the process will be carried on whether or not they both avail themselves of it.

(iv) As soon as peace and order have been sufficiently restored in Palestine steps will be taken to carry out this policy of giving the people of Palestine an increasing part in the government of their country, the objective being to place Palestinians in charge of all the Departments of Government, with the assistance of British advisers and subject to the control of the High Commissioner. With this object in view His Majesty's Government will be prepared immediately to arrange that Palestinians shall be placed in charge of certain Departments, with British advisers. The Palestinian heads of Departments will sit on the Executive Council, which advises the High Commissioner. Arab and Jewish representatives will be invited to serve as heads of Departments approximately in proportion to their respective populations. The number of Palestinians in charge of Departments will be increased as circumstances permit until all heads of Departments are Palestinians, exercising the administrative and advisory functions which are at present performed by British officials. When that stage is reached consideration will be given to the question of converting the Executive Council into a Council of Ministers with a consequential change in the status and functions of the Palestinian heads of Departments.

(v) His Majesty's Government make no proposals at this stage regarding the establishment of an elective legislature. Nevertheless they would regard this as an appropriate constitutional development, and, should public opinion in Palestine hereafter show itself in favour of such a development, they will be prepared, provided that local conditions permit, to establish the necessary machinery.

(vi) At the end of five years from the restoration of peace and order, an appropriate body representative of the people of Palestine and of His Majesty's Government will be set up to review the working of the constitutional arrangements during the transitional period and to consider and make recommendations regarding the Constitution of the independent Palestine State.

(vii) His Majesty's Government will require to be satisfied that in the treaty contemplated by sub-paragraph (i) or in the Constitution contemplated by sub-paragraph (vi) adequate provision has been made for:

(a) the security of, and freedom of access to, the Holy Places, and the protection of the interests and property of the various religious bodies

(b) the protection of the different communities in Palestine in accordance with the obligations of His Majesty's Government to both Arabs and Jews and for the special position in Palestine of the Jewish National Home

(c) such requirements to meet the strategic situation as may be regarded as necessary by His Majesty's Government in the light of the circumstances then existing

His Majesty's Government will also require to be satisfied that the interests of certain foreign countries in Palestine, for the preservation of which they are presently responsible, are adequately safeguarded.

(viii) His Majesty's Government will do everything in their power to create conditions which will enable the independent Palestine State to come into being within ten years. If, at the end of ten years, it appears to His Majesty's Government that, contrary to their hope, circumstances require the postponement of the establishment of the independent State, they will consult with representatives of the people of Palestine, the Council of the League of Nations and the neighbouring Arab States before deciding on such a postponement. If His Majesty's Government come to the conclusion that postponement is unavoidable, they will invite the co-operation of these parties in framing plans for the future with a view to achieving the desired objective at the earliest possible date.

14. ...they believe that they will be acting consistently with their Mandatory obligations to both Arabs and Jews, and in the manner best calculated to serve the interests of the whole people of Palestine by adopting the following proposals regarding immigration:

(i) Jewish immigration during the next five years will be at a rate which, if economic absorptive capacity permits, will bring the Jewish population up to approximately one-third of the total population of the country. Taking into account the expected natural increase of the Arab and Jewish populations, and the number of illegal Jewish immigrants now in the country, this would allow for the admission, as from the beginning of April this year, of some 75,000 immigrants over the next five years. These immigrants would, subject to the criterion of economic absorptive capacity, be admitted as follows:

(a) For each of the next five years a quota of 10,000 Jewish immigrants will be allowed, on the understanding that a shortage in any one year may be added to the quotas for subsequent years, within the five-year period, if economic absorptive capacity permits

(b) In addition, as a contribution towards the solution of the Jewish refugee problem, 25,000 refugees will be admitted as soon as the High Commissioner is satisfied that adequate provision for their maintenance is ensured, special consideration being given to refugee children and dependants

(ii) The existing machinery for ascertaining economic absorptive capacity will be retained, and the High Commissioner will have the ultimate responsibility for deciding the limits of economic capacity. Before each periodic decision is taken, Jewish and Arab representatives will be consulted.

(iii) After the period of five years no further Jewish immigration will be permitted unless the Arabs of Palestine are prepared to acquiesce in it.

(iv) His Majesty's Government are determined to check illegal immigration, and further preventive measures are being adopted. The numbers of any Jewish illegal immigrants who, despite these measures, may succeed in coming into the country and cannot be deported will be deducted from the yearly quotas.

15. His Majesty's Government are satisfied that, when the immigration over five years which is now contemplated has taken place they will not be justified in facilitating, nor will they be under any obligation to facilitate, the further development of the Jewish National Home by immigration regardless of the wishes of the Arab population.

16. The Administration of Palestine is required, under Article 6 of the Mandate, 'while ensuring that the rights and position of other sections of the population are not prejudiced', to encourage 'close settlement by Jews on the land', and no restriction has been imposed hitherto on the transfer of land from Arabs to Jews. The Reports of several expert Commissions have indicated that, owing to the natural growth of the Arab population and the steady sale in recent years of Arab land to Jews, there is now in certain areas no room for further transfers of Arab land, whilst in some other areas such transfers of land must be restricted if Arab cultivators are to maintain their existing standard of life and a considerable landless Arab population is not soon to be created. In these circumstances, the High Commissioner will be given general powers to prohibit and regulate transfers of land. These powers will date from the publication of this statement of Policy and the High Commissioner will retain them throughout the transitional period.

17. The policy of the Government will be directed towards the development of the land and the improvement, where possible, of methods of cultivation. In the light of such development it

BILTMORE PROGRAMME*
(11 May 1942)

Representatives of Zionist organizations, including the World Zionist Organization and the Jewish Agency, attended a six-day Extraordinary Zionist Conference, held at the Biltmore Hotel in New York, USA.

The following programme was approved by a Zionist Conference held in the Biltmore Hotel, New York City:

1. American Zionists assembled in this Extraordinary Conference reaffirm their unequivocal devotion to the cause of democratic freedom and international justice to which the people of the United States, allied with the other United Nations, have dedicated themselves, and give expression to their faith in the ultimate victory of humanity and justice over lawlessness and brute force.

2. This Conference offers a message of hope and encouragement to their fellow Jews in the Ghettos and concentration camps of Hitler-dominated Europe and prays that their hour of liberation may not be far distant.

3. The Conference sends its warmest greetings to the Jewish Agency Executive in Jerusalem, to the Va'ad Leumi, and to the whole Yishuv in Palestine, and expresses its profound admiration for their steadfastness and achievements in the face of peril and great difficulties...

4. In our generation, and in particular in the course of the past twenty years, the Jewish people have awakened and transformed their ancient homeland; from 50,000 at the end of the last war their numbers have increased to more than 500,000. They have made the waste places to bear fruit and the desert to blossom. Their pioneering achievements in agriculture and in industry, embodying new patterns of co-operative endeavour, have written a notable page in the history of colonization.

5. In the new values thus created, their Arab neighbours in Palestine have shared. The Jewish people in its own work of national redemption welcomes the economic, agricultural and national development of the Arab peoples and states. The Conference reaffirms the stand previously adopted at Congresses of the World Zionist Organization, expressing the readiness and the desire of the Jewish people for full co-operation with their Arab neighbours.

6. The Conference calls for the fulfilment of the original purpose of the Balfour Declaration and the Mandate which 'recognizing the historical connection of the Jewish people with Palestine' was to afford them the opportunity, as stated by President Wilson, to found there a Jewish Commonwealth.

The Conference affirms its unalterable rejection of the White Paper of May 1939 and denies its moral or legal validity. The White Paper seeks to limit, and in fact to nullify Jewish rights to immigration and settlement in Palestine, and, as stated by Mr Winston Churchill in the House of Commons in May 1939, constitutes 'a breach and repudiation of the Balfour Declaration'. The policy of the White Paper is cruel and indefensible in its denial of sanctuary to Jews fleeing from Nazi persecution; and at a time when Palestine has become a focal point in the war front of the United Nations, and Palestine Jewry must provide all available manpower for farm and factory and camp, it is in direct conflict with the interests of the allied war effort.

7. In the struggle against the forces of aggression and tyranny, of which Jews were the earliest victims, and which now menace the Jewish National Home, recognition must be given to the right of the Jews of Palestine to play their full part in the war effort and in the defence of their country, through a Jewish military force fighting under its own flag and under the high command of the United Nations.

8. The Conference declares that the new world order that will follow victory cannot be established on foundations of peace, justice and equality, unless the problem of Jewish homelessness is finally solved.

The Conference urges that the gates of Palestine be opened; that the Jewish Agency be vested with control of immigration into Palestine and with the necessary authority for upbuilding the country, including the development of its unoccupied and uncultivated lands; and that Palestine be established as a Jewish Commonwealth integrated in the structure of the new democratic world.

Then and only then will the age-old wrong to the Jewish people be righted.

* Text supplied by courtesy of Josef Fraenkel.

UN GENERAL ASSEMBLY RESOLUTION ON THE FUTURE GOVERNMENT OF PALESTINE (PARTITION RESOLUTION)
(29 November 1947)

The General Assembly,

Having met in special session at the request of the mandatory Power to constitute and instruct a special committee to prepare for the consideration of the question of the future government of Palestine at the second regular session;

Having constituted a Special Committee and instructed it to investigate all questions and issues relevant to the problem of Palestine, and to prepare proposals for the solution of the problem, and

Having received and examined the report of the Special Committee (document A/364) including a number of unanimous recommendations and a plan of partition with economic union approved by the majority of the Special Committee,

Considers that the present situation in Palestine is one which is likely to impair the general welfare and friendly relations among nations;

Takes note of the declaration by the mandatory Power that it plans to complete its evacuation of Palestine by 1 August 1948;

Recommends to the United Kingdom, as the mandatory Power for Palestine, and to all other Members of the United Nations the adoption and implementation, with regard to the future government of Palestine, of the Plan of Partition with Economic Union set out below;

Requests that

(a) The Security Council take the necessary measures as provided for in the plan for its implementation;

(b) The Security Council consider, if circumstances during the transitional period require such consideration, whether the situation in Palestine constitutes a threat to the peace. If it decides that such a threat exists, and in order to maintain international peace and security, the Security Council should supplement the authorization of the General Assembly by taking measures, under Articles 39 and 41 of the Charter, to empower the United Nations Commission, as provided in this resolution, to exercise in Palestine the functions which are assigned to it by this resolution;

(c) The Security Council determine as a threat to the peace, breach of the peace or act of aggression, in accordance with Article 39 of the Charter, any attempt to alter by force the settlement envisaged by this resolution;

(d) The Trusteeship Council be informed of the responsibilities envisaged for it in this plan;

Calls upon the inhabitants of Palestine to take such steps as may be necessary on their part to put this plan into effect;

Appeals to all Governments and all peoples to refrain from taking any action which might hamper or delay the carrying out of these recommendations...

Official Records of the second session of the General Assembly, Resolutions, p. 131.

THE DECLARATION OF THE ESTABLISHMENT OF THE STATE OF ISRAEL
(14 May 1948)

The Declaration was approved and signed by the 33 members of the Va'ad Leumi (National Council) at a meeting held in Tel Aviv on 14 May 1948, prior to the expiry of the Mandate for Palestine.

The Land of Israel was the birthplace of the Jewish people. Here their spiritual, religious and political identity was shaped. Here they first attained to statehood, created cultural values of national and universal significance and gave to the world the eternal Book of Books.

After being forcibly exiled from their land, the people kept faith with it throughout their Dispersion and never ceased to pray and hope for their return to it and for the restoration in it of their political freedom.

Impelled by this historic and traditional attachment, Jews strove in every successive generation to re-establish themselves in their ancient homeland. In recent decades they returned in their masses. Pioneers, defiant returnees, and defenders, they made deserts bloom, revived the Hebrew language, built villages and towns, and created a thriving community controlling its own economy and culture, loving peace but knowing how to defend itself, bringing the blessings of progress to all the country's inhabitants, and aspiring towards independent nationhood.

In the year 5657 (1897), at the summons of the spiritual father of the Jewish State, Theodor Herzl, the First Zionist Congress convened and proclaimed the right of the Jewish people to national rebirth in its own country.

This right was recognized in the Balfour Declaration of the 2nd November, 1917, and reaffirmed in the Mandate of the League of Nations which, in particular, gave international sanction to the historic connection between the Jewish people and Eretz-Israel and to the right of the Jewish people to rebuild its National Home.

The catastrophe which recently befell the Jewish people—the massacre of millions of Jews in Europe—was another clear demonstration of the urgency of solving the problem of its homelessness by re-establishing in Eretz-Israel the Jewish State, which would open the gates of the homeland wide to every Jew and confer upon the Jewish people the status of a fully privileged member of the community of nations.

Survivors of the Nazi holocaust in Europe, as well as Jews from other parts of the world, continued to migrate to Eretz-Israel, undaunted by difficulties, restrictions and dangers, and never ceased to assert their right to a life of dignity, freedom and honest toil in their national homeland.

In the Second World War the Jewish community of this country contributed its full share to the struggle of the freedom- and peace-loving nations against the forces of Nazi wickedness and, by the blood of its soldiers and its war effort, gained the right to be reckoned among the peoples who founded the United Nations.

On the 29th November, 1947, the United Nations General Assembly passed a resolution calling for the establishment of a Jewish State in Eretz-Israel; the General Assembly required the inhabitants of Eretz-Israel to take such steps as were necessary on their part for the implementation of that resolution. This recognition by the United Nations of the right of the Jewish people to establish their State is irrevocable.

This right is the natural right of the Jewish people to be masters of their own fate, like all other nations, in their own sovereign State.

Accordingly we, members of the National Council, representatives of the Jewish Community of Eretz-Israel and of the Zionist Movement, are here assembled on the day of the termination of the British Mandate over Eretz-Israel and, by virtue of our natural and historic right and on the strength of the resolution of the United Nations General Assembly, hereby declare the establishment of a Jewish state in Eretz-Israel, to be known as the State of Israel.

We declare that, with effect from the moment of the termination of the Mandate being tonight, the eve of Sabbath, the 6th Iyar, 5708 (15th May, 1948), until the establishment of the elected, regular authorities of the State in accordance with the Constitution which shall be adopted by the Elected Constituent Assembly not later than the 1st October 1948, the People's Council shall act as a Provisional Council of State, and its executive organ, the People's Administration, shall be the Provisional Government of the Jewish State, to be called 'Israel'.

The State of Israel will be open for Jewish immigration and for the Ingathering of the Exiles; it will foster the development of the country for the benefit of all its inhabitants; it will be based on freedom, justice and peace as envisaged by the prophets of Israel; it will ensure complete equality of social and political rights to all its inhabitants irrespective of religion, race or sex; it will guarantee freedom of religion, conscience, language, education and culture; it will safeguard the Holy Places of all religions; and it will be faithful to the principles of the Charter of the United Nations.

The State of Israel is prepared to co-operate with the agencies and representatives of the United Nations in implementing the resolution of the General Assembly of the 29th November, 1947, and will take steps to bring about the economic union of the whole of Eretz-Israel.

We appeal to the United Nations to assist the Jewish people in the building-up of its State and to receive the State of Israel into the community of nations.

We appeal—in the very midst of the onslaught launched against us now for months—to the Arab inhabitants of the State of Israel to preserve peace and participate in the upbuilding of the State on the basis of full and equal citizenship and due representation in all its provisional and permanent institutions.

We extend our hand to all neighbouring states and their peoples in an offer of peace and good neighbourliness, and appeal to them to establish bonds of co-operation and mutual help with the sovereign Jewish people settled in its own land. The State of Israel is prepared to do its share in a common effort for the advancement of the entire Middle East.

We appeal to the Jewish people throughout the Diaspora to rally round the Jews of Eretz-Israel in the tasks of immigration and upbuilding and to stand by them in the great struggle for the realization of the age-old dream—the redemption of Israel.

Placing our trust in the Almighty, we affix our signatures to this proclamation at this session of the provisional Council of State, on the soil of the Homeland, in the city of Tel Aviv, on this Sabbath eve, the 5th day of Iyar, 5708 (14th May, 1948).

English version as published on the website of the Knesset (www.knesset.gov.il/docs/eng/megilat_eng.htm).

UN GENERAL ASSEMBLY RESOLUTION 194 (III)
(11 December 1948)

The resolution's terms have been reaffirmed every year since 1948.

11. *Resolves* that the refugees wishing to return to their homes and live at peace with their neighbours should be permitted to do so at the earliest practicable date, and that compensation should be paid for the property of those choosing not to return and for the loss of or damage to property which, under principles of international law or in equity, should be made good by the Governments or authorities responsible; ...

Official Records of the third session of the General Assembly, Part I, Resolutions, p. 21.

UN GENERAL ASSEMBLY ON THE ADMISSION OF ISRAEL TO MEMBERSHIP IN THE UNITED NATIONS
(11 May 1949)

Having received the report of the Security Council on the application of Israel for membership of the United Nations,

Noting that, in the judgement of the Security Council, Israel is a peace-loving State and is able and willing to carry out the obligations contained in the Charter,

Noting that the Security Council has recommended to the General Assembly that it admit Israel to membership in the United Nations,

Noting furthermore the declaration by the State of Israel that it 'unreservedly accepts the obligations of the United Nations Charter and undertakes to honour them for the day when it becomes a Member of the United Nations',

Recalling its resolutions of 29 November 1947 and 11 December 1948 and taking note of the declarations and explanations made by the representative of the Government of Israel before the *ad hoc* Political Committee in respect of the implementation of the said resolutions,

The General Assembly,

Acting in discharge of its functions under Article 4 of the Charter and rule 125 of its rules of procedure,

1. *Decides* that Israel is a peace-loving State which accepts the obligations contained in the Charter and is able and willing to carry out those obligations;
2. *Decides* to admit Israel to membership in the United Nations.

Official Records of the third session of the General Assembly, Resolutions, p. 18.

UN GENERAL ASSEMBLY RESOLUTION ON THE INTERNATIONALIZATION OF JERUSALEM
(9 December 1949)

The General Assembly,
Having regard to its resolution 181 (II) of 29 November 1947 and 194 (III) of 11 December 1948,
Having studied the reports of the United Nations Conciliation Commission for Palestine set up under the latter resolution,
I. Decides
In relation to Jerusalem,
Believing that the principles underlying its previous resolutions concerning this matter, and in particular its resolution of 29 November 1947, represent a just and equitable settlement of the question,
1. To restate, therefore, its intention that Jerusalem should be placed under a permanent international regime, which should envisage appropriate guarantees for the protection of the Holy Places, both within and outside Jerusalem, and to confirm specifically the following provisions of General Assembly resolution 181 (II): (1) The City of Jerusalem shall be established as a *corpus separatum* under a special international regime and shall be administered by the United Nations; (2) The Trusteeship Council shall be designated to discharge the responsibilities of the Administering Authority...; and (3) The City of Jerusalem shall include the present municipality of Jerusalem plus the surrounding villages and towns, the most eastern of which shall be Abu Dis; the most southern, Bethlehem; the most western, Ein Karim (including also the built-up area of Motsa); and the most northern, Shu'fat, as indicated on the attached sketchmap;... [*Map not reproduced here—Ed.*]

Official Records of the fourth session of the General Assembly, Resolutions, p. 25.

LAW OF RETURN 5710-1950
(5 July 1950)

Legislation guaranteeing the right of immigration into Israel for all Jews was approved by the Knesset on 5 July 1950. [Subsequent amendments are not reproduced here.]

1. Every Jew has the right to come to this country as an oleh.
2. (a) Aliyah shall be by oleh's visa; (b) An oleh's visa shall be granted to every Jew who has expressed his desire to settle in Israel, unless the Minister of Immigration is satisfied that the applicant
(1) is engaged in an activity directed against the Jewish people; or
(2) is likely to endanger public health or the security of the State.
3.
(a) A Jew who has come to Israel and subsequent to his arrival has expressed his desire to settle in Israel may, while still in Israel, receive an oleh's certificate.
(b) The restrictions specified in section 2 (b) shall apply also to the grant of an oleh's certificate, but a person shall not be regarded as endangering public health on account of an illness contracted after his arrival in Israel.
4. Every Jew who has immigrated into this country before the coming into force of this Law, and every Jew who was born in this country, whether before or after the coming into force of this Law, shall be deemed to be a person who has come to this country as an oleh under this Law.
5. The Minister of Immigration is charged with the implementation of this Law and may make regulations as to any matter relating to such implementation and also as to the grant of oleh's visas and oleh's certificates to minors up to the age of 18 years.

UN SECURITY COUNCIL RESOLUTION 242
(22 November 1967)

The Security Council,
Expressing its continued concern with the grave situation in the Middle East,
Emphasizing the inadmissibility of the acquisition of territory by war and the need to work for a just and lasting peace in which every state in the area can live in security,
Emphasizing further that all Member States in their acceptance of the Charter of the United Nations have undertaken a commitment to act in accordance with Article 2 of the Charter,
1. *Affirms* that the fulfilment of Charter principles requires the establishment of a just and lasting peace in the Middle East which should include the application of both the following principles:
(i) Withdrawal of Israeli armed forces from territories occupied in the recent conflict;
(ii) Termination of all claims or states of belligerency and respect for the acknowledgement of the sovereignty, territorial integrity and political independence of every State in the area and their right to live in peace within secure and recognized boundaries free from threats or acts of force;
2. *Affirms further* the necessity
(a) For guaranteeing freedom of navigation through international waterways in the area;
(b) For achieving a just settlement of the refugee problem;
(c) For guaranteeing the territorial inviolability and political independence of every State in the area, through measures including the establishment of demilitarized zones;
3. *Requests* the Secretary-General to designate a Special Representative to proceed to the Middle East to establish and maintain contacts with the States concerned in order to promote agreement and assist efforts to achieve a peaceful and accepted settlement in accordance with the provisions and principles in this resolution;
4. *Requests* the Secretary-General to report to the Security Council on the progress of the efforts of the Special Representative as soon as possible.

UN Document S/RES/242 (1967).

UN SECURITY COUNCIL RESOLUTION 252
(21 May 1968)

Resolution 252 was the first Security Council resolution dealing specifically with the issue of Jerusalem. It was adopted by 13 votes to none; the USA and Canada abstained in the vote. [The two General Assembly resolutions, the Jordanian Permanent Representative's letter and the report of the Secretary-General, to which the introductory section refers, are not reproduced here.]

The Security Council,
Recalling General Assembly resolutions 2253 (ES-V) of 4 July 1967 and 2254 (ES-V) of 14 July 1967,
Having considered the letter of the Permanent Representative of Jordan on the situation in Jerusalem (S/8560) and the report of the Secretary-General (S/8146),
Having heard the statements made before the Council,
Noting that since the adoption of the above-mentioned resolutions Israel has taken further measures and actions in contravention of those resolutions,
Bearing in mind the need to work for a just and lasting peace,
Reaffirming that acquisition of territory by military conquest is inadmissible,
1. *Deplores* the failure of Israel to comply with the General Assembly resolutions mentioned above;
2. *Considers* that all legislative and administrative measures and actions taken by Israel, including expropriation of land and properties thereon, which tend to change the legal status of Jerusalem are invalid and cannot change that status;
3. *Urgently calls upon* Israel to rescind all such measures already taken and to desist forthwith from taking any further action which tends to change the status of Jerusalem;
4. *Requests* the Secretary-General to report to the Security Council on the implementation of the present resolution.

UN Document S/RES/252 (1968)

PALESTINIAN NATIONAL CHARTER (PLO COVENANT)

Resolutions of the Palestine National Council, July 1–17, 1968.

In September 1993 the Chairman of the Palestine Liberation Organization (PLO), Yasser Arafat, declared those articles of the PLO Covenant which deny Israel's right to exist or are inconsistent with the PLO's commitments to Israel under the terms of subsequent accords to be invalid. Revision of those articles, presented here in italics, was to be undertaken as part of the ongoing peace process. In April 1996 the Palestine National Council (PNC) voted to amend the PLO Covenant, thereby removing all clauses demanding the destruction of Israel. In December 1998, at a meeting of the PNC attended by US President Bill Clinton, the removal from the Covenant of all such clauses was reaffirmed.

The following is the complete and unabridged text of the Palestinian National Covenant, as published officially in English by the PLO.

Article I
Palestine is the homeland of the Arab Palestinian people; it is an indivisible part of the Arab homeland, and the Palestinian people are an integral part of the Arab nation.

Article II
Palestine, with the boundaries it had during the British Mandate, is an indivisible territorial unit.

Article III
The Palestinian Arab people possess the legal right to their homeland and have the right to determine their destiny after achieving the liberation of their country in accordance with their wishes and entirely of their own accord and will.

Article IV
The Palestinian identity is a genuine, essential, and inherent characteristic; it is transmitted from parents to children. The Zionist occupation and the dispersal of the Palestinian Arab people, through the disasters which befell them, do not make them lose their Palestinian identity and their membership in the Palestinian community, nor do they negate them.

Article V
The Palestinians are those Arab nationals who, until 1947, normally resided in Palestine regardless of whether they were evicted from it or have stayed there. Anyone born, after that date, of a Palestinian father—whether inside Palestine or outside it—is also a Palestinian.

Article VI
The Jews who had normally resided in Palestine until the beginning of the Zionist invasion will be considered Palestinians.

Article VII
That there is a Palestinian community and that it has material, spiritual, and historical connection with Palestine are indisputable facts. It is a national duty to bring up individual Palestinians in an Arab revolutionary manner. All means of information and education must be adopted in order to acquaint the Palestinian with his country in the most profound manner, both spiritual and material, that is possible. He must be prepared for the armed struggle and ready to sacrifice his wealth and his life in order to win back his homeland and bring about its liberation.

Article VIII
The phase in their history, through which the Palestinian people are now living, is that of national (watani) struggle for the liberation of Palestine. Thus the conflicts among the Palestinian national forces are secondary, and should be ended for the sake of the basic conflict that exists between the forces of Zionism and of imperialism on the one hand, and the Palestinian Arab people on the other. On this basis the Palestinian masses, regardless of whether they are residing in the national homeland or in diaspora (mahajir) constitute—both their organizations and the individuals—one national front working for the retrieval of Palestine and its liberation through armed struggle.

Article IX
Armed struggle is the only way to liberate Palestine. This is the overall strategy, not merely a tactical phase. The Palestinian Arab people assert their absolute determination and firm resolution to continue their armed struggle and to work for an armed popular revolution for the liberation of their country and their return to it. They also assert their right to normal life in Palestine and to exercise their right to self-determination and sovereignty over it.

Article X
Commando action constitutes the nucleus of the Palestinian popular liberation war. This requires its escalation, comprehensiveness, and the mobilization of all the Palestinian popular and educational efforts and their organization and involvement in the armed Palestinian revolution. It also requires the achieving of unity for the national (watani) struggle among the different groupings of the Palestinian people, and between the Palestinian people and the Arab masses, so as to secure the continuation of the revolution, its escalation, and victory.

Article XI
The Palestinians will have three mottoes: national (*wataniyya*) unity, national (*qawmiyya*) mobilization, and liberation.

Article XII
The Palestinian people believe in Arab unity. In order to contribute their share toward the attainment of that objective, however, they must, at the present stage of their struggle, safeguard their Palestinian identity and develop their consciousness of that identity, and oppose any plan that may dissolve or impair it.

Article XIII
Arab unity and the liberation of Palestine are two complementary objectives, the attainment of either of which facilitates the attainment of the other. Thus, Arab unity leads to the liberation of Palestine, the liberation of Palestine leads to Arab unity; and work towards the realization of one objective proceeds side by side with work towards the realization of the other.

Article XIV
The destiny of the Arab nation, and indeed Arab existence itself, depend upon the destiny of the Palestine cause. From this interdependence springs the Arab nation's pursuit of, and striving for, the liberation of Palestine. The people of Palestine play the role of the vanguard in the realization of this sacred (*qawmi*) goal.

Article XV
The liberation of Palestine, from an Arab viewpoint, is a national (qawmi) duty and it attempts to repel the Zionist and imperialist aggression against the Arab homeland, and aims at the elimination of Zionism in Palestine. Absolute responsibility for this falls upon the Arab nation—peoples and governments—with the Arab people of Palestine in the vanguard. Accordingly, the Arab nation must mobilize all its military, human, moral, and spiritual capabilities to participate actively with the Palestinian people in the liberation of Palestine. It must, particularly in the phase of the armed Palestinian revolution, offer and furnish the Palestinian people with all possible help, and material and human support, and make available to them the means and opportunities that will enable them to continue to carry out their leading role in the armed revolution, until they liberate their homeland.

Article XVI
The liberation of Palestine, from a spiritual point of view, will provide the Holy Land with an atmosphere of safety and tranquility, which in turn will safeguard the country's religious sanctuaries and guarantee freedom of worship and of visit to all, without discrimination of race, color, language, or religion. Accordingly, the people of Palestine look to all spiritual forces in the world for support.

Article XVII
The liberation of Palestine, from a human point of view, will restore to the Palestinian individual his dignity, pride, and

freedom. Accordingly the Palestinian Arab people look forward to the support of all those who believe in the dignity of man and his freedom in the world.

Article XVIII
The liberation of Palestine, from an international point of view, is a defensive action necessitated by the demands of self-defense. Accordingly the Palestinian people, desirous as they are of the friendship of all people, look to freedom-loving, and peace-loving states for support in order to restore their legitimate rights in Palestine, to re-establish peace and security in the country, and to enable its people to exercise national sovereignty and freedom.

Article XIX
The partition of Palestine in 1947 and the establishment of the state of Israel are entirely illegal, regardless of the passage of time, because they were contrary to the will of the Palestinian people and to their natural right in their homeland, and inconsistent with the principles embodied in the Charter of the United Nations, particularly the right to self-determination.

Article XX
The Balfour Declaration, the Mandate for Palestine, and everything that has been based upon them, are deemed null and void. Claims of historical or religious ties of Jews with Palestine are incompatible with the facts of history and the true conception of what constitutes statehood. Judaism, being a religion, is not an independent nationality. Nor do Jews constitute a single nation with an identity of its own; they are citizens of the states to which they belong.

Article XXI
The Arab Palestinian people, expressing themselves by the armed Palestinian revolution, reject all solutions which are substitutes for the total liberation of Palestine and reject all proposals aiming at the liquidation of the Palestinian problem, or its internationalization.

Article XXII
Zionism is a political movement organically associated with international imperialism and antagonistic to all action for liberation and to progressive movements in the world. It is racist and fanatic in its nature, aggressive, expansionist, and colonial in its aims, and fascist in its methods. Israel is the instrument of Zionist movement, and geographical base for world imperialism placed strategically in the midst of the Arab homeland to combat the hopes of the Arab nation for liberation, unity, and progress. Israel is a constant source of threat vis-à-vis peace in the Middle East and the whole world. Since the liberation of Palestine will destroy the Zionist and imperialist presence and will contribute to the establishment of peace in the Middle East, the Palestinian people look for the support of all the progressive and peaceful forces and urge them all, irrespective of their affiliations and beliefs, to offer the Palestinian people all aid and support in their just struggle for the liberation of their homeland.

Article XXIII
The demand of security and peace, as well as the demand of right and justice, require all states to consider Zionism an illegitimate movement, to outlaw its existence, and to ban its operations, in order that friendly relations among peoples may be preserved, and the loyalty of citizens to their respective homelands safeguarded.

Article XXIV
The Palestinian people believe in the principles of justice, freedom, sovereignty, self-determination, human dignity, and in the right of all peoples to exercise them.

Article XXV
For the realization of the goals of this Charter and its principles, the Palestine Liberation Organization will perform its role in the liberation of Palestine in accordance with the Constitution of this Organization.

Article XXVI
The Palestine Liberation Organization, representative of the Palestinian revolutionary forces, is responsible for the Palestinian Arab people's movement in its struggle—to retrieve its homeland, liberate and return to it and exercise the right to self-determination in it—in all military, political, and financial fields and also for whatever may be required by the Palestine case on the inter-Arab and international levels.

Article XXVII
The Palestine Liberation Organization shall co-operate with all Arab states, each according to its potentialities; and will adopt a neutral policy among them in the light of the requirements of the war of liberation; and on this basis it shall not interfere in the internal affairs of any Arab state.

Article XXVIII
The Palestinian Arab people assert the genuineness and independence of their national (wataniyya) revolution and reject all forms of intervention, trusteeship, and subordination.

Article XXIX
The Palestinian people possess the fundamental and genuine legal right to liberate and retrieve their homeland. The Palestinian people determine their attitude toward all states and forces on the basis of the stands they adopt vis-à-vis to the Palestinian revolution to fulfil the aims of the Palestinian people.

Article XXX
Fighters and carriers of arms in the war of liberation are the nucleus of the popular army which will be the protective force for the gains of the Palestinian Arab people.

Article XXXI
The Organization shall have a flag, an oath of allegiance, and an anthem. All this shall be decided upon in accordance with a special regulation.

Article XXXII
Regulations, which shall be known as the Constitution of the Palestinian [sic] Liberation Organization, shall be annexed to this Charter. It will lay down the manner in which the Organization, and its organs and institutions, shall be constituted; the respective competence of each; and the requirements of its obligation under the Charter.

Article XXXIII
This Charter shall not be amended save by [vote of] a majority of two-thirds of the total membership of the National Congress of the Palestine Liberation Organization [taken] at a special session convened for that purpose.

English rendition as published in Basic Political Documents of the Armed Palestinian Resistance Movement; Leila S. Kadi (Ed.), Palestine Research Centre, Beirut, December 1969, pp. 137–141.

UN SECURITY COUNCIL RESOLUTION ON JERUSALEM
(25 September 1971)

The resolution, No. 298 (1971), was passed nemine contradicente, *with the abstention of Syria.*

The Security Council,

Recalling its resolutions 252 (1968) of 21 May 1968, and 267 (1969) of 3 July 1969, and the earlier General Assembly resolution 2253 (ES-V) and 2254 (ES-V) of 4 and 14 July 1967, concerning measures and actions by Israel designed to change the status of the Israeli-occupied section of Jerusalem,

Having considered the letter of the Permanent Representative of Jordan on this situation in Jerusalem and the reports of the Secretary-General, and having heard the statements of the parties concerned in the question,

Recalling the principle that acquisition of territory by military conquest is inadmissible,

Noting with concern the non-compliance by Israel with the above-mentioned resolutions,

Noting with concern also that since the adoption of the above-mentioned resolutions Israel has taken further measures designed to change the status and character of the occupied section of Jerusalem,

1. *Reaffirms* its resolutions 252 (1968) and 267 (1969);

2. *Deplores* the failure of Israel to respect the previous resolutions adopted by the United Nations concerning measures and actions by Israel purporting to affect the status of the City of Jerusalem;

3. *Confirms* in the clearest possible terms that all legislative and administrative actions taken by Israel to change the status of the City of Jerusalem, including expropriation of land and properties, transfer of populations and legislation aimed at the incorporation of the occupied section, are totally invalid and cannot change that status;

4. *Urgently calls upon* Israel to rescind all previous measures and actions and to take no further steps in the occupied section of Jerusalem which may purport to change the status of the City, or which would prejudice the rights of the inhabitants and the interests of the international community, or a just and lasting peace;

5. *Requests* the Secretary-General, in consultation with the President of the Security Council and using such instrumentalities as he may choose, including a representative or a mission, to report to the Council as appropriate and in any event within 60 days on the implementation of the present resolution.

UN Document S/RES/298 (1971).

UN SECURITY COUNCIL RESOLUTION 338
(22 October 1973)

UN Resolutions between 1967 and October 1973 reaffirmed Security Council Resolution 242. In an attempt to end the fourth Middle East war, which had broken out between the Arabs and Israel on 6 October 1973, the UN Security Council passed the following Resolution:

The Security Council,

1. *Calls upon* all parties to the present fighting to cease all firing and terminate all military activity immediately, not later than 12 hours after the moment of the adoption of the decision, in the positions they now occupy;

2. *Calls upon* the parties concerned to start immediately after the ceasefire the implementation of Security Council Resolution 242 (1967) in all of its parts;

3. *Decides that*, immediately and concurrently with the ceasefire negotiations start between the parties concerned under appropriate auspices aimed at establishing a just and durable peace in the Middle East.

UN Document PR/73/29 (1973).

UN SECURITY COUNCIL RESOLUTION 340
(25 October 1973)

The Security Council,

Recalling its Resolutions 338 (1973) of 22 October 1973 and 339 (1973) of 23 October 1973,

Noting with regret the reported repeated violations of the ceasefire in non-compliance with Resolutions 338 (1973) and 339 (1973),

Noting with concern from the Secretary-General's report that the UN military observers have not yet been enabled to place themselves on both sides of the ceasefire line,

1. *Demands* that an immediate and complete ceasefire be observed and that the parties withdraw to the positions occupied by them at 16.50 hours GMT on 22 October 1973;

2. *Requests* the Secretary-General as an immediate step to increase the number of UN military observers on both sides;

3. *Decides* to set up immediately under its authority a UN emergency force to be composed of personnel drawn from member states of the UN, except the permanent members of the Security Council, and requests the Secretary-General to report within 24 hours on the steps taken to this effect;

4. *Requests* the Secretary-General to report to the Council on an urgent and continuing basis on the state of implementation of this Resolution, as well as Resolutions 338 (1973) and 339 (1973);

5. *Requests* all member states to extend their full co-operation to the UN in the implementation of this Resolution, as well as Resolutions 338 (1973) and 339 (1973).

UN Document PR/73/31 (1973).

DISENGAGEMENT AGREEMENT BETWEEN SYRIAN AND ISRAELI FORCES AND PROTOCOL TO AGREEMENT ON UNITED NATIONS DISENGAGEMENT OBSERVER FORCE (UNDOF)
(signed in Geneva, 31 May 1974)

(Annex A)

A. Israel and Syria will scrupulously observe the cease-fire on land, sea and air and will refrain from all military actions against each other, from the time of signing this document in implementation of the United Nations Security Council Resolution 338 dated 22 October 1973.

B. The military forces of Israel and Syria will be separated in accordance with the following principles:

1. All Israeli military forces will be west of a line designated line A on the map attached hereto *(reproduced below)*, except in Quneitra (Kuneitra) area, where they will be west of a line A-1.

2. All territory east of line A will be under Syrian administration and Syrian civilians will return to this territory.

3. The area between line A and the line designated as line B on the attached map will be an area of separation. In this area will be stationed UNDOF established in accordance with the accompanying Protocol.

4. All Syrian military forces will be east of a line designated as line B on the attached map.

5. There will be two equal areas of limitation in armament and forces, one west of line A and one east of line B as agreed upon.

C. In the area between line A and line A-1 on the attached map there shall be no military forces.

D. *Paragraph D deals with practical details of signing and implementation.*

E. Provisions of paragraphs A, B and C shall be inspected by personnel of the United Nations comprising UNDOF under the Agreement.

F. *Paragraphs F and G deal with repatriation of prisoners and return of bodies of dead soldiers.*

H. This Agreement is not a peace agreement. It is a step towards a just and durable peace on the basis of the Security Council Resolution 338 dated 22 October 1973.

A Protocol to the Disengagement Agreement outlined the functions of the United Nations Disengagement Observer Force (UNDOF).

RESOLUTION OF CONFERENCE OF ARAB HEADS OF STATE
(Rabat, 28 October 1974)

The Conference of the Arab Heads of State:

1. *Affirms* the right of the Palestinian people to return to their homeland and to self-determination.

2. *Affirms* the right of the Palestinian people to establish an independent national authority, under the leadership of the PLO in its capacity as the sole legitimate representative of the Palestine people, over all liberated territory. The Arab States are pledged to uphold this authority, when it is established, in all spheres and at all levels.

3. *Supports* the PLO in the exercise of its national and international responsibilities, within the context of the principle of Arab solidarity.

4. *Invites* the kingdom of Jordan, Syria and Egypt to formalize their relations in the light of these decisions and in order that they be implemented.

5. *Affirms* the obligation of all Arab States to preserve Palestinian unity and not to interfere in Palestinian internal affairs.

Sources: *Le Monde: Problèmes Politiques et Sociaux*, 7 March 1975; *Arab Report and Record*.

UN GENERAL ASSEMBLY RESOLUTION 3236 (XXIX)
(22 November 1974)

The General Assembly,

Having considered the question of Palestine,

Having heard the statement of the Palestinian Liberation Organization, the representative of the Palestinian people,

Having also heard other statements made during the debate,

Deeply concerned that no just solution to the problem of Palestine has yet been achieved and recognizing that the

REGIONAL INFORMATION

Documents on Palestine

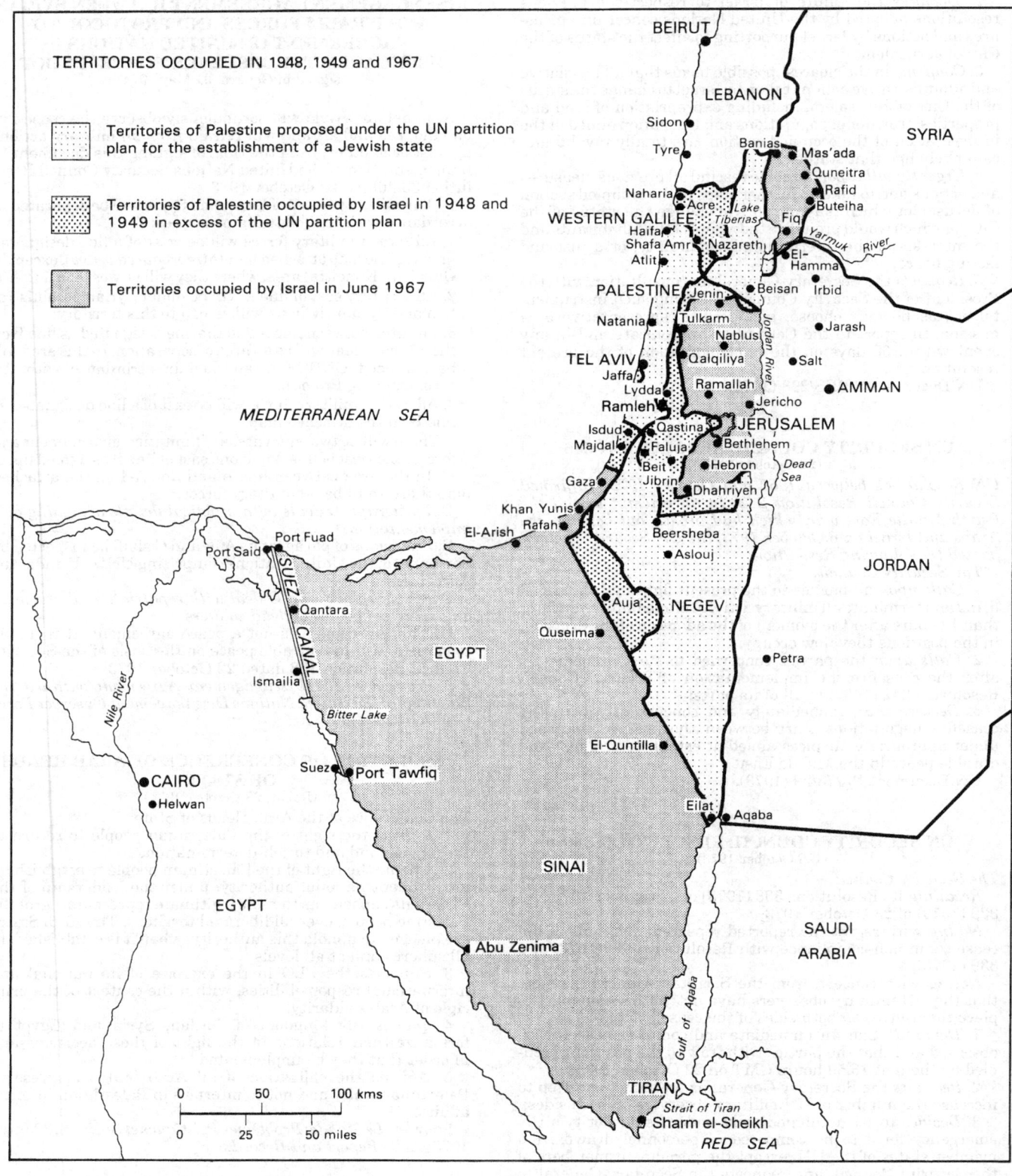

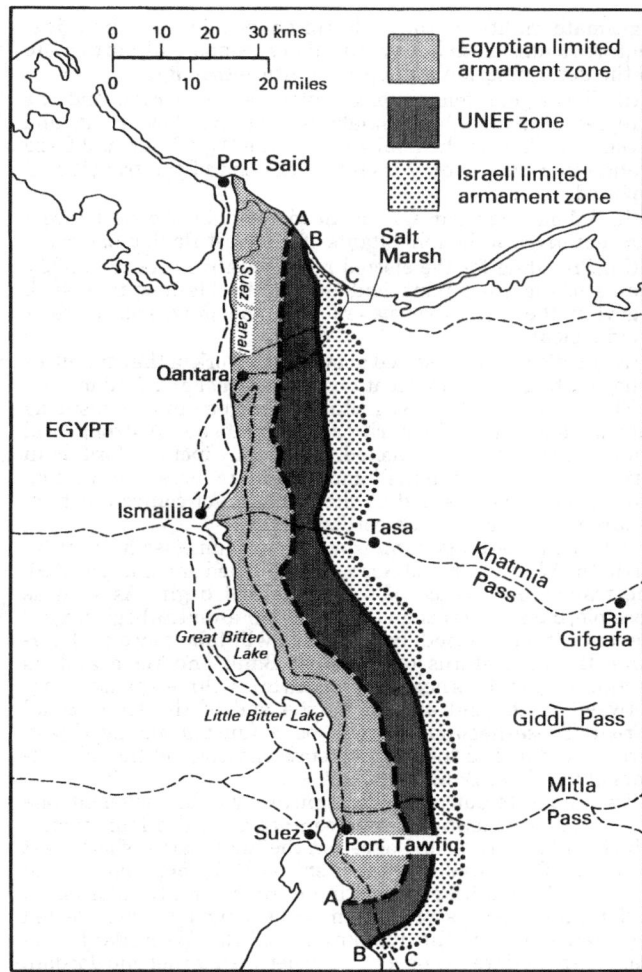

Disengagement Agreement of 18 January 1974 between Israel and Egypt

Disengagement Agreement of 31 May 1974 between Israel and Syria

problem of Palestine continues to endanger international peace and security,

Recognizing that the Palestinian people is entitled to self-determination in accordance with the Charter of the United Nations,

Expressing its grave concern that the Palestinian people has been prevented from enjoying its inalienable rights, in particular its right to self-determination,

Guided by the purposes and principles of the Charter,

Recalling its relevant resolutions which affirm the right of the Palestinian people to self-determination,

1. *Reaffirms* the inalienable rights of Palestinian people in Palestine, including:

(a) The right to self-determination without external interference

(b) The right to national independence and sovereignty

2. *Reaffirms also* the inalienable right of the Palestinians to return to their homes and property from which they have been displaced and uprooted, and calls for their return;

3. *Emphasizes* that full respect for and the realization of these inalienable rights of the Palestinian people are indispensable for the solution of the question of Palestine;

4. *Recognizes* that the Palestinian people is a principal party in the establishment of a just and durable peace in the Middle East;

5. *Further Recognizes* the right of the Palestinian people to regain its rights by all means in accordance with the purposes and principles of the Charter of the United Nations;

6. *Appeals* to all States and international organizations to extend their support to the Palestinian people in its struggle to restore its rights, in accordance with the Charter;

7. *Requests* the Secretary-General to establish contacts with the Palestinian Liberation Organization on all matters concerning the question of Palestine;

8. *Requests* the Secretary-General to report to the General Assembly at its thirtieth session on the implementation of the present resolution;

9. *Decides* to include the item 'Question of Palestine' in the provisional agenda of its thirtieth session.

UN Document BR/74/55 (1974).

CAMP DAVID: THE FRAMEWORK FOR PEACE IN THE MIDDLE EAST

Muhammad Anwar al-Sadat, President of the Arab Republic of Egypt, and Menachem Begin, Prime Minister of Israel, met with President Jimmy Carter of the USA at Camp David from 5 September to 17 September 1978, and agreed on the following framework for peace in the Middle East. They invited other parties to the Arab–Israeli conflict to adhere to it.

Preamble

The search for peace in the Middle East must be guided by the following:

The agreed basis for a peaceful settlement of the conflict between Israel and its neighbours in UN Security Council Resolution 242 in all its parts.

The historic initiative by President Sadat in visiting Jerusalem and the reception accorded to him by the Parliament, Government and people of Israel, and the reciprocal visit of Prime Minister Begin to Ismailia, the peace proposals made by both leaders, as well as the warm reception of these missions by the peoples of both countries, have created an unprecedented opportunity for peace which must not be lost if this generation and future generations are to be spared the tragedies of war.

The provisions of the Charter of the UN and the other accepted norms of international law and legitimacy now provide accepted standards for the conduct of relations between all states.

To achieve a relationship of peace, in the spirit of article 2 of the UN Charter, future negotiations between Israel and any neighbour prepared to negotiate peace and security with it, are necessary for the purpose of carrying out all the provisions and principles of Resolutions 242 and 338.

Peace requires respect for the sovereignty, territorial integrity and political independence of every state in the area and their right to live in peace within secure and recognized boundaries free from threats or acts of force. Progress toward that goal can accelerate movement towards a new era of reconciliation in the Middle East marked by co-operation in promoting economic development, in maintaining stability and in assuring security...

Framework

Taking these factors into account, the parties are determined to reach a just, comprehensive and durable settlement of the Middle East conflict through the conclusion of peace treaties based on Security Council Resolutions 242 and 338 in all their parts. Their purpose is to achieve peace and good neighbourly relations. They recognize that, for peace to endure, it must involve all those who have been most deeply affected by the conflict. They therefore agree that this framework as appropriate is intended by them to constitute a basis for peace not only between Egypt and Israel but also between Israel and each of its other neighbours which is prepared to negotiate peace with Israel on this basis. With that objective in mind, they have agreed to proceed as follows:

A. West Bank and Gaza

1. Egypt, Israel, Jordan and the representatives of the Palestinian people should participate in negotiations on the resolution of the Palestinian problem in all its aspects to achieve that objective, negotiations relating to the West Bank and Gaza should proceed in three stages.

(A) Egypt and Israel agree that, in order to ensure a peaceful and orderly transfer of authority, and taking into account the security concerns of all the parties, there should be transitional arrangements for the West Bank and Gaza for a period not exceeding five years. In order to provide full autonomy to the inhabitants, under these arrangements the Israeli military government and its civilian administration will be withdrawn as soon as a self-governing authority has been freely elected by the inhabitants of these areas to replace the existing military government.

To negotiate the details of transitional arrangement, the Government of Jordan will be invited to join the negotiations on the basis of this framework. These new arrangements should give due consideration to both the principle of self-government by the inhabitants of these territories and to the legitimate security concerns of the parties involved.

(B) Egypt, Israel and Jordan will agree on the modalities for establishing the elected self-governing authority in the West Bank and Gaza. The delegations of Egypt and Jordan may include Palestinians from the West Bank and Gaza or other Palestinians as mutually agreed. The parties will negotiate an agreement which will define the powers and responsibilities of the self-governing authority to be exercised in the West Bank and Gaza. A withdrawal of Israeli armed forces will take place and there will be a redeployment of the remaining Israeli forces into specified security locations.

The negotiations shall be based on all the provisions and principles of UN Security Council Resolution 242. The negotiations will resolve, among other matters, the location of the boundaries and the nature of the security arrangements. The solution from the negotiations must also recognize the legitimate rights of the Palestinian people and their just requirements. In this way, the Palestinians will participate in the determination of their own future through:

(i) The negotiations among Egypt, Israel, Jordan and the representatives of the inhabitants of the West Bank and Gaza to agree on the final status of the West Bank and Gaza and other outstanding issues by the end of the transitional period.

(ii) Submitting their agreement to a vote by the elected representatives of the inhabitants of the West Bank and Gaza.

(iii) Providing for the elected representatives of the inhabitants of the West Bank and Gaza to decide how they shall govern themselves consistent with the provisions of their agreement.

(iv) Participating as stated above in the work of the committee negotiating the peace treaty between Israel and Jordan.

The agreement will also include arrangements for assuring internal and external security and public order. A strong local police force will be established, which may include Jordanian citizens. In addition, Israeli and Jordanian forces will participate in joint patrols and in the manning of control posts to assure the security of the borders.

(C) When the self-governing authority (administrative council) in the West Bank and Gaza is established and inaugurated, the transitional period of five years will begin. As soon as possible, but not later than the third year after the beginning of the transitional period, negotiations will take place to determine the final status of the West Bank and Gaza and its relationship with its neighbours, and to conclude a peace treaty between Israel and Jordan by the end of the transitional period. These negotiations will be conducted among Egypt, Israel, Jordan and the elected representatives of the inhabitants of the West Bank and Gaza.

Two separate but related committees will be convened; one committee, consisting of representatives of the four parties which will negotiate and agree on the final status of the West Bank and Gaza, and its relationship with its neighbours, and the second committee, consisting of representatives of Israel and representatives of Jordan to be joined by the elected representatives of the inhabitants of the West Bank and Gaza, to negotiate the peace treaty between Israel and Jordan, taking into account the agreement reached on the final status of the West Bank and Gaza.

2. All necessary measures will be taken and provisions made to assure the security of Israel and its neighbours during the transitional period and beyond. To assist in providing such security, a strong local police force will be constituted by the self-governing authority. It will be composed of inhabitants of the West Bank and Gaza. The police will maintain continuing liaison on internal security matters with the designated Israeli, Jordanian and Egyptian officers.

3. During the transitional period, the representatives of Egypt, Israel, Jordan and the self-governing authority will constitute a continuing committee to decide by agreement on the modalities of admission of persons displaced from the West Bank and Gaza in 1967, together with necessary measures to prevent disruption and disorder. Other matters of common concern may also be dealt with by this committee.

4. Egypt and Israel will work with each other and with other interested parties to establish agreed procedures for a prompt, just and permanent implementation of the resolution of the refugee problem.

B. Egypt-Israel

1. Egypt and Israel undertake not to resort to the threat or the use of force to settle disputes. Any disputes shall be settled by peaceful means in accordance with the provisions of article 33 of the Charter of the UN.

2. In order to achieve peace between them, the parties agree to negotiate in good faith with a goal of concluding within three months from the signing of this framework a peace treaty between them, while inviting the other parties to the conflict to proceed simultaneously to negotiate and conclude similar peace treaties with a view to achieving a comprehensive peace in the area. The framework for the conclusion of a peace treaty between Egypt and Israel will govern the peace negotiations between them. The parties will agree on the modalities and the

timetable for the implementation of their obligations under the treaty.

Associated Principles

1. Egypt and Israel state that the principles and provisions described below should apply to peace treaties between Israel and each of its neighbours—Egypt, Jordan, Syria and Lebanon.

2. Signatories shall establish among themselves relationships normal to states at peace with one another. To this end, they should undertake to abide by all the provisions of the Charter of the UN. Steps to be taken in this respect include:
  (a) Full recognition;
  (b) Abolishing economic boycotts;
  (c) Guaranteeing that under their jurisdiction the citizens of the other parties shall enjoy the protection of the due process of law.

3. Signatories should explore possibilities for economic development in the context of final peace treaties, with the objective of contributing to the atmosphere of peace, co-operation, and friendship which is their common goal.

4. Claims commissions may be established for the mutual settlement of all financial claims.

5. The United States shall be invited to participate in the talks on matters related to the modalities of the implementation of the agreements and working out the time-table for the carrying out of the obligation of the parties.

6. The UN Security Council shall be requested to endorse the peace treaties and ensure that their provisions shall not be violated. The permanent members of the Security Council shall be requested to underwrite the peace treaties and ensure respect for their provisions. They shall also be requested to conform their policies and actions with the undertakings contained in this framework.

The second agreement signed at Camp David was a framework for the conclusion of a peace treaty between Egypt and Israel. The actual Treaty was signed on 26 March 1979, and is reproduced below.

THE PEACE TREATY BETWEEN EGYPT AND ISRAEL SIGNED IN WASHINGTON ON 26 MARCH 1979

The Government of the Arab Republic of Egypt and the Government of the State of Israel:

Preamble

Convinced of the urgent necessity of the establishment of a just, comprehensive and lasting peace in the Middle East in accordance with Security Council Resolutions 242 and 338;

Reaffirming their adherence to the 'Framework for Peace in the Middle East agreed at Camp David', dated 17 September 1978;

Noting that the aforementioned framework as appropriate is intended to constitute a basis for peace not only between Egypt and Israel but also between Israel and each of the other Arab neighbours which is prepared to negotiate peace with it on this basis;

Desiring to bring to an end the state of war between them and to establish a peace in which every state in the area can live in security;

Convinced that the conclusion of a treaty of peace between Egypt and Israel is an important step in the search for comprehensive peace in the area and for the attainment of the settlement of the Arab–Israeli conflict in all its aspects;

Inviting the other Arab parties to this dispute to join the peace process with Israel guided by and based on the principles of the aforementioned framework;

Desiring as well to develop friendly relations and co-operation between themselves in accordance with the UN Charter and the principles of international law governing international relations in times of peace;

Agree to the following provisions in the free exercise of their sovereignty, in order to implement the 'framework for the conclusion of a peace treaty between Egypt and Israel'.

Article I

1. The state of war between the parties will be terminated and peace will be established between them upon the exchange of instruments of ratification of this treaty.

2. Israel will withdraw all its armed forces and civilians from the Sinai behind the international boundary between Egypt and Mandated Palestine, as provided in the annexed protocol (annexed), and Egypt will resume the exercise of its full sovereignty over the Sinai.

3. Upon completion of the interim withdrawal provided for in Annex 1, the parties will establish normal and friendly relations, in accordance with Article III (3).

Article II

The permanent boundary between Egypt and Israel is the recognized international boundary between Egypt and the former Mandated Territory of Palestine, as shown on the map at Annex 2 (*not reproduced here—Ed.*), without prejudice to the issue of the status of the Gaza Strip. The parties recognize this boundary as inviolable. Each will respect the territorial integrity of the other, including their territorial waters and airspace.

Article III

1. The parties will apply between them the provisions of the Charter of the UN and the principles of international law governing relations among states in times of peace.
  In particular:
  A. They recognize and will respect each other's sovereignty, territorial integrity and political independence.
  B. They recognize and will respect each other's right to live in peace within their secure and recognized boundaries.
  C. They will refrain from the threat of use of force, directly or indirectly, against each other and will settle all disputes between them by peaceful means.

2. Each party undertakes to ensure that acts or threats of belligerency, hostility, or violence do not originate from and are not committed from within its territory, or by any forces subject to its control or by any other forces stationed on its territory, against the population, citizens or property of the other party. Each party also undertakes to refrain from organizing, instigating, inciting, assisting or participating in acts or threats of belligerency, hostility, subversion or violence against the other party, anywhere, and undertakes to ensure that perpetrators of such acts are brought to justice.

3. The parties agree that the normal relationship established between them will include full recognition, diplomatic, economic and cultural relations, termination of economic boycotts and discriminatory barriers to the free movement of people and goods, and will guarantee the mutual enjoyment by citizens of the due process of law. The process by which they undertake to achieve such a relationship parallel to the implementation of other provisions of this treaty is set out in the annexed protocol (Annex 3).

Article IV

1. In order to provide maximum security for both parties on the basis of reciprocity, agreed security arrangements will be established including limited force zones in Egyptian and Israeli territory, and UN forces and observers, described in detail as to nature and timing in Annex 1, and other security arrangements the parties may agree upon.

2. The parties agree to the stationing of UN personnel in areas described in Annex 1, the parties agree not to request withdrawal of the UN personnel and that these personnel will not be removed unless such removal is approved by the Security Council of the UN, with the affirmative vote of the five members, unless the parties otherwise agree.

3. A joint commission will be established to facilitate the implementation of the treaty, as provided for in Annex 1.

4. The security arrangements provided for in paragraphs 1 and 2 of this article may at the request of either party be reviewed and amended by mutual agreement of the parties.

Article V

Article V deals with rights of passage of shipping through the Suez Canal, the Strait of Tiran and the Gulf of Aqaba.

Article VI

1. This treaty does not affect and shall not be interpreted as affecting in any way the rights and obligations of the parties under the Charter of the UN.

2. The parties undertake to fulfil in good faith their obligations under this treaty, without regard to action or inaction of any other party and independently of any instrument external to this treaty.

3. They further undertake to take all the necessary measures for the application in their relations of the provisions of the multilateral conventions to which they are parties. Including the submission of appropriate notification to the Secretary-General of the UN and other depositories of such conventions.

4. The parties undertake not to enter into any obligation in conflict with this treaty.

5. Subject to Article 103 of the UN Charter, in the event of a conflict between the obligations of the parties under the present treaty and any of their other obligations, the obligations under this treaty will be binding and implemented.

Article VII

1. Disputes arising out of the application or interpretation of this treaty shall be resolved by negotiations.

2. Any such disputes which cannot be settled by negotiations shall be resolved by conciliation or submitted to arbitration.

Article VIII

The parties agree to establish a claims commission for the mutual settlement of all financial claims.

Article IX

1. This treaty shall enter into force upon exchange of instruments of ratification.

2. This treaty supersedes the agreement between Egypt and Israel of September 1975.

3. All protocols, annexes, and maps attached to this treaty shall be regarded as an integral part hereof.

4. The treaty shall be communicated to the Secretary-General of the UN for registration in accordance with the provisions of Article 102 of the Charter of the UN.

Annex 1—military and withdrawal arrangements

Israel will complete withdrawal of all its armed forces and civilians from Sinai within three years of the date of exchange of instruments of ratification of the treaty. The withdrawal will be accomplished in two phases, the first, within nine months, to a line east of Al Arish and Ras Muhammad; the second to behind the international boundary. During the three-year period, Egypt and Israel will maintain a specified military presence in four delineated security zones (see map—*not reproduced here—Ed.*), and the UN will continue its observation and supervisory functions. Egypt will exercise full sovereignty over evacuated territories in Sinai upon Israeli withdrawal. A joint commission will supervise the withdrawal, and security arrangements can be reviewed when either side asks but any change must be by mutual agreement.

Annex 2—maps (*not reproduced here*)

Annex 3—normalization of relations

Ambassadors will be exchanged upon completion of the interim withdrawal. All discriminatory barriers and economic boycotts will be lifted and, not later than six months after the completion of the interim withdrawal, negotiations for a trade and commerce agreement will begin. Free movement of each other's nationals and transport will be allowed and both sides agree to promote 'good neighbourly relations'. Egypt will use the airfields left by Israel near Al Arish, Rafah, Ras al-Naqb and Sharm al-Shaikh, only for civilian aircraft. Road, rail, postal, telephone, wireless and other forms of communications will be opened between the two countries on completion of interim withdrawal.

Exchange of Letters

Negotiations on the West Bank and Gaza—Negotiations on autonomy for the West Bank and Gaza will begin within one month of the exchange of the instruments of ratification. Jordan will be invited to participate and the Egyptian and Jordanian delegations may include Palestinians from the West Bank and Gaza, or other Palestinians as mutually agreed. If Jordan decides not to take part, the negotiations will be held by Egypt and Israel. The objective of the negotiations is the establishment of a self-governing authority in the West Bank and Gaza 'in order to provide full autonomy to the inhabitants'.

Egypt and Israel hope to complete negotiations within one year so that elections can be held as soon as possible. The self-governing authority elected will be inaugurated within one month of the elections at which point the five year transitional period will begin. The Israeli military Government and its civilian administration will be withdrawn, Israeli armed forces withdrawn and the remaining forces redeployed 'into specified security locations'.

UN SECURITY COUNCIL RESOLUTION ON ISRAELI SETTLEMENTS
(1 March 1980)

The resolution, No. 465, was adopted unanimously by the 15 members of the Council. The USA repudiated its vote in favour of the resolution on 3 March 1980.

The Security Council, taking note of the reports of the Commission of the Security Council established under resolution 446 (1979) to examine the situation relating to the settlements in the Arab territories occupied since 1967, including Jerusalem, contained in documents S/13450 and S/13679,

—Taking note also of letters from the permanent representative of Jordan (S/13801) and the permanent representative of Morocco, Chairman of the Islamic Group (S/13802),

—Strongly deploring the refusal by Israel to co-operate with the Commission and regretting its formal rejection of resolutions 446 (1979) and 452 (1979),

—Affirming once more that the fourth Geneva Convention relative to the protection of civilian persons in time of war of 12 August 1949 is applicable to the Arab territories occupied by Israel since 1967, including Jerusalem,

—Deploring the decision of the Government of Israel to officially support Israeli settlement in the Palestinian and other Arab territories occupied since 1967,

—Deeply concerned over the practices of the Israeli authorities in implementing that settlement policy in the occupied Arab territories, including Jerusalem, and its consequences for the local Arab and Palestinian population,

—Taking into account the need to consider measures for the impartial protection of private and public land and property, and water resources,

—Bearing in mind the specific status of Jerusalem and, in particular, the need for protection and preservation of the unique spiritual and religious dimension of the holy places in the city,

—Drawing attention to the grave consequences which the settlement policy is bound to have on any attempt to reach a comprehensive, just and lasting peace in the Middle East,

—Recalling pertinent Security Council resolutions, specifically resolutions 237 (1967) of 14 June 1967, 252 (1968) of 21 May 1968, 267 (1969) of 3 July 1969, 271 (1969) of 15 September 1969 and 298 (1971) of 25 September 1971, as well as the consensus statement made by the President of the Security Council on 11 November 1976,

—Having invited Mr Fahd Qawasmah, Mayor of Al-Khalil (Hebron), in the occupied territories, to supply it with information pursuant to rule 39 of provisional rules of procedure,

1. Commends the work done by the Commission in preparing the report contained in document S/13679,

2. Accepts the conclusions and recommendations contained in the above-mentioned report of the Commission,

3. Calls upon all parties, particularly the Government of Israel, to co-operate with the Commission,

4. Strongly deplores the decision of Israel to prohibit the free travel of Mayor Fahd Qawasmah in order to appear before the Security Council, and requests Israel to permit his free travel to the United Nations headquarters for that purpose,

5. Determines that all measures taken by Israel to change the physical character, demographic composition, institutional structure or status of the Palestinian and other Arab territories occupied since 1967, including Jerusalem, or any part thereof, have no legal validity and that Israel's policy and practices of settling parts of its population and new immigrants in those

territories constitute a flagrant violation of the Fourth Geneva Convention relative to the protection of civilian persons in time of war and also constitute a serious obstruction to achieving a comprehensive, just and lasting peace in the Middle East,

6. Strongly deplores the continuation and persistence of Israel in pursuing those policies and practices and calls upon the Government and people of Israel to rescind those measures, to dismantle the existing settlements and in particular to cease, on an urgent basis, the establishment, construction and planning of settlements in the Arab territories occupied since 1967, including Jerusalem,

7. Calls upon all states not to provide Israel with any assistance to be used specifically in connection with settlements in the occupied territories,

8. Requests the Commission to continue to examine the situation relating to settlements in the Arab territories occupied since 1967 including Jerusalem, to investigate the reported serious depletion of natural resources, particularly the water resources, with a view of ensuring the protection of those important natural resources of the territories under occupation, and to keep under close scrutiny the implementation of the present resolution,

9. Requests the Commission to report to the Security Council before 1 September 1980, and decides to convene at the earliest possible date thereafter in order to consider the report and the full implementation of the present resolution.

PRESIDENT CARTER'S STATEMENT REPUDIATING US VOTE IN SUPPORT OF UN SECURITY COUNCIL RESOLUTION 465
(3 March 1980)

I want to make it clear that the vote of the US in the Security Council of the UN does not represent a change in our position regarding the Israeli settlements in the occupied areas nor regarding the status of Jerusalem.

While our opposition to the establishment of the Israeli settlements is long-standing and well-known, we made strenuous efforts to eliminate the language with reference to the dismantling of settlements in the resolution. This call for dismantling was neither proper nor practical. We believe that the future disposition of the existing settlements must be determined during the current autonomy negotiations.

As to Jerusalem, we strongly believe that Jerusalem should be undivided with free access to the holy places for all faiths, and that its status should be determined in the negotiations for a comprehensive peace settlement.

The US vote in the UN was approved with the understanding that all references to Jerusalem would be deleted. The failure to communicate this clearly resulted in a vote in favour of the resolution rather than abstention.

THE FAHD PLAN

In August 1981 Crown Prince Fahd of Saudi Arabia launched an eight-point peace plan for the Middle East. During the remainder of 1981 some Arab states showed their support, but failure to agree on the 'Fahd Plan' caused the break-up of the Fez Arab Summit in November only a few hours after it had opened. The plan is as follows:

1. Israel to withdraw from all Arab territory occupied in 1967, including Arab Jerusalem.
2. Israeli settlements built on Arab land after 1967 to be dismantled.
3. A guarantee of freedom of worship for all religions in holy places.
4. An affirmation of the right of the Palestinian Arab people to return to their homes, and compensation for those who do not wish to return.
5. The West Bank and Gaza Strip to have a transitional period under the auspices of the United Nations for a period not exceeding several months.
6. An independent Palestinian state should be set up with Jerusalem as its capital.
7. All states in the region should be able to live in peace.
8. The UN or member-states of the UN to guarantee carrying-out of these principles.

THE SHULTZ PLAN

At the beginning of February 1988 the Government of the USA announced a new plan for the resolution of the Palestine issue, which came to be known as the 'Shultz Plan', after the US Secretary of State, George Shultz. The presentation of the plan followed more than a year of diplomatic activity during which the idea of an international peace conference under the auspices of the UN, which had been agreed in principle by Shimon Peres, the Israeli Minister of Foreign Affairs, and King Hussein of Jordan, had won increasing support. The main provisions of the plan, as they were subsequently clarified, were for a six-month period of negotiations between Israel and a joint Jordanian/Palestinian delegation, to determine the details of a transitional autonomy arrangement for the West Bank and the Gaza Strip, which would last for three years; during the transitional period a permanent settlement would be negotiated by the Israeli and Jordanian/Palestinian delegations; both sets of negotiations would run concurrently with and, if necessary, with reference to, an international peace conference, involving the five permanent members of the UN Security Council and all the interested parties (including the Palestinians in a joint Jordanian/Palestinian delegation), which, like the separate Israeli-Jordanian/Palestinian negotiations, would be conducted on the basis of all the participants' acceptance of UN Security Council Resolutions 242 and 338, but would have no power to impose a settlement.

On 6 March 1988 the Israeli newspaper, Yedioth Aharonoth, published a photocopy of a letter from George Shultz to the Israeli Prime Minister, Itzhak Shamir, containing details of his peace proposals. The contents of the letter, identical versions of which were believed to have been delivered to the Governments of Egypt, Jordan and Syria, were as follows:

Dear Mr Prime Minister,

I set forth below the statement of understandings which I am convinced is necessary to achieve the prompt opening of negotiations on a comprehensive peace. This statement of understandings emerges from discussions held with you and other regional leaders. I look forward to the letter of reply of the government of Israel in confirmation of this statement.

The agreed objective is a comprehensive peace providing for the security of all the States in the region and for the legitimate rights of the Palestinian people.

Negotiations will start on an early date certain between Israel and each of its neighbors which is willing to do so. Those negotiations could begin by May 1, 1988. Each of these negotiations will be based on United Nations Security Council Resolutions 242 and 338, in all their parts. The parties to each bilateral negotiation will determine the procedure and agenda of their negotiation. All participants in the negotiations must state their willingness to negotiate with one another.

As concerns negotiations between the Israeli delegation and Jordanian-Palestinian delegation, negotiations will begin on arrangements for a transitional period, with the objective of completing them within six months. Seven months after transitional negotiations begin, final status negotiations will begin, with the objective of completing them within one year. These negotiations will be based on all the provisions and principles of the United Nations Security Council Resolution 242. Final status talks will start before the transitional period begins. The transitional period will begin three months after the conclusion of the transitional agreement and will last for three years. The United States will participate in both negotiations and will promote their rapid conclusion. In particular, the United States will submit a draft agreement for the parties' consideration at the outset of the negotiations on transitional arrangements.

Two weeks before the opening of negotiations, an international conference will be held. The Secretary-General of the United Nations will be asked to issue invitations to the parties involved in the Arab–Israeli conflict and the five permanent members of the United Nations Security Council. All participants in the conference must accept United Nations Security Council Resolutions 242 and 338, and renounce violence and terrorism. The parties to each bilateral negotiations may refer reports on the status of their negotiations to the conference, in a manner to be agreed. The conference will not be able to impose solutions or veto agreements reached.

Palestinian representation will be within the Jordanian-Palestinian delegation. The Palestinian issue will be addressed in the negotiations between the Jordanian-Palestinian and Israeli delegations. Negotiations between the Israeli delegation and the Jordanian-Palestinian delegation will proceed independently of any other negotiations.

This statement of understandings is an integral whole. The United States understands that your acceptance is dependent on the implementation of each element in good faith.

Sincerely yours,
George P. Shultz.

DECLARATION OF PALESTINIAN INDEPENDENCE

In November 1988 the 19th session of the PNC culminated in the declaration 'in the name of God and the Palestinian Arab people' of the independent State of Palestine, with the Holy City of Jerusalem as its capital. The opportunity for the PLO to assert sovereignty over a specific area arose through the decision of King Hussein of Jordan, in July 1988, to sever Jordan's 'administrative and legal links' with the West Bank. The Declaration of Independence cited UN General Assembly Resolution 181 of 1947, which partitioned Palestine into two states, one Arab and one Jewish, as providing the legal basis for the right of the Palestinian Arab people to national sovereignty and independence. At the end of the session, the PNC issued a political statement. Details of the Declaration of Independence, and of the political statement, set out below, are taken from an unofficial English-language translation of the proceedings, distributed by the PLO.

'The National Council proclaims, in the name of God and the Palestinian Arab people, the establishment of the State of Palestine on our Palestinian land, with the Holy City of Jerusalem as its capital.

The State of Palestine is the state of Palestinians wherever they may be. In it they shall develop their national and cultural identity and enjoy full equality in rights. Their religious and political beliefs and their human dignity shall be safeguarded under a democratic parliamentary system of government built on the freedom of opinion; and on the freedom to form parties; and on the protection of the rights of the minority by the majority and respect of the decisions of the majority by the minority; and on social justice and equal rights, free of ethnic, religious, racial or sexual discrimination; and on a constitution that guarantees the rule of law and the independence of the judiciary; and on the basis of total allegiance to the centuries-old spiritual and civilizational Palestinian heritage of religious tolerance and coexistence.

The State of Palestine is an Arab state, an integral part of the Arab nation and of that nation's heritage, its civilization and its aspiration to attain its goals of liberation, development, democracy and unity. Affirming its commitment to the Charter of the League of Arab states and its insistence on the reinforcement of joint Arab action, the State of Palestine calls on the people of its nation to assist in the completion of its birth by mobilizing their resources and augmenting their efforts to end the Israeli occupation.

The State of Palestine declares its commitment to the principles and objectives of the United Nations, and to the Universal Declaration of Human Rights, and to the principles and policy of non-alignment.

The State of Palestine, declaring itself a peace-loving state committed to the principles of peaceful coexistence, shall strive with all states and peoples to attain a permanent peace built on justice and respect of rights, in which humanity's constructive talents can prosper, and creative competition can flourish, and fear of tomorrow can be abolished, for tomorrow brings nothing but security for the just and those who regain their sense of justice.

As it struggles to establish peace in the land of love and peace, the State of Palestine exhorts the United Nations to take upon itself a special responsibility for the Palestinian Arab people and their homeland; and exhorts the peace-loving, freedom-cherishing peoples and states of the world to help it attain its objectives and put an end to the tragedy its people are suffering by providing them with security and endeavouring to end the Israeli occupation of the Palestinian territories.

The State of Palestine declares its belief in the settlement of international and regional disputes by peaceful means in accordance with the Charter and resolutions of the United Nations; and its rejection of threats of force or violence or terrorism and the use of these against its territorial integrity and political independence or the territorial integrity of any other state, without prejudice to its natural right to defend its territory and independence.

The Palestine National Council resolves:

First: On the Escalation and Continuity of the *Intifada*

A. To provide all the means and capabilities needed to escalate our people's *intifada* in various ways and on various levels to guarantee its continuation and intensification.

B. To support the popular institutions and organizations in the occupied Palestinian territories.

C. To bolster and develop the Popular Committees and other specialized popular and trade union bodies, including the attack group and the popular army, with a view to expanding their role and increasing their effectiveness.

D. To consolidate the national unity that emerged and developed during the *intifada*.

E. To intensify efforts on the international level for the release of the detainees, the repatriation of the deportees, and the termination of the organized, official acts of repression and terrorism against our children, our women, our men, and our institutions.

F. To call on the United Nations to place the occupied Palestinian land under international supervision for the protection of our people and the termination of the Israeli occupation.

G. To call on the Palestinian people outside our homeland to intensify and increase their support, and to expand the family-assistance program.

H. To call on the Arab nation, its people, forces, institutions and governments, to increase their political, material and informational support of the *intifada*.

I. To call on all free and honorable people worldwide to stand by our people, our revolution, our *intifada* against the Israeli occupation, the repression, and the organized, fascist official terrorism to which the occupation forces and the armed fanatic settlers are subjecting our people, our universities, our institutions, our national economy, and our Islamic and Christian holy places.

Second: In the Political Field

Proceeding from the above, the Palestine National Council, being responsible to the Palestinian people, their national rights and their desire for peace as expressed in the Declaration of Independence issued on November 15, 1988; and in response to the humanitarian quest for international entente, nuclear disarmament and the settlement of regional conflicts by peaceful means, affirms the determination of the Palestine Liberation Organization to arrive at a political settlement of the Arab–Israeli conflict and its core, the Palestinian issue, in the framework of the UN Charter, the principles and rules of international legitimacy, the edicts of international law, the resolutions of the United Nations, the latest of which are Security Council Resolutions 605, 607 and 608, and the resolutions of the Arab summits, in a manner that assures the Palestinian Arab people's right to repatriation, self-determination and the establishment of their independent state on their national soil, and that institutes arrangements for the security and peace of all states in the region.

Towards the achievement of this, the Palestine National Council affirms:

1. The necessity of convening an international conference on the issue of the Middle East and its core, the Palestinian issue, under the auspices of the United Nations and with the participation of the permanent members of the Security Council and all parties to the conflict in the region, including, on an equal footing, the Palestine Liberation Organization, the sole legitimate representative of the Palestinian people; on the understanding that the international conference will be held on the basis of Security Council Resolutions 242 and 338 and the safeguarding of the legitimate national rights of the Palestinian people, foremost among which is the right to

self-determination, in accordance with the principles and provisions of the UN Charter as they pertain to the right of peoples to self-determination, and the inadmissibility of the acquisition of others' territory by force or military conquest, and in accordance with the UN resolutions relating to the Palestinian issue.

2. The withdrawal of Israel from all the Palestinian and Arab territories it occupied in 1967, including Arab Jerusalem.

3. The annulment of all expropriation and annexation measures and the removal of the settlements established by Israel in the Palestinian and Arab territories since 1967.

4. Endeavouring to place the occupied Palestinian territories, including Arab Jerusalem, under the supervision of the United Nations for a limited period, to protect our people, to create an atmosphere conducive to the success of the proceedings of the international conference toward the attainment of a comprehensive political settlement and the achievement of peace and security for all on the basis of mutual consent, and to enable the Palestinian state to exercise its effective authority in these territories.

5. The settlement of the issue of the Palestinian refugees in accordance with the pertinent United Nations resolutions.

6. Guaranteeing the freedom of worship and the right to engage in religious rites for all faiths in the holy place in Palestine.

7. The Security Council shall draw up and guarantee arrangements for the security of all states concerned and for peace between them, including the Palestinian state.

The Palestine National Council confirms its past resolutions that the relationship between the fraternal Jordanian and Palestinian peoples is a privileged one and that the future relationship between the states of Jordan and Palestine will be built on confederal foundations, on the basis of the two fraternal peoples' free and voluntary choice, in consolidation of the historic ties that bind them and the vital interests they hold in common.

The National Council also renews its commitment to the United Nations resolutions that affirm the right of peoples to resist foreign occupation, imperialism and racial discrimination, and their right to fight for their independence; and it once more announces its rejection of terrorism in all its forms, including state terrorism, emphasizing its commitment to the resolutions it adopted in the past on this subject, and to the resolutions of the Arab summit in Algiers in 1988, and to UN Resolutions 42/159 of 1967 and 61/40 of 1985, and to what was stated in this regard in the Cairo Declaration of 7/11/85.

Third: In the Arab and International Fields

The Palestine National Council emphasizes the importance of the unity of Lebanon in its territory, its people and its institutions, and stands firmly against the attempts to partition the land and disintegrate the fraternal people of Lebanon. It further emphasizes the importance of the joint Arab effort to participate in a settlement of the Lebanese crisis that helps crystallize and implement solutions that preserve Lebanese unity. The Council also stresses the importance of consecrating the right of the Palestinians in Lebanon to engage in political and informational activity and to enjoy security and protection; and of working against all the forms of conspiracy and aggression that target them and their right to work and live; and of the need to secure the conditions that assure them the ability to defend themselves and provide them with security and protection.

The Palestine National Council affirms its solidarity with the Lebanese nationalist Islamic forces in their struggle against the Israeli occupation and its agents in the Lebanese South; expresses its pride in the allied struggle of the Lebanese and Palestinian peoples against the aggression and toward the termination of the Israeli occupation of parts of the South; and underscores the importance of bolstering this kinship between our people and the fraternal, combative people of Lebanon.

And on this occasion, the Council addresses a reverent salute to the long-suffering people of our camps in Lebanon and its South, who are enduring the aggression, massacres, murder, starvation, air raids, bombardments and sieges perpetrated against the Palestinian camps and Lebanese villages by the Israeli army, air force and navy, aided and abetted by hireling forces in the region; and it rejects the resettlement conspiracy, for the Palestinians' homeland is Palestine.

The Council emphasizes the importance of the Iraq-Iran cease-fire resolution toward the establishment of a permanent peace settlement between the two countries and in the Gulf Region; and calls for an intensification of the efforts being exerted to ensure the success of the negotiations toward the establishment of peace on stable and firm foundations; affirming, on this occasion, the price of the Palestinian Arab people and the Arab nation as a whole in the steadfastness and triumphs of fraternal Iraq as it defended the eastern gate of the Arab nation.

The National Council also expresses its deep pride in the stand taken by the peoples of our Arab nation in support of our Palestinian Arab people and of the Palestine Liberation Organization and of our people's *intifada* in the occupied homeland; and emphasizes the importance of fortifying the bonds of combat among the forces, parties and organizations of the Arab national liberation movement, in defense of the right of the Arab nation and its peoples to liberation, progress, democracy and unity. The Council calls for the adoption of all measures needed to reinforce the unity of struggle among all members of the Arab national liberation movement.

The Palestine National Council, as it hails the Arab states and thanks them for their support of our people's struggle, calls on them to honour the commitments they approved at the summit conference in Algiers in support of the Palestinian people and their blessed *intifada*. The Council, in issuing this appeal, expresses its great confidence that the leaders of the Arab nation will remain, as we have known them, a bulwark of support for Palestine and its people.

The Palestine National Council reiterates the desire of the Palestine Liberation Organization for Arab solidarity as the framework within which the Arab nation and its states can organize themselves to confront Israel's aggression and American support of that aggression, and within which Arab prestige can be enhanced and the Arab role strengthened to the point of influencing international policies to the benefit of Arab rights and causes.

The Palestine National Council expresses its deep gratitude to all the states and international forces and organizations that support the national rights of the Palestinians; affirms its desire to strengthen the bonds of friendship and co-operation with the Soviet Union, the People's (Republic of) China, the other socialist countries, the non-aligned states, the Islamic states, the African states, the Latin American states and the other friendly states; and notes with satisfaction the signs of positive evolution in the positions of some West European states and Japan in the direction of support for the rights of the Palestinian people, applauds this development, and urges intensified efforts to increase it.

The National Council affirms the fraternal solidarity of the Palestinian people and the Palestine Liberation Organization with the struggle of the peoples of Asia, Africa and Latin America for their liberation and the reinforcement of their independence; and condemns all American attempts to threaten the independence of the states of Central America and interfere in their affairs.

The Palestine National Council expresses the support of the Palestine Liberation Organization for the national liberation movements in South Africa and Namibia...

The Council notes with considerable concern the growth of the Israeli forces of fascism and extremism and the escalation of their open calls for the implementation of the policy of annihilation and individual and collective expulsion of our people from their homeland, and calls for intensified efforts in all areas to confront this fascist peril. The Council at the same time expresses its appreciation of the role and courage of the Israeli peace forces as they resist and expose the forces of fascism, racism and aggression, support our people's struggle and their valiant *intifada* and back our people's right to self-determination and the establishment of an independent state. The Council confirms its past resolutions regarding the reinforcement and development of relations with these democratic forces.

The Palestine National Council also addresses itself to the American people, calling on them all to strive to put an end to the American policy that denies the Palestinian people's national rights, including their sacred right to self-determination, and urging them to work toward the adoption of policies that conform to the Declaration of Human Rights and the international conventions and resolutions and serve the quest for peace in the Middle East and security for all its peoples, including the Palestinian people.

The Council charges the Executive Committee with the task of completing the formation of the Committee for the Perpetuation of the Memory of the Martyr-Symbol Abu Jihad, which shall initiate its work immediately upon the adjournment of the Council.

The Council sends its greetings to the United Nations Committee on the Exercise of the Inalienable Rights of the Palestinian People, and to the fraternal and friendly international and non-governmental institutions and organizations, and to the journalists and media that have stood and still stand by our people's struggle and *intifada*.

The National Council expresses deep pain at the continued detention of hundreds of combatants from among our people in a number of Arab countries, strongly condemns their continued detention, and calls upon those countries to put an end to these abnormal conditions and release those fighters to play their role in the struggle.

In conclusion, the Palestine National Council affirms its complete confidence that the justice of the Palestinian cause and of the demands for which the Palestinian people are struggling will continue to draw increasing support from honorable and free people around the world; and also affirms its complete confidence in victory on the road to Jerusalem, the capital of our independent Palestinian state.'

DECLARATION OF PRINCIPLES ON PALESTINIAN SELF-RULE
(13 September 1993)

The Government of the State of Israel and the Palestinian team (in the Jordanian-Palestinian delegation to the Middle East Peace Conference) (the 'Palestinian Delegation') representing the Palestinian people, agree that it is time to put an end to decades of confrontation and conflict, recognize their mutual legitimate and political rights, and strive to live in peaceful coexistence and mutual dignity and security and achieve a just, lasting and comprehensive peace settlement and historic reconciliation through the agreed political process.

Accordingly, the two sides agree to the following principles:

Article I
Aim of the negotiations

The aim of the Israeli-Palestinian negotiations within the current Middle East peace process is, among other things, to establish a Palestinian Interim Self-Government Authority, the elected Council, (the 'Council') for the Palestinian people in the West Bank and the Gaza Strip, for a transitional period not exceeding five years, leading to a permanent settlement based on Security Council Resolutions 242 and 338.

It is understood that the interim arrangements are an integral part of the overall peace process and that final status negotiations will lead to the implementation of Security Council Resolutions 242 and 338.

Article II
Framework for the interim period

The agreed framework for the interim period is set forth in the Declaration of Principles.

Article III
Elections

1. In order that the Palestinian people in the West Bank and Gaza Strip may govern themselves according to democratic principles, direct, free and general political elections will be held for the Council under agreed supervision and international observation, while the Palestinian police will ensure public order.

2. An agreement will be concluded on the exact mode and conditions of the elections in accordance with the protocol attached as Annex I, with the goal of holding the elections not later than nine months after the entry into force of this Declaration of Principles.

3. These elections will constitute a significant interim preparatory step toward the realization of the legitimate rights of the Palestinian people and their just requirements.

Article IV

Jurisdiction of the Council will cover West Bank and Gaza Strip territory, except for issues that will be negotiated in the permanent status negotiations. The two sides view the West Bank and the Gaza Strip as a single territorial unit, whose integrity will be preserved during the interim period.

Article V
Transitional period and permanent status negotiations

1. The five-year transitional period will begin upon the withdrawal from the Gaza Strip and Jericho area.

2. Permanent status negotiations will commence as soon as possible, but not later than the beginning of the third year of the interim period, between the Government of Israel and the Palestinian people representatives.

3. It is understood that these negotiations shall cover remaining issues, including Jerusalem, refugees, settlements, security arrangements, borders, relations and co-operation with other neighbours, and other issues of common interest.

4. The two parties agree that the outcome of the permanent status negotiations should not be prejudiced or pre-empted by agreements reached for the interim period.

Article VI
Preparatory transfer of powers and responsibilities

1. Upon the entry into force of this Declaration of Principles and the withdrawal from the Gaza Strip and Jericho area, a transfer of authority from the Israeli military government and its Civil Administration to the authorized Palestinians for this task, as detailed herein, will commence. This transfer of authority will be of preparatory nature until the inauguration of the Council.

2. Immediately after the entry into force of this Declaration of Principles and the withdrawal from the Gaza Strip and Jericho area, with the view to promoting economic development in the West Bank and Gaza Strip, authority will be transferred to the Palestinians in the following spheres: education and culture, health, social welfare, direct taxation, and tourism. The Palestinian side will commence in building the Palestinian police force, as agreed upon. Pending the inauguration of the Council, the two parties may negotiate the transfer of additional powers and responsibilities as agreed upon.

Article VII
Interim agreement

1. The Israeli and Palestinian delegations will negotiate an agreement on the interim period (the 'Interim Agreement').

2. The Interim Agreement shall specify, among other things, the structure of the Council, the number of its members, and the transfer of powers and responsibilities from the Israeli military government and its Civil Administration to the Council. The Interim Agreement shall also specify the Council's executive authority, legislative authority in accordance with Article IX below, and the independent Palestinian judicial organs.

3. The Interim Agreement shall include arrangements, to be implemented upon the inauguration of the Council, for the assumption by the Council of all of the powers and responsibilities transferred previously in accordance with Article VI above.

4. In order to enable the Council to promote economic growth, upon its inauguration, the Council will establish, among other things, a Palestinian Electricity Authority, a Gaza Sea Port Authority, a Palestinian Development Bank, a Palestinian Export Promotion Board, a Palestinian Environmental Authority, a Palestinian Land Authority and a Palestinian Water Administration Authority, and any other authorities agreed upon, in accordance with the Interim Agreement that will specify their powers and responsibilities.

5. After the inauguration of the Council, the Civil Administration will be dissolved, and the Israeli military government will be withdrawn.

Article VIII
Public order and security

In order to guarantee public order and internal security for the Palestinians of the West Bank and the Gaza Strip, the Council will establish a strong police force, while Israel will continue to carry the responsibility for defending against external threats, as well as the responsibility for overall security of the Israelis to protect their internal security and public order.

Article IX
Laws and military orders

1. The Council will be empowered to legislate, in accordance with the Interim Agreement, within all authorities transferred to it.
2. Both parties will review jointly laws and military orders presently in force in remaining spheres.

Article X
Joint Israeli-Palestinian liaison committee

In order to provide for a smooth implementation of this Declaration of Principles and any subsequent agreements pertaining to the interim period, upon the entry into force of this Declaration of Principles, a Joint Israeli-Palestinian Liaison Committee will be established in order to deal with issues requiring co-ordination, other issues of common interest, and disputes.

Article XI
Israeli-Palestinian co-operation in economic fields

Recognizing the mutual benefit of co-operation in promoting the development of the West Bank, the Gaza Strip and Israel, upon the entry into force of this Declaration of Principles, an Israeli-Palestinian Economic Co-operation Committee will be established in order to develop and implement in a co-operative manner the programmes identified in the protocols attached as Annex III and Annex IV.

Article XII
Liaison and co-operation with Jordan and Egypt

The two parties will invite the Governments of Jordan and Egypt to participate in establishing further liaison and co-operation arrangements between the Government of Israel and the Palestinian representatives, on one hand, and the Governments of Jordan and Egypt, on the other hand, to promote co-operation between them. These arrangements will include the constitution of a Continuing Committee that will decide by agreement on the modalities of the admission of persons displaced from the West Bank and Gaza Strip in 1967, together with necessary measures to prevent disruption and disorder. Other matters of common concern will be dealt with by this Committee.

Article XIII
Redeployment of Israeli forces

1. After the entry into force of this Declaration of Principles, and not later than the eve of elections for the Council, a redeployment of Israeli military forces in the West Bank and the Gaza Strip will take place, in addition to withdrawal of Israeli forces carried out in accordance with Article XIV.
2. In redeploying its military forces, Israel will be guided by the principle that its military forces should be redeployed outside the populated areas.
3. Further redeployments to specified locations will be gradually implemented commensurate with the assumption of responsibility for public order and internal security by the Palestinian police force pursuant to Article VIII above.

Article XIV
Israeli withdrawal from the Gaza Strip and Jericho area

Israel will withdraw from the Gaza Strip and Jericho area, as detailed in the protocol attached as Annex II.

Article XV
Resolution of disputes

1. Disputes arising out of the application or interpretation of this Declaration of Principles, or any subsequent agreements pertaining to the interim period, shall be resolved by negotiations through the Joint Liaison Committee to be established pursuant to Article X above.
2. Disputes which cannot be settled by negotiations may be resolved by a mechanism of conciliation to be agreed upon by the parties.
3. The parties may agree to submit to arbitration disputes relating to the interim period, which cannot be settled through conciliation. To this end, upon the agreement of both parties, the parties will establish an Arbitration Committee.

Article XVI
Israel-Palestinian co-operation concerning regional programs

Both parties view the multilateral working groups as an appropriate instrument for promoting a 'Marshall Plan,' the regional programs and other programs, including special programs for the West Bank and Gaza Strip, as indicated in the protocol attached as Annex IV.

Article XVII
Miscellaneous provisions

1. This Declaration of Principles will enter into force one month after its signing.
2. All protocols annexed to this Declaration of Principles and Agreed Minutes pertaining thereto shall be regarded as an integral part hereof.

Annex 1—protocol on the mode and conditions of elections

1. Palestinians of Jerusalem who live there will have the right to participate in the election process, according to an agreement between the two sides.
2. In addition, the election agreement should cover, among other things, the following issues:

a. the system of elections,

b. the mode of the agreed supervision and international observation and their personal composition, and

c. rules and regulations regarding election campaign, including agreed arrangements for the organizing of mass media, and the possibility of licensing a broadcasting and TV station.

3. The future status of displaced Palestinians who were registered on 4th June 1967 will not be prejudiced because they are unable to participate in the election process due to practical reasons.

Annex 2—protocol on withdrawal of Israeli forces from the Gaza Strip and Jericho Area

1. The two sides will conclude and sign within two months from the date of entry into force of this Declaration of Principles, an agreement on the withdrawal of Israeli military forces from the Gaza Strip and Jericho area. This agreement will include comprehensive arrangements to apply in the Gaza Strip and the Jericho area subsequent to the Israeli withdrawal.
2. Israel will implement an accelerated and scheduled withdrawal of Israeli military forces from the Gaza Strip and Jericho area, beginning immediately with the signing of the agreement on the Gaza Strip and Jericho area and to be completed within a period not exceeding four months after the signing of this agreement.
3. The above agreement will include, among other things:

a. Arrangements for a smooth and peaceful transfer of authority from the Israeli military government and its Civil Administration to the Palestinian representatives.

b. Structure, powers and responsibilities of the Palestinian authority in these areas, except, external security, settlements, Israelis, foreign relations, and other subjects mutually agreed upon.

c. Arrangements for assumption of internal security and public order by the Palestinian police force consisting of police officers recruited locally and from abroad (holding Jordanian passports and Palestinian documents issued by Egypt). Those who will participate in the Palestinian police force coming from abroad should be trained as police and police officers.

d. A temporary international or foreign presence, as agreed upon.

e. Establishment of a joint Palestinian-Israeli co-ordination and co-operation committee for mutual security purposes.

f. An economic development and stabilization program, including the establishment of an Emergency Fund, to encourage foreign investment, and financial and economic support. Both sides will co-ordinate and co-operate jointly and unilaterally with regional and international parties to support these aims.

g. Arrangements for a safe passage for persons and transportation between the Gaza Strip and Jericho area.

4. The above agreement will include arrangements for co-ordination between both parties regarding passages:
   a. Gaza–Egypt; and
   b. Jericho–Jordan.

5. The offices responsible for carrying out the powers and responsibilities of the Palestinian authority under this Annex II and Article VI of the Declaration of Principles will be located in the Gaza Strip and in the Jericho area pending the inauguration of the Council.

6. Other than these agreed arrangements, the status of the Gaza Strip and Jericho area will continue to be an integral part of the West Bank and Gaza Strip, and will not be changed in the interim period.

PROTOCOL ON ISRAELI-PALESTINIAN CO-OPERATION IN ECONOMIC AND DEVELOPMENT PROGRAMS

The two sides agree to establish an Israeli-Palestinian Continuing Committee for Economic Co-operation, focusing, among other things, on the following:

1. Co-operation in the field of water, including a Water Development Program prepared by experts from both sides, which will also specify the mode of co-operation in the management of water resources in the West Bank and Gaza Strip, and will include proposals for studies and plans on water rights of each party, as well as on the equitable utilization of joint water resources for implementation in and beyond the interim period.

2. Co-operation in the field of electricity, including an Electricity Development Program, which will also specify the mode of co-operation for the production, maintenance, purchase and sale of electricity resources.

3. Co-operation in the field of energy, including an Energy Development Program, which will provide for the exploitation of oil and gas for industrial purposes, particularly in the Gaza Strip and in the Negev, and will encourage further joint exploitation of other energy resources. This Program may also provide for the construction of a Petrochemical industrial complex in the Gaza Strip and the construction of oil and gas pipelines.

4. Co-operation in the field of finance, including a Financial Development and Action Program for the encouragement of international investment in the West Bank and the Gaza Strip, and in Israel, as well as the establishment of a Palestinian Development Bank.

5. Co-operation in the fields of transport and communications, including a Program, which will define guidelines for the establishment of a Gaza Sea Port Area, and will provide for the establishing of transport and communications lines to and from the West Bank and the Gaza Strip to Israel and to other countries. In addition, this Program will provide for carrying out the necessary construction of roads, railways, communications lines, etc.

6. Co-operation in the field of trade, including studies, and Trade Promotion Programs, which will encourage local, regional and inter-regional trade, as well as a feasibility study of creating free trade zones in the Gaza Strip and in Israel, mutual access to these zones, and co-operation in other areas related to trade and commerce.

7. Co-operation in the field of industry, including industrial Development Programs, which will provide for the establishment of joint Israeli-Palestinian Research and Development Centers, will promote Palestinian-Israeli joint ventures, and provide guidelines for co-operation in the textile, food, pharmaceutical, electronics, diamonds, computer and science-based industries.

8. A program for co-operation in, and regulation of, labour relations and co-operation in social welfare issues.

9. A Human Resources Development and Co-operation Plan, providing for joint Israeli-Palestinian workshops and seminars, and for the establishment of joint vocational training centres, research institutes and data banks.

10. An Environmental Protection Plan, providing for joint and/or co-ordinated measures in this sphere.

11. A program for developing co-ordination and co-operation in the field of communication and media.

12. Any other programs of mutual interest.

PROTOCOL ON ISRAELI-PALESTINIAN CO-OPERATION CONCERNING REGIONAL DEVELOPMENT PROGRAMS

1. The two sides will co-operate in the context of the multilateral peace efforts in promoting a Development Program for the region, including the West Bank and the Gaza Strip, to be initiated by the G-7. The parties will request the G-7 to seek the participation in this program of other interested states, such as members of the Organization for Economic Co-operation and Development, regional Arab states and institutions, as well as members of the private sector.

2. The Development Program will consist of two elements:
   a) an Economic Development Program for the West Bank and the Gaza Strip
   b) a Regional Economic Development Program

A. *The Economic Development Program for the West Bank and the Gaza Strip* will consist of the following elements:
(1) A Social Rehabilitation Program, including a Housing and Construction Program
(2) A Small and Medium Business Development Plan
(3) An Infrastructure Development Program (water, electricity, transportation and communications, etc.)
(4) A Human Resources Plan
(5) Other programs

B. *The Regional Economic Development Program* may consist of the following elements:
(1) The establishment of a Middle East Development Fund, as a first step, and a Middle East Development Bank, as a second step
(2) The development of a joint Israeli-Palestinian-Jordanian Plan for co-ordinated exploitation of the Dead Sea area
(3) The Mediterranean Sea (Gaza)—Dead Sea Canal
(4) Regional Desalinization and other water development projects
(5) A regional plan for agricultural development, including a co-ordinated regional effort for the prevention of desertification
(6) Interconnection of electricity grids
(7) Regional co-operation for the transfer, distribution and industrial exploitation of gas, oil and other energy resources
(8) A regional Tourism, Transportation and Telecommunications Development Plan
(9) Regional co-operation in other spheres

3. The two sides will encourage the multilateral working groups, and will co-ordinate towards its success. The two parties will encourage international activities, as well as pre-feasibility and feasibility studies, within the various multilateral working groups.

AGREED MINUTES TO THE DECLARATION OF PRINCIPLES ON INTERIM SELF-GOVERNMENT ARRANGEMENTS

A. *General Understandings and Agreements*

Any powers and responsibilites transferred to the Palestinians pursuant to the Declaration of Principles prior to the inauguration of the Council will be subject to the same principles pertaining to Article IV, as set out in these Agreed Minutes below.

B. *Specific Understandings and Agreements*

Article IV

It is understood that:

1. Jurisdiction of the Council will cover West Bank and Gaza Strip territory, except for issues that will be negotiated in the permanent status negotiations: Jerusalem, settlements, military locations and Israelis.

2. The Council's jurisdiction will apply with regard to the agreed powers, responsibilities, spheres and authorities transferred to it.

Article VI (2)

It is agreed that the transfer of authority will be as follows:

(1) The Palestinian side will inform the Israeli side of the names of the authorized Palestinians who will assume the powers, authorities and responsibilities that will be transferred to the Palestinians according to the Declaration of Principles in the following fields: education and culture, health, social welfare, direct taxation, tourism, and any other authorities agreed upon.

(2) It is understood that the rights and obligations of these offices will not be affected.

(3) Each of the spheres described above will continue to enjoy existing budgetary allocations in accordance with arrangements to be mutually agreed upon. These arrangements also will provide for the necessary adjustments required in order to take into account the taxes collected by the direct taxation office.

(4) Upon the execution of the Declaration of Principles, the Israeli and Palestinian delegations will immediately commence negotiations on a detailed plan for the transfer of authority on the above offices in accordance with the above understandings.

Article VII (2)

The Interim Agreement will also include arrangements for co-ordination and co-operation.

Article VII (5)

The withdrawal of the military government will not prevent Israel from exercising the powers and responsibilities not transferred to the Council.

Article VIII

It is understood that the Interim Agreement will include arrangements for co-operation and co-ordination between the two parties in this regard. It is also agreed that the transfer of powers and responsibilities to the Palestinian police will be accomplished in a phased manner, as agreed in the Interim Agreement.

Article X

It is agreed that, upon the entry into force of the Declaration of Principles, the Israeli and Palestinian delegations will exchange the names of the individuals designated by them as members of the Joint Israeli-Palestinian Liaison Committee.

It is further agreed that each side will have an equal number of members in the Joint Committee. The Joint Committee will reach decisions by agreement. The Joint Committee may add other technicians and experts, as necessary. The Joint Committee will decide on the frequency and place or places of its meetings.

Annex II

It is understood that, subsequent to the Israeli withdrawal, Israel will continue to be responsible for external security, and for internal security and public order of settlements and Israelis. Israeli military forces and civilians may continue to use roads freely within the Gaza Strip and the Jericho area.

Article XVI

Israeli-Palestinian Co-operation Concerning Regional Programs

Both parties view the multilateral working groups as an appropriate instrument for promoting a 'Marshall Plan,' the regional programs and other programs, including special programs for the West Bank and Gaza Strip, as indicated in the protocol attached as Annex IV.

Article XVII

Miscellaneous Provisions

1. This Declaration of Principles will enter into force one month after its signing.

2. All protocols annexed to this Declaration of Principles and Agreed Minutes pertaining thereto shall be regarded as an integral part hereof.

THE CAIRO AGREEMENT ON THE GAZA STRIP AND JERICHO
(4 May 1994)

The Government of the State of Israel and the Palestine Liberation Organization (hereinafter 'the PLO'), the representative of the Palestinian people;

Preamble

Within the framework of the Middle East peace process initiated at Madrid in October 1991;

Reaffirming their determination to live in peaceful co-existence, mutual dignity and security, while recognizing their mutual legitimate and political rights;

Reaffirming their desire to achieve a just, lasting and comprehensive peace settlement through the agreed political process;

Reaffirming their adherence to the mutual recognition and commitments expressed in the letters dated September 9, 1993, signed by and exchanged between the Prime Minister of Israel and the Chairman of the PLO;

Reaffirming their understanding that the interim self-government arrangements, including the arrangements to apply in the Gaza Strip and the Jericho Area contained in this Agreement, are an integral part of the whole peace process and that the negotiations on the permanent status will lead to the implementation of Security Council Resolutions 242 and 338;

Desirous of putting into effect the Declaration of Principles on Interim Self-Government Arrangements signed at Washington, D.C. on September 13, 1993, and the agreed minutes thereto (hereinafter 'The Declaration of Principles'), and in particular the protocol on withdrawal of Israeli forces from the Gaza Strip and the Jericho Area:

Hereby agree to the following arrangements regarding the Gaza Strip and the Jericho Area:

Article I

DEFINITIONS

For the purpose of this Agreement:

a. The Gaza Strip and the Jericho Area are delineated on Map Nos. 1 and 2 attached to this Agreement (*Maps not reproduced—Ed.*)

b. 'The settlements' means the Gush Katif and Erez settlement areas, as well as the other settlements in the Gaza Strip, as shown on attached Map No. 1

c. 'The military installation area' means the Israeli military installation area along the Egyptian border in the Gaza Strip, as shown on Map No. 1; and

d. The term 'Israelis' shall also include Israeli statutory agencies and corporations registered in Israel

Article II

SCHEDULED WITHDRAWAL OF ISRAELI MILITARY FORCES

1. Israel shall implement an accelerated and scheduled withdrawal of Israeli military forces from the Gaza Strip and from the Jericho Area to begin immediately with the signing of this Agreement. Israel shall complete such withdrawal within three weeks from this date.

2. Subject to the arrangements included in the Protocol concerning withdrawal of Israeli military forces and security arrangements attached as Annex I, the Israeli withdrawal shall include evacuating all military bases and other fixed installations to be handed over to the Palestinian Police, to be established pursuant to Article IX below (hereinafter 'the Palestinian Police').

3. In order to carry out Israel's responsibility for external security and for internal security and public order of settlements and Israelis, Israel shall, concurrently with the withdrawal, redeploy its remaining military forces to the settlements and the military installation area, in accordance with the provisions of this Agreement. Subject to the provisions of this Agreement, this redeployment shall constitute full

implementation of Article XIII of the Declaration of Principles with regard to the Gaza Strip and the Jericho Area only.

4. For the purposes of this Agreement, 'Israeli military forces' may include Israeli police and other Israeli security forces.

5. Israelis, including Israeli military forces, may continue to use roads freely within the Gaza Strip and the Jericho Area. Palestinians may use public roads crossing the settlements freely, as provided for in Annex I.

6. The Palestinian Police shall be deployed and shall assume responsibility for public order and internal security of Palestinians in accordance with this Agreement and Annex I.

Article III

TRANSFER OF AUTHORITY

1. Israel shall transfer authority as specified in this Agreement from the Israeli military government and its Civil Administration to the Palestinian Authority, hereby established, in accordance with Article V of this Agreement, except for the authority that Israel shall continue to exercise as specified in this Agreement.

2. As regards the transfer and assumption of authority in civil spheres, powers and responsibilities shall be transferred and assumed as set out in the Protocol concerning civil affairs attached as Annex II.

3. Arrangements for a smooth and peaceful transfer of the agreed powers and responsibilities are set out in Annex II.

4. Upon the completion of the Israeli withdrawal and the transfer of powers and responsibilities as detailed in Paragraphs 1 and 2 above and in Annex II, the Civil Administration in the Gaza Strip and the Jericho Area will be dissolved and the Israeli military government will be withdrawn. The withdrawal of the military government shall not prevent it from continuing to exercise the powers and responsibilities specified in this Agreement.

5. A joint Civil Affairs Co-ordination and Co-operation Committee (hereinafter 'the CAC') and two joint regional civil affairs subcommittees for the Gaza Strip and the Jericho Area respectively shall be established in order to provide for co-ordination and co-operation in civil affairs between the Palestinian Authority and Israel, as detailed in Annex II.

6. The offices of the Palestinian Authority shall be located in the Gaza Strip and the Jericho Area pending the inauguration of the council to be elected pursuant to the Declaration of Principles.

Article IV

STRUCTURE AND COMPOSITION OF THE PALESTINIAN AUTHORITY

1. The Palestinian Authority will consist of one body of 24 members which shall carry out and be responsible for all the legislative and executive powers and responsibilities transferred to it under this Agreement, in accordance with this article, and shall be responsible for the exercise of judicial functions in accordance with Article VI, subparagraph 1.b of this Agreement.

2. The Palestinian Authority shall administer the departments transferred to it and may establish, within its jurisdiction, other departments and subordinate administrative units as necessary for the fulfilment of its responsibilities. It shall determine its own internal procedures.

3. The PLO shall inform the Government of Israel of the names of the members of the Palestinian Authority and any change of members. Changes in the membership of the Palestinian Authority will take effect upon an exchange of letters between the PLO and the Government of Israel.

4. Each member of the Palestinian Authority shall enter into office upon undertaking to act in accordance with this Agreement.

Article V

JURISDICTION

1. The authority of the Palestinian Authority encompasses all matters that fall within its territorial, functional and personal jurisdiction, as follows:

a. The territorial jurisdiction covers the Gaza Strip and the Jericho Area territory, as defined in Article I, except for settlements and the military installation area. Territorial jurisdiction shall include land, subsoil and territorial waters, in accordance with the provisions of this Agreement.

b. The functional jurisdiction encompasses all powers and responsibilities as specified in this Agreement. This jurisdiction does not include foreign relations, internal security and public order of settlements and the military installation area and Israelis, and external security.

c. The personal jurisdiction extends to all persons within the territorial jurisdiction referred to above, except for Israelis, unless otherwise provided in this Agreement.

2. The Palestinian Authority has, within its authority, legislative, executive and judicial powers and responsibilities, as provided for in this Agreement.

3.a. Israel has authority over the settlements, the military installation area, Israelis, external security, internal security and public order of settlements, the military installation area and Israelis, and those agreed powers and responsibilities specified in this Agreement.

b. Israel shall exercise its authority through its military government, which for that end, shall continue to have the necessary legislative, judicial and executive powers and responsibilities, in accordance with international law. This provision shall not derogate from Israel's applicable legislation over Israelis in personam.

4. The exercise of authority with regard to the electromagnetic sphere and airspace shall be in accordance with the provisions of this Agreement.

5. The provisions of this article are subject to the specific legal arrangements detailed in the Protocol concerning legal matters attached as Annex III. Israel and the Palestinian Authority may negotiate further legal arrangements.

6. Israel and the Palestinian Authority shall co-operate on matters of legal assistance in criminal and civil matters through the legal subcommittee of the CAC.

Article VI

POWERS AND RESPONSIBILITIES OF THE PALESTINIAN AUTHORITY

1. Subject to the provisions of this Agreement, the Palestinian Authority, within its jurisdiction:

a. has legislative powers as set out in Article VII of this Agreement, as well as executive powers;

b. will administer justice through an independent judiciary;

c. will have, inter alia, power to formulate policies, supervise their implementation, employ staff, establish departments, authorities and institutions, sue and be sued and conclude contracts; and

d. will have, inter alia, the power to keep and administer registers and records of the population, and issue certificates, licenses and documents.

2.a. In accordance with the Declaration of Principles, the Palestinian Authority will not have powers and responsibilities in the sphere of foreign relations, which sphere includes the establishment abroad of embassies, consulates or other types of foreign missions and posts or permitting their establishment in the Gaza Strip or the Jericho Area, the appointment of or admission of diplomatic and consular staff, and the exercise of diplomatic functions.

b. Notwithstanding the provisions of this paragraph, the PLO may conduct negotiations and sign agreements with states or international organizations for the benefit of the Palestinian Authority in the following cases only:

(1) Economic agreements, as specifically provided in Annex IV of this Agreement;

(2) Agreements with donor countries for the purpose of implementing arrangements for the provision of assistance to the Palestinian Authority;

(3) Agreements for the purpose of implementing the regional development plans detailed in Annex IV of the Declaration of Principles or in agreements entered into in the framework of the multilateral negotiations; and

(4) Cultural, scientific and education agreements.

c. Dealings between the Palestinian Authority and representatives of foreign states and international organizations, as well as the establishment in the Gaza Strip and the Jericho Area of representative offices other than those described in subparagraph 2.a, above, for the purpose of implementing the agreements referred to in subparagraph 2.b above, shall not be considered foreign relations.

Article VII

LEGISLATIVE POWERS OF THE PALESTINIAN AUTHORITY

1. The Palestinian Authority will have the power, within its jurisdiction, to promulgate legislation, including basic laws, laws, regulations and other legislative acts.

2. Legislation promulgated by the Palestinian Authority shall be consistent with the provisions of this Agreement.

3. Legislation promulgated by the Palestinian Authority shall be communicated to a legislation subcommittee to be established by the CAC (hereinafter 'the Legislation Subcommittee'). During a period of 30 days from the communication of the legislation, Israel may request that the Legislation Subcommittee decide whether such legislation exceeds the jurisdiction of the Palestinian Authority or is otherwise inconsistent with the provisions of this Agreement.

4. Upon receipt of the Israeli request, the Legislation Subcommittee shall decide, as an initial matter, on the entry into force of the legislation pending its decision on the merits of the matter.

5. If the Legislation Subcommittee is unable to reach a decision with regard to the entry into force of the legislation within 15 days, this issue will be referred to a Board of Review. This Board of Review shall be comprised of two judges, retired judges or senior jurists (hereinafter 'Judges'), one from each side, to be appointed from a compiled list of three judges proposed by each.

6. Legislation referred to the Board of Review shall enter into force only if the Board of Review decides that it does not deal with a security issue which falls under Israel's responsibility, that it does not seriously threaten other significant Israeli interests protected by this Agreement and that the entry into force of the legislation could not cause irreparable damage or harm.

7. The Legislation Subcommittee shall attempt to reach a decision on the merits of the matter within 30 days from the date of the Israeli request. If this subcommittee is unable to reach such a decision within this period of 30 days, the matter shall be referred to the joint Israeli-Palestinian Liaison Committee referred to in Article XV below (hereinafter 'the Liaison Committee'). This Liaison Committee will deal with the matter immediately and will attempt to settle it within 30 days.

8. Where the legislation has not entered into force pursuant to paragraphs 5 or 7 above, this situation shall be maintained pending the decision of the Liaison Committee on the merits of the matter, unless it has decided otherwise.

9. Laws and military orders in effect in the Gaza Strip or the Jericho Area prior to the signing of this Agreement shall remain in force, unless amended or abrogated in accordance with this Agreement.

Article VIII

ARRANGEMENTS FOR SECURITY AND PUBLIC ORDER

1. In order to guarantee public order and internal security for the Palestinians of the Gaza Strip and the Jericho Area, the Palestinian Authority shall establish a strong police force, as set out in Article IX below. Israel shall continue to carry the responsibility for defence against external threats, including the responsibility for protecting the Egyptian border and the Jordanian line, and for defence against external threats from the sea and from the air, as well as the responsibility for overall security of Israelis and settlements, for the purpose of safeguarding their internal security and public order, and will have all the powers to take the steps necessary to meet this responsibility.

2. Agreed security arrangements and co-ordination mechanisms are specified in Annex I.

3. A Joint Co-ordination and Co-operation committee for mutual security purposes (hereinafter 'the JSC'), as well as three joint district co-ordination and co-operation offices for the Gaza District, the Khan Younis District and the Jericho District respectively (hereinafter 'the DCOS') are hereby established as provided for in Annex I.

4. The security arrangements provided for in this Agreement and in Annex I may be reviewed at the requests of either party and may be amended by mutual agreement of the parties. Specific review arrangements are included in Annex I.

Article IX

THE PALESTINIAN DIRECTORATE OF POLICE FORCE

1. The Palestinian Authority shall establish a strong police force, the Palestinian Directorate of Police Force (hereinafter 'the Palestinian Police'). The duties, functions, structure, deployment and composition of the Palestinian Police, together with provisions regarding its equipment and operation, are set out in Annex I, Article III. Rules of conduct governing the activities of the Palestinian Police are set out in Annex I, Article VIII.

2. Except for the Palestinian Police referred to in this article and the Israeli military forces, no other armed forces shall be established or operate in the Gaza Strip or the Jericho Area.

3. Except for the arms, ammunition and equipment of the Palestinian Police described in Annex I, Article III, and those of the Israeli military forces, no organization or individual in the Gaza Strip and the Jericho Area shall manufacture, sell, acquire, possess, import or otherwise introduce into the Gaza Strip or the Jericho Area any firearms, ammunition, weapons, explosives, gunpowder or any related equipment, unless otherwise provided for in Annex I.

Article X

PASSAGES

Arrangements for co-ordination between Israel and the Palestinian Authority regarding the Gaza-Egypt and Jericho-Jordan passages, as well as any other agreed international crossings, are set out in Annex 1.

Article XI

SAFE PASSAGE BETWEEN THE GAZA STRIP AND THE JERICHO AREA

Arrangements for safe passage of persons and transportation between the Gaza Strip and the Jericho Area are set out in Annex I, Article IX.

Article XII

RELATIONS BETWEEN ISRAEL AND THE PALESTINIAN AUTHORITY

1. Israel and the Palestinian Authority shall seek to foster mutual understanding and tolerance and shall accordingly abstain from incitement, including hostile propaganda, against each other and, without derogating from the principle of freedom of expression, shall take legal measures to prevent such incitement by any organizations, groups or individuals within their jurisdiction.

2. Without derogating from the other provisions of this agreement, Israel and the Palestinian Authority shall co-operate in combating criminal activity which may affect both sides, including offences related to trafficking in illegal drugs

and psychotropic substances, smuggling, and offences against property, including offences related to vehicles.

Article XIII

ECONOMIC RELATIONS

The economic relations between the two sides are set out in the Protocol on Economic Relations signed in Paris on April 29, 1994 and the appendixes thereto, certified copies of which are attached as Annex IV, and will be governed by the relevant provisions of this agreement and its annexes.

Article XIV

HUMAN RIGHTS AND THE RULE OF LAW

Israel and the Palestinian Authority shall exercise their powers and responsibilities pursuant to this Agreement with due regard to internationally-accepted norms and principles of human rights and the rule of law.

Article XV

THE JOINT ISRAELI-PALESTINIAN LIAISON COMMITTEE

1. The Liaison Committee established pursuant to Article X of the Declaration of Principles shall ensure the smooth implementation of this Agreement. It shall deal with issues requiring co-ordination, other issues of common interest and disputes.
2. The Liaison Committee shall be composed of an equal number of members from each party. It may add other technicians and experts as necessary.
3. The Liaison Committee shall adopt its rules of procedure, including the frequency and place or places of its meetings.
4. The Liaison Committee shall reach its decision by agreement.

Article XVI

LIAISON AND CO-OPERATION WITH JORDAN AND EGYPT

1. Pursuant to Article XII of the Declaration of Principles, the two parties shall invite the governments of Jordan and Egypt to participate in establishing further Liaison and Co-operation Arrangements between the Government of Israel and the Palestinian Representatives on the one hand, and the governments of Jordan and Egypt on the other hand, to promote co-operation between them. These arrangements shall include the constitution of a Continuing Committee.
2. The Continuing Committee shall decide by agreement on the modalities of admission of persons displaced from the West Bank and the Gaza Strip in 1967, together with necessary measures to prevent disruption and disorder.
3. The Continuing Committee shall deal with other matters of common concern.

Article XVII

SETTLEMENT OF DIFFERENCES AND DISPUTES

Any difference relating to the application of this agreement shall be referred to the appropriate co-ordination and co-operation mechanism established under this agreement. The provisions of Article XV of the Declaration of Principles shall apply to any such difference which is not settled through the appropriate co-ordination and co-operation mechanism, namely:
1. Disputes arising out of the application or interpretation of this agreement or any subsequent agreements pertaining to the interim period shall be settled by negotiations through the Liaison Committee.
2. Disputes which cannot be settled by negotiations may be settled by a mechanism of conciliation to be agreed between the parties.
3. The parties may agree to submit to arbitration disputes relating to the interim period, which cannot be settled through conciliation. To this end, upon the agreement of both parties, the parties will establish an arbitration committee.

Article XVIII

PREVENTION OF HOSTILE ACTS

Both sides shall take all measures necessary in order to prevent acts of terrorism, crime and hostilities directed against each other, against individuals falling under the other's authority and against their property, and shall take legal measures against offenders. In addition, the Palestinian side shall take all measures necessary to prevent such hostile acts directed against the settlements, the infrastructure serving them and the military installation area, and the Israeli side shall take all measures necessary to prevent such hostile acts emanating from the settlements and directed against Palestinians.

Article XIX

MISSING PERSONS

The Palestinian Authority shall co-operate with Israel by providing all necessary assistance in the conduct of searches by Israel within the Gaza Strip and the Jericho Area for missing Israelis, as well as by providing information about missing Israelis. Israel shall co-operate with the Palestinian Authority in searching for, and providing necessary information about, missing Palestinians.

Article XX

CONFIDENCE-BUILDING MEASURES

With a view to creating a positive and supportive public atmosphere to accompany the implementation of this agreement, and to establish a solid basis of mutual trust and good faith, both parties agree to carry out confidence-building measures as detailed herewith:
1. Upon the signing of this agreement, Israel will release, or turn over, to the Palestinian Authority within a period of 5 weeks, about 5,000 Palestinian detainees and prisoners, residents of the West Bank and the Gaza Strip. Those released will be free to return to their homes anywhere in the West Bank or the Gaza Strip. Prisoners turned over to the Palestinian Authority shall be obliged to remain in the Gaza Strip or the Jericho Area for the remainder of their sentence.
2. After the signing of this Agreement, the two parties shall continue to negotiate the release of additional Palestinian prisoners and detainees, building on agreed principles.
3. The implementation of the above measures will be subject to the fulfilment of the procedures determined by Israeli law for the release and transfer of detainees and prisoners.
4. With the assumption of Palestinian Authority, the Palestinian side commits itself to solving the problem of those Palestinians who were in contact with the Israeli authorities. Until an agreed solution is found, the Palestinian side undertakes not to prosecute these Palestinians or to harm them in any way.
5. Palestinians from abroad whose entry into the Gaza Strip and the Jericho Area is approved pursuant to this agreement, and to whom the provisions of this article are applicable, will not be prosecuted for offences committed prior to September 13, 1993.

Article XXI

TEMPORARY INTERNATIONAL PRESENCE

1. The parties agree to a temporary international or foreign presence in the Gaza Strip and the Jericho Area (hereinafter 'the TIP'), in accordance with the provisions of this article.
2. The TIP shall consist of 400 qualified personnel, including observers, instructors and other experts, from 5 or 6 of the donor countries.
3. The two parties shall request the donor countries to establish a special fund to provide finance for the TIP.

4. The TIP will function for a period of 6 months. The TIP may extend this period, or change the scope of its operation, with the agreement of the two parties.

5. The TIP shall be stationed and operative within the following cities and villages: Gaza, Khan Younis, Rafah, Deir al-Balah, Jabalya, Absan, Beit Hanun and Jericho.

6. Israel and the Palestinian Authority shall agree on a special protocol to implement this article, with the goal of concluding negotiations with the donor countries contributing personnel within two months.

Article XXII

RIGHTS, LIABILITIES AND OBLIGATIONS

1.a. The transfer of all powers and responsibilities to the Palestinian Authority, as detailed in Annex II, includes all related rights, liabilities and obligations arising with regard to acts or omissions which occurred prior to the transfer. Israel will cease to bear any financial responsibility regarding such acts or omissions and the Palestinian Authority will bear all financial responsibility for these and for its own functioning.
b. Any financial claim made in this regard against Israel will be referred to the Palestinian Authority.
c. Israel shall provide the Palestinian Authority with the information it has regarding pending and anticipated claims brought before any court or tribunal against Israel in this regard.
d. Where legal proceedings are brought in respect of such a claim, Israel will notify the Palestinian Authority and enable it to participate in defending the claim and raise any arguments on its behalf.
e. In the event that an award is made against Israel by any court or tribunal in respect of such a claim, the Palestinian Authority shall reimburse Israel the full amount of the award.
f. Without prejudice to the above, where a court or tribunal hearing such a claim finds that liability rests solely with an employee or agent who acted beyond the scope of the powers assigned to him or her, unlawfully or with wilful malfeasance, the Palestinian Authority shall not bear financial responsibility.
2. The transfer of authority in itself shall not affect rights, liabilities and obligations of any person or legal entity, in existence at the date of signing of this Agreement.

Article XXIII

FINAL CLAUSES

1. This Agreement shall enter into force on the date of its signing.
2. The arrangements established by this Agreement shall remain in force until and to the extent superseded by the Interim Agreement referred to in the Declaration of Principles or any other Agreement between the parties.
3. The five-year Interim Period referred to in the Declaration of Principles commences on the date of the signing of this Agreement.
4. The parties agree that, as long as this Agreement is in force, the security fence erected by Israel around the Gaza Strip shall remain in place and that the line demarcated by the fence, as shown on attached Map No. 1, shall be authoritative only for the purpose of this Agreement.
5. Nothing in this Agreement shall prejudice or pre-empt the outcome of the negotiations on the Interim Agreement or on the Permanent Status to be conducted pursuant to the Declaration of Principles. Neither party shall be deemed, by virtue of having entered into this Agreement, to have renounced or waived any of its existing rights, claims or positions.
6. The two parties view the West Bank and the Gaza Strip as a single territorial unit, the integrity of which will be preserved during the Interim Period.
7. The Gaza Strip and the Jericho Area shall continue to be an integral part of the West Bank and the Gaza Strip, and their status shall not be changed for the period of this Agreement. Nothing in this Agreement shall be considered to change this status.
8. The preamble to this Agreement, and all Annexes, Appendices and Maps attached hereto, shall constitute an integral part hereof. *[Maps not reproduced here: Ed]*

TREATY OF PEACE BETWEEN THE STATE OF ISRAEL AND THE HASHEMITE KINGDOM OF JORDAN
(26 October 1994)

The Treaty was signed by Prime Minister Itzhak Rabin of Israel and the Jordanian premier, Abd al-Salam Majali, in Washington, DC, USA, and was witnessed by President Bill Clinton of the USA. The agreement included 30 Articles, and five Annexes (not reproduced here) dealing with international boundaries, border crossings, and co-operation on the issues of water, crime and drug trafficking, and the environment.

The Government of the State of Israel and the Government of the Hashemite Kingdom of Jordan:

Preamble
BEARING in mind the Washington Declaration, signed by them on 25th July 1994, and which they are both committed to honour;
AIMING at the achievement of a just, lasting and comprehensive peace in the Middle East based on Security Council resolutions 242 and 338 in all their aspects;
BEARING in mind the importance of maintaining and strengthening peace based on freedom, equality, justice and respect for fundamental human rights, thereby overcoming psychological barriers and promoting human dignity;
REAFFIRMING their faith in the purposes and principles of the Charter of the United Nations and recognising their right and obligation to live in peace with each other as well as with all states, within secure and recognised boundaries;
DESIRING to develop friendly relations and co-operation between them in accordance with the principles of international law governing international relations in time of peace;
DESIRING as well to ensure lasting security for both their States and in particular to avoid threats and the use of force between them;
BEARING in mind that in their Washington Declaration of 25th July, 1994, they declared the termination of the state of belligerency between them;
DECIDING to establish peace between them in accordance with this Treaty of Peace;
HAVE AGREED as follows:

Article I

ESTABLISHMENT OF PEACE

Peace is hereby established between the State of Israel and the Hashemite Kingdom of Jordan (the 'Parties') effective from the exchange of the instruments of ratification of this Treaty.

Article II

GENERAL PRINCIPLES

The Parties will apply between them the provisions of the Charter of the United Nations and the principles of international law governing relations among states in times of peace. In particular:
1. They recognise and will respect each other's sovereignty, territorial integrity and political independence;
2. They recognise and will respect each other's right to live in peace within secure and recognised boundaries;
3. They will develop good neighbourly relations of co-operation between them to ensure lasting security, will refrain from the threat or use of force against each other and will settle all disputes between them by peaceful means;
4. They respect and recognise the sovereignty, territorial integrity and political independence of every state in the region;
5. They respect and recognise the pivotal role of human development and dignity in regional and bilateral relationships;

6. They further believe that within their control, involuntary movements of persons in such a way as to adversely prejudice the security of either Party should not be permitted.

Article III

INTERNATIONAL BOUNDARY

1. The international boundary between Israel and Jordan is delimited with reference to the boundary definition under the Mandate as is shown in Annex I (a—see below), on the mapping materials attached thereto and co-ordinates specified therein.

2. The boundary, as set out in Annex I (a), is the permanent, secure and recognized international boundary between Israel and Jordan, without prejudice to the status of any territories that came under Israeli military government control in 1967.

3. The Parties recognise the international boundary, as well as each other's territory, territorial waters and airspace, as inviolable, and will respect and comply with them.

4. The demarcation of the boundary will take place as set forth in Appendix (I) to Annex I and will be concluded not later than nine months after the signing of the Treaty.

5. It is agreed that where a boundary follows a river, in the event of natural changes in the course of the flow of the river as described in Annex I (a), the boundary shall follow the new course of the flow. In the event of any other changes the boundary shall not be affected unless otherwise agreed.

6. Immediately upon the exchange of the instruments of ratification of this Treaty, each Party will deploy on its side of the international boundary as defined in Annex I (a).

7. The Parties shall, upon the signature of this Treaty, enter into negotiations to conclude, within 9 months, an agreement on the delimitation of their maritime boundary in the Gulf of Aqaba.

8. Taking into account the special circumstances of the Nayarharim/Baqura area, which is under Jordanian sovereignty, with Israeli private ownership rights, the Parties agreed to apply the provisions set out in Annex I (b).

9. With respect to the Zofar/Al-Ghamr area, the provisions set out in Annex I (c) will apply.

Article IV

SECURITY

1.
 a. Both Parties, acknowledging that mutual understanding and co-operation in security-related matters will form a significant part of their relations and will further enhance the security of the region, take upon themselves to base their security relations on mutual trust, advancement of joint interests and co-operation, and to aim towards a regional framework of partnership in peace.

 b. Towards that goal the Parties recognise the achievements of the European Community and European Union in the development of the Conference on Security and Co-operation in Europe (CSCE) and commit themselves to the creation, in the Middle East, of a CSCME (Conference on Security and Co-operation in the Middle East). This commitment entails the adoption of regional models of security successfully implemented in the post World War era (along the lines of the Helsinki process) culminating in a regional zone of security and stability.

2. The obligations referred to in this Article are without prejudice to the inherent right of self-defence in accordance with the United Nations Charter.

3. The Parties undertake, in accordance with the provisions of this Article, the following:
 a. to refrain from the threat or use of force or weapons, conventional, non-conventional or of any other kind, against each other, or of other actions or activities that adversely affect the security of the other Party;
 b. to refrain from organising, instigating, inciting, assisting or participating in acts or threats of belligerency, hostility, subversion or violence against the other Party;
 c. to take necessary and effective measures to ensure that acts or threats of belligerency, hostility, subversion or violence against the other Party do not originate from, and are not committed within, through or over their territory (hereinafter the term 'territory' includes the airspace and territorial waters).

4. Consistent with the era of peace and with the efforts to build regional security and to avoid and prevent aggression and violence, the Parties further agree to refrain from the following:
 a. joining or in any way assisting, promoting or co-operating with any coalition, organisation or alliance with a military or security character with a third party, the objectives or activities of which include launching aggression or other acts of military hostility against the other Party, in contravention of the provisions of the present Treaty.
 b. allowing the entry, stationing and operating on their territory, or through it, of military forces, personnel or materiel of a third party, in circumstances which may adversely prejudice the security of the other Party.

5. Both Parties will take necessary and effective measures, and will co-operate in combating terrorism of all kinds. The Parties undertake:
 a. to take necessary and effective measures to prevent acts of terrorism, subversion or violence from being carried out from their territory or through it and to take necessary and effective measures to combat such activities and all their perpetrators.
 b. without prejudice to the basic rights of freedom of expression and association, to take necessary and effective measures to prevent the entry, presence and co-operation in their territory of any group or organisation, and their infrastructure, which threatens the security of the other Party by the use of or incitement to the use of, violent means.
 c. to co-operate in preventing and combating cross-boundary infiltrations.

6. Any question as to the implementation of this Article will be dealt with through a mechanism of consultations which will include a liaison system, verification, supervision, and where necessary, other mechanisms, and higher level consultation. The details of the mechanism of consultations will be contained in an agreement to be concluded by the Parties within 3 months of the exchange of the instruments of ratification of this Treaty.

7. The Parties undertake to work as a matter of priority, and as soon as possible in the context of the Multilateral Working Group on Arms Control and Regional Security, and jointly, towards the following:
 a. the creation in the Middle East of a region free from hostile alliances and coalitions;
 b. the creation of a Middle East free from weapons of mass destruction, both conventional and non-conventional, in the context of a comprehensive, lasting and stable peace, characterised by the renunciation of the use of force, reconciliation and goodwill.

Article V

DIPLOMATIC AND OTHER BILATERAL RELATIONS

1. The Parties agree to establish full diplomatic and consular relations and to exchange resident ambassadors within one month of the exchange of the instruments of ratification of this Treaty.

2. The Parties agree that the normal relationship between them will further include economic and cultural relations.

Article VI

WATER

With the view to achieving a comprehensive and lasting settlement of all the water problems between them:

1. The Parties agree mutually to recognise the rightful allocations of both of them in Jordan River and Yarmouk River waters and Araba/Arava ground water in accordance with the agreed acceptable principles, quantities and quality as set out in Annex II, which shall be fully respected and complied with.

2. The Parties, recognising the necessity to find a practical, just and agreed solution to their water problems and with the view that the subject of water can form the basis for the advancement of co-operation between them, jointly undertake to ensure that the management and development of their water

resources do not, in any way, harm the water resources of the other Party.

3. The Parties recognise that their water resources are not sufficient to meet their needs. More water should be supplied for their use through various methods, including projects of regional and international co-operation.

4. In light of paragraph 3 of this Article, with the understanding that co-operation in water-related subjects would be to the benefit of both Parties, and will help alleviate their water shortages, and that water issues along their entire boundary must be dealt with in their totality, including the possibility of trans-boundary water transfers, the Parties agree to search for ways to alleviate water shortage and to co-operate in the following fields:

   a. development of existing and new water resources, increasing the water availability including co- operation on a regional basis as appropriate, and minimising wastage of water resources through the chain of their uses;
   b. prevention of contamination of water resources;
   c. mutual assistance in the alleviation of water shortages;
   d. transfer of information and joint research and development in water-related subjects, and review of the potentials for enhancement of water resources development and use.

5. The implementation of both Parties' undertakings under this Article is detailed in Annex II.

Article VII

ECONOMIC RELATIONS

1. Viewing economic development and prosperity as pillars of peace, security and harmonious relations between states, peoples and individual human beings, the Parties, taking note of understandings reached between them, affirm their mutual desire to promote economic co-operation between them, as well as within the framework of wider regional economic co-operation.

2. In order to accomplish this goal, the Parties agree to the following:

   a. to remove all discriminatory barriers to normal economic relations, to terminate economic boycotts directed at each other, and to co-operate in terminating boycotts against either Party by third parties;
   b. recognising that the principle of free and unimpeded flow of goods and services should guide their relations, the Parties will enter into negotiations with a view to concluding agreements on economic co-operation, including trade and the establishment of a free trade area, investment, banking, industrial co-operation and labour, for the purpose of promoting beneficial economic relations, based on principles to be agreed upon, as well as on human development considerations on a regional basis. These negotiations will be concluded no later than 6 months from the exchange of the instruments of ratification of this Treaty.
   c. to co-operate bilaterally, as well as in multilateral forums, towards the promotion of their respective economies and of their neighbourly economic relations with other regional parties.

Article VIII

REFUGEES AND DISPLACED PERSONS

1. Recognising the massive human problems caused to both Parties by the conflict in the Middle East, as well as the contribution made by them towards the alleviation of human suffering, the Parties will seek to further alleviate those problems arising on a bilateral level.

2. Recognising that the above human problems caused by the conflict in the Middle East cannot be fully resolved on the bilateral level, the Parties will seek to resolve them in appropriate forums, in accordance with international law, including the following:

   a. in the case of displaced persons, in a quadripartite committee together with Egypt and the Palestinians;
   b. in the case of refugees, i) in the framework of the Multilateral Working Group on Refugees; and ii) in negotiations, in a framework to be agreed, bilateral or otherwise, in conjunction with and at the same time as the permanent status negotiations pertaining to the territories referred to in Article 3 of this Treaty;
   c. through the implementation of agreed United Nations programmes and other agreed international economic programmes concerning refugees and displaced persons, including assistance to their settlement.

Article IX

PLACES OF HISTORICAL AND RELIGIOUS SIGNIFICANCE

1. Each party will provide freedom of access to places of religious and historical significance.

2. In this regard, in accordance with the Washington Declaration, Israel respects the present special role of the Hashemite Kingdom of Jordan in Muslim Holy shrines in Jerusalem. When negotiations on the permanent status will take place, Israel will give high priority to the Jordanian historic role in these shrines.

3. The Parties will act together to promote interfaith relations among the three monotheistic religions, with the aim of working towards religious understanding, moral commitment, freedom of religious worship, and tolerance and peace.

Article X

CULTURAL AND SCIENTIFIC EXCHANGES

The Parties, wishing to remove biases developed through periods of conflict, recognise the desirability of cultural and scientific exchanges in all fields, and agree to establish normal cultural relations between them. Thus, they shall, as soon as possible and not later than 9 months from the exchange of the instruments of ratification of this Treaty, conclude the negotiations on cultural and scientific agreements.

Article XI

MUTUAL UNDERSTANDING AND GOOD NEIGHBOURLY RELATIONS

1. The Parties will seek to foster mutual understanding and tolerance based on shared historic values, and accordingly undertake:

   a. to abstain from hostile or discriminatory propaganda against each other, and to take all possible legal and administrative measures to prevent the dissemination of such propaganda by any organisation or individual present in the territory of either Party;
   b. as soon as possible, and not later than 3 months from the exchange of the instruments of ratification of this Treaty, to repeal all adverse or discriminatory references and expressions of hostility in their respective legislation;
   c. to refrain in all government publications from any such references or expressions;
   d. to ensure mutual enjoyment by each other's citizens of due process of law within their respective legal systems and before their courts.

2. Paragraph 1 (a) of this Article is without prejudice to the right to freedom of expression as contained in the International Covenant on Civil and Political Rights.

3. A joint committee shall be formed to examine incidents where one Party claims there has been a violation of this Article.

Articles XII–XXIV

Articles XII–XXIV deal with co-operation between the two countries in the areas of crime and illegal drugs, transportation and roads, access to ports, civil aviation, posts and telecommunications, tourism, the environment, energy, development of the Jordan Rift Valley area, health, agriculture, joint development of the towns of Aqaba (Jordan) and Eilat (Israel), and the settlement of financial claims.

Article XXV

RIGHTS AND OBLIGATIONS

1. This Treaty does not affect and shall not be interpreted as affecting, in any way, the rights and obligations of the Parties under the Charter of the United Nations.

2. The Parties undertake to fulfil in good faith their obligations under this Treaty, without regard to action or inaction of any other party and independently of any instrument inconsistent with this Treaty. For the purposes of this paragraph each Party represents to the other that in its opinion and interpretation there is no inconsistency between their existing treaty obligations and this Treaty.

3. They further undertake to take all the necessary measures for the application in their relations of the provisions of the multilateral conventions to which they are parties, including the submission of appropriate notification to the Secretary General of the United Nations and other depositories of such conventions.

4. Both Parties will also take all the necessary steps to abolish all pejorative references to the other Party, in multilateral conventions to which they are parties, to the extent that such references exist.

5. The Parties undertake not to enter into any obligation in conflict with this Treaty.

6. Subject to Article 103 of the United Nations Charter, in the event of a conflict between the obligations of the Parties under the present Treaty and any of their other obligations, the obligations under this Treaty will be binding and implemented.

Articles XXVI–XXX

Articles XXVI–XXX deal with provisions for the ratification and implementation of the Treaty, interim measures, the settlement of disputes arising out of the application or interpretation of the Treaty, and the registration of the agreement.

ISRAELI-PALESTINIAN INTERIM AGREEMENT ON THE WEST BANK AND THE GAZA STRIP
(28 September 1995)

The Interim Agreement was signed by the Chairman of the PLO, Yasser Arafat, and the Israeli Minister of Foreign Affairs, Shimon Peres, in Washington, DC, USA. The Agreement was witnessed by representatives of the USA, Russia, Egypt, Jordan, Norway and the European Union (EU). Considerable additional detail was contained in seven annexes (not reproduced here) to the Agreement (the most expansive of which—Annex I—concerned redeployment and security arrangements) and a map (also not reproduced here) in which the boundaries of first-phase redeployment areas 'A' and 'B' were defined.

The Government of the State of Israel and the Palestine Liberation Organization (hereinafter the 'PLO'), the representative of the Palestinian people;

Preamble

WITHIN the framework of the Middle East peace process initiated at Madrid in October 1991;

REAFFIRMING their determination to put an end to decades of confrontation and to live in peaceful coexistence, mutual dignity and security, while recognizing their mutual legitimate and political rights;

REAFFIRMING their desire to achieve a just, lasting and comprehensive peace settlement and historic reconciliation through the agreed political process;

RECOGNIZING that the peace process and the new era that it has created, as well as the new relationship established between the two Parties as described above, are irreversible, and the determination of the two Parties to maintain, sustain and continue the peace process;

RECOGNIZING that the aim of the Israeli-Palestinian negotiations within the current Middle East peace process is, among other things, to establish a Palestinian Interim Self-Government Authority, i.e. the elected Council (hereinafter 'the Council' or 'the Palestinian Council'), and the elected Ra'ees of the Executive Authority, for the Palestinian people in the West Bank and the Gaza Strip, for a transitional period not exceeding five years from the date of signing the Agreement on the Gaza Strip and the Jericho Area (hereinafter 'the Gaza-Jericho Agreement') on May 4, 1994, leading to a permanent settlement based on Security Council Resolutions 242 and 338;

REAFFIRMING their understanding that the interim self-government arrangements contained in this Agreement are an integral part of the whole peace process, that the negotiations on the permanent status, that will start as soon as possible but not later than May 4, 1996, will lead to the implementation of Security Council Resolutions 242 and 338, and that the Interim Agreement shall settle all the issues of the interim period and that no such issues will be deferred to the agenda of the permanent status negotiations;

REAFFIRMING their adherence to the mutual recognition and commitments expressed in the letters dated September 9, 1993, signed by and exchanged between the Prime Minister of Israel and the Chairman of the PLO;

DESIROUS of putting into effect the Declaration of Principles on Interim Self-Government Arrangements signed at Washington, DC on September 13, 1993, and the Agreed Minutes thereto (hereinafter 'the DOP') and in particular Article III and Annex I concerning the holding of direct, free and general political elections for the Council and the Ra'ees of the Executive Authority in order that the Palestinian people in the West Bank, Jerusalem and the Gaza Strip may democratically elect accountable representatives;

RECOGNIZING that these elections will constitute a significant interim preparatory step toward the realization of the legitimate rights of the Palestinian people and their just requirements and will provide a democratic basis for the establishment of Palestinian institutions;

REAFFIRMING their mutual commitment to act, in accordance with this Agreement, immediately, efficiently and effectively against acts or threats of terrorism, violence or incitement, whether committed by Palestinians or Israelis;

FOLLOWING the Gaza-Jericho Agreement; the Agreement on Preparatory Transfer of Powers and Responsibilities signed at Erez on August 29, 1994 (hereinafter 'the Preparatory Transfer Agreement'); and the Protocol on Further Transfer of Powers and Responsibilities signed at Cairo on August 27, 1995 (hereinafter 'the Further Transfer Protocol'); which three agreements will be superseded by this Agreement;

HEREBY AGREE as follows:

CHAPTER 1—THE COUNCIL

Article I

TRANSFER OF AUTHORITY

1. Israel shall transfer powers and responsibilities as specified in this Agreement from the Israeli military government and its Civil Administration to the Council in accordance with this Agreement. Israel shall continue to exercise powers and responsibilities not so transferred.

2. Pending the inauguration of the Council, the powers and responsibilities transferred to the Council shall be exercised by the Palestinian Authority established in accordance with the Gaza-Jericho Agreement, which shall also have all the rights, liabilities and obligations to be assumed by the Council in this regard. Accordingly, the term 'Council' throughout this Agreement shall, pending the inauguration of the Council, be construed as meaning the Palestinian Authority.

3. The transfer of powers and responsibilities to the police force established by the Palestinian Council in accordance with Article XIV below (hereinafter 'the Palestinian Police') shall be accomplished in a phased manner, as detailed in this Agreement and in the Protocol concerning Redeployment and Security Arrangements attached as Annex I to this Agreement (hereinafter 'Annex I').

4. As regards the transfer and assumption of authority in civil spheres, powers and responsibilities shall be transferred and assumed as set out in the Protocol Concerning Civil Affairs attached as Annex III to this Agreement (hereinafter 'Annex III').

5. After the inauguration of the Council, the Civil Administration in the West Bank will be dissolved, and the Israeli military government shall be withdrawn. The withdrawal of

the military government shall not prevent it from exercising the powers and responsibilities not transferred to the Council.

6. A Joint Civil Affairs Co-ordination and Co-operation Committee (hereinafter 'the CAC'), Joint Regional Civil Affairs Subcommittees, one for the Gaza Strip and the other for the West Bank, and District Civil Liaison Offices in the West Bank shall be established in order to provide for co-ordination and co-operation in civil affairs between the Council and Israel, as detailed in Annex III.

7. The offices of the Council, and the offices of its Ra'ees and its Executive Authority and other committees, shall be located in areas under Palestinian territorial jurisdiction in the West Bank and the Gaza Strip.

Article II

ELECTIONS

1. In order that the Palestinian people of the West Bank and the Gaza Strip may govern themselves according to democratic principles, direct, free and general political elections will be held for the Council and the Ra'ees of the Executive Authority of the Council in accordance with the provisions set out in the Protocol concerning Elections attached as Annex II to this Agreement (hereinafter 'Annex II').

2. These elections will constitute a significant interim preparatory step towards the realization of the legitimate rights of the Palestinian people and their just requirements and will provide a democratic basis for the establishment of Palestinian institutions.

3. Palestinians of Jerusalem who live there may participate in the election process in accordance with the provisions contained in this Article and in Article VI of Annex II (Election Arrangements concerning Jerusalem).

4. The elections shall be called by the Chairman of the Palestinian Authority immediately following the signing of this Agreement to take place at the earliest practicable date following the redeployment of Israeli forces in accordance with Annex I, and consistent with the requirements of the election timetable as provided in Annex II, the Election Law and the Election Regulations, as defined in Article I of Annex II.

Article III

STRUCTURE OF THE PALESTINIAN COUNCIL

1. The Palestinian Council and the Ra'ees of the Executive Authority of the Council constitute the Palestinian Interim Self-Government Authority, which will be elected by the Palestinian people of the West Bank, Jerusalem and the Gaza Strip for the transitional period agreed in Article I of the DOP.

2. The Council shall possess both legislative power and executive power, in accordance with Articles VII and IX of the DOP. The Council shall carry out and be responsible for all the legislative and executive powers and responsibilities transferred to it under this Agreement. The exercise of legislative powers shall be in accordance with Article XVIII of this Agreement (Legislative Powers of the Council).

3. The Council and the Ra'ees of the Executive Authority of the Council shall be directly and simultaneously elected by the Palestinian people of the West Bank, Jerusalem and the Gaza Strip, in accordance with the provisions of this Agreement and the Election Law and Regulations, which shall not be contrary to the provisions of this Agreement.

4. The Council and the Ra'ees of the Executive Authority of the Council shall be elected for a transitional period not exceeding five years from the signing of the Gaza-Jericho Agreement on May 4, 1994.

5. Immediately upon its inauguration, the Council will elect from among its members a Speaker. The Speaker will preside over the meetings of the Council, administer the Council and its committees, decide on the agenda of each meeting, and lay before the Council proposals for voting and declare their results.

6. The jurisdiction of the Council shall be as determined in Article XVII of this Agreement (Jurisdiction).

7. The organization, structure and functioning of the Council shall be in accordance with this Agreement and the Basic Law for the Palestinian Interim Self-Government Authority, which Law shall be adopted by the Council. The Basic Law and any regulations made under it shall not be contrary to the provisions of this Agreement.

8. The Council shall be responsible under its executive powers for the offices, services and departments transferred to it and may establish, within its jurisdiction, ministries and subordinate bodies, as necessary for the fulfillment of its responsibilities.

9. The Speaker will present for the Council's approval proposed internal procedures that will regulate, among other things, the decision-making processes of the Council.

Article IV

SIZE OF THE COUNCIL

The Palestinian Council shall be composed of 82 representatives and the Ra'ees of the Executive Authority, who will be directly and simultaneously elected by the Palestinian people of the West Bank, Jerusalem and the Gaza Strip.

Article V

THE EXECUTIVE AUTHORITY OF THE COUNCIL

1. The Council will have a committee that will exercise the executive authority of the Council, formed in accordance with paragraph 4 below (hereinafter 'the Executive Authority').

2. The Executive Authority shall be bestowed with the executive authority of the Council and will exercise it on behalf of the Council. It shall determine its own internal procedures and decision making processes.

3. The Council will publish the names of the members of the Executive Authority immediately upon their initial appointment and subsequent to any changes.

4.a. The Ra'ees of the Executive Authority shall be an ex officio member of the Executive Authority

b. All of the other members of the Executive Authority, except as provided in subparagraph c. below, shall be members of the Council, chosen and proposed to the Council by the Ra'ees of the Executive Authority and approved by the Council

c. The Ra'ees of the Executive Authority shall have the right to appoint some persons, in number not exceeding twenty percent of the total membership of the Executive Authority, who are not members of the Council, to exercise executive authority and participate in government tasks. Such appointed members may not vote in meetings of the Council

d. Non-elected members of the Executive Authority must have a valid address in an area under the jurisdiction of the Council

Article VI

OTHER COMMITTEES OF THE COUNCIL

1. The Council may form small committees to simplify the proceedings of the Council and to assist in controlling the activity of its Executive Authority.

2. Each committee shall establish its own decision-making processes within the general framework of the organization and structure of the Council.

Article VII

OPEN GOVERNMENT

1. All meetings of the Council and of its committees, other than the Executive Authority, shall be open to the public, except upon a resolution of the Council or the relevant committee on the grounds of security, or commercial or personal confidentiality.

2. Participation in the deliberations of the Council, its committees and the Executive Authority shall be limited to their

respective members only. Experts may be invited to such meetings to address specific issues on an ad hoc basis.

Article VIII

JUDICIAL REVIEW

Any person or organization affected by any act or decision of the Ra'ees of the Executive Authority of the Council or of any member of the Executive Authority, who believes that such act or decision exceeds the authority of the Ra'ees or of such member, or is otherwise incorrect in law or procedure, may apply to the relevant Palestinian Court of Justice for a review of such activity or decision.

Article IX

POWERS AND RESPONSIBILITIES OF THE COUNCIL

1. Subject to the provisions of this Agreement, the Council will, within its jurisdiction, have legislative powers as set out in Article XVIII of this Agreement, as well as executive powers.

2. The executive power of the Palestinian Council shall extend to all matters within its jurisdiction under this Agreement or any future agreement that may be reached between the two Parties during the interim period. It shall include the power to formulate and conduct Palestinian policies and to supervise their implementation, to issue any rule or regulation under powers given in approved legislation and administrative decisions necessary for the realization of Palestinian self-government, the power to employ staff, sue and be sued and conclude contracts, and the power to keep and administer registers and records of the population, and issue certificates, licenses and documents.

3. The Palestinian Council's executive decisions and acts shall be consistent with the provisions of this Agreement.

4. The Palestinian Council may adopt all necessary measures in order to enforce the law and any of its decisions, and bring proceedings before the Palestinian courts and tribunals.

5.a. In accordance with the DOP, the Council will not have powers and responsibilities in the sphere of foreign relations, which sphere includes the establishment abroad of embassies, consulates or other types of foreign missions and posts or permitting their establishment in the West Bank or the Gaza Strip, the appointment of or admission of diplomatic and consular staff, and the exercise of diplomatic functions.

b. Notwithstanding the provisions of this paragraph, the PLO may conduct negotiations and sign agreements with states or international organizations for the benefit of the Council in the following cases only:

(1) Economic agreements, as specifically provided in Annex V of this Agreement;

(2) Agreements with donor countries for the purpose of implementing arrangements for the provision of assistance to the Council;

(3) Agreements for the purpose of implementing the regional development plans detailed in Annex IV of the DOP or in agreements entered into in the framework of the multilateral negotiations; and

(4) Cultural, scientific and educational agreements.

c. Dealings between the Council and representatives of foreign states and international organizations, as well as the establishment in the West Bank and the Gaza Strip of representative offices other than those described in subparagraph 5.a above, for the purpose of implementing the agreements referred to in subparagraph 5.b above, shall not be considered foreign relations.

6. Subject to the provisions of this Agreement, the Council shall, within its jurisdiction, have an independent judicial system composed of independent Palestinian courts and tribunals.

CHAPTER 2—REDEPLOYMENT AND SECURITY ARRANGEMENTS

Article X

REDEPLOYMENT OF ISRAELI MILITARY FORCES

1. The first phase of the Israeli military forces redeployment will cover populated areas in the West Bank—cities, towns, villages, refugee camps and hamlets—as set out in Annex I, and will be completed prior to the eve of the Palestinian elections, i.e., 22 days before the day of the elections.

2. Further redeployments of Israeli military forces to specified military locations will commence after the inauguration of the Council and will be gradually implemented commensurate with the assumption of responsibility for public order and internal security by the Palestinian Police, to be completed within 18 months from the date of the inauguration of the Council as detailed in Articles XI (Land) and XIII (Security), below and in Annex I.

3. The Palestinian Police shall be deployed and shall assume responsibility for public order and internal security for Palestinians in a phased manner in accordance with Article XIII (Security) below and Annex I.

4. Israel shall continue to carry the responsibility for external security, as well as the responsibility for overall security of Israelis for the purpose of safeguarding their internal security and public order.

5. For the purpose of this Agreement, 'Israeli military forces' includes Israeli Police and other Israeli security forces.

Article XI

LAND

1. The two sides view the West Bank and the Gaza Strip as a single territorial unit, the integrity and status of which will be preserved during the interim period.

2. The two sides agree that West Bank and Gaza Strip territory, except for issues that will be negotiated in the permanent status negotiations, will come under the jurisdiction of the Palestinian Council in a phased manner, to be completed within 18 months from the date of the inauguration of the Council, as specified below:

a. Land in populated areas (Areas A and B), including government and Al Waqf land, will come under the jurisdiction of the Council during the first phase of redeployment.

b. All civil powers and responsibilities, including planning and zoning, in Areas A and B, set out in Annex III, will be transferred to and assumed by the Council during the first phase of redeployment.

c. In Area C, during the first phase of redeployment Israel will transfer to the Council civil powers and responsibilities not relating to territory, as set out in Annex III.

d. The further redeployments of Israeli military forces to specified military locations will be gradually implemented in accordance with the DOP in three phases, each to take place after an interval of six months, after the inauguration of the Council, to be completed within 18 months from the date of the inauguration of the Council.

e. During the further redeployment phases to be completed within 18 months from the date of the inauguration of the Council, powers and responsibilities relating to territory will be transferred gradually to Palestinian jurisdiction that will cover West Bank and Gaza Strip territory, except for the issues that will be negotiated in the permanent status negotiations.

f. The specified military locations referred to in Article X, paragraph 2 above will be determined in the further redeployment phases, within the specified time-frame ending not later than 18 months from the date of the inauguration of the Council, and will be negotiated in the permanent status negotiations.

3. For the purpose of this Agreement and until the completion of the first phase of the further redeployments:

a. 'Area A' means the populated areas delineated by a red line and shaded in brown on attached map No. 1 (*not reproduced here—Ed.*);

b. 'Area B' means the populated areas delineated by a red line and shaded in yellow on attached map No. 1, and the built-up area of the hamlets listed in Appendix 6 to Annex I; and

c. 'Area C' means areas of the West Bank outside Areas A and B, which, except for the issues that will be negotiated in the permanent status negotiations, will be gradually transferred to Palestinian jurisdiction in accordance with this Agreement.

Article XII

ARRANGEMENTS FOR SECURITY AND PUBLIC ORDER

1. In order to guarantee public order and internal security for the Palestinians of the West Bank and the Gaza Strip, the Council shall establish a strong police force as set out in Article XIV below. Israel shall continue to carry the responsibility for defence against external threats, including the responsibility for protecting the Egyptian and Jordanian borders, and for defence against external threats from the sea and from the air, as well as the responsibility for overall security of Israelis and Settlements, for the purpose of safeguarding their internal security and public order, and will have all the powers to take the steps necessary to meet this responsibility.

2. Agreed security arrangements and co-ordination mechanisms are specified in Annex I.

3. A Joint Co-ordination and Co-operation Committee for Mutual Security Purposes (hereinafter 'the JSC'), as well as Joint Regional Security Committees (hereinafter 'RSCs') and Joint District Co-ordination Offices (hereinafter 'DCOs'), are hereby established as provided for in Annex I.

4. The security arrangements provided for in this Agreement and in Annex I may be reviewed at the request of either Party and may be amended by mutual agreement of the Parties. Specific review arrangements are included in Annex I.

5. For the purpose of this Agreement, 'the Settlements' means, in the West Bank—the settlements in Area C; and in the Gaza Strip—the Gush Katif and Erez settlement areas, as well as the other settlements in the Gaza Strip, as shown on attached map No. 2 (*not reproduced—Ed.*).

Article XIII

SECURITY

1. The Council will, upon completion of the redeployment of Israeli military forces in each district, as set out in Appendix 1 to Annex I, assume the powers and responsibilities for internal security and public order in Area A in that district.

2.a. There will be a complete redeployment of Israeli military forces from Area B. Israel will transfer to the Council and the Council will assume responsibility for public order for Palestinians. Israel shall have the overriding responsibility for security for the purpose of protecting Israelis and confronting the threat of terrorism.

b. In Area B the Palestinian Police shall assume the responsibility for public order for Palestinians and shall be deployed in order to accommodate the Palestinian needs and requirements in the following manner:

(1) The Palestinian Police shall establish 25 police stations and posts in towns, villages, and other places listed in Appendix 2 to Annex I and as delineated on map No. 3 (*not reproduced—Ed.*). The West Bank RSC may agree on the establishment of additional police stations and posts, if required.

(2) The Palestinian Police shall be responsible for handling public order incidents in which only Palestinians are involved.

(3) The Palestinian Police shall operate freely in populated places where police stations and posts are located, as set out in paragraph b(1) above.

(4) While the movement of uniformed Palestinian policemen in Area B outside places where there is a Palestinian police station or post will be carried out after co-ordination and confirmation through the relevant DCO, three months after the completion of redeployment from Area B, the DCOs may decide that movement of Palestinian policemen from the police stations in Area B to Palestinian towns and villages in Area B on roads that are used only by Palestinian traffic will take place after notifying the DCO.

(5) The co-ordination of such planned movement prior to confirmation through the relevant DCO shall include a scheduled plan, including the number of policemen, as well as the type and number of weapons and vehicles intended to take part. It shall also include details of arrangements for ensuring continued co-ordination through appropriate communication links, the exact schedule of movement to the area of the planned operation, including the destination and routes thereto, its proposed duration and the schedule for returning to the police station or post.

The Israeli side of the DCO will provide the Palestinian side with its response, following a request for movement of policemen in accordance with this paragraph, in normal or routine cases within one day and in emergency cases no later than 2 hours.

(6) The Palestinian Police and the Israeli military forces will conduct joint security activities on the main roads as set out in Annex I.

(7) The Palestinian Police will notify the West Bank RSC of the names of the policemen, number plates of police vehicles and serial numbers of weapons, with respect to each police station and post in Area B.

(8) Further redeployments from Area C and transfer of internal security responsibility to the Palestinian Police in Areas B and C will be carried out in three phases, each to take place after an interval of six months, to be completed 18 months after the inauguration of the Council, except for the issues of permanent status negotiations and of Israel's overall responsibility for Israelis and borders.

(9) The procedures detailed in this paragraph will be reviewed within six months of the completion of the first phase of redeployment.

Article XIV

THE PALESTINIAN POLICE

1. The Council shall establish a strong police force. The duties, functions, structure, deployment and composition of the Palestinian Police, together with provisions regarding its equipment and operation, as well as rules of conduct, are set out in Annex I.

2. The Palestinian police force established under the Gaza-Jericho Agreement will be fully integrated into the Palestinian Police and will be subject to the provisions of this Agreement.

3. Except for the Palestinian Police and the Israeli military forces, no other armed forces shall be established or operate in the West Bank and the Gaza Strip.

4. Except for the arms, ammunition and equipment of the Palestinian Police described in Annex I, and those of the Israeli military forces, no organization, group or individual in the West Bank and the Gaza Strip shall manufacture, sell, acquire, possess, import or otherwise introduce into the West Bank or the Gaza Strip any firearms, ammunition, weapons, explosives, gunpowder or any related equipment, unless otherwise provided for in Annex I.

Article XV

PREVENTION OF HOSTILE ACTS

1. Both sides shall take all measures necessary in order to prevent acts of terrorism, crime and hostilities directed against each other, against individuals falling under the other's authority and against their property, and shall take legal measures against offenders.

2. Specific provisions for the implementation of this Article are set out in Annex I.

Article XVI

CONFIDENCE BUILDING MEASURES

With a view to fostering a positive and supportive public atmosphere to accompany the implementation of this Agreement, to establish a solid basis of mutual trust and good faith, and in order to facilitate the anticipated co-operation and new relations between the two peoples, both Parties agree to carry out confidence building measures as detailed herewith:

1. Israel will release or turn over to the Palestinian side, Palestinian detainees and prisoners, residents of the West Bank and the Gaza Strip. The first stage of release of these prisoners and detainees will take place on the signing of this Agreement and the second stage will take place prior to the date of the elections. There will be a third stage of release of detainees and prisoners. Detainees and prisoners will be released from among categories detailed in Annex VII (Release of Palestinian Prisoners and Detainees). Those released will be free to return to their homes in the West Bank and the Gaza Strip.

2. Palestinians who have maintained contact with the Israeli authorities will not be subjected to acts of harassment, violence, retribution or prosecution. Appropriate ongoing measures will be taken, in co-ordination with Israel, in order to ensure their protection.

3. Palestinians from abroad whose entry into the West Bank and the Gaza Strip is approved pursuant to this Agreement, and to whom the provisions of this Article are applicable, will not be prosecuted for offences committed prior to September 13, 1993.

CHAPTER 3—LEGAL AFFAIRS

Article XVII

JURISDICTION

1. In accordance with the DOP, the jurisdiction of the Council will cover West Bank and Gaza Strip territory as a single territorial unit, except for:
    a. Issues that will be negotiated in the permanent status negotiations: Jerusalem, settlements, specified military locations, Palestinian refugees, borders, foreign relations and Israelis; and
    b. Powers and responsibilities not transferred to the Council.

2. Accordingly, the authority of the Council encompasses all matters that fall within its territorial, functional and personal jurisdiction, as follows:
    a. The territorial jurisdiction of the Council shall encompass Gaza Strip territory, except for the Settlements and the Military Installation Area shown on map No. 2, and West Bank territory, except for Area C which, except for the issues that will be negotiated in the permanent status negotiations, will be gradually transferred to Palestinian jurisdiction in three phases, each to take place after an interval of six months, to be completed 18 months after the inauguration of the Council. At this time, the jurisdiction of the Council will cover West Bank and Gaza Strip territory, except for the issues that will be negotiated in the permanent status negotiations.
    Territorial jurisdiction includes land, subsoil and territorial waters, in accordance with the provisions of this Agreement.
    b. The functional jurisdiction of the Council extends to all powers and responsibilities transferred to the Council, as specified in this Agreement or in any future agreements that may be reached between the Parties during the interim period.
    c. The territorial and functional jurisdiction of the Council will apply to all persons, except for Israelis, unless otherwise provided in this Agreement.
    d. Notwithstanding subparagraph a. above, the Council shall have functional jurisdiction in Area C, as detailed in Article IV of Annex III.

3. The Council has, within its authority, legislative, executive and judicial powers and responsibilities, as provided for in this Agreement.

4.a. Israel, through its military government, has the authority over areas that are not under the territorial jurisdiction of the Council, powers and responsibilities not transferred to the Council and Israelis.
    b. To this end, the Israeli military government shall retain the necessary legislative, judicial and executive powers and responsibilities, in accordance with international law. This provision shall not derogate from Israel's applicable legislation over Israelis in personam.

5. The exercise of authority with regard to the electromagnetic sphere and air space shall be in accordance with the provisions of this Agreement.

6. Without derogating from the provisions of this Article, legal arrangements detailed in the Protocol Concerning Legal Matters attached as Annex IV to this Agreement (hereinafter 'Annex IV') shall be observed. Israel and the Council may negotiate further legal arrangements.

7. Israel and the Council shall co-operate on matters of legal assistance in criminal and civil matters through a legal committee (hereinafter 'the Legal Committee'), hereby established.

8. The Council's jurisdiction will extend gradually to cover West Bank and Gaza Strip territory, except for the issues to be negotiated in the permanent status negotiations, through a series of redeployments of the Israeli military forces. The first phase of the redeployment of Israeli military forces will cover populated areas in the West Bank—cities, towns, refugee camps and hamlets, as set out in Annex I—and will be completed prior to the eve of the Palestinian elections, i.e. 22 days before the day of the elections. Further redeployments of Israeli military forces to specified military locations will commence immediately upon the inauguration of the Council and will be effected in three phases, each to take place after an interval of six months, to be concluded no later than eighteen months from the date of the inauguration of the Council.

Article XVIII

LEGISLATIVE POWERS OF THE COUNCIL

1. For the purposes of this Article, legislation shall mean any primary and secondary legislation, including basic laws, laws, regulations and other legislative acts.

2. The Council has the power, within its jurisdiction as defined in Article XVII of this Agreement, to adopt legislation.

3. While the primary legislative power shall lie in the hands of the Council as a whole, the Ra'ees of the Executive Authority of the Council shall have the following legislative powers:
    a. The power to initiate legislation or to present proposed legislation to the Council;
    b. The power to promulgate legislation adopted by the Council; and
    c. The power to issue secondary legislation, including regulations, relating to any matters specified and within the scope laid down in any primary legislation adopted by the Council.

4.a. Legislation, including legislation which amends or abrogates existing laws or military orders, which exceeds the jurisdiction of the Council or which is otherwise inconsistent with the provisions of the DOP, this Agreement, or of any other agreement that may be reached between the two sides during the interim period, shall have no effect and shall be void ab initio.
    b. The Ra'ees of the Executive Authority of the Council shall not promulgate legislation adopted by the Council if such legislation falls under the provisions of this paragraph.

5. All legislation shall be communicated to the Israeli side of the Legal Committee.

6. Without derogating from the provisions of paragraph 4 above, the Israeli side of the Legal Committee may refer for the attention of the Committee any legislation regarding which Israel considers the provisions of paragraph 4 apply, in order to discuss issues arising from such legislation. The Legal Committee will consider the legislation referred to it at the earliest opportunity.

Article XIX

HUMAN RIGHTS AND THE RULE OF LAW

Israel and the Council shall exercise their powers and responsibilities pursuant to this Agreement with due regard to internationally-accepted norms and principles of human rights and the rule of law.

Article XX

RIGHTS, LIABILITIES AND OBLIGATIONS

1.a. Transfer of powers and responsibilities from the Israeli military government and its civil administration to the Council, as detailed in Annex III, includes all related rights, liabilities and obligations arising with regard to acts or omissions which occurred prior to such transfer. Israel will cease to bear any financial responsibility regarding such acts or omissions and the Council will bear all financial responsibility for these and for its own functioning.
b. Any financial claim made in this regard against Israel will be referred to the Council.
c. Israel shall provide the Council with the information it has regarding pending and anticipated claims brought before any court or tribunal against Israel in this regard.
d. Where legal proceedings are brought in respect of such a claim, Israel will notify the Council and enable it to participate in defending the claim and raise any arguments on its behalf.
e. In the event that an award is made against Israel by any court or tribunal in respect of such a claim, the Council shall immediately reimburse Israel the full amount of the award.
f. Without prejudice to the above, where a court or tribunal hearing such a claim finds that liability rests solely with an employee or agent who acted beyond the scope of the powers assigned to him or her, unlawfully or with willful malfeasance, the Council shall not bear financial responsibility.
2.a. Notwithstanding the provisions of paragraphs 1.d through 1.f above, each side may take the necessary measures, including promulgation of legislation, in order to ensure that such claims by Palestinians, including pending claims in which the hearing of evidence has not yet begun, are brought only before Palestinian courts or tribunals in the West Bank and the Gaza Strip, and are not brought before or heard by Israeli courts or tribunals.
b. Where a new claim has been brought before a Palestinian court or tribunal subsequent to the dismissal of the claim pursuant to subparagraph a. above, the Council shall defend it and, in accordance with subparagraph 1.a above, in the event that an award is made for the plaintiff, shall pay the amount of the award.
c. The Legal Committee shall agree on arrangements for the transfer of all materials and information needed to enable the Palestinian courts or tribunals to hear such claims as referred to in sub-paragraph b. above, and, when necessary, for the provision of legal assistance by Israel to the Council in defending such claims.
3. The transfer of authority in itself shall not affect rights, liabilities and obligations of any person or legal entity, in existence at the date of signing of this Agreement.
4. The Council, upon its inauguration, will assume all the rights, liabilities and obligations of the Palestinian Authority.
5. For the purpose of this Agreement, 'Israelis' also includes Israeli statutory agencies and corporations registered in Israel.

Article XXI

SETTLEMENT OF DIFFERENCES AND DISPUTES

Any difference relating to the application of this Agreement shall be referred to the appropriate co-ordination and co-operation mechanism established under this Agreement. The provisions of Article XV of the DOP shall apply to any such difference which is not settled through the appropriate co-ordination and co-operation mechanism, namely:
1. Disputes arising out of the application or interpretation of this Agreement or any related agreements pertaining to the interim period shall be settled through the Liaison Committee.
2. Disputes which cannot be settled by negotiations may be settled by a mechanism of conciliation to be agreed between the Parties.
3. The Parties may agree to submit to arbitration disputes relating to the interim period, which cannot be settled through conciliation. To this end, upon the agreement of both Parties, the Parties will establish an Arbitration Committee.

CHAPTER 4—CO-OPERATION

Article XXII

RELATIONS BETWEEN ISRAEL AND THE COUNCIL

1. Israel and the Council shall seek to foster mutual understanding and tolerance and shall accordingly abstain from incitement, including hostile propaganda, against each other and, without derogating from the principle of freedom of expression, shall take legal measures to prevent such incitement by any organizations, groups or individuals within their jurisdiction.
2. Israel and the Council will ensure that their respective educational systems contribute to the peace between the Israeli and Palestinian peoples and to peace in the entire region, and will refrain from the introduction of any motifs that could adversely affect the process of reconciliation.
3. Without derogating from the other provisions of this Agreement, Israel and the Council shall co-operate in combating criminal activity which may affect both sides, including offenses related to trafficking in illegal drugs and psychotropic substances, smuggling, and offenses against property, including offenses related to vehicles.

Article XXIII

CO-OPERATION WITH REGARD TO TRANSFER OF POWERS AND RESPONSIBILITIES

In order to ensure a smooth, peaceful and orderly transfer of powers and responsibilities, the two sides will co-operate with regard to the transfer of security powers and responsibilities in accordance with the provisions of Annex I, and the transfer of civil powers and responsibilities in accordance with the provisions of Annex III.

Article XXIV

ECONOMIC RELATIONS

The economic relations between the two sides are set out in the Protocol on Economic Relations, signed in Paris on April 29, 1994, and the Appendices thereto, and the Supplement to the Protocol on Economic Relations, all attached as Annex V, and will be governed by the relevant provisions of this Agreement and its Annexes.

Article XXV

CO-OPERATION PROGRAMMES

1. The Parties agree to establish a mechanism to develop programmes of co-operation between them. Details of such co-operation are set out in Annex VI.
2. A Standing Co-operation Committee to deal with issues arising in the context of this co-operation is hereby established as provided for in Annex VI.

Article XXVI

THE JOINT ISRAELI-PALESTINIAN LIAISON COMMITTEE

1. The Liaison Committee established pursuant to Article X of the DOP shall ensure the smooth implementation of this Agreement. It shall deal with issues requiring co-ordination, other issues of common interest and disputes.
2. The Liaison Committee shall be composed of an equal number of members from each Party. It may add other technicians and experts as necessary.
3. The Liaison Committee shall adopt its rules of procedures, including the frequency and place or places of its meetings.
4. The Liaison Committee shall reach its decisions by agreement.
5. The Liaison Committee shall establish a subcommittee that will monitor and steer the implementation of this

Agreement (hereinafter 'the Monitoring and Steering Committee'). It will function as follows:

a. The Monitoring and Steering Committee will, on an ongoing basis, monitor the implementation of this Agreement, with a view to enhancing the co-operation and fostering the peaceful relations between the two sides.

b. The Monitoring and Steering Committee will steer the activities of the various joint committees established in this Agreement (the JSC, the CAC, the Legal Committee, the Joint Economic Committee and the Standing Co-operation Committee) concerning the ongoing implementation of the Agreement, and will report to the Liaison Committee.

c. The Monitoring and Steering Committee will be composed of the heads of the various committees mentioned above.

d. The two heads of the Monitoring and Steering Committee will establish its rules of procedures, including the frequency and places of its meetings.

Article XXVII

LIAISON AND CO-OPERATION WITH JORDAN AND EGYPT

1. Pursuant to Article XII of the DOP, the two Parties have invited the Governments of Jordan and Egypt to participate in establishing further liaison and co-operation arrangements between the Government of Israel and the Palestinian representatives on the one hand, and the Governments of Jordan and Egypt on the other hand, to promote co-operation between them. As part of these arrangements a Continuing Committee has been constituted and has commenced its deliberations.

2. The Continuing Committee shall decide by agreement on the modalities of admission of persons displaced from the West Bank and the Gaza Strip in 1967, together with necessary measures to prevent disruption and disorder.

3. The Continuing Committee shall also deal with other matters of common concern.

Article XXVIII

MISSING PERSONS

1. Israel and the Council shall co-operate by providing each other with all necessary assistance in the conduct of searches for missing persons and bodies of persons which have not been recovered, as well as by providing information about missing persons.

2. The PLO undertakes to co-operate with Israel and to assist it in its efforts to locate and to return to Israel Israeli soldiers who are missing in action and the bodies of soldiers which have not been recovered.

CHAPTER 5—MISCELLANEOUS PROVISIONS

Article XXIX

SAFE PASSAGE BETWEEN THE WEST BANK AND THE GAZA STRIP

Arrangements for safe passage of persons and transportation between the West Bank and the Gaza Strip are set out in Annex I.

Article XXX

PASSAGES

Arrangements for co-ordination between Israel and the Council regarding passage to and from Egypt and Jordan, as well as any other agreed international crossings, are set out in Annex I.

Article XXXI

FINAL CLAUSES

1. This Agreement shall enter into force on the date of its signing.

2. The Gaza-Jericho Agreement, the Preparatory Transfer Agreement and the Further Transfer Protocol will be superseded by this Agreement.

3. The Council, upon its inauguration, shall replace the Palestinian Authority and shall assume all the undertakings and obligations of the Palestinian Authority under the Gaza-Jericho Agreement, the Preparatory Transfer Agreement, and the Further Transfer Protocol.

4. The two sides shall pass all necessary legislation to implement this Agreement.

5. Permanent status negotiations will commence as soon as possible, but not later than May 4, 1996, between the Parties. It is understood that these negotiations shall cover remaining issues, including: Jerusalem, refugees, settlements, security arrangements, borders, relations and co-operation with other neighbours, and other issues of common interest.

6. Nothing in this Agreement shall prejudice or preempt the outcome of the negotiations on the permanent status to be conducted pursuant to the DOP. Neither Party shall be deemed, by virtue of having entered into this Agreement, to have renounced or waived any of its existing rights, claims or positions.

7. Neither side shall initiate or take any step that will change the status of the West Bank and the Gaza Strip pending the outcome of the permanent status negotiations.

8. The two Parties view the West Bank and the Gaza Strip as a single territorial unit, the integrity and status of which will be preserved during the interim period.

9. The PLO undertakes that, within two months of the date of the inauguration of the Council, the Palestinian National Council will convene and formally approve the necessary changes in regard to the Palestinian Covenant, as undertaken in the letters signed by the Chairman of the PLO and addressed to the Prime Minister of Israel, dated September 9, 1993 and May 4, 1994.

10. Pursuant to Annex I, Article IX of this Agreement, Israel confirms that the permanent check-points on the roads leading to and from the Jericho Area (except those related to the access road leading from Mousa Alami to the Allenby Bridge) will be removed upon the completion of the first phase of redeployment.

11. Prisoners who, pursuant to the Gaza-Jericho Agreement, were turned over to the Palestinian Authority on the condition that they remain in the Jericho Area for the remainder of their sentence, will be free to return to their homes in the West Bank and the Gaza Strip upon the completion of the first phase of redeployment.

12. As regards relations between Israel and the PLO, and without derogating from the commitments contained in the letters signed by and exchanged between the Prime Minister of Israel and the Chairman of the PLO, dated September 9, 1993 and May 4, 1994, the two sides will apply between them the provisions contained in Article XXII, paragraph 1, with the necessary changes.

13.a. The Preamble to this Agreement, and all Annexes, Appendices and maps attached hereto (*not reproduced—Ed.*), shall constitute an integral part hereof.

b. The Parties agree that the maps (*not reproduced—Ed.*) attached to the Gaza-Jericho Agreement as

a. map No. 1 (The Gaza Strip), an exact copy of which is attached to this Agreement as map No. 2 (in this Agreement 'map No. 2');

b. map No. 4 (Deployment of Palestinian Police in the Gaza Strip), an exact copy of which is attached to this Agreement as map No. 5 (in this Agreement 'map No. 5'); and

c. map No. 6 (Maritime Activity Zones), an exact copy of which is attached to this Agreement as map No. 8 (in this Agreement 'map No. 8')

are an integral part hereof and will remain in effect for the duration of this Agreement.

14. While the Jeftlik area will come under the functional and personal jurisdiction of the Council in the first phase of redeployment, the area's transfer to the territorial jurisdiction of the Council will be considered by the Israeli side in the first phase of the further redeployment phases.

THE WYE RIVER MEMORANDUM
(23 October 1998)

The Wye River Memorandum was signed by Israeli Prime Minister Benjamin Netanyahu and Palestinian (National) Authority (PA) President Yasser Arafat, and witnessed by US President Bill Clinton, on 23 October 1998 at the Wye Plantation, Maryland, USA. The Memorandum was to enter into force 10 days after this date. An attachment to the Memorandum detailed a 'time line' for the implementation of the terms of the Interim Agreement and the Memorandum.

The following are steps to facilitate implementation of the Interim Agreement on the West Bank and Gaza Strip of September 28, 1995 (the 'Interim Agreement') and other related agreements including the Note for the Record of January 17, 1997 (hereinafter referred to as 'the prior agreements') so that the Israeli and Palestinian sides can more effectively carry out their reciprocal responsibilities, including those relating to further redeployments and security respectively. These steps are to be carried out in a parallel phased approach in accordance with this Memorandum and the attached time line. They are subject to the relevant terms and conditions of the prior agreements and do not supersede their other agreements.

I. FURTHER REDEPLOYMENTS

A. Phase One and Two Further Redeployments

1. Pursuant to the Interim Agreement and subsequent agreements, the Israeli side's implementation of the first and second F.R.D. will consist of the transfer to the Palestinian side of 13% from Area C as follows:

1% to Area (A)
12% to Area (B)

The Palestinian side has informed that it will allocate an area/areas amounting to 3% from the above Area (B) to be designated as Green Areas and/or Nature Reserves. The Palestinian side has further informed that they will act according to the established scientific standards, and that therefore there will be no changes in the status of these areas, without prejudice to the rights of the existing inhabitants in these areas including Bedouins; while these standards do not allow new construction in these areas, existing roads and buildings may be maintained.

The Israeli side will retain in these Green Areas/Nature Reserves the overriding security responsibility for the purpose of protecting Israelis and confronting the threat of terrorism. Activities and movements of the Palestinian Police forces may be carried out after co-ordination and confirmation; the Israeli side will respond to such requests expeditiously.

2. As part of the foregoing implementation of the first and second F.R.D., 14.2% from Area (B) will become Area (A).

B. Third Phase of Further Redeployments

With regard to the terms of the Interim Agreement and of Secretary Christopher's letters to the two sides of January 17, 1997 relating to the further redeployment process, there will be a committee to address this question. The United States will be briefed regularly.

II. SECURITY

In the provisions on security arrangements of the Interim Agreement, the Palestinian side agreed to take all measures necessary in order to prevent acts of terrorism, crime and hostilities directed against the Israeli side, against individuals falling under the Israeli side's authority and against their property, just as the Israeli side agreed to take all measures necessary in order to prevent acts of terrorism, crime and hostilities directed against the Palestinian side, against individuals falling under the Palestinian side's authority and against their property. The two sides also agreed to take legal measures against offenders within their jurisdiction and to prevent incitement against each other by any organizations, groups or individuals within their jurisdiction.

Both sides recognize that it is in their vital interests to combat terrorism and fight violence in accordance with Annex I of the Interim Agreement and the Note for the Record. They also recognize that the struggle against terror and violence must be comprehensive in that it deals with terrorists, the terror support structure, and the environment conducive to the support of terror. It must be continuous and constant over a long-term, in that there can be no pauses in the work against terrorists and their structure. It must be co-operative in that no effort can be fully effective without Israeli-Palestinian co-operation and the continuous exchange of information, concepts, and actions.

Pursuant to the prior agreements, the Palestinian side's implementation of its responsibilities for security, security co-operation, and other issues will be as detailed below during the time periods specified in the attached time line:

A. Security Actions

1. Outlawing and Combating Terrorist Organizations

a. The Palestinian side will make known its policy of zero tolerance for terror and violence against both sides.

b. A work plan developed by the Palestinian side will be shared with the U.S. and thereafter implementation will begin immediately to ensure the systematic and effective combat of terrorist organizations and their infrastructure.

c. In addition to the bilateral Israeli-Palestinian security co-operation, a U.S.-Palestinian committee will meet biweekly to review the steps being taken to eliminate terrorist cells and the support structure that plans, finances, supplies and abets terror. In these meetings, the Palestinian side will inform the U.S. fully of the actions it has taken to outlaw all organizations (or wings of organizations, as appropriate) of a military, terrorist or violent character and their support structure and to prevent them from operating in areas under its jurisdiction.

d. The Palestinian side will apprehend the specific individuals suspected of perpetrating acts of violence and terror for the purpose of further investigation, and prosecution and punishment of all persons involved in acts of violence and terror.

e. A U.S.-Palestinian committee will meet to review and evaluate information pertinent to the decisions on prosecution, punishment or other legal measures which affect the status of individuals suspected of abetting or perpetrating acts of violence and terror.

2. Prohibiting Illegal Weapons

a. The Palestinian side will ensure an effective legal framework is in place to criminalize, in conformity with the prior agreements, any importation, manufacturing or unlicensed sale, acquisition or possession of firearms, ammunition or weapons in areas under Palestinian jurisdiction.

b. In addition, the Palestinian side will establish and vigorously and continuously implement a systematic programme for the collection and appropriate handling of all such illegal items in accordance with the prior agreements. The U.S. has agreed to assist in carrying out this programme.

c. A U.S.-Palestinian-Israeli committee will be established to assist and enhance co-operation in preventing the smuggling or other unauthorized introduction of weapons or explosive materials into areas under Palestinian jurisdiction.

3. Preventing Incitement

a. Drawing on relevant international practice and pursuant to Article XXII (1) of the Interim Agreement and the Note for the Record, the Palestinian side will issue a decree prohibiting all forms of incitement to violence or terror, and establishing mechanisms for acting systematically against all expressions or threats of violence or terror. This decree will be comparable to the existing Israeli legislation which deals with the same subject.

b. A U.S.-Palestinian-Israeli committee will meet on a regular basis to monitor cases of possible incitement to violence or terror and to make recommendations and reports on how to prevent such incitement. The Israeli, Palestinian and U.S. sides will each appoint a media specialist, a law enforcement representative, an educational specialist and a current or former elected official to the committee.

B. Security Co-operation

The two sides agree that their security co-operation will be based on a spirit of partnership and will include, among other things, the following steps:

1. Bilateral Co-operation
There will be full bilateral security co-operation between the two sides which will be continuous, intensive and comprehensive.

2. Forensic Co-operation
There will be an exchange of forensic expertise, training, and other assistance.

3. Trilateral Committee
In addition to the bilateral Israeli-Palestinian security co-operation, a high-ranking U.S.-Palestinian-Israeli committee will meet as required and not less than biweekly to assess current threats, deal with any impediments to effective security co-operation and co-ordination and address the steps being taken to combat terror and terrorist organizations. The committee will also serve as a forum to address the issue of external support for terror. In these meetings, the Palestinian side will fully inform the members of the committee of the results of its investigations concerning terrorist suspects already in custody and the participants will exchange additional relevant information. The committee will report regularly to the leaders of the two sides on the status of co-operation, the results of the meetings and its recommendations.

C. Other Issues

1. Palestinian Police Force
a. The Palestinian side will provide a list of its policemen to the Israeli side in conformity with the prior agreements.

b. Should the Palestinian side request technical assistance, the U.S. has indicated its willingness to help meet their needs in co-operation with other donors.

c. The Monitoring and Steering Committee will, as part of its functions, monitor the implementation of this provision and brief the U.S.

2. PLO Charter
The Executive Committee of the Palestine Liberation Organization and the Palestinian Central Council will reaffirm the letter of 22 January 1998 from PLO Chairman Yasser Arafat to President Clinton concerning the nullification of the Palestinian National Charter provisions that are inconsistent with the letters exchanged between the PLO and the Government of Israel on 9–10 September 1993. PLO Chairman Arafat, the Speaker of the Palestine National Council, and the Speaker of the Palestinian Council will invite the members of the PNC, as well as the members of the Central Council, the Council, and the Palestinian Heads of Ministries to a meeting to be addressed by President Clinton to reaffirm their support for the peace process and the aforementioned decisions of the Executive Committee and the Central Council.

3. Legal Assistance in Criminal Matters
Among other forms of legal assistance in criminal matters, the requests for arrest and transfer of suspects and defendants pursuant to Article II (7) of Annex IV of the Interim Agreement will be submitted (or resubmitted) through the mechanism of the Joint Israeli-Palestinian Legal Committee and will be responded to in conformity with Article II (7) (f) of Annex IV of the Interim Agreement within the twelve week period. Requests submitted after the eighth week will be responded to in conformity with Article II (7) (f) within four weeks of their submission. The U.S. has been requested by the sides to report on a regular basis on the steps being taken to respond to the above requests.

4. Human Rights and the Rule of Law
Pursuant to Article XI (1) of Annex I of the Interim Agreement, and without derogating from the above, the Palestinian Police will exercise powers and responsibilities to implement this Memorandum with due regard to internationally accepted norms of human rights and the rule of law, and will be guided by the need to protect the public, respect human dignity, and avoid harassment.

III. INTERIM COMMITTEES AND ECONOMIC ISSUES

1. The Israeli and Palestinian sides reaffirm their commitment to enhancing their relationship and agree on the need actively to promote economic development in the West Bank and Gaza. In this regard, the parties agree to continue or to reactivate all standing committees established by the Interim Agreement, including the Monitoring and Steering Committee, the Joint Economic Committee (JEC), the Civil Affairs Committee (CAC), the Legal Committee, and the Standing Co-operation Committee.

2. The Israeli and Palestinian sides have agreed on arrangements which will permit the timely opening of the Gaza Industrial Estate. They also have concluded a 'Protocol Regarding the Establishment and Operation of the International Airport in the Gaza Strip During the Interim Period'.

3. Both sides will renew negotiations on Safe Passage immediately. As regards the southern route, the sides will make best efforts to conclude the agreement within a week of the entry into force of this Memorandum. Operation of the southern route will start as soon as possible thereafter. As regards the northern route, negotiations will continue with the goal of reaching agreement as soon as possible. Implementation will take place expeditiously thereafter.

4. The Israeli and Palestinian sides acknowledge the great importance of the Port of Gaza for the development of the Palestinian economy, and the expansion of Palestinian trade. They commit themselves to proceeding without delay to conclude an agreement to allow the construction and operation of the port in accordance with the prior agreements. The Israeli-Palestinian Committee will reactivate its work immediately with a goal of concluding the protocol within sixty days, which will allow commencement of the construction of the port.

5. The two sides recognize that unresolved legal issues adversely affect the relationship between the two peoples. They therefore will accelerate efforts through the Legal Committee to address outstanding legal issues and to implement solutions to these issues in the shortest possible period. The Palestinian side will provide to the Israeli side copies of all of its laws in effect.

6. The Israeli and Palestinian sides will launch a strategic economic dialogue to enhance their economic relationship. They will establish within the framework of the JEC an Ad Hoc Committee for this purpose. The committee will review the following four issues: (1) Israeli purchase tax; (2) co-operation in combating vehicle theft; (3) dealing with unpaid Palestinian debts; and (4) the impact of Israeli standards as barriers to trade and the expansion of the A1 and A2 lists. The committee will submit an interim report within three weeks of the entry into force of this Memorandum, and within six weeks will submit its conclusions and recommendations to be implemented.

7. The two sides agree on the importance of continued international donor assistance to facilitate implementation by both sides of agreements reached. They also recognize the need for enhanced donor support for economic development in the West Bank and Gaza. They agree jointly to approach the donor community to organize a Ministerial Conference before the end of 1998 to seek pledges for enhanced levels of assistance.

IV. PERMANENT STATUS NEGOTIATIONS

The two sides will immediately resume permanent status negotiations on an accelerated basis and will make a determined effort to achieve the mutual goal of reaching an agreement by May 4, 1999. The negotiations will be continuous and without interruption. The U.S. has expressed its willingness to facilitate these negotiations.

V. UNILATERAL ACTIONS

Recognizing the necessity to create a positive environment for the negotiations, neither side shall initiate or take any step that will change the status of the West Bank and the Gaza Strip in accordance with the Interim Agreement.

SHARM EL-SHEIKH MEMORANDUM ON THE IMPLEMENTATION TIMELINE OF OUTSTANDING COMMITMENTS OF AGREEMENTS SIGNED AND THE RESUMPTION OF PERMANENT STATUS NEGOTIATIONS (WYE TWO)
(4 September 1999)

The implementation of the Wye River Memorandum having stalled under the Netanyahu administration in Israel, in September 1999 the new Israeli Prime Minister, Ehud Barak, and the PA President, Yasser Arafat, met in the Egyptian resort of Sharm el-Sheikh to discuss the possible reactivation of the Memorandum. On 4 September the two leaders signed the Sharm el-Sheikh Memorandum (also known as Wye Two), which detailed a revised timetable for the outstanding provisions of the October 1998 Memorandum. The Memorandum was witnessed by President Hosni Mubarak for Egypt, Secretary of State Madeleine Albright for the USA, and King Abdullah of Jordan.

The Government of the State of Israel and the Palestine Liberation Organization (PLO) commit themselves to full and mutual implementation of the Interim Agreement and all other agreements concluded between them since September 1993 (hereinafter 'the prior agreements'), and all outstanding commitments emanating from the prior agreements. Without derogating from the other requirements of the prior agreements, the two sides have agreed as follows:

1. Permanent Status Negotiations

a. In the context of the implementation of the prior agreements, the two sides will resume the Permanent Status negotiations in an accelerated manner and will make a determined effort to achieve their mutual agenda, i.e. the specific issues reserved for Permanent Status negotiators and other issues of common interest.

b. The two sides reaffirm their understanding that the negotiations on the Permanent Status will lead to the implementation of Security Council Resolutions 242 and 338.

c. The two sides will make a determined effort to conclude a Framework Agreement on all Permanent Status issues in five months from the resumption of the Permanent Status negotiations.

d. The two sides will conclude a comprehensive agreement on all Permanent Status issues within one year from the resumption of the Permanent Status negotiations.

e. Permanent Status negotiations will resume after the implementation of the first stage of release of prisoners and the second stage of the First and Second Further Redeployments and not later than September 13, 1999. In the Wye River Memorandum, the United States has expressed its willingness to facilitate these negotiations.

2. Phase One and Phase Two of the Further Redeployments

The Israeli side undertakes the following with regard to Phase One and Phase Two of the Further Redeployments:

a. On September 5, 1999, to transfer 7% from Area C to Area B.

b. On November 15, 1999, to transfer 2% from Area B to Area A and 3% from Area C to Area B.

c. On January 20, 2000, to transfer 1% from Area C to Area A, and 5.1% from Area B to Area A.

3. Release of Prisoners

a. The two sides shall establish a joint committee that shall follow up on matters related to the release of Palestinian prisoners.

b. The Government of Israel shall release Palestinian and other prisoners who committed their offences prior to September 13, 1993, and were arrested prior to May 4, 1994. The Joint Committee shall agree on the names of those who will be released in the first two stages. Those lists shall be recommended to the relevant Authorities through the Monitoring and Steering Committee.

c. The first stage of release of prisoners shall be carried out on September 5, 1999 and shall consist of 200 prisoners. The second stage of release of prisoners shall be carried out on October 8, 1999 and shall consist of 150 prisoners.

d. The joint committee shall recommend further lists of names to be released to the relevant Authorities through the Monitoring and Steering Committee.

e. The Israeli side will aim to release Palestinian prisoners before next Ramadan.

4. Committees

a. The Third Further Redeployment Committee shall commence its activities not later than September 13, 1999.

b. The Monitoring and Steering Committee, all Interim Committees (i.e. Civil Affairs Committee, Joint Economic Committee, Joint Standing Committee, legal committee, people to people), as well as Wye River Memorandum committees shall resume and/or continue their activity, as the case may be, not later than September 13, 1999. The Monitoring and Steering Committee will have on its agenda, inter alia, the Year 2000, Donor/PA projects in Area C, and the issue of industrial estates.

c. The Continuing Committee on displaced persons shall resume its activity on October 1, 1999 (Article XXVII, Interim Agreement).

d. Not later than October 30, 1999, the two sides will implement the recommendations of the Ad-hoc Economic Committee (article III-6, Wye River Memorandum).

5. Safe Passage

a. The operation of the Southern Route of the Safe Passage for the movement of persons, vehicles, and goods will start on October 1, 1999 (Annex I, Article X, Interim Agreement) in accordance with the details of operation, which will be provided for in the Safe Passage Protocol that will be concluded by the two sides not later than September 30, 1999.

b. The two sides will agree on the specific location of the crossing point of the Northern Route of the Safe Passage as specified in Annex I, Article X, provision c-4, in the Interim Agreement not later than October 5, 1999.

c. The Safe Passage Protocol applied to the Southern Route of the Safe Passage shall apply to the Northern Route of the Safe Passage with relevant agreed modifications.

d. Upon the agreement on the location of the crossing point of the Northern Route of the Safe Passage, construction of the needed facilities and related procedures shall commence and shall be ongoing. At the same time, temporary facilities will be established for the operation of the Northern Route not later than four months from the agreement on the specific location of the crossing-point.

e. In between the operation of the Southern crossing point of the Safe Passage and the Northern crossing point of the Safe Passage, Israel will facilitate arrangements for the movement between the West Bank and the Gaza Strip, using non-Safe Passage routes other than the Southern Route of the Safe Passage.

f. The location of the crossing points shall be without prejudice to the Permanent Status negotiations (Annex I, Article X, provision e, Interim Agreement).

6. Gaza Sea Port

The two sides have agreed on the following principles to facilitate and enable the construction works of the Gaza Sea Port. The principles shall not prejudice or pre-empt the outcome of negotiations on the Permanent Status:

a. The Israeli side agrees that the Palestinian side shall commence construction works in and related to the Gaza Sea Port on October 1, 1999.

b. The two sides agree that the Gaza Sea Port will not be operated in any way before reaching a joint Sea Port protocol on all aspects of operating the Port, including security.

c. The Gaza Sea Port is a special case, like the Gaza Airport, being situated in an area under the responsibility of the Palestinian side and serving as an international passage. Therefore, with the conclusion of a joint Sea Port Protocol, all activities and arrangements relating to the construction of the Port shall be in accordance with the provisions of the Interim Agreement, especially those relating to international passages, as adapted in the Gaza Airport Protocol.

d. The construction shall ensure adequate provision for effective security and customs inspection of people and goods, as well as the establishment of a designated checking area in the Port.

e. In this context, the Israeli side will facilitate on an ongoing basis the works related to the construction of the Gaza Sea Port, including the movement in and out of the Port of vessels, equipment, resources, and material required for the construction of the Port.

f. The two sides will co-ordinate such works, including the designs and movement, through a joint mechanism.

7. Hebron Issues

a. The Shuhada Road in Hebron shall be opened for the movement of Palestinian vehicles in two phases. The first phase has been carried out, and the second shall be carried out not later than October 30, 1999.

b. The wholesale market Hasbahe will be opened not later than November 1, 1999, in accordance with arrangements which will be agreed upon by the two sides.

c. A high-level Joint Liaison Committee will convene not later than September 13, 1999 to review the situation in the Tomb of the Patriarchs/Al Haram Al Ibrahimi (Annex I, Article VII, Interim Agreement and as per the January 15, 1998 US Minute of Discussion).

8. Security

a. The two sides will, in accordance with the prior agreements, act to ensure the immediate, efficient and effective handling of any incident involving a threat or act of terrorism, violence or incitement, whether committed by Palestinians or Israelis. To this end, they will co-operate in the exchange of information and co-ordinate policies and activities. Each side shall immediately and effectively respond to the occurrence of an act of terrorism, violence or incitement and shall take all necessary measures to prevent such an occurrence.

b. Pursuant to the prior agreements, the Palestinian side undertakes to implement its responsibilities for security, security co-operation, ongoing obligations and other issues emanating from the prior agreements, including, in particular, the following obligations emanating from the Wye River Memorandum:

1. continuation of the programme for the collection of the illegal weapons, including reports.

2. apprehension of suspects, including reports.

3. forwarding of the list of Palestinian policemen to the Israeli side not later than September 13, 1999.

4. beginning of the review of the list by the Monitoring and Steering Committee not later than October 15, 1999.

9. The two sides call upon the international donor community to enhance its commitment and financial support to the Palestinian economic development and the Israeli-Palestinian peace process.

10. Recognizing the necessity to create a positive environment for the negotiations, neither side shall initiate or take any step that will change the status of the West Bank and the Gaza Strip in accordance with the Interim Agreement.

11. Obligations pertaining to dates which occur on holidays or Saturdays shall be carried out on the first subsequent working day.

This memorandum will enter into force one week from the date of its signature.

It is understood that, for technical reasons, implementation of Article 2a and the first stage mentioned in Article 3c will be carried out within a week from the signing of this Memorandum.

REPORT OF THE SHARM EL-SHEIKH FACT-FINDING COMMITTEE (THE MITCHELL REPORT)

Violence between Israeli forces and Palestinians broke out in late September 2000, following a visit by the leader of Israel's Likud party, Ariel Sharon, to the site of the Temple Mount/Haram al-Sharif, in East Jerusalem. A period of intense international diplomatic activity ensued, in an attempt to bring about an end to the violent confrontations which had swiftly spread throughout the West Bank and Gaza Strip. On 14 October UN Secretary-General Kofi Annan secured the agreement of the Israeli Prime Minister, Ehud Barak, and the PA President, Yasser Arafat, to lead delegations to a summit meeting in Sharm el-Sheikh, Egypt, with mediation by US President Bill Clinton. The summit duly proceeded on 16 October, concluding the following day with what Clinton termed agreement on 'immediate concrete measures' to end the violence. (Subsequent truce agreements, based on understandings brokered by Clinton at Sharm el-Sheikh, failed to hold, however.) Agreement was reached at the summit on the formation of a US-appointed international fact-finding commission to investigate the clashes. The committee—chaired by former US Senator George Mitchell and comprising also former President Süleyman Demirel of Turkey, Norwegian Minister of Foreign Affairs Thorbjørn Jagland, former US Senator Warren Rudman, and the High Representative for the Common Foreign and Security Policy of the European Union, Javier Solana—was appointed by Clinton in early November. Reproduced below is the full text of the committee's report, published on 20 May 2001. [Footnotes—principally references to statements and submissions of the Government of Israel and the PLO, which made submissions to the committee on behalf of the Palestinians—have been omitted].

SUMMARY OF RECOMMENDATIONS

The Government of Israel and the Palestinian Authority (PA) must act swiftly and decisively to halt the violence. Their immediate objectives then should be to rebuild confidence and resume negotiations.

During this mission our aim has been to fulfil the mandate agreed at Sharm el-Sheikh. We value the support given our work by the participants at the summit, and we commend the parties for their co-operation. Our principal recommendation is that they recommit themselves to the Sharm el-Sheikh spirit and that they implement the decisions made there in 1999 and 2000. We believe that the summit participants will support bold action by the parties to achieve these objectives.

The restoration of trust is essential, and the parties should take affirmative steps to this end. Given the high level of hostility and mistrust, the timing and sequence of these steps are obviously crucial. This can be decided only by the parties. We urge them to begin the process of decision immediately.

Accordingly, we recommend that steps be taken to:

End the Violence

The Government of Israel and the PA should reaffirm their commitment to existing agreements and undertakings and should immediately implement an unconditional cessation of violence.

The Government of Israel and PA should immediately resume security co-operation.

Rebuild Confidence

The PA and Government of Israel should work together to establish a meaningful 'cooling-off period' and implement additional confidence-building measures, some of which were detailed in the October 2000 Sharm el-Sheikh Statement and some of which were offered by the US on January 7, 2001 in Cairo [see Recommendations section for further description].

The PA and Government of Israel should resume their efforts to identify, condemn and discourage incitement in all its forms.

The PA should make clear through concrete action to Palestinians and Israelis alike that terrorism is reprehensible and unacceptable, and that the PA will make a 100 percent effort to prevent terrorist operations and to punish perpetrators. This effort should include immediate steps to apprehend and incarcerate terrorists operating within the PA's jurisdiction.

The Government of Israel should freeze all settlement activity, including the 'natural growth' of existing settlements.

The Government of Israel should ensure that the IDF [*Israel Defence Forces*] adopt and enforce policies and procedures encouraging non-lethal responses to unarmed demonstrators, with a view to minimizing casualties and friction between the two communities.

The PA should prevent gunmen from using Palestinian populated areas to fire upon Israeli populated areas and IDF positions. This tactic places civilians on both sides at unnecessary risk.

The Government of Israel should lift closures, transfer to the PA all tax revenues owed, and permit Palestinians who had been employed in Israel to return to their jobs; and should ensure that security forces and settlers refrain from the destruction of homes and roads, as well as trees and other agricultural property in Palestinian areas. We acknowledge the Government of Israel's position that actions of this nature have been taken for security reasons. Nevertheless, the economic effects will persist for years.

The PA should renew co-operation with Israeli security agencies to ensure, to the maximum extent possible, that Palestinian workers employed within Israel are fully vetted and free of connections to organizations and individuals engaged in terrorism.

The PA and Government of Israel should consider a joint undertaking to preserve and protect holy places sacred to the traditions of Jews, Muslims, and Christians.

The Government of Israel and PA should jointly endorse and support the work of Palestinian and Israeli non-governmental organizations involved in cross-community initiatives linking the two peoples.

Resume Negotiations

In the spirit of the Sharm el-Sheikh agreements and understandings of 1999 and 2000, we recommend that the parties meet to reaffirm their commitment to signed agreements and mutual understandings, and take corresponding action. This should be the basis for resuming full and meaningful negotiations.

INTRODUCTION

On October 17, 2000, at the conclusion of the Middle East Peace Summit at Sharm el-Sheikh, Egypt, the President of the United States spoke on behalf of the participants (the Government of Israel, the Palestinian Authority, the Governments of Egypt, Jordan, and the United States, the United Nations, and the European Union). Among other things, the President stated that:

The United States will develop with the Israelis and Palestinians, as well as in consultation with the United Nations Secretary-General, a committee of fact-finding on the events of the past several weeks and how to prevent their recurrence. The committee's report will be shared by the US President with the UN Secretary-General and the parties prior to publication. A final report shall be submitted under the auspices of the US President for publication.

On November 7, 2000, following consultations with the other participants, the President asked us to serve on what has come to be known as the Sharm el-Sheikh Fact-Finding Committee. In a letter to us on December 6, 2000, the President stated that:

The purpose of the Summit, and of the agreement that ensued, was to end the violence, to prevent its recurrence, and to find a path back to the peace process. In its actions and mode of operation, therefore, the Committee should be guided by these overriding goals... [T]he Committee should strive to steer clear of any step that will intensify mutual blame and finger-pointing between the parties. As I noted in my previous letter, 'the Committee should not become a divisive force or a focal point for blame and recrimination but rather should serve to forestall violence and confrontation and provide lessons for the future'. This should not be a tribunal whose purpose is to determine the guilt or innocence of individuals or of the parties; rather, it should be a fact-finding committee whose purpose is to determine what happened and how to avoid it recurring in the future.

After our first meeting, held before we visited the region, we urged an end to all violence. Our meetings and our observations during our subsequent visits to the region have intensified our convictions in this regard. Whatever the source, violence will not solve the problems of the region. It will only make them worse. Death and destruction will not bring peace, but will deepen the hatred and harden the resolve on both sides. There is only one way to peace, justice, and security in the Middle East, and that is through negotiation.

Despite their long history and close proximity, some Israelis and Palestinians seem not to fully appreciate each other's problems and concerns. Some Israelis appear not to comprehend the humiliation and frustration that Palestinians must endure every day as a result of living with the continuing effects of occupation, sustained by the presence of Israeli military forces and settlements in their midst, or the determination of the Palestinians to achieve independence and genuine self-determination. Some Palestinians appear not to comprehend the extent to which terrorism creates fear among the Israeli people and undermines their belief in the possibility of co-existence, or the determination of the Government of Israel to do whatever is necessary to protect its people.

Fear, hate, anger, and frustration have risen on both sides. The greatest danger of all is that the culture of peace, nurtured over the previous decade, is being shattered. In its place there is a growing sense of futility and despair, and a growing resort to violence.

Political leaders on both sides must act and speak decisively to reverse these dangerous trends; they must rekindle the desire and the drive for peace. That will be difficult. But it can be done and it must be done, for the alternative is unacceptable and should be unthinkable.

Two proud peoples share a land and a destiny. Their competing claims and religious differences have led to a grinding, demoralizing, dehumanizing conflict. They can continue in conflict or they can negotiate to find a way to live side-by-side in peace.

There is a record of achievement. In 1991 the first peace conference with Israelis and Palestinians took place in Madrid to achieve peace based on UN Security Council Resolutions 242 and 338. In 1993, the Palestine Liberation Organization (PLO) and Israel met in Oslo for the first face-to-face negotiations; they led to mutual recognition and the Declaration of Principles (signed by the parties in Washington, D.C. on September 13, 1993), which provided a road map to reach the destination agreed in Madrid. Since then, important steps have been taken in Cairo, in Washington, and elsewhere. Last year the parties came very close to a permanent settlement.

So much has been achieved. So much is at risk. If the parties are to succeed in completing their journey to their common destination, agreed commitments must be implemented, international law respected, and human rights protected. We encourage them to return to negotiations, however difficult. It is the only path to peace, justice and security.

DISCUSSION

It is clear from their statements that the participants in the summit of last October hoped and intended that the outbreak of violence, then less than a month old, would soon end. The US President's letters to us, asking that we make recommendations on how to prevent a recurrence of violence, reflect that intention.

Yet the violence has not ended. It has worsened. Thus the overriding concern of those in the region with whom we spoke is to end the violence and to return to the process of shaping a sustainable peace. That is what we were told, and were asked to address, by Israelis and Palestinians alike. It was the message conveyed to us as well by President Mubarak of Egypt, King Abdullah of Jordan, and UN Secretary-General Annan.

Their concern must be ours. If our report is to have effect, it must deal with the situation that exists, which is different from that envisaged by the summit participants. In this report, we will try to answer the questions assigned to us by the Sharm el-Sheikh summit: What happened? Why did it happen?

In light of the current situation, however, we must elaborate on the third part of our mandate: How can the recurrence of violence be prevented? The relevance and impact of our work, in the end, will be measured by the recommendations we make concerning the following:

Ending the Violence.
Rebuilding Confidence.
Resuming Negotiations.

WHAT HAPPENED?

We are not a tribunal. We complied with the request that we do not determine the guilt or innocence of individuals or of the parties. We did not have the power to compel the testimony of witnesses or the production of documents. Most of the information we received came from the parties and, understandably, it largely tended to support their arguments.

In this part of our report, we do not attempt to chronicle all of the events from late September 2000 onward. Rather, we discuss only those that shed light on the underlying causes of violence.

In late September 2000, Israeli, Palestinian, and other officials received reports that Member of the Knesset (now Prime Minister) Ariel Sharon was planning a visit to the Haram al-Sharif/Temple Mount in Jerusalem. Palestinian and US officials urged then Prime Minister Ehud Barak to prohibit the visit. Mr Barak told us that he believed the visit was intended to be an internal political act directed against him by a political opponent, and he declined to prohibit it.

Mr Sharon made the visit on September 28 accompanied by over 1,000 Israeli police officers. Although Israelis viewed the visit in an internal political context, Palestinians saw it as highly provocative to them. On the following day, in the same place, a large number of unarmed Palestinian demonstrators and a large Israeli police contingent confronted each other. According to the US Department of State, 'Palestinians held large demonstrations and threw stones at police in the vicinity of the Western Wall. Police used rubber-coated metal bullets and live ammunition to disperse the demonstrators, killing 4 persons and injuring about 200'. According to the Government of Israel, 14 Israeli policemen were injured.

Similar demonstrations took place over the following several days. Thus began what has become known as the 'Al-Aqsa Intifada' (Al-Aqsa being a mosque at the Haram al-Sharif/Temple Mount).

The Government of Israel asserts that the immediate catalyst for the violence was the breakdown of the Camp David negotiations on July 25, 2000 and the 'widespread appreciation in the international community of Palestinian responsibility for the impasse'. In this view, Palestinian violence was planned by the PA leadership, and was aimed at 'provoking and incurring Palestinian casualties as a means of regaining the diplomatic initiative.'

The Palestine Liberation Organization (PLO) denies the allegation that the intifada was planned. It claims, however, that 'Camp David represented nothing less than an attempt by Israel to extend the force it exercises on the ground to negotiations', and that 'the failure of the summit, and the attempts to allocate blame on the Palestinian side only added to the tension on the ground...'

From the perspective of the PLO, Israel responded to the disturbances with excessive and illegal use of deadly force against demonstrators; behavior which, in the PLO's view, reflected Israel's contempt for the lives and safety of Palestinians. For Palestinians, the widely seen images of the killing of 12-year-old Muhammad al-Durra in Gaza on September 20, shot as he huddled behind his father, reinforced that perception.

From the perspective of the Government of Israel, the demonstrations were organized and directed by the Palestinian leadership to create sympathy for their cause around the world by provoking Israeli security forces to fire upon demonstrators, especially young people. For Israelis, the lynching of two military reservists, First Sergeant Vadim Novesche and First Corporal Yosef Avrahami, in Ramallah on October 12, reflected a deep-seated Palestinian hatred of Israel and Jews.

What began as a series of confrontations between Palestinian demonstrators and Israeli security forces, which resulted in the Government of Israel's initial restrictions on the movement of people and goods in the West Bank amd Gaza Strip (closures), has since evolved into a wider array of violent actions and responses. There have been exchanges of fire between built-up areas, sniping incidents and clashes between Israeli settlers and Palestinians. There have also been terrorist acts and Israeli reactions thereto (characterized by the Government of Israel as counter-terrorism), including killings, further destruction of property and economic measures. Most recently, there have been mortar attacks on Israeli locations and IDF ground incursions into Palestinian areas.

From the Palestinian perspective, the decision of Israel to characterize the current crisis as 'an armed conflict short of war' is simply a means 'to justify its assassination policy, its collective punishment policy, and its use of lethal force'. From the Israeli perspective, 'The Palestinian leadership have instigated, orchestrated and directed the violence. It has used, and continues to use, terror and attrition as strategic tools'.

In their submissions, the parties traded allegations about the motivation and degree of control exercised by the other. However, we were provided with no persuasive evidence that the Sharon visit was anything other than an internal political act; neither were we provided with persuasive evidence that the PA planned the uprising.

Accordingly, we have no basis on which to conclude that there was a deliberate plan by the PA to initiate a campaign of violence at the first opportunity; or to conclude that there was a deliberate plan by the Government of Israel to respond with lethal force.

However, there is also no evidence on which to conclude that the PA made a consistent effort to contain the demonstrations and control the violence once it began; or that the Government of Israel made a consistent effort to use non-lethal means to control demonstrations of unarmed Palestinians. Amid rising anger, fear, and mistrust, each side assumed the worst about the other and acted accordingly.

The Sharon visit did not cause the 'Al-Aqsa Intifada'. But it was poorly timed and the provocative effect should have been foreseen; indeed it was foreseen by those who urged that the visit be prohibited. More significant were the events that followed: the decision of the Israeli police on September 29 to use lethal means against the Palestinian demonstrators; and the subsequent failure, as noted above, of either party to exercise restraint.

WHY DID IT HAPPEN?

The roots of the current violence extend much deeper than an inconclusive summit conference. Both sides have made clear a profound disillusionment with the behavior of the other in failing to meet the expectations arising from the peace process launched in Madrid in 1991 and then in Oslo in 1993. Each side has accused the other of violating undertakings and undermining the spirit of their commitment to resolving their political differences peacefully.

Divergent Expectations

We are struck by the divergent expectations expressed by the parties relating to the implementation of the Oslo process. Results achieved from this process were unthinkable less than 10 years ago. During the latest round of negotiations, the parties were closer to a permanent settlement than ever before.

None the less, Palestinians and Israelis alike told us that the promise on which the Oslo process is based—that tackling the hard 'permanent status' issues be deferred to the end of the process—has gradually come under serious pressure. The step-by-step process agreed to by the parties was based on the assumption that each step in the negotiating process would lead to enhanced trust and confidence. To achieve this, each party would have to implement agreed-upon commitments and abstain from actions that would be seen by the other as attempts to abuse the process in order to predetermine the shape of the final outcome. If this requirement is not met, the Oslo road map cannot successfully lead to its agreed destination. Today, each side blames the other for having ignored this fundamental aspect, resulting in a crisis in confidence. This problem became even more pressing with the opening of permanent status talks.

The Government of Israel has placed primacy on moving toward a Permanent Status Agreement in a non-violent atmosphere, consistent with commitments contained in the agreements between the parties. 'Even if slower than was initially envisaged, there has, since the start of the peace process in Madrid in 1991, been steady progress towards the goal of a Permanent Status Agreement without the resort to violence on a scale that has characterized recent weeks'. The 'goal' is the

Permanent Status Agreement, the terms of which must be negotiated by the parties.

The PLO view is that delays in the process have been the result of an Israeli attempt to prolong and solidify the occupation. Palestinians 'believed that the Oslo process would yield an end to Israeli occupation in five years', the time frame for the transitional period specified in the Declaration of Principles. Instead there have been, in the PLO's view, repeated Israeli delays culminating in the Camp David summit, where, 'Israel proposed to annex about 11.2% of the West Bank (excluding Jerusalem)…' and offered unacceptable proposals concerning Jerusalem, security and refugees. 'In sum, Israel's proposals at Camp David provided for Israel's annexation of the best Palestinian lands, the perpetuation of Israeli control over East Jerusalem, a continued Israeli military presence on Palestinian territory, Israeli control over Palestinian natural resources, airspace and borders, and the return of fewer than 1% of refugees to their homes.'

Both sides see the lack of full compliance with agreements reached since the opening of the peace process as evidence of a lack of good faith. This conclusion led to an erosion of trust even before the permanent status negotiations began.

Divergent Perspectives

During the last seven months, these views have hardened into divergent realities. Each side views the other as having acted in bad faith; as having turned the optimism of Oslo into the suffering and grief of victims and their loved ones. In their statements and actions, each side demonstrates a perspective that fails to recognize any truth in the perspective of the other.

The Palestinian Perspective

For the Palestinian side, 'Madrid' and 'Oslo' heralded the prospect of a State, and guaranteed an end to the occupation and a resolution of outstanding matters within an agreed time frame. Palestinians are genuinely angry at the continued growth of settlements and at their daily experiences of humiliation and disruption as a result of Israel's presence in the Palestinian territories. Palestinians see settlers and settlements in their midst not only as violating the spirit of the Oslo process, but also as an application of force in the form of Israel's overwhelming military superiority, which sustains and protects the settlements.

The Interim Agreement provides that 'the two parties view the West Bank and Gaza as a single territorial unit, the integrity and status of which will be preserved during the interim period'. Coupled with this, the Interim Agreement's prohibition on taking steps which may prejudice permanent status negotiations denies Israel the right to continue its illegal expansionist settlement policy. In addition to the Interim Agreement, customary international law, including the Fourth Geneva Convention, prohibits Israel (as an occupying power) from establishing settlements in occupied territory pending an end to the conflict.

The PLO alleges that Israeli political leaders 'have made no secret of the fact that the Israeli interpretation of Oslo was designed to segregate the Palestinians in non-contiguous enclaves, surrounded by Israeli military-controlled borders, with settlements and settlement roads violating the territories' integrity'. According to the PLO, 'In the seven years since the [Declaration of Principles], the settler population in the West Bank, excluding East Jerusalem and the Gaza Strip, has doubled to 200,000, and the settler population in East Jerusalem has risen to 170,000. Israel has constructed approximately 30 new settlements, and expanded a number of existing ones to house these new settlers.'

The PLO also claims that the Government of Israel has failed to comply with other commitments such as the further withdrawal from the West Bank and the release of Palestinian prisoners. In addition, Palestinians expressed frustration with the impasse over refugees and the deteriorating economic circumstances in the West Bank and Gaza Strip.

The Israeli Perspective

From the Government of Israel perspective, the expansion of settlement activity and the taking of measures to facilitate the convenience and safety of settlers do not prejudice the outcome of permanent status negotiations.

Israel understands that the Palestinian side objects to the settlements in the West Bank and Gaza Strip. Without prejudice to the formal status of the settlements, Israel accepts that the settlements are an outstanding issue on which there will have to be agreement as part of any permanent status resolution between the sides. This point was acknowledged and agreed upon in the Declaration of Principles of 13 September 1993 as well as other agreements between the two sides. There has in fact been a good deal of discussion on the question of settlements between the two sides in the various negotiations toward a permanent status agreement.

Indeed, Israelis point out that at the Camp David summit and during subsequent talks the Government of Israel offered to make significant concessions with respect to settlements in the context of an overall agreement.

Security, however, is the key Government of Israel concern. The Government of Israel maintains that the PLO has breached its solemn commitments by continuing the use of violence in the pursuit of political objectives. 'Israel's principal concern in the peace process has been security. This issue is of overriding importance… [S]ecurity is not something on which Israel will bargain or compromise. The failure of the Palestinian side to comply with both the letter and spirit of the security provisions in the various agreements has long been a source of disturbance in Israel.'

According to the Government of Israel, the Palestinian failure takes several forms: institutionalized anti-Israel, anti-Jewish incitement; the release from detention of terrorists; the failure to control illegal weapons; and the actual conduct of violent operations, ranging from the insertion of riflemen into demonstrations to terrorist attacks on Israeli civilians. The Government of Israel maintains that the PLO has explicitly violated its renunciation of terrorism and other acts of violence, thereby significantly eroding trust between the parties. The Government of Israel perceives 'a thread, implied but nonetheless clear, that runs throughout the Palestinian submissions. It is that Palestinian violence against Israel and Israelis is somehow explicable, understandable, legitimate'.

END THE VIOLENCE

For Israelis and Palestinians alike the experience of the past several months has been intensely *personal*. Through relationships of kinship, friendship, religion, community and profession, virtually everyone in both societies has a link to someone who has been killed or seriously injured in the recent violence. We were touched by their stories. During our last visit to the region, we met with the families of Palestinian and Israeli victims. These individual accounts of grief were heart-rending and indescribably sad. Israeli and Palestinian families used virtually the same words to describe their grief.

When the widow of a murdered Israeli physician—a man of peace whose practice included the treatment of Arab patients—tells us that it seems that Palestinians are interested in killing Jews for the sake of killing Jews, Palestinians should take notice. When the parents of a Palestinian child killed while in his bed by an errant .50 calibre bullet draw similar conclusions about the respect accorded by Israelis to Palestinian lives, Israelis need to listen. When we see the shattered bodies of children we know it is time for adults to stop the violence.

With widespread violence, both sides have resorted to portrayals of the other in hostile stereotypes. This cycle cannot be easily broken. Without considerable determination and readiness to compromise, the rebuilding of trust will be impossible.

Cessation of Violence

Since 1991, the parties have consistently committed themselves, in all their agreements, to the path of non-violence. They did so most recently in the two Sharm el-Sheikh summits of September 1999 and October 2000. To stop the violence now, the PA and Government of Israel need not 'reinvent the wheel'. Rather, they should take immediate steps to end the violence, reaffirm their mutual commitments, and resume negotiations.

Resumption of Security Co-operation

Palestinian security officials told us that it would take some time—perhaps several weeks—for the PA to reassert full control over armed elements nominally under its command and to exert decisive influence over other armed elements operating in Palestinian areas. Israeli security officials have not disputed these assertions. What is important is that the PA make an all out effort to enforce a complete cessation of violence and that it be clearly seen by the Government of Israel as doing so. The Government of Israel must likewise exercise a 100 percent effort to ensure that potential friction points, where Palestinians come into contact with armed Israelis, do not become stages for renewed hostilities.

The collapse of security co-operation in early October reflected the belief by each party that the other had committed itself to a violent course of action. If the parties wish to attain the standard of 100 percent effort to prevent violence, the immediate resumption of security co-operation is mandatory.

We acknowledge the reluctance of the PA to be seen as facilitating the work of Israeli security services absent an explicit political context (i.e. meaningful negotiations) and under the threat of Israeli settlement expansion. Indeed, security co-operation cannot be sustained without such negotiations and with ongoing actions seen as prejudicing the outcome of negotiations. However, violence is much more likely to continue without security co-operation. Moreover, without effective security co-operation, the parties will continue to regard all acts of violence as officially sanctioned.

In order to overcome the current deadlock, the parties should consider how best to revitalize security co-operation. We commend current efforts to that end. Effective co-operation depends on recreating and sustaining an atmosphere of confidence and good personal relations.

It is for the parties themselves to undertake the main burden of day-to-day co-operation, but they should remain open to engaging the assistance of others in facilitating that work. Such outside assistance should be by mutual consent, should not threaten good bilateral working arrangements, and should not act as a tribunal or interpose between the parties. There was good security co-operation until last year that benefited from the good offices of the US (acknowledged by both sides as useful), and was also supported indirectly by security projects and assistance from the European Union. The role of outside assistance should be that of creating the appropriate framework, sustaining goodwill on both sides, and removing friction where possible. That framework must be seen to be contributing to the safety and welfare of both communities if there is to be acceptance by those communities of these efforts.

REBUILD CONFIDENCE

The historic handshake between Chairman Arafat and the late Prime Minister Rabin at the White House in September 1993 symbolized the expectation of both parties that the door to the peaceful resolution of differences had been opened. Despite the current violence and mutual loss of trust, both communities have repeatedly expressed a desire for peace. Channelling this desire into substantive progress has proved difficult. The restoration of trust is essential, and the parties should take affirmative steps to this end. Given the high level of hostility and mistrust, the timing and sequence of these steps are obviously crucial. This can be decided only by the parties. We urge them to begin the process of decision immediately.

Terrorism

In the September 1999 Sharm el-Sheikh Memorandum, the parties pledged to take action against 'any threat or act of terrorism, violence or incitement'. Although all three categories of hostilities are reprehensible, it was no accident that 'terrorism' was placed at the top of the list.

Terrorism involves the deliberate killing and injuring of randomly selected non-combatants for political ends. It seeks to promote a political outcome by spreading terror and demoralization throughout a population. It is immoral and ultimately self defeating. We condemn it and we urge that the parties co-ordinate their security efforts to eliminate it.

In its official submissions and briefings, the Government of Israel has accused the PA of supporting terrorism by releasing incarcerated terrorists, by allowing PA security personnel to abet, and in some cases to conduct, terrorist operations, and by terminating security co-operation with the Government of Israel. The PA vigorously denies the accusations. But Israelis hold the view that the PA's leadership has made no real effort over the past seven months to prevent anti-Israeli terrorism. The belief is, in and of itself, a major obstacle to the rebuilding of confidence.

We believe that the PA has a responsibility to help rebuild confidence by making clear to both communities that terrorism is reprehensible and unacceptable, and by taking all measures to prevent terrorist operations and to punish perpetrators. This effort should include immediate steps to apprehend and incarcerate terrorists operating within the PA's jurisdiction.

Settlements

The Government of Israel also has a responsibility to help rebuild confidence. A cessation of Palestinian–Israeli violence will be particularly hard to sustain unless the Government of Israel freezes all settlement construction activity. The Government of Israel should also give careful consideration to whether settlements that are focal points for substantial friction are valuable bargaining chips for future negotiations or provocations likely to preclude the onset of productive talks.

The issue is, of course, controversial. Many Israelis will regard our recommendation as a statement of the obvious, and will support it. Many will oppose it. But settlement activities must not be allowed to undermine the restoration of calm and the resumption of negotiations.

During the half-century of its existence, Israel has had the strong support of the United States. In international forums, the US has at times cast the only vote on Israel's behalf. Yet, even in such a close relationship there are some differences. Prominent among those differences is the US Government's long-standing opposition to the Government of Israel's policies and practices regarding settlements. As the then Secretary of State, James A. Baker, III, commented on May 22, 1991:

Every time I have gone to Israel in connection with the peace process, on each of my four trips, I have been met with the announcement of new settlement activity. This does violate United States policy. It's the first thing that Arabs—Arab Governments, the first thing that the Palestinians in the territories—whose situation is really quite desperate—the first thing they raise when we talk to them. I don't think there is any bigger obstacle to peace than the settlement activity that continues not only unabated but at an enhanced pace.

The policy described by Secretary Baker, on behalf of the Administration of President George H.W. Bush, has been, in essence, the policy of every American administration over the past quarter century.

Most other countries, including Turkey, Norway, and those of the European Union, have also been critical of Israeli settlement activity, in accordance with their views that such settlements are illegal under international law and not in compliance with previous agreements.

On each of our two visits to the region there were Israeli announcements regarding expansion of settlements, and it was almost always the first issue raised by Palestinians with whom we met. During our last visit, we observed the impact of 6,400 settlers on 140,000 Palestinians in Hebron and 6,500 settlers on over 1,100,000 Palestinians in the Gaza Strip. The Government of Israel describes its policy as prohibiting new settlements but permitting expansion of existing settlements to accommodate 'natural growth'. Palestinians contend that there is no distinction between 'new' and 'expanded' settlements; and that, except for a brief freeze during the tenure of Prime Minister Itzhak Rabin, there has been a continuing, aggressive effort by Israel to increase the number and size of settlements.

The subject has been widely discussed within Israel. The *Ha'aretz* English Language Edition editorial of April 10, 2001 stated:

A government which seeks to argue that its goal is to reach a solution to the conflict with the Palestinians through peaceful means, and is trying at this stage to bring an end to the violence and terrorism, must announce an end to construction in the settlements.

The circumstances in the region are much changed from those which existed nearly 20 years ago. Yet, President Reagan's words remain relevant: 'The immediate adoption of a settlement freeze by Israel, more than any other action, could create the confidence needed [...]'

Beyond the obvious confidence-building qualities of a settlement freeze, we note that many of the confrontations during this conflict have occurred at points where Palestinians, settlers, and security forces protecting the settlers, meet. Keeping both the peace and these friction points will be very difficult.

Reducing Tension

We were told by both Palestinians and Israelis that emotions generated by the many recent deaths and funerals have fuelled additional confrontations, and, in effect, maintained the cycle of violence. We cannot urge one side or the other to refrain from demonstrations. But both sides must make clear that violent demonstrations will not be tolerated. We can and do urge that both sides exhibit a greater respect for human life when demonstrators confront security personnel. In addition, a renewed effort to stop the violence might feature, for a limited time, a 'cooling off' period during which public demonstrations at or near friction points will be discouraged in order to break the cycle of violence. To the extent that demonstrations continue, we urge that demonstrators and security personnel keep their distance from one another to reduce the potential for lethal confrontation.

Actions and Responses

Members of the Committee staff witnessed an incident involving stone throwing in Ramallah from the perspectives, on the ground, of both sides. The people confronting one another were mostly young men. The absence of senior leadership on the IDF side was striking. Likewise, the absence of responsible security and other officials counselling restraint on the Palestinian side was obvious.

Concerning such confrontations, the Government of Israel takes the position that 'Israel is engaged in an armed conflict short of war. This is not a civilian disturbance or a demonstration or a riot. It is characterized by live-fire attacks on a *significant scale* [emphasis added]...[T]he attacks are carried out by a well-armed and organized militia...' Yet, the Government of Israel acknowledges that of some 9,000 'attacks' by Palestinians against Israelis, 'some 2,700 [about 30 percent] involved the use of automatic weapons, rifles, hand guns, grenades, [and] explosives of other kinds'.

Thus, for the first three months of the current uprising, most incidents *did not* involve Palestinian use of firearms and explosives. B'Tselem *[the Israeli Information Centre for Human Rights in the Occupied Territories]* reported that, 'according to IDF figures, 73 percent of the incidents [from September 29 to December 2, 2000] did not include Palestinian gunfire. Despite this, it was in these incidents that most of the Palestinians [were] killed and wounded...' Altogether, nearly 500 people were killed and over 10,000 injured over the past seven months; the overwhelming majority in both categories were Palestinian. Many of these deaths were avoidable, as were many Israeli deaths.

Israel's characterization of the conflict, as noted above, is overly broad, for it does not adequately describe the variety of incidents reported since late September 2000. Moreover, by thus defining the conflict, the IDF has suspended its policy of mandating investigations by the Department of Military Police Investigations whenever a Palestinian in the territories dies at the hands of an IDF soldier in an incident not involving terrorism. In the words of the Government of Israel, 'Where Israel considers that there is reason to investigate particular incidents, it does so, although, given the circumstances of armed conflict, it does not do so routinely'. We believe, however, that by abandoning the blanket 'armed conflict short of war' characterization and by re-instituting mandatory military police investigations, the Government of Israel could help mitigate deadly violence and help rebuild mutual confidence. Notwithstanding the danger posed by stone-throwers, an effort should be made to differentiate between terrorism and protests.

Controversy has arisen between the parties over what Israel calls the 'targeting of individual enemy combatants'. The PLO describes these actions as 'extra-judicial executions', and claims that Israel has engaged in an 'assassination policy' that is 'in clear violation of Article 32 of the Fourth Geneva Convention...' The Government of Israel states that, 'whatever action Israel has taken has been taken firmly within the bounds of the relevant and accepted principles relating to the conduct of hostilities'.

With respect to demonstrations, the Government of Israel has acknowledged 'that individual instances of excessive response may have occurred. To a soldier or a unit coming under Palestinian attack, the equation is not that of the Israeli army versus some stone throwing Palestinian protesters. It is a personal equation'.

We understand this concern, particularly since rocks can maim or even kill. It is no easy matter for a few young soldiers, confronted by large numbers of hostile demonstrators, to make fine legal distinctions on the spot. Still, this 'personal equation' must fit within an organizational ethic; in this case, *The Ethical Code of the Israel Defence Forces*, which states, in part:

The sanctity of human life in the eyes of the IDF servicemen will find expression in all of their actions, in deliberate and meticulous planning, in safe and intelligent training and in proper execution of their mission. In evaluating the risk to self and others, they will use the appropriate standards and will exercise constant care to limit injury to life to the extent required to accomplish the mission.

Those required to respect the IDF ethical code are largely draftees, as the IDF is a conscript force. Active duty enlisted personnel, non-commissioned officers and junior officers—the categories most likely to be present at friction points—are young, often teenagers. Unless more senior career personnel or reservists are stationed at friction points, no IDF personnel present in these sensitive areas have experience to draw upon from previous violent Israeli–Palestinian confrontations. We think it is essential, especially in the context of restoring confidence by minimizing deadly confrontations, that the IDF deploy more senior, experienced soldiers to these sensitive points.

There were incidents where IDF soldiers have used lethal force, including live ammunition and modified metal-cored rubber rounds, against unarmed demonstrators throwing stones. The IDF should adopt crowd-control tactics that minimize the potential for deaths and casualties, withdrawing metal-cored rubber rounds from general use and using instead rubber baton rounds without metal cores.

We are deeply concerned about the public safety implications of exchanges of fire between populated areas, in particular between Israeli settlements and neighbouring Palestinian villages. Palestinian gunmen have directed small arms fire at Israeli settlements and at nearby IDF positions from within or adjacent to civilian dwellings in Palestinian areas, thus endangering innocent Israeli and Palestinian civilians alike. We condemn the positioning of gunmen within or near civilian dwellings. The IDF often responds to such gunfire with heavy calibre weapons, sometimes resulting in deaths and injuries to innocent Palestinians. An IDF officer told us at the Ministry of Defence on March 23, 2001 that, 'When shooting comes from a building we respond, and sometimes there are innocent people in the building'. Obviously, innocent people are injured and killed during exchanges of this nature. We urge that such provocations cease and that the IDF exercise maximum restraint in its responses if they do occur. Inappropriate or excessive uses of force often lead to escalation.

We are aware of IDF sensitivities about these subjects. More than once we were asked: 'What about Palestinian rules of engagement? What about a Palestinian code of ethics for their military personnel?' These are valid questions.

On the Palestinian side there are disturbing ambiguities in the basic areas of responsibility and accountability. The lack of control exercised by the PA over its own security personnel and armed elements affiliated with the PA leadership is very troubling. We urge the PA to take all necessary steps to establish a clear and unchallenged chain of command for armed personnel operating under its authority. We recommend that the PA institute and enforce effective standards of conduct and accountability, both within the uniformed ranks and between the police and the civilian political leadership to which it reports.

Incitement

In their submissions and briefings to the Committee, both sides expressed concerns about hateful language and images emanating from the other, citing numerous examples of hostile sectarian and ethnic rhetoric in the Palestinian and Israeli media, in school curricula and in statements by religious leaders, politicians and others.

We call on the parties to renew their formal commitments to foster mutual understanding and tolerance and to abstain from incitement and hostile propaganda. We condemn hate language and incitement in all its forms. We suggest that the parties be particularly cautious about using words in a manner that suggests collective responsibility.

Economic and Social Impact of Violence

Further restrictions on the movement of people and goods have been imposed by Israel on the West Bank and the Gaza Strip. These closures take three forms: those which restrict movement between the Palestinian areas and Israel; those (including curfews) which restrict movement within the Palestinian areas; and those which restrict movement from the Palestinian areas to foreign countries. These measures have disrupted the lives of hundreds of thousands of Palestinians; they have increased Palestinian unemployment to an estimated 40 percent, in part by preventing some 140,000 Palestinians from working in Israel; and have stripped away about one-third of the Palestinian gross domestic product. Moreover, the transfer of tax and customs duty revenues owed to the PA by Israel has been suspended, leading to a serious fiscal crisis in the PA.

Of particular concern to the PA has been the destruction by Israeli security forces and settlers of tens of thousands of olive and fruit trees and other agricultural property. The closures have had other adverse effects, such as preventing civilians from access to urgent medical treatment and preventing students from attending school.

The Government of Israel maintains that these measures were taken in order to protect Israeli citizens from terrorism. Palestinians characterize these measures as 'collective punishment'. The Government of Israel denies the allegations:

Israel has not taken measures that have had an economic impact simply for the sake of taking such measures or for reasons of harming the Palestinian economy. The measures have been taken for reasons of security. Thus, for example, the closure of the Palestinian territories was taken in order to prevent, or at least minimize the risks of, terrorist attacks...The Palestinian leadership has made no attempt to control this activity and bring it to an end.

Moreover, the Government of Israel points out that violence in the last quarter of 2000 cost the Israeli economy $1.2 billion [US $1,200m.], and that the loss continues at a rate of approximately $150 million per month.

We acknowledge Israel's security concerns. We believe, however, that the Government of Israel should lift closures, transfer to the PA all revenues owed, and permit Palestinians who have been employed in Israel to return to their jobs. Closure policies play into the hands of extremists seeking to expand their constituencies and thereby contribute to escalation. The PA should resume co-operation with Israeli security agencies to ensure that Palestinian workers employed within Israel are fully vetted and free of connections to terrorists and terrorist organizations.

International development assistance has from the start been an integral part of the peace process, with an aim to strengthen the socio-economic foundations for peace. This assistance today is more important than ever. We urge the international community to sustain the development agenda of the peace process.

Holy Places

It is particularly regrettable that places such as the Temple Mount/Haram al-Sharif in Jerusalem, Joseph's Tomb in Nablus, and Rachel's Tomb in Bethlehem have been the scenes of violence, death and injury. These are places of peace, prayer and reflection which must be accessible to all believers.

Places deemed holy by Muslims, Jews, and Christians merit respect, protection and preservation. Agreements previously reached by the parties regarding holy places must be upheld. The Government of Israel and the PA should create a joint initiative to defuse the sectarian aspect of their political dispute by preserving and protecting such places. Efforts to develop inter-faith dialogue should be encouraged.

International Force

One of the most controversial subjects raised during our inquiry was the issue of deploying an international force to the Palestinian areas. The PA is strongly in favour of having such a force to protect Palestinian civilians and their property from the IDF and from settlers. The Government of Israel is just as adamantly opposed to an 'international protection force', believing that it would prove unresponsive to Israeli security concerns and interfere with bilateral negotiations to settle the conflict.

We believe that to be effective such a force would need the support of both parties. We note that international forces deployed in this region have been or are in a position to fulfil their mandates and make a positive contribution only when they were deployed with the consent of all of the parties involved.

During our visit to Hebron we were briefed by personnel of the Temporary International Presence in Hebron (TIPH), a presence to which both parties have agreed. The TIPH is charged with observing an explosive situation and writing reports on their observations. If the parties agree, as a confidence-building measure, to draw upon TIPH personnel to help them manage other friction points, we hope that TIPH contributors could accommodate such a request.

Cross-Community Initiatives

Many described to us the near absolute loss of trust. It was all the more inspiring, therefore, to find groups (such as the Parent's Circle and the Economic Co-operation Foundation) dedicated to cross-community understanding in spite of all that has happened. We commend them and their important work.

Regrettably, most of the work of this nature has stopped during the current conflict. To help rebuild confidence, the Government of Israel and PA should jointly endorse and support the work of Israeli and Palestinian non-governmental organizations (NGOs) already involved in confidence-building through initiatives linking both sides. It is important that the PA and Government of Israel support cross-community organizations and initiatives, including the provision of humanitarian assistance to Palestinian villages by Israeli NGOs. Providing travel permits for participants is essential. Co-operation between the humanitarian organizations and the military/security services of the parties should be encouraged and institutionalized.

Such programmes can help build, albeit slowly, constituencies for peace among Palestinians and Israelis and can provide safety nets during times of turbulence. Organizations involved in this work are vital for translating good intentions into positive actions.

RESUME NEGOTIATIONS

Israeli leaders do not wish to be perceived as 'rewarding violence'. Palestinian leaders do not wish to be perceived as 'rewarding occupation'. We appreciate the political constraints on leaders of both sides. Nevertheless, if the cycle of violence is to be broken and the search for peace resumed, there needs to be a new bilateral relationship incorporating both security co-operation and negotiations.

We cannot prescribe to the parties how best to pursue their political objectives. Yet the construction of a new bilateral relationship solidifying and transcending an agreed cessation of violence requires intelligent risk-taking. It requires, in the first instance, that each party again be willing to regard the other as a *partner*. Partnership, in turn, requires at this juncture something more than was agreed in the Declaration of Principles and in subsequent agreements. Instead of declaring the peace process to be 'dead', the parties should determine how they will conclude their common journey along their agreed 'road map', a journey which began in Madrid and continued—in spite of problems—until very recently.

To define a starting point is for the parties to decide. Both parties have stated that they remain committed to their mutual agreements and undertakings. It is time to explore further implementation. The parties should declare their intention to meet on this basis, in order to resume full and meaningful negotiations, in the spirit of their undertakings at Sharm el-Sheikh in 1999 and 2000.

Neither side will be able to achieve its principal objectives unilaterally or without political risk. We know how hard it is for leaders to act—especially if the action can be characterized by political opponents as a concession—without getting something in return. The PA must—as it has at previous critical junctures—take steps to reassure Israel on security matters. The Government of Israel must—as it has in the past—take steps to reassure the PA on political matters. Israelis and Palestinians should avoid, in their own actions and attitudes, giving extremists, common criminals and revenge seekers the final say in defining their joint future. This will not be easy if deadly incidents occur in spite of effective co-operation. Notwithstanding the daunting difficulties, the very foundation of the trust required to re-establish a functioning partnership consists of each side making such strategic reassurances to the other.

RECOMMENDATIONS

The Government of Israel and the PA must act swiftly and decisively to halt the violence. Their immediate objectives then should be to rebuild confidence and resume negotiations. What we are asking is not easy. Palestinians and Israelis—not just their leaders, but two publics at large—have lost confidence in one another. We are asking political leaders to do, for the sake of their people, the politically difficult: to lead without knowing how many will follow.

During this mission our aim has been to fulfil the mandate agreed at Sharm el-Sheikh. We value the support given our work by the participants at the summit, and we commend the parties for their co-operation. Our principal recommendation is that they recommit themselves to the Sharm el-Sheikh spirit, and that they implement the decisions made there in 1999 and 2000. We believe that the summit participants will support bold action by the parties to achieve these objectives.

End the Violence

The Government of Israel and the PA should reaffirm their commitment to existing agreements and undertakings and should immediately implement an unconditional cessation of violence.

Anything less than a complete effort by both parties to end the violence will render the effort itself ineffective, and will likely be interpreted by the other side as evidence of hostile intent.

The Government of Israel and PA should immediately resume security co-operation.

Effective bilateral co-operation aimed at preventing violence will encourage the resumption of negotiations. We are particularly concerned that, absent effective, transparent security co-operation, terrorism and other acts of violence will continue and may be seen as officially sanctioned whether they are or not. The parties should consider widening the scope of security co-operation to reflect the priorities of both communities and to seek acceptance for these efforts from those communities.

We acknowledge the PA's position that security co-operation presents a political difficulty absent a suitable political context, i.e., the relaxation of stringent Israeli security measures combined with ongoing, fruitful negotiations. We also acknowledge the PA's fear that, with security co-operation in hand, the Government of Israel may not be disposed to deal forthrightly with Palestinian political concerns. We believe that security co-operation cannot long be sustained if meaningful negotiations are unreasonably deferred, if security measures 'on the ground' are seen as hostile, or if steps are taken that are perceived as provocative or as prejudicing the outcome of negotiations.

Rebuild Confidence

The PA and Government of Israel should work together to establish a meaningful 'cooling-off period' and implement additional confidence-building measures, some of which were proposed in the October 2000 Sharm el-Sheikh Statement and some of which were offered by the US on January 7, 2001 in Cairo.

The PA and Government of Israel should resume their efforts to identify, condemn and discourage incitement in all its forms.

The PA should make clear through concrete action to Palestinians and Israelis alike that terrorism is reprehensible and unacceptable, and that the PA will make a 100 percent effort to prevent terrorist operations and to punish perpetrators. This effort should include immediate steps to apprehend and incarcerate terrorists operating within the PA's jurisdiction.

The Government of Israel should freeze all settlement activity, including the 'natural growth' of existing settlements.

The kind of security co-operation desired by the Government of Israel cannot for long co-exist with settlement activity described very recently by the European Union as causing 'great concern' and by the US as 'provocative'.

The Government of Israel should give careful consideration to whether settlements which are focal points for substantial friction are valuable bargaining chips for future negotiations, or provocations likely to preclude the onset of productive talks.

The Government of Israel may wish to make it clear to the PA that a future peace would pose no threat to the territorial contiguity of a Palestinian State to be established in the West Bank and the Gaza Strip.

The IDF should consider withdrawing to positions held before September 28, 2000 which will reduce the number of friction points and the potential for violent confrontations.

The Government of Israel should ensure that the IDF adopt and enforce policies and procedures encouraging non-lethal responses to unarmed demonstrators, with a view to minimizing casualties and friction between the two communities. The IDF should:

Re-institute, as a matter of course, military police investigations into Palestinian deaths resulting from IDF actions in the Palestinian territories in incidents not involving terrorism. The IDF should abandon the blanket characterization of the current uprising as 'an armed conflict short of war', which fails to discriminate between terrorism and protest.

Adopt tactics of crowd-control that minimize the potential for deaths and casualties, including the withdrawal of metal-cored rubber rounds from general use.

Ensure that experienced, seasoned personnel are present for duty at all times at known friction points.

Ensure that the stated values and standard operating procedures of the IDF effectively instil the duty of caring for Palestinians in the West Bank and Gaza Strip as well as Israelis living there, consistent with The Ethical Code of the IDF.

The Government of Israel should lift closures, transfer to the PA all tax revenues owed, and permit Palestinians who had been employed in Israel to return to their jobs; and should ensure that security forces and settlers refrain from the destruction of homes and roads, as well as trees and other agricultural property in Palestinian areas. We acknowledge the Government of Israel's position that actions of this nature have been taken for security reasons. Nevertheless, their economic effects will persist for years.

The PA should renew co-operation with Israeli security agencies to ensure, to the maximum extent possible, that Palestinian workers employed within Israel are fully vetted and free of connections to organizations and individuals engaged in terrorism.

The PA should prevent gunmen from using Palestinian populated areas to fire upon Israeli populated areas and IDF positions. This tactic places civilians on both sides at unnecessary risk.

The Government of Israel and IDF should adopt and enforce policies and procedures designed to ensure that the response to any gunfire emanating from Palestinian populated areas minimizes the danger to the lives and property of Palestinian civilians, bearing in mind that it is probably the objective of gunmen to elicit an excessive IDF response.

The Government of Israel should take all necessary steps to prevent acts of violence by settlers.

The parties should abide by the provisions of the Wye River Agreement prohibiting illegal weapons.

The PA should take all necessary steps to establish a clear and unchallenged chain of command for armed personnel operating under its authority.

The PA should institute and enforce effective standards of conduct and accountability, both within the uniformed ranks and between the police and the civilian political leadership to which it reports.

The PA and Government of Israel should consider a joint undertaking to preserve and protect holy places sacred to the traditions of Muslims, Jews, and Christians. An initiative of this nature might help to reverse a disturbing trend: the increasing use of religious themes to encourage and justify violence.

The Government of Israel and PA should jointly endorse and support the work of Palestinian and Israeli non-governmental organizations (NGOs) involved in cross-community initiatives linking the two peoples. It is important that these activities, including the provision of humanitarian aid to Palestinian villages by Israeli NGOs, receive the full backing of both parties.

Resume Negotiations

We reiterate our belief that a 100 percent effort to stop the violence, an immediate resumption of security co-operation and an exchange of confidence-building measures are all important for the resumption of negotiations. Yet none of these steps will long be sustained absent a return to serious negotiations.

It is not within our mandate to prescribe the venue, the basis or the agenda of negotiations. However, in order to provide an effective political context for practical co-operation between the parties, negotiations must not be unreasonably deferred and they must, in our view, manifest a spirit of compromise, reconciliation and partnership, notwithstanding the events of the past seven months.

In the spirit of the Sharm el-Sheikh agreements and understandings of 1999 and 2000, we recommend that the parties meet to reaffirm their commitment to signed agreements and mutual understandings, and take corresponding action. This should be the basis for resuming full and meaningful negotiations.

The parties are at a crossroads. If they do not return to the negotiating table, they face the prospect of fighting it out for years on end, with many of their citizens leaving for distant shores to live their lives and raise their children. We pray they make the right choice. That means stopping the violence now. Israelis and Palestinians have to live, work, and prosper together. History and geography have destined them to be neighbours. That cannot be changed. Only when their actions are guided by this awareness will they be able to develop the vision and reality of peace and shared prosperity.

UN SECURITY COUNCIL RESOLUTION 1397
(12 March 2002)

Resolution 1397 affirmed for the first time the UN Security Council's 'vision' of both Israeli and Palestinian states. It was the first US-sponsored resolution on the Middle East for some 25 years, and was adopted by 14 votes to none; Syria abstained in the vote.

The Security Council,

Recalling all its previous relevant resolutions, in particular resolutions 242 (1967) and 338 (1973),

Affirming a vision of a region where two States, Israel and Palestine, live side by side within secure and recognized borders,

Expressing its grave concern at the continuation of the tragic and violent events that have taken place since September 2000, especially the recent attacks and the increased number of casualties,

Stressing the need for all concerned to ensure the safety of civilians,

Stressing also the need to respect the universally accepted norms of international humanitarian law.

Welcoming and encouraging the diplomatic efforts of special envoys from the United States of America, the Russian Federation, the European Union and the United Nations Special Co-ordinator and others, to bring about a comprehensive, just and lasting peace in the Middle East,

Welcoming the contribution of Saudi Crown Prince Abdullah,

1. *Demands* immediate cessation of all acts of violence, including all acts of terror, provocation, incitement and destruction;

2. *Calls upon* the Israeli and Palestinian sides and their leaders to co-operate in the implementation of the Tenet work plan and Mitchell Report recommendations with the aim of resuming negotiations on a political settlement;

3. *Expresses* support for the efforts of the Secretary-General and others to assist the parties to halt the violence and to resume the peace process;

4. *Decides* to remain seized of the matter.

UN Document S/Res/1397 (2002).

A PERFORMANCE-BASED ROADMAP TO A PERMANENT TWO-STATE SOLUTION TO THE ISRAELI–PALESTINIAN CONFLICT
(30 April 2003)

The 'roadmap' was presented to both Israeli and Palestinian leaders on 30 April 2003, having been drafted in late 2002 by the Quartet group, comprising the UN, the USA, the EU and Russia. Publication of the roadmap, which was intended to lead to an immediate resumption of Israeli-Palestinian negotiations, followed the naming of a new Palestinian Cabinet by the recently appointed Palestinian Prime Minister, Mahmoud Abbas.

The following is a performance-based and goal-driven roadmap, with clear phases, timelines, target dates, and benchmarks aiming at progress through reciprocal steps by the two parties in the political, security, economic, humanitarian, and institution-building fields, under the auspices of the Quartet [the United States, European Union, United Nations, and Russia]. The destination is a final and comprehensive settlement of the Israel–Palestinian conflict by 2005, as presented in President Bush's speech of 24 June, and welcomed by the EU, Russia and the UN in the 16 July and 17 September Quartet Ministerial statements.

A two-state solution to the Israeli–Palestinian conflict will only be achieved through an end to violence and terrorism, when the Palestinian people have a leadership acting decisively against terror and willing and able to build a practising democracy based on tolerance and liberty, and through Israel's readiness to do what is necessary for a democratic Palestinian state to be established, and a clear, unambiguous acceptance by both parties of the goal of a negotiated settlement as described below. The Quartet will assist and facilitate implementation of the plan, starting in Phase I, including direct discussions between the parties as required. The plan establishes a realistic timeline for implementation. However, as a performance-based plan, progress will require and depend upon the good faith efforts of the parties, and their compliance with each of the obligations outlined below. Should the parties perform their obligations rapidly, progress within and through the phases may come sooner than indicated in the plan. Non-compliance with obligations will impede progress.

A settlement, negotiated between the parties, will result in the emergence of an independent, democratic, and viable Palestinian state living side by side in peace and security with Israel and its other neighbors. The settlement will resolve the Israeli–Palestinian conflict, and end the occupation that began in 1967, based on the foundations of the Madrid Conference, the principle of land for peace, UNSCRs 242, 338 and 1397, agreements previously reached by the parties, and the initiative of Saudi Crown Prince Abdullah—endorsed by the Beirut Arab League Summit—calling for acceptance of Israel as a neighbor living in peace and security, in the context of a comprehensive settlement. This initiative is a vital element of international efforts to promote a comprehensive peace on all tracks, including the Syrian-Israeli and Lebanese-Israeli tracks.

The Quartet will meet regularly at senior levels to evaluate the parties' performance on implementation of the plan. In each phase, the parties are expected to perform their obligations in parallel, unless otherwise indicated.

PHASE I: ENDING TERROR AND VIOLENCE, NORMALIZING PALESTINIAN LIFE, AND BUILDING PALESTINIAN INSTITUTIONS—PRESENT TO MAY 2003

In Phase I, the Palestinians immediately undertake an unconditional cessation of violence according to the steps outlined below; such action should be accompanied by supportive measures undertaken by Israel. Palestinians and Israelis resume security co-operation based on the Tenet work plan to end violence, terrorism, and incitement through restructured and effective Palestinian security services. Palestinians undertake comprehensive political reform in preparation for statehood, including drafting a Palestinian constitution, and free, fair and open elections upon the basis of those measures. Israel takes all necessary steps to help normalize Palestinian life. Israel withdraws from Palestinian areas occupied from September 28, 2000 and the two sides restore the status quo that existed at that time, as security performance and co-operation progress. Israel also freezes all settlement activity, consistent with the Mitchell report.

At the outset of Phase I:

Palestinian leadership issues unequivocal statement reiterating Israel's right to exist in peace and security and calling for an immediate and unconditional ceasefire to end armed activity and all acts of violence against Israelis anywhere. All official Palestinian institutions end incitement against Israel.

Israeli leadership issues unequivocal statement affirming its commitment to the two-state vision of an independent, viable, sovereign Palestinian state living in peace and security alongside Israel, as expressed by President Bush, and calling for an immediate end to violence against Palestinians everywhere. All official Israeli institutions end incitement against Palestinians.

SECURITY

Palestinians declare an unequivocal end to violence and terrorism and undertake visible efforts on the ground to arrest, disrupt, and restrain individuals and groups conducting and planning violent attacks on Israelis anywhere.

Rebuilt and refocused Palestinian Authority security apparatus begins sustained, targeted, and effective operations aimed at confronting all those engaged in terror and dismantlement of terrorist capabilities and infrastructure. This includes commencing confiscation of illegal weapons and consolidation of security authority, free of association with terror and corruption.

GOI [*Government of Israel*] takes no actions undermining trust, including deportations, attacks on civilians; confiscation and/or demolition of Palestinian homes and property, as a punitive measure or to facilitate Israeli construction; destruction of Palestinian institutions and infrastructure; and other measures specified in the Tenet work plan.

Relying on existing mechanisms and on-the-ground resources, Quartet representatives begin informal monitoring and consult with the parties on establishment of a formal monitoring mechanism and its implementation.

Implementation, as previously agreed, of US rebuilding, training and resumed security co-operation plan in collaboration with outside oversight board (US–Egypt–Jordan). Quartet support for efforts to achieve a lasting, comprehensive cease-fire.

All Palestinian security organizations are consolidated into three services reporting to an empowered Interior Minister.

Restructured/retrained Palestinian security forces and IDF counterparts progressively resume security co-operation and other undertakings in implementation of the Tenet work plan, including regular senior-level meetings, with the participation of US security officials.

Arab states cut off public and private funding and all other forms of support for groups supporting and engaging in violence and terror.

All donors providing budgetary support for the Palestinians channel these funds through the Palestinian Ministry of Finance's Single Treasury Account.

As comprehensive security performance moves forward, IDF withdraws progressively from areas occupied since September 28, 2000 and the two sides restore the status quo that existed prior to September 28, 2000. Palestinian security forces redeploy to areas vacated by IDF.

PALESTINIAN INSTITUTION-BUILDING

Immediate action on credible process to produce draft constitution for Palestinian statehood. As rapidly as possible, constitutional committee circulates draft Palestinian constitution, based on strong parliamentary democracy and cabinet with empowered prime minister, for public comment/debate. Constitutional committee proposes draft document for submission after elections for approval by appropriate Palestinian institutions.

Appointment of interim prime minister or cabinet with empowered executive authority/decision-making body.

GOI fully facilitates travel of Palestinian officials for PLC and Cabinet sessions, internationally supervised security retraining, electoral and other reform activity, and other supportive measures related to the reform efforts.

Continued appointment of Palestinian ministers empowered to undertake fundamental reform. Completion of further steps to achieve genuine separation of powers, including any necessary Palestinian legal reforms for this purpose.

Establishment of independent Palestinian election commission. PLC reviews and revises election law.

Palestinian performance on judicial, administrative, and economic benchmarks, as established by the International Task Force on Palestinian Reform.

As early as possible, and based upon the above measures and in the context of open debate and transparent candidate selection/electoral campaign based on a free, multi-party process, Palestinians hold free, open, and fair elections.

GOI facilitates Task Force election assistance, registration of voters, movement of candidates and voting officials. Support for NGOs involved in the election process.

GOI reopens Palestinian Chamber of Commerce and other closed Palestinian institutions in East Jerusalem based on a commitment that these institutions operate strictly in accordance with prior agreements between the parties.

HUMANITARIAN RESPONSE

Israel takes measures to improve the humanitarian situation. Israel and Palestinians implement in full all recommendations of the Bertini report to improve humanitarian conditions, lifting curfews and easing restrictions on movement of persons and goods, and allowing full, safe, and unfettered access of international and humanitarian personnel.

AHLC [*Ad-Hoc Liaison Committee*] reviews the humanitarian situation and prospects for economic development in the West Bank and Gaza and launches a major donor assistance effort, including to the reform effort.

GOI and PA continue revenue clearance process and transfer of funds, including arrears, in accordance with agreed, transparent monitoring mechanism.

CIVIL SOCIETY

Continued donor support, including increased funding through PVOs/NGOs [*private voluntary organizations/non-governmental organizations*], for people to people programs, private sector development and civil society initiatives.

SETTLEMENTS

GOI immediately dismantles settlement outposts erected since March 2001.

Consistent with the Mitchell Report, GOI freezes all settlement activity (including natural growth of settlements).

PHASE II: TRANSITION—JUNE 2003–DECEMBER 2003

In the second phase, efforts are focused on the option of creating an independent Palestinian state with provisional borders and attributes of sovereignty, based on the new constitution, as a way station to a permanent status settlement. As has been noted, this goal can be achieved when the Palestinian people have a leadership acting decisively against terror, willing and able to build a practicing democracy based on tolerance and liberty. With such a leadership, reformed civil institutions and security structures, the Palestinians will have the active support of the Quartet and the broader international community in establishing an independent, viable, state.

Progress into Phase II will be based upon the consensus judgment of the Quartet of whether conditions are appropriate to proceed, taking into account performance of both parties. Furthering and sustaining efforts to normalize Palestinian lives and build Palestinian institutions, Phase II starts after Palestinian elections and ends with possible creation of an independent Palestinian state with provisional borders in 2003. Its primary goals are continued comprehensive security performance and effective security co-operation, continued normalization of Palestinian life and institution-building, further building on and sustaining of the goals outlined in Phase I, ratification of a democratic Palestinian constitution, formal establishment of office of prime minister, consolidation of political reform, and the creation of a Palestinian state with provisional borders.

International Conference: Convened by the Quartet, in consultation with the parties, immediately after the successful conclusion of Palestinian elections, to support Palestinian economic recovery and launch a process, leading to establishment of an independent Palestinian state with provisional borders.

Such a meeting would be inclusive, based on the goal of a comprehensive Middle East peace (including between Israel and Syria, and Israel and Lebanon), and based on the principles described in the preamble to this document.

Arab states restore pre-*intifada* links to Israel (trade offices, etc.).

Revival of multilateral engagement on issues including regional water resources, environment, economic development, refugees, and arms control issues.

New constitution for democratic, independent Palestinian state is finalized and approved by appropriate Palestinian institutions. Further elections, if required, should follow approval of the new constitution.

Empowered reform cabinet with office of prime minister formally established, consistent with draft constitution.

Continued comprehensive security performance, including effective security co-operation on the bases laid out in Phase I.

Creation of an independent Palestinian state with provisional borders through a process of Israeli-Palestinian engagement, launched by the international conference. As part of this process, implementation of prior agreements, to enhance maximum territorial contiguity, including further action on settlements in conjunction with establishment of a Palestinian state with provisional borders.

Enhanced international role in monitoring transition, with the active, sustained, and operational support of the Quartet.

Quartet members promote international recognition of Palestinian state, including possible UN membership.

PHASE III: PERMANENT STATUS AGREEMENT AND END OF THE ISRAELI-PALESTINIAN CONFLICT— 2004–2005

Progress into Phase III, based on consensus judgment of Quartet, and taking into account actions of both parties and Quartet monitoring. Phase III objectives are consolidation of reform and stabilization of Palestinian institutions, sustained, effective Palestinian security performance, and Israeli-Palestinian negotiations aimed at a permanent status agreement in 2005.

Second International Conference: Convened by Quartet, in consultation with the parties, at beginning of 2004 to endorse agreement reached on an independent Palestinian state with provisional borders and formally to launch a process with the active, sustained, and operational support of the Quartet, leading to a final, permanent status resolution in 2005, including on borders, Jerusalem, refugees, settlements; and, to support progress toward a comprehensive Middle East settlement between Israel and Lebanon and Israel and Syria, to be achieved as soon as possible.

Continued comprehensive, effective progress on the reform agenda laid out by the Task Force in preparation for final status agreement.

Continued sustained and effective security performance, and sustained, effective security co-operation on the bases laid out in Phase I.

International efforts to facilitate reform and stabilize Palestinian institutions and the Palestinian economy, in preparation for final status agreement.

Parties reach final and comprehensive permanent status agreement that ends the Israel–Palestinian conflict in 2005, through a settlement negotiated between the parties based on UNSCR 242, 338, and 1397, that ends the occupation that began in 1967, and includes an agreed, just, fair, and realistic solution to the refugee issue, and a negotiated resolution on the status of Jerusalem that takes into account the political and religious concerns of both sides, and protects the religious interests of Jews, Christians, and Muslims worldwide, and fulfils the vision of two states, Israel and sovereign, independent, democratic and viable Palestine, living side-by-side in peace and security.

Arab state acceptance of full normal relations with Israel and security for all the states of the region in the context of a comprehensive Arab-Israeli peace.

THE GOVERNMENT RESOLUTION REGARDING THE DISENGAGEMENT PLAN
(6 June 2004)

The Israeli Cabinet approved the plan for Israel's disengagement from Palestinians in the Gaza Strip and the northern West Bank on 6 June 2004. The proposals, which were originally outlined by Prime Minister Ariel Sharon at the annual Herzliya Conference in December 2003, required Israel to dismantle most military installations and all 21 Israeli settlements in the Gaza Strip, and to withdraw from four settlements in the West Bank. The Knesset endorsed the plan on 25 October 2004, and the first stage of disengagement entered formal effect from 17 August 2005. The Israel Defence Forces were reported to have completed their withdrawals from the Gaza Strip and the four West Bank settlements, within the framework of the Disengagement Plan, on 12 September and 22 September 2005, respectively. (For further details, see Israel and the Palestinian Territories.)

Addendum A—Revised Disengagement Plan—Main Principles

1. BACKGROUND—POLITICAL AND SECURITY IMPLICATIONS

The State of Israel is committed to the peace process and aspires to reach an agreed resolution of the conflict based upon the vision of US President George Bush. The State of Israel believes that it must act to improve the current situation. The State of Israel has come to the conclusion that there is currently no reliable Palestinian partner with which it can make progress in a two-sided peace process. Accordingly, it has developed a plan of revised disengagement (hereinafter—the plan), based on the following considerations:

One. The stalemate dictated by the current situation is harmful. In order to break out of this stalemate, the State of Israel is required to initiate moves not dependent on Palestinian co-operation.

Two. The purpose of the plan is to lead to a better security, political, economic and demographic situation.

Three. In any future permanent status arrangement, there will be no Israeli towns and villages in the Gaza Strip. On the other hand, it is clear that in the West Bank, there are areas which will be part of the State of Israel, including major Israeli population centers, cities, towns and villages, security areas and other places of special interest to Israel.

Four. The State of Israel supports the efforts of the United States, operating alongside the international community, to promote the reform process, the construction of institutions and the improvement of the economy and welfare of the Palestinian residents, in order that a new Palestinian leadership will emerge and prove itself capable of fulfilling its commitments under the Roadmap.

Five. Relocation from the Gaza Strip and from an area in Northern Samaria should reduce friction with the Palestinian population.

Six. The completion of the plan will serve to dispel the claims regarding Israel's responsibility for the Palestinians in the Gaza Strip.

Seven. The process set forth in the plan is without prejudice to the relevant agreements between the State of Israel and the Palestinians. Relevant arrangements shall continue to apply.

Eight. International support for this plan is widespread and important. This support is essential in order to bring the Palestinians to implement in practice their obligations to combat terrorism and effect reforms as required by the Roadmap, thus enabling the parties to return to the path of negotiation.

2. MAIN ELEMENTS

A. THE PROCESS:

The required preparatory work for the implementation of the plan will be carried out (including staff work to determine criteria, definitions, evaluations, and preparations for required legislation).

Immediately upon completion of the preparatory work, a discussion will be held by the Government in order to make a decision concerning the relocation of settlements, taking into consideration the circumstances prevailing at that time—whether or not to relocate, and which settlements.

The towns and villages will be classified into four groups, as follows:

1) Group A—Morag, Netzarim, Kfar Darom
2) Group B—the villages of Northern Samaria (Ganim, Kadim, Sa-Nur and Homesh)
3) Group C—the towns and villages of Gush Katif
4) Group D—the villages of the Northern Gaza Strip (Elei Sinai, Dugit and Nissanit)

It is clarified that, following the completion of the aforementioned preparations, the Government will convene periodically in order to decide separately on the question of whether or not to relocate, with respect to each of the aforementioned groups.

3. The continuation of the aforementioned process is subject to the resolutions that the Government will pass, as mentioned above in Article 2, and will be implemented in accordance with the content of those resolutions.

3.1 *The Gaza Strip*

1) The State of Israel will evacuate the Gaza Strip, including all existing Israeli towns and villages, and will redeploy outside the Strip. This will not include military deployment in the area of the border between the Gaza Strip and Egypt ('the Philadelphi Route') as detailed below.

2) Upon completion of this process, there shall no longer be any permanent presence of Israeli security forces in the areas of Gaza Strip territory which have been evacuated.

3.2 *The West Bank*

3) The State of Israel will evacuate an area in Northern Samaria (Ganim, Kadim, Sa-Nur and Homesh), and all military installations in this area, and will redeploy outside the vacated area.

4) Upon completion of this process, there shall no longer be any permanent presence of Israeli security forces in this area.

5) The move will enable territorial contiguity for Palestinians in the Northern Samaria area.

6) The State of Israel will assist, together with the international community, in improving the transportation infrastructure in the West Bank in order to facilitate the contiguity of Palestinian transportation.

7) The process will facilitate normal life and Palestinian economic and commercial activity in the West Bank.

3.3 The intention is to complete the planned relocation process by the end of 2005.

THE SECURITY FENCE:

The State of Israel will continue building the Security Fence, in accordance with the relevant decisions of the Government. The route will take into account humanitarian considerations.

3. SECURITY SITUATION FOLLOWING THE RELOCATION

One. The Gaza Strip:

1) The State of Israel will guard and monitor the external land perimeter of the Gaza Strip, will continue to maintain exclusive authority in Gaza air space, and will continue to exercise security activity in the sea off the coast of the Gaza Strip.

2) The Gaza Strip shall be demilitarized and shall be devoid of weaponry, the presence of which does not accord with the Israeli-Palestinian agreements.

3) The State of Israel reserves its fundamental right of self-defense, both preventive and reactive, including where necessary the use of force, in respect of threats emanating from the Gaza Strip.

Two. The West Bank:

1) Upon completion of the evacuation of the Northern Samaria area, no permanent Israeli military presence will remain in this area.

2) The State of Israel reserves its fundamental right of self-defense, both preventive and reactive, including where necessary the use of force, in respect of threats emanating from the Northern Samaria area.

3) In other areas of the West Bank, current security activity will continue. However, as circumstances require, the State of Israel will consider reducing such activity in Palestinian cities.

4) The State of Israel will work to reduce the number of internal check-points throughout the West Bank.

4. MILITARY INSTALLATIONS AND INFRASTRUCTURE IN THE GAZA STRIP AND NORTHERN SAMARIA

In general, these will be dismantled and evacuated, with the exception of those which the State of Israel decides to transfer to another party.

5. SECURITY ASSISTANCE TO THE PALESTINIANS

The State of Israel agrees that by co-ordination with it, advice, assistance and training will be provided to the Palestinian security forces for the implementation of their obligations to combat terrorism and maintain public order, by American, British, Egyptian, Jordanian or other experts, as agreed therewith. No foreign security presence may enter the Gaza Strip and/or the West Bank without being co-ordinated with and approved by the State of Israel.

6. THE BORDER AREA BETWEEN THE GAZA STRIP AND EGYPT (PHILADELPHI ROUTE)

The State of Israel will continue to maintain a military presence along the border between the Gaza Strip and Egypt (Philadelphi Route). This presence is an essential security requirement. At certain locations, security considerations may require some widening of the area in which the military activity is conducted.

Subsequently, the evacuation of this area will be considered. Evacuation of the area will be dependent, inter alia, on the security situation and the extent of co-operation with Egypt in establishing a reliable alternative arrangement.

If and when conditions permit the evacuation of this area, the State of Israel will be willing to consider the possibility of the establishment of a seaport and airport in the Gaza Strip, in accordance with arrangements to be agreed with Israel.

7. REAL ESTATE ASSETS

In general, residential dwellings and sensitive structures, including synagogues, will not remain. The State of Israel will aspire to transfer other facilities, including industrial, commercial and agricultural ones, to a third, international party which will put them to use for the benefit of the Palestinian population that is not involved in terror.

The area of the Erez industrial zone will be transferred to the responsibility of an agreed upon Palestinian or international party.

The State of Israel will explore, together with Egypt, the possibility of establishing a joint industrial zone on the border of the Gaza Strip, Egypt and Israel.

8. CIVIL INFRASTRUCTURE AND ARRANGEMENTS

Infrastructure relating to water, electricity, sewage and telecommunications will remain in place.

In general, Israel will continue, for full price, to supply electricity, water, gas and petrol to the Palestinians, in accordance with current arrangements.

Other existing arrangements, such as those relating to water and the electro-magnetic sphere shall remain in force.

9. ACTIVITY OF CIVILIAN INTERNATIONAL ORGANIZATIONS

The State of Israel recognizes the great importance of the continued activity of international humanitarian organizations and others engaged in civil development, assisting the Palestinian population.

The State of Israel will co-ordinate with these organizations arrangements to facilitate their activities.

The State of Israel proposes that an international apparatus be established (along the lines of the AHLC), with the agreement of Israel and international elements which will work to develop the Palestinian economy.

10. ECONOMIC ARRANGEMENTS

In general, the economic arrangements currently in operation between the State of Israel and the Palestinians shall remain in force. These arrangements include, inter alia:

One. The entry and exit of goods between the Gaza Strip, the West Bank, the State of Israel and abroad.

Two. The monetary regime.

Three. Tax and customs envelope arrangements.

Four. Postal and telecommunications arrangements.

Five. The entry of workers into Israel, in accordance with the existing criteria.

In the longer term, and in line with Israel's interest in encouraging greater Palestinian economic independence, the State of Israel expects to reduce the number of Palestinian workers entering Israel, to the point that it ceases completely. The State of Israel supports the development of sources of employment in the Gaza Strip and in Palestinian areas of the West Bank, by international elements.

11. INTERNATIONAL PASSAGES

a. The International Passage Between the Gaza Strip and Egypt
  1) The existing arrangements shall continue.
  2) The State of Israel is interested in moving the passage to the 'three borders' area, south of its current location. This would need to be effected in co-ordination with the Government of Egypt. This move would enable the hours of operation of the passage to be extended.

b. The International Passages Between the West Bank and Jordan:
The existing arrangements shall continue.

12. EREZ CROSSING POINT

The Erez crossing point will be moved to a location within Israel in a time frame to be determined separately by the Government.

13. CONCLUSION

The goal is that implementation of the plan will lead to improving the situation and breaking the current deadlock. If and when there is evidence from the Palestinian side of its willingness, capability and implementation in practice of the fight against terrorism, full cessation of terrorism and violence and the institution of reform as required by the Roadmap, it will be possible to return to the track of negotiation and dialogue.

Addendum C—Format of the Preparatory Work for the Revised Disengagement Plan

1. A process of relocation involves many significant personal repercussions for the relocated residents. In implementing the plan, the Government of Israel is obliged to consider the implications for the relocated residents, assist them, and ease the process for them as much as possible. The difficulties and sensitivities involved in the process must be born in mind by the Government and by those who implement the process.

2. The Government of Israel attributes great importance to conducting a dialogue with the population designated for relocation, regarding various issues relating to the implementation of the plan—including with respect to relocation and compensation—and will act to conduct such a dialogue.

ESTABLISHING AN ORGANIZATIONAL FRAMEWORK

3. An organizational framework will be established with the purpose of addressing and assisting in all matters related to the implementation of the plan.

4. The Ministerial Committee for National Security (The Security Cabinet) will accompany and direct the Revised Disengagement Plan, including acceleration of the construction of the Security Fence, with the exception of the decisions concerning relocation (Article 2.A (2) and (3) in Addendum A).

The Security Cabinet will be responsible for the implementation of this Government Resolution.

5. A Steering Committee is hereby established that will be responsible for co-ordinating the issues pertaining to the Revised Disengagement Plan. The Steering Committee will report to the Security Cabinet on its activities, and bring before it issues which require a decision by the political echelon. The Steering Committee will include the following members:

One. Head of the National Security Council—Chairman

Two. Representatives of the Ministry of Defense, the IDF and the Israel Police

Three. Director-General of the Prime Minister's Office

Four. Director-General of the Ministry of Finance

Five. Director-General of the Ministry of Justice

Six. Director-General of the Ministry of Foreign Affairs

Seven. Director-General of the Ministry of Industry, Trade and Labor

Eight. Director-General of the Ministry of Agriculture and Rural Development

Nine. Director-General of the Ministry of National Infrastructures

Ten. Director-General of the Ministry of the Interior

Eleven. Director-General of the Ministry of Construction and Housing

6. A Committee on Relocation, Compensation, and Alternative Settlement is hereby established which will be charged with the task of preparing legislation regarding relocation and compensation, as well as details of the principles and indexes

for compensation, including incentives, advance payments, and compensatory aspects of relocation alternatives in priority areas, in accordance with Government policy. The Committee's recommendations will be presented to the Security Cabinet and serve as a basis for the draft bill on this issue.

This committee will constitute the exclusive authorized body for the co-ordination and conducting of dialogue with the population designated for relocation and compensation, and with all other bodies related to the issue of compensation—until the completion of the legislation. The Committee will be able to establish professional sub-committees, as it deems necessary, for the sake of fulfilling its tasks. The committee will include the following members:

One. Director-General of the Ministry of Justice—Chairman
Two. Representative of the Ministry of Finance
Three. Representative of the Ministry of Industry, Trade and Labor
Four. Representative of the Ministry of Agriculture and Rural Development
Five. Representative of the Prime Minister's Office

7. The Jewish Agency for Israel, as a body involved in settlement, will act in accordance with instructions from the Steering Committee and in co-ordination with the Committee on Relocation, Compensation and Alternative Settlement. The role of the Jewish Agency will be to carry out the activities required for alternative settlement, either agricultural or communal, for those among the relocated civilian population who so desire.

8. a. An Executive Administration is hereby established in the Prime Minister's Office which will be subordinate to the Steering Committee. Its task will be to implement this Government Resolution with regard to the relocation of civilians and compensation.

Two. The Executive Administration will be authorized to grant advance payments to those eligible for compensation—which will be counted against the compensation to be owed to them—according to terms that will be determined by the Committee on Relocation, Compensation, and Alternative Settlement, and in accordance with the instructions and procedures established by the said Committee.

Three. The Head of the Executive Administration will hold the rank of Ministry Director-General.

9. All Government ministries and other governmental bodies will forward, without delay, all information required for the aforementioned organizational frameworks to fulfill their tasks.

LEGISLATION

10. a. The Ministry of Justice will formulate and the Prime Minister will submit, as soon as possible, a draft bill to the Ministerial Committee for Legislation, which will include provisions regarding relocation and compensation for those eligible, as well as the authority necessary for this purpose.

Two. Soon thereafter, the Government will submit the bill to the Knesset.

Three. The IDF Military Commanders in the Areas will issue the Security Legislation necessary for the implementation of the Government's Resolutions.

BUDGET

11. a. Within one month of the adoption of this Resolution, the Director of the Budget Division of the Ministry of Finance, in co-ordination with the Director-General of the Prime Minister's Office and the Director-General of the Ministry of Justice, will allocate the required budget and other resources necessary for the Steering Committee, the Committee on Relocation, Compensation and Alternative Settlement, the Executive Administration and the Jewish Agency to carry out their activities.

Two. The 2005 Budget and subsequent budgets will be adjusted periodically to conform with the process and Government Resolutions on this issue.

Three. For the sake of commencing its activities, the Executive Administration will be allocated, in the first stage, 10 staff positions.

TRANSITION INSTRUCTIONS

12. During the interim period from the date this Resolution is passed, the following instructions will apply to the towns, villages and areas included in the plan (hereafter—the towns and villages), for the purpose of making preparations on the one hand, while maintaining normal and continuous daily life on the other:

One. Municipal and communal activities related to the course of normal life and services to which residents are entitled will continue unaffected, including services provided by the regional council, as well as security, education, welfare, telecommunications, mail, public transportation, electricity, water, gas, petrol, health services, banks and all other services customarily provided to towns and villages prior to this Resolution.

Two. Government plans for construction and development that have yet to commence will not be advanced for implementation.

Three.

Four. Nothing stated in this Resolution is intended to undermine Government Resolution no. 150, dated August 2, 1996, regarding other areas. The aforementioned Government Resolution no. 150 will also apply to towns and villages for the purpose of approval prior to planning and land allocation.

EXCEPTIONAL CASES COMMITTEE

13. An Exceptional Cases Committee will be established which will be authorized to permit the implementation of any plan which was frozen, in accordance with the provisions above, and authorized to decide not to advance plans even if their implementation has already commenced, following an examination of each individual case, and in keeping with criteria that it shall establish.

The Exceptional Cases Committee will be headed by the Director-General of the Prime Minister's Office, and will include the Directors-General of the Ministries of Finance and Justice.

Decisions of the Exceptional Cases Committee may be appealed to the Security Cabinet, in any instance where they are brought before it by a member of the Government.

PRINCIPLES FOR COMPENSATION

14. a. The date which determines the right for compensation is the date of the adoption of this Government Resolution.

b. Those entitled to compensation will receive fair and suitable compensation, as will be set out in the law legislated for this purpose.

JOINT UNDERSTANDING ON NEGOTIATIONS (ANNAPOLIS CONFERENCE)
(27 November 2007)

Following a series of preparatory meetings between US officials and Israeli and Palestinian delegations, an international peace meeting intended officially to relaunch the Middle East peace process was held under US auspices in Annapolis, Maryland, USA, on 27 November 2007. Members of the international Quartet group and the League of Arab States (Arab League) attended the talks, and Syria notably sent a low-level delegation. At the close of the meeting US President George W. Bush read a statement of 'joint understanding' between the Israeli Prime Minister, Ehud Olmert, and the PA Executive President, Mahmoud Abbas, who both expressed their commitment to achieving a final settlement of the outstanding issues of contention between Israelis and Palestinians by the end of 2008.

The representatives of the Government of the State of Israel and the Palestine Liberation Organization (PLO), represented respectively by Prime Minister Ehud Olmert and President Mahmoud Abbas, in his capacity as Chairman of the PLO Executive Committee and President of the Palestinian Authority, have convened in Annapolis, Maryland, under the auspices of President George W. Bush of the United States of America, and with the support of the participants of this international conference, having concluded the following Joint Understanding:

We express our determination to bring an end to bloodshed, suffering and decades of conflict between our peoples, to usher in a new era of peace, based on freedom, security, justice, dignity, respect and mutual recognition, to propagate a culture of peace and non-violence, and to confront terrorism and incitement, whether committed by Palestinians or Israelis.

In furtherance of the goal of two states, Israel and Palestine, living side by side in peace and security:

We agree to immediately launch good faith bilateral negotiations in order to conclude a peace treaty resolving all outstanding issues, including all core issues, without exception, as specified in previous agreements.

We agree to engage in vigorous, ongoing and continuous negotiations, and shall make every effort to conclude an agreement before the end of 2008.

For this purpose, a steering committee, led jointly by the head of the delegation of each party, will meet continuously, as agreed.

The steering committee will develop a joint work plan and establish and oversee the work of negotiations teams to address all issues, to be headed by one lead representative from each party.

The first session of the steering committee will be held on 12 December 2007.

President Abbas and Prime Minister Olmert will continue to meet on a bi-weekly basis to follow up the negotiations in order to offer all necessary assistance for their advancement.

The parties also commit to immediately implement their respective obligations under the Performance-Based Road Map to a Permanent Two-State Solution to the Israel-Palestinian Conflict, issued by the Quartet on 30 April 2003 (hereinafter, 'the Roadmap') and agree to form an American, Palestinian and Israeli mechanism, led by the United States, to follow up on the implementation of the Roadmap. The parties further commit to continue the implementation of the ongoing obligations of the Roadmap until they reach a peace treaty. The United States will monitor and judge the fulfillment of the commitments of both sides of the Roadmap.

Unless otherwise agreed by the parties, implementation of the future peace treaty will be subject to the implementation of the Roadmap, as judged by the United States.

In conclusion, we express our profound appreciation to the President of the United States and his Administration, and to the participants of this international conference, for their support for our bilateral peace process.

APPLICATION OF PALESTINE FOR ADMISSION TO MEMBERSHIP IN THE UNITED NATIONS
(23 September 2011)

On 23 September 2011, despite opposition from Israel and criticism from Hamas, PA Executive President Abbas presented an application for full membership in the UN on behalf of the 'State of Palestine'. However, on 11 November the Security Council announced that it was unable to recommend the application for consideration by the General Assembly, as only eight of the Council's 15 members were prepared to vote in favour. (An application to membership in the UN must receive the support of at least nine Security Council members, provided that none of the five permanent members indicate their opposition. The USA had previously stated that it would veto the Palestinian application at any formal vote.) On 29 November 2012 the General Assembly approved Resolution A/RES/67/19, which proposed to upgrade the status of the PA (as the 'State of Palestine') to that of a non-member observer state.

Note by the Secretary-General

In accordance with rule 135 of the rules of procedure of the General Assembly and rule 59 of the provisional rules of procedure of the Security Council, the Secretary-General has the honour to circulate herewith the attached application of Palestine for admission to membership in the United Nations, contained in a letter received on 23 September 2011 from its President (see annex I). He also has the honour to circulate a further letter, dated 23 September 2011, received from him at the same time (see annex II).

Annex I—Letter Received on 23 September 2011 from the President of Palestine to the Secretary-General

I have the profound honour, on behalf of the Palestinian people, to submit this application of the State of Palestine for admission to membership in the United Nations.

This application for membership is being submitted based on the Palestinian people's natural, legal and historic rights and based on United Nations General Assembly Resolution 181 (II) of 29 November 1947 as well as the Declaration of Independence of the State of Palestine of 15 November 1988 and the acknowledgement by the General Assembly of this Declaration in Resolution 43/177 of 15 December 1988.

In this connection, the State of Palestine affirms its commitment to the achievement of a just, lasting and comprehensive resolution of the Israeli-Palestinian conflict based on the vision of two States living side by side in peace and security, as endorsed by the United Nations Security Council and General Assembly and the international community as a whole and based on international law and all relevant United Nations resolutions.

For the purpose of this application for admission, a declaration made pursuant to rule 58 of the provisional rules of procedure of the Security Council and rule 134 of the rules of procedure of the General Assembly is appended to this letter (see enclosure).

I should be grateful if you would transmit this letter of application and the declaration to the Presidents of the Security Council and the General Assembly as soon as possible.

(Signed) Mahmoud Abbas
President of the State of Palestine
Chairman of the Executive Committee of the Palestine Liberation Organization

Declaration

In connection with the application of the State of Palestine for admission to membership in the United Nations, I have the honour, in my capacity as the President of the State of Palestine and as the Chairman of the Executive Committee of the Palestine Liberation Organization, the sole legitimate representative of the Palestinian people, to solemnly declare that the State of Palestine is a peace-loving nation and that it accepts the obligations contained in the Charter of the United Nations and solemnly undertakes to fulfill them.

(Signed) Mahmoud Abbas
President of the State of Palestine
Chairman of the Executive Committee of the Palestine Liberation Organization

Annex II—Letter Dated 23 September 2011 from the President of Palestine to the Secretary-General

After decades of displacement, dispossession and the foreign military occupation of my people and with the successful culmination of our State-building program, which has been endorsed by the international community, including the Quartet of the Middle East Peace Process, it is with great pride and honour that I have submitted to you an application for the admission of the State of Palestine to full membership in the United Nations.

On 15 November 1988, the Palestine National Council (PNC) declared the Statehood of Palestine in exercise of the Palestinian people's inalienable right to self-determination. The Declaration of Independence of the State of Palestine was acknowledged by the United Nations General Assembly in Resolution 43/177 of 15 December 1988. The right of the Palestinian people to self-determination and independence and the vision of a two-State solution to the Israeli-Palestinian conflict have been firmly established by General Assembly in numerous resolutions, including, *inter alia*, Resolutions 181 (II) (1947), 3236 (XXIX) (1974), 2649 (XXV) (1970), 2672 (XXV) (1970), 65/16 (2010) and 65/202 (2010) as well as by United Nations Security Council Resolutions 242 (1967), 338 (1973) and 1397 (2002) and by the International Court of Justice Advisory Opinion of 9 July 2004 (on the Legal Consequences of the Construction of a Wall in the Occupied Palestinian Territory). Furthermore, the vast majority of the international community has stood in support of our inalienable rights as a people, including to statehood, by according bilateral recognition to the State of Palestine on the basis of the 4 June 1967 borders, with East Jerusalem as its capital, and the number of such recognitions continues to rise with each passing day.

Palestine's application for membership is made consistent with the rights of the Palestine refugees in accordance with international law and the relevant United Nations resolutions, including General Assembly Resolution 194 (III) (1948), and with the status of the Palestine Liberation Organization as the sole legitimate representative of the Palestinian people.

The Palestinian leadership reaffirms the historic commitment of the Palestine Liberation Organization of 9 September 1993. Further, the Palestinian leadership stands committed to resume negotiations on all final status issues—Jerusalem, the Palestine refugees, settlements, borders, security and water—on the basis of the internationally endorsed terms of reference, including the relevant United Nations resolutions, the Madrid principles, including the principle of land for peace, the Arab Peace Initiative and the Quartet Roadmap, which specifically requires a freeze of all Israeli settlement activities.

At this juncture, we appeal to the United Nations to recall the instructions contained in General Assembly Resolution 181 (II) (1947) and that 'sympathetic consideration' be given to application of the State of Palestine for admission to the United Nations.

Accordingly, I have had the honour to present to Your Excellency the application of the State of Palestine to be a full member of the United Nations as well as a declaration made pursuant to rule 58 of the provisional rules of procedure of the Security Council and rule 134 of the rules of procedure of the General Assembly. I respectfully request that this letter be conveyed to the Security Council and the General Assembly without delay.

(Signed) Mahmoud Abbas
President of the State of Palestine
Chairman of the Executive Committee of the Palestine Liberation Organization
UN Document S/2011/592 (2011).

PALESTINIAN DECLARATION ACCEPTING THE JURISDICTION OF THE INTERNATIONAL CRIMINAL COURT
(31 December 2014)

The PA (as the 'State of Palestine') acceded to the International Criminal Court (ICC) on 2 January 2015, with jurisdiction backdated to 13 June 2014. The following is a reproduction of the formal declaration of acceptance of ICC jurisdiction submitted by the PA, along with the formal instruments of accession.

In conformity with Article 12, paragraph 3, of the Rome Statute of the International Criminal Court, ('the Statute'), the Government of the State of Palestine hereby recognizes the jurisdiction of the Court for the purpose of identifying, prosecuting and judging authors and accomplices of crimes within the jurisdiction of the Court committed in the occupied Palestinian territory, including East Jerusalem, since June 13, 2014.

This declaration is without prejudice to any other declaration the State of Palestine may decide to lodge in the future.

Accordingly, the State of Palestine undertakes to cooperate with the Court without delay or exception, in accordance with Chapter IX of the Statute.

This declaration shall be valid for an unspecified period of time and shall enter into force upon its signature.

(Signed) Mahmoud Abbas
President of the State of Palestine
Reproduced from the website of the ICC (www.icc-cpi.int/iccdocs/PIDS/press/Palestine_A_12-3.pdf).

CALENDARS IN THE MIDDLE EAST AND NORTH AFRICA

The Islamic Calendar

The Islamic era dates from 16 July 622 CE, which was the beginning of the Arab year in which the *Hijra* ('flight' or migration) of the prophet Muhammad (the founder of Islam), from Mecca to Medina (in modern Saudi Arabia), took place. The Islamic or *Hijri* Calendar is lunar, each year having 354 or 355 days, the extra day being intercalated 11 times every 30 years. Accordingly, the beginning of the *Hijri* year occurs earlier in the Gregorian Calendar by a few days each year. Dates are reckoned in terms of the *anno Hegirae* (AH) or year of the Hegira (*Hijra*). The Islamic year 1445 AH began on 19 July 2023.

The year is divided into the following months:

1. Muharram	30 days	7. Rajab	30 days
2. Safar	29 days	8. Shaaban	29 days
3. Rabia I	30 days	9. Ramadan	30 days
4. Rabia II	29 days	10. Shawwal	29 days
5. Jumada I	30 days	11. Dhu'l-Qa'da	30 days
6. Jumada II	29 days	12. Dhu'l-Hijja	29 or 30 days

The *Hijri* Calendar is used for religious purposes throughout the Islamic world and is the official calendar in Saudi Arabia. In most Arab countries it is used in conjunction with the Gregorian Calendar for official purposes, but in Türkiye (formerly Turkey) and Egypt the Gregorian Calendar has replaced it.

PRINCIPAL ISLAMIC FESTIVALS

New Year: 1st Muharram. The first 10 days of the year are regarded as holy, especially the 10th.

Ashoura: 10th Muharram. Celebrates the first meeting of Adam and Eve after leaving Paradise, also the ending of the Flood and the death of Husain, grandson of the Prophet Muhammad. The feast is celebrated with fairs and processions.

Mouloud or Yum al-Nabi (Birth of Muhammad): Celebrated by Sunni Muslims on 12th Rabia I. Shi'a Muslims celebrate the Birth of Muhammad on 17th Rabia I.

Leilat al-Meiraj (Ascension of Muhammad): 27th Rajab.

Ramadan (Month of Fasting):

Eid al-Fitr or Eid al-Saghir or Küçük Bayram (The Small Feast): Three days beginning 1st Shawwal. This celebration follows the constraint of the Ramadan fast.

Eid al-Adha or Eid al-Kabir or Büyük Bayram (The Great Feast, Feast of the Sacrifice): Four days beginning on 10th Dhu'l-Hijja. The principal Islamic festival, commemorating Abraham's sacrifice and coinciding with the pilgrimage to Mecca. Celebrated by the sacrifice of a sheep, by feasting and by donations to the poor.

Islamic Year	1444 AH	1445 AH	1446 AH
New Year	30 July 2022	19 July 2023	7 July 2024
Ashoura	8 August 2022	28 July 2023	16 July 2024
Mouloud	8 October 2022	27 September 2023	15 September 2024
Leilat al-Meiraj	18 February 2023	8 February 2024	27 January 2025
Ramadan begins	23 March 2023	11 March 2024	1 March 2025
Eid al-Fitr	21 April 2023	10 April 2024	30 March 2025
Eid al-Adha	28 June 2023	16 June 2024	6 June 2025

Note: Local determinations may vary by one day from those given here.

The Iranian Calendar

The Iranian Calendar, introduced in 1925, was based on the Islamic Calendar, adapted to the solar year. Iranian New Year (*Now Ruz* or *Norouz*) occurs at the vernal equinox, which usually falls on 21 March in the Gregorian Calendar. In Iran it was decided to base the calendar on the coronation of Cyrus the Great, in place of the *Hijra*, from 1976, and the year beginning 21 March 1976 became 2535. During 1978, however, it was decided to revert to the former system of dating. The year 1402 began on 21 March 2023.

The Iranian year is divided into the following months:

1. Favardine	31 days	7. Mehr	30 days
2. Ordibehecht	31 days	8. Aban	30 days
3. Khordad	31 days	9. Azar	30 days
4. Tir	31 days	10. Dey	30 days
5. Mordad	31 days	11. Bahman	30 days
6. Chariver	31 days	12. Esfand	29 or 30 days

The Iranian Calendar is used for all purposes in Iran, except the determining of Islamic religious festivals, for which the lunar Islamic Calendar is used.

The Hebrew Calendar

The Hebrew Calendar is solar with respect to the year but lunar with respect to the months. The normal year has 353–355 days in 12 lunar months, but seven times in each 19 years an extra month of 30 days (*Adar II*) is intercalated after the normal month of Adar to adjust the calendar to the solar year. New Year (*Rosh Hashanah*) usually falls in September of the Gregorian calendar, but the day varies considerably. The year 5784 began on 15 September 2023.

The months are as follows:

1. Tishri	30 days	7. Nisan	30 days
2. Marcheshvan	29 or 30 days	8. Iyyar	29 days
3. Kislev	29 or 30 days	9. Sivan	30 days
4. Tebeth	29 days	10. Tammuz	29 days
5. Shebat	30 days	11. Av	30 days
6. Adar	29 days	12. Ellul	29 days
(Adar II)	30 days		

The Hebrew Calendar is used to determine the dates of Jewish religious festivals only. The civil year begins with the month Tishri, while the ecclesiastical year commences on the first day of Nisan.

RESEARCH INSTITUTES

ASSOCIATIONS AND INSTITUTES STUDYING THE MIDDLE EAST AND NORTH AFRICA*

ARGENTINA

Sección Interdisciplinaria de Estudios de Asia y Africa: Facultad de Filosofía y Letras, Universidad de Buenos Aires, Moreno 350, 1091 Buenos Aires; tel. and fax (11) 4345-8196; e-mail asiayafrica09@yahoo.com.ar; internet www.museoetnografico.filo.uba.ar; f. 1982; research and lectures; Dir Prof. MÓNICA BERÓN.

ARMENIA

Institute of Oriental Studies of the National Academy of Sciences of Armenia: 24/4 Marshal Bagramyan Ave, 0019 Yerevan; tel. (1) 58-33-82; e-mail info@orient.sci.am; internet orient.sci.am; f. 1971; specializes in the history and philology of the Near and Middle East, and South and Far East; Dir Assoc. Prof. ROBERT P. GHAZARYAN; publ. *Bulletin of the Institute of Oriental Studies*.

AUSTRALIA

Centre for Arab and Islamic Studies: The Australian National University, Canberra, ACT 2601; tel. (2) 6125-4982; fax (2) 6125-5410; e-mail cais@anu.edu.au; internet cais.anu.edu.au; research into the politics, history, political economy, international relations, strategic and defence issues and religion of the Middle East and Central Asia; Dir Prof. KARIMA LAACHIR; publ. conference proceedings, occasional papers and monographs.

Middle East Studies Forum (MESF): Alfred Deakin Institute for Citizenship and Globalisation, Deakin University, 221 Burwood Hwy, Burwood, Vic 3125; e-mail mesf@deakin.edu.au; internet www.mesf.org.au; hosts projects and scholarship in the field of Middle East and Central Asian studies and languages; Convenor Prof. SHAHRAM AKBARZADEH.

AUSTRIA

Gesellschaft für Turkologie, Osmanistik und Türkeiforschung e.V. (GTOT): c/o Institut für Orientalistik, Universität Wien, Spitalgasse 2, Hof 4, 1090 Vienna; e-mail yavuz.koese@univie.ac.at; internet www.gtot.org; f. 2011; Pres. Prof. Dr YAVUZ KÖSE; publ. *Diyâr. Journal of Ottoman, Turkish and Middle Eastern Studies* (2 a year).

Institut für Orientalistik der Universität Wien: Spitalgasse 2, Hof 4.1, 1090 Vienna; tel. (1) 427-74-34-01; e-mail orientalistik@univie.ac.at; internet orientalistik.univie.ac.at; library of 26,200 vols; Head of Dept Assoc. Prof. Dr VERONIKA RITT-BENMIMOUN; publ. *Wiener Zeitschrift für die Kunde des Morgenlandes* (annually), *Archiv für Orientforschung*.

AZERBAIJAN

Institute of Oriental Studies: Academy of Sciences, Pr. H Cavid 115, Baku; tel. and fax (12) 538-87-55; fax (12) 539-23-51; e-mail info@orientalstudies.az; internet www.orientalstudies.az; f. 1958; research into social, political, economic and cultural development of Oriental countries and their relations with Azerbaijan; history of Islam; philology; Dir GOVKHAR BAKHSHALI BAKHSHALIYEVA.

BELGIUM

Association Egyptologique Reine Elisabeth: Parc du Cinquantenaire, 10, 1000 Brussels; tel. (2) 741-73-64; fax (2) 733-77-35; e-mail aere.egke@kmkg-mrah.be; internet www.aere-egke.be; f. 1923 to encourage Egyptian studies; fmrly Fondation Égyptologique Reine Elisabeth; 480 mems; library of 90,000 vols; Chair. Comte ARNOUL D'ARSCHOT SCHOONHOVEN; Dirs LUC LIMME, ALAIN MARTIN; publ. *Chronique d'Egypte*, *Bibliotheca Aegyptiaca*, *Papyrologica Bruxellensia*, *Bibliographie Papyrologique sur fiches*, *Monumenta Aegyptiaca*, *Rites égyptiens*, *Papyri Bruxellenses Graecae*, *Monographies Reine Elisabeth*, *Médecine égyptienne*.

Middle East and North Africa Research Group (MENARG): University of Ghent, Universiteitsstraat 8, 9000 Gent; tel. (9) 264-69-15; fax (9) 264-69-97; e-mail menarg@ugent.be; internet www.ugent.be/ps/conflict-ontwikkeling/en/research/menarg; dedicated to production of new knowledge about and critical insight into politics, society and economy in contemporary Middle East and North Africa; Dir SAMI ZEMNI.

---

*See also Regional Organizations—Education; Arts and Culture

Nederlands-Vlaams Instituut in Cairo (see under Egypt).

CHINA, PEOPLE'S REPUBLIC

Institute of Middle East Studies: China Institutes of Contemporary International Relations, A2 Wanshousi, Haidian, Beijing 100081; tel. (10) 88547395; fax (10) 68418641; internet www.cicir.ac.cn; Dir Dr NIU XINCHUN.

Middle East Studies Institute (MESI): Shanghai International Studies University, Bldg 6, 550 Dalian Rd, Shanghai 200083; tel. (21) 35373278; fax (21) 35373332; e-mail mideastweb@126.com; internet mideast.shisu.edu.cn; f. 1980 as Center for Middle East Culture Studies; Dir Prof. JUN DING; publ. *Arab World Studies* (6 a year), *Asian Journal of Middle Eastern and Islamic Studies* (4 a year), *Reports on Middle East Development* (annually).

CUBA

Centro de Estudios de Africa y del Medio Oriente (Centre for African and Middle Eastern Studies): Avda 3ra, 1805, entre 18 y 20, Miramar, Playa, Havana; tel. and fax (7) 22-1222; e-mail ceamo@ceniai.inf.cu; internet www.nodo50.org/ceamo; f. 1979; scientific non-governmental asscn; aims to expand the study of Africa and the Middle East and the impact of their cultures in Cuba, as well as Cuban policy towards these regions; organizes postgraduate courses, seminars, lectures and workshops; library includes 5,000 books, 4,000 documents and 500 periodicals; publ. journal *Revista de Africa y Medio Oriente* (2 a year, in English and Spanish), bulletins, research papers and books.

CYPRUS

Cyprus American Archaeological Research Institute (CAARI): 11 Andreas Demitriou St, Nicosia 1066; tel. (2) 456414; fax (2) 671147; e-mail admin@caari.org.cy; internet www.caari.org; f. 1978 to promote the study of Cypriot archaeology, as well as the history and culture of the Eastern Mediterranean; affiliated to the American Schools of Oriental Research (see under USA); hosts lectures, seminars and symposia; Dir Dr LINDY CREWE; library includes 9,000 books and monographs, 4,600 bound off-prints and 4,000 documents; publ. *CAARI News* (4 a year), newsletter on events around the world relevant to Cypriot archaeology and related history and art.

Economics Research Centre of the University of Cyprus (CypERC): POB 20537, Nicosia 1678; tel. (2) 893214; fax (2) 895027; e-mail erc@ucy.ac.cy; internet www.erc.ucy.ac.cy; independent research body focused on subjects pertinent to the Cyprus and European economy; Dir Dr ELENA ANDREOU.

CZECH REPUBLIC

Orientální ústav AV ČR (Oriental Institute of the Academy of Sciences of the Czech Republic): Pod Vodárenskou věží 4, 182 08 Prague 8; tel. (2) 66053111; e-mail orient@orient.cas.cz; internet www.orient.cas.cz; f. 1922; research in Asian studies; Dir Dr TÁŇA DLUHOŠOVÁ; publ. *Archiv orientální* (3 a year), *Nový Orient* (3 a year).

DENMARK

Center for Mellemøst-Studier (Centre for Contemporary Middle East Studies): University of Southern Denmark, Main Campus, Odense University, Campusvej 55, 5230 Odense M; tel. 65-50-21-83; e-mail middle-east@sdu.dk; internet www.sdu.dk/middle-east; f. 1983; national centre for interdisciplinary research in cultures and societies of the contemporary Middle East; library of 3,000 vols and 90 periodicals; Head of Dept DIETRICH JUNG.

EGYPT

Academy of the Arabic Language: 15 Aziz Abaza St, Cairo 11211 (Zamalek); tel. (2) 7362002; e-mail acc@idsc.net.eg; internet www.arabicacademy.org.eg; f. 1932; library of 60,000 vols and periodicals; Pres. ABDEL WAHAB ABDEL HAFEZ (acting); publ. *Review* (2 a year), books on reviving Arabic heritage, council and conference proceedings, biographies of mems of Academy, lexicons and directories of scientific and technical terms.

Al-Ahram Center for Political and Strategic Studies (ACPSS): Al-Ahram Foundation, al-Galaa St, Cairo; tel. (2) 25786037; fax (2)

27703229; e-mail acpss1@ahram.org.eg; internet acpss.ahram.org.eg; f. 1968; research into international relations, politics and economics; particular emphasis on Arab–Israeli relations; 35-mem. research team; library of 10,000 vols and 130 periodicals; Dir Dr MOHAMED FAYEZ FARHAT; publs incl. *The Arab Strategic Report* (annually), *Strategic Economic Directions* (annually), *The State of Religion in Egypt Report* (annually), *Strategic Papers* (monthly), *Al-Ahram Strategic File* (monthly), *Israeli Digest* (monthly), *Strategic Readings* (monthly), *Egyptian Affairs* (quarterly), *Iran Digest* (monthly).

American Research Center in Egypt: 2 Midan Simón Bolívar, Cairo 11461 (Garden City); tel. (2) 27948239; fax (2) 27953052; e-mail cairo@arce.org; internet www.arce.org; and 909 North Washington St, Suite 320, Alexandria, VA 22314, USA; tel. (703) 721-3479; e-mail info@arce.org; f. 1948 by American universities to promote research by US and Canadian scholars in all phases of Egyptian civilization, incl. archaeology, art history, humanities and social sciences; grants and fellowships available; 31 institutional mems and 1,250 individual mems; Exec. Dir Dr LOUISE BERTINI; publ. *Journal* (annually).

Economic Research Forum (ERF): 21 al-Sad al-Aaly St, Dokki, Giza 12311; tel. (2) 33318600; fax (2) 33318604; e-mail erf@erf.org.eg; internet www.erf.org.eg; promotes high-quality economic research that contributes to inclusive and sustainable devt in the Arab countries, Iran and Türkiye (fmrly Turkey); Chair. HASSAN ALY; Man. Dir. IBRAHIM EL-BADAWI; publ. *Middle East Deveopment Journal* (2 a year).

Institut Dominicain d'Etudes Orientales (Dominican Institute for Oriental Studies): Priory of the Dominican Fathers, POB 18, 1 Sharia Masna al-Tarabish, Abbasiyah, Cairo 11381; tel. (2) 24857825; e-mail secretariat@ideo-cairo.org; internet www.ideo-cairo.org; f. 1953; library of 160,000 vols; Dir EMMANUEL PISANI; publ. *Mélanges de L'Institut Dominicain d'Etudes Orientales—Midéo* (every 18 months), *Les Cahiers du Midéo* (series).

Institut d'Egypte: 13 Sharia Sheikh Rihane, Cairo; f. 1798; studies literary, artistic and scientific questions relating to Egypt and neighbouring countries; 120 mems, 50 assoc. mems, 50 corresponding mems; library of 160,000 vols; Pres. Prof. M. HAFEZ; publ. *Bulletin* (annually), *Mémoires* (irregular).

Institut Français d'Archéologie Orientale (French Institute of Oriental Archaeology): 37 Sharia Sheikh Ali Youssef, Qasr al-Aïny 11562, Cairo 11441; tel. (2) 27900255; e-mail direction@ifao.egnet.net; internet www.ifao.egnet.net; f. 1880; excavations, research and publications; library of 82,000 vols; Chair. JULIEN LOISEAU; Dir LAURENT COULON; publ. *Annales Islamologiques*, *Bulletin Critique des Annales Islamologiques*, etc.

Institute of Arab Research and Studies: POB 229, 1 Sharia Arab Advocates Union, Cairo (Garden City); tel. (2) 7951648; fax (2) 7962543; e-mail info@iars.net; internet www.iars.net; f. 1953; research and studies into contemporary Arab affairs; international relations; library service; affiliated to the Arab League Educational, Cultural and Scientific Org.; Dir Prof. Dr MOHAMED MOSTAFA KAMAL; publ. *Journal of Arab Research and Studies* (annually).

Middle East Research and Futuristic Studies Centre: Sharia el-Khalifa el-Mahmoun, Ain Shams University, Cairo 11566; e-mail merc.director@asu.edu.eg; internet www.asu.edu.eg/merc; f. 1967; organizes conferences, symposia, lectures and training courses; Dir Dr HATEM EL-ABD; publs include *Middle East Affairs* (quarterly) and *Middle East Research Periodical* (bi-annual).

National Centre for Middle East Studies: POB 18, 1 Sharia Qasr el-Nil, Bab el-Louk, Cairo 11513; tel. (2) 770041; fax (2) 770063; e-mail ncmes2010@yahoo.com; internet ncmes.org; f. 1989; research into peace process, arms control and conflict resolution; publ. *Middle East Papers* (3 a year).

Nederlands-Vlaams Instituut in Cairo (NVIC) (Netherlands-Flemish Institute in Cairo): POB 50, 1 Sharia Dr Mahmoud Azmi, Cairo 11211 (Zamalek); tel. (2) 27382520; fax (2) 27382523; e-mail info@nvic.leidenuniv.nl; internet www.nvic.leidenuniv.nl; f. 1971; fmrly Netherlands Institute for Archaeology and Arabic Studies in Cairo; Dir Dr RUDOLF DE JONG; library and publs in the field of Arabic Studies, Egyptology, archaeology and Coptology.

Société Archéologique d'Alexandrie (Archaeological Society of Alexandria): POB 815, 6 Sharia Mahmoud Moukhtar, Alexandria 21111; tel. and fax (3) 4860650; e-mail info@asalex.org; internet asalex.org/index.html; f. 1893; 248 mems; Pres. Prof. Dr MONA HAGGAG; publ. *Bulletins*, *Mémoires*, *Monuments de l'Egypte Gréco-Romaine*, *Cahiers*, *Publications Spéciales*, *Archaeological and Historical Studies*.

Société Egyptienne d'Economie Politique, de Statistique et de Législation: BP 732, 16 ave Ramses, Cairo; tel. (2) 5750797; fax (2) 5743491; e-mail espesl@hotmail.com; f. 1909; 1,550 mems; library of 50,000 vols; Pres. Prof. Dr AHMAD F. SURUR; Sec.-Gen. Prof. Dr MOUSTAFA K. EL-SAID; Library Dir SALEM S. ZAID; publ. *Revue L'Egypte Contemporaine* (quarterly in Arabic, French and English).

Society for Coptic Archaeology: 222 ave Ramses, Cairo 11517; tel. (2) 4861299; e-mail sac1934.info@gmail.com; f. 1934; 360 mems; library of 19,600 vols; Pres. (vacant); Sec.-Gen. Dr MOURAD MAGDI WAHBA; publ. *Bulletin* (annually), *Fouilles*, *Bibliothèque d'Art et d'Archéologie*, *Textes et Documents*.

FINLAND

Suomen Itämainen Seura (Finnish Oriental Society): c/o Dept of World Cultures, University of Helsinki, POB 59, 00014 Helsinki; e-mail sihteeri@suomenitamainenseura.org; internet www.suomenitamainenseura.org; f. 1917; Pres. SAANA SVÄRD; publ. *Studia Orientalia*, *Studia Orientalia Electronica*.

FRANCE

Centre d'Etudes Euro-Arabe: 42 ave Montaigne, 75008 Paris; tel. 1-53-57-43-20; fax 1-53-57-43-21; e-mail ceeaparis@ceea.com; internet www.ceea.com; f. 1992; research into politics, history, security and economics of the Middle East; promotes European-Arab relationships in various fields; rep. office in Beirut, Lebanon; Pres. Dr SALEH BIN BAKR AL-TAYAR; Dir Dr MEHDI CHEHADE; publ. various research papers and a periodic newsletter in French, Arabic and English.

Département d'Etudes Orientales: Université de la Sorbonne Nouvelle (Paris III), 8 ave de Saint-Mandé, 75012 Paris; e-mail dept-eo@sorbonne-nouvelle.fr; internet www.univ-paris3.fr/dept-eahii; Dir OLIVER BAST.

Fondation Nationale des Sciences Politiques: 27 rue Saint-Guillaume, 75337 Paris Cedex 07; tel. 1-45-49-50-50; fax 1-42-22-31-26; e-mail webmestre@sciences-po.fr; internet www.sciences-po.fr; f. 1945; eight research centres; library incl. 650,000 books and 4,500 periodicals; Pres. LAURENCE BERTRAND DORLÉAC.

Institut du Monde Arabe (Institute of the Arab World): 1 rue des Fossés Saint Bernard, pl. Mohammed V, 75005 Paris Cedex 05; tel. 1-40-51-38-38; e-mail rap@imarabe.org; internet www.imarabe.org; f. 1980; Pres. JACK LANG; publ. *Al-Moukhtarat* and *Qantara* (both quarterly).

Institut National des Langues et Civilisations Orientales (National Institute of Oriental Languages and Civilizations): 65 rue des Grands Moulins, CS21351, 75214 Paris Cedex 13; tel. 1-81-70-10-14; e-mail communication@inalco.fr; internet www.inalco.fr; f. 1795; faculties of languages and world civilizations; c. 8,000 students, 235 teachers and lecturers (2022); library of 550,000 vols and 9,600 periodicals; Pres. JEAN-FRANÇOIS HUCHET; High International Studies (DHEI), Dept of International Business (CPEI), Automatic Languages Treatment (TAL), Multilingual Engineering (IM); publ. *Livret de l'Etudiant* (annually), various Oriental studies and periodicals.

Institut de Papyrologie de la Sorbonne: Université de Paris-Sorbonne, IUFM de Paris, 10 rue Molitor, 75016 Paris; tel. and fax 1-40-50-25-88; e-mail institut-papyrologie@paris-sorbonne.fr; internet www.papyrologie.paris-sorbonne.fr; f. 1920; library of 10,300 vols and 25 periodicals; Dir BENOÎT LAUDENBACH.

Institut de Recherches et d'Etudes sur le Monde Arabe et Musulman (Institute of Research and Studies on the Arab and Muslim World): Université d'Aix-Marseille I et III, Maison Méditerranéenne des Sciences de l'Homme, 5 rue du Château de l'Horloge, BP 647, 13097 Aix-en-Provence Cedex 2; tel. 4-42-52-41-62; e-mail secretariat.iremam@mmsh.univ-aix.fr; internet iremam.cnrs.fr; library of 65,000 vols and 250 periodicals (60 in Arabic); Dir RICHARD JACQUEMOND; publ. *L'Année du Maghreb*, *Revue des Mondes Musulmans et de la Méditerranée*, etc.

Société Asiatique: Palais de l'Institut, 23 quai Conti, 75006 Paris; tel. and fax 1-44-41-43-10; e-mail societeasiatique@yahoo.fr; internet www.aibl.fr/societe-asiatique; f. 1822; more than 700 mems; library of 90,000 vols and 200 periodicals; Pres. OLIVIER PICARD; publ. *Journal Asiatique* (2 a year), *Cahiers de la Société Asiatique*.

GEORGIA

Giorgi Tsereteli Institute of Oriental Studies: G. Tsereteli St, 0162, Tbilisi; tel. (32) 23-38-85; e-mail giorgi.sanikidze@iliauni.edu.ge; internet iliauni.edu.ge/en/iliauni/institutebi-451/g-weretlis-agmosavletmcodneobis-instituti-742; f. 1960; affiliated with Ilia State University since 2010; researches languages, history and culture of Near, Middle and Far East; Dir Prof. GIORGI SANIKIDZE.

GERMANY

Centre for Applied Research in Partnership with the Orient (CARPO): Kaiser-Friedrich-St 13, 53113 Bonn; tel. (228) 52265670; e-mail info@carpo-bonn.org; internet carpo-bonn.org; f. 2014; independent research into political, economic and social aspects of the Middle East, in partnership with experts from the region; also offers consultancy services to policymakers; Pres. MARIE-CHRISTINE HEINZE.

Centrum für Nah- und Mittelost-Studien (CNMS): Philipps-Universität Marburg, Gebäude F|14, Deutschhausstr. 12, 35032 Marburg; tel. (6421) 2824946; fax (6421) 2824829; e-mail cnms@uni-marburg.de; internet www.uni-marburg.de/de/cnms; f. 2006; interdisciplinary centre for study of the Middle East region; covers contemporary social and economic studies, as well as philology, history, and Islamic and cultural studies; Dir Prof. Dr NILS P. HEESSEL.

Deutsche Arbeitsgemeinschaft Vorderer Orient (DAVO): Centre for Research on the Arab World (CERAW), University of Mainz, 55099 Mainz; tel. (6131) 3922701; fax (6131) 3924736; e-mail davo@geo.uni-mainz.de; internet www.davo1.de; f. 1993; interdisciplinary asscn of more than 1,300 scholars, students and others interested in contemporary research on the Middle East and North Africa; Pres. Prof. Dr GÜNTER MEYER; publ. journal *DAVO-Nachrichten* (bi-annual) and weekly e-mail list with latest news on international Middle Eastern studies.

Deutsche Morgenländische Gesellschaft: Theologische Fakultät, Fürstengraben 6, 07737 Jena; tel. (36) 41941114; e-mail peter.stein@uni-jena.de; internet www.dmg-web.de; f. 1845; Chair. Prof. Dr STEFAN WENINGER; publ. *Zeitschrift* (2 a year) and *Abhandlungen für die Kunde des Morgenlandes*.

GIGA Institut für Nahost-Studien (GIGA Institute of Middle East Studies): Neuer Jungfernstieg 21, 20354 Hamburg; tel. (40) 42825523; fax (40) 42825547; e-mail imes@giga-hamburg.de; internet www.giga-hamburg.de/de/institute/giga-institut-f%c3%bcr-nahost-studien/; f. 2007; affiliated to Leibniz-Institut für Globale und Regionale Studien (German Institute of Global and Area Studies); devoted to research in politics, social sciences and economics of the Near and Middle East and North Africa; library of c. 33,000 books and 230 periodicals; Dir Prof. Dr AMRITA NARLIKAR; publ. *Focus Nahost* (monthly).

Institut für Altorientalistik (Institute for Ancient Near Eastern Studies): Freie Universität Berlin, Fabeckstr. 23–25, 14195 Berlin; tel. (30) 83853347; e-mail altorientalistik@geschkult.fu-berlin.de; internet geschkult.fu-berlin.de/e/altorient; f. 1950; Dir Prof. Dr EVA CANCIK-KIRSCHBAUM.

Institut für Orient und Asienwissenschaften (IOA): Brühlerstr. 7, 53119 Bonn; tel. (228) 737223; e-mail japanologie@uni-bonn.de; internet ioa.uni-bonn.de; f. 1959 (1887 Berlin); Dir of Institute Prof. Dr HARALD MEYER.

Nah- und Mittelost Verein e.V. (German Near and Middle East Association): Kronenstr. 1, 10117 Berlin; tel. (30) 2064100; fax (30) 20641010; e-mail numov@numov.de; internet www.numov.de; f. 1934; 600 mems; Hon. Chair. Dr JOHANN ERICH WILMS; Exec. Dir HELENE RANG; publ. *WirtschaftsForum Nah-und Mittelost* (bi-monthly).

Stiftung Zentrum für Türkeistudien (Centre for Studies on Türkiye): Universität Duisburg-Essen, Altendorferstr. 3, 45127 Essen; tel. (201) 31980; fax (201) 3198333; e-mail zfti@zfti.de; internet www.zfti.de; f. 1985; aims to promote German-Turkish relations and improve knowledge about Türkiye (fmrly Turkey) and Turkish migrants in Europe; Chair. SERAP GÜLER; Dir Prof. Dr HACI HALIL USLUCAN; publ. periodicals and working papers.

TürkeiEuropaZentrum (TEZ): Universität Hamburg, Edmund-Siemers-Allee 1, Flügel Ost, 20146 Hamburg; tel. (40) 428385891; e-mail tez.aai@uni-hamburg.de; internet www.aai.uni-hamburg.de/tuerkeieuropa.html; f. 2008; promotes interdisciplinary research on Türkiye (fmrly Turkey) and the Ottoman Empire; part of Asia-Africa Institute; Dir Dr JANINA KAROLEWSKI.

INDIA

Asiatic Society of Mumbai: Town Hall, Shahid Bhagat Singh Rd, Mumbai 400 023; tel. (22) 22660956; fax (22) 2665139; e-mail asiaticsociety1804@gmail.com; internet asiaticsociety.org.in; f. 1804 as Bombay Literary Society; in 1973 established the Dr P. V. Kane Research Institute for Oriental Studies (later renamed the Dr P. V. Kane Institute for Post Graduate Studies and Research—affiliated to the University of Bombay); promotes and publ. research in culture, art and literature of Asia (both general and specifically Indian); offers scholarships and fellowships; holds seminars and lectures on current, historical and cultural affairs; 100,000 books, 12,000 old coins and 1,300 maps; Pres. Prof. VISPI BALAPORIA; publs include *Journal* (annually), reports, critical annotated texts of rare Sanskrit and Pali MSS.

Centre of Middle East Studies: O.P. Jindal Global University, Narela Rd, Sonipat 131 001; e-mail cmes@jgu.edu.in; internet jgu.edu.in/jsia/middle-east-studies; f. 2016; Dir Dr ABDUL FATTAH AMMOURAH; publ. *Siasat Al-Insaf: The Middle Eastern Review*.

Jindal Center for Israel Studies (JCIS): O.P. Jindal Global University, Office 397, 3rd Floor, T3 Bldg, Narela Rd, Sonipat 131 001; tel. (130) 4091714; e-mail kjangid@jgu.edu.in; internet jgu.edu.in/jsia/jindal-center-for-israel-studies; f. 2012; aims to build a research colloquium on Israeli History, Politics, Society and Culture, as well as on Israel-Jewish Diaspora Relations; to advance knowledge of India–Israel bilateral engagement; Co-ordinator Prof. Dr KHINVRAJ JANGID.

IRAN

British Institute of Persian Studies: 1623 Dr Shariati St, Gholhak, Tehran 19396-13661; e-mail bips@thebritishacademy.ac.uk; internet www.bips.ac.uk; f. 1961; cultural institute, with emphasis on history and archaeology; approx. 260 mems; library of c. 14,000 vols; Pres. Prof. CHARLES MELVILLE; publ. *Iran* (2 a year).

Institute for Political and International Studies (IPIS): Shahid Bahonar Ave, Shahid Aghaii St, Tajrish, Tehran; POB 19395-1793, Tehran; tel. (21) 22802641; e-mail info@ipis.ir; internet www.ipis.ir; f. 1983; research and information on Iran's foreign policy and international relations; emphasis on Middle East, Persian (Arabian) Gulf, Europe, South-East Asia and Central Asia; affiliated to the Ministry of Foreign Affairs; Pres. Dr MUHAMMAD HASSAN SHEIKH AL-ISLAMI; publ. *Central Asia and the Caucasus* (quarterly), *Iranian Journal of International Affairs* (quarterly), *Iranian Journal of Foreign Policy* (quarterly).

IRAQ

Centre for Arab Gulf Studies: University of Basra, POB 49, Basra; tel. 7735069637; e-mail bsc@uobasrah.edu.iq; internet bsgcenter.uobasrah.edu.iq/index.php; f. 1974; research into economics, politics, strategic issues, geography, history, anthropology and culture of the Persian (Arabian) Gulf region; seriously damaged and much of its collection looted during the US-led military campaign to oust the regime of Saddam Hussain in 2003; Dir Dr QAIS NASSER RAHI; publ. *Arab Gulf Journal* (quarterly) and *The Gulf Economist* (quarterly).

Iraqi Academy of Sciences: Iraqi Academy of Sciences, POB 4023, Waziriya, Baghdad; tel. (1) 422-4202; fax (1) 422-2066; e-mail info@iraqacademy.iq; internet www.iraqacademy.iq; f. 1947 to maintain the Arabic language, to undertake research into Arabic history, Islamic heritage and the history of Iraq, and to encourage research in the modern arts and sciences; some of collection looted or destroyed during or after the US-led military intervention to oust the regime of Saddam Hussain in early 2003; Pres. Prof. Dr MUHAMMAD HUSSEIN AL-YASSIN; publ. *Journal of the Academy of Sciences* (quarterly, in Arabic; 2 a year, in Kurdish).

Middle East Research Institute (MERI): 646 Italian Village, Irbil, Kurdistan Region, Iraq; tel. (66) 264-9690; e-mail info@meri-k.org; internet www.meri.org; f. 2014; not-for-profit, independent foundation, focused on the economics, governance, politics and security issues of the Middle East region, especially those relating to Iraq and Iraqi Kurdistan; Pres. Prof. DLAWER ALA'ALDEEN.

ISRAEL

The Academy of the Hebrew Language: POB 90004, Giv'at Ram Campus, Jerusalem 9190401; tel. (2) 6493555; fax (2) 5617065; e-mail acad@vms.huji.ac.il; internet hebrew-academy.org.il; f. 1953; study and development of the Hebrew language and compilation of a historical dictionary; Pres. Prof. AHARON MAMAN; publ. *Zikhronot*, *Leshonenu* (quarterly), *Leshonenu La'am*, monographs and dictionaries.

W. F. Albright Institute of Archaeological Research (AIAR): POB 19096, 26 Salah el-Din St, Jerusalem 9119002; tel. (2) 6288956; fax (2) 6264424; e-mail albrightinstitute@aiar.org; internet www.aiar.org; f. 1900 by the American Schools of Oriental Research; research in Syro-Palestinian archaeology, Biblical studies, Near Eastern history and languages; sponsors excavations; library with c. 24,000 vols and 266 journal titles relating to all aspects of ancient Near Eastern studies, with a concentration on Syro-Palestinian archaeology and Semitic languages and literature; Chair. JOAN R. BRANHAM; Pres. J. P. DESSEL.

Arab Studies Society: Orient House Bldg, POB 20479, 10 Abu Obeidah ibn el-Jarah St, Jerusalem; tel. (2) 6273330; e-mail abushamseyeh@yahoo.com; internet www.orienthouse.org/arabstudies; f. 1980 to promote Arabic culture, in particular Palestinian thought and culture; works undertaken by 8 centres with 14 depts; library of c. 14,000 vols on Palestine and the Middle East; Dir ISHAQ BUDEIRI; publ. more than 100 books on culture and history of Jerusalem and Palestine.

Begin-Sadat Center for Strategic Studies: Bar-Ilan University, Bldg 109, Ramat Gan 529002; tel. (3) 5318959; fax (3) 5359195; e-mail besa.center@biu.ac.il; internet www.besacenter.org; f. 1993; research on Middle Eastern security; organizes conferences and workshops; Dir Prof. EITAN SHAMIR; publ. *BESA Middle East Security and Policy Studies*, *BESA Perspectives Papers*.

REGIONAL INFORMATION — Research Institutes

The Ben-Zvi Institute for the Study of Jewish Communities in the East: POB 7660, 14 Ibn Gabirol, Jerusalem 9107601; tel. (2) 5398888; fax (2) 5638310; e-mail ybz@ybz.org.il; internet www.ybz.org.il; f. 1947; sponsors research in the history and culture of Jewish communities in the East; owned by Yad Izhak Ben-Zvi and the Hebrew University of Jerusalem; library of MSS and printed books; Dir REHAV RUBIN; publ. *Ginzei Qedem* (annually), *Pe'amim—Studies in Oriental Jewry*, *Pe'amim* (quarterly), and monographs.

Couvent Saint Etienne des Pères Dominicains, Ecole Biblique et Archéologique Française: POB 19053, 83–85 Nablus Rd, Jerusalem 9119001; tel. (2) 5359050; e-mail directeur@ebaf.edu; internet www.ebaf.edu; f. 1890; research, Biblical and Oriental studies, exploration and excavation in Israel, Palestine and Jordan; Dir Frère JEAN-JACQUES PÉRENNÈS; library of 150,000 vols; publ. *Revue Biblique*, *Etudes Bibliques*, *Cahiers de la Revue Biblique*, *Bible in its Traditions*.

The Harry S. Truman Research Institute for the Advancement of Peace: Hebrew University of Jerusalem, Mount Scopus, Jerusalem 919051; tel. (2) 5882300; e-mail truman@savion.huji.ac.il; internet truman.huji.ac.il; f. 1965; fosters peace and advances co-operation in the Middle East and the peoples of the world through research; library of more than 1,500 periodicals; Chair., Academic Cttee Prof. RAYA MORAG; publ. works on the Middle East, Africa, Asia and Latin America.

Institute of Asian and African Studies: Hebrew University, Mount Scopus, Jerusalem 91905; tel. (2) 5883516; e-mail michal.biran1@mail.huji.ac.il; internet asia-africa.huji.ac.il; f. 1926 as the Institute of Oriental Studies; incorporates Max Schloessinger Memorial Foundation; studies of medieval and modern languages, culture and history of Middle East, Asia and Africa; Dir Prof. MICHAL BIRAN; publs incl. *Max Schloessinger Memorial Series*, *Collected Studies in Arabic and Islam Series*, *Jerusalem Studies in Arabic and Islam*, translation series and studies in classical Islam and Arabic language and literature, *Hebrew University Armenian Series*.

Institute for National Security Studies (INSS): 40 Haim Levanon St, Tel Aviv 6997556; tel. (3) 6400400; e-mail info@inss.org.il; internet www.inss.org.il; f. 2006; incorporates the fmr Jaffee Center for Strategic Studies (f. 1977); research into Middle Eastern strategic affairs; library of c. 6,000 vols; Dir Prof. MANUEL TRAJTENBERG; publ. *Strategic Survey for Israel* (annually), *Strategic Assessment* (quarterly), *Strategic Survey for Israel* (annually), *INSS Insight* (weekly).

Israel Democracy Institute (IDI): POB 4702, 4 Pinsker St, Jerusalem; tel. (2) 5300888; e-mail info@idi.org.il; internet www.idi.org.il; independent research centre and non-partisan think tank; Pres. YOHANAN PLESNER; publ. *The Israeli Democracy Index* (annual), plus articles, books, occasional papers and policy recommendations.

Israel Exploration Society: POB 7041, Jerusalem 9107001; tel. (2) 6257991; fax (2) 6247772; e-mail israelexplorationsociety@gmail.com; internet www.israelexplorationsociety.com; f. 1914; archaeological excavations and historical research, congresses and lectures; 4,000 mems; Dir Dr RONA AVISSAR LEWIS; publ. *Eretz-Israel* (Hebrew and English, commemorative series), *Qadmoniot* (Hebrew, bi-annual), *Israel Exploration Journal* (English, bi-annual), various books on archaeology (in Hebrew and English).

Israel/Palestine Center for Research and Information (IPCRI): POB 9321, Hebrew University, Jerusalem 91110; tel. (2) 6769460; fax (2) 6768011; e-mail office@ipcri.org; internet www.ipcri.org; f. 1988; jt Palestinian-Israeli organization; research into all aspects of the Israeli–Palestinian conflict; Co-Dirs NIVINE SANDOUKA (Palestine), LIEL MAGHEN (Israel).

Jerusalem University College: POB 1276, Mt Zion, Jerusalem 9101202; tel. (2) 6718628; fax (2) 6732717; e-mail admissions@juc.edu; internet www.juc.edu; f. 1957 as Institute of Holy Land Studies; Christian study centre, graduate and undergraduate studies in the history, languages, religions and cultures of Israel in the Middle Eastern context; Pres. Dr OLIVER HERSEY.

The Jewish-Arab Center (JAC): University of Haifa, Eshkol Tower, 23rd Floor, Haifa; tel. (4) 8240019; e-mail jewrab@univ.haifa.ac.il; internet jac.haifa.ac.il; f. 1972; promotes studies and research that contribute to mutual understanding between Jews and Arabs, and aims to influence conflict resolution in the Middle East; organizes conferences, symposia, lectures and seminars; Dir Dr DORON NAVOT; publ. *Al-Karmil* (annually).

The Kenyon Institute: POB 19283, 32 Mount of Olives Rd, Sheikh Jarrah, Jerusalem 91190; tel. (2) 5828101; e-mail info@kenyon-institute.org.uk; internet www.kenyon-institute.org.uk; f. 1919; part of Council for British Research in the Levant (CBRL); fmrly British School of Archaeology in Jerusalem and British Institute at Amman for Archaeology and History; promotes study of arts and social sciences relevant to the Levant; library of c. 10,000 vols and more than 100 periodicals; Dir Dr TOUFIC HADDAD; publ. *Levant* (3 a year), *Contemporary Levant* (2 a year), *Monographs*.

The Middle East & Central Asia Research Center: Ramat HaGolan St 65, Ariel; e-mail mecarc@ariel.ac.il; internet www.ariel.ac.il/wp/mecarc; comprises 4 research divisions, focused on: Israel, Palestine & Israeli Arabs; diplomacy and foreign policy; Iranian and Shi'a affairs; and national resilience; Chair. Dr GADI HITMAN.

The Middle East & Islamic Studies Association of Israel (MEISAI): Hebrew University, Mt Scopus, Jerusalem 91905; tel. (52) 4654520; e-mail meisai1949@gmail.com; internet www.meisai.org.il; f. 1949 as the Israel Oriental Society; lectures and symposia to study all aspects of contemporary Middle Eastern, Asian and African affairs; Pres. Prof. YITZHAK REITER; publ. *Hamizrah Hehadash (The New East)* (Hebrew—with English summary—annually), *Ruach Mizrahit (East Wind)* (Hebrew, electronic).

Moshe Dayan Center for Middle Eastern and African Studies/Shiloah Institute: Tel Aviv University, Ramat Aviv, Tel Aviv 69978; tel. (3) 6409100; fax (3) 6415802; e-mail dayancen@post.tau.ac.il; internet www.dayan.org; f. 1959; Dir Prof. UZI RABI; publ. *Bulletin* (2 a year).

Pontifical Biblical Institute: POB 497, 3 Paul Emile Botta St, Jerusalem 91004; tel. (2) 6252843; fax (2) 6241203; e-mail admipib@gmail.com; internet www.biblico.it/jerusalem.html; f. 1927; study of Biblical languages and Biblical archaeology, history, topography; in conjunction with Hebrew University of Jerusalem; seminar for postgraduate students, student tours; Dir Rev. Dr JOSEF MARIO BRIFFA.

Wilfrid Israel Museum: Kibbutz Hazorea 3658100; tel. (4) 9899566; fax (4) 9590860; e-mail info@wilfrid.org.il; internet www.wilfrid.org.il; f. 1947; opened 1951 in memory of late Wilfrid Israel; a cultural centre for reference, study and art exhibitions; houses Wilfrid Israel collection of Near and Far Eastern art and cultural materials; local archaeological exhibits from Neolithic to Byzantine times; science and art library; Dir ELISSA DVIR.

The Zalman Shazar Center: POB 10477, 2 Betar St, Jerusalem 9110401; tel. (2) 5650444; fax (2) 6712388; e-mail shazar@shazar.org.il; internet www.shazar.org.il; f. 1925 to promote the study of Jewish history and general history; 1,000 mems; CEO MICHAL SAGI; publishing arm, The Zalman Shazar Center for Jewish History, publ. *Zion* (quarterly), *Historia* (2 a year).

ITALY

Istituto per l'Oriente C. A. Nallino: Via A. Caroncini 19, 00197 Rome; tel. (06) 8084106; fax (06) 8079395; e-mail ipocan@ipocan.it; internet www.ipocan.it; f. 1921 as L'Istituto per l'Oriente; adopted current name in 1982 in honour of one of its founders, Carlo Alfonso Nallino; research into all aspects of bilateral and multilateral relations between Italy and the countries of the Near and Middle East; with particular emphasis on law, society and immigration; organizes courses on Arabic, Turkish and Persian languages and Arab-Islamic culture; library of c. 35,000 vols and 300 periodicals; Pres. Prof. CLAUDIO LO JACONO; publ. *Oriente Moderno* (monographic essays, catalogues and bibliographical reviews), *Eurasian Studies* (in collaboration with the Skilliter Centre for Ottoman Studies, Newnham College, University of Cambridge, UK), *Rassegna di Studi Etiopici* (in collaboration with University of Naples Orientale, Italy), *Quaderni di Studi Arabi*.

JAPAN

Ajia Keizai Kenkyusho (Institute of Developing Economies/Japan External Trade Organization): 3-2-2 Wakaba, Mihama-ku, Chibashi, Chiba 261-8545; tel. (43) 299-9536; fax (43) 299-9726; e-mail info@ide.go.jp; internet www.ide.go.jp; f. 1958; 250 mems; Pres. KYOJI FUKAO; library of 572,409 vols (2006); publ. *Ajia Keizai* (Japanese, monthly), *The Developing Economies* (English, quarterly), *Middle East Review* (English, annually), occasional papers in English.

Chuto Chosakai (Middle East Research Institute of Japan): Hirakawacho Court Bldg 6F, 1-1-6 Hirakawacho, Chiyoda-ku, Tokyo 102-0093; tel. (3) 6261-4554; fax (3) 6261-4550; internet www.meij.or.jp; f. 1960; Chair. MIKIO SASAKI; Pres. AKITAKA SAIKI; publ. *Chuto Kenkyu* (Journal of Middle Eastern Studies, 3 a year), *Chuto Nenkan* (Yearbook of Middle East and North Africa), *Newsletter*.

JIME Center (Japanese Institute of Middle Eastern Economies): The Institute of Energy Economics, Inui Bldg, Kachidoki, 10th Floor, 13-1, Kachidoki 1-chome Chuo-ku, Tokyo 104-0054; fax (3) 5547-0229; e-mail webmaster@jime.ieej.or.jp; internet jime.ieej.or.jp; f. 2005; provides in-depth analysis of the political, economic, social and cultural developments in the Middle East, as the leading supplier of global energy resources; Dir SHUJI HOSAKA; publ. *Chuto Dokobunseki* (Middle Eastern and Energy Bulletin, Japanese, monthly), *Gendai Chuto Kenkyu* (Contemporary Middle Eastern Studies, Japanese, quarterly) and news and research reports, *Chutoken Kenkyu Hokoku* (report of JIME research achievements, Japanese, monthly), *Kunibetsu Teiki Hokoku* (Japanese, quarterly).

Nippon Oriento Gakkai (The Society for Near Eastern Studies in Japan): Taimei Bldg 9A, 5th Floor, 3-22, Chiyoda-ku, Tokyo 101-0052; tel. and fax (3) 3291-7519; e-mail office@j-orient.com; internet www.j-orient.com; f. 1954; about 800 mems; Pres. JIRO KONDO; publ. *Oriento* (Japanese, 2 a year), *Orient* (European languages, annually).

JORDAN

Centre for Strategic Studies: University of Jordan, Amman 11942; tel. (6) 5300100; fax (6) 5355515; e-mail css@jcss.org; internet jcss.org; f. 1984; research on strategic, political, economic and social issues concerning Jordan and the Middle East; since the 1990s has also been concerned with democracy, political pluralism, the economy and the environment; has specialist units concerned with Iranian, Euro-Mediterranean and economic studies; organizes conferences, seminars and workshops; also conducts opinion polls; Dir Prof. ZAID EYADAT.

British Institute in Amman: 6 al-Baouneyah St, Qaiwar Complex, Jabal al-Lweibdeh, Amman 11191; tel. (2) 4622105; e-mail jordaninfo@cbrl.ac.uk; internet cbrl.ac.uk; part of Council for British Research in the Levant (CBRL); seeks to advance public education on the Levant through promotion and dissemination of research in the humanities, social sciences and related subjects; focuses on Cyprus, Israel, Jordan, Lebanon, Palestinian territories and the Syrian Arab Republic; Dir Dr CAROL PALMER.

Institut Français du Proche Orient (IFPO): 3 Ibrahim A. Zahri St, Amman; tel. (6) 4611171; fax (6) 4611170; e-mail admifpo.amman@gmail.com; internet www.ifporient.org; f. 2003 by merger of Institut Français d'Archéologie du Proche Orient, Institut Français d'Etudes Arabes de Damas and Centre d'Etudes et de Recherches sur le Moyen-Orient Contemporain; university research and documentation institution with sections also in Beirut, Lebanon, and Damascus, Syrian Arab Republic; library of c. 9,000 vols and 120 periodicals and a collection of 700 maps; Dir MYRIAM CATUSSE; Head, Jordan Office JULIE BONNÉRIC.

Al Urdun Al Jadid Research Centre (UJRC): POB 940631, Amman 11194; tel. (6) 5533112; fax (6) 5533118; internet www.ujrc-jordan.net; f. 1990; independent research centre seeking to consolidate role of civil society as an effective partner in promoting a sustainable democracy in Jordan and the Arab world, and in upholding the values of human rights, citizenship and equality, through scientific research, dialogue, conferences and workshops; also publ. proceedings (incl. research papers) and organizes training; Dir-Gen. HANI HOURANI; Exec. Dir HUSSEIN ABU RUMMAN; publ. *Civil Society Issues Magazine* (Arabic, monthly), *The Economic Policy Dialogue Newsletter* (English and Arabic, quarterly).

LEBANON

Centre for Arab Unity Studies: Al-Nahda Bldg, Basra St, Hamra, Beirut; tel. (1) 750084; e-mail info@caus.org.lb; internet www.caus.org.lb; f. 1975; fosters research into all aspects of Arab society with particular emphasis on pan-Arab projects; Gen. Dir LUNA ABUSWAIREH; publ. *Arab Journal of Political Science* (Arabic, quarterly), *Al-Mustaqbal al-Arabi* (Arabic, monthly), *Contemporary Arab Affairs* (English, quarterly), *Arab Journal of Economic Research* (Arabic, quarterly), *Idafat* (Arabic, quarterly).

Centre for Lebanese Studies: Atiyah Bldg, Level 3, Chouran, Beirut 1102–2801; tel. (1) 792028; e-mail info@lebanesestudies.com; internet www.lebanesestudies.com; f. 1984; seeks to promote independent academic research into the political, social, educational, historical, economic and cultural issues of Lebanon; affiliated to St Antony's College, University of Oxford, UK; also office in London, UK; Chair. BASIM ZIADEH; Dir Dr MAHA SHUAYB.

Institut Français du Proche Orient (IFPO): BP 11-1424, rue de Damas, Beirut; tel. (1) 420291; fax (1) 420295; e-mail secretariat.directeur@ifporient.org; internet www.ifporient.org; f. 2003 by merger of Institut Français d'Archéologie du Proche Orient, Institut Français d'Etudes Arabes de Damas and Centre d'Etudes et de Recherches sur le Moyen-Orient Contemporain; university research and documentation institution with sections also in Jordan, Iraq and Palestinian territories; contemporary and archaeological library of 35,000 vols and 800 periodicals and a collection of 3,500 maps; Dir MYRIAM CATUSSE.

Institute for Palestine Studies (IPS): BP 11-7164, Anis Nsouli St, Verdun, Beirut 1107 2230; tel. (1) 804959; fax (1) 814193; e-mail ipsbeirut@palestine-studies.org; internet www.palestine-studies.org; POB 487, 19 Emile Habibi St, 4th Fl. Al-Masion, Ramallah, Palestinian Territories; tel. (2) 2989108; e-mail ipsquds@palestine-studies.org; 3501 M St, NW, Washington, DC 20007; tel. (202) 599-4836; e-mail ipsdc@palestine-studies.org; f. 1963; independent non-profit Arab research organization; aims to promote better understanding of the Palestine problem and the Arab–Israeli conflict; library of more than 80,000 vols, microfilm collection, private papers, archives and photographs; Gen. Dir KHALED FARRAJ (Beirut); Dirs STEPHEN BENNETT (Washington, DC), ALA JARADAT (Ramallah);
publ. *Journal of Palestine Studies* (English, quarterly), *Jerusalem Quarterly* (English), *Majallat al-Dirasat al-Filastiniyah* (Arabic, quarterly), *Selections from the Hebrew Press* (Arabic, daily) and documentary series, reprints, research papers, etc.

Lebanese Center for Policy Studies (LCPS): BP 55-215, 10th Floor, Sadat Tower, Leon St, Beirut; tel. (1) 799301; fax (1) 799302; e-mail info@lcps-lebanon.org; internet www.lcps-lebanon.org; f. 1989; research into political, social and economic development; library facilities; Exec. Dir MAKRAM OUAISS; publ. *Abaad*, *The Beirut Review*, *The Lebanon Report*.

MAURITANIA

Centre for Strategies on Security in the Sahel-Sahara (Centre 4s): Tevragh Zeina, Nouakchott; internet newcentre4s.org; research into issues related to defence, security, terrorism, impact of competition for hydrocarbons and uranium, migration, illegal trafficking of goods and people in the Sahel-Sahara region; principal countries of interest include Algeria, Burkina Faso, Cabo Verde, Chad, Cameroon, The Gambia, Guinea, Guinea-Bissau, Mali, Mauritania, Niger, Nigeria and Senegal; Pres. AHMEDOU OULD-ABDALLAH.

THE NETHERLANDS

Amsterdam Centre for Middle East Studies: UvA/ACMES, c/o DR F. BOUSSAID & DR M. VOORHOEVE, Postbus 15578, 1001 NB Amsterdam; tel. (20) 6201579; fax (20) 6264479; e-mail ACMES@uva.nl; internet acmes.uva.nl; aims to strengthen and internationalize the Middle Eastern Studies profile of the University of Amsterdam; organizes lectures, classes, conferences and seminars; Co-Dirs Dr FARID BOUSSAID, Dr MAAIKE VOORHOEVE.

Nederlands-Vlaams Instituut in Cairo (NVIC) (Netherlands-Flemish Institute in Cairo): POB 12200, 2500 DD The Hague (see Egypt).

Netherlands Institute for the Near East (Nederlands Instituut voor het Nabije Oosten—NINO): Witte Singel 25, POB 9515, 2300 RA Leiden; tel. (71) 5272039; fax (71) 5272038; e-mail c.waerzeggers@hum.leidenuniv.nl; internet www.nino-leiden.nl; f. 1939; Dir Dr WILLEMIJN WAAL; library of c.44,000 vols and 300 periodicals; publ. *Uitgaven van het Nederlands Instituut voor het Nabije Oosten (PIHANS)*, *Egyptologische Uitgaven (EU)*, *Achaemenid History (AchHist)* (monographs), *Bibliotheca Orientalis (BiOr)*, *Anatolica*.

NORWAY

Centre for Islamic and Middle East Studies: University of Oslo, Department of Culture Studies and Oriental Languages, POB 1010, Blindern, N-0315 Oslo; tel. 22-85-71-91; e-mail brynjar.lia@ikos.uio.no; internet www.hf.uio.no/ikos/english/research/center/islamic-and-middle-east-studies; f. 2011; Chair. Assoc. Prof. TERESA PEPE; publ. *Journal of Arabic and Islamic Studies* (online).

Centre for Middle Eastern and Islamic Studies (SMI): University of Bergen, POB 7805, Bergen; tel. 55-58-23-00; fax 55-58-96-43; e-mail post@ahkr.uib.no; internet www.uib.no/smi; f. 1988; Chair. Prof. CHRISTIAN MAUDER; publ. *Bergen Studies on the Middle East and Africa* (monographs).

PAKISTAN

Islamic Research Institute: International Islamic University, Faisal Masjid, POB 1035, Islamabad; tel. (51) 2281289; fax (51) 2289777; e-mail dgiri@iiu.edu.pk; internet iri.iiu.edu.pk; f. 1960; conducts research in Islamic studies; organizes seminars and conferences on various aspects of Islam; library of 120,000 books and periodicals, 610 microfilms, 260 MSS, 1,035 photostats, 220 audio cassettes; Dir-Gen. Prof. Dr MUHAMMAD ZIA-UL-HAQ; publ. *Al-Dirasat al-Islamiyah* (Arabic, quarterly), *Islamic Studies* (English, quarterly), *Fikr O-Nazar* (Urdu, quarterly), also monographs, reports, etc.

PALESTINIAN TERRITORIES

Palestine Economic Policy Research Institute (MAS): Muin Bseiso St, al-Masyoun, POB 2426, Ramallah; tel. (2) 2987053; fax (2) 2987055; e-mail info@mas.ps; internet www.mas.ps; f. 1994; independent, not-for-profit institute; Dir-Gen. RAJA KHALIDI; publ. *Economic and Social Monitor* (Arabic and English, quarterly), in conjunction with the Palestinian Central Bureau of Statistics and the Palestinian Monetary Authority, and various studies and pamphlets on economic and social development in the Palestinian territories.

POLAND

Centrum Archeologii Śródziemnomorskiej (Research Centre for Mediterranean Archaeology): 69 Prosta St, 6th Floor, 00-838 Warsaw; tel. (22) 5531328; fax (22) 6284523; e-mail pcma@uw.edu.pl;

internet www.pcma.uw.edu.pl; f. 1956; research institute of Polish Academy of Sciences; documentation and publication of Polish excavations in the Middle East and antiquities in Polish museums; Dir Dr ARTUR OBŁUSKI; publ. *Polish Archaeology in the Mediterranean* (annually).

RUSSIAN FEDERATION

Institute of Asian and African Studies: ul. Mokhovaya 11, 125009 Moscow; tel. (495) 629-43-49; e-mail office@iaas.msu.ru; internet www.iaas.msu.ru; f. 1956 as Institute for Oriental Languages, renamed as above 1972; comprises three sections: philology, history, and social and economic studies, and research centres, incl. Centre for Arabic and Islamic Studies and Centre of Judaica; 250 mems; Dir Prof. ALEXEY A. MASLOV.

Russian Institute for Strategic Studies: Flotskaya, 15B, 125413 Moscow; tel. (495) 454-92-64; fax (495) 454-92-58; e-mail mail@riss.ru; internet riss.ru; provides analysis and research on Middle Eastern affairs to government bodies; Head FRADKOV M. EFIMOVICH.

SAUDI ARABIA

Arab Urban Development Institute: 8411 Abdullah bin Hudhafah al-Sahmi al-Safarat, Unit No. 1, Riyadh 12521-3803; tel. (1) 480-2555; fax (1) 480-2666; e-mail info@araburban.org; internet www.araburban.org; f. 1980; affiliated to the Arab Towns Org. (ATO); provides training, research, consultancy and documentation services to Arab cities and municipalities and mems of ATO for improving the Arab city and preserving its original character and Islamic cultural heritage; membership comprises more than 400 Arab cities and towns, representing 22 Arab states; library of 78,630 vols and 630 periodicals; Chair. ABDULLAH AL-ALI AL-NUAIM; publ. books and research papers.

Gulf Research Center: POB 2134, 19 Rayat al-Etihad St, Jeddah 21451; tel. (2) 651-1999; fax (2) 653-1375; e-mail info@grc.net; internet www.grc.net; f. 2000; conducts research into political, economic, social and security issues affecting the countries of the Cooperation Council for the Arab States of the Gulf (Gulf Cooperation Council) and the wider region of the Persian (Arabian) Gulf; organizes conferences and workshops; Chair. ABDULAZIZ SAGER; publ. *Gulf Monitor* (bi-monthly), *Journal of Gulf Studies*, books, research papers, policy analysis, studies, newsletters and bulletins.

Islamic Economics Institute: King Abdul Aziz University, POB 80214, Jeddah 21589; tel. (2) 695-2751; fax (2) 640-3458; e-mail iei@kau.edu.sa; internet iei.kau.edu.sa; f. 1977; research into all aspects of Islamic economics; library of 35,000 vols and 400 periodicals; Dir and Dean Dr MUHAMMAD BIN ABDULLAH NASSIF; publ. *Journal of King Abdul Aziz University: Islamic Economics* (2 a year).

King Faisal Center for Research and Islamic Studies: POB 51049, Riyadh 11543; tel. (1) 455-5504; fax (1) 465-9993; e-mail kfcris@kfcris.com; internet www.kfcris.com; f. 1983; part of King Faisal Foundation; seeks to preserve and promote Islamic heritage and to contribute to the advancement of Islamic societies by encouraging research and issue-related studies; library of c. 1m. vols, 3,500 periodicals, 25,000 MSS and 40,000 microfilms; Chair. Prince TURKI AL-FAISAL BIN ABDUL AZIZ AL SAUD; Sec.-Gen. MAHA BINT MOHAMMED AL-FAISAL; publ. *Journal of Linguistic Studies*, *Islam and Contemporary World*, *Issues* (English) and books.

SINGAPORE

Middle East Institute: National University of Singapore, Terrace Blk B, Level 6, Singapore 119620; tel. 65162380; e-mail contact.mei@nus.edu.sg; internet www.mei.nus.edu.sg; an autonomous research unit within the National University of Singapore; specializes in the study of the contemporary affairs of the Middle East; publishes commentaries, analytical articles and research papers; Chair. BILAHARI KAUSIKAN; Exec. Dir MICHELLE TEO.

SLOVAKIA

Institute of Oriental Studies: Slovak Academy of Sciences, Klemensova 19, 813 64 Bratislava; tel. (2) 5292-6326; fax (2) 5292-6326; e-mail kaoreast@savba.sk; internet www.orient.sav.sk; f. 1960; library of 16,777 vols and 55 periodicals; Dir Dr EMANUEL BEŠKA; publ. *Asian and African Studies* (2 a year).

SPAIN

Centro Superior de Estudios de Oriente Próximo y Egipto: Universidad Autónoma de Madrid, Facultad de Filosofía y Letras, Cantoblanco, 28049 Madrid; tel. (91) 4977670; e-mail ceae@uam.es; internet www.uam.es/uam/en/centro-superior-estudios-oriente-proximo-egipto; f. 1998; Dir CARMEN DEL CERRO LINARES; publ. *Isimu* (annually).

Instituto Egipcio de Estudios Islámicos (Egyptian Institute of Islamic Studies): Francisco de Asís Méndez Casariego 1, 28002 Madrid; tel. (91) 5639468; fax (91) 5638640; e-mail secretaria@institutoegipcio.com; internet institutoegipcio.es; f. 1950; works on both academic and cultural levels in the field of Arabic, Mediterranean and Hispanic cultures through its publications (incl. journals and books on Hispano-Arabic studies), courses, lectures, conferences, art gallery and library; Dir Dr RASHA ISMAIL; publ. *Revista del Instituto Egipcio de Estudios Islámicos* (annually).

Instituto de Lenguas y Culturas del Mediterráneo y Oriente Próximo (Institute of Languages and Cultures of the Mediterranean and Middle East): Albasanz 26–28, 28037 Madrid; tel. (91) 6022300; fax (91) 6022971; e-mail secretaria.ilc@cchs.csic.es; internet www.ilc.csic.es; f. 1985 as Instituto de Filología, following the amalgamation of four existing institutes (the Benito Arias Montano, Miguel Asín, Miguel de Cervantes and Antonio de Nebrija); renamed as above 2007; research groups incl. Medieval Jewish Culture, Arab Studies, Biblical Philology, Languages and Culture of the Ancient Near East; Dir AITOR IGARCÍA MORENO; publ. *Sefarad* (review of Hebrew, Sephardic and Near Eastern Studies, 2 a year), *Al-Qantara* (review of Arab Studies, 2 a year), *Emerita* (review of Linguistics and Classical Philology, 2 a year) and books.

SWEDEN

Centre for Advanced Middle East Studies: Faculty of Social Sciences, Lund University, POB 201, 22100, Lund; tel. (46) 222 92 67; e-mail info@cme.lu.se; internet www.cmes.lu.se; f. 2007; supports and co-ordinates multidisciplinary research into the Middle East region; Dir of Studies KARIN AGGESTAM; publ. *CyberOrient* and monographs.

Nordiska Afrikainstitutet (Nordic Africa Institute): POB 1703, 75147, Uppsala; tel. (18) 471 52 00; e-mail nai@nai.uu.se; internet www.nai.uu.se; f. 1962; research and documentation centre for contemporary African affairs, organizes seminars and publ. wide range of books and reports; library of 80,000 vols and 210 periodicals; Dir THÉRÈSE SJÖMANDER MAGNUSSON; publ. *NAI Policy Notes*, *Africa Now*, *Annual Report*, *Current African Issues* and monographs.

SWITZERLAND

Centre d'Etudes et de Recherche sur le Monde Arabe et Méditerranéen (CERMAM) (Study and Research Centre for the Arab and Mediterranean World): CP 1342, 1211 Geneva 1; tel. (22) 7000470; fax (22) 7410822; e-mail info@cermam.org; internet www.cermam.org; f. 2000; Dir HASNI ABIDI.

Schweizerische Asiengesellschaft (Swiss Asia Society): CH 3001, Haus der Akademien, Laupenstr. 7, Bern; tel. (31) 3069250; e-mail sagw@sagw.ch; internet www.sagw.ch; f. 1939; 175 mems; Pres. Prof. Dr CRISTINA URCHUEGUÍA; publ. *Asiatische Studien / Etudes Asiatiques* (4 a year), *Schweizer Asiatische Studien / Etudes Asiatiques Suisses* (Monographien und Studienhefte).

SYRIAN ARAB REPUBLIC

Institut Français du Proche Orient (IFPO): BP 344, Abou Roumaneh, Damascus; BP 344, Damascus; tel. (11) 3330214; fax (11) 3327887; e-mail contact@ifporient.org; internet www.ifporient.org; f. 2003 by merger of Institut Français d'Archéologie du Proche Orient, Institut Français d'Etudes Arabes de Damas and Centre d'Etudes et de Recherches sur le Moyen-Orient Contemporain; university research and documentation institution with sections also in Amman, Jordan, and Beirut, Lebanon; medieval and modern library of 90,000 vols, 650 periodicals and a collection of 7,000 maps; Dir MYRIAM CATUSSE.

TUNISIA

Institut des Belles Lettres Arabes: 12 rue Jamâa el-Haoua, 1008 Tunis BM; tel. (71) 560133; e-mail ibla@gnet.tn; internet ibla-tunis.org.tn; f. 1926; cultural centre and research library; publ. *IBLA* (2 a year) and special studies.

Institut de Recherche sur le Maghreb Contemporain: 20 rue Mohamed Ali Tahar, Mutuelleville, 1002 Tunis; tel. (71) 796722; e-mail direction@irmcmaghreb.org; internet www.irmcmaghreb.org; f. 1992; library of c. 30,000 vols and 87 periodicals (2016); Dir KATIA BOISSEVAIN.

TÜRKIYE

British Institute at Ankara: 154 Atatürk Bul., 06690 Çankaya, Ankara; tel. (312) 4275487; fax (312) 4280159; e-mail ankara.manager@biaa.ac.uk; internet www.biaa.ac.uk; f. 1948; library of c. 65,000 vols; Dir Dr LUTGARDE VANDEPUT; publ. *Anatolian Studies* (annually), *Heritage Turkey* (annually), and *BIAA Monographs*.

Deutsches Archäologisches Institut (German Archaeological Institute): İnönü Cad. 10, 34437 İstanbul; tel. (212) 3937600; fax

(212) 3937614; e-mail sekretariat.istanbul@dainst.de; internet www.dainst.org/dai/meldungen; f. 1929; library of c. 70,000 vols and 200 periodicals; archive of photographs; Pres. Prof. Dr FRIEDERIKE FLESS; publs incl. *Istanbuler Mitteilungen* (annually) and *Archäologische Mitteilungen aus Iran und Turan* (annually).

Institut Français d'Etudes Anatoliennes (French Institute of Anatolian Studies): Palais de France, Nuru Ziya Sok. 10, PK 54, 34433 Beyoğlu, İstanbul; tel. (212) 2441717; e-mail ifea@ifea-istanbul.net; internet www.ifea-istanbul.net; f. 1930; 15 scientific mems; library of c. 30,000 vols and 800 periodicals; Dir PHILIPPE BOURMAUD; publ. *Collection IFEA, Collection Varia Turcica, Collection Varia Anatolica, Anatolia Antiqua, Anatolia Moderna*.

Nederlands Instituut in Turkije/Hollanda Araştırma Enstitüsü (Netherlands Institute in Türkiye—NIT): PK 132, İstiklal Cad. 181, Nur-i Ziya Sok. 5, Beyoğlu 34431, İstanbul; tel. (212) 2939283; e-mail nit@nit-istanbul.org; internet www.nit-istanbul.org; f. 1958; administered by the Netherlands Institute for the Near East, Leiden (see under The Netherlands); library of 15,000 vols; Dir Dr FOKKE A. GERRITSEN; publ. *Publications de l'Institut Historique et Archéologique Néerlandais de Stamboul (PIHANS), Anatolica* (annually).

Orient-Institut Istanbul: Galip Dede Cad. 65, Şahkulu Mah., 34420 Beyoğlu, İstanbul; tel. (212) 2936067; fax (212) 2496359; e-mail oiist@oiist.org; internet www.oiist.org/en/institut; f. 1989, as extension of Orient-Institut Beirut (2009 as independent institution); research on Ottoman, Mediterranean, and Turkish culture, history, and society; library holds approx. 50,000 vols and 1,550 periodicals; affiliated with Max Weber Stiftung (Germany); Dir Prof. Dr CHRISTOPH K. NEUMANN (acting); publs *Istanbuler Texte und Studien, Newsletter* (2 a year), *Orient-Institut Studies, Pera-Blätter*.

Österreichisches Kulturforum Istanbul: Köybaşi Cad. 44, 34464 Yeniköy, İstanbul; tel. (212) 3638415; fax (212) 2622622; e-mail istanbul-kf@bmeia.gv.at; internet www.bmeia.gv.at/kf-istanbul; Dir SILVIA NEUREITER.

Türk Dil Kurumu (Turkish Language Institute): Atatürk Bul. 217, 06680 Çankaya, Ankara; tel. (312) 4575200; fax (312) 4680783; e-mail bilgi@tdk.gov.tr; internet www.tdk.gov.tr; f. 1932 as Türk Dili Tetkik Cemiyeti (Society for the Investigation of the Turkish Language), an independent body to carry out linguistic research and contribute to the natural development of the language; brought under govt control in 1983; 48 mems (2022); library of 45,272 vols; Pres. Prof. Dr OSMAN MERT; publ. *Türk Dili* (monthly), *Türk Dili Araştirmalari Yilliği-Belleten* (2 a year), *Türk Dünyası Dil ve Edebiyat Dergisi* (2 a year).

Türk Kültürünü Araştirma Enstitüsü (Institute for the Study of Turkish Culture): 17 Cad., 06490 Bahçelievler, Ankara; tel. (312) 2133100; fax (312) 2134135; e-mail tkaedernegi@hotmail.com; internet www.turkkulturu.org.tr; f. 1961; scholarly research into all aspects of Turkish culture; Dir Prof. Dr AHMET BICAN ERCILASUN; publ. *Türk Kültürü* (monthly), *Cultura Turcica* (annually), *Türk Kültürü Araştirmalari* (annually).

Türk Tarih Kurumu (Turkish Historical Society): Kizilay Sok. 1, 06100 Ankara; tel. (312) 3102368; fax (312) 3101698; e-mail ttkinfo@ttk.gov.tr; internet www.ttk.gov.tr; f. 1931; 40 mems; library of 228,685 vols; Pres. Prof. Dr BIROL ÇETIN; publ. *Belleten* (3 a year), *Belgeler* (annually).

UNITED ARAB EMIRATES

Emirates Centre for Strategic Studies and Research (ECSSR): POB 4567, Abu Dhabi; tel. (2) 4044444; fax (2) 4044442; e-mail info@ecssr.ae; internet www.ecssr.ae; f. 1994; research on political, economic, social and cultural issues pertaining to the Persian (Arabian) Gulf region; Dir-Gen. Dr SULTAN MOHAMMED AL-NUAIMI.

National Library and Archives: POB 5884, Presidential Court, Abu Dhabi; tel. (2) 4183333; fax (2) 4445811; e-mail cs@nla.ae; internet www.nla.ae; f. 1968; attached to UAE Presidential Court; research, data collection and analysis on aspects of the Persian (Arabian) Gulf region; Dir-Gen. HAMAD BIN ABDULRAHMAN AL-MIDFA; publ. *Liwa* (academic journal; 2 a year).

UNITED KINGDOM

Birmingham Centre for Islamic and Middle Eastern Studies: School of Philosophy, Theology and Religion, University of Birmingham, Edgbaston, Birmingham, B15 2TT; e-mail ptrschool@contacts.bham.ac.uk; internet www.birmingham.ac.uk/schools/ptr/departments/theologyandreligion/research/islamic/index.aspx; multi-disciplinary centre specializing in research and study related to Islam and the contemporary Middle East; publ. *Islam and Christian-Muslim Relations* (4 a year).

British Institute for Libyan and Northern African Studies (BILNAS): c/o British Academy, 10–11 Carlton House Terrace, London, SW1Y 5AH; e-mail gensec@bilnas.org; internet www.bilnas.org; f. 1969 as Society for Libyan Studies; promotes research into Libyan and North African archaeology, history and linguistics; Dir CORISANDE FENWICK; Pres. NICHOLAS BARTON; publ. journal *Libyan Studies* (annually).

British Institute for the Study of Iraq (Gertrude Bell Memorial): 10 Carlton House Terrace, London, SW1Y 5AH; tel. (20) 7969-5274; e-mail bisi@britac.ac.uk; internet www.bisi.ac.uk; f. 1932 to promote, support and undertake research in Iraq and neighbouring countries; charitable trust, funded in part by the British Academy and also from its own endowment; covers archaeology, history, anthropology, geography, language and other related domains from the earliest times until the present; has mems in 40 countries; Pres. JOHN CURTIS; publ. journal *Iraq* (journal, annually; c. 700), as well as occasional monographs.

British Society for Middle Eastern Studies (BRISMES): 71–75 Shelton St, Covent Garden, London, WC2H 9JQ; e-mail office@brismes.org; internet www.brismes.ac.uk; f. 1973; Vice-Pres. NEVE GORDON; publs include *British Journal of Middle Eastern Studies* (5 a year).

Centre of Islamic Studies (CIS): University of Cambridge, Faculty of Asian and Middle Eastern Studies, Sidgwick Ave, Cambridge, CB3 9DA; tel. (1223) 335103; fax (1223) 335110; e-mail cis@cis.cam.ac.uk; internet www.cis.cam.ac.uk; f. 1960; conducts research to develop critical awareness of the role of Islam in wider society; research and outreach programmes; Dir Prof. CHRIS YOUNG.

Centre for Jewish Studies: Department of Religions and Theology, University of Manchester, Samuel Alexander Bldg, Oxford Road, Manchester, M13 9PL; tel. (161) 2753614; e-mail cjs@manchester.ac.uk; internet www.manchesterjewishstudies.org; f. 1996; conducts research and facilitates study in the field of Jewish Studies; Co-Dirs Prof. DANIEL LANGTON, Dr JEAN-MARC DREYFUS, Prof. ALEX SAMELY; publ. *Melilah: Manchester Journal of Jewish Studies* (annual), *Journal of Semitic Studies* (2 a year).

Council for Arab-British Understanding (CAABU): Arab-British Centre, 1 Gough Sq., London, EC4A 3DE; tel. (20) 7832-1321; e-mail info@caabu.org; internet www.caabu.org; f. 1967; aims to promote understanding between Arab nations and the UK through four principal programmes: parliamentary, educational, working with the media and organizing events; nearly 1,000 mems; Chair. DAVID JONES; Dir CHRIS DOYLE.

Council for British Research in the Levant (CBRL): The British Academy, 10 Carlton House Terrace, London, SW1Y 5AH; tel. (20) 7969-5296; e-mail info@cbrl.ac.uk; internet cbrl.ac.uk; seeks to advance knowledge and understanding of the peoples and cultures of the Levant; produces and disseminates original, rigorous and independent scholarship in the humanities, social sciences and related fields; Dir Dr CAROL PALMER; publ. *Contemporary Levant* (2 a year), *Levant* (3 a year), *CBRL Bulletin* (annual) and monographs.

Egypt Exploration Society: 3 Doughty Mews, London, WC1N 2PG; tel. (20) 7242-1880; e-mail contact@ees.ac.uk; internet www.ees.ac.uk; f. 1882; library of 22,000 vols; c. 2,000 mems; Pres. Prof. DORIS BEHRENS-ABOUSEIF; Dir Dr CARL GRAVES; publs include *Excavation Memoirs, Archaeological Survey, Graeco-Roman Memoirs, Journal of Egyptian Archaeology, Texts from Excavations, Egyptian Archaeology*.

Institute of Arab and Islamic Studies: University of Exeter, Stocker Rd, Exeter, EX4 4ND; tel. (1392) 723365; e-mail iais@exeter.ac.uk; internet arabislamicstudies.exeter.ac.uk; f. 1999 by amalgamation of Centre for Arab Gulf Studies, Dept of Middle Eastern Studies and Centre for Mediterranean Studies; multi-disciplinary centre for Arab and Islamic studies; incorporates the Centre for Gulf Studies, the Centre for Kurdish Studies, the European Centre for Palestine Studies and the Centre for Persian and Iranian Studies; extensive library and documentation unit; Dir Prof. CHRISTINA PHILLIPS; publ. *Journal of Arabian Studies: Arabia, the Gulf, and the Red Sea* (2 a year).

Institute for Iranian Studies: School of History, University of St Andrews, St Katharine's Lodge, The Scores, St Andrews, KY16 9AL; tel. (1334) 463027; fax (1334) 462927; e-mail iran@st-andrews.ac.uk; internet iranian.wp.st-andrews.ac.uk; f. 2006 to promote research and teaching in all aspects of Iranian civilization and culture; library of 6,000 Persian-language books; Dir Dr TIM GREENWOOD.

Institute of Ismaili Studies: Aga Khan Centre, 10 Handyside St, London, N1C 4DN; tel. (20) 7756-2700; e-mail info@iis.ac.uk; internet www.iis.ac.uk; f. 1977 by HH the Aga Khan; promotes scholarship and learning on Islam, with an emphasis on Shi'ism in general and its Ismaili *tariqah* in particular, and a better understanding of their relationship with other faiths and societies; it also encourages an interdisciplinary approach to the study of Islamic history and thought; library of printed and audiovisual materials and MSS; Dir Dr ZAYN KASSAM.

Institute for Middle Eastern and Islamic Studies: School of Government and International Affairs, University of Durham, The Al-Qasimi Bldg, Elvet Hill Rd, Durham, DH1 3TU; tel. (191) 334-5675; e-mail c.a.jones@durham.ac.uk; internet www.dur.ac.uk/

imeis; f. 1962; teaches postgraduate programmes in political economy and international relations of the Middle East and North Africa, Middle Eastern and Islamic studies; organizes seminars, lectures and conferences; incorporates the Centre for Iranian Studies (f. 1999 to promote research and debate on Iran in the UK); documentation unit (f. 1970; now part of main university library) monitors economic, social and political devts in the region with some 200,000 documents; publ. programme of research monographs, occasional papers and bibliographies; Dir Prof. CLIVE JONES; publ. *Middle East Papers* (annually).

Iqbal Centre for Critical Muslim Studies: The Iqbal Centre for the Study of Contemporary Islam, School of Languages, Cultures and Societies, University of Leeds, Leeds, LS2 9JT; tel. (113) 3433422; e-mail m.sheikh@leeds.ac.uk; internet iqbalcentre.leeds.ac.uk; seeks to promote and support the research and teaching of Critical Muslim Studies and related fields; organizes lectures, seminars, conferences; publ. research monographs, papers, and audiovisual content; Dirs Dr MUSTAPHA SHEIKH, Dr TAJUL ISLAM, Prof. SALMAN SAYYID.

The Islamic Cultural Centre and The London Central Mosque: 146 Park Rd, London, NW8 7RG; tel. (20) 7724-3363; fax (20) 7724-0493; e-mail info@iccuk.org; internet www.iccuk.org; f. 1944 to provide information and guidance on Islam and Islamic culture and to provide facilities for Muslims residing in the UK; library of 20,000 vols in Arabic, English, Urdu and Persian; Dir-Gen. Dr AHMAD AL-DUBAYAN.

Islamic and Middle Eastern Studies (IMES): University of Edinburgh, 19 George Sq., Edinburgh, EH8 9LD; tel. (131) 650-4182; fax (131) 650-6804; e-mail imes@ed.ac.uk; internet www.imes.ed.ac.uk; incorporates the Prince Alwaleed bin Talal Centre for the Study of Islam in the Contemporary World (Dir Prof. HUGH GODDARD); Head of Dept Prof. INES AŠČERIĆ-TODD.

London School of Jewish Studies (LSJS): Schaller House, Wohl Campus for Jewish Learning, 44A Albert Rd, London, NW4 2SJ; tel. (20) 8203-6427; e-mail lsjsadmin@lsjs.ac.uk; internet www.lsjs.ac.uk; provides teacher training for educators in Jewish schools, and promotes lifelong learning and professional development; Dean Rabbi RAPHAEL ZARUM; Chief Exec. JOANNE GREENAWAY.

LSE Middle East Centre: PAN 10.01, Pankhurst House, Clement's Inn, London, WC2A 2AZ; tel. (20) 7955-7038; e-mail n.almanasfi@lse.ac.uk; internet www.lse.ac.uk/Middle-East-Centre; conducts and facilitates original research on the politics, societies and economics of the Middle East and North Africa; incorporates Kuwait Programme, Kurdish Studies Series, Social Movements and Popular Mobilisation in the MENA research network; Dir Dr MICHAEL MASON; publ. *MEC Paper Series, Kuwait Programme Papers, Conflict Research Programme–Iraq Papers*, plus various reports and event proceedings.

Maghreb Studies Association: c/o The Executive Secretary, MOHAMED BEN-MADANI, 45 Burton St, London, WC1H 9AL; tel. and fax (20) 7388-1840; e-mail ben-madani@maghreb-studies-association.co.uk; internet www.maghreb-studies-association.co.uk; f. 1981 to promote the study of and interest in the Maghreb; independent; organizes lectures and conferences; Chair. Prof. ALLAN CHRISTELOW; issues quarterly journal.

Middle East Centre: St Antony's College, 68 Woodstock Rd, Oxford, OX2 6JF; tel. (1865) 284780; fax (1865) 274529; e-mail mec@sant.ox.ac.uk; internet www.sant.ox.ac.uk/mec; f. 1957; Dir Prof. EUGENE ROGAN; library of 34,000 vols and archive of private papers and photographs; publ. St Antony's Middle East monographs.

The Muslim Institute: 109 Fulham Palace Rd, London, W6 8JA; internet www.musliminstitute.org; f. 1974; research and teaching programmes, academic and current affairs seminars; library of 6,000 vols; 800 mems; supplies publs of the Muslim Parliament of Great Britain.

Oxford Centre for Hebrew and Jewish Studies: The Clarendon Institute, Walton St, Oxford, OX1 2HG; tel. (1865) 610422; e-mail enquiries@ochjs.ac.uk; internet www.ochjs.ac.uk; f. 1972; Pres. Prof. JUDITH OLSZOWY-SCHLANGER; publ. *Journal of Jewish Studies* (2 a year).

Oxford Centre for Islamic Studies: Marston Rd, Oxford, OX3 0EE; tel. (1865) 618500; fax (1865) 248942; e-mail islamic.studies@oxcis.ac.uk; internet www.oxcis.ac.uk; f. 1985; Dir Dr FARHAN AHMAD NIZAMI; publ. *Journal of Islamic Studies* (3 a year).

Palestine Exploration Fund: 5–6 Dreadnought Walk, Greenwich, London, SE10 9FP; tel. (20) 7935-5379; fax (20) 7485-7438; e-mail execsec@pef.org.uk; internet www.pef.org.uk; f. 1865; the oldest organization in the world for the study of the archaeology, ancient history and geography of the southern Levant; extensive library; collections incl. archaeological, archival and photographic items; holds regular free public lectures at the British Museum; 615 subscribers; Chair. CASEY STRINE; Pres. JONATHAN N. TUBB; publ. *PEQ: The Palestine Exploration Quarterly* (4 a year), as well as annuals, monographs and photographic books.

Royal Asiatic Society of Great Britain and Ireland: 14 Stephenson Way, London, NW1 2HD; tel. (20) 7388-4539; e-mail info@royalasiaticsociety.org; internet www.royalasiaticsociety.org; f. 1823 for the study of the history, sociology, institutions, customs, languages and art of Asia; c. 700 mems; c. 700 subscribing libraries; library of 80,000 vols, as well as MSS, paintings, prints, drawings, photographs, maps and coins; affiliated societies in various Asian cities; Pres. Prof. S. ANSARI; Dir ALISON OHTA; publ. *Journal, Storey Bibliography of Persian Literature* and monographs.

Royal Society for Asian Affairs: 16 Old Queen St, London SW1H 9HP; tel. (20) 7235-5122; e-mail info@rsaa.org.uk; internet www.rsaa.org.uk; f. 1901; 1,200 mems with knowledge of the past or present Near, Middle and Far East and Central Asia; library of c. 5,500 vols; Chief Exec. MICHAEL RYDER; Chair. SOPHIE IBBOTSON; Pres. Prof. PETER FRANKOPAN; publ. journal *Asian Affairs* (4 a year).

The Saudi-British Society: The Saudi-British Society, 1 Gough Sq., London, EC4A 3DE; tel. (1372) 842788; fax (20) 7835-2088; e-mail secretary@saudibritishsociety.org.uk; internet www.saudibritishsociety.org.uk; f. 1987; non-political; Chair. Sir WILLIAM PATEY.

SOAS University of London: 10 Thornhaugh St, Russell Sq., London, WC1H 0XG; tel. (20) 7637-2388; e-mail comms@soas.ac.uk; internet www.soas.ac.uk; f. 1916; library of c. 1.2m. vols and 2,750 MSS; Dir Prof. ADAM HABIB; publ. *Bulletin of the School of Oriental and African Studies* (3 a year), *The Journal of African Law* (3 a year), *The China Quarterly*, and *South East Asia Research* (4 a year).

UNITED STATES OF AMERICA

American Institute for Maghrib Studies (AIMS): Center for Middle Eastern Studies, 845 N. Park Ave, Marshall Bldg, Room 470, POB 210158-B Tucson, AZ 85721-0158; tel. (520) 626-6498; fax (520) 621-9257; e-mail aims@aimsnorthafrica.org; internet aimsnorthafrica.org; f. 1984; promotes systematic study of North Africa among interested scholars, specialists, students and others concerned with the region; Pres. JAMES MILLER; Dir TERRY RYAN; publ. *The Journal of North African Studies* (6 a year).

America-Mideast Educational and Training Services, Inc (AMIDEAST): Suite 600, 2025 M St, NW, Washington, DC 20036-3363; tel. (202) 776-9600; fax (202) 776-7000; e-mail inquiries@amideast.org; internet www.amideast.org; f. 1951; private, non-profit org. that strengthens mutual understanding and co-operation between Americans and the peoples of the Middle East and North Africa through programmes of education, development and information, language training and academic exchange; headquarters in Washington, DC, with field offices in Egypt, Iraq, Jordan, Kuwait, Lebanon, Morocco, Oman, the Palestinian territories, Qatar, the Syrian Arab Republic, Tunisia, the United Arab Emirates and Yemen; Pres. and CEO THEODORE H. KATTOUF.

American Oriental Society: University of Michigan, 913 S University Ave, Ann Arbor, MI 48109-1190; tel. (734) 347-1259; e-mail jrodgers@umich.edu; internet www.americanorientalsociety.org; f. 1842; research into Oriental civilizations and Asian languages and literature; 1,350 mems; library of 23,500 vols; Pres. MARTIN KERN; publ. *Journal of the American Oriental Society* (quarterly), *AOS Monograph Series* (irregular), essay series and offprint series.

American Schools of Oriental Research: 209 Commerce St, Alexandria, VA 22314; tel. (703) 789-9229; e-mail info@asor.org; internet www.asor.org; f. 1900; 1,500 mems; supports activities of independent archaeological institutions abroad: The Albright Institute of Archaeological Research, Jerusalem, Israel, the American Center of Oriental Research in Amman, Jordan, and the Cyprus American Archaeological Research Institute in Nicosia, Cyprus; Pres. SHARON HERBERT; Exec. Dir ANDREW G. VAUGHN; publ. *Near Eastern Archaeology* (quarterly), *Bulletin* (biannually), *Journal of Cuneiform Studies* (annually), and *Ancient Near East Today* (weekly).

Arab Gulf States Institute in Washington (AGSIW): Suite 1060, 1050 Connecticut Ave, NW, Washington, DC 20036; tel. (202) 768-9922; fax (202) 768-9927; e-mail info@agsiw.org; internet www.agsiw.org; f. 2014; research into issues related to the Arab Gulf states and US interests in that region; Chair. FRANK G. WISNER; Pres. DOUGLAS A. SILLIMAN.

Center for Contemporary Arab Studies: 241 Intercultural Center, Georgetown University, 37th & O Sts, NW, Washington, DC 20057; tel. (202) 687-5793; fax (202) 687-7001; e-mail ccasinfo@georgetown.edu; internet ccas.georgetown.edu; f. 1975; active in postgraduate education, public affairs, outreach to pre-college educators; Dir JOSEPH SASSOON; publs on social, economic, political, cultural and development aspects of Arab world, newsletter (tri-annual) and occasional papers.

Center for Middle East Policy (CMEP): The Brookings Institution, 1775 Massachusetts Ave, NW, Washington, DC 20036; tel. (202) 797-6000; e-mail communications@brookings.edu; f. 2002;

specializes in research concerning US policy in the region; Dir NATAN SACHS; publ. *Middle East Memo*.

Center for Middle Eastern and North African Studies: University of Michigan, Suite 500, 500 Church St, Ann Arbor, MI 48109-1042; tel. (734) 647-4143; fax (734) 763-4765; e-mail cmenas@umich.edu; internet www.ii.umich.edu/cmenas; f. 1961; research into the ancient, medieval and modern cultures of the modern Middle East and North Africa, Near Eastern languages and literature; library includes 340,000 vols on Middle East and North Africa; Dir Assoc. Prof. RYAN SZPIECH; publ. *Newsletter* (quarterly).

Center for Middle Eastern Studies: University of Chicago, 5828 S University Ave, Chicago, IL 60637; e-mail oritb@uchicago.edu; internet www.cmes.uchicago.edu; f. 1965; research into medieval and modern cultures of North Africa and Western and Central Asia; Dir ORIT BASHKIN.

Center for Middle Eastern Studies (CMES): Harvard University, 38 Kirkland St, Cambridge, MA 02138; tel. (617) 495-4055; fax (617) 496-8584; e-mail cmes@fas.harvard.edu; internet cmes.fas.harvard.edu; f. 1954; research on Middle Eastern subjects and Islamic studies; Dir CEMAL KAFADAR; publ. *Middle East Monograph Series*, *Harvard Middle Eastern and Islamic Review*, *CMES News* (2 a year).

Center for Middle Eastern Studies: The University of Texas at Austin, 204 W 21st St (F9400), Austin, TX 78712-1029; tel. (512) 471-3881; fax (512) 471-7834; e-mail dmes@uts.cc.utexas.edu; internet liberalarts.utexas.edu/mes; f. 1960; comprehensive interdisciplinary programme in area studies and languages of the Middle East, with some 50 affiliated faculties; offers graduate and undergraduate degrees in Middle Eastern studies, incl. jt degree programmes with Business, Public Affairs, Communications, the School of Information, and Law; publ. books on the modern Middle East and translations of contemporary fiction and memoirs; Dept Man. BRETT BOWMAN.

Center for the Study of Muslim & Arab Worlds (CSMAW): California State University, 5500 University Parkway, San Bernardino, CA 92407-2318; tel. (909) 537-5814; e-mail csmaw@csusb.edu; internet www.csusb.edu/csmaw; dedicated to broadening and decolonizing knowledge of the Muslim, Islamicate and Arab worlds through teaching, research and community outreach; Dir Dr DANY DOUEIRI; publ. *Arab Studies Quarterly*.

Department of Near Eastern Languages and Cultures: Indiana University, 3050 Near Eastern Languages & Cultures Global and International Studies Bldg 3050, 355 North Jordan Ave, Bloomington, IN 47405-1105; tel. (812) 855-5993; fax (812) 855-8659; e-mail nelc@indiana.edu; internet melc.indiana.edu; graduate and undergraduate courses in Islamic studies, Middle Eastern literatures, religions, and cultures and civilizations, Byzantine studies, and Arabic, Turkish and Persian language and linguistics; Chair. Prof. STEPHEN VINSON.

Fares Center for Eastern Mediterranean Studies: The Fletcher School of Law and Diplomacy, Tufts University, 160 Packard Ave, Medford, MA 02155; tel. (617) 627-6560; fax (617) 627-3461; e-mail fares-center@tufts.edu; internet fletcher.tufts.edu/farescenter; f. 2001; seeks to promote greater understanding of the Eastern Mediterranean region; organizes and sponsors symposiums, conferences and seminars; Dir Prof. NADIM ROUHANA; publ. *Pharos* (annual newsletter), as well as occasional papers.

Harvard Museum of the Ancient Near East: 6 Divinity Ave, Cambridge, MA 02138; tel. (617) 495-4631; fax (617) 496-8904; e-mail hmane@harvard.edu; internet hmane.harvard.edu; f. 1889 as Harvard Semitic Museum; present name adopted in 2020; sponsors exploration and research in Western Asia; archaeological and ethnographic collections from ancient Near East; research collections open by appointment, museum open free to general public; Dir Dr PETER DER MANUELIAN.

Hoover Institution on War, Revolution and Peace: Stanford University, 434 Galvez Mall, Stanford, CA 94305-6003; tel. (650) 723-1754; e-mail schieron@stanford.edu; internet www.hoover.org; f. 1919; extensive library and archives on 20th century history, incl. important collection of the Middle East and North Africa; Dir CONDOLEEZZA RICE; publ. *Hoover Digest* (quarterly), *Strategika* (online), monographs, books, etc.

Institute for the Transregional Study of the Contemporary Middle East, North Africa and Central Asia (TRI): Princeton University, 104 Jones Hall, Princeton, NJ 08544; tel. (609) 258-2178; fax (609) 258-0204; e-mail tri@princeton.edu; internet www.princeton.edu/transregional; f. 1994; comparative study and research focused on development, economic, social and political issues, democratization and human rights in the Middle East, North Africa and Central Asia regions; Dir Prof. BERNARD HAYKEL.

Kurdish Political Studies Program, School of Politics, Security, and International Affairs (KPSP): College of Sciences, University of Central Florida, 4297 Andromeda Loop N., Room 302, Howard Phillips Hall, Orlando, FL 32816; tel. (407) 823-2040; e-mail kurdish@ucf.edu; internet sciences.ucf.edu/politics/kps; Chair., Advisory Bd GÜNEŞ MURAT TEZCÜR.

Middle East Center: University of Utah, Orson Spencer Hall, 215 S Central Campus Dr., Room 210, Salt Lake City, UT 84112; tel. (801) 581-6101; fax (801) 581-6105; e-mail ias@utah.edu; internet www.mec.utah.edu; f. 1960; co-ordinates programme in Middle East languages and area studies in 12 academic depts; focuses on study of Arabic, Hebrew, Persian, Turkish, anthropology, history and political science; annual summer programme for Utah educators in the Middle East; library of 150,000 vols; Dir CHRIS LOW.

Middle East Forum: Suite 3600, 1650 Market St, Philadelphia, PA 19103; tel. (215) 546-5406; e-mail info@meforum.org; internet www.meforum.org; f. 1994; right-wing think tank that seeks to promote US interests in the Middle East; Pres. DANIEL PIPES; Dir GREGG ROMAN; publ. *Middle East Quarterly*.

Middle East Institute: 1763 St, NW, Washington, DC, 20036; tel. (202) 785-1141; fax (202) 331-8861; e-mail info@mei.edu; internet www.mei.edu; f. 1946; non-profit org. that promotes understanding of the Middle East, North Africa, Central Asia and the Caucasus; sponsors classes in Arabic, Hebrew, Persian and Turkish; convenes political and economic programmes and an annual conference; houses scholars and experts in a public policy centre; George Camp Keiser Library houses 25,000 vols and more than 300 periodicals; Pres. and CEO PAUL SALEM; publ. *Middle East Journal* (quarterly).

The Middle East Institute: Columbia University, 606 W 122th St, Knox Hall, 3rd Floor, MC 9640, New York, NY 10027; tel. (212) 854-2201; e-mail mei@columbia.edu; internet www.mei.columbia.edu; f. 1954; graduate training programme on the modern Middle East for students seeking professional careers as regional specialists, research into problems of economics, govt, law and international relations of the Middle East countries, and their languages and history; library of more than 150,000 vols in Middle East vernaculars and equally rich in Western languages, incl. Russian; Dir Prof. BRINKLEY MESSIK; publ. *Comparative Studies of South Asia, Africa and the Middle East*.

Middle East Policy Council: Suite 512, 1730 M St, NW, Washington, DC 20036; tel. (202) 296-6767; fax (202) 296-5791; e-mail info@mepc.org; internet mepc.org; f. 1981 to expand public discussion and understanding of issues affecting US policy in the Middle East; Pres. RICHARD J. SCHMIERER; publ. *Middle East Policy* (quarterly).

Middle East Studies Association of North America: 3542 N Santa Rita Ave, Tucson, AZ 85705; tel. (520) 333-2577; fax (520) 207-3166; e-mail secretariat@mesana.org; internet www.mesana.org; f. 1966 to promote high standards of scholarship and instruction in Middle East studies, to facilitate communication among scholars through meetings and publications, and to foster co-operation among persons and organizations concerned with the scholarly study of the Middle East since the rise of Islam; more than 2,700 mems; Exec. Dir JEFFERY D. REGER; publ. *International Journal of Middle East Studies* (quarterly), *Bulletin* (bi-annual), *Newsletter* (quarterly), *The Review of Middle East Studies* (2 a year).

Middle East Studies Center: East Hall 322, Portland State University, POB 751, Portland, OR 97201-0751; tel. (503) 725-8278; e-mail mesctr@pdx.edu; internet www.pdx.edu/middle-east-studies; f. 1959; Middle East language and area studies, Arabic, Hebrew, Persian and Turkish languages and literatures; contemporary Turkish studies and Islamic studies programme; area classes in history, political science, geography, anthropology and sociology; Dir LINDSAY J. BENSTEAD.

Near East Foundation: Suite 710, 110 W Fayette St, Syracuse, NY 13202; tel. (315) 428-8670; e-mail info@neareast.org; internet www.neareast.org; f. 1915; provides and promotes environment and natural resource management; agriculture and rural development; food security; urban development and rehabilitation; microfinance; community-based and bank-guaranteed lending; employment and job creation; population-, health- and family-planning; adult literacy and education; women's participation; in Jordan, Lebanon, the West Bank and Gaza, Egypt, Sudan, Ethiopia, Djibouti, Morocco and Mali; Chair. NINA B. QUIGLEY; Co-Pres SIMONA CECI, JOHN ASHBY; publ. annual report online, printed brochures periodically.

Oriental Institute (OI): University of Chicago, 1155 E 58th St, Chicago, IL 60637; tel. (773) 702-9514; fax (773) 702-9853; e-mail oi-administration@uchicago.edu; internet oi.uchicago.edu; f. 1919; principally concerned with cultures and languages of the ancient Near East; extensive museum; Interim Dir THEO VAN DEN HOUT; extensive publication programme, incl. scholarly monographs, museum catalogues; also publ. *News and Notes* (bi-monthly), *Journal of Near Eastern Studies* (bi-annual).

Prince Alwaleed Bin Talal Center for Muslim-Christian Understanding (ACMCU): Georgetown University, Intercultural Center (ICC), Suite 260, 37 & O St, NW, Washington, DC 20057; tel. (202) 687-8375; fax (202) 687-8376; e-mail acmcu@georgetown.edu; internet acmcu.georgetown.edu; f. 1933 to improve relations between the Muslim world and the West, as well as between Islam and Christianity; renamed as above in 2005, following a substantial investment by HRH Prince Alwaleed bin Talal of Saudi Arabia; organizes academic programmes and publ. books and articles; Dir Prof. JONATHAN GRIBETZ.

Program in Near Eastern Studies: Princeton University, 110 Jones Hall, Princeton, NJ 08544-1008; tel. (609) 258-4427; fax (609) 258-9055; e-mail nes@princeton.edu; internet nesp.princeton.edu; f. 1947; research into all aspects of the modern Near East and North Africa; library of 340,000 vols; Dir Prof. MARINA RUSTOW; publ. *Princeton Studies on the Near East* (irregular), *Princeton Papers: Inter-disciplinary Journal of Middle Eastern Studies* (semi-annual).

Tahrir Institute for Middle East Policy (TIMEP): 1717 K St, NW 900, Washington, DC 20006; e-mail info@timep.org; internet www.timep.org; f. 2013; research and analysis on Middle East affairs, aimed at influencing US and European policy towards the region; seeks to promote local perspectives; Exec. Dir MAI EL-SADANY.

UCLA Center for Near Eastern Studies: University of California, 10286 Bunche Hall, Los Angeles, CA 90095-1480; tel. (310) 825-1181; e-mail cnes@international.ucla.edu; internet international.ucla.edu/cnes; f. 1957; social sciences, culture and language studies of the Near East since the rise of Islam; library of more than 500,000 vols and 10,000 MSS in Arabic, Armenian, Hebrew, Persian and Turkish; annual publication of series of colloquia and of Giorgio Levi Della Vida Award Conference in Islamic Studies vols; 100 associated faculty mems; Dir ALI BEHDAD; publ. monographs, conference papers, working papers, etc.

Washington Institute for Near East Policy: Suite 500, 1111 19th St, NW, Washington, DC 20036; tel. (202) 452-0650; fax (202) 223-5364; e-mail press@washingtoninstitute.org; internet www.washingtoninstitute.org; f. 1985; promotes scholarly research and informed debate on the Middle East; Exec. Dir ROBERT SATLOFF.

VATICAN CITY

Pontificio Istituto Orientale (Pontifical Oriental Institute): 7 Piazza Santa Maria Maggiore, 00185 Rome; tel. (06) 447-4170; e-mail info@orientale.it; internet www.orientale.it; f. 1917; library of 200,000 vols; Rector DAVID NAZAR; publ. *Orientalia Christiana Periodica, Orientalia Christiana Analecta, Concilium Florentinum (Documenta et Scriptores), Anaphorae Syriacae, Kanonika*.

YEMEN

Sana'a Center for Strategic Studies: Haddah St, nr Al-Misbahi Intersection, San'a; tel. (1) 444375; fax (1) 444316; e-mail info@sanaacenter.org; internet sanaacenter.org; independent policy and research centre; Chair. MAGED AL-MADHAJI; publ. policy papers and reports.

SELECT BIBLIOGRAPHY (BOOKS)

Books on the Middle East

See also bibliographies at end of relevant chapters in Part Two.

Abdel Ghafar, Adel. *China and North Africa: Between Economics, Politics and Security*. London, I. B. Tauris, 2022.

Abdo, Geneive. *The New Sectarianism: the Arab Uprisings and the Rebirth of the Shi'a-Sunni Divide*. New York, Oxford University Press, 2017.

Abu-Rabi, Ibrahim M. *Contemporary Arab Thought: Studies in Post-1967 Arab Intellectual History*. London, Pluto Press, 2003.

Acharya, Amitar. *US Military Strategy in the Gulf*. London, Routledge, 1989.

Adelson, Roger. *London and the Invention of the Middle East: Money, Power and War 1902–1922*. New Haven, CT, Yale University Press, 1995.

Adib-Moghaddam, Arshin. *On the Arab Revolts and the Iranian Revolution: Power and Resistance Today*. New York, Bloomsbury, 2013.

Afkhami, Mahnaz. *Faith and Freedom: Women's Human Rights in the Muslim World*. London, I. B. Tauris, 1996.

Aggestam, Karin, and Björkdahl, Annika (Eds). *Rethinking Peacebuilding: The Quest for Just Peace in the Middle East and the Western Balkans*. Abingdon, Routledge, 2014.

Ahmadi, Koroush. *Islands and International Politics in the Persian Gulf: Abu Musa and Tunbs in Strategic Context*. Abingdon, Routledge, 2008.

Ahmed, Akbar S., and Donnan, Hastings (Eds). *Islam, Globalization and Postmodernity*. London, Routledge, 1994.

Akbarzadeh, Shahram (Ed.). *Routledge Handbook of International Relations in the Middle East*. Abingdon, Routledge, 2019.

Akbarzadeh, Shahram, et al. (Eds). *American Democracy Promotion in the Changing Middle East: From Bush to Obama*. Abingdon, Routledge, 2013.

Ali, Tariq. *The Clash of Fundamentalisms: Crusades, Jihads and Modernity*. London, Verso, 2002.

Allain, Jean. *International Law in the Middle East: Closer to Power Than Justice*. Aldershot, Ashgate, 2004.

Allan, Tony. *The Middle East Water Question: Hydropolitics and the Global Economy*. London, I. B. Tauris, 2001.

Allin, Dana H., and Simon, Steven. *The Sixth Crisis: Iran, Israel, America and the Rumors of War*. New York, Oxford University Press, 2010.

Alpher, Yossi. *Winners and Losers in the 'Arab Spring': Profiles in Chaos*. Abingdon, Routledge, 2019.

Alsharek, A., Springborg, R., and Stewart, S. (Eds). *Popular Culture and Political Identity in the Arab Gulf States*. London, Saqi Books, 2008.

Aman, Mohammed M. *Middle East Conflicts & Reforms*. Washington DC, Westphalia Press, 2014.

Amir-Moezzi, Ali. *Spirituality and Islam: Belief and Practice in Shi'ism*. London, I. B. Tauris, 2008.

Andersen, Roy R., Seibert, Robert F., and Wagner, Jon G. *Politics and Change in the Middle East: Sources of Conflict and Accommodation*. Upper Saddle River, NJ, Prentice Hall, 2007.

Angrist, Michele Penner. *Party Building in the Modern Middle East*. Seattle, WA, University of Washington Press, 2006.

Aruri, Naseer Hasan, and Shuraydi, Mohammad A. (Eds). *Revising Culture, Reinventing Peace: The Influence of Edward W. Said*. Interlink Publishing Group, 2000.

Aruri, Naseer Hasan (Ed.). *Palestinian Refugees: The Right of Return*. London, Pluto Press, 2001.

Aslan, Reza. *No God but God: The Origins, Evolution and Future of Islam*. London, Arrow Books, revised edn, 2006.

Atwan, Abdel Bari. *The Secret History of al Qaeda*. Berkeley, CA, University of California Press, revised edn, 2008.

Ayubi, Nazih N. *Over-Stating the Arab State: Politics and Society in the Middle East*. London, I. B. Tauris, 1995.

Bahgat, Gawdat. *Proliferation of Nuclear Weapons in the Middle East*. Gainsville, FL, University Press of Florida, 2009.

Bailey, Sydney. *Four Arab–Israeli Wars and the Peace Process*. London, Macmillan, 1990.

Bakkour, Samer. *The End of the Middle East Peace Process: The Failure of US Diplomacy*. Abingdon, Routledge, 2022.

al-Barghouti, Tamim. *The Umma and the Dawla: The Nation State and the Arab Middle East*. London, Pluto Press, 2008.

Barkey, Henri. *The Politics of Economic Reform in the Middle East*. London, Macmillan, 1993.

Bauer, Alain, and Raufer, Xavier. *L'énigme Al-Qaida*. Paris, Éditions Jean-Claude Lattès, 2005.

Bazoobandi, Sara. *Political Economy of the Gulf Sovereign Wealth Funds: A Case Study of Iran, Kuwait, Saudi Arabia and the United Arab Emirates*. Abingdon, Routledge, 2013.

Beinin, Joel. *Workers and Peasants in the Modern Middle East*. Cambridge University Press, 2001.

Ben-Ami, Shlomo. *Scars of War, Wounds of Peace: The Israeli–Arab Tragedy*. London, Phoenix Press, revised edn, 2006.

Prophets without Honor: The 2000 Camp David Summit and the End of the Two-State Solution. Oxford, Oxford University Press, 2022.

Bengio, Ofra (Ed.). *Kurdish Awakening: Nation Building in a Fragmented Homeland*. Austin, TX, University of Texas Press, 2014.

Ben-Porat, Guy (Ed.). *The Failure of the Middle East Peace Process?* London, Macmillan, 2008.

Ben-Zvi, Abraham. *Decade of Transition: Eisenhower, Kennedy, and the Origins of the American-Israeli Alliance*. New York, Columbia University Press, 1999.

Bergen, Peter, and Tiedemann, Katherine (Eds). *Negotiating the Borders Between Terror, Politics and Religion*. New York, Oxford University Press, 2013.

Berry, Mike, and Philo, Greg. *Israel and Palestine: Competing Histories*. London, Pluto Press, 2006.

Bianquis, Th., Bosworth, C. E., Donzel, E. van, and Heinrichs, W. P. (Eds). *Encyclopaedia of Islam*. 10 vols. Leiden, Brill Academic Publishers, 2000.

Bickerton, Ian J., and Klausner, Carla L. *A History of the Arab–Israeli Conflict*. Abingdon, Routledge, 8th edn, 2018.

Bidwell, Robin (Ed.). *Dictionary of Modern Arab History*. London, Kegan Paul International, 1998.

Bill, J., and Springborg, R. *Politics in the Middle East*. London, HarperCollins, 5th edn, 2000.

Bin Huwaidin, Mohamed. *China's Relations with Arabia and the Gulf, 1949–1999*. London, Routledge, 2002.

Binder, Leonard. *The Ideological Revolution in the Middle East*. Melbourne, FL, Krieger Publishing, 1979.

Islamic Liberalism: A Critique of Development Ideologies. Chicago, IL, Chicago University Press, 1988.

von Bismarck, Helene. *British Policy in the Persian Gulf, 1961–1968: Conceptions of Informal Empire*. Basingstoke, Palgrave Macmillan, 2013.

Blanga, Yehuda U. *The US, Israel, and Egypt: Diplomacy in the Shadow of Attrition, 1969–70*. London, Routledge, 2019.

Bonine, Michael E. et al (Eds). *Is there a Middle East? The Evolution of a Geopolitical Concept*. Stanford, CA, Stanford University Press, 2012.

Bonne, Alfred. *The Economic Development of the Middle East*. Abingdon, Routledge, 2013.

Bonner, Michael. *Jihad in Islamic History: Doctrines and Practice*. Princeton, NJ, Princeton University Press, 2006.

Brachman, Jarret M. *Global Jihadism: Theory and Practice*. Abingdon, Routledge, 2008.

Bradley, John R. *After the Arab Spring: How Islamists Hijacked the Middle East Revolts*. Basingstoke, Palgrave Macmillan, 2012.

Brandell, Inga (Ed.). *State Frontiers: Borders and Boundaries in the Middle East*. London, I. B. Tauris, 2006.

Bregman, Ahron (Ed.). *Warfare in the Middle East since 1945*. Aldershot, Ashgate, 2008.

Bregman, Ahron, and El-Tahri, Jihan. *The Fifty Years' War: Israel and the Arabs*. London, Penguin and BBC Books, 1998.

Brenchley, Frank. *Britain and the Middle East: An Economic History, 1945–1987*. London, Lester Crook Academic Publishing, 1989.

Breslauer, George W. (Ed.). *Soviet Strategy in the Middle East*. London, Routledge, 1989.

REGIONAL INFORMATION

Select Bibliography (Books)

Browers, Michaelle L. *Political Ideology in the Arab World: Accommodation and Transformation.* Cambridge University Press, 2009.

Brown, Daniel. *Rethinking Tradition in Modern Islamic Thought.* Cambridge University Press, 1996.

Brown, L. Carl. *Religion and State: The Muslim Approach to Politics.* New York, Columbia University Press, 2000.

Diplomacy in the Middle East. London, I. B. Tauris, 2001.

Brown, Nathan J. *When Victory is Not an Option: Islamist Movements in Arab Politics.* Ithaca, NY, Cornell University Press, 2012.

Brown, Nathan, and Shahin, Emad el-Din (Eds). *The Struggle over Democracy in the Middle East: Regional Politics and External Policies.* Abingdon, Routledge, 2009.

Buchanan, Andrew S. *Peace with Justice: A History of the Israeli-Palestinian Declaration of Principles on Interim Self-Government Arrangements.* Basingstoke, St Martin's Press, 2000.

Bulloch, John. *The Making of a War: The Middle East from 1967–1973.* London, Longman, 1974.

Bulloch, John, and Morris, Harvey. *The Gulf War.* London, Methuen, 1990.

Saddam's War. London, Faber and Faber, 1991.

Burgat, François. *Face to Face with Political Islam.* London, I. B. Tauris, 1997.

Islamism in the Shadow of al-Qaeda. Austin, TX, University of Texas Press, 2008.

Burke, Jason. *Al-Qaeda: The True Story of Radical Islam.* London, Penguin, 2004.

Burton, Guy. *China and Middle East Conflicts: Responding to War and Rivalry from the Cold War to the Present.* Abingdon, Routledge, 2022.

Butenschøn, Nils A., and Meijer, Roel (Eds). *The Middle East in Transition: the Centrality of Citizenship.* Northampton, MA, Edward Elgar Publishers, 2018.

Butt, Gerald. *A Rock and a Hard Place: Origins of Arab-Western Conflict in the Middle East.* London, HarperCollins, 1994.

The Arabs: Myth and Reality. London, I. B. Tauris, 1998.

Butterworth, Charles E., and Zartman, I. William (Eds). *Between the State and Islam.* Cambridge, Cambridge University Press, 2001.

Carter, Hannah, and Ehteshami, Anoushiravan (Eds). *The Middle East's Relations with Asia and Russia.* London, Routledge, 2004.

Castellino, Joshua, and Cavanaugh, Kathleen A. *Minority Rights in the Middle East.* New York, Oxford University Press, 2013.

Cattan, J. *Evolution of Oil Concessions in the Middle East and North Africa.* Dobbs Ferry, NY, Oceana, 1967.

Cavatorta, Francesco, Storm, Lise, and Resta, Valeria (Eds). *Routledge Handbook on Political Parties in the Middle East and North Africa.* Abingdon, Routledge, 2021.

Challand, B. *Violence and Representation in the Arab Uprisings.* Cambridge, Cambridge University Press, 2023.

Chamlou, Nadereh. *Gender and Development in the Middle East and North Africa: Women in the Public Sphere.* Washington, DC, The World Bank, 2004.

Charountaki, Marianna. *The Kurds and US Foreign Policy: International Relations in the Middle East since 1945.* Abingdon, Routledge, 2014.

Chase, Anthony Tirado (Ed.). *Routledge Handbook on Human Rights and the Middle East and North Africa.* Abingdon, Routledge, 2017.

de Châtel, Francesca. *Water Sheikhs and Dam Builders: Stories of People and Water in the Middle East.* Edison, NJ, Transaction Publishing, 2008.

Choueiri, Youssef M. *Arab Nationalism: A History.* Oxford, Blackwell, 2001.

A Companion to the History of the Middle East. Oxford, Blackwell, 2005.

Clarke, Duncan. *Empires of Oil: Corporate Oil in Barbarian Worlds.* London, Profile, 2007.

Coates Ulrichsen, Kristian. *Insecure Gulf: The End of Certainty and the Transition to the Post-Oil Era.* New York, Columbia University Press, 2011.

(Ed.). *The Changing Security Dynamics of the Persian Gulf.* New York, Oxford University Press, 2017.

Cobham, David, and Dibeh, Ghassan (Eds). *Monetary Policy and Central Banking in the Middle East and North Africa.* Abingdon, Routledge, 2012.

Money in the Middle East and North Africa: Monetary Policy Frameworks and Strategies. Abingdon, Routledge, 2013.

Cohen, Michael J. *Palestine: Retreat from the Mandate.* London, Elek Books, 1978.

Commins, David. *The Gulf States: A Modern History.* London, I. B. Tauris, 2012.

Conrad, Lawrence J. (Ed.). *The Formation and Perception of the Modern Arab World, Studies by Marwan R. Buheiry.* Princeton, NJ, The Darwin Press, 1989.

Cook, David. *Understanding Jihad.* Berkeley, CA, University of California Press, 2005.

Cook, Stephen A. *Ruling But Not Governing: The Military and Political Development in Egypt, Algeria and Turkey.* Baltimore, MD, Johns Hopkins University Press, 2007.

Cooley, John K. *Green March, Black September: The Story of the Palestinian Arabs.* London, Frank Cass, 1973.

Corbin, Henry. *History of Islamic Philosophy.* London, Kegan Paul International, 1992.

Cordesman, Anthony H. *Weapons of Mass Destruction in the Middle East.* London, Brasseys, 1991.

Bahrain, Oman, Qatar, and The UAE: Challenges Of Security. Abingdon, Routledge, 2019.

Cordesman, Anthony H., and al-Rodhan, Khalid R. *The Changing Dynamics of Energy in the Middle East.* 2 vols. Westport, CT, Praeger Security International, 2006.

Costantini, Irene. *Statebuilding in the Middle East and North Africa: The Aftermath of Regime Change.* Abingdon, Routledge, 2018.

Courbage, Youssef, and Fargues, Philippe. *Christians and Jews under Islam.* London, I. B. Tauris, 1997.

Covarrubias, Jack, and Lansford, Tom (Eds). *Strategic Interests in the Middle East.* Aldershot, Ashgate, 2008.

Crone, Patricia. *Meccan Trade and the Rise of Islam.* Oxford, Basil Blackwell, 1987.

Cronin, Stephanie (Ed.). *Subalterns and Social Protest: History from Below in the Middle East and North Africa.* Abingdon, Routledge, 2007.

Cudsi, Alexander, and Dessouki, Ali E. Hillal (Eds). *Islam and Power.* London, Croom Helm, 1981.

Dabashi, Hamid. *The Arab Spring: The End of Postcolonialism.* London, Zed Books, 2012.

Daftary, Farhad. *A Short History of the Isma'lis: Traditions of a Muslim Community.* Edinburgh University Press, 1999.

Danahar, Paul. *The New Middle East: The World After the Arab Spring.* London, Bloomsbury, 2013.

Daniel, Norman. *Islam and the West: The Making of an Image.* Oneworld Publications, revised edn, 1993.

Davidson, Christopher M. *From Sheikhs to Sultanism: Statecraft and Authority in Saudi Arabia and the UAE.* London, Hurst & Co, 2021.

Dazi-Héni, Fatiha. *Monarchies et Sociétés d'Arabie, Le Temps des Confrontations.* Paris, Presses de la Fondation Nationale des Sciences Politiques, 2006.

Decobert, Christian. *Le mendiant et le combattant: l'institution de l'islam.* Paris, Editions du Seuil, 1991.

Dekmejian, R. H. *Islam in Revolution: Fundamentalism in the Arab World.* Syracuse, NY, Syracuse University Press, 1995.

DeLong-Bas, Natana J. *Wahhabi Islam: From Revival and Reform to Global Jihad.* London, I. B. Tauris, 2004.

Destani, Bejtullah D. *Minorities in the Middle East: Kurdish Communities 1918–1974.* 4 vols. Slough, Archive Editions, 2006.

Devji, Faisal. *Landscapes of the Jihad: Militancy, Morality, Modernity.* Ithaca, NY, Cornell University Press, 2005.

DeVore, Ronald M. (Ed.). *The Arab–Israeli Conflict: A Historical, Political, Social and Military Bibliography.* Oxford, Clio Press, 1977.

Dombroski, Kenneth R. *Peacekeeping in the Middle East as an International Regime.* Abingdon, Routledge, 2007.

Doumato, Eleanor A., and Posusney, Marsha P. (Eds). *Women and Globalization in the Arab Middle East: Gender, Economy and Society.* Boulder, CO, Lynne Rienner Publishers, 2003.

Dowek, Ephraim. *Israeli-Egyptian Relations, 1980–2000.* London, Frank Cass, 2001.

Droz-Vincent, Philippe. *Military Politics of the Contemporary Arab World.* Cambridge, Cambridge University Press, 2020.

Efrat, Moshe, and Bercovitch, Jacob. *Superpowers and Client States in the Middle East: The Imbalance of Influence.* London, Routledge, 1991.

Ehteshami, Anoushiravan. *Globalization and Geopolitics in the Middle East: Old Games, New Rules.* Abingdon, Routledge, 2007.

Dynamics of Change in the Persian Gulf: Political Economy, War and Revolution. Abingdon, Routledge, 2013.

Ehteshami, Anoushiravan, and Horesh, Niv. *How China's Rise is Changing the Middle East.* Abingdon, Routledge, 2019.

Ehteshami, Anoushiravan, and Nonneman, Gerd. *War and Peace in the Gulf: Domestic Politics and Regional Relations into the 1990s.* Reading, Ithaca Press, 1991.

Ehteshami, Anoushiravan, Rasheed, Amjed, and Beaujouan, Juline. *Islam, IS and the Fragmented State: The Challenges of Political Islam in the MENA Region.* Abingdon and New York, Routledge, 2020.

Eibl, Ferdinand. *Social Dictatorships: The Political Economy of the Welfare State in the Middle East and North Africa.* Oxford, Oxford University Press, 2020.

Eickelman, Dale F., and Piscatori, James. *Muslim Politics.* Princeton, NJ, Princeton University Press, 1996.

Elbadawi, Ibrahim, and Makdisi, Samir. (Eds). *Democracy in the Arab World: Explaining the Deficit.* Abingdon, Routledge, 2010.

Elkhafif, Mahmoud, Taghdisi-Rad, Sahar, and Elagraa, Mutasim. (Eds). *Economic and Trade Policies in the Arab World: Employment, Poverty Reduction and Integration.* Abingdon, Routledge, 2012.

Elon, Amos. *A Blood-Dimmed Tide: Dispatches from the Middle East.* London, Allen Lane, 2000.

Elsheshtawy, Yasser. *The Evolving Arab City: Tradition, Modernity and Urban Development.* Abingdon, Routledge, 2008.

Enayat, Hamid. *Modern Islamic Political Thought: The Response of the Shi'i and Sunni Muslims to the Twentieth Century.* London, Macmillan, 1982.

Enderlin, Charles. *Paix ou guerres. Les secrets des négociations israélo-arabes 1917–1995.* Paris, Fayard, 2003.

Engert, Stefan. *EU Enlargement and Socialization: Turkey and Cyprus.* Abingdon, Routledge, 2010.

Ennaji, Moha, and Sadiqi, Fatima. (Eds). *Gender and Violence in the Middle East.* Abingdon, Routledge, 2011.

Erdogan, Ayfer. *Arab Spring-Arab Fall: Divergent Transitions in post-2011 Tunisia and Egypt.* Lanham, Lexington Books, 2021.

Esposito, John L. (Ed.). *Voices of Resurgent Islam.* New York, Oxford University Press, 1983.

The Oxford Encyclopaedia of the Modern Islamic World. New York, Oxford University Press, Inc, 1995.

The Oxford History of Islam. New York, Oxford University Press, Inc, 2000.

Evron, Y., and Kowner, R. (Eds). *Israel-Asia Relations in the Twenty-First Century: The Search for Partners in a Changing World.* London, Routledge, 2023.

Faath, Sigrid (Ed.). *Anti-Americanism in the Islamic World.* London, C. Hurst & Co, 2006.

Fain, W. Taylor. *American Ascendance and British Retreat in the Persian Gulf Region.* New York, Palgrave Macmillan, 2008.

Fawcett, Louise. *International Relations of the Middle East.* Oxford, Oxford University Press, 2nd edn, 2009.

Feliu, Laura, and Izquierdo-Brichs, Ferran. *Communist Parties in the Middle East: 100 Years of History* (Europa Regional Perspectives). Abingdon, Routledge, 2019.

Feldman, Noah. *After Jihad: America and the Struggle for Islamic Democracy.* New York, Farrar, Straus and Giroux, 2004.

The Fall and Rise of the Islamic State. Princeton, NJ, Princeton University Press, 2008.

The Arab Winter: A Tragedy. Princeton, NJ, Princeton University Press, 2020.

Field, Michael. *Inside the Arab World.* Cambridge, MA, Harvard University Press, revised edn, 1998.

Findlay, Allan M. *The Arab World.* London, Routledge, 1996.

Fisher, S. N. *Social Forces in the Middle East.* Ithaca, NY, Cornell University Press, 3rd edn, 1977.

The Middle East: A History. New York, McGraw-Hill, 4th edn, 1990.

Fisher, W. B. *The Middle East—A Physical, Social and Regional Geography.* London, 7th edn, 1978.

Fisk, Robert. *The Great War for Civilisation: The Conquest of the Middle East.* London, HarperCollins, 2006.

Fox, J. W., Mourtada-Sabbah, N., and al-Mutawa, M. (Eds). *Globalization and the Gulf.* Abingdon, Routledge, 2006.

Freedman, Robert O. *The Middle East Enters the Twenty-first Century.* Gainesville, FL, University Press of Florida, 2002.

Freer, Courtney. *Rentier Islamism: The Influence of the Muslim Brotherhood in Gulf Monarchies.* Oxford, Oxford University Press, 2018.

Fuller, Graham E., and Lesser, Jan O. *A Sense of Siege: The Geopolitics of Islam and the West.* Boulder, CO, Westview Press, 1995.

Fulton, Jonathan, and Sim, Li-Chen (Eds). *External Powers and the Gulf Monarchies.* Abingdon, Routledge, 2018.

Fulton, Jonathan. *China's Relations with the Gulf Monarchies.* London, Routledge, 2018.

Routledge Handbook On China - Middle East Relations. Abingdon and New York, Routledge, 2022.

Galal, Ahmed, and Hoekman, Bernard. *Arab Economic Integration: Between Hope and Reality.* Washington, DC, Brookings Institution Press, 2003.

Gallagher, Nancy Elizabeth (Ed.). *Approaches to the History of the Middle East: Interviews with Leading Middle East Historians.* Reading, Garnet, 1995.

Garon, Lise. *Dangerous Alliances: Civil Society, the Media and Democratic Transition in North Africa.* London, Zed Books, 2003.

Gasiorowski, M., Long, D. E., and Reich, B. *The Government and Politics of the Middle East and North Africa.* Boulder, CO, Westview Press, 2007.

Gause, F. Gregory. *The International Relations of the Persian Gulf.* Cambridge, Cambridge University Press, 2009.

Gelber, Yoav. *Palestine 1948: War, Escape and the Emergence of the Palestinian Refugee Problem.* Brighton, Sussex Academic Press, 2001.

Gelvin, James L. *The Israeli–Palestinian Conflict: One Hundred Years of War.* Cambridge, Cambridge University Press, 2005.

Gerges, Fawaz A. *The Far Enemy: Why Jihad Went Global.* Cambridge University Press, 2005.

Gerner, Deborah J. *Understanding the Contemporary Middle East.* Boulder, CO, Lynne Rienner Publishers, 2000.

Gershoni, Israel, Erdem, Hakan, and Woköck, Ursula (Eds). *Histories of the Modern Middle East: New Directions.* Boulder, CO, Lynne Rienner Publishers, 2002.

Gershoni, Israel, and Jankowski, James (Eds). *Rethinking Nationalism in the Arab Middle East.* New York, Columbia University Press, 1998.

Gertel, Jörg, and Hexel, Ralf (Eds). *Coping with Uncertainty: Youth in the Middle East and North Africa.* London, Saqi Books, 2018.

Gervais, Victor, and van Genugten, Saskia (Eds). *Stabilising the Contemporary Middle East and North Africa: Regional Actors and New Approaches.* London, Palgrave Macmillan, 2020.

Ghareeb, Edmund, and Khadduri, Majid. *War in the Gulf, 1990–91: The Iraq–Kuwait Conflict and its Implications.* Oxford University Press, 1997.

Ghattas, Kim. *Black Wave: Saudi Arabia, Iran and the Rivalry That Unravelled the Middle East.* London, Wildfire, 2020.

Giacaman, George, and Jrund Lonning, Dag. *After Oslo: New Realities, Old Problems.* London, Pluto Press, 1998.

Gibb, H. A. R., and Bowen, Harold. *Islamic Society and the West.* London, 2 vols, 1950, 1957.

Gilbert, Martin. *The Routledge Atlas of the Arab–Israeli Conflict.* Abingdon, Routledge, 2005.

Gilsenan, Michael. *Recognizing Islam: Religion and Society in the Modern Middle East.* London, I. B. Tauris, 1990.

Gittings, John (Ed.). *Beyond the Gulf War: The Middle East and the New World Order.* London, Catholic Institute for International Relations, 1991.

Glassé, Cyril. *The Concise Encyclopedia of Islam.* London, revised edn, Stacey International, 2001.

Glubb, Lt-Gen. Sir John. *A Short History of the Arab Peoples.* London, Hodder and Stoughton, 1969.

Göçek, Fatma Müge (Ed.). *Women of the Middle East.* Abingdon, Routledge, 2016.

Golan, Galia, and Salem, Walid (Eds). *Non-State Actors in the Middle East: Factors for Peace and Democracy.* Abingdon, Routledge, 2013.

Goldschmidt Jr., Arthur (with Boum, Aomar). *A Concise History of the Middle East.* Abingdon, Routledge, 11th edn, 2019.

Gomaa, Ahmed M. *The Foundation of the League of Arab States.* London, Longman, 1977.

al-Gosaibi, Ghazi. *The Gulf Crisis—An Attempt to Understand.* London, Kegan Paul International, 1993.

Gowers, Andrew, and Walter, Tony. *Behind the Myth: Yasir Arafat and the Palestinian Revolution.* London, W. H. Allen, 1990.

Gresh, Alain, and Vidal, Dominique. *The New A–Z of the Middle East.* London, I. B. Tauris, 2004.

Grinberg, Lev Luis. *Politics and Violence in Israel/Palestine: Democracy versus Military Rule.* Abingdon, Routledge, 2011.

Grossman, Mark. *Encyclopaedia of the Persian Gulf War.* Santa Barbara, California, ABC-Clio, 1996.

Grunebaum, Gustave E. von (Ed.). *Unity and Variety in Muslim Civilisation.* Chicago, 1955.

Islam: Essays on the Nature and Growth of a Cultural Tradition. London, Routledge and Kegan Paul, 1961.

Modern Islam: the Search for Cultural Identity. London, 1962.

Guazzone, Laura, and Pioppi, Daniela (Eds). *The Arab State and Neo-liberal Globalization: The Restructuring of State Power in the Middle East.* Reading, Ithaca Press, 2009.

Habeck, Mary. *Knowing the Enemy: Jihadist Ideology and the War on Terror.* New Haven, CT, Yale University Press, 2007.

Haddad, Tania, and al-Hindy, Elie (Eds). *Religion and Civil Society in the Arab World: In the Vortex of Globalization and Tradition.* London, Routledge India, 2018.

Hafez, Mohammed M. *Why Muslims Rebel: Repression and Resistance in the Islamic World.* Boulder, CO, Lynne Rienner Publishers, revised edn, 2004.

Hakimian, Hassan, and Moshaver, Ziba (Eds). *The State and Global Change: The Political Economy of Change in the Middle East and North Africa.* Richmond, Curzon Press, 2001.

Halabi, Yakub. *US Foreign Policy in the Middle East: From Crises to Change.* Aldershot, Ashgate, 2009.

Halliday, Fred. *Nation and Religion in the Middle East.* Boulder, CO, Lynne Rienner Publishers, 2000.

Islam and the Myth of Confrontation: Religion and Politics in the Middle East. London, I. B. Tauris, revised edn, 2002.

The Middle East in International Politics: Power, Politics and Ideology. Cambridge University Press, 2005.

100 Myths about the Middle East. London, Saqi Books, 2005.

Halm, Heinz. *The Fatimids and their Traditions of Learning.* London, I. B. Tauris, 1997.

Halpern, Manfred. *The Politics of Social Change in the Middle East and North Africa.* Princeton, NJ, Princeton University Press, 1963.

Hanieh, Adam. *Capitalism and Class in the Gulf Arab States.* Basingstoke, Palgrave Macmillan, updated edn, 2014.

Harders, Cilja, and Legrenzi, Matteo (Eds). *Beyond Regionalism?* Aldershot, Ashgate, 2008.

Hardy, Roger. *Arabia after the Storm: Internal Stability of the Gulf Arab States.* London, Royal Institute of International Affairs, 1992.

Hare, William. *The Struggle for the Holy Land.* London, Madison Publishing, 1998.

Harris, Lillian Craig. *China Considers the Middle East.* London, I. B. Tauris, 1994.

Hart, Alan. *Arafat—Terrorist or Peacemaker?* London, Sidgwick and Jackson, 2nd edn, 1994.

Hartshorn, J. E. *Christianity in the Arab World.* Norwich, SCM Press, revised edn, 1998.

Haugbolle, Sune, and Hastrup, Anders (Eds). *The Politics of Violence, Truth and Reconciliation in the Arab Middle East.* Abingdon, Routledge, 2008.

Hayes, J. R. (Ed.). *The Genius of Arab Civilisation: Source of Renaissance.* New York University Press, 3rd edn, 1992.

Heikal, Mohammed. *Illusions of Triumph: An Arab View of the Gulf War.* London, HarperCollins, 1992.

Held, David, and Ulrichsen, Kristian (Eds). *The Transformation of the Gulf: Politics, Economics and the Global Order.* Abingdon, Routledge, 2011.

Heradstvelt, Daniel, and Hveem, Helge. *Oil in the Gulf: Obstacles to Democracy and Development.* Aldershot, Ashgate, 2004.

Hertog, Steffen, Luciani, Giacomo, and Valeri, Marc (Eds). *Business Politics in the Middle East.* London, C. Hurst & Co, 2013.

Herzog, Maj.-Gen. Chaim. *The War of Atonement.* London, Weidenfeld and Nicolson, 1975.

The Arab–Israeli Wars. London, Arms and Armour Press, 1982.

Hewedy, Amin. *Militarisation and Security in the Middle East.* London, Pinter, 1989.

Higgins, Rosalyn. *United Nations Peacekeeping 1946–67: Documents and Commentary*, Vol. I, *The Middle East.* Oxford University Press, 1969.

Hinnebusch, Raymond, and Gani, Jasmine (Eds). *The Routledge Handbook to the Middle East and North African State and States System.* Abingdon, Routledge, 2020.

Hiro, Dilip. *Inside the Middle East.* London, Routledge and Kegan Paul, 1981.

Islamic Fundamentalism. London, Paladin, 1988.

Sharing the Promised Land. An Interwoven Tale of Israelis and Palestinians. London, Hodder & Stoughton, 1996.

War Without End: The Rise Of Islamist Terrorism And Global Response. London, Routledge, 2002.

The Essential Middle East: A Comprehensive Guide. New York, Carroll & Graf Publishers, 2003.

Hirst, David. *Oil and Public Opinion in the Middle East.* New York, Praeger, 1966.

The Gun and the Olive Branch: The Roots of Violence in the Middle East. London, Faber, 1977.

Hitti, Philip K. *The Origins of the Druze People and Religion.* London, Saqi Books, 2007.

Hodgkin, E. C. *The Arabs.* Modern World Series, Oxford University Press, 1966.

(Ed.). *Two Kings in Arabia: Sir Reader Bullard's Letters from Jeddah.* Reading, Ithaca Press, 1999.

Holt, P. M., Lambton, A. K. S., and Lewis, B. (Eds). *The Cambridge History of Islam.* Vol. I, *The Central Islamic Lands.* Cambridge University Press, 1970; Vol. II, *The Further Islamic Lands, Islamic Society and Civilization.* Cambridge University Press, 1971.

Holthaus, Leonie. *Regimelegitimität und regionale Kooperation im Golf-Kooperationsrat (Gulf Cooperation Council).* Frankfurt am Main, Peter Lang, 2010.

Hourani, A. H. *Minorities in the Arab World.* London, 1947.

The Emergence of the Modern Middle East. London, Macmillan, 1981.

A History of the Arab Peoples. London, Faber and Faber, revised edn, 2005.

Islam in European Thought. Cambridge University Press, 1991.

Hourani, Albert, Khoury, Philip, and Wilson, Mary C. (Eds). *The Modern Middle East.* London, I. B. Tauris, 2004.

Hroub, Khaled (Ed.). *Political Islam: Ideology and Practice.* London, Saqi Books, 2009.

Hudson, Michael C. *Arab Politics: The Search for Legitimacy.* New Haven, CT, and London, Yale University Press, 1977/78.

Hurewitz, J. C. *Unity and Disunity in the Middle East.* New York, Carnegie Endowment for International Peace, 1952.

Middle East Dilemmas. New York, 1953.

Diplomacy in the Near and Middle East. Vol. I, *1535–1914*; Vol. II, *1914–1956.* Van Nostrand, 1956.

(Ed.). *Soviet-American Rivalry in the Middle East.* London, Pall Mall Press, and New York, Praeger, 1969.

Middle East Politics: The Military Dimension. London, Pall Mall Press, 1969.

Ibrahim, Badr el-Din A. *Economic Co-operation in the Gulf: Issues in the Economies of the Arab Gulf Cooperation Council States.* Abingdon, Routledge, 2012.

Inbar, Efraim, and Frisch, Hillel (Eds). *Radical Islam and National Society: Challenges and Responses.* Abingdon, Routledge, 2007.

International Institute for Strategic Studies. *Sources of Conflict in the Middle East.* London, Adelphi Papers, International Institute for Strategic Studies, 1966.

Domestic Politics and Regional Security: Jordan, Syria and Israel. London, Gower, International Institute for Strategic Studies, 1989.

Irwin, Robert. *For Lust of Knowing: The Orientalists and their Enemies.* London, Penguin, 2007.

Ismail, Salwa. *Rethinking Islamist Politics: Culture, the State and Islamism.* London, I. B. Tauris, 2006.

Israeli, Ofer. *Complex Effects of International Relations: Intended and Unintended Consequences of Human Actions in Middle East Conflicts.* Albany, NY, State University of New York Press, 2020.

Israeli, Raphael. *War, Peace and Terror in the Middle East.* London, Frank Cass, 2003.

Issawi, Charles. *An Economic History of the Middle East and North Africa.* London, Methuen, 1982.

Jaber, Faleh A., and Dawod, Hosham (Eds). *The Kurds: Nationalism and Politics.* London, Saqi Books, 2006.

Jägerskog, Anders, Schulz, Michael, and Swain, Ashok (Eds). *Routledge Handbook on Middle East Security.* Abingdon, Routledge, 2019.

Jansen, Johannes J. G. *The Dual Nature of Islamic Fundamentalism.* Ithaca, NY, Cornell University Press, 1997.

Jebnoun, Noureddine, et al (Eds). *Modern Middle East Authoritarianism: Roots, Ramifications, and Crisis.* Abingdon, Routledge, 2013.

Jebril, N., and Abunajela, M. A. (Eds). *Media and Democracy in the Middle East.* London, Routledge, 2023.

Jerichow, A. and Simonsen, J. B. (Eds). *Islam in a Changing World and the Middle East.* Richmond, Curzon Press, 1997.

Joffé, George (Ed.). *Islamic Radicalisation in Europe and the Middle East: Reassessing the Causes of Terrorism.* London, I. B. Tauris, 2012.

Johnson, Nels. *Islam and the Politics of Meaning in Palestinian Nationalism*. Henley-on-Thames, Kegan Paul International, 1983.

Jones, Jeremy. *Negotiating Change: The New Politics of the Middle East*. London, I. B. Tauris, 2006.

Kadhim, Abbas (Ed.). *Governance in the Middle East and North Africa: A Handbook*. Abingdon, Routledge, 2012.

Kaim, Markus. *Great Powers and Regional Orders: The United States and the Persian Gulf*. Aldershot, Ashgate, 2008.

Kamrava, Mehran. *The New Voices of Islam: Rethinking Politics and Modernity—A Reader*. Berkeley, CA, University of California Press, 2006.

Kane, Chen, and Murauskaite, Egle (Eds). *Regional Security Dialogue in the Middle East: Changes, Challenges and Opportunities*. Abingdon, Routledge, 2014.

Kapiszewski, Andrzej. *Nationals and Expatriates: Population and Labour Dilemmas of the Gulf Cooperation Council States*. Reading, Ithaca Press, 2000.

Karsh, Efraim. *Rethinking the Middle East*. London, Frank Cass, 2003.

Islamic Imperialism: A History. New Haven, CT, Yale University Press, revised edn, 2007.

Karsh, Efraim, and Kumaraswamy, P. R. *Israel, the Hashemites and the Palestinians: The Fateful Triangle*. London, Frank Cass, 2003.

Katz, Mark N. *Russia and Arabia: Soviet Foreign Policy toward the Arabian Peninsula*. Baltimore, MD, and London, Johns Hopkins University Press, 1986.

Kayal, Alawi D. *The Control of Oil: East–West Rivalry in the Persian Gulf*. London, Kegan Paul, 2002.

Kaye, Dalia Dassa. *Beyond the Handshake: Multilateral Cooperation in the Arab-Israeli Peace Process, 1991–96*. New York, Columbia University Press, 2001.

Keay, John. *The Arabs: A Living History*. London, Harvill, 1983.

Sowing the Wind: The Seeds of Conflict in the Middle East. London, John Murray, 2003.

Kéchichian, Joseph A. *Power and Succession in Arab Monarchies*. Boulder, CO, Lynne Rienner Publishers, 2008.

Keddie, Nikki R. *Women in the Middle East: Past and Present*. Princeton, NJ, Princeton University Press, 2006.

Kedourie, Elie. *Arabic Political Memoirs and Other Studies*. London, Frank Cass, 1974.

In the Anglo-Arab Labyrinth. 1976.

Islam in the Modern World and Other Studies. London, Mansell, 1980.

Kelly, J. B. *Eastern Arabian Frontiers*. London, Faber, 1963.

Arabia, the Gulf and the West: A Critical View of the Arabs and their Oil Policy. London, Weidenfeld and Nicolson, 1980.

Kemp, Geoffrey, and Harkavy, Robert. *The Strategic Geography of the Changing Middle East*. Washington, DC, Brookings Institution Press, 1996.

Kemp, Geoffrey, and Pressman, Jeremy. *Point of No Return: The Deadly Struggle for Middle East Peace*. Washington, DC, Brookings Institution Press, 1997.

Kepel, Gilles (trans. Antony Roberts). *Jihad: The Trail of Political Islam*. London, I. B. Tauris, 2002.

(trans. Pascale Ghazaleh). *The War for Muslim Minds: Islam and the West*. Cambridge, MA, Harvard University Press, 2004.

The Roots of Radical Islam. London, Saqi Books, revised edn, 2005.

Beyond Terror and Martyrdom: The Future of the Middle East. Cambridge, MA, Harvard University Press, 2008.

Kepel, Gilles, and Milelli, Jean-Pierre (Eds). *Al Qaeda in its Own Words*. Cambridge, MA, Harvard University Press, 2008.

Kerr, Malcolm. *The Arab Cold War 1958–1964*. Oxford University Press, 1965.

Khalaf, Abdulhadi, and Luciani, Giacomo (Eds). *Constitutional Reform and Political Participation in the Gulf*. Dubai, Gulf Research Centre, 2007.

Khalaf, Abdulhadi, al-Shehabi, Omar, and Hanieh, Adam (Eds). *Transit States: Labour, Migration and Citizenship in the Gulf*. London, Pluto Press, 2014.

Khalidi, Rashid. *Resurrecting Empire: Western Footprints and America's Perilous Path in the Middle East*. London, I. B. Tauris, 2005.

Khalil, Muhammad. *The Arab States and the Arab League* (historical documents). Beirut, Khayats.

Khalili, Laleh. *Politics of the Modern Arab World*. Abingdon, Routledge, 2008.

Khan, Muhammad Akram. *Islamic Economics and Finance: A Glossary*. Abingdon, Routledge, 2007.

Khatab, Sayed, and Bouma, Gary D. *Democracy in Islam*. Abingdon, Routledge, 2007.

Khatib, Dania Koleilat (Ed.). *The Syrian Crisis: Effects on the Regional and International Relations*. Singapore, Springer, 2021.

Khedir, Hewa Haji. *Social Capital, Civic Engagement and Democratization in Kurdistan*. Cham, Palgrave Macmillan, 2020.

Khuri, Fuad I. *Imams and Emirs: State, Religion and Sects in Islam*. London, Saqi Books, 1990.

Kingston, Paul W. T. *Britain and the Politics of Modernization in the Middle East, 1945–1958*. Cambridge University Press, 1996.

Kirk, George E. *The Middle East in the War*. London, 1953.

A Short History of the Middle East: From the Rise of Islam to Modern Times. New York, 1955.

Klein, Menachem. *Jerusalem: The Contested City*. New York University Press, 2001.

Kliot, Norit. *Water Resources and Conflict in the Middle East*. London, Routledge, 1994.

Koch, Christopher. *Gulf Security in the Twenty-First Century*. London, I. B. Tauris, 1997.

Korany, Bahgat, and Dessouki, Ali E. Hillal. *The Foreign Policies of Arab States: The Challenge of Globalization*. Cairo, American University in Cairo Press, revised edn, 2009.

Kotilaine, Jarmo T. *Sustainable Prosperity in the Arab Gulf: From Miracle to Method*. London, Routledge, 2023.

Kowner, R., Evron, Y., and Kumaraswamy, P. R. (Eds). *East-West Asia Relations in the 21st Century: From Bilateral to Interregional Relationships*. London, Routledge, 2023.

Kraetzschmar, Hendrik Jan (Ed.). *The Dynamics of Opposition Cooperation in the Arab World: Contentious Politics in Times of Change*. Abingdon, Routledge, 2013.

Kreutz, Andrej. *Russia in the Middle East: Friend or Foe?* Westport, CT, and London, Praeger Security International, 2006.

Kubbig, Bernd, and Fikenscher, Sven-Eric (Eds). *Arms Control and Missile Proliferation in the Middle East*. Abingdon, Routledge, 2011.

Kumar, Ravinder. *India and the Persian Gulf Region*. London, 1965.

Kurzman, Dan. *Genesis 1948: The First Arab–Israeli War*. London, Vallentine Mitchell, 1972.

Lacroix, Stéphane, and Filiu, Jean-Pierre (Eds). *Revisiting The Arab Uprisings: The Politics of a Revolutionary Moment*. London, Hurst & Co, 2018.

La Guardia, Anton. *Holy Land, Unholy War: Israelis and Palestinians*. London, John Murray, 2001.

Lahoud, Nelly, and Johns, Anthony H. (Eds). *Islam in World Politics*. Abingdon, Routledge, 2005.

Lall, Arthur. *The UN and the Middle East Crisis*. New York and London, 1968.

Lamport, Mark A., and Raheb, Mitri (Eds). *The Rowman & Littlefield Handbook of Christianity in the Middle East*. Lanham, MD, Rowman & Littlefield, 2020.

Landau, Emily B. *Arms Control in the Middle East: Cooperative Security Dialogue and Regional Constraints*. Brighton, Sussex Academic Press, 2006.

Lapidus, Ira M. *A History of Islamic Societies*. Cambridge University Press, 1989.

Laqueur, W. Z. *Communism and Nationalism in the Middle East*. London and New York, 1957.

Confrontation: The Middle-East War and World Politics. London, Wildwood, 1974.

(Ed.). *The Israel-Arab Reader*. New York and London, Penguin, 4th edn, 1984.

Laskier, M. M., Reguer, S., and Simon, R. S. *The Jews of the Middle East and North Africa in Modern Times*. Irvington, NY, Columbia University Press, 2003.

Lawrence, Quil. *Invisible Nation: How the Kurds' Quest for Statehood is Shaping Iraq and the Middle East*. New York, Walker & Company, 2008.

Lee, Robert D. *Religion and Politics in the Middle East: Identity, Ideology, Institutions, and Attitudes*. Boulder, CO, Westview Press, 2009.

Legrenzi, Matteo, and Momani, Bessma. (Eds). *Shifting Geo-Economic Power of the Gulf: Oil, Finance and Institutions*. Farnham, Ashgate, 2011.

Lenczowski, George. *The Middle East in World Affairs*. Ithaca, NY, Cornell University Press, 4th edn, 1980.

Lennon, A. T. J. (Ed.). *The Epicenter of Crisis: The New Middle East*. Washington, DC, Washington Quarterly Readers, 2008.

REGIONAL INFORMATION

Lesch, David W. (Ed.). *The Middle East and the United States: A Historical and Political Reassessment.* Boulder, CO, Westview Press, 4th edn, 2007.

Lewis, Bernard. *The Arabs in History.* Oxford University Press, 6th edn, 1993.

Shaping of the Modern Middle East. New York, Oxford University Press, 1994.

The Middle East: 2000 Years of History from the Rise of Christianity to the Present Day. London, Phoenix Press, revised edn, 2000.

What Went Wrong?: Western Impact and Middle Eastern Response. New York, Oxford University Press, 2001.

The Crisis of Islam: Holy War and Unholy Terror. London, Weidenfeld and Nicolson, 2004.

Logan, William S., and White, Paul J. (Eds). *Remaking the Middle East.* Oxford, Berg, 1997.

Longrigg, S. H. *Oil in the Middle East.* London, 3rd edn, 1968.

The Middle East: A Social Geography. London, 2nd revised edn, 1970.

Longrigg, S. H., and Jankowski, J. P. *The Geography of the Middle East.* Piscataway, NJ, Aldine Transaction, 2nd revised edn, 2009.

Louër, Laurence. *Transnational Shia Politics: Religious and Political Networks in the Gulf.* New York, Columbia University Press, 2008.

Louis, William Roger. *The British Empire in the Middle East 1945–51.* Oxford University Press, 1984.

Lundgren Jörum, Emma. *Beyond Syria's Borders: A History of Territorial Disputes in the Middle East.* London, I. B. Tauris, 2014.

Lust-Okar, E., and Zerhouni, S. (Eds). *Political Participation in the Middle East.* Boulder, CO, Lynne Rienner Publishers, 2008.

Lynch, Marc. *Voices of the New Arab Public: Iraq, al-Jazeera, and Middle East Politics Today.* New York, Columbia University Press, 2006.

The Arab Uprising: The Unfinished Revolutions of the New Middle East. New York, PublicAffairs, 2012.

Lynch, Marc, Schwedler, Jillian, and Yom, Sean (Eds). *The Political Science of the Middle East: Theory and Research since the Arab Uprisings.* Oxford, Oxford University Press, 2022.

Maalouf, Amin. *The Crusades Through Arab Eyes.* London, Saqi Books, 1984.

Mabon, Simon. *Houses Built on Sand: Violence, Sectarianism and Revolution in the Middle East.* Manchester, Manchester University Press, 2020.

Mackintosh-Smith, Tim. *Arabs: A 3,000 Year History of Peoples, Tribes and Empires.* New Haven, CT, Yale University Press, 2019.

Maddy-Weitzmann, Bruce. *A Century of Arab Politics: From the Arab Revolt to the Arab Spring.* Lanham, MD, Rowman & Littlefield Publishers, 2016.

Maddy-Weitzmann, Bruce, and Inbar, Efraim (Eds). *Religious Radicalism in the Greater Middle East.* London, Frank Cass, 1997.

Mahdavi, Mojtaba, and Keskin, Tugrul (Eds). *Rethinking China, the Middle East and Asia in a "Multiplex World".* Leiden and Boston, Brill, 2022.

Mahler, Gregory S., and Mahler, Alden R. W. *The Arab–Israeli Conflict: An Introduction and Documentary Reader.* Abingdon, Routledge, 2009.

Makris, G. P. *Islam in the Middle East: A Living Tradition.* Oxford, Blackwell, 2006.

Mallat, Chibli. *The Middle East into the Twenty-First Century: The Japan Lectures and Other Studies on the Arab–Israeli Conflict, the Gulf Crisis and Political Islam.* Reading, Ithaca Press, 1996.

Mandaville, Peter. *Global Political Islam.* Abingdon, Routledge, 2008.

Mansfield, Peter. *The Ottoman Empire and Its Successors.* London, Macmillan, 1973.

(Ed.). *The Middle East: A Political and Economic Survey.* London, Oxford University Press, 5th edn, 1980.

The Arabs. Penguin, 5th edn, 1992.

A History of the Middle East. Harmondsworth, Penguin, 2003.

Mansouri, Fethi (Ed.). *Australia and the Middle East: A Front-line Relationship.* London, I. B. Tauris, 2006.

Ma'oz, Moshe, and Sheffer, Gabriel. *Middle Eastern Minorities and Diasporas.* Brighton, Sussex Academic Press, 2002.

Marcel, Valerie. *Oil Titans: National Oil Companies in the Middle East.* Washington, DC, The Brookings Institution, 2005.

Martin Muqoz, Gema (Ed.). *Islam, Modernism and the West: Cultural and Political Relations at the end of the Millennium.* London, I. B. Tauris, 1997.

Mattar, Philip (Ed.). *Encyclopedia of the Palestinians.* London, Fitzroy Dearborn, 2000.

Matthiesen, Toby. *Sectarian Gulf: Bahrain, Saudi Arabia, and the Arab Spring That Wasn't.* Stanford, CA, Stanford University Press, Stanford Briefs, 2013.

Mehrava, Kamran. *Troubled Waters: Insecurity in the Persian Gulf.* Ithaca, NY, Cornell University Press, 2018.

Meijer, Roel (Ed.). *Cosmopolitanism, Identity and Authenticity in the Middle East.* Richmond, Curzon Press, 1999.

Menashri, David (Ed.). *Central Asia Meets the Middle East.* London, Frank Cass, 1998.

Mencütek, Zeynep Şahin. *Refugee Governance, State and Politics in the Middle East.* Abingdon, Routledge, 2020.

Mendelsohn, Everett. *A Compassionate Peace: A Future for Israel, Palestine and the Middle East.* New York, The Noonday Press, 1989.

Mengoni, Luisa, and Romagnoli, Alessandro. *The Economic Development Process in the Middle East and North Africa.* Abingdon, Routledge, 2013.

Meri, Josef W. *Medieval Islamic Civilization: An Encyclopedia.* Abingdon, Routledge, 2006.

Mernissi, Fatima. *Islam and Democracy—Fear of the Modern World.* London, Virago, 1993.

Meskell, Lynn. *Archaeology Under Fire: Nationalism, Politics and Heritage in the Eastern Mediterranean and Middle East.* London, Routledge, 1998.

Miles, Hugh. *Al-Jazeera: How Arab TV News Challenged America.* New York, Grove Press, 2005.

Miller, Rory. *Desert Kingdoms to Global Powers: The Rise of the Arab Gulf.* New Haven, CT, Yale University Press, 2019.

Milton-Edwards, Beverley. *Contemporary Politics in the Middle East.* Cambridge, Polity, 3rd edn, 2011.

Milton-Edwards, Beverley, and Hinchliffe, Peter. *Conflicts in the Middle East since 1945.* London, Routledge, 2001.

Mohs, Polly A. *Military Intelligence and the Arab Revolt.* Abingdon, Routledge, 2007.

Mojtahedzadeh, Pirouz. *Security and Territoriality in the Persian Gulf: A Maritime Political Geography.* Richmond, Curzon Press, 1999.

Moller, Bjorn (Ed.). *Oil and Water: Co-operative Security in the Persian Gulf.* London, I. B. Tauris, 2001.

Momen, Moojan. *An Introduction to Shi'i Islam.* New Haven, CT, Yale University Press, revised edn, 1987.

Mommer, Bernard. *Global Oil and the Nation State.* New York, Oxford University Press, Inc, 2002.

Monroe, Elizabeth. *Britain's Moment in the Middle East 1914–71.* London, Chatto and Windus, new edn, 1981.

Philby of Arabia. Reading, Ithaca Press, 1998.

Moore Henry, Clement, and Springborg, Robert. *Globalization and the Politics of Development in the Middle East.* Cambridge, Cambridge University Press, 2nd edn, 2010.

Mortimer, Edward. *Faith and Power: The Politics of Islam.* London, Faber, 1982.

Mostyn, T. *Censorship in Islamic Societies.* London, Saqi Books, 2002.

Muasher, Marwan. *The Arab Center: The Promise of Moderation.* New Haven, CT, Yale University Press, 2008.

Mumford, Andrew. *The West's War Against Islamic State: Operation Inherent Resolve in Syria and Iraq.* London, I. B. Tauris, 2021.

Munson, Henry, Jr. *Islam and Revolution in the Middle East.* New Haven, CT, and London, Yale University Press, 1988.

Murakami, Masahiro. *Managing Water for Peace in the Middle East: Alternative Strategies.* Tokyo, United Nations University Press, 1996.

Murden, Simon W. *Islam, the Middle East, and the New Global Hegemony.* Boulder, CO, Lynne Rienner Publishers, 2002.

Mühlberger, Wolfgang, and Alaranta, Toni (Eds). *Political Narratives in the Middle East and North Africa: Conceptions of Order and Perceptions of Instability.* Cham, Springer, 2020.

Nafi, Basheer M. and Taji-Farouki, Suha (Eds). *Islamic Thought in the Twentieth Century.* New York, Palgrave Macmillan, 2004.

Al-Na'im, Abdullahi Ahmed. *Islam and the Secular State: Negotiating the Future of Shari'a.* Cambridge, MA, Harvard University Press, 2008.

Nakash, Yitzhak. *Reaching for Power: The Shi'a in the Modern Arab World.* Princeton, NJ, Princeton University Press, 2007.

al-Naqeeb, Khaldoun. *Society and State in the Gulf and Arab Peninsula: A Different Perspective* (Routledge Library Editions: The Arab Nation). Abingdon, Routledge, 2012.

Nasr, Seyyed Hossein. *Science and Civilization in Islam*. Cambridge, MA, Harvard University Press, revised edn, 1987.

Nasr, Vali. *The Shia Revival: How Conflicts within Islam will Shape the Future*. New York, W. W. Norton and Co, 2007.

Meccanomics: The March of the New Muslim Middle Class. Oxford, Oneworld Publications, 2010.

Natali, Denise. *The Kurds and the State: Evolving National Identity in Iraq, Turkey and Iran*. Syracuse, NY, Syracuse University Press, 2005.

Navias, Martin. *Going Ballistic: The Build-up of Missiles in the Middle East*. London, Brassey's, 1993.

Niblock, Tim. *'Pariah' States and Sanctions in the Middle East: Iraq, Libya, Sudan*. Boulder, CO, Lynne Rienner Publishers, 2001.

Niblock, Tim, and Murphy, Emma. *Economic and Political Liberalism in the Middle East*. London, British Academic Press, 1993.

Nizameddin, Talal. *Russia and the Middle East*. London, C. Hurst & Co, 1999.

Noland, Marcus, and Pack, Howard. *The Arab Economies in a Changing World*. Washington, DC, Peterson Institute for International Economics, 2007.

Nonneman, Gerd. *Development, Administration and Aid in the Middle East*. London, Routledge, 1988.

(Ed.). *The Middle East and Europe: The Search for Stability and Integration*. London, Federal Trust, 1993.

(Ed.). *Analyzing Middle East Foreign Policies, and the Relationship with Europe*. Abingdon, Routledge, 2005.

Noorani, A. G. *Islam and Jihad: Prejudice and Reality*. London, Zed Books, 2002.

Noueihed, Lin, and Warren, Alex. *The Battle for the Arab Spring: Revolution, Counter-revolution and the Making of a New Era*. New Haven, CT, Yale University Press, 2012.

Nydell, Margaret K. *Understanding Arabs: A Guide for Westerners*. Yarmouth, ME, Intercultural Press, 1992.

O'Ballance, Edgar. *The Third Arab–Israeli War*. London, Faber and Faber, 1972.

Oren, Michael B. *Six Days of War: June 1967 and the Making of the Modern Middle East*. London and New York, Oxford University Press, 2002.

Orfy, Mohammed Moustafa. *NATO and the Middle East: The Geopolitical Context Post-9/11*. Abingdon, Routledge, 2014.

Osborne, Christine. *The Gulf States and Oman*. Abingdon, Routledge, 2018.

Owen, Roger. *The Middle East in the World Economy 1800–1914*. London, I. B. Tauris (1972), revised edn, 1993.

A History of Middle East Economies in the 20th Century. London, I. B. Tauris, 1998.

State, Power and Politics in the Making of the Modern Middle East. London, Routledge, 3rd edn, 2004.

Palmer, Alan. *The Decline and Fall of the Ottoman Empire*. London, John Murray, 1992.

Pantelides, Veronica S. *Arab Education 1956–1978: A Bibliography*. London, Mansell, 1982.

Pappé, Ilan. *The Modern Middle East* Abingdon, Routledge, 3rd edn, 2013.

Pargeter, Alison. *The Muslim Brotherhood: From Opposition to Power*. London, Saqi Books, 2013.

Parker, Richard B. *The October War—A Retrospective*. Gainesville, FL, University Press of Florida, 2001.

Parra, Francisco. *Oil Politics: A Modern History of Petroleum*. London, I. B. Tauris, 2003.

Paya, Ali. and Esposito, John L. (Eds). *Iraq, Democracy and the Future of the Muslim World*. Abingdon, Routledge, 2010.

Persson, Magnus. *Great Britain, the United States and the Security of the Middle East: The Formation of the Baghdad Pact*. Lund, Lund University Press, 1998.

Peters, F. E. *The Hajj: The Muslim Pilgrimage to Mecca and the Holy Places*. Princeton, NJ, Princeton University Press, 1995.

Phares, Walid. *The War of Ideas: Jihadism Against Democracy*. New York, Palgrave Macmillan, 2007.

Pipes, Daniel. *In the Path of God: Islam and Political Power*. New York, Basic Books, 1983.

Piscatori, James P. (Ed.). *Islam in the Political Process*. Cambridge University Press, 1983.

Islam in a World of Nation-States. Cambridge University Press, 1986.

Poliak, A. N. *Feudalism in Egypt, Syria, Palestine and the Lebanon, 1250–1900*. London, Luzac, for the Royal Asiatic Society, 1939.

Polk, W. R. *The Arab World Today*. Cambridge, MA, Harvard University Press, 1991.

(Ed. with Chambers, R. L.) *Beginnings of Modernization in the Middle East: The Nineteenth Century*. Chicago, IL, University of Chicago Press, 1969.

The Elusive Peace: The Middle East in the Twentieth Century. London, Frank Cass, 1980.

Porath, Y. *The Emergence of the Palestinian Arab National Movement 1918–1929*. London, Frank Cass, 1974.

Pratt, N. *Democracy and Authoritarianism in the Arab World*. Boulder, CO, Lynne Rienner Publishers, 2006.

Quandt, William B. *Peace Process: American Diplomacy and the Arab–Israeli Conflict since 1967*. Berkeley, CA, University of California Press, 2001.

Quigley, John B. *The Legality of a Jewish State: A Century of Debate Over Rights in Palestine*. Cambridge, Cambridge University Press, 2022.

Qumsiyeh, Mazin B. *Sharing the Land of Canaan: Human Rights and the Israel–Palestinian Struggle*. London, Pluto Press, 2004.

Rabinovich, Itamar. *Waging Peace: Israel and the Arabs, 1948–2003*. Princeton, NJ, Princeton University Press, 2004.

Randjbar-Daemi, Siavush, Sadeghi-Boroujerdi, Eskandar, and Banko, Lauren (Eds). *Political Parties in the Middle East*. Abingdon, Routledge, 2019.

Rasheed, Amjed. *Power and Paranoia in Syria-Iraq Relations: The Impact of Hafez Assad and Saddam Hussain*. London and New York, Routledge, 2023.

Reimer-Burgrova, Helena. *Politics of Violence and Fear in MENA*. Cham, Palgrave Macmillan, 2022.

Richards, A., and Waterbury, J. *A Political Economy of the Middle East*. Boulder, CO, Westview Press (1990 and 1996), 3rd edn (revised), 2007.

Rikhye, Maj.-Gen. I. J. *The Sinai Blunder*. London, Frank Cass, 1980.

Rivlin, B., and Szyliowicz, J. S. (Eds). *The Contemporary Middle East—Tradition and Innovation*. New York, Random House, 1965.

Rivlin, Paul. *Arab Economies in the Twenty-First Century*. Cambridge University Press, 2009.

Robson, Laura. *States of Separation: Transfer, Partition, and the Making of the Modern Middle East*. Oakland, CA, University of California Press, 2017.

Roded, Ruth (Ed.). *Women in Islam and the Modern Middle East: A Reader*. London, I. B. Tauris, 2007.

Rodinson, Maxime. *Islam and capitalisme*. Paris, Editions de Seuil, 1966.

Muhammad. London, Penguin, 1974.

The Arabs. Chicago, IL, University of Chicago Press (1981), revised edn, 1989.

Israel and the Arabs. London, Penguin, 1982.

Rogan, Eugene. *The Arabs: A History*. London, Allen Lane, 2009.

Rogan, Eugene L., and Shlaim, Avi (Eds). *The War for Palestine: Rewriting the History of 1948*. Cambridge University Press, 2001.

Rogerson, Barnaby. *The Prophet Muhammad: A Biography*. Boston, MA, Little Brown & Co, 2003.

Romano, David. *The Kurdish Nationalist Movement: Opportunity, Mobilization and Identity*. Cambridge University Press, 2006.

Romano, David, and Gurses, Mehmet (Eds). *Conflict, Democratization and the Kurds in the Middle East: Turkey, Iran, Iraq and Syria*. New York, Palgrave Macmillan, 2014.

Ronart, Stephan, and Ronart, Nandy. *Concise Encyclopaedia of Arabic Civilization*. Amsterdam, 1966.

Rondot, Pierre. *The Destiny of the Middle East*. London, Chatto & Windus, 1960.

Rosen, Lawrence. *Varieties of Muslim Experience: Encounters with Arab Political and Cultural Life*. Chicago, IL, Chicago University Press, 2008.

Rowe, Paul S. (Ed.). *Routledge Handbook of Minorities in the Middle East*. Abingdon, Routledge, 2018.

Roy, Olivier. *The Failure of Political Islam*. London, I. B. Tauris, 1995.

Globalized Islam: The Search for a New Ummah. New York, Columbia University Press, 2004.

The New Central Asia: Geopolitics and the Birth of Nations. London, I. B. Tauris, 2007.

The Politics of Chaos in the Middle East. London, C. Hurst & Co, 2008.

Rubin, Barry M. *The Arab States and the Palestine Conflict*. Syracuse, NY, Syracuse University Press, 1981.

(Ed.). *Conflict and Insurgency in the Contemporary Middle East*. Abingdon, Routledge, 2009.

(Ed.). *Security and Stability in the Middle East*. Abingdon, Routledge, 2011.

Russell, James A. *Critical Issues Facing the Middle East*. London, Macmillan, 2006.

Ruthven, Malise. *Islam in the World*. Harmondsworth, Penguin (1984), 2nd revised edn, 2000.

Fundamentalism: The Search for Meaning. Oxford, Oxford University Press, 2005.

Islam in the World. London, Granta Books, revised edn, 2006.

Saba Yared, Nazik. *Secularism and the Arab World*. London, Saqi Books, 2008.

Sabet, Amr G. E. *Islam and the Political: Theory, Governance and International Relations*. London, Pluto Press, 2008.

Sachar, Howard M. *Europe Leaves the Middle East 1936–1954*. London, Allen Lane, 1973.

Sadiki, Larbi. *The Search for Arab Democracy: Discourses and Counter Discourses*. New York, Columbia University Press, 2004.

Islamist Democracy: (Re)Visions of Polity and Society in the Arab Middle East. London, C. Hurst & Co, revised edn, 2007.

Rethinking Arab Democratization: Elections without Democracy. Oxford University Press, 2009.

Routledge Handbook of Middle East Politics. Abingdon, Routledge, 2020.

Sadiki, Larbi, and Saleh, Layla. *COVID-19 and Risk Society Across the MENA Region: Assessing Governance, Democracy, and Inequality*. London, I. B. Tauris, 2022.

Sadiki, Larbi, et al. (Eds). *Democratic Transition in the Middle East: Unmaking Power*. Abingdon, Routledge, 2012.

Said, Edward W. *The Question of Palestine*. London, Routledge, 1979 (reissued, Vintage, 1992).

Covering Islam. London, Routledge, 1982 (reissued, Vintage, 1997).

The End of the Peace Process: Oslo and After. New York, Pantheon Books, 2000.

Sajoo, Amyn B. (Ed.). *Civil Society in the Muslim World*. London, I. B. Tauris, 2004.

Sakr, Naomi (Ed.) *Women and Media in the Middle East: Power through Self-expression*. London, I. B. Tauris, 2004.

Salame, G. *Democracy without Democrats? The Renewal of Politics in the Muslim World*. London and New York, I. B. Tauris, 1994.

Salem, Paul (Ed.). *Conflict Resolution in the Arab World: Selected Essays*. Beirut, American University of Beirut Press, 1997.

Salhi, Zahia Smail (Ed.). *Gender and Diversity in the Middle East and North Africa*. Abingdon, Routledge, 2012.

Salhi, Zahi Smail, and Netton, Ian Richard. *The Arab Diaspora*. Abingdon, Routledge, 2005.

Salzman, Philip C., and Robinson Divine, Donna (Eds). *Postcolonial Theory and the Arab–Israel Conflict*. Abingdon, Routledge, 2008.

Satloff, Robert B. *The Politics Of Change In The Middle East*. Abingdon, Routledge, 2019.

Sayan, Serdar. *Economic Performance in the Middle East and North Africa: Institutions, Corruption and Reform*. Abingdon, Routledge, 2009.

Sayigh, Fatallah. *Le Désert et la Gloire*. Paris, Editions Gallimard, 1993.

Sayigh, Yusif A. *The Determinants of Arab Economic Development*. London, Croom Helm, 1977.

Arab Oil Policies in the 1970s. London, Croom Helm, 1983.

Elusive Development: From Dependence to Self-Reliance in the Arab Region. London, Routledge, 1991.

Schwedler, Jillian (Ed.). *Understanding the Contemporary Middle East*. Boulder, CO, Lynne Rienner Publishers, 4th edn, 2013.

Scott Appleby, R. (Ed.). *Spokesmen for the Despised: Fundamentalist Leaders of the Middle East*. Chicago, IL, University of Chicago Press, 1997.

Seale, Patrick. *The Struggle for Arab Independence: Riad el-Solh and the Makers of the Modern Middle East*. Cambridge, Cambridge University Press, 2010.

Sedgwick, Mark. *Islam and Muslims: A Guide to Diverse Experience in a Modern World*. Boston, MA, Intercultural Press, 2006.

Selby, Jan. *Water, Power & Politics in the Middle East. The Other Palestinian–Israeli Conflict*. London, I. B. Tauris, 2003.

Selvik, Kjetil, and Utvik, Bjørn Olav (Eds). *Oil States in the New Middle East: Uprisings and Stability*. Abingdon, Routledge, 2016.

Shaban, M. A. *The Abbasid Revolution*. Cambridge University Press, 1970.

Islamic History: A New Interpretation. 2 vols. Cambridge University Press, 1976–78.

Shadid, Muhammad K. *The United States and the Palestinians*. London, Croom Helm, 1981.

Shafik, Nemat. *Prospects for Middle East and North African Economies*. Basingstoke, Macmillan Press, 1997.

Shapland, Gregory. *Rivers of Discord: International Water Disputes in the Middle East*. London, C. Hurst & Co, 1997.

Sharabi, H. B. *Governments and Politics of the Middle East in the Twentieth Century*. London, Greenwood Press (1962), revised edn, 1987.

Sharnoff, Michael. *Nasser's War: Egypt's Response to the 1967 War with Israel*. Abingdon, Routledge, 2017.

Shay, Shaul. *The Shahids: Islam and Suicide Attacks*. Edison, NJ, Transaction Publishers, 2004.

Shehata, Samer. (Ed.). *Islamist Politics in the Middle East: Movements and Change*. Abingdon, Routledge, 2012.

Sheikh, Naveed Shahzad. *The New Politics of Islam*. Abingdon, Routledge, 2007.

Shlaim, Avi. *War and Peace in the Middle East*. New York and London, Penguin, 1995.

Israel and Palestine: Reappraisals, Revisions, Refutations. London, Verso, 2009.

Shlaim, Avi, and Sayigh, Y. (Eds). *The Cold War and The Middle East*. Oxford University Press, 1998.

Shulze, Reinhard. *A Modern History of the Islamic World*. London, I. B. Tauris, 2002.

Sid-Ahmad, Abd al-Salam, and Ehteshami, Anoushiravan (Eds). *Islamic Fundamentalism*. Boulder, CO, Westview Press, 1996.

Sid-Ahmad, Muhammad. *After the Guns Fell Silent*. London, Croom Helm, 1976.

Sivan, Emmanuel. *Radical Islam: Medieval Theology and Modern Politics*. New Haven, CT, Yale University Press, 1985.

Smith, Dan. *The State of the Middle East: An Atlas of Conflict and Resolution*. Berkeley, CA, University of California Press, 2006.

Sowell, Kirk H. *The Arab World. An Illustrated History*. New York, Hippocrene Books, 2004.

Springborg, Robert. *Political Economies of the Middle East and North Africa*. Cambridge, Polity Press, 2020.

Sriram, Chandra Lekha. *Transitional Justice in the Middle East and North Africa*. London, C. Hurst & Co, 2017.

Stark, Freya. *Dust in the Lion's Paw*. London and New York, 1961.

Stetter, Stephan (Ed.). *The Middle East and Globalization: Encounters and Horizons*. New York, Palgrave Macmillan, 2012.

Stewart, Dona J. *The Middle East Today: Political, Geographical and Cultural Perspectives*. Abingdon, Routledge, 2012.

Stewart, P. J. *Unfolding Islam*. Reading, Ithaca Press, 1995.

Stickley, Thomas (Ed.). *Man, Food and Agriculture in the Middle East*. Beirut, American University of Beirut Press, 1969.

Stocking, G. W. *Middle East Oil. A Study in Political and Economic Controversy*. Nashville, TN, Vanderbilt University Press, 1979.

Sultan, Nabil A., Weir, David, and Karake-Shalhoub, Zeinab (Eds). *The New Post-Oil Arab Gulf: Managing People and Wealth*. London, Saqi Books, 2011.

Sultany, Nimer. *Law and Revolution: Legitimacy and Constitutionalism after the Arab Spring*. Oxford, Oxford University Press, 2017.

Sumner, B. H. *Tsardom and Imperialism in the Far East and Middle East*. London, Oxford University Press, 1940.

Süsler, Buğra. *Turkey, the EU and the Middle East: Foreign Policy Cooperation and the Arab Uprisings*. London, Routledge, 2022.

Susser, Asher. *Israel, Jordan, and Palestine: the Two-state Imperative*. Waltham, MA, Brandeis University Press, 2012.

Susser, Asher, and Shmuelevitz, Aryeh (Eds). *The Hashemites in the Modern Arab World: Essays in Honour of the Late Professor Uriel Dann*. London, Frank Cass, 1995.

Szekely, Ora. *The Politics of Militant Group Survival in the Middle East: Resources, Relationships, and Resistance*. London, Palgrave Macmillan, 2017.

el-Tamimi, Abdul Malek Khalaf. *Water in The Arab World: The Politics and Economics of Access to Water Resources*. London, I. B. Tauris, 2010.

Tamimi, Azzam (Ed.). *Islam and Secularism in the Middle East*. London, C. Hurst & Co, 2000.

Taylor, Alan R. *The Arab Balance of Power*. Syracuse, NY, Syracuse University Press, 1982.

Taylor, Trevor. *The Middle East in the International System: Lessons from Europe and Implications for Europe*. London, Royal Institute of International Affairs, 1997.

Tempest, Paul (Ed.). *An Enduring Friendship: 400 Years of Anglo-Gulf Relations*. London, Stacey International, 2006.

Tétreault, Mary Ann, Okruhlik, Gwenn, and Kapiszewski, Andrzej (Eds). *Political Change in the Arab Gulf States: Stuck in Transition*. Boulder, CO, Lynne Rienner Publishers, 2011.

Thayer, P. W. (Ed.). *Tensions in the Middle East*. Baltimore, 1958.

Thomas, L. V., and Frye, R. N. *The United States and Turkey and Iran*. Cambridge, MA, 1951.

Toaldo, Mattia. *The Origins of the US War on Terror: Lebanon, Libya and American Intervention in the Middle East*. Abingdon, Routledge, 2012.

Trenin, Dmitri. *What is Russia up to in the Middle East?* Cambridge, Polity Press, 2017.

Trevelyan, Lord Humphrey. *The Middle East in Revolution*. London, Macmillan, 1970.

Trimingham, J. Spencer. *The Sufi Orders in Islam*. Oxford, Clarendon Press, 1971.

Tripp, Charles. *The Power and the People: Paths of Resistance in the Middle East*. New York, Cambridge University Press, 2013.

Tschirgi, Dan. *The American Search for Mideast Peace*. New York, Praeger, 1989.

Tynan, Caroline F. *Saudi Interventions in Yemen: A Historical Comparison of Ontological Insecurity*. London, Routledge, 2020.

Usher, Graham. *Dispatches from Palestine*. London, Pluto Press, 1999.

Vaner, S., Heradstveit, D., and Kazancigil, A. (Eds). *Sécularisation et Démocratisation dans les Sociétés Musulmanes*. Bern, Peter Lang, 2008.

Vassiliev, Alexei. *Russian Policy in the Middle East: From Messianism to Pragmatism*. Reading, Ithaca Press, 1993.

Vatikiotis, P. J. *Conflict in the Middle East*. London, George Allen and Unwin, 1971.

Islam and the State. London, Routledge, 1991.

Viorst, Milton. *Reaching for the Olive Branch: UNRWA and Peace in the Middle East*. Washington, DC, Middle East Institute, 1989.

Volpi, Frédéric. *Transnational Islam and Regional Security*. Abingdon, Routledge, 2007.

(Ed.). *Political Civility in the Middle East*. Abingdon, Routledge, 2011.

Volpi, Frédéric, and Cavatorta, Francesco (Eds). *Democratization in the Muslim World: Changing Patterns of Authority and Power*. Abingdon, Routledge, 2007.

Waines, David. *The Unholy War*. Wilmette, Medina Press, 1971.

An Introduction to Islam. Cambridge University Press, 1995.

Warren, David H. *Rivals in the Gulf: Yusuf al-Qaradawi, Abdullah Bin Bayyah, and the Qatar-UAE Contest Over the Arab Spring and the Gulf Crisis*. London, Routledge, 2021.

Warriner, Doreen. *Land and Poverty in the Middle East*. London, 1948.

Land Reform and Development in the Middle East: Study of Egypt, Syria and Iraq. London, 1962.

Wasserstein, Bernard. *Divided Jerusalem: The Struggle for the Holy City*. London, Profile, 2001.

Watkins, Eric (Ed.). *The Middle East Environment: Selected Papers of the 1995 Conference of the British Society for Middle Eastern Studies*. Cambridge, St Malo Press, 1995.

Islamic Political Thought: The Basic Concepts. Edinburgh University Press (1968), revised edn, 1987.

Wilson, Rodney. *Trade and Investment in the Middle East*. Macmillan Press, 1977.

Economic Development in the Middle East. Abingdon, Routledge, 2nd edn, 2012.

Winckler, Onn. *Arab Political Demography: Population Growth, Labour Migration, and Natalist Policies*. Brighton, Sussex Academic Press, 2009.

Wolf, Aaron T. *Hydropolitics Along the Jordan River: Scarce Water and its Impact on the Arab–Israeli Conflict*. Tokyo, United Nations University Press, 1996.

Worrall, James. *International Institutions of the Middle East: The GCC, Arab League, and Arab Maghreb Union*. Abingdon, Routledge, 2017.

Wright, Clifford A. *Facts and Fables: The Arab–Israeli conflict*. London, Kegan Paul International, 1989.

Wright, J. W., Jr (Ed.). *The Political Economy of Middle East Peace: The Impact of Competing Arab and Israeli Trade*. London, Routledge, 1999.

Wright, J. W., Jr, and Drake, Laura (Eds). *Economic and Political Impediments to Middle East Peace: Critical Questions and Alternative Scenarios*. New York, St Martin's Press, 1999.

Yamani, Mai (Ed.). *Cradle of Islam: The Hijaz and the Quest for an Arabian Identity*. London, I. B. Tauris, 2005.

Yergin, Daniel. *The Prize: The Epic Quest for Oil, Money and Power*. New York, Simon and Schuster (1990), revised edn, 1993.

Yom, Sean L. *From Resilience to Revolution: How Foreign Interventions Destabilize the Middle East*. New York, Columbia University Press, 2016.

Yom, Sean (Ed.). *The Societies of the Middle East and North Africa: Structures, Vulnerabilities, and Forces*. Abingdon, Routledge, 2019.

Youngs, Richard. *Europe and the Middle East: In the Shadow of September 11*. Boulder, CO, Lynne Rienner Publishers, 2006.

Zabad, Ibrahim. *Middle Eastern Minorities: The Impact of the Arab Spring*. Abingdon, Routledge, 2017.

Zahlan, Rosemarie Said. *The Making of the Modern Gulf States*. Reading, Ithaca Press, revised edn, 1999.

Palestine and the Gulf States: The Presence at the Table. Abingdon, Routledge, 2009.

Zeitoun, Mark. *Power and Water in the Middle East: The Hidden Politics of the Palestinian–Israeli Water Conflict*. London, I. B. Tauris, 2008.

Zekri, Slim (Ed.). *Water Policies in MENA Countries*. Cham, Springer, 2020.

Zubaida, Sami. *Law and Power in the Islamic World*. London, I. B. Tauris, 2005.

Books on North Africa

Abun-Nasr, Jamil M. *A History of the Maghreb*. Cambridge University Press, 1972.

Aghrout, Ahmed. *From Preferential Status to Partnership: The Euro-Maghreb Relationship*. Aldershot, Ashgate, 2000.

Ahmida, Ali A. *Beyond Colonialism and Nationalism in North Africa*. London, Macmillan, 2001.

Amin, Samir. *L'Economie du Maghreb*. 2 vols, Paris, Editions du Minuit, 1966.

The Maghreb in the Modern World. London, Penguin, 1971.

Amirah-Fernández, H., and Zoubir, Y. H. *North Africa: Politics, Regions, and the Limits of Transformation*. Abingdon, Routledge, 2008.

Balta, Paul. *Le Grand Maghreb*. Paris, Editions La Découverte, 1990.

Benichou Gottreich, Emily, and Schroeter, Daniel J. (Eds). *Jewish Culture and Society in North Africa*. Bloomington, IN, Indiana University Press, 2011.

Berque, Jacques. *Le Maghreb entre deux guerres*. Paris, Editions du Seuil, 2nd edn, 1967.

Bonnefous, Marc. *Le Maghreb: repères et rappels*. Paris, Editions du Centre des Hautes Etudes sur l'Afrique et l'Asie modernes de Paris, 1991.

Brown, Leon Carl (Ed.). *State and Society in Independent North Africa*. Washington, DC, Middle East Institute, 1966.

Brunel, Claire, and Hufbauer, Gary Clyde. *Maghreb Regional and Global Integration: A Dream to Be Fulfilled*. Washington, DC, Peterson Institute, 2008.

Cammett, Melani C. *Globalization and Business Politics in Arab North Africa*. New York, Cambridge University Press, 2007.

Capot-Rey, R. *Le Sahara français*. Paris, 1953.

Cavatorta, Francesco, and Merone, Fabio (Eds). *Salafism after the Arab Awakening: Contending with People's Power*. London, C. Hurst & Co, 2017.

Centre d'Etudes des Relations Internationales. *Le Maghreb et la communauté économique européenne*. Paris, Editions FNSP, 1965.

Clancy-Smith, Julia. *North Africa, Islam and the Mediterranean World*. London, Frank Cass, 2001.

Collinson, Sarah. *Shore to Shore: The Politics of Migration in Euro-Maghreb Relations*. London, Royal Institute of International Affairs, 1997.

Colombo, Silvia. *Political and Institutional Transition in North Africa: Egypt and Tunisia in Comparative Perspective*. London, Routledge, 2018.

Cordesman, Anthony H. *A Tragedy of Arms: Military and Security Developments in the Maghreb*. Westport, CT, Praeger, 2002.

REGIONAL INFORMATION — Select Bibliography (Books)

Damis, John. *Conflict in Northwest Africa: The Western Sahara Dispute*. Stanford, CA, Hoover Institution Press, 1983.

Duclos, J., Leca, J., and Duvignaud, J. *Les nationalismes maghrébins*. Paris, Centre d'Etudes des Relations Internationales, 1966.

Durand, Gwendal. *L'Organisation d'al-Qaïda au Maghreb islamique: réalité ou manipulations*. Paris, L'Harmattan, 2011.

Economic Commission for Africa. *Main Problems of Economic Co-operation in North Africa*. Tangier, 1966.

Ennaji, Moha (Ed.). *Multiculturalism and Democracy in North Africa: Aftermath of the Arab Spring*. Abingdon, Routledge, 2014.

Entelis, John P. *Islam, Democracy and the State in North Africa*. Bloomington, IN, Indiana University Press, 1997.

Evers Rasander, E., and Westerlund, David (Eds). *African Islam and Islam in Africa: Encounters Between Sufis and Islamists*. London, C. Hurst & Co, 1997.

el-Issawi, Fatima, and Cavatorta, Francesco (Eds). *The Unfinished Arab Spring: Micro-Dynamics of Revolts between Change and Continuity*. London, Gingko, 2020.

el-Fassi, Allal. (trans. H. Z. Nuseibeh). *The Independence Movements in Arab North Africa*. Washington, DC, 1954.

Fernandez Molina, Irene, and Hernando de Larramendi, Miguel (Eds). *Foreign Policy in North Africa: Navigating Global, Regional and Domestic Transformations*. Abingdon, Routledge, 2022.

Feuer, Sarah J. *Regulating Islam: Religion and the State in Contemporary Morocco and Tunisia*. Cambridge, Cambridge University Press, 2018.

Fontana, Iole. *EU Neighbourhood Policy in the Maghreb: Implementing the ENP in Tunisia and Morocco Before and After the Arab Uprisings*. Abingdon, Routledge, 2017.

Furlonge, Sir Geoffrey. *The Lands of Barbary*. London, John Murray, 1966.

García, Alejandro. *Historias del Sáhara. El mejor y el peor de los mundos*. Madrid, Los Libros de la Catarata, 2002.

Historia del Sáhara y su conflicto. Madrid, Los Libros de la Catarata, 2010.

Garon, Lise. *Dangerous Alliances: Civil Society, The Media and Democratic Transition in North Africa*. London, Zed Books, 2003.

Gautier, E. F. *Le Passé de l'Afrique du Nord*. Paris, 1937.

Germidis, Dimitri, with the help of Delapierre, Michel. *Le Maghreb, la France et l'enjeu technologique*. Paris, Editions Cujas, 1976.

Ghazi, Mahmud Ahmad. *The Sansusiyyah Movement of North Africa*. Islamabad, Shariah Academy, International Islamic University, 2001.

Gordon, D. C. *North Africa's French Legacy 1954–62*. Cambridge, MA, Harvard University Press, 1962.

Grewal, Sharan. *Soldiers of Democracy? Military Legacies and the Arab Spring*. Oxford, Oxford University Press, 2023.

Hahn, Lorna. *North Africa: From Nationalism to Nationhood*. Washington, DC, 1960.

Halverson, Jeffry R., and Greenberg, Nathaniel. *Islamists of the Maghreb*. Abingdon, Routledge, 2018.

Hermassi, Elbaki. *Leadership and National Development in North Africa*. Berkeley, CA, University of California Press, 1973.

Heseltine, N. *From Libyan Sands to Chad*. Leiden, 1960.

Hill, J. N. C. *Democratisation in the Maghreb*. Edinburgh, Edinburgh University Press, 2016.

Hüsken, Thomas. *Tribal Politics in the Borderland of Egypt and Libya*. Cham, Palgrave Macmillan, 2019.

Joffé, E. G. H. (Ed.). *North Africa: Nation, State and Region*. London, Routledge and University of London, 1993.

Joffé, George (Ed.). *Islamist Radicalisation in North Africa: Politics and Process*. Abingdon, Routledge, 2011.

North Africa's Arab Spring. Abingdon, Routledge, 2013.

Julien, Ch.-A. *Histoire de l'Afrique du nord*. 2 vols, Paris, 2nd edn, 1951–52.

History of North Africa: From the Arab Conquest to 1830. Revised by R. Le Tourneau. Ed. C. C. Stewart. London, Routledge and Kegan Paul, 1970.

Khaldoun, Ibn. *History of the Berbers*. Translated into French by Slane. 4 vols, Algiers, 1852–56.

Khalil, Andrea. *Crowds and Politics in North Africa: Tunisia, Algeria and Libya*. Abingdon, Routledge, 2014.

Knapp, Wilfrid. *North West Africa: A Political and Economic Survey*. Oxford University Press, 3rd edn, 1977.

La Guérivière, Jean de. *Amère Méditerranée: Le Maghreb et Nous*. Paris, Editions du Seuil, 2004.

Laremont, Ricardo (Ed.). *Revolution, Revolt and Reform in North Africa: The Arab Spring and Beyond*. Abingdon, Routledge, 2013.

Laskier, Michael M. *Israel and the Maghreb: From Statehood to Oslo*. Gainesville, FL, University Press of Florida; London, Eurospan, 2004.

Layachi, Azzedine. *The United States and North Africa: A Cognitive Approach to Foreign Policy*. New York and London, Praeger, 1990.

(Ed.). *Economic Crisis and Political Change in North Africa*. New York and London, Praeger, 1998.

Le Tourneau, Roger. *Evolution politique de l'Afrique du nord musulman*. Paris, 1962.

Liska, G. *The Greater Maghreb: From Independence to Unity?* Washington, DC, Center of Foreign Policy Research, 1963.

Maddy-Weitzman, Bruce. *The Berber Identity Movement and the Challenge to North African States*. Austin, TX, University of Texas Press, 2011.

Amazigh Politics in the Wake of the Arab Spring. Austin, University of Texas Press, 2022.

Maddy-Weitzman, B., and Zisenwine, D. (Eds). *The Maghrib in the New Century: Identity, Religion and Politics*. Gainesville, FL, University of Florida Press, 2008.

Martinez, Luis. *The State in North Africa: After the Arab Uprisings*. Oxford, Oxford University Press, 2020.

Mason, Robert. *The Gulf States and the Horn of Africa: Interests, Influences and Instability*. Manchester, Manchester University Press, 2022.

McDougall, James. (Ed.). *Nation, Society and Culture in North Africa*. London, Frank Cass, 2003.

Marçais, G. *La Berberie musulmane et l'Orient au moyen age*. Paris, 1946.

Metzger, Chantal. *Le Maghreb en guerre: 1939–1945*. Malakoff, Armand Collin, 2018.

Mezran, Karim K. *Negotiating National Identity: The Case of the Arab States of North Africa*. Rome, Antonio Pelicani, 2002.

Moore, C. H. *Politics in North Africa*. Boston, MA, Little, Brown, 1970.

Naylor, Phillip C. *North Africa: A History from Antiquity to the Present*. Austin, TX, University of Texas Press, 2009.

Nickerson, Jane S. *Short History of North Africa*. New York, 1961.

Özel, Işık. *State–Business Alliances and Economic Development: Turkey, Mexico and North Africa*. Abingdon, Routledge, 2014.

Parrinder, Geoffrey. *Religion in Africa*. London, Pall Mall Press, 1970.

Pazzanita, Anthony G. *Historical Dictionary of Western Sahara*. Lanham, MA, Scarecrow Press, 3rd edn, 2006.

Robana, Abderrahman. *The Prospects for an Economic Community in North Africa*. London, Pall Mall, 1973.

Rouis, Mustapha, and Tabor, Steven R. *Regional Economic Integration in the Middle East and North Africa: Beyond Trade Reform*. Washington, DC, The World Bank, 2013.

Rousseaux, Vanessa. *L'urbanisation au Maghreb: le langage des cartes*. Aix en Provence, Presses Universitaires d'Aix-Marseille, 2004.

Sahli, Mohamed Chérif. *Décoloniser l'histoire; introduction à l'histoire du Maghreb*. Paris, Maspero, 1965.

Sayeh, Ismail. *Les Sahraouis*. Paris, L'Harmattan, 1998.

Segura i Mas, Antoni. *El Magreb, del colonialismo al islamismo*. Barcelona, Universidad de Barcelona, 1994.

Shahin, Emad Eldin. *Political Ascent: Contemporary Islamic Movements in North Africa*. Boulder, CO, Westview Press, 1998.

Steel, R. (Ed.). *North Africa*. New York, Wilson, 1967.

Thurston, Alexander. *Jihadists of North Africa and the Sahel: Local Politics and Rebel Groups*. Cambridge, Cambridge University Press, 2020.

Tilmatine, Mohand, and Desrues, Thierry (Eds). *Les revendications amazighes dans la tourmente des "printemps arabes": trajectoires historiques et évolutions récentes des mouvements identitaires en Afrique du Nord*. Rabat, Centre Jacques-Berque, 2017.

Toynbee, Sir Arnold. *Between Niger and Nile*. Oxford University Press, 1965.

Trimingham, J. S. *The Influence of Islam upon Africa*. London, Longmans, and Beirut, Librairie du Liban, 1968.

Tvedt, Terje (Ed.). *The River Nile in the Post-Colonial Age*. Cairo, American University of Cairo Press, 2010.

Vermeren, Pierre. *Maghreb: la démocratie impossible?* Paris, Fayard, 2004.

Volpi, Frédéric. *Revolution and Authoritarianism in North Africa*. New York, Oxford University Press, 2014.

Weipert-Fenner, Irene, and Wolff, Jonas (Eds). *Socioeconomic Protests in MENA and Latin America: Egypt and Tunisia in Interregional Comparison*. Cham, Palgrave Macmillan, 2020.

White, Gregory. *A Comparative Political Economy of Tunisia and Morocco: On the Outside of Europe Looking in*. Albany, NY, State University of New York Press, 2001.

Willis, Michael. *Politics and Power in the Maghreb: Algeria, Tunisia and Morocco from Independence to the Arab Spring*. London, C. Hurst & Co, 2012.

Wippel, Steffen. *Wirtschaft, Politik und Raum: Territoriale und regionale Prozesse in der westlichen Sahara*. Berlin, Verlag Hans Schiler, 2012.

Yerkes, Sarah E. *Geopolitics and Governance in North Africa: Local Challenges, Global Implications*. Edinburgh, Edinburgh University Press, 2023.

Youssef, Adam. *Europe's Relations with North Africa: Politics, Economics and Security*. London, I. B. Tauris, 2017.

Zartman, I. William. *Government and Politics in North Africa*. London, Greenwood Press, revised edn, 1978.

(Ed.). *Man, State and Society in the Contemporary Maghreb*. London, Pall Mall, 1973.

Zhang, Chuchu. *Islamist Party Mobilization: Tunisia's Ennahda and Algeria's HMS Compared, 1989–2014*. Singapore, Palgrave Macmillan, 2020.

Zoubir, Yahia H. *North Africa in Transition: State, Society and Economic Transformation in the 1990s*. Gainesville, FL, University Press of Florida, 1999.

Zoubir, Yahia H., and Dris-Aït-Hamadouche, Louisa. *Global Security Watch—The Maghreb: Algeria, Libya, Morocco and Tunisia*. Santa Barbara, CA, Praeger, 2013.

Zoubir, Yahia H., and White, Gregory (Eds). *North African Politics: Change and Continuity*. Abingdon, Routledge, 2016.

Zunes, Stephen, and Mundy, Jacob. *Western Sahara: War, Nationalism, and Conflict Irresolution*. Syracuse, NY, Syracuse University Press, 2010.

Zweiri, M. *Arab-Iranian Relations Since the Arab Uprisings*. London, Routledge, 2023.

SELECT BIBLIOGRAPHY (PERIODICALS)

Al-Abhath: Publ. by American University of Beirut Press, POB 11-0236, Riad el-Solh, Beirut 1107 2020, Lebanon; e-mail alabhath@aub.edu.lb; internet www.aub.edu.lb/alabhath; f. 1948; annual publication specializing in Arab and Middle East studies; English and Arabic; Editors RAMZI BAALBAKI, BILAL ORFALI.

Acta Orientalia: c/o Institutt for Kulturstudier og Orientalske Språk, Universitetet i Oslo, POB 1010 Blindern, 0315 Oslo, Norway; tel. 22-85-80-39; e-mail c.p.zoller@ikos.uio.no; internet journals.uio.no/actaorientalia; f. 1922; publ. under auspices of the Oriental Societies of Denmark, Finland, Norway and Sweden; history, language, archaeology and religions of the Near and Far East and South Asia; Editor CLAUS PETER ZOLLER; annually.

Acta Orientalia Academiae Scientiarum Hungaricae: Institute of East Asian Studies, Eötvös Loránd University, H-1088 Budapest, Múzeum krt. 4F, Hungary; e-mail kosa.gabor@btk.elte.hu; internet akjournals.com/view/journals/062/062-overview.xml?rskey=vccDKS&result=1; f. 1950; English; Editor-in-Chief GÁBOR KÓSA; quarterly.

Africa Research Bulletin: Wiley-Blackwell, 9600 Garsington Rd, Oxford, OX4 2DQ, UK; tel. (1363) 775207; e-mail editors@africaresearch.co.uk; internet onlinelibrary.wiley.com/journal/14676346; f. 1964; monthly bulletins divided into Economic, Financial and Technical Series and Political, Social and Cultural Series; Editor VERONICA HOSKINS.

Anatolian Studies: BIAA, 10 Carlton House Terrace, London, SW1Y 5AH, UK; tel. (20) 7969-5204; fax (20) 7969-5401; e-mail biaa@britac.ac.uk; internet www.biaa.ac.uk/publications/item/name/anatolian-studies; f. 1948; annual of the British Institute at Ankara; covers the arts, humanities, social sciences and environmental sciences in Türkiye (fmrly Turkey); Editor NAOISE MAC SWEENEY; annually.

Anatolica: Nederlands Instituut voor het Nabije Oosten, POB 9515, 2300 RA Leiden, Netherlands; tel. (71) 5272036; e-mail ninopublications@hum.leidenuniv.nl; internet www.nino-leiden.nl/anatolica; f. 1967; publ. by the Netherlands Institute in Turkey in co-operation with the Netherlands Institute for the Near East (Nederlands Instituut voor het Nabije Oosten—NINO); Editor-in-Chief J. J. ROODENBERG; annually.

L'Année du Maghreb: Institut de Recherches et d'Études sur le Monde Arabe et Musulman (IREMAM), 5 rue du Château de l'Horloge, BP 647, 13094 Aix-en-Provence Cedex 2, France; tel. 4-42-52-49-64; fax 4-42-52-49-80; e-mail lannee.dumaghreb@gmail.com; internet anneemaghreb.revues.org; publ. by the Centre National de la Recherche Scientifique, CNRS Editions, 15 rue Malebranche, 75005 Paris, France; f. 1962 as Annuaire de l'Afrique du Nord; present name adopted 2005; year book contains special studies on current affairs and political science, report on a collective programme of social sciences research on North Africa, chronologies, chronicles, documentation and book reviews; Editors-in-Chief FRANÇOIS DUMASY, NESSIM ZNAIEN, ERIC GOBE.

Arab Studies Quarterly: Center for the Study of Muslim and Arab Worlds (CSMAW), California State University, 5500 University Parkway, San Bernardino, CA 92407, USA; e-mail aoude@hawaii.edu; internet www.plutojournals.com/asq; f. 1979; Editor IBRAHIM G. AOUDÉ; quarterly.

Arabica (Revue d'Etudes Arabes et Islamiques): Université Paris III, 13 rue de Santeuil, 75231 Paris Cedex 05, France; e-mail secretariat.arabica@gmail.com; internet brill.com/view/journals/arab/arab-overview.xml; f. 1954; publ. by Brill Academic Publishers, POB 9000, 2300 PA, Leiden, Netherlands; Editor FRÉDÉRIC LAGRANGE; quarterly.

Archiv für Orientforschung: c/o Institut für Orientalistik der Universität Wien, Spitalgasse 2, Hof 4.1, 1090 Vienna, Austria; fax (1) 427-79-434; e-mail michaela.weszeli@univie.ac.at; internet orientalistik.univie.ac.at/publikationen/afo; f. 1923; articles in English, German, French and Italian; Editors Prof. Dr HERMANN HUNGER, Prof. Dr MICHAEL JURSA, Prof. Dr. GEBHARD J. SELZ, Dr MICHAELA WESZELI.

Archiv Orientální (ArOr): Orientální ústav Akademie věd České republiky, Pod Vodárenskou věží 4, 182 08 Prague 8, Czech Republic; e-mail aror@orient.cas.cz; internet aror.orient.cas.cz; f. 1929; Editor-in-Chief SERGIO ALIVERNINI; 3 a year.

Asian Affairs: Royal Society for Asian Affairs, 16 Old Queen St, London, SW1H 9HP, UK; tel. (20) 7235-5122; e-mail info@rsaa.org.uk; internet rsaa.org.uk/journal; Editor BILL HAYTON; 4 a year.

Asian Journal of Middle Eastern and Islamic Studies (AJMEIS): Routledge, Taylor & Francis, 4 Park Sq., Milton Park, Abingdon, Oxon, OX14 4RN, UK; tel. (20) 8052-0500; e-mail enquiries@taylorandfrancis.com; internet www.tandfonline.com/toc/rmei20/current; journal of Middle East Studies Institute, Shanghai International Studies University (China, People's Republic); f. 2007 as Journal of Middle Eastern and Islamic Studies (in Asia); name changed as above in 2017; interdisciplinary journal focusing on the political, security, economic, energy, cultural, educational and demographic linkages between Asia and the Middle Eastern/Islamic worlds; Editors-in-Chief JUN DING, TIM NIBLOCK; 4 a year.

Belleten: Türk Tarih Kurumu (Turkish Historical Society), Kizilay Sok. 1, 06100 Ankara, Turkey; tel. (312) 3102368; fax (312) 3101698; e-mail belleten@ttk.gov.tr; internet belleten.gov.tr; f. 1937; history and archaeology of Türkiye; Editor Dr BIROL ÇETIN; 3 a year.

Bibliotheca Orientalis: Netherlands Institute for the Near East (Nederlands Instituut voor het Nabije Oosten—NINO), POB 9515, 2300 RA Leiden, Netherlands; tel. (71) 5272036; fax (71) 5272038; e-mail bior@hum.leidenuniv.nl; internet www.nino-leiden.nl/bior; f. 1943; Editors R. E. KON, A. VAN DER KOOIJ, L. LIMME, D. J. W. MEIJER, H. GZELLA, W. J. I. WAAL, M. STOL, C. WAERZEGGERS; 3 double issues a year.

British Journal of Middle Eastern Studies: 71–75 Shelton St, Covent Garden, London, WC2H 9JQ, UK; e-mail lloyd.ridgeon@glasgow.ac.uk; internet www.brismes.ac.uk/journal/the-british-journal-of-middle-eastern-studies; f. 1974 as British Society of Middle Eastern Studies Bulletin; publ. by Taylor & Francis for BRISMES; Editor Dr LLOYD RIDGEON; 4 a year.

Bulletin d'études orientales: Institut Français du Proche Orient, BP 344, Abou Roumaneh, Damascus, Syrian Arab Republic; tel. (11) 3330214; fax (11) 3327887; e-mail p.koetschet@ifporient.org; internet www.ifporient.org/publications/beo; f. 1922; Editor PAULINE KOETSCHET; annually.

Bulletin of the School of Oriental and African Studies: SOAS University of London, 10 Thornhaugh St, Russell Sq., London, WC1H 0XG, UK; e-mail bsoas@soas.ac.uk; internet journals.cambridge.org/jid_BSO; f. 1917; publ. by Cambridge University Press; publishes scholarly articles and book reviews on the history, languages and literatures, religions, arts and music of Asia, the Middle East and Africa; Editor Dr AYMAN SHIHADEH.

Les Cahiers de Tunisie: Faculté des Sciences Humaines et Sociales, Université de Tunis, 94 blvd de 9 Avril 1938, 1007 Tunis, Tunisia; tel. (71) 560-840; e-mail fshst@fshst.rnu.tn; internet www.digitalhumanities.com.tn/journals/1; f. 1953; research in humanities; Dir HAYET AMAMOU; quarterly.

The Cairo Review of Global Affairs: School of Global Affairs and Public Policy, American University in Cairo, AUC Ave, POB 74, New Cairo 11835, Egypt; tel. 26153649; e-mail info@thecairoreview.com; internet www.thecairoreview.com; Man. Editors FIRAS AL-ATRAQCHI, KARIM HAGGAG; quarterly.

Chuto Kenkyu (Journal of Middle Eastern Studies): The Middle East Research Institute of Japan, Hirakawacho Court 6F, 1-1-1 Hirakawacho, Chiyoda-ku, Tokyo 102-0093, Japan; tel. (3) 6261-4554; e-mail mideastij@hotmail.com; internet www.meij.or.jp/publication/chutoukenkyu; f. 1960; Japanese; 3 a year.

Le Commerce du Levant: POB 45-332, 3e étage, Immeuble l'Orient-Le Jour, route de Damas, Baabda, Hazmié, Lebanon; tel. (5) 952259; fax (5) 453644; e-mail redaction@lecommercedulevant.com; internet www.lecommercedulevant.com; economic; Editor-in-Chief SAHAR AL-ATTAR; monthly.

Contemporary Arab Affairs: 155 Grand Ave, Suite 400, Oakland, CA 94612–3758, USA; e-mail caa@caus.org.lb; internet brill.com/view/journals/jcaa/jcaa-overview.xml; f. 2008; journal of the Centre for Arab Unity Studies; modern Arab scholarship in the English language; Editor-in-Chief ALI E. HILLAL DESSOUKI; quarterly.

Contemporary Levant: Routledge, Taylor & Francis, 4 Park Sq., Milton Park, Abingdon, Oxon, OX14 4RN, UK; tel. (20) 8052-0500; e-mail contemporarylevant@cbrl.org.uk; internet www.tandfonline.com/toc/ycol20/current; publ. by Taylor & Francis on behalf of

Council for British Research in the Levant (CBRL); Editor-in-Chief Dr SARAH IRVING (Staffordshire Univ., UK); 2 a year.

The Cyprus Review: University of Nicosia, 46 Makedonitissas Ave, POB 24005, 1700 Nicosia, Cyprus; e-mail cy_review@unic.ac.cy; internet cyprusreview.org; f. 1989; publ. by Univ. of Nicosia; focuses on social, political and economic affairs of Cyprus; bi-annual; Editor-in-Chief Assc. Prof. CHRISTINA IOANNOU; Man. Editor Dr EMILIOS A. SOLOMOU.

Diyâr. Zeitschrift für Osmanistik, Türkei- und Nahostforschung (Journal of Ottoman, Turkish and Middle Eastern Studies): c/o Institut für Orientalistik der Universität Wien, Spitalgasse 2, Hof 4, 1090 Vienna, Austria; e-mail diyar@ergon-verlag.de; internet orientalistik.univie.ac.at/publikationen/diyar; in German, English and French; publ. by Ergon Verlag for Gesellschaft für Turkologie, Osmanistik und Turkeiforschung eV (Germany); Editor-in-Chief YAVUZ KÖSE (Univ. of Vienna, Austria); 2 a year.

Estudios de Asia y Africa: Centre for Asian and African Studies, El Colegio de México, Carretera Pichacho Ajusco 20, Ampliación Fuentes de Pedregal, México DF 14110, Mexico; tel. (5) 5449-3000; e-mail maleb@colmex.mx; internet estudiosdeasiayafrica.colmex.mx; f. 1966 as Estudios Orientales; present name adopted 1975; Editor ROBERTO EDUARDO GARCÍA FERNÁNDEZ; quarterly.

Hamizrah Hehadash (The New East): The Middle East & Islamic Studies Association of Israel (MEISAI), The Hebrew University, Jerusalem, Israel; e-mail meisai1949@gmail.com; internet www.meisai.org.il; f. 1949; Middle Eastern, Asian and African affairs; Hebrew, with English summary; annually.

Hesperis-Tamuda: Faculté des Lettres et des Sciences Humaines, Université Muhammad V, 3 ave Ibn Battouta, BP 1040, Rabat, Morocco; e-mail khalidbensrhir@gmail.com; internet www.hesperis-tamuda.com; f. 1921; history, anthropology, civilization of Maghreb and Western Islam, special reference to bibliography; Scientific Co-ordinator KHALID BEN-SRHIR; annually.

Indo-Iranian Journal: Brill, POB 9000, 2300 PA Leiden, Netherlands; tel. (71) 5353500; fax (71) 5317532; e-mail paalvast@brill.com; internet www.brill.com/iij; f. 1957; English, occasionally French and German; publishes papers on ancient and medieval Indian languages, literature, philosophy and religion, ancient and medieval Iran, and Tibet; Editors-in-Chief PETER BISSCHOP, JONATHAN SILK; quarterly.

International Journal of Middle East Studies: Cambridge University Press, One Liberty Plaza, 20th Floor, New York, NY 10006, USA; tel. (212) 337-5000; e-mail customer_service@cambridge.org; internet journals.cambridge.org/jid_mes; f. 1970; Journal of the Middle East Studies Asscn of North America; Editor JOEL GORDON; quarterly.

Iranian Studies: Routledge, Taylor & Francis, 4 Park Sq., Milton Park, Abingdon, Oxon, OX14 4RN, UK; tel. (20) 8052-0500; e-mail enquiries@taylorandfrancis.com; internet www.tandfonline.com/toc/cist20/current; f. 1967; journal of the Int. Society for Iranian Studies; Iranian and Persian history, literature and society; Editor SUSSAN SIAVOSH (Trinity Univ., USA); 6 a year.

Der Islam: Asien-Afrika-Institut, Universität Hamburg, Edmund-Siemers-Allee 1-Ost, 20146 Hamburg, Germany; tel. (40) 428385925; e-mail der_islam.aai@uni-hamburg.de; internet www.degruyter.com/view/j/islm; articles in English, German and French; Chief Editor Prof. Dr STEFAN HEIDEMANN; 2 a year.

Islamic Quarterly: The Islamic Cultural Centre and the London Central Mosque, 146 Park Rd, London, NW8 7RG, UK; tel. (20) 7724-3363; fax (20) 7724-0493; e-mail iq@iccuk.org; internet www.iccuk.org; f. 1954; Editor Dr AHMAD AL-DUBAYAN; quarterly.

Israel Affairs: Routledge, Taylor & Francis, 4 Park Sq., Milton Park, Abingdon, Oxon, OX14 4RN, UK; tel. (20) 8052-0500; e-mail enquiries@taylorandfrancis.com; internet www.tandfonline.com/toc/fisa20/current; f. 1994; Israeli history, politics, economics, art and literature; Editor EFRAIM KARSH (King's College London, UK); 6 a year.

Jeune Afrique: Groupe Jeune Afrique, 57 bis, rue d'Auteuil, 75016 Paris, France; tel. 1-44-30-19-60; e-mail service.client@jeuneafrique.com; internet www.jeuneafrique.com; f. 1960; Man. Dir AMIR BEN YAHMED; weekly.

Journal of the American Oriental Society: American Oriental Society, Harlan Hatcher Graduate Library, University of Michigan, 913 S University Ave, Ann Arbor, MI 48109-1190, USA; tel. (734) 347-1259; e-mail jrodgers@umich.edu; internet www.americanorientalsociety.org/publications/journal-of-the-american-oriental-society-jaos; f. 1842; Oriental civilizations and Asian languages and literature; Editor-in-Chief STEPHANIE PERI BEARMAN; quarterly.

Journal of Arabian Studies: Routledge, Taylor & Francis, 4 Park Sq., Milton Park, Abingdon, Oxon, OX14 4RN, UK; tel. (20) 8052-0500; e-mail enquiries@taylorandfrancis.com; internet www.tandfonline.com/toc/rjab20/current; f. 2011; history, politics, economics, art, literature of the Arabian peninsula; affiliated with Assn for Gulf and Arabian Peninsular Studies (AGAPS); Editors JAMES ONLEY (American University of Sharjah), GERD NONNEMAN (Georgetown University in Qatar); 2 a year.

Journal of Arabic and Islamic Studies: Department of Culture Studies and Oriental Languages, University of Oslo, POB 1010, Blindern, 0315 Oslo, Norway; tel. 22-85-67-83; e-mail stephan.guth@ikos.uio.no; internet journals.uio.no/JAIS; f. 1995; history, language, literature and culture of the Middle East and the wider Muslim world; Editors LUTZ EDZARD, STEPHAN GUTH; online only; annual.

Journal Asiatique: Société Asiatique, Palais de l'Institut, 23 quai Conti, 75006 Paris, France; Publr Peeters, Bondgenotenlaan 153, 3000 Leuven, Belgium; tel. and fax 1-16-23-51-70; e-mail contact@societeasiatique.fr; internet www.aibl.fr/societe-asiatique/publications-196/journal-asiatique; f. 1822; covers all phases of Oriental research; Editor GRÉGORY CHAMBON; 2 a year.

Journal of Contemporary Iraq & the Arab World: Intellect Books Ltd, The Mill, Parnall Rd, Fishponds, Bristol, BS16 3JG, UK; tel. (117) 958-9910; fax (117) 958-9911; e-mail info@intellectbooks.com; internet www.intellectbooks.com/journal-of-contemporary-iraq-the-arab-world; f. 2007; journal of the Int. Assn of Contemporary Iraqi Studies and Int. Assn of Middle Eastern Studies; Editors TAREQ ISMAEL (Univ. of Calgary, Canada), JACQUELINE ISMAEL (Univ. of Calgary, Canada); 3 a year.

Journal for Islamic Studies: Centre for Contemporary Islam, University of Cape Town, Dept of Religious Studies, Private Bag, Rondebosch 7701, South Africa; tel. (21) 6503828; fax (21) 6897575; e-mail sadiyya.shaikh@uct.ac.za; internet humanities.uct.ac.za/contemporary-islam; publishes original research on Islam as a world culture and civilization; covers religion, theology, law, history, culture, art, ethics, politics, international relations, philosophy and sociology; Chief Editor AUWAIS RAFUDEEN; annually.

Journal of the Middle East and Africa: Routledge, Taylor & Francis, 4 Park Sq., Milton Park, Abingdon, Oxon, OX14 4RN, UK; tel. (20) 8052-0500; e-mail enquiries@taylorandfrancis.com; internet www.tandfonline.com/toc/ujme20/current; publ. by Taylor & Francis on behalf of the Assn for the Study of the Middle East and Africa; Editor-in-Chief Dr FRANCK SALAMEH (Boston College, USA); 4 a year.

Journal of Modern Jewish Studies: Routledge, Taylor & Francis, 4 Park Sq., Milton Park, Abingdon, Oxon, OX14 4RN, UK; tel. (20) 8052-0500; e-mail enquiries@taylorandfrancis.com; internet www.tandfonline.com/toc/cmjs20/current; literature, history, religion and social studies; Editor YARON PELEG (Univ. of Cambridge, UK); 4 a year.

Journal of Muslim Minority Affairs: Routledge, Taylor & Francis, 4 Park Sq., Milton Park, Abingdon, Oxon, OX14 4RN, UK; tel. and fax (20) 8052-0500; e-mail enquiries@taylorandfrancis.com; internet www.tandfonline.com/journals/cjmm20; f. 1979; publ. by Routledge for the Institute of Muslim Minority Affairs, UK; Editor-in-Chief Dr SALEHA S. MAHMOOD; 4 a year.

Journal of Near Eastern Studies: Oriental Institute, University of Chicago, 1155 E 58th St, Chicago, IL 60637, USA; tel. (773) 702-9592; e-mail jnes@uchicago.edu; internet www.journals.uchicago.edu/JNES/home.html; f. 1884; owned by Univ. of Chicago Press; devoted to the ancient, medieval and pre-modern Near and Middle East, archaeology, languages, history, Islam; Editor JAMES F. OSBORNE; 2 a year.

The Journal of North African Studies: Routledge, Taylor & Francis, 4 Park Sq., Milton Park, Abingdon, Oxon, OX14 4RN, UK; tel. (20) 8052-0500; e-mail enquiries@taylorandfrancis.com; internet www.tandfonline.com/toc/fnas20/current; f. 1996; history, sociology, anthropology, economics and diplomacy; Editors ANDREA KHALIL (The City Univ. of New York, USA), SHANA COHEN (University of Cambridge, UK); 6 a year.

Journal of Palestine Studies: 3501 M St, NW, Washington, DC 20007, USA; e-mail jps@palestine-studies.org; internet www.palestine-studies.org; f. 1971; publ. by the Univ. of California Press for the Institute for Palestine Studies, Washington, DC; Palestinian affairs and the Arab–Israeli conflict; Editors RASHID I. KHALIDI, SHERENE SEIKALY; Man. Editor MARIA KHOURY; quarterly.

Levant: Routledge, Taylor & Francis, 4 Park Sq., Milton Park, Abingdon, Oxon, OX14 4RN, UK; tel. (20) 8052-0500; e-mail enquiries@taylorandfrancis.com; internet www.tandfonline.com/toc/ylev20/current; f. 1969; publ. by Taylor & Francis on behalf of the CBRL; archaeology and history (prehistory–Ottoman); Editor-in-Chief Dr CAROLINE MIDDLETON (CBRL); 3 a year.

Maghreb-Machrek: 12 rue du Quatre Septembre, 75002 Paris, France; tel. 1-42-86-55-65; fax 1-42-60-43-35; e-mail agpaedit@eska.fr; internet eska-publishing.com/fr/1323-maghreb-machrek; f. 1964; Editor-in-Chief JEAN-YVES MOISSERON (Institut de Recherche pour le Développement); quarterly.

The Maghreb Review: 45 Burton St, London, WC1H 9AL, UK; tel. and fax (20) 7388-1840; e-mail maghreb@maghrebreview.com; internet www.maghrebreview.com; f. 1976; covers the Maghreb, the Middle

REGIONAL INFORMATION — Select Bibliography (Periodicals)

East, Africa and Islamic studies; Editor MUHAMMAD BEN MADANI; quarterly.

Majallat a-Rabita: Communication and Public Information, Muslim World League, POB 537, Mecca al-Mukarramah 21955, Saudi Arabia; tel. (2) 530-9444; e-mail mwljournal@themwl.org; internet www.themwl.org; f. 1965; Arabic; Dir OSMAN ABU ZAYED OSMAN; monthly.

MEN: Middle East News Agency, POB 1165, 17 Sharia Hoda Sharawi, Cairo, Egypt; tel. (2) 3933000; fax (2) 3935055; e-mail webmaster@mena.org.eg; internet www.mena.org.eg; f. 1962; weekly economic news bulletin in English; Chair. ALI HASSAN.

Middle East Critique: Routledge, Taylor & Francis, 4 Park Sq., Milton Park, Abingdon, Oxon, OX14 4RN, UK; tel. (20) 8052-0500; e-mail enquiries@taylorandfrancis.com; internet www.tandfonline.com/toc/ccri20/current; f. 1992 as Critique: Critical Middle Eastern Studies; renamed as above 2009; promotes an academic and critical examination of the history and contemporary political, social, economic and cultural affairs of Middle Eastern countries; Editors ERIC J. HOOGLUND, MATTEO CAPASSO; 4 a year.

Middle East Development Journal: Routledge, Taylor & Francis, 4 Park Sq., Milton Park, Abingdon, Oxon, OX14 4RN, UK; tel. (20) 8052-0500; e-mail enquiries@taylorandfrancis.com; internet www.tandfonline.com/toc/rmdj20/current; journal of the Economic Research Forum (Cairo, Egypt); aims to deepen understanding of development in the Middle East and North Africa, and to strengthen the social science research community in the region; Man. Editor RAIMUNDO SOTO; 2 a year.

Middle East Economic Digest (MEED): POB 25960, GBS Bldg, 6th Floor, al-Falak St, Dubai Media City, Dubai, United Arab Emirates; tel. (4) 48180263; e-mail customerservice@meed.com; internet www.meed.com; f. 1957; weekly report on economic, business and political developments; Editor COLIN FOREMAN.

Middle East Economic Survey: Middle East Petroleum and Economic Publications (Cyprus), Alkeos 23, Engomi, 2404 Nicosia, Cyprus; tel. (22) 665434; e-mail info@mees.com; internet www.mees.com; f. 1957 (in Beirut); weekly review and analysis of energy, finance and banking, and political developments; Publr SALEH S. JALLAD; Man. Editor JAMES COCKAYNE.

The Middle East Journal: Middle East Institute, 1763 N St, NW, Washington, DC 20036-, USA; tel. (202) 785-1141; e-mail mej@mei.edu; internet www.mei.edu/education/middle-east-journal; journal devoted to the study of the modern-era Middle East; f. 1947; Editor JACOB PASSEL; quarterly.

The Middle East Observer: 41 Sherif St, Cairo, Egypt; tel. (2) 6670340; fax (2) 6670340; e-mail editors@meobserver.org; internet www.meobserver.org; f. 1954; economics; Chief Editor HESHAM ABD AL-RAOUF; Publr AHMAD FODA; weekly.

Middle East Policy: Middle East Policy Council, 1730 M St, NW, Suite 512, Washington, DC 20036, USA; tel. (202) 296-6767; fax (202) 296-5791; e-mail info@mepc.org; internet www.mepc.org; policy analysis; Editor ANNE JOYCE; quarterly.

Middle East Quarterly: Middle East Forum, Suite 3600, 1650 Market St, Philadelphia, PA 19103, USA; tel. (215) 546-5406; e-mail info@meforum.org; internet www.meforum.org/middle-east-quarterly; f. 1994; politics, economics and culture; Editor EFRAIM KARSH; quarterly.

Middle East Report: POB 10659, Chicago, IL 60610, USA; e-mail editor@merip.org; internet www.merip.org; f. 1971; publishing, education and research; Exec. Editor KATIE NATANEL; quarterly.

Middle Eastern Literatures: Routledge, Taylor & Francis, 4 Park Sq., Milton Park, Abingdon, Oxon, OX14 4RN, UK; tel. (20) 8052-0500; e-mail enquiries@taylorandfrancis.com; internet www.tandfonline.com/toc/came20/current; f. 1998; Editors HUDA FAKHREDDINE (Univ. of Pennsylvania, USA), CHARIS OLSZOK (Univ. of Cambridge, UK), NORA PARR (Freie Universität Berlin, Germany), ADAM TALIB (Durham Univ., UK); 3 a year.

Middle Eastern Studies: Routledge, Taylor & Francis, 4 Park Sq., Milton Park, Abingdon, Oxon, OX14 4RN, UK; tel. (20) 8052-0500; e-mail enquiries@taylorandfrancis.com; internet www.tandfonline.com/toc/fmes20/current; f. 1964; Editors SAUL KELLY, HELEN KEDOURIE; 6 a year.

The Muslim World: Macdonald Center, Hartford Seminary, 77 Sherman St, Hartford, CT 06105, USA; tel. (860) 509-9500; e-mail muwo@wiley.com; internet onlinelibrary.wiley.com/journal/14781913; f. 1911; Islamic studies in general and Muslim-Christian relations in past and present; Editor YAHYA MICHOT; quarterly.

The Muslim World League Journal: Press and Publications Dept, Muslim World League, POB 537, Mecca al-Mukarramah 21955, Saudi Arabia; tel. (12) 530-9444; e-mail mwljournal@themwl.org; internet www.themwl.org; monthly.

Nový Orient (New Orient): Orientální ústav Akademie věd České republiky, Pod Vodárenskou věží 4, 182 08 Prague 8, Czech Republic; tel. (2) 66053523; e-mail novor@orient.cas.cz; internet orient.cas.cz/en/editorial-activity/novy-orient/; f. 1945; Editor-in-Chief Dr JAKUB HRUBÝ; 3 a year.

Oil & Gas Journal: 1455 West Loop South, Suite 400, Houston, TX 77027, USA; e-mail ogj@omeda.com; internet www.ogj.com; f. 1902; publ. by PennWell Corpn; petroleum industry and business weekly; Editor-in-Chief CHRISTOPHER E. SMITH.

Oriente Moderno: Istituto per l'Oriente C. A. Nallino, Via A. Caroncini 19, 00197 Rome, Italy; tel. (06) 8084106; fax (06) 8079395; e-mail ipocan@ipocan.it; internet www.ipocan.it; f. 1921; articles, book reviews; Pres. Prof. CLAUDIO LO JACONO; 2 a year.

Palestine-Israel: Middle East Publications, POB 19839, Jerusalem 91197, Israel; tel. (2) 6282159; fax (2) 6273388; e-mail pij@pij.org; internet www.pij.org; f. 1994; independent journal publ. as a joint venture between Israelis and Palestinians; promotes dialogue between the two sides and offers critical analysis of regional issues; Editors ZIAD ABU ZAYYAD, HILLEL SCHENKER; quarterly.

Palestine Solidarité: Association France Palestine Solidarité, 21 rue Voltaire, 75011 Paris, France; tel. 1-43-72-15-79; e-mail afps@france-palestine.org; internet www.france-palestine.org; quarterly.

Persica: Dutch-Iranian Society, University of Leiden, Dept of Persian Studies, Witte Singel 24, POB 9515, 2300 RA Leiden, Netherlands; e-mail persica@hum.leidenuniv.nl; internet poj.peeters-leuven.be/content.php?journal_code=PERS&url=journal; f. 1963; publ. by Peeters; Editor Dr A. A. SEYED-GOHRAB; annually.

Petroleum Economist: 27 Furnival St, London, EC4A 1JQ, UK; tel. (20) 3409-2240; e-mail editorial@petroleum-economist.com; internet pemedianetwork.com/petroleum-economist; f. 1934; Editor-in-Chief PAUL HICKIN; monthly.

Revue d'assyriologie et d'archéologie orientale: c/o Dominique Charpin, 39 ave d'Alembert, 92160 Antony, France; tel. 1-42-37-27-97; e-mail dominique.charpin@college-de-france.fr; internet www.puf.com/Collections/Revue_Assyriologie-Arch%C3%A9ologie_orientale; f. 1884; Editor-in-Chief DOMINIQUE CHARPIN; annually.

Rivista degli Studi Orientali: Dipartimento di Studi Orientali, Facoltà di Lettere, Università Degli Studi, 'La Sapienza', P. le Aldo Moro 5, 00185 Rome, Italy; tel. (06) 49913802; fax (06) 4451209; e-mail giulia.tozzi@libraweb.net; internet rso.libraweb.net; publ. by Fabrizio Serra editore; Dir FRANCO D'AGOSTINO; quarterly.

Rocznik Orientalistyczny: Uniwersytet Warszawski, Krakowskie Przedmieście 26/28, 00-927 Warszawa, Poland; tel. (22) 5520343; e-mail rorient@pan.pl; internet journals.pan.pl/ro; f. 1915; Editor-in-Chief MAREK M. DZIEKAN; 2 a year.

Royal Asiatic Society of Great Britain and Ireland Journal: 14 Stephenson Way, London, NW1 2HD, UK; tel. (20) 7388-4539; e-mail info@royalasiaticsociety.org; internet www.royalasiaticsociety.org; f. 1823; covers all aspects of Oriental research; Pres. Prof. S. ANSARI; Editor DAUD ALI; 4 a year.

Saudi Aramco World: Aramco Services Co, 1200 Smith St, Two Allen Center, 35th Floor, Houston, TX 77002, USA; internet www.saudiaramcoworld.com; f. 1949; non-political information—culture, history, natural history, economics, etc.—of the Middle East; Editor RICHARD DOUGHTY; bi-monthly.

Studia Arabistyczne i Islamistyczne: Wydział Orientalistyczny, Uniwersytet Warszawski, Krakowskie Przedmieście 26/28, 00-927 Warszawa, Poland; tel. (22) 8263683; e-mail janusz.danecki@uw.edu.pl; internet www.orient.uw.edu.pl; f. 1993; Editor JANUSZ DANECKI; annually.

Studia Islamica: Brill Academic Publishers, POB 9000, 2300 PA, Leiden, Netherlands; tel. (71) 5353500; fax (71) 5317532; e-mail studiaislamicajournal@gmail.com; internet brill.com/view/journals/si/si-overview.xml; f. 1953; Editor HOUARI TOUATI; 2 a year.

Studia Orientalia: Finnish Oriental Society, c/o Lotta Aunio, POB 59, 00014 University of Helsinki, Helsinki, Finland; tel. (9) 635177; fax (9) 635017; e-mail tiedekirja@tsv.fi; internet www.suomenitamainenseura.org; Editor LOTTA AUNIO.

Turcica: Collège de France, Institut des Civilisations, 52 rue du Cardinal-Lemoine, 75005 Paris, France; tel. 1-44-27-18-89; e-mail turcica@college-de-france.fr; internet poj.peeters-leuven.be/content.php?journal_code=TURC&url=journal; f. 1969; all aspects of Turkish and Turkic culture; Editor Prof. MARC TOUTANT; annually.

Turkish Studies: Routledge, Taylor & Francis, 4 Park Sq., Milton Park, Abingdon, Oxon, OX14 4RN, UK; tel. (20) 8052-0500; e-mail enquiries@taylorandfrancis.com; internet www.tandfonline.com/toc/ftur20/current; f. 2000; Turkish history, politics, government, international relations, foreign policy; economic, religious, social, and all other issues; Editor PAUL KUBICEK (Oakland Univ., USA); 5 a year.

Vostok/Oriens (The East): Russian Academy of Sciences, 107031 Moscow, ul. Rozhdestvenka 12, Russia; tel. (495) 625-51-46; fax (495) 938-18-44; e-mail vostokauct@gmail.com; internet www.vostokoriens.ru; f. 1955; fmrly Sovetskoye Vostokovedeniye (Soviet

Oriental Studies); publ. by the History and Contemporaneity Asian-African Society, the Institute of Oriental Studies and Institute of Africa of the Russian Academy of Sciences; in Russian, with English summaries; Editor-in-Chief Dr VITALII V. NAUMKIN; 6 a year.

The Washington Report on Middle East Affairs: American Educational Trust, POB 53062, Washington, DC 20009, USA; tel. (202) 939-6050; fax (202) 265-4574; e-mail info@wrmea.org; internet www.wrmea.org; f. 1982; Exec. Editor DELINDA C. HANLEY; Man. Editor DALE SPRUSANSKY; 7 a year.

Die Welt des Islams (International Journal for the Study of Modern Islam): Brill Academic Publishers, POB 9000, 2300 PA, Leiden, Netherlands; tel. (71) 5353500; fax (71) 5317532; internet brill.com/view/journals/wdi/wdi-overview.xml; Seminar für Orientalistik der Ruhr-Universität Bochum, 44780 Bochum, Germany; fax (234) 3214671; e-mail emsupport@brill.com; f. 1951; contains articles in German, English and French on the contemporary Muslim world with special reference to history, society and culture; Editor RAINER BRUNNER (Centre National de la Recherche Scientifique, France).

Wiener Zeitschrift für die Kunde des Morgenlandes: Institut für Orientalistik der Universität Wien, Spitalgasse 2, Hof 4, 1090 Vienna, Austria; tel. (1) 427-74-34-01; e-mail orientalistik@univie.ac.at; internet orientalistik.univie.ac.at; in German, English and French; Editors ELLEN REHM, ELVIRA WAKELNIG; annually.

Zeitschrift der Deutschen Morgenländischen Gesellschaft: Fachgebiet Indologie und Tibetologie, Philipps-Universität Marburg, Deutschhausstr. 12, 35032 Marburg, Germany; tel. (6421) 2824741; e-mail steiner@uni-marburg.de; internet www.dmg-web.de; f. 1847; covers the history, languages and literature of the Orient; Editor Prof. Dr ROLAND STEINER; 2 a year.

INDEX OF REGIONAL ORGANIZATIONS

(Main reference only)

A

Access to COVID-19 Tools Accelerator, 1106
Accounting and Auditing Organization for Islamic Financial Institutions, 1169
Adaptation for Smallholder Agriculture Programme, 1099
Addis Ababa Action Agenda, 1092
Administrative Tribunal of the Arab League, 1146
Afreximbank, 1169
Africa Centres for Disease Control and Prevention, 1125
African Airlines Association, 1179
African-Asian Rural Development Organization, 1167
African Capacity Building Foundation, 1125
African Centre for Applied Research and Training in Social Development, 1178
African Civil Aviation Commission, 1125
African Commission on Human and Peoples' Rights, 1120
African Continental Free Trade Area, Secretariat, 1120
African Court of Human and Peoples' Rights, 1120
African Court of Justice and Human Rights, 1123
African Development Bank, 1115
African Parliamentary Union, 1172
African Petroleum Producers' Organization, 1166
African Regional Organization of ITUC, 1176
African Risk Capacity, 1125
African Standby Force, 1124
African Telecommunications Union, 1125
African Training and Research Centre in Administration for Development, 1167
African Union, 1119
African Union Agenda 2063, 1121
African Union Development Agency, 1120
African Union of Mutuals, 1178
Afro-Asian Peoples' Solidarity Organization, 1172
Afro-Asian Writers' Association, 1166
Agadir Agreement, 1167
Agri-Business Capital Fund, 1099
Agriculture, Land and Water Use Commission for the Near East, 1086
Al-Quds Fund, 1155
Alliance israélite universelle, 1171
Amnesty International, 1178
Arab Academy for Science, Technology and Maritime Transport, 1152
Arab Administrative Development Organization, 1152
Arab Air Carriers' Organization, 1179
Arab Atomic Energy Agency, 1152
Arab Authority for Agricultural Investment and Development, 1166
Arab Bank for Economic Development in Africa, 1167
Arab Bureau of Education for the Gulf States, 1171
Arab Center for the Studies of Arid Zones and Dry Lands, 1152
Arab Centre for Climate Change Policies, 1041
Arab Common Market for Electricity, 1148
Arab Company for Detergent Chemicals, 1154
Arab Energy Conference, 1154
Arab Federation for Oil and Gas Technologies, 1179
Arab Federation for Paper, Printing and Packaging Industries, 1179
Arab Fund for Economic and Social Development, 1126
Arab Fund for Technical Assistance to African Countries, 1146
Arab Gulf Programme for the United Nations Development Organizations, 1167
Arab Industrial Development, Standardization and Mining Organization, 1153
Arab Information and Communication Technology Union, 1179
Arab Inter-Parliamentary Union, 1173
Arab Investment and Export Credit Guarantee Corporation, 1153
Arab Labour Organization, 1153
Arab League, 1146
Arab League Central Boycott Office, 1146
Arab League Educational, Cultural and Scientific Organization, 1153
Arab Maritime Petroleum Transport Company, 1154
Arab Medical Association Against Cancer, 1177
Arab Monetary Fund, 1127
Arab Network of Nuclear Regulators, 1090
Arab Organization for Agricultural Development, 1153
Arab Organization for Human Rights, 1176
Arab Permanent Postal Commission, 1177
Arab Petroleum Investments Corporation, 1154
Arab Satellite Communications Organization, 1153
Arab Shipbuilding and Repair Yard Company, 1154
Arab States Broadcasting Union, 1153
Arab Strategy for Disaster Risk Reduction, 1148
Arab Towns Organization, 1178
Arab Trade Financing Program, 1128
Arab Trade Union Confederation, 1176
Arab Union of Electricity, 1171
Arab Women's Solidarity Association United, 1178
Asian-African Legal Consultative Organization, 1176
Asian Infrastructure Investment Bank, 1129
Association of Agricultural Research Institutions in the Near East and North Africa, 1166
Association of Arab Universities, 1171

B

Banque Arabe pour le Développement Economique en Afrique, 1167
Basel, Rotterdam and Stockholm Conventions, Secretariat, 1053
Black Sea Economic Cooperation, 1169

C

Caspian Summit, 1173
China/IFAD South-South Triangular Co-operation Facility, 1099
CIESM—The Mediterranean Science Commission, 1177
Codex Alimentarius Commission, 1086
Common Framework for Debt Treatments, 1170
Community of Sahel-Saharan States, 1168
Confederation of African Football, 1178
Conference on Interaction and Confidence Building Measures in Asia, 1173
Consultative Group on International Agricultural Research, 1166
Convention on Biological Diversity, 1057
Convention on International Trade in Endangered Species of Wild Flora and Fauna, 1059
Convention on the Conservation of Migratory Species of Wild Animals, 1059
Cooperation Council for the Arab States of the Gulf, 1131
Council for the Development of Social Science Research in Africa, 1178
Council of Arab and African States bordering the Red Sea and Gulf of Aden, 1168
Council of Arab Economic Unity, 1153

D

Deauville Partnership, 1116
Developing Eight, 1168
Doha Round, 1114

E

East Mediterranean Gas Forum, 1167
Economic and Social Commission for Western Asia, 1041
Economic Commission for Africa, 1038
Economic Cooperation Organization, 1138
Economic Research Forum, 1168
Equator Principles Association, 1169
European Bank for Reconstruction and Development, 1135
European-Mediterranean Seismological Centre, 1178
European Political Community, 1173
European Union, 1140
European Union of Arabic and Islamic Scholars, 1171

F

Facility for Refugees, Migrants, Forced Displacement and Rural Stability, 1099
FAO, 1081
FAO Desert Locust Control Committee, 1086
Fédération Internationale de Football Association, 1178
Federation of Arab Engineers, 1179

REGIONAL INFORMATION

Index of Regional Organizations

Federation of Islamic Medical Associations, 1177
Financial Action Task Force, 1170
Financial Intermediary Fund for Pandemic Prevention, Preparedness and Response, 1093
Financing Facility for Remittances, 1099
Fishery Committee for the Eastern Central Atlantic, 1086
Food and Agriculture Organization of the United Nations, 1081
Food Systems Summit, 1082
Fourth Arab Economic and Social Development Summit, 1147
Framework Convention for the Protection of the Marine Environment of the Caspian Sea, 1171

G

Gas Exporting Countries Forum, 1167
Gavi, the Vaccine Alliance, 1108
GEF Small Grants Programme, 1052
General Arab Insurance Federation, 1179
General Fisheries Commission for the Mediterranean, 1086
Global Acceleration Plan for Gender Equality, 1110
Global Alliance on Circular Economy and Resource Efficiency, 1054
Global Centre for Technology, Innovation and Sustainable Development, 1049
Global Compact for Safe, Orderly and Regular Migration, 1112
Global Compact on Refugees, 1060
Global Crisis Response Group, 1109
Global Donor Platform for Rural Development, 1100
Global Dryland Alliance, 1168
Global Environment Facility, 1056
Global Islamic Fund for Refugees, 1145
Global Outbreak Alert and Response Network, 1104
Global Pact for the Environment, 1056
Global Partnership on Marine Litter, 1055
Global Policy Centre for Resilient Ecosystems and Desertification, 1049
Global Strategy for Women's, Children's and Adolescents' Health, 1105
Global Vector Control Response Programme, 1105
Greater Arab Free Trade Area, 1147
Green Climate Fund, Secretariat, 1053
Group of 15, 1168
Group of 20, 1170
Group of 77, 1168
Group of Seven, 1173
Gulf Cooperation Council, 1131
Gulf International Bank, 1135
Gulf Investment Corporation, 1135
Gulf Organization for Industrial Consulting, 1179

I

Indian Ocean Rim Association, 1168
Indigenous Peoples Assistance Facility, 1099
Intergovernmental Group of 24 on International Monetary Affairs and Development, 1170
Intergovernmental Panel on Climate Change, 1057
Intergovernmental Science-Policy Platform on Biodiversity and Ecosystem Services, 1057
International African Institute, 1178
International Agency for Research on Cancer, 1109
International Arab Society of Certified Accountants, 1171
International Association of Jewish Lawyers and Jurists, 1176
International Atomic Energy Agency, 1087
International Bank for Reconstruction and Development, 1091
International Centre for Agricultural Research in the Dry Areas, 1166
International Centre for Settlement of Investment Disputes, 1095
International Civil Aviation Organization, 1112
International Confederation of Arab Trade Unions, 1176
International Coral Reef Initiative, 1172
International Criminal Court, 1176
International Criminal Police Organization, 1177
International Development Association, 1096
International Energy Agency, 1172
International Energy Forum, 1172
International Federation of Association Football, 1178
International Federation of Red Cross and Red Crescent Societies, 1178
International Finance Corporation, 1097
International Fund for Agricultural Development, 1098
International Grains Council, 1167
International Institute for Democracy and Electoral Assistance, 1174
International Islamic Fiqh Academy, 1159

International Islamic Trade Finance Corporation, 1145
International Labour Organization, 1112
International Land Coalition, 1100
International Maritime Organization, 1112
International Monetary Fund, 1100
International Olive Council, 1167
International Olympic Committee, 1179
International Organisation of Vine and Wine, 1166
International Organization for Migration, 1112
International Organization of La Francophonie, 1175
International Plant Protection Convention, Secretariat, 1166
International Renewable Energy Agency, 1172
International Resource Panel, 1057
International Solar Alliance, 1172
International Telecommunication Union, 1112
International Wool Textile Organization, 1167
Inter-Parliamentary Union, 1174
Islamic Centre for Development of Trade, 1159
Islamic Chamber of Commerce, Industry and Agriculture, 1160
Islamic Committee of the International Crescent, 1160
Islamic Corporation for the Development of the Private Sector, 1145
Islamic Corporation for the Insurance of Investment and Export Credit, 1145
Islamic Development Bank, 1143
Islamic Development Bank Institute, 1145
Islamic Financial Services Board, 1171
Islamic Observatory on Islamophobia, 1156
Islamic Organization for Food Security, 1160
Islamic Solidarity Fund, 1160
Islamic Solidarity Fund for Development, 1145
Islamic Solidarity Sports Federation, 1160
Islamic University of Technology, 1160
Islamic World Academy of Sciences, 1171
Islamic World Educational, Scientific and Cultural Organization, 1160
Istanbul International Centre for Private Sector in Development, 1049
IUCN—International Union for Conservation of Nature, 1172

J

Jeddah Amendment to the Djibouti Code of Conduct, 1112
Jewish Agency for Israel, 1174
Joint Comprehensive Plan of Action, 1134
Joint FAO/WHO Food Standards Programme, 1086
Joint SDG Fund, 1052
Joint UN Programme on HIV/AIDS, 1108

K

Kyoto Protocol, 1058

L

La Francophonie, 1175
League of Arab States, 1146

M

Médecins Sans Frontières, 1178
Mediterranean Action Plan on the Implementation of the Barcelona Convention, Secretariat, 1053
Middle East Council of Churches, 1177
MIKTA, 1174
Minamata Convention on Mercury, Secretariat, 1053
Multilateral Fund for the Implementation of the Montreal Protocol, Secretariat, 1053
Multilateral Investment Guarantee Agency, 1095
Multi-Partner Trust Fund Office, 1052
Muslim World League, 1177

N

Near East Forestry and Range Commission, 1086
Nile Basin Initiative, 1168
North African Regional Capability, 1124
North Atlantic Treaty Organization, 1174
Nuclear Non-Proliferation Treaty, 1134

O

Observer Group Golan, 1063
Observer Group Lebanon, 1064

Office of the Ombudsperson of the 1267/1989/2253 ISIL and al-Qa'ida Sanctions Committee, 1109
Office of the Special Envoy of the United Nations Secretary-General for Syria, 1068
Office of the Special Envoy of the United Nations Secretary-General for Yemen, 1070
Office of the United Nations High Commissioner for Human Rights, 1111
Office of the United Nations Special Coordinator for Lebanon, 1072
Office of the United Nations Special Coordinator for the Middle East Peace Process, 1073
OIC, 1155
OIC Declaration on Human Rights, 1155
OIC States Broadcasting Union, 1160
OIC Union of News Agencies, 1160
OPEC, 1161
OPEC Fund for International Development, 1164
Operation EUNAVFOR MED IRINI, 1142
Organisation for Economic Co-operation and Development, 1169
Organisation for the Prohibition of Chemical Weapons, 1175
Organisation Internationale de la Francophonie, 1175
Organisation of Southern Cooperation, 1171
Organization of Arab Petroleum Exporting Countries, 1154
Organization of Islamic Capitals and Cities, 1160
Organization of Islamic Cooperation, 1155
Organization of the Black Sea Economic Cooperation, 1169
Organization of the Petroleum Exporting Countries, 1161
Organization of Turkic States, 1175
Organization of World Heritage Cities, 1166
Oslo Governance Centre, 1049

P

Pan-African Agency of the Great Green Wall, 1126
Pan African University, 1126
Pan-African Youth Union, 1179
Pan-Arab Strategy for Promoting Renewable Energy, 1148
Paris Agreement, 1058
Parliamentary Assembly of Turkic States, 1175
Parliamentary Union of the OIC Member States, 1175
Partners in Population and Development, 1169
Partnership for Action on Green Economy, 1056
Peninsula Shield Force, 1132
Plastic Waste Partnership, 1055
Platform for Agricultural Risk Management, 1100
Programme for Infrastructure Development in Africa, 1120
Programme of Assistance to the Palestinian People, 1052

Q

Quadripartite Collaboration for One Health, 1105

R

Rabitat al-Alam al-Islami, 1177
Research Centre for Islamic History, Art and Culture, 1160
Revive the Spirit of Mosul Programme, 1113
Rural Poor Stimulus Facility, 1099
Rural Resilience Programme, 1099

S

Science, Technology and Innovation Organization, 1160
Second Islamic Summit on Science and Technology, 1057
Second United Nations Oceans Conference, 1051
Sendai Framework for Disaster Risk Reduction, 1110
Shanghai Cooperation Organisation, 1175
Silva Mediterranea, 1086
South Summit, 1168
Special Tribunal for Lebanon, 1114
Statistical, Economic and Social Research and Training Centre for Islamic Countries, 1160
Sustainable Development Goals, 1047
Sustainable Energy for All, 1172

U

UN Women, 1110
UNEP, 1052
UNEP International Environmental Technology Centre, 1053
UNEP Ozone Secretariat, 1053
UNESCO, 1112
UNESCO International Institute for Capacity Building in Africa, 1113
UNICEF, 1044
UNICEF Global Office of Innovation, 1044
UNICEF Innocenti, 1044
Union for the Mediterranean, 1176
Union of Arab Banks, 1171
Union of Arab Chambers, 1179
Union of Arab Olympic Committees, 1179
Union of Arab Securities Authorities, 1171
Union of the Arab Maghreb, 1169
United Nations 2030 Agenda for Sustainable Development, 1047
United Nations Assistance Mission for Iraq, 1073
United Nations Capital Development Fund, 1052
United Nations Children's Fund, 1044
United Nations Conference on Trade and Development, 1111
United Nations Convention on the Law of the Sea, 1053
United Nations Convention on the Rights of the Child, 1044
United Nations Convention Relating to the Status of Refugees, 1060
United Nations Convention Relating to the Status of Stateless Persons, 1061
United Nations Development Coordination Office, 1047
United Nations Development Programme, 1048
United Nations Disengagement Observer Force, 1063
United Nations Educational, Scientific and Cultural Organization, 1112
United Nations Entity for Gender Equality and the Empowerment of Women, 1110
United Nations Environment Programme, 1052
United Nations Framework Convention on Climate Change, 1058
United Nations Girls' Education Initiative, 1046
United Nations High Commissioner for Refugees, 1060
United Nations Human Settlements Programme, 1111
United Nations Industrial Development Organization, 1113
United Nations Interim Force in Lebanon, 1064
United Nations Mission for the Referendum in Western Sahara, 1065
United Nations Mission to Support the Hudaydah Agreement, 1072
United Nations Office for Disarmament Affairs, 1110
United Nations Office for Disaster Risk Reduction, 1110
United Nations Office for the Coordination of Humanitarian Affairs, 1110
United Nations Office on Drugs and Crime, 1110
United Nations Peacekeeping Force in Cyprus, 1067
United Nations Plan of Action to Prevent Violent Extremism, 1050
United Nations Population Fund, 1111
United Nations Relief and Works Agency for Palestine Refugees in the Near East, 1077
United Nations Scientific Committee on the Effects of Atomic Radiation, 1053
United Nations Support Mission in Libya, 1074
United Nations Truce Supervision Organization, 1068
United Nations Volunteers, 1052
Universal Postal Union, 1113

V

Vulnerable Twenty Group, 1171

W

WHO, 1103
WHO Academy, 1103
WHO Centre for Health Development, 1103
World Bank, 1096
World Council of Churches, 1177
World Economic Forum, 1169
World Food Programme, 1079
World Health Organization, 1103
World Heritage Programme, 1113
World Intellectual Property Organization, 1113
World Jewish Congress, 1177
World Medical Association, 1177
World Meteorological Organization, 1113
World Tourism Organization, 1114
World Trade Organization, 1114
World Union of Jewish Students, 1179
WWF International, 1172